THE AUTHORITY SINCE 1868

THE WORLD ALMANAC®

AND BOOK OF FACTS

2004

WORLD ALMANAC BOOKS

THE WORLD ALMANAC
ALMANAC
AND BOOK OF FACTS
2004

Editorial Director: William A. McGeveran Jr.
Managing Editor: Lori P. Wiesenfeld
Desktop Production Manager: Elizabeth J. Lazzara
Senior Editor: Kevin Seabrooke
Associate Editors: Erik C. Gopel, Christopher Larson
Desktop Publishing Associate: Lloyd Sabin
Contributing Editors: Elizabeth Barden, Richard Hantula, Jane Hogan, Michael J. Holley, Geoffrey M. Horn, Dr. Lee T. Shapiro, George W. Smith, Donald Young
Research: Sarah Janssen, Rachael Mason, Catherine McHugh
Cover: Bill SMITH STUDIO

WORLD ALMANAC EDUCATION GROUP
Chief Executive Officer, WRC Media Inc.: Martin E. Kenney Jr.
President: Robert Jackson
Publisher: Ken Park
Director–Purchasing and Production: Edward A. Thomas
Associate Editor: Ileana Parvulescu; **Desktop Publishing Assistant:** Michael Meyerhofer
Director of Indexing Services: Marjorie B. Bank; **Index Editor:** Walter Kronenberg
Facts On File World News Digest: Marion Farrier, Editor in Chief; Jonathan Taylor, Managing Editor
World Almanac Reference Database@ *FACTS*.com: Louise Bloomfield, Dennis La Beau

WORLD ALMANAC BOOKS
Vice President–Sales and Marketing: James R. Keenley
Marketing Coordinator: Sarah De Vos

We acknowledge with thanks the many helpful letters and e-mails from readers of THE WORLD ALMANAC. Because of the volume of mail, it is not possible to reply to each one. However, every communication is read by the editors, and all suggestions receive careful attention. THE WORLD ALMANAC's e-mail address is Walmanac@waegroup.com.

The first edition of THE WORLD ALMANAC, a 120-page volume with 12 pages of advertising, was published by the New York World in 1868. Annual publication was suspended in 1876. Joseph Pulitzer, publisher of the *New York World*, revived THE WORLD ALMANAC in 1886 with the goal of making it a "compendium of universal knowledge." It has been published annually since then. THE WORLD ALMANAC does not decide wagers.

COVER PHOTOS: © Globe, Masterfile; books, Mars Rover, dolphin, tank, Photos.com; China, Statue of Liberty, football, flags, Can. flag (Can. edition), hockey (Can. edition), PhotoDisc; train, UN, money, RCMP officer (Can. edition), Corel; Franklin, Amer. Philos. Soc.; clown fish, chameleon, PhotoDisc/Getty Images; sailors, eWire Collection/Getty Images; carnival masks, Corbis; Sorenstam, Hepburn, SARS masks (Can. edition), AP/Wide World Photos; Pres. Bush & Donald Rumsfeld, Dept. of Defense photo.

WORLD ALMANAC BOOKS
A Division of World Almanac Education Group, Inc.
A WRC Media Company
512 Seventh Avenue
New York, NY 10018

CONTENTS

The World Almanac
and Book of Facts
2004

THE TOP TEN NEWS STORIES OF 2003

1. **Saddam Hussein was deposed in Iraq** by an invasion led by the U.S. and Britain but without the support of UN Security Council permanent members France, Russia, and China. Continued sporadic resistance, sectarian issues, and the battered state of Iraq after years of war and sanctions made for a slow and difficult transition to Iraqi rule and economic reconstruction. Through Oct. 15, 215 U.S. and 38 British soldiers had been killed in hostile action. Iraqi casualties were difficult to determine, but both military and civilian casualties were much higher than coalition losses.

2. The **space shuttle** *Columbia* disintegrated during reentry Feb. 1, killing the 7 astronauts aboard and calling into question NASA's safety policies and the future of manned space flight.

3. The **U.S. economy continued** to grow at a steady pace and stock markets rallied through early Oct., although the number of jobs continued declining for much of the year. In an attempt to stimulate job creation, Pres. George W. Bush (R) succeeded in passing a new round of tax cuts, totaling $350 billion over 10 years. But a combination of previous tax cuts, economic sluggishness that held down tax receipts, and increased spending for the Iraq War and other initiatives produced a $374 billion deficit in the year ended Sept. 30, 2003.

4. The U.S., with Russia, the European Union, and the United Nations, Apr. 30, unveiled a **"road map" for peace in the Middle East,** but a cease-fire under the plan fell apart in Aug. By October, close to 900 Israelis and some 2,500 Palestinians had died in the last 3 years of heightened violence.

5. The U.S. continued to take the lead in the **international fight against terrorism**. Some leading al-Qaeda suspects, including suspected planners of the Sept. 11 attacks, were captured, but leader Osama bin Laden remained at large and was presumed alive. The U.S. passed a 2nd year since the Sept. 2001 attacks without sustaining a major terrorist strike. In Afghanistan, the government of Hamid Karzai remained in power, but the deposed Islamicist Taliban were increasing their resistance in the country's south.

6. The **campaign for the 2004 presidential election** was underway, with 9 Democrats (as of mid-Oct.) seeking their party's nomination to run against incumbent Pres. Bush.

7. Californians Oct. 7 voted 55%-45% to **recall Gov. Gray Davis** (D), held responsible for huge budget deficits, and elected actor **Arnold Schwarzenegger** (R) to replace him. Schwarzenegger won 49% of the vote in the replacement part of the ballot, which listed 134 other candidates. Lt. Gov. Cruz Bustamante (D) placed 2nd with 32%. Turnout was a relatively strong 60%.

8. On Aug. 14 electricity went out for about 50 million people in Ontario and 8 Northeast and Midwestern U.S. states. It was **the biggest blackout** ever to hit North America.

9. **Homosexual rights** advocates made major gains on several fronts including a U.S. Supreme Court decision striking down a state law banning consensual same-gender sexual relations, the Episcopal Church's Aug. 5 confirmation of Rev. V. Gene Robinson as its first openly gay bishop, and court rulings in Canada opening the way for same-sex marriages.

10. A newly identified disease, severe acute respiratory syndrome **(SARS),** reached epidemic proportions in China and spread around the globe, afflicting more than 8,000 people, disrupting international travel, and causing 774 deaths by July 31, according to the World Health Organization; the epidemic was declared over by then.

THE 2004 PRESIDENTIAL RACE AT A GLANCE

By Geoffrey M. Horn

Geoffrey M. Horn, a freelance writer and editor, is the author of The World Almanac Library of American Government.

More than 200 million Americans will be eligible to vote in the presidential election of Nov. 2, 2004. Analysis of recent trends suggests that 50-55% of them will actually cast ballots on Election Day. The Democrats will hold their nominating convention July 26-29 in Boston, and the Republicans will convene Aug. 30-Sept. 2 in New York City. In all likelihood, the two major-party nominees will have effectively been selected earlier, probably by mid-March.

As in 1992—the last time an incumbent Republican president named Bush was on the ballot—the Democrats entered the primary season with a large number of challengers and no clear front runner. By Oct. 15, 2003, the Democratic field included 9 candidates recognized by the national party. Eight had been campaigning at least since early 2003; the lone exception was retired Gen. Wesley Clark, who did not become a candidate until Sept. 17. One declared candidate, Sen. Bob Graham of Florida, dropped out of the race Oct. 6, citing organizational and fundraising problems. Several well-known Democrats, including former Vice Pres. Al Gore and Sen. Hillary Rodham Clinton of New York, ruled out running for president in 2004.

Unlike his father in 1992, Pres. George W. Bush faced no serious challenge in the Republican party primaries. Through Sept. 2003, the president raised about $85 million, more than 3 times as much money as his closest Democratic rival in fund-raising (Howard Dean). Bush campaign strategists set a fundraising goal of $200 million by Feb. 2004.

The following section includes brief biographies of Pres. Bush and his 9 Democratic challengers as of Oct. 15, 2003. As many as a dozen minor-party presidential candidates may also appear on ballots in Nov. 2004. Consumer advocate Ralph Nader, who won 2.7% of the popular vote in 2000 for the Green Party, said Oct. 2 he would decide by the end of 2003 whether to run again.

Under the Help America Vote Act, signed by Pres. Bush in Oct. 2002, states are to receive $3.9 billion over 3 years to help upgrade their voting systems and technology. While this process will take time to complete, some reforms were expected to be in place by the 2004 election, including the requirement that states provide provisional ballots to voters whose eligibility is in doubt.

PROFILES OF CANDIDATES
(as of Oct. 15, 2003; in alphabetical order)

Republican Candidate

Pres. George W. Bush

Full name: George Walker Bush. **Born:** July 6, 1946, New Haven, CT. **Current Home State:** TX. **Education:** Yale Univ., B.A., 1968; Harvard Univ., M.B.A., 1975. **Religious Affiliation:** Methodist. **Military Service:** Air Natl. Guard, 1968-73. **Marriage:** Laura Welch 1977; 2 children: Barbara, Jenna. **Family Net Worth** (est.*): Between $8.8 mil and $21.9 mil.

Career Highlights: Oil company exec., 1975-87; managing gen. partner, Texas Rangers baseball team, 1989-84; TX gov., 1995-2000; U.S. pres., 2001-present. **Campaign Funds** (to Sept. 30, 2003, as per FEC): $84.6 mil raised, $15.0 mil spent, $73.5 mil cash on hand.

Issues and Record: Much of the Bush presidency has been dominated by U.S. response to terrorist attacks of Sept. 11, 2001, including establishment of new Dept. of Homeland Security. U.S.-led coalitions ousted the Taliban regime in Afghanistan, Oct.-Dec. 2001, and rapidly toppled Saddam Hussein in Iraq, Mar.-Apr. 2003. Promoted "road map" for peace in Mideast. Passage in 2001 of 10-year, $1.35-tril tax-cut bill, other tax cuts in 2002 and 2003, and No Child Left Behind education measure formed the centerpiece of Bush's domestic program. Democrats accuse Bush of mismanaging the economy, and alienating the nation's allies. CNN/*USA Today*/Gallup polls registered a decline in the president's job approval rating from an astronomical 87%, Nov. 2-4, 2001, in the wake of the Sept. 11 terror attacks, to a moderate 55%, Oct. 6-8, 2003. In an interview May 6 with the *Dallas Morning News*, Vice Pres. Dick Cheney disclosed that he had been asked and had agreed to run again with Bush in 2004.

Campaign Sidelights: The Bush campaign reported raising a record $49.5 mil during July-Sept. 2003, more than the all the president's Democratic opponents combined. Bush's total included contributions from some 262,000 donors.

Website: www.georgewbush.com

Democratic Candidates

Gen. Wesley Clark (ret.)

Full name: Wesley Kanne Clark. **Born:** Dec. 23, 1944, in Chicago, IL. **Current Home State:** AR. **Education:** U.S. Military Acad., B.S., 1966; Oxford Univ. (Rhodes Scholar), M.A., 1968. **Religious Affiliation:** Rom. Catholic. **Military Service:** Army, 1966-2000; retired as 4-star general and Supreme Allied Commander, NATO; numerous decorations include Silver Star, Bronze Star, Purple Heart (wounded in Vietnam). **Marriage:** Gertrude Kingston 1967; child: Wesley, Jr. **Family Net Worth:*** No data available.

Career Highlights: Career military officer, 1966-2000; investment banker, military consultant and CNN commentator, 2000-03. **Campaign Funds** (to Sept. 30, 2003, as per FEC): $3.5 mil raised, $0.1 mil spent, $3.4 mil cash on hand.

Issues and Record: Emphasizes service record, including command of NATO troops during Kosovo war in 1999. Received the Presidential Medal of Freedom, the nation's highest civilian award, in 2000 from Pres. Bill Clinton. Describes himself as "pro-choice ... pro-affirmative action ... pro-environment ... pro-health." Opposed Iraq war as "reckless." Would rescind some Bush tax cuts on wealthiest to fund homeland security, aid state and local governments, and provide tax benefits for businesses that create jobs. Favors establishment of a voluntary Civilian Reserve corps that can be mobilized in time of emergency. Former military colleagues have called him brilliant but abrasive. Clark, who acknowledged voting for Richard Nixon in 1972 and Ronald Reagan in 1984, did not register as a Democrat until Oct. 6, 2003. Lieberman criticized Clark's realignment as a "journey of political convenience, not conviction."

Campaign Sidelights: Clark's candidacy originated in the Draft Clark movement, launched in Apr. 2003; since entering the race Sept. 17 at the top of the polls, the general has surrounded himself with aides to former Pres. Clinton.

Website: www.clark04.com

Howard Dean

Full name: Howard Brush Dean III. **Born:** Nov. 17, 1948, New York, NY. **Current Home State:** VT. **Education:** Yale Univ., B.A., 1971; Albert Einstein Coll. of Medicine, M.D., 1978. **Religious Affiliation:** Congregationalist. **Military Service:** None. **Marriage:** Judith Steinberg 1981; 2 children: Anne, Paul. **Family Net Worth** (est.*): Between $2.2 mil and $5.1 mil.

Career Highlights: Investment broker, 1972-74; resident, internal medicine, 1978-81; practicing physician, 1981-91; VT house of reps., 1983-86; lt. gov., 1986-91; gov., 1991-2003. **Campaign Funds** (to Sept. 30, 2003, as per FEC): $25.1 mil raised, $12.8 mil spent, $12.4 mil cash on hand.

Issues and Record: Early opponent of the Iraq war; now supports continued presence of U.S. and international troops, saying "failure in Iraq is not an option." Would repeal all Bush tax cuts to pay for expanded health insurance coverage, improved homeland security, and investments that create jobs. Calls himself a fiscal conservative who would restrict spending to balance the federal budget. As governor of Vermont in 2000, signed nation's first measure legalizing civil unions for gays, but opposes same-sex marriage. Distinguishes himself from more centrist opponents by saying he represents "the Democratic wing of the Democratic party" and portrays himself as a Washington outsider. Gephardt has attacked him for endorsing a 1995 GOP plan, backed by Newt Gingrich, to slow the growth of Medicare, and Lieberman and Kerry have criticized him for saying the U.S. should pursue an "even-handed" approach to the Israel-Palestinian dispute. Led in polls until Clark entered; draws the most attacks at debates, from more centrist candidates.

Campaign Sidelights: According to preliminary reports, Dean raised $14.8 mil during July-Sept. 2003, the most ever collected by a Democratic candidate in a single quarter. Dean received money from more than 168,000 individual contributors; about half the funds were donated via the Internet, which Dean has used as a highly effective organizing tool.

Website: www.deanforamerica.com

Sen. John Edwards

Full name: John Reid Edwards. **Born:** June 10, 1953, Seneca, SC. **Current Home State:** NC. **Education:** North Carolina State Univ., B.S., 1974; Univ. of North Carolina, Chapel Hill, J.D., 1977. **Religious Affiliation:** Methodist. **Military Service:** None. **Marriage:** (Mary) Elizabeth Anania 1977; 4 children: Catharine, Emma Claire, Jack, Wade (d. 1996). **Family Net Worth** (est.*): Between $8.7 mil and $36.5 mil.

Career Highlights: Attorney, 1977-98; U.S. senator, 1999-present. **Campaign Funds** (to Sept. 30, 2003, as per FEC): $14.5 mil raised, $9.7 mil spent, $4.8 mil cash on hand.

Issues and Record: Working class background offered as underpinning his populist theme. Supported resolution authorizing Iraq war but voted against Bush's $87 bil request for Iraq and Afghanistan, charging the president had failed "to create the kind of international coalition that can succeed in Iraq." Voted for USA Patriot Act but criticizes the way Attorney Gen. John Ashcroft has implemented it. Favors establishment of a new homeland intelligence agency to track down domestic terrorists. Would raise taxes on wealthiest Americans to fund credit of up to $5,000 for 1st-time home buyers. Would offer scholarships for prospective teachers who agree to teach in underserved areas. Pledges to extend health insurance coverage to every child.

Campaign Sidelights: A trial lawyer, Edwards made his reputation in a 1997 case by winning more than $30 mil in damages for a 9-year-old girl severely injured by a faulty swimming pool drain. He spent more than $6 mil of his own money to win his U.S. Senate seat in 1998. Edwards was on Gore's shortlist for the vice-presidential nomination in 2000. In Sept. 2003, he ruled out running for a 2nd Senate term in 2004.

Website: www.johnedwards2004.com

Rep. Dick Gephardt

Full name: Richard Andrew Gephardt. **Born:** Jan. 31, 1941, St. Louis, MO. **Current Home State:** MO. **Education:** Northwestern Univ., B.S., 1962; Univ. of Michigan, J.D., 1965. **Religious Affiliation:** Baptist. **Military Service:** Air Natl. Guard, 1965-71. **Marriage:** Jane Ann Byrnes 1966; 3 children: Matt, Chrissy, Kate. **Family Net Worth** (est.*): Between $134,000 and $614,000.

Career Highlights: Attorney, 1965-77; city alderman, St. Louis, 1971-76; member, U.S. House of Reps., 1977-present (3rd CD, South St. Louis); (House Dem. leader, 1989-2002); candidate for 1988 Dem. presid. nomination. **Campaign Funds** (to Sept. 30, 2003, as per FEC): $13.7 mil raised, $7.8 mil spent, $5.9 mil cash on hand.

Issues and Record: As Democratic leader in the House, helped draft congressional resolution authorizing Iraq war; voted for Bush's $87 bil aid request for Iraq and Afghanistan. Would rescind Bush tax cuts to help finance universal health care coverage, based on increased subsidies to employer-based plans. Proposes recruiting 2.5 million new teachers by establishing a Teacher Corps that would pay college loans of students who agree to teach for 5 years. Favors establishment of a variable international minimum wage, to be implemented through the World Trade Organization. Would launch "Apollo 21" program with goal of U.S. energy independence within a decade. Emphasizes longtime pro-labor record, including opposition to passage of NAFTA in 1993.

Campaign Sidelights: In a debate in Albuquerque Sept. 4, Gephardt used the phrase "a miserable failure" five separate times in describing Pres. Bush and his policies. To date has dominated the field in winning endorsements from labor unions.

Website: www.dickgephardt2004.com

Sen. John Kerry

Full name: John Forbes Kerry. **Born:** Dec. 11, 1943, Denver, CO. **Current Home State:** MA. **Education:** Yale Univ., B.A., 1966; Boston Coll., LL.B., 1976. **Religious Affiliation:** Rom. Catholic. **Military Service:** Navy, 1966-70 (Vietnam), Silver Star, Bronze Star, 3 Purple Hearts; Navy Reserves, 1972-78. **Marriage:** (1) Julia Thorne 1970, separated 1982, divorced 1988; 2 children: Alexandra, Vanessa. (2) Teresa Heinz 1995. **Family Net Worth** (est.*): Between $198.8 mil and $839 mil.

Career Highlights: Spokesman, Vietnam Veterans Against the War, 1971; asst. district attorney, Middlesex County, MA, 1976-79; lt. gov., 1982-84; U.S. senator, 1985-present . **Campaign Funds** (to Sept. 30, 2003, as per FEC): $16.8 mil raised, $11.9 mil spent, $7.9 mil cash on hand.

Issues and Record: Emphasizes military record and national security experience. Supported resolution authorizing war in Iraq but voted against Bush's $87 bil aid request for Iraq and Afghanistan. Says Pres. Bush "misled every one of us" about the war. Would keep Bush tax cuts for the middle class, repeal cuts for the wealthy. Would fund 4-year tuition for students at public colleges in exchange for 2 years of national service. Would reform health insurance by allowing Americans to buy into Federal Employees Health Benefits Program. Has promised to appoint only pro-choice judges to the Supreme Court. Has pledged not to use the Heinz family fortune for campaign spending.

Campaign Sidelights: A *Boston Globe* article Feb. 2 revealed that Kerry's ancestry on his father's side was Jewish rather than Irish, as had been assumed. A genealogy specialist hired by the *Globe* found that Kerry's grandfather, Fritz Kohn, was born to Jewish parents and changed his name to Frederick A. Kerry before coming to the U.S. in 1905. The senator's paternal grandmother, Ida Lowe, was also Jewish. Kerry called the article "a revelation."

Website: www.johnkerry.com

Rep. Dennis Kucinich

Full name: Dennis John Kucinich. **Born:** Oct. 8, 1946, Cleveland, OH. **Current Home State:** OH. **Education:** Case Western Reserve Univ., B.A., M.A., 1973. **Religious Affiliation:** Rom. Catholic. **Military Service:** None. **Marriage:** Divorced twice. **Family Net Worth** (est.*): Between $2,000 and $32,000.

Career Highlights: Cleveland city council, 1969-75, 1983-85; mayor, 1977-79; OH senate, 1994-96; U.S. House of Reps., 1997-present (10th CD, western Cleveland and suburbs). **Campaign Funds** (to Sept. 30, 2003, as per FEC): $3.4 mil raised, $2.6 mil spent, $0.8 mil cash on hand.

Issues and Record: Opposed war in Iraq and favors immediate withdrawal of U.S. troops ("We need to bring the UN in and get the U.S. out"). Would implement universal health care coverage based on a Canadian-style, single-payer plan. Favors U.S. pullout from NAFTA and the World Trade Organization. Would establish cabinet-level Department of Peace. Supports repeal of USA Patriot Act. Formerly an opponent of abortion, but now pledges to nominate only pro-choice judges to the Supreme Court. Raised in poverty, he became the youngest mayor of a major U.S. city in 1977; he barely survived a recall vote in 1978 but failed to win reelection in 1979 after letting Cleveland default on its debts rather than sell a city-owned power company.

Campaign Sidelights: Kucinich is a vegan, eating no meat or dairy. He was introduced to the diet by a woman friend, Yelena Boxer, and says he "became a vegan out of love."

Website: www.kucinich.us

Sen. Joe Lieberman

Full name: Joseph Isadore Lieberman. **Born:** Feb. 24, 1942, Stamford, CT. **Current Home State:** CT. **Education:** Yale Univ., B.A., 1964; LL.B., 1967. **Religious Affiliation:** Orthodox Jewish. **Military Service:** None. **Marriage:** (1) Betty Haas 1965; divorced 1981; 2 children: Matthew, Rebecca. (2) Hadassah Freilich Tucker 1983; 1 child: Hani. **Family Net Worth** (est.*): Between $320,000 and $1.5 mil.

Career Highlights: Attorney, 1967-70, 1980-82; CT senate, 1971-81; attorney. gen, 1983-89; U.S. Senate, 1989-present; Dem. vice-pres. nominee, 2000. **Campaign Funds** (to Sept. 30, 2003, as per FEC): $11.8 mil raised, $7.7 mil spent, $4.1 mil cash on hand.

Issues and Record: Supports the war in Iraq and the continued presence of U.S. troops there. Would revise Bush tax plan, raising rates on the wealthy and providing further benefits for the middle class. Would extend health insurance coverage to 32 mil uninsured Americans, in part by establishing MediKids insurance program open to all children from birth. Pledges to "return integrity and fairness to the White House." Would revamp fuel efficiency standards and encourage high-technology investments to end U.S. dependence on imported oil. Promises to create 10 mil jobs by providing incentives to the private sector. Has endorsed limited use of school vouchers. Seen as most conservative in the field of Democrats. Would be first Jewish president.

Campaign Sidelights: Lieberman likes to remind Democratic voters of the 2000 campaign, when he and Al Gore won the popular vote but fell short in the electoral college. At the 1st Democratic debate, held in South Carolina May 3, 2003, he said, "I know I can beat George Bush. Why? Al Gore and I already did it."

Website: www.joe2004.com

Carol Moseley Braun

Full name: Carol Elizabeth Moseley Braun. **Born:** Aug. 16, 1947, Chicago, IL. **Current Home State:** IL. **Education:** Univ. of Illinois, B.A., 1969; Univ. of Chicago, J.D., 1972. **Religious Affiliation:** Rom. Catholic. **Military Service:** None. **Marriage:** Michael Braun 1973, divorced 1986; 1 child: Matthew. **Family Net Worth (est.*):** Between $127,000 and $380,000.

Career Highlights: Asst. U.S. attorney, 1973-77; IL house of reps., 1978-88; recorder of deeds, Cook County, IL, 1988-92; U.S. senator, 1993-99; U.S. ambassador to New Zealand, 1999-2001. **Campaign Funds** (to Sept. 30, 2003, as per FEC): $0.34 mil raised, $0.31 mil spent, $0.03 mil cash on hand.

Issues and Record: Opposed war in Iraq but says U.S. needs to give troops "the support they need to get the job finished." Would provide universal health care coverage through a government-run, single-payer system. Opposes capital punishment. Favors repealing the USA Patriot Act. Would increase federal role in funding education to reduce reliance on local property taxes. In 1992, Moseley Braun became the 1st African-American woman to win a U.S. Senate seat; she lost her seat in Nov. 1998 amid charges, never prosecuted, of campaing irregularities. The lone woman among the major party candidates, she was endorsed by the National Organization for Women and the National Women's Political Caucus.

Campaign Sidelights: When asked by the *Chicago Tribune* after her Nov. 1998 defeat whether she would ever again run for office, Moseley Braun replied, "Read my lips: Not. Never. Nein. Nyet." Questioned about the quote by a CNN interviewer Sept. 22, 2003, she explained her change of heart by referring to an old song, "I'll Never Say Never Again, Again."

Website: www.carolforpresident.com

Rev. Al Sharpton

Full name: Alfred Charles Sharpton, Jr. **Born:** Oct. 3, 1954, Brooklyn, NY. **Current Home State:** NY. **Education:** Brooklyn College. **Religious Affiliation:** Pentecostal. **Military Service:** None. **Marriage:** Kathy Lee Jordan 1980; 2 children: Dominique, Ashley. **Family Net Worth*:** No data available.

Career Highlights: Ordained minister, 1964-present; community activist; founder and director, National Action Network, 1991-present. **Campaign Funds** (to Sept. 30, 2003, as per FEC): $0.26 mil raised, $0.24 mil spent, $0.02 mil cash on hand.

Issues and Record: Opposed Iraq war and wants rapid withdrawal of U.S. troops. Supports constitutional amendments that would establish public education, health care, and voting as fundamental rights; also favors revival of the Equal Rights Amendment for women. Would extend full representation or statehood to DC. Seeks to increase public participation in the political process. Supports affirmative action. Opposes capital punishment. Sharpton, highly controversial as a NY community activist in the late 1980s and early '90s, received the highest unfavorable rating (45%) of any Democratic candidate in a CNN/*USA Today*/Gallup poll taken Aug. 25-26, 2003. He has run unsuccessfully for the U.S. Senate in 1992 and 1994 and for New York City mayor in 1997.

Campaign Sidelights: Asked in a Sept. 9 debate to pick a favorite song, Sharpton—who was James Brown's tour manager in the 1970s—chose "Talking Loud and Saying Nothing," which he called "Brown's song about the Republican Party."

Website: www.al2004.org

*Net worth estimates are based on required financial disclosure statements (as available), as compiled by The Center for Public Integrity.

Presidential Primary and Caucus Dates, 2004

Source: Federal Election Commission

(As of Oct. 2003; dates are tentative and subject to change)

State	Primary Caucus	State	Primary Caucus	State	Primary Caucus
District of Columbia	Jan. 13	Hawaii	Feb. 24 (D)	Pennsylvania	Apr. 27
Iowa	Jan. 19	Idaho	Feb. 24 (D)	Indiana	May 4
New Hampshire	Jan. 27	Utah[1]	Feb. 27	North Carolina	May 4
Arizona	Feb. 3	California	Mar. 2	Nebraska	May 11
Delaware	Feb. 3	Connecticut	Mar. 2	West Virginia	May 11
Missouri	Feb. 3	Georgia	Mar. 2	Wyoming	May 15 (D)
New Mexico	Feb. 3 (D)	Maryland	Mar. 2	Arkansas	May 18
North Dakota	Feb. 3	Massachusetts	Mar. 2	Kentucky	May 18
Oklahoma	Feb. 3	Minnesota	Mar. 2	Oregon	May 18
South Carolina	Feb. 3	New York	Mar. 2	Idaho	May 25
Michigan	Feb. 7 (D)	Ohio	Mar. 2	Alabama	June 1
Maine	Feb. 8 (D)	Rhode Island	Mar. 2	New Mexico	June 1
District of Columbia	Feb. 10 (R)	Texas	Mar. 2	South Dakota	June 1
		Vermont	Mar. 2	Montana	June 8
Tennessee	Feb. 10	Washington	Mar. 2	New Jersey	June 8
Virginia	Feb. 10	Florida	Mar. 9	Alaska	Pending
District of Columbia	Feb. 14 (D)	Louisiana	Mar. 9	American Samoa	Pending
Nevada	Feb. 14 (D)	Mississippi	Mar. 9	Guam	Pending
Wisconsin	Feb. 17	Kansas	Mar. 13 (D)	Puerto Rico	Pending
		Illinois	Mar. 16	Virgin Islands	Pending
		Colorado	Apr. 13 (D)		

Note: (D) = Democratic; (R) = Republican. (1) The holding of the primary is dependent upon funding by the legislature.

Other U.S. Political Parties

Source: Federal Election Commission; World Almanac research

(As of Oct. 15, 2003; dates and details subject to change.)

Green Party. Share of 2000 pres. vote: 2.74%. Convention planned for June 24-27, 2004, Milwaukee, WI. *Website:* www.gp.org

Reform Party. Share of 2000 pres. vote: 0.42%. Convention date and location to be determined. *Website:* www.reformparty.org

Libertarian Party. Share of 2000 pres. vote: 0.36%. Convention planned for May 27-31, Atlanta, GA. *Website:* www.lp.org

Constitution Party. Share of 2000 pres. vote: 0.09%. Convention planned for June 22-27, 2004, Valley Forge, PA. *Website:* www.constitutionparty.com

Natural Law Party. Share of 2000 pres. vote: 0.08%. Convention date and location to be determined. *Website:* www.natural-law.org

SPECIAL SECTION: THE BABY BOOM GENERATION

The United States has more than 78 million baby boomers—people born between 1946 and 1964, a period of high birth rates in most industrialized countries following World War II. The oldest of the boomers came of age amid the political, social, and cultural upheavals of the 1960s; they contributed to these events, and were affected by them. Now the earliest boomers are approaching retirement age, and their departure from the workforce will likely reshape the U.S. economy; nearly 18 million boomers will turn 65 between 2011 and 2015 alone.

This special section opens with essays by two familiar voices from the Baby Boom generation, reflecting on how the changing years shaped their views and attitudes and those of their compatriots.

Following these essays is a timeline of events that helped form the experience of the boomers as they grew to maturity, plus a three-page statistical profile.

Baby Boomers
By Wendy Wasserstein

Playwright Wendy Wasserstein, who won both a Pulitzer Prize and a Tony for her play The Heidi Chronicles, *is a baby boomer herself, having been born in 1950.*

I was on an escalator in B. Altman's Department Store in New York City when I heard that President Kennedy had been shot. I was on my way to my high school bazaar, and I remember watching other people on the escalator burst into tears and hold each other. For any baby boomer, Kennedy's assassination was a pivotal point. In our young minds, Kennedy was the positive future: glamorous, cultivated, sexy, and almost, in a movie-star way, a perfect president. Kennedy would take America out of the 1950s' dreariness of suburban life, epitomized by television shows such as *Leave It to Beaver* and *Father Knows Best*, and into a sophisticated worldliness. He wouldn't just lead the country. He would take every single one of us with him to the next step. Kennedy was a media darling, and we were media babies.

Growing Up with TV

We were the first generation whose imaginations had been sculpted by television. For some boomers this meant TV as it evolved in the late 1960s and the 1970s; they became accustomed to the notion of half-siblings and step-parents, in shows like *The Partridge Family* or *The Brady Bunch*. But legions of earlier boomers like me were exposed to a steady stream of hard-core nuclear normal families, as in *Make Room for Daddy* and *The Donna Reed Show*. Later in life, as many of us found that our lives had evolved into re-marriage, or an acceptance of single life, or gay/lesbian partnerships, we could not help but contrast our living arrangements with a paradigm that went back to the 1950s idea of family: Daddy works and Mom is home in a shirt-waist dress, cooking delicious Ritz cracker pies in the split-level ranch home kitchen.

Boomers came of age in an optimistic America. We also came of age in an America obsessed with us. It was always "our" television and "our" music that mattered. We were the beginning of youth culture. And, as far as we were concerned, first was best: the best rock 'n roll ever was The Beatles and The Rolling Stones, the best movies were *The Graduate* and *Lawrence of Arabia*. Of course, we knew about the music that preceded us, like the blues and Frank Sinatra, and all the classic movies of the 30s and 40s. But the point was, even the great Hollywood directors like William Wyler, Billy Wilder, Alfred Hitchcock, and George Cukor led up to us: Stephen Spielberg, Martin Scorsese, and Cameron Crowe and what we could do. We were the ones who popularized the phrase, "Don't Trust Anyone Over Thirty."

Changing the World

If boomers excelled in self-importance, we had an excuse: important changes were taking place, and we were a big part of them. I remember being at Amherst College in 1969-70, the year of the nationwide campus strikes. Amherst, traditionally an all-male college, was conducting a temporary experiment with co-education. There were 23 women and 1,200 men at the college. Every morning, I would go into the dining hall and make my roommate Mary Jane a peanut butter and jelly sandwich and bring it back to her in the dorm because she was too shy to go herself and have 1,200 heads turn to look at her. Despite the awkwardness of the situation, what it brought home for me was that we were on the cusp of a huge change for men and women.

I remember busting into a faculty meeting at Amherst College with a few of the other 23 women students. The professors were deliberating about how to handle the pro-Kent State/anti-Vietnam War student strike. They wanted to support the protest, and were considering modifying the traditional grading system to make it easier for seniors to graduate and allow underclassmen to emerge from the strike without having destroyed their academic transcripts. "I think you also have to consider the position of women here," I told those professors, twisting my de rigeur long hair around my finger. "Even if we do stop the war, the real changes in this country are going to be the position of women."

A noted professor looked up at me and said, "Take your pitiable pleas elsewhere. You just want to remain at this college. We're doing important work here." We were all sent back to our various colleges, and Amherst remained a men's college until it co-educated a few years later.

During our lifetimes, we boomers have seen the evolution of the civil rights movement, the women's movement, and the gay movement. Those of us who came of age in the 60s, a turbulent but prosperous time in American history, witnessed new possibilities for individual exploration and growth. As groups were gaining political rights, so were individuals gaining self-definitions. The norms of our childhood were transformed: women succeeded in careers they hadn't been allowed to enter earlier, and there was greater acceptance of a variety of sexualities and conceptions of families. Furthermore, Lyndon Johnson signed the Civil Rights Act during our adolescence. That would become our definitive position on race.

Age Resistance

Because boomers came of age in a world fascinated by them, and partially created for them, we are often not the most cooperative when it comes to aging. We are, in fact, at the forefront of not just aging gracefully, but not aging at all. Against all odds, we will hold back the hands of time. Look at any boomer over 50 in Hollywood and I bet you can't tell that person is a day over 35. Even outside Hollywood boomers are spear-heading the movements for personal trainers, yoga, running, and if we could, drug-store Botox. Nobody loves a vitamin more than a baby boomer. Nobody can tell you more about their personal nutrition than a baby boomer. Baby boomer women have the best toned triceps of any generation ever; a boomer woman could probably lift a tall building more easily than Superman, and she could do it for six reps. The parents of baby boomers have lived longer than any other generation, so baby boomers are in the position of caring for the elderly just as their own children have left their nest. Watching loved ones deal with diseases of age, sometimes with dementia, makes baby boomers even more fearful of growing old themselves.

The thing about being a baby boomer is, somewhere we still believe that no one is going to do it better than we did. No one will be better than The Beatles, no one will be more glamorous than Jack Kennedy, no time will be as turbulent as the late 60s, no parents will be as difficult as ours were, and no psyches will be as interesting as ours still are. We see ourselves as the cultural standard of the 20th century. That is our glory. And our defining sorrow.

A View From Within
By Joyce Maynard

Joyce Maynard, in her autobiographical writings and her novels, has chronicled her generation and its experiences.

Born in the year 1953, I began life at a period when more babies were entering the U.S. population than at any time in the nation's history. Over the decades since then, our sheer numbers (not to mention our volubility and the confidence that comes with being part of a huge and much-vaunted majority) contributed to a sense, among my contemporaries and me, that whatever concerns were most pressing in our lives must be of paramount importance to the country as a whole.

To a surprising degree, this has proved true. In 1969, the nation looked upon the youth culture of Woodstock as a symbol—of the power of music, the pursuit of self expression, the values of peace, love, and community, and the rejection of "The Establishment"—even in the midst of torrential rain and an aftermath of foot-deep mud.

The following year, I was part of the first class of women at a prep school that had been closed to girls for close to 200 years. Then I entered an Ivy League university that had opened its doors to women only three years earlier. The boys of my year became the last participants in the draft lottery. But if they were the last in some things, they were the first in others: raised typically by mothers with potholders and plates of cookies in hand, they would love and marry women more ready to don work attire than aprons.

Blazing a Trail

The boomers seemed to be not so much following a well-worn path as blazing a trail: protesting a war with such vehemence that our generation would later be credited by many with ending it. Even if our mothers were something like June Cleaver (on TV's *Leave It to Beaver*), our reading matter leaned more toward Eldridge Cleaver (author of *Soul on Ice*). We grew up with the Civil Rights movement, and witnessed the landmark Supreme Court decision in *Roe* v. *Wade* not far from the time when many of us came into our own sexually active adulthood. We celebrated the passage of Title IX and Billie Jean King's defeat of Bobby Riggs in the much-heralded Battle of the Sexes Tennis showdown.

Many of us were cynical about our parents' values, and rejected anything that suggested tradition. For women, we were the first generation to assert that marriage and childbearing were not enough for us. Having entered the work force in huge numbers, we announced that we would have not simply jobs, but careers. (As for childbearing: that might have to wait. Given the population crisis, we might just adopt.)

Of course, as in any generation, some of us upheld traditional views and values, and some had no interest in politics, protests, or political action of any kind. But for the most part we were a generation of activists. We did not keep our views to ourselves; we proclaimed them and proselytized. Not always so good at listening, we were powerfully effective at making ourselves heard.

The music we favored, the clothes we wore, the TV shows and movies we watched, the way we styled or wore our hair (or left it to its own devices), and to some extent the way we voted represented a vast force that would shape, in many ways, the fashions and attitudes of the culture as a whole, not only in our youth, but for decades after—and still.

Signposts for Our Culture

In many ways, the generation I belong to has served as a signpost for our culture as a whole. As we have aged—married, had children, divorced, started careers, been down-sized, faced the challenges of aging parents, and our own aging as well—so, too, has the media addressed the issues of our lives, and government gone through the motions, at least, of addressing them. From LSD to Prozac to Viagra, our interests and needs helped define the shape of the marketplace.

The slogan "Never trust someone over 30" had to be abandoned as we crossed that divide ourselves. (Now, of course, 30 looks impossibly young.) These days, when market researchers look toward the baby boomers generation, it's menopause treatment, botox, retirement planning, and funeral plots they're offering up.

Despite the passage of time, one phenomenon has endured for most of us: our identification with youth and rebellion.

While we have entered the very mainstream culture many of us once rejected—facing the same realities our parents did, of raising families, needing to pay for college, etc.—we have held fiercely to a sense of ourselves as free-thinking and untraditional in ways our parents (shaped by the Depression and World War II) never had the luxury to be.

The 50-year-olds I know—lawyers and doctors, as well as carpenters, artists and homemakers—still reminisce about their days on the commune, or the summer they backpacked in Arizona, or India. Many of us still own the LPs (Rolling Stones, Led Zeppelin, James Brown, and of course the Beatles) we bought when we were young. We may not smoke pot anymore (though I could name plenty of 50-year-olds who do), but not so many of us can look our children in the eye and say "I never lit a joint, and you shouldn't either." This non-traditional spirit may be confined to a Deepak Chopra seminar or the choice to buy only organic vegetables, but it remains a part of boomers' go-your-own way perspective.

Generation Gap

Ironically, for many of us, we seem to have given birth to the most traditional and downright conservative generation of children since the years of American Bandstand. On a recent visit to my old prep school, sitting in on a class about the 60s, I was stunned to hear one student after another dismiss the views of the counter culture—a group they described their parents as having flirted with but ultimately rejected. After viewing a short documentary about Ken Kesey and West Coast communes, they came out in favor of "a good life"—as defined by "a nice home," "a secure career," and "money in the bank."

It is a humbling shock to see that the group to which the media and marketplace cater now is the young—and that's not us! A movie star aged 40 is over the hill as a romantic heroine. Mick Jagger may still be up on the stage, dancing, but it's not The Rolling Stones they're playing on the radio today. As for the Beatles: the hits of our youth have been transformed into soothing supermarket music.

Aging Boomers

Where, for my parents, the Depression hit as they were growing up, harder times have come to many baby boomers just at the moment we approach our "golden" age. The ease and comfort of the last few decades have caught up with us.

Now aging baby boomers look at an uncertain social security system and ask if retirement—a concept our youth-obsessed generation never gave much thought to—will even be possible. Will the generation that viewed itself as forever young and free have to be forever working?

Those of us who have made good money (and maybe lost it in the stock market) hold fewer illusions that a big house and a Lexus in the driveway are likely to bring happiness. Some of us who perhaps had no time for, or thought of, religion in our youth now seek out a spiritual life. What seems most precious to us these days is not career, success, or possessions, but time and (if available) the freedom to do the things we love, things that seem to hold meaning.

We hold onto our youth for dear life—with our spandex running gear and yoga classes, CDs of old James Taylor albums, and (for some of the men, and even some of the women) our mid-life, fertility-treatment-assisted babies and adopted second families. Having lived through failed marriages and difficult mid-life attempts to reconfigure something that might pass as a family, we know the preciousness—and rarity—of solid and loving relationships—with a partner, with our children, with our friends.

We may even dare to speak the words that 30 years ago would have seemed impossibly uncool. Whether you call it God, or just spirituality, whether sought in a church, or a hiking trail in the wilderness—if I were asked to name the abiding concern of my baby boom generation, as we enter or move toward our second half-century—at a moment when so much that we invested in may have evaporated, or proven insubstantial—it would probably be a quest for the meaning of life, and the hope, and faith, that one exists.

A GENERATION AGES:
TIMELINE: 1946-1985

	1946	1947	1948	1949	1950
Top Stories	Nazi war crimes trials Churchhill "iron curtain" speech Philippines independent from U.S.	Cold war tensions rise Marshall Plan, Truman Doctrine announced India, Pakistan win independence	Truman beats Dewey New countries: Israel, Communist N Korea West Berlin airlift Gandhi assassinated	China, led by Mao, becomes Communist NATO founded; Germany formally divided Apartheid in S Africa	Korean War begins Alger Hiss convicted of perjury in spy case Ralph Bunche wins Nobel Peace Prize
Firsts & Trends	G.I. Bill helps millions of WWII veterans Dr. Spock publishes *Baby & Child Care* Paris fashion: 1st bikini	Yeager breaks sound barrier in X-1 plane Dead Sea Scrolls Jackie Robinson ends baseball color bar	Desegregation of U.S. military ordered Transistor developed Polaroid camera Kinsey Report	Russians test A-bomb Abstract expressionist painting; cool jazz Air Force investigates UFO sightings	Credit cards, cable TV, Miltown tranquilizer introduced *Lonely Crowd* spotlights conformity
Arts & Sports	Films: *The Best Years of Our Lives; It's a Wonderful Life* Crosby, Sinatra, Como are popular crooners	Broadway: Brando smolders in *Streetcar Named Desire* *Diary of Anne Frank* TV: *Howdy Doody*	Olympic Games restart after 12-year gap Art: *Christina's World* Milton Berle ("Uncle Miltie") tops on TV	Books: George Orwell, *1984*; Shirley Jackson, "The Lottery" Arthur Miller drama *Death of a Salesman*	"Peanuts" comic strip Bette Davis in *All About Eve* "Goodnight Irene" TV: Sid Caesar

	1956	1957	1958	1959	1960
Top Stories	Ike wins 2nd term War in Suez Soviet bloc: Stalin denounced; Hungary uprising crushed	European Common Market created School integration crisis at Little Rock Ghana is independent	John XXIII is new pope King of Iraq overthrown U.S. troops in Lebanon Algeria crisis: French turn to De Gaulle	Revolution in Cuba: Castro takes power Nixon "kitchen debate" in Moscow; Khrushchev visits U.S.	Kennedy (JFK) beats Nixon in TV debate, national election Massacre in S Africa U-2 spy plane downed
Firsts & Trends	Interstate Highway System funded 1st neutrino observed Elvis tops pop charts, stars on *Ed Sullivan*	Sputnik space launch Cancer tied to smoking Kerouac's *On the Road* is "Beat" classic Frisbee marketed	Hula hoop Pinups: Brigitte Bardot, Marilyn Monroe Edd "Kookie" Byrnes, Ricky Nelson	New states: Alaska (49th); Hawaii (50th) TV quiz show scandals Pantyhose introduced Barbie dolls	Civil rights sit-ins 1st laser demonstrated 1st oral contraceptive ("the pill") in U.S. Twist is dance craze
Arts & Sports	Don Larsen pitches perfect game Musical: *My Fair Lady* Allen Ginsberg, *Howl* Huntley-Brinkley news	Althea Gibson wins Wimbledon, U.S. titles Musicals: *West Side Story; The Music Man* TV: *Leave It to Beaver*	Jim Brown, Johnny Unitas tops in NFL Films: Poitier & Curtis in *The Defiant Ones* Peggy Lee, "Fever"	Films: *Ben Hur*; French "new wave" cinema *Twilight Zone* on TV Plane crash kills Buddy Holly, Ritchie Valens	Scary movie: *Psycho* Musical: *Bye Bye Birdie* TV: *The Flintstones* Montreal wins 5th straight Stanley Cup

	1966	1967	1968	1969	1970
Top Stories	U.S. bombs N Vietnam Indira Gandhi in India Red Guards in China U.S. crime suspects get *Miranda* rights	Israel wins 6-Day War U.S. anti-Vietnam War protests mount Thurgood Marshall 1st black on Supreme Ct	Martin Luther King slain; riots follow Robert Kennedy killed Vietnam: Tet offensive, My Lai massacre	Men walk on moon Nixon inaugurated Ted Kennedy accident at Chappaquiddick Manson cult murders	Vietnam War spreads to Cambodia; 4 killed at Kent State Egypt: Nasser dies; Sadat is president
Firsts & Trends	U.S. begins listing endangered species Masters & Johnson sexuality study "Happenings" in NYC	1st heart transplant Twiggy is fashion icon SF "Summer of Love" Lombardi's Packers win 1st Super Bowl	Czech "Prague Spring" liberalization crushed Movements: student radicals; Black Power *Whole Earth Catalog*	Woodstock festival In vitro fertilization 1st microprocessor *Sesame Street* transforms children's TV	1st Earth Day held; EPA established Pop music transition: Hendrix, Joplin die; Beatles split, go solo
Arts & Sports	Russell leads Celtics to 8th straight crown TV: *Star Trek; Batman; Mission: Impossible* Beach Boys at peak	Ali rejects military draft Music: Motown, soul, acid-rock, *Sgt. Pepper* Films: *The Graduate, Bonnie & Clyde*	Films: *2001, Planet of the Apes* Lily Tomlin, Goldie Hawn on *Laugh-In* Rock musical: *Hair*	Namath's Jets, Amazin' Mets are winners Movie: *Butch Cassidy* (Newman & Redford) TV hit: *Brady Bunch*	"Doonesbury" debut TV: *Mary Tyler Moore; Odd Couple; MNF* Films: *Patton, Love Story*

	1976	1977	1978	1979	1980
Top Stories	U.S. bicentennial Carter defeats Ford Era ends in China: Mao, Zhou Enlai die FBI, CIA probed	Carter grants amnesty to draft evaders; focus on human rights Bert Lance scandal Panama Canal treaties	Israel-Egypt accords at Camp David John Paul II is pope Over 900 die in Jonestown murder-suicide	Islamic revolution in Iran; U.S. embassy seized, hostages held Soviets in Afghanistan, Inflation at 13.3%	U.S. boycotts Olympics Reagan beats Carter Iraq invades Iran John Lennon killed Mt. St. Helens erupts
Firsts & Trends	Supreme Ct. ends ban on death penalty 1st Apple computer Music trends: disco, reggae	CB radio craze Elvis is dead Eagles, Fleetwood Mac v. Talking Heads, Ramones	1st "test-tube baby" Louise Brown born Bakke court decision bars racial quotas Fad: exercise fashions	Thatcher is 1st woman PM in Britain Three Mile Island accident, *China Syndrome*	Cuban boat refugees Birth of CNN Carl Sagan, *Cosmos*, on PBS Top toy: Rubik's Cube
Arts & Sports	Gymnast Nadia Comaneci is Olympic star TV: *Charlie's Angels* Films: *Rocky; Network; Taxi Driver*	*Roots* TV miniseries Movies: *Star Wars; Annie Hall; Saturday Night Fever* Musical: *Annie*	Affirmed bests Alydar Punk rock: Sex Pistols, Clash, Elvis Costello Films: *Animal House; Superman; Grease*	1st *Star Trek* movie, *Kramer vs. Kramer* Musical: *Evita* Books: Wolfe, *The Right Stuff*	NBA: Jabbar wins 6th MVP; Bird & Magic Johnson are rookies TV: *Dallas* cliffhanger ("Who shot J.R.?")

The baby boom generation includes Americans born from 1946 (when millions of soldiers returned home to the U.S. from World War II) through 1964 (the last year of high birth rates). The following timeline highlights notable events and trends from 1946 to 1985, when the last of the boomers were turning 21.

1951	1952	1953	1954	1955	
Truman fires MacArthur Draft age drops to 18 Kefauver organized crime hearings Rosenbergs convicted	Eisenhower ("Ike") elected president Nixon gives "Checkers" TV speech Kenya Mau Mau terror	Korea truce accord Stalin dies in USSR Warren is Supreme Ct chief justice UK crowns Elizabeth II	Supreme Ct bars public school segregation Dienbienphu falls; French quit Indochina Nasser head of Egypt	Warsaw Pact formed Ike has heart attack Civil war in Vietnam AFL-CIO union merger Albert Einstein dies	Top Stories
22nd Amendment limits pres. to 2 terms CBS airs 1st network color TV broadcast UNIVAC computer	U.S. tests H-bomb Salk polio vaccine Puerto Rico becomes U.S. commonwealth "Theater of the absurd"	Hillary climbs Everest Double helix structure of DNA discovered Open-heart surgery Hefner starts *Playboy*	Army-McCarthy hearings Rock & roll era begins TV dinners introduced *Nautilus* is 1st U.S. nuclear submarine	Civil rights: Rosa Parks sparks bus boycott 1st Disneyland opens; *Mickey Mouse Club*; Davy Crockett craze	Firsts & Trends
I Love Lucy TV debut Book: J.D. Salinger's, *Catcher in the Rye* Giants beat Dodgers on Thomson homer	Movies: *High Noon*, *Singin' in the Rain* Book: Hemingway, *Old Man and the Sea* *Ozzie & Harriet* on TV	Top film love scene: *From Here to Eternity* Theater: *The Crucible* Yankees win 5th straight World Series	Mile run under 4 mins. Books: Tolkien, *Lord of the Rings*; Golding, *Lord of the Flies* Film: *On the Waterfront*	James Dean dies Nabokov, *Lolita* TV: *Captain Kangaroo* Dodgers win their 1st World Series	Arts & Sports

1961	1962	1963	1964	1965	
Berlin Wall erected Bay of Pigs fiasco Peace Corps created Congo crisis: Hammarskjold, Lumumba die	Cuban missile crisis, brink of nuclear war Vatican Council opens Civil war in Algeria Glenn orbits earth	JFK killed; Johnson (LBJ) is president Huge DC rally hears Martin Luther King, "I Have a Dream …"	LBJ beats Goldwater Gulf of Tonkin vote War on Poverty Brezhnev replaces Khrushchev in USSR	Congress OKs Voting Rights Act, Medicare Malcolm X murdered Watts riots Selma march	Top Stories
Kennedy "Camelot" era Boomer births peak Yuri Gagarin 1st human in space Pampers introduced	Rachel Carson, *Silent Spring*; Helen Gurley Brown; *Sex & the Single Girl* 1st Bond flick: *Dr. No*	Betty Friedan, *The Feminine Mystique* McDonald's sells its billionth burger Weight Watchers starts	Controversy: Warren Report on JFK killing Beatle-mania hits U.S. Clay (later Ali) beats Liston in title fight	Nader jump-starts consumer movement Warhol soup cans mark pop art heyday Miniskirts on the rise	Firsts & Trends
Maris hits 61 homers FCC chairman calls TV a "vast wasteland" Patsy Cline is #1 country music star	Wilt Chamberlain has record 100-pt game Films: Peck in *To Kill a Mockingbird*, O'Toole in *Lawrence of Arabia*	King & queen of folk music: Dylan & Baez Surf sound tops charts TV personalities: Julia Child, Johnny Carson	Film: *Dr. Strangelove* TV: *Gilligan's Island* Musicals: *Mary Poppins*; *Funny Girl* with Barbra Streisand	Rolling Stones single: "Satisfaction" Dylan goes electric Film: *Sound of Music* *Bonanza* tops on TV	Arts & Sports

1971	1972	1973	1974	1975	
UN admits Communist China, expels Taiwan Birth of Bangladesh 26th Amendment cuts voting age to 18	Nixon visits China, wins 2nd term despite Watergate Violence in N Ireland George Wallace shot	Vietnam cease-fire; U.S. exits, draft ends Wounded Knee Yom Kippur War Chile: Allende ousted	Facing impeachment, Nixon resigns, is pardoned by Ford Spy scandal topples Brandt in Germany	Vietnam, Laos, Cambodia go Communist Franco dies in Spain NYC fiscal crisis Jimmy Hoffa "missing"	Top Stories
Supreme Ct landmark cases: busing, Pentagon Papers *Ms.* magazine debut "Stairway to Heaven"	Apollo program ends Self-help: Atkins diet; *I'm O.K., You're O.K.* Bobby Fischer world chess champ	Watergate unravels; VP Agnew quits Arab oil embargo *Roe v. Wade* case legalizes abortion	Patty Hearst abducted Tallest building: Sears Tower in Chicago Aaron tops Ruth in HRs Streaking	1st space linkup marks U.S.-USSR détente *Saturday Night Live* with Belushi, Radner, Aykroyd, Chase	Firsts & Trends
Musicals: *Jesus Christ Superstar*; *Godspell* Singer-songwriters: Carole King, Joni Mitchell, Elton John	Munich Olympics: Terrorists kill 11 Israelis Title IX gives boost to women's sports Film: *The Godfather*	Sports champs: Secretariat, Billie Jean King *All in the Family*, *The Waltons* are TV hits Film: *American Graffiti*	TV: *Happy Days*; *Upstairs, Downstairs* Mel Brooks comedies: *Blazing Saddles, Young Frankenstein*	Ali TKOs Frazier in "Thrilla in Manila" Films: *Jaws; Rocky Horror Picture Show* Musical: *Chicago*	Arts & Sports

1981	1982	1983	1984	1985	
Assassination plots: Reagan, John Paul I survive; Sadat is slain in Egypt AIDS epidemic begins	Israel invades Lebanon Poland: Solidarity movement outlawed Britain & Argentina fight Falklands war	Lebanon bombs kill over 250 Americans U.S. invades Grenada S Korean jet KAL 007 shot down by USSR	Reagan reelected; Geraldine Ferraro is Dems' VP nominee India: Indira Gandhi killed; Bhopal disaster	Reagan aides covertly sell arms to Iran, help Nicaraguan contras *Achille Lauro* hijacking, other terrorist attacks	Top Stories
O'Connor is 1st female Supreme Ct justice 1st space shuttle flight IBM PC introduced Charles & Diana wed	DC: Vietnam Veterans Memorial dedicated Jarvik-7 artificial heart ERA defeated Jane Fonda workouts	1st U.S. woman in space: Sally Ride Michael Jackson's *Thriller* shatters album sales marks	NYC subway vigilante Jesse Jackson pushes "Rainbow Coalition" CDs replacing LPs, cassettes	Gorbachev, last Soviet leader, takes office Microsoft Windows 1.0 Madonna dominates pop music, fashion	Firsts & Trends
McEnroe tops in tennis Music videos on MTV Films: *Raiders of the Lost Ark; Chariots of Fire; Arthur*	Macho heroes: Eastwood, Stallone, Schwarzenegger Films: *E.T.; Tootsie* *Cheers* new TV sitcom	*60 Minutes, M*A*S*H* finale lead TV ratings Films: *The Big Chill*, Tom Cruise in *Risky Business*	Walter Payton, Dan Marino star in NFL Music: Springsteen, *Born in the U.S.A.* TV: *Cosby; Miami Vice*	Record breakers: Pete Rose (hits), Nolan Ryan (strikeouts) USA for Africa, "We Are the World"	Arts & Sports

THE BABY BOOMERS: A STATISTICAL PORTRAIT

The baby boom phenomenon (1946-64) began when the industrialized world experienced a sharp and sustained rise in fertility rates at the end of World War II. This rise is usually attributed to the return of millions of soldiers from battlefronts; in the U.S. alone, the number of men and women in uniform shrank from more than 12 million in 1945 to about 1.6 million in 1947. Reasons for the collapse of the baby boom in the mid-1960s are harder to pinpoint. Factors often cited include expanded educational opportunities for young women, which encouraged them to defer marriage and child-rearing; increased participation of females in the workplace; and widespread availability of oral contraceptives ("the Pill").

Third World countries did not experience the same kind of demographic shift. In developing countries, where birth rates are higher and average life spans shorter than in the industrialized world, young people consistently represent the dominant share of the population. This can be seen in the population "inverted pyramid" for Mexico, below. It stands in sharp contrast to the middle-aged spread pattern shaped in the U.S. first by the baby boom, and then by the "baby bust" of the late 1960s and the 1970s.

The Boomer Impact: Population Distribution, U.S. and Mexico, 2000

Source: U.S. Census Bureau. **Boldface Ages** = approx. age of boomers in 2000; numbers in millions

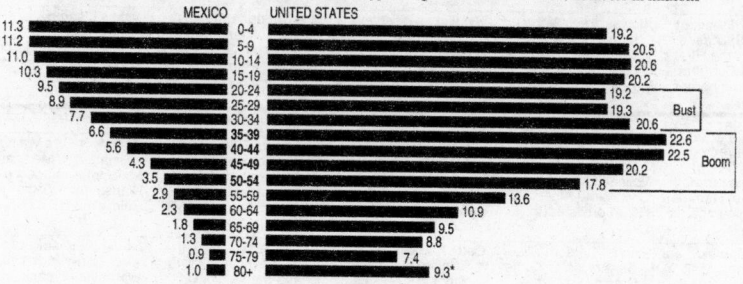

*Further breakdown within the 80+ group not available.

Most Populous Nations, Percent of 35-54-Year-Olds (2000)

Source: U.S. Census Bureau, Intl. Data Base ranked by % of 35-to-54-year-olds

Rank	Country	Total pop. (millions)	% Age 35-54	Rank	Country	Total pop. (millions)	% Age 35-54	Rank	Country	Total pop. (millions)	% Age 35-54
1.	Russia....	146.0	30.5	5.	Brazil......	175.6	23.0	9.	Pakistan...	141.6	16.3
2.	U.S......	282.3	29.5	6.	Indonesia..	224.1	22.5	10.	Nigeria....	123.7	15.5
3.	Japan....	126.7	27.7	7.	India......	1,002.7	21.1				
4.	China....	1,262.5	26.2	8.	Bangladesh	130.4	18.0				

Top 5 Urban Areas by Population, 1950-2015[1]

Source: UN Population Division, *World Urbanization Prospects: The 2001 Revision*

	1950		2001		2015[2]
1	New York, U.S................12.3	Tokyo, Japan 26.5		Tokyo, Japan 27.2
2	London, U.K. 8.7	São Paulo, Brazil.............18.3		Dhaka, Bangladesh...........22.8
3	Tokyo, Japan 6.9	Mexico City 18.3		Mumbai[3], India 22.6
4	Paris, France 5.4	New York, U.S. 16.8		São Paulo, Brazil..............21.2
5	Moscow, Soviet Union 5.4	Mumbai[3], India............16.5		Delhi, India.................20.9

(1) In millions. (2) Projected. (3) Name changed from Bombay.

Live Births in the U.S.: 1940–70

Source: U.S. National Center for Health Statistics

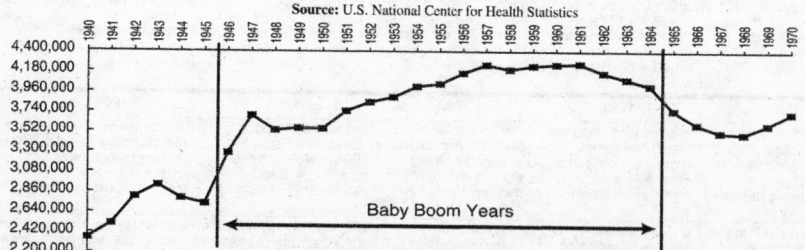

The Changing World of the Baby Boomers

When the first baby boomers were born in 1946, the populations of the world and the U.S. were less than half what they are today. Families sat around the radio for entertainment. In the U.S. a new house could be bought for $12,500, a new car for $1,400, and a loaf of bread for 10 cents; on the other hand, the annual salary averaged barely more than $3,000, and the minimum wage was 40 cents an hour. The first boomers were born at the dawn of the cold war, reached draft age during the Vietnam War, and had passed into middle age when the Soviet bloc fell apart at the end of the 1980s. They lived through the civil rights movement, the women's movement, and most recently the upsurge of radical Muslim fundamentalism.

Selected World Social and Economic Indicators, 1960-2000
Source: World Bank. World Development Indicators

	Date	World	U.S.	Countries by Income		
				High	Middle	Low
Population (millions)	1960	3,020.1	180.7	679.3	1,377.5	963.3
	1980	4,428.4	227.2	830.1	2,038.0	1,560.3
	2000	6,052.8	282.2	953.2	2,691.6	2,408.1
Urban (%)	1960	33.3	70.0	65.4	29.9	15.7
	1980	39.3	73.7	73.1	38.6	22.3
	2000	46.7	77.2	77.3	51.2	29.6
Birth rate	1960	31.2	23.7	21.3	25.6	46.1
(per 1,000 people)	1980	27.2	15.9	14.9	23.4	38.7
	2000	21.5	14.7	12.1	17.5	29.8
Death rate	1960	17.7	9.5	10.0	17.9	22.9
(per 1,000 people)	1980	10.4	8.8	8.8	8.0	14.3
	2000	9.0	8.7	8.6	7.6	10.7
Infant mortality rate	1960	119.3	26.0	34.8	118.0	148.1
(per 1,000 live births)	1980	78.1	12.6	12.4	54.2	110.4
	2000	56.8	6.9	5.5	31.7	81.6
Life expectancy at birth Female	1960	51.9	73.1	71.8	47.6	42.8
(years)	1980	64.8	77.5	77.2	68.0	53.3
	2000	68.5	80.0	81.0	72.0	59.6
Male	1960	48.6	66.6	66.3	44.0	42.7
	1980	60.7	70.0	70.5	63.5	52.0
	2000	64.6	74.3	74.5	67.1	57.8
Gross domestic product per capita	1960	2,607	13,115	9,745	739	218
(constant 1995 U.S.$)	1980	4,396	21,001	19,221	1,493	299
	2000	5,666	31,843	29,170	1,999	459
Electric power consumption	1980	1,445	8,914	5,559	578	106
(kwh per capita)	2000	2,175	12,332	8,615	1,407	307
Television sets (per 1,000 people)	1980	112.8	562.1	439.3	51.9	8.0
	2000	272.4	835.0	675.8	293.5	84.1

Boomers in the U.S.: A Generation in Motion

Congress passed a $33.5 billion road-building measure in 1956, launching the largest public works project in U.S. history—the Interstate Highway System. Construction of this network, linking nearly all major U.S. cities, accelerated several trends that have characterized the baby boom generation: growth of the suburbs, increased mobility of the population, and the triumph of the automobile.

According to Census data, in 1950 23.3% of Americans lived in suburbs, compared with 32.3% in cities, 43.9% in rural areas. The 1970 census marked the first one showing the suburban population predominant (37.2% suburban, 31.4% urban, 31.4% rural). By 1998, the figures were 49.9% suburban, 30.2% urban, 19.9% rural. In 1950 there were 49.2 million motor vehicles in the U.S.; by 2000 there were 225.8 million—more than the number of licensed drivers in 2000 (191 million). Air traffic also increased dramatically; rail traffic dropped.

Especially in the Sunbelt, extending from Florida through Texas, Arizona, and California, urban centers (recently labeled "boomburbs") that were small settlements before 1950 experienced phenomenal growth. The downside of urban sprawl and the proliferation of automobiles can be seen in the rush-hour traffic congestion in most major metropolitan areas.

Costs of Automobile Traffic Congestion in Selected U.S. Metropolitan Areas, 2000
Source: Texas Transportation Institute, 2002 Urban Mobility Study

	Freeway daily vehicle miles of travel		Annual person-hours of delay		Annual congestion cost		
					Per person	Delay and fuel cost	Fuel wasted (gal. per
Urbanized areas	Total miles (1,000s)	Per lane-mile of freeway	Total hours (1,000s)	Per person	($)	(mil. $)	person)
Total average	15,375	16,035	47,595	27	505	900	43
Chicago IL-Northwestern IN	48,400	18,160	221,300	27	505	4,095	43
Los Angeles CA	126,495	23,425	791,970	62	1,155	14,635	94
New York NY-Northeastern NJ	101,295	15,350	400,115	23	450	7,660	39
San Francisco-Oakland CA	47,980	20,550	167,200	41	795	3,210	67
Washington DC-MD-VA	34,535	18,320	123,190	35	655	2,325	56

Education, Income, and Employment Among U.S. Boomers

As the boomers moved through the school system, completing high school became the norm rather than the exception throughout the U.S. The percentage of women with 4 or more years of college soared—a change facilitated by the rise of the median age of first marriage among females from 20.4 years in 1964 to 24.5 years in 1994.

Measured in current dollars, boomers' family incomes more than doubled between 1980 and 2001, in part because of the large proportion of households in which both married partners were employed; measured in constant 2001 dollars, however, household incomes rose only 22.8% when the head of household was in the 45–54 age bracket, and 14.5% when the head of household was between the ages of 35 and 44.

U.S. Educational Attainment of Persons at Least 25 Years Old
Source: U.S. Census Bureau

	MALE			FEMALE		
	Under 5 years of elementary school	High school completion or higher	4 or more years of college	Under 5 years of elementary school	High school completion or higher	4 or more years of college
1950...	11.9%	31.5%	7.1%	9.8%	35.1%	5.0%
1960...	9.4	39.4	9.6	7.3	42.5	5.8
1965...	7.7	48.0	12.0	5.9	49.9	7.1
1970...	5.9	55.0	14.1	4.7	55.4	8.2
1975...	4.7	63.1	17.6	3.8	62.1	10.6
1980...	3.6	69.2	20.9	3.2	68.1	13.6
1985...	2.9	74.4	23.1	2.5	73.5	16.0
1990...	2.7	77.7	24.4	2.2	77.5	18.4
1995...	2.0	81.7	26.0	1.7	81.6	20.2
2000...	1.6	84.2	27.8	1.5	85.1	23.6

U.S. Boomer Attitudes

An AARP/Modern Maturity Survey of U.S. attitudes toward money and debt revealed significant differences between **early boomers** (born 1946–55), **late boomers** (born 1956–64), and 3 other demographic groups: the World War II generation (born before 1936), the "silent" generation (born 1936–45), and Generation X (born 1965–82). Other recent AARP surveys show that older boomers, whose political outlook was shaped by the Vietnam War and Watergate, remain skeptical about U.S. institutions, although in recent years they have adopted a somewhat more favorable view of government.

Attitudes Toward Wealth, 2000
Source: AARP

Main Things They Would Do With $1 Million

	Would like to be wealthy	Help family/ friends	Save and invest	Donate to charity	Pay off debt	Buy new house	Get education	Travel
All Groups	65%	23%	20%	14%	13%	10%	5%	4%
Generation X	75	14	26	10	15	14	5	4
Late boomers	74	17	23	13	16	10	9	5
Early boomers	65	25	18	13	17	9	5	4
Silent generation	58	31	18	18	12	5	3	4
WW II generation	38	38	7	24	4	5	2	3

Indebtedness by Generation, 2000
Source: AARP

	Owe money on credit card*	Owe money on a home mortgage	Owe money on a car loan		Owe money on credit card*	Owe money on a home mortgage	Owe money on a car loan
All Groups	42%	41%	35%	**Early baby boomers**	51	56	37
Generation X	42	29	44	Silent generation	39	51	32
Late baby boomers .	53	60	42	World War II........	19	15	11

*After paying most recent bill.

Older Boomers' Views of U.S. Institutions
Source: AARP, *Tracing Baby Boomer Attitudes Then and Now* (2002)

How much confidence boomers have in:	Boomers 1973-75			Boomers in 2002		
	A great deal	Only some	Hardly any	A great deal	Only some	Hardly any
Executive branch	15%	47%	36%	26%	54%	21%
Congress	16	63	20	13	62	27
U.S. Supreme Court...............	34	50	13	28	54	19
Statements by government leaders	3	38	56	6	64	30
Major companies	22	56	21	12	67	20
Educational system	36	54	10	20	65	16
Organized religion	30	48	19	13	62	25

The Aging Boomer Population

On average, the U.S. baby boomers who turned 45 in 2001 can expect to live over 30 more years (32.5 for men, 36.6 for women); those who turned 55 in 2001 can expect to live another 2½ decades. As the large U.S. boomer population ages, demands on nation's health care and retirement systems are certain to increase. A study published during the same year by Bradley C. Strunk and Paul B. Ginsburg calculates that annual health care spending per capita, measured in 2001 dollars, rises by an average of $152 for each year a boomer adds between the ages of 50 and 64.

Sources of Health Coverage, Persons 50-64[1]

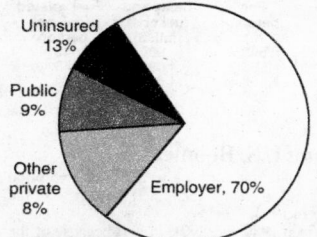

Uninsured 13%

Public 9%

Other private 8%

Employer, 70%

(1) As of 2000

Retirement Issues

A survey by the Employee Benefit Research Institute found that 72% of younger boomers (born 1955-64), but only 58% of older ones, were somewhat or very confident that they would have enough money for retirement. About 26% of younger boomers and 34% of older boomers said they had not actually saved for retirement.

As more and more baby boomers retire the social security system will be under increasing strain. The ratio of workers to those drawing benefits has already dropped sharply since 1950 (when there were 16.5 workers per beneficiary) to 3.3 in 2002, and is projected to fall below 3.0 by 2014. It is projected that in 2018 the Social Security trust fund will begin to decline each year, so that some kind of remedy—reduced benefits, higher contributions, or higher ages for eligibility—will become necessary.

With uncertainties about Social Security, pension plans organized by employers figure large in boomers' retirement thinking. Over the last 30 years, the percentage of pension plans classified as the "defined contribution" type has grown steadily. In these plans, employers and/or employees make specific contributions to retirement accounts, such as 401(k) plans. In 1998, 92% of pension plans were of this type, according to the EBRI and only 8% were "defined benefit" plans, under which employers agreed to pay a certain benefit amount to employees after retirement. In 1975, 67% of plans were defined contribution and 33% defined benefit.

The 10 Leading Causes of Death, Ages 45–64, 2001[1]
Source: U.S. National Center for Health Statistics

	Deaths	Rate[2]		Deaths	Rate[2]
All causes	411,545	638.1	5. Diabetes	14,815	23.0
1. Cancer	139,908	216.9	6. Chronic lower respiratory diseases	14,619	22.7
2. Heart diseases	98,048	152.0	7. Chronic liver disease and cirrhosis	12,813	19.9
3. Accidents (unintentional injuries) ..	19,965	31.0	8. Suicide....................	8,823	13.7
Motor vehicle accidents	8,663	13.4	9. AIDS	5,408	8.4
4. Cerebrovascular diseases	15,426	23.9	10. Kidney disease	5,141	8.0

(1) Preliminary.　(2) Per 100,000 population.

Antarctica: Exploring Earth's Last Frontier
By Dr. Jerri Nielsen

Dr. Jerri Nielsen went to the South Pole in November 1998 to serve as doctor at the Amundsen-Scott Research Station. While she was there she discovered she had breast cancer. Her best-selling book Ice Bound *describes her adventure.*

We lived in refrigerators, metal insulated buildings with meat locker doors to keep out the cold. Our outside world was covered in thin hoarfrost, a dusting of crystalline ice. A large geodesic Dome sheltered the small community from the unrelenting corrosive winds and drifts of winter. These drifts, which dwarfed structures and sometimes covered them, were not really snow. The polar plateau is a desert, with scant precipitation made up of ice crystals falling from a clear sky. The drifts were really masses of ice ripped from the surface in the dark storms of winter-ice that piled like huge dunes of sand wherever the wind met an obstacle. The accumulations had to be laboriously bulldozed away each spring. The floor of the Dome was ice—ice 2 miles thick. We had excavated catacombs and corridors to house the septic systems and utilities of the station. Inside the Dome the temperature was the same as outdoors, an annual mean temperature of –60 degrees Fahrenheit, at times dipping below –100 degrees F (the Dome, not heated itself, functions as an elaborate windbreak for the buildings inside it). The South Pole is at an elevation of 9,240 feet, and those who stay there experience physiological effects comparable to those of a much higher altitude because of the low barometric pressures of winter.

Like Nowhere Else

It is a place unlike anywhere else on Earth: living there was like living on a space station in a distant galaxy. There was one day and one night per year. Day was six months long, as was night. A period of twilight occurs as the intense sun, which spends the summer circling above, slowly spirals down. At that time the entire world, not just the western sky, is washed in the colors of the sunset. Then the sun slips below the horizon and darkness falls. What remains are the phases of the moon, the southern sky, and the Aurora Australis—the Antarctic counterpart to the Northern Lights—undulating above in spirals of green and white. I felt as I entered this place that I had fallen into a crevasse, a great abyss from which I would never return.

There, in a place where no noise enters from the outer world, with no deadlines, no news, and no contrived urgency, life and death seem so clear. Antarctica is a blank slate on which you can write your soul. The voice inside is more easily heard where you barely have what you need to get by. The drive to survive turns indifferent strangers into great friends. Many of the great Antarctic explorers returned to the Ice until it took their lives. I think I know why. Friendship is easier in a place where people need each other to live and the universal questions of human life seem simpler.

No Way Out

For 8 months out of the year there is no way in or out of the South Pole. It was during that period that I, the only medically trained person on the expedition, found a large mass in my right breast. I thought, "I gambled and I have lost. I will make the last year of my life the best." At first I hoped, as so many do, that I was wrong, that I would be all right. As it became obvious that I could die, I began to organize the medical department so that others could take over in my absence. Like others who have experienced community in a remote place, I tried to figure out how I could live long enough to impart my knowledge to people there so that they could go on. To my surprise, it was the community that organized to save me.

Combining an old microscope, a camera, and a computer we were able to project tissue samples to pathologists over the Internet. But we needed tissue, my tissue. Using a dried up potato and some thawed chicken to practice on, I taught a welder how to operate as my surgical assistant. That is how we learned that I had an aggressive type of breast cancer. The United States Air Force, at great risk, dropped medication by parachute. A mechanic served as my nurse, administering chemotherapy (he used a wristwatch to time each drop as I received it). The lifesaving treatment made me so ill that the National Science Foundation (NSF), my employ-ers, thought that I might not survive. This would leave the station without a physician. We decided that when the weather turned, they would attempt to get me out. No plane can land at the Pole in winter—the hydraulics do not function and jet fuel jells at very low temperatures. We had to wait until late spring. Then the Air Guard made a gallant rescue, flying in earlier than had ever been attempted.

Continents: Area, % of Earth's Land			
Australia	2,966,000 sq. mi.	7,682,300 sq. km.	(5%)
Europe*	4,063,000 sq. mi.	10,523,000 sq km.	(7%)
Antarctica	5,400,000 sq. mi.	14,000,000 sq. km.	(10%)
South America	6,884,000 sq. mi.	17,830,000 sq. km.	(12%)
North America	9,362,000 sq. mi.	24,247,000 sq. km.	(16%)
Africa	11,704,000 sq. mi.	30,313,000 sq. km.	(20%)
Asia*	17,120,000 sq. mi.	44,339,000 sq. km.	(30%)

*Europe here includes Russia W of Ural Mts. and Ural R., and European Turkey; these areas not included in Asia figures.

Why We Are There

Why do people voluntarily live under these ferocious conditions? We were there for science, like the 700 researchers in 2003 who conducted 141 projects managed by the National Science Foundation. The Polar Regions have been called the window to outer space. The long night, low temperatures, and dryness allow astronomical observations at certain wavelengths to be carried on more effectively there than anyplace else on Earth, and much more cheaply than in outer space. The remoteness of the South Pole from urbanization and other sources of contamination means that the air there is mixed and clean—it is Earth's background air and serves as an excellent baseline and source of comparison. Much important work in aeronomy (the study of the upper atmosphere) can best be done there. The regions have also been called the miners' canaries of the Earth: atmospheric changes can be detected first at the poles. (A large hole—a drastic thinning, actually—in the ozone layer was detected over Antarctica in 1985; it continues to be monitored closely.)

Research is also being done in medicine, biology, geology, and geophysics. Antarctica has a major role in the Earth's heat engine, affecting our climate. One of the NSF's goals is to sponsor research that benefits from the unique conditions found in Antarctica. Protected by international treaty as a place of peace and science, the continent is one of the first successful attempts at global government.

I went to the South Pole looking for adventure in the earth's last frontier. Now I know that the frontier is located neither in a place nor a time. The frontier is where it has always been and always will be, in the human mind.

Antarctica: The Cold Hard Facts
3rd-smallest continent (see box above), but still about 1.5 times the size of the U.S.; no indigenous population
98% ice-covered (the other 2% mostly barren rock on high mountains and in coastal areas)
Has 70% of world's fresh water locked in its ice cap; 90% of the world's ice
Not until 1840 was Antarctica identified as a large land mass or continent, rather than a group of islands
Coldest, windiest, driest continent:
• Lowest temperature yet recorded on earth, –129°F, July 21, 1983, at the Russian Vostok Station
• Strong winds flow downward from the interior toward the coast. Wind speed of 200 mph (320 kmph) recorded at Dumont d'Urville base in July 1972
• Average annual precipitation at Amundsen Research Station, 0.8 inches
Antarctic Treaty (1961) provides for scientific research and bars military uses. 27 nations conduct research on Antarctica; about 3,000-4,000 researchers in summer
See also World Exploration and Geography chapter.

Libraries in Today's World

By Maurice J. Freedman

Maurice J. Freedman, M.L.S., Ph.D., the director of the Westchester Library System (Ardsley, NY), was president of the American Library Association from 2002 to 2003.

When the Internet began its dramatic rise, many people drew the obvious implications—"you can't go wrong investing in dotcoms" was one, and "libraries are history" was another. Why would anyone need books or other library services, the reasoning went, when everything one needed to know was floating out there in cyberspace, ready to appear at the click of a mouse?

In fact, what we find today is the exact opposite of the prophecies of doom: public library usage is dramatically up in all of its main indicators. Not only has the Internet not put libraries out of business; it has contributed to their increased usage. Sometimes people go to libraries to gain free access to the Internet (or subscription Internet services) that they don't have at home. Often, after doing some research on the Internet, they go to the library to learn more about the subject, borrow books about it—or borrow that novel that sounded so fascinating.

But this heightened usage comes against a background of cutbacks in library support all across the U.S. The weakened economy has hit state and local governments hard, and all too frequently libraries, including school libraries, are first to fall prey to the budget-cutter's knife. This despite the fact that studies have repeatedly shown that student achievement is greater when there is a professional librarian heading a well-supported school library (or, as some would say, a media specialist in the media center).

Library Facts

According to the American Library Association:

- Americans go to some kind of library—school, public, or academic—more than twice as often as they go to the movies.
- Reference librarians answer more than 7 million questions weekly. Standing in a line single file, those 7 million questioners would reach all the way from Boston to San Francisco.
- There are more public libraries than McDonald's restaurants in the U.S.—a total of 16,220, including branches.
- Americans spend $7 billion a year on home video games; $1 billion a year is spent on all books, periodicals, and other materials for school libraries.

The Good News

Library usage *is* up. People are checking out more books (and videos and DVDs and everything else) than they used to, and coming to the library more often. Statistics collected by the National Center for Education Statistics show that circulation in the U.S. rose 22.9% from 1990 to 2000. In the same period, library visits more than doubled, increasing 126.1%. The number of reference questions handled by librarians jumped by 44.7%. And these increases have continued since 2000, according to the latest estimates.

What does this amount to on a local scale? To take the example of the public libraries in my own library system—that of Westchester County in New York state—total circulation grew by 8.8% between 2000 and 2001. Compared to the pre-Internet years, the 2001 circulation was 16.8% higher than in 1995, and 44.6% higher than in 1985. One Westchester library was closed for renovations for 5 weeks in 2002, yet still managed to rack up the highest circulation in its history. Now that people can reserve books, DVDs, and other library items via the Internet, the number of reserves filled has increased dramatically, to over 76,000 per month in 2003, compared with 4,000 per month in 1999 when the process required filling out and submitting a paper request form for each book.

An American Library Association poll in 2002 found that an overwhelming majority of those surveyed see libraries as dynamic places offering a range of activities for the whole family. Similar large numbers believe that libraries afford opportunity for education and self-improvement, and that free libraries serve "an essential role in our democracy and are needed now more than ever." Librarians, the poll found, are generally credited with techno-savvy and a position at the "forefront of the Information Age." In fact, the range of skills librarians must have at their fingertips has expanded with the increasing complexity of the world and of libraries: they must be experts at navigating the Internet, good storytellers, cheerful and sensitive advisers in the traditional task of helping people find a good book, and at the same time knowledgeable mentors in pointing people to the many resources libraries offer for finding employment, investigating health issues, and handling all the other concerns of our daily existence.

A study conducted by the Bill & Melinda Gates Foundation, looking at modern technology in libraries, found that 98-99% of all people surveyed want public access computers in public libraries.

The inescapable conclusion is that the American people love their public libraries. And they have even more reason for this now than they did in the past. With the consolidation that has occurred in the publishing industry, and the parallel concentration of media outlet ownership, the public library's importance looms even larger. It is preeminently the place where Americans can go at no charge to get all points of view, learn without externally opposed limits, and obtain the information they need to be an informed electorate.

The fact that public libraries are free has been at the heart of their importance to the nation. Because of unemployment, shrinking incomes, and less disposable cash, Americans have been flocking to their local public libraries. They go there for books, DVDs, CDs, newspapers, periodicals, a variety of other free programs and services, and sometimes just to be with other members of their community.

Providing access to the Internet, another free service, has proved a roaring success for public libraries. Thanks to federal, state, and local funding, and to the Gates Foundation, almost every public library in the U.S. offers one or more Internet terminals for public use. The "digital divide," the great gap between the information haves and have-nots, has narrowed as a result: people can use Internet-connected terminals in their local libraries to get at cyberspace's wealth of information. Additionally, public libraries make available online thousands of full-text periodicals, thus providing their communities with resources that dramatically expand the amount of information available. And in most cases, those with home or business Internet connections can access library resources whenever they like.

Tough Times for Libraries

Libraries around the U.S. have often been early victims or near victims of government cost-cutting:

- Oakland, CA, public libraries, responding to diminished book funds, have posted "wish lists" on Internet bookseller Amazon.com so that the public can select and easily contribute needed items.

- The interlibrary loan and reference services provided by the Colorado State Library—70,000 books loaned and 160,000 questions answered in 2001—was eliminated as of July 1, 2002.

- To meet a 5% budget cut in 2002, the Seattle Public Library closed its doors for its two slowest weeks in the year.

- The Franklin Public Library in Franklin, MA—said to be the first public lending library in the U.S.—faced closure in 2003. Thanks to national publicity, the town found money to keep the library open for another year. Still, the budget was reduced by 30%. (The library started in 1790 with a donation of 100 books from Benjamin Franklin.)

The Bad News

If people love libraries, and their mission is so vital, what's the matter? The answer is simple—money.

According to the American Association of School Libraries, certified library media specialists all over the country are being eliminated because of budget cuts and rejected referendums. And school libraries are sometimes simply disappearing: with decreased education funding and growing student populations, the libraries (or media centers) are being turned into classroom space. Meanwhile, reduced funds for buying books (while average hardcover prices have just about doubled in the last 18 years) means that in most states the average age of school library book collections dates to around 1980. In other words, half the books our children read contain information more than 20 years old.

This is having a drastic effect on children. Research shows that the poorest children have the least access to books and libraries; that the poorest schools have the poorest school libraries, and their students have the poorest achievement scores.

Bearing the burden of many of the cuts are librarians themselves. They face increased job insecurity and tightened purse strings. And this is not a case of lean years following years of plenty—the fact is, librarians have historically suffered from inequitable pay. Predominantly female, library staff members are paid substantially less than members of male-dominated occupations who are similarly qualified (or, in many cases, less qualified). Recognizing this situation at last, the ALA has created an Allied Professional Association to see that librarians and other staff who provide 21st century information services are compensated with 21st century salaries.

In response to this predicament, and to the harsh funding cuts that started in 2002 and continued with a vengeance into 2003, the ALA initiated the Campaign to Save America's Libraries. Together with grass-roots efforts by people all over the country, this has yielded some good results—good, at least, in that some of the cuts have been rescinded. However, increases have been rare. Libraries continue to have to make do with dollars shrunk by inflation, if they escape from cuts.

Hope for the Future

As dark as the picture is, we should not dwell on the negatives. The fact is, Americans use their libraries, they need them, and they love them. Library supporters have mobilized nationwide against the cuts and are actively promoting their cause. They are pleading the case repeatedly that library funding should increase rather than decrease during bad economic times. In some places, they already have been successful. Ultimately they will find mechanisms and apply the pressure that will enable libraries to provide the top-level information services that the American people have always wanted, and need more than ever to keep democracy strong.

Finding the Right College
By Edward B. Fiske and Bruce G. Hammond

Edward B. Fiske, former education editor of the New York Times, *has written widely on school reform and college admissions and is editor of the annual* Fiske Guide to Colleges. *Bruce G. Hammond is director of college counseling at Sandia Preparatory School in Albuquerque, NM, and is co-author, with Fiske, of* The Fiske Guide to Getting Into the Right College.

With the children of baby boomers swelling student populations at high schools across the U.S., more graduates are seeking higher education than ever before. According to the National Center for Education Statistics, undergraduate enrollment will reach a record 13.6 million in fall 2003, and the number is expected to continue rising. Although there is a place somewhere for every qualified student, competition has reached unprecedented levels, especially at the 75 or so institutions that accept fewer than half their applicants.

A Diverse System

Prospective college students in the U.S. can choose from a dazzling menu of choices. They range from tiny schools where students number in the dozens to massive ones with dorms that have their own ZIP codes; from colleges so remote that the nearest pavement is miles away to those surrounded by the high-rise growth of the largest cities; from schools where students wear prints and pastels to those where a preferred uniform is combat boots and chains. Yet all too many high school students limit themselves to a narrow list of choices. Many gravitate toward large, well-known institutions, but a small college may be a better fit because it can offer more contact with faculty and more access to extracurricular organizations. State schools with low sticker prices and lesser-known privates that give merit scholarships can also be a bargain for cost-conscious students. In any case, students should be encouraged to find the school that best matches their own interests and skills.

It's Academic

The most important factor in college admissions is the high school academic transcript that shows the courses taken and grades received. Grade point average is a big factor. At the same time, students wishing to be considered by the most selective colleges may need to excel in demanding courses, including College Board Advanced Placement (AP) courses or comparable offerings. These students should tackle a diverse curriculum that includes upper-level subjects such as physics and calculus.

Most colleges and universities require applicants to take either the SAT I or ACT test. The SAT I, preferred by many colleges on the east and west coasts, includes verbal and math sections and will be revised in March 2005 to include, among other changes, a writing section with an essay. The ACT, often preferred in the Midwest, and closer to material commonly covered in schools, includes English, math, reading, and science reasoning sections with an optional essay. In addition, about 80 of the nation's most selective institutions require or recommend that students take up to three hour-long SAT II: Subject Tests.

Standardized test scores are particularly important for students seeking academic scholarships or applying to large public universities because many decisions are based largely on scores and grades. To prepare for the SATs, students may consider taking the shorter PSATs during sophomore year. PSAT scores are used for selecting National Merit Scholarship semi-finalists. Many scholarship committees also use them to select candidates for merit awards.

Written recommendations from one or more teachers, and from a high school counselor, round out the list of common application requirements on the academic side.

The Personal Element

Most selective colleges ask applicants to describe extracurricular activities, employment, paid or volunteer work, and other out-of-school activities—with quality usually more important than quantity. What special skills, interests, and character and leadership qualities emerge from these descriptions? College admissions officers are looking to assemble a well-rounded class that includes students with a passion for, or distinction in, one or more activities.

Admissions Facts

Average acceptance rate at colleges and universities: 70%.

At the most selective schools, covering about 6% of all institutions, average acceptance rate was 40% or less.

Average yield rate for all colleges: 44%.

Colleges offering early action: 18%; colleges offering early decision 19%. 60-80% offer neither.

Wait lists used at 32% of institutions, usually the most selective schools and those with low yield rates. Of these, 60% accepted fewer than 10% of the students on their lists.

Source: *The State of College Admissions 2002-2003,* National Assoc. for College Admission Counseling (NACAC).

Many applications require students to complete a personal statement that is both a barometer of their writing ability and a window into their lives. The best essays reveal something important about the applicant that may not be apparent from the rest of the application.

Many colleges also ask for a short essay explaining why the student has chosen to apply. In an era when some students apply to ten colleges or more, the applicant who can write convincingly about why he or she has chosen a particular institution will stand a better chance of admission.

Early Decision

The admissions process is driven by deadlines, and students should settle on a list of colleges by the fall of 12th grade. A growing proportion of applicants to many selective schools apply via early decision (ED) or early action (EA). ED entails a binding commitment to attend if accepted; EA has no such commitment. Admissions statistics reveal that ED applicants have a better chance for admission, but early decision is controversial because it limits students' ability to explore new options during grade 12 or to negotiate financial aid offers. A few institutions, notably Yale and Stanford, have abandoned early decision in favor of early action, though with the stipulation that students may not apply EA or ED anywhere else.

Coaching

Increasing competition for access to well-known colleges and universities has fueled a steady increase in supplemental, fee-based counseling and coaching services. Many students willingly pay $1,000 or more for a coaching course or one-on-one tutoring to prepare for standardized tests, while others prepare on their own using books or software. Students are much more likely to improve from 1000 to 1200 after coaching than from 1200 to 1400, and college counselors often advise advanced students to prepare on their own. No solid evidence exists that a coaching course is better than good self-directed preparation.

Private Consultants

Some families hire consultants to coach students through the entire application process, often with the mistaken impression that such counselors can use influence to help a student gain admission. Independent counselors can be useful primarily for students who do not receive adequate counseling at their high school. Costs for these services vary widely.

Financial Aid

With the total cost of the most selective private institutions now at more than $35,000 per year, and rising tuitions at state colleges and universities, many families must seek financial assistance. Aid applicants are required to submit the Free Application for Federal Student Aid (FAFSA) as soon as possible after January 1. At some private colleges, they also must file the College Board's CSS/PROFILE® form. Students with significant financial need are advised to be wary of early decision programs and to apply to a broad range of colleges—thus allowing them to compare aid awards, and even appeal to First Choice U. on the basis of a more generous offer from another institution.

Deadlines You Should Know

November 1—Deadline to apply for early decision or early action at many colleges.

January 1—Application deadline at many colleges.

February 1—Deadline to File the Free Application for Federal Student Aid (FAFSA).

First Week of April—Date by which many colleges report admissions decisions.

May 1—Deadline for applicants to accept offers at many colleges, usually with a deposit required.

Ratings, Yields, and Campus Visits

Under heightened scrutiny from the general public and media outlets such as *U.S. News & World Report*—which ranks and rates colleges using various statistical measurements—colleges are more preoccupied than ever with maintaining the appearance of selectivity. This means they pay close attention to the average test scores of accepted students and attendees and the percentage of students they accept. The "yield," or percentage of accepted students who decide to attend, has also been an object of attention, though *U.S. News* has now dropped it from its ratings formula. Colleges are more likely to admit students who show interest by visiting the campus, having an interview, applying early, and maintaining contact with the admissions staff because they know from experience that these students are most likely to enroll. Of course, visiting the campus is very important anyway to give students a clearer idea of whether they really would like it there.

Diversity in Admissions

Minority college population (2000): 28%.

In June 2003 rulings involving the Univ. of Michigan, the Supreme Court, in the interest of diversity in the student body, upheld giving preference to minorities as part of "a highly individualized holistic review of each applicant's file" but rejected a system that automatically awarded favorable points to minority applicants.

Maintaining Perspective

Students and parents must work hard to avoid getting too caught up in the selectivity game. There are scores of colleges and universities that would be an excellent match for the needs, values, and learning style of any single applicant. Attending a prestigious college does not always increase earning potential or chances for future success, and is not the answer for everyone. The college search is best viewed as a voyage of discovery rather than a high-pressure scramble for admission to a short list of brand-name institutions.

For Further Reading

Publications

"America's Best Colleges," *U.S. News & World Report*. This magazine's widely read and controversial rankings are published every fall. Much of the material is available at www.usnews.com.

The College Finder, Steven Antonoff. Faucet Books. Offers lists of prominent programs in hundreds of categories.

Colleges That Change Lives, Loren Pope. Penguin Books. Profiles of 40 small colleges "that you should know about even if you aren't a straight A student."

The Fiske College Deadline Planner, Edward B. Fiske and Bruce G. Hammond. Sourcebooks. Comprehensive list of important deadlines for applicants.

The Fiske Guide to Colleges, Edward B. Fiske. Sourcebooks. A comprehensive look at the 300 "best and most interesting" colleges in the nation.

The Fiske Guide to Getting into the Right College, Edward B. Fiske and Bruce G. Hammond. Sourcebooks. Overview of the college selection process.

Four-Year Colleges, Petersons Publishing. Includes a variety of indexes, college profiles, and descriptions of academic programs.

The Gatekeepers, Jacques Steinberg. Viking Press. An insider's account of the admissions process at a prestigious liberal arts college.

Websites

www.act.org
The online home of ACT. Offers test registration services.

www.collegeboard.com
Offers test registration information and a college search feature.

www.fafsa.ed.gov
The federal government's web site for filing the Free Application for Federal Student Aid.

www.fastweb.com
The web's best free scholarship search site.

www.nacac.com
The National Association for College Admission Counseling. Wide variety of information on the subject.

www.number2.com
A web site offering free preparation materials for the SAT and ACT.

www.petersons.com
Contains online college search, test prep, and financial aid resources.

YEAR IN REVIEW

CHRONOLOGY OF EVENTS

Reported Month by Month, Oct. 16, 2002, to Oct. 16, 2003

OCTOBER 16-31, 2002

National

Congress Passes Bill to Improve Voting Procedures— The Senate, 92-2, **Oct. 16**, following the House's lead, approved a bill that would give $3.9 billion to the states to fix shortcomings in their election process. The bill was inspired by the chaos in Florida that left the result of the 2000 presidential election in doubt for a month. The money would be used to replace antiquated voting machines, train poll workers, and create accurate lists of registered voters. Pres. George W. Bush signed the legislation **Oct. 29**.

Senator Killed in Air Crash—Sen. Paul Wellstone (D, MN) was killed in a plane crash near Eveleth, MN, **Oct. 25**, along with 7 other passengers—his wife, Sheila; his daughter, Marcia Markuson; 3 aides; and 2 pilots. The Beech A100, known as a King Air, went down in a wooded area during a storm. Wellstone, one of the Senate's most liberal members, was in a close reelection campaign against former St. Paul mayor Norm Coleman (R).

International

North Korea Admits to Nuclear Arms Program—The Bush administration revealed **Oct. 16** that North Korea had acknowledged it was developing nuclear arms. The admission had come earlier in the month at a meeting in Pyongyang, after a U.S. diplomat confronted his hosts with evidence of a clandestine nuclear project; North Korea and the U.S. had agreed in 1994 that the former would freeze all development of nuclear weapons.

Israelis Killed in Continuing Violence—As Arab-Israeli violence continued, a sport utility vehicle carrying a bomb was crashed into a bus in northern Israel **Oct. 21**, killing 14 passengers; 50 others were wounded.

U.S. Presses for Action Against Hussein—On **Oct. 23**, the U.S. presented a resolution to the UN Security Council calling for military action against Iraq if Iraqi weapons of mass destruction were not eliminated and began a diplomatic initiative aimed at securing its passage. Earlier, on **Oct. 20**, Iraqi Pres. Saddam Hussein announced that in celebration of his **Oct. 15** reelection (unopposed), most prisoners would be freed. As thousands were released, many were killed in the chaos; relatives of some who did not emerge staged protests demanding to know their fate.

Chechens Seize Moscow Theater, Over 100 Hostages Die—About 50 armed Chechen militants occupied a theater in Moscow **Oct. 23** and seized some 800 hostages, demanding that Russia end its attacks on the province. After at least 33 hostages, mostly children, were released, the captors **Oct. 24** released the body of a woman they had killed. Russian troops attacked the theater **Oct. 26**, killing most of the Chechens, including their leader; 4 were taken alive. Russian authorities said the militants had threatened to start executing hostages; they had also planted explosives throughout the theater. The government said **Oct. 30** that 120 hostages had died, all but 2 from effects of a gas released by troops, which the authorities ultimately identified as an aerosol version of Fentanyl, a powerful pain-killer. The government came under criticism for allegedly failing to arrange prompt medical care for the drugged hostages, a charge it disputed.

U.S. Diplomat Slain in Jordan—On **Oct. 28**, Laurence Foley, an administrator of a U.S. development assistance program in Jordan, was assassinated inside his home in Amman, apparently by terrorists.

Leftist Elected President in Brazil Runoff—Luiz Inacio Lula da Silva, the first successful presidential candidate to rise from the working class, was elected president of Brazil **Oct. 27** in a runoff election. A member of the Workers' Party, he defeated Jose Serra of the governing party.

General

Vatican Rejects U.S. Bishops' Approach to Abuse— The Vatican **Oct. 18** found fault with the plan worked out by U.S. bishops for dealing with the abuse of minors by priests. An official letter from Cardinal Giovanni Battista Re to Bishop Wilton Gregory, president of the U.S. Conference of Catholic Bishops, said the agreement worked out at a bishops' conference in June did not sufficiently protect the rights of priests under Church law. The letter noted that the draft policy did not provide for a statute of limitations, and said it defined abuse too broadly, to include actions not involving physical force or contact. A commission composed of both Vatican and U.S. bishops was set up to review the plan.

Sniper Suspects Arrested—Two suspects, John Allen Williams, 41, a former soldier also known as John Allen Muhammad, and John Lee Malvo, a 17-year-old from Jamaica, were arrested **Oct. 24** in connection with a series of apparently random sniper shootings in the Washington, DC, area that left 10 people dead and 3 wounded over the period from Oct. 2 through Oct. 22. On **Oct. 23**, police said they were looking for the pair, and for a Chevrolet Caprice with a certain New Jersey license plate; the breakthrough followed phone tips and physical evidence allegedly linking the snipers to a Montgomery, AL, robbery. Early on **Oct. 24**, a traveler spotted the car parked at a rest stop off Interstate 70 near Frederick, MD, and at 3:30 a.m., police stormed the car, arresting the 2 occupants, who were asleep. Police found a Bushmaster XM-15 .223-caliber rifle in the auto, later identified as the weapon used in the shootings; the car had been modified for firing a rifle from the trunk. On **Oct. 25**, Montgomery County, MD, filed charges of first-degree murder against both. In the face of evidence possibly linking the suspects to earlier shootings elsewhere, other localities began to file charges as well.

> *"Tonight the people of the Washington metropolitan region are breathing a collective sigh of relief."*
>
> Montgomery County, MD, Executive Doug Duncan, **Oct. 24, 2002**, on the arrest of the two sniper suspects.

Anaheim Is Surprise Winner of World Series—The Anaheim Angels, in their 42nd season, won baseball's World Series **Oct. 27**, for their first time ever, with a 4-1 victory over the San Francisco Giants in the 7th and deciding game.

NOVEMBER 2002

National

Judge Approves Microsoft Settlement—Federal District Judge Colleen Kollar-Kotelly, in Washington, DC, **Nov. 1**, approved an antitrust settlement between the Microsoft Corp. and U.S. Justice Dept. The settlement, reached in November 2001, had prompted some state attorneys general to seek stiffer sanctions, most of which Kollar-Kotelly denied. She did add provisions requiring Microsoft to share more information with competitors on its Windows operating system and directed the company to set up a compliance committee composed of Microsoft board members. Aspects of the settlement the judge left in place barred the software giant from exclusive deals that would hurt competitors and called for Microsoft to treat manufacturers equally, not retaliating against companies that created competing software.

Republicans Retake Senate, Gain Seats in House—The Republican Party emerged from 2002 off-year elections, **Nov. 5**, with a majority in the Senate and an increased margin in the House. Democrats made slight gains in gubernatorial elections. An energetic nationwide campaign by Pres. George W. Bush, in which he appealed to voters to send him more allies, was credited with lifting the Republicans.

Before the election, Senate Democrats held a 50-49 majority (there was 1 independent). Afterward the GOP held 51 seats, the Democrats 47, with 1 independent, and an incumbent Democrat faced a runoff in Louisiana. In Missouri an appointed Democrat, Jean Carnahan, lost her seat to former House member Jim Talent. Another Democratic incumbent, Sen. Max Cleland, lost in Georgia to U.S. Rep. Saxby Chambliss (R), who made an issue of his opponent's failure to support Bush's version of a homeland security bill. In Minnesota, former Vice Pres. Walter Mondale (D), running as a stand-in for Sen. Paul Wellstone, who had died in a plane crash, lost to former St. Paul Mayor Norm Coleman (R). In Arkansas, however, Atty. Gen. Mark Pryor (D) ousted incumbent Sen. Tim Hutchinson (R), who had angered his conservative base by divorcing his wife and marrying a younger woman.

In the 435-member House, Republicans increased their total from 223 to 228, while Democrats ended up with 203. The seat of deceased Hawaii Rep. Patsy in the new Congress was to be decided in a special election. (Ed Case, D, had won a special election **Nov. 30** to complete the 5 remaining weeks in her term in the outgoing Congress.) Three other seats were also undecided. Redistricting following the 2000 census had created a number of open seats or ones in which incumbents were pitted against each other. In most other districts, incumbents won easily.

Democrats captured governorships from the GOP in Pennsylvania, Michigan, Illinois, and Wisconsin. Incumbent Govs. Gray Davis (D) and George Pataki (R) were reelected in California and New York, respectively. In Texas, Gov. Rick Perry (R), who had succeeded Bush when the latter was elected president, won a full term, and the president's brother Jeb Bush (R) was easily reelected governor of Florida, despite being a principal target of the Democrats.

> "It's been a very successful night for the Republican Party, for the president of the United States, and for the country at large."
>
> Sen. Bill Frist (R, TN), about the Republicans' victories on Election Day, **Nov. 5, 2002.**

SEC Chief Resigns Under Fire—Harvey Pitt, chairman of the Securities and Exchange Commission, submitted his resignation to Pres. Bush **Nov. 5**. Pitt's closeness to the accounting industry had proved embarrassing, and he was criticized for failing to reveal that William Webster, his choice to head the newly created Public Accounting Oversight Board, had headed the audit committee for U.S. Technologies, which was under criminal investigation. Pitt himself became the subject of investigations into his selection of board members. On **Nov. 12**, Webster resigned as head of the accounting board.

Pelosi Chosen to Lead House Democrats—Rep. Nancy Pelosi (CA) was elected by House Democrats **Nov. 14** to head their caucus in the new Congress, succeeding Dick Gephardt (MO), who resigned as leader after Democrats lost seats in the Nov. 5 election. Pelosi, the first woman to lead either party in the House, comes from the liberal wing of her party.

Bush Signs Homeland Security Bill—Pres. Bush **Nov. 25** signed the Homeland Security Bill on which Congress had just completed action. The new cabinet department, focused on internal security against terrorism, was to include all or part of 22 agencies under its umbrella. On the same day, Bush named former Pennsylvania Gov. Tom Ridge, who had headed up the homeland security effort for the past year, as secretary of the department. The bill had been over-

whelmingly approved by the Senate and House after being hung up for months over a dispute relating to the civil-service status of federal workers affected by the reorganization.

Bush appointed former Sec. of State Henry Kissinger chairman, **Nov. 27**, of a commission to investigate possible intelligence and security flaws prior to the Sept. 11 attacks.

International

CIA Missile Kills Top al-Qaeda Leader—The CIA **Nov. 3** used a missile fired from an unmanned aircraft to kill Qaed Salim Sinan al-Harethi, leader of the al-Qaeda terrorist organization in Yemen, along with 5 lesser operatives riding in the same automobile. The strike was the first of its kind to target al-Qaeda figures outside Afghanistan. On **Nov. 21**, U.S. officials announced that Abd al-Rahim al-Nashiri, said to be a principal planner of the 1998 U.S. embassy bombings in Africa, had been captured.

Party Tied to Islam Wins Turkish Elections—The Justice and Development Party, the outgrowth of an Islamic party, won the Turkish national elections **Nov. 3**, with 34% of the vote; the Republican People's Party drew 19%. The party of Prem. Bulent Ecevit got only 1.2% of the vote, not enough to qualify it for seats in Parliament. However, Recep Tayyip Erdogan, leader of the winning party, was constituionally barred from membership in Parliament because of a 1998 conviction for inciting hatred, and thus could not officially take office. Erdogan said his party was committed to secularism, joining the European Union, and good relations with the U.S.

Israeli Prime Minister Calls for New Elections, as Bombings Continue—Israeli Prime Min. Ariel Sharon **Nov. 5** called for new elections, to take place early in 2003. Sharon had found it increasingly difficult to maintain his leadership in a deeply fractured parliament. Former Prime Min. Benjamin Netanyahu, who joined the government **Nov. 6** as foreign minister, challenged Sharon for leadership of the Likud Party, but lost a **Nov. 28** primary, 56% to 40%. Meanwhile, among violent incidents on both sides, snipers in Hebron ambushed and killed 12 Israelis **Nov. 15**, and 11 Israelis were killed **Nov. 21** in a suicide bombing on a Jerusalem bus. On **Nov. 22** a British UN official was shot to death at a refugee camp in Jenin, in an apparent error by an Israeli soldier.

UN Security Council Gets Tough With Iraq—After weeks of negotiation, the UN Security Council **Nov. 8** voted unanimously, 15-0, to give Iraq a "final opportunity" to comply with previous disarmament resolutions. The resolution also established a strict timetable for full Iraqi cooperation with the UN weapons inspectors. Arab League foreign ministers, meeting **Nov. 10** in Beirut, supported the inspection of Iraq's weapons sites, but not a U.S.-led invasion if Iraq did not cooperate. On **Nov. 12**, the Iraqi parliament, under the control of Pres. Saddam Hussein, unanimously rejected the UN resolution; the next day, however, Iraq agreed to inspections, while reiterating claims that it did not have weapons of mass destruction.

At a NATO summit meeting in Prague, **Nov. 21**, leaders of the 19 member nations united in condemning Iraq. However, Germany remained opposed to war with Iraq. Speaking in Bucharest, Romania, **Nov. 23**, Bush appealed to a large crowd for support against Iraq. The first weapons inspectors arrived in Baghdad, the Iraqi capital, **Nov. 25**.

Bin Laden Possibly Heard on New Recording—A voice that U.S. officials identified as apparently that of terrorist leader Osama bin Laden was heard on an audiotape broadcast over the Al Jazeera TV channel **Nov. 12**. The 4-minute message threatened that other nations faced attack if they supported any U.S. invasion of Iraq.

Communist China Gets New Leadership—A transition to new leadership occurred at the 16th congress of the Chinese Communist Party. The long-anticipated retirement of Jiang Zemin as general secretary of the party and effective leader of the country was confirmed **Nov. 14**, but Jiang continued as head of the powerful Central Military Commission. In all, 6 members of the party's 7-member inner council were stepping down, and the body was expanded to 9 members. The only remaining incumbent, Hu Jintao, was promoted to general secretary **Nov. 15**. Prime Min. Zhu Rongji and Li Peng, the leader of parliament, also bowed out of their party council posts. The new Hu regime would have to deal with government corruption, rising unemployment, and demands for political change.

More Than 215 Die in Rioting Over Beauty Pageant— A decision by organizers to hold the Miss World beauty competition in Nigeria proved calamitous, as rioting by Muslims opposed to the pageant claimed more than 215 lives in the northern Nigerian city of Kaduna. The riots were particularly inflamed by an article **Nov. 14** in a Lagos newspaper speculating that the prophet Muhammad "would probably have chosen a wife" from among the contestants. On **Nov. 22**, the organizers announced that the pageant would be moved to London.

Terrorists Bomb Israeli-owned Hotel in Kenya—Israelis abroad were a target of terrorism on **Nov. 28**, when 3 suicide bombers demolished an Israeli-owned hotel in Kenya, near Mombasa; 10 Kenyans and 3 Israelis also lost their lives. Minutes earlier, 2 shoulder-fired missiles narrowly missed an Israeli jetliner carrying 261 Israelis, as it took off from the airport in Mombasa. In the wake of the attacks, more than 250 Israelis were flown back to Israel from Kenya. U.S. and Israeli officials suspected involvement by al-Qaeda, although Kenyan authorities, who held a dozen foreigners for questioning, reported no clear links.

General

Sniper Suspects Charged in Virginia—Murder charges were filed **Nov. 6** in Virginia against John Allen Muhammad and John Lee Malvo in connection with shootings in the region that had killed 10 and wounded 3. Shootings linked to the 2 had also occurred in Maryland and the District of Columbia, but Atty. Gen. John Ashcroft, **Nov. 7**, supported the choice of Virginia as a venue for trial, because it made the death penalty available for Malvo, who was 17.

Tornadoes Claim Heavy Toll in Mid-U.S.—Dozens of tornadoes swept through the central United States **Nov. 10**, killing more than 35 and causing widespread destruction. Among the hardest hit states were Tennessee (17 killed), Alabama (12 killed), and Ohio (5 killed).

U.S. Catholic Bishops OK New Plan in Abuse Cases— After the Vatican in October rejected portions of their original plan, U.S. Roman Catholic bishops in Washington, DC, **Nov. 13** agreed to revised rules for dealing with accusations of sexual abuse against minors by priests; the revisions were formulated by a committee of U.S. and Vatican bishops. The new plan provided that priests be judged by church tribunals under canon law. An accused priest would be suspended from duties immediately, pending resolution of his case, and bishops would not be permitted to transfer an accused priest to a new ministry in a new diocese. The definition of sexual abuse was narrowed, however, and an individual alleging abuse as a child would generally be required to file a complaint by age 28. The new plan was criticized by abuse victims.

DECEMBER 2002

National

Bush Shakes Up His Economic Team—Pres. George W. Bush **Dec. 6** obtained the resignation of 2 of his top economic advisers, Treasury Sec. Paul O'Neill and Lawrence Lindsey, chairman of the National Economic Council. On **Dec. 9**, Bush nominated Paul Snow, chairman of CSX Corp., a railroad conglomerate, as the new Treasury secretary. On **Dec. 12** he chose Stephen Friedman, former cochairman of Goldman Sachs Group, to succeed Lindsey. With the economy slumping, Bush reportedly saw a need for a new team to articulate administration policy.

On **Dec. 10**, Bush nominated William Donaldson, an investment banker and former chairman of the New York Stock Exchange, to succeed Harvey Pitt as chairman of the Securities and Exchange Commission. Pitt had resigned under pressure in November.

U.S. Economy at a Glance: Calendar Year 2002	
Unemployment rate	5.8%
Consumer prices (change over 2001)	+2.4%
Trade deficit	$418.04 bil.
Dow Jones high (Mar. 19)	10,635.30
Dow Jones closing (year end)	8341.63
Dow Jones low (Oct. 9)	7286.27
GDP (change over 2001)	+2.4%

Democrats Retain Senate Seat in Louisiana—U.S. Sen. Mary Landrieu (D) was reelected in a runoff in Louisiana, **Dec. 7**. Her victory meant that the new Senate would contain 51 Republicans, 48 Democrats, and 1 independent.

In another Louisiana runoff, **Dec. 7**, Rodney Alexander (D) narrowly prevailed to win a House seat from the 5th Congressional District. In Colorado, **Dec. 10**, following a recount, Bob Beauprez (R) was declared the winner in the state's new 7th CD. In Hawaii's 2nd CD, Ed Case (D), who had won a special election to fill the unexpired term of deceased U.S. Rep. Patsy Mink, was elected to a new term **Jan. 4**, 2003. The new House thus contained 229 Republicans, 205 Democrats, and 1 independent.

United Airlines Files for Bankruptcy—UAL Corp., the parent of United Airlines, filed for bankruptcy in Chicago **Dec. 9**. United, the largest U.S. airline ever to file for bankruptcy, said it was losing $22 million a day; the action came after the Air Transportation Stabilization Board, **Dec. 4**, rejected the company's request for $1.8 billion in loan guarantees, saying United's business plan was not sound. In bankruptcy the airline would continue to operate and would honor frequent flier miles. Executives **Dec. 10** called for reducing the size of the fleet and for further pay cuts.

Gore Rules Out 2004 Bid for Presidency—Former Vice Pres. Al Gore announced **Dec. 15** that he would not seek the Democratic nomination for president in 2004. Gore had narrowly lost the 2000 presidential election to George W. Bush. Public opinion polls showed that Gore had more support than any other likely candidate for the party nomination—other than former First Lady Hillary Rodham Clinton, who had pledged to fill out her Senate term, though she also appeared not to unequivocally rule out running.

Kissinger Resigns as Head of Terror Investigation— Former Sec. of State Henry Kissinger resigned **Dec. 13** as chair of the new National Commission on Terrorist Attacks. He said compliance with a congressional rule to disclose clients would jeopardize his consulting firm. On **Dec. 11**, former Sen. George Mitchell (D, ME) had resigned as vice chair, saying the position would take too much time and might require him to resign from his law firm; Democrats named former Rep. Lee Hamilton (D, IN) as vice chair. On **Dec. 16**, Pres. Bush named former New Jersey Gov. Thomas Kean (R) as the new chair.

Bush Announces Plan for Smallpox Vaccinations— Saying he believed hostile nations might have stockpiled the smallpox virus, Pres. Bush **Dec. 13** announced a plan calling for prompt mandatory vaccination of armed forces personnel. The vaccine would also be offered to health care workers, police officers, firefighters, and other emergency workers on a voluntary basis. Experts say that, despite their effectiveness, smallpox vaccinations can pose a serious risk to a few, perhaps 15 people out of every million.

U.S. to Build Missile Defense Shield—Pres. Bush **Dec. 17** ordered the Pentagon to proceed with construction by 2004 of a limited missile defense shield. The defensive shield had been discussed for years, but this was the first deadline to be set. Six land-based missile interceptors would be built in Alaska and California within 2 years; 10 more would be added in Alaska in 2005. Up to 20 smaller interceptors would be stationed on Navy ships.

Lott Resigns as Majority Leader After Furor—Sen. Trent Lott (R, MS), who had just been chosen by his Republican colleagues as majority leader in the new Senate, bowed out as leader **Dec. 20** amid a furor over a statement he made **Dec. 5**, at the 100th birthday party of retiring veteran Sen. Strom Thurmond (R, SC), appearing to praise his segregationist candidacy for president in 1948. As the comment achieved notoriety, Lott made a series of public apologies that failed to satisfy even some critics in his own party. Pres.

Bush **Dec. 12** deplored Lott's remark, though without calling for his resignation. On **Dec. 18**, Sec. of State Colin Powell and Gov. Jeb Bush of Florida both expressed concern, and the next day Sen. Bill Frist (R, TN) indicated he would challenge Lott for the post. On **Dec. 23**, Republicans elected Frist by acclamation. A physician, Frist was a comparative newcomer to the Senate, having been elected first in 1994.

> *"I want to say this about my state: When Strom Thurmond ran for president, we voted for him. We're proud of it. And if the rest of the country had followed our lead, we wouldn't have had all these problems over the years, either."*
>
> Sen. Trent Lott (R, MS), at Sen. Strom Thurmond's 100th birthday party **Dec. 5, 2002**, speaking about Thurmond's 1948 presidential bid as a proponent of segregation.

International

Weapons Inspectors Visit Sites in Iraq—UN weapons inspectors continued to visit sites in Iraq in search of evidence that Iraq was building or in possession of weapons of mass destruction. On **Dec. 3**, inspectors paid a surprise visit to one of Pres. Saddam Hussein's many vast palace complexes, which prompted an Iraqi complaint. On **Dec. 7**, Iraq issued a report required by the November UN resolution. The 12,000-page document purported to be a full account covering any programs related to production of weapons of mass destruction. Copies went to the UN inspection commission, the International Atomic Energy Agency (IAEA), and the 5 permanent UN Security Council members. By **Dec. 12**, 98 inspectors were searching Iraqi facilities.

Some 330 members of about 50 Iraqi opposition groups met in London, **Dec. 14-17** to plan for a new government in the event Hussein was ousted. They approved creating a transitional national assembly and 3-person executive council, to be followed by a new constitution and elections.

Sec. of State Powell said **Dec. 19** that Iraq was in "material breach" of UN resolutions, and risked war if it continued a pattern of lying and lack of cooperation that he found in the **Dec. 7** document. On **Dec. 23**, Iraq shot down an unmanned U.S. surveillance plane. On **Dec. 26**, after Iraqi planes crossed into a no-flight zone, U.S. and British planes bombed a military command center southeast of Baghdad.

Israeli-Palestinian Death Toll Continues to Rise—Among other incidents, Israeli forces killed 10 Palestinians, including 2 UN employees **Dec. 6**, during a raid on alleged terrorist targets in a refugee camp in Gaza. On **Dec. 27**, Palestinians shot and killed 4 Jewish seminary students in a West Bank settlement; 2 of the assailants were also killed.

Spain Seizes North Korean Ship with Missiles—Two Spanish warships **Dec. 9** stopped an unmarked North Korean cargo ship in the Gulf of Aden. Boarding the ship, the Spaniards found 15 Scud missiles, conventional warheads, and rocket fuel. Spain gave control of the ship to the U.S., which, however, determined, **Dec. 11**, that the missiles had been ordered by the government of Yemen. The U.S., which had long criticized North Korea for selling weapons, allowed the ship to deliver the missiles.

North Korea Continues Nuclear Development, Repudiating Restraints—North Korea said **Dec. 12** that it would reactivate a nuclear reactor idle since 1994. The Communist state had previously admitted to operating a clandestine nuclear-weapons program in violation of a 1994 international agreement; in response the U.S., Japan, South Korea, and the European Union had agreed to suspend fuel oil supplies. It was thought that the plant, in Yongbyon, could produce enough plutonium to make 1 or 2 nuclear weapons each year.

On **Dec. 22** North Korea confirmed reports by the IAEA that the regime had disabled monitors on the Yongbyon reactor and removed monitors from a pond where spent nuclear fuel rods were stored. North Korea **Dec. 23** started reopening a plutonium reprocessing plant. The regime warned the next day of an "uncontrollable catastrophe" if the U.S. failed to agree to negotiations on nuclear-related issues, and on **Dec. 27**, North Korea said it would expel all international nuclear inspectors.

European Union Opens Doors to 10 New Members—At a **Dec. 12-13** summit in Copenhagen, the European Union formally invited 10 nations to join its ranks in 2004. The 10 included the former Soviet republics of Estonia, Latvia, and Lithuania and formerly Communist Czech Republic, Hungary, Poland, Slovakia, and Slovenia, as well as Cyprus and Malta. However, EU leaders **Dec. 13** turned down Turkey's request to set a date for accession talks.

South Korea Elects a New President—Roh Moo Hyun, candidate of the ruling Millennium Democratic Party, was elected president of South Korea **Dec. 19**, succeeding Kim Dae Jung, who was ineligible for another term. Roh had pledged to follow Kim's policy of engagement with North Korea; his opponent, Lee Hoi Chang had favored suspending assistance to North Korea until it showed cooperation on arms control and other issues.

Iran, Russia Sign Accord on Nuclear Plant—Iran and Russia signed an agreement, **Dec. 25**, to complete a nuclear power plant in southern Iran. They also agreed to consider the building of a 2nd plant in Iran. Russia promised to provide fuel for the reactor. The U.S. opposed the accord, arguing that Iran had no need for peaceful uses of nuclear energy because of its large oil and gas reserves.

Chechen Rebels Bomb Government Offices, Kill 52—Chechen militants seeking independence from Russia drove a truck and an off-road vehicle toward pro-Russian Chechen government offices in Grozny, the Chechen capital, **Dec. 27**, setting off 2 bomb blasts. The blasts created a crater more than 12 feet deep and killed at least 52 people.

Kenyans Reject Ruling Party after 4 Decades—The political party of Pres. Daniel Arap Moi, which had led Kenya since independence in 1963, was decisively defeated in the **Dec. 29** presidential election. Moi, president for 24 years, was ineligible to run again under the constitution. His chosen successor, Uhuru Kenyatta, son of the country's first president, got only 20% of the vote, to 63% for opposition party leader Mwai Kibaki. The latter had served Moi as finance minister and vice president before breaking with him; he vowed to fight against corruption and poverty.

3 American Missionaries Slain in Yemen—A lone gunman, thought to be linked to the Yemeni group Islamic Jihad, killed 3 Americans working in a Baptist missionary hospital in Jibla, Yemen, **Dec. 30**; a 4th was shot and seriously injured. The gunman, a university student, was captured at the scene.

General

Cardinal Law, Under Fire, Resigns as Boston Archbishop—Cardinal Bernard Law, in an announcement made at the Vatican **Dec. 13**, resigned as archbishop of Boston. For a year he had been under growing criticism for allegedly protecting priests accused of abusing minors. On **Dec. 3**, personnel documents were released under court order; they revealed that the archdiocese had continued to assign priests to parishes even after multiple accusations of wrongdoing. On **Dec. 9**, 58 priests of the archdiocese released a letter calling on Law to step down, and the lay group Voice of the Faithful voted **Dec. 11** to join in this call. Some 450 plaintiffs were suing the archdiocese, seeking damages of about $100 million. In resigning, Law asked forgiveness from those "who have suffered from my shortcomings and mistakes."

Earlier, on **Dec. 10**, the Roman Catholic diocese of Manchester, NH, reached an agreement with state Atty. Gen. Philip McLaughlin, admitting responsibility for failing to protect children from abusive priests. Under the settlement, an accused priest would be removed from contact with minors and the diocese's compliance with its policies regarding abuse would be reviewed annually by the attorney general's office.

JANUARY 2003

National

Bush Proposes More Tax Cuts—Pres. George W. Bush **Jan. 7** proposed a new tax-cut package of $670 bil over 10 years. A major component was the elimination of the tax on stock dividends; Bush said that change was aimed at abolishing the double taxation of dividends. The president also called for putting into effect in 2003 the tax cuts for individuals approved by Congress in 2001 to take effect in 2006 and 2008. The Urban Institute and the Brookings Institution estimated that under Bush's proposal those whose income was in the top 1% would get 28% of the benefits, while the bottom 60% would get 8%.

Democrats Announce for the Presidency—Four Democrats announced they would run for president in 2004. They joined Sen. John Kerry (MA) and former Gov. Howard Dean (VT), who had already made their intentions known. Sen. John Edwards (NC) said **Jan. 2** that he would run; Rev. Al Sharpton, an African American activist from New York, declared his candidacy **Jan. 3**; Rep. Richard Gephardt (MO), who had been House minority leader until after the 2002 election, entered the contest **Jan. 4** (officially announced **Feb. 19**); and Sen. Joseph Lieberman (CT), Al Gore's running mate in 2000, announced his candidacy **Jan. 13**.

Illinois Governor Spares 171 on Death Row—On **Jan. 10** and **11**, a few days before leaving office, Gov. George Ryan (R) of Illinois spared the lives of 171 convicts sentenced to death. Ryan pardoned 4 whom he said had made false confessions after being beaten by police, cut sentences of 3 others to 40 years, and commuted sentences of the rest to life in prison without parole.

AOL's Founder Resigns, as Losses Mount—Steve Case, founder of America Online, announced **Jan. 12** that he was resigning as AOL chairman. On **Jan. 16**, AOL Time Warner CEO Richard Parsons took over Case's position. On **Jan. 30** AOL Time Warner stated it was writing down the value of AOL by $35 bil and of its cable division $10 bil, bringing the total loss of its assets since the disastrous 2001 merger of AOL and Time Warner to nearly $100 bil. The same day, Ted Turner resigned as vice chairman.

Ridge in Cabinet as First Homeland Security Secretary—The Senate, **Jan. 22**, approved, 94–0, Pres. Bush's nomination of Tom Ridge to be secretary of homeland security. Ridge, a former Pennsylvania governor, had been coordinating the national security effort since the Sept. 2001 attacks, but the cabinet department itself was not approved by Congress until Nov. 2002. Ridge was sworn in **Jan. 24**. On **Jan. 30**, John Snow was confirmed by the Senate as U.S. treasury secretary.

Bush Delivers State of the Union Address—Pres. Bush, **Jan. 28**, delivered the annual State of the Union address to a joint session of Congress. Seeking to address domestic concerns as part of his agenda, he restated his support for a broad new tax-cut package and called for strengthening Medicare and overhauling Social Security. He also called for a $15 bil program over 5 years to combat AIDS in Africa and the Caribbean (approved by Congress in May). He portrayed Iraqi Pres. Saddam Hussein as a tyrant who consistently evaded UN resolutions regarding weapons of mass destruction.

> "We will consult. But let there be no misunderstanding: If Saddam Hussein does not fully disarm, for the safety of our people and for the peace of the world, we will lead a coalition to disarm him."
>
> Pres. Bush, in the State of the Union Address, **Jan. 28, 2003**, on taking military action against Iraq.

International

General Strike Cripples Venezuela—On **Jan. 2**, Pres. Hugo Chavez of Venezuela proposed that other nations help resolve the internal crisis brought on by a devastating month-long general strike. Chavez appealed for international diplomacy to reach an agreement with business and labor leaders and retired military officers who opposed his regime. On **Jan. 3**, 2 were killed and dozens wounded in clashes between pro- and anti-government factions. Trying to help end the impasse, ex-Pres. Jimmy Carter met with Chavez and opposition leaders **Jan. 20**.

Brazil Swears in New President—On **Jan. 1**, Luiz Inacio Lula da Silva, leader of the left-wing Workers Party, was inaugurated as president of Brazil; Da Silva, who was elected by a landslide in Oct. 2002, promised "a new style of government," with a major focus on job creation.

Bombers Kill 22 in Tel Aviv—Two Palestinian suicide bombers killed themselves and 22 others **Jan. 5** in coordinated attacks in Tel Aviv. In retaliation, Israel, **Jan. 6**, barred Palestinian leaders from attending a conference in London. Fighting across Israel claimed the lives of 9 Palestinians and 2 Israelis **Jan. 12**, and 3 Israeli soldiers were shot and killed **Jan. 23** near Hebron. An Israeli attack on Gaza City **Jan. 26** claimed 12 lives.

North Korea Quits NPT—North Korea said **Jan. 10** that it was withdrawing from the 1970 Nuclear Nonproliferation Treaty. Claiming its use of nuclear energy would be peaceful, North Korea said it was acting in self-defense against the U.S., which it accused of hostile intentions. On **Jan. 11**, after 3 days of unofficial meetings with 2 North Korean diplomats, Gov. Bill Richardson (NM), a former U.S. ambassador to the UN, said the North Koreans wanted better relations with the U.S.

As UN Weapons Inspector Cites Iraqi Non-Cooperation, U.S. Amasses Troops in the Region—A major report by Hans Blix, chief UN inspector for chemical and biological weapons, presented **Jan. 27**, accused Iraq of failure to cooperate in accounting for and removing weapons of mass destruction. A more optimistic report the same day, by Mohamed El Baradei, chief inspector for atomic weapons, said his team had as yet found no evidence that Iraq was reviving its nuclear-weapons program. Earlier, on **Jan. 16**, inspectors found 12 empty warheads capable of carrying chemical weapons, and Iraq later said it had discovered 4 more such warheads. Iraq agreed **Jan. 20** to let scientists be interviewed privately by inspectors, but within the country.

Defense Sec. Donald Rumsfeld signed orders **Jan. 10-11** deploying 62,000 troops to the Persian Gulf region; on **Jan. 19** he noted, however, that the Bush administration might allow Hussein to seek a safe haven in another country as a means of avoiding a war. Britain **Jan. 11** deployed an aircraft carrier to the Gulf and said **Jan. 20** that it was sending 26,000 troops to the Gulf. France said **Jan. 20** that it would not support a UN resolution for military action. On **Jan. 30**, leaders of Britain and 7 other European nations, not including France or Germany, joined in an open letter to the *Wall Street Journal* calling on the international community to take a united stand against Iraq.

Israeli Voters Keep Sharon in Power—The Likud Party of Prime Min. Ariel Sharon retained power in parliamentary elections held in Israel **Jan. 28**. Likud emerged with 38 seats in the 120-member Knesset, to only 19 for the Labor Party, its longtime rival, led by Amran Mitzna.

Shoe Bomber Sentenced—U.S. District Court Judge William Young **Jan. 30** sentenced Richard C. Reid to life in prison for attempting to set off a plastic explosives in his shoes on a trans-Atlantic flight in Dec. 2001. Reid had pleaded guilty to the charges against him.

Explosion Kills 18 in Afghanistan—A bomb destroyed a bridge near an army post, killing 18 people on a bus **Jan. 31** in southern Afghanistan outside Kandahar; authorities blamed Taliban and al-Qaeda fugitives.

General

Ohio State Defeats Miami for Football Title—The Ohio State Buckeyes of the Big Ten Conference won the national intercollegiate (NCAA) Division 1–A football title **Jan. 3**, defeating the defending champions, the Miami Hurricanes, 31–24, in 2 overtimes. The game, the Fiesta Bowl, played in Tempe, AZ, matched the nation's only 2 unbeaten teams.

Serena Williams Holds 4 Top Tennis Titles at Once—Serena Williams **Jan. 25** became the 5th player ever to hold all 4 top women's professional tennis titles at the same time.

She did this by defeating her older sister, Venus, in the final of the Australian Open, 7–6 (4), 3–6, 6–4. In 2002, Serena had won the French, U.S., and Wimbledon titles.

Tampa Bay Routs Oakland in Super Bowl—The Tampa Bay Buccaneers claimed their first U.S. pro football title **Jan. 26** when they defeated the Oakland Raiders, 48–21, in Super Bowl XXXVII. The NFL championship game, played in San Diego, matched the winners of the National Conference (Bucs) and American Conference (Raiders). The Raiders quarterback and league MVP, Rich Gannon, threw 5 interceptions, 3 of which were run back for Buc touchdowns. Brad Johnson was the Tampa Bay quarterback.

FEBRUARY 2003

National

Space Shuttle Disintegrates, 7 Astronauts Die—The space shuttle *Columbia* broke apart in space **Feb. 1** over the southwestern U.S. after it had begun its descent toward a planned landing at Cape Canaveral, FL. All 7 crew members were killed. Debris was scattered over a wide area in Texas and Louisiana. The last voice communication from Air Force Col. Rick Husband, the commander, 16 minutes before the scheduled landing, had given no indication of trouble.

This was the 113th U.S. space shuttle mission, and the 2nd to end in tragedy. Flights by the 3 remaining shuttles were suspended. *Columbia* had been launched from the Kennedy Space Center at Cape Canaveral on **Jan. 16**. Its 80 scientific projects included many experiments on the impact of space travel on living organisms. The other 6 crew members were: Navy Cmdr. William McCool, Air Force Lt. Col. Michael Anderson, Navy Capt. David Brown, Navy Cmdr. Laurel Blair Salton Clark, Indian-born engineer Kalpana Chawla, and Israeli Air Force Col. Ilan Ramon—the first astronaut from his country. A memorial service was held at Cape Canaveral **Feb. 10**.

By **Feb. 18**, some 3,700 pieces of debris, including a nose cone and part of the left wing, had been found and taken to Cape Canaveral, still only a small portion of the vehicle. As investigations got underway, several theories were considered, including one that blamed material that had fallen off an external fuel tank after liftoff and struck the left wing.

> "My fellow Americans, this day has brought terrible news and great sadness to our country. At 9:00 A.M. this morning, Mission Control in Houston lost contact with our Space Shuttle Columbia. A short time later, debris was seen falling from the skies above Texas. The Columbia is lost; there are no survivors."
>
> Pres. Bush, addressing the nation about the Columbia explosion, **Feb. 1, 2003**.

Bush Budget Plan Projects Large Deficits—Pres. George W. Bush **Feb. 3** submitted a federal budget for the 2004 fiscal year. It included major new tax cuts and a big increase in defense spending, all previously proposed, and projected a deficit of $307.4 billion; the budget outline covering the next 5 years foresaw total deficits slightly exceeding $1 trillion. The cost of any war with Iraq was not included.

U.S. Raises Warning on Terrorist Attacks—Citing increased level of "chatter" in terrorist communications, the Bush administration **Feb. 7** temporarily raised the national terrorist threat alert level from yellow, for "elevated risk," to orange, or "high risk," the 2nd highest level out of 5. On **Feb. 10**, the Dept. of Homeland Security issued guidelines for preparing for an attack involving chemical, biological, or radiological weapons; the public was urged to keep some basic emergency supplies on hand, be able to seal windows and doors, and prepare a family communication plan. The level was changed back to yellow **Feb. 27**, as administration officials cited a drop in the level of chatter.

Leader of Islamic Charity Pleads Guilty to Fraud—The leader of an Islamic charity based in the U.S. admitted **Feb. 10** that he had illegally diverted donations made for humanitarian purposes to Islamic militants in Chechnya and Bosnia-Herzegovina. Enaam Arnaout entered his guilty plea in U.S. district court in Chicago.

Democratic Field Swells—On **Feb. 18**, two more Democrats, Former Sen. Carol Moseley Braun (IL) and Rep. Dennis Kucinich (OH), said they were forming exploratory committees preparatory to competing for the party's 2004 presidential nomination.

International

Havel Steps Down as Czech President—Vaclav Havel, the playwright who had led the intellectual resistance to Communist rule in Czechoslovakia, concluded his 2nd 5-year term as president of the Czech Republic, **Feb. 2**. He had been president of Czechoslovakia for 3 years before Slovakia split off in 1992. Vaclav Klaus, a former Czech prime minister and old rival of Havel, **Feb. 28**, won the presidency by 2 votes, getting 141 votes out of a possible 281 in voting in a combined session of Parliament.

Debate on a War Against Iraq Intensifies—As U.S. military forces moved into position for a strike against Iraq, a worldwide debate on the merits of war intensified. Sec. of State Colin Powell, addressing the UN Security Council **Feb. 5**, presented the administration's case for UN-endorsed military action. Drawing on intelligence information from a variety of sources, he said that the regime of Pres. Saddam Hussein had removed incriminating evidence from sites and intimidated its scientists in an effort to deceive UN inspectors; he also maintained that there were ties between Iraq and al-Qaeda terrorists and that Iraq harbored its own terrorist cell.

After he spoke, 10 East European countries voiced strong support for the U.S. position, but China, France, and Russia remained opposed to military action at the present. On **Feb. 6**, 3 NATO members—Belgium, France, and Germany—blocked deployment of military equipment to Turkey that the Turks could use in defense against an Iraqi attack.

Sec. of Defense Donald Rumsfeld **Feb. 6** approved deployment of the Army's 101st Airborne Division and the aircraft carrier *Kitty Hawk* to the Persian Gulf region. On **Feb. 9**, after inspectors met with Iraqi officials in Baghdad, Hans Blix, one of the chief inspectors, said Iraq was showing more signs of cooperation. Documents had been provided describing the destruction of anthrax and nerve agent stockpiles, and Iraq **Feb. 10** authorized surveillance overflights by U.S., French, and Russian planes. On **Feb. 13**, UN missile experts revealed that the range of Iraq's al-Samoud 2 rocket exceeded the 150-km (93-mi) limit imposed by the UN; given a deadline to destroy them, Iraq **Feb. 27** agreed to begin doing so.

On **Feb. 15**, millions of people opposing war demonstrated in cities around the world. Police in London and Rome estimated crowds there at 750,000 and 600,000, respectively. At least 200,000 reportedly turned out in Berlin, and at least 100,000 in Paris and New York. At least 150,000 rallied in San Francisco **Feb. 16**. Bush said he was not swayed by protesters and argued that no new UN resolution was needed to authorize an attack; however, the administration pursued efforts to get a second resolution, in apparent deference to British Prime Min. Tony Blair, who sought the resolution as backing.

NATO **Feb. 16** reached agreement on helping Turkey arm itself against a possible Iraqi attack, with assistance going not from NATO directly but through its Defense Planning Council. Meanwhile, Turkey, seeking U.S. financial support as a basis for its participation in the war, **Feb. 19** rejected a $26 billion U.S. aid package as inadequate.

North Korea Continues Its Nuclear Confrontation—North Korea said **Feb. 5** that its nuclear reactor at Yongbyon had resumed operation, but that it would be used only to generate electricity. Deputy Sec. of State Richard Armitage said **Feb. 4** that the administration would talk directly with North Korea after the inauguration of South Korea's new president. The U.S. director of Central Intelligence, George Tenet, said **Feb. 12** that North Korea had an untested ballistic missile that could threaten the western U.S.

Killings Blamed on Colombian Rebels—More than 30 people were killed and many others injured **Feb. 7** when a bomb exploded at a social club in Bogota; the attack was blamed on the country's largest guerrilla group, the Revolutionary Armed Forces of Colombia (FARC). FARC was also blamed in killings that occurred after a U.S.-operated plane reportedly involved in anti-drug activities crashed in southern Colombia **Feb. 13**. It was thought possible that the plane was downed by gunfire; also, a U.S. Defense Dept. contractor and a Colombian army sergeant were found shot to death, and the FARC later reported it had abducted 3 other U.S. contractors. A Colombian Army Black Hawk helicopter searching for guerrillas crashed in the northern Colombian mountains **Feb. 26**, killing all 23 soldiers on board.

New Bin Laden Tape Is Aired; Other Terrorism Developments—In an audiotape played on the Arab TV network Al Jazeera **Feb. 11**, a person claiming to be Osama bin Laden called for suicide attacks against the U.S. and its supporters. At Gatwick Airport, south of London, on **Feb. 13**, police arrested a Venezuelan man arriving from Colombia who was carrying a live hand grenade; he was charged with terrorism offenses **Feb. 17**.

Five judges in a Hamburg, Germany, court **Feb. 19** convicted a Moroccan in the Sept. 11, 2001, attacks on the U.S. The judges found that Mounir el-Motassadeq had assisted a Hamburg terrorist cell that included 3 of the Sept. 11 hijackers. He was found guilty of 3,066 counts of being an accessory to murder, and sentenced to 15 years.

Israeli-Palestinian Violence Continues—Sporadic violence between Israelis and Palestinians continued. A bombing in Gaza **Feb. 15** by the militant group Hamas killed 4 Israeli soldiers inside a tank. An explosion in Gaza City Feb. 16 killed 6 Hamas members. On **Feb. 17**, Israeli tanks demolished the Gaza home of a Hamas leader as soldiers killed 2 Palestinians. Israeli operations in the West Bank and Gaza **Feb. 19** left 12 Palestinians dead. By **Feb. 23**, at least 40 Palestinians had died in the wake of the Hamas bombing.

U.S. Troops to Fight Philippine Muslim Extremists—The Pentagon announced **Feb. 20** that 1,700 American troops would be sent to the Philippines to take on an extremist Muslim group, Abu Sayyaf, operating in the south. About 750 ground troops would participate, supported as needed by about 1,000 Marines on board 2 ships.

Archbishop of Canterbury Installed—In an elaborate ceremony, **Feb. 27**, Most Rev. Rowan Williams was enthroned in Canterbury cathedral, the mother church of Anglican Christianity, as 104th archbishop of Canterbury.

General

Waltrip Wins Rain-Shortened Daytona 500—Michael Waltrip won the Daytona 500 **Feb. 16**, completing 109 laps in a race that was normally 200 but was shortened by rain. Waltrip, driving a Chevrolet, led 68 of the laps.

Snowstorm Smothers Northeastern U.S.—A heavy storm swept through the Northeast **Feb. 16** and **17**, setting records for snow accumulation in many localities. Flooding, exposure, and collapsed buildings contributed to the deaths of 59 people. The heaviest snowfall, 48.5 inches, was reported in Garrett County, MD. Boston's 27.5 inches was a record. Thousands of airline flights were canceled.

21 Die at Chicago Club After Crowd Panics—A rush to the exits at a Chicago social club **Feb. 17** resulted in 21 people being crushed to death. About 50 others were injured. Witnesses said security guards at the 2nd-floor club, E2, had used pepper spray to break up a fight. In the ensuing stampede, the stairwell to the first floor became jammed. Other exits may have been locked or obstructed.

At Least 196 in South Korea Die in Arsonist's Subway Attack—A man reportedly angry at doctors who had treated him for a stroke ignited a fire on a subway train in Taegu, South Korea, **Feb. 18**, causing the deaths of at least 196 people, with many others injured and some listed as missing. Witnesses said he used a cigarette lighter to ignite a carton containing liquid. The arsonist, who survived, was arrested.

289 Killed in Crash of Iranian Military Plane—All 289 aboard an Iranian military transport plane, a Russian-made Ilyushin, were killed **Feb. 19** when it crashed in mountainous terrain in southeastern Iran. The passengers were members of the Islamic Revolutionary Guards.

Fire at Rhode Island Nightclub Kills 100—A fire at a nightclub in West Warwick, RI, **Feb. 20** enveloped and destroyed the building within minutes. The death toll reached 100 and many more were injured. Some 350 people were packed into the nightclub for a concert by the heavy metal band Great White. A pyrotechnic display had released a shower of white sparks which ignited sound-proofing materials near the stage; flames quickly spread.

Quake Kills Hundreds in China—An earthquake measuring 6.8 on the Richter scale flattened thousands of houses and other buildings **Feb. 24** in Xinjiang Uygur Autonomous Region in northwest China. By **Feb. 25** the death toll had reached more than 260, and many survivors were left homeless.

MARCH 2003

National

Senate Ratifies Nuclear Agreement With Russia—The U.S. Senate, **Mar. 6**, approved, 95–0, the Strategic Offensive Reductions Treaty signed in 2002 by Pres. George W. Bush and Pres. Vladimir Putin of Russia. The treaty required the 2 countries to reduce the number of their deployed nuclear warheads to between 1,700 and 2,200 by 2012. Each country now had about 6,000 warheads deployed. Ratification by the Russian parliament was still pending.

Drilling for Oil in Wildlife Refuge Rejected—The Senate **Mar. 19** rejected a proposal supported by the Bush administration to allow drilling for oil in the Alaska National Wildlife Refuge. The refuge was thought to contain huge oil reserves; conservationists argued that drilling would degrade the wilderness environment.

Senate Cuts Bush Tax Cut Plan—The tax-cut proposal put forth by Pres. Bush—the centerpiece of his economic recovery program—lost ground in the Senate, **Mar. 25**. The day before, the administration had said it would ask Congress for $74.7 billion to pay for the war in Iraq, and seek additional funds for foreign aid and domestic security. Concern over these costs won added support for an amendment to the 10-year tax bill, which cut the total package from $726 bil to $350 bil; it passed the Senate in this form, 51–48, with 3 Republicans in the majority.

Top Air Force Academy Officers Fired in Sexual Assault Scandal—The Air Force announced **Mar. 25** that it was replacing the 4 top officers at the U.S. Air Force Academy as a result of allegations by over 50 women cadets and former cadets that they had been raped or assaulted sexually during the past decade. The women claimed the academy had failed to protect them and had in fact investigated those filing complaints. An investigation into the charges was continuing.

U.S. Economy at a Glance: March 2003	
Unemployment rate	5.8%
Consumer prices (12 mo. change)	3.0%
Trade deficit (12 mos. through Mar.)	$449.6 bil.
Dow Jones high (1st quarter: Jan. 14)	8842.62
Dow Jones low (1st quarter: Mar. 11)	7524.06
Dow Jones closing (1st quarter)	7837.86
1st quarter GDP growth (annual rate)	1.4%

War With Iraq

Diplomacy Fails to Prevent Iraq War—Diplomatic efforts to continue UN weapons inspections in Iraq as a means of obtaining compliance with UN resolutions and averting military action proved unsuccessful. One of the chief inspectors, Hans Blix, reported **Mar. 1** that Iraq, while not proven to be in violation of its obligations to divest itself of weapons of mass destruction, had made little effort to assist inspectors. However, as directed by inspectors, Iraq began to destroy an arsenal of over 100 al-Samoud 2 missiles, whose range exceeded the 150-km (93-mi) UN-imposed limit.

Also on **Mar. 1**, Turkey's parliament refused to permit stationing of U.S. troops on its soil; meanwhile, Iraqi dissident groups, meeting in Kurdish-controlled northern Iraq, called for a transition to a parliamentary system of government.

Blix said **Mar. 5** that he wanted more time for inspections. France, Russia, and Germany indicated the same day that they would oppose a draft resolution submitted to the UN Security Council by the U.S., Britain, and Spain declaring that Iraq had missed its last chance to disarm peacefully. China, **Mar. 6,** also called for more time. Sec. of State Colin Powell said the U.S. could lead a coalition of willing nations that would disarm Iraq with or without UN authority.

The 3 sponsors of the draft resolution proposed a compromise **Mar. 7,** setting a **Mar. 17** deadline for Iraq to demonstrate cooperation in disarming, but France indicated it would veto any such resolution. Pres. George W. Bush, Prime Min. Tony Blair of Great Britain, and Prem. Jose Maria Aznar of Spain met in the Azores **Mar. 16** and declared that their diplomatic efforts to avert war would end the next day. On **Mar. 17,** when it was apparent that the Security Council would not approve their resolution, the 3 cosponsors withdrew it, and Bush warned that Pres. Saddam Hussein and his sons must leave Iraq within 48 hours, an ultimatum Hussein rejected. UN Sec. Gen. Kofi Annan **Mar. 17** ordered all UN personnel, including weapons inspectors, to evacuate Iraq.

The U.S. State Dept. **Mar. 18** listed 30 countries as members of a "coalition of the willing" supporting military intervention, and indicated that 15 other countries were supporting the effort but had asked not to be named. Only 3 countries in the coalition, the U.S., Britain, and Australia, were known to be providing troops. Canada had announced **Mar. 17** that it would not participate in the war. Turkey's parliament **Mar. 20** agreed to allow U.S. planes to cross Turkish airspace; the parliament also approved deployment of new Turkish troops in N. Iraq, but the U.S. and Britain were opposed to such a move.

U.S. and British Forces Invade Iraq—The U.S.-led military offensive aimed at ousting the regime of Saddam Hussein in Iraq got underway **Mar. 19.** The first strike occurred after dark, when about 40 Tomahawk cruise missiles descended on targets in Baghdad, in response to intelligence information that Hussein was at a meeting with other top leaders at a private house over a bunker in the southern part of the city. U.S. aircraft also took part in the raid. Iraq fired 3 missiles at U.S. bases in Kuwait; one landed harmlessly near a U.S. Marine camp, and 2 were knocked down by U.S. Patriot missiles. In a televised address, Pres. Bush announced the onset of the military campaign, named Operation Iraqi Freedom.

In early ground combat, units of the U.S. Army's 3rd Infantry Division and Marine 1st Expeditionary Force entered Iraq after dark **Mar. 20.** The division moved north toward Baghdad, while U.S. and British marines turned northeast toward Basra, Iraq's 2nd-largest city. In an aerial bombardment, part of what the Pentagon dubbed its "shock and awe" campaign, some 1,300 missiles and bombs rained down on military targets in Baghdad after dark on **Mar. 21.** The bombardment, which continued in succeeding days, was captured on live TV, as news channels followed the war on a continuing basis, aided by reports from "embedded" journalists traveling with troops. U.S. forces **Mar. 21** seized major oil fields near Basra.

A U.S. supply vehicle made a wrong turn in Nasiriyah **Mar. 22;** 7 Americans were believed ambushed and killed, and 5, including a woman, were captured. It was thought that some U.S. soldiers may have been executed after having been captured alive. The next day, 9 U.S. marines were killed in Nasiriyah, and Marines found 3,000 chemical warfare suits and masks at a hospital there. Hussein, appearing on Iraqi TV **Mar. 24** (whether live or on tape was uncertain), appealed to Iraqis to hold firm against the coalition. The Iraqis also shot down an Apache helicopter that day and captured 2 U.S. pilots, who were shown on Iraqi TV.

U.S. Troops Near Baghdad, British Take Umm Qasr, Special Forces in N. Iraq—Third Infantry soldiers were within 50 miles of Baghdad by **Mar. 24,** but a sandstorm impeded progress **Mar. 25-26.** Bombing of targets in the city and Republican Guard units defending it intensified, but there was

no assault on the city in late Mar. The 7th Cavalry reportedly killed Iraqis near Najaf, another city leading to Baghdad, **Mar. 25-26.** The Pentagon reported **Mar. 26** that 4,000 Iraqis had been taken prisoner.

British forces said **Mar. 25** that they had captured the Gulf port city of Umm Qasr, but Basra, nearby, had not fallen; its million residents were reported in desperate need of water; by the end of March aid workers had partially restored water supplies.

More than 1,000 members of the U.S. 173rd Airborne Brigade parachuted into northern Iraq **Mar. 26,** seeking to unite with anti-Hussein Kurds, who maintained a semiautonomous status there. The U.S. presence was apparently also designed to discourage Turkey from sending troops in to stem Kurdish nationalism. Kurds and U.S. special forces **Mar. 28** wrested a number of villages from the control of a militant Islamic group, Ansar al-Islam, reportedly linked to al-Qaeda.

Casualties Reported, Resistance Sometimes Heavy—The number of Iraqi military and civilian casualties was difficult to determine. According to figures reported **Apr. 1,** the U.S. by then had 46 soldiers dead, 7 captured, and 16 missing, while the British had 27 dead, and none missing or captured. Some coalition deaths were due to accidents, friendly fire, or other causes not attributable to enemy fire. Eight British soldiers and 4 U.S. marines died **Mar. 21** in a helicopter crash in Kuwait. Six British soldiers and one U.S. serviceman died **Mar. 22** when 2 copters collided. A U.S. missile **Mar. 23** mistakenly shot down a British fighter jet, killing the 2-man crew. A U.S. soldier was arrested **Mar. 23** after he allegedly threw grenades into 3 U.S. officers' tents in Kuwait; 14 soldiers were wounded, 2 fatally. Among civilian casualties, an American bomb **Mar. 24** hit a bus carrying mostly Syrians out of Iraq, killing 5 and wounding 10. Another bomb or missile, possibly of U.S. origin, killed 17 or more civilians in Baghdad, **Mar. 26.** And a blast in a Baghdad market **Mar. 28** killed more than 50 civilians, according to claims by Iraqi officials. Coalition forces stated that they did not target civilians and were largely successful in minimizing civilian casualties through precision bombing.

Scattered Iraqi resistance, particularly by "fedayeen" paramilitary forces, was heavy at times, and stretched-out supply lines came under frequent attacks, leading to what some observers characterized as delays in the progress of coalition forces toward entering Baghdad. Iraq introduced a new tactic **Mar. 29:** A suicide bomber blew up his taxi and killed 4 U.S. soldiers near Najaf. On **Mar. 30** an Iraqi spokesman said that 4,000 volunteers from 23 countries were ready to carry out suicide attacks. U.S. and British officials complained that Iraqi forces were resorting to tactics that violated military codes of conduct, such as disguising themselves in civilian clothes, pretending to surrender and then fighting, forcing civilians to act as human shields, and threatening them with death to prevent them from welcoming or cooperating with coalition forces.

Britain and U.S. Win Increased Domestic Support for War; Opinion Elsewhere More Negative—Polls taken shortly after war began showed a narrow majority of British supporting it. U.S. support was also increasing; for example, a *Newsweek* poll published **Mar. 29** found that 74% of Americans thought the Bush administration had a well-thought-out military plan; his job approval rating also climbed 15 points, to 68%. However, polls in many other countries showed large majorities opposed to the war, and there were anti-war demonstrations in major cities in the U.S., Britain, and around the world.

Prime Min. Tony Blair had won parliamentary support for British participation in the war, **Mar. 18,** when the House of Commons voted 412–149 to use "all means necessary" against Hussein. Clare Short, cabinet secretary for international development, who on **Mar. 9** had threatened to resign if Britain invaded Iraq without a 2nd UN resolution authorizing force, decided to stay on, but Robin Cook, leader of Commons, resigned **Mar. 17.**

International

Mastermind of Sept. 11 Attacks Seized in Pakistan—On **Mar. 1,** Pakistani counter-terrorism officials seized Khalid Sheikh Mohammed, believed to be the 3rd-ranking member of al-Qaeda and principal planner of the Sept. 11, 2001, terror attacks on the U.S. The U.S. had indicted him in 1995 in connection with a failed plot to bomb up to 12 airplanes over the Pacific Ocean. Also arrested were 2 others, one of whom allegedly had wired money from the United Arab Emirates to the Sept. 11 hijackers.

Tensions With North Korea Remain High—Four North Korean fighter planes **Mar. 2** intercepted a U.S. surveillance plane over the Sea of Japan, in international waters. The North Koreans followed the U.S. plane for 22 minutes, approaching as close as 50 feet, before returning home. On **Mar. 5,** a number of Democratic Party leaders, including former Sec. of State Madeleine Albright and former Defense Sec. William Perry, urged the administration to negotiate directly with North Korea, which it appeared reluctant to do. On **Mar. 10,** North Korea test-fired a 2nd ground-to-ship missile over the Sea of Japan.

Bombings in Philippines Blamed on Terrorists—Two bombings on the Philippines island of Mindanao **Mar. 4** were blamed on Islamic separatists. One explosion killed 21, including an American Baptist missionary, and injured 150; a 2nd explosion killed 1 person and injured 3. The Philippine military said **Mar. 14** that it had killed almost 200 separatist militants in 3 days of fighting on Mindanao.

Palestinians Name a Prime Minister—The Palestinian Legislative Council **Mar. 10** created the position of prime minister, and gave the office control over internal affairs. However, peace talks with Israel remained under control of Palestinian leader Yasir Arafat. Arafat had already announced **Mar. 6** that he would appoint his ally Mahmoud Abbas to the new post.

On **Mar. 5,** a Palestinian suicide bomber killed himself and 16 others on a bus in Haifa. The next day 11 Palestinians died and more than 100 were wounded in an Israeli attack on a refugee camp; the Israelis were seeking a Hamas leader and fighting broke out. The Israelis, firing from 2 helicopters, killed a Hamas leader and 3 bodyguards in a vehicle **Mar. 8,** and Israeli raids on Islamic Jihad militants and other targets in the West Bank **Mar. 13-14** took the lives of 10 Palestinians. On **Mar. 16,** an Israeli army bulldozer ran over and killed an American woman who had sought to prevent it from destroying a Palestinian home. A Palestinian suicide bomber **Mar. 30** killed himself and wounded 3 dozen others in an attack outside a café in Netanya.

Premier of Serbia Assassinated—Prem. Zoran Djindjic of Serbia died **Mar. 12** after being shot by assassins. Serbian leaders blamed the Zemun clan, an organized crime group. Its leader, Milorad Lukovic, had been angered by the premier's cooperation with the UN war crimes tribunal and his support for government reforms. Police **Mar. 13** reported that 40 arrests had been made. On **Mar. 18,** the Serbian parliament approved Zoran Zivkovic as Djindjic's successor.

Côte d'Ivoire Installs New Premier—Côte d'Ivoire, torn by civil war for 6 months, got a new premier, Seydou Diarra, **Mar. 10,** under a French-brokered peace accord for sharing power among government, opposition parties, and 3 rebel factions. Some 3,000 people had died during the civil war.

Turkey Gets New Premier at Critical Moment—Amid controversy over Turkey's role in the prospective war in Iraq, the country got a new premier. Recep Tayyip Erdogan, chairman of the ruling party, was chosen by parliament **Mar. 14** to succeed Abdullah Gul. Erdogan's party had won the November 2002 election, but he became eligible for the premiership only after a constitutional change allowed him to run for a seat in parliament, which he won.

General

Kidnapped Girl Found Alive in UT—Elizabeth Smart, 15, who had been abducted from her home in Salt Lake City, UT, in June 2002, was found alive on **Mar. 12.** She was in the custody of Brian Mitchell, a panhandler and self-described prophet, and his wife, Wanda Barzee, in the nearby town of Sandy. Mitchell had worked for one day at the Smart home in November 2001. A polygamist, he had been excommunicated from the Church of Jesus Christ of Latter-day Saints. The girl's rescue, following reports from people who had seen Mitchell linked to the abduction in a television report, raised question about police competence. On **Mar. 18,** charges were filed against Mitchell and Barzee.

> "It is nothing but a miracle. I just held her, held her all the way home."
>
> Ed Smart, whose 15-year-old daughter Elizabeth was found alive **Mar. 12, 2003,** after being kidnapped 9 months earlier.

Mysterious Illness Seen as Threat—A strange new illness that caused pneumonia-like symptoms became a cause for alarm. On **Mar. 15,** the World Health Organization issued an alert on what it called severe acute respiratory syndrome (SARS), which had spread from Asia to Europe and North America. By **Mar. 27,** 1,408 people in 14 countries had been stricken, and 53 had died, including at least 34 in China. The condition, characterized by high fever, dry cough, and difficult breathing, was thought to spread by sneezes and coughs.

Antiabortion Activist Found Guilty of Murder—James Kopp, an opponent of abortion, was found guilty by an Erie County (NY) judge of 2nd-degree murder **Mar. 18** in the shooting death of Dr. Barnett Slepian in 1998. Admitting the crime in 2002, Kopp claimed he had sought only to wound Slepian in order to prevent him from carrying out abortions. He had waived a jury trial.

Chicago **Named Best Movie of 2002—***Chicago,* a rousing musical set in the 1920s, was named **Mar. 23** as the best film of 2002 by the Academy of Motion Picture Arts and Sciences. The academy's annual awards ceremony in Hollywood was less flamboyant than usual because of the onset of the war against Iraq. In all, *Chicago* won 6 Oscars. Adrien Brody was named best actor for *The Pianist,* and Nicole Kidman best actress for *The Hours.* Roman Polanski was voted best director for *The Pianist.*

APRIL 2003

National

Senate, House at Odds Over Tax Cut—Disagreement among Republican leaders in the Senate and House added to the uncertainty over Pres. George W. Bush's tax-cut proposal. On **Apr. 10,** just before a Senate vote, Sen. Charles Grassley (R, IA) announced a compromise with 2 Republican senators who opposed the $726 bil cut Bush favored. The $350 bil compromise figure narrowly survived the budget-resolution vote, with Vice Pres. Richard Cheney breaking a tie for a 51–50 margin. Two Republicans voted against it. The same day, the House approved a budget resolution, 216-211, that provided for a $550 bil tax cut. Bush said **Apr. 15** that at least a $550 bil cut was essential to stimulate the economy.

Amber Alert Bill Signed—Pres. Bush **Apr. 30** signed so-called Amber Alert legislation, initiating a nationwide system aimed at promptly informing the public of child abductions over radio, TV, and electronic highway signs. The law, part of a package of child safety measures passed by Congress, was named after Amber Hagerman, a nine-year-old Texas child kidnapped and murdered in 1996.

War and Reconstruction in Iraq

U.S.-Led Coalition Routs Hussein's Iraqi Regime—The U.S.-led military coalition, consisting mainly of U.S. and British forces, crushed the armed forces of Iraq in fighting that lasted less than a month, with relatively few coalition casualties. After delays caused in part by sandstorms and thinly stretched supply lines, American forces were pressing toward Baghdad by the beginning of April. The U.S. Army's 3rd Infantry Division attacked the Republican Guard's Medina division north of Karbala and within 50 miles of Baghdad, **Apr. 1,** while the U.S. 1st Marine Division attacked the Baghdad division 70 miles southeast of the capital. Both were within 30 miles of Baghdad **Apr. 2.** Air assaults had reportedly reduced the divisions defending Baghdad by at least 50% by **Apr. 2**. Iraqi ground fire downed a U.S. Black Hawk helicopter **Apr. 2**, killing 7 crew members.

On **Apr. 3**, U.S. Marines, meeting some resistance, crossed the Tigris River and moved to within 25 miles of Baghdad. Most of Baghdad lost electrical power. U.S. forces encircled the city **Apr. 4** and gained control of the major airport. Iraqi TV broadcast 2 tapes of Pres. Saddam Hussein **Apr. 4**, but the dates the tapes were made were unclear. Iraqi troop losses were put at 2,000-3,000 **Apr. 5**, as the 3rd Infantry moved through southwest Baghdad; it reached the city center. A U.S. plane bombed a building in the Mansur neighborhood that day, after a report that Hussein and his 2 sons might be there. By **Apr. 8**, major government buildings had been occupied. Organized resistance melted away.

Two journalists were killed and 3 wounded **Apr. 8** when a U.S. tank fired at the Palestine Hotel in Baghdad; U.S. officials said the forces were responding to enemy fire. A U.S. attack that same day hit the Baghdad offices of the Arabic-language television network Al Jazeera, near the Iraqi Information Ministry, killing another journalist. After being stalled for weeks, British forces moved into Basra, in the south, on **Apr. 6**. By **Apr. 7**, organized Iraqi resistance had been wiped out.

Three U.S. soldiers were killed at a highway checkpoint **Apr. 4** when 2 Iraqi women set off a car bomb in a suicide attack. Meanwhile, on **Apr. 1**, U.S. forces announced the rescue from an Iraqi hospital of injured Army Pfc. Jessica Lynch, one of a group of soldiers from the 50th Maintenance Company who had been ambushed near Nasiriyah **Mar. 22**. U.S. officials said that some human remains found when Lynch was rescued were apparently those of soldiers in the same convoy. On **Apr. 13**, five other members of that unit, along with two U.S. soldiers from an Apache helicopter downed **Mar. 24**, were found alive by U.S. troops north of Baghdad after being abandoned by their captors.

On the northern front, Turkey **Apr. 2** agreed to let the U.S. transport food and nonmilitary supplies through its territory. In a friendly fire accident **Apr. 6**, U.S. planes bombed a convoy of U.S. and Kurdish troops, killing 18 Kurds. On **Apr. 10**, Kurdish fighters captured Kirkuk, a major city near the northern oil fields. Turkish leaders expressed concern about Kurdish advances near the oil fields. U.S. and U.S. Special Forces took Mosul, Iraq's 3rd-largest city, **Apr. 11**. Marines captured Tikrit, hometown of Pres. Saddam Hussein, **Apr. 14**, and U.S. military officials declared that the principal fighting was over.

> "It's a little sobering. When you're training for this, you joke about it, you can't wait for the real thing. Then when you see it, when you see the real thing, you never want to see it again."
>
> U.S. Marine Capt. *Sal Aguilar*, in a field in Baghdad surrounded by dead Iraqi people, **April 2003**.

As War Ebbs, Looting Spreads, Reconstruction Begins—With the collapse of the Hussein regime, chaos was widespread in major cities; electrical power and other services were disrupted, and there were shortages of water and medical supplies. The U.S. **Apr. 6** flew Ahmed Chalabi, leader of the Iraqi National Congress (a London-based organization of anti-Hussein groups) and 500-700 Iraqi fighters to southern Iraq. The postwar mood was generally exuberant, as when Iraqis, helped by Americans, toppled a 20-ft statue of Hussein in Baghdad's Firdos Square, **Apr. 9**.

Looting became widespread, with Hussein's palaces and government buildings prime targets. Raids on hospitals added to the medical crisis. In Baghdad, the National Museum of Antiquities lost valuable artifacts, some dating back to the dawn of civilization. In Najaf, an Iraqi mob stormed a mosque **Apr. 10** and killed 2 Shiite clerics. After the Kurds captured Kirkuk, there was looting directed mainly at non-Kurdish ethnic groups, and some Baath party members were victims of revenge killings. U.S. Marines and Iraqi policemen began joint security patrols in Baghdad **Apr. 14**.

Lt. Gen. Jay Garner (ret.), head of the Office of Reconstruction and Humanitarian Assistance, arrived in Baghdad **Apr. 14**, to head reconstruction and transition efforts. He

met **Apr. 15** with Iraqi leaders. Quietly entering Baghdad **Apr. 21**, he pledged to restore essential services.

Hundreds of thousands of Shiites journeyed to Karbala **Apr. 22-23** to participate in an annual Shiite religious observation banned under Hussein; many participants called for Americans to leave Iraq. On **Apr. 27**, U.S. forces arrested Muhammad Mohsen Zobeidi, who had proclaimed himself mayor of Baghdad.

About 300 Iraqis met in Baghdad **Apr. 28** under the sponsorship of the U.S. and Britain and decided to call a national conference within a month that would choose a transitional government.

No WMDs Are Found in Iraq So Far—The belief by the Bush administration and others that the Hussein regime had weapons of mass destruction was the primary stated justification for the invasion of Iraq. As fighting subsided, reports were being investigated, but no verified WMDs had been found as of the end of April. Suspicious materials in drums at a military training site near were found to be, **Apr. 9**, chemicals used in pesticides. After denying that Iraq had any WMDs, Gen. Amir al-Saadi, the regime's top science adviser, turned himself in to U.S. forces **Apr. 12**.

Many Top Aides to Hussein Are Captured—U.S. military officials **Apr. 11** listed 55 figures prominent in the Hussein regime who were being sought. Each was identified as a card in a deck, with Hussein being the ace of spades. His whereabouts remained unknown.

One who was not on the list, Mohammed Abul Abbas, a Palestinian known as Abu Abbas, was arrested **Apr. 15**. An Italian court had convicted him in absentia in 1986 for his leading role in the 1985 hijacking of the *Achille Lauro* cruise ship, during which a U.S. citizen was killed.

On **Apr. 17**, U.S. special forces captured Hussein's half brother, Barzan Ibrahim al-Tikriti, a former intelligence chief and one of the 55. Another, Hikmat Mizban Ibrahim al-Azzawi, a former finance minister, was arrested **Apr. 18**. Emad Husayn Abdullah al-Ani, who had helped develop a lethal nerve agent in the 1980s, turned himself that day. By **Apr. 23**, 11 of the 55 were in custody. Tariq Aziz, the regime's deputy foreign minister and a veteran diplomat, surrendered to U.S. forces **Apr. 24**.

U.S. Leaders Warn Syria, Iran—Pres. Bush said **Apr. 13** that Syria had chemical weapons and was accepting Iraqi leaders. On **Apr. 14**, Sec. of State Powell said the U.S. would consider "measures of a diplomatic, economic, or other nature" to deal with Syria. Defense Sec. Donald Rumsfeld said the same day that some Iraqi leaders had been allowed to enter Syria, and warned Syria not to harbor them. Syria claimed **Apr. 14** that it did not have weapons of mass destruction and said it would not allow WMDs or Iraqi leaders into Syria from Iraq. Rumsfeld said **Apr. 15** that the U.S. was shutting down an Iraq-to-Syria oil pipeline that violated UN sanctions. The Bush administration said it had warned Iran not to interfere with efforts to form a government in Iraq; some Iranians were reportedly crossing into Iraq to agitate for an Islamic state.

Shootings at Anti-U.S. Rallies Fuel Tensions—Iraqis said that 15 people died, and about 65 were wounded, after U.S. soldiers opened fire on a crowd holding an anti-U.S. demonstration **Apr. 28** in Falluja. U.S. officials said the soldiers were responding to gunfire from the crowd; Iraqis at the scene disputed this. In another disputed incident there **Apr. 30**, U.S. troops fired into an anti-U.S. crowd; Iraqis claimed two people were shot dead. Earlier, on **Apr. 15-16**, U.S. forces had shot Iraqis in protesting crowds in Mosul; estimates of deaths ranged from 10 to 17; again, U.S. soldiers said they had responded to fire.

International

Killings Reported in Congolese Villages—Based on reports by witnesses, UN officials said **Apr. 6** that at least 966 people had been killed **Apr. 3** in a dozen Congolese villages in an area rich with minerals. The attacking force was unknown; various factions had been fighting in the region. The UN estimate of dead was later lowered to 150-350.

Bin Laden Purportedly Calls for "Martyrdom"—The Associated Press **Apr. 7** received a taped message reportedly by terrorist leader Osama bin Laden. The speaker called on his Islamic supporters to seek martyrdom through suicide attacks on Americans and Britons.

Israel Attacks Kills Hamas Leader—Missiles from Israeli helicopter gunships killed Said Al-din al-Arabid, a local leader of the militant Hamas group, in Gaza City **Apr. 8.** The strike killed at least 5 other Palestinians and wounded at least 47. Other Israeli military actions on **Apr. 3** and **Apr. 19** resulted in a total of 13 Palestinian deaths.

North Korea Exits Nuclear Nonproliferation Treaty—Making good on its January announcement, North Korea **Apr. 10** formally withdrew from the Nuclear Nonproliferation Treaty. It became the first signatory to withdraw from the treaty. U.S. and North Korean officials met in Beijing, **Apr. 23** to discuss the status of North Korea's weapons program. On **Apr. 24,** the North Koreans said they had nuclear weapons and had begun making bomb-grade plutonium. The talks broke off **Apr. 25.**

Nigeria's President Reelected—Olusegun Obasanjo, president of Nigeria, Africa's most populous country, was reelected **Apr. 19,** with a reported 62% of the vote. His nearest challenger charged fraud, and gunfights between factions erupted in one city. International monitors expressed concern **Apr. 21** about fraud and intimidation in some parts of Nigeria.

New Palestinian Cabinet and Prime Minister Are Chosen; Road Map Conveyed—After a 10-day stalemate, Palestinian leader Yasir Arafat and his choice for prime minister, Mahmoud Abbas, reached agreement **Apr. 23** on the makeup of a new cabinet. It included several Arafat loyalists. On **Apr. 29** the Palestinian parliament voted to approve the new prime minister and government, a key step in moving toward a U.S.-backed peace plan. Early on **Apr. 30,** a Palestinian suicide bomber killed himself and three others outside a pub in Tel Aviv; over 50 were wounded. Despite the incident, the peace process reached a new stage the same day, as the peace plan, aiming to establish Palestinian statehood by 2005, was presented to the Israelis and Palestinians. The so-called road map, drawn up in collaboration with the European Union, Russia, and the UN, laid out conditions Israelis and Palestinians must meet to form a future Palestinian state.

U.S. Sets Military Withdrawal from Saudi Arabia—U.S. officials said **Apr. 29** that the U.S. military presence in Saudi Arabia would be virtually eliminated in the next few months, with all combat troops withdrawn. Some 400-500 U.S. soldiers would remain for training purposes.

Suspected al-Qaeda Terrorists Captured—Pakistani authorities **Apr. 30** announced the arrests of six suspected al-Qaeda members, including Whalid ba Attash, also known as Tawfiq bin Attash or Khallad, claimed to have been a key figure behind the 2000 bombing of the USS *Cole* and the Sept. 11, 2001, attacks on the U.S.

General

SARS Continues to Spread—Initial efforts to contain the newly identified ailment known as severe acute respiratory syndrome (SARS) were unsuccessful. In Hong Kong, **Apr. 1,** authorities evacuated 240 residents of a housing complex where 213 people had developed flu-like symptoms resembling those of SARS. Schools were closed in Hong Kong, where many people were wearing masks. The World Health Organization, **Apr. 2,** advised travelers to stay away from Hong Kong and China's Guangdong province, where the ailment had apparently originated. Chinese Health Min. Zhang Wenkang claimed **Apr. 3** that SARS in China was essentially under control. The government admitted **Apr. 20** that it had substantially understated its total of SARS cases. The disease's death rate was a subject of debate, with estimates ranging from 3% up to 15%. Canada reported 97 likely cases, including 10 deaths, mostly in or near Toronto. In a move that angered Canadian officials, the WHO **Apr. 23** added Toronto to a list of places travelers should avoid; the advisory was rescinded a week later. Reported cases in Beijing rose rapidly late in the month to 1,199 by **Apr. 28.** Thousands of people rioted in Chagugang

that day after a report spread that a building there would become a ward for patients.

Syracuse Wins NCAA Basketball Title—Syracuse won the NCAA men's basketball championship **Apr. 7,** defeating Kansas, 81–78, in New Orleans. The Orangemen, en route to their first title, had knocked off 2 of the 4 No. 1 regional seeds, Oklahoma and Texas. Syracuse freshman Carmelo Anthony, who led tournament scoring with 121 points, including 20 in the final game, was named the most outstanding player in the Final Four.

The women's basketball title went to Connecticut, which defeated Tennessee, 73–68, in Atlanta **Apr. 9.** The winners' Diana Taurasi was the national women's player of the year.

Canadian Wins Masters Title—Mike Weir won a one-hole playoff with Len Mattiace to take the Masters golf tournament in Augusta, GA, **Apr. 13.** Both had finished regulation play at 281, 7 under par. Tiger Woods, seeking his 3rd straight Masters title, finished at 290. Weir was the first Canadian to win any of golf's 4 major tournaments.

Martha Burk, chair of the National Council of Women's Organizations, had sought without success to get the Augusta National Golf Club to admit women members. She and 40 supporters protested near the front gate of the course **Apr. 12.** Burk had also brought pressure on sponsors; the Club gave them up, and the tournament was telecast without commercials.

MAY 2003

National

Court Rules on Campaign Finance Law—A 3-judge panel of a U.S. Court of Appeals in Washington, DC, **May 2,** struck down parts of the campaign finance reform law approved by Congress in 2002. The judges eased the ban on so-called soft money, saying it could be raised for party-building efforts such as registering voters, though it still could not be used by groups indirectly attacking or endorsing candidates. Both sides planned appeals.

Democrats Debate Issues—Nine Democrats seeking their party's nomination for president in 2004 debated in Columbia, SC, **May 3.** U.S. Rep. Richard Gephardt (MO) proposed scrapping Pres. George W. Bush's tax cuts and using the money to finance tax credits to help companies pay for employee health insurance. Other candidates, including Sen. Joseph Lieberman (CT), dismissed this proposal as too much big spending. Sen. John Kerry (MA) criticized former Gov. Howard Dean (VT) for his opposition to the war in Iraq. Sen. Bob Graham (FL), who had already been campaigning, formally declared his candidacy **May 6.**

Pres. Bush formally filed re-election papers **May 16.**

Democrats Flee Texas to Kill Redistricting Bill—More than 50 Democrats in the Texas House crossed the boundary into Oklahoma **May 11-12** to leave the House without a quorum and thus prevent action on a redistricting bill unfavorable to their party.

Heat Kills 19 Packed Into Truck—Nineteen among 70-100 people packed into a truck operated by smugglers of illegal aliens were found dead from the heat, or died later, after sheriff's deputies, **May 14,** opened the door of the truck, parked outside Victoria, TX; the occupants included illegals from Mexico, Guatemala, and El Salvador. The driver and 3 others were charged the next day with conspiracy to smuggle, transport, and conceal undocumented immigrants.

Congress Approves Tax Cut Measure—Congress completed action on the tax-reduction bill supported by Pres. Bush, though with major modifications. Bush had called for $726 bil in cuts; the final total, approved by a Senate-House conference committee **May 21,** provided just $318 bil over 10 years, though the reduction was partly from earlier phase-outs of tax cuts that might eventually be renewed. The House (231-200) and Senate (51-50 on Vice Pres. Dick Cheney's tie-breaking vote) approved the conference report **May 23;** it was signed **May 28.** The law lowered tax rates for capital gains and dividends to 15% for most taxpayers, but only for 5 years. It immediately reduced tax rates for upper- and middle-income taxpayers. For the next 2 years, it gave a tax break to married couples and increased the tax credit for children. Critics complained that millions of low-income people would not benefit from the new cuts.

In other economic news, the U.S. dollar was declining sharply against major world currencies, and reports from the Dept. of Labor, **May 15-16**, showed a decline in wholesale and consumer prices, raising speculation that the economy could possibly enter a rare period of deflation.

Whitman Resigns as EPA Administrator—Former NJ Gov. Christine Todd Whitman, head of the Environmental Protection Agency, announced **May 21** that she would resign in June. More of an environmentalist than other members of the administration, she had enjoyed mixed success in promoting her agenda.

Judges Void $145 Bil Award to Smokers—A 3-judge panel of a Florida district court **May 21** threw out a record $145 bil punitive damage award against cigarette manufacturers by a jury in 2000. The judges ruled that the trial judge should not have allowed an estimated 300,000 smokers to file a class-action suit.

Microsoft, AOL Time Warner Reach Pact—Under a legal settlement agreed **May 29**, Microsoft would pay AOL Time Warner $750 mil to end a private antitrust suit brought by Netscape (a unit of AOL). Microsoft also would give AOL access to some of its key software. The accord, described as ending a long-running war between the giant companies, called for cooperation on new technology and joint efforts against electronic piracy.

Stock Market Continues Rise—The Dow Jones Industrial Average closed at 8850 points on **May 30**, the last trading day in May, up 4.4% since May 1. The end of the Iraq war and good prospects for some companies had helped buoy the stock market to its 3rd straight month of gains.

Bush Trip Begins—Pres. Bush visited Poland, **May 31**, in the first leg of a European and Mideast trip aimed at improving relations with Europe and promoting a "road map" toward Palestinian-Israeli peace.

International

Bush Declares End to Combat in Iraq—Pres. George W. Bush, speaking from the deck of the aircraft carrier *Abraham Lincoln*, declared **May 1** that combat operations had ended in Iraq. He called the "liberation of Iraq . . . a crucial advance in the campaign against terror." Bush, sharing the piloting responsibilities, had flown in a Navy jet to the carrier, off the coast of California.

> *"Major combat operations in Iraq have ended. In the battle of Iraq, the United States and our allies have prevailed."*
>
> Pres. Bush, on the USS *Abraham Lincoln*, **May 1, 2003**.

As of **Apr. 30**, U.S. forces had suffered a reported 138 deaths in the Iraq conflict, and British troops had 32 dead. The U.S. total included 23 deaths not due to hostilities. A total of 548 U.S. soldiers were wounded in action. U.S. and British officials did not attempt to estimate Iraqi casualties. As reported later, on **June 11**, the Associated Press conducted a survey of hospitals in Iraq and concluded that, counting only recorded deaths in hospitals and only cases that could be adequately documented, at least 3,249 civilians in Iraq died from war-related causes between the onset of the war and Apr. 20, when fighting was dying down.

As the search for weapons of mass destruction in Iraq continued, U.S. officials said **May 6** that a tractor-trailer found in northern Iraq in April might have been used as a mobile lab for chemical or biological weapons. Officials said **May 12** that they had custody of Rihab Rashjid Taha, a microbiologist nicknamed Dr. Germ who had played a major role in Iraq's biological weapons program; the chief of staff of Iraq's army was also in custody as of **May 13**. On **May 28**, Bush administration officials concluded that 2 tractor-trailer units, including one found in April, were designed to produce deadly biological weapons, but there was no evidence that they had been used for that purpose.

As civil disorder continued in Iraq, Pres. Bush **May 6**, in an apparent shakeup, named L. Paul Bremer III, a retired diplomat, as his envoy in Iraq, with authority over the chief

figure in the reconstruction, Lt. Gen. Jay Garner (ret.). Gen. Tommy Franks, U.S. military commander in Iraq, said **May 11** that the former ruling Baath Party had been dissolved, and on **May 16** Bremer banned 15,000 to 30,000 senior Baath leaders from holding government jobs. Some 10,000 Shiite Muslims demonstrated in Baghdad May 19 against the U.S presence.

In northern Iraq, clashes between Kurds and Arabs began **May 15** and continued several days; 9 people were killed in Kirkuk.

A UN Security Council resolution, adopted 14-0 **May 22**, lifted sanctions imposed on Iraq after the 1991 Gulf War. It put the U.S. and Britain in control of Iraq "until an internationally recognized representative government is established." They would administer the sale of oil and the disbursement of oil income to rebuild the nation.

Sec. of State Colin Powell, in Syria **May 3**, asked Pres. Bashar al-Assad to detain any former Iraqi leaders who had entered Syria and prevent Iraqi weapons from being brought into Syria. He called on Syria to stop supporting militant organizations that opposed Israel.

On **May 28**, after 4 U.S. soldiers had been killed in a few days, U.S. officials said that a larger military force than previously planned would be kept in Iraq.

Rumsfeld Announces End of Major Afghan Combat—Meeting with Pres. Hamid Karzai in Kabul, Afghanistan, **May 1**, Sec. of Defense Donald Rumsfeld declared that U.S. military forces had concluded major combat operations there. The Taliban regime, which had sheltered the al-Qaeda terrorists, had been ousted more than a year earlier. Some 8,000 U.S. soldiers and a 5,500-member International Security Assistance Force remained.

A plane crash in Turkey, **May 26**, killed all 74 aboard, including 62 Spanish soldiers returning from peacekeeping duties in Afghanistan.

India, Pakistan Resume Ties—Prime Min. Atal Bihari Vajpayee of India announced **May 2** that India was restoring diplomatic relations and transportation connections with Pakistan. Prime Min. Zafarullah Khan Jamali of Pakistan reciprocated, **May 6**, and said Pakistan would reduce tariffs on 70 Indian imports. However, Pakistan's **May 5** offer to eliminate its nuclear weapons if India did the same was rejected by Vajpayee 2 days later.

Mideast Adversaries Support "Road Map" to Peace—A so-called road map, designed to point the way to peace and a Palestinian state by 2005, got some support from both Israel and the Palestinians. Sec. of State Colin Powell met separately **May 11** with Israeli Prime Min. Ariel Sharon and new Palestinian Prime Min. Mahmoud Abbas. Sharon said his government would not support the plan, issued **Apr. 30**, until the Palestinian Authority stopped anti-Israeli violence, but he did back the plan's goal of a Palestinian state. Abbas accepted the plan, and Powell urged him to act decisively to disarm militant groups. Syria, Jordan, Egypt, and Saudi Arabia also backed the plan.

Sharon and Abbas met for 3 hours **May 17**, and Sharon, **May 23**, went farther than before in support of the road map, saying he was "prepared to accept the steps" in the plan. This followed reassurances by the U.S. that it would "fully and seriously" address Israeli security concerns. The Israeli cabinet **May 25**, for the first time, officially accepted the Palestinian claim to eventual statehood.

Violence and unrest continued. In the first 2 weeks of May, 29 Palestinians were killed by Israeli forces; then 5 suicide attacks **May 17-19** killed 12 Israelis and 5 bombers, leading Sharon to postpone a U.S. trip. Continuing Israeli military operations resulted in 11 more Palestinian deaths **May 15-21**.

2nd British Cabinet Minister Resigns—Clare Short, first secretary for international development under British Prime Min. Tony Blair, and an opponent of the war, resigned **May 12**. She criticized his support for what she considered an insufficient role for the UN in reconstruction of Iraq. Blair named Baroness Valerie Amos as her successor; she was the first black woman to serve in a British cabinet.

75 Killed in Chechnya in 2 Suicide Bombings—At least 75 people were killed and hundreds injured in 2 explosions in Chechnya, where a revolt against Russia continued. Explosives detonated from a truck in Znamenskoye **May 12** killed at least 59 and destroyed 6 apartment houses and 3 government buildings. On **May 14** in Iliskhan-Yurt a woman detonated explosives apparently intended to kill Akhmed Kadyrov, Russian administrator in Chechnya; he survived, but 16 others, including 4 of his bodyguards, died.

Suicide Bombers Kill 34 in Saudi Capital—Four bomb attacks, initiated almost simultaneously overnight, **May 12-13** in Riyadh, killed 9 attackers and 25 others, 9 of them Americans. Three of the targets were residential compounds where foreigners lived. The attackers got past guards, rammed their vehicles through gates, and set off explosives. The Saudi government said **May 13** that it believed that Khaled al-Jehani, a member of al-Qaeda, had masterminded the attacks. U.S. officials said **May 15** that the Saudis had ignored appeals for more security at potential Western targets. U.S. and Saudi officials said **May 19** that al-Qaeda was planning more Saudi and U.S. attacks, and U.S., British, and German embassies in Riyadh were closed **May 20**.

Argentina Gets a President After Rival Quits Race—The contest for president of Argentina ended abruptly **May 14** when former Pres. Carlos Saul Menem, trailing badly in polls, dropped out, leaving Nestor Kirchner, governor of Santa Cruz province, as winner by default. Both belong to the Peronist party. In the first round of voting, **Apr. 27**, Menem had run slightly ahead of Kirchner. The latter, the first president to come from Patagonia, was sworn in **May 25**.

Terror Bombings Claim 41 Lives in Morocco—On **May 16**, Morocco joined the list of countries targeted by suicidal terrorists. Five nearly simultaneous explosions in Casablanca killed 29 innocent people, plus 12 of the 14 bombers. About 100 were injured. Most victims died at the Casa de Espana, a social club and restaurant. In an audiotape released in February, a speaker thought to be terrorist leader Osama bin Laden had warned that Morocco and Saudi Arabia were "ready for liberation." Moroccan security forces arrested scores of suspected militants.

General

Bennett Found to Have Gambled Heavily—William J. Bennett, a former education secretary known as a crusader against moral permissiveness and author of the best-seller *The Book of Virtues*, was revealed in news reports **May 2** to have gambled heavily in casinos for a number of years. According to casino sources, Bennett had lines of credit at several casinos and may have lost millions of dollars in all. While acknowledging that he had done "too much gambling" he said he had not gambled more than he could afford to lose and did not put his family at risk.

Funny Cide Wins Kentucky Derby, Preakness—Funny Cide won the first 2 jewels in horse-racing's Triple Crown, beginning with the Kentucky Derby in Louisville, KY, **May 3**. Under jockey Jose Santos, the 12-1 underdog defeated the favorite, Empire Maker, by 1.75 lengths in 2 min, 1.19 sec. Funny Cide, the first gelding to win the derby since 1929, went on to run away with the Preakness, **May 17** in Baltimore, winning by 9.75 lengths, the 2nd biggest margin in the race's history.

Record Number of Tornadoes Kill 48—Storms transporting tornadoes rolled through the Midwest and South in early May, bringing death to 48, injuring hundreds, and leveling hundreds of buildings. The total of 400 tornadoes between **May 4** and **11** was twice the previous weekly U.S. record. Pres. George W. Bush, who declared disaster areas in 6 states, visited the devastated town of Pierce City, MO, **May 13**. The death tolls were highest in Missouri (18), Tennessee (15), and Kansas (7).

SARS Deaths—The World Health Organization (WHO) reported **May 8** that the recently identified severe acute respiratory syndrome (SARS) had been found in 31 countries, with a total of 7,053 cases so far, and 506 deaths. The United States **May 6** reported 63 cases of the disease so far, with no deaths. The WHO **May 8** added Taiwan's capital, Taipei, and 2 new Chinese areas to the list of places travelers should avoid. In Beijing, 16,436 people had been quarantined as of **May 6**. On **May 2** the Univ. of California at Berkeley barred 500 Asian students from attending its summer session.

Russia **May 8** identified its first likely SARS case and closed some border crossings with China. Responding to criticism that news of the disease had been suppressed, China **May 13** ordered local officials to promptly and accurately report threats to public health. At least 120 officials had been fired or disciplined for failing to respond properly to the disease. Taiwanese officials **May 12** fired the head of a hospital for failing to deal with the epidemic properly. Taiwan quarantined 2 hospitals and said **May 15** that it had 264 probable cases and 30 deaths. The WHO **May 14** dropped Toronto from the list of places where SARS was spreading, but a cluster of new cases was reported, and a WHO travel alert was reinstated. At a Toronto school, 2,000 students, teachers, and staff members were quarantined **May 28** after a student showed SARS symptoms.

Plane Door Opens, Scores Fall to Their Deaths—The main cargo door of a cargo jet opened at a height of 33,000 feet over the Congo, **May 8**, and an unknown number of people were sucked out of the plane. The Russian-built Ilyushin 76 was flying from Kinshasa to Lubumbashi. There were no records to indicate the number aboard, but it was estimated at 200, with the number of dead between 60 and 170. Survivors held on to ropes and netting inside the plane.

Times Documents Reporter's Deceptions—The *New York Times* **May 11** devoted more than 4 full pages to a story documenting major deceptions and inaccuracies by one of its reporters, Jayson Blair. He had resigned from the staff May 1, after the *Washington Post* reported allegations that he had plagiarized an Apr. 18 *San Antonio Express-News* article in a *Times* piece published **Apr. 26**.

In its **May 11** story the *Times* noted serious errors in half of the 73 national articles Blair had written since October, including cases where he made up quotations altogether and lifted accounts and information from other news organizations. He included datelines for many articles that falsely indicated he had been to places he never went to.

Jonathan Landman, the *Times* metropolitan editor, had warned in an email in April 2002, "We have to stop Jayson from writing for the *Times*. Right now." Despite warnings of problems with Blair, he continued to win top assignments. Critics blamed the *Times* for failure to monitor its reporting adequately, and some argued that Blair had been advanced quickly and avoided close scrutiny partly because he was black.

In another incident, a Pulitzer Prize-winning writer for the *Times*, Rick Bragg, resigned from the paper **May 28** after questions were raised about his reliance on a freelance journalist whom he did not credit.

Olympic Bombing Suspect Arrested—Eric Rudolph, accused of planting a bomb during the 1996 Olympics in Atlanta, GA, and of attacks on abortion clinics and a gay nightclub, was arrested in Murphy, NC, **May 31**. A woman died in the Olympic Park bombing, and a police officer was killed in another of the attacks attributed to Rudolph, long the subject of an FBI manhunt.

Earthquake in Algeria Takes Heavy Toll—A magnitude-6.8 earthquake shook the vicinity of Algiers, Algeria, **May 21**, claiming more than 2,260 lives and leaving more than 10,000 people injured.

Woman Golfer Competes in Men's Tournament—For the first time in 59 years, **May 22**, a woman competed in a men's PGA event. The golfer, Annika Sorenstam, a native of Sweden, was regarded as the best current female player. In the 2 rounds that she played in the Bank of America Colonial tournament, in Fort Worth, TX, she posted a 5-over-par 145, too high to qualify for the last 2 rounds.

Brazilian Driver Wins Indy 500—Gil de Ferran won the 500-mile automobile race in Indianapolis **May 25**. He edged out Helio Castroneves, the 2001 and 2002 winner and a fellow Brazilian, by 0.2990 seconds.

JUNE 2003
National

FCC Eases Rules on Media Ownership—In a controversial decision, **June 2**, the Federal Communications Commission voted 3-2 to eliminate a rule barring a media company from owning both a TV station and a newspaper in the same market. A revised FCC rule barred any one company from owning TV stations reaching more than 45% of TV households nationwide (up from 35%).

Defendants Found Guilty of Aiding Terrorists—Two defendants in a U.S. district court in Detroit were found guilty **June 3** of conspiring to provide support to terrorists. A 3rd was convicted of document fraud. All were Moroccans. A 4th defendant was acquitted. Prosecutors said the defendants, seized shortly after Sept. 11, 2001, had conspired to assist in attacks on U.S. tourist sites and U.S. military sites abroad.

Martha Stewart Indicted on Stock-Sale Charges—Martha Stewart, founder of a highly successful media and home furnishings company, was indicted in a U.S. district court in New York City **June 4** on charges of conspiracy, obstruction of justice, and securities fraud. The charges related to what prosecutors contended were attempts to cover up circumstances of her sale of ImClone stock after she had allegedly received inside information unfavorable to the company. Stewart pleaded not guilty on the same day, and stepped down as chair and CEO of Martha Stewart Living Omnimedia. Her former stockbroker, Peter Bacanovic, was also indicted **June 4**. Samuel Waksal, founder and former CEO of ImClone, had pleaded guilty to 6 criminal charges; on **June 10** he was sentenced to 7 years and 3 months in prison and fined $4.3 mil for securities fraud, perjury, and obstruction of justice.

Congress Takes 2nd Look at New Tax Cut Law—Soon after Pres. George W. Bush signed new tax cuts into law, Congress began to consider changes. At the last minute, Republicans had deleted a child tax credit that would have benefited 6.5 million low-income families, and reports indicated that 8 million taxpayers would receive no benefits from the cuts. On **June 5**, the Senate voted, 94-2, to restore the child tax credit to low-income families. Meanwhile, House Republican leaders **June 10** unveiled a broader $82 bil bill that provided new tax credits to couples making up to $200,000 a year.

Unemployment Hits 9-Year High—The Labor Dept. reported **June 6** that the May unemployment rate stood at 6.1%, the highest since 1994. A net total of 2.5 million jobs had been lost since February 2001. On **June 25**, the Federal Reserve Board lowered the key federal funds rate, the overnight loan rate between banks, to 1.0%, its lowest since 1958.

Head of Catholic Sex Abuse Oversight Board Resigns; Phoenix Bishop Resigns—Frank Keating, a former governor of Oklahoma, resigned **June 16** as head of a board set up by Roman Catholic bishops to oversee their compliance with sexual abuse policies they adopted in 2002. Keating, in comments published in the Los Angeles Times **June 12**, had compared the behavior of some bishops to members of the Mafia, saying they listened too much to their lawyers and not enough to their hearts. Some board members viewed his comments as exaggerated or abrasive. In his resignation letter, Keating denounced some bishops for resisting grand jury subpoenas and suppressing names of abusing priests.

Bishop Thomas O'Brien resigned **June 18** as head of the Phoenix, AZ, diocese, 2 days after being charged with leaving the scene of a **June 14** accident in which his car struck a pedestrian, who was killed. Earlier, on **May 3**, he had signed agreements with Maricopa County Attorney Richard Romley admitting that he had concealed cases of sexual abuse by priests and agreeing to outside oversight of diocesan actions dealing with alleged sex abuse by priests.

Arrest Reported in Brooklyn Bridge Plot—Federal officials **June 19** announced the arrest 3 months earlier of Iyman Faris, a Columbus (OH) truck driver who, they said, was involved in a terrorist plot to destroy the Brooklyn Bridge. The driver, a naturalized U.S. citizen from Pakistan,

had allegedly met terrorist leader Osama bin Laden and sent messages to al-Qaeda officials discussing how to sever the suspension cables. He had agreed to plead guilty in May to charges of providing support to terrorists.

Supreme Court Upholds Affirmative Action— In a historic decision **June 23**, the Supreme Court, by a 5-4 margin, upheld an affirmative action program at the Univ. of Michigan providing preference to minorities for admission to the law school. At the same time, the Court, 6-3, struck down an affirmative action program for Michigan's undergraduate college which had provided preference to minorities according to a strict numerical formula.

Under the undergraduate program, all black, Hispanic, and Native American applicants were automatically awarded 20 points (on a scale of 150), which meant that almost all qualified minority members were admitted, while many qualified whites were not. The Bush administration had advocated the invalidation of both Michigan programs as thinly disguised quota systems.

> *"In order to cultivate a set of leaders with legitimacy in the eyes of the citizenry, it is necessary that the path to leadership be visibly open to talented and qualified individuals of every race and ethnicity."*
>
> Justice Sandra Day O'Connor, in the **June 23, 2003**, Supreme Court decision upholding affirmative action in admissions to the Univ. of Michigan law school.

Justices Uphold Internet Pornography Law—In *U.S.* v. *American Library Association*, the Supreme Court **June 23** upheld, 6-3, the Children's Internet Protection Act, which required federally funded libraries to block obscene Intenet computer network material on computers to which minors have access.

Citing Privacy, High Court Protects Gay Sex—The Supreme Court **June 26** gave a major boost to the gay rights movement when it struck down a Texas state law that forbade sexual activity between same-sex partners. In *Lawrence* v. *Texas the Court*, 6-3, overturned the law that made it illegal for people of the same sex (though not of opposite sexes) to engage in sodomy. Kansas, Missouri, and Oklahoma had similar laws. Nine other states had anti-sodomy laws applying to both same-sex and opposite-sex partners. All these laws were effectively invalidated.

In his majority opinion, Justice Anthony Kennedy wrote that homosexuals were entitled to respect and that the state "cannot demean their existence . . . by making their private sexual conduct a crime." In dissent, Justice Antonin Scalia objected that all morals legislation related to sexual conduct was now called into question and that allowing same-sex marriage would be a logical next step. The ruling overturned the court's 1986 decision in *Bowers* v. *Hardwick*, upholding a Georgia law against sodomy.

U.S. Economy at a Glance: June 2003	
Unemployment rate	6.4%
Consumer prices (12 mo. change)	2.1%
Trade deficit (12 mos. through June)	$467.3 bil
Dow Jones high (1st quarter: June 17)	9323.02
Dow Jones low (1st quarter: Apr. 1)	8069.86
2nd quarter GDP growth (annual rate)	3.3%

International

War, Terror on Agenda of Industrial Nations' Leaders—Presidents and prime ministers of the world's 8 leading industrial nations held their annual summit meeting in Evian, France, **June 1-3**. Presidents George W. Bush and Jacques Chirac of France, who had differed sharply on the Iraq war, greeted each other coldly, but said **June 2** that they were prepared to move ahead together. A summit communiqué June 2 called terrorism and weapons of mass destruction the "pre-eminent threat to international security."

Saudis Arrest Top al-Qaeda Figure—Saudi officials **June 26** announced the arrest of Ali Abd al-Rahman al-Faqasi al-Ghamdi, also known as Abu Bakr al-Azdi, suspected of overseeing May bombings in Riyadh that killed 34 people. Ghamdi was believed to be a senior al-Qaeda figure, and to have been plotting further attacks.

Coalition Forces in Iraq Come Under Attack—Although Pres. Bush had declared the combat phase of the war essentially ended, ambushes and other hit-and-run attacks continued to cause casualties among U.S. and British troops. U.S. deaths were running at about one per day during much of June. On **June 24**, 6 British soldiers were killed after being ambushed north of Basra.

Against that backdrop, the allies struggled to establish self-government in Iraq. On **June 1**, abandoning a plan to soon create a large national assembly, they announced that they would appoint an advisory council of 25 to 30 Iraqis.

U.S. forces raided private homes in Thuluya, north of Baghdad, **June 9-10**, and held 400 residents for questioning. Another strike was launched at a terrorist training camp northwest of Baghdad, **June 12**; 68 Iraqis were killed, and 70 surface-to-air missiles were reportedly found. Raids in and near Baghdad continued **June 16-17**, and another raid near Tikrit **June 18** turned up 50 of Saddam Hussein's security personnel, as well as $8.5 mil in cash. An explosion along an oil pipeline in north-central Iraq, **June 12**, was attributed to sabotage. There were later reports of the destruction of electrical transformers and high-tension cables. A 2nd oil pipeline explosion occurred **June 21**; 2 more occurred within days.

U.S. forces **June 18** announced the capture of Abid Hamid Mahmoud al-Tikriti, Hussein's secretary and a key adviser. Defense Dept. officials said **June 20** that he had told interrogators that Hussein and his 2 sons survived the war, and that the sons had fled to Syria. In a firefight along the Iraq-Syria border, **June 18**, U.S. Special Operations forces wounded 5 Syrian guards.

Missing Weapons in Iraq Provoke Heated Debate—The search for weapons of mass destruction (WMDs) in Iraq remained inconclusive, provoking debate. UN weapons inspector Hans Blix said in a **June 2** report that inspectors prior to the war had been unable to prove or disprove the presence of WMDs. Under fire in Parliament, Prime Min. Tony Blair of Britain said the same day he remained "100 percent behind the evidence" of Iraq's weapons. On **June 3**, a House of Commons committee began an investigation into how British intelligence information was used to justify the war. A declassified Sept. 2002 report by the U.S. Defense Intelligence Agency, released **June 6**, found "no reliable information on whether Iraq is producing and stockpiling chemical weapons." National Security Adviser Condoleezza Rice acknowledged **June 8** that Bush's claim in his State of the Union address that Iraq tried to buy uranium from Niger was based on documents discovered to have been forged.

Ontario Court Legalizes Gay Marriage—A 3-member panel of the Ontario Court of Appeal **June 10** ordered provincial officials to extend full marriage rights to same-sex couples, ruling unanimously that the common-law definition of marriage as a male-female union was unconstitutional. The decision followed similar rulings by Canadian provincial courts in Quebec and British Columbia, but the new order was unique in taking immediate effect, prompting some homosexual couples to wed in the province that day. Prime Min. Jean Chretien **June 17** indicated that the federal government would not appeal the decision and promised legislation that would legalize gay marriage nationwide.

Mideast Peace Effort Advances Despite Violence—The so-called road map to peace, appeared to gain momentum in late June when Palestinian militant groups announced a conditional truce and Israeli forces pulled out of much of the Gaza strip. On **June 29**, Hamas and Islamic Jihad, two groups responsible for many bombings, said they would suspend attacks for 3 months, and the al-Aksa Martyrs Brigade agreed to suspend attacks for 6 months. Israeli forces pulled out of most of the Gaza Strip **June 30**, ending a blockade of the key highway that had started in 2000. However, the future of the June 29 cease-fire remained in doubt.

Pres. Bush had met **June 3** in Egypt with Saudi Crown Prince Abdullah, Prime Min. Hosni Mubarak of Egypt, the kings of Bahrain and Jordan, and Palestinian Prime Min. Mahmoud Abbas. Bush reaffirmed his commitment to an independent Palestine. On **June 4**, Bush met with Abbas and Prime Min. Ariel Sharon in Jordan. Abbas declared that the

uprising by Muslim militants "must end," and Sharon vowed to remove unauthorized outposts of Jewish settlements in the West Bank. Israeli soldiers dismantled a settlement at Mitzpeh Yitzhar **June 19**, as settlers protested.

Earlier events had not looked positive for the peace effort. Tens of thousands of Israelis opposed to the plan demonstrated in Jerusalem **June 4**. At a Gaza border crossing, **June 8**, 3 Palestinians killed 4 Israeli soldiers and wounded 4 before they were killed. A 5th Israeli soldier was killed in Hebron **June 8**. On **June 10**, Israeli helicopters fired missiles into a car in Gaza occupied by Abdel Aziz al-Rantisi, 2nd-ranking leader of Hamas; he was injured and a bodyguard and bystander killed. In other military action, 5 Palestinians were killed by Israeli forces **June 10**. The next day Israeli helicopters killed 4 Hamas members in Gaza; 5 bystanders also died. Missiles from Israeli gunships **June 12** killed a suspected Hamas militant along with 2 family members and 4 others. Meanwhile, a suicide bomber killed himself and 17 Israeli civilians in an explosion on a Jerusalem bus, **June 11**.

Liberian President Indicted for War Crimes—A war crimes tribunal announced **June 4** that it had indicted Pres. Charles Taylor of Liberia. The Special Court for Sierra Leone was a joint UN-Sierra Leone tribunal established to try people accused of war crimes in connection with the civil war that ended there in 2002. Taylor was accused of "bearing the greatest responsibility" for the war, which cost as many as 200,000 lives. Taylor, in Ghana when the indictment was announced, returned to Liberia before he could be arrested.

Civil war continued in Liberia, with 2 rebel groups menacing the capital, Monrovia. On **June 9**, French special forces transported 535 foreign nationals by helicopter to a ship offshore. On **June 17**, the rebel groups agreed to stop fighting, but the cease-fire was soon broken. On **June 25**, U.S. officials allowed thousands of refugees to enter the U.S. diplomatic compound in Monrovia, but shells from the attacking rebel forces exploded in the compound, causing injuries.

18 Killed in Terror Bombing Near Chechnya—In Russia's North Ossetia-Alania republic, near Chechnya, a suicide bomber killed herself and at least 17 others at a bus stop, **June 5**. Many of the dead were service personnel.

Bomb Kills 4 German Peacekeepers in Kabul—On **June 7**, an explosion in a vehicle next to a bus killed 4 German peacekeeping soldiers and one Afghan bystander, and wounded 31 others.

North Korea Defends Need for Nuclear Weapons—North Korea said **June 9** that it needed to develop nuclear weapons because it could then save money by decreasing the size of its conventional forces. The regime said it did not intend to use nuclear blackmail.

The U.S. and South Korea agreed **June 5** that U.S. forces along the demilitarized zone along the North-South border (14,000 of 37,000 troops in the country) would be redeployed south of Seoul. U.S. troops had been at the DMZ since the end of the Korean War in 1953.

General

New Respiratory Epidemic Appears to Fade—The World Health Organization said **June 5** that the severe acute respiratory syndrome (SARS) epidemic was apparently beginning to wane. In China, where about 150 new cases had been reported daily in early May, only 7 cases were reported between **June 1** and **12**. WHO lifted its last travel advisories, for mainland China **June 12**, for Taiwan **June 17**, and for Hong Kong **June 23**, and listed only Taiwan and Toronto as areas where SARS was still spreading.

2 Top New York Times Editors Resign—A scandal involving an errant reporter led to the resignation, **June 5**, of the 2 top editors of the *New York Times*. Howell Raines, the executive editor, and Gerald Boyd, the managing editor, quit **June 5**, about a month after Jayson Blair had resigned leaving a trail of fabricated reporting. Many *Times* staff members thought that Raines and Boyd had shown favoritism toward Blair and had failed to act quickly in the face of obvious problems. *Times* publisher Arthur Sulzberger Jr. announced **June 5** that Joseph Lelyveld, Raines's predecessor, would be executive editor on an interim basis.

Funny Cide Fails in Bid to Win Triple Crown—Empire Maker won the Belmont Stakes in Elmont, NY, **June 7**, thwarting a bid by Funny Cide to win horse racing's Triple Crown. Funny Cide had won the Kentucky Derby and Preakness in May. Empire Maker covered the 1.5-mile distance in 2 minutes and 28.26 seconds, just ahead of Ten Most Wanted, with Funny Cide 5 lengths back in 3rd.

New Jersey Devils Win Stanley Cup—The New Jersey Devils won hockey's Stanley Cup, **June 9**, when they defeated the Anaheim Mighty Ducks, 3-0, in the 7th and deciding game of their series. Rookie forward Mike Rupp scored the first goal, and he assisted 2 others scored by Jeff Friesen. The Ducks' goalie, Jean-Sebastien Giguere, who had a 1.62 goals-against average per game in 21 playoff games, was named most valuable player for the playoffs.

2 Blockbusters Hit the Stands—The publishing industry got a lift in June with 2 blockbuster best-sellers. Sen. Hillary Clinton (D, NY) brought out her memoir, *Living History*, **June 9**, and sold 200,000 copies the first day, beginning at midnight at many bookstores. Most interest focused on her reaction to the news that her husband, Pres. Bill Clinton, had lied to her about his relationship with an intern, Monica Lewinsky. The former first lady had received an $8 mil advance from Simon & Schuster.

The 5th book in the Harry Potter series by J.K. Rowling, *Harry Potter and the Order of the Phoenix*, hit mobbed bookstores **June 21**, again beginning at midnight. The book, which continued the adventures of the young wizard, now 15 years old, sold some 5 mil copies the first day alone.

U.S. Open Golf Winner Ties Record—Jim Furyk won the men's U.S. Open golf title **June 15** with a record-tying total of 272. Only 2 other U.S. Open golfers had scored as low. He was 8 under par on the course in Olympia, IL. Furyk had never won any of the 4 major tournaments.

San Antonio Wins Pro Basketball Title—The San Antonio Spurs, playing at home, won the championship of the National Basketball Assn. **June 15**, 4 games to 2, by defeating the New Jersey Nets, 88-77. Spurs' co-captains Tim Duncan and David Robinson combined for 34 points and 37 rebounds. The Nets led at one time by 9 points, only to see the Spurs score the next 19 points.

JULY 2003

National

Unemployment and Deficit Estimates Rise—The Labor Dept. reported **July 3** that June unemployment had climbed to a 9-year high of 6.4%. Since Feb. 2001, the economy had lost almost 2.6 mil jobs. The White House Office of Management and Budget **July 15** foresaw a $455 bil deficit for 2003 fiscal year, $475 bil for fiscal 2004; the highest previous deficit had been $290 bil in fiscal 1992. Fed Chairman Alan Greenspan told a House committee **July 15** that he was optimistic about the economy but that the Fed would keep interest rates low. He told a Senate committee **July 16** that mushrooming budget deficits could slow economic growth.

White House Admits Mistake in Iraq Nuclear Claim—The White House became embroiled in a dispute over a sentence in the January State of the Union speech, in which Pres. George W. Bush said the British government had "learned that Saddam Hussein recently sought significant quantities of uranium [for nuclear weapons] from Africa." Subsequently, key documents supporting this claim had proved to be forgeries. On **July 6**, in the New York Times, retired diplomat Joseph Wilson IV wrote that the Bush administration had sent him to Niger in 2002 to investigate the claim but that his conclusion that it was likely bogus apparently did not reach top officials. An unattributed White House statement **July 7** said the claim "should not have been included" in the speech.

CIA Director George Tenet **July 11** accepted responsibility for the sentence as having been cleared by his agency. National Security Adviser Condoleezza Rice and Defense Sec. Donald Rumsfeld argued that the January statement remained technically accurate, as being the British conclusion. British Prime Min. Tony Blair said **July 14** that his government stood by the British intelligence on the issue. Bush's deputy national security adviser, Stephen Hadley, said **July 22** that he had received 2 CIA memos warning about a lack of evidence, but had forgotten them.

2nd Test Supports Theory on Shuttle Disaster—A 2nd simulation test conducted by NASA **July 7** supported the theory that a piece of insulating foam from an external tank had fallen off and created a hole in the heat shield of the space shuttle Columbia. On reentry into the atmosphere, it was concluded, superheated gases had entered the wing, causing the shuttle's disintegration on Feb. 1. In the test, in the Southwest Research Institute in San Antonio, TX, a piece of foam was fired at a wing at 530 mph; it created a hole about 16x16 inches.

Bush Routs Rivals in Fund-Raising, as Campaign Continues—In reports filed with the Federal Election Commission **July 15**, Pres. Bush had a huge lead over the Democratic aspirants. He raised $34.4 million in the 2nd quarter. Former Gov. Howard Dean (VT) led the Democrats with $7.6 mil; Sen. John Kerry (MA) placed 2nd with $5.9 mil. Dean, a harsh critic of the Iraq war, was showing success at using the Internet to raise money and recruit volunteers.

All but 3 of the 9 current Democratic candidates appeared at a **July 14** forum sponsored by the NAACP; NAACP Pres. Kweisi Mfume excoriated the absentees—Sen. Joseph Lieberman (CT), Rep. Richard Gephardt (MO), and Rep. Dennis Kucinich (OH). At a **July 15** forum conducted by the Human Rights Campaign, a gay rights organization, 3 of the candidates—Kucinich, former Sen. Carol Moseley Braun (IL), and the Rev. Al Sharpton—endorsed gay marriage.

Blair Addresses Congress—Speaking to a joint session of Congress **July 17**, British Prime Min. Blair defended the coalition decision to invade Iraq. He said that even if weapons of mass destruction were not found, "history will forgive" the allies because a brutal dictator had been overthrown. He admonished his listeners, "Don't give up on Europe. Work with it."

California Governor Faces Recall Election—Gov. Gray Davis (D), elected to a 2nd term as governor of California only 8 months earlier, learned **July 23** that he would soon face an election seeking to remove him from office; a separate question on the ballot would allow voters to choose a successor should he be recalled. Sec. of State Kevin Shelley announced he had certified the validity of 1.3 million signatures for the recall vote, 400,000 more than required by law; the vote was set for Oct. 7. Many Californians were shocked by the state's huge $38 bil budget deficit, and its belated disclosure, and many believed Davis had mishandled the 2000 state energy crisis. The campaign for the recall election was financed in large part by U.S. Rep. Darrell Issa (R), who also planned to be a gubernatorial candidate.

Report on Sept. 11 Cites Intelligence Failures—A report from the Senate and House intelligence committees on the Sept. 11, 2001, terror attack, released **July 24**, said that the FBI and CIA had disregarded warnings that al-Qaeda planned to strike directly at the U.S. and had failed to take note of "significant and relevant" information on some of the hijackers. Although the agencies circulated internal warnings of a possible plot, they missed chances to deny entry to or arrest prospective hijackers or to perform surveillance. A lengthy account in the report identifying a possible role by a foreign country was kept classified; Saudi Arabia was believed to be the country. In statements **July 24**, Pres. Bush and FBI Director Robert Mueller claimed the U.S. government had done much since the attack to prevent a recurrence.

Banks Agree to Fines for Enron Fraud—The 2 largest U.S. banks, J.P. Morgan Chase and Citigroup, agreed **July 28** to pay nearly $300 mil in fines and penalties to settle charges they had aided Enron in deceiving investors as to its financial health, even while performing no transactions that were technically illegal.

International

Middle East Quieter as Talks Continue—Discussions among Middle East leaders and U.S. officials aimed at advancing the so-called road map to peace continued in July, and violence between Israelis and Palestinians declined.

Prime ministers Ariel Sharon of Israel and Mahmoud Abbas of the Palestinian Authority met in Jerusalem **July 1.** On **July 2,** Israeli forces withdrew to the edge of Bethlehem but continued to surround the city. Pres. George W. Bush July 25 met with Abbas at the White House for the first time; he echoed Abbas's concern over Israel's erection of a security fence cutting into Palestinian areas, while at the same time calling for compromises on both sides. At a meeting in Washington, DC, **July 29** between Bush and Sharon, Sharon rebuffed calls to halt construction of the fence and called for progress by Palestinians in curbing terrorism; Bush reaffirmed commitment to Israel's security, while calling for Sharon to show restraint. Prior to the Bush-Sharon meeting, the Israeli cabinet **July 27** agreed to free a few hundred jailed Islamic militants, but none with "blood on their hands."

50 Killed in Attack on Mosque in Pakistan—Three attackers killed 50 people at a Shiite mosque in Quetta, Pakistan, **July 4.** First they opened fire and then one set off a grenade strapped to his waist. The 3 attackers also died, and dozens of people were wounded; Sunni Muslim militants were suspected.

Suicide Bombers Kill 14 in Moscow—A **July 5** explosion at a rock-music festival on the outskirts of Moscow killed 14 people in addition to the 2 bombers. Both bombers were women; one was identified as Chechen.

Liberian Civil War Continues, as President Clings to Power—Pres. Charles Taylor of Liberia delayed in making good on a promise to resign, as rebel forces scored victories and casualties mounted. A cease-fire barely held in early July as government soldiers and rebels roamed the capital, Monrovia, looting and committing random acts of violence. Taylor said **July 6** that he had accepted an invitation to go into exile in Nigeria, but then said he would not depart until a multinational peacekeeping force took over. Meanwhile, a U.S. Defense Dept. delegation arrived in Monrovia, **July 7,** to investigate humanitarian and security problems and the Americans were welcomed enthusiastically in the streets. Pres. Bush said, **July 8,** that he had not decided what role the U.S. would play in stabilizing the nation, founded in the 1800s by freed American slaves.

The cease-fire was decisively broken **July 19,** when one rebel group attacked the capital in force. Twenty-one U.S. marines landed in Monrovia **July 21** to protect the U.S. embassy, hit by mortar fire that day. Pres. Bush **July 25** ordered a naval force that included 2,300 marines to sail to a position off the coast. Continued heavy fighting in the capital caused hundreds of civilian casualties, and a 2nd major rebel group engaged government forces in the city of Buchanan.

Iraqi Governing Council Starts Work—On **July 7,** leading Iraqi political groups endorsed a U.S. plan for a governing council. A 37-member council began its work that day, and L. Paul Bremer III, civilian administrator for Iraq, introduced a new national currency. The governing council, representing all major ethnic and religious groups, met in Baghdad **July 13.** It was granted authority to operate government ministries, name diplomats, approve a budget, and create a commission to draft a new constitution. A Shiite politician was appointed **July 30** as the first to serve in a rotating presidency.

Bush Visits 5 African Countries—Pres. Bush and First Lady Laura Bush began a visit to 5 sub-Saharan African nations **July 7.** Earlier, the president had repeatedly urged Pres. Taylor of Liberia to resign to spare his nation more violence. Bush had also announced a plan to provide $100 mil in counterterrorism aid to 5 East African countries. During the trip Bush also emphasized his proposals to spend $15 bil in Africa to suppress AIDS and $5 bil in African countries progressing toward democracy and capitalism.

In Senegal, Bush met with leaders of 8 countries and the Bushes visited Goree Island, whence one million slaves had been taken to America. The president called slavery "one of the greatest crimes of history." He met with Pres. Thabo Mbeki in South Africa **July 9,** supporting his diplomatic efforts to mediate a violent civil confrontation in Zimbabwe. The next day he met with Pres. Festus Mogae in Botswana, where the adult HIV/AIDS infection rate was estimated at

39%, highest in the world. Bush's last stops, **July 11-12,** were in Uganda and Nigeria.

North Korea Says It Is Building Nuclear Bombs—North Korean diplomats indicated **July 8** that the Communist regime had enough plutonium for 6 nuclear bombs and that building of the weapons was underway; the diplomats said that they had finished reprocessing fuel rods on June 30 and had begun to produce weapons using the fuel. A stalemate over nuclear negotiations showed signs of resolution **July 31,** when the Bush administration said North Korea appeared ready to agree to multilateral talks, as the U.S. had been urging.

U.S. Troops Suffer Continuing Casualties in Iraq — Opponents of the U.S. occupation of Iraq, including supporters of the overthrown Iraqi regime, continued to launch attacks on U.S. troops. Gen. John Abizaid, new head of the U.S. Central Command, **July 16** described Iraqi resistance as a "classical guerrilla-type campaign"; by **July 30** a total of 50 U.S. troops had been killed in hostile fire since the end of major combat operations was announced May 1. On **July 4,** U.S. forces killed 11 Iraqis who had attempted a highway ambush. At a graduation ceremony **July 5** for U.S.-trained Iraqi policemen, a bomb killed 7 of the recruits and wounded 74. In an audiotape played **July 4** by the Al Jazeera network, a voice believed to be Saddam Hussein's urged Iraqis to resist the coalition forces.

Gen. Tommy Franks, who retired **July 7** as head of U.S. Central Command, told a Senate committee **July 9** that the U.S. military force in Iraq likely could not be reduced "for the foreseeable future." Defense Sec. Donald Rumsfeld told the committee U.S. operations in Iraq were costing $3.9 bil a month. Gen. Ricardo Sanchez, coalition ground commander in Iraq, said **July 20** that 8 battalions of Iraqis would be trained and become the first part of an Iraqi defense force.

British Scientist in Iraq Dispute Commits Suicide—British scientist David Kelly, a government adviser and former UN weapons inspector in Iraq, was found dead, an apparent suicide, **July 18.** Kelly had emerged as the most likely source for a May BBC report, which claimed that a Sept. 2002 intelligence dossier, presented to Parliament to buttress claims that Iraq had weapons of mass destruction, had been "sexed up" at the insistence of government communications director Alistair Campbell. The dossier had warned that Iraq could deploy chemical and biological weapons within 45 minutes. A 2nd report to Parliament, in Feb. 2003, proved to have been based in part on an old university doctoral thesis picked off the Internet and used without attribution.

A report by the House of Commons Foreign Affairs Committee, **July 7,** had cleared Campbell and British Prime Min. Blair of attempts to manipulate intelligence. But after the Defense Ministry said **July 10** that Kelly had been a BBC source, the committee had reopened its investigation. Testifying **July 15,** Kelly, receiving a harsh interrogation, said he did not believe he had been the principal BBC source. The Defense Ministry said Kelly had been reprimanded for talking to the BBC. The BBC **July 20** said Kelly had been the principal source for their report. Some members of Parliament called on Blair and Campbell to resign.

U.S. Troops Kill 2 Sons of Saddam Hussein—Tipped off by an informer, U.S. soldiers laid siege to a home in Mosul in northern Iraq, **July 22,** and in a gun battle killed its 4 occupants, including 2 once powerful sons of deposed Pres. Saddam Hussein. The brothers, Uday and Qusay, were notorious for their sadism and corruption. Qusay had run the Special Republican Guard, and Uday, found with $400,000 in U.S. currency, led a paramilitary organization, the Saddam Fedayeen. An informant was to receive the two $15 mil rewards offered for the brothers. Seeking to convince Iraqis that the brothers were in fact dead, the U.S. released photographs of their bodies **July 24.** On a videotape released **July 29,** a voice purporting to be that of Saddam Hussein praised the sons as martyrs for the cause. With their deaths, 36 of the 55 former Iraqi leaders on the U.S. "most wanted" list had now been killed or captured. U.S. forces launched continuing raids in the Tikrit area, capturing suspected loyalists of Saddam Hussein as they hunted for Saddam himself.

General

Vatican Appoints New Boston Archbishop—The Vatican announced **July 1** that the Bishop Sean O'Malley would succeed Cardinal Bernard Law as Roman Catholic archbishop of Boston; he was installed **July 30**. O'Malley, a Capuchin friar, had been named bishop of the troubled Palm Beach, FL, diocese in Sept. 2002; he was regarded as a peacemaker and at the same time as a traditionalist. Law had resigned amid widespread criticism for allegedly protecting priests who had abused children; nearly 500 alleged victims were suing the archdiocese, which was also suffering financially from reduced contributions. Massachusetts Atty. Gen. Thomas Reilly **July 23** made public an investigation concluding that at least 789 children had been abused by 250 priests and other church personnel in the archdiocese since 1940. He said an "institutional culture" of secrecy had protected the abusers.

SARS Epidemic Contained—The World Health Organization reported **July 5** that the "human chains" of transmission for severe acute respitory syndrome (SARS) appeared to be broken and removed the last country, Taiwan, from a list of places with recent local transmission. WHO said about 200 SARS patients remained hospitalized around the world. Through **July 31**, WHO later estimated a total of 8,098 people had contracted SARS, and 774 had died of it.

Serena Williams Retains Title—Serena Williams held on to her Wimbledon tennis women's singles title **July 5**, defeating older sister Venus, 4-6, 6-4, 6-2, in a rematch of the 2002 finals. Roger Federer of Switzerland won the men's singles title **July 6**, defeating Mark Philippoussis of Australia, 7-6, 6-2, 7-6. At age 46, Martina Navratilova won her 20th Wimbledon title (tying her with Billie Jean King for the most ever) **July 6**, when she teamed with Leander Paes of India for the mixed-doubles championship.

Twins Joined at Head Die After Operation—Doctors in Singapore **July 8** separated 29-year-old twins who had been joined at the head since birth. However, the 54-hour operation failed after doctors were unable to stop the loss of blood, and both women died. The Iranian sisters, Laden and Laleh Bijani, both law school graduates, had determinedly sought the operation despite the serious risks involved.

Basketball Star Indicted for Sexual Assault—Kobe Bryant of the Los Angeles Lakers was charged with one count of sexual assault **July 18**. A young woman had filed a complaint against him **July 1**, following their meeting at a lodge in Edwards, CO. Bryant, who was married and the father of an infant daughter, admitted he had had sex with the woman, but claimed it was consensual.

Golfer Scores Open Upset—Ben Curtis of Kent, OH, achieved a big upset **July 20**, winning the British Open golf championship in his first appearance ever in one of the major tournaments. Curtis, ranked 396th in the world, posted a one-under-par 283, becoming the first golfer to win a "major" on his first try; he won $1.1 mil in prize money.

Councilman Shot Dead in New York's City Hall—A member of the New York City Council was shot dead at a council meeting **July 23** inside City Hall in lower Manhattan. James Davis, a councilman from Brooklyn, and Othniel Askew, who was planning to challenge him in the next election, had entered the building together without having to pass through metal detectors; within minutes after their arrival, Askew shot Davis several times with a pistol, before Askew in turn was shot dead by a police officer.

Armstrong Wins Tour de France for 5th Time—Lance Armstrong **July 27** became only the 2nd cyclist ever to win the Tour de France for the 5th time in a row. He finished 61 seconds ahead of Jan Ullrich of Germany in 83 hours, 41 minutes, and 12 seconds.

Bush, Vatican Condemn Same-Sex Unions—On July 30 Pres. Bush, while calling for "respect" for each individual, took a stand against gay marriage. The president said, "I believe a marriage is between a man and a woman, and I think we ought to codify that one way or the other." The Vatican **July 31** issued a strongly worded document condemning any legislation recognizing same-sex unions or permitting homosexual couples to adopt children.

AUGUST 2003

National

California Recall Campaign Underway—California's recall election campaign for governor got underway in August, with 135 challengers meeting the state's modest legal requirements to be placed on the ballot. On Election Day, Oct. 7, voters would first be asked whether to recall Gov. Gray Davis (D); if Davis failed to win a majority, whoever won a plurality on the 2nd part of the ballot would become governor. Arnold Schwarzenegger (R), well-known as a movie actor and former "Mr. Universe," announced his candidacy **Aug. 6** on Jay Leno's NBC-TV *Tonight* show. Rep. Darrell Issa (R), who had largely funded the campaign for the recall, dropped out of the contest **Aug. 7**. Bill Simon (R), an unsuccessful candidate in 2002, left the contest **Aug. 23**; State Sen. Tom McClintock remained as a leading Republican candidate. Many prominent Democrats, including Sen. Diane Feinstein (D), declined to run. Lt. Gov. Cruz Bustamente (D) had urged against recall but put himself forth as a candidate in case the recall went through. Peter Ueberroth (R), the former baseball commissioner, was running as an independent, as was political columnist Arianna Huffington. There were many unconventional candidates, including Larry Flynt, publisher of *Hustler* magazine; former TV child star Gary Coleman; and porno film actress Mary Carey. The unpopular Davis **Aug. 1** had signed a compromise state budget agreement that slashed spending and borrowing in order to reduce a huge $38 bil deficit. He charged **Aug. 19** that the recall was part of a Republican plot to steal elections.

Blackout Leaves 50 Million in the Dark—A power failure spread rapidly through Ohio, Michigan, and the Northeast, as well as eastern Canada, on **Aug. 14**. Some 50 million people in 8 states and the province of Ontario were left without electricity for as long as 2 days. Power went out shortly after 4 PM, affecting homes and businesses, traffic lights and trains. In New York City, the most populous place affected, all power had been restored by the evening of **Aug. 15**, but subways could not run until the next morning. Many airports closed and 1,700 flights were canceled. Water supplies were at risk in Cleveland and Detroit. Looting and other criminal activity remained at a minimum, and fewer than 10 deaths were blackout-related.

On **Aug. 19**, the U.S. and Canada agreed to conduct a joint investigation. Pres. George W. Bush said, **Aug. 19**, that the blackout was "a wake-up call for the need to modernize our electricity delivery systems."

Alabama Justice Defies Courts on Ten Commandments—Alabama Chief Justice Roy Moore lost a confrontation with courts over display of a rock inscribed with the Ten Commandments in the lobby of the State Supreme Court in Montgomery. A federal judge, finding a violation of separation of church and state, threatened to fine him if he did not remove it. Moore's appeal to the U.S. Supreme Court was rejected **Aug. 20**. He refused to comply and was buttressed by hundreds of supporters, who flocked to the building. On **Aug. 21**, the 8 associate justices of the Alabama Supreme Court ordered the monument removed. Moore was suspended for defying the court order.

Report on Shuttle Disaster Indicts NASA—A board investigating the Feb. 1 *Columbia* shuttle disaster issued a report **Aug. 26** that severely criticized the National Aeronautics and Space Administration. The *Columbia* Accident Investigation Board concluded that the immediate cause of the explosion was a piece of insulating foam that broke off from the external fuel tank and, at a speed of 545 mph, hit the leading edge of the left wing 82 seconds into the flight, creating a 100-square-inch hole through which hot gases entered. The board cited a "broken safety culture" at NASA—including schedule pressures, insufficient funding, and competing priorities. NASA engineers had been aware of the foam incident after takeoff and made known their concerns, but management had disregarded them. The board suggested that a rescue mission could have been attempted if NASA had moved quickly enough.

International

Suicide Bomber Kills 50 at Russian Hospital—A suicide bomber rammed a truck through the gates of a military hospital in Mozdok, in North Ossetia, in Russia, **Aug. 1**; the bomb he detonated killed 50 people; Russian officials blamed Chechen separatists.

Al-Qaeda's No. 2 Leader Warns U.S.—In a tape first heard publicly **Aug. 3**, a speaker believed to be Ayman al-Zawahiri, 2nd in command in al-Qaeda, warned the U.S. not to harm prisoners held at Guantanamo Bay, Cuba, and threatened continuing attacks.

Bomb at Indonesia Hotel Kills 12; Other Suspects Prosecuted—A bomb exploded in a car at the J. W. Marriott Hotel in Jakarta, Indonesia, **Aug. 5**, killing 12 and wounding 150. The hotel was frequented by Americans. Authorities said the bomb had been detonated with the use of a cellular phone. On **Aug. 19**, Indonesian police named 16 suspects in the hotel bombing; 10 were in custody.

On **Aug. 7** Amrozi bin Nurhasyim was convicted in the Oct. 2002 bombing of 2 nightclubs in Bali, Indonesia. He had confessed to buying explosives for one of the bombs and a van used to transport them. On **Aug. 12** Thai police arrested Nurjaman Riduan Isamuddin, believed to be an architect of the Bali bombings. He was also thought to have been involved in the Sept., 2001 terrorist attack, among others.

Irish Militant Convicted of Terrorism—The reputed leader of the Real Irish Republican Army, an offshoot of the Provisional IRA, was convicted in Dublin **Aug. 6** of directing terrorism and belonging to an illegal group. The defendant, Michael McKevitt, convicted in a Special Criminal Court, was sentenced **Aug. 7** to total of 26 years in prison.

Violence on the Rise in Afghanistan—Violence blamed on Taliban resistance fighters and rival warlords took a heavy death toll in Afghanistan in August. The UN suspended field work in S Afghanistan **Aug. 10** after attacks on aid workers. More than 50 people were killed throughout the country Aug. 12 and 13, including 15 when a bomb exploded on a bus. Fifteen guerrillas and 5 soldiers died in a clash near the Pakistan border. Nine police officers were killed in an ambush in eastern Afghanistan, **Aug. 19**.

British Investigate Suicide of Weapons Scientist—An official investigation into the suicide of an expert on Iraqi weapons got underway in Britain **Aug. 11**. The scientist, David Kelly, had been a basic source for a BBC report suggesting that the government manipulated evidence concerning Iraq's supposed weapons of mass destruction. Alastair Campbell, a top aide to Prime Min. Tony Blair, testified **Aug. 19** that he had not exaggerated intelligence information on Iraqi weapons; Blair, testifying **Aug. 28**, also denied that the government "sexed up" the dossier. On **Aug. 29**, Campbell resigned.

Peacekeepers Enter Liberia as President Flees—The violent reign of Pres. Charles Taylor of Liberia ended **Aug. 11** when he flew into exile in Nigeria. Peacekeepers seeking to stop fighting between government and rebel troops were already moving into the capital, Monrovia. The UN Security Council, **Aug. 1**, had called for a multinational peacekeeping force. The Economic Community of West African States (ECOWAS) quickly put together a small force, mostly Nigerians, which began arriving in Monrovia **Aug. 4**. Seven U.S. marines, arriving from 3 U.S. Navy ships offshore, entered Monrovia **Aug. 6** to assess the situation.

Taylor, **Aug. 7**, said he would transfer power to Vice Pres. Moses. In a parting shot, Taylor **Aug. 10** said he was being "forced into exile by the world superpower" and vowed he would be back. Rebels **Aug. 14** handed over to ECOWAS

the port facilities, permitting delivery of food. In Ghana, **Aug. 18**, representatives of the Liberian government, 2 rebel armies, and unarmed opposition groups signed a peace agreement that provided for an interim government to be established in October.

Libya to Pay Relatives of Plane Bomb Victims—Libya said **Aug. 15**, in a letter to the UN Security Council, that it accepted responsibility for the bombing of a Pan Am airliner over Lockerbie, Scotland, in 1988, that claimed 270 lives. Libya agreed to pay reparations that could total $2.7 bil. An initial $4 mil would go to each family when UN sanctions against Libya were lifted, another $4 mil if U.S. sanctions were lifted, and a final $2 mil if the U.S. State Dept. dropped Libya from its list of countries sponsoring terrorism. Diplomats from Libya, the U.S., and Britain had worked out the settlement.

Cycle of Violence Resumes in Middle East—Optimism about the future of Israeli-Palestinian relations was dimmed **Aug. 19** when a bomb detonated on a bus in Jerusalem and killed 21, including the bomber. Another 100 people were wounded. No attack had occurred in Jerusalem since Palestinian militants had declared a cease-fire June 29. Both Hamas and Islamic Jihad claimed responsibility, the latter as retaliation for Israel's killing **Aug. 14** of Mohammed Sidr, the organization's military leader. Israel **Aug. 19** halted efforts to advance the so-called road map to peace, and on **Aug. 20** arrested 17 in Hebron in connection with the bombing. An Israeli missile strike **Aug. 21** killed a Hamas political leader and 2 bodyguards in Gaza City; Hamas and Islamic Jihad abandoned their declared cease-fire. Pres. George W. Bush **Aug. 22** ordered a freeze on the assets of 6 top Hamas leaders and 5 charities said to support Hamas. On **Aug. 24**, Israeli forces killed 4 Hamas members in Gaza City.

On **Aug. 4**, after an Israeli woman and her daughter were wounded by gunfire, Israel said it would halt plans to pull its military out of some West Bank towns. Palestinian Prime Min. Mahoud Abbas **Aug. 5** canceled a meeting with Prime Min. Ariel Sharon after Israel indicated it would release only a small number of the Palestinian prisoners it was holding. (The Israelis freed 330 **Aug. 6**.) Two suicide bombers killed themselves and 2 Israelis and wounded 17 **Aug. 12** in Israel and Gaza.

Bomb Wrecks UN Headquarters in Iraq; Iraq Casualties Mount—On **Aug. 19**, a suicide bomber driving a cement mixer loaded with up to 1,500 pounds of explosives dealt a severe blow to the international effort to aid Iraq. The explosives detonated next to the UN Headquarters in Baghdad, killing 22 and wounding more than 100. Those killed included Sergio Vieira de Mello, the senior UN representative in Iraq. The building, the former Canal Hotel, was only lightly guarded. The UN said **Aug. 20** that it would continue its work but reduce its staff; the World Bank and International Monetary Fund began withdrawing staffs the same day. No group claimed responsibility for the attack.

Earlier, on **Aug. 7**, 19 were killed and at least 65 wounded when a car bomb exploded outside the Jordanian embassy in Baghdad. Jordan had allowed the U.S. to station several thousand troops in Jordan during the war. In Basra, **Aug. 9-10**, British soldiers confronted Iraqis rioting in protest over shortages of power and fuel. The soldiers fired rubber bullets into one crowd **Aug. 9**. The UN Security Council Aug. 14 welcomed appointment of a governing council in Iraq but did not grant formal recognition. On **Aug. 15** and **17**, saboteurs blew up sections of a pipeline carrying oil to Turkey. A mortar attack on a prison outside Baghdad, **Aug. 16**, killed 6 prisoners and wounded 59. A U.S. soldier shot and killed a Reuters cameraman at the prison **Aug. 17**; he thought his camera was a rocket-propelled grenade. A bomb in Baghdad ruptured a water main in Baghdad, **Aug. 17**, cutting off water to 300,000 homes. Three British soldiers were killed **Aug. 23** while on patrol in Basra. U.S. officials said, **Aug. 19**, that former Vice Pres. Taha Yassin Ramadan, a close adviser to ex-Pres. Saddam Hussein, had been captured.

By **Aug. 29**, 282 U.S. service personnel had died in Iraq from all causes; of those, 143 were killed after **May 1**, the day that Bush had proclaimed major combat over, including 67 in hostile action

Car Bomb Targets Shiite Mosque in Iraq—A car bomb exploded **Aug. 29** at the Imam Ali Mosque in the Shiite holy city of Najaf during Friday prayers, killing more than 80 worshippers, including a leading moderate Shiite cleric, Ayatollah Mohammed Baqir al-Hakim. Followers of al-Hakim blamed supporters of Saddam Hussein for the bombing, though an audiotaped statement attributed to Hussein, aired **Sept. 1**, denied responsibility.

Explosions Hit Mumbai—Two bombs, placed in taxis, exploded in a shopping district in Mumbai (Bombay), India, **Aug. 25**, killing more than 50 and wounding over 100. Officials suspected Islamic militants.

North Korea Issues Nuclear Warning—On **Aug. 28**, during 6-nation talks in Beijing, a representative of North Korea said that Communist state would prove it had nuclear weapons by conducting a nuclear test. The talks, which involved representatives of the U.S., China, Japan, Russia, and South Korea, were aimed at defusing tensions in the region brought on by advances in North Korea's nuclear-weapons activities. The other nations hoped that North Korea would drop its nuclear plans in return for food and other aid from other countries; the summit concluded **Aug. 29** with an agreement to hold more talks.

General

Murder of College Athlete Leads to Apparent Coverup—The unexplained murder of a member of the Baylor Univ. men's basketball team continued to make headlines. The player, Patrick Dennehy, had been reported missing **June 19**. His roommate, Carlton Dodson, a former teammate, was arrested for murder **July 21**, and a body found near Waco, TX, **July 25**, with 2 bullet wounds was identified as Dennehy's. Tapes recorded on **July 30-31** and **Aug. 1** appeared to reveal that basketball coach Dave Bliss had advised assistant coaches and players to depict Dennehy as a drug dealer—an apparent attempt to conceal the fact that Bliss had paid money to Dennehy. Baylor Pres. Robert Sloan, after learning that players had used drugs and failed drug tests, **Aug. 8** accepted the resignations of Bliss and Athletic Director Tom Stanton.

Divided Episcopalians Approve Gay Bishop—The election of the first openly homosexual Episcopal bishop threatened to create a schism within the Episcopal Church in the U.S. and the international Anglican Communion. The House of Deputies, **Aug. 3**, and the House of Bishops, **Aug. 5**, approved the election of the Rev. V. Gene Robinson as bishop of the New Hampshire diocese. The latter approval came after 2 last-minute accusations about Robinson's conduct failed to survive an investigation. Some delegates at the Minneapolis (MN) convention said they would appeal Robinson's election to the archbishop of Canterbury.

Heat Wave in Europe Kills Thousands—Record high temperatures were reported in some European countries in August, and thousands of heat-related deaths were reported, mostly in France. On **Aug. 10**, Britain recorded its hottest day ever, 100.6 degrees F. Switzerland reported a new all-time high, 107.6 degrees F, on **Aug. 11**. Prem. Jean-Pierre Raffarin of France declared a medical state of emergency **Aug. 14**, allowing hospitals to recall staff from vacations to assist patients suffering from heatstroke and dehydration; heat related deaths in France were estimated at more than 10,000. Dr. Lucien Abenhaim, French director general of health, resigned **Aug. 18** amid criticism.

Abusive Ex-Priest Murdered in Prison—A former priest who had been in the forefront of the sexual-abuse scandal in the Roman Catholic Church was strangled at a state prison in Shirley, MA, **Aug. 23**, apparently by another inmate, while both were under protective custody. The ex-priest, John Geoghan, convicted of groping a 10-year-old boy, had faced pending criminal and civil charges involving 130 alleged victims. Authorities said Joseph Druce, a convicted murderer, would be charged in the killing of Geoghan. Authorities had reportedly been warned that Druce could be planning to kill Geoghan; an investigation was under way.

SEPTEMBER 2003
National

Bush Withdraws Nomination for Judgeship—A long struggle over the nomination of Miguel Estrada to a U.S. court of appeals ended **Sept. 4** when Pres. George W. Bush withdrew his name. Bush had nominated Estrada, a Honduran immigrant who became assistant solicitor general in the Justice Dept., in May 2001. Senate Democrats, who argued that Estrada's views were too conservative, had blocked the nomination through filibuster.

Bush Asks $87 Bil for Iraq—Pres. Bush, in a TV address **Sept. 7**, asked Congress for $87 bil to pay for the occupation and reconstruction of Iraq over the next year. Of that, $66 bil would go for the cost of military and intelligence operations in Iraq and Afghanistan, and about $20 bil for the economic recovery of Iraq. Many in Congress were uneasy over the cost and opposed the $20 bil, arguing that U.S. taxpayers should not have to bear that cost without Iraqi assistance.

Ex-Enron Officer Gets Prison Sentence—Ben Glisan Jr., Enron's former treasurer, pleaded guilty **Sept. 10** in U.S. district court in Houston to criminal wire fraud. He had sought to conceal almost $1 bil in company losses in an off-balance-sheet partnership. Judge Kenneth Hoyt sentenced him to 5 years in prison; he was also required to give up $938,000 in profits from his illegal transaction.

Clark Enters Presidential Race—Gen. Wesley Clark (ret.) said **Sept. 17** that he would seek the Democratic presidential nomination. Clark, a West Point graduate and decorated Vietnam veteran, was later supreme commander of NATO.

Three candidates for the Democratic nomination who had been campaigning for months officially declared their intentions. Announcing **Sept. 2** in South Carolina, Sen. John Kerry (MA) said Pres. Bush had a "radical vision" of government that favored the rich. Declaring his candidacy **Sept. 16**, Sen. John Edwards (NC) called Bush a champion of the rich. Former Sen. Carol Moseley Braun declared officially **Sept. 22**.

A flurry of mid-September polls showed that Bush's job-approval rating had declined to around 50% and that several Democratic aspirants might run strongly against him. Clark said **Sept. 18** that he "probably" would have voted for an October 2002 congressional resolution authorizing Bush to attack Iraq, but the next day he backtracked. On **Sept. 23**, Rep. Richard Gephardt (MO) received his 13th labor-union endorsement, from the 840,000-member Laborers International Union of North America. On **Sept. 25**, all 10 current Democratic candidates joined in a debate in New York City. Several criticized Dean, who was widely regarded as the front-runner, based on polls.

Stock Exchange CEO Resigns After Outcry—Richard Grasso, chairman and CEO of the New York Stock Exchange, resigned under fire, **Sept. 17**. On **Sept. 2**, William Donaldson, chairman of the Securities and Exchange Commission, had ordered the NYSE to provide details of Grasso's retirement package. Grasso in 2003 was taking $139.5 mil in deferred pay and retirement benefits. He said **Sept. 9** that he would forgo $48 mil in additional income due to him in the next 4 years.

California Recall Vote to Proceed—A final legal hurdle to the scheduled Oct. 7 gubernatorial recall election in California was cleared **Sept. 23**, when the U.S. 9th Circuit Court of Appeals overturned a ruling by a 3-judge court panel that the vote should be postponed because punch-card voting machines were unreliable. Former baseball commissioner Peter Ueberroth left the race **Sept. 9**; maverick liberal candidate Arianna Huffington dropped out **Sept. 30**.

Probe of CIA Leak Begun—Attorney Gen. John Ashcroft, **Sept. 30**, announced that the Justice Dept. was launching an internal investigation into whether and which administration officials may have acted illegally in leaking the identity of a CIA agent married to a former diplomat, Joseph C. Wilson IV; Wilson had criticized the administration for allegedly manipulating intelligence information to justify war with Iraq. Democrats called instead for an independent investigation.

Three Detained in Guantanamo Spy Inquiries—By **Sept. 30**, 3 persons working at the U.S. Guantanamo Bay prison camp in Cuba had been arrested and charged with espionage. The three included a Muslim chaplain, an Arabic translator (both members of the military), and a civilian translator. More than 650 al-Qaeda and Taliban suspects remained in custody, without charges, at Guantanamo.

U.S. Economy at a Glance: September 2003	
Unemployment rate	6.1%
Consumer prices (12 mos. change)	1.5%
Trade deficit (12 mos. through July)	$474.5 bil.
Dow Jones high (3rd quarter: Sept. 16)	9659.34
Dow Jones low (3rd quarter: July 10)	9036.04

International

U.S. Seeks Support for Iraq Peacekeeping, Encounters Problems—The United States, **Sept. 3**, began circulating a UN Security Council resolution that would authorize putting peacekeepers from many nations in Iraq. On **Sept. 4**, however, French Pres. Jacques Chirac of France and German Chancellor Gerhard Schroeder opposed the draft; the latter said stability could only be achieved by having the UN take charge of the process.

On **Sept. 1**, the Iraqi governing council had named a 25-member cabinet that would begin to assume responsibility for running government departments. On **Sept. 13**, French Foreign Min. Dominique de Villepin urged that an Iraqi interim government be established within a month that would report to the UN; Sec. of State Colin Powell, in Baghdad the next day, called the proposal unrealistic.

Britain announced **Sept. 8** that it would send 1,200 more troops to Iraq. On **Sept. 12**, U.S. soldiers, in error, fired on U.S.-trained Iraqi policemen in Falluja, killing or mortally wounding 10. Three U.S. soldiers were killed in an ambush near Tikrit **Sept. 18**.

On **Sept. 17**, modifying past statements, Pres. Bush said, "We've had no evidence that Saddam Hussein was involved with September the 11th." Sen. Edward Kennedy (D, MA) charged the next day that the war was a "fraud . . . made up in Texas" to give Republicans a political boost.

On **Sept. 19**, former Iraqi Defense Min. Gen. Sultan Hashem Ahmed al-Tai surrendered to U.S. authorities in Mosul. Akila al-Hashemi, one of 3 women on the Iraqi governing council, was shot near her home in Baghdad; she died **Sept. 25**. A bomb exploded outside UN headquarters in Baghdad **Sept. 22**, killing the bomber and a guard and wounding 19. The UN said **Sept. 25** that it was withdrawing more staff from Iraq.

The annual series of speeches by world leaders to the UN General Assembly began in New York **Sept. 23**. Sec. Gen. Kofi Annan said that unilateralism and preemptive action threatened to undermine the UN mission; Pres. Bush defended the use of force in Iraq, and appealed to other nations to help rebuild Iraq and Afghanistan. He said the U.S. would support an expanded UN role in Iraq, including the running of elections and the training of civil servants. Pres. Chirac urged the transfer of power to the Iraqis on a "realistic timetable." Sec. Powell **Sept. 25** set a 6-month deadline for Iraqi leaders to complete a new constitution.

Palestinian Prime Minister Resigns; Israel Threatens Arafat—The short stormy tenure of Mahmoud Abbas as the Palestinian prime minister ended **Sept. 6** with his resignation. He complained of a lack of support from Palestinian leaders, and of a failure by Israel to adhere to the so-called road map to peace. Yasir Arafat, leader of the Palestinian Authority, had resisted Abbas's efforts to get more control over the Palestinian security services. Ahmed Qurei, speaker of the Palestinian parliament, **Sept. 10** accepted Arafat's nomination to become prime minister.

On **Sept. 6**, Israeli planes bombed the home of Sheikh Ahmed Yassin, cofounder of the militant organization Hamas, wounding him and 14 others. Palestinian suicide bombers killed 13 Israelis in 2 attacks **Sept. 9**. In a statement issued **Sept. 11**, the 11-member Israeli security cabinet suggested that Palestinian leader Yasir Arafat might be expelled from Palestinian territory. Sec. of State Colin Powell warned **Sept. 12** that such a move might just make Arafat more of a hero.

Up to 200 Taliban Militia Killed in Afghanistan—Amid reports that supporters of the ousted Taliban regime in Afghanistan were reorganizing, U.S. military forces accelerated their military operations. Lt. Gen. John Vines, the U.S. commander, said **Sept. 7** that up to 200 Taliban fighters had been killed in clashes during the past 2 weeks. Sec. of Defense Donald Rumsfeld met in Kabul **Sept. 7** with Pres. Hamid Karzai.

World Trade Talks Collapse in Mexico—Trade negotiations in Cancun, Mexico, aimed at helping developing nations collapsed, **Sept. 14**. Representatives of 146 countries had come together **Sept. 10** for a meeting of the World Trade Organization, seeking to open markets and increase free trade. Poor countries sought to dissuade wealthier countries from spending nearly $300 bil annually for agricultural subsidies, which they contended hurt their small farmers. The meeting ended in stalemate.

Swedish Voters Reject Euro as Currency—In a **Sept. 14** referendum, 56% of Swedish voters rejected a proposal to adopt the euro as the national currency. Twelve of the 15 European Union members now used the euro; the vote kept Sweden, along with Britain and Denmark, outside the euro zone. A leading euro advocate, Swedish Foreign Min. Anna Lindh, was stabbed in a Stockholm department store, **Sept. 10**, and died the next day; her assailant escaped.

Putin Rebuffs Bush on Iran Nuclear Reactor—At a joint news conference with Pres. Bush at Camp David, MD, **Sept. 27**, Russian Pres. Vladimir Putin said his country would go on with its plan to help Iran build a nuclear reactor. For 2 years, Pres. Bush had sought to persuade Putin to end the $800 mil commercial nuclear contract, concerned that materials for the program could be used to build weapons.

General

Roddick Wins U.S. Tennis Open Men's Title—Fourth-seeded Andy Roddick won the men's singles title **Sept. 7** at the U.S. Open tennis tournament in Queens, NY. It was the first grand-slam title for the 21-year-old American, who defeated Juan Carlos Ferrero of Spain, the 3rd seed, 6-3, 7-6, 6-3. On **Sept. 6**, Justine Henin-Hardenne won the women's singles title, defeating fellow Belgian Kim Clijsters, 7-5, 6-1. Serena and Venus Williams, the sisters who had been dominating women's tennis, did not compete because of injuries.

Archdiocese Settles With Abuse Victims—On **Sept. 9**, the Roman Catholic archdiocese of Boston and lawyers representing about 550 victims of sexual abuse by priests announced a settlement that could run to $85 mil. A mediator would divide up the money. $80,000 to $300,000 per victim, based on the circumstances of the abuse. The archdiocese would also pay for psychological counseling.

Hurricane Claims 40 Lives—Hurricane Isabel struck the North Carolina coast **Sept. 18** and plowed inland, causing at least 40 deaths; property damage was put at $5 bil. Virginia had the highest death toll, at least 23. At sea, Isabel had winds in excess of 150 miles per hour, but winds declined to less than 100 mph by the time the storm made landfall. Extensive flooding occurred in many coastal cities, including Baltimore and Annapolis, MD. Some 4 mil people lost electric power, and federal government offices in Washington, DC, largely closed down. Isabel dissipated over Lake Erie **Sept. 19**.

> "Floyd went up to my house, but Isabel came right in."
> Edenton, NC, resident *Isabelle Ann Bruce*, describing the damage to her house from Hurricane Isabel as compared to that from Hurricane Floyd in 1999.

Pope Names 31 New Cardinals—Pope John Paul II **Sept. 28** announced the appointment of 31 new cardinals, to be officially installed in ceremonies Oct. 21. The 31 included one who was not named (apparently because he lived in a country where his security could be threatened) and one from the U.S., Archbishop Joseph Rigali of Philadelphia. The additions increased to about 135 the number of cardinals under 80 and eligible to vote for a new pope.

OCTOBER 1-16, 2003

National

Judge Bars Death Penalty in Terrorism Trial—A federal judge ruled **Oct. 2**, that prosecutors of alleged terrorist Zacarias Moussaoui could not seek the death penalty or link Moussaoui to the Sept. 11, 2001, attacks because they had not allowed him to interview captured top al-Qaeda operatives held overseas who might provide helpful testimony.

Employment Report Shows Job Growth—The Labor Dept. reported **Oct. 3** that 57,000 new jobs had been created in September—for the first job growth in 8 months. The unemployment rate, which had risen to 6.4% in June, held steady with August's figure at 6.1%. On **Oct. 9**, the Congressional Budget Office estimated that the budget deficit for the 2003 fiscal year would be $374 bil, the largest-ever in dollar terms, although, at 3.5% of gross domestic product, a smaller fraction of the nation's economy than some deficits of the 1980s and early 1990s.

The Dow Jones Industrial Average closed **Oct. 15** at 9,803, after having posted fairly steady advances from a 2003 low of around 7,400 in mid-March.

Californians Recall Governor; Schwarzenegger Elected—In a political earthquake, California voters **Oct. 7** voted to recall their governor from office and replace him with actor-turned-gubernatorial candidate Arnold Schwarzenegger. Gov. Gray Davis (D), who had been elected to a 2nd term just 11 months earlier, was removed by a margin of 55% to 45%, in an election in which 8 mil Californians participated. From a huge field of 135 candidates, voters gave 49% of the vote to Schwarzenegger (R), an Austrian-born former bodybuilder who had won worldwide fame as an action movie star; his closest rival, Lt. Gov. Cruz Bustamante (D), received 32%.

Davis had fallen into wide disfavor because of a $38 bil budget deficit and his perceived mishandling of the state's energy crisis. Schwarzenegger, considered a moderate conservative, vowed to work with Californians to resolve the budget crisis; in his campaign he said he would work to repeal a recent increase in the state vehicle tax and would avoid raising new taxes. He won easily, despite a *Los Angeles Times* story, **Oct. 2**, reporting claims by women that he had made unwanted sexual advances to them in years past. Schwarzenegger acknowledged he had often been on "rowdy movie sets," and apologized for having "behaved badly sometimes." His wife, Maria Shriver, a TV journalist and niece of former Pres. John F. Kennedy, had strongly defended Schwarzenegger's suitability for office.

"Do Not Call" List Challenges Telemarketers—The national "do not call" list, aimed at blocking unwanted phone solicitations by telemarketers, **Oct. 9** resumed accepting requests from people to add their numbers. The Federal Trade Commission had already received 52 mil requests to put numbers on the list. The future of the list was uncertain, however, because of legal challenges, on free-speech grounds.

Democratic Hopefuls Debate in Phoenix—Ten Democrats vying for their party's presidential nomination met for a debate in Phoenix, AZ. **Oct. 9**. Retired Gen. Wesley Clark, the newest candidate, drew criticism from several rivals. They focused especially on recent apparently contradictory statements by Clark, who first said he would have supported a congressional resolution authorizing the invasion of Iraq, and then said he would not. The number of contenders dropped to 9 on **Oct. 6**, when Sen. Bob Graham (FL) withdrew. Polls had shown him getting only single-digit support. Rep. Dennis Kucinich (OH), who had been campaigning for months, officially declared **Oct. 13**.

International

Search for Weapons in Iraq Continues—David Kay, the U.S. government's chief weapons inspector in Iraq, testified to Congress **Oct. 2** that his team had yet to find conclusive evidence of weapons of mass destruction in that country, though he said Saddam Hussein's regime had sought to develop the weapons, forbidden to it under UN Security Council resolutions. Kay said that his team might need up to 9 months to complete its work.

Bomber Kills 19; Israel Retaliates in Syria—A suicide bomber set off an explosion at a restaurant in Haifa, in northern Israel, **Oct. 4**, killing herself and 19 others. Israel retaliated **Oct. 5** with an air attack on a facility 10 miles northwest of Damascus, Syria. Israel said the site was a terrorist training camp used by Hamas and Islamic Jihad; Syria denied this and asked the Security Council to condemn Israel's attack, its first inside Syria since the 1973 war.

Israeli forces killed 8 Palestinians in fighting **Oct. 10** and 11 during a raid into Rafah refugee camp in the Gaza Strip; the Israelis were after tunnels which they claimed were used to smuggle weapons. 3 Americans were killed and 1 wounded **Oct. 15** when a bomb exploded under a diplomatic convoy in the Gaza Strip.

Bombings Add to Death Toll in Iraq—In 2 incidents in Iraq on **Oct. 6**, 3 U.S. soldiers and an Iraqi translator were killed and another soldier was wounded. On **Oct. 9**, a vehicle crashed through the gates of a police station in Baghdad and exploded, killing at least 8 others. The same day, a U.S. soldier was killed by a rocket-propelled grenade northeast of Baghdad, and a Spanish diplomat was shot dead outside his Baghdad home. A bomb outside the Turkish embassy in Baghdad **Oct. 14** killed the bomber and one bystander.

UN Passes Iraq Resolution—The UN Security Council **Oct. 16** unanimously passed a U.S. and British-backed resolution endorsing a U.S.-led multinational force in Iraq. The measure urged UN members to support the Iraq occupation with troops and money, and called on the Iraq Governing Council to present, by Dec. 15, a timetable for preparing a new constitution. Russia, France, and Germany indicated dissatisfaction that the resolution did not accelerate the pace for a transfer of power or provide a stronger UN rule, and said they would not commit troops or new funds. But the unanimous resolution was seen as a victory for the U.S. government and a sign of lessened tension between the U.S. and some of its traditional European allies over Iraq.

General

Rush Limbaugh Admits Painkiller Addiction—Conservative radio talk show host Rush Limbaugh announced on the air **Oct. 10** that he was addicted to prescription painkillers, and said he would enter a rehabilitation center. Earlier, on **Oct. 1**, Limbaugh had resigned as an ESPN football comentator, after controversy arose when he said that a black NFL quarterback, Donovan McNabb, "got a lot of credit...he didn't deserve" because of his race.

China Sends Man into Space—China **Oct. 15** became the 3rd country in the world, after Russia and the U.S., to launch a man into space. Yang Liwei landed safely **Oct. 16**, after orbiting the Earth 14 times in his *Shenzhou 5* craft.

Yankees, Marlins Capture Pennants—The Florida Marlins **Oct. 15** defeated the Chicago Cubs in Chicago by a score of 9-6 to win the National League Pennant in the deciding 7th game, coming from behind both in the game and in the series, which they had trailed 3 games to 1 at one point. The next day, **Oct. 16**, the New York Yankees won the 7th game of their series with the Boston Red Sox, coming from behind, then breaking a tie in the bottom of the 11th inning, to post a 6-5 victory over their longtime rivals and win the American League pennant.

10 Die as Ferry in New York City Strikes Pier—A ferry in New York City, transporting passengers from Manhattan, slammed into a pier on Staten Island **Oct. 15**, causing the death of 10 people and injuring dozens of others, a few of whom lost limbs. The boat struck a maintenance pier 400 feet from the nearest ferry slip; the pilot, Asst. Capt. Richard Smith, fled to his home on Staten Island where he reportedly attempted suicide. An investigation was underway.

Pope Celebrates Jubilee—Pope John Paul II **Oct. 16** celebrated the 25th anniversary of his being named head of the Roman Catholic Church, at a mass in St. Peter's Square in Rome. Now 83 years old, and unable to walk on his own or speak at length, the frail pope asked Catholics to pray for him to have the strength to continue as their leader. Thousands of worshippers attended the mass, paying tribute to a man who had served longer than all but 3 other popes in the church's history.

Notable Supreme Court Decisions, 2002-2003

During the Supreme Court's 2002-2003 term, which ended June 26, 71 decisions were announced, of which 14, or about 20% (down from 28% in 2001-02 and about 1/3 in 2000-01) were decided by 5-4 votes. Chief Justice William H. Rehnquist and Justices Antonin Scalia and Clarence Thomas tended to vote as a conservative bloc, often finding themselves at odds with the court's liberal wing—Justices Ruth Bader Ginsburg, Stephen G. Breyer, John Paul Stevens, and David H. Souter. Justices Sandra Day O'Connor and Anthony M. Kennedy were considered swing votes, though the majority of their votes were with the conservatives in close cases. Following are some of the major rulings of the term.

Criminal Law: The justices June 26 ruled, 6-3, that a Texas law banning sodomy between consenting adults of the same sex was unconstitutional. A 5-4 majority overturned the court's ruling in *Bowers v. Hardwick* (1986), and held that antisodomy laws violated the 14th Amendment's due process clause by depriving defendants of their personal liberty *[Lawrence v. Texas]*.

The court Apr. 29 upheld, 5-4, a law requiring that illegal immigrants convicted of crimes be detained during deportation proceedings, but ruled, 6-3, that the detained immigrants could still pursue habeas corpus petitions in the federal court system *[Demore v. Kim]*.

The court, in two 5-4 rulings, Mar. 5, held that California's "three-strikes" law, which dramatically increased penalties for those convicted of a third felony offense, did not constitute cruel and unusual punishment *[Ewing v. California* and *Lockyer v. Andrade]*.

Speech and Press: The justices June 23 upheld, 6-3, the Children's Internet Protection Act, which required federally funded libraries to block or filter obscene Internet computer network material on computers to which minors had access *[U.S. v. American Library Association]*.

The court Feb. 26 ruled, 8-1, that antiabortion protestors who blockaded abortion clinics could not be prosecuted under the Racketeering and Corrupt Organizations Act (RICO), a federal law designed to fight organized crime *[Scheidler v. National Organization for Women (NOW)* and *Operation Rescue v. NOW]*.

The justices June 16 upheld, 7-2, a ban on direct financial contributions to the campaigns of federal political candidates by nonprofit issue-advocacy corporations *[Federal Election Commission v. Beaumont]*.

The court Apr. 7 ruled, 6-3, that states could outlaw cross-burning without violating the First Amendment's free speech guarantee, arguing that the act historically implied a threat of violence. A 7-2 majority struck down a Virginia cross-burning ban, however, on the grounds that it did not give defendants the opportunity to demonstrate a purely ideological and nonviolent intent *[Virginia v. Black]*.

Civil Rights: The justices June 26 ruled, 5-4, that the 1965 Voting Rights Act allowed Southern states to redraw legislative districts to reduce the number of districts in which blacks and other minorities formed large voting majorities, as long as the intent was to widen their political influence, not dilute it *[Georgia v. Ashcroft]*.

The court June 23 held, 5-4, that the individualized consideration of race as a positive factor in university admissions was a constitutionally acceptable means of achieving diversity *[Grutter v. Bollinger]*. In a linked case, the court ruled, 6-3, that automatically assigning points toward admission to all members of underrepresented racial and ethnic minorities was a violation of the 14th Amendment's equal protection guarantee *[Gratz v. Bollinger]*.

Labor Issues: The court June 9 unanimously ruled that workers seeking to sue their employers for discrimination could rely on circumstantial—as opposed to direct—evidence to show that race, sex, religion, or national origin had been a motivating factor in a dismissal or other job-related decision *[Desert Palace Inc. v. Costa]*.

The justices May 27 ruled, 6-3, that states could be sued for violations of the 1993 federal Family and Medical Leave Act. The court rejected claims of state immunity under the 11th Amendment, arguing that the leave act was enforcing the 14th Amendment's equal protection clause by seeking to remedy gender discrimination in the workplace *[Nevada Department of Human Resources v. Hibbs]*.

Copyrights and Trademarks: The court Mar. 4 unanimously ruled that the owners of well-known brands needed to demonstrate some blurring or disparagement of a brand image, but not lost sales or profits, in order to obtain an injunction against the use of a similar mark by another company *[Moseley v. V Secret Catalogue Inc.]*.

The court Jan. 15 voted, 7-2, to uphold the Sonny Bono Copyright Extension Act, a 1998 law that extended the terms of existing copyrights by 20 years in order to bring U.S. law into line with European standards *[Eldred v. Ashcroft]*.

Personal Injury and Damages: The justices on Apr. 7 voted, 6-3, to limit the size of punitive damages awards, suggesting that the ratio of punitive to compensatory damages should range between 10 to one and one to one in order to avoid violating the Constitution's due process guarantees *[State Farm v. Campbell]*.

Health Care: The court May 19 voted, 6-3, to lift an injunction against a Maine program that sought to negotiate drug discounts for the uninsured by using state Medicaid-related drug purchases as leverage with pharmaceutical companies *[Pharmaceutical Research and Manufacturers of America v. Walsh]*.

The 2003 Nobel Prizes

The 2003 Nobel Prize winners were announced Oct. 2-10. Each prize consisted of a large solid gold medal and a cash award of 10 million Swedish kronor (about $1.32 million).

Chemistry: Peter Agre and Roderick MacKinnon of the U.S. shared the award for helping to discover the structures, or "channels," in cell walls that allowed cells to ferry water and salts into and out of the body.

Economics: The Royal Swedish Academy of Sciences awarded the Nobel Memorial Prize in Economic Science to Robert F. Engle of the U.S. and Clive W. J. Granger of the U.K. for their statistical work in measuring investment risks.

Literature: J. M. Coetzee was the 2nd South African writer to win the Swedish Academy of Letters prize. Coetzee is the author of 7 novels, 2 of which won Britain's Booker Prize. His 1980 novel *Waiting for the Barbarians*, in spare yet eloquent language, depicted the historical situation in South Africa before the abolition of apartheid.

Peace: Shirin Ebadi of Iran, a lawyer and activist, became the first Muslim woman, and the 3rd Muslim ever, to win the Nobel Peace Prize, for her work supporting democracy and human rights. Her efforts focused especially on the rights of women and children. On Oct. 10, after learning she had won the prize, Ebadi held a press conference at which she called for the release of Iranian political prisoners and also criticized U.S. intervention in Muslim countries.

Physics: Vitaly L. Ginzburg of Russia and Alexei A. Abrikosov, a Russian-born American, each received one-third of the award for their work in electrical superconductivity. Anthony J. Leggett, a British-born American, received the other third for his research in superfluidity, the ability of certain fluids to flow without producing any friction.

Physiology or Medicine: Paul C. Lauterbur of the U.S. and Sir Peter Mansfield of the U.K. were honored for their work in developing magnetic resonance imaging (MRI). Used for scanning human bodily tissue (especially the brain and spinal cord), MRI does not employ potentially damaging radiation as have older technologies, such as X rays.

Offbeat News Stories, 2003

Give Me Latte, or . . . Coffee aficionados in Seattle were all steamed up in summer 2003 over Initiative 77—popularly known as the "latte tax." The proposed 10-cent-a-cup tax would be imposed only on espresso-based beverages—the brews that made Starbucks (based in Seattle) famous. Proceeds would go to early childhood education programs for low-income families. Seattle's latte fans campaigned passionately against the initiative, even staging a costumed reenactment of the Boston Tea Party where activists tossed burlap coffee sacks (balloon-filled) into a local lake. In the end the initiative went down in defeat.

Running, A-monk. Sometimes the path to enlightenment is literally thousands of miles long. Buddhist priest Genshin Fujinami, 44, now known as a "marathon monk," completed a 7-year, 24,800-mile spiritual journey through Japan's Hiei Mountains in September. The Tendai-sect ritual dates back to the 8th century and details explicitly the paces and distances for every period of the pilgrimage. According to temple officials, the journey is itself believed to be a path to enlightenment, and though attempted by many it has been survived by only 11 since the end of World War II. Traditionally, those who fail to make it to the end must take their own life.

Amore al Telefono. Italian private investigators are pointing to a new betrayer of extramarital affairs—the now ubiquitous cell phone. Tomponzi Investigations, the country's largest private investigation firm, conducted a survey that revealed that about 90% of cheating spouses were caught by evidence on their own wireless phones. The firm released "Five Golden Rules" to avoid being caught red-handed, which included deleting all text messages, "even the most beautiful," and practicing normal work conversations in front of a mirror to throw a spouse off-track in case an amorous call arrives while in his or her presence.

Letters to God. Hundreds of people annually write their prayers and problems down on paper and mail it to a simple address: "God, Jerusalem, Israel." These letters go first to the Israeli post office's Dead Letters Department, which sees an influx every year around Yom Kippur, the day of atonement. The Dead Letters postal workers see that each piece of mail (collected in a velvet bag) is taken to the Western Wall and posted into a crack, where visitors traditionally insert notes with prayers and wishes.

Cabbage for One. Everyone knows it's important to finish your vegetables, so when Japanese retailer Aeon Co. Ltd. determined that it's difficult for single people to do justice to large vegetables, they decided to look for a solution. In November the company began selling dwarf varieties of large vegetables at 270 stores, including quarter-size cabbages and half-size Japanese radishes. According to the latest census, 41% of households in Japan are single-person residences.

Special Delivery. For Charles D. McKinley, there's no place like home. He was so desperate to see his family in Dallas, TX, that he shipped himself there from New York City in a wooden crate that measured 42" x 36" x 15"—a tight fit for his 5' 8", 170-lb. frame. The two-day trip began at the warehouse where McKinley worked, when a co-worker nailed him into the crate. From there, he was loaded onto a truck and taken to a pressurized, heated cargo plane in New Jersey, which flew him to Niagara Falls, NY, then Fort Wayne, IN, and finally to Dallas. He was then loaded onto a truck which delivered the crate directly to his parents' home. There was no clue that the box, which supposedly contained a computer and clothing, held a person, until the delivery driver unloaded the crate and saw a pair of eyes through a crack. Thinking the box held a dead body, he promptly called police, and McKinley was arrested on unrelated charges, after spending only a few minutes with his stunned parents. He was later charged with violating a federal law prohibiting stowaway travel.

A Sign of Things to Come? Nowadays advertising is ubiquitous. Ads have saturated daily life, appearing on every available surface—including hats, shirts, and shoes—as well as in every print and electronic medium in existence. Perhaps it's only a matter of time before they're broadcast directly into people's brains. A British company called Cunning Stunts has taken sort of a step in that direction, by allowing university students to use their heads, but not their brains, to make money. The premise is simple. A vegetable dye is used to apply a brand name logo to the students' foreheads. The "walking billboards" are paid about $140 a week. In return, they must promise not to alter or remove the logo and must spend a minimum of 3 hours "out and about."

If You Bring it, Will They Come? The Colossal Colon Tour—featuring a 40-foot-long, 4-foot-tall model of a human colon—was making a 20-city tour of the U.S. from February to November 2003 to promote colorectal cancer awareness and prevention. Visitors can either crawl through the giant colon to see examples of various colon diseases or view them through windows. To make the experience as realistic as possible, its creators used actual footage from a colonoscopy. The Colossal Colon is the brainchild of Molly McMaster, herself a colorectal cancer survivor.

The "Grandma Scholarship." For a college student today, $325 might cover the cost of books or lab fees for a semester. But for Rebecca Dupont, a check for that amount will cover tuition for a whole year at Hood College in Frederick, MD. At a time when average tuition at a four-year private college easily exceeds $16,000 a year, Dupont is paying exactly what her grandmother, a 1948 Hood graduate, paid. She is one of seven students awarded a "heritage scholarship" that charges them the same first-year tuition as a parent or grandparent was assessed years ago.

Miscellaneous Facts

Daily Jam, Part 1. The Toyota Motor Corp. urged the 28,000 employees at its headquarters near Tokyo, Japan, to stop driving to work and take public transportation. Each weekday morning, a 1-to-2 mile, hour-long traffic jam builds up in front of Toyota City, Aichi, about 155 miles from Tokyo.

Daily Jam, Part 2. According to a study by the Texas Transportation Institute, the average U.S. driver spent 51 hours a year stuck in traffic in 2001. That's up 4 hours over 1996. The study estimated the cost in wasted time and gas at $69.5 billion. Los Angeles led the list of most congested cities with 90 hours per driver, followed by San Francisco (68 hours), Denver (64 hours), and Miami (63 hours).

Mile High, No Really. Denver is still the "Mile High City," but its official plaque on the steps of the state Capitol was moved 5 steps—3 feet lower than the old marker denoting 1 mile above sea level. The marker draws thousands of tourists every year and Denver trademarked the term in 1998. Using more precise technology the new plaque was positioned within 2 millimeters of the 5,280-foot mark.

A Lot of Crickets, by Jiminy. By gluing micro-transmitters to individual insects, the U.S. Dept. of Agriculture tracked swarms containing millions of 2-inch Mormon Crickets across the West in the summer. Researchers found the crickets walked over 1.25 miles per day in bands 3 miles deep and a mile across—eating most plants in their path.

Bye-bye Old Beetle. One of the most popular cars in U.S. history, the original Volkswagen Beetle, reached the end of the line in Puebla, Mexico, July 30. Though not sold in the U.S. since 1978, Beetles were made and used in several countries. Mexico used them as taxis and police cars.

Say Cheese! Americans eat 30 lbs. of cheese a year, according to the USDA, up from 6 lbs. in 1944. Pizza is the largest source of cheese in the U.S. diet. According to the National Assoc. of Pizzeria Operators, pizzerias bought $2.5 billion worth of pizza cheese in 2002.

Biggest Bite. Not too surprisingly, alligators are the champs of chomp, according to a study done by a Univ. of Florida zoologist. Gators, which can clamp down with as much as 2,290 pounds of force, can out-bite lions, dusky shark, and hyenas.

Notable Quotes in 2003

Iraq Conflict

"They should be given the time to do their work and all of us, the council and the assembly, must realize that time will be necessary, a reasonable amount of time. I'm not saying forever, but they do need time to get their work done, and I suspect the council will allow that to be done."

UN Sec. Gen Kofi Annan, Jan. 27, referring to UN weapons inspectors in Iraq.

"Some have said we must not act until the threat is imminent. Since when have terrorists and tyrants announced their intentions, politely putting us on notice before they strike? If this threat is permitted to fully and suddenly emerge, all actions, all words, and all recriminations would come too late. Trusting in the sanity and restraint of Saddam Hussein is not a strategy, and it is not an option."

Pres. George W. Bush, in the State of the Union Address, Jan. 28, on taking military action against Iraq.

"I truly question the judgment of any president who can say that a massive unprovoked military attack on a nation, which is over 50% children, is 'in the highest moral traditions of our country.'"

Sen. Robert Byrd, in the Senate, Feb. 12.

"France and Germany have the same point of view on this crisis. Any decision belongs to the Security Council and the Security Council alone."

French Pres. Jacques Chirac at a Jan. 22 meeting with German Chancellor Gerhard Schroeder.

"You're thinking of Europe as Germany and France. I don't. I think that's old Europe. . . . Look at vast numbers of other countries in Europe. They're not with France and Germany on this. They're with the United States."

U.S. Defense Sec. Donald Rumsfeld, Jan. 22, responding to a question about opposition in Europe to U.S. policy on Iraq.

"This is not the time to falter. This is the time . . . to show that we will stand up for what we know to be right, to show that we will confront the tyrannies and dictatorships and terrorists who put our way of life at risk, to show at the moment of decision that we have the courage to do the right thing."

U.K. Prime Min. Tony Blair arguing in the House of Commons Mar. 18 for a motion to disarm Iraq "by all means necessary."

"In this battle, we have fought for the cause of liberty and for the peace of the world. Our nation and our coalition are proud of this accomplishment, yet it is you, the members of the United States military, who achieved it. Your courage, your willingness to face danger for your country and for each other made this day possible."

Pres. Bush, May 1, announcing the end of major combat in Iraq, aboard the aircraft carrier USS *Abraham Lincoln*.

"The British government has learned that Saddam Hussein recently sought significant quantities of uranium from Africa."

Pres. Bush, in his Jan. 28 State of the Union address.

"Knowing all that we know now, the reference to Iraq's attempt to acquire uranium from Africa should not have been included in the State of the Union speech."

A senior *Bush administration official*, in a statement July 7 authorized by the White House.

"There was no imminent threat. This was made up in Texas, announced in January to the Republican leadership, that war was going to take place and was going to be good politically. This whole thing was a fraud."

Sen. Edward Kennedy (D, MA) in a Sept. 18 interview.

"To try to gauge just how out of touch the Democrat leadership is on the war on terror, just close your eyes and try to imagine Ted Kennedy landing that Navy jet on the deck of that aircraft carrier. I don't know about you; I certainly don't want to see Teddy Kennedy in a Navy flight suit anytime soon."

House majority leader *Tom DeLay* (R, TX), July 25.

National News

"The facts that I have seen in reviewing each and every one of these cases raised questions not only about the innocence of people on death row, but about the fairness of the death penalty system as a whole. Our capital system is haunted by the demon of error: error in determining guilt and error in determining who among the guilty deserves to die."

Gov. George Ryan (R, IL), Jan. 11, on his commutation of all death sentences in his state.

"Jobs are created when the economy grows; the economy grows when Americans have more money to spend and invest; and the best and fairest way to make sure Americans have that money is not to tax it away in the first place."

Pres. Bush, in the State of the Union Address, Jan. 28.

"We think it's upside-down economics: it does too little to stimulate the economy now and does too much to weaken our economic future. It will create huge, permanent deficits that will raise interest rates, stifle growth, hinder homeownership, and cut off the avenues of opportunity that have let so many work themselves up from poverty."

Gov. Gary Locke (D, WA), in the Democratic response to the State of the Union Address, Jan. 28.

"I want to make something very, very clear at this point: We don't want individuals or families to start sealing their doors or their windows."

Sec. of Homeland Security, Tom Ridge, in Feb. 2003, days after officials recommended that Americans prepare emergency kits containing duct tape and plastic sheeting to cover windows in case of a terrorist attack.

"I'm sort of on record as not being in favor of marriage, period, for myself. I've done one marriage, and I think I'll stay out of the marriage business. I've got other things to worry about."

New York City Mayor Michael Bloomberg, at the gay and lesbian pride parade June 30, when asked whether he supported gay marriage.

"Say *hasta la vista* to Gray Davis."

Actor Arnold Schwarzenegger, announcing on *The Tonight Show*, Aug. 6, that he was running for governor in the California recall election.

"On January 16th, we saw our loved ones launch into a brilliant, cloud-free sky. Their hearts were full of enthusiasm, pride in country, faith in their God, and a willingness to accept risk in the pursuit of knowledge—knowledge that might improve the quality of life for all mankind. *Columbia*'s 16-day mission of scientific discovery was a great success, cut short by mere minutes—yet it will live on forever in our memories."

Excerpt from a statement from the families of those lost on the space shuttle *Columbia*, Feb. 3.

International

"You may not like the word, but what's happening is occupation."

Israeli Prime Min. Ariel Sharon, May 26, describing the situation in West Bank and Gaza.

"You have to look at history as an evolution of society."

Canadian Prime Min. Jean Chrétien, on his country's new policy providing full marriage rights for same-sex couples.

"I found the mass murderers I was looking for, and I have outlived all of them. . . . My work is done."

94-year-old *Nazi hunter Simon Wiesenthal*, explaining his retirement in the Austrian magazine *Format* in April.

"I'm not very happy about the future of Mount Everest. At the base camp, there are 1,000 people there, with some 500 tents, and a booze place for drinks and all the other comforts. Just sitting around in a big base camp, knocking back cans of beer, I don't particularly regard as mountaineering."

Sir Edmund Hillary, who, along with Tenzing Norgay, was the first to reach the summit of Mt. Everest; in Nepal in May for the 50th anniversary of his feat.

Lighter Side

"At my age, celebrating means getting into bed for a good nap."

95-year-old *Don Flickinger*, May 3, on receiving his associate's degree, which he had started in 1928.

"I hear kids crying in the background. There's nothing we can do. They're gone."

Roto-Rooter dispatcher Margie Valadez, who received dozens of calls from parents of kids who flushed pet fish down the toilet to return them to the ocean, after seeing a fish freed in a similar way in the movie *Finding Nemo*.

OBITUARIES

Deaths, Oct. 16, 2002–Oct. 15, 2003

A

Agnelli, Giovanni, 81, longtime head of Italy's Fiat auto company; Turin, Italy, Jan. 24, 2003.

Amin, Idi, 78(?), Ugandan military ruler, 1971-79; under his rule an estimated 300,000 people were killed; Jidda, Saudi Arabia, Aug. 16, 2003.

Arledge, Roone, 71, TV executive who revolutionized sports coverage at ABC and ran the news division for 2 decades; New York, NY, Dec. 5, 2002.

Armstrong, Garner Ted, 73, TV evangelist who founded 2 churches after being excommunicated from Worldwide Church of God by his father; Tyler, TX, Sept. 15, 2003.

Atkins, Dr. Robert C., 72, cardiologist who promoted a controversial diet high in fats and proteins, low in carbohydrates; New York, NY, Apr. 17, 2003.

Axelrod, George, 81, who wrote *The Seven Year Itch* (1952) and screenplays for *Breakfast at Tiffany's* (1961) and *The Manchurian Candidate* (1962); Los Angeles, CA, June 21, 2003.

B

Berio, Luciano, 77, versatile Italian modernist composer; Rome, Italy, May 27, 2003.

Berrigan, Philip, 79, former Catholic priest who helped lead the radical anti-war movement in the Vietnam era; Baltimore, MD, Dec. 6, 2002.

Bloom David, 39, NBC TV reporter, coanchor; died of natural causes while covering war in Iraq, Apr. 6, 2003.

Bonds, Bobby, 57, 3-time All-Star major league baseball player, 1968-81; father of Barry Bonds; San Carlos, CA, Aug. 23, 2003.

Bracken, Eddie, 87, character actor whose films included *The Miracle of Morgan's Creek* and *Hail the Conquering Hero* (both 1944); Montclair, NJ, Nov. 14, 2002.

Brinkley, David, 82, TV newscaster and commentator whose broadcasts with Chet Huntley on NBC (1956-70) sparked a new era in TV journalism; later (1981-97) he anchored Sunday's *This Week With David Brinkley* on ABC; Houston, TX, June 11, 2003.

Bronson, Charles, 81, action-film star in Europe and later Hollywood; known especially for his 1974 *Death Wish* vengeance film and its sequels; Los Angeles, CA, Aug. 30, 2003.

Brooks, Herb, 66, coach who guided the U.S. Olympic hockey team's "miracle on ice" victory in 1980 winter games; near Minneapolis, MN, Aug. 11, 2003.

Buchholz, Horst, 69, German actor who made his mark in Hollywood in such films as *The Magnificent Seven* (1960); Berlin, Germany, Mar. 3, 2003.

C

Carter, Benny, 95, one of jazz's greatest alto saxophonists; also a composer, bandleader, and civil rights activist; Los Angeles, CA, July 12, 2003.

Carter, Nell, 54, singer and actress who won a Tony for *Ain't Misbehavin'* (1978) and played the housekeeper in TV's *Gimme a Break!* (1981-87); Beverly Hills, CA, Jan. 23, 2003.

Cash, Johnny, 71, country music icon, known as "The Man in Black"; recorded 1,500 songs and sold more than 50 million records in a nearly 5-decade-long career; Nashville, TN, Sept. 12, 2003.

Cash, June Carter, 73, country music singer and songwriter; wife of Johnny Cash; Nashville, TN, May 15, 2003.

Chaikin, Joseph, 67, actor and director known for his experimental theater; New York, NY, June 22, 2003.

Coburn, James, 74, character actor whose films included *The Magnificent Seven* (1960) and *Affliction* (1998); Los Angeles, CA, Nov. 18, 2002.

Coors, Joseph, 85, beer company magnate; backer of conservative causes; Rancho Mirage, CA, Mar. 15, 2003.

Cronyn, Hume, 91, veteran Canadian-born actor; he and wife Jessica Tandy made up a renowned acting team; Fairfield, CT, June 15, 2003.

Cruz, Celia, 77, Cuban-born singer, for many years the undisputed queen of salsa; Fort Lee, NJ, July 16, 2003.

D

DeBusschere, Dave, 62, basketball Hall of Famer whose defensive prowess sparked New York Knicks NBA championships in 1970 and 1973; New York, NY, May 14, 2003.

Dillon, C. Douglas, 93, Wall Street financier, diplomat, and U.S. treasury secretary, 1961-65; New York, NY, Jan. 10, 2003.

Doby, Larry, 79, baseball Hall of Famer; in 1947 became 1st black player in the American League; Montclair, NJ, June 18, 2003.

E

Eban, Abba, 87, Israeli UN representative in 1949, later served as foreign minister; also a scholarly author; Petah Tikva, Israel, Nov. 17, 2002.

Ebsen, Buddy, 95, vaudevillian; star of 1930s movie musicals; later played the patriarch of TV's "Beverly Hillbillies" and detective Barnaby Jones; Torrance, CA, July 6, 2003.

F

Falkenburg, Jinx, 84, cover-girl model during World War II; later a talk-show pioneer with husband Tex McCrary; Manhasset, NY, Aug. 27, 2003.

Fast, Howard, 88, author of *Freedom Road* (1944) and other historical novels; Old Greenwich, CT, Mar. 12, 2003.

Fiedler, Leslie, 85, provocative literary critic best known for *Love and Death in the American Novel* (1960); Buffalo, NY, Jan. 29, 2003.

Freeman, Orville L., 84, former Minnesota governor and U.S. agriculture secretary; Minneapolis, MN, Feb. 20, 2003.

G

Galtieri, Leopoldo, 76, military ruler who in 1982 led Argentina into war with Britain over the Falkland Islands; Buenos Aires, Argentina, Jan. 12, 2003.

Gardner, Herb, 68, comic playwright who wrote *A Thousand Clowns* (1962) and *I'm Not Rappaport* (1985); New York, NY, Sept. 24, 2003.

Gavilan, Kid, 77, flamboyant former world welterweight champ (1951-54); Miami, FL, Feb. 13, 2003.

Getty Jr., J. Paul, 70, U.S. oil-fortune heir who settled in Britain in the 1970s and gave away over $200 million; London, England, Apr. 17, 2003.

Gibb, Maurice, 53, 1 of the 3 brothers who made up the Bee Gees; Miami Beach, FL, Jan. 12, 2003.

Gibson, Althea, 76, women's tennis pro who in 1957 became the first black player to win both Wimbledon and the U.S. national tennis championship (1957); East Orange, NJ, Sept. 28, 2003.

Giroud, Françoise, 86, French journalist who in the 1970s was France's 1st minister of women's affairs; Paris, France, Jan. 19, 2003.

Green, Adolph, 87, lyricist of Broadway musicals like *Bells Are Ringing* (1956), and the film musical *Singin' in the Rain* (1952); New York, NY, Oct. 24, 2002.

Guy, Billy, 66, an original member of the Coasters rock group; Las Vegas, NV, Nov. 12, 2002.

H

Hackett, Buddy, 78, popular comedian of nightclubs, theater, and TV; he also appeared in over 20 films; Malibu, CA, June 30, 2003.

Harris, Richard, 72, hard-living Irish-born actor whose films ranged from *Camelot* (1967) to *Harry Potter and the Sorcerer's Stone* (2001); London, England, Oct. 25, 2002.

Heilbrun, Carolyn, 77, Columbia professor, feminist literary scholar, and mystery writer (as Amanda Cross); by suicide, New York, NY, Oct. 9, 2003.

Heiskell, Andrew, 87, chairman of Time Inc. from 1960 to 1980; later helped raise large sums for charity; Darien, CT, July 6, 2003.

Helms, Richard, 89, 1st career intelligence professional to serve as director of the CIA (1966-72); Washington, DC, Oct. 22, 2002.

Hepburn, Katharine, 96, legendary actress whose films included *The Philadelphia Story* (1940), *The African Queen* (1952), and *Guess Who's Coming to Dinner* (1967)—one of her record 4 Oscar-winning roles; Old Saybrook, CT, June 29, 2003.

Hill, George Roy, 81, director of such classics as *Butch Cassidy and the Sundance Kid* (1969) and *The Sting* (1973); New York, NY, Dec. 27, 2002.

Hiller, Dame Wendy, 90, British actress who won a 1958 supporting actress Oscar for *Separate Tables*; Beaconsfield, England, May 14, 2003.

Hines, Gregory, 57, stellar tap dancer who had a major crossover career as a stage, screen, and TV actor; Los Angeles, CA, Aug. 9, 2003.

Hines, Jerome, 81, bass vocalist who sang with NYC Metropolitan Opera for 41 years; New York, NY, Feb. 4, 2003.

Hirschfeld, Al, 99, artist known for his caricatures of theater personalities; New York, NY, Jan. 20, 2003.

Hope, Bob, 100, legendary comedian, renowned for his rapid-fire one-liners; he flourished on radio and TV and in the movies (often paired with Bing Crosby), entertained U.S. troops overseas from the 1940s till the 1990s, often hosted Hollywood's Oscars; Toluca Lake, CA, July 27, 2003.

J

Jackson, Maynard H., 65, Democratic mayor of Atlanta, GA (1973-81, 1989-93); Arlington, VA, June 23, 2003.

Jam Master Jay (Jason Mizell), 37, disc jockey who helped Run-DMC break into mainstream music; murdered in New York, NY, Oct. 30, 2002.

Jenkins, Roy (Lord Jenkins of Hillhead), 82, British politician; cofounded the Social Democratic Party; East Hendred, England, Jan. 5, 2003.

K

Kazan, Elia, 94, director responsible for the world theater premiere of *A Streetcar Named Desire* (1947) and the film classics *Gentleman's Agreement* (1947) and *On the Waterfront* (1954); New York, NY, Sept. 28, 2003.

Kempson, Rachel, 92, British actress and matriarch of the Redgrave acting family; Millbrook, NY, May 24, 2003.

Kerr, Jean, 80, author of the best-seller *Please Don't Eat the Daisies* (1957); married to theater critic Walter Kerr; White Plains, NY, Jan. 5, 2003.

Kroc, Joan, 75, former owner of the San Diego Padres, widow of McDonald's Corp. founder Ray Kroc; Rancho Santa Fe, CA, Oct. 12, 2003.

L

Long, Russell B., 84, Democratic senator from Louisiana, 1948-87; son of Louisiana politician Huey Long; Washington, DC, May 9, 2003.

Longden, Johnny, 96, star jockey; won the 1943 Triple Crown aboard Count Fleet; Banning, CA, Feb. 14, 2003.

Longford, Lady Elizabeth, 96, historian, biographer, and matriarch of a British literary dynasty; Hurst Green, England, Oct. 23, 2002.

M

MacKenzie, Gisele, 76, Canadian-born singer, well known to TV audiences of the 1950s and 1960s; Burbank, CA, Sept. 5, 2003.

Maddox, Lester G., 87, Georgia restaurateur elected governor as a segregationist in 1967; later softened his stance; Atlanta, GA, June 25, 2003.

Mann, Herbie, 73, innovative jazz flutist; drew upon a host of international styles, from Brazilian to Japanese; Pecos, NM, July 1, 2003.

Marinho, Roberto, 98, Brazilian media magnate; produced telenovelas (soap operas) seen around the world; Rio de Janeiro, Brazil, Aug. 6, 2003.

Matta, Roberto, 90 or 91, Chilean artist whose haunting surrealist canvasses influenced U.S. abstract expressionists; Tarquinia, Italy, Nov. 23, 2002.

Mauldin, Bill, 81, cartoonist whose bedraggled Willie and Joe were icons for U.S. troops during World War II; Newport Beach, CA, Jan. 22, 2003.

McClendon, Sarah, 92, veteran White House reporter from Texas; Washington, DC, Jan. 8, 2003.

McCrary, Tex, 92, PR man who with wife Jinx Falkenburg was a talk-show pioneer in the 1940s and 1950s; New York, NY, July 29, 2003.

Merton, Robert K., 92, Columbia Univ. sociologist who coined the term "role model" and pioneered focus groups; New York, NY, Feb. 23, 2003.

Moynihan, Daniel Patrick, 76, diplomat and 4-term Democratic senator from New York (1977-2001), esteemed for his writing and research in social policy; Washington, DC, Mar. 26, 2003.

N

Ne Win, 91, military ruler of Burma (now Myanmar), 1962-88; Yangon, Myanmar, Dec. 5, 2002.

Neilson, Roger, 69, National Hockey League coach who pioneered the use of videotape in analyzing hockey; Peterborough, Canada, June 22, 2003.

O

O'Bannon, Frank, 73, Indiana Democrat who had been governor of his state since 1997; Chicago, IL, Sept. 8, 2003.

O'Connor, Donald, 78, actor and dancer best known for his 1950s "Francis the Talking Mule" movies and the movie musical Singin' in the Rain (1952); Woodland Hills, CA, Sept. 27, 2003.

Olatunji, Babatunde, 75, Nigerian-born drummer and bandleader who helped inspire Afro-jazz fusion in the 1960s; Salinas, CA, Apr. 6, 2003.

Omarr, Sydney, 76, astrologer of the Hollywood stars; Santa Monica, CA, Jan. 2, 2003.

P

Palmer, Robert, 54, British singer and songwriter who won a best male rock vocal Grammy in 1986 for "Addicted to Love"; Paris, France, Sept. 26, 2003.

Parker, Suzy, 69, 1950s model who paved the way for the "supermodels" to come; Montecito, CA, May 3, 2003.

PayCheck, Johnny, 64, rebellious country music singer best known for his 1977 recording of "Take This Job and Shove It"; Nashville, TN, Feb. 18, 2003.

Peck, Gregory, 87, dignified Hollywood star who played a journalist fighting anti-Semitism in Gentleman's Agreement (1947) and attorney Atticus Finch in To Kill a Mockingbird (1962), for which he won an Oscar; Los Angeles, CA, June 12, 2003.

Phillips, Sam, 80, founder of Sun Records, who recorded a young Elvis Presley and discovered other pioneer artists; Memphis, TN, July 30, 2003.

Plimpton, George, 76, founding editor of the Paris Review; a "participatory journalist" who tried everything from pro football to trapeze acrobatics; New York, NY, Sept. 26, 2003.

Prigogine, Ilya, 86, Russian-born Belgian chemist who won a 1977 Nobel Prize for work in thermodynamics; Brussels, Belgium, May 28, 2003.

R

Rawls, John, 81, Harvard philosopher, known for A Theory of Justice (1971); Lexington, MA, Nov. 24, 2002.

Regan, Donald T., 84, Pres. Reagan's treasury secretary (1981-85) and White House chief of staff (1985-87); Williamsburg, VA, June 10, 2003.

Riefenstahl, Leni, 101, German film director known for the Nazi propaganda documentaries Triumph of the Will (1935) and Olympia (1938); Poecking, Germany, Sept. 8, 2003.

Ritter, John, 54, comic actor in TV's "Three's Company" (1977-84); was starring in the TV sitcom "8 Simple Rules...for Dating My Teenage Daughter"; Burbank, CA, Sept. 11, 2003.

Ritts, Herb, 50, photographer known for his flattering images of celebrities and glorification of young, athletic bodies; Los Angeles, CA, Dec. 26, 2002.

Rogers, (Mr.) Fred, 74, who as puppeteer, producer, and host of the PBS TV show Mister Rogers' Neighborhood (1968-2001) offered low-key friendly fun and guidance to young children; Pittsburgh, PA, Feb. 27, 2003.

Rostow, Eugene V., 89, Yale law school dean turned presidential adviser; helped shape Vietnam-era foreign policy; Alexandria, VA, Nov. 25, 2002.

Rostow, Walt W., 85, economic historian who was a leading advocate and planner of U.S. military action in Vietnam; Austin, TX, Feb. 13, 2003.

S

Sadruddin Aga Khan, Prince, 70, philanthropist, environmentalist, and longtime UN High Commissioner for Refugees (1965-1977); Boston, MA, May 12, 2003.

Said, Edward, 67, Columbia Univ. literary scholar and critic; a leading advocate of the Palestinian cause; New York, NY, Sept. 25, 2003.

Sankoh, Foday, 65, leader of a Sierra Leone rebel group; in UN custody awaiting trial on war-crimes charges; Freetown, Sierra Leone, July 29, 2003.

Santamaria, Mongo, 80, Cuban-born conga player and percussionist; Miami, FL, Feb. 1, 2003.

Schlesinger, John, 77, British film director of the Oscar-winning Midnight Cowboy (1969) and Sunday, Bloody Sunday (1971); Palm Springs, CA, July 25, 2003.

Schramm, Tex, 83, innovative general manager of the Dallas Cowboys football team (1960-89); Dallas, TX, July 15, 2003.

Scott, Martha, 88, actress who created the role of Emily in the 1938 Broadway production of Our Town; Los Angeles, CA, May 28, 2003.

Segundo, Compay, 95, Cuban singer, guitarist, and songwriter; Havana, Cuba, July 13, 2003.

Shoemaker, Bill, 73, Hall of Fame jockey who rode 4 Kentucky Derby winners, won 8,833 times in all; San Marino, CA, Oct. 12, 2003.

Simmons, Richard W., 89, actor who played the title character in the 1950s TV series Sergeant Preston of the Yukon; Oceanside, CA, Jan. 11, 2003.

Simone, Nina, 70, jazz and blues singer and activist dubbed "The High-Priestess of Soul"; Carry-le-Rouet, France, Apr. 21, 2003.

Sisulu, Walter, 90, Nelson Mandela's closest associate in the African National Congress; South Africa, May 5, 2003.

Stack, Robert, 84, actor best known as 1930s crime fighter Eliot Ness in TV's "The Untouchables" (1959-63); Los Angeles, CA, May 14, 2003.

Steig, William, 95, cartoonist for The New Yorker and author of children's books, including Shrek, basis of a popular movie; Boston, MA, Oct. 3, 2003.

Strummer, Joe, 50, guitarist and vocalist with the British punk-rock band The Clash; Broomfield, England, Dec. 22, 2002.

T

Teller, Edward, 95, Hungarian-born nuclear physicist sometimes referred to as the father of the hydrogen bomb; Stanford, CA, Sept. 9, 2003.

Thatcher, Sir Denis, 88, British oil executive married to Margaret Thatcher; London, England, June 26, 2003.

Thurmond, Strom, 100, South Carolina governor (1947-51), segregationist presidential candidate (1948), longest-serving U.S. senator (1954-56, 1957-2003); Edgefield, SC, June 26, 2003.

Trevor-Roper, Hugh, 89, British historian; praised for The Last Days of Hitler (1947); erred in the 1980s by authenticating forged Hitler diaries; Oxford, England, Jan. 26, 2003.

U

Uris, Leon, 78, best-selling author of Exodus (1958) and other historical epics; Shelter Island, NY, June 21, 2003.

W

Wellstone, Paul, 58, liberal Democrat from Minnesota who had served in the Senate since 1991; in plane crash near Eveleth, MN, Oct. 25, 2002.

White, Barry, 58, rhythm and blues singer whose seductive versions of 1970s ballads made him a disco-era superstar; Los Angeles, CA, July 4, 2003.

Wilson, Sloan, 83, novelist who wrote the 1955 best-seller The Man in the Gray Flannel Suit; Colonial Beach, VA, May 25, 2003.

Winsor, Kathleen, 83, romance novelist who wrote Forever Amber (1944); New York, NY, May 26, 2003.

Z

Zevon, Warren, 56, singer and songwriter known for wry ballads about morbid characters; Los Angeles, CA, Sept. 7, 2003.

Ziegler, Ronald L., 63, presidential press secretary throughout the Nixon administration (1969-74); Coronado, CA, Feb. 10, 2003.

Zindel, Paul, 66, young-adult novelist and playwright; won Pulitzer for The Effect of Gamma Rays on Man-in-the-Moon Marigolds; New York, NY, Mar. 27, 2003.

Historical Anniversaries

1904 — 100 Years Ago

U.S. Supreme Court rules Jan. 4 that **citizens of Puerto Rico** are not aliens and cannot be refused access to the continental U.S.

Baltimore's business center is destroyed by fire Feb. 7-8.

Russia and **Japan** officially declare war against each other on Feb. 10, two days after a Japanese attack on the Russian fleet in a Manchurian port.

On Mar. 14, U.S. Supreme Court orders the breakup of J.P. Morgan and Edward Heary Harriman's Northern Securities Company, **halting consolidation** of the nation's **railroads**.

Britain and **France** settle key disputes and agree on closer relations under the **Entente Cordiale**, signed Apr. 8.

Andrew Carnegie, Apr. 15, establishes a hero fund amounting to $5 mil. to reward those who risk their lives rescuing others, and support the survivors of those heroes.

A fire on the *General Slocum* excursion steamer on New York's East River, June 15, kills over 1,000 people, most of them women and children from the Little Germany neighborhood.

William K. Vanderbilt sponsors the first organized automobile race, the **Vanderbilt Cup**, Oct 8.

The first section of the **New York subway system** opens Oct. 27, running from the Brooklyn Bridge north to 145th St. and Broadway.

Theodore Roosevelt is reelected to the presidency Nov. 8, defeating Democrat Alton B. Parker.

In his annual message to Congress Dec. 6, Roosevelt issues what becomes known as the **Roosevelt Corollary** to the **Monroe Doctrine**, stating that the U.S. can intervene to end "intolerable conditions" in the Western Hemisphere.

Art. Claude Monet's *Houses of Parliament*; Gustav Klimt's *The Water Serpents*; Gutzon Borglum's *Mares of Diomedes*.

Literature. Ellen Glasgow's *The Deliverance*; Henry James's *The Golden Bowl*; O. Henry's *Cabbages and Kings*; Jack London's *The Sea Wolf*. Anton Chekhov dies July 15.

Movies. *The Impossible Voyage*, by Georges Méliès, a hand-colored film based on the play by Jules Verne.

Music. Gustav Mahler's *Symphony No. 5*; Richard Wagner's *Parsifal* is performed by the Metropolitan Opera Company amid reviews criticizing its eroticism.

Nonfiction. Ida M. Tarbell's *The History of the Standard Oil Company*; Lincoln Steffens's *The Shame of the Cities*.

Popular Songs. "Meet Me in St. Louis, Louis" by Frederick Mills and Andrew Sterling; "Yankee Doodle Boy" by George M. Cohan.

Science and Technology. Louis Cartier invents the wristwatch; Ambrose Fleming invents the vacuum tube diode (radio tube); Thomas Morgan's experiments with fruit flies lead to the discovery of sex-linked gene mutations; Benjamin Holt constructs first gasoline-powered tractor.

Sports. The Olympic Games are held in the U.S. for the first time, in St. Louis, July 1-Nov. 23, with 12 countries participating. New York Giants manager John McGraw refuses to allow his team to play in the World Series against Boston, citing conflicts with American League management. Denton T. "Cy" Young pitches the first perfect game of the modern era, May 5.

Theatre. *Sunday*, starring Ethel Barrymore; *Mrs. Wiggs of the Cabbage Patch*.

Miscellaneous. A woman is arrested for smoking in an open car on New York City's Fifth Ave. The Louisiana Purchase Exposition in St. Louis, a world's fair, introduces ice cream cones and iced tea. Jujitsu vogue spreads, spurred on by Pres. Roosevelt.

1954 — 50 Years Ago

On Feb. 2, Pres. Eisenhower officially reports detonation of the **first hydrogen bomb**, which took place at Eniwetok Attol in 1952.

Five U.S. representatives are wounded by gunshots fired from the gallery in the House by Puerto Rican independence supporters Mar. 1.

The controversial **Army-McCarthy hearings** are conducted and televised Apr. 23-June 17. Sen. Joseph McCarthy is officially censured by the Senate Dec. 2.

The **Geneva Conference** meets Apr. 26-July 21 and reaches agreements for an armistice and political settlement in Indochina.

U.S. Supreme Court rules unanimously May 17 that racial segregation in public schools violates the 14th Amendment in **Brown v. Board of Education of Topeka.**

Robert Oppenheimer, head of the Manhattan Project, is dismissed from government service June 29 because of suspected Communist associations.

Pres. Eisenhower proposes his four-point **highway modernization** program on July 12.

On Sept. 3 Eisenhower signs the **Espionage and Sabotage Act of 1954**, authorizing the death penalty as punishment for peacetime sabotage.

Work begins Sept. 6 on the **first nuclear power plant** in the U.S., located near Pittsburgh.

The Tonight Show debuts on TV Sept. 27, with host Steve Allen.

Gamal Abdel Nasser assumes the presidency of Egypt Nov. 19.

Prices on the **New York Stock Exchange** Dec. 31 are the **highest** quoted since 1929; volume of shares traded during 1954 is the highest since 1933.

Art. Jackson Pollock's *White Light*; Diego Rivera's *The Painter's Studio*; Norman Rockwell's *Girl at Mirror*. Henri Matisse dies Nov. 3.

Literature. William Faulkner's *A Fable*; William Golding's *Lord of the Flies*; Mac Hyman's *No Time for Sergeants*; J.R.R. Tolkien's *The Fellowship of the Ring* and *The Two Towers*. Ernest Hemingway wins the Nobel Prize for Literature; Colette dies Aug. 3.

Movies. *On the Waterfront* starring Marlon Brando; Alfred Hitchcock's *Rear Window* starring James Stewart and Grace Kelly; *The Barefoot Contessa* starring Humphrey Bogart and Ava Gardner; Federico Fellini's *La Strada*.

Music. Igor Stravinsky's *Four Russian Peasant Songs*; Aaron Copland's *The Tender Land*; Roy Harris's *Symphonic Fantasy*.

Nonfiction. Albert Einstein's *Ideas and Opinions*; Joseph Wood Krutch's *The Measure of Man*.

Popular Songs. Elvis Presley's "That's All Right (Mama)"; The Chordettes' "Mr. Sandman"; Joe Turner's "Shake Rattle and Roll"; The Penguins' "Earth Angel"; "Hernando's Hideaway" from the musical *Pajama Game*.

Science and Technology. Jonas Salk's polio vaccine is given to 500,000 schoolchildren in test areas; RCA begins marketing color TVs; first successful kidney transplant performed by Joseph Edward Murray at Boston's Peter Bent Brigham Hospital.

Sports. Roger Bannister is the first to break the 4-minute mile (3:59.4), May 6, at the Iffley Road track in Oxford, England. U.S. Open golf tournament won by Ed Furgol; Mildred "Babe" Didrikson Zaharias wins U.S. Women's Open golf tournament; New York Giants win the World Series in four straight games over the Cleveland Indians; LaSalle defeats Bradley 92-76 for NCAA championship; *Sports Illustrated* begins publication Aug. 16.

Theatre. *The Confidential Clerk* by T.S. Eliot; Sandy Wilson's *The Boy Friend* starring Julie Andrews; Herman Wouk's *The Caine Mutiny Court-Martial* starring Henry Fonda and Lloyd Nolan; Maxwell Anderson's *The Bad Seed* starring Patty McCormack and Eileen Heckart. Joseph Papp founds the New York Shakespeare Festival.

Miscellaneous. Sun Myung Moon founds the Unification Church, May 1. Actor Lionel Barrymore dies Nov. 15. On Dec. 27 U.S. Air Force officials announce a **new land speed record** of 632 mph, set by an experimental rocket-powered sled.

UNITED STATES GOVERNMENT

EXECUTIVE BRANCH	LEGISLATIVE BRANCH	JUDICIAL BRANCH
PRESIDENT **Vice President** **Executive Office of the President** White House Office Office of the Vice President Council of Economic Advisers Council on Environmental Quality National Security Council Office of Administration Office of Management and Budget Office of National Drug Control Policy Office of Policy Development Office of Science and Technology Policy Office of the U.S. Trade Representative	**CONGRESS** **Senate House** Architect of the Capitol U.S. Botanic Garden General Accounting Office Government Printing Office Library of Congress Congressional Budget Office	**Supreme Court of the United States** Courts of Appeals District Courts Territorial Courts Court of International Trade Court of Federal Claims Tax Court Court of Appeals for Veterans Claims Administrative Office of the Courts Federal Judicial Center Sentencing Commission

The Bush Administration
As of Oct. 2003; mailing addresses are for Washington, DC.
Terms of office of the president and vice president: Jan. 20, 2001, to Jan. 20, 2005.

President — George W. Bush receives an annual salary of $400,000 (taxable), and an annual expense allowance of $50,000 (nontaxable) for costs resulting from official duties. In addition, up to $100,000 a year may be spent on travel expenses and $19,000 on official entertainment (both nontaxable), available for expenditures within the Executive Office of the President.
Website: www.whitehouse.gov/president; *E-mail:* president@whitehouse.gov
Vice President — Dick Cheney receives an annual salary of $198,600 (taxable), plus $90,000 for official entertainment expenses (nontaxable).
Website: www.whitehouse.gov/vicepresident; *E-mail:* vice.president@whitehouse.gov

The Cabinet Department Heads
(Salary: $171,900 per year)
Secretary of State — Colin L. Powell
Secretary of the Treasury — John Snow
Secretary of Defense — Donald H. Rumsfeld
Attorney General — John Ashcroft
Secretary of the Interior — Gale Norton
Secretary of Agriculture — Ann M. Veneman
Secretary of Commerce — Donald L. Evans
Secretary of Labor — Elaine L. Chao
Secretary of Health and Human Services — Tommy Thompson
Secretary of Housing and Urban Development — Mel Martinez
Secretary of Transportation — Norman Y. Mineta
Secretary of Energy — Spencer Abraham
Secretary of Education — Roderick R. Paige
Secretary of Veterans Affairs — Anthony Principi
Secretary of Homeland Security — Tom Ridge

The White House Staff
1600 Pennsylvania Ave. NW 20500
Website: www.whitehouse.gov
Chief of Staff to the President — Andrew H. Card Jr.
Asst. to the President & Deputy Chief of Staff — Joseph W. Hagin II
Asst. to the President & Deputy Chief of Staff — Harriet Miers
Assistants to the President:
  Counsel to the President — Alberto R. Gonzalez
  Deputy Counsel to the President — David Leitch
  Domestic Policy Council — Margaret Spellings
  Homeland Security Advisor — John Gordon
  Presidential Personnel — Dina Powell
  Press Secretary — Scott McClellan
  Legislative Affairs — David Hobbs
  Communications — Dan Bartlett
  National Economic Council — Stephen Friedman, dir.
  Intergovernmental Affairs — Ruben S. Barrales
  National Security — Condoleezza Rice
  Staff Secretary — Brett Kavanaugh
  Political Affairs — Matt Schlapp
  Public Liaison — Lezlee Westine
  Cabinet Secretary — Brian Montgomery
  Director of Presidential Scheduling — Bradley Blakeman
  Director of Speechwriting — Michael Gerson
  Chief of Staff to the First Lady — Andrea Ball
    E-mail: first.lady@whitehouse.gov
  Senior Advisor to the President — Karl Rove

Director of Advance — Greg Jenkins
Management, Admin., & Oval Office Operations — Linda Gambatesa
Faith-Based and Community Initiatives — Jim Towey
Office of National AIDS Policy — Carol Thompson, act. dir.

Executive Agencies
Council of Economic Advisers — Dr. N. Gregory Mankiw, chair
  Website: www.whitehouse.gov/cea
Office of Administration — Tim Campen, dir.
  Website: www.whitehouse.gov/oa
Office of Science & Technology Policy — Dr. John H. Marburger
  Website: www.ostp.gov
Office of Natl. Drug Control Policy — John P. Walters, dir.
  Website: www.whitehousedrugpolicy.gov
Office of Management and Budget — Joshua B. Bolten, dir.
  Website: www.whitehouse.gov/omb
U.S. Trade Representative — Robert B. Zoellick
  Website: www.ustr.gov
Council on Environ. Quality — James L. Connaughton, chair
  Website: www.whitehouse.gov/ceq

Department of State
2201 C St. NW 20520
Website: www.state.gov
Secretary of State — Colin L. Powell
Deputy Secretary — Richard L. Armitage
Chief of Staff — Lawrence Wilkerson
U.S. Ambassador to the United Nations — John D. Negroponte
U.S. Agency for Intl. Dev. — Andrew S. Natsios
Under Sec. for Political Affairs — Marc Grossman
Under Sec. for Management — Grant S. Green Jr.
Under Sec. for Global Affairs — Paula J. Dobriansky
Under Sec. for Economic, Business, & Agricultural Affairs — Alan P. Larson
Under Sec. for Arms Control & International Security Affairs — John R. Bolton
Under Sec. for Public Diplomacy & Public Affairs — Patricia de Stacy Harrison, act.
Policy Planning Director — Mitchell B. Reiss
Chief of Protocol — Donald B. Ensenat
Inspector General — vacant
Legal Adviser — William H. Taft IV
Counterterrorism — J. Cofer Black
War Crimes Issues — Pierre-Richard Prosper
Director General of the Foreign Service & Director of Human Resources — W. Robert Pearson

Assistant Secretaries for:
Administration — Willliam A. Eaton
African Affairs — Walter H. Kansteiner
Arms Control — Stephen G. Rademaker
Civil Rights — Barbara Pope
Consular Affairs — Maura Harty
Democracy, Human Rights, & Labor — Lorne W. Craner
Diplomatic Security — Francis X. Taylor
East Asian & Pacific Affairs — James A. Kelly
Economic & Business Affairs — Earl Anthony Wayne
Educational & Cultural Affairs — Patricia de Stacy Harrison
European & Eurasian Affairs — Elizabeth A. Jones
Intelligence & Research — Carl W. Ford Jr.
International Narcotics & Law Enforcement Affairs — Robert Charles
International Organization Affairs — Kim Holmes
Legislative Affairs — Paul V. Kelly
Near Eastern Affairs — William Joseph Burns
Nonproliferation — John Stern Wolf
Oceans, International Environmental, & Scientific Affairs — John F. Turner
Political-Military Affairs — Lincoln P. Bloomfield
Population, Refugees, & Migration — Arthur E. Dewey
Public Affairs — Richard A. Boucher
Resource Management — Christopher B. Burnham
South Asian Affairs — Christina B. Rocca
Verification & Compliance — Paula A. DeSutter
Western Hemisphere Affairs — Roger F. Noriega

Department of the Treasury
1500 Pennsylvania Ave. NW 20220
Website: www.ustreas.gov
Secretary of the Treasury — John W. Snow
Deputy Sec. of the Treasury — vacant
Under Sec. for Domestic Finance — Peter R. Fisher
Under Sec. for International Affairs — John B. Taylor
General Counsel — vacant
Inspector General — Jeffrey Rush Jr.
Inspector General for Tax Administration — Pam Gardiner, act.
Assistant Secretaries for:
Economic Policy — Mark Warshawsky, act.
Financial Institutions — Wayne A. Abernathy
Fiscal Affairs — Donald Hammond
International Affairs — Randy K. Quarles
Legislative Affairs — John Duncan
Management — Teresa Mullett Russel
Public Affairs — Rob Nichols
Tax Policy — Pamela F. Olson
Treasurer of the U.S. — vacant
Bureaus:
Alcohol and Tobacco Tax and Trade — Arthur J. Libertucci, dir.
Comptroller of the Currency — John Hawke Jr., comm.
Engraving & Printing — Tom Ferguson, dir.
Financial Management Service — Richard Gregg, comm.
Internal Revenue Service — Mark W. Everson, comm.
Mint — Henrietta Holmsman Fore
Office of Thrift Supervision — James Gilleron
Public Debt — Van Zeck, comm.

Department of Defense
The Pentagon 20301
Website: www.defenselink.mil
Secretary of Defense — Donald H. Rumsfeld
Deputy Secretary — Paul D. Wolfowitz
Under Sec. for Acquis. and Technol. — Michael Wynne, act.
Under Sec. for Personnel & Readiness — David S. C. Chu
Under Sec. for Policy — Douglas J. Feith
Assistant Secretaries for:
Command, Control, Communications, & Intelligence — John P. Stenbit
Force Management — Charles S. Abell
Health Affairs — William Winkenwerder Jr., MD
International Security Affairs — Peter W. Rodman
International Security Policy — Dr. J. D. Crouch II
Legislative Affairs — Powell A. Moore
Public Affairs — Lawrence Di Rita, act.
Reserve Affairs — Thomas F. Hall

Special Operations & Low-Intensity Conflict — Thomas W. O'Connell
Program Analysis & Evaluation — Ken Krieg
Inspector General — Joseph E. Schmitz
Comptroller — Dov S. Zakheim
General Counsel — William J. Haynes II
Intelligence Oversight — George B. Lotz II
Operational Test & Evaluation — Thomas P. Christie, dir.
Chairman, Joint Chiefs of Staff — Gen. Richard B. Myers
Secretary of the Army — Les Brownlee, act.
Secretary of the Navy — Hansford T. Johnson, act.
Commandant of the Marine Corps — Gen. Michael W. Hagee
Secretary of the Air Force — James G. Roche

Department of Justice
Constitution Ave. & 10th St. NW 20530
Website: www.usdoj.gov
Attorney General — John Ashcroft
Deputy Attorney General — Larry Thompson
Associate Attorney General — Robert D. McCallum Jr.
Office of Dispute Resolution — Jeffrey M. Senger
Solicitor General — Theodore B. Olson
Office of Inspector General — Glenn Fine
Assistants:
Antitrust Division — R. Hewitt Pate
Civil Division — Peter D. Keisler
Civil Rights Division — R. Alexander Acosta
Criminal Division — Christopher Wray, act.
Environ. & Nat. Resources Division — Thomas Sansonetti
Justice Programs — Deborah Daniels
Legal Counsel — Edward Whelan, act.
Legislative Affairs — William E. Moschella
Legal Policy — vacant
Tax Division — Eileen O'Connor
Executive Secretariat — Kathie Harting
Office of Public Affairs — Barbara Comstock
Office of Information & Privacy — Richard L. Huff/Daniel J. Metcalfe
Community Oriented Policing Services — Carl R. Peed
Federal Bureau of Investigation — Robert S. Mueller III
Exec. Off. for Immigration Review — Kevin D. Rooney, dir.
Bureau of Prisons — Harley G. Lappin
Community Relations Service — Sharee M. Freeman, dir.
Drug Enforcement Admin. — Karen P. Tandy
Office of Intelligence Policy & Review — James Baker
Office of Professional Responsibility — H. Marshall Jarrett, counsel
Exec. Off. for U.S. Trustees — Lawrence Friedman, dir.
Foreign Claims Settlement Comm. — Mauricio J. Tamargo
Exec. Office for U.S. Attorneys — Guy A. Lewis, dir.
Pardon Attorney — Roger C. Adams
U.S. Parole Commission — Edward F. Reilly Jr.
U.S. Marshals Service — Benigno G. Reyna
U.S. Natl. Cen. Bureau of INTERPOL — James M. Sullivan
Office of Intergovernmental and Public Liaison — Lori Sharpe Day
Office of Tribal Justice — Tracy Toulou
Violence Against Women Office — Diane Stewart
National Drug Intelligence Center — Michael T. Horn, dir.

Department of the Interior
1849 C St. NW 20240
Website: www.doi.gov
Secretary of the Interior — Gale Norton
Deputy Secretary — J. Steven Griles
Assistant Secretaries for:
Fish, Wildlife, & Parks — Craig Manson
Indian Affairs — Aurene M. Martin
Land & Minerals — Rebecca W. Watson
Policy, Management, & Budget — P. Lynn Scarlett
Water & Science — Bennett Raley
Bureau of Land Management — Kathleen Clarke
Bureau of Reclamation — John W. Keys III
Fish & Wildlife Service — Steven A. Williams
Geological Survey — Charles Groat
Minerals Management Service — R.M. "Johnnie" Burton
National Park Service — Fran P. Mainella, dir.
Surf. Mining Reclam. & Enforcement — Jeffrey Jarrett
Communications — Eric Ruff, dir.
Congressional & Legislative Affairs — David L. Bernhardt

Solicitor — William G. Myers
External Affairs — Kit Kimball
Exec. Secretariat & Regulatory Affairs — Fay Iudicello

Department of Agriculture
1400 Independence Ave. SW 20250
Website: www.usda.gov

Secretary of Agriculture — Ann M. Veneman
Deputy Secretary — James R. "Jim" Moseley
Under Secretaries for:
  Farm & Foreign Agric. Services — J. B. Penn
  Food, Nutrition, & Consumer Services — Eric M. Bost
  Food Safety — Elsa A. Murano
  Marketing & Regulatory Progs. — William T. Hawks
  Natural Resources & Environment — Mark E. Rey
  Research, Education, & Economics — Joseph Jen
  Rural Development — Tom Dorr
Assistant Secretaries for:
  Administration — John Surina, act.
  Civil Rights — Vernon Parker
  Congressional Relations — Mary Waters
General Counsel — Nancy S. Bryson
Inspector General — Phyllis Fong
Chief Financial Officer — Edward R. McPherson
Chief Information Officer — Scott Charbo
Chief Economist — Keith Collins
Press Secretary — Alisa Harrison

Department of Commerce
1401 Constitution Ave. NW 20230
Website: www.commerce.gov

Secretary of Commerce — Donald L. Evans
Deputy Secretary — Samuel Bodman
Chief of Staff — Phil Bond
General Counsel — Ted Kassinger
Assistant Secretaries:
  Chief Financial Officer & Asst. Secretary for
    Admin. — Otto Wolff
  Economic Development Admin. — David Sampson
  Export Admin. — Jim Jochun
  Export Enforcement — Michael Garcia
  Import Administration — Faryar Shirzad
  Legislative and Intergovernmental Affairs — Brenda Becker
  Market Access & Compliance — William Lash
  National Telecomm. Information Administration —
    Michael D. Gallagher, act.
  Oceans & Atmosphere — James Mahoney
  Trade Development — Linda Conlin
  U.S. & Foreign Commercial Service — Maria Cino, dir.
Bureau of the Census — Charles Louis Kincannon
Under Sec. for Oceans & Atmosphere — Vice Admiral
  Conrad Lautenbacher
Under Sec. for Industry & Security — Kenneth Juster
Under Sec. for International Trade — Grant Aldonas
Under Sec. for Economics and Statistics Admin. —
  Kathleen Cooper
Under Sec. for Patent & Trademark Office — James Rogan
Under Sec. for Technology — Phil Bond
Natl. Institute of Standards & Tech. — Arden Bement
Minority Business Dev. Agency — Ronald Langston
Public Affairs — Ron Bonjean

Department of Labor
200 Constitution Ave. NW 20210
Website: www.dol.gov

Secretary of Labor — Elaine L. Chao
Deputy Secretary — vacant
Chief of Staff — Steven J. Law
Assistant Secretaries for:
  Admin. & Management — Patrick Pizzella
  Congressional & Intergov. Affairs — Kristine Iverson
  Employment & Training — Emily Stover DeRocco
  Employment Standards — Victoria Lipnic
  Occupational Safety & Health — John Henshaw
  Mine Safety & Health — David Lauriski
  Employee Benefits Security Admin. — Ann Combs
  Policy — Christopher Spear
  Public Affairs — Lisa Krusa, act.
  Veterans Employment & Training — Frederico Juarbe Jr.
Solicitor of Labor — Howard M. Radzely, act.

Bureau of International Affairs — vacant
Women's Bureau — Shinae Chun
Inspector General — Gordon S. Heddell
Bureau of Labor Statistics — Kathleen P. Utgoff

Department of Health and Human Services
200 Independence Ave. SW 20201
Website: www.os.dhhs.gov

Secretary of Health & Human Services — Tommy Thompson
Deputy Secretary — Claude A. Allen
Chief of Staff — Scott Whitaker
Assistant Secretaries for:
  Aging — Josefina Carbonell
  Children & Families — Wade F. Horn
  Health — Richard Carmona, act.
  Legislation — vacant
  Administration & Management — Ed Sontag
  Planning & Evaluation — Ann-Marie Lynch, act.
  Public Affairs — Kevin Keane
General Counsel — Alex Azar II
Inspector General — Janet Rehnquist
Office for Civil Rights — Richard M. Campanelli
Surgeon General — Richard Carmona
Centers for Medicare and Medicaid Services — Tom Scully

Department of Housing and Urban Development
451 7th St. SW 20410
Website: www.hud.gov

Secretary of Housing & Urban Development — Mel Martinez
Deputy Secretary — Alphonso R. Jackson
Chief of Staff — Frank R. Jimenez
Assistant Secretaries for:
  Community Planning & Development — Roy A. Bernardi
  Congressional & Intergov. Relations — Stephen B. Nesmith
  Fair Housing & Equal Opportunity — Carolyn Y. Peoples
  Administration — Vickers B. Meadows
  Housing & Federal Housing Comm. — John C. Weicher
  Policy Development & Research — vacant
  Public & Indian Housing — Michael Liu
General Counsel — Richard A. Hauser
Inspector General — Kevin M. Donohue
Chief Financial Officer — vacant
Government National Mortgage Assn. — Ronald Rosenfeld
Off. of Federal Housing Enterprise Oversight — vacant

Department of Transportation
400 7th St. SW 20590
Website: www.dot.gov

Secretary of Transportation — Norman Y. Mineta
Deputy Secretary — vacant
Assistant Secretaries for:
  Administration — Vincent Taylor
  Aviation & International Affairs — Michael W. Reynolds
  Budget & Programs — Donna McLean
  Governmental Affairs — Nicole Nason
  Public Affairs — Leonardo Alcivar
  Transportation Policy — Emil H. Frankel
Federal Aviation Admin. — Marion C. Blakey
Federal Highway Admin. — Mary Peters
Federal Railroad Admin. — Allan Rutter
Maritime Admin. — Capt. William Schubert
Natl. Highway Traffic Safety Admin. — Dr. Jeffrey W.
  Runge
Federal Transit Admin. — Jennifer L. Dorn
Research & Special Programs Admin. — Samuel G. Bonasso
St. Lawrence Seaway Devel. Corp. — Albert Jacquez

Department of Energy
1000 Independence Ave. SW 20585
Website: www.energy.gov

Secretary of Energy — Spencer Abraham
Deputy Secretary — Kyle McSlarrow
Under Secretary — Robert Card
Chief of Staff — Joseph McMonigle
General Counsel — Lee Otis
Inspector General — Gregory Friedman
Assistant Secretaries for:
  Administration & Human Resource Management —
    Richard Farrell
  Congressional & Intergov. Affairs — vacant
  Defense Programs — vacant

Energy Efficiency & Renewable Energy — David Garman
Environment, Safety, & Health — Beverly Cook
Environmental Management — Jessie Roberson
Fossil Energy — Carl Michael Smith
International Affairs — Vicky A. Bailey
Oversight & Performance Assurance — Glenn Podonsky
Nuclear Energy — Bill Magwood
Energy Information Admin. — Guy F. Caruso
Economic Impact & Diversity — Theresa Speake
Hearings & Appeals — George Breznay, dir.
Science & Technology — Walter L. Warnick, dir.
Civilian Radioactive Waste Management — Margaret Chu
National Nuclear Security Admin. — Linton Brooks
Chief Financial Officer — Bruce Carnes
Energy Advisory Board — Craig R. Reed
Office of Public Affairs — Jeanne Lopatto

Department of Education
400 Maryland Ave., SW 20202
Website: www.ed.gov

Secretary of Education — Roderick R. Paige
Deputy Secretary — Eugene W. Hickok, act.
Chief of Staff — John M. Danielson
Inspector General — John P. Higgins Jr.
General Counsel — Brian W. Jones
Assistant Secretaries for:
  Adult & Vocational Education — vacant
  Civil Rights — Gerald Reynolds
  Institute of Education Sciences — Grover J. "Russ" Whitehurst
  Elementary & Secondary Educ. — Ronald Tomalis, act.
  Intergov. & Interagency Affairs — Laurie M. Rich
  Legislative & Congressional Affairs — Karen A. Johnson
  Postsecondary Education — Sally L. Stroup
  Special Educ. & Rehab. Services — Robert H. Pasternack
Bilingual Education & Minority Language Affairs — Maria Hernandez Ferrier
Rehab. Services Admin. — Joanne M. Wilson, comm.
Education Statistics — Dr. Gary Phillips, act. comm.

Department of Veterans Affairs
810 Vermont Ave. NW 20420
Website: www.va.gov

Secretary of Veterans Affairs — Anthony Principi
Deputy Secretary — Leo Mackay Jr.
Assistant Secretaries for:
  Congressional Affairs — Gordon Mansfield
  Management — William H. Campbell

Human Resources & Admin. — vacant
Policy & Planning — Claude Kicklighter
Public & Intergovernmental Affairs — vacant
Inspector General — Richard J. Griffin
Under Sec. for Benefits — Daniel L. Cooper
Under Sec. for Health — Robert H. Roswell, M.D.
Under Sec. for Memorial Affairs — John W. Nicholson
General Counsel — Tim McClain
Board of Veterans Appeals — Eligah Dane Clark, chair
Board of Contract Appeals — Gary Krump, chair
Small & Disadvantaged Business Utilization — Scott S. Denniston, dir.
Veterans Service Organization Liaison — Allen F. Kent

Department of Homeland Security
Nebraska Ave. 20528
Website: www.dhs.gov/dhspublic

Secretary of Homeland Security — Tom Ridge
Under Sec. for Border & Trans. Sec. — Asa Hutchinson
Under Sec. for Emergency Preparedness & Response — Michael Brown
Under Sec. for Info. Analysis & Infrastructure Protection — Frank Libutti
Under Sec. for Management — Janet Hale
Under Sec. for Science & Tech. — Dr. Charles E. McQueary
Assistant Secretaries for:
  Public Affairs — Susan K. Neely
  Bur. of Immigration & Customs Enforcement — Michael J. Garcia
  Infrastructure Protection — Robert P. Liscouski
  Policy & Planning of BTS — C. Stewart Verdery
U.S. Coast Guard Commandant — Adm. Thomas H. Collins
U.S. Secret Service — W. Ralph Basham, dir.
Inspector General — Clark Kent Ervin, act.
Bur. of Citizenship & Immigration Services — Eduardo Aguirre Jr., dir.
Office of Natl. Capital Region Coordination — Michael F. Byrne, dir.
Officer for Civil Rights & Civil Liberties — Daniel W. Sutherland
General Counsel — Joe D. Whitley
Chief Privacy Officer — Nuala O'Connor Kelly
Chief Information Officer — Steven I. Cooper
Chief Financial Officer — Bruce Marshall Carnes
Chief Human Capital Officer — Ronald J. James
Customs & Border Protection — Robert C. Bonner, comm.

Notable U.S. Government Agencies

Source: *The U.S. Government Manual*; National Archives and Records Administration; World Almanac research
All addresses are Washington, DC, unless otherwise noted; as of Oct. 2003
* = independent agency

Bureau of Alcohol, Tobacco, Firearms and Explosives — Bradley A. Buckles, dir. (Dept. of Justice, 650 Mass. Ave NW, 20226). *Website:* www.atf.treas.gov
Bureau of the Census — Charles Louis Kincannon, dir. (Dept. of Commerce, 4700 Silver Hill Rd., 20233). *Website:* www.census.gov
Bureau of Citizenship & Immigration Services — Eduardo Aguirre Jr., dir. (Dept. of Homeland Security, 425 I St. NW, 20536).
Bureau of Economic Analysis — J. Steven Landefeld, dir. (Dept. of Commerce, 1441 L St. NW, 20230). *Website:* www.bea.gov
Bureau of Indian Affairs — Aurene M. Martin, act. asst. sec. (Dept. of the Interior, 1849 C St. NW, 20240). *Website:* www.doi.gov/bureau-indian-affairs.html
Bureau of Prisons — Harley G. Lappin, dir. (Dept. of Justice, 320 First St. NW, 20534). *Website:* www.bop.gov
Centers for Disease Control & Prevention — Dr. Julie Louise Gerberding, dir. (Dept. of HHS, 1600 Clifton Rd., Atlanta, GA 30333). *Website:* www.cdc.gov
***Central Intelligence Agency** — George J. Tenet, dir. (Wash., DC 20505). *Website:* www.cia.gov
***Commission on Civil Rights** — Mary Frances Berry, chair (624 9th St. NW, 20425). *Website:* www.usccr.gov

***Commodity Futures Trading Commission** — James E. Newsome, chair (3 Lafayette Centre, 1155 21st St. NW, 20581). *Website:* www.cftc.gov
***Consumer Product Safety Commission** — Hal Stratton, chair (East-West Towers, 4330 East-West Hwy., Bethesda, MD 20814). *Website:* www.cpsc.gov
***Environmental Protection Agency** — Marianne Lamont Horinko, acting adm. (Ariel Rios Bldg., 1200 Pennsylvania Ave. NW, 20460). *Website:* www.epa.gov
***Equal Employment Opportunity Commission** — Cari M. Dominguez, chair (1801 L St. NW, 20507). *Website:* www.eeoc.gov
***Export-Import Bank of the United States** — Philip Merrill, pres. and chair (811 Vermont Avenue NW, 20571). *Website:* www.exim.gov
***Farm Credit Administration** — Michael M. Reyna, chair, Farm Credit Administration Board (1501 Farm Credit Drive, McLean, VA 22102). *Website:* www.fca.gov
Federal Aviation Administration — Marion C. Blakey, adm. (Dept. of Trans., 800 Independence Ave. SW, 20591). *Website:* www.faa.gov
Federal Bureau of Investigation — Robert S. Mueller III, dir. (Dept. of Justice, 935 Pennsylvania Ave. NW, 20535). *Website:* www.fbi.gov

°**Federal Communications Commission** — Michael K. Powell, chair (445 12th St. SW, 20554). *Website:* www.fcc.gov

°**Federal Deposit Insurance Corporation** — Donald E. Powell, chair (550 17th St. NW, 20429). *Website:* www.fdic.gov

°**Federal Election Commission** — Ellen L. Weintraub, chair (999 E St. NW, 20463).*Website:* www.fec.gov

°**Federal Emergency Management Agency** — Michael D. Brown, under sec. (500 C St. SW, 20472). *Website:* www.fema.gov

°**Federal Energy Regulatory Commission** — Pat Wood III, chair (888 1st St. NE, 20426). *Website:* www.ferc.gov

Federal Highway Administration — Mary E. Peters, adm. (Dept. of Trans., 400 7th St. SW, 20590). *Website:* www.fhwa.dot.gov

°**Federal Maritime Commission** — Steven R. Blust, chair (800 N. Capitol St. NW, 20573). *Website:* www.fmc.gov

°**Federal Mine Safety & Health Review Commission** — Michael F. Duffy, chair (601 New Jersey Ave. NW, 20001). *Website:* www.fmshrc.gov

°**Federal Reserve System** — Alan Greenspan, chair, Board of Governors (20th St. & Constitution Ave. NW, 20551). *Website:* www.federalreserve.gov

°**Federal Trade Commission** — Timothy J. Muris, chair (600 Pennsylvania Ave. NW, 20580). *Website:* www.ftc.gov

Fish & Wildlife Service — Steven A. Williams, dir. (Dept. of the Interior, 1849 C St. NW, 20240). *Website:* www.fws.gov

Food and Drug Administration — Mark McClellan, comm. (Dept. of HHS, 5600 Fishers Lane, Rockville, MD 20857). *Website:* www.fda.gov

Forest Service — Dale N. Bosworth, chief (Dept. of Agriculture, 201 14th St. SW, 20024). *Website:* www.fs.fed.us

General Accounting Office — (cong. agency) David Michael Walker, comptroller gen. (441 G St. NW, 20548). *Website:* www.gao.gov

°**General Services Administration** — Stephen A. Perry, adm. (1800 F St. NW, 20405). *Website:* www.gsa.gov

Government Printing Office — (cong. agency) Bruce R. James, public printer (732 N. Capitol St. NW, 20401). *Website:* www.gpoaccess.gov

°**Inter-American Foundation** — Frank Yturria, chair (901 N Stuart St., 10th floor, Arlington, VA 22203). *Website:* www.iaf.gov

Internal Revenue Service — Mark W. Everson, comm. (Dept. of Treas., 1111 Constitution Ave. NW, 20224). *Website:* www.irs.gov

Library of Congress — (cong. agency) Dr. James H. Billington, Librarian of Congress (101 Indep. Ave. SE, 20540). *Website:* www.loc.gov

°**National Aeronautics and Space Administration** — Sean O'Keefe, adm. (300 E St. SW, 20546). *Website:* www.nasa.gov

°**National Archives & Records Administration** — John W. Carlin, archivist (700 Pennsylvania Ave. NW, 20408). *Website:* www.nara.gov

°**National Endowment for the Arts** — Dana Gioia, chair (1100 Pennsylvania Ave. NW, 20506). *Website:* www.arts.gov

°**National Endowment for the Humanities** — Bruce Cole, chair (1100 Pennsylvania Ave. NW, 20506). *Website:* www.neh.fed.us

National Institutes of Health — Dr. Elias Zerhouni, dir. (Dept. of HHS, 9000 Rockville Pike, Bethesda, MD 20892). *Website:* www.nih.gov

°**National Labor Relations Board** — Robert J. Battista, chair (1099 14th St. NW, 20570). *Website:* www.nlrb.gov

National Oceanic and Atmospheric Administration — Vice Adm. Conrad C. Lautenbacher Jr., adm. (Dept. of Commerce, 14th & Constitution Ave. NW, 20230). *Website:* www.noaa.gov

National Park Service — Fran B. Mainella, dir. (Dept. of the Interior, 1849 C St. NW, 20240). *Website:* www.nps.gov

°**National Railroad Passenger Corp. (Amtrak)** — David Gunn, pres. and CEO (60 Mass. Ave. NE, 20002). *Website:* www.amtrak.com

°**National Science Foundation** — Dr. Rita Colwell, dir., National Science Foundation; Dr. Warren M. Washington, chair, National Science Board (4201 Wilson Blvd., Arlington, VA 22230).*Website:* www.nsf.gov

°**National Transportation Safety Board** — Ellen Engleman, chair (490 L'Enfant Plaza SW, 20594). *Website:* www.ntsb.gov

°**Nuclear Regulatory Commission** — Nils J. Diaz, chair (11555 Rockville Pike, Rockville, MD 20852). *Website:* www.nrc.gov

Occupational Safety & Health Administration — John L. Henshaw, asst. sec. (Dept. of Labor, 200 Constitution Ave. NW, 20210).*Website:* www.osha.gov

°**Occupational Safety & Health Review Commission** — James M. Stephens, chair (1120 20th St. NW, 9th Floor, 20036). *Website:* www.oshrc.gov

°**Office of Government Ethics** — Amy L. Comstock, dir. (1201 New York Ave. NW, Suite 500, 20005). *Website:* www.usoge.gov

°**Office of Personnel Management** — Kay Coles James, dir. (1900 E St. NW, 20415-0001). *Website:* www.opm.gov

°**Office of Special Counsel** — vacant (1730 M St. NW, Suite 300, 20036). *Website:* www.osc.gov

°**Peace Corps** — Gaddi H. Vasquez, dir. (1111 20th St., NW, 20526). *Website:* www.peacecorps.gov

°**Postal Rate Commission** — George A. Omas, chair (1333 H St. NW, Suite 300, 20268). *Website:* www.prc.gov

°**Securities and Exchange Commission** — William H. Donaldson, chair (450 5th St. NW, 20549). *Website:* www.sec.gov

°**Selective Service System** — Lewis C. Brodsky, act. dir. (National Headquarters, 1515 Wilson Blvd., Arlington, VA 22209-2425). *Website:* www.sss.gov

°**Small Business Administration** — Hector V. Barreto, adm. (409 Third St. SW, 20416). *Website:* www.sba.gov

Smithsonian Institution — (quasi-official agency) Lawrence M. Small, sec. (PO Box 37012, SI Building, Rm. 153, MRCOIO, 20013). *Website:* www.si.edu

°**Social Security Administration** — Jo Anne B. Barnhart, comm. (6401 Security Blvd., Baltimore, MD 21235). *Website:* www.ssa.gov

Surgeon General — Dr. Richard Carmona (Dept. of HHS, 5600 Fishers Ln., Rm. 18-66, Rockville, MD 20857). *Website:* www.surgeongeneral.gov

°**Tennessee Valley Authority** — Glenn L. McCollough Jr., chair, Board of Directors (400 W. Summit Hill Dr., Knoxville, TN 37902, and One Mass. Ave. NW, Suite 300, 20444). *Website:* www.tva.gov

°**Trade and Development Agency** — Thelma J. Askey, dir. (1000 Wilson Blvd. Ste. 1600, Arlington, VA 22209). *Website:* www.tda.gov

United States Coast Guard — Adm. Thomas H. Collins, commandant (Dept. of Homeland Security, 2100 2nd St. SW, 20593). *Website:* www.uscg.mil

United States Customs and Border Protection — Robert C. Bonner, comm. (Dept. of Homeland Security, 1300 Pennsylvania Ave. NW, 20229). *Website:* www.customs.gov

United States Geological Survey — Charles G. Groat, dir. (Dept. of the Interior, 12201 Sunrise Valley Dr., Reston, VA 20192). *Website:* www.usgs.gov

°**United States International Trade Commission** — Deanna Tanner Okun, chair (500 E St. SW, 20436). *Website:* www.usitc.gov

United States Mint — Henrietta Holsman Fore, dir. (Dept. of Treas., U.S. Mint Headquarters, 801 9th St., NW, 20002). *Website:* www.usmint.gov

°**United States Postal Service** — John E. Potter, Postmaster General (475 L'Enfant Plaza SW, 20260). *Website:* www.usps.gov

United States Secret Service — W. Ralph Bashman, dir. (Dept. of Homeland Security, 950 H St. NW, 20223). *Website:* www.secretservice.gov

CABINETS OF THE U.S.

The U.S. Cabinet and Its Role

The heads of major executive departments of government constitute the Cabinet. This institution, not provided for in the U.S. Constitution, developed as an advisory body out of the desire of presidents to consult on policy matters. Aside from its advisory role, the Cabinet as a body has no function and wields no executive authority. Individual members exercise authority as heads of their departments, reporting to the president.

In addition to the heads of federal departments as listed below, the Cabinet commonly includes other officials designated by the president as of Cabinet rank.

The officials so designated by Pres. George W. Bush include: Vice Pres. Dick Cheney, Chief of Staff to the President Andrew H. Card Jr., Environmental Protection Agency Acting Administrator Marianne Lamont Horinko, Office of Management and Budget Director Joshua B. Bolten, Office of National Drug Control Policy Director John Walters, and United States Trade Representative Robert B. Zoellick.

The Cabinet meets at times set by the president. Members of Pres. Bush's Cabinet listed in this chapter are as of Oct. 15, 2003.

Secretaries of State

The Department of Foreign Affairs was created by act of Congress on July 27, 1789, and the name changed to Department of State on Sept. 15, 1789.

President	Secretary	Home	Apptd.
Washington	Thomas Jefferson	VA	1789
	Edmund Randolph	VA	1794
	Timothy Pickering	PA	1795
Adams, J.	Timothy Pickering	PA	1797
	John Marshall	VA	1800
Jefferson.	James Madison	VA	1801
Madison	Robert Smith	MD	1809
	James Monroe	VA	1811
Monroe	John Quincy Adams	MA	1817
Adams, J.Q.	Henry Clay	KY	1825
Jackson	Martin Van Buren	NY	1829
	Edward Livingston	LA	1831
	Louis McLane	DE	1833
	John Forsyth	GA	1834
Van Buren	John Forsyth	GA	1837
Harrison, W.H.	Daniel Webster	MA	1841
Tyler	Daniel Webster	MA	1841
	Abel P. Upshur	VA	1843
	John C. Calhoun	SC	1844
Polk	John C. Calhoun	SC	1845
	James Buchanan	PA	1845
Taylor	James Buchanan	PA	1849
	John M. Clayton	DE	1849
Fillmoe	John M. Clayton	DE	1850
	Daniel Webster	MA	1850
	Edward Everett	MA	1852
Pierce	William L. Marcy	NY	1853
Buchanan	William L. Marcy	NY	1857
	Lewis Cass	MI	1857
	Jeremiah S. Black	PA	1860
Lincoln	Jeremiah S. Black	PA	1861
	William H. Seward	NY	1861
Johnson, A.	William H. Seward	NY	1865
Grant	Elihu B. Washburne	IL	1869
	Hamilton Fish	NY	1869
Hayes	Hamilton Fish	NY	1877
	William M. Evarts	NY	1877
Garfield	William M. Evarts	NY	1881
	James G. Blaine	ME	1881
Arthur	James G. Blaine	ME	1881
	F.T. Frelinghuysen	NJ	1881
Cleveland	F.T. Frelinghuysen	NJ	1885
	Thomas F. Bayard	DE	1885
Harrison, B.	Thomas F. Bayard	DE	1889
Harrison, B.	James G. Blaine	ME	1889
	John W. Foster	IN	1892
Cleveland	Walter Q. Gresham	IN	1893
	Richard Olney	MA	1895
McKinley	Richard Olney	MA	1897
	John Sherman	OH	1897
	William R. Day	OH	1898
	John Hay	DC	1898
Roosevelt, T.	John Hay	DC	1901
	Elihu Root	NY	1905
	Robert Bacon	NY	1909
Taft	Robert Bacon	NY	1909
	Philander C. Knox	PA	1909
Wilson	Philander C. Knox	PA	1913
	William J. Bryan	NE	1913
	Robert Lansing	NY	1915
	Bainbridge Colby	NY	1920
Harding	Charles E. Hughes	NY	1921
Coolidge	Charles E. Hughes	NY	1923
	Frank B. Kellogg	MN	1925
Hoover	Frank B. Kellogg	MN	1929
	Henry L. Stimson	NY	1929
Roosevelt, F.D.	Cordell Hull	TN	1933
	E.R. Stettinius Jr.	VA	1944
Truman	E.R. Stettinius Jr.	VA	1945
	James F. Byrnes	SC	1945
	George C. Marshall	PA	1947
	Dean G. Acheson	CT	1949
Eisenhower	John Foster Dulles	NY	1953
	Christian A. Herter	MA	1959
Kennedy	Dean Rusk	NY	1961
Johnson, L.B.	Dean Rusk	NY	1963
Nixon	William P. Rogers	NY	1969
	Henry A. Kissinger	DC	1973
Ford	Henry A. Kissinger	DC	1974
Carter	Cyrus R. Vance	NY	1977
	Edmund S. Muskie	ME	1980
Reagan	Alexander M. Haig Jr.	CT	1981
	George P. Shultz	CA	1982
Bush, G.H.W.	James A. Baker 3rd	TX	1989
	Lawrence S. Eagleburger	MI	1992
Clinton	Warren M. Christopher	CA	1993
	Madeleine K. Albright	DC	1997
Bush, G.W.	Colin L. Powell	NY	2001

Secretaries of the Treasury

The Treasury Department was organized by act of Congress on Sept. 2, 1789.

President	Secretary	Home	Apptd.
Washington	Alexander Hamilton	NY	1789
	Oliver Wolcott	CT	1795
Adams, J.	Oliver Wolcott	CT	1797
	Samuel Dexter	MA	1801
Jefferson	Samuel Dexter	MA	1801
	Albert Gallatin	PA	1801
Madison	Albert Gallatin	PA	1809
	George W. Campbell	TN	1814
	Alexander J. Dallas	PA	1814
	William H. Crawford	GA	1816
Monroe	William H. Crawford	GA	1817
Adams, J.Q.	Richard Rush	PA	1825
Jackson	Samuel D. Ingham	PA	1829
	Louis McLane	DE	1831
	William J. Duane	PA	1833
	Roger B. Taney	MD	1833
	Levi Woodbury	NH	1834
Van Buren	Levi Woodbury	NH	1837
Harrison, W.H.	Thomas Ewing	OH	1841
Tyler	Thomas Ewing	OH	1841
	Walter Forward	PA	1841
	John C. Spencer	NY	1843
	George M. Bibb	KY	1844
Polk	Robert J. Walker	MS	1845
Taylor	William M. Meredith	PA	1849
Fillmore	Thomas Corwin	OH	1850
Pierce	James Guthrie	KY	1853
Buchanan	Howell Cobb	GA	1857
	Phillip F. Thomas	MD	1860
	John A. Dix	NY	1861
Lincoln	Salmon P. Chase	OH	1861
	William P. Fessenden	ME	1864
	Hugh McCulloch	IN	1865
Johnson, A.	Hugh McCulloch	IN	1865

President	Secretary	Home	Apptd.	President	Secretary	Home	Apptd.
Grant	George S. Boutwell	MA	1869	Roosevelt, F.D.	William H. Woodin	NY	1933
	William A. Richardson	MA	1873		Henry Morgenthau, Jr.	NY	1934
	Benjamin H. Bristow	KY	1874	Truman	Fred M. Vinson	KY	1945
	Lot M. Morrill	ME	1876		John W. Snyder	MO	1946
Hayes	John Sherman	OH	1877	Eisenhower	George M. Humphrey	OH	1953
Garfield	William Windom	MN	1881		Robert B. Anderson	CT	1957
Arthur	Charles J. Folger	NY	1881	Kennedy	C. Douglas Dillon	NJ	1961
	Walter Q. Gresham	IN	1884	Johnson, L.B.	C. Douglas Dillon	NJ	1963
	Hugh McCulloch	IN	1884		Henry H. Fowler	VA	1965
Cleveland	Daniel Manning	NY	1885		Joseph W. Barr	IN	1968
	Charles S. Fairchild	NY	1887	Nixon	David M. Kennedy	IL	1969
Harrison, B.	William Windom	MN	1889		John B. Connally	TX	1971
	Charles Foster	OH	1891		George P. Shultz	IL	1972
Cleveland	John G. Carlisle	KY	1893		William E. Simon	NJ	1974
McKinley	Lyman J. Gage	IL	1897	Ford	William E. Simon	NJ	1974
Roosevelt, T.	Lyman J. Gage	IL	1901	Carter	W. Michael Blumenthal	MI	1977
	Leslie M. Shaw	IA	1902		G. William Miller	RI	1979
	George B. Cortelyou	NY	1907	Reagan	Donald T. Regan	NY	1981
Taft	Franklin MacVeagh	IL	1909		James A. Baker 3rd	TX	1985
Wilson	William G. McAdoo	NY	1913		Nicholas F. Brady	NJ	1988
	Carter Glass	VA	1918	Bush, G.H.W.	Nicholas F. Brady	NJ	1989
	David F. Houston	MO	1920	Clinton	Lloyd Bentsen	TX	1993
Harding	Andrew W. Mellon	PA	1921		Robert E. Rubin	NY	1995
Coolidge	Andrew W. Mellon	PA	1923		Lawrence H. Summers	CT	1999
Hoover	Andrew W. Mellon	PA	1929	Bush, G.W.	Paul H. O'Neill	PA	2001
	Ogden L. Mills	NY	1932		John W. Snow	PA	2003

Secretaries of Defense

The Department of Defense, originally designated the National Military Establishment, was created on Sept. 18, 1947. It is headed by the secretary of defense, who is a member of the president's Cabinet. The departments of the army, of the navy, and of the air force function within the Defense Department, and since 1947 the secretaries of these departments have not been members of the president's Cabinet.

President	Secretary	Home	Apptd.	President	Secretary	Home	Apptd.
Truman	James V. Forrestal	NY	1947	Ford	James R. Schlesinger	VA	1974
	Louis A. Johnson	WV	1949		Donald H. Rumsfeld	IL	1975
	George C. Marshall	PA	1950	Carter	Harold Brown	CA	1977
	Robert A. Lovett	NY	1951	Reagan	Caspar W. Weinberger	CA	1981
Eisenhower	Charles E. Wilson	MI	1953		Frank C. Carlucci	PA	1987
	Neil H. McElroy	OH	1957	Bush, G.H.W.	Richard B. Cheney	WY	1989
	Thomas S. Gates Jr.	PA	1959	Clinton	Les Aspin	WI	1993
Kennedy	Robert S. McNamara	MI	1961		William J. Perry	CA	1994
Johnson, L.B.	Robert S. McNamara	MI	1963		William S. Cohen	ME	1997
	Clark M. Clifford	MD	1968	Bush, G.W.	Donald H. Rumsfeld	IL	2001
Nixon	Melvin R. Laird	WI	1969				
	Elliot L. Richardson	MA	1973				
	James R. Schlesinger	VA	1973				

Secretaries of War

The War Department (which included jurisdiction over the navy until 1798) was created by act of Congress on Aug. 7, 1789, and Gen. Henry Knox was commissioned secretary of war under that act on Sept. 12, 1789.

President	Secretary	Home	Apptd.	President	Secretary	Home	Apptd.
Washington	Henry Knox	MA	1789	Grant	John A. Rawlins	IL	1869
	Timothy Pickering	PA	1795		William T. Sherman	OH	1869
	James McHenry	MD	1796		William W. Belknap	IA	1869
Adams, J.	James McHenry	MD	1797		Alphonso Taft	OH	1876
	Samuel Dexter	MA	1800		James D. Cameron	PA	1876
Jefferson	Henry Dearborn	MA	1801	Hayes	George W. McCrary	IA	1877
Madison	William Eustis	MA	1809		Alexander Ramsey	MN	1879
	John Armstrong	NY	1813	Garfield	Robert T. Lincoln	IL	1881
	James Monroe	VA	1814	Arthur	Robert T. Lincoln	IL	1881
	William H. Crawford	GA	1815	Cleveland	William C. Endicott	MA	1885
Monroe	John C. Calhoun	SC	1817	Harrison, B.	Redfield Proctor	VT	1889
Adams, J.Q.	James Barbour	VA	1825		Stephen B. Elkins	WV	1891
	Peter B. Porter	NY	1828	Cleveland	Daniel S. Lamont	NY	1893
Jackson	John H. Eaton	TN	1829	McKinley	Russel A. Alger	MI	1897
	Lewis Cass	MI	1831		Elihu Root	NY	1899
	Benjamin F. Butler	NY	1837	Roosevelt, T.	Elihu Root	NY	1901
Van Buren	Joel R. Poinsett	SC	1837		William H. Taft	OH	1904
Harrison, W.H.	John Bell	TN	1841		Luke E. Wright	TN	1908
Tyler	John Bell	TN	1841	Taft	Jacob M. Dickinson	TN	1909
	John C. Spencer	NY	1841		Henry L. Stimson	NY	1911
	James M. Porter	PA	1843	Wilson	Lindley M. Garrison	NJ	1913
	William Wilkins	PA	1844		Newton D. Baker	OH	1916
Polk	William L. Marcy	NY	1845	Harding	John W. Weeks	MA	1921
Taylor	George W. Crawford	GA	1849	Coolidge	John W. Weeks	MA	1923
Fillmore	Charles M. Conrad	LA	1850		Dwight F. Davis	MO	1925
Pierce	Jefferson Davis	MS	1853	Hoover	James W. Good	IL	1929
Buchanan	John B. Floyd	VA	1857		Patrick J. Hurley	OK	1929
	Joseph Holt	KY	1861	Roosevelt, F.D.	George H. Dern	UT	1933
Lincoln	Simon Cameron	PA	1861		Harry H. Woodring	KS	1937
	Edwin M. Stanton	PA	1862		Henry L. Stimson	NY	1940
Johnson, A.	Edwin M. Stanton	PA	1865	Truman	Robert P. Patterson	NY	1945
	John M. Schofield	IL	1868		Kenneth C. Royall[1]	NC	1947

(1) Last member of the Cabinet with this title. The War Department became the Department of the Army and became a branch of the Department of Defense in 1947.

Secretaries of the Navy

The Navy Department was created by act of Congress on Apr. 30, 1798.

President	Secretary	Home	Apptd.	President	Secretary	Home	Apptd.
Adams, J.	Benjamin Stoddert	MD	1798	Johnson, A.	Gideon Welles	CT	1865
Jefferson.	Benjamin Stoddert	MD	1801	Grant	Adolph E. Borie	PA	1869
	Robert Smith	MD	1801		George M. Robeson	NJ	1869
Madison	Paul Hamilton	SC	1809	Hayes	Richard W. Thompson	IN.	1877
	William Jones	PA.	1813		Nathan Goff Jr.	WV	1881
	Benjamin W. Crowninshield	MA	1814	Garfield	William H. Hunt	LA	1881
Monroe	Benjamin W. Crowninshield	MA	1817	Arthur	William E. Chandler	NH	1882
	Smith Thompson	NY	1818	Cleveland.	William C. Whitney	NY	1885
	Samuel L. Southard	NJ.	1823	Harrison, B.	Benjamin F. Tracy	NY	1889
Adams, J.Q.	Samuel L. Southard	NJ.	1825	Cleveland.	Hilary A. Herbert	AL	1893
Jackson	John Branch	NC	1829	McKinley	John D. Long	MA.	1897
	Levi Woodbury	NH	1831	Roosevelt, T.	John D. Long	MA.	1901
	Mahlon Dickerson	NJ.	1834		William H. Moody	MA.	1902
Van Buren	Mahlon Dickerson	NJ.	1837		Paul Morton	IL.	1904
	James K. Paulding	NY	1838		Charles J. Bonaparte	MD.	1905
Harrison, W.H.	George E. Badger	NC	1841		Victor H. Metcalf	CA	1906
Tyler	George E. Badger	NC	1841		Truman H. Newberry	MI	1908
	Abel P. Upshur	VA	1841	Taft.	George von L. Meyer.	MA.	1909
	David Henshaw	MA	1843	Wilson	Josephus Daniels	NC	1913
	Thomas W. Gilmer	VA	1844	Harding	Edwin Denby	MI	1921
	John Y. Mason	VA	1844	Coolidge	Edwin Denby	MI	1923
Polk	George Bancroft.	MA	1845		Curtis D. Wilbur	CA	1924
	John Y. Mason	VA	1846	Hoover	Charles Francis Adams	MA.	1929
Taylor	William B. Preston	VA	1849	Roosevelt, F.D.	Claude A. Swanson	VA	1933
Fillmore	William A. Graham	NC	1850		Charles Edison	NJ	1940
	John P. Kennedy	MD	1852		Frank Knox	IL.	1940
Pierce	James C. Dobbin	NC	1853		James V. Forrestal.	NY	1944
Buchanan	Isaac Toucey	CT	1857	Truman	James V. Forrestal[1]	NY	1945
Lincoln	Gideon Welles	CT	1861				

(1) Last member of Cabinet with this title. The Navy Department became a branch of the Department of Defense when the latter was created on Sept. 18, 1947.

Attorneys General

The Office of Attorney General was established by act of Congress on Sept. 24, 1789. It officially reached Cabinet rank in Mar. 1792, when the first attorney general, Edmund Randolph, attended his initial Cabinet meeting. The Department of Justice, headed by the attorney general, was created June 22, 1870.

President	Attorney General	Home	Apptd.	President	Attorney General	Home	Apptd.
Washington	Edmund Randolph.	VA	1789	Cleveland.	Richard Olney.	MA	1893
	William Bradford	PA	1794		Judson Harmon	OH	1895
	Charles Lee.	VA	1795	McKinley	Joseph McKenna	CA.	1897
Adams, J.	Charles Lee.	VA	1797		John W. Griggs.	NJ	1898
Jefferson.	Levi Lincoln.	MA.	1801		Philander C. Knox.	PA.	1901
	John Breckenridge	KY	1805	Roosevelt, T.	Philander C. Knox.	PA.	1901
	Caesar A. Rodney.	DE	1807		William H. Moody	MA	1904
Madison	Caesar A. Rodney.	DE	1807		Charles J. Bonaparte	MD	1906
	William Pinkney.	MD.	1811	Taft.	George W. Wickersham	NY.	1909
	Richard Rush.	PA	1814	Wilson	J.C. McReynolds.	TN.	1913
Monroe	Richard Rush.	PA	1817		Thomas W. Gregory	TX.	1914
	William Wirt.	VA	1817		A. Mitchell Palmer.	PA.	1919
Adams, J.Q.	William Wirt.	VA	1825	Harding	Harry M. Daugherty	OH	1921
Jackson	John M. Berrien.	GA	1829	Coolidge	Harry M. Daugherty	OH	1923
	Roger B. Taney.	MD.	1831		Harlan F. Stone.	NY.	1924
	Benjamin F. Butler.	NY	1833		John G. Sargent.	VT.	1925
Van Buren	Benjamin F. Butler.	NY	1837	Hoover.	William D. Mitchell	MN	1929
	Felix Grundy	TN	1838	Roosevelt, F.D.	Homer S. Cummings	CT	1933
	Henry D. Gilpin.	PA	1840		Frank Murphy	MI	1939
Harrison, W.H.	John J. Crittenden	KY	1841		Robert H. Jackson	NY.	1940
Tyler	John J. Crittenden	KY	1841		Francis Biddle.	PA.	1941
	Hugh S. Legare	SC	1841	Truman	Thomas C. Clark.	TX.	1945
	John Nelson	MD.	1843		J. Howard McGrath.	RI	1949
Polk	John Y. Mason.	VA	1845		J.P. McGranery.	PA.	1952
	Nathan Clifford.	ME.	1846	Eisenhower	Herbert Brownell Jr.	NY.	1953
	Isaac Toucey	CT	1848		William P. Rogers.	MD	1957
Taylor	Reverdy Johnson.	MD.	1849	Kennedy	Robert F. Kennedy	MA	1961
Fillmore	John J. Crittenden	KY	1850	Johnson, L.B.	Robert F. Kennedy	MA	1963
Pierce	Caleb Cushing.	MA	1853		N. de B. Katzenbach.	IL.	1964
Buchanan	Jeremiah S. Black.	PA	1857		Ramsey Clark.	TX.	1967
	Edwin M. Stanton.	PA	1860	Nixon	John N. Mitchell.	NY.	1969
Lincoln	Edward Bates	MO.	1861		Richard G. Kleindienst.	AZ.	1972
	James Speed	KY	1864		Elliot L. Richardson.	MA	1973
Johnson, A.	James Speed	KY	1865		William B. Saxbe	OH	1974
	Henry Stanbery.	OH	1866	Ford.	William B. Saxbe	OH	1974
	William M. Evarts.	NY	1868		Edward H. Levi.	IL.	1975
Grant	Ebenezer R. Hoar.	MA	1869	Carter	Griffin B. Bell.	GA	1977
	Amos T. Akerman.	GA	1870		Benjamin R. Civiletti.	MD	1979
	George H. Williams.	OR	1871	Reagan	William French Smith.	CA.	1981
	Edwards Pierrepont.	NY	1875		Edwin Meese 3rd	CA.	1985
	Alphonso Taft.	OH	1876		Richard Thornburgh.	PA	1988
Hayes	Charles Devens.	MA	1877	Bush, G.H.W.	Richard Thornburgh.	PA	1989
Garfield.	Wayne MacVeagh.	PA	1881		William P. Barr.	NY.	1991
Arthur	Benjamin H. Brewster.	PA	1882	Clinton	Janet Reno.	FL	1993
Cleveland	Augustus Garland.	AR	1885	Bush, G.W.	John Ashcroft.	MO	2001
Harrison, B.	William H. H. Miller.	IN.	1889				

Secretaries of the Interior

The Department of the Interior was created by act of Congress on Mar. 3, 1849.

President	Secretary	Home	Apptd.
Taylor	Thomas Ewing	OH	1849
Fillmore	Thomas M. T. McKennan	PA	1850
	Alex H. H. Stuart	VA	1850
Pierce	Robert McClelland	MI	1853
Buchanan	Jacob Thompson	MS	1857
Lincoln	Caleb B. Smith	IN	1861
	John P. Usher	IN	1863
Johnson, A.	John P. Usher	IN	1865
	James Harlan	IA	1865
	Orville H. Browning	IL	1866
Grant	Jacob D. Cox	OH	1869
	Columbus Delano	OH	1870
	Zachariah Chandler	MI	1875
Hayes	Carl Schurz	MO	1877
Garfield	Samuel J. Kirkwood	IA	1881
Arthur	Henry M. Teller	CO	1882
Cleveland	Lucius Q.C. Lamar	MS	1885
	William F. Vilas	WI	1888
Harrison, B.	John W. Noble	MO	1889
Cleveland	Hoke Smith	GA	1893
	David R. Francis	MO	1896
McKinley	Cornelius N. Bliss	NY	1897
	Ethan A. Hitchcock	MO	1898
Roosevelt, T.	Ethan A. Hitchcock	MO	1901
	James R. Garfield	OH	1907
Taft	Richard A. Ballinger	WA	1909
	Walter L. Fisher	IL	1911
Wilson	Franklin K. Lane	CA	1913
	John B. Payne	IL	1920
Harding	Albert B. Fall	NM	1921
	Hubert Work	CO	1923
Coolidge	Hubert Work	CO	1923
	Roy O. West	IL	1929
Hoover	Ray Lyman Wilbur	CA	1929
Roosevelt, F.D.	Harold L. Ickes	IL	1933
Truman	Harold L. Ickes	IL	1945
	Julius A. Krug	WI	1946
	Oscar L. Chapman	CO	1949
Eisenhower	Douglas McKay	OR	1953
	Fred A. Seaton	NE	1956
Kennedy	Stewart L. Udall	AZ	1961
Johnson, L.B.	Stewart L. Udall	AZ	1963
Nixon	Walter J. Hickel	AK	1969
	Rogers C.B. Morton	MD	1971
Ford	Rogers C.B. Morton	MD	1971
	Stanley K. Hathaway	WY	1975
	Thomas S. Kleppe	ND	1975
Carter	Cecil D. Andrus	ID	1977
Reagan	James G. Watt	CO	1981
	William P. Clark	CA	1983
	Donald P. Hodel	OR	1985
Bush, G.H.W.	Manuel Lujan	NM	1989
Clinton	Bruce Babbitt	AZ	1993
Bush, G.W.	Gale Norton	CO	2001

Secretaries of Agriculture

The Department of Agriculture was created by act of Congress on May 15, 1862. On Feb. 8, 1889, its commissioner was renamed secretary of agriculture and became a member of the Cabinet.

President	Secretary	Home	Apptd.
Cleveland	Norman J. Colman	MO	1889
Harrison, B.	Jeremiah M. Rusk	WI	1889
Cleveland	J. Sterling Morton	NE	1893
McKinley	James Wilson	IA	1897
Roosevelt, T.	James Wilson	IA	1901
Taft	James Wilson	IA	1909
Wilson	David F. Houston	MO	1913
	Edwin T. Meredith	IA	1920
Harding	Henry C. Wallace	IA	1921
Coolidge	Henry C. Wallace	IA	1923
	Howard M. Gore	WV	1924
	William M. Jardine	KS	1925
Hoover	Arthur M. Hyde	MO	1929
Roosevelt, F.D.	Henry A. Wallace	IA	1933
	Claude R. Wickard	IN	1940
Truman	Clinton P. Anderson	NM	1945
	Charles F. Brannan	CO	1948
Eisenhower	Ezra Taft Benson	UT	1953
Kennedy	Orville L. Freeman	MN	1961
Johnson, L.B.	Orville L. Freeman	MN	1963
Nixon	Clifford M. Hardin	IN	1969
	Earl L. Butz	IN	1971
Ford	Earl L. Butz	IN	1974
	John A. Knebel	VA	1976
Carter	Bob Bergland	MN	1977
Reagan	John R. Block	IL	1981
	Richard E. Lyng	CA	1986
Bush, G.H.W.	Clayton K. Yeutter	NE	1989
	Edward Madigan	IL	1991
Clinton	Mike Espy	MS	1993
	Dan Glickman	KS	1995
Bush, G.W.	Ann M. Veneman	CA	2001

Secretaries of Commerce and Labor

The Department of Commerce and Labor, created by Congress on Feb. 14, 1903, was divided by Congress Mar. 4, 1913, into separate departments of Commerce and Labor. The secretary of each was made a Cabinet member.

Secretaries of Commerce and Labor

President	Secretary	Home	Apptd.
Roosevelt, T.	George B. Cortelyou	NY	1903
	Victor H. Metcalf	CA	1904
	Oscar S. Straus	NY	1906
Taft	Charles Nagel	MO	1909

Secretaries of Labor

President	Secretary	Home	Apptd.
Wilson	William B. Wilson	PA	1913
Harding	James J. Davis	PA	1921
Coolidge	James J. Davis	PA	1923
Hoover	James J. Davis	PA	1929
	William N. Doak	VA	1930
Roosevelt, F.D.	Frances Perkins	NY	1933
Truman	L.B. Schwellenbach	WA	1945
	Maurice J. Tobin	MA	1949
Eisenhower	Martin P. Durkin	IL	1953
	James P. Mitchell	NJ	1953
Kennedy	Arthur J. Goldberg	IL	1961
	W. Willard Wirtz	IL	1962
Johnson, L.B.	W. Willard Wirtz	IL	1963
Nixon	George P. Shultz	IL	1969
	James D. Hodgson	CA	1970
	Peter J. Brennan	NY	1973
Ford	Peter J. Brennan	NY	1974
	John T. Dunlop	CA	1975
	W.J. Usery Jr.	GA	1976
Carter	F. Ray Marshall	TX	1977

President	Secretary	Home	Apptd.
Reagan	Raymond J. Donovan	NJ	1981
	William E. Brock	TN	1985
	Ann D. McLaughlin	DC	1987
Bush, G.H.W.	Elizabeth Hanford Dole	NC	1989
	Lynn Martin	IL	1991
Clinton	Robert B. Reich	MA	1993
	Alexis M. Herman	AL	1997
Bush, G.W.	Elaine L. Chao	KY	2001

Secretaries of Commerce

President	Secretary	Home	Apptd.
Wilson	William C. Redfield	NY	1913
	Joshua W. Alexander	MO	1919
Harding	Herbert C. Hoover	CA	1921
Coolidge	Herbert C. Hoover	CA	1923
	William F. Whiting	MA	1928
Hoover	Robert P. Lamont	IL	1929
	Roy D. Chapin	MI	1932
Roosevelt, F.D.	Daniel C. Roper	SC	1933
	Harry L. Hopkins	NY	1939
	Jesse Jones	TX	1940
	Henry A. Wallace	IA	1945
Truman	Henry A. Wallace	IA	1945
	W. Averell Harriman	NY	1947
	Charles Sawyer	OH	1948
Eisenhower	Sinclair Weeks	MA	1953
	Lewis L. Strauss	NY	1958
	Frederick H. Mueller	MI	1959
Kennedy	Luther H. Hodges	NC	1961

President	Secretary	Home	Apptd.	President	Secretary	Home	Apptd.
Johnson, L.B....	Luther H. Hodges	NC	1963	Carter	Juanita M. Kreps.	NC	1977
	John T. Connor	NJ	1965		Philip M. Klutznick	IL	1979
	Alex B. Trowbridge.	NJ	1967	Reagan	Malcolm Baldrige	CT	1981
	Cyrus R. Smith	NY	1968		C. William Verity Jr.	OH	1987
Nixon	Maurice H. Stans	MN	1969	Bush, G.H.W...	Robert A. Mosbacher	TX	1989
	Peter G. Peterson	IL	1972		Barbara H. Franklin.	PA	1992
	Frederick B. Dent.	SC	1973	Clinton	Ronald H. Brown	DC	1993
Ford	Frederick B. Dent.	SC	1974		Mickey Kantor	CA	1996
	Rogers C.B. Morton.	MD	1975		William M. Daley	IL	1997
	Elliot L. Richardson	MA	1975		Norman Y. Mineta	CA	2000
				Bush, G.W.	Donald L. Evans	TX	2001

Secretaries of Housing and Urban Development

The Department of Housing and Urban Development was created by act of Congress on Sept. 9, 1965.

President	Secretary	Home	Apptd.	President	Secretary	Home	Apptd.
Johnson, L.B....	Robert C. Weaver	WA	1966	Carter	Patricia Roberts Harris	DC	1977
	Robert C. Wood.	MA	1969		Moon Landrieu	LA	1979
Nixon	George W. Romney	MI	1969	Reagan	Samuel R. Pierce Jr.	NY	1981
	James T. Lynn	OH	1973	Bush, G.H.W...	Jack F. Kemp	NY	1989
Ford	James T. Lynn	OH	1974	Clinton	Henry G. Cisneros	TX	1993
	Carla Anderson Hills	CA	1975		Andrew M. Cuomo	NY	1997
				Bush, G.W.	Mel Martinez	FL	2001

Secretaries of Transportation

The Department of Transportation was created by act of Congress on Oct. 15, 1966.

President	Secretary	Home	Apptd.	President	Secretary	Home	Apptd.
Johnson, L.B....	Alan S. Boyd	FL	1966	Reagan	Andrew L. Lewis Jr.	PA	1981
Nixon	John A. Volpe	MA	1969		Elizabeth Hanford Dole.	NC	1983
	Claude S. Brinegar	CA	1973		James H. Burnley	NC	1987
Ford	Claude S. Brinegar	CA	1974	Bush, G.H.W...	Samuel K. Skinner	IL	1989
	William T. Coleman Jr.	PA	1975		Andrew H. Card Jr.	MA	1992
Carter	Brock Adams	WA	1977	Clinton	Federico F. Peña.	CO.	1993
	Neil E. Goldschmidt	OR	1979		Rodney E. Slater	AR	1997
				Bush, G.W.	Norman Y. Mineta	CA	2001

Secretaries of Energy

The Department of Energy was created by federal law on Aug. 4, 1977.

President	Secretary	Home	Apptd.	President	Secretary	Home	Apptd.
Carter	James R. Schlesinger	VA	1977	Bush, G.H.W...	James D. Watkins	CA	1989
	Charles Duncan Jr.	WY	1979	Clinton	Hazel R. O'Leary	MN	1993
Reagan.	James B. Edwards.	SC	1981		Federico F. Peña.	CO.	1997
	Donald P. Hodel	OR	1982		Bill Richardson	NM	1998
	John S. Herrington	CA	1985	Bush, G.W.	Spencer Abraham.	MI	2001

Secretaries of Health, Education, and Welfare

The Department of Health, Education, and Welfare was created by Congress on Apr. 11, 1953. On Sept. 27, 1979, it was divided by Congress into the departments of Education and of Health and Human Services, with the secretary of each being a Cabinet member.

President	Secretary	Home	Apptd.	President	Secretary	Home	Apptd.
Eisenhower	Oveta Culp Hobby	TX	1953	Nixon	Robert H. Finch	CA	1969
	Marion B. Folsom	NY	1955		Elliot L. Richardson.	MA	1970
	Arthur S. Flemming	OH	1958		Caspar W. Weinberger	CA	1973
Kennedy	Abraham A. Ribicoff	CT	1961	Ford	Caspar W. Weinberger	CA	1974
	Anthony J. Celebrezze	OH	1962		Forrest D. Mathews.	AL	1975
Johnson, L.B....	Anthony J. Celebrezze	OH	1963	Carter	Joseph A. Califano Jr.	DC	1977
	John W. Gardner	NY	1965		Patricia Roberts Harris	DC	1979
	Wilbur J. Cohen	MI	1968				

Secretaries of Health and Human Services

President	Secretary	Home	Apptd.	President	Secretary	Home	Apptd.
Carter	Patricia Roberts Harris	DC	1979	Reagan	Otis R. Bowen.	IN	1985
Reagan.	Richard S. Schweiker	PA	1981	Bush, G.H.W...	Louis W. Sullivan	GA	1989
	Margaret M. Heckler	MA	1983	Clinton	Donna E. Shalala	WI	1993
				Bush, G.W.	Tommy Thompson	WI	2001

Secretaries of Education

President	Secretary	Home	Apptd.	President	Secretary	Home	Apptd.
Carter	Shirley Hufstedler	CA	1979	Bush, G.H.W...	Lauro F. Cavazos	TX	1989
Reagan.	Terrel Bell	UT	1981		Lamar Alexander	TN	1991
	William J. Bennett	NY	1985	Clinton	Richard W. Riley	SC	1993
	Lauro F. Cavazos.	TX	1988	Bush, G.W.	Roderick R. Paige.	TX	2001

Secretaries of Veterans Affairs

The Department of Veterans Affairs was created on Oct. 25, 1988, when Pres. Ronald Reagan signed a bill that made the Veterans Administration into a Cabinet department, effective Mar. 15, 1989.

President	Secretary	Home	Apptd.	President	Secretary	Home	Apptd.
Bush, G.H.W...	Edward J. Derwinski	IL	1989	Clinton	Togo D. West Jr.	NC	1998
Clinton	Jesse Brown	IL	1993		Hershel W. Gober (acting)	AR	2000
				Bush, G.W.	Anthony Principi	CA	2001

Department of Homeland Security

The Department of Homeland Security was created by act of Congress on Nov. 25, 2002. Pres. George W. Bush in 2003 appointed Thomas Ridge of Pennsylvania as its first secretary.

CONGRESS

The One Hundred and Eighth Congress With Official 2002 Election Results

Source: Clerk of the House of Representatives; as of Oct. 15, 2003

The 108th Congress convened on Jan. 7, 2003.

The Senate

Rep., 51; Dem., 48; Ind., 1; Total, 100. Boldface denotes the 2002 election winner. *Incumbent.

Terms are for 6 years and end Jan. 3 of the year preceding the senator's name in the following table. Annual salary, $154,700; President Pro Tempore, Majority Leader, and Minority Leader, $171,900. To be eligible for the Senate, one must be at least 30 years old, a U.S. citizen for at least 9 years, and a resident of the state from which chosen. Congress must meet annually on Jan. 3, unless it has, by law, appointed a different day.

The address is U.S. Senate, Washington DC 20510; the telephone number is 202-224-3121; the website is www.senate.gov

Senate officials in 2003 were: President Pro Tempore, Ted Stevens (AK); Majority Leader, Bill Frist (TN); Majority Whip, Mitch McConnell (KY); Minority Leader, Tom Daschle (SD); Minority Whip, Harry Reid (NV).

D–Democrat; R–Republican; I–Independent; LB–Libertarian; RF–Reform

Term ends	Senator (Party); Service from[1]	2002 Election		Term ends	Senator (Party); Service from[1]	2002 Election
	Alabama				**Kansas**	
2005	Richard Shelby (R); 1/6/87			2005	Sam Brownback (R); 11/27/96	
2009	**Jeff Sessions* (R)**; 1/7/97	792,561		2009	**Pat Roberts* (R)**; 1/7/97	641,075
	Susan Parker (D)	538,878			Steven A. Rosile (LB)	70,725
	Alaska				**Kentucky**	
2005	Lisa Murkowski (R); 12/20/02			2005	Jim Bunning (R); 1/6/99	
2009	**Ted Stevens* (R)**; 12/24/68	179,435		2009	**Mitch McConnell* (R)**; 1985	731,679
	Frank Vondersaar (D)	24,133			Lois Combs Weinberg (D)	399,634
	Arizona				**Louisiana**	
2005	John McCain (R); 1/6/87			2005	John B. Breaux (D); 1/6/87	
2007	Jon Kyl(R); 1/4/95			2009	**Mary L. Landrieu* (D)**[2]; 1/7/97	638,654
	Arkansas				Suzanne Haik Terrell (R)[2]	596,642
2005	Blanche Lambert Lincoln (D); 1/6/99				**Maine**	
2009	**Mark Pryor (D)**; 1/7/03	433,386		2007	Olympia J. Snowe (R); 1/4/95	
	Tim Hutchinson* (R)	370,735		2009	**Susan M. Collins* (R)**; 1/7/97	295,041
	California				Chellie Pingree (D)	209,858
2005	Barbara Boxer (D); 1993				**Maryland**	
2007	Dianne Feinstein (D); 11/10/92			2005	Barbara Ann Mikulski (D); 1/6/87	
	Colorado			2007	Paul S. Sarbanes (D); 1977	
2005	Ben Nighthorse Campbell (R); 1993				**Massachusetts**	
2009	**Wayne Allard* (R)**; 1/7/97	717,893		2007	Edward M. Kennedy (D); 11/7/62	
	Tom Strickland (D)	648,130		2009	**John F. Kerry* (D)**; 1/2/85	1,605,976
	Connecticut				Michael E. Cloud (LB)	369,807
2005	Christopher J. Dodd (D); 1981				**Michigan**	
2007	Joe Lieberman (D); 1989			2007	Debbie Stabenow (D); 2001	
	Delaware			2009	**Carl Levin* (D)**; 1979	1,896,614
2007	Thomas R. Carper (D); 2001				Andrew Raczkowski (R)	1,185,545
2009	**Joseph Biden* (D)**; 1973	135,253			**Minnesota**	
	Raymond J. Clatworthy (R)	94,793		2007	Mark Dayton (D); 2001	
	Florida			2009	**Norm Coleman (R)**; 1/7/03	1,116,697
2005	Bob Graham (D); 1/6/87				Walter F. Mondale (D)	1,067,246
2007	Bill Nelson (D); 2001				**Mississippi**	
	Georgia			2007	Trent Lott (R); 1989	
2005	Zell Miller (D); 7/24/00			2009	**Thad Cochran* (R)**; 12/27/78	533,269
2009	**Saxby Chambliss (R)**; 1/7/03	1,071,352			Shawn O'Hara (RF)	97,226
	Max Cleland* (D)	932,422			**Missouri**	
	Hawaii			2005	Christopher (Kit) Bond (R); 1/6/87	
2005	Daniel K. Inouye (D); 1963			2009	**Jim Talent (R)**; 11/23/02	935,032
2007	Daniel K. Akaka (D); 4/28/90				Jean Carnahan (D)	913,778
	Idaho				**Montana**	
2005	Mike Crapo (R); 1/6/99			2007	Conrad Burns (R); 1989	
2009	**Larry E. Craig* (R)**; 1991	266,215		2009	**Max Baucus* (D)**; 12/15/78	204,853
	Alan Blinken (D)	132,975			Mike Taylor (R)	103,611
	Illinois				**Nebraska**	
2005	Peter G. Fitzgerald (R); 1/6/99			2007	Ben Nelson (D); 2001	
2009	**Richard J. Durbin* (D)**; 1/7/97	2,103,766		2009	**Chuck Hagel* (R)**; 1/7/97	397,438
	Jim Durkin (R)	1,325,703			Charlie A. Matulka (D)	70,290
	Indiana				**Nevada**	
2005	Evan Bayh (D); 1/6/99			2005	Harry Reid (D); 1/6/87	
2007	Richard G. Lugar (R); 1977			2007	John Ensign (R); 2001	
	Iowa				**New Hampshire**	
2005	Chuck Grassley (R); 1981			2005	Judd Gregg (R); 1993	
2009	**Tom Harkin* (D)**; 1985	554,278		2009	**John Sununu (R)**; 1/7/03	227,229
	Greg Ganske (R)	447,892			Jeanne Shaheen (D)	207,478

Term ends	Senator (Party); Service from[1]	2002 Election
New Jersey		
2007	Jon S. Corzine (D); 2001	
2009	**Frank Lautenberg (D)**; 1/7/03	**1,138,193**
	Douglas R. Forrester (R)	928,439
New Mexico		
2007	Jeff Bingaman (D); 1983	
2009	**Pete V. Domenici* (R)**; 1973	**314,193**
	Gloria Tristani (D)	168,863
New York		
2005	Charles E. Schumer (D); 1/6/99	
2007	Hillary Rodham Clinton (D); 2001	
North Carolina		
2005	John Edwards (D); 1/6/99	
2009	**Elizabeth H. Dole (R)**; 1/7/03	**1,248,664**
	Erskine B. Bowles (D)	1,047,983
North Dakota		
2005	Byron L. Dorgan (D); 12/14/92	
2007	Kent Conrad (D); 1/6/87	
Ohio		
2005	George V. Voinovich (R); 1/6/99	
2007	Mike DeWine (R); 1/4/95	
Oklahoma		
2005	Don Nickles (R); 1981	
2009	**James M. Inhofe* (R)**; 11/21/94	**583,579**
	David Walters (D)	369,789
Oregon		
2005	Ron Wyden (D); 2/6/96	
2009	**Gordon Smith* (R)**; 1/7/97	**712,287**
	Bill Bradbury (D)	501,898
Pennsylvania		
2005	Arlen Specter (R); 1981	
2007	Rick Santorum (R); 1/4/95	
Rhode Island		
2007	Lincoln D. Chafee (R); 11/2/99	
2009	**John F. Reed* (D)**; 1/7/97	**253,774**
	Robert G. Tingle (R)	69,808
South Carolina		
2005	Ernest Hollings (D); 11/9/66	

Term ends	Senator (Party); Service from[1]	2002 Election
2009	**Lindsey Graham (R)**; 1/7/03	**600,010**
	Alex Sanders (D)	487,359
South Dakota		
2005	Tom Daschle (D); 1/6/87	
2009	**Tim Johnson* (D)**; 1/7/97	**167,481**
	John Thune (R)	166,949
Tennessee		
2007	Bill Frist (R); 1/4/95	
2009	**Lamar Alexander (R)**; 1/7/03	**891,498**
	Bob Clement (D)	728,232
Texas		
2007	Kay Bailey Hutchison (R); 6/5/93	
2009	**John Cornyn (R)**; 12/2/02	**2,496,243**
	Ron Kirk (D)	1,955,758
Utah		
2005	Robert F. Bennett (R); 1993	
2007	Orrin G. Hatch (R); 1977	
Vermont		
2005	Patrick Leahy (D); 1975	
2007	James M. Jeffords (I); 1989	
Virginia		
2007	George F. Allen (R); 2001	
2009	**John W. Warner* (R)**; 1/2/79	**1,229,894**
	Nancy B. Spannaus (I)	145,102
Washington		
2005	Patty Murray (D); 1993	
2007	Maria Cantwell (D); 2001	
West Virginia		
2007	Robert C. Byrd (D); 1959	
2009	**John D. Rockefeller IV* (D)**; 1/15/85	**275,281**
	Jay Wolfe (R)	160,902
Wisconsin		
2005	Russ Feingold (D); 1993	
2007	Herbert H. Kohl (D); 1989	
Wyoming		
2007	Craig Thomas (R); 1/4/95	
2009	**Michael B. Enzi* (R)**; 1/7/97	**133,710**
	Joyce Jansa Corcoran (D)	49,570

(1) Jan. 3, unless otherwise noted. (2) Lousiana law requires a candidate to receive more than 50% of the vote to win an election. Because no candidate received a majority of the vote in the November 2002 election, a runoff was held Dec. 7 between the top 2 vote getters, Mary Landrieu and Suzanne Haik Terrell, with the results shown in the table.

The House of Representatives

Rep., 229; Dem., 205; Ind., 1; Total 435. Boldface denotes the 2002 election winner. *Incumbent.

Terms are for 2 years ending Jan. 3, 2005. Annual salary, $154,700; Speaker of the House, $198,600; Majority Leader and Minority Leader, $171,900. To be eligible for membership, a person must be at least 25 years of age, a U.S. citizen for at least 7 years, and a resident of the state from which he or she is chosen. The address is U.S. House of Representatives, Washington, DC 20515; the telephone number is 202-224-3121. The website is www.house.gov

House officials in 2003 were: Speaker, J. Dennis Hastert (IL); Majority Leader, Tom DeLay (TX); Majority Whip, Roy Blunt (MO); Minority Leader, Nancy Pelosi (CA); Minority Whip, Steny Hoyer (MD).

Note: As a result of the 2000 census, new districts were added in the following states: Arizona, California, Colorado, Florida, Georgia, Nevada, North Carolina, and Texas; these are marked as **new** in the table below. The following states lost districts: Connecticut, Illinois, Indiana, Michigan, Mississippi, New York, Ohio, Oklahoma, Pennsylvania, and Wisconsin. Many other districts were redrawn.

D=Democrat; **R**=Republican; **C**=Conservative; **CN**=Constitution; **CPF**=Constitution Party of Florida; **GR**=Green; **I**=Independent; **IN**=Independence; **L**=Liberal; **LB**=Libertarian; **RTL**=Right to Life; **UC**=United Citizens; **WG**=Wisconsin Green

Dist.	Representative (Party)	2002 Election
Alabama		
1	**Jo Bonner* (R)**	**108,102**
	Judy McCain Belk (D)	67,507
2	**Terry Everett* (R)**	**129,233**
	Charles Woods (D)	55,495
3	**Mike Rogers* (R)**	**91,169**
	Joe Turnham (D)	87,351
4	**Robert B. Aderholt* (R)**	**139,705**
	Tony Hughes McLendon (L)	20,858
5	**Robert E. (Bud) Cramer, Jr.*(D)**	**143,029**
	Stephen P. Engel (R)	48,226
6	**Spencer Bachus* (R)**	**178,171**
	J. Holden McAllister (LB)	19,639
7	**Artur Davis (D)**	**153,735**
	Lauren Orth McCay (LB)	12,100

Dist.	Representative (Party)	2002 Election
Alaska		
	Don Young* (R)	**169,685**
	Clifford Greene (D)	39,357
Arizona		
New 1	**Rick Renzi (R)**	**85,967**
	George Cordova (D)	79,730
2	**Trent Franks (R)**	**100,359**
	Randy Camacho (D)	61,217
3	**John B. Shadegg* (R)**	**104,847**
	Charles Hill (D)	47,173
4	**Ed Pastor* (D)**	**44,517**
	Jonathan Barnert (R)	18,381
5	**J. D. Hayworth* (R)**	**103,870**
	Craig Columbus (D)	61,559

Dist.	Representative (Party)	2002 Election
6	Jeff Flake* (R)............	103,094
	Deborah Thomas (D)............	49,355
New 7	Raúl M. Grijalva (D)............	61,256
	Ross Hieb (R)............	38,474
8	Jim Kolbe* (R)............	126,930
	Mary Judge Ryan (D)............	67,328

Arkansas

Dist.	Representative (Party)	2002 Election
1	Marion Berry* (D)............	129,701
	Tommy Robinson (R)............	64,357
2	Vic Snyder* (D)............	142,752
	Ed Garner (write-in)............	10,874
3	John Boozman* (R)............	141,478
	George N. Lyne............	1,577
4	Mike Ross* (write-in) (D)............	119,633
	Jay Dickey (R)............	77,904

California

Dist.	Representative (Party)	2002 Election
1	Mike Thompson* (D)............	118,669
	Lawrence R. Wiesner (R)............	60,013
2	Wally Herger* (R)............	117,747
	Mike Johnson (D)............	52,455
3	Doug Ose* (R)............	121,732
	Howard Beeman (D)............	67,136
4	John T. Doolittle* (R)............	147,997
	Mark A. Norberg (D)............	72,860
5	Robert T. Matsui* (D)............	92,726
	Richard Frankhuizen (R)............	34,749
6	Lynn C. Woolsey* (D)............	139,750
	Paul L. Erickson (R)............	62,052
7	George Miller* (D)............	97,849
	Charles R. Hargrave (R)............	36,584
8	Nancy Pelosi* (D)............	127,684
	G. Michael German (R)............	20,063
9	Barbara Lee* (D)............	135,893
	Jerald Udinsky (R)............	25,333
10	Ellen O. Tauscher* (D)............	126,390
	Sonia Esther Harden (LB)............	40,807
11	Richard W. Pombo* (R)............	104,921
	Elaine Shaw (D)............	69,035
12	Tom Lantos* (D)............	105,597
	Michael Moloney (R)............	38,381
13	Fortney Pete Stark* (D)............	86,495
	Syed R. Mahmood (R)............	26,852
14	Anna G. Eshoo* (D)............	117,055
	Joseph Henry Nixon (R)............	48,346
15	Michael M. Honda* (D)............	87,482
	Linda Rae Hermann (R)............	41,251
16	Zoe Lofgren* (D)............	72,370
	Douglas Adams McNea (R)............	32,451
17	Sam Farr* (D)............	101,632
	Clint C. Engler (R)............	40,334
18	Dennis A. Cardoza (D)............	56,181
	Dick Monteith (R)............	47,528
19	George Radanovich* (R)............	106,209
	John Veen (D)............	47,403
20	Calvin M. Dooley* (D)............	47,627
	Andre Minuth (R)............	25,628
New 21	Devin Nunes (R)............	87,544
	David G. LaPere (D)............	32,584
22	William M. Thomas* (R)............	120,473
	Jaime A. Corvera (D)............	38,988
23	Lois Capps* (D)............	95,752
	Beth Rogers (R)............	62,604
24	Elton Gallegly* (R)............	120,585
	Fern Rudin (D)............	58,755
25	Howard P. "Buck" McKeon* (R).....	80,775
	Bob Conaway (D)............	38,674
26	David Dreier* (R)............	95,360
	Marjorie Mikels (D)............	50,081
27	Brad Sherman* (D)............	79,815
	Robert M. Levy (R)............	48,996
28	Howard L. Berman* (D)............	73,771
	David R. Hernandez, Jr. (R)............	23,926
29	Adam B. Schiff* (D)............	76,036
	Jim Scileppi (R)............	40,616
30	Henry A. Waxman* (D)............	130,604
	Tony D. Goss (R)............	54,989

Dist.	Representative (Party)	2002 Election
31	Xavier Becerra* (D)............	54,569
	Luis Vega (R)............	12,674
32	Hilda L. Solis* (D)............	58,530
	Emma E. Fischbeck (R)............	23,366
33	Diane E. Watson* (D)............	97,779
	Andrew Kim (R)............	16,699
34	Lucille Roybal-Allard* (D)...........	48,734
	Wayne Miller (R)............	17,090
35	Maxine Waters* (D)............	72,401
	Ross Moen (R)............	18,094
36	Jane Harman* (D)............	88,198
	Stuart Johnson (R)............	50,328
37	Juanita Millender-McDonald* (D)....	63,445
	Oscar A. Velasco (R)............	20,154
38	Grace F. Napolitano* (D)............	62,600
	Alex A. Burrola (R)............	23,126
39	Linda T. Sanchez* (D)............	52,256
	Tim Escobar (R)............	38,925
40	Edward R. Royce* (R)............	92,422
	Christina Avalos (D)............	40,265
41	Jerry Lewis* (R)............	91,326
	Keith Alan Johnson (D)............	40,155
42	Gary G. Miller* (R)............	98,476
	Richard Waldron (D)............	42,090
43	Joe Baca*(D)............	45,374
	Wendy C. Neighbor (R)............	20,821
44	Ken Calvert* (R)............	76,686
	Louis Vandenberg (D)............	38,021
45	Mary Bono* (R)............	87,101
	Elle K. Kurpiewski (D)............	43,692
46	Dana Rohrabacher* (R)............	108,807
	Gerrie Schipske (D)............	60,890
47	Loretta Sanchez* (D)............	42,501
	Jeff Chavez (R)............	24,346
48	Christopher Cox* (R)............	122,884
	John L. Graham (D)............	51,058
49	Darrell E. Issa* (R)............	94,594
	Karl W. Dietrich (LB)............	26,891
50	Randy "Duke" Cunningham* (R)......	111,095
	Del G. Stewart (D)............	55,855
51	Bob Filner* (D)............	59,541
	Maria Guadalupe Garcia (R)............	40,430
52	Duncan Hunter* (R)............	118,561
	Peter Moore-Kochlacs (D)............	43,526
53	Susan A. Davis* (D)............	72,252
	Bill VanDeWeghe (R)............	43,891

Colorado

Dist.	Representative (Party)	2002 Election
1	Diana DeGette* (D)............	111,718
	Ken Chlouber (R)............	49,884
2	Mark Udall* (D)............	123,504
	Sandy Hume (R)............	75,564
3	Scott McInnis* (R)............	143,433
	Denis Berckefeldt (D)............	68,160
4	Marilyn N. Musgrave (R)............	115,359
	Stan Matsunaka (D)............	87,499
5	Joel Hefley* (R)............	128,118
	Curtis Imrie (D)............	45,587
6	Thomas G. Tancredo* (R)............	158,851
	Lance Wright (D)............	71,327
New 7	Bob Beauprez (R)............	81,789
	Mike Feeley (D)............	81,668

Connecticut

Dist.	Representative (Party)	2002 Election
1	John B. Larson* (D)............	134,698
	Phil Steele (R)............	66,968
2	Rob Simmons* (R)............	117,434
	Joe Courtney (D)............	99,674
3	Rosa L. DeLauro* (D)............	121,557
	Richter Elser (R)............	54,757
4	Christopher Shays* (R)............	113,197
	Stephanie H. Sanchez (D)............	62,491
5	Nancy Johnson* (R)............	113,626
	Jim Maloney (D)............	90,616

Delaware

	Representative (Party)	2002 Election
	Michael N. Castle* (R)............	164,605
	Micheal C. Miller (D)............	61,011

Dist.	Representative (Party)	2002 Election
Florida		
1	Jeff Miller* (R)	152,635
	Bert Oram (D)	51,972
2	Allen Boyd* (D)	152,164
	Tom McGurk (R)	75,275
3	Corrine Brown* (D)	88,462
	Jennifer Carroll (R)	60,747
4	Ander Crenshaw* (R)	171,152
	Charles S. Knause (write-in)	509
5	Ginny Brown-Waite (R)	121,998
	Karen L. Thurman* (D)	117,758
6	Cliff Stearns* (R)	141,570
	David E. Bruderly (D)	75,046
7	John L. Mica* (R)	142,147
	Wayne Hogan (D)	96,444
8	Ric Keller* (R)	123,497
	Eddie Diaz (D)	66,099
9	Michael Bilirakis* (R)	169,369
	Chuck Kalogianis (D)	67,623
10	C. W. Bill Young* (R)	Unopposed
11	Jim Davis* (D)	Unopposed
12	Adam H. Putnam* (R)	Unopposed
13	Katherine Harris (R)	139,048
	Jan Schneider (D)	114,739
14	Porter J. Goss* (R)	Unopposed
15	Dave Weldon* (R)	146,414
	Jim Tso (D)	85,433
16	Mark Foley* (R)	176,171
	Jack McLain (CPF)	47,169
17	Kendrick B. Meek (D)	113,749
	Michael Italie (write-in)	73
18	Ileana Ros-Lehtinen* (R)	103,512
	Ray Chote (D)	42,852
19	Robert Wexler* (D)	156,747
	Jack Merkl (R)	60,477
20	Peter Deutsch* (D)	Unopposed
21	Lincoln Diaz-Balart* (R)	Unopposed
22	E. Clay Shaw, Jr.* (R)	131,930
	Carol A. Roberts (D)	83,265
23	Alcee L. Hastings* (D)	96,347
	Charles Laurie (R)	27,986
New 24	Tom Feeney (R)	135,576
	Harry Jacobs (D)	83,667
New 25	Mario Diaz-Balart (R)	81,845
	Annie Betancourt (D)	44,757
Georgia		
1	Jack Kingston* (R)	103,661
	Don Smart (D)	40,026
2	Sanford D. Bishop, Jr.* (D)	102,925
3	Jim Marshall (D)	75,394
	Calder Clay (R)	73,866
4	Denise L. Majette (D)	118,045
	Cynthia Van Auken (R)	35,202
5	John Lewis* (D)	116,259
6	Johnny Isakson* (R)	163,525
	Jeff Weisberger (D)	41,204
7	John Linder* (R)	138,997
	Mike Berlon (D)	37,124
8	Mac Collins* (R)	142,505
	A. Petrakopoulos (D)	39,422
9	Charlie Norwood* (R)	123,313
	Barry Irwin (D)	45,974
10	Nathan Deal* (R)	129,242
	Roger Kahn (D)	65,007
11	Phil Gingrey (R)	69,427
New 12	Max Burns (R)	77,479
	Champ Walker (D)	62,904
13	David Scott (D)	70,011
	Clay Cox (R)	47,405
Hawaii		
1	Neil Abercrombie* (D)	131,673
	Mark Terry (R)	45,032
2	Ed Case[1] (D)	33,002
	Matt Matsunaga (D)	23,050

Dist.	Representative (Party)	2002 Election
Idaho		
1	C. L. "Butch" Otter* (R)	120,743
	Betty Richardson (D)	80,269
2	Michael K. Simpson* (R)	135,605
	Edward Kinghorn (D)	57,769
Illinois		
1	Bobby L. Rush *(D)	149,068
	Raymond G. Wardingley (R)	29,776
2	Jesse L. Jackson, Jr.* (D)	151,443
	Doug Nelson (R)	32,567
3	William O. Lipinski * (D)	156,042
4	Luis V. Gutierrez* (D)	67,339
	Anthony J. "Tony" Lopez-Cisneros (R)	12,778
5	Rahm Emanuel (D)	106,514
	Mark A. Augusti (R)	46,008
6	Henry J. Hyde* (R)	113,174
	Tom Berry (D)	60,698
7	Danny K. Davis* (D)	137,933
	Mark Tunney (R)	25,280
8	Philip M. Crane (R)	95,275
	Melissa L. Bean (D)	70,626
9	Janice D. Schakowsky* (D)	118,642
	Nicholas M. Duric (R)	45,307
10	Mark Steven Kirk* (R)	128,611
	Henry H. "Hank" Perritt, Jr. (D)	58,300
11	Jerry Weller* (R)	124,192
	Keith S. Van Duyne (D)	68,893
12	Jerry F. Costello* (D)	131,580
	David Sadler (R)	58,440
13	Judy Biggert* (R)	139,546
	Tom Mason (D)	59,069
14	J. Dennis Hastert* (R)	135,198
	Laurence J. Quick (D)	47,165
15	Timothy V. Johnson* (R)	134,650
	Joshua T. Hartke (D)	64,131
16	Donald A. Manzullo* (R)	133,339
	John Kutsch (D)	55,488
17	Lane Evans* (D)	127,093
	Peter Calderone (R)	76,519
18	Ray LaHood* (R)	192,567
19	John Shimkus* (R)	133,956
	David D. Phelps* (D)	110,517
Indiana		
1	Peter J. Visclosky* (D)	90,443
	Mark J. Leyva (R)	41,909
2	Chris Chocola (R)	95,081
	Jill Long Thompson (D)	86,253
3	Mark E. Souder* (R)	92,566
	Jay Rigdon (D)	50,509
4	Steve Buyer* (R)	112,760
	Bill Abbott (D)	41,314
5	Dan Burton* (R)	129,442
	Katherine Fox Carr (D)	45,283
6	Mike Pence* (R)	118,436
	Melina Ann Fox (D)	63,871
7	Julia M. Carson* (D)	77,478
	Brose A. McVey (R)	64,379
8	John N. Hostettler* (R)	98,952
	Bryan L. Hartke (D)	88,763
9	Baron P. Hill* (D)	96,654
	Mike Sodrel (R)	87,169
Iowa		
1	Jim Nussle* (R)	112,280
	Ann Hutchinson (D)	83,779
2	James A. Leach* (R)	108,130
	Julie Thomas (D)	94,767
3	Leonard L. Boswell* (D)	115,367
	Stan Thompson (D)	97,285
4	Tom Latham (R)	115,430
	John Norris (D)	90,784
5	Steve King (R)	113,257
	Paul Shomshor (D)	68,853

Dist.	Representative (Party)	2002 Election
Kansas		
1	**Jerry Moran* (R)**	**189,976**
	Jack Warner (LB)	18,585
2	**Jim Ryun* (R)**	**127,477**
	Dan Lykins (D)	79,160
3	**Dennis Moore* (D)**	**110,095**
	Adam Taff (R)	102,882
4	**Todd Tiahrt* (R)**	**115,691**
	Carlos Nolla (D)	70,656
Kentucky		
1	**Ed Whitfield* (R)**	**117,600**
	Klint Alexander (D)	62,617
2	**Ron Lewis* (R)**	**122,773**
	David L. Williams (D)	51,431
3	**Anne M. Northup* (R)**	**118,228**
	Jack Conway (D)	110,846
4	**Ken Lucas* (D)**	**87,776**
	Geoff Davis (R)	81,651
5	**Harold "Hal" Rogers* (R)**	**137,986**
	Sidney Jane Bailey (D)	38,254
6	**Ernie Fletcher* (R)**	**115,622**
	Gatewood Galbraith (I)	41,753
Louisiana		
1	**David Vitter* (R)**	**147,117**
	Monica L. Monica (R)	20,268
2	**William J. Jefferson* (D)**	**90,310**
	Irma Muse Dixon (D)	28,480
3	**W. J. (Billy) Tauzin* (R)**	**130,323**
	William Beier (other)	12,964
4	**Jim McCrery* (R)**	**114,649**
	John Milkovich (D)	42,340
5	**Rodney Alexander (D)**	**52,952**
	Lee Fletcher (R)	45,278
6	**Richard H. Baker* (R)**	**146,932**
	"Rick" Moscatello (other)	27,898
7	**Chris John* (D)**	**138,659**
	Roberto Valletta (other)	21,051

In Louisiana, all candidates of all parties ran against each other on Nov. 5, 2002, in a non-partisan primary. Candidates who received more than 50% of the vote were declared elected. Because no candidate received a majority of the vote in District 5, a runoff was held Dec. 7, 2002, between the top 2 vote getters.

Dist.	Representative (Party)	2002 Election
Maine		
1	**Thomas H. Allen* (D)**	**172,646**
	Steven Joyce (R)	97,931
2	**Michael H. Michaud (D)**	**116,868**
	Kevin L. Raye (R)	107,849
Maryland		
1	**Wayne T. Gilchrest* (R)**	**192,004**
	Amy D. Tamlyn (D)	57,986
2	**C. A. Dutch Ruppersberger (D)**	**105,718**
	Helen Delich Bentley (R)	88,954
3	**Benjamin L. Cardin* (D)**	**145,589**
	Scott Conwell (R)	75,721
4	**Albert Russell Wynn* (D)**	**131,644**
	John B. Kimble (R)	34,890
5	**Steny H. Hoyer* (D)**	**137,903**
	Joseph T. Crawford (R)	60,758
6	**Roscoe G. Bartlett (R)**	**147,825**
	Donald M. DeArmon (D)	75,575
7	**Elijah E. Cummings* (D)**	**137,047**
	Joseph E. Ward (R)	49,172
8	**Chris Van Hollen (D)**	**112,788**
	Constance A. Morella* (R)	103,587
Massachusetts		
1	**John W. Olver* (D)**	**137,841**
	Matthew W. Kinnaman (R)	66,061
2	**Richard E. Neal* (D)**	**153,387**
	Other	1,341
3	**James P. McGovern* (D)**	**155,697**

Dist.	Representative (Party)	2002 Election
4	**Barney Frank* (D)**	**166,125**
5	**Martin T. Meehan* (D)**	**122,562**
	Charles McCarthy (R)	69,337
6	**John F. Tierney* (D)**	**162,900**
	Mark C. Smith (R)	75,462
	Blank/Scattering	14,252
7	**Edward J. Markey* (D)**	**170,968**
	Blank/Scattering	61,976
8	**Michael E. Capuano* (D)**	**111,861**
	Blank/Scattering	42,923
9	**Stephen F. Lynch* (D)**	**168,055**
	Blank/Scattering	66,890
10	**William D. Delahunt* (D)**	**179,238**
	Luis Gonzaga (R)	79,624
Michigan		
1	**Bart Stupak* (D)**	**150,701**
	Don Hooper (R)	69,254
2	**Peter Hoekstra* (R)**	**156,937**
	Jeffrey Wrisley (D)	61,749
3	**Vernon J. Ehlers* (R)**	**153,131**
	Kathryn Lynnes (D)	61,987
4	**Dave Camp* (R)**	**149,090**
	Lawrence Hollenbeck (D)	65,950
5	**Dale E. Kildee* (D)**	**158,709**
	Clint Foster (LB)	9,344
6	**Fred Upton* (R)**	**126,936**
	Gary Giguere, Jr. (D)	53,793
7	**Nick Smith* (R)**	**121,142**
	Mike Simpson (D)	78,412
8	**Mike Rogers* (R)**	**156,525**
	Frank McAlpine (D)	70,920
9	**Joe Knollenberg* (R)**	**141,102**
	David Fink (D)	96,856
10	**Candice S. Miller (R)**	**137,339**
	Carl Marlinga (D)	77,053
11	**Thaddeus G. McCotter (R)**	**126,050**
	Kevin Kelley (D)	87,402
12	**Sander M. Levin* (D)**	**140,970**
	Harvey Dean (R)	61,502
13	**Carolyn C. Kilpatrick* (D)**	**120,869**
	Raymond Warner (LB)	11,072
14	**John Conyers, Jr.* (D)**	**145,285**
	Dave Stone (R)	26,544
15	**John D. Dingell* (D)**	**136,518**
	Martin Kaltenbach (R)	48,626
Minnesota		
1	**Gil Gutknecht* (R)**	**163,570**
	Steve Andreasen (D)	92,165
2	**John Kline (R)**	**152,970**
	Bill Luther* (D)	121,121
3	**Jim Ramstad* (R)**	**213,334**
	Darryl Stanton (D)	82,575
4	**Betty McCollum* (D)**	**164,597**
	Clyde Billington (R)	89,705
5	**Martin Olav Sabo* (D)**	**171,572**
	Daniel Nielsen Mathias (R)	66,271
6	**Mark R. Kennedy* (R)**	**164,747**
	Janet Robert (D)	100,738
7	**Collin C. Peterson* (D)**	**170,234**
	Dan Stevens (R)	90,342
8	**James L. Oberstar* (D)**	**194,909**
	Bob Lemen (R)	88,673
Mississippi		
1	**Roger F. Wicker* (R)**	**95,404**
	Rex N. Weathers (D)	32,318
2	**Bennie G. Thompson* (D)**	**89,913**
	Clinton B. LeSueur (R)	69,711
3	**Charles W. "Chip" Pickering* (R)**	**139,329**
	Ronnie Shows* (D)	76,184
4	**Gene Taylor* (D)**	**121,742**
	Karl Cleveland Mertz (R)	34,373

Dist.	Representative (Party)	2002 Election
Missouri		
1	Wm. Lacy Clay* (D)	133,946
	Richard Schwadron (R)	51,755
2	W. Todd Akin* (R)	167,057
	John Hogan (D)	77,223
3	Richard A. Gephardt* (D)	122,181
	Catherine S. Enz (R)	80,551
4	Ike Skelton* (D)	142,204
	James A. (Jim) Noland Jr. (R)	64,451
5	Karen McCarthy* (D)	122,645
	Steve Gordon (R)	60,245
6	Sam Graves* (R)	131,151
	Cathy Rinehart (D)	73,202
7	Roy Blunt* (R)	149,519
	Ron Lapham (D)	45,964
8	Jo Ann Emerson* (R)	135,144
	Gene Curtis (D)	50,686
9	Kenny C. Hulshof* (R)	146,032
	Donald M. (Don) Deichman (D)	61,126
Montana		
	Dennis R. Rehberg* (R)	214,100
	Steve Kelly (D)	108,233
Nebraska		
1	Doug Bereuter* (R)	133,013
	Robert Eckerson (LB)	22,831
2	Lee Terry* (R)	89,917
	Jim Simon (D)	46,843
3	Tom Osborne* (R)	163,939
	Jerry Hickman (LB)	12,017
Nevada		
1	Shelley Berkley* (D)	64,312
	Lynette Maria Boggs-McDonald (R)	51,148
2	Jim Gibbons* (R)	149,574
	Travis O. Souza (D)	40,189
New 3	Jon C. Porter (R)	100,378
	Dario Herrera (D)	66,659
New Hampshire		
1	Jeb Bradley (R)	128,993
	Martha Fuller Clark (D)	85,426
2	Charles Bass* (R)	125,804
	Katrina Swett (D)	90,479
New Jersey		
1	Robert E. Andrews* (D)	121,846
	Timothy Haas (I)	9,543
2	Frank A. LoBiondo* (R)	116,834
	Steven A. Farkas (D)	47,735
3	Jim Saxton* (R)	123,375
	Richard Strada (D)	64,364
4	Christopher H. Smith* (R)	115,293
	Mary Brennan (D)	55,967
5	Scott Garrett (R)	118,881
	Anne Sumers (D)	76,504
6	Frank Pallone, Jr.* (D)	91,379
	Ric Medrow (R)	42,479
7	Mike Ferguson* (R)	106,055
	Tim Carden (D)	74,879
8	Bill Pascrell, Jr.* (D)	88,101
	Jared Silverman (R)	40,318
9	Steven R. Rothman* (D)	97,108
	Joseph Glass (R)	42,088
10	Donald M. Payne* (D)	86,433
	Andrew Wirtz (R)	15,913
11	Rodney P. Frelinghuysen* (R)	132,938
	Vij Pawar (D)	48,477
12	Rush D. Holt* (D)	104,806
	DeForest "Buster" Soaries (R)	62,938
13	Robert Menendez* (D)	72,605
	James Geron (R)	16,852
New Mexico		
1	Heather Wilson* (R)	95,711
	Richard M. Romero (D)	77,234
2	Steve Pearce (R)	79,631
	John Arthur Smith (D)	61,916
3	Tom Udall (D)	122,921

Dist.	Representative (Party)	2002 Election
New York		
1	Timothy H. Bishop (D)	84,276
	Felix J. Grucci, Jr. (R)	81,524
2	Steve J. Israel* (D)	85,451
	Joseph P. Finley* (R)	59,117
3	Peter T. King* (R)	121,537
	Stuart L. Finz (D)	46,022
4	Carolyn McCarthy* (D)	94,806
	Marilyn F. O'Grady (R)	72,822
5	Gary L. Ackerman* (D)	68,773
	Perry S. Reich (C)	5,718
6	Gregory W. Meeks* (D)	72,799
	Rey Clarke (IN)	2,632
7	Joseph Crowley* (D)	50,967
	Kevin Brawley (R)	18,572
8	Jerrold L. Nadler* (D)	81,002
	Jim Farrin (R)	19,674
9	Anthony D. Weiner* (D)	60,737
	Alfred F. Donohue (R)	31,698
10	Edolphus Towns* (D)	73,859
	Herbert F. Ryan (C)	1,639
11	Major R. Owens* (D)	76,917
	Susan Cleary (R)	11,149
12	Nydia M. Velázquez* (D)	48,408
	Cesar Estevez (C)	2,119
13	Vito Fossella* (R)	72,204
	Arne M. Mattsson (D)	29,366
14	Carolyn B. Maloney* (D)	95,931
	Anton Srdanovic (R)	31,548
15	Charles B. Rangel* (D)	84,367
	Jessie A. Fields (R)	11,008
16	José E. Serrano* (D)	50,716
	Frank Dellavalle	4,366
17	Eliot L. Engel* (D)	77,535
	C. Scott Vanderhoef (R)	42,634
18	Nita M. Lowey* (D)	98,957
	Michael J. Reynolds (RTL)	8,558
19	Sue W. Kelly* (R)	121,129
	Janine M. H. Selendy (D)	44,967
20	John E. Sweeney* (R)	140,238
	Frank Stoppenbach (D)	45,878
21	Michael R. McNulty* (D)	161,329
	Charles B. Rosenstein (R)	53,525
22	Maurice D. Hinchey* (D)	113,280
	Eric Hall (R)	58,088
23	John M. McHugh (R)	124,682
24	Sherwood L. Boehlert *(R)	108,017
	David W. Walrath (C)	32,991
25	James T. Walsh* (R)	144,610
	Stephanie Aldersley (D)	53,290
26	Thomas M. Reynolds* (R)	135,089
	Ayesha F. Nariman (D)	41,140
27	Jack Quinn* (R)	120,117
	Peter Crotty (D)	47,811
28	Louise McIntosh Slaughter* (D)	99,057
	Henry F. Wojtaszek (R)	59,547
29	Amo Houghton* (R)	127,657
	Kisun J. Peters (D)	37,128
North Carolina		
1	Frank W. Ballance, Jr. (D)	93,157
	Greg Dority (R)	50,907
2	Bob Etheridge* (D)	100,121
	Joseph L. Ellen (R)	50,965
3	Walter B. Jones* (R)	131,448
	Gary Goodson (LB)	13,486
4	David E. Price* (D)	132,185
	Tuan A. Nguyen (R)	78,095
5	Richard Burr* (R)	137,879
	David Crawford (D)	58,558
6	Howard Coble* (R)	151,430
	Tara Grubb (LB)	16,067
7	Mike McIntyre* (D)	118,543
	James R. Adams (R)	45,537
8	Robin Hayes* (R)	80,298
	Chris Kouri (D)	66,819
9	Sue Wilkins Myrick* (R)	140,095
	Ed McGuire (D)	49,974

Dist.	Representative (Party)	2002 Election
10	Cass Ballenger* (R)	102,768
	Ron Daugherty (D)	65,587
11	Charles H. Taylor* (R)	112,335
	Sam Neill (D)	86,664
12	Melvin L. Watt* (D)	98,821
	Jeff Kish (R)	49,588
New 13	Brad Miller (D)	100,287
	Carolyn W. Grant (R)	77,688

North Dakota

Dist.	Representative (Party)	2002 Election
	Earl Pomeroy* (D)	121,073
	Rick Clayburgh (R)	109,957

Ohio

Dist.	Representative (Party)	2002 Election
1	Steve Chabot* (R)	110,760
	Greg Harris (D)	60,168
2	Rob Portman* (R)	139,218
	Charles W. Sanders (D)	48,785
3	Michael R. Turner (R)	111,630
	Rick Carne (D)	78,307
4	Michael Oxley* (R)	120,001
	Jim Clark (D)	57,726
5	Paul E. Gillmor* (R)	126,286
	Roger Anderson (D)	51,872
6	Ted Strickland* (D)	113,972
	Mike Halleck (R)	77,643
7	David L. Hobson* (R)	113,252
	Kara Anastasio (D)	45,568
8	John A. Boehner* (R)	119,947
	Jeff Hardenbrook (D)	49,444
9	Marcy Kaptur* (D)	132,236
	Ed Emery (R)	46,481
10	Dennis J. Kucinich* (D)	129,997
	Jon A. Heben (R)	41,778
11	Stephanie Tubbs Jones (D)	116,590
	Patrick A. Pappano (R)	36,146
12	Patrick J. Tiberi* (R)	116,982
	Edward Brown (D)	64,707
13	Sherrod Brown* (D)	123,025
	Ed Oliveros (R)	55,357
14	Steven C. LaTourette* (R)	134,413
	Dale Blanchard (D)	51,846
15	Deborah Pryce (R)	108,193
	Mark Brown (D)	54,286
16	Ralph Regula* (R)	129,734
	Jim Rice (D)	58,644
17	Timothy J. Ryan (D)	94,441
	Ann Womer Benjamin (R)	62,188
18	Robert W. Ney* (R)	125,546

Oklahoma

Dist.	Representative (Party)	2002 Election
1	John Sullivan* (R)	119,566
	Doug Dodd (D)	90,649
2	Brad Carson* (D)	146,748
	Kent Pharaoh (R)	51,234
3	Frank D. Lucas* (R)	148,206
	Robert T. Murphy (I)	47,884
4	Tom Cole (R)	106,452
	Darryl Roberts (D)	91,322
5	Ernest J. Istook, Jr.* (R)	121,374
	Lou Barlow (D)	63,208

Oregon

Dist.	Representative (Party)	2002 Election
1	David Wu* (D)	149,215
	Jim Greenfield (R)	80,917
2	Greg Walden* (R)	181,295
	Peter Buckley (D)	64,991
3	Earl Blumenauer* (D)	156,851
	Sarah Seale (R)	62,821
4	Peter A. DeFazio* (D)	168,150
	Liz VanLeeuwen (R)	90,523
5	Darlene Hooley* (D)	137,713
	Brian J. Boquist (R)	113,441

Pennsylvania

Dist.	Representative (Party)	2002 Election
1	Robert A. Brady* (D)	121,076
	Marie G. Delany (R)	17,444
2	Chaka Fattah* (D)	150,623
	Thomas G. Dougherty (R)	20,988
3	Phil English* (R)	116,763
	Anndrea M. Benson (GR)	33,554

Dist.	Representative (Party)	2002 Election
4	Melissa A. Hart* (R)	130,534
	Stevan Drobac, Jr. (D)	71,674
5	John E. Peterson* (R)	124,942
	Thomas A. Martin (LB)	18,078
6	Jim Gerlach (R)	103,648
	Dan Wofford (D)	98,128
7	Curt Weldon* (R)	146,296
	Peter A. Lennon (D)	75,055
8	James C. Greenwood* (R)	127,475
	Timothy T. Reece (D)	76,178
9	Bill Shuster* (R)	124,184
	John R. Henry (D)	50,558
10	Don Sherwood* (R)	152,017
	Kurt J. Shotko (GR)	11,613
11	Paul E. Kanjorski* (D)	93,758
	Louis J. Barletta (R)	71,543
12	John P. Murtha* (D)	124,201
	Bill Choby (R)	44,818
13	Joseph M. Hoeffel* (D)	107,945
	Melissa Brown (R)	100,295
14	Michael F. Doyle* (D)	123,323
	Write-in	89
15	Patrick J. Toomey* (R)	98,493
	Edward J. O'Brien (D)	73,212
16	Joseph R. Pitts* (R)	119,046
	Will Todd (GR)	8,720
17	Tim Holden* (D)	103,483
	George W. Gekas (R)	97,802
18	Tim Murphy (R)	119,885
	Jack Machek (D)	79,451
19	Todd Russell Platts* (R)	143,097
	Ben Price (GR)	7,900

Rhode Island

Dist.	Representative (Party)	2002 Election
1	Patrick J. Kennedy* (D)	95,286
	David W. Rogers (R)	59,370
2	James R. Langevin* (D)	129,390
	John O. Matson (R)	37,767

South Carolina

Dist.	Representative (Party)	2002 Election
1	Henry E. Brown, Jr.* (R)	127,562
	James E. Dunn, (UC)	9,841
2	Joe Wilson* (R)	144,149
	Mark Whittington (UC)	17,189
3	J. Gresham Barrett* (R)	119,644
	George L. Brightharp (D)	55,743
4	Jim DeMint* (R)	122,422
	Peter J. Ashy (D)	52,635
5	John M. Spratt, Jr.* (D)	121,912
	Doug Kendall (LB)	11,013
6	James E. Clyburn* (D)	116,586
	Gary McLeod (R)	55,760

South Dakota

Dist.	Representative (Party)	2002 Election
	William J. Janklow (R)	180,023
	Stephanie Herseth (D)	153,656

Tennessee

Dist.	Representative (Party)	2002 Election
1	William L. Jenkins* (R)	127,300
	Write-in	1,586
2	John J. Duncan, Jr.* (R)	146,887
	John Greene (D)	37,035
3	Zach Wamp* (R)	112,254
	John Wolfe (D)	58,824
4	Lincoln Davis (D)	95,989
	Janice Bowling (R)	85,680
5	Jim Cooper (D)	108,903
	Robert Duvall (R)	56,825
6	Bart Gordon* (D)	117,034
	Robert L. Garrison (R)	57,401
7	Marsha Blackburn (R)	138,314
	Tim Barron (D)	51,790
8	John S. Tanner* (D)	117,811
	Mat McClain (R)	45,853
9	Harold E. Ford, Jr.* (D)	120,904
	Tony Rush (I)	23,208

Texas

Dist.	Representative (Party)	2002 Election
1	Max Sandlin* (D)	86,384
	John Lawrence (R)	66,654
2	Jim Turner* (D)	85,492
	Van Brookshire (R)	53,656

Dist.	Representative (Party)	2002 Election
3	Sam Johnson* (R)	113,974
	Manny Molera (D)	37,503
4	Ralph M. Hall* (D)	97,304
	John Graves (R)	67,939
5	Jeb Hensarling (R)	81,439
	Ron Chapman (D)	56,330
6	Joe Barton* (R)	115,396
	Felix Alvarado (D)	45,404
7	John Abney Culberson* (R)	96,795
	Drew Parks (LB)	11,674
8	Kevin Brady* (R)	140,575
	Gil Guillory (LB)	10,351
9	Nick Lampson* (D)	86,710
	Paul Williams (R)	59,635
10	Lloyd Doggett* (D)	114,428
	Michele Messina (LB)	21,196
11	Chet Edwards* (D)	74,678
	Ramsey Farley (R)	68,236
12	Kay Granger* (R)	121,208
	Edward A. Hanson (LB)	10,723
13	Mac Thornberry* (R)	119,401
	Zane Reese (D)	31,218
14	Ron Paul* (R)	102,905
	Corby Windham (D)	48,224
15	Rubén Hinojosa* (D)	66,311
16	Silvestre Reyes* (D)	72,383
17	Charles W. Stenholm* (D)	84,136
	Rob Beckham (R)	77,622
18	Sheila Jackson Lee* (D)	99,161
	Phillip J. Abbott (R)	27,980
19	Randy Neugebauer[2] (R)	28,546
	Mike Conaway (R)	27,959
20	Charles A. Gonzalez* (D)	68,685
21	Lamar S. Smith* (R)	161,836
	John Courage (D)	56,206
22	Tom DeLay* (R)	100,499
	Tim Riley (D)	55,716
23	Henry Bonilla* (R)	77,573
	Henry Cuellar (D)	71,067
24	Martin Frost* (D)	73,002
	Mike Rivera Ortega (R)	38,332
25	Chris Bell (D)	63,590
	Tom Reiser (R)	50,041
26	Michael C. Burgess (R)	123,195
	Paul William LeBon (D)	37,485
27	Solomon P. Ortiz* (D)	68,559
	Pat Ahumada (R)	41,004
28	Ciro D. Rodriguez* (D)	71,393
	Gabriel Perales, Jr. (R)	26,973
29	Gene Green* (D)	55,760
	Paul Hansen (LB)	2,833
30	Eddie Bernice Johnson* (D)	88,980
	Ron Bush (R)	28,981
New 31	John R. Carter (R)	111,556
	David Bagley (D)	44,183
New 32	Pete Sessions* (R)	100,226
	Pauline K. Dixon (D)	44,886

Utah
Dist.	Representative (Party)	2002 Election
1	Rob Bishop (R)	109,265
	Dave Thomas (D)	66,104
2	Jim Matheson* (D)	110,764
	John Swallow (R)	109,123
3	Chris Cannon* (R)	103,598
	Nancy Jane Woodside (D)	44,533

Vermont
| | Bernard Sanders* (I) | 144,880 |
| | William "Bill" Meub (R) | 72,813 |

Virginia
Dist.	Representative (Party)	2002 Election
1	Jo Ann Davis* (R)	113,168
	Write-in	4,829
2	Edward L. Schrock* (R)	103,807
	D. C. Amarasinghe (GR)	20,589
3	Robert C. Scott* (D)	87,521
	Write-in	3,552
4	J. Randy Forbes* (R)	108,733
	Write-in	2,308
5	Virgil H. Goode, Jr.* (R)	95,360
	Meredith M. Richards (D)	54,805
6	Bob Goodlatte* (R)	105,530
	Write-in	3,202
7	Eric Cantor* (R)	113,658
	Ben L. "Cooter" Jones (D)	49,854
8	James P. Moran* (D)	102,759
	Scott C. Tate (R)	64,121
9	Rick Boucher* (D)	100,075
	J. Katzen (R)	52,076
10	Frank R. Wolf* (R)	115,917
	John B. Stevens, Jr. (D)	45,464
11	Tom Davis* (R)	135,379
	Frank W. Creel (CN)	26,892

Washington
Dist.	Representative (Party)	2002 Election
1	Jay Inslee* (D)	114,087
	Joe Marine (R)	84,696
2	Rick Larsen* (D)	101,219
	Norma Smith (R)	92,528
3	Brian Baird* (D)	119,264
	Joseph Zarelli (R)	74,065
4	Doc Hastings* (R)	108,257
	Craig Mason (D)	53,572
5	George R. Nethercutt, Jr.* (R)	126,757
	Bart Haggin (D)	65,146
6	Norman D. Dicks* (D)	126,116
	Bob Lawrence (R)	61,584
7	Jim McDermott* (D)	156,300
	Carol Thorne Cassady (R)	46,256
8	Jennifer Dunn* (R)	121,633
	Heidi Behrens-Benedict (D)	75,931
9	Adam Smith* (D)	95,805
	Sarah Casada (R)	63,146

West Virginia
1	Alan B. Mollohan* (D)	110,941
2	Shelley Moore Captio*(R)	98,276
	Jim Humphreys (D)	65,400
3	Nick Joe Rahall, II* (D)	87,783
	Paul E. Chapman (R)	37,229

Wisconsin
1	Paul Ryan* (R)	140,176
	Jeffrey C. Thomas (D)	63,895
2	Tammy Baldwin* (D)	163,313
	Ron Greer (R)	83,694
3	Ron Kind* (D)	131,038
	Bill Arndt (R)	69,955
4	Gerald D. Kleczka* (D)	122,031
	Brian Verdin (WG)	18,324
5	F. James Sensenbrenner, Jr.* (R)	191,224
	Robert Raymond (I)	29,567
6	Tom Petri* (R)	169,834
	Scattering	1,327
7	David R. Obey* (D)	146,364
	Joe Rothbauer (R)	81,518
8	Mark Green* (R)	152,745
	Andrew M. Becker (D)	50,284

Wyoming
| | Barbara Cubin* (R) | 110,229 |
| | Ron Akin (D) | 65,961 |

The following members of Congress are nonvoting: Aníbal Acevedo-Vilá (Popular Democratic Party), resident commissioner, Puerto Rico; Eleanor Holmes Norton (D), District of Columbia; Madeleine Bordallo (D), Guam; Eni F. H. Faleomavaega (D), American Samoa; Donna M. Christian-Christensen (D) Virgin Islands.

(1) Although Patsy Takemoto Mink died on Sept. 28, 2002, the Hawaii Supreme Court ruled that her name would remain on the ballot for the Nov. 5, 2002, election; she was the winner with 56% of the vote. A special election was held Nov. 30, 2002, to fill the seat for the remainder of the term; Ed Case (D) won with 51% of the vote. In a special election for the new Congress, Jan. 4, 2003, Ed Case was again the winner, as shown in the table. More than 40 names were on the ballot; the top 2 vote-getters are shown. (2) Randy Neugebauer won a special election June 3, 2003, to fill the seat left vacant by the resignation of Larry Combest May 31, 2003.

Congressional Committees

(as of Oct. 2003)

Rep. = Republican; Dem. = Democrat

Senate Standing Committees

Agriculture, Nutrition, and Forestry
Chairman: Thad Cochran, MS
Ranking Dem.: Tom Harkin, IA

Appropriations
Chairman: Ted Stevens, AK
Ranking Dem.: Robert C. Byrd, WV

Armed Services
Chairman: John W. Warner, VA
Ranking Dem.: Carl Levin, MI

Banking, Housing, and Urban Affairs
Chairman: Richard C. Shelby, AL
Ranking Dem.: Paul S. Sarbanes, MD

Budget
Chairman: Don Nickles, OK
Ranking Dem.: Kent Conrad, ND

Commerce, Science, and Transportation
Chairman: John McCain, AZ
Ranking Dem.: Ernest Hollings, SC

Energy and Natural Resources
Chairman: Pete V. Domenici, NM
Ranking Dem.: Jeff Bingaman, NM

Environment and Public Works
Chairman: James M. Inhofe, OK
Ranking: James M. Jeffords, VT

Finance
Chairman: Chuck Grassley, IA
Ranking Dem.: Max Baucus, MT

Foreign Relations
Chairman: Richard G. Lugar, IN
Ranking Dem.: Joseph R. Biden Jr., DE

Governmental Affairs
Chairman: Susan Collins, ME
Ranking Dem.: Joe Lieberman, CT

Health, Education, Labor, and Pensions
Chairman: Judd Gregg, NH
Ranking Dem.: Edward M. Kennedy, MA

Indian Affairs
Chairman: Ben Nighthorse Campbell, CO
Ranking Dem.: Daniel K. Inouye, HI

Judiciary
Chairman: Orrin G. Hatch, UT
Ranking Dem.: Patrick Leahy, VT

Rules and Administration
Chairman: Trent Lott, MS
Ranking Dem.: Christopher J. Dodd, CT

Small Business and Entrepreneurship
Chairman: Olympia Snowe, ME
Ranking Dem.: John F. Kerry, MA

Veterans' Affairs
Chairman: Arlen Specter, PA
Ranking Dem.: Bob Graham, FL

Senate Special Committee

Aging
Chairman: Larry E. Craig, ID
Ranking Dem.: John B. Breaux, LA

Senate Select Committees

Ethics
Chairman: George V. Voinovich (Rep., OH)
Vice Chairman: Harry Reid (Dem., NV)

Intelligence
Chairman: Pat Roberts (Rep., KS)
Vice Chairman: John D. Rockefeller IV (Dem., WV)

Joint Committees of Congress

Economic
Chairman: Senator Robert F. Bennett (Rep., UT)
Vice Chairman: Representative Jim Saxton (Rep., NJ)

Library
Chairman: Senator Ted Stevens (Rep., AK)
Vice Chairman: Representative Vernon Ehlers (Rep., MI)

Printing
Chairman: Representative Bob Ney (Rep., OH)
Vice Chairman: Senator Saxby Chambliss (Rep., GA)

Taxation
Chairman: Representative Bill Thomas (Rep., CA)
Vice Chairman: Senator Charles E. Grassley (Rep., IA)

House Standing Committees

Agriculture
Chairman: Bob Goodlatte, VA
Ranking Dem.: Charlie Stenholm, TX

Appropriations
Chairman: C. W. Bill Young, FL
Ranking Dem.: David R. Obey, WI

Armed Services
Chairman: Duncan Hunter, CA
Ranking Dem.: Ike Skelton, MO

Budget
Chairman: Jim Nussle, IA
Ranking Dem.: John Spratt, SC

Education and the Workforce
Chairman: John A. Boehner, OH
Ranking Dem.: George Miller, CA

Energy and Commerce
Chairman: W.J. "Billy" Tauzin, LA
Ranking Dem.: John D. Dingell, MI

Financial Services
Chairman: Michael G. Oxley, OH
Vice Chair: Sue W. Kelly

Government Reform
Chairman: Tom Davis, VA
Vice Chair: Christopher Shays, CT

House Administration
Chairman: Bob Ney, OH
Ranking Dem.: John B. Larson, CT

International Relations
Chairman: Henry J. Hyde, IL
vice Chair: Christopher H. Smith, NJ

Judiciary
Chairman: F. James Sensenbrenner, Jr., WI
Ranking Dem.: John Conyers, Jr., MI

Resources
Chairman: Richard Pombo, CA
Ranking Dem.: Nick J. Rahall II, WV

Rules
Chairman: David Dreier, CA
Vice Chair: Porter Goss, FL

Science
Chairman: Sherwood L. Boehlert, NY
Ranking Dem.: Ralph M. Hall, TX

Small Business
Chairman: Donald A. Manzullo, IL
Ranking Dem.: Nydia M. Velazquez, NY

Standards of Official Conduct
Chairman: Joel Hefley, CO
Ranking Dem.: Alan B. Mollohan, WV

Transportation and Infrastructure
Chairman: Don E. Young, AK
Ranking Dem.: James L. Oberstar, MN

Veterans' Affairs
Chairman: Christopher H. Smith, NJ
Ranking Dem.: Lane A. Evans, IL

Ways and Means
Chairman: Bill Thomas, CA
Ranking Dem.: Charles B. Rangel, NY

House Select Committee

Intelligence
Chairman: Porter Goss, FL
Ranking Dem.: Jane Harman, CA

Homeland Security
Chairman: Christopher Cox, CA
Ranking Dem.: Jim Turner, TX

Congress divides its tasks among some 250 committees and subcommittees. Standing committees generally have legislative jurisdiction and operate with subcommittees that handle work in specific areas. Select and joint committees are chiefly for oversight or housekeeping. The chair of each House or Senate committee and a majority of its members come from the majority party, which, as of Oct. 2003, was the Republican Party in both the Senate and the House.

Floor Leaders in the U.S. Senate Since the 1920s

Majority Leaders				Minority Leaders			
Name	Party	State	Tenure	Name	Party	State	Tenure
Charles Curtis[1]	R	KS	1925-1929	Oscar W. Underwood[2]	D	AL	1920-1923
James E. Watson	R	IN	1929-1933	Joseph T. Robinson	D	AR	1923-1933
Joseph T. Robinson	D	AR	1933-1937	Charles L. McNary	R	OR	1933-1944
Alben W. Barkley	D	KY	1937-1947	Wallace H. White	R	ME	1944-1947
Wallace H. White	R	ME	1947-1949	Alben W. Barkley	D	KY	1947-1949
Scott W. Lucas	D	IL	1949-1951	Kenneth S. Wherry	R	NE	1949-1951
Ernest W. McFarland	D	AZ	1951-1953	Henry Styles Bridges	R	NH	1951-1953
Robert A. Taft	R	OH	1953	Lyndon B. Johnson	D	TX	1953-1955
William F. Knowland	R	CA	1953-1955	William F. Knowland	R	CA	1955-1959
Lyndon B. Johnson	D	TX	1955-1961	Everett M. Dirksen	R	IL	1959-1969
Mike Mansfield	D	MT	1961-1977	Hugh D. Scott	R	PA	1969-1977
Robert C. Byrd	D	WV	1977-1981	Howard H. Baker Jr.	R	TN	1977-1981
Howard H. Baker Jr.	R	TN	1981-1985	Robert C. Byrd	D	WV	1981-1987
Robert J. Dole	R	KS	1985-1987	Robert J. Dole	R	KS	1987-1995
Robert C. Byrd	D	WV	1987-1989	Thomas A. Daschle	D	SD	1995-2001[3]
George J. Mitchell	D	ME	1989-1995	Trent Lott	R	MS	(3)
Robert J. Dole	R	KS	1995-1996	Bill Frist	R	TN	2002-2003[3]
Trent Lott	R	MS	1996-2001[3]	Thomas A. Daschle	D	SD	2003-
Thomas A. Daschle	D	SD	2001-2003[3]				
Bill Frist	R	TN	2003-				

Note: The offices of party (majority and minority) leaders in the Senate did not evolve until the early 20th century. (1) First Republican to be designated floor leader. (2) First Democrat to be designated floor leader. (3) Starting Jan. 3, 2001, the Senate was split 50-50; with Al Gore (D) as outgoing vice pres. with the deciding vote, Thomas A. Daschle (D) became majority leader and Trent Lott (R) was now minority leader. From Jan. 20, 2001, with Dick Cheney (R) installed as vice pres., the positions were reversed. From June 6, 2001, the switch of Sen. James Jeffords (VT) from Republican to Independent meant the Democrats had a majority; Daschle resumed as majority leader, Lott as minority leader. Lott resigned as party leader Dec. 20, 2002, and Bill Frist was elected to replace him in the 108th Congress; since Republicans now had a majority, Frist became majority leader as of Jan. 7, 2003, with Daschle as minority leader.

Speakers of the House of Representatives
(through Oct. 2003)

Party designations: A, American; D, Democratic; DR, Democratic-Republican; F, Federalist; R, Republican; W, Whig

Name	Party	State	Tenure	Name	Party	State	Tenure
Frederick Muhlenberg	F	PA	1789-1791	James G. Blaine	R	ME	1869-1875
Jonathan Trumbull	F	CT	1791-1793	Michael C. Kerr	D	IN	1875-1876
Frederick Muhlenberg	F	PA	1793-1795	Samuel J. Randall	D	PA	1876-1881
Jonathan Dayton	F	NJ	1795-1799	Joseph W. Keifer	R	OH	1881-1883
Theodore Sedgwick	F	MA	1799-1801	John G. Carlisle	D	KY	1883-1889
Nathaniel Macon	DR	NC	1801-1807	Thomas B. Reed	R	ME	1889-1891
Joseph B. Varnum	DR	MA	1807-1811	Charles F. Crisp	D	GA	1891-1895
Henry Clay	DR	KY	1811-1814	Thomas B. Reed	R	ME	1895-1899
Langdon Cheves	DR	SC	1814-1815	David B. Henderson	R	IA	1899-1903
Henry Clay	DR	KY	1815-1820	Joseph G. Cannon	R	IL	1903-1911
John W. Taylor	DR	NY	1820-1821	Champ Clark	D	MO	1911-1919
Philip P. Barbour	DR	VA	1821-1823	Frederick H. Gillett	R	MA	1919-1925
Henry Clay	DR	KY	1823-1825	Nicholas Longworth	R	OH	1925-1931
John W. Taylor	D	NY	1825-1827	John N. Garner	D	TX	1931-1933
Andrew Stevenson	D	VA	1827-1834	Henry T. Rainey	D	IL	1933-1935
John Bell	D	TN	1834-1835	Joseph W. Byrns	D	TN	1935-1936
James K. Polk	D	TN	1835-1839	William B. Bankhead	D	AL	1936-1940
Robert M. T. Hunter	D	VA	1839-1841	Sam Rayburn	D	TX	1940-1947
John White	W	KY	1841-1843	Joseph W. Martin Jr.	R	MA	1947-1949
John W. Jones	D	VA	1843-1845	Sam Rayburn	D	TX	1949-1953
John W. Davis	D	IN	1845-1847	Joseph W. Martin Jr.	R	MA	1953-1955
Robert C. Winthrop	W	MA	1847-1849	Sam Rayburn	D	TX	1955-1961
Howell Cobb	D	GA	1849-1851	John W. McCormack	D	MA	1962-1971
Linn Boyd	D	KY	1851-1855	Carl Albert	D	OK	1971-1977
Nathaniel P. Banks	A	MA	1856-1857	Thomas P. O'Neill Jr.	D	MA	1977-1987
James L. Orr	D	SC	1857-1859	James Wright	D	TX	1987-1989
William Pennington	R	NJ	1860-1861	Thomas S. Foley	D	WA	1989-1995
Galusha A. Grow	R	PA	1861-1863	Newt Gingrich	R	GA	1995-1999
Schuyler Colfax	R	IN	1863-1869	J. Dennis Hastert	R	IL	1999-
Theodore M. Pomeroy	R	NY	1869				

Political Divisions of the U.S. Senate and House of Representatives, 1901-2003

Source: *Congressional Directory;* Senate Library

Note: all figures reflect immediate post-election party breakdown; **boldface** denotes party in majority immediately after election.

Congress	Years	SENATE					HOUSE OF REPRESENTATIVES				
		Total Sens.	Demo-crats	Repub-licans	Other parties	Vacant	Total Members	Demo-crats	Repub-licans	Other parties	Vacant
57th	1901-03	90	29	**56**	3	2	357	153	**198**	5	1
58th	1903-05	90	32	**58**			386	178	**207**		1
59th	1905-07	90	32	**58**			386	136	**250**		
60th	1907-09	92	29	**61**		2	386	164	**222**		
61st	1909-11	92	32	**59**		1	391	172	**219**		
62nd	1911-13	92	42	**49**		1	391	**228**	162	1	
63rd	1913-15	96	**51**	44	1		435	**290**	127	18	
64th	1915-17	96	**56**	39	1		435	**231**	193	8	3
65th	1917-19	96	**53**	42	1		435	210[1]	**216**	9	
66th	1919-21	96	47	**48**	1		435	191	**237**	7	
67th	1921-23	96	37	**59**			435	132	**300**	1	2
68th	1923-25	96	43	**51**	2		435	207	**225**	3	
69th	1925-27	96	40	**54**	1	1	435	183	**247**	5	
70th	1927-29	96	47	**48**	1		435	195	**237**	3	

Congress	Years	Total Sens.	Demo-crats	SENATE Repub-licans	Other parties	Vacant	Total Members	Demo-crats	Repub-licans	Other parties	Vacant
71st	1929-31	96	39	56	1		435	163	267	1	4
72nd	1931-33	96	47	48	1		435	216²	218	1	
73rd	1933-35	96	59	36	1		435	313	117	5	
74th	1935-37	96	69	25	2		435	322	103	10	
75th	1937-39	96	75	17	4		435	333	89	13	
76th	1939-41	96	69	23	4		435	262	169	4	
77th	1941-43	96	66	28	2		435	267	162	6	
78th	1943-45	96	57	38	1		435	222	209	4	
79th	1945-47	96	57	38	1		435	243	190	2	
80th	1947-49	96	45	51			435	188	246	1	
81st	1949-51	96	54	42			435	263	171	1	
82nd	1951-53	96	48	47	1		435	234	199	2	
83rd	1953-55	96	46	48	2		435	213	221	1	
84th	1955-57	96	48	47	1		435	232	203		
85th	1957-59	96	49	47			435	234	201		
86th	1959-61	98	64	34			436³	283	153		
87th	1961-63	100	64	36			437⁴	262	175		
88th	1963-65	100	67	33			435	258	176		1
89th	1965-67	100	68	32			435	295	140		
90th	1967-69	100	64	36			435	248	187		
91st	1969-71	100	58	42			435	243	192		
92nd	1971-73	100	54	44	2		435	255	180		
93rd	1973-75	100	56	42	2		435	242	192	1	
94th	1975-77	100	60	37	2		435	291	144	1	
95th	1977-79	100	61	38	1		435	292	143		
96th	1979-81	100	58	41	1		435	277	158		
97th	1981-83	100	46	53	1		435	242	192	1	
98th	1983-85	100	46	54			435	269	166		
99th	1985-87	100	47	53			435	253	182		
100th	1987-89	100	55	45			435	258	177		
101st	1989-91	100	55	45			435	260	175		
102nd	1991-93	100	56	44			435	267	167	1	
103rd	1993-95	100	57	43			435	258	176	1	
104th	1995-97	100	48	52			435	204	230	1	
105th	1997-99	100	45	55			435	207	227	1	
106th	1999-2001	100	45	55			435	211	223	1	
107th	2001-03	100	50	50⁵			435	212	221	2	
108th	2003-05	100	48	51	1		435	205	229	1	

(1) Democrats organized the House with help of other parties. (2) Democrats organized House because of Republican deaths. (3) Proclamation declaring Alaska a state issued Jan. 3, 1959. (4) Proclamation declaring Hawaii a state issued Aug. 21, 1959. (5) While the Senate was split 50-50, control was held by whichever party had an incumbent vice president. Republican Sen. James M. Jeffords (VT) changed his party designation to Independent on June 6, 2001, switching control of the Senate to Democrats from Republicans.

Congressional Bills Vetoed, 1789-2003

Source: Senate Library

President	Regular vetoes	Pocket vetoes	Total vetoes	Vetoes overridden	President	Regular vetoes	Pocket vetoes	Total vetoes	Vetoes overridden
Washington	2	—	2	—	Benjamin Harrison	19	25	44	1
John Adams	—	—	—	—	Cleveland²	42	128	170	5
Jefferson	—	—	—	—	McKinley	6	36	42	—
Madison	5	2	7	—	Theodore Roosevelt	42	40	82	1
Monroe	1	—	1	—	Taft	30	9	39	1
John Q. Adams	—	—	—	—	Wilson	33	11	44	6
Jackson	5	7	12	—	Harding	5	1	6	—
Van Buren	—	1	1	—	Coolidge	20	30	50	4
William Harrison	—	—	—	—	Hoover	21	16	37	3
Tyler	6	4	10	1	Franklin Roosevelt	372	263	635	9
Polk	2	1	3	—	Truman	180	70	250	12
Taylor	—	—	—	—	Eisenhower	73	108	181	2
Fillmore	—	—	—	—	Kennedy	12	9	21	—
Pierce	9	—	9	5	Lyndon Johnson	16	14	30	—
Buchanan	4	3	7	—	Nixon	26	17	43	7
Lincoln	2	4	6	—	Ford	48	18	66	12
Andrew Johnson	21	8	29	15	Carter	13	18	31	2
Grant	45	48	93	4	Reagan	39	39	78	9
Hayes	12	1	13	1	George H. W. Bush³	29	15	44	1
Garfield	—	—	—	—	Clinton⁴	36	1	37	2
Arthur	4	8	12	1	George W. Bush⁵	—	—	—	—
Cleveland¹	304	110	414	2	Total³,⁴	1,484	1,065	2,549	106

— = 0. (1) First term only. (2) Second term only. (3) Excluded from the figures are 2 additional bills, which Pres. George H. W. Bush claimed to be vetoed but Congress considered enacted into law because the president failed to return them to Congress during a recess period. (4) Does not include line-item vetoes, which were ruled unconstitutional by the Supreme Court on June 25, 1998. (5) As of Oct. 15, 2003.

Librarians of Congress

Librarian	Served	Appointed by President	Librarian	Served	Appointed by President
John J. Beckley	1802-1807	Jefferson	Herbert Putnam	1899-1939	McKinley
Patrick Magruder	1807-1815	Jefferson	Archibald MacLeish	1939-1944	F. D. Roosevelt
George Watterston	1815-1829	Madison	Luther H. Evans	1945-1953	Truman
John Silva Meehan	1829-1861	Jackson	L. Quincy Mumford	1954-1974	Eisenhower
John G. Stephenson	1861-1864	Lincoln	Daniel J. Boorstin	1975-1987	Ford
Ainsworth Rand Spofford	1864-1897	Lincoln	James H. Billington	1987-	Reagan
John Russell Young	1897-1899	McKinley			

U.S. SUPREME COURT

(data as of Oct. 2003)

Justices of the U.S. Supreme Court

The Supreme Court comprises the chief justice of the U.S. and 8 associate justices, all appointed for life by the president with advice and consent of the Senate. Names of chief justices are in **boldface.** Salaries: chief justice, $198,600; associate justice, $190,100. The U.S. Supreme Court Bldg. is at 1 First St. NE, Washington, DC 20543. The Court website is www.supremecourtus.gov

Members at start of 2003-2004 term (Oct. 6, 2003): Chief justice: William H. Rehnquist; assoc. justices: Stephen G. Breyer, Ruth Bader Ginsburg, Anthony M. Kennedy, Sandra Day O'Connor, Antonin Scalia, David H. Souter, John Paul Stevens, Clarence Thomas.

Name, apptd. from	Service Term	Yrs	Born	Died	Name, apptd. from	Service Term	Yrs	Born	Died
John Jay, NY	1789-1795	5	1745	1829	Joseph McKenna, CA	1898-1925	26	1843	1926
John Rutledge, SC[1]	1789-1791	1	1739	1800	Oliver W. Holmes, MA	1902-1932	29	1841	1935
William Cushing, MA	1789-1810	20	1732	1810	William R. Day, OH	1903-1922	19	1849	1923
James Wilson, PA	1789-1798	8	1742	1798	William H. Moody, MA	1906-1910	3	1853	1917
John Blair, VA	1789-1796	6	1732	1800	Horace H. Lurton, TN	1909-1914	4	1844	1914
James Iredell, NC	1790-1799	9	1751	1799	Charles E. Hughes, NY[1]	1910-1916	5	1862	1948
Thomas Johnson, MD	1791-1793	1	1732	1819	Willis Van Devanter, WY	1910-1937	26	1859	1941
William Paterson, NJ	1793-1806	13	1745	1806	Joseph R. Lamar, GA	1910-1916	5	1857	1916
John Rutledge, SC[2, 3]	1795	—	1739	1800	**Edward D. White,** LA[2]	1910-1921	10	1845	1921
Samuel Chase, MD	1796-1811	15	1741	1811	Mahlon Pitney, NJ	1912-1922	10	1858	1924
Oliver Ellsworth, CT	1796-1800	4	1745	1807	James C. McReynolds, TN	1914-1941	26	1862	1946
Bushrod Washington, VA	1798-1829	31	1762	1829	Louis D. Brandeis, MA	1916-1939	22	1856	1941
Alfred Moore, NC	1799-1804	4	1755	1810	John H. Clarke, OH	1916-1922	5	1857	1945
John Marshall, VA	1801-1835	34	1755	1835	**William H. Taft,** CT	1921-1930	8	1857	1930
William Johnson, SC	1804-1834	30	1771	1834	George Sutherland, UT	1922-1938	15	1862	1942
Henry B. Livingston, NY	1806-1823	16	1757	1823	Pierce Butler, MN	1922-1939	16	1866	1939
Thomas Todd, KY	1807-1826	18	1765	1826	Edward T. Sanford, TN	1923-1930	7	1865	1930
Joseph Story, MA	1811-1845	33	1779	1845	Harlan F. Stone, NY[1]	1925-1941	16	1872	1946
Gabriel Duval, MD	1811-1835	22	1752	1844	**Charles E. Hughes,** NY[2]	1930-1941	11	1862	1948
Smith Thompson, NY	1823-1843	20	1768	1843	Owen J. Roberts, PA	1930-1945	15	1875	1955
Robert Trimble, KY	1826-1828	2	1777	1828	Benjamin N. Cardozo, NY	1932-1938	6	1870	1938
John McLean, OH	1829-1861	32	1785	1861	Hugo L. Black, AL	1937-1971	34	1886	1971
Henry Baldwin, PA	1830-1844	14	1780	1844	Stanley F. Reed, KY	1938-1957	19	1884	1980
James M. Wayne, GA	1835-1867	32	1790	1867	Felix Frankfurter, MA	1939-1962	23	1882	1965
Roger B. Taney, MD	1836-1864	28	1777	1864	William O. Douglas, CT	1939-1975	36[4]	1898	1980
Philip P. Barbour, VA	1836-1841	4	1783	1841	Frank Murphy, MI	1940-1949	9	1890	1949
John Catron, TN	1837-1865	28	1786	1865	**Harlan F. Stone,** NY[2]	1941-1946	5	1872	1946
John McKinley, AL	1837-1852	15	1780	1852	James F. Byrnes, SC	1941-1942	1	1879	1972
Peter V. Daniel, VA	1841-1860	19	1784	1860	Robert H. Jackson, NY	1941-1954	12	1892	1954
Samuel Nelson, NY	1845-1872	27	1792	1873	Wiley B. Rutledge, IA	1943-1949	6	1894	1949
Levi Woodbury, NH	1845-1851	5	1789	1851	Harold H. Burton, OH	1945-1958	13	1888	1964
Robert C. Grier, PA	1846-1870	23	1794	1870	**Fred M. Vinson,** KY	1946-1953	7	1890	1953
Benjamin R. Curtis, MA	1851-1857	6	1809	1874	Tom C. Clark, TX	1949-1967	18	1899	1977
John A. Campbell, AL	1853-1861	8	1811	1889	Sherman Minton, IN	1949-1956	7	1890	1965
Nathan Clifford, ME	1858-1881	23	1803	1881	**Earl Warren,** CA	1953-1969	16	1891	1974
Noah H. Swayne, OH	1862-1881	18	1804	1884	John Marshall Harlan, NY	1955-1971	16	1899	1971
Samuel F. Miller, IA	1862-1890	28	1816	1890	William J. Brennan Jr., NJ	1956-1990	33	1906	1997
David Davis, IL	1862-1877	14	1815	1886	Charles E. Whittaker, MO	1957-1962	5	1901	1973
Stephen J. Field, CA	1863-1897	34	1816	1899	Potter Stewart, OH	1958-1981	23	1915	1985
Salmon P. Chase, OH	1864-1873	8	1808	1873	Byron R. White, CO	1962-1993	31	1917	2002
William Strong, PA	1870-1880	10	1808	1895	Arthur J. Goldberg, IL	1962-1965	3	1908	1990
Joseph P. Bradley, NJ	1870-1892	21	1813	1892	Abe Fortas, TN	1965-1969	4	1910	1982
Ward Hunt, NY	1872-1882	9	1810	1886	Thurgood Marshall, NY	1967-1991	24	1908	1993
Morrison R. Waite, OH	1874-1888	14	1816	1888	**Warren E. Burger,** VA	1969-1986	17	1907	1995
John M. Harlan, KY	1877-1911	34	1833	1911	Harry A. Blackmun, MN	1970-1994	24	1908	1999
William B. Woods, GA	1880-1887	6	1824	1887	Lewis F. Powell Jr., VA	1971-1987	16	1907	1998
Stanley Matthews, OH	1881-1889	7	1824	1889	William H. Rehnquist, AZ[1]	1971-1986	15	1924	
Horace Gray, MA	1881-1902	20	1828	1902	John Paul Stevens, IL	1975-		1920	
Samuel Blatchford, NY	1882-1893	11	1820	1893	Sandra Day O'Connor, AZ	1981-		1930	
Lucius Q.C. Lamar, MS	1888-1893	5	1825	1893	**William H. Rehnquist,** AZ[2]	1986-		1924	
Melville W. Fuller, IL	1888-1910	21	1833	1910	Antonin Scalia, VA	1986-		1936	
David J. Brewer, KS	1889-1910	20	1837	1910	Anthony M. Kennedy, CA	1988-		1936	
Henry B. Brown, MI	1890-1906	15	1836	1913	David H. Souter, NH	1990-		1939	
George Shiras Jr., PA	1892-1903	10	1832	1924	Clarence Thomas, VA	1991-		1948	
Howell E. Jackson, TN	1893-1895	2	1832	1895	Ruth Bader Ginsburg, DC	1993-		1933	
Edward D. White, LA[1]	1894-1910	16	1845	1921	Stephen G. Breyer, MA	1994-		1938	
Rufus W. Peckham, NY	1895-1909	13	1838	1909					

(1) Later, chief justice, as listed. (2) Formerly assoc. justice. (3) Named as acting chief justice; confirmation rejected by the Senate. (4) Longest term of service.

> ▶ **IT'S A FACT:** When the Supreme Court is in session, the Justices enter the courtroom promptly at 10 AM, and those present must stand until all Justices are seated, following the traditional chant from the marshal: "The Honorable, the Chief Justice and the Associate Justices of the Supreme Court of the United States. Oyez! Oyez! Oyez! All persons having business before the honorable, the Supreme Court of the United States, are admonished to draw near and give their attention, for the Court is now sitting. God save the United States and this honorable Court."

STATE GOVERNMENT
Governors of States and Puerto Rico
As of Oct. 15, 2003.

State	Capital, ZIP Code	Governor	Party	Term years	Term expires	Annual salary[1]
Alabama	Montgomery 36130	Bob Riley	Rep.	4	Jan. 2007	$96,361
Alaska	Juneau 99811	Frank Murkowski	Rep.	4	Dec. 2006	85,776
Arizona	Phoenix 85007	Janet Napolitano	Dem.	4	Jan. 2007	95,000
Arkansas	Little Rock 72201	Mike Huckabee	Rep.	4	Jan. 2007	75,296
California	Sacramento 95814	Gray Davis[2]	Dem.	4	Jan. 2007	175,000
Colorado	Denver 80203	Bill Owens	Rep.	4	Jan. 2007	90,000
Connecticut	Hartford 06106	John G. Rowland	Rep.	4	Jan. 2007	150,000
Delaware	Dover 19901	Ruth Ann Minner	Dem.	4	Jan. 2005	114,000
Florida	Tallahassee 32399	Jeb Bush	Rep.	4	Jan. 2007	124,575
Georgia	Atlanta 30334	Sonny Perdue	Rep.	4	Jan. 2007	127,303
Hawaii	Honolulu 96813	Linda Lingle	Rep.	4	Dec. 2006	94,780
Idaho	Boise 83720	Dirk Kempthorne	Rep.	4	Jan. 2007	98,500
Illinois	Springfield 62706	Rod R. Blagojevich	Dem.	4	Jan. 2007	150,691
Indiana	Indianapolis 46204	Joseph E. Kernan	Dem.	4	Jan. 2005	95,000
Iowa	Des Moines 50319	Tom Vilsack	Dem.	4	Jan. 2007	104,795
Kansas	Topeka 66612	Kathleen Sebelius	Dem.	4	Jan. 2007	98,331
Kentucky	Frankfort 40601	Paul Patton	Dem.	4	Dec. 2003	107,130
Louisiana	Baton Rouge 70804	M. J. "Mike" Foster Jr.	Rep.	4	Jan. 2004	95,000
Maine	Augusta 04333	John E. Baldacci	Dem.	4	Jan. 2007	70,000
Maryland	Annapolis 21401	Robert L. Ehrlich Jr.	Rep.	4	Jan. 2007	135,000
Massachusetts	Boston 02133	Mitt Romney	Rep.	4	Jan. 2007	135,000
Michigan	Lansing 48909	Jennifer M. Granholm	Dem.	4	Jan. 2007	177,000
Minnesota	St. Paul 55155	Tim Pawlenty	Rep.	4	Jan. 2007	114,506
Mississippi	Jackson 39205	Ronnie Musgrove	Dem.	4	Jan. 2004	122,160
Missouri	Jefferson City 65102	Bob Holden	Dem.	4	Jan. 2005	120,087
Montana	Helena 59620	Judy Martz	Rep.	4	Jan. 2005	93,089
Nebraska	Lincoln 68509	Mike Johanns	Rep.	4	Jan. 2007	85,000
Nevada	Carson City 89710	Kenny C. Guinn	Rep.	4	Jan. 2007	117,000
New Hampshire	Concord 03301	Craig Benson	Rep.	2	Jan. 2005	100,690
New Jersey	Trenton 08625	James E. McGreevey	Dem.	4	Jan. 2006	157,000
New Mexico	Santa Fe 87503	Bill Richardson	Dem.	4	Jan. 2007	110,000
New York	Albany 12224	George E. Pataki	Rep.	4	Jan. 2007	179,000
North Carolina	Raleigh 27603	Mike Easley	Dem.	4	Jan. 2005	118,430
North Dakota	Bismarck 58505	John Hoeven	Rep.	4	Jan. 2005	87,216
Ohio	Columbus 43266	Bob Taft	Rep.	4	Jan. 2007	122,800
Oklahoma	Oklahoma City 73105	Brad Henry	Dem.	4	Jan. 2007	110,299
Oregon	Salem 97310	Ted Kulongoski	Dem.	4	Jan. 2007	93,600
Pennsylvania	Harrisburg 17120	Edward G. Rendell	Dem.	4	Jan. 2007	142,142
Rhode Island	Providence 02903	Donald L. Carcieri	Rep.	4	Jan. 2007	105,000
South Carolina	Columbia 29211	Mark Sanford	Rep.	4	Jan. 2007	106,078
South Dakota	Pierre 57501	Mike Rounds	Rep.	4	Jan. 2007	98,250
Tennessee	Nashville 37243	Phil Bredesen	Dem.	4	Jan. 2007	85,000
Texas	Austin 78711	Rick Perry	Rep.	4	Jan. 2007	115,345
Utah	Salt Lake City 84114	Michael O. Leavitt	Rep.	4	Jan. 2005	100,600
Vermont	Montpelier 05609	James H. Douglas	Rep.	2	Jan. 2005	127,456
Virginia	Richmond 23219	Mark R. Warner	Dem.	4	Jan. 2006	124,855
Washington	Olympia 98504	Gary Locke	Dem.	4	Jan. 2005	142,286
West Virginia	Charleston 25305	Bob Wise	Dem.	4	Jan. 2005	90,000
Wisconsin	Madison 53707	Jim Doyle	Dem.	4	Jan. 2007	131,768
Wyoming	Cheyenne 82002	Dave Freudenthal	Dem.	4	Jan. 2007	105,000
Puerto Rico	San Juan 00936	Sila Calderón	PDP[3]	4	Jan. 2005	70,000

(1) Salary in effect in 2003. (2) In a recall election Oct. 7, 2003, Davis was voted out as governor, and Arnold Schwarzenegger was elected to replace him. He was expected to take office in Nov. (3) Popular Democratic Party.

State Officials, Salaries, Party Membership
As of Oct. 15, 2003; I=independent

Alabama
Governor — Bob Riley, R, $96,361
Lt. Gov. — Lucy Baxley, D, $12 per day, plus $50 per day expenses, plus $3,780 per mo expenses
Atty. Gen. — William Pryor, R, $163,429
Sec. of State — Nancy L. Worley, D, $71,500
Treasurer — Kay Ivey, R, $71,500
Auditor — Beth Chapman, R, $71,500
Legislature: meets annually at Montgomery 1st Tues. in Mar., 1st year of term of office; 1st Tues. in Feb., 2nd and 3rd yr; 2nd Tues. in Jan., 4th yr. Members receive $10 per day salary, plus $50 per day and $2,280 per mo expenses.
Senate — Dem., 25; Rep., 10. Total, 35
House — Dem., 63; Rep., 42. Total, 105

Alaska
Governor — Frank Murkowski, R, $85,776
Lt. Gov — Loren D. Leman, R, $80,040
Atty. General — Gregg Renkes, R, $91,200
Legislature: meets annually in Jan. at Juneau for 120 days with a 10-day extension possible upon 2/3 vote. Members receive $24,012 annually, plus $202 per diem.
Senate — Dem., 8; Rep., 12. Total, 20
House — Dem., 13; Rep., 27. Total, 40

Arizona
Governor — Janet Napolitano, D, $95,000
Sec. of State — Jan Brewer, R, $70,000
Atty. Gen. — Terry Goddard, D, $90,000
Treasurer — David Petersen, R, $70,000
Legislature: meets annually in Jan. at Phoenix. Each member receives an annual salary of $24,000 plus a per diem.
Senate — Dem., 13; Rep., 17. Total, 30
House — Dem., 20; Rep., 39; 1 ind. Total, 60

Arkansas
Governor — Mike Huckabee, R, $75,296
Lt. Gov. — Winthrop P. Rockefeller, R, $36,392
Sec. of State — Charlie Daniels, D, $47,060
Atty. Gen. — Mike Beebe, D, $62,746
Treasurer — Gus Wingfield, D, $47,060
Auditor — Jim Wood, D, $47,060
General Assembly: meets odd years in Jan. at Little Rock. Members receive $13,751 annually.
Senate — Dem., 27; Rep., 8. Total, 35
House — Dem., 70; Rep., 30. Total, 100

California
Governor — Gray Davis[1], D, $175,000
Lt. Gov. — Cruz Bustamante, D, $131,250
Sec. of State — Kevin Shelley, D, $131,250
Controller — Steve Westly, D, $140,000
Treasurer — Phil Angelides, D, $140,000
Atty. Gen. — Bill Lockyer, D, $148,750
Legislature: meets at Sacramento on the 1st Mon. in Dec. of even-numbered years; each session lasts 2 years. Members receive $99,000 annually, plus $121 per diem.
Senate — Dem., 25; Rep., 15. Total, 40
Assembly — Dem., 48; Rep., 32. Total, 80
(1) Arnold Schwarzenegger (R) elected Oct. 7, 2003, to replace Davis in Nov.

Colorado
Governor — Bill Owens, R, $90,000
Lt. Gov. — Jane Norton, R, $68,500
Sec. of State — Donetta Davidson, R, $68,500
Atty. Gen. — Ken Salazar, D, $80,000
Treasurer — Mike Coffman, R, $68,500
General Assembly: meets annually in Jan. at Denver. Members receive $30,000 annually plus $99 per diem for attendance at interim committee meetings.
Senate — Dem., 17; Rep., 18. Total, 35
House — Dem., 28; Rep., 37. Total, 65

Connecticut
Governor — John G. Rowland, R, $150,000
Lt. Gov. — M. Jodi Rell, R, $110,000
Sec. of State — Susan Bysiewicz, D, $110,000
Treasurer — Denise Nappier, D, $110,000
Comptroller — Nancy S. Wyman, D, $110,000
Atty. Gen. — Richard Blumenthal, D, $110,000
General Assembly: meets annually odd years in Jan. and even years in Feb., at Hartford. Members receive $28,000 annually, plus $5,500 (senator), $4,500 (representative) per year for expenses.
Senate — Dem., 21; Rep., 15. Total, 36
House — Dem., 95; Rep., 56. Total, 151

Delaware
Governor — Ruth Ann Minner, D, $114,000
Lt. Gov. — John C. Carney Jr., D, $62,400
Sec. of State — Harriet Smith Windsor, D, $106,000
Atty. Gen. — M. Jane Brady, R, $116,700
Treasurer — Jack A. Markell, D, $94,000
General Assembly: meets annually the 2nd Tues. in Jan. and continues each Tues., Wed., and Thurs. until June 30, at Dover. Members receive $34,800 annually.
Senate — Dem., 13; Rep., 8. Total, 21
House — Dem., 12; Rep., 29. Total, 41

Florida
Governor — Jeb Bush, R, $124,575
Lt. Gov. — Toni Jennings, R, $119,390
Chief Financial Officer — Tom Gallagher, R, $123,331
Atty. Gen. — Charlie Crist, R, $123,331
Comm. of Agriculture — Charles Bronson, R, $123,331
Legislature: meets annually at Tallahassee. Members receive $29,916 annually, plus expense allowance.
Senate — Dem., 14; Rep., 26. Total, 40
House — Dem., 39; Rep., 81. Total, 120

Georgia
Governor — Sonny Perdue, R, $127,303
Lt. Gov. — Mark Taylor, D, $83,148
Sec. of State — Cathy Cox, D, $112,776
Atty. Gen. — Thurbert Baker, D, $125,871
General Assembly: meets annually at Atlanta on 2nd Mon. in Jan. Members receive $16,200 annually ($128 per diem and $7,000 annual expense reimbursement).
Senate — Dem., 26; Rep., 30. Total, 56
House — Dem., 107; Rep., 72; 1 ind. Total, 180

Hawaii
Governor — Linda Lingle, R, $94,780
Lt. Gov. — James R. Aiona Jr., R, $90,041
Atty. Gen. — Mark J. Bennett, $85,302
Comptroller — Russ K. Saito, $85,302
Dir. of Budget & Finance — Georgina K. Kawamura, $85,302
Legislature: meets annually on 3rd Wed. in Jan. at Honolulu. Members receive $32,000 annually; presiding officers $37,000.
Senate — Dem., 22; Rep., 3. Total, 25
House — Dem., 36; Rep., 15. Total, 51

Idaho
Governor — Dirk Kempthorne, R, $98,500
Lt. Gov. — Jim Risch, R, $26,750
Sec. of State — Ben Ysursa, R, $82,500
Treasurer — Ron Crane, R, $82,500
Atty. Gen. — Lawrence Wasden, R, $91,500
Legislature: meets annually the Mon. on or nearest Jan. 9 at Boise. Members receive $15,646 annually, plus $99 per day during session if required to maintain a 2nd residence, $38 if no 2nd residence; plus $50 per day when engaged in legislative business when legislature is not in session.
Senate — Dem., 7; Rep., 28. Total, 35
House — Dem., 16; Rep., 54. Total, 70

Illinois
Governor — Rod R. Blagojevich, D, $150,691
Lt. Gov. — Patrick Quinn, D, $115,235
Sec. of State — Jesse White, D, $132,963
Comptroller — Daniel Hynes, D, $115,235
Atty. Gen. — Lisa Madigan, D, $132,963
Treasurer — Judy Baar Topinka, R, $115,235
General Assembly: meets annually in Nov. and Jan. at Springfield. Members receive $57,619 annually.

Indiana
Senate — Dem., 32; Rep., 26; 1 ind. Total, 59
House — Dem., 66; Rep., 52. Total, 118

Indiana
Governor — Joseph E. Kernan, D, $95,000
Lt. Gov. — vacant
Sec. of State — Todd Rokita, R, $66,000
Atty. Gen. — Steve Carter, R, $79,400
Treasurer — Tim Berry, R, $66,000
Auditor — Connie Kay Nass, R, $66,000
General Assembly: meets annually on the Tues. after 2nd Mon. in Jan. at Indianapolis. Members receive $11,600 annually, plus $112 per day in session, $25 per day while not in session.
Senate — Dem., 18; Rep., 32. Total, 50
House — Dem., 51; Rep., 49. Total, 100

Iowa
Governor — Tom Vilsack, D, $104,795
Lt. Gov. — Sally Pederson, D, $74,781
Sec. of State — Chester J. Culver, D, $85,790
Atty. Gen. — Tom Miller, D, $102,794
Treasurer — Michael L. Fitzgerald, D, $85,790
Auditor — David A. Vaudt, R, $85,790
Sec. of Agriculture — Patty Judge, D, $85,790
General Assembly: meets annually in Jan. at Des Moines. Members receive $21,381 annually, plus expense allowance.
Senate — Dem., 21; Rep., 29. Total, 50
House — Dem., 47; Rep., 53. Total, 100

Kansas
Governor — Kathleen Sebelius, D, $98,331
Lt. Gov. — John Moore, D, $111,523
Sec. of State — Ron Thornburgh, R, $76,389
Atty. Gen. — Phill Kline, R, $87,845
Treasurer — Lynn Jenkins, R, $76,389
Insurance Commissioner — Sandy Praeger, R, $76,389
Legislature: meets annually on the 2nd Mon. of Jan. at Topeka. Members receive $78.75 per day salary, plus $85 per day expenses in session, plus $5,400 total allowance.
Senate — Dem., 10; Rep., 30. Total, 40
House — Dem., 45; Rep., 80. Total, 125

Kentucky
Governor — Paul Patton, D, $107,130
Lt. Gov. — Steve Henry, D, $91,075
Sec. of State — John Y. Brown III, D, $91,075
Atty. Gen. — A. B. Chandler III, D, $88,941
Treasurer — Jonathan Miller, D, $91,075
Auditor — Ed Hatchett, D, $91,075
Sec. of Economic Dev. — Gene Strong, $162,750
General Assembly: meets annually on the 1st Tues. after the 1st Mon. in Jan. at Frankfort. Members receive $166 per day, plus $94 per day expenses during session and $1,554 per month for expenses for interim.
Senate — Dem., 16; Rep., 22. Total, 38
House — Dem., 65; Rep., 35. Total, 100

Louisiana
Governor — M. J. "Mike" Foster Jr., R, $95,000
Lt. Gov. — Kathleen Babineaux Blanco, D, $85,000
Sec. of State — W. Fox McKeithen, R, $85,000
Atty. Gen. — Richard Ieyoub, D, $85,000
Treasurer — John Kennedy, D, $85,000
Legislature: meets in odd-numbered years at Baton Rouge starting last Mon. in Mar., for 60 legislative days of 85 calendar days; meets in even-numbered years on last Mon. in Apr. for 30 days of 45 calendar days. Members receive $16,800 annually, plus $97 per day expenses while in session and $500 per month as an unvouchered expense allowance.
Senate — Dem., 27; Rep., 12. Total, 39
House — Dem., 75; Rep., 30. Total, 105

Maine
Governor — John E. Baldacci, D, $70,000
Sec. of State — Dan A. Gwadosky, D, $81,952
Atty. Gen. — G. Steven Rowe, D, $89,502
Treasurer — Dale McCormick, D, $81,349
State Auditor — Gail M. Chase, D, $90,293
Legislature: meets in odd-numbered years at Augusta on first Wed. in Dec.; meets in even-numbered years on Wed. after first Tues. in Jan. Members receive $11,384 for first regular session, $8,131 for 2nd, plus a daily expense allowance.
Senate — Dem., 18; Rep., 17. Total, 35
House — Dem., 80; Rep., 67; 3 unenrolled; 1 Green. Total, 151

Maryland
Governor — Robert L. Ehrlich Jr., R, $135,000
Lt. Gov. — Michael S. Steele, R, $112,500
Comptroller — William Donald Schaefer, D, $112,500
Atty. Gen. — J. Joseph Curran Jr., D, $112,500
Sec. of State — R. Karl Aumann, R, $78,750
Treasurer — Nancy Kopp, D, $112,500

General Assembly: meets 90 consecutive days annually beginning on 2nd Wed. in Jan. at Annapolis. Members receive $34,500 annually, plus expenses.
Senate — Dem., 33; Rep., 14. Total, 47
House — Dem., 98; Rep., 43. Total, 141

Massachusetts
Governor — Willard "Mitt" Romney[1], R, $135,000
Lt. Gov. — Kerry Healey[1], R, $120,000
Sec. of the Commonwealth — William F. Galvin, D, $120,000
Atty. Gen. — Thomas F. Reilly, D, $122,500
Treasurer — Tim P. Cahill, D, $120,000
State Auditor — A. Joseph DeNucci, D, $120,000
General Court (legislature): meets Jan. annually in Boston. Members receive $49,710 annually.
Senate — Dem., 34; Rep., 6. Total, 40
House — Dem., 136; Rep., 23; 1 ind. Total, 160
(1) Does not accept salary.

Michigan
Governor — Jennifer M. Granholm, D, $177,000
Lt. Gov. — John Cherry, D, $123,900
Sec. of State — Terry Lynn Land, R, $124,900
Atty. Gen. — Michael Cox, R, $124,900
Treasurer — Jay B. Rising, $153,000
Legislature: meets annually in Jan. at Lansing. Members receive $79,650 annually.
Senate — Dem., 16; Rep., 22. Total, 38
House — Dem., 48; Rep., 62. Total, 110

Minnesota
(DFL=Democratic-Farmer-Labor Party)
Governor — Tim Pawlenty, R, $114,506
Lt. Gov. — Carol Molnau, R, $78,197
Sec. of State — Mary Kiffmeyer, R, $90,227
Atty. Gen. — Michael Hatch, DFL, $114,288
Auditor — Patricia Awada, R, $102,258
Legislature: meets for a total of 120 days within every 2 years, at St. Paul. Members receive $31,141 annually, plus expense allowance during session.
Senate — DFL, 35; Rep., 31; 1 ind. Total, 67
House — DFL, 53; Rep., 81. Total, 134

Mississippi
Governor — Ronnie Musgrove, D, $122,160
Lt. Gov. — Amy Tuck, R, $60,000
Sec. of State — Eric Clark, D, $90,000
Atty. Gen. — Mike Moore, D, $108,960
Treasurer — Marshall Bennett, D, $90,000
Auditor — Phil Bryant, R, $90,000
Legislature: meets annually in Jan. at Jackson. Members receive $10,000 per regular session, plus travel allowance, and $1,500 per month when not in session.
Senate — Dem., 29; Rep., 23. Total, 52
House — Dem., 81; Rep., 38; 3 ind. Total, 122

Missouri
Governor — Bob Holden, D, $120,087
Lt. Gov. — Joe Maxwell, D, $77,184
Sec. of State — Matt Blunt, R, $96,455
Atty. Gen. — Jeremiah W. Nixon, D, $104,332
Treasurer — Nancy Farmer, D, $96,455
State Auditor — Claire McCaskill, D, $96,455
General Assembly: meets annually at Jefferson City beginning 1st Wed. after 1st Mon. in Jan. Members receive $31,351 annually.
Senate — Dem., 13; Rep., 20; 1 vacancy. Total, 34
House — Dem., 72; Rep., 90; 1 vacancy. Total, 163

Montana
Governor — Judy Martz, R, $93,089
Lt. Gov. — Karl Ohs, R, $66,724
Sec. of State — Bob Brown, R, $72,085
Atty. Gen. — Mike McGrath, D, $82,549
Legislative Assembly: meets odd years in Jan. at Helena. Members receive $76.80 per legislative day, plus $90.31 per day for expenses while in session.
Senate — Dem., 21; Rep., 29. Total, 50
House — Dem., 47; Rep., 53. Total, 100

Nebraska
Governor — Mike Johanns, R, $85,000
Lt. Gov. — David Heineman, R, $60,000
Sec. of State — John A. Gale, R, $65,000
Atty. Gen. — Jon Bruning, R, $75,000
Treasurer — Lorelee Byrd, R, $60,000
State Auditor — Kate Witek, R, $60,000
Legislature: Unicameral body composed of 49 members who are elected on a nonpartisan ballot and are called senators; meets annually in Jan. at Lincoln. Members receive $12,000 annually, plus expenses.

Nevada
Governor — Kenny C. Guinn, R, $117,000
Lt. Gov. — Lorraine Hunt, R, $50,000
Sec. of State — Dean Heller, R, $80,000

Controller — Kathy Augustine, R, $80,000
Atty. Gen. — Brian Sandoval, R, $110,000
Treasurer — Brian Krolicki, R, $80,000
Legislature: meets at Carson City odd years starting on 1st Mon. in Feb. for 120 days. Members receive $130 per day salary, plus $85 per day expenses, while in session.
Senate — Dem., 8; Rep., 13. Total, 21
Assembly — Dem., 23; Rep., 19. Total, 42

New Hampshire
Governor — Craig Benson, R, $100,690
Sec. of State — William M. Gardner, D, $87,380
Atty. Gen. — Peter W. Heed, R, $97,370
Treasurer — Michael A. Ablowich, R, $78,640
General Court (Legis.): meets every year in Jan. at Concord. Members receive $200, presiding officers $250, biannually.
Senate — Dem., 6; Rep., 18. Total, 24
House — Rep., 277; Dem., 119; 1 ind.; 4 vacancies. Total, 400

New Jersey
Governor — James E. McGreevey, D, $157,000
Sec. of State — Regena L. Thomas, D, $137,165
Atty. Gen. — Peter Harvey, D, $137,165
Treasurer — John E. McCormac, $137,165
Legislature: meets throughout the year at Trenton. Members receive $35,000 annually, except president of Senate and speaker of Assembly, who receive 1/3 more.
Senate — Dem., 20; Rep., 20. Total, 40
Assembly — Dem., 42; Rep., 37; 1 Green. Total, 80

New Mexico
Governor — Bill Richardson, D, $110,000
Lt. Gov. — Diane D. Denish, D, $85,000
Sec. of State — Rebecca Vigil-Giron, D, $85,000
Atty. Gen. — Patricia Madrid, D, $95,000
Treasurer — Robert E. Vigil, D, $85,000
Auditor — Domingo P. Martinez, D, $85,000
Commissioner of Public Lands — Patrick Lyons, R, $90,000
Legislature: meets starting on the 3rd Tues. in Jan. at Santa Fe; odd years for 60 days, even years for 30 days. Members receive $145 per day while in session.
Senate — Dem., 24; Rep., 18. Total, 42
House — Dem., 43; Rep., 27. Total, 70

New York
Governor — George E. Pataki, R, $179,000
Lt. Gov. — Mary O. Donohue, R, $151,500
Sec. of State — Randy A. Daniels, R, $120,800
Comptroller — Alan G. Hevesi, D, $151,500
Atty. Gen. — Eliot Spitzer, D, $151,500
Legislature: meets annually on the 1st Wed. after the 1st Mon. in Jan. at Albany. Members receive $79,500 annually, plus $138 per day expenses.
Senate — Dem., 24; Rep., 38. Total, 62
Assembly — Dem., 103; Rep., 47. Total, 150

North Carolina
Governor — Mike Easley, D, $118,430
Lt. Gov. — Beverly Perdue, D, $104,523
Sec. of State — Elaine F. Marshall, D, $104,523
Atty. Gen. — Roy Cooper, D, $104,523
Treasurer — Richard H. Moore, D, $104,523
General Assembly: meets odd years starting on the 3rd Wed. following the 2nd Mon. in Jan. at Raleigh. Members receive $13,951 annually and a $559 monthly expense allowance, plus travel and other allowances in session. Also meets in even years for a short session (about 6-8 weeks), usually in May.
Senate — Dem., 28; Rep., 22. Total, 50
House — Dem., 59; Rep., 61. Total, 120

North Dakota
Governor — John Hoeven, R, $87,216
Lt. Gov. — John S. Dalrymple III, R, $67,708
Sec. of State — Alvin A. Jaeger, R, $68,018
Atty. Gen. — Wayne Stenehjem, R, $74,668
Treasurer — Kathi Gilmore, D, $64,233
Legislative Assembly: meets odd years in Jan. at Bismarck. Members receive $250 per month salary, plus $125 per calendar day salary during session and $45 per day expenses, plus any additional state or local taxes on lodging, with a limit of $650 per month.
Senate — Dem., 16; Rep., 31. Total, 47
House — Dem., 28; Rep., 66. Total, 94

Ohio
Governor — Bob Taft, R, $122,800
Lt. Gov. — Jennette Bradley, R, $64,375
Sec. of State — J. Kenneth Blackwell, R, $90,725
Atty. Gen. — Jim Petro, R, $90,725
Treasurer — Joseph T. Deters, R, $90,725
Auditor — Betty D. Montgomery, R, $90,725
General Assembly: begins odd years at Columbus starting on 1st Mon. in Jan. Members receive $51,674 annually.
Senate — Dem., 11; Rep., 22. Total, 33
House — Dem., 37; Rep., 62. Total, 99

Oklahoma
Governor — Brad Henry, D, $110,299
Lt. Gov. — Mary Fallin, R, $85,500
Sec. of State — M. Susan Savage, D, $90,000
Atty. Gen. — Drew Edmondson, D, $103,109
Treasurer — Robert Butkin, D, $87,875
Auditor — Jeff A. McMahan, D, $87,875
Legislature: meets annually at noon the first Mon. in Feb. at Oklahoma City. In odd-numbered years, the session includes one day (1st Tuesday after 1st Monday) in Jan. Members receive $38,400 annually.
Senate — Dem., 28; Rep., 20. Total, 48
House — Dem., 53; Rep., 48. Total, 101

Oregon
Governor — Ted Kulongoski, D, $93,600
Sec. of State — Bill Bradbury, D, $72,000
Atty. Gen. — Hardy Myers, D, $77,200
Treasurer — Randall Edwards, D, $72,000
Legislative Assembly: meets odd years in Jan. at Salem. Members receive $1,283 monthly, $85 expenses per day during session and when attending meetings during the interim, plus between $450 and $750 expense account during interim.
Senate — Dem., 15; Rep., 15. Total, 30
House — Dem., 25; Rep., 35. Total, 60

Pennsylvania
Governor — Edward G. Rendell, D, $142,142
Lt. Gov. — Catherine Baker Knoll, D, $119,399
Sec. of the Commonwealth — Pedro A. Cortés, D, $102,343
Atty. Gen. — Mike Fisher, R, $118,262
Treasurer — Barbara Hafer, R, $118,262
General Assembly: convenes annually on the 1st Tues. in Jan. at Harrisburg. Members receive $64,638.05 annually, plus expenses.
Senate — Dem., 21; Rep., 29. Total, 50
House — Dem., 94; Rep., 109. Total, 203

Rhode Island
Governor — Donald L. Carcieri, R, $105,000
Lt. Gov. — Charles J. Fogarty, D, $88,500
Sec. of State — Matthew A. Brown, D, $88,500
Atty. Gen. — Patrick C. Lynch, D, $94,000
Treasurer — Paul J. Tavares, D, $88,500
General Assembly: meets annually in Jan. at Providence. Members receive $10,000 annually.
Senate — Dem., 32; Rep., 6. Total, 38
House — Dem., 63; Rep., 11; 1 ind. Total, 75

South Carolina
Governor — Mark Sanford, R, $106,078
Lt. Gov. — R. Andre Bauer, R, $46,545
Sec. of State — Mark Hammond, R, $92,007
Comptroller — Richard A. Engstrom, R, $92,007
Atty. Gen. — Henry McMaster, R, $92,007
Treasurer — Grady L. Patterson Jr., D, $92,007
General Assembly: meets annually on the 2nd Tues. in Jan. at Columbia. Members receive $10,400 annually, plus $130 per day for expenses.
Senate — Dem., 21; Rep., 25. Total, 46
House — Dem., 52; Rep., 72. Total, 124

South Dakota
Governor — Mike Rounds, R, $98,250
Lt. Gov. — Dennis M. Daugaard, R, $13,404
Sec. of State — Chris Nelson, R, $66,757
Treasurer — Vernon L. Larson, R, $66,757
Atty. Gen. — Larry Long, R, $83,425
Auditor — Rich Sattgast, R, $66,757
Comm. of School & Public Lands — Bryce Healy, D, $66,757
Legislature: meets annually beginning the 2nd Tues. in Jan. at Pierre, for 40-day session in odd-numbered years, and 35-day session in even-numbered years. Members receive $12,000 per 2-year term plus $110 per legislative day or $110 for a statute committee.
Senate — Dem., 9; Rep., 26. Total, 35
House — Dem., 21; Rep., 49. Total, 70

Tennessee
Governor — Phil Bredesen[1], D, $85,000
Lt. Gov. — John S. Wilder, D, $49,500
Sec. of State — Riley C. Darnell, D, $131,124
Treasurer — Steve Adams, D, $131,124
Comptroller — John Morgan, D, $131,124
Atty. Gen. — Paul Summers, D, $121,728
General Assembly: meets annually on the 2nd Tues. in Jan. at Nashville. Members receive $16,500 annual salary, plus $128 per day expenses while in session.
Senate — Dem., 18; Rep., 15. Total, 33
House — Dem., 57; Rep., 42. Total, 99
(1) Does not accept salary.

Texas
Governor — Rick Perry, R, $115,345
Lt. Gov. — David Dewhurst, R, $7,200
Sec. of State — Geoffrey Connor, R, $117,516
Comptroller — Carole Keeton Strayhorn, R, $92,217
Atty. Gen. — Greg W. Abbott, R, $92,217
Railroad Commissioners — Michael L. Williams, R, Chair; Victor G. Carrillo, R; Charles R. Matthews, R; $92,217
Legislature: meets odd years in Jan. at Austin. Members receive $7,200 annually, plus $125 per day expenses while in session.
Senate — Dem., 12; Rep., 19. Total, 31
House — Dem., 62; Rep., 88. Total, 150

Utah
Governor — Michael O. Leavitt, R, $100,600
Lt. Gov. — Olene S. Walker, R, $78,200
Atty. Gen. — Mark Shurtleff, R, $84,600
Auditor — Auston G. Johnson, R, $80,700
Treasurer — Edward T. Alter, R, $78,200
Legislature: convenes for 45 days on 3rd Mon. in Jan. each year at Salt Lake City. Members receive $120 per day, plus $38 a day expenses.
Senate — Dem., 7; Rep., 22. Total, 29
House — Dem., 19; Rep., 56. Total, 75

Vermont
Governor — James H. Douglas, R, $127,456
Lt. Gov. — Brian E. Dubie, R, $54,103
Sec. of State — Deborah L. Markowitz, D, $80,818
Atty. Gen. — William H. Sorrell, D, $96,752
Treasurer — Jeb (George B.) Spaulding, D, $80,818
Auditor — Elizabeth M. Ready, D, $80,818
General Assembly: meets in Jan. at Montpelier (annual and biennial session). Members receive $536 per week while in session plus $105 per day for special session, plus expenses.
Senate — Dem., 19; Rep., 11. Total, 30
House — Dem., 69; Rep., 74; Progressive, 4; 2 ind.; 1 vacancy. Total, 150

Virginia
Governor — Mark R. Warner, D, $124,855
Lt. Gov. — Timothy M. Kaine, D, $36,321
Atty. Gen. — Jerry W. Kilgore, R, $110,667
Sec. of the Commonwealth — Anita A. Rimler, D, $131,370
Treasurer — Jody M. Wagner, D, $115,188
General Assembly: meets annually in Jan. at Richmond. Members receive $18,000 (senate), $17,640 (assembly) annually, plus expense and mileage allowances.
Senate — Dem., 17; Rep., 23. Total, 40
House — Dem., 33; Rep., 63; 2 ind.; 2 vacancies. Total, 100

Washington
Governor — Gary Locke, D, $142,286
Lt. Gov. — Brad Owen, D, $74,377
Sec. of State — Sam Reed, R, $99,708
Atty. Gen. — Christine Gregoire, D, $129,351
Treasurer — Mike Murphy, D, $99,708
Legislature: meets annually in Jan. at Olympia. Members receive $33,556 annually, plus $82 per diem while in session, and $82 per diem for attending meetings during interim.
Senate — Dem., 24; Rep., 25. Total, 49
House — Dem., 52; Rep., 46. Total, 98

West Virginia
Governor — Bob Wise, D, $90,000
Sec. of State — Joe Manchin III, D, $65,000
Atty. Gen. — Darrell McGraw, D, $75,000
Treasurer — John D. Perdue, D, $70,000
Comm. of Agric. — Gus R. Douglass, D, $70,000
Auditor — Glen B. Gainer III, D, $70,000
Legislature: meets annually in Jan. at Charleston, except after gubernatorial elections, when the legislature meets in Feb. Members receive $15,000 annually.
Senate — Dem., 24; Rep., 10. Total, 34
House — Dem., 75; Rep., 25. Total, 100

Wisconsin
Governor — Jim Doyle, D, $131,768
Lt. Gov. — Barbara Lawton, D, $65,579
Sec. of State — Douglas La Follette, D, $62,549
Treasurer — Jack Voight, R, $62,549
Atty. Gen. — Peggy A. Lautenschlager, D, $127,868
Legislature: meets in Jan. at Madison. Members receive $45,569 annually, plus $88 per day expenses.
Senate — Dem., 15; Rep., 18. Total, 33
Assembly — Dem., 40; Rep., 59. Total, 99

Wyoming
Governor — Dave Freudenthal, D, $105,000
Sec. of State — Joseph B. Meyer, R, $92,000
Atty. Gen. — Patrick J. Crank, R, $95,000
Treasurer — Cynthia Lummis, R, $92,000
State Auditor — Max Maxfield, R, $92,000
Legislature: meets odd years in Jan., even years in Feb., at Cheyenne. Members receive $125 per day while in session, plus $80 per day for expenses.
Senate — Dem., 10; Rep., 20. Total, 30
House — Dem., 15; Rep., 45. Total, 60

VITAL STATISTICS

Recent Trends in Vital Statistics

Source: National Center for Health Statistics, U.S. Dept. of Health and Human Services; latest years available

Highlights

Provisional U.S. data for 2002 reported by the National Center for Health Statistics show that birth rates were at an all-time low. The teen birth rate declined for the 11th straight year, dropping to 42.9 births per 1,000 women aged 15-19 years in 2002; this was a 28% reduction since 1990. Marriage rates declined for 2002, while divorce rates rose marginally (by 0.1 percentage point), according to provisional 2002 data. Life expectancy for all Americans at birth rose to 77.2 years in 2001, an all-time high and an increase of nearly 2 years since 1990.

Births

An estimated 4,022,000 babies were born in the U.S. in 2002, a drop from 4,025,933 births in 2001. The birth rate declined to 13.9 per 1,000 total population in 2002 from 14.1 in 2001; it was the lowest birth rate reported for the U.S. since national data were first collected in 1909. The fertility rate (number of live births per 1,000 women aged 15-44 years) dropped to an estimated 64.8 for 2002, down from the 2001 rate of 65.3.

Deaths

The number of deaths during 2002 was estimated at 2,436,000, up from 2,416,425 in 2001. The provisional data

for 2002 showed a death rate of 8.4 per 1,000 population, down marginally from the previous year. The infant mortality rate was 6.9 infant deaths per 1,000 live births in 2002, up from 6.8 in 2001.

Natural Increase

As a result of natural increase (the excess of births over deaths) by itself, an estimated 1,586,000 persons were added to the population in 2002. The rate of increase (5.5 per 1,000 population) was down very slightly from the revised figure of 5.6 for 2001.

Marriages

An estimated 2,254,000 marriages were performed in 2002, compared with 2,345,000 in 2001. The provisional marriage rate for 2002 (7.8 per 1,000 population) was down from the 2001 rate of 8.2.

Divorces

The provisional 2002 data give a divorce rate of 4.0 per 1,000 population, up from 3.9 in 2001. Data are incomplete, however. The NCHS no longer includes divorce data for California, Indiana, Louisiana, and Oklahoma.

Births and Deaths in the U.S.

Source: National Center for Health Statistics, U.S. Dept. of Health and Human Services

| | BIRTHS | | DEATHS | | | BIRTHS | | DEATHS | |
| | Total | | Total | | | Total | | Total | |
Year	number	Rate	number	Rate	Year	number	Rate	number	Rate
1960	4,257,850	23.7	1,711,982	9.5	1995	3,899,589	14.6	2,312,132	8.7
1970	3,731,386	18.4	1,921,031	9.5	1996	3,891,494	14.4	2,314,690	8.6
1980	3,612,258	15.9	1,989,841	8.8	1997	3,880,894	14.2	2,314,245	8.5
1990	4,092,994	16.7	2,148,463	8.6	1998	3,941,553	14.3	2,337,256	8.5
1991	4,094,566	16.2	2,169,518	8.6	1999	3,959,417	14.2	2,391,399	8.6
1992	4,049,024	15.8	2,175,613	8.5	2000	4,058,814	14.4	2,403,351	8.5
1993	4,000,240	15.4	2,268,553	8.7	2001	4,025,933	14.1	2,416,425	8.5
1994	3,952,767	15.0	2,278,994	8.7	2002 (P)	4,022,000	13.9	2,436,000	8.4

(P) = provisional data. **NOTE:** Statistics cover only events occurring within the U.S. and exclude fetal deaths. Rates per 1,000 population; enumerated as of Apr. 1 for 1960 and 1970; estimated as of July 1 for all other years. Beginning 1970 statistics exclude births and deaths occurring among nonresidents of the U.S. Data include revisions. Birth and death rates for years in the 1990s revised on basis of the 2000 Census.

Marriage and Divorce Rates, 1920-2002

Source: National Center for Health Statistics, U.S. Dept. of Health and Human Services

The U.S. marriage rate dipped during the Depression and peaked sharply just after World War II; the trend after that has been more gradual. The divorce rate has generally risen since the 1920s; it peaked at 5.3 per 1,000 in 1981, before declining somewhat. The graph below shows marriage and divorce rates per 1,000 population since 1920. (Recent divorce rates calculated excluding data (and populations) from the non-reporting states California, Indiana, Louisiana, and Oklahoma; incomplete reporting from Oklahoma may lead to slight underestimation of marriage rate. Some data are provisional.)

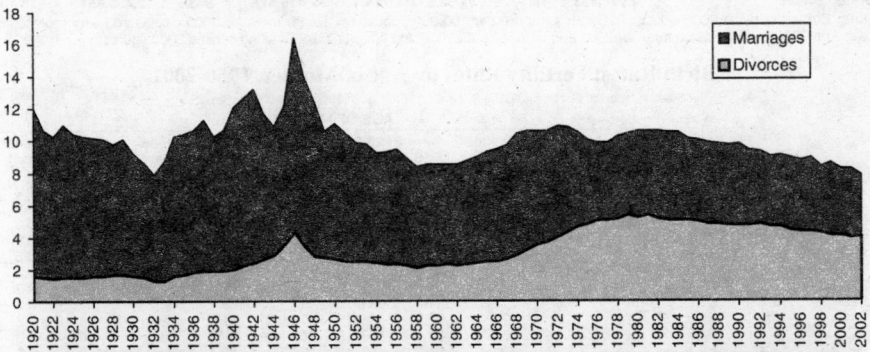

■ Marriages
□ Divorces

Births and Deaths, by States, 2000-2001

Source: National Center for Health Statistics, U.S. Dept. of Health and Human Services

	LIVE BIRTHS 2001 Number	Rate	2000 Number	Rate	DEATHS 2001 Number	Rate	2000 Number	Rate
Alabama	60,454	13.5	63,299	14.2	45,316	1,014.0	45,062	1,027.0
Alaska	10,003	15.8	9,974	15.9	2,974	469.4	2,914	468.4
Arizona	85,597	16.1	85,273	16.6	41,058	773.7	40,500	829.5
Arkansas	37,010	13.7	37,783	14.1	27,759	1,030.1	28,217	1,095.2
California	527,759	15.3	531,959	15.7	234,044	676.4	229,551	682.5
Colorado	67,007	15.1	65,438	15.2	28,294	638.5	27,288	659.7
Connecticut	42,648	12.4	43,026	12.6	29,827	868.4	30,129	913.8
Delaware	10,749	13.5	11,051	14.1	7,112	892.8	6,875	902.0
District of Columbia	7,625	13.3	7,666	13.4	5,951	1,037.1	6,001	1,157.7
Florida	205,793	12.6	204,125	12.8	167,269	1,021.6	164,395	1,072.2
Georgia	133,526	15.9	132,644	16.2	64,485	767.2	63,870	804.1
Hawaii	17,072	13.9	17,551	14.5	8,394	684.1	8,290	703.0
Idaho	20,688	15.7	20,366	15.7	9,753	738.5	9,563	751.1
Illinois	184,064	14.7	185,036	14.9	105,430	842.1	106,634	875.1
Indiana	86,459	14.1	87,699	14.4	55,198	900.9	55,469	928.1
Iowa	37,619	12.8	38,266	13.1	27,791	947.9	28,060	975.2
Kansas	38,869	14.4	39,666	14.8	24,647	912.1	24,717	927.2
Kentucky	54,658	13.4	56,029	13.9	39,861	979.7	39,504	991.2
Louisiana	65,352	14.6	67,898	15.2	41,757	934.1	41,138	940.3
Maine	13,759	10.7	13,603	10.7	12,421	967.0	12,354	981.6
Maryland	73,218	13.6	74,316	14.0	43,839	813.9	43,753	838.4
Massachusetts	81,077	12.7	81,614	12.9	56,754	886.6	56,681	913.6
Michigan	133,427	13.3	136,171	13.7	86,424	863.7	86,953	876.7
Minnesota	67,562	13.6	67,604	13.7	37,735	757.0	37,690	780.7
Mississippi	42,282	14.8	44,075	15.5	28,259	988.2	28,654	1,028.1
Missouri	75,464	13.4	76,463	13.7	54,982	975.3	54,865	997.1
Montana	10,970	12.1	10,957	12.1	8,265	912.9	8,096	911.8
Nebraska	24,820	14.4	24,646	14.4	15,174	882.2	14,992	897.5
Nevada	31,382	15.0	30,829	15.4	16,285	776.3	15,261	811.6
New Hampshire	14,656	11.6	14,609	11.8	9,815	779.4	9,697	797.5
New Jersey	115,795	13.6	115,632	13.7	74,710	877.8	74,800	911.7
New Mexico	27,128	14.8	27,223	15.0	14,129	771.7	13,425	768.1
New York	254,026	13.3	258,737	13.6	159,240	834.4	158,203	865.5
North Carolina	118,185	14.4	120,311	14.9	70,934	864.4	71,935	928.5
North Dakota	7,629	12.0	7,676	12.0	6,048	950.1	5,856	930.6
Ohio	151,570	13.3	155,472	13.7	108,027	948.5	108,125	959.4
Oklahoma	50,118	14.4	49,782	14.4	34,682	999.6	35,079	1,037.8
Oregon	45,322	13.0	45,804	13.4	30,158	868.2	29,552	884.5
Pennsylvania	143,495	11.7	146,281	11.9	129,729	1,054.4	130,813	1,091.5
Rhode Island	12,713	12.0	12,505	11.9	10,021	945.7	10,027	1,006.6
South Carolina	55,756	13.7	56,114	14.0	36,612	901.3	36,948	941.5
South Dakota	10,483	13.8	10,345	13.7	6,923	912.9	7,021	952.3
Tennessee	78,340	13.6	79,611	14.0	55,151	959.2	55,246	998.4
Texas	365,410	17.1	363,414	17.4	152,779	714.9	149,939	735.4
Utah	47,959	21.0	47,353	21.2	12,662	555.7	12,364	571.2
Vermont	6,366	10.4	6,500	10.7	5,201	848.5	5,127	857.6
Virginia	98,884	13.7	98,938	14.0	56,280	782.0	56,282	807.4
Washington	79,570	13.3	81,036	13.7	44,642	744.9	43,941	756.2
West Virginia	20,428	11.3	20,865	11.5	20,967	1,164.2	21,114	1,171.5
Wisconsin	69,072	12.8	69,326	12.9	46,628	862.5	46,461	877.4
Wyoming	6,115	12.4	6,253	12.7	4,029	816.	3,920	815.1
United States	**4,025,933**	**14.1**	**4,058,814**	**14.4**	**2,416,425**	**848.5**	**2,403,351**	**873.1**

Note: Births are per 1,000 population. Death rates are per 100,000 population. Death rates for 2000 calculated using projections based on 1990 census; death rates for 2001 and birth rates for 2000 and 2001 calculated using census 2000 figures.

Birth Rates; Fertility Rates by Age of Mother, 1950-2001

Source: National Center for Health Statistics, U.S. Dept. of Health and Human Services

	Birth rate[1]	Fertility rate[2]	10-14 years	AGE OF MOTHER 15-19 years Total	15-17	18-19	20-24 years	25-29 years	30-34 years	35-39 years	40-44 years	45-49 years
						Live births per 1,000 women by age group						
1950	24.1	106.2	1.0	81.6	40.7	132.7	196.6	166.1	103.7	52.9	15.1	1.2
1960	23.7	118.0	0.8	89.1	43.9	166.7	258.1	197.4	112.7	56.2	15.5	0.9
1970	18.4	87.9	1.2	68.3	38.8	114.7	167.8	145.1	73.3	31.7	8.1	0.5
1980	15.9	68.4	1.1	53.0	32.5	82.1	115.1	112.9	61.9	19.8	3.9	0.2
1990	16.7	70.9	1.4	59.9	37.5	88.6	116.5	120.2	80.8	31.7	5.5	0.2
1991	16.2	69.3	1.4	61.8	38.6	94.0	115.3	117.2	79.2	31.9	5.5	0.2
1992	15.8	68.4	1.4	60.3	37.6	93.6	113.7	115.7	79.6	32.3	5.9	0.3
1993	15.4	67.0	1.4	59.0	37.5	91.1	111.3	113.2	79.9	32.7	6.1	0.3
1994	15.0	65.9	1.4	58.2	37.2	90.2	109.2	111.0	80.4	33.4	6.4	0.3
1995	14.6	64.6	1.3	56.0	35.5	87.7	107.5	108.8	81.1	34.0	6.6	0.3
1996	14.4	64.1	1.2	53.5	33.3	84.7	107.8	108.6	82.1	34.9	6.8	0.3
1997	14.2	63.6	1.1	51.3	31.4	82.1	107.3	108.3	83.0	35.7	7.1	0.4
1998	14.3	64.3	1.0	50.3	29.9	80.9	108.4	110.2	85.2	36.9	7.4	0.4
1999	14.2	64.4	0.9	48.8	28.2	79.1	107.9	111.2	87.1	37.8	7.4	0.4
2000	14.4	65.9	0.9	47.7	26.9	78.1	109.7	113.5	91.2	39.7	8.0	0.5
2001	14.1	65.3	0.8	45.3	24.7	76.1	106.2	113.4	91.9	40.6	8.1	0.5

(1) Live births per 1,000 population. (2) Live births per 1,000 women 15-44 years of age.

Nonmarital Childbearing in the U.S., 1970-2001
Source: National Center for Health Statistics, U.S. Dept. of Health and Human Services

Race of Mother	1970	1975	1980	1985	1990	1994	1995	1996	1997	1998	1999	2000	2001
	Percent of live births to unmarried mothers												
All races	10.7	14.3	18.4	22.0	28.0	32.6	32.2	32.4	32.4	32.8	33.0	33.2	33.5
White	5.5	7.1	11.2	14.7	20.4	25.4	25.3	25.7	25.8	26.3	26.8	27.1	27.7
Black	37.5	49.5	56.1	61.2	66.5	70.4	69.9	69.8	69.2	69.1	68.9	68.5	68.4
American Indian or Alaska Native	22.4	32.7	39.2	46.8	53.6	57.0	57.2	58.0	58.7	59.3	58.9	58.4	59.7
Asian or Pacific Islander	—	—	7.3	9.5	13.2	16.2	16.3	16.7	15.6	15.6	15.4	14.8	14.9
Hispanic origin (selected states)[1,2]	—	—	23.6	29.5	36.7	43.1	40.8	40.7	40.9	41.6	42.2	42.7	42.5
White, non-Hispanic (selected states)[1]	—	—	9.6	12.4	16.9	20.8	21.2	21.5	21.5	21.9	22.1	22.1	22.5
Black, non-Hispanic (selected states)[1]	—	—	57.3	62.1	66.7	70.7	70.0	70.0	69.4	69.3	69.1	68.7	68.6
Births to unmarried mothers (1,000s)	399	448	666	828	1,165	1,290	1,254	1,260	1,257	1,294	1,309	1,347	1,349
Maternal age	Percent distribution of live births to unmarried mothers												
Under 20 years	50.1	52.1	40.8	33.8	30.9	30.5	30.9	30.4	30.7	30.1	29.3	28.0	26.6
20–24 years	31.8	29.9	35.6	36.3	34.7	34.8	34.5	34.2	34.9	35.6	36.4	37.4	38.2
25 years and over	18.1	18.0	23.5	29.9	34.4	34.6	34.7	35.3	34.4	34.3	34.3	34.6	35.2
	Live births per 1,000 unmarried women 15–44 years of age[3]												
All races and origins	26.4	24.5	29.4	32.8	43.8	46.9	45.1	44.8	44.0	44.3	44.4	45.2	45.0
White[4]	13.9	12.4	18.1	22.5	32.9	38.3	37.5	37.6	37.0	37.5	38.1	38.9	39.2
Black[4]	95.5	84.2	81.1	77.0	90.5	82.1	75.9	74.4	73.4	73.3	71.5	72.5	70.1
Hispanic origin (selected states)[1,2]	—	—	—	—	89.6	101.2	95.0	93.2	91.4	90.1	93.4	97.3	98.0
White, non-Hispanic	—	—	—	—	28.5	28.2	28.3	27.0	27.4	27.9	27.9	27.7

— Data not available. (1) Data for Hispanics and non-Hispanics are affected by expansion of the reporting area for an Hispanic-origin item on the birth certificate and by immigration. The states in the reporting area increased from 22 in 1980, to 23 and the District of Columbia in 1983, 48 and DC by 1990, and 50 and DC by 1993. (2) Includes mothers of all races. (3) Rates computed by relating births to unmarried mothers, regardless of mother's age, to unmarried women 15–44 years of age. (4) For 1970 and 1975, birth rates are by race of child.

Top 20 Countries for U.S. Foreign Adoptions, 1991-2002
Source: Holt International Children's Service

Country	2002	2001	2000	1999	1998	1997	1996	1995	1994	1993	1992	1991
China	5,053	4,681	5,053	4,101	4,206	3,597	3,333	2,130	787	330	206	61
Russia	4,939	4,279	4,269	4,348	4,491	3,816	2,454	1,896	1,530	746	324	0
Guatemala	2,219	1,609	1,518	1,002	911	788	427	449	436	512	418	329
South Korea	1,779	1,770	1,794	2,008	1,829	1,654	1,516	1,666	1,795	1,775	1,840	1,818
Ukraine	1,106	1,246	659	321	180	NA	1	4	164	273	55	0
Kazakhstan	819	672	399	113	NA	NA	0	0	0	0	0	0
Vietnam	766	737	724	709	603	425	354	318	220	110	22	37
India	466	543	503	499	478	349	380	371	412	331	352	445
Colombia	334	266	246	231	351	233	255	350	351	426	404	521
Bulgaria	260	297	214	221	151	148	163	110	97	133	91	9
Cambodia	254	407	402	249	249	66	32	10	3	1	15	60
Philippines	221	219	173	195	200	163	229	298	314	360	357	393
Haiti	187	192	131	96	121	144	68	49	61	51	16	49
Belarus	169	129	NA	NA	NA	NA	NA	NA	NA	NA	NA	NA
Romania	168	782	1,122	895	406	621	555	275	199	97	121	2,594
Ethiopia	105	158	95	103	96	82	44	63	54	30	37	15
Poland	101	86	83	97	77	78	62	30	94	70	109	92
Thailand	67	74	88	77	84	NA	55	53	47	69	86	131
Peru	65	NA	NA	NA	NA	NA	NA	NA	NA	NA	NA	NA
Mexico	61	73	106	137	168	152	76	83	85	91	91	97

NA = Not available. Note: Totals are for U.S. Government fiscal years.

Numbers of Multiple Births in the U.S., 1990-2001
Source: National Center for Health Statistics, U.S. Dept. of Health and Human Services

The general upward trend in multiple births reflects greater numbers of births to older women and increased use of fertility drugs.

Year	Twins	Triplets	Quadruplets	Quintuplets and higher	Year	Twins	Triplets	Quadruplets	Quintuplets and higher
1990	93,865	2,830	185	13	1997	104,137	6,148	510	79
1992	95,372	3,547	310	26	1998	110,670	6,919	627	79
1993	96,445	3,834	277	57	1999	114,307	6,742	512	67
1994	97,064	4,233	315	46	2000	118,916	6,742	506	77
1995	96,736	4,551	365	57	2001	121,246	6,885	501	85
1996	100,750	5,298	560	81					

10 Leading Causes of Infant Death in the U.S., 2001
Source: National Center for Health Statistics, U.S. Dept. of Health and Human Services

Cause	Number	Rate[1]	% change 2000-2001[2]
Congenital malformations, deformations, and chromosomal abnormalities	5,513	136.9	-3.3
Disorders relating to short gestation and low birthweight, not elsewhere classified	4,410	109.5	1.1
Sudden infant death syndrome	2,234	55.5	-10.8
Newborn affected by maternal complications of pregnancy	1,499	37.2	7.5
Newborn affected by complications of placenta, cord, and membranes	1,018	25.3	-3.4
Respiratory distress of newborn	1,011	25.1	2.0
Accidents (unintentional injuries)	976	24.2	11.5
Bacterial sepsis[3] of newborn	696	17.3	-8.5
Diseases of the circulatory system	622	15.4	-5.5
Intrauterine hypoxia and birth asphyxia	534	13.3	-14.2
All other causes	9,055	224.9	NA
All causes	27,568	684.8	-0.9

NA = Not applicable. (1) Infant deaths per 100,000 live births. (2) Refers to change in mortality rates from 2000 to 2001. (3) Toxic condition resulting from the spread of bacteria.

U.S. Infant Mortality Rates, by Race and Sex, 1960-2001

Source: National Center for Health Statistics, U.S. Dept. of Health and Human Services

Year	ALL RACES Total	Male	Female	WHITE Total	Male	Female	BLACK Total	Male	Female
1960	26.0	29.3	22.6	22.9	26.0	19.6	44.3	49.1	39.4
1970	20.0	22.4	17.5	17.8	20.0	15.4	32.6	36.2	29.0
1980	12.6	13.9	11.2	11.0	12.3	9.6	21.4	23.3	19.4
1985	10.6	11.9	9.3	9.3	10.6	8.0	18.2	19.9	16.5
1986	10.4	11.5	9.1	8.9	10.0	7.8	18.0	20.0	16.0
1987	10.1	11.2	8.9	8.6	9.6	7.6	17.9	19.6	16.0
1988	10.0	11.0	8.9	8.5	9.5	7.4	17.6	19.0	16.1
1989	9.8	10.8	8.8	8.1	9.0	7.1	18.6	20.0	17.2
1990	9.2	10.3	8.1	7.6	8.5	6.6	18.0	19.6	16.2
1991	8.9	10.0	7.8	7.3	8.3	6.3	17.6	19.4	15.7
1992	8.5	9.4	7.6	6.9	7.7	6.1	16.8	18.4	15.3
1993	8.4	9.3	7.4	6.8	7.6	6.0	16.5	18.3	14.7
1994	8.0	8.8	7.2	6.6	7.2	5.9	15.8	17.5	14.1
1995	7.6	8.3	6.8	6.3	7.0	5.6	15.1	16.3	13.9
1996	7.3	8.0	6.6	6.1	6.7	5.4	14.7	16.0	13.3
1997	7.2	8.0	6.5	6.0	6.7	5.4	14.2	15.5	12.8
1998	7.2	7.8	6.5	6.0	6.5	5.4	14.3	15.7	12.8
1999	7.1	7.7	6.4	5.8	6.4	5.2	14.6	15.9	13.2
2000	6.9	7.6	6.2	5.7	6.2	5.1	14.1	15.5	12.6
2001	6.8	7.5	6.1	5.7	6.2	5.1	14.0	15.5	12.5

Note: Rates per 1,000 live births.

Years of Life Expected at Birth in U.S., 1900-2001

Source: National Center for Health Statistics, U.S. Dept. of Health and Human Services

Year[1]	ALL RACES Total	Male	Female	WHITE Total	Male	Female	BLACK Total	Male	Female
1900	47.3	46.3	48.3	47.6	46.6	48.7	NA	NA	NA
1910	50.0	48.4	51.8	50.3	48.6	52.0	NA	NA	NA
1920	54.1	53.6	54.6	54.9	54.4	55.6	NA	NA	NA
1930	59.7	58.1	61.6	61.4	59.7	63.5	NA	NA	NA
1940	62.9	60.8	65.2	64.2	62.1	66.6	NA	NA	NA
1950	68.2	65.6	71.1	69.1	66.5	72.2	NA	NA	NA
1960	69.7	66.6	73.1	70.6	67.4	74.1	NA	NA	NA
1970	70.8	67.1	74.7	71.7	68.0	75.6	64.1	60.0	68.3
1975	72.6	68.8	76.6	73.4	69.5	77.3	68.8	62.4	71.3
1980	73.7	70.0	77.5	74.4	70.7	78.1	68.1	63.8	72.5
1985	74.7	71.2	78.2	75.3	71.9	78.7	69.3	65.0	73.4
1986	74.8	71.3	78.3	75.4	72.0	78.8	69.1	64.8	73.4
1987	75.0	71.5	78.4	75.6	72.2	78.9	69.1	64.7	73.4
1988	74.9	71.5	78.3	75.6	72.3	78.9	68.9	64.4	73.2
1989	75.1	71.7	78.5	75.9	72.5	79.2	68.8	64.3	73.3
1990	75.4	71.8	78.8	76.1	72.9	79.4	69.1	64.5	73.6
1991	75.5	72.0	78.9	76.3	72.9	79.2	69.3	64.6	73.8
1992	75.5	72.1	78.9	76.4	73.0	79.5	69.6	65.0	73.9
1993	75.5	72.1	78.9	76.3	73.0	79.5	69.2	64.6	73.7
1994	75.7	72.4	79.0	76.5	73.3	79.6	69.5	64.9	73.9
1995	75.8	72.5	78.9	76.5	73.4	79.6	69.6	65.2	73.9
1996	76.1	73.1	79.1	76.8	73.9	79.7	70.2	66.1	74.2
1997	76.5	73.6	79.4	77.1	74.3	79.9	71.1	67.2	74.7
1998	76.7	73.8	79.5	77.3	74.5	80.0	71.3	67.6	74.8
1999	76.7	73.9	79.4	77.3	74.6	79.9	71.4	67.8	74.7
2000	76.9	74.1	79.5	77.4	74.8	80.0	71.7	68.2	74.9
2001	77.2	74.4	79.8	77.7	75.0	80.2	72.2	68.6	75.5

NA = Not available. (1) Data prior to 1940 for death-registration states only.

U.S. Life Expectancy at Selected Ages, 2001

Source: National Center for Health Statistics, U.S. Dept. of Health and Human Services

Exact age in years	ALL RACES[1] Both sexes	Male	Female	WHITE Both sexes	Male	Female	BLACK Both sexes	Male	Female
0	77.2	74.4	79.8	77.7	75.0	80.2	72.2	68.6	75.5
1	76.7	74.0	79.3	77.1	74.5	79.6	72.2	68.6	75.4
5	72.8	70.1	75.4	73.2	70.6	75.7	68.3	64.8	71.5
10	67.9	65.2	70.4	68.3	65.6	70.8	63.4	59.8	66.6
15	52.9	60.2	65.5	63.3	60.7	65.8	58.5	54.9	61.7
20	58.1	55.5	60.6	58.5	56.0	60.9	53.7	50.3	56.8
25	53.4	50.9	55.7	53.8	51.3	56.1	49.1	45.8	52.0
30	48.6	46.2	50.9	49.0	46.6	51.2	44.5	41.4	47.2
35	43.9	41.5	46.0	44.2	41.9	46.3	39.9	36.9	42.5
40	39.2	37.0	41.3	39.5	37.3	41.6	35.5	32.5	38.0
45	34.7	32.5	36.6	34.9	32.8	36.9	31.2	28.4	33.6
50	30.3	28.2	32.1	30.5	28.4	32.3	27.1	24.4	29.3
55	26.0	24.0	27.7	26.1	24.2	27.8	23.3	20.8	25.3
60	21.9	20.1	23.4	22.0	20.2	23.5	19.7	17.5	21.5
65	18.1	16.4	19.4	18.2	16.5	19.5	16.4	14.4	17.9
70	14.6	13.1	15.7	14.6	13.2	15.7	13.5	11.7	14.7
75	11.5	10.2	12.4	11.5	10.2	12.3	10.8	9.3	11.7
80	8.8	7.7	9.4	8.7	7.7	9.3	8.6	7.3	9.2
85	6.5	5.7	6.9	6.4	5.6	6.7	6.7	5.7	7.0
90	4.8	4.2	5.0	4.6	4.1	4.8	5.1	4.5	5.3
95	3.6	3.2	3.7	3.4	3.0	3.4	3.9	3.6	4.0
100	2.7	2.5	2.8	2.4	2.3	2.5	3.0	2.9	3.0

(1) Includes races other than white and black.

The 10 Leading Causes of Death in the U.S., 2001
Source: National Center for Health Statistics, U.S. Dept. of Health and Human Services

	Number	Death rate[1]	% of deaths		Number	Death rate[1]	% of deaths
ALL CAUSES	2,416,425	848.5	100.0	5. Accidents	101,537	35.7	4.2
1. Heart disease	700,142	245.8	29.0	6. Diabetes mellitus	71,372	25.1	3.0
2. Cancer	553,768	194.4	22.9	7. Influenza and pneumonia	62,034	21.8	2.6
3. Stroke	163,538	57.4	6.8	8. Alzheimer's disease	53,852	18.9	2.2
4. Chronic lower respiratory diseases	123,013	43.2	5.1	9. Kidney disease	39,480	13.9	1.6
				10. Blood poisoning	32,238	11.3	1.3

(1) Per 100,000 population.

U.S. Abortions, by State, 1992-2000
Source: Alan Guttmacher Institute, New York, NY

	Reported abortions[1]			Rate per 1,000 women[2]			% change
	1992	1996	2000	1992	1996	2000	1996-2000[3]
U.S. TOTAL	1,528,930	1,360,160	1,312,990	25.7	22.4	21.3	-5
Alabama	17,450	15,150	13,830	18.1	15.5	14.3	-8
Alaska	2,370	2,040	1,660	16.6	14.2	11.7	-18
Arizona	20,600	19,310	17,940	23.4	19.2	16.5	-14
Arkansas	7,130	6,200	5,540	13.5	11.2	9.8	-12
California	304,220	237,830	236,060	41.8	32.8	31.2	-5
Colorado	19,880	18,310	15,530	23.6	19.9	15.9	-20
Connecticut	19,720	16,230	15,240	25.9	21.9	21.1	-4
Delaware	5,730	4,090	5,440	34.9	24.0	31.3	31
District of Columbia	21,320	15,220	9,800	134.6	104.5	68.1	-39
Florida	84,680	94,050	103,050	29.3	30.7	31.9	4
Georgia	39,680	37,320	32,140	23.7	20.8	16.9	-19
Hawaii	12,190	6,930	5,630	46.4	26.8	22.2	-17
Idaho	1,710	1,600	1,950	7.3	6.1	7.0	15
Illinois	68,420	69,390	63,690	25.2	25.3	23.2	-8
Indiana	15,840	14,850	12,490	12.0	11.1	9.4	-15
Iowa	6,970	5,780	5,970	11.3	9.3	9.8	5
Kansas	12,570	10,630	12,270	22.4	18.6	21.4	15
Kentucky	10,000	8,470	4,700	11.4	9.5	5.3	-44
Louisiana	13,600	14,740	13,100	13.5	14.5	13.0	-10
Maine	4,200	2,700	2,650	14.8	9.8	9.9	1
Maryland	31,260	31,310	34,560	26.2	26.2	29.0	11
Massachusetts	40,660	41,160	30,410	28.1	28.8	21.4	-26
Michigan	55,580	48,780	46,470	25.1	22.1	21.6	-2
Minnesota	16,180	14,660	14,610	15.6	13.7	13.5	-2
Mississippi	7,550	4,490	3,780	12.4	7.1	6.0	-17
Missouri	13,510	10,810	7,920	11.5	9.0	6.6	-27
Montana	3,300	2,900	2,510	18.5	15.4	13.5	-12
Nebraska	5,580	4,460	4,250	15.6	12.2	11.6	-4
Nevada	13,300	15,450	13,740	43.0	41.7	32.2	-23
New Hampshire	3,890	3,470	3,010	14.6	12.9	11.2	-13
New Jersey	55,320	63,100	65,780	30.5	34.9	36.3	4
New Mexico	6,410	5,470	5,760	17.7	14.1	14.7	4
New York	195,390	167,600	164,630	45.7	39.7	39.1	-2
North Carolina	36,180	33,550	37,610	22.2	19.5	21.0	8
North Dakota	1,490	1,290	1,340	10.7	9.2	9.9	7
Ohio	49,520	42,870	40,230	19.5	17.1	16.5	-3
Oklahoma	8,940	8,400	7,390	12.5	11.6	10.1	-13
Oregon	16,060	15,050	17,010	23.9	21.2	23.5	11
Pennsylvania	49,740	39,520	36,570	18.6	15.0	14.3	-5
Rhode Island	6,990	5,420	5,600	29.5	23.3	24.1	3
South Carolina	12,190	9,940	8,210	14.2	11.4	9.3	-18
South Dakota	1,040	1,030	870	6.9	6.5	5.5	-15
Tennessee	19,060	17,990	19,010	16.2	14.6	15.2	4
Texas	97,400	91,270	89,160	23.0	20.2	18.8	-7
Utah	3,940	3,700	3,510	9.2	7.5	6.6	-11
Vermont	2,900	2,300	1,660	21.5	17.3	12.7	-27
Virginia	35,020	29,940	28,780	22.6	19.0	18.1	-5
Washington	33,190	26,340	26,200	27.7	20.9	20.2	-3
West Virginia	3,140	2,610	2,540	7.8	6.6	6.8	3
Wisconsin	15,450	14,160	11,130	13.5	12.2	9.6	-21
Wyoming	460	280	100	4.4	2.6	1.0	-64

(1) Rounded to the nearest 10. (2) Aged 15-44 years old. (3) Percentage change in the rate.

Contraceptive Use in the U.S.
Source: National Center for Health Statistics, U.S. Dept. of Health and Human Services; as of 1995; results of a new survey will be published in 2004.

Percent of women in each age group

	15-44	15-19	20-24	25-29	30-34	35-39	40-44
Using any method	64.2	29.8	63.4	69.3	72.7	72.9	71.5
Female sterilization	17.8	0.1	2.5	11.8	21.4	29.8	35.6
Male sterilization	7.0	—	0.7	3.1	7.6	13.6	14.5
Pill	17.3	13.0	33.1	27.0	20.7	8.1	4.2
Implant	0.9	0.8	2.4	1.4	0.5	0.2	0.1
Injectable	1.9	2.9	3.9	2.9	1.3	0.8	0.2
Intrauterine device (IUD)	0.5	—	0.2	0.5	0.6	0.7	0.9
Diaphragm	1.2	0.0	0.4	0.6	1.7	2.2	1.9
Condom	13.1	10.9	16.7	16.8	13.4	12.3	8.8
Female condom	0.0	—	0.1	—	—	—	—
Periodic abstinence	1.5	0.4	0.6	1.2	2.3	2.1	1.8
Natural family planning	0.2	—	0.1	0.2	0.3	0.4	0.2
Withdrawal	2.0	1.2	2.1	2.6	2.1	2.3	1.4
Other methods[1]	1.0	0.3	0.9	1.2	1.3	0.9	1.8

(1) Includes morning-after pill, foam, cervical cap, Today sponge, suppository, jelly or cream (without diaphragm), and other methods not shown separately.

U.S. Median Age at First Marriage, 1890-2002
Source: Bureau of the Census, U.S. Dept. of Commerce

Year[1]	Men	Women	Year[1]	Men	Women	Year[1]	Men	Women	Year[1]	Men	Women	Year[1]	Men	Women
2002	26.9	25.3	1996	27.1	24.8	1991	26.3	24.1	1970	23.2	20.8	1930	24.3	21.3
2001	26.9	25.1	1995	26.9	24.5	1990	26.1	23.9	1965	22.8	20.6	1920	24.6	21.2
2000	26.8	25.1	1994	26.7	24.5	1985	25.5	23.3	1960	22.8	20.3	1910	25.1	21.6
1999	26.9	25.1	1993	26.5	24.5	1980	24.7	22.0	1950	22.8	20.3	1900	25.9	21.9
1998	26.7	25.0	1992	26.5	24.4	1975	23.5	21.1	1940	24.3	21.5	1890	26.1	22.0
1997	26.8	25.0												

(1) Figures after 1940 based on Current Population Survey data; figures for 1900-40 based on decennial censuses.

Cigarette Use in the U.S., 1985-2002
Source: Substance Abuse and Mental Health Services Administration (SAMHSA), U.S. Dept. of Health and Human Services
(percentage reporting use in the month prior to the survey; figures exclude persons under age 12)

	1985	1999	2000	2001	2002	Race/Ethnicity	1985	1999	2000	2001	2002
TOTAL	38.7	25.8	24.9	24.9	26.0	White	38.9	27.0	25.9	26.1	26.9
Sex						Black	38.0	22.5	23.3	23.9	25.3
Male	43.4	28.3	26.9	27.1	28.7	Hispanic	40.0	22.6	20.7	20.9	23.0
Female	34.5	23.4	23.1	23.0	23.4	Education[2]					
Age group						Non-high school graduate	37.3	39.9	32.4	33.8	35.2
12-17	29.4	14.9	13.4	13.0	13.0	High school graduate	37.0	36.4	31.1	32.1	32.3
18-25	47.4	39.7	38.3	39.1	40.8	Some college	32.6	32.5	27.7	26.7	29.0
26-34	45.7	24.9[1]	24.2[1]	24.2[1]	25.2[1]	College graduate	23.0	18.2	13.9	13.8	14.5
35 and older	35.5	NA	NA	NA	NA						

NA = Not available. (1) Figures are for all persons aged 26 and older. (2) Estimates for Education are for persons aged 18 and older.

Drug Use in the General U.S. Population, 2002
Source: Substance Abuse and Mental Health Services Administration (SAMHSA), U.S. Dept. of Health and Human Services

According to the Substance Abuse and Mental Health Services Administration's 2002 National Survey on Drug Use and Health, an estimated 108 million Americans 12 years of age and older (46.0%) had used an illicit drug at least once during their lifetimes, 14.9% had used one during the previous year, and 8.3% had used one in the most recent month.

The rate of current illicit drug use (in the past month) in 2002 was 10.3% for men; for women it was 6.4%. An estimated 29.9% of Americans 12 or older (70.3 million) used an illicit drug other than marijuana at least once in their life. Some changes made to the survey meant that the 2002 data could not be directly compared to earlier estimates.

The Substance Abuse and Mental Health Services Administration's Drug Abuse Warning Network (DAWN) reported 670,307 drug-related episodes in hospital emergency departments in the coterminous U.S in 2002, or 261 episodes per 100,000 population—unchanged from 2001. Cocaine was a factor in 30% of these. Alcohol in combination with illegal drug use was a factor in 31%. (Alcohol-related episodes were only reported to DAWN when alcohol was used in combination with a reportable drug.)

Drug Use: America's Middle and High School Students, 2002
Source: Monitoring the Future, Univ. of Michigan Inst. for Social Research and National Inst. on Drug Abuse

Use of illicit drugs by American young people dropped for a number of drugs in 2002, according to the University of Michigan's 28th annual survey of high school seniors and 12th annual survey of 8th and 10th graders. Use of Ecstasy, after climbing sharply since 1998, dropped for all grades surveyed. Marijuana and LSD also declined.

Alcohol use declined for all grade levels while remaining quite widespread: 19.6% of 8th graders had consumed alcohol in the past 30 days, 35.4% of 10th graders and 48.6% of 12th graders. Cigarette smoking, which had gone up in the mid-90s, continued its decline of recent years. For 8th graders, 10.7% had smoked in the past 30 days (down 1.5 points from 2001), while 17.7% of 10th graders (down 3.6 points) and 26.7% of 12th graders (down 2.8 points) had smoked in the past 30 days.

Compared to 2001, all 3 grade levels showed lower percentages of students who had used any illicit drug in the past 30 days. For 8th graders, 10.4% said they had done this (a drop of 1.2 percentage points from the year before), and for 10th graders the percentage was down 1.9 points, with 20.8% saying they had used illicit drugs in the past 30 days. 12th graders showed a marginal decline, with 25.4% of high school seniors admitting use in the most recent period, a drop of 0.4 points from 2001. For all grade levels, the percentages using any illicit drugs were substantially higher than in 1992, when 6.8% of 8th graders, 11.0% of 10th graders, and 14.4% of 12th graders had used illicit drugs.

Percentages of students who had used an illicit drug at some time in the past year (as opposed to the last 30 days) followed a similar pattern, with drops of about 2 points for 8th and 10th graders, and of half a point for seniors. The 2002 percentages of students using drugs at some time in the past year were: 17.7% for 8th graders (compared to 12.9% in 1992), 34.8% for 10th graders (20.4% in 1992), and 41.0% for 12th graders (27.1% in 1992).

Marijuana remained the most commonly used illegal drug for all 3 grade levels. In 2002, the proportion of students that reported using marijuana the past year or in the past 30 days dropped by about 2 points from 2001 for 10th graders (2002 numbers: 30.3% had used in the past year, and 17.8% in the past 30 days). For both 8th graders and 12th graders, 30-day and annual use of marijuana declined by a little less than a percentage point; in 2002, 14.6% of 8th graders and 36.2% of 12th graders had used marijuana in the past year, while 8.3% of 8th graders and 21.5% of 12th graders had used in the past 30 days. Use of marijuana on a daily basis went down 0.6 points for 10th graders—to 3.9% in 2002—while 1.2% of 8th graders (a minimal 0.1 point drop from 2001) used marijuana daily, and 6.0% of 12th graders (up 0.1 points) did so.

Use of Ecstasy declined for all three grades. Of 8th graders, 1.4% had used the drug in the past 30 days, and 2.9 in the past year (drops of 0.5 and 0.6 points, respectively). For 10th graders, the numbers were 1.8% in the past 30 days (down 0.8 points) and 4.9% in the past year (down 1.3 points), while for seniors the 2002 figures were 2.4 in the past 30 days (down 0.4 points) and 7.4 in the past year (down 1.8 points). LSD use declined for all 3 grades in both the 30-day and annual categories; 0.7% of students in all 3 grades had used the drug in the past 30 days (drops of 0.3 points for 8th graders, 0.8 points for 10th graders, and 1.6 points for 12th graders). Use of hallucinogens other than LSD exhibited modest declines for all 3 grade levels both for use ever in one's lifetime and for use in the past year. Use of several categories of drugs remained basically unchanged in 2002; among these were heroin, narcotics other than heroin, and cocaine. Crack cocaine use in the past year showed a small rise for 10th-graders.

About 15,100 8th graders, 14,300 10th graders, and 12,900 seniors from 394 schools took part in the survey. The survey missed the 3-6% of a class group that drops out of school early, and about 9-17% who were absentees. These populations tend to have higher rates of drug use overall.

Drug Use: America's High School Seniors, 1975-2002

Source: *Monitoring the Future*, Univ. of Michigan Inst. for Social Research and National Inst. on Drug Abuse

PERCENTAGE EVER USED

	Class of 1975	Class of 1980	Class of 1985	Class of 1990	Class of 1995	Class of 1997	Class of 1998	Class of 1999	Class of 2000	Class of 2001	Class of 2002	'01-'02 change
Marijuana/hashish	47.3	60.3	54.2	40.7	41.7	49.6	49.1	49.7	48.8	49.0	47.8	−1.1
Inhalants[1]	NA	17.3	18.1	18.5	17.8	16.9	16.5	16.0	14.2	13.0	11.7	−1.4
Amyl & butyl nitrites	NA	11.1	7.9	2.1	1.5	2.0	2.7	1.7	0.8	1.9	1.5	−0.4
Hallucinogens[2]	NA	15.6	12.1	9.7	12.7	15.1	14.1	13.7	13.0	14.7	12.0	−2.7
LSD	11.3	9.3	7.5	8.7	11.7	13.6	12.6	12.2	11.1	10.9	8.4	−2.5
PCP	NA	9.6	4.9	2.8	2.7	3.9	3.9	3.4	3.4	3.5	3.1	−0.5
Ecstasy	NA	NA	NA	NA	NA	6.9	5.8	8.0	11.0	11.7	10.5	−1.2
Cocaine	9.0	15.7	17.3	9.4	6.0	8.7	9.3	9.8	8.6	8.2	7.8	−0.4
Crack	NA	NA	NA	3.5	3.0	3.9	4.4	4.6	3.9	3.7	3.8	+0.1
Heroin[3]	2.2	1.1	1.2	1.3	1.6	2.1	2.0	2.0	2.4	1.8	1.7	−0.1
Other opiates[4]	9.0	9.8	10.2	8.3	7.2	9.7	9.8	10.2	10.6	9.9	10.1	+0.2
Stimulants[4,5]	22.3	26.4	26.2	17.5	15.3	16.5	16.4	16.3	15.6	16.2	16.8	+0.5
Sedatives[4]	18.2	14.9	11.8	7.5	7.6	8.7	9.2	9.5	NA	NA	NA	NA
Barbiturates[4]	16.9	11.0	9.2	6.8	7.4	8.1	8.7	8.9	9.2	8.7	9.5	+0.9
Methaqualone[4]	8.1	9.5	6.7	2.3	1.2	1.7	1.6	1.8	NA	NA	NA	NA
Tranquilizers[4]	17.0	15.2	11.9	7.2	7.1	7.8	8.5	9.3	8.9	9.2	11.4	+1.2
Alcohol[6]	90.4	93.2	92.2	89.5	80.7	81.7	81.4	80.0	80.3	79.7	78.4	−1.3
Cigarettes	73.6	71.0	68.8	64.4	64.2	65.4	65.3	64.6	62.5	61.0	57.2	−3.9
Steroids	NA	NA	NA	2.9	2.3	2.4	2.7	2.9	2.5	3.7	4.0	+0.3

NA = Not available. (1) Adjusted for underreporting of amyl and butyl nitrites. (2) Adjusted for underreporting of PCP. (3) Reflects use with or without injection. (4) Includes only drug use that was not under a doctor's orders. (5) Data for 1990-2002 are not directly comparable to prior years. (6) Data for 1994-2002 are not directly comparable to prior years.

Alcohol Use by 8th and 12th Graders, 1980-2002

Source: *Monitoring the Future*, Univ. of Michigan Inst. for Social Research and National Inst. on Drug Abuse

	1980	1990	1991	1992	1993	1994	1995	1996	1997	1998	1999	2000	2001	2002
ALCOHOL[1]				Percent using alcohol in the month before the survey										
All 12th graders	72.0	57.1	54.0	51.3	51.0	50.1	51.3	50.8	52.7	52.0	51.0	50.0	49.8	48.6
Male	77.4	61.3	58.4	55.8	54.9	55.5	55.7	54.8	56.2	57.3	55.3	54.0	54.7	52.3
Female	66.8	52.3	49.0	46.8	46.7	45.2	47.0	46.9	48.9	46.9	46.8	46.1	45.1	45.1
White	75.4	63.8	60.0	56.8	55.6	54.0	54.5	54.8	56.4	57.7	56.3	55.1	55.3	54.0
Black	47.6	35.8	33.7	31.7	32.4	33.8	35.2	36.5	34.3	33.3	32.2	30.0	29.4	30.1
All 8th graders	—	—	25.1	26.1	26.2	25.5	24.6	26.2	24.5	23.0	24.0	22.4	21.5	19.6
Male	—	—	26.3	26.3	26.7	26.5	25.0	26.6	25.2	24.0	24.8	22.5	22.3	19.1
Female	—	—	23.8	25.9	26.1	24.7	24.0	25.8	23.9	21.9	23.3	22.0	20.6	20.0
White	—	—	—	26.6	27.1	25.3	25.4	26.6	26.7	24.8	24.7	24.7	23.2	21.5
Black	—	—	—	18.6	19.7	19.4	18.7	18.1	17.9	16.1	16.0	16.0	15.0	14.8
HEAVY ALCOHOL[2]				Percent heavily using the 2 weeks before the survey										
All 12th graders	41.2	32.2	29.8	27.9	27.5	28.2	29.8	30.2	31.3	31.5	30.8	30.0	29.7	28.6
Male	52.1	39.1	37.8	35.6	34.6	37.0	36.9	37.0	37.9	39.2	38.1	36.7	36.0	34.2
Female	30.5	24.4	21.2	20.3	20.7	20.2	23.0	23.5	24.4	24.0	23.6	23.5	23.7	23.0
White	44.3	36.6	34.6	32.1	31.3	31.5	32.3	33.4	35.1	36.4	35.7	34.6	34.5	33.7
Black	17.7	14.4	11.7	11.3	12.6	14.4	14.9	15.3	13.4	12.3	12.3	11.5	11.8	11.5
All 8th graders	—	—	12.9	13.4	13.5	14.5	14.5	15.6	14.5	13.7	15.2	14.1	13.2	12.4
Male	—	—	14.3	13.9	14.8	16.0	15.1	16.5	15.3	14.4	16.4	14.4	13.7	12.5
Female	—	—	11.4	12.8	12.3	13.0	13.9	14.5	13.5	12.7	13.9	13.6	12.4	12.1
White	—	—	—	12.7	12.6	12.9	13.9	15.1	15.1	14.1	14.3	14.9	13.8	12.7
Black	—	—	—	9.6	10.7	11.8	10.8	10.4	9.8	9.0	9.9	10.0	9.0	9.4

— Data not available. **Note:** *Monitoring the Future* study excludes high school dropouts (about 3-6% of the class group, according to a 1996 report) and absentees (about 16-17% of 12th graders and about 9-10% of 8th graders). High school dropouts and absentees have higher alcohol usage than those included in the survey. (1) In 1993 the alcohol question was changed to indicate that a "drink" meant "more than a few sips." (2) Five or more drinks in a row at least once in the prior 2-week period.

U.S. Motor Vehicle Accidents

Source: National Safety Council

Motor vehicle deaths in the U.S. in 2002 totaled 44,000, a 1% increase from 2001 (after showing a similar 1% hike from 2000 to 2001). However, since miles driven increased about 2% from 2001 to 2002, the mileage death rate was down 1% for 2002 from the previous year.

Among the estimated 193,300,000 licensed drivers in 2002, there were slightly more male drivers than female (96,800,000 male vs 96,500,000 female; 50.1% male), but males accounted for 62% of all miles driven. About 18,600,000 male drivers and 12,100,000 female drivers were involved in an accident in 2002. Male drivers were also involved in many more fatal accidents than female drivers; about 38,900 men and 13,800 women drivers were involved in fatal accidents. The rate of involvement was also substantially higher for men (22 per billion miles driven) than for women (13).

About 54% of motor-vehicle deaths in 2002 occurred during the day, when more people were driving. Based on mileage, however, night-time was far more dangerous, with a death rate more than 2.5 times that of day-time driving.

In 2001, about 41% of all traffic fatalities involved an intoxicated (blood alcohol concentration of 0.08 or greater) or alcohol-impaired driver or nonoccupant. (In 1991 alcohol-related fatalities accounted for 49% of all traffic deaths.) Of the 17,448 alcohol-related traffic fatalities in 2001 (a 0.4% increase from 2000, but a 13% drop from 1991), an estimated 14,933 occurred in accidents where a driver or nonoccupant was intoxicated; the remainder involved a driver or nonoccupant (pedestrian, bicyclist, etc.) who had been drinking but was not legally intoxicated. Alcohol was a factor in about 7% of all traffic accidents.

	Deaths 2002	% change from 2001	Rate 2002[1]
All motor vehicle accidents	44,000	+1	15.7
Collision between motor vehicles	18,200	−1	6.5
Collision with fixed object	13,500	+5	4.8
Pedestrian accidents	5,700	−7	2.0
Noncollision accidents	5,500	+6	2.0
Collision with pedal cycle	700	−13	0.2
Collision with railroad train	300	0	0.1
Other collision (animal, animal-drawn vehicles)	100	0	(2)

(1) Deaths per 100,000 population. (2) Death rate was less than 0.05.

Improper Driving Reported in Accidents, 2000-2002

Source: National Safety Council

Type	Percentage of fatal accidents			Percentage of injury accidents			Percentage of all accidents		
	2002	2001	2000	2002	2001	2000	2002	2001	2000
Improper driving	59.5	59.5	61.6	54.7	57.1	60.3	50.3	54.1	57.8
Speed too fast or unsafe	21.9	23.0	18.6	12.6	14.6	16.3	10.1	11.7	13.6
Right of way	17.4	17.9	10.1	18.9	18.5	19.9	16.4	18.3	20.1
Failed to yield	10.1	9.4	4.6	14.3	13.8	15.0	11.4	11.7	12.7
Disregarded signal	4.0	4.9	8.2	3.3	3.4	1.3	3.4	4.7	2.2
Passed stop sign	3.3	3.6	3.8	1.3	1.3	3.6	1.6	1.9	5.3
Drove left of center	5.7	6.3	0.7	0.9	0.9	1.1	0.7	0.9	1.0
Improper overtaking	1.0	0.9	0.9	0.5	0.6	2.0	0.8	0.8	2.4
Made improper turn	0.5	0.8	0.7	1.2	1.8	0.6	1.7	2.3	0.9
Followed too closely	0.4	0.4	0.9	2.8	4.2	4.3	3.8	5.4	5.7
Other improper driving	12.5	10.2	9.0	17.9	16.5	16.1	16.8	14.7	14.1
No improper driving stated	40.5	40.5	38.4	45.3	42.9	39.7	49.7	45.9	42.2

Note: Based on reports from 8 state traffic authorities. When a driver was under the influence of alcohol or drugs, the accident was considered a result of the driver's physical condition—not a driving error. For this reason, accidents in which the driver was reported to be under the influence are included under "no improper driving stated."

Principal Types of Accidental Deaths in the U.S., 1970-2002

Source: National Safety Council

Year	Motor vehicle	Falls	Poisoning	Drowning	Fires, flames, smoke	Ingestion of food, object	Firearms	Mechanical Suffocation
1970	54,633	16,926	5,299	7,860	6,718	2,753	2,406	NA
1980	53,172	13,294	4,331	7,257	5,822	3,249	1,955	NA
1985	45,901	12,001	5,170	5,316	4,938	3,551	1,649	NA
1990	46,814	12,313	5,803	4,685	4,175	3,303	1,416	NA
1991	43,536	12,662	6,434	4,818	4,120	3,240	1,441	NA
1992	40,982	12,646	7,082	3,542	3,958	3,182	1,409	NA
1993	41,893	13,141	8,537	3,807	3,900	3,160	1,521	NA
1994	42,524	13,450	8,994	3,942	3,986	3,065	1,356	NA
1995	43,363	13,986	9,072	4,350	3,761	3,185	1,225	NA
1996	43,649	14,986	9,510	3,959	3,741	3,206	1,134	NA
1997	43,458	15,447	10,163	4,051	3,490	3,275	981	NA
1998	43,501	16,274	10,801	4,406	3,255	3,515	866	NA
1999	42,401	13,162[3]	12,186[3]	3,529[3]	3,348	3,885	824	1,618[3]
2000[1]	43,354	13,322	12,757	3,482	3,377	4,313	776	1,335
2001[1]	43,700	14,300	14,000	3,300	3,400	4,000	800	1,200
2002[2]	44,000	14,500	15,700	3,000	2,900	4,200	800	1,300
Death rates per 100,000 population								
1970	26.8	8.3	2.6	3.9	3.3	1.4	1.2	NA
1980	23.4	5.9	1.9	3.2	2.6	1.4	0.9	NA
1985	19.3	5.0	2.2	2.2	2.1	1.5	0.7	NA
1990	18.8	4.9	2.3	1.9	1.7	1.3	0.6	NA
1991	17.3	5.0	2.6	1.8	1.6	1.3	0.6	NA
1992	16.1	5.0	2.7	1.4	1.6	1.2	0.6	NA
1993	16.3	5.1	3.4	1.5	1.5	1.2	0.6	NA
1994	16.3	5.2	3.5	1.5	1.5	1.2	0.5	NA
1995	16.5	5.3	3.4	1.7	1.4	1.2	0.5	NA
1996	16.5	5.6	3.5	1.5	1.4	1.2	0.4	NA
1997	16.2	5.8	3.8	1.5	1.3	1.2	0.4	NA
1998	16.1	6.0	4.0	1.6	1.2	1.3	0.3	NA
1999	15.5	4.8[3]	4.5[3]	1.3[3]	1.2	1.4	0.3	0.6[3]
2000[1]	15.7	4.8	4.6	1.3	1.2	1.6	0.3	0.5
2001[1]	15.7	5.1	5.0	1.2	1.2	1.4	0.3	0.4
2002[2]	15.7	5.2	5.6	1.1	1.0	1.5	0.3	0.5

NA = Not available. Note: There were 13,100 other accidental deaths in 2002. (1) Revised figures. (2) Preliminary figures. (3) Data for this year and later not comparable with earlier data because of classification changes.

Risk Behaviors in High School Students, 2001

Source: CDC, Youth Risk Behavior Surveillance—United States, 2001

		Percent rarely or never wear seatbelts[1]			Percent rarely or never wear bicycle helmets[2]			Percent who rode with a driver who had been drinking alcohol[3]		
		Female	Male	Total	Female	Male	Total	Female	Male	Total
Race										
	Non-Hispanic White	9.7	17.7	13.6	81.1	85.5	83.6	29.4	31.2	30.3
	Non-Hispanic Black	12.2	20.3	16.1	90.4	90.9	90.7	24.2	31.2	27.6
	Hispanic	11.3	17.7	14.5	86.9	90.6	88.9	39.3	37.1	38.3
Grade										
	9	10.8	19.4	14.9	80.4	86.0	83.3	31.3	29.2	30.4
	10	10.3	16.6	13.3	81.5	85.0	83.5	29.9	31.5	30.6
	11	9.7	17.5	13.6	86.2	87.7	87.1	25.4	32.8	29.1
	12	9.4	18.6	13.9	85.1	87.1	86.3	31.3	34.5	32.8
	Total	10.2	18.1	14.1	82.6	86.3	84.7	29.6	31.8	30.7

(1) When riding in a car or truck driven by someone else. (2) Among the 65.1% of students who rode bicycles during the 12 months preceding the survey. (3) One or more times during the 30 days preceding the survey.

WORLD ALMANAC QUICK QUIZ

Unmarried mothers accounted for about what fraction of live births in the U.S. as of 2001?

 (a) 1/5   (b) 1/4   (c) 1/3   (d) 1/2

For the answer look in this chapter, or see page 1008.

Sexual Activity of High School Students, 2001
Source: CDC, *Youth Risk Behavior Surveillance—United States, 2001*

	Ever had sexual intercourse			First sexual intercourse before age 13			Currently sexually active[1]			Responsible sexual behavior[2]		
	Female	Male	Total	Female	Male	Total	Female	Male	Total	Female	Male	Total
Race/Ethnicity												
White[3]	41.3	45.1	43.2	3.3	6.2	4.7	32.3	30.0	31.3	84.2	89.3	86.6
Black[3]	53.4	68.8	60.8	7.6	25.7	16.3	39.5	52.3	45.6	84.8	85.9	85.2
Hispanic	44.0	53.0	48.4	4.1	11.4	7.6	34.5	37.3	35.9	82.1	85.2	83.6
Grade												
9	29.1	40.5	34.4	5.4	13.7	9.2	19.9	25.9	22.7	93.5	92.2	92.8
10	39.3	42.2	40.8	4.7	10.6	7.5	30.7	28.6	29.7	85.4	91.4	88.3
11	49.7	54.0	51.9	2.9	6.4	4.6	38.1	37.8	38.1	82.1	87.0	84.5
12	60.1	61.0	60.5	2.2	5.0	3.6	51.0	44.6	47.9	70.1	81.9	75.8
Total	42.9	48.5	45.6	4.0	9.3	6.6	33.4	33.4	33.4	83.9	88.5	86.1

(1) Sexual intercourse during the 3 months preceding the survey. (2) This includes students who had never had sexual intercourse, had had sexual intercourse but not during the 3 months preceeding the survey, or had used a condom the last time they had sexual intercourse during the 3 months preceding the survey. (3) Non-Hispanic.

Death Rates[1] for Suicide at Selected Ages, 1960, 1980, 2000
Source: *Health, United States, 2003*, National Center for Health Statistics, U.S. Dept. of Health and Human Services

	2000			1980			1960		
AGE	BOTH SEXES	MALE	FEMALE	BOTH SEXES	MALE	FEMALE	BOTH SEXES	MALE	FEMALE
15-24	10.2	17.1	3.0	12.3	20.2	4.3	5.2	8.2	2.2
25-44	13.4	21.3	5.4	15.6	24.0	7.7	12.2	17.9	6.6
45-64	13.5	21.3	6.2	15.9	23.7	8.9	22.0	34.4	10.2
65 and older	15.2	31.1	4.0	17.6	35.0	6.1	24.5	44.0	8.4
All ages	10.4	17.7	4.0	12.2	19.9	5.7	12.5	20.0	5.6

(1) Per 100,000 population.

Deaths in the U.S. Involving Firearms, by Age, 2000
Source: National Safety Council

	All ages	Under 5	5-14	15-19	20-24	25-44	45-64	65-74	75 & over
Total firearms deaths[1]	28,663	59	377	2,606	3,969	11,147	6,223	1,941	2,341
Male	24,582	37	302	2,323	3,583	9,366	5,154	1,684	2,133
Female	4,081	22	75	283	386	1,781	1,069	257	208
Unintentional	776	19	67	107	95	284	128	41	35
Male	671	11	62	97	86	234	113	34	34
Female	105	8	5	10	9	50	15	7	1
Suicides	16,586	0	110	897	1,370	5,644	4,691	1,700	2,174
Male	14,454	0	90	793	1,250	4,780	3,977	1,528	2,036
Female	2,132	0	20	104	120	864	714	172	138
Homicides	10,801	40	187	1,549	2,414	4,980	1,326	184	121
Male	9,006	26	138	1,381	2,167	4,137	996	108	53
Female	1,795	14	49	168	247	843	330	76	68
Undetermined[2]	230	0	10	26	45	91	38	11	9
Male	190	0	9	25	37	73	29	9	8
Female	40	0	1	1	8	18	9	2	1

(1) Total includes firearms deaths by legal intervention. These deaths totaled 270 in 2000. (2) "Undetermined" means that the intention involved (whether accident, suicide, or homicide) could not be determined.

Home Accident Deaths in the U.S., 1950-2002
Source: National Safety Council

Year	Total	Falls	Poisoning	Fires, burns[1]	Suffoc.: ingesting object	Suffoc.: mechanical	Firearms	Drowning	Natural heat/cold	All other
1950	29,000	14,800	2,550	5,000	(2)	1,600	950	(2)	(2)	4,100
1960	28,000	12,300	2,450	6,350	1,850	1,500	1,200	(2)	(2)	2,550
1970	27,000	9,700	4,100	5,600	1,800[3]	1,100[3]	1,400[3]	(2)	(2)	3,300[3]
1980	22,800	7,100	3,200	4,800	2,000	500	1,100	(2)	(2)	4,100[4]
1990	21,500	6,700	4,500	3,400	2,300	600	800	(2)	(2)	3,200
1995	27,200	8,400	7,000	3,500	1,500	800	900	900	(2)	4,200
1996	27,500	9,000	7,300	3,500	1,500	800	800	900	(2)	3,700
1997	27,700	9,100	7,800	3,200	1,500	800	700	900	(2)	3,500
1998	29,000	9,500	8,400	2,900	1,800	800	600	1,000	(2)	4,000
1999[3]	30,500	7,600	9,300	3,000	1,900	1,100	600	900	700	5,400
2000[5]	29,200	7,100	9,800	2,700	2,100	1,000	500	1,000	400	4,600
2001[5]	31,600	8,100	11,000	2,700	2,100	1,000	600	900	500	4,700
2002[6]	33,300	8,000	12,500	2,200	2,300	1,100	500	900	400	5,400

(1) Includes deaths resulting from conflagration, regardless of nature of injury. (2) Included under "All other" category. (3) Data for this year and later not comparable with earlier data because of classification changes. (4) Includes about 1,000 deaths attributed to summer heat wave. (5) Revised figures. (6) Data are preliminary.

Worldwide Airline Fatalities, 1986-2002[1]
Source: National Safety Council

Year	Aircraft accidents[2]	Passenger deaths	Death rate[3]	Year	Aircraft accidents[2]	Passenger deaths	Death rate[3]	Year	Aircraft accidents[2]	Passenger deaths	Death rate[3]
1986 . .	24	641	0.04	1992 . .	28	1,070	0.06	1998 . .	20	904	0.03
1987 . .	25	900	0.06	1993 . .	33	864	0.04	1999 . .	21	499	0.02
1988 . .	29	742	0.04	1994 . .	27	1,170	0.05	2000 . .	18	757	0.03
1989 . .	29	879	0.05	1995 . .	25	711	0.03	2001[4] . .	13	577	0.02
1990 . .	27	544	0.03	1996 . .	24	1,146	0.05	2002[5] . .	14	791	0.03
1991 . .	29	638	0.03	1997 . .	25	921	0.04				

(1) Some figures have been revised from previous figures. (2) Involving 1 or more passenger fatalities only. (3) Passenger deaths per 100 mil passenger kilometers. (4) Excluding accidents caused by terrorism or sabotage. (5) Preliminary.

U.S. Fires, 2002
Source: National Fire Protection Assn.

Fires

- Public fire departments responded to 1,687,500 fires in 2002, a decrease of 2.7% from 2001.
- There were 519,000 structure fires in 2002, a marginal decrease of 0.5% from the 2001 figure.
- 77% of all structure fires, or 401,000 fires, occurred in residential properties.
- Fires in vehicles dropped 6.3% from the previous year, totalling 329,500 in 2002.
- There were 839,000 fires in outside properties, a decline of 2.6% from 2001.

Civilian deaths

- There were 3,380 civilian fire deaths in 2002. This was a decrease of 9.8% from the year before (after excluding from the 2001 total the deaths that occurred because of the 9/11 terrorist attack).
- The number of civilian fire deaths in the home dropped by 14.1%, to 2,670. This was the lowest number since the National Fire Protection Association adopted new survey methodology in 1977. Some 79% of all fire deaths were in the home.
- Nationwide, someone died in a home fire every 156 minutes.

Civilian injuries

- There were an estimated 18,425 civilian fire injuries in 2002, a decrease of 9.2% from 2001 (the civilian injuries of 9/11 are excluded from the calculation). In 2001 there were an estimated 21,100 civilian fire injuries, of which 800 were linked to 9/11. These estimates are traditionally low because of underreporting of civilian fire injuries to the fire service.
- Residential properties were the site of 14,050 civilian fire injuries in 2002, and nonresidential structure fires accounted for 1,550 injuries.
- Nationwide, a civilian was injured in a fire every 28 minutes.

Property damage

- Property damage from fires amounted to an estimated $10,337,000,000 in 2002, a decrease of 2.2% from 2001 (excluding events of 9/11 from the calculations).
- Structure fires accounted for $8,742,000,000 of property damage.
- Property loss in residential properties came to $6,055,000,000 for 2002.

Intentionally set fires

- There were an estimated 44,500 intentionally set structure fires in 2002, a decrease of 2.2% from the 2001 number.
- Intentionally set structure fires resulted in 350 civilian deaths in 2002, a 6.1% increase over 2001, if the events of 9/11 are excluded from the calculation. Property damage from intentionally set structure fires totalled $919,000,000, a drop of 9.2% from the 2001 figure (again, excluding 9/11 damage).
- The number of intentionally set vehicle fires in 2002 was 41,000, up 3.8% from 2001. The 2002 intentionally set vehicle fires caused an estimated $222,000,000 in property damage, an increase of 1.4% from 2001.

Physicians by Age, Sex, and Specialty, 2001
Source: American Medical Assn., as of Dec. 31, 2001

	Total Physicians[1]		Under 35 yrs		35-44 yrs		45-54 yrs		55-64 yrs	
	Male	Female	Male	Female	Male	Female	Male	Female	Male	Female
All Specialties.........	630,253	205,903	81,681	57,226	142,783	68,567	159,752	48,703	108,166	18,052
Aerospace Medicine......	457	31	10	2	74	9	157	15	102	5
Allergy & Immunology	3,126	944	135	132	671	339	934	289	780	125
Anaesthesiology........	29,080	7,687	2,956	1,124	10,412	2,942	8,778	2,171	4,355	1,051
Cardiovascular Disease...	19,930	1,796	1,737	328	5,656	729	6,662	539	3,790	146
Child Psychiatry........	3,748	2,686	222	252	970	988	1,148	862	831	363
Colon/Rectal Surgery.....	1,073	104	63	27	318	54	346	21	214	2
Dermatology..........	6,476	3,351	641	846	1,335	1,289	1,876	878	1,675	256
Diagnostic Radiology	17,639	4,489	3,094	1,103	4,850	1,690	5,303	1,309	3,375	323
Emergency Medicine	19,597	4,767	4,043	1,602	5,281	1,573	6,738	1,218	2,607	305
Family Practice........	52,672	22,391	8,320	7,769	13,920	8,051	17,794	5,096	6,841	1,104
Forensic Pathology	404	179	28	20	73	56	131	65	85	22
Gastroenterology	10,028	1,031	856	204	3,124	462	3,436	294	1,909	66
General Practice	11,891	2,275	43	15	534	246	2,003	707	2,893	719
General Preventive Med. ..	1,216	635	111	104	359	249	358	207	195	48
General Surgery........	33,114	4,421	6,655	1,975	7,152	1,424	7,464	802	6,407	157
Internal Medicine	100,613	40,181	19,388	13,360	26,218	14,161	29,505	9,403	15,108	2,416
Medical Genetics	219	198	25	33	63	64	68	67	39	27
Neurological Surgery	4,773	239	682	80	1,129	83	1,190	63	1,024	10
Neurology.............	10,049	2,830	949	557	2,633	1,072	3,391	872	2,009	241
Nuclear Medicine	1,210	262	70	25	217	72	371	98	315	50
Obstetrics/Gynecology....	26,010	15,032	2,087	4,866	5,228	5,259	7,670	3,450	6,245	1,098
Occupational Medicine....	2,376	484	2	4	285	140	807	218	499	73
Ophthalmology..........	15,664	2,820	1,523	680	3,700	1,084	4,339	768	3,756	210
Orthopedic Surgery	22,056	857	3,381	297	5,505	312	5,893	198	4,692	37
Otolaryngology.........	8,746	915	1,240	289	2,183	364	2,146	216	2,001	29
Pathology-Anat./Clin.....	12,753	5,612	964	796	2,664	1,864	3,571	1,681	2,905	882
Pediatric Cardiology......	1,203	433	143	79	399	208	315	78	204	41
Pediatrics............	32,735	32,265	5,947	10,472	7,905	10,602	9,015	7,244	5,879	2,916
Physical Med./Rehab.	4,513	2,235	662	411	1,727	858	1,146	562	552	268
Plastic Surgery........	5,747	675	403	131	1,576	261	1,719	211	1,400	58
Psychiatry.............	27,793	12,223	1,932	1,904	4,906	3,496	7,375	3,727	6,744	1,909
Public Health	1,276	509	1	3	94	69	350	175	309	106
Pulmonary Diseases	7,980	1,225	909	283	2,332	564	2,875	270	1,350	69
Radiation Oncology	3,141	917	383	149	959	346	858	262	632	128
Radiology............	7,560	1,194	493	103	1,625	383	1,292	356	2,180	243
Thoracic Surgery	4,884	142	185	10	1,258	65	1,400	58	1,210	8
Transplantation Surgery...	64	8	1	–	33	5	21	3	6	–
Urology...............	10,039	358	1,042	134	2,316	138	2,538	75	2,617	6
Not Classified..........	24,795	13,519	7,194	5,342	10,041	5,301	3,517	1,680	2,404	866
Unspecified	5,138	2,308	2,774	1,433	1,048	463	723	271	277	89

(1) Includes physicians 65 and older, "Inactive," "Address Unknown," and certain specialties with very few practitioners

U.S. Health Expenditures, 1960-2001

Source: *Health, United States, 2003*, National Center for Health Statistics, U.S. Dept. of Health and Human Services

	1960	1970	1980	1990	1995	1998	1999	2000	2001
					Amount in billions				
National health expenditures	$26.7	$73.1	$245.8	$696.0	$990.1	$1,150.0	$1,219.7	$1,310.0	$1,424.5
					Percent distribution				
Health services and supplies	93.6	92.2	95.0	96.2	96.7	96.7	96.6	96.4	96.4
Personal health care	87.6	86.5	87.3	87.6	87.4	87.8	87.3	86.8	86.8
Hospital care	34.4	37.8	41.3	36.5	34.7	32.9	32.3	31.8	31.7
Professional services	31.3	28.3	27.4	31.2	32.0	32.7	32.5	32.4	32.5
Physician and clinical services. . .	20.1	19.1	19.2	22.6	22.3	22.3	22.2	22.0	22.0
Other professional services	1.5	1.0	1.5	2.6	2.9	3.1	3.0	3.0	3.0
Dental services	7.4	6.4	5.4	4.5	4.5	4.6	4.6	4.6	4.6
Other personal health care	2.4	1.7	1.3	1.4	2.3	2.6	2.8	2.8	2.9
Nursing home and home health	3.4	6.1	8.2	9.4	10.6	10.7	10.0	9.6	9.3
Home health care.	0.2	0.3	1.0	1.8	3.1	2.9	2.6	2.4	2.3
Nursing home care.	3.2	5.8	7.2	7.6	7.5	7.7	7.3	7.2	6.9
Retail outlet sales of medical products	18.6	14.3	10.5	10.5	10.2	11.5	12.5	13.0	13.4
Prescription drugs	10.0	7.5	4.9	5.8	6.1	7.6	8.6	9.3	9.9
Other medical products	8.5	6.8	5.6	4.7	4.0	4.0	3.9	3.7	3.5
Government administration and net cost of private health insurance	4.5	3.8	4.9	5.7	6.1	5.6	6.0	6.2	6.3
Government public health activities[1] . .	1.5	1.9	2.7	2.9	3.2	3.3	3.4	3.4	3.3
Investment	6.4	7.8	5.0	3.8	3.3	3.3	3.4	3.6	3.6
Research	2.6	2.7	2.2	1.8	1.7	1.8	1.9	2.2	2.3
Construction.	3.8	5.2	2.8	2.0	1.6	1.5	1.4	1.4	1.3
			Average annual percent change from previous year shown						
National health expenditures	—	10.6	12.9	11.0	7.3	5.1	6.1	7.4	8.7
Health services and supplies	—	10.4	13.2	11.1	7.4	5.1	6.0	7.1	8.7
Personal health care	—	10.5	13.0	11.0	7.3	5.3	5.5	6.9	8.7
Hospital care	—	11.7	13.9	9.6	6.2	3.3	4.1	5.8	8.3
Professional services	—	9.5	12.5	12.4	7.9	5.9	5.6	7.1	8.8
Physician and clinical services. . .	—	10.1	12.9	12.8	7.0	5.2	5.2	6.9	8.6
Other professional services	—	6.6	17.1	17.5	9.5	7.6	3.3	5.8	9.1
Dental services	—	9.1	11.1	9.0	7.1	6.1	6.1	7.7	8.0
Other personal health care	—	7.2	10.0	11.4	18.9	9.6	11.3	9.1	11.5
Nursing home and home health	—	17.2	16.3	12.5	10.0	5.3	-0.6	3.0	5.2
Home health care.	—	14.5	26.9	18.1	19.4	3.2	-3.7	-1.8	4.5
Nursing home care.	—	17.4	15.4	11.5	7.2	6.1	0.5	4.7	5.5
Retail outlet sales of medical products	—	7.8	9.4	11.1	6.5	9.7	14.6	12.1	11.9
Prescription drugs	—	7.5	8.2	12.8	8.6	12.8	19.7	16.4	15.7
Other medical products	—	8.1	10.6	9.2	3.8	4.6	4.9	2.7	2.4
Government administration and net cost of private health insurance	—	8.6	15.9	12.7	8.6	2.1	13.7	10.3	11.2
Government public health activities[1] . .	—	13.2	17.4	11.6	9.2	6.5	7.7	7.7	5.3
Investment	—	12.9	7.9	8.0	4.3	5.5	7.3	16.2	9.0
Research	—	10.9	10.8	8.8	6.2	6.2	14.5	24.1	12.7
Construction.	—	14.1	6.1	7.3	2.4	4.6	-0.9	5.8	3.2

Note: Numbers may not add to totals because of rounding. (1) Includes personal care services delivered by government public health agencies.

Ownership of Life Insurance in the U.S. and Assets of U.S. Life Insurance Companies, 1940-2002

Source: American Council of Life Insurers
(amounts in millions)

Year	PURCHASES OF LIFE INSURANCE				INSURANCE IN FORCE					Assets
	Ordinary	Group	Industrial	Total	Ordinary	Group	Industrial	Credit	Total	
1940	$6,689	$691	$3,350	$10,730	$79,346	$14,938	$20,866	$380	$115,530	$30,802
1950	17,326	6,068	5,402	28,796	149,116	47,793	33,415	3,844	234,168	64,020
1960	52,883	14,645	6,880	74,408	341,881	175,903	39,563	29,101	586,448	119,576
1970	122,820	63,690[1]	6,612	193,122[1]	734,730	551,357	38,644	77,392	1,402,123	207,254
1975	188,003	95,190[1]	6,729	289,922[1]	1,083,421	904,695	39,423	112,032	2,139,571	289,304
1980	385,575	183,418	3,609	572,602	1,760,474	1,579,355	35,994	165,215	3,541,038	479,210
1985	910,944	319,503[2]	722	1,231,169[2]	3,247,289	2,561,595	28,250	215,973	6,053,107	825,901
1990	1,069,660	459,271	220	1,529,151	5,366,982	3,753,506	24,071	248,038	9,392,597	1,408,208
1991	1,041,508	573,953[1]	198	1,615,659[1]	5,677,777	4,057,606	22,475	228,478	9,986,336	1,551,201
1992	1,048,135	440,143	222	1,488,500	5,941,810	4,240,919	20,973	202,090	10,405,792	1,664,531
1993	1,101,327	576,823	149	1,678,299	6,428,434	4,456,338	20,451	199,518	11,104,741	1,839,127
1994	1,056,976	560,232	257	1,617,465	6,429,811	4,443,179	18,947	189,398	11,081,335	1,942,273
1995	1,039,102	537,828	156	1,577,086	6,872,252	4,604,856	18,134	201,083	11,696,325	2,143,544
1996	1,089,137	614,565	130	1,703,832	7,407,682	5,067,804	18,064	210,746	12,704,296	2,327,924
1997	1,203,552	688,589	128	1,892,269	7,854,570	5,279,042	17,991	212,255	13,363,858	2,579,078
1998	1,324,565	739,508	106	2,064,179	8,505,894	5,735,273	17,365	212,917	14,471,449	2,826,522
1999[3] . . .	1,399,848	966,858	—	2,508,019	9,172,397	6,110,218	—	213,453	15,496,069	3,070,653
2000[3] . . .	1,593,907	921,001	—	2,681,234	9,376,370	6,376,127	—	200,770	15,953,267	3,181,736
2001[3] . . .	1,600,471	1,172,080	—	2,938,702	9,345,723	6,765,074	—	178,851	16,289,648	3,269,019
2002[3] . . .	1,752,941	1,013,728	—	2,888,817	9,311,729	6,876,075	—	158,534	16,346,338	3,380,000

— = Data not available. Ordinary purchases, ordinary in force, and group in force numbers were revised for 1994-97. (1) Includes Servicemen's Group Life Insurance, which amounted to $17.1 billion in 1970, $1.7 billion in 1975, and $166.7 billion in 1991. (2) Includes Federal Employees' Group Life Insurance of $10.8 billion. (3) For 1999 and later, category of "ordinary" is combined with data for "industrials." Also, totals for purchases from 1999 on include the category "Credit," not listed here.

Health Insurance Coverage,[1] by State, 1990, 2000, 2002

Source: Bureau of the Census, U.S. Dept. of Commerce

	2002 Not covered[2]	2002 % not covered	2000 Not covered[2]	2000 % not covered	1990 Not covered[2]	1990 % not covered		2002 Not covered[2]	2002 % not covered	2000 Not covered[2]	2000 % not covered	1990 Not covered[2]	1990 % not covered
AL..	564	12.7	582	13.3	710	17.4	MT..	139	15.3	150	16.8	115	14.0
AK..	119	18.7	117	18.7	77	15.4	NE..	174	10.2	154	9.1	138	8.5
AZ..	916	16.8	869	16.7	547	15.5	NV..	418	19.7	344	16.8	201	16.5
AR..	440	16.3	379	14.3	421	17.4	NH..	125	9.9	103	8.4	107	9.9
CA.	6,398	18.2	6,299	18.5	5,683	19.1	NJ..	1,197	13.9	1,021	12.2	773	10.0
CO.	720	16.1	620	14.3	495	14.7	NM..	388	21.1	435	24.2	339	22.2
CT.	356	10.5	330	9.8	226	6.9	NY..	3,042	15.8	3,056	16.3	2,176	12.1
DE.	79	9.9	72	9.3	96	13.9	NC..	1,368	16.8	1,084	13.6	883	13.8
DC.	74	13.0	78	14.0	109	19.2	ND..	69	10.9	71	11.3	40	6.3
FL..	2,843	17.3	2,829	17.7	2,376	18.0	OH..	1,344	11.9	1,248	11.2	1,123	10.3
GA.	1,354	16.1	1,166	14.3	971	15.3	OK..	601	17.3	641	18.9	574	18.6
HI..	123	10.0	113	9.4	81	7.3	OR..	511	14.6	433	12.7	360	12.4
ID..	233	17.9	199	15.4	159	15.2	PA..	1,380	11.3	1,047	8.7	1,218	10.1
IL..	1,767	14.1	1,704	13.9	1,272	10.9	RI...	104	9.8	77	7.4	105	11.1
IN..	797	13.1	674	11.2	587	10.7	SC..	500	12.5	480	12.1	550	16.2
IA..	277	9.5	253	8.8	225	8.1	SD..	85	11.5	81	11.0	81	11.6
KS..	280	10.4	289	10.9	272	10.8	TN..	614	10.8	615	10.9	673	13.7
KY..	548	13.6	545	13.6	480	13.2	TX..	5,556	25.8	4,748	22.9	3,569	21.1
LA..	820	18.4	789	18.1	797	19.7	UT..	310	13.4	281	12.5	156	9.0
ME.	144	11.3	138	10.9	139	11.2	VT..	66	10.7	52	8.6	54	9.5
MD.	730	13.4	547	10.4	601	12.7	VA..	962	13.5	814	11.6	996	15.7
MA.	644	9.9	549	8.7	530	9.1	WA..	850	14.2	792	13.5	557	11.4
MI..	1,158	11.7	901	9.2	865	9.4	WV..	255	14.6	250	14.1	249	13.8
MN.	397	7.9	399	8.1	389	8.9	WI..	538	9.8	406	7.6	321	6.7
MS.	465	16.7	380	13.6	531	19.9	WY..	86	17.7	76	15.7	58	12.5
MO.	646	11.6	524	9.5	665	12.7	U.S.	43,574	15.2	39,804	14.2	34,719	13.9

(1) For population, all ages, including those 65 or over, an age group largely covered by Medicare. (2) In thousands.

Persons Not Covered by Health Insurance, by Selected Characteristics, 2002

Source: Bureau of the Census, U.S. Dept. of Commerce

	Number[1]	%		Number[1]	%
Total.............	43,574	15.2	Naturalized citizen	2,251	17.5
Sex			Not a citizen	8,935	43.3
Male.........................	23,327	16.7	**Region**		
Female.......................	20,246	13.9	Northeast.....................	7,057	13.0
Race and Ethnicity			Midwest......................	7,533	11.7
White........................	33,320	14.2	South	17,773	17.5
Non-Hispanic..................	20,782	10.7	West	11,210	17.1
Black........................	7,429	19.9	**Household Income**		
Asian and Pacific Islander........	2,447	18.1	Less than $25,000	14,776	23.5
Hispanic[2]....................	12,756	32.4	$25,000 to $49,999............	14,638	19.3
Age			$50,000 to $74,999............	6,904	11.8
Under 18 years	8,531	11.6	$75,000 or more...............	7,256	8.2
18 to 24 years	8,128	29.6	**Education** (18 years and older)		
25 to 34 years	9,769	24.9	Total	35,042	16.5
35 to 44 years	7,781	17.7	No high school diploma	9,768	28.0
45 to 64 years	9,106	13.5	High school graduate only	12,671	18.8
65 years and over	258	0.8	Some college, no degree	6,214	15.0
Nativity			Associate degree	1,981	12.1
Native	32,388	12.8	Bachelor's degree or higher	4,408	8.4
Foreign born	11,186	33.4			

(1) In thousands. (2) Persons of Hispanic origin may be of any race.

Health Coverage for Persons Under 65, by Characteristics, 1984, 1999-2001

Source: *Health, United States, 2003*, National Center for Health Statistics, U.S. Dept. of Health and Human Services

	PRIVATE INSURANCE 1984	PRIVATE INSURANCE 1999[3]	PRIVATE INSURANCE 2000	PRIVATE INSURANCE 2001	MEDICAID[1] 1984	MEDICAID[1] 1999[3]	MEDICAID[1] 2000	MEDICAID[1] 2001	NOT COVERED[2] 1984	NOT COVERED[2] 1999[3]	NOT COVERED[2] 2000	NOT COVERED[2] 2001
Age					Percent of each population group							
Under 18 years..............	72.6	68.8	67.0	66.7	11.9	18.1	19.4	21.2	13.9	11.9	12.4	11.0
18-44 years	76.5	72.0	70.9	70.6	5.1	5.7	5.6	6.3	17.1	21.0	22.0	21.7
45-64 years	83.3	79.3	78.7	78.6	3.4	4.4	4.5	4.7	9.6	12.2	12.7	12.3
Race and Hispanic origin[4,5]												
White, non-Hispanic.........	82.4	80.3	79.3	79.2	3.7	6.0	6.3	7.0	11.8	12.1	12.5	11.9
Black, non-Hispanic	59.4	58.2	57.0	57.6	19.1	18.7	19.3	20.3	19.7	19.4	20.0	19.2
All Hispanic	57.1	50.3	49.0	47.6	12.2	14.1	14.2	16.0	29.1	33.9	35.4	34.8
Percent of poverty level[4]												
Below 100%................	33.0	26.1	25.8	25.6	30.5	36.8	37.2	39.0	34.7	34.4	34.2	33.3
100-149%.................	61.8	40.1	39.5	39.6	7.5	18.6	20.3	23.5	27.0	35.8	36.5	32.4
150-199%.................	77.2	59.4	58.4	57.0	3.1	9.8	10.8	13.3	17.4	27.7	27.3	26.4
200% or more..............	91.6	88.7	87.2	87.1	0.6	2.0	2.3	2.6	5.8	7.7	8.7	8.4
Geographic region[4]												
Northeast	80.7	77.1	76.5	76.5	8.5	10.1	10.5	10.8	10.1	12.2	12.1	11.6
Midwest	80.9	80.2	78.9	78.1	7.2	7.3	7.9	9.0	11.1	11.5	12.3	11.7
South	74.5	68.0	67.0	66.3	5.0	8.9	9.4	10.7	17.4	19.8	20.4	20.0
West	72.3	68.9	67.1	68.6	6.9	10.3	10.2	10.6	17.8	18.6	20.2	18.6

Note: Data based on household interviews of a sample of the civilian noninstitutionalized population. Percents do not add to 100 because other types of health insurance (e.g., Medicare, military) are not shown and persons with both private insurance and Medicaid appear in both columns. (1) Includes Medicaid or other public assistance. In 2001, the age-adjusted percent of the population under 65 covered by Medicaid was 7.9%; 1.2% were covered by state-sponsored health plans and 1.2% were covered by State Children's Health Insurance Program (SCHIP). (2) Includes persons not covered by private insurance, Medicaid or other public assistance, Medicare, or military plans. (3) In 1997 the questionnaire changed compared with previous years. (4) Age adjusted. (5) Changed reporting methods make percentages for race before 1999 not strictly comparable with those from 1999 on.

Enrollment in Health Maintenance Organizations (HMOs), 1976-2002

Source: *Health, United States, 2003*, National Center for Health Statistics, U.S. Dept. of Health and Human Services

	1976	1980	1990	1995	1996	1997	1998	1999	2000	2001	2002
					Number of enrolled in millions						
TOTAL	6.0	9.1	33.0	50.9	59.1	66.8	76.6	81.3	80.9	79.5	76.1
Model type[1]											
Individual practice assoc.[2]	0.4	1.7	13.7	20.1	26.0	26.7	32.6	32.8	33.4	33.1	31.6
Group[3]	5.6	7.4	19.3	13.3	14.1	11.0	13.8	15.9	15.6	15.0	15.0
Mixed	—	—	—	17.6	19.0	29.0	30.1	32.6	32.3	30.9	29.6
Federal program[4]											
Medicaid[5]	—	0.3	1.2	3.5	4.7	5.6	7.8	10.4	10.8	11.4	12.8
Medicare	—	0.4	1.8	2.9	3.7	4.8	5.7	6.5	6.6	6.1	5.4
					Percent of population enrolled in HMOs						
TOTAL	2.8	4.0	13.4	19.4	22.3	25.2	28.6	30.1	30.0	28.3	26.4
Geographic region											
Northeast	2.0	3.1	14.6	24.4	25.9	32.4	37.8	36.7	36.5	35.1	33.4
Midwest	1.5	2.8	12.6	16.4	18.8	19.5	22.7	23.3	23.2	21.7	20.6
South	0.4	0.8	7.1	12.4	15.2	17.9	21.0	23.9	22.6	21.0	19.8
West	9.7	12.2	23.2	28.6	33.2	36.4	39.1	41.4	41.7	40.7	38.2

— = Not available. **Note:** Data as of June 30 in 1976-80, Jan. 1 from 1990 onwards. HMOs in Guam included starting in 1994; Puerto Rico, 1998; Guam HMO enrollment was 34,000 in 2002 and Puerto Rico enrollment was 1,825,000 in 2002. Open-ended enrollment in HMO plans, amounting to 8 million on Jan. 1, 2002, included from 1994 onwards. (1) Enrollment may not equal total because some plans did not report these characteristics. (2) This type of HMO contracts with an association of physicians from various settings (a mixture of solo and group practices) to provide health services. (3) Group includes staff, group, and network model types. (4) Enrollment by Medicaid or Medicare beneficiaries, where the Medicaid or Medicare program contracts directly with the HMO to pay the premium. (5) Data for 1990 and later include enrollment in managed-care health insuring organizations.

Health Care Visits, by Selected Characteristics, 1997, 2001

Source: Centers for Disease Control and Prevention, National Center for Health Statistics.
National Health Interview Survey, family core and sample adult questionnaires.

	No visits		1-3 visits		4-9 visits		10 or more visits	
	1997	2001	1997	2001	1997	2001	1997	2001
					Percent distribution			
All persons	16.5	16.5	46.2	45.8	23.6	24.4	13.7	13.3
Age								
Under 6 years	5.0	5.5	44.9	45.8	37.0	37.9	13.0	10.8
6–17 years	15.3	14.6	58.7	58.9	19.3	20.5	6.8	6.1
18–24 years	22.0	25.4	46.8	44.7	20.0	19.5	11.2	10.5
25–44 years	21.6	22.6	46.7	46.5	18.7	18.7	13.0	12.2
45–54 years	17.9	17.1	43.9	44.9	23.4	23.6	14.8	14.4
55–64 years	15.3	13.3	41.3	39.6	26.7	28.9	16.7	18.2
65–74 years	9.8	8.1	36.9	35.8	31.6	33.5	21.6	22.6
75 years and over	7.7	5.8	31.8	28.2	33.8	38.1	26.6	27.9
Sex								
Male	21.3	21.3	47.1	46.5	20.6	21.6	11.0	10.7
Female	11.8	11.9	45.4	45.1	26.5	27.1	16.3	15.9
Race and Hispanic origin								
White, non-Hispanic	14.7	14.3	46.6	46.4	24.4	25.4	14.3	13.9
Black, non-Hispanic	16.9	16.4	46.1	46.4	23.1	24.0	13.8	13.1
Hispanic[1]	24.9	27.0	42.3	40.2	20.3	20.7	12.5	12.0
Geographic region								
Northeast	13.2	11.8	45.9	47.2	26.0	26.6	14.9	14.3
Midwest	15.9	14.9	47.7	47.2	22.8	24.0	13.6	13.9
South	17.2	17.7	46.1	45.2	23.3	24.4	13.5	12.8
West	19.1	20.5	44.8	44.1	22.8	22.8	13.3	12.7

NOTE: Covers visits to doctor's offices, emergency departments, and home visits. (1) Persons of Hispanic origin may be of any race.

Major Reasons Given by Patients for Emergency Room Visits, 2001

Source: National Center for Health Statistics, U.S. Dept. of Health and Human Services

Rank	Principal reason for visit	Number of visits (1,000)	Percent distribution
	ALL VISITS	107,490	100.0
1.	Stomach pain, cramps, and spasms	6,828	6.4
2.	Chest pain and related symptoms	5,669	5.3
3.	Fever	4,265	4.0
4.	Headache, pain in head	3,172	3.0
5.	Cough	3,065	2.9
6.	Back symptoms	2,648	2.5
7.	Shortness of breath	2,535	2.4
8.	Pain, site not referable to a specific body system	2,389	2.2
9.	Symptoms referable to throat	2,354	2.2
10.	Vomiting	2,272	2.1
11.	Lacerations and cuts—upper extremity	2,238	2.1
12.	Earache or ear infection	1,885	1.8
13.	Accident, not otherwise specified	1,678	1.6
14.	Motor vehicle accident, type of injury unspecified	1,640	1.5
15.	Labored or difficult breathing (dyspnea)	1,551	1.4
16.	Injury, other and unspecified type—head, neck, and face	1,538	1.4
17.	Vertigo—dizziness	1,452	1.4
18.	Leg symptoms	1,423	1.3
19.	Skin rash	1,397	1.3
20.	Neck symptoms	1,392	1.3
	ALL OTHER REASONS	56,101	52.2

Top 20 Reasons Given by Patients for Physicians' Office Visits, 2001
Source: National Center for Health Statistics, U.S. Dept. of Health and Human Services

Rank		Number of visits (1,000)	Total	Female	Male
	ALL VISITS	880,487	100.0	100.0	100.0
1.	General medical examination	68,844	7.8	7.4	8.5
2.	Progress visit, not otherwise specified	39,783	4.5	4.4	4.7
3.	Cough	27,062	3.1	2.7	3.6
4.	Postoperative visit	23,995	2.7	2.7	2.5
5.	Routine prenatal examination	19,848	2.3	3.8	. . .
6.	Medication, other and unspecified kind	16,457	1.9	1.9	1.8
7.	Symptoms referable to throat	15,082	1.7	1.8	1.5
8.	Back symptoms	13,707	1.6	1.5	1.7
9.	Stomach pain, cramps, and spasms	13,594	1.5	1.6	1.5
10.	Vision dysfunctions	13,555	1.5	1.5	1.6
11.	Knee symptoms	12,743	1.4	1.4	1.5
12.	Diabetes mellitus	12,502	1.4	1.1	1.9
13.	Well-baby examination	12,361	1.4	1.2	1.7
14.	Skin rash	12,088	1.4	1.3	1.5
15.	Fever	10,910	1.2	1.0	1.5
16.	Gynecological examination	10,782	1.2	2.1	. . .
17.	Hypertension	10,467	1.2	1.1	1.3
18.	Headache, pain in head	9,876	1.1	1.2	1.0
19.	Nasal congestion	9,592	1.1	0.9	1.4
20.	Earache or ear infection	9,449	1.1	1.2	0.9
	ALL OTHER REASONS	517,791	58.8	57.8	60.2

Drugs Most Frequently Prescribed in Physicians' Offices, 2001
Source: National Center for Health Statistics, U.S. Dept. of Health and Human Services; *Physicians' Desk Reference*; in thousands

Rank	Name of drug (principal generic substance)[1]	Times prescribed	Therapeutic use
1.	Lipitor (atorvastatin calcium)	21,223	Lowers cholesterol
2.	Celebrex (celecoxib)	17,608	Anti-inflammatory agent
3.	Vioxx (rofecoxib)	15,265	Anti-inflammatory agent
4.	Claritin (loratadine)	14,640	Antihistamine
5.	Lasix (furosemide)	13,834	Diuretic, antihypertensive
6.	Synthroid (levothyroxine)	13,667	Thyroid hormone therapy
7.	Premarin (estrogens)	13,023	Estrogen replacement therapy
8.	Tylenol (acetaminophen)	12,626	Analgesic (for pain relief)
9.	Prednisone	12,234	Steroid replacement therapy, anti-inflammatory agent
10.	Albuterol sulfate	12,044	Antiasthmatic/bronchodilator
11.	Prilosec (omeprazole)	11,054	For duodenal or gastric ulcer
12.	A.S.A. (acetylsalicylic acid, aspirin)	10,875	Analgesic (for pain relief)
13.	Aspirin	10,791	Analgesic (for pain relief)
14.	Zocor (simvastatin)	10,468	Lowers cholesterol
15.	Paxil	10,218	Antidepressant
16.	Atenolol	10,098	For high blood pressure
17.	Amoxicillin	9,940	Antibiotic
18.	Zoloft (sertraline hydrochloride)	9,750	Antidepressant
19.	Norvasc (amlodipine besylate)	9,748	For high blood pressure
20.	Glucophage (metformin)	9,663	Blood glucose regulator
	ALL OTHER	1,065,016	

(1) The trade or generic name used by the physician on the prescription or other medical records. The use of trade names is for identification only and does not imply endorsement by the Public Health Service or the U.S. Dept. of Health and Human Services.

Hospitals and Nursing Homes in the U.S., 2001
Source: *Hospital Statistics™* 2003 edition, Health Forum, LLC, An American Hospital Association Company, copyright 2003; *Health, United States, 2003*
For information on choosing a nursing home, go to the website www.medicare.gov/nursing/overview.asp

STATE	Hospitals[1]	% of beds occupied[1]	Nursing homes	% of beds occupied	STATE	Hospitals[1]	% of beds occupied[1]	Nursing homes	% of beds occupied
AL	107	59	228	91.2	MT	53	65	103	78.1
AK	19	58	15	72.3	NE	84	60	230	83.4
AZ	61	64	139	79.9	NV	24	68	46	79.6
AR	83	58	250	74.5	NH	28	61	83	90.4
CA	384	67	1,342	81.5	NJ	78	69	364	87.1
CO	66	61	223	83.8	NM	35	58	80	87.6
CT	35	74	254	91.9	NY	212	77	669	93.9
DE	5	74	42	83.4	NC	111	69	413	87.9
DC	10	73	21	91.3	ND	40	58	87	92.9
FL	202	61	727	83.3	OH	166	62	998	77.8
GA	147	62	361	91.3	OK	108	58	379	69.1
HI	23	74	45	91.4	OR	60	60	145	72.8
ID	40	54	84	72.5	PA	205	68	766	87.5
IL	192	61	854	75.5	RI	11	71	97	87.6
IN	110	57	560	73.8	SC	62	71	179	88.6
IA	116	59	466	78.0	SD	50	64	112	91.9
KS	133	53	380	80.4	TN	123	55	349	88.9
KY	103	61	304	89.4	TX	411	61	1,182	69.3
LA	125	57	332	77.5	UT	42	56	92	72.8
ME	37	64	126	89.8	VT	14	65	44	90.6
MD	49	73	251	83.1	VA	87	69	277	86.4
MA	80	73	506	89.7	WA	84	60	268	82.7
MI	145	65	434	83.8	WV	57	63	139	90.6
MN	133	68	427	93.2	WI	121	61	419	84.2
MS	96	60	199	89.9	WY	24	54	39	82.2
MO	117	60	545	70.5	U.S.	4,908	64	16,675	82.5

(1) Community hospitals (excludes federal hospitals, hospital units of institutions, facilities for the mentally retarded, and alcoholism and chemical dependency hospitals).

Expected New Cancer Cases and Deaths, by Sex, for Leading Sites, 2003

Source: American Cancer Society

The estimates of expected new cases are offered as a rough guide only. They exclude basal and squamous cell skin cancers and in situ carcinomas, except urinary bladder. Carcinoma in situ of the breast accounts for about 55,700 new cases annually, melanoma carcinoma in situ for about 37,700. More than 1 million cases of basal cell and squamous cell cancer, which are highly curable forms of skin cancer, occur annually. About 2,200 nonmelanoma skin cancer deaths are included among deaths expected in all sites.

EXPECTED NEW CASES

Both sexes		Women		Men	
Prostate	220,900	Breast	211,300	Prostate	220,900
Breast	212,600	Lung	80,100	Lung	91,800
Lung	171,900	Colorectal	74,700	Colorectal	72,800
Colorectal	147,500	Uterine corpus (endometrium)	40,100	Urinary bladder	42,200
Urinary bladder	57,400	Ovary	25,400	Melanoma-skin	29,900
ALL SITES	1,334,100	ALL SITES	658,800	ALL SITES	675,300

EXPECTED DEATHS

Both sexes		Women		Men	
Lung	157,200	Lung	68,800	Lung	88,400
Colorectal	57,100	Breast	39,800	Prostate	28,900
Breast	40,200	Colorectal	28,800	Colorectal	28,300
Pancreas	30,000	Pancreas	15,300	Pancreas	14,700
Prostate	28,900	Ovary	14,300	Non-Hodgkin's lymphoma	12,200
ALL SITES	556,500	ALL SITES	270,600	ALL SITES	285,900

U.S. Cancer Incidence for Top 15 Sites, 1992-2000

Source: Surveillance, Epidemiology, and End Results (SEER) Program, National Cancer Institute

	Rate[1]	Average yearly % change		Rate[1]	Average yearly % change		Rate[1]	Average yearly % change
ALL SITES	477.7	-0.7	Urinary bladder	20.4	-0.1	Oral cavity and pharynx	11.3	-2.0
Prostate	180.6	-3.1	Non-Hodgkin's			Pancreas	11.1	-0.4
Breast (female)	132.5	+0.8	lymphoma	19.1	0.0	Kidney and renal pelvis	10.8	+1.3
Lung	64.0	-1.2	Ovary	17.0	-0.8	Stomach	9.3	-1.3
Colon and rectum	54.5	-0.6	Melanoma of the skin	15.7	+2.5	Thyroid	6.4	+3.4
Corpus and Uterus	24.5	-0.1	Leukemia	12.4	-1.3			

(1) Per 100,000 population; rates for prostate, breast, corpus and uterus, and ovary are sex-specific; rates age-adjusted to the 2000 population, and so not comparable with previously published rates; annual average for 8-year period.

U.S. Cancer Mortality for Top 15 Sites, 1992-2000

Source: Surveillance, Epidemiology, and End Results (SEER) Program, National Cancer Institute

	Rate[1]	Average yearly % change[2]		Rate[1]	Average yearly % change[2]		Rate[1]	Average yearly % change[2]
ALL SITES	206.5	-1.0	Ovary	9.0	-0.8	Liver and intrahepatic bile		
Lung	57.6	-0.8	Non-Hodgkin's lymphoma	8.5	0.0	duct	4.4	+2.1
Prostate	35.3	-3.4	Leukemia	7.8	-0.5	Urinary bladder	4.4	-0.3
Breast (female)	29.2	-2.4	Stomach	5.1	-2.8	Esophagus	4.3	+0.6
Colon and rectum	22.0	-1.7	Brain and other nervous			Kidney and renal pelvis	4.2	-0.3
Pancreas	10.6	-0.1	system	4.7	-0.7	Myeloma (bone marrow)	3.9	-0.3

(1) Per 100,000 population; rates age-adjusted to the 2000 population, and so not comparable with previously published rates; annual average for 8-year period. (2) For 1992-2000.

Cardiovascular Diseases Statistical Summary, 2001

Source: American Heart Association

Prevalence — An estimated 63,800,000 Americans had one or more forms of heart and blood vessel disease in 2001.

• hypertension (high blood pressure) — 50,000,000
• coronary heart disease — 13,200,000
• stroke — 4,800,000
• congestive heart failure — 5,000,000

Mortality — 931,108 in 2001 (38.5% of all deaths).

• Someone died from cardiovascular disease every 33 seconds in the U.S. in 2001.

Congenital or inborn heart defects — Mortality from such heart defects was 4,109 in 2001.

Coronary heart disease (heart attack and angina pectoris) — caused 502,189 deaths in 2001.

• 13,200,000 Americans had a history of heart attack and/or angina pectoris.
• As many as 1,200,000 Americans had coronary attacks in 2001.

Congestive heart failure — killed 52,828 in 2001.

Stroke — killed 163,538 Americans in 2001.

Rheumatic heart disease — killed 3,489 in 2001.

Transplant Waiting List, Oct. 2003*

Source: United Network for Organ Sharing

Type of transplant	Patients waiting
Kidney	55,869
Liver	17,267
Pancreas	1,448
Kidney-pancreas	2,402
Intestine	163
Heart	3,585
Heart-lung	184
Lung	3,899
Total[1]	82,839

Transplants Performed, 2002

Source: United Network for Organ Sharing

Type of transplant	Number
Kidney	14,775
Liver	5,329
Pancreas	554
Kidney-pancreas	905
Intestine	107
Heart	2,155
Heart-lung	33
Lung	1,042
Total	24,900

* As of Oct. 13, 2003. (1) Some patients are waiting for more than one organ; therefore total number of patients waiting is less than the sum of patients waiting for each organ.

AIDS Deaths and New AIDS Cases in the U.S., 1985-2002

Source: *Health, United States, 2003;* National Center for Health Statistics, U.S. Dept. of Health and Human Services

	Percent Distribution	All Years[2]	1985	1990	1995	1999	2000	2001	2002	2002 rate[3]
TOTAL DEATHS[1]	—	501,669	6,981	31,988	52,254	18,454	17,347	17,402	16,371	NA
All races	—	831,112	8,159	41,448	70,412	44,580	40,282	41,450	42,745	15.0
				NEW AIDS CASES						
All males, 13 years and over	100.0	676,609	7,504	36,179	56,689	34,013	30,135	30,663	31,644	28.0
Race White, non-Hispanic	47.7	322,920	4,746	20,825	26,028	12,691	11,314	11,054	11,221	13.9
Black, non-Hispanic	35.4	239,650	1,710	10,239	20,833	14,830	13,082	13,764	14,310	111.9
Hispanic[4]	15.6	105,628	992	4,743	9,111	6,043	5,275	5,318	5,543	39.3
American Indian or Alaska Native[5]	0.3	2,203	7	81	197	135	136	149	155	17.3
Asian or Pacific Islander[5]	0.8	5,666	49	264	489	295	291	348	381	8.2
Age 13-19 years	0.4	2,632	27	107	223	131	145	184	199	1.4
20-29 years	15.4	104,174	1,501	6,921	8,387	3,972	3,327	3,291	3,433	17.5
30-39 years	44.7	302,420	3,588	16,668	25,684	14,410	12,543	12,082	12,101	56.2
40-49 years	27.8	188,299	1,634	8,828	16,151	10,836	9,648	10,261	10,658	49.5
50-59 years	8.7	58,745	597	2,645	4,692	3,479	3,387	3,633	3,959	24.9
60 years and over	3.0	20,339	157	1,010	1,562	1,185	1,085	1,212	1,294	6.5
All females, 13 years and over	100.0	145,696	524	4,544	12,978	10,312	9,958	10,617	10,951	9.2
Race White, non-Hispanic	22.0	32,000	143	1,228	3,042	1,896	1,859	1,993	1,930	2.3
Black, non-Hispanic	61.2	89,130	280	2,557	7,586	6,711	6,489	6,963	7,339	50.0
Hispanic[4]	15.9	23,145	98	726	2,236	1,599	1,462	1,543	1,561	11.8
American Indian or Alaska Native[5]	0.3	509	2	9	38	40	70	42	42	4.5
Asian or Pacific Islander[5]	0.6	832	1	20	73	61	74	67	68	1.4
Age 13-19 years	1.4	1,995	5	67	157	166	170	171	203	1.5
20-29 years	20.6	29,996	178	1,117	2,676	1,886	1,750	1,717	1,819	9.6
30-39 years	43.6	63,504	232	2,087	5,934	4,234	3,973	4,145	3,991	18.7
40-49 years	24.1	35,168	45	780	3,059	2,789	2,857	3,147	3,377	15.3
50-59 years	7.0	10,243	26	274	818	916	867	999	1,150	6.9
60 years and over	3.3	4,790	38	219	334	321	341	438	411	1.5
All children, under 13 years	100.0	8,807	131	725	745	255	189	170	150	0.3
Race White, non-Hispanic	18.2	1,601	26	157	117	30	32	30	23	0.1
Black, non-Hispanic	61.6	5,422	87	390	483	171	122	111	99	1.2
Hispanic[4]	19.1	1,685	18	169	135	49	30	26	24	0.2
American Indian or Alaska Native[5]	0.4	31	0	5	2	2	1	0	0	0.2
Asian or Pacific Islander[5]	0.7	58	0	4	5	2	3	3	4	0.2
Age Under 1 year	36.9	3,249	54	298	258	87	61	47	46	1.1
1-12 years	63.1	5,558	77	427	487	168	128	123	104	0.2

NA = Not available. **Note:** The definition of AIDS cases for reporting purposes was expanded in 1985, 1987, and 1993, as more was learned about the spectrum of human immunodeficiency virus-associated diseases. Data exclude residents of U.S. territories. Figures were updated Dec. 31, 2002 to include delayed case reports and may differ from previous reports of *Health, United States.* (1) Based on preliminary figures presented at the National HIV Prevention Conference, July 2003. (2) Revised figures; includes cases and deaths prior to 1985 and for years not shown. Through Dec. 2002. (3) Rate is per 100,000 pop. (4) Persons of Hispanic origin may be of any race. (5) Excludes persons of Hispanic origin.

New AIDS Cases in the U.S., 1985-2001, by Transmission Category

Source: *Health, United States, 2002,* CDC, National Center for HIV, STD, and TB Prevention, Div. of HIV/AIDS Prevention

TRANSMISSION CATEGORY	Percent distribution	All years[1]	1985	1990	1995	1998	1999	2000	1st ½ 2001
All males 13 years and older	100.0	629,429	7,504	36,193	56,776	35,104	34,094	30,251	14,304
Men who have sex with men	56.8	357,583	5,348	23,658	30,944	16,878	15,632	13,648	6,241
Injecting drug use	21.0	132,238	1,103	6,923	13,376	7,440	6,893	5,554	2,215
Men who have sex with men and injecting drug use	7.6	48,132	661	2,943	4,185	2,224	1,929	1,587	657
Hemophilia/coagulation disorder	0.8	4,893	68	332	438	153	143	93	45
Heterosexual contact[2]	4.5	28,430	32	715	2,924	2,723	2,947	2,537	1,077
Sex with injecting drug user	1.4	8,931	25	454	871	645	634	514	228
Transfusion[3]	0.8	4,944	102	440	319	151	137	146	54
Undetermined[4]	8.5	53,209	190	1,182	4,550	5,535	5,413	6,686	4,015
All females 13 years and older	100.0	129,005	524	4,547	12,998	10,410	10,352	9,979	4,698
Injecting drug use	40.3	52,009	287	2,347	5,426	3,251	2,985	2,545	954
Hemophilia/coagulation disorder	0.2	278	3	15	29	24	13	5	3
Heterosexual contact[2]	39.8	51,339	119	1,538	5,555	4,401	4,397	4,025	1,680
Sex with injecting drug user	15.1	19,437	82	1,030	1,923	1,249	1,135	976	383
Transfusion[3]	2.9	3,754	63	330	253	126	131	151	42
Undetermined[4]	16.8	21,625	52	317	1,735	2,608	2,826	3,253	2,019

Note: The definition of AIDS cases for reporting purposes was expanded in 1985, 1987, and 1993, as more was learned about the spectrum of human immunodeficiency virus-associated diseases. Data exclude residents of U.S. territories. Figures were updated June 30, 2001 to include temporarily delayed case reports and may differ from previous reports of *Health, United States.* (1) Includes cases prior to 1985 and for years not shown. (2) Includes persons who have had heterosexual contact with a person with human immunodeficiency virus (HIV) infection or at risk of HIV infection. (3) Receipt of blood transfusion, blood components, or tissue. (4) Includes persons for whom risk information is incomplete, persons still under investigation, men reported only to have had heterosexual contact with prostitutes, and interviewed persons for whom no specific risk is identified.

HEALTH
Basic First Aid
Source: American Red Cross

NOTE: This information is not intended to be a substitute for formal training. It is recommended that you contact your local American Red Cross chapter to sign-up for a First Aid/CPR/AED course.

It is important to get medical assistance as soon as possible, but knowing what to do until a doctor or other trained person gets to the scene can save a life, especially in cases of severe bleeding, stoppage of breathing, poisoning, and shock.

People with special medical problems, such as diabetes, cardiovascular disease, epilepsy, or allergy, are urged to wear some sort of emblem identifying the problem, as a safeguard against receiving medication that might be harmful or even fatal. Emblems may be obtained from Medic Alert Foundation, 2323 Colorado Ave., Turlock, CA 95382; 888-633-4298.

Animal bite — Wash wound with soap under running water and apply antibiotic ointment and dressing. When possible, the animal should be caught alive for rabies testing.

Asphyxiation — Call 9-1-1, or the local emergency number, then start rescue breathing.

Bleeding — Elevate the wound above the heart if possible. Apply direct pressure to the wound with sterile compress until bleeding stops. Call 9-1-1, or the local emergency number if bleeding is severe.

Burn — If mild, with skin unbroken and no blisters, flush with cool water until pain subsides. Apply a loose sterile dry dressing if necessary. If severe, call 9-1-1 or the local emergency number. Apply sterile compresses and keep patient comfortably warm until advanced medical assistance arrives. Do not try to clean burn or break blisters.

Chemical in eye — Call or have someone call 9-1-1 or the local emergency number. With the victim's head turned to the side, continuously flush the injured eye with water, letting the water run away from the other eye.

Choking — See **Abdominal Thrust**.

Convulsions — Place person on back on bed or rug. Loosen clothing. Turn head to side. Do not place a blunt object between the patient's teeth. If convulsions do not stop, get medical attention immediately.

Cut (minor) — Apply mild antiseptic and sterile compress after washing with soap under warm running water.

Fainting — If victim feels faint, lower him or her to the ground. Lay the victim down on his or her back. If there are no signs of a spinal injury or nausea, elevate the victim's legs approximately 12 inches. Loosen any restrictive clothing and check for any other signs of injury. Call 9-1-1 or the local emergency number if the victim remains unconscious for more than a few minutes.

Foreign body in eye — Try to remove the object by having the victim blink several times. If the object doesn't come out, try gently flushing the eye with water. Do not rub the eye. If the object still doesn't come out, the victim should receive professional medical attention.

Frostbite — Handle frostbitten area gently. Do not rub. Soak affected area in warm water (100–105° F). Do not allow frostbitten area to touch the container. Soak until frostbitten part looks red and feels warm. Loosely bandage with dry, sterile dressings. If fingers or toes are frostbitten, put sterile gauze between them.

Heat Stroke and Heat Exhaustion — Remove the victim from the heat. Loosen any tight clothing and apply cool, wet cloths to the skin. If the victim is conscious give him or her cool water, to drink slowly. Call 9-1-1 or the local emergency number if the victim becomes unconscious.

Hypothermia — Call 9-1-1 or the local emergency number. Move victim to a warm place. Remove wet clothing and dry victim, if necessary. Warm victim gradually by wrapping the person in warm blankets or clothing. Apply heat pads or other heat sources if available, but not directly to the body. Give the victim warm, non-alcoholic and decaffeinated liquids to drink.

Loss of Limb — If a limb is severed, it is important to properly protect the limb so that it can possibly be reattached. After the victim is cared for, the limb should be wrapped in a sterile gauze or clean material and placed in a clean plastic bag, garbage can or other suitable container. Pack ice around the limb on the OUTSIDE of the bag to keep the limb cold. Call ahead to the hospital to alert staff there of the situation.

Poisoning — Call 9-1-1 or the local emergency number and Poison Control Center (800-222-1222) and follow their directions. Do not give the victim any food or drink or induce vomiting, unless specified by the Poison Control Center.

Shock (injury-related) — Monitor breathing and consciousness. Help the victim rest as comfortably as possible. If uncertain as to his or her injuries, keep the victim flat on the back. Otherwise elevate feet and legs 12 inches. Maintain normal body temperature; if the weather is cold or damp, place blankets or extra clothing over and under the victim; if weather is hot, provide shade.

Snakebite — Call 9-1-1 or the local emergency number. Wash the injury. Keep the area still and at a lower level than the heart. Keep the victim quiet. If the victim cannot get professional medical help within 30 minute, consider using a snakebite kit if available.

Sprains and fractures — Apply ice to reduce swelling and pain. Do not try to straighten or move broken limbs. Apply a splint to immobilize the injured area if the victim must be transported. If you suspect a serious injury, call 9-1-1 or the local emergency number.

Sting from insect — If possible, remove stinger by scraping it away or using tweezers. Wash the area with soap and water; cover it to keep it clean. Apply a cold pack to reduce pain and swelling. Call 9-1-1 or the local emergency number immediately if body swells, patient collapses, or you know that the victim is allergic to the sting.

Unconsciousness — Call 9-1-1 or the local emergency number immediately. If the person has signs of circulation, place him or her in the recovery position (i.e., lying on his or her side, with head supported, so that the airway is open —but do not move if a spinal injury is suspected).

Abdominal Thrust (Heimlich Maneuver)

The recommended first aid for conscious choking victims is the abdominal thrust, also known as the Heimlich maneuver, after its creator, Dr. Henry Heimlich.

- Get behind the victim and wrap your arms around him or her about 1-2 inches above the navel.
- Make a fist with one hand and place it, with the thumb knuckle pressing inward at the abdomen.
- Grasp the fist with the other hand and give upward thrusts until object is removed or help arrives.

Rescue Breathing

- Determine consciousness by tapping the victim on the shoulder and asking loudly, "Are you okay?"
- Tilt the victim's head back so that the chin is pointing upward. Do not press on the soft tissue under the chin, as this might obstruct the airway. If you suspect that an accident victim might have neck or back injuries, open the airway by placing the tips of your index and middle fingers on the corners of the person's jaw, and your thumbs on the victim's cheekbones, to lift the jaw forward without tilting the head.
- Place your cheek and ear close to the victim's mouth and nose. Look at the chest to see if it rises and falls. Listen and feel for air to be exhaled for about 5 seconds.
- If there is no breathing, pinch the victim's nostrils shut with the thumb and index finger of your hand that is pressing on the victim's forehead. Another way to prevent leakage of air when the lungs are inflated is to press your cheek against the victim's nose.
- Blow air into the mouth by taking a deep breath and then sealing your mouth tightly around the victim's mouth. Initially, give 2 rescue (approx. 2 seconds each) breaths.
- Watch for the victim's chest to see if it rises.
- Stop when the chest is expanded. Raise your mouth; turn your head to the side and listen for exhalation.
- Watch the chest to see if it falls. Check for signs of circulation, including movement or coughing in response to the rescue breaths. If there are signs of circulation, but no breathing, continue rescue breathing. If there are no signs of circulation, begin CPR.
- Repeat giving 1 breath every 5 seconds until the victim starts breathing or advanced medical help arrives and takes over. Recheck for breathing and movement about every minute.

Note: Infants (up to 1 year) and children (1 to 8 years) should be treated as described above, except for the following:
- Do not tilt the head as far back as an adult's head.
- Both the mouth and nose of an infant should be sealed by the mouth.
- Blow into the infant's mouth and nose once every 3 seconds with less pressure and volume than for a child.

Heart and Blood Vessel Disease

Sources: American Heart Association, 7272 Greenville Ave., Dallas, TX 75231-4596; phone: (800) 242-8721; Centers for Disease Control and Prevention; National Institutes of Health

Warning Signs

Of Heart Attack
- Uncomfortable pressure, fullness, squeezing, or pain in the center of the chest lasting 2 minutes or longer
- Pain may radiate to the shoulder, arm, neck, or jaw
- Sweating may accompany pain or discomfort
- Nausea and vomiting also may occur
- Shortness of breath, dizziness, or fainting may accompany other signs
- The American Heart Association advises immediate action at the onset of these symptoms. More than half of heart attack victims die within 1 hour of the onset of symptoms.

Of Stroke
- Sudden numbness or weakness of face, arm or leg, especially on one side of the body
- Sudden confusion, trouble speaking or understanding
- Sudden trouble seeing in one or both eyes
- Sudden trouble walking, dizziness, loss of balance or coordination
- Sudden severe headache with no known cause
- Prompt treatment of stroke can be a major factor in controlling the effects.

Some Major Risk Factors

Blood pressure—High blood pressure, or hypertension, increases the risk of stroke, heart attack, kidney failure, and congestive heart failure. It affects people of all races, sexes, ethnic origins, and ages. Various causes can trigger this often symptomless disease, and it is recommended that individuals have a blood pressure reading at least once every 2 years (more often if advised by a physician).

A blood pressure reading is really two measurements in one, with one written over the other, such as 122/78. The **upper number (systolic pressure)** represents the amount of pressure in the blood vessels when the heart contracts (beats) and pushes blood through the circulatory system. The **lower number (diastolic pressure)** represents the pressure in the blood vessels between beats, when the heart is resting. According to National Institutes of Health guidelines, a blood pressure reading below 120/80 is considered normal, and readings from 120/80 to 139/89 are considered either "normal" or "prehypertension."

High blood pressure is divided into 2 stages:
Stage 1 is 140-159 (systolic) and 90-99 (diastolic);
Stage 2 is 160 or higher (systolic) and 100 or higher (diastolic).
Individuals with diabetes or chronic kidney disease are considered to have high blood pressure if they have a read-ing of 130/80 or higher. The diagnosis can be based on either the systolic or the diastolic reading, whichever is higher.

High blood pressure usually cannot be cured, but it can be controlled in a variety of ways, including lifestyle modifications and medication. Treatment always should be at the direction and under the supervision of a physician.

Cholesterol—Cholesterol is a waxy fat-like substance found in all cells of the body. It is produced by the body and also comes in some foods. The body needs some cholesterol, but excess levels increase the risk of heart disease. High cholesterol itself does not cause symptoms, so many people are unaware that they have a problem.

There are 2 kinds of cholesterol: LDL (low-density lipoprotein), often called "bad" cholesterol, leads to narrowing of the arteries; HDL (high-density lipoprotein), known as "good" cholesterol, helps reduce this risk.

National Institutes of Health guidelines classify total cholesterol levels (determined by a blood test) of less than 200 mg/dl as desirable, 200-239 as borderline high, and 240 and above as high. About 37 mil Americans have a cholesterol level of 240 mg/dl or higher. LDL levels of less than 100 are considered optimal, 130-159 as borderline high, 160-189 as high, and 190 and over as very high. For HDL, levels of 60 mg/dl and above are considered protective against heart disease, while levels under 40 mg/dl are considered a major risk factor for heart disease.

Like high-blood pressure, high cholestrol can be controlled by life-style modification and medication, and should be treated under supervision of a physician.

Triglycerides, another form of fat in the blood, can also raise the risk of heart disease. Levels that are borderline high (150-199) or high (200 or more) may need treatment.

Diabetes—Diabetes is a major risk factor for heart disease; 2/3 to 3/4 of people with diabetes mellitus die of some form of heart or blood vessel disease. See also "Diabetes" in this chapter.

Smoking—Cigarette smokers have more than twice the risk of heart attack and 2-4 times the risk of sudden cardiac death as nonsmokers. Young smokers have a higher risk for early death from stroke. See also "Some Benefits of Quitting Smoking" in this chapter.

Obesity—Using a body mass index (BMI) of 25 and higher for overweight and 30 and higher for obesity, an estimated 131 mil Americans age 20 and over are overweight and 62 mil are obese. See also "Weight Guidelines for Adults" in this chapter.

Examples of Moderate[1] Amounts of Exercise

Source: *Physical Activity and Health: A Report of the Surgeon General*, U.S. Dept. of Health and Human Services, 1996

ACTIVITY	TIME[2]	ACTIVITY	TIME[2]	ACTIVITY	TIME[2]
Washing windows or floors	45-60	Bicycling 5 mi	30	Basketball (playing a game)	15-20
Playing touch football	30-45	Dancing fast (social)	30	Bicycling 4 mi	15
Wheeling self in wheelchair	30-40	Raking leaves	30	Jumping rope	15
Walking 1¾ mi (20 min/mi)	35	Walking 2 mi (15 min/mi)	30	Running 1½ mi (10 min/mi)	15
Basketball (shooting baskets)	30	Swimming laps	20	Shoveling snow	15

Note: The activities are arranged from less vigorous, and using more time, to more vigorous, and using less time. (1) A "moderate" amount of physical activity uses about 150 calories (kcal), or 1,000 if done daily for a week. (2) Activities can be performed at various intensities; the suggested durations, in minutes; based on the expected intensity of effort.

Finding Your Target Heart Rate

Source: Carole Casten, EdD, *Aerobics Today;* Peg Jordan, RN, Aerobics and Fitness Assoc. of America

The target heart rate is the heartbeat rate a person should have during aerobic exercise (such as running, fast walking, cycling, or cross-country skiing) to get the full benefit of the exercise for cardiovascular conditioning.

First, determine the intensity level at which one would like to exercise. A sedentary person may want to begin an exercise regimen at the 60% level and work up gradually to the 70% level. Athletes and highly fit individuals must work at an 85% or higher level to receive benefits.

Second, calculate the target heart rate. One common way is by using the American College of Sports Medicine Method.

To obtain cardiovascular fitness benefits from aerobic exercise, it is recommended that an individual participate in an aerobic activity at least 3-5 times a week for 20-30 minutes per session, although cardiac patients and very sedentary individuals can obtain benefits with shorter periods (15-20 minutes). Generally, training changes occur in 4-6 weeks, but they can occur in as little as 2 weeks.

Using the American College of Sports Medicine Method to calculate one's target heart rate, an individual should subtract his or her age from 220, then multiply by the desired intensity level of the workout. Then divide the answer by 6 for a 10-second pulse count. (The 10-second pulse count is useful for checking whether the target heart rate is being achieved during the workout. One can easily check one's pulse—at the wrist or side of the neck—counting the number of beats in 10 seconds.)

For example, a 20-year-old wishing to exercise at 70% intensity would employ the following steps:

Maximum Heart Rate	220 − 20 = 200
Target Heart Rate	200 × .70 = 140
10-second Pulse Count	140/6 = 23

To work at the desired level of intensity, this 20-year-old would strive for a target heart rate of 140 beats per minute, or a 10-second pulse count of 23.

Cancer Prevention

Source: American Cancer Society, 1599 Clifton Road NE, Atlanta, GA 30329-4251; phone: (800) 227-2345

PRIMARY PREVENTION: Modifiable determinants of cancer risk.

Smoking	Lung cancer mortality rates are about 22 times higher for current male smokers, and 12 times higher for current female smokers, than for those who have never smoked. Smoking accounts for about 30% of all cancer deaths in the U.S. Tobacco use is responsible for nearly 1 in 5 deaths in the U.S. Smoking is associated with cancer of the lung, mouth, nasal cavities, pharynx, larynx, esophagus, stomach, pancreas, liver, uterine cervix, kidney, bladder, and myeloid leukemia.
Nutrition and Diet	Risk for colon, rectum, breast (among postmenopausal women), kidney, prostate, and endometrial cancers increases in obese people. While a diet high in fat may be a factor in the development of certain cancers, particularly cancer of the colon and rectum, prostate, and endometrium, the link between obesity and cancer is more the result of an imbalance between caloric intake and energy expenditure than fat per se. Eating 5 or more servings of fruits and vegetables each day, and eating other foods from plant sources (especially grains and beans), may reduce risk for many cancers. Physical activity can help protect against some cancers, and help to maintain a healthy weight.
Sunlight	Many of the one million skin cancers that are expected to be diagnosed in 2001 could have been prevented by protection from the sun's rays. Epidemiological evidence shows that sun exposure is a major factor in the development of melanoma and that the incidence rates are increasing around the world.
Alcohol	Heavy drinking, especially when accompanied by cigarette smoking or smokeless tobacco use, increases risk of cancers of the mouth, larynx, pharynx, esophagus, and liver. Studies have also noted an association between regular alcohol consumption and an increased risk of breast cancer.
Smokeless Tobacco	Use of chewing tobacco or snuff increases risk of cancers of the mouth and pharynx. The excess risk of cancer of the cheek and gum may reach nearly 50-fold among long-term snuff users.
Estrogen	Estrogen replacement therapy (ERT) to control menopausal symptoms can increase the risk of endometrial cancer. However, adding progesterone to estrogen (hormone replacement therapy, or HRT) helps to minimize this risk. Most studies suggest that long-term use (5 years or more) of HRT after menopause increases the risk of breast cancer, and recent studies suggest that risks from taking HRT exceed benefits. The benefits and risks of the use of HRT or ERT by menopausal women should be discussed carefully by the woman and her doctor.
Radiation	Excessive exposure to ionizing radiation can increase cancer risk. Medical and dental X rays are adjusted to deliver the lowest dose possible without sacrificing image quality. Excessive radon exposure in the home may increase lung cancer risk, especially in cigarette smokers. If levels are found to be too high, remedial actions should be taken.
Environmental Hazards	Exposure to various chemicals (including benzene, asbestos, vinyl chloride, arsenic, and aflatoxin) increases risk of various cancers. Risk of lung cancer from asbestos is greatly increased when combined with smoking.

Cancer-Detection Guidelines

Source: American Cancer Society, 1599 Clifton Road NE, Atlanta, GA 30329-4251; phone: (800) 227-2345

SECONDARY PREVENTION: Steps to diagnose a cancer or precursor as early as possible after it has developed.

For people having periodic health examinations, a cancer-related checkup should include health counseling and, depending on a person's age, might include examinations for cancers of the thyroid, oral cavity, skin, lymph nodes, testes, and ovaries, as well as for some nonmalignant diseases. Special tests for certain cancer sites for individuals at average risk are recommended as outlined below:

Breast Cancer	Yearly mammograms starting at age 40 and continuing for as long as a woman is in good health. Breast clinical physical exams should be part of a periodic health exam, about every three years for women in their 20s and 30s and every year for women 40 and over. Women should report any breast change promptly to their health care providers. Breast self-exam is an option for women starting in their 20s. Women at increased risk (e.g., family history, genetic tendency, past breast cancer) should speak with their doctors about the benefits and limitations of starting mammography screening earlier, having additional tests (e.g., breast ultrasound or MRI), or having more frequent exams.
Cervical Cancer	Women should begin cervical cancer screening about 3 years after they begin having vaginal intercourse, but no later than when they are 21 years old. Screening should be done every year with the regular Pap test or every 2 years using the newer liquid-based Pap test. Beginning at age 30, women who have had 3 normal Pap test results in a row may get screened every 2 to 3 years. Women who have certain risk factors such as diethylstilbestrol (DES) exposure before birth, HIV infection, or a weakened immune system due to organ transplant, chemotherapy, or chronic steroid use should continue to be screened annually. Another reasonable option for women over 30 is to get screened every 3 years (but no more frequently) with either the conventional or liquid-based Pap test, *plus* the HPV DNA test. Women 70 years of age or older who have had 3 or more normal Pap tests in a row and no abnormal Pap test results in the last 10 years may choose to stop having cervical cancer screening. Women with a history of cervical cancer, DES exposure before birth, HIV infection or a weakened immune system should continue to have screening as long as they are in good health. Women who have had a total hysterectomy (removal of the uterus and cervix) may also choose to stop having cervical cancer screening, unless the surgery was done as a treatment for cervical cancer or precancer. Women who have had a hysterectomy without removal of the cervix should continue to follow the guidelines above.
Colorectal Cancer	Beginning at age 50, both men and women should follow one of these testing schedules: Yearly fecal occult blood test, or Flexible sigmoidoscopy every five years, or Yearly fecal occult blood test, plus flexible sigmoidoscopy every 5 years, or Colonoscopy every 10 years, or Double-contrast barium enema every 5-10 years.
Endometrial Cancer	For women with or at high risk of hereditary nonpolyposis colon cancer (HNPCC), annual screening including endometrial biopsy should be obtained beginning at age 35.
Prostate Cancer	Both Prostate-Specific Antigen (PSA) and Digital Rectal Examination (DRE) should be offered annually, beginning at age 50, to men who have at least a 10-year life expectancy. Men at high risk, such as African-Americans and men who have a first-degree relative (father, brother, or son) diagnosed with prostate cancer at an early age, should begin testing at age 45. Health care professionals should give men the opportunity to openly discuss the benefits and risks of testing at annual checkups. Men should actively participate in the decision by learning about prostate cancer and the pros and cons of early detection and treatment of prostate cancer, so that they can make an informed decision about testing.
Skin Cancer	Adults should practice skin self-exam regularly. Suspicious lesions should be evaluated promptly by a physician.

Breast Cancer

Source: American Cancer Society, Inc., 1599 Clifton Road NE, Atlanta, GA 30329-4251; phone: (800) 227-2345

It is estimated that, in 2003, about 211,300 women and 1,300 men in the United States will be diagnosed with breast cancer, and about 40,200 women and 400 men will die from it. Breast cancer is the second largest cause of cancer death for women in the U.S. (lung cancer ranks first), but mortality rates have been declining, especially among younger women, probably because of earlier detection and improved treatment.

The risk for breast cancer increases as a woman ages. The risk is also higher for women with a personal or family history; a long menstrual history (menstrual periods that started early and ended late in life); recent use of oral contraceptives (birth control pills) long-term use of postmenopausal hormone replacement therapy; and no children or no live birth until age 30 or older. Other risk factors for the disease include alcohol consumption and obesity. Inherited mutations such as in the BRCA1 and BRCA2 genes greatly increase a woman's risk for breast cancer, but these mutations probably account for less than 10% of all breast cancers. By far, the majority of women who develop breast cancer have no family history.

Breast cancer is often manifested first as an abnormality that appears on a mammogram, which is a special type of x-ray. Physical signs and symptoms that show up later, which may be detectable by a woman or her doctor, include a breast lump and, less commonly, breast thickening, swelling, distortion, or tenderness; skin irritation or dimpling; or pain, scaliness, or retraction of the nipple. Breast pain is more commonly associated with benign (noncancerous) conditions.

Studies show that **early detection** increases survival and treatment options. The American Cancer Society (ACS) recommends yearly mammograms starting at age 30. Breast clinical physical exams should be part of a periodic health exam, about every 3 years for women in their 20s and 30s and every year for women 40 and over. Women should report any breast change promptly to their health care providers. Breast self-exam is an option for women starting in their 20s. Women who may be at increased risk for the disease because of family history, genetic tendency, or past breast cancer should speak with their doctors about the benefits and limitations of starting mammography screening earlier, having additional tests (e.g. breast ultrasound or MRI), or having more frequent exams. Although most breast lumps that are detected are noncancerous, any suspicious lump needs to be biopsied.

Treatment for breast cancer may involve lumpectomy (local removal of a tumor), mastectomy (surgical removal of the breast), radiation therapy, chemotherapy, hormone therapy, immunotherapy, or some combination of these. For early-stage breast cancer, long-term survival rates following lumpectomy plus radiation therapy are similar to survival rates after modified radical mastectomy.

Numerous **drugs** that may **prevent** breast cancer or improve its treatment are being studied. One is **tamoxifen**, a synthetic hormone that blocks the action of estrogen in the breast. Already used for treating breast cancer, it has been shown to reduce the likelihood of developing the disease in women considered at higher than average risk, including women age 60 and older. Unfortunately, tamoxifen also has dangerous side effects, such as increased risk of uterine cancer and blood clots in the lungs. Research is also being done on another drug, **raloxifene**, which is approved for preventing osteoporosis in postmenopausal women. It is now being directly compared to tamoxifen in a large clinical study to evaluate its effect on breast cancer risk.

Trends in Daily Use of Cigarettes, for U.S. 8th, 10th, and 12th Graders

Source: *Monitoring the Future*, Univ. of Michigan Inst. for Social Research and National Inst. on Drug Abuse

(percent who smoked daily in last 30 days; change 2001-2002 in percentage points)

	8th grade						10th grade						12th grade					
	1998	1999	2000	2001	2002	'01-'02 change	1998	1999	2000	2001	2002	'01-'02 change	1998	1999	2000	2001	2002	'01-'02 change
TOTAL........	8.8	8.1	7.4	5.5	5.1	−0.3	15.8	15.9	14.0	12.2	10.1	−2.1	22.4	23.1	20.6	19.0	16.9	−2.1
Sex............																		
Male........	8.1	7.4	7.0	5.9	5.4	−0.6	14.7	15.6	13.7	12.4	9.4	−3.1	22.7	23.6	20.9	18.4	17.2	−1.2
Female......	9.0	8.4	7.5	4.9	4.9	0.0	16.8	15.9	14.1	11.9	10.8	−1.1	21.5	22.2	19.7	18.9	16.1	−2.8
College plans ..																		
None or under 4 yrs......	25.2	25.2	21.7	17.7	17.1	−0.6	31.7	32.1	28.8	27.3	22.9	−4.5	34.6	34.2	31.7	30.1	27.6	−2.5
Complete 4 yrs.	6.6	5.9	5.6	3.9	3.9	0.0	12.9	13.2	11.6	9.6	7.9	−1.7	18.4	19.5	16.6	15.5	13.8	−1.7
Region																		
Northeast	6.1	7.2	6.9	6.1	3.7	−2.4	18.7	17.7	14.1	11.0	8.3	−2.6	23.4	23.2	22.8	21.9	18.4	−3.5
North central..	11.2	11.5	9.0	6.4	5.7	−0.7	17.3	19.6	16.3	13.2	11.5	−1.7	27.8	25.9	23.6	25.2	22.5	−2.7
South	10.2	8.5	7.8	6.1	6.6	+0.5	17.1	16.3	15.7	14.3	11.3	−3.0	21.8	24.2	19.4	15.5	16.6	+1.1
West........	5.8	3.8	4.9	2.6	2.9	+0.3	8.8	9.1	7.8	7.0	7.8	+0.8	15.5	17.3	16.9	13.4	9.5	−3.9
Race/Ethnicity[1]																		
White	10.4	9.7	9.0	7.5	6.0	−1.4	20.3	19.1	17.7	15.5	13.3	−2.2	28.3	26.9	25.7	23.8	21.8	−2.0
Black	3.8	3.8	3.2	2.8	2.8	0.0	5.8	5.3	5.2	5.2	5.0	−0.2	7.4	7.7	8.0	7.5	6.4	−1.1
Hispanic.....	8.4	8.5	7.1	5.0	4.4	−0.7	9.4	9.1	8.8	7.4	6.4	−1.1	13.6	14.0	15.7	12.0	9.2	−2.9

(1) For each of these groups, data for the specified year and previous year have been combined to increase sample size and thus provide a more reliable estimate.

Some Benefits of Quitting Smoking

Source: American Cancer Society, Inc., 1599 Clifton Road NE, Atlanta, GA 30329-4251; phone: (800) 227-2345

Within 20 Minutes
• Blood pressure drops to a level close to that before the last cigarette
• Temperature of hands and feet increases to normal
Within 8 Hours
• Carbon monoxide level in the blood drops to normal
Within 24 Hours
• Chance of heart attack decreases
Within 2 Weeks to 3 Months
• Circulation improves
• Lung function increases up to 30%
Within 1 to 9 Months
• Coughing, sinus congestion, fatigue, and shortness of breath decrease

• Cilia regain normal function in the lungs, increasing the ability to handle mucus, clean the lungs, reduce infection
Within 1 Year
• Excess risk of coronary heart disease is half that of a smoker's
Within 5 Years
• Stroke risk is reduced to that of a nonsmoker 5-15 years after quitting
Within 10 Years
• Lung cancer death rate about half that of a continuing smoker's
• Risk of cancer of the mouth, throat, esophagus, bladder, kidney, and pancreas decreases
Within 15 Years
• Risk of coronary heart disease is that of a nonsmoker's

Diabetes

Source: American Diabetes Association, 1701 N Beauregard St., Alexandria, VA 22311; phone: (800) 342-2383

Diabetes is a chronic disease in which the body does not produce or properly use **insulin**, a hormone needed to convert sugar, starches, and other foods into energy necessary for daily life. Both genetics and environment appear to play roles in the onset of diabetes. This disease, which has no cure, is the 5th-leading cause of death by disease in the U.S. According to death certificate data, diabetes contributed to 210,000 deaths in 1999. It is estimated that there are 17 million Americans with diabetes, 5.9 million of whom are undiagnosed.

In 1997, the American Diabetes Association issued **new guidelines for diagnosing diabetes**. The recommendations include: lowering the acceptable level of blood sugar in a fasting glucose test from 140 mg of glucose/deciliter of blood to 126 mg/deciliter; testing all adults 45 years and older, and then every 3 years if normal; and testing at a younger age, or more frequently, in high-risk individuals. The American Diabetes Association supports studies that have proven that detection at an earlier stage and modest lifestyle changes will help prevent or delay complications of diabetes.

There are 2 major types of diabetes:

Type 1 (formerly known as insulin dependent, or juvenile diabetes). The body produces very little or no insulin; disease most often begins in childhood or early adulthood. People with type 1 diabetes must take daily insulin injections to stay alive.

Type 2 (formerly known as non-insulin dependent, or adult-onset diabetes). The body does not produce enough or cannot properly use insulin. It is the most common form of the disease (90-95% of cases in people over age 20) and often begins later in life.

Warning Signs of Diabetes

Type 1 Diabetes (usually occurs suddenly):

frequent urination	unusual weight loss
unusual thirst	extreme fatigue
extreme hunger	irritability

Type 2 Diabetes (occurs less suddenly):

any type 1 symptoms	cuts/bruises slow to heal
frequent infections	tingling/numbness in hands or feet
blurred vision	recurring skin, gum, or bladder infections

Pre-Diabetes

Among U.S. adults 40-74 years of age, at least 16.0 million (15.6% of the population) have **pre-diabetes**, the state that occurs when a person's blood glucose levels are higher than normal but not high enough for a diagnosis of diabetes.

In a recent study, about 11% of people with pre-diabetes developed type 2 diabetes during each year of the study. Other studies show that most people with pre-diabetes develop type 2 diabetes in 10 years.

Complications of Diabetes

People often have diabetes many years before it is diagnosed. During that time, serious complications have a chance to develop. Potential complications include:

Blindness. Diabetes is the leading cause of blindness in people ages 20-74. Each year, from 12,000 to 24,000 people lose their sight because of diabetes.

Kidney disease. 10% to 21% of all people with diabetes develop kidney disease. In 1999, more than 38,160 people initiated treatment for end-stage renal disease (kidney failure) because of diabetes.

Amputations. Diabetes is the most frequent cause of nontraumatic lower limb amputations. The risk of a leg amputation is 15 to 40 times greater for a person with diabetes than for the average American. Each year, an estimated 80,000 people lose a foot or leg as a result of complications brought on by diabetes.

Heart disease and stroke. People with diabetes are 2 to 4 times more likely to have heart disease (more than 77,000 deaths due to heart disease annually). And they are 2 to 4 times more likely to suffer a stroke.

Health-care and related costs for the treatment of the disease, added to the cost of lost productivity, total more than $130 billion annually in the U.S.

Alzheimer's Disease

Source: Alzheimer's Association, 225 N Michigan Ave., 17th Fl., Chicago, IL 60601-7633; phone: (800) 272-3900; www.alz.org

Alzheimer's disease, the most common form of dementia, is a progressive, degenerative disease of the brain in which nerve cells deteriorate and die for unknown reasons. Its first symptoms usually involve impaired memory and confusion about recent events. As the disease advances, it results in greater impairment of memory, thinking, behavior, and physical health.

The **rate of progression** of Alzheimer's varies, ranging from 3 to 20 years; the average length of time from onset of symptoms until death is 8 years. Eventually, affected individuals lose their ability to care for themselves and become susceptible to infections of the lungs, urinary tract, or other organs as they grow progressively more debilitated.

Alzheimer's disease affects an estimated 4.5 million Americans, striking men and women of all ethnic groups. Although most people diagnosed with Alzheimer's are older than age 60, some cases occur in people in their 40s and 50s. By age 65, an estimated 10 percent of the population has Alzheimer's, and the disease affects almost half of those over 85. In the United States, annual costs of diagnosis, treatment, and long-term care are estimated at $100 billion.

Diagnosis involves a comprehensive evaluation that may include a complete health history, a physical examination, neurological and mental status assessments, and other testing as needed. Skilled health care professionals can generally diagnose Alzheimer's with about 90 percent accuracy. Other conditions that can cause similar symptoms include depression, drug interactions, nutritional imbalances, infections such as AIDS, meningitis, and syphilis, and other forms of dementia, such as those associated with stroke, Huntington's disease, Parkinson's disease, frontotemporal dementia, and vascular disease. Absolute confirmation of diagnosis requires a brain biopsy or autopsy.

Treatments for cognitive and behavioral symptoms are available, but no intervention has yet been developed that prevents Alzheimer's or reverses its course. Providing care for people with Alzheimer's is physically and psychologically demanding. Nearly 70 percent of affected individuals live at home, where family or friends care for them. In advanced stages of the disease, many individuals require care in a nursing home. Nearly half of all nursing home residents in the United States have Alzheimer's.

People with Alzheimer's need a safe, stable environment and a regular daily schedule offering appropriate stimulation. Physical exercise and social interaction are important, as is proper nutrition. Security is also a consideration, because many people with Alzheimer's tend to wander. An identification bracelet listing the person's name, address, and condition may help ensure the safe return of an individual who wanders.

Warning Signs of Alzheimer's Disease

• Recent memory loss that affects job performance
• Inability to learn new information
• Difficulty with everyday tasks such as cooking or dressing oneself
• Inability to remember simple words
• Use of inappropriate words when communicating
• Disorientation of time and place
• Poor or decreased judgment
• Problems with abstract thinking
• Putting objects in inappropriate places
• Rapid changes in mood or behavior
• Increased irritability, anxiety, depression, confusion, and restlessness
• Prolonged loss of initiative

Acquired Immune Deficiency Syndrome

Source: Centers for Disease Control and Prevention; www.cdc.gov

AIDS (Acquired Immune Deficiency Syndrome), is caused by the human immunodeficiency virus (**HIV**). HIV kills or disables crucial cells of the immune system, progressively destroying the body's ability to fight disease.

HIV is commonly spread through unprotected sexual contact with an infected partner. HIV is also spread through contact with infected blood. Where modern screening techniques are used it is rare to contract HIV from transfusion, but it can be contracted when intravenous drug users share syringes. Though HIV can be spread through semen, vaginal fluids, and breast milk, there is no evidence it can be spread through saliva. About one-quarter of untreated HIV-positive pregnant women transmit HIV to their fetuses, but with drug treatment that risk can be reduced to about 1%. Studies have indicated no evidence of HIV transmission through casual contact such as the sharing of food utensils, towels and bedding, telephones, or toilet seats.

Some people experience flu-like symptoms a short time after infection with HIV, and scientists estimate that about half of those infected with HIV develop more serious, often chronic symptoms within ten years. Even when symptoms are not present, HIV is active in the body, multiplying, infecting, and killing CD4+ T cells, or "T-helper cells," the crucial immune cells that signal other cells in the immune system to perform their functions.

The term **AIDS** applies to the most advanced stages of HIV infection. According to the official definition set by the Centers for Disease Control and Prevention (CDC), an HIV-infected person with fewer than 200 CD4+ T cells can be said to have AIDS. (Healthy adults usually have 1,000 or more). An HIV-infected person, regardless of T cell count, is diagnosed with AIDS if he or she develops one of 26 conditions that typically affect people with advanced HIV. Most of these conditions are "opportunistic infections" that occur when the immune system is so ravaged by HIV that the body cannot fight off certain bacteria, viruses and microbes.

Months or years prior to the onset of AIDS, many people experience such symptoms as swollen glands, lack of energy, fevers and sweats, and skin rashes. People with full-blown AIDS may develop infections of the intestinal tract, lungs, brain, eyes, and other organs, with a variety of symptoms, and may become severely debilitated. They also are prone to developing certain cancers, especially those caused by viruses, such as Kaposi's sarcoma, cervical cancer, and lymphoma. Children with AIDS may have delayed development or failure to thrive.

HIV is primarily **detected** by testing a person's blood for the presence of antibodies (disease-fighting proteins) to HIV. In about 5% of infected individuals, HIV antibodies take as long as six months after exposure to reach detectable levels, but in most cases the antibodies are detectable in about six weeks. HIV testing may also be performed on oral fluid and urine samples.

The **U.S. Food and Drug Administration** has approved a number of **drugs** that may slow down the growth of HIV in the body and treat the infections and cancers associated with AIDS. The first group of drugs used to treat HIV, called nucleoside analog reverse transcriptase inhibitors (NRTIs), include the drug zidovudine (commonly known as AZT). Non-nucleoside reverse transcriptase inhibitors (NNRTIs) have also been approved to treat HIV. A third class of drugs, called protease inhibitors, are also approved for HIV. In 2003 the FDA granted accelerated approval of Fuzeon for use with other anti-HIV drugs to treat advanced cases of infection. Fuzeon was the first among a new class of medications called fusion inhibitors; drugs in this class interfered with HIV's entry into cells by hindering the fusion of viral and cellular membranes.

Patients are typically given a combination of different drugs, because HIV can much more easily become resistant to a single drug. While these drugs extend the period between HIV infection and serious illness, they do not prevent the spread of the disease to others, and can have severe side effects.

Since there is no vaccine or cure for AIDS, the only protection is to avoid activities that carry a risk. When it cannot be known with certainty whether a sexual partner has HIV, the virus that causes AIDS, the CDC recommends abstinence (the only certain protection), mutual monogamy with an uninfected partner, or correct and consistent use of male latex condoms.

Allergies and Asthma

Source: Asthma and Allergy Foundation of America, 1233 20th St., NW, Suite 402, Washington, DC 20036; phone: (800) 7-ASTHMA; www.aafa.org

One out of five Americans suffers from **allergies**. People with allergies have extra-sensitive immune systems that react to normally harmless substances. Allergens that may produce this reaction include plant pollens, dust mites, or animal dander; plants such as poison ivy; certain drugs, such as penicillin; and certain foods such as eggs, milk, nuts, or seafood.

The tendency to develop allergies is usually inherited, and allergies usually begin to appear in childhood, but they can show up at any age. Common allergies for infants include food allergies and eczema (patches of dry skin). Older children and adults may often develop allergic rhinitis (hay fever), a reaction to an inhaled allergen; common symptoms include nasal congestion, runny nose, and sneezing.

It is best to avoid contact with the allergen, if feasible. In some cases, medications such as antihistamines are used to decrease the reaction, and there are treatments aimed at gradually desensitizing the patient to the allergen. Other effective allergy treatments include decongestants, eye drops, and ointments.

Some people with allergies also have **asthma**, and allergens are a common asthma trigger. Asthma is a disease of chronic inflammation, affecting the passages that carry air into and out of the lungs. It is most often seen in children but can develop at any age.

People with asthma have inflamed, supersensitive airways that tighten and become filled with mucus during an asthma episode. Wheezing, difficulty in breathing, tightening of the chest, and coughing are common symptoms. Asthma can progress through stages to become life-threatening if not controlled. Emergency symptoms of asthma include a bluish cast to the face and lips, severe anxiety, increased pulse rate, and sweating.

Besides common allergens, tobacco smoke, cold air, and pollution can trigger an asthma attack, as can viral infections or physical exercise that taxes the breathing. Of course, an accurate diagnosis by a physician is important. Although there is no cure for asthma or allergies, they can be controlled with medications and lifestyle changes. Allergy vaccines are available which can be effective in many patients.

Arthritis

Source: Arthritis Foundation, 1330 West Peachtree Street, Atlanta, GA 30309; phone: (800) 283-7800; www.arthritis.org

The term "arthritis" refers to more than 100 different diseases that cause pain, stiffness, swelling, and restricted movement in joints. The condition is usually chronic. The Centers for Disease Control and Prevention (CDC) reported in 2002 that nearly 70 million adults suffer from arthritis and/or chronic joint symptoms. The cause for most types of arthritis is unknown; scientists are studying the roles played by genetics, lifestyle, and the environment.

Symptoms of arthritis may develop either slowly or suddenly. A visit to the doctor is indicated when pain, stiffness, or swelling in a joint or difficulty in moving a joint persists for more than two weeks. To make a diagnosis of arthritis, the doctor records the patient's symptoms and examines joints, looking for any swelling or limited movement. In addition, the doctor checks for other signs often seen with arthritis, such as rashes, mouth sores, or eye involvement. Finally, the doctor may test the blood, urine, or joint fluid, or take X rays of the joints.

Medications to treat arthritis include drugs that relieve pain and swelling, such as analgesics, anti-inflammatory drugs, biologic response modifiers, glucocorticoids, or disease-modifying antirheumatic drugs, which tend to slow the disease process. Most treatment programs call for exercise; use of heat or cold; and joint-protection techniques (such as avoiding excess stress on joints, using assistive devices, and controlling weight). In some cases, surgery can help when other treatments fail.

Of the three most prevalent forms of arthritis, **osteoarthritis** is the most common, affecting more than 20 million Americans; it usually occurs after age 45. In this type, which is also called degenerative arthritis, the protective cartilage of joints is lost and changes occur in the bone, leading to

pain and stiffness. It usually occurs in the fingers, knees, feet, hips, and back.

Fibromyalgia, another common arthritis condition, affects more than 2 million Americans and affects more women than men. In this form, widespread pain and tenderness occur in muscles and their attachments to the bone. Common symptoms include fatigue, disturbed sleep, stiffness, and psychological distress.

Rheumatoid arthritis, which also affects more than 2 million people in the U.S., is one of the most serious and disabling forms of the disease. In this type, which is also more common in women, inflammation of the joints leads to damage of the cartilage and bone. The areas of the body that can be affected are the hands, wrists, feet, knees, ankles, shoulders, neck, jaw, and elbows.

Other forms of arthritis and related conditions include lupus, gout, ankylosing spondylitis, and scleroderma; also related are bursitis and tendinitis, which may result from injuring or overusing a joint.

Depression

Source: National Institute of Mental Health

Depression is a serious illness that affects thoughts, feelings, and the ability to function in everyday life. It strikes across all age groups, and often goes unrecognized or inadequately treated. A study released in 2003 by the National Institites of Health estimated that 13-14 million Americans suffer from depression in any given year and that over 16% have depression at some point in life. Young people are among those at risk; the study found that in a one-year period 3 times as many persons with depression were from 18 to 29 years old as were 60 or older.

Nearly twice as many women as men suffer from a depressive illness in a given year. Although conventional wisdom holds that depression is most closely associated with menopause, in fact, the childbearing years are marked by the highest rates of depression, followed by the years prior to menopause. The influence of hormones on depression in women has been an active area of NIMH research.

In a given year, 1-2% of people over age 65 living in the community (outside of institutions) suffer from major depression. Depression frequently occurs with other physical illnesses, including heart disease, stroke, cancer, and diabetes. It is not a normal part of aging.

In cases of depression, the treatments that are available will alleviate symptoms, and more people with depression now do seek the help they need. But many depressed people—and those around them—still fail to realize that they have an illness or could benefit from medical help. The 2003 NIH study also concluded that more than half of those seeking help do not get adequate treatment, often because they consult family practioners who do not deal aggressively enough with the problem.

Symptoms and Types of Depression

Symptoms of depression include the following:
• persistent sad mood;
• loss of interest or pleasure in activities once enjoyed;
• significant change in appetite or body weight;
• difficulty sleeping or oversleeping;
• physical slowing or agitation;
• loss of energy;
• feelings of worthlessness or inappropriate guilt;
• difficulty thinking or concentrating;
• recurrent thoughts of death or suicide.

A diagnosis of *major depressive disorder* (or *unipolar major depression*) is made if an individual has 5 or more of these symptoms during the same two-week period. Unipolar major depression typically comes to the fore in episodes that recur during a person's lifetime.

Bipolar disorder (or *manic-depressive illness*) is characterized by episodes of major depression as well as episodes of mania—abnormally and persistently elevated mood or irritability, accompanied by such symptoms as inflated self-esteem, less need for sleep, increased talkativeness, racing

thoughts, distractibility, agitation, and excessive involvement in pleasurable activities that have a high potential for painful consequences. While sharing some of the features of major depression, bipolar disorder is a distinct illness.

Dysthymic disorder (or *dysthymia*), a less severe yet typically more chronic form of depression, is diagnosed when a depressed mood persists for at least two years in adults (one year in children or adolescents) and is accompanied by at least 2 other depressive symptoms. Many people with dysthymic disorder also experience major depressive episodes.

In contrast to the normal experiences of sadness, loss, or passing moods, depression is extreme and persistent and can interfere significantly with an individual's ability to function. A recent study sponsored by the World Health Organization and the World Bank found unipolar major depression to be the leading cause of disability in the U.S. and worldwide.

Treatments for Depression

A variety of **drugs** are used to treat depression. These drugs influence the functioning of certain neurotransmitters in the brain, primarily serotonin and norepinephrine, known as monoamines. Older drugs—so-called tricyclic antidepressants (TCAs) and monoamine oxidase inhibitors (MAOIs)—affect the functioning of both of these neurotransmitters. But they can have strong side effects or, in the case of MAOIs, require dietary restrictions. Newer medications, such as the selective serotonin reuptake inhibitors (SSRIs), have fewer side effects. All of these medications can be effective, but some people respond to one type and not another.

NIMH research has shown that certain types of **psychotherapy**, particularly cognitive-behavioral therapy (CBT) and interpersonal therapy (IPT), can help relieve depression. CBT helps patients change the negative styles of thinking and behaving often associated with depression. IPT focuses on working through disturbed personal relationships that may contribute to depression. Both kinds of psychotherapy work by changing the way the brain functions. Studies of adults have shown that while psychotherapy alone is rarely sufficient to treat moderate to severe depression, it may provide relief in combination with antidepressant drugs.

Electroconvulsive therapy (ECT) has been found effective in treating 80-90% of cases of severe depression. ECT involves producing a seizure in the brain of a patient under general anesthesia by applying electrical stimulation to the brain through electrodes placed on the scalp. Memory loss and other cognitive problems are common, but typically short-lived, side effects.

For more information, start with the website www.nimh. nih.gov/publicat/depressionmenu.cfm

Autism

Source: National Center on Birth Defects and Developmental Disabilities, Centers for Disease Control and Prevention;
National Dissemination Center for Children With Disabilities

Autism is the common name for a group of so-called autism spectrum disorders (ASDs), certain developmental disabilities associated with an abnormality of the brain. These include autistic disorder, pervasive developmental disorder-not otherwise specified (PDD-NOS), and Asperger's syndrome. Autism is identified more commonly today than in the past; whether it is more common is not known. The National Dissemination Center for Children With Disabilities estimates that it affects 5 to 15 children per 1,000. Symptoms typically start to appear very early in childhood and last throughout life. Males are 4 times more likely than females to be autistic.

Autism covers a wide range of behavior; symptoms vary, and a symptom may appear strong in one person, mild or absent in another. In general, autistic people have unusual ways of learning, paying attention, and reacting; most have some problem with social and communications skills. They may prefer to be alone and have trouble understanding others' feelings. About 40% do not talk at all; others have echolalia, meaning they repeat what others say to them. Their voices may sound flat or they may seem unable to control how loudly or softly they talk. Some autistic people can speak well but have difficulty listening to what others say. Autistic people may tend to repeat certain behaviors and may not want to vary daily routines. They may develop complex abilities more readily than simpler ones. For example, autistic children may be able to read very long words but not identify the sound the letter *p* makes.

The cause of autism is unknown; possible factors being explored by researchers include neurological damage and biochemical imbalance in the brain. There is no known cure, but doctors believe that early and intensive training can help autistic children develop new skills and learn better how to talk, play, interact, and learn. Special education programs are available starting at the age of three. While medicines have been effective in relieving some symptoms of autism, behavioral training is currently the most effective form of treatment.

For further information see www.cdc.gov/ncbddd/dd/ddautism.htm and www.nichcy.org/pubs/factshe/fs1txt.htm#orgs

SARS

Source: Centers for Disease Control and Prevention (CDC); World Health Organization

Severe Acute Respiratory Syndrome (SARS) is a sometimes-fatal viral respiratory illness, considered by the World Health Organization to be the first severe, readily transmissible new disease of the 21st century. The first cases of what was later recognized as SARS appeared in Guangdong Prov., China, in Nov. 2002; the disease was reported to WHO in Feb. 2003, and in that month appeared in Hong Kong. From there it spread to Vietnam, Singapore, and other countries. Within a few months it spread to more than 2 dozen countries in Asia, Europe, and North and South America.

Public health responses, including isolating individuals with the disease, helped to contain the outbreak, and by late July no new cases were being reported. There were a total of 8,098 cases and 774 deaths by July 31, 2003, according to the WHO. The worst outbreaks occurred in China (5,327 cases, 349 deaths), Hong Kong (1755 cases, 299 deaths), Taiwan (346 cases, 37 deaths), Canada (251 cases, 43 deaths), and Singapore (238 cases, 33 deaths). The U.S. had 29 cases and no deaths.

Caused by a previously unrecognized coronavirus, called SARS-associated coronavirus (SARS-CoV), the illness typically begins with a high fever. Headache, general discomfort, and body aches are other possible symptoms. A dry cough may appear after 2-7 days. Diarrhea affects 10%-20% of patients. Most patients develop pneumonia, and 10%-20% require mechanical ventilation. There are several laboratory tests that can detect SARS-CoV.

It is believed that SARS spreads by close person-to-person contact, in particular from respiratory droplets produced when an infected individual coughs or sneezes; these droplets can cause infection if they land on the eyes, nose, or mouth (mucous membranes) of a person standing nearby. Kissing, sharing eating utensils, or touching a contaminated surface could also lead to infection. It is considered possible that the virus may also spread by air or other ways not yet known. The CDC recommends that SARS be treated in the same way as any serious community-acquired atypical pneumonia would be treated.

Organ and Tissue Donation

Source: U.S. Dept of Health and Human Services

Each year, over 20,000 Americans receive organ transplants that save or enhance their lives, but about 6,000 others die while waiting for a transplant. At present over 80,000 people are on the waiting list for transplants, and there is an acute shortage of available organs to transplant. A similar situation exists with regard to tissue. In Apr. 2001, Health and Human Services Sec. Tommy G. Thompson announced a "Gift of Life Donation Initiative" aimed at encouraging organ donation. The HHS plan included enlisting the cooperation of major corporations, issuing a model donor card (which would identify its carrier as someone wishing to donate organs and/or tissue), support for creation of a national medal to be presented to families of donors, and investigation of donor registries as a way of ensuring that an individual's intent to donate is communicated.

HHS, the American Medical Association, and other groups stress that individuals wishing to donate organs/tissues should inform their families, so that they know this when the issue is brought up by medical personnel. Prospective donors should also carry a signed organ donor card, and indicate their intentions on their driver's license. The organs that can be donated are the heart, kidneys, pancreas, lungs, liver, and intestines. The tissues are bone marrow, cornea, skin, heart valves, and connective tissue.

Officials stress that an agreement to donate one's organs after death will not affect the quality of medical care and that the process does not disfigure the body or prevent an open-casket funeral. There is no cost to the donor's family; all costs are borne by the recipient. A number of factors determine patients' priority in receiving an organ, such as blood and tissue type, medical urgency, location, and time on the waiting list. Organs and tissues cannot be bought or sold; this is illegal.

For more information, and a link to an organ donor card, go to www.organdonor.gov/faq.html or call UNOS (the United Network for Organs Sharing) at 1-888-894-6361.

▶ ***IT'S A FACT:*** In 1992 the American Academy of Pediatrics recommended that infants be put to sleep on their back (or on their side, but this alternative was later taken back) as a means of lowering the risk of SIDS, or Sudden Infant Death Syndrome. The National Institute of Child Health & Human Development endorsed the recommendation with a "Back to Sleep" campaign launched in 1994. SIDS deaths in the U.S. declined by more than 50% between 1992 and 2003. This result has been attributed in part to changing practices based on the recommendation. Research into the cause of SIDS is continuing.

Spending on Health in the 50 Most Populous Countries

Source: The World Health Report 2002, The World Health Organization

Country	Total spending on health as % of GDP	Per capita total spending on health[1]	Country	Total spending on health as % of GDP	Per capita total spending on health[1]
Afghanistan	1.0	$8	Myanmar	2.2	$153
Algeria	3.6	64	Nepal	5.4	12
Argentina	8.6	658	Nigeria	2.2	8
Australia	8.3	1,698	North Korea	2.1	18
Bangladesh	3.8	14	Pakistan	4.1	18
Brazil	8.3	267	Peru	4.8	100
Canada	9.1	2,058	Philippines	3.4	33
China	5.3	45	Poland	6.0	246
Colombia	9.6	186	Romania	2.9	48
Congo, Dem. Rep. of the	1.5	9	Russia	5.3	92
Egypt	3.8	51	Saudi Arabia	5.3	448
Ethiopia	4.6	5	South Africa	8.8	255
France	9.5	2,057	South Korea	6.0	584
Germany	10.6	2,422	Spain	7.7	1,073
Ghana	4.2	11	Sudan	4.7	13
India	4.9	23	Tanzania	5.9	12
Indonesia	2.7	19	Thailand	3.7	71
Iran	5.5	258	Turkey	5.0	150
Iraq	3.7	375	Uganda	3.9	10
Italy	8.1	1,498	Ukraine	4.1	26
Japan	7.8	2,908	United Kingdom	7.3	1,747
Kenya	8.3	28	**United States**	**13.0**	**4,499**
Malaysia	2.5	101	Uzbekistan	3.7	30
Mexico	5.4	311	Venezuela	4.7	233
Morocco	4.5	50	Vietnam	5.2	21

(1) At average exchange rates.

Complementary and Alternative Medicine

Source: National Center for Complementary and Alternative Medicine, National Institutes of Health (NIH)

Complementary and alternative medicine (CAM) comprises a wide variety of healing philosophies, approaches, and therapies. It includes treatments and health care practices not widely taught in medical schools, not generally used in hospitals, and not usually reimbursed by health insurance companies. While some scientific evidence exists regarding some therapies, for most there are key questions that are yet to be answered through well-designed scientific studies--questions such as whether they are safe and whether they work for the diseases or medical conditions for which they are used. The National Institutes of Health cautions people not to seek alternative therapies without the consultation of a licensed health care provider.

The National Center for Complementary and Alternative Medicine (NCCAM), a part of the National Institutes of Health, distinguishes between **complementary medicine**, used together with conventional medicine (as, for instance, the use of aromatherapy to lessen discomfort after surgery) and **alternative medicine**, used in place of conventional medicine (as, for instance, adopting a special diet to treat cancer instead of using the conventional approaches of chemotherapy, radiation, or surgery). The list of what is considered to be CAM changes continually, as therapies proven to be safe and effective become adopted into conventional health care and as new approaches to health care emerge. Worldwide, only about 10-30% of health care is provided by conventional practitioners; the remaining 70-90% involves alternative practices. An estimated 1 in 3 Americans uses some form of alternative medicine.

The NCCAM classifies CAM in 5 categories:

Alternative medical systems are built upon complete systems of theory and practice. Often, these systems have evolved apart from and earlier than the conventional medical approach used in the U.S. Examples of alternative medical systems that have developed in Western cultures include homeopathic medicine and naturopathic medicine. Systems that have developed in non-Western cultures include traditional Chinese medicine and Ayurveda.

Mind-body medicine uses a variety of techniques designed to enhance the mind's capacity to affect bodily function and symptoms. Some techniques that were considered CAM in the past have become mainstream (for example, patient support groups and cognitive-behavioral therapy). Other mind-body techniques are still considered CAM, including meditation, prayer, mental healing, and therapies that use creative outlets such as art, music, or dance.

Biologically based therapies in CAM use substances found in nature, such as herbs, foods, and vitamins. Some examples include dietary supplements, herbal products, and other so-called "natural" but as yet scientifically unproven therapies (for example, using shark cartilage to treat cancer).

Manipulative and body-based methods in CAM are based on manipulation and/or movement of one or more parts of the body. Some examples include chiropractic or osteopathic manipulation and massage.

Energy therapies involve the use of energy fields. They are of two types:

—*Biofield therapies* are intended to affect energy fields that purportedly surround and penetrate the human body. The existence of such fields has not yet been proven. Some forms of energy therapy manipulate biofields by applying pressure and/or manipulating the body by placing the hands in, or through, these fields. Examples include qi gong, Reiki, and Therapeutic Touch.

—*Bioelectromagnetic-based therapies* involve the unconventional use of electromagnetic fields, such as pulsed fields, magnetic fields, or alternating current or direct current fields.

Top-Selling Medicinal Herbs in the U.S., 1998–2002[1]

Source: *Nutrition Business Journal;* dollars in millions

Herb	1998	1999	2000	2001	2002	Herb	1998	1999	2000	2001	2002
Echinacea	$214	$220	$202	$214	$188	St. John's wort	$315	$243	$164	$122	$ 86
Noni/Morinda	22	33	87	112	187	Green tea	22	23	39	68	74
Garlic	203	183	170	177	173	Milk thistle	35	43	46	59	63
Ginkgo Biloba	307	311	246	213	163	Other single herbs	783	1,003	925	1,016	1,300
Saw palmetto	107	121	127	142	133	Total single herbs	2,255	2,416	2,241	2,370	2,585
Ginseng	222	199	169	150	116	Combination herbs	1,666	1,693	1,896	2,026	1,717
Soy	25	38	65	97	102	**Total**	**$3,920**	**$4,110**	**$4,136**	**$4,397**	**$4,302**

(1) Sales numbers do not include nonmedicinal use.

Alternative Health Services in the U.S., 2002

Source: *Nutrition Business Journal*

Health care practice	Practitioners Licensed	Lay or other	Total revenues[1]	Health care practice	Practitioners Licensed	Lay or other	Total revenues[1]
Chiropractic	68,400	3,700	$15,510	Naturopathy	2,600	3,200	$ 680
Traditional Chinese				Osteopathy	42,400	1,000	—
medicine	13,300	15,500	3,610	Nurses/MDs	657,000	41,000	160
Acupuncture	17,100	5,200	2,290	Others	—	19,570	650
Homeopathy	1,100	5,700	520	**Total**	**873,900**	**290,870**	**$ 31,920**
Massage therapy	72,000	196,000	8,500				

(1) In millions of dollars.

Food Guide Pyramid

The Food Guide Pyramid was developed by the U.S. Dept. of Agriculture and was last revised in 2000. The Pyramid is an outline of what to eat each day. It is not meant as a rigid prescription, but as a general guide to help in choosing a healthful diet. It calls for eating a variety of foods to get needed nutrients and, at the same time, the right amount of calories to maintain or improve your weight.

The Pyramid focuses heavily on fat because most Americans' diets are too high in fat, especially saturated fat. Some nutritionists, however, argue the Pyramid puts too much stress on carbohydrates, such as bread and pasta, while underemphasizing the role of unsaturated fats and protein in a healthy diet. In Sept. 2003 the Dept. of Agriculture solicited comments on proposed revisions to the Pyramid that would take into greater account the sedentary lifestyle of most Americans and the dangers of obesity; possible changes under consideration include listing amounts in cups and ounces instead of servings and offering a range of calorie levels with appropriate levels of food intake for each.

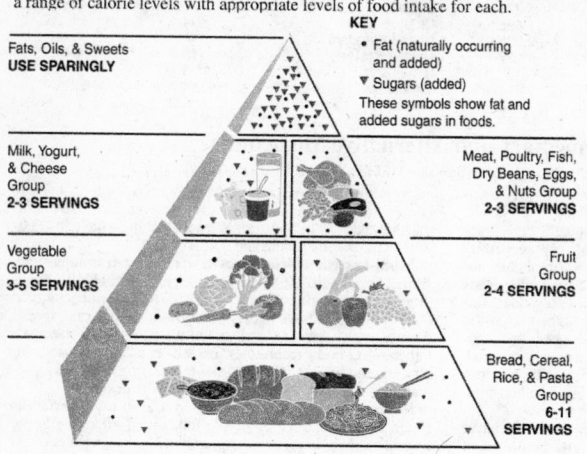

KEY

- ▼ Fat (naturally occurring and added)
- ▼ Sugars (added)

These symbols show fat and added sugars in foods.

What Counts as a Serving?

Bread, Cereal, Rice, and Pasta
1 slice of bread
1 ounce of ready to-eat cereal
½ cup of cooked cereal, rice, or pasta

Vegetable
1 cup of raw leafy vegetables
½ cup of other vegetables, cooked or chopped raw
¾ cup of vegetable juice

Fruit
1 medium apple, banana, orange
½ cup of chopped, cooked, or canned fruit
¾ cup of fruit juice

Milk, Yogurt, and Cheese
1 cup of milk or yogurt
1-1/2 ounces of natural cheese
2 ounces of process cheese

Meat, Poultry, Fish, Dry Beans, Eggs, and Nuts
2-3 ounces of cooked lean meat, poultry, or fish
½ cup of cooked dry beans or 1 egg counts as 1 ounce of lean meat.
2 tablespoons of peanut butter or $^1/_3$ cup of nuts count as 1 ounce of meat.

Food and Nutrition

In a report issued in Sept. 2002, the Food and Nutrition Board of the National Academy of Sciences' Institute of Medicine recommended increased levels of physical activity and more flexible guidelines for eating. Adults and children should engage in moderately intense physical activity for an hour a day, the study said, a level twice the minimum goal set by the 1996 Surgeon General's report. Caloric intake should be geared to activity level, offering recommended calorie totals for individuals according to a scheme that takes into account height, weight, sex, and four different exertion levels (for example, a daily average of 1,800-2,000 calories was recommended for a 30-year-old woman weighing 111-150 pounds and 5 feet 5 inches tall with a sedentary lifestyle, while a very active woman, with other characteristics the same, might consume 2,500-2,800 calories a day).

The study said carbohydrates should make up 45-65% of an adult's calories, with fat providing 20-35% and protein 10-35%. The ranges were intended to allow people to accommodate their preferences while making healthy and realistic choices. Guidelines for children were similar, although the range for fat was slightly higher: it was recommended that 25-40% of a child's calories come from fat. Adults and children, it said, should have at least 130 grams of carbohydrates a day to provide necessary glucose for brain functions; most people, however, consume much more. The study contained the Food and Nutrition Board's first specific recommendations for daily intake of fiber [see below] and reaffirmed earlier recommended levels for protein, 0.8

grams per kilogram of body weight for adults. The report noted that mono- and polyunsaturated fats can play a positive role in the diet, while cautioning against saturated fats and excessive intake of added sugar.

The study was called *Dietary Reference Intakes for Energy, Carbohydrates, Fiber, Fat, Protein and Amino Acids (Macronutrients)*. Earlier Food and Nutrition Board reports had set Dietary Reference Intakes (DRIs) for vitamins and minerals. The DRIs, based on extensive scientific research, were intended to promote health at all stages of life, and not just guard against nutritional deficiencies.

PROTEIN

Proteins, composed of amino acids, are essential to good nutrition. They build, maintain, and repair the body. Best sources: eggs, milk, fish, meat, poultry, soybeans, nuts. High-quality proteins such as eggs, meat, or fish supply all 8 amino acids needed in the diet. Plant foods can be combined to meet protein needs as well: whole grain breads and cereals, rice, oats, soybeans, other beans, split peas, and nuts.

FATS

Fats provide energy by furnishing calories to the body, and they also carry vitamins A, D, E, and K. They are the most concentrated source of energy in the diet. Best sources of polyunsaturated and monounsaturated fats: margarine, vegetable/plant oils, nuts. Meats, cheeses, butter, cream, egg yolks, lard are concentrated sources of saturated fats.

CARBOHYDRATES

Carbohydrates provide energy for body function and activity by supplying immediate calories. The carbohydrate group includes sugars, starches, fiber, and starchy vegetables. Best sources: grains, legumes, potatoes, vegetables, fruits.

FIBER

The portion of plant foods that our bodies cannot digest is known as fiber. There are 2 basic types: *insoluble* ("roughage") and *soluble*. Insoluble fibers help move food materials through the digestive tract; soluble fibers tend to slow them down. Both types absorb water, thus prevent and treat constipation by softening and increasing the bulk of the undigested food components passing through the digestive tract. Soluble fibers have also been reported to be helpful in reducing blood cholesterol levels. Best sources: beans, bran, fruits, whole grains, vegetables. New recommendations from the Food and Nutrition Board call for men 50 and younger to have 38 grams of fiber a day and women to have 25 grams; 30 and 21 grams a day are proposed, respectively, for older men and women (because of reduced food intake). Fiber is also recommended for children and teenagers.

WATER

Water dissolves and transports other nutrients throughout the body, aiding the processes of digestion, absorption, circulation, and excretion. It helps regulate body temperature.

VITAMINS

Vitamin A—promotes good eyesight and helps keep the skin and mucous membranes resistant to infection. Best sources: liver, sweet potatoes, carrots, kale, cantaloupe, turnip greens, collard greens, broccoli, fortified milk.

Vitamin B_1 (thiamine)—prevents beriberi. Essential to carbohydrate metabolism and health of nervous system. Best sources: pork, enriched cereals, grains, soybeans, nuts.

Vitamin B_2 (riboflavin)—protects the skin, mouth, eyes, eyelids, and mucous membranes. Essential to protein and energy metabolism. Best sources: milk, meat, poultry, cheese, broccoli, spinach.

Vitamin B_6 (pyridoxine)—important in the regulation of the central nervous system and in protein metabolism. Best sources: whole grains, meats, fish, poultry, nuts, brewers' yeast.

Vitamin B_{12} (cobalamin)—needed to form red blood cells. Best sources: meat, fish, poultry, eggs, dairy products.

Niacin—maintains health of skin, tongue, digestive system. Best sources: poultry, peanuts, fish, enriched flour and bread.

Folic acid (folacin)—required for normal blood cell formation, growth, and reproduction and for important chemical reactions in body cells. Best sources: yeast, orange juice, green leafy vegetables, wheat germ, asparagus, broccoli, nuts.

Other B vitamins—biotin, pantothenic acid.

Vitamin C (ascorbic acid)—maintains collagen, a protein necessary for the formation of skin, ligaments, and bones. It helps heal wounds and mend fractures and aids in resisting some types of viral and bacterial infections. Best sources: citrus fruits and juices, cantaloupe, broccoli, brussels sprouts, potatoes and sweet potatoes, tomatoes, cabbage.

Vitamin D—important for bone development. Best sources: sunlight, fortified milk and milk products, fish-liver oils, egg yolks.

Vitamin E (tocopherol)—helps protect red blood cells. Best sources: vegetable oils, wheat germ, whole grains, eggs, peanuts, margarine, green leafy vegetables.

Vitamin K—necessary for formation of prothrombin, which helps blood to clot. Also made by intestinal bacteria. Best dietary sources: green leafy vegetables, tomatoes.

MINERALS

Calcium—works with phosphorus in building and maintaining bones and teeth. Best sources: milk and milk products, cheese, blackstrap molasses, some types of tofu.

Phosphorus—performs more functions than any other mineral, and plays a part in nearly every chemical reaction in the body. Best sources: cheese, milk, meats, poultry, fish, tofu.

Iron—Necessary for the formation of myoglobin, which is a reservoir of oxygen for muscle tissue, and hemoglobin, which transports oxygen in the blood. Best sources: lean meats, beans, green leafy vegetables, shellfish, enriched breads and cereals, whole grains.

Other minerals—chromium, cobalt, copper, fluorine, iodine, magnesium, manganese, molybdenum, potassium, selenium, sodium, sulfur, and zinc.

Understanding Food Label Claims

Source: Food Labeling Education Information Center, Beltville, MD

The federal Nutrition Labeling and Education Act of 1990 provides that manufacturers can make certain claims on processed food labels only if they meet the definitions specified here:

SUGAR

Sugar free: less than 0.5 g per serving

No added sugar; Without added sugar; No sugar added:

- No sugars added during processing or packing, including ingredients that contain sugars (for example, fruit juices, applesauce, or dried fruit).
- Processing does not increase sugar content above the amount naturally in the ingredients. (A functionally insignificant increase in sugars is acceptable from processes used for purposes other than increasing sugar content.)
- The food for which it substitutes normally contains added sugars.

Reduced sugar: at least 25% less sugar than reference food

CALORIES

Low calorie: 40 calories or less per serving; if the serving is 30 g or less or 2 tablespoons or less, 40 calories or less per 50 g of food

Calorie free: under 5 calories per serving

Reduced or Fewer calories: at least 25% fewer calories than reference food

FAT

Fat free: less than 0.5 g of fat per serving

Saturated fat free: less than 0.5 g of saturated fat per serving, and the level of trans fatty acids does not exceed 1% of total fat

Low fat: 3 g or less per serving and, if the serving is 30 g or less or 2 tbs or less, per 50 g of the food .

Low saturated fat: 1 g or less per serving and not more than 15% of calories from saturated fatty acids

Reduced or Less fat: at least 25% less per serving than reference food

CHOLESTEROL

Cholesterol free: less than 2 mg of cholesterol and 2 g or less of saturated fat per serving

Low cholesterol: 20 mg or less and 2 g or less of saturated fat per serving and, if

the serving is 30 g or less or 2 tbs or less, per 50 g of the food

Reduced or Less cholesterol: at least 25% less than reference food

SODIUM

Sodium free: less than 5 mg per serving

Low sodium: 140 mg or less per serving and, if the serving is 30 g or less or 2 tbs or less, per 50 g of the food

Very low sodium: 35 mg or less per serving and, if the serving is 30 g or less or 2 tbs or less, per 50 g of the food

Reduced or Less sodium: at least 25% less per serving than reference food

FIBER

High fiber: 5 g or more per serving. (Also, must meet low-fat definition, or must state level of total fat.)

Good source of fiber: 2.5 g to 4.9 g per serving

More or Added fiber: at least 2.5 g more per serving than reference food

Nutritive Value of Food (Calories, Proteins, etc.)

Source: *Home and Garden Bulletin No. 72;* U.S. Dept. of Agriculture

FOOD	Measure	Grams	Food Energy (calories)	Protein (grams)	Fat (grams)	Saturated fats (grams)	Carbohydrate (grams)	Calcium (milligrams)	Iron (milligrams)	Sodium (milligrams)	Vitamin A (I.U.)	Ascorbic Acid (milligrams)
DAIRY PRODUCTS												
Cheese, cheddar, cut pieces	1 oz.	28	115	7	9	6.0	T	204	0.2	176	300	0
Cheese, cottage, small curd	1 cup	210	215	26	9	6.0	6	126	0.3	850	340	T
Cheese, cream	1 oz.	28	100	2	10	6.2	1	23	0.3	84	400	0
Cheese, Swiss	1 oz.	28	95	7	7	4.5	1	219	0.2	388	230	0
Half-and-half	1 tbsp.	15	20	T	2	1.1	1	16	T	6	70	T
Cream, sour	1 tbsp.	12	25	T	3	1.6	1	14	T	6	90	T
Milk, whole	1 cup	244	150	8	8	5.1	11	291	0.1	120	310	2
Milk, nonfat (skim)	1 cup	245	85	8	T	0.3	12	302	0.1	126	500	2
Milkshake, chocolate	10 oz.	283	355	9	8	4.8	60	374	0.9	314	240	0
Ice cream, hardened	1 cup	133	270	5	14	8.9	32	176	0.1	116	540	1
Sherbet	1 cup	193	270	2	4	2.4	59	103	0.3	88	190	4
Yogurt, fruit-flavored	8 oz.	227	230	10	2	1.6	43	345	0.2	133	100	1
EGGS												
Fried in margarine	1	46	90	6	7	1.9	1	25	0.7	162	390	0
Hard-cooked	1	50	75	6	5	1.6	1	25	0.6	62	280	0
Scrambled (milk added) in margarine	1	61	100	7	7	2.2	1	44	0.7	171	420	T
FATS & OILS												
Butter, salted	1 tbsp.	14	100	T	11	7.1	T	3	T	116	430	0
Margarine, salted	1 tbsp.	14	100	T	11	2.2	T	4	T	132	460	0
Olive oil	1 tbsp.	14	125	0	14	1.9	0	0	0	0	0	0
Salad dressing, blue cheese	1 tbsp.	15	75	1	8	1.5	1	12	T	164	30	T
Salad dressing, French, regular	1 tbsp.	16	85	T	9	1.4	1	2	T	188	T	T
Salad dressing, French, low calorie	1 tbsp.	16	25	T	2	0.2	2	6	T	306	T	T
Salad dressing, italian	1 tbsp.	15	80	T	9	1.3	1	1	T	162	30	T
Mayonnaise	1 tbsp.	14	100	T	11	1.7	T	3	0.1	80	40	0
FISH, MEAT, POULTRY												
Clams, raw, meat only	3 oz.	85	65	11	1	0.3	2	59	2.6	102	90	9
Crabmeat, canned	1 cup	135	135	23	3	0.5	1	61	1.1	1,350	50	0
Fish sticks, frozen, reheated	1 fish stick	28	70	6	3	0.8	4	11	0.3	53	20	0
Salmon canned (pink), solids and liquid	3 oz.	85	120	17	5	0.9	0	167	0.7	443	60	0
Sardines, Atlantic, canned in oil, drained solids	3 oz.	85	175	20	9	2.1	0	371	2.6	425	190	0
Shrimp, French fried	3 oz.	85	200	16	10	2.5	11	61	2.0	384	90	0
Trout, broiled, with butter and lemon juice.	3 oz.	85	175	21	9	4.1	T	26	1.0	122	230	1
Tuna, canned in oil	3 oz.	85	165	24	7	1.4	0	7	1.6	303	70	0
Bacon, broiled or fried crisp.	3 slices	19	110	6	9	3.3	T	2	0.3	303	0	6
Ground beef, broiled, regular	3 oz.	85	245	20	18	6.9	0	9	2.1	70	T	0
Roast beef, relatively lean (lean only)	2.6 oz.	75	150	22	5	1.9	0	3	1.5	46	T	0
Beef steak, lean and fat.	3 oz.	85	240	23	15	6.4	0	9	2.6	53	T	0
Beef & vegetable stew.	1 cup	245	220	16	11	4.4	15	29	2.9	292	5,690	17
Lamb, chop, broiled loin, lean and fat	2.8 oz.	80	235	22	16	7.3	0	16	1.4	62	T	0
Liver, beef, fried.	3 oz.	85	185	23	7	2.5	7	9	5.3	90	30,690	23
Ham, light cure, roasted, lean and fat	3 oz.	85	205	18	14	5.1	0	6	0.7	1,009	0	0
Pork, chop, broiled, lean and fat	3.1 oz.	87	275	24	19	7.0	0	3	0.7	61	10	T
Bologna	2 slices	57	180	7	16	6.1	2	7	0.9	581	0	12
Frankfurter, cooked	1	45	145	5	13	4.8	1	5	0.5	504	0	12
Sausage, pork link, cooked	1 link	13	50	3	4	1.4	T	4	0.2	168	0	T
Veal, cutlet, braised or broiled.	3 oz.	85	185	23	9	4.1	0	9	0.8	56	T	0
Chicken, drumstick, fried, bones removed	2.5 oz.	72	195	16	11	3.0	6	12	1.0	194	60	0
Chicken, roasted, half breast, without skin	3 oz.	86	140	27	3	0.9	0	13	0.9	64	20	0
Turkey, roasted, chopped light and dark meat	1 cup	140	240	41	7	2.3	0	35	2.5	98	0	0
Frankfurter, chicken, cooked	1	45	115	6	9	2.5	3	43	0.9	616	60	0
FRUITS & FRUIT PRODUCTS												
Apple, raw, 2-3/4 in. diam.	1	138	80	T	T	0.1	21	10	0.2	1	70	8
Apple juice	1 cup	248	115	T	T	T	29	17	0.9	7	T	2
Apricots, raw	3	106	50	1	T	T	12	15	0.6	1	2,770	11
Banana, raw	1	114	105	1	1	0.2	27	7	0.4	1	90	10
Cherries, sweet, raw	10	68	50	1	1	0.1	11	10	0.3	T	150	5
Cranberry juice cocktail, sweetened	1 cup	253	145	T	T	T	38	8	0.4	10	10	108
Fruit cocktail, canned, in heavy syrup	1 cup	255	185	1	T	T	48	15	0.7	15	520	5
Grapefruit, raw, medium, white	1/2	120	40	1	T	T	10	14	0.1	T	10	41
Grapes, Thompson seedless.	10	50	35	T	T	0.1	9	6	0.1	1	40	5
Lemonade, frozen, unsweetened	6 oz.	244	55	1	T	0.1	16	20	0.3	2	30	77
Cantaloupe, 5-in. diam.	1/2	267	95	2	1	0.1	22	29	0.6	24	8,610	113
Orange, 2-5/8 in. diam.	1	131	60	1	T	T	15	52	0.1	T	270	70
Orange juice, frozen, diluted	1 cup	249	110	2	T	T	27	22	0.2	2	190	97
Peach, raw, 2-1/2 in. diam.	1	87	35	1	T	T	10	4	0.1	T	470	6
Raisins, seedless.	1	145	435	5	1	0.2	115	71	3.0	17	10	5
Strawberries, whole	1 cup	149	45	1	1	T	10	21	0.6	1	40	84
Tomatoes, raw	1	123	25	1	T	T	5	9	0.6	10	1,390	22
Watermelon, 4 by 8 in. wedge	1 piece	482	155	3	2	0.3	35	39	0.8	10	1,760	46
GRAIN PRODUCTS												
Bagel, plain	1	68	200	7	2	0.3	38	29	1.8	245	0	0
Biscuit, 2 in. diam., from home recipe	1	28	100	2	5	1.2	13	47	0.7	195	10	T
Bread, pita, enriched, white, 6-1/2 in. diam	1 pita	60	165	6	1	0.1	12	15	0.7	124	0	0
Bread, white, enriched	1 slice	25	65	1	1	0.3	12	32	0.7	129	T	T
Bread, whole-wheat.	1 slice	28	70	3	1	0.4	13	20	1.0	180	T	T
Oatmeal or rolled oats, without added salt	1 cup	234	145	6	2	0.4	25	19	1.6	2	40	0
Bran flakes (40% bran), added sugar, salt, iron, vitamins.	1 oz.	28	90	4	1	0.1	22	14	8.1	264	1,250	0
Corn flakes, added sugar, salt, iron, vitamins	1 oz.	28	110	2	T	T	24	1	1.8	351	1,250	15
Rice, puffed, added iron, thiamine, niacin	1 oz.	28	110	2	T	T	25	4	1.8	340	1,250	15
Wheat, shredded, plain, 1 biscuit or 2/3 cup	1 oz.	28	100	3	1	0.1	23	11	1.2	3	0	0
Bulgur, uncooked.	1 cup	170	600	19	3	1.2	129	49	9.5	7	0	0
Cake, angel food, 1/12 of cake	1	53	125	3	T	T	29	44	0.2	269	0	0
Cupcake, 2-1/2 in. diam., with chocolate icing	1	35	120	2	4	1.8	20	21	0.7	92	50	T
Plain sheet cake with white, uncooked frosting, 1/9 of cake	1	121	445	4	14	4.6	77	61	1.2	275	240	T

FOOD	Measure	Grams	Food Energy (calories)	Protein (grams)	Fat (grams)	Saturated fats (grams)	Carbohydrate (grams)	Calcium (milligrams)	Iron (milligrams)	Sodium (milligrams)	Vitamin A (I.U.)	Ascorbic Acid (milligrams)
Fruitcake, dark, 1/32 of loaf	1	43	165	2	7	1.5	25	41	1.2	67	50	16
Cake, pound, 1/17 of loaf	1	29	110	2	5	3.0	15	8	0.5	108	160	0
Cheesecake, 1/12 of 9-in. diam. cake	1	92	280	5	18	9.9	26	52	0.4	204	230	5
Brownies, with nuts, from commercial recipe	1	25	100	1	4	1.6	16	13	0.6	59	70	T
Cookies, chocolate chip, from home recipe	4	40	185	2	11	3.9	26	13	1.0	82	20	0
Crackers, graham, 2-1/2 in. squares	2	14	60	1	1	0.4	11	6	0.4	86	0	0
Crackers, saltines	4	12	50	1	1	0.5	9	3	0.5	165	0	0
Danish pastry, round piece	1	57	220	4	12	3.6	26	60	1.1	218	60	T
Doughnut, cake type	1	50	210	3	12	2.8	24	22	1.0	192	20	T
Macaroni, firm stage (hot)	1 cup	130	190	7	1	0.1	39	14	2.1	1	0	0
Muffin, bran, commercial mix	1	45	140	3	4	1.3	24	27	1.7	385	100	0
Muffin, corn, from home recipe	1	45	145	3	5	1.5	21	66	0.9	169	80	T
Noodles, enriched, cooked	1 cup	160	200	7	2	0.5	37	16	2.6	3	110	0
Pie, apple, 1/6 of pie	1	158	405	3	18	4.6	60	13	1.6	476	50	2
Pie, cherry, 1/6 of pie	1	158	410	4	18	4.7	61	22	1.6	480	700	0
Pie, lemon meringue, 1/6 of pie	1	140	355	5	14	4.3	53	20	1.4	395	240	4
Pie, pecan, 1/6 of pie	1	138	575	7	32	4.7	71	65	4.6	305	220	0
Popcorn, air-popped, plain	1 cup	8	30	1	T	T	6	1	0.2	T	10	0
Pretzels, stick	10	3	10	T	T	T	2	1	0.1	48	0	0
Rolls, enriched, brown & serve	1	28	85	2	2	0.5	14	33	0.8	155	T	T
Rolls, frankfurter & hamburger	1	40	115	3	2	0.5	20	54	1.2	241	T	T
Tortillas, corn	1	30	65	2	1	0.1	13	42	0.6	1	80	0
LEGUMES, NUTS, SEEDS												
Beans, Black	1 cup	171	225	15	1	0.1	41	47	2.9	1	T	0
Beans, Great Northern, cooked	1 cup	180	210	14	1	0.1	38	90	4.9	13	0	0
Peanuts, roasted in oil, salted	1 cup	145	840	39	71	9.9	27	125	2.8	626	0	0
Peanut butter	1 tbsp.	16	95	5	8	1.4	3	5	0.3	75	0	0
Refried beans, canned	1 cup	290	295	18	3	0.4	51	141	5.1	1,228	0	17
Tofu	1 piece	120	85	9	5	0.7	3	108	2.3	8	0	0
Sunflower seeds, hulled	1 oz.	28	160	6	14	1.5	5	33	1.9	1	10	T
MIXED FOODS												
Chop suey with beef and pork, home recipe	1 cup	250	300	26	17	4.3	13	60	4.8	1,053	600	33
Enchilada	1	230	235	20	16	7.7	24	97	3.3	1,332	2,720	T
Pizza, cheese, 1/8 of 15-in.-diam. pizza	1	120	290	15	9	4.1	39	220	1.6	699	750	2
Spaghetti with meatballs & tomato sauce	1 cup	248	330	19	12	3.9	39	124	3.7	1,009	1,590	22
SUGARS & SWEETS												
Candy, caramels	1 oz.	28	115	1	3	2.2	22	42	0.4	64	T	T
Candy, milk chocolate	1 oz.	28	145	2	9	5.4	16	50	0.4	23	30	T
Fudge, chocolate	1 oz.	28	115	1	3	2.1	21	22	0.3	54	T	T
Gelatin dessert, from prepared powder	1/2 cup	120	70	2	0	0.0	17	2	T	55	0	0
Candy, hard	1 oz.	28	110	0	0	0.0	28	T	0.1	7	0	0
Honey	1 tbsp.	21	65	T	0	0.0	17	1	0.1	1	0	T
Jams & preserves	1 tbsp.	20	55	T	T	0.0	14	4	0.2	2	T	T
Popsicle, 3 fl. oz.	1	95	70	0	0	0.0	18	0	T	11	0	0
Sugar, white, granulated	1 tbsp.	12	45	0	0	0.0	12	T	T	T	0	0
VEGETABLES												
Asparagus, spears, cooked from raw	4 spears	60	15	2	T	T	3	14	0.4	2	500	16
Beans, green, from frozen, cuts	1 cup	135	35	2	T	T	8	61	1.1	18	710	11
Broccoli, raw from raw	1 spear	180	50	5	1	0.1	10	82	2.1	20	2,540	113
Cabbage, raw, coarsely shredded or sliced	1 cup	70	15	1	T	T	4	33	0.4	13	90	33
Carrots, raw, 7-1/2 by 1-1/8 in.	1	72	30	1	T	T	7	19	0.4	25	20,250	7
Cauliflower, cooked, drained, from raw	1 cup	125	30	2	T	T	6	34	0.5	8	20	69
Celery, raw	1 stalk	40	5	T	T	T	1	14	0.2	35	50	3
Collards, cooked from raw	1 cup	190	60	2	T	0.1	5	148	0.8	36	4,220	19
Corn, sweet, yellow, cooked from raw	1 ear	77	85	3	1	0.2	19	2	0.5	13	170	5
Eggplant, cooked, steamed	1 cup	96	25	1	T	T	6	6	0.3	3	60	1
Lettuce, iceberg, chopped	1 cup	55	5	1	T	T	1	10	0.3	5	180	2
Lettuce, looseleaf (such as romaine)	1 cup	56	10	1	T	T	2	38	0.8	5	1,060	10
Mushrooms, raw	1 cup	70	20	1	T	T	3	4	0.9	3	0	2
Onions, raw, chopped	1 cup	160	55	2	T	0.1	12	40	0.6	3	0	13
Peas, green, frozen, cooked	1 cup	160	125	8	T	0.1	23	38	2.5	139	1,070	16
Potatoes, baked, peeled	1	156	145	3	T	T	34	8	0.5	8	0	20
Potatoes, frozen, French fried (oven-heated)	10	50	110	2	4	2.1	17	5	0.7	16	0	5
Potatoes, mashed, milk added	1 cup	210	160	4	1	0.7	37	55	0.6	636	40	14
Potato chips	10	20	105	1	7	1.8	10	5	0.2	94	0	8
Potato salad	1 cup	250	360	7	21	3.6	28	48	1.6	1,323	520	25
Spinach, drained, cooked from raw	1 cup	180	40	5	T	0.1	7	245	6.4	126	14,740	18
Sweet potatoes, baked in skin, peeled	1	114	115	2	T	T	28	32	0.5	11	24,880	28
Vegetable juice cocktail, canned	1 cup	242	45	2	T	T	11	27	1.0	883	2,830	67
MISCELLANEOUS												
Beer, regular	12 fl. oz.	360	150	1	0	0.0	13	14	0.1	18	0	0
Gin, rum, vodka, whisky, 86 proof	1½ fl. oz.	42	105	0	0	0.0	T	T	T	T	0	0
Wine, table, white	3½ fl. oz.	102	80	T	0	0.0	3	9	0.3	5	(1)	0
Cola-type beverage	12 fl. oz.	369	160	0	0	0.0	41	11	0.2	18	0	0
Ginger ale	12 fl. oz	366	125	0	0	0.0	32	11	0.1	29	0	0
Coffee, brewed	6 fl. oz.	180	T	T	T	T	T	4	T	2	0	0
Tea, brewed	8 fl. oz.	240	T	T	T	T	T	0	T	7	0	0
Catsup	1 tbsp.	15	15	T	T	T	4	3	0.1	156	210	2
Mustard, prepared, yellow	1 tsp.	5	5	T	T	T	T	4	0.1	63	0	T
Olives, canned, green	4 medium	13	15	T	2	0.2	T	8	0.2	312	40	0
Pickles, dill, whole	1	65	5	T	T	T	1	17	0.7	928	70	4
Relish, finely chopped, sweet	1 tbsp.	15	20	T	T	T	5	3	0.1	107	20	1
Soup, tomato, prepared with milk	1 cup	248	160	6	6	2.9	22	159	1.8	932	850	68
Soup, chicken noodle, prepared with water	1 cup	241	75	4	2	0.7	9	17	0.8	1,106	710	T
Soup, green pea, prepared with water	1 cup	250	165	9	3	1.4	27	28	2.0	988	200	2
Soup, vegetarian, prepared with water	1 cup	241	70	2	2	0.3	12	22	1.1	822	3,010	1

T — Indicates trace. (1) Value not determined. **NOTE:** Values shown here for these foods may be from several different manufacturers and, therefore, may differ somewhat from the values provided by one source.

U.S. Per Capita Consumption of Selected Foods, 1910-2000

Source: Economic Research Service, U.S. Dept. of Agriculture

	Whole milk[1]	Low-fat & skim milk[1]	Butter[2]	Margarine[2]	Red meat[2]	Poultry[2]	Fish & shellfish[2]
1910	25.18	7.05	18.4	1.6	96.0	11.8	11.2
1940	29.24	4.72	17.0	2.4	92.4	12.3	11.0
1970	25.48	5.78	5.4	10.8	131.9	33.8	11.7
2000	8.05	14.42	4.5	8.3	113.7	66.9	15.2

(1) Gallons. (2) Pounds.

Dietary Requirements

The Food and Nutrition Board of the National Academy of Sciences' Institute of Medicine, in reports published from 1997 to 2001, set **Dietary Reference Intakes (DRIs)** for vitamins and elements (often called minerals). The DRIs, based on recent scientific research, establish daily consumption values that aim to optimize health at all stages of life, not just to guard against nutritional deficiencies.

The DRIs include 4 categories of values. The **Recommended Dietary Allowance (RDA)** gives an intake that meets the nutrient requirements of almost all (97-98%) healthy individuals in a specified group. The **Estimated Average Requirement (EAR)** is the intake that meets the estimated nutrient need of half the individuals in a specified group, while the **Adequate Intake (AI)** is the value given when adequate scientific evidence is not available to calculate an EAR. For healthy breastfed infants, the AI is the mean intake; for other life stage groups the AI is thought to cover the needs of all individuals in the group, but lack of data or uncertainty in the data prevents the percentage of individuals covered from being specified with confidence. The **Tolerable Upper Intake Level (UL)** designates the maximum intake that is unlikely to pose risks of adverse health effects in almost all healthy individuals in a specified group; taking the nutrient above that level could be bad for one's health. RDAs and AIs may both be used as goals for individual intake.

The following two tables give the RDA or, where not available, the AI, followed by an asterisk(*).

Recommended Levels for Vitamins

Source: Food and Nutrition Board, National Academy of Sciences—Institute of Medicine, 2001

in milligrams per day (mg/d) or in micrograms per day (μg/d); asterisks denote levels defined as "adequate intake" (AI).

	Vitamin A (μg/d)[1]	Vitamin C (mg/d)	Vitamin D (μg/d)[2]	Vitamin E (mg/d)	Vitamin K (μg/d)	Thiamin (mg/d)	Riboflavin (mg/d)	Niacin (mg/d)[3]	Vitamin B6 (mg/d)	Folate (μg/d)[4]	Vitamin B12 (μg/d)	Pantothenic Acid (mg/d)	Biotin (μg/d)	Choline (mg/d)[5]
Infants														
0-6 mos	400*	40*	5*	4*	2.0*	0.2*	0.3*	2*	0.1*	65*	0.4*	1.7*	5*	125*
7-12 mos	500*	50*	5*	5*	2.5*	0.3*	0.4*	4*	0.3*	80*	0.5*	1.8*	6*	150*
Children														
1-3 yrs	300	15	5*	6	30*	0.5	0.5	6	0.5	150	0.9	2*	8*	200*
4-8 yrs	400	25	5*	7	55*	0.6	0.6	8	0.6	200	1.2	3*	12*	250*
Males														
9-13 yrs	600	45	5*	11	60*	0.9	0.9	12	1.0	300	1.8	4*	20*	375*
14-18 yrs	900	75	5*	15	75*	1.2	1.3	16	1.3	400	2.4	5*	25*	550*
19-30 yrs	900	90	5*	15	120*	1.2	1.3	16	1.3	400	2.4	5*	30*	550*
31-50 yrs	900	90	5*	15	120*	1.2	1.3	16	1.3	400	2.4	5*	30*	550*
51-70 yrs	900	90	10*	15	120*	1.2	1.3	16	1.7	400	2.4[6]	5*	30*	550*
over 70 yrs	900	90	15*	15	120*	1.2	1.3	16	1.7	400	2.4[6]	5*	30*	550*
Females														
9-13 yrs	600	45	5*	11	60*	0.9	0.9	12	1.0	300	1.8	4*	20*	375*
14-18 yrs	700	65	5*	15	75*	1.0	1.0	14	1.2	400[7]	2.4	5*	25*	400*
19-30 yrs	700	75	5*	15	90*	1.1	1.1	14	1.3	400[7]	2.4	5*	30*	425*
31-50 yrs	700	75	5*	15	90*	1.1	1.1	14	1.3	400[7]	2.4	5*	30*	425*
51-70 yrs	700	75	10*	15	90*	1.1	1.1	14	1.5	400	2.4[6]	5*	30*	425*
over 70 yrs	700	75	15*	15	90*	1.1	1.1	14	1.5	400	2.4[6]	5*	30*	425*
Pregnancy														
18 yrs. or less	750	80	5*	15	75*	1.4	1.4	18	1.9	600[8]	2.6	6*	30*	450*
19-30 yrs	770	85	5*	15	90*	1.4	1.4	18	1.9	600[8]	2.6	6*	30*	450*
31-50 yrs	770	85	5*	15	90*	1.4	1.4	18	1.9	600[8]	2.6	6*	30*	450*
Lactation														
18 yrs. or less	1,200	115	5*	19	75*	1.4	1.6	17	2.0	500	2.8	7*	35*	550*
19-30 yrs	1,300	120	5*	19	90*	1.4	1.6	17	2.0	500	2.8	7*	35*	550*
31-50 yrs	1,300	120	5*	19	90*	1.4	1.6	17	2.0	500	2.8	7*	35*	550*

NOTE: For healthy breastfed infants, the AI is the mean intake. The AI for other life stage and gender groups is believed to cover needs of all individuals in the group, but lack of data or uncertainty in the data prevent being able to specify with confidence the percentage of individuals covered by this intake. (1) As retinol activity equivalents. (2) In the absence of adequate exposure to sunlight. (3) As niacin equivalents (NE). 1 mg of niacin = 60 mg of tryptophan; 0-6 months = preformed niacin (not NE). (4) As dietary folate equivalents (DFE). 1 DFE = 1 μg food folate = 0.6 μg of folic acid from fortified food or as a supplement consumed with food = 0.5 μg of a supplement taken on an empty stomach. (5) Although AIs have been set for choline, there are few data to assess whether a dietary supply of choline is needed at all stages of the life cycle, and it may be that the choline requirement can be met by endogenous synthesis at some of these stages. (6) Because 10-30% of older people may malabsorb food-bound B_{12}, it is advisable for those older than 50 years to meet their RDA mainly by consuming foods fortified with B_{12} or a supplement containing B_{12}. (7) In view of evidence linking folate intake with neural tube defects in the fetus, it is recommended that all women capable of becoming pregnant consume 400 μg from supplements or fortified foods in addition to intake of food folate from a varied diet. (8) It is assumed that women will continue consuming 400 μg from supplements or fortified food until their pregnancy is confirmed and they enter prenatal care, which ordinarily occurs after the end of the periconceptional period—the critical time for formation of the neural tube.

Recommended Levels for Elements (Minerals)

Source: Food and Nutrition Board, National Academy of Sciences—Institute of Medicine, 2001

in milligrams per day (mg/d) or in micrograms per day (µg/d); asterisks denote levels defined as "adequate intake" (AI).

	Calcium (mg/d)	Chromium (µg/d)	Copper (µg/d)	Fluoride (mg/d)	Iodine (µg/d)	Iron (mg/d)	Magnesium (mg/d)	Manganese (mg/d)	Molybdenum (µg/d)	Phosphorus (mg/d)	Selenium (µg/d)	Zinc (mg/d)
Infants												
0-6 mos	210*	0.2*	200*	0.01*	110*	0.27*	30*	0.003*	2*	100*	15*	2*
7-12 mos	270*	5.5*	220*	0.5*	130*	11	75*	0.6*	3*	275*	20*	3
Children												
1-3 yrs	500*	11*	340	0.7*	90	7	80	1.2*	17	460	20	3
4-8 yrs	800*	15*	440	1*	90	10	130	1.5*	22	500	30	5
Males												
9-13 yrs	1,300*	25*	700	2*	120	8	240	1.9*	34	1,250	40	8
14-18 yrs	1,300*	35*	890	3*	150	11	410	2.2*	43	1,250	55	11
19-30 yrs	1,000*	35*	900	4*	150	8	400	2.3*	45	700	55	11
31-50 yrs	1,000*	35*	900	4*	150	8	420	2.3*	45	700	55	11
51-70 yrs	1,200*	30*	900	4*	150	8	420	2.3*	45	700	55	11
over 70 yrs	1,200*	30*	900	4*	150	8	420	2.3*	45	700	55	11
Females												
9-13 yrs	1,300*	21*	700	2*	120	8	240	1.6*	34	1,250	40	8
14-18 yrs	1,300*	24*	890	3*	150	15	360	1.6*	43	1,250	55	9
19-30 yrs	1,000*	25*	900	3*	150	18	310	1.8*	45	700	55	8
31-50 yrs	1,000*	25*	900	3*	150	18	320	1.8*	45	700	55	8
51-70 yrs	1,200*	20*	900	3*	150	8	320	1.8*	45	700	55	8
over 70 yrs	1,200*	20*	900	3*	150	8	320	1.8*	45	700	55	8
Pregnancy												
18 yrs or less	1,300*	29*	1,000	3*	220	27	400	2.0*	50	1,250	60	12
19-30 yrs	1,000*	30*	1,000	3*	220	27	350	2.0*	50	700	60	11
31-50 yrs	1,000*	30*	1,000	3*	220	27	360	2.0*	50	700	60	11
Lactation												
18 yrs or less	1,300*	44*	1,300	3*	290	10	360	2.6*	50	1,250	70	13
19-30 yrs	1,000*	45*	1,300	3*	290	9	310	2.6*	50	700	70	12
31-50 yrs	1,000*	45*	1,300	3*	290	9	320	2.6*	50	700	70	12

Weight Guidelines for Adults

Source: Clinical Guidelines on the Identification, Evaluation, and Treatment of Overweight and Obesity in Adults, National Heart, Lung, and Blood Institute, National Institutes of Health, 1998; Health, United States, 2003

Guidelines on identification, evaluation, and treatment of overweight and obesity in adults were released in June 1998 by the National Heart, Lung, and Blood Institute (NHLBI), in cooperation with the National Institute of Diabetes and Digestive and Kidney Diseases. The guidelines, based on research into risk factors in heart disease, stroke, and other conditions, define degrees of overweight and obesity in terms of **body mass index (BMI)**, which is based on weight and height and is strongly correlated with total body fat content. A BMI of 25-29 is said to indicate **overweight**; a BMI of 30 or above is said to indicate **obesity**. Weight reduction is advised for persons with a BMI of 25 or higher. (Previous guidelines have been less stringent.) Factors such as a large waist circumference, high blood pressure or cholesterol, and a family history of obesity-related disease may increase risk.

Despite the advantages of controlling one's weight, the percentage of Americans who are overweight or obese has risen greatly in recent decades, according to figures in Health, United States, 2003, the latest survey of the country's health in a series published annually by the National Center for Health Statistics. In 1999-2000, only 33.6% of adult Americans (20-74 years old) had a healthy weight (BMI of 18.5 to less than 25), while 64.5% were overweight or obese, and 30.9%, or nearly a third, were obese. In 1976-80, by contrast, 49.6% of adults had a healthy weight, and 47.4% were overweight or obese, with 15.1%—half the 1999-2000 figure—exhibiting obesity. (A small percentage of Americans have a BMI of under 18.5.)

Children and adolescents showed a similar pattern. In 1999-2000, 15.3% of children aged 6-11 were overweight or obese, compared with 6.5% in 1976-80. For adolescents (12-19 years in age), the numbers were 15.5% in 1999-2000, compared with 5.0% in the earlier period.

Health, United States, 2003, noted that the prevalence of diagnosed diabetes had increased markedly in recent years—to 6.5% of the adult population in 2002, up from 5.3% in 1997. The rise was attributed, in part, to the increase in overweight and obesity.

The table given here shows the BMI for certain heights and weights. For weight reduction tips, write to the NHLBI Information Center, PO Box 30105, Bethesda, MD 20824-0105. See also the NHLBI website: www.nhlbi.nih.gov/index.htm

Weight (lbs)

Height	HEALTHY						OVERWEIGHT					OBESE								
4'10"	91	96	100	105	110	115	119	124	129	134	138	143	148	153	158	162	167	172	177	181
4'11"	94	99	104	109	114	119	124	128	133	138	143	148	153	158	163	168	173	178	183	188
5'0"	97	102	107	112	118	123	128	133	138	143	148	153	158	163	168	174	179	184	189	194
5'1"	100	106	111	116	122	127	132	137	143	148	153	158	164	169	174	180	185	190	195	201
5'2"	104	109	115	120	126	131	136	142	147	153	158	164	169	175	180	186	191	196	202	207
5'3"	107	113	118	124	130	135	141	146	152	158	163	169	175	180	186	191	197	203	208	214
5'4"	110	116	122	128	134	140	145	151	157	163	169	174	180	186	192	197	204	209	215	221
5'5"	114	120	126	132	138	144	150	156	162	168	174	180	186	192	198	204	210	216	222	228
5'6"	118	124	130	136	142	148	155	161	167	173	179	186	192	198	204	210	216	223	229	235
5'7"	121	127	134	140	146	153	159	166	172	178	185	191	198	204	211	217	223	230	236	242
5'8"	125	131	138	144	151	158	164	171	177	184	190	197	203	210	216	223	230	236	243	249
5'9"	128	135	142	149	155	162	169	176	182	189	195	203	209	216	222	229	236	243	250	257
5'10"	132	139	146	153	160	167	174	181	188	195	202	209	216	222	229	236	243	250	257	264
5'11"	136	143	150	157	165	172	179	186	193	200	208	215	222	229	236	243	250	257	265	272
6'0"	140	147	154	162	169	177	184	191	199	206	213	221	228	235	242	250	258	265	272	279
6'1"	144	151	159	166	174	182	189	197	204	212	219	227	235	242	250	257	265	272	280	288
6'2"	148	155	163	171	179	186	194	202	210	218	225	233	241	249	256	264	272	280	287	295
6'3"	152	160	168	176	184	192	200	208	216	224	232	240	248	256	264	272	279	287	295	303
6'4"	156	164	172	180	189	197	205	213	221	230	238	246	254	263	271	279	287	295	304	312
BMI[1]	19	20	21	22	23	24	25	26	27	28	29	30	31	32	33	34	35	36	37	38

(1) The BMI numbers apply to both men and women. Some very muscular people may have a high BMI without health risks.

Where to Get Help

Source: Based on *Health & Medical Year Book.* © by Collier Newfield, Inc.: additional data, World Almanac research

Listed here are some of the major U.S. and Canadian organizations providing information about good health practices generally, or about specific conditions and how to deal with them. (Canadian sources are identified as such.) Where a toll-free number is not available, an address is given when possible.

Some entries conclude with an e-mail address for the organization and/or an address for its Internet site, where you can also obtain useful information. In addition to these selected sites, there is a vast array of medical information on the Internet; however, it is very important to be certain that the source of information is reliable and accurate. Always check with a physician before embarking on any new health-related undertaking.

General Sources

Centers for Disease Control and Prevention Voice Information System
800-311-3435
Recorded information about public health topics, such as AIDS and Lyme disease. Also, you can request to talk with a CDC expert or have information faxed to you.
Website: www.cdc.gov

National Health Information Center
800-336-4797; in Maryland, 301-565-4167
Phone numbers for more than 1,000 health-related organizations in the United States. Printed materials offered.
E-mail: nhicinfo@health.org
Website: www.health.gov/NHIC

National Institutes of Health
301-496-4000
Free information, including the latest research findings, on many diseases.
E-mail: NIHinfo@OD.NIH.GOV
Website: www.nih.gov

Tel-Med
Check the phone book for local listings or call Tel-Med at 909-478-0330.
Recorded information on over 600 health topics. Online medical reference library in English and Spanish. Sponsored by local medical societies, health organizations, or hospitals.
E-mail: telmed@ix.netcom.com
Website: www.tel-med.com

Aging

National Association of Area Agencies on Aging's Eldercare Locator Line
800-677-1116
Information and assistance on a wide range of services and programs including adult day-care and respite services, consumer fraud, hospital and nursing home information, legal services, elder abuse/protective services, Medicaid/Medigap information, tax assistance, and transportation.
Hours 9 AM-8 PM EST M-F.
Website: www.eldercare.gov

National Institute on Aging
800-222-2225
Information and publications about disabling conditions, support groups, and community resources.
Hours: M-F 8:30-5:00 EST
E-mail: karpf@nia.nih.gov
Website: www.nia.nih.gov

AIDS

AIDSinfo
800-HIV-0440
Information on federally and privately sponsored clinical trials for patients with AIDS or HIV; treatment information ofr people with aids, their families and health care providers
E-mail: ContactUs@aidsinfo.nih.gov
Website: www.aidsinfo.nih.gov

Canadian AIDS Society
613-230-3580
Written materials and referrals.
Website: www.cdnaids.ca
E-mail: CASinfo@cdnaids.ca

Centers for Disease Control and Prevention National AIDS/HIV Hotline
800-342-AIDS 24 hours; in Spanish, 800-344-SIDA, everyday, 8 AM-2 AM; for the hearing impaired, 800-AIDS-TTY, M-F, 10 AM-10 PM
Information on the prevention and spread of AIDS, along with referrals.
E-mail: hivmail@cdc.gov
Website: www.cdc.gov/hiv/hivinfo/nah.htm

Alcoholism and Drug Abuse

Wellplace
800-821-4357, 24 hours
Referrals to local facilities
Website: www.wellplace.com

Alcoholics Anonymous
212-870-3400
Worldwide support groups for alcoholics. Check phone book for local chapters.
Websites: www.alcoholics-anonymous.org or www.AA.org

American Council on Alcoholism
800-527-5344
Treatment referrals and counseling for recovering alcoholics.
E-mail: aca2@earthlink.net
Website: www.aca-usa.org

National Clearinghouse for Alcohol and Drug Information
800-729-6686
Provides written materials on alcohol and drug-related subjects.
E-mail: info@health.org
Website: www.health.org

National Council on Alcoholism and Drug Dependence Hopeline
800-622-2255
Advisory and referral service.
Website: www.ncadd.org
E-mail: national@ncadd.org

DrugHelp
800-DRUGHELP
Answers questions on substance abuse and provides referrals to treatment centers. Operates 24 hours.
Website: www.drughelp.org

Alzheimer's Disease

Alzheimer's Association
800-272-3900
Gives referrals to local chapters and support groups; offers information on publications available from the association.
E-mail: info@alz.org
Website: www.alz.org

Alzheimer's Society of Canada
416-488-8772
Gives phone numbers for local support chapters. Publishes support materials.
E-mail: info@alzheimer.ca
Website: www.alzheimer.ca

Amyotrophic Lateral Sclerosis

ALS Association
818-880-9007
Information about ALS (Lou Gehrig's Disease) and referrals to ALS specialists, local chapters and support groups.
Website: www.alsa.org

Arthritis

Arthritis Foundation
800-283-7800
Information, publications, and referrals to local groups.
Website: www.arthritis.org

Arthritis Society (Canada)
393 University Ave., Suite 1700
Toronto, ON M5G 1E6
416-979-7228; in Ontario only, 800-321-1433
Phone numbers for local chapters.
E-mail: info@arthritis.ca
Website: www.arthritis.ca

National Arthritis and Musculoskeletal and Skin Diseases Information Clearinghouse
877-226-4267
Subject searches and resource referrals.
E-mail: niamsinfo@mail.nih.gov
Website: www.niams.nih.gov

Asthma and Allergies
See also **Lung Diseases**

Asthma and Allergy Foundation of America
800-7-ASTHMA
Information; education; links to support groups.
E-mail: info@aafa.org
Website: www.aafa.org

American Academy of Allergy, Asthma, and Immunology Referral Line
800-822-ASMA, 24 hours
Patient information and referrals for asthma and allergies.
E-mail: info@aaaai.org
Website: www.aaaai.org

Autism

Autism Society of America
301-657-0881 or 800-3AUTISM
Information about autism, referral to local chapters.
E-mail: info@autism-society.org
Website: www.autism-society.org

Blindness and Eye Care

Canadian National Institute for the Blind
416-486-2500 or contact your local chapter.
National office offers training and library with braille books and audiotapes. Local chapters provide core services: orientation in mobility, sight enhancement, counseling, referrals, career aid, technology services.
Website: www.cnib.ca

Foundation Fighting Blindness
888-394-3937; for the hearing impaired, TDD 800-683-5555
Answers questions about retinal degenerative diseases; has written materials.
E-mail: info@blindness.org
Website: www.blindness.org

Library of Congress National Library Service for the Blind and Physically Handicapped
800-424-8567; in Washington, DC, 202-707-5100; for the hearing impaired, TDD 202-707-0744
Information on libraries that offer talking books and books in braille.
E-mail: nls@loc.gov
Website: lcweb.loc.gov/nls

National Association for Parents of the Visually Impaired
800-562-6265
Support and information for parents of individuals who are visually impaired.
E-mail: napci@perkins.org
Website: www.napvi.org

Blood Disorders

Cooley's Anemia Foundation
800-522-7222
Information on patient care and support groups; makes referrals to local chapters.
E-mail: info@cooleysanemia.org
Website: www.thalassemia.org

Sickle Cell Disease Association of America
800-421-8453; in California, 310-216-6363
Genetic counseling and information packet.
Website: www.sicklecelldisease.org
E-mail: scdaa@sicklecelldisease.org

Burns

Phoenix Society
800-888-2876
Counseling for burn survivors and information on self-help services for burn survivors and their families.
E-mail: info@phoenix-society.org
Website: www.phoenix-society.org

Cancer

American Cancer Society
800-ACS-2345
Publications and information about cancer and coping with cancer; makes referrals to local chapters for support services.
E-mail: ACS@aol.com
Website: www.cancer.org

Canadian Cancer Information Service
888-939-3333 or 416-961-7223
Information on prevention, treatment, drugs, clinical trails, local services.
E-mail: info@cis.cancer.ca
Website: www.cancer.ca

National Cancer Institute's Cancer Information Service
800-4-CANCER
Information about clinical trials, treatments, symptoms, prevention, referrals to support groups, and screening. Includes chat online info inquiries.
Website: cis.nci.nih.gov

Y-Me Breast Cancer Support Program
800-221-2141, 24 hours; 800-986-9505 Spanish, 24-hours
Information and literature on breast cancer, counseling, and referrals.
Website: www.y-me.org

Cerebral Palsy

Ontario Federation for Cerebral Palsy
Ontario only: 877-244-9686; 416-244-9686
Canada does not have a national cerebral palsy organization, but the provincial organizations offer information on housing, services, and coping with life, and each one will provide contact numbers for the others.
E-mail: info@ofcp.on.ca
Website: www.ofcp.on.ca

United Cerebral Palsy Associations
877-835-7335, (TTY) 202-973-7197; in Washington, DC, 202-776-0406
Written materials.
Website: www.ucpa.org

Child Abuse
See *Domestic Violence*

Children

American Academy of Pediatrics
847-434-4000
Child-care publications and materials; referrals to pediatricians.
E-mail: kidsdocs@aap.org
Website: www.aap.org

National Center for Missing and Exploited Children
800-843-5678; for the hearing impaired, 800-826-7653. Operates 24 hours.
Hotline for reporting missing children and sightings of missing children.
Website: www.missingkids.org

Chronic Fatiguev Syndrome

CFIDS Association of America
800-442-3437
Literature and a list of support groups.
E-mail: info@cfids.org
Website: www.cfids.org

Crisis

National Runaway Switchboard
800-621-4000
Crisis intervention and referrals for runaways. Runaways can leave messages for parents, and vice versa. Operates 24 hours.
E-mail: info@nrscrisisline.org
Website: www.nrscrisisline.org

Cystic Fibrosis

Canadian Cystic Fibrosis Foundation
416-485-9149; 800-378-2233 in Canada only.
Information and brochures; makes referrals to local chapters.
E-mail: info@cysticfibrosis.ca
Website: www.cysticfibrosis.ca

Cystic Fibrosis Foundation
800-FIGHT-CF
Answers questions and offers literature and referrals to local clinics.
E-mail: info@cff.org
Website: www.cff.org

Diabetes

American Diabetes Association
800-342-2383
Information about diabetes, nutrition, exercise, and treatment; offers referrals.
E-mail: asleADA@diabetes.org
Website: www.diabetes.org

Canadian Diabetes Association
416-363-3373; 800-226-8464 in Canada only.
Information about diabetes and its management.
E-mail: info@diabetes.ca
Website: www.diabetes.ca

Juvenile Diabetes Foundation Hotline
800-533-2873
Answers questions, provides literature (some in Spanish). Offers referrals to local chapters, physicians, and clinics.
E-mail: info@jdf.org
Website: www.jdf.org

Digestive Diseases

Crohn's and Colitis Foundation of America
800-932-2423
Educational materials; offers referrals to local chapters, which can provide referrals to support groups and physicians.
E-mail: info@ccfa.org
Website: www.ccfa.org

Crohn's and Colitis Foundation of Canada
416-920-5035; in Canada only, 800-387-1479
Will send out educational materials upon request.
E-mail: ccfc@ccfc.ca
Website: www.ccfc.ca

Domestic Violence

Childhelp's USA National Child Abuse Hotline
800-4-A-CHILD
Crisis intervention, professional counseling, referrals to local groups and shelters for runaways, and literature. Operates 24 hours.
Website: www.childhelpusa.org

National Council on Child Abuse and Family Violence
800-799-7233, (TTY) 800-787-3244
Information and referrals.
E-mail: info@NCCAFV.org
Website: www.nccafv.org

Down Syndrome

National Down Syndrome Congress
800-232-6372; in Georgia, 770-604-9500
Answers questions on all aspects of Down syndrome. Provides referrals.
E-mail: info@ndsccenter.org
Website: www.ndsccenter.org

National Down Syndrome Society
800-221-4602; 212-460-9330 (NYC)
E-mail: info@ndss.org
Website: www.ndss.org

Drug Abuse
See *Alcoholism and Drug Abuse*

Dyslexia

International Dyslexia Association
800-ABCD-123; in Maryland, 410-296-0232
Information on testing, tutoring, and computers used to aid people with dyslexia and related disorders.
E-mail: info@interdys.org
Website: www.interdys.org

Eating Disorders

National Association of Anorexia Nervosa and Associated Disorders
847-831-3438
Written materials, referrals to health professionals treating eating disorders, telephone counseling, offers self-help groups and information on how to set up a self-help group.
E-mail: anad20@aol.com
Website: www.anad.org

Endometriosis

Endometriosis Association
800-992-ENDO; An answering machine for callers to request information.
E-mail: endo@endometriosisassn.org
Website: www.endometriosisassn.org

Epilepsy

Epilepsy and Seizure Disorder Service at the Epilepsy Foundation of America
800-332-1000, Mon. through Thurs.
Information and referrals to local chapters.
Website: www.efa.org

Food Safety and Nutrition

Meat and Poultry Hotline of the U.S. Department of Agriculture's Food, Safety, and Inspection Service
800-535-4555
Information on prevention of food-borne illness and the proper handling, preparation, storage, labeling, and cooking of meat, poultry, and eggs.
E-mail: MPHotline.fsis@usda.gov
Website: www.foodsafety.gov

FDA Center for Food Safety and Applied Nutrition Outreach & Information Center
800-SAFE-FOOD
Information on how to buy and use food products and on their proper handling and storage, women's health, and cosmetics & colors. Callers may speak to food specialists, Mon. through Fri., 10 am to 4 PM (EST).
Website: www.cfsan.fda.gov

Headaches

National Headache Foundation
888-NHF-5552
Literature on headaches and treatment.
E-mail: info@headaches.org
Website: www.headaches.org

Heart Disease and Stroke

American Heart Association
800-242-8721
Information, publications, and referrals to organizations.
Website: www.americanheart.org

National Institute of Neurological Disorders and Stroke
800-352-9424
Literature and information.
Website: www.ninds.nih.gov

National Stroke Association
800-787-6537
Information on support networks for stroke victims and their families; referrals to local support groups.
Website: www.stroke.org

Hospices

Children's Hospice International
800-242-4453; in Virginia, 703-684-0330
Information, referrals to children's hospices.
E-mail: info@chionline.org
Website: www.chionline.org

Hospice Education Institute Hospicelink
800-331-1620; in Maine, 207-255-8800
Information, referrals to local programs.
E-mail: hospiceall@aol.com
Website: www.hospiceworld.org

Huntington's Disease

Huntington's Disease Society of America
800-345-4372; in New York, 212-242-1968
Information and referrals to physicians and support groups.
E-mail: hdsainfo@hdsa.org
Website: www.hdsa.org

Impotence

Impotence Information Center
800-843-4315
Information on treatment of impotence, incontinence, and prostate problems.

Kidney Diseases

Kidney Foundation of Canada
514-369-4806; in Canada only, 800-361-7494
Educational materials and general information.
Website: www.kidney.ca

National Kidney and Urologic Diseases Information Clearinghouse
301-654-4415, 800-981-5390
Information, referrals to organizations.
Website: www.niddk.nih.gov

National Kidney Foundation
800-622-9010, 212-889-2210
Information and referrals.
E-mail: info@kidney.org
Website: www.kidney.org

Lead Exposure

National Lead Information Center
800-424-LEAD
Recommendations (in English and Spanish) for reducing a child's exposure to lead. Referrals to state and local agencies.
Website: www.epa.gov/lead

Liver Diseases

American Liver Foundation
800-465-7837; 800-443-7872
Information on hepatitis, liver disease, and gallbladder disease.
E-mail: info@liverfoundation.org
Website: www.liverfoundation.org

Lung Diseases

See also *Asthma and Allergies*
American Lung Association
Check the phone book for local listings or call the national office at 800-LUNG-USA for automatic connection to the office nearest you. Answers questions about asthma and lung diseases; publications and referrals.
E-mail: info@lungusa.org
Website: www.lungusa.org
Lung Line Information Service at the National Jewish Medical and Research Center
800-222-LUNG; outside the U.S.: 303-388-4461
Answers questions on asthma, emphysema, allergies, smoking, and other respiratory and immune system disorders.
E-mail: lungline@njc.org
Website: www.njc.org

Lupus

Lupus Foundation of America
800-558-0121; 202-349-1155
Sends information to those who leave name and address on answering machine.
E-mail: info@lupus.org
Website: www.lupus.org

Lyme Disease

Lyme Disease Foundation
800-525-5000, 24 hours
Written information; doctor referrals.
E-mail: lymefind@aol.com
Website: www.lyme.org

Mental Health

Depression and Bipolar Support Alliance
800-826-3632
Support for patients and families, provides publications, and makes referrals to affiliated organizations.
E-mail: questions@dbsalliance.org
Website: www.dbsalliance.org
National Foundation for Depressive Illness
800-239-1265, 24 hours
Recorded message describing the symptoms of depression and offering an address for more information and physician referral.
Website: www.depression.org
National Institute of Mental Health
301-443-4513, toll free 866-615-6464
Information on a range of topics, from children's mental disorders to schizophrenia, depression, eating disorders, and others.
E-mail: nimhinfo@nih.gov
Website: www.nimh.nih.gov
National Mental Health Association
800-969-6642
Referrals to mental health groups.
E-mail: infoctr@nmha.org
Website: www.nmha.org

Multiple Sclerosis

Multiple Sclerosis Society of Canada
416-922-6065, 800-268-7582 in Canada only.
Counseling, literature, and referrals to local chapters.
E-mail: info@mssociety.ca
Website: www.mssociety.ca
National Multiple Sclerosis Society
800-344-4867
Information about local chapters.
Website: www.nationalmssociety.org

Muscular Dystrophy

Muscular Dystrophy Association
800-572-1717
Written materials on 40 neuromuscular diseases, including muscular dystrophy. Will give information over the phone about such matters as MDA clinics, support groups, summer camps, and wheelchair purchase assistance.
E-mail: mda@mdausa.org
Website: www.mdausa.org

Nutrition

See *Food Safety and Nutrition*

Organ Donation

Living Bank
800-528-2971, 24 hours
A registry and referral service for people wanting to commit organs to transplantation or research.
E-mail: info@livingbank.org
Website: www.livingbank.org

Osteoporosis

National Osteoporosis Foundation
800-223-9994, in Washington, DC, 202-223-2226
Information packet available on request.
Website: www.nof.org

Pain

National Chronic Pain Outreach Association
540-862-9437
Information packet available on request.
Website: www.chronicpain.org

Parkinson's Disease

National Parkinson Foundation
800-327-4545; in Miami, 305-547-6666
Answers questions, makes physician referrals, and provides written information in English and Spanish.
E-mail: mailbox@parkinson.org
Website: www.parkinson.org
Parkinson Society Canada
800-565-3000, Canada only; 416-227-9700
Information; referrals to support groups.
E-mail: General.info@parkinson.ca
Website: www.parkinson.ca

Plastic Survgery

Plastic Surgery Information Service
888-475-2784
Referrals to board-certified plastic surgeons in the U.S. and Canada; general information.
Website: www.plasticsurgery.org

Polio

Post-Polio Health International
314-534-0475
Information on coping with the late effects of polio; referrals to other organizations.
E-mail: info@post-polio.org
Website: www.post-polio.org

Prostate Problems

American Foundation for Urologic Disease
800-242-2383
Information and publications.
E-mail: admin@afud.org
Website: www.afud.org

Rare Disorders

National Organization for Rare Disorders
800-999-6673
Information on diseases and networking programs; referrals to organizations for specific disorders.
E-mail: orphan@rarediseases.org
Website: www.rarediseases.org

Rehabilitation

National Rehabilitation Information Center
800-34-NARIC; in Maryland, 301-459-5900; TTY 301-459-5984
Research referrals and information on rehabilitation issues.
E-mail: naricinfo@heitechservices.com
Website: www.naric.com

Scleroderma

United Scleroderma Foundation
800-722-4673
Referrals to local support groups and treatment centers, as well as information on scleroderma and related skin disorders.
E-mail: sfinfo@scleroderma.org
Website: www.scleroderma.org

Sexually Transmitted Diseases

See also *AIDS*
National STD Hotline
800-227-8922
Information; confidential referrals.
E-mail: std-hivnet@ashastd.org
Website: www.ashastd.org

Sjogren's Syndrome

Sjogren's Syndrome Foundation
800-475-6473;
Provides an answering machine for callers to request treatment literature.
Website: www.sjogrens.org

Skin Problems

National Psoriasis Foundation
800-723-9166
Information and referrals.

E-mail: getinfo@npfusa.org
Website: www.psoriasis.org

Speech and Hearing

American Speech-Language-Hearing Association Action Center
800-638-8255 (also TTY)
Materials on speech and language disorders and hearing impairment; referrals.
E-mail: actioncenter@asha.org
Website: www.asha.org
Canadian Hard of Hearing Association
800-263-8068, Canada only; TTY 613-526-2692; 613-526-1584
Publications; answers general questions.
E-mail: chhanational@chha.ca
Website: www.chha.ca
Dial a Hearing Screening Test
800-222-EARS
Answers questions on hearing problems. Makes referrals to local telephone numbers for a two-minute hearing test. Also to ear, nose, and throat specialists and to organizations that can provide specialized ear and hearing aid information. 9 AM-5 PM EST
Hearing Aid Helpline
800-521-5247, ext. 333
Information and distributes a directory of hearing aid specialists certified by the International Hearing Society.
Website: www.ihsinfo.org
National Center for Stuttering
800-221-2483; 212-532-1460
Information on stuttering in all age groups.
E-mail: martin.schwartz@nyu.edu
Website: www.stuttering.com
Stuttering Foundation of America
800-992-9392
Referrals to speech pathologists; resource lists, publications.
E-mail: stutter@stutteringhelp.org
Website: www.stutteringhelp.org

Spinal Injuries

National Spinal Cord Injury Association
800-962-9629; 301-214-4006
Peer counseling; referrals to local chapters and other organizations.
Website: www.spinalcord.org

Stroke

See *Heart Disease and Stroke*

Sudden Infant Death Syndrome

American Sudden Infant Death Syndrome Institute
800-232-SIDS
Answers questions; literature; referrals to other organizations.
E-mail: prevent@sids.org
Website: www.sids.org
National SIDS Foundation
800-221-SIDS; in Maryland, 410-653-8226
Literature on medical information, referrals, and support groups.
E-mail: info@sidsalliance.org
Website: www.sidsalliance.org

Tourette Syndrome

Tourette Syndrome Association
718-224-2999
Printed information.
E-mail: ts@tsa-usa.org
Website: tsa-usa.org

Urinary Incontinence

National Association for Continence
800-BLADDER
Information on bladder control, services available for incontinence, and assistive devices.
E-mail: memberservices@nafc.org
Website: www.nafc.org
Simon Foundation for Continence
800-23-SIMON
Support and literature on incontinence.
E-mail: Simoninfo@simonfoundation.org
Website: www.simonfoundation.org

Women's Health

National Women's Health Network
202-347-1140; 202-628-7814
Information and referrals on more than 70 women's health concerns.
Website: www.womenshealthnetwork.org
National Women's Health Resource Center
877-986-9472
A national clearinghouse for women's health information.
Website: www.healthywomen.org

ECONOMICS

Consumer Price Index

The Consumer Price Index (CPI) is a measure of the average change in prices over time of one or more kinds of basic consumer goods and services.

From Jan. 1978, the Bureau of Labor Statistics began publishing CPIs for 2 population groups: (1) a CPI for all urban consumers (CPI-U), which covers about 87% of the total population; and (2) a CPI for urban wage earners and clerical workers (CPI-W), which covers about 32% of the total population. The CPI-U includes, in addition to wage earners and clerical workers, groups such as professional, managerial, and technical workers, the self-employed, short-term workers, the unemployed, retirees, and others not in the labor force.

The CPI is based on prices of food, clothing, shelter, and fuels; transportation fares; charges for doctors' and dentists' services; drug prices; and prices of other goods and services bought for day-to-day living. The index currently measures price changes from a designated reference period, 1982-84, which equals 100.0. Use of this reference period began in Jan. 1988.

U.S. Consumer Price Indexes, 2002-2003

Source: Bureau of Labor Statistics, U.S. Dept. of Labor

(Data are semiannual averages of monthly figures. For all urban consumers; 1982-84 = 100; % change not annualized)

	1st half 2002	% change 2nd half 2001 to 1st half 2002	2nd half 2002	% change 1st half 2002 to 2nd half 2002	1st half 2003	% change 2nd half 2002 to 1st half 2003
ALL ITEMS	178.9	0.8	180.9	1.1	183.3	1.3
Food, beverages	176.5	1.0	177.1	0.3	179.1	1.1
Housing	179.2	1.1	181.4	1.2	184.0	1.1
Apparel	125.1	−0.3	122.9	−1.8	121.4	−1.2
Transportation	151.4	−0.7	154.3	1.9	158.1	2.5
Medical care	282.4	2.5	288.8	2.3	294.5	2.0
Recreation[1]	106.1	0.9	106.3	0.2	107.4	1.0
Education and communication[1]	106.8	0.4	109.0	2.1	109.2	0.2
Other goods, services	290.8	1.5	295.7	1.7	297.6	0.6
Services	208.1	3.1	211.5	1.6	215.0	1.7
SPECIAL INDEXES						
All items less food	179.4	0.7	181.7	1.3	184.2	1.4
Commodities less food	135.7	−1.1	136.3	0.4	137.4	0.8
Nondurables	160.2	0.3	161.9	1.1	164.8	1.8
Energy	118.1	−4.8	125.3	0.8	135.7	8.3
All items less energy	186.9	1.2	188.4	0.9	190.0	0.8

(1) Dec. 1997 = 100.

U.S. Consumer Price Indexes (CPI-U),[1] Annual Percent Change, 1990-2002

Source: Bureau of Labor Statistics, U.S. Dept. of Labor

	1990	1991	1992	1993	1994	1995	1996	1997	1998	1999	2000	2001	2002
ALL ITEMS	5.4	4.2	3.0	3.0	2.6	2.8	3.0	2.3	1.6	2.2	3.4	2.8	1.6
Food	5.8	2.9	1.2	2.2	2.4	2.8	3.3	2.6	2.2	2.1	2.3	3.2	1.8
Shelter	5.4	4.5	3.3	3.0	3.1	3.2	3.2	3.1	3.3	2.9	3.3	3.7	3.7
Rent, residential	5.6	6.1	2.5	2.3	2.5	2.5	2.7	2.9	3.2	3.1	3.6	4.5	4.0
Fuel and other utilities	3.5	3.3	2.2	3.0	1.0	0.7	3.1	2.6	−1.8	0.2	7.1	8.9	−4.4
Apparel and upkeep	4.6	3.7	2.5	1.4	−0.2	−1.0	−0.2	0.9	0.1	−1.3	−1.8	−2.6
Private transportation	5.2	2.6	2.2	2.3	3.1	3.7	2.7	0.7	−2.2	1.9	6.1	0.6	−0.8
New cars	1.8	3.8	2.5	2.4	3.4	2.2	1.7	0.2	−0.6	−0.3	−0.1	−0.5	−1.2
Gasoline	14.1	−1.8	−0.2	−1.3	0.5	1.6	6.1	−0.1	−13.4	9.3	28.5	−3.6	−6.5
Public transportation	10.1	4.4	1.7	10.3	3.0	2.3	3.4	2.6	1.9	3.9	6.0	0.5	−1.5
Medical care	9.0	8.7	7.4	5.9	4.8	4.5	3.5	2.8	3.2	3.5	4.1	4.6	4.7
Entertainment, Recreation[2,3]	4.7	4.5	2.8	2.5	2.9	2.5	3.4	2.1	1.5	0.9	1.3	1.5	1.2
Education[3]	—	—	—	—	6.3	5.6	5.3	5.0	4.9	4.8	5.1	5.3	6.3
Commodities	5.2	4.2	2.0	1.9	1.7	1.9	2.6	1.4	0.1	1.8	3.3	1.0	−0.7

(1) The Consumer Price Index CPI-U measures the average change in prices of goods and services purchased by all urban consumers. 1982-1984 = 100. (2) The Bureau of Labor Statistics reclassified Entertainment as Recreation in 1997. (3) Dec. 1997 = 100.

Consumer Price Index, 1915-2003

Source: Bureau of Labor Statistics, U.S. Dept. of Labor

(1967 = 100. Annual averages of monthly figures, specified for all urban consumers.)

Prices as measured by the U.S. Consumer Price Index have risen steadily since World War II. What cost $1.00 in 1967 (the reference year) cost about 30 cents in 1915, 54 cents in 1945, and $5.49 by 2003.

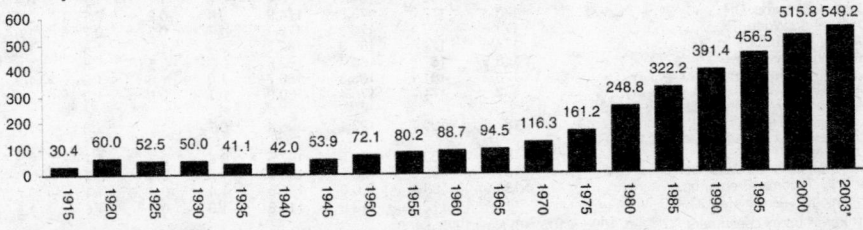

1915	1920	1925	1930	1935	1940	1945	1950	1955	1960	1965	1970	1975	1980	1985	1990	1995	2000	2003*
30.4	60.0	52.5	50.0	41.1	42.0	53.9	72.1	80.2	88.7	94.5	116.3	161.2	248.8	322.2	391.4	456.5	515.8	549.2

*Average for 1st half 2003.

U.S. Consumer Price Indexes for Selected Items and Groups, 1970-2002

Source: Bureau of Labor Statistics, U.S. Dept. of Labor

(1982-84 = 100, unless otherwise noted. Annual averages of monthly figures. For all urban consumers.)

	1970	1975	1980	1985	1990	1995	1998	1999	2000	2001	2002
ALL ITEMS	38.8	53.8	82.4	107.6	130.7	152.4	163.0	166.6	172.2	177.1	179.9
Food and beverages	40.1	60.2	86.7	105.6	132.1	148.9	161.1	164.6	168.4	173.6	176.8
Food	39.2	59.8	86.8	105.6	132.4	148.4	160.7	164.1	167.8	173.1	176.2
Food at home	39.9	61.8	88.4	104.3	132.3	148.8	161.1	164.2	167.9	173.4	175.6
Cereals and bakery products	37.1	62.9	83.9	107.9	140.0	167.5	181.1	185.0	188.3	193.8	198.0
Meats, poultry, fish, and eggs	44.6	67.0	92.0	100.1	130.0	138.8	147.3	147.9	154.5	161.3	162.1
Dairy products	44.7	62.6	90.9	103.2	126.5	132.8	150.8	159.6	160.7	167.1	168.1
Fruits and vegetables	37.8	56.9	82.1	106.4	149.0	177.7	198.2	203.1	204.6	212.2	220.9
Sugar and sweets	30.5	65.3	90.5	105.8	124.7	137.5	150.2	152.3	154.0	155.7	159.0
Fats and oils	39.2	73.5	89.3	106.9	126.3	137.3	146.9	148.3	147.4	155.7	155.4
Nonalcoholic beverages	27.1	41.3	91.4	104.3	113.5	131.7	133.0	134.3	137.8	139.2	139.2
Other foods	39.6	58.9	83.6	106.4	131.2	151.1	165.5	168.9	172.2	176.0	177.1
Food away from home	37.5	54.5	83.4	108.3	133.4	149.0	161.1	165.1	169.0	173.9	178.3
Alcoholic beverages	52.1	65.9	86.4	106.4	129.3	153.9	165.7	169.7	174.7	179.3	183.6
Housing	36.4	50.7	81.1	107.7	128.5	148.5	160.4	163.9	169.6	176.4	180.3
Shelter	35.5	48.8	81.0	109.8	140.0	165.7	182.1	187.3	193.4	200.6	208.1
Rent of primary residence	46.5	58.0	80.9	111.8	138.4	157.8	172.1	177.5	183.9	192.1	199.7
Fuel and other utilities	29.1	45.4	75.4	106.5	111.6	123.7	128.5	128.8	137.9	150.2	143.6
Gas (piped) and electricity	25.4	40.1	71.4	107.1	109.3	119.2	121.2	120.9	128.0	142.4	134.4
Household furnishings and operations	46.8	63.4	86.3	103.8	113.3	123.0	126.6	126.7	128.2	129.1	128.3
Apparel	59.2	72.5	90.9	105.0	124.1	132.0	133.0	131.3	129.6	127.3	124.0
Men's and boys'	62.2	75.5	89.4	105.0	120.4	126.2	131.8	131.1	129.7	125.7	121.7
Women's and girls'	71.8	85.5	96.0	104.9	122.6	126.9	126.0	123.3	121.5	119.3	115.8
Footwear	56.8	69.6	91.8	102.3	117.4	125.4	128.0	125.7	123.8	123.0	121.4
Transportation	37.5	50.1	83.1	106.4	120.5	139.1	141.6	144.4	153.3	154.3	152.9
Private	37.5	50.6	84.2	106.2	118.8	136.3	137.9	140.5	149.1	150.0	148.8
New vehicles	53.0	62.9	88.4	106.1	121.4	139.0	143.4	142.9	142.8	142.1	140.0
Used cars and trucks	31.2	43.8	62.3	113.7	117.6	156.5	150.6	152.0	155.8	158.7	152.0
Gasoline	27.9	45.1	97.5	98.6	101.0	99.8	91.6	100.1	128.6	124.0	116.0
Public	35.2	43.5	69.0	110.5	142.6	175.9	190.3	197.7	209.6	210.6	207.4
Medical care	34.0	47.5	74.9	113.5	162.8	220.5	242.1	250.6	260.8	272.8	285.6
Entertainment/Recreation[1,2]	47.5	62.0	83.6	107.9	132.4	153.9	101.1	102.0	103.3	104.9	106.2
Other goods and services	40.9	53.9	75.2	114.5	159.0	206.9	237.7	258.3	271.1	282.6	293.2
Tobacco products	43.1	54.7	72.0	116.7	181.5	225.7	274.8	355.8	394.9	425.2	461.5
Personal care	43.5	57.9	81.9	106.3	130.4	147.1	156.7	161.1	165.6	170.5	174.7
Personal care products	42.7	58.0	79.6	107.6	128.2	143.1	148.3	151.8	153.7	155.1	154.7
Personal care services	44.2	57.7	83.7	108.9	132.8	151.5	166.0	171.4	178.1	184.3	188.4

(1) Dec. 1997 = 100. (2) Entertainment was reclassified as Recreation in 1997.

Consumer Price Indexes by Region and Selected Cities, 2001-2003[1]

Source: Bureau of Labor Statistics, U.S. Dept. of Labor

(1982-84 = 100, unless otherwise noted)

	Semiannual averages				Percent change from preceding semiannual average			
	2nd half 2001	1st half 2002	2nd half 2002	1st half 2003	2nd half 2001	1st half 2002	2nd half 2002	1st half 2003
U.S. CITY AVERAGE	177.5	178.9	180.9	183.3	0.5	0.8	1.1	1.3
Northeast urban	184.9	186.9	189.5	192.2	0.6	1.1	1.4	1.4
Size A—More than 1,500,000	186.2	188.4	191.2	194.0	0.8	1.2	1.5	1.5
Size B/C—50,000 to 1,500,000[2]	110.6	111.3	112.5	114.1	0.2	0.6	1.1	1.4
Midwest urban	172.9	173.8	175.9	177.8	0.1	0.5	1.2	1.1
Size A—More than 1,500,000	174.6	176.2	178.2	179.8	0.2	0.9	1.1	0.9
Size B/C—50,000 to 1,500,000[2]	110.3	110.3	111.5	113.0	-0.1	0	1.1	1.3
Size D—Nonmetro. (less than 50,000)	166.7	167.5	169.9	172.0	-0.1	0.5	1.4	1.2
South urban	171.4	172.3	174.3	176.7	0.3	0.5	1.2	1.4
Size A—More than 1,500,000	172.5	173.5	175.7	178.4	0.8	0.6	1.3	1.5
Size B/C—50,000 to 1,500,000[2]	109.6	110.2	111.4	112.8	0	0.5	1.1	1.3
Size D—Nonmetro. (less than 50,000)	169.4	170.0	172.6	174.8	-0.4	0.4	1.5	1.3
West urban	182.1	184.0	185.5	188.2	1.1	1.0	0.8	1.5
Size A—More than 1,500,000	184.2	186.3	188.1	191.0	1.0	1.1	1.0	1.5
Size B/C—50,000 to 1,500,000[2]	111.7	112.6	113.0	114.6	1.0	0.8	0.4	1.4
SELECTED AREAS								
Atlanta, GA	176.4	177.6	178.9	181.1	0.2	0.7	0.7	1.2
Boston–Brockton–Nashua, MA–NH–ME–CT	192.6	194.4	198.7	201.9	1.1	0.9	2.2	1.6
Chicago–Gary–Kenosha, IL–IN–WI	178.2	180.1	180.1	183.8	-0.2	1.1	1.2	0.9
Cleveland–Akron, OH	173.3	172.9	173.8	174.9	0.4	-0.2	0.5	0.6
Dallas–Fort Worth, TX	171.8	172.1	173.3	176.1	1.7	0.2	0.7	1.6
Detroit–Ann Arbor–Flint, MI	174.6	177.6	180.3	182.2	0.3	1.7	1.5	1.1
Houston–Galveston–Brazoria, TX	158.6	157.8	160.7	162.8	-0.2	-0.5	1.8	1.3
L.A.–Riverside–Orange County, CA	178.2	181.1	183.3	186.7	1.0	1.6	1.2	1.9
Miami–Fort Lauderdale, FL	173.6	174.7	176.4	180.0	0.7	0.6	1.0	2.0
New York, NY–Northern NJ–Long Island, NY–NJ–CT–PA	187.8	190.7	193.1	196.4	0.7	1.5	1.3	1.7
Philadelphia–Wilmington–Atlantic City, PA–DE–NJ–MD	182.1	183.3	186.5	187.5	0.9	0.7	1.7	0.5
San Francisco–Oakland–San Jose, CA	191.1	192.3	193.7	196.8	1.3	0.6	0.7	1.6
Seattle–Tacoma–Bremerton, WA	186.9	188.3	190.3	191.6	1.4	0.7	1.1	0.7
Washington–Baltimore, DC–MD–VA–WV[3]	111.1	112.1	113.9	115.6	1.3	0.9	1.6	1.5

(1) For all urban consumers. (2) Dec. 1996 = 100. (3) Nov. 1996 = 100.

Percentage Change in Consumer Prices in Selected Countries

Source: International Monetary Fund

(annual averages)

COUNTRY	1975-1980	1980-1985	1992-1993	1993-1994	1994-1995	1995-1996	1996-1997	1997-1998	1998-1999	1999-2000	2000-2001R	2001-2002
Canada	8.7	7.4	1.8	0.2	2.2	1.6	1.6	1.0	1.7	2.7	2.5	2.2
France	10.5	9.6	2.1	1.7	1.8	2.0	1.2	0.7	0.5	1.7	1.6	1.9
Germany	4.1	3.9	4.1	3.0	1.8	1.5	1.8	1.0	0.6	1.9	2.5	1.3
Italy	16.3	13.7	4.5	4.0	5.2	4.0	2.0	2.0	1.7	2.5	2.8	2.5
Japan	6.5	2.7	1.3	0.7	-0.1	0.1	1.7	0.6	-0.3	-0.7	-0.7	-0.9
Spain	18.6	12.2	4.6	4.7	4.7	3.6	2.0	1.8	2.3	3.4	3.6	3.1
Sweden	10.5	9.0	4.6	2.2	2.5	0.5	0.5	-0.1	0.5	0.9	2.4	2.2
Switzerland	2.3	4.3	3.3	0.8	1.8	0.8	0.5	0.1	0.7	1.5	1.0	0.6
United Kingdom	14.4	7.2	1.6	2.5	3.4	2.4	3.1	3.4	1.6	3.0	1.8	1.6
United States	8.9	5.5	3.0	2.6	2.8	3.0	2.3	1.6	2.2	3.4	2.8	1.6

R = Revised.

Index of Leading Economic Indicators

Source: The Conference Board

The index of leading economic indicators is used to project the U.S. economy's performance. The index is made up of 10 measurements of economic activity that tend to change direction in advance of the overall economy. The index has predicted economic downturns from 8 to 20 months in advance and recoveries from 1 to 10 months in advance; however, it can be inconsistent, and has occasionally shown "false signals" of recessions.

Components

Average weekly hours of production workers in manufacturing
Average weekly initial claims for unemployment insurance, state programs
Manufacturers' new orders for consumer goods and materials, adjusted for inflation
Vendor performance (slower deliveries diffusion index)
Manufacturers' new orders, nondefense capital goods industries, adjusted for inflation
New private housing units authorized by local building permits
Stock prices, 500 common stocks
Money supply: M-2, adjusted for inflation
Interest rate spread, 10-yr Treasury bonds less federal funds
Consumer expectations (researched by Univ. of Michigan)

U.S. Gross Domestic Product, Gross National Product, Net National Product, National Income, and Personal Income

Source: Bureau of Economic Analysis, U.S. Dept. of Commerce

(billions of current dollars)

	1960	1970	1980	1990	2000R	2001	2002
GROSS DOMESTIC PRODUCT	—	—	—	$5,546.1	$9,824.6	$10,082.2	$10,446.2
GROSS NATIONAL PRODUCT	$515.3	$1,015.5	$2,732.0	5,567.8	9,848.0	10,104.1	10,436.7
Less: Consumption of fixed capital	46.4	88.8	303.8	602.7	1,228.9	1,329.3	1,393.5
Equals: Net national product	468.9	926.6	2,428.1	4,965.1	8,619.1	8,774.8	9,043.2
Less: Indirect business tax and nontax liability	45.3	94.0	213.3	444.0	753.6	774.8	800.4
Business transfer payments	2.0	4.1	12.1	26.8	43.7	42.5	44.1
Statistical discrepancy	-2.8	-1.1	4.9	7.8	-128.5	-117.3	-116.7
Plus: Subsidies less current surplus of government enterprises	0.4	2.9	5.7	4.5	34.1	47.3	32.5
Equals: National income	424.9	832.6	2,203.5	4,491.0	7,984.4	8,122.0	8,347.9
Less: Corporate profits with inventory valuation and capital consumption adjustments	49.5	74.7	177.2	380.6	788.1	731.6	787.4
Net interest	11.3	41.2	200.9	463.7	611.5	649.8	684.2
Contributions for social insurance	21.9	62.2	216.5	503.1	701.3	726.1	747.5
Wage accruals less disbursements	0.0	0.0	0.0	0.1	0.0	0.0	0.0
Plus: Personal interest income	27.5	81.8	312.6	666.3	1,077.0	1,091.3	1,078.5
Personal dividend income	24.9	69.3	271.9	698.2	375.7	409.2	433.8
Government transfer payments to persons	12.9	22.2	52.9	144.4	1,037.3	1,137.0	1,252.9
Business transfer payments to persons	2.0	4.1	12.1	21.3	33.0	33.4	35.1
Equals: PERSONAL INCOME	409.4	831.8	2,258.5	4,673.8	8,406.6	8,685.3	8,929.1

R = Revised.

U.S. Gross Domestic Product

Source: Bureau of Economic Analysis, U.S. Dept. of Commerce

(billions of current dollars)

	1992	2002	2nd Quarter 2003[1]		1992	2002	2nd Quarter 2003[1]
Gross domestic product	6,318.9	10,446.2	10,793.9	Net exports of goods and services	-27.9	-423.6	-502.0
Personal consumption expenditures	4,209.7	7,303.7	7,595.6	Exports	636.8	1,014.9	1,030.8
Durable goods	470.8	871.9	900.3	Goods	448.7	703.6	711.0
Nondurable goods	1,322.9	2,115.0	2,202.2	Services	188.1	311.3	319.8
Services	2,415.9	4,316.8	4,493.1	Imports	664.6	1,438.5	1,532.7
Gross private domestic investment	866.6	1,593.2	1,610.1	Goods	544.9	1,192.1	1,273.3
Fixed investment	851.6	1,589.3	1,632.1	Services	119.8	246.4	259.5
Nonresidential	626.1	1,117.4	1,119.9	Government consumption expenditures and gross investment	1,270.5	1,972.9	2,090.2
Structures	172.2	269.3	258.5	Federal	534.5	693.7	779.7
Equipment and software	453.9	848.1	861.4	National defense	378.5	447.4	518.6
Residential	225.5	471.9	512.2	Nondefense	156	246.3	261.1
Change in private inventories	15.0	3.9	-22.1	State and local	736.0	1,279.2	1,310.5

(1) Seasonally adjusted at annual rates.

Countries With Highest Gross Domestic Product and Per Capita GDP[1]

Source: Central Intelligence Agency, *The World Factbook 2003*

Gross Domestic Product
(billions of dollars; 2002 estimates)

Per Capita Gross Domestic Product[3]
(dollars; 2002 estimates unless otherwise noted)

Gross Domestic Product		Per Capita Gross Domestic Product	
1. U.S. $10,400	21. Thailand $429	1. Luxembourg . . $44,000	21. Liechtenstein . $25,000[5]
2. China[2] 5,700	22. Taiwan 406	2. U.S. 37,600	22. Italy 25,000
3. Japan 3,550	23. Argentina 391	3. San Marino . . . 34,600[4]	23. Singapore . . . 24,000
4. India 2,660	24. Poland 368	4. Norway 31,800	24. U.A.E. 22,000
5. Germany 2,184	25. Philippines 356	5. Switzerland . . . 31,700	25. Qatar 21,500
6. France 1,540	26. Pakistan 311	6. Ireland 30,500	26. Spain 20,700
7. U.K. 1,520	27. Belgium 297	7. Canada 29,400	27. New Zealand . . 20,200
8. Italy 1,438	28. Colombia 268	8. Belgium 29,000	28. South Korea . . 19,400
9. Russia 1,350	29. Egypt 268	9. Denmark 29,000	29. Andorra . . . . . 19,000[6]
10. Brazil 1,340	30. Saudi Arabia . . 242	10. Japan 28,000	30. Greece 19,000
11. South Korea . . . 931	31. Bangladesh . . . 239	11. Austria 27,700	31. Israel 19,000
12. Canada 923	32. Switzerland 231	12. Australia 27,000	32. Brunei 18,600
13. Mexico 900	33. Sweden 227	13. Monaco . . . . . . 27,000[5]	33. Portugal 18,000
14. Spain 828	34. Austria 226	14. Netherlands . . 26,900	34. Slovenia 18,000
15. Indonesia 663	35. Ukraine 218	15. Germany 26,600	35. Taiwan 18,000
16. Australia 528	36. Malaysia 210	16. Finland 26,200	36. The Bahamas . 17,000
17. Turkey 468	37. Greece 201	17. France 25,700	37. Malta 17,000
18. Iran 456	38. Vietnam 183	18. Sweden 25,400	38. Czech Republic 15,300
19. Netherlands . . . 434	39. Portugal 182	19. U.K. 25,300	39. Cyprus 15,000
20. South Africa . . . 432	40. Algeria 167	20. Iceland 25,000	40. Kuwait 15,000

(1) U.S. data from *The World Factbook* may differ from data from the U.S. Bureau of Economic Analysis. International GDP estimates derive from purchasing power parity calculations, which involve the use of intl. dollar price weights applied to quantities of goods and services produced in a given economy. (2) Hong Kong had a GDP of $180.0 billion and a per capita GDP of $25,000 in 2001; Macao had a GDP of $8.6 billion and a per capita GDP of $18,500 in 2002. (3) These territories or former territories (as well as Hong Kong, above) had large per capita GDPs: Bermuda (UK, 2002) $35,200, Cayman Islands (UK, 2002) $35,000, Aruba (Neth., 2002) $28,000, Guam (U.S., 2000) $21,000, Greenland (Den., 2001) $20,000, Faroe Islands (Den., 2001) $22,000, Macao (China, 2001) $17,600, Gibraltar (UK, 1997) $17,500. (4) 2001 est. (5) 1999 est. (6) 2000 est.

U.S. National Income by Industry[1]

Source: Bureau of Economic Analysis, U.S. Dept. of Commerce

(billions of current dollars)

	1960	1970	1980	1990	1995	1998	1999	2000	2001	2002
National income without capital consumption adjustment	$428.6	$835.1	$2,263.9	$4,640.5	$5,884.4	$7,013.2	$7,424.5	$7,958.7	$8,053.5	$8,182.7
Domestic industries	425.1	827.8	2,216.3	4,611.6	5,864.0	7,016.6	7,401.8	7,935.3	8,031.5	8,192.2
Private industries	371.6	695.4	1,894.5	3,929.0	5,039.9	6,101.6	6,448.5	6,928.0	6,969.4	7,076.2
Agriculture, forestry, fisheries .	17.8	25.9	61.4	89.0	86.9	102.4	111.3	109.7	111.1	109.5
Mining	5.6	8.4	43.8	40.8	45.7	54.2	48.6	62.9	69.5	58.9
Construction	22.5	47.4	126.6	230.5	266.7	349.6	389.4	422.9	438.9	443
Manufacturing	125.3	215.6	532.1	879.0	1,058.5	1,145.4	1,180.5	1,250.7	1,132.2	1,123.5
Durable goods	73.4	127.7	313.7	498.1	606.8	671.0	688.0	729.2	640.5	629.1
Nondurable goods	52.0	87.9	218.4	380.9	451.6	474.4	492.6	521.4	491.8	494.4
Transportation, public utilities .	35.8	64.4	177.3	330.5	440.7	495.9	511.4	530.5	529.9	515
Transportation	18.5	31.5	85.8	138.7	183.9	224.6	234.0	243.7	236.6	236.6
Communications	8.2	17.6	48.1	94.2	129.4	142.8	144.1	149.4	148.4	137
Electric, gas, sanitary services	9.1	86.8	43.4	97.6	127.3	128.5	133.2	137.4	144.9	141.5
Wholesale trade	25.0	47.5	143.3	266.0	328.2	420.5	444.4	481.1	458.4	467.1
Retail trade	41.3	79.9	189.4	385.3	481.8	585.6	619.3	659.1	686.1	704.3
Finance, insurance, real estate	51.3	96.4	279.5	738.5	1,013.5	1,309.5	1,379.3	1,521.5	1,571.1	1,636.5
Services	46.9	109.8	341.0	969.5	1,318.1	1,638.6	1,764.2	1,889.8	1,972.0	2,018.4
Government	53.5	132.4	321.8	682.6	824.2	915.1	953.3	1,007.3	1,062.1	1,116.0

(1) Figures may not add because of rounding. Total national income also includes income from outside the U.S.

U.S. National Income by Type of Income[1]

Source: Bureau of Economic Analysis, U.S. Dept. of Commerce.

(billions of current dollars)

	1960	1970	1980	1990	1995	1998	1999	2000[R]	2001	2002
NATIONAL INCOME[2]	427.5	837.5	2,243.0	4,642.1	5,876.7	7,041.4	7,468.7	7,984.4	8,122.0	8347.9
Compensation of employees	296.4	617.2	1,651.7	3,351.0	4,202.5	4,989.6	5,308.8	5,723.4	5,874.9	5977.4
Wage and salary accruals	272.8	551.5	1,377.4	2,754.6	3,441.1	4,192.1	4,475.6	4,836.3	4,950.6	5003.7
Government	49.2	117.1	261.2	516.8	622.7	692.7	724.2	768.9	810.8	852.8
Other	223.7	434.3	1,116.2	2,237.9	2,818.4	3,499.4	3,751.4	4,067.4	4,139.8	4150.9
Supplements to wages and salaries	23.6	65.7	274.3	596.4	761.4	797.5	833.2	887.1	924.3	973.7
Employer contributions for social insurance	9.3	23.8	88.9	206.5	264.5	306.9	323.0	342.9	353.9	363.0
Other labor income	14.4	41.9	185.4	390.0	497.0	490.6	510.2	544.2	570.4	610.6
Proprietors' income with inventory valuation and capital consumption adjustments	51.9	79.8	177.6	381.0	497.7	623.8	678.4	714.8	727.9	756.5
Farm	11.4	14.3	13.1	31.1	22.2	25.6	27.7	22.6	19.0	12.9
Nonfarm	40.4	65.5	164.5	349.9	475.5	598.2	650.7	692.2	708.8	743.7
Rental income of persons with capital consumption adjustment	16.2	20.3	31.3	49.1	117.9	138.6	149.1	146.6	137.9	142.4
Corporate profits with inventory valuation and capital consumption adjustments . .	52.3	81.6	198.5	408.6	668.8	777.4	805.8	788.1	731.6	787.4
Corporate profits with inventory valuation adjustment	51.4	74.0	209.3	388.6	650.2	739.4	757.9	767.3	675.1	658.3
Profits before tax	51.5	80.6	251.4	401.5	668.5	721.1	762.1	782.3	670.2	665.2
Profits tax liability	22.7	34.4	84.8	140.6	211.0	238.8	247.8	259.4	199.3	213.3
Profits after tax	28.8	46.2	166.6	260.9	457.5	482.3	514.3	522.9	470.9	451.9
Dividends	13.4	24.3	64.1	165.6	254.2	348.7	328.4	376.1	409.6	434.3

	1960	1970	1980	1990	1995	1998	1999	2000R	2001	2002
Undistributed profits	15.5	21.9	102.6	95.3	203.3	133.6	185.9	146.8	61.2	17.6
Inventory valuation adjustment	−0.2	−6.6	−42.1	−12.9	−18.3	18.3	−4.2	−15.0	5.0	−6.9
Net interest	**10.7**	**38.4**	**183.9**	**452.4**	**389.8**	**511.9**	**526.6**	**611.5**	**649.8**	**684.2**

R = revised. (1) Figures do not add, because of rounding and incomplete enumeration. (2) National income is the aggregate of labor and property earnings that arises in the production of goods and services. It is the sum of employee compensation, proprietors' income, rental income, adjusted corporate profits, and net interest. It measures the total factor costs of goods and services produced by the economy. Income is measured before deduction of taxes. Total national income figures include adjustments not itemized.

Selected Personal Consumption Expenditures in the U.S., 1995-2002[1]

Source: Bureau of Economic Analysis, U.S. Dept. of Commerce
(billions of dollars)

	1995	1996	1997	1998	1999	2000	2001	2002
Personal consumption expenditures	$4,969.0	$5,237.5	$5,529.3	$5,856.0	$6,246.5	$6,683.7	$6,987.0	$7,303.7
Food and tobacco	802.5	834.1	862.0	906.9	964.7	1,027.2	1,068.7	1,110.7
Food purchased for off-premise consumption	459.8	476.7	486.5	507.9	537.7	568.6	589.0	604.4
Purchased meals and beverages	287.5	300.5	316.6	335.4	351.5	376.5	393.2	414.6
Food furnished to employees (incl. milit.) and produced/consumed on farms	8.5	8.7	9.0	9.3	9.6	9.9	10.2	10.4
Tobacco products	46.7	48.2	49.8	54.4	65.9	72.2	76.3	81.3
Clothing, accessories, and jewelry	317.3	333.3	348.0	367.2	391.2	409.8	412.6	424.1
Shoes	37.1	38.8	40.1	42.4	44.7	46.3	47.0	48.8
Clothing and accessories except shoes	210.4	219.5	231.3	242.0	256.1	267.1	267.9	275.5
Women's and children's	135.5	140.8	148.0	154.6	164.1	171.9	172.6	178.0
Men's and boys'	74.9	78.6	83.3	87.4	92.0	95.2	95.3	97.6
Jewelry and watches	38.1	40.3	41.2	44.3	48.5	51.1	51.0	53.2
Other	31.7	34.7	35.5	38.5	41.9	45.3	46.7	NA
Personal care (toilet articles, barbershops, health clubs)	67.4	71.6	76.1	79.9	84.0	87.8	89.1	90.9
Housing	740.8	772.5	810.5	859.7	912.6	960.0	1,014.5	1,071.5
Owner-occupied nonfarm dwellings–space rent	529.3	555.4	585.5	625.0	666.4	704.9	751.0	799.3
Tenant-occupied nonfarm dwellings–rent	177.0	180.6	186.1	194.0	202.8	207.8	217.1	225.1
Rental value of farm dwellings	6.0	6.2	6.4	6.7	7.2	7.6	8.0	8.1
Other	28.5	30.2	32.5	34.0	36.1	39.6	38.5	38.9
Household operation	555.0	589.2	617.8	642.9	677.7	723.9	747.3	756.3
Furniture, including mattresses and bedsprings	47.5	50.9	53.8	56.7	60.3	64.4	64.0	66.7
Kitchen and other household appliances	29.1	30.0	30.8	32.1	34.1	35.7	36.1	37.3
China, glassware, tableware, and utensils	23.8	25.4	27.2	29.1	31.4	33.3	34.1	35.5
Other durable house furnishings	47.7	50.5	53.5	57.1	61.6	65.1	66.4	68.6
Semidurable house furnishings	29.7	31.0	33.1	34.5	36.8	38.3	38.7	39.8
Cleaning and polishing preparations, and miscellaneous household supplies and paper products	47.3	49.8	51.4	53.5	56.9	59.3	61.7	64.4
Stationery and writing supplies	17.7	18.8	20.0	21.3	22.6	23.4	23.5	23.9
Household utilities (oil, gas, electricity, water, sanitary)	175.0	185.0	188.1	186.2	190.1	209.2	221.7	148.2
Telephone and telegraph	87.8	97.1	105.0	112.9	122.3	130.6	136.5	137.9
Other	49.4	50.7	55.1	59.7	61.5	64.5	64.6	257.0
Medical care	888.6	932.3	984.4	1,041.7	1,097.9	1,171.1	1,270.2	1,366.7
Drug preparations and sundries	92.1	100.3	110.6	122.1	139.2	156.3	176.4	196.0
Ophthalmic products and orthopedic appliances	15.8	17.6	19.1	20.6	21.6	22.9	21.6	22.1
Physicians	192.4	199.1	208.8	220.5	230.3	244.3	266.7	285.4
Dentists	46.5	48.4	51.9	55.1	58.3	62.7	67.5	73.1
Other professional services	112.9	119.7	125.9	132.1	137.0	142.8	153.5	163.3
Hospitals and nursing homes	370.9	390.8	408.9	427.8	445.8	471.5	509.6	544.4
Health insurance	58.0	56.6	59.3	63.6	65.7	70.6	75.0	82.3
Personal business	406.8	435.1	489.0	529.8	575.2	632.5	634.3	665.1
Transportation	560.3	594.6	626.7	649.9	707.8	768.9	794.8	810.4
User-operated transportation	517.8	550.2	578.9	599.2	654.7	711.9	742.0	761.1
New autos	82.2	81.9	82.5	87.9	98.4	105.5	105.9	103.2
Net purchases of used autos	50.0	51.4	53.1	54.9	57.7	59.4	60.6	58.6
Other motor vehicles	80.2	84.3	89.0	104.5	118.7	125.9	149.0	168.1
Tires, tubes, accessories, and other parts	36.9	38.7	39.6	41.5	44.4	45.9	45.8	46.2
Repair, greasing, washing, parking, storage, rental, and leasing	122.2	134.2	146.3	153.6	165.1	175.5	181.6	186.4
Gasoline and oil	113.3	124.2	128.1	114.8	129.3	164.4	162.1	173.5
Bridge, tunnel, ferry, and road tolls	3.4	3.7	4.0	4.0	4.4	4.6	4.9	5.1
Insurance	29.7	31.8	36.3	38.0	36.8	30.7	32.1	35.0
Purchased local transportation	10.4	11.2	11.6	12.3	12.4	12.7	13.2	13.3
Mass transit systems	7.1	7.7	7.8	8.3	8.6	9.1	9.5	9.5
Taxicab	3.2	3.5	3.7	4.1	3.8	3.6	3.7	3.8
Purchased intercity transportation	32.1	33.3	36.2	38.4	40.7	44.3	39.7	36.0
Railway	0.6	0.6	0.7	0.7	0.7	0.8	0.9	0.9
Bus	1.6	1.8	1.8	1.9	2.0	1.5	1.5	1.5
Airline	25.5	26.2	29.0	30.8	32.7	36.7	32.4	29.3
Other	4.3	4.7	4.7	4.9	5.3	5.2	4.8	4.3
Recreation	401.6	429.6	456.6	489.1	526.5	564.7	593.9	620.1
Books, maps, magazines, sheet music	49.3	52.5	55.4	59.2	63.3	67.4	70.3	70.8
Wheel goods, toys, sports and photographic equipment and supplies, boats, and pleasure aircraft	85.7	91.1	96.0	102.7	110.8	118.0	127.5	131.4
Video and audio goods, including musical instruments, and computer goods	77.0	80.0	83.7	90.3	98.1	106.3	105.6	110.6
Other (plants/seeds, clubs, spectator admissions, etc.)	189.8	205.9	221.5	236.9	254.3	272.9	290.4	NA
Education and research	114.5	122.3	130.5	140.2	152.1	164.0	174.9	185.6
Religious and welfare activities	134.9	146.8	149.5	163.9	172.9	190.1	199.6	213.7
Foreign travel and other, net	−20.7	−24.1	−21.8	−15.1	−16.0	−16.1	−12.9	−11.2
Foreign travel by U.S. residents	54.1	57.6	63.6	68.8	72.3	80.9	76.3	76.1
Expenditures abroad by U.S. residents	2.3	2.2	2.9	3.1	3.2	3.3	3.6	NA
Less: Expenditures in the United States by nonresidents	75.4	82.4	86.7	85.4	89.6	98.3	90.6	89.9
Less: Personal remittances in kind to nonresidents	1.6	1.5	1.6	1.6	1.9	2.0	2.2	NA

NA = Not available. (1) Subtotals may not add to total, due to rounding.

U.S. Per Capita Money Income, 1967-2001

Source: Bureau of the Census, U.S. Dept. of Commerce

Year	Current dollars	2001 dollars	Year	Current dollars	2001 dollars	Year	Current dollars	2001 dollars	Year	Current dollars	2001 dollars
1967....	$2,464	$11,067	1985....	$11,013	$17,280	1996	$18,136	$20,372	1999	$21,181	$22,499
1970....	3,177	12,543	1990....	14,387	18,894	1997	19,241	21,162	2000	22,346	22,970
1975....	4,818	13,972	1995....	17,227	19,871	1998	20,120	21,821	2001	22,851	22,851
1980....	7,787	15,844									

Distribution of U.S. Total Personal Income[1]

Source: Bureau of Economic Analysis, U.S. Dept. of Commerce; in billions of current dollars

Year	Personal income	Personal taxes and nontax payments	Disposable personal income	Personal outlays	Personal Savings Amount	As pct. of disposable income
1960.................	$411.7	$48.7	$362.9	$339.6	$23.3	6.4%
1965.................	555.8	61.9	493.9	456.2	37.8	7.6
1970.................	836.1	109.0	727.1	666.1	61.0	8.4
1975.................	1,315.6	156.4	1,159.2	1,054.8	104.4	9.0
1980.................	2,285.7	312.4	1,973.3	1,811.5	161.8	8.2
1985.................	3,439.6	437.7	3,002.0	2,795.8	206.2	6.9
1990.................	4,791.6	624.8	4,166.8	3,958.1	208.7	5.0
1995.................	6,072.1	795.0	5,277.0	5,097.2	179.8	3.4
1998.................	7,391.0	1,070.9	6,320.0	6,054.7	265.4	4.2
1999.................	7,777.3	1,159.2	6,618.0	6,457.2	160.9	2.4
2000.................	8,406.6	1,286.4	7,120.2	6,918.6	201.5	2.8
2001.................	8,685.3	1,292.1	7,393.2	7,223.5	169.7	2.3
2002.................	8,929.1	1,113.6	7,815.5	7,524.5	291.0	3.7

(1) Personal income minus taxes/nontax payments=disposable income; disposable income minus outlays=savings. Figures may not add because of rounding.

Banks in the U.S.—Number, Deposits

Source: Federal Deposit Insurance Corp. (as of Dec. 31, 2002)

Comprises all FDIC-insured commercial and savings banks, including savings and loan institutions (S&Ls).

	TOTAL NUMBER OF BANKS				TOTAL DEPOSITS (millions of dollars)				
	ALL BANKS	Commercial banks[1] Natl.	State	Non-members	All savings	ALL DEPOSITS	Commercial banks[1] Natl.	State	Non-members	All savings
Year										
1935...	15,295	5,386	1,001	7,735	1,173	$45,102[2]	$24,802	$13,653	$5,669	$978[2]
1940...	15,772	5,144	1,342	6,956	2,330	67,494	35,787	20,642	7,040	4,025
1945...	15,969	5,017	1,864	6,421	2,667	151,524	77,778	41,865	16,307	15,574
1950...	16,500	4,958	1,912	6,576	3,054	171,963	84,941	41,602	19,726	25,694
1955...	17,001	4,692	1,847	6,698	3,764	235,211	102,796	55,739	26,198	50,478
1960...	17,549	4,530	1,641	6,955	4,423	310,262	120,242	65,487	34,369	90,164
1965...	18,384	4,815	1,405	7,327	4,837	467,633	185,334	78,327	51,982	151,990
1970...	18,205	4,621	1,147	7,743	4,694	686,901	285,436	101,512	95,566	204,367
1975...	18,792	4,744	1,046	8,595	4,407	1,157,648	450,308	143,409	187,031	376,900
1980...	18,763	4,425	997	9,013	4,328	1,832,716	656,752	191,183	344,311	640,470
1985...	18,033	4,959	1,070	8,378	3,626	3,140,827	1,241,685	354,585	521,628	1,022,739
1990...	15,158	3,979	1,009	7,355	2,815	3,637,292	1,558,915	397,797	693,438	987,142
1995...	11,970	2,858	1,042	6,040	2,030	3,769,477	1,695,817	614,924	716,829	741,907
1998...	10,463	2,456	994	5,324	1,689	4,386,298	2,137,946	810,471	733,027	704,855
1999...	10,221	2,363	1,010	5,207	1,641	4,538,036	2,154,259	899,252	777,264	707,261
2000...	9,905	2,230	991	5,094	1,590	4,914,808	2,250,464	1,032,110	894,000	738,234
2001...	9,631	2,137	972	4,971	1,533	5,189,444	2,384,462	1,079,388	927,772	797,822
2002...	9,354	2,077	950	4,861	1,439	5,568,508	2,565,771	1,152,380	971,730	878,627

(1) "Nonmembers" are banks that are not members of the Federal Reserve System; "National" and "State" institutions are members.
(2) Figures for 1935 do not include data for S&Ls (not available).

50 Largest U.S. Bank Holding Companies

Source: *American Banker* (as of Dec. 31, 2002)

Company Name	Total Assets ($ in thousands)	Company Name	Total Assets ($ in thousands)
Citigroup Inc., New York, NY	$1,097,190,000	Northern Trust Corp., Chicago, IL	$39,478,200
J.P. Morgan Chase & Co., New York, NY	758,800,000	Mellon Financial Corp., Pittsburgh, PA	36,231,000
Bank of America Corp., Charlotte, NC	660,458,000	Union Planters Corp., Memphis, TN	34,144,363
Wells Fargo & Co., San Francisco, CA	349,259,000	Popular Inc., San Juan, PR	33,660,352
Wachovia Corp., Charlotte, NC	341,839,000	M&T Bank Corp., Buffalo, NY	33,174,525
Bank One Corp., Chicago, IL	277,383,000	Marshall & Ilsley Corp., Milwaukee, WI	32,874,642
Washington Mutual Inc., Seattle, WA	268,298,000	Huntington Bancshares Inc., Columbus, OH.	27,578,710
FleetBoston Financial Corp., Boston, MA ..	190,453,000	Zions Bancorp., Salt Lake City, UT	26,565,689
U.S. Bancorp, Minneapolis, MN	180,027,000	Compass Bancshares Inc., Birmingham, AL.	23,884,709
National City Corp., Cleveland, OH	118,258,415	First Tennessee National Corp., Memphis, TN·	23,823,095
SunTrust Banks Inc., Atlanta, GA	117,322,523	Banknorth Group Inc., Portland, ME	23,418,941
State Street Corp., Boston, MA	85,794,000	GreenPoint Financial Corp., New York, NY ..	21,814,000
KeyCorp, Cleveland, OH	85,202,000	Astoria Financial Corp., Lake Success, NY..	21,697,829
Fifth Third Bancorp, Cincinnati, OH	80,894,448	National Commerce Financial Corp.,	
BB&T Corp., Winston-Salem, NC	80,216,816	Memphis, TN.	21,472,116
Bank of New York Co. Inc., New York, NY ...	77,564,000	North Fork Bancorp Inc., Melville, NY......	21,413,101
Golden West Financial Corp., Oakland, CA..	68,405,828	Synovus Financial Corp., Columbus, GA ...	19,036,246
PNC Financial Services Group Inc.,		Hibernia Corp., New Orleans, LA	17,392,661
Pittsburgh, PA.	66,377,000	Provident Financial Group Inc., Cincinnati, OH	16,721,191
Comerica Inc., Detroit, MI	53,301,000	Commerce Bancorp Inc., Cherry Hill, NJ	16,403,981
SouthTrust Corp., Birmingham, AL.........	50,570,856	Colonial BancGroup Inc., Montgomery, AL..	15,822,355
Regions Financial Corp., Birmingham, AL ..	47,938,840	Associated Banc-Corp, Green Bay, WI	15,043,275
Charter One Financial Inc., Cleveland, OH ..	41,896,072	Hudson City Bancorp Inc., Paramus, NJ	14,144,604
AmSouth Bancorp., Birmingham, AL.......	40,571,272	Webster Financial Corp., Waterbury, CT	13,468,004
UnionBanCal Corp., San Francisco, CA.	40,169,773	Commerce Bancshares Inc., Kansas City, MO	13,308,415
Sovereign Bancorp Inc., Philadelphia, PA ...	39,524,193	Commercial Federal Corp., Omaha, NE	13,081,467

U.S. Bank Failures, 1934-2002

Source: Federal Deposit Insurance Corp.

Comprises all FDIC-insured commercial and savings banks, including savings and loan institutions (S&Ls) 1980 and after.

Year	Closed or assisted	Year	Closed or assisted	Year	Closed or assisted	Year	Closed or assisted	Year	Closed or assisted	Year	Closed or assisted
1934	9	1959	3	1969	9	1979	10	1987	262	1995	8
1935	26	1960	1	1970	7	1980	22	1988	465	1996	6
1936	69	1961	5	1971	7	1981	40	1989	534	1997	1
1937	77	1963	2	1972	2	1982	119	1990	382	1998	3
1938	74	1964	7	1973	6	1983	99	1991	271	1999	8
1939	60	1965	5	1975	13	1984	106	1992	181	2000	7
1940	43	1966	7	1976	17	1985	180	1993	50	2001	4
1955	5	1967	4	1978	7	1986	204	1994	15	2002	11

World's 50 Largest Banking Companies[1]

Source: *American Banker* (as of Dec. 31, 2002)

	Assets[2] (millions)		Assets[2] (millions)
Mizuho Holdings, Japan	$1,135,553	Lloyds TSB Group PLC, UK	$406,886
Citigroup, U.S.	1,097,190	Rabobank Group, Netherlands	392,819
Sumitomo Mitsui Financial Group, Japan	872,962	Dexia, Belgium	367,874
UBS AG, Switzerland	852,190	Wells Fargo & Co., U.S.	349,259
Allianz AG, Germany	850,356	Wachovia Corp., U.S.	341,839
Deutsche Bank, Germany	791,674	Reasona Holdings Inc., Japan	332,892
J.P. Morgan Chase & Co., U.S.	758,800	Abbey National PLC, UK	331,121
HSBC Holdings PLC, U.K.	757,406	Banco Santander Central Hispano, Spain	324,378
ING Group NV, Netherlands	751,711	BBV Argenteria, Spain	293,156
BNP Paribas, France	744,627	Intesa, Italy	280,733
Mitsubishi Tokyo Financial Group, Japan	742,896	Bank One Corp., U.S.	277,383
Bayerische Hypo-und Vereinsbanken AG, Germany	704,626	Washington Mutual Corp., U.S.	268,298
Credit Suisse Group, Switzerland	682,602	Nordea AB, Sweden	261,241
Royal Bank of Scotland Group, UK	663,279	Credit Lyonnais SA, France	256,729
Bank of America Corp., U.S.	660,458	Westdeutsche Landesbank Girozentrale, Germany	249,810
Barclays PLC, UK	648,807	Almanij NV, Belgium	249,391
UFJ Holdings, Japan	590,898	Royal Bank of Canada, Canada	240,154
ABN Amro Holding NV, Netherlands	581,850	Eurohypo AG, Germany	237,166
HBOS PLC, UK	571,616	KBC Bank, Belgium	232,670
Credit Agricole SA, France	530,144	Danske Bank SA, Denmark	230,579
Societe Generale, France	525,994	UniCredito Italiano SpA, Italy	223,674
Fortis, Netherlands	509,227	San Paolo Imi SpA, Italy	213,615
Axa, France	466,134	National Australia Bank, Australia	204,349
Commerzbank AG, Germany	437,407	Norddeutsche Landesbank, Germany	206,675
Norinchukin Bank, Japan	433,630	FleetBoston Financial Corp., U.S.	190,453

(1) Includes bank holding companies and commercial and savings banks. (2) Currency conversion based on Exchange rates on Dec. 31 or at end of fiscal year.

Federal Deposit Insurance Corporation (FDIC)

The Federal Deposit Insurance Corporation (FDIC) is the independent deposit insurance agency created by Congress to maintain stability and public confidence in the nation's banking system. In its unique role as deposit insurer of banks and savings associations, and in cooperation with other federal and state regulatory agencies, the FDIC seeks to promote the safety and soundness of insured depository institutions in the U.S. financial system by identifying, monitoring, and addressing risks to the deposit insurance funds. The FDIC aims at promoting public understanding and sound public policies by providing financial and economic information and analyses. It seeks to minimize disruptive effects from the failure of banks and savings associations, and to ensure fairness in the sale of financial products and the provision of financial services.

To maintain its insurance funds, the FDIC assesses depository institutions insurance premiums twice a year. The amount of the premium is based on the institution's balance of insured deposits for the preceding two quarters and the institution's risk to the insurance fund. The Corporation may borrow from the U.S. Treasury, not to exceed $30 billion outstanding, but the agency has made no such borrowings since it was organized in 1933. The FDIC's Bank Insurance Fund was $32.8 billion (unaudited) and the Savings Association Insurance Fund stood at $12.1 billion (unaudited), as of June 30, 2003.

Federal Reserve Board Discount Rate

The discount rate is the rate of interest set by the Federal Reserve that member banks are charged when borrowing money through the Federal Reserve System. Includes any changes through August 2003.

Effective date	Rate
1980:	
Feb. 15	13
May 30	12
June 13	11
July 28	10
Sept. 26	11
Nov. 17	12
Dec. 5	13
1981:	
May 5	14
Nov. 2	13
Dec. 4	12
1982:	
July 20	11½
Aug. 2	11
Aug. 16	10
Aug. 27	10
Oct. 12	9½
Dec. 15	8½
1984:	
April 9	9
Nov. 21	8½
Dec. 24	8
1985:	
May 20	7½
1986:	
March 7	7
April 21	6½
July 11	6
Aug. 21	5½
1987:	
Sept. 4	6
1988:	
Aug. 9	6½
1989:	
Feb. 24	7
1990:	
Dec. 18	6½
1991:	
Apr. 30	5½
Sept. 13	5
Nov. 6	4½
Dec. 20	3½
1992:	
July 2	3
1994:	
May 17	½
Aug. 16	4
Nov. 15	4¾
1995:	
Feb. 1	5
1996:	
Jan. 31	5
1998:	
Oct. 15	4¾
Nov. 17	4½
1999:	
Aug. 24	4¾
Nov. 16	5
2000:	
Feb. 2	5¼
Mar. 21	5½
May 16	6
2001:	
Jan. 3	5¾
Jan. 31	5
Mar. 20	4½
Apr. 18	4
May 15	3½
June 27	3¼
Aug. 21	3
Sept. 17	2½
Oct. 2	2
Dec. 11	1¼
2002	
Nov. 6	¾
2003	
Jan. 9[1]	2¼, 2¾
June 25[1]	2, 2½

(1) The Federal Reserve approved a new system for lending directly to banks, effective Jan. 9, 2003. The discount rate was replaced with two new rates, the *primary credit rate* and *secondary credit rate*. The primary credit rate (listed first) is available to banks in generally sound financial condition. The secondary credit (listed second) rate is given to banks that do not qualify for the primary credit rate. Both are extended for very short terms, usually overnight. Under the new system, financially sound institutions are not required to exhaust all funds before borrowing from the Fed. The new Jan. 9 rates reflected the changed Federal Reserve policy but not an overall increase in interest rates. For example, the widely followed "federal funds" rate was left unchanged at 1¼%. As of June 25, it was 1%.

Federal Reserve System

The Federal Reserve System is the central bank for the U.S. The system was established on Dec. 23, 1913, originally to give the country an elastic currency, to provide facilities for discounting commercial paper, and to improve the supervision of banking. Since then, the system's responsibilities have been broadened. Over the years, stability and growth of the economy, a high level of employment, stability in the purchasing power of the dollar, and reasonable balance in transactions with other countries have come to be recognized as primary objectives of governmental economic policy.

The Federal Reserve System consists of the Board of Governors, the 12 District Reserve Banks and their branch offices, and the Federal Open Market Committee. Several advisory councils help the board meet its varied responsibilities.

The hub of the system is the 7-member Board of Governors in Washington. The members of the board are appointed by the president and confirmed by the Senate, to serve 14-year terms. The president also appoints the chairman and vice chairman of the board from among the board members for 4-year terms that may be renewed. As of Oct. 2003 the board members were: Alan Greenspan, Chair; Roger W. Ferguson Jr., Vice Chair; Edward M. Gramlich; Susan Schmidt Bies; Mark W. Olson; Ben S. Bernanke; and Donald L. Kohn.

The board is the policy-making body. In addition to those responsibilities, it supervises the budget and operations of the Reserve Banks, approves the appointments of their presidents, and appoints 3 of each District Bank's directors, including the chairman and vice chairman of each Reserve Bank's board.

The 12 Reserve Banks and their branch offices serve as the decentralized portion of the system, carrying out day-to-day operations such as circulating currency and coin and providing fiscal agency functions and payments mechanism services. The District Banks are in Boston, New York, Philadelphia, Cleveland, Richmond, Atlanta, Chicago, St. Louis, Minneapolis, Kansas City, Dallas, and San Francisco.

The system's principal function is monetary policy, which it controls using 3 tools: reserve requirements, the discount rate, and open market operations. Uniform reserve requirements, set by the board, are applied to the transaction accounts and nonpersonal time deposits of all depository institutions.

Responsibility for setting the discount rate (the interest rate at which depository institutions can borrow money from the Reserve Banks) is shared by the Board of Governors and the Reserve Banks. Changes in the discount rate are recommended by the individual boards of directors of the Reserve Banks and are subject to approval by the Board of Governors.

The most important tool of monetary policy is open market operations (the purchase and sale of government securities). Responsibility for influencing the cost and availability of money and credit through the purchase and sale of government securities lies with the Federal Open Market Committee (FOMC), which is composed of the 7 members of the Board of Governors, the president of the Federal Reserve Bank of New York, and 4 other Federal Reserve Bank presidents, who each serve one-year terms on a rotating basis. The committee bases its decisions on economic and financial developments and outlook, setting yearly growth objectives for key measures of money supply and credit. The decisions of the committee are carried out by the Domestic Trading Desk of the Federal Reserve Bank of New York.

The Federal Reserve Act prescribes a Federal Advisory Council, consisting of 1 member from each Federal Reserve District, who is elected annually by the Board of Directors of each of the 12 Federal Reserve Banks. The council meets with the Federal Reserve Board 4 times a year to discuss business and financial conditions, as well as to make advisory recommendations.

The Consumer Advisory Council is a statutory body, including both consumer and creditor representatives, which advises the Board of Governors on its implementation of consumer regulations and other consumer-related matters.

Following the congressional passage of the Monetary Control Act of 1980, the Federal Reserve System's Board of Governors established the Thrift Institutions Advisory Council to provide information and perspectives on the special needs and problems of thrift institutions. This group is composed of representatives of mutual savings banks, savings and loan associations, and credit unions.

Website: www.federalreserve.gov

United States Mint

Source: United States Mint, U.S. Dept. of the Treasury

The United States Mint was created on Apr. 2, 1792, by an act of Congress, which established the U.S. national coinage system. Supervision of the mint was a function of the secretary of state, but in 1799 the mint became an independent agency reporting directly to the president. The mint was made a statutory bureau of the Treasury Department in 1873, with a director appointed by the president to oversee its operations.

The mint manufactures and ships all U.S. coins for circulation to Federal Reserve banks and branches, which in turn issue coins to the public and business community through depository institutions. The mint also safeguards the Treasury Department's stored gold and silver, as well as other monetary assets.

The composition of dimes, quarters, and half dollars, traditionally produced from silver, was changed by the Coinage Act of 1965, which mandated that these coins from here on in be minted from a cupronickel-clad alloy and reduced the silver content of the half dollar to 40%. In 1970, legislative action mandated that the half dollar and a dollar coin be minted from the same alloy.

The Eisenhower dollar was minted from 1971 through 1978, when legislation called for the minting of the smaller Susan B. Anthony dollar coin. The Anthony dollar, which was minted from 1979 through 1981, marked the first time that a woman, other than a mythical figure, appeared on a U.S. coin produced for general circulation. Authorized by the U.S. Dollar Coin Act of 1997 to replace the Susan B. Anthony dollar in 2000, is the Golden Dollar Coin. Golden in color, with a smooth edge and wide border, the obverse side depicts Sacagawea (a Shoshone woman who helped guide Lewis and Clark) and her infant son. The reverse shows an American eagle and 17 stars, one for each of the states at the time of the Lewis and Clark expedition.

Mint headquarters are in Washington, DC. Mint production facilities are in Philadelphia, Denver, San Francisco, and West Point, NY. In addition, the mint is responsible for the U.S. Bullion Depository at Fort Knox, KY.

Proof coin sets, silver proof coin sets, and uncirculated coin sets are available from the mint. The mint also produces ongoing series of national and historic medals in honor of significant persons, events, and sites.

Since 1982, the mint has produced the following congressionally authorized commemorative coins: 1982 George Washington half dollar; 1984 U.S. Olympic coins; 1986 U.S. Statue of Liberty coins; 1987 Bicentennial of the U.S. Constitution coins; 1989 U.S. Congressional coins; 1990 Eisenhower Centennial coin; 1991 United Services Organization 59th Anniversary coin; 1991 Korean War Memorial coin; 1991 Mount Rushmore Anniversary coins; 1992 U.S. Olympic coins; 1992 White House 200th Anniversary coin; 1992 Christopher Columbus Quincentenary coins; 1993 Bill of Rights coins; 1993 World War II 50th Anniversary coins; 1994 World Cup USA coins; Thomas Jefferson 250th Anniversary coin; U.S. Veterans coins (featuring the Prisoner of War coin, Vietnam Veterans Memorial coin, and Women in Military Service for America coin); Bicentennial of the U.S. Capitol Commemorative Silver Dollar; 1995 Civil War Battlefield coins; 1995/1996 U.S. Olympic Games of the Atlanta Centennial Games; 1997 U.S. Botanic Garden Silver

Dollar; 1997 Franklin Delano Roosevelt Gold coin; 1997 Gold and Silver Jackie Robinson Commemorative coins; 1997 National Law Enforcement Memorial Silver Dollar; Black Revolutionary War Patriots Silver Dollar; Robert F. Kennedy Silver Dollar; National Law Enforcement Officers Memorial Silver Dollar; 1999 Yellowstone National Park Silver Dollar; 1999 George Washington five-dollar gold coin; the Dolley Madison Silver Dollar; 2000 U.S. Leif Ericson Proof Silver Dollar; 2000 Icelandic Leif Ericson Proof Silver Krønur; the 2000 Library of Congress Commemorative Coin Program featuring the Proof Silver Dollar and the Proof Bi-metallic Gold and Platinum $10 coin; the 2001 American Buffalo Proof Siver Dollar; the 2001 U.S. Capitol Visitor Center Commemorative Coin Program, featuring the Half Dollar Clad Proof coin, the Proof Silver Dollar, and the Proof Gold $5 coin; the 2002 Olympic Winter Games Silver Dollar and Gold $5 coins, and 2002 West Point Bicentennial

Commemorative Silver Dollar; the 2003 First Flight Centennial Commemorative coins (Gold, Silver, and Clad).

The congressionally authorized American Eagle gold, platinum, and silver bullion coins are available through dealers worldwide. The gold and platinum eagles are sold in one-ounce, half-ounce, quarter-ounce, and one-tenth-ounce sizes. The American eagle silver bullion coin contains one troy ounce of .999 fine silver and is priced according to the daily market value of silver. These coins also are available directly from the mint in proof condition, separately priced.

The mint offers free public tours and operates sales centers at the U.S. mints in Denver and Philadelphia; it also operates a sales center at Union Station, in Washington, DC.

Further information is available from the U.S. Mint, Customer Care Center, 801 9th St., NW, Washington, DC 20220. Telephone number: (800) USA-MINT.
Website: www.usmint.gov

Denominations of U.S. Currency

Since 1969 the largest denomination of U.S. currency that has been issued is the $100 bill. As larger-denomination bills reach the Federal Reserve Bank, they are removed from circulation. Because some discontinued currency is expected to be in the hands of holders for many years, the description of the various denominations below is continued.

Amt.	Portait	Embellishment on Back	Amt.	Portait	Embellishment on Back
$1	Washington	Great Seal of U.S.	$100	B. Franklin	Independence Hall
2	Jefferson	Signers of Declaration	500	McKinley	Ornate denominational marking
5	Lincoln	Lincoln Memorial	1,000	Cleveland	Ornate denominational marking
10	Hamilton	U.S. Treasury	5,000	Madison	Ornate denominational marking
20	Jackson	White House	10,000	Salmon Chase	Ornate denominational marking
50	Grant	U.S. Capitol	100,000*	Wilson	Ornate denominational marking

*For use only in transactions between Federal Reserve System and Treasury Department.

New Commemorative State Quarters, 1999-2008

Source: United States Mint, U.S. Dept. of the Treasury

Beginning in Jan. 1999, a series of five quarter dollars with new reverses are being issued each year through 2008, celebrating each of the 50 states. To make room on the reverse of the commemorative quarters for each state's design, certain design elements have been moved, thereby creating a new obverse design as well. The coins are being issued in the sequence the states became part of the Union (date each state entered the union is shown below).

1999	2000	2001	2002	2003
Delaware Dec. 7, 1787	Massachusetts Feb. 6, 1788	New York July 26, 1788	Tennessee June 1, 1796	Illinois Dec. 3, 1818
Pennsylvania Dec. 12, 1787	Maryland Apr. 28, 1788	North Carolina Nov. 21, 1789	Ohio Mar. 1, 1803	Alabama Dec. 14, 1819
New Jersey Dec. 18, 1787	South Carolina May 23, 1788	Rhode Island May 29, 1790	Louisiana Apr. 30, 1812	Maine Mar. 15, 1820
Georgia Jan. 2, 1788	New Hampshire June 21, 1788	Vermont Mar. 4, 1791	Indiana Dec. 11, 1816	Missouri Aug. 10, 1821
Connecticut Jan. 9, 1788	Virginia June 25, 1788	Kentucky June 1, 1792	Mississippi Dec. 10, 1817	Arkansas June 15, 1836

2004	2005	2006	2007	2008
Michigan Jan. 26, 1837	California Sept. 9, 1850	Nevada Oct. 31, 1864	Montana Nov. 8, 1889	Oklahoma Nov. 16, 1907
Florida Mar. 3, 1845	Minnesota May 11, 1858	Nebraska Mar. 1, 1867	Washington Nov. 11, 1889	New Mexico Jan. 6, 1912
Texas Dec. 29, 1845	Oregon Feb. 14, 1859	Colorado Aug. 1, 1876	Idaho July 3, 1890	Arizona Feb. 14, 1912
Iowa Dec. 28, 1846	Kansas Jan. 29, 1861	North Dakota Nov. 2, 1889	Wyoming July 10, 1890	Alaska Jan. 3, 1959
Wisconsin May 29, 1848	West Virginia J une 20, 1863	South Dakota Nov. 2, 1889	Utah Jan. 4, 1896	Hawaii Aug. 21, 1959

Portraits on U.S. Treasury Bills, Bonds, Notes, and Savings Bonds

Denomination	Savings bonds	Treasury bills*	Treasury bonds*	Treasury notes*
$50	Washington		Jefferson	
75	Adams			
100	Jefferson		Jackson	
200	Madison			
500	Hamilton		Washington	
1,000	B. Franklin	H. McCulloch	Lincoln	Lincoln
5,000	P. Revere	J. G. Carlisle	Monroe	Monroe
10,000	J. Wilson	J. Sherman	Cleveland	Cleveland
50,000	C. Glass			
100,000		A. Gallatin	Grant	Grant
1,000,000		O. Wolcott	T. Roosevelt	T. Roosevelt
100,000,000				Madison
500,000,000				McKinley

*The U.S. Treasury discontinued issuing treasury bill, bond, and note certificates in 1986. Since then, all issues of marketable treasury securities have been available only in book-entry form, although some certificates remain in circulation.

> **IT'S A FACT:** According to the U.S. Secret Service, in 1995 fewer than 1% of counterfeit notes detected in the U.S. were created digitally. By 2002, this number had risen by 40%.

U.S. Currency and Coin

Source: Financial Management Service, U.S. Dept. of the Treasury (June 30, 2003)

Amounts Outstanding and in Circulation

Currency	Total currency and coin	Total currency	Federal Reserve notes[1]	U.S. notes	Currency no longer issued
Amounts outstanding	$801,910,239,078	$767,356,305,220	$766,845,226,896	$260,472,666	$250,605,658
Less amounts held by:					
Treasury	304,112,857	20,010,857	19,792,658	20,739	197,460
Federal Reserve banks	108,234,784,035	107,292,888,062	107,292,886,625	50	1,387
Amounts in circulation	$693,371,342,186	$660,043,406,301	$659,532,547,613	$260,451,877	$250,406,811

Coins[2]		Total	Dollars[3]	Fractional coins
Amounts outstanding		$34,553,933,858	$3,500,209,008	$31,053,724,850
Less amounts held by:				
Treasury		284,102,000	275,214,000	8,888,000
Federal Reserve banks		941,895,973	142,889,793	799,006,180
Amounts in circulation		$33,327,935,885	$3,082,105,215	$30,245,830,670

(1) Issued on or after July 1, 1929. (2) Excludes coins sold to collectors at premium prices. (3) Includes $481,781,898 in standard silver dollars.

Currency in Circulation by Denominations

(June 30, 2003)

Denomination	Total currency in circulation	Federal Reserve notes[1]	U.S. notes	Currency no longer issued
$1	$7,859,958,822	$7,714,441,001	$143,481	$145,374,340
$2	1,320,297,544	1,187,976,202	132,308,766	12,576
$5	9,130,373,135	8,991,624,100	109,525,910	29,223,125
$10	14,288,442,110	14,266,768,950	5,950	21,667,210
$20	100,145,035,940	100,124,931,360	3,380	20,101,200
$50	57,500,583,650	57,489,090,200	-	11,493,450
$100	469,484,877,000	469,444,422,300	18,464,300	21,990,400
$500	142,690,500	142,506,500	-	184,000
$1,000	165,952,000	165,747,000	-	205,000
$5,000	1,755,000	1,700,000	-	55,000
$10,000	3,440,000	3,340,000	-	100,000
Fractional parts	485	—	—	485
Partial notes[2]	115	—	90	25
TOTAL CURRENCY	**$660,043,406,301**	**$659,532,547,613**	**$260,451,877**	**$250,406,811**

(1) Issued on or after July 1, 1929. (2) Represents the value of certain partial denominations not presented for redemption.

Comparative Totals of Money in Circulation — Selected Dates

Date	Dollars (in millions)	Per capita[1]	Date	Dollars (in millions)	Per capita[1]
April 30, 2003	$688.772.0	$2,368.17	June 30, 1970	$54,351.0	$265.39
Mar. 31, 2002	641,909.0	2,238.45	June 30, 1965	39,719.8	204.14
Mar. 30, 2001	585.916.0	2,121.82	June 30, 1960	32,064.6	177.47
Mar. 31, 2000	562,949.0	2,050.00	June 30, 1955	30,229.3	182.90
Mar. 31, 1999	517,829.0	1,902.21	June 30, 1950	27,156.3	179.03
Mar. 31, 1998	474,979.0	1,762.42	June 30, 1945	26,746.4	191.14
Mar. 31, 1997	444,534.0	1,664.58	June 30, 1940	7,847.5	59.40
Mar. 31, 1996	416,280.0	1,573.15	June 30, 1935	5,567.1	43.75
Mar. 31, 1995	401,610.0	1,531.39	June 30, 1930	4,522.0	36.74
Mar. 31, 1990	257,664.4	1,028.71	June 30, 1925	4,815.2	41.56
June 30, 1985	185,890.7	778.58	June 30, 1920	5,467.6	51.36
June 30, 1980	127,097.2	558.28	June 30, 1915	3,319.6	33.01
June 30, 1975	81,196.4	380.08	June 30, 1910	3,148.7	34.07

(1) Based on Bureau of the Census estimates of population. The requirement for a gold reserve against U.S. notes was repealed by Public Law 90-269, approved Mar. 18, 1968. Silver certificates issued on and after July 1, 1929, became redeemable from the general fund on June 24, 1968. The amount of security after those dates has been reduced accordingly.

New U.S. Currency Designs

On Mar. 25, 1996, the U.S. Treasury issued a redesigned $100 note incorporating many new and modified anti-counterfeiting features. It was the first of the U.S. currency series to be redesigned. A new $50 note was issued Oct. 27, 1997, a new $20 bill was released into circulation Sept. 24, 1998, and new $10 and $5 notes were issued May 24, 2000; a new $1 note with a more modest redesign was to come next. Old notes are being removed from circulation as they are returned to the Federal Reserve.

The new $100 bill has a larger portrait, moved off-center; a watermark (seen only when held up to the light) to the right of the portrait, depicting the same person (Benjamin Franklin); a security thread that glows red when exposed to ultraviolet light in a dark environment; color-shifting ink that changes from green to black when viewed at different angles, to appear in the numeral on the lower, front right-hand corner of the bill; microprinting in the numeral in the note's lower, front left-hand corner and on the portrait; and other features for security, machine authenti-

cation, and processing of the currency. The redesigned $5, $10, $20, and $50 bills incorporate the same features as the $100 bill, with the notable addition of a low-vision feature, a large (14-mm high, as compared to 7.8-mm on the old design), dark numeral on a light background on the back of the note. (The security thread glows yellow in the $50, green in the $20, orange in the $10, and blue in the $5. There is no color-shifting ink on the $5 note.) More new currency information is available on the U.S. Treasury's website: www.ustreas.gov

On Oct. 9, 2003, the U.S. Treasury introduced a new $20 note, using background colors for the first time since 1905. The new note features subtle shades of green, blue, and peach. The notes have a security thread running vertically up one side, with "USA TWENTY" and a small U.S. flag; the thread glows green under UV light. Other security features include a watermark similar to the portrait of Andrew Jackson and color-shifting ink in the number "20" in the lower right corner on the note's face.

> ▶ **IT'S A FACT:** The estimated federal budget deficit of $374 billion for fiscal year 2003 and the estimated one-year deficit increase of $216 billion between fiscal years 2002 and 2003 are both the largest in dollar value in U.S. history. (However, at 3.5% of GDP, the 2003 deficit is still smaller relative to the size of the economy than deficits of the mid-1980s and early 1990s.)

Summary of Receipts, Outlays, and Surpluses or Deficits, 1936-2003

Source: Financial Management Service, U.S. Dept. of the Treasury

(millions of current dollars)

Fiscal Year[1]	Receipts	Outlays	Surplus or Deficit (–)[2]	Fiscal Year[1]	Receipts	Outlays	Surplus or Deficit (–)[2]
1936	$3,923	$8,228	$–4,304	1971	$187,139	$210,172	$–23,033
1937	5,387	7,580	–2,193	1972	207,309	230,681	–23,373
1938	6,751	6,840	–89	1973	230,799	245,707	–14,908
1939	6,295	9,141	–2,846	1974	263,224	269,359	–6,135
1940	6,548	9,468	–2,920	1975	279,090	332,332	–53,242
1941	8,712	13,653	–4,941	1976	298,060	371,779	–73,719
1942	14,634	35,137	–20,503	Transition quarter[3]	81,232	95,973	–14,741
1943	24,001	78,555	–54,554	1977	355,559	409,203	–53,644
1944	43,747	91,304	–47,557	1978	399,561	458,729	–59,168
1945	45,159	92,712	–47,553	1979	463,302	503,464	–40,162
1946	39,296	55,232	–15,936	1980	517,112	590,920	–73,808
1947	38,514	34,496	4,018	1981	599,272	678,209	–78,936
1948	41,560	29,764	11,796	1982	617,766	745,706	–127,940
1949	39,415	38,835	580	1983	600,562	808,327	–207,764
1950	39,443	42,562	–3,119	1984	666,467	851,781	–185,324
1951	51,616	45,514	6,102	1985	734,057	946,316	–212,260
1952	66,167	67,686	–1,519	1986	769,091	990,231	–221,140
1953	69,608	76,101	–6,493	1987	854,143	1,003,804	–149,661
1954	69,701	70,855	–1,154	1988	908,166	1,063,318	–155,151
1955	65,451	68,444	–2,993	1989	990,701	1,144,020	–153,319
1956	74,587	70,640	3,947	1990	1,031,308	1,251,776	–220,469
1957	79,990	76,578	3,412	1991	1,054,265	1,323,757	–269,492
1958	79,636	82,405	–2,769	1992	1,090,453	1,380,794	–290,340
1959	79,249	92,098	–12,849	1993	1,153,226	1,408,532	–255,306
1960	92,492	92,191	301	1994	1,257,451	1,460,553	–203,102
1961	94,388	97,723	–3,335	1995	1,351,495	1,515,412	–163,917
1962	99,676	106,821	–7,146	1996	1,452,763	1,560,094	–107,331
1963	106,560	111,316	–4,756	1997	1,578,955	1,600,911	–21,957
1964	112,613	118,528	–5,915	1998	1,721,421	1,652,224	+70,039
1965	116,817	118,228	–1,411	1999	1,827,302	1,704,942	+124,360
1966	130,835	134,532	–3,698	2000	2,025,060	1,788,143	+236,917
1967	148,822	157,464	–8,643	2001[R]	1,991,044	1,863,769	+127,021
1968	152,973	178,134	–25,161	2002[R]	1,853,296	2,010,962	–157,666
1969	186,882	183,640	3,242	2003[E]	1,783,000	2,157,000	–374,000
1970	192,807	195,649	–2,842				

R = Revised. E = Estimated. (1) Fiscal years 1936 to 1976 end June 30; after 1976, fiscal years end Sept. 30. (2) May not equal difference between figures shown, because of rounding. (3) Transition quarter covers July 1, 1976-Sept. 30, 1976.

Budget Receipts and Outlays, 1789-1935

Source: U.S. Dept. of the Treasury; annual statements for years ending June 30 unless otherwise noted

(thousands of dollars)

Yearly Average	Receipts	Outlays	Yearly Average	Receipts	Outlays	Yearly Average	Receipts	Outlays
1789-1800[1]	$5,717	$5,776	1861-1865	$160,907	$683,785	1901-1905	$559,481	$535,559
1801-1810[2]	13,056	9,086	1866-1870	447,301	377,642	1906-1910	628,507	639,178
1811-1820[2]	21,032	23,943	1871-1875	336,830	287,460	1911-1915	710,227	720,252
1821-1830[2]	21,928	16,162	1876-1880	288,124	255,598	1916-1920	3,483,652	8,065,333
1831-1840[2]	30,461	24,495	1881-1885	366,961	257,691	1921-1925	4,306,673	3,578,989
1841-1850[2]	28,545	34,097	1886-1890	375,448	279,134	1926-1930	4,069,138	3,182,807
1851-1860	60,237	60,163	1891-1895	352,891	363,599	1931-1935	2,770,973	5,214,874
			1896-1900	434,877	457,451			

(1) Average for period March 4, 1789, to Dec. 31, 1800. (2) Years from 1801 to 1842 end Dec. 31; average for 1841-1850 is for the period Jan. 1, 1841, to June 30, 1850.

Public Debt of the U.S.

Source: Bureau of Public Debt, U.S. Dept. of the Treasury; World Almanac research

Fiscal year	Debt (billions)	Debt per cap. (dollars)	Interest paid (billions)	% of federal outlays	Fiscal year	Debt (billions)	Debt per cap. (dollars)	Interest paid (billions)	% of federal outlays
1870	$2.4	$61.06	—	—	1983	$1,377.2	$5,870	$128.8	15.9
1880	2.0	41.60	—	—	1984	1,572.3	6,640	153.8	18.1
1890	1.1	17.80	—	—	1985	1,823.1	7,598	178.9	18.9
1900	1.2	16.60	—	—	1986	2,125.3	8,774	190.2	19.2
1910	1.1	12.41	—	—	1987	2,350.3	9,615	195.4	19.5
1920	24.2	228	—	—	1988	2,602.3	10,534	214.1	20.1
1930	16.1	131	—	—	1989	2,857.4	11,545	240.9	21.0
1940	43.0	325	$1.0	10.5	1990	3,233.3	13,000	264.8	21.1
1950	256.1	1,688	5.7	13.4	1991	3,665.3	14,436	285.5	21.6
1955	272.8	1,651	6.4	9.4	1992	4,064.6	15,846	292.3	21.2
1960	284.1	1,572	9.2	10.0	1993	4,411.5	17,105	292.5	20.8
1965	313.8	1,613	11.3	9.6	1994	4,692.8	18,025	296.3	20.3
1970	370.1	1,814	19.3	9.9	1995	4,974.0	18,930	332.4	22.0
1975	533.2	2,475	32.7	9.8	1996	5,224.8	19,805	344.0	22.0
1976	620.4	2,852	37.1	10.0	1997	5,413.1	20,026	355.8	22.2
1977	698.8	3,170	41.9	10.2	1998	5,526.2	20,443	363.8	22.0
1978	771.5	3,463	48.7	10.6	1999	5,656.3	20,746	353.5	20.7
1979	826.5	3,669	59.8	11.9	2000	5,674.2	20,591	362.0	20.3
1980	907.7	3,985	74.9	12.7	2001	5,807.5	20,353	359.5	19.3
1981	997.9	4,338	95.6	14.1	2002	6,228.2	21,589	332.5	16.5
1982	1,142.0	4,913	117.4	15.7	2003[1]	6,783.2	23,230	318.1	14.7

Note: As of end of fiscal year. Through 1976 the fiscal year ended June 30. From 1977 on, the fiscal year ends Sept. 30. (1) Estimated.

U.S. Budget Receipts and Outlays, 1998-2003

Source: Financial Management Service, U.S. Dept. of the Treasury; Congressional Budget Office

As of Oct. 2003, the estimate from the Congressional Budget Office of the total U.S. budget deficit for the fiscal year 2003 was $374 billion, or 3.5% of GDP. This is more than double the deficit for fiscal year 2002, which was $158 billion, or 1.5% of GDP.

(in millions of current dollars; many figures do not add to totals because of independent rounding or omitted subcategories, including some subcategories with negative values.)

	Fiscal 1998[1]	Fiscal 1999[1]	Fiscal 2000[1]	Fiscal 2001[1]	Fiscal 2002[1]	Fiscal 2003[1,2]
NET RECEIPTS						
Individual income taxes	$828,597	$879,480	$1,004,461	$994,339	$858,345	$789,972
Corporation income taxes	188,677	184,680	207,288	151,075	148,044	125,308
Social insurance taxes and contributions:						
Federal old-age and survivors insurance	358,784	383,559	411,676	434,057	440,541	—
Federal disability insurance	57,016	60,910	68,907	73,463	74,780	—
Federal hospital insurance	119,863	132,268	135,528	149,650	149,049	—
Railroad retirement fund	4,353	4,143	4,336	4,272	4,177	—
Total employment taxes and contributions	540,015	580,880	620,447	661,442	668,548	687,832
Other insurance and retirement:						
Unemployment	27,484	26,480	27,641	27,812	27,620	34,230
Federal employees retirement	4,261	4,399	4,693	4,647	4,533	—
Non-federal employees	74	73	70	66	61	—
Total social insurance taxes and contributions	571,835	611,832	652,851	693,967	700,761	726,593
Excise taxes	57,669	70,412	68,866	66,232	66,989	67,085
Estate and gift taxes	24,076	27,782	29,010	28,400	26,507	21,962
Customs duties	18,297	18,336	19,913	19,616	18,602	20,023
Deposits of earnings by Federal Reserve Banks	24,540	25,917	32,293	26,124	23,683	23,565
All other miscellaneous receipts	5,027	5,112	5,807	11,426	10,366	11,144
Net Budget Receipts	1,721,421	1,827,302	2,025,038	1,990,930	1,853,296	1,783,000
NET OUTLAYS						
Legislative Branch	2,600	2,612	2,913	3,029	3,230	3,926
The Judiciary	3,463	3,793	4,087	4,409	4,824	5,109
Executive Office of the President:						
The White House Office	46	51	53	52	58	—
Office of Management and Budget	56	59	64	64	71	—
Total Executive Office	236	416	284	280	496	1,324
International Assistance Program:						
International security assistance	4,950	5,405	6,534	6,783	7,982	—
Multilateral assistance	1,850	1,857	1,759	2,166	2,187	—
Agency for International Development	2,435	2,337	2,622	2,764	3,682	—
International Development Assistance	2,494	2,410	2,953	2,895	3,752	—
Total International Assistance Program	8,980	10,061	12,083	11,767	13,309	16,732
Agriculture Department:						
Food stamp program	20,141	19,005	18,295	19,097	22,069	—
Farm Service Agency	10,421	19,508	33,353	22,974	17,519	—
Forest Service	3,399	3,423	3,978	4,225	5,438	—
Total Agriculture Department	53,950	62,839	75,728	68,156	68,989	76,995
Commerce Department:						
Bureau of the Census	542	1,131	4,214	1,025	628	—
Total Commerce Department	4,047	5,036	7,931	5,017	5,322	6,079
Defense Department—Military:						
Military personnel	68,976	69,503	75,950	73,977	86,802	—
Operation and maintenance	93,473	96,420	105,871	112,019	130,167	—
Procurement	48,207	48,824	51,616	54,991	62,511	—
Research, development, test, evaluation	37,421	37,362	37,608	40,462	44,388	—
Military construction	6,046	5,519	5,111	4,978	5,055	—
Total Defense Department—Military	256,124	261,379	281,233	290,980	332,116	408,578
Defense Department—Civil	31,216	32,008	32,019	34,161	35,159	40,159
Education Department	31,498	32,435	33,308	35,959	46,285	59,693
Energy Department	14,444	16,054	15,010	16,420	17,772	19,493
Health and Human Services Department:						
Public Health Service	23,680	25,554	28,281	32,667	36,597	—
Centers for Medicare and Medicaid Services[3]	379,950	390,181	413,124	450,751	243,001	—
Food and Drug Administration	838	951	1,023	1,075	1,127	—
National Institutes of Health	12,501	13,815	15,415	17,254	20,450	—
Total Health and Human Services Dept.	350,571	359,700	382,627	426,444	466,104	508,405
Homeland Security Department	—	—	—	—	—	35,845
Housing and Urban Development Department	30,224	32,736	30,830	33,937	31,880	38,048
Interior Department	7,232	7,814	8,036	8,024	9,641	10,385
Justice Department:						
Federal Bureau of Investigation	2,949	3,040	3,088	20,810	3,556	—
Drug Enforcement Administration	1,099	1,203	1,339	3,208	1,602	—
Immigration and Naturalization Service[4]	3,593	3,775	4,163	4,558	5,340	—
Federal Prison System	2,682	3,204	3,708	4,205	4,746	—
Total Justice Department	16,169	18,318	19,561	20,810	24,197	21,459
Labor Department:						
Unemployment Trust Fund	23,408	24,870	24,149	31,530	62,211	—
Total Labor Department	30,002	32,459	31,354	39,280	64,252	70,700
State Department	5,373	6,463	6,849	7,446	9,453	11,009
Transportation Department:						
Federal Aviation Administration	9,242	9,507	9,561	10,731	13,096	—
Total Transportation Department	39,467	41,836	46,030	54,075	61,282	51,532
Treasury Department:						
Internal Revenue Service	33,153	37,087	37,986	38,695	46,996	—
Interest on the public debt	363,824	353,511	362,118	359,508	332,537	324,634
Total Treasury Department	390,094	386,703	390,813	389,944	374,516	373,647
Veterans Affairs Department	41,776	43,169	47,087	45,043	50,881	58,300
Environmental Protection Agency	6,288	6,752	7,236	7,390	7,451	8,051

	Fiscal 1998[1]	Fiscal 1999[1]	Fiscal 2000[1]	Fiscal 2001[1]	Fiscal 2002[1]	Fiscal 2003[1,2]
General Services Administration	$1,095	$–46	$25	$–8	$–271	$1,011
National Aeronautics and Space Administration	14,206	13,665	13,442	14,094	14,429	14,798
Office of Personnel Management	46,307	47,515	48,660	50,915	52,512	55,794
Small Business Administration	–78	58	–422	–569	492	1,567
Social Security Administration	408,202	419,790	441,810	461,748	488,694	508,676
Other independent agencies:						
Corporation for Natl. and Community Service	591	609	684	757	793	—
Corporation for Public Broadcasting	250	281	316	360	375	—
District of Columbia	818	–2,910	312	539	927	—
Equal Employment Opportunity Commission	244	255	290	289	324	—
Export-Import Bank of the U.S.	–208	–159	–743	–1,749	–140	—
Federal Communications Commission	1,769	3,293	4,073	4,011	5,253	—
Federal Deposit Insurance Corporation	–4,122	–5,025	–2,837	–1,220	–353	—
Legal Services Corporation	285	298	301	320	333	—
National Archives & Records Adm.	210	225	201	217	268	—
National Foundation on the Arts and Humanities	207	217	218	223	227	—
National Labor Relations Board	177	182	198	220	230	—
National Science Foundation	3,188	3,285	3,487	3,691	4,187	4,921
Nuclear Regulatory Commission	38	37	33	31	40	—
Railroad Retirement Board	4,837	4,830	4,992	5,541	5,425	—
Securities and Exchange Commission	–231	–255	–506	–330	–536	—
Smithsonian Institution	488	486	517	561	616	—
Tennessee Valley Authority	–784	2	–307	–662	124	—
Total other independent agencies	**10,653**	**6,943**	**10,526**	**12,581**	**15,874**	**—**
Undistributed offsetting receipts	–161,036	–159,080	–172,844	–190,946	–201,149	–211,901
NET BUDGET OUTLAYS	**$1,652,224**	**$1,704,942**	**$1,788,045**	**$1,863,909**	**$2,010,962**	**$2,157,000**
Less net receipts	1,721,421	1,827,302	2,025,038	1,990,930	1,853,296	1,783,000
DEFICIT (-) OR SURPLUS (+)	**$+70,039**	**$+124,360**	**$+236,993**	**$+127,021**	**$–157,666**	**$–374,000**

— = Not available. (1) Fiscal year ends Sept. 30. (2) Figures for some agencies are preliminary. (3) Formerly the Health Care Financing Adm. (4) As of Jan. 2003, transferred to Homeland Security Dept.

State Finances: Revenue, Expenditures, Debt, and Taxes

Source: Census Bureau, U.S. Dept. of Commerce
(fiscal year 2001)

STATE	Revenue (millions)	Expenditures (millions)	Debt (millions)	Per capita debt	Per capita taxes	Per capita expenditures
Alabama	$17,860	$16,718	$5,577	$1,248	$1,510	$3,741
Alaska	6,186	9,047	4,507	7,109	2,255	14,270
Arizona	15,489	17,143	3,711	699	1,575	3,230
Arkansas	10,330	10,597	2,842	1,054	1,851	3,932
California	176,081	170,470	62,343	1,802	2,614	4,927
Colorado	19,774	15,686	4,917	1,110	1,708	3,540
Connecticut	17,750	18,189	19,027	5,539	2,881	5,295
Delaware	5,114	4,312	3,889	4,879	2,644	5,410
Florida	46,371	50,265	18,613	1,137	1,523	3,070
Georgia	25,250	27,860	7,520	895	1,709	3,314
Hawaii	6,591	6,792	5,301	4,320	2,859	5,536
Idaho	5,286	4,952	2,342	1,773	1,937	3,748
Illinois	47,348	45,170	30,248	2,416	1,849	3,608
Indiana	20,767	21,584	8,518	1,390	1,651	3,523
Iowa	10,255	12,271	2,542	867	1,759	4,185
Kansas	8,713	10,197	2,184	808	1,846	3,774
Kentucky	18,550	17,331	8,348	2,052	1,930	4,259
Louisiana	17,811	16,410	7,977	1,785	1,610	3,671
Maine	5,207	5,738	4,211	3,280	2,078	4,469
Maryland	20,939	21,484	11,661	2,165	2,003	3,989
Massachusetts	29,304	32,435	42,149	6,585	2,691	5,067
Michigan	43,347	46,658	20,114	2,010	2,225	4,663
Minnesota	26,135	24,612	5,624	1,128	2,715	4,937
Mississippi	11,693	11,727	3,819	1,335	1,661	4,101
Missouri	20,134	18,888	11,373	2,018	1,568	3,351
Montana	4,224	4,048	2,740	3,027	1,652	4,473
Nebraska	5,944	6,111	1,800	1,046	1,766	3,553
Nevada	6,644	6,747	3,387	1,615	1,827	3,216
New Hampshire	4,575	4,411	5,608	4,454	1,394	3,504
New Jersey	42,788	37,660	29,728	3,493	2,262	4,425
New Mexico	9,099	9,174	4,305	2,351	2,186	5,010
New York	112,439	106,599	80,385	4,212	2,351	5,586
North Carolina	32,203	31,627	9,998	1,218	1,901	3,854
North Dakota	3,373	2,898	1,549	2,432	1,829	4,549
Ohio	52,803	47,880	18,748	1,646	1,722	4,204
Oklahoma	12,746	11,416	5,986	1,725	1,828	3,290
Oregon	18,219	16,321	6,418	1,848	1,697	4,699
Pennsylvania	45,887	51,488	19,249	1,565	1,835	4,185
Rhode Island	5,483	5,351	5,833	5,503	2,120	5,048
South Carolina	16,865	18,079	9,560	2,354	1,579	4,451
South Dakota	3,171	2,690	2,216	2,923	1,289	3,549
Tennessee	17,344	18,385	3,388	589	1,399	3,198
Texas	65,525	64,686	16,816	787	1,377	3,027
Utah	9,132	9,253	4,023	1,765	1,787	4,060
Vermont	3,143	3,371	2,326	3,794	2,533	5,499
Virginia	22,760	26,787	12,963	1,801	1,818	3,722
Washington	23,646	27,824	12,607	2,104	2,116	4,643
West Virginia	8,297	7,300	4,092	2,272	1,901	4,054
Wisconsin	18,826	24,857	12,172	2,252	2,177	4,598
Wyoming	2,880	2,645	1,346	2,725	2,277	5,355
ALL STATES[1]	**$1,180,304**	**$1,184,146**	**$576,599**	**$2,025**	**$1,966**	**$4,159**

(1) Totals may not add because of rounding.

State and Local Government Receipts and Current Expenditures

Source: Bureau of Economic Analysis, U.S. Dept. of Commerce

(billions of current dollars)

	1999	2000	2001	2002
RECEIPTS	**$1,144.1**	**$1,214.2**	**$1,261.3**	**$1,304.90**
Personal tax and nontax receipts	255.8	2,77.5	281.2	266.6
Income taxes	199.7	2,18.1	218.7	200.7
Nontaxes	36.1	39.0	41.9	45.1
Other	20.0	20.4	20.6	20.7
Corporate profits tax accruals	34.8	35.6	29.1	33.5
Indirect business tax and nontax accruals	612.7	644.5	664.4	689.8
Sales taxes	300.6	314.3	321.2	333.5
Property taxes	239.2	248.1	257.4	267.8
Other	72.9	82.1	85.8	88.5
Contributions for social insurance	9.7	9.2	9.2	9.4
Federal grants-in-aid	231.0	247.5	277.4	305.7
CURRENT EXPENDITURES	**1,105.8**	**1,196.2**	**1,292.6**	**1,356.40**
Consumption expenditures	864.7	937.9	993.7	1,034.5
Transfer payments to persons	252.7	271.3	304.4	335.6
Net interest paid	−0.7	−2.8	−2.1	−2.0
Interest paid	78.7	81.4	83.3	85.2
Less: Interest received by government	79.4	84.2	85.4	87.1
Less: Dividends received by government	0.4	0.4	0.4	0.5
Subsidies less current surplus of government enterprises	−10.5	−9.7	−3.1	−11.2
Subsidies	0.4	0.4	7.8	0.8
Less: Current surplus of government enterprises	10.9	10.2	10.9	12
Less: Wage accruals less disbursements	0.0	0.0	0.0	0.0
CURRENT SURPLUS or DEFICIT (−)	**38.3**	**18.0**	**−31.3**	**−51.5**

State and Local Government Current Expenditures, by Function

Source: Bureau of Economic Analysis, U.S. Dept. of Commerce

(billions of dollars)

	1980	1985	1990	1995	1998	1999	2000	2001
State and local	**$307.8**	**$447.0**	**$660.8**	**$902.5**	**$1,033.7**	**$1,105.8**	**$1,196.2**	**$1,292.6**
General public service	**26.3**	**39.3**	**59.4**	**83.6**	**100.3**	**107.6**	**117.1**	**124.3**
Executive and legislative	4.4	6.5	9.9	12.4	15.0	16.2	17.7	18.9
Tax collection and financial management	8.9	14.6	20.1	26.5	29.2	31.6	34.9	34.6
Net interest paid	−5.5	−8.0	−6.4	0.2	—	−1.1	−3.2	−2.5
Other	18.5	26.3	35.9	44.4	56.1	60.9	67.8	73.4
Public order and safety	**32.4**	**53.7**	**84.5**	**118.9**	**144.1**	**154.7**	**168.7**	**181.8**
Police	14.4	22.3	32.2	44.5	55.1	59.2	65.1	71.5
Fire	5.9	9.3	13.4	17.3	20.5	21.5	23.2	24.8
Law courts	5.7	9.2	14.9	20.6	25.2	27.2	29.5	31.2
Prisons	6.4	13.0	24.1	36.5	43.3	46.7	51.0	54.3
Economic affairs	**36.9**	**47.7**	**58.5**	**72.1**	**81.1**	**87.1**	**95.0**	**107.8**
General economic and labor affairs	7.1	7.4	10.1	12.0	13.8	14.5	15.5	16.2
Agriculture	1.9	1.8	3.7	4.1	4.4	5.0	5.7	5.6
Energy	−1.2	−3.2	−5.4	−6.6	−7.3	−8.0	−8.7	−2.1
Natural resources	2.8	4.2	5.9	8.3	8.6	9.1	9.9	10.7
Transportation	27.7	40.9	52.2	66.1	74.9	80.0	86.4	91.7
Highways	24.7	34.7	43.5	54.6	62.1	66.1	71.8	76.1
Air	−0.3	−0.6	−1.3	−1.7	−2.2	−2.4	−2.5	−2.3
Water	—	—	—	−0.1	−0.2	−0.2	−0.2	−0.3
Transit and railroad	3.3	6.8	10.0	13.3	15.3	16.4	17.4	18.2
Other	−1.4	−4.3	−8.1	−11.8	−13.3	−13.5	−13.8	−14.2
Housing and community services	**4.0**	**2.3**	**4.4**	**3.7**	**6.0**	**6.0**	**7.8**	**7.5**
Water	−0.4	−1.9	−2.4	−3.6	−4.8	−5.4	−5.5	−5.6
Sewerage	1.8	1.5	0.4	−0.7	−1.1	−1.2	−1.2	−1.4
Sanitation	2.4	2.8	4.5	5.3	6.0	6.4	7.0	7.0
Other	0.3	−0.1	1.9	2.7	6.0	6.2	7.5	7.4
Health	**41.2**	**62.3**	**106.2**	**179.6**	**196.7**	**215.6**	**236.5**	**268**
Recreation and culture	**4.1**	**6.5**	**9.4**	**12.2**	**13.9**	**14.7**	**16.1**	**16.8**
Education	**129.8**	**187.7**	**269.1**	**341.6**	**398**	**421**	**449.5**	**474.8**
Elementary and secondary	97.0	140.5	203.5	261.2	307.2	325.3	347.3	366.3
Higher	24.7	36.1	49.5	58.1	65.3	68.4	72.6	77.0
Libraries	1.6	2.5	3.7	4.7	5.8	6.2	6.6	6.9
Other	6.5	8.6	12.5	17.6	19.7	21.1	22.9	24.6
Income security	**33.0**	**47.4**	**69.1**	**90.8**	**93.6**	**99.1**	**105.5**	**111.6**
Disability	3.1	5.4	10.4	13.0	13.4	13.5	13.9	14.3
Welfare and social services	29.9	42.0	58.7	77.8	80.2	85.6	91.6	97.2

WORLD ALMANAC QUICK QUIZ

If you paid $1.00 for an item in the U.S. in 1967, what could you expect to pay in 2003 (based on Consumer Price Index)?

  (a) $2.75   (b) $3.40   (c) $5.49   (d) $7.28

For the answer look in this chapter, or see page 1008.

Top U.S. Charities by Donations, 2002[1]

Source: The Chronicle of Philanthropy
(in millions of dollars)

Rank	Organization	Private Support[2]	Total Income
1	American National Red Cross (Washington, DC)	$1,736.4	$4,087.4
2	Salvation Army (Alexandria, VA)	1,372.0	2,147.4
3	Gifts In Kind International (Alexandria, VA)	793.2	795.7
4	American Cancer Society (Atlanta, GA)	777.4	789.4
5	Fidelity Investments Charitable Gift Fund (Boston, MA)	735.5	758.2
6	Lutheran Services in America (St. Paul, MN)	723.3	8,030.8
7	YMCA of the USA (Chicago, IL)	713.9	4,271.7
8	Nature Conservancy (Arlington, VA)	628.3	972.4
9	University of Southern California (Los Angeles, CA)	585.2	NA
10	Feed the Children (Oklahoma City, OK)	547.0	553.4
11	United Way of New York City (New York, NY)	498.0	523.1
12	America's Second Harvest (Chicago, IL)	485.1	487.9
13	Harvard University (Cambridge, MA)	477.6	2,362.2
14	Stanford University (Palo Alto, CA)	$454.8	$2,511.8
15	Boys and Girls Clubs of America (Atlanta, GA)	453.7	1,079.4
16	American Heart Association (Dallas, TX)	437.5	525.7
17	World Vision (Federal Way, WA)	437.1	553.0
18	AmeriCares Foundation (New Canaan, CT)	412.7	413.5
19	Habitat for Humanity International (Americus, GA)	411.9	718.4
20	Cornell University (Ithaca, NY)	363.0	1,876.0
21	Campus Crusade for Christ International (Orlando, FL)	346.7	386.8
22	Goodwill Industries International (Bethesda, MD)	337.8	2,055.2
23	Food for the Poor (Deerfield Beach, FL)	320.8	351.9
24	University of Pennsylvania (Philadelphia, PA)	319.7	2,714.4
25	The Johns Hopkins University (Baltimore, MD)	318.7	2,412.9

(1) Preliminary. (2) Private support consists of donations from individuals, foundations, and corporations. Total income also includes government funding and fees charged.

Consumer Credit Outstanding, 2000-2002

Source: Federal Reserve System
(billions of dollars)
Estimated amounts of credit outstanding as of end of year. Not seasonally adjusted.

	2000	2001	2002		2000	2001	2002
TOTAL	$1,593.1	$1,701.9	$1,932.9	Credit unions	$22.2	$22.3	$22.2
Major Holders				Savings institutions	16.6	17.8	16.2
Commercial banks	541.5	558.4	587.2	Nonfinancial business	42.4	29.8	19.2
Finance companies	219.8	236.6	237.8	Pools of securitized assets[1]	356.1	401.1	410.4
Credit unions	184.4	189.6	195.7	**Nonrevolving**	1,034.6	1,126.4	1,194.9
Fed. government and Sallie Mae	104.0	119.5	129.6	Commercial banks	323.4	333.5	356.2
Savings institutions	64.6	69.1	68.5	Finance companies	182.9	206.6	198.8
Nonfinancial business	82.7	68.0	56.9	Credit unions	162.2	167.3	173.5
Pools of securitized assets[1]	500.1	580.3	657.2	Fed. government and Sallie Mae	104.0	119.5	129.6
Major Types of Credit[2]				Savings institutions	48.0	51.3	52.3
Revolving	693.0	727.3	738.0	Nonfinancial business	40.2	38.2	-37.7
Commercial banks	218.1	224.9	231.0	Pools of securitized assets[1]	173.9	209.9	246.8
Finance companies	37.6	31.5	38.9				

NA = Not applicable. (1) Outstanding balances of pools upon which securities have been issued; these balances are no longer carried on the balance sheets of the loan originators. (2) Includes estimates for holders that do not separately report consumer credit holding by type.

> ► **IT'S A FACT:** According to cardweb.com, American households with at least one credit card owed an average balance of $8,940 at the end of 2002. Approximately 39% of credit-card holders pay off their entire outstanding balance each month, but over 20% do not pay more than the required monthly minimum payment.

Leading U.S. Businesses in 2002

Source: Data from FORTUNE Magazine
(millions of dollars in revenues)

Advertising, Marketing
Omnicom Group	$7,536
Interpublic Group	6,204

Aerospace
Boeing	$54,069
United Technologies	28,212
Lockheed Martin	26,806
Honeywell Intl.	22,274
Northrop Grumman	17,837
Raytheon	16,962
General Dynamics	13,863
Textron	10,658

Airlines
AMR	$17,299
UAL	14,286
Delta Air Lines	13,305
NWA	9,489
Continental Airlines	8,402
US Airways Group	6,977
Southwest Airlines	5,522
Alaska Air Group	2,224
America West Holdings	2,047

Apparel
Nike	$9,893
VF	5,182
Jones Apparel Group	4,341
Levi Strauss	4,137
Liz Claiborne	3,718
Reebok International	3,128

Polo Ralph Lauren	$2,364
Kellwood	2,205
Warnaco Group	1,549
Phillips-Van Heusen	1,405

Automotive Retailing, Services
AutoNation	$19,479
United Auto Group	7,577
Sonic Automotive	7,415

Beverages
Coca-Cola	$19,564
Coca-Cola Enterprises	16,889
Anheuser-Busch	13,566
The Pepsi Bottling Group	9,216
Adolph Coors	3,776
Pepsi Americas	3,240
Constellation Brands	2,821

Building Materials, Glass
Owens-Corning	$4,872
USG	3,468
Armstrong Holdings	3,172
Vulcan Materials	2,797
Martin-Marietta Materials	1,497
Texas Industries	1,345

Chemicals
Dow Chemical	$27,609
E. I. du Pont de Nemours	24,522
PPG Industries	8,067
Ashland	7,792
Rohm & Haas	5,727

Commercial Banks
Citigroup	$100,789
Bank of America Corp.	45,732
J.P. Morgan Chase	43,372
Wells Fargo	28,473
Wachovia Corp.	23,591
Bank One Corp.	22,171
Fleet Boston	15,868
U.S. Bancorp	15,422

Computer and Data Services
Electronic Data Systems	$21,782
Computer Sciences	11,426
First Data	7,636
Science Applications Intl.	6,104
Unisys	5,607
Affiliated Computer Srvs.	3,063

Computer Peripherals
EMC	$5,438
Lexmark International	4,356
Maxtor	3,780

Computers, Office Equipment
IBM	$83,132
Hewlett-Packard	56,588
Dell Computer	35,404
Xerox	15,849
Sun Microsystems	12,496
Apple	5,742
NCR	5,585

Computer Software

Microsoft	$28,365
Oracle	9,673
Computer Assoc. Intl	2,964

Diversified Financials

General Electric	$131,698
Fannie Mae	52,901
Freddie Mac	39,663
American Express	23,807
Household International	14,672

Electronics, Electrical Equip.

Emerson Electronic	$13,824
Whirlpool	11,016
Eaton	7,209
SPX	5,046

Energy

American Electric Power	$15,583
TXU	14,086
El Paso	12,616
Cynergy	11,990
Reliant Resources	11,654

Engineering, Construction

Fluor	$10,190
Jacobs Engineering Grp.	4,556

Entertainment

AOL Time Warner	$41,780
Walt Disney	25,329
Viacom	24,606

Food

ConAgra	$27,630
PepsiCo	25,112
Sara Lee	17,628
H. J. Heinz	9,431
Kellogg	8,304
General Mills	7,949
Smithfield Foods	7,356
Campbell Soup	6,133
Land O'Lakes	5,847
Dole Food	4,392

Food and Drug Stores

Kroger	$51,760
Albertson's	35,916
Safeway	32,399
Walgreen	28,261
CVS	24,182
Publix	15,931
Rite Aid	15,171
Winn-Dixie Stores	12,943

Food Production

Archer Daniels Midland	$23,454
Tyson Foods	23,367
Dean	9,213

Food Services

McDonald's	$15,406
Yum Brands	7,757
Darden Restaurants	4,369
Starbucks	3,289

Forest and Paper Products

International Paper	$24,976
Georgia-Pacific	23,271
Weyerhaeuser	18,521
MeadWestvaco	7,489
Boise Cascade	7,412

Furniture

Leggett & Platt	$4,272
Steelcase	3,090
Furniture Brands Int'l.	2,398
La-Z-Boy	2,154

General Merchandisers

Wal-Mart Stores	$246,525
Target	43,917
Sears Roebuck	41,366
Kmart	32,765
J. C. Penney	32,347
Federated Dept. Stores	15,435
May Dept. Stores	13,491

Health Care

UnitedHealth Group	$25,020
Cigna	19,915
Aetna	19,879
HCA	19,729
WellPoint Health Networks	17,339
Tenet Healthcare	13,913

Anthem	$13,282
Express Scripts	13,187

Hotels, Casinos, Resorts

Marriott International	$10,619
Park Place Entertainment	4,652
Harrah's	4,172
MGM Mirage	4,031

Household and Personal Products

Procter & Gamble	$40,238
Kimberly-Clark	13,566
Colgate-Palmolive	9,294
Gillette	8,453
Avon Products	6,228
Estee Lauder	4,744
Clorox	4,061

Industrial and Farm Equip.

Caterpillar	$20,152
Deere	13,947
Illinois Tool Works	9,812
American Standard	7,795
Parker Hannifin	6,149

Insurance—Life, Health (Mutual)

New York Life	$24,721
Mass. Mutual Life Ins.	20,247
TIAA-CREF	19,971
Northwestern Mutual	15,916
Guardian Life of America	8,136

Insurance—Life, Health (Stock)

MetLife	$34,055
Prudential Financial	26,797
AFLAC	10,257
UnumProvident	9,560
John Hancock Fin. Svcs.	8,911

Insurance—Property, Casualty (Mutual)

State Farm Insurance	$49,654
Auto-Owners Insurance	3,514
Sentry Insurance Group	1,826
Amica Mutual Insurance	1,444
Federated Mutual Insurance	1,421

Insurance—Property, Casualty (Stock)

American International Group	$67,723
Berkshire Hathaway	42,353
Allstate	29,579
Loews	16,898
Nationwide	15,949

Mail, Pkg., Freight Delivery

United Parcel Service	$31,272
FedEx	20,607

Metals

Alcoa	$20,618
United States Steel	6,949
Nucor	4,802
AK Steel Holding	4,340
Phelps Dodge	3,722
Bethlehem Steel	3,572

Mining, Crude-Oil Production

Occidental Petroleum	$7,429
Unocal	5,297

Motor Vehicles and Parts

General Motors	$186,763
Ford Motor	163,360
Delphi	27,427
Johnson Controls	20,103
Visteon	18,395

Network and Other Communications

Motorola	$26,679
Cisco Systems	18,915
Lucent Technologies	13,568

Petroleum Refining

Exxon Mobil	$182,466
ChevronTexaco	92,043
ConocoPhilips	58,394
Marathon Oil	27,470

Pharmaceuticals

Merck	$51,790
Johnson & Johnson	36,298
Pfizer	35,281
Bristol-Myers Squibb	18,119
Abbott Laboratories	17,685
Pharmacia	16,929
Wyeth	14,584

Eli Lilly	11,078
Schering-Plough	10,180

Pipelines

Williams	$9,391
Plains All Amer. Pipeline	8,384

Publishing & Printing

Gannett	$6,422
Tribune	5,384
McGraw-Hill	4,788
R.R. Donnelley & Sons	4,755
New York Times	3,079
Knight-Ridder	2,842

Railroads

Union Pacific	$12,491
Burlington Northern Santa Fe	8,979
CSX	8,152
Norfolk Southern	6,270

Scientific, Photo., and Control Equip.

Eastman Kodak	$12,841
Agilent Technologies	6,010

Securities

Morgan Stanley/Dean Witter	$32,415
Merrill Lynch	28,253
Goldman Sachs Group	22,854
Lehman Bros. Holdings	16,781

Semiconductors and Other Electron.

Intel	$26,764
Solectron	12,276
Sanmina-SCI Systems	8,762

Specialty Retailers

Home Depot	$58,247
Costco Wholesale	38,763
Lowe's	26,491
Best Buy	19,597
Gap	14,455
Circuit City Stores	12,792
TJX	11,981
Staples	11,596
Office Depot	11,438
Toys "R" Us	11,305

Telecommunications

Verizon	$67,625
AT&T	46,727
SBC Communications	43,138
Sprint	27,180
BellSouth	22,440
AT&T Wireless Services	15,632
Qwest Communications	15,487

Temporary Help

Manpower	$10,611
Kelly Services	4,324

Textiles

Mohawk Industries	$4,522
WestPoint Stevens	1,811

Tobacco

Altria	$62,182
R.J. Reynolds Tobacco	6,211
Universal	2,500

Toys, Sporting Goods

Mattel	$4,885
Hasbro	2,816

Transportation Equipment

Harley-Davidson	$4,091
Brunswick	3,712

Utilities: Gas and Electric

Duke Energy	$15,663
Exelon	14,955
PG&E Corp.	13,784
First Energy	12,152
Edison International	11,838
Southern	10,549

Waste Management

Waste Management	$11,142
Allied Waste Industries	5,517
Republic Services	2,365

Wholesalers (Diversified)

Genuine Parts	$8,259
W. W. Grainger	4,644
Wesco International	3,326
Fisher Scientific	3,238
Hughes Supply	3,066
Ace Hardware	3,029

25 U.S. Corporations With Largest Revenues in 2002
Source: FORTUNE Magazine
(millions of dollars)

Company, headquarters	Revenues	Company, headquarters	Revenues
Wal-Mart Stores, Bentonville, AR	$246,525	Hewlett-Packard, Palo Alto, CA	$56,588
General Motors, Detroit, MI	186,763	Boeing, Chicago, IL	54,069
ExxonMobil, Irving, TX	182,466	Fannie Mae, Washington, DC	52,901
Ford Motor, Dearborn, MI	163,630	Merck, Whitehouse Station, NJ	51,790
General Electric, Fairfield, CT	131,698	Kroger, Cincinnati, OH	51,760
Citigroup, New York, NY	100,789	Cardinal Health, Dublin, OH	51,136
ChevronTexaco, San Ramon, CA	92,043	McKesson, San Francisco, CA	50,006
IBM, Armonk, NY	83,132	State Farm Insurance, Bloomington, IL	49,654
American International Group, New York, NY	67,723	AT&T, Bedminster, NJ	46,727
Verizion Communications, New York, NY	67,625	Bank of America Corp., Charlotte, NC	45,732
Altria Group, New York, NY	62,182	AmerisourceBergen, Chesterbrook, PA	45,235
ConocoPhilips, Houston, TX	58,394	Target, Minneapolis, MN	43,917
Home Depot, Atlanta, GA	58,247		

Fastest-Growing U.S. Franchises in 2002[1]
Source: *Entrepreneur* Magazine

Company	Business	Minimum start-up cost[2]
Curves for Women	Women's fitness and weight loss centers	$25,600
Subway	Submarine sandwiches and salads	52,000
7-Eleven, Inc.	Convenience stores	varies
Taco Bell Corp.	Mexican quick-service restaurant	3,000,000
Jani-King	Commercial cleaning	11,300
McDonald's	Hamburgers, chicken, salads	489,900
Jan-Pro Franchising Int'l, Inc.	Commercial cleaning	1,000
Baskin-Robbins USA Co.	Ice cream & yogurt	132,800
The Quizno's Franchise Co.	Submarine sandwiches, soups, salads	208,400
KFC Corp.	Chicken	1,100,000
CleanNet USA, Inc.	Commercial office cleaning	3,900
Results! Travel	Travel services	11,000
RE/MAX Int'l., Inc.	Real estate	20,000
WSI Internet	Internet services	40,000
Dunkin' Donuts	Donuts & baked goods	255,700
GNC Franchising, Inc.	Vitamin and nutrition stores	132,700
Great Clips, Inc.	Family hair salons	94,600
Snap-on Tools	Professional tools & equipment	20,700
Action Int'l.	Business coaching, consulting, and training	50,000
Allegra Network LLC.	Printing center	256,000
Gumball Gourmet	Gumball machine kiosks	24,800
Comfort Keepers	Non-medical in-home senior care	39,000
The UPS Store	Postal/business/communications services	141,100
Jazzercise	Dance/exercise classes	1,800
Cinnabon	Cinnamon rolls	232,500

(1) Ranked by number of new franchise units added. (2) Not including franchise fee, which varies.

Largest Corporate Mergers or Acquisitions in U.S.
Source: Securities Data Co.
(as of Oct. 2003; * denotes an announced merger or acquisition not yet complete; year = year effective or announced)

Company	Acquirer	Dollars (in billions)	Year	Company	Acquirer	Dollars (in billions)	Year
Time Warner	America Online, Inc.	$181.6	2001	AT&T Broadband & Internet Services	Comcast Corp.	$30.0	2001
Warner-Lambert	Pfizer Inc.	88.8	2000	Electronic Data Syst.	shareholders	29.7	1996
Mobil Corp.	Exxon Corp.	86.4	1999	First Chicago NBD.	BANC ONE Corp.	29.6	1998
Citicorp	Travelers Group Inc.	72.6	1998	RJR Nabisco	Kohlberg Kravis Roberts	29.4	1989
Ameritech Corp	SBC Communications Inc.	72.4	1999	Pharmacia & Upjohn	Monsanto Co.	26.9	2000
GTE Corp.	Bell Atlantic Corp.	71.3	2000	Associates First Capital	shareholders	26.6	1998
Tele-Communications	AT&T	69.9	1999	Conoco	Phillips Petroleum	24.8	2002
AirTouch Communications	Vodafone Group PLC	65.8	1999	Lucent Technologies (AT&T)	shareholders	24.1	1996
BankAmerica Corp.	NationsBank Corp.	61.6	1998	Bestfoods	Unilever PLC	23.7	2000
Pharmacia Corp.	Pfizer, Inc.	61.3	2003	Compaq Computer	Hewlett-Packard	23.5	2002
US West	Qwest Communication	56.3	2000	Amer. General Corp.	American Int'l. Group	23.4	2001
Amoco Corp.	British Petroleum Co. PLC	55.0	1998	AMFM, Inc.	Clear Channel Communications	22.7	2000
MediaOne Group	AT&T	51.9	2000	Pacific Telesis Group	SBC Communications, Inc.	22.4	1997
Liberty Media Group (AT&T)	shareholders	46.0	2001	General Re Corp.	Berkshire Hathaway Inc.	22.3	1998
Texaco	Chevron	43.3	2001	US Bancorp, MN	Firstar Corp.	21.1	2001
MCI Communications	WorldCom Inc.	41.4	1998	Ascend Communications	Lucent Technologies.	21.1	1999
SDL Inc.	JDS Uniphase Corp.	41.0	2001	Network Solutions, Inc.	VeriSign, Inc.	20.8	2000
CBS Corp.	Viacom.	40.9	2000	Waste Management	USA Waste Services	20.0	1998
Chrysler Corp.	Daimler-Benz AG.	40.5	1998	Nabisco Holdings	Philip Morris	19.4	2000
Wells Fargo & Co.	Norwest Corp.	34.4	1998	AT&T Wireless Serv.	shareholders	18.8	2001
VoiceStream Wireless Corp.	Deutsche Telekom AG	34.1	2001	Capital Cities/ABC Inc.	Walt Disney	18.3	1996
ARCO	BP Amoco PLC	33.7	2000	SunAmerica Inc.	American Int'l. Group	18.1	1999
J.P. Morgan & Co.	Chase Manhattan	33.6	2000	Manulife Financial	John Hancock Financial Services*	11.0	2003
US West Media Group	shareholders	31.7	1998	General Electric	Vivendi Universal*.	9.5	2003
Agilent Technologies	shareholders	31.2	2000				
Associates First Capital	Citigroup	31.0	2000				
NYNEX	Bell Atlantic	30.8	1997				

2003 Federal Corporate Tax Rates

Taxable Income Amount	Tax Rate	Taxable Income Amount	Tax Rate	Taxable Income Amount	Tax Rate
Not more than $50,000	15%	$100,001 to $335,000	39%	$15,000,001 to $18,333,333 .	38%
$50,001 to $75,000	25%	$335,001 to $10,000,000.....	34%	More than $18,333,333.....	35%
$75,001 to $100,000	34%	$10,000,001 to $15,000,000 .	35%		

Personal service corporations (used by incorporated professionals such as attorneys and doctors) pay a flat rate of 35%.

U.S. Capital Gains Tax, 1960-2003

Source: George W. Smith IV, CPA, Partner, George W. Smith & Company, P.C.

The following shows the maximum tax rate on net long-term capital gains for individuals since 1960.

Year	Max %	Year	Max %	Year	Max %	Year	Max %	Year	Max %	Year	Max %
1960...	25.0	1971...	32.5	1978...	28.0	1987 ...	28.0	1990 ...	28.0	1999 ...	20.0[5]
1970...	29.5	1972...	35.0[1]	1981...	20.0	1988 ...	33.0[2]	1997 ...	20.0[4]	2001 ...	20/18[6]

(1) From 1972 to 1976, the interplay of minimum tax and maximum tax resulted in a marginal rate of 49.125%. (2) Statutory maximum of 28%, but "phase-out" notch increased marginal rate to 33%; interplay of all "phase-outs" could have increased the effective marginal rate to 49.5%. (3) The Budget Act of 1990 increased the statutory rate to 31% and capped the marginal rate at 28%; however, some taxpayers faced effective marginal rates of more than 34% because of the phase-out of personal exemptions and itemized deductions. (4) New rate is for those who, after July 28, 1997, sell capital assets held for more than 18 mos (12 mos for sales after Dec. 31, 1997). A 10% capital gains rate applies to individuals in the 15% income tax bracket. (Those who, after July 28, 1997, but before Jan. 1, 1998, sell capital assets held between 12 and 18 mos will be taxed at the old top rate of 28%. Those who sold capital assets after May 6, 1997, but before July 29, 1997, will be taxed at the 20% rate, so long as such assets were held for at least a year.) (5) The IRS Restructuring and Reform Act of 1998 repealed the more-than-18-month holding period for sales after Dec. 31, 1997. Beginning Jan. 1, 1998, capital assets need only be held 12 months to have the 20%/10% capital gains rates apply. (6) For capital assets bought after Dec. 31, 2000, and held for more than 5 years, the 20% minimum capital gains rate will be lowered to 18%. The 10% rate will be lowered to 8%, regardless of when the assets were bought. This provision was repealed in 2003. (7) The maximum capital gains rate for capital assets held more than one year and sold on or after May 6, 2003, was decreased to 15%. The 10% bracket was reduced to 5%. The capital gains rate for the sale of collectibles such as antiques remains at 28%, and the sale of certain depreciable real estate is taxed at a maximum of 25%.

Global Stock Markets

Source: The Conference Board; not seasonally adjusted

Stock price indexes (1990[1]=100):	June 1, 1960	June 1, 1970	June 1, 1980	June 1, 1990	June 1, 2000	June 1, 2001	June 1, 2002	Jan. 1 2003	June 1 2003
United States	17.1	21.9	34.3	107.6	437.2	368.0	297.5	257.2	292.9
Japan	4.4	7.3	23.8	110.8	60.4	45.0	36.8	28.9	31.5
Germany	36.1	27.5	30.5	111.1	407.9	358.2	259.1	162.5	190.4
France	16.3	15.6	23.8	112.0	354.7	287.5	214.5	161.6	169.7
United Kingdom	8.2	11.6	24.9	108.2	279.9	252.0	209.1	159.1	182.1
Italy	28.9	20.6	15.9	117.3	309.0	254.1	196.7	162.6	181.1
Canada	14.8	25.0	60.3	103.6	298.0	226.1	208.9	192.0	204.1

(1) 12-month average.

U.S. Holdings of Foreign Stocks[1]

Source: Bureau of Economic Analysis, U.S. Dept. of Commerce

(billions of dollars)

	2000	2001	2002		2000	2001	2002
Western Europe	$1,118.4	$934.2	$777.5	Latin America...............	$66.6	$59.3	$53.2
Of which: United Kingdom	411.7	350.0	299.2	Of which: Argentina...........	3.7	0.7	0.6
Finland...........	52.7	51.3	42.4	Brazil.............	24.2	21.8	20.0
France	137.2	112.2	93.9	Mexico............	28.0	26.3	23.8
Germany	76.7	72.2	58.1				
Ireland...........	31.3	28.4	22.9	Other W. Hemisphere	170.7	172.4	148.6
Italy	42.5	33.7	27.4	Of which: Bermuda	108.1	118.9	98.3
Netherlands	147.9	112.8	89.7	Netherlands Antilles ..	23.1	14.5	10.7
Spain	38.4	32.5	26.7				
Sweden	36.0	24.3	19.3	Other countries and territories	190.8	186.5	155.7
Switzerland	94.9	75.6	65.3	Of which: Australia	43.4	37.1	30.4
				Hong Kong	34.3	30.2	23.8
Canada	108.6	89.6	69.7	Singapore	24.9	21.4	16.9
Japan....................	197.8	170.7	140.5	TOTAL HOLDINGS...........	1,852.9	1,612.7	1,345.2

(1) As of year end.

Gold Reserves of Central Banks and Governments

Source: International Financial Statistics, IMF; million fine troy ounces

Year end	All countries[1]	United States	Belgium	Canada	France	Germany[2]	Italy	Japan	Nether- lands	Switzer- land	United Kingdom
1975	1,018.71	274.71	42.17	21.95	100.93	117.61	82.48	21.11	54.33	83.20	21.03
1980	952.99	264.32	34.18	20.98	81.85	95.18	66.67	24.23	43.94	83.28	18.84
1985	949.39	262.65	34.18	20.11	81.85	95.18	66.67	24.33	43.94	83.28	19.03
1990	939.01	261.91	30.23	14.76	81.85	95.18	66.67	24.23	43.94	83.28	18.94
1995	908.79	261.70	20.54	3.41	81.85	95.18	66.67	24.23	34.77	83.28	18.43
1996	906.10	261.66	15.32	3.09	81.85	95.18	66.67	24.23	34.77	83.28	18.43
1997	890.57	261.64	15.32	3.09	81.89	95.18	66.67	24.23	27.07	83.28	18.42
1998	966.15	261.61	9.52	2.49	102.37	118.98	83.36	24.23	33.83	83.28	23.00
1999	967.07	261.67	8.30	1.81	97.25	111.52	78.83	24.23	31.57	83.28	20.55
2000	952.09	261.61	8.30	1.18	97.25	111.52	78.83	24.55	29.32	77.79	15.67
2001	942.76	262.00	8.30	1.05	97.25	111.52	78.83	24.60	28.44	70.68	11.42
2002	930.56	262.00	8.29	.60	97.25	110.79	78.83	24.60	27.38	61.62	10.09

(1) Covers IMF members with reported gold holdings. For countries not listed above, see International Monetary Fund's *International Financial Statistics Report*. (2) West Germany prior to 1991.

Record One-Day Gains and Losses on the Dow Jones Industrial Average

Source: Dow Jones & Co., Inc.; as of Sept. 30, 2003

GREATEST POINT GAINS / GREATEST POINT LOSSES

Rank	Date	Close	Net Chg	% Chg	Rank	Date	Close	Net Chg	% Chg
1.	3/16/2000	10630.60	499.19	4.93	1.	9/17/2001	8920.70	−684.81	−7.13
2.	7/24/2002	8191.29	488.95	6.35	2.	4/14/2000	10305.77	−617.78	−5.66
3.	7/29/2002	8711.88	447.49	5.41	3.	10/27/1997	7161.15	−554.26	−7.18
4.	4/5/2001	9918.05	402.63	4.23	4.	8/31/1998	7539.07	−512.61	−6.37
5.	4/18/2001	10615.83	399.10	3.91	5.	10/19/1987	1738.74	−508.00	−22.61
6.	9/8/1998	8020.78	380.53	4.98	6.	3/12/2001	10208.25	−436.37	−4.10
7.	10/15/2002	8255.68	378.28	4.80	7.	7/19/2002	8019.26	−390.23	−4.64
8.	9/24/2001	8603.86	368.05	4.47	8.	9/20/2001	8376.21	−382.92	−4.37
9.	10/1/2002	7938.79	346.86	4.57	9.	10/12/2000	10034.58	−379.21	−3.64
10.	5/16/2001	11215.92	342.95	3.15	10.	3/7/2000	9796.03	−374.47	−3.68

GREATEST % GAINS / GREATEST % LOSSES

Rank	Date	Close	Net Chg	% Chg	Rank	Date	Close	Net Chg	% Chg
1.	3/15/1933	62.10	8.26	15.34	1.	12/12/1914	54.00	−17.42	−24.39
2.	10/6/1931	99.34	12.86	14.87	2.	10/19/1987	1738.74	−508.00	−22.61
3.	10/30/1929	258.47	28.40	12.34	3.	10/28/1929	260.64	−38.33	−12.82
4.	9/21/1932	75.16	7.67	11.36	4.	10/29/1929	230.07	−30.57	−11.73
5.	10/21/1987	2027.85	186.84	10.15	5.	11/6/1929	232.13	−25.55	−9.92
6.	8/3/1932	58.22	5.06	8.69	6.	12/18/1899	58.27	−5.57	−8.72
7.	2/11/1932	78.60	6.80	9.47	7.	8/12/1932	63.11	−5.79	−8.40
8.	11/14/1929	217.28	18.59	9.36	8.	3/14/1907	76.23	−6.89	−8.29
9.	12/18/1931	80.69	6.90	9.35	9.	10/26/1987	1793.93	−156.83	−8.04
10.	2/13/1932	85.82	7.22	9.19	10.	7/21/1933	88.71	−7.55	−7.84

Dow Jones Industrial Average, 1963-2002

High	Date	YEAR	Low		Low		High	Date	YEAR	Low		Low
Dec. 18	767.21	1963	Jan. 2	646.79			Nov. 29	1287.20	1983	Jan. 3	1027.04	
Nov. 18	891.71	1964	Jan. 2	766.08			Jan. 6	1286.64	1984	July 24	1086.57	
Dec. 31	969.26	1965	June 28	840.59			Dec. 16	1553.10	1985	Jan. 4	1184.96	
Feb. 9	995.15	1966	Oct. 7	744.32			Dec. 2	1955.57	1986	Jan. 22	1502.29	
Sept. 25	943.08	1967	Jan. 3	786.41			Aug. 25	2722.42	1987	Oct. 19	1738.74	
Dec. 3	985.21	1968	Mar. 21	825.13			Oct. 21	2183.50	1988	Jan. 20	1879.14	
May 14	968.85	1969	Dec. 17	769.93			Oct. 9	2791.41	1989	Jan. 3	2144.64	
Dec. 29	842.00	1970	May 6	631.16			July 16	2999.75	1990	Oct. 11	2365.10	
Apr. 28	950.82	1971	Nov. 23	797.97			Dec. 31	3168.83	1991	Jan. 9	2470.30	
Dec. 11	1036.27	1972	Jan. 26	889.15			June 1	3413.21	1992	Oct. 9	3136.58	
Jan. 11	1051.70	1973	Dec. 5	788.31			Dec. 29	3794.33	1993	Jan. 20	3241.95	
Mar. 13	891.66	1974	Dec. 6	577.60			Jan. 31	3978.36	1994	Apr. 4	3593.35	
July 15	881.81	1975	Jan. 2	632.04			Dec. 13	5216.47	1995	Jan. 30	3832.08	
Sept. 21	1014.79	1976	Jan. 2	858.71			Dec. 27	6560.91	1996	Jan. 10	5032.94	
Jan. 3	999.75	1977	Nov. 2	800.85			Aug. 6	8259.31	1997	Apr. 11	6391.69	
Sept. 8	907.74	1978	Feb. 28	742.12			Nov. 23	9374.27	1998	Aug. 31	7539.07	
Oct. 5	897.61	1979	Nov. 7	796.67			Dec. 31	11497.12	1999	Jan. 22	9120.67	
Nov. 20	1000.17	1980	Apr. 21	759.13			Jan. 14	11722.98	2000	Mar. 7	9796.03	
Apr. 27	1024.05	1981	Sept. 25	824.01			May 21	11337.92	2001	Sept. 21	8235.84	
Dec. 27	1070.55	1982	Aug. 12	776.92			Mar. 19	10635.25	2002	Oct. 9	7286.27	

Milestones of the Dow Jones Industrial Average

(as of Sept. 30, 2003)

First close over...

Level	Date	Level	Date	Level	Date	Level	Date
100	Jan. 12, 1906	7000	Feb. 13, 1997	8700	Mar. 16, 1998	10100	Apr. 8, 1999
500	Mar. 12, 1956	7500	June 10, 1997	8800	Mar. 19, 1998	10300	Apr. 12, 1999*
1000	Nov. 14, 1972	8000	July 16, 1997	8900	Mar. 20, 1998	10400	Apr. 14, 1999
1500	Dec. 11, 1985	8100	July 24, 1997	9000	Apr. 6, 1998	10500	Apr. 21, 1999
2000	Jan. 8, 1987	8200	July 30, 1997	9100	Apr. 14, 1998	10700	Apr. 22, 1999*
2500	July 17, 1987	8100	July 24, 1997	9200	May 13, 1998	10800	Apr. 27, 1999
3000	April 17, 1991	8200	July 30, 1997	9300	July 16, 1998	11000	May 3, 1999*
3500	May 19, 1993	8300	Feb. 12, 1998	9500	Jan. 6, 1999*	11100	May 13, 1999
4000	Feb. 23, 1995	8400	Feb. 18, 1998	9600	Jan. 8, 1999	11200	July 12, 1999
4500	June 16, 1995	8300	Feb. 12, 1998	9700	Mar. 5, 1999	11300	Aug. 25, 1999
5000	Nov. 21, 1995	8400	Feb. 18, 1998	9800	Mar. 11, 1999	11400	Dec. 23, 1999
5500	Feb. 8, 1996	8500	Feb. 27, 1998	9900	Mar. 15, 1999	11500	Jan. 7, 2000
6000	Oct. 14, 1996	8600	Mar. 10, 1998	10000	Mar. 29, 1999	11700	Jan. 14, 2000*
6500	Nov. 25, 1996						

*9400, 10200, 10600, 10900, and 11600 are not listed because the Dow had risen another 100 points or more by the time the market closed for the day.

Components of the Dow Jones Averages

(as of Sept. 30, 2003)

Dow Jones Industrial Average

Alcoa	DuPont	IBM	Microsoft Corp.*
Altria Group	Eastman Kodak Co.	Intel Corp.*	Procter & Gamble Co.
American Express Co.	Exxon Mobil Corp.	International Paper Co.	SBC Communications
AT&T Corp.	General Electric Co.	J.P. Morgan Chase & Co.	3M Company
Boeing Co.	General Motors Corp.	Johnson & Johnson	United Technologies Corp.
Caterpillar	Hewlett-Packard Co.	McDonald's Corp.	Wal-Mart Stores
Citigroup	Home Depot	Merck & Co.	Walt Disney Co.
Coca-Cola	Honeywell International		

Dow Jones Utility Average

AES Corp.	Duke Energy Corp.	PG&E Corp.
American Electric Power Co.	Edison International	Public Service Enterprise Group
CenterPoint Energy	Exelon Corp.	Southern Co.
Consolidated Edison	FirstEnergy Corp.	TXU
Dominion Resources	NiSource	Williams Cos.

Dow Jones Transportation Average

Alexander & Baldwin	Expeditors International of Washington,	Roadway Corp.
AMR (American Airlines) Corp.	Inc.	Ryder System
Burlington Northern Santa Fe Corp.	FedEx Corp.	Southwest Airlines Co.
CNF	GATX Corp.	Union Pacific Corp.
Continental Airlines	J.B. Hunt Transportation Services	United Parcel Service
CSX	Norfolk Southern Corp.	USF Corp.
Delta Air Lines	Northwest Airlines Corp.	Yellow Corp.

NOTE: United Parcel Service was added to the Dow Jones Transportation Average on Dec. 6, 2002. In Apr. 2003, United Airlines stock was removed from the NYSE after trading below $1 for 30 consecutive trading days. Airborne, Inc., was dropped from the index Aug. 15, 2003, after most of the company was bought out by DHS. Expeditors International of Washington, Inc., was added in its place.

Record One-Day Gains and Losses on the Nasdaq Stock Market

Source: Nasdaq Stock Market; as of September 30, 2003

	GREATEST POINT GAINS			GREATEST % GAINS			GREATEST POINT LOSSES			GREATEST % LOSSES	
Rank	Date	Change	Rank	Date	% Change	Rank	Date	Change	Rank	Date	% Change
1.	1/3/2001	324.83	1.	1/3/2001	14.17%	1.	4/14/2000	−355.49	1.	10/19/1987	−11.35%
2.	12/5/2000	274.05	2.	12/5/2000	10.48%	2.	4/3/2000	−349.15	2.	4/14/2000	−9.67%
3.	4/18/2000	254.41	3.	4/5/2001	8.92%	3.	4/12/2000	−286.27	3.	10/20/1987	−9.00%
4.	5/30/2000	254.37	4.	4/18/2001	8.12%	4.	4/10/2000	−258.25	4.	10/26/1987	−9.00%
5.	10/19/2000	247.04	5.	5/30/2000	7.94%	5.	1/4/2000	−229.46	5.	8/31/1998	−8.56%
6.	10/13/2000	242.09	6.	10/13/2000	7.87%	6.	3/14/2000	−200.61	6.	4/3/2000	−7.64%
7.	6/2/2000	230.88	7.	10/19/2000	7.79%	7.	5/10/2000	−200.28	7.	1/2/2001	−7.23%
8.	4/25/2000	228.75	8.	5/8/2002	7.78%	8.	5/23/2000	−199.66	8.	12/20/2000	−7.12%
9.	4/17/2000	217.87	9.	12/22/2000	7.56%	9.	10/25/2000	−190.22	9.	4/12/2000	−7.06%
10.	6/1/2000	181.59	10.	10/21/1987	7.34%	10.	3/29/2000	−189.22	10.	10/27/1997	−7.02%

Nasdaq Stock Market, 1971-2002

High	YEAR	Low	High	YEAR	Low	High	YEAR	Low	High	YEAR	Low
114.12	1971	99.68	152.29	1979	117.84	456.27	1987	288.49	1072.82	1995	740.53
135.15	1972	113.65	208.29	1980	124.09	397.54	1988	329.00	1328.45	1996	978.17
136.84	1973	88.67	223.96	1981	170.80	487.60	1989	376.87	1748.62	1997	1194.39
96.53	1974	54.87	241.63	1982	158.92	470.30	1990	322.93	2200.63	1998	1357.09
88.00	1975	60.70	329.11	1983	229.88	586.35	1991	352.85	4090.61	1999	2193.13
97.88	1976	78.06	288.41	1984	223.91	676.95	1992	545.85	5048.62	2000	2332.78
105.05	1977	93.66	325.53	1985	245.82	790.56	1993	645.02	2892.36	2001	1387.06
139.25	1978	99.09	411.21	1986	322.14	803.93	1994	691.23	2059.38	2002	1114.11

Milestones of the Nasdaq Stock Market

Source: Nasdaq Stock Market; as of Sept. 30, 2003

First close over...		First close over...		First close over...	
100	Feb. 8, 1971	1,000	July 17, 1995	3,500	Dec. 3, 1999
200	Nov. 13, 1980	1,500	July 11, 1997	4,000	Dec. 29, 1999
300	May 6, 1986	2,000	July 16, 1998	4,500	Feb. 17, 2000
400	May 30, 1986	2,500	Jan. 29, 1999	5,000	Mar. 9, 2000
500	Apr. 12, 1991	3,000	Nov. 3, 1999		

Standard & Poor's 500 Index, 1991-2003

Source: *Facts On File World News Digest;* monthly closing levels

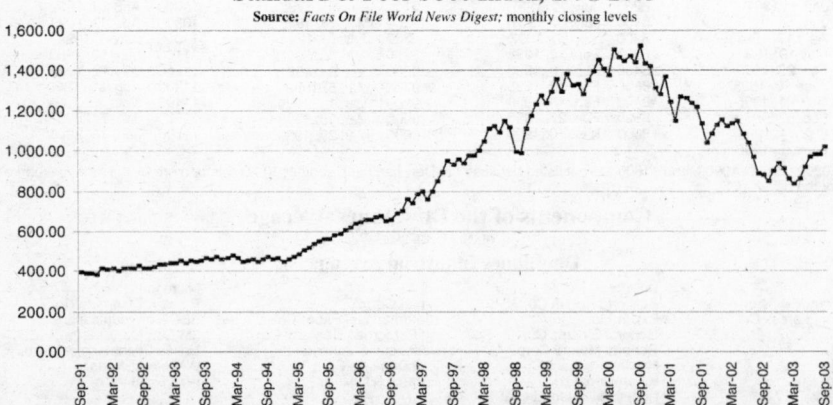

Most Active Common Stocks in 2002

New York Exchange Volume (millions of shares)		American Exchange Volume (millions of shares)		NASDAQ Volume (millions of shares)	
Lucent Technologies Inc.	5,572.20	Nabors Industries Limited	513.0	Cisco Systems, Inc.	19,993.8
Tyco International	5,267.20	IVAX Corp.	325.9	Sun Microsystems, Inc.	17,540.0
General Electric Co.	5,221.60	Devon Energy Corp.	278.6	Intel Corp.	14,859.2
AOL Time Warner, Inc.	4,514.50	Grey Wolf, Inc.	182.3	Oracle Corp.	12,672.1
Nortel Networks Corp.	4,293.20	Wyndham International, Inc.	112.8	Microsoft Corp.	9,901.4
Citigroup, Inc.	3,823.40	Impac Mortgage Holdings, Inc.	92.9	Applied Materials, Inc.	8,635.8
Pfizer, Inc	3,411.20	Apex Mortgage Capital, Inc.	91.4	JDS Uniphase Corp.	6,933.0
EMC Corp.	3,204.90	C-3D Digital, Inc.	89.9	Nextel Communications, Inc.	6,249.3
AT&T Corp.	3,093.60	Anworth Asset Mortgage Corp.	81.0	Dell Computer Corp.	6,172.2
AT&T Wireless Services, Inc.	2,711.10	USURF America, Inc.	78.7	Brocade Communications Systems, Inc.	4,332.0

Average Yields of Long-Term Treasury, Corporate, and Municipal Bonds

Source: Office of Market Finance, U.S. Dept. of the Treasury

Period	Treasury 30-year bonds[1]	New Aa corporate bonds[2]	New Aa municipal bonds[3]	Period	Treasury 30-year bonds[1]	New Aa corporate bonds[2]	New Aa municipal bonds[3]	Period	Treasury 30-year bonds[1]	New Aa corporate bonds[2]	New Aa municipal bonds[3]
1986				**1992**				**1998**			
June	7.57	9.39	7.87	June	7.84	8.45	6.49	Jun	5.70	6.43	5.12
Dec.	7.37	8.87	6.87	Dec.	7.44	8.12	6.22	Dec	5.06	6.13	4.98
1987				**1993**				**1999**			
June	8.57	9.64	7.79	June	6.81	7.48	5.63	Jun.	6.04	7.21	5.37
Dec.	9.12	10.22	7.96	Dec.	6.25	7.22	5.35	Dec.	6.35	7.55	5.95
1988				**1994**				**2000**			
June	9.00	10.08	7.78	June	7.40	8.16	6.11	June	5.93	7.75	5.80
Dec.	9.01	10.05	7.61	Dec.	7.87	8.66	6.80	Dec.	5.49	7.21	5.22
1989				**1995**				**2001**			
June	8.27	9.24	7.02	June	6.57	7.42	5.84	June	5.67	7.11	5.20
Dec.	7.90	9.23	6.98	Dec.	6.06	7.02	5.45	Dec.	5.48	6.80	5.25
1990				**1996**				**2002**			
June	8.46	9.69	7.24	June	7.06	8.00	6.02	June	5.66	6.57	5.09
Dec.	8.24	9.55	7.09	Dec.	6.55	7.45	5.64	Dec.	5.06	5.93	4.85
1991				**1997**				**2003**			
June	8.47	9.37	7.13	June	6.77	7.71	5.53	Jan.	5.07	5.87	4.90
Dec.	7.70	8.55	6.69	Dec.	5.99	6.68	5.19	March	4.90	NA	4.76
								June	4.45	NA	4.33

NA = Not available. (1) Treasury bond rate is for a 30-year maturity prior to Feb. 2002 and for 25-year and above long-term average thereafter. (2) Treasury series based on 3-week moving average of reoffering yields of new corporate bonds rated Aa by Moody's Investors Service with an original maturity of at least 20 years. Treasury discontinued yield index after Jan. 31, 2003. (3) Index of new reoffering yields on 20-year general obligations rated Aa by Moody's Investors Service.

Performance of Mutual Funds by Type, 2003

Source: Thomson Financial, Rockville, MD. 800-232-2285

(data for periods ending Sept. 30)

Fund Type/Fund Objective	AVERAGE ANNUAL RETURN			Fund Type/Fund Objective	AVERAGE ANNUAL RETURN		
	1–year	3–year	5–year		1–year	3–year	5–year
Diversified Stock				Asset Allocation–Global	18.98%	–3.89%	4.10%
Aggressive Growth	28.39%	–19.20%	2.61%	Balanced–Domestic	15.66	–2.10	3.33
Equity Income	20.48	–2.33	2.90	Balanced–Global	22.37	–2.37	4.75
Growth–Domestic	23.61	–12.07	1.92	**Bond**			
Growth & Income	21.19	–5.85	2.41	Corporate–High Yield	24.71	3.25	2.95
Mid Cap	27.25	–7.46	7.94	Corporate–Investment Grade	6.73	7.90	5.53
S&P 500 Index	20.61	–9.57	0.47	Convertible	23.31	–3.28	7.06
Small Cap	31.38	–3.40	8.96	General Bd–Investment Grade	6.12	7.45	5.62
Specialty Stock				General Bd–Long	7.63	7.75	5.75
Sector–Energy/Natural Res	21.10	1.09	9.07	General Bd–Short & Interm.	5.24	6.48	5.32
Sector–Financial Services	24.29	3.31	7.51	General Mortgage	2.85	6.59	5.53
Sector–Precious Metals	42.35	36.85	15.63	**Global Income**	15.29	8.60	6.00
Sector–Health/Biotechnology	24.00	–8.68	9.12	Loan Participation	9.09	3.47	3.97
Sector–Other	10.89	–7.12	1.72	Multi–Sector Bond	13.66	7.70	5.48
Sector–Real Estate	25.72	13.59	11.75	US Government/Agency	2.36	6.96	5.03
Sector–Tech/Communications	58.19	–30.05	–0.09	US Government–Long	3.21	8.21	5.40
Sector–Utilities	21.45	–13.39	–1.02	US Government–Short & Interm.	2.63	6.56	5.17
World Stock				US Treasury	3.30	8.25	5.90
Emerging Market Equity	43.56	1.42	10.50	**Municipal Bond**			
Global Equity	26.04	–8.61	3.78	Municipal–High Yield	4.43	5.96	3.70
Non–US Equity	25.53	–8.98	3.22	Municipal–Insured	2.66	6.72	4.66
Emerging Market Income	38.59	15.67	19.66	Municipal–National	2.95	6.30	4.27
Hybrid				Municipal–Single State	2.67	6.46	4.31
Asset Allocation–Domestic	16.14	–2.84	3.09				

> ► **IT'S A FACT:** Single-day trading volume on the New York Stock Exchange reached the 1 million mark in 1886. Over 100 years later, in 1997, this number reached 1 billion; by 2001 it had reached 2 billion. As of Sept. 2003 the record for highest trading volume on a single day was on July 24, 2002, when about 2.77 billion shares were traded.

Chicago Board of Trade, Contracts Traded 1992, 2002

Source: Chicago Board of Trade

	1992	2002	% change 1992-2002		1992	2002	% change 1992-2002
FUTURES GROUP				Stock index	2,215	234,219	99.1
Agricultural	31,783,316	54,080,291	41.2	Metals	20,105	0	
Financial............	89,121,811	213,277,300	58.2	**Total options**	**28,701,626**	**67,566,482**	**57.5**
Stock index..........	360,879	8,925,704	96.0	**COMBINED FUTURES AND OPTIONS**			
Metals...............	63,548	17,201	-269.4	Agricultural	36,928,711	66,668,748	44.6
Total futures	**121,329,766**	**276,316,047**	**56.1**	Financial	112,655,672	268,021,106	58.0
OPTIONS GROUP				Stock index[1]	363,094	9,159,923	96.0
Agricultural...........	5,145,395	12,588,457	59.1	Metals	83,653	17,201	-386.3
Financial............	23,533,861	54,743,806	57.0	**GRAND TOTAL**.......	**150,031,392**	**343,882,529**	**56.4**

(1) Now called the Equity Index, and composed of 6 Dow Jones Indexes; not comparable to Stock Index shown for 1992.

U.S. Mutual Fund Shareholders[1]

Source: The Investment Company Institute

Shareholder Characteristics, 2001			Households owning mutual funds (in	
Median age[2]........................	46			
Median annual household Income	$62,100			
Median household financial assets	$100,000	Year	millions)[3]	
Median number of funds owned.........	4	1980	4.6	
Median year of first fund purchase......	1990	1984	10.2	
Employed[2]	78%	1988	22.2	
Married or living with a partner	67%	1992	25.8	
Spouse or partner employed.........	77%	1994	30.2	
Four-year college degree or more[2]	52%	1996	36.8	
Owning:		1998	44.4	
Equity funds..................	88%	1999	48.4	
Bond funds	37%	2000	50.6	
Hybrid funds	34%	2001	54.2	
Money market funds	48%			

(1) Data include households owning mutual funds inside and outside employer-sponsored retirement plans. (2) Refers to the household's responding financial decision maker for mutual fund investments. (3) Data from 1980-1988 exclude households owning mutual funds solely through employer-sponsored retirement plans.

Distribution of Financial Assets of U.S. Families[1]

Source: Federal Reserve System (by type of asset, in percent)

Type of financial asset	1989	1992	1995	1998	2001	Type of financial asset	1989	1992	1995	1998	2001
Transaction accounts........	19.0	17.5	13.9	11.4	11.5	Retirement accounts	21.5	25.7	28.1	27.6	28.4
Certificates of deposit........	10.2	8.0	5.6	4.3	3.1	Cash value of life insurance ..	6.0	5.9	7.2	6.4	5.3
Savings bonds	1.5	1.1	1.3	0.7	0.7	Other managed assets	6.6	5.4	5.9	8.6	10.6
Bonds....................	10.2	8.4	6.3	4.3	4.6	Other	4.8	3.8	3.3	1.7	1.9
Stocks....................	15.0	16.5	15.6	22.7	21.6	Financial assets as a					
Mutual funds (excluding money market funds).....	5.3	7.6	12.7	12.4	12.2	percentage of total assets	30.5	31.6	36.7	40.7	42.0

(1) Data from the triennial *Survey of Consumer Finances.*

Stock Ownership of U.S. Families, by Income & Age, 1989, 1995, 1998, & 2001[1]

Source: Federal Reserve System
(in percent, except as noted)

All families		Families having direct or indirect stock holdings[2]				Median value of portfolios for families with stock holdings (thousands of 2001 dollars)				Stock holdings as share of financial assets[3]			
		1989	1995	1998	2001	1989	1995	1998	2001	1989	1995	1998	2001
		31.7%	40.4%	48.9%	51.9%	$11.7	$16.9	$27.2	$34.3	27.8%	39.9%	53.9%	56.0%
Annual Income (in thousands of dollars):	Under $20	3.3	6.5	10.0	12.4	NA	4.3	5.4	7.0	13.6	14.2	20.4	36.9
	$20-40	15.2	24.7	30.8	33.5	8.3	7.3	10.9	7.5	10.0	26.7	29.7	34.9
	$40-60	28.6	41.5	50.2	52.1	6.3	7.2	13.1	15.0	16.7	28.4	37.9	46.4
	$60-80	44.0	54.3	69.3	75.7	8.0	14.6	20.4	28.5	21.7	35.6	45.7	51.7
	$80-90	57.6	69.7	77.9	82.0	13.1	28.9	49.0	64.6	26.1	41.3	50.4	57.4
	$90-100	76.9	80.0	90.4	89.6	53.7	69.3	146.5	247.7	34.3	45.4	62.5	60.4
By age of family head (years):	Under 35	22.4	36.6	40.8	48.9	4.1	5.9	7.6	7.0	20.2	27.2	44.8	52.6
	35-44	39.0	46.4	56.7	59.5	7.1	11.6	21.8	27.5	29.3	39.5	54.6	57.3
	45-54	41.8	48.9	58.6	59.2	18.1	30.0	41.4	50.0	33.5	42.6	55.7	59.1
	55-64	36.2	40.0	55.9	57.1	25.3	35.8	51.2	81.2	27.6	44.2	58.4	56.1
	65-74	26.7	34.4	42.7	39.2	27.9	39.3	61.0	150.0	26.0	35.8	51.3	55.1
	75 +	25.9	27.9	29.4	34.2	34.4	23.1	65.3	120.0	25.0	39.8	48.7	51.4

NA = Not available. (1) Data from the triennial *Survey of Consumer Finances.* (2) Indirect holdings are those in mutual funds, retirement accounts, and other managed assets. (3) Among stock holding families.

The Richest 400

The Sept. 30, 2003, issue of *Forbes* contained the magazine's latest annual roster of the 400 wealthiest Americans. Here are the top ten (with *Forbes's* estimate of their net worth):

    1.   Microsoft chief Bill Gates, $46 bil.
    2.   Berkshire Hathaway magnate Warren Buffett $36 bil.
    3.   Microsoft co-founder Paul Allen, $22 bil.
   4-8. Heirs of Wal-Mart founder Sam Walton—Alice L. Walton, Helen R. Walton, Jim C. Walton, John T. Walton,S. Robson Walton, each $20.5 bil.
    9.   Oracle chief Larry Ellison, $18 bil.
  10. Dell computer chief Michael Dell, $13 bil.

The total estimated net worth of all 400 on the list came to $955 bil, up from $872 bil in 2002, but still below their $1.2 tril total net worth in 2000.

Minerals

Source: Geological Survey, U.S. Dept. of the Interior, as of mid-2003; minerals.usgs.gov/minerals

Aluminum: the second-most-abundant metallic element in the earth's crust. Bauxite is the main source of aluminum. Guinea, Australia, and Jamaica have about 60% of the world's reserves. Main uses in the U.S. are transportation (35%), packaging (25%), and construction (15%).

Chromium: most of the world's production of chromite ore is in India, Kazakhstan, and South Africa. The metallurgical industry uses about 90% of the chromite consumed in the world; the chemical industry, 6%.

Cobalt: used in superalloys for jet engines, chemicals, permanent magnets, tool steels, and cemented carbides for cutting tools. Australia, Canada, Congo (Kinshasa), Cuba, Russia, and Zambia account for most of the world cobalt production.

Construction Aggregates: construction sand and gravel and crushed stone are two of the most accessible natural resources in the world. Construction sand and gravel is produced in every U.S. State, and crushed stone is mined in every state except Delaware. They are used in construction, agriculture, chemicals, and metallurgy and are produced worldwide.

Copper: main uses of copper in the U.S. are in building construction (46%), electrical and electronic products (23%), consumer and general products (11%), industrial machinery and equipment (10%), and transportation (10%). The leading mine producers are Chile, Indonesia, the U.S. (in Arizona, Utah, and New Mexico), Australia, Peru, Canada, and China.

Gold: used in the U.S. in jewelry and the arts (84%), dentistry (8%), electrical and electronics (7%), and other industrial (1%). South Africa has about half of the world's resources; significant quantities are also present in the U.S. (mined in most western States and Alaska), Australia, Russia, Uzbekistan, Canada, and Brazil.

Gypsum: used in wallboard and plaster products, cement production, and agriculture. Leading producers are the U.S., Iran, Canada, Spain, China, and Mexico.

Iron ore: the source of primary iron for the world's iron and steel industries. Major iron ore producers include Brazil, Australia, China, India, Russia, Ukraine, and the U.S.

Lead: Australia, China, the U.S., and Peru are the world's largest producers of lead. Major end uses in the U.S. are transportation (with 75% used in batteries, bearings, casting metals, and solders), other batteries, construction sheeting, sporting ammunition, and power cable coverings. The U.S. produces and consumes about 22% and 23%, respectively, of the world's lead metal (primary and recycled).

Manganese: essential to iron and steel production. South Africa and Ukraine have over 80% of the world's identified resources.

Nickel: vital to the stainless steel industry; and used to make superalloys. Leading producers are Russia, Australia, Canada, New Caledonia, and Indonesia.

Platinum-Group Metals: this group consists of 6 metals: platinum, palladium, rhodium, ruthenium, iridium, and osmium. They commonly occur together in nature and are among the scarcest of the metallic elements. In the U.S., the automotive and chemical industries use PGMs mainly as catalysts. They also are consumed in electrical and electronic, dental, and medical industries. Russia and South Africa have most of the world's reserves.

Phosphate Rock: used in fertilizers, animal feed supplements, chemicals, and food. Phosphorus is an essential element for plant and animal nutrition. The U.S., Morocco, China, Russia, and Tunisia are the world's leading producers.

Salt: used in chemicals, highway deicing, industry, agriculture, food, and water treatment. Leading producers are the U.S., China, Germany, India, and Canada.

Silver: used in photography, electrical and electronic products, sterlingware, electroplated ware, and jewelry in the U.S. Silver is mined in more than 60 countries. Alaska and Nevada produce more than 70% of U.S. silver.

Soda Ash: a raw material for glass, chemicals, and detergents, it can be mined or produced synthetically. The U.S. is, by far, the world's leading producer of natural soda ash.

Sulfur: used in agricultural chemicals production, oil refining, metal mining, and many other industries. It is produced as a byproduct of oil refining, natural gas processing, and nonferrous metal smelting. Leading producers are the U.S., Canada, Russia, China, and Japan.

Titanium: ilmenite and rutile are the major mineral sources of titanium. About 95% of titanium minerals is used to produce TiO_2 pigments. The remainder is mainly used to produce metals, chemicals, and ceramics. Major mining operations are in Australia, Canada, Norway, and South Africa. U.S. mine production is in Florida and Virginia.

Zinc: used as a protective coating on steel, as diecastings, as an alloying metal with copper to make brass, and as a component of chemical compounds in rubber and paints. Leading producers are China, Australia, Peru, Canada, the U.S. (in Alaska, Missouri, and Tennessee), and Mexico.

World Mineral Reserve Base

Source: U.S. Geological Survey, U.S. Dept. of the Interior; as of year-end 2002

Mineral	Reserve Base[1]	Mineral	Reserve Base[1]
Aluminum	33,000 mil metric tons[2]	Nickel	140 mil metric tons
Chromium	7,100 mil metric tons[3]	Phosphate Rock	47,000 mil metric tons
Cobalt	13 mil metric tons	Platinum-Group Metals	73,000 metric tons
Copper	950 mil metric tons	Silver	430,000 metric tons
Gold	89,000 metric tons	Soda Ash (Natural)	40,000 mil metric tons
Iron Ore	330,000 mil metric tons	Titanium (ilmenite/rutile)	820 mil metric tons[4]
Lead	140 mil metric tons	Zinc	450 mil metric tons
Manganese	5,000 mil metric tons		

(1) Includes demonstrated reserves that are currently economic or marginally economic, plus some that are currently subeconomic. (2) Bauxite. (3) Chromite ore. (4) Titanium dioxide (TiO_2) content of ilmenite and rutile.

World Gold Production, 1975-2002[1]

Source: U.S. Geological Survey, U.S. Dept. of the Interior
(thousands of troy ounces)

Year	World prod.	Africa			North and South America				Other			
		South Africa	Ghana	Congo Dem. Rep.	United States	Canada	Mexico	Colombia	Australia	China	Philippines	USSR/Russia[2]
1975	38,476	22,938	524	116	1,052	1,654	145	309	527	NA	503	NA
1980	39,197	21,669	353	96	970	1,627	196	510	548	NA	753	8,425
1985	49,284	21,565	299	257	2,427	2,815	266	1,142	1,881	1,950	1,063	8,700
1990	70,207	19,454	541	299	9,458	5,447	311	944	7,849	3,215	791	9,710
1991	70,423	19,326	846	283	9,454	5,676	326	1,120	7,530	3,858	833	8,359
1992	73,530	19,743	998	225	10,617	5,189	318	1,033	7,825	4,501	730	8,232
1993	73,300	19,908	1,250	280	10,642	4,917	357	883	7,948	5,144	509	8,228
1994	72,500	16,650	1,400	357	10,500	4,710	447	668	8,237	4,240	870	8,173
1995	71,800	16,800	1,710	322	10,200	4,890	652	680	8,150	4,500	873	4,250
1996	73,600	16,000	1,580	264	10,500	5,350	787	710	9,310	4,660	970	3,960
1997	78,900	15,800	1,760	13	11,600	5,510	836	605	10,100	5,630	1,050	3,990
1998	80,400	14,900	2,330	5	11,800	5,320	817	605	10,000	5,720	1,090	3,690
1999	82,300	14,500	2,570	7	11,000	5,070	764	1,410	9,680	5,560	1,000	4,050
2000	82,900	13,800	2,320	2	11,300	5,020	848	1,190	9,530	5,790	965	4,600
2001	83,600	12,700	2,210	2	10,800	5,110	846	701	9,160	5,950	1,090	4,890
2002	82,000	12,800	2,240	2	9,580	4,790	663	669	8,780	6,110	1,290	5,080

(1) Figures are rounded. (2) Figures for 1975-94 are for USSR as constituted prior to Dec. 1991; after 1994, Russia only. NA = Not available.

U.S. Nonfuel Minerals Production

Source: U.S. Geological Survey, U.S. Dept. of the Interior

Production as measured by mine shipments, sales, or marketable production (including consumption by producers).

		1996	1997	1998	1999	2000	2001	2002
Beryllium (metal equivalent)	metric tons	211	231	243	200	180	100	80
Copper (recoverable content of ores, etc.)	thousand metric tons	1,920	1,940	1,860	1,600	1,440	1,340	1,140
Gold (recoverable content of ores, etc.)	metric tons	326.0	362.0	366.0	341.0	353.0	335	298
Iron ore, usable (includes byproduct material)	million metric tons	62.1	63.0	62.9	57.7	63.1	46.2	51.6
Lead (in concentrate)	thousand metric tons	426	448	481	503	457	454	440
Magnesium metal (primary)	thousand metric tons	133	125	106	W	W	W	W
Molybdenum (content of ore and concentrate)	metric tons	56,000	58,900	53,300	43,000	41,000	37,600	32,600
Nickel (content of ore and concentrate)	metric tons	1,333	—	—	—	—	—	—
Silver (recoverable content of ores, etc.)	metric tons	1,570	2,180	2,060	1,950	1,860	1,740	1,420
Zinc (recoverable content of ores, etc.)	thousand metric tons	586	592	709	808	786	799	754
Asbestos	thousand metric tons	10	7	6	7	5	5	3
Barite	thousand metric tons	662	692	476	434	392	400	420
Boron minerals	thousand metric tons	581	604	587	618	564	536	518
Bromine	million kilograms	227	247	230	239	228	212	222
Cement (portland, masonry, etc.)	thousand metric tons	79,266	82,582	83,931	86,600E	87,846	88,861	89,732
Clays	thousand metric tons	43,100	41,800	41,900	42,200	40,800	40,600	39,400
Diatomite	thousand metric tons	729	773	725	747	677	644	650
Feldspar	thousand metric tons	890	900E	820E	875E	790E	800E	790E
Fluorspar	thousand metric tons	8	—	—	—	—	NA	NA
Garnet (industrial)	metric tons	60,900	64,900	74,000	60,700	60,200	52,700	38,500
Gemstones	million dollars	43.6	25.0	14.3	16.1	17.2	15.1	12.6
Gypsum	thousand metric tons	17,500	18,600	19,000	22,400	19,500	16,300	15,700
Helium (extracted from natural gas)	million cubic meters	103	116	112.0	118E	117E	100E	85E
Helium (Grade A sold)	million cubic meters	95	107	112.0	108E	125E	137E	125E
Iodine	thousand kilograms	1,270	1,320	1,490	1,620	1,470	1,290	1,420
Lime	thousand metric tons	19,225	19,678	20,132	19,565	19,555	18,941	17,931
Mica (scrap & flake)	thousand metric tons	97	114	87	104	101	97	81
Peat	thousand metric tons	549	661	685	731	755	870	642
Perlite (sold and used by producers)	thousand metric tons	684	706	685	711	672	588	521
Phosphate rock (marketable product)	thousand metric tons	45,400	45,900	44,200	40,600	38,600	31,900	36,100
Potash (K2O equivalent)	thousand metric tons	1,390	1,400	1,300	1,200	1,300	1,200	1,200
Pumice and pumicite	thousand metric tons	612	577	583	643	697	618	956
Salt	thousand metric tons	42,900	40,600	40,800	41,000	43,300	42,200	37,700
Sand and gravel (construction)	thousand metric tons	914,000	961,000	1,080,000	1,080,000E	1,120	1,120	1,130
Sand and gravel (industrial)	thousand metric tons	27,800	28,500	28,200	28,900	28,400	27,900	28,000
Soda ash (sodium carbonate)	thousand metric tons	10,200	10,700	10,100	10,200	10,200	10,300	10,500
Sodium sulfate (natural)	thousand metric tons	306	318	290	NA	NA	NA	NA
Stone (crushed)	million metric tons	1,330	1,410	1,510	1,560E	1,560	1,600	1,520
Stone (dimension)	thousand metric tons	1,150	1,180	1,140	1,250E	1,254	1,280	1,300
Sulfur (in all forms)	thousand metric tons	12,000	12,000	11,600E	11,300	10,300	9,250	9,270
Talc	thousand metric tons	994	1,050	971	925	851	853	775

(W) Withheld to avoid disclosing company proprietary data. (—) No production. (E) Estimated. (NA) Not available.

U.S. Reliance on Foreign Supplies of Minerals

Source: U.S. Geological Survey, U.S. Dept. of the Interior

Mineral	% Imported in 2002	Major sources (1998-2001)	Major Uses
Arsenic (trioxide)	100%	China, Chile, Mexico	Wood preservatives, nonferrous alloys
Asbestos	100	Canada	Roofing products, gaskets, friction products
Bauxite & alumina	100	Australia, Guinea, Jamaica, Brazil	Aluminum production, refractories, abrasives, chemicals
Columbium (niobium)	100	Brazil, Canada, Germany, Estonia	Steelmaking, superalloys
Fluorspar	100	China, South Africa, Mexico	Hydrofluoric acid, aluminum fluoride, steelmaking
Graphite (natural)	100	China, Mexico, Canada, Brazil	Refractories, brake linings, pencils
Indium	100	China, Canada, France, Russia	Coatings, solders, alloys, electrical components
Manganese	100	South Africa, Gabon, Australia, Mexico	Steelmaking, batteries, agricultural chemicals
Mica, sheet (natural)	100	India, Belgium, Germany, China	Electronic & electrical equipment
Quartz crystal (industrial)	100	Brazil, Germany, Madagascar	Electronics, optical applications
Strontium	100	Mexico, Germany	Television picture tubes, ferrite magnets, pyrotechnics
Thallium	100	Belgium, Canada, France, Russia, United Kingdom	Electronics, alloys, glass
Vanadium	100	South Africa, Canada, China, Czech Republic	Steelmaking, catalysts
Yttrium	100	China, Japan, France, United Kingdom	Television phosphors, fluorescent lights, oxygen sensors, ceramics
Gemstones	99	Israel, Belgium, India	Jewelry, carvings, gem & mineral collections
Bismuth	95	Belgium, Mexico, China, United Kingdom	Pharmaceuticals, chemicals, alloys, metallurgical additives
Platinum	93	South Africa, United Kingdom, Germany, Russia	Catalysts, jewelry, dental & medical alloys
Diamond (natural industrial)	89	Switzerland, Russia, United Kingdom, Ireland	Abrasives
Stone (dimension)	88	Italy, Canada, India, Spain	Construction, monuments
Titanium mineral concentrates	82	South Africa, Australia, Canada, Ukraine	Pigment, welding rod coatings, metal, carbides, chemicals
Potash	80	Canada, Russia, Belarus, Germany	Fertilizers, chemicals
Tantalum	80	Australia, China, Japan, Thailand	Capacitors, superalloys, cemented carbide tools
Tin	79	Peru, China, Indonesia, Brazil, Bolivia	Solder, tinplate, chemicals, alloys
Barite	76	China, India, Canada, Thailand	Oil & gas well drilling fluids, chemicals

Mineral	% Imported in 2002	Major sources (1998-2001)	Major Uses
Iodine	76	Chile, Japan, Russia	Sanitation, pharmaceuticals, heat stabilizers, catalysts, animal feed
Cobalt	75	Finland, Norway, Russia, Canada	Superalloys, cemented carbides, magnetic alloys, chemicals
Tungsten	70	China, Russia	Cemented carbides, electrical & electronic components, tool steels, alloys
Palladium	69	Russia, South Africa, United Kingdom, Belgium	Catalysts, dental, electronics, electrical
Chromium	63	South Africa, Kazakhstan, Zimbabwe, Turkey, Russia	Steel, chemicals, refractories
Silver	61	Canada, Mexico, Peru, United Kingdom	Photography, electrical & electronic products, catalysts, brazing alloys, jewelry
Zinc	60	Canada, Mexico, Kazakhstan	Galvanizing, zinc-base alloys, brass & bronze
Rhenium	59	Chile, Kazakhstan, Germany, Russia	Superalloys, petroleum-reforming catalysts
Beryllium	55	Kazakhstan, Russia, Brazil, Philippines	Electrical & electronic components, computers, telecommunications
Magnesium metal	54	Canada, China, Russia, Israel	Aluminum-base alloys, automotive diecastings, desulfurizing iron & steel
Titanium (sponge)	54	Japan, Russia, Kazakhstan	Aerospace, armor, chemical processing, power generation, medical devices
Rare earths	53	China, France, Japan, Estonia	Catalysts, glass polishing, ceramics, magnets, metallurgy, phosphors
Peat	50	Canada	Horticulture, agriculture

Economic and Financial Glossary

Source: Reviewed by William M. Gentry, Graduate School of Business, Columbia University

Annuity contract: An investment vehicle sold by insurance companies. Annuity buyers can elect to receive periodic payments for the rest of their lives. Annuities provide insurance against outliving one's wealth.

Arbitrage: A form of hedged investment meant to capture slight differences in the prices of 2 related securities—for example, buying gold in London and selling it at a higher price in New York.

Balanced budget: A budget is balanced when receipts equal expenditures. When receipts exceed expenditures, there is a **surplus;** when they fall short of expenditures, there is a **deficit.**

Balance of payments: The difference between all payments, for some categories of transactions, made to and from foreign countries over a set period of time. A *favorable* balance of payments exists when more payments are coming in than going out; an *unfavorable* balance of payments obtains when the reverse is true. Payments may include gold, the cost of merchandise and services, interest and dividend payments, money spent by travelers, and repayment of principal on loans.

Balance of trade (trade gap): The difference between exports and imports, in both actual funds and credit. A nation's balance of trade is *favorable* when exports exceed imports and *unfavorable* when the reverse is true.

Bear market: A market in which prices are falling.

Bearer bond: A bond issued in bearer form rather than being registered in a specific owner's name. Ownership is determined by possession.

Bond: A written promise, or IOU, by the issuer to repay a fixed amount of borrowed money on a specified date and generally to pay interest at regular intervals in the interim.

Bull market: A market in which prices are on the rise.

Capital gain (loss): An increase (decrease) in the market value of an asset over some period of time. For tax purposes, capital gains are typically calculated from when an asset is bought to when it is sold.

Commercial paper: An extremely short-term corporate IOU, generally due in 270 days or less.

Convertible bond: A corporate bond (see below) that may be converted into a stated number of shares of common stock. Its price tends to fluctuate along with fluctuations in the price of the stock and with changes in interest rates.

Consumer price index (CPI): A statistical measure of the change in the price of consumer goods.

Corporate bond: A bond issued by a corporation. The bond normally has a stated life and pays a fixed rate of interest. Considered safer than the common or preferred stock of the same company.

Cost of living: The cost of maintaining a standard of living measured in terms of purchased goods and services. Inflation typically measures changes in the cost of living.

Cost-of-living adjustments: Changes in promised payments, such as retirement benefits, to account for changes in the cost of living.

Credit crunch (liquidity crisis): A situation in which cash for lending is in short supply.

Debenture: An unsecured bond backed only by the general credit of the issuing corporation.

Deficit spending: Government spending in excess of revenues, generally financed with the sale of bonds. A deficit increases the government debt.

Deflation: A decrease in the level of prices.

Depression: A long period of economic decline marked by low prices, high unemployment, and many business failures.

Derivatives: Financial contracts, such as options, whose values are based on, or *derived* from, the price of an underlying financial asset or indicator such as a stock or an interest rate.

Devaluation: The official lowering of a nation's currency, decreasing its value in relation to foreign currencies.

Discount rate: The rate of interest set by the Federal Reserve that member banks are charged when borrowing money through the Federal Reserve System.

Disposable income: Income after taxes that is available to persons for spending and saving.

Diversification: Investing in more than one asset in order to reduce the riskiness of the overall asset portfolio. By holding more than one asset, losses on some assets may be offset by gains realized on other assets.

Dividend: Discretionary payment by a corporation to its shareholders, usually in the form of cash or stock shares.

Dow Jones Industrial Average: An index of stock market prices, based on the prices of 30 companies, 28 of which are on the New York Stock Exchange.

Econometrics: The use of statistical methods to study economic and financial data.

Federal Deposit Insurance Corp. (FDIC): A U.S. government-sponsored corporation that insures accounts in national banks and other qualified institutions against bank failures.

Federal Reserve System: The entire banking system of the U.S., incorporating 12 Federal Reserve banks (one in each of 12 Federal Reserve districts), 25 Federal Reserve branch banks, all national banks, and state-chartered commercial banks and trust companies that have been admitted to its membership. The governors of the system greatly influence the nation's monetary and credit policies.

Full employment: The economy is said to be at full employment when everyone who wishes to work at the going wage-rate for his or her type of labor is employed, save only for the small amount of unemployment due to the time it takes to switch from one job to another.

Futures: A futures contract is an agreement to buy or sell a specific amount of a commodity or financial instrument at a particular price at a set date in the future. For example, futures based on a stock index (such as the Dow Jones Industrial Average) are bets on the future price of that group of stocks.

Golden parachute: Provisions in contracts of some high-level executives guaranteeing substantial severance benefits if they lose their position in a corporate takeover.

Government bond: A bond issued by the U.S. Treasury, considered a safe investment. These are divided into 2 categories—marketable and not marketable. *Savings bonds* cannot be bought and sold once the original purchase is made. Marketable bonds fall into several categories. *Treasury bills* are short-term U.S. obligations, maturing in 3, 6, or 12 months. *Treasury notes* mature in up to 10 years. *Treasury bonds* mature in 10 to 30 years. *Indexed bonds* are adjusted for inflation.

Greenmail: A company buying back its own shares for more than the going market price to avoid a threatened hostile takeover.

Gross domestic product (GDP): The market value of all goods and services that have been bought for final use during a period of time. It became the official measure of the size of the U.S. economy in 1991, replacing *gross national product (GNP)*, in use since 1941. GDP covers workers and capital employed within the nation's borders. GNP covers production by U.S. residents regardless of where it takes place. The switch aligned U.S. terminology with that of most other industrialized countries.

Hedge fund: A flexible investment fund for a limited number of large investors (the minimum investment is typically $1 million). Hedge funds use a variety of investment techniques, including those forbidden to mutual funds, such as short-selling and heavy leveraging.

Hedging: Taking 2 positions whose gains and losses will offset each other if prices change, in order to limit risk.

Individual retirement account (IRA): A self-funded tax-advantaged retirement plan that allows employed individuals to contribute up to a maximum yearly sum. With a *traditional* IRA, individuals contribute pre-tax earnings and defer income taxes until retirement. With a *Roth* IRA, individuals contribute after-tax earnings but do not pay taxes on future withdrawals (the interest is never taxed). *401(k) plans* are employer-sponsored plans similar to traditional IRAs, but having higher contribution limits.

Inflation: An increase in the level of prices.

Insider information: Important facts about the condition or plans of a corporation that have not been released to the general public.

Interest: The cost of borrowing money.

Investment bank: A financial institution that arranges the initial issuance of stocks and bonds and offers companies advice about acquisitions and divestitures.

Junk bonds: Bonds issued by companies with low credit ratings. They typically pay relatively high interest rates because of the fear of default.

Leading indicators: A series of 11 indicators from different segments of the economy used by the U.S. Commerce Department to predict when changes in the level of economic activity will occur.

Leverage: The extent to which a purchase was paid for with borrowed money. Amplifies the potential gain or loss for the purchaser.

Leveraged buyout (LBO): An acquisition of a company in which much of the purchase price is borrowed, with the debt to be repaid from future profits or by subsequently selling off company assets. A leveraged buyout is typically carried out by a small group of investors, often including incumbent management.

Liquid assets: Assets consisting of cash and/or items that are easily converted into cash.

Margin account: A brokerage account that allows a person to trade securities on credit. A **margin call** is a demand for more collateral on the account.

Money supply: The currency held by the public, plus checking accounts in commercial banks and savings institutions.

Mortgage-backed securities: Created when a bank, builder, or government agency gathers together a group of mortgages and then sells bonds to other institutions and the public. The investors receive their proportionate share of the interest payments on the loans as well as the principal payments. Usually, the mortgages in question are guaranteed by the government.

Municipal bond: Issued by governmental units such as states, cities, local taxing authorities, and other agencies. Interest is exempt from U.S.—and sometimes state and local—income tax. *Municipal bond unit investment trusts* offer a portfolio of many different municipal bonds chosen by professionals. The income is exempt from federal income taxes.

Mutual fund: A portfolio of professionally bought and managed financial assets in which you pool your money along with that of many other people. A share price is based on net asset value, or the value of all the investments owned by the funds, less any debt, and divided by the total number of shares. The major advantage, relative to investing individually in only a small number of stocks, is less risk—the holdings are spread out over many assets and if one or two do badly the remainder may shield you from the losses. *Bond funds* are mutual funds that deal in the bond market exclusively. *Money market mutual*

funds buy in the so-called money market—institutions that need to borrow large sums of money for short terms. These funds often offer special checking account advantages.

National debt: The debt of the national government, as distinguished from the debts of political subdivisions of the nation and of private business and individuals.

National debt ceiling: Total borrowing limit set by Congress beyond which the U.S. national debt cannot rise. This limit is periodically raised by congressional vote.

Option: A type of contractual agreement between a buyer and a seller to buy or sell shares of a security. A **call** option contract gives the right to purchase shares of a specific stock at a stated price within a given period of time. A **put** option contract gives the buyer the right to sell shares of a specific stock at a stated price within a given period of time.

Per capita income: The total income of a group divided by the number of people in the group.

Prime interest rate: The rate charged by banks on short-term loans to large commercial customers with the highest credit rating.

Producer price index: A statistical measure of the change in the price of wholesale goods. It is reported for 3 different stages of the production chain: crude, intermediate, and finished goods.

Program trading: Trading techniques involving large numbers and large blocks of stocks, usually used in conjunction with computer programs. Techniques include *index arbitrage,* in which traders profit from price differences between stocks and futures contracts on stock indexes, and *portfolio insurance,* which is the use of stock-index futures to protect stock investors from potentially large losses when the market drops.

Public debt: The total of a nation's debts owed by state, local, and national government. Increases in this sum, reflected in public-sector deficits, indicate how much of the nation's spending is being financed by borrowing rather than by taxation.

Recession: A mild decrease in economic activity marked by a decline in real (inflation-adjusted) GDP, employment, and trade, usually lasting from 6 months to a year, and marked by widespread decline in many sectors of the economy.

Savings Association Insurance Fund (SAIF): Created in 1989 to insure accounts in savings and loan associations up to $100,000.

Seasonal adjustment: Statistical changes made to compensate for regular fluctuations in data that are so great they tend to distort the statistics and make comparisons meaningless. For instance, seasonal adjustments are made for a slowdown in housing construction in midwinter and for the rise in farm income in the fall after summer crops are harvested.

Short-selling: Borrowing shares of stock from a brokerage firm and selling them, hoping to buy the shares back at a lower price, return them, and realize a profit from the decline in prices.

Stagnation: Economic slowdown in which there is little growth in the GDP, capital investment, and real income.

Stock: *Common stocks* are shares of ownership in a corporation. For publicly held firms, the stock typically trades on an exchange, such as the New York Stock Exchange; for closely held firms, the founders and managers own most of the stock. There can be wide swings in the prices of this kind of stock. *Preferred stock* is a type of stock on which a fixed dividend must be paid before holders of common stock are issued their share of the issuing corporation's earnings. Preferred stock is less risky than common stock. *Convertible preferred stock* can be converted into the common stock of the company that issued the preferred. *Over-the-counter stock* is not traded on the major or regional exchanges, but rather through dealers from whom you buy directly. *Blue chip* stocks are so called because they have been leading stocks for a long time. *Growth* stocks are from companies that reinvest their earnings, rather than pay dividends, with the expectation of future stock price appreciation.

Supply-side economics: A school of thinking about economic policy holding that lowering income tax rates will inevitably lead to enhanced economic growth and general revitalization of the economy.

Takeover: Acquisition of one company by another company or group by sale or merger. A *friendly takeover* occurs when the acquired company's management is agreeable to the merger; when management is opposed to the merger, it is a *hostile* takeover.

Tender offer: A public offer to buy a company's stock; usually priced at a premium above the market.

Zero coupon bond: A corporate or government bond that is issued at a deep discount from the maturity value and pays no interest during the life of the bond. It is redeemable at face value.

AGRICULTURE

U.S. Farms—Number and Acreage by State, 2000, 2002

Source: National Agricultural Statistics Service, U.S. Dept. of Agriculture

STATE	No. of farms (1,000) 2002	2000	Acreage in farms (mil.) 2002	2000	Acreage per farm 2002	2000	STATE	No. of farms (1,000) 2002	2000	Acreage in farms (mil.) 2002	2000	Acreage per farm 2002	2000
AL....	47	47	8.9	9.0	189.4	191.5	NE....	52	54	46.4	46.4	892.3	859.3
AK....	0.59	0.58	0.92	0.92	1,559.3	1,586.2	NV....	3	3	6.8	6.8	2,266.7	2,266.7
AZ....	7.3	7.5	26.5	26.7	3,630.1	3,560	NH....	3.1	3.1	0.41	0.42	132.3	135.5
AR....	48.5	48	14.6	14.6	301	304.2	NJ....	9.6	9.6	0.82	0.83	85.4	86.5
CA....	84	87.5	27.7	27.8	29.8	317.7	NM....	15	15.2	44	44	2,933.3	2,894.7
CO....	30	29.5	31.3	31.6	1,043.3	1,071.2	NY....	37	38	7.6	7.7	205.4	202.6
CT....	3.9	3.9	0.36	0.36	92.3	92.3	NC....	56	57	9.1	9.2	162.5	161.4
DE....	2.4	2.6	0.56	0.58	233.3	223.1	ND....	30	30.3	39.4	39.4	1,313.3	1,300.3
FL....	44	44	10.2	10.3	231.8	234.1	OH....	78	80	14.7	14.9	188.5	186.3
GA....	50	50	11	11.1	220	222	OK....	87	85	34	34	390.8	400
HI....	5.3	5.5	1.44	1.44	271.7	261.8	OR....	41	40	17.2	17.2	419.5	430
ID....	24	24.5	11.9	11.9	495.8	485.7	PA....	59	59	7.7	7.7	130.5	130.5
IL....	76	78	27.7	27.7	364.5	355.1	RI....	0.7	0.7	0.06	0.06	85.7	85.7
IN....	63	64	15.4	15.5	244.4	242.2	SC....	24.5	24	4.8	4.8	195.9	200
IA....	92.5	95	32.6	32.8	352.4	345.3	SD....	32.5	32.5	44	44	1,353.8	1,353.8
KS....	63	64	47.4	47.5	752.4	742.2	TN....	90	90	11.7	11.7	130	130
KY....	89	90	13.6	13.6	152.8	151.1	TX....	230	226	131	130	569.6	575.2
LA....	29	29.5	8.05	8.1	277.6	274.6	UT....	15	15.5	11.6	11.6	773.3	748.4
ME....	6.7	6.8	1.26	1.27	188.1	186.8	VT....	6.6	6.7	1.34	1.34	203	200
MD....	12.2	12.4	2.1	2.1	172.1	169.4	VA....	49	49	8.7	8.7	177.6	177.6
MA....	6	6.1	0.56	0.57	93.3	93.4	WA....	39	40	15.7	15.7	402.6	392.5
MI....	52	52	10.4	10.4	200	200	WV....	20.5	20.5	3.6	3.6	175.6	175.6
MN....	79	79	28.4	28.6	359.5	362	WI....	77	77	15.9	16.2	206.5	210.4
MS....	43	43	11	11.1	255.8	258.1	WY....	9.2	9.2	34.6	34.6	3,760.9	3,760.9
MO....	107	109	29.8	30	278.5	275.2							
MT....	28	27.6	56.7	56.7	2,025	2,054.3	U.S....	2,158	2,172	941	942	436	434

U.S. Farms, 1940-2002

Source: National Agricultural Statistics Service, U.S. Dept. of Agriculture

The number of U.S. farms increased slightly in 2002 (by about 0.1%), while the size of the average farm decreased slightly (by about 0.2%). Over the long term, numbers of U.S. farms have declined substantially, while average farm size has increased.

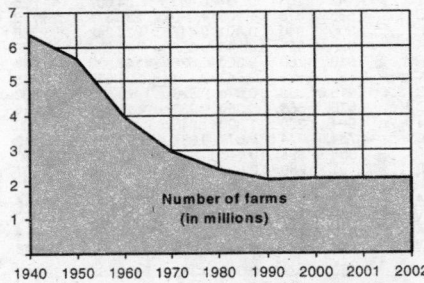

Number of farms (in millions)

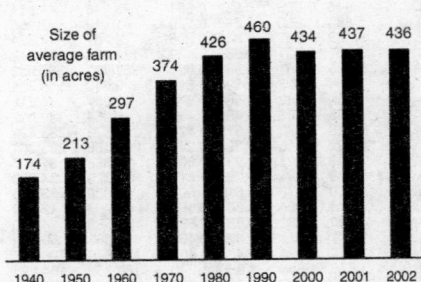

Size of average farm (in acres)

174, 213, 297, 374, 426, 460, 434, 437, 436

1940 1950 1960 1970 1980 1990 2000 2001 2002

Livestock on Farms in the U.S., 1900-2003

Source: National Agricultural Statistics Service, U.S. Dept. of Agriculture

(in thousands)

Year (On Jan. 1)	All cattle[1]	Milk cows	Sheep and lambs	Hogs and pigs[2]	Year (On Jan. 1)	All cattle[1]	Milk cows	Sheep and lambs	Hogs and pigs[2]
1900.....	59,739	16,544	48,105	51,055	1991	96,393	9,966	11,174	54,416
1910.....	58,993	19,450	50,239	48,072	1992	97,556	9,688	10,797	57,649
1920.....	70,400	21,455	40,743	60,159	1993	99,176	9,581	10,906	58,795
1930.....	61,003	23,032	51,565	55,705	1994	100,974	9,494	9,836	60,847
1940.....	68,309	24,940	52,107	61,165	1995	102,755	9,487	8,886	57,150
1950.....	77,963	23,853	29,826	58,937	1996	103,487	9,416	8,461	56,124
1955.....	96,592	23,462	31,582	50,474	1997	101,656	9,318	8,024	57,366
1960.....	96,236	19,527	33,170	59,026	1998	99,744	9,199	7,825	62,213
1965.....	109,000	16,981	25,127	56,106	1999	99,115	9,133	7,215	60,896
1970.....	112,369	12,091	20,423	57,046	2000	98,198	9,190	7,032	59,117
1975.....	132,028	11,220	14,515	54,693	2001	97,277	9,183	6,965	58,603
1980.....	111,242	10,758	12,699	67,318	2002	96,704	9,112	6,685	60,288
1985.....	109,582	10,777	10,716	54,073	2003	96,106	9,152	6,350	58,736
1990.....	95,816	10,015	11,358	53,788					

(1) From 1970, includes milk cows and heifers that have calved. (2) 1900-95, as of Dec. 1 of preceding year; 1996-2002 as of June 1 of same year.

> **IT'S A FACT:** In 1999, the average American ate 118 lbs. of red meat, down from 129 lbs. in 1970-1979 and 86 lbs. of poultry, up from 35 lbs. in the 1970s.

U.S. Meat Production and Consumption, 1940-2002

Source: Economic Research Service, U.S. Dept. of Agriculture

(in millions of pounds)

Year	Beef Production	Beef Consumption[2]	Veal Production	Veal Consumption[2]	Lamb and mutton Production	Lamb and mutton Consumption[2]	Pork Production	Pork Consumption[2]	All red meats[1] Production	All red meats[1] Consumption[2]	All Poultry Production	All Poultry Consumption[2]
1940.....	7,175	7,257	981	981	876	873	10,044	9,701	19,076	18,812	NA	NA
1950.....	9,534	9,529	1,230	1,206	597	596	10,714	10,390	22,075	21,721	3,174	3,097
1960.....	14,728	15,465	1,109	1,118	769	857	13,905	14,057	30,511	31,497	6,310	6,168
1970.....	21,684	23,451	588	613	551	669	14,699	14,957	37,522	39,689	10,193	9,981
1980.....	21,643	23,560	400	420	318	351	16,617	16,838	38,978	41,170	14,173	13,525
1990.....	22,743	24,030	327	325	363	397	15,354	16,025	38,787	40,778	23,468	22,152
1991.....	22,917	24,115	306	305	363	397	15,999	16,392	39,585	41,209	24,701	23,272
1992.....	23,086	24,262	310	311	348	388	17,233	17,462	40,977	42,423	26,201	24,394
1993.....	23,049	24,006	285	286	337	381	17,088	17,408	40,759	42,081	27,328	25,097
1994.....	24,386	25,128	293	291	308	346	17,696	17,812	42,683	43,577	29,113	25,754
1995.....	25,222	25,534	319	319	285	346	17,849	17,768	43,675	43,967	30,393	25,944
1996.....	25,525	25,861	378	378	268	333	17,117	16,797	43,288	43,369	32,015	26,760
1997.....	25,490	25,611	334	333	260	332	17,274	16,823	43,358	43,099	32,964	27,261
1998.....	25,760	26,305	262	265	251	360	19,010	18,308	45,283	45,237	33,352	27,821
1999.....	26,493	26,937	235	235	248	358	19,308	18,946	46,284	46,476	35,252	29,584
2000.....	26,888	27,338	225	225	234	354	18,952	18,643	46,299	46,560	36,073	30,508
2001.....	26,212	27,026	205	204	227	368	19,160	18,492	45,804	46,089	38,942	30,823
2002.....	27,192	27,878	205	v204	223	383	19,685	19,147	47,305	47,612	38,079	32,575

(1) Meats may not add to total because of rounding. (2) Consumption (also called total disappearance) is estimated as: production plus beginning stocks, plus imports, minus exports, minus ending stocks. NA = Not available.

Eggs: U.S. Production, Price, and Value, 2001-2002[1]

Source: National Agricultural Statistics Service, U.S. Dept. of Agriculture

STATE	Eggs produced 2001	Eggs produced 2002 (mil)	Price per dozen[2] 2001	Price per dozen[2] 2002 (dollars)	Value of Production 2001	Value of Production 2002 (1,000 dollars)	STATE	Eggs produced 2001	Eggs produced 2002 (mil)	Price per dozen[2] 2001	Price per dozen[2] 2002 (dollars)	Value of Production 2001	Value of Production 2002 (1,000 dollars)
AL....	2,359	2,281	1.350	1.560	265,388	296,530	NE....	3,001	2,977	0.382	0.341	95,532	84,596
AR....	3,431	3,329	1.060	1.070	303,072	296,836	NH....	43	46	0.851	0.783	3,021	2,975
CA....	5,998	6,124	0.472	0.392	235,921	200,051	NJ....	556	533	0.531	0.512	24,603	22,741
CO....	946	1,008	0.612	0.591	48,246	49,644	NY....	1,143	1,100	0.567	0.489	54,007	44,825
CT....	884	855	0.568	0.520	41,819	37,050	NC....	2,535	2,518	1.100	1.090	232,375	228,718
DE....	369	347	0.676	0.606	20,787	17,524	OH....	7,900	7,940	0.491	0.447	323,242	295,765
FL....	2,737	2,731	0.536	0.479	122,253	109,012	OK....	926	951	0.843	0.832	65,052	65,936
GA....	5,086	4,961	0.868	0.861	367,887	355,952	OR....	818	760	0.600	0.536	40,900	33,947
HI....	129.4	117.5	0.894	0.891	9,640	8,724	PA....	6,662	6,520	0.547	0.514	303,676	279,273
ID....	251	242	0.586	0.576	12,257	11,616	SC....	1,416	1,380	0.674	0.626	79,532	71,990
IL....	888	893	0.486	0.442	35,964	32,892	SD....	575	568	0.350	0.332	16,771	15,715
IN....	6,025	5,973	0.515	0.479	258,573	238,422	TN....	294	300	1.300	1.240	31,850	31,000
IA....	8,691	9,910	0.390	0.343	282,458	283,261	TX....	4,734	4,774	0.677	0.687	267,077	273,312
KY....	933	921	0.935	0.801	72,696	61,477	UT....	865	894	0.440	0.420	31,717	31,290
LA....	480	494	0.793	0.817	31,720	33,633	VT....	61	59	0.629	0.623	3,213	3,037
ME....	1,100	1,079	0.618	0.591	56,650	53,136	VA....	766	734	0.961	0.988	61,344	60,433
MD....	870	894	0.607	0.565	44,008	42,092	WA....	1,339	1,369	0.560	0.486	62,501	55,445
MA....	80	80	0.657	0.630	4,380	4,200	WV....	235	261	1.410	1.400	27,612	30,450
MI....	1,677	1,771	0.437	0.403	61,063	59,459	WI....	1,235	1,158	0.500	0.511	51,458	49,312
MN....	3,112	3,124	0.435	0.408	112,810	106,216	WY....	3.6	3.6	0.560	0.486	168	146
MS....	1,550	1,588	1.260	1.240	162,750	164,093							
MO....	1,789	1,837	0.507	0.497	75,585	76,082	Other[3]	1,155	1,189	0.359	0.335	41,488	39,867
MT....	95	104	0.410	0.460	3,246	3,987	U.S.[4]....	85,745	86,698	0.622	0.590	4,446,312	4,262,662

(1) Estimates cover the 12-month period from Dec. 1 of the previous year through Nov. 30. (2) Average of all eggs sold by producers, including hatching eggs. (3) AK, AZ, KS, NM, NV, ND, and RI combined to avoid disclosure of individual operations; totals listed under "other." (4) Total states may not equal U.S. total because of rounding.

Total U.S. Government Agricultural Payments, by State, 1990-2002

Source: Economic Research Service, U.S. Dept. of Agriculture

(in thousands of dollars)

STATE	1990	1995	1999	2000	2001	2002
Alabama	$82,226	$54,140	$179,505	$170,852	$230,734	$262,148
Alaska	1,117	1,735	1,766	1,672	2,173	1,829
Arizona	43,349	9,456	107,899	107,066	99,254	68,926
Arkansas	312,696	383,783	815,267	900,648	832,545	446,553
California	252,333	239,809	668,501	667,466	586,761	451,495
Colorado	236,723	167,661	374,202	351,116	319,599	188,414
Connecticut	2,123	2,382	8,708	18,143	7,540	4,916
Delaware	3,213	3,150	19,850	25,028	25,004	11,863
Florida	37,155	55,778	76,859	56,741	108,011	81,467
Georgia	130,593	67,332	361,827	380,057	427,261	652,789
Hawaii	519	947	820	11,927	3,860	1,802
Idaho	133,431	89,482	210,657	261,297	207,664	163,322
Illinois	506,603	543,753	1,798,822	1,943,916	1,849,769	612,706
Indiana	244,170	246,026	852,051	938,464	925,278	332,782
Iowa	753,733	786,652	2,061,881	2,302,094	1,971,677	737,107
Kansas	834,746	422,226	1,401,286	1,231,923	1,068,706	452,680
Kentucky	81,610	67,382	232,109	448,473	293,379	137,901
Louisiana	154,631	164,251	420,630	451,831	434,612	251,735
Maine	6,982	14,114	11,650	13,851	7,819	13,752

STATE	1990	1995	1999	2000	2001	2002
Maryland	$17,386	$15,241	$68,265	$88,470	$86,626	$48,338
Massachusetts	3,023	2,490	10,186	10,973	10,138	6,204
Michigan	168,831	151,055	401,436	381,056	352,766	188.513
Minnesota	511,759	467,807	1,409,859	1,502,230	1,242,141	480,483
Mississippi	185,969	133,544	440,837	463,901	517,007	249,758
Missouri	299,065	256,629	717,096	869,390	817,044	397,292
Montana	299,599	189,809	492,057	490,002	476,158	259,096
Nebraska	624,646	507,302	1,411,884	1,406,971	1,297,623	485,091
Nevada	5,347	4,264	2,676	3,918	5,864	11,121
New Hampshire	1,856	1,216	3,944	4,768	2,815	3,895
New Jersey	15,744	5,491	10,258	22,481	16,403	6,434
New Mexico	63,840	55,134	92,378	79,495	93,729	72,996
New York	59,304	43,563	120,397	159,876	114,039	158,174
North Carolina	73,255	41,476	290,453	447,096	330,730	268,132
North Dakota	545,378	296,215	975,583	1,170,234	944,591	381,658
Ohio	197,006	167,351	650,237	678,104	681,651	278,967
Oklahoma	319,040	164,662	532,263	439,851	392,822	308,822
Oregon	89,137	52,145	105,641	137,401	104,946	80,290
Pennsylvania	41,414	41,096	95,717	147,848	103,462	129,113
Rhode Island	191	317	877	1,218	292	697
South Carolina	62,637	34,586	127,788	144,499	130,287	64,019
South Dakota	332,851	245,016	791,124	789,895	715,264	281,256
Tennessee	91,029	47,405	227,205	298,873	247,485	107,178
Texas	974,702	643,119	1,961,835	1,647,066	1,703,168	986,216
Utah	34,897	25,045	30,521	36,181	39,754	45,719
Vermont	5,793	4,334	12,221	26,093	7,877	36,341
Virginia	32,378	25,967	100,980	152,452	117,158	153,790
Washington	205,425	116,062	270,594	352,503	298,784	214,138
West Virginia	6,049	5,268	11,269	23,509	9,842	5,683
Wisconsin	181,243	184,350	503,046	603,213	415,110	330,604
Wyoming	31,283	31,432	40,203	34,302	50,272	47,260
UNITED STATES	**$9,298,030**	**$7,279,451**	**$21,513,119**	**$22,896,433**	**$20,727,496**	**$10,961,465**

U.S. Federal Food Assistance Programs, 1990-2002[1]

Source: Food and Nutrition Service, U.S. Dept. of Agriculture
(in millions of dollars)

	1990	1995	1997	1998	1999	2000	2001	2002
Food stamps[2]	$15,491	$24,620	$21,487	$18,893	$17,698	$17,029	$17,800	$20,693
Puerto Rico nutrition asst.[3]	937	1,131	1,174	1,204	1,236	1,268	1,296	1,351
Natl. school lunch[4]	3,834	5,160	5,554	5,830	6,019	6,149	6,475	6,856
School breakfast[5]	596	1,048	1,214	1,272	1,345	1,393	1,450	1,567
WIC[6]	2,122	3,440	3,844	3,890	3,940	3,981	4,150	4,342
Summer food service[7]	164	237	244	263	268	267	272	263
Child/adult care[7]	813	1,464	1,572	1,553	1,621	1,684	1,738	1,855
Special milk	19	17	17	17	16	15	16	16
Nutrition for the elderly[4]	142	148	145	141	140	137	152	152
Food distrib. to Indian reserv.[7]	66	65	71	72	76	72	68	69
Commodity supp. food prog.[7]	85	99	99	94	98	95	103	112
Food dist.—charitable inst.[8]	104	64	6	9	3	2	7	16
Emergency food assistance[9]	334	135	192	234	270	225	377	434
TOTAL[10]	**$24,707**	**$37,628**	**$35,619**	**$33,472**	**$32,730**	**$32,317**	**$33,904**	**$37,726**

(1) All data are for fiscal (not calendar) years. (2) Includes federal share of state administrative expenses and other federal costs.
(3) Puerto Rico participated in the Food Stamp Program from FY 1975 until July 1982, when it initiated a separate grant program.
(4) Nutrition Services Incentive Program, formerly the Nutrition Program for the Elderly; includes cash payments and commodity costs (entitlement, bonus, and cash in lieu). (5) Excludes startup costs. (6) Includes the WIC Farmers Market Nutrition Program, program studies and special grants. (7) Includes commodity costs and administrative expenditures. (8) Includes summer camps. (9) Includes the Emergency Food Assistance Program (TEFAP) for all years, and the Soup Kitchens/Food Banks Program (1989-96). (10) Excludes Food Program Administration (federal) costs. Totals may not add because of rounding.

Farm Business Real Estate Debt Outstanding, by Lender Groups,[1] 1960-2002

Source: Economic Research Service, U.S. Dept. of Agriculture
(in millions of dollars)

Dec. 31	Total farm real estate debt[2]	AMOUNTS HELD BY PRINCIPAL LENDER GROUPS				
		Farm Credit System[2]	Farm Services Agency[3]	Life insurance companies[4]	All operating banks	Other[5]
1960	$11,310	$2,222	$624	$2,652	$1,356	$4,456
1970	27,506	6,420	2,180	5,123	3,329	10,455
1980	89,692	33,225	7,435	11,998	7,765	27,813
1985	100,076	42,169	9,821	11,273	10,732	25,775
1990	74,732	25,924	7,639	9,704	16,288	15,169
1991	74,944	25,305	7,041	9,546	17,417	15,632
1992	75,421	25,408	6,394	8,765	18,757	16,095
1993	76,036	24,900	5,837	8,985	19,595	16,719
1994	77,680	24,597	5,465	9,025	21,079	17,514
1995	79,287	24,851	5,055	9,092	22,277	18,012
1996	81,657	25,730	4,702	9,468	23,276	18,481
1997	85,359	27,098	4,373	9,699	25,240	18,950
1998	89,615	28,888	4,073	10,723	27,168	18,763
1999	94,226	30,302	3,872	11,490	29,799	18,763
2000	97,648	31,825	3,658	11,828	31,901	18,377
2001	103,101	35,253	3,586	12,003	33,358	18,687
2002[6]	110,841	40,359	3,371	12,287	35,544	19,127

(1) Excludes operator households. (2) Includes data for joint stock land banks and real estate loans by Agricultural Credit Assn. (3) Includes loans made directly by Farm Services Agency for farm ownership, soil, and water loans to individuals, Native American tribe land acquisition, grazing associations, and half of economic emergency loans. Also includes loans for rural housing on farm tracts and labor housing. (4) American Council of Life Insurance members. (5) Estimated by ERS, USDA. Includes Commodity Credit Corporation storage and drying facility loans. (6) Preliminary.

U.S. Farm Marketings by State, 2001-2002

Source: Economic Research Service, U.S. Dept. of Agriculture
(in thousands of dollars)

STATE	RANK, 2002	2002 FARM MARKETINGS Total	Crops	Livestock and products	2001 FARM MARKETINGS Total	Crops	Livestock and products
Alabama	(29)	$2,962,089	$583,811	$2,378,278	$3,519,731	$705,216	$2,814,515
Alaska	(49)	50,679	22,773	27,906	51,865	23,853	28,012
Arizona	(27)	2,997,195	1,903,139	1,094,056	2,574,698	1,409,090	1,165,608
Arkansas	(14)	4,526,611	1,574,866	2,951,745	5,131,964	1,624,569	3,507,395
California	(1)	26,106,640	19,865,008	6,241,632	25,892,319	18,545,880	7,346,439
Colorado	(12)	4,880,517	1,378,928	3,501,589	4,728,954	1,354,465	3,374,489
Connecticut	(43)	468,489	314,125	154,364	476,150	298,829	177,321
Delaware	(40)	723,513	177,184	546,329	847,718	185,719	661,999
Florida	(8)	6,848,253	5,609,028	1,239,225	6,415,882	4,957,896	1,457,986
Georgia	(15)	4,472,045	1,582,309	2,889,736	5,514,952	1,975,220	3,539,732
Hawaii	(41)	509,143	424,354	84,789	510,507	419,298	91,209
Idaho	(19)	3,933,672	1,935,141	1,998,531	3,847,926	1,787,513	2,060,413
Illinois	(6)	7,486,125	5,923,828	1,562,297	7,547,087	5,704,242	1,842,845
Indiana	(13)	4,799,545	3,248,526	1,551,019	5,105,437	3,235,048	1,870,389
Iowa	(3)	10,833,860	5,759,106	5,074,754	11,550,109	5,614,520	5,935,589
Kansas	(5)	7,861,794	2,536,465	5,325,329	8,121,044	2,585,380	5,535,664
Kentucky	(24)	3,111,713	1,151,034	1,960,679	3,548,328	1,280,795	2,267,533
Louisiana	(33)	1,773,423	1,159,374	614,049	1,817,088	1,115,957	701,131
Maine	(44)	442,394	211,923	230,471	485,064	210,774	274,290
Maryland	(36)	1,431,766	621,423	810,343	1,596,085	646,712	949,373
Massachusetts	(45)	380,274	297,024	83,250	366,611	272,925	93,686
Michigan	(22)	3,390,072	2,130,372	1,259,700	3,469,122	1,979,799	1,489,323
Minnesota	(7)	7,478,126	3,833,272	3,644,854	8,101,875	3,813,440	4,288,435
Mississippi	(28)	2,962,343	1,012,645	1,949,698	3,146,582	871,056	2,275,526
Missouri	(16)	4,401,882	2,099,829	2,302,053	4,824,141	2,144,809	2,679,332
Montana	(34)	1,687,481	701,983	985,498	1,785,002	657,248	1,127,754
Nebraska	(4)	9,588,658	3,764,363	5,824,295	9,488,580	3,402,349	6,086,231
Nevada	(47)	366,242	155,085	211,157	424,596	153,300	271,296
New Hampshire	(48)	147,573	91,297	56,276	155,478	89,644	65,834
New Jersey	(39)	855,727	663,118	192,609	821,070	617,316	203,754
New Mexico	(32)	1,956,978	574,926	1,382,052	2,215,122	545,019	1,670,103
New York	(25)	3,104,484	1,234,324	1,870,160	3,419,790	1,199,163	2,220,627
North Carolina	(9)	6,602,899	2,658,886	3,944,013	7,730,633	3,086,554	4,644,079
North Dakota	(23)	3,222,630	2,498,974	723,656	2,978,548	2,258,615	719,933
Ohio	(17)	4,276,038	2,645,811	1,630,227	4,682,011	2,818,473	1,863,538
Oklahoma	(21)	3,730,952	837,492	2,893,460	4,026,680	873,802	3,152,878
Oregon	(26)	3,102,265	2,294,134	808,131	3,122,641	2,297,688	824,953
Pennsylvania	(18)	4,042,439	1,360,038	2,682,401	4,454,979	1,308,750	3,146,229
Rhode Island	(50)	46,087	39,787	6,300	47,438	39,735	7,703
South Carolina	(35)	1,452,079	691,852	760,227	1,646,020	763,677	882,343
South Dakota	(20)	3,779,495	1,719,982	2,059,513	4,107,879	1,852,454	2,255,425
Tennessee	(31)	1,999,858	1,086,785	913,073	2,160,707	1,033,948	1,126,759
Texas	(2)	12,664,912	4,577,242	8,087,670	13,795,618	4,456,153	9,339,465
Utah	(37)	1,057,178	249,426	807,752	1,116,343	263,082	853,261
Vermont	(42)	476,352	76,178	400,174	556,779	66,719	490,060
Virginia	(30)	2,172,890	721,763	1,451,127	2,443,987	770,785	1,673,202
Washington	(11)	5,208,955	3,713,638	1,495,317	5,191,920	3,464,259	1,727,661
West Virginia	(46)	378,486	78,289	300,197	407,570	59,315	348,255
Wisconsin	(10)	5,318,908	1,550,606	3,768,302	5,896,293	1,432,106	4,464,187
Wyoming	(38)	875,784	126,213	749,571	982,545	145,086	837,459
UNITED STATES		$192,947,507	$99,467,672	$93,479,835	$202,849,408	$96,418,236	$106,431,172

Grain, Hay, Potato, Cotton, Soybean, Tobacco Production, by State, 2002

Source: National Agricultural Statistics Service, U.S. Dept. of Agriculture

STATE	Barley (1,000 bu)	Corn, grain (1,000 bu)	Cotton (Upland) (1,000 b)	All hay (1,000 t)	Oats (1,000 bu)	Potatoes (1,000 cwt)	Soybeans (1,000 bu)	Tobacco (1,000 lb)	All wheat (1,000 bu)
AL	—	15,840	575	1,760	—	554	3,720	—	2,400
AK	158	—	—	26	48	154	—	—	—
AZ	4,400	5,180	560	2,034	—	2,106	—	—	9,455
AR	—	34,840	1,650.00	3,595	—	—	96,480	—	38,640
CA	5,100	25,500	1,430.00	9,594	2,160	17,695	—	—	31,500
CO	7,200	112,320	—	3,003	464	30,189	—	—	38,700
CT	—	NE	—	115	—	—	—	3,148	—
DE	1,932	13,861	—	43	—	936	4,625	—	4,060
FL	—	3,264	83	784	—	9,659	248	11,960	301
GA	—	33,350	1,650.00	1,690	1,500	—	2,940	55,650	8,200
ID	53,960	8,000	—	5,608	1,750	133,385	—	—	87,660
IL	—	1,496,000	—	2,355	3,450	1,984	449,780	—	31,850
IN	—	631,620	—	1,596	868	728	235,750	8,000	17,490
IA	—	1,963,500	—	5,645	13,300	—	494,880	—	800
KS	238	290,000	76	6,965	3,120	986	58,420	—	267,300
KY	512	106,080	—	5,520	—	—	40,950	226,430	18,020
LA	—	68,320	750	1,125	—	—	20,800	—	8,800
ME	2,080	NE	—	234	2,610	16,960	—	—	—
MD	3,362	32,300	—	508	—	1,175	10,810	2,380	11,880
MA	—	NE	—	200	—	740	—	1,845	—
MI	988	232,300	—	3,700	4,160	13,878	78,155	—	32,830
MN	6,435	1,051,900	—	6,610	15,960	18,700	308,850	—	62,240

STATE	Barley (1,000 bu)	Corn, grain (1,000 bu)	Cotton (Upland) (1,000 b)	All hay (1,000 t)	Oats (1,000 bu)	Potatoes (1,000 cwt)	Soybeans (1,000 bu)	Tobacco (1,000 lb)	All wheat (1,000 bu)
MS	—	66,250	1,980.00	1,875	—	—	43,840	—	9,020
MO	—	283,500	610	7,840	1,680	1,296	170,000	3,055	34,200
MT	39,900	1,820	—	4,620	2,695	3,224	—	—	109,895
NE	215	940,800	—	5,950	2,365	8,611	176,330	—	48,640
NV	194	NE	—	1,519	—	2,584	—	—	405
NH	—	NE	—	87	—	—	—	—	—
NJ	222	4,060	—	210	—	689	2,231	—	1,856
NM	—	8,820	100	1,684	—	2,336	—	—	3,740
NY	470	43,650	—	3,726	3,630	5,500	4,416	—	7,424
NC	1,380	58,100	790	1.131	1,995	3,570	30,080	357,350	20,160
ND	57,040	114,425	—	3,920	12,760	23,460	86,790	—	216,610
OH	240	252,560	—	3,750	3,720	1,008	141,300	9,460	50,220
OK	—	24,700	200	5,030	1,110	—	7,000	—	98,000
OR	3,700	3,105	—	3,407	3,080	24,936	—	—	34,010
PA	4,440	59,160	—	3,560	7,015	2,590	9,100	6,815	9,990
RI	—	NE	—	15	—	90	—	—	—
SC	—	11,960	130	627	1,290	—	7,055	59,475	7,030
SD	1,845	304,000	—	4,800	4,500	330	126,790	—	42,235
TN	—	66,340	813	4,514	—	—	34,720	72,540	13,800
TX	—	205,660	5,000.00	13,850	7,040	5,360	6,020	—	78,300
UT	2,880	2,030	—	2,286	450	244	—	—	4,892
VT	—	NE	—	480	—	—	—	—	—
VA	3,080	20,130	99	2,050	—	1,386	10,120	66,180	10,710
WA	18,360	13,300	—	3,346	650	95,200	—	—	129,695
WV	—	3,150	—	1,061	—	—	629	1,950	336
WI	1,800	391,500	—	5,340	15,000	31,125	66,880	3,394	10,771
WY	4,900	4,464	—	1,600	810	—	—	—	2,376
US	226,873	9,007,659	16,496.00	150,962	119,132	463,214	2,729,709	889,632	1,616,441

NE = Not estimated; bu = bushels; b = bales (480-lbs); t = tons; cwt = hundredweight.

Production of Principal U.S. Crops, 1989-2002

Source: National Agricultural Statistics Service, U.S. Dept. of Agriculture

Year	Corn for grain (1,000 bu)	Oats (1,000 bu)	Barley (1,000 bu)	Sorghum for grain (1,000 bu)	All wheat (1,000 bu)	Rye (1,000 bu)	Flaxseed (1,000 bu)	Upland Cotton (1,000 b)	Cottonseed (1,000 t)
1989	7,531,953	373,587	404,203	615,420	2,036,618	13,647	1,215	12,196.6	4,677.4
1990	7,934,028	357,654	422,196	573,303	2,729,778	10,176	3,812	15,505.4	5,968.5
1991	7,474,765	243,851	464,326	584,860	1,980,139	9,734	6,200	17,614.3	6,925.5
1992	9,476,698	294,229	455,090	875,022	2,466,798	11,440	3,288	16,219.5	6,230.1
1993	6,336,470	206,770	398,041	534,172	2,396,440	10,340	3,480	16,134.6	6,343.2
1994	10,102,735	229,008	374,862	649,206	2,320,981	11,341	2,922	19,662.0	7,603.9
1995	7,373,876	162,027	359,562	460,373	2,182,591	10,064	2,211	17,532.2	6,848.7
1996	9,293,435	155,273	395,751	802,974	2,285,133	9,016	1,602	18,413.5	7,143.5
1997	9,206,832	167,246	359,878	633,545	2,481,466	8,132	2,420	18,245.0	6,934.6
1998	9,758,685	165,981	352,125	519,933	2,547,321	12,161	6,708	13,475.9	5,365.4
1999	9,430,612	146,193	280,292	595,166	2,299,010	11,038	7,864	16,293.7	6,354.0
2000	9,915,051	149,545	318,728	470,526	2,232,460	8,386	10,730	16,799.2	6,435.6
2001[1]	9,506,840	117,024	249,420	514,524	1,957,043	6,971	11,455	19,602.4	7,452.2
2002	9,007,659	119,132	226,873	369,758	1,616,441	6,985	12,569	16,496.0	6,419.3

Year	Tobacco (1,000 lb)	All hay (1,000 t)	Beans, dry edible (1,000 cwt)	Peas, dry edible (1,000 cwt)	Peanuts[2] (1,000 lb)	Soybeans[3] (1,000 bu)	Potatoes (1,000 cwt)	Sweet potatoes (1,000 cwt)
1989	1,367,188	144,706	23,729	3,883	3,989,995	1,923,666	370,444	11,358
1990	1,626,380	146,212	32,379	2,372	3,602,770	1,925,947	402,110	12,594
1991	1,664,372	152,073	33,765	3,715	4,926,570	1,986,539	417,622	11,203
1992	1,721,671	146,903	22,615	2,535	4,284,416	2,190,354	425,367	12,005
1993	1,613,319	146,799	21,913	3,292	3,392,415	1,870,958	428,693	11,053
1994	1,582,896	150,060	29,028	2,255	4,247,455	2,516,054	467,054	13,395
1995	1,268,538	154,166	30,812	4,765	4,247,455	2,176,814	443,606	12,906
1996	1,517,334	149,457	27,960	2,671	3,661,205	2,382,364	498,633	13,456
1997	1,787,399	152,536	29,370	5,752	3,539,380	2,688,750	467,091	13,327
1998	1,479,867	151,780	30,418	5,934	3,963,440	2,741,014	475,771	12,382
1999	1,292,692	159,707	33,085	4,773	3,829,490	2,653,758	478,216	12,234
2000	1,052,999	151,921	26,409	3,474	3,265,505	2,757,810	513,621	13,794
2001[1]	991,552	156,764	19,583	3,763	4,276,704	2,890,682	437,888	14,637
2002	889,632	150,962	29,974	4,242	3,320,490	2,729,709	463,214	12,498

Year	Rice (1,000 cwt)	Sugarcane (1,000 t)	Sugar beets (1,000 t)	Pecans[4] (1,000 lb)	Apples (1,000 t)	Grapes (1,000 t)	Peaches (1,000 t)	Oranges[5] (1,000 bx)	Grapefruit[5] (1,000 bx)
1989	154,487	29,426	25,131	250,500	4,958.4	5,930.9	1,181.5	209,050	69,500
1990	156,088	28,136	27,513	205,000	4,828.4	5,659.9	1,121.1	184,415	49,300
1991	159,367	30,252	28,203	299,000	4,853.4	5,555.9	1,347.8	178,950	55,500
1992	179,658	30,363	29,143	166,000	5,284.3	6,052.1	1,336.0	209,610	55,265
1993	156,110	31,101	26,249	365,000	5,342.4	6,023.2	1,330.1	255,760	68,375
1994	197,779	30,929	31,853	199,000	5,667.8	5,870.6	1,253.3	240,450	65,100
1995	173,871	30,944	27,954	268,000	5,292.5	5,922.3	1,150.8	263,605	71,050
1996	171,321	29,462	26,680	221,500	5,196.0	5,554.3	1,058.2	263,890	66,200
1997	182,992	31,709	29,886	335,000	5,161.9	7,290.9	1,312.3	292,620	70,200
1998	184,443	32,743	32,499	73,200	5,381.3	5,816.4	1,162.8	315,525	63,150
1999	206,027	35,299	33,420	203,100	5,223.3	6,234.8	1,216.7	224,580	61,200
2000	190,872	36,114	32,541	209,800	5,291.9	7,688.0	1,289.9	299,760	66,980
2001[1]	215,270	34,587	25,764	388,500	4,714.4	6,569.6	1,216.6	280,935	59,750
2002	210,960	35,932	27,550	172,900	4,277.8	7,364.0	1,287.7	283,760	58,660

(1) Revised. (2) Harvested for nuts. (3) Harvested for beans. (4) Utilized production only. (5) Crop year ending in year cited.

Average Prices Received by U.S. Farmers, 1940-2002

Source: National Agricultural Statistics Service, U.S. Dept. of Agriculture

Figures below represent dollars per 100 lb for hogs, beef cattle, veal calves, sheep, lamb, and milk (wholesale); dollars per head for milk cows; cents per lb for chickens, broilers, turkeys, and wool; cents per dozen for eggs; weighted calendar year prices for livestock and livestock products other than wool. For 1943-63, wool prices are weighted on marketing year basis. The marketing year was changed in 1964 from a calendar year to a Dec.-Nov. basis for hogs, chickens, broilers, and eggs.

Year	Hogs	Cattle (beef)	Calves (veal)	Sheep	Lambs	Milk cows	Milk	Chickens (excl. broilers)	Broilers	Turkeys	Eggs	Wool
1940...	5.39	7.56	8.83	3.95	8.10	61	1.82	13.0	17.3	15.2	18.0	28.4
1950...	18.00	23.30	26.30	11.60	25.10	198	3.89	22.2	27.4	32.8	36.3	62.1
1960...	15.30	20.40	22.90	5.61	17.90	223	4.21	12.2	16.9	25.4	36.1	42.0
1970...	22.70	27.10	34.50	7.51	26.40	332	5.71	9.1	13.6	22.6	39.1	35.4
1975...	46.10	32.20	27.20	11.30	42.10	412	8.75	9.9	26.3	34.8	54.5	44.8
1980...	38.00	62.40	76.80	21.30	63.60	1,190	13.05	11.0	27.7	41.3	56.3	88.1
1985...	44.00	53.70	62.10	23.90	67.70	860	12.76	14.8	30.1	49.1	57.1	63.3
1986...	49.30	52.60	61.10	25.60	69.00	820	12.51	12.5	34.5	47.1	61.6	66.8
1987...	51.20	61.10	78.50	29.50	77.60	920	12.54	11.0	28.7	34.8	54.9	91.7
1988...	42.30	66.60	89.20	25.60	69.10	990	12.26	9.2	33.1	38.6	52.8	138.0
1989...	42.50	69.50	90.80	24.40	66.10	1,030	13.56	14.9	36.6	40.9	68.9	124.0
1990...	53.70	74.60	95.60	23.20	55.50	1,160	13.74	9.3	32.6	39.4	70.9	80.0
1991...	49.10	72.70	98.00	19.70	52.20	1,100	12.27	7.1	30.8	38.4	67.8	55.0
1992...	41.60	71.30	89.00	25.80	59.50	1,130	13.15	8.6	31.8	37.7	57.6	74.0
1993...	45.20	72.60	91.20	28.60	64.40	1,160	12.84	10.0	34.0	39.0	63.4	51.0
1994...	39.90	66.70	87.20	30.90	65.60	1,170	13.01	7.6	35.0	40.4	61.4	78.0
1995...	40.50	61.80	73.10	28.00	78.20	1,130	12.78	6.5	34.4	41.6	62.4	104.0
1996...	51.90	58.70	58.40	29.90	82.20	1,090	14.75	6.6	38.1	43.3	74.9	70.0
1997...	52.90	63.10	78.90	37.90	90.30	1,100	13.36	7.7	37.7	39.9	70.3	84.0
1998...	34.40	59.60	78.80	30.60	72.30	1,120	15.41	8.0	39.3	38.0	65.5	60.0
1999...	30.30	63.40	87.70	31.10	74.50	1,280	14.38	7.1	37.1	40.8	62.2	38.0
2000...	42.30	68.60	104.00	34.30	79.80	1,340	12.40	5.7	33.6	40.7	61.8	33.0
2001[1]...	44.30	71.30	106.00	34.60	66.90	1,500	15.05	4.5	39.3	39.0	62.2	36.0
2002...	33.40	66.50	96.40	28.20	74.10	1,600	12.19	4.7	30.5	36.5	59.0	53.0

Figures below represent cents per lb for cotton, apples, and peanuts; dollars per bushel for oats, wheat, corn, barley, and soybeans; dollars per 100 lb for rice, sorghum, and potatoes; dollars per ton for cottonseed and baled hay; weighted crop year prices. The marketing year is described as follows: apples, June-May; wheat, oats, barley, hay, and potatoes, July-June; cotton, rice, peanuts, and cottonseed, Aug.-July; soybeans, Sept.-Aug.; and corn and sorghum grain, Oct.-Sept.

Year	Corn	Wheat	Upland cotton*	Oats	Barley	Rice	Soybeans	Sorghum	Peanuts	Cottonseed	Hay	Potatoes	Apples
1940...	0.62	0.67	9.8	0.30	0.39	1.80	0.89	0.87	3.7	21.70	9.78	0.85	NA
1950...	1.52	2.00	39.9	0.79	1.19	5.09	2.47	1.88	10.9	86.60	21.10	1.50	NA
1960...	1.00	1.74	30.1	0.60	0.84	4.55	2.13	1.49	10.0	42.50	21.70	2.00	2.7
1970...	1.33	1.33	21.9	0.62	0.97	5.17	2.85	2.04	12.8	56.40	26.10	2.21	6.5
1975...	2.54	3.55	51.1	1.45	2.42	8.35	4.92	4.21	19.0	97.00	52.10	4.48	8.8
1980...	3.11	3.91	74.4	1.79	2.86	12.80	7.57	5.25	25.1	129.00	71.00	6.55	12.1
1985...	2.23	3.08	56.8	1.23	1.98	6.53	5.05	3.45	24.4	66.00	67.60	3.92	17.3
1986...	1.50	2.42	51.5	1.21	1.61	3.75	4.78	2.45	29.2	80.00	59.70	5.03	19.1
1987...	1.94	2.57	63.7	1.56	1.81	7.27	5.88	3.04	28.0	82.50	65.00	4.38	12.7
1988...	2.54	3.72	55.6	2.61	2.80	6.83	7.42	4.05	28.0	118.00	85.20	6.02	17.4
1989...	2.36	3.72	63.6	1.49	2.42	7.35	5.69	3.75	28.0	105.00	85.40	7.36	13.9
1990...	2.28	2.61	67.1	1.14	2.14	6.68	5.74	3.79	34.7	121.00	80.60	6.08	20.9
1991...	2.37	3.00	56.8	1.21	2.10	7.58	5.58	4.01	28.3	71.00	71.20	4.96	25.1
1992...	2.07	3.24	53.7	1.32	2.04	5.89	5.56	3.38	30.0	97.50	74.30	5.52	19.5
1993...	2.50	3.26	58.1	1.36	1.99	7.98	6.40	4.13	30.4	113.00	84.70	6.18	18.4
1994...	2.26	3.45	72.0	1.22	2.03	6.78	5.48	3.80	28.9	101.00	86.70	5.58	18.6
1995...	3.24	4.55	75.4	1.67	2.89	9.15	6.72	5.69	29.3	106.00	82.20	6.77	24.0
1996...	2.71	4.30	69.3	1.96	2.74	9.96	7.35	4.17	28.1	126.00	95.80	4.93	20.8
1997...	2.43	3.38	65.2	1.60	2.38	9.70	6.47	3.95	28.3	121.00	100.00	5.62	22.1
1998...	1.90	2.65	64.2	1.10	1.98	8.50	5.35	3.10	25.7	129.00	84.60	5.24	17.1
1999...	1.82	2.48	45.0	1.12	2.13	5.93	4.63	2.80	25.4	89.00	76.90	5.77	21.3
2000...	1.85	2.62	49.8	1.10	2.11	5.61	4.54	3.37	27.4	105.00	84.60	5.08	17.8
2001[1]...	1.97	2.78	29.8	1.59	2.22	4.25	4.38	3.46	23.4	90.50	96.50	6.99	22.9
2002...	2.35	3.56	40.5	1.81	2.72	4.22	4.30	18.2		100.00	92.40	6.82	25.7

*Beginning in 1964, 480-lb net weight bales. NA = Not available. (1) Revised.

World Wheat, Rice, and Corn Production, 2002

Source: UN Food and Agriculture Organization; in metric tons

COUNTRY	Wheat	Rice[1]	Corn	COUNTRY	Wheat	Rice[1]	Corn
Afghanistan	2,686,000	388,000	298,000	Croatia..........	988,175	—	2,501,774
Algeria	1,502,000	300	1,100	Cuba...........	—	325,539	233,297
Argentina	12,500,000	713,449	14,710,352	Czech Rep.	3,866,470	—	616,234
Australia	9,385,000	1,275,000	521,000	Denmark	4,130,000	—	—
Austria	1,460,000	—	2,000,000	Dominican Rep....	—	730,705	30,267
Azerbaijan	1,692,818	16,640	128,029	Ecuador.........	13,635	1,283,390	386,320
Bangladesh	1,606,000	38,134,000	10,000	Egypt...........	6,183,210	5,600,000	6,800,000
Belarus.........	1,151,800	—	16,000	Ethiopia	1,250,000	—	2,600,000
Belgium-Lux.	1,708,000	—	515,000	Finland..........	568,600	—	—
Bolivia..........	143,480	248,211	724,613	France	38,986,000	105,000	16,013,000
Bosnia & Herz....	297,000	—	912,000	Germany	20,817,740	—	3,738,448
Brazil	2,925,890	10,489,400	35,478,716	Ghana	—	280,000	1,407,000
Bulgaria	4,888,648	9,500	1,206,000	Greece..........	2,033,000	167,000	2,014,000
Cambodia	—	3,740,002	168,060	Guatemala	9,072	39,916	1,050,140
Canada.........	15,689,900	—	9,065,300	Hungary.........	3,896,000	7,000	6,087,000
Chile...........	1,818,693	141,927	923,666	India...........	71,814,304	116,580,000	10,570,000
China	91,290,240	176,553,000	123,175,000	Indonesia........	—	51,603,748	9,277,258
Colombia	29,367	2,353,440	1,331,160	Iran	12,000,000	2,115,000	1,200,000
Côte d'Ivoire.....	—	818,000	625,000	Iraq	800,000	90,000	60,000

COUNTRY	Wheat	Rice[1]	Corn	COUNTRY	Wheat	Rice[1]	Corn
Israel	175,000	—	58,000	Romania	4,380,000	1,500	8,500,000
Italy	7,764,763	1,371,000	10,937,365	Russian Fed.	50,557,000	483,000	1,541,000
Japan	827,800	11,111,000	180	Saudi Arabia	1,800,000	—	4,000
Kazakhstan	12,699,975	199,089	435,208	Senegal	—	177,756	97,858
Kenya	280,000	45,000	2,800,000	Serbia & Mont.	2,245,030	—	5,597,207
Korea, North	130,000	2,190,000	1,651,000	Sierra Leone	—	250,000	10,000
Korea, South	2,800	6,650,000	60,000	Slovakia	1,554,420	—	753,840
Kyrgyzstan	1,305,548	19,029	428,154	Slovenia	175,000	—	255,000
Laos	—	2,410,000	113,000	South Africa	2,400,000	3,300	9,123,000
Lithuania	1,165,100	—	—	Spain	6,782,900	815,700	4,394,500
Madagascar	10,000	2,670,600	1,603,271	Sweden	2,116,600	—	—
Mexico	3,272,660	225,880	17,500,000	Switzerland	584,100	—	199,500
Morocco	3,356,680	16,780	198,880	Syria	4,775,440	—	231,888
Myanmar	103,000	21,900,000	660,000	Tanzania	77,000	514,000	2,700,500
Namibia	6,119	—	27,700	Thailand	800	25,945,000	4,170,000
Nepal	1,258,045	4,130,000	1,510,770	Turkey	21,000,000	400,000	2,500,000
Netherlands	1,057,000	—	158,000	Turkmenistan	2,023,000	45,000	11,000
New Zealand	355,000	—	156,549	Ukraine	20,550,000	80,000	4,171,000
Niger	6,300	76,400	6,377	United Kingdom	16,053,000	—	—
Nigeria	77,000	3,192,000	4,934,000	U.S.	43,992,312	9,568,996	228,805,088
Pakistan	18,226,100	6,343,000	1,689,000	Uzbekistan	4,956,000	143,100	232,000
Paraguay	355,000	100,684	783,499	Venezuela	560	790,000	1,805,000
Peru	186,256	2,124,060	2,099,485	Vietnam	—	34,063,500	2,314,700
Philippines	—	13,270,653	4,319,262	Zimbabwe	150,000	600	—
Poland	9,296,566	—	1,967,694				
Portugal	387,000	145,000	851,000	**World**	**572,878,902**	**576,280,153**	**602,589,189**

— production is small or nonexistent. Because not all countries are reported on this table, country totals do not add to world totals.
(1) Rice paddy.

Wheat, Rice, and Corn—Exports/Imports of 10 Leading Countries, 2001, 1995

Source: UN Food and Agriculture Organization; in metric tons

TOP EXPORTERS

Wheat

2001		1995	
U.S.	25,782,618	U.S.	32,420,000
Canada	17,658,856	Canada	16,960,000
France	15,621,317	France	16,310,000
Australia	15,542,103	Australia	7,818,000
Argentina	10,789,976	Argentina	6,913,286
Germany	5,710,406	Germany	3,681,597
Kazakhstan	3,022,663	Hungary	2,764,541
Ukraine	2,852,610	U.K.	2,669,090
India	2,649,381	Kazakhstan	2,485,588
Russian Fed.	1,635,710	Denmark	1,540,179

Rice

2001		1995	
Thailand	7,685,051	Thailand	6,197,990
Vietnam	3,729,000	India	4,913,156
U.S.	2,622,087	U.S.	3,083,609
Pakistan	2,423,858	Vietnam	1,988,000
India	2,193,736	Pakistan	1,852,267
China	2,011,320	Australia	541,848
Myanmar	939,160	Italy	523,898
Uruguay	811,178	Uruguay	462,471
Egypt	708,658	Argentina	390,091
Australia	615,223	Myanmar	353,800

Corn

2001		1995	
U.S.	47,943,762	U.S.	60,240,000
Argentina	10,909,613	France	6,474,138
France	7,046,438	Argentina	6,000,873
China	5,997,984	South Africa	1,508,450
Hungary	1,568,555	Hungary	600,950
South Africa	620,267	Canada	443,612
Germany	595,657	Belgium-Lux.	442,645
Brazil	565,949	Zimbabwe	287,818
Paraguay	563,739	Germany	244,000
Thailand	501,624	Paraguay	203,430

TOP IMPORTERS

Wheat

2001		1995	
Italy	7,526,750	China	12,601,814
Brazil	7,016,330	Brazil	6,135,235
Iran	6,438,950	Japan	5,965,296
Japan	5,521,251	Italy	5,078,844
Algeria	4,538,000	Egypt	5,069,599
Egypt	4,412,941	Indonesia	4,054,203
Spain	3,863,443	Algeria	3,504,679
South Korea	3,628,735	Iran	3,100,000
Mexico	3,385,801	Spain	2,757,498
Morocco	3,375,588	Belgium-Lux.	2,719,024

Rice

2001		1995	
Côte d'Ivoire	1,948,435	Indonesia	3,157,700
Nigeria	1,508,335	China	1,645,837
Iraq	950,000	Iran	1,633,000
Philippines	810,903	Bangladesh	995,946
Iran	778,369	Brazil	870,506
Saudi Arabia	765,044	South Korea	587,000
Brazil	699,385	U. Arab Em.	540,888
Senegal	682,072	Saudi Arabia	522,942
Japan	645,675	Côte d'Ivoire	483,688
Indonesia	642,168	South Africa	466,154

Corn

2001		1995	
Japan	16,221,654	Japan	16,580,000
South Korea	8,481,831	China	11,702,350
Mexico	6,174,028	South Korea	9,035,169
China	5,234,519	Spain	2,912,371
Egypt	4,797,234	Mexico	2,686,921
Canada	3,246,927	Egypt	2,425,162
Spain	2,735,458	Malaysia	2,383,267
Malaysia	1,974,512	Belg.-Lux.	1,815,945
Netherlands	1,915,731	Netherlands	1,589,800
Colombia	1,769,988	U.K.	1,501,563

Value of U.S. Agricultural Exports and Imports, 1977-2002

Source: Economic Research Service, U.S. Dept. of Agriculture
(in billions of dollars, except percent)

Year[1]	Trade surplus	Agric. exports	% of all exports	Agric. imports	% of all imports	Year[1]	Trade surplus	Agric. exports	% of all exports	Agric. imports	% of all imports
1977	10.6	24.0	20	13.4	9	1990	16.6	39.5	11	22.9	5
1978	13.4	27.3	21	13.9	8	1991	16.4	39.3	10	22.9	5
1979	15.8	32.0	19	16.2	8	1992	18.3	43.1	10	24.8	5
1980	23.2	40.5	19	17.3	7	1993	17.7	42.9	10	25.1	4
1981	26.4	43.8	19	17.3	7	1994	19.2	46.2	10	27.0	4
1982	23.6	39.1	18	15.5	6	1995	26.0	56.3	10	30.3	4
1983	18.5	34.8	18	16.3	7	1996	26.8	60.3	10	33.5	4
1984	19.1	38.0	18	18.9	6	1997	21.0	57.2	9	36.1	4
1985	11.5	31.2	.15	19.7	6	1998	14.9	51.8	8	36.9	4
1986	5.4	26.3	13	20.9	6	1999	10.7	48.4	8	37.7	4
1987	7.2	27.9	12	20.7	5	2000	12.2	51.2	7	39.0	3
1988	14.3	35.3	12	21.0	5	2001[2]	14.3	53.7	8	39.4	3
1989	18.1	39.7	12	21.6	5	2002[3]	11.1	53.0	8	41.9	4

(1) Fiscal year (Oct.-Sept.). (2) Revised. (3) Preliminary.

World Commercial Catch of Fish, Crustaceans, and Mollusks, by Major Fishing Areas, 1996-2001

Source: Food and Agriculture Organization of the United Nations (FAO)
(in thousands of metric tons; live weight)

AREA	1996	1997	1998	1999	2000	2001
Marine						
Pacific Ocean	63,452	62,657	57,047	63,631	65,524	63,298
Atlantic Ocean	25,237	26,385	25,606	25,648	26,049	26,386
Indian Ocean	8,432	8,777	8,940	9,100	9,284	9,204
Total Marine	**97,121**	**97,820**	**91,593**	**98,378**	**100,857**	**98,888**
Inland Waters						
Asia	19,501	21,104	22,431	24,397	25,577	26,861
Africa	1,950	2,018	2,134	2,245	2,406	2,414
Europe	838	821	856	901	886	821
N. America	564	600	597	627	618	618
S. America	448	465	477	524	556	579
Former USSR	412	388	432	507	498	412
Oceania	22	24	25	26	26	27
Total Inland	**23,323**	**25,032**	**26,520**	**28,720**	**30,070**	**31,320**
GRAND TOTAL	**120,444**	**122,852**	**118,113**	**127,098**	**130,927**	**130,207**

Note: Data for marine mammals and aquatic plants are excluded. Totals include areas or territories not shown. Details may not equal totals due to rounding.

Commercial Catch of Fish, Crustaceans, and Mollusks, for 20 Leading Countries, 1996-2001[1]

Source: Food and Agriculture Organization of the United Nations (FAO)
(in thousands of metric tons; live weight; ranked for 2001)

COUNTRY	2001	2000	1999	1998	1997	1996	COUNTRY	2001	2000	1999	1998	1997	1996
China	42,579	41,568	40,030	39,545	36,529	33,320	Philippines	2,380	2,281	2,201	2,146	2,136	2,133
Peru	7,996	10,665	8,437	4,346	7,877	9,522	Korean Rep.	2,282	2,146	2,423	2,354	2,596	2,772
India	5,965	5,689	5,592	5,245	5,379	5,258	Vietnam	2,010	1,952	1,854	1,653	1,573	1,461
Japan	5,521	5,752	5,961	6,030	6,733	6,763	Iceland	1,985	1,986	1,740	1,686	2,210	2,064
U.S.[2]	5,405	5,174	5,228	5,154	5,422	5,395	Bangladesh	1,687	1,661	1,579	1,354	1,262	1,194
Indonesia	5,068	4,929	4,736	4,595	4,453	4,291	Denmark	1,552	1,578	1,448	1,560	1,867	1,723
Chile	4,363	4,692	5,325	3,558	6,083	6,909	Mexico	1,475	1,368	1,251	1,216	1,529	1,495
Russian Fed.	3,718	4,048	4,210	4,518	4,715	4,730	Spain	1,397	1,289	1,511	1,529	1,389	1,363
Thailand	3,606	3,631	3,621	3,508	3,417	3,561	Malaysia	1,393	1,441	1,407	1,287	1,281	1,239
Norway	3,199	3,191	3,096	3,259	3,224	2,970	Taiwan	1,303	1,338	1,347	1,105	1,052	976

(1) Includes aquaculture. (2) Includes weight of clam, oyster, scallop, and other mollusk shells. This weight is not included in U.S. landings statistics shown elsewhere.

U.S. Commercial Landings of Fish and Shellfish, 1986-2002[1]

Source: U.S. Dept. of Commerce, Natl. Oceanic and Atmospheric Admin., Natl. Marine Fisheries Service

YEAR	Landings for human food		Landings for industrial purposes[2]		TOTAL	
	mil lb	mil dollars	mil lb	mil dollars	mil lb	mil dollars
1986	3,393	$2,641	2,638	$122	6,031	$2,763
1987	3,946	2,979	2,950	136	6,896	3,115
1988	4,588	3,362	2,604	158	7,192	3,520
1989	6,204	3,111	2,259	127	8,463	3,238
1990	7,041	3,366	2,363	156	9,404	3,522
1991	7,031	3,169	2,453	139	9,484	3,308
1992	7,618	3,531	2,019	147	9,637	3,678
1993	8,214	3,317	2,253	154	10,467	3,471
1994	7,936	3,751	2,525	95	10,461	3,846
1995	7,667	3,625	2,121	145	9,788	3,770
1996	7,474	3,355	2,091	132	9,565	3,487
1997	7,244	3,285	2,598	163	9,842	3,448
1998	7,173	3,009	2,021	119	9,194	3,128
1999	6,832	3,265	2,507	202	9,339	3,467
2000	6,912	3,398	2,157	152	9,069	3,550
2001	7,314	3,074	2,178	154	9,492	3,228
2002	7,205	2,940	2,192	152	9,397	3,092

Note: Data do not include products of aquaculture, except oysters and clams. (1) Statistics on landings are shown in round weight for all items except univalve and bivalve mollusks such as clams, oysters, and scallops, which are shown in weight of meats (excluding the shell). All data are preliminary. (2) Processed into meal, oil, solubles, and shell products or used as bait or animal food.

U.S. Domestic Landings, by Regions, 2001-2002[1]

Source: U.S. Dept. of Commerce, Natl. Oceanic and Atmospheric Admin., Natl. Marine Fisheries Service

REGION	2001		2002	
	1,000 lb	1,000 dollars	1,000 lb	1,000 dollars
New England	635,162	$646,447	583,915	$685,428
Middle Atlantic	217,975	172,503	206,697	170,134
Chesapeake	617,244	174,968	495,675	172,320
South Atlantic	199,554	176,488	214,799	173,429
Gulf	1,605,564	798,319	1,716,140	692,717
Pacific Coast and Alaska	6,173,671	1,187,106	6,138,249	1,130,633
Great Lakes	18,818	17,844	17,848	15,544
Hawaii	23,870	54,561	23,841	52,113
TOTAL	**9,491,858**	**$3,228,236**	**9,397,164**	**$3,092,318**

(1) Landings reported in round (live) weight items except for univalve and bivalve mollusks (e.g., clams, oysters, scallops), which are reported in weight of meats (excluding shell). Landings for Mississippi River Drainage Area states not included (not available).

EMPLOYMENT

Employment and Unemployment in the U.S., 1900-2002

Source: Bureau of Labor Statistics, U.S. Dept. of Labor

(civilian labor force, persons 16 years of age and older; annual averages; in thousands)

Year[1]	Employed	Unemployed	Unemployment rate	Year[1]	Employed	Unemployed	Unemployment rate
1900[2]	26,956	1,420	5.0%	1988	114,968	6,701	5.5%
1910[2]	34,599	2,150	5.9	1989	117,342	6,528	5.3
1920[2]	39,208	2,132	5.2	1990[3]	118,793	7,047	5.6
1930[2]	44,183	4,340	8.9	1991	117,718	8,628	6.8
1940[2]	47,520	8,120	14.6	1992	118,492	9,613	7.5
1950	58,918	3,288	5.0	1993	120,259	8,940	6.9
1955	62,170	2,852	4.4	1994[4]	123,060	7,996	6.1
1960	65,778	3,852	5.5	1995	124,900	7,404	5.6
1965	71,088	3,366	4.5	1996	126,708	7,236	5.4
1970	78,678	4,093	4.9	1997[5]	129,558	6,739	4.9
1975	85,846	7,929	8.5	1998[5]	131,463	6,210	4.5
1980	99,303	7,637	7.1	1999[6]	133,488	5,880	4.2
1985	107,150	8,312	7.2	2000[7]	136,891	5,692	4.0
1986	109,597	8,237	7.0	2001[7]	136,933	6,801	4.7
1987	112,440	7,425	6.2	2002[7]	136,485	8,378	5.8

(1) **Other unemployment rates (1905-1945):** 1905, 4.3; 1915, 8.5; 1925, 3.2; 1935, 20.3; 1936, 16.9; 1937, 14.3; 1938, 19.0; 1939, 17.2. 1945, 1.9; all for 14 years of age and older. (2) Persons 14 years of age and older. (3) Beginning in 1990, data incorporate 1990 census-based population controls, adjusted for estimated undercount. (4) Beginning in 1994, not strictly comparable with prior years, because of major redesign of the survey used. (5) Not strictly comparable with 1994-96 because of revisions in population controls used in household survey. (6) Data not strictly comparable with 1998 and earlier years because of further revisions in population controls used in household survey. (7) Beginning in Jan. 2000, not strictly comparable with earlier years because of revisions to the controls used in the survey.

Unemployment Insurance Data, by State, 2002

Source: Employment and Training Admin., U.S. Dept. of Labor; state programs only

STATE	Monetarily eligible claimants	First payments	Final payments	Initial claims	Benefits paid	Average weekly benefit	Employers subject to state law
AL..........	173,183	145,445	47,535	329,213	$299,060,192	$167.44	85,959
AK..........	53,557	48,722	20,353	102,717	98,332,699	193.34	16,457
AZ..........	159,261	124,941	54,006	257,047	369,965,757	176.21	107,559
AR..........	155,815	104,865	42,145	250,242	292,728,695	223.40	60,432
CA..........	1,739,707	1,401,507	670,842	3,064,317	5,820,095,724	217.24	987,442
CO..........	146,208	113,938	61,090	175,642	540,952,204	313.18	139,234
CT..........	233,767	162,293	53,821	282,760	679,637,228	286.90	96,648
DE..........	37,816	32,334	9,045	61,358	112,787,637	228.08	25,329
DC..........	23,723	18,349	13,563	23,608	124,756,122	289.70	26,404
FL..........	443,878	357,608	175,087	560,413	1,177,429,681	225.33	405,789
GA..........	372,184	260,128	119,533	578,475	759,529,040	238.73	194,505
HI..........	47,838	29,626	12,201	90,540	151,792,905	297.23	28,637
ID..........	69,327	59,570	21,031	132,892	173,306,234	231.70	40,306
IL..........	549,276	466,345	207,721	875,777	2,347,328,070	280.06	278,082
IN..........	246,568	198,718	86,800	382,677	578,522,698	254.58	125,060
IA..........	137,569	111,411	32,038	209,114	354,086,166	254.72	68,678
KS..........	109,772	83,381	32,110	180,868	318,658,675	276.37	67,582
KY..........	175,905	133,254	39,106	311,041	488,739,058	245.83	88,279
LA..........	129,299	98,791	38,377	221,241	290,129,167	197.25	94,730
ME..........	59,099	33,156	12,191	78,681	116,974,053	224.42	38,958
MD..........	197,806	130,496	47,272	272,692	474,107,885	240.94	133,729
MA..........	343,647	299,998	134,684	537,075	1,886,573,445	360.09	172,275
MI..........	582,497	471,730	180,235	917,839	1,820,860,703	276.49	211,644
MN..........	211,762	170,607	68,451	316,572	818,777,962	317.61	131,429
MS..........	108,318	76,970	29,437	194,192	187,314,743	168.49	53,408
MO..........	254,333	185,414	72,833	436,870	564,205,424	205.49	129,917
MT..........	36,067	26,361	9,955	60,269	70,196,525	187.07	33,217
NE..........	59,654	44,216	18,405	84,032	116,385,184	211.51	45,128
NV..........	104,247	85,757	39,522	183,149	338,075,510	232.13	46,971
NH..........	37,963	23,965	8,062	61,256	113,619,078	259.84	38,872
NJ..........	400,396	348,752	200,236	605,409	2,002,930,738	331.22	278,236
NM..........	47,304	37,385	15,611	74,925	126,690,340	207.09	41,630
NY..........	822,582	618,022	382,783	1,219,461	3,146,516,765	275.47	473,266
NC..........	475,047	372,683	135,370	1,032,295	1,066,002,194	258.98	177,152
ND..........	20,869	16,251	5,536	34,800	45,497,031	219.27	18,650
OH..........	454,581	355,347	130,169	807,022	1,443,057,890	251.05	231,436
OK..........	94,117	71,149	29,202	156,004	244,369,832	233.87	75,096
OR..........	228,926	174,847	78,869	478,436	826,039,740	276.90	100,185
PA..........	676,530	560,805	197,968	1,231,114	2,535,461,889	291.06	267,411
PR..........	131,597	116,070	67,696	219,510	257,287,910	106.91	50,976
RI..........	53,923	43,957	18,166	90,865	203,128,136	304.31	32,796
SC..........	201,116	145,555	60,595	387,526	410,218,124	208.11	89,312
SD..........	14,367	11,595	1,911	24,231	29,775,952	198.30	22,780
TN..........	237,866	219,541	86,369	452,155	591,050,951	209.57	109,318
TX..........	889,806	544,396	336,999	1,069,602	2,172,490,922	258.68	393,141
UT..........	82,394	63,729	27,512	102,950	245,346,105	275.41	55,166
VT..........	32,319	27,755	6,138	45,962	92,683,572	250.16	20,647
VI..........	3,820	3,249	1,610	3,895	19,003,070	288.89	3,073
VA..........	238,153	173,432	67,354	405,132	733,907,712	311.27	164,494
WA..........	385,052	280,946	111,233	640,192	1,487,011,760	328.63	196,123
WV..........	68,126	56,791	12,923	96,671	159,858,549	214.92	37,423
WI..........	361,533	329,518	82,176	719,232	946,629,189	247.17	122,207
WY..........	27,021	17,775	3,579	26,554	38,530,877	232.01	19,281
U.S.	12,947,491	10,089,446	4,417,456	21,156,512	$40,308,417,760	$256.76	6,952,455

Unemployment Rates, by Selected Country, 1970-2003

Source: Bureau of Labor Statistics, U.S. Dept. of Labor; civilian labor force, seasonally adjusted

Time period	U.S.	Australia	Canada	France	Germany[1]	Italy[2]	Japan	Sweden	UK
1970	4.9	1.6	5.7	2.5	0.5	3.2	1.2	1.5	3.1
1975	8.5	4.9	6.9	4.2	3.4	3.4	1.9	1.6	4.6
1980	7.1	6.1	7.5	6.5	2.8	4.4	2.0	2.0	7.0
1981	7.6	5.8	7.6	7.6	4.0	4.9	2.2	2.5	10.5
1982	9.7	7.2	11.0	8.3	5.6	5.4	2.4	3.1	11.3
1983	9.6	10.0	11.9	8.6	6.9[3]	5.9	2.7	3.5	11.8
1984	7.5	9.0	11.3	10.0	7.1	5.9	2.8	3.1	11.7
1985	7.2	8.3	10.7	10.5	7.2	6.0	2.6	2.8	11.2
1986	7.0	8.1	9.6	10.6	6.6	7.5[3]	2.8	2.6	11.2
1987	6.2	8.1	8.8	10.8	6.3	7.9	2.9	2.2[3]	10.3
1988	5.5	7.2	7.8	10.3	6.3	7.9	2.5	1.9	8.6
1989	5.3	6.2	7.5	9.6	5.7	7.8	2.3	1.6	7.2
1990	5.6[3]	6.9	8.1	9.1	5.0	7.0	2.1	1.8	6.9
1991	6.8	9.6	10.3	9.6	5.6	6.9[3]	2.1	3.1	8.8
1992	7.5	10.8	11.2	9.9[3]	6.7	7.3	2.2	5.6	10.1
1993	6.9	10.9	11.4	11.3	7.9	10.2[3]	2.5	9.3	10.5
1994	6.1[3]	9.7	10.4	11.8	8.5	11.2	2.9	9.6	9.7
1995	5.6	8.5	9.4	11.3	8.2	11.8	3.2	9.1	8.7
1996	5.4	8.6	9.6	11.9	8.9	11.7	3.4	9.9	8.2
1997	4.9	8.6	9.1	11.8	9.9	11.9	3.4	10.1	7.0
1998	4.5	8.0	8.3	11.3	9.4	12.0	4.1	8.4	6.3
1999	4.2	7.2	6.8	10.6	8.7	11.5	4.7	7.1	6.0
2000	4.0	6.3	6.1	9.1	8.1	10.7	4.8	5.8	5.5
2001	4.7	6.7	6.4	8.5	8.0	9.6	5.1	5.0	5.1
2002	5.8	6.3	7.0	8.8	8.4	9.1	5.4	5.2	5.2
2003 1st quarter	5.8	6.1	6.7	9.1	9.0	9.0	5.4	5.7	5.1
2003 2nd quarter	6.2	6.1	6.9	NA	9.2	8.9	5.4	6.1	NA

NA = Not available. **NOTE:** Some data for 2002-2003 are preliminary. For the sake of comparisons, U.S. unemployment rate concepts were applied to unemployment data for other countries. Quarterly figures for France and Germany were calculated by applying annual adjustment factors to current published data and are less precise indicators of unemployment under U.S. concepts than the annual figures. (1) For former West Germany only, through 1990; from 1991 on figures are for unified Germany and not adjusted by BLS. (2) Quarterly rates are for first month of quarter. (3) As a result of revisions in survey methodology, there are breaks in the data series for the U.S. (1994, 1997-2000), France (1992), Germany (1983, 1991), Italy (1986, 1991, 1993), and Sweden (1987); data prior to a survey change are not fully comparable to data after a survey change.

Employed Persons in the U.S., by Occupation and Sex, 1996, 2002

Source: Bureau of Labor Statistics, U.S. Dept. of Labor

(in thousands)

	Total 16 years and older		Men 16 years and older		Women 16 years and older	
	1996	2002	1996	2002	1996	2002
TOTAL	126,708	136,485	68,207	72,903	58,501	63,582
Managerial and professional specialty	36,497	42,482	18,744	21,037	17,754	21,445
Executive, administrative, and managerial	17,746	20,561	9,979	11,115	7,767	9,446
Officials and administrators, public administration	716	808	384	405	332	403
Other executive, administrative, and managerial	12,656	14,571	7,703	8,543	4,953	6,028
Management-related occupations	4,374	5,182	1,892	2,167	2,481	3,015
Professional specialty	18,752	21,921	8,764	9,922	9,987	11,999
Engineers	1,960	2,028	1,793	1,809	167	219
Mathematical and computer scientists	1,345	2,030	933	1,405	412	625
Natural scientists	536	545	379	354	157	192
Health diagnosing occupations	960	1,176	715	832	245	344
Health assessment and treating occupations	2,812	3,267	403	446	2,409	2,822
Teachers, college and university	889	1,015	502	582	387	433
Teachers, except college and university	4,724	5,652	1,207	1,411	3,517	4,242
Lawyers and judges	911	963	647	681	264	282
Other professional specialty occupations	4,616	5,245	2,186	2,403	2,430	2,842
Technical, sales, and administrative support	37,683	38,947	13,489	14,267	24,194	24,680
Technicians and related support	3,926	4,509	1,865	2,068	2,061	2,441
Sales occupations	15,404	16,254	7,782	8,285	7,622	7,969
Administrative support, including clerical	18,353	18,184	3,842	3,914	14,511	14,270
Service occupations	17,177	19,219	6,967	7,701	10,210	11,518
Precision production, craft, and repair	13,587	14,660	12,368	13,459	1,219	1,201
Mechanics and repairers	4,521	4,760	4,335	4,545	185	215
Construction trades	5,108	6,304	4,981	6,151	127	153
Other precision production, craft, and repair	3,959	3,596	3,052	2,764	906	832
Operators, fabricators, and laborers	18,197	17,697	13,750	13,675	4,447	4,022
Machine operators, assemblers, and inspectors	7,874	6,488	4,902	4,198	2,972	2,290
Transportation and material moving occupations	5,302	5,814	4,799	5,211	504	603
Motor vehicle operators	4,025	4,482	3,575	3,940	450	541
Other transportation and material moving occupations	1,277	1,332	1,223	1,271	54	61
Handlers, equipment cleaners, helpers, and laborers	5,021	5,395	4,049	4,265	971	1,129
Construction laborers	809	1,089	778	1,046	31	43
Other handlers, equipment cleaners, etc.	4,212	4,305	3,272	3,219	940	1,086
Farming, forestry, and fishing	3,566	3,480	2,889	2,765	677	716
Farm operators and managers	NA	1,168	NA	882	NA	286
Other farming, forestry, and fishing occupations	NA	2,313	NA	1,883	NA	430

NA = Not available. NOTE: Beginning in Jan. 2000, data reflect revised population controls used in the household survey. Totals may not add because of independent rounding.

Elderly in the Labor Force, 1890-2002

Source: Bureau of the Census, U.S. Dept. of Commerce

The percentage of men 65 years of age and older in the labor force steadily declined between 1890 and 1990 dropping 74% in 100 years, but then increased slightly by 2000. The percentage of women 65 or older in the work force has always been much lower than that of men; after ranging from about 6%-8% from 1890 to 1950, it has increased slightly to 8%-10% in recent decades.

(labor force participation rate; figs. for 1910 not available)

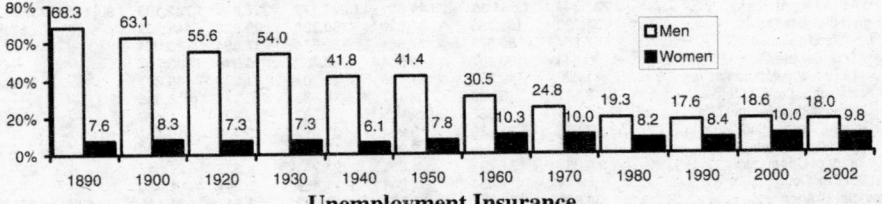

Unemployment Insurance

Source: Unemployment Insurance Service, U.S. Dept. of Labor

Unlike old-age and survivors insurance, which is entirely a federal program, unemployment insurance in the U.S. is a federal-state system that provides insured wage earners partial replacement for lost wages during a period of involuntary unemployment. The program protects most wage and salary workers. During fiscal year 2002, an estimated 127.7 million workers in commerce, industry, agriculture, and government were covered under the federal-state system.

Each state, as well as the District of Columbia, Puerto Rico, and the Virgin Islands, has its own law and operates its own program. The amount and duration of the weekly benefits are determined by state laws and are based on prior wages and length of employment. States are required to extend the duration of benefits when unemployment in the state rises to and remains above specified levels; costs of extended benefits are shared by the state and federal governments.

Under the Federal Unemployment Tax Act, the federal tax rate is 6.2% on the first $7,000 paid to each employee of employers with one or more employees in 20 weeks of the year or with a quarterly payroll of $1,500 or more. A credit of up to 5.4% is allowed for taxes paid under state unemployment in-

surance laws that meet certain criteria, for a net federal rate of 0.8%; subject employers also pay a state unemployment tax. Governmental agencies and certain nonprofit organizations are not subject to the federal tax; these employers reimburse states for benefits paid to former employees.

The secretary of labor certifies states for administrative grants to operate the program (under the Social Security Act) and for employer tax credit (under the Federal Unemployment Tax Act).

Benefits are financed solely by employer contributions, except in Alaska, New Jersey, and Pennsylvania, where employees also contribute. Benefits are paid through the states' public employment offices, at which unemployed workers must register for work and to which they must report regularly for referral to a possible job during the time when they are drawing weekly benefit payments.

In the 12 months leading up to Aug. 31, 2003, state unemployment insurance benefits totaled $41.6 bil, going to 10.2 million beneficiaries. For those 12 months, beneficiaries received an average weekly benefit of $261, which lasted an average of 16 weeks.

U.S. Unemployment Rates by Selected Characteristics, 2000-2003

Source: Bureau of Labor Statistics, U.S. Dept. of Labor

	2000	2001	2002	2003 Jan.	Feb.	Mar.	Apr.	May	June	July	Aug.	Sept.
Total (all civilian workers)	4.0	4.7	5.8	6.5	6.4	6.2	5.8	5.8	6.3	6.3	6.0	5.8
Men, 20 years and older	3.3	4.2	5.3	6.6	6.3	6.1	5.7	5.5	5.7	5.5	5.3	5.1
Women, 20 years and older	3.6	4.1	5.1	5.1	5.2	5.1	4.8	4.9	5.4	5.6	5.7	5.3
Both sexes, 16 to 19 years	13.1	14.7	16.5	17.8	17.9	17.9	17.2	18.0	22.3	18.7	15.2	17.0
White	3.5	4.2	5.1	5.8	5.6	5.5	5.1	5.1	5.6	5.5	5.3	5.0
Black	7.6	8.6	10.2	10.9	11.1	10.6	10.3	10.5	12.0	12.0	11.0	10.6
Hispanic origin	5.7	6.6	7.5	8.8	8.3	8.3	7.2	7.4	8.2	8.2	7.6	7.0
Married men, spouse present*	NA	NA	NA	3.5	3.6	3.8	3.7	3.9	4.4	3.9	3.8	3.7
Married women, spouse present*	NA	NA	NA	3.3	3.6	3.7	3.6	3.7	3.9	3.9	3.8	4.0
Women who maintain families	5.9	6.6	8.0	8.0	9.0	8.4	8.5	8.3	8.7	9.0	8.4	8.5
OCCUPATION												
Management, professional, and related occupations. . . .	1.8	2.3	3.0	3.2	3.1	2.9	2.9	3.0	3.5	3.7	3.6	3.2
Service occupations	5.2	5.8	6.6	7.4	7.8	7.9	7.1	6.5	6.9	6.6	6.9	6.7
Sales and office occupations	3.8	4.4	5.6	5.5	5.5	5.3	5.3	5.7	6.3	5.7	5.6	5.9
Natural resources, construction, and maintenance occupations	5.3	6.4	7.8	11.1	11.0	9.7	8.3	7.5	7.4	7.0	6.8	6.6
Production, transportation, and material moving occupations	5.1	6.4	7.6	9.0	8.5	8.6	8.0	8.1	8.7	8.5	7.5	6.9
INDUSTRY												
Nonagricultural, private wage, and salary workers	4.1	5.0	6.2	7.0	6.9	6.6	6.2	6.2	6.6	6.3	6.1	6.1
Mining	4.4	4.2	6.3	9.0	7.1	8.2	7.7	7.5	6.8	7.9	3.8	4.6
Construction	6.2	7.1	9.2	14.0	14.0	11.8	9.3	8.4	7.9	7.5	7.1	7.6
Manufacturing	3.5	5.2	6.7	7.2	6.7	6.8	6.7	6.5	7.0	6.9	6.7	6.8
Durable goods	3.2	5.2	6.9	7.8	6.9	6.7	7.3	6.9	7.3	7.4	6.9	7.3
Non durable goods	4.0	5.2	6.2	6.1	6.5	7.0	5.8	5.9	6.6	6.0	6.4	5.9
Wholesale and retail trade	4.3	4.9	6.1	6.7	6.1	5.9	6.0	6.2	6.9	6.6	5.6	5.9
Transportation and utilities	3.4	4.3	4.9	6.3	5.8	5.9	5.0	4.9	5.5	5.4	4.8	4.7
Information	3.2	4.9	6.9	6.7	8.6	7.4	7.3	6.9	6.4	5.9	6.1	7.0
Financial activities	2.4	2.9	3.5	3.6	3.4	4.0	3.6	3.6	4.0	3.1	3.7	3.3
Professional and business services	4.8	6.1	7.9	8.9	8.9	9.1	8.3	8.4	8.5	8.2	7.2	8.0
Education and health services	2.5	2.8	3.4	3.2	3.2	2.9	3.4	3.5	4.4	4.0	4.3	3.7
Leisure and hospitality	6.6	7.5	8.4	9.3	10.0	8.9	8.5	7.9	8.6	8.4	9.0	8.8
Other services	3.9	4.0	5.1	5.3	5.7	6.1	5.5	5.7	5.9	6.6	6.1	5.5
Agriculture and related	9.0	11.2	10.1	13.2	14.7	12.9	12.0	10.2	6.9	8.2	10.7	6.2
Government	2.1	2.2	2.5	2.8	2.4	2.6	2.2	2.4	3.5	3.8	3.7	2.7
Self-employed and unpaid family workers	2.1	2.1	2.6	3.0	3.0	2.7	2.4	2.6	2.7	2.5	2.7	2.6

* Numbers for married men and married women with spouse present are seasonally adjusted; other numbers are not seasonally adjusted. NA = Not available.

Civilian Employment of the Federal Government, March 2003

Source: Statistical Analysis and Services Division, U.S. Office of Personnel Management

(payroll in thousands of dollars)

	ALL AREAS Employment*	Payroll*	UNITED STATES Employment*	Payroll	WASH., D.C., MSA² Employment	Payroll	OVERSEAS Employment	Payroll
TOTAL, all agencies¹	**2,738,344**	**11,364,381**	**2,644,901**	**11,027,178**	**332,856**	**1,782,103**	**93,443**	**337,203**
Legislative Branch	**31,033**	**150,255**	**31,026**	**150,198**	**29,923**	**143,922**	**7**	**57**
Congress	17,564	80,074	17,564	80,074	17,564	80,074	—	—
U.S. Senate	6,544	30,767	6,544	30,767	6,544	30,767	—	—
House of Representatives	11,020	49,307	11,020	49,307	11,020	49,307	—	—
Architect of the Capitol	2,117	8,885	2,117	8,885	2,117	8,885	—	—
Congressional Budget Ofc	225	1,582	225	1,582	225	1,582	—	—
General Accounting Ofc	3,265	21,629	3,264	21,622	2,453	16,437	1	7
Government Printing Ofc	2,985	12,899	2,985	12,899	2,735	11,956	—	—
Library of Congress	4,357	21,791	4,351	21,741	4,328	21,647	6	50
U.S. Tax Court	241	1,454	241	1,454	241	1,454	—	—
Judicial Branch	**34,209**	**170,977**	**33,776**	**169,093**	**1,913**	**11,411**	**433**	**1,884**
Supreme Court	420	1,529	420	1,529	420	1,529	—	—
U.S. Courts	33,789	169,448	33,356	167,564	1,493	9,882	433	1,884
Executive Branch	**2,673,102**	**11,043,149**	**2,580,099**	**10,707,887**	**301,020**	**1,626,770**	**93,003**	**335,262**
Exec Ofc of the President	1,695	10,717	1,684	10,644	1,684	10,644	11	73
White House Office	404	1,988	404	1,988	404	1,988	—	—
Ofc of Vice President	24	135	24	135	24	135	—	—
Ofc of Mgmt & Budget	497	3,433	497	3,433	497	3,433	—	—
Ofc of Administration	215	1,234	215	1,234	215	1,234	—	—
Council Economic Advisors	27	147	27	147	27	147	—	—
Council Environmental Quality	19	126	19	126	19	126	—	—
Ofc of Policy Development	27	145	27	145	27	145	—	—
National Security Council	63	410	63	410	63	410	—	—
Ofc of Natl Drug Control	109	754	109	754	109	754	—	—
Ofc of U.S. Trade Rep	190	1,571	179	1,498	179	1,498	11	73
Executive Departments	1,686,647	7,236,642	1,600,574	6,928,953	230,705	1,236,906	86,073	307,689
State	31,916	170,295	12,520	64,628	10,988	53,609	19,396	105,667
Treasury	131,872	604,134	131,212	599,158	16,004	114,893	660	4,976
Defense, Total	664,446	2,397,998	610,132	2,250,371	62,391	239,932	54,314	147,627
Defense, Mil Function	639,096	2,329,425	584,853	2,181,897	61,476	237,599	54,243	147,528
Defense, Civ Function	25,350	68,573	25,279	68,474	915	2,333	71	99
Dept of the Army	230,166	635,741	207,264	569,903	18,875	40,570	22,902	65,838
Army, Mil Function	204,816	567,168	181,985	501,429	17,960	38,237	22,831	65,739
Army, Civil Function	25,350	68,573	25,279	68,474	915	2,333	71	99
Corps of Engineers	25,253	68,326	25,182	68,227	818	2,086	71	99
Dept of the Navy	183,932	744,351	175,527	710,250	24,667	99,826	8,405	34,101
Dept of the Air Force	150,958	610,740	144,637	585,186	4,829	19,524	6,321	25,554
Defense Logist. Agency	21,404	93,206	20,561	89,525	1,610	9,560	843	3,681
Other Defense Activities	77,986	313,960	62,143	295,507	12,410	70,452	15,843	18,453
Justice	101,392	622,644	99,650	610,823	21,690	137,540	1,742	11,821
Interior	71,005	295,256	70,664	294,018	7,916	41,754	341	1,238
Agriculture	98,879	408,017	97,667	403,718	11,644	63,634	1,212	4,299
Commerce	37,087	183,919	36,320	180,524	20,353	116,058	767	3,395
Labor	16,144	84,353	16,102	84,145	5,452	31,618	42	208
Health & Human Services	67,091	362,160	66,802	360,323	30,036	176,534	289	1,837
Housing & Urban Dev	10,643	59,435	10,551	58,938	3,398	20,776	92	497
Transportation	58,819	454,814	58,434	451,865	9,560	67,870	385	2,949
Energy	15,789	99,205	15,780	99,139	5,249	36,955	9	66
Education	4,592	27,096	4,585	27,065	3,253	19,795	7	31
Veterans Affairs	225,159	950,276	221,850	939,068	6,917	36,181	3,309	11,208
Homeland Security	151,813	517,040	148,305	505,170	15,854	79,757	3,508	11,870
Independent Agencies	984,760	3,795,790	977,841	3,768,290	68,631	379,220	6,919	27,500
Bd of Gov, Fed Rsrv Sys	1,748	11,305	1,748	11,305	1,748	11,305	—	—
Environmtl Protect Agcy	18,021	108,466	17,970	108,180	6,098	39,449	51	286
Equal Employ Opp Comm	2,679	14,098	2,669	14,055	645	3,877	10	43
Federal Communic Comm	2,048	13,290	2,046	13,274	1,723	11,437	2	16
Federal Deposit Ins Corp	5,468	38,277	5,459	38,223	1,921	14,744	9	54
Federal Trade Comm	1,058	6,858	1,058	6,858	913	5,856	—	—
General Svcs Admin	13,158	75,550	13,094	75,194	4,636	28,043	64	356
Natl Aero & Space Admin	18,831	119,494	18,814	119,374	4,199	27,564	17	120
Natl Fnd Arts & Humanities	377	2,162	377	2,162	377	2,162	—	—
Nuclear Regulatory Comm	3,009	20,876	3,009	20,876	2,085	14,825	—	—
Peace Corps	1,115	4,605	698	3,270	564	2,793	417	1,335
Securities & Exch. Comm	3,074	23,546	3,074	23,546	1,873	13,948	—	—
Small Business Adm	3,816	19,869	3,720	19,458	829	5,185	96	411
Smithsonian Inst	5,092	21,844	5,065	21,658	4,666	19,800	27	186
Social Security Admin	64,110	279,903	63,636	277,848	1,633	7,888	474	2,055
Tennessee Valley Authority	13,269	80,425	13,269	80,425	6	39	—	—
U.S. Postal Service	801,808	2,816,457	797,855	2,800,872	19,654	80,591	3,953	15,585

NOTE: * Denotes figures that are preliminary or are based in whole or part on figures for the previous month. (1) Totals include agencies not listed. (2) Metropolitan Statistical Area.

U.S. Occupational Illnesses, by Industry and Type of Illness, 2001

Source: Bureau of Labor Statistics, U.S. Dept. of Labor

(percent distribution)

| | All private sector[1] | GOODS PRODUCING | | | | SERVICE PRODUCING | | | | |
		Agriculture[2]	Mining[3]	Construction	Manufacturing	Trans. and pub. utilities[4]	Wholesale	Retail	Finance[5]	Service
Total [1,537,567 cases]	100.0	100.0	100.0	100.0	100.0	100.0	100.0	100.0	100.0	100.0
Nature of injury or illness:										
Sprains, strains	43.6	34.3	38.0	38.4	38.8	48.4	46.7	42.8	39.3	48.9
Bruises, contusions	8.9	9.9	10.7	6.8	8.0	9.4	10.2	10.4	7.4	8.8
Cuts, lacerations	7.5	9.9	6.7	11.8	8.8	4.2	6.4	10.1	6.0	4.3
Fractures	7.0	8.1	14.2	10.7	7.1	6.9	6.4	5.8	7.9	5.9
Heat burns	1.6	0.4	1.0	1.3	1.5	0.6	0.8	3.8	0.5	1.4
Carpal tunnel syndrome	1.7	0.4	0.6	0.7	3.5	0.8	1.5	1.3	5.8	1.4
Tendonitis	0.9	0.5	0.2	0.1	1.6	0.4	0.4	0.6	0.4	0.7
Chemical burns	0.6	0.5	0.4	0.6	1.0	0.4	0.4	0.6	0.4	0.6
Amputations	0.6	1.0	0.6	0.5	1.3	0.2	0.6	0.5	0.1	0.2
Multiple traumatic injuries	3.5	4.4	5.3	3.4	3.2	3.9	3.6	2.9	4.3	3.5
Part of body affected by the injury or illness:										
Head	6.5	8.5	5.3	7.5	7.2	5.9	5.4	6.2	7.2	6.0
Neck	1.8	1.1	2.3	1.2	1.5	1.9	1.8	1.6	1.3	2.5
Trunk	36.5	33.9	32.8	32.8	34.1	39.1	41.5	35.2	29.5	39.6
Upper extremities	23.1	23.8	23.0	24.8	31.4	16.3	19.9	25.5	23.9	17.9
Lower extremities	21.0	22.9	26.6	24.1	17.9	24.7	21.8	20.8	22.1	19.5
Body systems	1.4	1.1	1.2	1.2	1.2	1.4	0.7	1.1	3.5	1.9
Multiple parts	9.1	8.1	8.5	7.8	6.3	10.2	8.3	8.7	11.5	11.9
Source of injury or illness:										
Chemicals and chemical products	1.6	1.1	8.2	1.1	2.2	0.9	1.1	1.5	1.7	1.9
Containers	13.6	8.3	4.6	4.4	13.2	20.9	23.2	20.9	8.8	7.8
Furniture and fixtures	3.5	0.6	0.5	1.6	2.8	2.1	2.9	5.5	5.8	4.8
Machinery	6.3	7.5	10.8	6.4	11.6	2.4	6.3	6.2	6.0	3.8
Parts and materials	10.6	7.2	17.5	23.8	17.4	7.0	11.7	6.3	3.8	3.5
Worker motion or position	16.0	14.1	5.5	13.9	20.3	16.1	14.7	13.7	22.9	15.1
Floors, walkways, ground surfaces	17.2	14.3	17.2	18.5	10.9	17.0	13.6	20.1	29.3	20.2
Tools, instruments, and equipment	6.3	9.1	7.0	11.2	6.1	4.1	3.5	7.1	4.4	5.2
Vehicles	8.4	8.0	7.7	5.5	4.8	18.0	13.7	7.4	4.9	7.1
Health care patient	4.4	—	—	—	—	1.0	0.1	0.1	1.0	17.6
Event or exposure leading to injury or illness:										
Contact with objects and equipment	26.0	33.5	41.8	34.4	33.1	20.6	26.4	27.0	16.5	17.5
Struck by object	13.0	17.5	23.2	19.2	14.4	9.8	13.0	14.9	8.1	8.7
Struck against object	6.6	6.4	8.8	7.5	7.2	6.5	6.2	7.2	4.9	5.4
Caught in equipment or object	4.4	5.6	9.3	4.2	8.6	2.8	5.1	3.4	2.0	2.1
Fall to lower level	6.3	7.3	8.5	12.8	3.7	8.2	5.8	4.4	10.5	5.0
Fall on same level	11.9	8.1	8.5	7.4	7.9	9.3	9.1	16.8	19.2	16.0
Slip, trip, loss of balance—without fall	3.3	3.4	1.4	3.2	2.9	3.6	2.9	3.7	3.7	3.2
Overexertion	26.6	17.6	26.2	20.7	25.4	28.8	31.0	25.5	19.3	30.6
Overexertion in lifting	14.8	10.3	9.5	11.0	13.5	15.6	18.1	17.0	11.1	15.7
Repetitive motion	4.2	1.7	1.1	2.0	9.0	2.5	3.3	2.9	11.0	3.1
Exposure to harmful substances	4.4	3.8	3.9	3.4	5.1	3.5	2.1	5.8	3.8	4.9
Transportation accidents	4.3	5.1	2.9	3.7	1.9	9.1	6.9	2.9	3.4	4.5
Fires and explosions	0.2	0.1	0.3	0.5	0.2	0.2	0.6	0.3	—	0.1
Assaults and violent acts by person	1.1	—	0.1	0.1	0.1	0.4	0.1	0.9	1.9	3.4

NOTE: Dashes (—) indicate data are not available or do not meet publication guidelines. Because of rounding and classifications not shown, percentages may not add to 100. All injuries and illnesses reported involved days away from work. (1) Private sector includes all industries except government, but excludes farms with fewer than 11 employees. (2) Agriculture includes forestry and fishing, but excludes farms with fewer than 11 employees. (3) Data conforming to OSHA definitions for mining operators in coal, metal, and nonmetal mining are provided by the Mine Safety and Health Administration, U.S. Dept. of Labor. Independent mining contractors are excluded from the coal, metal, and nonmetal industries. Data for mining include establishments not governed by Mine Safety and Health Administration rules, such as those in oil and gas extraction. (4) Data for employers in railroad transportation are provided by the Federal Railroad Administration, U.S. Department of Transportation. (5) Finance includes insurance and real estate.

Fatal Occupational Injuries, 2002

Source: Bureau of Labor Statistics, U.S. Dept. of Labor

	FATALITIES Number	Percent		FATALITIES Number	Percent
TRANSPORTATION INCIDENTS	2,381	43	Struck by falling object	303	5
Highway	1,372	25	Struck by flying object	38	1
Collision between vehicles, mobile equipment	635	11	Caught in or compressed by equipment or objects	231	4
Vehicle struck stationary object or equipment	326	6	Caught in running equipment or machinery	110	2
Noncollision	373	7	Caught in or crushed in collapsing materials	116	2
Nonhighway (farm, industrial premises)	322	6	FALLS	714	13
Aircraft	192	3	EXPOSURE TO HARMFUL SUBSTANCE OR ENVIRONMENTS	538	10
Worker struck by a vehicle	356	6			
Water vehicle	71	1	Contact with electric current	289	5
Rail vehicle	64	1	Contact with overhead powerlines	122	2
ASSAULTS AND VIOLENT ACTS	840	15	Contact with temperature extremes	60	1
Homicides	609	11	Exposure to caustic, noxious, or allergenic substances	98	2
Shooting	469	8			
Stabbing	58	1	Inhalation of substance	49	1
Other, including bombing	82	1	Oxygen deficiency	90	2
Self-inflicted injuries	199	4	Drowning, submersion	60	1
CONTACT WITH OBJECTS AND EQUIPMENT	873	16	FIRES AND EXPLOSIONS	165	3
			OTHER EVENTS OR EXPOSURES	13	—
Struck by object	506	9	TOTAL	5,524	100

NOTE: Totals for categories may include subcategories not shown separately. Percentages based on incidence rate per total fatalities. Dashes (—) indicate less than 0.5% or unavailable data.

Hourly Compensation Costs[1], by Selected Country, 1975-2002

Source: Bureau of Labor Statistics, U.S. Dept. of Labor

(in U.S. dollars, compensation for production workers in manufacturing)

Country/Territory	1975	1985	1995	2002	Country/Territory	1975	1985	1995	2002
Australia	$5.62	$8.21	$15.56	$15.55	Luxembourg	$6.26	$7.49	$23.45	$18.91
Austria	4.51	7.58	25.32	21.07	Mexico	1.47	1.59	1.65	2.38
Belgium	6.41	8.97	27.62	22.79	Netherlands	6.58	8.75	24.12	21.74
Canada	5.96	10.95	16.10	16.02	New Zealand	3.15	4.38	9.91	8.89
Denmark	6.28	8.13	24.98	24.23	Norway	6.77	10.37	24.38	27.40
Finland	4.66	8.25	24.32	21.56	Portugal	1.58	1.53	5.37	—
France	4.52	7.52	19.38	17.42	Singapore	0.84	2.47	7.33	7.27
Germany[2]	6.29	9.50	31.57	26.18	Spain	2.53	4.66	12.80	12.04
Greece	1.69	3.66	9.06	—	Sri Lanka	0.28	0.28	0.48	—
Hong Kong[3]	0.76	1.73	4.91	5.83	Sweden	7.18	9.66	21.44	20.18
Ireland	3.05	5.99	13.78	15.09	Switzerland	6.09	9.66	29.3	24.11
Israel	2.25	4.06	10.54	12.14	Taiwan	0.38	1.49	5.85	5.41
Italy	4.67	7.63	16.22	14.93	United Kingdom	3.37	6.27	13.78	17.47
Japan	3.00	6.34	23.73	18.83	United States	6.36	13.01	17.19	21.33
Korea, South	0.32	1.23	7.29	9.16					

— Data not available. (1) Compensation includes all direct pay (including bonuses, etc.), paid benefits, and for some countries, labor taxes. (2) 1975 and 1985 data are for area covered by the former West Germany. 1995 and 2002 is for unified Germany. (3) Now part of China.

U.S Median Weekly Earnings, Second Quarter 2003*

Source: Bureau of Labor Statistics, U.S. Dept. of Labor

Age, Race, and Hispanic or Latino ethnicity	Total Number of workers (in thousands)	Median weekly earnings	Men Number of workers (in thousands)	Median weekly earnings	Women Number of workers (in thousands)	Median weekly earnings
TOTAL						
16 years and over	100,442	$616	56,111	$692	44,332	$547
16 to 24 years	11,041	380	6,206	391	4,835	366
16 to 19 years	1,724	307	980	317	744	292
20 to 24 years	9,317	396	5,225	406	4,091	384
25 years and over	89,401	659	49,905	743	39,497	582
25 to 54 years	76,297	656	42,841	735	33,457	581
25 to 34 years	24,810	588	14,267	616	10,543	542
35 to 44 years	27,101	687	15,376	775	11,726	589
45 to 54 years	24,386	726	13,198	854	11,188	603
55 years and over	13,104	685	7,064	798	6,040	591
55 to 64 years	11,300	710	6,072	833	5,228	606
65 years and over	1,804	537	992	622	812	427
WHITE[1]						
16 years and over	82,145	631	47,028	712	35,117	561
16 to 24 years	9,125	383	5,244	394	3,881	368
25 years and over	73,020	679	41,784	766	31,236	591
25 to 54 years	61,844	676	35,695	759	26,149	590
55 years and over	11,176	698	6,089	821	5,087	597
BLACK OR AFRICAN AMERICAN[1]						
16 years and over	11,879	509	5,471	540	6,408	489
16 to 24 years	1,249	363	593	368	656	354
25 years and over	10,630	534	4,879	584	5,752	507
25 to 54 years	9,397	527	4,309	580	5,087	503
55 years and over	1,234	582	569	602	664	553
ASIAN[1]						
16 years and over	4,242	678	2,414	759	1,828	606
16 to 24 years	324	404	191	391	133	435
25 years and over	3,918	725	2,223	804	1,695	622
25 to 54 years	3,421	727	1,924	796	1,497	638
55 years and over	497	672	299	848	198	521
HISPANIC AND LATINO						
16 years and over	13,624	430	8,597	456	5,027	399
16 to 24 years	2,152	341	1,367	350	785	328
25 years and over	11,472	464	7,230	488	4,242	417
25 to 54 years	10,519	458	6,643	482	3,875	416
55 years and over	953	514	587	567	367	447
Occupation						
Managerial, professional, and related occupations	35,730	$877	17,666	$1,048	18,065	$753
Management, business, and financial operations occupations	14,798	956	8,124	1,140	6,674	786
Professional and related occupations	20,932	837	9,542	988	11,391	734
Service occupations	13,184	398	6,568	451	6,616	365
Sales and office occupations	25,396	545	9,619	662	15,777	502
Sales and related occupations	9,986	598	5,676	733	4,310	455
Office and administrative support occupations	15,410	522	3,943	583	11,468	512
Natural resources, construction, and maintenance occupations	10,891	611	10,433	616	458	454
Farming, fishing, and forestry occupations	736	357	552	379	185	327
Construction and extraction occupations	5,889	598	5,770	600	119	535

Occupation	Total Number of workers (in thousands)	Median weekly earnings	Men Number of workers (in thousands)	Median weekly earnings	Women Number of workers (in thousands)	Median weekly earnings
Installation, maintenance, and repair occupations	4,265	$668	4,111	$669	154	$656
Production, transportation, and material moving occupations	15,241	510	11,825	562	3,416	399
Production occupations	8,600	504	6,041	573	2,560	399
Transportation and material moving occupations	6,641	517	5,784	547	857	396

*Not seasonally adjusted; figures are for median usual weekly earnings of full-time wage and salary workers. (1) Persons who selected this race group only; persons who selected more than one race group are not included.

Federal Minimum Hourly Wage Rates Since 1950

Source: Bureau of Labor Statistics, U.S. Dept. of Labor

The Fair Labor Standards Act of 1938 and subsequent amendments provide for minimum wage-coverage applicable to nonprofessional workers in specified nonsupervisory employment categories.

EFFECTIVE DATE	NONFARM WORKERS Under laws prior to 1966[1]	Percent of avg. earnings[2]	Under 1966 and later provis.[3]	FARM WORKERS[4]	EFFECTIVE DATE	NONFARM WORKERS Under laws prior to 1966[1]	Percent of avg. earnings[2]	Under 1966 and later provis.[3]	FARM WORKERS[4]
Jan. 25, 1950...	$0.75	54	NA	NA	Jan. 1, 1976....	$2.30	46	$2.20	$2.00
Mar. 1, 1956...	1.00	52	NA	NA	Jan. 1, 1977....	(5)	(5)	2.30	2.20
Sept. 3, 1961...	1.15	50	NA	NA	Jan. 1, 1978....	2.65	44	2.65	2.65
Sept. 3, 1963...	1.25	51	NA	NA	Jan. 1, 1979....	2.90	45	2.90	2.90
Feb. 1, 1967...	1.40	50	$1.00	$1.00	Jan. 1, 1980....	3.10	43	3.10	3.10
Feb. 1, 1968...	1.60	54	1.15	1.15	Jan. 1, 1981....	3.35	42	3.35	3.35
Feb. 1, 1969...	(5)	(5)	1.30	1.30	Apr. 1, 1990....	3.80[6]	35	3.80	3.80[6]
Feb. 1, 1970...	(5)	(5)	1.45	(5)	Apr. 1, 1991....	4.25[6]	38	4.25	4.25[6]
Feb. 1, 1971...	(5)	(5)	1.60	(5)	Oct. 1, 1996....	4.75[7]	37	4.75	4.75[7]
May 1, 1974...	2.00	46	1.90	1.60	Sept. 1, 1997...	5.15[7]	39	5.15	5.15[7]
Jan. 1, 1975...	2.10	45	2.00	1.80					

NA = not applicable. (1) Applies to workers covered prior to 1961 Amendments and, after Sept. 1965, to workers covered by 1961 Amendments. Rates set by 1961 Amendments were: Sept. 1961, $1.00; Sept. 1964, $1.15; and Sept. 1965, $1.25. (2) Percent of gross average hourly earnings of production workers in manufacturing. (3) Applies to workers newly covered by Amendments of 1966, 1974, and 1977, and Title IX of Education Amendments of 1972. (4) Included in coverage as of 1966, 1974, and 1977 Amendments. (5) No change in rate. (6) Training wage for workers age 16-19 in first 6 months of first job: Apr. 1, 1990, $3.35; Apr. 1, 1991, $3.62. The training wage expired Mar. 31, 1993. (7) Under 1996 legislation, a subminimum training wage of $4.25 an hour was established for employees under 20 years of age during their first 90 consecutive calendar days of employment with an employer. For workers receiving gratuities, the minimum wage remained $2.13 per hour.

Top 15 U.S. Metropolitan Areas, by Average Annual Salary, 2001

Source: Bureau of Labor Statistics, U.S. Dept. of Labor

Rank	Metropolitan area	Average annual salary[1]	Rank	Metropolitan area	Average annual salary[1]
1.	San Jose, CA	$65,926	9.	Oakland, CA.......................	$45,944
2.	San Francisco, CA..................	59,761	10.	Boston-Worcester-Lawrence-Lowell- Brockton, MA-NH..................	45,768
3.	New York, NY	58,963	11.	Trenton, NJ	45,746
4.	New Haven-Bridgeport-Danbury-Stamford- Waterbury, CT.....................	52,177	12.	Seattle-Bellevue-Everett, WA	45,326
5.	Middlesex-Somerset-Hunterdon, NJ	49,830	13.	Bergen-Passaic, NJ	44,667
6.	Newark, NJ	47,713	14.	Boulder-Longmont, CO	44,313
7.	Jersey City, NJ....................	47,621	15.	Hartford, CT	43,882
8.	Washington, DC-MD-VA-WV	47,584			

NOTE: Jacksonville, NC, recorded the **lowest average annual pay** among U.S. metropolitan areas in 2001—$21,393—followed by Brownsville-Harlingen-San Benito, TX ($22,146), McAllen-Edinburg-Mission, TX ($22,317), Yuma, AZ ($22,482), and Myrtle Beach, SC ($24,012). The nationwide metropolitan average was $37,897. (1) Data are preliminary and include workers covered by Unemployment Insurance and Unemployment Compensation for Federal Employees programs.

Average Hours and Earnings of U.S. Production Workers, 1969-2002[1]

Source: Bureau of Labor Statistics, U.S. Dept. of Labor

(annual averages)

	Weekly hours	Hourly earnings	Weekly earnings		Weekly hours	Hourly earnings	Weekly earnings
1969................	37.5	$3.22	$120.75	1986	34.7	$8.92	$309.52
1970................	37.0	3.40	125.80	1987	34.7	9.13	316.81
1971................	36.8	3.63	133.58	1988	34.6	9.43	326.28
1972................	36.9	3.90	143.91	1989	34.5	9.80	338.10
1973................	36.9	4.14	152.77	1990	34.3	10.19	349.29
1974................	36.4	4.43	161.25	1991	34.1	10.50	358.06
1975................	36.0	4.73	170.28	1992	34.2	10.76	367.83
1976................	36.1	5.06	182.67	1993	34.3	11.03	378.40
1977................	35.9	5.44	195.30	1994	34.5	11.32	390.73
1978................	35.8	5.87	210.15	1995	34.3	11.64	399.53
1979................	35.6	6.33	225.35	1996	34.3	12.03	412.74
1980................	35.2	6.84	240.77	1997	34.5	12.49	431.25
1981................	35.2	7.43	261.54	1998	34.5	13.00	448.04
1982................	34.7	7.86	272.74	1999	34.3	13.47	462.49
1983................	34.9	8.19	285.83	2000	34.3	14.00	480.41
1984................	35.1	8.48	297.65	2001	34.0	14.53	493.20
1985................	34.9	8.73	304.68	2002	33.9	14.95	506.22

(1) Data refer to production workers in natural resources, mining and manufacturing, construction workers, and non-supervisory workers in the service industries. Figures may be revised.

Union Affiliation and Median Weekly Earnings of Wage and Salary Workers in the U.S., 1996, 2002

Source: Bureau of Labor Statistics, U.S. Dept. of Labor

SEX AND AGE	1996				2002			
	TOTAL	Members of unions[1]	Represented by unions[2]	Non-union	TOTAL	Members of unions[1]	Represented by unions[2]	Non-union
Total, 16 years and older ...	$490	$615	$610	$462	$609	$740	$734	$587
16 to 24 years	298	371	362	294	381	497	494	374
25 years and older	520	625	621	498	647	753	748	623
25 to 34 years	463	554	548	447	591	682	670	577
35 to 44 years	559	636	632	530	669	759	753	647
45 to 54 years	594	687	686	552	707	789	787	675
55 to 64 years	535	620	616	505	673	787	784	639
65 years and older	384	510	510	367	502	592	594	484
Men, 16 years and older ...	557	653	651	520	680	780	776	652
16 to 24 years	307	375	369	303	392	498	494	385
25 years and older	599	669	668	580	732	797	793	713
25 to 34 years	499	591	587	485	627	722	710	614
35 to 44 years	632	683	683	617	759	810	806	747
45 to 54 years	698	718	721	682	808	831	831	796
55 to 64 years	643	667	664	633	799	836	838	779
65 years and older	477	589	593	424	583	610	616	576
Women, 16 years and older.	418	549	543	398	530	667	662	510
16 to 24 years	284	358	339	280	366	495	494	361
25 years and older	444	560	555	420	570	679	674	542
25 to 34 years	415	497	495	405	531	624	619	517
35 to 44 years	463	561	556	439	573	669	666	548
45 to 54 years	481	620	616	445	603	730	726	581
55 to 64 years	420	524	523	395	574	706	705	542
65 years and older	334	417	413	321	428	550	551	414

Note: Data refer to the sole or principal job of full-time workers. Excluded are self-employed workers regardless of whether or not their businesses are incorporated. (1) Including members of an employee association similar to a union. (2) Including members of a labor union or employee association similar to a union, and others whose jobs are covered by a union or an employee-association contract.

Work Stoppages (Strikes and Lockouts) in the U.S., 1960-2002

Source: Bureau of Labor Statistics, U.S. Dept. of Labor; involving 1,000 workers or more

Year	Number of stoppages[1]	Workers involved[1] (thousands)	Work days idle[1] (thousands)	Year	Number of stoppages[1]	Workers involved[1] (thousands)	Work days idle[1] (thousands)
1960........	222	896	13,260	1986	69	533	11,861
1965........	268	999	15,140	1987	46	174	4,481
1970........	381	2,468	52,761	1988	40	118	4,381
1971........	298	2,516	35,538	1989	51	452	16,996
1972........	250	975	16,764	1990	44	185	5,926
1973........	317	1,400	16,260	1991	40	392	4,584
1974........	424	1,796	31,809	1992	35	364	3,989
1975........	235	965	17,563	1993	35	182	3,981
1976........	231	1,519	23,962	1994	45	322	5,020
1977........	298	1,212	21,258	1995	31	192	5,771
1978........	219	1,006	23,774	1996	37	273	4,889
1979........	235	1,021	20,409	1997	29	339	4,497
1980........	187	795	20,844	1998	34	387	5,116
1981........	145	729	16,908	1999	17	73	1,996
1982........	96	656	9,061	2000	39	394	20,419
1983........	81	909	17,461	2001	29	99	1,151
1984........	62	376	8,499	2002	19	46	660
1985........	54	324	7,079				

(1) Numbers cover stoppages that began in the year indicated. Days of idleness include all stoppages in effect. Workers are counted more than once if they are involved in more than 1 stoppage during the year.

Work Stoppages Involving 5,000 Workers or More Beginning in 2002

Strikes and lockouts were at historic lows in 2002, as measured by the number of workers idled and number of workdays lost. There were 19 major stoppages beginning in 2002, idling 46,000 workers and resulting in 660,000 workdays lost; in 2001, 29 major stoppages had involved 99,000 workers and resulted in 1.2 million days lost. The only action in which more than 5,000 workers participated was the stoppage involving the Pacific Maritime Association and the International Longshore and Warehouse Union. From Sept. 27 to Oct. 9, 2002, 10,500 workers stayed off the job, resulting in 98,000 workdays lost.

Labor Union Directory

Source: Bureau of Labor Statistics, U.S. Dept. of Labor; AFL-CIO; World Almanac research.

(*) Independent union; all others affiliated with AFL-CIO.

Actors and Artistes of America, Associated (AAAA), 165 W 46th St., Suite 500, New York, NY 10036; founded 1919; Theodore Bikel, Pres.; no individual members, 8 National Performing Arts Unions are affiliates; approx. 100,000 combined membership.

Actors' Equity Association, 165 W 46th St., New York, NY 10036; founded 1913; Patrick Quinn, Pres. (since 2000); 40,000 active members.

Air Line Pilots Association, 535 Herndon Pkwy., Herndon, VA 20170; founded 1931; Capt. Duane Woerth, Pres. (since 1999); 66,000+ members, 43 airlines.

American Federation of Labor & Congress of Industrial Organizations (AFL-CIO), 815 16th St. NW, Washington, DC 20006; founded 1955; John J. Sweeney, Pres. (since 1995); 13 mil. members.

Automobile, Aerospace & Agricultural Implement Workers of America, International Union, United (UAW), 8000 E Jefferson Ave., Detroit, MI 48214; founded 1935; Ron Gettelfinger, Pres. (since 2002); 710,000 active (500,000 ret.) members, 950+ locals.

Bakery, Confectionery, Tobacco Workers and Grain Millers International Union (BCTGM), 10401 Connecticut Ave., Kensington, MD 20895; founded 1886; Frank Hurt, Pres. (since 1992); 120,000 members.

Boilermakers, Iron Ship Builders, Blacksmiths, Forgers and Helpers, International Brotherhood of (IBBISB/BF&H), 753 State Ave., Suite 565, Kansas City, KS 66101; founded 1880; Newton B. Jones, Int'l Pres. (since 2003); 100,000+ members, 420 locals.

Bricklayers and Allied Craftworkers, International Union of (BAC), 1776 Eye St. NW, Washington, DC 20006; founded 1865; John J. Flynn, Pres. (since 1999); 100,000 members, 200 locals.

***Carpenters and Joiners of America, United Brotherhood of,** 101 Constitution Ave., NW, Washington, DC 20001; founded 1881; Douglas J. McCarron, Pres. (since 1995); 520,000 members, 1,000 locals.

Communications Workers of America (IUE-CWA), 501 3rd St. NW, Washington, DC 20001; founded 1938; Morton Bahr, Pres. (since 1985); 700,000+ members, 1,200 locals. (Merged with the Intl. Union of Electronic, Electrical, Salaried, Machine, and Furniture Workers 10/1/00.)

***Education Association, National,** 1201 16th St. NW, Washington, DC 20036; founded 1857; Reg Weaver, Pres. (since 2002); 2.7 mil. members, 14,000+ affiliates.

Electrical Workers, International Brotherhood of (IBEW), 1125 15th St. NW, Washington, DC 20005; founded 1891; Edwin D. Hill, Pres. (since 2001); 780,000 members, 1,019 locals.

Engineers, International Union of Operating (IUOE), 1125 17th St. NW, Washington, DC 20036; founded 1896; Frank Hanley, Pres. (since 1990); 400,000 members, 170 locals.

Farm Workers of America, United (UFW), 29700 Woodford-Tehachapi Rd., PO Box 62, Keene, CA 93531; founded 1962; Arturo S. Rodriguez, Pres. (since 1993); 50,000 members.

***Federal Employees, Federal District 1, National Federation of (NFFE FD1, IAMAW, AFL-CIO),** 1016 16th St. NW, Washington, DC 20036; founded 1917; Richard N. Brown, Pres. (1998); 120,000 members, 290 locals.

Fire Fighters, International Association of, 1750 New York Ave. NW, Washington, DC 20006; founded 1918; Harold Schaitberger, Pres. (since 2000); 260,000 members, 2,700 locals.

Firemen and Oilers, National Conference of, 1023 15th St. NW, 10th Floor, Washington, DC 20035; founded 1898; George J. Francisco, Jr., Pres.; 26,000 members, 133 locals.

Flight Attendants, Association of, 1275 K St. NW, 5th floor, Washington, DC 20005; founded 1945; Patricia A. Friend, Int'l Pres.; 50,000 members, 26 carriers.

Food and Commercial Workers International Union, United (UFCW), 1775 K St. NW, Washington, DC 20006-1598; founded 1979 following merger; Douglas H. Dority, Intl. Pres. (since 1994); 1.4 mil. members, 997 locals.

Glass, Molders, Pottery, Plastics & Allied Workers Intl. Union (GMP), 608 E Baltimore Pike, PO Box 607, Media, PA 19063; founded 1842; James H. Rankin, Pres. (since 1997); 51,000 members, 370 locals.

Government Employees, American Federation of (AFGE), 80 F St. NW, Washington, DC 20001; founded 1932; John Gage, Pres. (since 2003); 600,000 members, 1,100 locals.

Graphic Communications International Union (GCIU), 1900 L St. NW, Washington, DC 20036; founded 1983; George Tedeschi, Pres. (since 2003); 150,000 members, 321 locals.

Hotel Employees and Restaurant Employees International Union, 1219 28th St. NW, Washington, DC 20007; John W. Wilhelm, Gen. Pres. (since 1998); 265,000 members, 111 locals.

Iron Workers, International Association of Bridge, Structural, Ornamental and Reinforcing, 1750 New York Ave. NW, Suite 400, Washington, DC 20006; founded 1896; Joseph Hunt, Gen. Pres. (since 2001); 120,000 members, 242 locals.

Laborers' International Union of North America (LIUNA), 905 16th St. NW, Washington, DC 20006-1765; founded 1903; Terence M. O'Sullivan, Pres. (since 2000); 800,000 members.

Letter Carriers, National Association of (NALC), 100 Indiana Ave. NW, Washington, DC 20001-2144; founded 1889; William H. Young, Pres. (since 2002); 305,000 members, 2,723 locals.

Locomotive Engineers, Brotherhood of (BLE), 1370 Ontario St., Cleveland, OH 44113; founded 1863; Don M. Hahs, Pres. (since 2001); 59,000 members, 600+ divisions.

Longshore & Warehouse Union, International (ILWU), 1188 Franklin St., San Francisco, CA 94109-6800; founded 1937; James Spinosa, Pres. (since 2000); 43,500 members, 60 locals.

Longshoremen's Association, International (ILA), 17 Battery Pl., Suite 930, New York, NY 10004; founded 1892; John M. Bowers, Pres. (since 1987); 65,000 members.

Machinists and Aerospace Workers, International Association of (IAMAW), 9000 Machinists Pl., Upper Marlboro, MD 20772; founded 1888; R. Thomas Buffenbarger, Pres. (since 1997); 780,000 members, 1,194 locals.

Maintenance of Way Employees, Brotherhood of (BMWE), 26555 Evergreen Rd., Suite 200, Southfield, MI 48076; founded 1887; M. A. "Mac" Fleming, Pres. (since 1990); 55,000 members, 790 locals.

Marine Engineers' Beneficial Assn. (MEBA), 444 N Capitol St. NW, Suite 800, Washington, DC 20001; founded 1875; Ron Davis, Pres. (since 2002).

Mine Workers of America, United (UMWA), 8315 Lee Highway, Fairfax, VA 22031; founded 1890; Cecil E. Roberts, Pres. (since 1995); 130,000 members, 600 locals.

Musicians of the United States and Canada, American Federation of (AFM), 1501 Broadway, Suite 600, New York, NY 10036; founded 1896; Thomas F. Lee, Pres. (since 2001); 125,000 members, 250+ locals.

Needletrades, Industrial, and Textile Employees, Union of (UNITE), 1710 Broadway, New York, NY 10019; founded 1995; Bruce S. Raynor, Pres. (since 2001); 250,000 members, 900 locals.

Newspaper Guild-Communications Workers of America (CWA), The, 501 3rd St. NW, Suite 250, Washington, DC 20001; founded 1933; Linda K. Foley, Pres. (since 1995); 34,000 members, 90 locals.

***Nurses Association, American (ANA),** 600 Maryland Ave. SW, Suite 100-W, Washington, DC 20024; founded 1897; Barbara Blakeney, Pres.; 2.6 mil. members, 54 constituent state & territorial assns.

Office and Professional Employees International Union (OPEIU), 265 W 14th St., Suite 610, New York, NY 10011; founded 1945 (AFL Charter); Michael Goodwin, Pres. (since 1994); 145,000 members, 200 locals.

PACE International Union, AFL-CIO, CLC (PACE), PO Box 1475, Nashville, TN 37202; founded 1884; Boyd D. Young, Pres. (since 1999); 320,000 members, 1,500 locals.

Painters and Allied Trades, International Union of (IUPAT), 1750 New York Ave. NW, Washington, DC 20006; founded 1887; James A. Williams, Gen. Pres.; 140,000 members, 425 locals.

Plasterers' and Cement Masons' International Association of the United States and Canada, Operative, 14405 Laurel Pl., Suite 300, Laurel, MD 20707; founded 1864; John J. Dougherty, Pres.; 40,000 members, 100 locals.

Plumbing and Pipe Fitting Industry of the United States and Canada, United Association of Journeymen and Apprentices of the, 901 Massachusetts Ave. NW, PO Box 37800, Washington, DC 20013; founded 1889; Martin J. Maddaloni, Gen. Pres. (since 1997); 326,000 members, 321 locals.

*__Police, National Fraternal Order of,__ 1410 Donelson Pike, A-17, Nashville, TN 37217; Chuck Canterbury, Natl. Pres. (since 2003); 308,000 members, 2,100+ affiliates.

Police Associations, International Union of, 1421 Prince St., Suite 400, Alexandria, VA 22314; Samuel Cabral, Pres. (since 1995); 80,000 members, 500 locals.

*__Postal Supervisors, National Association of,__ 1727 King St., Suite 400, Alexandria, VA 22314-2753; Vincent Palladino, Pres. (since 1992); 36,000 members, 400 locals.

Postal Workers Union, American (APWU), 1300 L St. NW, Washington, DC 20005; founded 1971; William Burrus, Pres. (since 2001); 366,000 members, 1,600+ locals.

Roofers, Waterproofers & Allied Workers, United Union of, 1660 L St. NW, Suite 800, Washington, DC 20036; founded 1906; John Martini, Intl. Pres.; 22,000 members.

*__Rural Letter Carriers' Association, National,__ 1630 Duke St., 4th Fl., Alexandria, VA 22314; founded 1903; Dale Holton, Pres.; 100,000 members; 50 state org.

Seafarers International Union of North America (SIU), 5201 Auth Way, Camp Springs, MD 20746; founded 1938; Michael Sacco, Pres. (since 1988); 85,000 members, 18 affiliates.

*__Security, Police, and Fire Professionals of America (SPFPA),__ 25510 Kelly Rd., Roseville, MI 48066; founded 1948; David L. Hickey, Pres. (since 2000); 12,000 members, 200 locals.

Service Employees International Union (SEIU), 1313 L St. NW, Washington, DC 20005; founded 1921; Andrew L. Stern, Pres. (since 1996); 1.6 million members, 350 locals.

Sheet Metal Workers' International Association (SMWIA), 1750 New York Ave. NW, Washington, DC 20006; founded 1888; Michael J. Sullivan, Pres. (since 1999); 150,000 members, 194 locals.

State, County, and Municipal Employees, American Federation of (AFSCME), 1625 L St. NW, Washington, DC 20036; Gerald W. McEntee, Pres. (since 1981); 1.4 mil. members, 3,617 locals.

Steelworkers of America, United (USWA), 5 Gateway Center, Pittsburgh, PA 15222; founded 1936; Leo W. Gerard, Pres. (since 2001); 1.2 mil. members, 1,800 locals.

Teachers, American Federation of (AFT), 555 New Jersey Ave. NW, Washington, DC 20001; founded 1916; Sandra Feldman, Pres. (since 1997); 1 mil.+ members, 3,000 locals.

Teamsters, International Brotherhood of (IBT), 25 Louisiana Ave. NW, Washington, DC 20001; founded 1903; James P. Hoffa, Gen. Pres. (since 1999); 1.4 mil. members, 569 locals.

Television and Radio Artists, American Federation of, (AFTRA) 260 Madison Ave., 7th fl., New York, NY 10016; founded 1937; John Connolly, Natl. Pres. (since 2001); 80,000 members, 35 locals.

Theatrical Stage Employees, Moving Picture Technicians, Artists and Allied Crafts of the United States, its Territories, and Canada, International Alliance of (IATSE), 1430 Broadway, 20th floor, New York, NY 10018; founded 1893; Thomas C. Short, Pres. (since 1994); 104,000 members, 555+ locals.

Transit Union, Amalgamated (ATU), 5025 Wisconsin Ave. NW, Washington, DC 20016; founded 1892; Warren S. George, Pres. (since 2003); 165,000 members, 285 locals.

Transportation-Communications International Union (TCU), 3 Research Place, Rockville, MD 20850; founded 1899; Robert A. Scardelletti, Pres. (since 1991); 100,000 members.

Transportation Union, United (UTU), 14600 Detroit Ave., Cleveland, OH 44107; founded 1969; Byron A. Boyd Jr., Pres. (since 2001); 125,000 members, 680 locals.

Transport Workers Union of America, 1700 Broadway, New York, NY 10019; founded 1934; Sonny Hall, Int'l. Pres. (since 1993); 125,000+ members, 92 locals.

*__Treasury Employees Union, National (NTEU),__ 1750 H St. NW, Washington, DC 20006; founded 1938; Colleen M. Kelley, Natl. Pres. (since 1999); 155,000 represented, 270+ chapters.

*__University Professors, American Association of (AAUP),__ 1012 14th St. NW, Suite 500, Washington, DC 20005; founded 1915; Jane Buck, Pres.; 45,000 members, 600 chapters.

Utility Workers Union of America (UWUA), 815 16th St. NW, Washington, DC 20006; founded 1945; Donald Wightman, Pres. (since 1996); 43,000 members, 250 locals.

U.S. Union Membership, 1930-2002

Source: Bureau of Labor Statistics, U.S. Dept. of Labor

Year	Labor force[1] (thousands)	Union members[2] (thousands)	Percentage of labor force	Year	Labor force[1] (thousands)	Union members[2] (thousands)	Percentage of labor force
1930....	29,424	3,401	11.6	1989	103,480	16,960	16.4
1935....	27,053	3,584	13.2	1990	103,905	16,740	16.1
1940....	32,376	8,717	26.9	1991	102,786	16,568	16.1
1945....	40,394	14,322	35.5	1992	103,688	16,390	15.8
1950....	45,222	14,267	31.5	1993	105,067	16,598	15.8
1955....	50,675	16,802	33.2	1994	107,989	16,748	15.5
1960....	54,234	17,049	31.4	1995	110,038	16,360	14.9
1965....	60,815	17,299	28.4	1996	111,960	16,269	14.5
1970....	70,920	19,381	27.3	1997	114,533	16,110	14.1
1975....	76,945	19,611	25.5	1998	116,730	16,211	13.9
1980....	90,564	19,843	21.9	1999	118,963	16,477	13.9
1985....	94,521	16,996	18.0	2000	120,786	16,258	13.5
1986....	96,903	16,975	17.5	2001*....	122,482	16,387	13.4
1987....	99,303	16,913	17.0	2002	122,007	16,107	13.2
1988....	101,407	17,002	16.8				

(1) Does not include agricultural employment; from 1985, does not include self employed or unemployed persons. (2) From 1930 to 1980, includes dues-paying members of traditional trade unions, regardless of employment status; after that includes employed only. From 1985, includes members of employee associations that engage in collective bargaining with employers. * Revised to reflect Census 2000-based population controls.

WORLD ALMANAC QUICK QUIZ

Rank these countries by hourly compensation costs for manufacturing production workers in 2002, lowest cost to highest:

    (a) Taiwan   (b) South Korea   (c) Mexico   (d) Singapore

For the answer look in this chapter, or see page 1008.

CRIME

Measuring Crime

The U.S. Dept. of Justice administers 2 statistical programs to measure the magnitude, nature, and impact of crime in the U.S. Because of a difference in focus and methodology, their results are not strictly comparable.

The **Uniform Crime Report (UCR)** program, conducted through the Federal Bureau of Investigation, was designed to provide statistics for law enforcement administration, operation, and management. It collects information on the crimes of homicide, forcible rape, robbery, aggravated assault, burglary, larceny-theft, motor vehicle theft, and arson, as they are reported to law enforcement authorities. A preliminary annual report is released each spring, and a more final report on the same period is released in the following year.

The **National Crime Victimization Survey (NCVS)** is conducted annually by the Bureau of Justice Statistics through interviews with members of a nationally representative sample of households, who report on on their experience of crime. It complements the UCR by providing alternate information about crimes, including those not reported to police. In contrast to the UCR, it does not cover murder or arson.

Further explanation of the NCVS and UCR is available at: www.ojp.usdoj.gov/bjs/abstract/ntmc.htm

Uniform Crime Reports for 2002
Source: FBI, *Uniform Crime Reports*, 2002, preliminary

Serious crimes, including murder and arson, reported to law enforcement agencies in the U.S. decreased 0.2% from 2001 to 2002, according to preliminary figures from the Federal Bureau of Investigation's Uniform Crime Reporting Program, released June 16, 2003. This represented a reversal from the 2.1% increase in 2001, which was the first such increase since 1991. Reported crime in the U.S. had been steady in 2000, and had gone down 7.8% in 1999, 5% in 1998, 2% in 1997, 3% in 1996, 1% in both 1994 and 1995, 2% in 1993, and 3% in 1992.

Reported serious crime is measured by the Crime Index, which includes 4 violent crimes and 3 property crimes. From 2001 to 2002, based on preliminary statistics, violent crime decreased by 1.4%, and property crime remained unchanged from 2001. In the violent crime category, robberies fell by 1.2%, while murder and forcible rape rose 0.8% and 4.0%, respectively. Aggravated assault declined by 2.0%.

Overall property crime in 2002 was unchanged from 2001. While burglary increased 1.5%, and motor vehicle theft was up 1.2%, larceny-theft fell 0.7%. Reports of arson, which is not included in the Crime Index proper, decreased by 3.7%.

In 2002, Crime Index totals decreased in 3 of the 4 major regions of the U.S. Crimes were down 3.3% in the Northeast, 0.1% in the South, and 2.1% in the Midwest. Law enforcement agencies reported a 2.9% increase in the West.

By city populations, cities with populations of 50,000 to 99,999 or 100,000 to 249,999 showed increases of 1.2% and 0.7%, respectively, from 2001. Cities with populations of 250,000 to 499,999 showed a decrease of 1.9%. In cities with over 1 million people, there was a 0.6% decrease, and in those with fewer than 10,000, a 1.2% decrease. The Crime Index also rose 1.8% in suburban counties and 0.4% in rural counties.

National Crime Victimization Survey for 2002
Source: Bureau of Justice Statistics, U.S. Dept. of Justice

The NCVS estimated that there were about 23 million victimizations of Americans age 12 and up in 2002 (including those unreported), down from 24.2 million in 2001. This is the lowest number since the NCVS was initiated in 1973; in that year there were an estimated 44 million victimizations. According to this survey, the violent crime rate in 2002 fell 8% from 2001, and the property crime rate went down 4.7%. These decreases continued trends that began in 1994; between 1993 and 2002, violent crime, as reflected in NCVS statistics, fell 54%, and property crime 50%. According to NCVS estimates, only about half of all violent crimes and 40% of property crimes in 2002 were reported to the police.

Criminal Victimization, 2001-2002
Source: National Crime Victimization Survey, U.S. Dept. of Justice

	Number of victimizations		Victimization rates[1]		
Type of Crime	2001	2002	2001	2002	% change, 2001-2002
All Crimes	24,216,000	23,036,000	NA	NA	NA
Personal Crimes	5,932,000	5,497,000	25.9	23.7	−8.5
Crimes of violence	5,744,000	5,341,000	25.1	23.1	−8.0
Rape	84,000	90,000	0.4	0.4	0.0
Attempted rape	63,000	77,000	0.3	0.3	0.0
Sexual assault	102,000	80,000	0.4	0.3	−25.0
Robbery[2]	427,000	386,000	1.9	1.7	−10.5
With injury[2]	174,000	170,000	0.8	0.7	−12.5
Aggravated assault[3]	1,222,000	990,000	5.3	4.3	−18.9
Simple assault[4]	3,643,000	3,591,000	15.9	15.5	−2.5
Personal theft[5]	188,000	155,000	0.8	0.7	−12.5
Property Crimes	18,284,000	17,539,000	166.9	159.0	−4.7
Household burglary[2]	2,687,000	2,597,000	24.5	23.5	−4.1
Motor vehicle theft[2]	724,000	781,000	6.6	7.1	7.6
Theft[2]	13,672,000	13,040,000	124.8	118.2	−5.3

NA = Not applicable (1) Per 1,000 persons age 12 or older or per 1,000 households. (2) Refers to completed crimes, and does not include attempted crimes. (3) Attack with a weapon or involving serious injury. (4) Attack without a weapon resulting in no injury, minor injury, or undetermined injury requiring less than 2 days hospitalization. (5) Purse snatching and pocket picking.

Federal Bureau of Investigation

The Federal Bureau of Investigation was created July 26, 1908, and was referred to as Office of Chief Examiner. It became the Bureau of Investigation (Mar. 16, 1909), United States Bureau of Investigation (July 1, 1932), Division of Investigation (Aug. 10, 1933), and Federal Bureau of Investigation (July 1, 1935).

Director	Assumed office	Director	Assumed office	Director	Assumed office
Stanley W. Finch	July 26, 1908	J. Edgar Hoover	Dec. 10, 1924	John E. Otto, act.	May 26, 1987
A(lexander) Bruce Bielaski	Apr. 30, 1912	L. Patrick Gray, act.	May 3, 1972	William S. Sessions	Nov. 2, 1987
William E. Allen, act.	Feb. 10, 1919	William D. Ruckelshaus,		Floyd I. Clarke, act.	July 19, 1993
William J. Flynn	July 1, 1919	act.	Apr. 27, 1973	Louis J. Freeh	Sept. 1, 1993
William J. Burns	Aug. 22, 1921	Clarence M. Kelley	July 9, 1973	Thomas J. Pickard, act.	June 25, 2001
J. Edgar Hoover, act.	May 10, 1924	William H. Webster	Feb. 23, 1978	Robert S. Mueller III	Sept. 4, 2001

IT'S A FACT: Of males who reported being robbed in 2002, 74% said the perpetrator was a stranger, according to the National Crime Victimization Survey. For women this figure was 43%.

Crime in the U.S., 1982-2001[1]

Source: FBI, *Uniform Crime Reports*, 2001, final statistics; additional data may be available at www.fbi.gov/ucr/ucr.htm

Year	Population[2]	Crime Index (total)	Violent crime[3]	Property crime[3]	Murder and non-negligent manslaughter[1]	Forcible rape	Robbery	Aggravated assault	Burglary	Larceny-theft
				NUMBER OF REPORTED OFFENSES						
1982—231,664,458...		12,974,400	1,322,390	11,652,000	21,010	78,770	553,130	669,480	3,447,100	7,142,500
1983—233,791,994...		12,108,630	1,258,087	10,850,543	19,308	78,918	506,567	653,294	3,129,851	6,712,759
1984—235,824,902...		11,881,755	1,273,282	10,608,476	18,692	84,233	485,008	685,349	2,984,434	6,591,874
1985—237,923,795...		12,430,357	1,327,767	11,102,590	18,976	87,671	497,874	723,246	3,073,348	6,926,380
1986—240,132,887...		13,211,869	1,489,169	11,722,700	20,613	91,459	542,775	834,322	3,241,410	7,257,153
1987—242,288,918...		13,508,708	1,483,999	12,024,709	20,096	91,111	517,704	855,088	3,236,184	7,499,851
1988—244,498,982...		13,923,086	1,566,221	12,356,865	20,675	92,486	542,968	910,092	3,218,077	7,705,872
1989—246,819,230...		14,251,449	1,646,037	12,605,412	21,500	94,504	578,326	951,707	3,168,170	7,872,442
1990—249,464,396...		14,475,613	1,820,127	12,655,486	23,438	102,555	639,271	1,054,863	3,073,909	7,945,670
1991—252,153,092...		14,872,883	1,911,767	12,961,116	24,703	106,593	687,732	1,092,739	3,157,150	8,142,228
1992—255,029,699...		14,438,191	1,932,274	12,505,917	23,760	109,062	672,478	1,126,974	2,979,884	7,915,199
1993—257,782,608...		14,144,794	1,926,017	12,218,777	24,526	106,014	659,870	1,135,607	2,834,808	7,820,909
1994—260,327,021...		13,989,543	1,857,670	12,131,873	23,326	102,216	618,949	1,113,179	2,712,774	7,879,812
1995—262,803,276...		13,862,727	1,798,792	12,063,935	21,606	97,470	580,509	1,099,207	2,593,784	7,997,710
1996—265,228,572...		13,493,863	1,688,540	11,805,323	19,645	96,252	535,594	1,037,049	2,506,400	7,904,685
1997—267,783,607...		13,194,571	1,636,096	11,558,475	18,208	96,153	498,534	1,023,201	2,460,526	7,743,760
1998—270,248,003...		12,485,714	1,533,887	10,951,820	16,974	93,144	447,186	976,583	2,332,735	7,376,311
1999—272,690,813...		11,634,378	1,426,044	10,208,334	15,522	89,411	409,371	911,740	2,100,739	6,955,520
2000—281,421,906...		11,608,070	1,425,486	10,182,584	15,586	90,178	408,016	911,706	2,050,992	6,971,590
2001—284,796,887...		11,849,006	1,436,611	10,412,395	15,980	90,491	422,921	907,219	2,109,767	7,076,171
				PERCENT CHANGE: NUMBER OF OFFENSES						
2001/2000		2.1	0.8	2.3	2.5	0.3	3.7	−0.5	2.9	1.5
2001/1997		−10.2	−12.2	−9.9	−12.2	−5.9	−15.2	−11.3	−14.3	−8.6
2001/1992		−17.9	−25.7	−16.7	−32.7	−17.0	−37.1	−19.5	−29.2	−10.6
				RATE PER 100,000 INHABITANTS						
1982............		5,600.5	570.8	5,029.7	9.1	34	238.8	289	1,488.0	3,083.1
1983............		5,179.2	538.1	4,641.1	8.3	33.8	216.7	279.4	1,338.7	2,871.3
1984............		5,038.4	539.9	4,498.5	7.9	35.7	205.7	290.6	1,265.5	2,795.2
1985............		5,224.5	558.1	4,666.4	8.0	36.8	209.3	304	1,291.7	2,911.2
1986............		5,501.9	620.1	4,881.8	8.6	38.1	226	347.4	1,349.8	3,022.1
1987............		5,575.5	612.5	4,963.0	8.3	37.6	213.7	352.9	1,335.7	3,095.4
1988............		5,694.5	640.6	5,054.0	8.5	37.8	222.1	372.2	1,316.2	3,151.7
1989............		5,774.0	666.9	5,107.1	8.7	38.3	234.3	385.6	1,283.6	3,189.6
1990............		5,802.7	729.6	5,073.1	9.4	41.1	256.3	422.9	1,232.2	3,185.1
1991............		5,898.4	758.2	5,140.2	9.8	42.3	272.7	433.4	1,252.1	3,229.1
1992............		5,661.4	757.7	4,903.7	9.3	42.8	263.7	441.9	1,168.4	3,103.6
1993............		5,487.1	747.1	4,740.0	9.5	41.1	256	440.5	1,099.7	3,033.9
1994............		5,373.8	713.6	4,660.2	9.0	39.3	237.8	427.6	1,042.1	3,026.9
1995............		5,274.9	684.5	4,590.5	8.2	37.1	220.9	418.3	987	3,043.2
1996............		5,087.6	636.6	4,451.0	7.4	36.3	201.9	391	945	2,980.3
1997............		4,927.3	611	4,316.3	6.8	35.9	186.2	382.1	918.8	2,891.8
1998............		4,620.1	567.6	4,052.6	6.3	34.5	165.5	361.4	863.2	2,729.5
1999............		4,266.5	523	3,743.6	5.7	32.8	150.1	334.3	770.4	2,550.7
2000............		4,124.8	506.5	3,618.3	5.5	32	145	324	728.8	2,477.3
2001............		4,160.5	504.4	3,656.1	5.6	31.8	148.5	318.5	740.8	2,484.6
				PERCENT CHANGE: RATE PER 100,000 INHABITANTS						
2001/2000		0.9	−0.4	1.0	1.3	−0.8	2.4	−1.7	1.6	0.3
2001/1997		−15.6	−17.4	−15.3	−17.5	−11.5	−20.2	−16.6	−19.4	−14.1
2001/1992		−26.5	−33.4	−25.4	−39.8	−25.7	−43.7	−27.9	−36.6	−19.9

(1) The murder and nonnegligent homicides that occurred as a result of the attacks of Sept. 11, 2001, are not included in this table. (2) Populations are Bureau of the Census provisional estimates as of July 1 for each year except 1990 and 2000, which are decennial census counts. (3) Violent crimes are offenses of murder, forcible rape, robbery, and aggravated assault. Property crimes are offenses of burglary, larceny-theft, and motor vehicle theft.

Law Enforcement Officers, 2001

Source: FBI, *Uniform Crime Reports*, 2001; later data may be available at www.fbi.gov/ucr/ucr.htm

The U.S. law enforcement community employed an average of 2.5 full-time officers for every 1,000 inhabitants as of Oct. 31, 2001.

Including full-time civilian employees, the overall law enforcement employee rate was 3.5 per 1,000 inhabitants, according to 13,530 city, county, and state police agencies. These agencies collectively offered law enforcement service covering a population of about 268 million, employing 659,104 officers and 279,926 civilians.

The law enforcement employee average for all cities nationwide was 3.1 per 1,000 inhabitants. The highest rate was 4.7 per 1,000 inhabitants, in cities with populations of 1,000,000 or more. Suburban and rural counties had average rates of 4.4 and 4.2, respectively.

Regionally, the law enforcement employee rate was 3.6 in the Northeast, 3.5 in the South, 2.8 in the Midwest, and 2.4 in the West. Both nationally and in cities, males constituted 88.8% of all sworn employees. In rural counties, 91.9% of the officers were males, while in suburban counties males accounted for 87.1%.

Civilians made up 29.8% of the total U.S. law enforcement employee force. They represented 23.2% of the police employees in cities, 39.3% in both rural and suburban counties. Females accounted for 62.7% of all civilian employees.

Seventy law enforcement officers were feloniously slain in the line of duty in 2001, 19 more than in 2000. Another 78 officers were killed as a result of accidents occurring while performing official duties, 6 fewer than in the previous year.

U.S. Crime Rates by Region, Geographic Division, and State, 2001

Source: FBI, *Uniform Crime Reports*, 2001; final statistics later data available at www.fbi.gov/ucr/ucr.htm

(rate per 100,000 population)

	Total rate	Violent crime[1]	Property crime[2]	Murder	Rape	Robbery	Aggra-vated assault	Burglary	Larceny-theft	Motor vehicle theft
U.S. TOTAL	4,160.5	504.4	3,656.1	5.6	31.8	148.5	318.5	740.8	2,484.6	430.6
Northeast	3,006.9	429.7	2,577.2	4.2	22.5	149.8	253.2	470.0	1,788.4	318.8
New England	3,025.7	353.6	2,672.2	2.4	27.1	88.9	235.2	508.8	1,808.0	355.3
Connecticut	3,117.9	335.5	2,782.4	3.1	18.7	122.1	191.7	501.0	1,920.0	361.4
Maine	2,688.2	111.5	2,576.7	1.4	25.3	20.5	64.2	536.1	1,910.7	129.9
Massachusetts	3,098.6	479.5	2,619.1	2.3	29.1	101.5	346.6	508.4	1,674.5	436.2
New Hampshire . . .	2,321.6	170.3	2,151.3	1.4	36.4	35.3	97.2	388.3	1,593.1	170.0
Rhode Island	3,684.9	309.6	3,375.3	3.7	39.3	93.1	173.5	644.4	2,254.7	476.2
Vermont	2,769.3	105.0	2,664.2	1.1	17.5	17.5	69.0	513.8	2,026.8	123.6
Middle Atlantic	3,000.3	456.5	2,543.7	4.9	20.8	171.3	259.5	456.4	1,781.4	305.9
New Jersey	3,225.3	390.1	2,835.2	4.0	15.1	166.3	204.7	551.7	1,839.0	444.4
New York	2,925.1	516.0	2,409.1	5.0	18.7	192.3	300.0	422.9	1,732.2	254.0
Pennsylvania	2,961.1	410.4	2,550.7	5.3	28.2	142.4	234.5	442.3	1,817.8	290.7
Midwest	3,981.1	432.0	3,549.1	5.3	35.1	128.3	263.3	677.7	2,491.5	379.9
East North Central . . .	3,985.8	463.3	3,522.5	6.0	36.4	146.9	274.0	699.9	2,424.0	398.7
Illinois	4,097.8	636.9	3,460.8	7.9	31.5	199.2	398.3	631.6	2,438.3	390.8
Indiana	3,831.4	371.8	3,459.6	6.8	28.1	117.3	219.7	699.3	2,408.8	351.6
Michigan	4,081.5	554.7	3,526.8	6.7	52.7	129.5	365.8	721.0	2,269.2	536.6
Ohio	4,177.6	351.9	3,825.7	4.0	39.3	151.2	157.4	852.1	2,602.3	371.3
Wisconsin	3,321.2	231.1	3,090.1	3.6	21.1	82.3	124.2	498.5	2,319.1	272.5
West North Central . .	3,970.1	358.5	3,611.5	3.6	31.9	84.9	238.2	625.6	2,650.0	336.0
Iowa	3,301.2	269.1	3,032.1	1.7	22.2	39.5	205.7	577.6	2,266.2	188.3
Kansas	4,321.4	404.8	3,916.6	3.4	35.1	89.9	276.4	761.3	2,858.9	296.3
Minnesota	3,583.7	264.4	3,319.3	2.4	45.0	75.6	141.4	512.8	2,504.3	302.3
Missouri	4,776.1	541.3	4,234.9	6.6	24.6	138.0	372.1	763.4	2,973.9	497.6
Nebraska	4,329.6	304.3	4,025.3	2.5	25.2	65.8	210.8	569.7	3,076.8	378.8
North Dakota	2,417.7	79.6	2,338.1	1.1	25.8	9.5	43.2	341.2	1,825.7	171.2
South Dakota	2,332.0	154.8	2,177.2	0.9	46.4	13.6	93.8	408.0	1,661.5	107.7
South	4,760.9	579.9	4,181.0	6.7	33.6	159.7	380.0	926.8	2,826.7	427.6
South Atlantic	4,762.2	615.9	4,146.2	6.3	31.1	174.5	403.9	908.8	2,798.8	438.7
Delaware	4,052.8	611.4	3,441.4	2.9	52.8	145.2	410.6	646.1	2,446.2	349.0
District of Columbia .	7,709.6	1,736.7	5,972.8	40.6	32.9	689.6	973.7	876.3	3,755.2	1,341.3
Florida	5,569.7	797.2	4,772.5	5.3	40.5	200.5	550.9	1,073.7	3,150.4	548.4
Georgia	4,646.3	497.0	4,149.3	7.1	26.0	171.8	292.1	856.4	2,844.5	448.3
Maryland	4,866.8	783.0	4,083.8	8.3	27.0	251.6	496.1	773.1	2,715.0	595.8
North Carolina	4,938.0	494.3	4,443.7	6.2	25.4	162.5	300.2	1,244.6	2,898.0	301.1
South Carolina	4,752.7	720.3	4,032.4	6.3	34.0	130.7	549.3	906.5	2,762.7	363.3
Virginia	3,178.3	291.3	2,886.9	5.1	24.6	95.4	166.2	439.7	2,185.1	262.1
West Virginia	2,559.5	279.4	2,280.1	2.2	17.8	39.2	220.2	532.8	1,568.8	178.5
East South Central . .	4,248.4	483.5	3,764.9	7.5	34.1	130.6	311.3	914.7	2,501.6	348.6
Alabama	4,319.4	438.6	3,880.8	8.5	30.7	125.1	274.4	910.4	2,687.8	282.7
Kentucky	2,938.1	257.0	2,681.1	4.7	27.8	80.7	143.8	651.9	1,799.3	229.8
Mississippi	4,185.2	350.1	3,835.1	9.9	40.1	115.3	184.8	1,043.4	2,460.3	331.5
Tennessee	5,152.8	745.3	4,407.5	7.4	38.3	178.0	521.6	1,040.2	2,874.8	492.5
West South Central . .	5,033.7	572.1	4,461.5	6.8	37.4	150.7	377.2	962.9	3,047.0	451.6
Arkansas	4,134.2	452.8	3,681.4	5.5	33.1	81.0	333.2	824.5	2,585.0	271.9
Louisiana	5,338.1	687.0	4,651.1	11.2	31.4	176.1	468.3	1,040.2	3,125.2	485.7
Oklahoma	4,607.0	512.3	4,094.7	5.3	42.9	79.4	384.6	999.2	2,732.2	363.3
Texas	5,152.7	572.8	4,579.9	6.2	38.3	165.8	362.5	958.3	3,140.1	481.4
West	4,354.9	520.3	3,834.7	5.5	33.3	150.0	331.5	736.4	2,518.5	579.7
Mountain	4,743.2	449.3	4,293.9	5.2	36.7	116.9	290.5	794.0	2,929.1	570.8
Arizona	6,077.4	540.3	5,537.1	7.5	28.6	167.1	337.1	1,032.9	3,520.6	983.6
Colorado	4,218.9	350.7	3,868.2	3.6	43.7	80.5	222.9	645.9	2,747.1	475.2
Idaho	3,133.4	243.1	2,890.3	2.3	32.2	18.5	190.1	568.3	2,141.2	180.8
Montana	3,688.7	352.4	3,336.3	3.8	20.8	25.4	302.4	405.8	2,729.2	201.3
Nevada	4,266.0	586.8	3,679.2	8.5	41.9	234.2	302.2	840.9	2,140.1	698.1
New Mexico	5,324.0	781.1	4,542.8	5.4	46.5	147.3	581.9	1,068.9	3,083.7	390.2
Utah	4,243.0	234.1	4,008.9	3.0	39.5	52.7	139.0	608.2	3,113.8	286.9
Wyoming	3,517.6	257.3	3,260.4	1.8	30.9	17.0	207.5	501.8	2,617.8	140.8
Pacific	4,196.9	549.1	3,647.8	5.5	32.0	163.4	348.2	712.9	2,351.4	583.4
Alaska	4,236.2	588.3	3,647.9	6.1	78.9	81.0	422.3	605.9	2,629.6	412.4
California	3,902.9	617.0	3,286.0	6.4	28.9	187.1	394.6	672.4	2,022.2	591.4
Hawaii	5,386.1	254.6	5,131.5	2.6	33.4	93.3	125.3	911.6	3,669.2	550.7
Oregon	5,044.1	306.7	4,737.4	2.4	33.8	79.2	191.3	767.3	3,542.7	427.4
Washington	5,151.9	355.0	4,796.8	3.0	43.4	99.1	209.5	885.5	3,258.7	652.6
Puerto Rico	1,826.1	297.0	1,529.1	19.4	4.9	208.3	64.4	519.1	680.8	329.3

Note: Offense totals are based on all reporting agencies and estimates for unreported areas. Totals may not add because of rounding. (1) Violent crimes are murder, forcible rape, robbery, and aggravated assault. (2) Property crimes are burglary, larceny-theft, and motor vehicle theft. Data not included for property crime of arson.

Sentences vs. Time Served for Selected Crimes

Source: Bureau of Justice Statistics, *Truth in Sentencing in State Prisons*, 1999

The following is a comparison of the average maximum sentence lengths (excluding both life and death sentences) and the actual time served for selected state-court convictions.

Type of offense	Avg. sentence	Avg. time served[1]	Type of offense	Avg. sentence	Avg. time served[1]
All violent	7 years, 1 month	3 years, 3 months	Robbery	7 years, 8 months	3 years, 4 months
Homicide	15 years	7 years	Negligent manslaughter	8 years, 1 month	3 years, 5 months
Rape	9 years, 8 months	5 years, 1 month	Assault	5 years, 1 month	2 years, 4 months
Other sexual assault . . .	6 years, 9 months	3 years, 3 months	Other	5 years, 7 months	2 years, 5 months

(1) Includes jail credit and prison time.

State and Federal Prison Population, Death Penalty, 2001-2002[1]

Source: Bureau of Justice Statistics, U.S. Dept. of Justice

The total number of prisoners under the jurisdiction of federal or state adult correctional authorities was 1,440,655 at year-end 2002. Overall, the U.S. prison population grew 2.6%, which was less than the average annual growth of 3.6% since 1995, but represented the biggest growth in 3 years. At year-end 2002, state and federal prisons housed 63% of the incarcerated population (1,361,258 out of 2,166,260). Jails, which are locally operated and typically hold persons awaiting trial and those with sentences of a year or less, held most of the remainder (665,475); juvenile and military facilities, territorial prisons, jails in Indian country, and facilities of the Bureau of Immigration and Customs Enforcement (formerly the INS) held the rest. The rate of incarceration in prisons was 476 sentenced inmates per 100,000 U.S. residents, up from 411 in 1995 (1 in every 110 men and 1 in every 1,656 women were sentenced prisoners under the jurisdiction of state or federal authorities). The number of persons under sentence of death at the end of 2001 dropped slightly from 3,593 to 3,581; 66 prisoners were executed—19 fewer than the previous year.

	SENTENCED PRISONERS			DEATH PENALTY, 2001		
	2002	2001	% change 2001-2002	Under sentence of death	Executions	Death penalty
U.S. TOTAL	1,380,370	1,345,217	2.6	3,581	66	—
Federal institutions	143,040	136,509	4.8	19	2	Yes
State institutions	1,237,330	1,208,708	2.4	3,562	64	38
Northeast	165,783	163,635	1.3	270	0	—
Connecticut	14,082	13,276	6.1	7	0	Yes
Maine	1,817	1,641	10.7	—	—	No
Massachusetts	8,947	9,355	-4.4	—	—	No
New Hampshire	2,451	2,392	2.5	0	0	Yes
New Jersey[2]	27,891	28,142	-0.9	16	0	Yes
New York	67,065	67,533	-0.7	6	0	Yes
Pennsylvania	40,164	38,057	5.5	241	0	Yes
Rhode Island	2,045	1,926	6.2	—	—	No
Vermont	1,321	1,313	0.6	—	—	No
Midwest	244,226	239,948	1.8	486	10	—
Illinois[2]	42,693	44,348	-3.7	158	0	Yes
Indiana	21,542	20,883	3.2	36	2	Yes
Iowa[2]	8,398	7,962	5.5	—	—	No
Kansas[2]	8,935	8,577	4.2	4	0	Yes
Michigan	50,591	48,849	3.6	—	—	No
Minnesota	7,129	6,606	7.9	—	—	No
Missouri	30,080	28,736	4.7	73	7	Yes
Nebraska	3,972	3,865	2.8	7	0	Yes
North Dakota	1,025	1,027	-0.2	—	—	No
Ohio[2]	45,646	45,281	0.8	203	1	Yes
South Dakota	2,891	2,781	4.0	5	0	Yes
Wisconsin	21,324	21,033	1.4	—	—	No
South	552,795	539,774	2.4	1,907	50	—
Alabama	27,532	26,138	5.3	186	0	Yes
Arkansas	12,999	12,496	4.0	40	1	Yes
Delaware	3,659	4,033	-9.3	14	2	Yes
Florida	75,204	72,404	3.9	372	1	Yes
Georgia	47,424	45,904	3.3	116	4	Yes
Kentucky	15,572	15,104	3.1	36	0	Yes
Louisiana	35,736	35,810	-0.2	88	0	Yes
Maryland	23,274	22,842	1.9	16	0	Yes
Mississippi	21,397	20,476	4.5	62	0	Yes
North Carolina	28,772	27,628	4.1	216	5	Yes
Oklahoma[2]	23,385	22,780	2.7	113	18	Yes
South Carolina	22,837	21,606	5.7	73	0	Yes
Tennessee[2]	24,989	23,671	5.6	96	0	Yes
Texas[2]	151,782	153,056	-0.8	453	17	Yes
Virginia	33,729	31,662	6.5	26	2	Yes
West Virginia	4,504	4,164	8.2	—	—	No
West	274,526	265,351	3.5	899	4	—
Alaska	2,577	2,196	17.3	—	—	No
Arizona	28,008	26,463	5.8	126	0	Yes
California	160,329	157,295	1.9	603	1	Yes
Colorado	18,833	17,448	7.9	6	0	Yes
Hawaii	3,840	3,670	4.6	—	—	No
Idaho	6,204	5,984	3.7	21	0	Yes
Montana	3,290	3,328	-1.1	6	0	Yes
Nevada	10,478	10,233	2.4	86	1	Yes
New Mexico	5,772	5,408	6.7	3	1	Yes
Oregon	12,075	11,368	6.2	26	0	Yes
Utah	5,461	5,254	3.9	11	0	Yes
Washington	15,922	15,020	6.0	9	1	Yes
Wyoming	1,737	1,684	3.1	2	0	Yes

Note: The District of Columbia had transferred its sentenced felons to the Federal Bureau of Prisons, as of Dec. 31, and no longer operates a prison system. (1) All information applies to Dec. 31 of the year indicated. (2) Includes some inmates sentenced to one year or less.

▶ **IT'S A FACT:** According to the Bureau of Justice Statistics, at year-end 2002, 23 state prison systems were operating above capacity. Idaho reported the lowest occupied capacity at 71%, while Alabama had the highest at 201%. The federal system was operating at 133% of capacity.

Prison Situation Among the States and in the Federal System, 2002

Source: *Prisoners in 2002*, Bureau of Justice Statistics, U.S. Dept. of Justice; July 2003

10 largest prison populations, 2002	Number of inmates	10 highest incarceration rates, 2002	Prisoners per 100,000 residents[1]	10 largest % increases in prison population			
				Growth 2001-2002	% annual increase	Growth since 1995	% increase
Federal	163,528	Louisiana	794	Maine	11.5	North Dakota	88.4
California	162,317	Mississippi	743	Rhode Island	8.6	Idaho	86.4
Texas	162,003	Texas	692	Colorado	7.9	Oregon	85.3
Florida	75,210	Oklahoma	692	Connecticut	7.9	West Virginia	81.4
New York	67,065	Alabama	612	Minnesota	7.9	Mississippi	74.7
Michigan	50,591	South Carolina	555	West Virginia	7.8	Federal	71.0
Georgia	47,445	Georgia	552	Vermont	7.0	Colorado	70.2
Ohio	45,646	Missouri	529	Virginia	6.5	Montana	64.6
Illinois	42,693	Arizona	513	Arizona	6.0	Tennessee	64.3
Pennsylvania	40,168	Michigan	501	Washington	6.0	Utah	58.4

(1) Prisoners with sentences of more than 1 year. The Federal Bureau of Prisons and the District of Columbia are excluded.

Executions, by State and Method, 1977-2002

Source: Bureau of Justice Statistics, *Capital Punishment 2001*, Dec. 2002;
Death Penalty Information Center, NAACP Legal Defense and Education Fund, *Death Row, U.S.A.*

	Lethal injection	Electro-cution	Lethal gas	Firing squad	Hanging		Lethal injection	Electro-cution	Lethal gas	Firing squad	Hanging
TOTAL U.S.	820	654	150	11	2	3	Missouri	59	59	0	0	0	0
Federal govt.	2	2	0	0	0	0	Montana	2	2	0	0	0	0
Alabama	25	1	24	0	0	0	Nebraska	3	0	3	0	0	0
Arizona	22	20	0	2	0	0	Nevada	9	8	0	1	0	0
Arkansas	24	23	1	0	0	0	New Mexico	1	1	0	0	0	0
California	10	8	0	2	0	0	North Carolina	23	21	0	2	0	0
Colorado	1	1	0	0	0	0	Ohio	5	5	0	0	0	0
Delaware	13	12	0	0	0	1	Oklahoma	55	55	0	0	0	0
Florida	51	7	44	0	0	0	Oregon	2	2	0	0	0	0
Georgia	31	8	23	0	0	0	Pennsylvania	3	3	0	0	0	0
Idaho	1	1	0	0	0	0	South Carolina	28	23	5	0	0	0
Illinois	12	12	0	0	0	0	Tennessee	1	1	0	0	0	0
Indiana	9	6	3	0	0	0	Texas	289	289	0	0	0	0
Kentucky	2	1	1	0	0	0	Utah	6	4	0	0	2	0
Louisiana	27	7	20	0	0	0	Virginia	87	61	26	0	0	0
Maryland	3	3	0	0	0	0	Washington	4	2	0	0	0	2
Mississippi	6	2	0	4	0	0	Wyoming	1	1	0	0	0	0

Note: Table shows methods used since 1977. Lethal injection was used in 80% of total executions. 17 states—Alabama, Arizona, Arkansas, California, Delaware, Florida, Georgia, Indiana, Kentucky, Louisiana, Mississippi, Nevada, North Carolina, South Carolina, Utah, Virginia, and Washington—have employed 2 methods. 18 states had no executions during the period.

Total Estimated Arrests, 2001

Source: FBI, *Uniform Crime Reports*, 2001

Total, all arrests[1,2]	13,699,254	Vandalism	270,645
Murder and nonnegligent manslaughter	13,653	Weapons; carrying, possessing, etc.	165,896
Forcible rape	27,270	Prostitution and commercialized vice	80,854
Robbery	108,400	Sex offenses (except forcible rape	
Aggravated assault	477,809	and prostitution)	91,828
Burglary	291,444	Drug abuse violations	1,586,902
Larceny-theft	1,160,821	Gambling	11,112
Motor vehicle theft	147,451	Offenses against the family and children	143,683
Arson	18,749	Driving under the influence	1,434,852
Violent crime[3]	**627,132**	Liquor laws	610,591
Property crime[4]	**1,618,465**	Drunkenness	618,668
Crime Index total[5]	**2,245,597**	Disorderly conduct	621,394
Other assaults	1,315,807	Vagrancy	27,935
Forgery and counterfeiting	113,741	All other offenses	3,618,164
Fraud	323,308	Suspicion	3,955
Embezzlement	20,157	Curfew and loitering law violations	142,889
Stolen property; buying, receiving, possessing	121,972	Runaways	133,259

(1) Does not include suspicion. (2) Because of rounding, the figures may not add to total. (3) Violent crimes are offenses of murder, forcible rape, robbery, and aggravated assault. (4) Property crimes are offenses of burglary, larceny-theft, and arson. (5) Includes arson.

Historic Assassinations Since 1865

1865—Apr. 14. U.S. Pres. Abraham Lincoln shot by John Wilkes Booth, a well-known actor with Confederate sympathies, at Ford's Theater in Washington, DC; died Apr. 15.

1881—Mar. 13. Alexander II, of Russia.—July 2. U.S. Pres. James A. Garfield shot by Charles J. Guiteau, a disappointed office seeker, in Washington, DC; died Sept. 19.

1894—June 24. Pres. Sadi Carnot of France, by Italian anarchist, Sante Caserio, in Lyon.

1898—Sept. 10. Empress Elizabeth of Austria, stabbed by Italian anarchist Luigi Luccheni.

1900—July 29. Umberto I, king of Italy.

1901—Sept. 6. U.S. Pres. William McKinley in Buffalo, NY; died Sept. 14. Leon Czolgosz executed for the crime.

1908—Feb. 1. King Carlos I of Portugal and his son Luis Felipe, in Lisbon.

1913—Feb. 23. Mexican Pres. Francisco I. Madero and Vice Pres. Jose Pino Suarez.—Mar. 18. George, king of Greece.

1914—June 28. Archduke Francis Ferdinand of Austria-Hungary and his wife in Sarajevo, Bosnia, by Gavrilo Princip.

1916—Dec. 30. Grigori Rasputin, powerful Russian monk.

1918—July 12. Grand Duke Michael of Russia, at Perm.—July 16. Nicholas II, abdicated as czar of Russia; his wife, the Czarina Alexandra; their son, Czarevitch Alexis; their daughters, Grand Duchesses Olga, Tatiana, Marie, Anastasia; and 4 members of their household, executed by Bolsheviks at Ekaterinburg.

1920—May 20. Mexican Pres. Gen. Venustiano Carranza in Tlaxcalantongo.

1922—Aug. 22. Michael Collins, Irish revolutionary.—Dec. 16. Polish Pres.Gabriel Narutowicz in Warsaw.

1923—July 20. Gen. Francisco "Pancho" Villa, ex-rebel leader, in Parral, Mexico.

1928—July 17. Gen. Alvaro Obregon, president-elect of Mexico, in San Angel, Mexico.

1932—May 6. Pres. Paul Doumer of France shot by Russian émigré, Pavel Gorgulov, in Paris.

1934—July 25. In Vienna, Austrian Chancellor Engelbert Dollfuss by Nazis.

1935—Sept. 8. U.S. Sen. Huey P. Long shot in Baton Rouge, LA, by Dr. Carl Austin Weiss; died Sept. 10.

1940—Aug. 20. Leon Trotsky (Lev Bronstein), 63, exiled Russian war minister, near Mexico City, by Ramon Mercador del Rio, a Spaniard.

1948—Jan. 30. Mohandas K. Gandhi, 78, shot in New Delhi, India, by Nathuram Vinayak Godse.—Sept. 17. Count Folke Bernadotte, UN mediator for Palestine, by Jewish extremists in Jerusalem.

1951—July 20. King Abdullah ibn Hussein of Jordan.—Oct. 16. Prime Min. Liaquat Ali Khan of Pakistan shot in Rawalpindi.

1956—Sept. 21. Pres. Anastasio Somoza of Nicaragua, shot in Leon; died Sept. 29.

1957—July 26. Pres. Carlos Castillo Armas of Guatemala, in Guatemala City by one of his own guards.

1958—July 14. King Faisal of Iraq; his uncle, Crown Prince Abdullah; and July 15, Prem. Nuri as-Said, by rebels in Baghdad.

1959—Sept. 25. Prime Min. Solomon Bandaranaike of Ceylon, by Buddhist monk in Colombo.

1961—Jan. 17. Ex-Prem. Patrice Lumumba of the Congo, in Katanga Province.—May 30. Dominican dictator Rafael Leonidas Trujillo Molina, near Ciudad Trujillo.

1963—June 12. Medgar W. Evers, NAACP's Mississippi field secretary, shot dead by Byron De La Beckwith in Jackson, MS.—Nov. 2. Pres. Ngo Dinh Diem of South Vietnam and his brother, Ngo Dinh Nhu, in a military coup.—Nov. 22. U.S. Pres. John F. Kennedy shot while riding in motorcade in Dallas, TX; accused gunman Lee Harvey Oswald was murdered by Jack Ruby while awaiting trial.

1965—Jan. 21. Iranian Prem. Hassan Ali Mansour in Tehran; 4 executed.—Feb. 21. Malcolm X, black nationalist, shot in New York City.

1966—Sept. 6. Prime Min. Hendrik F. Verwoerd of South Africa stabbed to death in parliament at Cape Town.

1968—Apr. 4. Rev. Dr. Martin Luther King Jr. fatally shot in Memphis, TN; James Earl Ray convicted of crime.—June 5. Sen. Robert F. Kennedy (D, NY) shot in Los Angeles; Sirhan Sirhan, convicted of crime.

1971—Nov. 28. Prime Min. Wasfi Tal of Jordan, in Cairo, by Palestinian guerrillas.

1973—Mar. 2. U.S. Amb. Cleo A. Noel Jr., U.S. Charge d'Affaires George C. Moore, and Belgian Charge d'Affaires Guy Eid killed by Palestinian guerrillas in Khartoum, Sudan.

1974—Aug. 19. U.S. Amb. to Cyprus, Rodger P. Davies, killed by sniper's bullet in Nicosia.

1975—Feb. 11. Pres. Richard Ratsimandrava, of Madagascar, shot in Tananarive.—Mar. 25. King Faisal of Saudi Arabia shot by nephew Prince Musad Abdel Aziz, in royal palace in Riyadh.—Aug. 15. Bangladesh Pres. Sheik Mujibur Rahman killed in coup.

1976—Feb. 13. Nigerian head of state, Gen. Murtala Ramat Mohammed, by self-styled "young revolutionaries."

1977—Mar. 16. Kamal Jumblat, Lebanese Druse chieftain, shot near Beirut.—Mar. 18. Congo Pres. Marien Ngouabi shot in Brazzaville.

1978—July 9. Former Iraqi Prem. Abdul Razak Al-Naif shot in London.

1979—Feb. 14. U.S. Amb. Adolph Dubs shot by Afghan Muslim extremists in Kabul.—Aug. 27. Lord Mountbatten, World War II hero, and 2 others killed when a bomb exploded on his fishing boat off the coast of Co. Sligo, Ire. IRA claimed responsibility.—Oct. 26. South Korean Pres. Park Chung Hee and 6 bodyguards fatally shot by Kim Jae Kyu, head of South Korean CIA, and 5 aides in Seoul.

1980—Apr. 12. Liberian Pres. William R. Tolbert slain in military coup.—Sept. 17. Former Nicaraguan Pres. Anastasio Somoza Debayle shot in Paraguay.

1981—Oct. 6. Egyptian Pres. Anwar al-Sadat shot by commandos while reviewing a military parade in Cairo; 7 others killed, 28 wounded; 4 convicted as assassins and executed.

1982—Sept. 14. Lebanese Pres.-elect Bashir Gemayel killed by bomb in east Beirut.

1983—Aug. 21. Philippine opposition leader Benigno Aquino Jr. shot by gunman at Manila International Airport.

1984—Oct. 31. Indian Prime Min. Indira Gandhi shot and killed by 2 Sikh bodyguards, in New Delhi.

1986—Feb. 28. Swedish Prem. Olof Palme shot by gunman on Stockholm street.

1987—June 1. Lebanese Prem. Rashid Karami killed when bomb exploded aboard a helicopter.

1988—Apr. 16. PLO military chief Khalil Wazir (Abu Jihad) gunned down by Israeli commandos in Tunisia.

1989—Aug. 18. Colombian presidential candidate Luis Carlos Galan killed by Medellín cartel drug traffickers at campaign rally in Bogotá.—Nov. 22. Lebanese Pres. Rene Moawad killed when bomb exploded next to his motorcade.

1990—Mar. 22. Presidential candidate Bernando Jamamillo Ossa shot by gunman at airport in Bogotá.

1991—May 21. Rajiv Gandhi, former prime min. of India, killed by bomb during election rally in Madras.

1992—June 29. Mohammed Boudiaf, pres. of Algeria, shot by gunman in Annaba.

1993—May 1. Ranasinghe Premadasa, pres. of Sri Lanka, killed by bomb in Colombo.

1994—Mar. 23. Luis Donaldo Colosio Murrieta, Mexican presidential candidate, shot by gunman Mario Aburto Martinez.
—Apr. 6. Burundian Pres. Cyprien Ntaryamira and Rwandan Pres. Juvenal Habyarimana killed, with 8 others, when their plane was apparently shot down.

1995—Nov. 4. Yitzhak Rabin, prime min. of Israel, shot by gunman Yigal Amir at peace rally in Tel Aviv.

1996—Oct. 2. Andrei Lukanov, former Bulgarian prime minister, shot outside his home by an unidentified gunman.

1998—Feb. 6. Claude Erigmac, prefect of Corsica, shot in the back while walking to a concert, by two unidentified gunmen.—Apr. 26. Guatemalan Rom. Catholic Bishop Juan Gerardi Conedera, human rights champion, found beaten to death in Guatemala City; 4 persons convicted, June 8, 2001.

1999—Mar. 23. Paraguayan Vice-Pres. Luis Maria Argaña, ambushed and shot to death, along with his driver, by four unidentified assailants.—Apr. 9. Niger's Pres. Ibrahim Bare Mainassara, ambushed and killed by dissident soldiers.—Oct. 27. Armenia's Prime Min. Vazgen Sarkissian, along with 7 others, was shot to death during a session of Parliament.

2000—Jan. 15. Serbian paramilitary leader Zeljko Raznjatovic (alias Arkan), with 2 others, shot and killed by unidentified gunman in Belgrade hotel lobby; 4 suspects later charged with the killing.— June 8. Brig. Gen. Stephen Saunders, Britain's senior military representative in Greece, shot and killed by 2 men on motorcycle, while driving a car in an Athens suburb.

2001—Jan. 16. Congolese Pres. Laurent Kabila, shot to death by a bodyguard at his presidential palace in the capital, Kinshasa.—June 1. Nepal's King Birendra, Queen Aiswarya, and 7 other royals fatally shot by Crown Prince Dipendra, who also fatally wounded himself.—Sept. 9. Afghan Northern Alliance (anti-Taliban) guerrilla leader Ahmed Shah Massoud, fatally injured in suicide-attack bombing in N. Afghanistan by 2 Arabs posing as journalists; died Sept. 15.—Sept. 24. Colombian culture minister Consuelo Araujo, kidnapped, later slain, by Revolutionary Armed Forces guerrillas.—Oct. 14. Abdel Rahman Hamad, a leader of Palestinian militant group Hamas, shot dead by Israeli military snipers.—Oct. 17. Israeli tourism minister Rehavam Zeevi, fatally shot; Popular Front for the Liberation of Palestine (PFLP) claimed responsibility.—Dec. 23. Nigerian Justice Min. Bola Ige, shot dead at his home in Ibadan.

2002—Feb. 14. Afghanistan's aviation and tourism minister, Abdul Rahman, beaten and stabbed to death at Kabul airport.—May 6. Dutch right-wing politician Pim Fortuyn shot dead outside a radio station in Hilversum, the Netherlands; Volkert van der Graaf, an animal rights activist, later sentenced to 18 years for the murder.—July 6. Afghan Vice Pres. Haji Abdul Qadir, shot dead outside his office in Kabul.—July 23. Salah Sherhada, a founder of the armed wing of Hamas, killed along with 14 civilians in an assassination air strike on Gaza City by an Israeli fighter jet.

2003—Mar. 12. Serbian Prime Min. Zoran Djindjic, shot dead by snipers outside governement headquarters in Belgrade.— Mar. 23. Abdul Majid Dar, ex-commander of Islamic militant group in Kashmir, killed by rival separatist gunmen while in secret negotiations with Indian gov.—Apr. 10. Shiite Muslim cleric Abdul Majid al-Khoei attacked by crowd, hacked to death at Imam Ali mosque in Najaf, Iraq.—Apr. 17. Sergei Yushenkov, former Russian legislator and Liberal Party head, shot dead outside apartment in Moscow.—Aug. 29. Prominent Shiite Muslim cleric Bakir al-Hakim killed in car bombing at Imam Ali mosque in Najaf, Iraq; several foreign suspects with al-Qaeda connections arrested.—Sept. 10. Swedish Foreign Min. Anna Lindh stabbed to death in dept. store in Stockholm.

Assassination Attempts

1912—Oct. 14. Former U.S. Pres. Theodore Roosevelt shot and wounded by demented man in Milwaukee, WI.

1933—Feb. 15. In Miami, FL, Joseph Zangara, anarchist, shot at Pres.-elect Franklin D. Roosevelt, but a woman seized his arm, and the bullet fatally wounded Mayor Anton J. Cermak, of Chicago, who died Mar. 6.

1944—July 20. Adolf Hitler was injured when a bomb, planted by a German officer, exploded in Hitler's headquarters. One aide was killed and 12 were injured in the explosion.

1950—Nov. 1. In an attempt to assassinate Pres. Harry Truman, 2 members of a Puerto Rican nationalist movement— Griselio Torresola and Oscar Collazo—tried to shoot their way into Blair House. Torresola was killed, and a White House policeman, Pvt. Leslie Coffelt, was fatally shot.

1970—Nov. 27. Pope Paul VI unharmed by knife-wielding assailant who attempted to attack him in Manila airport.

1972—May 15. Alabama Gov. George Wallace shot in Laurel, MD, by Arthur Bremer; seriously crippled.

1975—Sept. 5. Pres. Gerald R. Ford unharmed when a Secret Service agent grabbed a pistol aimed at him by Lynette (Squeaky) Fromme, a Charles Manson follower, in Sacramento.—Sept. 22. Pres. Ford again unharmed when Sara Jane Moore fired a revolver at him in San Francisco; a bystander helped deflect the shot.

1980—May 29. Civil rights leader Vernon E. Jordan Jr. shot and wounded in Ft. Wayne, IN.

1981—Jan. 16. Irish political activist Bernadette Devlin McAliskey and her husband shot and seriously wounded by 3 members of a Protestant paramilitary group in Co. Tyrone, Ire.—Mar. 30. Pres. Ronald Reagan, along with Press Sec. James Brady, Secret Service agent Timothy J. McCarthy, and Washington, DC, policeman Thomas Delahanty shot and seriously wounded by John W. Hinckley Jr. in Washington, DC.—May 13. Pope John Paul II and 2 bystanders shot and wounded by Mehmet Ali Agca, an escaped Turkish murderer, in St. Peter's Square, Rome.

1982—May 12. Pope John Paul II unharmed after guards overpowered a man with a knife, in Fatima, Portugal.

1984—Oct. 12. British Prime Min. Margaret Thatcher unharmed when a bomb, said to have been planted by the IRA, exploded at the Grand Hotel in Brighton, England, during a Conservative Party conference. Four died, including a member of Parliament.

1986—Sept. 7. Chilean Pres. Gen. Augusto Pinochet Ugarte escaped unharmed when his motorcade was attacked by rebels using rockets, bazookas, grenades, and rifles.

1995—June 26. Egyptian Pres. Hosni Mubarak unharmed when gunmen fired on his motorcade in Addis Ababa, Ethiopia. Four died, including 2 Ethiopian police officers.

1997—Feb. 12. Colombian Pres. Ernesto Samper Pizano unharmed when a bomb exploded on a runway in Barran-

quilla as his plane was preparing to land.—Apr. 30. Tajik Pres. Imamali Rakhmanov injured when a grenade was thrown at him.

1998—Feb. 9. Georgian Pres. Eduard A. Shevardnadze unharmed when gunmen fired on his motorcade in Tbilisi, Georgia. Three died, including 2 bodyguards and 1 assailant.

2000—Sept. 18. Armed men attempted to assassinate Côte d'Ivoire military leader Gen. Robert Guei in a predawn raid.

2002—Apr. 8. Afghan Defense Min. Muhammad Qassim Fahim, unharmed after bomb exploded in a Jalalabad marketplace as his motorcade passed. 5 others were killed.—Apr. 14. Leading Colombian presidential candidate Alvaro Uribe Velez unharmed after bomb exploded under parked bus as his motorcade passed in Barranquilla; 3 bystanders were killed.—May 6. Gulbuddin Hekmatyar, an Afghan warlord opposed to Karzai's interim government, survived an attempt on his life made outside Kabul by the CIA.—July 14. French Pres. Jacques Chirac, unharmed after Maxime Brunerie, a gunman with ties to neo-Nazi groups, fired at his open-top jeep during a Bastille Day parade in Paris.—Sept. 5. Afghan Pres. Hamid Karzai, unharmed after Abdul Rahman, apparently operating in connection with the Taliban, opened fire on his car in Kandahar.—Nov. 25. Turkmenistan Pres. Saparmurat Niyazov unharmed after gunmen open fire on his motorcade in Ashgabat.

2003—Mar 1. Akhmed Kadyrov, administrative head of Chechnya, unharmed when his motorcade was fired on by rebels in Argun, Chechnya. 7 others were killed.—June 10. Abdel Aziz al-Rantisi, 2nd-in-command of militant group Hamas, wounded in Gaza when Israeli helicopters fired missiles at his car.—Sept. 6. Hamas cofounder Sheikh Ahmed Yassin wounded when Israeli planes bombed his home.

Notable U.S. Kidnappings Since 1924

Robert Franks, 13, in Chicago, **May 22, 1924**, by 2 youths, Richard Loeb and Nathan Leopold, who killed boy. Demand for $10,000 ignored. Loeb died in prison; Leopold paroled 1958.

Charles A. Lindbergh Jr., 20 mos. old, in Hopewell, NJ, **Mar. 1, 1932**; found dead **May 12**. Ransom of $50,000 paid to man identified as Bruno Richard Hauptmann, 35, paroled German convict who entered U.S. illegally. Hauptmann was convicted after spectacular trial at Flemington, and electrocuted in Trenton, NJ, prison, **Apr. 3, 1936**.

William A. Hamm Jr., 39, in St. Paul, **June 15, 1933**. $100,000 paid. Alvin Karpis given life, paroled in 1969.

Charles F. Urschel, in Oklahoma City, **July 22, 1933**. Released **July 31** after $200,000 paid. George "Machine Gun" Kelly and 5 others sentenced to life.

Brooke L. Hart, 22, in San Jose, CA. Thomas Thurmond and John Holmes arrested after demanding $40,000 ransom. When Hart's body was found in San Francisco Bay, **Nov. 26, 1933**, a mob attacked the jail and lynched the 2 kidnappers.

George Weyerhaeuser, 9, in Tacoma, WA, **May 24, 1935**. Returned home **June 1** after $200,000 paid. Kidnappers given 20 to 60 years.

Charles Mattson, 10, in Tacoma, WA, **Dec. 27, 1936**. Found dead **Jan. 11, 1937**. Kidnapper asked $28,000, but failed to contact for delivery.

Arthur Fried, in White Plains, NY, **Dec. 4, 1937**. Body not found. Two kidnappers executed.

Robert C. Greenlease, 6, taken from Kansas City, MO, school **Sept. 28, 1953**, held for $600,000. Body was found Oct. 7. Bonnie Brown Heady and Carl A. Hall pleaded guilty and were executed.

Peter Weinberger, 32 days old, Westbury, NY, **July 4, 1956**, for $2,000 ransom, not paid. Child found dead. Angelo John LaMarca, 31, convicted, executed.

Lee Crary, 8, in Everett, WA, **Sept. 22, 1957**; $10,000 ransom, not paid. He escaped after 3 days, led police to George E. Collins, who was convicted.

Frank Sinatra Jr., 19, from hotel room in Lake Tahoe, CA, **Dec. 8, 1963**. Released **Dec. 11** after his father paid $240,000 ransom. Three men sentenced to prison.

Barbara Jane Mackle, 20, abducted **Dec. 17, 1968**, from Atlanta, GA, motel; found unharmed 3 days later, buried in a coffin-like box 18 inches underground, after her father had paid $500,000 ransom; Gary Steven Krist sentenced to life, Ruth Eisenmann-Schier to 7 years.

Mrs. Roy Fuchs, 35, and 3 children held hostage 2 hours, **May 14, 1969**, in Long Island, NY, released after her husband, a bank manager, paid kidnappers $129,000 in bank funds; 4 men arrested, ransom recovered.

Virginia Piper, 49, abducted **July 27, 1972**, from her home in suburban Minneapolis; found unharmed near Duluth 2 days later after husband paid $1 million ransom.

Patricia "Patty" Hearst, 19, taken from her Berkeley, CA, apartment **Feb. 4, 1974**. "Symbionese Liberation Army" captors demanded her father, publisher Randolph Hearst, give

millions to the area's poor. Implicated in a San Francisco bank holdup, **Apr. 15**. The FBI, **Sept. 18, 1975**, captured her and others; they were indicted on various charges. Patricia Hearst convicted of bank robbery, **Mar. 20, 1976**; released from prison under executive clemency, **Feb. 1, 1979**. In 1978, William and Emily Harris were sentenced to 10 years to life for the kidnapping; both were paroled in 1983.

J. Reginald Murphy, 40, an editor of *Atlanta* (GA) *Constitution*, kidnapped **Feb. 20, 1974**; freed **Feb. 22** after newspaper paid $700,000 ransom. William A. H. Williams arrested; most of the money recovered.

E. B. Reville, Hepzibah, GA, banker, and wife, Jean, kidnapped **Sept. 30, 1974**. Ransom of $30,000 paid. He was found alive; Jean Reville was found dead **Oct. 2**.

Jack Teich, Kings Point, NY, steel executive, seized **Nov. 12, 1974**; released **Nov. 19** after payment of $750,000.

Adam Walsh, 6, abducted from a Hollywood, FL, department store, **July 27, 1981**. Although his severed head was found 2 weeks later, his body was never recovered. John Walsh, Adam's father, became active in raising awareness about missing children.

Sidney J. Reso, oil company executive, seized **Apr. 29, 1992**; died **May 3**; Arthur D. Seale and wife, Irene, arrested **June 19**. Arthur Seale pleaded guilty, sentenced to life in prison; Irene Seale sentenced to 20-year prison term.

Polly Klaas, 12, Petaluma, CA, abducted at knife point, **Oct. 1, 1993**, during a slumber party at her home. Police arrested Richard Allen Davis on **Nov. 30**; he led them to her body, found **Dec. 4** in wooded area of Cloverdale, CA. Davis found guilty **June 18, 1996**, and sentenced to death **Sept. 26**.

Marshall I. Wais, 79, owner of 2 San Francisco steel companies, kidnapped **Nov. 19, 1996**, from his San Francisco home. Released unharmed the same day after $500,000 ransom paid; Thomas William Taylor and Michael K. Robinson arrested the same day.

Daniel Pearl, 38, reporter for *Wall Street Journal*, disappeared **Jan. 23, 2002**, while researching story in Karachi, Pakistan. His captors **Jan. 27** sent an e-mail demanding release of suspected Taliban and al-Qaeda fighters held by the U.S. British-born militant Ahmad Omar Saeed Sheikh **Feb. 14** admitted to organizing the kidnapping and said Pearl was dead. Sheikh and 3 others were convicted **July 15** of kidnapping and murder by a judge in Hyderabad.

Danielle van Dam, 7, discovered missing from her parents' San Diego home **Feb. 2, 2002**; body found **Feb. 27**. Neighbor David Westerfield convicted of her murder **Aug. 21** and sentenced to death **Jan. 7, 2003**.

Elizabeth Smart, 14, was abducted from her home in Salt Lake City, UT, **June 5, 2002**, allegedly by Brian D. Mitchell and forced to live with Mitchell and wife Wanda for nine months in various U.S. cities; found walking down street with captors in Sandy, UT, 15 miles from Smart family home, when passersby spotted Mitchell, **Mar. 12, 2003**.

NATIONAL DEFENSE

Chief Commanding Officers of the U.S. Military

Chairman, Joint Chiefs of Staff
Gen. Richard B. Myers (USAF)

Vice Chairman
Gen. Peter Pace (USN)

The Joint Chiefs of Staff consists of the Chairman and Vice Chairman of the Joint Chiefs of Staff; the Chief of Staff, U.S. Army; the Chief of Naval Operations; the Chief of Staff, U.S. Air Force; and the Commandant of the Marine Corps.

Army

Chief of Staff	Date of Rank
Gen. Peter J. Schoomaker	Oct. 4, 1997

Other Generals	
Abizaid, John	June 27, 2003
Brown, Bryan D.	Aug. 25, 2003
Hendrix, John W.	Nov. 23, 1999
Hill, James T.	Aug. 18, 2002
Kern, Paul J.	Oct. 30, 2001
Kernan, William F.	July 2000
Schwartz, Thomas A.	Aug. 31, 1998

Air Force

Chief of Staff	Date of Rank
Gen. John P. Jumper	Nov. 17, 1997

Other Generals	
Begert, William J.	May 1, 2001
Cook, Donald G.	Dec, 17, 2001
Eberhart, Ralph E.	Aug. 1, 1997
Foglesong, Robert H.	Nov. 5, 2001
Handy, John W.	July 1, 2000
Holland, Charles R.	Dec. 1, 2000
Hornburg, Hal M.	Aug. 1, 2000
Lord, Lance W.	Apr. 19, 2002
Lyles, Lester L.	July 1, 1999
Martin, Gregory S.	June 1, 2000
Myers, Richard B.	Sept. 1, 1997
Wald, Charles F.	Jan. 1, 2003

Navy

Chief of Naval Operations	Date of Rank
Adm. Vernon E. Clark	Nov. 1, 1999

Other Admirals	
Bowman, Frank L. (submariner)	Oct. 1, 1996
Doran, Walter F. (surface warfare)	May 4, 2002
Ellis, James O., Jr. (aviator)	Jan. 1, 1999
Fallon, William J. (aviator)	Nov. 1, 2000
Fargo, Thomas B. (submariner)	Dec. 1, 1999
Giambastiani, Edmund P., Jr. (submariner)	Oct. 2, 2002
Johnson, Gregory G. (aviator)	Feb. 1, 2002
Mullen, Michael G.	NA
Natter, Robert J. (surface warfare)	Sept. 1, 2000

Marine Corps

Commandant of the Marine Corps (CMC)	Date of Rank
Gen. Michael W. Hagee	Jan. 13, 2003

Other Generals	
Nyland, William L.	Sept. 4, 2002
Pace, Peter	Nov. 1, 2000

Coast Guard

Commandant, with rank of Admiral	Date of Rank
Thomas H. Collins	May 30, 2002

Vice Commandant, with rank of Vice Admiral	
Thomas J. Barrett	May 30, 2002

Unified Combatant Commands Commanders in Chief

U.S. European Command, Stuttgart-Vaihingen, Germany — Gen. James L. Jones (USMC)

U.S. Pacific Command, Honolulu, HI — Adm. Thomas B. Fargo (USN)

U.S. Joint Forces Command, Norfolk, VA — Adm. Edmund P Giambastiani

U.S. Special Operations Command, MacDill AFB, Florida — Gen. Bryan D. Brown (U.S. Army)

U.S. Transportation Command, Scott AFB. Illinois — Gen. John W. Handy (USAF)

U.S. Central Command, MacDill AFB, Florida — Gen. John Abizaid (U.S. Army)

U.S. Southern Command, Miami, FL — Gen. James T. Hill (U.S. Army)

U.S. Northern Command, Peterson AFB, Colorado — Gen. Ralph E. Eberhart (USAF)

U.S. Strategic Command, Offutt AFB, Nebraska — Adm. James O. Ellis Jr. (USN)

North Atlantic Treaty Organization International Commands

NATO Headquarters:
Chairman, NATO Military Committee — Gen. Harald Kujat (Germany)

Strategic Command:
Allied Command Operations (ACO) — Gen. James L. Jones (USMC), Supreme Allied Commander, Europe

Subordinate Commands:
Allied Forces South Europe (AFSOUTH) — Adm. Gregory G. Johnson (USN), Commander-in-Chief, South

Allied Forces North Europe (AFNORTH) — Gen. Sir John Deverell KCB OBE (Royal Army, UK), Commander-in-Chief, North

Allied Command Atlantic (ACLANT) — Adm. Ian Forbes (Royal Navy, UK), Supreme Allied Commander, Atlantic

Western Atlantic (WESTLANT) — Adm. Robert J. Natter (USN), Commander-in-Chief, Western Atlantic

Southern Atlantic (SOUTHLANT) — Vice Adm. Americo da Silva Santos (Portuguese Navy), Commander-in-Chief, Southern Atlantic

Eastern Atlantic (EASTLANT) — Adm. Sir Jonathan Band (Royal Navy, UK), Commander-in-Chief, Eastern Atlantic

Strategic Command: Allied Command Transformation (ACT) — Adm. Edmund P. Giambastiani (USN), Supreme Allied Commander Transformation

Principal U.S. Military Training Centers

Army

Name, PO address	ZIP	Nearest city	Name, PO address	ZIP	Nearest city
Aberdeen Proving Ground, MD	21005	Aberdeen	Fort Lee, VA	23801	Petersburg
Carlisle Barracks, PA	17013	Carlisle	Fort McClellan, AL.	36205	Anniston
Fort Benning, GA	31905	Columbus	Fort Rucker, AL	36362	Dothan
Fort Bliss, TX	79916	El Paso	Fort Sill, OK.	73503	Lawton
Fort Bragg, NC	28307	Fayetteville	Fort Leonard Wood, MO	65473	St. Robert
Fort Gordon, GA.	30905	Augusta	Joint Readiness Training Center,		
Fort Huachuca, AZ	85613	Sierra Vista	Ft. Polk, LA	71459	Leesville
Fort Jackson, SC	29207	Columbia	National Training Center, Ft. Irwin, CA	92311	Barstow, CA
Fort Knox, KY.	40121	Radcliff	The Judge Advocate General's Legal		
Fort Leavenworth, KS	66027	Leavenworth	Center and School, VA	22903	Charlottesville

Navy

Name, PO address	ZIP	Nearest city	Name, PO address	ZIP	Nearest city
Naval Education & Training Ctr.	32508	Pensacola, FL	Naval Submarine School	06349	Groton, CT
Naval Air Training Center	78419	Corpus Christi,TX	Naval Training Ctr., Great Lakes	60088	N. Chicago, IL
Training Command Fleet	92113	San Diego, CA	Naval War College	02841	Newport, RI
Naval Aviation Schools Command	32508	Pensacola, FL	Naval Air Tech. Training Ctr.	32508	Pensacola, FL
Naval Education & Training Ctr.	02841	Newport, RI	Fleet Antisubmarine Warfare	92147	San Diego, CA
Naval Post Graduate School	93943	Monterey, CA			

Marine Corps

Name, PO address	ZIP	Nearest city	Name, PO address	ZIP	Nearest city
MCB Camp Lejeune, NC	28542	Jacksonville	MCAS Cherry Point, NC	28533	Havelock
MCBCamp Pendleton, CA	92055	Oceanside	MCAS Miramar, CA	92145	San Diego
MCB Kaneohe Bay, HI	96863	Kailua	MCAS New River, NC	28545	Jacksonville
MCAGCCTwentynine Palms, CA	92278	Palm Springs	MCAS Beaufort, SC	29904	Beaufort
MCCDC Quantico, VA	22134	Quantico	MCAS Yuma, AZ	85369	Yuma
MCRD Parris Island, SC	29905	Beaufort	MCMWTC Bridgeport, CA	93517	Bridgeport
MCRD San Diego, CA	92140	San Diego			

MCB = Marine Corps Base. MCCDC = Marine Corps Combat Development Command. MCAS = Marine Corps Air Station. MCRD = Marine Corps Recruit Depot. MCAGCC = Marine Corps Air-Ground Combat Center. MCMWTC = Marine Corps Mountain Warfare Training Center.

Air Force

Name, PO address	ZIP	Nearest city	Name, PO address	ZIP	Nearest city
Goodfellow AFB, TX	76908	San Angelo	Maxwell AFB, AL	36112	Montgomery
Keesler AFB, MS	39534	Biloxi	Sheppard AFB, TX	76311	Wichita Falls
Lackland AFB, TX	78236	San Antonio			

All are Air Education and Training Command Bases.

Personal Salutes and Honors, U.S.

The U.S. **national salute**, 21 guns, is also the salute to a national flag. U.S. independence is commemorated by the salute to the Union—one gun for each state—fired at noon July 4, at all military posts provided with suitable artillery.

A 21-gun salute on arrival and departure, with 4 ruffles and flourishes, is rendered to the **president** of the United States, to a former president, and to a president-elect. The national anthem or "Hail to the Chief," as appropriate, is played for the president, and the national anthem for the others. A 21-gun salute on arrival and departure, with 4 ruffles and flourishes, also is rendered to the **sovereign or chief of state of a foreign country** or a member of a reigning royal family, and the national anthem of his or her country is played. The music is considered an inseparable part of the salute and immediately follows the ruffles and flourishes without pause. For the Honors March, generals receive the "General's March," admirals receive the "Admiral's March," and all others receive the 32-bar medley of "The Stars and Stripes Forever."

GRADE, TITLE, OR OFFICE	SALUTE (IN GUNS) Arriving	Leaving	Ruffles and flourishes	Music
Vice president of United States	19		4	Hail, Columbia
Speaker of the House	19		4	Honors March
U.S. or foreign ambassador	19		4	Nat. anthem of official
Premier or prime minister	19		4	Nat. anthem of official
Secretary of Defense, Army, Navy, or Air Force	19	19	4	Honors March
Other cabinet members, Senate president pro tempore, governor, or chief justice of U.S.	19		4	Honors March
Chairman, Joint Chiefs of Staff	19	19	4	
Army chief of staff, chief of naval operations, Air Force chief of staff, Marine commandant	19	19	4	Honors March
General of the Army, general of the Air Force, fleet admiral	19	19	4	
Generals, admirals	17	17	4	
Assistant secretaries of Defense, Army, Navy, or Air Force	17	17	4	Honors March
Chair of a committee of Congress	17		4	Honors March

OTHER SALUTES (on arrival only) include: 15 guns, with 3 ruffles and flourishes, for U.S. envoys or ministers and foreign envoys or ministers accredited to the U.S.; 15 guns, for a lieutenant general or vice admiral; 13 guns, with 2 ruffles and flourishes, for a major general or rear admiral (upper half) and for U.S. ministers resident and ministers resident accredited to the U.S.; 11 guns, with 1 ruffle and flourish, for a brigadier general or rear admiral (lower half) and for U.S. charges d'affaires and like officials accredited to the U.S.; 11 guns, no ruffles and flourishes, for consuls general accredited to the U.S.

Military Units, U.S. Army and Air Force

ARMY UNITS. Squad: In infantry usually 4-10 enlisted personnel under a staff sergeant. **Platoon:** In infantry 3-4 squads under a lieutenant. **Company:** Headquarters section and 3-4 platoons under a captain. (Company-size unit in the artillery is a battery; in the cavalry, a troop.) **Battalion:** Hdqts. and 3-5 companies under a lieutenant colonel. (Battalion-size unit in the cavalry is a squadron.) **Brigade:** Hdqts. and 3 or more battalions under a colonel. **Division:** Hdqts. and 3 brigades with artillery, combat support, and combat service support units under a major general. **Army Corps:** Two or more divisions with corps troops under a lieutenant general. **Field Army:** Hdqts. and 2 or more corps with field Army troops under a general.

AIR FORCE UNITS. Flight: Numerically designated flights are the lowest level unit in the Air Force. They are used primarily where there is a need for small mission elements to be incorporated into an organized unit. **Squadron:** A squadron is the basic unit in the Air Force. It is used to designate the mission units in operational commands. **Group:** The group is a flexible unit composed of 2 or more squadrons whose functions may be operational, support, or administrative in nature. **Wing:** An operational wing normally has 2 or more assigned mission squadrons in an area such as combat, flying training, or airlift. **Numbered Air Forces:** Normally an operationally oriented agency, the numbered air force is designed for the control of 2 or more wings with the same mission and/or geographical location. **Major Command:** A major subdivision of the Air Force that is assigned a major segment of the USAF mission. Major Command is composed of 3 or more numbered air forces.

The Federal Service Academies

U.S. Military Academy, West Point, NY. Founded 1802. Awards BS degree and Army commission for a 5-year service obligation. For admissions information, write Admissions Office, Bldg. 606, USMA, West Point, NY 10996.

U.S. Naval Academy, Annapolis, MD. Founded 1845. Awards BS degree and Navy or Marine Corps commission for a 5-year service obligation. For admissions information, write Candidate Guidence Office, Naval Academy, Annapolis, MD 21402-5018.

U.S. Air Force Academy, Colorado Springs, CO. Founded 1954. Awards BS degree and Air Force commission for a 6-year service obligation. For admissions information, write Registrar, U.S. Air Force Academy, CO 80840-5025.

U.S. Coast Guard Academy, New London, CT. Founded 1876. Awards BS degree and Coast Guard commission for a 5-year service obligation. For admissions information, write Director of Admissions, Coast Guard Academy, New London, CT 06320-8103.

U.S. Merchant Marine Academy, Kings Point, NY. Founded 1943. Awards BS degree, a license as a deck, engineer, or dual officer, and a U.S. Naval Reserve commission. Service obligations vary according to options taken by the graduate. For admissions information, write Admission Office, U.S. Merchant Marine Academy, Kings Point, NY 11024.

U.S. Army, Navy, Air Force, Marine Corps, and Coast Guard Insignia

Source: Dept. of the Army, Dept. of the Navy, Dept. of the Air Force, U.S. Dept. of Defense

Army

General of the Armies — Gen. John J. Pershing (1860-1948), the only person to have held this rank, in life, was authorized to prescribe his own insignia, but never wore in excess of four stars. The rank originally was established posthumously by Congress for George Washington in 1799, and he was promoted to the rank by joint resolution of Congress, approved by Pres. Gerald Ford, Oct. 19, 1976.

General of the Army — Five silver stars fastened together in a circle and the coat of arms of the United States in gold color metal with shield and crest enameled.

General	Four silver stars
Lieutenant General	Three silver stars
Major General	Two silver stars
Brigadier General	One silver star
Colonel	Silver eagle
Lieutenant Colonel	Silver maple leaf
Major	Gold maple leaf
Captain	Two silver bars
First Lieutenant	One silver bar
Second Lieutenant	One gold bar

Warrant Officers

Grade Five — Silver bar with 4 enamel silver squares
Grade Four — Silver bar with 4 enamel black squares
Grade Three — Silver bar with 3 enamel black squares
Grade Two — Silver bar with 2 enamel black squares
Grade One — Silver bar with 1 enamel black square

Noncommissioned Officers

Sergeant Major of the Army (E-9) — Three chevrons above 3 arcs, with an American Eagle centered on the chevrons, flanked by 2 stars—one star on each side of the eagle. Also wears distinctive red and white shield collar insignia.

Command Sergeant Major (E-9) — Three chevrons above 3 arcs with a 5-pointed star with a wreath around the star between the chevrons and arcs.

Sergeant Major (E-9) — Three chevrons above 3 arcs with a 5-pointed star between the chevrons and arcs.

First Sergeant (E-8) — Three chevrons above 3 arcs with a lozenge between the chevrons and arcs.

Master Sergeant (E-8) — Three chevrons above 3 arcs.

Sergeant First Class (E-7) — Three chevrons above 2 arcs.

Staff Sergeant (E-6) — Three chevrons above 1 arc.

Sergeant (E-5) — Three chevrons.

Corporal (E-4) — Two chevrons.

Specialists

Specialist (E-4) — Eagle device only.

Other enlisted

Private First Class (E-3) — One chevron above one arc.
Private (E-2) — One chevron.
Private (E-1) — None.

Air Force

Insignia for Air Force officers are identical to those of the Army. Insignia for enlisted personnel are worn on both sleeves and consist of a star and an appropriate number of rockers. Chevrons appear above 5 rockers for the top 3 noncommissioned officer ranks, as follows (in ascending order): Master Sergeant, 1 chevron; Senior Master Sergeant, 2 chevrons; and Chief Master Sergeant, 3 chevrons. The insignia of the Chief Master Sergeant of the Air Force has 3 chevrons and a wreath around the star design.

Navy

The following stripes are worn on the lower sleeves of the Service Dress Blue uniform. They are of gold embroidery.

Rank	Insignia
Fleet Admiral*	1 two inch with 4 one-half inch
Admiral	1 two inch with 3 one-half inch
Vice Admiral	1 two inch with 2 one-half inch
Rear Admiral (upper half)	1 two inchwith 1 one-half inch
Rear Admiral (lower half)	1 two inch
Captain	4 one-half inch
Commander	3 one-half inch
Lieutenant Commander	2 one-half inch with 1 one-quarter inch between
Lieutenant	2 one-half inch
Lieutenant (j.g.)	1 one-half inch with one-quarter inch above
Ensign	1 one-half inch

Warrant Officer-W-4 — ½″ stripe with 1 break
Warrant Officer W-3 — ½″ stripe with 2 breaks, 2″ apart
Warrant Officer W-2 — ½″ stripe with 3 breaks, 2″ apart

Enlisted personnel (noncommissioned petty officers)—A rating badge worn on the upper left sleeve, consisting of a spread eagle, appropriate number of chevrons, and centered specialty mark.

*The rank of Fleet Admiral is reserved for wartime use only.

Marine Corps

Marine Corps' distinctive cap and collar ornament is the Marine Corps Emblem—a combination of the American eagle, a globe, and an anchor. Marine Corps and Army officer insignia are similar. Marine Corps enlisted insignia, although basically similar to the Army's, feature crossed rifles beneath the chevrons. Marine Corps enlisted rank insignia are as follows:

Sergeant Major of the Marine Corps (E-9) — Same as Sergeant Major (below) but with Marine Corps emblem in the center with a 5-pointed star on both sides of the emblem.

Sergeant Major (E-9) — Three chevrons above 4 rockers with a 5-pointed star in the center.

Master Gunnery Sergeant (E-9) — Three chevrons above 4 rockers with a bursting bomb insignia in the center.

First Sergeant (E-8) — Three chevrons above 3 rockers with a diamond in the middle.

Master Sergeant (E-8) — Three chevrons above 3 rockers with crossed rifles in the middle.

Gunnery Sergeant (E-7) — Three chevrons above 2 rockers with crossed rifles in the middle.

Staff Sergeant (E-6) — Three chevrons above 1 rocker with crossed rifles in the middle.

Sergeant (E-5) — Three chevrons above crossed rifles.

Corporal (E-4) — Two chevrons above crossed rifles.

Lance Corporal (E-3) — One chevron above crossed rifles.

Private First Class (E-2) — One chevron.

Private (E-1) — None.

Coast Guard

Coast Guard insignia follow Navy custom, with certain minor changes such as the officer cap insignia. The Coast Guard shield is worn on both sleeves of officers and on the right sleeve of all enlisted personnel.

WORLD ALMANAC QUICK QUIZ

What percent of U.S. armed forces on active duty in 2003 were women?

(a) 4%   (b) 9%   (c) 15%   (d) 22%

For the answer look in this chapter, or see page 1008.

U.S. Army Personnel on Active Duty[1]

Source: Dept. of the Army, U.S. Dept. of Defense

Date[2]	Total strength[3]	Commissioned officers			Warrant officers		Enlisted personnel		
		Total	Male	Female[4]	Male[5]	Female	Total	Male	Female
1940.........	267,767	17,563	16,624	939	763	—	249,441	249,441	—
1942.........	3,074,184	203,137	190,662	12,475	3,285	—	2,867,762	2,867,762	—
1943.........	6,993,102	557,657	521,435	36,222	21,919	—	6,413,526	6,358,200	55,325
1944.........	7,992,868	740,077	692,351	47,726	36,893	10	7,215,888	7,144,601	71,287
1945.........	8,266,373	835,403	772,511	62,892	56,216	44	7,374,710	7,283,930	90,780
1946.........	1,889,690	257,300	240,643	16,657	9,826	18	1,622,546	1,605,847	16,699
1950.........	591,487	67,784	63,375	4,409	4,760	22	518,921	512,370	6,551
1955.........	1,107,606	111,347	106,173	5,174	10,552	48	985,659	977,943	7,716
1960.........	871,348	91,056	86,832	4,224	10,141	39	770,112	761,833	8,279
1965.........	967,049	101,812	98,029	3,783	10,285	23	854,929	846,409	8,520
1970.........	1,319,735	143,704	138,469	5,235	23,005	13	1,153,013	1,141,537	11,476
1975.........	781,316	89,756	85,184	4,572	13,214	22	678,324	640,621	37,703
1980 (Sept. 30) .	772,661	85,339	77,843	7,496	13,265	113	673,944	612,593	61,351
1985 (Sept. 30) .	776,244	94,103	83,563	10,540	15,296	288	666,557	598,639	67,918
1990 (Mar. 31) ..	746,220	91,330	79,520	11,810	15,177	470	639,713	567,015	72,698
1995.........	521,036	72,646	62,250	10,396	12,053	599	435,807	377,832	57,975
1996 (May 31) ..	493,330	68,850	58,875	9,975	11,456	660	408,511	351,669	56,842
1997 (May 31) ..	487,297	67,986	58,270	9,716	11,021	719	403,072	342,817	60,255
1998.........	491,707	67,048	56,650	10,398	10,989	661	402,000	345,149	56,851
1999.........	479,100	66,613	56,952	9,661	10,767	757	388,211	329,803	58,408
2000.........	471,633	66,344	56,391	9,953	10,608	781	393,900	333,947	59,953
2001.........	478,918	64,809	54,570	10,239	10,575	795	398,983	336,264	62,719
2002.........	485,536	66,446	55,715	10,731	10,900	812	404,363	341,794	62,569
2003.........	496,067	80,754[6]	NA	NA	NA	NA	411,013	NA	NA

NA = Not available. (1) Represents strength of the active Army, including Philippine Scouts, retired Regular Army personnel on extended active duty, and National Guard and Reserve personnel on extended active duty; excludes U.S. Military Academy cadets, contract surgeons, and National Guard and Reserve personnel not on extended active duty. (2) June 30, unless otherwise noted. (3) Data for 1940 to 1946 include personnel in the Army Air Forces and its predecessors (Air Service and Air Corps). (4) Includes women doctors, dentists, and Medical Service Corps officers for 1946 and subsequent years, women in the Army Nurse Corps for all years, and the Women's Army Corps and Women's Medical Specialists Corps (dietitians, physical therapists, and occupational specialists) for 1943 and subsequent years. (5) Act of Congress approved Apr. 27, 1926, directed the appointment as warrant officers of field clerks still in active service. Includes flight officers as follows: 1943, 5,700; 1944, 13,615; 1945, 31,117; 1946, 2,580.

U.S. Navy Personnel on Active Duty

Source: Dept. of the Navy, U.S. Dept. of Defense
(As of June 30, 2003)

Date	Officers	Nurses	Enlisted	Officer Candidates	Total	Date	Officers	Nurses	Enlisted	Officer Candidates	Total
1940 (June) .	13,162	442	144,824	2,569	160,997	1995 (May) ..	61,075	—	402,626	—	463,701
1945 (June) .	320,293	11,086	2,988,207	61,231	3,380,817	1996 (June) ..	60,013	—	376,595	—	436,608
1950 (June) .	42,687	1,964	331,860	5,037	381,538	1997 (June) ..	57,341	—	340,616	—	397,957
1960 (June) .	67,456	2,103	544,040	4,385	617,984	1998 (Sept.) ..	55,007	—	326,196	—	381,203
1970 (June) .	78,488	2,273	605,899	6,000	692,660	1999 (June) ..	55,726	—	322,372	—	378,098
1980 (June)[1] .	63,100	—	464,100	—	527,200	2000 (Oct.) ..	53,698	—	320,212	—	373,910
1990 (Sept.) .	74,429	—	530,133	—	604,562	2001 (Aug.) ..	54,177	—	317,100	—	375,618
1993 (Mar.) ..	66,787	—	445,409	—	512,196	2002 (June) ..	55,506	—	324,712	—	384,576
1994 (Apr.) ..	64,430	—	418,378	—	482,808	2003 (June) ..	55,852	—	321,739	3,188	380,779

(1) Starting in 1980, "Nurses" are included with "Officers," and "Officer Candidates" are included with "Enlisted."

U.S. Marine Corps Personnel on Active Duty

Source: Dept. of the Marines, U.S. Dept. of Defense
(As of June 30, 2003)

Year	Officers	Enlisted	Total	Year	Officers	Enlisted	Total	Year	Officers	Enlisted	Total
1940 ...	1,800	26,545	28,345	1991 ...	19,753	174,287	194,040	1998 ..	17,984	154,648	172,632
1945 ...	37,067	437,613	474,680	1992 ...	19,132	165,397	184,529	1999 ..	17,892	155,250	173,142
1950 ...	7,254	67,025	74,279	1993 ...	18,878	161,205	180,083	2000 ..	17,897	154,744	172,641
1960 ...	16,203	154,418	170,621	1994 ...	18,430	159,949	178,379	2001 ..	18,072	152,559	170,631
1970 ...	24,941	234,796	259,737	1995 ...	18,017	153,929	171,946	2002 ..	18,472	154,913	173,385
1980 ...	18,198	170,271	188,469	1996 ...	18,146	154,141	172,287	2003 ..	18,908	160,814	179,722
1990 ...	19,958	176,694	196,652	1997 ...	18,089	154,240	172,329				

U.S. Air Force Personnel on Active Duty

Source: Air Force Dept., U.S. Dept. of Defense
(as of June 30, 2003)

Year[1]	Strength	Year[1]	Strength	Year[1]	Strength	Year[1]	Strength	Year[1]	Strength	Year[1]	Strength
1918 ..	195,023	1942 ..	764,415	1960 ..	814,213	1991 ..	510,432	1996 ..	389,400	2000 ..	357,777
1920 ..	9,050	1943 ..	2,197,114	1970 ..	791,078	1992 ..	470,315	1997 ..	378,681	2001 ..	351,935
1930 ..	13,531	1944 ..	2,372,292	1980 ..	557,969	1993 ..	444,351	1998 ..	363,479	2002 ..	369,721
1940 ..	51,165	1945 ..	2,282,259	1986 ..	608,200	1994 ..	426,327	1999 ..	357,929	2003 ..	373,116
1941 ..	152,125	1950 ..	411,277	1990 ..	535,233	1995 ..	400,051				

(1) Prior to 1947, data are for U.S. Army Air Corps and Air Service of the Signal Corps.

U.S. Coast Guard Personnel on Active Duty

Source: U.S. Coast Guard, U.S. Dept. of Defense
(as of July 2003)

Year	Total	Officers	Cadets	Enlisted	Year	Total	Officers	Cadets	Enlisted	Year	Total	Officers	Cadets	Enlisted
1970 ..	37,689	5,512	653	31,524	1994 .	37,284	7,401	881	29,002	1999 .	35,266	7,135	880	27,251
1980 .	39,381	6,463	877	32,041	1995 .	36,731	7,489	841	28,401	2000 .	35,712	7,154	863	27,695
1985 .	38,595	6,775	733	31,087	1996 .	35,229	7,270	830	27,129	2001 .	35,328	7,112	631	27,585
1990 .	37,308	6,475	820	29,860	1997 .	34,717	7,079	868	26,770	2002 .	37,166	7,267	694	29,205
1992 .	39,185	7,348	919	30,918	1998 .	34,890	7,140	805	26,945	2003 .	39,000	7,532	983	30,859
1993 .	38,832	7,724	691	30,417										

Chairmen of the Joint Chiefs of Staff, 1949-2003

Gen. of the Army Omar N. Bradley, USA . . 8/16/49 –8/14/53
Adm. Arthur W. Radford, USN . . . . 8/15/53 – 8/14/57
Gen. Nathan F. Twining, USAF. . . . . 8/15/57 – 9/30/60
Gen. Lyman L. Lemnitzer, USA . . . . 10/1/60 – 10/30/62
Gen. Maxwell D. Taylor, USA . . . . 10/1/62 – 7/3/64
Gen. Earle G. Wheeler, USA . . . . 7/3/64 – 7/2/70
Adm. Thomas H. Moorer, USN . . . . 7/3/70 – 6/30/74
Gen. George S. Brown, USAF . . . . 7/1/74 – 6/20/78

Gen. David C. Jones, USAF . . . . 6/21/78 – 6/18/82
Gen. John W. Vessey, Jr., USA . . . . 6/18/82 – 9/30/85
Adm. William J. Crowe, Jr., USN . . . . 10/1/85 – 9/30/89
Gen. Colin L. Powell, USA. . . . . 10/1/89 – 9/30/93
Gen. John M. Shalikashvili, USA. . . . . 10/1/93 – 9/30/97
Gen. Henry H. Shelton, USA. . . . . 10/1/97 – 9/30/01
Gen. Richard B. Myers . . . . 10/1/01 –

Women in the U.S. Armed Forces

Source: U.S. Dept. of Defense, U.S. Census Bureau

Women in the Army, Navy, Air Force, Marines, and Coast Guard are fully integrated with male personnel. Expansion of military women's programs began in the Department of Defense in fiscal year 1973.

Admission of women to the service academies began in the fall of 1976.

Under rules instituted in 1993, women were allowed to fly combat aircraft and serve aboard warships. Women remained restricted from service in ground combat units.

Between Apr. 1993 and July 1994, almost 260,000 positions in the armed forces were opened to women. By the mid-1990s, 80% of all jobs and more than 90% of all career fields in the military had been opened to women. By mid-2000, women made up 14% of the armed forces. This figure had grown to 15.1% by Jan. 2003, with about 212,000 women on active duty.

Women Active Duty Troops in 2003

Service	% Women
Army.	15.4
Navy.	14.5
Marines	5.7
Air Force.	19.3
Coast Guard.	11.0

Women on Active Duty, All Services[*]: 1973-2003

Year	% Women	Year	% Women
1973 . .	2.5	1993. . .	11.6
1975 . .	4.6	2000. . .	14.4
1981 . .	8.9	2003. . .	15.1
1987 . .	10.2		

[*]Not incl. the Coast Guard, which is not a part of the Defense Dept. and is now a part of the Dept. of Homeland Security.

For Further Information on the U.S. Armed Forces

Army — Office of the Chief of Public Affairs, Attention: Media Relations Division—MRD, Army 1500, Wash., DC 20310-1500. **Website:** www.army.mil
Navy — Chief of Information, 1200 Navy Pentagon, Wash., DC 20350-1200. **Website:** www.navy.mil
Air Force — Office of Public Affairs, 1690 Air Force, Pentagon, Wash., DC 20330-1690. **Website:** www.af.mil

Marine Corps — Marine Corps Headquarters , Division of Public Affairs, U.S. Marine Corps, Wash., DC 20380-1775. **Website:** www.usmc.mil
Coast Guard — Commandant (G-IPA), U.S. Coast Guard, 2100 Second St. SW, Wash., DC 20593-0001. **Website:** www.uscg.mil

Additional information on all the U.S. Armed Forces branches, as well as many other related organizations, can be accessed through DefenseLINK, the official Internet site of the Dept. of Defense: www.defenselink.mil

African American Service in U.S. Wars

American Revolution. About 5,000 African Americans served in the Continental Army, mostly in integrated units, some in all-black combat units.
Civil War. Some 200,000 African Americans served in the Union Army; 38,000 were killed, and 22 won the Medal of Honor (the nation's highest award).
World War I. About 367,000 African Americans served in the armed forces, 100,000 in France.
World War II. Over 1 mil African Americans served in the armed forces; all-black fighter and bomber AAF units and infantry

divisions gave distinguished service. (By 1954, armed forces were completely desegregated.)
Korean War. Approximately 3,100 African Americans lost their lives in combat.
Vietnam War. 274,937 African Americans served in the armed forces (1965-74); 5,681 were killed in combat.
Persian Gulf War. About 104,000 African Americans served in the Kuwaiti theater—20% of all U.S. troops, compared with 8.7% of all troops for World War II and 9.8% for Vietnam.
Iraq War. 57 African-American military deaths (as of Sept. 2003).

Defense Contracts, 2002

Source: U.S. Dept. of Defense

(in thousands of dollars)

Listed are the 50 companies (including their subsidiaries) or organizations receiving the largest dollar volume of prime contract awards from the U.S. Department of Defense during fiscal year 2002.

Lockheed Martin.	$16,997,272	Textron.	$908,785	Dell Computer Corp.	$504,969
Boeing	16,551,756	Triwest Healthcare Alliance .	823,741	The Titan Corporation.	501,630
Northrop Grumman	8,732,668	Computer Sciences	807,671	Jacobs Engineering Group . .	486,024
Raytheon	6,995,085	URS Corporation	800,825	Halliburton.	483,670
General Dynamics	6,962,131	Booz Allen & Hamilton	687,553	Mitre	474,294
United Technologies.	3,607,184	GM GDLS Defense Group. .	678,307	Aerospace Corporation	473,061
Science Applications Intl. . . .	2,074,920	Alliant Techsystems.	674,013	Electronic Data Systems . . .	468,395
TRW.	2,026,546	Boeing Sikorsky		Stewart & Stevenson	
Health Net	1,691,430	Comanche Team	661,832	Services	439,939
L-3 Communications		Cardinal Health	649,582	Johnson Controls.	434,210
Holding.	1,660,048	North American Airlines. . . .	622,199	Longbow Limited Liability . .	411,099
General Electric	1,559,979	Oshkosh Truck.	601,664	WorldCom	403,530
United Defense Industries . .	1,514,163	Exxon Mobil	570,877	Javelin Joint Venture	401,438
Dyncorp	1,359,408	N.V. Koninklijke		Government of Canada.	394,578
Humana.	1,304,691	Nederlandesche	539,104	FedEx Corp.	385,781
Honeywell International	1,278,371	Veritas Capital		Harris	381,477
BAE Systems PLC.	1,115,608	Management LLC	521,866	International Business	
Bechtel Group, Inc..	1,029,712	Washington Group		Machines.	379,892
ITT Industries	994,167	International.	505,916	Johns Hopkins University . .	370,572

U.S. Veteran Population, 2003

Source: U.S. Dept. of Veterans Affairs; as of December 2002

TOTAL VETERANS IN CIVILIAN LIFE[1]	**25,179,316**
Total wartime veterans[2]	**18,790,522**
Total Gulf War	3,783,414
Gulf War with service in Vietnam era	338,942
Gulf War with no prior wartime service	3,444,472
Total Vietnam era	8,210,925
Vietnam era with service in Korean conflict	248,825
Vietnam era with no prior wartime service	7,492,934

Total Korean conflict	3,580,249
Korean conflict with service in WWII	305,374
Korean conflict with no prior wartime service	2,895,826
World War II	4,369,925
Total peacetime veterans	**6,388,925**
Service between Vietnam era and Gulf War only	3,469,042
Service between Korean conflict and Vietnam era only	2,723,365
Other peacetime	196,387

NOTE: Details may not add to total shown because of rounding. (1) There are an indeterminate number of Mexican Border period veterans. (2) The total for "wartime veterans" consists only of veterans from each listed war that had no prior wartime service. Figures are for U.S. veterans worldwide. Source: VetPop2001, VA Office of the Actuary.

Veterans Compensation and Pension Case Payments

Source: Office of Policy Planning and Preparedness, Dept. of Veterans Affairs

Fiscal year	Living veteran cases	Deceased veteran cases	Total cases	Total expenditures (dollars)	Fiscal year	Living veteran cases	Deceased veteran cases	Total cases	Total expenditures (dollars)
1900	752,510	241,019	993,529	$138,462,130	1990	2,746,329	837,596	3,583,925	$14,674,411,000
1910	602,622	318,461	921,083	159,974,056	1995	2,668,576	661,679	3,330,255	17,765,045,000
1920	419,627	349,916	769,543	316,418,030	1996	2,671,026	637,232	3,308,258	17,055,809,000
1930	542,610	298,223	840,833	418,432,809	1997	2,666,785	613,976	3,280,761	19,284,287,000
1940	610,122	239,176	849,298	429,138,465	1998	2,668,030	594,782	3,262,812	20,164,598,000
1950	2,368,238	658,123	3,026,361	2,009,462,298	1999	2,673,167	578,508	3,251,675	21,023,864,000
1960	3,008,935	950,802	3,959,737	3,314,761,383	2000	2,672,407	563,754	3,236,161	21,963,216,000
1970	3,127,338	1,487,176	4,614,514	5,253,839,611	2001	2,669,156	548,589	3,217,745	23,198,139,000
1980	3,195,395	1,450,785	4,646,180	11,046,637,368	2002	2,744,866	539,796	3,284,662	25,407,916,000

Directors of the Central Intelligence Agency

In 1942, Pres. Franklin D. Roosevelt established the Office of Strategic Services (OSS); it was disbanded in 1945. In 1946, Pres. Harry Truman established the Central Intelligence Group (CIG) to operate under the National Intelligence Authority (NIA). A 1947 law replaced the NIA with the National Security Council and the CIG with the Central Intelligence Agency.

Director	Served	Appointed by President	Director	Served	Appointed by President
Adm. Sidney W. Souers	1946	Truman	William E. Colby	1973-1976	Nixon
Gen. Hoyt S. Vandenberg	1946-1947	Truman	George Bush	1976-1977	Ford
Adm. Roscoe H. Hillenkoetter	1947-1950	Truman	Adm. Stansfield Turner	1977-1981	Carter
Gen. Walter Bedell Smith	1950-1953	Truman	William J. Casey	1981-1987	Reagan
Allen W. Dulles	1953-1961	Eisenhower	William H. Webster	1987-1991	Reagan
John A. McCone	1961-1965	Kennedy	Robert M. Gates	1991-1993	Bush
Adm. William F. Raborn Jr.	1965-1966	Johnson	R. James Woolsey	1993-1995	Clinton
Richard Helms	1966-1973	Johnson	John M. Deutch	1995-1997	Clinton
James R. Schlesinger	1973	Nixon	George J. Tenet	1997-	Clinton

The Medal of Honor

The Medal of Honor is the highest military award for bravery that can be given to any individual in the United States. The first Army Medals were awarded on Mar. 25, 1863, and the first Navy Medals went to sailors and Marines on Apr. 3, 1863.

On Dec. 21, 1861, Pres. Abraham Lincoln signed into law a bill to create the Navy Medal of Honor. Lincoln later (July 14, 1862) approved a resolution providing for the presentation of Medals of Honor to enlisted men of the Army and Voluntary Forces, making it a law. The law was amended on March 3, 1863, to extend its provisions to include officers as well as enlisted men.

The Medal of Honor is awarded in the name of Congress to a person who, while a member of the armed forces, distinguishes himself or herself conspicuously by gallantry and intrepidity at the risk of life above and beyond the call of duty while engaged in an action against any enemy of the United States; while engaged in military operations involving conflict with an opposing foreign force; or while serving with friendly foreign forces engaged in an armed conflict against an opposing armed force in which the United States is not a belligerent party. The deed performed must have been one of personal bravery or self-sacrifice so conspicuous as to clearly distinguish the individual above his or her comrades and must have involved risk of life. Incontestable proof of the performance of service is required, and each recommendation for award of this decoration is considered on the standard of extraordinary merit.

Prior to World War I, the 2,625 Army Medal of Honor awards up to that time were reviewed to determine which past awards met new stringent criteria. The Army removed 911 names from the list, most of them former members of a volunteer infantry group during the Civil War who had been induced to extend their enlistments when they were promised the medal. However, in 1977 a medal was restored to Dr. Mary Walker, and in 1989 medals were restored to Buffalo Bill Cody and 7 other Indian scouts.

Since then, Medals of Honor have been awarded for:

World War I	124	Korean War	131
Peacetime (1920-40)	18	Vietnam War	245
World War II	441	Somalia	2

The figure for World War II includes 7 African-American soldiers who were awarded Medals of Honor (6 of them posthumously) in Jan. 1997. Previously, no black soldier had received the medal for World War II service; an Army inquiry begun in 1993 concluded that the prevailing political climate and Army practices of the time had prevented proper recognition of heroism on the part of black soldiers in that war. In June, 2002, 22 Asian Americans received the award for World War II service.

The most recent recipient was Humbert "Rocky" Versace, who was awarded the medal posthumously on July 8, 2002. Versace spent 23 months as a prisoner of the Viet Cong, distinguishing himself by resisting interrogation and demanding humane treatment for his fellow captives. He was executed by his captors in Sept. 1965.

Active Duty U.S. Military Personnel Strengths, Worldwide, 2003

Source: U.S. Dept. of Defense

(as of Sept. 30, 2002)

U.S. TERRITORIES & SPEC. LOCATIONS		Portugal	992	**NORTH AFRICA, NEAR EAST, & SOUTH ASIA***	
U.S., 48 contiguous states	969,215	Serbia (incl. Kosovo)	2,804		
Alaska	15,906	Spain	2,621	Afghanistan	0
Hawaii	34,608	Turkey	1,587	Bahrain	1,560
Guam	3,149	United Kingdom	10,258	Diego Garcia	548
Puerto Rico	2,592	Afloat	5,003	Egypt	433
Transients	27,863	**Regional Total[1]**	**112,548**	Kuwait	567
Afloat	127,767			Saudi Arabia	776
Regional Total[1]	**1,181,150**	**EAST ASIA & PACIFIC**		Afloat	588
		Australia	171	**Regional Total[1]**	**4,820**
EUROPE		Japan	41,848		
Belgium	1,458	Korea, South	37,743	**OTHER WESTERN HEMISPHERE**	
Bosnia and Herzegovina	3,082	Singapore	167		
Germany	68,701	Thailand	125	Canada	148
Greece	593	Afloat	16,090	Cuba (Guantánamo)	549
Iceland	1,665	**Regional Total[1]**	**96,385**	Honduras	402
Italy	12,466			Afloat	324
Macedonia, F.Y.R. of	146	**SUB-SAHARAN AFRICA TOTAL[1]**	**263**	**Regional Total[1]**	**1,913**
Netherlands	629				
Norway	123	**FORMER SOVIET UNION TOTAL**	**129**	**TOTAL WORLDWIDE[2]**	**1,411,634**

*Special Forces personnel involved in Operation Enduring Freedom in Afghanistan not reported by Dept. of Defense. (1) Countries and areas with fewer than 100 assigned U.S. military members not listed; regional totals include personnel stationed in those countries and areas not shown. (2) Total worldwide also includes undistributed personnel.

Nations With Largest Armed Forces, by Active-Duty Troop Strength[1]

Source: *The Military Balance, 2002-2003* (International Institute for Strategic Studies, published by Oxford University Press, UK)

	Troop strength		Defense expend. ($ bil)	Tanks (MBT) (army only)	Navy Cruisers/ Frigates/ Destroyers	Sub-marines	Combat aircraft	
	Active troops (thousands)	Reserve troops					FGA (air force only)	Fighters
1. CHINA	2,270	500–600	46	7,010	42F/21D	69	838+	948+
2. UNITED STATES	1,414	1,259	322.4	7,620	27C/35F/55D*	72	3,000+ aircraft	
3. India	1,298	535	14.2	7,782	11F/8D*	16	510	155
4. N. Korea	1,082	4,700	2	3,500	3F	26	541 FGA/FTR	
5. RUSSIA	988	20,000	63.7	43,740	7C/10F/14D*	53	606	908
6. S. Korea	686	4,500	11.2	2,300	9F/6D	20	468 FGA/FTR	
7. Pakistan	620	513	2.4	2,100	8F	10	110	202
8. Turkey	514	378	7.2	4,205	19F	13	485 FGA/FTR	
9. Iran	520	350	4.7	1,565	3F	6	186	57
10. Vietnam	484	3,000–4,000	2.4	1,315	6F	2	65	124
11. Egypt	443	254	4.3	3,600	10F/1D	4	133	333
12. Iraq[2]	389	650	1.4	2,600	—	—	130	180
13. Taiwan	370	1,657	10.4	900+	11D/21F	4	386	57
14. Myanmar	444	—	1.1	178	—	—	60	22
15. Syria	319	354	1.9	4,700	2F	—	168	312
16. Germany	296	390	26.9	2,490	12F/2D	14	446 aircraft	
17. Thailand	306	200	1.8	320	12F	—	133	—
18. Ukraine	302	1,000	4.9	3,905	1C/2	1	63	277
19. Indonesia	297	400	0.86	—	17F	2	31	12
20. Brazil	287	1,115	10.5	178	14F	4	80	18
21. FRANCE	260	100	32.9	786	1C/3D/30F	10	449 aircraft	
22. Ethiopia	252	—	0.58	300	—	—	55	—
23. Japan	239	47	39.5	1,040	44D/10F	16	40	280
24. Italy	216	65	21	1,018	1C/4D/14F	6	261 aircraft	
25. United Kingdom	210	256	34.7	594	11D/21F	16	332 aircraft	
26. Poland	163	234	3.4	1,150	1D/3F	4	179	22
27. Saudi Arabia	124	—	24.3	1,050	4F	—	100	180
28. Morocco	196	150	1.3	744	2F	—	53	15
29. Mexico	192	300	5.7	—	3D/8F	—	107 aircraft	
30. Eritrea	172	120	0.17	100	—	—	17 aircraft[3]	

Nations with known strategic nuclear capability are shown in all capital letters. India and Pakistan HAVE tested nuclear devices. MBT = main battle tank. FGA = fighter, ground attack; rgt = regiment; sqn = squadron (12-24 aircraft); wg = wing (72 fighter aircraft). *Denotes navies with aircraft carriers, as follows: United States 12, United Kingdom 3, France 1, India 1, Italy 1, Russian 1, Brazil 1, Spain 1, Thailand 1. (1) All figures are for Aug. 2002, except Defense Expenditure, which is for 2001. (2) Figures are before war in Mar. 2003. (3) Serviceability in doubt. — = not available.

Nuclear Arms Treaties and Negotiations: A Historical Overview

Aug. 5, 1963—Limited Test Ban Treaty signed in Moscow by U.S., USSR, and Britain; prohibited testing of nuclear weapons in space, above ground, and under water.

Jan. 27, 1967—Outer Space Treaty banned the introduction of other weapons of mass destruction in space.

July 1, 1968—Nuclear Nonproliferation Treaty, with U.S., USSR, and Great Britain as major signers, limited spread of nuclear material for military purposes by agreement not to help nonnuclear nations get or make nuclear weapons.

May 26, 1972—Strategic Arms Limitation Treaty (SALT I) signed in Moscow by U.S. and USSR. This short-term agreement imposed a 5-year freeze on both testing and deployment of intercontinental ballistic missiles (ICBMs) as well as submarine-launched ballistic missiles (SLBMs). In the area of defensive nuclear weapons, the separate **ABM Treaty**, signed on the same occasion, limited antiballistic missiles to 2 sites of 100 antiballistic missile launchers in each country (amended in 1974 to 1 site in each country).

July 3, 1974—ABM Treaty Revision (protocol on anti-ballistic missile systems) and **Threshold Test Ban Treaty** on limiting underground testing of nuclear weapons to 150 kilotons were signed by U.S. and USSR in Moscow.

Sept. 1977—U.S. and USSR agreed to continue to abide by **SALT I**, despite its expiration date.

June 18, 1979—SALT II signed in Vienna by the U.S. and USSR, constrained offensive nuclear weapons, limiting each side to 2,400 missile launchers and heavy bombers; ceiling to apply until Jan. 1, 1985. Treaty also set a subceiling of 1,320 ICBMs and SLBMs with multiple warheads on each side. SALT II never reached the Senate floor for ratification because Pres. Jimmy Carter withdrew support following Dec. 1979 Soviet invasion of Afghanistan.

Dec. 8, 1987—Intermediate-Range Nuclear Forces (INF) Treaty signed in Washington, DC, by U.S. and USSR, eliminating all U.S. and Soviet intermediate- and shorter-range nuclear missiles from Europe and Asia. Ratified, with conditions, by U.S. Senate May 27, 1988; by USSR June 1, 1988. Entered into force June 1, 1988.

July 31, 1991—Strategic Arms Reduction Treaty (START I) signed in Moscow by USSR and U.S. to reduce strategic offensive arms by about 30% in 3 phases over 7 years. START I was the first treaty to mandate reductions by the superpowers. Treaty was approved by U.S. Senate Oct. 1, 1992.

With the Soviet Union breakup in Dec. 1991, 4 former Soviet republics became independent nations with strategic nuclear weapons—Russia, Ukraine, Kazakhstan, and Belarus. The last 3 agreed in principle in 1992 to transfer their nuclear weapons to Russia and ratify START I. The Russian Supreme Soviet voted to ratify, Nov. 4, 1992, but Russia decided not to provide instruments of ratification until the other 3 republics ratified START I and acceded to the Nuclear Nonproliferation Treaty (NPT) as nonnuclear nations. By late 1994, all 3 nations had done so, and NPT entered into force on Dec. 5, 1994.

Jan. 3, 1993—START II signed in Moscow by U.S. and Russia, called for both sides to reduce their long-range nuclear arsenals to about one-third of their then-current levels within a decade and disable and dismantle launching systems. The U.S. ratified START II Jan. 26, 1996; Russia ratified it Apr. 13, 2000. On Sept. 26, 1997, the U.S. and Russia signed an agreement that would delay the dismantling of launching systems under START II to the end of 2007.

Sept. 24, 1996—Comprehensive Test Ban Treaty (CTBT) signed by U.S. and Russia. The CTBT banned all nuclear weapon tests and other nuclear explosions. It was intended to help prevent the nuclear powers from developing more advanced weapons, while limiting the ability of other states to acquire such devices. As of Oct. 2003, the CTBT had been signed by 169 nations, including China, Russia, the U.S., the U.K, and France; ratified by 105, including France, Russia, and the U.K., but not the U.S. or China. Enters into force after 44 nuclear-capable states ratify it. As of Oct. 1, 2003, 32 of the 44 had done so.

Sept. 1997—ABM Treaty amended to allow greater flexibility in development of shorter-range nuclear weapons.

May 24, 2002—Nuclear Arms Reduction Pact (Treaty of Moscow) signed by U.S. and Russia in Moscow, committed both countries to cutting nuclear arsenals to 1,700 to 2,200 warheads each, down from about 6,000, by 2012. No intermediate timetable established, but joint committee set up for monitoring implementation; either side allowed to back out with 90 days notice. Ratified by U.S. Senate, Mar. 6, 2003.

June 2002—U.S. formally withdrew from the **ABM Treaty**, effective June 13, with the intent of developing a defensive missile system. Russia, June 14, announced its withdrawal from **START II**, stating that U.S. withdrawal from the ABM Treaty effectively invalidated START II.

Jan. 10, 2003—N. Korea withdrew from Nuclear Nonproliferation Treaty.

Monthly Military Pay Scale[1]

Source: U.S. Dept. of Defense; effective Jan. 1, 2003

Grade	<2	2	4	6	8	10	12	14	16	18	20	22	24	26
Commissioned officers														
O-10..	NA	NA	NA	NA	NA	NA	NA	NA	NA	NA	$12,078	$12,137	$12,389	$12,829
O-9 ...	NA	NA	NA	NA	NA	NA	NA	NA	NA	NA	10,564	10,716	10,936	11,320
O-8..	$7,475	$7,719	$7,927	$8,129	$8,468	$8,547	$8,869	$8,961	$9,238	$9,639	10,009	10,256	10,256	10,256
O-7 ...	6,211	6,499	6,739	6,931	7,121	7,340	7,559	7,780	8,469	9,051	9,051	9,051	9,051	9,097
O-6 ...	4,603	5,057	5,389	5,410	5,641	5,672	5,672	5,995	6,564	6,899	7,233	7,424	7,616	7,990
O-5 ...	3,838	4,323	4,679	4,865	4,977	5,223	5,403	5,636	5,992	6,162	6,329	6,520	6,520	6,520
O-4 ...	3,311	3,833	4,146	4,383	4,638	4,955	5,201	5,373	5,471	5,528	5,528	5,528	5,528	5,528
O-3 ...	2,911	3,300	3,884	4,070	4,274	4,406	4,623	4,736	4,736	4,736	4,736	4,736	4,736	4,736
O-2 ...	2,515	2,865	3,411	3,481	3,481	3,481	3,481	3,481	3,481	3,481	3,481	3,481	3,481	3,481
O-1 ...	2,184	2,273	2,747	2,747	2,747	2,747	2,747	2,747	2,747	2,747	2,747	2,747	2,747	2,747
Commissioned officers with over 4 years active duty service as enlisted member or warrant officer														
O-3E..	NA	NA	3,884	4,070	4,274	4,406	4,623	4,806	4,911	5,054	5,054	5,054	5,054	5,054
O-2E..	NA	NA	3,411	3,481	3,592	3,779	3,923	4,031	4,031	4,031	4,031	4,031	4,031	4,031
O-1E..	NA	NA	2,747	2,934	3,042	3,153	3,262	3,411	3,411	3,411	3,411	3,411	3,411	3,481
Warrant officers														
W-5...	NA	NA	NA	NA	NA	NA	NA	NA	NA	NA	5,169	5,347	5,525	5,703
W-4...	3,008	3,236	3,420	3,578	3,734	3,891	4,045	4,204	4,356	4,512	4,664	4,823	4,978	5,138
W-3...	2,747	2,862	3,017	3,141	3,282	3,467	3,581	3,772	3,916	4,058	4,202	4,266	4,407	4,548
W-2...	2,417	2,555	2,763	2,838	2,993	3,149	3,264	3,377	3,454	3,580	3,706	3,831	3,957	3,957
W-1...	2,134	2,309	2,501	2,663	2,782	2,888	3,007	3,085	3,203	3,321	3,410	3,410	3,410	3,410
Enlisted members														
E-9 ...	NA	NA	NA	NA	NA	3,564	3,645	3,747	3,867	3,987	4,181	4,344	4,506	4,757
E-8 ...	NA	NA	NA	NA	2,975	3,061	3,141	3,238	3,342	3,530	3,626	3,788	3,878	4,099
E-7 ...	2,069	2,258	2,428	2,516	2,668	2,753	2,838	2,990	3,066	3,139	3,183	3,332	3,428	3,671
E-6 ...	1,771	1,948	2,117	2,204	2,401	2,477	2,562	2,637	2,663	2,710	2,710	2,710	2,710	2,710
E-5 ...	1,625	1,734	1,904	2,037	2,152	2,237	2,283	2,283	2,283	2,283	2,283	2,283	2,283	2,283
E-4 ...	1,503	1,580	1,749	1,824	1,824	1,824	1,824	1,824	1,824	1,824	1,824	1,824	1,824	1,824
E-3 ...	1,356	1,442	1,528	1,528	1,528	1,528	1,528	1,528	1,528	1,528	1,528	1,528	1,528	1,528
E-2 ...	1,290	1,290	1,290	1,290	1,290	1,290	1,290	1,290	1,290	1,290	1,290	1,290	1,290	1,290
E-1>4[2]	1,150	1,150	1,150	1,150	1,150	1,150	1,150	1,150	1,150	1,150	1,150	1,150	1,150	1,150
E-1<4[2]	1,064	NA	NA	NA	NA	NA	NA	NA	NA	NA	NA	NA	NA	NA

NA = Not applicable. (1) Basic pay is limited for O-7 to O-10 to $11,874.90 per month, and for O-6 and below to $10,449.90 per month. (2) E-1>4 = E-1 grade personnel with 4 or more months service. E-1<4 = E-1 grade personnel with less than 4 months service.

Casualties in Principal Wars of the U.S.

Source: U.S. Dept. of Defense, U.S. Coast Guard

Data prior to World War I are based on incomplete records in many cases. Casualty data are confined to dead and wounded personnel and, therefore, exclude personnel captured or missing in action who were subsequently returned to military control. Dash (—) indicates information is not available. off. = officers.

WAR	Branch of service	Number serving	CASUALTIES			
			Battle deaths	Other deaths	Wounds not mortal[7]	Total[13]
Revolutionary War	Total	—	4,435	—	6,188	10,623
1775-83	Army	184,000	4,044	—	6,004	10,048
	Navy	to	342	—	114	456
	Marines	250,000	49	—	70	119
War of 1812	Total	286,730[8]	2,260	—	4,505	6,765
1812-15	Army	—	1,950	—	4,000	5,950
	Navy	—	265	—	439	704
	Marines	—	45	—	66	111
Mexican War	Total	78,789[8]	1,733	11,550	4,152	17,435
1846-48	Army	—	1,721	11,550	4,102	17,373
	Navy	—	1	—	3	4
	Marines	—	11	—	47	58
	Coast Guard[12]	71 off.	—	—	—	—
Civil War						
Union forces	Total	2,213,363[8]	140,415	224,097	281,881	646,392
1861-65	Army	2,128,948	138,154	221,374	280,040	639,568
	Navy	—	2,112	2,411	1,710	6,233
	Marines	84,415	148	312	131	591
Confederate forces	Total	—	74,524	59,297	—	133,821
(estimate)[1]	Army	600,000	—	—	—	—
1863-66	Navy	to	—	—	—	—
	Marines	1,500,000	—	—	—	—
	Coast Guard[12]	219 off.	1	—	—	1
Spanish-American War	Total	307,420	385	2,061	1,662	4,108
1898	Army[3]	280,564	369	2,061	1,594	4,024
	Navy	22,875	10	0	47	57
	Marines	3,321	6	0	21	27
	Coast Guard[12]	660	0	—	—	—
World War I	Total	4,743,826	53,513	63,195	204,002	320,710
April 6, 1917 - Nov. 11, 1918	Army[4]	4,057,101	50,510	55,868	193,663	300,041
	Navy	599,051	431	6,856	819	8,106
	Marines	78,839	2,461	390	9,520	12,371
	Coast Guard	8,835	111	81	—	192
World War II	Total	16,353,659	292,131	115,185	671,846	1,079,162
Dec. 7, 1941 - Dec. 31, 1946[2]	Army[5]	11,260,000	234,874	83,400	565,861	884,135
	Navy[6]	4,183,466	36,950	25,664	37,778	100,392
	Marines	669,100	19,733	4,778	68,207	91,718
	Coast Guard	241,093	574	1,343	—	1,917
Korean War[9]	Total	5,764,143	33,667	3,249	103,284	140,200
June 25, 1950 - July 27, 1953	Army	2,834,000	27,709	2,452	77,596	107,757
	Navy	1,177,000	493	160	1,576	2,226
	Marines	424,000	4,267	339	23,744	28,353
	Air Force	1,285,000	1,198	298	368	1,864
	Coast Guard	44,143	—	—	—	—
Vietnam War[10]	Total	8,752,000	47,393	10,800	153,363	211,556
Aug. 4, 1964 - Jan. 27, 1973	Army	4,368,000	30,929	7,272	96,802	135,003
	Navy	1,842,000	1,631	931	4,178	6,740
	Marines	794,000	13,085	1,753	51,392	66,230
	Air Force	1,740,000	1,741	842	931	3,514
	Coast Guard	8,000	7	2	60	69
Persian Gulf War	Total	467,939[11]	148	151	467	766
1991	Army	246,682	98	105	—	203
	Navy	98,852	6	14	—	20
	Marines	71,254	24	26	—	50
	Air Force	50,751	20	6	—	26
	Coast Guard	400	—	—	—	—
Iraq War[14]	Total	269,363	196[15]	113[15]	1,268	1,577
2003	Army	99,664	131	84[15]	974	1,189
	Navy	61,018	4	3[15]	10	17
	Marines	66,166	57	25	279	361
	Air Force	42,515	4	1	5	10
	Coast Guard	1,250	—	—	—	—

(1) Authoritative statistics for the Confederate forces are not available. An estimated 26,000-31,000 Confederate personnel died in Union prisons. (2) Data are for Dec. 1, 1941, through Dec. 31, 1946, when hostilities were officially terminated by Presidential Proclamation; few battle deaths or wounds not mortal were incurred after Japanese acceptance of Allied peace terms on Aug. 14,1945. Numbers serving Dec. 1, 1941-Aug. 31, 1945, were: Total—14,903,213; Army—10,420,000; Navy—3,883,520; Marine Corps—599,693. (3) Number serving covers the period April 21-Aug. 13, 1898, while dead and wounded data are for the period May 1-Aug. 31, 1898. Active hostilities ceased on Aug. 13, 1898, but ratifications of the treaty of peace were not exchanged between the U.S. and Spain until April 11, 1899. (4) Includes Army Air Forces battle deaths and wounds not mortal, as well as casualties suffered by American forces in northern Russia to Aug. 25, 1919, and in Siberia to April 1, 1920. Other deaths covered the period April 1, 1917-Dec. 31, 1918. (5) Includes Army Air Forces. (6) Battle deaths and wounds not mortal include casualties incurred in Oct. 1941 due to hostile action. (7) Marine Corps data for Iraq War, World War II, the Spanish-American War, and prior wars represent the number of individuals wounded, whereas all other data in this column represent the total number (incidence) of wounds. (8) As reported by Commissioner of Pensions in his Annual Report for Fiscal Year 1903. (9) As a result of an ongoing Dept. of Defense review of available Korean War casualty record information, updates to previously reported figures for battle deaths and other deaths are reflected in this table. (10) Number serving covers the period Aug. 4, 1964-Jan. 27, 1973 (date of ceasefire). Includes casualties incurred in Mayaguez Incident. Wounds not mortal exclude 150,332 persons not requiring hospital care. (11) Estimated. (12) Actually the U.S. Revenue Cutter Services, predecessor to the U.S. Coast Guard. (13) Totals do not include categories for which no data are listed. (14) Including deaths from May 1, 2003 (declared end of major combat) through Sept. 25, 2003. Military deaths through Apr. 30 only totaled 155 combat-related and 23 other. (15) 14 Army and 1 Navy deaths whose status was under review are included in these figures.

Homeland Security

On Nov. 25, 2002, Pres. George W. Bush signed a measure creating a cabinet-level **Department of Homeland Security (DHS)**. It became operational on Jan. 24, 2003, headed by Sec. Tom Ridge, a former Pennsylvania governor (1995-2001).

The main **objectives** of the DHS are to prevent terrorist attacks within the U.S., reduce the vulnerability to attacks, and minimize the effects of such attacks should they occur. The DHS is responsible for border and transportation security, protecting critical infrastructure, coordinating emergency response activities, and overseeing research and development for homeland security efforts. The new department also responds to natural disasters.

Following the attacks of Sept. 11, 2001, Pres. Bush created a small-scale advisory office known as the Office of Homeland Security. When a congressional inquiry in the summer of 2002 revealed extensive failures in intelligence gathering and communication, sentiment grew in favor of creating a large agency that could coordinate anti-terrorism efforts. The final plan passed by Congress in Nov. 2002 called for the integration of 22 federal agencies from many different departments.

The DHS is organized into 5 directorates: Border and Transportation Security, Emergency Preparedness, Science and Technology, Information Analysis and Infrastructure Protection, and Management, the administrative arm of the department. The U.S. Coast Guard, Secret Service, and Bureau of Citizenship and Immigration Services (formerly part of the INS) became part of DHS as discrete entities, separate from the directorates. The fiscal year 2004 budget for the new department was $36.2 billion.

Emergency Preparedness

In Feb. 2003, the DHS launched its public service "Ready" campaign in association with the Ad Council and the Sloan Foundation. People are advised to take 3 steps.

1. Make a Kit. Make a home emergency supply kit with at least 3 days worth of essential provisions for "sheltering-in-place," and assemble a lightweight version in case evacuation is necessary. Kits should include 1 gallon of water per person per day. Provide enough easily prepared canned or dried foods. In colder climates, supply warm clothes and a sleeping bag for each member of the family.

Kits should contain a first-aid kit, flashlight, battery-powered radio, extra batteries, toiletries, and any needed medical presciptions. They should include a filter mask (available in hardware stores) or other covering to use as a filter when breathing. Duct tape and heavy-duty garbage bags or plastic sheeting should be available in case it is necessary to seal windows and doors.

2. Make a Plan. Form a communication plan, with designated contacts for each family member. Provisions should be made both for staying in place and for evacuating.

Shelter-in-place. Designate in advance an interior room, or one with the fewest windows and doors, for shelter. In an emergency, if there is heavy debris in the air or authorities deem the air contaminated, close windows, doors, vents, and fireplace dampers, and turn off air conditioners, forced-air heating systems, exhaust fans, and clothes dryers. Take family members and emergency supplies to a selected room and seal doors and windows as needed. Follow TV or radio broadcasts, or the Internet, for further instructions.

Evacuation. Create an evacuation plan with a specific meeting place for family members. Keep at least half a tank of gas in the car at all times, and learn alternate driving routes, as well as alternate means of transportation in your area. If the air is contaminated, drive with the windows and vents closed and keep the air conditioning or heater off.

Work and School. Talk to schools and employers about emergency plans and how they will communicate with families in emergencies.

3. Be Informed. What to do depends partly on the nature of the threat.

Biological Threat. If a biological danger is reported, keep in contact with TV, radio, or the Internet for news and advice. If you become aware of a release of an unknown substance nearby, get away and cover your mouth and nose with layers of fabric that can filter the air but still allow breathing. Wash with soap and water, and seek medical attention.

Chemical Threat. In the event of a chemical attack, leave the contaminated area immediately, if you can safely do so. Signs of a chemical attack in the area may include people with symptoms such as watery eyes, twitching, choking, difficulty breathing, or loss of coordination. Listen to news reports. If you believe you may have been exposed to a chemical agent, remove clothes promptly and wash with soap and water. Do not scrub chemical into skin. Be sure to seek medical attention.

Explosions. If there is an explosion, take shelter from the blast under a desk or table. Leave the building or area when feasible; check for fire, and never use elevators.

Nuclear Blast. In case of a nuclear blast, take cover immediately, preferably below ground. Decide whether to shelter-in-place or evacuate; bear in mind that the more shielding and distance between you and the blast, and the less time of exposure, the more you reduce your risk.

Further Information: FEMA publishes a handbook, *Are You Ready? A Guide to Citizen Preparedness*, which can be obtained electronically at www.fema.gov/areyouready, or in print by calling 1-800-480-2520. You can also visit www.ready.gov or call 1-800-BE-READY.

SECURITY ADVISORIES

The **Homeland Security Advisory System**, established on Mar. 12, 2002, indicates the estimated threat level for a terrorist attack in the U.S.; state and local authorities may have separate alert systems and criteria.

Low (Green). Governments should refine and exercise pre-planned protective measures and train personnel, assess and update vulnerabilities, and take steps to reduce them.

Guarded (Blue). In addition to the above, authorities should check communications with emergency response and command locations, review emergency response procedures, and provide public information as needed.

Elevated (Yellow). Authorities should also increase surveillance of critical locations, coordinate emergency plans with nearby jurisdictions, implement response plans as appropriate.

High (Orange). Authorities should coordinate with federal, state, and local law enforcement agencies, or National Guard or other armed service; take additional precautions at public events, including possible cancellation; prepare to execute contingency procedures and move to alternate locations; restrict access to threatened facilities.

Severe (Red). Authorities should increase or redirect personnel to address critical emergency needs; assign or pre-position emergency response and specialty teams; monitor, redirect, or limit access to transportation systems; close public and government facilities.

As of Oct. 2003, the national threat level had reached "high" 4 times (on the basis of world events, monitored communications and surveillance, and information from captured al-Qaeda): Sept. 10-24, 2002, around the anniversary of Sept. 11; Feb. 7-27, 2003, based on threats of attacks during the Haj pilgrimage in Mecca; Mar. 17-Apr. 16, 2003, during the Iraq War; and May 20-30, following bombings in Saudi Arabia and Morocco, and as a precaution for Memorial Day. When the Iraq War was launched in Mar. 2003, the federal government implemented Operation Liberty Shield, a series of measures that included increased Coast Guard patrols and surveillance, airspace restrictions in key areas, increased airport security, monitoring of suspected terrorists, and stepped-up security at oil refineries, chemical facilities, nuclear reactors, bridges, tunnels, and electrical grids. As of Oct. 1, 2003, the nation was on "elevated" alert. New York City was at "high" alert as it had been since the system was established.

ENERGY

U.S. Energy Overview, 1960-2002

Source: Energy Information Administration, U.S. Dept. of Energy, *Annual Energy Review 2002*; in quadrillion Btu

	1960	1965	1970	1975	1980	1985	1990	1995	2000	2001	2002P
Production	42.80	50.68	63.50	61.36	67.24	67.65	70.73	71.16	71.22	71.37	70.95
Fossil fuels	39.87	47.24	59.19	54.73	59.01	57.54	58.53	57.44	57.25	58.11	56.99
Coal	10.82	13.06	14.61	14.99	18.60	19.33	22.46	22.03	22.62	23.05	22.55
Natural gas (dry)	12.66	15.78	21.67	19.64	19.91	16.98	18.33	19.08	19.66	20.23	19.56
Crude oil[1]	14.93	16.52	20.40	17.73	18.25	18.99	15.57	13.89	12.36	12.28	12.31
Natural gas plant liquids (NGPL)	1.46	1.88	2.51	2.37	2.25	2.24	2.18	2.44	2.61	2.55	2.56
Nuclear electric power	0.01	0.04	0.24	1.90	2.74	4.08	6.10	7.08	7.86	8.03	8.15
Hydroelectric pumped storage[2]	(3)	(3)	(3)	(3)	(3)	(3)	−0.04	−0.03	−0.06	−0.09	−0.90
Renewable energy	2.93	3.40	4.08	4.72	5.49	6.03	6.13	6.69	6.16	5.32	5.90
Conventional hydroelectric power[4]	1.61	2.06	2.63	3.15	2.90	2.97	3.05	3.21	2.81	2.20	2.67
Geothermal energy	(*)	(*)	0.02	0.07	0.11	0.20	0.34	0.29	0.32	0.31	0.30
Wood, waste, alcohol[5]	1.32	1.34	1.43	1.50	2.49	2.86	2.66	3.07	2.90	2.68	2.76
Solar	NA	NA	NA	NA	NA	(*)	0.06	0.07	0.07	0.07	0.06
Wind	NA	NA	NA	NA	NA	(*)	0.03	0.03	0.06	0.07	0.11
Imports	4.19	5.89	8.34	14.03	15.80	11.78	18.82	22.26	28.97	30.15	29.04
Coal	0.01	(*)	(*)	0.02	0.03	0.05	0.07	0.24	0.31	0.49	0.42
Natural gas	0.16	0.47	0.85	0.98	1.01	0.95	1.55	2.90	3.87	4.07	4.10
All crude oil and petroleum prods.[6]	4.00	5.40	7.47	12.95	14.66	10.61	17.12	18.88	24.53	25.40	24.31
Other[7]	0.02	0.01	0.02	0.08	0.10	0.17	0.08	0.24	0.26	0.19	0.20
Exports	1.48	1.83	2.63	2.32	3.69	4.20	4.75	4.51	4.01	3.76	3.65
Coal	1.02	1.38	1.94	1.76	2.42	2.44	2.77	2.32	1.53	1.27	1.03
Natural gas	0.01	0.03	0.07	0.07	0.05	0.06	0.09	0.16	0.25	0.38	0.52
All crude oil and petroleum prods.[6]	0.43	0.39	0.55	0.44	1.16	1.66	1.82	1.99	2.15	2.04	2.04
Other[7]	0.01	0.03	0.08	0.05	0.07	0.04	0.07	0.05	0.08	0.06	0.06
Consumption	45.09	54.02	67.84	71.99	78.29	76.42	84.61	91.22	98.94	96.32	97.35
Fossil fuels	42.14	50.58	63.52	65.36	69.98	66.22	72.46	77.49	85.00	83.13	83.49
Coal	9.84	11.58	12.27	12.66	15.42	17.48	19.17	20.09	22.58	21.90	22.18
Coal coke net imports	−0.01	−0.02	−0.06	0.01	−0.04	−0.01	0.01	0.06	0.07	0.03	0.06
Natural gas[8]	12.39	15.77	21.80	19.95	20.39	17.83	19.73	22.78	23.95	22.87	23.06
Petroleum[9]	19.92	23.25	29.52	32.73	34.20	30.92	33.55	34.55	38.40	38.33	38.18
Nuclear electric power	0.01	0.04	0.24	1.90	2.74	4.08	6.10	7.08	7.86	8.01	8.15
Hydroelectric pumped storage[2]	(3)	(3)	(3)	(3)	(3)	(3)	−0.04	−0.03	−0.06	−0.09	−0.09
Renewable energy	2.93	3.40	4.08	4.72	5.49	6.03	6.13	6.67	6.16	5.32	5.90
Conventional hydroelectric power[4]	1.61	2.06	2.63	3.16	2.90	2.97	3.05	3.21	2.81	2.20	2.67
Geothermal energy	(*)	(*)	0.01	0.07	0.11	0.20	0.34	0.29	0.32	0.31	0.30
Wood, waste, alcohol[5]	1.32	1.34	1.43	1.50	2.49	2.86	2.66	3.07	2.91	2.68	2.76
Solar energy	NA	NA	NA	NA	NA	(*)	0.06	0.07	0.07	0.07	0.06
Wind energy	NA	NA	NA	NA	NA	(*)	0.03	0.03	0.06	0.07	0.11

(1) Incl. lease condensate. (2) Total pumped storage facility production minus energy used for pumping. (3) Included in conventional hydroelectric power. (4) Starting in 1990, pumped storage is removed and expanded coverage of industrial use of hydroelectric power is included. (5) Substituted in 2000 for former "Biofuels" category; figures for 1960-99 were recalculated. Alcohol is ethanol blended into motor gasoline. (6) Incl. imports of crude oil for the Strategic Petroleum Reserve, which began in 1977. (7) Coal coke and small amts. of electricity transmitted across borders with Canada and Mexico. (8) Incl. supplemental gaseous fuels. (9) Petroleum products supplied, incl. natural gas plant liquids and crude oil burned as fuel. NA = Not available. P = preliminary. (*) = Less than 0.005 quadrillion Btu. Some figures here have been revised.

U.S. Energy Flow, 2002[1]

Source: Energy Information Administration, U.S. Dept. of Energy, *Annual Energy Review 2002*; in quadrillion Btu

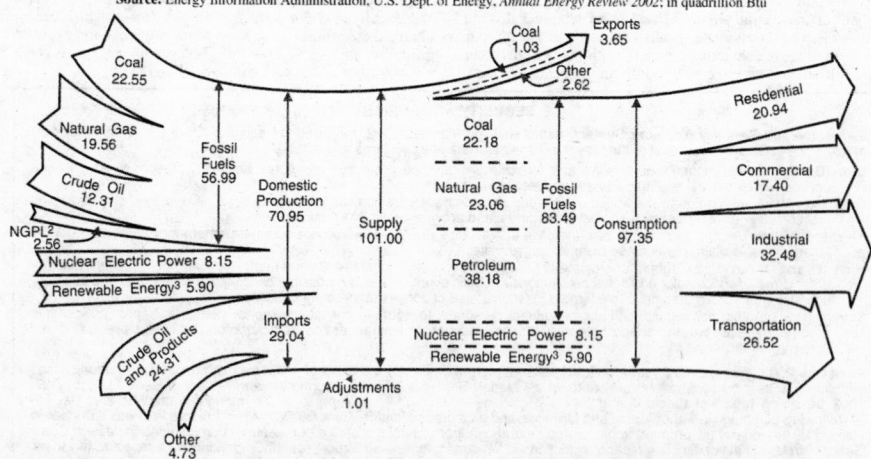

(1) Preliminary figures. (2) Natural Gas Plant Liquids. (3) Conv. hydroelectric power; wood, waste, and ethanol blended into gasoline; geothermal, solar, and wind. Some totals may not add due to rounding.

World Energy Consumption and Production Trends, 2001
Source: Energy Information Administration, U.S. Dept. of Energy, International Energy Database, Sept. 2003

The world's **consumption** of primary energy—petroleum, natural gas, coal, net hydroelectric, nuclear, geothermal, solar, wind, and wood and waste electric power, and other wood and waste (primarily for the United States)—increased from 399 quadrillion Btu in 2000 to 403 quadrillion Btu in 2001.

The 30 countries of the Organization for Economic Co-operation and Development (OECD), which includes some of the world's largest economies (the United States, Japan, and Germany), continued to dominate global energy use. OECD nations accounted for 57% of the world's primary energy consumption in 2001.

World **production** of primary energy increased from 396 quadrillion Btu in 2000 to 403 quadrillion Btu in 2001. World production of petroleum in 2001 was almost 75 million barrels per day, or 155 quadrillion Btu; petroleum remained the most heavily used source of energy.

In 2001, 3 countries—the United States, Russia, and China—were the world's leading producers (38%) and consumers (41%) of energy. Russia and the United States alone supplied 29% of the world total. The United States alone accounted for 24% of the world's energy consumption. The United States consumed 35% more energy than it produced—an imbalance of 25 quadrillion Btu.

World's Major Consumers of Primary Energy, 2001
Source: Energy Information Administration, U.S. Dept. of Energy, *International Energy Annual 2001*; quadrillion Btu

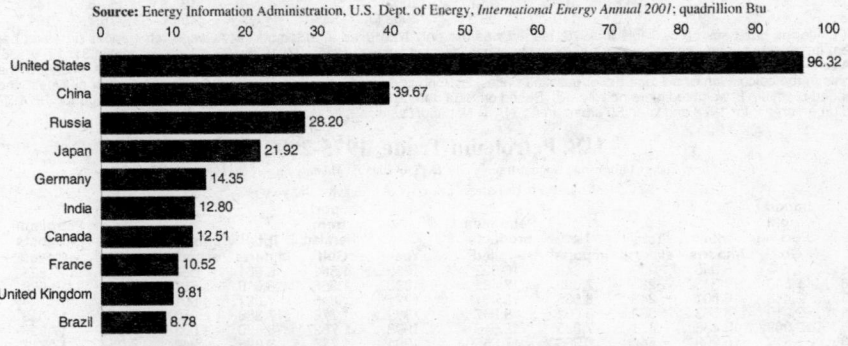

World's Major Producers of Primary Energy, 2001
Source: Energy Information Administration, U.S. Dept. of Energy. *International Energy Annual 2001*; quadrillion Btu

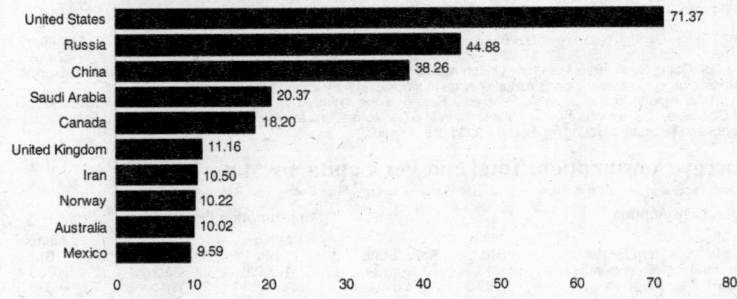

Gasoline Retail Prices in Selected Countries, 1990-2002
Source: Energy Information Administration, U.S. Dept. of Energy
(average price of unleaded regular gas; dollars per gallon, including taxes)

Year	Australia	Brazil	Canada	China	Germany	Japan	Mexico	Taiwan	U.S.
1990	NA	$3.82	$1.87	NA	$2.65	$3.17	$1.00	$2.49	$1.16
1991	$1.96	2.91	1.92	NA	2.90	3.46	1.29	2.39	1.14
1992	1.89	2.92	1.73	NA	3.27	3.59	1.50	2.42	1.13
1993	1.73	2.40	1.57	NA	3.07	4.02	1.56	2.27	1.11
1994	1.84	2.80	1.45	$0.96	3.52	4.39	1.48	2.14	1.11
1995	1.95	2.16	1.53	1.03	3.96	4.43	1.12	2.23	1.15
1996	2.12	2.31	1.61	1.03	3.94	3.65	1.26	2.15	1.23
1997	2.05	2.61	1.62	1.07	3.54	3.27	1.47	2.23	1.23
1998	1.63	2.80	1.38	1.08	3.34	2.82	1.50	1.86	1.06
1999	1.72	NA	1.51	NA	3.42	3.27	1.80	1.86	1.17
2000	1.94	NA	1.86	NA	3.45	3.74	2.02	2.15	1.51
2001	1.71	NA	1.72	NA	3.40	3.35	2.21	2.01	1.46
2002	1.76	NA	3.67	NA	3.67	3.15	NA	NA	1.36

NA = Not available.

Gasoline Retail Prices, U.S. City Average, 1974-2003

Source: Energy Information Administration, U.S. Dept. of Energy, *Monthly Energy Review*, Aug. 2003

(cents per gallon, including taxes)

AVERAGE	Leaded regular	Unleaded regular	Unleaded premium	All types[1]	AVERAGE	Leaded regular	Unleaded regular	Unleaded premium	All types[1]
1974	53.2	NA	NA	NA	1989	99.8	102.1	119.7	106.0
1975	56.7	NA	NA	NA	1990	114.9	116.4	134.9	121.7
1976	59.0	61.4	NA	NA	1991	NA	114.0	132.1	119.6
1977	62.2	65.6	NA	NA	1992	NA	112.7	131.6	119.0
1978	62.6	67.0	NA	65.2	1993	NA	110.8	130.2	117.3
1979	85.7	90.3	NA	88.2	1994	NA	111.2	130.5	117.4
1980	119.1	124.5	NA	122.1	1995	NA	114.7	133.6	120.5
1981[2]	131.1	137.8	147.0[3]	135.3	1996	NA	123.1	141.3	128.8
1982	122.2	129.6	141.5	128.1	1997	NA	123.4	141.6	129.1
1983	115.7	124.1	138.3	122.5	1998	NA	105.9	125.0	111.5
1984	112.9	121.2	136.6	119.8	1999	NA	116.5	135.7	122.1
1985	111.5	120.2	134.0	119.6	2000	NA	151.0	169.3	156.3
1986	85.7	92.7	108.5	93.1	2001	NA	146.1	165.7	153.1
1987	89.7	94.8	109.3	95.7	2002	NA	135.8	157.8	144.1
1988	89.9	94.6	110.7	96.3	2003 (Jan.-June)	NA	159.6	178.2	164.7

Until unleaded gas became available in 1976, leaded was the only type used in automobiles. Average retail prices (in cents per gallon) for selected years preceding those in the table above were as follows: 1950: .27; 1955: .29; 1960: .31; 1965: .31; 1970: .36. (1) Also includes types of motor gasoline not shown separately. (2) In Sept. 1981, the Bureau of Labor Statistics changed the weights in the calculation of average motor gasoline prices. Starting in Sept. 1981, gasohol is included in average for all types, and unleaded premium is weighted more heavily. (3) Based on Sept. through Dec. data only. **NOTE:** Geographic coverage for 1974-77 is 56 urban areas; for 1978 and later, 85 urban areas. NA = Not applicable.

U.S. Petroleum Trade, 1975-2002

Source: Energy Information Administration, U.S. Dept. of Energy, *Monthly Energy Review*, Aug. 2003

(in thousands of barrels per day; average for the year)

Year	Imports from Persian Gulf[1]	Total imports	Total exports	Net imports[2]	Petroleum products supplied[3]	Year	Imports from Persian Gulf[1]	Total imports	Total exports	Net imports[2]	Petroleum products supplied[3]
1975	1,165	6,056	209	5,846	16,322	1989	1,861	8,061	859	7,202	17,325
1976	1,840	7,313	223	7,090	17,461	1990	1,966	8,018	857	7,161	16,988
1977	2,448	8,807	243	8,565	18,431	1991	1,845	7,627	1,001	6,626	16,714
1978	2,219	8,363	362	8,002	18,847	1992	1,778	7,888	950	6,938	17,033
1979	2,069	8,456	471	7,985	18,513	1993	1,782	8,620	1,003	7,618	17,237
1980	1,519	6,909	544	6,365	17,056	1994	1,728	8,996	942	8,054	17,718
1981	1,219	5,996	595	5,401	16,058	1995	1,573	8,835	949	7,886	17,725
1982	696	5,113	815	4,298	15,296	1996	1,604	9,478	981	8,498	18,309
1983	442	5,051	739	4,312	15,231	1997	1,755	10,162	1,003	9,158	18,620
1984	506	5,437	722	4,715	15,726	1998	2,136	10,708	945	9,764	18,917
1985	311	5,067	781	4,286	15,726	1999	2,464	10,852	940	9,912	19,519
1986	912	6,224	785	5,439	16,281	2000	2,488	11,459	1,040	10,419	19,701
1987	1,077	6,678	764	5,914	16,665	2001	2,761	11,871	971	10,900	19,649
1988	1,541	7,402	815	6,587	17,283	2002	2,269	11,530	984	10,546	19,761

(1) Bahrain, Iran, Iraq, Kuwait, Qatar, Saudi Arabia, and the United Arab Emirates. (2) Net imports are total imports minus total exports. (3) Basically includes domestic production and imports minus change in stocks, refinery imports, and exports. **Notes:** Beginning in Oct. 1977, imports for the Strategic Petroleum Reserves are included. U.S. geographic coverage includes the 50 states and the District of Columbia. U.S. exports include shipments to U.S. territories, and imports include receipts from U.S. territories. Figures in this table may not add because of rounding. Some figures are revised.

Energy Consumption, Total and Per Capita, by State, 2000

Source: Energy Information Administration, U.S. Dept. of Energy, State Energy Data Report 2000

Total Consumption

Rank/State	Trillion Btu	Rank/State	Trillion Btu
1. Texas	11,588.6	28. Mississippi	1,143.8
2. California	8,518.7	29. Iowa	1,099.3
3. Pennsylvania	4,779.9	30. Arkansas	1,083.7
4. New York	4,620.0	31. Oregon	1,079.7
5. Illinois	4,417.9	32. Kansas	1,035.7
6. Ohio	4,001.8	33. Connecticut	863.0
7. Louisiana	3,965.2	34. West Virginia	744.0
8. Florida	3,943.8	35. Utah	718.2
9. Michigan	3,121.9	36. Nevada	632.8
10. Indiana	2,777.6	37. Alaska	627.3
11. Georgia	2,769.9	38. New Mexico	620.7
12. New Jersey	2,706.6	39. Montana	594.5
13. North Carolina	2,501.9	40. Nebraska	583.5
14. Virginia	2,303.6	41. Maine	561.2
15. Washington	2,173.8	42. Idaho	511.1
16. Tennessee	2,025.9	43. Wyoming	417.1
17. Alabama	1,977.3	44. North Dakota	365.4
18. Kentucky	1,868.2	45. New Hampshire	329.1
19. Wisconsin	1,799.7	46. Delaware	302.6
20. Massachusetts	1,722.8	47. Hawaii	264.8
21. Minnesota	1,688.0	48. Rhode Island	250.4
22. Missouri	1,659.2	49. South Dakota	246.0
23. Maryland	1,520.1	50. District of Columbia	166.2
24. South Carolina	1,477.1	51. Vermont	164.6
25. Oklahoma	1,400.5	**TOTAL U.S.**	**98,216.2**
26. Arizona	1,215.8		
27. Colorado	1,199.9		

Consumption Per Capita

Rank/State	Million Btu	Rank/State	Million Btu
1. Alaska	1,000.6	28. Georgia	338.4
2. Louisiana	887.3	29. Wisconsin	335.5
3. Wyoming	844.7	30. South Dakota	325.9
4. Montana	659.0	31. Virginia	325.4
5. North Dakota	569.0	32. New Jersey	321.7
6. Texas	555.8	33. Utah	321.6
7. Kentucky	462.2	34. Nevada	316.7
8. Indiana	456.8	35. Oregon	315.6
9. Alabama	444.6	36. Michigan	314.1
10. Maine	440.1	37. North Carolina	310.8
11. West Virginia	411.4	38. Missouri	296.5
12. Oklahoma	405.9	39. District of Columbia	290.6
13. Arkansas	405.4	40. Maryland	287.0
14. Mississippi	402.1	41. Colorado	279.0
15. Idaho	395.0	42. Massachusetts	271.3
16. Pennsylvania	389.2	43. Vermont	270.4
17. Delaware	386.1	44. New Hampshire	266.3
18. Kansas	385.3	45. Connecticut	253.4
19. Iowa	375.7	46. California	251.5
20. Washington	368.8	47. Florida	246.8
21. South Carolina	368.2	48. New York	243.5
22. Tennessee	356.1	49. Rhode Island	238.8
23. Illinois	355.7	50. Arizona	237.0
24. Ohio	352.5	51. Hawaii	218.6
25. Minnesota	343.1	**TOTAL U.S.**	**349.0**
26. New Mexico	341.2		
27. Nebraska	341.0		

WORLD ALMANAC QUICK QUIZ

Which of the following countries relies the most (by percentage) on nuclear energy as a source for electricity?
(a) China   (b) France   (c) United States   (d) Bulgaria
For the answer look in this chapter, or see page 1008.

World Crude Oil and Natural Gas Reserves, Jan. 1, 2002

Sources: Energy Information Administration, U.S. Dept. of Energy, *U.S. Crude Oil, Natural Gas, and Natural Gas Liquids Reserves, Nov. 2002; Oil and Gas Journal (OGJ)*, Dec. 2001; *World Oil (WO)*, Aug. 2002

Region/Country	Crude oil (billion barrels) OGJ	Crude oil (billion barrels) WO	Natural gas (trillion cubic feet) OGJ	Natural gas (trillion cubic feet) WO
North America	**54.2**	**50.9**	**272.7**	**282.1**
Canada	4.9	5.4	59.7	59.7
Mexico	26.9	23.1	29.5	39.0
United States	22.4	22.4	183.5	183.5
Central & South America	**96.0**	**69.1**	**253.0**	**250.2**
Argentina	3.0	2.9	27.5	26.8
Barbados	(1)	NA	(1)	NA
Bolivia	0.4	0.5	24.0	27.4
Brazil	8.5	8.6	7.8	7.9
Chile	0.2	(1)	3.5	1.3
Colombia	1.8	1.9	4.3	5.0
Cuba	0.8	0.3	2.5	0.5
Ecuador	2.1	2.6	3.7	3.9
Guatemala	0.5	NA	0.1	NA
Peru	0.3	0.9	8.7	8.7
Suriname	0.1	NA	0.0	NA
Trinidad and Tobago	0.7	0.7	23.5	19.7
Venezuela	77.7	50.2	147.6	149.2
Western Europe	**17.3**	**17.7**	**160.7**	**182.4**
Austria	0.1	0.1	0.9	0.8
Croatia	0.1	0.1	1.2	1.2
Denmark	1.1	1.3	2.7	3.1
France	0.1	0.1	0.4	0.5
Germany	0.4	0.3	12.1	9.0
Greece	(1)	NA	(1)	NA
Ireland	0.0	NA	0.7	NA
Italy	0.6	0.6	8.1	6.7
Netherlands	0.1	0.1	62.5	57.0
Norway	9.4	10.3	44.0	77.2
Spain	(1)	NA	(1)	NA
Turkey	0.3	0.3	0.3	0.3
United Kingdom	4.9	4.6	26.0	24.5
Yugoslavia	0.1	NA	1.7	NA
Eastern Europe & Former USSR	**58.4**	**67.1**	**1,967.9**	**1,950.5**
Albania	0.2	0.2	0.1	0.1
Bulgaria	(1)	(1)	0.2	0.1
Czech Republic	(1)	(1)	0.1	0.1
Slovakia	(1)	NA	0.5	NA
Hungary	0.1	0.1	1.3	2.3
Poland	0.1	0.1	5.1	5.8
Romania	1.0	1.2	3.6	4.3
Azerbaijan	1.2	NA	4.4	NA
Kazakhstan	5.4	NA	65.0	NA
Russia	48.6	53.9	1,680.0	1,700.0
Turkmenistan	0.5	NA	101.0	NA
Ukraine	0.4	NA	39.6	NA
Uzbekistan	0.6	NA	66.2	NA
Middle East	**685.6**	**662.5**	**1,974.6**	**2,367.9**
Bahrain	0.1	NA	3.2	NA
Iran	89.7	99.1	812.3	939.4
Iraq	112.5	115.0	109.8	112.6
Israel	(1)	NA	1.5	NA
Jordan	(1)	NA	0.2	NA
Kuwait	96.5	98.8	52.7	56.6
Oman	5.5	5.9	29.3	30.5
Qatar	15.2	13.8	508.5	757.7
Saudi Arabia	261.8	261.7	219.5	228.2
Syria	2.5	2.3	8.5	8.5
United Arab Emirates	97.8	62.8	212.1	204.1
Yemen	4.0	2.4	16.9	17.0
Africa	**76.7**	**94.9**	**394.8**	**477.1**
Algeria	9.2	17.0	159.7	175.0
Angola	5.4	6.0	1.6	4.0
Benin	(1)	NA	(1)	NA
Cameroon	0.4	NA	3.9	NA
Congo (Brazzaville)	1.5	1.6	3.2	4.2
Congo (Kinshasa)	0.2	NA	(1)	NA
Côte d'Ivoire (Ivory Coast)	0.1	NA	1.1	NA
Egypt	2.9	3.7	35.2	54.1
Equatorial Guinea	(1)	1.1	1.3	3.5
Ethiopia	(1)	NA	0.9	NA
Gabon	2.5	2.4	1.2	3.5
Ghana	(1)	NA	0.8	NA
Libya	29.5	30.0	46.4	46.9
Madagascar	0.0	NA	0.0	NA
Morocco	(1)	NA	(1)	NA
Mozambique	0.0	NA	4.5	NA
Namibia	0.0	NA	2.2	NA
Nigeria	24.0	30.0	124.0	159.0
Rwanda	0.0	NA	2.0	NA
Somalia	0.0	NA	0.2	NA
South Africa	(1)	NA	(1)	NA
Sudan	0.6	0.7	3.0	4.0
Tanzania	0.0	NA	0.8	NA
Tunisia	0.3	0.5	2.8	2.7
Asia & Oceania	**43.8**	**56.5**	**433.3**	**419.9**
Afghanistan	0.0	NA	3.5	NA
Australia	3.5	3.8	90.0	80.0
Bangladesh	0.1	NA	10.6	NA
Brunei	1.4	1.2	13.8	8.4
Burma	0.1	0.2	10.0	12.2
China	24.0	29.5	48.3	42.8
India	4.8	3.8	22.9	15.4
Indonesia	5.0	9.2	92.5	87.5
Japan	0.1	NA	1.4	NA
Malaysia	3.0	4.5	75.0	82.5
New Zealand	0.1	0.1	2.1	2.1
Pakistan	0.3	0.3	25.1	24.1
Papua New Guinea	0.2	0.5	12.2	15.0
Philippines	0.2	0.2	3.7	3.7
Taiwan	(1)	NA	2.7	NA
Thailand	0.5	0.6	12.7	13.3
Vietnam	0.6	2.2	6.8	6.8
World total	**1,032.0**	**1,018.7**	**5,457.1**	**5,930.2**

NOTE: NA=Not available. Data for Kuwait and Saudi Arabia include one-half of the reserves in the Neutral Zone between Kuwait and Saudi Arabia. All reserve figures except those for the former USSR and natural gas reserves in Canada are *proved reserves.* Former USSR and Canadian natural gas figures include amounts understood as *proved,* and some *probable reserves.* Totals may not equal sum of components due to inclusion of small "other" amounts and independent rounding. (1) Less than 50 million barrels of crude oil or less than 50 million cubic feet of natural gas.

Production of Crude Oil, by Major States, 2002

Source: Energy Information Administration, *Petroleum Supply Annual 2002*
(thousand barrels)

State	Total	State	Total	State	Total	State	Total
1. Texas[1]	411,985	9. North Dakota	30,993	17. Michigan	7,219	25. South Dakota	1,214
2. Alaska[1]	359,335	10. Mississippi	18,015	18. Ohio	6,004	26. Nevada	553
3. California[1]	258,010	11. Colorado	17,734	19. Florida	3,656	27. Tennessee	275
4. Louisiana[1]	93,477	12. Montana	16,855	20. Kentucky	2,679	28. New York	165
5. Oklahoma	66,642	13. Utah	13,676	21. Nebraska	2,779	29. Missouri	95
6. New Mexico	67,041	14. Illinois	12,051	22. Indiana	1,962	30. Arizona	63
7. Wyoming	54,717	15. Alabama	8,631	23. Pennsylvania	2,233	31. Virginia	22
8. Kansas	32,721	16. Arkansas	7,344	24. West Virginia	1,382	**U.S. TOTAL**	**2,097,124**

(1) Includes the following offshore production (thous. bbls.): Texas (1,274), Alaska (104,837), California (16,294), Louisiana (11,002).

U.S. Crude Oil Imports by Selected Country, 1988-2003

Source: Energy Information Administration, Petroleum Supply Monthly, Sept. 2003; ranked by 2003 totals

(thousand barrels per day)

	1988	1990	1995	1996	1997	1998	1999	2000	2001	2002	2003[1]
Saudi Arabia*	911	1,195	1,260	1,248	1,293	1,404	1,387	1,523	1,611	1,519	1,870
Mexico	674	689	1,027	1,207	1,360	1,321	1,254	1,313	1,394	1,500	1,528
Canada*	681	643	1,040	1,075	1,198	1,266	1,178	1,348	1,356	1,445	1,492
Venezuela*	439	666	1,151	1,303	1,394	1,377	1,150	1,223	1,291	1,201	1,054
Nigeria*	607	784	621	595	689	689	623	875	842	589	801
Iraq*	343	514	0	1	89	336	725	620	795	459	432
Angola	203	236	360	344	425	465	357	295	321	321	376
United Kingdom	254	155	341	216	169	161	284	291	244	405	370
Kuwait*	80	79	213	235	253	300	246	263	327	216	211
Russia[2]	0	1	14	18	3	9	21	7	0	85	186
Norway	62	96	258	293	288	221	263	302	281	348	162
Colombia	106	140	207	226	270	349	452	318	260	235	158
Gabon[3]	15	64	229	184	230	207	168	143	140	143	125
Ecuador[4]	33	38	96	96	114	98	114	125	113	100	105
Algeria*	58	63	27	8	6	10	25	1	11	30	87
Trinidad and Tobago	71	76	62	58	56	53	40	56	51	68	72
Brazil	0	0	0	0	0	0	0	5	13	58	37
Malaysia	19	40	6	8	8	25	21	29	15	9	22
Australia	59	47	16	25	31	31	31	49	34	51	20
Indonesia*	186	98	64	44	51	50	70	36	40	50	16
China	82	77	53	57	48	42	13	33	13	20	12
United Arab Emirates*	23	9	5	3	0	3	0	3	21	10	10
Total Arab-OPEC	1,415	1,864	1,505	1,496	1,641	2,053	2,385	2,410	2,675	2,243	2,611
Total OPEC	2,696	3,514	3,341	3,438	3,775	4,169	4,228	4,544	4,848	4,083	4,482
Total Non-OPEC	2,411	2,381	3,889	4,070	4,450	4,537	4,502	4,526	4,480	5,058	4,929
TOTAL	5,107	5,894	7,230	7,508	8,225	8,706	8,731	9,071	9,328	9,140	9,411

* Denotes OPEC members. (1) Jan.-July average. (2) May include oil from USSR states for 1988 and 1992. (3) Gabon withdrew from OPEC Dec. 31, 1994. Imports after Jan. 1, 1995, appear in Non-OPEC totals. (4) Ecuador withdrew from OPEC Dec. 31, 1992. Imports after Jan. 1, 1994, appear in Non-OPEC totals.

World Nuclear Power Summary, 2002

Source: International Atomic Energy Agency, Power Reactor Information System, May 2003

Country	Reactors in operation		Reactors under construction		Nuclear electricity supplied in 2002		Total operating experience[2]	
	No. of units	Total MW(e)	No. of units	Total MW(e)	TW(e).h[1]	% of nation's total	Years	Months
Argentina	2	935	1	692	5.39	7.23	48	7
Armenia	1	376	—	—	2.09	40.54	35	3
Belgium	7	5,760	—	—	44.74	57.32	184	7
Brazil	2	1,901	—	—	13.84	3.99	23	3
Bulgaria	4	2,722	—	—	20.22	47.30	125	2
Canada	14	10,018	—	—	70.96	12.32	461	2
China	7	5,318	4	3,275	23.45	1.43	31	6
Czech Republic	6	3,468	—	—	18.74	24.54	68	10
Finland	4	2,656	—	—	21.44	29.81	95	4
France	59	63,073	—	—	415.50	77.97	1,287	2
Germany	19	21,283	—	—	162.25	29.85	629	1
Hungary	4	1,755	—	—	12.79	36.14	70	2
India	14	2,503	7	3,420	17.76	3.68	209	5
Iran	—	—	2	2,111	—	—	0	0
Japan	54	44,287	3	3,696	313.81	34.47	1,070	4
Korea, North	—	—	1	1,040	—	—	0	0
Korea, South	18	14,890	2	1,920	113.07	38.62	202	7
Lithuania	2	2,370	—	—	12.90	80.12	34	6
Mexico	2	1,360	—	—	9.35	4.07	21	11
Netherlands	1	450	—	—	3.69	4.00	58	0
Pakistan	2	425	—	—	1.80	2.54	33	10
Romania	1	655	1	655	5.11	10.33	6	6
Russia	30	20,793	3	2,825	129.98	15.98	731	4
Slovakia	6	2,408	2	776	17.95	65.41	97	0
Slovenia	1	676	—	—	5.31	40.74	21	3
South Africa	2	1,800	—	—	11.99	5.87	36	3
Spain	9	7,574	—	—	60.28	25.76	210	2
Sweden	11	9,432	—	—	65.57	45.75	300	1
Switzerland	5	3,200	—	—	25.69	39.52	138	10
Taiwan	6	4,884	2	2,700	33.94	20.53	128	1
Ukraine	13	11,207	4	3,800	73.38	45.66	266	10
United Kingdom	31	12,252	—	—	81.08	22.43	1,301	8
United States	104	98,230	—	—	780.06	20.34	2,767	8
TOTAL	441	358,661	32	26,910	2,574.17	—	10,696	4

(1) 1 terawatt-hour [TW(e).h] = 10^6 megawatt-hour [MW(e).h]. For an average power plant, 1 TW(e).h = 0.39 megatons of coal equivalent (input) and 0.23 megatons of oil equivalent (input). (2) Through Dec. 31, 2002.

Nations Most Reliant on Nuclear Energy, 2002

Source: International Atomic Energy Agency, Sept. 2003

(Nuclear electricity generation as % of total electricity generated)

Country	%	Country	%	Country	%	Country	%	Country	%
Lithuania	80.1	Ukraine	45.7	Korea, Republic of	38.6	Spain	25.8	Canada	12.3
France	78.0	Sweden	45.7	Hungary	36.1	Czech Republic	24.5	Romania	10.3
Belgium	57.3	Slovenia	40.7	Japan	34.5	United Kingdon	22.4	Argentina	7.2
Slovakia	54.7	Armenia	40.5	Germany	29.9	**United States**	20.3	South Africa	5.9
Bulgaria	47.3	Switzerland	39.5	Finland	29.8	Russia	16.0	Mexico	4.1

U.S. Nuclear Reactor Units and Power Plant Operations, 1978-2002
Source: Energy Information Administration, U.S. Dept. of Energy, Annual Energy Review 2002

	Number of reactor units						Total design capacity (million KWs)	Nuclear-based electricity generation (million net KW-hrs)	Nuclear portion of domestic electricity generation (percent)
	Licensed for operation		Construction permits		On order	Shutdowns	Total		
	Operable	In startup	Granted	Pending					
1978	70	0	88	32	5	1	195	191	276,403	12.5
1979	69	0	90	24	3	1	185	180	255,155	11.4
1980	71	1	82	12	3	0	168	162	251,116	11.0
1981	75	0	76	11	2	0	163	157	272,674	11.9
1982	78	2	60	3	2	1	144	134	282,773	12.6
1983	81	3	53	0	2	0	138	129	293,677	12.7
1984	87	6	38	0	2	0	132	123	327,634	13.6
1985	96	3	30	0	2	0	130	121	383,691	15.5
1986	101	7	19	0	2	0	128	119	414,038	16.6
1987	107	4	14	0	2	2	127	119	455,270	17.7
1988	109	3	12	0	0	0	123	115	526,973	19.5
1989	111	1	10	0	0	2	121	113	529,402	17.8
1990	112	0	8	0	0	1	119	111	576,974	19.0
1991	111	0	8	0	0	1	119	111	612,642	19.9
1992	109	0	8	0	0	2	117	111	618,841	20.1
1993	110	0	7	0	0	0	116	110	610,367	19.1
1994	109	0	7	0	0	1	116	110	640,492	19.7
1995	109	1	6	0	0	0	116	110	673,402	20.1
1996	109	0	6	0	0	1	116	110	674,729	19.6
1997	107	0	3	0	0	2	110	102	628,644	18.0
1998	104	0	3	0	0	3	107	99	673,702	18.6
1999	104	0	0	0	0	0	104	NA	728,198	19.7
2000	104	0	0	0	0	0	104	NA	753,893	19.8
2001	104	0	0	0	0	0	104	NA	768,826	20.6
2002[1]	104	0	0	0	0	0	104	NA	780,064	20.3

NA = Not available. (1) Preliminary

Major U.S. Coal Producers, 2002[1]
Source: Energy Information Administration, U.S. Dept. of Energy

Rank	Company Name	Production (thousand short tons)	Percent of total production	Rank	Company Name	Production (thousand short tons)	Percent of total production
1.	Peabody Coal Sales Co.	149,602	13.7	15.	BHP Minerals Group	15,106	1.4
2.	Kennecott Energy & Coal Co.	111,088	10.2	16.	Pittsburg & Midway Coal Mining Co	14,471	1.3
3.	Arch Coal, Inc.	110,759	10.1	17.	Alpha Natural Resources, LLC	12,284	1.1
4.	RAG American Coal Holding, Inc.	70,234	6.4	18.	James River Coal Co.	11,138	1.0
5.	Consol Energy Inc.	61,534	5.6	19.	Peter Kiewit/Kennecott	10,028	0.9
6.	A.T. Massey Coal Co., Inc.	43,498	4.0	20.	PacifiCorp	9,766	0.9
7.	Vulcan Partners, L.P.	42,218	3.9	21.	Andalex Resources, Inc.	6,803	0.6
8.	Horizon Natural Resources Inc.	39,509	3.6	22.	Transalta Centralia Mining LLC.	5,827	0.5
9.	North American Coal Corp.	29,537	2.7	23.	Cumberland Resources Corp.	5,665	0.5
10.	TXU Corporation	23,670	2.2	24.	Alcoa, Inc.	5,574	0.5
11.	Westmoreland Mining LLC	20,075	1.8	25.	U.S. Steel Mining Co., LLC	5,469	*
12.	Robert Murray	19,839	1.8		All other coal producers	233,391	21.3
13.	Black Beauty Coal Co.	18,891	1.7				
14.	Alliance Coal, LLC	18,304	1.7		U.S. Total	1,094,283	100.0

Note: The company is the firm controlling the coal, particularly the sale of the coal. Usually it is also the owner of the mine. *The unit of measure is less than 0.5 or percent change is less than 0.1%. (1) Preliminary.

Major U.S. Coal Mines, 2002[1]
Source: Energy Information Administration, U.S. Dept. of Energy

Rank	Mine Name/Company	Mine Type	State	Production (short tons)
1.	North Antelope Rochelle Comple/Powder River Coal Company	Surface	Wyoming	74,792,642
2.	Black Thunder/Thunder Basin Coal Company, LLC	Surface	Wyoming	65,125,564
3.	Cordero Mine/Cordero Mining Co.	Surface	Wyoming	38,277,100
4.	Jacobs Ranch Mine/Jacobs Ranch Coal Company	Surface	Wyoming	31,728,341
5.	Antelope Coal Mine/Antelope Coal Company	Surface	Wyoming	26,808,505
6.	Caballo Mine/Caballo Coal Company	Surface	Wyoming	25,967,932
7.	Eagle Butte Mine/RAG Coal West, Inc.	Surface	Wyoming	24,901,828
8.	North Rochelle/Triton Coal Company LLC	Surface	Wyoming	23,883,760
9.	Buckskin Mine/Triton Coal Company	Surface	Wyoming	18,334,186
10.	Belle Ayr Mine/RAG Coal West Incorporated	Surface	Wyoming	17,431,329
11.	Freedom Mine/The Coteau Properties Company	Surface	North Dakota	15,653,071
12.	Decker Mine/Decker Coal Co.	Surface	Montana	10,028,398
13.	Rosebud #6 Mine&Crusher & Conv/Western Energy Company	Surface	Montana	10,015,036
14.	Bailey Mine/Consol Pennsylvania Coal Company	Underground	Pennsylvania	9,660,905
15.	Enlow Fork Mine/Consol Pennsylvania Coal Company	Underground	Pennsylvania	9,569,787
16.	Spring Creek Company/Spring Creek Coal Company	Surface	Montana	8,925,368
17.	Kayenta/Peabody Western Coal Company	Surface	Arizona	8,233,863
18.	Navajo Mine/BHP Navajo Coal Company	Surface	New Mexico	8,099,216
19.	Falkirk Mine/The Falkirk Mining Company	Surface	North Dakota	7,621,709
20.	Sufco/Canyon Fuel Company LLC	Underground	Utah	7,600,348
21.	Foidel Creek Mine/Twentymile Coal Company	Underground	Colorado	7,573,438
22.	Beckville Strip/TXU Mining Company LP	Surface	Texas	7,246,826
23.	Jewett Mine/Northwestern Resources Company	Surface	Texas	6,730,459
24.	Cumberland Mine/RAG Cumberland Resources LP	Underground	Pennsylvania	6,636,700
25.	Emerald Mine #1/RAG Emerald Resources LP	Underground	Pennsylvania	6,564,616
	All Other Mines			616,872,134
	U.S. Total			1,094,283,061

Note: The company is the firm operating the mine. (1) Preliminary.

ENVIRONMENT

Greenhouse Effect and Global Warming

Source: U.S. Environmental Protection Agency

The Earth naturally absorbs incoming solar radiation and emits thermal radiation back into space. Some of the thermal radiation is trapped by so-called greenhouse gases in the atmosphere, which increases warming of the Earth's surface and atmosphere. Levels of carbon dioxide (CO_2), a naturally occurring greenhouse gas, are higher now than at any time during the past 400,000 years for which concentrations can be determined from ice cores drilled in Greenland and Antarctica; they began rising in the past 2 centuries as a result of activities such as the burning of fossil fuels (coal, oil, natural gas) and deforestation. Water vapor, methane (CH_4), nitrous oxide (N_2O), and ozone (O_3) are also naturally occurring greenhouse gases. Greenhouse gases that are mostly human-made include chlorofluorocarbons (CFCs), hydrochlorofluorocarbons (HCFCs), hydrofluorocarbons (HFCs), perfluorocarbons (PFCs), and sulfur hexafluoride (SF_6). Several nongreenhouse gases (carbon monoxide [CO], oxides of nitrogen [NOx], and nonmethane volatile organic compounds [NMVOCs]) contribute indirectly to the greenhouse effect by producing greenhouse gases during chemical transformations or by influencing the atmospheric lifetimes of greenhouse gases.

In the past 2 centuries, atmospheric concentrations of CO_2, CH_4, and N_2O have increased by about 30%, 145%, and 15%, respectively. This buildup is believed by many scientists to be the major cause of higher than normal average global temperatures in the 1990s and into the 21st century; 2002 was the 2nd-warmest year on record. The hottest was 1998, the 3rd-hottest 2001, and 9 of the 10 hottest on record have occurred since 1990. Over the 20th century, Earth's average temperature has risen by about 1° F, and the last quarter century has shown a higher level of increase; some scientists believe that the global temperature could rise by 2° to 6° F over the 21st century. This global warming could speed the melting of polar ice caps, inundate coastal lowlands, and cause major changes in crop production and in natural habitat. Reports in 2003 of glaciers melting at Glacier National Park and elsewhere were viewed by some scientists as consequences of greenhouse warming. A study by World Health Organization scientists released in Sept. 2003 said that problems brought about by global warming, such as increased malaria (caused by the expanded range of malaria-carrying mosquitos) and malnutrition (caused by agricultural disruptions from climate change), might currently cause 160,000 deaths a year, mostly in developing nations, and that this number could double by 2020. The U.S. is the world's leading producer of CO_2, followed by China, Russia, Japan, India, and Germany.

In Dec. 1997, at a UN summit on global warming in Kyoto, Japan, delegates from over 150 nations adopted a treaty to limit emissions of CO_2, CH_4, N_2O, HFCs, PFCs, and SF_6. The so-called Kyoto Protocol called for cutting emissions 5.2% below 1990 levels by 2012 for all 38 industrialized countries that signed the accord. Developing nations were not bound. The 15 EU nations agreed to binding reductions of 8%, the U.S. to 7%, and Japan to 6%.

The U.S. signed the treaty on Nov. 12, 1998, but Pres. Bill Clinton did not send it to the Senate for ratification because of dim prospects for approval. The Bush administration opposes the treaty, calling it unfair to developed countries and anti-growth. A report submitted to the UN by the administration in May 2002 acknowledged a link between human activity and global warming, forecasting a 43% increase in U.S. greenhouse gas emissions from 2000 to 2020. However, the administration favored a voluntary approach, including tax incentives, rather than mandatory controls. At a meeting in Bonn, Germany, in July 2001, delegates agreed, despite U.S. opposition, on binding guidelines and timetables for achieving the Kyoto-mandated reductions. High-emissions nations could meet their targets by purchasing pollution credits from nations that exceed targets, and gain credits for "sinks," such as forests and croplands, that absorb CO_2 from the atmosphere. For the protocol to take effect it had to be ratified by countries responsible for at least 55% of developed nations' greenhouse emissions in 1990; by Sept. 2003 this had not happened, as neither the U.S. (accounting for 36%) nor Russia (accounting for 17%), had ratified it.

U.S. Greenhouse Gas Emissions From Human Activities, 1990-2001

Source: U.S. Environmental Protection Agency

GAS AND SOURCE	1990	1995	1996	1997	1998	1999	2000	2001
Carbon dioxide (CO_2)	**5,003.7**	**5,334.4**	**5,514.8**	**5,595.4**	**5,614.2**	**5,680.7**	**5,883.1**	**5,794.8**
Fossil fuel combustion	4,814.8	5,141.5	5,325.8	5,400.0	5,420.5	5,488.8	5,692.2	5,614.9
Methane (CH_4)	**644.0**	**650.0**	**636.8**	**629.5**	**622.7**	**615.5**	**613.4**	**605.9**
Landfills	212.1	216.1	212.1	207.5	202.4	203.7	205.8	202.9
Natural gas systems	122.0	127.2	127.4	126.0	124.0	120.3	121.2	117.3
Enteric fermentation[1]	117.9	123.0	120.5	118.3	116.7	116.6	115.7	114.8
Coal mining	87.1	73.5	68.4	68.1	67.9	63.7	60.9	60.7
Nitrous oxide (N_2O)	**397.6**	**430.9**	**441.7**	**440.9**	**436.8**	**430.0**	**429.9**	**424.6**
Agricultural soil management	267.5	284.1	293.2	298.2	299.2	297.0	294.6	294.3
Hydrofluorocarbons (HFCs), perfluorocarbons (PFCs), and sulfur hexafluoride (SF_6)[2]	**94.4**	**99.5**	**113.6**	**116.8**	**127.6**	**120.3**	**121.0**	**111.0**
TOTAL U.S. EMISSIONS	**6,139.6**	**6,514.9**	**6,707.0**	**6,782.6**	**6,801.3**	**6,849.5**	**7,047.4**	**6,936.2**
NET U.S. EMISSIONS[3]	**5,066.8**	**5,450.7**	**5,646.0**	**5,942.0**	**5,970.9**	**6,008.5**	**6,212.7**	**6,098.1**

Note: Emissions given in terms of equivalent emissions of carbon dioxide (CO_2), using units of teragrams of carbon dioxide equivalents (Tg CO_2 Eq.). (1) Digestive process of ruminant animals, such as cattle and sheep, producing methane as a by-product. (2) These gases have extremely high global warming potential, and PFCs and SF_6 have long atmospheric lifetimes. (3) Total emissions minus carbon dioxide absorbed by forests or other means.

U.S. Greenhouse Gas Emissions, 2001

Source: U.S. Environmental Protection Agency

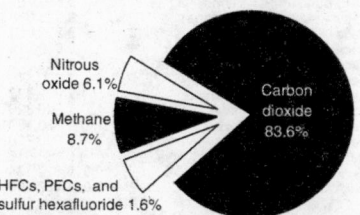

Nitrous oxide 6.1%
Methane 8.7%
HFCs, PFCs, and sulfur hexafluoride 1.6%
Carbon dioxide 83.6%

World Carbon Dioxide Emissions From the Use of Fossil Fuels, 2001

Source: U.S. Energy Information Administration

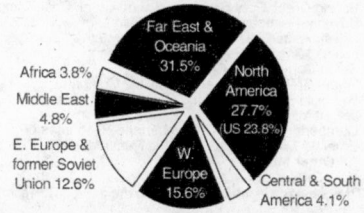

Far East & Oceania 31.5%
Africa 3.8%
Middle East 4.8%
E. Europe & former Soviet Union 12.6%
North America 27.7% (US 23.8%)
W. Europe 15.6%
Central & South America 4.1%

Average Global Temperatures, 1900-2002
Source: National Oceanic and Atmospheric Administration; in degrees Fahrenheit

1900-09 .. 56.5	1930-39 .. 57.0	1950-59 .. 57.1	1970-79 .. 57.0	1990-99...57.6	2001 .....57.8
1910-19 .. 56.6	1940-49 .. 57.1	1960-69 .. 57.1	1980-89.. 57.4	2000 .....57.6	2002 .....57.9
1920-29 .. 56.7					

Toxics Release Inventory, U.S., 2000-2001
Source: U.S. Environmental Protection Agency

Releases of toxic chemicals into the environment, by manner of release and industry sector; pollutant transfers by destination of transfer. For the core set of chemicals for which reports have been made since 1988, there has been a 54.5% drop in total on- and off-site releases between 1988 and 2001. Totals below may not add because of rounding.

	2000 mil lb	2001 mil lb		2000	2001
Pollutant releases			**Top industries, total releases**[1]		
Air releases	1,915	1,678	Metal mining	NA	46%
Surface water releases	267	220	Electric utilities	NA	17
Underground injection	270	209	Chemicals	NA	9
On-site land releases...............	3,824	3,085	Primary metals	NA	9
Off-site releases	490	522	Hazardous waste/solvent recovery.....	NA	4
TOTAL on- and off-site releases	**6,767**	**5,715**	Paper	NA	3
Pollutant transfers			All others.........................	NA	12
To recycling......................	1,877	1,695	**Top carcinogens, air/water/land releases**[1]		mil lb
To energy recovery	810	840	Styrene..........................	NA	48
To treatment	279	280	Dichloromethane....................	NA	22
To publicly owned treatment works....	341	340	Formaldehyde......................	NA	22
Other transfers....................	1	2	Acetaldehyde	NA	13
Off-site to disposal.................	582	600	Trichloroethylene	NA	9
TOTAL...........................	**3,891**	**3,757**	Ethylbenzene	NA	8

NA = Not available. (1) The EPA lowered reporting thresholds for lead and lead compounds for the year 2001. For pollutant releases and pollutant transfers the EPA released comparable statistics for 2000 and 2001; comparable numbers were not available at press time for releases by industry and top carcinogens.

Top 10 States, Total Toxics Releases, 2001
Source: U.S. Environmental Protection Agency

State	2001 mil lb	State	2001 mil lb	State	2001 mil lb	State	2001 mil lb
Nevada............	783	Alaska	522	Pennsylvania.......	207	North Carolina.......	148
Utah..............	767	Texas.............	271	Indiana............	206	**U.S. Total***	**6,158**
Arizona...........	607	Ohio..............	255	Tennessee........	149		

*Total includes District of Columbia, Puerto Rico, American Samoa, Guam, Northern Marianas, and the Virgin Islands.

Air Pollution
Source: World Bank, *World Development Indicators 2001*

Air pollution is a major threat to health and the environment. **Winter smog**—made up of soot, dust, and sulfur dioxide—is associated with increases in deaths. Prolonged exposure to **particulate pollution** can lead to chronic respiratory illnesses and exacerbate heart disease. It causes an estimated 500,000 premature deaths in the world each year.

Emissions of sulfur dioxide and nitrogen oxides lead to **acid rain**, which spreads over long distances, upsetting the chemical balance of soils, trees, and plants. Direct exposure to high levels of sulfur dioxide or acid deposition causes **defoliation**.

Where **coal** is a primary fuel, high levels of urban air pollution may result. If the coal has a high sulfur content, widespread acid deposition may result. Combustion of **petroleum** products is another important cause of air pollution.

Air Pollution in Selected World Cities[1]

In this table, **particulate matter** refers to smoke, soot, dust, and liquid droplets from combustion that are in the air—specifically, to particulates less than 10 microns in diameter capable of reaching deep into the respiratory tract. The level of particulates, an important indicator of air quality, is significantly affected by the state of technology and pollution controls. **Sulfur dioxide** is a pollutant formed when fossil fuels containing sulfur are burned. **Nitrogen dioxide** is a poisonous, pungent gas formed when nitric oxide combines with hydrocarbons and sunlight, producing a photochemical reaction. Nitrogen oxides are emitted by bacteria, nitrogenous fertilizers, aerobic decomposition of organic matter, biomass combustion, and, especially, burning fuel for vehicles and industrial activities.

Data are based on reports from urban monitoring sites. Annual means (measured in micrograms per cubic meter, mpcm) are average concentrations observed at various sites; resulting figures give a general indication of air quality, but results should be interpreted with caution. World Health Organization standards for acceptable air quality are 50 mpcm for sulfur dioxide and 40 mpcm for nitrogen dioxide; the WHO has set no guidelines for acceptable levels of suspended particulate matter.

City and Country	Particulate matter	Sulfur dioxide	Nitrogen dioxide	City and Country	Particulate matter	Sulfur dioxide	Nitrogen dioxide
Accra, Ghana............	31	NA	NA	Milan, Italy.............	36	31	248
Amsterdam, Netherlands....	37	10	58	Montreal, Canada	22	10	42
Athens, Greece	50	34	64	Moscow, Russia	27	109	NA
Bangkok, Thailand........	82	11	23	Mumbai (Bombay), India....	79	33	39
Barcelona, Spain	43	11	43	Nairobi, Kenya............	49	NA	NA
Beijing, China...........	106	90	122	New York, NY............	23	26	79
Berlin, Germany	25	18	26	Oslo, Norway.............	23	8	43
Cairo, Egypt.............	178	69	NA	Paris, France.............	15	14	57
Cape Town, South Africa....	15	21	72	Prague, Czech Republic	27	14	33
Caracas, Venezuela........	18	33	57	Quito, Ecuador	34	22	NA
Chicago, IL.............	27	14	57	Rio de Janeiro, Brazil	40	129	NA
Cordoba, Argentina	52	NA	97	Rome, Italy	35	NA	NA
Delhi, India.............	187	24	41	Seoul, South Korea........	45	44	60
Kolkata (Calcutta), India.....	153	49	34	Sofia, Bulgaria	83	39	122
London, UK	23	25	77	Sydney, Australia	22	28	81
Los Angeles, CA	38	9	74	Tokyo, Japan.............	43	18	68
Manila, Philippines..........	60	33	NA	Toronto, Canada..........	26	17	43
Mexico City, Mexico........	69	74	130	Warsaw, Poland	49	16	32

NA = Not available. (1) Data for particulates are for 1999 and come from the World Bank study, "The Human Cost of Air Pollution: New Estimates for Developing Countries;" data for sulfur dioxide and nitrogen dioxide are derived from WHO's Healthy Cities Air Management Information System and the World Resources Institute and were collected in 1998 or, if earlier, are the latest available.

Emissions of Principal Air Pollutants in the U.S., 1970-2001

Source: U.S. Environmental Protection Agency, Office of Air Quality Planning and Standards; in thousand short tons; estimated

Source	1970	1975	1980	1985	1990	1995	1998	1999	2000	2001
Carbon monoxide......	204,043	188,398	185,407	176,844	154,189	126,777	115,382	117,229	123,568	120,759
Nitrogen oxides[1].......	26,883	26,377	27,079	25,757	25,530	24,956	24,349	23,671	23,199	22,349
Volatile org. compounds[1]	34,659	30,765	31,106	27,404	24,116	22,041	18,783	19,378	19,704	17,963
Particulate matter[2]....	13,023	7,556	7,013	41,324	27,758	25,819	22,900	21,632	24,699	24,104
Sulfur dioxide.........	31,218	28,043	25,925	23,307	23,078	18,619	18,947	17,651	16,317	15,790
TOTAL[3]............	**309,826**	**281,139**	**276,530**	**294,636**	**254,671**	**218,212**	**200,361**	**399,922**	**207,487**	**321,724**

(1) Ozone, a major air pollutant and the primary constituent of smog, is not emitted directly to the air but is formed by sunlight acting on emissions of nitrogen oxides and volatile organic compounds. (2) PM-10, particulates 10 microns or smaller in diameter. (3) Totals are rounded, as are components of totals.

Carbon Monoxide Emission Estimates, 1970-2001

Source: U.S. Environmental Protection Agency, Office of Air Quality Planning and Standards; in thousand short tons

Source	1970	1975	1980	1985	1990	1995	1998	1999	2000	2001
Fuel combustion, elec. util.	237	276	322	291	363	372	450	619	502	492
Industrial processes[1]...	10,610	8,304	7,700	5,893	5,572	5,631	4,890	3,528	3,562	3,700
Transportation	174,603	167,884	160,512	153,217	131,704	107,755	96,936	93,225	92,239	99,502
Forest wildfires........	5,620	2,165	5,396	2,957	5,928	1,469	2,627	7,524	17,878	7,136
TOTAL[2]............	**204,043**	**188,398**	**185,407**	**176,844**	**154,189**	**126,777**	**115,382**	**117,229**	**123,568**	**120,759**

(1) Includes industrial fuel combustion, chemical and allied manufacturing, metals processing, and petroleum and other industrial sectors. (2) Totals may not add because of rounding or because all categories are not listed.

Nitrogen Oxides Emission Estimates, 1970-2001

Source: U.S. Environmental Protection Agency, Office of Air Quality Planning and Standards; in thousand short tons

Source	1970	1975	1980	1985	1990	1995	1998	1999	2000	2001
Fuel combustion, elec. util.	4,900	5,694	7,024	6,127	6,663	6,384	6,231	5,665	5,311	4,891
Industrial processes[1]...	5,099	4,546	4,110	4,009	3,832	3,910	3,879	3,632	3,469	3,487
Transportation	15,277	15,029	14,845	14,508	13,375	12,989	12,777	12,767	12,560	12,405
TOTAL[2]............	**26,883**	**26,377**	**27,079**	**25,757**	**25,530**	**24,956**	**24,349**	**23,671**	**23,199**	**22,349**

(1) Includes industrial fuel combustion, chemical and allied manufacturing, metals processing, and petroleum and other industrial sectors. (2) Totals may not add because of rounding or because all categories are not listed.

Particulate Matter (PM-10) Emissions, 1970-2001*

Source: U.S. Environmental Protection Agency, Office of Air Quality Planning and Standards

Source	1970	1975	1980	1985	1990	1995	1998	1999	2000	2001
Fuel combustion, elec. util.	1,775	1,191	879	280	295	268	229	265	692	663
Industrial processes[1]...	8,310	4,267	3,433	1,199	1,198	1,130	812	961	967	997
Transportation	645	666	689	712	716	644	589	589	552	535
TOTAL[2]............	**13,023**	**7,556**	**7,013**	**41,324**	**27,758**	**25,819**	**22,900**	**21,632**	**24,699**	**24,104**

*PM-10 refers to particulates equal or smaller than 10 microns in diameter, and so capable of entering deep into the respiratory tract. (1) Includes industrial fuel combustion, chemical and allied manufacturing, metals processing, and petroleum and other industrial sectors. (2) Totals may not add because of rounding or because all categories are not listed.

Air Quality of Selected U.S. Metropolitan Areas, 1993-2002

Source: U.S. Environmental Protection Agency, Office of Air Quality Planning and Standards

Data indicate the number of days metropolitan statistical areas failed to meet acceptable air-quality standards. All figures were revised based on new standards set in 1998.

Metropolitan statistical area	1993	1994	1995	1996	1997	1998	1999	2000*	2001*	2002*
Atlanta, GA...........	36	15	36	28	33	52	67	34	18	24
Bakersfield, CA........	97	105	107	110	58	78	144	132	125	152
Baltimore, MD.........	48	40	36	28	30	51	40	19	32	42
Boston, MA–NH........	2	6	7	4	7	8	10	1	12	16
Chicago, IL...........	4	13	24	7	10	12	19	2	22	21
Dallas, TX............	12	24	29	10	27	33	25	22	16	15
Denver, CO...........	6	3	5	2	0	9	5	3	8	8
Detroit, MI............	5	11	14	13	11	17	20	15	27	26
El Paso, TX...........	7	6	3	6	2	6	5	4	9	13
Fresno, CA...........	59	55	61	70	75	67	133	131	138	152
Houston, TX..........	27	41	66	28	47	38	52	42	29	23
Las Vegas, NV–AZ.....	3	3	3	14	4	5	8	2	1	6
Los Angeles–Long Beach, CA....	134	139	113	94	60	56	56	87	88	80
Miami, FL............	6	1	2	4	1	3	8	7	2	1
Minneapolis–St. Paul, MN–WI.....	0	2	5	0	0	1	1	2	2	1
New Haven–Meriden, CT..........	12	13	14	8	19	9	19	9	15	25
New York, NY..........	11	16	21	14	23	18	25	19	19	31
Orange County, CA.....	25	15	9	9	3	6	14	31	31	19
Philadelphia, PA–NJ....	62	37	38	38	38	37	32	22	29	33
Phoenix–Mesa, AZ.....	14	10	22	15	12	14	10	10	8	8
Pittsburgh, PA	14	22	27	12	21	39	40	29	52	53
Riverside–San Bernardino, CA.....	168	150	125	118	107	96	123	145	155	145
Sacramento, CA.......	20	37	41	44	17	29	69	45	49	69
St. Louis, MO–IL.......	9	33	38	23	15	24	31	18	17	34
Salt Lake City–Ogden, UT...	5	17	5	14	2	19	8	15	15	18
San Diego, CA.........	59	46	48	31	14	33	33	31	31	20
San Francisco, CA.....	0	0	2	0	0	0	10	4	12	17
Seattle–Bellevue–Everett, WA....	0	3	2	6	1	3	6	7	3	6
Ventura, CA..........	43	63	66	62	45	29	24	31	25	11
Washington, DC–MD–VA–WV.....	52	22	32	18	30	47	39	11	22	34

* Includes fine particles less than or equal to 2.5 mm in diameter.

> ► **IT'S A FACT:** The phasing out of leaded gasoline caused lead emissions in the U.S. to drop about 94% between 1983 and 2002. The number of children with elevated levels of lead in their blood fell from an estimated 3-4 million in the late 1970s to 434,000 in the 1990s, according to the Environmental Protection Agency. However, lead from old paint, contaminated dust and soil, and some industrial processes continued to be a source of some concern.

Hazardous Waste Sites in the U.S., 2003

Source: U.S. Environmental Protection Agency, *National Priorities List*, Sept. 2003

State/Territory	Total proposed Gen	Fed	Total final Gen	Fed	Total	State/Territory	Total proposed Gen	Fed	Total final Gen	Fed	Total
Alabama	2	0	10	3	15	New Hampshire	1	0	18	1	20
Alaska	0	0	1	5	6	New Jersey	3	0	105	8	116
Arizona	0	0	7	2	9	New Mexico	1	0	10	1	12
Arkansas	0	0	12	0	12	New York	1	0	86	4	91
California	2	0	73	24	99	North Carolina	0	0	27	2	29
Colorado	2	0	13	3	18	North Dakota	0	0	0	0	0
Connecticut	1	0	14	1	16	Ohio	4	2	26	3	35
Delaware	0	0	14	1	15	Oklahoma	1	0	9	1	11
District of Columbia	0	0	0	1	1	Oregon	1	0	9	2	12
Florida	1	0	45	6	52	Pennsylvania	2	0	88	6	96
Georgia	1	0	12	2	15	Rhode Island	0	0	10	2	12
Hawaii	0	0	1	2	3	South Carolina	0	0	23	2	25
Idaho	3	0	4	2	9	South Dakota	0	0	1	1	2
Illinois	4	1	36	4	45	Tennessee	0	1	9	3	13
Indiana	1	0	28	0	29	Texas	2	0	39	4	45
Iowa	1	0	12	1	14	Utah	4	0	11	4	19
Kansas	1	1	9	1	12	Vermont	0	0	9	0	9
Kentucky	0	0	13	1	14	Virginia	0	0	19	11	30
Louisiana	2	0	12	1	15	Washington	0	0	33	14	47
Maine	0	0	9	3	12	West Virginia	0	0	7	2	9
Maryland	1	0	9	9	19	Wisconsin	1	0	39	0	40
Massachusetts	1	0	24	7	32	Wyoming	0	0	1	1	2
Michigan	1	1	67	0	69	American Samoa	0	0	0	0	0
Minnesota	0	0	22	2	24	Commonwealth of Marianas	0	0	0	0	0
Mississippi	2	0	2	0	4	Guam	0	0	1	1	2
Missouri	0	0	22	3	25	Puerto Rico	0	0	9	0	9
Montana	1	0	14	0	15	Trust Territories	0	0	0	0	0
Nebraska	0	0	10	1	11	Virgin Islands	0	0	2	0	2
Nevada	0	0	1	0	1	Total	48	6	1,087	158	1,299

Note: Gen = general superfund sites; Fed = federal facility sites.

Renewable Water Resources

Source: Food and Agriculture Organization, United Nations

Globally, water supplies are abundant, but they are unevenly distributed among and within countries. In some areas, water withdrawals are so high, relative to supply, that surface water supplies are shrinking and groundwater reserves are being depleted faster than they can be replenished by precipitation. The U.S. has a total of 3,069.4 cubic kilometers of internal renewable water resources, or 10,837 cubic meters per capita. Totals for the world are 43,764 cubic kilometers, or 7,243 cubic meters per capita. These numbers, and those in the tables below, were published by the Food and Agriculture Organization in 2003; the tables draw upon studies done over a number of years and use 2000 population data.

Countries With Most Resources

(ranked by per capita resources)

Country	Total cubic km	Cubic meters per capita	Country	Total cubic km	Cubic meters per capita	Country	Total cubic km	Cubic meters per capita
Iceland	170.0	609,319	Norway	382.0	85,478	Panama	148.0	51,814
Guyana	241.0	316,689	Belize	18.6	82,102	Venezuela	1,233.2	51,021
Suriname	122.0	292,566	Liberia	232.0	79,643	Colombia	2,132.0	50,635
Congo, Republic of.	832.0	275,679	Bolivia	622.5	74,743	Brazil	8,233.0	48,314
Papua New Guinea	801.0	166,563	Peru	1,913.0	74,546	Bhutan	95.0	45,564
Gabon	164.0	133,333	Laos	333.6	63,184	Uruguay	139.0	41,654
Solomon Islands	44.7	100,000	Paraguay	336.0	61,135	Central African		
Canada	2,902.0	94,353	Chile	922.0	60,614	Republic	144.4	38,849
New Zealand	327.0	86,554	Equatorial Guinea	26.0	56,893	Nicaragua	196.7	38,787

Countries With Least Resources*

(ranked by per capita resource, starting with the lowest)

Country/ Territory	Total cubic km	Cubic meters per capita	Country/ Territory	Total cubic km	Cubic meters per capita	Country/ Territory	Total cubic km	Cubic meters per capita
Kuwait	0.0	10	Jordan	0.9	179	Burundi	3.6	566
Gaza Strip, Palestine	0.1	52	Bahrain	0.1	181	Saint Kitts and Nevis	0.0	621
United Arab Emirates	0.2	58	Yemen	4.1	223	Rwanda	5.2	683
Bahamas	0.0	66	Israel	1.7	276	Cape Verde	0.3	703
Qatar	0.1	94	Barbados	0.1	301	Antigua and Barbuda	0.1	800
Maldives	0.0	103	Oman	1.0	388	Egypt	58.3	859
Libya	0.6	113	Algeria	14.3	473	Morocco	29.0	971
Saudi Arabia	2.4	118	Djibouti	0.3	475	Kenya	30.2	985
Malta	0.1	129	Tunisia	4.6	482	Cyprus	0.8	995
Singapore	0.6	149						

* Data not available from all nations.

WORLD ALMANAC QUICK QUIZ

Rank from highest to lowest, by how much carbon monoxide each of these sources emitted in the U.S. in 2001:

(a) forest wildfires   (b) combustion for electric utilities   (c) cars and other forms of transportation   (d) industrial sources

For the answer look in this chapter, or see page 1008.

Watersheds in the U.S.

Source: U.S. Environmental Protection Agency

A **watershed** is a water drainage area, or land areas bounded by ridges that catch rain and snow and drain to rivers, lakes, and groundwater within the drainage area. In a comprehensive assessment of watersheds in the continental U.S. released in Sept. 1999, the Environmental Protection Agency (EPA) concluded that 15% of the 2,262 watersheds had good water quality, 36% had moderate water quality, and 23% had less acceptable water quality. There was insufficient information to characterize the remaining 26%. The data indicate that polluted runoff from urban and rural areas is a major contributor to water quality problems, threatening water quality even in currently healthy watersheds.

The EPA categorized the watersheds by combining nationally available data from 15 databases, from both public and private sources, into a single Index of Watershed Indicators. The indicators include 7 to assess watershed quality and 8 to assess vulnerability to degradation from pollution. You can find information about your own watershed by going to the following website: www.epa.gov/surf3/index.html

U.S. List of Endangered and Threatened Species

Source: Fish and Wildlife Service, U.S. Dept. of Interior; as of Sept. 1, 2003

Group	Endangered U.S.	Endangered Foreign	Threatened U.S.	Threatened Foreign	Total species[1]	U.S. species with recovery plans	Group	Endangered U.S.	Endangered Foreign	Threatened U.S.	Threatened Foreign	Total species[1]	U.S. species with recovery plans
Mammals	65	251	9	17	342	54	Crustaceans	18	0	3	0	21	13
Birds	78	175	14	6	273	77	**Animal subtotal**	388	516	129	39	1,072	399
Reptiles	14	64	22	15	115	32	Flowering plants	571	1	144	0	716	574
Amphibians	12	8	9	1	30	14	Conifers & cycads	2	0	1	2	5	2
Fishes	71	11	44	0	126	96	Ferns and allies	24	0	2	0	26	26
Clams	62	2	8	0	72	57	Lichens	2	0	0	0	2	2
Snails	21	1	11	0	33	22	**Plant subtotal**	599	1	147	2	749	604
Insects	35	4	9	0	48	29							
Arachnids	12	0	0	0	12	5	**GRAND TOTAL**	987	517	276	41	1,821	1,003

(1) Some species are classified as both endangered and threatened. The table tallies these "dual status" species only once, as endangered, except for the olive ridley sea turtle, which is dual status but tallied as a U.S. threatened species. The other dual status species, all tallied as endangered, are: (U.S.) chinook salmon, gray wolf, green sea turtle, piping plover, roseate tern, sockeye salmon, steelhead, Steller sea-lion; (non-U.S.) argali, chimpanzee, leopard, saltwater crocodile.

Some Endangered Animal Species

Source: Fish and Wildlife Service, U.S. Dept. of the Interior

Common name	Scientific name	Range
Albatross, Amsterdam	Diomedia amsterdamensis	Amsterdam Island, Indian Ocean
Antelope, giant sable	Hippotragus niger variani	Angola
Armadillo, giant	Pridontes maximus	Venezuela, Guyana to Argentina
Babirusa	Babyrousa babyrussa	Indonesia
Bandicoot, desert	Perameles eremiana	Australia
Bat, gray	Myotis grisescens	Central, southeastern U.S.
Bear, brown (grizzly)	Ursus arctos arctos	Palearctic
Bison, wood	Bison bison athabascae	Canada, northwestern U.S.
Bobcat, Mexican	Felis rufus escuinapae	Central Mexico
Caiman, black	Melanosuchus niger	Amazon basin
Camel, Bactrian	Camelus bactrianus	Mongolia, China
Caribou, woodland	Rangifer tarandus caribou	U.S., Canada
Cheetah	Acinonyx jubatus	Africa to India
Chimpanzee, pygmy	Pan paniscus	Congo (formerly Zaire)
Condor, California	Gymnogyps californianus	U.S. (AZ, CA, OR), Mexico (Baja California)
Crane, whooping	Grus americana	Canada, Mexico, U.S. (Rocky Mts. to Carolinas)
Crocodile, American	Crocodylus acutus	U.S. (FL), Mexico, Caribbean Sea, Central and S America
Deer, Columbian white-tailed	Odocoileus virginianus leucurus	U.S. (OR, WA)
Dolphin, Chinese river	Lipotes vexillifer	China
Dugong	Dugong dugon	East Africa to southern Japan
Elephant, Asian	Elephas maximus	S central and southeastern Asia
Fox, northern swift	Vulpes velox hebes	U.S., Canada
Frog, Goliath	Conraua goliath	Cameroon, Equatorial Guinea, Gabon
Gorilla	Gorilla gorilla	Central and W Africa
Hartebeest, Tora	Alcelaphus buselaphus tora	Egypt, Ethiopia, Sudan
Hawk, Hawaiian	Buteo solitarius	U.S. (HI)
Hyena, brown	Hyaena brunnea	Southern Africa
Impala, black-faced	Aepyceros melampus petersi	Angola, Namibia
Kangaroo, Tasmanian forester	Macropus giganteus tasmaniensis	Australia (Tasmania)
Leopard	Panthera pardus	Africa and Asia
Lion, Asiatic	Panthera leo persica	Turkey to India
Manatee, West Indian	Trichechus manatus	Southeastern U.S., Caribbean Sea, S America
Monkey, spider	Ateles geoffroyi frontatus	Costa Rica, Nicaragua
Ocelot	Felis pardalis	U.S. (AZ, TX) to Central and S America
Orangutan	Pongo pygmaeus	Borneo, Sumatra
Ostrich, West African	Struthio camelus spatzi	W Sahara
Otter, marine	Lutra felina	Peru south to Straits of Magellan
Panda, giant	Ailuropoda melanoleuca	China
Panther, Florida	Felis concolor coryi	U.S. (LA, AR east to SC, FL)
Parakeet, golden	Aratinga guarouba	Brazil
Parrot, imperial	Amazona imperialis	West Indies (Dominica)
Penguin, Galapagos	Spheniscus mendiculus	Ecuador (Galapagos Islands)
Puma, eastern	Puma concolor couguar	Eastern N America
Python, Indian	Python molurus molurus	Sri Lanka, India
Rat-kangaroo, brush-tailed	Bettongia penicillata	Australia
Rhinoceros, black	Diceros bicornis	Sub-Saharan Africa
Rhinoceros, northern white	Ceratotherium simum cottoni	Congo (formerly Zaire), Sudan, Uganda, Central African Republic
Salamander, Chinese giant	Andrias davidianus davidianus	Western China

Common name	Scientific name	Range
Sea-lion, Steller	Eumetopias jubatus	Alaska, Russia
Sheep, bighorn	Ovis canadensis	California
Squirrel, Carolina northern flying	Glaucomys sabrinus coloratus	U.S. (NC, TN)
Tiger	Panthera tigris	Asia
Tortoise, Galapagos	Geochelone elephantopus	Ecuador (Galapagos Islands)
Turtle, Plymouth red-bellied	Pseudemys rubriventris bangsi	U.S. (MA)
Whale, gray	Eschrichtius robustus	N Pacific Ocean
Whale, humpback	Megaptera novaeangliae	Oceania
Wolf, red	Canis rufus	Southeastern U.S. to central TX
Woodpecker, ivory-billed	Campephilus principalis	S central and southeastern U.S., Cuba
Yak, wild	Bos grunniens mutus	China (Tibet), India
Zebra, mountain	Equus zebra zebra	South Africa

Classification

Source: *Funk & Wagnalls New Encyclopedia*

In biology, classification is the identification, naming, and grouping of organisms into a formal system. The 2 fields that are most directly concerned with classification are taxonomy and systematics. Although the 2 disciplines overlap considerably, taxonomy is more concerned with nomenclature (naming) and with constructing hierarchical systems, and systematics with uncovering evolutionary relationships. Two kingdoms of living forms, Plantae and Animalia, have been recognized since Aristotle established the first taxonomy in the 4th century BC. In addition, there are the following 3 kingdoms: Protista (one-celled organisms), Monera (bacteria and blue-green algae; also known as the kingdom Procaryotae), and Fungi. The 7 basic categories of classification (from most general to most specific) are: kingdom, phylum (or division), class, order, family, genus, and species. Below are 2 examples:

ZOOLOGICAL HIERARCHY

Kingdom	Phylum	Class	Order	Family	Genus	Species name	Common name
Animalia	Chordata	Mammalia	Primates	Hominidae	Homo	Homo sapiens	Human

BOTANICAL HIERARCHY

Kingdom	Division'	Class	Order	Family	Genus	Species name	Common name
Plantae	Magnoliophyta	Magnoliopsida	Magnoliales	Magnoliaceae	Magnolia	M. virginiana	Sweet Bay

* In botany, the division is generally used in place of the phylum.

Gestation, Longevity, and Incubation of Animals

Information reviewed by Ronald M. Nowak, author *Walker's Mammals of the World* (6th ed., Johns Hopkins University Press, 1999). Average longevity figures supplied by Ronald T. Reuther. These apply to animals in captivity; the potential life span of animals is rarely attained in nature. Figures on gestation and incubation are averages based on estimates.

ANIMAL	Gestation (days)	Average longevity (years)	Maximum longevity (yr-mo)	ANIMAL	Gestation (days)	Average longevity (years)	Maximum longevity (yr-mo)
Ass	365	12	47	Leopard	98	12	23
Baboon	187	20	45	Lion	100	15	30
Bear: Black	219	18	36-10	Monkey (rhesus)	166	15	37
Grizzly	225	25	50	Moose	240	12	27
Polar	240	20	45	Mouse (meadow)	21	3	4
Beaver	105	5	50	Mouse (dom. white)	19	3	6
Bison	285	15	40	Opossum (American)	13	1	5
Camel	406	12	50	Pig (domestic)	112	10	27
Cat (domestic)	63	12	28	Puma	90	12	20
Chimpanzee	230	20	60	Rabbit (domestic)	31	5	13
Chipmunk	31	6	10	Rhinoceros (black)	450	15	45-10
Cow	284	15	30	Rhinoceros (white)	480	20	50
Deer (white-tailed)	201	8	20	Sea lion (California)	350	12	34
Dog (domestic)	61	12	20	Sheep (domestic)	154	12	20
Elephant (African)	660	35	70	Squirrel (gray)	44	10	23-6
Elephant (Asian)	645	40	77	Tiger	105	16	26-3
Elk	250	15	26-8	Wolf (maned)	63	5	15-8
Fox (red)	52	7	14	Zebra (Grant's)	365	15	50
Giraffe	457	10	36-2				
Goat (domestic)	151	8	18	**Incubation time (days)**			
Gorilla	258	20	54	Chicken			21
Guinea pig	68	4	8	Duck			30
Hippopotamus	238	41	61	Goose			30
Horse	330	20	50	Pigeon			18
Kangaroo (gray)	36	7	24	Turkey			26

Speeds of Animals

Source: *Natural History* magazine. © The American Museum of Natural History

ANIMAL	mph	ANIMAL	mph	ANIMAL	mph
Cheetah	70	Mongolian wild ass	40	Human	27.89
Pronghorn antelope	61	Greyhound	39.35	Elephant	25
Wildebeest	50	Whippet	35.50	Black mamba snake	20
Lion	50	Rabbit (domestic)	35	Six-lined race runner (lizard)	18
Thomson's gazelle	50	Mule deer	35	Wild turkey	15
Quarterhorse	47.5	Jackal	35	Squirrel	12
Elk	45	Reindeer	32	Pig (domestic)	11
Cape hunting dog	45	Giraffe	32	Chicken	9
Coyote	43	White-tailed deer	30	Spider (Tegenaria atrica)	1.17
Gray fox	42	Wart hog	30	Giant tortoise	0.17
Hyena	40	Grizzly bear	30	Three-toed sloth	0.15
Zebra	40	Cat (domestic)	30	Garden snail	0.03

Note: Most of these measurements are for maximum speeds over approximate quarter-mile distances. Exceptions are the lion and elephant, whose speeds were clocked in the act of charging; the whippet, which was timed over a 200-yd course; the cheetah, timed over a 100-yd distance; and the black mamba, six-lined race runner, spider, giant tortoise, three-toed sloth, and garden snail, which were measured over various small distances.

Major Venomous Animals

Snakes

Asian pit viper — from 2 ft to 5 ft long; throughout Asia; reactions and mortality vary, but most bites cause tissue damage, and mortality is generally low.

Australian brown snake — 4 ft to 7 ft long; very slow onset of cardiac or respiratory distress; moderate mortality, but because death can be sudden and unexpected, it is the most dangerous of the Australian snakes; antivenom.

Barba Amarilla or fer-de-lance — up to 7 ft long; from tropical Mexico to Brazil; severe tissue damage common; moderate mortality; antivenom.

Black mamba — up to 14 ft long, fast-moving; S and C Africa; rapid onset of dizziness, difficulty breathing, erratic heartbeat; mortality high, nears 100% without antivenom.

Boomslang — less than 6 ft long; in African savannahs; rapid onset of nausea and dizziness, often followed by slight recovery and then sudden death from internal hemorrhaging; bites rare, mortality high; antivenom.

Bushmaster — up to 12 ft long; wet tropical forests of C and S America; few bites occur, but mortality rate is high.

Common or Asian cobra — 4 ft to 8 ft long; throughout southern Asia; considerable tissue damage, sometimes paralysis; mortality probably not more than 10%; antivenom.

Copperhead — less than 4 ft long; from New England to Texas; pain and swelling; very seldom fatal; antivenom seldom needed.

Coral snake — 2 ft to 5 ft long; in Americas south of Canada; bite may be painless; slow onset of paralysis, impaired breathing; mortalities rare, but high without antivenom and mechanical respiration.

Cottonmouth water moccasin — up to 5 ft long; wetlands of southern U.S. from Virginia to Texas. Rapid onset of severe pain, swelling; mortality low, but tissue destruction can be extensive; antivenom.

Death adder — less than 3 ft long; Australia; rapid onset of faintness, cardiac and respiratory distress; at least 50% mortality without antivenom.

Desert horned viper — in dry areas of Africa and western Asia; swelling and tissue damage; low mortality; antivenom.

European viper — 1 ft to 3 ft long; bleeding and tissue damage; mortality low; antivenom.

Gaboon viper — more than 6 ft long; fat; 2-in. fangs; south of the Sahara; massive tissue damage, internal bleeding; few recorded bites.

King cobra — up to 16 ft long; throughout southern Asia; rapid swelling, dizziness, loss of consciousness, difficulty breathing, erratic heartbeat; mortality varies sharply with amount of venom involved, but most bites involve nonfatal amounts; antivenom.

Krait — up to 5 ft long; in SE Asia; rapid onset of sleepiness; numbness; as much as 50% mortality even with use of antivenom.

Puff adder — up to 5 ft long; fat; south of the Sahara and throughout the Middle East; rapid large swelling, great pain, dizziness; moderate mortality, often from internal bleeding; antivenom.

Rattlesnake — 2 ft to 6 ft long; throughout W Hemisphere; rapid onset of severe pain, swelling; mortality low, but amputation of affected digits is sometimes necessary; antivenom. Mojave rattler may produce temporary paralysis.

Ringhals, or spitting, cobra — 5 ft to 7 ft long; southern Africa; squirts venom through holes in front of fangs as a defense; venom is severely irritating, can cause blindness.

Russell's viper or tic-polonga — more than 5 ft long; throughout Asia; internal bleeding; bite reports common; moderate mortality rate; antivenom.

Saw-scaled or carpet viper — as much as 2 ft long; in dry areas from India to Africa; severe bleeding, fever; high mortality, causes more human fatalities than any other snake; antivenom.

Sea snakes — throughout Pacific, Indian oceans except NE Pacific; almost painless bite, variety of muscle pain, paralysis; mortality rate low, many bites not envenomed; some antivenoms.

Sharp-nosed pit viper or one hundred pace snake — up to 5 ft long; in S Vietnam, Taiwan, and China; the most toxic of Asian pit vipers; very rapid onset of swelling and tissue damage, internal bleeding; moderate mortality; antivenom.

Taipan — up to 11 ft long; in Australia and New Guinea; rapid paralysis with severe breathing difficulty; mortality nears 100% without antivenom.

Tiger snake — 2 ft to 6 ft long; S Australia; pain, numbness, mental disturbances with rapid onset of paralysis; may be the deadliest of all land snakes, although antivenom is quite effective.

Yellow or Cape cobra — 7 ft long; in S Africa; most toxic venom of any cobra; rapid onset of swelling, breathing and cardiac difficulties; mortality is high without treatment; antivenom.

Note: Not all bites by venomous snakes are actually envenomed. Any animal bite, however, carries the danger of tetanus, and anyone suffering a venomous snake bite should seek medical attention. Antivenoms do not cure; they are only an aid in the treatment of bites. Mortality rates above are for envenomed bites; low mortality, c. 2% or less; moderate, 2%-5%; high, 5%-15%.

Lizards

Gila monster — as much as 24 in. long, with heavy body and tail; in high desert in SW U.S. and N Mexico; immediate severe pain and transient low blood pressure; no recent mortality.

Mexican beaded lizard — similar to Gila monster, Mexican west coast; reaction and mortality rate similar to Gila monster.

Insects

Ants, bees, wasps, hornets, etc. Global distribution. Usual reaction is piercing pain in area of sting. Not directly fatal, except in cases of massive multiple stings. However, many people suffer allergic reactions — swelling and rashes — and a few may die within minutes from severe sensitivity to the venom (anaphylactic shock).

Spiders, Scorpions

Atrax spider — also known as funnel web spider; several varieties, often large; in Australia; slow onset of breathing, circulation difficulties; low mortality; antivenom.

Black widow — small, round-bodied with red hourglass marking; the widow and its relatives are found in tropical and temperate zones; severe musculoskeletal pain, weakness, breathing difficulty, convulsions; may be more serious in small children; low mortality; antivenom. The **redback** spider of Australia has the hourglass marking on its back, rather than on its front, but is otherwise identical to the black widow.

Brown recluse, or fiddleback, spider — small, oblong body; throughout U.S.; pain with later ulceration at place of bite; in severe cases fever, nausea, and stomach cramps; ulceration may last months; very low mortality.

Scorpion — crablike body with stinger in tail, various sizes, many varieties throughout tropical and subtropical areas; various symptoms may include severe pain spreading from the wound, numbness, severe agitation, cramps; severe reaction may include respiratory failure; low mortality, usually in children; antivenoms.

Tarantula — large, hairy spider found around the world; the American tarantula, and probably all other tarantulas, are harmless to humans, though their bite may cause some pain and swelling.

Sea Life

Cone-shell — mollusk in small, beautiful shell; in the S Pacific and Indian oceans; shoots barbs into victims; paralysis; low mortality.

Octopus — global distribution, usually in warm waters; all varieties produce venom, but only a few can cause death; rapid onset of paralysis with breathing difficulty.

Portuguese man-of-war — jellyfishlike, with tentacles up to 70 ft long; in most warm water areas; immediate severe pain; not directly fatal, though shock may cause death in rare cases.

Sea wasp — jellyfish, with tentacles up to 30 ft long, in the S Pacific; very rapid onset of circulatory problems; high mortality because of speed of toxic reaction; antivenom.

Stingray — several varieties of differing sizes; found in tropical and temperate seas and some fresh water; severe pain, rapid onset of nausea, vomiting, breathing difficulties; wound area may ulcerate, gangrene may appear; seldom fatal.

Stonefish — brownish fish that lies motionless as a rock on bottom in shallow water; throughout S Pacific and Indian oceans; extraordinary pain, rapid paralysis; low mortality; antivenom available; amount determined by number of puncture wounds; warm water relieves pain.

Major U.S. Public Zoological Parks

Source: *World Almanac* questionnaire, 2003; budget and attendance in millions; figures latest available

Zoo	Budget	Attendance	Acres	Species	Some major attractions/information
Arizona-Sonora Desert Museum (Tucson, AZ)	$6.0	0.5	100	300+	Desert Loop Trail, Hummingbird Aviary, Pollination Gardens (520) 883-2702; www.desertmuseum.org
Audubon Zoo (New Orleans)	NA	0.9	58	350+	Jaguar Jungle, Monkey Treehouse, white tigers (866) ITS-AZOO; www.audubonzoo.org
Baltimore Zoo	NA	0.6	161	305	Children's zoo, African Watering Hole, Keeper Encounters (410) 396-7102; www.baltimorezoo.org
Bronx Zoo/Wildlife Conservation Park (N.Y.C.)	38.0	2.2	265	500+	Tiger Mountain, Congo Gorilla Forest, Jungle World (718) 367-1010; www.bronxzoo.com
Brookfield Zoo (Chicago area)	48.0	2.0	216	479	Family Play Zoo, Living Coast, Habitat Africa, Tropic World (708) 485-0263; www.brookfieldzoo.org
Buffalo (NY) Zoological Gardens	4.8	0.4	24	200	Indian Rhino Pavilion, Gorilla Rainforest, Vanishing Animals (716) 837-3900; www.buffalozoo.org
Cincinnati Zoo and Botanical Garden	20.0	1.2	75	542	Vanishing Giants, Jungle Trails, Manatee Springs (800) 94-HIPPO; www.cincinnatizoo.org
Cleveland Metroparks Zoo	13.0	1.2	168	625	Rainforest, Wolf Wilderness, Australian Adventure (216) 661-6500; www.clemetzoo.com
Columbus Zoo and Aquarium (Powell, OH)	20.0	1.3	580	700	Manatee Coast, Discovery Reef, African Forest (800) MONKEYS; www.colszoo.org
Dallas Zoo	13.0	0.6	95	400	Endangered Tiger Habitat, Wilds of Africa, Children's Zoo (214) 670-5656; www.dallaszoo.org
Denver Zoo	15.3	1.7	80	715	Komodo Dragon habitat, okapi, black rhino, primates (303) 376-4800; www.denverzoo.org
Detroit Zoological Park (Royal Oak, MI)	12.8	1.3	125	581	Arctic Ring of Life, Wild Adventure, Natl. Amphibian Center (248) 398-0900; www.detroitzoo.org
The Houston Zoo	17.0	1.5	55	700+	Wortham World of Primates, koalas, komodo dragons (713) 533-6500; www.houstonzoo.org
Lincoln Park Zoological Gardens (Chicago)	17.0	3.0	35	208	Farm-in-the-Zoo, Kovler Lion House, Primate House (312) 742-2000; www.lpzoo.org
Los Angeles Zoo and Botanical Gardens	16.0	1.5	80	370	Dragons of Komodo, Chimpanzees of Mahale Mountains (323) 644-6400; www.lazoo.org
Louisville (KY) Zoo	10.0	0.8	134	402	African Petting Zoo, Islands Exhibit, Gorilla Forest (502) 459-2181; www.louisvillezoo.org
Memphis (TN) Zoo	8.0	0.7	70+	500+	China Exhibit, Cat Country, Primate Canyon (901) 276-WILD; www.memphiszoo.org
Miami Metrozoo	9.0	0.5	300	325	Komodo dragons, meerkats, Dr. Wilde's Rainforest Museum (305) 251-0400; www.zsf.org
Milwaukee County Zoo	19.1	1.3	192	395	Apes of Africa, Siberian Tigers, Lake Wisconsin Exhibit (414) 771-3040; www.milwaukeezoo.org
Minnesota Zoo (Apple Valley)	16.6	1.0	485	400+	Meerkats of the Kalahari, Dolphin shows, Tiger Lair (800) 366-7811; www.mnzoo.org
The National Zoo (Washington, DC)	28.6	3.0	163	475	Giant pandas, Sumatran tigers, Great Cats Exchange (202) 673-4800; www.fonz.org
North Carolina Zoo	15.0	0.7	1,448	250	On the Wing Bird Show, Deep Sea the Ride, Polar Bears (800) 488-0444; www.nczoo.org
Oklahoma City Zoological Park & Botanical Garden	10.5	0.7	110	600	Aquaticus, Cat Forest, Lion Overlook, Great EscApe (405) 424-3344; www.okczoo.com
Omaha's Henry Doorly Zoo	16.0	1.4	130	800	World's largest nocturnal exhibit, indoor rain forest, aquarium (402) 733-8401; www.omahazoo.org
Oregon Zoo (Portland)	28.6	1.3	64	200	Penguinarium, Africa Rainforest, Steller Cove (503) 226-1561; www.oregonzoo.org
Philadelphia Zoo	19.1	1.2	42	330	PECO Primate Reserve, Reptile and Amphibian House (215) 243-1100; www.phillyzoo.org
Phoenix (AZ) Zoo	15.0	1.2	125	250	Arizona Trail, Discovery Trail, Africa Trail, Tropics Trail (602) 273-1341; www.phoenixzoo.org
Point Defiance Zoo & Aquarium (Tacoma, WA)	6.4	0.4	27	300	Polar bears, sharks, elephants, leopards, petting farm (253) 591-5337; www.pdza.org
Rio Grande Zoo (Albuquerque, NM)	9.0	1.0	64	200	Animals of Africa, Australia, and the Americas, waterfalls (505) 764-6200; www.cabq.gov/biopark
Riverbanks Zoo & Garden (Columbia, SC)	6.2	0.9	170	375+	Ndoki Forest, Koala Knockabout, African Plains, Birdhouse (803) 779-8717; www.riverbanks.org
St. Louis Zoo	33.9	2.7	90	767	Big Cat Country, Jungle of the Apes, Monsanto Insectarium (314) 781-0900; www.stlzoo.org
San Diego Wild Animal Park	NA	1.7	1,800	400+	Condor Ridge, Heart of Africa, Wgasa Bush Line Railway (760) 747-8702; www.sandiegozoo.org/wap/ visitor_info.html
San Diego Zoo	NA	3.5	100	800+	Panda research station, Polar Bear Plunge, Gorilla Tropics (619) 234-3153; www.sandiegozoo.org
San Francisco Zoo	16.0	0.9	100	225	Gorilla World, Koala Crossing, Penguin Island, Lemur Forest (415) 753-7080; www.sfzoo.org
Toledo (OH) Zoo	15.0	1.0	62	700	Hippoquarium, Frogtown, Arctic Encounter, Africa! (419) 385-5721; www.toledozoo.org
Tulsa (OK) Zoo and Living Museum	3.9	0.6	82	450	North American Rain Forest, Elephant Encounter (918) 669-6600; www.tulsazoo.org
Woodland Park Zoo (Seattle)	21.0	1.0	9	290	Baby Asian elephant, Tropical Rain Forest, Northern Trail (206) 684-4800; www.zoo.org
Zoo Atlanta	15.8	0.7	39	221	Gorillas of the Ford African Rain Forest, Orkin Children's Zoo (404) 624-5600; www.zooatlanta.org

Note: NA = Not available.

Major Canadian Public Zoological Parks

Source: *World Almanac* questionnaire, 2003; budget in millions of dollars (Canadian), attendance in millions; figures latest available.

Zoo	Budget	Atten-dance	Acres	Species	Some major attractions/information
Assiniboine Park Zoo (Winnipeg)	$2.4	0.4	90	360	Snow leopards, polar and grizzly bears, Tropical House *(204) 986-2327;* www.zoosociety.com
Calgary Zoo	NA	0.9	136	254	Botanical Garden, Prehistoric Park, Canadian Wilds *(403) 232-9300;* www.calgaryzoo.ab.ca
Granby Zoo (Quebec)	11.7	0.5	100	225	Exotic Animal collection, AMAZOO water park *(877) GRANBYZOO;* www.zoogranby.ca
Toronto Zoo	31.0	1.2	710	500	Gorilla Rainforest, African Savanna, polar bears *(416) 392-5900;* www.torontozoo.com

Top 50 American Kennel Club Registrations

Source: American Kennel Club, New York, NY; covers (new) dogs registered during calendar year shown

Breed	Rank (2002)	Number registered (2002)	Rank (2001)	Number registered (2001)	Breed	Rank (2002)	Number registered (2002)	Rank (2001)	Number registered (2001)
Labrador Retriever	1	154,616	1	165,970	English Springer Spaniel	27	9,128	27	10,180
Golden Retriever	2	56,124	2	62,497	Great Dane	28	8,975	28	9,629
German Shepherd Dog	3	46,963	3	51,625	Weimaraner	29	8,774	29	8,964
Beagle	4	44,610	5	50,419	Brittany	30	7,846	31	8,465
Dachshund	5	42,571	4	50,478	West Highland White				
Yorkshire Terrier	6	37,277	6	42,025	Terrier	31	7,814	30	8,716
Boxer	7	34,340	8	37,035	Collie	32	6,252	33	7,340
Poodle	8	33,917	7	40,550	Pekingese	33	5,822	32	7,798
Chihuahua	9	28,466	9	36,627	Mastiff	34	5,797	37	5,434
Shih Tzu	10	28,294	10	33,240	Australian Shepherd	35	5,789	35	6,158
Miniature Schnauzer	11	23,926	13	27,587	Lhasa Apso	36	5,259	34	6,584
Pomeranian	12	23,061	12	28,495	Saint Bernard	37	5,188	36	5,722
Rottweiler	13	22,196	11	29,269	Papillon	38	4,547	40	4,438
Pug	14	21,774	15	23,769	Chinese Shar-Pei	39	4,437	38	5,416
Cocker Spaniel	15	20,655	14	25,445	Cavalier King Charles				
Shetland Sheepdog	16	17,453	16	20,899	Spaniel	40	4,028	44	3,612
Boston Terrier	17	15,983	18	18,100	Akita	41	3,987	39	4,904
Bulldog	18	15,810	19	15,501	Chesapeake Bay				
Miniature Pinscher	19	15,230	17	19,072	Retriever	42	3,829	41	4,400
Maltese	20	13,049	20	15,214	Cairn Terrier	43	3,812	42	4,333
Siberian Husky	21	12,350	21	14,915	Scottish Terrier	44	3,516	43	3,958
German Shorthaired					Newfoundland	45	3,121	50	2,911
Pointer	22	12,174	22	12,884	Vizsla	46	3,106	45	3,235
Doberman Pinscher	23	11,829	24	12,570	Bullmastiff	47	2,900	49	2,987
Basset Hound	24	10,789	23	12,850	Airedale Terrier	48	2,841	46	3,055
Pembroke Welsh Corgi	25	9,921	26	10,344	Bloodhound	49	2,804	48	3,010
Bichons Frise	26	9,706	25	10,969	Great Pyrenee	50	2,773	47	3,033

Cat Breeds, 2003

Source: The Cat Fanciers' Association, Manasquan, NJ

Only a small percentage of house cats in the U.S. are pedigreed or registered with one of the official registering bodies. The largest is the Cat Fanciers' Assn., Inc., with 685 member clubs. The Cat Fanciers' Association recognized 40 breeds as of Oct. 1, 2003 (in order of registration totals): Persian, Maine Coon, Exotic, Siamese, Abyssinian, Oriental, Birman, American Shorthair, Tonkinese (tied with American Shorthair), Burmese, Scottish Fold, Cornish Rex, Ragdoll, Devon Rex, Norwegian Forest Cat, Ocicat, Russian Blue, British Shorthair, Colorpoint Shorthair, Somali, Manx, Egyptian Mau, Japanese Bobtail, Turkish Angora, Sphynx, Chartreux, Selkirk Rex, American Curl, American Bobtail, Siberian, European Burmese, Bombay, Singapura, Turkish Van, Javanese, Korat, Balinese, Havana Brown, American Wirehair, and La Perm.

Frontier Forests

Only 1/5 of the Earth's forest cover from 8,000 years ago survives unfragmented, in large unspoiled tracts called **frontier forests**. These forests are big enough to provide stable habitats for a rich diversity of plant and animal species. Most are in the far north or the tropics (2/3 of their acreage is in Russia, Canada, or Brazil); most are also under threat from development or other causes.

Trees of the U.S.

Source: American Forests, Washington, DC

Approximately 826 native and naturalized species of trees are grown in the U.S. The oldest living tree is believed to be a bristlecone pine tree in California named Methuselah, estimated to be 4,700 years old. The world's largest known living tree, the General Sherman giant sequoia in California, weighs more than 6,167 tons—as much as 41 blue whales or 740 elephants. Listed here are 10 largest National Champion trees selected by American Forests.

10 Largest National Champion Trees

Tree Type	Girth at 4.5 ft. (in.)	Height (ft.)	Crown Spread (ft.)	Total Points	Location
Giant sequoia (Gen. Sherman tree)	1,024	261	108	1,312	Sequoia National Park, CA
Coast redwood	950	321	80	1,291	Jedidiah Smith State Park, CA
Western redcedar	761	159	45	931	Olympic National Park, WA
Sitka spruce	707	191	96	922	Olympic National Park, WA
Coast Douglas-fir	505	281	71	804	Olympic National Forest, WA
Bluegum eucalyptus	586	141	126	759	Petrolia, CA
Common baldcypress	644	83	85	748	Cat Island, LA
California-laurel	546	108	118	684	Grass Valley, CA
Sugar pine	442	232	29	681	Dorrington, CA
Port-Orford-cedar	451	219	39	680	Siskiyou National Forest, OR

DISASTERS

As of Oct. 1, 2003. Listings in this chapter are selective and may not include acts of terrorism, war related disasters, or disasters with relatively low fatalities.

Some Notable Shipwrecks Since 1854

(Figures indicate estimated lives lost. Does not include most military disasters.)

1854, Mar.—City of Glasgow; Brit. steamer missing in N Atlantic; 480.

1854, Sept. 27—Arctic; U.S. (Collins Line) steamer sunk in collision with French steamer *Vesta* near Cape Race; 285-351.

1856, Jan. 23—Pacific; U.S. (Collins Line) steamer missing in N Atlantic; 186-286.

1858, Sept. 23—Austria; German steamer destroyed by fire in N Atlantic; 471.

1863, Apr. 27—Anglo-Saxon; Brit. steamer wrecked at Cape Race; 238.

1865, Apr. 27—Sultana; Mississippi River steamer blew up near Memphis, TN; 1,450.

1869, Oct. 27—Stonewall; steamer burned on Mississippi River below Cairo, IL; 200.

1870, Jan. 25—City of Boston; Brit. (Inman Line) steamer vanished between New York and Liverpool; 177.

1870, Oct. 19—Cambria; Brit. steamer wrecked off N Ireland; 196.

1872, Nov. 7—Mary Celeste; U.S. half-brig sailed from New York for Genoa; found abandoned; loss of life unknown.

1873, Jan. 22—Northfleet; Brit. steamer foundered off Dungeness, England; 300.

1873, Apr. 1—Atlantic; Brit. (White Star) steamer wrecked off Nova Scotia; 585.

1873, Nov. 23—Ville du Havre; French steamer sank after collision with Brit. sailing ship *Loch Earn;* 226.

1875, May 7—Schiller; German steamer wrecked off Scilly Isles; 312.

1875, Nov. 4—Pacific; U.S. steamer sank after collision off Cape Flattery; 236.

1878, Sept. 3—Princess Alice; Brit. steamer sank after collision in Thames River; 700.

1878, Dec. 18—Byzantin; French steamer sank after collision in Dardanelles; 210.

1881, May 24—Victoria; steamer capsized in Thames River, Canada; 200.

1883, Jan. 19—Cimbria; German steamer sank in collision with Brit. steamer *Sultan* in North Sea; 389.

1887, Nov. 15—Wah Yeung; Brit. steamer burned at sea; 400.

1890, Feb. 17—Duburg; Brit. steamer wrecked, China Sea; 400.

1890, Sept. 19—Ertogrul; Turkish frigate wrecked off Japan; 540.

1891, Mar. 17—Utopia; Brit. steamer sank in collision with Brit. ironclad *Anson* off Gibraltar; 562.

1895, Jan. 30—Elbe; German steamer sank in collision with Brit. steamer *Craithie* in North Sea; 332.

1895, Mar. 11—Reina Regenta; Spanish cruiser foundered near Gibraltar; 400.

1898, Feb. 15—Maine; U.S. battleship blown up in Havana Harbor; 260.

1898, July 4—La Bourgogne; French steamer sank in collision with Brit. sailing ship *Cromartyshire* off Nova Scotia; 549.

1898, Nov. 26—Portland; U.S. steamer wrecked off Cape Cod; 157.

1904, June 15—General Slocum; excursion steamer burned in East River, New York City; 1,030.

1904, June 28—Norge; Danish steamer wrecked on Rockall Island, Scotland; 620.

1906, Aug. 4—Sirio; Italian steamer wrecked off Cape Palos, Spain; 350.

1908, Mar. 23—Matsu Maru; Japanese steamer sank in collision near Hakodate, Japan; 300.

1909, Aug. 1—Waratah; Brit. steamer, Sydney to London, vanished; 300.

1910, Feb. 9—General Chanzy; French steamer wrecked off Minorca, Spain; 200.

1911, Sept. 25—Liberté; French battleship exploded at Toulon; 285.

1912, Mar. 5—Principe de Asturias; Spanish steamer wrecked off Spain; 500.

1912, Apr. 14-15—Titanic; Brit. (White Star) steamer hit iceberg in N Atlantic; 1,503.

1912, Sept. 28—Kichemaru; Japanese steamer sank off Japanese coast; 1,000.

1914, May 29—Empress of Ireland; Brit. (Canadian Pacific) steamer sunk in collision with Norwegian collier in St. Lawrence River; 1,014.

1915, May 7—Lusitania; Brit. (Cunard Line) steamer torpedoed and sunk by German submarine off Ireland; 1,198.

1915, July 24—Eastland; excursion steamer capsized in Chicago River; 844.

1916, Feb. 26—Provence; French cruiser sank in Mediterranean; 3,100.

1916, Mar. 3—Principe de Asturias; Spanish steamer wrecked near Santos, Brazil; 558.

1916, Aug. 29—Hsin Yu; Chinese steamer sank off Chinese coast; 1,000.

1917, Dec. 6—Mont Blanc, Imo; French ammunition ship and Belgian steamer collided in Halifax Harbor; 1,600.

1918, Apr. 25—Kiang-Kwan; Chinese steamer sank in collision off Hankow; 500.

1918, July 12—Kawachi; Japanese battleship blew up in Tokayama Bay; 500.

1918, Oct. 25—Princess Sophia; Canadian steamer sank off Alaskan coast; 398.

1919, Jan. 17—Chaonia; French steamer lost in Straits of Messina, Italy; 460.

1919, Sept. 9—Valbanera; Spanish steamer lost off Florida coast; 500.

1921, Mar. 18—Hong Kong; steamer wrecked in South China Sea; 1,000.

1922, Aug. 26—Niitaka; Japanese cruiser sank in storm off Kamchatka, USSR; 300.

1924, June 12—USS Mississippi; U.S. battleship; explosions in gun turret, off San Pedro, CA; 48.

1927, Oct. 25—Principessa Mafalda; Italian steamer blew up, sank off Porto Seguro, Brazil; 314.

1928, Nov. 12—Vestris; Brit. steamer sank off Virginia; 113.

1934, Sept. 8—Morro Castle; U.S. steamer, Havana to New York, burned off Asbury Park, NJ; 134.

1939, May 23—Squalus; U.S. submarine sank off Portsmouth, NH; 26.

1939, June 1—Thetis; submarine sank, Liverpool Bay; 99.

1942, Feb. 18—Truxtun and Pollux; U.S. destroyer and cargo ship ran aground, sank off Newfoundland; 204.

1942, Oct. 2—Curacao; Brit. cruiser sank after collision with liner *Queen Mary;* 338.

1944, Dec. 17-18—3 U.S. Third Fleet destroyers sank during typhoon in Philippine Sea; 790.

1947, Jan. 19—Himera; Greek steamer hit a mine off Athens; 392.

1947, Apr. 16—Grandcamp; French freighter exploded in Texas City, TX, harbor, starting fires; 576+.

1948, Nov.—Chinese army evacuation ship exploded and sank off S Manchuria; 6,000.

1948, Dec. 3—Kiangya; Chinese refugee ship wrecked in explosion S of Shanghai; 1,100+.

1949, Sept. 17—Noronic; Canadian Great Lakes Cruiser burned at Toronto dock; 130.

1952, Apr. 26—Hobson and Wasp; U.S. destroyer and aircraft carrier collided in Atlantic; 176.

1954, May 26—Pennington; sank off Rhode Island; 103.

1954, Sept. 26—Toya Maru; Japanese ferry sank in Tsugaru Strait, Japan; 1,172.

1956, July 26—Andrea Doria and Stockholm; Italian liner and Swedish liner collided off Nantucket; 51.

1957, July 14—Eshghabad; Soviet ship ran aground in Caspian Sea; 270.

1960, Dec. 19—Constellation; U.S. aircraft carrier caught fire in Brooklyn Navy Yard, NY; 49.

1961, Apr. 8—Dara; British ocean liner exploded in Persian Gulf; 236.

1961, July 8—Save; Portuguese ship ran aground off Mozambique; 259.

1963, Apr. 10—Thresher; U.S. Navy atomic submarine sank in N Atlantic; 129.

1964, Feb. 10—Australian destroyer *Voyager* sank after collision with aircraft carrier *Melbourne* off New South Wales; 82.

1965, Nov. 13—Yarmouth Castle; Panamanian registered cruise ship burned and sank off Nassau; 89.

1967, July 29—Forrestal; U.S. aircraft carrier caught fire off N Vietnam; 134.

1968, Jan. 25—Dakar; Israeli submarine vanished in Mediterranean Sea; 69.

1968, late May—Scorpion; U.S. nuclear submarine sank in Atlantic near Azores; 99 (located Oct. 31).

1969, June 2—Evans; U.S. destroyer cut in half by Australian carrier *Melbourne,* S China Sea; 74.

1970, Mar. 4—Eurydice; French submarine sank in Mediterranean near Toulon; 57.

1970, Dec. 15—Namyong-Ho; South Korean ferry sank in Korea Strait; 308.

1974, May 1—Motor launch capsized off Bangladesh; 250.

1974, Sept. 26—Soviet destroyer sank in Black Sea; 200+.

1975, Nov. 10—Edmund Fitzgerald; U.S. cargo ship sank during storm on Lake Superior; 29.

1976, Oct. 20—George Prince and Frosta; ferryboat and Norwegian tanker collided on Mississippi R. at Luling, LA; 77.

1976, Dec. 25—Patria; Egyptian liner caught fire and sank in the Red Sea; 100.

1979, Aug. 14—23 yachts competing in Fastnet yacht race sank or abandoned during storm in S Irish Sea; 18.

1981, Jan. 27—Tamponas II; Indonesian passenger ship caught fire and sank in Java Sea; 580.

1981, May 26—Nimitz; U.S. Marine combat jet crashed on deck of U.S. aircraft carrier; 14.

1983, Feb. 12—Marine Electric; coal freighter sank during storm off Chincoteague, VA; 33.

1983, May 25—10th of Ramadan; Nile steamer caught fire and sank in Lake Nasser; 357.

1986, Apr. 20—ferry sank near Barisal, Bangladesh; 262.

1986, Aug. 31—Soviet passenger ship *Admiral Nakhimov* and Soviet freighter *Pyotr Vasev* collided in Black Sea; 398.

1987, Mar. 6—British ferry capsized off Zeebrugge, Belgium; 189.

1987, Dec. 20—Philippine ferry *Dona Paz* and oil tanker *Victor* collided in Tablas Strait; 4,341.

1988, Aug. 6—Indian ferry capsized on Ganges R.; 400+.

1989, Apr. 19—USS Iowa; explosion in gun turret; 47.

1989, Apr. 7—Komsolets; Soviet submarine; sank after fire off Norwegian coast; 42.

1989, Aug. 20—Brit. barge *Bowbelle* struck Brit. pleasure cruiser *Marchioness* on Thames R. in central London; 56.

1989, Sept. 10—Romanian pleasure boat and Bulgarian barge collided on Danube R.; 161.

1991, Apr. 10—Auto ferry and oil tanker collided outside Livorno Harbor, Italy; 140.

1991, Dec. 14—Salem Express; ferry rammed coral reef near Safaga, Egypt; 462.

1993, Feb. 17—Neptune; ferry capsized off Port-au-Prince, Haiti; 500+.

1993, Oct. 10—West Sea Ferry; capsized in Yellow Sea near W South Korea during storm; 285.

1994, Sept. 28—Estonia; ferry sank in Baltic Sea; 1,049.

1996, May 21—Bukoba; ferry sank in Lake Victoria (Africa); 500.

1997, Feb. 20—Tamil refugee boat sank off Sri Lanka; 165.

1997, Mar. 28—Albanian refugee boat sank in Adriatic Sea after being rammed by Italian navy warship *Sibilla*; 83.

1997, Sept. 8—Pride of la Gonâve; Haitian ferry sank off Montrouis, Haiti; 200+.

1998, Apr. 4—passenger boat capsized off coast near Ibaka beach, Nigeria; 280.

1998, Sept. 2—2 passenger boats capsized on Lake Kivu, near Bukavu, Congo; 200+.

1998, Sept. 18—ferry sank S of Manila; 97.

1999, Feb. 6—Harta Rimba; cargo ship sank off Indonesia; 280+.

1999, Mar. 26—passenger boat overturned off coast, Sierra Leone; 150+.

1999, Apr. 2—passenger ferry sank off coast of Nigeria; 100+.

1999, May 1—amphibious excursion boat sank in Lake Hamilton, AR; 13.

1999, May 8—passenger ferry capsized off Bangladesh; 200+.

1999, Nov. 24—Dashun; passenger ferry capsized near Yantai, China; 280.

2000, May 3—2 ferries capsized, Meghna R., Bangladesh; 72+.

2000, June 29—overloaded ferry capsized in storm off Sulawesi Island, Indonesia; 500+.

2000, Aug. 12—Kursk; Russian submarine sank in Barents Sea; 118.

2000, Sept. 26—Express Samina; Greek ferry sank off Paros, Greece; 81+.

2001, Feb. 9—Ehime Maru; Japanese trawler sunk by surfacing U.S. submarine *Greeneville*, near Hawaii; 9.

2001, Dec. 22—North Korean spy ship sank after exchanging fire with Japanese coast guard; 15.

2001, Oct. 19—Indonesian fishing boat overloaded with asylum-seekers sank off Java's south coast; 350+.

2002, May 4—Bangladesh ferry sank, Meghna R.; 370+.

2002, May 26—barge struck Interstate highway bridge over Arkansas R. in Oklahoma; 13+.

2002, Sept. 26—overloaded Senegalese ferry capsized in ocean off The Gambia; 1,863.

2003, Mar. 23—overloaded ferry capsized in Lake Tanganyika off Burundi; 111+.

2003, Apr. 4—ferry sank near Chhatak in Bangladesh; 80+.

2003, Apr. 21—2 ferries capsized in storms in Bangladesh on Meghna and Buriganga rivers; 180+.

2003, May 2 (reported)—Chinese submarine accident off Shandong prov.; 70.

2003, July 8—overcrowded ferry sank near Chandpur in the Bangladesh River; c. 400.

Some Notable Aircraft Disasters Since 1937

Date	Aircraft	Site of accident	Deaths
1937, May 6	German zeppelin Hindenburg	Burned at mooring, Lakehurst, NJ	36*
1944, Aug. 23	U.S. Air Force B-24 Liberator bomber	Hit school, Freckleton, England	61*
1945, July 28	U.S. Army B-25	Hit Empire State Building, New York, NY	14*
1952, Dec. 20	U.S. Air Force C-124	Fell, burned, Moses Lake, WA	87
1953, Mar. 3	Canadian Pacific Comet Jet	Karachi, Pakistan	11[1]
1953, June 18	U.S. Air Force C-124	Crashed, burned near Tokyo	129
1955, Oct. 6	United Airlines DC-4	Crashed in Medicine Bow Peak, WY	66
1955, Nov. 1	United Airlines DC-6B	Exploded, crashed near Longmont, CO	44[2]
1956, June 20	Venezuelan Super-Constellation	Crashed in Atlantic off Asbury Park, NJ	74
1956, June 30	TWA Super-Const., United DC-7	Collided over Grand Canyon, AZ	128
1960, Dec. 16	United DC-8 jet, TWA Super-Const.	Collided over New York City	134[3]
1962, Mar. 16	Flying Tiger Super-Constellation	Vanished in W Pacific	107
1962, June 3	Air France Boeing 707 jet	Crashed on takeoff from Paris	130
1962, June 22	Air France Boeing 707 jet	Crashed in storm, Guadeloupe, W.I.	113
1963, June 3	Chartered Northwest Airlines DC-7	Crashed in Pacific off British Columbia	101
1963, Nov. 29	Trans-Canada Airlines DC-8F	Crashed after takeoff from Montreal	118
1964, Mar. 1	Paradise Airlines Constellation	Crashed on approach in heavy weather	85
1965, May 20	Pakistani Boeing 720-B	Crashed at Cairo, Egypt, airport	121
1965, Sept. 17	Pan Am Boeing 707-121B	Crashed into mountains on approach to Montserrat, France	30
1966, Jan. 24	Air India Boeing 707 jetliner	Crashed on Mont Blanc, France-Italy	117
1966, Feb. 4	All-Nippon Boeing 727	Plunged into Tokyo Bay	133
1966, Mar. 5	BOAC Boeing 707 jetliner	Crashed on Mount Fuji, Japan	124
1966, Dec. 24	U.S. military-chartered CL-44	Crashed into village in South Vietnam	129*
1967, Apr. 20	Swiss Britannia turboprop	Crashed at Nicosia, Cyprus	126
1967, July 19	Piedmont Boeing 727, Cessna 310	Collided in air, Hendersonville, NC	82
1968, Apr. 20	S. African Airways Boeing 707	Crashed on takeoff, Windhoek, South-West Africa	122
1968, May 3	Braniff International Electra	Crashed in storm near Dawson, TX	85
1969, Mar. 16	Venezuelan DC-9	Crashed after takeoff from Maracaibo, Venezuela	155[4]
1969, Dec. 8	Olympic Airways DC-6B	Crashed near Athens in storm	93
1970, Feb. 15	Dominican DC-9	Crashed into sea on takeoff from Santo Domingo	102
1970, July 3	British chartered jetliner	Crashed near Barcelona, Spain	112
1970, July 5	Air Canada DC-8	Crashed near Toronto International Airport	108
1970, Aug. 9	Peruvian turbojet	Crashed after takeoff from Cuzco, Peru	101*
1970, Nov. 14	Southern Airways DC-9	Crashed in mountains near Huntington, WV	75[5]
1971, July 30	All-Nippon Boeing 727 and Japanese Air Force F-86	Collided over Morioka, Japan	162[6]
1971, Sept. 4	Alaska Airlines Boeing 727	Crashed into mountain near Juneau, AK	111
1972, Aug. 14	East German Ilyushin-62	Crashed on takeoff, East Berlin	156
1972, Oct. 13	Aeroflot Ilyushin-62	Crashed near Moscow	176
1972, Dec. 3	Chartered Spanish airliner	Crashed on takeoff, Canary Islands	155
1972, Dec. 29	Eastern Airlines Lockheed Tristar	Crashed on approach to Miami Intl. Airport	101
1973, Jan. 22	Chartered Boeing 707	Burst into flames during landing, Kano Airport, Nigeria	176
1973, Feb. 21	Libyan jetliner	Shot down by Israeli fighter planes over Sinai	108
1973, Apr. 10	British Vanguard turboprop	Crashed during snowstorm at Basel, Switzerland	104
1973, June 3	Soviet Supersonic TU-144	Crashed near Goussainville, France	14[7]
1973, July 11	Brazilian Boeing 707	Crashed on approach to Orly Airport, Paris	122
1973, July 31	Delta Airlines jetliner	Crashed, landing in fog at Logan Airport, Boston	89
1973, Dec. 23	French Caravelle jet	Crashed in Morocco	106
1974, Mar. 3	Turkish DC-10 jet	Crashed at Ermenonville near Paris	346

Date	Aircraft	Site of accident	Deaths
1974, Apr. 23	Pan American 707 jet	Crashed in Bali, Indonesia	107
1974, Dec. 1	TWA-727	Crashed in storm, Upperville, VA	92
1974, Dec. 4	Dutch-chartered DC-8	Crashed in storm near Colombo, Sri Lanka	191
1975, Apr. 4	Air Force Galaxy C-5A	Crashed near Saigon, S Viet., after takeoff (carrying orphans)	172
1975, June 24	Eastern Airlines 727 jet	Crashed in storm, JFK Airport, NY	113
1975, Aug. 3	Chartered 707	Hit mountainside, Agadir, Morocco	188
1976, Sept. 10	Brit. Airways Trident, Yug. DC-9	Collided near Zagreb, Yugoslavia	176
1976, Sept. 19	Turkish 727	Hit mountain, S Turkey	155
1976, Oct. 13	Bolivian 707 cargo jet	Crashed in Santa Cruz, Bolivia	100[8]
1977, Mar. 27	KLM 747, Pan American 747	Collided on runway, Tenerife, Canary Islands	583[9]
1977, Nov. 19	TAP Boeing 727	Crashed on Madeira	130
1977, Dec. 4	Malaysian Boeing 737	Hijacked, then exploded in mid-air over Straits of Johore	100
1977, Dec. 17	U.S. DC-3	Crashed after takeoff at Evansville, IN	29[10]
1978, Jan. 1	Air India 747	Exploded, crashed into sea off Bombay	213
1978, Sept. 25	Boeing 727, Cessna 172	Collided in air, San Diego, CA	150
1978, Nov. 15	Chartered DC-8	Crashed near Colombo, Sri Lanka	183
1979, May 25	American Airlines DC-10	Crashed after takeoff at O'Hare Intl. Airport, Chicago	275[11]
1979, Aug. 17	Two Soviet Aeroflot jetliners	Collided over Ukraine	173
1979, Nov. 26	Pakistani Boeing 707	Crashed near Jidda, Saudi Arabia	156
1979, Nov. 28	New Zealand DC-10	Crashed into mountain in Antarctica	257
1980, Mar. 14	Polish Ilyushin 62	Crashed making emergency landing, Warsaw	87[12]
1980, Aug. 19	Saudi Arabian Tristar	Burned after emergency landing, Riyadh	301
1981, Dec. 1	Yugoslavian DC-9	Crashed into mountain in Corsica	178
1982, Jan. 13	Air Florida Boeing 737	Crashed into Potomac R. after takeoff	78
1982, July 9	Pan Am Boeing 727	Crashed after takeoff in Kenner, LA	153[13]
1983, Sept. 1	S. Korean Boeing 747	Shot down after violating Soviet airspace	269
1983, Nov. 27	Colombian Boeing 747	Crashed near Barajas Airport, Madrid	183
1985, Feb. 19	Spanish Boeing 727	Crashed into Mt. Oiz, Spain	148
1985, June 23	Air-India Boeing 747	Crashed into Atlantic Ocean S of Ireland	329
1985, Aug. 2	Delta Air Lines L-1011	Crashed at Dallas-Ft. Worth Intl. Airport	137
1985, Aug. 12	Japan Air Lines Boeing 747	Crashed into Mt. Ogura, Japan	520[14]
1985, Dec. 12	Arrow Air DC-8	Crashed after takeoff in Gander, Newfoundland	256[15]
1986, Mar. 31	Mexican Boeing 727	Crashed NW of Mexico City	166
1986, Aug. 31	Aeromexico DC-9	Collided with Piper PA-28 over Cerritos, CA	82[16]
1987, May 9	Polish Ilyushin 62M	Crashed after takeoff in Warsaw, Poland	183
1987, Aug. 16	Northwest Airlines MD-82	Crashed after takeoff in Romulus, MI	156
1987, Nov. 28	S. African Boeing 747	Crashed into Indian Ocean near Mauritius	159
1987, Nov. 29	S. Korean Boeing 707	Exploded over Thai-Burmese border	155
1988, Mar. 17	Colombian Boeing 707	Crashed into mountainside near Venezuela border	137
1988, July 3	Iranian A300 Airbus	Shot down by U.S. Navy warship *Vincennes* over Pers. Gulf	290
1988, Dec. 21	Pan Am Boeing 747	Exploded and crashed in Lockerbie, Scotland	270[17]
1989, Feb. 8	U.S. Boeing 707	Crashed into mountain in Azores Islands off Portugal	144
1989, June 7	Suriname DC-8	Crashed near Paramaribo Airport, Suriname	168
1989, July 19	United Airlines DC-10	Crashed while landing in Sioux City, IA	111
1989, Sept. 19	French DC-10	Exploded in air over Niger	171
1990, Jan. 25	Avianca Air Boeing 707	Crashed on landing, JFK Airport, NY	73
1990, Feb. 14	Indian Airlines Airbus 320	Crashed and burned landing in Bangalore, India	91
1990, Oct. 2	Chinese airline Boeing 737, 707	Hijacked; 737 jet landing in Guangzhou, crashed into 707	132
1991, May 26	Lauda-Air Boeing 767-300	Exploded over rural Thailand	223
1991, July 11	Nigerian DC-8	Crashed while landing at Jidda, Saudi Arabia	261
1991, Oct. 5	Indonesian military transport	Crashed after takeoff from Jakarta	137*
1992, July 31	Thai Airbus A-300-310	Crashed into mountain S. of Kathmandu, Nepal	113
1992, Oct. 4	El Al Boeing 747-200F	Crashed into 2 apartment bldgs., Amsterdam, Netherlands	120*
1993, Feb. 8	Iran Air TU-154	Collided in air with military plane	132
1993, Mar. 5	Macedonian Pal Air Fokker 100	Crashed after takeoff in snowstorm in Skopje, Macedonia	
1994, Jan. 3	Aeroflot TU-154	Crashed and exploded after takeoff in Irkhutsk, Russia	125[18]
1994, Apr. 26	China Airlines Airbus A-300-600R	Crashed at Japan's Nagoya Airport	264
1994, June 16	China Northwest Airlines TU-154	Crashed 10 min. after takeoff	160
1994, Sept. 8	USAir Boeing 737-300	Crashed in Aliquippa, PA, near Pittsburgh Intl. Airport	132
1994, Oct. 31	American Eagle ATR-72-210	Crashed in field near Roselawn, IN	68
1995, Aug. 11	Aviateca Boeing 737	Crashed into Chichontepec volcano, El Salvador	65
1995, Dec. 18	Zairian passenger jet	Crashed in Angola, location disputed	136
1995, Dec. 20	American Airlines Boeing 757	Crashed into mountain 50 mi N of Cali, Colombia	160
1996, Jan. 8	Antonova 32 cargo jet	Crashed into central market, Kinshasa, Zaire	350+*
1996, Feb. 6	Turkish Boeing 757	Crashed into Atlantic Ocean, off Dominican Republic	189
1996, Apr. 25	T-43, a military version of a Boeing 737	Crashed into mountain near Dubrovnik, Croatia	35[19]
1996, May 11	ValuJet DC-9	Crashed into the Florida Everglades after takeoff	110
1996, July 17	Trans World Airlines Boeing 747	Exploded and crashed in Atlantic Ocean, off Long Isl., NY	230
1996, Aug. 29	Vnukovo TU-154	Crashed into mountain on Arctic island of Spitsbergen	141
1996, Oct. 2	Aeroperu Boeing 757	Crashed in Pacific after takeoff from Lima, Peru	70
1996, Oct. 31	Brazilian TAM Fokker-100	Crashed into houses in São Paulo, Brazil	98[20]
1996, Nov. 7	Nigerian Boeing 727	Crashed into a lagoon 40 mi SE of Lagos, Nigeria	143
1996, Nov. 12	Saudi Arabian Boeing 747, Kazakh Ilyushin-76 cargo plane	Collided in midair near New Delhi, India	349[21]
1996, Nov. 23	Ethiopian Boeing 767	Hijacked, then crashed in Indian Ocean off the Comoros	127
1997, Jan. 9	Comair Embraer 120	Crashed on approach into Detroit Metro. Airport	29
1997, Feb. 4	2 Sikorsky CH-53 transport helicopters	Collided in midair over northern Galilee, Israel	73
1997, May 8	China Southern Airlines Boeing 737	Crashed on approach into Shenzhen's Huangtian Airport	35
1997, July 11	Cubana de Aviación Antonov-24	Crashed into the Caribbean off SE Cuba	44
1997, Aug. 6	Korean Air Boeing 747-300	Crashed into jungle on Guam on approach into airport	228
1997, Sept. 3	Vietnamese Airlines TU-134	Crashed on approach into Phnom Penh airport	64
1997, Sept. 14	U.S. C-141 cargo plane, Ger. TU-154	Collided in midair off SW Africa	33
1997, Sept. 26	Indonesian Airbus A-300	Crashed near Medan, Indonesia, airport	234
1997, Oct. 10	Austral Airlines DC-9-32	Crashed and exploded near Neuvo Berlin, Uruguay	74
1997, Dec. 6	Russian AN-124 transport cargo plane	Crashed into apartment complex near Irkutsk, Siberia	67*
1997, Dec. 15	Chartered TU-154 from Tajikistan	Crashed in desert near Sharja, U.A.E., airport	85
1997, Dec. 17	Chartered Yakovlev-42 from Ukraine	Crashed in mountains near Katerini, Greece	70
1997, Dec. 19	SilkAir Boeing 737-300	Crashed in Musi River, Sumatra, Indonesia	104
1998, Jan. 14	Afghan cargo plane	Crashed into mountain, SW Pakistan	50+
1998, Feb. 2	Cebu Pacific Air DC-9-32	Crashed into mountain near Cagayan de Oro, Philippines	104
1998, Feb. 16	China Airlines Airbus 300-622R	Crashed on approach to airport, Taipei, Taiwan	203[22]

Date	Aircraft	Site of accident	Deaths
1998, Apr. 20	Air France Boeing 727-200	Crashed into mountain after takeoff from Bogotá, Colombia	53
1998, Sept. 2	Swissair MD-11	Crashed into Atlantic Ocean off Halifax, Nova Scotia	229
1998, Sept. 25	Pauknair BAE146	Crashed into hillside in Morocco	38
1998, Oct. 11	Congo Air Lines Boeing 727	Shot down by rebels in Kindu, Congo	40
1998, Dec. 11	Thai Airways Airbus A310-200	Crashed short of runway at Surat Thani airport, S Thailand	101
1999, Feb. 24	China Southwest Airlines TU-154	Crashed on approach to Wenzhou airport, eastern China	61
1999, Sept. 1	LAPA Boeing 737-200	Crashed on takeoff from Jorge Newbery Airport, Buenos Aires	74[23]
1999, Oct. 31	EgyptAir Boeing 767-300	Crashed off Nantucket, MA	217
2000, Jan. 31	Alaska Airlines MD-83	Crashed into Pacific Ocean NW of Malibu, CA	88
2000, Apr. 19	Air Philippines Boeing 737-200	Crashed by Davao airport	131
2000, May 21	Chartered Jetstream 31	Crashed near Wilkes-Barre, PA	19
2000, July 25	Air France Concorde	Crashed into hotel after takeoff from Paris	113[24]
2000, Aug. 23	Gulf Air Airbus A320	Crashed into Persian Gulf near Manama, Bahrain	143
2000, Oct. 31	Singapore Airlines 747-400	Crashed immediately after takeoff, Taipei, Taiwan	81
2000, Oct. 31	Chartered Antonov 26	Exploded after takeoff in northern Angola	50
2000, Nov. 15	Chartered Antonov 24	Crashed after takeoff from Luanda, Angola	40+
2001, Jan. 27	Chartered Beechcraft King Air 200	Crashed after takeoff from Boulder, CO	10[25]
2001, Mar. 3	C23 Sherpa mil. transp.	Crashed in storm, central GA	21
2001, Apr. 7	M-17 helicopter	Crashed into mountain S. of Hanoi, Vietnam	16[26]
2001, July 3	Vladivostokavia Tu-154	Crashed on approach to landing at Irkutsk, Russia	145
2001, Sept. 11	2 Boeing 767s, 2 Boeing 757s	see below[27]	265[27]
2001, Oct. 4	Sibir Airlines Tupelov Tu-154	Crashed into Black Sea, struck by errant Ukrainian missile	78
2001, Oct. 8	Twin-engine Cessna, Scandinavian Airlines System (SAS) jetliner	Collided in heavy fog during takeoff from Milan, Italy	118*
2001, Nov. 12	American Airlines Airbus A-300	Crashed after takeoff from JFK Airport, New York, NY	265*
2002, Jan. 17	Petroproduccion Fairchild FH-227E	Crashed into mountain in S Colombia	26
2002, Jan. 28	Ecuadoran airline Boeing 727-100	Crashed in Andes mountains in southern Colombia	92
2002, Feb. 12	Iran Air Tours Tu-154	Crashed before landing in Khorramabad, Iran	119
2002, Apr. 15	Air China Boeing 767-200	Crashed into hillside amid rain and fog near Pusan, South Korea	122
2002, Apr. 18	4-seat Rockwell Commander	Crashed into Pirelli building, tallest skyscraper in Milan, Italy	3*
2002, May 4	EAS Airlines BAC 1-11-500	Crashed in suburb of Kano, Nigeria, shortly after takeoff	148+*
2002, May 7	China Northern MD-82	Plunged into Yellow Sea near Dalian, China, after fire in cabin	112
2002, May 25	China Airlines Boeing 747-200	Broke apart in mid-air and plunged into Taiwan Strait	225
2002, July 1	Bashkirian Airlines Tu-154, DHL (Ger. cargo) Boeing 757	Collided over S Germany	71
2002, July 4	Prestige Airlines Cargo Boeing B-707	Crashed short of runway in Bangui, Central African Rep.	25
2002, July 27	Ukraine Air Force Sukhoi SU-27	Crashed into spectators at airshow in Lviv, Ukraine	85
2002, Aug. 19	Russian Mi-26 helicopter	Troop-carrier hit by Chechen missile near Grozny	127
2002, Dec. 23	Aeromist Kharkiv Antonov AN-140	Crashed into mountain in fog approaching Isfahan, Iran	46
2003, Jan. 8	Air Midwest, Beechcraft 1900D	Crashed after takeoff at Charlotte, N.C.	21
2003, Jan. 8	Turkish Airlines Avro RJ-100	Crashed on landing in Diyarbakir, Turkey	75
2003, Jan. 9	TANS Airlines Fokker 28 Fellowship	Crashed into mountain near Chachopoyas, Peru	46
2003, Feb. 19	Iranian Guard Ilyushin IL-76	Troop-carrying plane crashed into mountain near Kerman, Iran	289
2003, Mar. 6	Air Algerie Boeing 737	Crashed on takeoff at Tamanrasset, Algeria	102
2003, May 8	Congolese Army IL-76	On flight from Kinshasa door opened, passengers sucked out	60-170(?)
2003, May 26	Ukrain.-Medit. Airlines Yak. 42D	Crashed into mountain in fog approaching Trabzon, Turkey	75
2003, June 30	Algerian Air Force Lockheed C-130H Hercules	Military plane crashed into houses in Blida, Algeria killing 4 onboard and 11 on the ground.	15
2003, July 8	Sudan Airways, Boeing 737-2J8C	Crashed into hillside after takeoff from Port Sudan Airport	116
2003, July 19	Ryan Blake Air Charter, Swearington SA-226TC Metro II	Crashed into eastern slope of Mt. Kenya, killing 12 American tourists and the 2 pilots	14
2003, Aug. 24	Tropical Airways Let 410UVP-E	Crashed after takeoff in Haiti, because of overloading.	21

*Including those on ground and in buildings. (1) First fatal crash of commercial jet plane. (2) Caused by bomb planted by John G. Graham in insurance plot to kill his mother, a passenger. (3) Incl. all 128 aboard planes and 6 on ground. (4) Killed 84 on plane and 71 on ground. (5) Incl. 43 Marshall Univ. football players and coaches. (6) Airliner-fighter crash; pilot of fighter parachuted to safety, was arrested for negligence. (7) First supersonic plane crash; killed 6 crew and 8 on ground; there were no passengers. (8) Crew of 3 killed; 97, mostly children, killed on the ground. (9) World's worst airline disaster. (10) Incl. Univ. of Evansville basketball team. (11) Incl. 2 on ground. Highest death toll in U.S. aviation history. (12) Incl. 22 members of U.S. boxing team. (13) Incl. 8 on ground. (14) Worst single-plane disaster. (15) Incl. 248 members of U.S. 101st Airborne Division. (16) Incl. 15 on ground. (17) Incl. 11 on ground. (18) Incl. 1 on ground. (19) Incl. U.S. Sec. of Commerce Ron Brown. (20) Incl. 2 on ground. (21) World's worst midair collision. (22) Incl. 6 on ground. (23) Incl. 10 on ground. (24) World's first Concorde crash; deaths incl. 5 on ground. (25) Incl. 7 players and staff of Oklahoma State Univ. men's basketball team. (26) Carried U.S. mil. personnel, searching for MIAs from Vietnam War. (27) 4 planes were hijacked and crashed, with all on board (265, including 19 hijackers) killed: American Airlines Flight 11, a Boeing 767-200, with 81 passengers plus 11 crew, crashed into Tower 1 of the World Trade Center in NYC; United Airlines Flight 175, a Boeing 767-200, with 56 passengers plus 9 crew, crashed into Tower 2 of the World Trade Center; American Airlines Flight 77, a Boeing 757-200, with 58 passengers plus 6 crew, crashed into the Pentagon outside Washington, DC; United Air Lines Flight 93, a Boeing 757-200, with 37 passengers and 7 crew, crashed near Shanksville, PA. About 2,600 people on the ground died at the 2 World Trade Center towers, and 125 in the Pentagon.

Some Notable Railroad Disasters

Date	Location	Deaths	Date	Location	Deaths
1876, Dec. 29	Ashtabula, OH	92	1908, Sept. 25	Young's Point, MT	21
1880, Aug. 11	Mays Landing, NJ	40	1909, Jan. 15	Dotsero, CO	21
1887, Aug. 10	Chatsworth, IL.	81	1910, Mar. 1	Wellington, WA	96
1888, Oct. 10	Mud Run, PA	55	1910, Mar. 21	Green Mountain, IA	55
1889, June 12	Amagh, Ireland	80	1911, Aug. 25	Manchester, NY	29
1891, June 14	Nr. Basel, Switzerland	100	1912, July 4	East Corning, NY	39
1896, July 30	Atlantic City, NJ.	60	1912, July 5	Ligonier, PA	23
1903, Dec. 23	Laurel Run, PA	53	1914, Aug. 5	Tipton Ford, MO	43
1904, Aug. 7	Eden, CO	96	1914, Sept. 15	Lebanon, MO	28
1904, Sept. 24	New Market, TN	56	1915, May 22	Nr. Gretna, Scotland	227
1906, Mar. 16	Florence, CO	35	1916, Mar. 29	Amherst, OH	27
1906, Oct. 28	Atlantic City, NJ.	40	1917, Sept. 28	Kellyville, OK	23
1906, Dec. 30	Washington, DC	53	1917, Dec. 12	Modane, France	543
1907, Jan. 2	Volland, KS	33	1917, Dec. 20	Shepherdsville, KY	46
1907, Jan. 19	Fowler, IN	29	1918, June 22	Ivanhoe, IN	68
1907, Feb. 16	New York, NY	22	1918, July 9	Nashville, TN	101
1907, Feb. 23	Colton, CA	26	1918, Nov. 1	Brooklyn, NY	97
1907, May 11	Lompoc, CA	36	1919, Jan. 12	South Byron, NY	22
1907, July 20	Salem, MI	33	1919, Dec. 20	Onawa, ME	23

Date	Location	Deaths	Date	Location	Deaths
1921, Feb. 27	Porter, IN.	37	1972, Oct. 30	Chicago, IL	45
1921, Dec. 5	Woodmont, PA	27	1974, Aug. 30	Zagreb, Yugoslavia	153
1922, Aug. 5	Sulphur Spring, MO	34	1975, Feb. 28	London subway train	41
1922, Dec. 13	Humble, TX.	22	1977, Jan. 18	Granville, Australia.	83
1923, Sept. 27	Lockett, WY.	31	1981, June 6	Bihar, India.	800+
1925, June 16	Hackettstown, NJ	50	1982, Jan. 27	El Asnam, Algeria	130
1925, Oct. 27	Victoria, MS	21	1982, July 11	Tepic, Mexico.	120
1926, Sept. 5	Waco, CO	30	1983, Feb. 19	Empalme, Mexico	100
1937, July 16	Nr. Patna, India.	107	1985, Feb. 23	Madhya Pradesh, India	50
1938, June 19	Saugus, MT	47	1985, Aug. 3	southern France	35
1939, Aug. 12	Harney, NV	24	1987, July 2	Kasumbalesha Shaba, Zaire	125
1939, Dec. 22	Near Magdeburg, Germany	132	1988, June 27	Paris train station, Gare de Lyon	57
1939, Dec. 22	Near Friedrichshafen, Germany	99	1988, Dec. 12	London, England	115
1940, Apr. 19	Little Falls, NY.	31	1989, Jan. 15	Maizdi Khan, Bangladesh	110+
1940, July 31	Cuyahoga Falls, OH	43	1989, June 9	train collided with bus in S Russia	31
1943, Aug. 29	Wayland, NY.	27	1990, Jan. 4	Sindh Prov., Pakistan.	210+
1943, Sept. 6	Frankford Junction, Philad. PA	79	1991, May 14	Shigaraki, Japan	42
1943, Dec. 16	Between Rennert and Buie, NC	72	1993, Sept. 22	Big Bayou Conot, AL	47
1944, Jan. 16	Leon Prov., Spain.	500	1994, Mar. 8	Nr. Durban, South Africa	63
1944, Mar. 2	Salerno, Italy.	521	1994, Sept. 22	Tolunda, Angola.	300
1944, July 6	High Bluff, TN.	35	1995, Aug. 20	Firozabad, India.	358
1944, Aug. 4	Near Stockton, GA	47	1996, Feb. 16	Silver Spring, MD.	11
1944, Sept. 14	Dewey, IN.	29	1997, Mar. 3	Punjab State, Pakistan	125
1944, Dec. 31	Bagley, UT.	50	1997, Mar. 31	Huarte Arakil, Spain	21
1945, Aug. 9	Michigan, ND	34	1997, Apr. 29	Hunan, China.	58
1946, Mar. 20	Aracaju, Mexico	185	1997, May 4	Rwanda	100+
1946, Apr. 25	Naperville, IL.	45	1997, Sept. 14	Central India	77
1947, Feb. 18	Gallitzin, PA.	24	1998, June 3	Eschede, Germany	102
1949, Oct. 22	Nr. Dwor, Poland.	200+	1998, Feb. 19	Yaounde, Cameroon	100+
1950, Feb. 17	Rockville Centre, NY.	31	1999, Mar. 15	Bourbonnais, IL	11
1950, Sept. 11	Coshocton, OH	33	1999, Mar. 24	Nairobi, Kenya	32+
1950, Nov. 22	Richmond Hill, NY.	79	1999, Aug. 2	Gauhati, India	285+
1951, Feb. 6	Woodbridge, NJ	84	1999, Oct. 5	London, England	31
1952, Mar. 4	Nr. Rio de Janeiro, Brazil	119	2000, Jan. 4	Rena, Norway	35
1952, July 9	Rzepin, Poland	160	2000, July 28	São Paulo, Brazil	12
1952, Oct. 8	Harrow, England	112	2000, Nov. 11	Kaprun, Austria	155
1953, Mar. 27	Conneaut, OH.	21	2001, Feb. 28	Great Heck, England	13
1955, Apr. 3	Guadalajara, Mexico.	300	2001, Mar. 18	Nr. Des Moines, IA.	1
1956, Jan. 22	Los Angeles, CA.	30	2001, June 22	Cochin, India	64
1957, Sept. 1	Kendal, Jamaica	178	2001, Sept. 1	Indonesia	40
1957, Sept. 29	Montgomery, W Pakistan	250	2002, Feb. 20	South of Cairo, Egypt.	373
1957, Dec. 4	London, England.	90	2002, Apr. 18	Seville, FL	4
1958, May 8	Rio de Janeiro, Brazil	128	2002, Apr. 23	Placentia, CA.	2
1958, Sept. 15	Elizabethport, NJ	48	2002, May 25	Muamba, Mozambique	196+
1960, Nov. 14	Pardubice, Czech.	110	2002, June 24	Igandu, Tanzania	281+
1962, Jan. 8	Woerden, Netherlands	91	2002, Sept. 10	Bihar, India.	118
1962, May 3	Tokyo, Japan.	163	2002, Nov. 6	Nancy, France	12
1963, Nov. 9	Yokohama, Japan	120+	2003, Jan. 3	Maharashtra, India.	18
1964, July 26	Porto, Portugal	94	2003, Feb. 1	NW Zimbabwe.	46
1967, July 6	Madgeburg, Germany	94	2003, May 8	near Lake Balaton in Hungary	33
1970, Feb. 1	Buenos Aires, Argentina	236	2003, May 15	Ludhiana, India.	36
1972, June 16	Vierzy, France	107	2003, June 3	Spain, Albacete province.	19
1972, July 21	Seville, Spain	76	2003, June 22	Rajapur, India	33
1972, Oct. 6	Saltillo, Mexico	208	2003, July 2	Andhra Pradesh, India.	22

Some Notable U.S. Tornadoes Since 1925

Date	Location	Deaths	Date	Location	Deaths
1925, Mar. 18	MO, IL, IN.	689	1969, Jan. 23	MS.	32
1927, Apr. 12	Rock Springs, TX	74	1971, Feb. 21	Mississippi delta	110
1927, May 9	AR, Poplar Bluff, MO.	92	1973, May 26-27	South, Midwest (series)	47
1927, Sept. 29	St. Louis, MO	90	1974, Apr. 3-4	AL, GA, TN, KY, OH	315
1930, May 6	Hill, Navarro, Ellis Co., TX.	41	1977, Apr. 4	AL, MS, GA	22
1932, Mar. 21	AL (series of tornadoes)	268	1979, Apr. 10	TX, OK.	60
1936, Apr. 5	MS, GA.	455	1984, Mar. 28	NC, SC	57
1936, Apr. 6	Gainesville, GA.	203	1985, May 31	NY, PA, OH, Ont. (series)	75
1938, Sept. 29	Charleston, SC	32	1987, May 22	Saragosa, TX.	29
1942, Mar. 16	Central to NE Mississippi	75	1989, Nov. 15	Huntsville, AL.	18
1942, Apr. 27	Rogers and Mayes Co., OK	52	1990, Aug. 28	Northern IL	25
1944, June 23	OH, PA, WV, MD.	150	1991, Apr. 26	KS, OK.	23
1945, Apr. 12	OK-AR	102	1992, Nov. 21-23	South, Midwest	26
1947, Apr. 9	TX, OK, KS.	169	1994, Mar. 27-28	AL, TN, GA, NC, SC (series)	52
1948, Mar. 19	Bunker Hill and Gillespie, IL	33	1995, May 6-7	Southern OK, northern TX	23
1949, Jan. 3	LA and AR	58	1997, Mar. 1	Central AR	26
1952, Mar. 21	AR, MO, TN (series)	208	1997, May 27	Jarrell, TX	27
1953, May 11	Waco, TX	114	1998, Feb. 22-23	Central FL	42
1953, June 8	MI, OH	142	1998, Mar. 20	Northeast GA.	12
1953, June 9	Worcester and vicinity, MA	90	1998, Mar. 24	Eastern India	145
1953, Dec. 5	Vicksburg, MS.	38	1998, Apr. 8	AL, GA, MS	39
1955, May 25	KS, MO, OK, TX	115	1999, May 3-4	OK, KS.	42
1957, May 20	KS, MO	48	2000, Feb. 14	Southwest GA	22+
1958, June, 4	NW Wisconsin	30	2000, Mar. 28	TX	5
1959, Feb. 10	St. Louis, MO	21	2000, July 14	Alberta	11
1960, May 5, 6	Southeastern OK, AR	30	2000, Dec. 16	AL	12
1962, Mar. 31	Milton, FL	17	2001, Feb. 24	Pontotoc, MS	8
1965, Apr. 11	IN, IL, OH, MI, WI	271	2001, Nov. 23-24	AL, MS (series).	13
1966, Mar. 3	Jackson, MS	57	2002, Apr. 27-28	IL, KY, MD, MO	6
1966, Mar. 3	MS, AL	61	2002, Nov. 9-11	AL, MS, OH, PA, TN	36
1967, Apr. 21	IL, MI.	33	2003, Mar. 20	GA	6
1968, May 15	Midwest.	71	2003, May 4-11	TN, MO, KS, IL, OK, WV, AL	48

Principal U.S. Mine Disasters Since 1900

Source: Bureau of Mines, U.S. Dept. of the Interior; Mine Safety and Health Admin., U.S. Dept. of Labor
(All are bituminous-coal mines unless otherwise noted.)

Date	Location	Deaths	Date	Location	Deaths
1900, May 1	Scofield, UT	200	1922, Nov. 6	Spangler, PA	77
1902, May 19	Coal Creek, TN	184	1922, Nov. 22	Dolomite, AL	90
1902, July 10	Johnstown, PA	112	1923, Feb. 8	Dawson, NM	120
1903, June 30	Hanna, WY.	169	1923, Aug. 14	Kemmerer, WY	99
1904, Jan. 25	Cheswick, PA	179	1924, Mar. 8	Castle Gate, UT.	171
1905, Feb. 26	Virginia City, AL.	112	1924, Apr. 28	Benwood, WV	119
1907, Jan. 29	Stuart, WV	84	1926, Jan. 13	Wilburton, OK	91
1907, Dec. 6	Monongah, WV.	361	1927, Apr. 30	Everettville, WV	97
1907, Dec. 19	Jacobs Creek, PA	239	1928, May 19	Mather, PA.	195
1908, Nov. 28	Marianna, PA	154	1930, Nov. 5	Millfield, OH	82
1909, Nov. 13	Cherry, IL	259	1940, Jan. 10	Bartley, WV	91
1910, Jan. 31	Primero, CO	75	1947, Mar. 25	Centralia, IL	111
1910, May 5	Palos, AL.	90	1951, Dec. 21	West Frankfort, IL	119
1910, Nov.8	Delagua, CO	79	1959, Jan. 22	Port Griffith, PA	12
1911, Apr. 8	Littleton, AL	128	1968, Nov. 20	Farmington, WV.	78
1911, Dec. 9	Briceville, TN.	84	1970, Dec. 30	Hyden, KY.	38
1912, Mar. 26	Jed, WV	83	1972, May 2	Kellogg, ID[1]	91
1913, Apr. 23	Finleyville, PA	96	1976, Mar. 9	Oven Fork, KY.	15
1913, Oct. 22	Dawson, NM	263	1981, Apr. 15	Redstone, CO	15
1914, Apr. 28	Eccles, WV	181	1981, Dec. 8	Whitwell, TN	13
1915, Mar. 2	Layland, WV	112	1984, Dec. 19	Huntington, UT	27
1917, Apr. 27	Hastings, CO	121	1989, Sept. 13	Sturgis, KY.	10
1917, June 8	Butte, MT[1]	163	2001, Sept. 23	Brookwood, AL	13
1919, June 5	Wilkes-Barre, PA[2]	92			

Note: World's worst mine disaster killed 1,549 workers in Manchuria, Apr. 25, 1942. (1) Metal mine. (2) Anthracite mine.

Some Notable Hurricanes, Typhoons, Blizzards, Other Storms

H.—hurricane; T.—typhoon

Date	Location	Deaths	Date	Location	Deaths
1888, Mar. 11-14	Blizzard, eastern U.S.	400	1972, June 19-29	H. Agnes, FL to NY	118
1900, Sept. 8	H., Galveston, TX	8,000+	1972, Dec. 3	T. Theresa, Philippines	169
1906, Sept. 19-24	H., LA, MS.	350	1973, June-Aug.	Monsoon rains, India	1,217
1906, Sept. 18	T., Hong Kong	10,000	1974, June 11	Storm Dinah, Luzon Isl., Phil.	71
1915, Aug. 16	H., Galveston, TX	275	1974, July 11	T. Gilda, Japan, S. Korea.	108
1915, Sept. 29	H. LA	500	1974, Sept. 19-20	H. Fifi, Honduras	2,000
Sept. 14, 1919	Florida Keys through Gulf to TX	800-900	1974, Dec. 25	Cyclone leveled Darwin, Austral.	50
1926, Sept. 11-22	H., FL, AL	243	1975, Sept. 13-27	H. Eloise, Caribbean, NE U.S.	71
1926, Oct. 20	H., Cuba	600	1976, May 20	T. Olga, floods, Philippines	215
1928, Sept. 6-20	H., southern FL	2,500+	1978, Oct. 27	T. Rita, Philippines	c. 400
1930, Sept. 3	H., Dominican Republic	2,000	1979, Aug. 30 -		
1935, Aug. 29-			Sept. 7	H. David, Caribbean, E U.S.	1,100
Sept. 10	H., Caribbean, southeastern U.S.	400+	1980, Aug. 4-11	H. Allen, Caribbean, TX	272
1937, Sept. 2	T., "The Great Typhoon," Hong Kong	10,000+	1981, Nov. 25	T. Irma, Luzon Isl., Philippines	176
1938, Sept. 21	H., Long Island, NY; New England	600	1983, June	Monsoon, India.	900
1940, Nov. 11-12	Blizzard, NE, Midwest U.S.	144	1984, Sept. 2	T. Ike, S Philippines	1,363
1942, Oct. 15-16	H., Bengal, India	40,000	1985, May 25	Cyclone, Bangladesh	10,000
1944, Sept. 9-16	H., NC to New England.	46	1985, Oct. 26-		
1947, Dec. 26	Blizzard, NYC, N Atlantic states	55	Nov. 6	H. Juan, SE U.S.	97
1952, Oct. 22	T., Philippines	440	1987, Nov. 25	T. Nina, Philippines	650
1954, Aug. 30	H. Carol, northeastern U.S.	68	1988, Sept. 10-17	H. Gilbert, Caribbean, Gulf of Mexico	260
1954, Oct. 5-18	H. Hazel, E Canada, U.S.; Haiti.	347	1989, Sept. 16-22	H. Hugo, Caribbean, SE U.S.	504
1955, Aug. 12-13	H. Connie, NC, SC, VA, MD	43	1990, May 6-11	Cyclones, SE India.	450
1955, Aug. 7-21	H. Diane, eastern U.S.	400	1991, Apr. 30	Cyclone, Bangladesh	139,000
1955, Sept. 19	H. Hilda, Mexico	200	1991, Nov. 5	Tropical storm, Philippines	7,000+
1955, Sept. 22-28	H. Janet, Caribbean	500	1992, Aug. 24-26	H. Andrew, southern FL, LA	58
1956, Feb. 1-29	Blizzard, W Europe	1,000	1993, Mar. 13-14	Blizzard, E U.S.	200
1957, June 25-30	H. Audrey, TX to AL.	390	1993, June	Monsoon, Bangladesh	2,000
1958, Feb. 15-16	Blizzard, NE U.S.	171	1994, Nov. 8-18	Storm Gordon, Caribbean, FL	830
1959, Sept. 17-19	T. Sarah, Japan, South Korea	2,000	1995, Oct. 2-4	H. Opal, S Mexico, FL, AL	59
1959, Sept. 26-27	T. Vera, Honshu, Japan.	4,466	1995, Nov. 2-3	T. Angela, Philippines	600+
1960, Sept. 4-12	H. Donna, Caribbean, E U.S.	148	1996, Jan. 7-8	Blizzard, NE U.S.	100
1961, Sept. 11-14	H. Carla, TX.	46	1996, July 8-13	H. Bertha, Carib., E U.S.	15
1961, Oct. 31	H. Hattie, Br. Honduras	400	1996, Aug. 22	Blizzard, Himalayas, N India.	239
1962, Sept. 1	T. Wanda, Hong Kong	130-200	1996, Aug. 29-		
1963, May 28-29	Windstorm, Bangladesh	22,000	Sept. 6	H. Fran, Carib., NC, VA, WV.	30
1963, Oct. 4-8	H. Flora, Caribbean	6,000	1996, Sept. 9-10	H. Hortense, Caribbean.	24
1964, Oct. 4-7	H. Hilda, LA, MS, GA.	38	1996, Sept. 9	T. Sally, S China.	114
1964, June 30	T. Winnie, N Philippines	107	1996, Nov. 6	Cyclone, Andhra Pradesh, India	1,000+
1964, Sept. 5	T. Ruby, Hong Kong and China.	735	1996, Nov. 24-25	Ice storms, TX to MO.	26
1965, May 11-12	Windstorm, Bangladesh	17,000	1996, Dec. 25	Tropical storm, E Malaysia	100+
1965, June 1-2	Windstorm, Bangladesh	30,000	1997, May 19	Cyclone, Bangladesh	108
1965, Sept. 7-12	H. Betsy, FL, MS, LA.	74	1997, July 2	Storms, southeastern MI	16
1965, Dec. 15	Windstorm, Bangladesh	10,000	1997, Aug. 18	Typhoon, Taiwan	24
1966, June 4-10	H. Alma, Honduras, SE U.S.	51	1997, Oct. 8-10	H. Pauline, SW Mexico.	230
1966, Sept. 24-30	H. Inez, Carib., FL, Mexico	293	1998, Feb. 4-6	Blizzard, KY, WV	10+
1967, July 9	T. Billie, SW Japan	347	1998, June 9	Cyclone, Gujarat, India.	1,320
1967, Sept. 5-23	H. Beulah, Carib., Mex., TX.	54	1998, Aug.	Monsoon, Bangladesh	326
1967, Dec. 12-20	Blizzard, SW U.S.	51	1998, Sept. 21-23	H. Georges, Caribbean, FL Keys, U.S. Gulf Coast	600+
1968, Nov. 18-28	T. Nina, Philippines	63			
1969, Aug. 17-18	H. Camille, MS, LA	256	1998, Oct. 27-29	H. Mitch, Honduras, Nicaragua, Guatemala, El Salvador.	10,866+
1970, Sept. 15	T. Georgia, Philippines	300			
1970, Oct. 14	T. Sening, Philippines	583	1999, Sept. 4-17	H Floyd, Bahamas, E seaboard, U.S.	69+
1970, Oct. 15	T. Titang, Philippines	526	1999, Oct. 29	Cyclone, E India.	9,392
1970, Nov. 13	Cyclone, Bangladesh	300,000	1999, Dec. 26-29	Gales, France, Switzerland, Germany	120
1971, Aug. 1	T. Rose, Hong Kong	130	2000, Dec. 27	Winter storm, TX, OK, AR	40+

Date	Location	Deaths	Date	Location	Deaths
2001, June 6-17	Tropical storm *Allison*, SE U.S.	47	2002, Aug.-Sept.	T *Rusa*, North & South Korea	115+
2001, July 30	Typhoon, Taiwan	200	2003, Feb. 16-17	Blizzard, E seaboard U.S.	59
2001, Oct. 8-9	H *Iris*, Belize	22	2003, Sept. 2	T. Dujuan, southern China	32
2001, Nov. 2-5	H *Michelle*, Cuba, Jamaica	17	2003, Sept. 12	T. *Maemi*, South Korea	100+
2001, Nov. 6-12	T *Lingling*, S Philip., cent. Vietnam	220+	2003, Sept. 7-19	H. *Isabel*, NC, VA, MD, E seaboard, U.S.	40+
2002, July 1-11	T *Chata'an*, Micron., Philip., Japan	70+			

Some Notable Floods, Tidal Waves

Date	Location	Deaths	Date	Location	Deaths
1228	Holland	100,000	1982, Sept. 17-21	El Salvador, Guatemala	1,300+
1642	China	300,000	1984, Aug-Sept.	South Korea	200+
1883, Aug. 27	Indonesia	36,000	1985, July 19	Dam collapse, N Italy	361
1887	Huang He River, China	900,000	1987, Aug.-Sept.	N Bangladesh	1,000+
1889, May 31	Johnstown, PA	2,209	1988, Sept.	N India	1,000+
1903, June 15	Heppner, OR	325	1993, July-Aug.	Midwest	48
1911	Chang Jiang River, China	100,000	1994, July	GA, AL	32
1913, Mar. 25-27	OH, IN	732	1995, Jan. 30- Feb. 9	NW Europe	40
1915, Aug. 17	Galveston, TX	275	1995, July	NE China	1,200
1928, Mar. 13	Dam collapse, Saugus, CA	450	1995, Aug. 19	SW Morocco	136
1928, Sept. 13	Lake Okeechobee, FL	2,000	1995, Dec. 25	KwaZulu Natal, South Africa	166
1931, Aug.	Huang He River, China	3,700,000	1996, Feb. 17	Biak Isl., Indonesia	105
1937, Jan. 22	OH, MS Valleys	250	1996, April	Afghanistan	100+
1939	N China	200,000	1996, June-July	S China	950+
1946, Apr. 1	HI, AK	159	1996, Aug. 7	Pyrenees Mts., Spain	71
1947, Sept. 20	Honshu Island, Japan	1,900	1996, Dec.-		
1951, Aug.	Manchuria	1,800	1997, Jan.	Northwestern U.S.	29
1953, Jan. 31	W Europe	2,000	1997, Mar.	Ohio R. Valley	35
1954, Aug. 17	Farahzad, Iran	2,000	1997, July	Poland, Czech Republic	98
1955, Oct. 7-12	India, Pakistan	1,700	1997, Nov.	Spanish-Portuguese border	31+
1959, Nov. 1	W Mexico	2,000	1997, Nov.	Bardera, Somalia	1,300+
1959, Dec. 2	Frejus, France	412	1998, Jan.	Kenya	86
1960, Oct. 10	Bangladesh	6,000	1998, Feb.	California to Tijuana, Mexico	30+
1960, Oct. 31	Bangladesh	4,000	1998, Mar.	SW Pakistan	300+
1962, Feb. 17	North Sea coast, Germany	343	1998, July-Aug.	China	4,150
1962, Sept. 27	Barcelona, Spain	445	1998, July-Sept.	Bangladesh	1,441
1963, Oct. 9	Dam collapse, Vaiont, Italy	1,800	1998, July 17	Papua New Guinea	3,000
1966, Nov. 3-4	Florence, Venice, Italy	113	1998, Aug. 24	S Texas, Mexico	16
1967, Jan. 18-24	E Brazil	894	1999, Aug. 1-4	South Korea, Philippines,	
1967, Mar. 19	Rio de Janeiro, Brazil	436		Vietnam, Thailand	188+
1967, Nov. 26	Lisbon, Portugal	464	1999, Sept.-Oct.	NE Mexico	350+
1968, Aug. 7-14	Gujarat State, India	1,000	1999, Oct.-Dec.	Central Vietnam	700+
1968, Oct. 7	NE India	780	1999, Feb. 6-11	Botswana	70+
1969, Jan. 18-26	Southern CA	100	1999, Dec.	Venezuela	9,000+
1969, Mar. 17	Mundau Valley, Alagoas, Braz.	218	2000, Feb.-Mar.	Madagascar	150+
1969, Aug. 20-22	Western VA	189	2000, Feb.-Mar.	Mozambique	700
1969, Sept. 15	South Korea	250	2000, May 17	Timor Island	50+
1969, Oct. 1-8	Tunisia	500	2000, Aug. 2	Himachal Pradesh, India	120+
1970, May 20	Central Romania	160	2000, Aug. 2	Bhutan	200+
1970, July 22	Himalayas, India	500	2000, Sept. 19-30	India, Bangladesh	1,000+
1971, Feb. 26	Rio de Janeiro, Brazil	130	2000, Oct. 12-17	France, Brit., Italy, Switz.	35
1972, Feb. 26	Buffalo Creek, WV	118	2001, Jan.-Feb.	Mozambique	84+
1972, June 9	Rapid City, SD	236	2001, Aug.-Nov.	S Vietnam and Cambodia	360+
1972, Aug. 7	Luzon Isl., Philippines	454	2001, Aug. 1-6	Taiwan	100+
1972, Aug. 19-31	Pakistan	1,500	2001, Aug. 10-12	NE Iran	247
1974, Mar. 29	Tubaro, Brazil	1,000	2001, Aug.	Northern Thailand	170
1974, Aug. 12	Monty-Long, Bangladesh	2,500	2001, Nov. 9-10	Northern Algeria	711+
1976, June 5	Teton Dam collapse, ID	11	2001, Dec. 23-31	Rio de Janeiro	66
1976, July 31	Big Thompson Canyon, CO	139	2002, Jan. 30-Feb. 15	Java Isl., Indonesia	147
1976, Nov. 17	East Java, Indonesia	136	2002, Feb. 19	La Paz, Bolivia	65
1977, July 19-20	Johnstown, PA	68	2002, Apr.-May	E Africa	150+
1977, Nov. 6	Toccoa, GA	39	2002, early May	MO, IL, IN, WV, VA KY	20
1978, June-Sept.	N India	1,200	2002, Apr.-Aug.	China	800+
1979, Jan.-Feb.	Brazil	204	2002, July-Aug.	India, Nepal, Bangladesh	1,100+
1979, July 17	Lomblen Isl., Indonesia	539	2002, Aug.	Russia	110
1979, Aug. 11	Morvi, India	15,000	2002, Aug.	Germany, Hungary, Austria,	
1980, Feb. 13-22	Southern CA, AZ	26		Czech Rep.	100+
1981, Apr.	N China	550	2003, Feb. 16-18	Pakistan	25
1981, July	Sichuan, Hubei Prov., China	1,300	2003, May 17-27	Sri Lanka	250
1982, Jan. 23	Nr. Lima, Peru	600	2003, Aug 29-Aug.	Kassala, Sudan	12
1982, May 12	Guangdong, China	430	2003, Aug.-mid-Sept.	E India	200+

Some Major Earthquakes

Source: Global Volcanism Network, Smithsonian Institution; U.S. Geological Survey, Dept. of the Interior; World Almanac research

Magnitude of earthquakes (Mag.) is measured on the Richter scale; each higher number represents a tenfold increase in energy. Adopted in 1935, the scale is applied to earthquakes as far back as reliable seismograms are available.

Date	Location	Deaths	Mag.	Date	Location	Deaths	Mag.
526, May 20	Antioch, Syria	250,000	NA	1737, Oct. 11	India, Calcutta	300,000	NA
856	Corinth, Greece	45,000	"	1755, June 7	N Persia	40,000	"
1057	Chihli, China	25,000	"	1755, Nov. 1	Lisbon, Portugal	60,000	8.75*
1169, Feb. 11	Near Mt. Etna, Sicily	15,000[1]	"	1783, Feb. 4	Calabria, Italy	30,000	NA
1268	Cilicia, Asia Minor	60,000	"	1797, Feb. 4	Quito, Ecuador	41,000	"
1290, Sept. 27	Chihli, China	100,000	"	1811-12	New Madrid, MO (series)	NA	8.7*
1293, May 20	Kamakura, Japan	30,000	"	1822, Sept. 5	Asia Minor, Aleppo	22,000	NA
1531, Jan. 26	Lisbon, Portugal	30,000	"	1828, Dec. 28	Echigo, Japan	30,000	"
1556, Jan. 24	Shaanxi, China	830,000	"	1868, Aug. 13-15	Peru, Ecuador	40,000	"
1667, Nov.	Shemaka, Caucasia	80,000	"	1875, May 16	Venezuela, Colombia	16,000	"
1693, Jan. 11	Catania, Italy	60,000	"	1886, Aug. 31	Charleston, SC	60	6.6
1730, Dec. 30	Hokkaido, Japan	137,000	"	1896, June 15	Japan, sea wave	27,120	NA

Date	Location	Deaths	Mag.
1905, Apr. 4	Kangra, India	19,000	8.6
1906, Apr. 18-19	San Francisco, CA	503[2]	8.3
1906, Aug. 17	Valparaiso, Chile	20,000	8.6
1907, Oct. 21	Central Asia	12,000	8.1
1908, Dec. 28	Messina, Italy	83,000	7.5
1915, Jan. 13	Avezzano, Italy	29,980	7.5
1918, Oct. 11	Mona Passage, P.R.	116	7.5
1920, Dec. 16	Gansu, China	200,000	8.6
1923, Sept. 1	Yokohama, Japan	143,000	8.3
1925, Mar. 16	Yunnan, China	5,000	7.1
1927, May 22	Nan-Shan, China	200,000	8.3
1932, Dec. 25	Gansu, China	70,000	7.6
1933, Mar. 2	Japan	2,990	8.9
1933, Mar. 10	Long Beach, CA	115	6.2
1934, Jan. 15	India, Bihar-Nepal	10,700	8.4
1935, Apr. 21	Taiwan (Formosa)	3,276	7.4
1935, May 30	Quetta, India	50,000	7.5
1939, Jan. 25	Chillan, Chile	28,000	8.3
1939, Dec. 26	Erzincan, Turkey	30,000	8.0
1946, Dec. 20	Honshu, Japan	1,330	8.4
1948, June 28	Fukui, Japan	5,390	7.3
1949, Aug. 5	Pelileo, Ecuador	6,000	6.8
1950, Aug. 15	Assam, India	1,530	8.7
1953, Mar. 18	NW Turkey	1,200	7.2
1956, June 10-17	N Afghanistan	2,000	7.7
1957, July 2	N Iran	1,200	7.4
1957, Dec. 13	W Iran	1,130	7.3
1960, Feb. 29	Agadir, Morocco	12,000	5.9
1960, May 21-30	S Chile	5,000	9.5
1962, Sept. 1	NW Iran	12,230	7.3
1963, July 26	Skopje, Yugoslavia	1,100	6.0
1964, Mar. 27	Alaska	131	9.2
1966, Aug. 19	E Turkey	2,520	7.1
1968, Aug. 31	NE Iran	12,000	7.3
1970, Jan. 5	Yunnan Prov., China	15,621	7.7
1970, Mar. 28	W Turkey	1,100	7.3
1970, May 31	N Peru	66,000	7.8
1971, Feb. 9	San Fernando Val., CA	65	6.6
1972, Apr. 10	S Iran	5,054	7.1
1972, Dec. 23	Managua, Nicaragua	5,000	6.2
1974, Dec. 28	Pakistan (9 towns)	5,200	6.3
1975, Sept. 6	Turkey (Lice, etc.)	2,300	6.7
1976, Feb. 4	Guatemala	23,000	7.5
1976, May 6	NE Italy	1,000	6.5
1976, June 25	Irian Jaya, New Guinea	422	7.1
1976, July 27	Tangshan, China	255,000	8.0
1976, Aug. 16	Mindanao, Philippines	8,000	7.8
1976, Nov. 24	NW Iran-USSR border	5,000	7.3
1977, Mar. 4	Romania	1,500	7.2
1977, Aug. 19	Indonesia	200	8.0
1977, Nov. 23	NW Argentina	100	8.2
1978, Sept. 16	NE Iran	15,000	7.8
1979, Sept. 12	Indonesia	100	8.1
1979, Dec. 12	Colombia, Ecuador	800	7.9
1980, Oct. 10	NW Algeria	3,500	7.7
1980, Nov. 23	S Italy	3,000	7.2
1981, June 11	S Iran	3,000	6.9
1981, July 28	S Iran	1,500	7.3
1982, Dec. 13	W Arabian Peninsula	2,800	6.0
1983, May 26	N Honshu, Japan	81	7.7
1983, Oct. 30	E Turkey	1,342	6.9
1985, Mar. 3	Chile	146	7.8
1985, Sept. 19	Michoacan, Mexico	4,200+	8.1
1986, Oct. 10	El Salvador	1,000+	5.5
1987, Mar. 6	Colombia-Ecuador	4,000+	7.0
1988, Aug. 20	India-Nepal border	1,450	6.6
1988, Nov. 6	China-Burma border	1,000	7.3
1988, Dec. 7	Soviet Armenia	55,000	7.0
1989, Oct. 17	San Francisco Bay area	62	7.1
1990, May 30	N Peru	115	6.3
1990, June 20	W Iran	40,000+	7.7
1990, July 16	Luzon, Philippines	1,621	7.8
1991, Feb. 1	Pakistan, Afgh. border	1,200	6.8
1991, Oct. 19	N India	2,000	7.0
1992, Mar. 13, 15	E Turkey	4,000	6.2/6.0
1992, June 28	S California	1	7.5/6.6
1992, Dec. 12	Flores Isl., Indonesia	2,500	7.5
1993, July 12	off Hokkaido, Japan	200+	7.7
1992, Sept. 1	SW Nicaragua	116	7.0
1992, Oct. 12	Cairo, Egypt	450	5.9
1993, Sept. 30	Maharashtra, S India	9,748[3]	6.3
1994, Jan. 17	Northridge, CA	61	6.8
1994, Feb. 15	S Sumatra, Indon.	215	7.0
1994, June 6	Cauca, SW Colombia	1,000	6.8
1994, Aug. 19	N Algeria	164	6.0
1995, Jan. 16	Kobe, Japan	5,502	6.9
1995, May 27	Sakhalin Isl., Russia	1,989	7.5
1995, Oct. 1	SW Turkey	73	6.0
1996, Feb. 3	SW China	200+	7.0
1996, Feb. 17	Irian Jaya, Indonesia	53	7.5
1997, Feb. 4	Turkmen.-Iran border	79	6.6
1997, Feb. 27	W Pakistan	100+	7.3
1997, Feb. 28	NW Iran	1,000+	6.1
1997, May 10	N Iran	1,560	7.5
1997, July 9	NE Venezuela	82	6.9
1997, Sept. 26	Central Italy	11	5.5/5.7
1998, Jan. 10	Zhangbei, China	50	6.2
1998, Feb. 4, 8	Takhar province, NE Afghanistan	2,323	6.1
1998, May 22	Central Bolivia	105	6.5
1998, May 30	NE Afghanistan	4,700+	6.9
1998, June 27	Adana, Turkey	144	6.3
1999, Jan. 25	Armenia, Colombia	1,185+	6.0
1999, Feb. 11	Central Afghanistan	60	6.0
1999, Mar. 28	Uttar Pradesh, India	87	6.8
1999, Aug. 17	Western Turkey	17,200+	7.4
1999, Sept. 7	Athens, Greece	143	5.9
1999, Sept. 21	Taichung, Taiwan	2,474	7.6
1999, Nov. 12	Duzce, Turkey	675+	7.2
2000, June 4	Sumatra, Indonesia	103	7.9
2001, Jan. 13	San Vicente, El Salvador	800+	7.6
2001, Jan. 26	Gujarat, India	20,000+	7.9
2001, Feb. 13	San Vicente, El Salvador	255	6.6
2001, June 23	Arequipa, Peru	102	8.1
2002, Feb. 3	Central Turkey	44+	6.5
2002, Mar. 3	N Afghanistan	166	7.4
2002, Mar. 25-26	Nahrin, N Afghanistan	1,000+	6.1
2002, Apr. 1	E New Guinea	36	5.0
2002, Apr. 12	Hindu Kush, Afghanistan	50+	5.9
2002, June 22	W Iran	261+	6.5
2002, Oct. 31	S Italy	29	5.9
2003, Jan. 22	Colima, Mexico	29	7.6
2003, Feb. 24	S Xinjiang prov., China	261	6.4
2003, May 1	E Turkey	177	6.4
2003, May 21	N Algeria	2,200+	6.8

(*) estimated from earthquake intensity. NA = Not available. (1) Once thought to have been a volcanic eruption; evidence indicates a destructive earthquake and tsunami occurred on this date. (2) With subsequent fires, death toll rose to 700; some estimates of the death toll are much higher. (3) Official death toll as released by Indian government. Other sources reported estimates of about 30,000 deaths.

On Feb. 17, 2003, 21 people were crushed to death when a panic-stricken crowd tried to exit the E-2 nightclub in the South Side area of Chicago. On June 29, 2003, a 3rd-story porch in the Lincoln Park section of Chicago collapsed and hit a porch below, plunging both into an alley; 12 people were killed.

Some Notable Fires Since 1920

(See also Some Notable Explosions Since 1920.)

Date	Location	Deaths	Date	Location	Deaths
1923, May 17	Camden, SC, school	76	1949, Apr. 5	Effingham, IL, hospital	77
1924, Dec. 24	Babb's Switch, OK, school	35	1950, Jan. 7	Davenport, IA, Mercy Hospital	41
1929, May 15	Cleveland, OH, clinic	125	1953, Mar. 29	Largo, FL, nursing home	35
1930, Apr. 21	Columbus, OH, penitentiary	320	1953, Apr. 16	Chicago, metalworking plant	35
1931, July 24	Pittsburgh, PA, home for aged	48	1957, Feb. 17	Warrenton, MO, home for aged	72
1934, Dec. 11	Hotel Kerns, Lansing, MI	34	1958, Mar. 19	New York, NY, loft building	24
1938, May 16	Atlanta, GA, Terminal Hotel	35	1958, Dec. 1	Chicago, parochial school	95
1940, Apr. 23	Natchez, MS, dance hall	198	1958, Dec. 16	Bogota, Colombia, store	83
1942, Nov. 28	Cocoanut Grove, Boston	491	1959, June 23	Stalheim, Norway, resort hotel	34
1942, Dec. 12	St. John's, Nfld., hostel	100	1960, Mar. 12	Pusan, Korea, chemical plant	68
1943, Sept. 7	Gulf Hotel, Houston, TX	55	1960, July 14	Guatemala City, mental hospital	225
1944, July 6	Ringling Circus, Hartford, CT	168	1960, Nov. 13	Amude, Syria, movie theater	152
1946, June 5	LaSalle Hotel, Chicago	61	1961, Jan. 6	Thomas Hotel, San Francisco	20
1946, Dec. 7	Winecoff Hotel, Atlanta	119	1961, Dec. 8	Hartford, CT, hospital	16
1946, Dec. 12	NY, NY, ice plant, tenement	37	1961, Dec. 17	Niteroi, Brazil, circus	323

Date	Location	Deaths
1963, May 4	Diourbel, Senegal, theater	64
1963, Nov. 18	Surfside Hotel, Atlantic City, NJ	25
1963, Nov. 23	Fitchville, OH, rest home	63
1963, Dec. 29	Roosevelt Hotel, Jacksonville, FL	22
1964, May 8	Manila, apartment bldg.	30
1964, Dec. 18	Fountaintown, IN, nursing home	20
1965, Mar. 1	LaSalle, Quebec, apartment	28
1965, Aug. 11-16	Watts riot fires, CA	30+
1966, Mar. 11	Numata, Japan, 2 ski resorts	31
1966, Aug. 13	Melbourne, Australia, hotel	29
1966, Oct. 17	New York, NY, bldg. (firefighters)	12
1966, Dec. 7	Erzurum, Turkey, barracks	68
1967, Feb. 7	Montgomery, AL, restaurant	25
1967, May 22	Brussels, Belgium, store	322
1967, July 16	Jay, FL, state prison	37
1968, May 11	Vijayawada, India, wedding hall	58
1969, Dec. 2	Notre Dame, Can., nursing home	54
1970, Jan. 9	Marietta, OH, nursing home	27
1970, Nov. 1	Grenoble, France, dance hall	145
1970, Dec. 20	Tucson, AZ, hotel	28
1971, Mar. 6	Burghoezli, Switzerland, psychiatric clinic	28
1971, Dec., 25	Seoul, South Korea, hotel	162
1972, May 13	Osaka, Japan, nightclub	116
1972, July 5	Sherborne, England, hospital	30
1973, June 24	New Orleans, LA, bar	32
1973, Aug. 3	Isle of Man, Eng., amusement park	51
1973, Sept. 1	Copenhagen, Denmark, hotel	35
1973, Nov. 29	Kumamoto, Japan, dept. store	107
1973, Dec. 2	Seoul, South Korea, theater	50
1974, Feb. 1	São Paulo, Brazil, bank building	189
1974, June 30	Port Chester, NY, discotheque	24
1974, Nov. 3	Seoul, S. Korea, hotel, disco	88
1975, Dec. 12	Mina, Saudi Arabia, tent city	138
1976, Oct. 24	Bronx, NY, social club	25
1977, Feb. 25	Moscow, Russia, Rossiya hotel	45
1977, May 28	Southgate, KY, nightclub	164
1977, June 9	Abidjan, Ivory Coast, nightclub	41
1977, June 26	Columbia, TN, jail	42
1977, Nov. 14	Manila, Philippines, hotel	47
1978, Jan. 28	Kansas City, Coates House Hotel	16
1978, Aug. 19	Abadan, Iran, movie theater	425+
1979, July 14	Saragossa, Spain, hotel	80
1979, Dec. 31	Chapais, Quebec, social club	42
1980, May 20	Kingston, Jamaica, nursing home	157
1980, Nov. 21	MGM Grand Hotel, Las Vegas	84
1980, Dec. 4	Stouffer Inn, Harrison, NY	26
1981, Jan. 9	Keansburg, NJ, boarding home	30
1981, Feb. 10	Las Vegas Hilton	8
1981, Feb. 14	Dublin, Ireland, discotheque	44
1982, Sept. 4	Los Angeles, apartment house	24
1982, Nov. 8	Biloxi, MS, county jail	29
1983, Feb. 13	Turin, Italy, movie theater	64
1983, Dec. 17	Madrid, Spain, discotheque	83
1984, May 11	Great Adventure Amusement Pk., NJ	8
1985, Apr. 21	Tabaco, Phil., movie theater	44
1985, Apr. 26	Buenos Aires, Argentina, hospital	79
1985, May 11	Bradford, England, soccer stadium	53
1986, Dec. 31	Puerto Rico, Dupont Plaza Hotel	96
1987, May 6-June 2	N China, forest fire	193
1987, Nov. 17	London, England, subway	30
1988, Mar. 20	Lashio, Burma, 2,000 buildings	134
1990, Mar. 25	Bronx, NY, social club	87
1991, Mar. 3	Addis Ababa, Ethiopia, munitions dump	260+
1991, Sept. 3	Hamlet, NC, processing plant	25
1991, Oct. 20-21	Oakland, Berkeley, CA, wildfire	24
1993, Apr. 19	Waco, TX, cult compound	72
1994, May 10	Bangkok, Thailand, toy factory	213
1994, July 4-10	Glenwood Springs, CO (firefighters)	14
1994, Dec. 10	Karamay, China, theater	300
1994, Nov. 2	Durunka, Egypt, burning fuel flood	500
1995, Oct. 28	Baku, Azerbaijan, subway train	300
1995, Dec. 23	Mandi Dabwali, India, school	500+
1996, Mar. 19	Quezon City, Philippines, nightclub	150+
1996, Mar. 28	Bogor, Indonesia, shopping mall	78
1996, Oct. 22	Caracas, Venezuela, jail	25
1996, Nov. 20	Hong Kong, building	39
1997, Feb. 23	Baripada, India, worship site	164
1997, Apr. 15	Mina, Saudi Arabia, encampment	343
1997, June 7	Thanjavur, India, temple	60+
1997, June 13	New Delhi, India, movie theater	60
1997, July 11	Pattaya, Thailand, hotel	90
1997, Sept. 29	Children's home, near Colina, Chile	30
1998, Dec. 3	Manila, Philippines, orphanage	28
1999, Mar. 24	France and Italy, Mont Blanc tunnel	40
1999, Oct. 30	Inchon, S. Korea, karaoke salon	55+
2000, Mar. 17	Kanungu, Uganda, church	530
2000, Oct. 20	Mexico City, Mexico, nightclub	20
2000, Dec. 25	Luoyang, China, shopping center	309
2001, Jan. 1	Volendam, Netherlands, cafe	10
2001, Mar. 6	Central China, school	41
2001, Mar. 26	Machakos, Kenya, school	64
2001, Aug. 6	Madras, India, home for mentally ill	27
2001, Aug. 18	Quezon City, Philippines, hotel	73
2001, Sept. 1	Tokyo, Japan, nightclub	44
2001, Oct. 24	Swiss Alps, St. Gotthard Tunnel	11
2001, Dec. 29	Lima, Peru, fireworks accident	291
2002, Mar. 11	Mecca, Saudi Arabia, girls' school	15
2002, June 16	Beijing, China, internet cafe	24
2002, July 7	Donetsk region, Ukraine, coal mine	34+
2002, July 20	Lima, Peru, disco	25+
2002, July 31	Donetsk region, Ukraine, coal mine	20
2003, Feb. 20	Warwick, RI, nightclub (pyrotechnics)	100
2003, Sept. 15	Riyadh, Saudi Arabia at al-Haer prison	94

Some Notable Explosions Since 1920

(See also Principal U.S. Mine Disasters Since 1900.) Many bombings related to political conflicts and terrorism are not included.

Date	Location	Deaths
1920, Sept. 16	Wall Street, NY, NY, bomb	30
1921, Sept. 21	Chem. storage facility, Oppau, Ger.	561
1924, Jan. 3	Food plant, Pekin, IL	42
1927, May 18	Bath school, Lansing, MI	38
1928, April 13	Dance hall, West Plains, MO.	40
1937, Mar. 18	New London, TX, school	311
1940, Sept. 12	Hercules Powder, Kenvil, NJ	55
1942, June 5	Ordnance plant, Elwood, IL	49
1944, Apr. 14	Bombay, India, harbor	700
1944, July 17	Port Chicago, CA, pier	322
1944, Oct. 21	Liquid gas tank, Cleveland	135
1947, Apr. 16	Texas City, TX, pier	576
1948, July 28	Farben works, Ludwigshafen, Ger.	184
1950, May 19	Munitions barges, S. Amboy, NJ	30
1956, Aug. 7	Dynamite trucks, Cali, Colombia	1,100
1958, Apr. 18	Sunken munitions ship, Okinawa, Japan	40
1958, May 22	Nike missiles, Leonardo, NJ	10
1959, Apr. 10	World War II bomb, Philippines	38
1959, June 28	Rail tank cars, Meldrim, GA	25
1959, Aug. 7	Dynamite truck, Roseburg, OR	13
1959, Nov. 2	Jamuri Bazar, India, explosives	46
1959, Dec. 13	2 apt. bldgs., Dortmund, Ger.	26
1960, Mar. 4	Belgian munitions ship, Havana, Cuba	100
1962, Oct. 3	Telephone Co. office, NY, NY	23
1963, Jan. 2	Packing plant, Terre Haute, IN	16
1963, Mar. 9	Dynamite plant, S. Africa	45
1963, Aug. 13	Explosives dump, Gauhaiti, India	32
1963, Oct. 31	State Fair Coliseum, Indianapolis, IN	73
1964, July 23	Bone, Algeria, harbor munitions	100
1965, Mar. 4	Gas pipeline, Natchitoches, LA	17
1965, Aug. 9	Missile silo, Searcy, AR	53
1965, Oct. 21	Bridge, Tila Bund, Pakistan	80
1965, Oct. 30	Cartagena, Colombia	48
1965, Nov. 24	Armory, Keokuk, IA	20
1967, Dec. 25	Apartment bldg., Moscow, USSR	20
1968, Apr. 6	Sports store, Richmond, IN	43
1970, Apr. 8	Subway construction, Osaka, Japan	73
1971, June 24	Tunnel, Sylmar, CA	17
1973, Feb., 10	Liquid gas tank, Staten Island, NY	40
1975, Dec. 27	Coal mine, Chasnala, India	431
1976, Apr. 13	Lapua, Finland, munitions works	40
1977, Nov. 11	Freight train, Iri, South Korea	57
1977, Dec. 22	Grain elevator, Westwego, LA	35
1978, Feb. 24	Derailed tank car, Waverly, TN	12
1978, July 11	Propylene tank truck, Spanish campsite	150
1980, Oct. 23	School, Ortuella, Spain	64
1982, Apr. 25	Antiques exhibition, Todi, Italy	33
1982, Nov. 2	Salang Tunnel, Afghanistan	1,000+
1984, Feb. 25	Oil pipeline, Cubatao, Brazil	508
1984, June 21	Naval supply depot, Severomorsk, USSR	200+
1984, Nov. 19	Gas storage area, NE Mexico City	334
1984, Dec. 3	Chemical plant, Bhopal, India	3,849
1984, Dec. 5	Coal mine, Taipei, Taiwan	94
1985, June 25	Fireworks factory, Hallett, OK	21
1988, Apr. 10	Pakistani army ammunitions dump near Rawalpindi and Islamabad	100
1988, July 6	Oil rig, North Sea	167
1989, June 3	Gas pipeline, between Ufa, Asha, USSR	650+
1992, Mar. 3	Coal mine, Kozlu, Turkey	270+
1992, Apr. 22	Sewer, Guadalajara, Mexico	190
1992, May 9	Coal mine, Plymouth, Nova Scotia	26
1993, Feb. 26	World Trade Center, NY, NY	6
1994, July 18	Jewish com. center, Buenos Aires, Arg.	100
1995, Apr. 19	Fed'l. office building, Oklahoma City	168
1995, Apr. 29	Subway construction, South Korea	110
1995, Nov. 13	Military facility, Riyadh, Saudi Arabia	7
1996, Jan. 31	Bank, Colombo, Sri Lanka	53
1996, Feb. 25	Jerusalem and Ashkelon, Israel	27

Date	Location	Deaths	Date	Location	Deaths
1996, Mar. 3-4	Jerusalem and Tel Aviv, Israel	33	2000, July 16	Oil pipeline, Warri, Nigeria	30
1996, June 25	U.S. military housing complex, near	19	2000, Aug. 19	Train derailed in Nairobi, Kenya	25
	Dhahran, Saudi Arabia	19	2000, Aug. 20	Natural gas pipeline, Carlsbad, NM	10
1996, July 24	Train, Colombo, Sri Lanka	86	2000, Sept. 9	Truck explodes in Urumqi, China	60
1996, Nov. 16	Russian military apartment, Dagestan		2000, Sept. 13	Bomb, Jakarta, Indonesia	15
	region, Russia	68	2000, Sept. 19	Bomb, Islamabad, Pakistan	16
1996, Nov. 21	Building, San Juan, Puerto Rico	29	2000, Oct. 12	U.S. destroyer, Yemen	17
1996, Nov. 27	Coal mine, Shanxi province, China	91+	2001, Mar. 6	School, Wanzai County China	41
1996, Dec. 30	Train, Assam, India	59+	2001, Apr. 21	Coal mine, Shaanxi, China	51
1997, Jan. 18	Near courthouse, Lahore, Pakistan	25	2001, June 1	Dance club, Tel Aviv, Israel	21
1997, Mar. 19	Ammunition depot, Jalalabad, Afgh.	16	2001, July 17	Coal mine, Guanxi, China	76+
1997, July 8	Train, Punjab, India	36	2001, Aug. 19	Coal mine, Donetsk region, Ukraine	52
1997, Nov. 19	Car, Hyderabad, India	23	2001, Sept. 21	Chem. plant, Toulouse, France	29
1997, Dec. 2	Coal mine, Novokuznetsk, Siberia	68	2002, Jan. 21	Volcanic lava causes gas station blast	
1998, Jan. 17	Coal mine, Sokobanja, Serbia	29		in Goma, Dem. Rep. of the Congo	50+
1998, Feb. 14	Oil tankers (2), Yaounde, Cameroon	120	2002, Jan. 27	Munitions dump, Lagos, Nigeria	1,000+
1998, Feb. 14	17 bombs, Coimbatore, India	50	2002, Mar. 21	Car bomb near U.S. embassy, Lima, Peru	9
1998, Mar. 5	Bus, Colombo, Sri Lanka	32	2002, Apr. 11	Truck nr. synagogue, Djerba, Tunisia	17
1998, Apr. 4	Coal mine, Donetsk, Ukraine	63	2002, Apr. 21	Bomb, dept. store, Mindanao, Philip.	14
1998, Aug. 7	Bomb, U.S. emb., Nairobi, Kenya	213	2002, Apr. 26	Bomb at mosque, central Pakistan	12
	Bomb, U.S. emb., Dar-es-Salaam, Tanz	11	2002, May 8	Bomb on bus outside hotel, Karachi, Pak.	14
1998, Aug. 15	Car bomb, Omagh, Ireland	29	2002, May 9	Land mine at parade, Kaspiisk, Russia	34+
1998, Sept. 8	Two buses, Sao Paulo, Brazil	59	2002, June 14	Car bomb outside U.S. consulate,	
1998, Oct. 17	Oil pipeline, Jesse, Nigeria	700+		Karachi, Pak.	12
1999, May 16	Fuel truck, Punjab province, Pakistan	75	2002, June 18	Bomb on bus, Jerusalem, Israel	20
1999, July 29	Gold mine, Carletonville, S. Africa	17	2002, July 5	Bomb in market, Larba, Algeria	35+
1999, Sept. 10	Apartment building, Moscow	94	2002, Aug. 9	Explosion, Jalalabad, Afghanistan	25+
1999, Sept. 13	Apartment building, Moscow	118	2002, Sept. 5	Car bomb, Kabul, Afghanistan	30
1999, Sept. 16	Apartment building, Moscow	18	2002, Oct. 12	Bombings of nightclubs in Bali, Indon.	202
1999, Sept. 26	Fireworks factory, Celaya, Mexico	56	2003, Aug. 5	Car bomb at hotel in Jakarta, Indon.	12
2000, Feb. 25	Bombs on 2 buses, Ozamis, Philip.	41	2003, Aug. 19	Truck bomb, UN headquarters, Baghdad.	22
2000, Mar. 11	Coal mine, Krasnodon, Ukraine	80	2003, Aug. 25	Bombs in 2 taxis, Mumbai (Bombay), India.	52
2000, Apr. 16	Airport hangar, Congo, Dem. Rep. of	100+	2003, Aug. 29	Explosion at mosque in Najaf, Iraq	80+

Notable Nuclear Accidents

Oct. 7, 1957 — A fire in the Windscale plutonium production reactor N of Liverpool, England, released radioactive material; later blamed for 39 cancer deaths.

Jan. 3, 1961 — A reactor at a federal installation near Idaho Falls, ID, killed 3 workers. Radiation contained.

Oct. 5, 1966 — A sodium cooling system malfunction caused a partial core meltdown at the Enrico Fermi demonstration breeder reactor, near Detroit, MI. Radiation contained.

Jan. 21, 1969 — A coolant malfunction from an experimental underground reactor at Lucens Vad, Switzerland, released radiation into a cavern, which was then sealed.

Mar. 22, 1975 — Fire at the Brown's Ferry reactor in Decatur, AL, caused dangerous lowering of cooling water levels.

Mar. 28, 1979 — The worst commercial nuclear accident in the U.S. occurred as equipment failures and human mistakes led to a loss of coolant and a partial core meltdown at the Three Mile Island reactor in Middletown, PA.

Feb. 11, 1981 — 8 workers were contaminated when 100,000 gallons of radioactive coolant fluid leaked into containment building of TVA's Sequoyah 1 plant in Tennessee.

Apr. 25, 1981 — Some 100 workers were exposed to radiation during repairs of a nuclear plant at Tsuruga, Japan.

Jan. 6, 1986 — A cylinder of nuclear material burst after being improperly heated at a Kerr-McGee plant at Gore, OK. One worker died; 100 were hospitalized.

Apr. 26, 1986 — In the worst nuclear accident in the history of nuclear power, fires and explosions resulting from an unauthorized experiment at the Chernobyl nuclear power plant near Kiev, USSR (now in Ukraine), left at least 31 dead in the immediate aftermath and spread radioactive material over much of Europe. An estimated 135,000 people were evacuated from the region, some of which was uninhabitable for years. As a result of the radiation released, tens of thousands of excess cancer deaths (as well as increased birth defects) were expected.

Sept. 30, 1999 — Japan's worst nuclear accident ever occurred at a uranium-reprocessing facility in Tokaimura, NE of Tokyo, when workers accidentally overloaded a container with uranium, thereby exposing workers and area residents to extremely high radiation levels.

On Dec. 24, 1984, in the worst industrial accident in history, more than 3,000 people were killed within hours when toxic gas leaked from a storage tank in a Union Carbide insecticide factory in a heavily populated section of Bhopal, India. An estimated 14,000 or more people were eventually killed, and more than 100,000 suffered injuries, including severe damage to eyes, lungs, and kidneys.

Record Oil Spills

The number of tons can be multiplied by 7 to estimate roughly the number of barrels spilled; the exact number of barrels in a ton varies with the type of oil. Each barrel contains 42 gallons.

Name, place	Date	Cause	Tons
Ixtoc I oil well, S Gulf of Mexico	June 3, 1979	Blowout	600,000
Nowruz oil field, Persian Gulf	Feb. 1983	Blowout	600,000 (est.)
Atlantic Empress & Aegean Captain, off Trinidad and Tobago	July 19, 1979	Collision	300,000
Castillo de Bellver, off Cape Town, South Africa	Aug. 6, 1983	Fire	250,000
Amoco Cadiz, near Portsall, France	Mar. 16, 1978	Grounding	223,000
Torrey Canyon, off Land's End, England	Mar. 18, 1967	Grounding	119,000
Sea Star, Gulf of Oman	Dec. 19, 1972	Collision	115,000
Urquiola, La Coruna, Spain	May 12, 1976	Grounding	100,000
Hawaiian Patriot, N Pacific	Feb. 25, 1977	Fire	99,000
Othello, Tralhavet Bay, Sweden	Mar. 20, 1970	Collision	60,000-100,000

Other Notable Oil Spills

Name, place	Date	Cause	Gallons
Persian Gulf	began Jan. 23, 1991	Spillage by Iraq	130,000,000[1]
Braer, off Shetland Islands	Jan. 5, 1993	Grounding	26,000,000
Prestige, off N Spain	Nov. 13-19, 2002	Ship broke in half	22,600,000
Aegean Sea, off N Spain	Dec. 3, 1992	Unknown	21,500,000
Sea Empress, off SW Wales	Feb. 15, 1996	Grounding	18,000,000
World Glory, off South Africa	June 13, 1968	Hull failure	13,524,000
Exxon Valdez, Prince William Sound, AK	Mar. 24, 1989	Grounding	10,080,000
Keo, off MA	Nov. 5, 1969	Hull failure	8,820,000
Storage tank, Sewaren, NJ	Nov. 4, 1969	Tank rupture.	8,400,000
Ekofisk oil field, North Sea	Apr. 22, 1977	Well blowout	8,200,000

(1) Est. by Saudi Arabia. Some estimates as low as 25 mil gal.

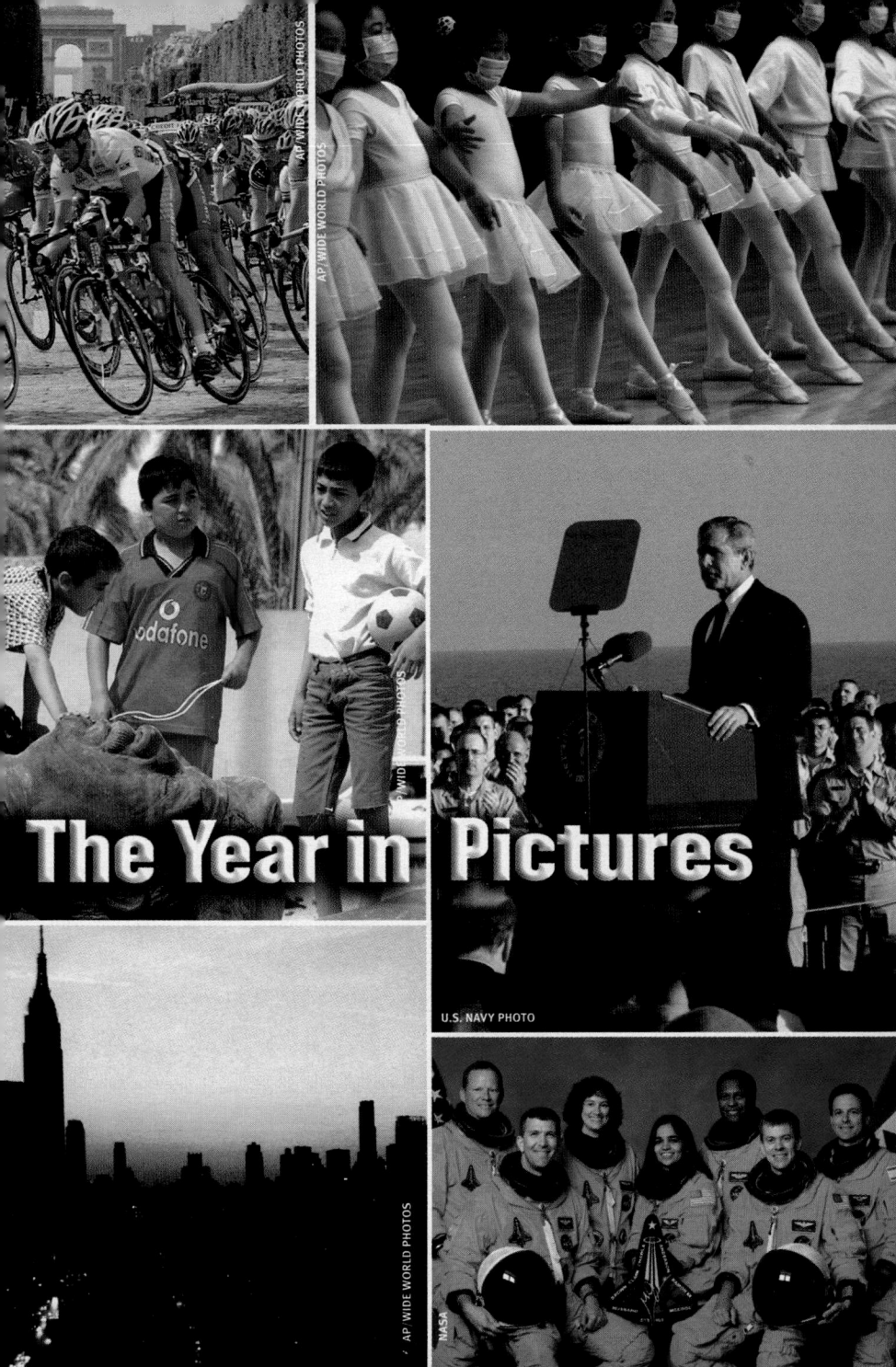

The Year in Pictures

AP/ WIDE WORLD PHOTOS

NO A LA GUERRA

NO WAR

AP/ WIDE WORLD PHOTOS

▲ WAR BEGINS

On Mar. 19 U.S.-led forces began a war against Iraq aimed at removing Saddam Hussein from power. The war started with massive air strikes against Baghdad, seen a week later engulfed in fire and smoke.

▲ AGAINST THE WAR

Opponents of the war staged large-scale demonstrations, like this one, Mar. 30, in Puerto de Santa Maria, Spain, near a U.S. naval base.

AP/ WIDE WORLD PHOTOS

AP/ WIDE WORLD PHOTOS

▲ ALLIES CONFER

Britain was the major U.S. ally; here British Prime Min. Tony Blair (left) meets with Pres. George W. Bush at Camp David.

▲ OTHER LEADERS DISSENT

Russian Pres. Vladimir Putin (center), French Pres. Jacques Chirac (left), and German Chancellor Gerhard Schröder, shown at a press conference in St. Petersburg, Russia, had sought continued UN weapons inspections rather than launching war.

▲ SWIFT ADVANCE
The ground offensive by U.S. and British troops progressed rapidly, meeting fairly light resistance; here 2 Marines defend a recently seized military compound in Baghdad.

▲ FALL OF SADDAM
Iraqi children inspect a toppled statue of Saddam Hussein on Apr. 12, three days after Baghdad came under U.S. control.

◄ NATION IN DISARRAY
As the regime collapsed, occupying troops failed to stem widespread looting and disorder; here a man carts off furniture looted from houses in the city of Basra.

War in Iraq

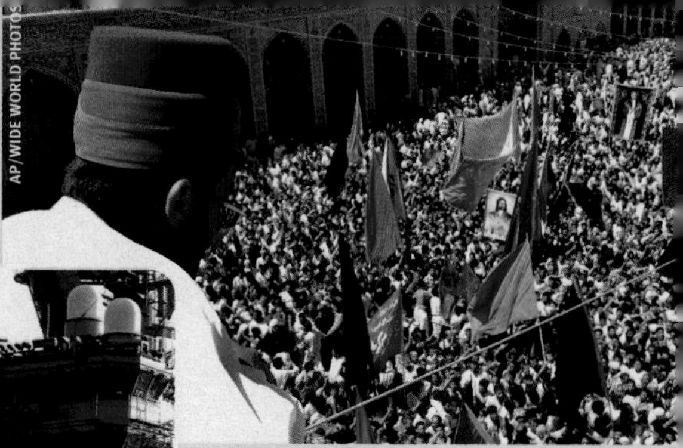
AP/WIDE WORLD PHOTOS

▲ **SHIITES COME TOGETHER**
Throngs of Shiite Muslim pilgrims gather at a shrine in Karbala on Apr. 23 for the first time in decades; their annual pilgrimage there had been forbidden under Saddam Hussein.

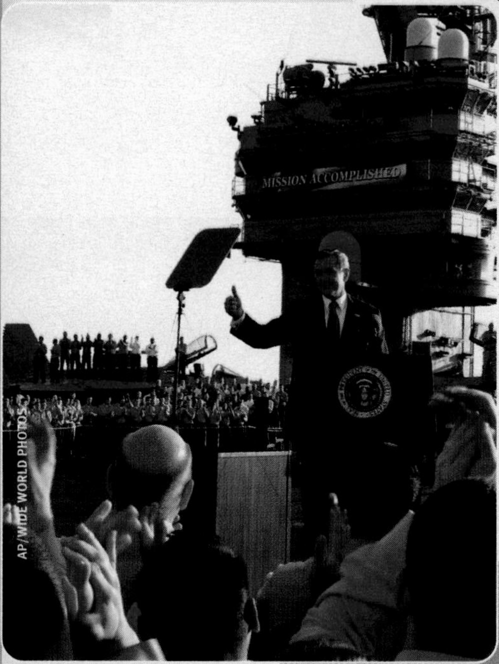
MISSION ACCOMPLISHED
AP/WIDE WORLD PHOTOS

▲ **MAJOR COMBAT DECLARED OVER**
After flying in on a Navy jet, Pres. Bush declared the end of major combat in Iraq May 1, aboard the aircraft carrier USS *Abraham Lincoln* off the California coast.

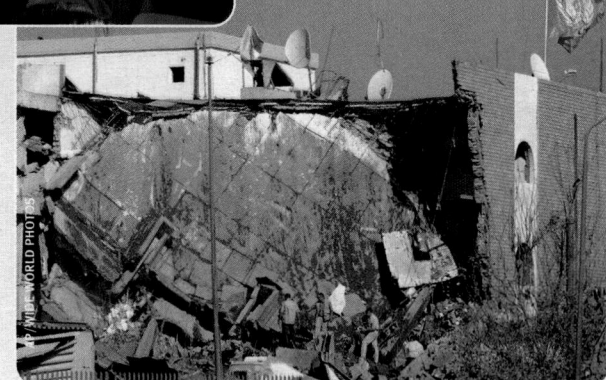

AP/WIDE WORLD PHOTOS

▲ **OPPOSITION CONTINUES**
Despite the end of large-scale combat, insurgents continued to inflict casualties on U.S. and British troops and commit acts of sabotage. In a significant escalation on Aug. 19, a truck bomb attack on UN headquarters in Baghdad (above) killed more than 20 people, including the UN special representative, Sergio Vieira de Mello.

◀ THE BIG BLACKOUT

In the biggest power failure ever to hit North America, electricity went out on Thursday afternoon, Aug. 14, disrupting life for millions of people in Ontario and 8 Northeast and Midwestern states. Here, New York City shown after sundown. Power returned sporadically, with Detroit the last to recover, early Sunday morning.

AP/WIDE WORLD PHOTOS

NASA

AP/WIDE WORLD PHOTOS

AP/WIDE WORLD PHOTOS

▲ COLUMBIA LOST

The space shuttle *Columbia* disintegrated during reentry Feb. 1, leaving a debris trail across the Texas sky. The ill-fated *Columbia* crew in a photo from a camera recovered in the wreckage (clockwise from left): Kalpana Chawla, David Brown, William McCool, Michael Anderson, Ilan Ramon, Laurel Clark, and Rick Husband.

▲ GAY BISHOP

Rev. V. Gene Robinson, seen here with his partner, Mark Andrew (right), and his daughter, Ella, was set to become the first openly gay Episcopal bishop following his election as bishop of New Hampshire and its ratification at a convention in Minneapolis. His selection, hailed by many, left the church sharply split.

197

◀ **TOTAL RECALL**

With California swamped by budget problems, Gov. Gray Davis (shown above, right, at a rally in San Francisco, with U.S. House Minority Leader Nancy Pelosi, D-CA), faced a recall election. Some 135 candidates were on the ballot to replace him if he was voted out. Among them was actor Arnold Schwarzenegger; here, supporters rally at the state capitol on his behalf.

▲ **DEMOCRATIC LINEUP**

From left to right, presidential candidates Rep. Dennis Kucinich (OH), Rep. Dick Gephardt (MO), Rev. Al Sharpton (NY), Sen. Joe Lieberman (CT), former Sen. Carol Moseley Braun (IL), former Gov. Howard Dean (VT), Sen. John Edwards (NC), Sen. Bob Graham (FL), and Sen. John Kerry (MA), pose prior to a May 3 debate at the Univ. of South Carolina. Ret. Gen. Wesley Clark entered the race in mid-September.

▲ **CHECK'S IN THE MAIL**

Pres. Bush speaks in front of a sample child tax credit check in Philadelphia—a day before mailing began July 25. The checks were part of Bush's $350 billion tax-cut package signed into law May 28.

DAVID JAMES

AP/WIDE WORLD PHOTOS

▲ CHICAGO!

Chicago took home 6 Oscars on Mar. 23, including Best Picture. Shown here is Catherine Zeta-Jones, in her Oscar-winning role as entertainer-murderess Velma Kelly.

▲ AMERICAN IDOL II

Singer Ruben Studdard (right), 2nd-season winner of TV's reality talent-contest show *American Idol*, jokes with runner-up Clay Aiken on stage after the May 21 finale.

AP/WIDE WORLD PHOTOS

PAUL KOLNIK

CLAY PATRICK McBRIDE, JR.

▲ WINNERS' CIRCLE

From left to right, at the 75th Academy Awards Mar. 23: Chris Cooper (*Adaptation*) and Catherine Zeta-Jones (*Chicago*) took home the Best Supporting awards, while Nicole Kidman (*The Hours*) and Adrien Brody (*The Pianist*) won Best Acting honors.

▲ CAN'T STOP THE BEAT

Hairspray stars Harvey Fierstein and Marissa Jaret Winokur, as Edna and Tracy Turnblad, with cast members. The Broadway musical version of John Waters' cult film won 8 Tonys June 8.

▲ GRAMMYS GALORE

Jazzy newcomer Norah Jones took away 5 Grammys on Feb. 24—including album, song, and record of the year. Her album *Come Away With Me* won 8 awards.

199

Farewells

◄ **MR. (FRED) ROGERS**
Fred Rogers, creator and host of the acclaimed PBS TV children's show *Mister Rogers' Neighborhood*, died Feb. 27 at 74.

▲ **BOB HOPE**
On a USO tour in 1970, legendary comedian Bob Hope entertains sailors of the U.S. 6th Fleet *Saratoga* in Gaeta, Italy. He died July 27 at 100.

STROM THURMOND
Veteran former Sen. Strom Thurmond (SC), who died June 26 at 100, is shown here after his 1948 nomination for president by the Dixiecrat party. ►

▲ **GREGORY PECK**
Quietly dignified screen actor Gregory Peck won an Oscar for his favorite role, as Atticus Finch in *To Kill a Mockingbird* (1962). He died June 12 at 87.

◄ **DAVID BRINKLEY**
TV newsman David Brinkley died June 11 at 82. Brinkley (left) co-anchored the pioneering *Huntley-Brinkley Report* with Chet Huntley from 1956 to 1970.

▲ **CELIA CRUZ**
For years the undisputed queen of salsa, Celia Cruz died July 16 at 77.

◄ **JOHNNY CASH**
Country music star Johnny Cash, shown here in 1985, died Sept. 12 at 71.

KATHARINE HEPBURN
Screen legend Katharine Hepburn died June 29 at 96. Hepburn, shown here in 1940's *The Philadelphia Story*, won a record 4 best actress Oscars. ►

NOTED PERSONALITIES

Widely Known Americans of the Present

Political leaders, journalists, other widely known living persons. As of Oct. 1, 2003. Excludes many in categories listed elsewhere in Noted Personalities, such as Writers of the Present and Entertainment Personalities of the Present, or in the Sports section. Includes some figures active in American life but not U.S. citizens.

Spencer Abraham, b 6/12/52 (East Lansing, MI), energy sec.
Roger Ailes, b 5/15/40 (Warren, OH), TV exec.
Madeleine K. Albright, b 5/15/37 (Prague, Czech.), former sec. of state.
Edwin ("Buzz") Aldrin, b 1/20/30 (Montclair, NJ), former astronaut, 2nd person on the Moon.
Lamar Alexander, b 7/3/40 (Maryville, TN), senator; former TN gov., presid. candidate.
Paul Allen, b 121/53 (Mercer Is., WA), co-founder of Microsoft.
Christiane Amanpour, b 1/12/58 (London, Eng.), TV journalist.
Richard K. Armey, b 7/7/40 (Cando, ND), former U.S. rep., House majority leader.
Neil Armstrong, b 8/5/30 (Wapakoneta, OH), former astronaut, 1st person on Moon.
John Ashcroft, b 5/9/42 (Chicago), attorney general.
Bruce Babbitt, b 6/27/38 (Los Angeles), former AZ gov., interior sec.
F. Lee Bailey, b 6/10/33 (Waltham, MA), attorney.
Russell Baker, b 8/14/25 (Loudoun Co., VA), columnist.
Dave Barry, b 7/3/47 (Armonk, NY), humorist.
Marion Barry, b 3/6/36 (Itta Bena, MS), former Wash., DC, mayor.
Gary Bauer, b 5/4/46 (Covington, KY), political activist.
William Bennett, b 7/31/43 (Brooklyn, NY), author, former education secretary.
Lloyd Bentsen, b 2/11/21 (Mission, TX), former senator, treasury sec., vice-presid. nominee.
Samuel ("Sandy") Berger, b 10/28/45 (Sharon, CT), former national security adviser.
Chris Berman, b 5/10/55 (Greenwich, CT), sportscaster.
Carl Bernstein, b 2/14/44 (Wash., DC), journalist, author.
Jeff Bezos, b 1/12/64 (Albuquerque, NM), founder and CEO of Amazon.com.
Joseph R. Biden Jr., b 11/20/42 (Scranton, PA), senator (DE).
James H. Billington, b 6/1/29 (Bryn Mawr, PA), librarian of Congress.
Wolf Blitzer, b 1948 (Augsburg, Germany), TV journalist.
Harold Bloom, b 7/11/30 (NYC), literary critic.
Michael R. Bloomberg, b 2/14/42 (Medford, MA), NYC mayor; financial information/media entrepreneur.
Roy Blunt, b 1/10/50 (Niangu, MO), U.S. House majority whip.
Julian Bond, b 1/14/40 (Nashville), civil rights leader.
David Bonior, b 6/6/45 (Detroit), former U.S. rep., House minority whip.
Daniel Boorstin, b 10/1/14 (Atlanta), historian, former librarian of Congress.
Barbara Boxer, b 11/11/40 (Brooklyn, NY), senator (CA).
Bill Bradley, b 7/28/43 (Crystal City, MO), former senator (NJ), basketball player, presid. candidate.
Ed Bradley, b 6/22/41 (Philadelphia), TV journalist.
James Brady, b 8/29/40 (Centralia, IL), former presid. press sec.; gun control advocate.
Carol Moseley Braun, b 8/16/47 (Chicago, IL), former senator, ambassador; 2003 presidential contender.
L. Paul Bremer III, b 9/30/41 (Hartford, CT), diplomat, top U.S. civilian administrator in Iraq.
Jimmy Breslin, b 10/17/30 (Jamaica, Queens, NY), columnist, author.
Stephen Breyer, b 8/15/38 (San Francisco), Sup. Ct. justice.
David Broder, b 9/11/29 (Chicago Heights, IL), journalist.
Tom Brokaw, b 2/6/40 (Webster, SD), TV anchor.
Vincent Brooks, b 1958(?) (Anchorage, AK), U.S. Army spokesman during Iraq war.
Joyce Brothers, b 9/20/28 (NYC), psychologist.

Aaron Brown, b 11/10/48 (Hopkins, MN), CNN anchor.
Jerry (Edmund G.) Brown Jr., b 4/7/38 (San Francisco), Oakland mayor; former CA gov., pres. candidate.
Willie Brown, b 3/20/34 (Mineola, TX), San Francisco mayor.
Pat Buchanan, b 11/2/38 (Wash., DC), journalist, former presid. candidate.
Art Buchwald, b 10/20/25 (Mt. Vernon, NY), humorist.
William F. Buckley Jr., b 11/24/25 (NYC), columnist, author.
Warren Buffett, b 8/30/30 (Omaha), investor.
Dan Burton, b 6/21/38 (Indianapolis), U.S. representative.
Barbara Bush, b 6/8/25 (Rye, NY), former first lady.
Barbara Bush, b 11/25/81 (Dallas, TX), daughter of Pres. George W. Bush.
George H. W. Bush, b 6/12/24 (Milton, MA), former president.
George W. Bush, b 7/6/46 (New Haven, CT), U.S. president.
Jeb Bush, b 2/11/53 (Houston), FL governor.
Jenna Bush, b 11/25/81 (Dallas, TX), daughter of Pres. George W. Bush.
Laura Bush, b 11/4/46 (Midland, TX), first lady.
Cruz Bustamante, b 1/4/53 (Dinuba, CA), CA lieut. gov., 2003 gov. recall election candidate.
Robert Byrd, b 11/20/17 (N. Wilkesboro, NC), senator (WV), former majority leader.
Peter Camejo, b 12/31/39 (NYC), Green Party leader, 2003 CA gov. recall election candidate.
Andrew Card, b 5/10/47 (Brockton, MA), White House chief of staff.
Tucker Carlson, b 5/16/69 (San Francisco), journalist, TV commentator.
Richard Carmona, b 11/22/49 (NYC), surgeon general.
Jimmy Carter, b 10/1/24 (Plains, GA), former president; won 2002 Nobel Peace Prize.
Rosalynn Carter, b 8/18/27 (Plains, GA), former first lady.
Stephen Carter, b 10/26/54 (Washington, D.C.), author, law professor.
James Carville Jr., b 10/25/44 (Fort Benning, GA), TV political commentator.
Steve Case, b 8/21/58 (Honolulu, HI), former AOL Time Warner chairman.
Oleg Cassini, b 4/11/13 (Paris, France), fashion designer.
Elaine Chao, b 3/26/53 (Taipei, Taiwan), labor sec.
Dick Cheney, b 1/30/41 (Lincoln, NE), U.S. vice president.
Lynne Cheney, b 8/14/41 (Casper, WY), political commentator, wife of Dick Cheney.
Julia Child, b 8/15/12 (Pasadena, CA), TV chef, author.
Noam Chomsky, b 12/7/28 (Philadelphia), linguist; activist.
Connie Chung, b 8/20/46 (Wash., DC), TV journalist.
Liz Claiborne, b 3/31/29 (Brussels, Belg.), fashion designer.
Wesley Clark, b 12/23/44 (Chicago), retired general, former NATO commander in Europe; 2004 presid. contender.
Bill Clinton, b 8/19/46 (Hope, AR), former U.S. president.
Chelsea Clinton, b 2/27/80 (Little Rock, AR), daughter of former Pres. Clinton and Hillary Rodham Clinton.
Hillary Rodham Clinton, b 10/26/47 (Chicago), senator (NY), former first lady.
Johnnie L. Cochran Jr., b 10/2/37 (Shreveport, LA), attorney.
Gary Condit, b 4/21/48 (Salina, OK), former U.S. representative (CA); figure in scandal.
Bob Costas, b 3/22/52 (Queens, NYC), TV journalist.
Ann Coulter, b 12/8/61 (New Canaan, CT), political commentator, author.
Katie Couric, b 1/7/57 (Arlington, VA), TV journalist.
Walter Cronkite, b 11/4/16 (St. Joseph, MO), former TV journalist.

Mario Cuomo, b 6/15/32 (Queens, NY), former NY gov.
Richard M. Daley, b 4/24/42 (Chicago), Chicago mayor.
Thomas Daschle, b 12/9/47 (Aberdeen, SD), Senate minority leader.
Gray Davis, b 12/26/42 (NYC), CA gov.; object of 2003 recall bid.
Howard Dean, b 11/17/48 (NYC), former VT gov., 2004 pres. contender.
Oscar de la Renta, b 7/22/36 (Santo Domingo, Dominican Rep.), fashion designer.
Tom DeLay, b 4/8/47 (Laredo, TX), House majority leader.
Michael Dell, b 2/23/65 (Houston, TX), founder, CEO of Dell computers.
Alan Dershowitz, b 9/1/38 (Brooklyn, NY), attorney.
Barry Diller, b 2/2/42 (San Francisco), TV exec.
Lou Dobbs, b 9/24/45 (Childress, TX), TV journalist.
Christopher Dodd, b 5/27/44 (Willimantic, CT), senator.
Elizabeth Hanford Dole, b 7/29/36 (Salisbury, NC), senator; former Red Cross pres., cabinet member, presid. contender.
Robert Dole, b 7/22/23 (Russell, KS), former Senate majority leader, presid. nominee.
Pete Domenici, b 5/7/32 (Albuquerque, NM), senator.
Sam Donaldson, b 3/11/34 (El Paso, TX), TV journalist.
Elizabeth Drew, b 11/16/35 (Cincinnati), journalist.
Matt Drudge, b 10/27/67 (MD), internet journalist.
Michael S. Dukakis, b 11/3/33 (Brookline, MA), former MA gov., presid. nominee.
Roger Ebert, b 6/18/42 (Urbana, IL), film critic.
Marian Wright Edelman, b 6/6/39 (Bennettsville, SC), children's rights advocate.
John Edwards, b 6/10/53 (Robbins, NC), senator; 2004 presid. contender.
Edward Egan, b 4/2/32 (Oak Park, IL), cardinal, archbishop of New York.
Michael Eisner, b 3/7/42 (Mt. Kisco, NY), Disney Co. exec.
Lawrence Ellison, b 1944, Oracle Corp. founder, exec.
Don(ald) Evans, b 7/27/46 (Houston), commerce sec.
Rev. Jerry Falwell, b 8/11/33 (Lynchburg, VA), TV evangelist, religious educator.
Louis Farrakhan, b 5/11/33 (Roxbury, MA), Nation of Islam leader.
Russell Feingold, b 3/2/53 (Janesville, WI), senator.
Dianne Feinstein, b 6/22/33 (San Francisco), senator.
Geraldine Ferraro, b 8/26/35 (Newburgh, NY), former U.S. representative, vice-presid. nominee.
Carly Fiorina, b 9/6/54 (Austin, TX), CEO of Hewlett-Packard.
Bobby Fisher, b 3/9/43 (Chicago, IL), chess prodigy.
Ari Fleischer b 1960, former White House press secretary.
Larry Flynt, b 11/1/42 (Salyersville, KY), publisher; 2003 CA gov. recall election candidate.
Shelby Foote, b 11/17/16 (Greenville, MS), historian.
Steve (Malcolm) Forbes Jr., b 7/18/47 (Morristown, NJ), publisher, former presid. candidate.
Betty Ford, b 4/8/18 (Chicago), former first lady.
Gerald R. Ford, b 7/14/13 (Omaha), former president.
Steve Fossett, b 4/22/1944 (California), adventurer, balloonist.
Al Franken, b 5/21/51 (NYC), humorist, political writer.
John Hope Franklin, b 1/2/15 (Rentiesville, OK), historian.
Tommy R. Franks, b 6/17/45 (Wynnewood, OK), gen., formercommander in chief U.S. Central Command.
Betty Friedan, b 2/4/21 (Peoria, IL), author, feminist.
Milton Friedman, b 7/31/12 (Bklyn, NY), economist.
Thomas Friedman, b 7/20/53 (Minneapolis), columnist, author.
Bill Frist, b 8/19/42 (Nashville, TN), Senate majority leader; physician.
John Kenneth Galbraith, b 10/15/08 (Iona Station, Ont.), economist, author, former amb. to India.
Bill Gates, b 10/28/55 (Seattle), Microsoft exec.
Henry Louis Gates Jr., b 9/16/50 (Keyser, WV), scholar.
David Geffen, b 2/21/43 (Brooklyn, NY), entertainment exec.
Richard Gephardt, b 1/31/41 (St. Louis, MO), former House party leader; presid. contender.
Louis Gerstner, b 3/1/42 (Mineola, NY), retired IBM exec.
Ed Gillespie b 1962 (?) (Brown Hills, NJ), Republican National Committee chair.
Newt Gingrich, b 6/17/43 (Harrisburg, PA), former House Speaker.
Ruth Bader Ginsburg, b 3/15/33 (Bklyn, NY), Sup. Ct. justice.
Rudolph Giuliani, b 5/28/44 (Bklyn, NY), former NYC mayor.
John Glenn, b 7/18/21 (Cambridge, OH), former senator, astronaut.
Ellen Goodman, b 4/11/41 (Newton, MA), columnist.
Doris Kearns Goodwin, b 1/4/43 (Rockville Centre, NY), historian, TV commentator.
Berry Gordy, b 11/28/29 (Detroit), Motown founder.
Al Gore Jr., b 3/31/48 (Wash., DC), former senator, U.S. vice president, presid. candidate.
Tipper Gore, b 8/19/48 (Wash., DC), wife of Al Gore.
Rev. Billy Graham, b 11/7/18 (Charlotte, NC), evangelist.
Bob Graham, b 4/9/36 (Dade Co., FL), U.S. senator, former FL gov; 2004 presidential contender.

(William) Franklin Graham, b 7/14/52 (Asheville, NC), evangelist, son of Billy Graham.
Phil Gramm, b 7/8/42 (Ft. Benning, GA), former senator (TX), presid. contender.
Jennifer Granholm, b 2/5/59 (Brit. Columbia, Can.), MI governor, former state atty. gen.
Richard Grasso, b 1946(?) (Queens, NY), former NYSE chair; quit when high pay aroused furor.
Andrew Greeley, b 2/5/28 (Oak Park, IL), priest, sociologist, writer.
Jeff Greenfield, b 6/10/43 (NYC), TV journalist.
Alan Greenspan, b 3/6/26 (NYC), Fed chairman.
Wilton Gregory, b 12/7/47 (Chicago), chairman, U.S. Conference of Catholic Bishops; bishop of Belleville, IL.
Andrew Grove, b 9/2/36 (Budapest, Hungary), Intel exec.
Bryant Gumbel, b 9/29/48 (New Orleans), TV journalist.
James Hahn, b 7/3/50 (Los Angeles), mayor of Los Angeles.
David Halberstam, b 4/10/34 (NYC), journalist, author.
Pete Hamill, b 6/24/35 (Brooklyn, NY), journalist, author.
Paul Harvey, b 9/4/18 (Tulsa, OK), radio journalist.
J. Dennis Hastert, b 1/2/42 (Aurora, IL), House Speaker.
Orrin Hatch, b 3/22/34 (Homestead Park, PA), senator (UT).
Hugh Hefner, b 4/9/26 (Chicago), publisher.
Jesse Helms, b 10/18/21 (Monroe, NC), former senator.
Leona Helmsley, b c1920 (NYC), real estate exec.
Heloise, b 4/15/51 (Waco, TX), advice columnist.
Tommy Hilfiger, b 3/24/51 (Elmira, NY), fashion designer.
Anita Hill, b 7/30/56 (Morris, OK), legal scholar, complainant against Clarence Thomas.
Christopher Hitchens, b 4/13/49 (Portsmouth, England), journalist, author.
James P. Hoffa, b 5/19/41, (Detroit), Teamsters Union head.
Richard Holbrooke, b 4/24/41 (Scarsdale, NY), former U.S. rep. to UN.
David Horowitz, b 1/10/39 (NYC), consumer advocate, columnist, author.
Steny H. Hoyer, b 6/14/39 (NYC), U.S. House minority whip.
Arianna Huffington, b 7/15/50 (Greece), columnist, 2003 CA gov. recall election dropout.
H. Wayne Huizenga, b 12/29/39 (Evergreen Park, IL), entrepreneur, sports exec.
Kay Bailey Hutchison, b 7/22/43 (Galveston, TX), senator.
Henry J. Hyde, b 4/18/24 (Chicago), U.S. representative.
Lee Iacocca, b 10/15/24 (Allentown, PA), former auto exec.
Carl Icahn, b 1936 (Queens, NY), financier.
Don Imus, b 7/23/40 (Riverside, CA), talk-show host.
Patricia Ireland, b 10/19/45 (Oak Park, IL), feminist leader.
Molly Ivins, b 8/30/44 (Monterey, CA), author, columnist.
Rev. Jesse Jackson, b 10/8/41 (Greenville, SC), civil rights leader, former presid. contender.
James Jeffords, b 5/11/34 (Rutland, VT), senator.
Peter Jennings, b 7/29/38 (Toronto, Can.), TV anchor.
Steven Jobs, b 2/24/55 (San Francisco), Apple Computer exec.
Jasper Johns, b 5/15/30 (Augusta, GA), artist.
Lady Bird Johnson, b 12/22/12 (Karnack, TX), former first lady.
Vernon E. Jordan Jr., b 8/15/35 (Atlanta), attorney, former presid. adviser, civil rights leader.
Donna Karan, b 10/2/48 (Forest Hills, NY), fashion designer.
John R. Kasich, b 5/13/52 (McKees Rocks, PA), former U.S. representative (OH).
Jeffrey Katzenberg, b 12/21/50 (NYC), entertainment exec.
Garrison Keillor, b 8/7/42 (Anoka, MN), author, broadcaster.
Jack Kemp, b 7/13/35 (Los Angeles), former vice-presid. nominee, HUD sec., pro football quarterback.
Anthony M. Kennedy, b 7/23/36 (Sacramento, CA), Sup. Ct. justice.
Edward M. Kennedy, b 2/22/32 (Brookline, MA), senator.
Bob (Joseph Robert) Kerrey, b 8/27/43 (Lincoln, NE), former senator.
John Kerry, b 12/11/43 (Denver), senator (MA), 2004 presid. contender.
Jack Kevorkian, b 5/26/28 (Pontiac, MI), physican, assisted-suicide activist.
Coretta Scott King, b 4/27/27 (Marion, AL), civil rights leader, widow of Martin Luther King Jr.
Larry King, b 11/19/33 (Brooklyn, NY), TV talk show host.
Michael Kinsley, b 3/9/51 (Detroit), editor, political commenator.
Jeane J. Kirkpatrick, b 11/19/26 (Duncan, OK), political scientist, former ambassador to UN.

Henry Kissinger, b 5/27/23 (Fuerth, Germany), former sec. of state, nat. security adviser; won 1973 Nobel Peace Prize.
Calvin Klein, b 11/19/42 (Bronx, NYC), fashion designer.
Philip H. Knight, b 2/24/38 (Portland, OR), CEO of Nike.
Edward I. Koch, b 12/12/24 (NYC), former NYC mayor.
C. Everett Koop, b 10/14/16 (Brooklyn, NY), former surgeon general.
Ted Koppel, b 2/8/40 (Lancashire, England), TV journalist.
Larry Kramer, b 6/25/35 (Bridgeport, CT), AIDS activist, writer.
William Kristol, b 12/23/52 (NYC), editor, columnist.
Dennis Kucinich, b 10/8/46 (Cleveland, OH), U.S. representative, 2004 presidential contender.
Brian Lamb, b 10/9/41 (Lafayette, IN), cable TV exec., journalist.
Estee Lauder, b 7/1/08 (NYC), founder, cosmetics and fragrance firm.
Matt Lauer, b 12/30/57 (NYC), TV journalist.
Ralph Lauren, b 10/14/39 (Bronx, NY), fashion designer.
Bernard F. Law, b 11/4/31 (Torreon, Mexico), cardinal, former archbishop of Boston, figure in church scandal.
Kenneth L. Lay, b 4/15/42 (Tyrone, MO), former CEO of Enron, linked to corporate accounting scandals.
Patrick Leahy, b 3/31/40 (Montpelier, VT), senator.
Norman Lear, b 7/27/22 (New Haven, CT), TV producer, political activist.
Jim Lehrer, b 5/19/34 (Wichita, KS), TV journalist, author.
James Levine, b 6/23/43 (Cincinnati) conductor.
Monica Lewinsky, b 7/23/73 (San Francisco), former White House intern, key figure in White House scandal.
Joseph Lieberman, b 2/24/42 (Stamford, CT), senator, former vice presid. candidate; 2004 presid. contender.
Daniel Liebeskind, b 1946 (Lodz, Poland), architect, involved in World Trade Center project.
Rush Limbaugh, b 1/12/51 (Cape Girardeau, MO), radio talk-show host.
Gary Locke, b 1/21/50 (Seattle), WA gov.
Trent Lott, b 10/9/41 (Grenada, MS), senator, former Senate party leader.
Shannon Lucid, b 1/14/43 (Shanghai, China), NASA scientist, astronaut.
Richard G. Lugar, b 4/4/32 (Indianapolis), senator.
Jessica Lynch, b 4/26/83 (Palestine, WV), rescued Iraq war POW.
John Madden, b 4/10/36 (Austin, MN), sportscaster.
Roger Mahoney, b 2/27/36 (Hollywood, CA), cardinal archbishop of Los Angeles.
Mel(quiades) Martinez, b 10/23/46 (Sagua la Grande, Cuba), housing and urban development sec.
Janet Maslin, b 8/12/49 (NYC), film critic, author.
Mary Matalin, b 8/19/53 (Chicago), political commentator.
Chris Matthews, b 12/18/45 (Philadelphia), TV journalist.
Terry McAuliffe, b 1957 (Syracuse, NY), Democratic national chairman.
John McCain, b 8/29/36 (Panama Canal Zone), senator (AZ); former presid. contender.
Scott McClellan, b 1968(?) (Austin, TX), White House press secretary.
Tom McClintock, b 7/10/56 (Thousand Oaks, CA), 2003 CA state sen., 2003 gov. recall election candidate.
Mitch McConnell, b 2/20/42 (S. Louisville, KY), Senate majority whip
David McCullough, b 7/7/33 (Pittsburgh, PA), historian, biographer.
John McLaughlin, b 3/29/27 (Providence, RI), TV journalist.
George McGovern, b 7/19/22 (Avon, SD), former senator, presid. nominee.
Dr. Phil McGraw, b 9/1/50 (Vinita, OK), talk-show host, motivational speaker, author.
Robert S. McNamara, b 6/9/16 (San Francisco), former defense sec., World Bank head.
Russell Means, b 11/10/39 (Pine Ridge Indian Reserv., SD), Native American activist.
Kweisi Mfume, b 10/24/48 (Baltimore), civil rights leader, former U.S. representative.
Kate Michelman, b 8/4/42 (New Jersey), abortion-rights activist.
Kate Millett, b 9/14/34 (St. Paul, MN), author, feminist.
Norman Mineta, b 11/12/31 (San Jose, CA), transportation sec.
George Mitchell, b 8/20/33, (Waterville, ME), former Senate majority leader.
Walter Mondale, b 1/5/28 (Ceylon, MN), former vice pres., senator, presid. nominee.
Bill Moyers, b 6/5/34 (Hugo, OK), TV journalist, author.
Robert S. Mueller III, b 8/7/44 (NYC), FBI director.
Rupert Murdoch, b 3/11/31 (Melbourne, Aust.), media exec.
Richard B. Myers, b 3/1/42 (Kansas City, MO), chairman of the Joint Chiefs of Staff.
Ralph Nader, b 2/27/34 (Winsted, CT), consumer advocate, former presid. candidate.
John Negroponte, b 7/21/39 (London, Eng.), U.S. representative to UN.
Don Nickles, b 12/6/48 (Ponca City, OK), U.S. Senator, former party whip.

Peggy Noonan, b 9/7/50 (Brooklyn, NY), columnist, speechwriter.
Oliver North, b 10/7/43 (San Antonio, TX), radio talk-show host, former National Security Council aide.
Eleanor Holmes Norton, b 6/13/37 (Wash., DC), U.S. House delegate.
Gale Norton, b 3/11/54 (Wichita, KS), interior sec.
Robert Novak, b 2/26/31 (Joliet, IL), journalist.
Sam Nunn, b 9/8/38 (Perry, GA), former senator.
Sandra Day O'Connor, b 3/26/30 (El Paso, TX), Sup. Ct. justice.
Sean O'Keefe, b 1/27/56 (LA), NASA head.
Sean O'Malley, b 6/29/44 (Lakewood, OH), Rom. Cath. archbishop of Boston.
Paul O'Neill, b 12/4/35 (Pittsburgh), former treasury sec.
Bill O'Reilly, b 9/10/49 (NYC), TV commentator, host.
Michael Ovitz, b 12/4/46 (Encino, CA), entertainment exec.
Clarence Page, b 6/2/47 (Dayton; OH), columnist, TV commentator.
Camille Paglia, b 4/2/47 (Endicott, NY), scholar, author.
Rod(erick) Paige, b 6/17/33 (Monticello, MS), education sec.
Leon F. Panetta, b 6/28/38 (Monterey, CA), former White House chief of staff, U.S. representative.
Rosa Parks, b 2/4/13 (Tuskegee, AL), civil rights activist.
Richard Parsons, b 4/4/48 (NYC), Time Warner CEO.
George Pataki, b 6/24/45 (Peekskill, NY), NY gov.
Jane Pauley, b 10/31/50 (Indianapolis), TV journalist.
Nancy Pelosi, b 3/26/41 (Baltimore, MD), House minority leader.
H. Ross Perot, b 6/27/30 (Texarkana, TX), entrepreneur, former presid. nominee.
Alvin F. Poussaint, b 5/15/34 (NYC), child psychiatrist.
Colin Powell, b 4/5/37 (NYC), sec. of state; former national security adviser, Joint Chiefs of Staff chairman.
Anthony Principi, b 4/16/44 (Bronx, NY), sec. of veterans affairs.
Dan Quayle, b 2/4/47 (Indianapolis), former U.S. vice pres., senator, presid. contender.
Anna Quindlen, b 7/8/53 (Philadelphia), author, columnist.
Marc Racicot, b 7/24/48 (Thompson Falls, MT), former Republican national chairman, former (MT) gov., campaign manager for Pres. Bush's 2004 reelection bid.
Dan Rather, b 10/31/31 (Wharton, TX), TV anchor.
Nancy Reagan, b 7/6/21 (NYC), former first lady.
Ronald Reagan, b 2/6/11 (Tampico, IL), former president.
Sumner Redstone, b 5/27/23 (Boston), media exec.
Ralph Reed, b 6/24/61 (Portsmouth, VA), political adviser.
William Rehnquist, b 10/1/24 (Milwaukee), Sup. Ct. chief justice.
Robert B. Reich, b 6/24/46 (Scranton, PA), economist, former labor sec.
Harry Reid, b 12/2/39 (Searchlight, NV), Senate minority whip.
Janet Reno, b 7/21/38 (Miami, FL), former attorney general.
Condoleezza Rice, b 11/14/54 (Birmingham, AL), national security advisor.
Ann Richards, b 9/1/33 (Lakeview, TX), former TX gov.
Bill Richardson, b 11/15/47 (Pasadena, CA), NM gov., former energy sec., UN ambassador, congressman.
Sally K. Ride, b 5/26/51 (Encino, CA), former astronaut.
Tom (Thomas Joseph) Ridge, b 8/26/45 (Munhall, PA), sec. of homeland security; former PA gov.
Justin Rigali, b 4/19/35 (Los Angeles, CA), archbishop of Philadelphia, named a cardinal.
Geraldo Rivera, b 7/4/43 (NYC), TV journalist.
Cokie Roberts, b 12/27/43 (New Orleans), TV journalist.
Rev. Oral Roberts, b 1/24/18 (nr. Ada, OK), TV evangelist, educator.
Rev. Pat Robertson, b 3/22/30 (Lexington, VA), religious broadcasting exec, former presid. contender.
David Rockefeller, b 6/12/15 (NYC), banker.
John D. "Jay" Rockefeller 4th, b 6/18/37 (NYC), senator (WV), former WV gov.
Laurance S. Rockefeller, b 5/26/10 (NYC), philanthropist.
Al Roker, b 8/20/54 (Queens, NY), TV weather person.
Mitt Romney, b 3/12/47 (Detroit), MA gov, former Olympics organizer.
Andy Rooney, b 1/14/19 (Albany, NY), TV commentator.
Charlie Rose, b 1/5/42 (Henderson, NC), TV journalist.
Karl Rove, b 12/25/50 (Denver) political consultant.
Louis Rukeyser, b 1/30/33 (NYC), TV journalist, financial analyst.
Donald Rumsfeld, b 7/9/32 (Chicago), defense sec.
Tim Russert, b 5/7/50 (Buffalo, NY), TV journalist.
Morley Safer, b 11/8/31 (Toronto, Can.), TV journalist.
William Safire, b 12/17/29 (NYC), columnist.
Diane Sawyer, b 12/22/45 (Glasgow, KY), TV journalist.
Antonin Scalia, b 3/11/36 (Trenton, NJ), Sup. Ct. justice.
Phyllis Schlafly, b 8/15/24 (St. Louis, MO) political activist.
Arthur Schlesinger Jr., b 10/15/17 (Columbus, OH), historian.
Caroline Kennedy Schlossberg, b 11/27/57 (NY, NY), author, daughter of Pres. Kennedy.
Patricia Schroeder, b 7/30/40 (Portland, OR), former U.S. representative.
Rev. Robert Schuller, b 9/16/26 (Alton, IA), TV evangelist.
Charles Schumer, b 11/23/50 (Brooklyn, NY), senator.

Arnold Schwarzenegger, b 7/30/47 (Thal, Styria, Austria), actor, 2003 CA gov. recall election candidate.
H. Norman Schwarzkopf, b 8/22/34 (Trenton, NJ), former military leader.
Willard Scott, b 3/7/34 (Alexandria, VA), TV weather person.
Alan H. ("Bud") Selig, b 7/30/34 (Milwaukee), baseball comm.
Donna E. Shalala, b 2/14/41 (Cleveland), former sec. of health and human services.
Gene Shalit, b 3/25/32 (NYC), TV film critic.
Al Sharpton, b 10/3/54 (Brooklyn, NYC), activist, civil rights leader; 2004 presid. contender.
Maria Shriver, b 11/6/55 (Chicago), TV journalist.
George P. Shultz, b 12/13/20 (NYC), former sec. of state, other cabinet posts.
O. J. Simpson, b 7/9/47 (San Francisco), former football star, murder defendant.
Liz Smith, b 2/2/23 (Ft. Worth, TX), gossip columnist.
John Snow, b 8/2/39 (Toledo, OH), treasury sec; former CFX CEO.
George Soros, b 8/12/30 (Budapest, Hungary), financier, philanthropist.
David H. Souter, b 9/17/39 (Melrose, MA), Sup. Ct. justice.
Arlen Specter, b 2/12/30 (Wichita, KS), senator (PA).
Kenneth Starr, b 7/21/46 (Vernon, TX), former Whitewater independent counsel.
Shelby Steele, b 1/1/46 (Chicago), scholar, critic.
George Steinbrenner, b 7/4/30 (Rocky River, OH), NY Yankees owner.
Gloria Steinem, b 3/25/34 (Toledo, OH), author, feminist.
George Stephanopoulos, b 2/10/61 (Fall River, MA), TV journalist, former presid. adviser.
David J. Stern, b 9/22/42 (NYC), basketball comm.
John Paul Stevens, b 4/20/20 (Chicago), Sup. Ct. justice.
Ted Stevens, b 11/18/23 (Indianapolis, IN), Senator (AK), Senate president pro tempore.
Martha Stewart, b 8/3/41 (Nutley, NJ), homemaking adviser, entrepreneur, facing trial in insider-trading case.
Arthur Ochs Sulzberger Jr., b 9/22/51 (Mt. Kisco, NY), newspaper publisher.
John H. Sununu, b 7/2/39 (Havana, Cuba), political commentator, former White House chief of staff.
John J. Sweeney, b 5/5/34 (NYC), AFL-CIO pres.
Paul Tagliabue, b 11/24/40 (Jersey City, NJ), football comm.
George Tenet, b 1/5/53 (Queens, NY), CIA director.
Clarence Thomas, b 6/23/48 (Savannah, GA), Sup. Ct. justice.
Helen Thomas, b 8/4/20 (Winchester, KY), journalist.
Fred Thompson, b 8/19/42 (Sheffield, AL), former senator; actor.
Hunter S. Thompson, b 7/18/37 (Louisville, KY), journalist.
Tommy G. Thompson, b 11/19/41 (Elroy, WI), sec. of health and human services, former WI gov.
Laurence Tisch, b 3/15/23 (NYC), entertainment exec.

Margaret Truman, b 2/17/24 (Independence, MO), author, daughter of Pres. Truman.
Donald Trump, b 6/14/1946 (NYC), real estate exec.
Ted Turner, b 11/19/38 (Cincinnati), TV exec, philanthropist.
Peter Ueberroth, b 9/2/37 (Chicago), sports & travel exec.
Jack Valenti, b 9/5/21 (Houston), movie industry exec.
Abigail Van Buren, b 7/4/18 (Sioux City, IA), advice columnist.
Gloria Vanderbilt, 2/20/24 (NYC), fashion designer, heiress.
Greta Van Susteren, b 6/11/54 (Appleton, WI), lawyer, TV commentator.
Ann M. Veneman, b 6/29/49 (Sacramento, CA), agriculture sec.
Jesse Ventura, b 7/15/51 (Minneapolis), former wrestler, MN governor.
Paul Volcker, b 9/5/27 (Cape May, NJ), economist, former Fed chairman.
Mike Wallace, b 5/9/18 (Brookline, MA), TV journalist.
Barbara Walters, b 9/25/31 (Boston), TV journalist.
James Watson, b 4/6/28 (Chicago), biochemist, DNA pioneer, co-winner 1962 Nobel Prize.
J. C. Watts Jr., b 11/18/57 (Eufaula, OK), former U.S. representative, Republican Conference chair (GOPAC).
Dr. Andrew Weil, b 6/8/42 (Philadelphia), health adviser.
Sanford I. Weill, b 3/16/33 (Brooklyn, NY), CEO of Citigroup.
Caspar Weinberger, b 8/18/17 (San Francisco), business exec, former defense sec., other cabinet posts.
Harvey Weinstein, b 3/19/52 (NYC), movie executive.
Jack Welch, b 11/19/35 (Peabody, MA), former General Electric CEO.
Jann Wenner, b 1/7/46 (NYC), publisher, founder Rolling Stone.
Cornel West, b 6/23/53 (Tulsa, OK), scholar, critic.
Ruth Westheimer, b 6/4/28 (Frankfurt am Main, Germany), human sexuality expert.
Christine Todd Whitman, b 9/26/46 (NYC), former EPA head, NJ gov.
Meg Whitman, b 8/4/56 (Cold Spring Harbor, NY), eBay pres. and CEO.
Elie Wiesel, b 9/30/28 (Sighet, Romania), scholar, author, 1986 Nobel Peace Prize winner.
L. Douglas Wilder, b 1/17/31 (Richmond, VA), former VA gov.
George Will, b 5/4/41 (Champaign, IL), journalist, author.
Jody Williams, b 10/9/50 (Brattleboro, VT), anti-landmine activist, 1997 Nobel Peace Prize winner.
Oprah Winfrey, b 1/29/54 (Kosciusko, MS), TV and media personality, businessperson, actress.
Paul Wolfowitz, b 12/22/43 (NYC), deputy defense secretary.
Bob Woodward, b 3/26/43 (Geneva, IL), journalist, author.
Paula Zahn, b 2/24/56 (Omaha, NE), TV journalist.
Robert B. Zoellick, b 1953 (Naperville, IL), U.S. trade representative.
Mortimer Zuckerman, b 6/4/37 (Montreal, Quebec), publisher, columnist.

Widely Known World Personalities of the Present

Living Non-Americans only. Excludes current heads of state or government (see Nations chapter) and most others covered elsewhere, such as in Widely Known Americans, Entertainers and Writers lists, or Sports Personalities.

Crown Prince Abdullah, b 1924 (Riyadh, Saudi Ar.), de facto ruler of Saudi Arabia; heir to throne
Gerry Adams, b 10/6/48 (Belfast, N. Ireland), Sinn Fein leader
Prince Albert, b 3/14/58 (Monte Carlo, Monaco), crown prince of Monaco (son of Prince Rainier and Princess Grace)
Theo Albrecht, b 3/28/22 (Schonebeck, Ger.), German billionaire, CEO of Aldi
Giulio Andreotti, b 1/14/19 (Rome, Italy), former Italian prime min.
Prince Andrew, b 2/19/60 (London, Eng.), Duke of York (2nd son of Queen Elizabeth II)
Kofi Annan, b 4/8/38 (Kumasi, Ghana), UN sec.-gen.; 2001 Nobel laureate
Princess Anne, b 8/15/50 (London, Eng.), Princess Royal (daughter of Queen Elizabeth II)
Corazon Aquino, b 1/25/33 (Manila, Philip.), former pres. of Philippines
Yasir Arafat, b 8/27/29 (Gaza Strip), head of Palestinian Authority; 1994 Nobel laureate
Oscar Arias Sánchez, b 9/13/41 (Heredia, Costa Rica), former Costa Rican pres., peace negotiator, 1987 Nobel laureate
Giorgio Armani, b 7/11/34 (Piacenza, Italy), fashion designer
Ehud Barak, b 2/12/42 (Mishmar Ha-Sharon Kibbutz, Israel), former Israeli prime min.
Ahmed Ben Bella, b 1916 (?) (Marnia, Algeria), 1st Algerian prime min.; revolutionary leader
Boris Berezovsky, b 1/23/46 (Moscow, USSR), businessman, politician
Tim Berners-Lee, b 6/8/55 (London, Eng.), World Wide Web inventor
Benazir Bhutto, b 6/21/53 (Karachi, Pak.), former prime min. of Pakistan
Osama bin Laden, b 1957 (?) (Riyadh, Saudi Ar.), leader of al-Qaeda terrorist organization
Hans Blix, b 6/28/28 (Uppsala, Sweden), UN weapons inspector

Fernando Botero, b 1932 (Medellín, Col.), Colombian artist
Boutros Boutros-Ghali, b 11/14/22 (Cairo, Egypt), former UN sec.-gen.
Richard Branson, b 7/18/50 (S. London, Eng.), British Virgin Records and Airways founder; explorer
(Leonard) James Callaghan, b 3/27/12 (Portsmouth, Hampshire, Eng.), former British prime min.
Kim Campbell, b 3/10/47 (Port Alberni, British Columbia, Can.), former Canadian prime min.
Pierre Cardin, b 7/7/22 (Venice, Italy), fashion designer
Princess Caroline, b 1/23/57 (Monte Carlo, Monaco), Monaco royal (older daughter of Prince Rainier and Princess Grace)
Violeta de Chamorro, b 10/18/29 (Rivas, Nicar.), former Nicaraguan pres.
Prince Charles, b 11/14/48 (London, Eng.), Prince of Wales (eldest son of Queen Elizabeth II); heir to British throne
Christo (Javacheff), b 6/13/35 (Gabrovo, Bulg.), artist
Joe (Charles Joseph) Clark, b 6/5/39 (High River, Alberta, Can.), former Canadian prime min.
King Constantine II, b 6/2/40 (Psychiko, Greece), former king of Greece
Mairead Corrigan-McGuire, b 1/27/44 (Belfast, N. Ireland), British peace activist, 1976 Nobel laureate
Francis Crick, b 6/8/16 (Northampton, Eng.), codiscoverer of DNA structure; 1962 Nobel laureate
Dalai Lama (Tenzin Gyatso), b 7/6/35 (Taktser, Amdo, Tibet), Buddhist leader; 1989 Nobel laureate
Jacques Derrida, b 7/15/30 (El Biar, Algeria), French deconstructionist philosopher
Iain Duncan Smith, b 4/9/54 (Edinburgh, Scot.), British Conservative opposition leader
Jean Claude Duvalier ("Baby Doc"), b 7/3/51 (Port-au-Prince, Haiti), former Haitian dictator
Bulent Ecevit, b 5/28/25 (Constantinople [Istanbul] Turkey), former Turkish premier

Prince Edward, b 10/9/35 (London, Eng.), Earl of Essex (3rd son of Queen Elizabeth II)
Prince Felipe, b 1/30/68 (Madrid, Spain), heir to Spanish throne
Sarah Ferguson, b 10/15/58 (London, Eng.), Duchess of York; ex-wife of Prince Andrew
David Frost, b 4/7/39 (Tenterden, Eng.), British journalist, interviewer
Alberto Fujimori, b 7/28/38 (Lima, Peru), ousted pres. of Peru
Valery Giscard d'Estaing, b 2/2/26 (Koblenz, Ger.), former French pres.
Jane Goodall, b 4/3/34 (London, Eng.), British anthropologist
Mikhail Gorbachev, b 3/2/31 (Privolnoye, USSR), former Soviet pres.; 1990 Nobel laureate
Prince Henry ("Harry") of Wales, b 9/15/84 (London, Eng.), son of Prince Charles; 3rd in line to British throne
Vaclav Havel, b 10/5/36 (Prague, Czech.), former Czech pres.; playwright
Stephen Hawking, b 1/8/42 (Oxford, Eng.), theoretical physicist; science writer
Edward Heath, b 7/9/16 (St. Peters-in-Thanet, Kent, Eng.), former British prime min.
Sir Edmund Hillary, b 7/20/19 (Auckland, New Zeal.), 1st to reach summit of Mt. Everest, with Tenzing Norgay, 1953
David Hockney, b 7/9/37 (Bradford, Eng.), artist
John Hume, b 1/18/37 (Derry, N. Ireland), Unionist politician; 1998 Nobel laureate
Saddam Hussein, b 4/28/37 (Tikrit, Iraq), former Iraqi ruler
Jiang Zemin, b 8/17/26 (Yangzhou, Jiangsu Prov., China), former pres. of China
Pope John Paul II (Karol Wojtyla), b 5/18/20 (Wadowice, Pol.), head of Rom. Cath. church
Garry Kasparov, b 4/13/63 (Baku, Azerbaijan, USSR), former world chess champion
Kim Dae Jung, b 12/3/25 (near Mokpo, S. Korea), former S. Korean dissident, opposition leader, pres.; 2000 Nobel laureate
F.W. (Frederik Willem) de Klerk, b 3/18/36 (Johannesburg, S. Africa), former S. African pres.; 1993 Nobel laureate
Helmut Kohl, b 4/3/30 (Ludwigshafen, Ger.), former German chancellor
Vladimir Kramnik, b 7/25/75 (Tuapse, Russia, USSR), world chess champion
Hans Kung, b 3/19/28 (Sursee, Switz.), Swiss Rom. Cath. theologian
Richard Leakey, b 12/19/44 (Nairobi, Kenya), Kenyan anthropologist
Claude Lévi-Strauss, b 11/28/08 (Brussels, Belg.), French anthropologist, structuralist
José López Portillo, b 6/16/20 (Mexico City, Mex.), former Mexican pres.
John Major, b 3/29/43 (Wimbledon, Eng.), former British prime min.
Nelson Mandela, b 7/18/18 (Transkei, S. Africa), former pres. of S. Africa; 1993 Nobel laureate
Imelda Marcos, b 7/2/29 (Manila, Philip.), former first lady of Philippines
Peter Max, b 10/19/37 (Berlin, Ger.), German artist, designer
Heather Mills McCartney b 1968 (Washington, Tyne and Wear, Eng.), model, land mine activist, wife of former Beatle Paul McCartney
Jean-Marie Messier, b 12/13/56 (Grenoble, Fr.), CEO of Vivendi Universal
Empress Michiko, b 10/20/34 (Tokyo, Jap.), empress of Japan
Slobodan Milosevic, b 8/20/41 (Pozarevac, Serbia, Yugoslavia), former Yugoslav pres.; charged with war crimes
Sun Myung Moon, b 1/6/20 (Kwangju Sangsa Ri, N. Korea), Unification Church founder
Brian Mulroney, b 3/20/39 (Baie-Corneau, Quebec, Can.), former Canadian prime min.
Prince Naruhito, b 2/23/60 (Tokyo, Jap.), crown prince of Japan
Benjamin Netanyahu, b 10/21/49 (Tel-Aviv, Israel), former Israeli prime min.

Queen Noor (Lisa Halaby), 8/23/51 (Washington, DC), American-born widow of Jordan's King Hussein
Manuel Noriega, 2/11/34 (Panama City, Pan.), ousted Panamanian pres., jailed in Miami
Mullah Muhammad Omar, b 1959 (Nodeh, Afghan.), Afghan Taliban leader
Yoko Ono, b 2/18/33 (Tokyo, Japan), widow of former Beatle John Lennon; musician
Daniel Ortega Saavedra, b 11/11/45 (La Libertad, Nicar.), former Nicaraguan pres., Sandinista leader
Camilla Parker Bowles, b 7/17/47 (London, Eng.), companion of Prince Charles
Jean-Marie le Pen, b 6/20/28 (La Trinite-sur-Mer, Fr.), French right-wing politician
Shimon Peres, b 8/21/23 (Wolozyn, Pol.), former Israeli prime min.; 1994 Nobel laureate
Javier Perez de Cuellar, b 1/19/20 (Lima, Peru), former UN sec.-gen.
Prince Philip, b 6/10/21 (Corfu, Greece), Duke of Edinburgh; (husband of Queen Elizabeth II)
Augusto Pinochet Ugarte, b 11/25/15 (Valparaiso, Chile), former Chilean ruler
Gerhard Richter, b 2/9/32 (Dresden, Ger.), artist
Mary Robinson, b 5/21/44 (Ballina, Co. Mayo, Ireland), former Irish pres., UN High Commissioner for Human Rights
Erno Rubik, b 7/13/44 (Budapest, Hung.), Rubik's Cube inventor
Yves Saint Laurent, b 8/1/36 (Oran, Algeria), fashion designer
Carlos Salinas de Gortari, b 4/3/48 (Mexico City, Mex.), former Mexican pres.
Princess Stephanie, b 2/1/65 (Monte Carlo, Monaco), Monaco royal (younger daughter of Prince Rainier and Princess Grace)
Jack Straw, b 8/3/46 (Buckhurst Hill, Essex, Eng.), British foreign sec.
Suharto, b 6/8/21 (Kemusa Argamulja, Java), former longtime Indonesian ruler
Aung San Suu Kyi, b 6/19/45 (Rangoon, Burma), political activist, 1991 Nobel laureate, under effective house arrest
Charles Taylor, b 1/28/48 (near Monrovia, Liberia), resigned 2003 as Liberian pres.
Valentina Tereshkova, b 3/6/37 (Maslennikovo, Russia, USSR), 1st woman in space
Dame Margaret Thatcher, b 10/13/25 (Grantham, Eng.), former British prime min.
David Trimble, b 10/15/44 (Belfast, N. Ireland), former N. Ireland first minister, 1998 Nobel laureate
John Napier Turner, b 6/7/29 (Richmond, Surrey, Eng.), former Canadian prime min.
Desmond Tutu, b 10/7/31 (Klerksdorp, Transvaal, S. Africa), former S. African archbishop; 1984 Nobel laureate
Dominique de Villepin, b 11/14/53 (Rabat, Morocco), French foreign minister
Kurt Waldheim, b 12/21/18 (St. Andra-Wordern, Austria), former UN sec.-gen. and Austrian pres.
Lech Walesa, b 9/29/43 (Popowo, Pol.), Solidarity leader; 1983 Nobel laureate
Simon Wiesenthal, b 12/31/08 (Buczacz, Austr.-Hung.), pursuer of Nazi war criminals
Prince William (of Wales), b 6/21/82 (London, Eng.), son of Prince Charles; 2nd in line to British throne
Betty Williams, b 5/22/43 (Belfast, N. Ireland), British peace activist, 1976 Nobel laureate
Rowan Williams, b 6/14/50 (Swansea, Eng.), Archbishop of Canterbury
Boris Yeltsin, b 2/1/31 (Butka, USSR), former Russian pres.
Muhammad Zahir Shah, b 10/15/14 (Kabul, Afghan.), former king of Afghanistan
Ayman al-Zawahri, b 6/19/51 (Cairo, Egypt), reputed No. 2 al-Qaeda leader

African-Americans of the Past

See also other categories.

Ralph David Abernathy, 1926-90, organizer, 1957, pres., 1968, Southern Christian Leadership Conf.
Crispus Attucks, c1723-70, leader of group of colonists that clashed with British soldiers in 1770 Boston Massacre.
Benjamin Banneker, 1731-1806, inventor, astronomer, mathematician, gazetteer.
Daisy Bates, 1920?-99, Arkansas, civil rights leader who fought for school integration.
James P. Beckwourth, 1798-c1867, western fur trader, scout; Beckwourth Pass in N California named for him.
Mary McCleod Bethune, 1875-1955, adviser to FDR and Truman; founder, pres., Bethune-Cookman College.
Henry Blair, 19th cent., pioneer inventor; obtained patents for a corn-planter, 1834, and cotton-planter, 1836.

Edward Bouchet, 1852-1918, first black to earn a PhD at a U.S. university (Yale, 1876).
Tom Bradley, 1917-98, first African-American mayor of L.A.
Sterling A. Brown, 1901-89, poet, literature professor; helped establish African-American literary criticism.
William Wells Brown, 1815-84, memoirist, ex-slave; first African American to publish a novel, 1853.
Ralph Bunche, 1904-71, first black to win the Nobel Peace Prize, 1950; undersecretary of the UN, 1950.
Stokely Carmichael (Kwame Toure), 1941-98, black power activist.
George Washington Carver, 1864-1943, botanist, chemist, and educator; transformed the economy of the South.
Charles Waddell Chesnutt, 1858-1932, author known for his short stories, such as in *The Conjure Woman (1899).*

Eldridge Cleaver, 1935-98, revolutionary social critic; former "minister of information" for Black Panthers; *Soul on Ice.*

James Cleveland, 1931-91, composer, musician, singer; first black gospel artist to appear at Carnegie Hall.

Countee Cullen, 1903-46, poet, prominent in the Harlem Renaissance of the 1920s; *The Black Christ.*

Benjamin O. Davis Jr., 1912-2002, leader of World War II black aviators, first African-American general in U.S. Air Force.

Benjamin O. Davis Sr., 1877-1970, first African-American general, 1940, in U.S. Army.

William L. Dawson, 1886-1970, Illinois congressman, first black chairman of a major U.S. House committee.

Aaron Douglas, 1900-79, "father of black American art."

Frederick Douglass, 1817-95, author, editor, orator, diplomat; edited abolitionist weekly *The North Star.*

St. Clair Drake, 1911-90, black studies pioneer, *Black Metropolis* (1945), with Horace R. Cayton.

Charles Richard Drew, 1904-50, physician, pioneered in development of blood banks.

William Edward Burghardt (W.E.B.) Du Bois, 1868-1963, historian, sociologist; an NAACP founder, 1909.

Paul Laurence Dunbar, 1872-1906, poet, novelist; won fame with *Lyrics of Lowly Life,* 1896.

Jean Baptiste Point du Sable, c1750-1818, pioneer trader and first settler of Chicago, 1779.

Medgar Evers, 1925-63, Mississippi civil rights leader; campaigned to register black voters; assassinated.

James Farmer, 1920-99, civil rights leader; founded Congress of Racial Equality.

Henry O. Flipper, 1856-1940, first African-American to graduate, 1877, from West Point.

Marcus Garvey, 1887-1940, founded Universal Negro Improvement Assn., 1911.

Ewart Guinier, 1911-90, trade unionist; first chairman of Harvard Univ.'s Dept. of African American Studies.

Prince Hall, 1735-1807, activist; founded black Freemasonry; served in American Revolutionary war.

Jupiter Hammon, c1720-1800, poet; first African-American to have his works published, 1761.

Lorraine Hansberry, 1930-65, playwright; won New York Drama Critics Circle Award, 1959; *A Raisin in the Sun.*

William H. Hastie, 1904-76, first black federal judge, appointed 1937; governor of Virgin Islands, 1946-49.

Matthew A. Henson, 1866-1955, member of Peary's 1909 expedition to the North Pole; placed U.S. flag at the pole.

Chester Himes, 1909-84, novelist; *Cotton Comes to Harlem.*

William A. Hinton, 1883-1959, physician, developed tests for syphilis; first black prof., 1949, at Harvard Med. School.

Charles Hamilton Houston, 1895-1950, lawyer, Howard University instructor, champion of minority rights.

Langston Hughes, 1902-67, poet, lyric writer, author; a major influence in 1920s Harlem Renaissance.

Daniel James Jr., 1920-78, first black 4-star general, 1975; commander, North American Air Defense Command.

Henry Johnson, 1897-1929, first American decorated by France in WW1 with the Croix de Guerre.

James Weldon Johnson, 1871-1938, poet, novelist, diplomat; lyricist for *Lift Every Voice and Sing.*

Barbara Jordan, 1936-96, congresswoman, orator, educator.; first black woman to win a seat in the Texas senate, 1966.

Ernest Everett Just, 1883-1941, marine biologist; studied egg development; author, *Biology of Cell Surfaces,* 1941.

Rev. Martin Luther King Jr., 1929-68, civil rights leader; led 1956 Montgomery, AL, boycott; founder, pres., Southern Christian Leadership Conference, 1957; Nobel laureate (1964); assassinated.

Lewis H. Latimer, 1848-1928, associate of Edison; supervised installation of first electric street lighting in NYC.

Mickey Leland, 1944-89, U.S. representative from Texas, 1978 until death; chairman of Congressional Black Caucus.

Henry Lewis, 1932-1996, (U.S.) conductor; first black conductor and musical director of major American orchestra.

Malcolm X (Little), 1925-65, Black Muslim, black nationalist leader; promoted black pride; assassinated.

Thurgood Marshall, 1908-93, first black U.S. solicitor general, 1965; first black justice of U.S. Sup. Ct., 1967-91.

Jan Matzeliger, 1852-89, invented lasting machine, patented 1883, which revolutionized the shoe industry.

Benjamin Mays, 1895-1984, educator, civil rights leader; headed Morehouse College, 1940-67.

Ronald McNair, 1950-86, physicist, astronaut; killed in *Challenger* explosion.

Dorie Miller, 1919-43, Navy hero of Pearl Harbor attack.

Elijah Muhammad, 1897-1975, founded Nation of Islam, 1931.

Pedro Alonzo Niño, navigator of Columbus's *Niña,* 1492.

Frederick D. Patterson, 1901-88, founder of United Negro College Fund, 1944.

Harold R. Perry, 1916-91, first black American Roman Catholic bishop in the 20th cent.

Adam Clayton Powell Jr., 1908-72, early civil rights leader, congressman, 1945-69.

Joseph H. Rainey, 1832-87, first black elected to U.S. House, 1869, from South Carolina.

A. Philip Randolph, 1889-1979, organized Brotherhood of Sleeping Car Porters, 1925; an organizer of 1941 and 1963 March on Washington movements.

Hiram R. Revels, 1822-1901, first African-American U.S. senator, elected in Mississippi, served 1870-71.

Norbert Rillieux, 1806-94; invented a vacuum pan evaporator, 1846, revolutionizing sugar-refining industry.

Paul Robeson, 1898-1976, actor, singer, civil rights activist; ostracized by conservatives in the 1950s.

Jackie Robinson, 1919-72, first African-American in major league baseball, 1947, and the Baseball Hall of Fame, 1962.

Carl T. Rowan, 1925-2000, reporter, columnist, author.

Bayard Rustin, 1910-87, an organizer of the 1963 March on Washington; exec. director, A. Philip Randolph Institute.

Peter Salem, at the Battle of Bunker Hill, June 17, 1775, shot and killed British commander Maj. John Pitcairn.

Carl Stokes, 1927-1996, first black mayor of a major American city (Cleveland), 1967-72.

Willard Townsend, 1895-1957, organized the United Transport Service Employees (redcaps), 1935.

Sojourner Truth, 1797-1883, born Isabella Baumfree; preacher, abolitionist; worked for black educ. opportunity.

Harriet Tubman, 1823-1913, Underground Railroad conductor, nurse and spy for Union Army in the Civil War.

Nat Turner, 1800-31, led most significant of more than 200 slave revolts in U.S., in Southampton, VA; hanged.

Booker T. Washington, 1856-1915, founder, 1881, and first pres. of Tuskegee Institute; *Up From Slavery.*

Harold Washington, 1922-87, first black mayor of Chicago.

Robert C. Weaver, 1907-97, first African-American appointed to cabinet; secretary of HUD.

Phillis Wheatley, c1753-84, poet; 2d American woman and first black woman to be published, 1770.

Walter White, 1893-1955, exec. sec., NAACP, 1931-55.

Roy Wilkins, 1901-81, exec. director, NAACP, 1955-77.

Daniel Hale Williams, 1858-1931, surgeon; performed one of first two open-heart operations, 1893.

Granville T. Woods, 1856-1910, invented third-rail system now used in subways, and automatic air brake.

Carter G. Woodson, 1875-1950, historian; founded Assn. for the Study of Negro Life and History.

Frank Yerby, 1916-91, first best-selling African-American novelist; *The Foxes of Harrow.*

Coleman A. Young, 1918-97, first Afr.-Amer. mayor of Detroit, 1974-93.

Architects and Some of Their Achievements

Max Abramovitz, b 1908, Avery Fisher Hall, NYC; U.S. Steel Bldg. (now USX Towers), Pittsburgh, PA.

Henry Bacon, 1866-1924, Lincoln Memorial, Wash., DC.

Pietro Belluschi, 1899-1994, Juilliard School, Lincoln Center, Pan Am, now MetLife, Bldg. (with Walter Gropius), NYC.

Marcel Breuer, 1902-81, Whitney Museum of American Art (with Hamilton Smith), NYC.

Charles Bulfinch, 1763-1844, State House, Boston; Capitol (part), Wash., DC.

Gordon Bunshaft, 1909-90, Lever House, Park Ave, NYC; Hirshhorn Museum, Wash., DC.

Daniel H. Burnham, 1846-1912, Union Station, Wash. DC; Flatiron Bldg., NYC.

Irwin Chanin, 1892-1988, theaters, skyscrapers, NYC.

Lucio Costa, 1902-98, master plan for city of Brasilia, with Oscar Niemeyer.

Ralph Adams Cram, 1863-1942, Cath. of St. John the Divine, NYC; U.S. Military Acad. (part), West Point, NY.

R. Buckminster Fuller, 1895-1983, U.S. Pavilion (geodesic domes), Expo 67, Montreal.

Frank O. Gehry, b 1929, Guggenheim Museum, Bilbao, Spain; Experience Music Project, Seattle, WA.

Cass Gilbert, 1859-1934, Custom House, Woolworth Bldg., NYC; Supreme Court Bldg., Wash., DC.

Bertram G. Goodhue, 1869-1924, Capitol, Lincoln, NE; St. Thomas's Church, St. Bartholomew's Church, NYC.

Michael Graves, b 1934, Portland Bldg., Portland, OR; Humana Bldg., Louisville, KY.

Walter Gropius, 1883-1969, Pan Am Bldg. (now MetLife Bldg.) (with Pietro Belluschi), NYC.

Lawrence Halprin, b 1916, Ghirardelli Sq., San Francisco; Nicollet Mall, Minneapolis; FDR Memorial, Wash., DC.

Peter Harrison, 1716-75, Touro Synagogue, Redwood Library, Newport, RI.

Wallace K. Harrison, 1895-1981, Metropolitan Opera House, Lincoln Center, NYC.

Thomas Hastings, 1860-1929, NY Public Library (with John Carrère), Frick Mansion, NYC.

James Hoban, 1762-1831, White House, Wash., DC.

Raymond Hood, 1881-1934, Rockefeller Center (part), Daily News, NYC; Tribune, Chicago, IL.

Richard M. Hunt, 1827-95, Metropolitan Museum (part), NYC; National Observatory, Wash., DC.

Helmut Jahn, b 1940, United Airlines Terminal, O'Hare Airport, Chicago.

William Le Baron Jenney, 1832-1907, Home Insurance (demolished 1931), Chicago, IL.

Philip C. Johnson, b 1906, AT&T headquarters (now 550 Madison Ave.), NYC; Transco Tower, Houston, TX.

Albert Kahn, 1869-1942, General Motors Bldg., Detroit, MI.

Louis Kahn, 1901-74, Salk Laboratory, La Jolla, CA; Yale Art Gallery, New Haven, CT.

Christopher Grant LaFarge, 1862-1938, Roman Catholic Chapel, West Point, NY.

Benjamin H. Latrobe, 1764-1820, Capitol (part), Wash., DC; State Capitol Bldg., Richmond, VA.

Le Corbusier, (Charles-Edouard Jeanneret), 1887-1965, Salvation Army Hostel and Swiss Dormitory, both Paris; master plan for cities of Algiers and Buenos Aires.

William Lescaze, 1896-1969, Philadelphia Savings Fund Society; Borg-Warner Bldg., Chicago.

Maya Lin, b 1959, Vietnam Veterans Memorial, Wash., DC.

Charles Rennie Mackintosh, 1868-1928, Glasgow School of Art; Hill House, Helensburgh.

Bernard R. Maybeck, 1862-1957, Hearst Hall, Univ. of CA, Berkeley; First Church of Christ Scientist, Berkeley, CA.

Charles F. McKim, 1847-1909, Public Library, Boston; Columbia Univ. (part), NYC.

Charles M. McKim, b 1920, KUHT-TV Transmitter Bldg., Lutheran Church of the Redeemer, Houston, TX.

Richard Meier, b 1934, Getty Center Museum, Los Angeles, CA; High Museum of Art, Atlanta, GA.

Ludwig Mies van der Rohe, 1886-1969, Seagram Bldg., (with Philip C. Johnson), NYC; National Gallery, Berlin.

Robert Mills, 1781-1855, Washington Monument, Wash., DC.

Charles Moore, 1925-93, Sea Ranch, near San Francisco; Piazza d'Italia, New Orleans, LA.

Richard J. Neutra, 1892-1970, Mathematics Park, Princeton, NJ; Orange Co. Courthouse, Santa Ana, CA.

Oscar Niemeyer, b 1907, government buildings, Brasilia Palace Hotel, all Brasilia.

Gyo Obata, b 1923, Natl. Air & Space Museum, Smithsonian Inst., Wash., DC; Dallas-Ft. Worth Airport.

Frederick L. Olmsted, 1822-1903, Central Park, NYC; Fairmount Park, Philadelphia, PA.

I(eoh) M(ing) Pei, b 1917, East Wing, Natl. Gallery of Art, Wash., DC; Pyramid, The Louvre, Paris; Rock & Roll Hall of Fame and Museum, Cleveland, OH.

Cesar Pelli, b 1926, World Financial Center, Carnegie Hall Tower, NYC; Petronas Twin Towers, Malaysia.

William Pereira, 1909-85, Cape Canaveral; Transamerica Bldg., San Francisco, CA.

John Russell Pope, 1874-1937, National Gallery, Wash., DC.

John Portman, b 1924, Peachtree Center, Atlanta, GA.

George Browne Post, 1837-1913, NY Stock Exchange; Capitol, Madison, WI.

James Renwick Jr., 1818-95, Grace Church, St. Patrick's Cath., NYC.; Corcoran (now Renwick) Gallery, Wash., DC.

Henry H. Richardson, 1838-86, Trinity Church, Boston, MA.

Kevin Roche, b 1922, Oakland Museum, Oakland, CA; Fine Arts Center, University of Massachusetts, Amherst.

James Gamble Rogers, 1867-1947, Columbia-Presbyterian Medical Center, NYC; Northwestern Univ., Evanston, IL.

John Wellborn Root, 1887-1963, Palmolive Bldg., Chicago; Hotel Statler, Wash., DC.

Paul Rudolph, 1918-97, Jewitt Art Center, Wellesley Colllege, MA; Art & Architecture Bldg., Yale Univ., New Haven, CT.

Eero Saarinen, 1910-61, Gateway to the West Arch, St. Louis, MO; Trans World Flight Center, NYC.

Louis Skidmore, 1897-1962, Atomic Energy Commission town site, Oak Ridge, TN; Terrace Plaza Hotel, Cincinnati, OH.

Clarence S. Stein, 1882-1975, Temple Emanu-El, NYC.

Edward Durell Stone, 1902-78, U.S. Embassy, New Delhi, India; (H. Hartford) Gallery of Modern Art, NYC.

Louis H. Sullivan, 1856-1924, Auditorium Bldg., Chicago, IL.

Richard Upjohn, 1802-78, Trinity Church, NYC.

Max O. Urbahn, 1912-95, Vehicle Assembly Bldg., Cape Canaveral, FL.

Robert Venturi, b 1925, Gordon Wu Hall, Princeton, NJ; Mielparque Nikko Kirifuri Resort, Japan.

Ralph T. Walker, 1889-1973, NY Telephone Bldg. (now NYNEX); IBM Research Lab, Poughkeepsie, NY.

Roland A. Wank, 1898-1970, Cincinnati Union Terminal, OH; head architect (1933-44), Tennessee Valley Authority.

Stanford White, 1853-1906, Washington Arch in Washington Square Park, first Madison Square Garden, NYC.

Frank Lloyd Wright, 1867-1959, Imperial Hotel, Tokyo; Guggenheim Museum, NYC; Marin County Civic Center, San Rafael; Kaufmann "Fallingwater" house, Bear Run, PA.; Taliesen West, Scottsdale, AZ.

William Wurster, 1895-1973, Ghirardelli Sq., San Francisco; Cowell College, UC, Berkeley, CA.

Minoru Yamasaki, 1912-86, World Trade Center, NYC.

Artists, Photographers, and Sculptors of the Past

Artists are painters unless otherwise indicated.

Berenice Abbott, 1898-1991, (U.S.) photographer. Documentary of New York City, Changing New York (1939).

Ansel Easton Adams, 1902-84, (U.S.) photographer. Landscapes of the American Southwest.

Washington Allston, 1779-1843, (U.S.) landscapist. Belshazzar's Feast.

Albrecht Altdorfer, 1480-1538, (Ger.) landscapist.

Andrea del Sarto, 1486-1530, (It.) frescoes. Madonna of the Harpies.

Fra Angelico, c1400-55, (It.) Renaissance muralist. Madonna of the Linen Drapers' Guild.

Diane Arbus, 1923-71, (U.S.) photographer. Disturbing images.

Alexsandr Archipenko, 1887-1964, (U.S.) sculptor. Boxing Match, Medranos.

Eugène Atget, 1856-1927, (Fr.) photographer. Paris life.

John James Audubon, 1785-1851, (U.S.) Birds of America.

Hans Baldung-Grien, 1484-1545, (Ger.) Todentanz.

Ernst Barlach, 1870-1938, (Ger.) Expressionist sculptor. Man Drawing a Sword.

Frederic-Auguste Bartholdi, 1834-1904, (Fr.) Liberty Enlightening the World, Lion of Belfort.

Fra Bartolommeo, 1472-1517, (It.) Vision of St. Bernard.

Romare Bearden, 1911-88, (U.S.) collage and other media. The Visitation.

Aubrey Beardsley, 1872-98, (Br.) illustrator. Salome, Lysistrata, Morte d'Arthur, Volpone.

Max Beckmann, 1884-1950, (Ger.) Expressionist. The Descent From the Cross.

Gentile Bellini, 1426-1507, (It.) Renaissance. Procession in St. Mark's Square.

Giovanni Bellini, 1428-1516, (It.) St. Francis in Ecstasy.

Jacopo Bellini, 1400-70, (It.) Crucifixion.

George Wesley Bellows, 1882-1925, (U.S.) sports artist, portraitist, landscapist. Stag at Sharkey's, Edith Clavell.

Thomas Hart Benton, 1889-1975, (U.S.) American regionalist. Threshing Wheat, Arts of the West.

Gianlorenzo Bernini, 1598-1680, (It.) Baroque sculpture. The Assumption.

Albert Bierstadt, 1830-1902, (U.S.) landscapist. The Rocky Mountains, Mount Corcoran.

George Caleb Bingham, 1811-79, (U.S.) Fur Traders Descending the Missouri.

William Blake, 1752-1827, (Br.) engraver. Book of Job, Songs of Innocence, Songs of Experience.

Rosa Bonheur, 1822-99, (Fr.) The Horse Fair.

Pierre Bonnard, 1867-1947, (Fr.) Intimist. The Breakfast Room, Girl in a Straw Hat.

Gutzon Borglum, 1871-1941, (U.S.) sculptor. Mt. Rushmore Memorial.

Hieronymus Bosch, 1450-1516, (Flem.) religious allegories. The Crowning With Thorns.

Sandro Botticelli, 1444-1510, (It.) Renaissance. Birth of Venus, Adoration of the Magi, Guiliano de'Medici.

Margaret Bourke-White, 1906-71, (U.S.) photographer, photojournalist. WW2, USSR, rural South during the Depression.

Mathew Brady, c1823-96, (U.S.) photographer. Official photographer of the Civil War.

Constantin Brancusi, 1876-1957, (Romanian-Fr.) Nonobjective sculptor. Flying Turtle, The Kiss.

Georges Braque, 1882-1963, (Fr.) Cubist. Violin and Palette.

Pieter Bruegel the Elder, c1525-69, (Flem.) *The Peasant Dance, Hunters in the Snow, Magpie on the Gallows.*
Pieter Bruegel the Younger, 1564-1638, (Flem.) *Village Fair, The Crucifixion.*
Edward Burne-Jones, 1833-98, (Br.) Pre-Raphaelite artist-craftsman. *The Mirror of Venus.*
Alexander Calder, 1898-1976, (U.S.) sculptor. *Lobster Trap and Fish Tail.*
Julia Cameron, 1815-79, (Br.) photographer. Considered one of the most important portraitists of the 19th cent.
Robert Capa (Andrei Friedmann), 1913-54, (Hung.-U.S.) photographer. War photojournalist; invasion of Normandy.
Michelangelo Merisi da Caravaggio, 1573-1610, (It.) Baroque. *The Supper at Emmaus.*
Emily Carr, 1871-1945, (Can.) landscapist. *Blunden Harbour, Big Raven, Rushing Sea of Undergrowth.*
Carlo Carrà, 1881-1966, (It.) Metaphysical school. *Lot's Daughters, The Enchanted Room.*
Mary Cassatt, 1844-1926, (U.S.) Impressionist. *The Cup of Tea, Woman Bathing, The Boating Party.*
George Catlin, 1796-1872, (U.S.) American Indian life. *Gallery of Indians, Buffalo Dance.*
Benvenuto Cellini, 1500-71, (It.) Mannerist sculptor, goldsmith. *Perseus and Medusa.*
Paul Cézanne, 1839-1906, (Fr.) *Card Players, Mont-Sainte-Victoire With Large Pine Trees.*
Marc Chagall, 1887-1985, (Russ.) Jewish life and folklore. *I and the Village, The Praying Jew.*
Jean Simeon Chardin, 1699-1779, (Fr.) still lifes. *The Kiss, The Grace.*
Frederick Church, 1826-1900, (U.S.) Hudson River school. *Niagara, Andes of Ecuador.*
Giovanni Cimabue, 1240-1302, (It.) Byzantine mosaicist. *Madonna Enthroned With St. Francis.*
Claude Lorrain (Claude Gellé), 1600-82, (Fr.) ideal-landscapist. *The Enchanted Castle.*
Thomas Cole, 1801-48, (U.S.) Hudson River school. *The Ox-Bow, In the Catskills.*
John Constable, 1776-1837, (Br.) landscapist. *Salisbury Cathedral From the Bishop's Grounds.*
John Singleton Copley, 1738-1815, (U.S.) portraitist. *Samuel Adams, Watson and the Shark.*
Lovis Corinth, 1858-1925, (Ger.) Expressionist. *Apocalypse.*
Jean-Baptiste-Camille Corot, 1796-1875, (Fr.) landscapist. *Souvenir de Mortefontaine, Pastorale.*
Correggio, 1494-1534, (It.) Renaissance muralist. *Mystic Marriages of St. Catherine.*
Gustave Courbet, 1819-77, (Fr.) Realist. *The Artist's Studio.*
Lucas Cranach the Elder, 1472-1553, (Ger.) Protestant Reformation portraitist. *Luther.*
Imogen Cunningham, 1883-1976, (U.S.) photographer, portraitist. Plant photography.
Nathaniel Currier, 1813-88, and **James M. Ives,** 1824-95, (both U.S.) lithographers. *A Midnight Race on the Mississippi, American Forest Scene—Maple Sugaring.*
John Steuart Curry, 1897-1946, (U.S.) Americana, murals. *Baptism in Kansas.*
Salvador Dalí, 1904-89, (Sp.) Surrealist. *Persistence of Memory, The Crucifixion.*
Honoré Daumier, 1808-79, (Fr.) caricaturist. *The Third-Class Carriage.*
Jacques-Louis David, 1748-1825, (Fr.) Neoclassicist. *The Oath of the Horatii.*
Arthur Davies, 1862-1928, (U.S.) Romantic landscapist. *Unicorns, Leda and the Dioscuri.*
Willem de Kooning, 1904-1997, (U.S.) abstract expressionist. *Excavation, Woman I, Door to the River.*
Edgar Degas, 1834-1917, (Fr.) *The Ballet Class.*
Eugène Delacroix, 1798-1863, (Fr.) Romantic. *Massacre at Chios, Liberty Leading the People.*
Paul Delaroche, 1797-1856, (Fr.) historical themes. *Children of Edward IV.*
Luca Della Robbia, 1400-82, (It.) Renaissance terracotta artist. *Cantoria* (singing gallery), Florence cathedral.
Donatello, 1386-1466, (It.) Renaissance sculptor. *David, Gattamelata.*
Jean Dubuffet, 1902-85, (Fr.) painter, sculptor, printmaker. *Group of Four Trees.*
Marcel Duchamp, 1887-1968, (Fr.) Dada artist. *Nude Descending a Staircase, No. 2.*
Raoul Dufy, 1877-1953, (Fr.) Fauvist. *Chateau and Horses.*
Asher Brown Durand, 1796-1886, (U.S.) Hudson River school. *Kindred Spirits.*
Albrecht Dürer, 1471-1528, (Ger.) Renaissance painter, engraver, woodcuts. *St. Jerome in His Study, Melencolia I.*
Anthony van Dyck, 1599-1641, (Flem.) Baroque portraitist. *Portrait of Charles I Hunting.*
Thomas Eakins, 1844-1916, (U.S.) Realist. *The Gross Clinic.*
Alfred Eisenstaedt, 1898-1995, (Ger.-U.S.) photographer, photojournalist. Famous photo, V-J Day, Aug. 14, 1945.
Peter Henry Emerson, 1856-1936, (Br.) photographer. Promoted photography as an independent art form.

Jacob Epstein, 1880-1959, (Br.) religious and allegorical sculptor. *Genesis, Ecce Homo.*
Jan van Eyck, c1390-1441, (Flem.) naturalistic panels. *Adoration of the Lamb.*
Roger Fenton, 1819-68, (Br.) photographer. Crimean War.
Anselm Feuerbach, 1829-80, (Ger.) Romantic Classicist. *Judgment of Paris, Iphigenia.*
John Bernard Flannagan, 1895-1942, (U.S.) animal sculptor. *Triumph of the Egg.*
Jean-Honoré Fragonard, 1732-1806, (Fr.) Rococo. *The Swing.*
Daniel Chester French, 1850-1931, (U.S.) *The Minute Man of Concord;* seated *Lincoln,* Lincoln Memorial, Wash., DC.
Caspar David Friedrich, 1774-1840, (Ger.) Romantic landscapes. *Man and Woman Gazing at the Moon.*
Thomas Gainsborough, 1727-88, (Br.) portraitist. *The Blue Boy, The Watering Place, Orpin the Parish Clerk.*
Alexander Gardner, 1821-82, (U.S.) photographer. Civil War; railroad construction; Great Plains Indians.
Paul Gauguin, 1848-1903, (Fr.) Post-impressionist. *The Tahitians, Spirit of the Dead Watching.*
Lorenzo Ghiberti, 1378-1455, (It.) Renaissance sculptor. Gates of Paradise baptistery doors, Florence.
Alberto Giacometti, 1901-66, (Swiss) attenuated sculptures of solitary figures. *Man Pointing.*
Giorgione, c1477-1510, (It.) Renaissance. *The Tempest.*
Giotto di Bondone, 1267-1337, (It.) Renaissance. *Presentation of Christ in the Temple.*
François Girardon, 1628-1715, (Fr.) Baroque sculptor of classical themes. *Apollo Tended by the Nymphs.*
Vincent van Gogh, 1853-90, (Dutch) *The Starry Night, L'Arlesienne, Bedroom at Arles, Self-Portrait.*
Arshile Gorky, 1905-48, (U.S.) Surrealist. *The Liver Is the Cock's Comb.*
Francisco de Goya y Lucientes, 1746-1828, (Sp.) *The Naked Maja, The Disasters of War* (etchings).
El Greco, 1541-1614, (Sp.) *View of Toledo, Assumption of the Virgin.*
Horatio Greenough, 1805-52, (U.S.) Neo-classical sculptor.
Matthias Grünewald, 1480-1528, (Ger.) mystical religious themes. *The Resurrection.*
Frans Hals, c1580-1666, (Dutch) portraitist. *Laughing Cavalier, Gypsy Girl.*
Austin Hansen, 1910-96, (U.S.) photographer. Harlem, NY, life.
Childe Hassam, 1859-1935, (U.S.) Impressionist. *Southwest Wind, July 14 Rue Daunon.*
Edward Hicks, 1780-1849, (U.S.) folk painter. *The Peaceable Kingdom.*
Lewis Wickes Hine, 1874-1940, (U.S.) photographer. Studies of immigrants, children in industry.
Hans Hofmann, 1880-1966, (U.S.) early abstract Expressionist. *Spring, The Gate.*
William Hogarth, 1697-1764, (Br.) caricaturist. *The Rake's Progress.*
Katsushika Hokusai, 1760-1849, (Jpn.) printmaker. *Crabs.*
Hans Holbein the Elder, 1460-1524, (Ger.) late Gothic. *Presentation of Christ in the Temple.*
Hans Holbein the Younger, 1497-1543, (Ger.) portraitist. *Henry VIII, The French Ambassadors.*
Winslow Homer, 1836-1910, (U.S.) naturalist painter, marine themes. *Marine Coast, High Cliff.*
Edward Hopper, 1882-1967, (U.S.) realistic urban scenes. *Nighthawks, House by the Railroad.*
Horst P. Horst, 1906-99, (Ger.) fashion, celebrity photographer.
Jean-Auguste-Dominique Ingres, 1780-1867, (Fr.) Classicist. *Valpincon Bather.*
George Inness, 1825-94, (U.S.) luminous landscapist. *Delaware Water Gap.*
William Henry Jackson, 1843-1942, (U.S.) photographer. American West, building of Union Pacific Railroad.
Donald Judd, 1928-94, (U.S.) sculptor, major Minimalist.
Frida Kahlo, 1907-54, (Mex.) painter; *Self-Portrait With Monkey.*
Vasily Kandinsky, 1866-1944, (Russ.) Abstractionist. *Capricious Forms, Improvisation 38* (second version).
Paul Klee, 1879-1940, (Swiss) Abstractionist. *Twittering Machine, Pastoral, Death and Fire.*
Gustav Klimt, 1862-1918, (Austrian) cofounder of Vienna Secession Movement, *The Kiss.*
Oscar Kokoschka, 1886-1980, (Austrian) Expressionist. *View of Prague, Harbor of Marseilles.*
Kathe Kollwitz, 1867-1945, (Ger.) printmaker, social justice themes. *The Peasant War.*
Gaston Lachaise, 1882-1935, (U.S.) figurative sculptor. *Standing Woman.*
John La Farge, 1835-1910, (U.S.) muralist. *Red and White Peonies, The Ascension.*
Sir Edwin (Henry) Landseer, 1802-73, (Br.) painter, sculptor. *Shoeing, Rout of Comus.*
Dorothea Lange, 1895-1965, (U.S.) photographer. Depression photographs, migrant farm workers.
Fernand Léger, 1881-1955, (Fr.) machine art. *The Cyclists.*
Leonardo da Vinci, 1452-1519, (It.) *Mona Lisa, Last Supper, The Annunciation.*

Emanuel Leutze, 1816-68, (U.S.) historical themes. *Washington Crossing the Delaware.*
Roy Lichtenstein, 1923-97, (U.S.) pop artist.
Jacques Lipchitz, 1891-1973, (Fr.) Cubist sculptor. *Harpist.*
Filippino Lippi, 1457-1504, (It.) Renaissance.
Fra Filippo Lippi, 1406-69, (It.) Renaissance. *Coronation of the Virgin, Madonna and Child With Angels.*
Morris Louis, 1912-62, (U.S.) abstract Expressionist. *Signa, Stripes, Alpha-Phi.*
Rene Magritte, 1898-1967, (Belgian) Surrealist. *The Descent of Man, The Betrayal of Images.*
Aristide Maillol, 1861-1944, (Fr.) sculptor. *L'Harmonie.*
Édouard Manet, 1832-83, (Fr.) forerunner of Impressionism. *Luncheon on the Grass, Olympia.*
Andrea Mantegna, 1431-1506, (It.) Renaissance frescoes. *Triumph of Caesar.*
Franz Marc, 1880-1916, (Ger.) Expressionist. *Blue Horses.*
John Marin, 1870-1953, (U.S.) Expressionist seascapes. *Maine Island.*
Reginald Marsh, 1898-1954, (U.S.) satirical artist. *Tattoo and Haircut.*
Masaccio, 1401-28, (It.) Renaissance. *The Tribute Money.*
Henri Matisse, 1869-1954, (Fr.) Fauvist. *Woman With the Hat.*
Michelangelo Buonarroti, 1475-1564, (It.) *Pietà, David, Moses, The Last Judgment,* Sistine Chapel ceiling.
Jean-Francois Millet, 1814-75, (Fr.) painter of peasant subjects. *The Gleaners, The Man With a Hoe.*
Joan Miró, 1893-1983, (Sp.) Exuberant colors, playful images. *Catalan landscape, Dutch Interior.*
Amedeo Modigliani, 1884-1920, (It.) *Reclining Nude.*
Piet Mondrian, 1872-1944, (Dutch) Abstractionist. *Composition With Red, Yellow and Blue.*
Claude Monet, 1840-1926, (Fr.) Impressionist. *The Bridge at Argenteuil, Haystacks.*
Henry Moore, 1898-1986, (Br.) sculptor of large-scale, abstract works. *Reclining Figure* (several).
Gustave Moreau, 1826-98, (Fr.) Symbolist. *The Apparition, Dance of Salome.*
James Wilson Morrice, 1865-1924, (Can.) landscapist. *The Ferry, Quebec, Venice, Looking Over the Lagoon.*
William Morris, 1834-1896, (Br.) decorative artist, leader of the Arts and Crafts movement.
Grandma Moses, 1860-1961, (U.S.) folk painter. *Out for the Christmas Trees, Thanksgiving Turkey.*
Edvard Munch, 1863-1944, (Nor.) Expressionist. *The Cry.*
Bartolome Murillo, 1618-82, (Sp.) Baroque religious artist. *Vision of St. Anthony, The Two Trinities.*
Eadweard Muybridge, 1830-1904, (Br.-U.S.) photographer. Studies of motion, *Animal Locomotion.*
Nadar (Gaspar-Félix Tournachon), 1820-1910, (Fr.) photographer, caricaturist, portraitist. Invented photo-essay.
Barnett Newman, 1905-70, (U.S.) abstract Expressionist. *Stations of the Cross.*
Isamu Noguchi, 1904-88, (U.S.) abstract sculptor, designer. *Kouros, BirdC(MU),* sculptural gardens.
Georgia O'Keeffe, 1887-1986, (U.S.) Southwest motifs. *Cow's Skull: Red, White, and Blue, The Shelton With Sunspots.*
José Clemente Orozco, 1883-1949, (Mex.) frescoes. *House of Tears, Pre-Columbian Golden Age.*
Timothy H. O'Sullivan, 1840-82, (U.S.) Civil War photographer.
Charles Willson Peale, 1741-1827, (U.S.) Amer. Revolutionary portraitist. *The Staircase Group,* U.S. presidents.
Rembrandt Peale, 1778-1860, (U.S.) portraitist. Thomas Jefferson.
Pietro Perugino, 1446-1523, (It.) Renaissance. *Delivery of the Keys to St. Peter.*
Pablo Picasso, 1881-1973, (Sp.) painter, sculptor. *Guernica; Dove; Head of a Woman; Head of a Bull, Metamorphosis.*
Piero della Francesca, c1415-92, (It.) Renaissance. *Duke of Urbino, Flagellation of Christ.*
Camille Pissarro, 1830-1903, (Fr.) Impressionist. *Boulevard des Italiens, Morning, Sunlight; Bather in the Woods.*
Jackson Pollock, 1912-56, (U.S.) abstract Expressionist. *Autumn Rhythm.*
Nicolas Poussin, 1594-1665, (Fr.) Baroque pictorial classicism. *St. John on Patmos.*
Maurice B. Prendergast, c1860-1924, (U.S.) Post-impressionist water colorist. *Umbrellas in the Rain.*
Pierre-Paul Prud'hon, 1758-1823, (Fr.) Romanticist. *Crime Pursued by Vengeance and Justice.*
Pierre Cecile Puvis de Chavannes, 1824-98, (Fr.) muralist. *The Poor Fisherman.*
Raphael Sanzio, 1483-1520, (It.) Renaissance. *Disputa, School of Athens, Sistine Madonna.*
Man Ray, 1890-1976, (U.S.) Dada artist. *Observing Time, The Lovers, Marquis de Sade.*
Odilon Redon, 1840-1916, (Fr.) Symbolist painter, lithographer. *In the Dream, Vase of Flowers.*
Rembrandt van Rijn, 1606-69, (Dutch) *The Bridal Couple, The Night Watch.*
Frederic Remington, 1861-1909, (U.S.) painter, sculptor. Portrayer of the American West, *Bronco Buster.*

Pierre-Auguste Renoir, 1841-1919, (Fr.) Impressionist. *The Luncheon of the Boating Party, Dance in the Country.*
Joshua Reynolds, 1723-92, (Br.) portraitist. *Mrs. Siddons as the Tragic Muse.*
Herb Ritts, 1952-2002, (U.S.) photographer. Nudes, celebrities.
Diego Rivera, 1886-1957, (Mex.) frescoes. *The Fecund Earth.*
Larry Rivers, 1923-2002, (U.S.) painter, sculptor, often realistic; *Dutch Masters* series.
Henry Peach Robinson, 1830-1901 (Br.) photographer. A leader of "high art" photography.
Norman Rockwell, 1894-1978, (U.S.) painter, illustrator. *Saturday Evening Post* covers.
Auguste Rodin, 1840-1917, (Fr.) sculptor. *The Thinker.*
Mark Rothko, 1903-70, (U.S.) abstract Expressionist. *Light, Earth and Blue.*
Georges Rouault, 1871-1958, (Fr.) Expressionist. *Three Judges.*
Henri Rousseau, 1844-1910, (Fr.) primitive exotic themes. *The Snake Charmer.*
Theodore Rousseau, 1812-67, (Swiss-Fr.) landscapist. *Under the Birches, Evening.*
Peter Paul Rubens, 1577-1640, (Flem.) Baroque. *Mystic Marriage of St. Catherine.*
Jacob van Ruisdael, c1628-82, (Dutch) landscapist. *Jewish Cemetery.*
Charles M. Russell, 1866-1926, (U.S.) Western life.
Salomon van Ruysdael, c1600-70, (Dutch) landscapist. *River With Ferry-Boat.*
Albert Pinkham Ryder, 1847-1917, (U.S.) seascapes and allegories. *Toilers of the Sea.*
Augustus Saint-Gaudens, 1848-1907, (U.S.) memorial statues. *Farragut, Mrs. Henry Adams (Grief).*
Andrea Sansovino, 1460-1529, (It.) Renaissance sculptor. *Baptism of Christ.*
Jacopo Sansovino, 1486-1570, (It.) Renaissance sculptor. *St. John the Baptist.*
John Singer Sargent, 1856-1925, (U.S.) Edwardian society portraitist. *The Wyndham Sisters, Madam X.*
George Segal, 1924-2000, (U.S.) sculptor of life-sized figures realistically depicting daily life.
Georges Seurat, 1859-91, (Fr.) Pointillist. *Sunday Afternoon on the Island of La Grande Jatte.*
Gino Severini, 1883-1966, (It.) Futurist and Cubist. *Dynamic Hieroglyph of the Bal Tabarin.*
Ben Shahn, 1898-1969, (U.S.) social and political themes. *Sacco and Vanzetti* series, *Seurat's Lunch, Handball.*
Charles Sheeler, 1883-1965, (U.S.) abstractionist.
David Alfaro Siqueiros, 1896-1974, (Mex.) political muralist. *March of Humanity.*
David Smith, 1906-65, (U.S.) welded metal sculpture. *Hudson River Landscape, Zig, Cubi* series.
Edward Steichen, 1879-1973, (U.S.) photographer. Credited with transforming photography into an art form.
Alfred Stieglitz, 1864-1946, (U.S.) photographer, editor; helped create acceptance of photography as art.
Paul Strand, 1890-1976, (U.S.) photographer. People, nature, landscapes.
Gilbert Stuart, 1755-1828, (U.S.) portraitist. George Washington, Thomas Jefferson, James Madison.
Thomas Sully, 1783-1872, (U.S.) portraitist. *Col. Thomas Handasyd Perkins, The Passage of the Delaware.*
William Henry Fox Talbot, 1800-77, (Br.) photographer. *Pencil of Nature,* early photographically illustrated book.
George Tames, 1919-94, (U.S.) photographer. Chronicled presidents, political leaders.
Yves Tanguy, 1900-55, (Fr.) Surrealist. *Rose of the Four Winds, Mama, Papa Is Wounded!*
Giovanni Battista Tiepolo, 1696-1770, (It.) Rococo frescoes. *The Crucifixion.*
Jacopo Tintoretto, 1518-94, (It.) Mannerist. *The Last Supper.*
Titian, c1485-1576, (It.) Renaissance. *Venus and the Lute Player, The Bacchanal.*
Jose Rey Toledo, 1916-94, (U.S.) Native American artist. Captured the essence of tribal dances on canvas.
Henri de Toulouse-Lautrec, 1864-1901, (Fr.) *At the Moulin Rouge.*
John Trumbull, 1756-1843, (U.S.) historical themes. *The Declaration of Independence.*
J(oseph) M(allord) W(illiam) Turner, 1775-1851, (Br.) Romantic landscapist. *Snow Storm.*
Paolo Uccello, 1397-1475, (It.) Gothic-Renaissance. *The Rout of San Romano.*
Maurice Utrillo, 1883-1955, (Fr.) Impressionist. *Sacre-Coeur de Montmartre.*
John Vanderlyn, 1775-1852, (U.S.) Neo-classicist. *Ariadne Asleep on the Island of Naxos.*
Diego Velázquez, 1599-1660, (Sp.) Baroque. *Las Meninas, Portrait of Juan de Pareja.*
Jan Vermeer, 1632-75, (Dutch) interior genre subjects. *Young Woman With a Water Jug.*
Paolo Veronese, 1528-88, (It.) devotional themes, vastly peopled canvases. *The Temptation of St. Anthony.*
Andrea del Verrocchio, 1435-88, (It.) Floren. sculptor. *Colleoni.*

Maurice de Vlaminck, 1876-1958, (Fr.) Fauvist landscapist. *Red Trees.*
Andy Warhol, 1928-87, (U.S.) Pop Art. *Campbell's Soup Cans, Marilyn Diptych.*
Antoine Watteau, 1684-1721, (Fr.) Rococo painter of "scenes of gallantry." *The Embarkation for Cythera.*
George Frederic Watts, 1817-1904, (Br.) painter and sculptor of grandiose allegorical themes. *Hope.*
Benjamin West, 1738-1820, (U.S.) realistic historical themes. *Death of General Wolfe.*

Edward Weston, 1886-1958, (U.S.) photographer. Landscapes of American West.
James Abbott McNeill Whistler, 1834-1903, (U.S.) *Arrangement in Grey and Black, No. 1: The Artist's Mother.*
Archibald M. Willard, 1836-1918, (U.S.) *The Spirit of '76.*
Grant Wood, 1891-1942, (U.S.) Midwestern regionalist. *American Gothic, Daughters of Revolution.*
Ossip Zadkine, 1890-1967, (Russ.) School of Paris sculptor. *The Destroyed City, Musicians, Christ.*

Business Leaders and Philanthropists of the Past

Giovanni Agnelli, 1921-2003, (It.) industrialist, principal shareholder of Fiat.
Walter Annenberg, 1908-2002, (U.S.) publisher, founder *TV Guide,* philanthropist.
Elizabeth Arden (F. N. Graham), 1884-1966, (U.S.) Canadian-born founder of cosmetics empire.
Philip D. Armour, 1832-1901, (U.S.) industrialist; streamlined meatpacking.
John Jacob Astor, 1763-1848, (U.S.) German-born fur trader, banker, real estate magnate; at death, richest in U.S.
Francis W. Ayer, 1848-1923, (U.S.) ad industry pioneer.
August Belmont, 1816-90, (U.S.) German-born financier.
James B. (Diamond Jim) Brady, 1856-1917, (U.S.) financier, philanthropist, legendary bon vivant.
Adolphus Busch, 1839-1913, (U.S.) German-born businessman; established brewery empire.
Asa Candler, 1851-1929, (U.S.) founded Coca-Cola Co.
Andrew Carnegie, 1835-1919, (U.S.) Scottish-born industrialist; philanthropist; founded Carnegie Steel Co.
Tom Carvel, 1908-89, (Gr.-U.S.) founded ice cream chain.
William Colgate, 1783-1857, (Br.-U.S.) Br.-born businessman, philanthropist; founded soap-making empire.
Jay Cooke, 1821-1905, (U.S.) financier; sold $1 billion in Union bonds during Civil War.
Peter Cooper, 1791-1883, (U.S.) industrialist, inventor, philanthropist; founded Cooper Union (1859).
Ezra Cornell, 1807-74, (U.S.) businessman, philanthropist; headed Western Union, established university.
Erastus Corning, 1794-1872, (U.S.) financier; headed N.Y. Central.
Charles Crocker, 1822-88, (U.S.) railroad builder, financier.
Samuel Cunard, 1787-1865, (Can.) pioneered trans-Atlantic steam navigation.
Marcus Daly, 1841-1900, (U.S.) Irish-born copper magnate.
W. Edwards Deming, 1900-93, (U.S.) quality-control expert who revolutionized Japanese manufacturing.
Walt Disney, 1901-66, (U.S.) pioneer in cinema animation; built entertainment empire.
Herbert H. Dow, 1866-1930, (U.S.) founder of chemical co.
James Duke, 1856-1925, (U.S.) founded American Tobacco, Duke Univ.
Eleuthere I. du Pont, 1771-1834, (Fr.-U.S.) gunpowder manufacturer; founded one of the largest business empires.
Thomas C. Durant, 1820-85, (U.S.) railroad official, financier.
William C. Durant, 1861-1947, (U.S.) industrialist; formed General Motors.
George Eastman, 1854-1932, (U.S.) inventor; manufacturer of photographic equipment.
Marshall Field, 1834-1906, (U.S.) merchant; founded Chicago's largest department store.
Harvey Firestone, 1868-1938, (U.S.) founded tire company.
Avery Fisher, 1906-94, (U.S.) industrialist, philanthropist, founded Fisher electronics.
Henry M. Flagler, 1830-1913, (U.S.) financier; helped form Standard Oil; developed Florida as resort state.
Malcolm Forbes, 1919-90, (U.S.) magazine publisher.
Henry Ford, 1863-1947, (U.S.) auto maker; developed first popular low-priced car.
Henry Ford 2nd, 1917-87, (U.S.) headed auto company founded by grandfather.
Henry C. Frick, 1849-1919, (U.S.) steel and coke magnate; had prominent role in development of U.S. Steel.
Jakob Fugger (Jakob the Rich), 1459-1525, (Ger.) headed leading banking, trading house, in 16th-cent. Europe.
Alfred C. Fuller, 1885-1973, (U.S.) Canadian-born businessman; founded brush company.
Elbert H. Gary, 1846-1927, (U.S.) one of the organizers of U.S. Steel; chaired board of directors, 1903-27.
Jean Paul Getty, 1892-1976, (U.S.) founded oil empire.
Amadeo Giannini, 1870-1949, (U.S.) founded Bank of America.
Stephen Girard, 1750-1831, (U.S.) French-born financier, philanthropist; richest man in U.S. at his death.
Leonard H. Goldenson, 1905-99, (U.S.) turned ABC into major TV network.
Jay Gould, 1836-92, (U.S.) railroad magnate, financier.
Hetty Green, 1834-1916, (U.S.) financier, the "witch of Wall St."; richest woman in U.S. in her day.
William Gregg, 1800-67, (U.S.) launched textile industry in S.

Meyer Guggenheim, 1828-1905, (U.S.) Swiss-born merchant, philanthropist; built merchandising, mining empires.
Armand Hammer, 1898-1990, (U.S.) headed Occidental Petroleum; promoted U.S.-Soviet ties.
Edward H. Harriman, 1848-1909, (U.S.) railroad financier, administrator; headed Union Pacific.
Henry J. Heinz, 1844-1919, (U.S.) founded food empire.
James J. Hill, 1838-1916, (U.S.) Canadian-born railroad magnate, financier; founded Great Northern Railway.
Conrad N. Hilton, 1888-1979, (U.S.) hotel chain founder.
Howard Hughes, 1905-76, (U.S.) industrialist, aviator, movie maker.
H. L. Hunt, 1889-1974, (U.S.) oil magnate.
Collis P. Huntington, 1821-1900, (U.S.) railroad magnate.
Henry E. Huntington, 1850-1927, (U.S.) railroad builder, philanthropist.
Walter L. Jacobs, 1898-1985, (U.S.) founder of the first rental car agency, which later became Hertz.
Howard Johnson, 1896-1972, (U.S.) founded restaurants.
Henry J. Kaiser, 1882-1967, (U.S.) industrialist; built empire in steel, aluminum.
Minor C. Keith, 1848-1929, (U.S.) railroad magnate; founded United Fruit Co.
Will K. Kellogg, 1860-1951, (U.S.) businessman, philanthropist; founded breakfast food co.
Richard King, 1825-85, (U.S.) cattleman; founded half-million-acre King Ranch in Texas.
William S. Knudsen, 1879-1948, (U.S.) Danish-born auto industry executive.
Samuel H. Kress, 1863-1955, (U.S.) businessman, art collector, philanthropist; founded "dime store" chain.
Ray A. Kroc, 1902-84, (U.S.) founded McDonald's fast-food chain.
Alfred Krupp, 1812-87, (Ger.) armaments magnate.
William Levitt, 1907-94, (U.S.) industrialist, "suburb maker".
Thomas Lipton, 1850-1931, (Scot.) merchant, tea empire.
James McGill, 1744-1813, (Scot.-Can.) founded university.
Andrew W. Mellon, 1855-1937, (U.S.) financier, industrialist; benefactor of National Gallery of Art.
Charles E. Merrill, 1885-1956, (U.S.) financier; developed firm of Merrill Lynch.
John Pierpont Morgan, 1837-1913, (U.S.) most powerful figure in finance and industry at the turn of the cent.
Akio Morita, 1921-99, (Japan) co-founded Sony Corp.
Malcolm Muir, 1885-1979, (U.S.) created *Business Week* magazine; headed *Newsweek,* 1937-61.
Samuel Newhouse, 1895-1979, (U.S.) publishing and broadcasting magnate; built communications empire.
Aristotle Onassis, 1906-75, (Gr.) shipping magnate.
William S. Paley, 1901-90, (U.S.) built CBS communic. empire.
George Peabody, 1795-1869, (U.S.) merchant, financier, philanthropist.
James C. Penney, 1875-1971, (U.S.) businessman; developed department store chain.
William C. Procter, 1862-1934, (U.S.) headed soap co.
John D. Rockefeller, 1839-1937, (U.S.) industrialist; established Standard Oil.
John D. Rockefeller Jr., 1874-1960, (U.S.) philanthropist; established foundation; provided land for UN.
Meyer A. Rothschild, 1743-1812, (Ger.) founded international banking house.
Thomas Fortune Ryan, 1851-1928, (U.S.) financier; a founder of American Tobacco.
Edmond J. Safra, 1932-99, (U.S.) founded Republic National Bank of New York.
David Sarnoff, 1891-1971, (U.S.) broadcasting pioneer; established first radio network, NBC.
Richard Sears, 1863-1914, (U.S.) founded mail-order co.
Werner von Siemens, 1816-92, (Ger.) industrialist; inventor.
Alfred P. Sloan, 1875-1966, (U.S.) industrialist, philanthropist; headed General Motors.
A. Leland Stanford, 1824-93, (U.S.) railroad official, philanthropist; founded university.
Nathan Straus, 1848-1931, (U.S.) German-born merchant, philanthropist; headed Macy's.
Levi Strauss, c1829-1902, (U.S.) pants manufacturer.
Clement Studebaker, 1831-1901, (U.S.) wagon, carriage (maker).
Gustavus Swift, 1839-1903, (U.S.) pioneer meatpacker.

Gerard Swope, 1872-1957, (U.S.) industrialist, economist; headed General Electric.
Dave Thomas, 1932-2002, (U.S.) Wendy's founder.
James Walter Thompson, 1847-1928, (U.S.) ad executive.
Alice Tully, 1902-93, (U.S.) philanthropist, arts patron.
Theodore N. Vail, 1845-1920, (U.S.) organized Bell Telephone system; headed AT&T.
Cornelius Vanderbilt, 1794-1877, (U.S.) financier; established steamship, railroad empires.
Henry Villard, 1835-1900, (U.S.) German-born railroad executive, financier.
George Westinghouse, 1846-1914, (U.S) inventor, manufacturer; organized Westinghouse Electric Co., 1886.
Charles R. Walgreen, 1873-1939, (U.S.) founded drugstore chain.

DeWitt Wallace, 1889-1981, (U.S.) and **Lila Wallace,** 1889-1984, (U.S.) cofounders of *Reader's Digest* magazine.
Sam Walton, 1918-92, (U.S.) founder of Wal-Mart stores.
John Wanamaker, 1838-1922, (U.S.) pioneered department-store merchandising.
Aaron Montgomery Ward, 1843-1913, (U.S.) established first mail-order firm.
Thomas J. Watson, 1874-1956, (U.S.) IBM head, 1914-56.
John Hay Whitney, 1905-82, (U.S.) publisher, sportsman, philanthropist.
Charles E. Wilson, 1890-1961, (U.S.) auto industry exec., public official.
Frank W. Woolworth, 1852-1919, (U.S.) created 5 & 10 chain.
William Wrigley Jr., 1861-1932, (U.S.) founded Wrigley chewing gum company.

American Cartoonists

Reviewed by Lucy Shelton Caswell, Professor and Curator, Cartoon Research Library, Ohio State University

Scott Adams, b 1957, Dilbert.
Charles Addams, 1912-88, macabre cartoons.
Brad Anderson, b 1924, Marmaduke.
Sergio Aragones, b 1937, *MAD Magazine.*
Peter Arno, 1904-68, *The New Yorker.*
Tex Avery, 1908-80, animator, Bugs Bunny, Porky Pig.
George Baker, 1915-75, The Sad Sack.
Carl Barks, 1901-2000, Donald Duck comic books.
C. C. Beck, 1910-89, Captain Marvel.
Dave Berg, 1920-2002, *Mad Magazine.*
Jim Berry, b 1932, Berry's World.
Herb Block (Herblock), 1909-2001, political cartoonist.
George Booth, b 1926, *The New Yorker.*
Berkeley Breathed, b 1957, Bloom County.
Dik Browne, 1917-89, Hi & Lois, Hagar the Horrible.
Marjorie Buell, 1904-93, Little Lulu.
Ernie Bushmiller, 1905-82, Nancy.
Milton Caniff, 1907-88, Terry & the Pirates, Steve Canyon.
Al Capp, 1909-79, Li'l Abner.
Roz Chast, b 1954, *The New Yorker.*
Paul Conrad, 1924, political cartoonist.
Roy Crane, 1901-77, Captain Easy, Buz Sawyer.
Robert Crumb, b 1943, underground cartoonist.
Shamus Culhane, 1908-96, animator.
Jay N. Darling (Ding), 1876-1962, political cartoonist.
Jack Davis, b 1926, *MAD Magazine.*
Jim Davis, b 1945, Garfield.
Billy DeBeck, 1890-1942, Barney Google.
Rudolph Dirks, 1877-1968, The Katzenjammer Kids.
Walt Disney, 1901-66, produced animated cartoons, created Mickey Mouse, Donald Duck.
Steve Ditko, b 1927, Spider-Man.
Mort Drucker, b 1929, *MAD Magazine.*
Will Eisner, b 1917, The Spirit.
Jules Feiffer, b 1929, political cartoonist.
Bud Fisher, 1884-1954, Mutt & Jeff.
Ham Fisher, 1900-55, Joe Palooka.
Max Fleischer, 1883-1972, Betty Boop.
Hal Foster, 1892-1982, Tarzan, Prince Valiant.
Fontaine Fox, 1884-1964, Toonerville Folks.
Isadore "Friz" Freleng, 1905-95, animator, Yosemite Sam, Porky Pig, Sylvester and Tweety Bird.
Rube Goldberg, 1883-1970, Boob McNutt.
Chester Gould, 1900-85, Dick Tracy.
Harold Gray, 1894-1968, Little Orphan Annie.
Matt Groening, b 1954, Life in Hell, The Simpsons.
Cathy Guisewite, b 1950, Cathy.
Bill Hanna, 1910-2001, & **Joe Barbera,** b 1911, animators, Tom & Jerry, Yogi Bear, Flintstones.
Johnny Hart, b 1931, BC, Wizard of Id.
Oliver Harrington, 1912-95, Bootsie.
Alfred Harvey, 1913-94, created Casper the Friendly Ghost.
Jimmy Hatlo, 1898-1963, Little Iodine.
John Held Jr., 1889-1958, Jazz Age.
George Herriman, 1881-1944, Krazy Kat.
Harry Hershfield, 1885-1974, Abie the Agent.
Al Hirschfeld, 1903-2003, *N.Y. Times* theater caricaturist.
Burne Hogarth, 1911-96, Tarzan.
Helen Hokinson, 1900-49, *The New Yorker.*
Nicole Hollander, b 1939, Sylvia.
Chuck Jones, 1912-2002, animator, Bugs Bunny, Porky Pig.
Mike Judge, b. 1962, Beavis and Butt-head, King of the Hill.
Bob Kane, b 1916-98, Batman.
Bil Keane, b 1922, The Family Circus.
Walt Kelly, 1913-73, Pogo.

Hank Ketcham, 1920-2001, Dennis the Menace.
Ted Key, b 1912, Hazel.
Frank King, 1883-1969, Gasoline Alley.
Jack Kirby, 1917-94, Fantastic Four, The Incredible Hulk.
Rollin Kirby, 1875-1952, political cartoonist.
B(ernard) Kliban, 1935-91, cat books.
Edward Koren, b 1935, *The New Yorker.*
Harvey Kurtzman, 1921-93, *MAD Magazine.*
Walter Lantz, 1900-94, Woody Woodpecker.
Gary Larson, b 1950, The Far Side.
Mell Lazarus, b 1929, Momma, Miss Peach.
Stan Lee, b 1922, Marvel Comics.
David Levine, b 1926, *N.Y. Review of Books* caricatures.
Doug Marlette, b 1949, political cartoonist, Kudzu.
Don Martin, 1931-2000, *MAD Magazine.*
Bill Mauldin, 1921-2003, political cartoonist.
Jeff MacNelly, 1947-2000, political cartoonist, Shoe.
Winsor McCay, 1872-1934, Little Nemo.
John T. McCutcheon, 1870-1949, political cartoonist.
Aaron McGruder, b 1974, The Boondocks.
George McManus, 1884-1954, Bringing Up Father.
Dale Messick, b 1906, Brenda Starr.
Norman Mingo, 1896-1980, Alfred E. Neuman.
Bob Montana, 1920-75, Archie.
Dick Moores, 1909-86, Gasoline Alley.
Willard Mullin, 1902-78, sports cartoonist; Dodgers "Bum," Mets "Kid."
Russell Myers, b 1938, Broom Hilda.
Thomas Nast, 1840-1902, political cartoonist; Republican elephant and Democratic donkey.
Pat Oliphant, b 1935, political cartoonist.
Frederick Burr Opper, 1857-1937, Happy Hooligan.
Richard Outcault, 1863-1928, Yellow Kid, Buster Brown.
Brant Parker, b 1920, Wizard of Id.
Trey Parker, b 1969?, animator, co-creator of *South Park.*
Mike Peters, b 1943, cartoonist, Mother Goose & Grimm.
George Price, 1901-95, *The New Yorker.*
Antonio Prohias, 1921(?)-98, Spy vs. Spy.
Alex Raymond, 1909-56, Flash Gordon, Jungle Jim.
Forrest (Bud) Sagendorf, 1915-94, Popeye.
Art Sansom, 1920-91, The Born Loser.
Charles Schulz, 1922-2000, Peanuts.
Elzie C. Segar, 1894-1938, Popeye.
Joe Shuster, 1914-92, & **Jerry Siegel,** 1914-96, Superman.
Sidney Smith, 1887-1935, The Gumps.
Otto Soglow, 1900-75, Little King.
Art Spiegelman, b 1948, Raw, Maus.
William Steig, b 1907, *The New Yorker.*
Matt Stone, b 1971?, animator, co-creator of South Park.
Paul Szep, b 1941, political cartoonist.
James Swinnerton, 1875-1974, Little Jimmy, Canyon Kiddies.
Paul Terry, 1887-1971, animator of Mighty Mouse.
Bob Thaves, b 1924, Frank and Ernest.
James Thurber, 1894-61, *The New Yorker.*
Garry Trudeau, b 1948, Doonesbury.
Mort Walker, b 1923, Beetle Bailey.
Bill Watterson, b 1958, Calvin and Hobbes.
Russ Westover, 1887-1966, Tillie the Toiler.
Signe Wilkinson, b 1950, political cartoonist.
Frank Willard, 1893-1958, Moon Mullins.
J. R. Williams, 1888-1957, The Willets Family, Out Our Way.
Gahan Wilson, b 1930, *The New Yorker.*
Tom Wilson, b 1931, Ziggy.
Art Young, 1866-1943, political cartoonist.
Chic Young, 1901-73, Blondie.

Economists, Educators, Historians, and Social Scientists of the Past

For Psychologists see Scientists of the Past.

Brooks Adams, 1848-1927, (U.S.) historian, political theoretician; *The Law of Civilization and Decay.*

Henry Adams, 1838-1918, (U.S.) historian, autobiographer; *History of the United States of America, The Education of Henry Adams.*

Francis Bacon, 1561-1626, (Eng.) philosopher, essayist, and statesman; championed observation and induction.

George Bancroft, 1800-91, (U.S.) historian; wrote 10-volume *History of the United States.*

Jack Barbash, 1911-94, (U.S.) labor economist who helped create the AFL-CIO.

Henry Barnard, 1811-1900, (U.S.) public school reformer.

Charles A. Beard, 1874-1948, (U.S.) historian; *The Economic Basis of Politics.*

Bede (the Venerable), c673-735, (Br.) scholar, historian; *Ecclesiastical History of the English People.*

Ruth Benedict, 1887-1948, (U.S.) anthropologist; studied Indian tribes of the Southwest.

Sir Isaiah Berlin, 1909-97, (Br.) philosopher, historian; *The Age of Enlightenment.*

Louis Blanc, 1811-82, (Fr.) Socialist leader and historian.

Sarah G. Blanding, 1899-1985, (U.S.) head of Vassar College, 1946-64.

Leonard Bloomfield, 1887-1949, (U.S.) linguist; *Language.*

Franz Boas, 1858-1942, (U.S.) German-born anthropologist; studied American Indians.

Van Wyck Brooks, 1886-1963, (U.S.) historian; critic of New England culture, especially literature.

Edmund Burke, 1729-97, (Ir.) British parliamentarian and political philosopher; *Reflections on the Revolution in France.*

Nicholas Murray Butler, 1862-1947, (U.S.) educator; headed Columbia Univ., 1902-45; Nobel Peace Prize, 1931.

Joseph Campbell, 1904-87, (U.S.) author, editor, teacher; wrote books on mythology, folklore.

Thomas Carlyle, 1795-1881, (Sc.) historian, critic; *Sartor Resartus, Past and Present, The French Revolution.*

Edward Channing, 1856-1931, (U.S.) historian; wrote 6-volume *History of the United States.*

Henry Steele Commager, 1902-98, (U.S.) historian, educator; wrote *The Growth of the American Republic.*

John R. Commons, 1862-1945, (U.S.) economist, labor historian; *Legal Foundations of Capitalism.*

James B. Conant, 1893-1978, (U.S.) educator, diplomat; *The American High School Today.*

Benedetto Croce, 1866-1952, (It.) philosopher, statesman, and historian; *Philosophy of the Spirit.*

Bernard A. De Voto, 1897-1955, (U.S.) historian; wrote trilogy on American West; edited Mark Twain manuscripts.

Melvil Dewey, 1851-1931, (U.S.) devised decimal system of library-book classification.

Emile Durkheim, 1858-1917, (Fr.) a founder of modern sociology; *The Rules of Sociological Method.*

Charles Eliot, 1834-1926, (U.S.) educator, Harvard president.

Friedrich Engels, 1820-95, (Ger.) political writer; with Marx wrote the *Communist Manifesto.*

Irving Fisher, 1867-1947, (U.S.) economist; contributed to the development of modern monetary theory.

John Fiske, 1842-1901, (U.S.) historian and lecturer; popularized Darwinian theory of evolution.

Charles Fourier, 1772-1837, (Fr.) utopian socialist.

Giovanni Gentile, 1875-1944, (It.) philosopher, educator; reformed Italian educational system.

Sir James George Frazer, 1854-1941, (Br.) anthropologist; studied myth in religion; *The Golden Bough.*

Henry George, 1839-97, (U.S.) economist, reformer; led single-tax movement.

Edward Gibbon, 1737-94, (Br.) historian; *The History of the Decline and Fall of the Roman Empire.*

Francesco Guicciardini, 1483-1540, (It.) historian; *Storia d'Italia,* principal historical work of the 16th cent.

Thomas Hobbes, 1588-1679, (Eng.) philosopher, political theorist; *Leviathan.*

Richard Hofstadter, 1916-70, (U.S.) historian; *The Age of Reform.*

John Holt, 1924-85, (U.S.) educator and author.

John Maynard Keynes, 1883-1946, (Br.) economist; principal advocate of deficit spending.

Russell Kirk, 1918-94, (U.S.), social philosopher; *The Conservative Mind.*

Alfred L. Kroeber, 1876-1960, (U.S.) cultural anthropologist; studied Indians of North and South America.

Christopher Lasch, 1932-94, (U.S.) social critic, historian; *The Culture of Narcissism.*

James L. Laughlin, 1850-1933, (U.S.) economist; helped establish Federal Reserve System.

Lucien Lévy-Bruhl, 1857-1939, (Fr.) philosopher; studied the psychology of primitive societies; *Primitive Mentality.*

John Locke, 1632-1704, (Eng.) philosopher and political theorist; *Two Treatises of Government.*

Thomas B. Macaulay, 1800-59, (Br.) historian, statesman.

Niccolò Machiavelli, 1469-1527, (It.) writer, statesman. *The Prince.*

Bronislaw Malinowski, 1884-1942, (Pol.) considered the father of social anthropology.

Thomas R. Malthus, 1766-1834, (Br.) economist; famed for *Essay on the Principle of Population.*

Horace Mann, 1796-1859, (U.S.) pioneered modern public school system.

Karl Mannheim, 1893-1947, (Hung.) sociologist, historian; *Ideology and Utopia.*

Karl Marx, 1818-83, (Ger.) political theorist, proponent of Communism; *Communist Manifesto, Das Kapital.*

Giuseppe Mazzini, 1805-72, (It.) political philosopher.

William H. McGuffey, 1800-73, (U.S.) whose *Reader* was a mainstay of 19th-cent. U.S. public education.

George H. Mead, 1863-1931, (U.S.) philosopher, social psychologist.

Margaret Mead, 1901-78, (U.S.) cultural anthropologist; popularized field; *Coming of Age in Samoa.*

Alexander Meiklejohn, 1872-1964, (U.S.) Br.-born educator; championed academic freedom and experimental curricula.

James Mill, 1773-1836, (Sc.) philosopher, historian, economist; a proponent of utilitarianism.

Perry G. Miller, 1905-63, (U.S.) historian; interpreted 17th-cent. New England.

Theodor Mommsen, 1817-1903, (Ger.) historian; *The History of Rome.*

Ashley Montagu, 1905-99, (Eng.) anthropologist; *The Natural Superiority of Women.*

Charles-Louis Montesquieu, 1689-1755, (Fr.) social philosopher; *The Spirit of Laws.*

Maria Montessori, 1870-1952, (It.) educator, physician; started Montessori method of student self-motivation.

Samuel Eliot Morison, 1887-1976, (U.S.) historian; chronicled voyages of early explorers.

Lewis Mumford, 1895-1990, (U.S.) sociologist, critic; *The Culture of Cities.*

Gunnar Myrdal, 1898-1987, (Swed.) economist, social scientist; *Asian Drama: An Inquiry Into the Poverty of Nations.*

Joseph Needham, 1900-95, (Br.) scientific historian; *Science and Civilization in China.*

Allan Nevins, 1890-1971, (U.S.) historian, biographer; *The Ordeal of the Union.*

José Ortega y Gasset, 1883-1955, (Sp.) philosopher; advocated control by elite; *The Revolt of the Masses.*

Robert Owen, 1771-1858, (Br.) political philosopher, reformer; pioneer in cooperative movement.

Thomas (Tom) Paine, 1737-1809, (U.S.) political theorist, writer. *Common Sense.*

Vilfredo Pareto, 1848-1923, (It.) economist, sociologist.

Francis Parkman, 1823-93, (U.S.) historian; *France and England in North America.*

Elizabeth P. Peabody, 1804-94, (U.S.) education pioneer; founded 1st kindergarten in U.S., 1860.

William Prescott, 1796-1859, (U.S.) early American historian; *The Conquest of Peru.*

Pierre Joseph Proudhon, 1809-65, (Fr.) social theorist; father of anarchism; *The Philosophy of Property.*

François Quesnay, 1694-1774, (Fr.) economic theorist.

David Ricardo, 1772-1823, (Br.) economic theorist; advocated free international trade.

David Riesman, 1909-2002, (U.S.) sociologist, coauthor *The Lonely Crowd.*

Jean-Jacques Rousseau, 1712-78, (Fr.) social philosopher; the father of romantic sensibility; *Confessions.*

Edward Sapir, 1884-1939, (Ger.-U.S.) anthropologist; studied ethnology and linguistics of U.S. Indian groups.

Ferdinand de Saussure, 1857-1913, (Swiss) a founder of modern linguistics.

Hjalmar Schacht, 1877-1970, (Ger.) economist.

Joseph Schumpeter, 1883-1950, (Czech.-U.S.) economist, sociologist.

Elizabeth Seton, 1774-1821, (U.S.) nun; est. parochial school education in U.S.; first native-born American saint.

George Simmel, 1858-1918, (Ger.) sociologist, philosopher; helped establish German sociology.

Adam Smith, 1723-90, (Br.) economist; advocated laissez-faire economy, free trade; *The Wealth of Nations.*

Jared Sparks, 1789-1866, (U.S.) historian, educator, editor; *The Library of American Biography.*

Oswald Spengler, 1880-1936, (Ger.) philosopher and historian; *The Decline of the West.*

William G. Sumner, 1840-1910, (U.S.) social scientist, economist; laissez-faire economy, Social Darwinism.

Hippolyte Taine, 1828-93, (Fr.) historian; basis of naturalistic school; *The Origins of Contemporary France.*

A(lan) J(ohn) P(ercivale) Taylor, 1906-89, (Br.) historian; *The Origins of the Second World War.*

Nikolaas Tinbergen, 1907-88, (Dutch-Br.) ethologist; pioneer in study of animal behavior.

Alexis de Tocqueville, 1805-59, (Fr.) political scientist, historian; *Democracy in America.*

Francis E. Townsend, 1867-1960, (U.S.) led old-age pension movement, 1933.

Arnold Toynbee, 1889-1975, (Br.) historian; *A Study of History,* sweeping analysis of hist. of civilizations.

George Trevelyan, 1838-1928, (Br.) historian, statesman; favored "literary" over "scientific" history; *History of England.*

Barbara Tuchman, 1912-89, (U.S.) author of popular history books, *The Guns of August, The March of Folly.*

Frederick J. Turner, 1861-1932, (U.S.) historian, educator; *The Frontier in American History.*

Thorstein B. Veblen, 1857-1929, (U.S.) economist, social philosopher; *The Theory of the Leisure Class.*

Giovanni Vico, 1668-1744, (It.) historian, philosopher; regarded by many as first modern historian; *New Science.*

Izaak Walton, 1593-1683, (Eng.) wrote biographies; political-philosophical study of fishing, *The Compleat Angler.*

Sidney J., 1859-1947, and **Beatrice**, 1858-1943, **Webb**, (Br.) leading figures in Fabian Society and Labor Party.

Max Weber, 1864-1920, (Ger.) sociologist; *The Protestant Ethic and the Spirit of Capitalism.*

Emma Hart Willard, 1787-1870, (U.S.) pioneered higher education for women.

C. Vann Woodward, 1908-99, (U.S.) historian; *The Strange Career of Jim Crow.*

American Journalists of the Past

Reviewed by Dean Mills, Dean, Missouri School of Journalism

See also African-Americans, Business Leaders, Cartoonists, Writers of the Past.

Franklin P. Adams (F.P.A.), 1881-1960, humorist; wrote column "The Conning Tower."

Martin Agronsky, 1915-99, broadcast journalist; developed Agronsky & Company.

Joseph W. Alsop, 1910-89, and **Stewart Alsop**, 1914-74, Washington-based political analysts, columnists.

Brooks Atkinson, 1894-1984, theater critic.

James Gordon Bennett, 1795-1872, editor and publisher; founded *NY Herald.*

James Gordon Bennett, 1841-1918, succeeded father, financed expeditions, founded afternoon paper.

Elias Boudinot, d 1839, founding editor of first Native American newspaper in U.S., *Cherokee Phoenix* (1828-34).

David Brinkley, 1920-2003, co-anchor of NBC's *Huntley-Brinkley Report,* host of ABC's *This Week With David Brinkley.*

Margaret Bourke-White, 1904-71, photojournalist.

Arthur Brisbane, 1864-1936, editor; helped introduce "yellow journalism" with sensational, simply written articles.

Heywood Broun, 1888-1939, author, columnist; founded American Newspaper Guild.

Herb Caen, 1916-97, longtime columnist for *San Francisco Chronicle* and *Examiner.*

John Campbell, 1653-1728, published *Boston News-Letter,* first continuing newspaper in the American colonies.

Jimmy Cannon, 1909-73, syndicated sports columnist.

John Chancellor, 1927-96, TV journalist; anchored *NBC Nightly News.*

Harry Chandler, 1864-1944, *Los Angeles Times* publisher, 1917-41; made it a dominant force.

Marquis Childs, 1903-90, reporter and columnist for *St. Louis Post-Dispatch* and United Feature syndicate.

Craig Claiborne, 1920-2000, *NY Times* food editor and critic; key in internationalizing American taste.

Elizabeth Cochrane (Nellie Bly), pioneer woman journalist, investig. reporter, noted for series on trip around the world.

Charles Collingwood, 1917-85, CBS news correspondent, foreign affairs reporter, documentary host.

Howard Cosell, 1920-95, TV and radio sportscaster.

Gardner Cowles, 1861-1946, founded newspaper chain.

Cyrus Curtis, 1850-1933, publisher of *Saturday Evening Post, Ladies' Home Journal, Country Gentleman.*

Charles Anderson Dana, 1819-97, editor, publisher; made *NY Sun* famous for its news reporting.

Elmer (Holmes) Davis, 1890-1958, *NY Times* editorial writer; radio commentator.

Richard Harding Davis, 1864-1916, war correspondent, travel writer, fiction writer.

Benjamin Day, 1810-89, published *NY Sun* beginning in 1833, introducing penny press to the U.S.

Frederick Douglass, 1817-95, ex-slave, social reformer, newspaper editor.

Finley Peter Dunne, 1867-1936, humorist, social critic, wrote "Mr. Dooley" columns.

Mary Baker Eddy, 1821-1910, founded Christian Science movement and *Christian Science Monitor.*

Rowland Evans Jr., 1921-2001, Washington columnist and commentator.

Marshall Field III, 1893-1956, retail magnate, *Chicago Sun* founder.

Doris Fleeson, 1901-70, war correspondent, columnist.

James Franklin, 1697-1735, printer, pioneer journalist, publisher of *New England Courant* and *Rhode Island Gazette.*

Fred W. Friendly, 1915-98, radio, TV reporter, announcer, producer, executive, collaborator with Edward R. Murrow.

Margaret Fuller, 1810-50, social reformer, transcendentalist, critic and foreign correspondent for *NY Tribune.*

Frank E. Gannett, 1876-1957, founded newspaper chain.

William Lloyd Garrison, 1805-79, abolitionist; publisher of *The Liberator.*

Sarah McClendon, 1910-2003, (U.S.) veteran White House correspondent.

Elizabeth Meriwether Gilmer (Dorothy Dix), 1861-1951, reporter, pioneer of the advice column genre.

Edwin Lawrence Godkin, 1831-1902, founder of *The Nation,* editor of *N.Y. Evening Post.*

Katharine Graham, 1917-2001, publisher of the *Washington Post.*

Sheilah Graham, 1904-89, Hollywood gossip columnist.

Horace Greeley, 1811-72, editor and politician; founded *NY Tribune.*

Meg Greenfield, 1930-1999, *Newsweek* columnist, editorial page editor Wash. Post.

Gilbert Hovey Grosvenor, 1875-1966, longtime editor of *National Geographic* magazine.

John Gunther, 1901-70, *Chicago Daily News* foreign correspondent, author.

Sarah Josepha Buell Hale, 1788-1879, first female magazine editor, (Ladies' Magazine, later *Godey's Lady's Book*)

Benjamin Harris, 1673-1716, publisher (1690) of *Publick Occurrences,* 1st newspaper in the American colonies; suppressed after one issue.

William Randolph Hearst, 1863-1951, founder of Hearst newspaper chain and one of the pioneer yellow journalists.

Gabriel Heatter, 1890-1972, radio commentator.

John Hersey, 1914-98, foreign correspondent for *Time, Life,* and *The New Yorker,* author.

Marguerite Higgins, 1920-66, reporter, war correspondent.

Hedda Hopper, 1885-1966, Hollywood gossip columnist.

Roy Howard, 1883-1964, editor, executive, Scripps-Howard papers and United Press (later United Press International).

Chet (Chester Robert) Huntley, 1911-74, co-anchor of NBC's *Huntley-Brinkley Report.*

Ralph Ingersoll, 1900-85, editor, *Fortune, Time, Life* exec.

H. V. (Hans von) Kaltenborn, 1878-1965, radio commentator, reporter.

Murray Kempton, 1917-97, reporter, columnist for magazines and newspapers, including *NY Post.*

John S. Knight, 1894-1981, editor, publisher; founded Knight newspaper group, which merged into Knight-Ridder.

Joseph Kraft, 1942-86, foreign policy columnist.

Arthur Krock, 1886-1974, *NY Times* political writer, Washington bureau chief.

Charles Kuralt, 1934-97, TV anchor and host of CBS "On the Road" feature stories about life in the U.S.

Ann Landers, real name Eppie Lederer, 1918-2002, advice columnist.

David Lawrence, 1888-1973, reporter, columnist, publisher; founded *U.S. News & World Report.*

Frank Leslie, 1821-80, engraver and publisher of newspapers and magazines, notably *Leslie's Illustrated Newspaper.*

Alexander Liberman, 1912-99, editorial director for Conde Nast magazines.

A(bbott) J(oseph) Liebling, 1904-63, foreign correspondent, critic, principally with *The New Yorker.*

Walter Lippmann, 1889-1974, political analyst, social critic, columnist, author.

Peter Lisagor, 1915-76, Washington bureau chief, *Chicago Daily News;* broadcast commentator.

David Ross Locke, 1833-88, humorist, satirist under pseudonym P.V. Nasby; owned *Toledo (Ohio) Blade.*

Elijah Parish Lovejoy, 1802-37, abolitionist editor in St. Louis and in Alton, IL; killed by proslavery mob.

Clare Booth Luce, 1903-87, war correspondent for *Life;* diplomat, playwright.

Henry R. Luce, 1898-1967, founded *Time, Fortune, Life, Sports Illustrated.*

C(harles) K(enny) McClatchy, 1858-1936 founder of McClatchy newspaper chain.

Samuel McClure, 1857-1949, founder (1893) of *McClure's Magazine*, famous for its investigative reporting.

Anne O'Hare McCormick, 1889-1954, foreign correspondent, first woman on *NY Times* editorial board.

Robert R. McCormick, 1880-1955, editor, publisher, executive of *Chicago Tribune* and *NY Daily News*.

Dwight Macdonald, 1906-1982, reporter, social critic for *The New Yorker, The Nation, Esquire*.

Ralph McGill, 1893-1969, crusading editor and publisher of *Atlanta Constitution*.

O(scar) O(dd) McIntyre, 1884-1938, feature writer, syndicated columnist concentrating on everyday life in New York City.

Don Marquis, 1878-1937, humor columnist for *NY Sun* and *N.Y. Tribune*; wrote "archy and mehitabel" stories.

Robert Maynard, 1937-97, first African-American editor and then owner of major U.S. paper, the *Oakland Tribune*.

Joseph Medill, 1823-99, longtime editor of *Chicago Tribune*.

H(enry) L(ouis) Mencken, 1880-1956, reporter, editor, columnist with *Baltimore Sun* papers; anti-establishment viewpoint.

Edwin Meredith, 1876-1928, founder of magazine company.

Frank A. Munsey, 1854-1925, owner, editor, and publisher of newspapers and magazines, including *Munsey's Magazine*.

Edward R. Murrow, 1908-65, broadcast reporter, news analyst; reported from Britain in WW2; hosted *See It Now, Person to Person*.

William Rockhill Nelson, 1841-1915, cofounder, editor, and publisher, *Kansas City Star*.

Adolph S. Ochs, 1858-1935, publisher; built *NY Times* into a leading newspaper.

Louella Parsons, 1881-1972, Hollywood gossip columnist.

Drew (Andrew Russell) Pearson, 1879-1969, investigative reporter and columnist.

(James) Westbrook Pegler, 1894-1969, reporter, columnist.

Shirley Povich, 1905-98, sports columnist.

Joseph Pulitzer, 1847-1911, *NY World* publisher; founded Columbia Journalism School, Pulitzer Prizes.

Joseph Pulitzer II, 1885-1955, longtime *St. Louis Post-Dispatch* editor, publisher; built it into major paper.

Ernie (Ernest Taylor) Pyle, 1900-45, reporter, war correspondent; killed in WW2.

Henry Raymond, 1820-69, cofounder, editor, *NY Times*.

Harry Reasoner, 1923-91, TV reporter, anchor.

John Reed, 1887-1920, reporter, foreign correspondent famous for coverage of Bolshevik Revolution.

Whitelaw Reid, 1837-1912, longtime editor, *NY Tribune*.

James Reston, 1909-95 *NY Times* political reporter, columnist.

Frank Reynolds, 1923-83, TV reporter, anchor.

(Henry) Grantland Rice, 1880-1954, sportswriter.

Jacob Riis, 1849-1914, reporter, photographer; exposed slum conditions in *How the Other Half Lives*.

Max Robinson, 1939-88, TV journalist, first African-American to anchor network news, 1978.

Harold Ross, 1892-1951, founder, editor, The *New Yorker*.

Mike Royko, 1932-97, columnist for *Chicago Sun-Times* and *Chicago Tribune*.

(Alfred) Damon Runyon, 1884-1946, sportswriter, columnist; stories collected in *Guys and Dolls*.

John B. Russwurm, 1799-1851, cofounded (1827) nation's first black newspaper, *Freedom's Journal*, in NYC.

Adela Rogers St. Johns, 1894-1988, reporter, sportswriter for Hearst newspapers.

Harrison Salisbury, 1908-93, reporter, foreign correspondent; a Soviet specialist.

E(dward) W(yllis) Scripps, 1854-1926, founded first large U.S. newspaper chain, pioneered syndication.

Eric Sevareid, 1912-92, war correspondent, radio newscaster, TV commentator.

William L. Shirer, 1904-93, broadcaster, foreign correspondent; wrote *The Rise and Fall of the Third Reich*.

Howard K. Smith, 1914-2002, broadcast journalist.

Red (Walter) Smith, 1905-82, sportswriter.

Edgar P. Snow, 1905-71, correspondent, expert on Chinese Communist movement.

Lawrence Spivak, 1900-94, co-creator, moderator, producer of *Meet the Press*.

(Joseph) Lincoln Steffens, 1866-1936, muckraking journalist.

I(sidor) F(einstein) Stone, 1907-89, one-man editor of *I.F. Stone's Weekly*.

Arthur Hays Sulzberger, 1891-1968, longtime publisher of *N.Y. Times*.

C(yrus) L(eo) Sulzberger, 1912-93, *N.Y. Times* foreign correspondent and columnist.

David Susskind, 1920-87, TV producer, public affairs talk-show host (*Open End*).

John Cameron Swayze, 1906-95, newscaster, anchor of *Camel News Caravan*.

Herbert Bayard Swope, 1882-1958, war correspondent and editor of *N.Y. World*.

Ida Tarbell, 1857-1944, muckraking journalist.

Isaiah Thomas, 1750-1831, printer, publisher, cofounder of revolutionary journal, *Massachusetts Spy*.

Lowell Thomas, 1892-1981, radio newscaster, world traveler.

Dorothy Thompson, 1894-1961, foreign correspondent, columnist, radio commentator.

Ida Bell Wells-Barnett, 1862-1931, African-American reporter, editor, anti-lynching crusader.

William Allen White, 1868-1944, editor, publisher; made *Emporia (KS) Gazette* known worldwide.

Walter Winchell, 1897-1972, reporter, columnist, broadcaster of celebrity news.

John Peter Zenger, 1697-1746, printer and journalist; acquitted in precedent-setting libel suit (1735).

Military and Naval Leaders of the Past

Reviewed by Alan C. Aimone, USMA Library

Creighton Abrams, 1914-74, (U.S.) commanded forces in Vietnam, 1968-72.

Alexander the Great, 356-323 B.C., (Maced.) conquered Persia and much of the world known to Europeans.

Harold Alexander, 1891-1969, (Br.) led Allied invasion of Italy, 1943, WW2.

Ethan Allen, 1738-89, (U.S.) headed Green Mountain Boys; captured Ft. Ticonderoga, 1775, Amer. Rev.

Edmund Allenby, 1861-1936, (Br.) in Boer War, WW1; led Egyptian expeditionary force, 1917-18.

Benedict Arnold, 1741-1801, (U.S.) victorious at Saratoga; tried to betray West Point to British, Amer. Rev.

Henry "Hap" Arnold, 1886-1950, (U.S.) commanded Army Air Force in WW2.

John Barry, 1745-1803, (U.S.) won numerous sea battles during Amer. Rev.

Belisarius, c505-565, (Byzant.) won remarkable victories for Byzantine Emperor Justinian I.

Pierre Beauregard, 1818-93, (U.S.) Confed. general, ordered bombardment of Ft. Sumter that began Civil War.

Gebhard von Blücher, 1742-1819, (Ger.) helped defeat Napoleon at Waterloo.

Napoleon Bonaparte, 1769-1821, (Fr.) defeated Russia and Austria at Austerlitz, 1805; invaded Russia, 1812; defeated at Waterloo, 1815.

Edward Braddock, 1695-1755, (Br.) commanded forces in French and Indian War.

Omar N. Bradley, 1893-1981, (U.S.) headed U.S. ground troops in Normandy invasion, 1944, WW2.

John Burgoyne, 1722-92, (Br.) defeated at Saratoga, Amer. Rev.

Julius Caesar, 100-44 BC, (Rom.) general and politician; conquered in Gaul; overthrew Roman Republic.

Claire Lee Chennault, 1893-1958, (U.S.) headed Flying Tigers in WW2.

Mark W. Clark, 1896-1984, (U.S.) helped plan N African invasion in WW2; commander of UN forces, Korean War.

Karl von Clausewitz, 1780-1831, (Pruss.) military theorist.

Lucius D. Clay, 1897-1978, (U.S.) led Berlin airlift, 1948-49.

Henry Clinton, 1738-95, (Br.) commander of forces in Amer. Rev., 1778-81.

Cochise, c1815-74, (Nat. Am.) chief of Chiricahua band of Apache Indians in Southwest.

Charles Cornwallis, 1738-1805, (Br.) victorious at Brandywine, 1777; surrendered at Yorktown, Amer. Rev.

Hernan Cortes, 1485-1547, (Sp.) led Spanish conquistadors in the defeat of the Aztec empire, 1519-28.

Crazy Horse, 1849-77, (Nat. Am.) Sioux war chief victorious at battle of Little Bighorn.

George Armstrong Custer, 1839-76, (U.S.) U.S. army officer defeated and killed at battle of Little Bighorn.

Moshe Dayan, 1915-81, (Isr.) directed campaigns in the 1967, 1973 Arab-Israeli wars.

Stephen Decatur, 1779-1820, (U.S.) naval hero of Barbary wars, War of 1812.

Anton Denikin, 1872-1947, (Russ.) led White forces in Russian civil war.

George Dewey, 1837-1917, (U.S.) destroyed Spanish fleet at Manila, 1898, Span.-Amer. War.

Karl Doenitz, 1891-1980, (Ger.) submarine com. in chief and naval commander, WW2.

Jimmy Doolittle, 1896-1993, (U.S.) led 1942 air raid on Tokyo and other Japanese cities in WW2.

Hugh C. Dowding, 1883-1970, (Br.) headed RAF, 1936-40, WW2.

Jubal Early, 1816-94, (U.S.) Confed. general, led raid on Washington, 1864, Civil War.

Dwight D. Eisenhower, 1890-1969, (U.S.) commanded Allied forces in Europe, WW2.

David Farragut, 1801-70, (U.S.) Union admiral, captured New Orleans, Mobile Bay, Civil War.

Ferdinand Foch, 1851-1929, (Fr.) headed victorious Allied armies, 1918, WW1.

Nathan Bedford Forrest, 1821-77, (U.S.) Confed. general, led raids against Union supply lines, Civil War.

Frederick the Great, 1712-86, (Pruss.) led Prussia in Seven Years War.

Horatio Gates, 1728-1806, (U.S.) commanded army at Saratoga, Amer. Rev.

Genghis Khan, 1162-1227, (Mongol) unified Mongol tribes and subjugated much of Asia, 1206-21.

Geronimo, 1829-1909, (Nat. Am.) leader of Chiricahua band of Apache Indians.

Charles G. Gordon, 1833-85, (Br.) led forces in China, Crimean War; killed at Khartoum.

Ulysses S. Grant, 1822-85, (U.S.) headed Union army, Civil War, 1864-65; forced Lee's surrender, 1865.

Nathanael Greene, 1742-86, (U.S.) defeated British in Southern campaign, 1780-81.

Heinz Guderian, 1888-1953, (Ger.) tank theorist, led panzer forces in Poland, France, Russia, WW2.

Che (Ernesto) Guevara, 1928-67, (Arg.) guerrilla leader; prominent in Cuban revolution; killed in Bolivia.

Gustavus Adolphus, 1594-1632, (Swed.) King; military tactician; reformer; led forces in Thirty Years' War.

Douglas Haig, 1861-1928, (Br.) led British armies in France, 1915-18, WW1.

William F. Halsey, 1882-1959, (U.S.) defeated Japanese fleet at Leyte Gulf, 1944, WW2.

Hannibal, 247-183 B.C., (Carthag.) invaded Rome, crossing Alps, in Second Punic War, 218-201 B.C.

Sir Arthur Travers Harris, 1895-1984, (Br.) led Britain's WW2 bomber command.

Richard Howe, 1726-99, (Br.) commanded navy in Amer. Rev., 1776-78; June 1 victory against French, 1794.

William Howe, 1729-1814, (Br.) commanded forces in Amer. Rev., 1776-78.

Isaac Hull, 1773-1843, (U.S.) sunk British frigate Guerriere, War of 1812.

Thomas (Stonewall) Jackson, 1824-63, (U.S.) Confed. general, led Shenandoah Valley campaign, Civil War.

Joseph Joffre, 1852-1931, (Fr.) headed Allied armies, won Battle of the Marne, 1914, WW1.

Chief Joseph, c1840-1904, (Nat. Am.) chief of the Nez Percé, led his tribe across 3 states seeking refuge in Canada; surrendered about 30 mi from Canadian border.

John Paul Jones, 1747-92, (U.S.) commanded Bonhomme Richard in victory over Serapis, Amer. Rev., 1779.

Stephen Kearny, 1794-1848, (U.S.) headed Army of the West in Mexican War.

Albert Kesselring, 1885-1960 (Ger.) field marshal who led the defense of Italy in WW2.

Ernest J. King, 1878-1956, (U.S.) key WW2 naval strategist.

Horatio H. Kitchener, 1850-1916, (Br.) led forces in Boer War; victorious at Khartoum; organized army in WW1.

Henry Knox, 1750-1806, (U.S.) general in Amer. Rev.; first sec. of war under U.S. Constitution.

Lavrenti Kornilov, 1870-1918, (Russ.) commander-in-chief, 1917; led counter-revolutionary march on Petrograd.

Thaddeus Kosciusko, 1746-1817, (Pol.) aided Amer. Rev.

Walter Krueger, 1881-1967, (U.S.) led Sixth Army in WW2 in Southwest Pacific.

Mikhail Kutuzov, 1745-1813, (Russ.) fought French at Borodino, Napoleonic Wars, 1812; abandoned Moscow; forced French retreat.

Marquis de Lafayette, 1757-1834, (Fr.) fought in, secured French aid for Amer. Rev.

T(homas) E. Lawrence (of Arabia), 1888-1935, (Br.) organized revolt of Arabs against Turks in WW1.

Henry (Light-Horse Harry) Lee, 1756-1818, (U.S.) cavalry officer in Amer. Rev.

Robert E. Lee, 1807-70, (U.S.) Confed. general defeated at Gettysburg, Civil War; surrendered to Grant, 1865.

Curtis LeMay, 1906-90, (U.S.) Air Force commander in WW2, Korean War, and Vietnam War.

Lyman Lemnitzer, 1899-1988, (U.S.) WW2 hero, later general, chairman of Joint Chiefs of Staff.

James Longstreet, 1821-1904, (U.S.) aided Lee at Gettysburg, Civil War.

Maurice, Count of Nassau, 1567-1625, (Dutch) military innovator; led forces in Thirty Years' War.

Douglas MacArthur, 1880-1964, (U.S.) commanded forces in SW Pacific in WW2; headed occupation forces in Japan, 1945-51; UN commander in Korean War.

Erich von Manstein, 1887-1973, (Ger.) served WW1-2, planned inv. of France (1940), convicted of war crimes.

Carl Gustaf Mannerheim, 1867-1951, (Finn.) army officer and pres. of Finland 1944-46.

Francis Marion, 1733-95, (U.S.) led guerrilla actions in South Carolina during Amer. Rev.

Duke of Marlborough, 1650-1722, (Br.) led forces against Louis XIV in War of the Spanish Succession.

George C. Marshall, 1880-1959, (U.S.) chief of staff in WW2; authored Marshall Plan.

George B. McClellan, 1826-85, (U.S.) Union general, commanded Army of the Potomac, 1861-62, Civil War.

George Meade, 1815-72, (U.S.) commanded Union forces at Gettysburg, Civil War.

Billy Mitchell, 1879-1936, (U.S.) WW1 air-power advocate; court-martialed for insubordination, later vindicated.

Helmuth von Moltke, 1800-91, (Ger.) victorious in Austro-Prussian, Franco-Prussian wars.

Louis de Montcalm, 1712-59, (Fr.) headed troops in Canada, French and Indian War; defeated at Quebec, 1759.

Bernard Law Montgomery, 1887-1976, (Br.) stopped German offensive at Alamein, 1942, WW2; helped plan Normandy.

Daniel Morgan, 1736-1802, (U.S.) victorious at Cowpens, 1781, Amer. Rev.

Louis Mountbatten, 1900-79, (Br.) Supreme Allied Commander of SE Asia, 1943-46, WW2.

Joachim Murat, 1767-1815, (Fr.) led cavalry at Marengo, Austerlitz, and Jena, Napoleonic Wars.

Horatio Nelson, 1758-1805, (Br.) naval commander, destroyed French fleet at Trafalgar.

Michel Ney, 1769-1815, (Fr.) commanded forces in Switz., Aust., Russ., Napoleonic Wars; defeated at Waterloo.

Chester Nimitz, 1885-1966, (U.S.) commander of naval forces in Pacific in WW2.

George S. Patton, 1885-1945, (U.S.) led assault on Sicily, 1943, Third Army invasion of Europe, WW2.

Oliver Perry, 1785-1819, (U.S.) won Battle of Lake Erie in War of 1812.

John Pershing, 1860-1948, (U.S.) commanded Mexican border campaign, 1916, Amer. Expeditionary Force, WW1.

Henri Philippe Pétain, 1856-1951, (Fr.) defended Verdun, 1916; headed Vichy government in WW2.

George E. Pickett, 1825-75, (U.S.) Confed. general famed for "charge" at Gettysburg, Civil War.

Charles Portal, 1893-1971, (Br.) chief of staff, Royal Air Force, 1940-45, led in Battle of Britain.

Hyman Rickover, 1900-86, (U.S.) father of nuclear navy.

Matthew Bunker Ridgway, 1895-1993, (U.S.) commanded Allied ground forces in Korean War.

Erwin Rommel, 1891-1944, (Ger.) headed Afrika Korps, WW2.

Gerd von Rundstedt, 1875-1953, (Ger.) supreme commander in West, 1942-45, WW2.

Aleksandr Samsonov, 1859-1914, (Russ.) led invasion of E Prussia, WW1, defeated at Tannenberg, 1914.

Winfield Scott, 1786-1866, (U.S.) hero of War of 1812; headed forces in Mexican War, took Mexico City.

Philip Sheridan, 1831-88, (U.S.) Union cavalry officer, headed Army of the Shenandoah, 1864-65, Civil War.

William T. Sherman, 1820-91, (U.S.) Union general, sacked Atlanta during "march to the sea," 1864, Civil War.

Carl Spaatz, 1891-1974, (U.S.) directed strategic bombing against Germany, later Japan, in WW2.

Raymond Spruance, 1886-1969, (U.S.) victorious at Midway Island, 1942, WW2.

Joseph W. Stilwell, 1883-1946, (U.S.) headed forces in the China, Burma, India theater in WW2.

J.E.B. Stuart, 1833-64, (U.S.) Confed. cavalry commander, Civil War.

Aleksandr Suvorov, 1729-1800, (Rus.) commanded Allied Russian and Austrian armies against Ottoman Turks in Russo-Turkish War.

George H. Thomas, 1816-70, (U.S.) saved Union army at Chattanooga, 1863; won at Nashville, 1864, Civil War.

Semyon Timoshenko, 1895-1970, (USSR) defended Moscow, Stalingrad, WW2; led winter offensive, 1942-43.

Alfred von Tirpitz, 1849-1930, (Ger.) responsible for submarine blockade in WW1.

Sebastien Le Prestre de Vauban, 1633-1707, (Fr.) innovative military engineer and theorist.

Jonathan M. Wainwright, 1883-1953, (U.S.) forced to surrender on Corregidor, 1942, WW2.

George Washington, 1732-99, (U.S.) led Continental army, 1775-83, Amer. Rev.

Archibald Wavell, 1883-1950, (Br.) commanded forces in N and E Africa, and SE Asia in WW2.

Anthony Wayne, 1745-96, (U.S.) captured Stony Point, 1779, Amer. Rev.

Duke of Wellington, 1769-1852, (Br.) defeated Napoleon at Waterloo, 1815.

James Wolfe, 1727-59, (Br.) captured Quebec from French, 1759, French and Indian War.

Isoroku Yamamoto, 1884-1943, (Jpn.) com. in chief of Japanese fleet and naval planner before and during WW2.

Georgi Zhukov, 1895-1974, (Russ.) defended Moscow, 1941, led assault on Berlin, 1945, WW2.

Philosophers and Religious Figures of the Past

Excludes most biblical figires. For Greeks and Romans, see also Historical Figures chapter.

Lyman Abbott, 1835-1922, (U.S.) clergyman, reformer; advocate of Christian Socialism.

Pierre Abelard, 1079-1142, (Fr.) philosopher, theologian, teacher; used dialectic method to support Christian beliefs.

Mortimer Adler, 1902-2001, (U.S.) philosopher, helped create "Great Books" program.

Felix Adler, 1851-1933, (U.S.) German-born founder of the Ethical Culture Society.

(St.) Anselm, c1033-1109, (It.) philosopher-theologian, church leader; "ontological argument" for God's existence.

(St.) Thomas Aquinas, 1225-74, (It.) preeminent medieval philosopher-theologian; *Summa Theologica.*

Aristotle, 384-322 BC, (Gr.) pioneering wide-ranging philosopher, logician, ethician, naturalist.

(St.) Augustine, 354-430, (N Africa) philosopher, theologian, bishop; *Confessions, City of God, On the Trinity.*

J. L. Austin, 1911-60, (Br.) ordinary-language philosopher.

Averroes (Ibn Rushd), 1126-98, (Sp.) Islamic philosopher, physician.

Avicenna (Ibn Sina), 980-1037, (Iran.) Islamic philosopher, scientist.

A(lfred) J(ules) Ayer, 1910-89, (Br.) philosopher; logical positivist; *Language, Truth, and Logic.*

Roger Bacon, c1214-94, (Eng.) philosopher and scientist.

Bahaullah (Mirza Husayn Ali), 1817-92, (Pers.) founder of Baha'i faith.

Karl Barth, 1886-1968, (Swiss) theologian; a leading force in 20th-cent. Protestantism.

Thomas à Becket, 1118-70, (Eng.) archbishop of Canterbury; opposed Henry II; murdered by King's men.

(St.) Benedict, c480-547, (It.) founded the Benedictines.

Jeremy Bentham, 1748-1832, (Br.) philosopher, reformer; enunciated utilitarianism.

Henri Bergson, 1859-1941, (Fr.) philosopher of evolution.

George Berkeley, 1685-1753, (Ir.) idealist philosopher, churchman.

John Biddle, 1615-62, (Eng.) founder of English Unitarianism.

Jakob Boehme, 1575-1624, (Ger.) theosophist and mystic.

Dietrich Bonhoeffer, 1906-1945 (Ger.) Lutheran theologian, pastor; executed as opponent of Nazis.

William Brewster, 1567-1644, (Eng.) headed Pilgrims.

Emil Brunner, 1889-1966, (Swiss) Protestant theologian.

Giordano Bruno, 1548-1600, (It.) philosopher, pantheist.

Martin Buber, 1878-1965, (Ger.) Jewish philosopher, theologian; *I and Thou.*

Buddha (Siddhartha Gautama), c563-c483 BC, (Indian) philosopher; founded Buddhism.

John Calvin, 1509-64, (Fr.) theologian; a key figure in the Protestant Reformation.

Rudolph Carnap, 1891-1970, (U.S.) German-born analytic philosopher; a founder of logical positivism.

William Ellery Channing, 1780-1842, (U.S.) clergyman; early spokesman for Unitarianism.

Auguste Comte, 1798-1857, (Fr.) philosopher; originated positivism.

Confucius, 551-479 BC, (Chin.) founder of Confucianism.

John Cotton, 1584-1652, (Eng.) Puritan theologian.

Thomas Cranmer, 1489-1556, (Eng.) churchman; wrote much of *Book of Common Prayer.*

René Descartes, 1596-1650, (Fr.) philosopher, mathematician; "father of modern philosophy." *Discourse on Method, Meditations on First Philosophy.*

John Dewey, 1859-1952, (U.S.) philosopher, educator; instrumentalist theory of knowledge; helped inaugurate progressive education movement.

Denis Diderot, 1713-84, (Fr.) philosopher, encyclopedist.

John Duns Scotus, c1266-1308, (Sc.) Franciscan philosopher and theologian.

Mary Baker Eddy, 1821-1910, (U.S.) founder of Christian Science; *Science and Health.*

Jonathan Edwards, 1703-58, (U.S.) preacher, theologian; "Sinners in the Hands of an Angry God."

(Desiderius) Erasmus, c1466-1536, (Dutch) Renaissance humanist; *On the Freedom of the Will.*

Johann Fichte, 1762-1814, (Ger.) idealist philosopher.

Michel Foucault, 1926-84, (Fr.) structuralist philosopher, historian.

George Fox, 1624-91, (Br.) founder of Society of Friends.

(St.) Francis of Assisi, 1182-1226, (It.) founded Franciscans.

al-Ghazali, 1058-1111, Islamic philosopher.

Georg W. F. Hegel, 1770-1831, (Ger.) idealist philosopher; *Phenomenology of Mind.*

Martin Heidegger, 1889-1976, (Ger.) existentialist philosopher; affected many fields; *Being and Time.*

Johann G. Herder, 1744-1803, (Ger.) philosopher, cultural historian; a founder of German Romanticism.

Thomas Hobbes, 1588-1679, (Eng.) philosopher, political theorist; *Leviathan.*

David Hume, 1711-76, (Sc.) empiricist philosopher; *Enquiry Concerning Human Understanding.*

Jan Hus, 1369-1415, (Czech.) religious reformer.

Edmund Husserl, 1859-1938, (Ger.) philosopher; founded the phenomenological movement.

Thomas Huxley, 1825-95, (Br.) philosopher, educator.

William Inge, 1860-1954, (Br.) theologian; explored mystic aspects of Christianity.

William James, 1842-1910, (U.S.) philosopher, psychologist; pragmatist; studied religious experience.

Karl Jaspers, 1883-1969, (Ger.) existentialist philosopher.

Joan of Arc, 1412-1431, (Fr.) national heroine and a patron saint of France; key figure in the Hundred Years' War.

Immanuel Kant, 1724-1804, (Ger.) philosopher; founder of modern critical philosophy; *Critique of Pure Reason.*

Thomas à Kempis, c1380-1471, (Ger.) monk, devotional writer; *Imitation of Christ,* attributed to him.

Soren Kierkegaard, 1813-55, (Dan.) religious philosopher; pre-existentialist; *Either/Or, The Sickness Unto Death.*

John Knox, 1505-72, (Sc.) leader of the Protestant Reformation in Scotland.

Lao-Tzu, 604-531 BC, (Chin.) philosopher; considered the founder of the Taoist religion.

Gottfried von Leibniz, 1646-1716, (Ger.) rationalistic philosopher, logician, mathematician.

John Locke, 1632-1704, (Eng.) political theorist, empiricist philosopher; *Essay Concerning Human Understanding.*

(St.) Ignatius Loyola, 1491-1556, (Sp.) founder of the Jesuits; *Spiritual Exercises.*

Martin Luther, 1483-1546, (Ger.) leader of the Protestant Reformation, founded Lutheran church.

Jean-Francois Lyotard, 1924-98, (Fr.) postmodern philosopher, lecturer; *The Post-Modern Condition.*

Maimonides, 1135-1204, (Sp.) major Jewish philosopher.

Gabriel Marcel, 1889-1973, (Fr.) Roman Catholic existentialist philosopher, dramatist, and critic.

Jacques Maritain, 1882-1973, (Fr.) Neo-Thomist philosopher.

Cotton Mather, 1663-1728, (U.S.) defender of orthodox Puritanism; founded Yale, 1701.

Philipp Melanchthon, 1497-1560, (Ger.) theologian, humanist; an important voice in the Reformation.

Maurice Merleau-Ponty, 1908-61, (Fr.) existentialist philosopher; *Phenomenology of Perception.*

Thomas Merton, 1915-68, (U.S.) Trappist monk, spiritual writer; *The Seven Storey Mountain.*

John Stuart Mill, 1806-73, (Br.) philosopher, economist; libertarian political theorist; *Utilitarianism.*

Muhammad, c570-632, (Arab) the prophet of Islam.

Dwight Moody, 1837-99, (U.S.) evangelist.

G(eorge) E(dward) Moore, 1873-1958, (Br.) philosopher; *Principia Ethica,* "A Defense of Common Sense."

Elijah Muhammad, 1897-1975, (U.S.) leader of the Black Muslim sect.

Heinrich Muhlenberg, 1711-87, (Ger.) organized the Lutheran Church in America.

John H. Newman, 1801-90, (Br.) Roman Catholic convert, cardinal; led Oxford Movement; *Apologia pro Vita Sua.*

Reinhold Niebuhr, 1892-1971, (U.S.) Protestant theologian.

Richard Niebuhr, 1894-1962 (U.S.) Protestant theologian.

Friedrich Nietzsche, 1844-1900, (Ger.) philosopher; *The Birth of Tragedy, Beyond Good and Evil, Thus Spake Zarathustra.*

Robert Nozick, 1938-2002, (U.S.) political philosopher; *Anarchy, State, and Utopia.*

Blaise Pascal, 1623-62, (Fr.) philosopher, mathematician; *Pensées.*

(St.) Patrick, c389-c461, (Br.) brought Christianity to Ireland.

(St.) Paul, ?-c67, a key proponent of Christianity; his epistles are first Christian theological writing.

Norman Vincent Peale, 1898-1993, (U.S.) minister, author; *The Power of Positive Thinking.*

C(harles) S. Peirce, 1839-1914, (U.S.) philosopher, logician; originated concept of pragmatism, 1878.

Plato, c428-347 BC, (Gr.) philosopher; wrote classic Socratic dialogues; argued for universal truths and independent reality of ideas or forms; *Republic.*

Plotinus, 205-70, (Rom.) a founder of neo-Platonism; *Enneads.*

W(illard) V(an) O(rman) Quine, 1908-2001, (U.S.) philosopher, logician; "On What There Is."

John Rawls, 1922-2002, (U.S.) politcial philosopher; A Theory of Justice (1971).

Josiah Royce, 1855-1916, (U.S.) idealist philosopher

Bertrand Russell, 1872-1970, (Br.) philosopher, logician; one of the founders of modern logic; a prolific popular writer.

Charles T. Russell, 1852-1916, (U.S.) founder of Jehovah's Witnesses.

Gilbert Ryle, 1900-76, (Br.) analytic philosopher; *The Concept of Mind.*

George Santayana, 1863-1952, (U.S.) philosopher, writer, critic; *The Sense of Beauty, The Realms of Being.*

Jean-Paul Sartre, 1905-80, (Fr.) philosopher, novelist, playwright. *Nausea, No Exit, Being and Nothingness.*

Friedrich von Schelling, 1775-1854, (Ger.) philosopher of romantic movement.

Friedrich Schleiermacher, 1768-1834, (Ger.) theologian; a founder of modern Protestant theology.

Arthur Schopenhauer, 1788-1860, (Ger.) philosopher; *The World as Will and Idea.*

Albert Schweitzer, 1875-1965, (Ger.) theologian, social philosopher, medical missionary.

Joseph Smith, 1805-44, (U.S.) founded Latter-Day Saints (Mormon) movement, 1830.

Socrates, 469-399 BC, (Gr.) influential philosopher immortalized by Plato.

Herbert Spencer, 1820-1903, (Br.) philosopher of evolution.

Baruch de Spinoza, 1632-77, (Dutch) rationalist philosopher; *Ethics.*

Billy Sunday, 1862-1935, (U.S.) evangelist.

Pierre Teilhard de Chardin, 1881-1955, (Fr.) Jesuit priest, paleontologist, philosopher-theologian; *The Divine Milieu.*

Daisetz Teitaro Suzuki, 1870-1966, (Jpn.) Buddhist scholar.

(St.) Theresa of Lisieux, 1873-97. (Fr.) Carmelite nun revered for everyday sanctity; *The Story of a Soul.*

Emanuel Swedenborg, 1688-1772, (Swed.) philosopher, mystic.

Paul Tillich, 1886-1965, (U.S.) German-born philosopher and theologian; brought depth psychology to Protestantism.

John Wesley, 1703-91, (Br.) theologian, evangelist; founded Methodism.

Alfred North Whitehead, 1861-1947, (Br.) philosopher, mathematician; *Process and Reality.*

William of Occam, c1285-c1349 (Eng.) medieval scholastic philosopher; nominalist.

Roger Williams, c1603-83, (U.S.) clergyman; championed religious freedom and separation of church and state.

Ludwig Wittgenstein, 1889-1951, (Austrian) philosopher; major influence on contemporary language philosophy; *Tractatus Logico-Philosophicus, Philosophical Investigations.*

John Woolman, 1720-72, (U.S.) Quaker social reformer, abolitionist, writer; *The Journal.*

John Wycliffe, 1320-84, (Eng.) theologian, reformer.

(St.) Francis Xavier, 1506-52, (Sp.) Jesuit missionary, "Apostle of the Indies."

Brigham Young, 1801-77, (U.S.) Mormon leader after Smith's assassination; colonized Utah.

Huldrych Zwingli, 1484-1531, (Swiss) theologian; led Swiss Protestant Reformation.

Political Leaders of the Past

(U.S. presidents, vice presidents, Supreme Ct. justices, signers of Decl. of Indep. ; listed elsewhere.)

Abu Bakr, 573-634, Muslim leader, first caliph, chosen successor to Muhammad.

Dean Acheson, 1893-1971, (U.S.) sec. of state; architect of cold war foreign policy.

Samuel Adams, 1722-1803, (U.S.) patriot, Boston Tea Party firebrand.

Konrad Adenauer, 1876-1967, (Ger.) first West German chancellor.

Emilio Aguinaldo, 1869-1964, (Philip.) revolutionary; fought against Spain and the U.S.

Akbar, 1542-1605, greatest Mogul emperor of India.

Carl Albert, 1908-2000 (U.S.) House rep. from OK, Speaker, 1971-76.

Salvador Allende Gossens, 1908-1973, (Chilean) Marxist pres. 1970-73; ousted and died in coup.

Idi Amin, 1925-2003 (Uganda), Ugandan ruler from 1971 to 1979, blamed for hundreds of thousands of deaths.

Hafez al Assad, 1930-2000 (Syr.), Syrian ruler from 1970.

Herbert H. Asquith, 1852-1928, (Br.) liberal prime min.; instituted major social reform.

Atahualpa, ?-1533, Inca (ruling chief) of Peru.

Kemal Ataturk, 1881-1938, (Turk.) founded modern Turkey.

Clement Attlee, 1883-1967, (Br.) Labour party leader, prime min.; enacted natl. health, nationalized many industries.

Stephen F. Austin, 1793-1836, (U.S.) led Texas colonization.

Mikhail Bakunin, 1814-76, (Rus.) revolutionary; leading exponent of anarchism.

Arthur J. Balfour, 1848-1930, (Br.) foreign sec. under Lloyd George; issued Balfour Declaration backing Zionism.

Bernard M. Baruch, 1870-1965, (U.S.) financier, govt. adviser.

Fulgencio Batista y Zaldívar, 1901-73, (Cub.) Cuban pres. (1940-44, 1952-59), overthrown by Castro.

Lord Beaverbrook, 1879-1964, (Br.) financier, statesman, newspaper owner.

Menachem Begin, 1913-92, (Isr.) Israeli prime min., shared 1978 Nobel Peace Prize.

Eduard Benes, 1884-1948, (Czech.) pres. during interwar and post-WW2 eras.

David Ben-Gurion, 1886-1973, (Isr.) first prime min. of Israel, 1948-53, 1955-63.

Thomas Hart Benton, 1782-1858, (U.S.) Missouri senator; championed agrarian interests and westward expansion.

Aneurin Bevan, 1897-1960, (Br.) Labour party leader.

Ernest Bevin, 1881-1951, (Br.) Labour party leader, foreign minister; helped lay foundation for NATO.

Otto von Bismarck, 1815-98, (Ger.) statesman known as the Iron Chancellor; uniter of Germany, 1870.

James G. Blaine, 1830-93, (U.S.) Republican politician, diplomat; influential in Pan-American movement.

Léon Blum, 1872-1950, (Fr.) socialist leader, writer; headed first Popular Front government.

Simón Bolívar, 1783-1830, (Venez.) S. Amer. Revolutionary who liberated much of the continent from Spanish rule.

William E. Borah, 1865-1940, (U.S.) isolationist senator; helped block U.S. membership in League of Nations.

Cesare Borgia, 1476-1507, (It.) soldier, politician; an outstanding figure of the Italian Renaissance.

Willy Brandt, 1913-92, (Ger.) statesman, chancellor of West Germany, 1969-74; promoted East/West peace, *Ostpolitik.*

Leonid Brezhnev, 1906-82, (USSR) Soviet leader, 1964-82.

Aristide Briand, 1862-1932, (Fr.) foreign min.; chief architect of Locarno Pact and anti-war Kellogg-Briand Pact.

William Jennings Bryan, 1860-1925, (U.S.) Democratic, populist leader, orator; 3 times lost race for presidency.

Ralph Bunche, 1904-71, (U.S.) a founder and key diplomat of United Nations for more than 20 years.

John C. Calhoun, 1782-1850, (U.S.) political leader; champion of states' rights and a symbol of the Old South.

Robert Castlereagh, 1769-1822, (Br.) foreign sec.; guided Grand Alliance against Napoleon.

Camillo Benso Cavour, 1810-61, (It.) statesman; largely responsible for uniting Italy under the House of Savoy.

Nicolae Ceausescu, 1918-89, (Roman.) Communist leader, head of state 1967-89; executed.

Austen Chamberlain, 1863-1937, (Br.) statesman; helped finalize Locarno Treaties, both 1925.

Neville Chamberlain, 1869-1940, (Br.) Conservative prime min. whose appeasement of Hitler led to Munich Pact.

Chiang Kai-shek, 1887-1975, (Chin.) Nationalist Chinese pres. whose government was driven from mainland to Taiwan.

Winston Churchill, 1874-1965, (Br.) prime min., soldier, author; guided Britain through WW2.

Galeazzo Ciano, 1903-44, (It.) fascist foreign minister; helped create Rome-Berlin Axis, executed by Mussolini.

Henry Clay, 1777-1852, (U.S.) "The Great Compromiser," one of the most influential pre-Civil War political leaders.

Georges Clemenceau, 1841-1929, (Fr.) twice prem., Wilson's antagonist at Paris Peace Conference after WW1.

DeWitt Clinton, 1769-1828, (U.S.) political leader; responsible for promoting idea of the Erie Canal.

Robert Clive, 1725-74, (Br.) first administrator of Bengal; laid foundation for British Empire in India.

Jean Baptiste Colbert, 1619-83, (Fr.) statesman; influential under Louis XIV, created the French navy.

Bettino Craxi, 1934-2000, (It.) Italy's first post-WWII Socialist premier.

Oliver Cromwell, 1599-1658, (Br.) Lord Protector of England, led parliamentary forces during Civil War.

Curzon of Kedleston, 1859-1925, (Br.) viceroy of India, foreign sec.; major force in post-WW1 world.

Édouard Daladier, 1884-1970, (Fr.) Radical Socialist politician, arrested by Vichy, interned by Germans until 1945.

Richard J. Daley, 1902-1976, (U.S.) Chicago mayor.

Georges Danton, 1759-94, (Fr.) leading French Rev. figure.

Jefferson Davis, 1808-89, (U.S.) pres. of the Confederacy.

Charles G. Dawes, 1865-1951, (U.S.) statesman, banker; advanced plan to stabilize post-WW1 German finances.

Alcide De Gasperi, 1881-1954, (It.) prime min.; founder of Christian Democratic party.

Charles De Gaulle, 1890-1970, (Fr.) general, statesman; first pres. of the Fifth Republic.

Deng Xiaoping, 1904-97, (Chin.) "paramount leader" of China; backed economic modernization.

Eamon De Valera, 1882-1975, (Ir.-U.S.) statesman; led fight for Irish independence.

Thomas E. Dewey, 1902-71, (U.S.) NY governor; twice loser in try for presidency.

Ngo Dinh Diem, 1901-63, (Viet.) South Vietnamese pres.; assassinated in government takeover.

Everett M. Dirksen, 1896-1969, (U.S.) Senate Republican minority leader, orator.

Benjamin Disraeli, 1804-81, (Br.) prime min.; considered founder of modern Conservative party.

Engelbert Dollfuss, 1892-1934, (Austrian) chancellor; assassinated by Austrian Nazis.

Andrea Doria, 1466-1560, (It.) Genoese admiral, statesman; called "Father of Peace" and "Liberator of Genoa."

Stephen A. Douglas, 1813-61, (U.S.) Democratic leader, orator; opposed Lincoln for the presidency.

Alexander Dubcek, 1921-92, (Czech.) statesman whose attempted liberalization was crushed, 1968.

John Foster Dulles, 1888-1959, (U.S.) sec. of state under Eisenhower, cold war policy-maker.

Abba Eban, 1915-2002, (Isr.) diplomat, foreign minister 1966-74.

Friedrich Ebert, 1871-1925, (Ger.) Social Democratic movement leader; 1st pres., Weimar Republic, 1919-25.

Sir Anthony Eden, 1897-1977, (Br.) foreign sec., prime min. during Suez invasion of 1956.

Ludwig Erhard, 1897-1977, (Ger.) economist, West German chancellor; led nation's economic rise after WW2.

Amintore Fanfani, 1908-99, (It.) six-time premier of Italy.

Joao Baptista de Figueiredo, 1918-99, (Braz.) president of Brazil, restored the nation's democracy.

Hamilton Fish, 1808-93, (U.S.) sec. of state, successfully mediated disputes with Great Britain, Latin America.

James V. Forrestal, 1892-1949, (U.S.) sec. of navy, first sec. of defense.

Francisco Franco, 1892-1975, (Sp.) leader of rebel forces during Spanish Civil War and longtime ruler of Spain.

Benjamin Franklin, 1706-90, (U.S.) printer, publisher, author, inventor, scientist, diplomat.

Louis de Frontenac, 1620-98, (Fr.) governor of New France (Canada); encouraged explorations, fought Iroquois.

J. William Fulbright, 1905-95, (U.S.) U.S. senator; leading figure in U.S. foreign policy during cold war years.

Hugh Gaitskell, 1906-63, (Br.) Labour party leader; major force in reversing its stand for unilateral disarmament.

Albert Gallatin, 1761-1849, (U.S.) sec. of treasury; instrumental in negotiating end of War of 1812.

Léon Gambetta, 1838-82, (Fr.) statesman, politician; one of the founders of the Third Republic.

Indira Gandhi, 1917-84, (In.) daughter of Jawaharlal Nehru, prime min. of India, 1966-77, 1980-84; assassinated.

Mohandas K. Gandhi, 1869-1948, (In.) political leader, ascetic; led movement against British rule; assassinated.

Giuseppe Garibaldi, 1807-82, (It.) patriot, soldier; a leader in the Risorgimento, Italian unification movement.

William E. Gladstone, 1809-98, (Br.) prime min. 4 times; dominant force of Liberal party from 1868 to 1894.

Paul Joseph Goebbels, 1897-1945, (Ger.) Nazi propagandist, master of mass psychology.

Barry Goldwater, 1909-98 (U.S.) conservative U.S. senator and 1964 Republican presid. nominee.

Klement Gottwald, 1896-1953, (Czech.) Communist leader; ushered Communism into his country.

Alexander Hamilton, 1755-1804, (U.S.) first treasury sec.; champion of strong central government.

Dag Hammarskjold, 1905-61, (Swed.) statesman; UN sec.-general.

Hassan II, King, 1929-99, (Moroc.) ruler of Morocco,1962-99.

John Hay, 1838-1905, (U.S.) sec. of state; primarily associated with Open Door Policy toward China.

Patrick Henry, 1736-99, (U.S.) major revolutionary figure, remarkable orator.

Édouard Herriot, 1872-1957, (Fr.) Radical Socialist leader; twice prem., pres. of National Assembly.

Theodor Herzl, 1860-1904, (Hung.) founded modern Zionism.

Heinrich Himmler, 1900-45, (Ger.) head of Nazi SS and Gestapo.

Paul von Hindenburg, 1847-1934, (Ger.) field marshal, WW1; 2nd pres. of Weimar Republic, 1925-34.

Adolf Hitler, 1889-1945, (Ger.) dictator; built Nazism, launched WW2, presided over the Holocaust.

Ho Chi Minh, 1890-1969, (Viet.) N Vietnamese pres., Vietnamese Communist leader.

Harry L. Hopkins, 1890-1946, (U.S.) New Deal administrator; closest adviser to FDR during WW2.

Edward M. House, 1858-1938, (U.S.) diplomat; confidential adviser to Woodrow Wilson.

Samuel Houston, 1793-1863, (U.S.) leader of struggle to win control of Texas from Mexico.

Cordell Hull, 1871-1955, (U.S.) sec. of state, 1933-44; initiated reciprocal trade to lower tariffs, helped organize UN.

Hubert H. Humphrey, 1911-78, (U.S.) Minnesota Democrat; senator; vice pres., pres. candidate.

Hussein, King, 1935-99 (Jordan), peacemaker; ruler of Jordan, 1952-99.

Jinnah, Muhammad Ali, 1876-1948, (Pak.) founder, first governor-general of Pakistan.

Benito Juarez, 1806-72, (Mex.) rallied his country against foreign threats, sought to create democratic, federal republic.

Constantine Karamanlis, 1907-98, (Gr.) Greek prime min. (1955-63, 1974-80); restored democracy; later president.

Frank B. Kellogg, 1856-1937, (U.S.) sec. of state; negotiated Kellogg-Briand Pact to outlaw war.

Robert F. Kennedy, 1925-68, (U.S.) attorney general, senator; assassinated while seeking presidency.

Aleksandr Kerensky, 1881-1970, (Russ.) headed provisional government after Feb. 1917 revolution.

Ayatollah Ruhollah Khomeini, 1900-89, (Iranian), religious-political leader, spearheaded overthrow of shah, 1979.

Nikita Khrushchev, 1894-1971, (USSR) prem., first sec. of Communist party; initiated de-Stalinization.

Kim Il Sung, 1912-94, (Korean) N Korean dictator, 1948-94.

Lajos Kossuth, 1802-94, (Hung.) principal figure in 1848 Hungarian revolution.

Pyotr Kropotkin, 1842-1921, (Russ.) anarchist; championed the peasants but opposed Bolshevism.

Kublai Khan, c1215-94, Mongol emperor; founder of Yüan dynasty in China.

Béla Kun, 1886-c1939, (Hung.) member of 3d Communist Internat.; tried to foment worldwide revolution.

Robert M. LaFollette, 1855-1925, (U.S.) Wisconsin public official; leader of progressive movement.

Fiorello La Guardia, 1882-1947, (U.S.) colorful NYC reform mayor.

Pierre Laval, 1883-1945, (Fr.) politician, Vichy foreign min.; executed for treason.

Andrew Bonar Law, 1858-1923, (Br.) Conservative party politician; led opposition to Irish home rule.

Vladimir Ilyich Lenin (Ulyanov), 1870-1924, (Russ.) revolutionary; founded Bolshevism; Soviet leader 1917-24.

Ferdinand de Lesseps, 1805-94, (Fr.) diplomat, engineer; conceived idea of Suez Canal.

Rene Levesque, 1922-87, (Can.) prem. of Quebec, 1976-85; led unsuccessful separatist campaign.

Maxim Litvinov, 1876-1951, (Pol.-Russ.) revolutionary, commissar of foreign affairs; favored cooperation with West.

Liu Shaoqi, c1898-1974, (Chin.) Communist leader; fell from grace during Cultural Revolution.

David Lloyd George, 1863-1945, (Br.) Liberal party prime min.; laid foundations for modern welfare state.

Henry Cabot Lodge, 1850-1924, (U.S.) Republican senator; led opposition to participation in League of Nations.

Huey P. Long, 1893-1935, (U.S.) Louisiana political demagogue, governor; assassinated.

Rosa Luxemburg, 1871-1919, (Ger.) revolutionary; leader of the German Social Democratic party and Spartacus party.

J. Ramsay MacDonald, 1866-1937, (Br.) first Labour party prime min. of Great Britain.

Harold Macmillan, 1895-1986, (Br.) prime min. of Great Britain, 1957-63.

Joseph R. McCarthy, 1908-57, (U.S.) senator, extremist in searching out alleged Communists and pro-Communists.

Makarios III, 1913-77, (Cypriot) Greek Orthodox archbishop; first pres. of Cyprus.

Mao Zedong, 1893-1976, (Chin.) chief Chinese Marxist theorist, revolutionary, political leader; led Chinese revolution establishing his nation as Communist state.

Jean Paul Marat, 1743-93, (Fr.) revolutionary, politician; identified with radical Jacobins; assassinated.

José Martí, 1853-95, (Cub.) patriot, poet; leader of Cuban struggle for independence.

Jan Masaryk, 1886-1948, (Czech.) foreign min.; died by mysterious alleged suicide following Communist coup.

Thomas G. Masaryk, 1850-1937, (Czech.) statesman, philosopher; first pres. of Czechoslovak Republic.

Jules Mazarin, 1602-61, (Fr.) cardinal, statesman; prime min. under Louis XIII and queen regent Anne of Austria.

Giuseppe Mazzini, 1805-72, (It.) reformer dedicated to Risorgimento movement for renewal of Italy.

Tom Mboya, 1930-69, (Kenyan) political leader; instrumental in securing independence for Kenya.

Cosimo I de' Medici, 1519-74, (It.) Duke of Florence, grand duke of Tuscany.

Lorenzo de' Medici, the Magnificent, 1449-92, (It.) merchant prince; a towering figure in Italian Renaissance.

Catherine de Médicis, 1519-89, (Fr.) queen consort of Henry II, regent of France; influential in Catholic-Huguenot wars.

Golda Meir, 1898-1978, (Isr.) a founder of the state of Israel and prime min., 1969-74.

Klemens W. N. L. Metternich, 1773-1859, (Austrian) statesman; arbiter of post-Napoleonic Europe.

François Mitterrand, 1916-96, (Fr.) pres. of France, 1981-95.

Mobutu Sese Seko, 1930-97, (Zaire) longtime ruler of Zaire (now Congo) (1965-97); exiled after rebellion.

Guy Mollet, 1905-75, (Fr.) socialist politician, resistance leader.

Henry Morgenthau Jr., 1891-1967, (U.S.) sec. of treasury; fundraiser for New Deal and U.S. WW2 activities.

Gouverneur Morris, 1752-1816, (U.S.) statesman, diplomat. financial expert, helped plan decimal coinage.

Daniel Patrick Moynihan 1927-2003, (U.S.) senator, diplomat, social scientist and author.

Benito Mussolini, 1883-1945, (It.) leader of the Italian fascist state; assassinated.

Imre Nagy, c1896-1958, (Hung.) Communist prem.; assassinated after Soviets crushed 1956 uprising.

Gamal Abdel Nasser, 1918-70, (Egypt) leader of Arab unification, 2nd Egyptian pres.

Jawaharlal Nehru, 1889-1964, (In.) prime min.; guided India through its early years of independence.

Kwame Nkrumah, 1909-72, (Ghan.) 1st prime min., 1957-60, and pres., 1960-66, of Ghana.

Frederick North, 1732-92, (Br.) prime min.; his inept policies led to loss of American colonies.

Daniel O'Connell, 1775-1847, (Ir.) political leader; known as The Liberator.

Julius K. Nyerere, 1923?-99, (Tanz.) founding father, 1st pres., 1962-85, of Tanzania.

Omar, c581-644, Muslim leader; 2nd caliph, led Islam to become an imperial power.

Thomas P. (Tip) O'Neill Jr., 1912-94, (U.S.) U.S. congressman, Speaker of the House, 1977-86.

Ignace Paderewski, 1860-1941, (Pol.) statesman, pianist; composer, briefly prime min., an ardent patriot.

Viscount Palmerston, 1784-1865, (Br.) Whig-Liberal prime min., foreign min.; embodied British nationalism.

Andreas George Papandreou, 1919-1996, (Gk.) leftist politician; served 2 times as prem. (1981-89, 1993-96).

Georgios Papandreou, 1888-1968, (Gk.) Republican politician; served 3 times as prime min.

Franz von Papen, 1879-1969, (Ger.) politician; major role in overthrow of Weimar Republic and rise of Hitler.

Charles Stewart Parnell, 1846-1891, (Ir.) nationalist leader; "uncrowned king of Ireland."

Lester Pearson, 1897-1972, (Can.) diplomat, Liberal party leader, prime min.

Robert Peel, 1788-1850, (Br.) reformist prime min., founder of Conservative party.

Eva (Evita) Perón, 1919-52 (Arg.) highly influential 2nd wife of Juan Perón.

Juan Perón, 1895-1974, (Arg.) dynamic pres. of Argentina (1946-55, 1973-74).

Joseph Pilsudski, 1867-1935, (Pol.) statesman; instrumental in reestablishing Polish state in the 20th cent.

Charles Pinckney, 1757-1824, (U.S.) founding father; his Pinckney plan largely incorporated into Constitution.

Christian Pineau, 1905-95, (Fr.) leader of French Resistance during WW2; French foreign min., 1956-58.

William Pitt, the Elder, 1708-78, (Br.) statesman; the "Great Commoner," transformed Britain into imperial power.

William Pitt, the Younger, 1759-1806, (Br.) prime min. during French Revolutionary wars.

Georgi Plekhanov, 1857-1918, (Russ.) revolutionary, social philosopher; called "father of Russian Marxism."

Raymond Poincaré, 1860-1934, (Fr.) 9th pres. of the Republic; advocated harsh punishment of Germany after WW1.

Pol Pot, 1925-98, (Camb.) leader of Khmer Rouge; ruled Cambodia, 1975-79; responsible for mass deaths.

Georges Pompidou, 1911-74, (Fr.) Gaullist political leader; pres. 1969-74.

Grigori Potemkin, 1739-91, (Russ.) field marshal; favorite of Catherine II.

Yitzhak Rabin, 1922-95, (Isr.) military, political leader; prime min. of Israel, 1974-77, 1992-95; assassinated.

Edmund Randolph, 1753-1813, (U.S.) attorney; prominent in drafting, ratification of constitution.

John Randolph, 1773-1833, (U.S.) Southern planter; strong advocate of states' rights.

Jeannette Rankin, 1880-1973, (U.S.) pacifist; first woman member of U.S. Congress.

Walter Rathenau, 1867-1922, (Ger.) industrialist, statesman.

Sam Rayburn, 1882-1961, (U.S.) Democratic leader; representative for 47 years, House Speaker for 17.

Paul Reynaud, 1878-1966, (Fr.) statesman; prem. in 1940 at the time of France's defeat by Germany.

Syngman Rhee, 1875-1965, (Korean) first pres. of S Korea.

Cecil Rhodes, 1853-1902, (Br.) imperialist, industrial magnate; established Rhodes scholarships in his will.

Cardinal de Richelieu, 1585-1642, (Fr.) statesman, known as "red eminence;" chief minister to Louis XIII.

Maximilien Robespierre, 1758-94, (Fr.) leading figure in French Revolution and Reign of Terror.

Nelson Rockefeller, 1908-79, (U.S.) Republican governor of NY, 1959-73; U.S. vice pres., 1974-77.

George W. Romney, 1907-95, (U.S.) auto exec.; 3-term Republican governor of Michigan.

Eleanor Roosevelt, 1884-1962, (U.S.) influential First Lady, humanitarian, UN diplomat.

Elihu Root, 1845-1937, (U.S.) lawyer, statesman, diplomat; leading Republican supporter of the League of Nations.

Dean Rusk, 1909-95, (U.S.) statesman; sec. of state, 1961-69.

John Russell, 1792-1878, (Br.) Liberal prime min. during the Irish potato famine.

Anwar al-Sadat, 1918-81, (Egypt.) pres., 1970-1981; promoted peace with Israel; Nobel laureate; assassinated.

António de Oliveira Salazar, 1889-1970, (Port.) longtime dictator.

José de San Martin, 1778-1850, S Amer. revolutionary; protector of Peru.

Eisaku Sato, 1901-75, (Jpn.) prime min.; presided over Japan's post-WW2 emergence as major world power.

Abdul Aziz Ibn Saud, c1880-1953, (Saudi Arabia) king of Saudi Arabia, 1932-53.

Robert Schuman, 1886-1963, (Fr.) statesman; founded European Coal and Steel Community.

Carl Schurz, 1829-1906, (U.S.) German-American political leader, journalist, orator, dedicated reformer.

Kurt Schuschnigg, 1897-1977, (Austrian) chancellor; unsuccessful in stopping Austria's annexation by Germany.

William H. Seward, 1801-72, (U.S.) anti-slavery activist; as U.S. sec. of state purchased Alaska.

Carlo Sforza, 1872-1952, (It.) foreign min., anti-fascist.

Sitting Bull, c1831-90, (Nat. Am.) Sioux leader in Battle of Little Bighorn over George A. Custer, 1876.

Alfred E. Smith, 1873-1944, (U.S.) NY Democratic governor; first Roman Catholic to run for presidency.

Margaret Chase Smith, 1897-1995, (U.S.) congresswoman, senator; 1st woman elected to both houses of Congress.

Jan C. Smuts, 1870-1950, (S. African) statesman, philosopher, soldier, prime min.

Paul Henri Spaak, 1899-1972, (Belg.) statesman, socialist leader.

Joseph Stalin, 1879-1953, (USSR) Soviet dictator, 1924-53; instituted forced collectivization, massive purges, and labor camps, causing millions of deaths.

Edwin M. Stanton, 1814-69, (U.S.) sec. of war, 1862-68.

Edward R. Stettinius Jr., 1900-49, (U.S.) industrialist, sec. of state who coordinated aid to WW2 allies.

Adlai E. Stevenson, 1900-65, (U.S.) Democratic leader, diplomat, Illinois governor, presidential candidate.

Henry L. Stimson, 1867-1950, (U.S.) statesman; served in 5 administrations, foreign policy adviser in 30s and 40s.

Gustav Stresemann, 1878-1929, (Ger.) chancellor, foreign minister; strove to regain friendship for post-WW1 Germany.

Sukarno, 1901-70, (Indon.) dictatorial first pres. of the Indonesian republic.

Sun Yat-sen, 1866-1925, (Chin.) revolutionary; leader of Kuomintang, regarded as the father of modern China.

Robert A. Taft, 1889-1953, (U.S.) conservative Senate leader, called "Mr. Republican."

Charles de Talleyrand, 1754-1838, (Fr.) statesman, diplomat; the major force of the Congress of Vienna of 1814-15.

U Thant, 1909-74 (Bur.) statesman, UN sec.-general.

Norman M. Thomas, 1884-1968, (U.S.) social reformer; 6 times Socialist party presidential candidate.

Josip Broz Tito, 1892-1980, (Yug.) pres. of Yugoslavia from 1953, WW2 guerrilla chief, postwar rival of Stalin.

Palmiro Togliatti, 1893-1964, (It.) major Italian Communist leader.

Hideki Tojo, 1885-1948, (Jpn.) statesman, soldier; prime min. during most of WW2.

François Toussaint L'Ouverture, c1744-1803, (Haitian) patriot, martyr; thwarted French colonial aims.

Leon Trotsky, 1879-1940, (Russ.) revolutionary, founded Red Army, expelled from party in conflict with Stalin; assassinated.

Pierre Elliott Trudeau, 1919-2000, (Can.) longtime liberal prime minister of Canada, 1968-79, 1980-84; achieved native Canadian constitution.

Rafael L. Trujillo Molina, 1891-1961, (Dom.) dictator of Dominican Republic, 1930-61; assassinated.

Moise K. Tshombe, 1919-69, (Cong.) pres. of secessionist Katanga, prem. of Congo.

William M. Tweed, 1823-78, (U.S.) politician boss of Tammany Hall, NYC's Democratic political machine.

Walter Ulbricht, 1893-1973, (Ger.) Communist leader of German Democratic Republic.

Arthur H. Vandenberg, 1884-1951, (U.S.) senator; proponent of bipartisan anti-Communist foreign policy.

Eleutherios Venizelos, 1864-1936, (Gk.) most prominent Greek statesman of early 20th cent.

Hendrik F. Verwoerd, 1901-66, (S. African) prime min.; rigorously applied apartheid policy despite protest.

George Wallace, 1919-98, (U.S.) former segregationist governor of Alabama and presid. candidate.

Robert Walpole, 1676-1745, (Br.) statesman; generally considered Britain's first prime min.

Daniel Webster, 1782-1852, (U.S.) orator, politician; advocate of business interests during Jacksonian agrarianism.

Chaim Weizmann, 1874-1952, (Russ.-Isr.) Zionist leader, scientist; first Israeli pres.

Wendell L. Willkie, 1892-1944, (U.S.) Republican who tried to unseat FDR when he ran for his 3d term.

Harold Wilson, 1916-95, (Br.) Labour party leader; prime min., 1964-70, 1974-76.

Emiliano Zapata, c1879-1919, (Mex.) revolutionary; major influence on modern Mexico.

Todor Zhivkov, 1911-98, (Bulg.) Communist ruler of Bulgaria from 1954 until ousted in a 1989 coup.

Zhou Enlai, 1898-1976, (Chin.) diplomat, prime min.; a leading figure of the Chinese Communist party.

Scientists of the Past

Revised by Peter Barker, Prof. & Chair. Dept. of the Hist. of Science. Univ. of Oklahoma

For pre-modern scientists see also Philosophers and Religious Figures of the Past and Historical Figures chapter.

Albertus Magnus, c1200-1280, (Ger.) theologian, philosopher; helped found medieval study of natural science.

Alhazen (Ibn al-Haytham), c965-ca.1040, mathematician, astronomer; optical theorist.

Andre-Marie Ampère, 1775-1836, (Fr.) mathematician, chemist; founder of electrodynamics.

John V. Atanasoff, 1903-95, (U.S.) physicist; co-invented Atanasoff-Berry Computer (1939-41), regarded in law as the original "automatic electronic digital computer".

Amedeo Avogadro, 1776-1856, (It.) chemist, physicist; proposed that equal volumes of gas contain equal numbers of molecules, permitting determination of molecular weights.

John Bardeen, 1908-91, (U.S.) double Nobel laureate in physics (transistor, 1956; superconductivity, 1972).

A. H. Becquerel, 1852-1908, (Fr.) physicist; discovered radioactivity in uranium (1896).

Alexander Graham Bell, 1847-1922, (U.S.) inventor; first to patent and commercially exploit the telephone (1876).

Daniel Bernoulli, 1700-82, (Swiss) mathematician; developed fluid dynamics and kinetic theory of gases.

Clifford Berry, 1918-1963, (U.S.) collaborated with Atanasoff on the ABC computer (1939-41).

Jöns Jakob Berzelius, 1779-1848, (Swed.) chemist; developed modern chemical symbols and formulas, discovered selenium and thorium.

Henry Bessemer, 1813-98, (Br.) engineer; invented Bessemer steel-making process.

Bruno Bettelheim, 1903-90, (Austrian-U.S.) psychoanalyst specializing in autistic and other disturbed children; *Uses of Enchantment* (1976).

Louis Blériot, 1872-1936, (Fr.) engineer; monoplane pioneer, first Channel flight (1909).

Franz Boas, 1858-1942, (Ger.-U.S.) founded modern anthropology; studied Pacific Coast tribes.

Niels Bohr, 1885-1962, (Dan.) atomic and nuclear physicist; founded quantum mechanics.

Max Born, 1882-1970, (Ger.) atomic and nuclear physicist; helped develop quantum mechanics.

Satyendranath Bose, 1894-1974, (Indian) physicist; forerunner of modern quantum theory for integral-spin particles.

Louis de Broglie, 1892-1987, (Fr.) physicist; proposed quantum wave-particle duality.

Robert Bunsen, 1811-99, (Ger.) chemist; pioneered spectroscopic analysis; discovered rubidium, caesium.

Luther Burbank, 1849-1926, (U.S.) naturalist; developed plant breeding into a modern science.

Vannevar Bush, 1890-1974, (U.S.) electrical engineer; developed differential analyzer, an early analogue computer; headed WWII Office of Scientific Res. and Dev.

Marvin Camras, 1916-95, (U.S.) inventor, electrical engineer; invented magnetic tape recording.

Alexis Carrel, 1873-1944, (Fr.) surgeon, biologist; developed methods of suturing blood vessels and transplanting organs.

Rachel Carson, 1907-64, (U.S.) marine biologist, environmentalist; *Silent Spring* (1962).

George Washington Carver, c1864-1943, (U.S.) agricultural scientist, nutritionist; improved and pioneered new uses for peanuts and sweet potatoes.

James Chadwick, 1891-1974, (Br.) physicist; discovered the neutron (1932); led British Manhattan Project group in U.S. (1943-45).

Albert Claude, 1898-1983, (Belg.-U.S.) a founder of modern cell biology; determined role of mitochondria.

Nicolaus Copernicus, 1473-1543, (Pol.) first modern astronomer to propose sun as center of the planets' motions.

Jacques Yves Cousteau, 1910-1997, (Fr.) oceanographer; co-inventor, with E. Gagnan, of the Aqualung (1943).

Seymour Cray, 1925-96, (U.S.) computer industry pioneer; developed supercomputers.

Marie, 1867-1934 (Pol.-Fr.) and **Pierre Curie**, 1859-1906, (Fr.) physical chemists; pioneer investigators of radioactivity, discovered radium and polonium (1898).

Gottlieb Daimler, 1834-1900, (Ger.) engineer, inventor; pioneer automobile manufacturer.

John Dalton, 1766-1844, (Br.) chemist, physicist; formulated atomic theory, made first table of atomic weights.

Charles Darwin, 1809-82, (Br.) naturalist; established theory of organic evolution; *Origin of Species* (1859).

Lee De Forest, 1873-1961, (U.S.) inventor of triode, pioneer in wireless telegraphy, sound pictures, television.

Max Delbruck, 1906-81, (Ger.-U.S.) founded molecular biology.

Rudolf Diesel, 1858-1913, (Ger.) mechanical engineer; patented Diesel engine (1892).

Theodosius Dobzhansky, 1900-75, (Russ.-U.S.) biologist; reconciled genetics and natural selection contributing to "modern synthesis" in evolution.

Christian Doppler, 1803-53, (Austrian) physicist; showed change in wave frequency caused by motion of source, now known as Doppler effect.

J. Presper Eckert Jr., 1919-95, (U.S.) co-inventor, with Mauchly, of the ENIAC computer (1943-45).

Thomas A. Edison, 1847-1931, (U.S.) inventor; held more than 1,000 patents, including incandescent electric lamp.

Paul Ehrlich, 1854-1915, (Ger.) medical researcher in immunology and bacteriology; pioneered antitoxin production.

Albert Einstein, 1879-1955, (Ger.-U.S.) theoretical physicist; founded relativity theory, replacing Newton's theories of space, time, and gravity. Proved $E=mc^2$ (1905).

John F. Enders, 1897-1985, (U.S.) virologist, helped discover vaccines against polio, measles, mumps and chicken pox.

Erik Erikson, 1902-94, (U.S.) psychoanalyst, author; theory of developmental stages of life, *Childhood and Society* (1950).

Leonhard Euler, 1707-83, (Swiss) mathematician, physicist; pioneer of calculus, revived ideas of Fermat.

Gabriel Fahrenheit, 1686-1736, (Ger.) physicist; improved thermometers and introduced Fahrenheit temperature scale.

Michael Faraday, 1791-1867, (Br.) chemist, physicist; discovered electrical induction and invented dynamo (1831).

Philo T. Farnsworth, 1906-71, (U.S.) inventor; built first television system (San Francisco, 1928).

Pierre de Fermat, 1601-65, (Fr.) mathematician; founded modern theory of numbers.

Enrico Fermi, 1901-54, (It.-U.S.) nuclear physicist; demonstrated first controlled chain reaction (Chicago, 1942).

Richard Feynman, 1918-88, (U.S.) theoretical physicist, author; founder of Quantum Electrodynamics (QED).

Alexander Fleming, 1881-1955, (Br.) bacteriologist; discovered penicillin (1928).

Jean B. J. Fourier, 1768-1830, (fr.) introduced method of analysis in math and physics known as Fourier Series.

Sigmund Freud, 1856-1939, (Austrian) psychiatrist; founder of psychoanalysis. *Interpretation of Dreams* (1901).

Erich Fromm, 1900-1980, (U.S.) psychoanalyst. *Man for Himself* (1947).

Galileo Galilei, 1564-1642, (It.) physicist; used telescope to vindicate Copernicus, founded modern science of motion.

Luigi Galvani, 1737-98, (It.) physiologist; studied electricity in living organisms.

Carl Friedrich Gauss, 1777-1855, (Ger.) math. physicist; completed work of Fermat and Euler in number theory.

Joseph Gay-Lussac, 1778-1850, (Fr.) chemist, physicist; investigated behavior of gases, discovered boron.

Josiah W. Gibbs, 1839-1903, (U.S.) theoretical physicist, chemist; founded chemical thermodynamics.

Robert H. Goddard, 1882-1945, (U.S.) physicist; invented liquid fuel rocket (1926).

George W. Goethals, 1858-1928, (U.S.) chief engineer who completed Panama Canal (1907-14).

William C. Gorgas, 1854-1920, (U.S.) physician; pioneer in prevention of yellow fever and malaria.

Stephen Jay Gould, 1941-2002, (U.S.) paleontologist, evolutionary biologist, writer.

Ernest Haeckel, 1834-1919, (Ger.) zoologist, evolutionist; early Darwinist, introduced concept of "ecology."

Otto Hahn, 1879-1968, (Ger.) chemist; with Meitner discovered nuclear fission (1938).

Edmund Halley, 1656-1742, (Br.) astronomer; predicted return of 1682 comet ("Halley's Comet") in 1759.

William Harvey, 1578-1657, (Br.) physician, anatomist; discovered circulation of the blood (1628).

Werner Heisenberg, 1901-76, (Ger.) physicist; developed matrix mechanics and uncertainty principle (1927).

Hermann von Helmholtz, 1821-94, (Ger.) physicist, physiologist; formulated principle of conservation of energy.

William Herschel, 1738-1822, (Ger.-Br.) astronomer; discovered Uranus (1781).

Heinrich Hertz, 1857-94, (Ger.) physicist; discovered radio waves and photo-electric effect (1886-7).

David Hilbert, 1862-1943, (Ger.) mathematician; contributed to algebra, calculus and foundational studies (formalism).

Edwin P. Hubble, 1889-1953, (U.S.) astronomer; discovered observational evidence of expanding universe.

Alexander von Humboldt, 1769-1859, (Ger.) naturalist, author; explored S America, created ecology.

Edward Jenner, 1749-1823, (Br.) physician; pioneered vaccination, introduced term "virus."

James Joule, 1818-89, (Br.) physicist; found relation between heat and mechanical energy (conservation of energy).

Carl Jung, 1875-1961, (Swiss) psychiatrist; founder of analytical psychology.

Sister Elizabeth Kenny, 1886-1952, (Austral.) nurse; developed treatment for polio.

Johannes Kepler, 1571-1630, (Ger.) astronomer; discovered laws of planetary motion.

Al-Khawarizmi, early 9th cent., (Arab.), mathematician; regarded as founder of algebra.

Robert Koch, 1843-1910 (Ger.) bacteriologist; isolated bacterial causes of tuberculosis and other diseases.

Georges Köhler, 1946-95, (Ger.) immunologist; with Cesar Milstein he developed monoclonal antibody technique.

Jacques Lacan, 1901-81, (Fr.) controversial influential psychoanalyst.

Joseph Lagrange, 1736-1813, (Fr.) geometer, astronomer; showed that gravity of earth and moon cancels creating stable points in space around them.

Jean B. Lamarck, 1744-1829, (Fr.) naturalist; forerunner of Darwin in evolutionary theory.

Pierre Simon de Laplace, 1749-1827, (Fr.) astronomer, physicist; proposed nebular origin for solar system.

Antoine Lavoisier, 1743-94, (Fr.) a founder of mod. chemistry.

Ernest O. Lawrence, 1901-58, (U.S.) physicist; invented the cyclotron.

Jerome Lejeune, 1927-94, (Fr.) geneticist; discovered chromosomal cause of Down syndrome (1959).

Louis 1903-72, and **Mary Leakey,** 1913-96, (Br.) early hominid paleoanthropologists; discovered remains in Africa.

Anton van Leeuwenhoek, 1632-1723, (Dutch) founder of microscopy.

Kurt Lewin, 1890-1947, (Ger.-U.S.) social psychologist; studied human motivation and group dynamics.

Justus von Liebig, 1803-73, (Ger.) founded quantitative organic chemistry.

Joseph Lister, 1827-1912, (Br.) physician; pioneered antiseptic surgery.

Hendrik Lorentz, 1853-1928 (Neth.), physicist, developed electron theory of matter, contributed to theory of relativity.

Konrad Lorenz, 1903-89, (Austrian) ethologist; pioneer in study of animal behavior.

Percival Lowell, 1855-1916, (U.S.) astronomer; predicted the existence of Pluto.

Louis, 1864-1948, and **Auguste Lumière,** 1862-1954, (Fr.) invented cinematograph and made first motion picture (1895).

Guglielmo Marconi, 1874-1937, (It.) physicist; developed wireless telegraphy.

John W. Mauchly, 1907-80, (U.S.) co-inventor, with Eckert, of computer ENIAC (1943-45).

James Clerk Maxwell, 1831-79, (Br.) physicist; unified electricity and magnetism; electromagnetic theory of light.

Maria Goeppert Mayer, 1906-72, (Ger.-U.S.) physicist; developed shell model of atomic nuclei.

Barbara McClintock, 1902-92, (U.S.) geneticist; showed that some genetic elements are mobile.

Lise Meitner, 1878-1968. (Austrian) co-discoverer, with Hahn, of nuclear fission (1938).

Gregor J. Mendel, 1822-84, (Austrian) botanist, monk; his experiments became the foundation of modern genetics.

Dmitri Mendeleyev, 1834-1907, (Russ.) chemist; established Periodic Table of the Elements.

Franz Mesmer, 1734-1815, (Ger.) physician; introduced hypnotherapy.

Albert A. Michelson, 1852-1931, (U.S.) physicist; invented interferometer.

Robert A. Millikan, 1868-1953, (U.S.) physicist; measured electronic charge.

Thomas Hunt Morgan, 1866-1945, (U.S.) geneticist, embryologist; established role of chromosomes in heredity.

Isaac Newton, 1642-1727, (Br.) natural philosopher; discovered laws of gravitation, motion; with Leibniz, founded calculus.

Robert N. Noyce, 1927-90, (U.S.) invented microchip.

J. Robert Oppenheimer, 1904-67, (U.S.) physicist; scientific director of Manhattan project.

Wilhelm Ostwald, 1853-1932, (Ger.) chemist, philosopher; main founder of modern physical chemistry.

Louis Pasteur, 1822-95, (Fr.) chemist; showed that germs cause disease and fermentation, originated pasteurization.

Linus C. Pauling, 1901-94, (U.S.) chemist; studied chemical bonds; campaigned for nuclear disarmament.

Jean Piaget, 1896-1980, (Swiss) psychologist; four-stage theory of intellectual development in children.

Max Planck, 1858-1947, (Ger.) physicist; introduced quantum hypothesis (1900).

Jules Henri Poincaré, 1854-1912 (Fr.), mathematician, founded algebraic topology, many other discoveries in math and physics

Walter S. Reed, 1851-1902, (U.S.) army physician; proved mosquitoes transmit yellow fever.

Theodor Reik, 1888-1969, (Austrian-U.S.) psychoanalyst, major Freudian disciple.

Bernhard Riemann, 1826-66, (Ger.) mathematician; developed non-Euclidean geometry used by Einstein.

Wilhelm Roentgen, 1845-1923, (Ger.) physicist; discovered X-rays (1895).

Carl Rogers, 1902-87, (U.S.) psychotherapist, author; originated nondirective therapy.

Ernest Rutherford, 1871-1937, (Br.) physicist; pioneer investigator of radioactivity, identified the atomic nucleus.

Albert B. Sabin, 1906-93, (Russ.-U.S.), developed oral polio live-virus vaccine.

Carl Sagan, 1934-96, (U.S.) astronomer, author.

Jonas Salk, 1914-95, (U.S.) developed first successful polio vaccine, widely used in U.S. after 1955.

Giovanni Schiaparelli, 1835-1910, (It.) astronomer; reported canals on Mars.

Erwin Schrödinger, 1887-1961, (Austrian) physicist; developed wave equation for quantum systems.

Glenn T. Seaborg, 1912-99, (U.S.) chemist, Nobel Prize winner (1951); codiscoverer of plutonium.

Harlow Shapley, 1885-1972, (U.S.) astronomer; mapped galactic clusters and position of Sun in our own galaxy.

B(urrhus) F(rederick) Skinner, 1904-89, (U.S.) psychologist; leading advocate of behaviorism.

Roger W. Sperry, 1913-94, (U.S.) neurobiologist; established different functions of right and left sides of brain.

Benjamin Spock, 1903-98, (U.S.) pediatrician, child care expert; *Common Sense Book of Baby and Child Care.*

Charles P. Steinmetz, 1865-1923, (Ger.-U.S.) electrical engineer; developed basic ideas on alternating current.

Leo Szilard, 1898-1964, (Hung.-U.S.) physicist; helped on Manhattan project, later opposed nuclear weapons.

Edward Teller, 1908-2003, (Hung.-U.S.) physicist, aided on Manhattan project, had key role in development of H-bomb.

Nikola Tesla, 1856-1943, (Serb.-U.S.) invented a number of electrical devices including a.c. dynamos, transformers and motors.

William Thomson (Lord Kelvin), 1824-1907, (Br.) physicist; aided in success of transatlantic telegraph cable (1865); proposed Kelvin absolute temperature scale.

Alan Turing, 1912-54, (Br.) mathematician; helped develop basis for computers.

Rudolf Virchow, 1821-1902, (Ger.) pathologist; pioneered the modern theory that diseases affect the body through cells.

Alessandro Volta, 1745-1827, (It.) physicist; electricity pioneer.

Werner von Braun, 1912-77, (Ger.-U.S.) developed rockets for warfare and space exploration.

John Von Neumann, 1903-57, (Hung.-U.S.) mathematician; originated game theory; basic design for modern computers.

Alfred Russell Wallace, 1823-1913, (Br.) naturalist; proposed concept of evolution independently of Darwin.

John B. Watson, 1878-1958, (U.S.) psychologist; a founder of behaviorism.

James E. Watt, 1736-1819, (Br.) mechanical engineer, inventor; invented modern steam engine (1765).

Alfred L. Wegener, 1880-1930, (Ger.) meteorologist, geophysicist; postulated continental drift.

Norbert Wiener, 1894-1964, (U.S.) mathematician; founder of cybernetics.

Sewall Wright, 1889-1988, (U.S.) evolutionary theorist; helped found population genetics.

Wilhelm Wundt, 1832-1920, (Ger.) founder of experimental psychology.

Ferdinand von Zeppelin, 1838-1917, (Ger.) soldier, aeronaut, airship designer.

Social Reformers, Activists, and Humanitarians of the Past

Jane Addams, 1860-1935, (U.S.) cofounder of Hull House; won Nobel Peace Prize, 1931.

Susan B. Anthony, 1820-1906, (U.S.) a leader in temperance, anti-slavery, and woman suffrage movements.

Thomas Barnardo, 1845-1905, (Br.) social reformer; pioneered in care of destitute children.

Clara Barton, 1821-1912, (U.S.) organized American Red Cross.

Henry Ward Beecher, 1813-87, (U.S.) clergyman, abolitionist.

Amelia Bloomer, 1818-94, (U.S.) suffragette, social reformer.

William Booth, 1829-1912, (Br.) founded Salvation Army.

John Brown, 1800-59, (U.S.) abolitionist who led murder of 5 pro-slavery men, was hanged.

Frances Xavier (Mother) Cabrini, 1850-1917, (It.-U.S.) Italian-born nun; founded charitable institutions; first American canonized as a saint, 1946.

Carrie Chapman Catt, 1859-1947, (U.S.) suffragette.

Cesar Chavez, 1927-93, (U.S.) labor leader; helped establish United Farm Workers of America.

Clarence Darrow, 1857-1938, (U.S.) lawyer; defender of "underdog," opponent of capital punishment.

Dorothy Day, 1897-1980, (U.S.) founder of Catholic Worker movement.

Eugene V. Debs, 1855-1926, (U.S.) labor leader; led Pullman strike, 1894; 4-time Socialist presidential candidate.

Dorothea Dix, 1802-87, (U.S.) crusader for mentally ill.

Thomas Dooley, 1927-61, (U.S.) "jungle doctor," noted for efforts to supply medical aid to developing countries.

Marjory Stoneman Douglas, 1890-1998, (U.S.) writer and environmentalist; campaigned to save Florida Everglades.

William Lloyd Garrison, 1805-79, (U.S.) abolitionist.

Emma Goldman, 1869-1940, (Russ.-U.S.) published anarchist *Mother Earth,* birth-control advocate.

Samuel Gompers, 1850-1924, (U.S.) labor leader.

Michael Harrington, 1928-89, (U.S.) exposed poverty in affluent U.S. in *The Other America,* 1963.

Sidney Hillman, 1887-1946, (U.S.) labor leader; helped organize CIO.

Samuel G. Howe, 1801-76, (U.S.) social reformer; changed public attitudes toward the handicapped.

Helen Keller, 1880-1968, (U.S.) crusader for better treatment for the handicapped; deaf and blind herself.

Maggie Kuhn, 1905-95, (U.S.) founded Gray Panthers, 1970.

William Kunstler, 1919-95, (U.S.) civil liberties attorney.

John L. Lewis, 1880-1969, (U.S.) labor leader; headed United Mine Workers, 1920-60.

Karl Menninger, 1893-1990, (U.S.) with brother William founded Menninger Clinic and Menninger Foundation.

Lucretia Mott, 1793-1880, (U.S.) reformer, pioneer feminist.

Philip Murray, 1886-1952, (U.S.) Scottish-born labor leader.

Florence Nightingale, 1820-1910, (Br.) founder of modern nursing.

Emmeline Pankhurst, 1858-1928, (Br.) woman suffragist.

Walter Reuther, 1907-70, (U.S.) labor leader; headed UAW.

Jacob Riis, 1849-1914, (U.S.) crusader for urban reforms.

Margaret Sanger, 1883-1966, (U.S.) social reformer; pioneered the birth-control movement.

Earl of Shaftesbury (A. A. Cooper), 1801-85, (Br.) social reformer.

Elizabeth Cady Stanton, 1815-1902, (U.S.) woman suffrage pioneer.

Lucy Stone, 1818-93, (U.S.) feminist, abolitionist.

Mother Teresa of Calcutta, 1910-97, (Alban.) nun; founded order to care for sick, dying poor; 1979 Nobel Peace Prize.

Philip Vera Cruz, 1905-94, (Filipino-U.S.) helped to found the United Farm Workers Union.

William Wilberforce, 1759-1833, (Br.) social reformer; prominent in struggle to abolish the slave trade.

Frances E. Willard, 1839-98, (U.S.) temperance, women's rights leader.

Mary Wollstonecraft, 1759-97, (Br.) wrote *Vindication of the Rights of Women.*

Writers of the Present

Name (Birthplace)	Birthdate
Chinua Achebe (Ogidi, Nigeria)	11/16/30
Richard Adams (Newbury, Eng.)	5/9/20
Edward Albee (Wash., DC)	3/12/28
Isabel Allende (Lima, Peru)	8/2/42
Martin Amis (Oxford, Eng.)	8/25/49
Maya Angelou (St. Louis, MO)	4/4/28
Piers Anthony (Oxford, Eng.)	8/6/34
Jeffrey Archer (Somerset, Eng.)	4/15/40
Oscar Arias Sanchez (Heredia, Costa Rica)	9/13/41
John Ashbery (Rochester, NY)	7/28/27
Margaret Atwood (Ottawa, Ont.)	11/18/39
David Auburn (Chicago, IL)	1969
Louis Auchincloss (Lawrence, NY)	9/27/17
Jean Auel (Chicago, IL)	2/18/36
Paul Auster (Newark, NJ)	2/3/47
Alan Ayckbourn (Hampstead, Eng.)	4/12/39
Russell Banks (Newton, MA)	3/28/40
John Barth (Cambridge, MD)	5/27/30
Ann Beattie (Wash., DC)	9/8/47
Saul Bellow (Lachine, Que.)	6/10/15
Peter Benchley (NYC)	5/8/40
John Berendt (Syracuse, NY)	12/5/39
Thomas Berger (Cincinnati, OH)	7/20/24
Judy Blume (Elizabeth, NJ)	2/ 12/38
T. Coraghessan Boyle (Peekskill, NY)	12/2/47
Ray Bradbury (Waukegan, IL)	8/22/20
Barbara Taylor Bradford (Leeds, Eng.)	5/10/33
Rita Mae Brown (Hanover, PA)	11/28/44
Christopher Buckley (NYC)	1952
Robert Olen Butler (Granite City, IL)	1/20/45
A. S. Byatt (Sheffield, England)	8/24/36
Hortense Calisher (NYC)	12/20/11
Ethan Canin (Ann Arbor, MI)	7/19/60
Peter Carey (Bacchus-Marsh, Victoria, Australia)	5/7/43
Michael Chabon (Washington, DC)	5/24/63
Sandra Cisneros (Chicago, IL)	12/20/54
Tom Clancy (Baltimore, MD)	4/12/47
Mary Higgins Clark (NYC)	12/24/31
Arthur C. Clarke (Minehead, Eng.)	12/16/17
Beverly Cleary (McMinnville, OR)	4/12/16
Paulo Coelho (Rio de Janeiro, Brazil)	8/24/47
Billy Collins (NYC)	3/22/41
Jackie Collins (London, Eng.)	10/4/41?
Evan S. Connell (Kansas City, MO)	8/17/24
Pat Conroy (Atlanta, GA)	10/26/45
Robin Cook (NYC)	5/4/40
Patricia Cornwell (Miami, FL)	6/9/56
Harry Crews (Alma, GA)	6/6/35
Michael Crichton (Chicago, IL)	10/23/42
Michael Cunningham (Cincinnati, Ohio)	11/6/52
Don DeLillo (NYC)	11/20/36
Nelson DeMille (NYC)	8/23/43
Joan Didion (Sacramento, CA)	12/5/34
E. L. Doctorow (NYC)	1/6/31
Takako Doi (Hyogo, Jap.)	11/30/28
Rita Dove (Akron, OH)	8/28/52
Roddy Doyle (Dublin, Ireland)	5/58
John Gregory Dunne (Hartford, CT)	5/25/32
Umberto Eco (Alessandria, Italy)	1/5/32
Bret Easton Ellis (Los Angeles, CA)	3/7/64

Name (Birthplace)	Birthdate
James Ellroy (Los Angeles)	3/4/48
Louise Erdrich (Little Falls, MN)	7/6/54
Laura Esquivel (Mexico City, Mexico)	9/30/50
Ken Follet (Cardiff, Wales)	6/5/49
Dario Fo (San Giano, Italy)	3/26/26
Horton Foote (Wharton, TX)	3/14/16
Richard Ford (Jackson, MS)	2/16/44
Frederick Forsyth (Ashford, Eng.)	8/25/38
John Fowles (Leigh-on-Sea, Eng.)	3/31/26
Paula Fox (NYC)	4/22/23
Dick Francis (Tenby, Pembrokeshire, Wales)	10/31/20
Jonathan Franzen (Western Springs, IL)	8/17/59
Michael Frayn (London, Eng.)	9/8/33
Marilyn French (NYC)	11/21/29
Brian Friel (Omagh, County Tyrone, N. Ireland)	1/9/29
Carlos Fuentes (Panama City, Panama)	11/11/28
Ernest J. Gaines (Oscar, LA)	1/15/33
Gabriel Garcia Marquez (Aracataca, Colombia)	3/6/28
Frank Gilroy (Bronx, NY)	10/13/25
Gail Godwin (Birmingham, AL)	6/18/37
William Goldman (Highland Park, IL)	8/12/31
Nadine Gordimer (Springs, S. Africa)	11/20/23
Mary Gordon (Far Rockaway, Long Island, NY)	12/8/49
Sue Grafton (Louisville, KY)	4/24/40
Günter Grass (Danzig, now Gdansk, Poland)	10/16/27
Shirley Ann Grau (New Orleans, LA)	7/8/29
John Grisham (Jonesboro, AR)	2/8/55
John Guare (NYC)	2/5/38
Arthur Hailey (Luton, Eng.)	4/5/20
David Hare (St. Leonards, Sussex, Eng.)	6/5/47
Robert Hass (San Francisco, CA)	3/1/41
Vaclav Havel (Prague, Czech.)	10/5/36
Seamus Heaney (Mossbawn, Cty. Derry, N. Ireland)	4/13/39
Mark Helprin (NYC)	6/28/47
Oscar Hijuelos (NYC)	8/24/51
Tony Hillerman (Sacred Heart, OK)	5/27/25
S. E. Hinton (Tulsa, OK)	1948
Alice Hoffman (NYC)	3/16/52
John Irving (Exeter, NH)	3/2/42
John Jakes (Chicago, IL)	3/31/32
P. D. James (Oxford, Eng.)	8/3/20
Erica Jong (NYC)	3/26/42
Garrison Keillor (Anoka, MN)	8/7/42
Thomas Keneally (Sydney, Austral.)	10/7/35
William Kennedy (Albany, NY)	1/16/28
Jamaica Kincaid (St. Johns, Antigua)	5/25/49
Stephen King (Portland, ME)	9/21/47
Barbara Kingsolver (Annapolis, MD)	4/8/55
Maxine Hong Kingston (Stockton, CA)	10/27/40
Galway Kinnell (Providence, RI)	2/1/27
Dean Koontz (Everett, PA)	7/9/45
Judith Krantz (NYC)	1/9/28
Maxine Kumin (Philadelphia, PA)	6/6/25
Milan Kundera (Brno, Czechoslovakia)	4/1/29
Tony Kushner (NYC)	7/16/56
David Leavitt (Pittsburgh, PA)	6/23/61
John Le Carré (Poole, Eng.)	10/19/31
Harper Lee (Monroeville, AL)	
Ursula K. Le Guin (Berkeley, CA)	10/21/29
Madeleine L'Engle (NYC)	11/29/18

Name (Birthplace)	Birthdate
Elmore Leonard (New Orleans, LA)	10/11/25
Doris Lessing (Kermanshah, Persia)	10/22/19
Ira Levin (NYC)	8/27/29
David Lodge (South London, Eng.)	1/28/35
Alison Lurie (Chicago, IL)	9/3/26
Naguib Mahfouz (Cairo, Egypt)	12/11/11
Norman Mailer (Long Branch, NJ)	1/31/23
David Mamet (Chicago, IL)	11/30/47
Bobbie Ann Mason (nr. Mayfield, KY)	5/1/40
Peter Matthiessen (NYC)	5/22/27
Armistead Maupin (Wash., DC)	4/13/44
Ed McBain (real name Evan Hunter) (NYC)	10/15/26
Cormac McCarthy (Providence, RI)	7/20/33
Frank McCourt (Brooklyn, NY)	8/19/30
Colleen McCullough (Wellington, N.S.W.)	6/1/37
Alice McDermott (Brooklyn, NY)	6/27/53
Ian McEwan (Aldershot, England)	6/21/48
Thomas McGuane (Wyandotte, MI)	12/11/39
Terry McMillan (Port Huron, MI)	10/18/51
Larry McMurtry (Wichita Falls, TX)	6/3/36
Terrence McNally (St. Petersburg, FL)	11/3/39
John McPhee (Princeton, NJ)	3/8/31
Arthur Miller (NYC)	10/17/15
Czeslaw Milosz (Szetejnie, Lithuania)	6/30/11
Toni Morrison (Lorain, OH)	2/18/31
Walter Mosley (Los Angeles, CA)	1/12/52
Alice Munro (Wingham, Ont.)	7/10/31
Haruki Murakami (Kyoto, Japan)	1/12/49
V. S. Naipaul (Chaguanas, Trinidad)	8/17/32
Joyce Carol Oates (Lockport, NY)	6/16/38
Edna O'Brien (Tuamgraney, Ir.)	12/15/30
Tim O'Brien (Austin, MN)	10/1/46
Kenzaburo Oe (Ose-mura, now Uchiko, Ehime, Shikoku, Japan)	1/31/35
Michael Ondaatje (Colombo, Sri Lanka)	9/12/43
Cynthia Ozick (NYC)	4/17/28
Grace Paley (NYC)	12/11/22
Suzan-Lori Parks (Fort Knox, KY)	1963
Marge Piercy (Detroit, MI)	3/31/36
Robert Pinsky (Long Branch, NJ)	10/20/40
Harold Pinter (Hackney, East London, Eng.)	10/10/30
Reynolds Price (Macon, NC)	2/1/33
Richard Price (Bronx, NY)	10/12/49
E. Annie Proulx (Norwich, CT)	8/22/35
Philip Pullman (Norwich, Eng.)	10/19/46
Thomas Pynchon (Glen Cove, Long Island, NY)	5/8/37
David Rabe (Dubuque, IA)	3/10/40
Ishmael Reed (Chattanooga, TN)	2/22/38
Ruth Rendell (London, England)	2/17/30

Name (Birthplace)	Birthdate
Anne Rice (New Orleans, LA)	10/4/41
Adrienne Rich (Baltimore, MD)	5/16/29
Nora Roberts (Washington, DC)	10/10/50
Philip Roth (Newark, NJ)	3/19/33
J.K. Rowling (Chipping Sodbury, Eng.)	7/31/65
Salman Rushdie (Bombay, India)	6/19/47
Richard Russo (Johnstown, NY)	7/15/49
J. D. Salinger (NYC)	1/1/19
Jose Saramago (Azinhaga, Portugal)	11/16/22
David Sedaris (Johnson City, NY)	12/26/56
Vikram Seth (Calcutta, India)	6/20/52
Sidney Sheldon (Chicago, IL)	2/11/17
Sam Shepard (Ft. Sheridan, IL)	11/5/43
Claude Simon (Tananarive, Madagascar)	10/10/13
Neil Simon (Bronx, NY)	7/4/27
Jane Smiley (Los Angeles, CA)	9/26/49
Aleksandr Solzhenitsyn (Kislovodsk, Russia)	12/11/18
Susan Sontag (NYC)	1/16/33
Wole Soyinka (Abeokuta, Nigeria)	7/13/34
Mickey Spillane (Brooklyn, NY)	3/9/18
Danielle Steel (NYC)	8/14/47
Richard Stern (NYC)	2/25/28
Mary Stewart (Sunderland, Eng.)	9/17/16
R(obert) L(awrence) Stine (Columbus, OH)	10/8/43
Tom Stoppard (Zlin, Czech.)	7/3/37
William Styron (Newport News, VA)	6/11/25
Wislawa Szymborska (Kornik, Poland)	7/2/23
Amy Tan (Oakland, CA)	2/19/52
Paul Theroux (Medford, MA)	4/10/41
Scott F. Turow (Chicago, IL)	4/12/49
Anne Tyler (Minneapolis, MN)	10/25/41
John Updike (Shillington, PA)	3/18/32
Mario Vargas Llosa (Arequipa, Peru)	3/28/36
Gore Vidal (West Point, NY)	10/3/25
Paula Vogel (Wash., DC)	11/16/51
Kurt Vonnegut Jr. (Indianapolis, IN)	11/11/22
Derek Walcott (Castries, Saint Lucia)	1/23/30
Alice Walker (Eatonton, GA)	2/9/44
Robert James Waller (Rockford, IA)	8/1/39
Joseph Wambaugh (East Pittsburgh, PA)	1/22/37
Wendy Wasserstein (Brooklyn, NY)	10/18/50
Edmund White (Cincinnati, OH)	1/19/40
August Wilson (Pittsburgh, PA)	4/27/45
Lanford Wilson (Lebanon, MO)	4/13/37
Tom Wolfe (Richmond, VA)	3/2/31
Tobias Wolff (Birmingham, AL)	6/19/45
Herman Wouk (NYC)	5/27/15
Yevgeny Yevtushenko (Irkutsk, Russia)	7/18/33

Writers of the Past

See also Journalists of the Past, and Greeks and Romans in Historical Figures chapter.

Alice Adams, 1926-99, (U.S.) novelist, short-story writer. *Superior Woman.*

James Agee, 1909-55, (U.S.) novelist. *A Death in the Family.*

S(hmuel) Y(osef) Agnon, 1888-1970, (Is.) Hebrew novelist. *Only Yesterday.*

Conrad Aiken, 1889-1973, (U.S.) poet, critic. *Ushant.*

Anna Akhmatova, 1889-1966, (Russ.) poet. *Requiem.*

Louisa May Alcott, 1832-88, (U.S.) novelist. *Little Women.*

Sholom Aleichem, 1859-1916, (Russ.) Yiddish writer. *Tevye's Daughter, The Old Country.*

Vicente Aleixandre, 1898-1984, (Sp.) poet. *La destrucción o el amor, Dialogolos del conocimiento.*

Horatio Alger, 1832-1899, (U.S.) "rags-to-riches" books.

Jorge Amado, 1912-2001, (Brazil) novelist. *Dona Flor and Her Two Husbands, The Violent Land.*

Eric Ambler, 1909-98, (Br.) suspense novelist. *A Coffin for Dimitrios.*

Kingsley Amis, 1922-95, (Br.) novelist, critic. *Lucky Jim.*

Hans Christian Andersen, 1805-75, (Dan.) author of fairy tales. *The Ugly Duckling.*

Maxwell Anderson, 1888-1959, (U.S.) playwright. *What Price Glory?, High Tor, Winterset, Key Largo.*

Sherwood Anderson, 1876-1941, (U.S.) short-story writer. "Death in the Woods;" *Winesburg, Ohio.*

Reinaldo Arenas, 1943-1990, (Cuba) novelist, short-story writer. *Before Night Falls.*

Ludovico Ariosto, 1474-1533, (It.) poet. *Orlando Furioso.*

Matthew Arnold, 1822-88, (Br.) poet, critic. "Thrysis," "Dover Beach," "Culture and Anarchy."

Isaac Asimov, 1920-92, (U.S.) versatile writer, espec. of science-fiction. *I Robot.*

Miguel Angel Asturias, 1899-1974, (Guatemala) novelist. *El Señor Presidente.*

W(ystan) H(ugh) Auden, 1907-73, (Br.) poet, playwright, literary critic. "The Age of Anxiety."

Jane Austen, 1775-1817, (Br.) novelist. *Pride and Prejudice, Sense and Sensibility, Emma, Mansfield Park.*

Isaac Babel, 1894-1941, (Russ.) short-story writer, playwright. *Odessa Tales, Red Cavalry.*

James Baldwin, 1924-87, author, playwright. *The Fire Next Time, Blues for Mister Charlie.*

Honoré de Balzac, 1799-1850, (Fr.) novelist. *Le Père Goriot, Cousine Bette, Eugénie Grandet.*

James M. Barrie, 1860-1937, (Br.) playwright, novelist. *Peter Pan, Dear Brutus, What Every Woman Knows.*

Charles Baudelaire, 1821-67, (Fr.) poet. *Les Fleurs du Mal.*

L(yman) Frank Baum, 1856-1919, (U.S.) *Wizard of Oz* series.

Simone de Beauvoir, 1908-86, (Fr.) novelist, essayist. *The Second Sex, Memoirs of a Dutiful Daughter.*

Samuel Beckett, 1906-89, (Ir.) novelist, playwright. *Waiting for Godot, Endgame* (plays); *Murphy, Watt, Molloy* (novels).

Brendan Behan, 1923-64, (Ir.) playwright. *The Quare Fellow, The Hostage, Borstal Boy.*

Robert Benchley, 1889-1945, (U.S.) humorist.

Stephen Vincent Benét, 1898-1943, (U.S.) poet, novelist. *John Brown's Body.*

John Berryman, 1914-72, (U.S.) poet. *Homage to Mistress Bradstreet.*

Ambrose Bierce, 1842-1914, (U.S.) short-story writer, journalist. *In the Midst of Life, The Devil's Dictionary.*

Elizabeth Bishop, 1911-79, (U.S.) poet. *North and South—A Cold Spring.*

William Blake, 1757-1827, (Br.) poet, artist. *Songs of Innocence, Songs of Experience.*

Aleksandr Blok, 1880-1921, (Russ.) poet. "The Twelve", "The Scythians."

IT'S A FACT: The remains of Alexandre Dumas, author of *The Three Musketeers, The Count of Monte Cristo,* and other enduringly popular novels, were installed in the Pantheon in Paris (the final resting place of many of France's luminaries), 200 years after his birth on July 24, 1802. Despite his great popularity, he had not been judged worthy of burial in the Pantheon. Scholars said this may have been because his writings were considered entertainments rather than great literature and, possibly, in part, because he was the grandson of a black Haitian slave.

Giovanni Boccaccio, 1313-75, (It.) poet. *Decameron.*
Heinrich Böll, 1917-85, (Ger.) novelist, short-story writer. *Group Portrait With Lady.*
Jorge Luis Borges, 1900-86, (Arg.) short-story writer, poet, essayist. *Labyrinths.*
James Boswell, 1740-95, (Sc.) biographer. *The Life of Samuel Johnson.*
Pierre Boulle, (1913-94), (Fr.) novelist. *The Bridge Over the River Kwai, Planet of the Apes.*
Paul Bowles, 1910-99, (U.S.) novelist, short-story writer. The Sheltering Sky.
Anne Bradstreet, c1612-72, (U.S.) poet. *The Tenth Muse Lately Sprung Up in America.*
Bertolt Brecht, 1898-1956, (Ger.) dramatist, poet. *The Three-penny Opera, Mother Courage and Her Children.*
Charlotte Brontë, 1816-55, (Br.) novelist. *Jane Eyre.*
Emily Brontë, 1818-48, (Br.) novelist. *Wuthering Heights.*
Elizabeth Barrett Browning, 1806-61, (Br.) poet. *Sonnets From the Portuguese, Aurora Leigh.*
Joseph Brodsky, 1940-96, (Russ.-U.S.) poet. *A Part of Speech, Less Than One, To Urania.*
Robert Browning, 1812-89, (Br.) poet. "My Last Duchess," "Fra Lippo Lippi," *The Ring and The Book.*
Pearl S. Buck, 1892-1973, (U.S.) novelist. *The Good Earth.*
Mikhail Bulgakov, 1891-1940, (Russ.) novelist, playwright. *The Heart of a Dog, The Master and Margarita.*
John Bunyan, 1628-88, (Br.) writer. *Pilgrim's Progress.*
Anthony Burgess, 1917-93, (Br.) author. *A Clockwork Orange.*
Frances Hodgson Burnett, 1849-1924, (Br.) novelist. *The Secret Garden.*
Robert Burns, 1759-96, (Sc.) poet. "Flow Gently, Sweet Afton," "My Heart's in the Highlands," "Auld Lang Syne."
Edgar Rice Burroughs, 1875-1950, (U.S.) novelist. "Tarzan" books.
William S. Burroughs, 1914-97, (U.S.) novelist. *Naked Lunch.*
George Gordon, Lord Byron, 1788-1824, (Br.) poet. *Don Juan, Childe Harold, Manfred, Cain.*
Pedro Calderon de la Barca, 1600-81, (Sp.) playwright. *Life Is a Dream.*
Italo Calvino, 1923-85, (It.) novelist, short-story writer. *If on a Winter's Night a Traveler.*
Luis Vaz de Camoes, 1524?-80 (Port.) poet. *The Lusiads.*
Albert Camus, 1913-60, (Fr.) writer. *The Stranger, The Fall.*
Elias Canetti, 1905-94, (Bulg.) novelist, essayist. *Auto-da-Fe.*
Karel Capek, 1890-1938, (Czech.) playwright, novelist, essayist. *R.U.R. (Rossum's Universal Robots).*
Truman Capote, 1924-84, (U.S.) author. *Other Voices, Other Rooms, Breakfast at Tiffany's, In Cold Blood.*
Lewis Carroll (Charles Dodgson), 1832-98, (Br.) writer, mathematician. *Alice's Adventures in Wonderland.*
Giacomo Casanova, 1725-98, (It.) adventurer, memoirist.
Willa Cather, 1873-1947, (U.S.) novelist. *O Pioneers!, My Antonia, Death Comes for the Archbishop.*
Constantine Cavafy, 1863-1933, (Gr.) poet. "Ithaka," "Sensual Pleasures."
Camilo Jose Cela, 1916-2001, (Sp.) novelist. *The Family of Pascual Duarte, The Hive.*
Miguel de Cervantes Saavedra, 1547-1616, (Sp.) novelist, dramatist, poet. *Don Quixote.*
Raymond Chandler, 1888-1959, (U.S.) writer of detective fiction. Philip Marlowe series.
Geoffrey Chaucer, c1340-1400, (Br.) poet. *The Canterbury Tales, Troilus and Criseyde.*
John Cheever, 1912-82, (U.S.) novelist, short-story writer. *The Wapshot Scandal,* "The Country Husband."
Anton Chekhov, 1860-1904, (Russ.) short-story writer, dramatist. *Uncle Vanya, The Cherry Orchard, The Three Sisters.*
G(ilbert) K(eith) Chesterton, 1874-1936, (Br.) critic, novelist, relig. apologist. Father Brown series of mysteries.
Kate Chopin, 1851-1904, (U.S.) writer. *The Awakening.*
Agatha Christie, 1890-1976, (Br.) mystery writer; created Miss Marple, Hercule Poirot; *And Then There Were None., Murder on the Orient Express, Murder of Roger Ackroyd.*
James Clavell, 1924-94, (Br.-U.S.) novelist. *Shogun, King Rat.*
Jean Cocteau, 1889-1963, (Fr.) writer, visual artist, filmmaker. *The Beauty and the Beast, Les Enfants Terribles.*
Samuel Taylor Coleridge, 1772-1834, (Br.) poet, critic. "Kubla Khan," "The Rime of the Ancient Mariner."
(Sidonie) Colette, 1873-1954, (Fr.) novelist. *Claudine, Gigi.*
Wilkie Collins, 1824-89, (Br.) Novelist. *The Moonstone.*
Joseph Conrad, 1857-1924, (Br.) novelist. *Lord Jim, Heart of Darkness, The Nigger of the Narcissus.*
James Fenimore Cooper, 1789-1851, (U.S.) novelist. *Leatherstocking Tales, The Last of the Mohicans.*

Pierre Corneille, 1606-84, (Fr.) dramatist. *Medeé, Le Cid.*
Hart Crane, 1899-1932, (U.S.) poet. "The Bridge."
Stephen Crane, 1871-1900, (U.S.) novelist, short-story writer. *The Red Badge of Courage,* "The Open Boat."
E. E. Cummings, 1894-1962, (U.S.) poet. *Tulips and Chimneys.*
Roald Dahl, 1916-90, (Br.-U.S.) writer. *Charlie and the Chocolate Factory, James and the Giant Peach.*
Gabriele D'Annunzio, 1863-1938, (It.) poet. novelist, dramatist. *The Child of Pleasure, The Intruder, The Victim.*
Dante Alighieri, 1265-1321, (It.) poet. *The Divine Comedy.*
Robertson Davies, 1913-95, (Can.) novelist, playwright, essayist. Salterton, Deptford, and Cornish trilogies.
Daniel Defoe, 1660-1731, (Br.) writer. *Robinson Crusoe, Moll Flanders, Journal of the Plague Year.*
Charles Dickens, 1812-70, (Br.) novelist. *David Copperfield, Oliver Twist, Great Expectations, A Tale of Two Cities.*
Philip K. Dick, 1928-82, (U.S.) science fiction writer. *Do Androids Dream of Electric Sheep?*
James Dickey, 1923-1997, (U.S.) poet, novelist. *Deliverance.*
Emily Dickinson, 1830-86, (U.S.) lyric poet. "Because I could not stop for Death . . .," "Success is counted sweetest . . ."
Isak Dinesen (Karen Blixen), 1885-1962, (Dan.) author. *Out of Africa, Seven Gothic Tales, Winter's Tales.*
John Donne, 1573-1631, (Br.) poet, divine. *Songs and Sonnets.*
José Donoso, 1924-96, (Chil.) surreal novelist and short-story writer. *The Obscene Bird of Night.*
John Dos Passos, 1896-1970, (U.S.) novelist. *U.S.A.*
Fyodor Dostoyevsky, 1821-81, (Russ.) novelist. *Crime and Punishment, The Brothers Karamazov, The Possessed.*
Arthur Conan Doyle, 1859-1930, (Br.) novelist. Sherlock Holmes mystery stories.
Theodore Dreiser, 1871-1945, (U.S.) novelist. *An American Tragedy, Sister Carrie.*
John Dryden, 1631-1700, (Br.) poet, dramatist, critic. *All for Love, Mac Flecknoe, Absalom and Achitophel.*
Alexandre Dumas, 1802-70, (Fr.) novelist, dramatist. *The Three Musketeers, The Count of Monte Cristo.*
Alexandre Dumas (fils), 1824-95, (Fr.) dramatist, novelist. *La Dame aux Camélias, Le Demi-Monde.*
Lawrence Durrell, 1912-90, (Br.) novelist, poet. *Alexandria Quartet.*
Ilya G. Ehrenburg, 1891-1967, (Russ.) writer. *The Thaw.*
George Eliot (Mary Ann Evans or Marian Evans), 1819-80, (Br.) novelist. *Silas Marner, Middlemarch.*
T(homas) S(tearns) Eliot, 1888-1965, (Br.) poet, critic. *The Waste Land,* "The Love Song of J. Alfred Prufrock."
Stanley Elkin, 1930-95, (U.S.) novelist, short story writer. *George Mills.*
Ralph Ellison, 1914-94, (U.S.), writer. *Invisible Man.*
Ralph Waldo Emerson, 1803-82, (U.S.) poet, essayist. "Brahma," "Nature," "The Over-Soul," "Self-Reliance."
James T. Farrell, 1904-79, (U.S.) novelist. *Studs Lonigan.*
William Faulkner, 1897-1962, (U.S.) novelist. *Sanctuary, Light in August, The Sound and the Fury, Absalom, Absalom!*
Edna Ferber, 1887-1968, (U.S.) novelist, short-story writer, playwright. *So Big, Cimarron, Show Boat.*
Henry Fielding, 1707-54, (Br.) novelist. *Tom Jones.*
F(rancis) Scott Fitzgerald, 1896-1940, (U.S.) short-story writer, novelist. *The Great Gatsby, Tender Is the Night.*
Gustave Flaubert, 1821-80, (Fr.) novelist. *Madame Bovary.*
Ian Fleming, 1908-64, (Br.) novelist; James Bond spy thrillers.
Ford Madox Ford, 1873-1939, (Br.) novelist, critic, poet. *The Good Soldier.*
C(ecil) S(cott) Forester, 1899-1966, (Br.) writer. Horatio Hornblower novels.
E(dward) M(organ) Forster, 1879-1970, (Br.) novelist. *A Passage to India, Howards End.*
Anatole France, 1844-1924, (Fr.) writer. *Penguin Island, My Friend's Book, The Crime of Sylvestre Bonnard.*
Robert Frost, 1874-1963, (U.S.) poet. "Birches," "Fire and Ice," "Stopping by Woods on a Snowy Evening."
William Gaddis, 1922-98, (U.S.) novelist. *The Recognitions.*
John Galsworthy, 1867-1933, (Br.) novelist, dramatist. *The Forsyte Saga.*
Federico Garcia Lorca, 1898-1936, (Sp.) poet, dramatist. *Blood Wedding.*
Erle Stanley Gardner, 1889-1970, (U.S.) mystery writer; created Perry Mason.
Jean Genet, 1911-86, (Fr.) playwright, novelist. *The Maids.*
Kahlil Gibran, 1883-1931, (Lebanese-U.S.) mystical novelist, essayist, poet. *The Prophet.*
André Gide, 1869-1951, (Fr.) writer. *The Immoralist, The Pastoral Symphony, Strait Is the Gate.*
Allen Ginsberg, 1926-1997, (U.S.) Beat poet. "Howl."

Jean Giraudoux, 1882-1944, (Fr.) novelist, dramatist. *Electra, The Madwoman of Chaillot, Ondine, Tiger at the Gate.*

Johann Wolfgang von Goethe, 1749-1832, (Ger.) poet, dramatist, novelist. *Faust, Sorrows of Young Werther.*

Nikolai Gogol, 1809-52, (Russ.) short-story writer, dramatist, novelist. *Dead Souls, The Inspector General.*

William Golding, 1911-93, (Br.) novelist. *Lord of the Flies.*

Oliver Goldsmith, 1728-74, (Br.-Ir.) dramatist, novelist. *The Vicar of Wakefield, She Stoops to Conquer.*

Maxim Gorky, 1868-1936, (Russ.) dramatist, novelist. *The Lower Depths.*

Robert Graves, 1895-1985, (Br.) poet, classical scholar, novelist. *I, Claudius; The White Goddess.*

Thomas Gray, 1716-71, (Br.) poet. "Elegy Written in a Country Churchyard," "The Progress of Poesy."

Julien Green, 1900-98, (U.S.-Fr.) expatriate American, French novelist. *Moira, Each Man in His Darkness.*

Graham Greene, 1904-91, (Br.) novelist. *The Power and the Glory, The Heart of the Matter, The Ministry of Fear.*

Zane Grey, 1872-1939, (U.S.) writer of Western stories.

Jakob Grimm, 1785-1863, (Ger.) philologist, folklorist; with brother **Wilhelm**, 1786-1859, collected *Grimm's Fairy Tales.*

Alex Haley, 1921-92, (U.S.) author. *Roots.*

Dashiell Hammett, 1894-1961, (U.S.) detective-story writer; created Sam Spade. *The Maltese Falcon, The Thin Man.*

Knut Hamsun, 1859-1952 (Nor.) novelist. *Hunger.*

Thomas Hardy, 1840-1928, (Br.) novelist, poet. *The Return of the Native, Tess of the D'Urbervilles, Jude the Obscure.*

Joel Chandler Harris, 1848-1908, (U.S.) Uncle Remus stories.

Moss Hart, 1904-61, (U.S.) playwright. *Once in a Lifetime, You Can't Take It With You, The Man Who Came to Dinner.*

Bret Harte, 1836-1902, (U.S.) short-story writer, poet. *The Luck of Roaring Camp.*

Jaroslav Hasek, 1883-1923, (Czech.) writer, playwright. *The Good Soldier Schweik.*

John Hawkes, 1925-98, (U.S.) experimental fiction writer. *The Goose on the Grave, Blood Oranges.*

Nathaniel Hawthorne, 1804-64, (U.S.) novelist, short-story writer. *The Scarlet Letter,* "Young Goodman Brown."

Heinrich Heine, 1797-1856, (Ger.) poet. *Book of Songs.*

Robert Heinlein, 1907-88, (U.S.) science fiction writer. *Stranger in a Strange Land.*

Joseph Heller, 1923-99, (U.S.) novelist. *Catch-22.*

Lillian Hellman, 1905-84, (U.S.) playwright, author of memoirs. *The Little Foxes, An Unfinished Woman, Pentimento.*

Ernest Hemingway, 1899-1961, (U.S.) novelist, short-story writer. *A Farewell to Arms, For Whom the Bell Tolls.*

O. Henry (W. S. Porter), 1862-1910, (U.S.) short-story writer. "The Gift of the Magi."

George Herbert, 1593-1633, (Br.) poet. "The Altar," "Easter Wings."

Zbigniew Herbert, 1924-98, (Pol.) poet. "Apollo and Marsyas."

Robert Herrick, 1591-1674, (Br.) poet. "To the Virgins to Make Much of Time."

James Herriot (James Alfred Wight), 1916-95, (Br.) novelist, veterinarian. *All Creatures Great and Small.*

John Hersey, 1914-93, (U.S.) novelist, journalist. *Hiroshima, A Bell for Adano.*

Hermann Hesse, 1877-1962, (Ger.) novelist, poet. *Death and the Lover, Steppenwolf, Siddhartha.*

James Hilton, 1900-54, (Br.) novelist. *Lost Horizon.*

Oliver Wendell Holmes, 1809-94, (U.S.) poet, novelist. *The Autocrat of the Breakfast-Table.*

Gerard Manley Hopkins, 1844-89, (Br.) poet. "Pied Beauty."

A(lfred) E. Housman, 1859-1936, (Br.) poet. *A Shropshire Lad.*

William Dean Howells, 1837-1920, (U.S.) novelist, critic. *The Rise of Silas Lapham.*

Langston Hughes, 1902-67, (U.S.) poet, playwright. *The Weary Blues, One-Way Ticket, Shakespeare in Harlem.*

Ted Hughes, 1930-98, (Br.) British poet laureate, 1984-98. *Crow, The Hawk in the Rain.*

Victor Hugo, 1802-85, (Fr.) poet, dramatist, novelist. *Notre Dame de Paris, Les Misérables.*

Zora Neale Hurston, 1903-60, (U.S.) writer, folklorist. *Their Eyes Were Watching God, Mules and Men.*

Aldous Huxley, 1894-1963, (Br.) writer. *Brave New World.*

Henrik Ibsen, 1828-1906, (Nor.) dramatist, poet. *A Doll's House, Ghosts, The Wild Duck, Hedda Gabler.*

William Inge, 1913-73, (U.S.) playwright. *Picnic; Come Back, Little Sheba; Bus Stop.*

Eugene Ionesco, 1910-94, (Fr.) surrealist dramatist. *The Bald Soprano, The Chairs.*

Washington Irving, 1783-1859, (U.S.) writer. "Rip Van Winkle," "The Legend of Sleepy Hollow."

Christopher Isherwood, 1904-1986, (Br.) novelist, playwright. *The Berlin Stories.*

Shirley Jackson, 1919-65, (U.S.) writer. "The Lottery."

Henry James, 1843-1916, (U.S.) novelist, short-story writer, critic. *The Portrait of a Lady, The Ambassadors, Daisy Miller.*

Robinson Jeffers, 1887-1962, (U.S.) poet. *Tamar and Other Poems, Medea.*

Samuel Johnson, 1709-84, (Br.) author, scholar, critic. *Dictionary of the English Language, Vanity of Human Wishes.*

Ben Jonson, 1572-1637, (Br.) dramatist, poet. *Volpone.*

James Joyce, 1882-1941, (Ir.) writer. *Ulysses, Dubliners, A Portrait of the Artist as a Young Man, Finnegans Wake.*

Ernst Junger, 1895-1998, (Ger.) novelist, essayist. *The Peace, On the Marble Cliff.*

Franz Kafka, 1883-1924, (Ger.) novelist, short-story writer. *The Trial, The Castle, The Metamorphosis.*

George S. Kaufman, 1889-1961, (U.S.) playwright. *The Man Who Came to Dinner, You Can't Take It With You, Stage Door.*

Yasunari Kawabata, 1899-1972, (Japan) novelist. *The Sound of the Mountains.*

Nikos Kazantzakis, 1883-1957, (Gk.) novelist. *Zorba the Greek, A Greek Passion.*

Alfred Kazin, 1915-98 (U.S.) author, critic, teacher. *On Native Grounds.*

John Keats, 1795-1821, (Br.) poet. "Ode on a Grecian Urn," "Ode to a Nightingale," "La Belle Dame Sans Merci."

Jack Kerouac, 1922-1969, (U.S.), author, Beat poet. *On the Road, The Dharma Bums,* "Mexico City Blues."

Joyce Kilmer, 1886-1918, (U.S.) poet. "Trees."

Rudyard Kipling, 1865-1936, (Br.) author, poet. "The White Man's Burden," "Gunga Din," *The Jungle Book.*

Jean de la Fontaine, 1621-95, (Fr.) poet. *Fables choisies.*

Pär Lagerkvist, 1891-1974, (Swed.) poet, dramatist, novelist. *Barabbas, The Sybil.*

Selma Lagerlöf, 1858-1940, (Swed.) novelist. *Jerusalem, The Ring of the Lowenskolds.*

Alphonse de Lamartine, 1790-1869, (Fr.) poet, novelist, statesman. *Méditations poétiques.*

Charles Lamb, 1775-1834, (Br.) essayist. *Specimens of English Dramatic Poets, Essays of Elia.*

Giuseppe di Lampedusa, 1896-1957, (It.) novelist. *The Leopard.*

William Langland, c1332-1400, (Eng.) poet. *Piers Plowman.*

Ring Lardner, 1885-1933, (U.S.) short-story writer, humorist.

Louis L'Amour, 1908-88, (U.S.) western author, screenwriter. *Hondo, The Cherokee Trail.*

D(avid) H(erbert) Lawrence, 1885-1930, (Br.) novelist. *Sons and Lovers, Women in Love, Lady Chatterley's Lover.*

Halldor Laxness, 1902-98, (Icelandic) novelist. *Iceland's Bell.*

Mikhail Lermontov, 1814-41, (Russ.) novelist, poet. "Demon," *Hero of Our Time.*

Alain-René Lesage, 1668-1747, (Fr.) novelist. *Gil Blas de Santillana.*

Gotthold Lessing, 1729-81, (Ger.) dramatist, philosopher, critic. *Miss Sara Sampson, Minna von Barnhelm.*

C(live) S(taples) Lewis, 1898-1963, (Br.) critic, novelist, religious writer. *Allegory of Love; The Lion, the Witch and the Wardrobe; Out of the Silent Planet.*

Sinclair Lewis, 1885-1951, (U.S.) novelist. *Babbitt, Main Street, Arrowsmith, Dodsworth.*

Li Po, 701-762 (China) poet. "Song Before Drinking," "She Spins Silk."

Vachel Lindsay, 1879-1931, (U.S.) poet. *General William Booth Enters Into Heaven, The Congo.*

Hugh Lofting, 1886-1947, (Br.) writer. Dr. Doolittle series.

Jack London, 1876-1916, (U.S.) novelist, journalist. *Call of the Wild, The Sea-Wolf, White Fang.*

Henry Wadsworth Longfellow, 1807-82, (U.S.) poet. *Evangeline, The Song of Hiawatha.*

Lope de Vega, 1562-1635, (Sp.) playwright. *The Sheep Well.*

Amy Lowell, 1874-1925, (U.S.) poet, critic. "Lilacs."

James Russell Lowell, 1819-91, (U.S.) poet, editor. *Poems, The Biglow Papers.*

Robert Lowell, 1917-77, (U.S.) poet. "Lord Weary's Castle."

Joaquim Maria Machado de Assis, 1839-1908, (Brazil) novelist, poet. *The Posthumous Memoirs of Bras Cubas.*

Archibald MacLeish, 1892-1982, (U.S.) poet. *Conquistador.*

Bernard Malamud, 1914-86, (U.S.) short-story writer, novelist. "The Magic Barrel," *The Assistant, The Fixer.*

Stéphane Mallarmé, 1842-98, (Fr.) poet. *Poésies.*

Sir Thomas Malory, ?-1471, (Br.) writer. *Morte d'Arthur.*

Andre Malraux, 1901-76, (Fr.) novelist. *Man's Fate.*

Osip Mandelstam, 1891-1938, (Russ.) poet. *Stone, Tristia.*

Thomas Mann, 1875-1955, (Ger.) novelist. *Buddenbrooks, The Magic Mountain,* "Death in Venice."

Katherine Mansfield, 1888-1923, (Br.) short-story writer. "Bliss."

Christopher Marlowe, 1564-93, (Br.) dramatist, poet. *Tamburlaine the Great, Dr. Faustus, The Jew of Malta.*

Andrew Marvell, 1621-78, (Br.) poet. "To His Coy Mistress."

John Masefield, 1878-1967, (Br.) poet. "Sea Fever," "Cargoes," *Salt Water Ballads.*

Edgar Lee Masters, 1869-1950, (U.S.) poet, biographer. *Spoon River Anthology.*

W(illiam) Somerset Maugham, 1874-1965, (Br.) author. *Of Human Bondage, The Moon and Sixpence.*

Guy de Maupassant, 1850-93, (Fr.) novelist, short-story writer. "A Life," "Bel-Ami," "The Necklace."

François Mauriac, 1885-1970, (Fr.) novelist, dramatist. *Viper's Tangle, The Kiss to the Leper.*

Vladimir Mayakovsky, 1893-1930, (Russ.) poet, dramatist. *The Cloud in Trousers.*

Mary McCarthy, 1912-89, (U.S.) critic, novelist, memoirist. *Memories of a Catholic Girlhood.*

Carson McCullers, 1917-67, (U.S.) novelist. *The Heart Is a Lonely Hunter, Member of the Wedding.*

Herman Melville, 1819-91, (U.S.) novelist, poet, *Moby-Dick, Typee. Billy Budd, Omoo.*

George Meredith, 1828-1909, (Br.) novelist, poet. *The Ordeal of Richard Feverel, The Egoist.*

Prosper Mérimée, 1803-70, (Fr.) author. *Carmen.*

James Merrill, 1926-95, (U.S.) poet. *Divine Comedies.*

James Michener, 1907-97, (U.S.) novelist. *Tales of the South Pacific.*

Edna St. Vincent Millay, 1892-1950, (U.S.) poet. *The Harp Weaver and Other Poems.*

Henry Miller, 1891-1980, (U.S.) erotic novelist. *Tropic of Cancer.*

A(lan) A(lexander) Milne, 1882-1956, (Br.) author. *Winnie-the-Pooh.*

John Milton, 1608-74, (Br.) poet, writer. *Paradise Lost, Comus. Lycidas, Areopagitica.*

Mishima Yukio (Hiraoka Kimitake), 1925-70, (Jpn.) writer. *Confessions of a Mask.*

Gabriela Mistral, 1889-1957, (Chil.) poet. *Sonnets of Death.*

Margaret Mitchell, 1900-49, (U.S.) novelist. *Gone With the Wind.*

Jean Baptiste Molière, 1622-73, (Fr.) dramatist. *Tartuffe, Le Misanthrope, Le Bourgeois Gentilhomme.*

Ferenc Molnár, 1878-1952, (Hung.) dramatist, novelist. *Liliom, The Guardsman, The Swan.*

Michel de Montaigne, 1533-92, (Fr.) essayist. *Essais.*

Eugenio Montale, 1896-1981, (It.) poet.

Brian Moore, 1921-99, (Ir.-U.S.) novelist. *The Lonely Passion of Judith Hearne.*

Clement C. Moore, 1779-1863, (U.S.) poet, educator. *"A Visit From Saint Nicholas."*

Marianne Moore, 1887-1972, (U.S.) poet.

Alberto Moravia, 1907-90, (It.) novelist, short-story writer. *The Time of Indifference.*

Sir Thomas More, 1478-1535, (Br.) writer, statesman, saint. *Utopia.*

Wright Morris, 1910-98 (U.S.) novelist. *My Uncle Dudley.*

Murasaki Shikibu, c978-1026, (Jpn.) novelist. *The Tale of Genji.*

Iris Murdoch, 1919-99 (Br.), novelist, philosopher. *The Sea, The Sea.*

Alfred de Musset, 1810-57, (Fr.) poet, dramatist. *La Confession d'un Enfant du Siècle.*

Vladimir Nabokov, 1899-1977, (Russ.-U.S.) novelist. *Lolita, Pale Fire.*

R.K. Narayan, 1906-2001, (India), novelist, *The Guide.*

Ogden Nash, 1902-71, (U.S.) poet of light verse.

Pablo Neruda, 1904-73, (Chil.) poet. *Twenty Love Poems and One Song of Despair, Toward the Splendid City.*

Patrick O'Brian, 1914-2000, (Br.) historical novelist. *Master and Commander, Blue at the Mizzen.*

Sean O'Casey, 1884-1964, (Ir.) dramatist. *Juno and the Paycock, The Plough and the Stars.*

Frank O'Connor (Michael Donovan), 1903-66, (Ir.) short-story writer. *"Guests of a Nation".*

Flannery O'Connor, 1925-64, (U.S.) novelist, short-story writer. *Wise Blood, "A Good Man Is Hard to Find."*

Clifford Odets, 1906-63, (U.S.) playwright. *Waiting for Lefty, Awake and Sing, Golden Boy, The Country Girl.*

John O'Hara, 1905-70, (U.S.) novelist, short-story writer. *From the Terrace, Appointment in Samarra, Pal Joey.*

Omar Khayyam, c1028-1122, (Per.) poet. *Rubaiyat.*

Eugene O'Neill, 1888-1953, (U.S.) playwright. *Emperor Jones, Anna Christie, Long Day's Journey Into Night.*

George Orwell, 1903-50, (Br.) novelist, essayist. *Animal Farm, Nineteen Eighty-Four.*

John Osborne, 1929-95, (Br.) dramatist, novelist. *Look Back in Anger, The Entertainer.*

Wilfred Owen, 1893-1918 (Br.) poet. *"Dulce et Decorum Est."*

Dorothy Parker, 1893-1967, (U.S.) poet, short-story writer. *Enough Rope, Laments for the Living.*

Boris Pasternak, 1890-1960, (Russ.) poet, novelist. *Doctor Zhivago.*

Alan Paton, 1903-88, (S. Africa) novelist. *Cry, the Beloved Country.*

Octavio Paz, 1914-98, (Mex.) poet, essayist. *The Labyrinth of Solitude, They Shall Not Pass!, The Sun Stone.*

Samuel Pepys, 1633-1703, (Br.) public official, diarist.

S(idney) J(oseph) Perelman, 1904-79, (U.S.) humorist. *The Road to Miltown, Under the Spreading Atrophy.*

Charles Perrault, 1628-1703, (Fr.) writer. *Tales From Mother Goose (Sleeping Beauty, Cinderella).*

Petrarch (Francesco Petrarca), 1304-74, (It.) poet. *Africa, Trionfi, Canzoniere.*

Luigi Pirandello, 1867-1936, (It.) novelist, dramatist. *Six Characters in Search of an Author.*

Sylvia Plath, 1932-63, (U.S.) author, poet. *The Bell Jar.*

Edgar Allan Poe, 1809-49, (U.S.) poet, short-story writer, critic. *"Annabel Lee," "The Raven," "The Purloined Letter."*

Alexander Pope, 1688-1744, (Br.) poet. *The Rape of the Lock, The Dunciad, An Essay on Man.*

Katherine Anne Porter, 1890-1980, (U.S.) novelist, short-story writer. *Ship of Fools.*

Chaim Potok, 1929-2002, (U.S.) novelist. *The Chosen.*

Ezra Pound, 1885-1972, (U.S.) poet. *Cantos.*

Anthony Powell, 1905-2000, (Br.) novelist. *A Dance to the Music of Time* series.

J(ohn) B. Priestley, 1894-1984, (Br.) novelist, dramatist. *The Good Companions.*

Marcel Proust, 1871-1922, (Fr.) novelist. *Remembrance of Things Past.*

Aleksandr Pushkin, 1799-1837, (Russ.) poet, novelist. *Boris Godunov, Eugene Onegin.*

Mario Puzo, 1920-99, (U.S.) novelist. *The Godfather.*

François Rabelais, 1495-1553, (Fr.) writer. *Gargantua.*

Jean Racine, 1639-99, (Fr.) dramatist. *Andromaque, Phèdre, Bérénice, Britannicus.*

Ayn Rand, 1905-82, (Russ.-U.S.) novelist, moral theorist. *The Fountainhead, Atlas Shrugged.*

Terence Rattigan, 1911-77, (Br.) playwright. *Separate Tables, The Browning Version.*

Erich Maria Remarque, 1898-1970, (Ger.-U.S.) novelist. *All Quiet on the Western Front.*

Samuel Richardson, 1689-1761, (Br.) novelist. *Pamela; or Virtue Rewarded.*

Rainer Maria Rilke, 1875-1926, (Ger.) poet. *Life and Songs, Duino Elegies, Poems From the Book of Hours.*

Arthur Rimbaud, 1854-91, (Fr.) poet. *A Season in Hell.*

Edwin Arlington Robinson, 1869-1935, (U.S.) poet. *"Richard Cory," "Miniver Cheevy," Merlin.*

Theodore Roethke, 1908-63, (U.S.) poet. *Open House, The Waking, The Far Field.*

Romain Rolland, 1866-1944, (Fr.) novelist, biographer. *Jean-Christophe.*

Pierre de Ronsard, 1524-85, (Fr.) poet. *Sonnets pour Hélène, La Franciade.*

Christina Rossetti, 1830-94, (Br.) poet. *"When I Am Dead, My Dearest."*

Dante Gabriel Rossetti, 1828-82, (Br.) poet, painter. *"The Blessed Damozel."*

Edmond Rostand, 1868-1918, (Fr.) poet, dramatist. *Cyrano de Bergerac.*

Damon Runyon, 1880-1946, (U.S.) short-story writer, journalist. *Guys and Dolls, Blue Plate Special.*

John Ruskin, 1819-1900, (Br.) critic, social theorist. *Modern Painters, The Seven Lamps of Architecture.*

Antoine de Saint-Exupéry, 1900-44, (Fr.) writer. *Wind, Sand and Stars, The Little Prince.*

Saki, or H(ector) H(ugh) Munro, 1870-1916, (Br.) writer. *The Chronicles of Clovis.*

George Sand (Amandine Lucie Aurore Dupin), 1804-76, (Fr.) novelist. *Indiana, Consuelo.*

Carl Sandburg, 1878-1967, (U.S.) poet. *The People, Yes; Chicago Poems, Smoke and Steel, Harvest Poems.*

William Saroyan, 1908-81, (U.S.) playwright, novelist. *The Time of Your Life, The Human Comedy.*

Nathalie Sarraute, 1900-99, (Fr.) Nouveau Roman novelist. *Tropisms.*

May Sarton, 1914-95, (Belg.-U.S.) poet, novelist. *Encounter in April, Anger.*

Dorothy L. Sayers, 1893-1957, (Br.) mystery writer; created Lord Peter Wimsey.

Richard Scarry, 1920-94, (U.S.) author of children's books. *Richard Scarry's Best Story Book Ever.*

Friedrich von Schiller, 1759-1805, (Ger.) dramatist, poet, historian. *Don Carlos, Maria Stuart, Wilhelm Tell.*

Sir Walter Scott, 1771-1832, (Sc.) novelist, poet. *Ivanhoe.*

Jaroslav Seifert, 1902-86, (Czech.) poet.

Dr. Seuss (Theodor Seuss Geisel), 1904-91, (U.S.) children's book author and illustrator. *The Cat in the Hat.*

William Shakespeare, 1564-1616, (Br.) dramatist, poet. *Romeo and Juliet, Hamlet, King Lear, Julius Caesar,* sonnets.

Karl Shapiro, 1913-2000, (U.S.) poet. *"Elegy for a Dead Soldier".*

George Bernard Shaw, 1856-1950, (Ir.-Br.) playwright, critic. *St. Joan, Pygmalion, Major Barbara, Man and Superman.*

Mary Wollstonecraft Shelley, 1797-1851, (Br.) novelist, feminist. *Frankenstein. The Last Man.*

Percy Bysshe Shelley, 1792-1822, (Br.) poet. *Prometheus Unbound, Adonais, "Ode to the West Wind," "To a Skylark."*

Richard B. Sheridan, 1751-1816, (Br.) dramatist. *The Rivals, School for Scandal.*

Robert Sherwood, 1896-1955, (U.S.) playwright, biographer. *The Petrified Forest, Abe Lincoln in Illinois.*

Mikhail Sholokhov, 1906-84, (Russ.) writer. *The Silent Don.*

Georges Simenon (Georges Sims), 1903-89, (Belg.-Fr.) mystery writer; created Inspector Maigret.

Upton Sinclair, 1878-1968, (U.S.) novelist. *The Jungle.*

Isaac Bashevis Singer, 1904-91, (Pol.-U.S.) novelist, short-story writer, in Yiddish. *The Magician of Lublin.*

C(harles) P(ercy) Snow, 1905-80, (Br.) novelist, scientist. *Strangers and Brothers, Corridors of Power.*

Stephen Spender, 1909-95, (Br.) poet, critic, novelist. *Twenty Poems,* "Elegy for Margaret."

Edmund Spenser, 1552-99, (Br.) poet. *The Faerie Queen.*

Johanna Spyri, 1827-1901, (Swiss) children's author. *Heidi.*

Christina Stead, 1903-83, (Austral.) novelist, short-story writer. *The Man Who Loved Children.*

Richard Steele, 1672-1729, (Br.) essayist, playwright, began the *Tatler* and *Spectator. The Conscious Lovers.*

Gertrude Stein, 1874-1946, (U.S.) writer. *Three Lives.*

John Steinbeck, 1902-68, (U.S.) novelist. *The Grapes of Wrath, Of Mice and Men, The Winter of Our Discontent.*

Stendhal (Marie Henri Beyle), 1783-1842, (Fr.) novelist. *The Red and the Black, The Charterhouse of Parma.*

Laurence Sterne, 1713-68, (Br.) novelist. *Tristram Shandy.*

Wallace Stevens, 1879-1955, (U.S.) poet. *Harmonium, The Man With the Blue Guitar, Notes Toward a Supreme Fiction.*

Robert Louis Stevenson, 1850-94, (Br.) novelist, poet, essayist. *Treasure Island, A Child's Garden of Verses.*

Bram Stoker, 1845-1910, (Br.) writer. *Dracula.*

Rex Stout, 1886-1975, (U.S.) mystery writer; created Nero Wolfe.

Harriet Beecher Stowe, 1811-96, (U.S.) novelist. *Uncle Tom's Cabin.*

Lytton Strachey, 1880-1932, (Br.) biographer, critic. *Eminent Victorians. Queen Victoria, Elizabeth and Essex.*

August Strindberg, 1849-1912, (Swed.) dramatist, novelist. *The Father, Miss Julie, The Creditors.*

Jonathan Swift, 1667-1745, (Br.) satirist, poet. *Gulliver's Travels,* "A Modest Proposal."

Algernon C. Swinburne, 1837-1909, (Br.) poet, dramatist. *Atalanta in Calydon.*

John M. Synge, 1871-1909, (Ir.) poet, dramatist. *Riders to the Sea, The Playboy of the Western World.*

Rabindranath Tagore, 1861-1941, (In.) author, poet. *Sadhana, The Realization of Life, Gitanjali.*

Booth Tarkington, 1869-1946, (U.S.) novelist. *Seventeen.*

Peter Taylor, 1917-94, (U.S.) novelist. *A Summons to Memphis.*

Sara Teasdale, 1884-1933, (U.S.) poet. *Helen of Troy and Other Poems, Rivers to the Sea.*

Alfred, Lord Tennyson, 1809-92, (Br.) poet. *Idylls of the King, In Memoriam,* "The Charge of the Light Brigade."

William Makepeace Thackeray, 1811-63, (Br.) novelist. *Vanity Fair, Henry Esmond, Pendennis.*

Dylan Thomas, 1914-53, (Welsh) poet. *Under Milk Wood, A Child's Christmas in Wales.*

Henry David Thoreau, 1817-62, (U.S.) writer, philosopher, naturalist. *Walden,* "Civil Disobedience."

James Thurber, 1894-1961, (U.S.) humorist; "The Secret Life of Walter Mitty," *My Life and Hard Times.*

J(ohn) R(onald) R(euel) Tolkien, 1892-1973, (Br.) writer. *The Hobbit, Lord of the Rings* trilogy.

Leo Tolstoy, 1828-1910, (Russ.) novelist, short-story writer. *War and Peace, Anna Karenina,* "The Death of Ivan Ilyich."

Anthony Trollope, 1815-82, (Br.) novelist. *The Warden, Barchester Towers,* the Palliser novels.

Ivan Turgenev, 1818-83, (Russ.) novelist, short-story writer. *Fathers and Sons, First Love, A Month in the Country.*

Amos Tutuola, 1920-97, (Nigerian) novelist. *The Palm-Wine Drunkard, My Life in the Bush of Ghosts.*

Mark Twain (Samuel Clemens), 1835-1910, (U.S.) novelist, humorist. *The Adventures of Huckleberry Finn, Tom Sawyer; Life on the Mississippi.*

Sigrid Undset, 1881-1949, (Nor.) novelist, poet. *Kristin Lavransdatter.*

Paul Valéry, 1871-1945, (Fr.) poet, critic. *La Jeune Parque, The Graveyard by the Sea.*

Paul Verlaine, 1844-96, (Fr.) Symbolist poet. *Songs Without Words.*

Jules Verne, 1828-1905, (Fr.) novelist. *Twenty Thousand Leagues Under the Sea.*

François Villon, 1431-63?, (Fr.) poet. *The Lays, The Grand Testament.*

Voltaire (F.M. Arouet), 1694-1778, (Fr.) writer of "philosophical romances"; philosopher, historian; *Candide.*

Robert Penn Warren, 1905-89, (U.S.) novelist, poet, critic. *All the King's Men.*

Evelyn Waugh, 1903-66, (Br.) novelist. *The Loved One, Brideshead Revisited, A Handful of Dust.*

H(erbert) G(eorge) Wells, 1866-1946, (Br.) novelist. *The Time Machine, The Invisible Man, The War of the Worlds.*

Eudora Welty, 1909-2001, (U.S.) Southern short story writer. "Why I Live at the P.O," "The Ponder Heart."

Rebecca West, 1893-1983, (Br.) novelist, critic, journalist. *Black Lamb and Grey Falcon.*

Edith Wharton, 1862-1937, (U.S.) novelist. *The Age of Innocence, The House of Mirth, Ethan Frome.*

E(lwyn) B(rooks) White, 1899-1985, (U.S.) essayist, novelist. *Charlotte's Web, Stuart Little.*

Patrick White, 1912-90, (Austral.) novelist. *The Tree of Man.*

T(erence) H(anbury) White, 1906-64, (Br.) author. *The Once and Future King, A Book of Beasts.*

Walt Whitman, 1819-92, (U.S.) poet. *Leaves of Grass.*

John Greenleaf Whittier, 1807-92, (U.S.) poet, journalist. *Snow-Bound.*

Oscar Wilde, 1854-1900, (Ir.) novelist, playwright. *The Picture of Dorian Gray, The Importance of Being Earnest.*

Laura Ingalls Wilder, 1867-1957, (U.S.) novelist. Little House on the Prairie series of children's books.

Thornton Wilder, 1897-1975, (U.S.) playwright. *Our Town, The Skin of Our Teeth, The Matchmaker.*

Tennessee Williams, 1911-83, (U.S.) playwright. *A Streetcar Named Desire, Cat on a Hot Tin Roof, The Glass Menagerie.*

William Carlos Williams, 1883-1963, (U.S.) poet, physician. *Tempers, Al Que Quiere! Paterson,* "This Is Just to Say."

Edmund Wilson, 1895-1972, (U.S.) critic, novelist. *Axel's Castle, To the Finland Station.*

P(elham) G(renville) Wodehouse, 1881-1975, (Br.-U.S.) humorist. The "Jeeves" novels, *Anything Goes.*

Thomas Wolfe, 1900-38, (U.S.) novelist. *Look Homeward, Angel; You Can't Go Home Again.*

Virginia Woolf, 1882-1941, (Br.) novelist, essayist. *Mrs. Dalloway, To the Lighthouse, A Room of One's Own.*

William Wordsworth, 1770-1850, (Br.) poet. "Tintern Abbey," "Ode: Intimations of Immortality," *The Prelude.*

Richard Wright, 1908-60, novelist, short-story writer. *Native Son, Black Boy, Uncle Tom's Children.*

Elinor Wylie, 1885-1928, (U.S.) poet. *Nets to Catch the Wind.*

William Butler Yeats, 1865-1939, (Ir.) poet, playwright. "The Second Coming," *The Wild Swans at Coole.*

Émile Zola, 1840-1902, (Fr.) novelist. *Nana, Thérèsè Raquin.*

Poets Laureate

There is no record of the origin of the office of Poet Laureate of England. Henry III (1216-72) reportedly had a Versificator Regis, or King's Poet, paid 100 shillings a year. Other poets said to have filled the role include Geoffrey Chaucer (d 1400), Edmund Spenser (d 1599), Ben Jonson (d 1637), and Sir William d'Avenant (d 1668).

The first official English poet laureate was John Dryden, appointed 1668, for life (as was customary). Then came Thomas Shadwell, in 1689; Nahum Tate, 1692; Nicholas Rowe, 1715; Rev. Laurence Eusden, 1718; Colley Cibber, 1730; William Whitehead, 1757; Rev. Thomas Warton, 1785; Henry James Pye, 1790; Robert Southey, 1813; William Wordsworth, 1843; Alfred, Lord Tennyson, 1850; Alfred Austin, 1896; Robert Bridges, 1913; John Masefield, 1930; C. Day Lewis, 1968; Sir John Betjeman, 1972; Ted Hughes, 1984; Andrew Motion, 1999.

In U.S., appointment is by Librarian of Congress and is not for life: Robert Penn Warren, appointed 1986; Richard Wilbur, 1987; Howard Nemerov, 1988; Mark Strand, 1990; Joseph Brodsky, 1991; Mona Van Duyn, 1992; Rita Dove, 1993; Robert Hass, 1995; Robert Pinsky, 1997; Stanley Kunitz, 2000; Billy Collins, 2001; Louise Gluck, 2003.

Composers of Classical and Avant Garde Music

Carl Philipp Emanuel Bach, 1714-88, (Ger.) Cantatas, passions, numerous keyboard and instrumental works.

Johann Christian Bach, 1735-82, (Ger.) Concertos, operas, sonatas.

Johann Sebastian Bach, 1685-1750, (Ger.) St. Matthew Passion, The Well-Tempered Clavier.

Samuel Barber, 1910-81, (U.S.) Adagio for Strings, Vanessa.

Béla Bartók, 1881-1945, (Hung.) Concerto for Orchestra, The Miraculous Mandarin.

Amy Beach (Mrs. H. H. A. Beach), 1867-1944, (U.S.) The Year's at the Spring, Fireflies, The Chambered Nautilus.

Ludwig van Beethoven, 1770-1827, (Ger.) Concertos (Emperor), sonatas (Moonlight, Pathetique), 9 symphonies.

Vincenzo Bellini, 1801-35, (It.) I Puritani, La Sonnambula, Norma.

Alban Berg, 1885-1935, (Austrian) Wozzeck, Lulu.

Hector Berlioz, 1803-69, (Fr.) Damnation of Faust, Symphonie Fantastique, Requiem.

Leonard Bernstein, 1918-90, (U.S.) Chichester Psalms, Jeremiah Symphony, Mass.

Georges Bizet, 1838-75, (Fr.) Carmen, Pearl Fishers.

Ernest Bloch, 1880-1959, (Swiss-U.S.) Macbeth (opera), Schelomo, Voice in the Wilderness.

Luigi Boccherini, 1743-1805, (It.) Chamber music and guitar pieces.

Alexander Borodin, 1833-87, (Russ.) Prince Igor, In the Steppes of Central Asia, Polovtzian Dances.

Pierre Boulez, b 1925, (Fr.) LeVisage nuptial, Edats/Multiple, Domaines.

Johannes Brahms, 1833-97, (Ger.) Liebeslieder Waltzes, Acad. Festival Overture, chamber music, 4 symphonies.
Benjamin Britten, 1913-76, (Br.) Peter Grimes, Turn of the Screw, A Ceremony of Carols, War Requiem.
Anton Bruckner, 1824-96, (Austrian) 9 symphonies.
Dietrich Buxtehude, 1637-1707, (Dan.) Organ works, vocal music.
William Byrd, 1543-1623, (Br.) Masses, motets.
John Cage, 1912-92, (U.S.) Winter Music, Fontana Mix.
Emmanuel Chabrier, 1841-94, (Fr.) Le Roi Malgré Lui, Espana.
Gustave Charpentier, 1860-1956, (Fr.) Louise.
Frédéric Chopin, 1810-49, (Pol.) Mazurkas, waltzes, etudes, nocturnes, polonaises, sonatas.
Aaron Copland, 1900-90, (U.S.) Appalachian Spring, Fanfare for the Common Man, Lincoln Portrait.
Claude Debussy, 1862-1918, (Fr.) Pelleas et Melisande, La Mer, Prelude to the Afternoon of a Faun.
Gaetano Donizetti, 1797-1848, (It.) Elixir of Love, Lucia di Lammermoor, Daughter of the Regiment.
Paul Dukas, 1865-1935, (Fr.) Sorcerer's Apprentice.
Antonin Dvorak, 1841-1904, (Czech.) Songs My Mother Taught Me, Symphony in E Minor (From the New World).
Edward Elgar, 1857-1934, (Br.) Enigma Variations, Pomp and Circumstance.
Manuel de Falla, 1876-1946, (Sp.) El Amor Brujo, La Vida Breve, The Three-Cornered Hat.
Gabriel Faurè, 1845-1924, (Fr.) Requiem, Elègie for Cello and Piano.
Cesar Franck, 1822-90, (Belg.) Symphony in D minor, Violin Sonata.
George Gershwin, 1898-1937, (U.S.) Rhapsody in Blue, An American in Paris, Porgy and Bess.
Philip Glass, b 1937, (U.S.) Einstein on the Beach, The Voyage.
Mikhail Glinka, 1804-57, (Russ.) A Life for the Tsar, Ruslan and Ludmilla.
Christoph W. Gluck, 1714-87, (Ger.) Alceste, Iphigène en Tauride.
Charles Gounod, 1818-93, (Fr.) Faust, Romeo and Juliet.
Edvard Grieg, 1843-1907, (Nor.) Peer Gynt Suite, Concerto in A minor for piano.
George Frideric Handel, 1685-1759, (Ger.-Br.) Messiah, Water Music.
Howard Hanson, 1896-1981, (U.S.) Symphonies No. 1 (Nordic) and No: 2 (Romantic).
Roy Harris, 1898-1979, (U.S.) Symphonies.
(Franz) Joseph Haydn, 1732-1809, (Austrian) Symphonies (Clock, London, Toy), chamber music, oratorios.
Paul Hindemith, 1895-1963, (U.S.) Mathis der Maler.
Gustav Holst, 1874-1934, (Br.) The Planets.
Arthur Honegger, 1892-1955, (Fr.) Judith, Le Roi David, Pacific 231.
Alan Hovhaness, 1911-2000, (U.S.) Symphonies, Magnificat.
Engelbert Humperdinck, 1854-1921, (Ger.) Hansel and Gretel.
Charles Ives, 1874-1954, (U.S.) Concord Sonata, symphonies.
Aram Khachaturian, 1903-78, (Russ.) Ballets, piano pieces, Sabre Dance.
Zoltán Kodaly, 1882-1967, (Hung.) Háry János, Psalmus Hungaricus.
Fritz Kreisler, 1875-1962, (Austrian) Caprice Viennois, Tambourin Chinois.
Edouard Lalo, 1823-92, (Fr.) Symphonie Espagnole.
Ruggero Leoncavallo, 1857-1919, (It.) Pagliacci.
Franz Liszt, 1811-86, (Hung.) 20 Hungarian rhapsodies, symphonic poems.
Edward MacDowell, 1861-1908, (U.S.) To a Wild Rose.
Gustav Mahler, 1860-1911, (Austrian) Das Lied von der Erde; 9 complete symphonies.
Pietro Mascagni, 1863-1945, (It.) Cavalleria Rusticana.
Jules Massenet, 1842-1912, (Fr.) Manon, Le Cid, Thaïs.
Felix Mendelssohn, 1809-47, (Ger.) A Midsummer Night's Dream, Songs Without Words, violin concerto.
Gian-Carlo Menotti, b 1911, (It.-U.S.) The Medium, The Consul, Amahl and the Night Visitors.

Claudio Monteverdi, 1567-1643, (It.) Opera, masses, madrigals.
Modest Moussorgsky, 1839-81, (Russ.) Boris Godunov, Pictures at an Exhibition.
Wolfgang Amadeus Mozart, 1756-91, (Austrian) Chamber music, concertos, operas (Magic Flute, Marriage of Figaro), 41 symphonies.
Jacques Offenbach, 1819-80, (Fr.) Tales of Hoffmann.
Carl Orff, 1895-1982, (Ger.) Carmina Burana.
Johann Pachelbel, 1653-1706, (Ger.) Canon and Fugue in D major.
Ignacy Paderewski, 1860-1941, (Pol.) Minuet in G.
Niccolò Paganini, 1782-1840, (It.) Caprices for violin solo.
Giovanni Palestrina, c1525-94, (It.) Masses, madrigals.
Krzystof Penderecki, b 1933, (Pol.) Psalmus, Polymorphia, De natura sonoris.
Francis Poulenc, 1899-1963, (Fr.) Dialogues des Carmèlites.
Mel Powell, 1923-98, (U.S.) Duplicates: A Concerto for Two Pianos and Orchestra, Cantilena Concertante.
Sergei Prokofiev, 1891-1953, (Russ.) Classical Symphony, Love for Three Oranges, Peter and the Wolf.
Giacomo Puccini, 1858-1924, (It.) La Boheme, Manon Lescaut, Tosca, Madama Butterfly.
Henry Purcell, 1659-95, (Eng.) Dido and Aeneas.
Sergei Rachmaninoff, 1873-1943, (Russ.) Concertos, preludes (Prelude in C sharp minor), symphonies.
Maurice Ravel, 1875-1937, (Fr.) Boléro, Daphnis et Chloè, Piano Concerto in D for Left Hand Alone.
Nikolai Rimsky-Korsakov, 1844-1908, (Russ.) Golden Cockerel, Scheherazade, Flight of the Bumblebee.
Gioacchino Rossini, 1792-1868, (It.) Barber of Seville, Othello, William Tell.
Camille Saint-Saëns, 1835-1921, (Fr.) Carnival of Animals (The Swan), Samson and Delilah, Danse Macabre.
Alessandro Scarlatti, 1660-1725, (It.) Cantatas, oratorios, operas.
Domenico Scarlatti, 1685-1757, (It.) Harpsichord works.
Alfred Schnittke, 1934-98, (Sov.-Ger.) Life With an Idiot.
Arnold Schoenberg, 1874-1951, (Austrian) Pelleas and Melisande, Pierrot Lunaire, Verklärte Nacht.
Franz Schubert, 1797-1828, (Austrian) Chamber music (Trout Quintet), lieder, symphonies (Unfinished).
Robert Schumann, 1810-56, (Ger.) Die Frauenliebe und Leben, Träumerei.
Dimitri Shostakovich, 1906-75, (Russ.) Symphonies, Lady Macbeth of the District Mzensk.
Jean Sibelius, 1865-1957, (Finn.) Finlandia.
Bedrich Smetana, 1824-84, (Czech.) The Bartered Bride.
Karlheinz Stockhausen, b 1928, (Ger.) KontraPunkte, Kontakte for Electronic Instruments.
Richard Strauss, 1864-1949, (Ger.) Salome, Elektra, Der Rosenkavalier, Thus Spake Zarathustra.
Igor Stravinsky, 1882-1971, (Russ.) Noah and the Flood, The Rake's Progress, The Rite of Spring.
Toru Takemitsu, 1930-96, (Jpn.) Requiem for Strings, Dorian Horizon.
Peter I. Tchaikovsky, 1840-93, (Russ.) Nutcracker, Swan Lake, The Sleeping Beauty.
Virgil Thomson, 1896-1989, (U.S.) Opera, film music, Four Saints in Three Acts.
Dmitri Tiomkin, 1894-1979, (Russ.-U.S.) film scores, including High Noon.
Sir Michael Tippett, 1905-98, (Br.) A Child of Our Time, The Midsummer Marriage, The Knot Garden.
Ralph Vaughan Williams, 1872-1958, (Eng.) Fantasiz on a Theme by Thomas Tallis, symphonies, vocal music.
Giuseppe Verdi, 1813-1901, (It.) Aida, Rigoletto, Don Carlo, Il Trovatore, La Traviata, Falstaff, Macbeth.
Heitor Villa-Lobos, 1887-1959, (Brazil) Bachianas Brasileiras.
Antonio Vivaldi, 1678-1741, (It.) Concerto grossos (The Four Seasons).
Richard Wagner, 1813-83, (Ger.) Rienzi, Tannhäuser, Lohengrin, Tristan and Isolde.
Carl Maria von Weber, 1786-1826, (Ger.) Der Freischutz.

Composers of Operettas, Musicals, and Popular Music

Richard Adler, b 1921, (U.S.) Pajama Game; Damn Yankees.
Milton Ager, 1893-1979, (U.S.) I Wonder What's Become of Sally; Hard Hearted Hannah; Ain't She Sweet?
Arthur Altman, 1910-94, (U.S.) All or Nothing at All.
Leroy Anderson, 1908-75, (U.S.) Sleigh Ride, Blue Tango, Syncopated Clock.
Paul Anka, b 1941, (Can.) My Way; Tonight Show theme.
Harold Arlen, 1905-86, (U.S.) Stormy Weather; Over the Rainbow; Blues in the Night; That Old Black Magic.
Burt Bacharach, b 1928, (U.S.) Raindrops Keep Fallin' on My Head; Walk on By; What the World Needs Now Is Love.
Ernest Ball, 1878-1927, (U.S.) Mother Machree; When Irish Eyes Are Smiling.
Irving Berlin, 1888-1989, (U.S.) Annie Get Your Gun; Call Me Madam; God Bless America; White Christmas.

Leonard Bernstein, 1918-90, (U.S.) On the Town; Wonderful Town; Candide; West Side Story.
Eubie Blake, 1883-1983, (U.S.) Shuffle Along; I'm Just Wild About Harry.
Jerry Bock, b 1928, (U.S.) Mr. Wonderful; Fiorello; Fiddler on the Roof; The Rothschilds.
Carrie Jacobs Bond, 1862-1946, (U.S.) I Love You Truly.
Nacio Herb Brown, 1896-1964, (U.S.) Singing in the Rain; You Were Meant for Me; All I Do Is Dream of You.
Hoagy Carmichael, 1899-1981, (U.S.) Stardust; Georgia on My Mind; Old Buttermilk Sky.
George M. Cohan, 1878-1942, (U.S.) Give My Regards to Broadway; You're a Grand Old Flag; Over There.
Cy Coleman, b 1929, (U.S.) Sweet Charity; Witchcraft.
John Frederick Coots, 1895-1985, (U.S.) Santa Claus Is Coming to Town; You Go to My Head; For All We Know.

Noel Coward, 1899-1973, (Br.) *Bitter Sweet;* Mad Dogs and Englishmen; Mad About the Boy.

Neil Diamond, b 1941, (U.S.) I'm a Believer; Sweet Caroline.

Walter Donaldson, 1893-1947, (U.S.) My Buddy; Carolina in the Morning; Makin' Whoopee.

Vernon Duke, 1903-69, (U.S.) April in Paris.

Bob Dylan, b 1941, (U.S.) Blowin' in the Wind.

Gus Edwards, 1879-1945, (U.S.) School Days; By the Light of the Silvery Moon; In My Merry Oldsmobile.

Sherman Edwards, 1919-81, (U.S.) See You in September; Wonderful! Wonderful!

Duke Ellington, 1899-1974, (U.S.) Sophisticated Lady; Satin Doll; It Don't Mean a Thing; Solitude.

Sammy Fain, 1902-89, (U.S.) I'll Be Seeing You; Love Is a Many-Splendored Thing.

Fred Fisher, 1875-1942, (U.S.) Peg O' My Heart; Chicago.

Stephen Collins Foster, 1826-64, (U.S.) My Old Kentucky Home; Old Folks at Home, Beautiful Dreamer.

Rudolf Friml, 1879-1972, (Czech-U.S.) *The Firefly; Rose Marie; Vagabond King; Bird of Paradise.*

John Gay, 1685-1732, (Br.) *The Beggar's Opera.*

George Gershwin, 1898-1937, (U.S.) Someone to Watch Over Me; I've Got a Crush on You; Embraceable You.

Morton Gould, 1913-96, (U.S.) Fall River Suite, Holocaust Suite, Spirituals for Orchestra, Stringmusic.

Ferde Grofe, 1892-1972, (U.S.) Grand Canyon Suite.

Marvin Hamlisch, b 1944, (U.S.) The Way We Were; Nobody Does It Better; *A Chorus Line.*

Ray Henderson, 1896-1970, (U.S.) *George White's Scandals;* That Old Gang of Mine; Five Foot Two, Eyes of Blue.

Victor Herbert, 1859-1924, (Ir.-U.S.) *Mlle. Modiste; Babes in Toyland; The Red Mill; Naughty Marietta; Sweethearts.*

Jerry Herman, b 1933, (U.S.) *Hello Dolly; Mame.*

Brian Holland, b 1941, **Lamont Dozier,** b 1941, **Eddie Holland,** b 1939, (all U.S.) Heat Wave; Stop! In the Name of Love; Baby, I Need Your Loving.

Antonio Carlos Jobim, 1927-94, (Brazil) *The Girl From Ipanema; Desafinado; One Note Samba.*

Billy (William Martin) Joel, b 1949, (U.S.) Just the Way You Are; Honesty; Piano Man.

Scott Joplin, 1868-1917, (U.S.) Maple Leaf Rag; *Treemonisha.*

John Kander, b 1927, (U.S.) *Cabaret; Chicago; Funny Lady.*

Jerome Kern, 1885-1945, (U.S.) *Sally; Sunny; Show Boat.*

Carole King, b 1942, (U.S.) Will You Love Me Tomorrow?; Natural Woman; One Fine Day; Up on the Roof.

Burton Lane, 1912-1997, (U.S.) *Finian's Rainbow.*

Franz Lehar, 1870-1948, (Hung.) *Merry Widow.*

Jerry Leiber, & **Mike Stoller,** both b 1933, (both U.S.) Hound Dog; Searchin'; Yakety Yak; Love Me Tender.

Mitch Leigh, b 1928, (U.S.) *Man of La Mancha.*

John Lennon, 1940-80, & **Paul McCartney,** b 1942, (both Br.) I Want to Hold Your Hand; She Loves You.

Jay Livingston, 1915-2001 (U.S.) Mona Lisa; Que Sera, Sera.

Andrew Lloyd Webber, b 1948, (Br.) *Jesus Christ Superstar; Evita; Cats; The Phantom of the Opera.*

Frank Loesser, 1910-69, (U.S.) *Guys and Dolls; Where's Charley?; The Most Happy Fella;* How to Succeed....

Frederick Loewe, 1901-88, (Austrian-U.S.) *Brigadoon; Paint Your Wagon; My Fair Lady; Camelot.*

Henry Mancini, 1924-94, (U.S.) Moon River; Days of Wine and Roses; Pink Panther Theme.

Barry Mann, b 1939, & **Cynthia Weil,** b 1937, (both U.S.) You've Lost That Loving Feeling.

Jimmy McHugh, 1894-1969, (U.S.) Don't Blame Me; I'm in the Mood for Love; I Feel a Song Coming On.

Alan Menken, b 1949, (U.S.) *Little Shop of Horrors, Beauty and the Beast.*

Joseph Meyer, 1894-1987, (U.S.) If You Knew Susie; California, Here I Come; Crazy Rhythm.

Chauncey Olcott, 1858-1932, (U.S.) Mother Machree.

Jerome "Doc" Pomus, 1925-91, (U.S.) Save the Last Dance for Me; A Teenager in Love.

Cole Porter, 1893-1964, (U.S.) *Anything Goes; Kiss Me Kate; Can Can; Silk Stockings.*

Smokey Robinson, b 1940, (U.S.) Shop Around; My Guy; My Girl; Get Ready.

Richard Rodgers, 1902-79, (U.S.) *Oklahoma!; Carousel; South Pacific; The King and I; The Sound of Music.*

Sigmund Romberg, 1887-1951, (Hung.) *Maytime; The Student Prince; Desert Song; Blossom Time.*

Harold Rome, 1908-93, (U.S.) *Pins and Needles; Call Me Mister; Wish You Were Here; Fanny; Destry Rides Again.*

Vincent Rose, b 1880-1944, (U.S.) Avalon; Whispering; Blueberry Hill.

Harry Ruby, 1895-1974, (U.S.) Three Little Words; Who's Sorry Now?

Arthur Schwartz, 1900-84, (U.S.) *The Band Wagon;* Dancing in the Dark; By Myself; That's Entertainment.

Neil Sedaka, b 1939, (U.S.) Breaking Up Is Hard to Do.

Paul Simon, b 1942, (U.S.) Sounds of Silence; I Am a Rock; Mrs. Robinson; Bridge Over Troubled Waters.

Stephen Sondheim, b 1930, (U.S.) *A Little Night Music; Company; Sweeney Todd; Sunday in the Park With George.*

John Philip Sousa, 1854-1932, (U.S.) *El Capitan;* Stars and Stripes Forever.

Oskar Straus, 1870-1954, (Austrian) *Chocolate Soldier.*

Johann Strauss, 1825-99, (Austrian) *Gypsy Baron; Die Fledermaus;* waltzes: Blue Danube; Artist's Life.

Charles Strouse, b 1928, (U.S.) *Bye Bye, Birdie; Annie.*

Jule Styne, 1905-94, (Br.-U.S.) *Gentlemen Prefer Blondes; Bells Are Ringing; Gypsy; Funny Girl.*

Arthur S. Sullivan, 1842-1900, (Br.) *H.M.S. Pinafore; Pirates of Penzance; The Mikado.*

Deems Taylor, 1885-1966, (U.S.) *Peter Ibbetson.*

Harry Tobias, 1905-94, (U.S.) I'll Keep the Lovelight Burning.

Egbert van Alstyne, 1882-1951, (U.S.) In the Shade of the Old Apple Tree; Memories; Pretty Baby.

Jimmy Van Heusen, 1913-90, (U.S.) Moonlight Becomes You; Swinging on a Star; All the Way; Love and Marriage.

Albert von Tilzer, 1878-1956, (U.S.) I'll Be With You in Apple Blossom Time; Take Me Out to the Ball Game.

Harry von Tilzer, 1872-1946, (U.S.) Only a Bird in a Gilded Cage; On a Sunday Afternoon.

Fats Waller, 1904-43, (U.S.) Honeysuckle Rose; Ain't Misbehavin'.

Harry Warren, 1893-1981, (U.S.) You're My Everything; We're in the Money; I Only Have Eyes for You.

Jimmy Webb, b 1946, (U.S.) Up, Up and Away; By the Time I Get to Phoenix; Didn't We?; Wichita Lineman.

Kurt Weill, 1900-50, (Ger.-U.S.) *Threepenny Opera; Lady in the Dark; Knickerbocker Holiday; One Touch of Venus.*

Percy Wenrich, 1887-1952, (U.S.) When You Wore a Tulip; Moonlight Bay; Put On Your Old Gray Bonnet.

Richard A. Whiting, 1891-1938, (U.S.) Till We Meet Again; Sleepytime Gal; Beyond the Blue Horizon; My Ideal.

John Williams, b 1932, (U.S.) *Jaws; E.T.; Star Wars* series; *Raiders of the Lost Ark* series.

Meredith Willson, 1902-84, (U.S.) *The Music Man.*

Stevie Wonder, b 1950, (U.S.) You Are the Sunshine of My Life; Signed, Sealed, Delivered, I'm Yours.

Vincent Youmans, 1898-1946, (U.S.) *Two Little Girls in Blue; Wildflower; No, No, Nanette; Hit the Deck; Rainbow; Smiles.*

Lyricists

Howard Ashman, 1950-91, (U.S.) Little Shop of Horrors; The Little Mermaid.

Johnny Burke, 1908-84, (U.S.) Misty; Imagination.

Irving Caesar, 1895-1996, (U.S.) Swanee; Tea for Two; Just a Gigolo.

Sammy Cahn, 1913-93, (U.S.) High Hopes; Love and Marriage; The Second Time Around; It's Magic.

Leonard Cohen, b 1934, (Can.) Suzanne; Stranger Song.

Betty Comden, b 1919, (U.S.) and **Adolph Green,** 1915-2002, (U.S.) The Party's Over; Just in Time; New York, New York.

Hal David, b 1921, (U.S.) What the World Needs Now Is Love.

Buddy De Sylva, 1895-1950, (U.S.) When Day Is Done; Look for the Silver Lining; April Showers.

Howard Dietz, 1896-1983, (U.S.) Dancing in the Dark; You and the Night and the Music; That's Entertainment.

Al Dubin, 1891-1945, (U.S.) Tiptoe Through the Tulips; Anniversary Waltz; Lullaby of Broadway.

Fred Ebb, b 1936, (U.S.) Cabaret; Zorba; Woman of the Year.

Ray Evans, b 1915 (U.S.) Mona Lisa; Que Sera, Sera.

Dorothy Fields, 1905-74, (U.S.) On the Sunny Side of the Street; Don't Blame Me; The Way You Look Tonight.

Ira Gershwin, 1896-1983, (U.S.) The Man I Love; Fascinating Rhythm; S'Wonderful; Embraceable You.

William S. Gilbert, 1836-1911, (Br.) The Mikado; H.M.S. Pinafore; Pirates of Penzance.

Gerry Goffin, b 1939, (U.S.) Will You Love Me Tomorrow; Take Good Care of My Baby; Up on the Roof.

Mack Gordon, 1905-59, (Pol.-U.S.) You'll Never Know; The More I See You; Chattanooga Choo-Choo.

Oscar Hammerstein II, 1895-1960, (U.S.) Ol' Man River; Oklahoma; Carousel.

E. Y. (Yip) Harburg, 1898-1981, (U.S.) Brother, Can You Spare a Dime; April in Paris; Over the Rainbow.

Lorenz Hart, 1895-1943, (U.S.) Isn't It Romantic; Blue Moon; Lover; Manhattan; My Funny Valentine.

DuBose Heyward, 1885-1940, (U.S.) Summertime.

Gus Kahn, 1886-1941, (U.S.) Memories; Ain't We Got Fun.

Alan J. Lerner, 1918-86, (U.S.) Brigadoon; My Fair Lady; Camelot; Gigi; On a Clear Day You Can See Forever.

Johnny Mercer, 1909-76, (U.S.) Blues in the Night; Come Rain or Come Shine; Laura; That Old Black Magic.

Bob Merrill, 1921-98, (U.S.) People; (How Much Is That) Doggie in the Window.

Jack Norworth, 1879-1959, (U.S.) Take Me Out to the Ball Game; Shine On Harvest Moon.
Mitchell Parish, 1901-93, (U.S.) Stardust; Stairway to the Stars.
Andy Razaf, 1895-1973, (U.S.) Honeysuckle Rose; Ain't Misbehavin'; S'posin'.

Leo Robin, 1900-84, (U.S.) Thanks for the Memory; Hooray for Love; Diamonds Are a Girl's Best Friend.
Paul Francis Webster, 1907-84, (U.S.) Secret Love; The Shadow of Your Smile; Love Is a Many-Splendored Thing.
Jack Yellen, 1892-1991, (U.S.) Down by the O-HI-O; Ain't She Sweet; Happy Days Are Here Again.

Blues and Jazz Artists of the Past

Julian "Cannonball" Adderley, 1928-75, alto sax
Nat Adderley, 1931-2000, cornet
Henry "Red" Allen, 1908-67, trumpet
Louis "Satchmo" Armstrong, 1901-71, trumpet, singer, bandleader
Albert Ayler, 1936-70, tenor sax, alto sax
Mildred Bailey, 1907-51, singer
Chet Baker, 1929-88, trumpet, singer
Count Basie, 1904-84, bandleader, piano, composer
Sidney Bechet, 1897-1959, soprano sax, clarinet
Bix Beiderbecke, 1903-31, cornet, composer, piano
Bunny Berigan, 1908-42, trumpet
Barney Bigard, 1906-80, clarinet
Eubie Blake, 1883-1983, composer, piano
Art Blakey, 1919-90, drums, bandleader
Jimmy Blanton, 1921-42, bass
Charles "Buddy" Bolden, 1877-1931, cornet, pioneer bandleader
Lester Bowie, 1941-99, trumpet, composer, bandleader
Big Bill Broonzy, 1893-1958, blues singer, guitar
Clifford Brown, 1930-56, trumpet
Ray Brown, 1926-2002, bass
Don Byas, 1912-72, tenor sax
Charlie Byrd, 1925-99, guitarist; popularized bossa nova
Cab Calloway, 1907-94, bandleader, singer
Harry Carney, 1910-74, baritone sax, clarinet
Betty Carter, 1930-98, jazz singer
Sidney "Big Sid" Catlett, 1910-51, drums
Doc Cheatham, 1905-97, trumpet
Don Cherry, 1936-95, trumpet
Charlie Christian, 1916-42, guitar
Kenny "Klook" Clarke, 1914-85, drums
Buck Clayton, 1911-91, trumpet
Al Cohn, 1925-88, tenor sax
Cozy Cole, 1909-81, drums
John Coltrane, 1926-67, tenor sax, soprano sax, composer
Eddie Condon, 1905-73, guitar, bandleader
Tadd Dameron, 1917-65, piano, composer
Eddie "Lockjaw" Davis, 1921-86, tenor sax
Miles Davis, 1926-91, trumpet, composer
Wild Bill Davison, 1906-89, cornet
Paul Desmond, 1924-77, alto sax
Vic Dickenson, 1906-84, trombone
Willie Dixon, 1915-92, blues composer, bass
Johnny Dodds, 1892-1940, clarinet
Warren "Baby" Dodds, 1898-1959, drums
Eric Dolphy, 1928-64, alto sax, bass clarinet, flute
Jimmy Dorsey, 1904-57, alto sax, bandleader
Tommy Dorsey, 1905-56, trombone, bandleader
Billy Eckstine, 1914-93, singer, bandleader
Harry "Sweets" Edison, 1915-99, trumpet
Roy Eldridge, 1911-89, trumpet, singer
Duke Ellington, 1899-1974, piano, bandleader, composer
Bill Evans, 1929-80, piano
Gil Evans, 1912-88, composer, arranger, piano
Art Farmer, 1928-99, trumpet, flugelhorn
Ella Fitzgerald, 1917-96, singer
Tommy Flanagan, 1930-2001, piano
Erroll Garner, 1921-77, piano, composer
Stan Getz, 1927-91, tenor sax
Dizzy Gillespie, 1917-93, trumpet, composer, singer
Benny Goodman, 1909-86, clarinet, bandleader
Dexter Gordon, 1923-90, tenor sax
Stéphane Grappelli, 1908-97, violin
Bobby Hackett, 1915-76, trumpet, cornet
Lionel Hampton, 1908-2002, vibraphone, bandleader
W. C. Handy, 1873-1958, composer
Jimmy Harrison, 1900-31, trombone
Coleman Hawkins, 1904-69, tenor sax
Fletcher Henderson, 1898-1952, bandleader, arranger
Woody Herman, 1913-87, clarinet, alto sax, bandleader
Jay C. Higginbotham, 1906-73, trombone
Earl "Fatha" Hines, 1903-83, piano
Milt Hinton, 1910-2000, bass
Al Hirt, 1922-99, trumpet
Johnny Hodges, 1906-70, alto sax
Billie Holiday, 1915-59, singer
John Lee Hooker, 1917-2001, blues guitar, singer
Sam "Lightnin'" Hopkins, 1912-82, blues singer, guitar
Howlin' Wolf, 1910-1976, blues singer, harmonica, guitar
Alberta Hunter, 1895-1984, singer
Mahalia Jackson, 1911-72, gospel singer
Milt Jackson, 1923-99, vibraphone

Elmore James, 1918-63, blues singer, guitar
Blind Lemon Jefferson, 1897-1930, blues singer, guitar
Bunk Johnson, 1879-1949, trumpet
J.J. Johnson, 1924-2001, trombone
James P. Johnson, 1891-1955, piano, composer
Robert Johnson, 1912-38, blues singer, guitar
Jo Jones, 1911-85, drums
Philly Joe Jones, 1923-85, drums
Thad Jones, 1923-86, cornet, bandleader, composer
Scott Joplin, 1868-1917, ragtime composer
Louis Jordan, 1908-75, singer, alto sax
Stan Kenton, 1911-79, bandleader, composer, piano
Albert King, 1923-92, blues guitar
John Kirby, 1908-52, bandleader, bass
Rahsaan Roland Kirk, 1936-77, saxophones, composer
Gene Krupa, 1909-73, drums, bandleader
Scott LaFaro, 1936-61, bass
Huddie Ledbetter (Lead Belly), 1888-1949, folk and blues singer, guitar
John Lewis, 1920-2001, piano, Modern Jazz Quartet founder
Mel Lewis, 1929-90, drums, bandleader
Jimmie Lunceford, 1902-47, bandleader
Machito (Frank Grillo), 1912-84, Latin percussion, singer, bandleader
Shelly Manne, 1920-84, drums, bandleader
Jimmy McPartland, 1907-91, trumpet
Carmen McRae, 1920-94, singer
Glenn Miller, 1904-44, trombone, bandleader
Charles Mingus, 1922-79, bass, composer, bandleader
Thelonious Monk, 1917-82, piano, composer
Wes Montgomery, 1925-68, guitar
"Jelly Roll" Morton, 1885-1941, composer, piano
Bennie Moten, 1894-1935, piano, bandleader
Gerry Mulligan, 1927-96, baritone sax, composer
"Fats" Navarro, 1923-50, trumpet
Red Nichols, 1905-65, cornet, bandleader
Red Norvo, 1908-99, vibraphone, xylophone, bandleader
Arturo "Chico" O'Farrill, 1921-2001, Latin composer, arranger
King Oliver, 1885-1938, cornet, band leader
Sy Oliver, 1910-88, arranger, composer
Kid Ory, 1886-1973, trombone, bandleader
Oran "Hot Lips" Page, 1908-54, trumpet, singer
Charlie "Bird" Parker, 1920-55, alto sax, composer
Joe Pass, 1929-94, guitar
Art Pepper, 1925-82, alto sax
Oscar Pettiford, 1922-60, bass
Bud Powell, 1924-66, piano
Chano Pozo, 1915-48, Cuban percussion, singer
Louis Prima, 1911-78, singer, bandleader
Tito Puente, 1923-2000, Latin percussion, bandleader
Gertrude "Ma" Rainey, 1886-1939, blues singer
Don Redman, 1900-64, composer, arranger
Django Reinhardt, 1910-53, guitar
Buddy Rich, 1917-87, drums
Red Rodney, 1928-94, trumpet
Jimmy Rowles, 1918-96, piano
Jimmy Rushing, 1903-72, blues and jazz singer
Pee Wee Russell, 1906-69, clarinet
Zoot Sims, 1925-85, tenor sax
Zutty Singleton, 1898-1975, drums
Bessie Smith, 1894-1937, blues singer
Clarence "Pinetop" Smith, 1904-29, piano, singer; boogie woogie pioneer
Willie "The Lion" Smith, 1897-1973, piano, composer
Muggsy Spanier, 1906-67, cornet
Sonny Stitt, 1924-82, tenor sax, alto sax
Billy Strayhorn, 1915-67, composer, piano; Duke Ellington collaborator
Sun Ra, 1915?-93, bandleader, piano, composer
Art Tatum, 1910-56, piano
Art Taylor, 1929-95, drums
Jack Teagarden, 1905-64, trombone, singer
Mel Torme, 1925-99, singer ("the Velvet Fog")
Dave Tough, 1908-48, drums
Lennie Tristano, 1919-78, piano, composer
Joe Turner, 1911-85, blues singer
Sarah Vaughan, 1924-90, singer
Joe Venuti, 1904-78, violin
T-Bone Walker, 1910-75, blues guitar
Thomas "Fats" Waller, 1904-43, piano, singer, composer
Dinah Washington, 1924-63, singer
Grover Washington Jr., 1943-99, pop-jazz sax, composer
Ethel Waters, 1896-1977, jazz and blues singer

Muddy Waters, 1915-83, blues singer, songwriter
Julius Watkins, 1921-77, French horn
Chick Webb, 1902-39, bandleader, drums
Ben Webster, 1909-73, tenor sax
Junior Wells, 1934-98, blues singer, harmonica
Paul Whiteman, 1890-1967, bandleader
Charles "Cootie" Williams, 1910-85, trumpet, bandleader
Joe Williams, 1918-99, singer
Mary Lou Williams, 1910-81, piano, composer

Tony Williams, 1945-97, drums
John Lee "Sonny Boy" Williamson, 1914-48, blues singer, harmonica
Sonny Boy Williamson ("Rice" Miller), 1900?-65, blues singer, harmonica
Teddy Wilson, 1912-86, piano
Kai Winding, 1922-83, trombone
Jimmy Yancey, 1894-1951, piano
Lester "Pres" Young, 1909-59, tenor sax

Noted Country Music Artists of the Past and Present

Roy Acuff, 1903-92, fiddler, singer, songwriter; "Wabash Cannon Ball"
Alabama (Randy Owen, 1949- ; Jeff Cook, 1949- ; Teddy Gentry, 1952- ; Mark Herndon, 1955-) "Feels So Right"
Eddy Arnold, 1918- , singer, guitarist, the "Tennessee Plowboy"
Chet Atkins, 1924-2001, guitarist, composer, producer, helped create the "Nashville sound"
Gene Autry, 1907-98, first great singing movie cowboy; "Back in the Saddle Again"
Garth Brooks, 1962- , singer, songwriter; "Friends in Low Places"
Brooks & Dunn (Kix Brooks, 1955- ; Ronnie Dunn, 1953-) "Hard Workin' Man"
Boudleaux and Felice Bryant (Boudleaux, 1920-87; Felice, 1925-), songwriting team; "Hey Joe"
Glen Campbell, 1936- , singer, instrumentalist, TV host; "Gentle on My Mind," "Rhinestone Cowboy"
Mary Chapin Carpenter, 1958- , singer, songwriter; "I Feel Lucky"
Carter Family (original members, **"Mother"** Maybelle 1909-78; A.P., 1891-1960, Sara, 1898-1979) "Wildwood Flower"
Johnny Cash, 1932-2003, singer, songwriter; "I Walk the Line," "Ring of Fire," "Folsom Prison Blues"
Patsy Cline, 1932-63, singer; "Walkin' After Midnight," "Crazy," "Sweet Dreams"
John Denver, 1943-97, singer, songwriter; "Rocky Mountain High"
Dixie Chicks (Natalie Maines, 1974- ; Martie Seidel, 1969- ; Emily Erwin Robison, 1972-) "Wide Open Spaces," "Fly"
Dale Evans (Lucille Wood Smith), 1912-2001, singer, actress, married Roy Rogers
Flatt & Scruggs (Lester Flatt, 1914-79; Earl Scruggs, 1924-), guitar-banjo duo and soloists; "Foggy Mountain Breakdown"
Red Foley, 1910-68, singer; "Chattanoogie Shoe Shine Boy"
Tennessee Ernie Ford, 1919-91, singer, TV host; "Sixteen Tons"
Lefty Frizzell, 1928-75, singer, guitarist; "Long Black Veil"
Vince Gill, 1957- , singer, songwriter; "When I Call Your Name"
Merle Haggard, 1937- , singer, songwriter; "Okie from Muskogee"
Emmylou Harris, 1947- , singer, songwriter, folk-country crossover artist; "If I Could Only Win Your Love"
Faith Hill, 1967- , singer, songwriter, married Tim McGraw; "Wild One," "This Kiss," "Breathe"
Waylon Jennings, 1937–2002, singer, songwriter, "outlaw country" pioneer; "Luckenbach, Texas"
George Jones, 1931- , singer, songwriter; "Why Baby Why"
The Judds (Naomi, 1946- ; Wynonna, 1964-), mother-daughter duo; Wynonna also a solo act
Alison Krauss, 1971– , bluegrass fiddler, singer, bandleader; "When You Say Nothing at All"
Kris Kristofferson, 1936- , singer, songwriter, actor; "Me and Bobby McGee"
Brenda Lee, 1944- , singer; "I'm Sorry"
Patty Loveless, 1957- , singer, songwriter; "How Can I Help You Say Goodbye"
Lyle Lovett, 1957- , singer, songwriter, bandleader, actor; "Cowboy Man"
Loretta Lynn, 1935- , singer, songwriter; "Coal Miner's Daughter"

Kathy Mattea, 1959- , singer, songwriter; "Eighteen Wheels and a Dozen Roses"
Reba McEntire, 1955- , singer, songwriter, actress; "Whoever's in New England"
Tim McGraw, 1967- , singer; "It's Your Love," with wife, Faith Hill
Roger Miller, 1936-92, singer, songwriter; "King of the Road"
Ronnie Milsap, 1944- , singer, songwriter; "There's No Gettin' Over Me"
Bill Monroe, 1911-96, singer, songwriter, mandolin player, "father of bluegrass music"; "Mule Skinner Blues"
Patsy Montana, 1908-96, yodeling/singing cowgirl; "I Want to Be a Cowboy's Sweetheart"
Willie Nelson, 1933- , singer, songwriter, actor; "On the Road Again"
Mark O'Connor, 1961- , fiddler, country-classical crossover composer
Dolly Parton, 1946- , singer, songwriter, actress; "Dollywood" theme park; "Here You Come Again," "9 to 5"
Minnie Pearl, 1912-96, comedienne, Grand Ole Opry star
Charley Pride, 1938- , singer, 1st African-American country star; "Kiss an Angel Good Mornin'"
Jim Reeves, 1923-64, singer, songwriter; "Four Walls"
Charlie Rich, 1932-95, singer, songwriter called the "Silver Fox"; "The Most Beautiful Girl"
LeAnn Rimes, 1982- , singer; "Blue"
Tex Ritter, 1905-74, singer, songwriter; "Jingle, Jangle, Jingle"
Marty Robbins, 1925-82, singer, songwriter; "A White Sport Coat and a Pink Carnation"
Jimmie Rodgers, 1897-1933, singer, songwriter; "T for Texas"
Kenny Rogers, 1938- , singer, songwriter, actor; "The Gambler"
Roy Rogers (Leonard Slye), 1911-98, singer, actor, "King of the Cowboys," sang with Sons of the Pioneers
Fred Rose, 1898-1954, singer, songwriter, producer; "Blue Eyes Cryin' in the Rain"
Ricky Skaggs, 1954- , singer, songwriter, bandleader; "Don't Cheat in Our Hometown"
George Strait, 1952- , singer, bandleader; "Ace in the Hole"
Merle Travis, 1917-83, singer, guitarist, songwriter; "Divorce Me C.O.D."
Randy Travis, 1959- , singer, songwriter; "Forever and Ever, Amen"
Ernest Tubb, 1914-84, singer, songwriter, guitarist; "Walking the Floor Over You"
Shania Twain, 1965- , singer, songwriter; "You're Still the One"
Conway Twitty, 1933-93, singer, songwriter; "Hello Darlin' "
Dottie West, 1932-91, singer, songwriter; "Here Comes My Baby"
Hank Williams Jr., 1949- , singer, songwriter; "Bocephus," "All My Rowdy Friends (Have Settled Down)"
Hank Williams Sr., 1923-53, singer, songwriter; "Your Cheatin' Heart"
Bob Wills, 1905-75, Western Swing fiddler, singer, bandleader, songwriter; "New San Antonio Rose"
Tammy Wynette, 1942-98, singer; "Stand By Your Man"
Trisha Yearwood, 1964- , singer, songwriter; "How Do I Live"
Dwight Yoakam, 1957- , singer, songwriter, actor; "Ain't That Lonely Yet"

Dance Figures of the Past

Source: Reviewed by Gary Parks, Reviews editor, *Dance* magazine

Alvin Ailey, 1931-89, (U.S.) modern dancer, choreographer; melded modern dance and Afro-Caribbean techniques.
Frederick Ashton, 1904-88, (Br.) ballet choreographer; director of Great Britain's Royal Ballet, 1963-70.
Fred Astaire, 1899-1987, (U.S.) dancer, actor; teamed with dancer/actress Ginger Rogers (1911-95) in movie musicals.
George Balanchine, 1904-83, (Russ.-U.S.) ballet choreographer, teacher; most influential exponent of the neoclassical style; founded, with Lincoln Kirstein, School of American Ballet and New York City Ballet.
Carlo Blasis, 1803-78, (It.) ballet dancer, choreographer, writer; his teaching methods are standards of classical dance.
August Bournonville, 1805-79, (Dan.) ballet dancer, choreographer, teacher; exuberant, light style.
Gisella Caccialanza, 1914-97, (U.S.) ballerina, charter member of Balanchine's American Ballet.

Enrico Cecchetti, 1850-1928, (It.) ballet dancer, leading dancer of Russia's Imperial Ballet; his technique was basis for Britain's Imperial Soc. of Teachers of Dancing.
Gower Champion, 1921-80, (U.S.) dancer, choreographer, director; with his wife **Marge,** b 1923, (U.S.) choreographed, danced in Broadway musicals and films.
John Cranko, 1927-73, (S. African) choreographer; created narrative ballets based on literary works.
Agnes de Mille, 1909-93, (U.S.) ballerina, choreographer; known for using American themes, she choreographed the ballet *Rodeo* and the musical *Oklahoma.*
Dame Ninette DeValois, 1898-2001, (Br.) choreographer, founding director London's Royal Ballet; *The Rake's Progress.*
Sergei Diaghilev, 1872-1929, (Russ.) impresario; founded Les Ballet Russes; saw ballet as an art unifying dance, drama, music, and decor.

Alexandra Danilova, 1903-97, (Russ.) ballerina; noted teacher at the School of American Ballet.

Isadora Duncan, 1877-1927, (U.S.) expressive dancer who united free movement with serious music; one of the founders of modern dance.

Fanny Elssler, 1810-84, (Austrian) ballerina of the Romantic era; known for dramatic skill, sensual style.

Michel Fokine, 1880-1942, (Russ.) ballet dancer, choreographer, teacher; rejected strict classicism in favor of dramatically expressive style.

Margot Fonteyn, 1919-91, (Br.) prima ballerina, Royal Ballet of Great Britain; famed performance partner of Rudolf Nureyev.

Bob Fosse, 1927-87, (U.S.) jazz dancer, choreographer, director; Broadway musicals and film.

Serge Golovine, 1924-98, (Fr.) ballet dancer with Grand Ballet du Marquis de Cuevas; choreographer.

Martha Graham, 1893-1991, (U.S.) modern dancer, choreographer; created and codified her own dramatic technique.

Martha Hill, 1901-95, (U.S.) educator; leading figure in modern dance; founded American Dance Festival.

Gregory Hines, 1946-2003, (U.S.) tap-dance innovator and master of improvisation.

Doris Humphrey, 1895-1958, (U.S.) modern dancer, choreographer, writer, teacher.

Robert Joffrey, 1930-88, (U.S.) ballet dancer, choreographer; cofounded with **Gerald Arpino,** b 1928, (U.S.), the Joffrey Ballet.

Kurt Jooss, 1901-79, (Ger.) choreographer, teacher; created expressionist works using modern and classical techniques.

Tamara Karsavina, 1885-1978, (Russ.) prima ballerina of Russia's Imperial Ballet and Diaghilev's Ballets Russes; partner of Nijinsky.

Nora Kaye, 1920-87, (U.S.) ballerina with Metropolitan Opera Ballet and Ballet Theater (now American Ballet Theatre).

Lincoln Kirstein, 1907-96 (U.S.) brought ballet as an art form to U.S.; founded, with George Balanchine, School of American Ballet and New York City Ballet.

Serge Lifar, 1905-86, (Russ.-Fr.) prem. danseur, choreographer; director of dance at Paris Opera 1930-45, 1947-58.

José Limón, 1908-72, (Mex.-U.S.) modern dancer, choreographer, teacher; developed technique based on Humphrey.

Catherine Littlefield, 1908-51, (U.S.) ballerina, choreographer, teacher; pioneer of American ballet.

Léonide Massine, 1896-1979, (Russ.-U.S.) ballet dancer, choreographer; his "symphonic ballet" used concert music previously thought unsuitable for dance.

Kenneth MacMillan, 1929-92, (Br.) dancer, choreographer; directed Royal Ballet of Great Britain 1970-77.

Vaslav Nijinsky, 1890-50, (Russ.) prem. danseur, choreographer; leading member of Diaghilev's Ballets Russes; his ballets were revolutionary for their time.

Alwin Nikolais, 1910-93, (U.S.) modern choreographer; created dance theater utilizing mixed media effects.

Jean-George Noverre, 1727-1810, (Fr.) ballet choreographer, teacher, writer; "Shakespeare of the Dance."

Rudolf Nureyev, 1938-93, (Russ.) prem. danseur, choreographer; leading male dancer of his generation; director of dance at Paris Opera, 1983-89.

Ruth Page, 1903-91, (U.S.) ballerina, choreographer; danced and directed ballet at Chicago Lyric Opera.

Anna Pavlova, 1881-1931, (Russ.) prima ballerina; toured with her own company to world acclaim.

Marius Petipa, 1818-1910, (Fr.) ballet dancer, choreographer; ballet master of the Imperial Ballet; established Russian classicism as leading style of late 19th cent.

Pearl Primus, 1919-95, (Trinidad-U.S.) modern dancer, choreographer, scholar; combined African, Caribbean, and African-American styles.

Jerome Robbins, 1918-98, (U.S.) choreographer, director, dancer; *The King and I, West Side Story, Fiddler on the Roof; Gypsy.*

Bill (Bojangles) Robinson, 1878-1949, (U.S.) famed tap dancer; called King of Tapology on stage and screen.

Ruth St. Denis, 1877-1968, (U.S.) influential interpretive dancer, choreographer, teacher.

Ted Shawn, 1891-1972, (U.S.) modern dancer, choreographer; formed dance company and school with Ruth St. Denis; established Jacob's Pillow Dance Festival.

Marie Taglioni, 1804-84, (It.) ballerina, teacher; in title role of *La Sylphide* established image of the ethereal ballerina.

Antony Tudor, 1908-87, (Br.) choreographer, teacher; exponent of the "psychological ballet."

Galina Ulanova, 1910-98, (Russ.) revered ballerina with Bolshoi Ballet.

Agrippina Vaganova, 1879-1951, (Russ.) ballet teacher, director; codified Soviet ballet technique that developed virtuosity; called "queen of variations."

Mary Wigman, 1886-1973, (Ger.) modern dancer, choreographer, teacher; influenced European expressionist dance.

Opera Singers of the Past

Frances Alda, 1883-1952, (N.Z.) soprano
Pasquale Amato, 1878-1942, (It.) baritone
Marian Anderson, 1897-1993, (U.S.) contralto
Jussi Björling, 1911-60, (Swed.) tenor
Lucrezia Bori, 1887-1960, (It.) soprano
Maria Callas, 1923-77, (U.S.) soprano
Emma Calvé, 1858-1942, (Fr.) soprano
Enrico Caruso, 1873-1921, (It.) tenor
Feodor Chaliapin, 1873-1938, (Russ.) bass
Boris Christoff, 1914-93, (Bulg.) bass
Giuseppe De Luca, 1876-1950, (It.) baritone
Fernando De Lucia, 1860-1925, (It.) tenor
Edouard De Reszke, 1853-1917, (Pol.) bass
Jean De Reszke, 1850-1925, (Pol.) tenor
Emmy Destinn, 1898-1930, (Czech.) soprano
Emma Eames, 1865-1952, (U.S.) soprano
(Carlo Broschi) Farinelli, 1705-82, (It.) castrato
Geraldine Farrar, 1882-1967, (U.S.) soprano
Eileen Farrell, 1920-2002, (U.S.) soprano
Kathleen Ferrier, 1912-53, (Eng.) contralto
Kirsten Flagstad, 1895-1962, (Nor.) soprano
Olive Fremstad, 1871-1951, (Swed.-U.S.) soprano
Amelita Galli-Curci, 1882-1963, (It.) soprano
Mary Garden, 1874-1967, (Br.) soprano
Beniamino Gigli, 1890-1957, (It.) tenor
Tito Gobbi, 1913-84, (It.) baritone
Giulia Grisi, 1811-69, (It.) soprano
Frieda Hempel, 1885-1955, (Ger.) soprano
Jerome Hines, 1921-2003, (U.S.) bass
Maria Jeritza, 1887-1982, (Czech.) soprano
Alexander Kipnis, 1891-1978, (Russ.-U.S.) bass
Alfredo Kraus, 1927-99, (Sp.) tenor
Luigi Lablache, 1794-1858, (It.) bass
Lilli Lehmann, 1848-1929, (Ger.) soprano

Lotte Lehmann, 1888-1976, (Ger.-U.S.) soprano
Jenny Lind, 1820-87, (Swed.) soprano
Maria Malibran, 1808-36, (Sp.) mezzo-soprano
Giovanni Martinelli, 1885-1969, (It.) tenor
John McCormack, 1884-1945, (Ir.) tenor
Nellie Melba, 1861-1931, (Austral.) soprano.
Lauritz Melchior, 1890-1973, (Dan.) tenor
Zinka Milanov, 1906-89, (Yugo.) soprano
Lillian Nordica, 1857-1914, (U.S.) soprano
Giuditta Pasta, 1797-1865, (It.) soprano
Adelina Patti, 1843-1919, (It.) soprano
Peter Pears, 1910-86, (Eng.) tenor
Jan Peerce, 1904-84, (U.S.) tenor
Ezio Pinza, 1892-1957, (It.) bass
Lily Pons, 1898-1976, (Fr.) soprano
Rosa Ponselle, 1897-1981, (U.S.) soprano
Hermann Prey, 1929-98, (Ger.) baritone.
Elisabeth Rethberg, 1894-1976, (Ger.) soprano
Giovanni Battista Rubini, 1794-1854, (It.) tenor
Leonie Rysanek, 1926-1998, (Austrian) soprano
Bidú Sayão, 1902-99, (Braz.) soprano
Friedrich Schorr, 1888-1953, (Hung.) bass-baritone
Marcella Sembrich, 1858-1935, (Pol.) soprano
Eleanor Steber, 1916-90, (U.S.) soprano
Ferruccio Tagliavini, 1913-95, (It.) tenor
Luisa Tetrazzini, 1871-1940, (It.) soprano
Lawrence Tibbett, 1896-1960, (U.S.) baritone
Tatiana Troyanos, 1938-93, (U.S.) mezzo-soprano
Richard Tucker, 1913-75, (U.S.) tenor
Pauline Viardot, 1821-1910, (Fr.) mezzo-soprano
William Warfield, 1920-2002, (U.S.) bass-baritone
Leonard Warren, 1911-60, (U.S.) baritone
Ljuba Welitsch, 1913-96, (Bulg.) soprano
Wolfgang Windgassen, 1914-74, (Ger.) tenor

Rock and Roll, Rhythm and Blues, and Rap Artists

Titles in quotation marks are singles; others are albums.

Aaliyah: "More than a Woman"
Paula Abdul: "Straight Up"
*AC/DC (2003): "Back in Black"
Bryan Adams: "Cuts Like a Knife"
*Aerosmith (2001): "Sweet Emotion"
Christina Aguilera: "What a Girl Wants"
Alice In Chains: "Heaven Beside You"
*The Allman Brothers Band (1995): "Ramblin' Man"
*The Animals (1994): "House of the Rising Sun"
Paul Anka: "Lonely Boy"
Fiona Apple: "Criminal"
Ashanti: "Foolish"
The Association: "Cherish"
Frankie Avalon: "Venus"
The B-52s: "Love Shack"
Bachman Turner Overdrive: "Takin' Care of Business"
Backstreet Boys: "I Want it That Way"
Bad Company: "Can't Get Enough"
Erykah Badu: "On and On"
*La Vern Baker (1991): "I Cried a Tear"
*Hank Ballard and the Midnighters (1990): "Work With Me, Annie"
*The Band (1994): "The Weight"
Barenaked Ladies: "One Week"
*The Beach Boys (1988): "Good Vibrations"
Beastie Boys: "(You Gotta) Fight for Your Right (to Party)"
*The Beatles (1988): Sgt. Pepper's Lonely Hearts Club Band
Beck: "Loser"
*The Bee Gees (1997): "Stayin' Alive"
Pat Benatar: "Hit Me With Your Best Shot"
Ben Folds Five: "Brick"
*Chuck Berry (1986): "Johnny B. Goode"
The Big Bopper: "Chantilly Lace"
Björk: "Human Behavior"
The Black Crowes: "Hard to Handle"
Black Sabbath: "Paranoid"
*Bobby "Blue" Bland (1992): "Turn On Your Love Light"
Mary J. Blige: My Life
Blind Faith: "Can't Find My Way Home"
Blink-182: "All the Small Things"
The B-52s: "Love Shack"
Blondie: "Heart of Glass"
Blood, Sweat, and Tears: "Spinning Wheel"
Blues Traveler: "Run-Around"
Gary "U.S." Bonds: "Quarter to Three"
Bon Jovi: "Livin' on a Prayer"
*Booker T. and the M.G.'s (1992): "Green Onions"
Earl Bostic: "Flamingo"
Boston: "More Than A Feeling"
*David Bowie (1996): "Space Oddity"
Boyz II Men: "I'll Make Love to You"
Toni Braxton: "Un-Break My Heart"
*James Brown (1986): "Papa's Got a Brand New Bag"
*Ruth Brown (1993): "Lucky Lips"
Jackson Browne: "Doctor My Eyes"
*Buffalo Springfield (1997): "For What It's Worth"
*Jimmy Buffett: "Margaritaville"
*Solomon Burke (2001): "Over and Over (Huggin' and Lovin')"
Bush: "Glycerine"
*The Byrds (1991): "Turn! Turn! Turn!"
Mariah Carey: "Vision of Love"
The Carpenters: "(They Long to Be) Close to You"
The Cars: "Shake It Up"
*Johnny Cash (1992): "I Walk the Line"
*Ray Charles (1986): "Georgia on My Mind"
Cheap Trick: "Surrender"
Chicago: "Saturday in the Park"
Chubby Checker: "The Twist"
*Eric Clapton (2000): "Layla"
*The Clash (2003): "Rock the Casbah"
*The Coasters (1987): "Yakety Yak"
*Eddie Cochran (1987): "Summertime Blues"
Joe Cocker: "With a Little Help From My Friends"
Collective Soul: "The World I Know"
Phil Collins: "Against All Odds"
*Sam Cooke (1986): "You Send Me"
Coolio: "Gangsta's Paradise"
Alice Cooper: "School's Out"
*Elvis Costello and the Attractions (2003): "Alison"
Counting Crows: "Mr. Jones"
*Cream (1993): "Sunshine of Your Love"
Creed: "Arms Wide Open"
*Creedence Clearwater Revival (1993): "Proud Mary"
*Crosby, Stills, and Nash (1997): "Suite: Judy Blue Eyes"
Sheryl Crow: "All I Want to Do"
The Cure: "Boys Don't Cry"
The Crystals: "Da Doo Ron Ron"
Cypress Hill: "Insane in the Brain"

Danny and the Juniors: "At the Hop"
*Bobby Darin (1990): "Splish Splash"
Spencer Davis Group: "Gimme Some Lovin' "
Deep Purple: "Smoke on the Water"
Def Leppard: "Photograph"
Depeche Mode: "Strange Love"
Destiny's Child: "Survivor"
*Bo Diddley (1987): "Who Do You Love?"
*Dion and the Belmonts (1989): "A Teenager in Love"
Celine Dion: "Because You Loved Me"
Dire Straits: "Money for Nothing"
DMX: "What's My Name"
*Fats Domino (1986): "Blueberry Hill"
Donovan: "Mellow Yellow"
The Doobie Brothers: "What a Fool Believes"
*The Doors (1993): "Light My Fire"
Dr. Dre: "Nothin' But a 'G' Thang"
*The Drifters (1988): "Save the Last Dance for Me"
Duran Duran: "Hungry Like the Wolf"
*Bob Dylan (1988): "Like a Rolling Stone"
*The Eagles (1998): "Hotel California"
*Earth, Wind, and Fire (2000): "Shining Star"
*Duane Eddy (1994): "Rebel-Rouser"
Missy Elliott: "Sock It 2 Me"
Emerson, Lake, and Palmer: "Lucky Man"
Eminem: "The Real Slim Shady"
En Vogue: "Hold On"
Enya: Shepherd Moons
The Eurythmics: "Sweet Dreams (Are Made of This)"
Everclear: "Father Of Mine"
*The Everly Brothers (1986): "Wake Up, Little Susie"
50 Cent (Curtis Jackson): Get Rich Or Die Tryin'
The Five Satins: "In the Still of the Night"
*The Flamingos (2001): "I Only Have Eyes for You"
*Fleetwood Mac (1998): Rumours
The Foo Fighters: "I'll Stick Around"
Foreigner: "Double Vision"
*The Four Seasons (1990): "Sherry"
*The Four Tops (1990): "I Can't Help Myself (Sugar Pie, Honey Bunch)"
*Aretha Franklin (1987): "Respect"
Nelly Furtado: "I'm Like a Bird"
Peter Gabriel: "Shock the Monkey"
Marvin Gaye (1987): "I Heard It Through the Grapevine"
Genesis: "No Reply at All"
Goo Goo Dolls: "Iris"
Grand Funk Railroad: "We're an American Band"
Grand Master Flash and the Furious Five: "The Message"
*The Grateful Dead (1994): "Uncle John's Band"
Macy Gray: "I Try"
*Al Green (1995): "Let's Stay Together"
Green Day: "Time of Your Life"
The Guess Who: "American Woman"
Guns N' Roses: "Sweet Child o' Mine"
*Bill Haley and His Comets (1987): "Rock Around the Clock"
Hall and Oates: "Kiss on My List"
Hanson: "MMMBop"
Juliana Hatfield: "Spin the Bottle"
*Isaac Hayes (2002): "Theme from 'Shaft'"
Heart: "Barracuda"
*Jimi Hendrix (1992): "Purple Haze"
Lauryn Hill: "Doo-Wop (That Thing)"
Hole: "Doll Parts"
*Buddy Holly (1986): "Peggy Sue"
*John Lee Hooker (1991): "Boogie Chillen"
Hootie and the Blowfish: Cracked Rear View
Whitney Houston: "I Will Always Love You"
*The Impressions (1991): "For Your Precious Love"
Indigo Girls: "Closer to Fine"
INXS: "Need You Tonight"
*The Isley Brothers (1992): "It's Your Thing"
*The Jackson Five (1997): "ABC"
Janet Jackson: Rhythm Nation
*Michael Jackson (2001): Thriller
*Etta James (1993): "At Last"
Tommy James & The Shondells: "Crimson and Clover"
Jane's Addiction: "Jane Says"
Ja Rule: Venni, Vetti, Vecci
Jay and the Americans: "This Magic Moment"
Jay-Z: "Can I Live"
*Jefferson Airplane (1996): "White Rabbit"
Jethro Tull: Aqualung
Joan Jett: "I Love Rock 'n' Roll"
Jewel: "You Were Meant for Me"
*Billy Joel (1999): "Piano Man"
*Elton John (1994): "Candle in the Wind"
*Little Willie John (1996): "Sleep"
*Janis Joplin (1995): "Me and Bobby McGee"

Journey: "Don't Stop Believin'"
K.C. and the Sunshine Band: "Get Down Tonight"
R. Kelly: "I Can't Sleep Baby (If I)"
Alicia Keys: "Fallin'"
Kid Rock: "Cowboy"
*__B.B. King (1987):__ "The Thrill Is Gone"
Carole King: Tapestry
*__The Kinks (1990):__ "You Really Got Me"
Kiss: "Rock 'n' Roll All Night"
*__Gladys Knight and the Pips (1996):__ "Midnight Train to Georgia"
Korn: "Blind"
Lenny Kravitz: "Are You Gonna Go My Way?"
*__Led Zeppelin (1995):__ "Stairway to Heaven"
*__Brenda Lee (2002):__ "I'm Sorry"
*__John Lennon (1994):__ "Imagine"
*__Jerry Lee Lewis (1986):__ "Whole Lotta Shakin' Going On"
Lil' Kim: "No Matter What They Say"
Limp Bizkit: "Break Stuff"
Linkin Park: "One Step Closer"
Little Anthony and the Imperials: "Tears on My Pillow"
*__Little Richard (1986):__ "Tutti Frutti"
Live: "Lightning Crashes"
L. L. Cool J: "Mama Said Knock You Out"
Jennifer Lopez: "Love Don't Cost aThing"
*__The Lovin' Spoonful (2000):__ "Summer in the City"
*__Frankie Lymon and the Teenagers (1993):__ "Why Do Fools Fall in Love?"
Lynyrd Skynyrd: "Free Bird"
Madonna: "Material Girl"
*__The Mamas and the Papas (1998):__ "Monday, Monday"
Aimee Mann: "Save Me"
Marilyn Manson: "Beautiful People"
*__Bob Marley (1994):__ Exodus
*__Martha and the Vandellas (1995):__ "Dancin' in the Streets"
The Marvelettes: "Please, Mr. Postman"
Matchbox 20: "Push"
Dave Matthews Band: "Don't Drink the Water"
*__Curtis Mayfield (1999):__ "Superfly"
*__Paul McCartney (1999):__ "Band on the Run"
Don McLean: "American Pie"
*__Clyde McPhatter (1987):__ "A Lover's Question"
Meat Loaf: "Paradise by the Dashboard Light"
John (Cougar) Mellencamp: "Jack and Diane"
Men at Work: "Who Can It Be Now?"
Metallica: "Enter Sandman"
George Michael: "Faith"
*__Joni Mitchell (1997):__ "Big Yellow Taxi"
Moby: "Bodyrock"
The Monkees: "I'm a Believer"
Moody Blues: "Nights in White Satin"
*__The Moonglows (2000):__ "Blue Velvet"
Alanis Morissette: "Ironic"
*__Van Morrison (1993):__ "Brown-Eyed Girl"
Nelly: Country Grammar
*__Ricky Nelson (1987):__ "Hello, Mary Lou"
Nine Inch Nails: "Closer"
Nirvana: Nevermind
No Doubt: Rock Steady
The Notorious B.I.G.: "Mo Money Mo Problems"
'N Sync: "Bye, Bye, Bye"
Oasis: "Wonderwall"
The Offspring: "Pretty Fly (for a White Guy)"
*__Roy Orbison (1987):__ "Oh, Pretty Woman"
Ozzy Osbourne: "Crazy Train"
*__Parliament/Funkadelic (1997):__ "One Nation Under a Groove"
Pearl Jam: "Jeremy"
*__Carl Perkins (1987):__ "Blue Suede Shoes"
Peter, Paul, and Mary: "Leaving on a Jet Plane"
*__Tom Petty and the Heartbreakers (2002):__ "Refugee"
Liz Phair: Exile in Guyville
Phish: "Sample in a Jar"
*__Wilson Pickett (1991):__ "Land of 1,000 Dances"
Pink: Missundazstood!
*__Pink Floyd (1996):__ The Wall
*__Gene Pitney (2002):__ "Only Love Can Break a Heart"
*__The Platters (1990):__ "The Great Pretender"
Poco: "Crazy Love"
*__The Police (2003):__ "Every Breath You Take"
Iggy Pop: "Lust for Life"
*__Elvis Presley (1986):__ "Love Me Tender"
The Pretenders: "Brass in Pocket"
*__Lloyd Price (1998):__ "Stagger Lee"
Prince (The Artist): "Purple Rain"
Procol Harum: "A Whiter Shade of Pale"
Public Enemy: "Fight the Power"
Puff Daddy and the Family: No Way Out
*__Queen (2001):__ "Bohemian Rhapsody"
Radiohead: "Creep"
Rage Against the Machine: "Bulls on Parade"
*__Bonnie Raitt (2000):__ "Something to Talk About"

*__The Ramones (2002):__ "I Wanna Be Sedated"
*__Otis Redding (1989):__ "(Sittin' on) the Dock of the Bay"
Red Hot Chili Peppers: "Under the Bridge"
*__Jimmy Reed (1991):__ "Ain't That Loving You, Baby?"
Lou Reed: "Walk on the Wild Side"
R.E.M.: "Losing My Religion"
REO Speedwagon: "Can't Fight This Feeling"
Busta Rhymes: "What's It Gonna Be?"
*__The Righteous Brothers (2003):__ "You've Lost That Lovin' Feelin'"
Johnny Rivers: "Poor Side of Town"
*__Smokey Robinson and the Miracles (1987):__ "Shop Around"
*__The Rolling Stones (1989):__ "Satisfaction"
The Ronettes: "Be My Baby"
Linda Ronstadt: "You're No Good"
Run-D.M.C.: "Raisin' Hell"
Rush: "Tom Sawyer"
Sade: "Smooth Operator"
Salt-N-Pepa: "Shoop"
*__Sam and Dave (1992):__ "Soul Man"
*__Santana (1998):__ "Black Magic Woman"
Seal: "Kiss From a Rose"
Neil Sedaka: "Breaking Up Is Hard to Do"
Bob Seger: "Old Time Rock & Roll"
The Sex Pistols: "Anarchy in the U.K."
Shaggy: "It Wasn't Me"
Shakira: "Whenever, Wherever"
Tupac Shakur: "How Do U Want It"
*__Del Shannon (1999):__ "Runaway"
*__The Shirelles (1996):__ "Soldier Boy"
Carly Simon: "You're So Vain"
*__Paul Simon (1987):__ "50 Ways to Leave Your Lover"
*__Simon and Garfunkel (1990):__ "Bridge Over Troubled Water"
Sisqo: "Thong Song"
*__Sly and the Family Stone (1993):__ "Everyday People"
Smashing Pumpkins: "Today"
Patti Smith: "Because the Night"
Will Smith: "Gettin' Jiggy With It"
The Smiths: "This Charming Man"
Snoop Dogg: "Gin and Juice"
Sonic Youth: "Bull in the Heather"
Soundgarden: "Black Hole Sun"
Britney Spears: "Hit Me Baby One More Time"
Spice Girls: "Wannabe"
*__Dusty Springfield (1999):__ "I Only Want to Be With You"
*__Bruce Springsteen (1999):__ "Born to Run"
Squeeze (2001): "Tempted"
*__Staple Singers (1999):__ "I'll Take You There"
*__Steely Dan (2001):__ "Rikki Don't Lose That Number"
Steppenwolf: "Born to Be Wild"
*__Rod Stewart (1994):__ "Maggie Mae"
Sting: "If You Love Somebody, Set Them Free"
Styx: "Come Sail Away"
Sublime: "What I Got"
The Sugar Hill Gang: "Rapper's Delight"
Donna Summer: "Bad Girls"
*__The Supremes (1988):__ "Stop! In the Name of Love"
*__Talking Heads (2002):__ "Once in a Lifetime"
*__James Taylor (2001):__ "You've Got a Friend"
*__The Temptations (1989):__ "My Girl"
Three Dog Night: "Joy to the World"
TLC: "Waterfalls"
T. Rex: "Bang a Gong (Get It On)"
*__Big Joe Turner (1987):__ "Shake, Rattle & Roll"
*__Ike and Tina Turner (1991):__ "Proud Mary"
*__Tina Turner (1991):__ "What's Love Got to Do With It?"
The Turtles: "Happy Together"
U2: "With or Without You"
Usher: "You Make Me Wanna"
*__Ritchie Valens (2001):__ "La Bamba"
Van Halen: "Running With the Devil"
Stevie Ray Vaughan: "Crossfire"
*__The Velvet Underground (1996):__ "Sweet Jane"
*__Gene Vincent1 (1998):__ "Be-Bop-A-Lula"
Tom Waits: "Downtown Train"
The Wallflowers: "One Headlight"
Dionne Warwick: "I Say a Little Prayer"
*__Muddy Waters (1987):__ "I Can't Be Satisfied"
Mary Wells: "My Guy"
*__The Who (1990):__ Tommy
Lucinda Williams: Car Wheels on a Gravel Road
*__Jackie Wilson (1987):__ "That's Why"
*__Stevie Wonder (1989):__ "You Are the Sunshine of My Life"
Wu-Tang Clan: "Protect Ya Neck"
*__The Yardbirds (1992):__ "For Your Love"
Yes: "Roundabout"
*__Neil Young (1995):__ "Down by the River"
*__The Young Rascals/The Rascals (1997):__ "Good Lovin' "
*Frank Zappa/Mothers of Invention (1995): Sheik Yerbouti
ZZ Top: "Legs"

* Inducted into Rock and Roll Hall of Fame as performer between 1986 and 2003; year is in parentheses. (1) Only individual performer is in Rock and Roll Hall of Fame.

Entertainment Personalities of the Present

Living actors, musicians, dancers, singers, producers, directors, radio-TV performers.

Name	Birthplace	Birthdate
Abbado, Claudio	Milan, Italy	6/26/33
Abdul, Paula	San Fernando, CA	6/19/62
Abraham, F. Murray	Pittsburgh, PA	10/24/39
Adams, Bryan	Kingston, Ontario	11/5/59
Adams, Don	New York, NY	4/19/26
Adams, Edie	Kingston, PA	4/16/29
Adams, Mason	Brooklyn, New York, NY	2/26/19
Adjani, Isabelle	Paris, France	6/27/55
Affleck, Ben	Berkeley, CA	8/15/72
Aguilera, Christina	Staten Is., New York, NY	12/18/80
Agutter, Jenny	Taunton, Somerset, England	12/20/52
Aiello, Danny	New York, NY	6/20/33
Aiken, Clay	Raleigh, NC	11/30/78
Aimee, Anouk	Paris, France	4/27/32
Albanese, Licia	Bari, Italy	7/22/13
Alberghetti, Anna Maria	Pesaro, Italy	5/15/36
Albert, Eddie	Rock Island, IL	4/22/08
Albert, Marv	Brooklyn, New York, NY	6/12/41
Alda, Alan	New York, NY	1/28/36
Alexander, Jane	Boston, MA	10/28/39
Alexander, Jason	Newark, NJ	9/23/59
Allen, Debbie	Houston, TX.	1/16/50
Allen, Joan	Rochelle, IL	8/20/56
Allen, Karen	Carrollton, IL	10/5/51
Allen, Tim	Denver, CO	6/13/53
Allen, Woody	Brooklyn, NY	12/1/35
Alley, Kirstie	Wichita, KS	1/12/51
Allman, Gregg	Nashville, TN	12/8/47
Allyson, June	Bronx, New York, NY.	10/7/17
Alonso, Maria Conchita	Cienfuegos, Cuba	6/29/57
Alpert, Herb	Los Angeles, CA	3/31/35
Altman, Robert	Kansas City, MO	2/20/25
Almodóvar, Pedro	Calzada de Calatrava, Spain	9/25/51
Ambrose, Lauren	New Haven, CT	2/20/78
Ames, Ed	Malden, Boston, MA	7/9/27
Amos, John	Newark, NJ	12/27/41
Amos, Tori	Newton, NC	8/22/63
Anderson, Gillian	Chicago, IL.	8/9/68
Anderson, Harry	Newport, RI	10/14/52
Anderson, Ian	Dunfermline, Scotland	8/10/47
Anderson, Kevin	Gurnee, IL	1/13/60
Anderson, Loni	St. Paul, MN.	8/5/46
Anderson, Lynn	Grand Forks, ND	9/26/47
Anderson, Melissa Sue	Berkeley, CA	9/26/62
Anderson, Pamela	Comox, Vancouver Island, BC	7/1/67
Anderson, Richard	Long Branch, NJ	8/8/26
Anderson, Richard Dean	Minneapolis, MN	1/23/50
Anderson, Wes	Houston, TX.	5/1/69
Andersson, Bibi	Stockholm, Sweden.	11/11/35
Andress, Ursula	Bern, Switzerland.	3/19/36
Andrews, Anthony	London, England	1/12/48
Andrews, Julie	Walton-on-Thames, Surrey, England.	10/1/35
Andrews, Patty	Minneapolis, MN	2/16/20
Aniston, Jennifer	Sherman Oaks, CA	2/11/69
Anka, Paul	Ottawa, Ontario	7/30/41
Ann-Margret	Stockholm, Sweden	4/28/41
Antonioni, Michelangelo	Ferrara, Italy	9/29/12
Apple, Fiona	New York, NY	9/13/77
Applegate, Christina	Los Angeles, CA	11/25/71
Archer, Anne	Los Angeles, CA	8/25/47
Arkin, Adam	Brooklyn, NY	8/19/56
Arkin, Alan	New York, NY	3/26/34
Arnaz, Desi, Jr.	Hollywood, CA.	1/19/53
Arnaz, Lucie	Hollywood, CA.	7/17/51
Arness, James	Minneapolis, MN	5/26/23
Arnold, Eddy	Henderson, TN	5/15/18
Arnold, Tom	Ottumwa, IA	3/6/59
Arquette, Patricia	Chicago, IL.	4/8/68
Arquette, Rosanna	New York, NY	8/10/59
Arroyo, Martina	Harlem, New York, NY.	2/2/37
Arthur, Beatrice	New York, NY.	5/13/23
Ashanti (Douglas)	Glen Cove, NY.	10/13/80
Ashley, Elizabeth	Ocala, FL	8/30/39
Asner, Ed	Kansas City, KS.	11/15/29
Assante, Armand	New York, NY	10/4/49
Astin, John	Baltimore, MD	3/30/30
Atkinson, Rowan	Newcastle-Upon-Tyne, England	1/6/55
Attenborough, Richard	Cambridge, England	8/29/23
Auberjonois, Rene	New York, NY	6/1/40
Austin, Patti	New York, NY	8/10/48
Autry, Alan	Shreveport, LA.	7/31/52
Avalon, Frankie	Philadelphia, PA	9/18/39
Aykroyd, Dan	Ottawa, Ontario	7/1/52
Azaria, Hank	Forest Hills, Queens, NY	4/25/64
Aznavour, Charles	Paris, France	5/22/24
Babyface (Kenneth Edmonds)	Indianapolis, IN.	4/10/59
Bacall, Lauren	Bronx, New York, NY	9/16/24
Bacon, Kevin	Philadelphia, PA	7/8/58
Badalucco, Michael	Brooklyn, NY.	12/20/54
Badu, Erykah	Dallas, TX.	2/26/71
Baez, Joan	Staten Island, NY	1/9/41
Bain, Conrad	Lethbridge, Alberta.	2/4/23
Baio, Scott	Brooklyn, NY.	9/22/61
Baker, Anita	Toledo, OH	1/26/58
Baker, Carroll	Johnstown, PA	5/28/31
Baker, Diane	Hollywood, CA.	2/25/38
Baker, Joe Don	Groesbeck, TX.	2/12/36
Baker, Kathy	Midland, TX	6/8/50
Baker, Kenny	Birmingham, England.	8/24/34
Bakula, Scott	St. Louis, MO	10/9/54
Baldwin, Alec	Massapequa, NY	4/3/58
Baldwin, Daniel	Massapequa, NY	10/5/60
Baldwin, Stephen	Massapequa, NY	5/12/66
Baldwin, William	Massapequa, NY	2/21/63
Bale, Christian	Pembrokeshire, Wales	1/30/74
Ballard, Kaye	Cleveland, OH	11/20/26
Bancroft, Anne	Bronx, New York, NY	9/17/31
Banderas, Antonio	Málaga, Spain	8/10/60
Banks, Tyra	Los Angeles, CA.	12/4/73
Bannon, Jack	Los Angeles, CA.	6/14/40
Baranski, Christine	Buffalo, NY.	5/2/52
Bardem, Javier	Las Palmas, Canary Islands.	3/1/69
Bardot, Brigitte	Paris, France	9/28/34
Barker, Bob	Darrington, WA.	12/12/23
Barkin, Ellen	Bronx, New York, NY	4/16/55
Barrie, Barbara	Chicago, IL.	5/23/31
Barry, Gene	New York, NY.	6/14/19
Barrymore, Drew	Los Angeles, CA.	2/22/75
Bartoli, Cecilia	Rome, Italy.	6/4/66
Baryshnikov, Mikhail	Riga, Latvia	1/28/48
Basinger, Kim	Athens, GA.	12/8/53
Bass, Lance	Laurel, MS	5/4/79
Bassett, Angela	Harlem, New York, NY	8/16/58
Bassey, Shirley	Cardiff, Wales.	1/8/37
Bateman, Jason	Rye, NY	1/14/69
Bateman, Justine	Rye, NY	2/19/66
Bates, Alan	Allestree, England	2/17/34
Bates, Kathy	Memphis, TN	6/28/48
Battle, Kathleen	Portsmouth, OH	8/13/48
Baxter, Meredith	Los Angeles, CA.	6/21/47
Bean, Orson	Burlington, VT.	7/22/28
Beatty, Ned	Louisville, KY	7/6/37
Beatty, Warren	Richmond, VA.	3/30/37
Beck (Hansen)	Los Angeles, CA.	7/8/70
Beck, Jeff	Wallington, Surrey, England.	6/24/44
Beck, John	Chicago, IL	1/28/43
Beckinsale, Kate	London, England	7/26/73
Bedelia, Bonnie	New York, NY.	3/25/48
Begley, Ed, Jr.	Los Angeles, CA.	9/16/49
Behar, Joy	Brooklyn, NY.	10/7/43
Belafonte, Harry	Harlem, New York, NY	3/1/27
Bel Geddes, Barbara	New York, NY.	10/31/22
Bell, Art	Pahrump, NV	6/17/45
Bell, Catherine	London, England	8/14/68
Bello, Maria	Norristown, PA.	4/18/67
Belmondo, Jean-Paul	Neuilly-sur-Seine, France	4/9/33
Belushi, Jim	Chicago, IL.	6/15/54
Belzer, Richard	Bridgeport, CT	8/4/44
Benatar, Pat	Brooklyn, NY.	1/10/53
Benedict, Dirk	Helena, MT.	3/1/45
Benigni, Roberto	Misericordia, Italy	10/27/52
Bening, Annette	Topeka, KS.	5/29/58
Benjamin, Richard	New York, NY.	5/22/38
Bennett, Tony	Astoria, Queens, NY.	8/3/26
Benson, George	Pittsburgh, PA	3/22/43
Benson, Robby	Dallas, TX.	1/21/56
Berenger, Tom	Chicago, IL.	5/31/50
Bergen, Candice	Beverly Hills, CA.	5/9/46
Bergen, Polly	Knoxville, TN	7/14/30
Bergman, Ingmar	Uppsala, Sweden	7/14/18
Berlinger, Warren	Brooklyn, NY.	8/31/37
Berman, Lazar	Leningrad, Russia.	2/26/30
Berman, Shelley	Chicago, IL.	2/3/26
Bernard, Crystal	Dallas, TX.	9/30/64
Bernhard, Sandra	Flint, MI.	6/6/55
Bernsen, Corbin	N. Hollywood, CA	9/7/54
Berry, Chuck	St. Louis, MO	10/18/26
Berry, Halle	Cleveland, OH	8/14/66
Berry, Ken	Moline, IL	11/3/33
Bertinelli, Valerie	Wilmington, DE.	4/23/60
Bertolucci, Bernardo	Parma, Italy	3/16/40

Name	Birthplace	Birthdate
Bialik, Mayim	San Diego, CA	12/12/75
Biggs, Jason	Pompton Plains, NJ	5/12/78
Bikel, Theodore	Vienna, Austria	5/2/24
Billingsley, Barbara	Los Angeles, CA	12/22/22
Binoche, Juliette	Paris, France	3/9/64
Birch, Thora	Beverly Hills, CA	3/11/82
Birney, David	Washington, DC	4/23/39
Bishop, Joey	Bronx, NY	2/3/18
Bisset, Jacqueline	Weybridge, England	9/13/44
Bissett, Josie	Seattle, WA	10/5/70
Björk (Gudmundsdottir)	Reykjavik, Iceland	11/21/65
Black, Clint	Long Branch, NJ	2/4/62
Black, Jack	Los Angeles, CA	4/7/69
Black, Karen	Park Ridge, IL	7/1/42
Blades, Ruben	Panama City, Panama	7/16/48
Blair, Janet	Altoona, PA	4/23/21
Blair, Linda	St. Louis, MO	1/22/59
Blair, Selma	Southfield, MI	6/23/72
Blake, Robert	Nutley, NJ	9/18/33
Blanchett, Cate	Melbourne, Australia	5/14/69
Bledsoe, Tempestt	Chicago, IL	8/1/73
Bleeth, Yasmine	New York, NY	6/14/68
Blethyn, Brenda	Ramsgate, Kent, England	2/20/46
Blige, Mary J.	Bronx, NY	1/11/71
Bloom, Claire	London, England	2/15/31
Bloom, Orlando	Canterbury, England	1/13/77
Blyth, Ann	Mt. Kisco, NY	8/16/28
Bochco, Steven	New York, NY	12/16/43
Bogdanovich, Peter	Kingston, NY	7/30/39
Bogosian, Eric	Woburn, MA	4/24/53
Bologna, Joseph	Brooklyn, NY	12/30/38
Bolton, Michael	New Haven, CT	2/26/53
Bonet, Lisa	San Francisco, CA	11/16/67
Bonham Carter, Helena	London, England	5/26/66
Bon Jovi, Jon	Sayreville, NJ	3/2/62
Bono (Vox)	Dublin, Ireland	5/10/60
Boone, Debby	Hackensack, NJ	9/22/56
Boone, Pat	Jacksonville, FL	6/1/34
Boreanaz, David	Buffalo, NY	5/16/71
Borgnine, Ernest	Hamden, CT	1/24/17
Bosco, Philip	Jersey City, NJ	9/26/30
Bosley, Tom	Chicago, IL	10/1/27
Bosson, Barbara	Charleroi, PA	11/1/39
Bostwick, Barry	San Mateo, CA	2/24/45
Bottoms, Timothy	Santa Barbara, CA	8/30/51
Bowen, Julie	Baltimore, MD	3/3/70
Bowie, David	London, England	1/8/47
Boxleitner, Bruce	Elgin, IL	5/12/50
Boy George	Bexleyheath, England	6/14/61
Boyle, Lara Flynn	Davenport, IA	3/24/70
Boyle, Peter	Philadelphia, PA	10/18/33
Bracco, Lorraine	Brooklyn, NY	10/2/55
Braff, Zach	S. Orange, NJ	4/6/75
Branagh, Kenneth	Belfast, N. Ireland	12/10/60
Brandauer, Klaus Maria	Steiermark, Austria	6/22/44
Brando, Marlon	Omaha, NE	4/3/24
Brandy (Norwood)	McComb, MS	2/11/79
Braschi, Nicoletta	Cesena, Italy	8/10/60
Bratt, Benjamin	San Francisco, CA	12/16/63
Braugher, Andre	Chicago, Il	7/1/62
Braxton, Toni	Severn, MD	10/7/66
Brendon, Nicholas	Los Angeles, CA	4/12/71
Brennan, Eileen	Los Angeles, CA	9/3/35
Brenner, David	Philadelphia, PA	2/4/45
Brewer, Teresa	Toledo, OH	5/7/31
Bridges, Beau	Hollywood, CA	12/9/41
Bridges, Jeff	Los Angeles, CA	12/4/49
Brightman, Sarah	Berkhamstead, England	8/14/60
Brimley, Wilford	Salt Lake City, UT	9/27/34
Brinkley, Christie	Malibu, CA	2/2/54
Broadbent, Jim	Lincolnshire, England	5/24/49
Broderick, Matthew	New York, NY	3/21/62
Brolin, James	Los Angeles, CA	7/18/40
Brooks, Albert	Beverly Hills, CA	7/22/47
Brooks, Garth	Tulsa, OK	2/7/62
Brooks, James L.	North Bergen, NJ	5/9/40
Brooks, Mel	Brooklyn, NY	6/28/26
Brosnan, Pierce	Navan, Co. Meath, Ireland	5/16/53
Brown, Blair	Washington, DC	4/23/46
Brown, Bobby	Roxbury, Boston, MA	2/5/69
Brown, Bryan	Panania, Australia	6/23/47
Brown, James	Barnwell, SC	5/3/33
Browne, Jackson	Heidelberg, Germany	10/9/48
Browne, Roscoe Lee	Woodbury, NJ	5/2/25
Brubeck, Dave	Concord, CA	12/6/20
Bryson, Peabo	Greenville, SC	4/13/51
Buckley, Betty	Ft. Worth, TX	7/3/47
Buffett, Jimmy	Pascagoula, MS	12/25/46
Bujold, Genevieve	Montreal, Quebec	7/1/42
Bullock, Sandra	Arlington, VA	7/26/64
Bumbry, Grace	St. Louis, MO	1/4/37

Name	Birthplace	Birthdate
Bundchen, Gisele	Horizontina, Brazil	7/20/80
Burghoff, Gary	Bristol, CT	5/24/43
Burke, Delta	Orlando, FL	7/30/56
Burnett, Carol	San Antonio, TX	4/26/33
Burns, Edward	Woodside, Queens, NY	1/29/68
Burrows, Darren E.	Winfield, KS	9/12/66
Burstyn, Ellen	Detroit, MI	12/7/32
Burton, LeVar	Landstuhl, W Germany	2/16/57
Burton, Tim	Burbank, CA	8/25/58
Buscemi, Steve	Brooklyn, NY	12/13/57
Busey, Gary	Goose Creek, TX	6/29/44
Busfield, Timothy	Lansing, MI	6/12/57
Butler, Brett	Montgomery, AL	1/30/58
Buttons, Red	Bronx, NY	2/5/19
Buzzi, Ruth	Westerly, RI	7/24/36
Bynes, Amanda	Thousand Oaks, CA	4/3/86
Byrne, David	Dumbarton, Scotland	5/14/52
Byrne, Gabriel	Dublin, Ireland	5/12/50
Caan, James	Bronx, NY	3/26/40
Caballe, Montserrat	Barcelona, Spain	4/12/33
Caesar, Sid	Yonkers, NY	9/8/22
Cage, Nicolas	Long Beach, CA	1/7/64
Cain, Dean	Mt. Clemens, MI	7/31/66
Caine, Michael	London, England	3/14/33
Caldwell, Sarah	Maryville, MO	3/6/24
Caldwell, Zoe	Hawthorne, Australia	9/14/33
Cameron, James	Kapuskasing, Ontario	8/16/54
Cameron, Kirk	Panorama City, CA	10/12/70
Camp, Hamilton	London, England	10/30/34
Campanella, Joseph	New York, NY	11/21/27
Campbell, Bruce	Royal Oak, MI	6/22/58
Campbell, Glen	Delight, AR	4/22/36
Campbell, Naomi	South London, England	5/22/70
Campbell, Neve	Guelph, Ontario	10/3/73
Campion, Jane	Waikanae, New Zealand	4/30/54
Cannell, Stephen J.	Pasadena, CA	2/5/41
Cannon, Dyan	Tacoma, WA	1/4/37
Capshaw, Kate	Ft. Worth, TX	11/3/53
Cara, Irene	New York, NY	3/18/64
Cardinale, Claudia	Tunis, Tunisia	4/15/39
Carey, Drew	Cleveland, OH	5/23/58
Carey, Mariah	Huntington, NY	3/27/70
Cariou, Len	Winnipeg, Canada	9/30/39
Carlin, George	Bronx, New York, NY	5/12/37
Carlisle Hart, Kitty	New Orleans, LA	9/3/10
Carlyle, Robert	Glasgow, Scotland	4/14/61
Carmen, Eric	Cleveland, OH	8/11/49
Carney, Art	Mt. Vernon, NY	11/4/18
Caron, Leslie	Boulogne, France	7/1/31
Carpenter, John	Carthage, NY	1/16/48
Carpenter, Mary Chapin	Princeton, NJ	2/21/58
Carr, Vikki	El Paso, TX	7/19/41
Carradine, David	Hollywood, CA	12/8/36
Carradine, Keith	San Mateo, CA	8/8/49
Carreras, Jose	Barcelona, Spain	12/5/46
Carrere, Tia	Honolulu, HI	1/2/67
Carrey, Jim	Newmarket, Ontario	1/17/62
Carroll, Diahann	Bronx, NY	7/17/35
Carroll, Pat	Shreveport, LA	5/5/27
Carson, Johnny	Corning, IA	10/23/25
Carson, Lisa Nicole	Brooklyn, NY	7/12/69
Carter, Dixie	McLemoresville, TN	5/25/39
Carter, Jack	Brooklyn, New York, NY	6/24/23
Carter, Lynda	Phoenix, AZ	7/24/51
Carter, Nick	Jamestown, NY	1/28/80
Carter, Ron	Ferndale, MI	5/4/37
Cartwright, Nancy	Kettering, OH	10/25/59
Caruso, David	Forest Hills, Queens, NY	1/17/56
Carvey, Dana	Missoula, MT	6/2/55
Cash, Rosanne	Memphis, TN	5/24/55
Cassidy, David	New York, NY	4/12/50
Castellaneta, Dan	Chicago, IL	9/10/58
Cates, Phoebe	New York, NY	7/16/63
Cattrall, Kim	Liverpool, England	8/21/56
Cavanagh, Tom	Ottawa, Canada	10/26/68
Cavett, Dick	Gibbon, NE	11/19/36
Chabert, Lacey	Purvis, MS	9/30/82
Chalke, Sarah	Ottawa, Ontario	8/27/76
Chamberlain, Richard	Beverly Hills, CA	3/31/34
Chan, Jackie	Hong Kong	4/7/54
Channing, Carol	Seattle, WA	1/31/21
Channing, Stockard	New York, NY	2/13/44
Chaplin, Geraldine	Santa Monica, CA	7/31/44
Chapman, Tracy	Cleveland, OH	3/30/64
Charisse, Cyd	Amarillo, TX	3/8/21
Charles, Ray	Albany, GA	9/23/30
Charo	Murcia, Spain	1/15/41
Chase, Chevy	New York, NY	10/8/43
Chasez, Joshua (J.C.)	Washington, DC	8/8/76
Cheadle, Don	Kansas City, MO	11/29/64

Name	Birthplace	Birthdate
Checker, Chubby	Spring Gulley, SC	10/3/41
Cher	El Centro, CA.	5/20/46
Chianese, Dominic	Bronx, NY	2/24/31
Chiklis, Michael	Lowell, MA	8/30/63
Cho, Margaret	San Francisco	12/5/68
Chong, Rae Dawn	Vancouver, British Columbia	2/28/61
Chong, Thomas	Edmonton, Alberta	5/24/38
Chow Yun-Fat	Hong Kong	5/18/55
Christensen, Hayden	Vancouver, British Columbia	4/19/81
Christensen, Helena	Copenhagen, Denmark	12/25/68
Christie, Julie	Chukua, Assam, India	4/14/40
Christopher, William	Evanston, IL.	10/20/32
Church, Charlotte	Llandaff, Cardiff, Wales	2/21/86
Church, Thomas Haden	El Paso, TX	6/17/61
Clapton, Eric	Surrey, England.	3/30/45
Clark, Anthony	Lynchburg, VA	4/4/64
Clark, Dick	Mt. Vernon, NY	11/30/29
Clark, Petula	Ewell, Surrey, England	11/15/32
Clark, Roy	Meherrin, VA	4/15/33
Clarkson, Kelly	Burleson, TX	4/24/82
Clay, Andrew Dice	Brooklyn, NY	9/29/58
Clayburgh, Jill	New York, NY	4/30/44
Cleese, John	Weston-super-Mare, England.	10/27/39
Cliburn, Van	Shreveport, LA.	7/12/34
Clooney, George	Lexington, KY	5/6/61
Close, Glenn	Greenwich, CT.	3/19/47
Coen, Ethan	St. Louis Park, MN.	9/21/57
Coen, Joel	St. Louis Park, MN.	11/29/54
Cole, Gary	Park Ridge, IL	9/20/57
Cole, Natalie	Los Angeles, CA	2/6/50
Cole, Olivia	Memphis, TN	11/26/42
Cole, Paula	Manchester, CT	4/5/68
Coleman, Dabney	Austin, TX	1/3/32
Coleman, Gary	Zion, IL.	2/8/68
Coleman, Ornette	Fort Worth, TX .	3/19/30
Collette, Toni	Blacktown, Australia	11/1/72
Collins, Joan	London, England	5/23/33
Collins, Judy	Seattle, WA	5/1/39
Collins, Pauline	Exmouth, England	9/3/40
Collins, Phil	London, England	1/30/51
Collins, Stephen	Des Moines, IA	10/1/47
Colvin, Shawn	Vermillion, SD	1/10/56
Combs, Sean "P. Diddy"	Harlem, NY	11/4/69
Comden, Betty	Brooklyn, NY	5/3/19
Connelly, Jennifer	Catskill Mountains, NY.	12/12/70
Connery, Sean	Edinburgh, Scotland	8/25/30
Connick, Harry, Jr.	New Orleans, LA	9/11/67
Connors, Mike	Fresno, CA.	8/15/25
Conrad, Robert	Chicago, IL.	3/1/35
Conroy, Frances	Monroe, GA.	11/13/53
Constantine, Michael	Reading, PA.	5/22/27
Conti, Tom	Paisley, Scotland	11/22/41
Conway, Tim	Willoughby, OH	12/15/33
Cook, Barbara	Atlanta, GA	10/25/27
Cooke, Alistair	Manchester, England.	11/20/08
Coolidge, Rita	Nashville, TN	5/1/45
Coolio	Los Angeles, CA	8/1/63
Cooper, Alice	Detroit, MI	2/4/48
Cooper, Jackie	Los Angeles, CA	9/15/21
Copperfield, David	Metuchen, NJ.	9/16/56
Coppola, Francis Ford	Detroit, MI	4/7/39
Coppola, Sofia	New York, NY	5/12/71
Corbett, John	Wheeling, WV	5/9/61
Corbin, Barry	Lamesa, TX.	10/16/40
Cord, Alex	Floral Park, NY	5/3/33
Corea, Chick	Chelsea, MA	6/12/41
Corelli, Franco	Ancona, Italy	4/8/23
Corley, Pat	Dallas, TX.	6/1/30
Corwin, Jeff	Halifax, Nova Scotia	7/11/67
Cosby, Bill	Philadelphia, PA	7/12/37
Costas, Bob	Queens, New York, NY	3/22/52
Costello, Elvis	London, England	8/25/54
Costner, Kevin	Compton, CA	1/18/55
Courtenay, Tom	Hull, England	2/25/37
Cowell, Simon	London, England	10/7/59
Cox, Nikki	Los Angeles, CA	6/2/78
Cox, Ronny	Cloudcroft, NM.	7/23/38
Cox Arquette, Courteney	Birmingham, AL	6/15/64
Coyote, Peter	New York, NY	10/10/42
Crain, Jeanne	Barstow, CA.	5/25/25
Crawford, Cindy	DeKalb, IL	2/20/66
Crawford, Michael	Salisbury, England.	1/19/42
Crespin, Regine	Marseilles, France	2/23/26
Crosby, David	Los Angeles, CA	8/14/41
Cross, Ben	London, England	12/16/47
Crouse, Lindsay	New York, NY	5/12/48
Crow, Sheryl	Kennett, MO.	2/11/62
Crowe, Cameron	Palm Springs, CA	7/13/57
Crowe, Russell	Wellington, New Zealand .	4/7/64
Crowell, Rodney	Houston, TX.	8/17/50
Crudup, Billy	Manhasset, NY	7/8/68

Name	Birthplace	Birthdate
Cruise, Tom	Syracuse, NY	7/3/62
Cruz, Penelope	Madrid, Spain	4/28/74
Crystal, Billy	Long Beach, NY	3/14/47
Culkin, Kieran	New York, NY.	9/30/82
Culkin, Macaulay	New York, NY.	8/26/80
Culkin, Rory	New York, NY.	7/21/89
Cullum, John	Knoxville, TN	3/2/30
Culp, Robert	Oakland, CA.	8/16/30
Cummings, Constance	Seattle, WA	5/15/10
Curry, Tim	Cheshire, England	4/19/46
Curtin, Jane	Cambridge, MA.	9/6/47
Curtis, Jamie Lee	Los Angeles, CA.	11/22/58
Curtis, Tony	New York, NY.	6/3/25
Cusack, Joan	New York, NY.	10/11/62
Cusack, John	Evanston, IL.	6/28/66
Cyrus, Billy Ray	Flatwoods, KY	8/25/61
Dafoe, Willem	Appleton, WI	7/22/55
Dahl, Arlene	Minneapolis, MN.	8/11/28
Dale, Jim	Rothwell, England.	8/15/35
Dalton, Abby	Las Vegas, NV	8/15/32
Dalton, Timothy	Colwyn Bay, Wales.	3/21/46
Daltrey, Roger	London, England	3/1/44
Daly, Carson	Santa Monica, CA.	6/22/73
Daly, Timothy	New York, NY.	3/1/56
Daly, Tyne	Madison, WI	2/21/46
Damon, Matt	Cambridge, MA.	10/8/70
Damone, Vic	Brooklyn, NY.	6/12/28
Danes, Claire	New York, NY.	4/12/79
Daniels, Anthony	Salisbury, England	2/21/46
D'Angelo	Richmond, VA.	2/11/74
D'Angelo, Beverly	Columbus, OH	11/15/54
Dangerfield, Rodney	Babylon, NY	11/22/21
Daniels, Charlie	Wilmington, NC.	10/28/36
Daniels, Jeff	Athens, GA.	2/19/55
Daniels, William	Brooklyn, NY.	3/31/27
Danner, Blythe	Rosemont, PA	2/3/43
Danson, Ted	San Diego, CA.	12/29/47
Danza, Tony	Brooklyn, New York, NY.	4/21/51
Darby, Kim	Hollywood, CA.	7/8/48
David, Larry	Brooklyn, NY.	7/2/47
Davidson, John	Pittsburgh, PA.	12/13/41
Davis, Ann B.	Schenectady, NY	5/5/26
Davis, Clifton	Chicago, IL.	10/4/45
Davis, Geena	Wareham, MA.	1/21/56
Davis, Judy	Perth, Australia	4/23/55
Davis, Kristin	Boulder, CO	2/24/65
Davis, Mac	Lubbock, TX	1/21/42
Davis, Ossie	Cogdell, GA	12/18/17
Dawber, Pam	Farmington Hills, MI	10/18/51
Dawson, Richard	Gosport, Hampshire, England	11/20/32
Dawson, Rosario	Bronx, New York, NY	5/9/79
Day, Doris	Cincinnati, OH	4/3/24
Day, Laraine	Roosevelt, UT.	10/13/17
Day-Lewis, Daniel	London, England	4/29/57
Dean, Jimmy	Plainview, TX	8/10/28
Dearie, Blossom	E. Durham, NY	4/28/26
DeCarlo, Yvonne	Vancouver, BC	9/1/22
Dee, Frances	Los Angeles, CA.	11/26/07
Dee, Ruby	Cleveland, OH	10/27/24
Dee, Sandra	Bayonne, NJ.	4/23/42
DeFranco, Buddy	Camden, NJ.	2/17/23
DeGeneres, Ellen	Metairie, LA	1/26/58
DeHaven, Gloria	Los Angeles, CA.	7/23/25
De Havilland, Olivia	Tokyo, Japan	7/1/16
Delaney, Kim	Philadelphia, PA.	11/29/61
Delany, Dana	New York, NY.	3/13/56
DeLaurentiis, Dino	Torre Annunziata, Italy	8/8/19
Delon, Alain	Sceaux, France	11/8/35
Del Toro, Benicio	Santurce, Puerto Rico	2/19/67
DeLuise, Dom	Brooklyn, NY.	8/1/33
Demme, Jonathan	Baldwin, NY	2/22/44
De Mornay, Rebecca	Santa Rosa, CA	8/29/62
Dench, Judi	York, England.	12/9/34
Deneuve, Catherine	Paris, France	10/22/43
De Niro, Robert	New York, NY.	8/17/43
Dennehy, Brian	Bridgeport, CT	7/9/38
Denver, Bob	New Rochelle, NY	1/9/35
DePalma, Brian	Newark, NJ.	9/11/40
Depardieu, Gerard	Chateauroux, France	12/27/48
Depp, Johnny	Owensboro, KY	6/9/63
Derek, Bo	Long Beach, CA.	11/20/56
Dern, Bruce	Winnetka, IL.	6/4/36
Dern, Laura	Santa Monica, CA.	2/10/67
Devane, William	Albany, NY	9/5/39
DeVito, Danny	Neptune, NJ	11/17/44
DeWitt, Joyce	Wheeling, WV.	4/23/49
Dey, Susan	Pekin, IL.	12/10/52
Diamond, Neil	Brooklyn, NY.	1/24/41
Diaz, Cameron	San Diego, CA	8/30/72

Name	Birthplace	Birthdate
DiCaprio, Leonardo	Hollywood, CA	11/11/74
Dick, Andy	Charleston, SC	12/21/65
Dickinson, Angie	Kulm, ND	9/30/31
Diddley, Bo	McComb, MS	12/30/28
Diesel, Vin	New York, NY	7/18/67
Diggs, Taye	Essex Co., NJ	1/2/72
Diller, Phyllis	Lima, OH	7/17/17
Dillman, Bradford	San Francisco, CA	4/14/30
Dillon, Matt	New Rochelle, NY	2/18/64
Dion, Celine	Charlemagne, Quebec	3/30/68
Dobson, Kevin	Queens, New York, NY	3/18/43
Dogg, Snoop	Long Beach, CA	10/20/71
Doherty, Shannen	Memphis, TN	4/12/71
Dolenz, Mickey	Los Angeles, CA	3/8/45
Domingo, Placido	Madrid, Spain	1/21/41
Domino, Fats	New Orleans, LA	2/26/28
Donahue, Phil	Cleveland, OH	12/21/35
D'Onofrio, Vincent	Brooklyn, NY	6/30/59
Donovan (Leitch)	Glasgow, Scotland	5/10/46
Dorn, Michael	Luling, TX	12/9/52
Dorough, Howie	Orlando, FL	8/22/73
Dotrice, Roy	Guernsey, England	5/26/23
Douglas, Kirk	Amsterdam, NY	12/9/16
Douglas, Michael	New Brunswick, NJ	9/25/44
Dow, Tony	Hollywood, CA	4/13/45
Down, Lesley-Ann	London, England	3/17/54
Downey, Robert, Jr.	New York, NY	4/4/65
Downey, Roma	Derry, Northern Ireland	5/6/60
Downs, Hugh	Akron, OH	2/14/21
Drescher, Fran	Flushing, Queens, NY	9/30/57
Drew, Ellen	Kansas City, MO	11/23/15
Dreyfuss, Richard	Brooklyn, NY	10/29/47
Driver, Minnie	London, England	1/31/70
Dryer, Fred	Hawthorne, CA	7/6/46
Duchovny, David	New York, NY	8/7/60
Duff, Hilary	Houston, TX	9/28/87
Duffy, Julia	Minneapolis, MN	6/27/51
Duffy, Patrick	Townsend, MT	3/17/49
Dukakis, Olympia	Lowell, MA	6/20/31
Duke, Patty	Elmhurst, NY	12/14/46
Dullea, Keir	Cleveland, OH	5/30/36
Dunaway, Faye	Bascom, FL	1/14/41
Duncan, Lindsay	Edinburgh, Scotland	11/7/50
Duncan, Sandy	Henderson, TX	2/20/46
Dunham, Katherine	Glen Ellyn, IL	6/22/10
Dunne, Griffin	New York, NY	6/8/55
Dunst, Kirsten	Point Pleasant, NJ	4/30/82
Durbin, Deanna	Winnipeg, Manitoba	12/4/21
Durning, Charles	Highland Falls, NY	2/28/23
Dussault, Nancy	Pensacola, FL	6/30/36
Dutton, Charles S.	Baltimore, MD	1/30/51
Duvall, Robert	San Diego, CA	1/5/31
Duvall, Shelley	Houston, TX	7/7/49
Dylan, Bob	Duluth, MN	5/24/41
Dylan, Jakob	New York, NY	12/9/69
Dysart, Richard	Brighton, MA	3/30/29
Dzundza, George	Rosenheim, Germany	7/19/45
Easton, Sheena	Bellshill, Scotland	4/27/59
Eastwood, Clint	San Francisco, CA	5/31/30
Ebert, Roger	Urbana, IL	6/18/42
Eden, Barbara	Tucson, AZ	8/23/34
Edwards, Anthony	Santa Barbara, CA	7/19/62
Edwards, Blake	Tulsa, OK	7/26/22
Edwards, Ralph	Merino, CO	6/13/13
Ehle, Jennifer	Winston-Salem, NC	12/29/69
Eichhorn, Lisa	Reading, PA	2/4/52
Eikenberry, Jill	New Haven, CT	1/21/47
Ekberg, Anita	Malmo, Sweden	9/29/31
Ekland, Britt	Stockholm, Sweden	10/6/42
Elam, Jack	Miami, AZ	11/13/16
Electra, Carmen	Cincinnati, OH	4/20/72
Elfman, Jenna	Los Angeles, CA	9/30/71
Elizabeth, Shannon	Houston, TX	9/7/73
Elizondo, Hector	New York, NY	12/22/36
Elliott, Bob	Boston, MA	3/26/23
Elliott, Chris	New York, NY	5/31/60
Elliott, Sam	Sacramento, CA	8/9/44
Elvira	Manhattan, KS	9/17/51
Eminem	St. Joseph, MO	10/17/72
Enberg, Dick	Mt. Clemens, MI	1/9/35
Englund, Robert	Glendale, CA	6/6/49
Enya	Gweedore, Ireland	5/17/61
Ephron, Nora	New York, NY	5/19/41
Estefan, Gloria	Havana, Cuba	9/1/57
Estevez, Emilio	New York, NY	5/12/62
Estrada, Erik	New York, NY	3/16/49
Etheridge, Melissa	Leavenworth, KS	5/29/61
Evans, Linda	Hartford, CT	11/18/42
Evans, Robert	New York, NY	6/29/30
Everett, Chad	South Bend, IN	6/11/36

Name	Birthplace	Birthdate
Everett, Rupert	Norfolk, England	5/29/59
Everly, Don	Brownie, KY	2/1/37
Everly, Phil	Chicago, IL	1/19/39
Evigan, Greg	South Amboy, NJ	10/14/53
Fabares, Shelley	Santa Monica, CA	1/19/44
Fabian (Forte)	Philadelphia, PA	2/6/43
Fabio	Milan, Italy	3/15/61
Fabray, Nanette	San Diego, CA	10/27/20
Fairchild, Morgan	Dallas, TX	2/3/50
Faison, Donald	New York, NY	6/22/74
Falana, Lola	Philadelphia, PA	9/11/43
Falco, Edie	Brooklyn, NY	7/5/63
Falk, Peter	New York, NY	9/16/27
Fallon, Jimmy	Brooklyn, NY	9/19/74
Farentino, James	Brooklyn, NY	2/24/38
Fargo, Donna	Mt. Airy, NC	11/10/49
Farina, Dennis	Chicago, IL	2/29/44
Farr, Jamie	Toledo, OH	7/1/34
Farrell, Mike	St. Paul, MN	2/6/39
Farrelly, Bob	Cumberland, RI	1958
Farrelly, Peter	Phoenixville, PA	12/17/56
Farrow, Mia	Los Angeles, CA	2/9/45
Fatone, Joey	Brooklyn, New York, NY	1/28/77
Faustino, David	Los Angeles, CA	3/3/74
Fawcett, Farrah	Corpus Christi, TX	2/2/47
Feinstein, Michael	Columbus, OH	9/7/56
Feldon, Barbara	Pittsburgh, PA	3/12/41
Feldshuh, Tovah	New York, NY	12/27/52
Feliciano, Jose	Lares, Puerto Rico	9/10/45
Fenn, Sherilyn	Detroit, MI	2/1/65
Ferrell, Conchata	Charleston, WV	3/28/43
Ferrell, Will	Irvine, CA	7/16/67
Ferrer, Mel	Elberon, NJ	8/25/17
Fey, Tina	Upper Darby, PA	5/18/70
Fiedler, John	Platteville, WI	2/3/25
Field, Sally	Pasadena, CA	11/6/46
Fiennes, Joseph	Salisbury, England	5/27/70
Fiennes, Ralph	Suffolk, England	12/22/62
Fierstein, Harvey	Brooklyn, NY	6/6/54
Fincher, David	Denver, CO	1962
Finney, Albert	Salford, England	5/9/36
Fiorentino, Linda	Philadelphia, PA	3/9/60
Firth, Colin	Grayshott, England	9/10/60
Firth, Peter	Bradford, Yorkshire, England	10/27/53
Fischer-Dieskau, Dietrich	Berlin, Germany	5/28/25
Fishburne, Laurence	Augusta, GA	7/30/61
Fisher, Carrie	Beverly Hills, CA	10/21/56
Fisher, Eddie	Philadelphia, PA	8/10/28
Fitzgerald, Geraldine	Dublin, Ireland	11/24/13
Flack, Roberta	Black Mountain, NC	2/10/39
Flanagan, Fionnula	Dublin, Ireland	12/10/41
Fleming, Rhonda	Hollywood, CA	8/10/23
Fletcher, Louise	Birmingham, AL	7/22/34
Flockhart, Calista	Freeport, IL	11/11/64
Florek, Dann	Flat Rock, MI	5/1/50
Foch, Nina	Leyden, Netherlands	4/20/24
Fogelberg, Dan	Peoria, IL	8/13/51
Fogerty, John	Berkeley, CA	5/28/45
Foley, Dave	Etobicoke, Ontario	1/4/63
Fonda, Bridget	Los Angeles, CA	1/27/64
Fonda, Jane	New York, NY	12/21/37
Fonda, Peter	New York, NY	2/23/40
Fontaine, Joan	Tokyo, Japan	10/22/17
Ford, Faith	Alexandria, LA	9/14/64
Ford, Glenn	Sainte-Christine, Quebec	5/1/16
Ford, Harrison	Des Plaines, IL	7/13/42
Forman, Milos	Caslav, Czechoslovakia	2/18/32
Forsythe, John	Penns Grove, NJ	1/29/18
Foster, Jodie	Los Angeles, CA	11/19/62
Fox, James	London, England	5/19/39
Fox, Matthew	Crowheart, WY	7/14/66
Fox, Michael J.	Edmonton, Alberta	6/9/61
Fox, Vivica A.	Indianapolis, IN	7/30/64
Foxworth, Robert	Houston, TX	11/1/41
Foxworthy, Jeff	Atlanta, GA	9/6/58
Foxx, Jamie	Terrell, TX	12/13/67
Frampton, Peter	Kent, England	4/22/50
Franciosa, Anthony	East Harlem, NY, NY	10/25/28
Francis, Anne	Ossining, NY	9/16/30
Francis, Connie	Newark, NJ	12/12/38
Franken, Al	New York, NY	5/21/51
Franklin, Aretha	Memphis, TN	3/25/42
Franklin, Bonnie	Santa Monica, CA	1/6/44
Franz, Dennis	Maywood, IL	10/28/44
Fraser, Brendan	Indianapolis, IN	12/3/68
Freeman, Al, Jr.	San Antonio, TX	3/21/34
Freeman, Mona	Baltimore, MD	6/9/26
Freeman, Morgan	Memphis, TN	6/1/37
French, Dawn	Holyhead, Wales	10/11/57
Fricker, Brenda	Dublin, Ireland	2/17/45

Name	Birthplace	Birthdate	Name	Birthplace	Birthdate
Friedkin, William	Chicago, IL	8/29/39	Green, Al	Forrest City, AR	4/13/46
Frost, David	Tenterden, England	4/7/39	Green, Seth	Overbrook Park, PA	2/8/74
Fry, Stephen	London, England	8/24/57	Green, Tom	Pembroke, Ontario	7/30/71
Fuentes, Daisy	Havana, Cuba	11/17/66	Greene, Shecky	Chicago, IL	4/8/26
Fuller, Robert	Troy, NY	7/29/34	Greenwood, Bruce	Noranda, Quebec	8/12/56
Funicello, Annette	Utica, NY	10/22/42	Gregory, Cynthia	Los Angeles, CA	7/8/46
Furlong, Edward	Pasadena, CA	8/2/77	Gregory, Dick	St. Louis, MO	10/12/32
Furtado, Nelly	Victoria, British Columbia	12/2/78	Grey, Jennifer	New York, NY	3/26/60
			Grey, Joel	Cleveland, OH	4/11/32
Gabor, Zsa Zsa	Budapest, Hungary	2/6/17	Grier, David Alan	Detroit, MI	6/30/55
Gabriel, John	Niagara Falls, NY	5/25/31	Grier, Pam	Winston-Salem, NC	5/26/49
Gabriel, Peter	Surrey, England	2/13/50	Griffin, Merv	San Mateo, CA	7/6/25
Galway, James	Belfast, N. Ireland	12/8/39	Griffith, Andy	Mount Airy, NC	6/1/26
Gandolfini, James	Westwood, NJ	9/18/61	Griffith, Melanie	New York, NY	8/9/57
Garagiola, Joe	St. Louis, MO	2/12/26	Griffiths, Rachel	New Castle, Australia	2/20/68
Garber, Victor	London, Ont.	3/16/49	Grimes, Tammy	Lynn, MA	1/30/34
Garcia, Andy	Havana, Cuba	4/12/56	Grint, Rupert	Hertfordshire, England	8/24/88
Garfunkel, Art	Queens, New York, NY	11/5/41	Grizzard, George	Roanoke Rapids, NC	4/1/28
Garland, Beverly	Santa Cruz, CA	10/17/26	Grodin, Charles	Pittsburgh, PA	4/21/35
Garner, James	Norman, OK	4/7/28	Grosbard, Ulu	Antwerp, Belgium	1/9/29
Garner, Jennifer	Houston, TX	4/17/72	Gross, Michael	Chicago, IL	6/21/47
Garofalo, Janeane	Newton, NJ	9/28/64	Guest, Christopher	New York, NY	2/5/48
Garr, Teri	Lakewood, OH	12/11/49	Guillaume, Robert	St. Louis, MO	11/30/37
Garrett, Betty	St. Joseph, MO	5/23/19	Gumbel, Greg	New Orleans, LA	5/3/46
Garrett, Brad	Woodland Hills, CA	4/14/60	Guthrie, Arlo	Brooklyn, New York, NY	7/10/47
Garth, Jennie	Urbana, IL	4/3/72	Guttenberg, Steve	Brooklyn, New York, NY	8/24/58
Gatlin, Larry	Seminole, TX	5/2/48	Guy, Buddy	Lettsworth, LA	7/30/36
Gavin, John	Los Angeles, CA	4/8/31	Guy, Jasmine	Boston, MA	3/10/64
Gayle, Crystal	Paintsville, KY	1/9/51	Gyllenhaal, Jake	Los Angeles, CA	12/19/80
Gaynor, Mitzi	Chicago, IL	9/4/31			
Gazzara, Ben	New York, NY	8/28/30	Hackman, Gene	San Bernardino, CA	1/30/30
Geary, Anthony	Coalville, UT	5/29/47	Hagen, Uta	Gottingen, Germany	6/12/19
Geary, Cynthia	Jackson, MS	3/21/65	Haggard, Merle	Bakersfield, CA	4/6/37
Gedda, Nicolai	Stockholm, Sweden	7/11/25	Hagman, Larry	Fort Worth, TX	9/21/31
Gellar, Sarah Michelle	New York, NY	4/14/77	Haid, Charles	San Francisco, CA	6/2/43
Gere, Richard	Philadelphia, PA	8/31/49	Haines, Connie	Savannah, GA	1/20/22
Getty, Estelle	New York, NY	7/25/23	Hale, Barbara	DeKalb, IL	4/18/22
Ghostley, Alice	Eve, MO	8/14/26	Hall, Arsenio	Cleveland, OH	2/12/55
Giannini, Giancarlo	La Spezia, Italy	8/1/42	Hall, Daryl	Pottstown, PA	10/11/49
Gibb, Barry	Isle of Man, England	9/1/46	Hall, Deidre	Milwaukee, WI	10/31/47
Gibb, Robin	Isle of Man, England	12/22/49	Hall, Michael C.	Raleigh, NC	2/1/71
Gibbons, Leeza	Irmo, SC	3/26/57	Hall, Monty	Winnipeg, Manitoba	8/25/21
Gibbs, Marla	Chicago, IL	6/14/31	Hall, Tom T.	Olive Hill, KY	5/25/36
Gibson, Deborah	Brooklyn, New York, NY	8/31/70	Halliwell, Geri	Watford, England	8/6/72
Gibson, Henry	Germantown, PA	9/21/35	Hamill, Mark	Oakland, CA	9/25/51
Gibson, Mel	Peekskill, NY	1/3/56	Hamilton, George	Memphis, TN	8/12/39
Gibson, Thomas	Charleston, SC	7/3/62	Hamilton, Linda	Salisbury, MD	9/26/56
Gifford, Frank	Santa Monica, CA	8/16/30	Hamlin, Harry	Pasadena, CA	10/30/51
Gifford, Kathie Lee	Neuilly-sur-Seine, France	8/16/53	Hammer	Oakland, CA	3/29/63
Gilbert, Sara	Santa Monica, CA	1/29/75	Hammond, Darrell	Melbourne, FL	10/8/60
Gilbert, Melissa	Los Angeles, CA	5/8/64	Hancock, Herbie	Chicago, IL	4/12/40
Gilberto, Astrud	Salvador, Brazil	3/30/40	Hanks, Tom	Concord, CA	7/9/56
Gili, Vince	Norman, OK	4/12/57	Hanley, Daryl	Chicago, IL	12/3/60
Gillette, Anita	Baltimore, MD	8/16/36	Hannigan, Alyson	Washington, DC	3/24/74
Gilley, Mickey	Natchez, MS	3/9/36	Hanson, Curtis	Reno, NV	3/24/45
Gilliam, Terry	Minneapolis, MN	11/22/40	Hanson, Isaac	Tulsa, OK	11/17/80
Gilpin, Peri	Waco, TX	5/27/61	Hanson, Taylor	Tulsa, OK	3/14/83
Ginty, Robert	New York, NY	11/14/48	Hanson, Zac	Tulsa, OK	10/22/85
Givens, Robin	New York, NY	11/27/64	Harden, Marcia Gay	La Jolla, CA	8/14/59
Glaser, Paul Michael	Cambridge, MA	3/25/43	Hardison, Kadeem	New York, NY	7/24/66
Glenn, Scott	Pittsburgh, PA	1/26/42	Harewood, Dorian	Dayton, OH	8/6/50
Gless, Sharon	Los Angeles, CA	5/31/43	Harmon, Angie	Highland Park, TX	8/10/72
Glover, Crispin	New York, NY	9/20/64	Harmon, Mark	Burbank, CA	9/2/51
Glover, Danny	San Francisco, CA	7/22/47	Harper, Jessica	Chicago, IL	10/10/49
Glover, Savion	Newark, NJ	11/19/73	Harper, Tess	Mammoth Springs, AR	8/15/50
Godard, Jean Luc	Paris, France	12/3/30	Harper, Valerie	Suffern, NY	8/22/40
Goldberg, Whoopi	New York, NY	11/13/55	Harrelson, Woody	Midland, TX	7/23/61
Goldblum, Jeff	Pittsburgh, PA	10/22/52	Harrington, Pat	New York, NY	8/13/29
Goldthwait, Bobcat	Syracuse, NY	5/26/62	Harris, Barbara	Evanston, IL	7/25/35
Goldwyn, Tony	Los Angeles, CA	5/20/60	Harris, Ed	Tenafly, NJ	11/28/50
Gooding, Cuba, Jr.	Bronx, NY	1/2/68	Harris, Emmylou	Birmingham, AL	4/2/47
Goodman, John	Afton, MO	6/20/52	Harris, Julie	Grosse Pte. Park, MI	12/2/25
Gordon-Levitt, Joseph	Los Angeles, CA	2/17/81	Harris, Neil Patrick	Albuquerque, NM	6/15/73
Gorme, Eydie	Bronx, NY	8/16/32	Harris, Rosemary	Ashby, England	9/19/30
Gorshin, Frank	Pittsburgh, PA	4/5/34	Harris, Steve	Chicago, IL	12/3/65
Gossett, Louis, Jr.	Brooklyn, NY	5/27/36	Harrison, Gregory	Avalon, CA	5/31/50
Gould, Elliott	Brooklyn, NY	8/29/38	Harry, Deborah	Miami, FL	7/1/45
Gould, Harold	Schenectady, NY	12/10/23	Hart, Mary	Madison, SD	11/8/50
Goulet, Robert	Lawrence, MA	11/26/33	Hart, Melissa Joan	Sayville, NY	4/18/76
Gowdy, Curt	Green River, WY	7/31/19	Hartley, Hal	Lindenhurst, NY	11/3/59
Graham, Heather	Milwaukee, WI	1/29/70	Hartley, Mariette	New York, NY	6/21/40
Grammer, Kelsey	St. Thomas, Virgin Isl.	2/21/55	Hartman, David	Pawtucket, RI	5/19/35
Granger, Farley	San Jose, CA	7/1/25	Hartman Black, Lisa	Houston, TX	6/1/56
Grant, Amy	Augusta, GA	11/25/60	Hartnett, Josh	San Francisco, CA	7/21/78
Grant, Hugh	London, England	9/9/60	Hasselhoff, David	Baltimore, MD	7/17/52
Grant, Lee	New York, NY	10/31/27	Hatcher, Teri	Sunnyvale, CA	12/8/64
Graves, Peter	Minneapolis, MN	3/18/26	Hathaway, Anne	Brooklyn, NY	11/12/82
Gray, Linda	Santa Monica, CA	9/12/40	Hauer, Rutger	Breukelen, Netherlands	1/23/44
Gray, Macy	Canton, OH	9/6/70	Haver, June	Rock Island, IL	6/10/26
Gray, Spaulding	Barrington, RI	6/5/41	Havoc, June	Seattle, WA	11/8/16
Grayson, Kathryn	Winston-Salem, NC	2/9/22	Hawke, Ethan	Austin, TX	11/6/70

Name	Birthplace	Birthdate
Hawn, Goldie	Washington, DC.	11/21/45
Hayden, Melissa	Toronto, Ontario.	4/25/23
Hayek, Salma	Coatzacoalcos, Mexico	9/2/66
Hayes, Isaac	Covington, TN	8/20/42
Hayes, Sean	Glen Ellyn, IL	6/26/70
Haynes, Roy	Roxbury, Boston, MA.	3/13/26
Hays, Robert	Bethesda, MD	7/24/47
Head, Anthony Stewart.	North London, England	2/20/54
Heard, John	Washington, DC.	3/7/46
Hearn, George	St. Louis, MO.	6/18/34
Heaton, Patricia	Bay Village, OH	3/4/58
Heche, Anne	Aurora, OH.	5/25/69
Hedren, Tippi	Lafayette, MN	1/19/31
Helfgott, David	Melbourne, Australia	5/19/47
Helgenberger, Marg	Fremont, NE	11/16/58
Helmond, Katherine	Galveston, TX	7/5/34
Hemingway, Mariel	Mill Valley, CA	11/22/61
Hemmings, David	Guildford, England	11/18/41
Hemsley, Sherman	Philadelphia, PA	2/1/38
Henderson, Florence	Dale, IN	2/14/34
Henderson, Skitch	Birmingham, England	1/27/18
Henley, Don	Gilmer, TX	7/22/47
Henner, Marilu	Chicago, IL	4/6/52
Hennessy, Jill	Edmonton, Alberta	11/25/68
Henry, Buck	New York, NY	12/9/30
Herman, Pee-Wee	Peekskill, NY	8/27/52
Herrmann, Edward	Washington, DC.	7/21/43
Hershey, Barbara	Hollywood, CA	2/5/48
Hesseman, Howard	Lebanon, OR	2/27/40
Heston, Charlton	Evanston, IL.	10/4/24
Hetfield, James	Downey, CA.	8/3/63
Hewitt, Jennifer Love	Waco, TX.	2/21/79
Hildegarde	Adell, WI	2/1/06
Hill, Arthur	Melfort, Sask.	8/1/22
Hill, Dulé	Orange, NJ	5/3/74
Hill, Faith	Jackson, MS	9/21/67
Hill, Lauryn	South Orange, NJ	5/25/75
Hill, Steven	Seattle, WA	2/24/22
Hillerman, John	Denison, TX.	12/20/32
Hines, Cheryl	Miami Beach, FL	9/21/65
Hingle, Pat	Denver, CO	7/19/24
Hirsch, Judd	New York, NY	3/15/35
Ho, Don	Kakaako, Oahu, HI.	8/13/30
Hoffman, Dustin	Los Angeles, CA	8/8/37
Hoffman, Philip Seymour	Fairport, NY	7/23/67
Hogan, Paul	Lightning Ridge, New South Wales, Australia.	10/8/39
Holbrook, Hal	Cleveland, OH	2/17/25
Holder, Geoffrey	Port of Spain, Trinidad.	8/1/30
Holliday, Polly	Jasper, AL	7/2/37
Holliman, Earl	Delhi, LA	9/11/28
Holly, Lauren	Bristol, PA	10/28/63
Holm, Celeste	New York, NY	4/29/19
Holm, Ian	Ilford, England	9/12/31
Holmes, Katie	Toledo, OH	12/18/78
Hooks, Jan	Decatur, GA.	4/23/57
Hopkins, Anthony	Port Talbot, South Wales.	12/31/37
Hopkins, Bo.	Greenville, SC	2/2/42
Hopkins, Telma	Louisville, KY.	10/28/48
Hopper, Dennis	Dodge City, KS	5/17/36
Horne, Lena	Brooklyn, NY	6/30/17
Horne, Marilyn.	Bradford, PA	1/16/34
Hornsby, Bruce	Williamsburg, VA	11/23/54
Horsley, Lee	Muleshoe, TX.	5/15/55
Horton, Robert	Los Angeles, CA	7/29/24
Hoskins, Bob.	Suffolk, England.	10/26/42
Houston, Whitney	Newark, NJ	8/9/63
Howard, Ken	El Centro, CA.	3/28/44
Howard, Ron	Duncan, OK	3/1/54
Howell, C. Thomas	Van Nuys, CA	12/7/66
Howes, Sally Ann	London, England	7/20/30
Hudson, Kate	Los Angeles, CA	4/19/79
Hughes, Barnard.	Bedford Hills, NY	7/16/15
Hulce, Tom	Whitewater, WI	12/6/53
Humperdinck, Engelbert	Madras, India.	5/2/36
Humphries, Barry	Melbourne, Australia	2/17/34
Hunt, Bonnie	Chicago, IL.	9/22/64
Hunt, Helen	Culver City, CA	6/15/63
Hunt, Linda	Morristown, NJ.	4/2/45
Hunter, Holly	Conyers, GA	3/20/58
Hunter, Tab	New York, NY	7/11/31
Hurley, Elizabeth	Hampshire, England	6/10/65
Hurt, John	Chesterfield, England	1/22/40
Hurt, Mary Beth	Marshalltown, IA	9/26/48
Hurt, William	Washington, DC.	3/20/50
Hussey, Ruth	Providence, RI	10/30/14
Huston, Anjelica	Santa Monica, CA	7/8/51
Hutton, Betty	Battle Creek, MI	2/26/21
Hutton, Lauren	Charleston, SC	11/17/43
Hutton, Timothy	Malibu, CA	8/16/60
Hyman, Earle	Rocky Mount, NC.	10/11/26

Name	Birthplace	Birthdate
Ian, Janis	New York, NY.	4/7/51
Ice Cube	Los Angeles, CA.	6/15/69
Ice-T	Newark, NJ	2/16/58
Idle, Eric	S. Shields, England	3/29/43
Idol, Billy	Middlesex, England	11/30/55
Iglesias, Enrique	Madrid, Spain	5/8/75
Iglesias, Julio	Madrid, Spain	9/23/43
Iler, Robert	New York, NY	3/2/85
Iman	Mogadishu, Somalia	7/25/55
Imbruglia, Natalie	Sydney, Australia	2/4/75
Imperioli, Michael	Mount Vernon, NY	1/1/66
Imus, Don	Riverside, CA	7/23/40
Ingram, James	Akron, OH.	2/16/56
Innes, Laura	Pontiac, MI	8/16/59
Ireland, Kathy	Glendale, CA	3/20/63
Irons, Jeremy	Isle of Wight, England.	9/19/48
Irving, Amy	Palo Alto, CA	9/10/53
Irving, George S.	Springfield, MA.	11/1/22
Irwin, Bill	Santa Monica, CA.	4/11/50
Irwin, Steve	Beerwah, Queensland, Australia	2/22/62
Ivey, Judith.	El Paso, TX	9/4/51
Ivory, James	Berkeley, CA.	6/7/28
Jackee (Harry)	Winston-Salem, NC	8/14/56
Jackman, Hugh	Sydney, Australia	10/12/68
Jackson, Anne	Allegheny, PA	9/3/26
Jackson, Glenda	Birkenhead, England	5/9/36
Jackson, Janet.	Gary, IN	5/16/66
Jackson, Jermaine	Gary, IN	12/11/54
Jackson, Jonathan	Orlando, FL	5/11/82
Jackson, Joshua	Vancouver, Brit. Columbia	6/11/78
Jackson, Kate	Birmingham, AL	10/29/48
Jackson, La Toya	Gary, IN	5/29/56
Jackson, Michael	Gary, IN	8/29/58
Jackson, Peter	Wellington, New Zealand	10/31/61
Jackson, Samuel L.	Chattanooga, TN	12/21/48
Jacobi, Derek	London, England	10/22/38
Jagger, Mick	Dartford, England	7/26/43
James, Etta	Los Angeles, CA.	1/25/38
James, Kevin	Mineola, NY	4/26/65
Janis, Conrad	New York, NY	2/11/28
Janney, Allison	Boston, MA.	11/19/60
Janssen, Famke	Amsterdam, Netherlands	11/5/65
Jardine, Al	Lima, OH	9/3/42
Jarmusch, Jim	Akron, OH.	1/22/53
Jarreau, Al	Milwaukee, WI	3/12/40
Jarrette, Keith	Allentown, PA.	5/8/45
Jeffreys, Anne	Goldsboro, NC	1/26/23
Jett, Joan	Philadelphia, PA.	9/22/60
Jewel (Kilcher)	Payson, UT.	5/23/74
Jewison, Norman	Toronto, Ontario	7/21/26
Jillian, Ann	Cambridge, MA.	1/29/50
Jillette, Penn	Greenfield, MA	3/5/55
Joel, Billy	Bronx, NY	5/9/49
John, Elton	Pinner, Middlesex, England	3/25/47
Johns, Glynis	Durban, S Africa	10/5/23
Johnson, Arte	Benton Harbor, MI	1/20/34
Johnson, Beverly	Buffalo, NY	10/13/52
Johnson, Don	Flatt Creek, MO	12/15/49
Johnson, Van	Newport, RI.	8/25/16
Johnston, Bruce	Chicago, IL.	6/24/44
Johnston, Kristen	Washington, DC	9/20/67
Jolie, Angelina	Los Angeles, CA.	6/4/75
Jones, Charlie	Ft. Smith, AR	11/9/30
Jones, Cherry	Paris, TN.	11/21/56
Jones, Davy	Manchester, England	12/30/45
Jones, Dean	Morgan City, AL	1/25/31
Jones, Elvin	Pontiac, MI	9/9/27
Jones, Gemma	London, England	12/4/42
Jones, George	Saratoga, TX	9/12/31
Jones, Grace	Spanishtown, Jamaica	5/19/52
Jones, Jack	Hollywood, CA	1/14/38
Jones, James Earl	Arkabutla, MS.	1/17/31
Jones, Jennifer	Tulsa, OK.	3/2/19
Jones, Norah	New York, NY.	3/30/79
Jones, Quincy	Chicago, IL.	3/14/33
Jones, Shirley	Smithton, PA	3/31/34
Jones, Star.	Badin, NC.	3/24/62
Jones, Tom	Pontypridd, Wales	6/7/40
Jones, Tommy Lee	San Saba, TX.	9/15/46
Jonze, Spike	Rockville, MD.	10/22/69
Jourdan, Louis	Marseilles, France	6/19/19
Jovovich, Milla	Kiev, Ukraine	12/17/75
Judd, Ashley	Granada Hills, CA.	4/19/68
Judd, Naomi	Ashland, KY.	1/11/46
Judd, Wynonna	Ashland, KY.	5/30/64
Kaczmarek, Jane	Milwaukee, WI	12/21/55
Kanaly, Steve	Burbank, CA.	3/14/46
Kane, Carol	Cleveland, OH	6/18/52

Name	Birthplace	Birthdate
Kaplan, Gabe	Brooklyn, NY	3/31/45
Karlen, John	Brooklyn, NY	5/28/33
Karn, Richard	Seattle, WA	2/17/56
Karras, Alex	Gary, IN	7/15/35
Kasem, Casey	Detroit, MI	4/27/32
Kattan, Chris	Sherman Oaks, CA	10/19/70
Kavner, Julie	Burbank, CA	9/7/51
Kazan, Lainie	New York, NY	5/15/42
Keach, Stacy	Savannah, GA	6/2/41
Keaton, Diane	Santa Ana, CA	1/5/46
Keaton, Michael	Pittsburgh, PA	9/9/51
Keel, Howard	Gillespie, IL	4/13/19
Keener, Catherine	Miami FL	3/23/59
Keeshan, Bob	Lynbrook, NY.	6/27/27
Keitel, Harvey	Brooklyn, NY	5/13/39
Keith, David	Knoxville, TN	5/8/54
Keith, Penelope	Sutton, Surrey, England.	4/2/40
Kellerman, Sally	Long Beach, CA.	6/2/37
Kelly, R(obert)	Chicago, IL.	1/8/69
Kennedy, George	New York, NY	2/18/25
Kennedy, Jamie	Upper Darby, PA	5/25/70
Kennedy, Jayne	Washington, DC.	10/27/51
Kenny G	Seattle, WA.	6/5/56
Kent, Allegra	Santa Monica, CA	8/11/37
Kercheval, Ken	Wolcottville, IN.	7/15/35
Kerns, Joanna	San Francisco, CA.	2/12/53
Kerr, Deborah	Helensburgh, Scotland	9/30/21
Kessel, Barney	Muskogee, OK.	10/17/23
Keys, Alicia	New York, NY	1/25/81
Khan, Chaka	Great Lakes, IL	3/23/53
Kidder, Margot	Yellowknife, N.W.T.	10/17/48
Kidman, Nicole	Honolulu, HI.	6/20/67
Kilborn, Craig	Kansas City, KS.	8/24/62
Kilmer, Val	Los Angeles, CA	12/31/59
Kimbrough, Charles	St. Paul, MN.	5/23/36
Kimmel, Jimmy	Brooklyn, NY	11/13/67
King, Alan	Brooklyn, NY	12/26/27
King, B. B.	Itta Bena, MS.	9/16/25
King, Carole	Brooklyn, NY	2/9/42
King, Larry	Brooklyn, NY	11/19/33
King, Perry	Alliance, OH.	4/30/48
Kingsley, Ben	Scarborough, England.	12/31/43
Kingston, Alex	London, England	3/11/63
Kinnear, Greg	Logansport, IN	6/17/63
Kinney, Kathy	Stevens Point, WI	11/3/53
Kinski, Nastassja	Berlin, W. Germany	1/24/60
Kirby, Bruno	New York, NY	4/28/49
Kirkland, Gelsey	Bethlehem, PA.	12/29/52
Kirkpatrick, Chris	Clarion, PA.	10/17/71
Kitt, Eartha	North, SC	1/17/27
Klein, Robert	Bronx, New York, NY	2/8/42
Kline, Kevin	St. Louis, MO.	10/24/47
Klugman, Jack	Philadelphia, PA	4/27/22
Knight, Gladys	Atlanta, GA	5/28/44
Knight, Shirley	Goessel, KS.	7/5/36
Knight, Wayne	New York, NY	8/7/55
Knightley, Keira	Teddington, England	3/26/85
Knotts, Don	Morgantown, WV	7/21/24
Knowles, Beyoncé	Houston, TX.	9/4/81
Konitz, Lee	Chicago, IL.	10/13/27
Kopell, Bernie	New York, NY	6/21/33
Korman, Harvey	Chicago, IL.	2/15/27
Kotto, Yaphet	New York, NY	11/15/37
Krakowski, Jane	Parsippany, NJ	10/11/68
Krause, Peter	Alexandria, MN	8/12/65
Kristofferson, Kris	Brownsville, TX	6/22/36
Kudrow, Lisa	Encino, CA.	7/30/63
Kurtz, Swoosie	Omaha, NE	9/6/44
Kutcher, Ashton	Cedar Rapids, IA	2/7/78
Kwan, Nancy	Hong Kong.	5/19/39
LaBelle, Patti	Philadelphia, PA.	5/24/44
LaBeouf, Shia	Los Angeles, CA	6/11/86
Ladd, Cheryl	Huron, SD	7/12/51
Ladd, Diane	Meridian, MS.	11/29/32
Lagasse, Emeril	Fall River, MA.	10/15/59
Lahti, Christine	Royal Oak, MI	4/4/50
Laine, Cleo	Southall, England.	10/28/27
Laine, Frankie	Chicago, IL.	3/30/13
Lake, Ricki	Hastings-on-Hudson, NY.	9/21/68
Lamas, Lorenzo	Santa Monica, CA	1/20/58
Lambert, Christopher	Great Neck, NY	3/29/57
Landau, Martin	Brooklyn, NY	6/20/28
Landis, John	Chicago, IL.	8/3/50
Lane, Diane	New York, NY	1/22/65
Lane, Nathan	Jersey City, NJ.	2/3/56
lang, k.d.	Consort, Alberta	11/2/61
Lang, Stephen	Queens, New York, NY	7/11/52
Lange, Hope	Redding Ridge, CT	11/28/31
Lange, Jessica	Cloquet, MN.	4/20/49
Langella, Frank	Bayonne, NJ	1/1/40
Langford, Frances	Lakeland, FL.	4/4/14
Lansbury, Angela	London, England	10/16/25
LaPaglia, Anthony	Adelaide, Australia	1/31/59
Laredo, Ruth	Detroit, MI.	11/20/37
Larroquette, John	New Orleans, LA	11/25/47
LaSalle, Eriq	Hartford, CT	6/23/62
Lauper, Cyndi	Brooklyn, NY.	6/20/53
Laurie, Piper	Detroit, MI.	1/22/32
Lavigne, Avril	Napanee, Ontario	9/27/84
Lavin, Linda	Portland, ME.	10/15/37
Law, Jude	London, England	12/29/72
Lawless, Lucy	Mount Albert, New Zealand .	3/29/68
Lawrence, Carol	Melrose Park, IL.	9/5/34
Lawrence, Joey	Montgomery, PA.	4/20/76
Lawrence, Martin	Frankfurt, Germany	4/16/65
Lawrence, Steve	Brooklyn, NY.	7/8/35
Lawrence, Vicki	Inglewood, CA	3/26/49
Leach, Robin	London, England	8/29/41
Leachman, Cloris	Des Moines, IA.	4/30/26
Lear, Norman	New Haven, CT	7/27/22
Learned, Michael	Washington, DC	4/9/39
Leary, Denis	Worcester, MA	8/18/57
LeBlanc, Matt	Newton, MA	7/25/67
LeBon, Simon	Bushey, England	10/27/58
Ledger, Heath	Perth, Australia.	4/4/79
Lee, Ang	Pingtung, Taiwan	10/23/54
Lee, Brenda	Lithonia, GA	12/11/44
Lee, Christopher	London, England	5/27/22
Lee, Michele	Los Angeles, CA.	6/24/42
Lee, Spike	Atlanta, GA.	3/20/57
Leeves, Jane	London, England	4/18/61
Legrand, Michel	Paris, France	2/24/32
Leguizamo, John	Bogota, Colombia	7/22/64
Leibman, Ron	New York, NY.	10/11/37
Leigh, Janet	Merced, CA.	7/6/27
Leigh, Jennifer Jason	Hollywood, CA	2/5/62
Leighton, Laura	Iowa City, IA .	7/24/68
Lennox, Annie	Aberdeen, Scotland	12/25/54
Leno, Jay	New Rochelle, NY	4/28/50
Leonard, Robert Sean	Westwood, NJ	2/28/69
Leoni, Tea	New York, NY	2/25/66
Leslie, Joan	Detroit, MI.	1/26/25
Leto, Jared	Bossier City, LA	12/26/71
Letterman, David	Indianapolis, IN.	4/12/47
Levine, James	Cincinnati, OH	6/23/43
Levinson, Barry	Baltimore, MD.	4/6/42
Levy, Eugene	Hamilton, Ontario	12/17/46
Lewis, Al	New York, NY.	4/30/10
Lewis, Huey	New York, NY.	7/5/50
Lewis, Jerry	Newark. NJ.	3/16/26
Lewis, Jerry Lee	Ferriday, LA	9/29/35
Lewis, John	La Grange, IL	5/30/20
Lewis, Juliette	San Fernando Valley, CA .	6/21/73
Lewis, Richard	Brooklyn, NY.	6/29/47
Li, Jet	Beijing, China	4/26/63
Light, Judith	Trenton, NJ.	2/9/49
Lightfoot, Gordon	Orillia, Ontario.	11/17/38
Lil' Kim	Brooklyn, NY.	7/11/75
Linden, Hal	Bronx, New York, NY	3/20/31
Ling, Lisa	Sacramento, CA	8/30/73
Linkletter, Art	Moose Jaw, Saskatchewan .	7/17/12
Linn-Baker, Mark	St. Louis, MO	6/17/54
Linney, Laura	New York, NY	2/5/64
Liotta, Ray	Newark, NJ.	12/18/55
Lithgow, John.	Rochester, NY	10/19/45
Little, Rich	Ottawa, Ontario	11/26/38
Little Richard	Macon, GA	12/5/32
Littrell, Brian	Lexington, KY.	2/20/75
Liu, Lucy	Queens, NY	12/2/68
L. L. Cool J.	St. Albans, Queens, NY	1/14/68
Lloyd, Christopher	Stamford, CT	10/22/38
Lloyd, Emily	North London, England	9/29/70
Lloyd Webber, Andrew	London, England	3/22/48
Locke, Sondra	Shelbyville, TN	5/28/47
Lockhart, June	New York, NY.	6/25/25
Locklear, Heather	Westwood, CA	9/25/61
Loggia, Robert	Staten Island, NY	1/3/30
Loggins, Kenny	Everett, WA	1/7/48
Lohan, Lindsay	New York, NY	7/2/86
Lollobrigida, Gina	Subiaco, Italy	7/4/27
Lom, Herbert	Prague, Czechoslovakia.	1/9/17
Lonergan, Kenneth	New York, NY.	1963
Long, Nia	Brooklyn, NY.	10/30/70
Long, Shelley	Ft. Wayne, IN	8/23/49
Lopez, Jennifer	Bronx, NY	7/24/70
Loren, Sophia	Rome, Italy	9/20/34
Loring, Gloria	New York, NY.	12/10/46
Loudon, Dorothy	Boston, MA.	9/17/33
Louis-Dreyfus, Julia	New York, NY.	1/13/61
Love, Courtney	San Francisco, CA .	7/9/64
Love, Mike	Baldwin Hills, CA .	3/15/41

Name	Birthplace	Birthdate
Lovett, Lyle	Klein, TX	11/1/57
Lovitz, Jon	Tarzana, CA	7/21/57
Loveless, Patty	Pikeville, KY	1/4/57
Lowe, Rob	Charlottesville, VA	3/17/64
Lowell, Carey	Huntington, NY	2/11/61
Lucas, George	Modesto, CA	5/14/44
Lucci, Susan	Scarsdale, NY	12/23/48
Luckinbill, Laurence	Ft. Smith, AR	11/21/34
Ludwig, Christa	Berlin, Germany	3/16/24
Luhrmann, Baz	Sydney, Australia	9/17/62
Lumet, Sidney	Philadelphia, PA	6/25/24
LuPone, Patti	Northport, NY	4/21/49
Lynch, David	Missoula, MT	1/20/46
Lynley, Carol	New York, NY	2/13/42
Lynn, Loretta	Butcher Hollow, KY	4/14/35
Lynne, Shelby	Quantico, VA	10/22/68
Lyonne, Natasha	Great Neck, NY	4/4/79
Ma, Yo-Yo	Paris, France	10/7/55
Maazel, Lorin	Neuilly-sur-Seine, France	3/6/30
Mac, Bernie	Chicago, IL	10/5/58
MacArthur, James	Los Angeles, CA	12/8/37
Macchio, Ralph	Huntington, NY	11/4/62
MacCorkindale, Simon	Ely, England	2/12/52
MacDowell, Andie	Gaffney, SC	4/21/58
MacGraw, Ali	Pound Ridge, NY	4/1/38
MacLachlan, Kyle	Yakima, WA	2/22/59
MacLaine, Shirley	Richmond, VA	4/24/34
MacLeod, Gavin	Mt. Kisco, NY	2/28/31
MacNee, Patrick	London, England	2/6/22
MacNeil, Cornell	Minneapolis, MN	9/24/22
MacNicol, Peter	Dallas, TX	4/10/54
MacPherson, Elle	Sydney, Australia	3/29/64
Macy, Bill	Revere, MA	5/18/22
Macy, William H.	Miami, FL	3/13/50
Madden, John	Austin, MN	4/10/36
Madigan, Amy	Chicago, IL	9/11/50
Madonna (Ciccone)	Bay City, MI	8/16/58
Maguire, Tobey	Santa Monica, CA	6/27/75
Maher, Bill	New York, NY	1/20/56
Mahoney, John	Manchester, England	6/20/40
Majors, Lee	Wyandotte, MI	4/23/39
Malden, Karl	Gary, IN	3/22/12
Malick, Terrence	Ottawa, IL	11/30/43
Malick, Wendie	Buffalo, NY	12/13/50
Malkovich, John	Christopher, IL	12/9/53
Malone, Dorothy	Chicago, IL	1/30/25
Mamet, David	Chicago, IL	11/30/47
Manchester, Melissa	Bronx, NY	2/15/51
Mandel, Howie	Toronto, Ontario	11/29/55
Mandrell, Barbara	Houston, TX	12/25/48
Mangione, Chuck	Rochester, NY	11/29/40
Manheim, Camryn	Caldwell, NJ	3/8/61
Manilow, Barry	Brooklyn, NY	6/17/46
Manoff, Dinah	New York, NY	1/25/58
Manson, Marilyn	Canton, OH	1/5/69
Mantegna, Joe	Chicago, IL	11/13/47
Marceau, Marcel	Strasbourg, France	3/22/23
Margulies, Julianna	Spring Valley, NY	6/8/66
Marin, Cheech	Los Angeles, CA	7/13/46
Marinaro, Ed	New York, NY	3/31/50
Markova, Alicia	London, England	12/1/10
Marriner, Neville	Lincoln, England	4/15/24
Marsalis, Branford	New Orleans, LA	8/26/60
Marsalis, Wynton	New Orleans, LA	10/18/61
Marsh, Jean	London, England	7/1/34
Marshall, Garry	Bronx, New York, NY	11/13/34
Marshall, Penny	Bronx, New York, NY	10/15/42
Marshall, Peter	Huntington, WV	3/30/27
Martin, Dick	Detroit, MI	1/30/22
Martin, Jesse L.	Rocky Mount, VA	1/18/69
Martin, Kellie	Riverside, CA	10/16/75
Martin, Ricky	San Juan, Puerto Rico	12/24/71
Martin, Steve	Waco, TX	8/14/45
Martin, Tony	Oakland, CA	12/25/13
Martins, Peter	Copenhagen, Denmark	10/27/46
Mason, Jackie	Sheboygan, WI	6/9/34
Mason, Marsha	St. Louis, MO	4/3/42
Masterson, Mary Stuart	New York, NY	6/28/66
Mastrantonio, Mary Elizabeth	Lombard, IL	11/17/58
Masur, Kurt	Brieg, Germany	7/18/27
Masur, Richard	New York, NY	11/20/48
Mathers, Jerry	Sioux City, IA	6/2/48
Matheson, Tim	Glendale, CA	12/31/47
Mathis, Johnny	San Francisco, CA	9/30/35
Matlin, Marlee	Morton Grove, IL	8/24/65
Matthews, Dave	Johannesburg, South Africa	1/9/67
May, Elaine	Philadelphia, PA	4/21/32
Mayo, Virginia	St. Louis, MO	11/30/20
Mazursky, Paul	Brooklyn, NY	4/25/30

Name	Birthplace	Birthdate
McArdle, Andrea	Abington, PA	11/5/63
McBride, Patricia	Teaneck, NJ	8/23/42
McCallum, David	Glasgow, Scotland	9/19/33
McCambridge, Mercedes	Joliet, IL	3/17/18
McCarthy, Andrew	Westfield, NJ	11/29/62
McCarthy, Jenny	Chicago, IL	11/1/72
McCarthy, Kevin	Seattle, WA	2/15/14
McCartney, Paul	Liverpool, England	6/18/42
McCarver, Tim	Memphis, TN	10/16/41
McClanahan, Rue	Healdton, OK	2/21/34
McConaughey, Matthew	Uvalde, Texas	11/4/69
McCoo, Marilyn	Jersey City, NJ	9/30/43
McCormack, Eric	Toronto, Canada	4/18/63
McCormack, Mary	Plainsfield, NJ	2/8/69
McCrane, Paul	Philadelphia, PA	1/19/61
McDaniel, James	Washington, DC	3/25/58
McDermott, Dylan	Waterbury, CT	10/26/61
McDiarmid, Ian	Carnoustie, Tayside, Scotland	4/17/47
McDonald, Audra	Berlin, Germany	7/3/70
McDonnell, Mary	Wilkes-Barre, PA	4/28/52
McDormand, Frances	Illinois	6/23/57
McDowell, Malcolm	Leeds, England	6/13/43
McEntire, Reba	McAlester, OK	3/28/55
McFerrin, Bobby	New York, NY	3/11/50
McGavin, Darren	Spokane, WA	5/7/22
McGillis, Kelly	Newport Beach, CA	7/9/57
McGoohan, Patrick	Astoria, Queens, NY	3/19/28
McGovern, Elizabeth	Evanston, IL	7/18/61
McGovern, Maureen	Youngstown, OH	7/27/49
McGraw, Tim	Delhi, LA	5/1/67
McGregor, Ewan	Crieff, Scotland	3/31/71
McGuire, Al	New York, NY	9/7/31
McKean, Michael	New York, NY	10/17/47
McKechnie, Donna	Pontiac, MI	11/16/42
McKellen, Ian	Burnley, England	5/25/39
McLachlan, Sarah	Halifax, Nova Scotia	1/28/68
McLean, A.J.	West Palm Beach, FL	1/9/78
McMahon, Ed	Detroit, MI	3/6/23
McNichol, Kristy	Los Angeles, CA	9/11/62
McPartland, Marian	Stough, England	3/20/20
McRaney, Gerald	Collins, MS	8/19/47
Meadows, Jayne	Wu Chang, China	9/27/20
Meara, Anne	Brooklyn, NY	9/20/29
Meat Loaf	Dallas, TX	9/27/51
Mehta, Zubin	Bombay, India	4/29/36
Mellencamp, John	Seymour, IN	10/7/51
Meloni, Christopher	Washington, DC	4/2/61
Mendes, Sam	Redding, England	8/1/65
Mendes, Sergio	Niterol, Brazil	2/11/41
Mercer, Marian	Akron, OH	11/26/35
Merchant, Natalie	Jamestown, NY	10/26/63
Merrill, Dina	New York, NY	12/9/25
Merrill, Robert	Brooklyn, NY	6/4/19
Messing, Debra	Brooklyn, NY	8/15/68
Metcalf, Laurie	Carbondale, IL	6/16/55
Michael, George	London, England	6/25/63
Michaels, Al	Brooklyn, NY	11/12/44
Michaels, Lorne	Toronto, Canada	11/17/44
Midler, Bette	Paterson, NJ	12/1/45
Midori	Osaka, Japan	10/25/71
Milano, Alyssa	Brooklyn, NY	12/19/72
Miles, Sarah	Ingatestone, England	12/31/41
Miles, Vera	near Boise City, OK	8/23/29
Miller, Ann	Houston, TX	4/12/23
Miller, Dennis	Pittsburgh, PA	11/3/53
Miller, Mitch	Rochester, NY	7/4/11
Miller, Penelope Ann	Santa Monica, CA	1/13/64
Mills, Donna	Chicago, IL	12/11/43
Mills, Hayley	London, England	4/18/46
Mills, John	Suffolk, England	2/22/08
Milner, Martin	Detroit, MI	12/28/27
Milnes, Sherrill	Downers Grove, IL	1/10/35
Milsap, Ronnie	Robinsville, NC	1/16/44
Minghella, Anthony	Isle of Wight, England	1/6/54
Ming-Na	Macao	11/20/63
Minnelli, Liza	Los Angeles, CA	3/12/46
Minogue, Kylie	Melbourne, Australia	5/28/68
Mirren, Helen	London, England	7/26/46
Mitchell, Brian	Seattle, WA	10/31/58
Mitchell, Joni	Fort McLeod, Alberta	11/7/43
Moby	Harlem, New York, NY	9/11/65
Modine, Matthew	Loma Linda, CA	3/22/59
Moffat, Donald	Plymouth, England	12/26/30
Moffo, Anna	Wayne, PA	6/27/34
Molinaro, Al	Kenosha, WI	6/24/19
Moll, Richard	Pasadena, CA	1/13/43
Monica (Arnold)	College Park, GA	10/24/80
Montalban, Ricardo	Mexico City, Mexico	11/25/20
Moody, Ron	London, England	1/8/24

Name	Birthplace	Birthdate
Moore, Demi	Roswell, NM.	11/11/62
Moore, Julianne	Fort Bragg, NC.	12/3/60
Moore, Mandy	Nashua, NH.	4/10/84
Moore, Mary Tyler	Brooklyn, NY	12/29/36
Moore, Melba	New York, NY	10/29/45
Moore, Michael	Flint, MI	4/23/54
Moore, Roger	London, England	10/14/27
Moore, Terry	Los Angeles, CA	1/7/29
Moranis, Rick	Toronto, Ontario	4/18/54
Moreau, Jeanne	Paris, France	1/23/28
Moreno, Rita	Humacao, PR	12/11/31
Morgan, Harry	Detroit, MI	4/10/15
Moriarty, Michael	Detroit, MI	4/5/41
Morissette, Alanis	Ottawa, Ontario	6/1/74
Morita, Pat.	Isleton, CA.	6/28/32
Morris, Garrett.	New Orleans, LA	2/1/37
Morris, Howard	New York, NY	9/4/19
Morrison, Van	Belfast, N. Ireland	8/31/45
Morrissey	Manchester, England.	5/22/59
Morrow, Rob	New Rochelle, NY	9/21/62
Morse, David.	Beverly, MA	10/11/53
Morse, Robert	Newton, MA	5/18/31
Mortensen, Viggo	New York, NY	10/20/58
Morton, Joe	Brooklyn, NY	10/18/47
Morton, Samantha	Nottingham, Enlgand	5/13/77
Moses, William	Los Angeles, CA	11/17/59
Moss, Carrie-Anne	Vancouver, British Columbia	8/21/67
Moss, Kate	Croydon, Surrey, England	1/16/74
Mueller-Stahl, Armin	Tilsit, E. Prussia.	12/17/30
Muldaur, Diana	Brooklyn, NY	8/19/38
Mulgrew, Kate	Dubuque, IA.	4/29/55
Mull, Martin	Chicago, IL.	8/18/43
Mullally, Megan	Los Angeles, CA	11/12/58
Mulroney, Dermot	Alexandria, VA.	10/31/63
Muniz, Frankie	Ridgewood, NJ	12/5/85
Munsel, Patrice	Spokane, WA.	5/14/25
Murphy, Ben	Jonesboro, AR.	3/6/42
Murphy, Brittany	Atlanta, GA	11/10/77
Murphy, Eddie.	Brooklyn, NY	4/3/61
Murphy, Michael	Los Angeles, CA.	5/5/38
Murray, Anne	Springhill, Nova Scotia.	6/20/45
Murray, Bill	Wilmette, IL	9/21/50
Murray, Don	Hollywood, CA.	7/31/29
Musburger, Brent	Portland, OR	5/26/39
Muti, Riccardo	Naples, Italy.	7/28/41
Myers, Mike.	Scarborough, Ontario	5/25/63
Nabors, Jim.	Sylacauga, AL	6/12/30
Nagra, Parminder	Leicester, England.	10/5/75
Nash, Graham.	Blackpool, England	2/2/42
Naughton, James	Middletown, CT	12/6/45
Neal, Patricia	Packard, KY.	1/20/26
Nealon, Kevin	Bridgeport, CT	11/18/53
Neeson, Liam	Ballymena, N. Ireland	6/7/52
Neill, Sam	Ulster, N. Ireland	9/14/47
Nelligan, Kate	London, Ontario	3/16/51
Nelson, Craig T.	Spokane, WA.	4/4/46
Nelson, Ed	New Orleans, LA	12/21/28
Nelson, Judd	Portland, ME	11/28/59
Nelson, Tracy	Santa Monica, CA	10/25/63
Nelson, Willie	Abbott, TX	4/30/33
Nero, Peter	Brooklyn, NY	5/22/34
Nesmith, Mike	Houston, TX.	12/30/42
Nettleton, Lois.	Oak Park, IL	8/16/29
Neuwirth, Bebe	Newark, NJ	12/31/58
Neville, Aaron	New Orleans, LA	1/24/41
Newhart, Bob	Oak Park, IL.	9/5/29
Newman, Paul.	Cleveland, OH	1/26/25
Newman, Randy	New Orleans, LA	11/28/43
Newton, Wayne.	Norfolk, VA.	4/3/42
Newton-John, Olivia	Cambridge, England	9/26/48
Nicholas, Denise	Detroit, MI	7/12/44
Nicholas, Fayard	Philadelphia, PA	10/20/14
Nichols, Mike.	Berlin, Germany.	11/6/31
Nicholson, Jack.	Neptune, NJ.	4/22/37
Nicks, Stevie	Phoenix, AZ.	5/26/48
Nielsen, Connie	Copenhagen, Denmark	7/3/65
Nielsen, Leslie.	Regina, Sask.	2/11/26
Nilsson, Birgit	Vastra Karup, Sweden.	5/17/18
Nimoy, Leonard.	Boston, MA.	3/26/31
Nixon, Cynthia.	New York, NY	4/9/66
Nolte, Nick.	Omaha, NE	2/8/41
Noone, Peter.	Manchester, England.	11/5/47
Norman, Jessye	Augusta, GA	9/15/45
Norris, Chuck	Ryan, OK.	3/10/40
North, Sheree	Hollywood, CA.	1/17/33
Northam, Jeremy	Cambridge, Enlgand	12/1/61
Norton, Edward.	Columbia, MD	8/18/69
Noth, Christopher	Madison, WI.	11/13/54
Novak, Kim	Chicago, IL.	2/13/33
Nuyen, France	Marseilles, France	7/31/39
Oates, John	New York, NY.	4/7/49
O'Brian, Hugh	Rochester, NY	4/19/25
O'Brien, Conan	Brookline, MA.	4/18/63
O'Brien, Margaret	Los Angeles, CA.	1/15/37
Ocean, Billy	Fyzabad, Trinidad.	1/21/50
O'Connor, Frances	Oxford, England	6/12/69
O'Connor, Sinead	Glenageary, Ireland	12/8/66
Odetta	Birmingham, AL	12/31/30
O'Donnell, Chris.	Winnetka, IL	6/26/70
O'Donnell, Rosie	Commack, NY	3/21/62
O'Hara, Catherine	Toronto, Canada	3/4/54
O'Hara, Maureen	Dublin, Ireland	8/17/20
O'Herlihy, Dan	Wexford, Ireland.	5/1/19
Oldman, Gary	South London, England	3/21/58
Olin, Ken	Chicago, IL.	7/30/54
Olin, Lena	Stockholm, Sweden.	3/22/55
Olmos, Edward James.	E. Los Angeles, CA	2/24/47
Olsen, Ashley.	Sherman Oaks, CA.	6/13/86
Olsen, Mary-Kate.	Sherman Oaks, CA.	6/13/86
Olsen, Merlin	Logan, UT.	9/15/40
O'Neal, Ryan	Los Angeles, CA.	4/20/41
O'Neal, Tatum	Los Angeles, CA.	11/5/63
O'Neill, Ed	Youngstown, OH	4/12/46
Ontkean, Michael.	Vancouver, B.C.	1/24/46
Orbach, Jerry	Bronx, New York, NY	10/20/35
Ordoño, Tony	New York, NY.	4/3/44
Ormond, Julia	Epsom, England.	1/4/65
Osbourne, Jack	London, England	11/8/85
Osbourne, Kelly	London, England	10/27/84
Osbourne, Ozzy	Birmingham, England.	12/3/48
Osbourne, Sharon	London, England	10/10/52
O'Shea, Milo	Dublin, Ireland	6/2/26
Oslin, K.T.	Crossett, AR.	5/15/42
Osment, Haley Joel	Los Angeles, CA.	4/10/88
Osmond, Donny	Ogden, UT	12/9/57
Osmond, Marie	Ogden, UT	10/13/59
O'Toole, Annette	Houston, TX.	4/1/53
O'Toole, Peter	Connemara, Ireland	8/2/32
Owens, Buck	Sherman, TX	8/12/29
Oz, Frank.	Herford, England	5/25/44
Ozawa, Seiji	Shenyang, China	9/1/35
Paar, Jack	Canton, OH	5/1/18
Pacino, Al.	East Harlem, NY.	4/25/40
Packer, Billy	Wellsville, NY	2/25/40
Page, Bettie	Nashville, TN	4/22/23
Page, Jimmy	Heston, England.	1/9/44
Page, Patti	Claremore, OK.	11/8/27
Paget, Debra	Denver, CO.	8/19/33
Paige, Janis	Tacoma, WA.	9/16/22
Palance, Jack	Lattimer, PA	2/18/20
Palin, Michael	Sheffield, England	5/5/43
Palmer, Betsy	East Chicago, IN.	11/1/29
Palmer, Geoffrey	London, England	6/4/27
Palminteri, Chazz.	Bronx, NY.	5/15/51
Paltrow, Gwyneth.	Los Angeles, CA.	9/27/72
Pantoliano, Joe	Hoboken, NJ.	9/12/51
Papas, Irene	Chiliomodion, Greece.	3/9/26
Paquin, Anna	Wellington, New Zealand	7/24/82
Parker, Alan.	London, England	2/14/44
Parker, Eleanor	Cedarville, OH	6/26/22
Parker, Fess	Ft. Worth, TX	8/16/25
Parker, Jameson	Baltimore, MD.	11/18/47
Parker, Jean	Butte, MT	8/11/12
Parker, Mary-Louise	Fort Jackson, SC	8/2/64
Parker, Sarah Jessica	Nelsonville, OH.	3/25/65
Parsons, Estelle.	Lynn, MA	11/20/27
Parton, Dolly	Sevierville, TN	1/19/46
Patinkin, Mandy	Chicago, IL	11/30/52
Patric, Jason	Queens, NY	6/17/66
Patton, Will.	Charleston, SC.	6/14/54
Paul, Adrian	London, England	5/29/59
Paulson, Sarah	Tampa, FL	12/17/75
Pavarotti, Luciano	Modena, Italy.	10/12/35
Paxton, Bill.	Fort Worth, TX.	5/17/55
Pearce, Guy.	Ely, England.	10/5/67
Peet, Amanda	New York, NY.	1/11/72
Pendergrass, Teddy	Philadelphia, PA.	3/26/50
Penn, Arthur.	Philadelphia, PA.	9/27/22
Penn, Sean	Burbank, CA.	8/17/60
Penny, Joe.	London, England	9/14/56
Perez, Rosie	Brooklyn, NY.	9/6/64
Perkins, Elizabeth	Queens, NY	11/18/60
Perlman, Itzhak	Tel Aviv, Israel	8/31/45
Perlman, Rhea.	Brooklyn, NY.	3/31/48
Perlman, Ron.	New York, NY.	4/13/50
Perrine, Valerie	Galveston, TX.	9/3/43
Perry, Luke	Fredericktown, OH	10/11/66
Perry, Mathew	Williamstown, MA	8/19/69
Persoff, Nehemiah	Jerusalem, Israel	8/14/20
Pesci, Joe	Newark, NJ.	2/9/43

Name	Birthplace	Birthdate
Peters, Bernadette	Queens, NY	2/28/48
Peters, Brock	New York, NY	7/2/27
Peters, Roberta	Bronx, NY	5/4/30
Petersen, Wolfgang	Emden, Germany	3/14/41
Peterson, Oscar	Montreal, Quebec	8/15/25
Petty, Tom	Gainesville, FL	10/20/50
Pfeiffer, Michelle	Santa Ana, CA	4/29/58
Philbin, Regis	New York, NY	8/25/31
Phillippe, Ryan	New Castle, DE	9/10/74
Phillips, Lou Diamond	Subic Bay, Philippines	2/17/62
Phillips, Mackenzie	Alexandria, VA	11/10/59
Phillips, Michelle	Long Beach, CA	6/4/44
Phoenix, Joaquin	San Juan, Puerto Rico	10/28/74
Pickett, Wilson	Prattville, AL	3/18/41
Pierce, David Hyde	Albany, NY	4/3/59
Pinchot, Bronson	New York, NY	5/20/59
Pink (Alecia Moore)	Doylestown, PA	9/8/79
Pinkett Smith, Jada	Baltimore, MD	9/18/71
Pirner, David	Green Bay, WI	4/16/64
Piscopo, Joe	Passaic, NJ	6/17/51
Pitt, Brad	Shawnee, OK	12/18/63
Plant, Robert	W. Bromwich, England	8/20/48
Pleshette, Suzanne	New York, NY	1/31/37
Plowright, Joan	Brigg, England	10/28/29
Plummer, Amanda	New York, NY	3/23/57
Plummer, Christopher	Toronto, Ontario	12/13/27
Poitier, Sidney	Miami, FL	2/20/27
Polanski, Roman	Paris, France	8/18/33
Pollack, Sydney	Lafayette, IN	7/1/34
Ponti, Carlo	Milan, Italy	12/11/13
Pop, Iggy	Muskegon, MI	4/21/47
Portman, Natalie	Jerusalem, Israel	6/9/81
Posey, Parker	Baltimore, MD	11/8/68
Post, Markie	Palo Alto, CA	11/4/50
Poston, Tom	Columbus, OH	10/17/21
Potts, Annie	Nashville, TN	10/28/52
Povich, Maury	Bethesda, MD	1/17/39
Powell, Jane	Portland, OR	4/1/29
Powers, Stefanie	Hollywood, CA	11/2/42
Prentiss, Paula	San Antonio, TX	3/4/39
Presley, Priscilla	Brooklyn, NY	5/24/45
Preston, Billy	Houston, TX	9/9/46
Previn, Andre	Berlin, Germany	4/6/29
Price, Leontyne	Laurel, MS	2/10/27
Price, Ray	Perryville, TX	1/12/26
Pride, Charley	Sledge, MS	3/18/38
Priestley, Jason	Vancouver, Brit. Columbia	8/28/69
Prince (The Artist)	Minneapolis, MN	6/7/58
Prince, Faith	Augusta, GA	8/5/57
Principal, Victoria	Fukuoka, Japan	1/3/50
Prinze, Freddie, Jr.	Albuquerque, NM	3/8/76
Probst, Jeff	Wichita, KS	11/1/61
Prosky, Robert	Philadelphia, PA	12/13/30
Provine, Dorothy	Deadwood, SD	1/20/37
Pryce, Jonathan	Holywell, N. Wales	6/1/47
Pryor, Richard	Peoria, IL	12/1/40
Puck, Wolfgang	St. Veit, Austria	1/8/49
Pulliam, Keshia Knight	Newark, NJ	4/9/79
Pullman, Bill	Hornell, NY	12/17/53
Purcell, Sarah	Richmond, IN	10/8/48
Quaid, Dennis	Houston, TX	4/9/54
Quaid, Randy	Houston, TX	10/1/50
Queen Latifah	Newark, NJ	3/18/70
Quinn, Aidan	Chicago, IL	3/8/59
Quinn, Colin	Brooklyn, NY	8/15/59
Quinn, Martha	Albany, NY	5/11/59
Rachins, Alan	Cambridge, MA	10/3/42
Radcliffe, Daniel	London, England	7/23/89
Rae, Charlotte	Milwaukee, WI	4/22/26
Raffi	Cairo, Egypt	7/8/48
Rainer, Luise	Vienna, Austria	1/12/10
Raitt, Bonnie	Burbank, CA	11/8/49
Ramey, Samuel	Colby, KS	3/28/42
Ramone, Johnny	Long Island, NY	10/8/51
Ramone, Tommy	Budapest, Hungary	1/29/52
Randall, Tony	Tulsa, OK	2/26/20
Randolph, John	Bronx, NY	6/1/15
Randolph, Joyce	Detroit, MI	10/21/25
Raphael, Sally Jessy	Easton, PA	2/25/43
Rashad, Phylicia	Houston, TX	6/19/48
Ratzenberger, John	Bridgeport, CT	4/6/47
Rawls, Lou	Chicago, IL	12/1/35
Reagan, Ronald	Tampico, IL	2/6/11
Reddy, Helen	Melbourne, Australia	10/25/41
Redford, Robert	Santa Monica, CA	8/18/37
Redgrave, Lynn	London, England	3/8/43
Redgrave, Vanessa	London, England	1/30/37
Reed, Jerry	Atlanta, GA	3/20/37
Reed, Lou	Brooklyn, NY	3/2/42

Name	Birthplace	Birthdate
Reed, Rex	Ft. Worth, TX	10/2/38
Reese, Della	Detroit, MI	7/6/31
Reeve, Christopher	New York, NY	9/25/52
Reeves, Keanu	Beirut, Lebanon	9/2/64
Regalbuto, Joe	Brooklyn, NY	8/24/49
Reid, Tara	Wyckoff, NJ	11/8/75
Reid, Tim	Norfolk, VA	12/19/44
Reilly, Charles Nelson	New York, NY	1/13/31
Reilly, John C.	Chicago, IL	5/24/65
Reiner, Carl	Bronx, NY	3/20/22
Reiner, Rob	Bronx, NY	3/6/47
Reinhold, Judge	Wilmington, DE	5/21/57
Reinking, Ann	Seattle, WA	11/10/49
Reiser, Paul	New York, NY	3/30/57
Reitman, Ivan	Komarno, Czechoslovakia	10/26/46
Remini, Leah	Brooklyn, NY	6/15/70
Resnik, Regina	New York, NY	8/30/22
Reynolds, Burt	Waycross, GA	2/11/36
Reynolds, Debbie	El Paso, TX	4/1/32
Reznor, Trent	Mercer, PA	5/17/65
Rhames, Ving	Harlem, New York, NY	5/12/59
Rhymes, Busta	Brooklyn, NY	5/20/72
Ribisi, Giovanni	Los Angeles, CA	12/17/74
Ricci, Christina	Santa Monica, CA	2/12/80
Richards, Denise	Downers Grove, IL	2/17/71
Richards, Keith	Dartford, Kent, England	12/18/43
Richards, Michael	Culver City, CA	7/24/49
Richardson, Ian	Edinburgh, Scotland	4/7/34
Richardson, Kevin	Lexington, KY	10/3/71
Richardson, Miranda	Lancashire, England	3/3/58
Richardson, Natasha	London, England	5/11/63
Richardson, Patricia	Bethesda, MD	2/23/51
Richie, Lionel	Tuskegee, AL	6/20/49
Rickles, Don	Queens, NY	5/8/26
Rickman, Alan	Hammersmith, England	2/21/46
Riegert, Peter	New York, NY	4/11/47
Rigg, Diana	Doncaster, England	7/20/38
Rimes, LeAnn	Flowood, MS	8/28/82
Ringwald, Molly	Roseville, CA	2/18/68
Ripa, Kelly	Stratford, NJ	10/2/70
Rivera, Chita	Washington, DC	1/23/33
Rivera, Geraldo	New York, NY	7/4/43
Rivers, Joan	Brooklyn, NY	6/8/33
Roach, Max	New Land, NC	1/10/24
Robbins, Tim	W. Covina, CA	10/16/58
Roberts, Doris	St. Louis, MO	11/4/29
Roberts, Eric	Biloxi, MS	4/18/56
Roberts, Julia	Smyrna, GA	10/28/67
Roberts, Pernell	Waycross, GA	5/18/28
Roberts, Tony	New York, NY	10/22/39
Robertson, Cliff	La Jolla, CA	9/9/25
Robertson, Dale	Harrah, OK	7/14/23
Robinson, Smokey	Detroit, MI	2/19/40
Roche, Eugene	Boston, MA	9/22/28
Rochon, Lela	Torrance, CA	4/17/64
Rock, Chris	South Carolina	2/7/66
Rock, The (Dwayne Johnson)	Hayward, CA	5/2/72
Rodgers, Jimmy	Camas, WA	9/18/33
Rodriquez, Johnny	Sabinal, TX	12/10/51
Rogers, Kenny	Houston, TX	8/21/38
Rogers, Mimi	Coral Gables, FL	1/27/56
Rogers, Wayne	Birmingham, AL	4/7/33
Rohm, Elisabeth	Dusseldorf, Germany	4/28/73
Rollins, Henry	Washington, DC	2/13/61
Rollins, Sonny	Harlem, NY	9/7/30
Romano, Ray	Queens, NY	12/21/57
Romijn-Stamos, Rebecca	Berkeley, CA	11/6/72
Ronstadt, Linda	Tucson, AZ	7/15/46
Rooney, Mickey	Brooklyn, NY	9/23/20
Rose, Axl	Lafayette, IN	2/6/62
Rose Marie	New York, NY	8/15/25
Roseanne	Salt Lake City, UT	11/3/52
Ross, Diana	Detroit, MI	3/26/44
Ross, Katharine	Hollywood, CA	1/29/40
Rossdale, Gavin	London, England	10/30/67
Ross, Marion	Albert Lea, MN	10/25/28
Rossellini, Isabella	Rome, Italy	6/18/52
Rostropovich, Mstislav	Baku, Azerbaijan	3/27/27
Roth, David Lee	Bloomington, IN	10/10/55
Roth, Tim	London, England	5/14/61
Rotten, Johnny	London, England	1/31/56
Rourke, Mickey	Schenectady, NY	9/16/56
Routledge, Patricia	Birkenhead, England	2/17/29
Rowlands, Gena	Cambria, WI	6/19/36
Rubinstein, John	Beverly Hills, CA	12/8/46
Rudner, Rita	Miami, FL	9/17/56
Ruehl, Mercedes	Queens, NY	2/28/48
Ruffalo, Mark	Kenosha, WI	11/22/67
Rush, Barbara	Denver, CO	1/4/27
Rush, Geoffrey	Toowoomba, Australia	7/6/51

Name	Birthplace	Birthdate
Russell, Jane	Bemidji, MN	6/21/21
Russell, Ken	Southampton, England	7/3/27
Russell, Keri	Fountain Valley, CA	3/23/76
Russell, Kurt	Springfield, MA	3/17/51
Russel, Leon	Lawton, OK	4/2/41
Russell, Mark	Buffalo, NY	8/23/32
Russell, Nipsey	Atlanta, GA	10/13/24
Russell, Theresa	San Diego, CA	3/20/57
Russo, Rene	Burbank, CA	2/17/54
Rutherford, Ann	Toronto, Ontario	11/2/17
Ruttan, Susan	Oregon City, OR	9/16/50
Ryan, Meg	Fairfield, CT	11/19/61
Ryan, Roz	Detroit, MI	7/7/51
Rydell, Bobby	Philadelphia, PA	4/26/42
Ryder, Winona	Winona, MN	10/29/71
Sabato, Antonio, Jr.	Rome, Italy	2/29/72
Sade	Ibadan, Nigeria	1/16/59
Sagal, Katey	Hollywood, CA	1/19/53
Saget, Bob	Philadelphia, PA	5/17/56
Sahl, Mort	Montreal, Quebec	5/11/27
Saint, Eva Marie	Newark, NJ	7/4/24
St. James, Susan	Hollywood, CA	8/14/46
St. John, Jill	Los Angeles, CA	8/19/40
Sajak, Pat	Chicago, IL	10/26/46
Saks, Gene	New York, NY	11/8/21
Sales, Soupy	Franklinton, NC	1/8/26
Salonga, Lea	Manila, Philippines	2/22/71
Samms, Emma	London, England	8/28/60
Sandler, Adam	Brooklyn, NY	9/9/66
Sands, Julian	West Yorkshire, England	1/15/58
Sanford, Isabel	New York, NY	8/29/17
San Giacomo, Laura	West Orange, NJ	11/14/61
Santana, Carlos	Autlan, Mexico	7/20/47
Sarandon, Susan	New York, NY	10/4/46
Sarnoff, Dorothy	New York, NY	5/25/17
Sartain, Gailard	Tulsa, OK	9/18/46
Savage, Ben	Highland Park, IL	9/13/80
Savage, Fred	Highland Park, IL	7/9/76
Sawa, Devon	Vancouver, British Columbia	9/7/78
Saxon, John	Brooklyn, NY	8/5/35
Sayles, John	Schenectady, NY	9/28/50
Scaggs, Boz	Canton, OH	6/8/44
Scales, Prunella	Sutton Abinger, England	6/22/32
Scalia, Jack	Brooklyn, NY	11/10/51
Schallert, William	Los Angeles, CA	7/6/22
Scheider, Roy	Orange, NJ	11/10/35
Schell, Maria	Vienna, Austria	1/15/26
Schell, Maximilian	Vienna, Austria	12/8/30
Schenkel, Chris	Bippus, IN	8/21/23
Schiffer, Claudia	Rheinbach, Germany	8/25/70
Schneider, John	Mt. Kisco, NY	4/8/54
Schneider, Rob	San Francisco, CA	10/31/63
Schreiber, Liev	San Francisco, CA	10/4/67
Schroder, Rick	Staten Island, NY	4/13/70
Schwarzenegger, Arnold	Thal, Austria	7/30/47
Schwarzkopf, Elisabeth	Jarotschin, Poland	12/9/15
Schwimmer, David	Astoria, Queens, NY	11/2/66
Sciorra, Annabella	New York, NY	3/24/64
Scofield, Paul	Hurstpierpoint, England	1/21/22
Scolari, Peter	New Rochelle, NY	9/12/54
Scorsese, Martin	Flushing, Queens, NY	11/17/42
Scott, Lizabeth	Scranton, PA	9/29/22
Scott, Ridley	South Shields, England	11/30/37
Scott-Heron, Gil	Chicago, IL	4/1/49
Scott Thomas, Kristin	Redruth, England	5/24/60
Scotto, Renata	Savona, Italy	2/24/35
Scully, Vin	Bronx, NY	11/29/27
Seagal, Steven	Lansing, MI	4/10/51
Secor, Kyle	Tacoma, WA	5/31/58
Sedaka, Neil	Brooklyn, NY	3/13/39
Seeger, Pete	New York, NY	5/3/19
Segal, George	Great Neck, NY	2/13/34
Seidelman, Susan	Abington, PA	12/11/52
Seinfeld, Jerry	Brooklyn, NY	4/29/54
Sellecca, Connie	Bronx, NY	5/25/55
Selleck, Tom	Detroit, MI	1/29/45
Severinsen, Doc	Arlington, OR	7/7/27
Sevigny, Chloë	Springfield, MA	11/18/74
Sewell, Rufus	London, England	10/29/67
Seymour, Jane	Hillingdon, England	2/15/51
Shackelford, Ted	Oklahoma City, OK	6/23/46
Shaffer, Paul	Thunder Bay, Ontario	11/28/49
Shalhoub, Tony	Green Bay, WI	10/9/53
Shandling, Garry	Chicago, IL	11/29/49
Shankar, Ravi	Benares, India	4/7/20
Shannon, Molly	Shaker Heights, OH	9/16/64
Sharif, Omar	Alexandria, Egypt	4/10/32
Shatner, William	Montreal, Quebec	3/22/31
Shaughnessy, Charles	London, England	2/9/55
Shaver, Helen	St. Thomas, Ontario	2/24/51
Shaw, Artie	New York, NY	5/23/10
Shea, John	N. Conway, NH	4/14/49
Shearer, Harry	Los Angeles, CA	12/23/43
Shearer, Moira	Dumfermline, Scotland	1/17/26
Shearing, George	London, England	8/13/19
Sheedy, Ally	New York, NY	6/13/62
Sheen, Charlie	Los Angeles, CA	9/3/65
Sheen, Martin	Dayton, OH	8/3/40
Sheindlin, Judge Judy	Brooklyn, NY	10/21/42
Shelley, Carole	London, England	8/16/39
Shepard, Sam	Ft. Sheridan, IL	11/5/43
Shepherd, Cybill	Memphis, TN	2/18/50
Sheridan, Nicollette	Worthing, England	11/21/63
Shields, Brooke	New York, NY	5/31/65
Shire, Talia	Lake Success, NY	4/25/46
Short, Bobby	Danville, IL	9/15/24
Short, Martin	Hamilton, Ontario	3/26/50
Show, Grant	Detroit, MI	2/27/62
Shue, Andrew	Washington, DE	2/20/67
Shue, Elisabeth	Wilmington, DE	10/6/63
Shyamalan, M. Night	Pondicherry, India	8/6/70
Siepi, Cesare	Milan, Italy	2/10/23
Sigler, Jamie-Lynn	Jericho, NY	5/15/81
Sikking, James B.	Los Angeles, CA	3/5/34
Sills, Beverly	Brooklyn, NY	5/25/29
Silver, Ron	New York, NY	7/2/46
Silverman, Jonathan	Beverly Hills, CA	8/5/66
Silverstone, Alicia	Hillsborough, CA	10/4/76
Simmons, Gene	Haifa, Israel	8/25/49
Simmons, Jean	London, England	1/31/29
Simon, Carly	Riverdale, NY	6/25/45
Simon, Paul	Newark, NJ	10/13/41
Sinatra, Nancy	Jersey City, NJ	6/8/40
Sinbad	Benton Harbor, MI	11/10/56
Singleton, John	Los Angeles, CA	1/6/68
Singleton, Penny	Philadelphia, PA	9/15/08
Sinise, Gary	Blue Island, IL	3/17/55
Sirico, Tony	Brooklyn, NY	7/29/42
Sizemore, Tom	Detroit, MI	9/29/64
Skerritt, Tom	Detroit, MI	8/25/33
Skye, Ione	Hertfordshire, England	9/4/70
Slater, Christian	New York, NY	8/18/69
Slater, Helen	Massapequa, NY	12/15/63
Slezak, Erika	Hollywood, CA	8/5/46
Slick, Grace	Evanston, IL	10/30/39
Smirnoff, Yakov	Odessa, Ukraine	1/24/51
Smith, Allison	Bronx, NY	12/9/69
Smith, Jaclyn	Houston, TX	10/26/47
Smith, Keely	Norfolk, VA	3/9/32
Smith, Kevin	Red Bank, NJ	8/2/70
Smith, Maggie	Ilford, England	12/28/34
Smith, Will	West Philadelphia, PA	9/25/68
Smits, Jimmy	New York, NY	7/9/55
Smothers, Dick	Governor's Island, NY	11/20/38
Smothers, Tom	Governor's Island, NY	2/2/37
Snipes, Wesley	Orlando, FL	7/31/62
Snyder, Tom	Milwaukee, WI	5/12/36
Soderbergh, Steven	Atlanta, GA	1/14/63
Somers, Suzanne	San Bruno, CA	10/16/46
Sommer, Elke	Berlin, Germany	11/5/40
Sorbo, Kevin	Mound, MN	9/24/58
Sorvino, Mira	Tenafly, NJ	9/28/67
Sorvino, Paul	Brooklyn, NY	4/13/39
Soul, David	Chicago, IL	8/28/43
Spacek, Sissy	Quitman, TX	12/25/49
Spacey, Kevin	S. Orange, NJ	7/26/59
Spade, David	Birmingham, MI	7/22/64
Spader, James	Boston, MA	2/7/60
Spano, Joe	San Francisco, CA	7/7/46
Spears, Britney	Kentwood, LA	12/2/81
Spector, Phil	Bronx, NY	12/26/40
Spelling, Aaron	Dallas, TX	4/22/28
Spelling, Tori	Los Angeles, CA	5/16/73
Spencer, John	New York, NY	12/20/46
Spielberg, Steven	Cincinnati, OH	12/18/46
Spiner, Brent	Houston, TX	2/2/49
Springer, Jerry	London, England	2/13/44
Springfield, Rick	Sydney, Australia	8/23/49
Springsteen, Bruce	Freehold, NJ	9/23/49
Stafford, Jo	Coalinga, CA	11/12/18
Stahl, Richard	Detroit, MI	1/4/32
Stallone, Sylvester	New York, NY	7/6/46
Stamos, John	Cypress, CA	8/19/63
Stamp, Terence	Stepney, England	7/22/39
Stang, Arnold	Chelsea, MA	9/28/25
Stanton, Harry Dean	West Irvine, KY	7/14/26
Stapleton, Jean	New York, NY	1/19/23
Stapleton, Maureen	Troy, NY	6/21/25
Starr, Ringo	Liverpool, England	7/7/40
Steenburgen, Mary	Newport, AR	2/8/53
Stefani, Gwen	Anaheim, CA	10/3/69

Name	Birthplace	Birthdate
Stein, Ben	Washington, DC	11/25/44
Stephens, James	Mt. Kisco, NY	5/18/51
Stern, Daniel	Bethesda, MD	8/28/57
Stern, Howard	Roosevelt, NY	1/12/54
Sternhagen, Frances	Washington, DC	1/13/30
Stevens, Andrew	Memphis, TN	6/10/55
Stevens, Cat	London, England	7/21/48
Stevens, Connie	Brooklyn, NY	8/8/38
Stevens, Rise	Bronx, NY	6/11/13
Stevens, Stella	Hot Coffee, MS	10/1/36
Stevenson, Parker	Philadelphia, PA	6/4/52
Stewart, French	Albuquerque, NM	2/20/64
Stewart, Jon	Trenton, NY	11/28/62
Stewart, Patrick	Mirfield, England	7/13/40
Stewart, Rod	London, England	1/10/45
Stiers, David Ogden	Peoria, IL	10/31/42
Stiles, Julia	New York, NY	3/28/81
Stiller, Ben	New York, NY	11/30/65
Stiller, Jerry	Brooklyn, NY	6/8/27
Stills, Stephen	Dallas, TX	1/3/45
Sting	Newcastle, England	10/2/51
Stipe, Michael	Decatur, GA	1/4/60
Stockwell, Dean	North Hollywood, CA	3/5/36
Stoltz, Eric	Whittier, CA	9/30/61
Stone, Dee Wallace	Kansas City, KS	12/14/48
Stone, Oliver	New York, NY	9/15/46
Stone, Sharon	Meadville, PA	3/10/58
Stookey, Paul	Baltimore, MD	12/30/37
Storch, Larry	New York, NY	1/8/23
Storm, Gale	Bloomington, TX	4/5/22
Stowe, Madeleine	Eagle Rock, CA	8/18/58
Strait, George	Pearsall, TX	5/18/52
Strasser, Robin	New York, NY	5/7/45
Stratas, Teresa	Toronto, Ontario	5/26/38
Strathairn, David	San Francisco, CA	1/26/49
Strauss, Peter	Croton-on-Hudson, NY	2/20/47
Streep, Meryl	Summit, NJ	6/22/49
Streisand, Barbra	Brooklyn, NY	4/24/42
Stringfield, Sherry	Colorado Springs, CO	6/24/67
Stritch, Elaine	Detroit, Mi	2/2/26
Stroman, Susan	Wilmington, DE	10/17/54
Struthers, Sally	Portland, OR	7/28/48
Stuart, Gloria	Santa Monica, CA	7/4/10
Stuarti, Enzo	Rome, Italy.	3/3/25
Studdard, Ruben	Birmingham, AL	9/12/78
Sullivan, Susan	New York, NY	11/18/42
Sumac, Yma	Ichocan, Peru.	9/10/27
Summer, Donna	Dorchester, MA	12/31/48
Sutherland, Donald	St. John, New Brunswick	7/17/34
Sutherland, Joan	Sydney, Australia.	11/7/26
Sutherland, Kiefer	London, England	12/21/66
Suvari, Mena	Newport, RI	2/9/79
Swank, Hilary	Bellingham, WA.	7/30/74
Swayze, Patrick	Houston, TX.	8/18/52
Swinton, Tilda	London, England	11/5/60
Swit, Loretta	Passaic, NJ	11/4/37
Sykes, Wanda	Portsmouth, VA	3/7/64
T, Mr.	Chicago, IL.	5/21/52
Takei, George	Los Angeles, CA	4/20/37
Talichief, Maria	Fairfax, OK.	1/24/25
Tamblyn, Russ	Los Angeles, CA	12/30/34
Tarantino, Quentin	Knoxville, TN	3/27/63
Tautou, Audrey	Beaumont, France	8/9/78
Taylor, Billy	Greenville, SC	7/21/21
Taylor, Buck	Hollywood, CA.	5/13/38
Taylor, Elizabeth	London, England	2/27/32
Taylor, James	Boston, MA	3/12/48
Taylor, Rip	Washington, DC.	1/13/34
Taylor, Rod	Sydney, Australia.	1/11/30
Taymor, Julie	Newton, MA.	12/15/52
Te Kanawa, Kiri	Gisborne, New Zealand.	3/6/44
Tebaldi, Renata	Pesaro, Italy.	2/1/22
Teller	Philadelphia, PA	2/14/48
Temple Black, Shirley	Santa Monica, CA	4/23/28
Tennant, Victoria	London, England	9/30/50
Tennille, Toni	Montgomery, AL	5/8/43
Tesh, John	Garden City, NY.	7/9/52
Tharp, Twyla	Portland, IN	7/1/41
Thaxter, Phyllis	Portland, ME	11/20/21
Theron, Charlize	South Africa.	8/7/75
Thicke, Alan	Kirkland Lake, Ontario	3/1/47
Thiessen, Tiffani	Long Beach, CA.	1/23/74
Thomas, Jay	Kermit, TX	7/12/48
Thomas, Jonathan Taylor	Bethlehem, PA.	9/8/81
Thomas, Marlo	Deerfield, MI	11/21/38
Thomas, Michael Tilson	Hollywood, CA.	12/21/44
Thomas, Philip Michael	Columbus, OH.	5/26/49
Thomas, Richard	New York, NY	6/13/51
Thompson, Emma	London, England	4/15/59
Thompson, Jack	Sydney, Australia.	8/31/40

Name	Birthplace	Birthdate
Thompson, Lea	Rochester, MN	5/31/61
Thompson, Sada	Des Moines, IA	9/27/29
Thorne-Smith, Courtney	San Francisco, CA	11/8/67
Thornton, Billy Bob	Hot Springs, AR	8/4/55
Thurman, Uma	Boston, MA.	4/29/70
Tiegs, Cheryl	Breckenridge, MN.	9/25/47
Tierney, Maura	Boston, MA	2/3/65
Tillis, Mel	Tampa, FL	8/8/32
Tilly, Jennifer	Harbor City, CA	9/16/58
Tilly, Meg	Long Beach, CA	2/14/60
Timberlake, Justin	Memphis, TN	1/31/81
Todd, Richard	Dublin, Ireland	6/11/19
Tomei, Marisa	Brooklyn, NY.	12/4/64
Tomlin, Lily	Detroit, MI.	9/1/39
Tork, Peter	Washington, DC	2/13/42
Torn, Rip	Temple, TX.	2/6/31
Townsend, Robert	Chicago, IL	2/6/57
Townshend, Peter	Chiswick, England	5/19/45
Travanti, Daniel J.	Kenosha, WI.	3/7/40
Travers, Mary.	Louisville, KY	11/7/37
Travis, Nancy	Astoria, Queens, NY.	9/21/61
Travis, Randy.	Marshville, NC	5/4/59
Travolta, John	Englewood, NJ	2/18/54
Trebek, Alex	Sudbury, Ontario	7/22/40
Tritt, Travis.	Marietta, GA	2/9/63
Tucci, Stanley	Katonah, NY.	1/11/60
Tucker, Chris	Decatur, GA	8/31/72
Tucker, Michael	Baltimore, MD.	2/6/44
Tucker, Tanya	Seminole, TX	10/10/58
Tune, Tommy	Wichita Falls, TX.	2/28/39
Turlington, Christy	Walnut Creek, CA.	1/2/69
Turner, Janine	Lincoln, NE.	12/6/62
Turner, Kathleen	Springfield, MO.	6/19/54
Turner, Tina	Brownsville, TN.	11/26/39
Turturro, John	Brooklyn, NY.	2/28/57
Twain, Shania	Windsor, Ontario.	8/28/65
Twiggy (Lawson)	London, England	9/19/49
Tyler, Liv	New York, NY.	7/1/77
Tyler, Steven	Yonkers, NY	3/26/48
Tyson, Cicely	Harlem, NY.	12/19/33
Uecker, Bob	Milwaukee, Wi	1/26/35
Uggams, Leslie	New York, NY.	5/25/43
Ullman, Tracey	Slough, England	12/30/59
Ullmann, Liv	Tokyo, Japan	12/16/39
Ulrich, Skeet	New York, NY.	1/20/69
Underwood, Blair	Tacoma, WA.	8/25/64
Usher (Raymond IV)	Chattanooga,TN	10/14/78
Ustinov, Peter	London, England	4/16/21
Vaccaro, Brenda	Brooklyn, NY.	11/18/39
Vale, Jerry	Bronx, NY.	7/8/32
Valente, Caterina	Paris, France	1/14/31
Valley, Mark	Ogdensburg, NY.	12/24/64
Valli, Frankie	Newark, NJ.	5/3/37
Van Ark, Joan	New York, NY.	6/16/43
Vance, Courtney B.	Birmingham, MI	3/12/60
Van Damme, Jean-Claude	Brussels, Belgium.	10/18/60
Van Der Beek, James	Chesire, CT	3/8/77
Van Doren, Mamie	Rowena, SD.	2/6/31
Vandross, Luther	New York, NY.	4/20/51
Van Dyke, Dick	West Plains, MO.	12/13/25
Van Dyke, Jerry	Danville, IL.	7/27/31
Van Halen, Eddie	Nijmegen, Netherlands.	1/26/55
Van Patten, Dick	Queens, NY	12/9/28
Van Peebles, Mario	Mexico City, Mexico	1/15/57
Van Sant, Gus	Louisville, KY	7/24/52
Van Zandt, Steven	Boston, MA.	11/22/50
Vaughn, Robert	New York, NY.	11/22/32
Vaughn, Vince	Minneapolis, MN.	3/28/70
Vedder, Eddie	Evanston, IL	12/23/64
Vereen, Ben.	Miami, FL	10/10/46
Verrett, Shirley	New Orleans, LA	5/31/33
Vickers, Jon	Prince Albert, Sask.	10/29/26
Vieira, Meredith	Providence, RI	12/30/53
Vigoda, Abe	New York, NY.	2/24/21
Vincent, Jan-Michael	Denver, CO.	7/15/44
Vinton, Bobby	Canonsburg, PA.	4/16/35
Vitale, Dick	East Rutherford, NJ	6/9/39
Voight, Jon	Yonkers, NY	12/29/38
Von Stade, Frederica	Somerville, NJ	6/1/45
Von Sydow, Max	Lund, Sweden	4/10/29
Von Trier, Lars	Copenhagen, Denmark	4/30/56
Wagner, Jack	Washington, MO.	10/3/59
Wagner, Lindsay	Los Angeles, CA.	6/22/49
Wagner, Robert	Detroit, MI.	2/10/30
Wahl, Ken	Chicago, IL.	2/14/56
Wahlberg, Mark	Dorchester, MA.	6/5/71
Wain, Bea	Bronx, NY.	4/30/17

Name	Birthplace	Birthdate	Name	Birthplace	Birthdate
Waite, Ralph	White Plains, NY	6/22/28	Williamson, Nicol	Hamilton, Scotland	9/14/38
Waits, Tom	Pomona, CA	12/7/49	Willis, Bruce	Idar-Oberstein, W. Germany	3/19/55
Walden, Robert	New York, NY	9/25/43	Wilson, Brian	Hawthorne, CA.	6/20/42
Walken, Christopher	Astoria, Queens, NY	3/31/43	Wilson, Cassandra	Jackson, MS.	12/4/55
Wallace, Marcia	Creston, IA.	11/1/42	Wilson, Demond	Valdosta, GA	10/13/46
Wallach, Eli	Brooklyn, NY	12/7/15	Wilson, Elizabeth	Grand Rapids, MI	4/4/25
Walter, Jessica	Brooklyn, NY	1/31/40	Wilson, Luke	Dallas, TX.	9/21/71
Ward, Fred	San Diego, CA	12/30/42	Wilson, Nancy	Chillicothe, OH	2/20/37
Ward, Sela	Meridian, MS	7/11/56	Wilson, Owen	Dallas, TX.	11/18/68
Ward, Simon	Kent, London, England	10/19/41	Windom, William	New York, NY.	9/28/23
Warden, Jack	Newark, NJ	9/18/20	Winfield, Paul.	Los Angeles, CA.	5/22/41
Warfield, Marsha	Chicago, IL.	3/5/54	Winfrey, Oprah	Kosciusko, MS	1/29/54
Warner, Malcolm-Jamal	Jersey City, NJ.	8/18/70	Winger, Debra	Cleveland, OH	5/16/55
Warren, Lesley Ann	New York, NY	8/16/46	Winkler, Henry	New York, NY.	10/30/45
Warrick, Ruth	St. Joseph, MO	6/29/16	Winningham, Mare.	Phoenix, AZ	5/16/59
Warwick, Dionne	East Orange, NJ	12/12/40	Winslet, Kate	Reading, England.	10/5/75
Washington, Denzel	Mt. Vernon, NY	12/28/54	Winter, Johnny	Beaumont, TX	2/23/44
Waters, John	Baltimore, MD	4/22/46	Winters, Jonathan	Dayton, OH.	11/11/25
Waters, Roger	Great Bookham, England	9/6/44	Winters, Shelley	East St. Louis, IL.	8/18/22
Waterston, Sam	Cambridge, MA	11/15/40	Winwood, Steve	Birmingham, England.	5/12/48
Watson, Emily	London, England	1/14/67	Wiseman, Joseph	Montreal, Quebec.	5/15/18
Watson, Emma	Oxford, England.	4/15/90	Withers, Jane	Atlanta, GA.	4/12/26
Watts, Andre	Nuremberg, Germany	6/20/46	Witherspoon, Reese	Nashville, TN	3/22/76
Watts, Naomi	Shoreham, England.	9/28/68	Witt, Alicia	Worcester, MA	8/21/75
Wayans, Damon	New York, NY	9/4/60	Wolf, Scott	Boston, MA.	6/4/68
Wayans, Keenen Ivory	Brooklyn, NY	6/8/58	Wonder, Stevie	Saginaw, MI	5/13/50
Weathers, Carl	New Orleans, LA	1/14/48	Wong, Faye	Beijing, China	8/8/69
Weaver, Dennis	Joplin, MO	6/4/24	Woo, John	Guangzhou, China	5/1/46
Weaver, Fritz	Pittsburgh, PA	1/19/26	Wood, Elijah.	Cedar Rapids, IA	1/28/81
Weaver, Sigourney	New York, NY	10/8/49	Woodard, Alfre	Tulsa, OK	11/8/53
Weir, Peter	Sydney, Australia.	8/8/44	Woods, James	Vernal, UT	4/18/47
Weisz, Rachel	London, England	3/7/71	Woodward, Edward	Croyden, England.	6/1/30
Weitz, Bruce	Norwalk, CT.	5/27/43	Woodward, Joanne	Thomasville, GA	2/27/30
Welch, Raquel	Chicago, IL.	9/5/40	Wopat, Tom	Lodi, WI	9/9/51
Weld, Tuesday	New York, NY	8/27/43	Wray, Fay	Mountain View, Alberta.	9/15/07
Wells, Kitty	Nashville, TN	8/30/19	Wright, Martha	Seattle, WA	3/23/26
Wendt, George	Chicago, IL.	10/17/48	Wright, Max	Detroit, MI.	8/2/43
West, Adam	Walla Walla, WA	9/19/28	Wright, Steven	New York, NY.	12/6/55
West, Shane	Baton Rouge, LA	6/10/78	Wright, Teresa	New York, NY.	10/27/18
Wettig, Patricia	Cincinnati, OH	12/4/51	Wright Penn, Robin	Dallas, TX.	4/8/66
Whalley, Joanne	Manchester, England.	8/25/64	Wyatt, Jane	Campgaw, NJ.	8/12/12
Wheaton, Wil.	Burbank, CA	7/29/72	Wyle, Noah	Hollywood, CA.	6/4/71
Whitaker, Forest	Longview, TX.	7/15/61	Wyman, Bill	London, England	10/24/36
White, Betty	Oak Park, IL.	1/17/22	Wyman, Jane.	St. Joseph, MO.	1/4/14
White, Jaleel	Pasadena, CA	11/27/76			
White, Vanna	N. Myrtle Beach, SC	2/18/57	Yankovic, Weird Al	Lynwood, CA	10/23/59
Whitford, Bradley	Madison, WI	10/10/59	Yanni	Kalamata, Greece.	11/14/54
Whiting, Margaret	Detroit, MI	7/22/24	Yarborough, Glenn	Milwaukee, WI	1/12/30
Whitman, Stuart	San Francisco, CA.	2/1/26	Yarrow, Peter.	New York, NY.	5/31/38
Whitmore, James	White Plains, NY	10/1/21	Yearwood, Trisha.	Monticello, GA	9/19/64
Widmark, Richard	Sunrise, MN.	12/26/14	Yoakam, Dwight.	Pikesville, KY	10/23/56
Wiest, Dianne	Kansas City, MO	3/28/48	York, Michael	Fulmer, England.	3/27/42
Wilder, Gene	Milwaukee, WI	6/11/33	York, Susannah	London, England	1/9/41
Wilkinson, Tom	Leeds, England	12/12/48	Young, Alan	North Shields, England.	11/19/19
Williams, Andy	Wall Lake, IA	12/3/27	Young, Burt	New York, NY.	4/30/40
Williams, Barry	Santa Monica, CA	9/30/54	Young, Neil	Toronto, Ontario.	11/12/45
Williams, Billy Dee	Harlem, NY	4/6/37	Young, Sean	Louisville, KY	11/20/59
Williams, Cindy	Van Nuys, CA	8/22/47			
Williams, Esther	Los Angeles, CA	8/8/23	Zane, Billy	Chicago, IL.	2/24/66
Williams, Hal	Columbus, OH	12/14/38	Zeffirelli, Franco	Florence, Italy.	2/12/23
Williams, Hank, Jr.	Shreveport, LA.	5/26/49	Zellweger, Renee.	Katy, TX	4/25/69
Williams, JoBeth	Houston, TX.	12/6/48	Zemeckis, Robert.	Chicago, IL.	5/14/52
Williams, Lucinda	Lake Charles, LA	1/26/53	Zerbe, Anthony	Long Beach, CA.	5/20/36
Williams, Michelle	Kalispell, MT	9/9/80	Zeta-Jones, Catherine	Swansea, Wales.	9/25/69
Williams, Montel	Baltimore, MD	7/3/56	Zimbalist, Efrem, Jr.	New York, NY.	11/30/18
Williams, Paul	Omaha, NE	9/19/40	Zimbalist, Stephanie	New York, NY.	10/8/56
Williams, Robin	Chicago, IL.	7/21/51	Zimmer, Kim	Grand Rapids, MI	2/2/55
Williams, Treat	Rowayton, CT	12/1/51	Zukerman, Pinchas	Tel Aviv, Israel	7/16/48
Williams, Vanessa.	Tarrytown, NY	3/18/63	Zuniga, Daphne	San Francisco, CA.	10/28/62
Williamson, Kevin	New Bern, NC	3/14/65			

Entertainment Personalities of the Past

See also other lists for some deceased entertainers not included here.

Name	Born	Died	Name	Born	Died	Name	Born	Died
Aaliyah	1979	2001	Alda, Robert	1914	1986	Andrews, Laverne	1913	1967
Abbott, Bud	1895	1974	Alexander, Ben	1911	1969	Andrews, Maxine	1918	1995
Abbott, George	1887	1995	Allen, Fred	1894	1956	Angeli, Pier	1933	1971
Acuff, Roy	1903	1992	Allen, Gracie	1906	1964	Anita Louise	1915	1970
Adams, Joey	1911	1999	Allen, Mel	1913	1996	Arbuckle, Fatty (Roscoe)	1887	1933
Adams, Maude	1872	1953	Allen, Peter	1944	1992	Arden, Eve	1908	1990
Adler, Jacob P	1855	1926	Allen, Steve	1921	2000	Arlen, Richard.	1900	1976
Adler, Luther	1903	1984	Allgood, Sara	1883	1950	Arliss, George.	1868	1946
Adoree, Renee	1898	1933	Ameche, Don	1908	1993	Armetta, Henry	1888	1945
Agar, John.	1921	2002	Ames, Leon.	1903	1993	Armstrong, Louis	1901	1971
Aherne, Brian	1902	1986	Amsterdam, Morey	1909?	1996	Arnaz, Desi	1917	1986
Ailey, Alvin	1931	1989	Anderson, Judith.	1897	1992	Arnold, Edward	1890	1956
Akins, Claude	1918	1994	Anderson, Marian	1902	1993	Arquette, Cliff	1905	1974
Albertson, Frank	1909	1964	Andre the Giant.	1946	1993	Arthur, Jean	1900	1991
Albertson, Jack	1907	1981	Andrews, Dana	1909	1992	Ashcroft, Peggy	1907	1991

Name	Born	Died
Astaire, Fred	1899	1987
Astor, Mary	1906	1987
Atkins, Chet	1924	2001
Atwill, Lionel	1885	1946
Auer, Mischa	1905	1967
Aumont, Jean-Pierre	1911	2001
Austin, Gene	1900	1972
Autry, Gene	1907	1998
Axton, Hoyt	1938	1999
Ayres, Lew	1908	1996
Backus, Jim	1913	1989
Bailey, Pearl	1918	1990
Bainter, Fay	1892	1968
Baker, Josephine	1906	1975
Balanchine, George	1904	1983
Ball, Lucille	1911	1989
Balsam, Martin	1919	1996
Bancroft, George	1882	1956
Bankhead, Tallulah	1903	1968
Banks, Leslie	1890	1952
Bara, Theda	1890	1955
Barnes, Binnie	1903	1998
Barnum, Phineas T.	1810	1891
Barrymore, Ethel	1879	1959
Barrymore, John	1882	1942
Barrymore, Lionel	1878	1954
Barrymore, Maurice	1848	1905
Bartel, Paul	1938	2000
Barthelmess, Richard	1897	1963
Bartholomew, Freddie	1924	1992
Bartok, Eva	1926	1998
Barty, Billy	1924	2000
Basehart, Richard	1914	1984
Basie, Count	1904	1984
Bates, Clayton (Peg Leg)	1907	1998
Bates, Florence	1888	1954
Bavier, Francis	1902	1989
Baxter, Anne	1923	1985
Baxter, Warner	1889	1951
Beatty, Clyde	1904	1965
Beaumont, Hugh	1909	1982
Beavers, Louise	1902	1962
Beery, Noah, Sr.	1884	1946
Beery, Noah, Jr.	1913	1994
Beery, Wallace	1889	1949
Begley, Ed.	1901	1970
Bellamy, Ralph	1904	1991
Belushi, John	1949	1982
Benaderet, Bea	1906	1968
Bendix, William	1906	1964
Bennett, Constance	1904	1965
Bennett, Joan	1910	1990
Bennett, Michael	1943	1987
Benny, Jack	1894	1974
Benzell, Mimi	1924	1970
Beradino, John	1917	1996
Berg, Gertrude	1899	1966
Bergen, Edgar	1903	1978
Bergman, Ingrid	1915	1982
Berkeley, Busby	1895	1976
Berle, Milton	1908	2002
Bernardi, Herschel	1923	1986
Bernhardt, Sarah	1844	1923
Bernie, Ben	1893	1943
Bessell, Ted	1939	1996
Bickford, Charles	1889	1967
Big Bopper, The	1930	1959
Bing, Rudolf	1902	1997
Bissell, Whit	1909	1996
Bixby, Bill	1934	1993
Bjoerling, Jussi	1911	1960
Blackmer, Sidney	1895	1973
Blackstone, Harry	1885	1965
Blake, Amanda	1931	1989
Blaine, Vivian	1921	1995
Blanc, Mel	1908	1989
Blocker, Dan	1928	1972
Blondell, Joan	1909	1979
Blore, Eric	1888	1959
Blue, Ben	1901	1975
Blyden, Larry	1925	1975
Bogarde, Dirk	1920	1999
Bogart, Humphrey	1899	1957
Boland, Mary	1880	1965
Boles, John	1895	1969
Bolger, Ray	1904	1987
Bond, Ward	1903	1960
Bondi, Beulah	1892	1981
Bono, Sonny	1935	1998
Boone, Richard	1917	1981
Booth, Edwin	1833	1893
Booth, Junius Brutus	1796	1852
Booth, Shirley	1898	1992
Borge, Victor	1909	2000
Bow, Clara	1905	1965
Bowes, Maj. Edward	1874	1946
Bowman, Lee	1914	1979
Brown, Les	1912	2001
Boxcar Willie	1931	1999
Boyd, Stephen	1928	1977
Boyd, William	1898	1972
Boyer, Charles	1899	1978
Bracken, Eddie	1915	2002
Brady, Alice	1893	1939
Brand, Neville	1921	1992
Brazzi, Rossano	1916	1994
Brennan, Walter	1894	1974
Brent, George	1904	1979
Brett, Jeremy	1935	1995
Brice, Fanny	1891	1951
Bridges, Lloyd	1913	1998
Broderick, Helen	1891	1959
Bronson, Charles	1921	2003
Brooks, Foster	1912	2001
Brown, Joe E.	1892	1973
Bruce, Lenny	1925	1966
Bruce, Nigel	1895	1953
Bruce, Virginia	1910	1982
Brynner, Yul	1915	1985
Buchanan, Edgar	1903	1979
Buchholz, Horst	1933	2003
Buñuel, Luis	1900	1983
Buono, Victor	1938	1982
Burke, Billie	1885	1970
Burnette, Smiley	1911	1967
Burns, George	1896	1996
Burr, Raymond	1917	1993
Burton, Richard	1925	1984
Busch, Mae	1897	1946
Bushman, Francis X.	1883	1966
Butterworth, Charles	1896	1946
Byington, Spring	1893	1971
Cabot, Bruce	1904	1972
Cabot, Sebastian	1918	1977
Cagney, James	1899	1986
Calhern, Louis	1895	1956
Calhoun, Rory	1923	1999
Callas, Maria	1923	1977
Calloway, Cab	1907	1994
Cambridge, Godfrey	1933	1976
Campbell, Mrs. Patrick	1865	1940
Candy, John	1950	1994
Cantinflas	1911	1993
Cantor, Eddie	1892	1964
Capra, Frank	1897	1991
Carey, Harry	1878	1947
Carey, Macdonald	1913	1994
Carle, Frankie	1903	2001
Carpenter, Karen	1950	1983
Carradine, John	1906	1988
Carrillo, Leo	1880	1961
Carroll, Leo G.	1892	1972
Carroll, Madeleine	1906	1987
Carroll, Nancy	1905	1965
Carson, Jack	1910	1963
Carter, Benny	1907	2003
Carter, Nell	1948	2003
Caruso, Enrico	1873	1921
Casadesus, Gaby	1901	1999
Casals, Pablo	1876	1973
Cash, Johnny	1932	2003
Cash, June Carter	1929	2003
Cass, Peggy	1924	1999
Cassidy, Jack	1927	1976
Cassavetes, John	1929	1989
Castle, Irene	1893	1969
Castle, Vernon	1887	1918
Caulfield, Joan	1922	1991
Chaliapin, Feodor	1873	1938
Champion, Gower	1919	1980
Chandler, Jeff	1918	1961
Chaney, Lon	1883	1930
Chaney, Lon, Jr.	1905	1973
Chapin, Harry	1942	1981
Chaplin, Charles	1889	1977
Chapman, Graham	1941	1989
Chase, Ilka	1905	1978
Chatterton, Ruth	1893	1961
Cherrill, Virginia	1908	1996
Chevalier, Maurice	1888	1972
Clair, René	1898	1981
Clark, Bobby	1888	1960
Clark, Dane	1913	1998
Clark, Fred	1914	1968
Clayton, Jan	1917	1983
Clift, Montgomery	1920	1966
Cline, Patsy	1932	1963
Clooney, Rosemary	1928	2002
Clyde, Andy	1892	1967
Cobain, Kurt	1967	1994
Cobb, Lee J.	1911	1976
Coburn, Charles	1877	1961
Coburn, James	1928	2002
Coca, Imogene	1908	2001
Cochran, Steve	1917?	1965
Coco, James	1930	1987
Cody, Buffalo Bill	1846	1917
Cody, Iron Eyes	1907	1999
Cohan, George M.	1878	1942
Cohen, Myron	1902	1986
Colbert, Claudette	1903	1996
Cole, Nat "King"	1919	1965
Collins, Ray	1890	1965
Colman, Ronald	1891	1958
Columbo, Russ	1908	1934
Como, Perry	1912	2001
Conniff, Ray	1916	2002
Connors, Chuck	1921	1992
Conrad, William	1920	1994
Conried, Hans	1917	1982
Conte, Richard	1911	1975
Convy, Bert	1933	1991
Conway, Tom	1904	1967
Coogan, Jackie	1914	1984
Cook, Elisha, Jr.	1904	1995
Cooke, Sam	1935	1964
Cooper, Gary	1901	1961
Cooper, Gladys	1888	1971
Cooper, Melville	1896	1973
Corby, Ellen	1913	1999
Corey, Jeff	1914	2002
Corio, Ann	1914	1999
Cornell, Katharine	1893	1974
Correll, Charles ("Andy")	1890	1972
Costello, Dolores	1905	1979
Costello, Lou	1906	1959
Cotten, Joseph	1905	1994
Coward, Noel	1899	1973
Cox, Wally	1924	1973
Crabbe, Buster	1908	1983
Crane, Bob	1928	1978
Crawford, Broderick	1911	1986
Crawford, Joan	1904	1977
Cregar, Laird	1914	1944
Crenna, Richard	1926	2003
Crews, Laura Hope	1880	1942
Crisp, Donald	1880	1974
Croce, Jim	1942	1973
Cronyn, Hume	1911	2003
Crosby, Bing	1903	1977
Crothers, Scatman	1910	1986
Cruz, Celia	1925	2003
Cugat, Xavier	1900	1990
Cukor, George	1899	1983
Cullen, Bill	1920	1990
Cummings, Robert	1908	1990
Currie, Finlay	1878	1968
Curtis, Keene	1923	2002
Curtis, Ken	1916	1991
Cushing, Peter	1913	1994
Dailey, Dan	1914	1978
Dandridge, Dorothy	1923	1965
Daniell, Henry	1894	1963
Daniels, Bebe	1901	1971
Darin, Bobby	1936	1973
Darnell, Linda	1921	1965
Darwell, Jane	1879	1967
Da Silva, Howard	1909	1986
Davenport, Harry	1866	1949
Davies, Marion	1897	1961
Davis, Bette	1908	1989
Davis, Joan	1907	1961
Davis, Sammy Jr.	1925	1990
Day, Dennis	1917	1988
Dean, James	1931	1955
Defore, Don	1917	1993
Dekker, Albert	1905	1968
Del Rio, Dolores	1908	1983
Demarest, William	1892	1983
DeMille, Agnes	1905	1993
DeMille, Cecil B.	1881	1959

Name	Born	Died	Name	Born	Died	Name	Born	Died
Denison, Michael	1915	1998	Fields, W.C.	1879	1946	Graham, Virginia	1912	1998
Denning, Richard	1914	1998	Fields, Totie	1931	1978	Grahame, Gloria	1925	1981
Dennis, Sandy	1937	1992	Finch, Peter	1916	1977	Granger, Stewart	1913	1993
Denny, Reginald	1891	1967	Fine, Larry	1902	1975	Grant, Cary	1904	1986
Denver, John	1943	1997	Firkusny, Rudolf	1912	1994	Granville, Bonita	1923	1988
Derek, John	1926	1998	Fiske, Minnie Maddern	1865	1932	Gray, Dolores	1924	2002
DeSica, Vittorio	1901	1974	Fitzgerald, Barry	1888	1961	Greco, Jose	1918	2001
Devine, Andy	1905	1977	Flagstad, Kirsten	1895	1962	Green, Adolph	1915	2002
Dewhurst, Colleen	1924	1991	Fleming, Art	1924	1995	Greene, Lorne	1915	1987
De Wilde, Brandon	1942	1972	Fleming, Eric	1925	1966	Greenstreet, Sydney	1879	1954
De Wolfe, Billy	1907	1974	Flippen, Jay C.	1900	1971	Greenwood, Charlotte	1890	1978
Diamond, Selma	1920	1985	Flynn, Errol	1909	1959	Greer, Jane	1924	2001
Dietrich, Marlene	1901	1992	Flynn, Joe	1925	1974	Gregory, James	1911	2002
Digges, Dudley	1879	1947	Foley, Red	1910	1968	Griffith, David Wark	1874	1948
Disney, Walt	1901	1966	Fonda, Henry	1905	1982	Griffith, Hugh	1912	1980
Dix, Richard	1894	1949	Fontaine, Frank	1920	1978	Guardino, Harry	1925	1995
Dmytryk, Edward	1908	1999	Fontanne, Lynn	1887	1983	Guinness, Sir Alec	1914	2000
Donahue, Troy	1936	2001	Fonteyn, Margot	1919	1991	Guthrie, Woody	1912	1967
Donat, Robert	1905	1958	Ford, John	1895	1973	Gwenn, Edmund	1875	1959
Donlevy, Brian	1901?	1972	Ford, Paul	1901	1976	Gwynne, Fred	1926	1993
Dors, Diana	1931	1984	Ford, Tennessee Ernie	1919	1991			
Douglas, Melvyn	1901	1981	Ford, Wallace	1899	1966	Hackett, Buddy	1924	2003
Douglas, Paul	1907	1959	Forrest, Helen	1918	1999	Hackett, Joan	1934	1983
Dove, Billie	1900	1998	Fosse, Bob	1927	1987	Hale, Alan	1892	1950
Downey, Morton, Jr.	1933	2001	Foster, Phil	1914	1985	Hale, Alan, Jr.	1918	1990
Doyle, David	1929	1997	Foster, Preston	1901	1970	Haley, Bill	1925	1981
Drake, Alfred	1914	1992	Foxx, Redd	1922	1991	Haley, Jack	1899	1979
Draper, Ruth	1889	1956	Foy, Eddie	1857	1928	Hall, Huntz	1919	1999
Dresser, Louise	1881	1965	Franchi, Sergio	1933?	1990	Hamilton, Margaret	1902	1985
Dressler, Marie	1869	1934	Francis, Arlene	1908	2001	Hammerstein, Oscar	1847	1919
Drew, Mrs. John	1820	1897	Francis, Kay	1903	1968	Hampton, Lionel	1908	2002
Dru, Joanne	1923	1996	Franciscus, James	1934	1991	Hardwicke, Cedric	1893	1964
Duchin, Eddy	1909	1951	Frankenheimer, John	1930	2002	Hardy, Oliver	1892	1957
Duff, Howard	1917	1990	Frann, Mary	1943	1998	Harlow, Jean	1911	1937
Dumbrille, Douglass	1890	1974	Frawley, William	1893	1966	Harris, Phil	1904	1995
Dumont, Margaret	1889	1965	Frederick, Pauline	1885	1938	Harris, Richard	1930	2002
Duncan, Isadora	1878	1927	French, Victor	1934	1989	Harrison, George	1943	2001
Dunn, James	1905	1967	Friganza, Trixie	1870	1955	Harrison, Rex	1908	1990
Dunne, Irene	1898	1990	Frisco, Joe	1890	1958	Hart, William S.	1870	1946
Dunnock, Mildred	1904	1991	Froman, Jane	1907	1980	Hartman, Phil	1948	1998
Durante, Jimmy	1893	1980	Fuller, Samuel	1912	1997	Harvey, Laurence	1928	1973
Duryea, Dan	1907	1968	Funt, Allen	1914	1999	Hawkins, Jack	1910	1973
Duse, Eleanora	1858	1924	Furness, Betty	1916	1994	Hawkins, Screamin' Jay	1929	2000
Dvorak, Ann	1912	1979				Hawthorne, Nigel	1929	2001
			Gabin, Jean	1904	1976	Hayakawa, Sessue	1890	1973
Eagels, Jeanne	1894	1929	Gable, Clark	1901	1960	Hayden, Sterling	1916	1986
Ebsen, Buddy	1908	2003	Gabor, Eva	1920	1995	Hayes, Gabby	1885	1969
Eckstine, Billy	1914	1993	Garbo, Greta	1905	1990	Hayes, Helen	1900	1993
Eddy, Nelson	1901	1967	Garcia, Jerry	1942	1995	Hayes, Peter Lind	1915	1998
Edelman, Herb	1933	1996	Gardenia, Vincent	1922	1992	Hayward, Leland	1902	1971
Edwards, Cliff	1897	1971	Gardner, Ava	1922	1990	Hayward, Louis	1909	1985
Edwards, Gus	1879	1945	Garfield, John	1913	1952	Hayward, Susan	1917	1975
Edwards, Vince	1928	1996	Garland, Judy	1922	1969	Hayworth, Rita	1918	1987
Egan, Richard	1923	1987	Garson, Greer	1904	1996	Head, Edith	1907	1981
Ellington, Duke	1899	1974	Gassman, Vittorio	1922	2000	Healy, Ted	1896	1937
Elliot, Cass	1941	1974	Gaye, Marvin	1939	1984	Heckart, Eileen	1919	2001
Ellis, Mary	1897	2003	Gaynor, Janet	1906	1984	Heflin, Van	1910	1971
Elman, Mischa	1891	1967	Gebel-Williams, Gunther	1934	2001	Heifetz, Jascha	1901	1987
Errol, Leon	1881	1951	Geer, Will	1902	1978	Held, Anna	1873	1918
Evans, Dale	1912	2001	George, Gladys	1900	1954	Hemingway, Margaux	1955	1996
Evans, Edith	1888	1976	Gibb, Andy	1958	1988	Hendrix, Jimi	1942	1970
Evans, Maurice	1901	1989	Gibb, Maurice	1949	2003	Henie, Sonja	1912	1969
Ewell, Tom	1909	1994	Gibson, Hoot	1892	1962	Henreid, Paul	1908	1992
			Gielgud, John	1904	2000	Henson, Jim	1936	1990
Fadiman, Clifton	1904	1999	Gilbert, Billy	1894	1971	Hepburn, Audrey	1929	1993
Fairbanks, Douglas	1883	1939	Gilbert, John	1895	1936	Hepburn, Katharine	1907	2003
Fairbanks, Douglas, Jr.	1909	2000	Gilford, Jack	1907	1990	Hersholt, Jean	1886	1956
Falkenburg, Jinx	1919	2003	Gillette, William	1855	1937	Hewett, Christopher	1922	2001
Farley, Chris	1964	1997	Gingold, Hermione	1897	1987	Hickey, William	1928	1997
Farmer, Frances	1914	1970	Gish, Dorothy	1898	1968	Hickson, Joan	1906	1998
Farnsworth, Richard	1920	2000	Gish, Lillian	1893	1993	Hill, Benny	1925	1992
Farnum, Dustin	1870	1929	Gleason, Jackie	1916	1987	Hill, George Roy	1921	2002
Farnum, William	1876	1953	Gleason, James	1886	1959	Hiller, Wendy	1912	2003
Farrar, Geraldine	1882	1967	Gluck, Alma	1884	1938	Hines, Gregory	1946	2003
Farrell, Charles	1901	1990	Gobel, George	1919	1991	Hines, Jerome	1921	2003
Farrell, Eileen	1920	2002	Goddard, Paulette	1905	1990	Hirt, Al	1922	1999
Farrell, Glenda	1904	1971	Godfrey, Arthur	1903	1983	Hitchcock, Alfred	1899	1980
Fassbinder, Rainer Werner	1946	1982	Godunov, Alexander	1949	1995	Hobson, Valerie	1917	1998
Fay, Frank	1897	1961	Goldwyn, Samuel	1882	1974	Hodiak, John	1914	1955
Faye, Alice	1912	1998	Gomez, Thomas	1905	1971	Holden, Fay	1894	1973
Fazenda, Louise	1895	1962	Goodman, Benny	1909	1986	Holden, William	1918	1981
Feld, Fritz	1900	1993	Gorcey, Leo	1915	1969	Holliday, Judy	1922	1965
Feldman, Marty	1933	1982	Gordon, Gale	1906	1995	Holloway, Sterling	1905	1992
Fell, Norman	1924	1998	Gordon, Ruth	1896	1985	Holly, Buddy	1936	1959
Fellini, Federico	1920	1993	Gosden, Freeman ("Amos")	1899	1982	Holt, Jack	1888	1951
Fenneman, George	1919	1997	Gottschalk, Ferdinand	1869	1944	Holt, Tim	1918	1973
Ferrer, Jose	1912	1992	Gottschalk, Louis	1829	1869	Homolka, Oscar	1898	1978
Fetchit, Stepin	1898	1985	Gould, Glenn	1932	1982	Hooker, John Lee	1917	2001
Fiedler, Arthur	1894	1979	Gould, Morton	1913	1996	Hoon, Shannon	1967	1995
Field, Betty	1918	1973	Grable, Betty	1916	1973	Hope, Bob	1903	2003
Fields, Gracie	1898	1979	Graham, Martha	1894	1991	Hopkins, Miriam	1902	1972

Name	Born	Died
Hopper, DeWolf	1858	1935
Hopper, William	1915	1970
Horowitz, Vladimir	1904	1989
Horton, Edward Everett	1886	1970
Houdini, Harry	1874	1926
Houseman, John	1902	1988
Hovis, Larry	1936	2003
Howard (Horwitz), Curly	1903	1952
Howard, Eugene	1881	1965
Howard, Joe	1867	1961
Howard, Leslie	1890	1943
Howard (Horwitz), Moe	1897	1975
Howard (Horwitz), Shemp	1895	1955
Howard, Tom	1885	1955
Howard, Trevor	1916	1988
Howard, Willie	1885	1949
Hudson, Rock	1925	1985
Hull, Henry	1890	1977
Hull, Josephine	1886	1957
Humphrey, Doris	1895	1958
Hunter, Jeffrey	1925	1969
Hunter, Kim	1922	2002
Hunter, Ross	1921	1996
Husing, Ted	1901	1962
Huston, John	1906	1987
Huston, Walter	1884	1950
Hutchence, Michael	1960	1997
Hutton, Jim	1934	1979
Hutton, Robert	1920	1994
Hyde-White, Wilfrid	1903	1991
Ingram, Rex	1895	1969
Iturbi, Jose	1895	1980
Ireland, Jill	1936	1990
Ireland, John	1915	1992
Irving, Henry	1838	1905
Ives, Burl	1909	1995
Jack, Wolfman	1938	1995
Jackson, Joe	1875	1942
Jackson, Mahalia	1911	1972
Jackson, Milt	1922	1999
Jaeckel, Richard	1926	1997
Jaffe, Sam	1891	1984
Jagger, Dean	1903	1991
Jam Master Jay	1965	2003
James, Dennis	1917	1997
James, Harry	1916	1983
Janis, Elsie	1889	1956
Jannings, Emil	1886	1950
Janssen, David	1930	1980
Jenkins, Allen	1900	1974
Jennings, Waylon	1937	2002
Jessel, George	1898	1981
Jeter, Michael	1952	2003
Johnson, Ben	1918	1996
Johnson, Celia	1908	1982
Johnson, Chic	1892	1962
Johnson, J.J.	1924	2001
Jolson, Al	1886	1950
Jones, Brian	1942	1969
Jones, Buck	1889	1942
Jones, Carolyn	1933	1983
Jones, Henry	1912	1999
Jones, Spike	1911	1965
Joplin, Janis	1943	1970
Jordan, Richard	1938	1993
Jory, Victor	1902	1982
Joslyn, Allyn	1905	1981
Julia, Raul	1940	1994
Jump, Gordon	1932	2003
Jurado, Katy	1924	2002
Kahn, Madeline	1942	1999
Kane, Helen	1910	1966
Kanin, Garson	1912	1999
Karloff, Boris	1887	1969
Karns, Roscoe	1893	1970
Kaufman, Andy	1949	1984
Kaye, Danny	1913	1987
Kaye, Stubby	1918	1997
Kazan, Elia	1909	2003
Kean, Charles	1811	1868
Kean, Mrs. Charles	1806	1880
Kean, Edmund	1787	1833
Keaton, Buster	1895	1966
Keeler, Ruby	1910	1993
Keith, Brian	1921	1997
Kellaway, Cecil	1894	1973
Kelley, DeForest	1920	1999
Kelly, Emmett	1898	1979
Kelly, Gene	1912	1996
Kelly, Grace	1929	1982
Kelly, Jack	1927	1992
Kelly, Nancy	1921	1985
Kelly, Patsy	1910	1981
Kelton, Pert	1907	1968
Kendall, Kay	1926	1959
Kennedy, Arthur	1914	1990
Kennedy, Edgar	1890	1948
Kibbee, Guy	1886	1956
Kilbride, Percy	1888	1964
Kiley, Richard	1922	1999
Kirby, George	1923	1995
Kirby, Durward	1912	2000
Klemperer, Werner	1919	2000
Knight, Ted	1923	1986
Kostelanetz, Andre	1901	1980
Kovacs, Ernie	1919	1962
Kramer, Stanley	1913	2001
Kruger, Otto	1885	1974
Kubrick, Stanley	1928	1999
Kulp, Nancy	1921	1991
Kurosawa, Akira	1910	1998
Ladd, Alan	1913	1964
Lahr, Bert	1895	1967
Lake, Arthur	1905	1987
Lake, Veronica	1919	1973
Lamarr, Hedy	1913	2000
Lamas, Fernando	1915	1982
Lamour, Dorothy	1914	1996
Lancaster, Burt	1913	1994
Lanchester, Elsa	1902	1986
Lane, Pricilla	1917	1995
Landis, Carole	1919	1948
Landis, Jessie Royce	1904	1972
Landon, Michael	1936	1991
Lang, Fritz	1890	1976
Langdon, Harry	1884	1944
Langtry, Lillie	1853	1929
Lanza, Mario	1921	1959
LaRue, Lash (Alfred)	1917	1996
Lauder, Harry	1870	1950
Laughton, Charles	1899	1962
Laurel, Stan	1890	1965
Lawford, Peter	1923	1984
Lawrence, Gertrude	1898	1952
Lean, David	1908	1991
Lee, Bernard	1908	1981
Lee, Bruce	1940	1973
Lee, Canada	1907	1952
Lee, Gypsy Rose	1914	1970
Lee, Peggy	1920	2002
LeGallienne, Eva	1899	1991
Lehmann, Lotte	1888	1976
Leigh, Vivien	1913	1967
Leighton, Margaret	1922	1976
Lemmon, Jack	1925	2001
Lennon, John	1940	1980
Lenya, Lotte	1898	1981
Leonard, Eddie	1870	1941
Leonard, Sheldon	1907	1997
LeRoy, Mervyn	1900	1987
Levant, Oscar	1906	1972
Levene, Sam	1905	1980
Levenson, Sam	1911	1980
Lewis, Joe E.	1902	1971
Lewis, Shari	1934	1998
Lewis, Ted	1892	1971
Liberace	1919	1987
Lillie, Beatrice	1894	1989
Lind, Jenny	1820	1887
Lindfors, Viveca	1920	1995
Lindley, Audra	1918	1997
Linville, Larry	1939	2000
Little, Cleavon	1939	1992
Llewelyn, Desmond	1914	1999
Lloyd, Harold	1893	1971
Lloyd, Marie	1870	1922
Lockhart, Gene	1891	1957
Logan, Ella	1913	1969
Lombard, Carole	1909	1942
Lombardo, Guy	1902	1977
Long, Richard	1927	1974
Lopes, Lisa	1971	2002
Lopez, Vincent	1895	1975
Lord, Jack	1920?	1998
Lorne, Marion	1888	1968
Lorre, Peter	1904	1964
Lovejoy, Frank	1912	1962
Lowe, Edmund	1890	1971
Loy, Myrna	1905	1993
Lubitsch, Ernst	1892	1947
Ludden, Allen	1918	1981
Lugosi, Bela	1882	1956
Lukas, Paul	1894	1971
Lundigan, William	1914	1975
Lunt, Alfred	1892	1977
Lupino, Ida	1918	1995
Lymon, Frankie	1942	1968
Lynde, Paul	1926	1982
Lynn, Diana	1926	1971
MacDonald, Jeanette	1903	1965
Mack, Ted	1904	1976
MacKenzie, Gisele	1927	2003
MacLane, Barton	1902	1969
MacMurray, Fred	1908	1991
MacRae, Gordon	1921	1986
Macready, George	1909	1973
Madison, Guy	1922	1996
Magnani, Anna	1908	1973
Mancini, Henry	1924	1994
Main, Marjorie	1890	1975
Malle, Louis	1932	1995
Mann, Herbie	1930	2003
Mansfield, Jayne	1932	1967
Mantovani, Annunzio	1905	1980
Marais, Jean	1913	1998
March, Fredric	1897	1975
March, Hal	1920	1970
Marchand, Nancy	1928	2000
Marley, Bob	1945	1981
Marshall, Brenda	1915	1992
Marshall, E.G.	1910	1998
Marshall, Herbert	1890	1966
Martin, Dean	1917	1995
Martin, Mary	1913	1990
Martin, Ross	1920	1981
Marvin, Lee	1924	1987
Marx, Arthur (Harpo)	1888	1964
Marx, Herbert (Zeppo)	1901	1979
Marx, Julius (Groucho)	1890	1977
Marx, Leonard (Chico)	1886	1961
Marx, Milton (Gummo)	1893	1977
Mason, James	1909	1984
Massey, Daniel	1933	1998
Massey, Raymond	1896	1983
Mastroianni, Marcello	1924	1996
Matthau, Walter	1920	2000
Mature, Victor	1916	1999
Maxwell, Marilyn	1921	1972
Mayer, Louis B.	1885	1957
Mayfield, Curtis	1942	1999
Maynard, Ken	1895	1973
Mazurki, Mike	1909	1990
McCartney, Linda	1941	1998
McClure, Doug	1935	1995
McCormack, John	1884	1945
McCrary, Tex	1910	2003
McCrea, Joel	1905	1990
McDaniel, Hattie	1895	1952
McDowall, Roddy	1928	1998
McFarland, George "Spanky"	1928	1993
McGuire, Dorothy	1916	2001
McHugh, Frank	1899	1981
McIntire, John	1907	1991
McKay, Gardner	1932	2001
McKern, Leo	1920	2002
McLaglen, Victor	1883	1959
McMahon, Horace	1907	1971
McNeill, Don	1907	1979
McQueen, Butterfly	1911	1995
McQueen, Steve	1930	1980
Meadows, Audrey	1924	1996
Medford, Kay	1920	1980
Meek, Donald	1880	1946
Meeker, Ralph	1920	1989
Melba, Nellie	1861	1931
Melchior, Lauritz	1890	1973
Menjou, Adolphe	1890	1963
Menken, Helen	1902	1966
Menuhin, Yehudi	1916	1999
Mercouri, Melina	1925	1994
Mercury, Freddie	1946	1991
Meredith, Burgess	1909	1997
Merman, Ethel	1908	1984
Merrick, David	1911	2000
Merrill, Gary	1915	1990
Mifune, Toshiro	1920	1997

Name	Born	Died	Name	Born	Died	Name	Born	Died
Milland, Ray	1905	1986	Orbison, Roy	1936	1988	Reinhardt, Max	1873	1943
Miller, Glenn	1904	1944	Ormandy, Eugene	1899	1985	Remick, Lee	1935	1991
Miller, Marilyn	1898	1936	O'Sullivan, Maureen	1911	1998	Renaldo, Duncan	1904	1980
Miller, Roger	1936	1992	Ouspenskaya, Maria	1876	1949	Rennie, Michael	1909	1971
Mills, Harry	1913	1982	Owen, Reginald	1887	1972	Renoir, Jean	1894	1979
Minnevitch, Borrah	1903	1955				Rettig, Tommy	1941	1996
Mineo, Sal	1939	1976	Paderewski, Ignace	1860	1941	Reynolds, Marjorie	1923	1997
Mingus, Charles	1922	1979	Page, Geraldine	1924	1987	Rich, Charlie	1932	1995
Miranda, Carmen	1913	1955	Pakula, Alan	1928	1998	Richardson, Ralph	1902	1983
Mitchell, Cameron	1918	1994	Pallette, Eugene	1889	1954	Riddle, Nelson	1921	1985
Mitchell, Thomas	1892	1962	Palmer, Lilli	1914	1986	Ripperton, Minnie	1947	1979
Mitchum, Robert	1917	1997	Palmer, Robert	1949	2003	Ritchard, Cyril	1898	1977
Mix, Tom	1880	1940	Pangborn, Franklin	1894	1958	Ritter, John	1948	2003
Monica, Corbett	1930	1998	Parks, Bert	1914	1992	Ritter, Tex	1907	1974
Monroe, Marilyn	1926	1962	Parks, Larry	1914	1975	Ritter, Thelma	1905	1969
Monroe, Vaughn	1911	1973	Pasternack, Josef A.	1881	1940	Ritz, Al	1901	1965
Montand, Yves	1921	1991	Pastor, Tony (vaudevillian)	1837	1908	Ritz, Harry	1906	1986
Montez, Maria	1917	1951	Pastor, Tony (bandleader)	1907	1969	Ritz, Jimmy	1903	1985
Montgomery, Elizabeth	1933	1995	Patti, Adelina	1843	1919	Robards, Jason	1922	2000
Montgomery, George	1916	2000	Patti, Carlotta	1840	1889	Robbins, Jerome	1918	1998
Montgomery, Robert	1904	1981	Patrick, Gail	1911	1980	Robbins, Marty	1925	1982
Moore, Clayton	1914	1999	Pavlova, Anna	1885	1931	Robeson, Paul	1898	1976
Moore, Colleen	1900	1988	Paycheck, Johnny	1938	2003	Robinson, Bill	1878	1949
Moore, Dudley	1935	2002	Payne, John	1912	1989	Robinson, Edward G.	1893	1973
Moore, Grace	1901	1947	Pearl, Minnie	1912	1996	Rochester (E. Anderson)	1905	1977
Moore, Garry	1914	1993	Peck, Gregory	1916	2003	Roddenberry, Gene	1921	1991
Moore, Victor	1876	1962	Peerce, Jan	1904	1984	Rodgers, Jimmie	1897	1933
Moorehead, Agnes	1906	1974	Pendleton, Nat	1899	1967	Rogers, Buddy	1904	1999
Morgan, Dennis	1910	1994	Penner, Joe	1905	1941	Rogers, Fred	1928	2003
Morgan, Frank	1890	1949	Peppard, George	1928	1994	Rogers, Ginger	1911	1995
Morgan, Helen	1900	1941	Perkins, Anthony	1932	1992	Rogers, Roy	1911	1998
Morgan, Henry	1915	1994	Perkins, Carl	1932	1998	Rogers, Will	1879	1935
Morley, Robert	1908	1992	Perkins, Marlin	1905	1986	Roland, Gilbert	1905	1994
Morris, Chester	1901	1970	Peters, Jean	1926	2000	Rolle, Esther	1920?	1998
Morris, Greg	1934	1996	Peters, Susan	1921	1952	Rollins, Howard	1950	1996
Morris, Wayne	1914	1959	Phillips, John	1935	2001	Roman, Ruth	1924	1999
Morrison, Jim	1943	1971	Phoenix, River	1970	1993	Romero, Cesar	1907	1994
Morrow, Vic	1932	1982	Piaf, Edith	1915	1963	Rooney, Pat	1880	1962
Mostel, Zero	1915	1977	Pickens, Slim	1919	1983	Rose, Billy	1899	1966
Mowbray, Alan	1897	1969	Pickford, Mary	1893	1979	Rossellini, Roberto	1906	1977
Mulhare, Edward	1923	1997	Picon, Molly	1898	1992	Rowan, Dan	1922	1987
Mulligan, Gerry	1927	1996	Pidgeon, Walter	1897	1984	Rubinstein, Artur	1887	1982
Mulligan, Richard	1932	2000	Pinza, Ezio	1892	1957	Ruggles, Charles	1886	1970
Muni, Paul	1895	1967	Pitts, Zasu	1898	1963	Russell, Gail	1924	1961
Munshin, Jules	1915	1970	Plato, Dana	1964	1999	Russell, Harold	1914	2002
Murphy, Audie	1924	1971	Pleasence, Donald	1919	1995	Russell, Lillian	1861	1922
Murphy, George	1902	1992	Pons, Lily	1904	1976	Russell, Rosalind	1911	1976
Murray, Arthur	1895	1991	Ponselle, Rosa	1897	1981	Rutherford, Margaret	1892	1972
Murray, Kathryn	1906	1999	Porter, Nyree Dawn	1940	2001	Ryan, Irene	1903	1973
Murray, Mae	1885	1965	Powell, Dick	1904	1963	Ryan, Robert	1909	1973
			Powell, Eleanor	1912	1982			
Nagel, Conrad	1896	1970	Powell, William	1892	1984	Sabu	1924	1963
Naish, J. Carroll	1900	1973	Power, Tyrone	1913	1958	Sargent, Dick	1933	1994
Naldi, Nita	1898	1961	Preminger, Otto	1905	1986	St. Cyr, Lili	1917	1999
Nance, Jack	1943	1997	Presley, Elvis	1935	1977	St. Denis, Ruth	1877	1968
Natwick, Mildred	1908	1994	Preston, Robert	1918	1987	Sakall, S.Z.	1884	1955
Negri, Pola	1897	1987	Price, Vincent	1911	1993	Sale (Chic), Charles	1885	1936
Nelson, Harriet (Hilliard)	1909	1994	Prima, Louis	1911	1978	Sanders, George	1906	1972
Nelson, Ozzie	1906	1975	Prinze, Freddie	1954	1977	Savalas, Telly	1924	1994
Nelson, Rick	1940	1985	Prowse, Juliet	1936	1996	Schildkraut, Joseph	1895	1964
Nesbit, Evelyn	1885	1967	Puente, Tito	1923	2000	Schipa, Tito	1889	1965
Newley, Anthony	1931	1999	Pyle, Denver	1920	1997	Schlesinger, John	1926	2003
Newton, Robert	1905	1956				Schnabel, Artur	1882	1951
Nicholas, Harold	1924	2000	Quayle, Anthony	1913	1989	Schneider, Romy	1938	1982
Nijinsky, Vaslav	1890	1950	Questel, Mae	1908	1998	Scott, George C.	1927	1999
Nilsson, Anna Q.	1893	1974	Quinn, Anthony	1915	2001	Scott, Hazel	1920	1981
Niven, David	1909	1983	Quintero, José	1924	1999	Scott, Martha	1914	2003
Nolan, Lloyd	1902	1985				Scott, Randolph	1898	1987
Normand, Mabel	1894	1930	Rabb, Ellis	1930	1998	Scott, Zachary	1914	1965
Notorious B.I.G.	1972	1997	Rabbit, Eddie	1941	1998	Scott-Siddons, Mrs.	1843	1896
Novarro, Ramon	1899	1968	Radner, Gilda	1946	1989	Seberg, Jean	1938	1979
Nureyev, Rudolf	1938	1993	Raft, George	1895	1980	Seeley, Blossom	1892	1974
			Rains, Claude	1890	1967	Segovia, Andres	1893	1987
Oakie, Jack	1903	1978	Ralston, Esther	1902	1994	Selena	1971	1995
Oakley, Annie	1860	1926	Ramone, Dee Dee	1952	2002	Sellers, Peter	1925	1980
Oates, Warren	1928	1982	Ramone, Joey	1951	2001	Selznick, David O.	1902	1965
Oberon, Merle	1911	1979	Rampal, Jean-Pierre	1922	2000	Sennett, Mack	1884	1960
O'Brien, Edmond	1915	1985	Rathbone, Basil	1892	1967	Senor Wences	1896	1999
O'Brien, Pat	1899	1983	Ratoff, Gregory	1897	1960	Serling, Rod	1924	1975
O'Connell, Arthur	1908	1981	Ray, Aldo	1926	1991	Shakur, Tupac	1971	1996
O'Connell, Helen	1921	1993	Ray, Johnnie	1927	1990	Shaw, Robert (actor)	1927	1978
O'Connor, Carroll	1924	2001	Rayburn, Gene	1917	1999	Shaw, Robert (conductor)	1916	1999
O'Connor, Donald	1925	2003	Raye, Martha	1916	1994	Shawn, Ted	1891	1972
O'Connor, Una	1880	1959	Raymond, Gene	1908	1998	Shean, Al	1868	1949
O'Keefe, Dennis	1908	1968	Redding, Otis	1941	1967	Shearer, Norma	1902	1983
Oland, Warner	1880	1938	Redgrave, Michael	1908	1985	Sheridan, Ann	1915	1967
Olcott, Chauncey	1860	1932	Reed, Donna	1921	1986	Shore, Dinah	1917	1994
Oliver, Edna May	1883	1942	Reed, Oliver	1938	1999	Shubert, Lee	1875	1953
Olivier, Laurence	1907	1989	Reed, Robert	1932	1992	Shull, Richard B.	1929	1999
Olsen, Ole	1892	1963	Reeves, George	1914	1959	Siddons, Mrs. Sarah	1755	1831
O'Neill, James	1849	1920	Reeves, Steve	1926	2000	Sidney, Sylvia	1910	1999

Name	Born	Died	Name	Born	Died	Name	Born	Died
Signoret, Simone	1921	1985	Terry, Ellen	1847	1928	Warner, H. B.	1876	1958
Silverheels, Jay	1912	1980	Thalberg, Irving	1899	1936	Washington, Dinah	1924	1963
Silvers, Phil	1912	1985	Thaw, John	1942	2002	Waters, Ethel	1896	1977
Sim, Alastair	1900	1976	Thigpen, Lynne	1948	2003	Waxman, Al	1935	2001
Simmons, Richard	1948	2003	Thomas, Danny	1912	1991	Wayne, David	1914	1995
Simone, Nina	1933	2003	Thomas, John Charles	1892	1960	Wayne, John	1907	1979
Sims, Irene	1930	2001	Thorndike, Sybil	1882	1976	Webb, Clifton	1891	1966
Sinatra, Frank	1915	1998	Tibbett, Lawrence	1896	1960	Webb, Jack	1920	1982
Sinclair, Madge	1938	1995	Tierney, Gene	1920	1991	Weems, Ted	1901	1963
Siskel, Gene	1946	1999	Tiny Tim	1932?	1996	Weissmuller, Johnny	1904	1984
Sitka, Emil	1914	1998	Tippett, Sir Michael	1905	1998	Welk, Lawrence	1903	1992
Sjostrom, Victor	1879	1960	Todd, Michael	1909	1958	Welles, Orson	1915	1985
Skelton, Red	1913	1997	Tomlinson, David	1917	2000	Wellman, William	1896	1975
Skinner, Otis	1858	1942	Tone, Franchot	1903	1968	Werner, Oskar	1922	1984
Smith, Alexis	1921	1992	Torme, Mel	1925	1999	West, Mae	1893	1980
Smith, Buffalo Bob	1917	1998	Toscanini, Arturo	1867	1957	Weston, Jack	1924	1996
Smith, C. Aubrey	1863	1948	Tracy, Lee	1898	1968	Whale, James	1889	1957
Smith, Kate	1907	1986	Tracy, Spencer	1900	1967	Wheeler, Bert	1895	1968
Smith, Kent	1907	1985	Traubel, Helen	1903	1972	White, Barry	1944	2003
Snow, Hank	1914	1999	Travers, Henry	1874	1965	White, Jesse	1919	1997
Solti, George	1912	1997	Treacher, Arthur	1894	1975	White, Pearl	1889	1938
Sondergaard, Gale	1899	1985	Tree, Herbert Beerbohm	1853	1917	Whiteman, Paul	1891	1967
Sothern, Ann	1909	2001	Trevor, Claire	1909	2000	Whitty, May	1865	1948
Sousa, John Philip	1854	1932	Truex, Ernest	1890	1973	Wickes, Mary	1910	1995
Sparks, Ned	1884	1957	Truffaut, Francois	1932	1984	Wilde, Cornel	1918	1989
Springfield, Dusty	1939	1999	Tucker, Forrest	1919	1986	Wilder, Billy	1906	2002
Stack, Robert	1919	2003	Tucker, Richard	1913	1975	Wilding, Michael	1912	1979
Stander, Lionel	1908	1994	Tucker, Sophie	1884	1966	Williams, Bert	1877	1922
Stanley, Kim	1925	2001	Turner, Lana	1920	1995	Williams, Guy	1924	1989
Stanwyck, Barbara	1907	1990	Turpin, Ben	1874	1940	Williams, Hank Sr.	1923	1953
Steiger, Rod	1925	2002	Twelvetrees, Helen	1908	1959	Wills, Bob	1905	1975
Stern, Isaac	1920	2001	Twitty, Conway	1933	1993	Wills, Chill	1903	1978
Stevens, Craig	1918	2000				Wilson, Carl	1946	1998
Stevens, Inger	1934	1970	Urich, Robert	1947	2002	Wilson, Dennis	1944	1983
Stevens, Mark	1916	1994				Wilson, Dooley	1894	1953
Stevenson, McLean	1929	1996	Valens, Ritchie	1941	1959	Wilson, Flip	1933	1998
Stewart, James	1908	1997	Valentino, Rudolph	1895	1926	Wilson, Marie	1917	1972
Stickney, Dorothy	1896	1998	Vallee, Rudy	1901	1986	Windsor, Marie	1919	2000
Stokowski, Leopold	1882	1977	Van, Bobby	1928	1980	Winninger, Charles	1884	1969
Stone, Lewis	1879	1953	Vance, Vivian	1912	1979	Withers, Grant	1904	1959
Stone, Milburn	1904	1980	Van Fleet, Jo.	1922	1996	Wong, Anna May	1907	1961
Straight, Beatrice	1918	2001	Varney, Jim.	1949	2000	Wood, Natalie	1938	1981
Strasberg, Lee	1901	1982	Vaughan, Sarah	1924	1990	Wood, Peggy	1892	1978
Strasberg, Susan	1938	1999	Veidt, Conrad	1893	1943	Woolley, Monty	1888	1963
Sturges, Preston	1898	1959	Velez, Lupe	1908	1944	Worth, Irene	1916	2002
Sullivan, Margaret	1911	1960	Vera-Ellen	1926	1981	Wyler, William	1902	1981
Sullivan, Barry	1912	1994	Verdon, Gwen	1925	2000	Wynette, Tammy	1942	1998
Sullivan, Ed	1902	1974	Vernon, Jackie	1925	1987	Wynn, Ed	1886	1966
Sullivan, Francis L.	1903	1956	Villechaize, Herve	1943	1993	Wynn, Keenan	1916	1986
Summerville, Slim	1892	1946	Vincent, Gene	1935	1971			
Swanson, Gloria	1899	1983	Vicious, Sid.	1958	1979	Yankovic, Frank	1915	1998
Swarthout, Gladys.	1904	1969	Vinson, Helen	1907	1999	York, Dick	1929	1992
Switzer, Carl "Alfalfa"	1926	1959	Von Stroheim, Erich	1885	1957	Young, Clara Kimball	1890	1960
			Von Zell, Harry	1906	1981	Young, Gig	1913	1978
Talbot, Lyle	1904	1996				Young, Loretta	1913	2000
Talmadge, Norma	1893	1957	Walker, Junior	1942	1995	Young, Robert	1907	1998
Tamiroff, Akim	1899	1972	Walker, Nancy	1922	1992	Young, Roland	1887	1953
Tandy, Jessica	1909	1994	Walker, Robert	1918	1951	Youngman, Henny	1906	1998
Tanguay, Eva	1878	1947	Wallenda, Karl	1905	1978			
Tati, Jacques.	1908	1982	Walsh, J. T.	1943	1998	Zanuck, Darryl F.	1902	1979
Taylor, Deems.	1885	1966	Walsh, Raoul	1887	1980	Zappa, Frank	1940	1993
Taylor, Dub	1907	1994	Walston, Ray	1914	2001	Zevon, Warren	1947	2003
Taylor, Estelle	1899	1958	Walter, Bruno	1876	1962	Zinneman, Fred	1907	1997
Taylor, Laurette	1887	1946	Ward, Helen	1916	1998	Ziegfeld, Florenz	1869	1932
Taylor, Robert	1911	1969	Waring, Fred	1900	1984	Zukor, Adolph	1873	1976

Original Names of Selected Entertainers

EDIE ADAMS: Elizabeth Edith Enke
EDDIE ALBERT: Edward Albert Heimberger
ALAN ALDA: Alphonso D'Abruzzo
JASON ALEXANDER: Jay Greenspan
FRED ALLEN: John Sullivan
WOODY ALLEN: Allen Konigsberg
JUNE ALLYSON: Ella Geisman
JULIE ANDREWS: Julia Wells
EVE ARDEN: Eunice Quedens
BEATRICE ARTHUR: Bernice Frankel
JEAN ARTHUR: Gladys Greene
FRED ASTAIRE: Frederick Austerlitz
BABYFACE: Kenneth Edmonds
LAUREN BACALL: Betty Joan Perske
ERYKAH BADU: Erica Wright
ANNE BANCROFT: Anna Maria Italiano
GENE BARRY: Eugene Klass
PAT BENATAR: Patricia Andrejewski
TONY BENNETT: Anthony Benedetto

IRVING BERLIN: Israel Baline
JACK BENNY: Benjamin Kubelsky
JOEY BISHOP: Joseph Gottlieb
THE BIG BOPPER: Jiles Perry "J.P." Richardson
BONO (VOX): Paul Hewson
VICTOR BORGE: Borge Rosenbaum
DAVID BOWIE: David Robert Jones
BOY GEORGE: George Alan O'Dowd
FANNY BRICE: Fanny Borach
CHARLES BRONSON: Charles Buchinski
ALBERT BROOKS: Albert Einstein
MEL BROOKS: Melvin Kaminsky
GEORGE BURNS: Nathan Birnbaum
ELLEN BURSTYN: Edna Gilhooley
RICHARD BURTON: Richard Jenkins
RED BUTTONS: Aaron Chwatt
NICOLAS CAGE: Nicholas Coppola
MICHAEL CAINE: Maurice Micklewhite

MARIA CALLAS: Maria Kalogeropoulos
DIAHANN CARROLL: Carol Diahann Johnson
JACKIE CHAN: Chan Kwong-Sung
CYD CHARISSE: Tula Finklea
RAY CHARLES: Ray Charles Robinson
CHUBBY CHECKER: Ernest Evans
CHER: Cherilyn Sarkisian
PATSY CLINE: Virginia Patterson Hensley
LEE J. COBB: Leo Jacoby
CLAUDETTE COLBERT: Lily Chauchoin
ALICE COOPER: Vincent Furnier
DAVID COPPERFIELD: David Kotkin
HOWARD COSELL: Howard Cohen
ELVIS COSTELLO: Declan McManus
LOU COSTELLO: Louis Cristillo
PETER COYOTE: Peter Cohon
MICHAEL CRAWFORD: Michael Dumble-Smith

TOM CRUISE: Thomas Mapother IV
TONY CURTIS: Bernard Schwartz
VIC DAMONE: Vito Farinola
RODNEY DANGERFIELD: Jacob Cohen
BOBBY DARIN: Walden Robert Cassotto
DORIS DAY: Doris von Kappelhoff
YVONNE DE CARLO: Peggy Middleton
SANDRA DEE: Alexandra Zuck
JOHN DENVER: Henry John
Deutschendorf Jr.
BO DEREK: Mary Cathleen Collins
DANNY DEVITO: Daniel Michaeli
ANGIE DICKINSON: Angeline Brown
BO DIDDLEY: Elias Bates
PHYLLIS DILLER: Phyllis Driver
DMX: Earl TROY DONAHUE: Merle
Johnson Jr.
KIRK DOUGLAS: Issur Danielovitch
MELVYN DOUGLAS: Melvyn Hesselberg
BOB DYLAN: Robert Zimmerman
BARBARA EDEN: Barbara Huffman
ELVIRA: Cassandra Peterson
EMINEM: Marshall Mathers
ENYA: Eithne Ni Bhraonian
DALE EVANS: Frances Smith
CHAD EVERETT: Raymond Cramton
DOUGLAS FAIRBANKS: Douglas
Ullman
MORGAN FAIRCHILD: Patsy McClenny
JAMIE FARR: Jameel Farah
ALICE FAYE: Alice Jeanne Leppert
STEPIN FETCHIT: Lincoln Perry
W.C. FIELDS: William Claude Dukenfield
BARRY FITZGERALD: William Shields
JOAN FONTAINE: Joan de Havilland
JODIE FOSTER: Alicia Christian Foster
REDD FOXX: John Sanford
ANTHONY FRANCIOSA: Anthony
Papaleo
ARLENE FRANCIS: Arlene Kazanjian
CONNIE FRANCIS: Concetta Franconero
GRETA GARBO: Greta Gustafsson
VINCENT GARDENIA: Vincent
Scognamiglio
JOHN GARFIELD: Julius Garfinkle
JUDY GARLAND: Frances Gumm
JAMES GARNER: James Bumgarner
CRYSTAL GAYLE: Brenda Gayle Webb
KATHIE LEE GIFFORD: Kathie Epstein
WHOOPI GOLDBERG: Caryn Johnson
EYDIE GORME: Edith Gormezano
STEWART GRANGER: James Stewart
CARY GRANT: Archibald Leach
LEE GRANT: Lyova Rosenthal
JOEL GREY: Joe Katz
ROBERT GUILLAUME: Robert Williams
BUDDY HACKETT: Leonard Hacker
HAMMER: Stanley Kirk Burrell
JEAN HARLOW: Harlean Carpentier
REX HARRISON: Reginald Carey
LAURENCE HARVEY: Larushka Skikne
HELEN HAYES: Helen Brown
SUSAN HAYWARD: Edythe Marriner
RITA HAYWORTH: Margarita Cansino
PEE-WEE HERMAN: Paul Reubenfeld
CHARLTON HESTON: John Charlton
Carter
WILLIAM HOLDEN: William Beedle
BILLIE HOLIDAY: Eleanora Fagan
JUDY HOLLIDAY: Judith Tuvim
BOB HOPE: Leslie Townes Hope
HARRY HOUDINI: Ehrich Weiss
LESLIE HOWARD: Leslie Stainer
HOWLIN' WOLF: Chester Burnett
ROCK HUDSON: Roy Scherer Jr. (later
Fitzgerald)
ENGELBERT HUMPERDINCK: Arnold
Dorsey
KIM HUNTER: Janet Cole
BETTY HUTTON: Betty Thornberg
ICE CUBE: O'Shea Jackson
ICE-T: Tracy Morrow
BILLY IDOL: William Broad
DAVID JANSSEN: David Meyer
JAY-Z: Shawn Carter
ANN JILLIAN: Anne Nauseda
ELTON JOHN: Reginald Dwight

DON JOHNSON: Donald Wayne
AL JOLSON: Asa Yoelson
JENNIFER JONES: Phylis Isley
TOM JONES: Thomas Woodward
LOUIS JOURDAN: Louis Gendre
WYNONNA JUDD: Christina Ciminella
BORIS KARLOFF: William Henry Pratt
DANNY KAYE: David Kaminsky
DIANE KEATON: Diane Hall
MICHAEL KEATON: Michael Douglas
CHAKA KHAN: Yvette Stevens
CAROLE KING: Carole Klein
LARRY KING: Larry Zeiger
BEN KINGSLEY: Krishna Banji
NASTASSJA KINSKI: Nastassja
Naksyznyski
TED KNIGHT: Tadeus Wladyslaw
Konopka
CHERYL LADD: Cheryl Stoppelmoor
VERONICA LAKE: Constance Ockleman
HEDY LAMARR: Hedwig Kiesler
DOROTHY LAMOUR: Mary Leta Dorothy
Slaton
MICHAEL LANDON: Eugene Orowitz
MARIO LANZA: Alfredo Cocozza
QUEEN LATIFAH: Dana Owens
STAN LAUREL: Arthur Jefferson
STEVE LAWRENCE: Sidney Leibowitz
BRENDA LEE: Brenda Mae Tarpley
GYPSY ROSE LEE: Rose Louise Hovick
MICHELLE LEE: Michelle Dusiak
PEGGY LEE: Norma Egstrom
JANET LEIGH: Jeanette Morrison
VIVIEN LEIGH: Vivian Hartley
HUEY LEWIS: Hugh Cregg
JERRY LEWIS: Joseph Levitch
LIL' KIM: Kimberly Denise Jones
CAROLE LOMBARD: Jane Peters
JACK LORD: John Joseph Ryan
SOPHIA LOREN: Sophia Scicolone
PETER LORRE: Laszio Lowenstein
MYRNA LOY: Myrna Williams
BELA LUGOSI: Bela Ferenc Blasko
MOMS MABLEY: Loretta Mary Aitken
SHIRLEY MACLAINE: Shirley Beaty
ELLE MACPHERSON: Eleanor Gow
MADONNA: Madonna Louise Veronica
Ciccone
LEE MAJORS: Harvey Lee Yeary 2nd
KARL MALDEN: Mladen Sekulovich
BARRY MANILOW: Barry Alan Pincus
JAYNE MANSFIELD: Vera Jane Palmer
MARILYN MANSON: Brian Warner
FREDRIC MARCH: Frederick Bickel
PETER MARSHALL: Pierre LaCock
WALTER MATTHAU: Walter
Matuschanskayasky
DEAN MARTIN: Dino Crocetti
MEAT LOAF: Marvin Lee Aday
FREDDIE MERCURY: Frederick Bulsara
ETHEL MERMAN: Ethel Zimmerman
GEORGE MICHAEL: Georgios
Panayiotou
RAY MILLAND: Reginald Truscott-Jones
ANN MILLER: Lucille Collier
JONI MITCHELL: Roberta Joan
Anderson
MOBY: Richard Melville Hall
MARILYN MONROE: Norma Jean
Mortenson (later Baker)
YVES MONTAND: Ivo Livi
RON MOODY: Ronald Moodnick
DEMI MOORE: Demetria Guynes
GARRY MOORE: Thomas Garrison
Morfit
RITA MORENO: Rosita Alverio
HARRY MORGAN: Harry Bratsburg
MR. T: Lawrence Tero
PAUL MUNI: Muni Weisenfreund
MIKE NICHOLS: Michael Igor
Peschowsky
CHUCK NORRIS: Carlos Ray
NOTORIOUS B.I.G.: Christopher Wallace
HUGH O'BRIAN: Hugh Krampke
MAUREEN O'HARA: Maureen
Fitzsimons

OZZY OSBOURNE: John Michael
Osbourne
PATTI PAGE: Clara Ann Fowler
JACK PALANCE: Walter Palanuik
BERT PARKS: Bert Jacobson
MINNIE PEARL: Sarah Ophelia Cannon
BERNADETTE PETERS: Bernadette
Lazzaro
EDITH PIAF: Edith Gassion
SLIM PICKENS: Louis Lindley
MARY PICKFORD: Gladys Smith
STEFANIE POWERS: Stefania
Federkiewicz
PAULA PRENTISS: Paula Ragusa
ROBERT PRESTON: Robert Preston
Meservey
PRINCE (THE ARTIST): Prince Rogers
Nelson
DEE DEE RAMONE: Douglas Colvin
JOEY RAMONE: Jeffrey Hyman
JOHNNY RAMONE: John Cummings
TOMMY RAMONE: Tom Erdelyi
TONY RANDALL: Leonard Rosenberg
MARTHA RAYE: Margaret O'Reed
DONNA REED: Donna Belle Mullenger
DELLA REESE: Delloreese Patricia Early
BUSTA RHYMES: Trevor Smith Jr.
JOAN RIVERS: Joan Sandra Molinsky
EDWARD G. ROBINSON: Emmanuel
Goldenberg
THE ROCK: Dwayne Johnson
GINGER ROGERS: Virginia McMath
ROY ROGERS: Leonard Franklin Slye
MICKEY ROONEY: Joe Yule Jr.
JOHNNY ROTTEN: John Lydon
LILLIAN RUSSELL: Helen Leonard
MEG RYAN: Margaret Hyra
WINONA RYDER: Winona Horowitz
SADE: Helen Folsad Abu
SOUPY SALES: Milton Hines
SUSAN SARANDON: Susan Tomaling
SEAL: Samuel Sealhenry
RANDOLPH SCOTT: George Randolph
Crane
JANE SEYMOUR: Joyce Frankenberg
OMAR SHARIF: Michael Shalhoub
CHARLIE SHEEN: Carlos Irwin Estevez
MARTIN SHEEN: Ramon Estevez
BEVERLY SILLS: Belle Silverman
TALIA SHIRE: Talia Coppola
PHIL SILVERS: Philip Silversmith
SINBAD: David Atkins
"BUFFALO BOB" SMITH: Robert
Schmidt
SNOOP DOGGY DOG: Calvin Broadus
ANN SOTHERN: Harriette Lake
ROBERT STACK: Robert Modini
BARBARA STANWYCK: Ruby Stevens
JEAN STAPLETON: Jeanne Murray
RINGO STARR: Richard Starkey
CONNIE STEVENS: Concetta Ingolia
STING: Gordon Sumner
DONNA SUMMER: La Donna Gaines
RIP TAYLOR: Charles Elmer Jr.
ROBERT TAYLOR: Spangler Brugh
DANNY THOMAS: Muzyad Yakhoob,
later Amos Jacobs
TINY TIM: Herbert Khaury
RIP TORN: Elmore Rual Torn Jr.
RANDY TRAVIS: Randy Traywick
SOPHIE TUCKER: Sophia Kalish
TINA TURNER: Annie Mae Bullock
TWIGGY: Leslie Hornby
CONWAY TWITTY: Harold Lloyd Jenkins
RUDOLPH VALENTINO: Rudolpho
D'Antonguolla
FRANKIE VALLI: Frank Castelluccio
SID VICIOUS: John Simon Ritchie
JOHN WAYNE: Marion Morrison
CLIFTON WEBB: Webb Hollenbeck
RAQUEL WELCH: Raquel Tejada
GENE WILDER: Jerome Silberman
SHELLEY WINTERS: Shirley Schrift
STEVIE WONDER: Stevland Morris
JANE WYMAN: Sarah Jane Fulks
GIG YOUNG: Byron Barr
LORETTA YOUNG: Gretchen Michaels

ARTS AND MEDIA

Some Notable Movies, Sept. 2002 – Aug. 2003

Film	Stars	Director
28 Days Later	Cillian Murphy, Brendan Gleeson	Danny Boyle
8 Mile	Eminem, Kim Basinger, Mekhi Phifer, Brittany Murphy, Evan Jones	Curtis Hanson
About Schmidt	Jack Nicholson, Hope Davis, Dermot Mulroney, Kathy Bates	Alexander Payne
Adaptation	Nicolas Cage, Meryl Streep, Chris Cooper, Tilda Swinton, Cara Seymour	Spike Jonze
American Splendor	Paul Giamatti, Hope Davis, featuring Harvey Pekar	Shari Springer Berman & Robert Pulcini
American Wedding	Jason Biggs, Alyson Hannigan, Seann William Scott	Jesse Dylan
Anger Management	Jack Nicholson, Adam Sandler, Marisa Tomei, John Turturro	Peter Segal
Antwone Fisher	Derek Luke, Denzel Washington, Joy Bryant, Salli Richardson	Denzel Washington
Bad Boys II	Martin Lawrence, Will Smith, Gabrielle Union	Michael Bay
Barbershop	Ice Cube, Anthony Anderson, Cedric the Entertainer, Sean Patrick Thomas, Eve	Tim Story
Bend It Like Beckham	Parminder Nagra, Keira Knightley, Jonathan Rhys Meyers	Gurinder Chadha
Bowling for Columbine	Michael Moore	Michael Moore
Bruce Almighty	Jim Carrey, Morgan Freeman, Jennifer Aniston	Tom Shadyac
Catch Me If You Can	Leonardo DiCaprio, Tom Hanks, Christopher Walken, Martin Sheen, Nathalie Baye	Steven Spielberg
Charlie's Angels: Full Throttle	Cameron Diaz, Drew Barrymore, Lucy Liu	McG
Chicago	Richard Gere, Catherine Zeta-Jones, Queen Latifah, Renée Zellweger	Rob Marshall
Confessions of a Dangerous Mind	Drew Barrymore, George Clooney, Julia Roberts, Rutger Hauer, Sam Rockwell	George Clooney
Die Another Day	Pierce Brosnan, Halle Berry, Judi Dench, Toby Stephens, Rosamund Pike	Lee Tamahori
Far From Heaven	Julianne Moore, Dennis Quaid, Dennis Haysbert, Patricia Clarkson, Viola Davis	Todd Haynes
Finding Nemo	Alexander Gould, Albert Brooks, Ellen DeGeneres, Willem Dafoe, Brad Garrett	Andrew Stanton & Lee Unkrich
Freaky Friday	Jamie Lee Curtis, Lindsay Lohan	Mark Waters
Frida	Salma Hayek, Alfred Molina, Ashley Judd	Julie Taymor
Gangs of New York	Leonardo DiCaprio, Cameron Diaz, Daniel Day-Lewis, Jim Broadbent	Martin Scorsese
Harry Potter and the Chamber of Secrets	Daniel Radcliffe, Rupert Grint, Emma Watson, Kenneth Branagh, John Cleese	Chris Columbus
Holes	Shia La Beouf, Sigourney Weaver, Patricia Arquette, Jon Voight	Andrew Davis
The Hours	Meryl Streep, Nicole Kidman, Julianne Moore, Ed Harris, John C. Reilly	Stephen Daldry
The Hulk	Eric Bana, Jennifer Connelly, Nick Nolte	Ang Lee
The Italian Job	Mark Wahlberg, Charlize Theron, Edward Norton, Seth Green	F. Gary Gray
Johnny English	Rowan Atkinson, John Malkovich	Peter Howitt
The Lizzie McGuire Movie	Hilary Duff, Yani Gellman, Adam Lamberg, Ashlie Brillaut, Robert Carradine, Hallie Todd, Jake Thomas	Jim Fall
The Lord of the Rings: The Two Towers	Elijah Wood, Sean Astin, Viggo Mortensen, Ian McKellen, Christopher Lee, Liv Tyler	Peter Jackson
The Matrix: Reloaded	Keanu Reeves, Laurence Fishburne, Carrie-Anne Moss, Hugo Weaving, Jada Pinkett Smith	Andy & Larry Wachowski
A Mighty Wind	Christopher Guest, Eugene Levy, Michael McKean, Harry Shearer, Bob Balaban	Christopher Guest
Nowhere in Africa	Juliane Köhler, Merab Ninidze, Lea Kurka, Matthias Habich, Sidede Onyulo	Caroline Link
The Pianist	Adrien Brody, Thomas Kretschmann	Roman Polanski
Pirates of the Caribbean: Curse of the Black Pearl	Johnny Depp, Orlando Bloom, Geoffrey Rush, Keira Knightley	Gore Verbinski
Punch-Drunk Love	Adam Sandler, Emily Watson, Philip Seymour Hoffman, Luis Guzman	Paul Thomas Anderson
The Quiet American	Michael Caine, Brendan Fraser, Rade Serbedzija, Do Hai Yen	Phillip Noyce
Rabbit Proof Fence	Everlyn Sampi, Tianna Sansbury, Kenneth Branagh, Jason Clarke, David Gulpilil	Phillip Noyce
The Ring	Elijah Wood, Billy Boyd, Dominic Monaghan, Ian McKellen, Sean Astin	Gore Verbinski.
Seabiscuit	Tobey Maguire, Jeff Bridges, Chris Cooper	Gary Ross
Spirited Away	Daveigh Chase, Michael Chiklis, Susan Egan, Lauren Holly, Jason Marsden	Hayao Miyazaki
Spy Kids 3-D: Game Over	Daryl Sabara, Alexa Vega, Sylvester Stallone, Ricardo Montalban	Robert Rodriguez
Talk to Her	Javier Camara, Dario Grandinetti, Rosario Flores, Leonor Watling	Pedro Almodóvar
Terminator 3: Rise of the Machines	Arnold Schwarzenegger, Nick Stahl, Claire Danes	Jonathan Mostow
Whale Rider	Keisha Castle-Hughes, Rawiri Paratene, Cliff Curtis	Niki Caro
X2: X-Men United	Hugh Jackman, Patrick Stewart, Shawn Ashmore, Halle Berry, Alan Cumming, Bruce Davison, Famke Janssen, James Marsden, Ian McKellen, Anna Paquin, Rebecca Romijn-Stamos	Bryan Singer

50 Top-Grossing Movies, 2002

Source: *Variety.* box-office grosses in the U.S. and Canada during calendar year 2002

Rank	Title	Gross (millions)	Rank	Title	Gross (millions)	Rank	Title	Gross (millions)
1.	Spider-Man	$403.7	16.	Minority Report	$132.0	34.	We Were Soldiers	$78.1
2.	Star Wars: Episode II–Attack of the Clones	310.3	17.	The Lord of the Rings: The Fellowship of the Ring	130.9	35.	Barbershop	75.7
3.	The Lord of the Rings: The Two Towers	268.7	18.	The Ring	127.3	36.	The Rookie	75.6
4.	Harry Potter and the Chamber of Secrets	253.0	19.	Sweet Home Alabama	126.2	37.	Spirit: Stallion of Cimarron	73.2
5.	My Big Fat Greek Wedding	228.8	20.	Mr. Deeds	126.2	38.	Two Weeks Notice	72.2
6.	Signs	227.8	21.	The Bourne Identity	121.5	39.	John Q.	71.1
7.	Austin Powers in Goldmember	213.1	22.	The Sum of All Fears	118.5	40.	Divine Secrets of the Ya-Ya Sisterhood	69.6
8.	Men in Black 2	190.4	23.	8 Mile	115.4	41.	Insomnia	67.3
9.	Ice Age	176.4	24.	Black Hawk Down	108.3	42.	Changing Lanes	66.8
10.	Die Another Day	154.7	25.	Catch Me if You Can	104.7	43.	Stuart Little 2	64.8
11.	Scooby-Doo	153.3	26.	Road to Perdition	104.1	44.	Jackass: The Movie	64.2
12.	A Beautiful Mind	149.5	27.	Panic Room	95.3	45.	The Time Machine	56.7
13.	Lilo & Stitch	145.8	28.	Red Dragon	93.0	46.	The Count of Monte Cristo	54.2
14.	XXX	141.2	29.	The Scorpion King	90.5	47.	Unfaithful	52.8
15.	The Santa Clause 2	138.4	30.	Spy Kids 2	85.6	48.	Like Mike	51.4
			31.	Blade 2	81.7	49.	The Tuxedo	50.4
			32.	Snow Dogs	81.2	50.	Gangs of New York	50.1
			33.	Maid in Manhattan	78.7			

National Film Registry, 1989-2002

Source: National Film Registry, Library of Congress

"Culturally, historically, or esthetically significant" films placed on the registry. * = selected in 2002.

Abbott and Costello Meet Frankenstein (1948)
Adam's Rib (1949)
The Adventures of Robin Hood (1938)
The African Queen (1951)
Alien (1979)*
All About Eve (1950)
All My Babies (1953)*
All That Heaven Allows (1955)
All That Jazz (1979)
All Quiet on the Western Front (1930)
All the King's Men (1949)
An American in Paris (1951)
America, America (1963)
American Graffiti (1973)
A Movie (1958)
Annie Hall (1977)
The Apartment (1960)
Apocalypse Now (1979)
The Awful Truth (1937)
The Bad and the Beautiful (1952)*
Badlands (1973)
The Band Wagon (1953)
The Bank Dick (1940)
The Battle of San Pietro (1945)
Beauty and the Beast (1991)*
Ben-Hur (1926)
The Best Years of Our Lives (1946)
Big Business (1929)
The Big Parade (1925)
The Big Sleep (1946)
The Birth of a Nation (1915)
The Black Pirate (1926)
Blacksmith Scene (1893)
The Black Stallion (1979)*
Blade Runner (1982)
The Blood of Jesus (1941)
Bonnie and Clyde (1967)
Boyz N the Hood (1991)*
Bride of Frankenstein (1935)
The Bridge on the River Kwai (1957)
Bringing Up Baby (1938)
Broken Blossoms (1919)
Cabaret (1972)
Carmen Jones (1954)
Casablanca (1942)
Castro Street (1966)
Cat People (1942)
Chan Is Missing (1982)
The Cheat (1915)
Chinatown (1974)
Chulas Fronteras (1976)
Citizen Kane (1941)
The City (1939)
City Lights (1931)
Civilization (1916)
Cologne: From the Diary of Ray and Esther (1939)
The Conversation (1974)
The Cool World (1963)
Cops (1922)
A Corner in Wheat (1909)
The Crowd (1928)
Czechoslovakia 1968 (1968)
David Holzman's Diary (1968)
The Day the Earth Stood Still (1951)
Dead Birds (1964)
The Deer Hunter (1978)
Destry Rides Again (1939)
Detour (1946)
Dodsworth (1936)
The Docks of New York (1928)
Dog Star Man (1964)
Don't Look Back (1967)
Do the Right Thing (1989)
Double Indemnity (1944)
Dracula (1931)
Dr. Strangelove (or, How I Learned to Stop Worrying and Love the Bomb)(1964)
Duck Amuck (1953)
Duck Soup (1933)

Easy Rider (1969)
Eaux D'Artifice (1953)
El Norte (1983)
The Emperor Jones (1933)
The Endless Summer (1966)*
E.T.: The Extra-Terrestrial (1982)
Evidence of the Film (1913)
The Exploits of Elaine (1914)
The Fall of the House of Usher (1928)
Fantasia (1940)
Fatty's Tintype Tangle (1915)
Five Easy Pieces (1970)
Flash Gordon serial (1936)
Footlight Parade (1933)
Force of Evil (1948)
The Forgotten Frontier (1931)
42nd Street (1933)
The Four Horsemen of the Apocalypse (1921)
Frankenstein (1931)
Frank Film (1973)
Freaks (1932)
The Freshman (1925)
From Here to Eternity (1953)*
From the Manger to the Cross (1912)
From Stump to Ship (1930)*
Fuji (1974)*
Fury (1936)
The General (1927)
Gerald McBoing Boing (1951)
Gertie the Dinosaur (1914)
Gigi (1958)
The Godfather (1972)
The Godfather, Part II (1974)
The Gold Rush (1925)
Gone With the Wind (1939)
GoodFellas (1990)
The Graduate (1967)
The Grapes of Wrath (1940)
Grass (1925)
The Great Dictator (1940)
The Great Train Robbery (1903)
Greed (1924)
Gun Crazy (1949)
Gunga Din (1939)
Harlan County, U.S.A. (1976)
Harold and Maude (1972)
The Heiress (1949)
Hell's Hinges (1916)
High Noon (1952)
High School (1968)
Hindenburg Disaster Newsreel Footage (1937)
His Girl Friday (1940)
The Hitch-Hiker (1953)
Hoosiers (1986)
Hospital (1970)
The Hospital (1971)
The House in the Middle (1954)
How Green Was My Valley (1941)
How the West Was Won (1962)
The Hustler (1961)
I Am a Fugitive From a Chain Gang (1932)
The Immigrant (1917)
In the Heat of the Night (1967)*
In the Land of the Head-Hunters aka In the Land of the War Canoes (1914)
Intolerance (1916)
Invasion of the Body Snatchers (1956)
It (1927)
It Happened One Night (1934)
It's a Wonderful Life (1946)
The Italian (1915)
Jammin' the Blues (1944)
Jam Session (1942)
Jaws (1975)
Jazz on a Summer's Day (1959)
The Jazz Singer (1927)
Killer of Sheep (1977)
King: A Filmed Record . . .Montgomery to Memphis (1970)
King Kong (1933)

The Kiss (1896)
Kiss Me Deadly (1955)
Knute Rockne, All American (1940)
Koyaanisqatsi (1983)
The Lady Eve (1941)
Lady Windermere's Fan (1925)*
Lambchops (1929)
The Land Beyond the Sunset (1912)
Lassie Come Home (1943)
The Last of the Mohicans (1920)
The Last Picture Show (1972)
Laura (1944)
Lawrence of Arabia (1962)
The Learning Tree (1969)
Let's All Go to the Lobby (1957)
Letter From an Unknown Woman (1948)
The Life and Death of 9413—A Hollywood Extra (1928)
Life and Times of Rosie the Riveter (1980)
The Life of Emile Zola (1937)
Little Caesar (1930)
The Little Fugitive (1953)
Little Miss Marker (1934)
The Living Desert (1953)
The Lost World (1925)
Louisiana Story (1948)
Love Finds Andy Hardy (1938)
Love Me Tonight (1932)
Magical Maestro (1952)
The Magnificent Ambersons (1942)
The Maltese Falcon (1941)
The Manchurian Candidate (1962)
Manhattan (1921)
Manhattan (1979)
March of Time: Inside Nazi Germany—1938 (1938)
Marian Anderson: The Lincoln Memorial Concert (1939)
Marty (1955)
M*A*S*H (1970)
Master Hands (1936)
Mean Streets (1973)
Meet Me in St. Louis (1944)
Melody Ranch (1940)*
Memphis Belle (1944)
Meshes of the Afternoon (1943)
Midnight Cowboy (1969)
Mildred Pierce (1945)
The Miracle of Morgan's Creek (1944)
Miss Lulu Bett (1921)
Modern Times (1936)
Modesta (1956)
Morocco (1930)
Motion Painting No. 1 (1947)
Mr. Smith Goes to Washington (1939)
Multiple Sidosis (1970)
The Music Box (1932)
My Darling Clementine (1946)
My Man Godfrey (1936)
The Naked Spur (1953)
Nanook of the North (1922)
Nashville (1975)
National Lampoon's Animal House (1978)
Network (1976)
A Night at the Opera (1935)
The Night of the Hunter (1955)
Night of the Living Dead (1968)
Ninotchka (1939)
North by Northwest (1959)
Nothing but a Man (1964)
One Flew Over the Cuckoo's Nest (1975)
On the Waterfront (1954)
The Outlaw Josey Wales (1976)
Out of the Past (1947)
The Ox-Bow Incident (1943)
Pass the Gravy (1928)
Paths of Glory (1957)

The Pearl (1948)*
Peter Pan (1924)
Phantom of the Opera (1925)
The Philadelphia Story (1940)
Pinocchio (1940)
A Place in the Sun (1951)
Planet of the Apes (1968)
The Plow That Broke the Plains (1936)
Point of Order (1964)
The Poor Little Rich Girl (1917)
Porky in Wackyland (1938)
Powers of Ten (1978)
President McKinley Inauguration Footage (1901)
Primary (1960)
The Prisoner of Zenda (1937)
The Producers (1968)
Psycho (1960)
The Public Enemy (1931)
Pull My Daisy (1959)
Punch Drunks (1934)*
Raging Bull (1980)
Raiders of the Lost Ark (1981)
Rear Window (1954)
Rebel Without a Cause (1955)
Red River (1948)
Regeneration (1915)
Republic Steel Strike Riots Newsreel Footage (1937)
Return of the Secaucus 7 (1980)
Ride the High Country (1962)
Rip Van Winkle (1896)
The River (1937)
Road to Morocco (1942)
Roman Holiday (1953)
Rose Hobart (1936)
Sabrina (1954)*
Safety Last (1923)
Salesman (1969)
Salomé (1923)
Salt of the Earth (1954)
Scarface (1932)
The Searchers (1956)
Serene Velocity (1970)
Seventh Heaven (1927)
Shadow of a Doubt (1943)
Shadows (1959)
Shaft (1971)
Shane (1953)
She Done Him Wrong (1933)
Sherlock, Jr. (1924)
Sherman's March (1986)
Shock Corridor (1963)
The Shop Around the Corner (1940)
Show Boat (1936)
Singin' in the Rain (1952)
Sky High (1922)
Snow White (1933)
Snow White and the Seven Dwarfs (1937)
Some Like It Hot (1959)
The Sound of Music (1965)
Stagecoach (1939)
A Star Is Born (1954)
Star Theatre (1901)*
Star Wars (1977)
Steamboat Willie (1928)
Stranger Than Paradise (1984)*
A Streetcar Named Desire (1951)
Stormy Weather (1943)
Sullivan's Travels (1941)
Sunrise (1927)
Sunset Boulevard (1950)
Sweet Smell of Success (1957)
Tabu (1933)
Tacoma Narrows Bridge Collapse (1940)
The Tall T (1957)
Taxi Driver (1976)
The Ten Commandments (1956)
The Tell-Tale Heart (1953)
Tevye (1939)
Theodore Case Sound Tests: Gus Visser and His Singing Duck (1925)*

IT'S A FACT: Four of the top 25 highest-grossing films in U.S. history are animated: #8, *Finding Nemo* (2003), $334.1 mil.; #12, *The Lion King* (1994), $312.9 mil.; #21, *Shrek* (2001), $267.7 mil.; #25, *Monsters, Inc.* (2001), $255.8 mil.

The Thief of Bagdad (1924)	Tootsie (1982)	Vertigo (1958)	Will Success Spoil Rock
The Thin Blue Line (1988)	Topaz (1943-45)	Westinghouse Works 1904	Hunter? (1957)
The Thing From Another World	Top Hat (1935)	(1904)	The Wind (1928)
(1951)	Touch of Evil (1958)	West Side Story (1961)	Wings (1927)
The Thin Man (1934)	Trance and Dance in Bali (1939)	What's Opera, Doc? (1957)	Within Our Gates (1920)
This Is Cinerama (1952)*	The Treasure of the Sierra	Where Are My Children? (1916)	The Wizard of Oz (1939)
This Is Spinal Tap (1984)*	Madre (1948)	Why Man Creates (1968)*	Woman of the Year (1942)
Through Navajo Eyes (series)	Trouble in Paradise (1932)	Why We Fight	A Woman Under the Influence
(1966)*	Tulips Shall Grow (1942)	(Series/1943-45)	(1974)
To Be or Not To Be (1942)	Twelve O'Clock High (1949)	Wild and Wooly (1917)*	Woodstock (1970)
To Fly (1976)	2001: A Space Odyssey (1968)	The Wild Bunch (1969)	Yankee Doodle Dandy (1942)
To Kill a Mockingbird (1962)	Verbena Tragica (1939)	Wild River (1960)*	Zapruder Film (1963)

100 Best American Movies of All Time
Source: American Film Institute

Compiled in 1998 based on ballots sent to 1,500 figures, mostly from the film world. Criteria for judging included historical significance, critical recognition and awards, and popularity. The year each film was first released is in parentheses.

1. Citizen Kane (1941)
2. Casablanca (1942)
3. The Godfather (1972)
4. Gone With the Wind (1939)
5. Lawrence of Arabia (1962)
6. The Wizard of Oz (1939)
7. The Graduate (1967)
8. On the Waterfront (1954)
9. Schindler's List (1993)
10. Singin' in the Rain (1952)
11. It's a Wonderful Life (1946)
12. Sunset Boulevard (1950)
13. The Bridge on the River Kwai (1957)
14. Some Like It Hot (1959)
15. Star Wars (1977)
16. All About Eve (1950)
17. The African Queen (1951)
18. Psycho (1960)
19. Chinatown (1974)
20. One Flew Over the Cuckoo's Nest (1975)
21. The Grapes of Wrath (1940)
22. 2001: A Space Odyssey (1968)
23. The Maltese Falcon (1941)
24. Raging Bull (1980)
25. E.T.: The Extra-Terrestrial (1982)
26. Dr. Strangelove (1964)
27. Bonnie and Clyde (1967)
28. Apocalypse Now (1979)
29. Mr. Smith Goes to Washington (1939)
30. Treasure of the Sierra Madre (1948)
31. Annie Hall (1977)
32. The Godfather, Part II (1974)
33. High Noon (1952)
34. To Kill a Mockingbird (1962)
35. It Happened One Night (1934)
36. Midnight Cowboy (1969)
37. The Best Years of Our Lives (1946)
38. Double Indemnity (1944)
39. Doctor Zhivago (1965)
40. North by Northwest (1959)
41. West Side Story (1961)
42. Rear Window (1954)
43. King Kong (1933)
44. The Birth of a Nation (1915)
45. A Streetcar Named Desire (1951)
46. A Clockwork Orange (1971)
47. Taxi Driver (1976)
48. Jaws (1975)
49. Snow White and the Seven Dwarfs (1937)
50. Butch Cassidy and the Sundance Kid (1969)
51. The Philadelphia Story (1940)
52. From Here to Eternity (1953)
53. Amadeus (1984)
54. All Quiet on the Western Front (1930)
55. The Sound of Music (1965)
56. M*A*S*H (1970)
57. The Third Man (1949)
58. Fantasia (1940)
59. Rebel Without a Cause (1955)
60. Raiders of the Lost Ark (1981)
61. Vertigo (1958)
62. Tootsie (1982)
63. Stagecoach (1939)
64. Close Encounters of the Third Kind (1977)
65. The Silence of the Lambs (1991)
66. Network (1976)
67. The Manchurian Candidate (1962)
68. An American in Paris (1951)
69. Shane (1953)
70. The French Connection (1971)
71. Forrest Gump (1994)
72. Ben-Hur (1959)
73. Wuthering Heights (1939)
74. The Gold Rush (1925)
75. Dances With Wolves (1990)
76. City Lights (1931)
77. American Graffiti (1973)
78. Rocky (1976)
79. The Deer Hunter (1978)
80. The Wild Bunch (1969)
81. Modern Times (1936)
82. Giant (1956)
83. Platoon (1986)
84. Fargo (1996)
85. Duck Soup (1933)
86. Mutiny on the Bounty (1935)
87. Frankenstein (1931)
88. Easy Rider (1969)
89. Patton (1970)
90. The Jazz Singer (1927)
91. My Fair Lady (1964)
92. A Place in the Sun (1951)
93. The Apartment (1960)
94. Goodfellas (1990)
95. Pulp Fiction (1994)
96. The Searchers (1956)
97. Bringing Up Baby (1938)
98. Unforgiven (1992)
99. Guess Who's Coming to Dinner (1967)
100. Yankee Doodle Dandy (1942)

All-Time Top-Grossing American Movies[1]
Source: *Variety* magazine

Rank	Title (original release)	Gross[2]	Rank	Title (original release)	Gross[2]
1.	Titanic (1997)	$600.8	25.	Monsters, Inc. (2001)	$255.8
2.	Star Wars: Episode IV—A New Hope (1977)	461.0	26.	Batman (1989)	251.2
3.	E.T.: The Extra-Terrestrial (1982)	435.0	27.	Men in Black (1997)	250.7
4.	Star Wars: Ep. I—The Phantom Menace (1999)	431.1	28.	Toy Story 2 (1999)	245.9
5.	Spider-Man (2002)	403.7	29.	Raiders of the Lost Ark (1981)	242.4
6.	Jurassic Park (1993)	357.1	30.	Twister (1996)	241.7
7.	The Lord of the Rings: The Two Towers (2002)	339.8	31.	My Big Fat Greek Wedding (2002)	241.4
8.	Finding Nemo (2003)	334.1	32.	Bruce Almighty (2003)	241.4
9.	Forrest Gump (1994)	329.7	33.	Ghostbusters (1984)	238.6
10.	Harry Potter and the Sorcerer's Stone (2001)	317.6	34.	Beverly Hills Cop (1984)	234.8
11.	The Lord of the Rings: The Fellowship of the Ring (2001)	313.4	35.	Cast Away (2000)	233.6
12.	The Lion King (1994)	312.9	36.	The Exorcist (1973)	232.7
13.	Star Wars: Episode II—Attack of the Clones (2002)	310.7	37.	The Lost World: Jurassic Park (1997)	229.1
14.	Return of the Jedi (1983)	309.2	38.	Signs (2002)	228.0
15.	Independence Day (1996)	306.2	39.	Rush Hour 2 (2001)	226.2
16.	The Sixth Sense (1999)	293.5	40.	Mrs. Doubtfire (1993)	219.2
17.	The Empire Strikes Back (1980)	290.3	41.	Ghost (1990)	217.6
18.	Home Alone (1990)	285.8	42.	Aladdin (1992)	217.4
19.	Pirates of the Caribbean: The Curse of the Black Pearl (2003)	283.4	43.	Saving Private Ryan (1998)	216.2
			44.	Mission: Impossible 2 (2000)	215.4
20.	The Matrix: Reloaded (2003)	280.5	45.	X2: X-Men United (2003)	214.9
21.	Shrek (2001)	267.7	46.	Austin Powers in Goldmember (2002)	213.1
22.	Harry Potter and the Chamber of Secrets (2002)	262.0	47.	Back to the Future (1985)	208.2
23.	Dr. Seuss' How the Grinch Stole Christmas (2000)	260.0	48.	Austin Powers: The Spy Who Shagged Me (1999)	205.4
24.	Jaws (1975)	260.0	49.	Terminator 2: Judgment Day (1991)	204.8
			50.	Austin Powers in Goldmember (2002)	203.5

(1) Through Sept. 11, 2003. (2) Gross is in millions of absolute dollars based on box office sales in the U.S. and Canada. Rising ticket prices favor newer films, but older films have the advantage of reissues.

Most Popular Movie Videos/DVDs

Source: Alexander & Associates/Video Flash, New York, NY

Note: Year given to distinguish from other films with the same title.

ALL-TIME   2002

Top Ten Rentals All Time VHS[1]	Top Ten Purchase Titles VHS[3]	Top Ten Rental Titles 2002 VHS	Top Ten Purchase Titles 2002 VHS
1. Pretty Woman	1. The Lion King	1. The Fast and the Furious	1. Shrek
2. Top Gun	2. Forrest Gump	2. Training Day	2. Cinderella II: Dreams Come True
3. The Little Mermaid	3. Toy Story	3. Harry Potter and the Sorcerer's Stone	3. Atlantis: Lost Empire
4. Home Alone	4. Aladdin	4. Shrek	4. Pearl Harbor (2001)
5. Ghost	5. Jurassic Park	5. Rush Hour 2	5. The Princess Diaries
6. The Lion King	6. Pocahontas	6. Pearl Harbor (2001)	6. Rush Hour 2
7. Beauty and the Beast	7. Beauty and the Beast	7. Black Hawk Down	7. Harry Potter and the Sorcerer's Stone
8. Terminator II: Judgment Day	8. The Little Mermaid	8. The Lord of the Rings: The Fellowship of the Ring	8. How the Grinch Stole Christmas (2000)
9. Forrest Gump	9. Cinderella	9. Ocean's Eleven (2001)	9. Jurassic Park 3
10. Aladdin	10. 101 Dalmatians	10. The Others	10. Monsters, Inc.

DVD[2]	DVD[2]	DVD	DVD
1. The Fast and the Furious	1. Shrek	1. The Fast and the Furious	1. The Fast and the Furious
2. Gladiator (2000)	2. Gladiator (2000)	2. Training Day	2. Training Day
3. Shrek	3. A Knight's Tale	3. Black Hawk Down	3. Shrek
4. Training Day	4. The Matrix	4. The Lord of the Rings: The Fellowship of the Ring	4. American Pie 2
5. The Matrix	5. The Fast and the Furious	5. Pearl Harbor (2001)	5. A Knight's Tale
6. Black Hawk Down	6. The Mummy Returns (2001)	6. Harry Potter and the Sorcerer's Stone	6. Harry Potter and the Sorcerer's Stone
7. Pearl Harbor (2001)	7. Rush Hour 2	7. American Pie 2	7. Monsters, Inc.
8. The Lord of the Rings: The Fellowship of the Ring	8. Training Day	8. Shrek	8. Rush Hour 2
9. Harry Potter and the Sorcerer's Stone	9. Planet of the Apes (2001)	9. The Others	9. The Lord of the Rings: The Fellowship of the Ring
10. American Pie 2	10. Remember the Titans	10. Monsters, Inc.	10. Spider-Man (2002)

(1) Mar. 1, 1987, to Dec. 31, 2002. (2) Jan. 1, 2000, to Dec. 31, 2002. (3) Feb. 16, 1988, to Dec. 31, 2002.

Top 50 Record Long-Run Broadway Plays[1]

Source: The League of American Theatres and Producers, Inc., New York, NY

Title	Performances	Title	Performances	Title	Performances
1. Cats	7,485	18. Annie	2,377	35. Crazy For You	1,622
2. Les Misérables	6,680	19. Man of La Mancha	2,328	36. The Best Little Whorehouse in Texas	1,584
3. *The Phantom of the Opera	6,517	20. Abie's Irish Rose	2,327	37. Mary, Mary	1,572
4. A Chorus Line	6,137	21. *Cabaret (revival)	2,249	38. Evita	1,567
5. Oh! Calcutta! (revival)	5,959	22. Oklahoma!	2,212	39. Ain't Misbehavin'	1,565
6. Miss Saigon	4,092	23. Smokey Joe's Cafe	2,037	40. The Voice of the Turtle	1,557
7. *Beauty and the Beast	3,844	24. Pippin	1,944	41. Jekyll & Hyde	1,543
8. 42nd Street	3,486	25. South Pacific	1,925	42. Barefoot in the Park	1,530
9. Grease (original)	3,388	26. The Magic Show	1,920	43. Dreamgirls	1,521
10. Fiddler on the Roof	3,242	27. Gemini	1,819	44. Mame	1,508
11. Life With Father	3,224	28. Deathtrap	1,793	45. Grease (revival)	1,505
12. Tobacco Road	3,182	29. Harvey	1,775	46. Same Time, Next Year	1,453
13. *Rent	3,072	30. Dancin'	1,774	47. Arsenic and Old Lace	1,444
14. Hello, Dolly!	2,844	31. La Cage aux Folles	1,761	48. *Aida	1,444
15. *Chicago (revival)	2,843	32. Hair	1,750	49. The Sound of Music (Orig.)	1,443
16. My Fair Lady	2,717	33. The Wiz	1,672	50. Me and My Girl	1,420
17. *The Lion King	2,435	34. Born Yesterday	1,642		

*Still running Sept. 14, 2003. (1) Number of performances through Sept. 14, 2003.

Broadway Season Statistics, 1959-2003

Source: The League of American Theatres and Producers, Inc., New York, NY

Season	Gross (mil $)	Attendance (mil)	Playing Weeks	New Productions	Season	Gross (mil $)	Attendance (mil)	Playing Weeks	New Productions
1959-1960	46	7.9	1,156	58	1981-1982	223	10.1	1,455	48
1960-1961	44	7.7	1,210	48	1982-1983	209	8.4	1,258	50
1961-1962	44	6.8	1,166	53	1983-1984	227	7.9	1,097	36
1962-1963	44	7.4	1,134	54	1984-1985	209	7.3	1,078	33
1963-1964	40	6.8	1,107	63	1985-1986	190	6.5	1,041	34
1964-1965	50	8.2	1,250	67	1986-1987	208	7.1	1,039	41
1965-1966	54	9.6	1,295	68	1987-1988	253	8.1	1,113	30
1966-1967	55	9.3	1,269	69	1988-1989	262	8.1	1,108	33
1967-1968	59	9.5	1,259	74	1989-1990	282	8.0	1,070	40
1968-1969	58	8.6	1,209	67	1990-1991	267	7.3	971	28
1969-1970	53	7.1	1,047	62	1991-1992	293	7.4	905	37
1970-1971	55	7.4	1,107	49	1992-1993	328	7.9	1,019	34
1971-1972	52	6.5	1,157	55	1993-1994	356	8.1	1,066	39
1972-1973	45	5.4	889	55	1994-1995	406	9.0	1,120	33
1973-1974	46	5.7	907	43	1995-1996	436	9.5	1,146	38
1974-1975	57	6.6	1,101	54	1996-1997	499	10.6	1,349	37
1975-1976	71	7.3	1,136	55	1997-1998	558	11.5	1,442	33
1976-1977	93	8.8	1,349	54	1998-1999	588	11.7	1,441	39
1977-1978	114	9.6	1,433	42	1999-2000	603	11.4	1,464	37
1978-1979	134	9.6	1,542	50	2000-2001	666	11.9	1,484	28
1979-1980	146	9.6	1,540	61	2001-2002	643	11.0	1,434	28
1980-1981	197	11.0	1,544	60	2002-2003	721	11.4	1,544	36

Some Notable Non-Profit Theater Companies in the U.S
Source: Theatre Communications Group, Inc.

ACT Theatre	Seattle	WA	Lincoln Center Theater	New York	NY
Actors Theatre of Louisville	Louisville	KY	Long Wharf Theatre	New Haven	CT
Alabama Shakespeare Festival	Montgomery	AL	Manhattan Theatre Club	New York	NY
Alley Theatre	Houston	TX	McCarter Theatre Center	Princeton	NJ
Alliance Theatre Company	Atlanta	GA	Milwaukee Repertory Theater	Milwaukee	WI
American Conservatory Theater	San Francisco	CA	Missouri Repertory Theatre	Kansas City	MO
American Repertory Theatre	Boston	MA	North Shore Music Theatre	Beverly	MA
Arena Stage	Washington	DC	The Old Globe	San Diego	CA
Arizona Theatre Company	Tucson	AZ	Oregon Shakespeare Festival	Ashland	OR
Berkeley Repertory Theatre	Berkeley	CA	Paper Mill Playhouse	Millburn	NJ
Center Stage	Baltimore	MD	Pittsburgh Public Theater	Pittsburgh	PA
Center Theatre Group/Mark Taper Forum	Los Angeles	CA	The Public Theater	New York	NY
Chicago Shakespeare Theater	Chicago	IL	Repertory Theatre of St. Louis	St. Louis	MO
The Children's Theatre Company	Minneapolis	MN	Roundabout Theatre Company	New York	NY
Cincinnati Playhouse in the Park	Cincinnati	OH	San Jose Repertory Theatre	San Jose	CA
The Cleveland Play House	Cleveland	OH	Seattle Children's Theatre	Seattle	WA
Coconut Grove Playhouse	Miami	FL	Seattle Repertory Theatre	Seattle	WA
Dallas Theater Center	Dallas	TX	Second Stage Theatre	New York	NY
Denver Center Theatre Company	Denver	CO	The Shakespeare Theatre	Washington	DC
Geffen Playhouse	Los Angeles	CA	South Coast Repertory	Costa Mesa	CA
Goodman Theatre	Chicago	IL	Steppenwolf Theatre Company	Chicago	IL
Guthrie Theater	Minneapolis	MN	Studio Arena Theatre	Buffalo	NY
Hartford Stage Company	Hartford	CT	TheatreWorks	Palo Alto	CA
Huntington Theatre Company	Boston	MA	Trinity Repertory Company	Providence	RI
La Jolla Playhouse	La Jolla	CA	Utah Shakespearean Festival	Cedar City	UT

U.S. Symphony Orchestras[1]
Source: American Symphony Orchestra League, 33 West 60th St., New York, NY 10023

Symphony Orchestra[2]	Music Director[3]	Symphony Orchestra[2]	Music Director[3]
Alabama Symphony (AL)	Richard Westerfield	Louisville Orchestra (KY)	Uriel Segal
American (NY)	Steven Sloane	Memphis (TN)	David Loebel
Arkansas Symphony (AR)	David Itkin	Milwaukee (WI)	Andreas Delfs
Atlanta (GA)	Robert Spano	Minnesota (Minneapolis)	Osmo Vänskä
Austin (TX)	Peter Bay	Naples Philharmonic (FL)	Christopher Seaman
Baltimore (MD)	Yuri Temirkanov	Nashville Symphony (TN)	Kenneth D.
Baton Rouge Symphony (LA)	Timothy Muffitt		Schermerhorn
Boston (MA)	James Levine	National (Washington, DC)	Leonard Slatkin
Brooklyn Philharmonic (NY)	Robert Spano	New Jersey (Newark)	Zdenek Macal
Buffalo Philharmonic (NY)	JoAnn Falletta	New Mexico (Albuquerque)	Guillermo Figueroa
Charlotte (NC)	Christof Perick	New York Philharmonic (NYC)	Lorin Maazel
Chicago (IL)	Daniel Barenboim	North Carolina Symphony (Raleigh)	Gerhardt Zimmermann
Cincinnati (OH)	Paavo Järvi	Oklahoma City Philharmonic (OK)	Joel A. Levine
Cleveland Orchestra (OH)	Franz Welser-Möst	Omaha Symphony (NE)	Victor Yampolsky
Colorado (CO)	Marin Alsop	Orchestra of St. Luke's (NY)	Donald Runnicles
Colorado Springs (CO)	Lawrence Leighton Smith	Oregon Symphony (Portland)	James DePreist
Columbus (OH)	Alessandro Siciliani	Pasadena Symphony Association (CA)	Jorge Mester
Dallas (TX)	Andrew Litton	Philadelphia (PA)	Wolfgang Sawallisch
Dayton Philharmonic (OH)	Neal Gittleman	Phoenix Symphony (AZ)	Hermann Michael
Delaware Symphony (DE)	David Amato	Pittsburgh (PA)	Mariss Jansons
Detroit (MI)	Neeme Järvi	Portland (ME)	Toshiyuki Shimada
Evansville Philharmonic (IN)	Alfred Savia	Rhode Island Philharmonic (RI)	Larry Rachleff
Florida Orchestra (Tampa)	Stefan Sanderling	Richmond Symphony (VA)	Mark Russell Smith
Florida West Coast (FL)	Leif Bjaland	Rochester Philharmonic Orch. (NY)	Christopher Seaman
Fort Wayne Philharmonic (IN)	Edvard Tchivzhel	St. Louis (MO)	Itzhak Perlman
Fort Worth (TX)	Miguel Harth-Bedoya	St. Paul Chamber Orchestra (MN)	Andreas Delfs
Grand Rapids (MI)	David Lockington	San Antonio (TX)	Larry Rachleff
Grant Park (Chicago, IL)	Carlos Kalmar	San Diego Symphony (CA)	Jaha Ling
Hartford (CT)	Edward Cumming	San Francisco (CA)	Michael Tilson Thomas
Honolulu (HI)	Dr. Samuel Wong	Santa Rosa Symphony (CA)	Jeffrey Kahane
Houston (TX)	Hans Graf	Seattle (WA)	Gerard Schwarz
Indianapolis (IN)	Mario Venzago	Spokane (WA)	Fabio Mechetti
Jacksonville (FL)	Fabio Mechetti	Syracuse (NY)	Daniel Hege
Kansas City (MO)	Anne Manson	Toledo (OH)	Stefan Sanderling
Knoxville (TN)	Kirk Trevor	Tucson (AZ)	George Hanson
Long Beach (CA)	Enrique Arturo Diemecke	Utah (Salt Lake City)	Keith Lockhart
Los Angeles Chamber (CA)	Jeffrey Kahane	Virginia Symphony (VA)	JoAnn Falletta
Los Angeles Philharmonic (CA)	Esa-Pekka Salonen	West Virginia (Charleston)	Grant Cooper
Louisiana Philharmonic (New Orleans)	Klauspeter Seibel	Youngstown Symphony Orchestra (OH)	Isaiah Jackson

(1) Includes only orchestras with annual expenses $1.6 mil or greater. (2) If only place name is given, add Symphony Orchestra. (3) General title; listed is highest-ranking member of conducting personnel.

U.S. Opera Companies[1]
Source: OPERA America, 1156 15th Street NW, Washington, DC 20005-1704; as of May 2003.

Arizona Opera (Tucson); David Speers, gen. dir.
Atlanta Opera (GA); Alfred Kennedy, exec. dir.
Austin Lyric Opera (TX); Richard Buckley, art. dir.
Baltimore Opera Company (MD); Michael Harrison, gen. dir.
Boston Lyric Opera (MA); Janice Mancini Del Sesto, gen. dir.
Central City Opera (Denver, CO); Pelham Pearce, gen. dir.
Chicago Opera Theater (IL); Brian Dickie, gen. dir.
Cincinnati Opera (OH); Patricia K. Beggs, mng. dir.
Cleveland Opera (OH); David Bamberger, gen. dir.
Connecticut Grand Opera and Orchestra (Stamford, CT); Laurence Gilgore, gen. dir.

Connecticut Opera (Hartford); Willie Anthony Waters, gen./art. dir.
Dallas Opera (TX); Karen Stone, gen. dir.
Dayton Opera (OH); Justin Reiter, prod. man.
Des Moines Metro Opera, Inc. (IA); Jerilee M. Mace, exec. dir.
Florentine Opera Company, Inc. (Milwaukee, WI); Dennis Hanthorn, gen. dir.
Florida Grand Opera (Miami, FL); Robert M. Heuer, gen. dir.
Fort Worth Opera Association (TX); Darren Woods, gen. dir.
Glimmerglass Opera (Cooperstown, NY); Joanne Cossa, gen. dir.

Hawaii Opera Theatre (Honolulu); Henry Akina, gen./art. dir.
Houston Grand Opera (TX); David Gockley, gen. dir.
Indianapolis Opera (IN); John C. Pickett, exec. dir.
Kentucky Opera (Louisville); Deborah S. Sandler, gen. dir.
Knoxville Opera Company (TN); Francis Graffeo, gen. dir.
Los Angeles Opera (CA); Plácido Domingo, art. dir.
Lyric Opera of Chicago (IL); William Mason, gen. dir.
Lyric Opera of Kansas City (MO); Evan R. Luskin, gen. dir.
Metropolitan Opera (New York, NY); Joseph Volpe, gen. mgr.
Michigan Opera Theatre (Detroit); David DiChiera, gen. dir.
Minnesota Opera Company (Minneapolis); Kevin Smith, pres./ gen. dir.
Nashville Opera Association (TN); Carol Penterman, exec. dir.
New Orleans Opera Association (LA); Robert Lyall, gen. dir.
New York City Opera (NY); Paul Kellogg, gen. art. dir.
Opera Carolina (Charlotte, NC); James Meena, gen. dir.
Opera Colorado (Denver); Peter Russell, gen. dir.
Opera/Columbus (OH); Philip M. Dobard, mng. dir.
Opera Company of Philadelphia (PA); Robert B. Driver, artistic dir.
OperaDelaware (Wilmington); Leland P. Kimball III, gen. dir.
Opera Grand Rapids (MI); John Peter Jeffries, exec. dir.
Opera Memphis (TN); Michael Ching, gen./art. dir.
Opera Omaha, Inc. (NE); Joan Desens, exec. dir.

Opera Pacific (Irvine, CA); Martin G. Hubbard, exec. dir.
Opera Theatre of Saint Louis (MO); Charles MacKay, gen. dir.
Orlando Opera (FL); Robert Swedberg, gen. dir.
Palm Beach Opera, Inc. (FL); R. Joseph Barnett, gen. dir.
Pittsburgh Opera (PA); Mark Weinstein, gen. dir.
Portland Opera (OR); Robert Bailey, gen. dir.
San Diego Opera Association (CA); Ian D. Campbell, gen. dir.
San Francisco Opera (CA); Pamela Rosenberg, gen. dir.
Santa Fe Opera (NM); Richard Gaddes, gen. dir.
Sarasota Opera (FL); Susan T. Danis, exec. dir.
Seattle Opera (WA); Speight Jenkins, gen. dir.
Skyline Opera Theatre (Milwaukee, WI); Christopher Libby, man. dir.
Syracuse Opera (NY); Catherine Wolff, gen. dir.
Toledo Opera (OH); Renay Conlin, gen. dir.
Tri-Cities Opera Company (Binghamton, NY); Reed W. Smith, exec. dir.
Tulsa Opera (OK); Carol I. Crawford, gen. dir.
Utah Festival Opera (Logan); Michael Ballam, gen. dir.
Utah Symphony & Opera (Salt Lake City); Anne Ewers, gen. dir.
Virginia Opera (Norfolk); Keith Stava, gen./art. dir.
Washington Opera (DC); Plácido Domingo, art. dir.
Wolf Trap Opera Company (Vienna, VA); Kim Pensinger Witman, gen. dir.

(1) Includes only opera companies with budgets of $1 million or more.

Some Notable U.S. Dance Companies

Source: DanceUSA

Organization	City	State	Organization	City	State
Alabama Ballet	Birmingham	AL	Houston Ballet Foundation	Houston	TX
Alvin Ailey American Dance Theater	New York	NY	Hubbard Street Dance Chicago	Chicago	IL
American Ballet Theatre	New York	NY	James Sewell Ballet	Minneapolis	MN
American Repertory Ballet Company	New Brunswick	NJ	Joe Goode Performance Group	San Francisco	CA
American Repertory Dance Company	Los Angeles	CA	Joffrey Ballet of Chicago	Chicago	IL
Aspen Santa Fe Ballet	Aspen	CO	June Watanabe in Company	San Rafael	CA
Ballet Austin	Austin	TX	Kansas City Ballet	Kansas City	MO
Ballet Florida	W. Palm Beach	FL	Kathy Harty Gray Dance Theatre	Alexandria	VA
Ballet Hispanico of New York	New York	NY	Kerala Dance Theatre	Los Angeles	CA
Ballet Memphis	Cordova	TN	Kim Robards Dance	Denver	CO
Ballet San Jose Silicon Valley	San Jose	CA	Ko-Thi Dance Company	Milwaukee	WI
Ballet Tennessee	Chattanooga	TN	Lar Lubovitch Dance Company	New York	NY
Ballet Theatre of Maryland	Annapolis	MD	Lily Cai Chinese Dance Company	San Francisco	CA
Ballet West	Salt Lake City	UT	Limón Dance Company	New York	NY
BalletMet Columbus	Columbus	OH	Lizz Lerman Dance Exchange	Takoma Park	MD
Bebe Miller Company	New York	NY	Lori Belilove & Company	New York	NY
Betty Salamun's DANCECIRCUS	Milwaukee	WI	Luna Negra Dance Theatre	Chicago	IL
Bill T. Jones/Arnie Zane Dance Company	New York	NY	Madison Ballet	Madison	WI
Boston Ballet	Boston	MA	Malashock Dance & Company	San Diego	CA
Bowen McCauley Dance	Arlington	VA	Margaret Jenkins Dance Company	San Francisco	CA
Buglisi/Foreman Dance	New York	NY	Mark Morris Dance Group	Brooklyn	NY
Carolyn Dorfman Dance Company	Union	NJ	Meredith Monk/The House Foundation	New York	NY
Chamber Dance Project	Sleepy Hollow	NY	Milwaukee Ballet	Milwaukee	WI
Charleston Ballet Theatre	Charleston	SC	Montgomery Ballet	Montgomery	AL
Chen & Dancers	New York	NY	Moving Arts Dance Company	Walnut Creek	CA
Chitresh Das Dance Company	San Francisco	CA	Nai-Ni Chen Dance Company	Fort Lee	NJ
Cincinnati Ballet	Cincinnati	OH	Nancy Karp and Dancers	San Francisco	CA
Cleo Parker Robinson	Denver	CO	New York City Ballet	New York	NY
Collage Dance Theatre	Los Angeles	CA	ODC/San Francisco	San Francisco	CA
Colorado Ballet Company	Denver	CO	Ohio Ballet	Akron	OH
Company C	San Francisco	CA	Pacific Northwest Ballet	Seattle	WA
Contemporary Dance/Fort Worth	Fort Worth	TX	Parsons Dance Foundation, Inc.	New York	NY
Cunningham Dance Foundation	New York	NY	Paul Taylor Dance Foundation	New York	NY
Dance Alloy	Pittsburgh	PA	Pittsburgh Ballet Theatre	Pittsburgh	PA
Dance Consort: Mezzacappa-Gabrian	New York	NY	Randy James Dance Works	Highland Park	NJ
Dance Institute of Washington	Washington	DC	Richmond Ballet	Richmond	VA
Dances Patrelle	New York	NY	Rincones & Company	Washington	DC
Dance Theatre of Harlem	New York	NY	Sandra Organ Dance Company	Houston	TX
Dayton Ballet	Dayton	OH	San Francisco Ballet	San Francisco	CA
Dayton Contemporary Dance Company	Dayton	OH	Snappy Dance Theatre	Cambridge	MA
Demetrius Klein Dance Company	Lake Worth	FL	Stephen Petronio Company	New York	NY
Diavolo Dance Theater	Los Angeles	CA	Tap Fusion	New York	NY
Doug Varone & Dancers/DOVA, Inc.	New York	NY	Tennessee Children's Dance Ensemble	Knoxville	TN
EIKO & KOMA	New York	NY	Texas ballet Theater	Ft. Worth	OK
Elisa Monte Dance	New York	NY	Trinity Irish Dance Co.	Chicago	IL
Felice Lesser Dance Theater	New York	NY	Troika Ranch	Brooklyn	NY
Flamenco Vivo Carlota Santana	New York	NY	Tulsa Ballet Theatre	Tulsa	OK
Garth Fagan Dance	Rochester	NY	Urban Bush Women	Brooklyn	NY
Gina Gibney Dance Inc.	New York	NY	The Washington Ballet	Washington	DC
Harem of the Queen	Washington	DC	Yu Wei Dance Collection	Philadelphia	PA

Some Notable Museums

This unofficial list of some of the largest museums in the U.S. by budget was compiled with the assistance of the American Association of Museums, a national association representing the concerns of the museum community. Association members also include zoos, aquariums, arboretums, botanical gardens, and planetariums, but these are not included in *The World Almanac* listing. See also Major U.S. Public Zoological Parks and Major Canadian Public Zoological Parks.

Museum	City	State	Museum	City	State
American Museum of Natural History	New York	NY	Milwaukee Public Museum	Milwaukee	WI
Amon Carter Museum of Western Art	Ft. Worth	TX	Minneapolis Institute of Art	Minneapolis	MN
The Art Institute of Chicago	Chicago	IL	Museum of African American History	Detroit	MI
Autry Museum of Western Heritage	Los Angeles	CA	Museum of Contemporary Art	Los Angeles	CA
Brooklyn Museum of Art	Brooklyn	NY	Museum of Fine Arts	Boston	MA
Busch-Reisinger Museum	Cambridge	MA	Museum of Fine Arts	Houston	TX
California Academy of Science	San Francisco	CA	Museum of Modern Art	New York	NY
California Science Center	Los Angeles	CA	Museum of New Mexico	Santa Fe	NM
Carnegie Museums of Pittsburgh	Pittsburgh	PA	Museum of Science	Boston	MA
Chicago Historical Society	Chicago	IL	Mystic Seaport Museum	Mystic	CT
Children's Museum of Indianapolis	Indianapolis	IN	National Air & Space Museum	Washington	DC
Cincinnati Art Museum	Cincinnati	OH	National Baseball Hall of Fame and		
Cincinnati Museum Center	Cincinnati	OH	Museum, Inc.	Cooperstown	NY
Cleveland Museum of Art	Cleveland	OH	National Gallery of Art	Washington	DC
Colonial Williamsburg	Williamsburg	VA	National Museum of American History-		
Corning Museum of Glass	Corning	NY	Smithsonian Inst.	Washington	DC
Dallas Museum of Art	Dallas	TX	National Museum of Natural History	Washington	DC
Denver Art Museum	Denver	CO	Nelson-Atkins Museum of Art	Kansas City	MO
Denver Museum of Nature and Science	Denver	CO	New York Historical Society	New York	NY
Detroit Institute of Arts	Detroit	MI	New York State Museum	Albany	NY
Exploratorium	San Francisco	CA	The Newseum	Arlington	VA
The Field Museum of Natural History	Chicago	IL	Peabody Essex Museum	Salem	MA
Fine Arts Museum of San Francisco	San Francisco	CA	Pennsylvania Historical & Museum		
Franklin Institute	Philadelphia	PA	Commission	Harrisburg	PA
The Frick Collection	New York	NY	Philadelphia Museum of Art	Philadelphia	PA
Harvard University Art Museum	Cambridge	MA	Public Museum of Grand Rapids	Grand Rapids	MI
Henry F. Dupont Winterthur Museum	Winterthur	DE	Rock & Roll Hall of Fame and Museum Inc.	Cleveland	OH
Henry Ford Museum/Greenfield Village	Dearborn	MI	San Diego Museum of Art	San Diego	CA
High Museum of Art	Atlanta	GA	San Francisco Museum of Modern Art	San Francisco	CA
Houston Museum of Natural Science	Houston	TX	Science Museum of Minnesota	Saint Paul	MN
Jamestown-Yorktown Foundation	Williamsburg	VA	Scottsdale Museum of Contemp. Art	Scottsdale	AZ
Jewish Museum	New York	NY	St. Louis Science Center	St. Louis	MO
L.A. County Museum of Art	Los Angeles	CA	Toledo Museum of Art	Toledo	OH
Liberty Science Center, Liberty State Park	Jersey City	NJ	U.S. Holocaust Memorial Museum	Washington	DC
Maryland Academy of Sciences	Baltimore	MD	Univ. of Pennsylvania Museum	Philadelphia	PA
Maryland Science Center	Baltimore	MD	Virginia Museum of Fine Arts	Richmond	VA
Mashantucket Pequot Museum and			Wadsworth Atheneum	Hartford	CT
Research Center	Mashantucket	CT	Walker Art Center	Minneapolis	MN
Metropolitan Museum of Art	New York	NY	Whitney Museum of American Art	New York	NY

Best-Selling U.S. Magazines, 2002

Source: Audit Bureau of Circulations, Schaumburg, IL

General magazines, exclusive of groups and comics; also excluding magazines that failed to file reports to ABC by press time. Based on total average paid circulation during the 6 months ending Dec. 31, 2002.

Publication	Total paid circ.	Publication	Total paid circ.	Publication	Total paid circ.
1. Reader's Digest	11,944,898	34. Smithsonian	2,045,430	69. Popular Mechanics	1,220,205
2. TV Guide (U.S.)	9,061,639	35. U.S. News and World		70. Scholastic Parent and	
3. Better Homes and		Report	2,032,286	Child	1,210,559
Gardens	7,607,832	36. Money	1,992,438	71. Family Handyman	1,156,914
4. National Geographic	6,657,424	37. Ebony	1,841,715	72. Real Simple	1,140,500
5. Good Housekeeping	4,690,508	38. National Enquirer	1,775,318	73. Vanity Fair	1,131,144
6. Family Circle	4,601,708	39. Country Living	1,758,891	74. Stuff	1,130,466
7. Woman's Day	4,239,930	40. V.F.W. Magazine	1,735,061	75. Country Home	1,104,559
8. My Generation	4,152,410	41. Men's Health	1,695,554	76. U.S. Weekly	1,101,059
9. Time	4,109,962	42. InStyle	1,670,792	77. PC World	1,101,056
10. Ladies Home Journal	4,101,414	43. Entertainment Weekly	1,646,822	78. American Hunter	1,098,957
11. People Weekly	3,632,804	44. Shape	1,643,816	79. Elks Magazine	1,069,904
12. Westways	3,411,317	45. Woman's World	1,612,099	80. Scouting	1,066,757
13. Rosie	3,337,582	46. Teen People	1,603,138	81. Essence	1,061,681
14. Home and Away	3,308,292	47. Cooking Light	1,574,194	82. FHM (For Him	
15. Sports Illustrated	3,245,940	48. Golf Digest	1,564,475	Magazine)	1,061,122
16. Playboy	3,213,638	49. Endless Vacation	1,558,834	83. Elks Magazine	1,059,112
17. Prevention	3,150,017	50. ESPN The Magazine	1,550,138	84. Vim and Vigor	1,056,183
18. Newsweek	3,125,151	51. Field and Stream	1,544,039	85. Discover	1,048,079
19. Cosmopolitan	3,021,720	52. Family Fun	1,534,849	86. Michigan Living	1,046,394
20. Guideposts	2,656,622	53. Popular Science	1,485,911	87. Home	1,027,945
21. American Legion		54. Sunset	1,476,930	88. Kiplinger's Personal	
Magazine	2,633,675	55. American Rifleman	1,458,652	Finance	1,024,868
22. Via Magazine	2,632,589	56. Golf Magazine	1,410,001	89. Outdoor Life	1,021,595
23. Southern Living	2,563,757	57. First for Women	1,395,781	90. Elle	1,000,638
24. Maxim	2,512,090	58. Car and Driver	1,387,113	91. Businessweek North	
25. Seventeen	2,459,135	59. Star	1,385,323	America	987,369
26. Redbook	2,394,184	60. Health	1,360,525	92. Game Informer	981,542
27. Martha Stewart Living	2,359,328	61. Self	1,332,782	93. Victoria	969,180
28. Glamour	2,304,151	62. Bon Appetit	1,322,577	94. Travel & Leisure	962,768
29. O, The Oprah		63. Motor Trend	1,283,260	95. Gourmet	958,974
Magazine	2,261,570	64. Rolling Stone	1,272,739	96. Food & Wine	951,751
30. AAA Going Places	2,213,480	65. Vogue	1,257,787	97. Allure	949,669
31. YM	2,206,067	66. Fitness	1,253,392	98. Marie Claire	943,100
32. Parenting	2,136,283	67. Boy's Life	1,237,157	99. This Old House	940,628
33. Parents	2,091,782	68. PC Magazine	1,230,600	100. New Yorker	938,600

Some Notable New Books, 2002

Source: List published by American Library Association, Chicago, IL, 2003, for books published in 2002

Fiction

Book of Illusions, Paul Auster
Caramelo, Sandra Cisneros
The Shell Collector, Anthony Doerr
Miniatures, Norah Labiner
Lovely Green Eyes, Arnost Lustig
Atonement, Ian McEwan
By the Lake, John McGahern
In Revere in Those Days, Roland Merullo
Family Matters, Rohinton Mistry
Rouse Up, O Young Men of the New Age, Kenzaburo Oe
The Russian Debutante's Handbook, Gary Shteyngart
God's Fool, Mark Slouka

Poetry

Poems Seven: New and Complete Poetry, Alan Dugan
The Painted Bed, Donald Hall
Bellocq's Ophelia, Natasha Tretheway

Nonfiction

Complete Works, Isaac Babel
Selected Essays, John Berger
Blood Diamonds: Tracing the Deadly Path of the World's Most Precious Stones, Greg Campbell
Master of the Senate: The Years of Lyndon Johnson, Robert A. Caro
Complications: A Surgeon's Notes on an Imperfect Science, Atul Gawande
Can't Be Satisfied: The Life and Times of Muddy Waters, Robert Gordon
Theodore Rex, Edmund Morris
Lusitania: An Epic Tragedy, Diana Preston
Jesse James: Last Rebel of the Civil War, T.J. Stiles
The Future of the Past, Alexander Stille
The Future of Life, Edward O. Wilson

Young Adults Nonfiction

Nonfiction

Black Potatoes: The Story of the Great Irish Famine, 1845-1850, Susan Campbell Bartoletti
Phineas Gage: A Gruesome but True Story About Brain Science, John Fleischman
Hole in My Life, Jack Gantos
Meltdown: A Race Against Nuclear Disaster at Three Mile Island: A Reporter's Story, Wilborn Hampton
Fields of Fury: The American Civil War, James M. McPherson
Left for Dead: A Young Man's Search for Justice for the USS Indianapolis, Peter Nelson
19 Varieties of Gazelle: Poems of the Middle East, Naomi Shihab Nye
This Land Was Made For You and Me: The Life & Songs of Woody Guthrie, Elizabeth Partridge
Revenge of the Whale: The True Story of the Whaleship Essex, Nathaniel Philbrick
To Afghanistan and Back: A Graphic Travelogue, Ted Rall
The Gatekeepers: Inside the Admissions Process of a Premier College, Jacques Steinberg

Fiction

Before We Were Free, Julia Alvarez
Catalyst, Laurie Halse Anderson
Feed, M. T. Anderson

Shattered: Stories of Children and War, Edited by Jennifer Armstrong
Ashes of Roses, Mary Jane Auch
The Book of Fred: A Novel, Abby Bardi
Abarat, Clive Barker
Hanging on to Max, Margaret Bechard
Tithe: A Modern Faerie Tale, Holly Black
Year of the Hangman, Gary L. Blackwood
Remembrance, Theresa Breslin
Postcards from No Man's Land, Aidan Chambers
Things Not Seen, Andrew Clements
Gingerbread, Rachel Cohn
Mississippi Trial, 1955, Chris Crowe
Green Man: Tales from the Mythic Forest, Edited by Ellen Datlow & Terri Windling
Seven Wild Sisters, Charles de Lint
Born Confused, Tanuja Desai Hidier
This Lullaby, Sarah Dessen
Parvana's Journey, Deborah Ellis
Cat in Glass and Other Tales of the Unnatural, Nancy Etchemendy
Overboard, Elizabeth Fama
The House of the Scorpion, Nancy Farmer
Once Upon a Marigold, Jean Ferris
America, E. R. Frank
Better Than Running at Night, Hillary Frank
My Heartbeat, Garret Freymann-Weyr
Out of the Fire, Deborah Froese
Coraline, Neil Gaiman
Pictures of Hollis Woods, Patricia Reilly Giff
Shattering Glass, Gail Giles
Bronx Masquerade, Nikki Grimes
Dr. Franklin's Island, Ann Halam
Hoot, Carl Hiaasen
Search of the Moon King's Daughter, Linda Holeman
The Hunting of the Last Dragon, Sherryl Jordan
The Secret Life of Bees, Sue Monk Kidd
Stoner & Spaz, Ron Koertge
Son of the Mob, Gordon Korman
The Lightkeeper's Daughter, Iain Lawrence
The Dollmage, Martine Leavitt
The Kite Rider, Geraldine McCaughrean
Aimee, Mary Beth Miller
Lamb: The Gospel According to Biff, Christ's Childhood Pal, Christopher Moore
Big Mouth & Ugly Girl, Joyce Carol Oates
When My Name Was Keoko: A Novel of Korea in World War II, Linda Sue Park
Fresh Girl, Jaira Placide
What Happened to Lani Garver, Carol Plum-Ucci
Three Clams and an Oyster, Randy Powell
Stetson, S. L. Rottman
Motorcycle Ride on the Sea of Tranquility, Patricia Santana
Kotuku, Deborah Savage
The Lovely Bones: A Novel, Alice Sebold
Seven for a Secret, Mary C. Sheppard
Green Arrow: Quiver, Kevin Smith and Phil Hester
Lucy the Giant, Sherri L. Smith
Surviving the Applewhites, Stephanie Tolan
The Game, Teresa Toten
Strangers and Beggars: Stories, James Van Pelt
Hush, Jacqueline Woodson
Girl in a Cage, Jane Yolen and Robert J. Harris

Some Notable New Books for Children, 2002

Source: List published by American Library Association, Chicago, IL, 2003, for books published in 2002.

Younger Readers

"Slowly, Slowly, Slowly," said the Sloth, Eric Carle
Rap a Tap Tap: Here's Bojangles – Think of That!, Leo and Diane Dillon
Gossie & Gertie, Olivier Dunrea
Muncha! Muncha! Muncha!, Candace Fleming
Alphabet Under Construction, Denise Fleming
What Charlie Heard, Mordicai Gerstein
Henrietta and the Golden Eggs, Hanna Johansen
Gooney Bird Greene, Lois Lowry
Hondo & Fabian, Peter McCarty
I Stink!, Kate McMullan
7 X 9 = Trouble!, Claudia Mills
Head, Body, Legs: A Story from Liberia, Won-Ldy Paye and Margaret H. Lippert
My Friend Rabbit, Eric Rohmann

Duck on a Bike, David Shannon
Madlenka's Dog, Peter Sis
Get Well, Good Knight, Shelley Moore Thomas
Bear Snores On, Karma Wilson
Frida, Jonah Winter

Middle Readers

The Pot that Juan Built, Nancy Andrews-Goebel
Stand Tall, Joan Bauer
Togo, Robert J. Blake
Ruby Holler, Sharon Creech
Inventing the Future: A Photobiography of Thomas Alva Edison, Marfe Ferguson Delano
Georgie Lee, Sharon Phillips Denslow
Once Upon a Marigold, Jean Ferris
Up On Cloud Nine, Anne Fine

The Signers: The 56 Stories Behind the Declaration of Independence, Dennis Brindell Fradin
Confucius: The Golden Rule, Russell Freedman
The Thief Lord, Cornelia Funke
Coraline, Neil Gaiman
Pictures of Hollis Woods, Patricia Reilly Giff
Talkin' about Bessie: The Story of Aviator Elizabeth Coleman, Nikki Grimes
Journey to the River Sea, Eva Ibbotson
My Chinatown: One Year in Poems, Kam Mak
A Corner of the Universe, Ann Martin
Saffy's Angel, Hilary McKay
To Fly: The Story of the Wright Brothers, Wendie Old
Ella Fitzgerald: The Tale of a Vocal Virtuosa, Andrea Davis Pinkney
Degas and the Dance: The Painter and the Petits Rats, Perfecting their Art, Susan Goldman Rubin
When Marian Sang: The True Recital of Marian Anderson, The Voice of a Century, Pam Muñoz Ryan
Saladin: Noble Prince of Islam, Diane Stanley
Becoming Joe DiMaggio, Maria Testa
Surviving the Applewhites, Stephanie S. Tolan
Fossil Fish Found Alive: Discovering the Coelacanth, Sally M. Walker

Older Readers

Before We Were Free, Julia Alvarez
Crispin: The Cross of Lead, Avi
Six Days in October: The Stock Market Crash of 1929, Karen Blumenthal

Where the Action Was: Women War Correspondents in World War II, Penny Colman
Goddess of Yesterday, Caroline Cooney
The House of the Scorpion, Nancy Farmer
Phineas Gage: A Gruesome but True Story about Brain Science, John Fleischman
Hole in My Life, Jack Gantos
The Life and Death of Adolf Hitler, James Cross Giblin
Hoot, Carl Hiaasen
The Kite Rider, Geraldine McCaughrean
19 Varieties of Gazelle: Poems of the Middle East, Naomi Shihab Nye
When My Name Was Keoko: A Novel of Korea in World War II, Linda Sue Park
This Land Was Made for You and Me: The Life and Songs of Woody Guthrie, Elizabeth Partridge

All Ages

The Declaration of Independence, Sam Fink
Action Jackson, Jan Greenberg and Sandra Jordan
The Spider and the Fly, Mary Howitt
Fireboat: The Heroic Adventures of the John J. Harvey, Maira Kalman
Atlantic, G. Brian Karas
I Pledge Allegiance: The Pledge of Allegiance with Commentary, Bill Martin Jr. and Michael Sampson
Noah's Ark, Jerry Pinkney
Knick-Knack Paddywhack!, Paul O. Zelinsky.

Best-Selling Books, 2002

Source: *Publishers Weekly*

Rankings are based on copies "shipped and billed" in 2002, minus returns through early 2003.

Fiction

1. *The Summons*, John Grisham
2. *Red Rabbit*, Tom Clancy Putnam
3. *Remnant*, Jerry B. Jenkins and Tim LaHaye
4. *The Lovely Bones*, Alice Sebold
5. *Prey*, Michael Crichton
6. *Skipping Christmas*, John Grisham
7. *The Shelters of Stone*, Jean M. Auel
8. *Four Blind Mice*, James Patterson
9. *Everything's Eventual*, Stephen King
10. *The Nanny Diaries*, Emma McLaughlin and Nicola Kraus
11. *From a Buick 8*, Stephen King
12. *The Beach House*, James Patterson & Peter de Jonge
13. *Star Wars: Attack of the Clones*, R.A. Salvatore
14. *Nights in Rodanthe*, Nicholas Sparks
15. *Answered Prayers*, Danielle Steel

Nonfiction

1. *Self Matters*, Phillip C. McGraw
2. *A Life God Rewards*, Bruce Wilkinson with David Kopp
3. *Let's Roll!*, Lisa Beamer with Ken Abraham
4. *Guinness World Records 2003*, Guinness World Records Ltd.
5. *Who Moved My Cheese?*, Spencer Johnson
6. *Leadership*, Rudolph W. Giuliani
7. *Prayer of Jabez for Women*, Darlene Wilkinson
8. *Bush at War*, Bob Woodward
9. *Portrait of a Killer*, Patricia Cornwell
10. *Body for Life*, Bill Phillips
11. *I Hope You Dance*, Mark D. Sanders and Tia Sillers
12. *Stupid White Men*, Michael Moore
13. *Bringing Up Boys*, James Dobson
14. *Good to Great*, Jim Collins
15. *Get with the Program*, Bob Greene

Trade Paperbacks

1. *Fix-It and Forget-It Cookbook*, Dawn J. Ranck and Phyllis Pellman Good
2. *The Two Towers*, J.R.R. Tolkien
3. *The Lord of the Rings*, J.R.R. Tolkien
4. *The Return of the King*, J.R.R. Tolkien
5. *The Fellowship of the Ring*, J.R.R. Tolkien
6. *What to Expect When You're Expecting*, 3rd ed., Heidi Murkoff, Arlene Eisenberg, and Sandee Hathaway

7. *Sula*, Toni Morrison
8. *A Child Called It*, David Pelzer
9. *Empire Falls*, Richard Russo
10. *Fast Food Nation*, Eric Schlosser
11. *The Last Time They Met*, Anita Shreve
12. *The Hobbit*, J.R.R. Tolkien
13. *A Common Life*, Jan Karon
14. *Suzanne's Diary for Nicholas*, James Patterson
15. *Chicken Soup for the Mother's Soul II*, Edited by Canfield & Hansen et al.

Almanacs, Atlases, & Annuals

1. *The World Almanac and Book of Facts 2003*, Edited by Ken Park
2. *Guinness World Records 2002*, Edited by Antonia Cunningham
3. *The World Almanac and Book of Facts 2002*, Edited by Ken Park
4. *J.K. Lasser's Your Income Tax 2003*, J.K. Lasser
5. *The Ernst & Young Tax Guide 2003*, Ernst & Young
6. *AAA North American Road Atlas*
7. *The World Almanac for Kids 2003*, Edited by Kevin Seabrooke
8. *What Color Is Your Parachute 2003*, Richard Nelson Bolles

Mass Market

1. *The Summons*, John Grisham
2. *The Lord of the Rings: The Two Towers*, J.R.R. Tolkien
3. *Face the Fire*, Nora Roberts
4. *The Villa*, Nora Roberts
5. *Midnight Bayou*, Nora Roberts
6. *On the Street Where You Live*, Mary Higgins Clark
7. *The Lord of the Rings: The Fellowship of the Ring*, J.R.R. Tolkien
8. *The Hobbit*, J.R.R. Tolkien
9. *1st to Die*, James Patterson
10. *The Kiss*, Danielle Steel
11. *Violets Are Blue*, James Patterson
12. *Isle of Dogs*, Patricia Cornwell
13. *Table for Two*, Nora Roberts
14. *The Lord of the Rings: The Return of the King*, J.R.R. Tolkien
15. *The Black House*, Stephen King and Peter Straub

WORLD ALMANAC QUICK QUIZ

The U.S. magazines with the largest paid circulation, as of 2002, were *Reader's Digest* and *TV Guide*. What magazine ranked 3rd?

(a) *Better Homes & Gardens*   (b) *Family Circle*   (c) *People Weekly*   (d) *Sports Illustrated*

For the answer look in this chapter, or see page 1008.

Leading U.S. Daily Newspapers, 2002

Source: *2002 Editor & Publisher International Yearbook*
(Circulation as of Sept. 30, 2002; m = morning, e = evening)

As of Feb. 1, 2003, the number of U.S. daily newspapers had dropped to 1,457, for a net loss of 11 since Feb. 1, 2002. Average daily circulation for the 6 months ending Sept. 30, 2002, decreased by 391,889, down to 55.2 million from 55.6 million in the same period in 2001, for a decrease of about 0.7%. The overall number of Sunday papers held steady at 913. Average Sunday circulation for the 6 months ending Sept. 30, 2002, fell 310,065, or about 0.5%, from 59.1 million to 58.8 million.

Newspaper		Circulation	Newspaper		Circulation
1. Arlington (VA) *USA Today*	(m)	2,136,068	51. Oklahoma City (OK) *Daily Oklahoma*	(m)	199,581
2. New York (NY) *Wall Street Journal*	(m)	1,800.607	52. Norfolk (VA) *Virginian-Pilot*	(m)	195,866
3. New York (NY) *Times*	(m)	1,113,000	53. St. Paul (MN) *Pioneer Press*	(m)	194,870
4. Los Angeles (CA) *Times*	(m)	925,135	54. Hartford (CT) *Courant*	(m)	190,312
5. Washington (DC) *Post*	(m)	746,724	55. Omaha (NE) *World-Herald*	(all day)	190,218
6. New York (NY) *Daily News*	(m)	715,070	56. Cincinnati (OH) *Enquirer*	(m)	189,084
7. Chicago (IL) *Tribune*	(m)	679,327	57. Richmond (VA) *Times-Dispatch*	(m)	187,409
8. New York (NY) *Post*	(m)	590,061	58. Little Rock (AR) *Democrat-Gazette*	(m)	185,709
9. Long Island (NY) *Newsday*	(m)	578,809	59. Nashville (TN) *Tennessean*	(m)	184,106
10. Houston (TX) *Chronicle*	(m)	552,052	60. Austin (TX) *American-Statesman*	(m)	183,288
11. San Francisco (CA) *Chronicle*	(all day)	512,129	61. Walnut Creek (CA) *Contra Costa Times*	(m)	182,196
12. Dallas (TX) *Morning News*	(m)	505,724	62. Riverside (CA) *Press-Enterprise*	(m)	178,994
13. Chicago (IL) *Sun-Times*	(m)	479,584	63. Bergen County (NJ) *Record*	(m)	178,962
14. Boston (MA) *Globe*	(m)	467,745	64. Los Angeles (CA) *Daily News*	(m)	178,217
15. Phoenix (AZ) *Arizona Republic*	(m)	448,782	65. Rochester (NY) *Democrat and*		
16. Newark (NJ) *Star-Ledger*	(m)	408,557	*Chronicle*	(m)	172,124
17. Philadelphia (PA) *Inquirer*	(m)	373,892	66. Neptune (NJ) *Asbury Park Press*	(m)	168,718
18. Atlanta (GA) *Journal-Constitution*	(m)	371,161	67. Jacksonville (FL) *Times-Union*	(m)	168,558
19. Detroit (MI) *Free Press*	(m)	368,839	68. West Palm Beach (FL) *Post*	(m)	167,531
20. Cleveland (OH) *Plain Dealer*	(m)	363,750	69. Providence (RI) *Journal*	(m)	166,836
21. Portland (OR) *Oregonian*	(all day)	342,789	70. Las Vegas (NV) *Review-Journal*	(m)	164,848
22. Minneapolis (MN) *Star Tribune*	(m)	342,780	71. Raleigh (NC) *News & Observer*	(m)	163,460
23. San Diego (CA) *Union-Tribune*	(m)	342,447	72. Fresno (CA) *Bee*	(m)	158,286
24. St. Petersburg (FL) *Times*	(m)	333,557	73. Seattle (WA) *Post-Intelligencer*	(m)	157,558
25. Miami (FL) *Herald*	(m)	315,340	74. Memphis (TN) *Commercial Appeal*	(m)	156,513
26. Denver (CO) *Post*	(m)	305,060	75. Des Moines (IA) *Register*	(m)	152,633
27. Denver (CO) *Rocky Mountain News*	(m)	304,949	76. Philadelphia (PA) *Daily News*	(m)	150,154
28. Orange County (CA) *Register*	(m)	300,888	77. Chicago (IL) *Daily Herald*	(m)	149,882
29. Baltimore (MD) *Sun*	(m)	300,410	78. Birmingham (AL) *News*	(m)	145,571
30. St. Louis (MO) *Post-Dispatch*	(m)	287,424	79. Honolulu (HI) *Advertiser*	(all day)	143,696
31. Sacramento (CA) *Bee*	(m)	283,194	80. Toledo (OH) *Blade*	(m)	140,628
32. San Jose (CA) *Mercury News*	(m)	272,682	81. Grand Rapids (MI) *Press*	(e)	140,135
33. Kansas City (MO) *Star*	(m)	269,188	82. Tulsa (OK) *World*	(m)	139,383
34. Los Angeles (CA) *Investor's Business*			83. Westchester Co. (NY) *Journal News*	(m)	139,170
Daily	(m)	264,699	84. Salt Lake City (UT) *Tribune*	(m)	134,777
35. Orlando (FL) *Sentinel*	(all day)	256,520	85. Akron (OH) *Beacon Journal*	(m)	134,774
36. New Orleans (LA) *Times-Picayune*	(m)	255,994	86. Dayton (OH) *Daily News*	(m)	131,435
37. Indianapolis (IN) *Star*	(m)	254,624	87. Tacoma (WA) *News Tribune*	(m)	128,739
38. Columbus (OH) *Dispatch*	(m)	251,557	88. Los Angeles (CA) *La Opinion*	(m)	126,189
39. Pittsburgh (PA) *Post-Gazette*	(m)	243,091	89. Syracuse (NY) *Post-Standard*	(m)	123,836
40. Boston (MA) *Herald*	(m)	242,957	90. Greensburg (PA) *Tribune-Review*	(m)	119,338
41. Detroit (MI) *News*	(e)	242,391	91. Wilmington (DE) *News Journal*	(all day)	119,163
42. Milwaukee (WI) *Journal Sentinel*	(m)	242,234	92. Allentown (PA) *Morning Call*	(m)	118,859
43. Fort Lauderdale (FL) *Sun-Sentinel*	(m)	238,589	93. Columbia (SC) *State*	(m)	115,959
44. Charlotte (NC) *Observer*	(m)	235,759	94. Knoxville (TN) *News-Sentinel*	(m)	112,017
45. Seattle (WA) *Times*	(m)	224,140	95. Lexington (KY) *Herald-Leader*	(m)	108,892
46. Buffalo (NY) *News*	(all day)	223,957	96. Albuquerque (NM) *Journal*	(m)	108,344
47. San Antonio (TX) *Express-News*	(m)	220,998	97. Sarasota (FL) *Herald-Tribune*	(m)	106,594
48. Fort Worth (TX) *Star-Telegram*	(m)	218,975	98. Worcester (MA) *Telegram & Gazette*	(m)	102,978
49. Louisville (KY) *Courier-Journal*	(m)	217,396	99. Spokane (WA) *Spokesman-Review*	(m)	102,805
50. Tampa (FL) *Tribune*	(m)	214,178	100. Harrisburg (PA) *Patriot-News*	(m)	101,598

Leading Canadian Daily Newspapers, 2002

Source: *2002 Editor & Publisher International Yearbook*
(Circulation as of Sept. 30, 2002; m = morning)

Newspaper		Circulation	Newspaper		Circulation
Toronto (ON) *Star*	(m)	462,692	Montreal (QC) *La Presse*	(m)	183,301
Toronto (ON) *Globe and Mail*	(m)	317,138	Vancouver (BC) *Sun*	(m)	180,888
Montreal (QC) *Le Journal*	(m)	259,332	Vancouver (BC) *Province*	(m)	159,555
Toronto (ON) *National Post*	(m)	248,954	Montreal (QC) *Gazette*	(m)	141,500
Toronto (ON) *Sun*	(m)	201,640	Ottawa (ON) *Citizen*	(m)	133,455

Top 20 News/Information Websites, July 2003

Source: comScore Media Metrix, Inc.

Rank	Visitors[1]	Rank	Visitors[1]
1. AOL Proprietary News*	25,664	12. CBS Sites* (www.cbs.com)	6,033
2. MSNBC.com (www.msnbc.com)	24,168	13. BBC Sites* (www.bbc.co.uk)	5,388
3. CNN (www.cnn.com)	23,343	14. MSN Slate (www.slate.msn.com)	5,368
4. Yahoo! News (news.yahoo.com)	23,124	15. USATODAY Sites* (www.usatoday.com)	4,797
5. The Weather Channel (www.weather.com)	21,996	16. Discovery.com Sites* (www.discovery.com)	4,390
6. ABOUT.COM (www.about.com)	20,697	17. WASHINGTONPOST.COM	
7. Weatherbug.com Property (www.weatherbug.com)	14,561	(www.washingtonpost.com)	3,712
8. New York Times Digital* (www.nytimes.com)	9,774	18. FOXNEWS.COM (www.foxnews.com)	3,560
9. Knight Ridder Digital*	8,022	19. ACCUWEATHER.COM	
10. ABC News Digital* (abc.abcnews.go.com)	7,454	(wwwa.accuweather.com)	3,313
11. IBS Sites*	6,598	20. McClatchy Corporation*	3,271

(1) Number of unique visitors in thousands who visited website at least once in July 2002. *Represents an aggregation of commonly owned/branded domain names.

Top-Selling Albums of All-Time[1]

Source: Recording Industry Assn. of America, Washington, DC

Rank	Title, Artist	Sales (in millions)	Rank	Title, Artist	Sales (in millions)
1.	*Eagles/Their Greatest Hits 1971-1975*, Eagles	28.0		*Jagged Little Pill*, Alanis Morissette	16.0
2.	*Thriller*, Michael Jackson	26.0		*No Fences*, Garth Brooks	16.0
3.	*The Wall*, Pink Floyd	23.0		*Boston*, Boston	16.0
4.	*Led Zeppelin IV*, Led Zeppelin	22.0	18.	*Double Live*, Garth Brooks	15.0
5.	*Greatest Hits Volume I & Volume II*, Billy Joel	21.0		*The Beatles 1962 - 1966*, The Beatles	15.0
6.	*Rumours*, Fleetwood Mac	19.0		*Physical Graffiti*, Led Zeppelin	15.0
	Come On Over, Shania Twain	19.0		*Saturday Night Fever* (soundtrack), Bee Gees	15.0
	The Beatles, The Beatles	19.0		*Appetite For Destruction*, Guns 'N Roses	15.0
	Back In Black, AC/DC	19.0		*Dark Side of the Moon*, Pink Floyd	15.0
10.	*The Bodyguard* (soundtrack), Whitney Houston	17.0		*Born in the U.S.A.*, Bruce Springsteen	15.0
11.	*Greatest Hits*, Elton John	16.0	25.	*Bat Out of Hell*, Meat Loaf	14.0
	Hotel California, Eagles	16.0		*Backstreet Boys*, Backstreet Boys	14.0
	The Beatles 1967 - 1970, The Beatles	16.0		*Supernatural*, Santana	14.0
	Cracked Rear View, Hootie & the Blowfish	16.0		*Ropin' The Wind*, Garth Brooks	14.0

(1) As of Aug. 25, 2003; sales figures represent RIAA multi-platinum certifications, albums ranked by latest sales certification.

Songs of the Century

Source: National Endowment for the Arts and the Recording Industry Association of America

A list of 365 "Songs of the Century" was compiled in 2001, based on ballots sent to musicians, critics, industry professionals, elected officials, and amateur music fans, and was subsequently distributed to selected schools as part of a curriculum; the top 100 are listed below. Criteria for judging included historical significance and popularity of the song as the record and artist. (The list has attracted some controversy, because it is based on a relatively small number of returned ballots—about 200—and was said by some critics to give too little attention to recent pop music genres.) The year each song was first released is in parentheses.

1. "Over the Rainbow," Judy Garland (1939)
2. "White Christmas," Bing Crosby (1942)
3. "This Land Is Your Land," Woody Guthrie (1947)
4. "Respect," Aretha Franklin (1967)
5. "American Pie," Don McLean (1971)
6. "Boogie Woogie Bugle Boy," The Andrews Sisters (1941)
7. *West Side Story* (album), original cast (1957)
8. "Take Me Out to the Ball Game," Billy Murray (1908)
9. "You've Lost That Lovin' Feelin'," The Righteous Brothers (1965)
10. "The Entertainer," Scott Joplin (1902)
11. "In the Mood," Glenn Miller Orchestra (1939)
12. "Rock Around the Clock," Bill Haley & The Comets (1955)
13. "When the Saints Go Marching In," Louis Armstrong (1938)
14. "You Are My Sunshine," Jimmie Davis (1940)
15. "Mack the Knife," Bobby Darin (1959)
16. "Satisfaction," The Rolling Stones (1965)
17. "Take the 'A' Train," Duke Ellington Orchestra (1941)
18. "Blueberry Hill," Fats Domino (1956)
19. "God Bless America," Kate Smith (1939)
20. "Stars and Stripes Forever," John Philip Sousa's Band (1896)
21. "I Heard It Through the Grapevine," Marvin Gaye (1968)
22. "Dock of the Bay," Otis Redding (1968)
23. "I Left My Heart in San Francisco," Tony Bennett (1962)
24. "Good Vibrations," The Beach Boys (1967)
25. "Stand By Me," Ben E. King (1961)
26. "Stormy Weather," Lena Horne (1943)
27. "Johnny B. Goode," Chuck Berry (1958)
28. "I Want to Hold Your Hand," The Beatles (1964)
29. "Midnight Train to Georgia," Gladys Knight & The Pips (1973)
30. "Imagine," John Lennon (1971)
31. "Rudolph the Red Nosed Reindeer," Gene Autry (1949)
32. "The Twist," Chubby Checker (1960)
33. "Happy Trails," Roy Rogers & Dale Evans (1951)
34. "Your Cheatin' Heart," Hank Williams (1953)
35. "Swing Low Sweet Chariot," Fisk Jubilee Singers (1909)
36. *The Sound of Music* (album), original cast (1960)
37. "Round Midnight," Thelonius Monk (1948)
38. "What's Love Got to Do With It," Tina Turner (1984)
39. "Over There," The American Quartet (1917)
40. "Star Dust," Hoagy Carmichael (1928)
41. "Ain't Misbehavin'," Fats Waller (1929)
42. "Georgia on My Mind," Ray Charles (1960)
43. "Oh Pretty Woman," Roy Orbison (1964)
44. "Every Breath You Take," The Police (1983)
45. "My Girl," The Temptations (1965)
46. "Hotel California," The Eagles (1977)
47. "Happy Days Are Here Again," Ben Selvin Orchestra (1930)
48. "Stand By Your Man," Tammy Wynette (1968)
49. "Take Five," Dave Brubeck (1959)
50. "America the Beautiful," Louise Homer (1925)
51. "When a Man Loves a Woman," Percy Sledge (1966)
52. "Light My Fire," The Doors (1967)
53. "Stairway to Heaven," Led Zeppelin (1971)
54. "Sweet Georgia Brown," Ben Bernie Orchestra (1925)
55. "When You Wish Upon a Star," Cliff Edwards (1940)
56. "Yesterday"/"Act Naturally," The Beatles (1965)
57. "Louie Louie," The Kingsmen (1963)
58. "God Bless the Child," Billie Holiday (1941)
59. "Born in the USA," Bruce Springsteen (1975)
60. "The Girl from Ipanema," Stan Getz/Astrud Gilberto (1964)
61. "I Walk the Line," Johnny Cash (1956)
62. "The Star-Spangled Banner," John McCormick (1917)
63. "O Happy Day," The Edwin Hawkins Singers (1969)
64. "Great Balls of Fire," Jerry Lee Lewis (1957)
65. "What's Going On," Marvin Gaye (1971)
66. *Oklahoma* (album), original cast (1943)
67. "Zip-A-Dee-Doo-Dah," Johnny Mercer (1946)
68. "Don't Be Cruel"/"Hound Dog," Elvis Presley (1956)
69. "St. Louis Blues," W. C. Handy (1923)
70. "Yankee Doodle," Vess Ossman (1894)
71. "California Dreamin'," The Mamas & the Papas (1966)
72. "On the Road Again," Willie Nelson (1980)
73. "Auld Lang Syne," Frank Stanley (1907)
74. "Summertime," Sidney Bechet (1939)
75. "Theme from Shaft," Isaac Hayes (1971)
76. "Beat It," Michael Jackson (1983)
77. "Sentimental Journey," Les Brown Orchestra (1945)
78. "Blue Suede Shoes," Carl Perkins (1956)
79. "The Sound of Silence," Simon & Garfunkel (1965)
80. "Smells Like Teen Spirit," Nirvana (1992)
81. "It Had to Be You," Isham Jones Orchestra (1924)
82. "Minnie the Moocher," Cab Calloway (1931)
83. "Sixteen Tons," Tennessee Ernie Ford (1955)
84. "What a Wonderful World," Louis Armstrong (1967)
85. "Fire and Rain," James Taylor (1970)
86. "Y.M.C.A.," The Village People (1978)
87. "Heartbreak Hotel," Elvis Presley (1956)
88. "King of the Road," Roger Miller (1965)
89. "I Will Survive," Gloria Gaynor (1976)

90. "Ave Maria," Marian Anderson (1937)
91. "Begin the Beguine," Artie Shaw Orchestra (1938)
92. "Like a Rolling Stone," Bob Dylan (1965)
93. "Stop in the Name of Love," The Supremes (1965)
94. "Stayin' Alive," The Bee Gees (1978)
95. "1999," Prince (1982)
96. "Please Remember Me," Tim McGraw (1999)
97. *Porgy and Bess* (album), original cast (1935)
98. "Back in the Saddle Again," Gene Autry (1938)
99. "Shake, Rattle and Roll," Joe Turner (1954)
100. "In the Still of the Night," The Five Satins (1956)

Top-Grossing North American Concert Tours, 1985-2002
Source: Pollstar, Fresno, CA

Artist (Year)	Total gross[1]	Cities/Shows	Artist (Year)	Total gross[1]	Cities/Shows
1. The Rolling Stones (1994)	$121.2	43/60	11. U2 (1997)	$79.9	37/46
2. U2 (2001)	109.7	56/80	12. The Eagles (1994)	79.4	32/54
3. Pink Floyd (1994)	103.5	39/59	13. 'N Sync (2000)	76.4	64/86
4. Paul McCartney (2002)	103.3	43/53	14. The New Kids on the Block (1990)	74.1	122/152
5. The Rolling Stones (1989)	98.0	33/60	15. Cher (2002)	73.6	84/93
6. The Rolling Stones (1997)	89.3	26/33	16. Dave Matthews Band (2000)	68.2	43/63
7. The Rolling Stones (2002)	87.9	33/34	17. U2 (1992)	67.0	61/73
8. 'N Sync (2001)	86.8	36/43	18. Billy Joel/Elton John (2002)	65.5	14/34
9. Backstreet Boys (2001)	82.1	73/98	19. The Rolling Stones (1999)	64.7	26/34
10. Tina Turner (2000)	80.2	88/95	20. The Eagles (1995)	63.3	46/58

(1) In millions. Not adjusted for inflation.

U.S. Commercial Radio Stations, by Format, 1995-2003[1]
Source: M Street Corporation, Littleton, NH © 2002; counts are for June of each year

Primary format	2003	2002	2001	1999	1998	1997	1995
1. Country	2,100	2,131	2,190	2,306	2,368	2,491	2,613
2. News/Talk	1,812	1,179	1,139	1,159	1,131	1,111	1,036
3. Religion (Teaching, Variety)	850	332	356	363	356	404	418
4. Oldies	815	813	786	766	799	755	710
5. Spanish	711	603	574	536	493	474	427
6. Adult Contemporary (AC)	699	713	709	775	844	902	1,052
7. Contemporary Christian	581	164	164	167	164	159	132
8. Top 40	525	474	468	401	379	358	318
9. Adult Standards	506	547	569	595	561	551	470
10. Variety	451	41	39	39	43	50	62
11. Sports	429	388	338	256	251	220	148
12. Classic Rock	428	384	338	314	282	240	306
13. Hot AC	407	395	369	325	281	260	256
14. Soft AC	339	340	375	382	368	346	347
15. Alternative Rock	314	96	92	95	96	94	80
16. Rock	287	278	282	280	266	262	301
17. Black Gospel	267	254	264	257	238	208	147
18. Southern Gospel	262	240	255	269	273	255	239
19. Classic Hits	238	258	265	222	192	172	
20. R&B	207	193	183	166	171	169	184
Off Air	151	110	113	96	102	143	308
Changing format/not available	1	5	3	3	3	2	19
TOTAL STATIONS	**13,304**	**10,569**	**10,516**	**10,444**	**10,292**	**10,207**	**9,889**

(1) Data for 2000 unavailable.

Sales of Recorded Music and Music Videos, by Units Shipped and Value, 1993-2002
Source: Recording Industry Assn. of America, Washington, DC
(in millions, net after returns)

FORMAT	1993	1994	1995	1996	1997	1998	1999	2000	2001	2002	% CHANGE 2001-2002
Compact disc (CD)											
Units shipped	495.4	662.1	722.9	778.9	753.1	847.0	938.9	942.5	881.9	803.3	-8.9%
Dollar value	6,511.4	8,464.5	9,377.4	9,934.7	9,915.1	11,416.0	12,816.3	13,214.5	12,909.4	12,044.1	-6.7%
CD single											
Units shipped	7.8	9.3	21.5	43.2	66.7	56.0	55.9	34.2	17.3	4.5	-74.1%
Dollar value	45.8	56.1	110.9	184.1	272.7	213.2	222.4	142.7	79.4	19.6	-75.4%
Cassette											
Units shipped	339.5	345.4	272.6	225.3	172.6	158.5	123.6	76.0	45.0	31.1	-30.9%
Dollar value	2,915.8	2,976.4	2,303.6	1,905.3	1,522.7	1,419.9	1,061.6	626.0	363.4	209.8	-42.3%
Cassette single											
Units shipped	85.6	81.1	70.7	59.9	42.2	26.4	14.2	1.3	-1.5	-0.5	-68.8%
Dollar value	298.5	274.9	236.3	189.3	133.5	94.4	48.0	4.6	-5.3	-1.6	-70.3%
LP/EP											
Units shipped	1.2	1.9	2.2	2.9	2.7	3.4	2.9	2.2	2.3	1.7	-23.7%
Dollar value	10.6	17.8	25.1	36.8	33.3	34.0	31.8	27.7	27.4	20.5	-25.2%
Vinyl single											
Units shipped	15.1	11.7	10.2	10.1	7.5	5.4	5.3	4.8	5.5	4.4	-20.8%
Dollar value	51.2	47.2	46.7	47.5	35.6	25.7	27.9	26.3	31.4	24.9	-20.6%
Music video											
Units shipped	11.0	11.2	12.6	16.9	18.6	27.2	19.8	18.2	17.7	14.7	-17.2%
Dollar value	213.3	231.1	220.3	236.3	323.9	508.0	376.7	281.9	329.2	288.4	-12.4%
DVD audio											
Units shipped	—	—	—	—	—	—	—	—	0.3	0.4	63.8%
Dollar value	—	—	—	—	—	—	—	—	6.0	8.5	41.3%
DVD video*											
Units shipped	—	—	—	—	—	0.5	2.5	3.3	7.9	10.7	34.8%
Dollar value	—	—	—	—	—	12.2	66.3	80.3	190.7	236.3	23.9%
TOTAL UNITS	955.6	1,122.7	1,112.7	1,137.2	1,063.4	1,123.9	1,160.6	1,079.2	968.5	859.7	-11.2%
TOTAL VALUE	10,046.6	12,068.0	12,320.3	12,533.8	12,236.8	13,711.2	14,584.7	14,323.7	13,740.9	12,614.2	-8.2%

* While broken out for this chart, DVD Video Product is included in the Music Video totals.

Sales of Recorded Music and Music Videos, by Genre and Format, 1997-2002

Source: Recording Industry Assn. of America, Washington, DC

Breakdown is by percentage of sales revenue for all recorded music sold, ranked for 2002.

GENRE	2002	2001	2000	1999	1998	1997
Rock	24.7	24.4	24.8	25.2	25.7	32.5
Rap/Hip-Hop[1]	13.8	11.4	12.9	10.8	9.7	10.1
R&B/Urban[2]	11.2	10.6	9.7	10.5	12.8	11.2
Country	10.7	10.5	10.7	10.8	14.1	14.4
Pop	9.0	12.1	11.0	10.3	10.0	9.4
Religious[3]	6.7	6.7	4.8	5.1	6.3	4.5
Jazz	3.2	3.4	2.9	3.0	1.9	2.8
Classical	3.1	3.2	2.7	3.5	3.3	2.8
Soundtracks	1.1	1.4	0.7	0.8	1.7	1.2
Oldies	0.9	0.8	0.9	0.7	0.7	0.8
New Age	0.5	1.0	0.5	0.5	0.6	0.8

GENRE	2002	2001	2000	1999	1998	1997
Children's	0.4	0.5	0.6	0.4	0.4	0.9
Other[4]	8.1	7.9	8.3	9.1	7.9	5.7
FORMAT						
Compact disc (CD)	90.5	89.2	89.3	83.2	74.8	70.2
Cassette	2.4	3.4	4.9	8.0	14.8	18.2
Singles (all types)	1.9	2.4	2.5	5.4	6.8	9.3
Music Videos/ Digital Video Disc (DVD)[5]	0.7	1.1	0.8	0.9	1.0	0.6
Digital download[6]	0.5	0.2	NA	NA	NA	NA
LPs	0.7	0.6	0.5	0.5	0.7	0.7

(1) Includes Rap (10.5% in 2002) and Hip-Hop (3.3% in 2002). (2) Includes R&B, blues, dance, disco, funk, fusion, Motown, reggae, soul. (3) Includes Christian, Gospel, Inspirational, Religious, and Spiritual. (4) "Other" includes Ethnic, Standards, Big Band, Swing, Latin, Electronic, Instrumental, Comedy, Humor, Spoken Word, Exercise, Language, Folk, and Holiday Music. (5) 2001 is the first year that music video/ DVD was recorded separately from audio DVD (not shown). (6) 2001 is the first year that data was collected on digital download purchases.

Multi-Platinum and Platinum Awards for Recorded Music and Music Videos, 2002

Source: Recording Industry Assn. of America, Washington, DC

To achieve platinum status, an **album** must reach a minimum sale of 1 mil units in LPs, tapes, and CDs, with a manufacturer's dollar volume of at least $2 mil based on one-third of the suggested retail list price for each record, tape, or CD sold. To achieve multi-platinum status, an album must reach a minimum sale of at least 2 mil units in LPs, tapes, and CDs, with a manufacturer's dollar volume of at least $4 mil based on one-third of the list price.

Singles must sell 1 mil units to achieve a platinum award (created in 1976) and 2 mil to achieve a multi-platinum award (created in 1984). In 1999, the Diamond Award, honoring sales of 10 million or more copes of an album or single was introduced. EP singles count as 2 units. Double-CD sets count as 2 units. **Music videos** (long form) must sell 100,000 units to qualify for a platinum award and must sell more than 200,000 units for a multi-platinum award. **Video singles**, which must have a maximum running time of 15 minutes and no more than 2 songs per title, must sell 50,000 units to qualify for a platinum award and at least 100,000 units to qualify for a multi-platinum award.

Awards listed were for albums and singles released in 2002 and for music videos released at any time.

Albums, Multi-Platinum
(numbers in parentheses = millions sold)

A New Day Has Come, Celine Dion (2)
Ashanti, Ashanti (3)
Busted Stuff, The Dave Matthews Band (2)
The Blueprint 2: The Gift and the Curse, Jay-Z (3)
Come Away With Me, Norah Jones (2)
Cry, Faith Hill (2)
Drive, Alan Jackson (3)
8 Mile (soundtrack), various artists (3)
ELV1S: 30 #1 Hits, Elvis Presley (3)
The Eminem Show, Eminem (7)
Forty Licks, The Rolling Stones (3)
Home, Dixie Chicks (3)
Justified, Justin Timberlake (2)
Let Go, Avril Lavigne (4)
Nellyville, Nelly (5)
No Shoes, No Shirt, No Problems, Kenny Chesney (2)
The Rising, Bruce Springsteen (2)
Shaman, Santana (2)
Stripped, Christina Aguilera (2)
Unleashed, Toby Keith (2)

Albums, Platinum

Be Not Nobody, Vanessa Carlton
Believe, Disturbed
The Best of Both Worlds, R. Kelly & Jay-Z
By the Way, Red Hot Chili Peppers
C'mon, C'mon, Sheryl Crow
Come Home with Me, Cam'ron
Elton John's Greatest Hits: 1970-2002, Elton John
Full Moon, Brandy
It Had to Be You...The Great American Songbook, Rod Stewart
J to the L-O!: The Remixes, Jennifer Lopez
Juslisen, Musiq
The Last Temptation, Ja Rule
Melt, Rascal Flatts
More Than You Think You Are, Matchbox Twenty
MTV Unplugged 2.0, Lauryn Hill
Nirvana, Nirvana
Now That's What I Call Music! Vol. 9, various artists
Now That's What I Call Music! Vol. 10, various artists
O, Yeah! Ultimate Aerosmith Hits, Aerosmith
P. Diddy Presents: We Invented the Remix, various artists
Reanimation, Linkin Park
Spider-Man (soundtrack), various artists
3D, TLC
Totally Hits 2002, various artists
Ultimate Manilow, Barry Manilow

Undaground Legend, Lil' Flip
Under Construction, Missy Elliott
Under Rug Swept, Alanis Morissette
Untouchables, Korn
Watermelon, Chicken, & Gritz, Nappy Roots
WWE: The Anthology (soundtrack), various artists
The Very Best of Chicago: Only the Beginning, Chicago
The Young and the Hopeless, Good Charlotte

Music Videos, Platinum

All Access Europe, Eminem
All the Way: A Decade of Song and Video, Celine Dion
Band of Gypsies—Live at the Fillmore, Jimi Hendrix
Billy Graham Homecoming, Vol. 1, various artists
Billy Graham Homecoming, Vol. 2, various artists
The Black Sabbath Story, Vol. 1: 1970-1978, Black Sabbath
The Brand New Day Tour, Sting
Bring the Pain, Chris Rock
Chronicles, Rush
The Colour of My Love, Celine Dion
Deuce, Korn
Don't Blame Me, Ozzy Osbourne
Drowned World Tour 2001, Madonna
Frat Party at the Pankake Festival, Linkin Park
Hide'em in Your Heart, Vol. 2, Steve Green
Janet: Live in Hawaii, Janet Jackson
Live . . . and Alone, Melissa Etheridge
Live and Loud, Ozzy Osbourne
Live at Folsom Field, The Dave Matthews Band
Mark Lowry on Broadway, Mark Lowry
Memphis Homecoming, various artists
One Night Only, Elton John
Pop Odyssey Live, 'N Sync
Rivers of Joy, various artists
Sacred Fire Live, Santana
Shockumentary, Insane Clown Posse
The Up in Smoke Tour, various artists
The Wildlife Concert, John Denver
Woodstock 99, various artists
Worship, Michael W. Smith

Music Videos, Multi-Platinum

America: A Tribute to Heroes, various artists (2)
Britney—The Videos, Britney Spears (2)
The Concert for New York City, various artists (2)
Elevation Tour 2001: Live from Boston, U2 (2)
Listener Supported, The Dave Matthews Band (3)
Live on Broadway, Robin Williams (2)
Live in Concert, Sade (2)
Live from Las Vegas, Britney Spears (2)
Live in New York City, Bruce Springsteen (3)
We Will Rock You, Queen (2)

WORLD ALMANAC EDITORS' PICKS
FAVORITE PARLOR GAMES

The editors of *The World Almanac* have ranked the following as their favorite parlor games:

1. Scrabble ®
2. Trivial Pursuit ®
3. Monopoly ®
4. Pictionary ®
5. Chess
6. Charades
7. Bridge
8. Backgammon
9. Poker
10. Checkers

Readers are invited to submit their own lists for these and other Editors' Picks; see instructions on page 1007. Results will be published in *The World Almanac 2005.*

Top-Selling Video Games, 2002

Source: The NPDFunworldSM TRSTS® Service, The NPD Group, Inc., Port Washington, NY; ranked by units sold.

Platform, Title
1. Sony PlayStation 2, Grand Theft Auto: Vice City
2. Sony PlayStation 2, Grand Theft Auto 3
3. Sony PlayStation 2, Madden NFL 2003
4. Nintendo Game Boy Advance, Super Mario Advance 2
5. Sony PlayStation 2, Gran Turismo 3: A-Spec
6. Sony PlayStation 2, Medal Honor Frontline
7. Sony PlayStation 2, Spider-Man: The Movie
8. Sony PlayStation 2, Kingdom Hearts

Platform, Title
9. Microsoft Xbox, Halo
10. Nintendo GameCube, Super Mario Sunshine
11. Sony PlayStation 2, Tony Hawk's Pro Skater 4
12. Nintendo Game Boy Advance, Yu-Gi-Oh! Eternal
13. Nintendo Game Boy Advance, Dragonball Z: Goku
14. Sony PlayStation 2, Lord of the Rings: Two Towers
15. Nintendo Gameboy Color, Yu-Gi-Oh! Dark Duel

U.S. Television Set Owners, 2003

Source: Nielsen Media Research; March 2003

Of the 106.7 million homes (98% of U.S. households) that owned at least one TV set in 2003:

100% had color televisions	41% had 3 or more TV sets	70% received basic cable
34% had 2 TV sets	91% had a VCR	48% received premium cable

Some Television Addresses, Phone Numbers, Internet Sites

ABC, Inc.—American Broadcasting Co.
500 S. Buena Vista St.
Burbank, CA 91521; (818) 460-7477
Website: abc.go.com

CBS—Columbia Broadcasting System
51 W. 52nd St.
New York, NY 10019; (212) 975-4321
Website: www.cbs.com

Fox—Fox Network
Fox Entertainment Group
1211 Avenue of the Americas
New York, NY 10036; (212) 852-7111
Website: www.fox.com

NBC—National Broadcasting Co.
30 Rockefeller Plaza
New York, NY 10112; (212) 664-4444
Website: www.nbc.com

PBS—Public Broadcasting Service
1320 Braddock Place
Alexandria, VA 22314; (703) 739-5000
Website: www.pbs.org

UPN—United Paramount Network
11800 Wilshire Blvd.
Los Angeles, CA 90025; (310) 575-7000
Website: www.upn.com

WB—WB Television Network
4000 Warner Blvd., Bldg. 34R
Burbank, CA 91522; (818) 977-5000
Website: www.thewb.com

CABLE

ABCFAMILY—ABC Family Channel
500 S. Buena Vista St.
Burbank, CA 91521; (818) 560-1000
Website: www.ABCfamily.com

A&E—Arts & Entertainment Network
235 E 45th St.
New York, NY 10017; (212) 210-1400
Website: www.aetv.com

AMC—American Movie Classics
200 Jericho Quadrangle
Jericho, NY 11753; (516) 803-4300
Website: www.amctv.com

APL—Animal Planet
One Discovery Place
Silver Spring, MD 20910-3354;
(240) 662-0000
Website: www.animalplanet.com

BET—Black Entertainment Television
1 BET Plaza, 1235 W St. NE
Washington, DC 20018; (202) 608-2000
Website: www.bet.com

CNBC—Consumer News and Business Channel
2200 Fletcher Ave.
Fort Lee, NJ 07024; (201) 585-2622
Website: www.cnbc.com

CNN—Cable News Network
One CNN Center
Atlanta, GA 30303; (404) 827-1500
Website: www.cnn.com

COMEDY—Comedy Central
1775 Broadway
11th Floor
New York, NY 10019; (212) 767-8600
Website: www.comedycentral.com

C-SPAN—Cable Satellite Public Affairs Network
400 N Capitol St. NW, Suite 650
Washington, DC 20001; (202) 737-3220
Website: www.c-span.org

DISN—The Disney Channel
3800 W Alameda Ave.
Burbank, CA 91505; (818) 569-7500
Website: www.disneychannel.com

DSC—The Discovery Channel
Discovery Communications
One Discovery Place
Silver Spring, MD 20910-3354;
(240) 662-0000
Website: www.discovery.com

ESPN—ESPN, Inc.
ESPN Plaza, 935 Middle St.
Bristol, CT 06010; (860) 766-2000
Website: www.espn.com

FOOD—Food Network
1180 Avenue of the Americas, 11th Floor
New York, NY 10036; (212) 398-8836
Website: www.foodnetwork.com

HBO—Home Box Office
1100 Avenue of the Americas
New York, NY 10036; (212) 512-1000
Website: www.hbo.com

HIST—The History Channel
235 E. 45th St.
New York, NY 10017; (212) 210-1375
Website: www.historychannel.com

LIFE—Lifetime
309 W 49th St.
New York, NY 10019; (212) 424-7000
Website: www.lifetimetv.com

MSNBC—Microsoft NBC News
1 MSNBC Plaza
Secaucus, NJ 07094; (201) 583-0000
Website: www.msnbc.com

MTV—Music Television
MTV Networks, Inc.
1515 Broadway
New York, NY 10036; (212) 258-8000
Website: www.mtv.com

NICK—Nickelodeon
MTV Networks, Inc.
1515 Broadway
New York, NY 10036; (212) 258-8000
Website: www.nick.com

Spike TV
MTV Networks
1515 Broadway, 37th Floor
New York, NY 10036; (212) 846-8000
Websites: www.thenewtnn.com,
www.spiketv.com

TBS—Turner Broadcasting System
1050 Techwood Dr. NW
Atlanta, GA 30318
(404) 827-1700
Website: www.tbssuperstation.com

TLC—The Learning Channel
Discovery Communications
One Discovery Place
Silver Spring, MD 20910; (240) 662-2000
Website: tlc.discovery.com

TWC—The Weather Channel
300 Interstate North Parkway
Atlanta, GA 30339-2404; (770) 226-0000
Website: www.weather.com

USA—USA Network
USA Networks
1230 Avenue of the Americas
New York, NY 10020; (212) 413-5000
Website: www.usanetwork.com

Number of Cable TV Systems,[1] 1975-2002

Source: *Television and Cable Factbook*, Warren Publishing, Inc., Washington, DC; estimates as of Jan. 1

Year	Systems	Year	Systems	Year	Systems	Year	Systems	Year	Systems	Year	Systems
1975	3,506	1980	4,225	1985	6,600	1990	9,575	1995	11,218	2000	10,400
1976	3,681	1981	4,375	1986	7,500	1991	10,704	1996	11,119	2001	9,924
1977	3,832	1982	4,825	1987	7,900	1992	11,035	1997	10,950	2002	9,947
1978	3,875	1983	5,600	1988	8,500	1993	11,108	1998	10,845		
1979	4,150	1984	6,200	1989	9,050	1994	11,214	1999	10,700		

(1) The satellite-signal-receiving hardware, cable lines, and cable boxes that provide cable programming to homes within a geographic area.

Top 20 Cable TV Networks, 2003

Source: *Cable Television Developments*, Natl. Cable Television Assn., Feb 2003; ranked by number of subscribers

Rank	Network[1]	Subscribers (mil)	Rank	Network[1]	Subscribers (mil)
1.	TBS Superstation (1976)	87.7	11.	Spike TV (2003)[2]	85.8
2.	ESPN (1979)	86.7	12.	The Weather Channel (1982)	85.3
3.	C-SPAN (1979)	86.6	13.	MTV (Music Television) (1981)	84.9
4.	Discovery Channel (1985)	86.5		QVC (1986)*	84.9
5.	USA (1980)	86.3	15.	ABC Family Channel (2001)[3]	84.8
6.	CNN (Cable News Network) (1980)	86.2	16.	TLC (The Learning Channel) (1980)	84.7
	TNT (Turner Network Television) (1988)	86.2	17.	ESPN2 (1993)	84.5
8.	Lifetime Television (LIFE) (1984)	86.0	18.	CNBC (1989)	84.1
	Nickelodeon (1979)/Nick at Nite (1985)	86.0	19.	AMC (American Movie Classics) (1984)	83.9
10.	A&E Network (1984)	85.9	20.	VH1 (Music First) (1985)	83.7

Note: Data include noncable affiliates. *As of Jan. 2003. (1) Date in parentheses is year service began. (2) Formerly The Nashville Network (1983-2000); The National Network (2000-2003); The New TNN (2003). (3) Began 1977 as the Family Channel; FOX Family Channel (1998-2000).

U.S. Households With Cable Television, 1977-2002

Source: Nielsen Media Research

Year	Basic cable subscribers	As % of households with TVs	Year	Basic cable subscribers	As % of households with TVs	Year	Basic cable subscribers	As % of households with TVs
1977	12,168,450	16.6	1986	42,237,140	48.1	1995	62,956,470	65.7
1978	13,391,910	17.9	1987	44,970,880	50.5	1996	64,654,160	66.7
1979	14,814,380	19.4	1988	48,636,520	53.8	1997	65,929,420	67.3
1980	17,671,490	22.6	1989	52,564,470	57.1	1998	67,011,180	67.4
1981	23,219,200	28.3	1990	54,871,330	59.0	1999	68,537,980	68.0
1982	29,340,570	35.0	1991	55,786,390	60.6	2000	69,297,290	67.8
1983	34,113,790	40.5	1992	57,211,600	61.5	2001	72,958,180	69.2
1984	37,290,870	43.7	1993	58,834,440	62.5	2002	73,525,150	68.9
1985	39,872,520	46.2	1994	60,483,600	63.4			

Average U.S. Television Viewing Time, October 2002

Source: Nielsen Media Research (hours: minutes per week)

Group	Age	Total per week	M-F 7-10 AM	M-F 10 AM-4:00 PM	M-SUN 8-11 PM	SAT 7 AM-1 PM	M-F 11:30 PM-1 AM	Sunday 1-7:00 PM
	18+	35:17	5:11	5:11	9:42	0:54	1:37	1:09
	18-24	23:11	3:32	3:32	5:54	0:35	1:19	1:37
	25-54	33:16	4:25	4:25	9:16	0:55	1:39	1:34
Women	55+	44:01	7:16	7:16	12:04	1:01	1:40	1:55
	18+	21:31	1:40	3:36	9:10	0:50	1:37	1:58
	18-24	23:18	0:56	2:49	5:21	0:33	1:31	1:24
	25-54	30:25	1:29	2:56	8:55	0:51	1:38	1:56
Men	55+	39:39	2:25	5:26	11:29	0:57	1:35	2:19
Teens	12-17	21:00	0:50	1:53	5:54	0:49	0:52	1:16
Children	2-11	20:30	1:42	2:58	4:49	1:11	0:29	1:04
ALL VIEWERS		**30:35**	**1:52**	**3:59**	**8:27**	**0:55**	**1:22**	**1:38**

TV Viewing Shares, Broadcast Years 1990-2002[1]

Source: *Cable TV Facts*, Cable Advertising Bureau, New York, NY

	All Television Households[2]					All Cable Households[2]					Pay Cable Households[2]				
	'90	'95	'00	'01	'02	'90	'95	'00	'01	'02	'90	'95	'00	'01	'02
Network Affiliates[3]	55	48	44	42	39	46	41	40	37	35	43	38	37	35	33
Indep. TV Stations[4]	20	22	12	11	11	16	17	9	8	8	16	17	9	8	8
Public TV Stations	3	3	3	3	3	3	3	2	2	2	2	2	2	2	2
Basic Cable[5]	21	30	46	49	49	32	42	55	57	56	30	41	55	57	56
Pay Cable	6	6	6	6	6	10	8	7	7	7	18	15	11	11	12

Note: After 1998, Fox affiliates switched from Independent classification to Network Affiliates. (1) Broadcast years represent the 12-month period October-September. (2) Share figures refer to percentage of the viewing audience for all television viewing, 24 hours/day. As a result of multiset use and rounding of numbers, share figures add to more than 100. (3) Includes CBS, NBC, ABC, and FOX. (4) Includes WB, UPN, and PAX. (5) Includes ad-supported cable and all other cable (non-pay and non-ad-supported channels).

Favorite Syndicated Programs, 2002-2003

Source: Nielsen Media Research, Sept. 23, 2002- May 25, 2003

Average audience percentages, or ratings, are estimates of the percentage of TV-owning households watching a program.

Rank	Program	Avg. audience (%)	Rank	Program	Avg. audience (%)
1.	Wheel of Fortune	9.3	12.	Judge Judy	5.2
2.	Jeopardy!	7.3	13.	Seinfeld (weekend)	5.1
3.	Friends	7.0		ESPN NFL Regular Season 2	5.1
4.	Seinfeld (7:30 PM)	6.9	15.	MMN Home Team Baseball	5.0
5.	ESPN NFL Regular Season	6.4	16.	Dr. Phil Show	4.7
6.	Everybody Loves Raymond	6.2	17.	Wheel of Fortune (weekend)	4.5
7.	Seinfeld (weekend)	6.1	18.	Will & Grace	4.1
8.	Oprah Winfrey Show	5.9	19.	That 70s Show	3.7
9.	Entertainment Tonight	5.8		Warner Bros. Vol. 32	3.7
10.	Seinfeld (11:00 PM)	5.7	21.	Live with Regis and Kelly	3.6
11.	World Wrestling Entertainment	5.4			

Favorite Prime-Time Television Programs, 2002-2003

Source: Nielsen Media Research

Data are for regularly scheduled network programs in 2002-2003 season through May 22; ranked by average audience percentage. Average audience percentages, or ratings, are estimates of the percentage of all TV-owning households that are watching a particular program. Audience share percentages are estimates of the percentage of those watching TV that are tuned into a particular program. Tied programs are given the same rank.

Rank	Programs	Avg. Audience	Audience Share	Rank	Programs	Avg. Audience	Audience Share
1.	CSI	16.1	24	28.	King of Queens	8.5	13
2.	Friends	13.8	22	29.	Frasier	8.4	13
3.	Joe Millionaire	13.3	19	30.	NFL Monday Showcase	8.3	13
4.	E.R.	12.9	21		The Guardian	8.3	13
5.	American Idol –Tuesday	12.6	19	32.	My Big Fat Greek Life	8.0	13
6.	American Idol – Wednesday	12.5	19	33.	Big Brother 3 – Wednesday	7.8	12
7.	Survivor: Thailand	12.1	19		NYPD Blue	7.8	13
8.	Everybody Loves Raymond	11.9	18	35.	Fear Factor	7.7	12
9.	Survivor: Amazon	11.7	18	36.	Providence	7.6	14
	Law and Order	11.7	19	37.	Extreme Makeover – Wednesday	7.5	12
11.	NFL Monday Night Football	11.2	19	38.	Third Watch	7.4	11
12.	CSI: Miami	11.0	18		60 Minutes II (9 PM)	7.4	11
13.	Will & Grace	10.9	16		Dateline–Friday	7.4	13
14.	The Bachelorette	10.7	16	41.	60 Minutes II	7.3	12
15.	Scrubs	10.3	16		Simpsons	7.3	12
16.	Law and Order: SVU	10.0	18	43.	Frasier – Thursday (9:30 PM)	7.2	12
	Without a Trace	10.0	17		Crossing Jordan	7.2	12
18.	The Bachelor	9.6	15	45.	24	7.1	11
19.	60 Minutes	9.5	16		My Wife and Kids	7.1	12
	Judging Amy	9.5	16		Wanda at Large	7.1	11
21.	Still Standing	9.4	14	48.	CBS Sunday Movie	7.0	11
22.	Law & Order: Criminal Intent (10 PM)	9.3	15		Star Search–Wednesday	7.0	11
	Law & Order: Criminal Intent	9.3	14		Dateline NBC – Tuesday	7.0	12
24.	The West Wing	9.0	14		8 Simple Rules for Dating My Teenage Daughter	7.0	11
25.	JAG	8.9	14		Ed	7.0	11
26.	Good Morning Miami	8.7	13		Becker	7.0	11
27.	Yes, Dear	8.6	13				

* Program ran at 8:30 pm for 5 weeks.

All-Time Highest-Rated Television Programs

Source: Nielsen Media Research, Jan. 1961-April 2003

Estimates exclude unsponsored or joint network telecasts (e.g., presidential addresses) or programs under 30 minutes long. Ranked by rating (percentage of TV-owning households tuned in to the program).

Rank	Program	Telecast date	Network	Rating (%)	Avg. households (in thousands)
1.	M*A*S*H (last episode)	2/28/83	CBS	60.2	50,150
2.	Dallas (Who Shot J.R.?)	11/21/80	CBS	53.3	41,470
3.	Roots-Pt. 8	1/30/77	ABC	51.1	36,380
4.	Super Bowl XVI	1/24/82	CBS	49.1	40,020
5.	Super Bowl XVII	1/30/83	NBC	48.6	40,480
6.	XVII Winter Olympics - 2nd Wed.	2/23/94	CBS	48.5	45,690
7.	Super Bowl XX	1/26/86	NBC	48.3	41,490
8.	Gone With the Wind-Pt. 1	11/7/76	NBC	47.7	33,960
9.	Gone With the Wind-Pt. 2	11/8/76	NBC	47.4	33,750
10.	Super Bowl XII	1/15/78	CBS	47.2	34,410
11.	Super Bowl XIII	1/21/79	NBC	47.1	35,090
12.	Bob Hope Christmas Show	1/15/70	NBC	46.6	27,260
13.	Super Bowl XVIII	1/22/84	CBS	46.4	38,800
	Super Bowl XIX	1/20/85	ABC	46.4	39,390
15.	Super Bowl XIV	1/20/80	CBS	46.3	35,330
16.	Super Bowl XXX	1/28/96	NBC	46.0	44,150
	ABC Theater (The Day After)	11/20/83	ABC	46.0	38,550

Rank	Program	Telecast date	Network	Rating (%)	Avg. households (in thousands)
18.	Roots-Pt. 6.	1/28/77	ABC	45.9	32,680
	The Fugitive.	8/29/67	ABC	45.9	25,700
20.	Super Bowl XXI	1/25/87	CBS	45.8	40,030
21.	Roots-Pt. 5.	1/27/77	ABC	45.7	32,540
22.	Super Bowl XXVIII	1/30/94	NBC	45.5	42,860
	Cheers (last episode).	5/20/93	NBC	45.5	42,360
24.	Ed Sullivan.	2/9/64	CBS	45.3	23,240
25.	Super Bowl XXVII	1/31/93	NBC	45.1	41,990
26.	Bob Hope Christmas Show	1/14/71	NBC	45.0	27,050
27.	Roots-Pt. 3.	1/25/77	ABC	44.8	31,900
28.	Super Bowl XXXII	1/25/98	NBC	44.5	43,630
29.	Super Bowl XI	1/9/77	NBC	44.4	31,610
	Super Bowl XV.	1/25/81	NBC	44.4	34,540
31.	Super Bowl VI	1/16/72	CBS	44.2	27,450
32.	XVII Winter Olympics - 2nd Fri.	2/25/94	CBS	44.1	41,540
	Roots-Pt. 2.	1/24/77	ABC	44.1	31,400
34.	Beverly Hillbillies	1/8/64	CBS	44.0	22,570
35.	Roots-Pt. 4.	1/26/77	ABC	43.8	31,190
	Ed Sullivan.	2/16/64	CBS	43.8	22,445
37.	Super Bowl XXIII	1/22/89	NBC	43.5	39,320
38.	Academy Awards.	4/7/70	ABC	43.4	25,390
39.	Super Bowl XXXI	1/26/97	FOX	43.3	42,000
	Super Bowl XXXIV	1/30/00	ABC	43.3	43,620
41.	Thorn Birds-Pt. 3	3/29/83	ABC	43.2	35,990
42.	Thorn Birds-Pt. 4	3/30/83	ABC	43.1	35,900
43.	CBS NFC Championship	1/10/82	CBS	42.9	34,960
44.	Beverly Hillbillies	1/15/64	CBS	42.8	21,960
45.	Super Bowl VII.	1/14/73	NBC	42.7	27,670

Top-Rated TV Shows of Each Season, 1950-51 to 2002-2003

Source: Nielsen Media Research; regular series programs, Sept.-May season

Season	Program	Rating[1]	TV-owning households (in thousands)	Season	Program	Rating[1]	TV-owning households (in thousands)
1950-51	Texaco Star Theatre.	61.6	10,320	1977-78	Laverne & Shirley	31.6	72,900
1951-52	Godfrey's Talent Scouts.	53.8	15,300	1978-79	Laverne & Shirley	30.5	74,500
1952-53	I Love Lucy.	67.3	20,400	1979-80	60 Minutes.	28.2	76,300
1953-54	I Love Lucy.	58.8	26,000	1980-81	Dallas	31.2	79,900
1954-55	I Love Lucy.	49.3	30,700	1981-82	Dallas	28.4	81,500
1955-56	$64,000 Question.	47.5	34,900	1982-83	60 Minutes.	25.5	83,300
1956-57	I Love Lucy.	43.7	38,900	1983-84	Dallas	25.7	83,800
1957-58	Gunsmoke	43.1	41,920	1984-85	Dynasty	25.0	84,900
1958-59	Gunsmoke	39.6	43,950	1985-86	Cosby Show	33.8	85,900
1959-60	Gunsmoke	40.3	45,750	1986-87	Cosby Show	34.9	87,400
1960-61	Gunsmoke	37.3	47,200	1987-88	Cosby Show	27.8	88,600
1961-62	Wagon Train.	32.1	48,555	1988-89	Roseanne	25.5	90,400
1962-63	Beverly Hillbillies	36.0	50,300	1989-90	Roseanne	23.4	92,100
1963-64	Beverly Hillbillies	39.1	51,600	1990-91	Cheers.	21.6	93,100
1964-65	Bonanza.	36.3	52,700	1991-92	60 Minutes.	21.7	92,100
1965-66	Bonanza.	31.8	53,850	1992-93	60 Minutes.	21.6	93,100
1966-67	Bonanza.	29.1	55,130	1993-94	Home Improvement.	21.9	94,200
1967-68	Andy Griffith.	27.6	56,670	1994-95	Seinfeld.	20.5	95,400
1968-69	Rowan & Martin's Laugh-In	31.8	58,250	1995-96	E.R.	22.0	95,900
1969-70	Rowan & Martin's Laugh-In	26.3	58,500	1996-97	E.R.	21.2	97,000
1970-71	Marcus Welby, MD	29.6	60,100	1997-98	Seinfeld.	22.0	98,000
1971-72	All in the Family	34.0	62,100	1998-99	E.R.	17.8	99,400
1972-73	All in the Family	33.3	64,800	1999-2000	Who Wants to Be a Millionaire	18.6	100,800
1973-74	All in the Family	31.2	66,200				
1974-75	All in the Family	30.2	68,500	2000-01	Survivor II	17.4	102,200
1975-76	All in the Family	30.1	69,600	2001-02	Friends	15.3	105,500
1976-77	Happy Days	31.5	71,200	2002-03	CSI	16.1	106,700

(1) Rating is percent of TV-owning households tuned in to the program. Data prior to 1988-89 exclude Alaska and Hawaii.

100 Leading U.S. Advertisers, 2002

Source: Reprinted with permission from AdAge.com and the June 23, 2003, issue of *Advertising Age*, © Crain Communications Inc. 2002

(in millions of dollars)

Rank	Advertiser	Ad spending	Rank	Advertiser	Ad spending
1.	General Motors Corp.	3,652	11.	Sony Corp.	1,621
2.	AOL Time Warner.	2,923	12.	GlaxoSmithKline	1,554
3.	Procter & Gamble Co.	2,673	13.	Toyota Motor Corp.	1,553
4.	Pfizer.	2,566	14.	Verizon Communications	1,527
5.	Ford Motor Co.	2,252	15.	McDonald's Corp.	1,336
6.	DaimlerChrysler	2,032	16.	Viacom	1,260
7.	Walt Disney Co.	1,803	17.	Altria Group	1,206
8.	Johnson & Johnson.	1,799	18.	Honda Motor Co.	1,193
9.	Sears, Roebuck & Co.	1,661	19.	Merck & Co.	1,158
10.	Unilever.	1,640	20.	L'Oreal	1,118

Rank	Advertiser	Ad spending	Rank	Advertiser	Ad spending
21.	PepsiCo	1,114	61.	Albertson's	525
22.	J. C. Penney Co.	1,108	62.	Dell Computer Corp.	511
23.	SBC Communications	1,092	63.	Deutsche Telekom	509
24.	U. S. Government	1,083	64.	Kroger Co.	509
25.	Nestle	1,073	65.	Schering-Plough Corp.	508
26.	Nissan Motor Co.	967	66.	Gillette Co.	495
27.	Target Corp.	960	67.	Aventis	486
28.	General Mills	954	68.	SABMiller	459
29.	Microsoft Corp.	909	69.	Campbell Soup Co.	447
30.	Home Depot	885	70.	Lowe's Cos.	444
31.	AT&T Wireless	873	71.	Gap Inc.	434
32.	Sprint Corp.	863	72.	Kellogg Co.	429
33.	IBM Corp.	832	73.	Visa International	423
34.	Best Buy Co.	819	74.	Adolph Coors Co.	420
35.	AT&T Corp.	815	75.	Limited Brands	411
36.	Estee Lauder Cos.	805	76.	Berkshire Hathaway	399
37.	Diageo	798	77.	Cadbury Schweppes	396
38.	Anheuser-Busch Cos.	793	78.	Mitsubishi Motors	392
39.	Hewlett-Packard Co.	736	79.	Mattel	384
40.	Yum Brands	733	80.	MCI	371
41.	Cendant Corp.	727	81.	Bayer	371
42.	Wyeth	725	82.	Wendy's International	359
43.	News Corp.	716	83.	MasterCard International	358
44.	Federated Department Stores.	715	84.	Safeway	356
45.	ConAgra Foods	680	85.	Doctor's Associates	353
46.	May Department Stores Co.	656	86.	Kimberly-Clark Corp.	352
47.	Mars Inc.	653	87.	Intel Corp.	345
48.	Burger King Corp.	650	88.	Morgan Stanley	342
49.	Kmart Corp.	629	89.	Circuit City Stores	341
50.	Nike	624	90.	SC Johnson	341
51.	Wal-Mart Stores	618	91.	Colgate-Palmolive Co.	337
52.	Sara Lee Corp.	605	92.	United Parcel Service	331
53.	Volkswagen	602	93.	Hershey Foods Corp.	331
54.	Vivendi Universal	591	94.	Nextel Communications	320
55.	General Electric Co.	579	95.	Reckitt Benckiser	318
56.	Clorox Co.	572	96.	Kia Motors Corp.	316
57.	Novartis	569	97.	Kohl's Corp.	316
58.	Coca-Cola Co.	569	98.	Fortune Brands.	313
59.	Bristol-Myers Squibb	563	99.	Eastman Kodak Co.	312
60.	American Express Co.	542	100.	Office Depot	312

U.S. Ad Spending by Top Categories, 2002

Source: Reprinted with permission from AdAge.com and the June 23, 2003, issue of *Advertising Age*, © Crain Communications Inc. 2003

(in millions of dollars, Jan.-Dec. 2002)

Category	Total	Mag.	Sun. Mag.	News-paper	Nat'l News-paper	Out-door	Televison Net-work	Spot	Syndi-cated	Cable	Radio Net-work	Spot
Automotive	$16,365	$1,698	$32	$4,406	$323	$282	$2,448	$3,871	$171	$952	$58	$252
Retail	13,528	882	132	5,704	288	276	1,802	2,350	196	702	110	496
Movies, media & advertising	6,024	890	27	1,441	300	210	1,033	617	188	456	85	177
Food, beverages & confectionery	6,015	1,218	55	26	9	72	1,950	831	437	1,011	91	121
Medicines & proprietary remedies	5,445	1,237	126	166	29	9	2,039	328	504	802	91	50
Financial services	4,658	707	47	882	388	125	1,039	340	93	734	40	118
Telecommunications	4,297	227	3	1,085	172	115	781	664	87	430	21	220
Toiletries, cosmetics & personal care	4,200	1,426	27	8	5	12	1,226	162	341	461	28	13
Airline travel, hotels & resorts	3,800	770	44	1,166	295	275	257	468	26	307	38	64
Restaurants	3,741	37	3	89	8	184	1,166	1,296	183	364	24	120
Direct response companies	3,582	1,112	397	153	109	1	270	172	212	790	31	12
Home furnishings, appliances, supplies	2,674	678	39	16	6	5	779	124	163	366	20	10
Insurance & real estate	2,519	263	24	663	152	130	314	329	89	309	38	64
Computers, software, Internet	2,433	949	6	118	279	47	778	255	63	478	23	77
Government, politics, & organizations	2,200	198	34	243	69	87	274	369	40	137	26	92
Apparel	1,898	1,327	32	8	19	28	303	23	27	143	4	10
Beer, wine & liquor	1,703	398	6	19	14	149	545	124	22	182	9	48
Audio & video equipment & supplies	1,283	309	24	46	22	9	329	86	32	198	19	24
Sporting goods, toys, & games	1,248	353	2	18	8	5	350	31	59	373	5	5
Entertainment & events	1,199	81	3	502	71	105	6	341	2	38	2	18
Pets, pet foods, & supplies	400	108	12	2	1	1	182	24	39	88	< 1	3
Business & manufacturing equipment	377	127	5	5	28	6	70	12	15	53	13	2
Cigarettes, tobacco, & accessories	284	259	8	8	3	1	41	2	22	11	0	< 1
Gasoline & oil	241	35	1	4	8	4	47	28	10	55	3	26
Miscellaneous	5,820	1,129	67	953	327	244	610	1,254	171	853	56	142
Total	95,933	16,417	1,157	17,729	2,932	2,380	18,638	14,100	3,192	10,291	834	2,164

AWARDS — MEDALS — PRIZES

The Alfred B. Nobel Prize Winners, 1901-2002

Alfred B. Nobel (1833-96), inventor of dynamite, bequeathed $9 mil, the interest on which was to be distributed yearly to those judged to have most benefited humankind in physics, chemistry, medicine-physiology, literature, and the promotion of peace. Prizes were first awarded in 1901. The 1st Nobel Memorial Prize in Economic Science was awarded in 1969, funded by the central bank of Sweden. Each prize is now worth about $1 million. If year is omitted, no award was given. To find the 2003 winners, see Table of Contents.

Physics

2002 Raymond Davis Jr., Riccardo Giacconi, U.S.; Masatoshi Koshiba, Japan
2001 Eric A. Cornell, Carl E. Wieman, U.S.; Wolfgang Ketterle, Ger.
2000 Jack S. Kilby, U.S.; Zhores I. Alferov, Russ.
1999 Gerardus 't Hooft and Martinus J. G. Veltman, Netherlands
1998 Robert B. Laughlin, Horst L. Störmer, Daniel C. Tsui, U.S.
1997 Steven Chu, William D. Phillips, U.S.; Claude Cohen-Tannoudji, Fr.
1996 David M. Lee, Douglas D. Osheroff, Robert C. Richardson, U.S.
1995 Martin Perl, Frederick Reines, U.S.
1994 Bertram N. Brockhouse, Can.; Clifford G. Shull, U.S.
1993 Joseph H. Taylor, Russell A. Hulse, U.S.
1992 Georges Charpak, Pol.-Fr.
1991 Pierre-Giles de Gennes, Fr.
1990 Richard E. Taylor, Can.; Jerome I. Friedman, Henry W. Kendall, U.S.
1989 Norman F. Ramsey, U.S.; Hans G. Dehmelt, Ger.-U.S.; Wolfgang Paul, Ger.
1988 Leon M. Lederman, Melvin Schwartz, Jack Steinberger, U.S.
1987 K. Alex Müller, Swiss; J. Georg Bednorz, Ger.
1986 Ernest Ruska, Ger.; Gerd Binnig, Ger.; Heinrich Rohrer, Swiss
1985 Klaus von Klitzing, Ger.
1984 Carlo Rubbia, It.; Simon van der Meer, Dutch
1983 Subrahmanyan Chandrasekhar, William A. Fowler, U.S.
1982 Kenneth G. Wilson, U.S.
1981 Nicolaas Bloembergen, Arthur Schaalow, U.S.; Kai M. Siegbahn, Swed.
1980 James W. Cronin, Val L. Fitch, U.S.
1979 Steven Weinberg, Sheldon L. Glashow, U.S.; Abdus Salam, Pakistani
1978 Pyotr Kapitsa, USSR; Arno Penzias, Robert Wilson, U.S.
1977 John H. Van Vleck, Philip W. Anderson, U.S.; Nevill F. Mott, Br.

1976 Burton Richter, Samuel C.C. Ting, U.S.
1975 James Rainwater, U.S.; Ben Mottelson, U.S.-Dan.; Aage Bohr, Dan.
1974 Martin Ryle, Antony Hewish, Br.
1973 Ivar Giaever, U.S.; Leo Esaki, Jpn.; Brian D. Josephson, Br.
1972 John Bardeen, Leon N. Cooper, John R. Schrieffer, U.S.
1971 Dennis Gabor, Br.
1970 Louis Neel, Fr.; Hannes Alfven, Swed.
1969 Murray Gell-Mann, U.S.
1968 Luis W. Alvarez, U.S.
1967 Hans A. Bethe, U.S.
1966 Alfred Kastler, Fr.
1965 Richard P. Feynman, Julian S. Schwinger, U.S.; Shinichiro Tomonaga, Jpn.
1964 Nikolai G. Basov, Aleksander M. Prochorov, USSR; Charles H. Townes, U.S.
1963 Maria Goeppert-Mayer, Eugene P. Wigner, U.S.; J. Hans D. Jensen, Ger.
1962 Lev. D. Landau, USSR
1961 Robert Hofstadter, U.S.; Rudolf L. Mossbauer, Ger.
1960 Donald A. Glaser, U.S.
1959 Owen Chamberlain, Emilio G. Segre, U.S.
1958 Pavel Cherenkov, Ilya Frank, Igor Y. Tamm, USSR
1957 Tsung-dao Lee, Chen Ning Yang, U.S.
1956 John Bardeen, Walter H. Brattain, William Shockley, U.S.
1955 Polykarp Kusch, Willis E. Lamb, U.S.
1954 Max Born, Br.; Walter Bothe, Ger.
1953 Frits Zernike, Dutch
1952 Felix Bloch, Edward M. Purcell, U.S.
1951 Sir John D. Cockcroft, Br.; Ernest T. S. Walton, Ir.
1950 Cecil F. Powell, Br.
1949 Hideki Yukawa, Jpn.
1948 Patrick M. S. Blackett, Br.
1947 Sir Edward V. Appleton, Br.
1946 Percy W. Bridgman, U.S.

1945 Wolfgang Pauli, U.S.
1944 Isidor Isaac Rabi, U.S.
1943 Otto Stern, U.S.
1939 Ernest O. Lawrence, U.S.
1938 Enrico Fermi, It.-U.S.
1937 Clinton J. Davisson, U.S.; Sir George P. Thomson, Br.
1936 Carl D. Anderson, U.S.; Victor F. Hess, Aus.
1935 Sir James Chadwick, Br.
1933 Paul A. M. Dirac, Br.; Erwin Schrodinger, Austria
1932 Werner Heisenberg, Ger.
1930 Sir Chandrasekhara V. Raman, Indian
1929 Prince Louis-Victor de Broglie, Fr.
1928 Owen W. Richardson, Br.
1927 Arthur H. Compton, U.S.; Charles T. R. Wilson, Br.
1926 Jean B. Perrin, Fr.
1925 James Franck, Gustav Hertz, Ger.
1924 Karl M. G. Siegbahn, Swed.
1923 Robert A. Millikan, U.S.
1922 Niels Bohr, Dan.
1921 Albert Einstein, Ger.-U.S.
1920 Charles E. Guillaume, Fr.
1919 Johannes Stark, Ger.
1918 Max K. E. L. Planck, Ger.
1917 Charles G. Barkla, Br.
1915 Sir William H. Bragg, Sir William L. Bragg, Br.
1914 Max von Laue, Ger.
1913 Heike Kamerlingh-Onnes, Dutch
1912 Nils G. Dalen, Swed.
1911 Wilhelm Wien, Ger.
1910 Johannes D. van der Waals, Dutch
1909 Carl F. Braun, Ger.; Guglielmo Marconi, It.
1908 Gabriel Lippmann, Fr.
1907 Albert A. Michelson, U.S.
1906 Sir Joseph J. Thomson, Br.
1905 Philipp E. A. von Lenard, Ger.
1904 John W. Strutt, Lord Rayleigh, Br.
1903 Antoine Henri Becquerel, Pierre Curie, Fr.; Marie Curie, Pol.-Fr.
1902 Hendrik A. Lorentz, Pieter Zeeman, Dutch
1901 Wilhelm C. Roentgen, Ger.

Chemistry

2002 John B. Fenn, U.S.; Koichi Tanaka, Japan; Kurt Wüthrich, Switzerland
2001 K. Barry Sharpless, U.S.; William S. Knowles, U.S., Ryoji Noyori, Japan
2000 Alan J. Heeger, U.S.; Alan G. MacDiarmid, NZ-U.S.; Hideki Shirakawa, Japan
1999 Ahmed H. Zewail, U.S.
1998 Walter Kohn, U.S.; John A. Pople, Br.
1997 Paul D. Boyer, U.S., & John E. Walker, Br.; Jens C. Skou, Dan.
1996 Harold W. Kroto, Br.; Robert F. Curl Jr., Richard E. Smalley, U.S.
1995 Paul Crutzen, Dutch; Mario Molina, Mex.-U.S.; Sherwood Rowland, U.S.
1994 George A. Olah, U.S.
1993 Kary B. Mullis, U.S.; Michael Smith, Br.-Can.
1992 Rudolph A. Marcus, Can.-U.S.
1991 Richard R. Ernst, Swiss
1990 Elias James Corey, U.S.
1989 Thomas R. Cech, Sidney Altman, U.S.
1988 Johann Deisenhofer, Robert Huber, Hartmut Michel, Ger.
1987 Donald J. Cram, Charles J. Pedersen, U.S.; Jean-Marie Lehn, Fr.
1986 Dudley Herschbach, Yuan T. Lee, U.S.; John C. Polanyi, Can.

1985 Herbert A. Hauptman, Jerome Karle, U.S.
1984 Bruce Merrifield, U.S.
1983 Henry Taube, Can.
1982 Aaron Klug, S. Afr.
1981 Kenichi Fukui, Jpn.; Roald Hoffmann, U.S.
1980 Paul Berg, Walter Gilbert, U.S.; Frederick Sanger, Br.
1979 Herbert C. Brown, U.S.; George Wittig, Ger.
1978 Peter Mitchell, Br.
1977 Ilya Prigogine, Belg.
1976 William N. Lipscomb, U.S.
1975 John Cornforth, Austral.-Br.; Vladimir Prelog, Yugo.-Swiss
1974 Paul J. Flory, U.S.
1973 Ernst Otto Fischer, Ger.; Geoffrey Wilkinson, Br.
1972 Christian B. Anfinsen, Stanford Moore, LWilliam H. Stein, U.S.
1971 Gerhard Herzberg, Canadian
1970 Luis F. Leloir, Arg.
1969 Derek H. R. Barton, Br.; Odd Hassel, Nor.
1968 Lars Onsager, U.S.
1967 Manfred Eigen, Ger.; Ronald G. W. Norrish, George Porter, Br.
1966 Robert S. Mulliken, U.S.

1965 Robert B. Woodward, U.S.
1964 Dorothy C. Hodgkin, Br.
1963 Giulio Natta, It.; Karl Ziegler, Ger.
1962 John C. Kendrew, Max F. Perutz, Br.
1961 Melvin Calvin, U.S.
1960 Willard F. Libby, U.S.
1959 Jaroslav Heyrovsky, Czech.
1958 Frederick Sanger, Br.
1957 Sir Alexander R. Todd, Br.
1956 Sir Cyril N. Hinshelwood, Br.; Nikolai N. Semenov, USSR
1955 Vincent du Vigneaud, U.S.
1954 Linus C. Pauling, U.S.
1953 Hermann Staudinger, Ger.
1952 Archer J. P. Martin, Richard L. M. Synge, Br.
1951 Edwin M. McMillan, Glenn T. Seaborg, U.S.
1950 Kurt Alder, Otto P. H. Diels, Ger.
1949 William F. Giauque, U.S.
1948 Arne W. K. Tiselius, Swed.
1947 Sir Robert Robinson, Br.
1946 James B. Sumner, John H. Northrop, Wendell M. Stanley, U.S.
1945 Artturi I. Virtanen, Fin.
1944 Otto Hahn, Ger.
1943 Georg de Hevesy, Hung.
1939 Adolf F. J. Butenandt, Ger.; Leopold Ruzicka, Swiss
1938 Richard Kuhn, Ger.

1937 Walter N. Haworth, Br.;
     Paul Karrer, Swiss
1936 Peter J. W. Debye, Dutch
1935 Frederic & Irene Joliot-Curie, Fr.
1934 Harold C. Urey, U.S.
1932 Irving Langmuir, U.S.
1931 Friedrich Bergius, Karl Bosch, Ger.
1930 Hans Fischer, Ger.
1929 Sir Arthur Harden, Br.;
     Hans von Euler-Chelpin, Swed.
1928 Adolf O. R. Windaus, Ger.
1927 Heinrich O. Wieland, Ger.

1926 Theodor Svedberg, Swed.
1925 Richard A. Zsigmondy, Ger.
1923 Fritz Pregl, Austrian
1922 Francis W. Aston, Br.
1921 Frederick Soddy, Br.
1920 Walther H. Nernst, Ger.
1918 Fritz Haber, Ger.
1915 Richard M. Willstatter, Ger.
1914 Theodore W. Richards, U.S.
1913 Alfred Werner, Swiss
1912 Victor Grignard, Paul Sabatier, Fr.

1911 Marie Curie, Pol.-Fr.
1910 Otto Wallach, Ger.
1909 Wilhelm Ostwald, Ger.
1908 Ernest Rutherford, Br.
1907 Eduard Buchner, Ger.
1906 Henri Moissan, Fr.
1905 Adolf von Baeyer, Ger.
1904 Sir William Ramsay, Br.
1903 Svante A. Arrhenius, Swed.
1902 Emil Fischer, Ger.
1901 Jacobus H. van't Hoff, Dutch

Physiology or Medicine

2002 Sydney Brenner, John E. Sulston, Br.; H. Robert Horvitz, U.S.
2001 Leland H. Hartwell, U.S.; R. Timothy (Tim) Hunt, Sir Paul M. Nurse, Br.
2000 Arvid Carlsson, Swed.; Paul Greengard, U.S.; Eric R. Kandel, Aus-U.S.
1999 Günter Blobel, U.S.
1998 Robert F. Furchgott, Louis J. Ignarro, Ferid Murad, U.S.
1997 Stanley B. Prusiner, U.S.
1996 Peter C. Doherty, Austral.; Rolf M. Zinkernagel, Swiss
1995 Edward B. Lewis, Eric F. Wieschaus, U.S.; Christiane Nuesslein-Volhard, Ger.
1994 Alfred G. Gilman, Martin Rodbell, U.S.
1993 Phillip A. Sharp, U.S.; Richard J. Roberts, Br.
1992 Edmond H. Fisher, Edwin G. Krebs, U.S.
1991 Edwin Neher, Bert Sakmann, Ger.
1990 Joseph E. Murray, E. Donnall Thomas, U.S.
1989 J. Michael Bishop, Harold E. Varmus, U.S.
1988 Gertrude B. Elion, George H. Hitchings, U.S; Sir James Black, Br.
1987 Susumu Tonegawa, Jpn.
1986 Rita Levi-Montalcini, It.-U.S., Stanley Cohen, U.S.
1985 Michael S. Brown, Joseph L. Goldstein, U.S.
1984 Cesar Milstein, Br.-Arg.; Georges J. F. Koehler, Ger.; Niels K. Jerne, Br.-Dan.
1983 Barbara McClintock, U.S.
1982 Sune Bergstrom, Bengt Samuelsson, Swed.; John R. Vane, Br.
1981 Roger W. Sperry, David H. Hubel, Torsten N. Wiesel, U.S.
1980 Baruj Benacerraf, George Snell, U.S.; Jean Dausset, Fr.
1979 Allan M. Cormack, U.S.; Godfrey N. Hounsfield, Br.
1978 Daniel Nathans, Hamilton O. Smith, U.S.; Werner Arber, Swiss
1977 Rosalyn S. Yalow, Roger C.L. Guillemin, Andrew V. Schally, U.S.
1976 Baruch S. Blumberg, Daniel Carleton Gajdusek, U.S.

1975 David Baltimore, Howard Temin, U.S.; Renato Dulbecco, It.-U.S.
1974 Albert Claude, Lux.-U.S.; George Emil Palade, Rom.-U.S.; Christian Rene de Duve, Belg.
1973 Karl von Frisch, Ger.; Konrad Lorenz, Ger.-Aus.; Nikolaas Tinbergen, Br.
1972 Gerald M. Edelman, U.S.; Rodney R. Porter, Br.
1971 Earl W. Sutherland Jr., U.S.
1970 Julius Axelrod, U.S.; Sir Bernard Katz, Br.; Ulf von Euler, Swed.
1969 Max Delbrück, Alfred D. Hershey, Salvador Luria, U.S.
1968 Robert W. Holley, H. Gobind Khorana, Marshall W. Nirenberg, U.S.
1967 Ragnar Granit, Swed.; Haldan Keffer Hartline, George Wald, U.S.
1966 Charles B. Huggins, Francis Peyton Rous, U.S.
1965 François Jacob, Andre Lwoff, Jacques Monod, Fr.
1964 Konrad E. Bloch, U.S.; Feodor Lynen, Ger.
1963 Sir John C. Eccles, Austral.; Alan L. Hodgkin, Andrew F. Huxley, Br.
1962 Francis H. C. Crick, Maurice H. F. Wilkins, Br.; James D. Watson, U.S.
1961 Georg von Bekesy, U.S.
1960 Sir F. MacFarlane Burnet, Austral.; Peter B. Medawar, Br.
1959 Arthur Kornberg, Severo Ochoa, U.S.
1958 George W. Beadle, Edward L. Tatum, Joshua Lederberg, U.S.
1957 Daniel Bovet, It.
1956 Andre F. Cournand, Dickinson W. Richards Jr., U.S.; Werner Forssmann, Ger.
1955 Alex H. T. Theorell, Swed.
1954 John F. Enders, Frederick C. Robbins, Thomas H. Weller, U.S.
1953 Hans A. Krebs, Br.; Fritz A. Lipmann, U.S.
1952 Selman A. Waksman, U.S.
1951 Max Theiler, U.S.
1950 Philip S. Hench. Edward C. Kendall, U.S.; Tadeus Reichstein, Swiss
1949 Walter R. Hess, Swiss; Antonio Moniz, Port.

1948 Paul H. Müller, Swiss
1947 Carl F. Cori, Gerty T. Cori, U.S.; Bernardo A. Houssay, Arg.
1946 Hermann J. Muller, U.S.
1945 Ernst B. Chain, Sir Alexander Fleming, Sir Howard W. Florey, Br.
1944 Joseph Erlanger, Herbert S. Gasser, U.S.
1943 Henrik C. P. Dam, Dan.; Edward A. Doisy, U.S.
1939 Gerhard Domagk, Ger.
1938 Corneille J. F. Heymans, Belg.
1937 Albert Szent-Gyorgyi, Hung.-U.S.
1936 Sir Henry H. Dale, Br.; Otto Loewi, U.S.
1935 Hans Spemann, Ger.
1934 George R. Minot, William P. Murphy, G. H. Whipple, U.S.
1933 Thomas H. Morgan, U.S.
1932 Edgar D. Adrian, Sir Charles S. Sherrington, Br.
1931 Otto H. Warburg, Ger.
1930 Karl Landsteiner, U.S.
1929 Christiaan Eijkman, Dutch; Sir Frederick G. Hopkins, Br.
1928 Charles J. H. Nicolle, Fr.
1927 Julius Wagner-Jauregg, Austrian
1926 Johannes A. G. Fibiger, Dan.
1924 Willem Einthoven, Dutch
1923 Frederick G. Banting, Can.; John J. R. Macleod, Scot.
1922 Archibald V. Hill, Br.; Otto F. Meyerhof, Ger.
1920 Schack A. S. Krogh, Dan.
1919 Jules Bordet, Belg.
1914 Robert Barany, Aus.
1913 Charles R. Richet, Fr.
1912 Alexis Carrel, Fr.
1911 Allvar Gullstrand, Swed.
1910 Albrecht Kossel, Ger.
1909 Emil T. Kocher, Swiss
1908 Paul Ehrlich, Ger.; Elie Metchnikoff, Fr.
1907 Charles L. A. Laveran, Fr.
1906 Camillo Golgi, It.; Santiago Ramon y Cajal, Span.
1905 Robert Koch, Ger.
1904 Ivan P. Pavlov, Russ.
1903 Niels R. Finsen, Dan.
1902 Sir Ronald Ross, Br.
1901 Emil A. von Behring, Ger.

Literature

2002 Imre Kertész, Hung.
2001 Sir V.S. Naipaul, Br.
2000 Gao Xingjian, Chin.
1999 Günter Grass, Ger.
1998 José Saramago, Por.
1997 Dario Fo, It.
1996 Wislawa Szymborska, Pol.
1995 Seamus Heaney, Ir.
1994 Kenzaburo Oe, Jpn.
1993 Toni Morrison, U.S.
1992 Derek Walcott, W. Ind.
1991 Nadine Gordimer, S. Afr.
1990 Octavio Paz, Mex.
1989 Camilo José Cela, Span.
1988 Naguib Mahfouz, Egy.
1987 Joseph Brodsky, USSR-U.S.
1986 Wole Soyinka, Nig.
1985 Claude Simon, Fr.
1984 Jaroslav Siefert, Czech.
1983 William Golding, Br.
1982 Gabriel Garcia Marquez, Colombian-Mex.
1981 Elias Canetti, Bulg.-Br.
1980 Czeslaw Milosz, Pol.-U.S.
1979 Odysseus Elytis, Gk.

1978 Isaac Bashevis Singer, U.S.
1977 Vicente Aleixandre, Span.
1976 Saul Bellow, U.S.
1975 Eugenio Montale, It.
1974 Eyvind Johnson, Harry Edmund Martinson, Swed.
1973 Patrick White, Austral.
1972 Heinrich Böll, Ger.
1971 Pablo Neruda, Chil.
1970 Aleksandr I. Solzhenitsyn, USSR
1969 Samuel Beckett, Ir.
1968 Yasunari Kawabata, Jpn.
1967 Miguel Angel Asturias, Guat.
1966 Samuel Joseph Agnon, Isr.; Nelly Sachs, Swed.
1965 Mikhail Sholokhov, USSR
1964 Jean Paul Sartre, Fr. (declined)
1963 Giorgos Seferis, Gk.
1962 John Steinbeck, U.S.
1961 Ivo Andric, Yugo.
1960 Saint-John Perse, Fr.
1959 Salvatore Quasimodo, It.
1958 Boris L. Pasternak, USSR (declined)

1957 Albert Camus, Fr.
1956 Juan Ramon Jimenez, Span.
1955 Halldor K. Laxness, Ice.
1954 Ernest Hemingway, U.S.
1953 Sir Winston Churchill, Br.
1952 Francois Mauriac, Fr.
1951 Par F. Lagerkvist, Swed.
1950 Bertrand Russell, Br.
1949 William Faulkner, U.S.
1948 T.S. Eliot, Br.
1947 Andre Gide, Fr.
1946 Hermann Hesse, Ger.-Swiss
1945 Gabriela Mistral, Chil.
1944 Johannes V. Jensen, Dan.
1939 Frans E. Sillanpaa, Fin.
1938 Pearl S. Buck, U.S.
1937 Roger Martin du Gard, Fr.
1936 Eugene O'Neill, U.S.
1934 Luigi Pirandello, It.
1933 Ivan A. Bunin, USSR
1932 John Galsworthy, Br.
1931 Erik A. Karlfeldt, Swed.
1930 Sinclair Lewis, U.S.
1929 Thomas Mann, Ger.
1928 Sigrid Undset, Nor.

1927 Henri Bergson, Fr.	1917 Karl A. Gjellerup,	1908 Rudolf C. Eucken, Ger.
1926 Grazia Deledda, It.	Henrik Pontoppidan, Dan.	1907 Rudyard Kipling, Br.
1925 George Bernard Shaw, Ir.-Br.	1916 Verner von Heidenstam, Swed.	1906 Giosue Carducci, It.
1924 Wladyslaw S. Reymont, Pol.	1915 Romain Rolland, Fr.	1905 Henryk Sienkiewicz, Pol.
1923 William Butler Yeats, Ir.	1913 Rabindranath Tagore, Indian	1904 Frederic Mistral, Fr.;
1922 Jacinto Benavente, Span.	1912 Gerhart Hauptmann, Ger.	Jose Echegaray, Span.
1921 Anatole France, Fr.	1911 Maurice Maeterlinck, Belg.	1903 Bjornsterne Bjornson, Nor.
1920 Knut Hamsun, Nor.	1910 Paul J. L. Heyse, Ger.	1902 Theodor Mommsen, Ger.
1919 Carl F. G. Spitteler, Swiss	1909 Selma Lagerlof, Swed.	1901 Rene F. A. Sully Prudhomme, Fr.

Peace

2002 Jimmy Carter, U.S.	1974 Eisaku Sato, Jpn.; Sean MacBride, Ir.	1931 Jane Addams, Nicholas Murray
2001 UN; Kofi Annan, Ghana	1973 Henry Kissinger, U.S.;	Butler, U.S.
2000 Kim Dae Jung, S. Kor.	Le Duc Tho, N. Viet. (Tho declined)	1930 Nathan Soderblom, Swed.
1999 Doctors Without Borders	1971 Willy Brandt, Ger.	1929 Frank B. Kellogg, U.S.
(Médecins Sans Frontières), Fr.	1970 Norman E. Borlaug, U.S.	1927 Ferdinand E. Buisson, Fr.;
1998 John Hume, David Trimble, N. Ir.	1969 Intl. Labor Organization	Ludwig Quidde, Ger.
1997 Jody Williams, U.S.; International	1968 Rene Cassin, Fr.	1926 Aristide Briand, Fr.;
Campaign to Ban Landmines	1965 UN Children's Fund (UNICEF)	Gustav Stresemann, Ger.
1996 Bishop Carlos Ximenes Belo,	1964 Martin Luther King Jr., U.S.	1925 Sir J. Austen Chamberlain, Br.;
José Ramos-Horta, Timorese	1963 International Red Cross,	Charles G. Dawes, U.S.
1995 Joseph Rotblat, Pol.-Br.;	League of Red Cross Societies	1922 Fridtjof Nansen, Nor.
Pugwash Conference	1962 Linus C. Pauling, U.S.	1921 Karl H. Branting, Swed.;
1994 Yasir Arafat, Pal.; Shimon Peres,	1961 Dag Hammarskjold, Swed.	Christian L. Lange, Nor.
Yitzhak Rabin, Isr.	1960 Albert J. Luthuli, S. Afr.	1920 Leon V.A. Bourgeois, Fr.
1993 Frederik W. de Klerk,	1959 Philip J. Noel-Baker, Br.	1919 Woodrow Wilson, U.S.
Nelson Mandela, S. Afr.	1958 Georges Pire, Belg.	1917 International Red Cross
1992 Rigoberta Menchú, Guat.	1957 Lester B. Pearson, Can.	1913 Henri La Fontaine, Belg.
1991 Aung San Suu Kyi, Myanmarese	1954 Office of UN High Com. for	1912 Elihu Root, U.S.
1990 Mikhail S. Gorbachev, USSR	Refugees	1911 Tobias M.C. Asser, Dutch;
1989 Dalai Lama, Tibet	1953 George C. Marshall, U.S.	Alfred H. Fried, Austrian
1988 UN Peacekeeping Forces	1952 Albert Schweitzer, Fr.	1910 Permanent Intl. Peace Bureau
1987 Oscar Arias Sanchez, Costa Rican	1951 Leon Jouhaux, Fr.	1909 Auguste M. F. Beernaert, Belg.;
1986 Elie Wiesel, Rom.-U.S.	1950 Ralph J. Bunche, U.S.	Paul H. B. B. d'Estournelles
1985 Intl. Physicians for the Prevention	1949 Lord John Boyd Orr of	de Constant, Fr.
of Nuclear War, U.S.	Brechin Mearns, Br.	1908 Klas P. Arnoldson, Swed.;
1984 Bishop Desmond Tutu, S. Afr.	1947 Friends Service Council, Br.; Amer.	Fredrik Bajer, Dan.
1983 Lech Walesa, Pol.	Friends Service Committee, U.S.	1907 Ernesto T. Moneta, It.;
1982 Alva Myrdal, Swed.; Alfonso	1946 Emily G. Balch, John R. Mott, U.S.	Louis Renault, Fr.
Garcia Robles, Mex.	1945 Cordell Hull, U.S.	1906 Theodore Roosevelt, U.S.
1981 Office of UN High Com. for Refugees	1944 International Red Cross	1905 Baroness Bertha von
1980 Adolfo Perez Esquivel, Arg.	1938 Nansen International Office	Suttner, Austrian
1979 Mother Teresa of Calcutta, Alb.-Ind.	for Refugees	1904 Institute of International Law
1978 Anwar Sadat, Egy.;	1937 Viscount Cecil of Chelwood, Br.	1903 Sir William R. Cremer, Br.
Menachem Begin, Isr.	1936 Carlos de Saavedra Lamas, Arg.	1902 Elie Ducommun,
1977 Amnesty International	1935 Carl von Ossietzky, Ger.	Charles A. Gobat, Swiss
1976 Mairead Corrigan,	1934 Arthur Henderson, Br.	1901 Jean H. Dunant, Swiss;
Betty Williams, N. Ir.	1933 Sir Norman Angell, Br.	Frederic Passy, Fr.
1975 Andrei Sakharov, USSR		

Nobel Memorial Prize in Economic Science

2002 Daniel Kahneman, U.S. and Israel;	1992 Gary S. Becker, U.S.	1978 Herbert A. Simon, U.S.
Vernon L. Smith, U.S.	1991 Ronald H. Coase, Br.-U.S.	1977 Bertil Ohlin, Swed.;
2001 George A. Akerlof, A. Michael	1990 Harry M. Markowitz, William F.	James E. Meade, Br.
Spence, Joseph E. Stiglitz, U.S.	Sharpe, Merton H. Miller, U.S.	1976 Milton Friedman, U.S.
2000 James J. Heckman,	1989 Trygve Haavelmo, Nor.	1975 Tjalling Koopmans, Dutch-U.S.;
Daniel L. McFadden, U.S.	1988 Maurice Allais, Fr.	Leonid Kantorovich, USSR
1999 Robert A. Mundell, Can.	1987 Robert M. Solow, U.S.	1974 Gunnar Myrdal, Swed.;
1998 Amartya Sen, Indian	1986 James M. Buchanan, U.S.	Friedrich A. von Hayek, Austrian
1997 Robert C. Merton, U.S.;	1985 Franco Modigliani, It.-U.S.	1973 Wassily Leontief, U.S.
Myron S. Scholes, Can.-U.S.	1984 Richard Stone, Br.	1972 Kenneth J. Arrow, U.S.;
1996 James A. Mirrlees, Br.;	1983 Gerard Debreu, Fr.-U.S.	John R. Hicks, Br.
William Vickrey, Can.-U.S.	1982 George J. Stigler, U.S.	1971 Simon Kuznets, U.S.
1995 Robert E. Lucas Jr., U.S.	1981 James Tobin, U.S.	1970 Paul A. Samuelson, U.S.
1994 John C. Harsanyi, John F. Nash,	1980 Lawrence R. Klein, U.S.	1969 Ragnar Frisch, Nor.;
U.S.; Reinhard Selten, Ger.	1979 Theodore W. Schultz, U.S.;	Jan Tinbergen, Dutch
1993 Robert W. Fogel,	Sir Arthur Lewis, Br.	
Douglass C. North, U.S.		

Pulitzer Prizes in Journalism, Letters, and Music

Endowed by Joseph Pulitzer (1847-1911), publisher of the *New York World*, in a bequest to Columbia Univ. and awarded annually, in years shown, for work the previous year. Prizes are now $7,500 in each category, except Public Service (in Journalism), for which a medal is given. For letters and music, prizes in past years are listed; if a year is omitted, no award was given that year.

Journalism, 2003

Public Service: *Boston Globe,* for its coverage of sexual abuse by Roman Catholic priests.

Breaking News Reporting: *Eagle-Tribune* staff, Lawrence, MA, for stories on the accidental drowning of four boys in the Merrimack River.

Investigative Reporting: Clifford J. Levy, *NY Times,* for a series on abuse of mentally ill adults in state-regulated homes.

Explanatory Reporting: *Wall Street Journal* staff, for reports on the significance and impact of corporate scandals in the U.S.

Beat Reporting: Diana K. Sugg, *Baltimore Sun,* for stories on how complex medical issues affect people's lives.

National Reporting: Alan Miller and Kevin Sack, *LA Times,* for reporting on a military aircraft, dubbed the "Widow Maker," linked to the deaths of 45 pilots

Internat. Reporting: Kevin Sullivan and Mary Jordan, *Wash. Post,* for reports on conditions in Mexico's criminal justice system.

Feature Writing: Sonia I. Nazario, *LA Times,* for story on a Honduran boy's search for his mother, who had migrated to the U.S.

Commentary: Colbert I. King, *Wash. Post,* for columns about politics and power.

Criticism: Stephen Hunter, *Wash. Post,* for film criticism.

Editorial Writing: Cornelia Grumman, *Chicago Tribune,* for editorials against the death penalty.

Editorial Cartooning: David Horsey, *Seattle Post-Intelligencer.*

Breaking News Photog.: *Rocky Mountain News* photography staff, for images of Colorado's 2002 forest fires.

Feature Photog.: Don Bartletti, *LA Times,* for portrayal of perils faced by Central American youths migrating to the U.S.

Letters

Fiction

1918—Ernest Poole, *His Family*
1919—Booth Tarkington, *The Magnificent Ambersons*
1921—Edith Wharton, *The Age of Innocence*
1922—Booth Tarkington, *Alice Adams*
1923—Willa Cather, *One of Ours*
1924—Margaret Wilson, *The Able McLaughlins*
1925—Edna Ferber, *So Big*
1926—Sinclair Lewis, *Arrowsmith* (refused prize)
1927—Louis Bromfield, *Early Autumn*
1928—Thornton Wilder, *Bridge of San Luis Rey*
1929—Julia M. Peterkin, *Scarlet Sister Mary*
1930—Oliver LaFarge, *Laughing Boy*
1931—Margaret Ayer Barnes, *Years of Grace*
1932—Pearl S. Buck, *The Good Earth*
1933—T. S. Stribling, *The Store*
1934—Caroline Miller, *Lamb in His Bosom*
1935—Josephine W. Johnson, *Now in November*
1936—Harold L. Davis, *Honey in the Horn*
1937—Margaret Mitchell, *Gone With the Wind*
1938—John P. Marquand, *The Late George Apley*
1939—Marjorie Kinnan Rawlings, *The Yearling*
1940—John Steinbeck, *The Grapes of Wrath*
1942—Ellen Glasgow, *In This Our Life*
1943—Upton Sinclair, *Dragon's Teeth*
1944—Martin Flavin, *Journey in the Dark*
1945—John Hersey, *A Bell for Adano*
1947—Robert Penn Warren, *All the King's Men*
1948—James A. Michener, *Tales of the South Pacific*
1949—James Gould Cozzens, *Guard of Honor*
1950—A. B. Guthrie Jr., *The Way West*
1951—Conrad Richter, *The Town*
1952—Herman Wouk, *The Caine Mutiny*
1953—Ernest Hemingway, *The Old Man and the Sea*
1955—William Faulkner, *A Fable*
1956—MacKinlay Kantor, *Andersonville*
1958—James Agee, *A Death in the Family*
1959—Robert Lewis Taylor, *The Travels of Jaimie McPheeters*
1960—Allen Drury, *Advise and Consent*
1961—Harper Lee, *To Kill a Mockingbird*
1962—Edwin O'Connor, *The Edge of Sadness*
1963—William Faulkner, *The Reivers*
1965—Shirley Ann Grau, *The Keepers of the House*
1966—Katherine Anne Porter, *Collected Stories*
1967—Bernard Malamud, *The Fixer*
1968—William Styron, *The Confessions of Nat Turner*
1969—N. Scott Momaday, *House Made of Dawn*
1970—Jean Stafford, *Collected Stories*
1972—Wallace Stegner, *Angle of Repose*
1973—Eudora Welty, *The Optimist's Daughter*
1975—Michael Shaara, *The Killer Angels*
1976—Saul Bellow, *Humboldt's Gift*
1978—James Alan McPherson, *Elbow Room*
1979—John Cheever, *The Stories of John Cheever*
1980—Norman Mailer, *The Executioner's Song*
1981—John Kennedy Toole, *A Confederacy of Dunces*
1982—John Updike, *Rabbit Is Rich*
1983—Alice Walker, *The Color Purple*
1984—William Kennedy, *Ironweed*
1985—Alison Lurie, *Foreign Affairs*
1986—Larry McMurtry, *Lonesome Dove*
1987—Peter Taylor, *A Summons to Memphis*
1988—Toni Morrison, *Beloved*
1989—Anne Tyler, *Breathing Lessons*
1990—Oscar Hijuelos, *The Mambo Kings Play Songs of Love*
1991—John Updike, *Rabbit at Rest*
1992—Jane Smiley, *A Thousand Acres*
1993—Robert Olen Butler, *A Good Scent From a Strange Mountain*
1994—E. Annie Proulx, *The Shipping News*
1995—Carol Shields, *The Stone Diaries*
1996—Richard Ford, *Independence Day*
1997—Steven Millhauser, *Martin Dressler: The Tale of an American Dreamer*
1998—Philip Roth, *American Pastoral*
1999—Michael Cunningham, *The Hours*
2000—Jhumpa Lahiri, *Interpreter of Maladies*
2001—Michael Chabon, *The Amazing Adventures of Kavalier & Clay*
2002—Richard Russo, *Empire Falls*
2003—Jeffrey Eugenides, *Middlesex*

Drama

1918—Jesse Lynch Williams, *Why Marry?*
1920—Eugene O'Neill, *Beyond the Horizon*
1921—Zona Gale, *Miss Lulu Bett*
1922—Eugene O'Neill, *Anna Christie*
1923—Owen Davis, *Icebound*
1924—Hatcher Hughes, *Hell-Bent for Heaven*
1925—Sidney Howard, *They Knew What They Wanted*

1926—George Kelly, *Craig's Wife*
1927—Paul Green, *In Abraham's Bosom*
1928—Eugene O'Neill, *Strange Interlude*
1929—Elmer Rice, *Street Scene*
1930—Marc Connelly, *The Green Pastures*
1931—Susan Glaspell, *Alison's House*
1932—George S. Kaufman, Morrie Ryskind, and Ira Gershwin, *Of Thee I Sing*
1933—Maxwell Anderson, *Both Your Houses*
1934—Sidney Kingsley, *Men in White*
1935—Zoe Akins, *The Old Maid*
1936—Robert E. Sherwood, *Idiot's Delight*
1937—George S. Kaufman and Moss Hart, *You Can't Take It With You*
1938—Thornton Wilder, *Our Town*
1939—Robert E. Sherwood, *Abe Lincoln in Illinois*
1940—William Saroyan, *The Time of Your Life*
1941—Robert E. Sherwood, *There Shall Be No Night*
1943—Thornton Wilder, *The Skin of Our Teeth*
1945—Mary Chase, *Harvey*
1946—Russel Crouse and Howard Lindsay, *State of the Union*
1948—Tennessee Williams, *A Streetcar Named Desire*
1949—Arthur Miller, *Death of a Salesman*
1950—Richard Rodgers, Oscar Hammerstein 2nd and Joshua Logan, *South Pacific*
1952—Joseph Kramm, *The Shrike*
1953—William Inge, *Picnic*
1954—John Patrick, *Teahouse of the August Moon*
1955—Tennessee Williams, *Cat on a Hot Tin Roof*
1956—Frances Goodrich and Albert Hackett, *The Diary of Anne Frank*
1957—Eugene O'Neill, *Long Day's Journey Into Night*
1958—Ketti Frings, *Look Homeward, Angel*
1959—Archibald MacLeish, *J. B.*
1960—George Abbott, Jerome Weidman, Sheldon Harnick, and Jerry Bock, *Fiorello!*
1961—Tad Mosel, *All the Way Home*
1962—Frank Loesser and Abe Burrows, *How to Succeed in Business Without Really Trying*
1965—Frank D. Gilroy, *The Subject Was Roses*
1967—Edward Albee, *A Delicate Balance*
1969—Howard Sackler, *The Great White Hope*
1970—Charles Gordone, *No Place to Be Somebody*
1971—Paul Zindel, *The Effect of Gamma Rays on Man-in-the-Moon Marigolds*
1973—Jason Miller, *That Championship Season*
1975—Edward Albee, *Seascape*
1976—Michael Bennett, James Kirkwood, Nicholas Dante, Marvin Hamlisch, and Edward Kleban, *A Chorus Line*
1977—Michael Cristofer, *The Shadow Box*
1978—Donald L. Coburn, *The Gin Game*
1979—Sam Shepard, *Buried Child*
1980—Lanford Wilson, *Talley's Folly*
1981—Beth Henley, *Crimes of the Heart*
1982—Charles Fuller, *A Soldier's Play*
1983—Marsha Norman, *'night, Mother*
1984—David Mamet, *Glengarry Glen Ross*
1985—Stephen Sondheim and James Lapine, *Sunday in the Park With George*
1987—August Wilson, *Fences*
1988—Alfred Uhry, *Driving Miss Daisy*
1989—Wendy Wasserstein, *The Heidi Chronicles*
1990—August Wilson, *The Piano Lesson*
1991—Neil Simon, *Lost in Yonkers*
1992—Robert Schenkkan, *The Kentucky Cycle*
1993—Tony Kushner, *Angels in America: Millennium Approaches*
1994—Edward Albee, *Three Tall Women*
1995—Horton Foote, *The Young Man From Atlanta*
1996—Jonathan Larson, *Rent*
1998—Paula Vogel, *How I Learned to Drive*
1999—Margaret Edson, *Wit*
2000—Donald Margulies, *Dinner With Friends*
2001—David Auburn, *Proof*
2002—Suzan-Lori Parks, *Topdog/Underdog*
2003—Nilo Cruz, *Anna in the Tropics*

History (U.S.)

1917—J. J. Jusserand, *With Americans of Past and Present Days*
1918—James Ford Rhodes, *History of the Civil War*
1920—Justin H. Smith, *The War With Mexico*
1921—William Sowden Sims, *The Victory at Sea*
1922—James Truslow Adams, *The Founding of New England*
1923—Charles Warren, *The Supreme Court in United States History*
1924—Charles Howard McIlwain, *The American Revolution: A Constitutional Interpretation*
1925—Frederick L. Paxton, *A History of the American Frontier*
1926—Edward Channing, *A History of the U.S.*
1927—Samuel Flagg Bemis, *Pinckney's Treaty*
1928—V. L Parrington, *Main Currents in American Thought*

1929—Fred A. Shannon, *The Organization and Administration of the Union Army, 1861-65*
1930—Claude H. Van Tyne, *The War of Independence*
1931—Bernadotte E. Schmitt, *The Coming of the War, 1914*
1932—Gen. John J. Pershing, *My Experiences in the World War*
1933—Frederick J. Turner, *The Significance of Sections in American History*
1934—Herbert Agar, *The People's Choice*
1935—Charles McLean Andrews, *The Colonial Period of American History*
1936—Andrew C. McLaughlin, *The Constitutional History of the United States*
1937—Van Wyck Brooks, *The Flowering of New England*
1938—Paul Herman Buck, *The Road to Reunion, 1865-1900*
1939—Frank Luther Mott, *A History of American Magazines*
1940—Carl Sandburg, *Abraham Lincoln: The War Years*
1941—Marcus Lee Hansen, *The Atlantic Migration, 1607-1860*
1942—Margaret Leech, *Reveille in Washington*
1943—Esther Forbes, *Paul Revere and the World He Lived In*
1944—Merle Curti, *The Growth of American Thought*
1945—Stephen Bonsal, *Unfinished Business*
1946—Arthur M. Schlesinger Jr., *The Age of Jackson*
1947—James Phinney Baxter 3d, *Scientists Against Time*
1948—Bernard De Voto, *Across the Wide Missouri*
1949—Roy F. Nichols, *The Disruption of American Democracy*
1950—O. W. Larkin, *Art and Life in America*
1951—R. Carlyle Buley, *The Old Northwest: Pioneer Period 1815-1840*
1952—Oscar Handlin, *The Uprooted*
1953—George Dangerfield, *The Era of Good Feelings*
1954—Bruce Catton, *A Stillness at Appomattox*
1955—Paul Horgan, *Great River: The Rio Grande in North American History*
1956—Richard Hofstadter, *The Age of Reform*
1957—George F. Kennan, *Russia Leaves the War*
1958—Bray Hammond, *Banks and Politics in America—From the Revolution to the Civil War*
1959—Leonard D. White and Jean Schneider, *The Republican Era; 1869-1901*
1960—Margaret Leech, *In the Days of McKinley*
1961—Herbert Feis, *Between War and Peace: The Potsdam Conference*
1962—Lawrence H. Gibson, *The Triumphant Empire: Thunderclouds Gather in the West*
1963—Constance McLaughlin Green, *Washington: Village and Capital, 1800-1878*
1964—Sumner Chilton Powell, *Puritan Village: The Formation of a New England Town*
1965—Irwin Unger, *The Greenback Era*
1966—Perry Miller, *Life of the Mind in America*
1967—William H. Goetzmann, *Exploration and Empire: The Explorer and Scientist in the Winning of the American West*
1968—Bernard Bailyn, *The Ideological Origins of the American Revolution*
1969—Leonard W. Levy, *Origin of the Fifth Amendment*
1970—Dean Acheson, *Present at the Creation: My Years in the State Department*
1971—James McGregor Burns, *Roosevelt: The Soldier of Freedom*
1972—Carl N. Degler, *Neither Black nor White*
1973—Michael Kammen, *People of Paradox: An Inquiry Concerning the Origins of American Civilization*
1974—Daniel J. Boorstin, *The Americans: The Democratic Experience*
1975—Dumas Malone, *Jefferson and His Time*
1976—Paul Horgan, *Lamy of Santa Fe*
1977—David M. Potter, *The Impending Crisis*
1978—Alfred D. Chandler Jr., *The Visible Hand: The Managerial Revolution in American Business*
1979—Don E. Fehrenbacher, *The Dred Scott Case: Its Significance in American Law and Politics*
1980—Leon F. Litwack, *Been in the Storm So Long*
1981—Lawrence A. Cremin, *American Education: The National Experience, 1783-1876*
1982—C. Vann Woodward, ed., *Mary Chesnut's Civil War*
1983—Rhys L. Issac, *The Transformation of Virginia, 1740-1790*
1985—Thomas K. McCraw, *Prophets of Regulation*
1986—Walter A. McDougall, *The Heavens and the Earth*
1987—Bernard Bailyn, *Voyagers to the West*
1988—Robert V. Bruce, *The Launching of Modern American Science, 1846-1876*
1989—Taylor Branch, *Parting the Waters: America in the King Years, 1954-63*; and James M. McPherson, *Battle Cry of Freedom: The Civil War Era*
1990—Stanley Karnow, *In Our Image: America's Empire in the Philippines*
1991—Laurel Thatcher Ulrich, *A Midwife's Tale: The Life of Martha Ballard, based on her diary, 1785-1812*
1992—Mark E. Neely Jr., *The Fate of Liberty: Abraham Lincoln and Civil Liberties*
1993—Gordon S. Wood, *The Radicalism of the American Revolution*

1995—Doris Kearns Goodwin, *No Ordinary Time: Franklin and Eleanor Roosevelt: The Home Front in World War II*
1996—Alan Taylor, *William Cooper's Town: Power and Persuasion on the Frontier of the Early American Republic*
1997—Jack N. Rakove, *Original Meanings: Politics and Ideas in the Making of the Constitution*
1998—Edward J. Larson, *Summer for the Gods: The Scopes Trial and America's Continuing Debate Over Science and Religion*
1999—Edwin G. Burrows and Mike Wallace, *Gotham: A History of New York City to 1898*
2000—David M. Kennedy, *Freedom From Fear: The American People in Depression and War, 1929-1945*
2001—Joseph J. Ellis, *Founding Brothers: The Revolutionary Generation*
2002—Louis Menand, *The Metaphysical Club: A Story of Ideas in America*
2003—Rick Atkinson, *An Army at Dawn: The War in North Africa, 1942-1943*

Biography or Autobiography

1917—Laura E. Richards and Maude Howe Elliott, assisted by Florence Howe Hall, *Julia Ward Howe*
1918—William Cabell Bruce, *Benjamin Franklin, Self-Revealed*
1919—Henry Adams, *The Education of Henry Adams*
1920—Albert J. Beveridge, *The Life of John Marshall*
1921—Edward Bok, *The Americanization of Edward Bok*
1922—Hamlin Garland, *A Daughter of the Middle Border*
1923—Burton J. Hendrick, *The Life and Letters of Walter H. Page*
1924—Michael Pupin, *From Immigrant to Inventor*
1925—M. A. DeWolfe Howe, *Barrett Wendell and His Letters*
1926—Harvey Cushing, *Life of Sir William Osler*
1927—Emory Holloway, *Whitman: An Interpretation in Narrative*
1928—Charles Edward Russell, *The American Orchestra and Theodore Thomas*
1929—Burton J. Hendrick, *The Training of an American: The Earlier Life and Letters of Walter H. Page*
1930—Marquis James, *The Raven* (Sam Houston)
1931—Henry James, *Charles W. Eliot*
1932—Henry F. Pringle, *Theodore Roosevelt*
1933—Allan Nevins, *Grover Cleveland*
1934—Tyler Dennett, *John Hay*
1935—Douglas Southall Freeman, *R. E. Lee*
1936—Ralph Barton Perry, *The Thought and Character of William James*
1937—Allan Nevins, *Hamilton Fish: The Inner History of the Grant Administration*
1938—Divided between Odell Shepard, *Pedlar's Progress* (Bronson Alcott) and Marquis James, *Andrew Jackson*
1939—Carl Van Doren, *Benjamin Franklin*
1940—Ray Stannard Baker, *Woodrow Wilson, Life and Letters*
1941—Ola Elizabeth Winslow, *Jonathan Edwards*
1942—Forrest Wilson, *Crusader in Crinoline* (Harriet Beecher Stowe)
1943—Samuel Eliot Morison, *Admiral of the Ocean Sea* (Christopher Columbus)
1944—Carleton Mabee, *The American Leonardo: The Life of Samuel F. B. Morse*
1945—Russell Blaine Nye, *George Bancroft: Brahmin Rebel.*
1946—Linny Marsh Wolfe, *Son of the Wilderness* (John Muir)
1947—William Allen White, *Autobiography of William Allen White*
1948—Margaret Clapp, *Forgotten First Citizen: John Bigelow*
1949—Robert E. Sherwood, *Roosevelt and Hopkins*
1950—Samuel Flagg Bemis, *John Quincy Adams and the Foundations of American Foreign Policy*
1951—Margaret Louise Coit, *John C. Calhoun: American Portrait*
1952—Merlo J. Pusey, *Charles Evans Hughes*
1953—David J. Mays, *Edmund Pendleton, 1721-1803*
1954—Charles A. Lindbergh, *The Spirit of St. Louis*
1955—William S. White, *The Taft Story*
1956—Talbot F. Hamlin, *Benjamin Henry Latrobe*
1957—John F. Kennedy, *Profiles in Courage*
1958—Douglas Southall Freeman (Vols. I-VI) and John Alexander Carroll and Mary Wells Ashworth (Vol. VII), *George Washington*
1959—Arthur Walworth, *Woodrow Wilson: American Prophet*
1960—Samuel Eliot Morison, *John Paul Jones*
1961—David Donald, *Charles Sumner and the Coming of the Civil War*
1963—Leon Edel, *Henry James: Vols. 2-3*
1964—Walter Jackson Bate, *John Keats*
1965—Ernest Samuels, *Henry Adams*
1966—Arthur M. Schlesinger Jr., *A Thousand Days*
1967—Justin Kaplan, *Mr. Clemens and Mark Twain*
1968—George F. Kennan, *Memoirs (1925-1950)*
1969—B. L. Reid, *The Man From New York: John Quinn and His Friends*
1970—T. Harry Williams, *Huey Long*
1971—Lawrence Thompson, *Robert Frost: The Years of Triumph, 1915-1938*
1972—Joseph P. Lash, *Eleanor and Franklin*
1973—W. A. Swanberg, *Luce and His Empire*
1974—Louis Sheaffer, *O'Neill, Son and Artist*

1975—Robert A. Caro, *The Power Broker: Robert Moses and the Fall of New York*
1976—R.W.B. Lewis, *Edith Wharton: A Biography*
1977—John E. Mack, *A Prince of Our Disorder: The Life of T. E. Lawrence*
1978—Walter Jackson Bate, *Samuel Johnson*
1979—Leonard Baker, *Days of Sorrow and Pain: Leo Baeck and the Berlin Jews*
1980—Edmund Morris, *The Rise of Theodore Roosevelt*
1981—Robert K. Massie, *Peter the Great: His Life and World*
1982—William S. McFeely, *Grant: A Biography*
1983—Russell Baker, *Growing Up*
1984—Louis R. Harlan, *Booker T. Washington*
1985—Kenneth Silverman, *The Life and Times of Cotton Mather*
1986—Elizabeth Frank, *Louise Bogan: A Portrait*
1987—David J. Garrow, *Bearing the Cross: Martin Luther King Jr. and the Southern Christian Leadership Conference*
1988—David Herbert Donald, *Look Homeward: A Life of Thomas Wolfe*
1989—Richard Ellmann, *Oscar Wilde*
1990—Sebastian de Grazia, *Machiavelli in Hell*
1991—Steven Naifeh and Gregory White Smith, *Jackson Pollock: An American Saga*
1992—Lewis B. Puller Jr., *Fortunate Son: The Healing of a Vietnam Vet*
1993—David McCullough, *Truman*
1994—David Levering Lewis, *W.E.B. DuBois: Biography of a Race, 1868-1919*
1995—Joan D. Hedrick, *Harriet Beecher Stowe: A Life*
1996—Jack Miles, *God: A Biography*
1997—Frank McCourt, *Angela's Ashes: A Memoir*
1998—Katharine Graham, *Personal History*
1999—A. Scott Berg, *Lindbergh*
2000—Stacy Schiff, *Véra (Mrs. Vladimir Nabokov)*
2001—David Levering Lewis, *W.E.B. Du Bois: The Fight for Equality and the American Century, 1919-1963*
2002—David McCullough, *John Adams*
2003—Robert Caro, *The Years of Lyndon Johnson: Master of the Senate*

American Poetry

Before 1922, awards were funded by the Poetry Society.
1918—*Love Songs*, by Sara Teasdale;
1919—*Old Road to Paradise*, by Margaret Widdemer; *Corn Huskers*, by Carl Sandburg.
1922—Edwin Arlington Robinson, *Collected Poems*
1923—Edna St. Vincent Millay, *The Ballad of the Harp-Weaver; A Few Figs From Thistles; other works*
1924—Robert Frost, *New Hampshire: A Poem With Notes and Grace Notes*
1925—Edwin Arlington Robinson, *The Man Who Died Twice*
1926—Amy Lowell, *What's O'Clock*
1927—Leonora Speyer, *Fiddler's Farewell*
1928—Edwin Arlington Robinson, *Tristram*
1929—Stephen Vincent Benet, *John Brown's Body*
1930—Conrad Aiken, *Selected Poems*
1931—Robert Frost, *Collected Poems*
1932—George Dillon, *The Flowering Stone*
1933—Archibald MacLeish, *Conquistador*
1934—Robert Hillyer, *Collected Verse*
1935—Audrey Wurdemann, *Bright Ambush*
1936—Robert P. Tristram Coffin, *Strange Holiness*
1937—Robert Frost, *A Further Range*
1938—Marya Zaturenska, *Cold Morning Sky*
1939—John Gould Fletcher, *Selected Poems*
1940—Mark Van Doren, *Collected Poems*
1941—Leonard Bacon, *Sunderland Capture*
1942—William Rose Benet, *The Dust Which is God*
1943—Robert Frost, *A Witness Tree*
1944—Stephen Vincent Benet, *Western Star*
1945—Karl Shapiro, *V-Letter and Other Poems*
1947—Robert Lowell, *Lord Weary's Castle*
1948—W. H. Auden, *The Age of Anxiety*
1949—Peter Viereck, *Terror and Decorum*
1950—Gwendolyn Brooks, *Annie Allen*
1951—Carl Sandburg, *Complete Poems*
1952—Marianne Moore, *Collected Poems*
1953—Archibald MacLeish, *Collected Poems*
1954—Theodore Roethke, *The Waking*
1955—Wallace Stevens, *Collected Poems*
1956—Elizabeth Bishop, *Poems, North and South*
1957—Richard Wilbur, *Things of This World*
1958—Robert Penn Warren, *Promises: Poems 1954-1956*
1959—Stanley Kunitz, *Selected Poems 1928-1958*
1960—W. D. Snodgrass, *Heart's Needle*
1961—Phyllis McGinley, *Times Three: Selected Verse From Three Decades*
1962—Alan Dugan, *Poems*
1963—William Carlos Williams, *Pictures From Breughel*
1964—Louis Simpson, *At the End of the Open Road*
1965—John Berryman, *77 Dream Songs*
1966—Richard Eberhart, *Selected Poems*

1967—Anne Sexton, *Live or Die*
1968—Anthony Hecht, *The Hard Hours*
1969—George Oppen, *Of Being Numerous*
1970—Richard Howard, *Untitled Subjects*
1971—William S. Merwin, *The Carrier of Ladders*
1972—James Wright, *Collected Poems*
1973—Maxine Winokur Kumin, *Up Country*
1974—Robert Lowell, *The Dolphin*
1975—Gary Snyder, *Turtle Island*
1976—John Ashbery, *Self-Portrait in a Convex Mirror*
1977—James Merrill, *Divine Comedies*
1978—Howard Nemerov, *Collected Poems*
1979—Robert Penn Warren, *Now and Then: Poems 1976-1978*
1980—Donald Justice, *Selected Poems*
1981—James Schuyler, *The Morning of the Poem*
1982—Sylvia Plath, *The Collected Poems*
1983—Galway Kinnell, *Selected Poems*
1984—Mary Oliver, *American Primitive*
1985—Carolyn Kizer, *Yin*
1986—Henry Taylor, *The Flying Change*
1987—Rita Dove, *Thomas and Beulah*
1988—William Meredith, *Partial Accounts: New and Selected Poems*
1989—Richard Wilbur, *New and Collected Poems*
1990—Charles Simic, *The World Doesn't End*
1991—Mona Van Duyn, *Near Changes*
1992—James Tate, *Selected Poems*
1993—Louise Glück, *The Wild Iris*
1994—Yusef Komunyakaa, *Neon Vernacular*
1995—Philip Levine, *The Simple Truth*
1996—Jorie Graham, *The Dream of the Unified Field*
1997—Lisel Mueller, *Alive Together: New and Selected Poems*
1998—Charles Wright, *Black Zodiac*
1999—Mark Strand, *Blizzard of One*
2000—C. K. Williams, *Repair*
2001—Stephen Dunn, *Different Hours*
2002—Carl Dennis, *Practical Gods*
2003—Paul Muldoon, *Moy Sand and Gravel*

General Nonfiction

1962—Theodore H. White, *The Making of the President 1960*
1963—Barbara W. Tuchman, *The Guns of August*
1964—Richard Hofstadter, *Anti-Intellectualism in American Life*
1965—Howard Mumford Jones, *O Strange New World*
1966—Edwin Way Teale, *Wandering Through Winter*
1967—David Brion Davis, *The Problem of Slavery in Western Culture*
1968—Will and Ariel Durant, *Rousseau and Revolution*
1969—Norman Mailer, *The Armies of the Night*; Rene Jules Dubos, *So Human an Animal: How We Are Shaped by Surroundings and Events*
1970—Eric H. Erikson, *Gandhi's Truth*
1971—John Toland, *The Rising Sun*
1972—Barbara W. Tuchman, *Stilwell and the American Experience in China, 1911-1945*
1973—Frances FitzGerald, *Fire in the Lake: The Vietnamese and the Americans in Vietnam*; Robert Coles, *Children of Crisis, Volumes II & III*
1974—Ernest Becker, *The Denial of Death*
1975—Annie Dillard, *Pilgrim at Tinker Creek*
1976—Robert N. Butler, *Why Survive? Being Old in America*
1977—William W. Warner, *Beautiful Swimmers*
1978—Carl Sagan, *The Dragons of Eden*
1979—Edward O. Wilson, *On Human Nature*
1980—Douglas R. Hofstadter, *Gödel, Escher, Bach: An Eternal Golden Braid*
1981—Carl E. Schorske, *Fin-de-Siecle Vienna: Politics and Culture*
1982—Tracy Kidder, *The Soul of a New Machine*
1983—Susan Sheehan, *Is There No Place on Earth for Me?*
1984—Paul Starr, *Social Transformation of American Medicine*
1985—Studs Terkel, *The Good War*
1986—Joseph Lelyveld, *Move Your Shadow*; J. Anthony Lukas, *Common Ground*
1987—David K. Shipler, *Arab and Jew*
1988—Richard Rhodes, *The Making of the Atomic Bomb*
1989—Neil Sheehan, *A Bright Shining Lie: John Paul Vann and America in Vietnam*
1990—Dale Maharidge and Michael Williamson, *And Their Children After Them*
1991—Bert Holldobler and Edward O. Wilson, *The Ants*
1992—Daniel Yergin, *The Prize: The Epic Quest for Oil*
1993—Garry Wills, *Lincoln at Gettysburg*
1994—David Remnick, *Lenin's Tomb: The Last Days of the Soviet Empire*
1995—Jonathan Weiner, *The Beak of the Finch: A Story of Evolution in Our Time*
1996—Tina Rosenberg, *The Haunted Land: Facing Europe's Ghosts After Communism*
1997—Richard Kluger, *Ashes to Ashes: America's Hundred-Year Cigarette War, the Public Health, and the Unabashed Triumph of Philip Morris*

1998—Jared Diamond, *Guns, Germs, and Steel: The Fates of Human Societies*
1999—John McPhee, *Annals of the Former World*
2000—John W. Dower, *Embracing Defeat: Japan in the Wake of World War II*
2001—Herbert P. Bix, *Hirohito and the Making of Modern Japan*
2002—Diane McWhorter, *Carry Me Home: Birmingham, Alabama, the Climactic Battle of the Civil War Revolution*
2003—Samantha Power, *A Problem From Hell: America and the Age of Genocide*

Special Citation in Letters

1944—Richard Rodgers and Oscar Hammerstein II, for *Oklahoma!*
1957—Kenneth Roberts, for his historical novels
1960—*The Armada*, by Garrett Mattingly
1961—*American Heritage Picture History of the Civil War*
1973—*George Washington, Vols. I-IV*, by James Thomas Flexner
1977—Alex Haley, for *Roots*
1978—E.B. White
1984—Theodore Seuss Geisel (Dr. Seuss)
1992—Art Spiegelman, for *Maus*

Music

1943—William Schuman, *Secular Cantata No. 2, A Free Song*
1944—Howard Hanson, *Symphony No. 4, Op. 34*
1945—Aaron Copland, *Appalachian Spring*
1946—Leo Sowerby, *The Canticle of the Sun*
1947—Charles E. Ives, *Symphony No. 3*
1948—Walter Piston, *Symphony No. 3*
1949—Virgil Thomson, *Louisiana Story*
1950—Gian-Carlo Menotti, *The Consul*
1951—Douglas Moore, *Giants in the Earth*
1952—Gail Kubik, *Symphony Concertante*
1954—Quincy Porter, *Concerto for Two Pianos and Orchestra*
1955—Gian-Carlo Menotti, *The Saint of Bleecker Street*
1956—Ernest Toch, *Symphony No. 3*
1957—Norman Dello Joio, *Meditations on Ecclesiastes*
1958—Samuel Barber, *Vanessa*
1959—John La Montaine, *Concerto for Piano and Orchestra*
1960—Elliott Carter, *Second String Quartet*
1961—Walter Piston, *Symphony No. 7*
1962—Robert Ward, *The Crucible*
1963—Samuel Barber, *Piano Concerto No. 1*
1966—Leslie Bassett, *Variations for Orchestra*
1967—Leon Kirchner, *Quartet No. 3*
1968—George Crumb, *Echoes of Time and The River*
1969—Karel Husa, *String Quartet No. 3*
1970—Charles W. Wuorinen, *Time's Encomium*
1971—Mario Davidovsky, *Synchronisms No. 6*
1972—Jacob Druckman, *Windows*
1973—Elliott Carter, *String Quartet No. 3*
1974—Donald Martino, *Notturno*
1975—Dominick Argento, *From the Diary of Virginia Woolf*
1976—Ned Rorem, *Air Music*
1977—Richard Wernick, *Visions of Terror and Wonder*
1978—Michael Colgrass, *Deja Vu for Percussion and Orchestra*
1979—Joseph Schwantner, *Aftertones of Infinity*
1980—David Del Tredici, *In Memory of a Summer Day*

1982—Roger Sessions, *Concerto for Orchestra*
1983—Ellen T. Zwilich, *Three Movements for Orchestra*
1984—Bernard Rands, *Canti del Sole*
1985—Stephen Albert, *Symphony, RiverRun*
1986—George Perle, *Wind Quintet IV*
1987—John Harbison, *The Flight Into Egypt*
1988—William Bolcom, *12 New Etudes for Piano*
1989—Roger Reynolds, *Whispers Out of Time*
1990—Mel Powell, *Duplicates: A Concerto for Two Pianos and Orchestra*
1991—Shulamit Ran, *Symphony*
1992—Wayne Peterson, *The Face of the Night, The Heart of the Dark*
1993—Christopher Rouse, *Trombone Concerto*
1994—Gunther Schuller, *Of Reminiscences and Reflections*
1995—Morton Gould, *Stringmusic*
1996—George Walker, *Lilacs*
1997—Wynton Marsalis, *Blood on the Fields*
1998—Aaron Jay Kernis, *String Quartet No. 2*
1999—Melinda Wagner, *Concerto for Flute, Strings and Percussion*
2000—Lewis Spratlan, *Life is a Dream, Opera in Three Acts: Act II, Concert Version*
2001—John Corigliano, *Symphony No. 2 for String Orchestra*
2002—Henry Brant, *Ice Field*
2003—John Adams, *On the Transmigration of Souls*

Special Citation in Music

1974—Roger Sessions
1976—Scott Joplin
1982—Milton Babbitt
1985—William Schuman
1998—George Gershwin
1999—Edward Kennedy "Duke" Ellington

National Book Awards, 1950-2002

The National Book Awards (known as the American Book Awards from 1980 to 1986) are administered by the National Book Foundation and have been given annually since 1950. The prizes, each valued at $10,000, are awarded to U.S. citizens for works published in the U.S. in the 12 months prior to the nominations. In some years, multiple awards were given for nonfiction in various categories; in such cases, the history and biography (if any) or biography winner is listed. Selected additional awards in nonfiction are given in footnotes. Nonfiction winners in certain separate categories may not be shown.

Fiction

Year	Author, Title	Year	Author, Title
1950	Nelson Algren, *The Man With the Golden Arm*	1976	William Gaddis, *JR*
1951	William Faulkner, *The Collected Stories*	1977	Wallace Stegner, *The Spectator Bird*
1952	James Jones, *From Here to Eternity*	1978	Mary Lee Settle, *Blood Ties*
1953	Ralph Ellison, *Invisible Man*	1979	Tim O'Brien, *Going After Cacciato*
1954	Saul Bellow, *The Adventures of Augie March*	1980	William Styron, *Sophie's Choice*
1955	William Faulkner, *A Fable*	1981	Wright Morris, *Plains Song*
1956	John O'Hara, *Ten North Frederick*	1982	John Updike, *Rabbit Is Rich*
1957	Wright Morris, *The Field of Vision*	1983	Alice Walker, *The Color Purple*
1958	John Cheever, *The Wapshot Chronicle*	1984	Ellen Gilchrist, *Victory Over Japan*
1959	Bernard Malamud, *The Magic Barrel*	1985	Don DeLillo, *White Noise*
1960	Philip Roth, *Goodbye, Columbus*	1986	E.L. Doctorow, *World's Fair*
1961	Conrad Richter, *The Waters of Kronos*	1987	Larry Heinemann, *Paco's Story*
1962	Walker Percy, *The Moviegoer*	1988	Pete Dexter, *Paris Trout*
1963	J.F. Powers, *Morte d'Urban*	1989	John Casey, *Spartina*
1964	John Updike, *The Centaur*	1990	Charles Johnson, *Middle Passage*
1965	Saul Bellow, *Herzog*	1991	Norman Rush, *Mating*
1966	Katherine Anne Porter, *The Collected Stories*	1992	Cormac McCarthy, *All the Pretty Horses*
1967	Bernard Malamud, *The Fixer*	1993	E. Annie Proulx, *The Shipping News*
1968	Thornton Wilder, *The Eighth Day*	1994	William Gaddis, *A Frolic of His Own*
1969	Jerzy Kosinski, *Steps*	1995	Philip Roth, *Sabbath's Theater*
1970	Joyce Carol Oates, *Them*	1996	Andrea Barrett, *Ship Fever and Other Stories*
1971	Saul Bellow, *Mr. Sammler's Planet*	1997	Charles Frazier, *Cold Mounatin*
1972	Flannery O'Connor, *The Complete Stories*	1998	Alice McDermott, *Charming Billy*
1973	John Barth, *Chimera*	1999	Ha Jin, *Waiting*
1974	Thomas Pynchon, *Gravity's Rainbow*	2000	Susan Sontag, *In America*
1974	Isaac Bashevis Singer, *A Crown of Feathers*	2001	Jonathan Franzen, *The Corrections*
1975	Robert Stone, *Dog Soldiers*	2002	Julia Glass, *Three Junes*

Nonfiction

Year	Author, Title	Year	Author, Title
1950	Ralph L. Rusk, *Ralph Waldo Emerson*	1953	Bernard A. De Voto, *The Course of an Empire*
1951	Newton Arvin, *Herman Melville*	1954	Bruce Catton, *A Stillness at Appomattox*
1952	Rachel Carson, *The Sea Around Us*	1955	Joseph Wood Krutch, *The Measure of Man*

Year	Author, Title	Year	Author, Title
1956	Herbert Kubly, *An American in Italy*	1979	Arthur M. Schlesinger, Jr., *Robert Kennedy and His Times*
1957	George F. Kennan, *Russia Leaves the War*	1980	Tom Wolfe, *The Right Stuff*
1958	Catherine Drinker Bowen, *The Lion and the Throne*	1981	Maxine Hong Kingston, *China Men*
1959	J. Christopher Herold, *Mistress to an Age: A Life of Madame De Stael*	1982	Tracy Kidder, *The Soul of a New Machine*
1960	Richard Ellman, *James Joyce*	1983	Fox Butterfield, *China: Alive in the Bitter Sea*
1961	William L. Shirer, *The Rise and Fall of the Third Reich*	1984	Robert V. Remini, *Andrew Jackson and the Course of American Democracy, 1833-1845*
1962	Lewis Mumford, *The City in History: Its Origins, Its Transformations, and Its Prospects*	1985	J. Anthony Lukas, *Common Ground: A Turbulent Decade in the Lives of Three American Families*
1963	Leon Edel, *Henry James: Vol. II: The Conquest of London; Vol. III: The Middle Years*	1986	Barry Lopez, *Arctic Dreams*
1964	William H. McNeill, *The Rise of the West: A History of the Human Community*	1987	Richard Rhodes, *The Making of the Atom Bomb*
1965	Louis Fisher, *The Life of Lenin*	1988	Neil Sheehan, *A Bright Shining Lie: John Paul Vann and America in Vietnam*
1966	Arthur M. Schlesinger, Jr., *A Thousand Days: John F. Kennedy in the White House*	1989	Thomas L. Friedman, *From Beirut to Jerusalem*
1967	Peter Gay, *The Enlightenment, An Interpretation Vol I: The Rise of Modern Paganism*	1990	Ron Chernow, *The House of Morgan: An American Banking Dynasty and the Rise of Modern Finance*
1968	George F. Kennan, *Memoirs: 1925-1950*[1]	1991	Orlando Patterson, *Freedom*
1969	Winthrop D. Jordan, *White Over Black: American Attitudes Toward the Negro, 1550-1812*[2]	1992	Paul Monette, *Becoming a Man: Half a Life Story*
1970	T. Harry Williams, *Huey Long*[3]	1993	Gore Vidal, *United States: Essays 1952-1992*
1971	James MacGregor Burns, *Roosevelt: The Soldier of Freedom*	1994	Sherwin B. Nuland, *How We Die: Reflections on Life's Final Chapter*
1972	Joseph P. Lash, *Eleanor and Franklin: The Story of Their Relationship, Based on Eleanor Roosevelt's Private Papers*	1995	Tina Rosenberg, *The Haunted Land: Facing Europe's Ghosts After Communism*
1973	James Thomas Flexner, *George Washington, Vol. IV: Anguish and Farewell, 1793-1799*[4]	1996	James Carroll, *An American Requiem: God, My Father, and the War That Came Between Us*
1974	John Clive, *Macaulay, The Shaping of the Historian;* Douglas Day, *Malcolm Lowry: A Biography*[5]	1997	Joseph J. Ellis, *American Sphinx: The Character of Thomas Jefferson*
1975	Richard B. Sewall, *The Life of Emily Dickinson*[6]	1998	Edward Ball, *Slaves in the Family*
1976	David Brion Davis, *The Problem of Slavery in the Age of Revolution, 1770-1823*	1999	John W. Dower, *Embracing Defeat: Japan in the Wake of World War II*
1977	W.A. Swanberg, *Norman Thomas: The Last Idealist*[7]	2000	Nathaniel Philbrick, *In the Heart of the Sea: The Tragedy of the Whaleship Essex*
1978	W. Jackson Bate, *Samuel Johnson*[8]	2001	Andrew Solomon, *The Noonday Demon: An Atlas of Depression*
		2002	Robert A. Caro, *Master of the Senate: The Years of Lyndon Johnson*[8]

(1) Science, Philosophy, and Religion: Jonathan Kozol, *Death at an Early Age*. (2) Arts & Letters: Norman Mailer, *The Armies of the Night: History as a Novel, The Novel as History*. (3) Arts & Letters: Lillian Hellman, *An Unfinished Woman: A Memoir*. (4) Contemp. Affairs: Frances FitzGerald, *Fire in the Lake: The Vietnamese and the Americans in Vietnam*. (5) Arts & Letters: Pauline Kael, *Deeper Into the Movies*. (6) Arts & Letters: Roger Shattuck, *Marcel Proust*; Lewis Thomas, *The Lives of a Cell: Notes of a Biology Watcher*. (7) Contemp. Thought: Bruno Bettelheim, *The Uses of Enchantment: The Meaning and Importance of Fairy Tales*. (8) **Other National Book Awards, 2002:** Poetry: Ruth Stone, *In the Next Galaxy*. Young people's literature: Nancy Farmer, *The House of the Scorpion*. Medal for Distinguished Contr. to American Letters: Philip Roth.

The Man Booker Prize for Fiction, 1969-2002

The Booker Prize for fiction, established in 1968, is awarded annually in October for what is judged the best full-length novel written in English by a citizen of the UK, the Commonwealth, or the Irish Republic. In 2002 sponsorship of the award was taken over by Man Group PLC, the name was changed to the Man Booker Prize, and the amount was increased from £20,000 to £50,000. The prize money for being named to the shortlist of six was also increased to £2,500 (from £1,000).

1969—P. H. Newby, *Something to Answer For*
1970—Bernice Rubens, *The Elected Member*
1971—V. S. Naipaul, *In a Free State*
1972—John Berger, *G*
1973—J. G. Farrell, *The Siege of Krishnapur*
1974—Nadine Gordimer, *The Conservationist*; Stanley Middleton, *Holiday*
1975—Ruth Prawer Jhabvala, *Heat & Dust*
1976—David Storey, *Saville*
1977—Paul Scott, *Staying On*
1978—Iris Murdoch, *The Sea, The Sea*
1979—Penelope Fitzgerald, *Offshore*
1980—William Golding, *Rites of Passage*
1981—Salman Rushdie, *Midnight's Children*
1982—Thomas Keneally, *Schindler's Ark*
1983—J. M. Coetzee, *Life and Times of Michael K*
1984—Anita Brookner, *Hotel du Lac*
1985—Keri Hulme, *The Bone People*
1986—Kingsley Amis, *The Old Devils*
1987—Penelope Lively, *Moon Tiger*
1988—Peter Carey, *Oscar and Lucinda*
1989—Kazuo Ishiguro, *The Remains of the Day*
1990—A. S. Byatt, *Possession*
1991—Ben Okri, *The Famished Road*
1992—Michael Ondaatje, *The English Patient*; Barry Unsworth, *Sacred Hunger*
1993—Roddy Doyle, *Paddy Clarke Ha Ha Ha*
1994—James Kelman, *How Late It Was, How Late*
1995—Pat Barker, *The Ghost Road*
1996—Graham Swift, *Last Orders*
1997—Arundhati Roy, *The God of Small Things*
1998—Ian McEwan, *Amsterdam*
1999—J. M. Coetzee, *Disgrace*
2000—Margaret Atwood, *The Blind Assassin*
2001—Peter Carey, *True History of the Kelly Gang*
2002—Yann Martel, *Life of Pi*

Miscellaneous Book Awards
(Awarded in 2003, unless otherwise noted)

Academy of American Poets Awards. Academy Fellowship, $35,000 stipend: Sharon Olds. James Laughlin Award, $5,000: Vijay Seshadri, *The Long Meadow*. Walt Whitman Award, $5,000: Tony Tost, *Invisible Bride*. Harold Morton Landon Translation Award, $1,000: W. S. Merwin, *Sir Gawain and the Green Knight*. (2002): Lenore Marshall Poetry Prize, $25,000: Madeline DeFrees, *Blue Dusk*. Raiziss/de Palchi Translation Award (fellowship), $20,000: Michael Palma, *Selected Poems of Giovanni Raboni*. Wallace Stevens Award, for mastery in the art of poetry, $150,000: Ruth Stone.

American Academy of Arts and Letters. Gold Medal for Poetry: W.S. Merwin. Award of Merit for the Novel: Paula Fox. Academy Awards in Literature ($7,500 each): Andrea Barrett, Clark Blaise, Percival Everett, Hilary Masters, Lynne McMahon, Gregory Orr, Tom Sleigh, Anne Winters. E. M. Forster Award, $15,000: Andrew O'Hagan. Sue Kaufman Prize for First Fiction, $2,500: Gabe Hudson, *Dear Mr. President*. Richard and Hinda

Rosenthal Foundation Award, $5,000: Maile Meloy, *Half in Love*. Harold D. Vursell Memorial Award, $10,000: Thom Jones. Rome Fellowships in Literature, one-year residence at the American Academy in Rome, for 2003-2004: Joshua Weiner (poetry), Sarah Arvio (fiction). Mildred and Harold Strauss Livings (5-year $50,000 annual stipend): Gish Jen and Claire Messud.

Le Prix Goncourt, by Académie Goncourt: Pascal Quignard, *Les Ombres Errantes* (Wandering Shadows).

Bollingen Prize in Poetry, by the Yale Univ. Library: Adrienne Rich.

Edgar Awards, by the Mystery Writers of America: Grand Master award: Ira Levin. Best novel: *Winter and Night*, S.J. Rozan. Best first novel by an American author: *The Blue Edge of Midnight*, Jonathon King. Best paperback original: *Out of Sight*, T.J. MacGregor. Best Critical/Biographical: *The Mammoth Encyclopedia of Modern Crime Fiction*, Mike Ashley.

Golden Kite Awards, by Society of Children's Book Writers and Illustrators. Fiction: Jaira Placide, *Fresh Girl*. Nonfiction: Elizabeth Partridge, *This Land Was Made for You and Me: The Life and Songs of Woody Guthrie*. Picture-illustration: Marla Frazee, *Mrs. Biddlebox* (Linda Smith, author). Picture book text: Sarah Wilson, *George Hogglesberry, Grade School Alien* (Chad Cameron, illus.).

Hugo Awards, by the World Science Fiction Convention. Novel: *Hominids*, Robert J. Sawyer. Novella: *Coraline*, Neil Gaiman. Novelette: *Slow Life*, Michael Swanwick. Short story: "Falling onto Mars," Geoffrey A. Landis. John W. Campbell Award for Best New Writer: Wen Spencer, *Alien Taste*.

Nebula Awards, by the Science Fiction Writers of America. Grand Master award: Ursula K. Le Guin. Novel: *American Gods*, Neil Gaiman. Novella: *Bronte's Egg*, Richard Chwedyk. Novelette: *Hell Is the Absence of God*, Ted Chiang. Short story: "Creature," Carol Emshwiller.

Coretta Scott King Award, by American Library Assn., for African American authors and illustrators of outstanding books for

children and young adults. Author: Nikki Grimes, *Bronx Masquerade*. Illustrator: E. B. Lewis, *Talkin' About Bessie: The Story of Aviator Elizabeth Coleman* (Nikki Grimes, author).

Lincoln Prize, by Lincoln and Soldiers Institute at Gettysburg College, for contribution to Civil War studies, $20,000 and bust of Lincoln; George C. Rable, *Fredericksburg! Fredericksburg!*.

National Book Critics Circle Awards. Fiction: Ian McEwan, *Atonement*. Nonfiction: Samantha Power, "*A Problem from Hell*": *America and the Age of Genocide*. Criticism: William H. Gass, *Tests of Time*. Biography/Autobiography: Janet Browne, *Charles Darwin: The Power of Place, Vol. II*. Poetry: B.H. Fairchild, *Early Occult Memory Systems of the Lower Midwest*. Nona Balakian Citation for Excellence in Reviewing: Maureen N. McLane. Ivan Sandrof Lifetime Achievement Award: Richard Howard.

PEN/Faulkner Award, for fiction, $15,000: Sabina Murray, *The Caprices*.

Whitbread Book of the Year Award, by Whitbread PLC: £25,000: Clair Tomalin, *Samuel Pepys: The Unequalled Self*.

Newbery Medal Books, 1922-2003

The Newbery Medal is awarded annually by the Association for Library Service to Children, a division of the American Library Association, to the author of the most distinguished contribution to American literature for children.

Year Given	Book, Author	Year Given	Book, Author
1922	*The Story of Mankind*, Hendrik Willem van Loon	1964	*It's Like This, Cat*, Emily Cheney Neville
1923	*The Voyages of Dr. Dolittle*, Hugh Lofting	1965	*Shadow of a Bull*, Maja Wojciechowska
1924	*The Dark Frigate*, Charles Boardman Hawes	1966	*I, Juan de Pareja*, Elizabeth Borton de Trevino
1925	*Tales From Silver Lands*, Charles Joseph Finger	1967	*Up a Road Slowly*, Irene Hunt
1926	*Shen of the Sea*, Arthur Bowie Chrisman	1968	*From the Mixed-Up Files of Mrs. Basil E. Frankweiler*,
1927	*Smoky, the Cowhorse*, Will James		E. L. Konigsburg
1928	*Gay-Neck*, Dhan Gopal Mukerji	1969	*The High King*, Lloyd Alexander
1929	*The Trumpeter of Krakow*, Eric P. Kelly	1970	*Sounder*, William H. Armstrong
1930	*Hitty, Her First Hundred Years*, Rachel Field	1971	*The Summer of the Swans*, Betsy Byars
1931	*The Cat Who Went to Heaven*, Elizabeth Coatsworth	1972	*Mrs. Frisby and the Rats of NIMH*, Robert C. O'Brien
1932	*Waterless Mountain*, Laura Adams Armer	1973	*Julie of the Wolves*, Jean George
1933	*Young Fu of the Upper Yangtze*, Elizabeth Foreman Lewis	1974	*The Slave Dancer*, Paula Fox
1934	*Invincible Louisa*, Cornelia Lynde Meigs	1975	*M. C. Higgins the Great*, Virginia Hamilton
1935	*Dobry*, Monica Shannon	1976	*Grey King*, Susan Cooper
1936	*Caddie Woodlawn*, Carol Ryrie Brink	1977	*Roll of Thunder, Hear My Cry*, Mildred D. Taylor
1937	*Roller Skates*, Ruth Sawyer	1978	*Bridge to Terabithia*, Katherine Paterson
1938	*The White Stag*, Kate Seredy	1979	*The Westing Game*, Ellen Raskin
1939	*Thimble Summer*, Elizabeth Enright	1980	*A Gathering of Days*, Joan Blos
1940	*Daniel Boone*, James Daugherty	1981	*Jacob Have I Loved*, Katherine Paterson
1941	*Call It Courage*, Armstrong Sperry	1982	*A Visit to William Blake's Inn: Poems for Innocent
1942	*The Matchlock Gun*, Walter D. Edmonds		and Experienced Travelers*, Nancy Willard
1943	*Adam of the Road*, Elizabeth Janet Gray	1983	*Dicey's Song*, Cynthia Voigt
1944	*Johnny Tremain*, Esther Forbes	1984	*Dear Mr. Henshaw*, Beverly Cleary
1945	*Rabbit Hill*, Robert Lawson	1985	*The Hero and the Crown*, Robin McKinley
1946	*Strawberry Girl*, Lois Lenski	1986	*Sarah, Plain and Tall*, Patricia MacLachlan
1947	*Miss Hickory*, Carolyn S. Bailey	1987	*The Whipping Boy*, Sid Fleischman
1948	*Twenty-One Balloons*, William Pène Du Bois	1988	*Lincoln: A Photobiography*, Russell Freedman
1949	*King of the Wind*, Marguerite Henry	1989	*Joyful Noise: Poems for Two Voices*, Paul Fleischman
1950	*The Door in the Wall*, Marguerite de Angeli	1990	*Number the Stars*, Lois Lowry
1951	*Amos Fortune, Free Man*, Elizabeth Yates	1991	*Maniac Magee*, Jerry Spinelli
1952	*Ginger Pye*, Eleanor Estes	1992	*Shiloh*, Phyllis Reynolds Naylor
1953	*Secret of the Andes*, Ann Nolan Clark	1993	*Missing May*, Cynthia Rylant
1954	*. . . And Now Miguel*, Joseph Krumgold	1994	*The Giver*, Lois Lowry
1955	*The Wheel on the School*, Meindert DeJong	1995	*Walk Two Moons*, Sharon Creech
1956	*Carry On, Mr. Bowditch*, Jean Lee Latham	1996	*The Midwife's Apprentice*, Karen Cushman
1957	*Miracles on Maple Hill*, Virginia Sorensen	1997	*The View From Saturday*, E. L. Konigsburg
1958	*Rifles for Watie*, Harold Keith	1998	*Out of the Dust*, Karen Hesse
1959	*The Witch of Blackbird Pond*, Elizabeth George Speare	1999	*Holes*, Louis Sachar
1960	*Onion John*, Joseph Krumgold	2000	*Bud, Not Buddy*, Christopher Paul Curtis
1961	*Island of the Blue Dolphins*, Scott O'Dell	2001	*A Year Down Yonder*, Richard Peck
1962	*The Bronze Bow*, Elizabeth George Speare	2002	*A Single Shard*, Linda Sue Park
1963	*A Wrinkle in Time*, Madeleine L'Engle	2003	*Crispin: The Cross of Lead*, Avi

Caldecott Medal Books, 1938-2003

The Caldecott Medal is awarded annually by the Association for Library Service to Children, a division of the American Library Association, to the illustrator of the most distinguished American picture book for children.

Year Given	Book, Illustrator	Year Given	Book, Illustrator
1938	*Animals of the Bible*, Dorothy P. Lathrop	1952	*Finders Keepers*, Nicolas, pseud. (Nicholas Mordvinoff)
1939	*Mei Li*, Thomas Handforth	1953	*The Biggest Bear*, Lynd Ward
1940	*Abraham Lincoln*, Ingri & Edgar Parin d'Aulaire	1954	*Madeline's Rescue*, Ludwig Bemelmans
1941	*They Were Strong and Good*, Robert Lawson	1955	*Cinderella, or the Little Glass Slipper*, Marcia Brown
1942	*Make Way for Ducklings*, Robert McCloskey	1956	*Frog Went A-Courtin'*, Feodor Rojankovsky
1943	*The Little House*, Virginia Lee Burton	1957	*A Tree Is Nice*, Marc Simont
1944	*Many Moons*, Louis Slobodkin	1958	*Time of Wonder*, Robert McCloskey
1945	*Prayer for a Child*, Elizabeth Orton Jones	1959	*Chanticleer and the Fox*, Barbara Cooney
1946	*The Rooster Crows*, Maude & Miska Petersham	1960	*Nine Days to Christmas*, Marie Hall Ets
1947	*The Little Island*, Leonard Weisgard	1961	*Baboushka and the Three Kings*, Nicolas Sidjakov
1948	*White Snow, Bright Snow*, Roger Duvoisin	1962	*Once a Mouse*, Marcia Brown
1949	*The Big Snow*, Berta & Elmer Hader	1963	*The Snowy Day*, Ezra Jack Keats
1950	*Song of the Swallows*, Leo Politi	1964	*Where the Wild Things Are*, Maurice Sendak
1951	*The Egg Tree*, Katherine Milhous	1965	*May I Bring a Friend?*, Beni Montressor

Year Given	Book, Illustrator
1966	*Always Room for One More*, Nonny Hogrogian
1967	*Sam, Bang, and Moonshine*, Evaline Ness
1968	*Drummer Hoff*, Ed Emberley
1969	*The Fool of the World and the Flying Ship*, Uri Shulevitz
1970	*Sylvester and the Magic Pebble*, William Steig
1971	*A Story A Story*, Gail E. Haley
1972	*One Fine Day*, Nonny Hogrogian
1973	*The Funny Little Woman*, Blair Lent
1974	*Duffy and the Devil*, Margot Zemach
1975	*Arrow to the Sun*, Gerald McDermott
1976	*Why Mosquitoes Buzz in People's Ears*, Leo & Diane Dillon
1977	*Ashanti to Zulu: African Traditions*, Leo & Diane Dillon
1978	*Noah's Ark*, Peter Spier
1979	*The Girl Who Loved Wild Horses*, Paul Goble
1980	*Ox-Cart Man*, Barbara Cooney
1981	*Fables*, Arnold Lobel
1982	*Jumanji*, Chris Van Allsburg
1983	*Shadow*, Marcia Brown
1984	*The Glorious Flight: Across the Channel with Louis Bleriot*, Alice and Martin Provensen

Year Given	Book, Illustrator
1985	*Saint George and the Dragon*, Trina Schart Hyman
1986	*The Polar Express*, Chris Van Allsburg
1987	*Hey, Al*, Richard Egielski
1988	*Owl Moon*, John Schoenherr
1989	*Song and Dance Man*, Stephen Grammell
1990	*Lon Po Po: A Red-Riding Hood Story From China*, Ed Young
1991	*Black and White*, David Macaulay
1992	*Tuesday*, David Wiesner
1993	*Mirette on the High Wire*, Emily Arnold McCully
1994	*Grandfather's Journey*, Allen Say
1995	*Smoky Night*, David Diaz
1996	*Officer Buckle and Gloria*, Peggy Rathmann
1997	*Golem*, David Wisniewski
1998	*Rapunzel*, Paul O. Zelinsky
1999	*Snowflake Bentley*, Mary Azarian
2000	*Joseph Had a Little Overcoat*, Simms Taback
2001	*So You Want to be President?*, David Small
2002	*The Three Pigs*, David Wiesner
2003	*My Friend Rabbit*, Eric Rohmann

Journalism Awards, 2003

National Journalism Awards, by Scripps Howard Foundation, $2,500 each. Editorial writing: John McCormick, *Chicago Tribune*; human interest writing: Paula Bock, *Seattle Times*; environmental reporting (over 100,000 circ.): Sam Roe, *Chicago Tribune*; environmental reporting (under 100,000 circ.): Canon City Daily Record (CO); Public service reporting (over 100,000 circ.): *Baltimore Sun* (Jim Haner, Kimberly A.C. Wilson and John B. O'Donnell); public service reporting (under 100,000 circ.): *Albuquerque Tribune* (NM); commentary: Frank Cerabino, *Palm Beach Post* (FL). Photojournalism: Don Bartletti, *Los Angeles Times*; editorial cartooning: Clay Bennett, *Christian Science Monitor* (Boston); college cartooning: Steven Olexa, *Daily Beacon*, Univ. of Tennessee (Knoxville). Distinguished service to literacy: *Orlando Sentinel* (FL); distinguished service to First Amendment: Seth Rosenfeld, *San Francisco Chronicle*. Business/economics reporting: *Chicago Tribune*; web reporting: *The Sun* (CA). Electronic journalism—Small market radio: KOSU-FM (Stillwater, OK); large market radio: Minnesota Public Radio/American RadioWorks (Saint Paul); small market TV/cable: KEYE-TV (Austin, TX); large market TV/cable: KHOU-TV, Houston.

National Magazine Awards, by American Society of Magazine Editors and Columbia Univ. Graduate School of Journalism. Gen. excel., circ. over 2 mil: *Parenting*; 1 mil-2 mil: *ESPN The Magazine*; 500,000 to 1 mil: *The Atlantic Monthly*; 250,000-500,000: *Texas Monthly*; 100,000-250,000: *Architectural Record*; under 100,000: *Foreign Policy*. Personal service: *Outside*; leisure interests: *National Geographic Adventure*; feature writing: *Harper's Magazine*; fiction: *The New Yorker*; design: *Details*; photography: *Condé Nast Traveler*; reporting: *The New Yorker*; public interest: *The Atlantic Monthly*; profiles: *Sports Illustrated*; essays: *The American Scholar*; criticism/reviews: *Vanity Fair*; columns/commentary: *The Nation*; single-topic issue: *Scientific American*; gen. excellence online: *Slate* (slate.msn.com).

George Foster Peabody Awards, by Univ. of Georgia. *Terror on Tape*, CNN. *Bringing Down a Dictator*, York Zimmerman, Inc., presented on PBS. *9/11*, CBS Special Presentation, New York.

The Sonic Memorial Project, Lost and Found Sound from the Kitchen Sisters Productions, presented on NPR, and SonicMemorial.org by Picture Projects in collaboration with dotsperinch. *Nightline: The Survivors*, ABC News, New York. *Frontline: Shattered Dreams of Peace: The Road From Oslo*, SET Productions, C-Films Productions for WGBH, in association with FRANCE 2, ABU DHABI Television, and Tel Ad Israel. *File on 4: Export Controls*, BBC Radio 4. *The Hepatitis C Epidemic: A 15-Year Government Cover-Up*, Fuji Television Network, Inc., Japan. *Sounding the Alarm*, WISN-TV, Milwaukee, WI. *Fake Drugs, Real Lives*, WFAA-TV, Dallas, TX. *DNA Protects Men of Dishonor*, KPRC-TV, Houston, TX. *Nightline: Heart of Darkness*, ABC News, New York. *How High Is the Mountain*, Public Television Service Foundation, Taiwan. *The Yiddish Radio Project*, NPR and Sound Portrait Productions. *Stories of Home*, WBEZ/Chicago Public Radio. *EGG The Arts Show*, Thirteen/WNET (New York). *The Complete Angler*, ESPN. *Monkey Trial*, Nebraska ETV and The American Experience, WGBH (Boston). *The Rise and Fall of Jim Crow*, Thirteen/WNET (New York). *Bang Bang You're Dead*, Showtime from Viacom Productions and A Jersey Guys Production, Inc. *Almost Strangers*, BBC America with Talkback Productions, presented on BBC. *Stage on Screen: Beckett on Film*, Thirteen/WNET (New York). *Russell Simmons Presents Def Poetry*, HBO and Simmons/Lathan. *The Interrogation of Michael Crowe*, Court TV from JB Media and Hearst Entertainment. *Boomtown*, NBC/NBC Studios Inc. in association with DreamWorks Television. *ExxonMobil Masterpiece Theatre: Othello*, WGBH and London Weekend Television. *ExxonMobil Masterpiece Theatre's American Collection: Almost a Woman*, WGBH and ALT Films. *The Gathering Storm*, HBO and Scott Free Productions. *Boston Public/Chapter 37*, FOX from David E. Kelley Productions and 20th Century Fox Television Studios; *Six Feet Under*, HBO from Janollari Studios and Actual Size, Inc. in association with HBO Original Programming. *Door to Door*, TNT from Rosemont Productions International in association with Angel/Brown Productions.

Reuben Award, by National Cartoonists Society. For best cartoonist of 2002: Matt Groening.

The Spingarn Medal, 1915-2003

The Spingarn Medal has been awarded annually since 1915 (except in 1938) by the National Assoc. for the Advancement of Colored People for the highest achievement by an African American in the previous year.

1915 Ernest E. Just	1939 Marian Anderson	1960 Langston Hughes	1983 Lena Horne
1916 Charles Young	1940 Louis T. Wright	1961 Kenneth B. Clark	1984 Thomas Bradley
1917 Harry T. Burleigh	1941 Richard Wright	1962 Robert C. Weaver	1985 Bill Cosby
1918 William S. Braithwaite	1942 A. Philip Randolph	1963 Medgar W. Evers	1986 Dr. Benjamin L. Hooks
1919 Archibald H. Grimké	1943 William H. Hastie	1964 Roy Wilkins	1987 Percy E. Sutton
1920 W. E. B. Du Bois	1944 Charles Drew	1965 Leontyne Price	1988 Frederick D. Patterson
1921 Charles S. Gilpin	1945 Paul Robeson	1966 John H. Johnson	1989 Jesse Jackson
1922 Mary B. Talbert	1946 Thurgood Marshall	1967 Edward W. Brooke	1990 L. Douglas Wilder
1923 George W. Carver	1947 Dr. Percy L. Julian	1968 Sammy Davis Jr.	1991 Gen. Colin L. Powell
1924 Roland Hayes	1948 Channing H. Tobias	1969 Clarence M. Mitchell Jr.	1992 Barbara Jordan
1925 James W. Johnson	1949 Ralph J. Bunche	1970 Jacob Lawrence	1993 Dorothy I. Height
1926 Carter G. Woodson	1950 Charles H. Houston	1971 Leon H. Sullivan	1994 Maya Angelou
1927 Anthony Overton	1951 Mabel K. Staupers	1972 Gordon Parks	1995 John Hope Franklin
1928 Charles W. Chesnutt	1952 Harry T. Moore	1973 Wilson C. Riles	1996 A. Leon Higginbotham
1929 Mordecai W. Johnson	1953 Paul R. Williams	1974 Damon Keith	1997 Carl T. Rowan
1930 Henry A. Hunt	1954 Theodore K. Lawless	1975 Henry (Hank) Aaron	1998 Myrlie Evers-Williams
1931 Richard B. Harrison	1955 Carl Murphy	1976 Alvin Ailey	1999 Earl G. Graves Sr.
1932 Robert R. Moton	1956 Jack R. Robinson	1977 Alex Haley	2000 Oprah Winfrey
1933 Max Yergan	1957 Martin Luther King Jr.	1978 Andrew Young	2001 Vernon E. Jordan Jr.
1934 William T. B. Williams	1958 Daisy Bates and the	1979 Rosa L. Parks	2002 John Lewis
1935 Mary McLeod Bethune	Little Rock Nine	1980 Dr. Rayford W. Logan	2003 Constance Baker
1936 John Hope	1959 Edward Kennedy	1981 Coleman Young	Motley
1937 Walter White	(Duke) Ellington	1982 Dr. Benjamin E. Mays	

Miscellaneous Awards, 2003

American Academy of Arts and Letters. Gold Medal for Music: Ned Rorem. Award for Distinguished Service to the Arts: Leon Botstein. Arnold W. Brunner Memorial Prize in Architecture, $5,000: Elizabeth Diller and Ricardo Scofidio. Academy Awards, $7,500 each, in Architecture: Greg Lynn, Guy Nordenson, Andrew Zago; in Art: R. Crumb, Robert Lazzarini, Nancy Rubins, Gary Stephan, Richard Tuttle; in Music: Eric Chasalow, Zhou Long, Jeffrey Mumford, Roberto Sierra. Jimmy Ernst Award in Art, $5,000: Lester Johnson. Walter Hinrichsen Award (Music): Elliott Gyger. Charles Ives Fellowships in Music, $15,000: Daniel Kellog, Barbara White. Charles Ives Scholarships in Music, $7,500 each: Anthony Cheung, Jorge Villavicencio Grossmann, James Lee III, David T. Little, Keeril Makan, Melissa Mazzoli. Benjamin H. Danks Award in Music, $20,000: Kevin Puts. Goddard Lieberson Fellowships in Music, $12,500 each: Steven Weigt, Trevor Weston. Richard Rodgers Awards for the Musical Theater, $100,000: *The Tutor*, Andrew Gerle and Maryrose Wood (production), *Once Upon a Time in New Jersey*, Susan DiLallo and Stephen Weiner (development), *The Devil in the Flesh*, Jeffrey Lunden and Arthur Perlman (development). Richard and Hinda Rosenthal Foundation Award in Art, $5,000: Steve DiBenedetto.

National Humanities Medal (formerly **Charles Frankel Prize**), by National Endowment for the Humanities. $5,000 each: Frankie Hewitt, Iowa Writers' Workshop, Donald Kagan, Brian Lamb, Art Linkletter, Patricia MacLachlan, The Mount Vernon Ladies' Association of the Union, Thomas Sowell.

Fields Medal, International Mathematical Union, every 4 years: (2002) Vladimir Voevodsky, Laurent Lafforgue.

Intel Science Talent Search (formerly given by Westinghouse). First ($100,000 schol.): Jamie Elyce Rubin, Fort Myers,
FL; second ($75,000 schol.): Tianhui "Michael" Li, Portland, OR; third ($50,000 schol.): Anatoly Preygel, Germantown, MD.

National Inventor of the Year Awards, by Intellectual Property Owners. Dr. Warren M. Zapol, Chief of Anesthesia and Critical Care at Mass. General Hospital, and Dr. Claes Frostell, Head of Karolinska Institutet Danderyd Hospital, Stockholm, Sweden.

John F. Kennedy Center for the Performing Arts Awards. (2002) James Earl Jones, James Levine, Chita Rivera, Paul Simon, Elizabeth Taylor.

Library of the Year Award, by Gale Research, Inc., and Library Journal. Las Vegas-Clark County (NV) Public Library.

Congressional Gold Medal, by Congress. British Prime Min. Tony Blair.

Presidential Medal of Freedom, by the White House. Jacques Barzun, Julia Child, Roberto Clemente, Van Cliburn, Vaclav Havel, Charlton Heston, Edward Teller, Dave Thomas, Byron White, James Q. Wilson, John Wooden.

National Medal of the Arts, by the National Endowment for the Arts and the White House. Florence Knoll Bassett, Trisha Brown, Philippe de Montebello, Uta Hagen, Lawrence Halprin, Al Hirschfeld, George Jones, Ming Cho Lee, William "Smokey" Robinson Jr.

Pritzker Architecture Prize, by the Hyatt Foundation, $100,000: Jørn Utson, Denmark.

Teacher of the Year, by Council of Chief State School Officers and Scholastic, Inc.: Dr. Betsy Rogers, Leeds, AL.

Templeton Prize for Progress Toward Research or Discoveries about Spiritual Realities, by Templeton Foundation, £700,000 (about $1 million): Holmes Rolston III, Professor of Philosophy at Colorado St. University.

Miss America Winners, for 1921-2004

1921	Margaret Gorman, Washington, DC
1922-23	Mary Campbell, Columbus, Ohio
1924	Ruth Malcolmson, Philadelphia, Pennsylvania
1925	Fay Lamphier, Oakland, California
1926	Norma Smallwood, Tulsa, Oklahoma
1927	Lois Delander, Joliet, Illinois
1933	Marion Bergeron, West Haven, Connecticut
1935	Henrietta Leaver, Pittsburgh, Pennsylvania
1936	Rose Coyle, Philadelphia, Pennsylvania
1937	Bette Cooper, Bertrand Island, New Jersey
1938	Marilyn Meseke, Marion, Ohio
1939	Patricia Donnelly, Detroit, Michigan
1940	Frances Marie Burke, Philadelphia, Pennsylvania
1941	Rosemary LaPlanche, Los Angeles, California
1942	Jo-Caroll Dennison, Tyler, Texas
1943	Jean Bartel, Los Angeles, California
1944	Venus Ramey, Washington, D.C.
1945	Bess Myerson, New York City, New York
1946	Marilyn Buferd, Los Angeles, California
1947	Barbara Walker, Memphis, Tennessee
1948	BeBe Shopp, Hopkins, Minnesota
1949	Jacque Mercer, Litchfield, Arizona
1951	Yolande Betbeze, Mobile, Alabama
1952	Coleen Kay Hutchins, Salt Lake City, Utah
1953	Neva Jane Langley, Macon, Georgia
1954	Evelyn Margaret Ay, Ephrata, Pennsylvania
1955	Lee Meriwether, San Francisco, California
1956	Sharon Ritchie, Denver, Colorado
1957	Marian McKnight, Manning, South Carolina
1958	Marilyn Van Derbur, Denver, Colorado
1959	Mary Ann Mobley, Brandon, Mississippi
1960	Lynda Lee Mead, Natchez, Mississippi
1961	Nancy Fleming, Montague, Michigan
1962	Maria Fletcher, Asheville, North Carolina
1963	Jacquelyn Mayer, Sandusky, Ohio
1964	Donna Axum, El Dorado, Arkansas
1965	Vonda Kay Van Dyke, Phoenix, Arizona
1966	Deborah Irene Bryant, Overland Park, Kansas
1967	Jane Anne Jayroe, Laverne, Oklahoma
1968	Debra Dene Barnes, Moran, Kansas
1969	Judith Anne Ford, Belvidere, Illinois
1970	Pamela Anne Eldred, Birmingham, Michigan
1971	Phyllis Ann George, Denton, Texas
1972	Laurie Lea Schaefer, Columbus, Ohio
1973	Terry Anne Meeuwsen, DePere, Wisconsin
1974	Rebecca Ann King, Denver, Colorado
1975	Shirley Cothran, Fort Worth, Texas
1976	Tawney Elaine Godin, Yonkers, New York
1977	Dorothy Kathleen Benham, Edina, Minnesota
1978	Susan Perkins, Columbus, Ohio
1979	Kylene Barker, Galax, Virginia
1980	Cheryl Prewitt, Ackerman, Mississippi
1981	Susan Powell, Elk City, Oklahoma
1982	Elizabeth Ward, Russellville, Arkansas
1983	Debra Maffett, Anaheim, California
1984	Vanessa Williams*, Milwood, New York
	Suzette Charles, Mays Landing, New Jersey
1985	Sharlene Wells, Salt Lake City, Utah
1986	Susan Akin, Meridian, Mississippi
1987	Kellye Cash, Memphis, Tennessee
1988	Kaye Lani Rae Rafko, Monroe, Michigan
1989	Gretchen Carlson, Anoka, Minnesota
1990	Debbye Turner, Columbia, Missouri
1991	Marjorie Vincent, Oak Park, Illinois
1992	Carolyn Suzanne Sapp, Honolulu, Hawaii
1993	Leanza Cornett, Jacksonville, Florida
1994	Kimberly Aiken, Columbia, South Carolina
1995	Heather Whitestone, Birmingham, Alabama
1996	Shawntel Smith, Muldrow, Oklahoma
1997	Tara Dawn Holland, Overland Park, Kansas
1998	Kate Shindle, Evanston, Illinois
1999	Nicole Johnson, Roanoke, Virginia
2000	Heather Renee French, Maysville, Kentucky
2001	Angela Perez Baraquio, Honolulu, Hawaii
2002	Katie Harman, Gresham, Oregon
2003	Erika Harold, Urbana, Illinois
2004	Ericka Dunlap, Orlando, Florida

* Resigned July 23, 1984.

Entertainment Awards
Tony (Antoinette Perry) Awards, 2003

Play: *Take Me Out*
Musical: *Hairspray*
Book of a musical: Thomas Meehan & Mark O'Donnell, *Hairspray*
Actor, play: Brian Dennehy, *Long Day's Journey into Night*
Actress, play: Vanessa Redgrave, *Long Day's Journey into Night*
Actor, musical: Harvey Fierstein, *Hairspray*
Actress, musical: Marissa Jaret Winokur, *Hairspray*
Musical score: Scott Whittman & Marc Shaiman, *Hairspray*
Director, play: Joe Mantello, *Take Me Out*
Director, musical: Jack O'Brien, *Hairspray*
Play revival: *Long Day's Journey into Night*
Musical revival: *Nine The Musical*

Featured actor, play: Denis O'Hare, *Take Me Out*
Featured actress, play: Michele Pawk, *Hollywood Arms*
Featured actor, musical: Dick Latessa, *Hairspray*
Featured actress, musical: Jane Krakowski, *Nine The Musical*
Choreography: Twyla Tharp, *Movin' Out*
Costume design: William Ivey Long, *Hairspray*
Scenic design: Catherine Martin, *La Bohème*
Lighting design: Nigel Levings, *La Bohème*
Orchestrations: Stuart Malina & Billy Joel, *Movin' Out*
Lifetime achievement: Cy Feuer
Special Theatrical Event: *Russell Simmons' Def Poetry Jam on Broadway*
Regional Theater: The Children's Theatre Company

Tony Awards, 1948-2003

Year	Play	Musical	Year	Play	Musical
1948	Mister Roberts	No Award	1976	Travesties	A Chorus Line
1949	Death of a Salesman	Kiss Me Kate	1977	The Shadow Box	Annie
1950	The Cocktail Party	South Pacific	1978	Da	Ain't Misbehavin'
1951	The Rose Tattoo	Guys and Dolls	1979	The Elephant Man	Sweeney Todd
1952	The Fourposter	The King and I	1980	Children of a Lesser God	Evita
1953	The Crucible	Wonderful Town	1981	Amadeus	42nd Street
1954	The Teahouse of the August Moon	Kismet	1982	The Life and Adventures of Nicholas Nickelby	Nine
1955	The Desperate Hours	The Pajama Game	1983	Torch Song Trilogy	Cats
1956	The Diary of Anne Frank	Damn Yankees	1984	The Real Thing	La Cage aux Folles
1957	Long Day's Journey Into Night	My Fair Lady	1985	Biloxi Blues	Big River
1958	Sunrise at Campobello	The Music Man	1986	I'm Not Rappaport	The Mystery of Edwin Drood
1959	J.B.	Redhead	1987	Fences	Les Miserables
1960	The Miracle Worker	(tie) Fiorello!, The Sound of Music	1988	M. Butterfly	Phantom of the Opera
1961	Becket	Bye, Bye Birdie	1989	The Heidi Chronicles	Jerome Robbins' Broadway
1962	A Man for All Seasons	How to Succeed in Business Without Really Trying	1990	The Grapes of Wrath	City of Angels
1963	Who's Afraid of Virginia Woolf?	A Funny Thing Happened on the Way to the Forum	1991	Lost in Yonkers	The Will Rogers Follies
1964	Luther	Hello, Dolly!	1992	Dancing at Lughnasa	Crazy for You
1965	The Subject Was Roses	Fiddler on the Roof	1993	Angels in America: Millennium Approaches	Kiss of the Spider Woman
1966	Marat/Sade	Man of La Mancha	1994	Angels in America: Perestroika	Passion
1967	The Homecoming	Cabaret	1995	Love! Valour! Compassion!	Sunset Boulevard
1968	Rosencrantz and Guildenstern Are Dead	Hallelujah, Baby!	1996	Master Class	Rent
1969	The Great White Hope	1776	1997	The Last Night of Ballyhoo	Titanic
1970	Borstal Boy	Applause	1998	Art	The Lion King
1971	Sleuth	Company	1999	Side Man	Fosse
1972	Sticks and Bones	Two Gentleman of Verona	2000	Copenhagen	Contact
1973	That Championship Season	A Little Night Music	2001	Proof	The Producers
1974	The River Niger	Raisin	2002	Edward Albee's The Goat or Who Is Sylvia?	Thoroughly Modern Millie
1975	Equus	The Wiz	2003	Take Me Out	Hairspray

2003 Selected Prime-Time Emmy Awards (for 2002-2003 season)

Drama series: The West Wing, NBC
Comedy series: Everybody Loves Raymond, CBS
Miniseries: Steven Spielberg Presents Taken, Sci Fi
Variety, music, or comedy series: The Daily Show With Jon Stewart, Comedy Central
Variety, music, or comedy special: Cher: The Farewell Tour, NBC
Made-for-television movie: Door to Door, TNT
Lead actor, drama series: James Gandolfini, The Sopranos, HBO
Lead actress, drama series: Edie Falco, The Sopranos, HBO
Lead actor, comedy series: Tony Shalhoub, Monk, USA
Lead actress, comedy series: Debra Messing, Will & Grace, NBC
Lead actor, miniseries/movie: William H. Macy, Door to Door, TNT

Lead actress, miniseries/movie: Maggie Smith, My House in Umbria, HBO
Sup. actor, drama series: Joe Pantoliano, The Sopranos, HBO
Sup. actress, drama series: Tyne Daly, Judging Amy, CBS
Sup. actor, comedy series: Brad Garrett, Everybody Loves Raymond, CBS
Sup. actress, comedy series: Doris Roberts, Everybody Loves Raymond, CBS
Sup. actor, miniseries/movie: Ben Gazzara, Hysterical Blindness, HBO
Sup. actress, miniseries/movie: Gena Rowlands, Hysterical Blindness, HBO
Individual performance, variety series/music program: Wayne Brady, Whose Line Is It Anyway?, ABC
Reality/competition program: The Amazing Race, CBS
Bob Hope Humanitarian Award: Bill Cosby

2003 Selected Daytime Emmy Awards (for 2002-2003 season)

Drama series: As the World Turns, CBS
Actress: Susan Flannery, The Bold and the Beautiful, CBS
Actor: Maurice Benard, General Hospital, ABC
Sup. actress: Vanessa Marcil, General Hospital, ABC
Sup. actor: Benjamin Hendrickson, As the World Turns, CBS
Younger actress: Jennifer Finnigan, The Bold and the Beautiful, CBS
Younger actor: Jordi Vilasuso, Guiding Light, CBS
Drama series directing team: All My Children, ABC
Drama series writing team: General Hospital, ABC
Preschool children's series: Sesame Street, PBS
Children's series: Reading Rainbow, PBS

Performer in children's series: Shia LaBeouf, Even Stevens, Disney Channel
Performer in children's special: Ben Foster, Bang Bang You're Dead, Showtime
Game/audience participation show: Jeopardy!, syndicated
Game show host: Alex Trebek, Jeopardy!, syndicated
Talk Show: (tie) The View, ABC; The Wayne Brady Show, syndicated
Talk show host: Wayne Brady, The Wayne Brady Show, syndicated
Special class series: A Baby Story, The Learning Channel
Lifetime Achievement Award: Art Linkletter

Prime-Time Emmy Awards, 1952-2003

The National Academy of Television Arts and Science presented the first Emmy Awards in 1949. Through the years, award categories have changed, but since 1952, the Academy has recognized an outstanding comedy and drama each year.

Year Given	Comedy	Drama	Year Given	Comedy	Drama
1952	Red Skelton Show, NBC	Studio One, CBS	1959	Jack Benny Show, CBS	(3)
1953	I Love Lucy, CBS	Robert Montgomery Presents, NBC	1960	Art Carney Special, NBC	Playhouse 90, CBS
			1961	Jack Benny Show, CBS	Hallmark Hall of Fame: Macbeth, NBC
1954	I Love Lucy, CBS	The U.S. Steel Hour, ABC			
1955	Make Room for Daddy, ABC	The U.S. Steel Hour, ABC	1962	Bob Newhart Show, CBS	The Defenders, CBS
1956	Phil Silvers Show, CBS	Producer's Showcase, NBC	1963	Dick Van Dyke Show, CBS	The Defenders, CBS
1957	Phil Silvers Show, CBS	Requiem for a Heavyweight, CBS[1]	1964	Dick Van Dyke Show, CBS	The Defenders, CBS
1958	Phil Silvers Show, CBS	Gunsmoke, CBS	1965	Dick Van Dyke Show, CBS	Hallmark Hall of Fame: The Magnificent Yankee, NBC

Year Given	Comedy	Drama	Year Given	Comedy	Drama
1966	Dick Van Dyke Show, CBS	The Fugitive, ABC	1983	Cheers, NBC	Hill Street Blues, NBC
1967	The Monkees, NBC	Mission: Impossible, CBS	1984	Cheers, NBC	Hill Street Blues, NBC
1968	Get Smart, NBC	Mission: Impossible, CBS	1985	The Cosby Show, NBC	Cagney & Lacey, CBS
1969	Get Smart, NBC	NET Playhouse, NET	1986	Golden Girls, NBC	Cagney & Lacey, CBS
1970	My World and Welcome to It, NBC	Marcus Welby, M.D., ABC	1987	Golden Girls, NBC	L.A. Law, NBC
1971	All in the Family, CBS	The Bold Ones: "The Senator," NBC	1988	The Wonder Years, ABC	thirtysomething, ABC
1972	All in the Family, CBS	Masterpiece Theatre: Elizabeth R, PBS	1989	Cheers, NBC	L.A. Law, NBC
			1990	Murphy Brown, CBS	L.A. Law, NBC
1973	All in the Family, CBS	The Waltons, CBS	1991	Cheers, NBC	L.A. Law, NBC
1974	M*A*S*H, CBS	Masterpiece Theatre: Upstairs, Downstairs; PBS	1992	Murphy Brown, CBS	Northern Exposure, CBS
			1993	Seinfeld, NBC	Picket Fences, CBS
1975	Mary Tyler Moore Show, CBS	Masterpiece Theatre: Upstairs, Downstairs; PBS	1994	Frasier, NBC	Picket Fences, CBS
			1995	Frasier, NBC	NYPD Blue, ABC
1976	Mary Tyler Moore Show, CBS	Police Story, NBC	1996	Frasier, NBC	ER, NBC
1977	Mary Tyler Moore Show, CBS	Masterpiece Theatre: Upstairs, Downstairs; PBS	1997	Frasier, NBC	Law & Order, NBC
			1998	Frasier, NBC	The Practice, ABC
1978	All in the Family, CBS	The Rockford Files, NBC	1999	Ally McBeal, Fox	The Practice, ABC
1979	Taxi, ABC	Lou Grant, CBS	2000	Will & Grace, NBC	The West Wing, NBC
1980	Taxi, ABC	Lou Grant, CBS	2001	Sex and the City, HBO	The West Wing, NBC
1981	Taxi, ABC	Hill Street Blues, NBC	2002	Friends, NBC	The West Wing, NBC
1982	Barney Miller, ABC	Hill Street Blues, NBC	2003	Everybody Loves Raymond, CBS	The West Wing, NBC

(1) "Best Single Program of the Year," shown on Playhouse 90, which was named "Best New Series." (2) Beginning in 1959, Emmys awarded for work in the season encompassing the previous and current year. (3) Playhouse 90 (CBS) was best drama of 1 hour or longer; Alcoa-Goodyear Theatre (NBC) was best drama of less than 1 hour.

2003 Golden Globe Awards
(Awarded for work in 2002)

Film

Drama: The Hours
Musical/comedy: Chicago
Actress, drama: Nicole Kidman, The Hours
Actor, drama: Jack Nicholson, About Schmidt
Actress, musical/comedy: Renee Zellweger, Chicago
Actor, musical/comedy: Richard Gere, Chicago
Sup. actress, drama: Meryl Streep, Adaptation
Sup. actor, drama: Chris Cooper, Adaptation
Director: Martin Scorsese, Gangs of New York
Screenplay: Alexander Payne and Jim Taylor, About Schmidt
Foreign-language film: Talk to Her (Spain)
Original score: Elliot Goldenthal, Frida
Original Song: "The Hands That Built America," from Gangs of New York, U2
Cecil B. De Mille award for lifetime achievement: Gene Hackman

Television

Series, drama: The Shield, FX
Actress, drama: Edie Falco, The Sopranos, HBO
Actor, drama: Michael Chiklis, The Shield, FX
Series, musical/comedy: Curb Your Enthusiasm, HBO
Actress, musical/comedy: Jennifer Aniston, Friends, NBC
Actor, musical/comedy: Tony Shalhoub, Monk, USA
Miniseries, movie made for TV: The Gathering Storm, HBO
Actress, miniseries/movie: Uma Thurman, Hysterical Blindness, HBO
Actor, miniseries/movie: Albert Finney, The Gathering Storm, HBO
Sup. actress, miniseries/movie: Kim Cattrall, Sex and the City, HBO
Sup. actor, miniseries/movie: Donald Sutherland, Path to War, HBO

2003 People's Choice Awards
(Awarded for work in 2002)

Film

Picture: (tie) Spider-Man and Lord of the Rings: The Fellowship of the Ring
Drama: Lord of the Rings: The Fellowship of the Ring
Comedy: My Big Fat Greek Wedding
Actor: Mel Gibson
Actress: Julia Roberts

Television

Drama: CSI: Crime Scene Investigation
Comedy: Friends

Male performer: Ray Romano, Everybody Loves Raymond
Female performer: Jennifer Aniston, Friends
New comedy: 8 Simple Rules for Dating My Teenage Daughter
New drama: CSI: Miami
Daytime drama: Days of Our Lives
Reality program: Survivor: Thailand

Music

Male performer: Eminem
Female performer: Faith Hill
Group or band: (tie) Creed and Dixie Chicks

Academy Awards (Oscars) for 1927-2002

Year	Picture	Actor	Actress	Sup. Actor[1]	Sup. Actress[1]	Director
1927-28	Wings	Emil Jannings, The Way of All Flesh	Janet Gaynor, Seventh Heaven			Frank Borzage, Seventh Heaven; Lewis Milestone, Two Arabian Knights
1928-29	Broadway Melody	Warner Baxter, In Old Arizona	Mary Pickford, Coquette			Frank Lloyd, The Divine Lady
1929-30	All Quiet on the Western Front	George Arliss, Disraeli	Norma Shearer, The Divorcee			Lewis Milestone, All Quiet on the Western Front
1930-31	Cimarron	Lionel Barrymore, Free Soul	Marie Dressler, Min and Bill			Norman Taurog, Skippy
1931-32	Grand Hotel	Fredric March, Dr. Jekyll and Mr. Hyde; Wallace Beery The Champ (tie)	Helen Hayes, The Sin of Madelon Claudet			Frank Borzage, Bad Girl
1932-33	Cavalcade	Charles Laughton, The Private Life of Henry VIII	Katharine Hepburn, Morning Glory			Frank Lloyd, Cavalcade
1934	It Happened One Night	Clark Gable, It Happened One Night	Claudette Colbert, It Happened One Night			Frank Capra, It Happened One Night
1935	Mutiny on the Bounty	Victor McLaglen, The Informer	Bette Davis, Dangerous			John Ford, The Informer

Year	Picture	Actor	Actress	Sup. Actor[1]	Sup. Actress[1]	Director
1936	The Great Ziegfeld	Paul Muni Story of Louis Pasteur	Luise Rainer The Great Ziegfeld	Walter Brennan Come and Get It	Gale Sondergaard Anthony Adverse	Frank Capra Mr. Deeds Goes to Town
1937	Life of Emile Zola	Spencer Tracy Captains Courageous	Luise Rainer The Good Earth	Joseph Schildkraut Life of Emile Zola	Alice Brady In Old Chicago	Leo McCarey The Awful Truth
1938	You Can't Take It With You	Spencer Tracy Boys Town	Bette Davis Jezebel	Walter Brennan Kentucky	Fay Bainter Jezebel	Frank Capra You Can't Take It With You
1939	Gone With the Wind	Robert Donat Goodbye Mr. Chips	Vivien Leigh Gone With the Wind	Thomas Mitchell Stage Coach	Hattie McDaniel Gone With the Wind	Victor Fleming Gone With the Wind
1940	Rebecca	James Stewart The Philadelphia Story	Ginger Rogers Kitty Foyle	Walter Brennan The Westerner	Jane Darwell The Grapes of Wrath	John Ford The Grapes of Wrath
1941	How Green Was My Valley	Gary Cooper Sergeant York	Joan Fontaine Suspicion	Donald Crisp How Green Was My Valley	Mary Astor The Great Lie	John Ford How Green Was My Valley
1942	Mrs. Miniver	James Cagney Yankee Doodle Dandy	Greer Garson Mrs. Miniver	Van Heflin Johnny Eager	Teresa Wright Mrs. Miniver	William Wyler Mrs. Miniver
1943	Casablanca	Paul Lukas Watch on the Rhine	Jennifer Jones The Song of Bernadette	Charles Coburn The More the Merrier	Katina Paxinou For Whom the Bell Tolls	Michael Curtiz Casablanca
1944	Going My Way	Bing Crosby Going My Way	Ingrid Bergman Gaslight	Barry Fitzgerald Going My Way	Ethel Barrymore None But the Lonely Heart	Leo McCarey Going My Way
1945	The Lost Weekend	Ray Milland The Lost Weekend	Joan Crawford Mildred Pierce	James Dunn A Tree Grows in Brooklyn	Anne Revere National Velvet	Billy Wilder The Lost Weekend
1946	The Best Years of Our Lives	Fredric March The Best Years of Our Lives	Olivia de Havilland To Each His Own	Harold Russell The Best Years of Our Lives	Anne Baxter The Razor's Edge	William Wyler The Best Years of Our Lives
1947	Gentleman's Agreement	Ronald Colman A Double Life	Loretta Young The Farmer's Daughter	Edmund Gwenn Miracle on 34th Street	Celeste Holm Gentleman's Agreement	Elia Kazan Gentleman's Agreement
1948	Hamlet	Laurence Olivier Hamlet	Jane Wyman Johnny Belinda	Walter Huston Treasure of Sierra Madre	Claire Trevor Key Largo	John Huston Treasure of Sierra Madre
1949	All the King's Men	Broderick Crawford All the King's Men	Olivia de Havilland The Heiress	Dean Jagger Twelve O'Clock High	Mercedes McCambridge All the King's Men	Joseph L. Mankiewicz Letter to Three Wives
1950	All About Eve	Jose Ferrer Cyrano de Bergerac	Judy Holliday Born Yesterday	George Sanders All About Eve	Josephine Hull Harvey	Joseph L. Mankiewicz All About Eve
1951	An American in Paris	Humphrey Bogart The African Queen	Vivien Leigh A Streetcar Named Desire	Karl Malden A Streetcar Named Desire	Kim Hunter A Streetcar Named Desire	George Stevens A Place in the Sun
1952	The Greatest Show on Earth	Gary Cooper High Noon	Shirley Booth Come Back Little Sheba	Anthony Quinn Viva Zapata!	Gloria Grahame The Bad and the Beautiful	John Ford The Quiet Man
1953	From Here to Eternity	William Holden Stalag 17	Audrey Hepburn Roman Holiday	Frank Sinatra From Here to Eternity	Donna Reed From Here to Eternity	Fred Zinnemann From Here to Eternity
1954	On the Waterfront	Marlon Brando On the Waterfront	Grace Kelly The Country Girl	Edmond O'Brien The Barefoot Contessa	Eva Marie Saint On the Waterfront	Elia Kazan On the Waterfront
1955	Marty	Ernest Borgnine Marty	Anna Magnani The Rose Tattoo	Jack Lemmon Mister Roberts	Jo Van Fleet East of Eden	Delbert Mann Marty
1956	Around the World in 80 Days	Yul Brynner The King and I	Ingrid Bergman Anastasia	Anthony Quinn Lust for Life	Dorothy Malone Written on the Wind	George Stevens Giant
1957	The Bridge on the River Kwai	Alec Guinness The Bridge on the River Kwai	Joanne Woodward The Three Faces of Eve	Red Buttons Sayonara	Miyoshi Umeki Sayonara	David Lean The Bridge on the River Kwai
1958	Gigi	David Niven Separate Tables	Susan Hayward I Want to Live	Burl Ives The Big Country	Wendy Hiller Separate Tables	Vincente Minnelli Gigi
1959	Ben-Hur	Charlton Heston Ben-Hur	Simone Signoret Room at the Top	Hugh Griffith Ben-Hur	Shelley Winters Diary of Anne Frank	William Wyler Ben-Hur
1960	The Apartment	Burt Lancaster Elmer Gantry	Elizabeth Taylor Butterfield 8	Peter Ustinov Spartacus	Shirley Jones Elmer Gantry	Billy Wilder The Apartment
1961	West Side Story	Maximilian Schell Judgment at Nuremberg	Sophia Loren Two Women	George Chakiris West Side Story	Rita Moreno West Side Story	Jerome Robbins, Robert Wise West Side Story
1962	Lawrence of Arabia	Gregory Peck To Kill a Mockingbird	Anne Bancroft The Miracle Worker	Ed Begley Sweet Bird of Youth	Patty Duke The Miracle Worker	David Lean Lawrence of Arabia
1963	Tom Jones	Sidney Poitier Lilies of the Field	Patricia Neal Hud	Melvyn Douglas Hud	Margaret Rutherford The V.I.P.s	Tony Richardson Tom Jones
1964	My Fair Lady	Rex Harrison My Fair Lady	Julie Andrews Mary Poppins	Peter Ustinov Topkapi	Lila Kedrova Zorba the Greek	George Cukor My Fair Lady
1965	The Sound of Music	Lee Marvin Cat Ballou	Julie Christie Darling	Martin Balsam A Thousand Clowns	Shelley Winters A Patch of Blue	Robert Wise The Sound of Music

Year	Picture	Actor	Actress	Sup. Actor[1]	Sup. Actress[1]	Director
1966	A Man for All Seasons	Paul Scofield *A Man for All Seasons*	Elizabeth Taylor *Who's Afraid of Virginia Woolf?*	Walter Matthau *The Fortune Cookie*	Sandy Dennis *Who's Afraid of Virginia Woolf?*	Fred Zinnemann *A Man for All Seasons*
1967	In the Heat of the Night	Rod Steiger *In the Heat of the Night*	Katharine Hepburn *Guess Who's Coming to Dinner*	George Kennedy *Cool Hand Luke*	Estelle Parsons *Bonnie and Clyde*	Mike Nichols *The Graduate*
1968	Oliver!	Cliff Robertson *Charly*	Katharine Hepburn *The Lion in Winter;* Barbra Streisand *Funny Girl* (tie)	Jack Albertson *The Subject Was Roses*	Ruth Gordon *Rosemary's Baby*	Sir Carol Reed *Oliver!*
1969	Midnight Cowboy	John Wayne *True Grit*	Maggie Smith *The Prime of Miss Jean Brodie*	Gig Young *They Shoot Horses, Don't They?*	Goldie Hawn *Cactus Flower*	John Schlesinger *Midnight Cowboy*
1970	Patton	George C. Scott *Patton* (refused)	Glenda Jackson *Women in Love*	John Mills *Ryan's Daughter*	Helen Hayes *Airport*	Franklin Schaffner *Patton*
1971	The French Connection	Gene Hackman *The French Connection*	Jane Fonda *Klute*	Ben Johnson *The Last Picture Show*	Cloris Leachman *The Last Picture Show*	William Friedkin *The French Connection*
1972	The Godfather	Marlon Brando *The Godfather* (refused)	Liza Minnelli *Cabaret*	Joel Grey *Cabaret*	Eileen Heckart *Butterflies Are Free*	Bob Fosse *Cabaret*
1973	The Sting	Jack Lemmon *Save the Tiger*	Glenda Jackson *A Touch of Class*	John Houseman *The Paper Chase*	Tatum O'Neal *Paper Moon*	George Roy Hill *The Sting*
1974	The Godfather Part II	Art Carney *Harry and Tonto*	Ellen Burstyn *Alice Doesn't Live Here Anymore*	Robert DeNiro *The Godfather Part II*	Ingrid Bergman *Murder on the Orient Express*	Francis Ford Coppola *The Godfather Part II*
1975	One Flew Over the Cuckoo's Nest	Jack Nicholson *One Flew Over the Cuckoo's Nest*	Louise Fletcher *One Flew Over the Cuckoo's Nest*	George Burns *The Sunshine Boys*	Lee Grant *Shampoo*	Milos Forman *One Flew Over the Cuckoo's Nest*
1976	Rocky	Peter Finch *Network*	Faye Dunaway *Network*	Jason Robards *All the President's Men*	Beatrice Straight *Network*	John G. Avildsen *Rocky*
1977	Annie Hall	Richard Dreyfuss *The Goodbye Girl*	Diane Keaton *Annie Hall*	Jason Robards *Julia*	Vanessa Redgrave *Julia*	Woody Allen *Annie Hall*
1978	The Deer Hunter	Jon Voight *Coming Home*	Jane Fonda *Coming Home*	Christopher Walken *The Deer Hunter*	Maggie Smith *California Suite*	Michael Cimino *The Deer Hunter*
1979	Kramer vs. Kramer	Dustin Hoffman *Kramer vs. Kramer*	Sally Field *Norma Rae*	Melvyn Douglas *Being There*	Meryl Streep *Kramer vs. Kramer*	Robert Benton *Kramer vs. Kramer*
1980	Ordinary People	Robert DeNiro *Raging Bull*	Sissy Spacek *Coal Miner's Daughter*	Timothy Hutton *Ordinary People*	Mary Steenburgen *Melvin & Howard*	Robert Redford *Ordinary People*
1981	Chariots of Fire	Henry Fonda *On Golden Pond*	Katharine Hepburn *On Golden Pond*	John Gielgud *Arthur*	Maureen Stapleton *Reds*	Warren Beatty *Reds*
1982	Gandhi	Ben Kingsley *Gandhi*	Meryl Streep *Sophie's Choice*	Louis Gossett Jr. *An Officer and a Gentleman*	Jessica Lange *Tootsie*	Richard Attenborough *Gandhi*
1983	Terms of Endearment	Robert Duvall *Tender Mercies*	Shirley MacLaine *Terms of Endearment*	Jack Nicholson *Terms of Endearment*	Linda Hunt *The Year of Living Dangerously*	James L. Brooks *Terms of Endearment*
1984	Amadeus	F. Murray Abraham *Amadeus*	Sally Field *Places in the Heart*	Haing S. Ngor *The Killing Fields*	Peggy Ashcroft *A Passage to India*	Milos Forman *Amadeus*
1985	Out of Africa	William Hurt *Kiss of the Spider Woman*	Geraldine Page *The Trip to Bountiful*	Don Ameche *Cocoon*	Anjelica Huston *Prizzi's Honor*	Sydney Pollack *Out of Africa*
1986	Platoon	Paul Newman *The Color of Money*	Marlee Matlin *Children of a Lesser God*	Michael Caine *Hannah and Her Sisters*	Dianne Wiest *Hannah and Her Sisters*	Oliver Stone *Platoon*
1987	The Last Emperor	Michael Douglas *Wall Street*	Cher *Moonstruck*	Sean Connery *The Untouchables*	Olympia Dukakis *Moonstruck*	Bernardo Bertolucci *The Last Emperor*
1988	Rain Man	Dustin Hoffman *Rain Man*	Jodie Foster *The Accused*	Kevin Kline *A Fish Called Wanda*	Geena Davis *The Accidental Tourist*	Barry Levinson *Rain Man*
1989	Driving Miss Daisy	Daniel Day-Lewis *My Left Foot*	Jessica Tandy *Driving Miss Daisy*	Denzel Washington *Glory*	Brenda Fricker *My Left Foot*	Oliver Stone *Born on the Fourth of July*
1990	Dances With Wolves	Jeremy Irons *Reversal of Fortune*	Kathy Bates *Misery*	Joe Pesci *Goodfellas*	Whoopi Goldberg *Ghost*	Kevin Costner *Dances With Wolves*
1991	The Silence of the Lambs	Anthony Hopkins *The Silence of the Lambs*	Jodie Foster *The Silence of the Lambs*	Jack Palance *City Slickers*	Mercedes Ruehl *The Fisher King*	Jonathan Demme *The Silence of the Lambs*
1992	Unforgiven	Al Pacino *Scent of a Woman*	Emma Thompson *Howards End*	Gene Hackman *Unforgiven*	Marisa Tomei *My Cousin Vinny*	Clint Eastwood *Unforgiven*
1993	Schindler's List	Tom Hanks *Philadelphia*	Holly Hunter *The Piano*	Tommy Lee Jones *The Fugitive*	Anna Paquin *The Piano*	Steven Spielberg *Schindler's List*
1994	Forrest Gump	Tom Hanks *Forrest Gump*	Jessica Lange *Blue Sky*	Martin Landau *Ed Wood*	Dianne Wiest *Bullets Over Broadway*	Robert Zemeckis *Forrest Gump*
1995	Braveheart	Nicolas Cage *Leaving Las Vegas*	Susan Sarandon *Dead Man Walking*	Kevin Spacey *The Usual Suspects*	Mira Sorvino *Mighty Aphrodite*	Mel Gibson *Braveheart*
1996	The English Patient	Geoffrey Rush *Shine*	Frances McDormand *Fargo*	Cuba Gooding Jr. *Jerry Maguire*	Juliette Binoche *The English Patient*	Anthony Minghella *The English Patient*

Year	Picture	Actor	Actress	Sup. Actor[1]	Sup. Actress[1]	Director
1997	*Titanic*	Jack Nicholson *As Good As It Gets*	Helen Hunt *As Good As It Gets*	Robin Williams *Good Will Hunting*	Kim Basinger *L.A. Confidential*	James Cameron *Titanic*
1998	*Shakespeare in Love*	Roberto Benigni *Life Is Beautiful*	Gwyneth Paltrow *Shakespeare in Love*	James Coburn *Affliction*	Judi Dench *Shakespeare in Love*	Steven Spielberg *Saving Private Ryan*
1999	*American Beauty*	Kevin Spacey *American Beauty*	Hilary Swank *Boys Don't Cry*	Michael Caine *The Cider House Rules*	Angelina Jolie *Girl, Interrupted*	Sam Mendes *American Beauty*
2000	*Gladiator*	Russell Crowe *Gladiator*	Julia Roberts *Erin Brockovich*	Benicio Del Toro *Traffic*	Marcia Gay Harden *Pollock*	Steven Soderbergh *Traffic*
2001	*A Beautiful Mind*	Denzel Washington *Training Day*	Halle Berry *Monster's Ball*	Jim Broadbent *Iris*	Jennifer Connelly *A Beautiful Mind*	Ron Howard *A Beautiful Mind*
2002	*Chicago*	Adrien Brody *The Pianist*	Nicole Kidman *The Hours*	Chris Cooper *Adaptation*	Catherine Zeta-Jones *Chicago*	Roman Polanski *The Pianist*

(1) These awards not given until 1936.

OTHER 2002 OSCAR WINNERS: Animated film: *Spirited Away.* Foreign film: *Nowhere in Africa,* Germany. Original screenplay: Pedro Almodóvar, *Talk to Her.* Adapted screenplay: Ronald Harwood, *The Pianist.* Cinematography: Conrad L. Hall, *Road to Perdition.* Art direction: John Myhre (art direction) and Gordon Sim (set direction), *Chicago.* Film editing: Martin Walsh, *Chicago.* Original song: "Lose Yourself," *8 Mile*—music by Eminem, Jeff Bass, and Luis Resto; lyrics by Eminem. Original score: Elliot Goldenthal, *Frida.* Costume design: Colleen Atwood, *Chicago.* Makeup: John Jackson and Beatrice De Alba, *Frida.* Sound: Michael Minkler, Dominick Tavella, and David Lee, *Chicago.* Documentary feature: Michael Moore and Michael Donovan, *Bowling for Columbine.* Documentary short subject: Bill Guttentag and Robert David Port, *Twin Towers.* Short film, live: Martin Strange-Hansen and Mie Andreasen, *This Charming Man (Der Er En Yndig Mand).* Short film, animated: Eric Armstrong, *The Chubbchubbs!* Visual effects: Jim Rygiel, Joe Letteri, Randall William Cook, and Alex Funke, *The Lord of the Rings: The Two Towers.* Sound editing: Ethan Van der Ryn and Michael Hopkins, *The Lord of the Rings: The Two Towers.* Honorary Oscar: Peter O'Toole.

Other Film Awards

Year in parentheses is year awarded.

Cannes Film Festival Awards (2003), Feature Films—Palme d'Or (Golden Palm): *Elephant,* Gus Van Sant, U.S.; Grand Prize: *Uzak (Distant),* Nuri Bilge Ceylan, Turkey; Best Actress: Marie-Josée Croze, Canada, *Les Invasions Barbares (The Barbarian Invasions);* Best Actor: (tie) Muzaffer Özdemir, Emin Toprak, Turkey, *Uzak (Distant);* Best Director: Gus Van Sant, U.S., *Elephant;* Best Screenplay: Denys Arcand, Canada, *Les Invasions Barbares (The Barbarian Invasions);* Special Jury Prize: *Panj é asr (At Five in the Afternoon),* Samira Makhmalbaf, Iran; Camera d'Or (Golden Camera, first-time director): Christoffer Boe, Denmark, *Reconstruction;* Special Mention Camera d'Or: Sedigh Barmak, Afghanistan, *Osama.* Lifetime Achievement Award: Jeanne Moreau. Short Films—Palme d'Or: *Cracker Bag,* Glendyn Ivin, Australia; Jury Prize: *L'Homme Sans Tete (The Man Without a Head),* Juan Solanas, France.

Director's Guild of America Awards (2003), Feature film: Rob Marshall, *Chicago;* documentary: Tasha Oldham, *The Smith Family.*

Sundance Film Festival Awards (2003), Grand Jury Prize: (drama) *American Splendor,* Shari Springer Berman and Robert Pulcini; (documentary) *Capturing the Friedmans,* Andrew Jarecki. Directing Award: (drama) Catherine Hardwicke, *Thirteen;*

(documentary) Jonathan Karsh, *My Flesh and Blood.* Waldo Salt Screenwriting Award: Tom McCarthy, *The Station Agent.* Freedom of Expression Award: (documentary) *What I Want My Words to Do to You,* Judith Katz, Madeleine Gavin, and Gary Sunshine. Audience Award: (drama) *The Station Agent,* Tom McCarthy; (documentary) *My Flesh and Blood,* Jonathan Karsh; (world) *Whale Rider,* Niki Caro. Cinematography Award: (drama) Derek Cianfrance, *Quattro Noza;* (documentary) Dana Kupper, Gordon Quinn and Peter Gilbert, *Stevie.* Special Jury Awards: (dramatic performance) Patricia Clarkson, for *The Station Agent, Pieces of April,* and *All The Real Girls;* Charles Busch, for *Die Mommie Die;* (dramatic emotional truth) *All the Real Girls,* David Gordon Green and *What Alice Found,* A. Dean Bell; (documentary) *The Murder of Emmett Till,* Stanley Nelson, and *A Certain Kind of Death,* Blue Hadaegh and Grover Babcock. Alfred P. Sloan Feature Film Award: *Dopamine,* Mark Decena. International Filmmakers Awards: Yesim Ustaoglu, Turkey, *Waiting for the Clouds;* Juan Pablo Rebello and Pablo Stoll, Uruguay, *Whisky;* Michael Kang, U.S., *The Motel;* Mai Tominaga, Japan, *100% Pure Wool.* Short Filmmaking: (Jury Prize) *Terminal Bar,* Stefan Nadelman.

2003 Academy of Country Music Awards

Entertainer of the Year: Toby Keith
Album of the Year: *Drive,* Alan Jackson; Keith Stegall, producer; Arista Nashville
Single of the Year: "The Good Stuff," Kenny Chesney; Buddy Cannon, Norro Wilson, Kenny Chesney, producers; BNA Records
Top Female Vocalist: Martina McBride
Top Male Vocalist: Kenny Chesney
Top Vocal Duo: Brooks & Dunn
Top Vocal Group: Rascal Flatts
Top New Female Vocalist: Kellie Coffey
Top New Male Vocalist: Joe Nichols

Top New Vocal Duo or Group: Emerson Drive
Video of the Year: "Drive (For Daddy Gene)," Alan Jackson; Robin Rucker, producer; Steve Goldmann, director
Song of the Year: "I'm Movin' On," Rascal Flatts; written by Phillip Brian White, David Vincent Williams; Murrah Music Corp. BMI/Las Wagas, Songs of Megalex, WB Music Corp. ASCAP, publisher
Vocal Event of the Year: "Mendocino County Line," Willie Nelson with Lee Ann Womack; Matthew Serletic, producer
Pioneer Award: Alabama
Humanitarian Award: Lonestar
Special Achievement Award: George Strait

2003 MTV Video Music Awards

Video of the Year: Missy Elliott, "Work It"
Best Male Video: Justin Timberlake, "Cry Me a River"
Best Female Video: Beyonce Knowles, featuring Jay-Z, "Crazy in Love"
Best Group Video: Coldplay, "The Scientist"
Best Rap Video: 50 Cent, "In Da Club"
Best Dance Video: Justin Timberlake, "Rock Your Body"
Best Pop Video: Justin Timberlake, "Cry Me a River"
Best Rock Video: Linkin Park, "Somewhere I Belong"
Best Hip Hop Video: Missy Elliott, "Work It"
Best New Artist: 50 Cent, "In Da Club"
Breakthrough Video: Coldplay, "The Scientist"
Best R&B Video: Beyonce Knowles, featuring Jay-Z, "Crazy in Love"

Best Video From a Film: Eminem, "Lose Yourself" (8 Mile)
Best MTV2 Video: A.F.I., "Girls Not Grey"
Best Direction: Jamie Thraves for "The Scientist" (Coldplay)
Best Choreography: Frank Gatson Jr. & LaVelle Smith for "Crazy in Love" (Beyonce Knowles, featuring Jay-Z)
Best Art Direction: Chris Hopewell for "There There" (Radiohead)
Best Editing: Olivier Gajan for "Seven Nation Army" (The White Stripes)
Best Cinematography: Jean-Yves Escoffier for "Hurt" (Johnny Cash)
Best Special Effects: Shynola/Clear for "Go With the Flow" (Queens of the Stone Age)
Viewers' Choice: Good Charlotte, "Lifestyles of the Rich and Famous"

> **IT'S A FACT:** Only two films, *Life Is Beautiful* in 1998 and *Z* in 1969, have been nominated in both Best Foreign Language Film and Best Picture in the same year (*Z* won the Foreign Film Oscar; *Life Is Beautiful* won neither).

Grammy Awards

Source: National Academy of Recording Arts & Sciences

Selected Grammy Awards for 2002
(awarded Feb. 23, 2003)

Record of the Year (single): "Don't Know Why," Norah Jones
Album of the Year: *Come Away With Me*, Norah Jones
Song of the Year: "Don't Know Why," Jesse Harris, songwriter (Norah Jones)
New artist: Norah Jones
Pop vocal perf., female: "Don't Know Why," Norah Jones
Pop vocal perf., male: "Your Body Is A Wonderland," John Mayer
Pop vocal perf., duo/group: "Hey Baby," No Doubt
Pop vocal album, traditional: *Playin' With My Friends: Bennett Sings The Blues*, Tony Bennett
Pop instrumental album: *Just Chillin'*, Norman Brown
Pop vocal album: *Come Away With Me*, Norah Jones
Dance recording: "Days Go By," Dirty Vegas
Rock vocal perf., female: "Steve McQueen," Sheryl Crow
Rock vocal perf., male: "The Rising," Bruce Springsteen
Rock vocal perf., duo/group: "In My Place," Coldplay
Rock instrumental perf.: "Approaching Pavonis Mons by Balloon (Utopia Planitia)," The Flaming Lips
Hard rock perf.: "All My Life," Foo Fighters
Metal perf.: "Here To Stay," Korn
Rock song: "The Rising," Bruce Springsteen, songwriter (Bruce Springsteen)
Rock album: *The Rising*, Bruce Springsteen
R&B vocal perf., female: "He Think I Don't Know," Mary J. Blige
R&B vocal perf., male: "U Don't Have To Call," Usher
R&B vocal perf., duo/group: "Love's in Need of Love Today," Stevie Wonder & Take 6
R&B song: "Love of My Life (An Ode to Hip Hop)," Erykah Badu, Madukwu Chinwah, Rashid Lonnie Lynn, Robert Ozuna, James Poyser, Raphael Saadiq, Glen Standridge, songwriters (Erykah Badu Featuring Common)
R&B album: *Voyage To India*, India.Arie
R&B album, contemporary: *Ashanti*, Ashanti
Rap solo perf., female: "Scream a.k.a. Itchin'," Missy Elliott
Rap solo perf., male: "Hot in Herre," Nelly
Rap vocal perf., duo/group: "The Whole World," OutKast Featuring Killer Mike
Rap album: *The Eminem Show*, Eminem
Country vocal perf., female: "Cry," Faith Hill
Country vocal perf., male: "Give My Love to Rose," Johnny Cash
Country perf. with vocal, duo/group: "Long Time Gone," by Dixie Chicks
Country song: "Where Were You (When The World Stopped Turning)," Alan Jackson, songwriter (Alan Jackson)
Country album: *Home*, Dixie Chicks
Bluegrass album: *Lost in The Lonesome Pines*, Jim Lauderdale, Ralph Stanley, & The Clinch Mountain Boys
Jazz album, vocal: *Live in Paris*, Diana Krall
Jazz album, instr.: *Directions in Music*, Herbie Hancock, Michael Brecker, & Roy Hargrove
Jazz album, contemporary: *Speaking of Now*, Pat Metheny Group
Blues album, contemporary: *Don't Give Up on Me*, Solomon Burke
Blues album, traditional: *A Christmas Celebration of Hope*, B.B. King
Folk album, contemporary: *This Side*, Nickel Creek
Folk album, traditional: *Legacy*, Doc Watson, David Holt
Reggae album: *Jamaican E.T.*, Lee "Scratch" Perry
Latin pop album: *Caraluna*, Bacilos
Producer, non-classical: Arif Mardin
Classical album: *Vaughan Williams: A Sea Symphony (Sym. No. 1)*; Robert Spano, conductor, Atlanta Sym. Orch; Norman Mackenzie, chorus dir.; Thomas C. Moore, producer (Christine Goerke, soprano, & Brett Polegato, baritone; Atlanta Sym. Orch. Cho.)
Classical vocal perf.: *Bel Canto*, Renée Fleming, soprano
Opera recording: *Wagner: Tannhäuser*, Daniel Barenboim, conductor; Chor der Deutschen Staatsoper Berlin, Staatskapelle Berlin

Grammy Awards for 1958-2002

Record of the Year (single)	Year	Album of the Year
Domenico Modugno, "Nel Blu Dipinto Di Blu (Volare)"	1958	Henry Mancini, *The Music From Peter Gunn*
Bobby Darin, "Mack the Knife"	1959	Frank Sinatra, *Come Dance With Me*
Percy Faith, "Theme From a Summer Place"	1960	Bob Newhart, *Button Down Mind*
Henry Mancini, "Moon River"	1961	Judy Garland, *Judy at Carnegie Hall*
Tony Bennett, "I Left My Heart in San Francisco"	1962	Vaughn Meader, *The First Family*
Henry Mancini, "The Days of Wine and Roses"	1963	Barbra Streisand, *The Barbra Streisand Album*
Stan Getz, Astrud Gilberto, "The Girl From Ipanema"	1964	Stan Getz, Astrud Gilberto, *Getz/Gilberto*
Herb Alpert, "A Taste of Honey"	1965	Frank Sinatra, *September of My Years*
Frank Sinatra, "Strangers in the Night"	1966	Frank Sinatra, *A Man and His Music*
5th Dimension, "Up, Up and Away"	1967	The Beatles, *Sgt. Pepper's Lonely Hearts Club Band*
Simon & Garfunkel, "Mrs. Robinson"	1968	Glen Campbell, *By the Time I Get to Phoenix*
5th Dimension, "Aquarius/Let the Sunshine In"	1969	Blood Sweat and Tears, *Blood, Sweat and Tears*
Simon & Garfunkel, "Bridge Over Troubled Water"	1970	Simon & Garfunkel, *Bridge Over Troubled Water*
Carole King, "It's Too Late"	1971	Carole King, *Tapestry*
Roberta Flack, "The First Time Ever I Saw Your Face"	1972	George Harrison and friends, *The Concert for Bangla Desh*
Roberta Flack, "Killing Me Softly With His Song"	1973	Stevie Wonder, *Innervisions*
Olivia Newton-John, "I Honestly Love You"	1974	Stevie Wonder, *Fulfillingness' First Finale*
Captain & Tennille, "Love Will Keep Us Together"	1975	Paul Simon, *Still Crazy After All These Years*
George Benson, "This Masquerade"	1976	Stevie Wonder, *Songs in the Key of Life*
Eagles, "Hotel California"	1977	Fleetwood Mac, *Rumours*
Billy Joel, "Just the Way You Are"	1978	Bee Gees, *Saturday Night Fever*
The Doobie Brothers, "What a Fool Believes"	1979	Billy Joel, *52nd Street*
Christopher Cross, "Sailing"	1980	Christopher Cross, *Christopher Cross*
Kim Carnes, "Bette Davis Eyes"	1981	John Lennon, Yoko Ono, *Double Fantasy*
Toto, "Rosanna"	1982	Toto, *Toto IV*
Michael Jackson, "Beat It"	1983	Michael Jackson, *Thriller*
Tina Turner, "What's Love Got to Do With It"	1984	Lionel Richie, *Can't Slow Down*
USA for Africa, "We Are the World"	1985	Phil Collins, *No Jacket Required*
Steve Winwood, "Higher Love"	1986	Paul Simon, *Graceland*
Paul Simon, "Graceland"	1987	U2, *The Joshua Tree*
Bobby McFerrin, "Don't Worry, Be Happy"	1988	George Michael, *Faith*
Bette Midler, "Wind Beneath My Wings"	1989	Bonnie Raitt, *Nick of Time*
Phil Collins, "Another Day in Paradise"	1990	Quincy Jones, *Back on the Block*
Natalie Cole, with Nat "King" Cole, "Unforgettable"	1991	Natalie Cole, with Nat "King" Cole, *Unforgettable*
Eric Clapton, "Tears in Heaven"	1992	Eric Clapton, *Unplugged*
Whitney Houston, "I Will Always Love You"	1993	Whitney Houston, *The Bodyguard*
Sheryl Crow, "All I Wanna Do"	1994	Tony Bennett, *MTV Unplugged*
Seal, "Kiss From a Rose"	1995	Alanis Morissette, *Jagged Little Pill*
Eric Clapton, "Change the World"	1996	Celine Dion, *Falling Into You*
Shawn Colvin, "Sunny Came Home"	1997	Bob Dylan, *Time Out of Mind*
Celine Dion, "My Heart Will Go On"	1998	Lauryn Hill, *The Miseducation of Lauryn Hill*
Santana featuring Rob Thomas, "Smooth"	1999	Santana, *Supernatural*
U2, "Beautiful Day"	2000	Steely Dan, *Two Against Nature*
U2, "Walk On"	2001	Various Artists, *O Brother, Where Art Thou?*
Norah Jones, "Don't Know Why"	2002	Norah Jones, *Come Away With Me*

EDUCATION

U.S. Public Schools: Students, Staff, Spending, 1899-2001

Source: National Center for Education Statistics, U.S. Dept. of Education

	1899-1900	1919-20	1939-40	1959-60	1969-70	1979-80	1989-90	1999-2000	2000-2001
Population statistics (thousands)									
Total U.S. population[1].................	75,995	104.514	131,028	177,830	201,385	224,567	246.819	272,691	281,422
Population 5-17 years of age..........	21,573	27,571	30,151	43,881	52,386	48.041	44,947	51,257	53,118
Percentage 5-17 years of age..........	28.4	26.4	23.0	24.7	26.0	21.4	18.2	18.8	18.9
Enrollment (thousands)									
Elementary and secondary[2]............	15,503	21,578	25,434	36,087	45,550	41,651	40,543	46,587	47,223
Kindergarten & grades 1-8	14,984	19,378	18,833	27,602	32,513	28,034	29,152	33,488	33,709
Grades 9-12	519	2,200	6,601	8,485	13.037	13,616	11,390	13,369	13,514
Percentage pop. 5-17 enrolled...........	71.9	78.3	84.4	82.2	87.0	86.7	90.2	91.4	88.9
Percentage in high schools	3.3	10.2	26.0	23.5	28.6	32.7	28.1	28.5	28.6
High school graduates (thousands)	62	231	1,143	1,627	2,589	2,748	2,320	2,546	2,569
School term; staff									
Average school term (in days)	144.3	161.9	175.0	178.0	178.9	178.5	*	*	*
Total instructional staff (thousands)	*	678	912	1,457	2,286	2,406	2,986	3,819	3,888
Teachers, librarians, and other non-supervisory instructional staff (thousands)	423	657	875	1,393	2,195	2,300	2,860	3,682	3,747
Revenue and expenditures (millions)									
Total revenue	$220	$970	$2,261	$14,747	$40,267	$96,881	$208,548	$372,865	$400,919
Total expenditures	215	1,036	2,344	15,613	40,683	95,962	212,770	381,829	411,518
Current expenditures[3].............	180	861	1,942	12,329[5]	34,218[5]	86,984[5]	188,229[5]	323,809[5]	348,170[5]
Capital outlay	35	154	258	2,662	4,659	6,506	17,781	43,401	47,118
Interest on school debt	*	18	131	490	1,171	1,874	3,776	9,135	10,165
Others	*	3	13	133	636	598	2,983	5,484	6,065
Salaries and pupil cost									
Avg. annual salary of instruct. staff[4]......	$325	$871	$1,441	$5,174	$9,047	$16,715	$32,638	$43,768	$46,706
Expenditure per capita total pop...........	2.83	9.91	17.89	88	202	427	862	1,400	1,462
Current expenditure per pupil ADA[6].......	16.67	53.32	88.09	375	816	2,272	4,980	7,392	7,898

NOTE: Because of rounding, details may not add to totals. * = Data not collected. Prior to 1959-60, data do not include Alaska and Hawaii. (1) Population data for 1899-1900 are based on total population from the decennial census. From 1919-20 to 1959-60, population data are total population, including armed forces overseas, as of July 1 preceding the school year. Data for later years are for resident population that excludes armed forces overseas. (2) Data for 1899-1900 are school year enrollment; data for later years are fall enrollment. (3) In 1899-1900, includes interest on school debt. (4) Includes supervisors, principals, teachers, and nonsupervisory instructional staff. (5) Because of changes in the definition of "current expenditures," data for 1959-60 and later years are not entirely comparable with prior years. (6) ADA means average daily attendance.

Programs for the Disabled, 1990-2002

Source: Office of Special Education Programs, U.S. Dept. of Education
(Number of children from 6 to 21 years old served annually in educational programs for the disabled; in thousands)

Type of Disability	1990-91	1992-93	1993-94	1994-95	1995-96	1996-97	1997-98	1998-99	1999-2000	2000-01	2001-02
Learning disabilities	2,144	2,366	2,428	2,510	2,602	2,674	2,754	2,817	2,834	2,848	2,846
Speech impairments	988	998	1,018	1,020	1,027	1,049	1,064	1,075	1,081	1,085	1,084
Mental retardation	551	532	554	571	586	594	603	611	600	599	592
Emotional disturbance ..	391	402	415	428	439	446	454	463	469	472	476
Multiple disabilities.....	98	103	110	90	95	99	107	108	111	121	127
Hearing impairments ...	59	61	65	65	68	69	70	71	71	70	70
Orthopedic impairments.	49	53	57	60	63	66	67	69	71	73	73
Other health impairments	56	66	83	107	134	161	191	221	253	290	337
Visual impairments.....	24	24	25	25	25	26	26	26	65	25	25
Autism	—	16	19	23	29	34	43	54	65	78	97
Deaf-blindness	2	1	1	1	1	1	1	2	2	1	2
Traumatic brain injury...	—	4	5	7	10	10	12	13	14	15	21
Developmental delay*....	—	—	—	—	—	—	—	—	—	—	45
ALL DISABILITIES	**4,362**	**4,626**	**4,779**	**4,908**	**5,079**	**5,231**	**4,397**	**5,541**	**5,614**	**5,705**	**5,795**

NOTE: Counts based on reports from states and District of Columbia. Details may not add to totals because of rounding and/or incomplete enumeration. — = not available or reliable data. * Applicable only to ages 3-9.

Technology in U.S. Public Schools, 2003

Source: Quality Education Data, Inc., Denver, CO
(Number and percentage of schools in each category that have the technology indicated.)

	Total		Elementary[1]		Middle/Jr. High[2]		Senior High[3]		K-12[4]		Special Ed./Adult Ed.	
TOTAL SCHOOLS........	91,408	100%	55,753	100%	14,188	100%	19,164	100%	2,441	100%	2,292	100%
Schools with computers ...	81,582	89	50,832	91	12,685	89	16,466	86	1,859	76	1,596	70
By number of computers:												
1-10	3,713	4	2,461	4	248	2	581	3	52	2	423	18
11-20	5,242	6	3,735	7	445	3	790	4	140	6	272	12
21-50	16,354	18	11,676	21	1,809	13	2,455	13	438	18	414	18
51-100	22,033	24	15,708	28	3,123	22	2,949	15	546	22	252	11
100+	34,240	37	17,252	31	7,060	50	9,691	51	683	28	235	10
Schools with LANs[5]	58,656	64	34,945	63	9,743	69	13,307	69	1,532	63	658	29
By enrollment:												
100-299	12,852	14	8,090	15	1,125	8	3,157	16	723	30	478	21
300-499	17,305	19	13,094	23	1,978	14	2,187	11	404	17	46	2
500+	28,499	31	13,761	25	6,640	47	7,963	42	405	17	134	6
Schools with WANs[6] ...	37,281	41	22,921	41	6,311	44	7,654	40	595	24	393	17
By enrollment:												
100-299	6,625	7	4,380	8	525	4	1,432	7	235	10	287	13
300-499	12,008	13	9,317	17	1,395	10	1,270	7	182	7	26	1
500+	18,648	20	9,224	17	4,391	31	4,952	26	178	7	80	3

(1) Includes preschool and schools with grade spans of Preschool-3, K-6, K-8, and K-12. (2) Includes schools with grade spans of 4-8, 7-8, and 7-9. (3) Includes vocational, technical, and alternative high schools and schools with grade spans of 7-12, 9-12, and 10-12. (4) K-12 also included under Elementary schools. (5) LAN=Local area computer network. (6) WAN=Wide area computer network.

Students Per Computer in U.S. Public Schools, 1983-2002

Source: Quality Education Data, Inc., Denver, CO

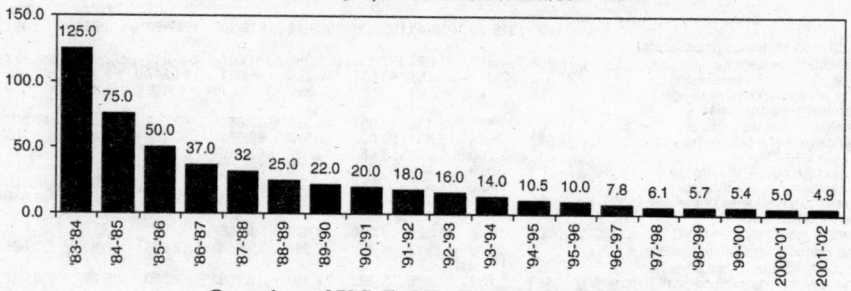

Overview of U.S. Public Schools, Fall 2001*

Source: National Center for Education Statistics, U.S. Dept. of Education; National Education Association

	Local school districts	Elementary schools[1]	Secondary schools[2]	Classroom teachers	Total enrollment	Pupils per teacher	Teacher's avg. pay[3]	Expend. per pupil[4]
Alabama	128	917	401	46,796	737,294	15.8	$39,268	$6,052
Alaska	53	193	92	8,026	134,358	16.7	49,418	9,998
Arizona	323	1,173	459	46,015	922,180	20.0	36,966	5,766
Arkansas	312	717	420	33,079	449,805	13.6	35,389	5,942
California	986	6,435	2,058	304,296	6,248,610	20.5	53,870	7,063
Colorado	178	1,188	385	44,182	742,145	16.8	40,222	7,082
Connecticut	166	877	217	41,773	570,228	13.7	54,300	10,525
Delaware	19	135	43	7,571	115,555	15.3	48,363	9,720
Dist. of Columbia	1	130	47	4,951	75,392	15.2	47,049	12,046
Florida	67	2,241	451	134,684	2,500,478	18.6	38,719	6,620
Georgia	180	1,589	339	92,732	1,470,634	15.9	44,073	7,431
Hawaii	1	204	57	11,007	184,546	16.8	41,951	7,106
Idaho	114	418	232	13,854	246,521	17.8	37,482	6,077
Illinois	893	3,197	983	129,600	2,071,391	16.0	50,000	8,672
Indiana	294	1,419	456	59,659	996,133	16.7	44,195	8,128
Iowa	371	1,045	428	34,906	485,932	13.9	38,230	7,340
Kansas	304	996	424	33,084	470,205	14.2	36,673	7,672
Kentucky	176	1,010	346	40,376	654,363	16.2	37,847	7,174
Louisiana	66	1,028	329	49,980	731,328	14.6	35,437	6,553
Maine	282	533	163	16,741	205,586	12.3	37,100	8,879
Maryland	24	1,089	256	53,774	860,640	16.0	46,200	8,829
Massachusetts	350	1,452	330	68,942	973,140	14.1	50,293	10,073
Michigan	554	2,739	851	98,849	1,730,668	17.5	52,037	9,031
Minnesota	417	1,276	753	53,081	851,384	16.0	43,330	7,960
Mississippi	152	587	319	31,214	493,507	15.8	32,800	5,535
Missouri	524	1,567	644	65,240	909,792	13.9	37,695	7,265
Montana	452	509	362	10,408	151,947	14.6	34,379	7,484
Nebraska	555	903	345	21,083	285,095	13.5	36,236	7,688
Nevada	17	386	126	19,276	356,814	18.5	41,524	6,150
New Hampshire	178	377	95	14,677	206,847	14.1	38,911	7,656
New Jersey	603	1,883	455	103,611	1,341,656	12.9	54,575	11,752
New Mexico	89	557	200	21,823	320,260	14.7	36,490	6,238
New York	703	3,119	937	209,128	2,872,132	13.7	53,081	11,887
North Carolina	121	1,749	377	85,684	1,315,363	15.4	42,959	6,824
North Dakota	222	331	204	8,035	106,047	13.2	31,709	6,467
Ohio	662	2,716	948	122,115	1,830,985	15.0	44,492	8,403
Oklahoma	543	1,223	589	41,632	622,139	14.9	35,412	6,458
Oregon	198	962	284	28,402	551,480	19.4	43,886	8,545
Pennsylvania	501	2,388	795	118,470	1,821,627	15.4	50,599	8,847
Rhode Island	36	265	64	11,104	158,046	14.2	49,758	10,116
South Carolina	89	844	281	46,617	691,078	14.8	38,943	7,210
South Dakota	176	461	276	9,370	127,542	13.6	31,295	6,581
Tennessee	138	1,223	344	58,358	925,030	15.9	38,554	6,108
Texas	1,040	5,077	1,780	282,847	4,163,447	14.7	39,293	7,039
Utah	40	510	246	22,211	484,677	21.8	37,414	5,029
Vermont	292	277	69	8,554	101,179	11.8	38,802	9,559
Virginia	137	1,482	406	89,314	1,163,091	13.0	41,262	7,664
Washington	296	1,413	617	52,534	1,009,200	19.2	43,483	7,312
West Virginia	55	597	196	20,139	282,885	14.0	36,751	8,148
Wisconsin	433	1,558	589	60,918	879,361	14.4	43,114	8,797
Wyoming	48	263	112	7,026	88,128	12.5	37,841	8,466
TOTAL U.S.	**14,559**	**65,228**	**22,180**	**2,997,748**	**47,687,871**	**15.9**	**$44,604**	**$7,898**

*Full-time elementary and secondary day schools only. (1) Includes schools below grade 9. (2) Includes schools with no grade lower than 7. (3) National Education Association estimate, Fall 2001. (4) Fall 2000.

Mathematics, Reading, and Science Achievement of U.S. Students

Source: National Assessment of Educational Progress, National Center for Education Statistics, U.S. Dept. of Education
Percent of students who scored at or above basic level in national tests.[1]

State[2]	GRADE 4 Math 1996	Math 2000	Reading 1998	Reading 2002	GRADE 8 Math 1996	Math 2000	Reading 1998	Reading 2002	Science 1996	Science 2000	State[2]	GRADE 4 Math 1996	Math 2000	Reading 1998	Reading 2002	GRADE 8 Math 1996	Math 2000	Reading 1998	Reading 2002	Science 1996	Science 2000
AL	48	57	56	52	45	52	67	64	47	51	MT	71	73	72	71	75	80	83	85	77	80
AK	65	NA	NA	NA	68	NA	NA	NA	65	NA	NE	70	67	NA	68	76	74	NA	83	71	70
AZ	57	58	51	51	57	62	72	68	55	57	NV	57	60	51	54	NA	58	70	62	NA	54
AR	54	56	54	58	52	52	68	72	55	54	NH	NA	NA	75	NA	NA	NA	NA	NA	NA	NA
CA	46	52	48	50	51	52	63	61	47	40	NJ	68	NA	NA	NA	NA	NA	NA	NA	NA	NA
CO	67	NA	69	NA	67	NA	76	NA	68	NA	NM	51	51	51	52	51	50	71	64	49	48
CT	75	77	76	74	70	72	81	76	68	65	NY	64	67	62	67	61	68	76	76	57	61
DE	54	NA	53	71	55	NA	64	81	51	NA	NC	64	76	58	67	56	70	74	76	56	56
DC	20	24	27	31	20	23	44	48	19	NA	ND	75	75	NA	71	77	77	NA	82	78	74
FL	55	NA	53	60	54	NA	67	72	51	NA	OH	NA	73	NA	68	NA	75	NA	82	NA	73
GA	53	58	54	59	51	55	68	70	49	52	OK	NA	69	66	60	NA	64	80	76	NA	62
HI	53	55	45	52	51	52	59	64	42	40	OR	65	65	58	66	67	71	78	80	68	67
ID	NA	71	NA	67	NA	71	NA	79	NA	73	PA	68	NA	NA	66	NA	NA	NA	77	NA	NA
IL	NA	66	NA	NA	NA	68	NA	NA	NA	62	RI	61	67	64	65	60	64	76	73	59	61
IN	72	78	74	68	68	76	NA	77	65	68	SC	48	60	53	58	48	55	66	68	45	50
IA	74	78	67	69	78	NA	NA	NA	71	NA	TN	58	60	57	58	53	53	71	71	53	57
KS	NA	76	70	68	NA	77	81	81	NA	NA	TX	69	77	59	62	59	68	74	73	55	53
KY	60	60	62	64	56	63	74	78	58	62	UT	69	70	62	69	70	68	77	75	70	68
LA	44	57	44	50	38	48	63	68	40	45	VT	67	73	NA	73	72	75	NA	82	70	74
ME	75	74	72	72	77	76	83	82	78	75	VA	62	73	62	71	58	67	78	80	59	63
MD	59	61	58	62	57	65	70	73	55	59	WA	67	NA	64	70	67	NA	76	78	61	NA
MA	71	79	70	80	68	76	79	81	69	74	WV	63	68	60	65	54	62	75	77	56	61
MI	68	72	62	64	67	70	NA	77	65	69	WI	74	NA	72	NA	75	NA	79	NA	73	NA
MN	76	78	69	73	75	80	81	NA	72	73	WY	64	73	64	68	68	70	76	78	71	71
MS	42	45	47	45	36	41	62	67	39	42	U.S.[2,3]	62	67	58	62	61	65	71	74	60	59
MO	66	72	61	66	64	67	75	82	64	68											

NA = Not administered. (1) Basic level denotes a partial mastery of prerequisite knowledge and skills fundamental for proficient work at each grade. (2) Excluding South Dakota, which did not participate. (3) Includes public schools only.

Revenues[1] for Public Elementary and Secondary Schools, by State, 2002-2003

Source: National Education Association; estimated; in thousands

STATE	Total	Federal Amount	Federal %	State Amount	State %	Local and intermediate Amount	Local %
Alabama	$4,646,517*	$497,526*	10.7*	$2,970,020*	63.9*	$1,178,971*	25.4*
Alaska	1,260,451	158,016	12.5	800,925	63.5	301,510	23.9
Arizona	6,816,904*	604,275*	8.9*	3,405,653*	50.0*	2,806,976*	41.2*
Arkansas	2,846,206	244,056	8.6	1,749,100	61.5	853,050	30.0
California	53,869,009	6,369,479	11.8	30,271,562	56.2	17,227,968	32.0
Colorado	6,091,236*	345,662*	5.7*	2,429,361*	39.9*	3,316,213*	54.4*
Connecticut	7,328,976*	372,625*	5.1*	3,114,094*	42.5*	3,842,257*	52.4*
Delaware	1,300,260	105,542	8.1	880,487	67.7	314,231	24.2
District of Columbia	861,294	147,800	17.2	0*	0	713,494	82.8
Florida	18,883,601	2,019,056	10.7	8,244,860	43.7	8,619,685	45.6
Georgia	14,278,081*	980,873*	6.9*	6,651,100*	46.6*	6,646,108*	46.5*
Hawaii	1,899,991	172,403	9.1	1,694,709	89.2	32,879	1.7
Idaho	1,650,000	150,000	9.1	1,000,000	60.6	500,000	30.3
Illinois	20,093,667	1,803,527	9.0	6,451,025	32.1	11,839,115	58.9
Indiana	9,675,535*	546,940*	5.7*	5,125,374*	53.0*	4,003,221*	41.4*
Iowa	4,013,494	236,285	5.9	1,992,545	49.6	1,784,664	44.5
Kansas	3,860,000	310,000	8.0	2,300,000	59.6	1,250,000	32.4
Kentucky	4,887,883	489,988	10.0	2,940,064	60.2	1,457,831	29.8
Louisiana	5,402,152	678,795	12.6	2,650,137	49.1	2,073,220	38.4
Maine	1,980,188	128,343	6.5	893,220	45.1	958,625	48.4
Maryland	8,172,931	505,869	6.2	2,943,596	36	4,723,466	57.8
Massachusetts	11,142,481*	606,434*	5.4*	5,262,423*	47.2*	5,273,623*	47.3*
Michigan	13,052,627*	606,816*	4.6*	10,677,908*	81.8*	1,767,903*	13.5*
Minnesota	8,351,734	467,213	5.6	6,210,521	74.4	1,674,000	20.0
Mississippi	3,281,844*	490,396*	14.9*	1,790,267*	54.6*	1,001,181*	30.5*
Missouri	7,805,873*	606,842*	7.8*	2,743,412*	35.1*	4,455,620*	57.1*
Montana	1,209,489	139,281	11.5	575,688	47.6	494,520	40.9
Nebraska	2,171,845	132,612	6.1	903,498	41.6	1,135,735	52.3
Nevada	2,833,823	163,992	5.8	814,600	28.7	1,855,231*	65.5
New Hampshire	1,947,079*	90,734*	4.7*	989,505*	50.8*	866,840*	44.5*
New Jersey	15,587,028*	435,765*	2.8*	5,762,962*	37.0*	9,388,301*	60.2*
New Mexico	2,556,277	354,301	13.9	1,886,790	73.8	315,186	12.3
New York	36,550,000	1,550,000	4.2	17,500,000	47.9	17,500,000	47.9
North Carolina	10,043,686*	773,708*	7.7*	7,231,497*	72.0*	2,038,480*	20.3*
North Dakota	742,204	94,301	12.7	308,361	41.5	339,542	45.7
Ohio	17,201,000*	1,043,673*	6.1*	7,423,406*	43.2*	8,733,921*	50.8*
Oklahoma	4,324,230*	482,714*	11.2*	2,493,178*	57.7*	1,348,339*	31.2*
Oregon	4,169,792	442,467	10.6	2,176,561	52.2	1,550,764	37.2
Pennsylvania	17,961,587*	902,798*	5.0*	7,175,397*	39.9*	9,883,393*	55.0*
Rhode Island	1,453,686*	56,913*	3.9*	545,275*	37.5*	851,498*	58.6*
South Carolina	6,200,155*	488,281*	7.9*	3,352,875*	54.1*	2,358,999*	38.0*

STATE	Total	Federal Amount	%	State Amount	%	Local and intermediate Amount	%
South Dakota	$949,533*	$138,566*	14.6*	$338,106*	35.6*	$472,862*	49.8*
Tennessee	5,539,106	582,949	10.5	2,651,441	47.9	2,304,716	41.6
Texas	35,310,001	3,271,069	9.3	14,412,652	40.8	17,626,280	49.9
Utah	3,007,531*	232,606*	7.7*	1,727,760*	57.4*	1,047,164*	34.8*
Vermont	1,125,183	71,432	6.3	803,077	71.4	250,674	22.3
Virginia	11,296,222*	652,813*	5.8*	5,113,635*	45.3*	5,529,774*	49.0*
Washington	8,639,088	874,499	10.1	5,402,690	62.5	2,361,899	27.3
West Virginia	2,665,587	287,172	10.8	1,591,776	59.7	786,639	29.5
Wisconsin	8,961,373	496,864	5.5	4,809,362	53.7	3,655,147	40.8
Wyoming	$970,940	$77,450	8.0	$485,990	50.1	$407,500	42.0
50 States and DC	$426,869,382	$33,481,720	7.8	$211,688,445	49.6	$181,719,217	42.6

*Indicates NEA estimate. (1) Included as revenue receipts are all appropriations from general funds of federal, state, county, and local governments; receipts from taxes levied for school purposes; income from permanent school funds and endowments; and income from leases of school lands and miscellaneous sources (interest on bank deposits, tuition, gifts, school lunch charges, etc.).

Enrollment in U.S. Public and Private Schools, 1899-2010*
Source: National Center for Education Statistics, U.S. Dept. of Education

School year[1]	Public school[2] enrollment	Private school[2] enrollment	% Private	School year[1]	Public school[2] enrollment	Private school[2] enrollment	% Private
1899-1900	15,503	1,352	8.7	1969-70.....	45,550	5,500[3]	12.1
1909-10	17,814	1,558	8.7	1979-80.....	41,651	5,000[3]	12.0
1919-20	21,578	1,699	7.9	1989-90.....	40,543	5,198	11.4
1929-30	25,678	2,651	10.3	1999-2000 ...	46,857	6,018	11.4
1939-40	25,434	2,611	10.3	2002-2003[4] ..	47,613	5,953	11.1
1949-50	25,111	3,380	13.5	2003-2004[4] ...	47,746	5,954	11.1
1959-60	35,182	5,675	16.1	2009-2010[4] ...	47,607	5,931	11.1

*Private includes all nonpublic schools, including religious schools. (1) Fall enrollment. (2) In thousands. (3) Estimated. (4) Projected.

U.S. Public High School Graduation Rates, 2000-2001
Source: National Center for Education Statistics, U.S. Dept. of Education

	Rate (%)[1]	Rank		Rate (%)[1]	Rank		Rate (%)[1]	Rank
Alabama...........	58.2	44	Louisiana.........	58.5	43	Ohio.............	70.9	26
Alaska	63.8	38	Maine..........	76.1	11	Oklahoma........	73.4	20
Arizona...........	70.5	28	Maryland........	74.4	18	Oregon..........	66.2	34
Arkansas........	73.2	21	Massachusetts......	75.3	13	Pennsylvania......	75.3	12
California........	68.7	31	Michigan........	74.7	16	Rhode Island.......	69.6	29
Colorado.........	69.3	30	Minnesota.......	82.3	5	South Carolina	48.0	51
Connecticut	72.9	23	Mississippi.......	56.9	47	South Dakota	71.9	25
Delaware	64.5	36	Missouri.........	72.5	24	Tennessee........	55.3	48
District of Columbia ..	57.2	46	Montana.........	77.3	10	Texas............	61.9	39
Florida	54.6	49	Nebraska........	80.0	6	Utah.............	83.3	3
Georgia	51.4	50	Nevada..........	68.6	32	Vermont..........	77.7	9
Hawaii...........	61.0	41	New Hampshire.....	75.3	14	Virginia	74.8	15
Idaho	78.0	8	New Jersey.......	88.3	1	Washington........	65.9	35
Illinois	70.9	27	New Mexico........	61.0	40	West Virginia	73.4	19
Indiana	67.8	33	New York	57.8	45	Wisconsin	78.2	7
Iowa	82.8	4	North Carolina	59.4	42	Wyoming	72.9	22
Kansas..........	74.5	17	North Dakota	84.0	2	TOTAL U.S.	67.3	
Kentucky.........	64.2	37						

NOTE: Data exclude ungraded pupils and have not been adjusted for interstate migration. (1) Graduates as percentage of fall 1997 9th-grade enrollment.

Teachers' Salaries in Upper Secondary Education, Selected Countries, 2001
Source: Organization for Economic Cooperation and Development

Annual statutory teachers' salaries in public institutions in upper secondary (senior high school) education, general programs, in equivalent U.S. dollars converted using PPPs[1]; ranked by starting salaries.

	Starting salary	Salary with 15 years' experience	Salary at top of scale		Starting salary	Salary with 15 years' experience	Salary at top of scale
Switzerland.....	$49,484	$63,893	$74,949	Tunisia[3]	$20,782	$20,977	$23,482
Germany	43,100	52,839	55,210	Greece..........	20,422	24,716	29,798
Spain	31,345	36,500	45,345	Portugal.........	19,585	28,974	52,199
Belgium (Fl.)....	30,544	44,085	52,990	New Zealand.....	17,544	33,941	33,941
Denmark........	30,103	40,019	42,734	Brazil	16,701	17,777	20,328
Belgium (Fr.).....	29,741	43,328	52,283	Paraguay	14,266	14,266	14,266
Norway	28,942	32,621	35,502	Malaysia[2]........	13,647	21,936	29,513
United States ...	28,806	41,708	49,862	Czech Republic ...	11,529	15,520	21,045
Netherlands	28,773	48,889	57,808	Chile	11,631	13,487	18,107
Australia	28,024	39,668	39,668	Philippines	10,777	11,896	12,811
Italy...........	25,400	31,959	39,561	Argentina	10,617	15,249	18,454
Korea (South)....	25,045	42,713	56,580	Turkey	9,162	11,180	16,473
Austria	24,742	34,516	52,692	Hungary........	7,704	11,260	14,809
France	24,016	31,507	45,501	Uruguay[4]	6,240	7,378	8,801
Ireland	23,861	37,234	41,977	Thailand........	6,057	14,886	28,390
England	23,297	36,864	36,864	Peru[2]	5,536	5,536	5,536
Iceland	23,282	29,546	32,306	Slovakia.........	5,319	6,604	9,267
Finland	23,104	32,429	34,314	Egypt...........	2,222	4,961	NA
Sweden	23,070	27,535	29,653	Indonesia........	1,219	2,234	3,535
Scotland	22,388	35,872	35,872				

NA = Not available. (1) Purchasing power parities (PPPs) are the rates of currency conversion that equalize the purchasing power of different currencies by eliminating the differences in price levels between countries. (2) Year of reference 2000. (3) Including additional bonuses. (4) Salaries for a position of 20 hours per week. Most teachers hold two positions.

Percent of Population with Upper Secondary Education, Selected Countries, 2001

Source: Organization for Economic Cooperation and Development

Percentage of the population ages 25-64 that received at least some upper secondary (senior high school) education

United States ... 88	Denmark...... 80	Australia 59	Peru[1] 44	Brazil[1]......... 26
Switzerland ... 87	Austria....... 77	Belgium 59	Italy 43	Turkey 24
Czech Republic . 86	New Zealand ... 76	Ireland........ 58	Argentina[1] 42	Mexico 22
Norway........ 86	Finland 74	Iceland........ 57	Spain 40	Paraguay[1]..... 22
Slovakia....... 85	Hungary 70	Luxembourg 53	Malaysia[1]....... 38	Indonesia 21
Germany 83	Korea 68	Greece 51	Jamaica........ 37	Portugal 20
Japan 83	Netherlands 65	Chile[1] 46	Philippines...... 36	Thailand[1] 18
Canada........ 82	France......... 64	Poland......... 46	Uruguay[1] 31	China 15
Sweden 81	United Kingdom . 63			

(1) Year of reference 2000.

Government Expenditure Per Student, Selected Countries, 2000

Source: Organization for Economic Cooperation and Development

Expenditure per student in U.S. dollars, converted using PPPs[1], on public and private institutions, by level of education, based on full-time equivalents

	Primary[2]	Secondary[3]		Primary[2]	Secondary[3]		Primary[2]	Secondary[3]
Argentina	1,598	2,382	Iceland.........	5,854	6,518	Philippines.......	573	587
Australia	4,967	6,894	India[4].........	268	540	Poland	2,105	NA
Austria	6,560	8,578	Indonesia......	137	416	Portugal	3,672	5,349
Belgium	4,310	6,889	Ireland.........	3,385	4,638	Russian Federation.	(5)	954
Brazil[4]........	928	890	Israel	4,351	5,518	Slovakia.........	1,308	1,927
Canada........	(5)	5,947	Italy	5,973	7,218	Spain	3,941	5,185
Chile	1,940	2,016	Jamaica........	NA	1,327	Sweden	6,336	6,339
Czech Republic ..	1,827	3,239	Japan	5,507	6,266	Switzerland	6,631	9,780
Denmark	7,074	7,726	Korea (South) ..	3,155	4,069	Thailand	1,111	935
Finland	4,317	6,094	Malaysia	1,235	2,238	Tunisia..........	(5)	2,280
France	4,486	7,636	Mexico	1,291	1,615	United Kingdom..	3,877	5,991
Germany	4,198	6,826	Netherlands	4,325	5,912	**United States**....	**6,995**	**8,855**
Greece.........	3,318	3,859	Norway	6,550	8,476	Uruguay.........	1,011	1,219
Hungary	2,245	2,446	Paraguay......	722	1,256	Zimbabwe	780	1,904

NA = Not available. (1) Purchasing power parities (PPPs) are the rates of currency conversion that equalize the purchasing power of different currencies by eliminating the differences in price levels between countries. (2) Elementary school age. (3) Junior high and upper secondary (senior high school) combined. (4) For 1999. (5) Data for primary and secondary combined.

Charges at U.S. Institutions of Higher Education, 1969-70 to 2001-2002

Source: National Center for Education Statistics, U.S. Dept. of Education

Figures for 1969-70 are average charges for full-time resident degree-credit students; figures for later years are average charges per full-time equivalent student. Room and board are based on full-time students. These figures are enrollment-weighted, according to the number of full-time-equivalent undergraduates, and thus vary from averages given elsewhere.

	TUITION AND FEES			BOARD RATES			DORMITORY CHARGES		
	All institutions	2-yr	4-yr	All institutions	2-yr	4-yr	All institutions	2-yr	4-yr
PUBLIC (in-state)									
1969-70	$323	$178	$427	$511	$465	$540	$369	$308	$395
1979-80	583	355	840	867	894	898	715	572	749
1989-90	1,356	756	2,035	1,635	1,581	1,728	1,513	962	1,561
1990-91	1,454	824	2,159	1,691	1,594	1,767	1,612	1,050	1,658
1991-92	1,624	937	2,410	1,780	1,612	1,852	1,731	1,074	1,789
1992-93	1,782	1,025	2,349	1,841	1,668	1,854	1,756	1,106	1,816
1993-94	1,942	1,125	2,537	1,880	1,681	1,895	1,873	1,190	1,934
1994-95	2,057	1,192	2,681	1,949	1,712	1,967	1,959	1,232	2,023
1995-96	2,179	1,239	2,848	2,020	1,681	2,045	2,057	1,297	2,121
1996-97	2,271	1,276	2,987	2,111	1,789	2,133	2,148	1,339	2,214
1997-98	2,360	1,314	3,110	2,228	1,795	2,263	2,225	1,401	2,301
1998-99	2,430	1,327	3,229	2,347	1,828	2,389	2,330	1,450	2,409
1999-2000	2,506	1,338	3,349	2,364	1,834	2,406	2,440	1,549	2,519
2000-2001	2,562	1,333	3,501	2,455	1,906	2,499	2,569	1,600	2,654
2001-2002[1]	2,727	1,379	3,746	2,597	2,036	2,642	2,721	1,722	2,811
PRIVATE									
1969-70	1,533	1,034	1,809	561	546	608	436	413	503
1979-80	3,130	2,062	3,811	955	924	1,078	827	769	999
1989-90	8,147	5,196	10,348	1,948	1,811	2,339	1,923	1,663	2,411
1990-91	8,772	5,570	11,379	2,074	1,989	2,470	2,063	1,744	2,654
1991-92	9,434	5,752	12,192	2,252	2,090	2,727	2,221	1,789	2,860
1992-93	9,942	6,059	10,294	2,344	1,875	2,354	2,348	1,970	2,362
1993-94	10,572	6,370	10,952	2,434	1,970	2,445	2,490	2,067	2,506
1994-95	11,111	6,914	11,481	2,509	2,023	2,520	2,587	2,233	2,601
1995-96	11,864	7,094	12,243	2,606	2,098	2,617	2,738	2,371	2,751
1996-97	12,498	7,236	12,881	2,663	2,181	2,672	2,878	2,537	2,889
1997-98	12,801	7,464	13,344	2,762	2,785	2,761	2,954	2,672	2,964
1998-99	13,428	7,854	13,973	2,865	2,884	2,865	3,075	2,581	3,091
1999-2000	14,081	8,235	14,588	2,882	2,922	2,881	3,224	2,808	3,237
2000-2001	15,000	9,067	15,470	2,993	3,000	2,993	3,374	2,722	3,392
2001-2002[1]	15,851	10,010	16,287	3,106	2,664	3,111	3,564	3,204	3,571

(1) Preliminary.

Top 20 Colleges and Universities in Endowment Assets, 2002[1]

Source: National Association of College and University Business Officers (NACUBO)

College/University	Endowment assets[2]	College/University	Endowment assets[2]
1. Harvard University	$17,169,757	11. Washington University	$3,517,104
2. Yale University	10,523,600	12. University of Pennsylvania	3,393,297
3. University of Texas System	8,630,679	13. University of Michigan	3,375,689
4. Princeton University	8,319,600	14. University of Chicago	3,255,368
5. Stanford University	7,613,000	15. Northwestern University	3,022,733
6. Massachusetts Institute of Technology	5,359,423	16. Rice University	2,939,804
7. Emory University	4,551,873	17. Duke University	2,927,478
8. Columbia University	4,208,373	18. Cornell University	2,853,742
9. University of California	4,199,067	19. University of Notre Dame	2,554,004
10. The Texas A&M University System and Foundations	3,743,442	20. Dartmouth College	2,186,610

NOTE: Market value of endowment assets, excluding pledges and working capital. (1) As of June 30, 2002. (2) In thousands.

U.S. Higher Education Trends: Bachelor's Degrees Conferred

Source: National Center for Education Statistics, U.S. Dept. of Education
Figures for 2003-2004 and 2009-2010 are projected.

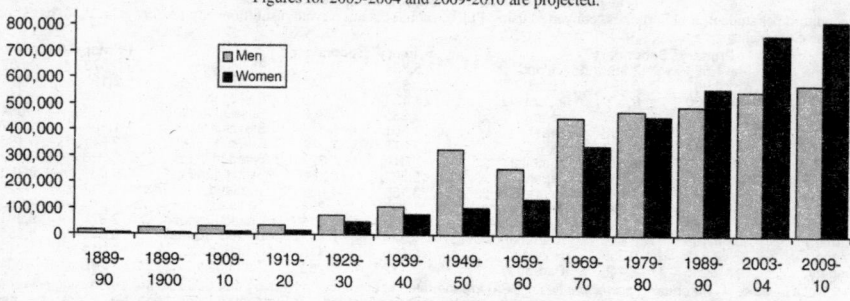

Financial Aid for College and Other Postsecondary Education

Reviewed by National Assoc. of Student Financial Aid Administrators

The cost of postsecondary education in the U.S. has increased in recent years, but financial aid, which may be in the form of grants (no repayment needed), loans, and/or work-study programs, is widely available to help families meet these expenses. Most aid is limited to family financial need as determined by standard formulas. Students interested in receiving aid are advised to apply, without making prior assumptions. Financial aid personnel at each school can provide information about programs available to students, steps to apply for them, and deadlines, all of which may vary.

First-time applicants for federal aid must file a Free Application for Federal Student Aid (FAFSA), generally as soon as possible after Jan. 1 for the academic year starting the following September. Figures provided must agree with federal income tax forms filed for the previous year. Other possible sources of aid include state governments, employers and unions, civic organizations, and the institutions themselves. There are also special federal programs that pay for postsecondary education in return for service: AmeriCorps (phone: 1-800-942-2677) and ROTC (phone: 1-800-USA-ROTC). Additional forms and certain fees may be required if a student is to be considered for institutional aid. Aid must be reapplied for annually.

A federal formula, based on information provided on the FAFSA, takes into account such factors as family after-tax income in the preceding calendar year, parental assets (excluding the parents' home) and length of time to retirement, and unusual expenses (such as very high medical expenses).

The resulting Expected Family Contribution, or EFC (which is divided among the family members—excluding parents—in college), is subtracted from the total cost of attendance for each person (including room and board or allowance for living costs) to determine financial need, and thus the maximum federal aid for which the family may be eligible. (Some institutions use a separate formula for need-based institutional aid.) Some schools guarantee to meet the full financial need of each admitted student; others try to do so but may fall short, depending on the availability of funds. Outside scholarships (even if non-need-based) are taken into account in determining need.

The aid package offered by each school may include one or more of the following resources: Federal Pell Grants, for those with greatest financial need; Federal Supplemental Educational Opportunity Grants, for those with relatively great financial need; grants from the school; Federal Work-Study or other work programs; low-interest Perkins loans; and subsidized and unsubsidized Stafford loans. For unsubsidized Stafford loans and all PLUS loans to parents, financial need is not a requirement. Loans have varying interest rates and other requirements. Repayment of Perkins and Stafford loans does not begin until after graduation; deferments are available under certain circumstances. For PLUS loans, parents must pass a credit check and begin repayment of both principal and interest while the student is still in school.

Certain federal income tax credits—dollar for dollar reductions of the amount of tax due—are available to families who meet income and other requirements; see the chapter on Taxes.

Rules for financial aid are complex and changeable. *The Student Guide*, a comprehensive resource on financial aid from the U.S. Dept. of Education, can be found at the website www.studentaid.ed.gov/students/publications/student_guide/index.html

Further information and FAFSA forms are available from the school or from the Federal Student Aid Information Center, PO Box 84, Washington, DC 20044; phone: 1-800-4-FED-AID, Mon.-Fri., 8 AM - 12 midnight Eastern Time. The Information Center also has a free booklet called *The EFC Formula Book.* FAFSA forms can be obtained online at www.fafsa.ed.gov

Average Salaries of U.S. College Professors, 2002-2003

Source: American Association of University Professors

TEACHING LEVEL		MEN Type of institution			WOMEN Type of institution		
		Public	Private/ Independent	Church-related	Public	Private/ Independent	Church-related
Doctoral level	Professor........	$93,880	$120,164	$102,104	$85,372	$109,326	$92,793
	Associate	66,433	78,823	71,306	62,077	73,788	66,367
	Assistant	57,062	69,980	60,350	52,238	61,875	55,351
Master's level	Professor........	75,181	80,881	76,293	72,706	77,290	69,614
	Associate	60,172	62,686	59,293	57,566	59,059	55,827
	Assistant	49,993	51,011	48,718	48,071	49,013	45,783
General 4-year	Professor	67,714	81,328	61,947	65,128	76,462	58,120
	Associate	55,518	58,290	50,518	53,395	56,169	48,631
	Assistant	46,375	48,015	42,428	44,711	46,797	41,682
2-year	Professor	67,300	54,892	NA	63,596	51,785	NA
	Associate	52,612	45,493	NA	50,771	42,148	NA
	Assistant	46,549	35,166	NA	44,814	36,624	NA

NA = Not available.

ACT (formerly American College Testing) Mean Scores and Characteristics of College-Bound Students, 1990-2003

Source: ACT, Inc.

(for school year ending in year shown)

SCORES[1]	Unit[1]	1990	1991	1992	1993	1994	1995	1996	1997	1998	1999	2000	2001	2002	2003
Composite Scores .	Points	20.6	20.6	20.6	20.7	20.8	20.8	20.9	21.0	21.0	21.0	21.0	21.0	20.8	20.8
Male..............	Points	21.0	20.9	20.9	21.0	20.9	21.0	21.0	21.1	21.2	21.1	21.2	21.1	20.9	21.0
Female	Points	20.3	20.4	20.5	20.5	20.7	20.7	20.8	20.8	20.9	20.9	20.9	20.9	20.7	20.8
English Score	Points	20.5	20.3	20.2	20.3	20.3	20.2	20.3	20.3	20.4	20.5	20.5	20.5	20.2	20.3
Male..............	Points	20.1	19.8	19.8	19.8	19.8	19.8	19.8	19.9	19.9	20.0	20.0	20.0	19.7	19.8
Female	Points	20.9	20.7	20.6	20.6	20.7	20.6	20.7	20.7	20.8	20.9	20.9	20.8	20.6	20.7
Math Score	Points	19.9	20.0	20.0	20.1	20.2	20.2	20.2	20.6	20.8	20.7	20.7	20.7	20.6	20.6
Male..............	Points	20.7	20.6	20.7	20.8	20.8	20.9	20.9	21.3	21.5	21.4	21.4	21.4	21.2	21.2
Female	Points	19.3	19.4	19.5	19.6	19.6	19.7	19.7	20.1	20.2	20.2	20.2	20.2	20.1	20.1
PARTICIPANTS															
Total Number	(1000s)	817	796	832	875	892	945	925	959	995	1,019	1,065	1,070	1,116	1,175
Male.............	Percent	46	45	45	45	45	44	44	44	43	43	43	43	44	44
White...........	Percent	79	79	79	79	79	80	79	74	76	72	72	71	69	68
Black...........	Percent	9	9	9	9	9	9	9	10	11	11	10	11	11	11
Composite Scores															
27 or above	Percent	12	11	12	12	13	13	13	14	14	14	14	14	13	14
18 or below	Percent	35	35	35	35	34	34	34	33	33	33	32	33	35	35

Note: Beginning with the Oct. 1989 test (1990 scores), an entirely new ACT Assessment was introduced. It is not possible to directly compare these data with data from earlier years. (1) Minimum point score, 1; maximum score, 36. Test scores and characteristics of college-bound students are based on the performance of all ACT-tested students who graduated in the spring of a given school year and took the ACT Assessment during junior or senior year of high school.

ACT Average Composite Scores by State, 2002-2003

Source: ACT, Inc.

STATE	Avg. Comp. Score	% Grads Taking ACT[1]	STATE	Avg. Comp. Score	% Grads Taking ACT[1]	STATE	Avg. Comp. Score	% Grads Taking ACT[1]	STATE	Avg. Comp. Score	% Grads Taking ACT[1]
Alabama......	20.1	73	Illinois........	20.2	100	Nebraska.....	21.7	73	Rhode Island..	21.7	6
Alaska	21.1	32	Indiana......	21.6	21	Nevada	21.3	34	South		
Arizona......	21.4	27	Iowa........	22.0	66	New			Carolina....	19.2	34
Arkansas	20.3	73	Kansas......	21.5	76	Hampshire..	22.2	8	South Dakota .	21.4	70
California ...	21.5	15	Kentucky	20.2	73	New Jersey...	21.2	6	Tennessee ...	20.4	74
Colorado.....	20.1	100	Louisiana	19.6	80	New Mexico ...	19.9	62	Texas	20.1	33
Connecticut .	22.1	7	Maine........	22.5	7	New York.....	22.3	15	Utah	21.3	67
Delaware	20.8	5	Maryland	20.7	12	North			Vermont	22.5	11
District of			Masschusetts.	22.3	10	Carolina.....	19.9	15	Virginia......	20.6	12
Columbia ..	17.5	30	Michigan	21.3	69	North Dakota .	21.3	80	Washington...	22.5	16
Florida	20.5	41	Minnesota	22.0	67	Ohio.........	21.4	64	West Virginia..	20.3	63
Georgia	19.8	22	Mississippi....	18.7	88	Oklahoma	20.5	69	Wisconsin ...	22.2	69
Hawaii	21.8	16	Missouri.....	21.4	69	Oregon	22.6	12	Wyoming.....	21.4	62
Idaho	21.2	60	Montana.....	21.7	52	Pennsylvania .	21.5	8	**U.S. AVG.....**	**20.8**	**40**

(1) Based on number of high school graduates in 2003, as projected by the Western Interstate Commission for Higher Education, and number of students in the class of 2003 who took the ACT.

SAT Mean Verbal and Math Scores of College-Bound Seniors, 1975-2003

Source: The College Board

(recentered scale; for school year ending in year shown)

	1975	1980	1985	1990	1995	1996	1997	1998	1999	2000	2001	2002	2003
Verbal Scores ...	512	502	509	500	504	505	505	505	505	505	506	504	507
Male...........	515	506	514	505	505	507	507	509	509	507	509	507	512
Female	509	498	503	496	502	503	503	502	502	504	502	502	503
Math Scores	498	492	500	501	506	508	511	512	511	514	514	516	519
Male...........	518	515	522	521	525	527	530	531	531	533	533	534	537
Female	479	473	480	483	490	492	494	496	495	498	498	500	503

NOTE: In 1995, the College Board recentered the scoring scale for the SAT by reestablishing the original mean score of 500 on the 200-800 scale. Earlier scores have been adjusted to account for this recentering.

SAT Mean Scores by State, 1990 and 1998-2003
Source: The College Board
(recentered scale; for school year ending in year shown)

STATE	1990 V	1990 M	1998 V	1998 M	1999 V	1999 M	2000 V	2000 M	2001 V	2001 M	2002 V	2002 M	2003 V	2003 M	% Grads Taking SAT[1]
Alabama	545	534	562	558	561	555	559	555	559	554	560	559	559	552	10
Alaska	514	501	521	520	516	514	519	515	514	510	516	519	518	518	55
Arizona	521	520	525	528	524	525	521	523	523	525	520	523	524	525	38
Arkansas	545	532	568	555	563	556	563	554	562	550	560	556	564	554	6
California	494	508	497	516	497	514	497	518	498	517	496	517	499	519	54
Colorado	533	534	537	542	536	540	534	537	539	542	543	548	551	553	27
Connecticut	506	496	510	509	510	509	508	509	509	510	509	509	512	514	84
Delaware	510	496	501	493	503	497	502	496	501	499	502	500	501	501	73
District of Columbia	483	467	488	476	494	478	494	486	482	474	480	473	484	474	77
Florida	495	493	500	501	499	498	498	500	498	499	496	499	498	498	61
Georgia	478	473	486	482	487	482	488	486	491	489	489	491	493	491	66
Hawaii	480	505	483	513	482	513	488	519	486	515	488	520	486	516	54
Idaho	542	524	545	544	542	540	540	541	543	542	539	541	540	540	18
Illinois	542	547	564	581	569	585	568	586	576	589	578	596	583	596	11
Indiana	486	486	497	500	496	498	498	501	499	501	498	503	500	504	63
Iowa	584	588	593	601	594	598	589	600	593	603	591	602	586	597	5
Kansas	566	563	582	585	578	576	574	580	577	580	578	580	578	582	9
Kentucky	548	541	547	550	547	547	548	550	550	550	550	552	554	552	13
Louisiana	551	537	562	558	561	558	562	558	564	562	561	559	563	559	8
Maine	501	490	504	501	507	503	504	500	506	500	503	502	503	501	70
Maryland	506	502	506	508	507	507	507	509	508	510	507	513	509	515	68
Massachusetts	503	498	508	508	511	511	511	513	511	515	512	516	516	522	82
Michigan	529	534	558	569	557	565	557	569	561	572	558	572	564	576	11
Minnesota	552	558	585	598	586	598	581	594	580	589	581	591	582	591	10
Mississippi	552	538	562	549	563	548	562	549	566	551	559	547	565	551	4
Missouri	548	541	570	573	572	572	572	577	577	577	574	580	582	583	8
Montana	540	542	543	546	545	546	543	546	539	539	541	547	538	543	26
Nebraska	559	562	565	571	568	571	560	571	562	568	561	570	573	578	8
Nevada	511	511	510	513	512	517	510	517	509	515	509	518	510	517	36
New Hampshire	518	510	523	520	520	518	520	519	520	516	519	519	522	521	75
New Jersey	495	498	497	508	498	510	498	513	499	513	498	513	501	515	85
New Mexico	554	546	554	551	549	542	549	543	551	542	551	543	548	540	14
New York	489	496	495	503	495	502	494	506	495	505	494	506	496	510	82
North Carolina	478	470	490	492	493	493	492	496	493	499	493	505	495	506	68
North Dakota	579	578	590	599	594	605	588	609	592	599	597	610	602	613	4
Ohio	526	522	536	540	534	568	533	539	534	539	533	540	536	541	28
Oklahoma	553	542	568	564	567	560	563	560	567	561	565	562	569	562	8
Oregon	515	509	528	528	525	525	527	527	526	526	524	528	526	527	57
Pennsylvania	497	490	497	495	498	495	498	497	500	499	498	500	500	502	73
Rhode Island	498	488	501	495	504	499	505	500	501	499	504	503	502	504	74
South Carolina	475	467	478	473	479	475	484	482	486	488	488	493	493	496	59
South Dakota	580	570	584	581	585	588	587	588	577	582	576	586	588	588	4
Tennessee	558	544	564	557	559	553	563	553	562	553	562	555	568	560	14
Texas	490	489	494	501	494	499	493	500	493	499	491	500	500	491	57
Utah	566	555	572	570	570	568	570	569	575	570	563	559	566	559	7
Vermont	507	493	508	504	514	506	513	508	511	506	512	510	515	512	70
Virginia	501	496	507	499	508	499	509	500	510	501	510	506	514	510	71
Washington	513	511	524	526	525	526	526	528	527	527	525	529	530	532	56
West Virginia	520	514	525	513	527	512	526	511	527	512	525	515	522	510	20
Wisconsin	552	559	581	594	584	595	584	597	584	596	583	599	585	594	7
Wyoming	534	538	548	546	546	551	545	545	547	545	531	537	548	549	11
NATIONAL AVG.	**500**	**501**	**505**	**512**	**505**	**511**	**505**	**514**	**506**	**514**	**504**	**516**	**507**	**519**	**48**

NOTE: In 1995, the College Board recentered the scoring scale for the SAT by reestablishing the original mean score of 500 on the 200-800 scale. The College Board states that comparing states or ranking them on the basis of SAT scores alone is invalid, and the College Board discourages doing so. (1) Based on number of high school graduates in 2003, as projected by the Western Interstate Commission for Higher Education, and number of students in the class of 2003 who took the SAT.

Average SAT Scores by Parental Education, 2003
Source: The College Board

(Deviation in points from mean score shown by highest level of educational attainment of test taker's parent. Mean 2003 verbal score was 507. Mean 2003 math score was 519.)

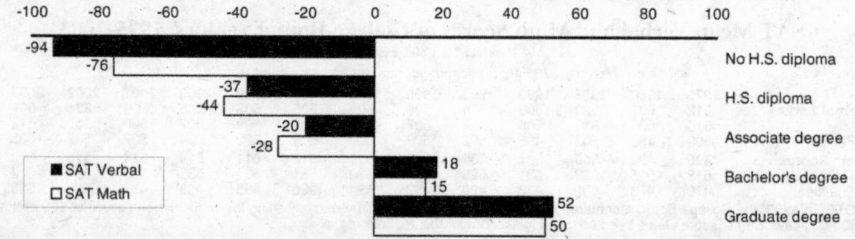

Top 50 Public Libraries in the U.S. and Canada, 2003

Source: Public Library Data Service, Statistical Report 2003, Public Library Association
Ranked at end of the 2002 fiscal year by population served.

Population served	Library name and location	No. of branches[1]	No. of holdings	Circulation	Annual acquisition expenditures
3,694,820	Los Angeles Public Library (CA)	67	5,765,741	13,090,726	$16,002,561
3,491,500	Los Angeles Public Library, County of (CA)	84	8,796,269	15,800,870	7,020,228
3,313,573	New York Public Library (NY)	80	6,647,603	15,097,886	11,850,608
2,896,016	Chicago Public Library (IL)	77	10,943,765	7,296,588	11,452,000
2,481,494	Toronto Public Library (ON)	97	7,573,955	29,224,857	8,601,569
2,465,326	Brooklyn Public Library (NY)	59	6,049,372	11,451,756	8,050,520
2,229,379	Queens Borough Public Library (NY)	62	9,151,020	16,803,725	8,811,802
1,953,631	Houston Public Library (TX)	37	4,713,879	6,085,583	6,331,109
1,916,466	Miami-Dade Public Library System (FL)	33	3,811,881	5,005,058	5,716,380
1,737,034	King County Library System (WA)	42	4,197,403	14,910,534	8,649,921
1,700,000	Broward County Libraries Division (FL)	36	2,482,553	8,394,685	6,041,252
1,517,550	Philadelphia, The Free Library of (PA)	54	6,219,231	7,024,391	8,002,171
1,488,600	San Antonio Public Library (TX)	18	1,935,036	4,863,676	2,817,722
1,373,947	Phoenix Public Library (AZ)	12	1,973,515	10,802,370	4,491,462
1,336,449	Carnegie Library of Pittsburgh (PA)	19	2,135,030	3,256,853	3,089,933
1,255,700	San Diego Public Library (CA)	33	3,199,014	6,995,244	3,926,917
1,227,024	Hawaii State Public Library System (HI)	49	3,356,529	7,155,643	3,174,613
1,219,147	Sacramento Public Library (CA)	24	2,053,904	4,809,397	3,757,200
1,200,817	Harris County Public Library (TX)	25	2,099,387	5,329,528	2,928,278
1,188,580	Dallas Public Library (TX)	22	5,844,333	4,915,119	3,553,207
1,166,096	Las Vegas-Clark County Library District (NV)	24	2,379,506	7,498,092	7,672,391
1,110,000	San Bernardino County Library (CA)	29	1,063,027	2,931,733	1,615,943
1,048,319	Providence Public Library (RI)	9	1,232,771	883,979	1,130,371
1,026,906	Tampa-Hillsborough County Public Library (FL)	21	2,026,358	5,013,714	4,105,384
1,020,003	Fairfax County Public Library (VA)	21	2,639,432	12,114,743	5,616,968
951,270	Detroit Public Library (MI)	24	7,314,712	1,151,952	2,275,666
950,265	Buffalo & Erie County Public Library (NY)	51	3,492,039	8,155,364	5,002,074
917,971	San Jose Public Library (CA)	17	2,108,284	11,635,850	4,517,000
904,987	Calgary Public Library (AB)	15	1,975,782	12,387,225	3,310,030
897,472	Memphis/Shelby County Public Library & Info. Ctr. (TN)	21	2,033,008	3,347,774	1,697,070
895,000	Orange County Library System (FL)	13	2,347,886	5,290,875	3,806,289
890,356	Tucson-Pima Public Library (AZ)	19	1,300,000	5,761,423	3,214,800
873,490	St. Louis County Library District (MO)	19	2,512,804	8,743,064	4,875,946
873,341	Montgomery County Dept. of Public Libraries (MD)	22	2,826,392	11,263,334	5,112,510
870,400	Contra Costa County Library (CA)	22	1,089,685	4,036,417	2,735,245
845,000	Atlanta-Fulton Public Library (GA)	30	2,479,718	3,054,633	3,376,652
835,362	Cincinnati & Hamilton County, The Public Lib. of (OH)	41	9,829,015	14,403,659	8,629,119
832,693	Indianapolis-Marion County Public Library (IN)	22	2,380,284	12,644,394	4,473,680
816,791	Prince George's County Memorial Library System (MD)	18	2,109,553	4,071,489	4,484,823
797,176	Columbus Metropolitan Library (OH)	20	2,928,785	15,323,568	7,105,981
793,600	San Francisco Public Library (CA)	26	2,236,464	6,328,889	5,461,096
790,000	Ottawa Public Library (ON)	33	2,339,950	7,601,022	2,688,140
778,879	Jacksonville Public Library (FL)	14	2,322,306	4,773,855	3,423,900
766,221	Palm Beach County Library System (FL)	14	1,197,332	5,714,696	4,149,040
754,292	Baltimore County Public Library (MD)	16	1,827,338	9,535,461	5,547,986
753,000	Charlotte & Mecklenburg County, Pub. Lib. of (NC)	22	1,761,548	6,404,831	2,839,576
740,974	Hennepin County Library (MN)	26	1,900,000	11,489,538	5,200,000
735,343	Rochester Public Library (NY)	10	1,201,262	1,838,233	1,253,620
693,604	Louisville Free Public Library (KY)	16	1,291,613	3,593,721	3,201,339
687,050	Kern County Library (CA)	24	1,039,831	1,839,343	1,308,018

(1) Main branch not included.

Number of Public Libraries and Operating Income, by State, 2001

Source: Public Libraries Survey, National Center for Education Statistics, U.S. Dept. of Education
(data for fiscal year 2001; operating income in thousands)

STATE	No. of libraries[1]	Operating income[2]	STATE	No. of libraries[1]	Operating income[2]	STATE	No. of libraries[1]	Operating income[2]
Alabama	283	$68,132	Kentucky	189	$79,874	Ohio	716	$682,412
Alaska	103	23,681	Louisiana	329	112,068	Oklahoma	210	63,440
Arizona	176	118,286	Maine	280	27,985	Oregon	210	112,473
Arkansas	209	38,704	Maryland	175	182,940	Pennsylvania	636	277,782
California	1,063	890,188	Massachusetts	490	220,510	Rhode Island	72	36,378
Colorado	243	167,910	Michigan	654	329,283	South Carolina	183	75,829
Connecticut	242	146,593	Minnesota	359	149,420	South Dakota	145	14,988
Delaware	37	16,059	Mississippi	237	37,393	Tennessee	285	75,791
District of			Missouri	363	153,728	Texas	825	319,354
Columbia	27	28,575	Montana	107	15,425	Utah	107	56,915
Florida	473	383,109	Nebraska	289	37,036	Vermont	190	13,408
Georgia	366	155,868	Nevada	87	62,888	Virginia	338	199,658
Hawaii	50	23,876	New Hampshire	238	35,575	Washington	320	233,162
Idaho	143	25,787	New Jersey	458	315,890	West Virginia	177	26,844
Illinois	786	512,341	New Mexico	101	28,885	Wisconsin	455	166,870
Indiana	430	245,243	New York	1,089	902,746	Wyoming	74	15,740
Iowa	561	73,270	North Carolina	379	156,375			
Kansas	373	77,092	North Dakota	89	8,837	**U.S. TOTAL**	16,421	$8,222,619

(1) Includes central libraries and branches. (2) Some totals may be underestimated because of nonresponse.

Four-Year Colleges and Universities

General Information for the 2002-2003 Academic Year

Source: Peterson's, part of The Thomson Corporation, Copyright 2003

These listings **include only accredited degree-granting institutions** in the United States and the U.S. territories **with a total enrollment of 1,000 or more.** Only **four-year** colleges and universities (which award a bachelor's degree as their highest undergraduate degree) are included. Data reported **only for institutions that provided updated information** on Peterson's Annual Survey of Undergraduate Institutions for the 2002-2003 academic year.

All institutions are coeducational except those where the ZIP code is followed directly by a number in parentheses. (1) = men only, (2) = primarily men, (3) = women only, (4) = primarily women.

The **Tuition & Fees** column shows the annual tuition and required fees for full-time students, or, where indicated, the tuition and standard fees per unit for part-time students. Where tuition varies according to residence, the figure is given for the most local resident and is coded: (A) = area residents, (S) = state residents; all other figures apply to all students regardless of residence. Where annual expenses are expressed as a lump sum (including full-time tuition, mandatory fees, and room and board), the figure is coded: (C) = comprehensive fee. **Rm. & Board** is the average cost for one academic year.

Control: 1 = independent (nonprofit), 2 = independent-religious, 3 = proprietary (profit-making), 4 = federal, 5 = state, 6 = commonwealth (Puerto Rico), 7 = territory (U.S. territories), 8 = county, 9 = district, 10 = city, 11 = state and local, 12 = state-related, 13 = private (unspecified). **Degree** means the highest degree offered (B = bachelor's, M = master's, F = first professional, D = doctorate).

Enrollment is the total number of matriculated undergraduate and (if applicable) graduate students.

Faculty is the total number of faculty members teaching undergraduate courses and (if available) graduate courses.

NA or a **dash** indicates category is inapplicable or data not available. **NR** indicates data not reported.

Name, address	Year Founded	Tuition & Fees	Rm. & Board	Control, Degree	Enrollment	Faculty
Abilene Christian Univ, Abilene, TX 79699-9100	1906	$12,430	$4,830	2-D	4,668	297
Acad of Art Coll, San Francisco, CA 94105-3410	1929	$12,060	$8,400	3-M	6,282	587
Adams State Coll, Alamosa, CO 81102	1921	$2,367 (S)	$5,607	5-M	2,417	138
Adelphi Univ, Garden City, NY 11530	1896	$16,980	$8,200	1-D	6,993	624
Adrian Coll, Adrian, MI 49221-2575	1859	$15,660	$5,440	2-B	1,021	102
Alabama Agr & Mech Univ, Huntsville, AL 35811	1875	$2,620 (S)	$4,500	5-D	5,914	374
Alabama State Univ, Montgomery, AL 36101-0271	1867	$2,904 (S)	$3,500	5-M	6,038	398
Albany State Univ, Albany, GA 31705-2717	1903	$2,554 (S)	$3,570	5-M	3,456	190
Albertus Magnus Coll, New Haven, CT 06511-1189	1925	$15,344	$7,110	2-M	2,325	69
Albion Coll, Albion, MI 49224-1831	1835	$20,700	$5,912	2-B	1,658	130
Albright Coll, Reading, PA 19612-5234	1856	$22,340	$6,809	2-M	2,087	139
Alcorn State Univ, Alcorn State, MS 39096-7500	1871	$4,440 (S)	$3,538	5-M	3,150	190
Alfred Univ, Alfred, NY 14802-1205	1836	$11,459 (S)	$8,478	1-D	2,419	216
Allegheny Coll, Meadville, PA 16335	1815	$23,380	$5,600	2-B	1,924	148
Alliant Intl Univ, San Diego, CA 92131-1799	1952	$14,820	$6,365	1-D	1,946	225
Alma Coll, Alma, MI 48801-1599	1886	$17,582	$6,336	2-B	1,317	133
Alvernia Coll, Reading, PA 19607-1799	1958	$15,150	$6,500	2-M	2,187	158
Alverno Coll, Milwaukee, WI 53234-3922 (3)	1887	$12,750	$4,960	2-M	1,999	199
Amberton Univ, Garland, TX 75041-5595	1971	$4,975	NA	2-M	1,648	39
American Coll of Computer & Information Sci, Birmingham, AL 35205 (2)	1988	$130	NA	3-M	10,696	23
American InterContinental Univ, Los Angeles, CA 90066	1982	$15,210	NA	3-M	1,293	121
American InterContinental Univ, Atlanta, GA 30328	1970	$25,000	NA	3-M	1,248	119
American InterContinental Univ, Atlanta, GA 30326-1016	1977	$13,950	$4,500	3-B	1,292	110
American Intl Coll, Springfield, MA 01109-3189	1885	$16,485	$8,232	1-D	1,565	155
American Public Univ System, Charles Town, WV 25414	1991	$9,000	NA	3-M	6,828	342
American Univ, Washington, DC 20016-8001	1893	$24,839	$9,746	2-D	11,052	951
American Univ of Puerto Rico, Bayamón, PR 00960-2037	1963	$4,640	NA	1-B	4,537	222
Amherst Coll, Amherst, MA 01002-5000	1821	$28,310	$7,380	1-B	1,618	207
Anderson Coll, Anderson, SC 29621-4035	1911	$13,115	$5,445	2-B	1,639	138
Anderson Univ, Anderson, IN 46012-3495	1917	$16,140	$5,620	2-D	2,506	233
Andrews Univ, Berrien Springs, MI 49104	1874	$14,570	$4,980	2-D	2,779	247
Angelo State Univ, San Angelo, TX 76909	1928	$2,506 (S)	$4,256	5-M	6,268	265
Anna Maria Coll, Paxton, MA 01612	1946	$17,710	$6,550	2-M	1,235	158
Appalachian State Univ, Boone, NC 28608	1899	$2,795 (S)	$4,333	5-D	14,178	892
Aquinas Coll, Grand Rapids, MI 49506-1799	1886	$16,400	$5,494	2-M	2,579	206
Arcadia Univ, Glenside, PA 19038-3295	1853	$21,270	$8,620	2-D	3,002	292
Argosy Univ-Sarasota, Sarasota, FL 34235-8246	1974	$345	NA	3	NA	NA
Arizona State Univ, Tempe, AZ 85287	1885	$2,585 (S)	$5,866	5-D	47,359	1,853
Arizona State Univ East, Mesa, AZ 85212	1995	$2,534 (S)	$4,544	5-M	3,126	90
Arizona State Univ West, Phoenix, AZ 85069-7100	1984	$2,585 (S)	NA	5-M	6,630	324
Arkansas State Univ, State University, AR 72467	1909	$4,480 (S)	$3,410	5-D	10,435	579
Arkansas Tech Univ, Russellville, AR 72801	1909	$3,256 (S)	$3,576	5-M	5,855	341
Armstrong Atlantic State Univ, Savannah, GA 31419-1997	1935	$2,392 (S)	$4,608	5-M	6,026	385
Art Ctr Coll of Design, Pasadena, CA 91103-1999	1930	$22,148	NA	1-M	1,505	407
The Art Inst of Atlanta, Atlanta, GA 30328	1949	$14,544	$5,490	3-B	2,437	146
The Art Inst of Colorado, Denver, CO 80203	1952	$330	NA	3-B	2,219	167
The Art Inst of Fort Lauderdale, Fort Lauderdale, FL 33316-3000	1968	$20,000	NA	3-B	3,500	110
The Art Inst of Phoenix, Phoenix, AZ 85021-2859	1995	$14,640	$5,595	3-B	1,218	80
The Art Inst of Portland, Portland, OR 97209	1963	$14,805	$5,250	3-B	1,108	99
Asbury Coll, Wilmore, KY 40390-1198	1890	$16,500	$4,204	2-M	1,314	143
Ashland Univ, Ashland, OH 44805-3702	1878	$17,270	$6,212	2-D	6,430	502
Assumption Coll, Worcester, MA 01609-1296	1904	$19,980	$4,850	2-M	2,380	200
Athens State Univ, Athens, AL 35611-1902	1822	$3,090 (S)	$900	5-B	2,528	111
Auburn Univ, Auburn University, AL 36849	1856	$3,784 (S)	$2,216	5-D	23,276	1,277
Auburn Univ Montgomery, Montgomery, AL 36124-4023	1967	$3,620 (S)	$4,610	5-D	5,104	308
Augsburg Coll, Minneapolis, MN 55454-1351	1869	$18,193	$5,690	2-M	2,994	294
Augustana Coll, Rock Island, IL 61201-2296	1860	$19,608	$5,586	2-B	2,261	198
Augustana Coll, Sioux Falls, SD 57197	1860	$16,088	$4,668	2-M	1,834	161
Augusta State Univ, Augusta, GA 30904-2200	1925	$2,384 (S)	$6,986	5-M	5,884	296
Aurora Univ, Aurora, IL 60506-4892	1893	$14,250	$5,514	1-D	3,316	110
Austin Coll, Sherman, TX 75090-4400	1849	$17,925	$6,822	2-M	1,281	118
Austin Peay State Univ, Clarksville, TN 37044-0001	1927	$3,446 (S)	$3,820	5-M	7,482	457
Averett Univ, Danville, VA 24541-3692	1859	$16,800	$5,150	2-M	2,739	272
Avila Univ, Kansas City, MO 64145-1698	1916	$14,160	$5,300	2-M	1,746	190
Azusa Pacific Univ, Azusa, CA 91702-7000	1899	$17,594	$5,314	2-D	7,693	927

Name, address	Year Founded	Tuition & Fees	Rm. & Board	Control Degree	Enrollment	Faculty
Babson Coll, Babson Park, MA 02457-0310.	1919	$26,000	$9,676	1-M	3,407	247
Baker Coll of Auburn Hills, Auburn Hills, MI 48326-1586	1911	$5,760	NA	1-B	2,596	115
Baker Coll of Cadillac, Cadillac, MI 49601	1986	$5,760	NA	1-B	1,174	73
Baker Coll of Clinton Township, Clinton Township, MI 48035-4701	1990	$5,760	NA	1-B	3,929	133
Baker Coll of Flint, Flint, MI 48507-5508.	1911	$5,760	$2,175	1-B	5,291	173
Baker Coll of Jackson, Jackson, MI 49202.	1994	$5,760	NA	1-B	1,392	90
Baker Coll of Muskegon, Muskegon, MI 49442-3497.	1888	$5,760	$2,100	1-B	3,422	145
Baker Coll of Owosso, Owosso, MI 48867-4400	1984	$5,760	$2,100	1-B	2,361	103
Baker Coll of Port Huron, Port Huron, MI 48060-2597	1990	$5,760	NA	1-B	1,363	95
Baldwin-Wallace Coll, Berea, OH 44017-2088.	1845	$17,432	$6,022	2-M	4,719	396
Ball State Univ, Muncie, IN 47306-1099.	1918	$4,700 (S)	$5,546	5-D	20,113	1,175
Bard Coll, Annandale-on-Hudson, NY 12504	1860	$27,450	$8,134	1-D	1,653	218
Barnard Coll, New York, NY 10027-6598 (3)	1889	$25,270	$10,140	1-B	2,297	292
Barry Univ, Miami Shores, FL 33161-6695.	1940	$20,320	$7,000	2-D	8,469	825
Barton Coll, Wilson, NC 27893-7000	1902	$13,084	$4,754	2-B	1,245	90
Bates Coll, Lewiston, ME 04240-6028	1855	$35,750 (C)	NA	1-B	1,738	183
Bayamón Central Univ, Bayamón, PR 00960-1725	1970	$4,015	NA	2-M	3,334	218
Baylor Univ, Waco, TX 76798.	1845	$18,430	$5,434	2-D	14,159	866
Bay Path Coll, Longmeadow, MA 01106-2292 (3)	1897	$15,934	$7,566	1-M	1,103	111
Becker Coll, Worcester, MA 01609.	1784	$14,520	$7,750	1-B	1,577	107
Belhaven Coll, Jackson, MS 39202-1789.	1883	$12,810	$4,990	2-M	2,021	204
Bellarmine Univ, Louisville, KY 40205-0671.	1950	$17,010	$5,300	2-M	2,332	222
Bellevue Univ, Bellevue, NE 68005-3098	1965	$4,270	NA	1-M	4,057	152
Belmont Univ, Nashville, TN 37212-3757.	1951	$14,450	$5,825	2-D	3,344	341
Beloit Coll, Beloit, WI 53511-5596	1846	$23,236	$5,268	1-B	1,281	126
Bemidji State Univ, Bemidji, MN 56601-2699	1919	$4,475 (S)	$4,597	5-M	4,941	328
Benedict Coll, Columbia, SC 29204	1870	$10,546	$5,434	2-B	3,005	168
Benedictine Coll, Atchison, KS 66002-1499	1859	$14,200	$5,630	2-M	1,375	64
Benedictine Univ, Lisle, IL 60532-0900.	1887	$16,660	$5,800	2-D	2,809	220
Bentley Coll, Waltham, MA 02452-4705	1917	$21,075	$9,350	1-M	5,648	452
Berea Coll, Berea, KY 40404 .	1855	$507	$4,303	1-B	1,578	162
Berklee Coll of Music, Boston, MA 02215-3693	1945	$19,696	$10,280	1-B	3,519	519
Bernard M. Baruch Coll of the City Univ of New York, New York, NY 10010-5585.	1919	$4,100 (S)	NA	11-D	15,361	1,054
Berry Coll, Mount Berry, GA 30149-0159.	1902	$14,260	$5,624	2-M	2,053	180
Bethel Coll, Mishawaka, IN 46545-5591	1947	$14,120	$4,380	2-M	1,746	109
Bethel Coll, St. Paul, MN 55112-6999	1871	$18,800	$6,380	2-M	3,091	303
Bethel Coll, McKenzie, TN 38201	1842	$9,030	$4,550	2-F	1,059	45
Bethune-Cookman Coll, Daytona Beach, FL 32114-3099	1904	$9,810	$6,130	2-B	2,584	192
Biola Univ, La Mirada, CA 90639-0001.	1908	$18,454	$5,930	2-D	4,593	366
Birmingham-Southern Coll, Birmingham, AL 35254 .	1856	$18,050	$5,940	2-M	1,407	133
Black Hills State Univ, Spearfish, SD 57799.	1883	$4,193 (S)	$3,127	5-M	3,747	192
Bloomfield Coll, Bloomfield, NJ 07003-9981.	1868	$12,300	$5,850	2-B	1,887	182
Bloomsburg Univ of Pennsylvania, Bloomsburg, PA 17815-1301	1839	$5,550 (S)	$4,776	5-M	8,039	393
Bluefield State Coll, Bluefield, WV 24701-2198	1895	$2,398 (S)	NA	5-B	2,831	207
Bluffton Coll, Bluffton, OH 45817-1196.	1899	$16,430	$5,636	2-M	1,110	106
Boise State Univ, Boise, ID 83725-0399.	1932	$3,251 (S)	$4,426	5-D	17,637	941
Boricua Coll, New York, NY 10032-1560	1974	$7,350	NA	1-M	1,520	116
Boston Coll, Chestnut Hill, MA 02467-3800	1863	$25,862	$8,990	2-D	13,510	NA
Boston Univ, Boston, MA 02215 .	1839	$27,414	$8,978	1-D	28,982	3,492
Bowdoin Coll, Brunswick, ME 04011 .	1794	$28,685	$7,305	1-B	1,657	191
Bowie State Univ, Bowie, MD 20715-9465.	1865	$5,025 (S)	$5,673	5-D	5,257	343
Bowling Green State Univ, Bowling Green, OH 43403.	1910	$6,502 (S)	6,490	5-D	18,773	1,045
Bradley Univ, Peoria, IL 61625-0002 .	1897	$16,110	$5,800	1-M	6,098	515
Brandeis Univ, Waltham, MA 02454-9110 .	1948	$28,165	$7,849	1-D	4,852	453
Brewton-Parker Coll, Mt. Vernon, GA 30445-0197.	1904	$300	NA	2-B	1,269	199
Briarcliffe Coll, Bethpage, NY 11714.	1966	$13,180	NA	3-B	2,742	164
Bridgewater Coll, Bridgewater, VA 22812-1599	1880	$16,990	$8,160	2-B	1,363	114
Bridgewater State Coll, Bridgewater, MA 02325-0001	1840	$3,735 (S)	$5,366	5-M	9,561	487
Brigham Young Univ, Provo, UT 84602-1001.	1875	$3,150	$4,874	2-D	32,408	2,066
Brigham Young Univ-Hawaii, Laie, HI 96762-1294.	1955	$2,490	$4,520	2-B	2,529	214
Brooklyn Coll of the City Univ of New York, Brooklyn, NY 11210-2889	1930	$3,553 (S)	NA	11-M	15,635	992
Brooks Inst of Photography, Santa Barbara, CA 93108-2399	1945	$20,250	NA	3-M	1,507	39
Brown Univ, Providence, RI 02912 .	1764	$28,480	$7,876	1-D	7,892	797
Bryant Coll, Smithfield, RI 02917-1284.	1863	$22,458	$8,546	1-M	3,390	229
Bryn Mawr Coll, Bryn Mawr, PA 19010-2899 (3)	1885	$26,220	$8,970	1-D	1,744	192
Bucknell Univ, Lewisburg, PA 17837 .	1846	$27,531	$6,052	1-M	3,587	317
Buena Vista Univ, Storm Lake, IA 50588 .	1891	$18,738	$5,230	2-M	1,345	112
Butler Univ, Indianapolis, IN 46208-3485 .	1855	$20,190	$6,710	1-F	4,326	435
Cabrini Coll, Radnor, PA 19087-3698.	1957	$19,220	$8,180	2-M	2,182	234
Caldwell Coll, Caldwell, NJ 07006-6195 .	1939	$16,100	$6,800	2-M	2,218	190
California Baptist Univ, Riverside, CA 92504-3206.	1950	$12,790	$5,360	2-M	2,165	187
California Coll for Health Sci, National City, CA 91950-6605 .	1978	$8,025	NA	3-M	5,458	19
California Coll of Arts & Crafts, San Francisco, CA 94107 .	1907	$21,920	$7,576	1-M	1,427	337
California Inst of Tech, Pasadena, CA 91125-0001 .	1891	$24,117	$7,560	1-D	2,120	324
California Inst of the Arts, Valencia, CA 91355-2340 .	1961	$22,955	$6,850	1-M	1,237	274
California Lutheran Univ, Thousand Oaks, CA 91360-2787 .	1959	$19,260	$6,920	-2-M	2,949	255
California Polytechnic State Univ, San Luis Obispo, San Luis Obispo, CA 93407 .	1901	$2,877 (S)	$7,119	5-M	18,453	1,268
California State Polytechnic Univ, Pomona, Pomona, CA 91768-2557 .	1938	$1,772 (S)	$6,626	5-M	19,821	1,217
California State Univ, Bakersfield, Bakersfield, CA 93311-1099.	1970	NR (S)	NA	5-M	7,741	551
California State Univ, Chico, Chico, CA 95929-0722 .	1887	$703 (S)	$6,973	5-M	16,246	1,014
California State Univ, Dominguez Hills, Carson, CA 90747-0001.	1960	$1,840 (S)	$7,340	5-M	13,504	762
California State Univ, Fresno, Fresno, CA 93740-8027 .	1911	$1,796 (S)	$8,949	5-D	21,209	1,319
California State Univ, Fullerton, Fullerton, CA 92834-9480 .	1957	$1,881 (S)	$4,027	5-M	32,143	1,886
California State Univ, Hayward, Hayward, CA 94542-3000 .	1957	$1,944 (S)	$3,705	5-M	13,240	761
California State Univ, Long Beach, Long Beach, CA 90840 .	1949	$1,744 (S)	$5,800	5-M	34,566	2,120
California State Univ, Los Angeles, Los Angeles, CA 90032-8530.	1947	$1,782 (S)	$6,399	5-D	20,675	1,155
California State Univ, Monterey Bay, Seaside, CA 93955-8001.	1994	$928 (S)	$5,700	5-M	3,020	280
California State Univ, Northridge, Northridge, CA 91330 .	1958	$1,814 (S)	$6,400	5-M	31,448	1,746
California State Univ, Sacramento, Sacramento, CA 95819-6048 .	1947	$1,891 (S)	$6,163	5-D	28,558	1,571
California State Univ, San Bernardino, San Bernardino, CA 92407-2397 .	1965	$2,568 (S)	$4,956	5-M	16,341	981
California State Univ, San Marcos, San Marcos, CA 92096-0001 .	1990	$2,048 (S)	NA	5-M	6,703	431
California State Univ, Stanislaus, Turlock, CA 95382.	1957	$1,879 (S)	$7,371	5-M	7,850	480

Name, address	Year Founded	Tuition & Fees	Rm. & Board	Control, Degree	Enrollment	Faculty
California Univ of Pennsylvania, California, PA 15419-1394	1852	$5,742 (S)	$5,176	5-M	6,082	374
Calumet Coll of Saint Joseph, Whiting, IN 46394-2195	1951	$9,000	NA	2-M	1,143	106
Calvin Coll, Grand Rapids, MI 49546-4388	1876	$16,775	$5,840	2-M	4,324	374
Cambridge Coll, Cambridge, MA 02138-5304	1971	$9,075	NA	1-M	2,700	331
Cameron Univ, Lawton, OK 73505-6377	1908	$2,520 (S)	$2,830	5-M	5,298	458
Campbellsville Univ, Campbellsville, KY 42718-2799	1906	$11,460	$4,740	2-M	1,811	186
Campbell Univ, Buies Creek, NC 27506	1887	$12,849	$4,550	2-D	4,098	302
Canisius Coll, Buffalo, NY 14208-1098	1870	$18,840	$7,540	2-M	5,041	469
Capella Univ, Minneapolis, MN 55402	1993	$14,250	NA	3-D	6,500	350
Capital Univ, Columbus, OH 43209-2394	1830	$20,500	$6,050	2-F	3,947	444
Cardinal Stritch Univ, Milwaukee, WI 53217-3985	1937	$13,580	$4,990	2-D	6,854	NA
Caribbean Univ, Bayamón, PR 00960-0493	1969	$3,000	NA	1-M	3,352	158
Carleton Coll, Northfield, MN 55057-4001	1866	$26,910	$5,535	1-B	1,932	231
Carlow Univ, Pittsburgh, PA 15213-3165 (4)	1929	$14,430	$5,710	2-M	2,070	225
Carnegie Mellon Univ, Pittsburgh, PA 15213-3891	1900	$27,116	$7,534	1-D	9,501	930
Carroll Coll, Helena, MT 59625-0002	1909	$13,928	$5,566	2-B	1,341	135
Carroll Coll, Waukesha, WI 53186-5593	1846	$17,380	$5,360	2-M	2,968	221
Carson-Newman Coll, Jefferson City, TN 37760	1851	$13,620	$4,800	2-M	2,205	199
Carthage Coll, Kenosha, WI 53140-1994	1847	$20,150	$6,070	2-M	2,520	161
Case Western Reserve Univ, Cleveland, OH 44106	1826	$22,730	$7,150	1-D	9,097	594
Castleton State Coll, Castleton, VT 05735	1787	$5,966 (S)	$6,014	5-M	1,725	170
Catawba Coll, Salisbury, NC 28144-2488	1851	$15,300	$5,200	2-M	1,557	129
The Catholic Univ of America, Washington, DC 20064	1887	$23,250	$9,002	2-D	5,527	670
Cazenovia Coll, Cazenovia, NY 13035-1084	1824	$15,860	$6,700	1-B	1,005	124
Cedar Crest Coll, Allentown, PA 18104-6196 (3)	1867	$19,915	$6,994	2-M	1,590	82
Cedarville Univ, Cedarville, OH 45314-0601	1887	$13,696	$5,010	2-M	3,005	247
Centenary Coll, Hackettstown, NJ 07840-2100	1867	$16,400	$6,850	2-M	1,857	107
Centenary Coll of Louisiana, Shreveport, LA 71134-1188	1825	$16,450	$5,550	2-M	1,038	126
Central Coll, Pella, IA 50219-1999	1853	$16,756	$5,796	2-B	1,659	143
Central Connecticut State Univ, New Britain, CT 06050-4010	1849	$4,770 (S)	$6,280	5-M	12,642	848
Central Methodist Coll, Fayette, MO 65248-1198	1854	$13,760	$4,920	2-M	1,361	112
Central Michigan Univ, Mount Pleasant, MI 48859	1892	$4,747 (S)	$5,524	5-D	28,159	1,045
Central Missouri State Univ, Warrensburg, MO 64093	1871	$4,410 (S)	$4,630	5-M	10,313	592
Central State Univ, Wilberforce, OH 45384	1887	$3,714 (S)	$5,208	5-M	1,400	127
Central Washington Univ, Ellensburg, WA 98926-7463	1891	$3,792 (S)	$5,410	5-M	9,202	504
Centre Coll, Danville, KY 40422-1394	1819	$19,125	$6,475	2-B	1,055	100
Chadron State Coll, Chadron, NE 69337	1911	$3,290 (S)	$3,655	5-M	2,712	121
Chaminade Univ of Honolulu, Honolulu, HI 96816-1578	1955	$13,165	$7,060	2-M	2,801	175
Champlain Coll, Burlington, VT 05402-0670	1878	$12,295	$8,400	1-M	2,508	218
Chapman Univ, Orange, CA 92866	1861	$24,590	$8,528	2-F	4,836	510
Charleston Southern Univ, Charleston, SC 29423-8087	1964	$14,456	$5,544	2-M	2,849	186
Charter Oak State Coll, New Britain, CT 06053-2142	1973	$125/credit (S)	NA	5-B	1,561	100
Chatham Coll, Pittsburgh, PA 15232-2826 (3)	1869	$19,742	$6,688	1-D	1,058	76
Chestnut Hill Coll, Philadelphia, PA 19118-2693 (4)	1924	$18,150	$7,270	2-D	1,535	246
Cheyney Univ of Pennsylvania, Cheyney, PA 19319-0200	1837	$5,033 (S)	$5,390	5-M	1,523	118
Chicago State Univ, Chicago, IL 60628	1867	$5,596 (S)	$5,700	5-M	7,158	438
Christian Brothers Univ, Memphis, TN 38104-5581	1871	$16,240	$4,770	2-M	1,989	243
Christopher Newport Univ, Newport News, VA 23606-2998	1960	$3,546 (S)	$6,350	5-M	5,391	335
The Citadel, The Military Coll of South Carolina, Charleston, SC 29409 (2)	1842	$4,946 (S)	$4,575	5-M	4,058	216
City Coll of the City Univ of New York, New York, NY 10031-9198	1847	$3,309 (S)	NA	11-F	10,119	951
City Univ, Bellevue, WA 98005	1973	$7,960	NA	1-M	7,124	1,095
Claflin Univ, Orangeburg, SC 29115	1869	$8,940	$5,000	2-B	1,546	120
Claremont McKenna Coll, Claremont, CA 91711	1946	$26,350	$8,740	1-B	1,024	148
Clarion Univ of Pennsylvania, Clarion, PA 16214	1867	$5,740 (S)	$4,344	5-M	6,541	347
Clark Atlanta Univ, Atlanta, GA 30314	1865	$12,862	$6,438	2-D	4,813	438
Clarke Coll, Dubuque, IA 52001-3198	1843	$16,190	$5,765	2-M	1,126	89
Clarkson Univ, Potsdam, NY 13699	1896	$23,500	$8,726	1-D	3,107	192
Clark Univ, Worcester, MA 01610-1477	1887	$25,865	$4,950	1-D	3,035	260
Clayton Coll & State Univ, Morrow, GA 30260-0285	1969	$2,606 (S)	NA	5-B	5,214	262
Clemson Univ, Clemson, SC 29634	1889	$6,034 (S)	$4,454	5-D	16,876	1,126
Cleveland State Univ, Cleveland, OH 44115	1964	$5,184 (S)	$5,880	5-D	15,974	905
Coastal Carolina Univ, Conway, SC 29528-6054	1954	$4,430 (S)	$5,610	5-M	5,980	353
Coe Coll, Cedar Rapids, IA 52402-5092	1851	$20,540	$5,610	2-M	1,325	129
Colby Coll, Waterville, ME 04901-8840	1813	$35,800 (C)	NA	1-B	1,830	197
Coleman Coll, La Mesa, CA 91942-1532	1963	$7,200	NA	1-M	1,022	101
Colgate Univ, Hamilton, NY 13346-1386	1819	$28,355	$6,775	1-M	2,837	293
Coll for Creative Studies, Detroit, MI 48202-4034	1926	$19,798	$3,300	1-B	1,204	226
Coll Misericordia, Dallas, PA 18612-1098	1924	$17,970	$7,400	2-M	1,984	189
Coll of Aeronautics, Flushing, NY 11369-1037 (2)	1932	$9,650	NA	1-B	1,316	60
Coll of Biblical Studies-Houston, Houston, TX 77036	1979	$3,800	NA	2-B	1,433	78
Coll of Charleston, Charleston, SC 29424-0001	1770	$4,556 (S)	$5,661	5-M	11,716	851
Coll of Mount St. Joseph, Cincinnati, OH 45233-1670	1920	$15,840	$6,020	2-M	2,067	211
Coll of Mount Saint Vincent, Riverdale, NY 10471-1093	1911	$18,180	$7,550	1-M	1,568	145
The Coll of New Jersey, Ewing, NJ 08628	1855	$7,516 (S)	$7,416	5-M	6,938	706
The Coll of New Rochelle, New Rochelle, NY 10805-2308 (3)	1904	$14,650	$7,150	1-M	2,853	255
Coll of Notre Dame of Maryland, Baltimore, MD 21210-2476 (3)	1873	$19,075	$7,600	2-M	3,148	86
Coll of Saint Benedict, Saint Joseph, MN 56374-2091 (4)	1887	$19,226	$5,789	2-B	2,072	159
Coll of St. Catherine, St. Paul, MN 55105-1789 (3)	1905	$18,362	$5,170	2-D	4,704	367
Coll of Saint Elizabeth, Morristown, NJ 07960-6989 (3)	1899	$16,375	$7,750	2-M	1,772	160
The Coll of Saint Rose, Albany, NY 12203-1419	1920	$14,640	$7,016	1-M	4,624	402
The Coll of St. Scholastica, Duluth, MN 55811-4199	1912	$18,216	$5,406	2-M	2,512	194
Coll of Santa Fe, Santa Fe, NM 87505-7634	1947	$18,284	$5,484	1-M	1,722	273
Coll of Staten Island of the City Univ of New York, Staten Island, NY 10314-6600	1955	$3,358 (S)	NA	11-M	12,087	721
Coll of the Holy Cross, Worcester, MA 01610-2395	1843	$26,440	$8,000	2-B	2,801	284
Coll of the Ozarks, Point Lookout, MO 65726	1906	$200	$2,840	2-B	1,348	110
The Coll of William & Mary, Williamsburg, VA 23187-8795	1693	$5,484 (S)	$5,489	5-D	7,645	737
The Coll of Wooster, Wooster, OH 44691-2363	1866	$25,040	$6,260	2-B	1,856	168
Colorado Christian Univ, Lakewood, CO 80226-7499	1914	$15,040	$5,320	2-M	1,801	118
The Colorado Coll, Colorado Springs, CO 80903-3294	1874	$26,333	$6,480	1-M	1,930	204
Colorado School of Mines, Golden, CO 80401-1887	1874	$6,380 (S)	$5,860	5-D	3,261	362
Colorado State Univ, Fort Collins, CO 80523-0015	1870	$3,435 (S)	$5,780	5-D	27,290	898
Colorado State Univ-Pueblo, Pueblo, CO 81001-4901	1933	$2,681 (S)	$5,624	5-M	5,531	240

Name, address	Year Founded	Tuition & Fees	Rm. & Board	Control, Degree	Enrollment	Faculty
Colorado Tech Univ, Colorado Springs, CO 80907-3896	1965	$9,438	NA	3-D	1,684	137
Columbia Coll, Columbia, MO 65216-0002	1851	$10,926	$4,666	2-M	1,038	85
Columbia Coll, New York, NY 10027	1754	$28,206	$9,736	1-B	4,109	NA
Columbia Coll, Columbia, SC 29203-5998 (3)	1854	$17,280	$5,245	2-M	1,474	152
Columbia Coll Chicago, Chicago, IL 60605-1996	1890	$14,104	$6,305	1-M	9,803	1,439
Columbia Intl Univ, Columbia, SC 29230-3122	1923	$11,690	$5,120	2-D	1,022	51
Columbia Southern Univ, Orange Beach, AL 36561	NR	$3,000	NA	3-M	2,200	45
Columbia Union Coll, Takoma Park, MD 20912-7796	1904	$14,548	$5,043	2-M	1,162	57
Columbia Univ, School of General Studies, New York, NY 10027-6939	1754	$27,267	$6,240	1-B	1,167	632
Columbia Univ, The Fu Foundation School of Engineering & Applied Sci, New York, NY 10027	1864	$28,206	$9,736	1-D	1,301	NA
Columbus Coll of Art & Design, Columbus, OH 43215-1758	1879	$17,660	$6,300	1-B	1,681	193
Columbus State Univ, Columbus, GA 31907-5645	1958	$2,466 (S)	$5,010	5-M	6,250	NA
Concord Coll, Athens, WV 24712-1000	1872	$2,962 (S)	$4,628	5-B	3,015	183
Concordia Coll, Moorhead, MN 56562	1891	$15,767	$4,310	2-B	2,775	254
Concordia Univ, Irvine, CA 92612-3299	1972	$17,990	$6,430	2-M	1,681	142
Concordia Univ, River Forest, IL 60305-1499	1864	$18,200	$5,400	2-D	1,802	157
Concordia Univ, St. Paul, MN 55104-5494	1893	$17,326	$5,530	2-M	1,921	391
Concordia Univ, Seward, NE 68434-1599	1894	$14,546	$4,388	2-M	1,425	123
Concordia Univ, Portland, OR 97211-6099	1905	$17,490	$4,400	2-M	1,074	103
Concordia Univ at Austin, Austin, TX 78705-2799	1926	$14,410	$6,150	2-M	1,076	86
Concordia Univ Wisconsin, Mequon, WI 53097-2402	1881	$15,575	$5,790	2-M	4,904	167
Connecticut Coll, New London, CT 06320-4196	1911	$35,625 (C)	NA	1-M	1,912	182
Converse Coll, Spartanburg, SC 29302-0006 (3)	1889	$17,860	$5,450	1-M	1,577	87
Coppin State Coll, Baltimore, MD 21216-3698	1900	$4,538 (S)	$5,814	5-M	4,003	202
Cornell Coll, Mount Vernon, IA 52314-1098	1853	$20,955	$5,800	2-B	1,001	108
Cornell Univ, Ithaca, NY 14853-0001	1865	$13,274 (S)	$8,980	1-D	19,575	1,792
Cornerstone Univ, Grand Rapids, MI 49525-5897	1941	$13,770	$5,218	2-F	2,450	133
Covenant Coll, Lookout Mountain, GA 30750	1955	$18,230	$5,260	2-M	1,221	73
Creighton Univ, Omaha, NE 68178-0001	1878	$18,882	$6,438	2-D	6,327	860
Crichton Coll, Memphis, TN 38111	1941	$10,920	$4,950	1-B	1,028	129
The Culinary Inst of America, Hyde Park, NY 12538-1499	1946	$16,940	$6,200	1-B	2,294	141
Cumberland Coll, Williamsburg, KY 40769-1372	1889	$11,458	$4,926	2-M	1,743	98
Cumberland Univ, Lebanon, TN 37087-3554	1842	$11,660	$4,290	1-M	1,463	123
Curry Coll, Milton, MA 02186-9984	1879	$19,650	$7,570	1-M	2,399	393
Daemen Coll, Amherst, NY 14226-3592	1947	$14,270	$6,700	1-F	2,027	193
Dakota State Univ, Madison, SD 57042-1799	1881	$3,774 (S)	$3,130	5-M	2,188	94
Dallas Baptist Univ, Dallas, TX 75211-9299	1965	$10,350	$4,140	2-M	4,417	344
Dalton State Coll, Dalton, GA 30720-3797	1963	$2,124 (S)	NA	5-B	3,647	179
Daniel Webster Coll, Nashua, NH 03063-1300	1965	$19,000	$7,440	1-B	1,058	61
Dartmouth Coll, Hanover, NH 03755	1769	$27,771	$8,217	1-D	5,495	640
Davenport Univ, Lansing, MI 48933-2197	1977	$8,656	NA	1-B	1,209	79
Davenport Univ, Grand Rapids, MI 49503	1866	$9,015	$7,410	1-M	2,216	111
Davenport Univ, Warren, MI 48092-5209	1985	$7,886	NA	1-M	2,486	114
Davenport Univ, Kalamazoo, MI 49006-2791	1977	$10,147	NA	1-B	1,063	110
Davenport Univ, Dearborn, MI 48126-3799	1985	$7,886	NA	1-M	3,138	190
David N. Myers Univ, Cleveland, OH 44115-1096	1848	$16,608	NA	1-M	1,177	165
Davidson Coll, Davidson, NC 28035	1837	$24,930	$7,094	2-B	1,645	168
Delaware State Univ, Dover, DE 19901-2277	1891	$4,216 (S)	$6,178	5-M	3,149	249
Delaware Valley Coll, Doylestown, PA 18901-2697	1896	$18,430	$6,870	1-M	1,995	172
Delta State Univ, Cleveland, MS 38733-0001	1924	$3,348 (S)	$3,180	5-D	3,826	273
Denison Univ, Granville, OH 43023	1831	$24,240	$6,880	1-B	2,099	190
DePaul Univ, Chicago, IL 60604-2287	1898	$17,850	$7,455	2-D	24,227	2,208
DePauw Univ, Greencastle, IN 46135-0037	1837	$22,840	$6,800	2-B	2,338	238
DeSales Univ, Center Valley, PA 18034-9568	1964	$17,340	$6,520	2-M	2,933	139
DeVry Coll of Tech, North Brunswick, NJ 08902-3362	1969	$10,265	NA	3-B	3,268	171
DeVry Inst of Tech, Long Island City, NY 11101	1998	$11,265	NA	3-B	2,052	124
DeVry Univ, Phoenix, AZ 85021-2995	1967	$10,155	NA	3-B	2,721	101
DeVry Univ, Fremont, CA 94555	1998	$11,265	NA	3-B	2,070	85
DeVry Univ, West Hills, CA 91304	1999	$10,755	NA	3-B	1,423	85
DeVry Univ, Long Beach, CA 90806	1984	$10,755	NA	3-B	2,629	131
DeVry Univ, Pomona, CA 91768-2642	1983	$10,755	NA	3-B	3,197	137
DeVry Univ, Orlando, FL 32839	2000	$10,755	NA	3-B	1,227	64
DeVry Univ, Alpharetta, GA 30004	1997	$10,155	NA	3-B	1,508	79
DeVry Univ, Decatur, GA 30030-2198	1969	$10,155	NA	3-B	2,950	139
DeVry Univ, Tinley Park, IL 60477	2000	$10,265	NA	3-B	1,928	103
DeVry Univ, Addison, IL 60101-6106	1982	$10,265	NA	3-B	3,028	162
DeVry Univ, Chicago, IL 60618-5994	1931	$10,265	NA	3-B	3,539	171
DeVry Univ, Kansas City, MO 64131-3698	1931	$10,155	NA	3-B	2,590	133
DeVry Univ, Columbus, OH 43209-2705	1952	$10,155	NA	3-B	3,632	157
DeVry Univ, Irving, TX 75063-2439	1969	$10,125	NA	3-B	3,163	181
Dickinson Coll, Carlisle, PA 17013-2896	1773	$28,640	$7,210	1-B	2,261	191
Dickinson State Univ, Dickinson, ND 58601-4896	1918	$2,798 (S)	$2,050	5-B	2,326	140
Dillard Univ, New Orleans, LA 70122-3097	1869	$10,865	$5,072	2-B	2,225	193
Doane Coll, Crete, NE 68333-2430	1872	$14,280	$4,300	2-M	1,015	127
Dominican Coll, Orangeburg, NY 10962-1210	1952	$15,650	$7,770	1-M	1,624	156
Dominican Univ, River Forest, IL 60305-1099	1901	$17,950	$5,600	2-M	2,776	204
Dominican Univ of California, San Rafael, CA 94901-2298	1890	$22,730	$9,780	2-M	1,653	244
Dordt Coll, Sioux Center, IA 51250-1697	1955	$14,880	$4,160	2-M	1,404	110
Dowling Coll, Oakdale, NY 11769-1999	1955	$14,700	$4,800	1-D	6,446	529
Drake Univ, Des Moines, IA 50311-4516	1881	$18,510	$5,490	1-D	5,092	369
Drew Univ, Madison, NJ 07940-1493	1867	$26,346	$7,288	2-D	2,487	164
Drexel Univ, Philadelphia, PA 19104-2875	1891	$18,413	$9,090	1-D	16,345	889
Drury Univ, Springfield, MO 65802-3791	1873	$13,214	$4,885	1-M	1,805	154
Duke Univ, Durham, NC 27708-0586	1838	$27,844	$7,921	2-D	12,488	NA
Duquesne Univ, Pittsburgh, PA 15282-0001	1878	$18,527	$7,170	2-D	9,595	827
D'Youville Coll, Buffalo, NY 14201-1084	1908	$13,336	$6,560	1-M	2,464	196
Earlham Coll, Richmond, IN 47374-4095	1847	$24,560	$5,416	2-F	1,193	167
East Carolina Univ, Greenville, NC 27858-4353	1907	$2,980 (S)	$5,090	5-D	20,577	1,120
East Central Univ, Ada, OK 74820-6899	1909	$2,371 (S)	$4,340	5-M	4,195	NA
Eastern Connecticut State Univ, Willimantic, CT 06226-2295	1889	$5,421 (S)	$6,614	5-M	5,215	346
Eastern Illinois Univ, Charleston, IL 61920-3099	1895	$4,648 (S)	$6,000	5-M	11,163	659
Eastern Kentucky Univ, Richmond, KY 40475-3102	1906	$2,928 (S)	$4,146	5-M	15,061	NA

Name, address	Year Founded	Tuition & Fees	Rm. & Board	Control, Degree	Enroll- ment	Faculty
Eastern Mennonite Univ, Harrisonburg, VA 22802-2462	1917	$16,370	$5,350	2-F	1,352	153
Eastern Michigan Univ, Ypsilanti, MI 48197	1849	$5,027 (S)	$5,597	5-D	24,195	1,224
Eastern Nazarene Coll, Quincy, MA 02170-2999	1918	$15,315	$5,215	2-M	1,228	48
Eastern New Mexico Univ, Portales, NM 88130	1934	$2,292 (S)	$4,540	5-M	3,607	199
Eastern Oregon Univ, La Grande, OR 97850-2899	1929	$4,305 (S)	$5,775	5-M	3,408	125
Eastern Univ, St. Davids, PA 19087-3696	1952	$16,780	$7,200	2-M	3,128	NA
Eastern Washington Univ, Cheney, WA 99004-2431	1882	$3,582 (S)	$5,025	5-D	9,924	492
East Stroudsburg Univ of Pennsylvania, East Stroudsburg, PA 18301-2999	1893	$5,502 (S)	$4,346	5-M	6,270	305
East Tennessee State Univ, Johnson City, TN 37614	1911	$3,311 (S)	$4,390	5-D	11,365	737
East Texas Baptist Univ, Marshall, TX 75670-1498	1912	$9,800	$3,456	2-B	1,496	123
East-West Univ, Chicago, IL 60605-2103	1978	$10,395	NA	1-B	1,113	79
Eckerd Coll, St. Petersburg, FL 33711	1958	$21,488	$5,686	2-B	1,608	134
Edgewood Coll, Madison, WI 53711-1997	1927	$15,100	$5,350	2-M	2,264	221
Edinboro Univ of Pennsylvania, Edinboro, PA 16444	1857	$5,464 (S)	$4,884	5-M	7,778	420
Edward Waters Coll, Jacksonville, FL 32209-6199	1866	$7,946	$5,742	2-B	1,320	49
Elizabethtown Coll, Elizabethtown, PA 17022-2298	1899	$21,350	$6,000	2-M	1,901	199
Elmhurst Coll, Elmhurst, IL 60126-3296	1871	$17,500	$5,796	2-M	2,490	263
Elmira Coll, Elmira, NY 14901	1855	$25,740	$8,080	1-B	1,547	110
Elon Univ, Elon, NC 27244-2010	1889	$15,505	$5,090	2-D	4,434	304
Embry-Riddle Aeronautical Univ, Prescott, AZ 86301-3720 (2)	1978	$19,930	$5,808	1-M	1,702	110
Embry-Riddle Aeronautical Univ, Daytona Beach, FL 32114-3900 (2)	1926	$19,960	$6,370	1-M	4,772	271
Embry-Riddle Aeronautical Univ, Extended Campus, Daytona Beach, FL 32114-3900 (2)	1970	$17,850	NA	1-M	9,173	3,103
Emerson Coll, Boston, MA 02116-4624	1880	$21,624	$9,542	1-D	4,529	375
Emmanuel Coll, Boston, MA 02115	1919	$18,100	$8,000	2-M	1,632	87
Emory & Henry Coll, Emory, VA 24327-0947	1836	$15,900	$6,050	2-M	1,003	97
Emory Univ, Atlanta, GA 30322-1100	1836	$26,932	$8,498	2-D	11,617	NA
Emporia State Univ, Emporia, KS 66801-5087	1863	$2,454 (S)	$4,046	5-D	6,005	266
Endicott Coll, Beverly, MA 01915-2096	1939	$16,460	$8,364	1-M	2,208	129
Evangel Univ, Springfield, MO 65802-2191	1955	$11,305	$4,130	2-M	1,666	144
The Evergreen State Coll, Olympia, WA 98505	1967	$3,591 (S)	$5,610	5-M	4,367	216
Excelsior Coll, Albany, NY 12203-5159	1970	$1,385	NA	1-M	20,492	NA
Fairfield Univ, Fairfield, CT 06824	1942	$24,555	$8,560	2-M	5,114	473
Fairleigh Dickinson Univ, Coll at Florham, Madison, NJ 07940-1099	1942	$19,074	$7,904	1-M	3,682	NA
Fairleigh Dickinson Univ, Metro Campus, Teaneck, NJ 07666-1914	1942	$19,074	$7,904	1-D	6,686	NA
Fairmont State Coll, Fairmont, WV 26554	1865	$2,766 (S)	$4,788	5-M	6,813	517
Farmingdale State Univ of New York, Farmingdale, NY 11735	1912	$4,240 (S)	$7,250	5-B	5,798	375
Fashion Inst of Tech, New York, NY 10001-5992	1944	$3,670 (S)	$6,138	11-M	10,855	966
Faulkner Univ, Montgomery, AL 36109-3398	1942	$9,300	$4,600	2-M	2,613	118
Fayetteville State Univ, Fayetteville, NC 28301-4298	1867	$2,052 (S)	$3,820	5-D	5,308	231
Felician Coll, Lodi, NJ 07644-2117	1942	$15,150	$7,200	2-M	1,717	163
Ferris State Univ, Big Rapids, MI 49307	1884	$5,852 (S)	$5,968	5-F	11,074	630
Fitchburg State Coll, Fitchburg, MA 01420-2697	1894	$3,688 (S)	$5,172	5-M	4,924	226
Five Towns Coll, Dix Hills, NY 11746-6055	1972	$12,820	$8,700	1-M	1,143	108
Flagler Coll, St. Augustine, FL 32085-1027	1968	$7,410	$4,450	1-B	1,973	155
Florida Agr & Mech Univ, Tallahassee, FL 32307-3200	1887	$2,794 (S)	$4,966	5-D	12,465	NA
Florida Atlantic Univ, Boca Raton, FL 33431-0991	1961	$2,786 (S)	$7,112	5-D	23,836	1,267
Florida Gulf Coast Univ, Fort Myers, FL 33965-6565	1991	$2,699 (S)	$7,000	5-M	4,799	180
Florida Inst of Tech, Melbourne, FL 32901-6975	1958	$20,900	$5,800	1-D	4,506	262
Florida Intl Univ, Miami, FL 33199	1965	$2,881 (S)	$7,180	5-D	33,451	1,320
Florida Metro Univ-Brandon Campus, Tampa, FL 33619	1890	$7,998	NA	3-M	1,350	64
Florida Metro Univ-Fort Lauderdale Campus, Fort Lauderdale, FL 33304-2522	1940	$7,998	NA	3-M	1,868	70
Florida Metro Univ-North Orlando Campus, Orlando, FL 32810-5674	1953	$7,998	NA	3-M	1,444	89
Florida Metro Univ-Pinellas Campus, Clearwater, FL 33759	1890	$7,998	NA	3-M	1,201	44
Florida Metro Univ-South Orlando Campus, Orlando, FL 32809	NR	$8,048	NA	3-M	1,964	77
Florida Metro Univ-Tampa Campus, Tampa, FL 33614-5899	1890	$7,848	NA	3-M	1,218	54
Florida Southern Coll, Lakeland, FL 33801-5698	1885	$15,078	$5,700	2-M	1,932	257
Florida State Univ, Tallahassee, FL 32306	1851	$2,538 (S)	$5,628	5-D	36,210	1,124
Fontbonne Univ, St. Louis, MO 63105-3098	1917	$13,714	$6,535	2-M	2,344	194
Fordham Univ, New York, NY 10458	1841	$23,540	$9,460	2-D	14,318	1,132
Fort Hays State Univ, Hays, KS 67601-4099	1902	$2,328 (S)	$4,843	5-M	6,392	300
Fort Lewis Coll, Durango, CO 81301-3999	1911	$2,632 (S)	$5,446	5-B	4,347	258
Fort Valley State Univ, Fort Valley, GA 31030-4313	1895	$3,150 (S)	$4,078	5-D	2,823	174
Framingham State Coll, Framingham, MA 01701-9101	1839	$3,334 (S)	$4,650	5-M	5,959	329
Franciscan Univ of Steubenville, Steubenville, OH 43952-1763	1946	$14,400	$5,200	2-M	2,253	189
Francis Marion Univ, Florence, SC 29501-0547	1970	$4,340 (S)	$4,082	5-M	3,496	204
Franklin & Marshall Coll, Lancaster, PA 17604-3003	1787	$27,280	$6,580	1-B	1,926	191
Franklin Coll, Franklin, IN 46131-2598	1834	$15,635	$5,280	2-B	1,048	99
Franklin Pierce Coll, Rindge, NH 03461-0060	1962	$21,380	$7,250	1-M	1,574	140
Franklin Univ, Columbus, OH 43215-5399	1902	$7,704	NA	1-M	5,808	425
Freed-Hardeman Univ, Henderson, TN 38340-2399	1869	$10,158	$5,170	2-M	1,927	117
Fresno Pacific Univ, Fresno, CA 93702-4709	1944	$17,592	$4,870	2-M	1,891	147
Friends Univ, Wichita, KS 67213	1898	$12,965	$3,890	1-M	3,190	225
Frostburg State Univ, Frostburg, MD 21532-1099	1898	$5,184 (S)	$5,619	5-M	5,457	357
Furman Univ, Greenville, SC 29613	1826	$21,264	$5,664	1-M	3,208	230
Gallaudet Univ, Washington, DC 20002-3625	1864	$9,660	$8,030	1-D	1,664	218
Gannon Univ, Erie, PA 16541-0001	1925	$16,670	$6,590	2-D	3,357	285
Gardner-Webb Univ, Boiling Springs, NC 28017	1905	$13,400	$4,980	2-D	3,821	132
Geneva Coll, Beaver Falls, PA 15010-3599	1848	$14,760	$6,130	2-M	1,919	143
George Fox Univ, Newberg, OR 97132-2697	1891	$18,875	$5,945	2-D	2,748	134
George Mason Univ, Fairfax, VA 22030-4444	1957	$5,158 (S)	$5,560	5-D	26,796	1,641
Georgetown Coll, Georgetown, KY 40324-1696	1829	$16,370	$5,190	2-M	1,673	128
Georgetown Univ, Washington, DC 20057	1789	$26,853	$9,682	2-D	12,856	948
The George Washington Univ, Washington, DC 20052	1821	$27,820	$9,110	1-D	23,019	1,626
Georgia Coll & State Univ, Milledgeville, GA 31061	1889	$3,138 (S)	$5,324	5-M	5,513	389
Georgia Inst of Tech, Atlanta, GA 30332-0001	1885	$3,616 (S)	$5,922	5-D	16,481	781
Georgian Court Coll, Lakewood, NJ 08701-2697 (3)	1908	$16,272	$6,600	2-M	2,871	242
Georgia Southern Univ, Statesboro, GA 30460	1906	$2,694 (S)	$4,620	5-D	15,075	701
Georgia Southwestern State Univ, Americus, GA 31709-4693	1906	$2,578 (S)	$3,926	5-M	2,508	149
Georgia State Univ, Atlanta, GA 30303-3083	1913	$3,472 (S)	$4,680	5-D	27,502	1,363
Gettysburg Coll, Gettysburg, PA 17325-1483	1832	$27,070	$6,640	2-B	2,377	268
Glenville State Coll, Glenville, WV 26351-1200	1872	$2,412 (S)	$4,440	5-B	2,184	166
Global Univ of the Assemblies of God, Springfield, MO 65804	1948	$2,040	NA	2-M	6,547	480

Name, address	Year Founded	Tuition & Fees	Rm. & Board	Control, Degree	Enrollment	Faculty
Golden Gate Univ, San Francisco, CA 94105-2968	1853	$9,600	NA	1-D	4,415	662
Goldey-Beacom Coll, Wilmington, DE 19808-1999	1886	$10,132	$3,937	1-M	1,400	49
Gonzaga Univ, Spokane, WA 99258	1887	$20,735	$5,960	2-D	5,529	494
Gordon Coll, Wenham, MA 01984-1899	1889	$19,100	$5,650	2-M	1,701	135
Goucher Coll, Baltimore, MD 21204-2794	1885	$23,250	$7,900	1-M	2,102	172
Governors State Univ, University Park, IL 60466-0975	1969	$2,920 (S)	NA	5-M	5,855	204
Grace Coll, Winona Lake, IN 46590-1294	1948	$12,466	$5,311	2-M	1,033	82
Graceland Univ, Lamoni, IA 50140	1895	$13,900	$4,530	2-M	2,297	106
Grambling State Univ, Grambling, LA 71245	1901	$2,716 (S)	$2,936	5-D	4,464	248
Grand Canyon Univ, Phoenix, AZ 85017-1097	1949	$14,500	$6,974	2-M	4,113	274
Grand Valley State Univ, Allendale, MI 49401-9403	1960	$5,056 (S)	$5,656	5-M	20,407	1,257
Grand View Coll, Des Moines, IA 50316-1599	1896	$14,194	$4,798	2-B	1,546	139
Grantham Univ, Slidell, LA 70460-6815 (2)	1951	$2,489	NA	3-B	2,500	12
Greensboro Coll, Greensboro, NC 27401-1875	1838	$14,650	$5,760	2-M	1,235	112
Greenville Coll, Greenville, IL 62246-0159	1892	$14,520	$5,400	2-M	1,239	104
Grinnell Coll, Grinnell, IA 50112-1690	1846	$23,530	$6,330	1-B	1,485	141
Grove City Coll, Grove City, PA 16127-2104	1876	$8,876	$4,626	2-B	2,288	167
Guilford Coll, Greensboro, NC 27410-4173	1837	$18,200	$5,780	2-B	1,801	141
Gustavus Adolphus Coll, St. Peter, MN 56082-1498	1862	$20,450	$5,170	2-B	2,536	238
Gwynedd-Mercy Coll, Gwynedd Valley, PA 19437-0901	1948	$16,700	$7,300	2-M	2,429	225
Hamilton Coll, Clinton, NY 13323-1296	1812	$28,760	$7,040	1-B	1,851	206
Hamline Univ, St. Paul, MN 55104-1284	1854	$19,213	$5,971	2-D	4,479	341
Hampden-Sydney Coll, Hampden-Sydney, VA 23943 (1)	1776	$19,893	$6,722	2-B	1,026	107
Hampshire Coll, Amherst, MA 01002	1965	$27,870	$7,294	1-B	1,267	118
Hampton Univ, Hampton, VA 23668	1868	$12,252	$5,828	1-D	5,790	400
Hannibal-LaGrange Coll, Hannibal, MO 63401-1999	1858	$9,960	$3,710	2-B	1,117	87
Hanover Coll, Hanover, IN 47243-0108	1827	$13,500	$5,500	2-B	1,050	102
Harding Univ, Searcy, AR 72149-0001	1924	$9,530	$4,650	2-M	5,095	275
Hardin-Simmons Univ, Abilene, TX 79698-0001	1891	$12,176	$3,699	2-F	2,291	181
Harrington Inst of Interior Design, Chicago, IL 60606 (4)	1931	$12,175	NA	3-B	1,125	100
Harris-Stowe State Coll, St. Louis, MO 63103-2136	1857	$3,040 (S)	NA	5-B	1,968	68
Hartwick Coll, Oneonta, NY 13820-4020	1797	$27,015	$7,050	1-B	1,397	152
Harvard Univ, Cambridge, MA 02138	1636	$27,448	$8,502	1-D	20,132	760
Haskell Indian Nations Univ, Lawrence, KS 66046-4800	1884	$210 (S)	$70	4-B	1,028	48
Hastings Coll, Hastings, NE 68901-7696	1882	$14,554	$4,398	2-M	1,078	108
Haverford Coll, Haverford, PA 19041-1392	1833	$27,260	$8,590	1-B	1,105	111
Hawai`i Pacific Univ, Honolulu, HI 96813-2785	1965	$10,368	$8,770	1-M	8,137	612
Heidelberg Coll, Tiffin, OH 44883-2462	1850	$13,672	$6,276	2-M	1,468	122
Henderson State Univ, Arkadelphia, AR 71999-0001	1890	$3,252 (S)	$3,936	5-M	3,444	210
Hendrix Coll, Conway, AR 72032-3080	1876	$14,900	$5,090	2-M	1,093	98
Heritage Coll, Toppenish, WA 98948-9599	1982	$6,400	NA	1-M	1,127	130
High Point Univ, High Point, NC 27262-3598	1924	$14,710	$6,610	2-M	2,750	212
Hillsdale Coll, Hillsdale, MI 49242-1298	1844	$15,300	$6,086	1-B	1,220	127
Hiram Coll, Hiram, OH 44234-0067	1850	$20,312	$6,820	2-B	1,134	137
Hobart & William Smith Colleges, Geneva, NY 14456-3397	1822	$27,348	$7,230	1-B	1,893	177
Hofstra Univ, Hempstead, NY 11549	1935	$16,542	$8,450	1-D	13,412	1,291
Hollins Univ, Roanoke, VA 24020-1603 (3)	1842	$18,450	$6,875	1-M	1,153	112
Holy Family Univ, Philadelphia, PA 19114-2094	1954	$14,490	NA	2-M	2,670	258
Hood Coll, Frederick, MD 21701-8575	1893	$20,275	$7,520	1-M	1,693	179
Hope Coll, Holland, MI 49422-9000	1866	$18,268	$5,688	2-B	3,035	282
Hope Intl Univ, Fullerton, CA 92831-3138	1928	$14,100	$5,092	2-M	1,204	62
Houghton Coll, Houghton, NY 14744	1883	$17,160	$5,600	2-B	1,394	101
Houston Baptist Univ, Houston, TX 77074-3298	1960	$11,355	$4,443	2-M	2,745	191
Howard Payne Univ, Brownwood, TX 76801-2715	1889	$10,500	$4,007	2-B	1,412	130
Howard Univ, Washington, DC 20059-0002	1867	$10,935	$5,570	1-D	10,517	1,547
Humboldt State Univ, Arcata, CA 95521-8299	1913	$2,461 (S)	$6,861	5-M	7,611	563
Hunter Coll of the City Univ of New York, New York, NY 10021-5085	1870	$3,365 (S)	$1,890	11-M	20,607	1,230
Huntington Coll, Huntington, IN 46750-1299	1897	$15,920	$5,680	2-M	1,016	95
Husson Coll, Bangor, ME 04401-2999	1898	$10,370	$5,510	1-M	1,868	103
Idaho State Univ, Pocatello, ID 83209	1901	$3,136 (S)	$4,410	5-D	13,350	596
The Illinois Inst of Art, Chicago, IL 60654	1916	$15,189	NA	3-B	1,950	160
The Illinois Inst of Art-Schaumburg, Schaumburg, IL 60173	NR	$15,364	$5,500	3-B	1,107	55
Illinois Inst of Tech, Chicago, IL 60616-3793	1890	$19,756	$5,944	1-D	6,199	535
Illinois State Univ, Normal, IL 61790-2200	1857	$5,036 (S)	$5,062	5-D	21,183	1,101
Illinois Wesleyan Univ, Bloomington, IL 61702-2900	1850	$24,540	$5,840	1-B	2,107	200
Immaculata Univ, Immaculata, PA 19345 (3)	1920	$16,400	$7,600	2-D	3,564	270
Indiana Inst of Tech, Fort Wayne, IN 46803-1297	1930	$15,590	$6,030	1-M	3,019	207
Indiana State Univ, Terre Haute, IN 47809-1401	1865	$4,216 (S)	$4,998	5-D	11,714	673
Indiana Univ Bloomington, Bloomington, IN 47405	1820	$5,315 (S)	$5,676	5-D	38,903	1,947
Indiana Univ East, Richmond, IN 47374-1289	1971	$3,789 (S)	NA	5-B	2,481	69
Indiana Univ Kokomo, Kokomo, IN 46904-9003	1945	$3,824 (S)	NA	5-M	2,772	74
Indiana Univ Northwest, Gary, IN 46408-1197	1959	$3,895 (S)	NA	5-M	4,893	349
Indiana Univ of Pennsylvania, Indiana, PA 15705-1087	1875	$5,541 (S)	$4,524	5-D	13,671	712
Indiana Univ-Purdue Univ Fort Wayne, Fort Wayne, IN 46805-1499	1917	$3,892 (S)	NA	5-M	11,757	640
Indiana Univ-Purdue Univ Indianapolis, Indianapolis, IN 46202-2896	1969	$4,715 (S)	$2,080	5-D	29,025	2,732
Indiana Univ South Bend, South Bend, IN 46634-7111	1922	$3,930 (S)	NA	5-M	7,457	498
Indiana Univ Southeast, New Albany, IN 47150-6405	1941	$3,865 (S)	NA	5-M	6,716	437
Indiana Wesleyan Univ, Marion, IN 46953-4974	1920	$14,420	$5,480	2-M	8,765	167
Inter American Univ of Puerto Rico, Aguadilla Campus, Aguadilla, PR 00605	1957	$3,484	NA	1-B	4,123	213
Inter American Univ of Puerto Rico, Barranquitas Campus, Barranquitas, PR 00794	1957	$3,840	NA	1-B	2,060	105
Inter American Univ of Puerto Rico, Guayama Campus, Guayama, PR 00785	1958	$1,682	NA	1-B	1,246	139
Inter American Univ of Puerto Rico, Metro Campus, San Juan, PR 00919-1293	1960	$3,866	NA	1-D	10,272	713
Inter American Univ of Puerto Rico, Ponce Campus, Mercedita, PR 00715-1602	1962	$4,200	NA	1-B	4,123	212
Inter American Univ of Puerto Rico, San Germán Campus, San Germán, PR 00683-5008	1912	$4,316	$2,400	1-D	5,972	322
Intl Acad of Design & Tech, Tampa, FL 33634-7350	1984	$15,120	NA	3-B	2,043	151
Intl Acad of Design & Tech, Chicago, IL 60602-9736	1977	$17,200	NA	3-B	2,309	167
Intl Coll, Naples, FL 34119	1990	$8,050	NA	1-M	1,349	97
Iona Coll, New Rochelle, NY 10801-1890	1940	$17,866	$9,700	2-M	4,449	374
Iowa State Univ of Sci & Tech, Ames, IA 50011	1858	$4,110 (S)	$5,020	5-D	27,898	1,625

Name, address	Year Founded	Tuition & Fees	Rm. & Board	Control, Degree	Enroll- ment	Faculty
Ithaca Coll, Ithaca, NY 14850-7020	1892	$21,102	$8,960	1-M	6,431	612
Jackson State Univ, Jackson, MS 39217	1877	$3,462 (S)	$4,676	5-D	7,783	422
Jacksonville State Univ, Jacksonville, AL 36265-1602	1883	$3,240 (S)	$2,875	5-M	8,930	411
Jacksonville Univ, Jacksonville, FL 32211-3394	1934	$16,780	$5,900	1-M	2,565	233
James Madison Univ, Harrisonburg, VA 22807	1908	$4,458 (S)	$5,794	5-D	15,965	978
Jamestown Coll, Jamestown, ND 58405	1883	$8,750	$3,850	2-B	1,185	65
John Brown Univ, Siloam Springs, AR 72761-2121	1919	$13,716	$5,070	2-M	1,708	109
John Carroll Univ, University Heights, OH 44118-4581	1886	$19,182	$6,564	2-M	4,294	397
John F. Kennedy Univ, Orinda, CA 94563-2603	1964	$13,092	NA	1-D	1,586	715
John Jay Coll of Criminal Justice of the City Univ of New York, New York, NY 10019-1093	1964	$3,459 (S)	NA	11-M	11,209	585
Johns Hopkins Univ, Baltimore, MD 21218-2699	1876	$27,690	$8,870	1-D	6,029	NA
Johnson & Wales Univ, North Miami, FL 33181	1992	$19,194	$6,288	1-B	2,145	90
Johnson & Wales Univ, Providence, RI 02903-3703	1914	$16,188	$6,777	1-D	9,630	403
Johnson & Wales Univ, Charleston, SC 29403	1984	$19,394	$4,860	1-B	1,497	55
Johnson C. Smith Univ, Charlotte, NC 28216-5398	1867	$12,444	$4,806	1-B	1,537	113
Johnson State Coll, Johnson, VT 05656-9405	1828	$5,876 (S)	$6,213	5-M	1,646	209
Jones Intl Univ, Englewood, CO 80112	1995	$880	NA	1-M	2,000	400
Judson Coll, Elgin, IL 60123-1498	1963	$16,050	$6,000	2-M	1,172	123
Juniata Coll, Huntingdon, PA 16652-2119	1876	$22,760	$6,290	2-B	1,345	120
Kalamazoo Coll, Kalamazoo, MI 49006-3295	1833	$21,603	$6,354	2-B	1,265	121
Kansas State Univ, Manhattan, KS 66506	1863	$3,444 (S)	$4,500	5-D	22,732	913
Kean Univ, Union, NJ 07083	1855	$5,840 (S)	$6,520	5-M	12,779	1,058
Keene State Coll, Keene, NH 03435	1909	$6,152 (S)	$5,430	5-M	4,962	393
Kennesaw State Univ, Kennesaw, GA 30144-5591	1963	$2,516 (S)	$3,105	5-M	15,655	703
Kent State Univ, Kent, OH 44242-0001	1910	$6,374 (S)	$5,570	5-D	23,504	1,300
Kentucky State Univ, Frankfort, KY 40601	1886	$2,846 (S)	$4,214	12-M	2,254	130
Kenyon Coll, Gambier, OH 43022-9623	1824	$28,710	$4,690	1-B	1,576	168
Kettering Univ, Flint, MI 48504-4898	1919	$20,333	$4,752	1-M	3,166	153
Keuka Coll, Keuka Park, NY 14478-0098	1890	$16,050	$7,600	2-M	1,124	84
King's Coll, Wilkes-Barre, PA 18711-0801	1946	$18,150	$7,550	2-M	2,188	183
Knox Coll, Galesburg, IL 61401	1837	$23,499	$5,760	1-B	1,121	107
Kutztown Univ of Pennsylvania, Kutztown, PA 19530-0730	1866	$5,477 (S)	$4,682	5-M	8,524	378
Lafayette Coll, Easton, PA 18042-1798	1826	$26,044	$8,069	2-B	2,300	226
LaGrange Coll, LaGrange, GA 30240-2999	1831	$13,226	$5,494	2-M	1,016	96
Lake Forest Coll, Lake Forest, IL 60045-2399	1857	$24,406	$5,764	1-M	1,341	146
Lakeland Coll, Sheboygan, WI 53082-0359	1862	$14,325	$5,441	2-M	3,586	52
Lake Superior State Univ, Sault Sainte Marie, MI 49783-1626	1946	$4,758 (S)	$5,548	5-B	3,219	221
Lamar Univ, Beaumont, TX 77710	1923	$3,076 (S)	$5,010	5-D	9,802	491
Lander Univ, Greenwood, SC 29649-2099	1872	$4,804 (S)	$4,548	5-M	2,947	202
Langston Univ, Langston, OK 73050-0907	1897	$2,557 (S)	$1,680	5-M	3,008	NA
La Roche Coll, Pittsburgh, PA 15237-5898	1963	$13,190	$6,474	2-M	1,981	223
La Salle Univ, Philadelphia, PA 19141-1199	1863	$21,420	$8,350	2-D	5,752	NA
Lasell Coll, Newton, MA 02466-2709	1851	$16,700	$8,300	1-M	1,048	130
La Sierra Univ, Riverside, CA 92515-8247	1922	$16,740	$4,560	2-D	1,758	95
Lawrence Tech Univ, Southfield, MI 48075-1058	1932	$13,290	$4,840	1-M	4,054	353
Lawrence Univ, Appleton, WI 54912-0599	1847	$23,667	$5,457	1-B	1,389	170
Lebanon Valley Coll, Annville, PA 17003-1400	1866	$21,200	$6,110	2-M	2,070	189
Lee Univ, Cleveland, TN 37320-3450	1918	$8,730	$4,950	2-M	3,711	275
Lehigh Univ, Bethlehem, PA 18015-3094	1865	$26,180	$7,530	1-D	6,686	495
Lehman Coll of the City Univ of New York, Bronx, NY 10468-1589	1931	$3,310 (S)	NA	11-M	9,510	702
Le Moyne Coll, Syracuse, NY 13214-1399	1946	$17,910	$7,250	2-M	3,288	280
Lenoir-Rhyne Coll, Hickory, NC 28603	1891	$16,450	$5,815	2-M	1,492	159
Lesley Univ, Cambridge, MA 02138-2790 (4)	1909	$19,700	$8,800	1-D	6,455	64
LeTourneau Univ, Longview, TX 75607-7001	1946	$14,190	$5,820	2-M	3,338	240
Lewis & Clark Coll, Portland, OR 97219-7899	1867	$23,730	$6,630	1-F	3,051	326
Lewis-Clark State Coll, Lewiston, ID 83501-2698	1893	$2,852 (S)	$3,880	5-B	3,117	180
Lewis Univ, Romeoville, IL 60446	1932	$15,250	$7,250	2-M	4,347	152
Liberty Univ, Lynchburg, VA 24502	1971	$12,020	$5,200	2-D	7,709	284
Lincoln Memorial Univ, Harrogate, TN 37752-1901	1897	$11,760	$4,380	1-M	2,201	135
Lincoln Univ, Jefferson City, MO 65102	1866	$3,638 (S)	$3,790	5-M	3,332	153
Lincoln Univ, Lincoln University, PA 19352	1854	$5,744 (S)	$5,584	12-M	1,998	171
Lindenwood Univ, St. Charles, MO 63301-1695	1827	$11,650	$5,600	2-M	6,937	330
Lindsey Wilson Coll, Columbia, KY 42728-1298	1903	$12,602	$5,484	2-M	1,588	107
Linfield Coll, McMinnville, OR 97128-6894	1849	$20,310	$6,553	2-B	1,599	158
Lipscomb Univ, Nashville, TN 37204-3951	1891	$11,356	$5,590	2-F	2,661	231
Lock Haven Univ of Pennsylvania, Lock Haven, PA 17745-2390	1870	$5,566 (S)	$4,996	5-M	4,574	248
Loma Linda Univ, Loma Linda, CA 92350	1905	$20,640	$2,780	2-D	3,427	1,365
Long Island Univ, Brooklyn Campus, Brooklyn, NY 11201-8423	1926	$16,377	$6,280	1-D	8,057	1,028
Long Island Univ, C.W. Post Campus, Brookville, NY 11548-1300	1954	$19,160	$7,400	1-D	10,644	1,129
Long Island Univ, Southampton Coll, Southampton, NY 11968-4198	1963	$19,230	$8,430	1-M	3,289	215
Longwood Univ, Farmville, VA 23909-1800	1839	$4,661 (S)	$5,070	5-M	4,178	214
Loras Coll, Dubuque, IA 52004-0178	1839	$17,949	$5,895	2-M	1,736	173
Louisiana Coll, Pineville, LA 71359-0001	1906	$9,050	$3,486	2-B	1,161	103
Louisiana State Univ & Agr & Mech Coll, Baton Rouge, LA 70803	1860	$3,536 (S)	$4,968	5-D	32,228	1,554
Louisiana State Univ Health Sci Ctr, New Orleans, LA 70112-2223	1931	$3,214 (S)	$2,748	5-D	2,851	3,000
Louisiana State Univ in Shreveport, Shreveport, LA 71115-2399	1965	$2,818 (S)	NA	5-M	4,228	259
Louisiana Tech Univ, Ruston, LA 71272	1894	$3,157 (S)	$3,345	5-D	11,257	475
Lourdes Coll, Sylvania, OH 43560-2898	1958	$14,600	NA	2-B	1,300	123
Loyola Coll in Maryland, Baltimore, MD 21210-2699	1852	$24,910	$7,670	2-D	6,144	520
Loyola Marymount Univ, Los Angeles, CA 90045-2659	1911	$22,016	$6,930	2-F	8,178	805
Loyola Univ Chicago, Chicago, IL 60611-2196	1870	$21,054	$7,900	2-D	13,061	1,979
Loyola Univ New Orleans, New Orleans, LA 70118-6195	1912	$20,106	$7,660	2-F	5,562	437
Lubbock Christian Univ, Lubbock, TX 79407-2099	1957	$10,992	$4,160	2-M	1,851	135
Luther Coll, Decorah, IA 52101-1045	1861	$20,310	$4,040	2-B	2,572	234
Luther Rice Bible Coll & Seminary, Lithonia, GA 30038-2454	1962	$3,050	NA	2-D	1,600	33
Lycoming Coll, Williamsport, PA 17701-5192	1812	$20,432	$5,624	2-B	1,418	112
Lynchburg Coll, Lynchburg, VA 24501-3199	1903	$21,515	$4,800	2-M	1,874	189
Lyndon State Coll, Lyndonville, VT 05851-0919	1911	$5,504 (S)	$5,782	5-M	1,315	133
Lynn Univ, Boca Raton, FL 33431-5598	1962	$22,750	$8,000	1-D	1,888	247
Macalester Coll, St. Paul, MN 55105-1899	1874	$23,772	$6,516	2-B	1,840	221
Macon State Coll, Macon, GA 31206-5144	1968	$1,490 (S)	NA	5-B	4,989	215
Madonna Univ, Livonia, MI 48150-1173	1947	$9,100	$5,444	2-M	3,808	292

Name, address	Year Founded	Tuition & Fees	Rm. & Board	Control/ Degree	Enrollment	Faculty
Malone Coll, Canton, OH 44709-3897	1892	$14,150	$5,830	2-M	2,137	189
Manchester Coll, North Manchester, IN 46962-1225	1889	$16,080	$6,340	2-M	1,140	93
Manhattan Coll, Riverdale, NY 10471	1853	$19,300	$8,100	2-M	3,208	264
Manhattanville Coll, Purchase, NY 10577-2132	1841	$23,040	$9,380	1-M	2,568	205
Mansfield Univ of Pennsylvania, Mansfield, PA 16933	1857	$5,674 (S)	$5,006	5-M	3,368	192
Marian Coll, Indianapolis, IN 46222-1997	1851	$16,560	$5,600	2-M	1,431	132
Marian Coll of Fond du Lac, Fond du Lac, WI 54935-4699	1936	$14,195	$4,800	2-M	2,672	141
Marietta Coll, Marietta, OH 45750-4000	1835	$20,112	$5,774	1-M	1,208	116
Marist Coll, Poughkeepsie, NY 12601-1387	1929	$17,882	$8,332	1-M	5,866	558
Marquette Univ, Milwaukee, WI 53201-1881	1881	$19,706	$6,350	2-D	11,042	1,002
Marshall Univ, Huntington, WV 25755	1837	$2,984 (S)	$5,298	5-D	13,788	730
Mars Hill Coll, Mars Hill, NC 28754	1856	$15,458	$5,700	2-B	1,275	150
Martin Luther Coll, New Ulm, MN 56073	1995	$11,710	$1,850	2-B	1,063	97
Mary Baldwin Coll, Staunton, VA 24401-3610 (4)	1842	$17,690	$6,450	2-M	1,625	129
Marygrove Coll, Detroit, MI 48221-2599 (4)	1905	$11,750	$5,800	2-M	6,465	77
Maryland Inst Coll of Art, Baltimore, MD 21217-4191	1826	$22,080	$6,880	1-M	1,363	207
Marymount Coll of Fordham Univ, Tarrytown, NY 10591-3796 (3)	1907	$17,210	$8,695	1-B	1,061	125
Marymount Manhattan Coll, New York, NY 10021-4597	1936	$16,292	$8,976	1-B	2,323	341
Marymount Univ, Arlington, VA 22207-4299	1950	$15,732	$6,920	2-M	3,638	356
Maryville Coll, Maryville, TN 37804-5907	1819	$18,835	$5,900	2-B	1,020	105
Maryville Univ of Saint Louis, St. Louis, MO 63141-7299	1872	$14,560	$6,300	1-M	3,265	313
Mary Washington Coll, Fredericksburg, VA 22401-5358	1908	$3,670 (S)	$5,318	5-M	4,835	335
Marywood Univ, Scranton, PA 18509-1598	1915	$18,450	$7,710	2-D	3,133	308
Massachusetts Coll of Art, Boston, MA 02115-5882	1873	$4,968 (S)	$9,800	5-M	2,120	172
Massachusetts Coll of Liberal Arts, North Adams, MA 01247-4100	1894	$4,197 (S)	$5,462	5-M	1,613	121
Massachusetts Coll of Pharmacy & Health Sci, Boston, MA 02115-5896	1823	$18,550	$9,580	1-D	2,130	136
Massachusetts Inst of Tech, Cambridge, MA 02139-4307	1861	$29,600	$8,710	1-D	10,317	1,949
The Master's Coll & Seminary, Santa Clarita, CA 91321-1200	1927	$16,620	$5,780	2-F	1,503	148
McDaniel Coll, Westminster, MD 21157-4390	1867	$23,260	$5,280	1-M	3,374	180
McKendree Coll, Lebanon, IL 62254-1299	1828	$14,200	$5,400	2-B	2,067	197
McMurry Univ, Abilene, TX 79697	1923	$12,018	$4,650	2-B	1,418	120
McNeese State Univ, Lake Charles, LA 70609	1939	$2,619 (S)	$3,788	5-M	8,029	392
Medaille Coll, Buffalo, NY 14214-2695	1875	$13,030	$5,950	1-M	2,000	232
Medgar Evers Coll of the City Univ of New York, Brooklyn, NY 11225-2298	1969	$3,430 (S)	NA	11-B	4,873	352
Medical Coll of Georgia, Augusta, GA 30912	1828	$3,356 (S)	$2,591	5-D	2,001	709
Medical Univ of South Carolina, Charleston, SC 29425-0002	1824	$6,732 (S)	NA	5-D	2,286	1,239
Mercer Univ, Macon, GA 31207-0003	1833	$19,728	$6,420	2-D	7,325	582
Mercy Coll, Dobbs Ferry, NY 10522-1189	1951	$10,000	$8,000	1-M	9,752	989
Mercyhurst Coll, Erie, PA 16546	1926	$16,980	$6,414	2-M	3,617	245
Meredith Coll, Raleigh, NC 27607-5298 (3)	1891	$18,065	$5,000	1-M	2,328	294
Merrimack Coll, North Andover, MA 01845-5800	1947	$19,000	$8,410	2-M	2,518	210
Mesa State Coll, Grand Junction, CO 81501	1925	$2,373 (S)	$6,037	5-M	5,560	333
Messiah Coll, Grantham, PA 17027	1909	$18,136	$6,130	2-B	2,895	266
Methodist Coll, Fayetteville, NC 28311-1420	1956	$14,970	$5,580	2-M	2,180	167
Metro Coll of New York, New York, NY 10013-1919 (4)	1964	$16,635	NA	1-M	1,665	224
Metro State Coll of Denver, Denver, CO 80217-3362	1963	$2,668 (S)	$567	5-B	19,413	1,000
Metro State Univ, St. Paul, MN 55106-5000	1971	$3,358 (S)	NA	5-M	6,419	619
Miami Intl Univ of Art & Design, Miami, FL 33132-1418	1965	$21,440	$5,800	3-M	1,016	93
Miami Univ, Oxford, OH 45056	1809	$7,600 (S)	$6,240	12-D	16,730	1,033
Michigan State Univ, East Lansing, MI 48824	1855	$6,101 (S)	$4,932	5-D	44,937	2,647
Michigan Tech Univ, Houghton, MI 49931-1295	1885	$6,455 (S)	$5,465	5-D	6,625	407
MidAmerica Nazarene Univ, Olathe, KS 66062-1899	1966	$12,910	$5,828	2-M	1,825	151
Middlebury Coll, Middlebury, VT 05753-6002	1800	$36,100 (C)	NA	1-D	2,297	232
Middle Tennessee State Univ, Murfreesboro, TN 37132	1911	$3,442 (S)	$4,060	5-D	21,163	1,010
Midway Coll, Midway, KY 40347-1120 (3)	1847	$10,950	$5,540	2-B	1,042	102
Midwestern State Univ, Wichita Falls, TX 76308	1922	$3,064 (S)	$4,434	5-M	6,218	312
Miles Coll, Birmingham, AL 35208	1905	$5,008	$3,800	2-B	1,807	131
Millersville Univ of Pennsylvania, Millersville, PA 17551-0302	1855	$5,547 (S)	$5,310	5-M	7,650	416
Millikin Univ, Decatur, IL 62522-2084	1901	$19,234	$6,123	2-M	2,496	260
Millsaps Coll, Jackson, MS 39210-0001	1890	$17,362	$6,364	2-M	1,251	100
Mills Coll, Oakland, CA 94613-1000 (3)	1852	$22,128	$8,500	1-D	1,176	158
Milwaukee School of Engineering, Milwaukee, WI 53202-3109 (2)	1903	$23,034	$5,445	1-M	2,586	271
Minnesota State Univ, Mankato, Mankato, MN 56001	1868	$3,981 (S)	$4,018	5-M	13,795	630
Minnesota State Univ, Moorhead, Moorhead, MN 56563-0002	1885	$3,388 (S)	$3,706	5-M	7,431	334
Minot State Univ, Minot, ND 58707-0002	1913	$2,806 (S)	$3,162	5-M	3,625	225
Mississippi Coll, Clinton, MS 39058	1826	$10,712	$4,680	2-F	3,227	243
Mississippi State Univ, Mississippi State, MS 39762	1878	$3,874 (S)	$6,080	5-D	16,610	1,082
Mississippi Univ for Women, Columbus, MS 39701-9998 (4)	1884	$3,298 (S)	$3,230	5-M	2,328	214
Mississippi Valley State Univ, Itta Bena, MS 38941-1400	1946	$3,410 (S)	$3,374	5-M	3,501	150
Missouri Baptist Univ, St. Louis, MO 63141-8660	1964	$11,310	$5,480	2-M	3,105	141
Missouri Southern State Coll, Joplin, MO 64801-1595	1937	$3,886 (S)	$4,000	5-B	5,782	297
Missouri Valley Coll, Marshall, MO 65340-3197	1889	$13,100	$5,200	2-B	1,600	103
Missouri Western State Coll, St. Joseph, MO 64507-2294	1915	$4,064 (S)	$3,804	5-B	5,197	330
Molloy Coll, Rockville Centre, NY 11571-5002	1955	$14,610	NA	1-M	2,893	324
Monmouth Coll, Monmouth, IL 61462-1998	1853	$18,600	$5,000	2-B	1,089	103
Monmouth Univ, West Long Branch, NJ 07764-1898	1933	$17,900	$7,240	1-M	6,035	493
Montana State Univ-Billings, Billings, MT 59101-0298	1927	$3,973 (S)	$3,430	5-M	4,407	242
Montana State Univ-Bozeman, Bozeman, MT 59717	1893	$3,807 (S)	$5,120	5-D	11,921	803
Montana State Univ-Northern, Havre, MT 59501-7751	1929	$3,608 (S)	$4,420	5-M	1,589	103
Montana Tech of The Univ of Montana, Butte, MT 59701-8997	1895	$4,350 (S)	$4,980	5-M	2,161	156
Montclair State Univ, Upper Montclair, NJ 07043-1624	1908	$5,741 (S)	$6,956	5-D	14,673	958
Montreat Coll, Montreat, NC 28757-1267	1916	$14,121	$4,442	2-M	1,070	90
Moody Bible Inst, Chicago, IL 60610-3284	1886	$1,586	$6,020	2-F	1,737	100
Moravian Coll, Bethlehem, PA 18018-6650	1742	$22,058	$7,095	2-F	2,049	180
Morehead State Univ, Morehead, KY 40351	1922	$2,926 (S)	$4,000	5-M	9,390	464
Morehouse Coll, Atlanta, GA 30314 (1)	1867	$13,618	$8,172	1-B	2,738	205
Morgan State Univ, Baltimore, MD 21251	1867	$4,698 (S)	$6,150	5-D	7,112	576
Morningside Coll, Sioux City, IA 51106-1751	1894	$15,460	$5,120	2-M	1,040	109
Morris Coll, Sumter, SC 29150-3599	1908	$6,993	$3,410	2-B	1,049	62
Mountain State Univ, Beckley, WV 25802-9003	1933	$4,560	$2,501	1-M	3,275	151
Mount Aloysius Coll, Cresson, PA 16630-1999	1939	$14,660	$5,440	2-M	1,311	117
Mount Holyoke Coll, South Hadley, MA 01075 (3)	1837	$27,708	$8,100	1-M	2,194	259
Mount Ida Coll, Newton Center, MA 02459-3310	1899	$16,296	$8,950	1-B	1,250	133

Name, address	Year Founded	Tuition & Fees	Rm. & Board	Control, Degree	Enrollment	Faculty
Mount Marty Coll, Yankton, SD 57078-3724	1936	$12,660	$4,600	2-M	1,123	102
Mount Mary Coll, Milwaukee, WI 53222-4597 (3)	1913	$14,165	$4,895	2-M	1,401	163
Mount Mercy Coll, Cedar Rapids, IA 52402-4797	1928	$15,300	$5,074	2-B	1,434	119
Mount Olive Coll, Mount Olive, NC 28365	1951	$10,010	$4,400	2-B	2,208	165
Mount Saint Mary Coll, Newburgh, NY 12550-3494	1960	$13,335	$6,520	1-M	2,541	171
Mount St. Mary's Coll, Los Angeles, CA 90049-1599 (4)	1925	$19,674	$7,832	2-M	1,988	251
Mount Saint Mary's Coll & Seminary, Emmitsburg, MD 21727-7799	1808	$21,000	$7,400	2-F	2,032	134
Mt. Sierra Coll, Monrovia, CA 91016	1990	$10,000	NA	3-B	1,100	50
Mount Union Coll, Alliance, OH 44601-3993	1846	$17,150	$5,070	2-B	2,372	216
Mount Vernon Nazarene Univ, Mount Vernon, OH 43050-9500	1964	$13,288	$4,527	2-M	2,337	197
Muhlenberg Coll, Allentown, PA 18104-5586	1848	$23,455	$6,295	2-B	2,470	226
Murray State Univ, Murray, KY 42071-0009	1922	$3,032 (S)	$4,420	5-M	9,915	548
Muskingum Coll, New Concord, OH 43762	1837	$14,800	$5,880	2-M	2,049	152
Naropa Univ, Boulder, CO 80302-6697	1974	$15,860	$8,400	1-M	1,201	136
Natl-Louis Univ, Chicago, IL 60603	1886	$15,651	$5,913	1-D	7,904	284
Natl Univ, La Jolla, CA 92037-1011	1971	$8,025	NA	1-M	17,865	1,574
Nazareth Coll of Rochester, Rochester, NY 14618-3790	1924	$16,376	$6,930	1-M	3,146	217
Nebraska Wesleyan Univ, Lincoln, NE 68504-2796	1887	$16,424	$4,530	2-M	1,684	142
Neumann Coll, Aston, PA 19014-1298	1965	$15,650	$7,260	2-M	2,221	174
Newbury Coll, Brookline, MA 02445	1962	$14,850	$7,500	1-B	1,472	89
New Coll of California, San Francisco, CA 94102-5206	1971	$10,220	NA	1-M	1,088	90
New Jersey City Univ, Jersey City, NJ 07305-1597	1927	$5,556 (S)	$6,198	5-M	9,099	599
New Jersey Inst of Tech, Newark, NJ 07102	1881	$7,906 (S)	$7,864	5-D	8,828	653
Newman Univ, Wichita, KS 67213-2097	1933	$12,040	$4,590	2-M	1,929	198
New Mexico Highlands Univ, Las Vegas, NM 87701	1893	$2,184 (S)	$5,638	5-M	3,225	134
New Mexico Inst of Mining & Tech, Socorro, NM 87801	1889	$2,911 (S)	$4,218	5-D	1,727	135
New Mexico State Univ, Las Cruces, NM 88003-8001	1888	$3,456 (S)	$4,422	5-D	15,243	937
New Orleans Baptist Theological Seminary, New Orleans, LA 70126-4858 (2)	1917	$3,050	NA	2-D	2,712	84
New School Bachelor of Arts, New School Univ, New York, NY 10011-8603	1919	$15,418	$9,896	1-D	1,292	NA
New York Inst of Tech, Old Westbury, NY 11568-8000	1955	$15,950	$7,680	1-F	9,155	820
New York Univ, New York, NY 10012-1019	1831	$26,646	$10,430	1-D	38,096	3,921
Niagara Univ, Niagara University, NY 14109	1856	$16,550	$7,300	2-M	3,446	293
Nicholls State Univ, Thibodaux, LA 70310	1948	$2,454 (S)	$3,352	5-M	7,314	278
Nichols Coll, Dudley, MA 01571-5000	1815	$19,723	$7,810	1-M	1,905	54
Norfolk State Univ, Norfolk, VA 23504	1935	$3,296 (S)	$5,588	5-D	6,839	457
North Carolina Agr & Tech State Univ, Greensboro, NC 27411	1891	$2,561 (S)	$4,768	5-D	9,115	458
North Carolina Central Univ, Durham, NC 27707-3129	1910	$3,032 (S)	$4,206	5-F	6,519	349
North Carolina State Univ, Raleigh, NC 27695	1887	$3,827 (S)	$5,796	5-D	29,940	1,685
North Central Coll, Naperville, IL 60566-7063	1861	$18,402	$6,045	2-M	2,533	196
North Central Univ, Minneapolis, MN 55404-1322	1930	$9,694	$4,250	2-B	1,163	88
North Dakota State Univ, Fargo, ND 58105	1890	$3,506 (S)	$4,175	5-D	11,146	593
Northeastern Illinois Univ, Chicago, IL 60625-4699	1961	$3,000 (S)	NA	5-M	11,409	623
Northeastern State Univ, Tahlequah, OK 74464-2399	1846	$2,425 (S)	$2,960	5-F	8,985	446
Northeastern Univ, Boston, MA 02115-5096	1898	$24,467	$9,660	1-D	18,507	1,112
Northern Arizona Univ, Flagstaff, AZ 86011	1899	$2,585 (S)	$5,156	5-D	19,907	1,328
Northern Illinois Univ, De Kalb, IL 60115-2854	1895	$4,802 (S)	$5,198	5-D	24,948	1,201
Northern Kentucky Univ, Highland Heights, KY 41099	1968	$3,216 (S)	$4,492	5-F	13,715	864
Northern Michigan Univ, Marquette, MI 49855-5301	1899	$4,128 (S)	$5,630	5-M	9,016	428
Northern State Univ, Aberdeen, SD 57401-7198	1901	$3,874 (S)	$3,234	5-M	3,020	110
North Georgia Coll & State Univ, Dahlonega, GA 30597-1001	1873	$2,616 (S)	$4,016	5-M	4,178	308
North Greenville Coll, Tigerville, SC 29688-1892	1892	$8,860	$5,030	2-B	1,486	123
North Park Univ, Chicago, IL 60625-4895	1891	$18,710	$6,520	2-D	2,181	121
Northwest Coll, Kirkland, WA 98083-0579	1934	$12,858	$5,996	2-M	1,120	82
Northwestern Coll, Orange City, IA 51041-1996	1882	$14,290	$4,130	2-B	1,313	118
Northwestern Coll, St. Paul, MN 55113-1598	1902	$17,400	$5,620	2-B	2,448	177
Northwestern Oklahoma State Univ, Alva, OK 73717-2799	1897	$2,323 (S)	$2,600	5-M	2,013	131
Northwestern State Univ of Louisiana, Natchitoches, LA 71497	1884	$2,645 (S)	$3,266	5-D	10,159	256
Northwestern Univ, Evanston, IL 60208	1851	$28,524	$8,967	1-D	16,032	1,142
Northwest Missouri State Univ, Maryville, MO 64468-6001	1905	$4,110 (S)	$4,556	5-M	6,514	247
Northwest Nazarene Univ, Nampa, ID 83686-5897	1913	$15,920	$4,440	2-M	1,470	90
Northwood Univ, Midland, MI 48640-2398	1959	$13,995	$6,270	1-M	3,627	66
Northwood Univ, Texas Campus, Cedar Hill, TX 75104-1204	1966	$13,995	$6,140	1-B	1,179	32
Norwich Univ, Northfield, VT 05663	1819	$18,209	$6,722	1-M	2,707	272
Notre Dame de Namur Univ, Belmont, CA 94002-1997	1851	$20,150	$9,370	2-M	1,799	176
Nova Southeastern Univ, Fort Lauderdale, FL 33314-7721	1964	$13,880	$6,484	1-D	21,619	1,372
Nyack Coll, Nyack, NY 10960-3698	1882	$13,790	$6,600	2-F	2,618	184
Oakland City Univ, Oakland City, IN 47660-1099	1885	$12,320	$4,560	2-D	1,897	150
Oakland Univ, Rochester, MI 48309-4401	1957	$5,031 (S)	$5,252	5-D	16,059	806
Oakwood Coll, Huntsville, AL 35896	1896	$10,194	$5,852	2-B	1,778	161
Oberlin Coll, Oberlin, OH 44074	1833	$28,050	$7,830	1-M	2,861	292
Occidental Coll, Los Angeles, CA 90041-3314	1887	$26,448	$7,448	1-M	1,832	201
Oglethorpe Univ, Atlanta, GA 30319-2797	1835	$19,440	$6,360	1-M	1,115	121
Ohio Dominican Univ, Columbus, OH 43219-2099	1911	$17,200	$5,500	2-M	2,317	163
Ohio Northern Univ, Ada, OH 45810-1599	1871	$23,310	$5,805	2-F	3,430	291
The Ohio State Univ, Columbus, OH 43210	1870	$5,664 (S)	$6,291	5-D	49,676	3,542
The Ohio State Univ at Lima, Lima, OH 45804-3576	1960	$3,927 (S)	NA	5-B	1,412	91
The Ohio State Univ at Marion, Marion, OH 43302-5695	1958	$3,927 (S)	NA	5-B	1,390	95
The Ohio State Univ-Mansfield Campus, Mansfield, OH 44906-1599	1958	$3,927 (S)	NA	5-B	1,495	64
The Ohio State Univ-Newark Campus, Newark, OH 43055-1797	1957	$3,927 (S)	NA	5-B	2,079	89
Ohio Univ, Athens, OH 45701-2979	1804	$6,336 (S)	$6,777	5-D	20,528	1,158
Ohio Univ-Chillicothe, Chillicothe, OH 45601-0629	1946	$3,564 (S)	NA	5-M	1,999	106
Ohio Univ-Eastern, St. Clairsville, OH 43950-9724	1957	$3,564 (S)	NA	5-B	1,118	114
Ohio Univ-Lancaster, Lancaster, OH 43130-1097	1968	$4,095 (S)	NA	5-M	1,744	104
Ohio Univ-Southern Campus, Ironton, OH 45638-2214	1956	$3,282 (S)	NA	5-M	1,746	155
Ohio Univ-Zanesville, Zanesville, OH 43701-2695	1946	$3,564 (S)	NA	5-M	1,635	155
Ohio Wesleyan Univ, Delaware, OH 43015	1842	$24,200	$7,010	2-B	1,935	183
Oklahoma Baptist Univ, Shawnee, OK 74804	1910	$11,040	$3,750	2-M	1,933	119
Oklahoma Christian Univ, Oklahoma City, OK 73136-1100	1950	$12,700	$4,500	2-M	1,718	204
Oklahoma City Univ, Oklahoma City, OK 73106-1402	1904	$12,000	$5,200	2-F	3,529	304
Oklahoma Panhandle State Univ, Goodwell, OK 73939-0430	1909	$2,172 (S)	$2,810	5-B	1,226	65
Oklahoma State Univ, Stillwater, OK 74078	1890	$3,025 (S)	$5,150	5-D	22,992	1,122
Old Dominion Univ, Norfolk, VA 23529	1930	$4,264 (S)	$5,498	5-D	20,105	879
Olivet Nazarene Univ, Bourbonnais, IL 60914-2271	1907	$14,980	$5,500	2-M	3,863	123

Name, address	Year Founded	Tuition & Fees	Rm. & Board	Control, Degree	Enroll- ment	Faculty
Oral Roberts Univ, Tulsa, OK 74171-0001	1963	$12,980	$5,570	2-D	3,542	289
Oregon Health & Sci Univ, Portland, OR 97239-3098	1974	$6,005 (S)	NA	12-D	1,849	836
Oregon Inst of Tech, Klamath Falls, OR 97601-8801	1947	$3,672 (S)	$5,515	5-B	3,139	203
Oregon State Univ, Corvallis, OR 97331	1868	$4,014 (S)	$5,976	5-D	18,789	789
Otis Coll of Art & Design, Los Angeles, CA 90045-9785	1918	$22,892	NA	1-M	1,001	185
Otterbein Coll, Westerville, OH 43081	1847	$20,133	$5,952	2-M	3,064	249
Ouachita Baptist Univ, Arkadelphia, AR 71998-0001	1886	$12,800	$4,600	2-B	1,653	163
Our Lady of Holy Cross Coll, New Orleans, LA 70131-7399	1916	$6,900	NA	2-M	1,390	115
Our Lady of the Lake Coll, Baton Rouge, LA 70808 (4)	1990	$250	NA	2-B	1,421	122
Our Lady of the Lake Univ of San Antonio, San Antonio, TX 78207-4689	1895	$15,076	$5,082	2-D	3,395	264
Pace Univ, New York, NY 10038	1906	$18,180	$7,590	1-D	14,095	1,190
Pacific Lutheran Univ, Tacoma, WA 98447	1890	$18,500	$5,870	2-M	3,385	275
Pacific Union Coll, Angwin, CA 94508-9707	1882	$17,355	$4,902	2-M	1,488	115
Pacific Univ, Forest Grove, OR 97116-1797	1849	$19,292	$5,379	1-D	2,414	136
Palm Beach Atlantic Univ, West Palm Beach, FL 33416-4708	1968	$14,850	$5,737	2-F	2,784	216
Palmer Coll of Chiropractic, Davenport, IA 52803-5287	1897	$18,945	NA	1-F	1,798	87
Park Univ, Parkville, MO 64152-3795	1875	$5,152	$5,180	1-M	10,123	765
Parsons School of Design, New School Univ, New York, NY 10011-8878	1896	$24,475	$9,396	1-M	2,958	757
Peirce Coll, Philadelphia, PA 19102-4699 (4)	1865	$11,200	NA	1-B	1,720	108
Pennsylvania Coll of Tech, Williamsport, PA 17701-5778	1965	$9,540 (S)	$5,942	12-B	5,963	436
The Pennsylvania State Univ Abington Coll, Abington, PA 19001-3918	1950	$8,238 (S)	NA	12-B	3,319	213
The Pennsylvania State Univ Altoona Coll, Altoona, PA 16601-3760	1939	$8,248 (S)	$5,660	12-B	3,885	269
The Pennsylvania State Univ at Erie, The Behrend Coll, Erie, PA 16563-0001	1948	$8,382 (S)	$5,660	12-M	3,710	268
The Pennsylvania State Univ Berks Campus of the Berks-Lehigh Valley Coll, Reading, PA 19610-6009	1924	$8,248 (S)	$5,660	12-B	2,471	175
The Pennsylvania State Univ Harrisburg Campus of the Capital Coll, Middletown, PA 17057-4898	1966	$8,362 (S)	$6,950	12-D	3,258	251
The Pennsylvania State Univ Schuylkill Campus of the Capital Coll, Schuylkill Haven, PA 17972-2208	1934	$8,110 (S)	$5,664	12-B	1,101	85
The Pennsylvania State Univ Univ Park Campus, University Park, PA 16802-1503	1855	$8,382 (S)	$5,560	12-D	41,445	2,478
Pepperdine Univ, Malibu, CA 90263-0002	1937	$26,370	$7,930	2-D	7,791	698
Peru State Coll, Peru, NE 68421	1867	$2,902 (S)	$4,010	5-M	1,687	87
Pfeiffer Univ, Misenheimer, NC 28109-0960	1885	$12,780	$5,120	2-M	1,892	117
Philadelphia Biblical Univ, Langhorne, PA 19047-2990	1913	$12,745	$5,650	2-F	1,425	124
Philadelphia Univ, Philadelphia, PA 19144-5497	1884	$18,804	$7,370	1-M	3,154	395
Piedmont Coll, Demorest, GA 30535-0010	1897	$12,500	$4,400	2-M	1,998	174
Pikeville Coll, Pikeville, KY 41501	1889	$9,000	$4,600	2-F	1,201	78
Pittsburg State Univ, Pittsburg, KS 66762	1903	$2,534 (S)	$2,003	5-M	6,751	269
Plattsburgh State Univ of New York, Plattsburgh, NY 12901-2681	1889	$4,229 (S)	$5,920	5-M	6,238	428
Plymouth State Coll, Plymouth, NH 03264-1595	1871	$5,856 (S)	$5,768	5-M	4,629	298
Point Loma Nazarene Univ, San Diego, CA 92106-2899	1902	$16,260	$6,380	2-M	2,998	281
Point Park Coll, Pittsburgh, PA 15222-1984	1960	$14,348	$6,098	1-M	3,132	339
Polytechnic Univ, Brooklyn Campus, Brooklyn, NY 11201-2990	1854	$24,480	$8,000	1-D	3,032	311
Polytechnic Univ of Puerto Rico, Hato Rey, PR 00919	1966	$5,190	NA	1-M	5,511	271
Pomona Coll, Claremont, CA 91711	1887	$26,020	$9,600	1-B	1,551	210
Pontifical Catholic Univ of Puerto Rico, Ponce, PR 00717-0777	1948	$4,458	$2,840	2-D	7,150	236
Portland State Univ, Portland, OR 97207-0751	1946	$102/credit(S)	NA	5-D	21,841	1,101
Prairie View A&M Univ, Prairie View, TX 77446-0519	1878	$3,232 (S)	$6,461	5-D	7,255	364
Pratt Inst, Brooklyn, NY 11205-3899	1887	$24,148	$8,186	1-F	4,439	763
Presbyterian Coll, Clinton, SC 29325	1880	$19,144	$5,508	2-B	1,217	113
Prescott Coll, Prescott, AZ 86301-2990	1966	$15,140	NA	1-M	1,031	59
Princeton Univ, Princeton, NJ 08544-1019	1746	$27,230	$7,842	1-D	6,790	990
Providence Coll, Providence, RI 02918	1917	$20,860	$8,120	2-M	5,275	321
Purchase Coll, State Univ of New York, Purchase, NY 10577-1400	1967	$4,227 (S)	$6,860	5-M	4,063	332
Purdue Univ, West Lafayette, IN 47907	1869	$5,580 (S)	$6,340	5-D	38,546	1,924
Purdue Univ Calumet, Hammond, IN 46323-2094	1951	$4,415 (S)	NA	5-M	8,863	291
Purdue Univ North Central, Westville, IN 46391-9542	1967	$3,590 (S)	NA	5-M	3,658	242
Queens Coll of the City Univ of New York, Flushing, NY 11367-1597	1937	$3,561 (S)	NA	11-M	16,604	1,120
Queens Univ of Charlotte, Charlotte, NC 28274-0002	1857	$15,650	$6,190	2-M	1,753	93
Quincy Univ, Quincy, IL 62301-2699	1860	$16,360	$5,320	2-M	1,192	102
Quinnipiac Univ, Hamden, CT 06518-1940	1929	$19,890	$8,980	1-F	6,951	452
Radford Univ, Radford, VA 24142	1910	$3,844 (S)	$5,442	5-M	9,242	536
Ramapo Coll of New Jersey, Mahwah, NJ 07430-1680	1969	$6,775 (S)	$7,722	5-M	5,494	352
Randolph-Macon Coll, Ashland, VA 23005-5505	1830	$20,045	$5,715	2-B	1,154	139
Reed Coll, Portland, OR 97202-8199	1908	$27,560	$7,380	1-M	1,389	128
Regis Coll, Weston, MA 02493 (3)	1927	$19,000	$8,675	2-M	1,045	98
Regis Univ, Denver, CO 80221-1099	1877	$19,550	$7,500	2-M	11,460	1,225
Reinhardt Coll, Waleska, GA 30183-2981	1883	$9,840	$5,380	2-B	1,118	113
Rensselaer Polytechnic Inst, Troy, NY 12180-3590	1824	$27,170	$8,902	1-D	7,687	476
Rhode Island Coll, Providence, RI 02908-1991	1854	$3,761 (S)	$6,136	5-D	8,758	636
Rhode Island School of Design, Providence, RI 02903-2784	1877	$24,765	$7,049	1-F	2,204	441
Rhodes Coll, Memphis, TN 38112-1690	1848	$22,938	$6,382	2-M	1,553	162
Rice Univ, Houston, TX 77251-1892	1912	$17,526	$7,480	1-D	4,785	783
The Richard Stockton Coll of New Jersey, Pomona, NJ 08240-0195	1969	$4,352 (S)	$6,290	5-M	6,538	359
Rider Univ, Lawrenceville, NJ 08648-3001	1865	$21,050	$8,060	1-M	5,469	459
Ringling School of Art & Design, Sarasota, FL 34234-5895	1931	$17,420	$8,544	1-B	1,015	115
Rivier Coll, Nashua, NH 03060-5086	1933	$18,355	$6,916	2-M	2,331	209
Roanoke Coll, Salem, VA 24153-3794	1842	$19,716	$6,338	2-B	1,822	163
Robert Morris Coll, Chicago, IL 60605	1913	$13,500	NA	1-B	5,231	349
Robert Morris Univ, Moon Township, PA 15108-1189	1921	$12,720	$6,752	1-D	4,726	301
Roberts Wesleyan Coll, Rochester, NY 14624-1997	1866	$15,774	$5,746	2-M	1,835	184
Rochester Inst of Tech, Rochester, NY 14623-5698	1829	$19,815	$7,527	1-D	14,634	1,148
Rockford Coll, Rockford, IL 61108-2393	1847	$20,210	$6,581	1-M	1,280	162
Rockhurst Univ, Kansas City, MO 64110-2561	1910	$16,380	$5,200	2-M	2,870	226
Rogers State Univ, Claremore, OK 74017-3252	1909	$1,839 (S)	$3,321	5-B	3,300	151
Roger Williams Univ, Bristol, RI 02809	1956	$21,110	$9,375	1-F	4,851	351
Rollins Coll, Winter Park, FL 32789-4499	1885	$24,958	$7,652	1-M	2,505	228
Roosevelt Univ, Chicago, IL 60605-1394	1945	$14,660	$6,500	1-D	7,321	662
Rose-Hulman Inst of Tech, Terre Haute, IN 47803-3920 (2)	1874	$23,425	$6,348	1-M	1,804	133
Rosemont Coll, Rosemont, PA 19010-1699 (3)	1921	$18,575	$8,000	2-M	1,066	171
Rowan Univ, Glassboro, NJ 08028-1701	1923	$6,658 (S)	$6,846	5-D	9,685	764
Rush Univ, Chicago, IL 60612-3832	1969	$14,880	$7,250	1-D	1,232	796

Name, address	Year Founded	Tuition & Fees	Rm. & Board	Control, Degree	Enrollment	Faculty
Rutgers, The State Univ of New Jersey, Camden, Camden, NJ 08102-1401	1927	$7,126 (S)	$7,106	5-F	5,248	380
Rutgers, The State Univ of New Jersey, Newark, Newark, NJ 07102	1892	$7,007 (S)	$7,570	5-D	10,346	604
Rutgers, The State Univ of New Jersey, New Brunswick, New Brunswick, NJ 08901-1281	1766	$7,308 (S)	$6,970	5-D	35,886	2,229
Sacred Heart Univ, Fairfield, CT 06432-1000	1963	$19,260	$8,430	2-M	6,028	454
Sage Coll of Albany, Albany, NY 12208-3425	1957	$14,320	$6,626	1-B	1,097	60
Saginaw Valley State Univ, University Center, MI 48710	1963	$4,940 (S)	$5,485	5-M	9,189	240
St. Ambrose Univ, Davenport, IA 52803-2898	1882	$16,650	$6,150	2-D	3,500	269
Saint Anselm Coll, Manchester, NH 03102-1310	1889	$22,160	$8,090	2-B	1,956	165
St. Augustine Coll, Chicago, IL 60640-3501	1980	$7,000	NA	1-B	1,769	164
Saint Augustine's Coll, Raleigh, NC 27604-2298	1867	$8,280	$4,960	2-B	1,502	118
St. Bonaventure Univ, St. Bonaventure, NY 14778-2284	1858	$17,925	$6,530	2-M	2,719	203
St. Cloud State Univ, St. Cloud, MN 56301-4498	1869	$3,998 (S)	$3,788	5-M	15,719	809
St. Edward's Univ, Austin, TX 78704-6489	1885	$13,620	$5,960	2-M	4,267	368
St. Francis Coll, Brooklyn Heights, NY 11201-4398	1884	$10,180	NA	2-B	2,512	233
Saint Francis Univ, Loretto, PA 15940-0600	1847	$18,024	$7,346	2-M	2,003	117
St. John Fisher Coll, Rochester, NY 14618-3597	1948	$17,550	$7,500	2-M	3,072	301
Saint John's Univ, Collegeville, MN 56321 (2)	1857	$19,226	$5,554	2-F	2,046	178
St. John's Univ, Jamaica, NY 11439	1870	$18,330	$9,700	2-D	19,288	1,219
Saint Joseph Coll, West Hartford, CT 06117-2700 (3)	1932	$19,610	$8,210	2-M	1,778	83
St. Joseph's Coll, New York, Brooklyn, NY 11205-3688	1916	$10,400	NA	1-M	1,198	139
St. Joseph's Coll, Suffolk Campus, Patchogue, NY 11772-2399	1916	$10,675	NA	1-M	3,653	295
Saint Joseph's Univ, Philadelphia, PA 19131-1395	1851	$22,545	$9,040	2-D	7,315	440
St. Lawrence Univ, Canton, NY 13617-1455	1856	$26,480	$7,755	1-M	2,293	202
Saint Leo Univ, Saint Leo, FL 33574-6665	1889	$13,170	$6,834	2-M	1,346	112
Saint Louis Univ, St. Louis, MO 63103-2097	1818	$21,008	$7,310	2-D	11,272	930
Saint Martin's Coll, Lacey, WA 98503-7500	1895	$17,890	$5,355	2-M	1,547	67
Saint Mary-of-the-Woods Coll, Saint Mary-of-the-Woods, IN 47876 (3)	1840	$16,370	$6,009	2-M	1,612	62
Saint Mary's Coll, Notre Dame, IN 46556 (3)	1844	$21,974	$7,289	2-B	1,492	189
Saint Mary's Coll of California, Moraga, CA 94575	1863	$20,885	$8,550	2-D	4,442	514
St. Mary's Coll of Maryland, St. Mary's City, MD 20686-3001	1840	$8,082 (S)	$6,613	5-B	1,823	177
Saint Mary's Univ of Minnesota, Winona, MN 55987-1399	1912	$15,695	$4,920	2-D	5,065	513
St. Mary's Univ of San Antonio, San Antonio, TX 78228-8507	1852	$15,227	$6,246	2-D	4,243	324
Saint Michael's Coll, Colchester, VT 05439	1904	$21,200	$7,255	2-M	2,637	194
St. Norbert Coll, De Pere, WI 54115-2099	1898	$19,084	$5,440	2-M	2,133	181
St. Olaf Coll, Northfield, MN 55057-1098	1874	$23,650	$4,850	2-B	3,041	322
Saint Peter's Coll, Jersey City, NJ 07306-5997	1872	$18,592	$7,800	2-M	3,054	261
St. Thomas Aquinas Coll, Sparkill, NY 10976	1952	$14,820	$8,260	1-M	2,140	150
St. Thomas Univ, Miami, FL 33054-6459	1961	$15,450	$5,040	2-F	2,365	242
Saint Vincent Coll, Latrobe, PA 15650-2690	1846	$18,430	$5,784	2-M	1,413	115
Saint Xavier Univ, Chicago, IL 60655-3105	1847	$15,930	$6,233	2-M	5,278	352
Salem Coll, Winston-Salem, NC 27108-0548 (3)	1772	$14,995	$8,870	2-M	1,027	86
Salem State Coll, Salem, MA 01970-5353	1854	$3,988 (S)	$5,248	5-M	8,793	529
Salisbury Univ, Salisbury, MD 21801-6837	1925	$6,214 (S)	$6,356	5-M	6,851	471
Salve Regina Univ, Newport, RI 02840-4192	1934	$19,410	$8,400	2-D	2,283	262
Samford Univ, Birmingham, AL 35229-0002	1841	$12,294	$4,994	2-D	4,366	408
Sam Houston State Univ, Huntsville, TX 77341	1879	$3,382 (S)	$4,090	5-D	13,091	537
San Diego State Univ, San Diego, CA 92182	1897	$2,014 (S)	$8,307	5-D	34,304	1,947
San Francisco State Univ, San Francisco, CA 94132-1722	1899	$1,826 (S)	$6,930	5-D	28,378	1,738
San Jose State Univ, San Jose, CA 95192-0001	1857	$2,059 (S)	$7,583	5-M	28,955	1,827
Santa Clara Univ, Santa Clara, CA 95053	1851	$24,185	$8,904	2-D	7,811	645
Sarah Lawrence Coll, Bronxville, NY 10708	1926	$29,360	$10,010	1-M	1,556	229
Savannah Coll of Art & Design, Savannah, GA 31402-3146	1978	$19,035	$8,175	1-M	5,792	316
Savannah State Univ, Savannah, GA 31404	1890	$2,628 (S)	$4,386	5-M	2,360	138
School of the Art Inst of Chicago, Chicago, IL 60603-3103	1866	$22,500	$6,825	1-M	2,698	491
School of the Museum of Fine Arts, Boston, MA 02115	1876	$20,103	$9,800	1-M	1,085	104
School of Visual Arts, New York, NY 10010-3994	1947	$17,830	$8,000	3-M	5,243	848
Seattle Pacific Univ, Seattle, WA 98119-1997	1891	$17,682	$6,660	2-D	3,684	283
Seattle Univ, Seattle, WA 98122	1891	$18,855	$7,902	2-D	6,337	460
Seton Hall Univ, South Orange, NJ 07079-2697	1856	$20,830	$9,268	2-D	9,596	841
Seton Hill Univ, Greensburg, PA 15601	1883	$17,370	$5,900	2-M	1,564	143
Shawnee State Univ, Portsmouth, OH 45662-4344	1986	$4,869 (S)	$5,421	5-B	3,606	263
Shaw Univ, Raleigh, NC 27601-2399	1865	$8,898	$5,488	2-M	2,683	234
Shenandoah Univ, Winchester, VA 22601-5195	1875	$17,510	$6,600	2-D	2,583	301
Shepherd Coll, Shepherdstown, WV 25443-3210	1871	$2,866 (S)	$4,738	5-B	4,676	337
Shippensburg Univ of Pennsylvania, Shippensburg, PA 17257-2299	1871	$5,502 (S)	$4,864	5-M	7,412	368
Siena Coll, Loudonville, NY 12211-1462	1937	$16,945	$7,010	2-B	3,405	313
Siena Heights Univ, Adrian, MI 49221-1796	1919	$13,630	$5,130	2-M	2,024	NA
Silver Lake Coll, Manitowoc, WI 54220-9319	1869	$14,350	$4,100	2-M	1,146	128
Simmons Coll, Boston, MA 02115 (3)	1899	$22,668	$9,100	1-D	3,315	351
Simpson Coll, Indianola, IA 50125-1297	1860	$16,649	$5,561	2-B	1,845	142
Simpson Coll & Graduate School, Redding, CA 96003-8606	1921	$14,760	$5,740	2-M	1,265	76
Skidmore Coll, Saratoga Springs, NY 12866-1632	1903	$27,980	$7,835	1-M	2,557	203
Slippery Rock Univ of Pennsylvania, Slippery Rock, PA 16057	1889	$5,548 (S)	$4,400	5-D	7,530	405
Smith Coll, Northampton, MA 01063 (3)	1871	$25,986	$8,950	1-D	3,121	303
Sojourner-Douglass Coll, Baltimore, MD 21205-1814 (4)	1980	$5,590	NA	1-M	1,124	136
Sonoma State Univ, Rohnert Park, CA 94928-3609	1960	$2,226 (S)	$7,294	5-M	8,162	590
South Carolina State Univ, Orangeburg, SC 29117-0001	1896	$4,556 (S)	$4,145	5-D	4,568	216
South Dakota School of Mines & Tech, Rapid City, SD 57701-3995	1885	$4,092 (S)	$3,484	5-D	2,447	125
South Dakota State Univ, Brookings, SD 57007	1881	$4,536 (S)	$3,586	5-D	9,952	508
Southeastern Coll of the Assemblies of God, Lakeland, FL 33801-6099	1935	$8,312	$4,606	2-B	1,458	101
Southeastern Louisiana Univ, Hammond, LA 70402	1925	$2,618 (S)	$3,720	5-M	15,205	682
Southeastern Oklahoma State Univ, Durant, OK 74701-0609	1909	$2,404 (S)	$2,670	5-M	4,033	226
Southeast Missouri State Univ, Cape Girardeau, MO 63701-4799	1873	$4,035 (S)	$4,938	5-M	9,534	517
Southern Adventist Univ, Collegedale, TN 37315-0370	1892	$12,800	$4,280	2-M	2,290	195
Southern Arkansas Univ-Magnolia, Magnolia, AR 71753	1909	$3,064 (S)	$3,220	5-M	3,013	165
Southern Connecticut State Univ, New Haven, CT 06515-1355	1893	$4,444 (S)	$6,537	5-M	12,219	744
Southern Illinois Univ Carbondale, Carbondale, IL 62901-6806	1869	$5,521 (S)	$4,903	5-D	21,873	1,112
Southern Illinois Univ Edwardsville, Edwardsville, IL 62026-0001	1957	$4,021 (S)	$5,364	5-F	12,708	742
Southern Methodist Univ, Dallas, TX 75275	1911	$21,942	$7,954	2-D	10,955	776
Southern Nazarene Univ, Bethany, OK 73008	1899	$11,990	$4,958	2-M	2,120	203
Southern New Hampshire Univ, Manchester, NH 03106-1045	1932	$17,656	$7,340	1-D	5,611	265

Name, address	Year Founded	Tuition & Fees	Rm. & Board	Control, Degree	Enrollment	Faculty
Southern Oregon Univ, Ashland, OR 97520	1926	$3,687 (S)	$5,665	5-M	5,478	320
Southern Polytechnic State Univ, Marietta, GA 30060-2896	1948	$2,452 (S)	$4,806	5-M	3,683	200
Southern Univ & Agr & Mech Coll, Baton Rouge, LA 70813	1880	$2,702 (S)	$4,306	5-D	8,572	546
Southern Univ at New Orleans, New Orleans, LA 70126-1009	1959	$2,160 (S)	NA	5-M	5,000	NA
Southern Utah Univ, Cedar City, UT 84720-2498	1897	$2,350 (S)	$5,224	5-M	5,881	305
Southern Wesleyan Univ, Central, SC 29630-1020	1906	$13,450	$4,700	2-M	2,301	225
Southwest Baptist Univ, Bolivar, MO 65613-2597	1878	$11,609	$3,700	2-M	3,534	295
Southwestern Adventist Univ, Keene, TX 76059	1894	$10,628	$5,020	2-M	1,191	92
Southwestern Assemblies of God Univ, Waxahachie, TX 75165-2397	1927	$8,648	$4,470	2-M	1,676	95
Southwestern Coll, Winfield, KS 67156-2499	1885	$13,922	$4,736	2-M	1,298	115
Southwestern Oklahoma State Univ, Weatherford, OK 73096-3098	1901	$2,448 (S)	$2,680	5-F	4,652	228
Southwestern Univ, Georgetown, TX 78626	1840	$17,570	$6,240	2-B	1,266	150
Southwest Missouri State Univ, Springfield, MO 65804-0094	1905	$4,708 (S)	$4,850	5-M	18,718	1,000
Southwest State Univ, Marshall, MN 56258-1598	1963	$4,091 (S)	$4,248	5-M	5,636	159
Southwest Texas State Univ, San Marcos, TX 78666	1899	$3,750 (S)	$5,524	5-D	25,055	1,033
Spalding Univ, Louisville, KY 40203-2188	1814	$12,946	$1,670	2-D	1,702	213
Spelman Coll, Atlanta, GA 30314-4399 (3)	1881	$12,675	$7,300	1-B	2,121	204
Spring Arbor Univ, Spring Arbor, MI 49283-9799	1873	$14,016	$5,080	2-M	3,124	91
Springfield Coll, Springfield, MA 01109-3797	1885	$18,690	$6,740	1-D	3,130	346
Spring Hill Coll, Mobile, AL 36608-1791	1830	$18,092	$6,540	2-M	1,467	122
Stanford Univ, Stanford, CA 94305-9991	1891	$27,204	$8,680	1-D	14,297	1,714
State Univ of New York at Albany, Albany, NY 12222-0001	1844	$4,820 (S)	$7,052	5-D	17,426	942
State Univ of New York at Binghamton, Binghamton, NY 13902-6000	1946	$4,717 (S)	$6,412	5-D	13,099	722
State Univ of New York at New Paltz, New Paltz, NY 12561	1828	$4,166 (S)	$6,110	5-M	8,019	611
State Univ of New York at Oswego, Oswego, NY 13126	1861	$4,194 (S)	$7,194	5-M	8,716	474
State Univ of New York Coll at Brockport, Brockport, NY 14420-2997	1867	$4,271 (S)	$6,520	5-M	8,862	603
State Univ of New York Coll at Buffalo, Buffalo, NY 14222-1095	1867	$4,109 (S)	$5,640	5-M	11,803	716
State Univ of New York Coll at Cortland, Cortland, NY 13045	1868	$4,265 (S)	$6,700	5-M	7,472	531
State Univ of New York Coll at Fredonia, Fredonia, NY 14063-1136	1826	$4,375 (S)	$5,800	5-M	5,301	418
State Univ of New York Coll at Geneseo, Geneseo, NY 14454-1401	1871	$4,440 (S)	$5,940	5-M	5,668	356
State Univ of New York Coll at Old Westbury, Old Westbury, NY 11568-0210	1965	$3,988 (S)	$5,837	5-B	3,142	216
State Univ of New York Coll at Oneonta, Oneonta, NY 13820-4015	1889	$4,306 (S)	$6,158	5-M	5,728	405
State Univ of New York Coll at Potsdam, Potsdam, NY 13676	1816	$4,215 (S)	$6,620	5-M	4,444	345
State Univ of New York Coll of Agriculture & Tech at Cobleskill, Cobleskill, NY 12043	1916	$4,261 (S)	$6,600	5-B	2,443	163
State Univ of New York Coll of Environmental Sci & Forestry, Syracuse, NY 13210-2779	1911	$3,862 (S)	$9,040	5-D	1,909	119
State Univ of New York Empire State Coll, Saratoga Springs, NY 12866-4391	1971	$3,555 (S)	NA	5-M	10,585	615
State Univ of New York Inst of Tech at Utica/Rome, Utica, NY 13504-3050	1966	$4,418 (S)	$6,560	5-M	2,628	168
State Univ of New York Upstate Medical Univ, Syracuse, NY 13210-2334	1950	$5,078 (S)	$7,785	5-D	1,136	695
State Univ of West Georgia, Carrollton, GA 30118	1933	$2,558 (S)	$4,244	5-D	9,673	455
Stephen F. Austin State Univ, Nacogdoches, TX 75962	1923	$2,486 (S)	$4,546	5-D	11,356	591
Stetson Univ, DeLand, FL 32723	1883	$22,380	$6,855	1-F	3,318	260
Stevens Inst of Tech, Hoboken, NJ 07030	1870	$24,750	$6,100	1-D	4,597	300
Stillman Coll, Tuscaloosa, AL 35403-9990	1876	$8,048	$4,236	2-B	1,458	86
Stonehill Coll, Easton, MA 02357-5510	1948	$19,908	$9,172	2-M	2,617	230
Stony Brook Univ, State Univ of New York, Stony Brook, NY 11794	1957	$4,358 (S)	$6,974	5-D	21,989	1,339
Strayer Univ, Washington, DC 20005-2603	1892	$8,930	NA	3-M	16,451	713
Suffolk Univ, Boston, MA 02108-2770	1906	$17,690	$10,290	1-D	5,941	602
Sullivan Univ, Louisville, KY 40205	1864	$11,695	$3,555	3-M	4,720	136
Sul Ross State Univ, Alpine, TX 79832	1920	$3,032 (S)	$3,850	5-M	1,954	133
Susquehanna Univ, Selinsgrove, PA 17870	1858	$22,240	$6,260	2-B	1,995	169
Swarthmore Coll, Swarthmore, PA 19081-1397	1864	$27,562	$8,530	1-B	1,479	200
Syracuse Univ, Syracuse, NY 13244-0003	1870	$23,424	$9,510	1-D	14,830	1,392
Tarleton State Univ, Stephenville, TX 76402	1899	$3,444 (S)	$4,896	5-M	8,320	453
Taylor Univ, Upland, IN 46989-1001	1846	$17,490	$5,130	2-B	1,869	157
Teikyo Post Univ, Waterbury, CT 06723-2540	1890	$16,500	$6,600	1-B	1,378	298
Temple Univ, Philadelphia, PA 19122-6096	1884	$8,062 (S)	$7,112	12-D	32,351	2,187
Tennessee State Univ, Nashville, TN 37209-1561	1912	$3,297 (S)	$3,600	5-D	8,881	531
Tennessee Tech Univ, Cookeville, TN 38505	1915	$3,288 (S)	$4,798	5-D	8,890	534
Texas A&M Intl Univ, Laredo, TX 78041-1900	1969	$3,301 (S)	$3,210	5-M	3,753	228
Texas A&M Univ, College Station, TX 77843	1876	$4,748 (S)	$6,030	5-D	45,083	2,276
Texas A&M Univ at Galveston, Galveston, TX 77553-1675	1962	$3,465 (S)	$4,692	5-M	1,556	120
Texas A&M Univ-Commerce, Commerce, TX 75429-3011	1889	$3,988 (S)	$4,786	5-D	8,487	548
Texas A&M Univ-Corpus Christi, Corpus Christi, TX 78412-5503	1947	$78/sem. hr.(S)	NA	5-D	7,607	439
Texas A&M Univ-Kingsville, Kingsville, TX 78363	1925	$2,982 (S)	$3,966	5-D	6,559	412
Texas A&M Univ-Texarkana, Texarkana, TX 75505-5518	1971	$2,004 (S)	NA	5-M	1,385	91
Texas Christian Univ, Fort Worth, TX 76129-0002	1873	$16,340	$5,302	2-D	8,074	599
Texas Lutheran Univ, Seguin, TX 78155-5999	1891	$14,550	$4,442	2-B	1,368	118
Texas Southern Univ, Houston, TX 77004-4584	1947	$2,298 (S)	$3,322	5-D	9,739	326
Texas Tech Univ, Lubbock, TX 79409	1923	$3,867 (S)	$5,497	5-D	27,569	1,067
Texas Wesleyan Univ, Fort Worth, TX 76105-1536	1890	$11,960	$5,242	2-F	2,813	226
Texas Woman's Univ, Denton, TX 76201 (4)	1901	$3,272 (S)	$4,683	5-D	8,694	443
Thiel Coll, Greenville, PA 16125-2181	1866	$13,428	$6,454	2-B	1,279	101
Thomas Edison State Coll, Trenton, NJ 08608-1176	1972	$3,025/year(S)	NA	5-M	9,225	NA
Thomas Jefferson Univ, Philadelphia, PA 19107	1824	$18,614	$8,440	1-M	2,272	212
Thomas More Coll, Crestview Hills, KY 41017-3495	1921	$14,600	$5,300	2-M	1,402	121
Tiffin Univ, Tiffin, OH 44883-2161	1888	$13,590	$5,900	1-M	1,533	232
Touro Coll, New York, NY 10010	1971	$10,400	$4,700	1-D	11,447	999
Touro Univ Intl, Cypress, CA 90630	NR	$7,200	NA	1-D	3,082	89
Towson Univ, Towson, MD 21252-0001	1866	$5,654 (S)	$6,322	5-D	17,481	1,288
Transylvania Univ, Lexington, KY 40508-1797	1780	$16,790	$5,940	2-B	1,109	92
Trevecca Nazarene Univ, Nashville, TN 37210-2877	1901	$11,960	$5,408	2-D	1,878	176
Trinity Christian Coll, Palos Heights, IL 60463-0929	1959	$14,640	$5,700	2-B	1,135	110
Trinity Coll, Hartford, CT 06106-3100	1823	$28,602	$7,380	1-M	2,298	251
Trinity Coll, Washington, DC 20017-1094 (3)	1897	$16,380	$7,170	2-M	1,645	184
Trinity Intl Univ, Deerfield, IL 60015-1284	1897	$16,530	$5,510	2-D	2,078	87
Trinity Univ, San Antonio, TX 78212-7200	1869	$17,364	$7,040	2-M	2,621	281
Tri-State Univ, Angola, IN 46703-1764	1884	$16,910	$5,250	1-M	1,267	94
Troy State Univ, Troy, AL 36082	1887	$3,532 (S)	$4,684	5-M	7,500	409
Troy State Univ Dothan, Dothan, AL 36303	1961	$3,532 (S)	NA	5-M	1,891	121

Name, address	Year Founded	Tuition & Fees	Rm. & Board	Control/ Degree	Enroll- ment	Faculty
Troy State Univ Montgomery, Montgomery, AL 36103-4419	1965	$3,290 (S)	NA	5-M	3,295	212
Truman State Univ, Kirksville, MO 63501-4221	1867	$4,200 (S)	$4,928	5-M	5,867	399
Tufts Univ, Medford, MA 02155	1852	$28,155	$8,310	1-D	9,432	1,154
Tulane Univ, New Orleans, LA 70118-5669	1834	$28,310	$7,394	1-D	12,759	962
Tusculum Coll, Greeneville, TN 37743-9997	1794	$13,700	$5,290	2-M	1,886	118
Tuskegee Univ, Tuskegee, AL 36088	1881	$11,310	$5,940	1-D	3,001	250
Union Coll, Schenectady, NY 12308-2311	1795	$27,514	$6,738	1-M	2,512	236
Union Inst & Univ, Cincinnati, OH 45206-1925	1969	$7,291	NA	1-D	2,801	286
Union Univ, Jackson, TN 38305-3697	1823	$13,700	$4,300	2-D	2,575	210
United States Air Force Acad, USAF Academy, CO 80840-5025 (2)	1954	$0 (C)	NA	4-B	4,219	531
United States Military Acad, West Point, NY 10996 (2)	1802	$0 (C)	NA	4-B	4,394	588
United States Naval Acad, Annapolis, MD 21402-5000 (2)	1845	$0 (C)	NA	4-B	4,309	598
Universidad del Turabo, Turabo, PR 00778-3030	1972	NA	NA	1-M	8,065	410
Universidad Metropolitana, Río Piedras, PR 00928-1150	1980	NA	NA	1-M	5,857	358
Univ at Buffalo, The State Univ of New York, Buffalo, NY 14260	1846	$4,850 (S)	$6,512	5-D	26,168	1,990
The Univ of Akron, Akron, OH 44325-0001	1870	$5,798 (S)	$5,959	5-D	24,348	1,647
The Univ of Alabama, Tuscaloosa, AL 35487	1831	$3,556 (S)	$4,232	5-D	19,584	1,062
The Univ of Alabama at Birmingham, Birmingham, AL 35294	1969	$3,880 (S)	$2,588	5-D	15,579	800
The Univ of Alabama in Huntsville, Huntsville, AL 35899	1950	$3,764 (S)	$4,700	5-D	7,045	461
Univ of Alaska Anchorage, Anchorage, AK 99508-8060	1954	$3,329 (S)	$6,030	5-M	15,843	1,297
Univ of Alaska Fairbanks, Fairbanks, AK 99775-7480	1917	$96/credit (S)	NA	5-D	7,661	678
Univ of Alaska Southeast, Juneau, AK 99801	1972	$3,090 (S)	$5,928	5-M	3,470	241
The Univ of Arizona, Tucson, AZ 85721	1885	$2,593 (S)	$6,568	5-D	36,847	1,411
Univ of Arkansas, Fayetteville, AR 72701-1201	1871	$4,456 (S)	$4,810	5-D	15,995	840
Univ of Arkansas at Fort Smith, Fort Smith, AR 72913-3649	1928	$1,830	NA	11-B	6,183	309
Univ of Arkansas at Little Rock, Little Rock, AR 72204-1099	1927	$4,210 (S)	$2,700	5-D	11,488	738
Univ of Arkansas at Monticello, Monticello, AR 71656	1909	$3,175 (S)	$3,100	5-M	2,482	131
Univ of Arkansas at Pine Bluff, Pine Bluff, AR 71601-2799	1873	$2,664 (S)	$4,382	5-M	3,144	217
Univ of Baltimore, Baltimore, MD 21201-5779	1925	$5,190 (S)	NA	5-D	4,792	332
Univ of Bridgeport, Bridgeport, CT 06601	1927	$16,466 (A)	$7,760	1-D	3,173	306
Univ of California, Berkeley, Berkeley, CA 94720-1500	1868	$4,895 (S)	$11,212	5-D	33,145	1,852
Univ of California, Davis, Davis, CA 95616	1905	$4,629 (S)	$8,522	5-D	28,269	1,950
Univ of California, Irvine, Irvine, CA 92697	1965	$4,739 (S)	$7,422	5-D	23,779	1,194
Univ of California, Los Angeles, Los Angeles, CA 90095	1919	$4,378 (S)	$9,480	5-D	37,599	2,427
Univ of California, Riverside, Riverside, CA 92521-0102	1954	$4,421 (S)	$8,232	5-D	15,934	768
Univ of California, San Diego, La Jolla, CA 92093	1959	$4,493 (S)	$8,066	5-D	23,548	1,092
Univ of California, Santa Barbara, Santa Barbara, CA 93106	1909	$3,853 (S)	$8,680	5-D	20,559	998
Univ of California, Santa Cruz, Santa Cruz, CA 95064	1965	$5,607 (S)	$10,389	5-D	14,139	691
Univ of Central Arkansas, Conway, AR 72035-0001	1907	$3,990 (S)	$3,600	5-D	8,553	515
Univ of Central Florida, Orlando, FL 32816	1963	$2,820 (S)	$6,212	5-D	38,598	1,557
Univ of Central Oklahoma, Edmond, OK 73034-5209	1890	$2,210 (S)	$3,600	5-M	14,099	713
Univ of Charleston, Charleston, WV 25304-1099	1888	$16,500	$4,850	1-M	1,004	104
Univ of Chicago, Chicago, IL 60637-1513	1891	$27,825	$8,728	1-D	12,556	1,861
Univ of Cincinnati, Cincinnati, OH 45221	1819	$6,936 (S)	$6,774	5-D	26,552	1,333
Univ of Colorado at Boulder, Boulder, CO 80309	1876	$3,575 (S)	$6,272	5-D	30,983	2,110
Univ of Colorado at Colorado Springs, Colorado Springs, CO 80918	1965	$4,082 (S)	$5,893	5-D	7,407	471
Univ of Colorado at Denver, Denver, CO 80217-3364	1912	$3,240 (S)	NA	5-D	NA	NA
Univ of Colorado Health Sci Ctr, Denver, CO 80262	1883	$5,392 (S)	NA	5-D	2,323	1,700
Univ of Connecticut, Storrs, CT 06269	1881	$6,800 (S)	$6,888	5-D	21,427	1,134
Univ of Dallas, Irving, TX 75062-4736	1955	$17,024	$6,304	2-D	3,170	227
Univ of Dayton, Dayton, OH 45469-1300	1850	$18,000	$5,600	2-D	10,126	801
Univ of Delaware, Newark, DE 19716	1743	$5,640 (S)	$5,822	12-D	20,676	1,406
Univ of Denver, Denver, CO 80208	1864	$23,259	$6,987	1-D	9,229	923
Univ of Detroit Mercy, Detroit, MI 48219-0900	1877	$16,050	$6,750	2-D	6,212	407
Univ of Dubuque, Dubuque, IA 52001-5099	1852	$16,155	$5,420	2-F	1,120	97
Univ of Evansville, Evansville, IN 47722-0002	1854	$18,230	$5,420	2-M	2,668	168
The Univ of Findlay, Findlay, OH 45840-3653	1882	$18,724	$6,792	2-M	4,591	340
Univ of Florida, Gainesville, FL 32611	1853	$2,581 (S)	$5,640	5-D	47,373	1,723
Univ of Georgia, Athens, GA 30602	1785	$3,616 (S)	$5,748	5-D	32,941	1,958
Univ of Guam, Mangilao, GU 96923	1952	NA	NA	7-M	3,748	230
Univ of Hartford, West Hartford, CT 06117-1599	1877	$21,550	$8,316	1-D	6,998	733
Univ of Hawaii at Hilo, Hilo, HI 96720-4091	1970	$2,426 (S)	$5,081	5-M	3,040	243
Univ of Hawaii at Manoa, Honolulu, HI 96822	1907	$3,349 (S)	$5,359	5-D	18,696	1,186
Univ of Houston, Houston, TX 77204	1927	$3,348 (S)	$5,694	5-D	34,443	1,587
Univ of Houston-Clear Lake, Houston, TX 77058-1098	1971	$3,568 (S)	NA	5-M	7,753	554
Univ of Houston-Downtown, Houston, TX 77002-1001	1974	$2,684 (S)	NA	5-M	10,528	528
Univ of Houston-Victoria, Victoria, TX 77901-4450	1973	$2,388 (S)	NA	5-M	2,183	108
Univ of Idaho, Moscow, ID 83844-2282	1889	$3,044 (S)	$4,680	5-D	12,419	611
Univ of Illinois at Chicago, Chicago, IL 60607-7128	1946	$6,442 (S)	$6,428	5-D	26,138	1,508
Univ of Illinois at Springfield, Springfield, IL 62703-5404	1969	$4,009 (S)	$6,370	5-D	4,451	258
Univ of Illinois at Urbana-Champaign, Champaign, IL 61820	1867	$5,748 (S)	$6,360	5-D	39,999	2,564
Univ of Indianapolis, Indianapolis, IN 46227-3697	1902	$15,820	$5,660	2-D	3,776	358
The Univ of Iowa, Iowa City, IA 52242-1316	1847	$4,993 (S)	$5,930	5-D	29,697	1,679
Univ of Kansas, Lawrence, KS 66045	1866	$3,484 (S)	$4,642	5-D	28,196	1,332
Univ of Kentucky, Lexington, KY 40506-0032	1865	$3,975 (S)	$4,050	5-D	25,741	NA
Univ of La Verne, La Verne, CA 91750-4443	1891	$19,500	$7,360	1-D	3,583	266
Univ of Louisiana at Lafayette, Lafayette, LA 70504	1898	$2,440 (S)	$2,896	5-D	16,006	576
Univ of Louisiana at Monroe, Monroe, LA 71209-0001	1931	$2,481 (S)	$5,080	5-D	8,965	NA
Univ of Louisville, Louisville, KY 40292-0001	1798	$4,344 (S)	$5,120	5-D	20,416	1,358
Univ of Maine, Orono, ME 04469	1865	$5,480 (S)	$5,922	5-D	11,135	708
The Univ of Maine at Augusta, Augusta, ME 04330-9410	1965	$4,290 (S)	NA	5-B	5,722	235
Univ of Maine at Farmington, Farmington, ME 04938-1990	1863	$4,482 (S)	$5,064	5-B	2,395	153
Univ of Maine at Machias, Machias, ME 04654-1321	1909	$4,390 (S)	$4,880	5-B	1,068	75
Univ of Maine at Presque Isle, Presque Isle, ME 04769-2888	1903	$3,850 (S)	$4,494	5-B	1,560	123
Univ of Mary, Bismarck, ND 58504-9652	1959	$9,400	$3,735	2-M	2,546	184
Univ of Mary Hardin-Baylor, Belton, TX 76513	1845	$10,640	$4,210	2-M	2,664	197
Univ of Maryland Baltimore County, Baltimore, MD 21250-5398	1963	$6,362 (S)	$6,780	5-D	11,711	763
Univ of Maryland, Coll Park, College Park, MD 20742	1856	$5,670 (S)	$7,241	5-D	34,740	2,146
Univ of Maryland Eastern Shore, Princess Anne, MD 21853-1299	1886	$4,537 (S)	$5,380	5-D	3,426	280
Univ of Maryland Univ Coll, Adelphi, MD 20783	1947	$5,064 (S)	NA	5-D	24,030	1,023

Name, address	Year Founded	Tuition & Fees	Rm. & Board	Control, Degree	Enroll- ment	Faculty
Univ of Massachusetts Amherst, Amherst, MA 01003	1863	$6,482 (S)	$5,630	5-D	24,062	1,256
Univ of Massachusetts Boston, Boston, MA 02125-3393	1964	$5,222 (S)	NA	5-D	12,719	850
Univ of Massachusetts Dartmouth, North Dartmouth, MA 02747-2300	1895	$5,164 (S)	$6,526	5-D	8,122	515
Univ of Massachusetts Lowell, Lowell, MA 01854-2881	1894	$5,213 (S)	$5,464	5-D	12,086	595
The Univ of Memphis, Memphis, TN 38152	1912	$3,792 (S)	$4,380	5-D	19,797	1,319
Univ of Miami, Coral Gables, FL 33124	1925	$24,810	$8,062	1-D	14,978	1,181
Univ of Michigan, Ann Arbor, MI 48109	1817	$7,277 (S)	$6,366	5-D	38,972	2,799
Univ of Michigan-Dearborn, Dearborn, MI 48128-1491	1959	$5,332 (S)	NA	5-M	8,725	503
Univ of Michigan-Flint, Flint, MI 48502-1950	1956	$4,752 (S)	NA	5-F	6,434	400
Univ of Minnesota, Crookston, Crookston, MN 56716-5001	1966	$6,422 (S)	$4,464	5-B	2,387	103
Univ of Minnesota, Duluth, Duluth, MN 55812-2496	1947	$6,467 (S)	$4,960	5-F	9,815	466
Univ of Minnesota, Morris, Morris, MN 56267-2134	1959	$7,259 (S)	$4,680	5-B	1,910	NA
Univ of Minnesota, Twin Cities Campus, Minneapolis, MN 55455-0213	1851	$6,280 (S)	$5,696	5-D	48,677	3,079
Univ of Mississippi, University, MS 38677	1844	$3,916 (S)	$5,200	5-D	13,135	NA
Univ of Mississippi Medical Ctr, Jackson, MS 39216-4505	1955	$2,850 (S)	$1,890	5-D	1,673	2,301
Univ of Missouri-Columbia, Columbia, MO 65211	1839	$5,552 (S)	$5,374	5-D	26,124	1,748
Univ of Missouri-Kansas City, Kansas City, MO 64110-2499	1929	$4,932 (S)	$5,235	5-D	13,881	910
Univ of Missouri-Rolla, Rolla, MO 65409-0910	1870	$5,650 (S)	$5,230	5-D	5,240	354
Univ of Missouri-St. Louis, St. Louis, MO 63121-4499	1963	$4,566 (S)	$5,400	5-D	15,658	661
Univ of Mobile, Mobile, AL 36663-0220	1961	$9,010	$5,000	2-M	2,003	170
The Univ of Montana-Missoula, Missoula, MT 59812-0002	1893	$3,988 (S)	$5,090	5-D	13,026	659
The Univ of Montana-Western, Dillon, MT 59725-3598	1893	$2,875 (S)	$4,500	5-B	1,142	67
Univ of Montevallo, Montevallo, AL 35115	1896	$4,334 (S)	$3,638	5-M	2,935	196
Univ of Nebraska at Kearney, Kearney, NE 68849-0001	1903	$3,383 (S)	$4,156	5-M	6,395	374
Univ of Nebraska at Omaha, Omaha, NE 68182	1908	$3,552 (S)	$4,517	5-D	14,451	849
Univ of Nebraska-Lincoln, Lincoln, NE 68588	1869	$4,125 (S)	$4,875	5-D	22,988	1,071
Univ of Nebraska Medical Ctr, Omaha, NE 68198	1869	$4,497 (S)	NA	5-D	2,724	831
Univ of Nevada, Las Vegas, Las Vegas, NV 89154-9900	1957	$2,736 (S)	$6,367	5-D	24,679	1,383
Univ of Nevada, Reno, Reno, NV 89557	1874	$2,622 (S)	$6,580	5-D	15,093	752
Univ of New England, Biddeford, ME 04005-9526	1831	$19,590	$7,560	1-F	3,097	189
Univ of New Hampshire, Durham, NH 03824	1866	$8,130 (S)	$5,882	5-D	14,248	717
Univ of New Hampshire at Manchester, Manchester, NH 03101-1113	1967	$5,541 (S)	NA	5-B	1,086	108
Univ of New Haven, West Haven, CT 06516-1916	1920	$20,735	$8,500	1-M	4,329	398
Univ of New Mexico, Albuquerque, NM 87131-2039	1889	$3,169 (S)	$5,300	5-D	24,593	1,372
Univ of New Orleans, New Orleans, LA 70148	1958	$3,026 (S)	$3,888	5-D	17,320	588
Univ of North Alabama, Florence, AL 35632-0001	1830	$3,820 (S)	$4,034	5-M	5,416	286
The Univ of North Carolina at Asheville, Asheville, NC 28804-3299	1927	$2,957 (S)	$4,650	5-M	3,391	271
The Univ of North Carolina at Chapel Hill, Chapel Hill, NC 27599	1789	$3,856 (S)	$5,805	5-D	26,028	1,469
The Univ of North Carolina at Charlotte, Charlotte, NC 28223-0001	1946	$2,948 (S)	$4,856	5-D	18,916	1,084
The Univ of North Carolina at Greensboro, Greensboro, NC 27412-5001	1891	$3,006 (S)	$4,656	5-D	13,918	856
The Univ of North Carolina at Pembroke, Pembroke, NC 28372-1510	1887	$2,365 (S)	$4,150	5-M	4,432	276
The Univ of North Carolina at Wilmington, Wilmington, NC 28403-3297	1947	$3,074 (S)	$5,378	5-D	10,729	618
Univ of North Dakota, Grand Forks, ND 58202	1883	$4,370 (S)	$3,987	5-D	12,423	593
Univ of Northern Colorado, Greeley, CO 80639	1890	$2,984 (S)	$5,560	5-D	12,434	605
Univ of Northern Iowa, Cedar Falls, IA 50614	1876	$4,117 (S)	$4,640	5-D	14,167	842
Univ of North Florida, Jacksonville, FL 32224-2645	1965	$2,757 (S)	$5,486	5-D	13,470	598
Univ of North Texas, Denton, TX 76203	1890	$3,217 (S)	$4,598	5-D	30,183	1,183
Univ of Notre Dame, Notre Dame, IN 46556	1842	$25,852	$6,510	2-D	11,311	1,171
Univ of Oklahoma, Norman, OK 73019-0390	1890	$2,929 (S)	$5,030	5-D	23,799	1,177
Univ of Oklahoma Health Sci Ctr, Oklahoma City, OK 73190	1890	$2,330 (S)	NA	5-D	2,935	347
Univ of Oregon, Eugene, OR 97403	1872	$4,230 (S)	$6,252	5-D	19,997	1,078
Univ of Pennsylvania, Philadelphia, PA 19104	1740	$27,988	$8,224	1-D	20,295	1,829
Univ of Phoenix-Colorado Campus, Lone Tree, CO 80124-5453	NR	$8,250	NA	3-D	2,783	383
Univ of Phoenix-Dallas Campus, Dallas, TX 75251	2001	$8,820	NA	3-D	1,449	118
Univ of Phoenix-Fort Lauderdale Campus, Fort Lauderdale, FL 33324-1393	NR	$8,340	NA	3-D	1,805	148
Univ of Phoenix-Hawaii Campus, Honolulu, HI 96813-4317	NR	$9,600	NA	3-D	1,264	181
Univ of Phoenix-Houston Campus, Houston, TX 77079-2004	2001	$8,820	NA	3-D	1,841	72
Univ of Phoenix-Jacksonville Campus, Jacksonville, FL 32216-0959	1976	$8,430	NA	3-D	1,590	166
Univ of Phoenix-Louisiana Campus, Metairie, LA 70001-2082	1976	$7,710	NA	3-D	1,893	152
Univ of Phoenix-Maryland Campus, Columbia, MD 21045-5424	NR	$9,600	NA	3-D	1,544	183
Univ of Phoenix-Metro Detroit Campus, Troy, MI 48098-2623	NR	$9,540	NA	3-D	3,318	388
Univ of Phoenix-Nevada Campus, Las Vegas, NV 89106-3797	1994	$8,520	NA	3-D	3,042	279
Univ of Phoenix-New Mexico Campus, Albuquerque, NM 87109-4645	NR	$8,190	NA	3-D	3,445	342
Univ of Phoenix-Northern California Campus, Pleasanton, CA 94588-3677	NR	$11,670	NA	3-D	5,513	741
Univ of Phoenix Online Campus, Phoenix, AZ 85034-7209	1989	$12,660	NA	3-D	48,118	11,834
Univ of Phoenix-Oregon Campus, Portland, OR 97223-8368	1976	$9,150	NA	3-D	1,536	187
Univ of Phoenix-Orlando Campus, Maitland, FL 32751	1996	$8,430	NA	3-D	1,395	138
Univ of Phoenix-Philadelphia Campus, Wayne, PA 19087-2121	1999	$10,800	NA	3-D	1,179	135
Univ of Phoenix-Phoenix Campus, Phoenix, AZ 85040-1958	1976	$8,400	NA	3-D	8,112	885
Univ of Phoenix-Puerto Rico Campus, Guaynabo, PR 00970-3870	1995	$4,950	NA	3-D	2,016	130
Univ of Phoenix-Sacramento Campus, Sacramento, CA 95833-3632	1993	$10,950	NA	3-D	3,468	304
Univ of Phoenix-San Diego Campus, San Diego, CA 92130-2092	1988	$10,200	NA	3-D	4,244	471
Univ of Phoenix-Southern Arizona Campus, Tucson, AZ 85712	1979	$8,100	NA	3-D	3,165	328
Univ of Phoenix-Southern California Campus, Fountain Valley, CA 92708-6027	1980	$11,100	NA	3-D	12,161	1,297
Univ of Phoenix-Southern Colorado Campus, Colorado Springs, CO 80919-2335	1999	$8,250	NA	3-D	1,256	146
Univ of Phoenix-Tampa Campus, Tampa, FL 33637-1920	NR	$8,100	NA	3-D	1,702	192
Univ of Phoenix-Utah Campus, Salt Lake City, UT 84123-4617	1984	$8,640	NA	3-D	3,168	305
Univ of Phoenix-Washington Campus, Seattle, WA 98188-7500	1997	$9,450	NA	3-D	1,826	225
Univ of Pittsburgh, Pittsburgh, PA 15260	1787	$8,528 (S)	$6,470	12-D	27,190	1,828
Univ of Pittsburgh at Bradford, Bradford, PA 16701-2812	1963	$8,452 (S)	$5,470	12-B	1,352	111
Univ of Pittsburgh at Greensburg, Greensburg, PA 15601-5860	1963	$8,468 (S)	$6,530	12-B	1,888	126
Univ of Pittsburgh at Johnstown, Johnstown, PA 15904-2990	1927	$8,480 (S)	$5,570	12-B	3,122	178
Univ of Portland, Portland, OR 97203-5798	1901	$20,740	$6,250	2-M	3,234	275
Univ of Puerto Rico at Arecibo, Arecibo, PR 00614-4010	1967	$1,245 (A)	$5,240	6-B	4,617	274
Univ of Puerto Rico at Humacao, Humacao, PR 00791	1962	$1,245 (A)	NA	6-B	4,507	284
Univ of Puerto Rico at Ponce, Ponce, PR 00732-7186	1970	$2,245 (S)	NA	6-B	3,837	201
Univ of Puerto Rico at Utuado, Utuado, PR 00641-2500	1979	$1,315 (S)	NA	6-B	1,766	106
Univ of Puerto Rico, Cayey Univ Coll, Cayey, PR 00736	1967	$1,245 (A)	NA	6-B	4,128	202
Univ of Puerto Rico, Mayagüez Campus, Mayagüez, PR 00681-9000	1911	$1,160 (S)	NA	6-D	12,414	761

Name, address	Year Founded	Tuition & Fees	Rm. & Board	Control, Degree	Enrollment	Faculty
Univ of Puerto Rico, Medical Sci Campus, San Juan, PR 00936-5067 (4)	1950	$1,620 (S)	NA	6-D	2,457	693
Univ of Puerto Rico, Río Piedras, San Juan, PR 00931	1903	$1,383 (S)	$4,940	6-D	21,666	1,793
Univ of Puget Sound, Tacoma, WA 98416	1888	$23,945	$6,140	1-D	2,846	262
Univ of Redlands, Redlands, CA 92373-0999	1907	$22,750	$8,114	1-M	2,180	260
Univ of Rhode Island, Kingston, RI 02881	1892	$5,854 (S)	$7,402	5-D	14,180	677
Univ of Richmond, University of Richmond, VA 23173	1830	$23,730	$4,940	1-F	3,774	340
Univ of Rio Grande, Rio Grande, OH 45674	1876	$9,486 (A)	$5,442	1-M	2,076	146
Univ of Rochester, Rochester, NY 14627-0250	1850	$26,077	$8,924	1-D	8,335	NA
Univ of St. Francis, Joliet, IL 60435-6169	1920	$16,030	$5,800	2-M	2,079	219
Univ of Saint Francis, Fort Wayne, IN 46808-3994	1890	$14,560	$5,240	2-M	1,709	193
Univ of St. Thomas, St. Paul, MN 55105-1096	1885	$19,468	$6,129	2-D	11,321	800
Univ of St. Thomas, Houston, TX 77006-4696	1947	$13,912	$6,070	2-D	5,154	270
Univ of San Diego, San Diego, CA 92110-2492	1949	$21,988	$9,130	2-D	7,126	670
Univ of San Francisco, San Francisco, CA 94117-1080	1855	$23,340	$9,350	2-D	8,194	644
Univ of Sci & Arts of Oklahoma, Chickasha, OK 73018	1908	$2,308 (S)	$2,790	5-B	1,490	88
The Univ of Scranton, Scranton, PA 18510	1888	$20,448	$8,770	2-M	4,728	378
Univ of Sioux Falls, Sioux Falls, SD 57105-1699	1883	$13,900	$4,100	2-D	1,405	97
Univ of South Alabama, Mobile, AL 36688-0002	1963	$3,410 (S)	$3,910	5-D	12,323	717
Univ of South Carolina, Columbia, SC 29208	1801	$4,984 (S)	$5,064	5-D	25,140	1,030
Univ of South Carolina Aiken, Aiken, SC 29801-6309	1961	$4,424 (S)	$4,060	5-M	3,416	227
Univ of South Carolina Spartanburg, Spartanburg, SC 29303-4999	1967	$4,788 (S)	$4,700	5-M	4,362	309
The Univ of South Dakota, Vermillion, SD 57069-2390	1862	$3,872 (S)	$3,278	5-D	8,873	295
Univ of Southern California, Los Angeles, CA 90089	1880	$26,954	$8,512	1-D	30,682	2,291
Univ of Southern Indiana, Evansville, IN 47712-3590	1965	$3,525 (S)	$4,940	5-M	9,675	559
Univ of Southern Maine, Portland, ME 04104-9300	1878	$4,861 (S)	$6,328	5-D	11,382	732
Univ of Southern Mississippi, Hattiesburg, MS 39406	1910	$3,874 (S)	$4,450	5-D	15,267	700
Univ of South Florida, Tampa, FL 33620-9951	1956	$2,734 (S)	$6,110	5-D	38,854	1,994
The Univ of Tampa, Tampa, FL 33606-1490	1931	$17,032	$6,132	1-M	4,265	320
The Univ of Tennessee, Knoxville, TN 37996	1794	$3,476 (S)	$4,912	5-D	27,971	1,491
The Univ of Tennessee at Chattanooga, Chattanooga, TN 37403-2598	1886	$3,550 (S)	$2,800	5-M	8,524	596
The Univ of Tennessee at Martin, Martin, TN 38238-1000	1900	$3,849 (S)	$4,480	5-M	5,714	377
The Univ of Texas at Arlington, Arlington, TX 76019	1895	$4,128 (S)	$4,607	5-D	23,821	990
The Univ of Texas at Austin, Austin, TX 78712-1111	1883	$3,950 (S)	$5,975	5-D	52,261	2,714
The Univ of Texas at Brownsville, Brownsville, TX 78520-4991	1973	$1,737 (A)	NA	5-M	9,973	537
The Univ of Texas at Dallas, Richardson, TX 75083-0688	1969	$4,775 (S)	$6,032	5-D	13,228	618
The Univ of Texas at El Paso, El Paso, TX 79968-0001	1913	$2,796 (S)	$4,255	5-D	17,232	910
The Univ of Texas at San Antonio, San Antonio, TX 78249-0617	1969	$3,920 (S)	$7,656	5-D	19,883	963
The Univ of Texas at Tyler, Tyler, TX 75799-0001	1971	$3,472 (S)	$2,907	5-M	4,241	297
The Univ of Texas Health Sci Ctr at Houston, Houston, TX 77225-0036	1972	$4,346 (S)	NA	5-D	3,335	1,115
The Univ of Texas Medical Branch, Galveston, TX 77555	1891	$44/cr. hr. (S)	NA	5-D	2,005	105
The Univ of Texas of the Permian Basin, Odessa, TX 79762-0001	1969	$3,398 (S)	$4,004	5-M	2,695	158
The Univ of Texas-Pan American, Edinburg, TX 78539-2999	1927	$2,719 (S)	$4,333	5-D	14,392	570
The Univ of Texas Southwestern Medical Ctr at Dallas, Dallas, TX 75390	1943	$2,345 (S)	NA	5-D	1,554	103
The Univ of the Arts, Philadelphia, PA 19102-4944	1870	$20,480	$5,300	1-M	2,091	479
Univ of the District of Columbia, Washington, DC 20008-1175	1976	$2,070 (S)	NA	9-M	5,470	456
Univ of the Incarnate Word, San Antonio, TX 78209-6397	1881	$14,328	$5,510	2-D	4,264	341
Univ of the Pacific, Stockton, CA 95211-0197	1851	$22,555	$7,198	1-D	5,886	648
Univ of the Sacred Heart, San Juan, PR 00914-0383	1935	$5,030	$1,800	2-M	5,229	352
Univ of the Sci in Philadelphia, Philadelphia, PA 19104-4495	1821	$19,338	$7,949	1-D	2,516	299
Univ of the South, Sewanee, TN 37383-1000	1857	$22,570	$6,290	2-D	1,449	169
Univ of the Virgin Islands, Charlotte Amalie, VI 00802-9990	1962	$2,860 (S)	$5,830	7-M	2,524	264
Univ of Toledo, Toledo, OH 43606-3398	1872	$5,849 (S)	$6,511	5-D	20,889	1,180
Univ of Tulsa, Tulsa, OK 74104-3189	1894	$14,990	$5,088	2-D	4,049	398
Univ of Utah, Salt Lake City, UT 84112-1107	1850	$3,324 (S)	$5,036	5-D	28,369	1,284
Univ of Vermont, Burlington, VT 05405	1791	$8,994 (S)	$6,378	5-D	10,314	685
Univ of Virginia, Charlottesville, VA 22903	1819	$4,780 (S)	$5,231	5-D	23,144	1,239
The Univ of Virginia's Coll at Wise, Wise, VA 24293	1954	$4,040 (S)	$5,401	5-B	1,632	102
Univ of Washington, Seattle, WA 98195	1861	$4,636 (S)	$6,570	5-D	39,246	3,383
The Univ of West Alabama, Livingston, AL 35470	1835	$3,498 (S)	$2,958	5-M	2,002	91
Univ of West Florida, Pensacola, FL 32514-5750	1963	$2,639 (S)	$6,000	5-D	9,185	546
Univ of Wisconsin-Eau Claire, Eau Claire, WI 54702-4004	1916	$3,722 (S)	$3,910	5-M	10,861	484
Univ of Wisconsin-Green Bay, Green Bay, WI 54311-7001	1968	$4,023 (S)	$3,700	5-M	5,255	259
Univ of Wisconsin-La Crosse, La Crosse, WI 54601-3742	1909	$3,804 (S)	$3,800	5-M	8,770	410
Univ of Wisconsin-Madison, Madison, WI 53706-1380	1848	$4,470 (S)	$5,940	5-D	41,515	NA
Univ of Wisconsin-Milwaukee, Milwaukee, WI 53201-0413	1956	$4,356 (S)	$4,400	5-D	24,587	NA
Univ of Wisconsin-Oshkosh, Oshkosh, WI 54901	1871	$3,670 (S)	$3,970	5-M	11,211	575
Univ of Wisconsin-Parkside, Kenosha, WI 53141-2000	1968	$3,532 (S)	$5,056	5-M	4,972	186
Univ of Wisconsin-Platteville, Platteville, WI 53818-3099	1866	$3,723 (S)	$3,978	5-M	6,017	289
Univ of Wisconsin-River Falls, River Falls, WI 54022-5001	1874	$3,876 (S)	$3,806	5-M	5,670	302
Univ of Wisconsin-Stevens Point, Stevens Point, WI 54481-3897	1894	$3,631 (S)	$3,816	5-M	8,954	440
Univ of Wisconsin-Stout, Menomonie, WI 54751	1891	$3,757 (S)	$3,830	5-M	7,902	392
Univ of Wisconsin-Superior, Superior, WI 54880-4500	1893	$3,928 (S)	$3,962	5-F	2,887	103
Univ of Wisconsin-Whitewater, Whitewater, WI 53190-1790	1868	$4,006 (S)	$3,570	5-M	10,796	511
Univ of Wyoming, Laramie, WY 82071	1886	$2,997 (S)	$5,120	5-D	12,745	647
Univ System Coll for Lifelong Learning, Concord, NH 03301	1972	$4,518 (S)	NA	11-B	1,823	458
Urbana Univ, Urbana, OH 43078-2091	1850	$13,540	$5,410	2-M	1,411	115
Ursinus Coll, Collegeville, PA 19426-1000	1869	$26,200	$6,600	2-B	1,340	147
Ursuline Coll, Pepper Pike, OH 44124-4398 (3)	1871	$15,900	$5,030	2-M	1,319	186
Utah State Univ, Logan, UT 84322	1888	$2,898 (S)	$4,180	5-D	22,848	763
Utica Coll, Utica, NY 13502-4892	1946	$19,118	$7,580	1-M	2,392	213
Valdosta State Univ, Valdosta, GA 31698	1906	$2,634 (S)	$4,680	5-D	9,919	567
Valley City State Univ, Valley City, ND 58072	1890	$2,202 (S)	$3,130	5-B	1,022	85
Valparaiso Univ, Valparaiso, IN 46383-6493	1859	$19,632	$5,130	2-F	3,661	328
Vanderbilt Univ, Nashville, TN 37240-1001	1873	$27,087	$9,060	1-D	10,712	938
Vanguard Univ of Southern California, Costa Mesa, CA 92626-6597	1920	$15,308	$5,458	2-M	1,540	138
Vassar Coll, Poughkeepsie, NY 12604	1861	$27,960	$7,340	1-M	2,472	301
Vermont Tech Coll, Randolph Center, VT 05061-0500	1866	$6,488 (S)	$5,782	5-B	1,256	133
Villa Julie Coll, Stevenson, MD 21153	1952	$12,798	$4,450	1-M	2,500	255
Villanova Univ, Villanova, PA 19085-1699	1842	$24,090	$8,330	2-D	10,489	857
Virginia Coll at Birmingham, Birmingham, AL 35209	1989	$10,100	NA	3-B	2,407	201
Virginia Commonwealth Univ, Richmond, VA 23284-9005	1838	$4,218 (S)	$5,750	5-D	26,009	1,935
Virginia Intermont Coll, Bristol, VA 24201-4298	1884	$13,863	$5,470	2-B	1,045	189

Name, address	Year Founded	Tuition & Fees	Rm. & Board	Control, Degree	Enrollment	Faculty
Virginia Military Inst, Lexington, VA 24450 (2)	1839	$5,582 (S)	$5,055	5-B	1,299	151
Virginia Polytechnic Inst & State Univ, Blacksburg, VA 24061	1872	$4,336 (S)	$4,070	5-D	27,662	1,491
Virginia State Univ, Petersburg, VA 23806-0001	1882	$3,804 (S)	$5,694	5-D	4,974	NA
Virginia Union Univ, Richmond, VA 23220-1170	1865	$11,630	$5,236	2-D	1,622	140
Virginia Wesleyan Coll, Norfolk, VA 23502-5599	1961	$19,200	$6,150	2-B	1,396	111
Viterbo Univ, La Crosse, WI 54601-4797	1890	$15,320	$5,110	2-M	2,331	183
Wagner Coll, Staten Island, NY 10301-4495	1883	$21,500	$7,000	1-M	2,180	188
Wake Forest Univ, Winston-Salem, NC 27109	1834	$24,750	$7,190	2-D	6,425	535
Walla Walla Coll, College Place, WA 99324-1198	1892	$16,944	$4,605	2-M	1,865	177
Walsh Coll of Accountancy & Business Administration, Troy, MI 48007-7006	1922	$7,100	NA	1-M	3,216	130
Walsh Univ, North Canton, OH 44720-3396	1958	$14,700	$8,750	2-M	1,648	177
Warner Southern Coll, Lake Wales, FL 33859	1968	$10,540	$5,060	2-M	1,132	105
Wartburg Coll, Waverly, IA 50677-0903	1852	$18,550	$5,180	2-B	1,695	167
Washburn Univ of Topeka, Topeka, KS 66621	1865	$3,656 (S)	$4,786	10-F	6,118	457
Washington & Jefferson Coll, Washington, PA 15301-4801	1781	$21,658	$5,992	1-B	1,209	108
Washington & Lee Univ, Lexington, VA 24450-0303	1749	$21,175	$5,913	1-F	2,130	209
Washington Coll, Chestertown, MD 21620-1197	1782	$24,300	$5,740	1-M	1,358	129
Washington State Univ, Pullman, WA 99164	1890	$5,268 (S)	$5,882	5-D	21,881	1,268
Washington Univ in St. Louis, St. Louis, MO 63130-4899	1853	$29,053	$9,240	1-D	12,767	1,062
Wayland Baptist Univ, Plainview, TX 79072-6998	1908	$8,450	$3,354	2-M	1,000	85
Waynesburg Coll, Waynesburg, PA 15370-1222	1849	$13,200	$5,050	2-M	1,714	118
Wayne State Coll, Wayne, NE 68787	1910	$3,014 (S)	$3,760	5-M	3,220	215
Wayne State Univ, Detroit, MI 48202	1868	$4,723 (S)	$6,100	5-D	31,167	1,735
Weber State Univ, Ogden, UT 84408-1001	1889	$2,426 (S)	$5,160	5-M	18,059	765
Webster Univ, St. Louis, MO 63119-3194	1915	$14,600	$6,120	1-D	6,890	1,947
Wellesley Coll, Wellesley, MA 02481 (3)	1870	$26,702	$8,242	1-B	2,300	306
Wentworth Inst of Tech, Boston, MA 02115-5998	1904	$14,300	$7,800	1-B	3,273	239
Wesleyan Univ, Middletown, CT 06459-0260	1831	$28,320	$7,610	1-D	3,192	348
Wesley Coll, Dover, DE 19901-3875	1873	$13,705	$6,200	2-M	2,254	92
West Chester Univ of Pennsylvania, West Chester, PA 19383	1871	$4,923 (S)	$5,146	5-M	12,584	773
Western Carolina Univ, Cullowhee, NC 28723	1889	$2,610 (S)	$3,596	5-D	7,033	493
Western Connecticut State Univ, Danbury, CT 06810-6885	1903	$2,648 (S)	$6,580	5-M	6,050	435
Western Illinois Univ, Macomb, IL 61455-1390	1899	$4,846 (S)	$5,062	5-M	13,461	689
Western Intl Univ, Phoenix, AZ 85021-2718	1978	$8,320	NA	3-M	3,751	243
Western Kentucky Univ, Bowling Green, KY 42101-3576	1906	$3,504 (S)	$4,052	5-M	17,818	1,072
Western Michigan Univ, Kalamazoo, MI 49008-5202	1903	$4,924 (S)	$6,128	5-D	29,732	1,189
Western New England Coll, Springfield, MA 01119-2654	1919	$17,754	$7,688	1-F	4,461	416
Western New Mexico Univ, Silver City, NM 88062-0680	1893	$2,289 (S)	NA	5-M	3,074	145
Western Oregon Univ, Monmouth, OR 97361-1394	1856	$3,720 (S)	$5,724	5-M	5,030	267
Western State Coll of Colorado, Gunnison, CO 81231	1901	$2,479 (S)	$5,680	5-B	2,320	120
Western Washington Univ, Bellingham, WA 98225-5996	1893	$3,702 (S)	$5,648	5-M	12,409	645
Westfield State Coll, Westfield, MA 01086	1838	$3,755 (S)	$4,762	5-M	5,188	275
West Liberty State Coll, West Liberty, WV 26074	1837	$2,748 (S)	$4,180	5-B	2,589	163
Westminster Coll, New Wilmington, PA 16172-0001	1852	$20,270	$5,990	2-M	1,576	141
Westminster Coll, Salt Lake City, UT 84105-3697	1875	$15,990	$4,820	1-M	2,353	247
Westmont Coll, Santa Barbara, CA 93108-1099	1937	$23,536	$7,922	2-B	1,323	128
West Texas A&M Univ, Canyon, TX 79016-0001	1909	$2,420 (S)	$4,215	5-M	6,781	293
West Virginia State Coll, Institute, WV 25112-1000	1891	$2,754 (S)	$4,400	5-B	4,992	282
West Virginia Univ, Morgantown, WV 26506	1867	$3,240 (S)	$5,572	5-D	23,492	1,071
West Virginia Univ Inst of Tech, Montgomery, WV 25136	1895	$3,488 (S)	$4,832	5-M	2,468	176
West Virginia Wesleyan Coll, Buckhannon, WV 26201	1890	$19,600	$5,200	2-M	1,597	154
Wheaton Coll, Wheaton, IL 60187-5593	1860	$771	NA	2-D	2,872	287
Wheaton Coll, Norton, MA 02766	1834	$27,330	$7,260	1-B	1,521	153
Wheeling Jesuit Univ, Wheeling, WV 26003-6295	1954	$18,100	$5,610	2-M	1,703	92
Whitman Coll, Walla Walla, WA 99362-2083	1859	$24,274	$6,550	1-B	1,454	183
Whittier Coll, Whittier, CA 90608-0634	1887	$22,178	$7,366	1-F	2,170	133
Whitworth Coll, Spokane, WA 99251-0001	1890	$18,798	$6,050	2-M	2,193	NA
Wichita State Univ, Wichita, KS 67260	1895	$3,055 (S)	$4,420	5-D	15,534	530
Widener Univ, Chester, PA 19013-5792	1821	$20,450	$8,050	1-D	5,828	398
Wilberforce Univ, Wilberforce, OH 45384	1856	$10,780	$5,320	2-B	1,190	70
Wilkes Univ, Wilkes-Barre, PA 18766-0002	1933	$18,860	$8,092	1-F	3,954	NA
Willamette Univ, Salem, OR 97301-3931	1842	$24,172	$6,400	2-F	2,420	279
William Carey Coll, Hattiesburg, MS 39401-5499	1906	$7,665	$3,285	2-M	2,301	195
William Jewell Coll, Liberty, MO 64068-1843	1849	$15,400	$4,550	2-B	1,168	128
William Paterson Univ of New Jersey, Wayne, NJ 07470-8420	1855	$6,400 (S)	$7,030	5-M	10,924	931
William Penn Univ, Oskaloosa, IA 52577-1799	1873	$13,654	$4,430	2-B	1,499	52
Williams Coll, Williamstown, MA 01267	1793	$26,520	$7,230	1-M	2,033	267
William Woods Univ, Fulton, MO 65251-1098	1870	$14,420	$5,700	2-M	1,813	58
Wilmington Coll, New Castle, DE 19720-6491	1967	$6,740	NA	1-D	7,277	584
Wilmington Coll, Wilmington, OH 45177	1870	$17,682	$6,490	2-M	1,262	131
Wingate Univ, Wingate, NC 28174-0159	1896	$14,550	$5,460	2-M	1,433	122
Winona State Univ, Winona, MN 55987-5838	1858	$4,165 (S)	$4,140	5-M	7,760	357
Winston-Salem State Univ, Winston-Salem, NC 27110-0003	1892	$2,326 (S)	$4,272	5-M	3,495	292
Winthrop Univ, Rock Hill, SC 29733	1886	$5,600 (S)	$4,470	5-M	6,459	435
Wittenberg Univ, Springfield, OH 45501-0720	1845	$23,760	$6,066	2-M	2,346	204
Wofford Coll, Spartanburg, SC 29303-3663	1854	$19,415	$5,780	2-B	1,085	103
Woodbury Univ, Burbank, CA 91504-1099	1884	$19,900	$6,874	1-M	1,404	206
Worcester Polytechnic Inst, Worcester, MA 01609-2280	1865	$26,360	$8,430	1-D	3,802	332
Worcester State Coll, Worcester, MA 01602-2597	1874	$3,273 (S)	$5,452	5-M	5,532	284
Wright State Univ, Dayton, OH 45435	1964	$5,361 (S)	$5,712	5-D	16,517	850
Xavier Univ, Cincinnati, OH 45207	1831	$18,020	$7,600	2-D	6,573	577
Xavier Univ of Louisiana, New Orleans, LA 70125-1098	1925	$10,900	$6,000	2-F	3,994	226
Yale Univ, New Haven, CT 06520	1701	$27,130	$8,240	1-D	11,378	1,346
Yeshiva Univ, New York, NY 10033-3201	1886	$19,510	$6,626	1-D	5,998	NA
York Coll of Pennsylvania, York, PA 17405-7199	1787	$8,000	$5,570	1-M	5,463	376
York Coll of the City Univ of New York, Jamaica, NY 11451-0001	1967	$3,442 (S)	NA	11-B	5,748	445
Youngstown State Univ, Youngstown, OH 44555-0001	1908	$5,472 (S)	$5,700	5-D	12,698	894

TRADE AND TRANSPORTATION

U.S. Trade With Selected Countries and Major Areas, 2002

Source: Office of Trade and Econ. Analysis, U.S. Dept. of Commerce

(in millions of dollars; countries ranked by amount of total trade with U.S.)

COUNTRY	Total Trade with U.S.	U.S. Exports to	Rank[1]	U.S. Imports from	Rank[1]	U.S. Trade Balance with	Rank[2]
Canada	$370,010.2	$160,922.6	1	$209,087.6	1	$–48,164.9	3
Mexico	232,086.1	97,470.3	2	134,615.8	2	–37,145.5	4
Japan	172,878.0	51,449.3	3	121,428.7	4	–69,979.4	2
China	147,320.3	22,127.8	7	125,192.5	3	–103,064.7	1
Germany	89,135.3	26,629.6	5	62,505.7	5	–35,876.1	5
U.K.	73,949.6	33,204.7	4	40,744.9	6	–7,540.2	16
Korea (South)	58,147.6	22,575.8	6	35,571.8	7	–12,996.1	10
Taiwan	50,529.7	18,381.8	9	32,147.9	8	–13,766.1	8
France	47,256.3	19,016.2	8	28,240.1	9	–9,223.9	13
Malaysia	34,352.6	10,343.7	16	24,008.9	11	–13,665.3	9
Italy	34,277.1	10,056.8	17	24,220.3	10	–14,163.5	7
Singapore	31,020.1	16,217.9	11	14,802.2	15	1,415.7	224
Ireland	29,182.8	6,745.1	21	22,437.7	12	–15,692.6	6
Netherlands	28,159.2	18,310.7	10	9,848.5	21	8,462.2	230
Brazil	28,156.6	12,376.0	15	15,780.6	13	–3,404.6	25
Belgium	23,132.6	13,325.8	12	9,806.8	22	3,519.0	228
Hong Kong	21,922.6	12,594.4	14	9,328.2	25	3,266.1	227
Thailand	19,653.1	4,860.2	23	14,792.9	16	–9,932.7	12
Australia	19,563.8	13,085.0	13	6,478.8	28	6,606.2	229
Venezuela	19,523.2	4,429.7	25	15,093.5	14	–10,663.8	11
Israel	19,442.4	7,026.7	20	12,415.7	18	–5,389.0	19
Philippines	18,255.9	7,276.0	19	10,979.9	20	–3,703.9	23
Saudi Arabia	17,930.6	4,780.7	24	13,149.9	17	–8,369.1	14
Switzerland	17,164.5	7,782.5	18	9,382.0	24	–1,599.4	36
India	15,919.4	4,101.1	27	11,818.3	19	–7,717.3	15
Sweden	12,369.3	3,153.0	30	9,216.3	26	–6,063.3	18
MAJOR AREA/GROUP							
North America	602,096.3	258,392.9	NA	343,703.4	NA	–85,310.5	NA
Western Europe	402,997.8	157,029.8	NA	245,968.0	NA	–88,938.2	NA
Euro Area	278,410.5	105,837.6	NA	172,572.9	NA	–66,735.3	NA
European Union (EU)	369,462.7	143,691.3	NA	225,771.4	NA	–82,080.2	NA
European Free Trade Association	25,181.7	9,422.5	NA	15,759.2	NA	–6,336.7	NA
Eastern Europe	21,494.1	6,596.6	NA	14,897.5	NA	–8,300.9	NA
Former Soviet Republics	12,728.8	4,111.5	NA	8,617.3	NA	–4,505.8	NA
OECD	401,307.7	156,244.7	NA	245,063.0	NA	–88,818.3	NA
Pacific Rim Countries	572,041.8	178,569.1	NA	393,472.7	NA	–214,903.6	NA
Asia/Near East	53,224.6	18,930.0	NA	34,294.6	NA	–15,364.6	NA
Asia/NICS	161,620.0	69,769.9	NA	91,850.1	NA	–22,080.2	NA
Asia/South	23,559.0	5,335.4	NA	18,223.6	NA	–12,888.2	NA
ASEAN	116,914.3	41,329.1	NA	75,585.2	NA	–34,256.1	NA
APEC	1,214,617.8	448,891.8	NA	765,726.0	NA	–316,834.3	NA
South/Central America	121,054.4	51,551.1	NA	69,503.3	NA	–17,952.2	NA
Twenty Latin American Republics	341,397.3	142,263.1	NA	199,134.2	NA	–56,871.1	NA
Central American Common Market	21,694.5	9,833.1	NA	11,861.4	NA	–2,028.3	NA
LAFTA	308,600.4	126,054.4	NA	182,546.0	NA	–56,491.6	NA
NATO	760,093.5	313,205.0	NA	446,888.5	NA	–133,683.6	NA
OPEC	72,056.5	18,811.9	NA	53,244.6	NA	–34,432.7	NA
WORLD TOTAL	**1,854,469.2**	**693,103.2**	**NA**	**1,161,366.0**	**NA**	**–468,262.8**	**NA**

(1) Rank shown is for column to the left. (2) Rank is by size of U.S. trade deficit; ranking includes territories as well as nations. NA = Not applicable. **Note:** Details may not equal totals because of rounding or incomplete enumeration.

Definitions of areas as used in the table: **North America**—Canada, Mexico. **Western Europe**—Andorra, Austria, Belgium, Bosnia and Herzegovina, Croatia, Cyprus, Denmark, Faroe Islands, Finland, France, Germany, Gibraltar, Greece, Iceland, Ireland, Italy, Liechtenstein, Luxembourg, Macedonia, Malta and Gozo, Monaco, Netherlands, Norway, Portugal, San Marino, Serbia & Montenegro, Slovenia, Spain, Svalbard/Jan Mayen Island, Sweden, Switzerland, Turkey, United Kingdom, Vatican City. **Euro Area**—Austria, Belgium, Finland, France, Germany, Greece, Ireland, Italy, Luxembourg, Netherlands, Portugal, Spain. **EU**—(European Union) Austria, Belgium, Denmark, Finland, France, Germany, Greece, Ireland, Italy, Luxembourg, Netherlands, Portugal, Spain, Sweden, United Kingdom. **EFTA**—(European Free Trade Association) Iceland, Liechtenstein, Norway, Switzerland. **Eastern Europe**—Albania, Armenia, Azerbaijan, Belarus, Bulgaria, Czech Republic, Estonia, Georgia, Hungary, Kazakhstan, Kyrgyzstan, Latvia, Lithuania, Moldova, Poland, Romania, Russia, Slovakia, Tajikistan, Turkmenistan, Ukraine, Uzbekistan. **Former Soviet Republics**—Armenia, Azerbaijan, Belarus, Estonia, Georgia, Kazakhstan, Kyrgyzstan, Latvia, Lithuania, Moldova, Russia, Tajikistan, Turkmenistan, Ukraine, Uzbekistan. **OECD**—(Organization for Economic Cooperation & Development in Europe) Austria, Belgium, Denmark, Finland, France, Germany, Greece, Iceland, Ireland, Italy, Liechtenstein, Luxembourg, Monaco, Netherlands, Norway, Portugal, San Marino, Spain, Svalbard/Jan Mayen Island, Switzerland, Turkey, United Kingdom. **Pacific Rim Countries/Territories**—Australia, Brunei, China, Indonesia, Japan, Macao, Malaysia, New Zealand, Papua New Guinea, Philippines, Singapore, South Korea, Taiwan. **Asia/Near East**—Bahrain, Iran, Israel, Jordan, Kuwait, Lebanon, Oman, Qatar, Saudi Arabia, Syria, U.A.E., Yemen. **Asia/NICS**—(Newly Industrialized Countries) Hong Kong (special administrative region of China), Singapore, South Korea, Taiwan. **Asia/South**—Afghanistan, Bangladesh, India, Nepal, Pakistan, Sri Lanka. **ASEAN**—(Association of Southeast Asian Nations) Brunei, Cambodia, Indonesia, Malaysia, Philippines, Singapore, Thailand. **APEC**—(Asia-Pacific Economic Cooperation) Australia, Brunei, Canada, Chile, China, Indonesia, Japan, Malaysia, Mexico, New Zealand, Papua New Guinea, Peru, Philippines, Russia, Singapore, South Korea, Taiwan, Thailand, Vietnam. **South/Central America**—Anguilla, Antigua and Barbuda, Argentina, Aruba, Bahamas, Barbados, Belize, Bermuda, Bolivia, Brazil, British Virgin Islands, Cayman Islands, Chile, Colombia, Costa Rica, Cuba, Dominica, Dominican Republic, Ecuador, El Salvador, Falkland Islands, French Guiana, Grenada, Guadeloupe, Guatemala, Guyana, Haiti, Honduras, Jamaica, Martinique, Montserrat, Netherland Antilles, Nicaragua, Panama, Paraguay, Peru, St. Kitts and Nevis, St. Lucia, St. Vincent and the Grenadines, Suriname, Trinidad and Tobago, Turks and Caicos Islands, Uruguay, Venezuela. **20 Latin American Republics**—Argentina, Bolivia, Brazil, Chile, Colombia, Costa Rica, Cuba, Dominican Republic, Ecuador, El Salvador, Guatemala, Haiti, Honduras, Mexico, Nicaragua, Panama, Paraguay, Peru, Uruguay, Venezuela. **Central American Common Market**—Costa Rica, El Salvador, Guatemala, Honduras, Nicaragua. **LAFTA**—(Latin American Free Trade Assn.) Argentina, Bolivia, Brazil, Chile, Colombia, Ecuador, Mexico, Paraguay, Peru, Uruguay, Venezuela. **NATO**—(North Atlantic Treaty Organization) Belgium, Canada, Denmark, France, Germany, Greece, Iceland, Ireland, Italy, Liechtenstein, Luxembourg, Monaco, Netherlands, Norway, Portugal, San Marino, Spain, Svalbard/Jan Mayan Island, Sweden, Switzerland, Turkey, United Kingdom. **OPEC**—(Organization of Petroleum Exporting Countries) Algeria, Indonesia, Iran, Iraq, Kuwait, Libya, Nigeria, Qatar, Saudi Arabia, United Arab Emirates, Venezuela.

U.S. Exports and Imports by Principal Commodity Groupings, 2002

Source: Office of Trade and Economic Analysis, U.S. Dept. of Commerce

(millions of dollars)

Items	Exports	Imports	Items	Exports	Imports
TOTAL	**$693,103**	**$1,161,366**	Jewelry	$2,087	$7,110
Agricultural commodities	**53,115**	**42,012**	Lighting, plumbing	1,333	5,566
Animal feeds	3,824	605	Metal manufactures[1]	11,170	16,681
Cereal flour	1,578	2,170	Metalworking machinery	4,140	5,104
Coffee	8	1,369	Nickel	421	933
Corn	5,108	137	Optical goods	2,132	2,836
Cotton, raw and linters	2,031	25	Paper and paperboard	9,551	14,435
Hides and skins	1,594	84	Photographic equipment	3,529	5,325
Live animals	636	2,093	Plastic articles[1]	6,820	9,138
Meat and preparations	6,356	4,269	Platinum	723	2,830
Oils/fats, vegetable	1,070	1,127	Pottery	83	1,697
Rice	769	162	Power generating mach.	32,430	33,922
Soybeans	5,734	28	Printed materials	4,429	3,960
Sugar	13	495	Records/magnetic media	4,414	5,279
Tobacco, unmanufactured	1,050	701	Rubber articles[1]	1,423	2,139
Vegetables and fruits	7,607	10,194	Rubber tires and tubes	2,232	4,765
Wheat	3,630	266	Scientific instruments	27,087	20,884
Manufactured goods	**544,913**	**974,576**	Ships, boats	1,200	1,325
ADP equipment; office machines	30,368	76,877	Silver and bullion	262	687
Airplane parts	14,309	4,986	Spacecraft	509	310
Airplanes	27,115	12,329	Specialized industrial machinery	23,532	18,401
Aluminum	2,947	6,757	Television, VCR, etc.	19,374	66,212
Artwork/antiques	977	5,194	Textile yarn, fabric	10,263	16,097
Basketware, etc.	3,842	6,564	Toys/games/sporting goods	2,985	22,067
Chemicals - cosmetics	5,870	4,195	Travel goods	277	4,402
Chemicals - dyeing	3,860	2,357	Vehicles	57,698	168,073
Chemicals - fertilizers	2,106	1,619	Watches/clocks/parts	236	3,203
Chemicals - inorganic	5,464	6,018	Wood manufactures	1,564	7,853
Chemicals - medicinal	15,732	24,748	**Mineral fuels**	**11,541**	**115,748**
Chemicals - organic	16,406	30,366	Coal	1,673	966
Chemicals - plastics	19,380	10,760	Crude oil	92	79,252
Chemicals[1]	12,348	6,168	Liquified propane/butane	471	1,250
Clothing	5,485	63,803	Mineral fuels, other	1,997	1,413
Copper	1,026	3,520	Natural gas	995	10,974
Electrical machinery	66,948	81,158	Petroleum preparations	6,009	20,748
Footwear	518	15,387	**Selected commodities**	**18,299**	**28,200**
Furniture and bedding	3,814	21,577	Alcoholic bev.,distilled	505	3,273
Gem diamonds	1,182	12,088	Cigarettes	1,466	316
General industrial machinery	30,075	35,200	Cork, wood, lumber	3,364	7,872
Glass	2,363	2,162	Crude fertilizers	1,520	1,275
Glassware	700	1,838	Fish and preparations	2,976	10,000
Gold, nonmonetary	3,244	2,428	Metal ores; scrap	4,626	3,101
Iron and steel mill products	5,252	12,951	Pulp and waste paper	3,842	2,363

(1) Those not specified elsewhere. **NOTE:** Not all products are listed in each commodity group.

Trends in U.S. Foreign Trade, 1790-2002

Source: Office of Trade and Economic Analysis, U.S. Dept. of Commerce

In 1790, U.S. exports and imports combined came to $43 million and there was a $3 million trade deficit. In 2002, U.S. exports and imports combined amounted to nearly $2 trillion, and the trade deficit, which had generally been climbing in recent years (after a century of trade surpluses), reached $468 billion, the highest total in history.

(in millions of dollars)

Year	Exports	Imports	Trade Balance	Year	Exports	Imports	Trade Balance	Year	Exports	Imports	Trade Balance
1790	$20	$23	$-3	1880	$836	$668	$168	1970	$42,681	$40,356	$2,325
1795	48	70	-22	1885	742	578	165	1975	107,652	98,503	9,149
1800	71	91	-20	1890	858	789	69	1980	220,626	244,871	-24,245
1805	96	121	-25	1895	808	732	76	1985	213,133	345,276	-132,143
1810	67	85	-19	1900	1,394	850	545	1990	394,030	495,042	-101,012
1815	53	113	-60	1905	1,519	1,118	401	1991	421,730	485,453	-63,723
1820	70	74	-5	1910	1,745	1,557	188	1992	448,164	532,665	-84,501
1825	91	90	1	1915	2,769	1,674	1,094	1993	465,091	580,659	-115,568
1830	72	63	9	1920	8,228	5,278	2,950	1994	512,626	683,256	-170,630
1835	115	137	-22	1925	4,910	4,227	683	1995	584,742	743,445	-158,703
1840	124	98	25	1930	3,843	3,061	782	1996	625,075	795,289	-170,214
1845	106	113	-7	1935	2,283	2,047	235	1997	689,182	870,671	-181,489
1850	144	174	-29	1940	4,021	2,625	1,396	1998	682,138	911,896	-229,758
1855	219	258	-39	1945	9,806	4,159	5,646	1999	695,797	1,024,618	-328,821
1860	334	354	-20	1950	9,997	8,954	1,043	2000	781,918	1,218,022	-436,104
1865	166	239	-73	1955	14,298	11,566	2,732	2001	729,100	1,140,999	-411,899
1870	393	436	-43	1960	19,659	15,073	4,586	2002	693,103	1,161,366	-468,263
1875	513	533	-20	1965	26,742	21,520	5,222				

The North American Free Trade Agreement (NAFTA)

NAFTA, a comprehensive plan for free trade between the U.S., Canada, and Mexico, took effect Jan. 1, 1994. Major provisions are:

Agriculture—Tariffs on all farm products are to be eliminated over 15 years. Domestic price-support systems may continue provided they do not distort trade.

Automobiles—By 2003, at least 62.5% of an automobile's value must have been produced in North America for it to qualify for duty-free status. Tariffs are to be phased out over 10 years.

Banking—U.S. and Canadian banks may acquire Mexican commercial banks accounting for as much as 8% of the industry's capital. All limits on ownership end in 2004.

Disputes—Special judges have jurisdiction to resolve disagreements within strict timetables.

Energy—Mexico continues to bar foreign ownership of its oil fields but, starting in 2004, U.S. and Canadian companies can bid on contracts offered by Mexican oil and electricity monopolies.

Environment—The trade agreement cannot be used to override national and state environmental, health, or safety laws.

Immigration—All 3 countries must ease restrictions on the movement of business executives and professionals.

Jobs—Barriers to limit Mexican migration to U.S. remain.

Patent and copyright protection—Mexico strengthened its laws providing protection to intellectual property.

Tariffs—Tariffs on 10,000 customs goods are to be eliminated over 15 years. One-half of U.S. exports to Mexico are to be considered duty-free within 5 years.

Textiles—A "rule of origin" provision requires most garments to be made from yarn and fabric that have been produced in North America. Most tariffs are being phased out over 5 years.

Trucking—Trucks were to have free access on crossborder routes and throughout the 3 countries by 1999, but the U.S. continued to impose restrictions on Mexican trucks. In 2001, an arbitration panel ruled that the U.S. restrictions were in violation of NAFTA. Pres. Bush in Nov. 2002 eased restrictions on Mexican trucks entering the U.S.

U.S. Trade With Mexico and Canada, 1993-2002

Source: Office of Trade and Economic Analysis, U.S. Dept. of Commerce

(U.S. exports to, imports from, Canada and Mexico in millions of dollars)

	MEXICO				CANADA		
Year	Exports	Imports	Trade Balance[1]	Year	Exports	Imports	Trade Balance[1]
1993	$41,581	$39,917	$1,664	1993	$100,444	$111,216	$-10,772
1994[2]	50,844	49,494	1,350	1994[2]	114,439	128,406	-13,968
1995	46,292	61,685	-15,393	1995	127,226	145,349	-18,123
1996	56,792	74,297	-17,506	1996	134,210	155,893	-21,682
1997	71,388	85,938	-14,549	1997	151,767	167,234	-15,467
1998	78,773	94,629	-15,857	1998	156,603	173,256	-16,653
1999	86,909	109,721	-22,812	1999	166,600	198,711	-32,111
2000	111,349	135,926	-24,577	2000	178,941	230,838	-51,897
2001	101,297	131,338	-30,041	2001	163,424	216,268	-52,844
2002	97,470	134,616	-37,146	2002	160,923	209,088	-48,165

(1) Totals may not add due to rounding. (2) NAFTA provisions began to take effect Jan. 1, 1994.

Foreign Exchange Rates, 1970-2002

Source: International Monetary Fund, Federal Reserve Board; Federal Reserve Board

(National currency units per dollar except as indicated; data are annual averages)

Note: As of 2002, the euro, the European Union's single currency, replaced the national currencies in the EU nations shown (Austria, Belgium, France, Germany, Greece, Ireland, Italy, Netherlands, Portugal, and Spain), as well as in Finland and Luxembourg.

Year	Australia[1] (dollar)	Austria (schilling)	Belgium (franc)	Canada (dollar)	Denmark (krone)	France (franc)	Germany[2] (deutsche mark)	Greece (drachma)
1970	1.1136	25.880	49.680	1.0103	7.489	5.5200	3.6480	30.00
1975	1.3077	17.443	36.799	1.0175	5.748	4.2876	2.4613	32.29
1980	1.1400	12.945	29.237	1.1693	5.634	4.2250	1.8175	42.62
1985	0.7003	20.690	59.378	1.3655	10.596	8.9852	2.9440	138.12
1990	0.7813	11.370	33.418	1.1668	6.189	5.4453	1.6157	158.51
1995	0.7415	10.081	29.480	1.3724	5.602	4.9915	1.4331	231.66
1998	0.6294	12.379	36.299	1.4835	6.701	5.8995	1.7597	295.53
1999	0.6453	0.9386[3]	0.9386[3]	1.4857	6.976	0.9386[3]	0.9386[3]	305.65
2000	0.5815	0.9232[3]	0.9232[3]	1.4855	8.095	0.9232[3]	0.9232[3]	365.92
2001	0.5169	0.8952[3]	0.8952[3]	1.5487	8.3323	0.8952[3]	0.8952[3]	0.8952[3]
2002	0.5437	0.9454[3]	0.9454[3]	1.5704	7.8862	0.9454[3]	0.9454[3]	0.9454[3]

Year	India (rupee)	Ireland[1] (pound)	Italy (lira)	Japan (yen)	Malaysia (ringgit)	Mexico (new peso)	Netherlands (guilder)	Norway (krone)
1970	7.576	2.3959	623	357.60	3.0900	—	3.5970	7.1400
1975	8.409	2.2216	653	296.78	2.4030	—	2.5293	5.2282
1980	7.887	2.0577	856	226.63	2.1767	—	1.9875	4.9381
1985	12.369	1.0656	1,909	238.54	2.4830	—	3.3214	8.5972
1990	17.504	1.6585	1,198	144.79	2.7049	2.8126	1.8209	6.2597
1995	32.427	1.6038	1,628.9	94.06	2.5044	6.4194	1.6057	6.3352
1998	41.259	1.4257	1,736.2	130.91	3.9244	9.1360	1.9837	7.5451
1999	43.055	1.0668	0.9386[3]	113.91	3.8000	9.5604	0.9386[3]	7.7992
2000	45.000	0.9232[3]	0.9232[3]	107.80	3.8000	9.4590	0.9232[3]	8.8131
2001	47.22	0.8952[3]	0.8952[3]	121.57	3.8000	9.337	0.8952[3]	8.9964
2002	48.63	0.9454[3]	0.9454[3]	125.22	3.8000	9.663	0.9454[3]	7.9839

Year	Portugal (escudo)	Singapore (dollar)	South Korea (won)	Spain (peseta)	Sweden (krona)	Switzerland (franc)	Thailand (baht)	UK[1] (pound)
1970	28.75	3.0800	310.57	69.72	5.1700	4.3160	21.000	2.3959
1975	25.51	2.3713	484.00	57.43	4.1530	2.5839	20.379	2.2216
1980	50.08	2.1412	607.43	71.76	4.2309	1.6772	20.476	2.3243
1985	170.39	2.2002	870.02	170.04	8.6039	2.4571	27.159	1.2963
1990	142.55	1.8125	707.76	101.93	5.9188	1.3892	25.585	1.7847
1995	151.11	1.4174	771.27	124.69	7.1333	1.1825	24.915	1.5785
1998	180.10	1.6736	1,401.44	149.40	7.9499	1.4498	41.359	1.6564
1999	0.9386[3]	1.6950	1,188.82	0.9386[3]	8.2624	1.5022	37.814	1.6182
2000	0.9232[3]	1.7250	1,130.90	0.9232[3]	9.1735	1.6904	40.210	1.5156
2001	0.8952[3]	1.7930	1,292.01	0.8952[3]	10.3425	1.6891	44.532	1.4396
2002	0.9454[3]	1.7908	1,250.31	0.9454[3]	9.7233	1.5567	43.019	1.5025

(1) U.S. dollars per unit of national currency. (2) West Germany before 1991. (3) Euro Area member, figures in euros per dollar. 1 EUR=13.7063 Aust. schillings, 40.3399 Bel. francs, 5.94573 Fin. markkas, 6.55957 Fr. francs, 1.95583 Ger. marks, 340.75 Gr. drachmas, .787564 Ir. pounds, 1936.27 It. lire, 40.3399 Lux. francs, 2.20371 Neth. guilders, 200.482 Port. escudos, 166.386 Sp. pesetas.

Foreign Direct Investment[1] in the U.S. by Selected Countries and Territories

Source: Bureau of Economic Analysis; U.S. Dept. of Commerce

(millions of dollars)

	1995	2000	2002		1995	2000	2002
ALL COUNTRIES[2]	$54,368	$1,256,867	$1,347,994	Other W. Hemisphere[3]	NA	$40,307	$35,374
Canada	6,481	114,309	92,041	Bahamas	0	1,254	1,332
Europe[3]	36,654	887,014	1,006,530	Bermuda	166	18,336	977
Austria	8	3,007	3,439	Netherlands Antilles	NA	3,807	4,680
Belgium	38	14,787	9,608	UK islands, Caribbean	64	15,191	25,502
Denmark	NA	4,025	1,924	Africa[3]	NA	2,700	2,344
Finland	0	8,875	7,212	South Africa	NA	704	540
France	1,217	125,740	170,619	Middle East[3]	500	6,506	6,766
Germany	14,155	122,412	137,036	Israel	NA	3,012	3,205
Ireland	106	25,523	26,179	Kuwait	31	908	989
Italy	NA	6,576	6,695	Lebanon	0	1	1
Liechtenstein	NA	319	259	Saudi Arabia	NA	NA	NA
Luxembourg	NA	58,930	34,349	United Arab Emirates	NA	64	68
Netherlands	855	138,894	154,753	Asia and Pacific[3]	9,169	192,647	188,023
Norway	14	2,665	3,416	Australia	2,488	18,775	24,470
Spain	147	5,068	4,739	Hong Kong	252	1,493	2,189
Sweden	NA	21,991	21,989	Japan	3,758	159,690	152,032
Switzerland	4,198	64,719	113,232	Korea, Republic of	1,257	3,110	2,439
United Kingdom	9,676	277,613	283,317	Malaysia	57	310	358
South and				New Zealand	NA	395	546
Central America[3]	NA	13,384	16,917	Philippines	NA	47	31
Brazil	5	882	971	Singapore	863	5,087	2,902
Mexico	146	7,462	7,857	Taiwan	286	3,174	2,311
Panama	0	3,819	5,668	European Union[4]	32,436	814,033	862,830
Venezuela	NA	792	4,447	OPEC[5]	504	4,330	7,923

(1) The book value of foreign direct investors' equity in, and net outstanding loans to, their U.S. affiliates. A U.S. affiliate is a U.S. business enterprise in which a single foreign direct investor owns at least 10% of the voting securities or the equivalent. (2) Total includes sources not reflected in regional subtotals. (3) Totals include countries or territories not shown. (4) The European Union comprises Austria, Belgium, Denmark, Finland, France, Germany, Greece, Ireland, Italy, Luxembourg, the Netherlands, Portugal, Spain, Sweden, and the United Kingdom. (5) Organization of Petroleum Exporting Countries: Algeria, Indonesia, Iran, Iraq, Kuwait, Libya, Nigeria, Qatar, Saudi Arabia, the United Arab Emirates, and Venezuela. NA = Not available.

U.S. Direct Investment[1] Abroad in Selected Countries and Territories

Source: Bureau of Economic Analysis, U.S. Dept. of Commerce

(millions of dollars)

	1990	2000	2002		1990	2000	2002
ALL COUNTRIES[2]	$424,086	$1,316,247	$1,520,965	Mexico	$9,398	$39,352	$58,074
Canada	67,033	132,472	152,522	Panama	7,409	30,758	20,003
Europe	211,194	687,320	796,913	Other	NA	1,618	1,336
Austria	889	2,872	3,988	Other Western			
Belgium	9,050	17,973	24,122	Hemisphere[3]	30,113	108,515	116,470
Czech Republic	NA	1,228	1,345	Bahamas	3,309	NA	NA
Denmark	1,597	5,270	7,688	Barbados	NA	2,141	1,487
Finland	551	1,342	1,397	Bermuda	21,737	60,114	68,856
France	18,874	42,628	43,978	Dominican Republic	NA	1,143	1,123
Germany	27,259	55,508	64,739	UK islands, Caribbean	4,800	33,451	29,252
Greece	288	795	1,056	Other	NA	11,665	15,751
Hungary	NA	1,920	2,460	Africa[3]	4,861	11,891	15,066
Ireland	6,880	35,903	41,636	Egypt	1,465	1,998	2,959
Italy	13,117	23,484	28,499	Nigeria	161	470	1,761
Luxembourg	1,390	27,849	35,727	South Africa	956	3,562	3,428
Netherlands	22,658	115,429	145,474	Middle East[3]	3,973	10,863	14,154
Norway	3,815	4,379	7,348	Israel	756	3,735	5,207
Poland	NA	3,884	4,750	Saudi Arabia	1,981	3,661	3,687
Portugal	598	2,664	3,394	United Arab Emirates	519	683	1,398
Russia	NA	1,147	617	Asia and Pacific[3]	61,869	207,125	269,947
Spain	7,704	21,236	23,884	Australia	14,846	34,838	36,337
Sweden	1,600	25,959	18,999	China	NA	11,140	10,294
Switzerland	25,199	55,377	70,051	Hong Kong	6,187	27,447	35,764
Turkey	494	1,826	1,888	India	513	2,379	3,678
United Kingdom	68,224	230,762	255,391	Indonesia	3,226	8,904	7,546
Other	NA	7,885	8,482	Japan	20,997	57,091	65,676
South America[3]	23,760	84,220	74,694	Korea, Republic of	2,178	8,968	12,192
Argentina	2,956	17,488	11,303	Malaysia	1,384	7,910	8,576
Brazil	14,918	36,717	31,715	New Zealand	3,131	4,271	4,383
Chile	1,368	10,052	11,625	Philippines	1,629	3,638	4,097
Colombia	1,728	3,693	3,735	Singapore	3,385	24,133	61,361
Ecuador	387	832	1,082	Taiwan	2,014	7,836	10,091
Peru	410	3,130	3,237	Thailand	1,585	5,824	6,883
Venezuela	1,490	10,531	10,819	European Union[4]	NA	609,674	699,970
Central America[3]	17,719	73,841	81,199	Eastern Europe[5]	NA	14,989	16,572
Costa Rica	NA	1,716	1,602	OPEC[6]	NA	28,545	30,831
Honduras	NA	399	184				

(1) The book value of U.S. direct investors' equity in, and net outstanding loans to, their foreign affiliates. A foreign affiliate is a foreign business enterprise in which a single U.S. investor owns at least 10% of the voting securities or the equivalent. (2) Total includes countries not reflected in regional totals. (3) Total includes countries not shown. (4) The European Union comprises Austria, Belgium, Denmark, Finland, France, Germany, Greece, Ireland, Italy, Luxembourg, the Netherlands, Portugal, Spain, Sweden, and the United Kingdom. (5) Eastern Europe consists of Albania, Armenia, Azerbaijan, Belarus, Bulgaria, Czech Rep., Estonia, Georgia, Hungary, Kazakhstan, Latvia, Lithuania, Moldova, Poland, Romania, Russia, Slovakia, Tajikistan, Turkmenistan, Ukraine, and Uzbekistan. (6) Organization of Petroleum Exporting Countries: Algeria, Indonesia, Iran, Iraq, Kuwait, Libya, Nigeria, Qatar, Saudi Arabia, the United Arab Emirates, and Venezuela. NA = not available.

U.S. International Transactions, 1965-2002

Source: Bureau of Economic Analysis, U.S. Dept. of Commerce; revised as of July 2003
(millions of dollars)

	1965	1970	1975	1980	1985	1990	1995	2001	2002
Exports of goods, services, and income[1]	$42,722	$68,387	$157,936	$344,440	$382,749	$700,455	$991,490	$1,284,942	$1,229,649
Merchandise bal. of payments basis[2]	26,461	42,469	107,088	224,250	215,915	389,307	575,871	718,712	681,874
Services	8,824	14,171	25,497	47,584	73,155	147,824	218,739	288,868	292,233
Income receipts on U.S.-owned assets abroad.	7,437	11,748	25,351	72,606	93,679	163,324	196,880	274,272	252,379
Imports of goods and services and income payments	-32,708	-59,901	-132,745	-333,774	-484,037	-757,758	-1,086,539	-1,632,072	-1,651,657
Merchandise balance of payments basis[2]	-21,510	-39,866	-98,185	-249,750	-338,088	-498,337	-749,431	-1,145,927	-1,164,746
Services	-9,111	-14,520	-21,996	-41,491	-72,862	-120,019	-147,036	-219,472	-227,399
Income payments on foreign assets in the U.S.	-2,088	-5,515	-12,564	-42,532	-73,087	-139,402	-190,072	-258,571	-251,108
Unilateral transfers, net	-4,583	-6,156	-7,075	-8,349	-22,700	-34,588	-34,046	-46,615	-58,853
Capital acct. transactions, net	NA	NA	NA	NA	NA	NA	NA	-1,062	-1,285
U.S. assets abroad, net (increase)/ capital outflow [−])	-5,716	-9,337	-39,703	-86,967	-39,889	-74,011	-307,207	-349,939	-178,985
U.S. official reserve assets, net	1,225	2,481	-849	-8,155	-3,858	-2,158	-9,742	-4,911	-3,681
U.S. government assets, other than official reserve assets, net	-1,605	-1,589	-3,474	-5,162	-2,821	2,307	-549	-486	-32
U.S. private assets, net	-5,336	-10,229	-35,380	-73,651	-33,211	-74,160	-296,916	-344,542	-175,272
Foreign assets in the U.S., net (increase/capital inflow [+])	742	6,359	17,170	62,612	146,383	140,992	451,234	765,531	706,983
Stat. discrepancy (sum of above items with sign reversed)	-457	-219	4,417	20,886	17,494	24,911	-14,931	-20,785	-45,852
Memorandum: Balance on current account	5,431	2,331	18,116	2,317	-123,987	-91,892	-129,095	-393,745	-480,861

NA = Not available. (1) Excludes transfers of goods and services under U.S. military grant programs. (2) Excludes exports of goods under U.S. military agency sales contracts identified in Census export documents, excludes imports of goods under direct defense expenditures identified in Census import documents, and reflects various other adjustments.

Merchant Fleets of the World by Flag of Registry, 2003

Source: Maritime Administration, U.S. Dept. of Commerce
Self-propelled oceangoing vessels of 1,000 gross deadweight tons and over, as of Jan. 1, 2003 (tonnage in thousands)

		All Vessels		Tanker		Dry Bulk Carrier		Container		Other[1]	
		No.	Tons	No.	Tons	No.	Tons	No.	Tons	No.	Tons
By Flag	Panama	4,860	189,521	1,170	63,397	1,509	93,822	564	18,570	1,617	13,733
	Liberia	1,454	75,924	557	41,445	311	18,781	342	11,589	244	4,109
	Greece	735	48,542	303	28,952	280	16,867	45	2,072	107	650
	Bahamas	1,036	46,098	254	28,660	168	9,519	82	2,377	532	5,541
	Malta	1,258	43,231	286	18,084	466	19,869	59	1,382	447	3,896
	Cyprus	1,157	36,322	155	7,169	437	21,658	133	3,220	432	4,274
	Singapore	854	32,871	414	17,197	126	9,199	175	4,450	139	2,026
	Norway (NIS)[2]	611	27,379	304	16,515	84	7,322	6	118	217	3,424
	Hong Kong	517	26,490	72	5,000	298	17,513	74	2,554	73	1,423
	China[3]	1,480	23,621	286	4,205	321	11,265	120	2,134	753	6,017
	Marshall Islands	324	22,872	135	14,817	93	5,690	62	1,677	34	686
	United States	426	13,853	120	6,552	18	797	90	3,292	198	3,212
	Japan	593	13,570	246	7,234	150	4,832	18	590	179	914
	Korea (South)	499	9,910	149	1,903	105	6,135	47	831	198	1,040
	India	284	9,685	101	5,316	101	3,900	8	152	74	316
	Italy	429	9,515	216	4,224	40	2,814	28	982	145	1,495
	Denmark (DIS)	280	8,903	85	3,876	5	264	74	4,329	116	434
	St. Vincent & the Grenadines	714	8,796	81	833	123	4,494	30	204	480	3,264
	Isle of Man	214	8,783	112	6,254	22	1,607	19	416	61	507
	Turkey	521	8,420	92	1,580	129	4,913	32	362	268	1,565
	All other	10,515	148,977	2,153	52,974	998	37,799	926	23,283	6,438	34,921
By Country[4]	Greece	2,915	148,873	807	64,967	1,301	72,285	146	4,709	661	6,913
	Japan	2,722	104,368	767	37,110	868	51,891	219	7,132	868	8,236
	China	2,033	43,629	314	7,200	578	24,398	210	4,401	931	7,630
	Norway	1,075	42,701	425	24,956	168	10,552	19	623	463	6,570
	Germany	2,024	40,252	179	6,488	156	6,097	793	21,382	896	6,285
	United States	890	40,247	337	27,378	115	5,563	84	2,893	354	4,412
	Hong Kong[3]	551	35,372	142	14,546	260	17,794	37	1,416	112	1,617
	Korea	755	25,067	215	7,638	178	13,422	97	2,486	265	1,521
	Taiwan	516	21,645	43	3,532	167	10,279	201	7,016	105	818
	Singapore	611	16,788	287	10,268	64	2,518	135	2,993	125	1,009
	Denmark	551	16,518	155	7,480	23	1,449	130	6,239	243	1,351
	United Kingdom	508	16,392	136	7,198	45	4,018	83	3,227	244	1,949
	Russia	1,661	14,751	389	>7,637	115	1,855	33	793	1,124	4,466
	Italy	466	12,200	232	5,160	66	4,509	13	322	155	2,209
	Saudi Arabia	93	10,963	74	10,588	1	2	1	68	17	305
	India	277	10,366	106	5,471	111	4,461	3	87	57	348
	Turkey	524	8,858	95	1,464	138	5,357	34	383	257	1,654
	Iran	125	7,247	32	4,428	43	1,915	7	179	43	725
	Sweden	291	6,901	123	5,345	8	67	0	0	160	1,490
	Belgium	116	6,863	61	4,736	16	1,859	2	13	37	255
	All Other	10,057	183,276	2,372	72,601	1,363	58,767	687	18,222	5,635	33,686
TOTAL ALL SHIPS		4,860	189,521	7,261	336,189	5,784	299,059	2,934	84,583	12,752	93,448

(1) Includes roll-on/roll-off, passenger, breakbulk ships, partial container ships, refrigerated cargo ships, barge carriers, and specialized cargo ships. (2) NIS = Norwegian International Ship Registry. (3) Excluding Hong Kong. (4) Based on parent company nationality.

50 Busiest U.S. Ports, 2001

Source: Corps of Engineers, Dept. of the Army, U.S. Dept. of Defense
(ports ranked by tonnage handled; all figures in tons)

Rank	Port Name	Total	Domestic	Foreign	Imports	Exports
1.	South Louisiana, LA, Port of	212,564,930	116,884,176	95,680,754	32,540,431	63,140,323
2.	Houston, TX	185,050,168	64,457,446	120,592,722	85,484,988	35,107,734
3.	New York, NY and NJ	137,484,344	70,217,807	67,266,537	59,225,608	8,040,929
4.	New Orleans, LA	85,628,353	35,331,809	50,296,544	27,074,274	23,222,270
5.	Beaumont, TX	79,130,510	17,147,005	61,983,505	56,720,246	5,263,259
6.	Corpus Christi, TX	77,575,699	23,654,308	53,921,391	44,987,020	8,934,371
7.	Huntington Tristate, WV	76,669,841	76,669,841	0	0	0
8.	Long Beach, CA	67,643,920	16,082,869	51,561,051	37,739,957	13,821,094
9.	Texas City, TX	62,270,351	18,140,825	44,129,526	40,303,834	3,825,692
10.	Baton Rouge, LA	61,415,441	40,764,561	20,650,880	14,218,892	6,431,988
11.	Plaquemines, LA, Port of	60,694,475	37,340,348	23,354,127	14,931,054	8,423,073
12.	Pittsburgh, PA	53,008,632	53,008,632	0	0	0
13.	Lake Charles, LA	52,845,128	20,924,852	31,920,276	27,743,104	4,177,172
14.	Los Angeles, CA	51,395,952	6,430,349	44,965,603	30,317,011	14,648,592
15.	Valdez, AK	50,977,318	50,974,668	2,650	3	2,647
16.	Mobile, AL	48,115,781	20,134,933	27,980,848	17,722,560	10,258,288
17.	Philadelphia, PA	46,372,067	13,429,272	32,942,795	32,419,856	522,939
18.	Tampa, FL	45,793,544	28,348,557	17,444,987	8,956,319	8,488,668
19.	Baltimore, MD	42,072,123	16,721,819	25,350,304	18,267,954	7,082,350
20.	Duluth-Superior, MN and WI	39,810,866	26,535,026	13,275,840	746,400	12,529,440
21.	Norfolk Harbor, VA	37,310,351	10,332,246	26,978,105	7,306,280	19,671,825
22.	St. Louis, MO and IL	34,432,125	34,432,125	0	0	0
23.	Portland, OR	31,339,470	14,327,674	17,011,796	4,149,181	12,862,615
24.	Freeport, TX	30,142,822	5,248,758	24,894,064	22,645,478	2,248,586
25.	Pascagoula, MS	29,549,416	11,063,170	18,486,246	15,289,831	3,196,415
26.	Portland, ME	28,491,727	2,042,550	26,449,177	26,248,688	200,489
27.	Charleston, SC	23,250,058	6,122,752	17,127,306	11,115,993	6,011,313
28.	Port Arthur, TX	22,802,479	7,672,180	15,130,299	12,531,490	2,598,809
29.	Chicago, IL	21,975,717	19,352,906	2,622,811	2,055,281	567,530
30.	Port Everglades, FL	21,915,409	12,297,426	9,617,983	7,430,214	2,187,769
31.	Paulsboro, NJ	21,261,036	8,342,319	12,918,717	12,811,269	107,448
32.	Richmond, CA	21,220,231	11,227,440	9,992,791	8,870,929	1,121,862
33.	Boston, MA	20,581,180	8,151,141	12,430,039	11,791,174	638,865
34.	Seattle, WA	20,546,494	5,625,803	14,920,691	7,695,732	7,224,959
35.	Tacoma, WA	20,523,372	8,147,262	12,376,110	3,992,637	8,383,473
36.	Savannah, GA	19,392,227	2,461,082	16,931,145	9,647,931	7,283,214
37.	Marcus Hook, PA	19,124,360	10,878,098	8,246,262	8,231,290	14,972
38.	Jacksonville, FL	17,809,488	8,866,314	8,943,174	8,046,653	896,521
39.	Detroit, MI	16,991,159	12,264,488	4,726,671	4,465,273	261,398
40.	Memphis, TN	16,907,072	16,907,072	0	0	0
41.	Anacortes, WA	16,769,260	14,759,243	2,010,017	1,076,267	933,750
42.	Honolulu, HI	16,562,200	11,772,360	4,789,840	4,270,069	519,771
43.	Cincinnati, OH	14,098,926	14,098,926	0	0	0
44.	Newport News, VA	13,859,969	7,181,734	6,678,235	1,580,578	5,097,657
45.	Indiana Harbor, IN	13,579,192	12,836,555	742,637	742,637	0
46.	San Juan, PR	12,805,025	7,592,310	5,212,715	4,757,423	455,292
47.	Oakland, CA	12,272,777	1,555,477	10,717,300	3,849,653	6,867,647
48.	Cleveland, OH	11,937,815	9,203,587	2,734,228	2,430,028	304,200
49.	Two Harbors, MN	11,874,606	11,874,606	0	0	0
50.	Ashtabula, OH	10,933,552	5,119,678	5,813,874	797,494	5,016,380

World Trade Organization (WTO)

Following World War II, the major world economic powers negotiated a set of rules for reducing and limiting trade barriers and settling trade disputes. These rules were called the General Agreement on Tariffs and Trade (GATT). Headquarters to oversee administration of the GATT were established in Geneva, Switzerland. Rounds of multilateral trade negotiations under the GATT were carried out periodically. The 8th round, begun in 1986 in Punta del Este, Uruguay, and dubbed the Uruguay Round, ended Dec. 15, 1993, when 117 countries completed a new trade-liberalization agreement. The name for the GATT was changed to the World Trade Organization (WTO), which officially came into being Jan. 1, 1995.

Leading Motor Vehicle Producers, 2002[1]

Source: Automotive News Data Center and Marketing Systems GmbH

	Total	Passenger Cars	Trucks		Total	Passenger Cars	Trucks
United States	12,328,306	5,027,425	7,300,881	Sweden	510,891	409,362	101,529
Japan	10,239,949	8,618,725	1,621,224	Czech Republic	460,183	454,418	5,765
Germany	5,469,564	5,122,894	346,700	Malaysia	446,604	380,050	66,554
France	3,660,985	3,284,000	376,985	South Africa	417,942	290,000	127,942
S. Korea	3,147,584	2,651,273	496,311	Poland	349,325	309,925	39,400
China	2,913,530	1,183,125	1,730,405	Australia	342,900	305,120	37,780
Spain	2,843,486	2,266,902	576,584	Indonesia	342,469	25,200	317,269
Canada	2,624,431	1,369,042	1,255,389	Turkey	340,117	197,750	142,367
United Kingdom	1,819,848	1,627,972	191,876	Taiwan	333,699	231,506	102,193
Mexico	1,815,190	1,139,685	673,505	Iran	305,671	260,000	45,671
Brazil	1,723,505	1,452,908	270,597	Portugal	252,488	182,573	69,915
Italy	1,428,901	1,125,764	303,137	Slovakia	235,860	235,700	160
Russia	1,264,946	1,001,526	263,420	Netherlands	225,240	182,368	42,872
Belgium	1,057,574	936,904	120,670	Argentina	159,311	111,250	48,061
India	859,927	722,600	137,327				
Thailand	540,071	145,000	395,071	**World Total**	**59,587,416**	**42,084,571**	**17,502,845**

(1) Totals include countries or territories not shown.

World Motor Vehicle Production, 1950-2002

Source: American Automobile Manufacturers Assn.; for 1998-2000: Automotive News Data Center and Marketing Systems GmbH
(in thousands)

Year	United States	Canada	W. Europe	Japan	Other	World total	U.S. % of world total
1950	8,006	388	1,991	32	160	10,577	75.7
1960	7,905	398	6,837	482	866	16,488	47.9
1970	8,284	1,160	13,049	5,289	1,637	29,419	28.2
1980	8,010	1,324	15,496	11,043	2,692	38,565	20.8
1985	11,653	1,933	16,113	12,271	2,939	44,909	25.9
1990	9,783	1,928	18,866	13,487	4,496	48,554	20.1
1991	8,811	1,888	17,804	13,245	5,180	46,928	18.8
1992	9,729	1,961	17,628	12,499	6,269	48,088	20.2
1993	10,898	2,246	15,208	11,228	7,205	46,785	23.3
1994	12,263	2,321	16,195	10,554	8,167	49,500	24.8
1995	11,985	2,408	17,045	10,196	8,349	49,983	24.0
1996	11,799	2,397	17,550	10,346	9,241	51,332	23.0
1997	12,119	2,571	17,773	10,975	10,024	53,463	22.7
1998	12,047	2,568	16,332	10,050	12,844	53,841	22.4
1999	13,107	3,042	17,603	9,985	14,050	57,787	22.7
2000	12,832	2,952	17,678	10,145	16,098	59,704	21.5
2001	11,518	2,535	17,825	9,777	16,170	57,705	19.7
2002	12,328	2,624	17,419	10,240	16,975	59,587	20.7

Note: Data for 1998-2001 may not be fully comparable with earlier years because derived from different source.

New Passenger Cars Imported Into the U.S., by Country of Origin,[1] 1970-2002

Source: Bureau of the Census, Foreign Trade Division

	Japan	Germany[2]	Italy	United Kingdom	Sweden	France	South Korea	Mexico	Canada	Total[3]
1970	381,338	674,945	42,523	76,257	57,844	37,114	NA	NA	692,783	2,013,420
1971	703,672	770,807	51,469	106,710	61,925	23,316	NA	0	802,281	2,587,484
1972	697,788	676,967	64,614	72,038	64,541	14,713	NA	9	842,300	2,485,901
1973	624,805	677,465	56,102	64,140	58,626	8,219	NA	4,469	871,557	2,437,345
1974	791,791	619,757	107,071	72,512	60,817	21,331	NA	3,914	817,559	2,572,557
1975	695,573	370,012	102,344	67,106	51,993	15,647	NA	0	733,766	2,074,653
1976	1,128,936	349,804	82,500	77,190	37,466	21,916	NA	0	825,590	2,536,749
1977	1,341,530	423,492	55,437	56,889	39,370	19,215	NA	NA	849,814	2,790,144
1978	1,563,047	416,231	69,689	54,478	56,140	28,502	NA	6	833,061	3,024,982
1979	1,617,328	495,565	72,456	46,911	65,907	27,887	NA	4	677,008	3,005,523
1980	1,991,502	338,711	46,899	32,517	61,496	47,386	NA	1	594,770	3,116,448
1981	1,911,525	234,052	21,635	12,728	68,042	42,477	NA	1	563,943	2,856,286
1982	1,801,185	259,385	9,402	13,023	89,231	50,032	NA	27	702,495	2,926,407
1983	1,871,192	239,807	5,442	17,261	114,726	40,823	NA	2	835,665	3,133,836
1984	1,948,714	335,032	8,582	19,833	114,854	37,788	NA	NA	1,073,425	3,559,427
1985	2,527,467	473,110	8,689	24,474	142,640	42,882	NA	13,647	1,144,805	4,397,679
1986	2,618,711	451,699	11,829	27,506	148,700	10,869	169,309	41,983	1,162,226	4,691,297
1987	2,417,509	377,542	8,648	50,059	138,565	26,707	399,856	126,266	926,927	4,589,010
1988	2,123,051	264,249	6,053	31,636	108,006	15,990	455,741	148,065	1,191,357	4,450,213
1989	2,051,525	216,881	9,319	29,378	101,571	4,885	270,609	133,049	1,151,122	4,042,728
1990	1,867,794	245,286	11,045	27,271	93,084	1,976	201,475	215,986	1,220,221	3,944,602
1991	1,762,347	171,097	2,886	14,862	62,905	1,727	186,740	249,498	1,109,248	3,612,665
1992	1,598,919	205,248	1,791	10,997	76,832	65	130,110	266,111	1,119,223	3,447,200
1993	1,501,953	180,383	1,178	20,029	58,742	23	122,943	299,634	1,371,856	3,604,361
1994	1,488,150	178,774	1,010	28,217	63,867	58	213,962	360,367	1,525,746	3,909,079
1995	1,114,360	204,932	1,031	42,450	82,593	14	131,718	462,800	1,552,691	3,624,428
1996	1,190,896	234,909	1,365	44,373	86,619	27	225,623	550,867	1,690,733	4,069,113
1997	1,387,812	300,489	1,912	43,691	79,780	67	222,568	544,075	1,731,209	4,378,295
1998	1,456,081	373,330	2,104	49,891	84,543	56	211,650	584,795	1,837,615	4,673,418
1999	1,707,277	461,061	1,697	68,394	83,399	186	372,965	639,878	2,170,427	5,639,616
2000	1,839,093	488,323	3,125	81,196	86,707	134	568,121	934,000	2,138,811	6,324,284
2001	1,790,346	494,131	2,580	82,487	92,439	92	633,769	861,853	1,855,789	6,065,138
2002	2,046,902	574,455	3,504	157,633	87,709	150	627,881	845,181	1,882,660	6,477,659

(1) Excludes passenger cars assembled in U.S. foreign trade zones. (2) Figures prior to 1991 are for West Germany. (3) Includes countries not shown separately.

Passenger Car Production, U.S. Plants, 2001-2002

Source: Ward's AutoInfoBank

	2001	2002		2001	2002
TOTAL U.S. CAR	4,879,119	5,027,425	Ford Motor Co.	989,868	1,072,389
Total Autoalliance	71,723	65,924	Total Ford	767,595	845,794
Mazda Mazda6	—	14,731	Focus	251,879	273,591
Mazda 626	46,707	32,872	Mustang	160,184	171,262
Mercury Cougar	25,016	18,321	Taurus	347,577	375,219
Total BMW	34,169	21,460	Thunderbird	7,955	25,722
Z3/M coupe	2,543	970	Total Lincoln	124,583	119,962
Z3/M roadster	31,626	10,664	Continental	17,923	12,703
Z4 roadster	—	9,826	LS	39,081	41,078
DaimlerChrysler	438,141	420,521	Town Car	67,579	66,181
Total Chrysler Group	171,665	147,206	Mercury Sable	97,690	106,633
Neon	30,700	9,945	General Motors	1,656,172	1,672,987
Neon (rh drive)	5,258	2,109	Total Buick	165,269	175,197
Prowler	3,002	329	LeSabre	135,338	142,647
Sebring sedan	82,108	84,803	Park Avenue	29,931	32,550
Sebring convertible	50,597	50,020	Total Cadillac	133,436	160,070
Total Dodge	266,476	273,315	CTS	1,424	47,072
Neon	145,718	156,988	DeVille	98,420	86,849
Stratus	118,871	114,849	Eldorado	8,171	2,721
Viper (est.)	1,887	1,478	Seville	25,421	23,428

	2001	2002		2001	2002
Total Chevrolet	**446,332**	**504,368**	Civic	236,029	219,134
Cavalier	240,830	264,937	Accord	363,232	336,231
Corvette	35,535	35,938	Civic	236,029	219,134
Malibu	169,967	203,493	**Mitsubishi**	**193,435**	**202,611**
Total Oldsmobile	**177,676**	**127,850**	Chrysler Sebring coupe	10,892	10,284
Alero	119,752	107,390	Dodge Stratus coupe	17,426	17,632
Aurora	19,420	7,217	Mitsubishi Eclipse	52,898	55,425
Intrigue	38,504	13,243	Mitsubishi Eclipse convertible	17,569	19,332
Total Pontiac	**458,034**	**461,146**	Mitsubishi Galant	94,650	99,938
Bonneville	46,795	38,397	NISSAN Altima	157,876	235,445
Grand Am	197,123	193,473	**NUMMI**	**188,967**	**205,306**
Grand Prix	131,105	145,813	Chevrolet Prizm	46,020	—
Sunfire	83,011	83,463	Pontiac Vibe	—	59,556
Total Saturn	**275,425**	**244,356**	Toyota Corolla	142,947	137,642
Ion	—	34,489	Toyota Voltz*	—	8,108
L series	103,516	98,899	**Subaru/Isuzu**	**103,010**	**102,813**
S series	171,909	110,968	Baja	—	9,688
Honda of America	**692,377**	**641,109**	Legacy	103,010	93,125
Total Acura	93,116	85,744	**Toyota Motor MFG**	**353,381**	**386,860**
CL	14,802	13,625	Avalon	81,321	75,250
TL	78,314	72,119	Camry	272,060	311,610
Total Honda Division	**599,261**	**555,365**			
Accord	363,232	336,231			

* For export only. (1) Company is a joint venture between Ford and Mazda. (2) NUMMI (New United Motor Manufacturing, Inc.) is a joint venture between GM and Toyota.

U.S. Car Sales by Vehicle Size and Type, 1985-2002

Source: Ward's Communications; percent of total U.S. sales

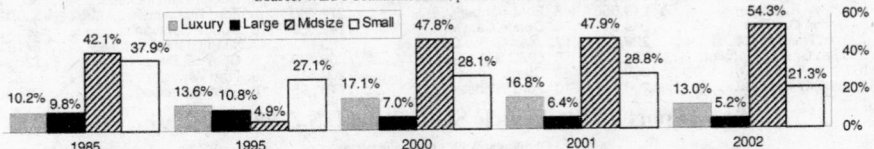

Domestic and Imported Retail Car Sales in the U.S., 1980-2002

Source: Ward's Communications

Calendar year	Domestic[1]	IMPORTS				Total U.S. sales	Import %	
		From Japan	From Germany	From other countries	Total imports		Total	Japan
1980	6,581,307	1,905,968	305,219	186,700	2,397,887	8,979,194	26.7	21.2
1981	6,208,760	1,858,896	282,881	185,502	2,327,279	8,536,039	27.3	21.8
1982	5,758,586	1,801,969	247,080	174,508	2,223,557	7,982,143	27.9	22.6
1983	6,795,295	1,915,621	279,748	191,403	2,386,772	9,182,067	26.0	20.9
1984	7,951,523	1,906,206	344,416	188,220	2,438,842	10,390,365	23.5	18.3
1985	8,204,542	2,217,837	423,983	195,925	2,837,745	11,042,287	25.7	20.1
1986	8,214,897	2,382,614	443,721	418,286	3,244,621	11,459,518	28.3	20.8
1987	7,080,858	2,190,405	347,881	657,465	3,195,751	10,276,609	31.1	21.3
1988	7,526,038	2,022,602	280,099	700,991	3,003,692	10,529,730	28.5	19.2
1989	7,072,902	1,897,143	248,561	553,660	2,699,364	9,772,266	27.6	19.4
1990	6,896,888	1,719,384	265,116	418,823	2,403,323	9,300,211	25.8	18.5
1991	6,136,757	1,500,309	192,776	344,814	2,037,899	8,174,656	24.9	18.4
1992	6,276,557	1,451,766	200,851	283,938	1,936,555	8,213,112	23.6	17.7
1993	6,741,667	1,328,445	186,177	261,570	1,776,192	8,517,859	20.9	15.6
1994	7,255,303	1,239,450	192,241	303,489	1,735,214	8,990,517	19.3	13.8
1995	7,128,712	981,462	207,555	317,269	1,506,257	8,634,964	17.4	11.4
1996	7,253,582	726,940	237,984	308,247	1,273,171	8,526,753	14.9	8.5
1997	6,916,769	726,104	297,028	332,173	1,355,305	8,272,074	16.4	8.8
1998	6,761,940	691,162	366,724	321,895	1,379,781	8,141,721	15.9	8.5
1999	6,979,357	757,568	466,870	494,489	1,718,927	8,698,284	21.1	8.7
2000	6,830,505	862,780	516,614	636,726	2,016,120	8,846,625	22.8	9.8
2001	6,494,104	914,018	510,290	737,003	2,161,311	8,655,415	25.0	10.6
2002	6,049,861	1,003,745	564,910	699,438	2,268,093	8,317,954	27.3	12.1

(1) Includes cars manufactured in Canada and Mexico.

U.S. Light-Vehicle Fuel Efficiency, 1975-2003

Source: Environmental Protection Agency, Office of Mobile Sources

After showing significant fuel-efficiency improvements from 1974 through 1985, both the categories of light-duty trucks (SUVs, minivans, vans, and light trucks) and cars have shown only small fuel-efficiency gains since 1985. In addition, light-duty trucks, which are less fuel-efficient than cars, have come to occupy an increasing proportion of the total light vehicle market, rising from only 19% in 1975 to an estimated 50.6% by 2002. This increase has been a major factor in the recent decline in the fuel efficiency of the average light vehicle sold. The average fuel economy of all light vehicles for model year 2003 was 24.4 miles per gallon, the highest in five years.

YEAR	Cars (MPG*)	Light-duty Trucks (MPG*)	All Light Vehicles (MPG*)	YEAR	Cars (MPG*)	Light-duty Trucks (MPG*)	All Light Vehicles (MPG*)
1975	15.8	13.7	15.3	1997	28.4	20.6	24.5
1980	23.5	18.6	22.5	1998	28.5	20.9	24.5
1985	27.0	20.6	25.0	1999	28.2	20.5	24.1
1990	27.8	20.7	25.2	2000	28.3	20.5	24.0
1994	28.0	20.8	24.6	2001	28.4	20.6	24.2
1995	28.3	20.5	24.7	2002	28.5	20.3	23.9
1996	28.3	20.8	24.8	2003	29.0	20.8	24.4

* MPG value represents laboratory city and highway fuel efficiency combined in a 55%/45% ratio.

Top-Selling Passenger Cars in the U.S. by Calendar Year, 1997-2002

Source: Ward's Communications

2002

1. Toyota Camry	434,145
2. Honda Accord	398,980
3. Ford Taurus	332,690
4. Honda Civic	313,159
5. Toyota Corolla	254,360
6. Ford Focus	243,199
7. Chevrolet Cavalier	238,225
8. Nissan Altima	201,822
9. Chevrolet Impala	198,918
10. Chevrolet Malibu	169,377
11. Buick Century	163,739
12. Pontiac Grand Am	150,818
13. Volkswagen Jetta	145,604
14. Ford Mustang	138,356
15. Buick LeSabre	135,916
16. Pontiac Grand Prix	130,141
17. Dodge Neon	126,118
18. Hyundai Elantra	120,638
19. Saturn S	117,533
20. BMW 3 Series	115,428

2001

1. Honda Accord	414,718
2. Toyota Camry	390,449
3. Ford Taurus	353,560
4. Honda Civic	331,780
5. Ford Focus	264,414
6. Toyota Corolla	245,023
7. Chevrolet Cavalier	233,298
8. Chevrolet Impala	208,395
9. Pontiac Grand Am	182,046
10. Chevrolet Malibu	176,583

2000

1. Toyota Camry	422,961
2. Honda Accord	404,515
3. Ford Taurus	382,035
4. Honda Civic	324,528
5. Ford Focus	286,166
6. Chevrolet Cavalier	236,803
7. Toyota Corolla	230,156
8. Pontiac Grand Am	214,923
9. Chevrolet Malibu	207,376
10. Saturn S	177,355

1999

1. Toyota Camry	448,162
2. Honda Accord	404,192
3. Ford Taurus	368,327
4. Honda Civic	318,308
5. Chevrolet Cavalier	272,122
6. Ford Escort	260,486
7. Toyota Corolla	249,128
8. Pontiac Grand Am	234,936
9. Chevrolet Malibu	218,540
10. Saturn S	207,977

Top-Selling Light Trucks in the U.S. by Calendar Year, 2000-2002

2002

1. Ford F Series	774,037
2. Chevy C/K Pickup/Silverado	648,040
3. Ford Explorer	433,847
4. Dodge Ram Pickup	396,934
5. Chevy Trailblazer	249,568
6. Dodge Caravan	244,911
7. Ford Ranger	226,094
8. Jeep Grand Cherokee	224,233
9. Chevy Tahoe	209,767
10. GMC Sierra	200,146

2001

1. Ford F Series	865,152
2. Chevy C/K Pickup/Silverado	708,386
3. Ford Explorer	415,921
4. Dodge Ram Pickup	344,538
5. Ford Ranger	272,460
6. Dodge Caravan	242,036
7. Jeep Grand Cherokee	223,612
8. GMC Sierra	206,930
9. Chevy Tahoe	202,319
10. Ford Windstar	179,595

2000

1. Ford F Series	820,248
2. Chevy C/K Pickup/Silverado	634,118
3. Ford Explorer	445,157
4. Dodge Ram Pickup	380,874
5. Ford Ranger	330,125
6. Dodge Caravan	285,739
7. Jeep Grand Cherokee	271,723
8. Chevy S Blazer	225,948
9. Ford Windstar	222,298
10. Ford Expedition	213,483

Sport Utility Vehicle Sales in the U.S., 1988-2002

Source: Ward's Communications

In 1988, 960,852 sport utility vehicles (SUVs) were sold in the United States, accounting for almost 19% of all light trucks and just over 6% of all sales of light vehicles (cars, SUVs, minivans, vans, pickup trucks, and trucks under 14,000 lbs.). In 2002, SUV sales increased 8.25% over the previous year to 4,100,015, or 24.3% of all light vehicles sold (48.1% of light trucks).

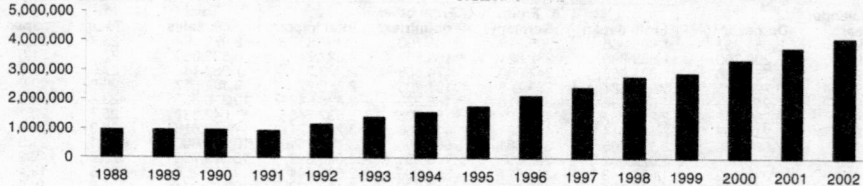

The Most Popular Colors, by Type of Vehicle, 2002 Model Year

Source: Du Pont Automotive Products

Luxury Cars

Color	Percent
Silver	32.1
White Metallic	17.7
White	11.8
Medium/Dark Blue	8.6
Black	8.5
Medium/Dark Gray	7.2
Medium Red	6.0
Gold	3.0
Medium/Dark Green	1.8
Light Brown	1.7
Other	1.6

Full Size/Intermediate Cars

Color	Percent
Silver	28.1
White	11.8
Light Brown	11.6
Black	11.2
Medium/Dark Blue	9.5
Medium Red	7.6
Medium Dark Gray	6.2
Medium Dark Green	5.3
Gold	3.4
Dark Red	2.6
Other	2.7

Compact/Sports Cars

Color	Percent
Silver	24.6
Black	14.3
Medium/Dark Blue	12.9
White	8.8
Bright Red	6.9
Medium/Dark Gray	6.7
Medium Red	5.5
Light Brown	4.3
Gold	4.1
Dark Red	2.6
Other	9.3

Light Trucks

Color	Percent
White	19.3
Silver	18.0
Black	12.4
Medium/Dark Blue	11.4
Medium Dark Gray	7.5
Medium/Red	7.1
Medium Dark Green	6.7
Light Brown	5.1
Bright Red	4.5
Gold	1.8
Other	6.2

Cars Registered in the U.S., 1900-2001[1]

Source: U.S. Dept. of Transportation, Federal Highway Administration

(includes automobiles for public and private use)

Year	Cars Registered	Year	Cars Registered	Year	Cars Registered	Year	Cars Registered
1900	8,000	1940	27,465,826	1975	106,705,934	1994	127,883,469
1905	77,400	1945	25,796,985	1980	121,600,843	1995	128,386,775
1910	458,377	1950	40,339,077	1985	127,885,193	1996	129,728,311
1915	2,332,426	1955	52,144,739	1990	133,700,497	1997	129,748,704
1920	8,131,522	1960	61,671,390	1991	128,299,601	1998	131,838,538
1925	17,481,001	1965	75,257,588	1992	126,581,148	1999	132,432,044
1930	23,034,753	1970	89,243,557	1993	127,327,189	2000	133,621,420
1935	22,567,827					2001	137,633,467

(1) There were no publicly owned vehicles before 1925; statistics also exclude military vehicles for all years. Alaska and Hawaii data included since 1960.

IT'S A FACT: According to the U.S. Dept. of Transportation's first National Household Travel Survey of the 21st century, cars outnumber drivers for the first time. The survey reports an average of 1.9 personal vehicles owned or available to U.S. households—but only 1.8 drivers per household. Among other findings: 8% of households have no vehicle, and 17% of adults reported using public transportation in the previous 2 months

Licensed Drivers, by Age, 1980-2001

Source: Federal Highway Administration, U.S. Dept. of Transportation

(in thousands)

AGE	1980 Male	Female	Total	1990 Male	Female	Total	2000 Male	Female	Total
(under 16)	52	41	93	23	20	43	13	12	25
16	1,001	822	1,823	769	674	1,443	697	666	1,363
17	1,530	1,260	2,790	1,136	996	2,132	1,124	1,067	2,192
18	1,763	1,484	3,247	1,378	1,217	2,595	1,426	1,329	2,755
19	1,900	1,643	3,542	1,608	1,429	3,037	1,593	1,493	3,086
(19 and under)	6,246	5,249	11,496	4,913	4,336	9,249	4,854	4,567	9,421
20	1,930	1,706	3,636	1,691	1,538	3,229	1,625	1,548	3,173
21	1,961	1,772	3,733	1,694	1,555	3,249	1,654	1,590	3,244
22	1,998	1,813	3,811	1,701	1,561	3,262	1,651	1,598	3,249
23	2,062	1,876	3,938	1,767	1,631	3,398	1,652	1,597	3,249
24	2,047	1,868	3,915	1,951	1,807	3,758	1,687	1,633	3,320
(20-24)	9,998	9,034	19,032	8,804	8,093	16,897	8,268	7,966	16,234
25-29	9,865	9,060	18,925	10,239	9,656	19,895	8,667	8,324	16,990
30-34	9,010	8,359	17,369	10,507	10,071	20,578	9,715	9,395	19,110
35-39	7,113	6,583	13,696	9,684	9,371	19,055	10,273	10,140	20,412
40-44	5,828	5,306	11,134	8,610	8,295	16,905	10,523	10,568	21,091
45-49	5,311	4,765	10,076	6,642	6,378	13,020	9,675	9,784	19,458
50-54	5,351	4,739	10,090	5,376	5,108	10,484	8,656	8,740	17,396
55-59	5,198	4,572	9,770	4,855	4,583	9,438	6,677	6,683	13,360
60-64	4,439	3,793	8,232	4,738	4,497	9,235	5,110	5,120	10,231
65-69	3,631	2,949	6,580	4,266	4,109	8,375	4,194	4,243	8,436
70 and over	5,195	3,699	8,894	7,159	6,726	13,885	9,181	9,955	19,136
70-74	NA	NA	NA	NA	NA	NA	3,651	3,814	7,465
75-79	NA	NA	NA	NA	NA	NA	2,825	3,087	5,912
80-84	NA	NA	NA	NA	NA	NA	1,723	1,930	3,653
85 and over	NA	NA	NA	NA	NA	NA	957	1,093	2,050
TOTAL	77,187	68,108	145,295	85,792	81,223	167,015	95,792	95,484	191,276

NA = not available.

Highway Speed Limits, by State

Source: Insurance Institute for Highway Safety

Under the National Highway System Designation Act, signed Nov. 28, 1995, by Pres. Bill Clinton, states were allowed to set their own highway speed limits, as of Dec. 8, 1995. Under federal legislation enacted in 1974 during the energy crisis, states had been, in effect, restricted to a National Maximum Speed Limit (NMSL) of 55 miles per hour (raised in 1987 to 65 mph on rural interstates).

Maximum posted speed limits, in miles per hour, are given by state in the table below. (Speeds shown in parentheses are for commercial trucks.) Most data current as of June 2003. For more information visit the Insurance Institute for Highway Safety website at www.hwysafety.org

STATE	Rural Interstate	Urban[1] Interstate	Limited[2] Access Roads	Other Roads	STATE	Rural Interstate	Urban[1] Interstate	Limited[2] Access Roads	Other Roads
AL	70	65	65	65	MT	75 (65)	65	70[3]	70[3]
AK	65	55	65	55	NE	75	65	65	60
AZ	75	55	55	55	NV	75	65	70	70
AR	70 (65)	55	60	55	NH	65	65	55	55
CA	70 (55)	65	70	65	NJ	65	55	65	55
CO	75	65	65	65	NM	75	75	65	55
CT	65	55	65	55	NY	65	65	65	55
DE	65	55	65	55	NC	70	70	70	55
FL	70	65	70	65	ND	75	75	70	65
GA	70	65	65	65	OH	65 (55)	65	55	55
HI	60	50	45	45	OK	75	70	70	70
ID	75 (65)	75	65	65	OR	65 (55)	55	55	55
IL	65 (55)	55	65	55	PA	65	55	65	55
IN	65 (60)	55	55	55	RI	65	55	55	55
IA	65	55	65	55	SC	70	70	60	55
KS	70	70	70	65	SD	75	75	65	65
KY	65	65	65	55	TN	70	70	70	65
LA	70	70	70	65	TX	75 (65)[3]	70[3]	75 (65)[3]	60 (55)[4]
ME	65	65	65	60	UT	75	65	75	65
MD	65	65	65	55	VT	65	55	50	50
MA	65	65	65	55	VA	65	65	65	55
MI	70 (55)	65	70	55	WA	70 (60)	60	60	60
MN	70	65	65	55	WV	70	55	65	55
MS	70	70	70	65	WI	65	65	65	55
MO	70	60	70	65	WY	75	60	65	65

(1) Urban interstates are determined from U.S. Census Bureau criteria, which may be adjusted by state and local governments to reflect planning and other issues. (2) Limited access roads are multiple-lane highways with restricted access via exit and entrance ramps rather than intersections. (3) Speed limit is 65 mph at night. (4) Speed limit is 55 mph at night. "Night" means from one-half hour after sunset to one-half hour before sunrise.

Selected Motor Vehicle Statistics

Source: Federal Highway Administration; U.S. Dept. of Transportation; Insurance Institute for Highway Safety

Driver's license age requirements, state gas tax, and safety belt laws as of July 2003; figures for 2001 where not specified.

STATE	Regular[1]	Learner's Permit	State gas tax cents/ gal.	Safety belt use law[11]	Licensed drivers per 1,000 resident pop.	Regist. motor vehicles per 1,000 pop.	Licensed drivers per motor vehicle	Gals. of fuel used per vehicle	Miles per gal.	Annual miles driven per vehicle	Vehicle miles per licensed driver
Alabama	17y, 6m	15	18	P	800	949	0.85	741	18.09	13,404	15,947
Alaska	16	14	8	S	753	941	0.81	662	11.94	7,898	9,998
Arizona	16	15y, 7m	18	S	692	747	0.90	800	16.03	12,820	14,325
Arkansas	16	14	21.7	S	734	692	1.07	1,074	14.70	15,792	15,002
California	17[2]	15	18	P	638	834	0.76	612	17.64	10,796	14,369
Colorado	17	15	22	S	764	1,052	0.71	567	16.31	9,240	13,064
Connecticut	18y	16	25	P	778	852	0.92	611	17.32	10,574	11,638
Delaware	16y, 10m[2]	15y, 10m	23	P	720	820	0.88	696	18.95	13,191	15,272
Dist. of Col.	18[3]	16	20	P	574	435	1.38	774	19.46	15,069	11,430
Florida	18	15	13.6	S	797	875	0.91	628	17.30	10,855	12,215
Georgia	18	15	7.5	P	713	871	0.81	854	17.29	14,771	18,495
Hawaii	16y[2]	15y, 6m	16	P	650	709	0.92	516	19.42	10,015	11,036
Idaho	16[4]	14y, 6m	25	S	693	1,002	0.69	652	16.32	10,634	15,700
Illinois	18[2]	15	19	S	629	790	0.80	648	16.11	10,449	13,194
Indiana	18	15	15	P	677	920	0.74	742	17.15	12,733	17,397
Iowa	17[2]	14	20	P	676	1,135	0.61	621	14.57	9,046	15,169
Kansas	16	14	21	S	696	865	0.81	714	16.92	12,080	15,046
Kentucky	16y, 6m[5]	15	16.4	S	682	892	0.77	826	15.44	12,758	16,781
Louisiana	17[6]	15	20	P	608	808	0.77	800	14.26	11,411	15,149
Maine	16y, 6m[2]	15	22	S	739	791	0.94	754	18.81	14,184	15,313
Maryland	17y, 7m[7]	15y, 9m	23.5	P	652	733	0.89	767	17.20	13,201	15,063
Massachusetts	18	16	21	S	726	815	0.90	612	16.67	10,199	11,498
Michigan	17[2]	14y, 9m	19	P	702	846	0.84	707	16.55	11,709	14,188
Minnesota	17[2]	15	20	S	602	916	0.66	720	16.27	11,713	18,013
Mississippi	16[8]	15	18.4	Sa	654	684	0.97	1,054	17.47	18,420	19,354
Missouri	18	15	17	Sa	690	747	0.92	951	16.91	16,073	17,511
Montana	15[9]	14y, 6m	27	S	757	1,142	0.68	675	14.35	9,690	14,650
Nebraska	17	15	24.5	S	741	953	0.79	757	14.64	11,082	14,284
Nevada	16[2]	15y, 6m	24.75	S	711	608	1.13	972	14.72	14,306	12,887
New Hampshire	18	15y, 6m	19.5	none	762	873	0.87	716	15.65	11,200	13,076
New Jersey	18y	16	10.5	P	679	776	0.89	735	14.22	10,444	12,025
New Mexico	16y, 6m[2]	16	18.5	P	677	781	0.89	930	17.50	16,264	18,862
New York	17[2]	16[10]	22	P	580	536	1.10	652	19.65	12,820	11,868
North Carolina	16y, 6m	15	24.1	P	731	755	0.97	834	17.76	14,819	15,563
North Dakota	16	14	21	S	710	1,115	0.66	728	14.05	10,225	15,869
Ohio	17[2]	15y, 6m	22	S	681	928	0.74	629	16.06	10,099	13,778
Oklahoma	16	15y, 6m	17	P	630	948	0.68	847	15.67	13,266	20,036
Oregon	17	15	24	S	741	875	0.85	646	17.53	11,317	13,572
Pennsylvania	17[2]	16	26	S	670	784	0.87	676	15.83	10,695	12,521
Rhode Island	17y, 6m[2]	16	29	Sa	630	722	0.88	607	17.22	10,453	12,100
South Carolina	16y, 6m	15	16	Sa	710	773	0.92	926	16.02	14,828	16,352
South Dakota	16	14	22	S	722	1,062	0.70	728	14.60	10,631	15,673
Tennessee	17	15	20	S	736	895	0.83	734	17.92	13,161	16,148
Texas	16y, 6[2]	15	20	P	626	673	0.93	968	15.55	15,058	16,154
Utah	17[7]	15y, 9m	24.5	Sa	670	772	0.87	752	17.80	13,388	15,678
Vermont	16y, 6m[2]	15	20	S	846	871	0.99	774	23.28	18,017	18,661
Virginia	18[2]	15, 6m	17.5	S	695	859	0.81	778	15.36	11,950	14,987
Washington	17[2]	15	23	p	719	865	0.83	627	16.52	10,362	12,663
West Virginia	17	15	25.65	S	728	806	0.94	765	17.76	13,577	14,969
Wisconsin	16y, 9[2]	15y, 6m	27.3	S	684	828	0.83	711	18.00	12,803	15,615
Wyoming	16	15	14	S	751	1,158	0.67	1,158	13.01	15,062	23,266
AVERAGE			18.4		680	809	0.84	725	16.64	12,071	14,542

NOTE: Many states are moving toward graduated licensing systems that phase in full driving privileges. During the learner's phase, driving generally is not permitted unless there is an adult supervisor. In an intermediate phase, young licensees not yet having unrestricted licenses may be allowed to drive unsupervised under certain conditions but not others. (1) Unrestricted operation of private passenger car. (2) Applicants under age 18 (19 in VA) must have completed an approved driver education course. (3) Learner's phase mandatory for all ages. Applicants under age 21 must complete a 6-month intermediate phase. (4) Applicants under age 17 must have completed an approved driver education course. (5) License holders under age 18 must complete a 4-hour course on safe driving within 1 yr. of receiving license (6) Applicants age 17 and older must have completed an educational program, but doesn't require behind-the-wheel training. (7) Initial applicants of any age must have completed an approved driver education course. (8) Applicants age 17 and older not subject to learner's permit and intermediate license requirements. (9) Applicants under age 16 must have completed an approved driver education course. (10) Driving in New York City is prohibited for all licensees under 18. (11) P = officer may stop vehicle for a violation (primary); S = an officer may issue seat belt citation only when vehicle is stopped for another moving violation (secondary). (a) Primary enforcement for children under a specified age: MS-8; MO-16; RI-13; SC, UT-19.

Road Mileage Between Selected U.S. Cities

	Atlanta	Boston	Chicago	Cincinnati	Cleveland	Dallas	Denver	Des Moines	Detroit	Houston
Atlanta, Ga.	...	1,037	674	440	672	795	1,398	870	699	789
Boston, Mass.	1,037	...	963	840	628	1,748	1,949	1,280	695	1,804
Chicago, Ill........	674	963	...	287	335	917	996	327	266	1,067
Cincinnati, Oh.	440	840	287	...	244	920	1,164	571	259	1,029
Cleveland, Oh.	672	628	335	244	...	1,159	1,321	652	170	1,273
Dallas Tex.	795	1,748	917	920	1,159	...	781	684	1,143	243
Denver, Col.	1,398	1,949	996	1,164	1,321	781	...	669	1,253	1,019
Detroit, Mich.	699	695	266	259	170	1,143	1,253	584	...	1,265
Houston, Tex.	789	1,804	1,067	1,029	1,273	243	1,019	905	1,265	...
Indianapolis, Ind. ...	493	906	181	106	294	865	1,058	465	278	987
Kansas City, Mo....	798	1,391	499	591	779	489	600	195	743	710
Los Angeles, Cal. .	2,182	2,979	2,054	2,179	2,367	1,387	1,059	1,727	2,311	1,538
Memphis, Tenn.	371	1,296	530	468	712	452	1,040	599	713	561
Milwaukee, Wis. ...	761	1,050	87	374	422	991	1,029	361	353	1,142
Minneapolis, Minn. .	1,068	1,368	405	692	740	936	841	252	671	1,157
New Orleans, La. ...	479	1,507	912	786	1,030	496	1,273	978	1,045	356
New York, N.Y.	841	206	802	647	473	1,552	1,771	1,119	637	1,608
Omaha, Neb.	986	1,412	459	693	784	644	537	132	716	865
Philadelphia, Pa. ...	741	296	738	567	413	1,452	1,691	1,051	573	1,508
Pittsburgh, Pa.	687	561	452	287	129	1,204	1,411	763	287	1,313
Portland Ore.	2,601	3,046	2,083	2,333	2,418	2,009	1,238	1,786	2,349	2,205
St. Louis, Mo.......	541	1,141	289	340	529	630	857	333	513	779
San Francisco	2,496	3,095	2,142	2,362	2,467	1,753	1,235	1,815	2,399	1,912
Seattle, Wash.	2,618	2,976	2,013	2,300	2,348	2,078	1,307	1,749	2,279	2,274
Tulsa, Okla.	772	1,537	683	736	925	257	681	443	909	478
Washington, DC....	608	429	671	481	346	1,319	1,616	984	506	1,375

	Indianapolis	Kansas City	Los Angeles	Louisville	Memphis	Milwaukee	Minneapolis	New Orleans	New York	Omaha
Atlanta, Ga.	493	798	2,182	382	371	761	1,068	479	841	986
Boston, Mass.	906	1,391	2,979	941	1,296	1,050	1,368	1,507	206	1,412
Chicago, Ill.	181	499	2,054	292	530	87	405	912	802	459
Cincinnati, Oh.	106	591	2,179	101	468	374	692	786	647	693
Cleveland Oh.	294	779	2,367	345	712	422	740	1,030	473	784
Dallas, Tex..	865	489	1,387	819	452	991	936	496	1,552	644
Denver, Col.	1,058	600	1,059	1,120	1,040	1,029	841	1,273	1,771	537
Detroit, Mich.	278	743	2,311	360	713	353	671	1,045	637	716
Houston, Tex.	987	710	1,538	928	561	1,142	1,157	356	1,608	865
Indianapolis, Ind. ...	...	485	2,073	111	435	268	586	796	713	587
Kansas City, Mo....	485	...	1,589	520	451	537	447	806	1,198	201
Los Angeles, Cal.. .	2,073	1,589	...	2,108	1,817	2,087	1,889	1,883	2,786	1,595
Memphis, Tenn.	435	451	1,817	367	...	612	826	390	1,100	652
Milwaukee, Wis. ...	268	537	2,087	379	612	...	332	994	889	493
Minneapolis, Minn. .	586	447	1,889	697	826	332	...	1,214	1,207	357
New Orleans, La. ...	796	806	1,883	685	390	994	1,214	...	1,311	1,007
New York, N.Y.	713	1,198	2,786	748	1,100	889	1,207	1,311	...	1,251
Omaha, Neb.	587	201	1,595	687	652	493	357	1,007	1,251	...
Philadelphia, Pa. ...	633	1,118	2,706	668	1,000	825	1,143	1,211	100	1,183
Pittsburgh, Pa.	353	838	2,426	388	752	539	857	1,070	368	895
Portland, Ore.	2,272	1,809	959	2,320	2,259	2,010	1,678	2,505	2,885	1,654
St. Louis, Mo.......	235	257	1,845	263	285	363	552	673	948	449
San Francisco	2,293	1,835	379	2,349	2,125	2,175	1,940	2,249	2,934	1,683
Seattle, Wash.	2,194	1,839	1,131	2,305	2,290	1,940	1,608	2,574	2,815	1,638
Tulsa, Okla.	631	248	1,452	659	401	757	695	647	1,344	387
Washington, DC....	558	1,043	2,631	582	867	758	1,076	1,078	233	1,116

	Philadephia	Pittsburgh	Portland	St. Louis	Salt Lake City	San Francisco	Seattle	Toledo	Tulsa	Wash., DC
Atlanta, Ga.	741	687	2,601	541	1,878	2,496	2,618	640	772	608
Boston, Mass.	296	561	3,046	1,141	2,343	3,095	2,976	739	1,537	429
Chicago, Ill.	738	452	2,083	289	1,390	2,142	2,013	232	683	671
Cincinnati, Oh.	567	287	2,333	340	1,610	2,362	2,300	200	736	481
Cleveland Oh.......	413	129	2,418	529	1,715	2,467	2,348	111	925	346
Dallas, Tex.	1,452	1,204	2,009	630	1,242	1,753	2,078	1,084	257	1,319
Denver, Col.	1,691	1,411	1,238	857	504	1,235	1,307	1,218	681	1,616
Detroit, Mich.	576	287	2,349	513	1,647	2,399	2,279	59	909	506
Houston, Tex.	1,508	1,313	2,205	779	1,438	1,912	2,274	1,206	478	1,375
Indianapolis, Ind. ...	633	353	2,272	235	1,504	2,293	2,194	219	631	558
Kansas City, Mo....	1,118	838	1,809	257	1,086	1,835	1,839	687	248	1,043
Los Angeles, Cal....	2,706	2,426	959	1,845	715	379	1,131	2,276	1,452	2,631
Memphis, Tenn.	1,000	752	2,259	285	1,535	2,125	2,290	654	401	867
Milwaukee, Wis. ...	825	539	2,010	363	1,423	2,175	1,940	319	757	758
Minneapolis, Minn. .	1,143	857	1,678	552	1,186	1,940	1,608	637	695	1,076
New Orleans, La. ...	1,211	1,070	2,505	673	1,738	2,249	2,574	986	647	1,078
New York, N.Y.'	100	368	2,885	948	2,182	2,934	2,815	578	1,344	233
Omaha, Neb.	1,183	895	1,654	449	931	1,683	1,638	681	387	1,116
Philadelphia, Pa. ...	...	288	2,821	868	2,114	2,866	2,751	514	1,264	133
Pittsburgh, Pa.	288	...	2,535	588	1,826	2,578	2,465	228	984	221
Portland, Ore.	2,821	2,535	...	2,060	767	636	172	2,315	1,913	2,754
St. Louis, Mo.	868	588	2,060	...	1,337	2,089	2,081	454	396	793
San Francisco	2,866	2,578	636	2,089	752	...	808	2,364	1,760	2,799
Seattle, Wash.	2,751	2,465	172	2,081	836	808	...	2,245	1,982	2,684
Tulsa, Okla.	1,264	984	1,913	396	1,172	1,760	1,982	850	...	1,189
Washington, DC....	133	221	2,754	793	2,047	2,799	2,684	447	1,189	...

Air Distances Between Selected World Cities in Statute Miles

Point-to-point measurements are usually from City Hall.

	Bangkok	Beijing	Berlin	Cairo	Cape Town	Caracas	Chicago	Hong Kong	Honolulu	Lima
Bangkok	...	2,046	5,352	4,523	6,300	10,555	8,570	1,077	6,609	12,244
Beijing	2,046	...	4,584	4,698	8,044	8,950	6,604	1,217	5,077	10,349
Berlin	5,352	4,584	...	1,797	5,961	5,238	4,414	5,443	7,320	6,896
Cairo	4,523	4,698	1,797	...	4,480	6,342	6,141	5,066	8,848	7,726
Cape Town	6,300	8,044	5,961	4,480	...	6,366	8,491	7,376	11,535	6,072
Caracas	10,555	8,950	5,238	6,342	6,366	...	2,495	10,165	6,021	1,707
Chicago	8,570	6,604	4,414	6,141	8,491	2,495	...	7,797	4,256	3,775
Hong Kong	1,077	1,217	5,443	5,066	7,376	10,165	7,797	...	5,556	11,418
Honolulu	6,609	5,077	7,320	8,848	11,535	6,021	4,256	5,556	...	5,947
London	5,944	5,074	583	2,185	5,989	4,655	3,958	5,990	7,240	6,316
Los Angeles	7,637	6,250	5,782	7,520	9,969	3,632	1,745	7,240	2,557	4,171
Madrid	6,337	5,745	1,165	2,087	5,308	4,346	4,189	6,558	7,872	5,907
Melbourne	4,568	5,643	9,918	8,675	6,425	9,717	9,673	4,595	5,505	8,059
Mexico City	9,793	7,753	6,056	7,700	8,519	2,234	1,690	8,788	3,789	2,639
Montreal	8,338	6,519	3,740	5,427	7,922	2,438	745	7,736	4,918	3,970
Moscow	4,389	3,607	1,006	1,803	6,279	6,177	4,987	4,437	7,047	7,862
New York	8,669	6,844	3,979	5,619	7,803	2,120	714	8,060	4,969	3,639
Paris	5,877	5,120	548	1,998	5,786	4,732	4,143	5,990	7,449	6,370
Rio de Janeiro	9,994	10,768	6,209	6,143	3,781	2,804	5,282	11,009	8,288	2,342
Rome	5,494	5,063	737	1,326	5,231	5,195	4,824	5,774	8,040	6,750
San Francisco	7,931	5,918	5,672	7,466	10,248	3,902	1,859	6,905	2,398	4,518
Singapore	883	2,771	6,164	5,137	6,008	11,402	9,372	1,605	6,726	11,689
Stockholm	5,089	4,133	528	2,096	6,423	5,471	4,331	5,063	6,875	7,166
Tokyo	2,865	1,307	5,557	5,958	9,154	8,808	6,314	1,791	3,859	9,631
Warsaw	5,033	4,325	322	1,619	5,935	5,559	4,679	5,147	7,366	7,215
Washington, DC	8,807	6,942	4,181	5,822	7,895	2,047	596	8,155	4,838	3,509

	London	Los Angeles	Madrid	Melbourne	Mexico City	Montreal	Moscow	New Delhi	New York	Paris
Bangkok	5,944	7,637	6,337	4,568	9,793	8,338	4,389	1,813	8,669	5,877
Beijing	5,074	6,250	5,745	5,643	7,753	6,519	3,607	2,353	6,844	5,120
Berlin	583	5,782	1,165	9,918	6,056	3,740	1,006	3,598	3,979	548
Cairo	2,185	7,520	2,087	8,675	7,700	5,427	1,803	2,758	5,619	1,998
Cape Town	5,989	9,969	5,308	6,425	8,519	7,922	6,279	5,769	7,803	5,786
Caracas	4,655	3,632	4,346	9,717	2,234	2,438	6,177	8,833	2,120	4,732
Chicago	3,958	1,745	4,189	9,673	1,690	745	4,987	7,486	714	4,143
Hong Kong	5,990	7,240	6,558	4,595	8,788	7,736	4,437	2,339	8,060	5,990
Honolulu	7,240	2,557	7,872	5,505	3,789	4,918	7,047	7,412	4,969	7,449
London	...	5,439	785	10,500	5,558	3,254	1,564	4,181	3,469	214
Los Angeles	5,439	...	5,848	7,931	1,542	2,427	6,068	7,011	2,451	5,601
Madrid	785	5,848	...	10,758	5,643	3,448	2,147	4,530	3,593	655
Melbourne	10,500	7,931	10,758	...	8,426	10,395	8,950	6,329	10,359	10,430
Mexico City	5,558	1,542	5,643	8,426	...	2,317	6,676	9,120	2,090	5,725
Montreal	3,254	2,427	3,448	10,395	2,317	...	4,401	7,012	331	3,432
Moscow	1,564	6,068	2,147	8,950	6,676	4,401	...	2,698	4,683	1,554
New York	3,469	2,451	3,593	10,359	2,090	331	4,683	7,318	...	3,636
Paris	214	5,601	655	10,430	5,725	3,432	1,554	4,102	3,636	...
Rio de Janeiro	5,750	6,330	5,045	8,226	4,764	5,078	7,170	8,753	4,801	5,684
Rome	895	6,326	851	9,929	6,377	4,104	1,483	3,684	4,293	690
San Francisco	5,367	347	5,803	7,856	1,887	2,543	5,885	7,691	2,572	5,577
Singapore	6,747	8,767	7,080	3,759	10,327	9,203	5,228	2,571	9,534	6,673
Stockholm	942	5,454	1,653	9,630	6,012	3,714	716	3,414	3,986	1,003
Tokyo	5,959	5,470	6,706	5,062	7,035	6,471	4,660	3,638	6,757	6,053
Warsaw	905	5,922	1,427	9,598	6,337	4,022	721	3,277	4,270	852
Washington, DC	3,674	2,300	3,792	10,180	1,885	489	4,876	7,500	205	3,840

	Rio de Janeiro	Rome	San Francisco	Singapore	Stockholm	Tehran	Tokyo	Vienna	Warsaw	Wash., DC
Bangkok	9,994	5,494	7,931	883	5,089	3,391	2,865	5,252	5,033	8,807
Beijing	10,768	5,063	5,918	2,771	4,133	3,490	1,307	4,648	4,325	6,942
Berlin	6,209	737	5,672	6,164	528	2,185	5,557	326	322	4,181
Cairo	6,143	1,326	7,466	5,137	2,096	1,234	5,958	1,481	1,619	5,822
Cape Town	3,781	5,231	10,248	6,008	6,423	5,241	9,154	5,656	5,935	7,895
Caracas	2,804	5,195	3,902	11,402	5,471	7,320	8,808	5,372	5,559	2,047
Chicago	5,282	4,824	1,859	9,372	4,331	6,502	6,314	4,698	4,679	596
Hong Kong	11,009	5,774	6,905	1,605	5,063	3,843	1,791	5,431	5,147	8,155
Honolulu	8,288	8,040	2,398	6,726	6,875	8,070	3,859	7,632	7,366	4,838
London	5,750	895	5,367	6,747	942	2,743	5,959	771	905	3,674
Los Angeles	6,330	6,326	347	8,767	5,454	7,682	5,470	6,108	5,922	2,300
Madrid	5,045	851	5,803	7,080	1,653	2,978	6,706	1,128	1,427	3,792
Melbourne	8,226	9,929	7,856	3,759	9,630	7,826	5,062	9,790	9,598	10,180
Mexico City	4,764	6,377	1,887	10,327	6,012	8,184	7,035	6,320	6,337	1,885
Montreal	5,078	4,104	2,543	9,203	3,714	5,880	6,471	4,009	4,022	489
Moscow	7,170	1,483	5,885	5,228	716	1,532	4,660	1,043	721	4,876
New York	4,801	4,293	2,572	9,534	3,986	6,141	6,757	4,234	4,270	205
Paris	5,684	690	5,577	6,673	1,003	2,625	6,053	645	852	3,840
Rio de Janeiro	...	5,707	6,613	9,785	6,683	7,374	11,532	6,127	6,455	4,779
Rome	5,707	...	6,259	6,229	1,245	2,127	6,142	477	820	4,497
San Francisco	6,613	6,259	...	8,448	5,399	7,362	5,150	5,994	5,854	2,441
Singapore	9,785	6,229	8,448	...	5,936	4,103	3,300	6,035	5,843	9,662
Stockholm	6,683	1,245	5,399	5,936	...	2,173	5,053	780	494	4,183
Tokyo	11,532	6,142	5,150	3,300	5,053	4,775	...	5,689	5,347	6,791
Warsaw	6,455	820	5,854	5,843	494	1,879	5,689	347	...	4,472
Washington, DC	4,779	4,497	2,441	9,662	4,183	6,341	6,791	4,438	4,472	...

100 MOST POPULOUS U.S. CITIES

Source: Bureau of Labor Statistics: employment; Bureau of Economic Analysis: per capita personal income; all other data from U.S. Census Bureau.

Included here are the 100 most populous U.S. cities, using 2002 Census Bureau estimates. Population rank indicated by figure in parentheses. Most data are for the city proper. Some statistics, where noted, apply to the whole Metropolitan Statistical Area (MSA). Employment figures are for 2002; per capita income figures for 2001. Mayors are as of Sept. 2003. Inc.=incorporated; est.=established.

Note: Websites are as of Sept. 2003 and subject to change.

Akron, Ohio

Population (2002): 214,349 (84); **Pop. density:** 3,452 per sq. mi; **Pop. change (1990-2002):** −4.0%. **Area:** 62.1 sq. mi. **Employment:** 107,817 employed; 7.6% unemployed. **Per capita income (MSA):** $29,953; increase (2000-2001): 2.4%.

.**Mayor:** Donald L. Plusquellic, Democrat

History: settled 1825; inc. as city 1865; located on Ohio-Erie Canal and is a port of entry; polymer center of the Americas.

Transportation: 1 airport; major trucking industry; Conrail, Amtrak; metro transit system. **Communications:** 1 TV, 8 radio stations; 1 daily newspaper. **Medical facilities:** 4 hosp.; specialized children's treatment center. **Educational facilities:** 4 univ. and colleges; 68 pub. schools. **Further information:** Greater Akron Chamber, One Cascade Plaza, 17th Floor, Akron, OH 44308; www.ci.akron.oh.us; www.greaterakronchamber.org

Albuquerque, New Mexico

Population (2002): 463,874 (35); **Pop. density:** 2,569 per sq. mi; **Pop. change (1990-2002):** +19.9. **Area:** 180.6 sq. mi. **Employment:** 243,224 employed; 4.4% unemployed. **Per capita income (MSA):** $27,030; increase (2000-2001): 4.8%.

Mayor: Martin Chavez, Democrat

History: founded 1706 by the Spanish; inc. 1890.

Transportation: 1 intl. airport; 1 railroad; 11 bus service/charters. **Communications:** 14 TV, 37 radio stations. **Medical facilities:** 6 major hosp. **Educational facilities:** 1 univ., 25 colleges. **Further information:** Albuquerque Convention & Visitors Bureau, PO Box 26866, Albuquerque, NM 87125-6866, 1-800-733-9918; www.itsatrip.org; www.cabq.gov-a-z.org

Anaheim, California

Population (2002): 332,642 (53); **Pop. density:** 6,802 per sq. mi; **Pop. change (1990-2002):** +24.8%. **Area:** 48.9 sq. mi. **Employment:** 164,219 employed; 5.4% unemployed. **Per capita income (MSA):** $36,647; increase (2000-2001): 3.4.

Mayor: Curt Pringle, Republican

History: founded 1857; inc. 1870; now known as home of The Disneyland Resort, the Mighty Ducks of Anaheim, and the Anaheim Angels.

Transportation: Amtrak, Metrolink (2 sta.), OCTA bus service, Greyhound. **Communications:** 2 TV, 2 radio stations (MSA). **Medical facilities:** 4 hosp.; 5 medical centers. **Educational facilities:** 13 univ. and colleges; 39 elem., 11 junior high, 10 high schools (MSA). **Further information:** City Hall, 200 South Anaheim Blvd., Ste. 733, Anaheim, CA 92805; www.anaheim.net

Anchorage, Alaska

Population (2002): 268,983 (65); **Pop. density:** 158 per sq. mi; **Pop. change (1990-2002):** +18.8%. **Area:** 1,697.2 sq. mi. **Employment:** 137,754 employed; 5.4% unemployed. **Per capita income (MSA):** $36,949; increase (2000-2001): 4.7%.

Mayor: Mark Begich, Democrat

History: founded 1914 as a construction camp for railroad; HQ of Alaska Defense Command, WWII; severely damaged in earthquake 1964, but now rebuilt and currently population center of Alaska.

Transportation: 1 intl. airport; 1 railroad; transit system, 1 port. **Communications:** 9 TV, 28 radio stations. **Medical facilities:** 4 hosp. **Educational facilities:** 3 univ., 1 college, 90 pub. schools. **Further information:** Anchorage Chamber of Commerce, 441 W. 5th Ave., Ste. 300, Anchorage, AK 99501-2309; www.ci.anchorage.ak.us; www.anchoragechamber.org

Arlington, Texas

Population (2002): 349,944 (50); **Pop. density:** 3,653 per sq. mi; **Pop. change (1990-2002):** +33.6%. **Area:** 95.8 sq. mi. **Employment:** 189,642 employed; 5.4% unemployed. **Per capita income (MSA):** $30,230; increase (2000-2001): 3.0%.

Mayor: Robert Clark, Non-Partisan

History: settled in 1840s between Dallas and Ft. Worth; inc. 1884.

Transportation: Dallas/Ft. Worth airport is 10 min. away; 11 railway lines; intercity transport system in planning stage. **Communications:** 11 TV, 44 radio stations. **Medical facilities:** 2 hosp. **Educational facilities:** 1 univ., 1 junior college; 60 pub. schools. **Further information:** Arlington Chamber of Commerce, 505 East Border, Arlington, TX 76010; www.ci.arlington.tx.us; www.arlingtontx.com

Atlanta, Georgia

Population (2002): 424,868 (41); **Pop. density:** 3,226 per sq. mi; **Pop. change (1990-2002):** +7.9%. **Area:** 131.7 sq. mi. **Employment:** 219,436 employed; 8.6% unemployed. **Per capita income (MSA):** $33,769; increase (2000-2001): 0.8%.

Mayor: Shirley Franklin, Democrat

History: founded as "Terminus" 1837; renamed Atlanta 1845; inc. 1847; played major role in Civil War; became permanent state capital 1877; birthplace of civil rights movement; host to 1996 Centennial Olympic Games.

Transportation: 1 intl. airport; 3 railroad lines; MARTA bus and rapid rail service. **Communications:** 14 TV, 56 radio stations; 29 cable TV cos. **Medical facilities:** 61 hosp.; VA hosp.; U.S. Centers for Disease Control and Prevention; American Cancer Society. **Educational facilities:** 43 colleges, univ., seminaries, junior colleges; 813 pub. schools (metro area). **Further information:** Metro Atlanta Chamber of Commerce, 235 Andrew Young Intl. Blvd. NW, Atlanta, GA 30303; www.atlantasmartcity.com; www.metroatlantachamber.com

Aurora, Colorado

Population (2002): 286,028 (60); **Pop. density:** 2,007 per sq. mi; **Pop. change (1990-2002):** +28.9%. **Area:** 142.5 sq. mi. **Employment:** 155,075 employed; 6.1% unemployed. **Per capita income (MSA):** $38,513; increase (2000-2001): 1.6%.

Mayor: Paul E. Tauer, Non-Partisan

History: located 5 mi east of Denver; early growth stimulated by presence of military bases; fast-growing trade, technology, and medical science center.

Transportation: adjacent to Denver Intl. Airport; 1 general aviation airport; bus system. **Communications:** 1 TV station. **Medical facilities:** Major pub. univ. medical center; 2 pub. hosp. **Educational facilities:** 1 univ., 4 community and junior colleges, 2 technical colleges; 68 pub. schools, 4 private schools. **Further information:** Aurora Planning Dept., 15151 E. Alameda Pkwy., Aurora, CO 80012; www.auroragov.org; www.aurorachamber.org

Austin, Texas

Population (2002): 671,873 (16); **Pop. density:** 2,671 per sq. mi; **Pop. change (1990-2002):** +35.9%. **Area:** 251.5 sq. mi. **Employment:** 382,981 employed; 6.2% unemployed. **Per capita income (MSA):** $31,511; decrease (2000-2001): −2.1%.

Mayor: Will Wynn, Non-Partisan

History: first permanent settlement 1835; capital of Rep. of Texas 1839; named after Stephen Austin; inc. 1840.

Transportation: 1 intl. airport; 2 railroads. **Communications:** 8 TV, 29 radio stations. **Medical facilities:** 13 hosp. **Educational facilities:** 5 univ. and colleges. **Further information:** Greater Austin Chamber, 210 Barton Springs Rd., Ste. 400, Austin, TX 78704; www.ci.austin.tx.us; www.austinchamber.org

Bakersfield, California

Population (2002): 260,969 (68); **Pop. density:** 2,307 per sq. mi; **Pop. change (1990-2002):** +41.9%. **Area:** 113.1 sq. mi. **Employment:** 95,465 employed; 8.7% unemployed. **Per capita income (MSA):** $21,021; increase (2000-2001): 2.3%.

Mayor: Harvey Hall, Non-Partisan

History: named after Col. Thomas Baker, an early settler; inc. 1898.

Transportation: 2 airports; 3 railroads; Amtrak; Greyhound buses; local bus system. **Communications:** 8 TV, 29 radio stations. **Medical facilities:** 9 major hosp.; 9 convalescent, 1 psychiatric, 3 physical rehab.; 5 urgent care facilities; 3 clinics. **Educational facilities:** 9 univ., 1 community college, 14 vocational schools, 1 adult school, 15 elem. school districts, 14 high schools (Kern County). **Further information:** Greater Bakersfield Chamber of Commerce, 1725 Eye St., PO Box 1947, Bakersfield, CA 93303; www.bakersfieldchamber.org

Baltimore, Maryland

Population (2002): 638,614 (18); **Pop. density:** 7,904 per sq. mi; **Pop. change (1990-2002):** −13.2%. **Area:** 80.8 sq. mi. **Employment:** 269,802 employed; 7.9% unemployed. **Per capita income (MSA):** $34,039; increase (2000-2001): 3.7%.

Mayor: Martin O'Malley, Democrat

History: founded by Maryland legislature 1729; inc. 1797; bombing of Ft. McHenry (1814) inspired Francis Scott Key to write "Star-Spangled Banner"; birthplace of America's railroads 1828; rebuilt after fire 1904; site of National Aquarium 1981.

Transportation: 1 major airport; 3 railroads; bus system; subway system; light rail system; Inner Harbor water taxi system; 2 underwater tunnels. **Communications:** 6 TV, 25 radio stations. **Medical facilities:** 31 hosp.; 2 major medical centers. **Educational facilities:** over 30 univ. and colleges; 186 pub. schools. **Further information:** Greater Baltimore Committee, 111 S. Calvert St., Ste. 1700, Baltimore, MD 21202-6180; www.ci.baltimore.md.us; www.baltimore.org

Baton Rouge, Louisiana

Population (2002): 225,702 (79); **Pop. density:** 2,939 per sq. mi; **Pop. change (1990-2002):** +1.5%. **Area:** 76.8 sq. mi. **Employment:** 109,643 employed; 5.9% unemployed. **Per capita income (MSA):** $26,032; increase (2000-2001): 3.2%.

Mayor: Bobby Simpson, Republican

History: claimed by Spain at time of Louisiana Purchase 1803; est. independence by rebellion 1810; inc. as town 1817; became state capital 1849; Union-held most of Civil War.

Transportation: 1 airport, 5 airlines; 1 bus line; 3 railroad trunk lines. **Communications:** 5 TV, 19 radio stations. **Medical facilities:** 5 hosp. **Educational facilities:** 2 univ.; 105 pub., 52 nonpublic schools. **Further information:** The Chamber of Greater Baton Rouge, PO Box 3217, Baton Rouge, LA 70821; www.baton-rouge.com/BatonRouge; www.brchamber.org

Birmingham, Alabama

Population (2002): 239,416 (72); **Pop. density:** 1,597 per sq. mi; **Pop. change (1990-2002):** −10.0%. **Area:** 149.9 sq. mi. **Employment:** 119,430 employed; 6.8% unemployed. **Per capita income (MSA):** $30,620; increase (2000-2001): 4.0%.

Mayor: Bernard Kincaid, Democrat

History: settled 1871 at the intersection of 2 major railroads within proximity of elements required for iron and steel production.

Transportation: 1 intl. airport; 4 major rail freight lines, Amtrak; 1 bus line; 75 truck line terminals; 5 air cargo cos.; 7 barge lines; 5 interstate highways. **Communications:** 7 TV, 32 radio stations; 1 educational TV, 1 educational radio station. **Medical facilities:** 16, including the Univ. of Alabama at Birmingham Medical Center; VA hosp. **Educational facilities:** 1 pub., 2 private univ.; 4 private colleges, 1 private law school. **Further information:** Birmingham Area Chamber of Commerce, 2027 First Ave. N, Birmingham, AL 35203; www.birminghamchamber.com; www.ci.bham.al.us

Boston, Massachusetts

Population (2002): 589,281 (20); **Pop. density:** 12,175 per sq. mi; **Pop. change (1990-2002):** +2.6%. **Area:** 48.4 sq. mi. **Employment:** 295,061 employed; 4.1% unemployed. **Per capita income (MSA):** $39,873; increase (2000-2001): 1.9%.

Mayor: Thomas M. Menino, Democrat

History: settled 1630 by John Winthrop; capital of Mass. Bay Colony; figured strongly in Am. Revolution, earning distinction as the "Cradle of Liberty"; inc. 1822.

Transportation: 1 major airport; 2 railroads; city rail and subway system; 3 underwater tunnels; port. **Communications:** 12 TV, 21 radio stations. **Medical facilities:** 31 hosp.; 8 major medical research centers. **Educational facilities:** 30 univ. and colleges. **Further information:** Greater Boston Convention and Visitors Bureau, 2 Copley Pl., Suite 105, Boston, MA 02116; www.bostonusa.org; www.gbcc.org

Buffalo, New York

Population (2002): 287,698 (59); **Pop. density:** 7,086 per sq. mi; **Pop. change (1990-2002):** −12.3%. **Area:** 40.6 sq. mi. **Employment:** 130,118 employed; 9.7% unemployed. **Per capita income (MSA):** $27,852; increase (2000-2001): 2.1%.

Mayor: Anthony M. Masiello, Democrat

History: settled 1780 by Seneca Indians; raided twice by British, War of 1812; served as western terminus for Erie Canal, became a center for trade and manufacturing; inc. 1832; last stop on the Underground Railroad; key point for Canada-U.S. political, trade, and social relations.

Transportation: 1 intl. airport; 4 Class I railroads; Amtrak metro rail system; water service to Great Lakes-St. Lawrence Seaway system and Atlantic seaboard. **Communications:** 11 TV, 12 radio stations. **Medical facilities:** 16 hosp., 40 research centers. **Educational facilities:** 15 colleges and univ.; 400 pub. and private schools. **Further information:** Buffalo Niagara Enterprise, 665 Main Street, Buffalo, NY 14203; www.ci.buffalo.ny.us; buffaloniagara.org

Chandler, Arizona

Population (2002): 202,016 (91); **Pop. density:** 834 per sq. mi; **Pop. change (1990-2002):** +122.7%. **Area:** 242.3 sq. mi. **Employment:** 76,116 employed; 4.2% unemployed. **Per capita income (MSA):** $28,337; increase (2000-2001): 1.2%.

Mayor: Boyd W. Dunn, Non-Partisan

History: town formed 1912; population doubled in 1990s as "the high-tech oasis of the Silicon Desert."

Transportation: 1 municipal airport; mass transit system. **Communications:** 2 TV, 3 newspapers. **Medical facilities:** 1 medical center. **Educational facilities:** 2 univ., 2 community coll.; 26 elem., 7 junior high, 4 high schools; 13 charter schools. **Further information:** Chandler Chamber, 25 South Arizona Pl., Suite 201, Chandler, AZ 85225; www.chandlerchamber.com; chandleraz.gov

Charlotte, North Carolina

Population (2002): 580,597 (21); **Pop. density:** 2,396 per sq. mi; **Pop. change (1990-2002):** +36.0%. **Area:** 242.3 sq. mi. **Employment:** 299,081 employed; 6.5% unemployed. **Per capita income (MSA):** $31,526; increase (2000-2001): 1.7%.

Mayor: Patrick McCrory, Republican

History: settled by Scotch-Irish immigrants 1740s; inc. 1768 and named after Queen Charlotte, George III's wife; scene of first major U.S. gold discovery 1799.

Transportation: 1 airport; 2 major railway lines; 1 bus line; 300 trucking firms. **Communications:** 7 TV, 26 radio stations. **Medical facilities:** 10 hosp., 2 medical centers. **Educational facilities:** 9 univ., 4 colleges, 88 elem. schools, 29 middle schools, 17 high schools. **Further information:** Chamber of Commerce, PO Box 32785, Charlotte, NC 28232; www.charlotte chamber. com

Chesapeake, Virginia

Population (2002): 206,665 (87); **Pop. density:** 607 per sq. mi; **Pop. change (1990-2002):** +36.0%. **Area:** 340.7 sq. mi. **Employment:** 107,008 employed; 3.3% unemployed. **Per capita income (MSA):** $27,452; increase (2000-2001): 4.4%.

Mayor: William E. Ward, Non-Partisan

History: region settled in 1620s with first English colonies on banks of Elizabeth River; home to Great Dismal Swamp Canal, first envisioned by George Washington in 1763; Battle of Great Bridge fought here Dec. 1775; inc. as a city 1963.

Transportation: Amtrak, freight rail service; bus service; 2 regional airports. **Communications:** 9 TV, 48 radio stations (serving Hampton Roads community). **Medical facilities:** 1 hosp. **Educational facilities:** 9 colleges and univ.; 49 pub. schools and educational centers. **Further information:** Hampton Roads Chamber of Commerce, Chesapeake Div., 400 Volvo Pky., Chesapeake, VA 23320; www.cityofchesapeake.net

Chicago, Illinois

Population (2002): 2,886,251 (3); **Pop. density:** 12,709 per sq. mi; **Pop. change (1990-2002):** +3.7%. **Area:** 227.1 sq. mi. **Employment:** 1,221,179 employed; 8.3% unemployed. **Per capita income (MSA):** $36,624; increase (2000-2001): 2.01%.

Mayor: Richard M. Daley, Democrat

History: site acquired from Indians 1795; significant white settlement began with opening of Erie Canal 1825; chartered as city 1837; boomed with arrival of railroads from east and canal to Mississippi R.; about one-third of city destroyed by fire 1871; major grain and livestock market.

Transportation: 3 airports; major railroad system, trucking industry. **Communications:** 9 TV, 31 radio stations. **Medical facilities:** over 123 hosp. **Educational facilities:** 95 insts. of higher learning. **Further information:** Chicagoland Chamber of Commerce, 1 IBM Plaza, Ste. 2800, Chicago, IL 60611; www.ci.chi.il.us; www.chicagolandchamber.com

Cincinnati, Ohio

Population (2002): 323,885 (55); **Pop. density:** 4,152 per sq. mi; **Pop. change (1990-2002):** −11.2%. **Area:** 78.0 sq. mi. **Employment:** 161,255 employed; 7.2% unemployed. **Per capita income (MSA):** $31,967; increase (2000-2001): 3.0%.

Mayor: Charlie Luken, Democrat

History: founded 1788 and named after the Society of Cincinnati, an organization of Revolutionary War officers; chartered as village 1802; inc. as city 1819.

Transportation: 1 intl. airport; 3 railroads; 1 bus system. **Communications:** 7 TV, 25 radio stations. **Medical facilities:** 27 hosp.; Children's Hosp. Medical Center; VA hosp. **Educational facilities:** 4 univ., 11 colleges, 8 technical & 2-year colleges. **Further information:** Chamber of Commerce, 300 Carew Tower, 441 Vine St., Cincinnati, OH 45202; www.cincinnatichamber.com; www.cincinnatiusa.org

Cleveland, Ohio

Population (2002): 467,851 (34); **Pop. density:** 6,029 per sq. mi; **Pop. change (1990-2002):** −7.4%. **Area:** 77.6 sq. mi. **Employment:** 180,893 employed; 12.5% unemployed. **Per capita income (MSA):** $31,807; increase (2000-2001): 1.8%.

Mayor: Jane Campbell, Democrat

History: surveyed in 1796; given recognition as village 1815, inc. as city 1836; annexed Ohio City 1854.

Transportation: 1 intl. airport; rail service; major port; rapid transit system. **Communications:** 9 TV, 21 radio stations. **Medical facilities:** 14 hosp. **Educational facilities:** 8 univ. and colleges; 127 pub. schools. **Further information:** Greater Cleveland Growth Assn., Tower City Center, 50 Pub. Square, Suite 200, Cleveland, OH 44113-2291; www.cleveland.oh.us; www.clevelandgrowth.com; www.city.cleveland.oh.us

Colorado Springs, Colorado

Population (2002): 371,182 (48); **Pop. density:** 1,999 per sq. mi; **Pop. change (1990-2002):** +31.1%. **Area:** 185.7 sq. mi. **Employment:** 194,226 employed; 6.6% unemployed. **Per capita income (MSA):** $29,280; decrease (2000-2001): −0.4%.

Mayor: Lionel Rivera, Non-Partisan

History: city founded in 1871 at the foot of Pike's Peak; inc. 1872.

Transportation: 1 municipal airport; 1 bus line. **Communications:** 9 TV, 28 radio stations. **Medical facilities:** 5 hosp. **Educational facilities:** 11 univ., 5 colleges. **Further information:** Chamber of Commerce, 2 N. Cascade, Ste. 110, Colorado Springs, CO 80901; www.springsgov.com; www.colorado springschamber.org

Columbus, Ohio

Population (2002): 725,228 (15); **Pop. density:** 3,449 per sq. mi; **Pop. change (1990-2002):** +14.0%. **Area:** 210.3 sq. mi. **Employment:** 390,893 employed; 5.2% unemployed. **Per capita income (MSA):** $31,343; increase (2000-2001): 2.0%.

Mayor: Michael B. Coleman, Democrat

History: first settlement 1797; laid out as new capital 1812 with current name; became city 1834.

Transportation: 6 airports; 2 railroads; 2 intercity bus lines. **Communications:** 8 TV, 29 radio stations. **Medical facilities:** 17 hosp. **Educational facilities:** 11 univ. and colleges; 8 technical/2-year schools; 129 pub. schools (67 elem., 21 middle, 14 high, 27 magnet). **Further information:** Greater Columbus Chamber of Commerce, 37 N. High St., Columbus, OH 43215. Experience Columbus, 90 N. High St., Columbus, OH 43215; www.experiencecolumbus.org

Corpus Christi, Texas

Population (2002): 278,520 (62); **Pop. density:** 1,802 per sq. mi; **Pop. change (1990-2002):** +7.8%. **Area:** 154.6 sq. mi. **Employment:** 126,272 employed; 6.1% unemployed. **Per capita income (MSA):** $24,280; increase (2000-2001): 2.8%.

Mayor: Samuel Loyd Neal, Non-Partisan

History: settled 1839 and inc. 1852.

Transportation: 1 intl. airport; 2 bus lines, metro bus system; 3 freight railroads. **Communications:** 6 TV, 17 radio stations. **Medical facilities:** 14 hosp. including a children's center. **Educational facilities:** 1 univ., 1 college. **Further information:** Corpus Christi Regional Economic Development Corp., PO Box 2724, Corpus Christi, TX 78403; www.ccredc.com; www.ci.corpus-christi.tx.us

Dallas, Texas

Population (2002): 1,211,467 (8); **Pop. density:** 3,537 per sq. mi; **Pop. change (1990-2002):** +20.3%. **Area:** 342.5 sq. mi. **Employment:** 637,827 employed; 9.1% unemployed. **Per capita income (MSA):** $34,697; decrease (2000-2001): −2.0%.

Mayor: Laura Miller, Democrat

History: first settled 1841; platted 1846; inc. 1871; developed as the financial and commercial center of Southwest; headquarters of regional Federal Reserve Bank; major center for distribution and high-tech manufacturing.

Transportation: 1 intl. airport, 1 regional airport; Amtrak; transit system. **Communications:** 17 TV, 52 radio stations. **Medical facilities:** 19 general hosp.; major medical center. **Educational facilities:** 218 pub. schools, 12 univ. and colleges, 3 community college campuses. **Further information:** Greater Dallas Chamber, Resource Center, 700 N. Pearl St., Ste. 1200, Dallas, TX 75201; www.dallaschamber.org; www.dallascityhall.com

Denver, Colorado

Population (2002): 560,415 (26); **Pop. density:** 3,653 per sq. mi; **Pop. change (1990-2002):** +19.9%. **Area:** 153.4 sq. mi. **Employment:** 279,122 employed; 6.9% unemployed. **Per capita income (MSA):** $38,513; increase (2000-2001): 1.6%.

Mayor: John W. Hickenlooper, Democrat

History: settled 1858 by gold prospectors and miners; inc. 1861; became territorial capital 1867; growth spurred by gold and silver boom; became financial, industrial, cultural center of Rocky Mt. region.

Transportation: 1 intl. airport, 3 corporate reliever airports; 5 rail freight lines, Amtrak; 1 bus line. **Communications:** 14 TV, 29 radio stations. **Medical facilities:** 20 hosp. **Educational facilities:** 15 four-yr. colleges and univ.; 8 two-yr. and community colleges. **Further information:** Denver Metro Chamber of Commerce, 1445 Market St., Denver, CO 80202-1729; www.denverchamber.org

Des Moines, Iowa

Population (2002): 198,076 (95); **Pop. density:** 2,613 per sq. mi; **Pop. change (1990-2002):** +2.5%. **Area:** 75.8 sq. mi. **Employment:** 124,765 employed; 4.5% unemployed. **Per capita income (MSA):** $32,991; increase (2000-2001): 3.8%.

Mayor: Preston Daniels, Democrat

History: Fort Des Moines built 1843; settled and inc. 1851; chartered as city 1857.

Transportation: 1 intl. airport; 7 bus lines; 4 railroads; metro bus system. **Communications:** 4 TV, 12 radio stations. **Medical facilities:** 6 hosp. **Educational facilities:** 2 univ., 6 colleges. **Further information:** Greater Des Moines Partnership, 700 Locust St., Ste. 100, Des Moines, IA 50309; www.desmoines metro.com; www.dmgov.org

Detroit, Michigan

Population (2002): 925,051 (10); **Pop. density:** 6,665 per sq. mi; **Pop. change (1990-2002):** −10.0%. **Area:** 138.8 sq. mi. **Employment:** 336,730 employed; 11.9% unemployed. **Per capita income (MSA):** $34,035; increase (2000-2001): 1.1%.

Mayor: Kwame M. Kilpatrick, Democrat

History: founded by French 1701; controlled by British 1760; acquired by U.S. 1796; destroyed by fire 1805; inc. as city 1815; capital of state 1837-47; auto manufacturing began 1890.

Transportation: 1 intl. airport, 1 general aviation airport; 10 railroads (4 Class I); major intl. port; pub. transit system. **Communications:** 4 TV, 6 radio stations. **Medical facilities:** 13 hosp.; 3 major medical centers. **Educational facilities:** 2 univ., 3 colleges, 1 community college. **Further information:** Detroit Regional Chamber, One Woodward Ave., PO Box 33840, Detroit, MI 48232-0840; www.detroitchamber.com

El Paso, Texas

Population (2002): 577,415 (22); **Pop. density:** 2,318 per sq. mi; **Pop. change (1990-2002):** +12.0%. **Area:** 249.1 sq. mi. **Employment:** 240,940 employed; 8.3% unemployed. **Per capita income (MSA):** $19,186; increase (2000-2001): 4.3%.

Mayor: Joe Wardy, Non-Partisan

History: first settled 1827; inc. 1873; arrival of railroad 1881 boosted city's population and industries.

Transportation: 1 intl. airport; 2 rail providers; 2 interstate highways; 4 intl. ports of entry. **Communications:** 12 TV, 21 radio stations. **Medical facilities:** 6 hosp.; 3 rehabilitation, 11 specialty centers. **Educational facilities:** 5 univ., 2 colleges (1 grad. only). **Further information:** Greater El Paso Chamber of Commerce, 10 Civic Center Plaza, El Paso, TX 79901; www.el paso.org

Fort Wayne, Indiana

Population (2002): 210,070 (85); **Pop. density:** 2,659 per sq. mi; **Pop. Change (1990-2002):** +3.5%. **Area:** 79.0 sq. mi. **Employment:** 96,024 employed; 6.4% unemployed. **Per capita income (MSA):** $27,819; decrease (2000-2001): −0.2%.

Mayor: Graham A. Richard, Democrat

History: French fort 1680; U.S. fort 1794; settled by 1832; inc. 1840 prior to Wabash-Erie canal completion 1843.

Transportation: 1 airport; 3 railroads; 6 bus lines. **Communications:** 5 TV, 21 radio stations. **Medical facilities:** 5 regional hosp.; VA hosp. **Educational facilities:** 5 univ., 4 colleges, 3 bus. schools; 86 pub. schools. **Further information:** Chamber of Commerce, 826 Ewing Street, Fort Wayne, IN 46802-2182; www.ft-wayne.in.us; www.fwchamber.org

Fort Worth, Texas

Population (2002): 567,516 (25); **Pop. density:** 1,940 per sq. mi; **Pop. change (1990-2002):** +26.6%. **Area:** 292.5 sq. mi. **Employment:** 268,232 employed; 8.1% unemployed. **Per capita income (MSA):** $20,230; increase (2000-2001): 3.0%.

Mayor: Mike Moncrief, Non-Partisan

History: established as military post 1849; inc. 1873; oil discovered 1917.

Transportation: 2 intl. airport, 1 industrial airport; 3 major railroads, Amtrak; local bus service; 1 transcontinental, 1 intrastate bus lines. **Communications:** 18 TV, 65 local radio stations. **Medical facilities:** 10 hosp.; 1 children's hosp.; 4 government hosp. **Educational facilities:** 5 univ. and colleges. **Further information:** Chamber of Commerce, 777 Taylor St. #900, Fort Worth, TX 76102; www.fortworthgov.org; www.fort worthchamber.com

Fremont, California

Population (2002): 206,856 (86); **Pop. density:** 2,697 per sq. mi; **Pop. change (1990-2002):** +19.3%. **Area:** 76.7 sq. mi. **Employment:** 108,281 employed; 4.7% unemployed. **Per capita income (MSA):** $39,963; decrease (2000-2001): −0.3%.

Mayor: Gus Morrison, Non-Partisan

History: area first settled by Spanish 1769; inc. 1956 with consolidation of 5 communities.

Transportation: intracity bus line; Bay Area Rapid Transit System (southern terminal). **Communications:** 1 radio station. **Medical facilities:** 1 hosp.; 2 major medical facilities; 18 clinics. **Educational facilities:** 1 community college; 42 pub. schools. **Further information:** Chamber of Commerce, 39488 Stevenson Place, Suite 100, Fremont, CA 94539; www.fremontbusiness.com

Fresno, California

Population (2002): 445,227 (36); **Pop. density:** 4,265 per sq. mi; **Pop. change (1990-2002):** +25.3%. **Area:** 104.4 sq. mi. **Employment:** 177,347 employed; 12.9% unemployed. **Per capita income (MSA):** $21,463; increase (2000-2001): 2.8%.

Mayor: Alan Autry, Non-Partisan

History: founded 1872; inc. as city 1885.

Transportation: 1 municipal airport; Amtrak; 1 bus line; intracity bus system. **Communications:** 15 TV, 23 radio stations. **Medical facilities:** 17 general hosp. **Educational facilities:** 9 colleges; 102 pub. schools. **Further information:** Greater Fresno Area Chamber of Commerce, PO Box 1469, Fresno, CA 93716-1469; www.fresnochamber.com; fresno-online.com

Garland, Texas

Population (2002): 219,646 (80); **Pop. density:** 3,847 per sq. mi; **Pop. change (1990-2002):** +21.5%. **Area:** 57.1 sq. mi. **Employment:** 118,574 employed; 6.2% unemployed. **Per capita income (MSA):** $34,697; decrease (2000-2001): −1.9%.

Mayor: Bob Day, Democrat

History: settled 1850s; inc. 1891.

Transportation: 30 min. from Dallas/Ft. Worth Intl. Airport; 2 railroads. **Communications:** 14 local TV (Dallas/Ft. Worth), 25+ radio stations. **Medical facilities:** 2 hosp.; 348 beds. **Educational facilities:** 3 univ., 2 community colleges; 64 pub. schools. **Further information:** Chamber of Commerce, 914 S. Garland Ave., Garland, TX 75040; www.garlandchamber.com

Glendale, Arizona

Population (2002): 230,564 (76); **Pop. density:** 4,139 per sq. mi; **Pop. change (1990-2002):** +52.8%. **Area:** 55.7 sq. mi. **Employment:** 118,500 employed; 5.6% unemployed. **Per capita income (MSA):** $28,337; increase (2000-2001): 1.2%.

Mayor: Elaine M. Scruggs, Non-Partisan

History: est. 1892; inc. 1910.

Transportation: 1 local airport, 30 min. from Phoenix Sky Harbor Intl. Airport. **Communications:** 12 TV stations, 40 radio stations. **Medical facilities:** 9 hosp. **Educational facilities:** 12 institutes of higher education, 9 pub. school districts. **Further information:** Chamber of Commerce, PO Box 249, 7105 N. 59th Ave., Glendale, AZ 85311; www.glendaleazchamber.org

Glendale, California

Population (2002): 199,430 (93); **Pop. density:** 6,517 per sq. mi; **Pop. change (1990-2002):** +10.8%. **Area:** 30.6 sq. mi. **Employment:** 90,724 employed, 6.4% unemployed. **Per capita income (MSA):** $20,611; increase (2000-2001): 3.4%.

Mayor: Frank Quintero, Non-Partisan

History: became a town in 1887; inc. 1906.

Transportation: near Los Angeles Intl. airport; 1 local airport; commuter trains, Amtrak; bus system. **Communications:** 21 TV, 70 radio stations. **Medical facilities:** 3 hosp; other facilities. **Educational facilities:** 1 community college; 26 pub. schools. **Further information:** City of Glendale Public Information Officer, 613 E. Broadway, Glendale, CA 91206; www.ci.glendale.ca.us

Grand Rapids, Michigan

Population (2002): 196,595 (99); **Pop. density:** 4,408 per sq. mi; **Pop. change (1990-2002):** +3.6%. **Area:** 44.6 sq. mi. **Employment:** 106,211 employed, 8.8% unemployed. **Per capita income (MSA):** $28,471; increase (2000-2001): 1.2%.

Mayor: John H. Logie, Non-Partisan

History: originally site of Ottawa Indian village; trading post 1826; became lumbering center and incorporated city 1850.

Transportation: 1 intl. airport; 3 rail carriers; Amtrak, Greyhound bus line; transit bus system. **Communications:** 8 TV, 39 radio stations. **Medical facilities:** 13 hosp. **Educational facilities:** 16 colleges; 19 pub. schools, 17 charter schools. **Further information:** Grand Rapids Area Chamber of Commerce, 111 Pearl St. NW, Grand Rapids, MI 49503; www.grandrapids.org

Greensboro, North Carolina

Population (2002): 228,217 (77); **Pop. density:** 2,180 per sq. mi; **Pop. change (1990-2002):** +19.1%. **Area:** 104.7 sq. mi. **Employment:** 115,367 employed; 6.7% unemployed. **Per capita income (MSA):** $28,774; increase (2000-2001): 0.2%.

Mayor: Keith Holliday, Non-Partisan

History: settled 1749; site of Revolutionary War conflict 1781 between Generals Nathanael Greene and Cornwallis; inc. 1807, origin of civil rights sit-in movement.

Transportation: 1 intl. airport; 2 railroads; Trailways/Greyhound bus service. **Communications:** all cable TV stations; 11 radio stations. **Medical facilities:** 4 hosp. **Educational facilities:** 2 univ., 4 colleges; 94 pub. schools. **Further information:** Chamber of Commerce, PO Box 3246, Greensboro, NC 27402; www.ci.greensboro.nc.us; www.greensboro.com

Henderson, Nevada

Population (2002): 206,153 (88); **Pop. density:** 2,587 per sq. mi; **Pop. change (1990-2002):** 216.6%. **Area:** 79.7 sq. mi. **Employment:** 65,456 employed; 4.6% unemployed. **Per capita income (MSA):** $27,916; increase (2000-2001): 0.5%.

Mayor: James B. Gibson, non-partisan.

History: early growth spurred by World War II magnesium mining; inc. 1953.

Transportation: Henderson Executive Airport; Citizens Area Transit (CAT) public transportation. **Communications:** 9 TV stations; 38 radio stations. **Medical facilities:** 3 hosp.; medical center facilities. **Educational facilities:** 5 coll.; 2 vocational schools; 23 elem., 5 middle, 6 high schools. **Further information:** City of Henderson Public Information Office, 240 Water St., Henderson, NV 89015; www.cityofhenderson.gov; www.hendersonchamber.com

Hialeah, Florida

Population (2002): 228,149 (78); **Pop. density:** 11,883 per sq. mi; **Pop. change (1990-2002):** +21.4%. **Area:** 19.2 sq. mi. **Employment:** 102,955 employed; 8.1% unemployed. **Per capita income (MSA):** $26,594; increase (2000-2001): 1.9%.

Mayor: Raul L. Martinez, Republican

History: founded 1917, inc. 1925; industrial and residential city NW of Miami; Hialeah Park Horse Racing Track.

Transportation: 5 mi from Miami Intl. Airport; access to Port of Miami; Amtrak; 2 rail freight lines; Metrorail, Metrobus systems. **Communications:** 5 TV, 7 radio stations. **Medical facilities:** 4 hosp. (30 more in the area). **Educational facilities:** 8 univ. and colleges, 25 pub., 39 private schools. **Further information:** Hialeah-Dade Development, Inc., 501 Palm Ave., Hialeah, FL 33010; www.ci.hialeah.fl.us; www.hddi.org

Honolulu, Hawaii

Population (2002): 378,155 (45); **Pop. density:** 4,413 per sq. mi; **Pop. change (1990-2002):** +0.3%. **Area:** 85.7 sq. mi. **Employment (MSA):** 396,069; employed, 3.9% unemployed. **Per capita income (MSA):** $21,115; increase (2000-2001): 2.3%.

Mayor: Jeremy Harris, Non-Partisan

History: harbor entered by Europeans 1778; declared capital of kingdom by King Kamehameha III 1850; Pearl Harbor naval base attacked by Japanese Dec. 7, 1941.

Transportation: 1 major airport; 3 commercial harbors. **Communications:** 12 TV, 36 radio stations. **Medical facilities:** 10 major medical centers. **Educational facilities:** 5 univ., 4 community colleges; 169 pub. schools, 88 private schools. **Further information:** Hawaii Visitors and Convention Bureau, 2270 Kalakaua Ave., 8th Fl., Honolulu, HI 96815; www.co.honolulu.hi.us; www.gohawaii.com

Houston, Texas

Population (2002): 2,009,834 (4); **Pop. density:** 3,469 per sq. mi; **Pop. change (1990-2002):** +18.4%. **Area:** 579.4 sq. mi. **Employment:** 1,004,150; employed, 7.2% unemployed. **Per capita income (MSA):** $35,872; increase (2000-2001): 4.0%.

Mayor: Lee P. Brown, Non-Partisan

History: founded 1836; inc. 1837; capital of Repub. of Texas 1837-39; developed rapidly after construction of channel to Gulf of Mexico 1914; world center of oil and natural gas technology.

Transportation: 3 commercial airports; 2 mainline railroads; major bus transit system; major intl. port. **Communications:** 16 TV, 63 radio stations. **Medical facilities:** 74 hosp. (Harris Co.); major medical center. **Educational facilities:** 34 univ. and colleges (Harris Co.) **Further information:** Greater Houston Partnership, 1200 Smith St., Houston, TX 77002-4400; www.houston.org; www.cityofhouston.gov

Indianapolis, Indiana

Population (2002): 783,612 (12); **Pop. density:** 2,168 per sq. mi; **Pop. change (1990-2002):** +7.1%. **Area:** 361.5 sq. mi. **Employment:** 414,735 employed; 5.4% unemployed. **Per capita income (MSA):** $31,960; increase (2000-2001): 2.6%.
Mayor: Bart Peterson, Democrat
History: settled 1820; became capital 1825.
Transportation: 1 intl. airport; 5 railroads; 3 interstate bus lines. **Communications:** 10 TV, 27 radio stations. **Medical facilities:** 17 hosp.; 1 major medical and research center. **Educational facilities:** 8 univ. and colleges; major pub. library system. **Further information:** Greater Indianapolis Chamber of Commerce, 111 Monument Circle, Ste. 1950, Indianapolis, IN 46204; www.ci.indianapolis.in.us; www.indychamber.com

Jacksonville, Florida

Population (2002): 762,461 (14); **Pop. density:** 1,006 per sq. mi; **Pop. change (1990-2002):** +20.1%. **Area:** 757.7 sq. mi. **Employment:** 368,604 employed; 5.8% unemployed. **Per capita income (MSA):** $29,625; increase (2000-2001): 1.6%.
Mayor: John Peyton, Republican
History: settled 1816 as Cowford; renamed after Andrew Jackson 1822; inc. 1832; rechartered 1851; scene of conflicts in Seminole and Civil wars.
Transportation: 1 intl. airport; 3 railroads; 2 interstate bus lines; 2 seaports. **Communications:** 7 TV, 34 radio stations. **Medical facilities:** 11 hosp. **Educational facilities:** 7 univ., 5 colleges, 2 community colleges; 233 pub. schools, 155 private schools. **Further information:** Chamber of Commerce, 3 Independent Drive, Jacksonville, FL 32202; www.expandinjax.com; www.myjaxchamber.com; www.coj.net

Jersey City, New Jersey

Population (2002): 240,100 (71); **Pop. density:** 16,114 per sq. mi; **Pop. change (1990-2002):** +5.1%. **Area:** 14.9 sq. mi. **Employment:** 106,114 employed; 10.0% unemployed. **Per capita income (MSA):** $28,584; increase (2000-2001): 1.7%.
Mayor: Glenn Cunningham, Democrat
History: site bought from Indians 1630; chartered as town by British 1668; scene of Revolutionary War conflict 1779; chartered under present name 1838; important station on Underground Railroad.
Transportation: Intercity bus and subway system; ferry service to Manhattan. **Communications:** see New York, NY. **Medical facilities:** 4 hosp. **Educational facilities:** 3 colleges.
Further information: Hudson County Chamber of Commerce, 660 Newark Ave., Ste. 220, Jersey City, NJ 07306; www.jerseycityonline.com

Kansas City, Missouri

Population (2002): 443,471 (37); **Pop. density:** 1,415 per sq. mi; **Pop. change (1990-2002):** +1.9%. **Area:** 313.5 sq. mi. **Employment:** 247,217 employed; 7.1% unemployed. **Per capita income (MSA):** $32,693; increase (2000-2001): 2.2%.
Mayor: Kay Barnes, Non-Partisan
History: settled by 1838 at confluence of the Missouri and Kansas rivers; inc. 1850.
Transportation: 1 intl. airport; a major rail center; more than 300 motor freight carriers; 7 barge lines. **Communications:** 9 TV, 43 radio stations. **Medical facilities:** 50 hosp.; 2 VA hosp. **Educational facilities:** 22 univ. and colleges. **Further information:** Greater Kansas City Chamber of Commerce, 911 Main St., Ste. 2600, Kansas City, MO 64105; www.kansascity.com; www.kcchamber.com

Las Vegas, Nevada

Population (2002): 508,604 (30); **Pop. density:** 4,489 per sq. mi; **Pop. change (1990-2002):** +95.7%. **Area:** 113.3 sq. mi. **Employment:** 264,885 employed; 5.6% unemployed. **Per capita income (MSA):** $27,916; increase (2000-2001): 0.5%.
Mayor: Oscar B. Goodman, Democrat
History: occupied by Mormons 1855-57; bought by railroad 1903; city of Las Vegas inc. 1911; gambling legalized 1931.
Transportation: 1 intl. airport; 1 railroad; bus system. **Communications:** 21 TV, 44 radio stations. **Medical facilities:** 11 hosp. **Educational facilities:** 1 univ., 2 state colleges; 277 pub. schools in area. **Further information:** Las Vegas Chamber of Commerce, 3720 Howard Hughes Parkway, Las Vegas, NV 89109-0937; www.lvchamber.com

Lexington, Kentucky

Population (2002): 263,618 (66); **Pop. density:** 927 per sq. mi; **Pop. change (1990-2002):** +17.0%. **Area:** 284.5 sq. mi. **Employment:** 136,158 employed; 3.5% unemployed. **Per capita income (MSA):** $28,849; increase (2000-2001): 0.9%.
Mayor: Teresa Ann Isaac, Non-Partisan
History: site was founded and named in 1775 by hunters after the site of the opening battle of the Revolutionary War at Lexington, Mass.; settled 1779; chartered 1782; inc. as a city 1832.

Transportation: 6 comm. airlines; 2 railroads; city buses. **Communications:** 5 TV, 20 radio stations. **Medical facilities:** 5 general, 5 specialized hosp. **Educational facilities:** 2 univ., 4 colleges, 53 public schools: 6 high schools, 10 middle schools, 35 elementary schools, 2 technology schools. **Further information:** Greater Lexington Chamber of Commerce, 330 E. Main St., Lexington, KY 40507; www.lexchamber.com

Lincoln, Nebraska

Population (2002): 232,362 (75); **Pop. density:** 3,115 per sq. mi; **Pop. change (1990-2002):** +20.6%. **Area:** 74.6 sq. mi. **Employment:** 133,693 employed; 6.3% unemployed. **Per capita income (MSA):** $20,872; increase (2000-2001): 5.4%.
Mayor: Coleen J. Seng, Non-Partisan
History: originally called Lancaster; chosen state capital 1867, renamed after Abraham Lincoln; inc. 1869.
Transportation: 1 airport; Greyhound; Amtrak, 2 railroads. **Communications:** 3 TV, 15 radio stations. **Medical facilities:** 6 hosp. including VA, rehabilitation facilities. **Educational facilities:** 3 univ., 3 voc.-tech./business colleges; 55 pub., 30 private schools, 3 focus programs. **Further information:** Chamber of Commerce, PO Box 83006, Lincoln, NE 68501-3006; www.lincoln.org; www.lcoc.com

Long Beach, California

Population (2002): 472,412 (33); **Pop. density:** 9,373 per sq. mi; **Pop. change (1990-2002):** +9.9%. **Area:** 50.4 sq. mi. **Employment:** 205,290; employed; 6.3% unemployed. **Per capita income (MSA):** $30,611; increase (2000-2001): 3.4%.
Mayor: Beverly O'Neill, Non-Partisan
History: settled as early as 1784 by Spanish; by 1884 present site developed on harbor; inc. 1888; oil discovered 1921.
Transportation: 1 airport; 3 railroads; major intl. port; 4 bus co. with 40 bus lines, light rail service. **Communications:** 1 radio station, 1 CATV franchise. **Medical facilities:** 5 hosp. **Educational facilities:** 1 univ., 1 community college (2 campuses); 87 pub. schools in district. **Further information:** Long Beach City Hall, 333 W. Ocean Blvd., Long Beach, CA 90802; www.ci.long beach.ca.us; www.lbchamber.com

Los Angeles, California

Population (2002): 3,798,981 (2); **Pop. density:** 8,098 per sq. mi; **Pop. change (1990-2002):** +9.0%. **Area:** 469.1 sq. mi. **Employment:** 1,739,747 employed; 7.7% unemployed. **Per capita income (MSA):** $30,611; increase (2000-2001): 3.4%.
Mayor: James K. Hahn, Democrat
History: founded by Spanish 1781; captured by U.S. 1846; inc. 1850; grew rapidly after coming of railroads, 1876 & 1885; Hollywood a district of L.A.
Transportation: 1 intl. airport; 3 railroads; major freeway system; intracity bus and rail system. **Communications:** 21 TV, 70 radio stations. **Medical facilities:** 822 hosp. and clinics in metro. area. **Educational facilities:** 192 univ. and colleges (incl. junior, community, and other); 1,678 pub. schools; 1,470 private schools. **Further information:** Los Angeles Area Chamber of Commerce, 350 S. Bixel St., PO Box 513696, Los Angeles, CA 90051-1696; www.ci.la.ca.us; www.lachamber.org

Louisville, Kentucky

Population (2002): 251,399 (69); **Pop. density:** 4,048 per sq. mi; **Pop. change (1990-2002):** –6.8%. **Area:** 62.1 sq. mi. **Employment:** 120,617 employed; 4.4% unemployed. **Per capita income (MSA):** $31,251; increase (2000-2001): 2.9%.
Mayor: Jerry Abramson, Democrat
History: settled 1778; named for Louis XVI of France; inc. 1828; base for Union forces in Civil War.
Transportation: 1 municipal airport, 2 private-craft airport; 1 terminal, 4 trunk-line railroads; metro bus line, Greyhound station; 5 barge lines. **Communications:** 6 TV, 21 radio stations, 2 educational. **Medical facilities:** 23 hosp. **Educational facilities:** 10 univ. and colleges, 32 business and vocational schools. **Further information:** Greater Louisville, Inc. Metro Chamber of Commerce, 614 W. Main St., Louisville, KY 40202; www.greater louisville.com

Lubbock, Texas

Population (2002): 203,715 (89); **Pop. density:** 1,775 per sq. mi; **Pop. change (1990-2002):** +9.1%. **Area:** 114.8 sq. mi. **Employment:** 105,731 employed; 3.1% unemployed. **Per capita income (MSA):** $24,788; decrease (2000-2001): –0.3%.
Mayor: Mark McDougal, Non-Partisan
History: settled 1879; laid out 1891; inc. 1909 through merger of two towns.
Transportation: 1 intl. airport; 2 railroads, bus line. **Communications:** 9 TV, 25 radio stations. **Medical facilities:** 7 hosp. **Educational facilities:** 3 univ., 1 junior college; 51 pub. schools. **Further information:** Chamber of Commerce, 1301 Broadway, Lubbock, TX 79401; www.ci. lubbock.tx.us; www.lubbockchamber.com

IT'S A FACT: According to legend, the California city of Modesto—new to the top 100—gained its name when it was being laid out in 1870 and prominent San Francisco banker William C. Ralston declined a proposal that the new town be named after him. A bystander commented that the "señor was much modesto," and the Spanish word for *modest* became the name of the town.

Madison, Wisconsin

Population (2002): 215,211 (83); **Pop. density:** 3,133 per sq. mi; **Pop. change (1990-2002):** +12.8%. **Area:** 68.7 sq. mi. **Employment:** 133,901 employed; 2.9% unemployed. **Per capita income (MSA):** $36,201; increase (2000-2001): 3.9%.
Mayor: Dave Cieslewicz, Non-Partisan
History: first white settlement 1832; selected as site for state capital, named after James Madison, 1836; chartered 1856.
Transportation: 2 airport, 11 airlines; 1 intracity, 3 intercity bus systems; 3 freight rail lines. **Communications:** 10 TV, 26 radio stations, 3 cable providers. **Medical facilities:** 6 hosp., 92 clinics. **Educational facilities:** 7 colleges and univ., including main branch of Univ. of Wisconsin; 30 elem. schools, 12 middle schools, 5 high schools. **Further information:** Greater Madison Chamber of Commerce, PO Box 71, Madison, WI 53701-0071; www.ci.madison.wi.us; www.madisonchamber.com

Memphis, Tennessee

Population (2002): 648,882 (17); **Pop. density:** 2,323 per sq. mi; **Pop. change (1990-2002):** +4.8%. **Area:** 279.3 sq. mi. **Employment:** 307,832 employed; 6.4% unemployed. **Per capita income (MSA):** $30,559; increase (2000-2001): 3.5%.
Mayor: Willie W. Herenton, Democrat
History: French, Spanish, and U.S. forts by 1797; settled by 1819; inc. as town 1826, as city 1840; surrendered charter to state 1879 after yellow fever epidemics; rechartered as city 1893.
Transportation: 1 intl. airport; 5 railroads; 1 bus system. **Communications:** 7 TV, 32 radio stations. **Medical facilities:** 20 hosp. **Educational facilities:** 17 univ. and colleges; 233 pub., 111 private schools. **Further information:** Memphis Regional Chamber, 22 N. Front St., Ste. 200, PO Box 224, Memphis, TN 38101-0224; www.ci.memphis.tn.us; www.memphis chamber.com

Mesa, Arizona

Population (2002): 426,841 (40); **Pop. density:** 3,415 per sq. mi; **Pop. change (1990-2002):** +47.1%. **Area:** 125.0 sq. mi. **Employment:** 218,183 employed; 4.8% unemployed. **Per capita income (MSA):** $28,337; increase (2000-2001): 1.2%.
Mayor: Keno Hawker, Non-Partisan
History: founded by Mormons 1878; inc. 1883; 20 minutes east of Phoenix Sky Harbor Intl. Airport; population boomed fivefold 1960-80.
Transportation: near Sky Harbor Intl. Airport in Phoenix, 2 local airports; metro bus service. **Medical facilities:** 5 major hosp. **Educational facilities:** 1 univ., 3 colleges; 85 pub. schools. **Further information:** Convention and Visitor's Bureau and Mesa Chamber of Commerce, 120 N. Center, Mesa, AZ 85201; www.ci.mesa.az.us; www.mesacvb.com; www.mesa chamber.org

Miami, Florida

Population (2002): 374,791 (47); **Pop. density:** 10,498 per sq. mi; **Pop. change (1990-2002):** +4.2%. **Area:** 35.7 sq. mi. **Employment:** 173,713 employed; 11.1% unemployed. **Per capita income (MSA):** $26,594; increase (2000-2001): 1.9%.
Mayor: Manuel A. Diaz, Independent
History: site of fort 1836; settlement began 1870; inc. 1896, modern city developed into financial and recreation center; land speculation in 1920s added to city's growth, as did Cuban, Central and South American, and Haitian immigration since 1960.
Transportation: 1 intl. airport; seaport; Amtrak, transit rail system; 2 bus lines; 65 truck lines. **Communications:** 9 commercial, 2 educational TV stations; 48 radio stations. **Medical facilities:** 8 hosp.; VA hosp. **Educational facilities:** 6 univ. and colleges. **Further information:** Miami-Dade Dept. of Planning, Development, and Regulation, Research Div., 111 NW 1st St., Ste. 1220, Miami, FL 33128; www.ci.miami.fl.us; www.greater miami.com

Milwaukee, Wisconsin

Population (2002): 590,895 (19); **Pop. density:** 6,149 per sq. mi; **Pop. change (1990-2002):** –6.0%. **Area:** 96.1 sq. mi. **Employment:** 247,629 employed; 9.6% unemployed. **Per capita income (MSA):** $33,780; increase (2000-2001): 2.7%.
Mayor: John O. Norquist, Democrat
History: Indian trading post by 1674; settlement began 1835; inc. as city 1848; famous beer industry.
Transportation: 1 intl. airport; 3 railroads; major port; 4 bus lines. **Communications:** 12 TV, 37 radio stations. **Medical facilities:** 8 hosp.; major medical center. **Educational facilities:** 7 univ. and colleges, 160 pub. schools. **Further information:** Greater Milwaukee Convention and Visitors' Bureau, 101 W.

Wisconsin Avenue, Suite 425, Milwaukee, WI 53202; www. milwaukee.org; www.ci.mil.wi.us; www.mmac.org

Minneapolis, Minnesota

Population (2002): 375,635 (46); **Pop. density:** 6,842 per sq. mi; **Pop. change (1990-2002):** +2.0%. **Area:** 54.9 sq. mi. **Employment:** 209,169 employed; 4.9% unemployed. **Per capita income (MSA):** $38,131; increase (2000-2001): 2.6%.
Mayor: R.T. Rybak, Democrat
History: site visited by Hennepin 1680; included in area of military reservations 1819; inc. 1867.
Transportation: 1 intl. airport; 5 railroads. **Communications:** 7 TV, 30 radio stations. **Medical facilities:** 7 hosp., incl. leading heart hosp. at Univ. of Minnesota. **Educational facilities:** 10 univ. and colleges; 121 pub., 28 private schools. **Further information:** City of Minneapolis Office of Pub. Affairs, 323M City Hall, 350 S. 5th Street, Minneapolis, MN 55415; www.ci.minneapolis.mn.us

Modesto, California

Population (2002): 203,555 (90); **Pop. density:** 5,686 per sq. mi; **Pop. change (1990-2002):** 22.3%. **Area:** 35.8 sq. mi. **Employment:** 88,700 employed; 10.2% unemployed. **Per capita income (MSA):** $22,677; decrease (2000-2001): –0.5%.
Mayor: Carmen Sabatino, Democrat
History: founded 1870 after the Gold Rush of 1849 brought an influx of settlers to the region; recent growth boosted by agriculture, immigration.
Transportation: 1 airport. **Communications:** 8 TV, 15 radio stations. **Medical facilities:** 2 hospitals. **Educational facilities:** 1 junior college, 6 public high schools. **Further information:** Modesto Convention & Visitor Bureau, 1150 Ninth St., Ste. C, PO Box 844, Modesto, CA 95353; www.modestocvb.org

Montgomery, Alabama

Population (2002): 201,425 (92); **Pop. density:** 1,296 per sq. mi; **Pop. change (1990-2002):** +5.6%. **Area:** 155.4 sq. mi. **Employment:** 93,394 employed; 5.0% unemployed. **Per capita income (MSA):** $26,830; increase (2000-2001): 2.9%.
Mayor: Bobby N. Bright, Democrat
History: inc. as town 1819, as city 1837; became state capital 1846; first capital of Confederacy 1861.
Transportation: 3 airlines; 2 railroads; 2 bus lines; Alabama R. navigable to Gulf of Mexico. **Communications:** 4 TV, 2 CATV, 1 public TV, 16 radio stations. **Medical facilities:** 3 major hosp.; VA and 32 clinics. **Educational facilities:** 8 colleges and univ.; 35 pub., 35 private schools. **Further information:** Montgomery Area Chamber of Commerce, PO Box 79, Montgomery, AL 36101; www.montgomerychamber.com

Nashville, Tennessee

Population (2002): 545,915 (27); **Pop. density:** 1,153 per sq. mi; **Pop. change (1990-2002):** +11.8%. **Area:** 473.3 sq. mi. **Employment:** 307,366 employed; 4.0% unemployed. **Per capita income (MSA):** $32,338; increase (2000-2001): 2.3%.
Mayor: Bill Purcell, Non-Partisan
History: settled 1779; first chartered 1806; became permanent state capital 1843; home of Grand Ole Opry.
Transportation: 1 airport; 1 railroad; bus line; transit system of buses and trolleys. **Communications:** 11 TV, 34 radio stations. **Medical facilities:** 14 hosp.; VA and speech-hearing center. **Educational facilities:** 17 universities and colleges, 129 pub. schools. **Further information:** Chamber of Commerce, 211 Commerce St., Ste 100, Nashville, TN 37201; www.nashville chamber.com

Newark, New Jersey

Population (2002): 277,000 (63); **Pop. density:** 11,639 per sq. mi; **Pop. change (1990-2002):** –0.6%. **Area:** 23.8 sq. mi. **Employment:** employed 104,062; 12.3% unemployed. **Per capita income (MSA):** $42,550; increase (2000-2001): 3.0%.
Mayor: Sharpe James, Democrat
History: settled by Puritans 1666; used as supply base by Washington 1776; inc. as town 1833, as city 1836.
Transportation: 1 intl. airport; 1 intl. seaport, 4 railroads; bus system; subways. **Communications:** 5 TV, 6 radio stations within city limits, 1 daily newspaper, 8 weekly papers. **Medical facilities:** 5 hosp. **Educational facilities:** 5 univ. and colleges; 58 pub. elementary schools, 13 junior and senior high schools, 10 special schools, 2 vocational schools, and 40 private schools. **Further information:** Newark Public Information Office, City of Newark, 920 Broad St., Newark, NJ 07102; www.ci.newark. nj.us; www.rbp.org

New Orleans, Louisiana

Population (2002): 473,681 (32); **Pop. density:** 2,623 per sq. mi; **Pop. change (1990-2002):** −4.7%. **Area:** 180.6 sq. mi. **Employment:** 180,472 employed; 6.2% unemployed. **Per capita income (MSA):** $28,048; increase (2000-2001): 6.3%.

Mayor: Ray Nagin, Democrat

History: founded by French 1718; became major seaport on Mississippi R.; acquired by U.S. as part of Louisiana Purchase 1803; inc. as city 1805; Battle of New Orleans was last battle of War of 1812.

Transportation: 2 airports; major railroad center; major intl. port. **Communications:** 8 TV, 26 radio stations. **Medical facilities:** 22 hosp.; 2 major research centers. **Educational facilities:** 10 univ. and 9 colleges. **Further information:** New Orleans Metropolitan Convention & Visitors Bureau, Inc., 1520 Sugar Bowl Dr., New Orleans, LA 70112; www.neworleanscvb.com; www.neworleansbusiness.net

New York, New York

Population (2002): 8,084,316 (1); **Pop. density:** 26,655 per sq. mi; **Pop. change (1990-2002):** +10.4%. **Area:** 303.3 sq. mi. **Employment:** 3,453,455 employed; 7.9% unemployed. **Per capita income (MSA):** $40,450; increase (2000-2001): 2.4%.

Mayor: Michael Bloomberg, Republican

History: trading post established 1624; British took control from Dutch 1664 and named city New York; briefly U.S. capital; Washington inaugurated as president 1789; under new charter, 1898, city expanded to include 5 boroughs: The Bronx, Brooklyn, Queens, and Staten Island, as well as Manhattan. Sept. 11, 2001, terrorist attack destroyed World Trade Center, killed about 2,800.

Transportation: 3 intl. airports serve area; 2 rail terminals; major subway network that includes 25 routes; 235 bus routes; ferry system; 4 underwater tunnels. **Communications:** 17 TV, 67 radio stations. **Medical facilities:** 79 hosp.; 6 academic medical centers. **Educational facilities:** 100 univ. and colleges; 1,198 pub. schools. **Further information:** Convention and Visitors Bureau, 810 Seventh Ave., New York, NY 10019; www.ci.nyc.ny.us; www.nycvisit.com

Norfolk, Virginia

Population (2002): 239,036 (73); **Pop. density:** 4,451 per sq. mi; **Pop. change (1990-2002):** −8.5%. **Area:** 53.7 sq. mi. **Employment:** 84,775 employed, 6.3% unemployed. **Per capita income (MSA):** $27,452; increase (2000-2001): 4.4%.

Mayor: Paul D. Fraim, Non-Partisan

History: founded 1682; burned by patriots to prevent capture by British during Revolutionary War; rebuilt and inc. as town 1805, as city 1845; site of world's largest naval base; major east coast commercial port and cruise terminal.

Transportation: 1 intl. airport; 2 railroads; Amtrak; bus system. **Communications:** 13 TV, 6 city-access TV, 27 radio stations. **Medical facilities:** 6 hosp. **Educational facilities:** 3 univ., 1 college, 1 medical school; 59 pub. schools. **Further information:** Norfolk Convention and Visitors Bureau, 232 E. Main St., Norfolk, VA 23510; www.norfolk.va.us; www.norfolkcvb.com

Oakland, California

Population (2002): 402,777 (42); **Pop. density:** 664 per sq. mi; **Pop. change (1990-2002):** +0.7%. **Area:** 56.1 sq. mi. **Employment:** 182,776 employed, 10.6% unemployed. **Per capita income (MSA):** $39,963; increase (2000-2001): −0.3%.

Mayor: Jerry Brown, Non-Partisan

History: area settled by Spanish 1820; inc. as city under present name 1854.

Transportation: 1 intl. airport; western terminus for 2 railroads; underground, 75-mi underwater subway. **Communications:** 1 TV, 3 radio stations in city. **Medical facilities:** 10 hosp. in MSA. **Educational facilities:** 12 East Bay colleges and univ.; 81 pub. schools. **Further information:** Oakland Metropolitan Chamber of Commerce, 475 14th St., Oakland, CA 94612-1903; www.oaklandchamber.com; www.oaklandnet.com

Oklahoma City, Oklahoma

Population (2002): 519,034 (29); **Pop. density:** 4,486 per sq. mi; **Pop. change (1990-2002):** +16.7%. **Area.** 607.0 sq. mi. **Employment:** 251,095 employed, 4.6% unemployed. **Per capita income (MSA):** $26,970; increase (2000-2001): 4.0%.

Mayor: Kirk Humphreys, Non-Partisan

History: settled during land rush in Midwest 1889; inc. 1890; became capital 1910; oil discovered 1928. Bomb in 1995 destroyed federal office bldg., killed 168 people.

Transportation: 1 intl. airport; 1 railroad; pub. transit system; 1 major bus lines. **Communications:** 6 TV, 19 radio stations. **Medical facilities:** 23 hosp. **Educational facilities:** 18 univ. and colleges; 100 pub., 36 private schools. **Further information:** Chamber of Commerce, Economic Development Division, 123 Park Ave., Oklahoma City, OK 73102; www.okcchamber.com; www.okccvb.org.

Omaha, Nebraska

Population (2002): 399,357 (43); **Pop. density:** 8,019 per sq. mi; **Pop. change (1990-2002):** +10.2%. **Area:** 115.7 sq. mi. **Employment:** 208,364 employed, 4.6% unemployed. **Per capita income (MSA):** $33,249; increase (2000-2001): 3.2%.

Mayor: Mike Fahey, Democrat

History: founded 1854; inc. 1857; large food-processing, telecommunications, information-processing center; home to more than 20 insurance companies.

Transportation: 11 major airlines; 3 major railroads; intercity bus line. **Communications:** 7 TV, 18 radio stations. **Medical facilities:** 11 hosp.; institute for cancer research. **Educational facilities:** 5 univ., 6 colleges; 243 pub., 78 private schools. **Further information:** Greater Omaha Chamber of Commerce, 1301 Harney St., Omaha, NE 68102; www.ci.omaha.ne.us; www.accessomaha.com

Philadelphia, Pennsylvania

Population (2002): 1,492,231 (5); **Pop. density:** 11,045 per sq. mi; **Pop. change (1990-2002):** −5.9%. **Area:** 135.1 sq. mi. **Employment:** 628,533 employed, 7.6% unemployed. **Per capita income (MSA):** $35,192; increase (2000-2001): 2.9%.

Mayor: John F. Street, Democrat

History: first settled by Swedes 1638; Swedes surrendered to Dutch 1654; settled by English and Scottish Quakers 1678; named Philadelphia 1682; chartered 1701; Continental Congresses convened 1774, 1775; Declaration of Independence signed here 1776; national capital 1790-1800; state capital 1683-1799.

Transportation: 1 major airport; 3 railroads; major freshwater port; subway, el, rail commuter, bus, and streetcar system. **Communications:** 2 major daily newspapers, 14 TV, 62 radio stations. **Medical facilities:** 42 hosp. **Educational facilities:** 28 univ. and colleges. **Further information:** Greater Philadelphia Chamber of Commerce, Business Information Center, 200 South Broad St., Suite 700, Philadelphia PA 19102; www.phila.gov; www.philachamber.com

Phoenix, Arizona

Population (2002): 1,371,960 (6); **Pop. density:** 2,889 per sq. mi; **Pop. change (1990-2002):** +34.3%. **Area:** 474.9 sq. mi. **Employment:** 774,246 employed; 38.7% unemployed. **Per capita income (MSA):** $28,337; increase (2000-2001): 1.2%.

Mayor: Skip Rimsza, Republican

History: settled 1870; inc. as city 1881; became territorial capital 1889.

Transportation: 1 intl. airport; 3 railroads; transcontinental bus line; pub. transit system. **Communications:** 12 TV, 17 radio stations. **Medical facilities:** 19 hosp., 1 medical research center. **Educational facilities:** 36 institutions of higher learning; 380 pub. schools (247 elem. and junior high schools, 35 senior high schools, 98 charter schools). **Further information:** Greater Phoenix Chamber of Commerce, 201 N. Central Ave., 27th fl., Phoenix, AZ 85073; www.phoenix.gov; www.phoenixchamber.com

Pittsburgh, Pennsylvania

Population (2002): 327,898 (54); **Pop. density:** 5,897 per sq. mi; **Pop. change (1990-2002):** −11.4%. **Area:** 55.6 sq. mi. **Employment:** 159,100 employed; 5.1% unemployed. **Per capita income (MSA):** $32,626; increase (2000-2001): 5.4%.

Mayor: Tom J. Murphy, Democrat

History: settled around Ft. Pitt 1758; inc. as city 1816; has one of the largest inland ports; by Civil War, already a center for iron production.

Transportation: 1 intl. airport; 20 railroads; 2 bus lines; trolley/subway system. **Communications:** 6 TV, 26 radio stations. **Medical facilities:** 35 hosp.; VA installation. **Educational facilities:** 3 univ., 6 colleges; 86 pub. schools. **Further information:** Greater Pittsburgh Convention & Visitors Bureau, Regional Enterprise Tower, 30th Floor, 425 Sixth Ave., Pittsburgh, PA 15219; Pittsburgh Regional Alliance, Regional Enterprise Tower, 36th Floor, 425 Sixth Ave., Pittsburgh, PA 15219; www.visitpittsburgh.com; www.pittsburghregion.com

Plano, Texas

Population (2002): 238,091 (74); **Pop. density:** 3,325 per sq. mi; **Pop. change (1990-2002):** +85.3%. **Area:** 71.6 sq. mi. **Employment:** 146,897 employed, 5.6% unemployed. **Per capita income (MSA):** $34,697; decrease (2000-2001): −1.9%.

Mayor: Pat Evans, Non-Partisan

History: settled 1846; inc. as city 1873.

Transportation: 1 bus line; 2 DART (Dallas Area Rapid Transit) stations. **Communications:** 2 TV, 2 radio stations. **Medical facilities:** 6 medical facilities. **Educational facilities:** 5 institutions of higher learning, 65 pub. schools. **Further information:** Plano Chamber of Commerce, PO Drawer 940287, Plano, TX 75094-0287; www.planotx.org; www.planochamber.org

Portland, Oregon

Population (2002): 539,438 (28); **Pop. density:** 4,017 per sq. mi; **Pop. change (1990-2002):** +11.0%. **Area:** 134.3 sq. mi. **Employment:** 258,054 employed; 9.0% unemployed. **Per capita income (MSA):** $31,971; increase (2000-2001): 0.5%.

Mayor: Vera Katz, Non-Partisan

History: settled by pioneers 1845; developed as trading center, aided by California Gold Rush 1849; city chartered 1851.

Transportation: 1 intl. airport; 2 major rail freight lines, Amtrak; mass transit bus, light rail, and street car system; marine port. **Com-munications:** 9 TV, 27 radio stations. **Medical facilities:** 12 hosp.; VA hosp. **Educational facilities:** 25 univ. and colleges, 1 community college. **Further information:** Portland Business Alliance, 520 SW Yamhill St., Ste. 100, Portland, OR 97204; www. portlandalliance.com

Raleigh, North Carolina

Population (2002): 306,944 (58); **Pop. density:** 2,678 per sq. mi; **Pop. change (1990-2002):** +39.3%. **Area:** 114.6 sq. mi. **Employment:** 179,037 employed; 6.2% unemployed. **Per capita income (MSA):** $32,998; increase (2000-2001): 1.0%.

Mayor: Charles Meeker, Democrat

History: named after Sir Walter Raleigh; site chosen for capital 1788; laid out 1792; inc. 1795; occupied by Gen. Sherman 1865.

Transportation: 1 intl. airport, 20 airlines, 12 commuter airlines; 3 railroads; 2 bus lines. **Communications:** 8 TV, 31 radio stations. **Medical facilities:** 3 hosp. **Educational facilities:** 6 univ. and colleges; 1 community college; 105 pub. schools (county). **Further information:** Chamber of Commerce, 800 S. Salisbury St., PO Box 2978, Raleigh, NC 27602; www.raleigh-wake.org; www.raleighchamber.org

Richmond, Virginia

Population (2002): 197,456 (97); **Pop. density:** 3,285 per sq. mi; **Pop. change (1990-2002):** -2.6%. **Area:** 60.1 sq. mi. **Employment:** 92,307 employed; 6.2% unemployed. **Per capita income (MSA):** $32,268; increase (2000-2001): 2.9%.

Mayor: Rudolph C. McCollum Jr., Democrat

History: first settled 1607; became capital of Commonwealth of Virginia, 1779; attacked by British under Benedict Arnold 1781; inc. as city 1782; capital of Confederate States of America, 1861-65.

Transportation: 1 intl. airport; 3 railroads; 1 intracity bus lines; deepwater terminal accessible to oceangoing ships. **Communications:** 4 TV, 28 radio stations. **Medical facilities:** Virginia Commonwealth Univ. Health Systems renowned for heart and kidney transplants; 8 hosp. **Educational facilities:** 8 univ. and colleges; 173 pub., 49 private schools. **Further information:** Chamber of Commerce, PO Box 12280, Richmond, VA 23241; www.ci.richmond.va.us; www.grcc.com

Riverside, California

Population (2002): 274,226 (64); **Pop. density:** 3,511 per sq. mi; **Pop. change (1990-2002):** +21.0%. **Area:** 78.1 sq. mi. **Employment:** 158,521 employed; 6.1% unemployed. **Per capita income (MSA):** $23,840; increase (2000-2001): 2.0%.

Mayor: Ronald O. Loveridge, Non-Partisan

History: founded 1870; inc. 1886; known for its citrus industry; home of the parent navel orange tree and the historic Mission Inn. **Transportation:** municipal airport, intl. airport nearby; rail freight lines, commuter line; trolley/bus system; interstate freeways. **Communications:** 15 TV, 47 radio stations. **Medical facilities:** 3 hosp.; many clinics. **Educational facilities:** 3 univ., 1 community college. **Further information:** Chamber of Commerce, 3985 University Avenue, Riverside, CA 92501; www.ci.riverside.ca.us; www.riverside-chamber.com

Rochester, New York

Population (2002): 217,158 (81); **Pop. density:** 6,066 per sq. mi; **Pop. change (1990-2002):** -5.9%. **Area:** 35.8 sq. mi. **Employment:** 105,794 employed; 10.0% unemployed. **Per capita income (MSA):** 29,870; increase (2000-2001): 3.5%.

Mayor: William A. Johnson Jr., Democrat

History: first permanent settlement 1812; inc. as village 1817, as city 1834; developed as Erie Canal town.

Transportation: 1 intl. airport; Amtrak; 2 bus lines; intracity transit service; Port of Rochester. **Communications:** 6 TV, 19 radio stations. **Medical facilities:** 8 general hosp. **Educational facilities:** 11 colleges, 3 community colleges. **Further information:** Greater Rochester Metro Chamber of Commerce, 55 St.

Paul St., Rochester, NY 14604-1391; www.rnychamber.com; www.ci.rochester.ny.us

Sacramento, California

Population (2002): 435,245 (38); **Pop. density:** 4,478 per sq. mi; **Pop. change (1990-2002):** +10.2%. **Area:** 97.2 sq. mi. **Employment:** 202,764 employed; 6.6% unemployed. **Per capita income (MSA):** $30,906; increase (2000-2001): 2.2%.

Mayor: Heather Fargo, Non-Partisan

History: settled 1839; important trading center during California Gold Rush 1840s; became state capital 1854.

Transportation: international, executive, and cargo airports; 2 mainline transcontinental rail carriers; bus and light rail system; Port of Sacramento. **Communications:** 8 TV, 34 radio stations; 3 cable TV cos. **Medical facilities:** 15 major hosp. **Educational facilities:** 7 colleges and univ., 5 community colleges, 81 pub. schools. **Further information:** Sacramento Metropolitan Chamber of Commerce, 917 Seventh St., Sacramento, CA 95814; www.metrochamber.org; www.sacramentocvb.org

St. Louis, Missouri

Population (2002): 338,353 (52); **Pop. density:** 5,466 per sq. mi; **Pop. change (1990-2002):** -14.7%. **Area:** 61.9 sq. mi. **Employment:** 145,050 employed; 9.6% unemployed. **Per capita income (MSA):** $32,666; increase (2000-2001): 3.0%.

Mayor: Francis Slay, Democrat

History: founded 1764 as a fur trading post by French; acquired by U.S. 1803; chartered as city 1822; became independent city 1876; lies on Mississippi R., near confluence with Missouri R.

Transportation: 2 intl. airports; 2d largest rail center, 7 trunk-line railroads; 3d largest inland port; Amtrak; Greyhound; bus & light rail; 32 barge lines, 550 motor freight carriers. **Communications:** 8 TV, 19 radio stations. **Medical facilities:** 8 hosp., incl. 2 teaching hosp.; VA hosp., 2 pediatric hosp. **Educational facilities:** 8 univ., 13 colleges and seminaries, 61 elem., 21 middle, 11 high schools. **Further information:** St. Louis Planning & Urban Design Agency, 1015 Locust St., Ste. 1200, St. Louis, MO 63101; stlouis.missouri.com

St. Paul, Minnesota

Population (2002): 284,037 (61); **Pop. density:** 5,379 per sq. mi; **Pop. change (1990-2002):** +4.3%. **Area:** 52.8 sq. mi. **Employment:** 141,812 employed; 5.1 unemployed. **Per capita income (MSA):** $38,131; increase (2000-2001): 2.6%.

Mayor: Randy C. Kelly, Democrat

History: founded in early 1840s as "Pig's Eye Landing"; became capital of the Minnesota territory 1849 and chartered as St. Paul 1854.

Transportation: 1 intl., 1 business airport; 6 major rail lines; 2 interstate bus lines; pub. transit system. **Communications:** 9 TV, 47 radio stations. **Medical facilities:** 6 hosp. **Educational facilities:** 5 univ., 5 colleges; 1 technical, 3 law schools, 1 art and design college; 65 public, 39 private schools. **Further information:** St. Paul Area Chamber of Commerce, 401 N. Robert St., Ste. 150, St. Paul, MN 55101; www.ci.stpaul.mn.us; www.saint paulchamber.com; www.stpaulcvb.org

St. Petersburg, Florida

Population (2002): 248,546 (70); **Pop. density:** 4,170 per sq. mi; **Pop. change (1990-2002):** +3.4%. **Area:** 59.6 sq. mi. **Employment:** 137,693 employed; 5.4% unemployed. **Per capita income (MSA):** $29,379; increase (2000-2001): 2.2%.

Mayor: Rick Baker, Non-Partisan

History: founded 1888; inc. 1903.

Transportation: 1 municipal, 2 intl. airports; Amtrak bus connection; county-wide public bus system; downtown 'looper' bus service, largest municipal marina in Florida; 1 cruise port. **Communications:** 17 TV, 41 radio stations in area, 2 daily newspapers. **Medical facilities:** 4 major hosp.; VA hosp. **Educational facilities:** 2 univ. and 1 college, 1 law school; 26 elem., 9 middle, 4 high schools; 100 private schools. **Further information:** City of St. Petersburg , PO Box 2842, St. Petersburg, FL 33731; www.stpete.com

San Antonio, Texas

Population (2002): 1,194,222 (9); **Pop. density:** 2,930 per sq. mi; **Pop. change (1990-2002):** +19.7%. **Area:** 407.6 sq. mi. **Employment:** 522,161 employed; 5.7% unemployed. **Per capita income (MSA):** $6,887; increase (2000-2001): 2.0%.

Mayor: Ed Garza, Non-Partisan

History: first Spanish garrison 1718; Battle at the Alamo in 1836; city subsequently captured by Texans; inc. 1837.

Transportation: 1 intl. airport; 4 railroads; 3 bus lines; pub. transit system. **Communications:** 12 TV, 42 radio stations. **Medical facilities:** 22 hosp.; major medical center. **Educational facilities:** 18 univ. and colleges; 16 pub. school districts. **Further information:** Chamber of Commerce, PO Box 1628, San Antonio, TX 78296; www.ci.sat.tx.us; www.sachamber.org

San Diego, California

Population (2002): 1,259,532 (7); **Pop. density:** 3,884 per sq. mi; **Pop. change (1990-2002):** +13.4%. **Area:** 324.3 sq. mi. **Employment:** 643,991 employed; 4.4% unemployed. **Per capita income (MSA):** $33,883; increase (2000-2001): 3.0%.

Mayor: Dick Murphy, Republican

History: claimed by the Spanish 1542; first mission est. 1769; scene of conflict during Mexican-American War 1846; inc. 1850.

Transportation: 1 major airport; 1 railroad; major freeway system; bus system; trolley system. **Communications:** 9 TV, 25 radio stations, 2 cable providers. **Medical facilities:** 17 hosp. **Educational facilities:** 25 colleges and univ.; 177 pub. schools. **Further information:** San Diego Regional Chamber of Commerce, 402 W. Broadway, Ste. 1000, San Diego, CA 92101; www.sannet.gov; www.sdchamber.org

San Francisco, California

Population (2002): 764,049 (13); **Pop. density:** 16,361 per sq. mi; **Pop. change (1990-2002):** +5.5%. **Area:** 46.7 sq. mi. **Employment:** 391,845; employed; 7.3% unemployed. **Per capita income (MSA):** $57,714; decrease (2000-2001): −1.7%.

Mayor: Willie L. Brown Jr., Non-Partisan

History: nearby Farallon Islands sighted by Spanish 1542; city settled by 1776; claimed by U.S. 1846; became a major city during California Gold Rush 1849; inc. as city 1850; earthquake devastated city 1906.

Transportation: 1 major airport; intracity railway system; 2 railway transit systems; bus and railroad service; ferry system; 1 underwater tunnel. **Communications:** 8 TV; 8 radio stations. **Medical facilities:** 16 hosp. **Educational facilities:** 18 univ. and colleges, 116 pub. schools, 5 charter schools. **Further information:** San Francisco Convention & Visitors Bureau, 201 3rd St., Ste. 900, San Francisco, CA 94103; www.ci.sf.ca.us; www.sf chamber.com; www.sfvisitor.org

San Jose, California

Population (2002): 900,443 (11); **Pop. density:** 5,148 per sq. mi; **Pop. change (1990-2002):** +15.0%. **Area:** 174.9 sq. mi. **Employment:** 443,571 employed; 9.8% unemployed. **Per capita income (MSA):** $51,579; decrease (2000-2001): −7.4%

Mayor: Ron Gonzales, Democrat

History: founded by the Spanish 1777 between San Francisco and Monterey; state cap. 1849-51; inc. 1850.

Transportation: 1 intl. airport; 2 railroads; light rail system; bus system. **Communications:** 9 TV, 15 radio stations. **Medical facilities:** 6 hosp. **Educational facilities:** 6 univ. and colleges. **Further information:** San Jose Convention and Visitors Bureau, 125 S. Market St., Ste. 300, San Jose, CA 95113; www.sanjose ca.gov; www.sanjose.org

Santa Ana, California

Population (2002): 343,413 (51); **Pop. density:** 12,672 per sq. mi; **Pop. change (1990-2002):** +16.7%. **Area:** 27.1 sq. mi. **Employment:** 162,905 employed; 7.4% unemployed. **Per capita income (MSA):** $36,647; increase (2000-2001): 3.4%

Mayor: Miguel Pulido, Non-Partisan

History: founded 1769; inc. as city 1869.

Transportation: 1 airport; 5 major freeways including main Los Angeles-San Diego artery; Amtrak. **Communications:** 14 TV, 28 radio stations. **Medical facilities:** 4 hosp. **Educational facilities:** 1 community college. **Further information:** Santa Ana Chamber of Commerce, 2020 N. Broadway, 2nd floor, Santa Ana, CA 92706; www.santaanachamber.com

Scottsdale, Arizona

Population (2002): 215,779 (82); **Pop. density:** 1,171 per sq. mi; **Pop. change (1990-2002):** +65.9%. **Area:** 184.2 sq. mi. **Employment:** 113,141 employed; 4.1% unemployed. **Per capita income (MSA):** $28,337; increase (2000-2001): 1.2%

Mayor: Mary Manross, Democrat

History: founded 1888 by Army Chaplain Winfield Scott; inc. June 25, 1951; Frank Lloyd Wright built winter home here (Taliesin West); slogan "West's Most Western Town," by Mayor Malcolm White adopted 1951.

Transportation: 1 intl. airport in area, 1 local airport; regional bus system; local bus system; taxi system. **Communications:** 12 TV, 45 radio stations. **Medical facilities:** 2 general hospitals; Mayo Clinic. **Educational facilities:** 1 univ. nearby, 1 community college; 3 unified school districts. **Further information:** Scottsdale Chamber of Commerce, 7343 Scottsdale Mall, Scottsdale, AZ 85251-4498; www.ci.scottsdale.az.us; www.scottsdalechamber.com

Seattle, Washington

Population (2002): 570,426 (24); **Pop. density:** 6,799 per sq. mi; **Pop. change (1990-2002):** +10.5%. **Area:** 83.9 sq. mi. **Employment:** 331,922 employed; 7.7% unemployed. **Per capita income (MSA):** $41,229; increase (2000-2001): 0.5%.

Mayor: Greg Nickels, Democrat

History: settled 1851; inc. 1869; suffered severe fire 1889; played prominent role during Alaska Gold Rush 1897; growth followed opening of Panama Canal 1914; center of aircraft industry WWII.

Transportation: 1 intl. airport; 2 railroads; ferries serve Puget Sound, Alaska, Canada. **Communications:** 7 TV, 39 radio stations. **Medical facilities:** 40 hosp. **Educational facilities:** 7 univ., 6 colleges, 11 community colleges. **Further information:** Greater Seattle Chamber of Commerce, 1301 5th Ave., Ste. 2400, Seattle, WA 98101-2611; www.ci.seattle.wa.us; www.seattlechamber.com

Shreveport, Louisiana

Population (2002): 199,033 (94); **Pop. density:** 1,930 per sq. mi; **Pop. change (1990-2002):** +0.3%. **Area:** 103.1 sq. mi. **Employment:** 85,853 employed; 7.6% unemployed. **Per capita income (MSA):** $24,812; increase (2000-2001): 3.4%.

Mayor: Keith Hightower, Democrat

History: founded 1836 near site of a 180-mi logjam cleared by Capt. Henry Shreve; inc. 1839; oil discovered 1905.

Transportation: 2 airports, over 40 flights daily; 3 bus lines. **Communications:** 6 TV, 20 radio stations. **Medical facilities:** 16 hosp. **Educational facilities:** 2 univ., 4 colleges; approx. 100 pub. schools. **Further information:** Chamber of Commerce, PO Box 20074, 400 Edwards St., Shreveport, LA 71120; www.shreveportchamber.com

Spokane, Washington

Population (2002): 196,305 (100); **Pop. density:** 3,396 per sq. mi; **Pop. change (1990-2002):** +10.2%. **Area:** 57.8 sq. mi. **Employment:** 95,114 employed, 7.8% unemployed. **Per capita income (MSA):** $26,107; increase (2000-2001): 0.5%.

Mayor: John Powers, Non-Partisan

History: settled 1872; inc. as village of Spokane Falls 1881, destroyed in fire 1889; reinc. as city of Spokane 1891.

Transportation: 1 intl. airport; 2 railroads; bus system. **Communications:** 5 TV, 25 radio stations. **Medical facilities:** 6 major hosp. **Educational facilities:** 9 univ. and colleges; 14 pub. school districts, 16 high schools. **Further information:** Spokane Regional Chamber of Commerce, 801 W. Riverside Ave., Spokane, WA 99201; www.spokanechamber.org

Stockton, California

Population (2002): 262,835 (67); **Pop. density:** 4,805 per sq. mi; **Pop. change (1990-2002):** +24.3%. **Area:** 54.7 sq. mi. **Employment:** 100,114; employed; 11.8% unemployed. **Per capita income (MSA):** $23,155; decrease (2000-2001): −0.2%.

Mayor: Gary Podesto, Non-Partisan

History: site purchased 1842; settled 1849; inc. 1850; chief distributing point for agric. products of San Joaquin Valley.

Transportation: 1 airport; deepwater inland seaport; 4 railroads; 2 bus lines, county bus system. **Communications:** 5 TV stations. **Medical facilities:** 4 hosp.; regional burn, cancer, heart centers. **Educational facilities:** 9 univ. and colleges; 58 pub. schools. **Further information:** Chamber of Commerce, 445 W. Weber Ave., Ste. 220, Stockton, CA 95203; www.stocktongov.com; www.stocktonchamber.org

Tacoma, Washington

Population (2002): 197,553 (96); **Pop. density:** 3,943 per sq. mi; **Pop. change (1990-2002):** +11.4%. **Area:** 50.1 sq. mi. **Employment:** 94,825; employed, 8.7% unemployed. **Per capita income (MSA):** $26,601; increase (2000-2001): 0.9%.

Mayor: Bill Baarsma, Non-Partisan.

History: first European explorer of area was British Capt. George Vancouver 1792; colonized by Hudson's Bay Co. at Ft. Nisqually 1833; inc. 1884.

Transportation: 1 intl. airport; 3 railroads; transit and light rail systems; Port of Tacoma. **Communications:** 6 TV stations. **Medical facilities:** 7 hosp.; Army Medical Center; VA facility. **Educational facilities:** 3 univ., 4 colleges. **Further information:** Tacoma-Pierce County Chamber, PO Box 1933, Tacoma, WA 98401; www.cityoftacoma.org; www.tacomachamber.org

Tampa, Florida

Population (2002): 315,140 (56); **Pop. density:** 2,811 per sq. mi; **Pop. change (1990-2002):** +8.4%. **Area:** 112.1 sq. mi. **Employment:** 185,076 employed, 5.4% unemployed. **Per capita income (MSA):** $29,379; increase (2000-2001): 2.2%.

Mayor: Pam Iorio, Non-Partisan

History: U.S. army fort on site 1824; inc. 1849; Ybor City National Historical Landmark district.

Transportation: 1 intl. airport; Port of Tampa; CSX rail, Amtrak Rail; bus system; downtown streetcar. **Communications:** 14 TV, 57 radio stations. **Medical facilities:** 26 hosp. **Educational facilities:** 6 univ. and colleges; 178 pub. schools. **Further information:** Greater Tampa Chamber of Commerce, 615 Channelside Drive, Ste. 108, P.O. Box 420, Tampa, FL 33601; www.tampachamber.com

Toledo, Ohio

Population (2002): 309,106 (57); **Pop. density:** 3,835 per sq. mi; **Pop. change (1990-2002):** –7.1%. **Area:** 80.6 sq. mi. **Employment:** 148,550 employed; 8.0% unemployed. **Per capita income (MSA):** $28,098; increase (2000-2001): 1.0%.

Mayor: Jack Ford, Democrat

History: site of Ft. Industry 1794; Battles of Ft. Meigs and Ft. Timbers 1812; figured in "Toledo War" 1835-36 between Ohio and Michigan over borders; inc. 1837.

Transportation: 7 major airlines; 4 railroads; 65 motor freight lines; 10 interstate bus lines. **Communications:** 7 TV, 22 radio stations. **Medical facilities:** 5 major hosp. complexes. **Educational facilities:** 6 univ. and colleges. **Further information:** Toledo Area Chamber of Commerce, 300 Madison Ave., Ste. 200, Toledo, OH 43604; www.toledochamber.com

Tucson, Arizona

Population (2002): 503,151 (31); **Pop. density:** 2,584 per sq. mi; **Pop. change (1990-2002):** +20.6%. **Area:** 194,7 sq. mi. **Employment:** 252,365 employed; 5.4% unemployed. **Per capita income (MSA):** $24,767; increase (2000-2001): 3.0%.

Mayor: Robert E. Walkup, Republican

History: settled 1775 by Spanish as a presidio; acquired by U.S. in Gadsden Purchase 1853; inc. 1877.

Transportation: 1 intl. airport; 2 railroads; 1 bus system, 1 trolley. **Communications:** 10 TV, 34 radio stations. **Medical facilities:** 12 hosp. **Educational facilities:** 2 univ., 1 community college; 216 pub. schools. **Further information:** Tucson Metropolitan Chamber of Commerce, PO Box 991, Tucson, AZ 85702; www.ci.tucson.az.us; www.tucsonchamber.org

Tulsa, Oklahoma

Population (2002): 391,908 (44); **Pop. density:** 2,146 per sq. mi; **Pop. change (1990-2002):** +6.7%. **Area:** 182.6 sq. mi. **Employment:** 214,528 employed; 5.8% unemployed. **Per capita income (MSA):** $30,650; increase (2000-2001): 4.0%.

Mayor: Bill LaFortune, Republican

History: settled in 1836 by Creek Indians; modern town founded 1882 and inc. 1898; oil discovered early 20th century; emerging as telecommunications hub.

Transportation: 1 intl. airport; 5 rail lines; 5 bus lines; transit bus system. **Communications:** 130 TV, 31 radio stations. **Medical facilities:** 10 hosp. **Educational facilities:** 8 univ. and colleges; 85 pub., 39 private schools. **Further information:** Tulsa Metro Chamber, 2 West 2nd Tower II, Ste. 150, Tulsa, OK 74103; www.tulsachamber.com; www.cityoftulsa.org

Virginia Beach, Virginia

Population (2002): 433,934 (39); **Pop. density:** 1,748 per sq. mi; **Pop. change (1990-2002):** +10.4%. **Area:** 248.3 sq. mi. **Employment:** 208,536 employed; 3.5% unemployed. **Per capita income (MSA):** $27,452; increase (2000-2001): 4.4%.

Mayor: Meyera E. Oberndorf, Independent

History: area founded by Capt. John Smith 1607; formed by merger with Princess Anne Co. 1963.

Transportation: 1 airport; 2 railroads; 1 bus line; pub. transit system. **Communications:** 8 TV, 44 radio stations. **Medical facilities:** 2 hosp. **Educational facilities:** 1 univ., 2 colleges; 86 pub. schools. **Further information:** Virginia Beach Dept. of Economic Development, 222 Central Park Ave., Suite 1000, Virginia Beach, VA 23462; www.yesvirginiabeach.com

Washington, District of Columbia

Population (2002): 570,898 (23); **Pop. density:** 9,298 per sq. mi; **Pop. change (1990-2002):** –5.9%. **Area:** 61.4 sq. mi. **Employment:** 284,553 employed, 6.4% unemployed. **Per capita income (MSA):** $41,754; increase (2000-2001): 3.0%.

Mayor: Anthony A. Williams, Democrat

History: U.S. capital; site at Potomac R. chosen by George Washington 1790 on land ceded from VA and MD (portion S of Potomac returned to VA 1846); Congress first met 1800; inc. 1802; sacked by British, War of 1812; one of the most important Civil War battles was fought at Ft. Stevens.

Transportation: 3 intl. airports in area; Amtrak, 6 other passenger & cargo rail lines; Metrobus/Metrorail transit system; bus line. **Communications:** 5 TV, 61 radio stations. **Medical facilities:** 16 hosp. **Educational facilities:** 10 univ. and colleges. **Further information:** DC Chamber of Commerce, 1213 K Street NW, Washington, DC 20005; www.dc.gov; www.dcchamber.org

Wichita, Kansas

Population (2002): 355,126 (49); **Pop. density:** 2,615 per sq. mi; **Pop. change (1990-2002):** +15.1%. **Area:** 135.8 sq. mi. **Employment:** 169,504 employed; 7.0% unemployed. **Per capita income (MSA):** $29,386; increase (2000-2001): 5.2%.

Mayor: Bob Knight, Non-Partisan

History: founded 1864; inc. 1871.

Transportation: 2 airports; 3 major rail freight lines; 2 bus lines. **Communications:** 80 TV, 34 radio stations. **Medical facilities:** 7 hosp., 2 psychiatric rehab. centers. **Educational facilities:** 3 univ., 1 medical school; 96 pub. schools. **Further information:** Chamber of Commerce, 350 W. Douglas Ave., Wichita, KS 67202; www.wichitakansas.org; www.wichita.gov.

Yonkers, New York

Population (2002): 197,234 (98); **Pop. density:** 10,897 per sq. mi; **Pop. change (1990-2002):** +4.8%. **Area:** 18.1 sq. mi. **Employment:** 89,879; employed, 5.7% unemployed. **Per capita income (MSA):** $40,450; increase (2000-2001): 2.4%.

Mayor: John Spencer, Republican

History: founded 1641 by the Dutch; inc. as town 1855; chartered as city 1872; directly north of NYC.

Transportation: intracity bus system; rail service. **Communications:** Daily newspaper; govt., public, educational access channels; also see New York, New York. **Medical facilities:** 3 hosp. **Educational facilities:** 3 colleges; 41 pub. schools. **Further information:** Chamber of Commerce, 20 S. Broadway, 12th fl., Yonkers, NY 10701; www.cityofyonkers.com; www.yonkerschamber.com; www.yonkersprogress.com

Fastest-Growing Big Cities*

City	2002 population	1990 population	% change
1. Henderson, NV	206,153	65,109	216.6
2. Chandler, AZ	202,016	90,703	122.7
3. Las Vegas, NV	508,604	259,834	95.7
4. Plano, TX	238,091	128,507	85.3
5. Scottsdale, AZ	215,779	130,086	65.9
6. Glendale, AZ	230,564	150,867	52.8
7. Mesa, AZ	426,841	290,212	47.1
8. Bakersfield, CA	260,969	183,959	41.9
9. Raleigh, NC	306,944	220,425	39.3
10. Phoenix, AZ	1,371,960	988,983	38.7

Fastest-Shrinking Big Cities*

City	2002 population	1990 population	% change
1. St. Louis, MO	338,353	396,685	–14.7
2. Baltimore, MD	638,614	736,014	–13.2
3. Buffalo, NY	287,698	327,931	–12.3
4. Pittsburgh, PA	327,898	370,139	–11.4
5. Cincinnati, OH	323,885	364,553	–11.2
6. Detroit, MI	925,051	1,027,946	–10.01
7. Birmingham, AL	239,416	265,940	–9.97
8. Norfolk, VA	239,036	261,250	–8.5
9. Cleveland, OH	467,851	505,450	–7.4
10. Toledo, OH	309,106	332,832	–7.1

*Among those with populations of 200,000 or more, based on 2002 U.S. Census Bureau estimates.

Percent of Population by Race and Hispanic Origin, 10 Largest Cities, 2000

City	White	Black or African-Amer.	Amer. Indian, Alaska Native	Asian	Hawaiian & Other Pacific Isl.	Some other race[1]	Two or more races	Hispanic or Latino (of any race)
1. New York, NY	44.7	26.6	0.5	9.8	0.1	13.4	4.9	27.0
2. Los Angeles, CA	46.9	11.2	0.8	10.0	0.2	25.7	5.2	46.5
3. Chicago, IL	42.0	36.8	0.4	4.3	0.1	13.6	2.9	26.0
4. Houston, TX	49.3	25.3	0.4	5.3	0.1	16.5	3.1	37.4
5. Philadelphia, PA	45.0	43.2	0.3	4.5	0.1	4.8	2.2	8.5
6. Phoenix, AZ	71.1	5.1	2.0	2.0	0.1	16.4	3.3	34.1
7. San Diego, CA	60.2	7.9	0.6	13.6	0.5	12.4	4.8	25.4
8. Dallas, TX	50.8	25.9	0.5	2.7	0.0	17.2	2.7	35.6
9. San Antonio, TX	67.7	6.8	0.8	1.6	0.1	19.3	3.7	58.7
10. Detroit, MI	12.3	81.6	0.3	1.0	0.0	2.5	2.3	5.0

(1) Persons who, instead of checking off a race shown, filled in a designation under "some other race."

STATES AND OTHER AREAS OF THE U.S.

Sources: Population: U.S. Commerce Dept., Bureau of the Census—Census 2000: April 1, 2000, and July 2002 est. (including armed forces stationed in the state). Area: Bureau of the Census, Geography Division; forested land: Agriculture Dept., Forest Service. Lumber production: Bureau of the Census, Industry Division; mineral production: Dept. of Interior, Office of Mineral Information; commercial fishing: Commerce Dept., Natl. Marine Fisheries Service; new private housing: Bureau of the Census, Residential Construction Branch. Personal per capita income: Commerce Dept., Bureau of Economic Analysis; sales tax: CCH Inc.; unemployment: Labor Dept., Bureau of Labor Statistics. Tourism: Tourism Industries/ITA, Tourism Works for America Report. Lottery figures (not all states have a lottery): *La Fleur's Lottery World.* Finance: Federal Deposit Insurance Corp. Federal employees: Labor Dept., Office of Personnel Management. Energy: Energy Dept., Energy Information Administration. Other information from sources in individual states.

NOTE: Population density is for land area only. Categories under racial distribution may not add to 100% due to rounding. "Nat. AK" includes Eskimos and Aleuts. **Hispanic population may be any race** and is dispersed among racial categories, besides being listed separately. Nonfuel mineral values for some states exclude small amounts to avoid disclosing proprietary data. Categories under employment distribution are not all-inclusive. **Famous Persons lists may include some nonnatives** associated with the state as well as persons born there. Website addresses listed may not be official state sites and are not endorsed by *The World Almanac;* all website addresses are subject to change.

Alabama

Heart of Dixie, Camellia State

People. Population (2002 est.): 4,486,508; rank: 23; **net change** (2001-2002): 0.4%. **Pop. density:** 88.4 per sq mi. **Racial distribution** (2000): 71.1% white; 26.0% black; 0.7% Asian; 0.5% Native American/Nat. AK; <0.1% Hawaiian/Pacific Islander; 0.7% other race; 2 or more races, 1.0%. **Hispanic pop.** (any race): 1.7%.

Geography. Total area: 52,419 sq mi; rank: 30. **Land area:** 50,744 sq mi; rank: 28. **Acres forested:** 23.0 mil. **Location:** East South Central state extending N-S from Tenn. to the Gulf of Mexico; E of the Mississippi River. **Climate:** long, hot summers; mild winters; generally abundant rainfall. **Topography:** coastal plains, including Prairie Black Belt, give way to hills, broken terrain; highest elevation, 2,407 ft. **Capital:** Montgomery.

Economy. Chief industries: pulp & paper, chemicals, electronics, apparel, textiles, primary metals, lumber and wood products, food processing, fabricated metals, automotive tires, oil and gas exploration. **Chief manuf. goods:** electronics, cast iron & plastic pipe, fabricated steel products, ships, paper products, chemicals, steel, mobile homes, fabrics, poultry processing, soft drinks, furniture, tires. **Chief crops:** cotton, greenhouse & nursery, peanuts, sweet potatoes, potatoes and other vegetables. **Livestock:** (Jan. 2003) 1.4 mil cattle/calves; 131,000 sheep/lambs; (Dec. 2002) 165,000 hogs/pigs; 15.3 mil chickens (excl. broilers); 1.1 bil broilers. **Timber/lumber** (est. 2002): 2.5 bil bd. ft.; pine, hardwoods. **Nonfuel minerals** (est. 2002): $968 mil.; cement (portland), stone (crushed), lime, sand and gravel (construction), cement (masonry). **Commercial fishing** (2001): $44.3 mil. **Chief port:** Mobile. **Principal internat. airports at:** Birmingham, Huntsville. **New private housing** (2002): 18,403 units/$2.0 bil. **Gross state product** (2001): $121.5 bil. **Employment dist.** (May 2003): 19% govt.; 19.6% trade/trans./util.; 15.8% mfg.; 9.8% ed./health serv.; 9.8% prof./bus. serv.; 8.2% leisure/hosp.; 5.2% finance; 5.4% constr.; 1.8% info. **Per cap. pers. income** (2002): $25,128. **Sales tax** (2003): 4%. **Tourism expends.** (2000): $5.3 bil. **Unemployment** (2002): 5.9%.

Finance. FDIC-insured commercial banks (2002): 151. **Deposits:** $139.4 bil. **FDIC-insured savings institutions** (2002): 12. **Assets:** $2.2 bil.

Federal govt. Fed. civ. employees (Mar. 2002): 35,545. **Avg. salary:** $55,429. **Notable fed. facilities:** Marshall Space Flight Ctr.; Maxwell/Gunter AFB; Ft. Rucker, Intern'l. Fertilizer Development Ctr.; Navy Station & U.S. Corps of Engineers; Redstone Arsenal.

Energy. Electricity production (est. 2002, kWh, by source): Coal: 71.5 bil; Petroleum: 130 mil; Gas: 11.2 bil; Hydroelectric: 8.8 bil; Nuclear: 31.9 bil.

State data. Motto: We dare defend our rights. **Flower:** Camellia. **Bird:** Yellowhammer. **Tree:** Southern Longleaf pine. **Song:** Alabama. **Entered union** Dec. 14, 1819; rank, 22nd. **State fair:** Regional and county fairs held in Sept. and Oct.; no state fair.

History. Alabama was inhabited by the Creek, Cherokee, Chickasaw, Alabama, and Choctaw peoples when the Europeans arrived. The first Europeans were Spanish explorers in the early 1500s. The French made the first permanent settlement on Mobile Bay, 1702. France later gave up the entire region to England under the Treaty of Paris, 1763. Spanish forces took control of the Mobile Bay area, 1780, and it remained Spanish until U.S. troops seized the area, 1813. Most of present-day Alabama was held by the Creeks until Gen. Andrew Jackson broke their power, 1814, and they were removed to Oklahoma Territory. The state seceded, 1861, and the Confederate states were organized Feb. 4, at Montgomery, the first capital; it was readmitted, 1868.

Tourist attractions. First White House of the Confederacy, Civil Rights Memorial, Alabama Shakespeare Festival, all Montgomery; Ivy Green, Helen Keller's birthplace, Tuscumbia; Civil Rights Museum, statue of Vulcan, Birmingham; Carver Museum, Tuskegee; W. C. Handy Home & Museum, Florence; Alabama Space and Rocket Center, Huntsville; Moundville State Monument, Moundville; Pike Pioneer Museum, Troy; USS *Alabama* Memorial Park, Mobile; Russell Cave Natl. Monument, near Bridgeport: a detailed record of occupancy by humans from about 10,000 BC to AD 1650.

Famous Alabamians. Hank Aaron, Tallulah Bankhead, Hugo L. Black, Paul "Bear" Bryant, George Washington Carver, Nat King Cole, William C. Handy, Bo Jackson, Helen Keller, Coretta Scott King, Harper Lee, Joe Louis, Willie Mays, John Hunt Morgan, Jim Nabors, Jesse Owens, Condoleezza Rice, George Wallace, Booker T. Washington, Hank Williams.

Tourist information. Bureau of Tourism and Travel, 401 Adams Avenue, Suite 126, Montgomery, AL 36104; 1-800-ALABAMA out of state. **Website:** www.alabamatravel.org/tourism.html

Website. www.alabama.gov

Alaska

The Last Frontier (unofficial)

People. Population (2002 est.): 643,786; rank: 47; **net change** (2001-2002): 1.6%. **Pop. density:** 1.1 per sq mi. **Racial distribution** (2000): 69.3% white; 3.5% black; 4.0% Asian; 15.6% Native American/Nat. AK; 0.5% Hawaiian/Pacific Islander; 1.6% other race; 2 or more races, 5.4%. **Hispanic pop.** (any race): 4.1%.

Geography. Total area: 663,267 sq mi; rank: 1. **Land area:** 571,951 sq mi; rank: 1. **Acres forested:** 126.9 mil. **Location:** NW corner of North America, bordered on E by Canada. **Climate:** SE, SW, and central regions, moist and mild; far north extremely dry. Extended summer days, winter nights, throughout. **Topography:** includes Pacific and Arctic mountain systems, central plateau, and Arctic slope. Mt. McKinley, 20,320 ft, is the highest point in North America. **Capital:** Juneau.

Economy. Chief industries: petroleum, tourism, fishing, mining, forestry, transportation, aerospace. **Chief manuf. goods:** fish products, lumber & pulp, furs. **Agriculture: Chief crops:** greenhouse products, barley, oats, hay, potatoes, lettuce, aquaculture. **Livestock:** (Jan. 2003) 11,500 cattle/calves; (Dec. 2002) 1,200 hogs/pigs. **Timber/lumber:** (est. 2002): (undisclosed); spruce, yellow cedar, hemlock. **Nonfuel minerals** (est. 2002): $1.0 bil.; zinc, gold, lead, silver, sand and gravel (construction). **Commercial Fishing** (2001): $869.9 mil. **Chief ports:** Anchorage, Dutch Harbor, Kodiak, Seward, Skagway, Juneau, Sitka, Valdez, Wrangell. **Principal internat. airports at:** Anchorage, Fairbanks, Juneau. **New private housing** (2002): 3,003 units/$469 mil. **Gross state product** (2001): $28.6 bil. **Employment distrib.** (May 2003): 27.5% govt.; 20.4% trade/trans./util.; 2.9% mfg.; 10.6% ed./health serv.; 7.8% prof./bus. serv.; 10.3% leisure/hosp.; 4.6% finance; 5.6% constr.; 2.3% info. **Per cap. pers. income** (2002): $32,151. **Sales tax:** (2003): none. **Unemployment** (2002): 7.7%. **Tourism expends.** (2000): $1.5 bil.

Finance. FDIC-insured commercial banks (2002): 6. **Deposits:** $4.8 bil. **FDIC-insured savings institutions** (2002): 2. **Assets:** $338 mil.

Federal govt. Fed. civ. employees (Mar. 2002): 11,248. **Avg. salary:** $51,269. **Notable fed. facilities:** Ft. Richardson; Ft. Wainwright; Elmendorf AFB; Eilson AFB.

Energy. Electricity production (est. 2002, kWh, by source): Coal: 204 mil; Petroleum: 751 mil; Gas: 2.9 bil; Hydroelectric: 1.6 bil; Other: 1 mil.

State data. Motto: North to the future. **Flower:** Forget-Me-Not. **Bird:** Willow ptarmigan. **Tree:** Sitka spruce. **Song:** Alaska's Flag. **Entered union** Jan. 3, 1959; rank, 49th. **State fair** at Palmer; late Aug.-early Sept.

History. Early inhabitants were the Tlingit-Haida people and tribes of the Athabascan family. The Aleut and Inuit (Eskimo), who arrived about 4,000 years ago from Siberia, lived in the coastal areas. Vitus Bering, a Danish explorer working for Russia, was the first European to land in Alaska, 1741. The first permanent Russian settlement was established on Kodiak Island, 1784. In 1799, the Russian-American Co. controlled the region, and the first chief manager, Aleksandr Baranov, set up headquarters at Archangel, near present-day Sitka. Sec. of State William H. Seward bought Alaska from Russia for $7.2 mil in 1867, a bargain some called "Seward's Folly." In 1896, gold was discovered in the Klondike region, and the famed gold rush began. Alaska became a territory in 1912.

Tourist attractions. Inside Passage; Portage Glacier; Mendenhall Glacier; Ketchikan Totems; Glacier Bay Natl. Park and Preserve; Denali Natl. Park, one of N. America's great wildlife sanctuaries, surrounding Mt. McKinley, N. America's highest peak; Mt. Roberts Tramway, Juneau; Pribilof Islands fur seal rookeries; restored St. Michael's Russian Orthodox Cathedral, Sitka; White Pass & Yukon Route railroad; Skagway; Katmai Natl. Park & Preserve.

Famous Alaskans. Tom Bodett, Susan Butcher, Ernest Gruening, Jewel (Kilcher), Gov. Tony Knowles, Sydney Laurence, Libby Riddles, Jefferson "Soapy" Smith.

Tourist information. Alaska Division of Tourism, PO Box 110801, Juneau, AK 99811-0801; 1-907-465-2012. **Website:** www.dced.state.ak.us/tourism

Website. www.state.ak.us

Arizona
Grand Canyon State

People. Population (2002 est.): 5,456,453; rank: 19; **net change** (2001-2002): 2.8%. **Pop. density:** 48.0 per sq mi. **Racial distribution** (2000): 75.5% white; 3.1% black; 1.8% Asian; 5.0% Native American/Nat. AK; 0.1% Hawaiian/Pacific Islander; 11.6% other race; 2 or more races, 2.9%. **Hispanic pop.** (any race): 25.3%.

Geography. Total area: 113,998 sq mi; rank: 6. **Land area:** 113,635 sq mi; rank: 6. **Acres forested:** 19.4 mil. **Location:** in the southwestern U.S. **Climate:** clear and dry in the southern regions and northern plateau; high central areas have heavy winter snows. **Topography:** Colorado plateau in the N, containing the Grand Canyon; Mexican Highlands running diagonally NW to SE; Sonoran Desert in the SW. **Capital:** Phoenix.

Economy. Chief industries: manufacturing, construction, tourism, mining, agriculture. **Chief manuf. goods:** electronics, printing & publishing, foods, prim. & fabric. metals, aircraft and missiles, apparel. **Chief crops:** cotton, lettuce, cauliflower, broccoli, sorghum, barley, corn, wheat, citrus fruits. **Livestock:** (Jan. 2003) 840,000 cattle/calves; (Dec. 2002) 143,000 hogs/pigs. **Timber/lumber** (est. 2002): 62 mil bd. ft.; pine, fir, spruce. **Nonfuel minerals** (est. 2002): $1.9 bil.; copper, sand and gravel (construction), cement (portland), molybdenum concentrates, stone (crushed). **Principal internat. airports at:** Phoenix, Tucson. **New private housing** (2002): 66,031 units/$8.6 bil. **Gross state product** (2001): $160.7 bil. **Employment distrib.** (May 2003): 17% govt.; 19.4% trade/trans./util.; 7.6% mfg.; 10.7% ed./health serv.; 13.8% prof./bus. serv.; 10.3% leisure/hosp.; 6.7% finance; 7.7% constr.; 2.1% info. **Per cap. pers. income** (2003): $26,183. **Sales tax** (2003): 5.6%. **Unemployment** (2002): 6.2%. **Tourism expends.** (2002): $10.6 bil. **Lottery** (2002): total sales: $294.8 mil; net income: $84.9 mil.

Finance. FDIC-insured commercial banks (2002): 43. **Deposits:** $18.6 bil. **FDIC-insured savings institutions** (2002): 3. **Assets:** $523 mil.

Federal govt. Fed. civ. employees (Mar. 2002): 29,932. **Avg. salary:** $47,960. **Notable fed. facilities:** Luke, Davis-Monthan AF bases; Ft. Huachuca Army Base; Yuma Proving Grounds.

Energy. Electricity production (est. 2002, kWh, by source): Coal: 38.0 bil; Petroleum: 50 mil; Gas: 5.3 bil; Hydroelectric: 7.4 bil; Nuclear: 30.9 bil; Other: 33 mil.

State data. Motto: Ditat Deus (God enriches). **Flower:** Blossom of the Saguaro cactus. **Bird:** Cactus wren. **Tree:** Paloverde. **Song:** Arizona. **Entered union** Feb. 14, 1912; rank, 48th. **State fair** at Phoenix; late Oct.-early Nov.

History. Anasazi, Mogollon, and Hohokam civilizations inhabited the area c 300 BC-AD 1300, later Pueblo peoples; Navajo and Apache came c 15th cent. Marcos de Niza, a Franciscan, and Estevanico, a former black slave, explored, 1539; Spanish explorer Francisco Vásquez de Coronado visited, 1540. Eusebio Francisco Kino, a Jesuit missionary, taught Indians 1692-1711, and left missions. Tubac, a Spanish fort, became the first European settlement, 1752. Spain ceded Arizona to Mexico, 1821. The U.S. took over, 1848, after the Mexican War. The area below the Gila River was obtained from Mexico in the Gadsden Purchase, 1853. Arizona

became a territory, 1863. Apache wars ended with Geronimo's surrender, 1886.

Tourist attractions. The Grand Canyon; Painted Desert; Petrified Forest Natl. Park; Canyon de Chelly; Meteor Crater; London Bridge, Lake Havasu City; Biosphere 2, Oracle; Navajo Natl. Monument; Sedona.

Famous Arizonans. Bruce Babbitt, Cochise, Alice Cooper, Geronimo, Barry Goldwater, Zane Grey, Carl Hayden, George W. P. Hunt, Helen Jacobs, Bil Keane, Percival Lowell, William H. Pickering, John J. Rhodes, Morris Udall, Stewart Udall, Frank Lloyd Wright.

Tourist information. Arizona Office of Tourism, Ste. 4015, 2702 N. 3rd St., Phoenix, AZ 85004; 1-800-520-3433. **Website:** www.arizonaguide.com

Website. www.az.gov

Arkansas
The Natural State, The Razorback State

People. Population (2002 est.): 2,710,079; rank: 33; **net change** (2001-2002): 0.6%. **Pop. density:** 52.0 per sq mi. **Racial distribution** (2000): 80.0% white; 15.7% black; 0.8% Asian; 0.8% Native American/Nat. AK; 0.1% Hawaiian/Pacific Islander; 1.5% other race; 2 or more races, 1.3%. **Hispanic pop.** (any race): 3.2%.

Geography. Total area: 53,179 sq mi; rank: 29. **Land area:** 52,068 sq mi; rank: 27. **Acres forested:** 18.8 mil. **Location:** in the west south-central U.S. **Climate:** long, hot summers, mild winters; generally abundant rainfall. **Topography:** eastern delta and prairie, southern lowland forests, and the northwestern highlands, which include the Ozark Plateaus. **Capital:** Little Rock.

Economy. Chief industries: manufacturing, agriculture, tourism, forestry. **Chief manuf. goods:** food products, chemicals, lumber, paper, plastics, electric motors, furniture, auto components, airplane parts, apparel, machinery, steel. **Chief crops:** rice, soybeans, cotton, tomatoes, grapes, apples, commercial vegetables, peaches, wheat. **Livestock:** (Jan. 2003) 1.8 mil cattle/calves; (Dec. 2002) 305,000 hogs/pigs; 22.8 mil chickens (excl. broilers); 1.2 bil broilers. **Timber/lumber** (est. 2002): 2.6 bil bd. ft.; oak, hickory, gum, cypress, pine. **Nonfuel minerals** (est. 2002): $543 mil.; bromine, stone (crushed), cement (portland), sand and gravel (construction), lime. **Chief ports:** Little Rock, Pine Bluff, Osceola, Helena, Fort Smith, Van Buren, Camden, Dardanelle, North Little Rock, West Memphis, Crossett, McGehee, Morrilton. **New private housing** (2002): 12,436 units/$1.2 bil. **Gross state product** (2001): $67.9 bil. **Employment distrib.** (May 2003): 17.3% govt.; 21% trade/trans./util.; 18.1% mfg.; 12% ed./health serv.; 8.7% prof./bus. serv.; 8% leisure/hosp.; 4.3% finance; 4.7% constr.; 1.7% info. **Per cap. pers. income** (2002): $23,512. **Sales tax** (2003): 5.125%. **Unemployment** (2002): 5.4%. **Tourism expends.** (2000): $3.8 bil.

Finance. FDIC-insured commercial banks (2002): 169. **Deposits:** $26.5 bil. **FDIC-insured savings institutions** (2002): 8. **Assets:** $3.6 bil.

Federal govt. Fed. civ. employees (Mar. 2002): 11,239. **Avg. salary:** $47,114. **Notable fed. facilities:** Nat'l. Ctr. for Toxicological Research, Jefferson; Pine Bluff Arsenal, Little Rock AFB.

Energy. Electricity production (est. 2002, kWh, by source): Coal: 23.0 bil; Petroleum: 137 mil; Gas: 1.7 bil; Hydroelectric: 3.6 bil; Nuclear: 14.6 bil.

State data. Motto: Regnat Populus (The people rule). **Flower:** Apple blossom. **Bird:** Mockingbird. **Tree:** Pine. **Song:** Arkansas. **Entered union** June 15, 1836; rank, 25th. **State fair** at Little Rock; late Sept.-early Oct.

History. Quapaw, Caddo, Osage, Cherokee, and Choctaw peoples lived in the area at the time of European contact. The first European explorers were de Soto, 1541; Marquette and Jolliet, 1673; and La Salle, 1682. The first settlement was by the French under Henri de Tonty, 1686, at Arkansas Post. In 1762, the area was ceded by France to Spain, then given back again, 1800, and was part of the Louisiana Purchase, 1803. It was made a territory, 1819. Arkansas seceded in 1861, only after the Civil War began; more than 10,000 Arkansans fought on the Union side.

Tourist attractions. Hot Springs Natl. Park (water ranging from 95°F-147°F); Eureka Springs; Ozark Folk Center, Blanchard Caverns, both near Mountain View; Crater of Diamonds (only U.S. diamond mine) near Murfreesboro; Toltec Mounds Archeological State Park, Little Rock; Buffalo Natl. River; Mid-America Museum, Hot Springs; Pea Ridge National Military Park, Pead Ridge; Tanyard Springs, Morrilton; Wiederkehr Wine Village, Wiederkehr Village.

Famous Arkansans. Daisy Bates, Dee Brown, Paul "Bear" Bryant, Glen Campbell, Johnny Cash, Hattie Caraway, Wesley Clark, Bill Clinton, "Dizzy" Dean, Orval Faubus, James W. Fulbright, John Grisham, John H. Johnson, Douglas MacArthur, John L. McClellan, James S. McDonnell, Scottie Pippen, Dick Powell, Brooks Robinson, Billy Bob Thornton, Winthrop Rockefeller, Mary Steenburgen, Edward Durell Stone, Sam Walton, Archibald Yell.

Tourist Information. Arkansas Dept. of Parks & Tourism, One Capitol Mall, Little Rock, AR 72201; 1-800-NATURAL. **Website:** www.arkansas.com
Website. www.state.ar.us

California
Golden State

People. Population (2002 est.): 35,116,033; rank: 1; **net change** (2001-2002): 1.5%. **Pop. density:** 225.2 per sq mi. **Racial distribution** (2000): 59.5%; white; 6.7% black; 10.9% Asian; 1.0% Native American/Nat. AK; 0.3% Hawaiian/Pacific Islander; 16.8% other race; 2 or more races, 4.7% **Hispanic pop.** (any race): 32.4%.

Geography. Total area: 163,696 sq mi; rank: 3. **Land area:** 155,959 sq mi; rank: 3. **Acres forested:** 40.2 mil. **Location:** on western coast of the U.S. **Climate:** moderate temperatures and rainfall along the coast; extremes in the interior. **Topography:** long mountainous coastline; central valley; Sierra Nevada on the east; desert basins of the southern interior; rugged mountains of the north. **Capital:** Sacramento.

Economy. Chief industries: agriculture, tourism, apparel, electronics, telecommunications, entertainment. **Chief manuf. goods:** electronic and electrical equip., computers, industrial machinery, transportation equip. and instruments, food. **Chief farm products:** milk and cream, grapes, cotton, flowers, oranges, rice, nursery products, hay, tomatoes, lettuce, strawberries, almonds, asparagus. **Livestock:** (Jan. 2003) 5.2 mil cattle/calves; 790,000 sheep/lambs; (Dec. 2002) 135,000 hogs/pigs; 26.3 mil chickens (excl. broilers). **Timber/lumber** (est. 2002): 2.9 bil bd. ft.; fir, pine, redwood, oak. **Nonfuel minerals** (est. 2002): $3.4 bil.; sand and gravel (construction), cement (portland), boron minerals, stone (crushed), gold. **Commercial fishing** (2001): $108.2 mil. **Chief ports:** Long Beach, Los Angeles, San Diego, Oakland, San Francisco, Sacramento, Stockton. **Principal internat. airports at:** Fresno, Los Angeles, Oakland, Ontario, Sacramento, San Diego, San Francisco, San Jose. **New private housing** (2002): 159,573 units/$26.9 bil. **Gross state product** (2001): $1,359.3 bil. **Employment distrib.** (May 2003): 17.2% govt.; 18.7% trade/trans./util.; 10.9% mfg.; 10.6% ed./health serv.; 14.5% prof./bus. serv.; 9.8% leisure/hosp.; 6% finance; 5.4% constr.; 3.3% info. **Per cap. pers. income** (2002): $32,996. **Sales tax** (2003): 7.25%. **Unemployment** (2002): 6.7%. **Tourism expends.** (2000): $78.1 bil. **Lottery** (2002): total sales: $2.9 bil; net income: $1 bil.

Finance. FDIC-insured commercial banks (2002): 286. **Deposits:** $305.9 bil. **FDIC-insured savings institutions** (2002): 39. **Assets:** $424.5 bil.

Federal govt. Fed. civ. employees (Mar. 2002): 138,684. **Avg. salary:** $56,171. **Notable fed. facilities:** Vandenberg, Beale, Travis AF bases; San Diego Naval Sta.; Pt. Loma Naval Sub Base; USMC Camp Pendleton; Lawrence Livermore Natl. Lab; Berkeley Natl. Lab; NASA Jet Propulsion Lab; Edwards AFB (NASA Dryden Flight Test Ctr., AF Flight Rest Ctr.; San Francisco Mint.

Energy. Electricity production (est. 2002, kWh, by source): Petroleum: 48 mil; Gas: 8.7 bil; Hydroelectric: 29.6 bil; Nuclear: 34.3 bil; Other: 204 mil.

State data. Motto: Eureka (I have found it). **Flower:** Golden poppy. **Bird:** California valley quail. **Tree:** California redwood. **Song:** I Love You, California. **Entered union** Sept. 9, 1850; rank, 31st. **State fair** at Sacramento; late Aug.-early Sept.

History. Early inhabitants included more than 100 different Native American tribes with multiple dialects. The first European explorers were Cabrillo, 1542, and Drake, 1579. The first settlement was the Spanish Alta California mission at San Diego, 1769, first in a string founded by Franciscan Father Junípero Serra. U.S. traders and settlers arrived in the 19th cent. and staged the Bear Flag revolt, 1846, in protest against Mexican rule; later that year U.S. forces occupied California. At the end of the Mexican War, Mexico ceded the territory to the U.S., 1848; that same year gold was discovered, and the famed gold rush began.

Tourist attractions. The *Queen Mary,* Long Beach; Palomar Mountain; Disneyland, Anaheim; Getty Center, Los Angeles; Tournament of Roses and Rose Bowl, Pasadena;

Universal Studios, Hollywood; Long Beach Aquarium of the Pacific; Golden State Museum, Sacramento; San Diego Zoo; Yosemite Valley; Lassen and Sequoia-Kings Canyon natl. parks; Lake Tahoe; Mojave and Colorado deserts; San Francisco Bay; Napa Valley; Monterey Peninsula; oldest living things on earth believed to be a stand of Bristlecone pines in the Inyo National Forest, est. 4,700 years old; world's tallest tree, 365-ft "National Geographic Society" coast redwood, in Humboldt Redwoods State Park.

Famous Californians. Edmund G. (Pat) Brown, Jerry Brown, Luther Burbank, Julia Child, Ted Danson, Cameron Diaz, Leonardo DiCaprio, Joe DiMaggio, Dianne Feinstein, John C. Fremont, Robert Frost, Tom Hanks, Bret Harte, William Randolph Hearst, Helen Hunt, Jack Kemp, Monica Lewinsky, Jack London, George Lucas, Mark McGwire, Aimee Semple McPherson, Marilyn Monroe, John Muir, Richard M. Nixon, George S. Patton Jr., Gregory Peck, Nancy Pelosi, Ronald Reagan, Sally K. Ride, William Saroyan, Father Junípero Serra, O.J. Simpson, Kevin Spacey, Leland Stanford, John Steinbeck, Shirley Temple, Earl Warren, Ted Williams, Serena Williams, Venus Williams, Tiger Woods.

California Division of Tourism. P.O. Box 1499, Sacramento, CA 95812-1499;1-800-GOCALIF. **Website:** www.go calif.ca.gov
Website. www.state.ca.us

Colorado
Centennial State

People. Population (2002 est.): 4,506,542; rank: 22; **net change** (2001-2002): 1.7%. **Pop. density:** 43.4 per sq mi. **Racial distribution** (2000): 82.8% white; 3.8% black; 2.2% Asian; 1.0% Native American/Nat. AK; 0.1% Hawaiian/Pacific Islander; 7.2% other race; 2 or more races, 2.8% **Hispanic pop.** (any race): 17.1%.

Geography. Total area: 104,094 sq mi; rank: 8. **Land area:** 103,718 sq mi; rank: 8. **Acres forested:** 21.6 mil. **Location:** in W central U.S. **Climate:** low relative humidity, abundant sunshine, wide daily, seasonal temp. ranges; alpine conditions in the high mountains. **Topography:** eastern dry high plains; hilly to mountainous central plateau; western Rocky Mountains of high ranges, with broad valleys, deep, narrow canyons. **Capital:** Denver.

Economy. Chief industries: manufacturing, construction, government, tourism, agriculture, aerospace, electronics equipment. **Chief manuf. goods:** computer equip. & instruments, foods, machinery, aerospace products. **Chief crops:** corn, wheat, hay, sugar beets, barley, potatoes, apples, peaches, pears, dry edible beans, sorghum, onions, oats, sunflowers, vegetables. **Livestock:** (Jan. 2003) 3.1 mil cattle/calves; 370,000 sheep/lambs; (Dec. 2002) 790,000 hogs/pigs; 4.8 mil chickens (excl. broilers). **Timber/lumber** (est. 2002): 135 mil bd. ft.; oak, ponderosa pine, Douglas fir. **Nonfuel minerals** (est. 2002): $619 mil.; sand and gravel (construction), cement (portland), stone (crushed), molybdenum concentrates, gold. **Principal internat. airport at:** Denver. **New private housing** (2002): 47,871 units/$6.4 bil. **Gross state product** (2001): $173.8 bil. **Employment distrib.** (May 2003): 16.7% govt.; 18.6% trade/trans./util.; 7.2% mfg.; 9.8% ed./health serv.; 13.2% prof./bus. serv.; 11.3% leisure/hosp.; 7% finance; 7.2% constr.; 4.1% info. **Per cap. pers. income** (2002): $33,276. **Sales tax** (2003): 2.9%. **Unemployment** (2002): 5.7%. **Tourism expends.** (2000): $10.2 bil. **Lottery** (2002): total sales: $408 mil; net income: $110 mil.

Finance. FDIC-insured commercial banks (2002): 169. **Deposits:** $37.4 bil. **FDIC-insured savings institutions** (2002): 10. **Assets:** $2.6 bil.

Federal govt. Fed. civ. employees (Mar. 2002): 32,257. **Avg. salary:** $57,399. **Notable fed. facilities:** U.S. Air Force Academy; U.S. Mint; Ft. Carson; Natl. Renewable Energy Labs; U.S. Rail Transportation Test Ctr.; Cheyenne Mtn. Operations Ctr. (NORAD, U.S. Space Comm.); Denver Federal Ctr.; Natl. Ctr. for Atmospheric Research; Natl. Instit. for Standards in Technology; Natl. Wildlife Res. Ctr.; NOAA Env. Technology Lab.

Energy. Electricity production (est. 2002, kWh, by source): Coal: 35.1 bil; Petroleum: 24 mil; Gas: 5.3 bil; Hydroelectric: 972 mil; Other: 60 mil.

State data. Motto: Nil Sine Numine (Nothing Without Providence). **Flower:** Rocky Mountain columbine. **Bird:** Lark bunting. **Tree:** Colorado blue spruce. **Song:** Where the Columbines Grow. **Entered union:** Aug. 1, 1876; rank 38th. **State fair** at Pueblo; mid-Aug.—early Sept.

▶ IT'S A FACT: Colorado claims 54 mountain peaks over 14,000 feet. The lowest elevation in the Centennial State is on the Arikaree River as it flows into Kansas, 3,315 feet above sea level. Colorado has the highest low point in the U.S.— higher than the high point of 18 other states.

History. Early civilization centered around the Mesa Verde c 2,000 years ago; later, Ute, Pueblo, Cheyenne, and Arapaho peoples lived in the area. The region was claimed by Spain, but passed to France. The U.S. acquired eastern Colorado in the Louisiana Purchase, 1803. Lt. Zebulon M. Pike explored the area, 1806, discovering the peak that bears his name. After the Mexican War, 1846-48, U.S. immigrants settled in the east, former Mexicans in the south. Gold was discovered in 1858, causing a population boom. Displaced Native Americans protested, resulting in the so-called Sand Creek Massacre, 1864, where more than 200 Cheyenne and Arapaho were killed. All Native Americans were later removed to Oklahoma Territory.

Tourist attractions. Rocky Mountain and Black Canyon of the Gunnison natl. parks; Aspen Ski Resort; Garden of the Gods, Colorado Springs; Great Sand Dunes, Dinosaur, and Colorado natl. monuments; Pikes Peak and Mt. Evans highways; Mesa Verde Natl. Park (ancient Anasazi Indian cliff dwellings); Grand Mesa Natl. Forest; mining towns of Central City, Silverton, Cripple Creek; Burlington's Old Town; Bent's Fort, outside La Junta; Georgetown Loop Historic Mining Railroad Park, Cumbres & Toltec Scenic Railroad; limited stakes gaming in Central City, Blackhawk, Cripple Creek, Ignacio, and Towaoe.

Famous Coloradans. Tim Allen, Frederick Bonfils, Henry Brown, Molly Brown, William N. Byers, M. Scott Carpenter, Lon Chaney, Jack Dempsey, Mamie Eisenhower, Douglas Fairbanks, Barney Ford, Scott Hamilton, Chief Ourey, "Baby Doe" Tabor, Lowell Thomas, Byron R. White, Paul Whiteman.

State Chamber of Commerce. 1776 Lincoln, Ste. 1200, Denver, CO 80203. Phone: 303-831-7411

Tourist information. Colorado Travel and Tourism Authority, P.O. Box 3524, Englewood, CO 80155; 1-800-COLORADO. **Website:** www.colorado.com

Website. www.colorado.gov

Connecticut
Constitution State, Nutmeg State

People. Population (2002 est.): 3,460,503; rank: 29; **net change** (2001-2002): 0.8%. **Pop. density:** 714.2 per sq mi. **Racial distribution** (2000): 81.6% white; 9.1% black; 2.4% Asian; 0.3% Native American/Nat. AK; <0.1% Hawaiian/Pacific Islander; 4.3% other race; 2 or more races, 2.2%. **Hispanic pop.** (any race): 9.4%.

Geography. Total area: 5,543 sq mi; rank: 48. **Land area:** 4,845 sq mi; rank: 48. **Acres forested:** 1.9 mil. **Location:** New England state in NE corner of the U.S. **Climate:** moderate; winters avg. slightly below freezing; warm, humid summers. **Topography:** western upland, the Berkshires, in the NW, highest elevations; narrow central lowland N-S; hilly eastern upland drained by rivers. **Capital:** Hartford.

Economy. Chief industries: manufacturing, retail trade, government, services, finances, insurance, real estate. **Chief manuf. goods:** aircraft engines and parts, submarines, helicopters, machinery and computer equipment, electronics and electrical equipment, medical instruments, pharmaceuticals. **Chief crops:** nursery stock, Christmas trees, mushrooms, vegetables, sweet corn, tobacco, apples. **Livestock:** (Jan. 2003) 61,000 cattle/calves; (Dec. 2002) 3,800 hogs/pigs; 3.8 mil chickens (excl. broilers). **Timber/lumber** (est. 2002): 45 mil bd. ft.; oak, birch, beech, maple. **Nonfuel minerals** (est. 2002): $142 mil.; stone (crushed), sand and gravel (construction), stone (dimension), clays (common), gemstones. **Commercial fishing** (2001): $31.1 mil. **Chief ports:** New Haven, Bridgeport, New London. **Principal internat. airport at:** Windsor Locks. **New private housing** (2002): 9,731 units/$1.6 bil. **Gross state product** (2001): $166.2 bil. **Employment distrib.** (May 2003): 15.1% govt.; 18.6% trade/trans./util.; 12.3% mfg.; 15.9% ed./health serv.; 12% prof./bus. serv.; 7.7% leisure/hosp.; 8.6% finance; 3.7% constr.; 2.4% info. **Per cap. pers. income** (2002): $42,706. **Sales tax** (2003): 6%. **Unemployment** (2002): 4.3%. **Tourism expends.** (2002): $7 bil. **Lottery** (2002): total sales: $907.9 mil; net income: $271.5 mil.

Finance. FDIC-insured commercial banks (2002): 26. **Deposits:** $3.1 bil. **FDIC-insured savings institutions** (2002): 41. **Assets:** $50.7 bil.

Federal govt. Fed. civ. employees (Mar. 2002): 6,669. **Avg. salary:** $56,376. **Notable fed. facilities:** U.S. Coast Guard Academy; Navy Sub Base New London.

Energy. Electricity production (est. 2002, kWh, by source): Petroleum: 8 mil; Hydroelectric: 32 mil; Other: 143 mil.

State data. Motto: Qui Transtulit Sustinet (He who transplanted still sustains). **Flower:** Mountain laurel. **Bird:** American robin. **Tree:** White oak. **Song:** Yankee Doodle. **Fifth** of the 13 original states to ratify the Constitution, Jan. 9, 1788. **State Fair:** largest fair at Durham, late Sept.; no state fair.

History. At the time of European contact, inhabitants of the area were Algonquian peoples, including the Mohegan and Pequot. Dutch explorer Adriaen Block was the first European visitor, 1614. By 1634, settlers from Plymouth Bay had started colonies along the Connecticut River; in 1637 they defeated the Pequots. The Colony of Connecticut was chartered by England, 1662, adding New Haven, 1665. In the American Revolution, Connecticut Patriots fought in most major campaigns, while Connecticut privateers captured British merchant ships.

Tourist attractions. Mark Twain House, Hartford; Yale University's Art Gallery, Peabody Museum, both in New Haven; Mystic Seaport; Mystic Marine Life Aquarium; P. T. Barnum Museum, Bridgeport; Gillette Castle, Hadlyme; U.S.S. *Nautilus* Memorial, Groton (1st nuclear-powered submarine); Mashantucket Pequot Museum & Research Center, Foxwoods Resort & Casino, both in Ledyard; Mohegan Sun, Uncasville; Lake Compounce, Bristol.

Famous "Nutmeggers." Ethan Allen, Phineas T. Barnum, Samuel Colt, Jonathan Edwards, Nathan Hale, Katharine Hepburn, Isaac Hull, Robert Mitchum, J. Pierpont Morgan, Ralph Nader, Israel Putnam, Wallace Stevens, Harriet Beecher Stowe, Mark Twain, Noah Webster, Eli Whitney.

Tourist information. Dept. of Economic and Community Development, 505 Hudson St., Hartford, CT 06106; 1-800-CTBOUND. **Website:** www.ctbound.org

Website. www.ct.gov

Delaware
First State, Diamond State

People. Population (2002 est.): 807,385; rank: 45; **net change** (2001-2002): 1.4%. **Pop. density:** 413.2 per sq mi. **Racial distribution** (2000): 74.6% white; 19.2% black; 2.1% Asian; 0.3% Native American/Nat. AK; <0.1% Hawaiian/Pacific Islander; 2.0% other race; 2 or more races, 1.7%. **Hispanic pop.** (any race): 4.8%.

Geography. Total area: 2,489 sq mi; rank: 49. **Land area:** 1,954 sq mi; rank: 49. **Acres forested:** 0.4 mil. **Location:** occupies the Delmarva Peninsula on the Atlantic coastal plain. **Climate:** moderate. **Topography:** Piedmont plateau to the N, sloping to a near sea-level plain. **Capital:** Dover.

Economy. Chief industries: chemicals, agriculture, finance, poultry, shellfish, tourism, auto assembly, food processing, transportation equipment. **Chief manuf. goods:** nylon, apparel, luggage, foods, autos, processed meats and vegetables, railroad & aircraft equipment. **Chief crops:** soybeans, potatoes, corn, mushrooms, lima beans, green peas, barley, cucumbers, wheat, corn, grain sorghum, greenhouse & nursery. **Livestock:** (Jan. 2003) 26,000 cattle/calves; (Dec. 2002) 22,000 hogs/pigs; 1.5 mil chickens (excl. broilers); 257.4 mil broilers. **Timber/lumber** (est. 2002): 12 mil bd. ft.; hardwoods and softwoods (except for southern yellow pine). **Nonfuel minerals** est. 2002): $17.5 mil.; sand and gravel (construction), magnesium compounds, gemstones. **Commercial fishing** (2001): $7.7 mil. **Chief ports:** Wilmington. **Principal internat. airport at:** Philadelphia/Wilmington. **New private housing** (2002): 6,331 units/$703 mil. **Gross state product** (2001): $40.5 bil. **Employment distrib.** (May 2003): 13.5% govt.; 18.7% trade/trans./util.; 8.4% mfg.; 12% ed./health serv.; 16.5% prof./bus. serv.; 9.1% leisure/hosp.; 9.2% finance; 5.9% constr.; 1.9% info. **Per cap. pers. income** (2002): $32,779. **Sales tax** (2003): none. **Unemployment** (2002): 4.2%. **Tourism expends.** (2000): $1.1 bil. **Lottery** (2002): total sales: $674 mil; net income: $292.4 mil.

Finance. FDIC-insured commercial banks (2002): 28. **Deposits:** $80.2 bil. **FDIC-insured savings institutions** (2002): 7. **Assets:** $42.7 bil.

Federal govt. Fed. civ. employees (Mar. 2002): 63,459. **Avg. salary:** $53,080. **Notable fed. facilities:** Dover AFB, Federal Wildlife Refuge, Bombay Hook.

Energy. Electricity production (est. 2002, kWh, by source): Petroleum: 135 mil; Gas: 15 mil.

State data. Motto: Liberty and independence. **Flower:** Peach blossom. **Bird:** Blue hen chicken. **Tree:** American holly. **Song:** Our Delaware. **First** of original 13 states to ratify the Constitution, Dec. 7, 1787. **State fair** at Harrington; end of July.

History. The Lenni Lenape (Delaware) people lived in the region at the time of European contact. Henry Hudson located the Delaware R., 1609, and in 1610, English explorer Samuel Argall entered Delaware Bay, naming the area after Virginia's governor, Lord De La Warr. The Dutch first settled near present Lewes, 1631, but the colony was destroyed by Indians. Swedes settled at Fort Christina (now Wilmington), 1638. Dutch settled anew, 1651, near New Castle and seized the Swedish settlement, 1655, only to lose all Delaware and New Netherland to the British, 1664. After 1682, Delaware became part of Pennsylvania, and in 1704 it was granted its own assembly. In 1776, it adopted a constitution as the state of Delaware. Although it remained in the Union during the Civil War, Delaware retained slavery until abolished by the 13th amendment in 1865.

Tourist attractions. Ft. Christina Monument, site of founding of New Sweden, Holy Trinity (Old Swedes) Church, erected 1698, the oldest Protestant church in the U.S. still in use, Wilmington; Hagley Museum, Winterthur Museum and Gardens, both near Wilmington; historic district, New Castle; John Dickinson "Penman of the Revolution" home, Dover; Rehoboth Beach, "nation's summer capital," Rehoboth; Dover Downs Intl. Speedway.

Famous Delawareans. Thomas F. Bayard, Henry Seidel Canby, E. I. du Pont, John P. Marquand, Howard Pyle, Caesar Rodney.

Chamber of Commerce. 1200 N. Orange St., Ste. 200, Wilmington, DE 19899-0671; 1-800-2VISITDE. **Website:** www.visitdelaware.net

Website. www.delaware.gov

Florida
Sunshine State

People. Population (2002 est.): 16,713,149; rank: 4; **net change** (2001-2002): 2.1%. **Pop. density:** 309.9 per sq mi. **Racial distribution** (2000): 78.0% white; 14.6% black; 1.7% Asian; 0.3% Native American/Nat. AK; 0.1% Hawaiian/Pacific Islander; 3.0% other race; 2 or more races, 2.4%. **Hispanic pop.** (any race): 16.8%.

Geography. Total area: 65,755 sq mi; rank: 22. **Land area:** 53,927 sq mi; rank: 26. **Acres forested:** 16.3 mil. **Location:** peninsula jutting southward 500 mi between the Atlantic and the Gulf of Mexico. **Climate:** subtropical N of Bradenton-Lake Okeechobee-Vero Beach line; tropical S of line. **Topography:** land is flat or rolling; highest point is 345 ft in the NW. **Capital:** Tallahassee.

Economy. Chief industries: tourism, agriculture, manufacturing, construction, services, international trade. **Chief manuf. goods:** electric & electronic equipment, transportation equipment, food, printing & publishing, chemicals, instruments, industrial machinery. **Chief crops:** citrus fruits, vegetables, melons, greenhouse and nursery products, potatoes, sugarcane, strawberries. **Livestock:** (Jan. 2003) 1.8 mil cattle/calves; (Dec. 2002) 35,000 hogs/pigs; 13.0 mil chickens (excl. broilers); 114.7 mil broilers. **Timber/lumber** (est. 2002): 888 mil bd. ft.; pine, cypress, cedar; 751 mil bd. ft. **Nonfuel minerals** (est. 2002): $2.0 bil.; phosphate rock, stone (crushed), cement (portland), sand and gravel (construction), cement (masonry). **Commercial fishing** (2001): $196.6 mil. Chief ports: Pensacola, Tampa, Manatee, Miami, Port Everglades, Jacksonville, St. Petersburg, Canaveral. **Principal internat. airports at:** Daytona Beach, Ft. Lauderdale/Hollywood, Ft. Myers, Jacksonville, Key West, Melbourne, Miami, Orlando, Panama City, St. Petersburg/Clearwater, Sarasota/Bradenton, Tampa, West Palm Beach. **New private housing** (2002): 185,431 units/$22.5 bil. **Gross state product** (2001): $491.5 bil. **Employment distrib.** (May 2003): 14.5% govt.; 20% trade/trans./util.; 5.4% mfg.; 12% ed./health serv.; 17.1% prof./bus. serv.; 11.4% leisure/hosp.; 6.6% finance; 6.1% constr.; 2.3% info. **Per cap. pers. income** (2002): $29,596. **Sales tax** (2003): 6%. **Unemployment** (2002): 5.5%. **Tourism expends.** (2000): $59.8 bil. **Lottery** (2002): total sales: $2.3 bil; net income: $926.5 mil.

Finance. FDIC-insured commercial banks (2002): 260. **Deposits:** $58.6 bil. **FDIC-insured savings institutions** (2002): 41. **Assets:** $27.9 bil.

Federal govt. Fed. civ. employees (Mar. 2002): 63,459. **Avg. salary:** $53,080. **Notable fed. facilities:** John F. Kennedy Space Ctr., NASA-Kennedy Space Ctr.'s Spaceport USA; Eglin AFB; MacDill AFB; Pensacola NAS; Jacksonville NAS; Mayport Naval Sta.

Energy. Electricity production (est. 2002, kWh, by source): Coal: 52.3 bil; Petroleum: 31.2 bil; Gas: 54.3 bil; Hydroelectric: 184 mil; Nuclear: 33.7 bil; Other: 118 mil.

State data. Motto: In God we trust. **Flower:** Orange blossom. **Bird:** Mockingbird. **Tree:** Sabal palmetto palm. **Song:** Old Folks at Home. **Entered union** Mar. 3, 1845; rank, 27th. **State fair** at Tampa; early Feb.

History. The original inhabitants of Florida included the Timucua, Apalachee, and Calusa peoples. Later the Seminole migrated from Georgia to Florida, becoming dominant there in the early 18th cent. The first European to see Florida was Ponce de León, 1513. France established a colony, Fort Caroline, on the St. John River, 1564. Spain settled St. Augustine, 1565, and Spanish troops massacred most of the French. Brit-

ain's Sir Francis Drake burned St. Augustine, 1586. In 1763, Spain ceded Florida to Great Britain, which held the area briefly, 1763-83, before returning it to Spain. After Andrew Jackson led a U.S. invasion, 1818, Spain ceded Florida to the U.S., 1819. The Seminole War, 1835-42, resulted in removal of most Native Americans to Oklahoma Territory. Florida seceded from the Union, 1861, and was readmitted in 1868.

Tourist attractions. Miami Beach; St. Augustine, oldest permanent European settlement in U.S.; Castillo de San Marcos, St. Augustine; Walt Disney World's Magic Kingdom, EPCOT Center, Disney-MGM Studios, and Animal Kingdom, all near Orlando; Sea World, Universal Studios, near Orlando; Spaceport USA, Kennedy Space Center; Everglades Natl. Park; Ringling Museum of Art, Ringling Museum of the Circus, both in Sarasota; Cypress Gardens, Winter Haven; Busch Gardens, Tampa; U.S. Astronaut Hall of Fame, Mariana Caverns; Church St. Station, Orlando; Silver Springs, Ocala.

Famous Floridians. Edna Buchanan, Jeb Bush, Marjory Stoneman Douglas, Henry M. Flagler, Carl Hiaasen, James Weldon Johnson, MacKinlay Kantor, John D. MacDonald, Chief Osceola, Claude Pepper, Henry B. Plant, A. Philip Randolph, Marjorie Kinnan Rawlings, Janet Reno, Joseph W. Stilwell, Charles P. Summerall, Ben Vereen.

Tourist information. Visit Florida, P.O. Box 1100, Tallahassee, FL 32302-1100, 1-850-488-5607; 1-888-735-2872 (1-888-7FLA-USA). **Website:** www.flausa.com

Website. www.myflorida.com

Georgia
Empire State of the South, Peach State

People. Population (2002 est.): 8,560,310; rank: 10; **net change** (2001-2002): 1.8%. **Pop. density:** 147.8 per sq mi. **Racial distribution** (2000): 65.1% white; 28.7% black; 2.1% Asian; 0.3% Native American/Nat. AK; 0.1% Hawaiian/Pacific Islander; 2.4% other race; 2 or more races, 1.4%. **Hispanic pop.** (any race): 5.3%.

Geography. Total area: 59,425 sq mi; rank: 24. **Land area:** 57,906 sq mi; rank: 21. **Acres forested:** 24.4 mil. **Location:** South Atlantic state. **Climate:** maritime tropical air masses dominate in summer; polar air masses in winter; E central area drier. **Topography:** most southerly of the Blue Ridge Mts. cover NE and N central; central Piedmont extends to the fall line of rivers; coastal plain levels to the coast flatlands. **Capital:** Atlanta.

Economy. Chief industries: services, manufacturing, retail trade. **Chief manuf. goods:** textiles, apparel, food, and kindred products, pulp & paper products. **Chief crops:** peanuts, cotton, corn, tobacco, hay, soybeans. **Livestock:** (Jan. 2003) 1.2 mil cattle/calves; (Dec. 2002) 345,000 hogs/pigs; 29.6 mil chickens (excl. broilers); 1290.5 bil broilers. **Timber/lumber** (est. 2002): 3 mil bd. ft.; pine, hardwood; 3.2 bil bd. ft. **Nonfuel minerals** (est. 2002): $1.5 bil.; clays (kaolin), stone (crushed), clays (fuller's earth), cement (portland), sand and gravel (construction). **Commercial fishing** (2001): $15.2 mil. **Chief ports:** Savannah, Brunswick. **Principal internat. airports at:** Atlanta, Savannah. **New private housing** (2002): $97,523 units/$10.0 bil. **Gross state product** (2001): $299.9 bil. **Employment distrib.** (May 2003): 15.6% govt.; 20.8% trade/trans./util.; 11.4% mfg.; 9.6% ed./health serv.; 14% prof./bus. serv.; 8.7% leisure/hosp.; 5.4% finance; 5.4% constr.; 3.3% info. **Per cap. pers. income** (2002): $28,821. **Sales tax** (2003): 4%. **Unemployment** (2002): 5.1%. **Tourism expends.** (2000): $15.5 bil. **Lottery** (2002): total sales: $2.3 bil; net income: $726.2 mil.

Finance. FDIC-insured commercial banks (2002): 319. **Deposits:** $124.7 bil. **FDIC-insured savings institutions** (2002): 22. **Assets:** $7.4 bil.

Federal govt. Fed. civ. employees (Mar. 2002): 64,343. **Avg. salary:** $51,598. **Notable fed. facilities:** Dobbins AFB; Ft. Benning; Ft. Gordon; Ft. Gillem; Ft. Stewart; King's Bay Naval Base; Moody AFB; Navy Supply Corps School; Ft. McPherson; Fed. Law Enforcement Training Ctr., Glynco, Robins AFB; Centers for Disease Control.

Energy. Electricity production (est. 2002, kWh, by source): Coal: 78.1 bil; Petroleum: 192 mil; Gas: 1.2 bil; Hydroelectric: 2.0 bil; Nuclear: 31.1 bil.

WORLD ALMANAC QUICK QUIZ

After the 13 original colonies, which state was the next to join the Union?

    (a) Louisiana   (b) Vermont
    (c) Alabama   (d) Maine

For the answer look in this chapter, or see page 1008.

State data. Motto: Wisdom, justice and moderation. **Flower:** Cherokee rose. **Bird:** Brown thrasher. **Tree:** Live oak. **Song:** Georgia On My Mind. **Fourth** of the 13 original states to ratify the Constitution, Jan. 2, 1788. **State fair** at Macon, 3rd week in Oct.

History. Creek and Cherokee peoples were early inhabitants of the region. The earliest known European settlement was the Spanish mission of Santa Catalina, 1566, on Saint Catherines Island. Gen. James Oglethorpe established a colony at Savannah, 1733, for the poor and religiously persecuted. Oglethorpe defeated a Spanish army from Florida at Bloody Marsh, 1742. In the American Revolution, Georgians seized the Savannah armory, 1775, and sent the munitions to the Continental Army. They fought seesaw campaigns with Cornwallis's British troops, twice liberating Augusta and forcing final evacuation by the British from Savannah, 1782. The Cherokee were removed to Oklahoma Territory, 1832-38, and thousands died on the long march, known as the Trail of Tears. Georgia seceded from the Union, 1861, and was invaded by Union forces, 1864, under Gen. William T. Sherman, who took Atlanta, Sept. 2, and proceeded on his famous "march to the sea," ending in Dec., in Savannah. Georgia was readmitted, 1870.

Tourist attractions. State Capitol, Stone Mt. Park, Six Flags Over Georgia, Kennesaw Mt. Natl. Battlefield Park, Martin Luther King Jr. Natl. Historic Site, Underground Atlanta, Jimmy Carter Library & Museum, all Atlanta; Chickamauga and Chattanooga Natl. Military Park, near Dalton; Chattahoochee Natl. Forest; alpine village of Helen; Dahlonega, site of America's first gold rush; Brasstown Bald Mt.; Lake Lanier; Franklin D. Roosevelt's Little White House, Warm Springs; Callaway Gardens, Pine Mt.; Andersonville Natl. Historic Site; Okefenokee Swamp, near Waycross; Jekyll Island; St. Simons Island; Cumberland Island Natl. Seashore; historic riverfront district, Savannah.

Famous Georgians. Kim Basinger, Griffin Bell, James Bowie, James Brown, Erskine Caldwell, Jimmy Carter, Ray Charles, Lucius D. Clay, Ty Cobb, James Dickey, John C. Fremont, Newt Gingrich, Joel Chandler Harris, "Doc" Holliday, Holly Hunter, Alan Jackson, Martin Luther King Jr., Gladys Knight, Sidney Lanier, Little Richard, Juliette Gordon Low, Margaret Mitchell, Sam Nunn, Flannery O'Connor, Otis Redding, Burt Reynolds, Julia Roberts, Jackie Robinson, Clarence Thomas, Travis Tritt, Ted Turner, Carl Vinson, Alice Walker, Herschel Walker, Joseph Wheeler, Joanne Woodward, Trisha Yearwood, Andrew Young.

Chamber of Commerce. 235 International Blvd., Atlanta, GA 30303; (404) 880-9000;   1-800-VISITGA. **Website:** www.georgia.org/tourism
Website. www.georgia.gov

Hawai'i
Aloha State

People. Population (2002 est.): 1,244,898; rank: 42; **net change** (2001-2002): 1.5%. **Pop. density:** 193.8 per sq mi. **Racial distribution** (2000): 24.3% white; 1.8% black; 41.6% Asian; 0.3% Native American/Nat. AK; 9.4% Hawaiian/Pacific Islander; 1.3% other race; 2 or more races, 21.4%. **Hispanic pop.** (any race): 7.2%.

Geography. Total area: 10,931 sq mi; rank: 43. **Land area:** 6,423 sq mi; rank: 47. **Acres forested:** 1.7 mil. **Location:** Hawaiian Islands lie in the North Pacific, 2,397 mi SW from San Francisco. **Climate:** subtropical, with wide variations in rainfall; Waialeale, on Kaua'i, wettest spot in U.S. (annual rainfall 460 in.) **Topography:** islands are tops of a chain of submerged volcanic mountains; active volcanoes: Mauna Loa, Kilauea. **Capital:** Honolulu.

Economy. Chief industries: tourism, defense, sugar, pineapples. **Chief manuf. goods:** processed sugar, canned pineapple, clothing, foods, printing & publishing. **Chief crops:** sugar, pineapples, macadamia nuts, fruits, coffee, vegetables, floriculture. **Livestock:** (Jan. 2003) 152,000 cattle/calves; (Dec. 2002) 24,000 hogs/pigs; 625,000 chickens (excl. broilers); 0.88 mil broilers. **Timber/lumber** (est. 2002): (undisclosed). **Nonfuel minerals** (est. 2002): $75.3 mil.; stone (crushed), sand and gravel (construction), gemstones. **Commercial fishing** (2001): $54.6 mil. **Chief ports:** Honolulu, Hilo, Kailua. **Principal internat. airports at:** Hilo, Honolulu, Kailua, Kahului. **New private housing** (2002): 5,902 units/$1.1 bil. **Gross state product** (2001): $43.7 bil. **Employment distrib.** (May 2003): 21.4% govt.; 19% trade/trans./util.; 2.7%

mfg.; 11.5% ed./health serv.; 12% prof./bus. serv.; 17.2% leisure/hosp.; 5% finance; 4.8% constr.; 2.1% info. **Per cap. pers. income** (2002): $30,001. **Sales tax** (2003): 4%. **Unemployment** (2002): 4.2%. **Tourism expends.** (2000): $15.1 bil.

Finance. FDIC-insured commercial banks (2002): 7. **Deposits:** $17.5 bil. **FDIC-insured savings institutions** (2002): 2. **Assets:** $7.1 bil.

Federal govt. Fed. civ. employees (Mar. 2002): 19,792. **Avg. salary:** $49,197. **Notable fed. facilities:** Pearl Harbor Naval Shipyard; Hickam AFB; Schofield Barracks; Ft. Shafter; Marine Corps Base-Kaneohe Bay; Barbers Point NAS; Wheeler AFB; Prince Kuhio Federal Bldg.

Energy. Electricity production (est. 2002, kWh, by source): Petroleum: 6.6 bil; Hydroelectric: 9 mil; Other: 2 mil.

State data. Motto: The life of the land is perpetuated in righteousness. **Flower:** Yellow hibiscus. **Bird:** Hawaiian goose. **Tree:** Kukui (Candlenut). **Song:** Hawai'i Pono'i. **Entered union** Aug. 21, 1959; rank, 50th. **State fair:** at O'ahu, late June.

History. Polynesians from islands 2,000 mi to the south settled the Hawaiian Islands, probably between AD 300 and AD 600. The first European visitor was British captain James Cook, 1778. Between 1790 and 1810, the islands were united politically under the leadership of a native king, Kamehameha I, whose four successors—all bearing the name Kamehameha—ruled the kingdom from his death, 1819, until the end of the dynasty, 1872. Missionaries arrived, 1820, bringing Western culture. King Kamehameha III and his chiefs created the first constitution and a legislature that set up a public school system. Sugar production began, 1835, and it became the dominant industry. In 1893, Queen Liliuokalani was deposed, and a republic was instituted, 1894, headed by Sanford B. Dole. Annexation by the U.S. came in 1898. The Japanese attack on Pearl Harbor, Dec. 7, 1941, brought the U.S. into World War II.

Tourist attractions. Hawaii Volcanoes, Haleakala natl. parks; Natl. Memorial Cemetery of the Pacific, Waikiki Beach, Diamond Head, Honolulu; U.S.S. *Arizona* Memorial, Pearl Harbor; Hanauma Bay; Polynesian Cultural Center, Laie; Nu'uanu Pali; Waimea Canyon; Wailoa and Wailuku River state parks.

Famous Islanders. Bernice Pauahi Bishop, Tia Carrere, Father Damien de Veuster, Don Ho, Duke Kahanamoku, King Kamehameha, Brook Mahealani Lee, Daniel K. Inouye, Jason Scott Lee, Queen Liliuokalani, Bette Midler, Ellison Onizuka.

Chamber of Commerce of Hawaii. 1132 Bishop St., Suite 200, Honolulu, HI 96813; (808) 545-4300; 1-800-GOHAWAII. **Website:** www.gohawaii.com
Website. www.hawaii.gov

Idaho
Gem State

People. Population (2002 est.): 1,341,131; rank: 39; **net change** (2001-2002): 1.6%. **Pop. density:** 16.2 per sq mi. **Racial distribution** (2000): 91.0% white; 0.4% black; 0.9% Asian; 1.4% Native American/Nat. AK; 0.1% Hawaiian/Pacific Islander; 4.2% other race; 2 or more races, 2.0%. **Hispanic pop.** (any race): 7.9%.

Geography. Total area: 83,570 sq mi; rank: 14. **Land area:** 82,747 sq mi; rank: 11. **Acres forested:** 21.6 mil. **Location:** northwestern Mountain state bordering on British Columbia. **Climate:** tempered by Pacific westerly winds; drier, colder, continental climate in SE; altitude an important factor. **Topography:** Snake R. plains in the S; central region of mountains, canyons, gorges (Hells Canyon, 7,900 ft, deepest in N. America); subalpine northern region. **Capital:** Boise.

Economy. Chief industries: manufacturing, agriculture, tourism, lumber, mining, electronics. **Chief manuf. goods:** electronic components, computer equipment, processed foods, lumber and wood products, chemical products, primary metals, fabricated metal products, machinery. **Chief crops:** potatoes, peas, dry beans, sugar beets, alfalfa seed, lentils, wheat, hops, barley, plums and prunes, mint, onions, corn, cherries, apples, hay. **Livestock:** (Jan. 2003) 2.0 mil cattle/calves; 260,000 sheep/lambs; (Dec. 2002) 22,000 hogs/pigs; 1.7 bil bd. ft. **Nonfuel minerals** (est. 2002): $307 mil.; phosphate rock, sand and gravel (construction), silver, molybdenum concentrates, stone (crushed). **Chief port:** Lewiston. **New private housing** (2002): 13,488 units/$1.6 bil. **Gross state product** (2001): $36.9 bil. **Employment distrib.** (May 2003): 20.5% govt.; 20% trade/trans./util.; 10.7% mfg.; 10.6%

ed./health serv.; 12.4% prof./bus. serv.; 9.6% leisure/hosp.; 4.6% finance; 6.6% constr.; 1.6% info. **Per cap. pers. income** (2002): $25,057. **Sales tax** (2003): 5%. **Unemployment** (2002): 5.8%. **Tourism expends.** (2000): $2.3 bil. **Lottery** (2002): total sales: $92.7 mil; net income: $15 mil.

Finance. FDIC-insured commercial banks (2002): 17. **Deposits:** $2.7 bil. **FDIC-insured savings institutions** (2002): 3. **Assets:** $912 mil.

Federal govt. Fed. civ. employees (Mar. 2002): 7,826. **Avg. salary:** $49,537. **Notable fed. facilities:** Idaho Natl. Engineering Lab; Mountain Home AFB.

Energy. Electricity production (est. 2002, kWh, by source): Gas: 37 mil; Hydroelectric: 8.1 bil.

State data. Motto: Esto Perpetua (It is perpetual). **Flower:** Syringa. **Bird:** Mountain bluebird. **Tree:** White pine. **Song:** Here We Have Idaho. **Entered union** July 3, 1890; rank, 43rd. **State fair** at Boise, late Aug.; at Blackfoot, early Sept.

History. Early inhabitants were Shoshone, Northern Paiute, Bannock, and Nez Percé peoples. White exploration of the region began with Lewis and Clark, 1805-6. Next came fur traders, setting up posts, 1809-34, and missionaries, 1830s-50s. Mormons made their first permanent settlement at Franklin, 1860. Idaho's gold rush began the same year and brought thousands of permanent settlers. Most remarkable of the Indian wars was the 1,700-mi trek, 1877, of Chief Joseph and the Nez Percé, pursued by U.S. troops through 3 states and caught just short of the Canadian border. The Idaho territory was organized, 1863. Idaho adopted a progressive constitution and became a state, 1890.

Tourist attractions. Hells Canyon, deepest gorge in N. America; World Center for Birds of Prey; Craters of the Moon; Sun Valley, in Sawtooth Mts.; Crystal Falls Cave; Shoshone Falls; Lava Hot Springs; Lake Pend Oreille; Lake Coeur d'Alene; Sawtooth Natl. Recreation Area; River of No Return Wilderness Area; Redfish Lake.

Famous Idahoans. William E. Borah, Frank Church, Fred T. Dubois, Chief Joseph, Ezra Pound, Sacagawea, Picabo Street, Lana Turner.

Tourist information. Department of Commerce, 700 W. State St., Boise, ID 83720; 1-800-842-5858. **Website:** www.visitid.org

Website. www.state.id.us

Illinois
Prairie State

People. Population (2002 est.): 12,600,620; rank: 5; **net change** (2001-2002): 0.6%. **Pop. density:** 226.7 per sq mi. **Racial distribution** (2000): 73.5% white; 15.1% black; 3.4% Asian; 0.2% Native American/Nat. AK; <0.1% Hawaiian/Pacific Islander; 5.8% other race; 2 or more races, 1.9%. **Hispanic pop.** (any race): 12.3%.

Geography. Total area: 57,914 sq mi; rank: 25. **Land area:** 55,584 sq mi; rank: 24. **Acres forested:** 4.3 mil. **Location:** East North Central state; western, southern, and eastern boundaries formed by Mississippi, Ohio, and Wabash rivers, respectively. **Climate:** temperate; typically cold, snowy winters, hot summers. **Topography:** prairie and fertile plains throughout; open hills in the southern region. **Capital:** Springfield.

Economy. Chief industries: services, manufacturing, travel, wholesale and retail trade, finance, insurance, real estate, construction, health care, agriculture. **Chief manuf. goods:** machinery, electric and electronic equipment, prim. & fabric. metals, chemical products, printing & publishing, food and kindred products. **Chief crops:** corn, soybeans, wheat, sorghum, hay. **Livestock:** (Jan. 2003) 1.4 mil cattle/calves; 68,000 sheep/lambs; (Dec. 2002) 4.1 mil hogs/pigs; 4.0 mil chickens (excl. broilers). **Timber/lumber** (est. 2002): 130 mil bd. ft.; oak, hickory, maple, cottonwood. **Nonfuel minerals** (est. 2002): $950 mil.; stone (crushed), cement (portland), sand and gravel (construction), sand and gravel (industrial), lime. **Commercial fishing** (2001): $14,000. Chief ports: Chicago. **Principal internat. airport at:** Chicago. **New private housing** (2002): 60,971 units/$8.5 bil. **Gross state product** (2001): $475.5 bil. **Employment distrib.** (May 2003): 14.7% govt.; 20.2% trade/trans./util.; 12.5% mfg.; 12.3% ed./health serv.; 13.3% prof./bus. serv.; 8.5% leisure/hosp.; 6.8% finance; 4.7% constr.; 2.5% info. **Per cap. pers. income** (2002): $33,404. **Sales tax** (2003): 6.25%. **Unemployment** (2002): 6.5%. **Tourism expends.** (2000): $23.7 bil. **Lottery** (2002): total sales: $1.6 bil; net income: $552.3 mil.

Finance. FDIC-insured commercial banks (2002): 677. **Deposits:** $341.6 bil. **FDIC-insured savings institutions** (2002): 110. **Assets:** $32.0 bil.

Federal govt. Fed. civ. employees (Mar. 2002): 40,347. **Avg. salary:** $58,232. **Notable fed. facilities:** Fermi Natl. Ac-

celerator Lab; Argonne Natl. Lab; Rock Island Arsenal; Great Lakes, Naval Training Station, Scott AFB.

Energy. Electricity production (est. 2002, kWh, by source): Coal: 20.5 bil; Petroleum: 48 mil; Gas: 337 mil; Hydroelectric: 64 mil.

State data. Motto: State sovereignty—national union. **Flower:** Native violet. **Bird:** Cardinal. **Tree:** White oak. **Song:** Illinois. **Entered union** Dec. 3, 1818; rank, 21st. **State fair** at Springfield, mid-Aug.; DuQuoin, late Aug.

History. Seminomadic Algonquian peoples, including the Peoria, Illinois, Kaskaskia, and Tamaroa, lived in the region at the time of European contact. Fur traders were the first Europeans in Illinois, followed shortly by Jolliet and Marquette, 1673, and La Salle, 1680, who built a fort near present-day Peoria. The first settlements were French, at Cahokia, near present-day St. Louis, 1699, and Kaskaskia, 1703. France ceded the area to Britain, 1763, and in 1778, American Gen. George Rogers Clark took Kaskaskia from the British without a shot. Defeat of Native American tribes in the Black Hawk War, 1832, and growth of railroads brought change to the area. In 1787, it became part of the Northwest Territory. Post-Civil War Illinois became a center for the labor movement as bitter strikes, such as the Haymarket Square riot, occurred in 1885-86.

Tourist attractions. Chicago museums and parks; Lincoln shrines at Springfield, New Salem, Sangamon County; Cahokia Mounds, Collinsville; Starved Rock State Park; Crab Orchard Wildlife Refuge; Mormon settlement at Nauvoo; Fts. Kaskaskia, Chartres, Massac (parks); Shawnee Natl. Forest, Southern Illinois; Illinois State Museum, Springfield; Dickson Mounds Museum, between Havana and Lewiston.

Famous Illinoisans. Jane Addams, John Ashcroft, Saul Bellow, Jack Benny, Ray Bradbury, Gwendolyn Brooks, William Jennings Bryan, St. Frances Xavier Cabrini, Hillary Rodham Clinton, Clarence Darrow, John Deere, Stephen A. Douglas, James T. Farrell, George W. Ferris, Marshall Field, Betty Friedan, Benny Goodman, Ulysses S. Grant, Dennis Hastert, Ernest Hemingway, Charlton Heston, Wild Bill Hickok, Henry J. Hyde, Abraham Lincoln, Vachel Lindsay, Edgar Lee Masters, Oscar Mayer, Cyrus McCormick, Ronald Reagan, Donald Rumsfeld, Carl Sandburg, Adlai Stevenson, James Watson, Frank Lloyd Wright, Philip Wrigley.

Tourist information. Illinois Dept. of Commerce and Community Affairs, 620 E. Adams St., Springfield, IL 62701; 1-800-2-CONNECT. **Website:** www.enjoyillinois.com

Website. www.illinois.gov

Indiana
Hoosier State

People. Population (2002 est.): 6,159,068; rank: 14; **net change** (2001-2002): 0.5%. **Pop. density:** 171.7 per sq mi. **Racial distribution** (2000): 87.5% white; 8.4% black; 1.0% Asian; 0.3% Native American/Nat. AK; <0.1% Hawaiian/Pacific Islander; 1.6% other race; 2 or more races, 1.2%. **Hispanic pop.** (any race): 3.5%.

Geography. Total area: 36,418 sq mi; rank: 38. **Land area:** 35,867 sq mi; rank: 38. **Acres forested:** 4.5 mil. **Location:** East North Central state; Lake Michigan on N border. **Climate:** 4 distinct seasons with a temperate climate. **Topography:** hilly southern region; fertile rolling plains of central region; flat, heavily glaciated north; dunes along Lake Michigan shore. **Capital:** Indianapolis.

Economy. Chief industries: manufacturing, services, agriculture, government, wholesale and retail trade, transportation and public utilities. **Chief manuf. goods:** primary metals, transportation equipment, motor vehicles & equip., industrial machinery & equipment, electronic & electric equipment. **Chief crops:** corn, soybeans, wheat, nursery and greenhouse products, vegetables, popcorn, fruit, hay, tobacco, mint. **Livestock:** (Jan. 2003) 880,000 cattle/calves; 50,000 sheep/lambs; (Dec. 2002) 3.2 mil hogs/pigs; 29.1 mil chickens (excl. broilers). **Timber/lumber** (est. 2002): 324 mil bd. ft.; oak, tulip, beech, sycamore. **Nonfuel minerals** (est. 2002): $740 mil; mostly crushed stone, portland and masonry cement, sand & gravel, lime. **Chief ports:** Burns Harbor, Portage; Southwind Maritime, Mt. Vernon; Clark Maritime, Jeffersonville. **Principal internat. airports at:** Indianapolis, Ft. Wayne. **New private housing** (2002): 39,596 units/$5.0 bil. **Gross state product** (2001): $189.9 bil. **Employment distrib.** (May 2003): 14.7% govt.; 20% trade/trans./util.; 20% mfg.; 12.2% ed./health serv.; 8.4% prof./bus. serv.; 9.3% leisure/hosp.; 4.8% finance; 4.9% constr.; 1.4% info. **Per cap. pers. income** (2002): $28,240. **Sales tax** (2003): 6%. **Unemployment** (2002): 5.1%. **Tourism expends.** (2000): $6.7 bil. **Lottery** (2002): total sales: $626.3 mil; net income: $169.4 mil.

Finance. FDIC-insured commercial banks (2002): 151. **Deposits:** $58.6 bil. **FDIC-insured savings institutions** (2002): 60. **Assets:** $14.9 bil.

Federal govt. Fed. civ. employees (Mar. 2002): 18,115. **Avg. salary:** $52,206. **Notable fed. facilities:** Nav. Surface Warfare Ctr., Crane Div.

Energy. Electricity production (est. 2002, kWh, by source): Coal: 109.8 bil; Petroleum: 454 mil; Gas: 1.7 bil; Hydroelectric: 411 mil.

State data. Motto: Crossroads of America. **Flower:** Peony. **Bird:** Cardinal. **Tree:** Tulip poplar. **Song:** On the Banks of the Wabash, Far Away. **Entered union** Dec. 11, 1816; rank, 19th. **State fair** at Indianapolis; mid-Aug.

History. When the Europeans arrived, Miami, Potawatomi, Kickapoo, Piankashaw, Wea, and Shawnee peoples inhabited the area. A French trading post was built, 1731-32, at Vincennes. La Salle visited the present South Bend area, 1679 and 1681. The first French fort was built near present-day Lafayette, 1717. France ceded the area to Britain, 1763. During the American Revolution, American Gen. George Rogers Clark captured Vincennes, 1778, and defeated British forces, 1779. At war's end, Britain ceded the area to the U.S. Miami Indians defeated U.S. troops twice, 1790, but were beaten, 1794, at Fallen Timbers by Gen. Anthony Wayne. At Tippecanoe, 1811, Gen. William H. Harrison defeated Tecumseh's Indian confederation. The Delaware, Potawatomi, and Miami were moved farther west, 1820-1850.

Tourist attractions. Lincoln Log Cabin Historic Site, near Charleston; George Rogers Clark Park, Vincennes; Wyandotte Cave; Tippecanoe Battlefield Memorial Park; Benjamin Harrison home; Indianapolis 500 raceway and museum, all Indianapolis; Indiana Dunes, near Chesterton; National College Football Hall of Fame, South Bend; Hoosier Nat'l. Forest, south-central Indiana.

Famous "Hoosiers." Larry Bird, Ambrose Burnside, Hoagy Carmichael, Jim Davis, James Dean, Eugene V. Debs, Theodore Dreiser, Paul Dresser, Jeff Gordon, Benjamin Harrison, Gil Hodges, Michael Jackson, David Letterman, John Mellencamp, Jane Pauley, Cole Porter, Gene Stratton Porter, Ernie Pyle, Dan Quayle, James Whitcomb Riley, Oscar Robertson, Red Skelton, Booth Tarkington, Kurt Vonnegut, Lew Wallace, Wendell L. Willkie, Wilbur Wright.

Chamber of Commerce. One North Capital, Suite 200, Indianapolis, IN 46204; 1-888-ENJOYIN. **Website:** www.in.gov/enjoyindiana

Website. www.ai.org

Iowa
Hawkeye State

People. Population (2002 est.): 2,936,760; rank: 30; **net change** (2001-2002): 0.2%. **Pop. density:** 52.6 per sq mi. **Racial distribution** (2000): 93.9% white; 2.1% black; 1.3% Asian; 0.3% Native American/Nat. AK; <0.1% Hawaiian/Pacific Islander; 1.3% other race; 2 or more races, 1.1%. **Hispanic pop.** (any race): 2.8%.

Geography. Total area: 56,272 sq mi; rank: 26. **Land area:** 55,869 sq mi; rank: 23. **Acres forested:** 2.1 mil. **Location:** West North Central state bordered by Mississippi R. on the E and Missouri R. on the W. **Climate:** humid, continental. **Topography:** Watershed from NW to SE; soil especially rich and level in the N central counties. **Capital:** Des Moines.

Economy. Chief industries: agriculture, communications, construction, finance, insurance, trade, services, manufacturing. **Chief manuf. goods:** processed food products, tires, farm machinery, electronic products, appliances, household furniture, chemicals, fertilizers, auto accessories. **Chief crops:** silage and grain corn, soybeans, oats, hay. **Livestock:** (Jan. 2003) 3.6 mil cattle/calves; 250,000 sheep/lambs; (Dec. 2002) 15.3 mil hogs/pigs; 46.2 mil chickens (excl. broilers). **Timber/lumber** (est. 2002): 77 mil bd. ft.; red cedar. **Nonfuel minerals** (est. 2002): $487 mil.; stone (crushed), cement (portland), sand and gravel (construction), gypsum (crude), lime. **Principal internat. airport** at: Des Moines. **Employment distrib.** (May 2003): 17.3% govt.; 20.7% trade/trans./util.; 15.2% mfg.; 13.3% ed./health serv.; 7.3% prof./bus. serv.; 8.7% leisure/hosp.; 6.4% finance; 4.6% constr.; 2.4% info. **Per cap. pers. income** (2002): $28,280. **Sales tax** (2003): 5%. **New private housing** (2002): 14,789 units/$1.7 bil. **Gross state product** (2001): $90.9 bil. **Unemployment** (2002): 4.0%. **Tourism expends.** (2000): $4.5 bil. **Lottery** (2002): total sales: $181.3 mil; net income: $48.2 mil.

Finance. FDIC-insured commercial banks (2002): 410. **Deposits:** $40.3 bil. **FDIC-insured savings institutions** (2002): 23. **Assets:** $5.3 bil.

Federal govt. Fed. civ. employees (Mar. 2002): 7,113. **Avg. salary:** $48,743. **Notable fed. facilities:** Ames Lab; Natl. Animal Disease Ctr.

Energy. Electricity production (est. 2002, kWh, by source): Coal: 34.1 bil; Petroleum: 50 mil; Gas: 421 mil; Hydroelectric: 926 mil; Nuclear: 4.6 bil; Other: 46 mil.

State data. Motto: Our liberties we prize, and our rights we will maintain. **Flower:** Wild rose. **Bird:** Eastern goldfinch. **Tree:** Oak. **Rock:** Geode. **Entered union** Dec. 28, 1846; rank, 29th. **State fair** at Des Moines; mid-Aug.

History. Early inhabitants were Mound Builders who dwelt on Iowa's fertile plains. Later, Woodland tribes including the Iowa and Yankton Sioux lived in the area. The first Europeans, Marquette and Jolliet, gave France its claim to the area, 1673. In 1762, France ceded the region to Spain, but Napoleon took it back, 1800. It became part of the U.S. through the Louisiana Purchase, 1803. Native American Sauk and Fox tribes moved into the area from states farther east but relinquished their land in defeat, after the 1832 uprising led by the Sauk chieftain Black Hawk. By mid-19th cent. they were forced to move on to Kansas. Iowa became a territory in 1838, and entered as a free state, 1846, strongly supporting the Union.

Tourist attractions. Herbert Hoover birthplace and library, West Branch; Effigy Mounds Natl. Monument, prehistoric Indian burial site, Marquette; Amana Colonies; Grant Wood's paintings and memorabilia, Davenport Municipal Art Gallery; Living History Farms, Des Moines; Adventureland, Altoona; Boone & Scenic Valley Railroad, Boone; Greyhound Parks, in Dubuque and Council Bluffs; Prairie Meadows horse racing, Altoona; riverboat cruises and casino gambling, Mississippi and Missouri Rivers; Iowa Great Lakes, Okoboji.

Famous Iowans. Tom Arnold, Johnny Carson, Marquis Childs, Buffalo Bill Cody, Mamie Dowd Eisenhower, Bob Feller, George Gallup, Susan Glaspell, James Norman Hall, Harry Hansen, Herbert Hoover, Ann Landers, Glenn Miller, Lillian Russell, Billy Sunday, James A. Van Allen, Abigail Van Buren, Carl Van Vechten, Henry Wallace, John Wayne, Meredith Willson, Grant Wood.

Tourist information. Division of Tourism, Iowa Dept. of Economic Development, 200 E. Grand Ave., Des Moines, IA 50309; 1-800-476-6035. **Website:** www.traveliowa.com

Website. www.iowa.gov

Kansas
Sunflower State

People. Population (2002 est.): 2,715,884; rank: 32; **net change** (2001-2002): 0.5%. **Pop. density:** 33.2 per sq mi. **Racial distribution** (2000): 86.1% white; 5.7% black; 1.7% Asian; 0.9% Native American/Nat. AK; 0.1% Hawaiian/Pacific Islander; 3.4% other race; 2 or more races, 2.1%. **Hispanic pop.** (any race): 7.0%.

Geography. Total area: 82,277 sq mi; rank: 15. **Land area:** 81,815 sq mi; rank: 13. **Acres forested:** 1.5 mil. **Location:** West North Central state, with Missouri R. on E. **Climate:** temperate but continental, with great extremes between summer and winter. **Topography:** hilly Osage Plains in the E; central region level prairie and hills; high plains in the W. **Capital:** Topeka.

Economy. Chief industries: manufacturing, finance, insurance, real estate, services. **Chief manuf. goods:** transportation equipment, machinery & computer equipment, food and kindred products, printing & publishing. **Chief crops:** wheat, sorghum, corn, hay, soybeans, sunflowers. **Livestock:** (Jan. 2003) 6.6 mil cattle/calves; 90,000 sheep/lambs; (Dec. 2002) 1.5 mil hogs/pigs. **Timber/lumber** (est. 2002): 12 mil bd. ft.; oak, walnut; 14 mil bd. ft. **Nonfuel minerals** (est. 2002): $661 mil.; cement (portland), helium (Grade-A), salt, stone (crushed), helium (crude). **Chief ports:** Kansas City. **Principal internat. airport** at: Kansas City. **New private housing** (2002): 12,983 units/$1.6 bil. **Gross state product** (2001): $87.2 bil. **Employment distrib.** (May 2003): 19.3% govt.; 19.9% trade/trans./util.; 13.2% mfg.; 11.9% ed./health serv.; 9.3% prof./bus. serv.; 8.1% leisure/hosp.; 5.2% finance; 4.8% constr.; 3.7% info. **Per cap. pers. income** (2002): $29,141. **Sales tax** (2003): 5.2%. **Unemployment** (2002): 5.1%. **Tourism expends.** (2000): $3.7 bil. **Lottery** (2002): total sales: $190.1 mil; net income: $55.2 mil.

Finance. FDIC-insured commercial banks (2002): 363. **Deposits:** $31.2 bil. **FDIC-insured savings institutions** (2002): 17. **Assets:** $12.1 bil.

Federal govt. Fed. civ. employees (Mar. 2002): 15,033. **Avg. salary:** $49,884. **Notable fed. facilities:** Fts. Riley, Leavenworth; Leavenworth Fed. Pen.; McConnell AFB; Colmery-O'Neal Veterans Hospital.

Energy. Electricity production (est. 2002, kWh, by source): Coal: 35.4 bil; Petroleum: 503 mil; Gas: 1.8 bil; Nuclear: 9.0 bil.

State data. Motto: Ad Astra per Aspera (To the stars through difficulties). **Flower:** Native sunflower. **Bird:** Western meadowlark. **Tree:** Cottonwood. **Song:** Home on the Range. **Entered union** Jan. 29, 1861; rank, 34th. **State fair** at Hutchinson; begins Friday after Labor Day.

History. When Coronado first explored the area, Wichita, Pawnee, Kansa, and Osage peoples lived there. These Native Americans—hunters who also farmed—were joined on the Plains by the nomadic Cheyenne, Arapaho, Comanche, and Kiowa about 1800. French explorers established trading between 1682 and 1739, and the U.S. took over most of the area in the Louisiana Purchase, 1803. After 1830, thousands of eastern Native Americans were removed to Kansas. Kansas became a territory, 1854. Violent incidents between pro- and antislavery settlers caused the territory to be known as "Bleeding Kansas." It eventually entered the Union as a free state, 1861. Railroad construction after the war made Abilene and Dodge City terminals of large cattle drives from Texas.

Tourist attractions. Eisenhower Center, Abilene; Agricultural Hall of Fame and Natl. Center, Bonner Springs; Dodge City-Boot Hill & Frontier Town; Old Cowtown Museum, Wichita; Ft. Scott and Ft. Larned, restored 1800s cavalry forts; Kansas Cosmosphere and Space Center, Hutchinson; Woodlands Racetrack, Kansas City; U.S. Cavalry Museum, Ft. Riley; NCAA Visitors Center, Shawnee; Heartland Park Raceway, Topeka.

Famous Kansans. Kirstie Alley, Roscoe "Fatty" Arbuckle, Ed Asner, Gwendolyn Brooks, John Brown, George Washington Carver, Wilt Chamberlain, Walter P. Chrysler, Glenn Cunningham, John Stuart Curry, Robert Dole, Amelia Earhart, Wyatt Earp, Dwight D. Eisenhower, Ron Evans, Maurice Greene, Wild Bill Hickok, Cyrus Holliday, Dennis Hopper, William Inge, Don Johnson, Walter Johnson, Nancy Landon Kassebaum, Buster Keaton, Emmett Kelly, Alf Landon, Edgar Lee Masters, Hattie McDaniel, Oscar Micheaux, Carry Nation, Georgia Neese-Gray, Charlie Parker, Gordon Parks, Jim Ryun, Barry Sanders, Vivian Vance, William Allen White, Jess Willard.

Tourist information. Kansas Dept. of Commerce & Housing, Travel and Tourism Div., 700 SW Harrison, Suite 1300, Topeka, KS 66601; 1-913-296-2009; 1-800-2KANSAS. **Website:** www.travelks.com

Website. www.accesskansas.org

Kentucky
Bluegrass State

People. Population (2002 est.): 4,092,891; rank: 26; **net change** (2001-2002): 0.6%. **Pop. density:** 103.0 per sq mi. **Racial distribution** (2000): 90.1% white; 7.3% black; 0.7% Asian; 0.2% Native American/Nat. AK; <0.1% Hawaiian/Pacific Islander; 0.6% other race; 2 or more races, 1.1%. **Hispanic pop.** (any race): 1.5%.

Geography. Total area: 40,409 sq mi; rank: 37. **Land area:** 39,728 sq mi; rank: 36. **Acres forested:** 12.7 mil. **Location:** East South Central state, bordered on N by Illinois, Indiana, Ohio; on E by West Virginia and Virginia; on S by Tennessee; on W by Missouri. **Climate:** moderate, with plentiful rainfall. **Topography:** mountainous in E; rounded hills of the Knobs in the N; Bluegrass, heart of state; wooded rocky hillsides of the Pennyroyal; Western Coal Field; the fertile Purchase in the SW. **Capital:** Frankfort.

Economy. Chief industries: manufacturing, services, finance, insurance and real estate, retail trade, public utilities. **Chief manuf. goods:** transportation & industrial machinery, apparel, printing & publishing, food products, electric & electronic equipment. **Chief crops:** tobacco, corn, soybeans. **Livestock:** (Jan. 2003) 2.3 mil cattle/calves; (Dec. 2002) 370,000 hogs/pigs; 6.2 mil chickens (excl. broilers); 269.9 mil broilers. **Timber/lumber** (est.2002): 691 mil bd. ft.; hardwoods, pines. **Nonfuel minerals** (est. 2002): $372 mil.; stone (crushed), lime, cement (portland), sand and gravel (construction), clays (ball). **Chief ports:** Paducah, Louisville, Covington, Owensboro, Ashland, Henderson County, Lyon County, Hickman-Fulton County. **Principal internat. airports at:** Covington/Cincinnati, Louisville. **New private housing** (2002): 19,459 units/$2.1 bil. **Gross state product** (2001): $120.3 bil. **Employment distrib.** (May 2003): 17.8% govt.; 20.5% trade/trans./util.; 15.1% mfg.; 12.7% ed./health serv.; 8.7% prof./bus. serv.; 8.9% leisure/hosp.; 4.8% finance; 4.6% constr.; 1.8% info. **Per cap. pers. income** (2002): $25,579. **Sales tax** (2003): 6%. **Unemployment** (2002): 5.6%. **Tourism expends.** (2000): $5.3 bil. **Lottery** (2002): total sales: $638.7 mil; net income: $172.7 mil.

Finance. FDIC-insured commercial banks (2002): 221. **Deposits:** $40.1 bil. **FDIC-insured savings institutions** (2002): 27. **Assets:** $3.1 bil.

Federal govt. Fed. civ. employees (Mar. 2002): 20,002. **Avg. salary:** $44,545. **Notable fed. facilities:** U.S. Gold Bullion Depository, Ft. Knox; Ft. Campbell; Fed. Correctional Institution, Lexington.

Energy. Electricity production (est. 2002, kWh, by source): Coal: 75.3 bil; Petroleum: 121 mil; Gas: 693 mil; Hydroelectric: 4.0 bil.

State data. Motto: United we stand, divided we fall. **Flower:** Goldenrod. **Bird:** Cardinal. **Tree:** Tulip Poplar. **Song:** My Old Kentucky Home. **Entered union** June 1, 1792; rank, 15th. **State fair** at Louisville, late Aug.

History. The area was predominantly hunting grounds for Shawnee, Wyandot, Delaware, and Cherokee peoples. Explored by Americans Thomas Walker and Christopher Gist, 1750-51, Kentucky was the first area west of the Alleghenies settled by American pioneers. The first permanent settlement was Harrodsburg, 1774. Daniel Boone blazed the Wilderness Trail through the Cumberland Gap and founded Ft. Boonesborough, 1775. Conflicts with Native Americans, spurred by the British, were unceasing until, during the American Revolution, Gen. George Rogers Clark captured British forts in Indiana and Illinois, 1778. In 1792, Virginia dropped its claims to the region, and it became the 15th state. Although officially a Union state, Kentuckians had divided loyalties during the Civil War and were forced to choose sides; its slaves were freed only after the adoption of the 13th Amendment to the U.S. Constitution, 1865.

Tourist attractions. Kentucky Derby; Louisville; Land Between the Lakes Natl. Recreation Area, Kentucky Lake and Lake Barkley; Mammoth Cave Natl. Park; Echo River, 360 ft below ground; Lake Cumberland; Lincoln's birthplace, Hodgenville; My Old Kentucky Home State Park, Bardstown; Cumberland Gap Natl. Historical Park, Middlesboro; Kentucky Horse Park, Lexington; Shaker Village, Pleasant Hill.

Famous Kentuckians. Muhammad Ali, John James Audubon, Alben W. Barkley, Daniel Boone, Louis D. Brandeis, John C. Breckinridge, Kit Carson, Albert B. "Happy" Chandler, Henry Clay, Jefferson Davis, D. W. Griffith, "Casey" Jones, Abraham Lincoln, Mary Todd Lincoln, Thomas Hunt Morgan, Carry Nation, Col. Harland Sanders, Diane Sawyer, Adlai Stevenson, Jesse Stuart, Zachary Taylor, Hunter S. Thompson, Robert Penn Warren, Whitney Young Jr.

Tourist Information. Kentucky Dept. of Travel, 500 Mero St., #2200, Frankfort, KY 40601; 1-800-225-TRIP. **Website:** www.kentuckytourism.com

Website. www.kentucky.gov

Louisiana
Pelican State

People. Population (2002 est.): 4,482,646; rank: 24; **net change** (2001-2002): 0.3%. **Pop. density:** 102.9 per sq mi. **Racial distribution** (2000): 63.9% white; 32.5% black; 1.2% Asian; 0.6% Native American/Nat. AK; <0.1% Hawaiian/Pacific Islander; 0.7% other race; 2 or more races, 1.1%. **Hispanic pop.** (any race): 2.4%.

Geography. Total area: 51,840 sq mi; rank: 31. **Land area:** 43,562 sq mi; rank: 33. **Acres forested:** 13.8 mil. **Location:** West South Central state on the Gulf Coast. **Climate:** subtropical, affected by continental weather patterns. **Topography:** lowlands of marshes and Mississippi R. flood plain; Red R. Valley lowlands; upland hills in the Florida Parishes; average elevation, 100 ft. **Capital:** Baton Rouge.

Economy. Chief industries: wholesale and retail trade, tourism, manufacturing, construction, transportation, communication, public utilities, finance, insurance, real estate, mining. **Chief manuf. goods:** chemical products, foods, transportation equipment, electronic equipment, petroleum products, lumber, wood, and paper. **Chief crops:** soybeans, sugarcane, rice, corn, cotton, sweet potatoes, pecans, sorghum, aquaculture. **Livestock:** (Jan. 2003) 850,000 cattle/calves; (Dec. 2002) 20,000 hogs/pigs; 2.6 mil chickens (excl. broilers). **Timber/lumber** (est. 2002): 1.3 bil bd. ft.; pines, hardwoods, oak. **Nonfuel minerals** (est. 2002): $294 mil.; salt, sand and gravel (construction), stone (crushed), sand and gravel (industrial), lime. **Commercial fishing** (2001): $342.4 mil. **Chief ports:** New Orleans, Baton Rouge, Lake Charles, Port of S. Louisiana (La Place), Shreveport, Plaquemine, St. Bernard, Alexandria. **Principal internat. airport at:** New Orleans. **New private housing** (2002): 18,425 units/ $1.9 bil. **Gross state product** (2001): $148.7 bil. **Employment distrib.** (May 2003): 20% govt.; 20.4% trade/trans./util.; 8.3% mfg.; 12.6% ed./health serv.; 9.2% prof./bus. serv.;

10.4% leisure/hosp.; 5.2% finance; 6.3% constr.; 1.6% info. **Per cap. pers. income** (2002): $25,446. **Sales tax** (2003): 4%. **Unemployment** (2002): 6.1%. **Tourism expends.** (2000): $9 bil. **Lottery** (2002): total sales: $311.6 mil; net income: $111 mil.

Finance. FDIC-insured commercial banks (2002): 140. **Deposits:** $36.6 bil. **FDIC-insured savings institutions** (2002): 32. **Assets:** $4.9 bil.

Federal govt. Fed. civ. employees (Mar. 2002): 19,877. **Avg. salary:** $49,216. **Notable federal facilities:** Strategic Petroleum Reserve, Michoud Assembly Plant, Southeast U.S. Agricultural Research Ctr., U.S. Army Corps of Engineers, all New Orleans; Ft. Polk (Joint Readiness Training Ctr.); Barksdale AFB; New Orleans NAS.

Energy. Electricity production (est. 2002, kWh, by source): Coal: 11.5 bil; Petroleum: 62 mil; Gas: 21.6 bil; Nuclear: 17.3 bil.

State data. Motto: Union, justice, and confidence. **Flower:** Magnolia. **Bird:** Eastern brown pelican. **Tree:** Cypress. **Song:** Give Me Louisiana. **Entered union** Apr. 30, 1812; rank, 18th. **State fair** at Shreveport; Oct.

History. Caddo, Tunica, Choctaw, Chitimacha, and Chawash peoples lived in the region at the time of European contact. Europeans Cabeza de Vaca and Panfilo de Narvaez first visited, 1530. The region was claimed for France by La Salle, 1682. The first permanent settlement was by the French at Biloxi, now in Mississippi, 1699. France ceded the region to Spain, 1762, took it back, 1800, and sold it to the U.S., 1803, in the Louisiana Purchase. During the American Revolution, Spanish Louisiana aided the Americans. Admitted as a state in 1812, Louisiana was the scene of the Battle of New Orleans, 1815.

Louisiana Creoles are descendants of early French and/or Spanish settlers. About 4,000 Acadians, French settlers in Nova Scotia, Canada, were forcibly transported by the British to Louisiana in 1755 (an event commemorated in Longfellow's "Evangeline") and settled near Bayou Teche; their descendants became known as Cajuns. Another group, the Islenos, were descendants of Canary Islanders brought to Louisiana by a Spanish governor in 1770. Traces of Spanish and French survive in local dialects.

Tourist attractions. Mardi Gras, French Quarter, Superdome, Dixieland jazz, Aquarium of the Americas, Audubon Zoo & Gardens, all New Orleans; Battle of New Orleans site; Longfellow-Evangeline Memorial Park, St. Martinville; Kent House Museum, Alexandria; Hodges Gardens, Natchitoches, USS *Kidd* Memorial, Baton Rouge.

Famous Louisianans. Louis Armstrong, Pierre Beauregard, Judah P. Benjamin, Braxton Bragg, Kate Chopin, Harry Connick Jr., Ellen DeGeneres, Lillian Hellman, Grace King, Bob Livingston, Huey Long, Wynton Marsalis, Leonidas K. Polk, Anne Rice, Henry Miller Shreve, Britney Spears, Edward D. White Jr.

Tourist information. Louisiana Office of Tourism, PO Box 94291, Baton Rouge, LA 70804-9291; 1-800-677-4082. **Website.** www.louisianatravel.com
Website. www.state.la.us

Maine
Pine Tree State

People. Population (2002 est.): 1,294,464; rank: 40; **net change** (2001-2002): 0.8%. **Pop. density:** 41.9 per sq mi. **Racial distribution** (2000): 96.9% white; 0.5% black; 0.7% Asian; 0.6% Native American/Nat. AK; <0.1% Hawaiian/Pacific Islander; 0.2% other race; 2 or more races, 1.0%. **Hispanic pop.** (any race): 0.7%.

Geography. Total area: 35,385 sq mi; rank: 39. **Land area:** 30,862 sq mi; rank: 39. **Acres forested:** 17.7 mil. **Location:** New England state at northeastern tip of U.S. **Climate:** Southern interior and coastal, influenced by air masses from the S and W; northern clime harsher, avg. over 100 in. snow in winter. **Topography:** Appalachian Mts. extend through state; western borders have rugged terrain; long sand beaches on southern coast; northern coast mainly rocky promontories, peninsulas, fjords. **Capital:** Augusta.

Economy. Chief industries: manufacturing, agriculture, fishing, services, trade, government, finance, insurance, real estate, construction. **Chief manuf. goods:** paper & wood products, transportation equipment. **Chief crops:** potatoes, aquaculture products. **Livestock:** (Jan. 2003) 97,000 cattle/calves; (Dec. 2002) 6,000 hogs/pigs; 5.8 mil chickens (excl. broilers). **Timber/lumber** (est. 2002): 988 mil bd. ft.; pine, spruce, fir. **Nonfuel minerals** (est. 2002): $106 mil.; sand and gravel (construction), cement (portland), stone (crushed), stone (dimension), cement (masonry). **Commercial fishing**

(2001): $241.4 mil. **Chief ports:** Searsport, Portland, Eastport. **Principal internat. airports at:** Bangor, Portland. **New private housing** (2002): 7,207 units/$899 mil. **Gross state product** (2001): $37.4 bil. **Employment distrib.** (May 2003): 17.8% govt.; 20% trade/trans./util.; 10.5% mfg.; 17.6% ed./health serv.; 8.5% prof./bus. serv.; 9.6% leisure/hosp.; 5.7% finance; 4.9% constr.; 1.9% info. **Per cap. pers. income** (2002): $27,744. **Sales tax** (2003): 5%. **Unemployment** (2002): 4.4%. **Tourism expends.** (2000): $2.1 bil. **Lottery** (2002): total sales: $157.9 mil; net income: $40.5 mil.

Finance. FDIC-insured commercial banks (2002): 15. **Deposits:** $19.1 bil. **FDIC-insured savings institutions** (2002): 24. **Assets:** $8.4 bil.

Federal govt. Fed. civ. employees (Mar. 2002): 8,450. **Avg. salary:** $50,058. **Notable fed. facilities:** Kittery Naval Shipyard; Brunswick NAS.

Energy. Electricity production (est. 2002, kWh, by source): Hydroelectric: 6 mil.

State data. Motto: Dirigo (I direct). **Flower:** White pine cone and tassel. **Bird:** Chickadee. **Tree:** Eastern white pine. **Song:** State of Maine Song. **Entered union** Mar. 15, 1820; rank, 23rd. **State fair:** at Bangor, late July; at Skowhegan, mid-Aug.

History. When the Europeans arrived, Maine was inhabited by Algonquian peoples including the Abnaki, Penobscot, and Passamaquoddy. Maine's rocky coast was believed to have been explored by the Cabots, 1498-99. French settlers arrived, 1604, at the St. Croix River, English, c 1607, on the Kennebec; both settlements failed. Maine was made part of Massachusetts, 1691. In the American Revolution, a Maine regiment fought at Bunker Hill. A British fleet destroyed Falmouth (now Portland), 1775, but the British ship *Margaretta* was captured near Machiasport. In 1820, Maine broke off and became a separate state.

Tourist attractions. Acadia Natl. Park, Bar Harbor, on Mt. Desert Island; Old Orchard Beach; Portland's Old Port; Kennebunkport; Common Ground Country Fair; Portland Headlight; Baxter State Pk.; Freeport/L. L. Bean.

Famous "Down Easters." Leon Leonwood (L.L.) Bean, James G. Blaine, Cyrus H. K. Curtis, Hannibal Hamlin, Sarah Jewett, Stephen King, Henry Wadsworth Longfellow, Sir Hiram and Hudson Maxim, Edna St. Vincent Millay, George Mitchell, Edmund Muskie, Judd Nelson, Edwin Arlington Robinson, Joan Benoit Samuelson, Liv Tyler, Kate Douglas Wiggin, Ben Ames Williams.

Chamber of Commerce and Industry. Maine Chamber & Business Alliance, 7 Community Dr., Augusta, ME 04330; 1-888-MAINE45 (from within the United States and Canada). **Website:** www.visitmaine.com
Website. www.state.me.us

Maryland
Old Line State, Free State

People. Population (2002 est.): 5,458,137; rank: 18; **net change** (2001-2002): 1.3%. **Pop. density:** 558.4 per sq mi. **Racial distribution** (2000): 64.0% white; 27.9% black; 4.0% Asian; 0.3% Native American/Nat. AK; <0.1% Hawaiian/Pacific Islander; 1.8% other race; 2 or more races, 2.0%. **Hispanic pop.** (any race): 4.3%.

Geography. Total area: 12,407 sq mi; rank: 42. **Land area:** 9,774 sq mi; rank: 42. **Acres forested:** 2.6 mil. **Location:** South Atlantic state stretching from the Ocean to the Allegheny Mts. **Climate:** continental in the west; humid subtropical in the east. **Topography:** Eastern Shore of coastal plain and Maryland Main of coastal plain, piedmont plateau, and the Blue Ridge, separated by the Chesapeake Bay. **Capital:** Annapolis.

Economy. Chief industries: manufacturing, biotechnology and information technology, services, tourism. **Chief manuf. goods:** electric and electronic equipment; food and kindred products, chemicals and allied products, printed materials. **Chief crops:** greenhouse and nursery products, soybeans, corn. **Livestock:** (Jan. 2003) 245,000 cattle/calves; (Dec. 2002) 45,000 hogs/pigs; 4.3 mil chickens (excl. broilers); 292.9 mil broilers. **Timber/lumber** (est. 2002): 268 mil bd. ft.; hardwoods. **Nonfuel minerals** (est. 2002): $375 mil.; stone (crushed), cement (portland), sand and gravel (construction), cement (masonry), stone (dimension). **Commercial fishing** (2001): $55.6 mil. **Chief port:** Baltimore. **Principal internat. airport at:** Baltimore. **New private housing** (2002): 29,293 units/$3.5 bil. **Gross state product** (2001): $195.0 bil. **Employment distrib.** (May 2003): 18.8% govt.; 18.4% trade/trans./util.; 6.1% mfg.; 13.6% ed./health serv.; 14.6% prof./bus. serv.; 8.9% leisure/hosp.; 6% finance; 6.7% constr.; 2% info. **Per cap. pers. income** (2002):

$36,298. **Sales tax** (2003): 5%. **Unemployment** (2002): 4.4%. **Tourism expends.** (2000): $8.8 bil. **Lottery** (2002): total sales: $1.3 bil; net income: $443.5 mil.

Finance. FDIC-insured commercial banks (2002): 73. **Deposits:** $37.2 bil. **FDIC-insured savings institutions** (2002): 56. **Assets:** $8.6 bil.

Federal govt. Fed. civ. employees (Mar. 2002): 102,707. **Avg. salary:** $65,814. **Notable fed. facilities:** U.S. Naval Academy; Natl. Agriculture Res. Ctr.; Ft. Meade, Aberdeen Proving Ground; Goddard Space Flight Ctr.; Natl. Institutes of Health; Natl. Inst. of Standards & Technology; Food & Drug Administration; Bureau of the Census; Natl. Naval Med. Ctr., Bethesda; Natl. Marine Fisheries Serv.; Natl. Oceanic and Atmospheric Admin.

Energy. Electricity production (est. 2002, kWh, by source): Petroleum: 28 mil; Gas: 3 mil.

State data. Motto: Fatti Maschii, Parole Femine (Manly deeds, womanly words). **Flower:** Black-eyed Susan. **Bird:** Baltimore oriole. **Tree:** White oak. **Song:** Maryland, My Maryland. **Seventh** of the original 13 states to ratify Constitution, Apr. 28, 1788. **State fair** at Timonium; late Aug.-early Sept.

History. Europeans encountered Algonquian-speaking Nanticoke and Piscataway and Iroquois-speaking Susquehannock when they first visited the area. Italian explorer Verrazano visited the Chesapeake region in the early 16th cent. English Capt. John Smith explored and mapped the area, 1608. William Claiborne set up a trading post on Kent Island in Chesapeake Bay, 1631. King Charles I granted land to Cecilius Calvert, Lord Baltimore, 1632; Calvert's brother Leonard, with about 200 settlers, founded St. Marys, 1634. The bravery of Maryland troops in the American Revolution, as at the Battle of Long Island, won the state its nickname "The Old Line State." In the War of 1812, when a British fleet tried to take Ft. McHenry, Marylander Francis Scott Key wrote "The Star-Spangled Banner," 1814. Although a slave-holding state, Maryland remained with the Union during the Civil War and was the site of the battle of Antietam, 1862, which halted Gen. Robert E. Lee's march north.

Tourist attractions. The Preakness at Pimlico track, Baltimore; The Maryland Million at Laurel Race Course; Ocean City; restored Ft. McHenry, near which Francis Scott Key wrote "The Star-Spangled Banner"; Edgar Allan Poe house, Ravens Football at Memorial Stadium, Camden Yards, Natl. Aquarium, Harborplace, all Baltimore; Antietam Battlefield, near Hagerstown; South Mountain Battlefield; U.S. Naval Academy, Annapolis; Maryland State House, Annapolis, 1772, the oldest still in legislative use in the U.S.

Famous Marylanders. John Astin, Benjamin Banneker, Tom Clancy, Jonathan Demme, Francis Scott Key, H. L. Mencken, Kweisi Mfume, Ogden Nash, Charles Willson Peale, William Pinkney, Edgar Allan Poe, Cal Ripken Jr., Babe Ruth, Upton Sinclair, Roger B. Taney, John Waters, Montel Williams.

Maryland Dept. of Business & Economic Development. 217 E. Redwood St., Baltimore, MD 21202; (410) 767-6870; 1-800-MDISFUN. **Website:** www.mdisfun.org **Website.** www.state.md.us

Massachusetts
Bay State, Old Colony

People. Population (2002 est.): 6,427,801; rank: 13; **net change** (2001-2002): 0.4%. **Pop. density:** 819.9 per sq mi. **Racial distribution** (2000): 84.5% white; 5.4% black; 3.8% Asian; 0.2% Native American/Nat. AK; <0.1% Hawaiian/Pacific Islander; 3.7% other race; 2 or more races, 2.3%. **Hispanic pop.** (any race): 6.8%.

Geography. Total area: 10,555 sq mi; rank: 44. **Land area:** 7,840 sq mi; rank: 45. **Acres forested:** 3.1 mil. **Location:** New England state along Atlantic seaboard. **Climate:** temperate, with colder and drier clime in western region. **Topography:** jagged indented coast from Rhode Island around Cape Cod; flat land yields to stony upland pastures near central region and gentle hilly country in west; except in west, land is rocky, sandy, and not fertile. **Capital:** Boston.

Economy. Chief industries: services, trade, manufacturing. **Chief manuf. goods:** electric and electronic equipment, instruments, industrial machinery and equipment, printing and publishing, fabricated metal products. **Chief crops:** cranberries, greenhouse, nursery, vegetables. **Livestock:** (Jan. 2003) 51,000 cattle/calves; (Dec. 2002) 16,500 hogs/pigs; 336,000 chickens (excl. broilers). **Timber/lumber** (est. 2002): (undisclosed); white pine, oak, other hard woods; **Nonfuel minerals** (est. 2002): $375 mil.; stone (crushed), cement (portland), sand and gravel (construction), cement (masonry), stone (dimension). **Commercial fishing** (2001): $280.3 mil.

Chief ports: Boston, Fall River, New Bedford, Salem, Gloucester, Plymouth. **Principal internat. airport at:** Boston. **New private housing** (2002): 17,465 units/$2.8 bil. **Gross state product** (2001): $287.8 bil. **Employment distrib.** (May 2003): 13.6% govt.; 17.8% trade/trans./util.; 10.3% mfg.; 17.8% ed./health serv.; 13.7% prof./bus. serv.; 9.1% leisure/hosp.; 7.1% finance; 4.2% constr.; 2.9% info. **Per cap. pers. income** (2002): $39,244. **Sales tax** (2003): 5%. **Unemployment** (2002): 5.3%. **Tourism expends.** (2000): $13.2 bil. **Lottery** (2002): total sales: $4.2 bil; net income: $899.2 mil.

Finance. FDIC-insured commercial banks (2002): 39. **Deposits:** $83.4 bil. **FDIC-insured savings institutions** (2002): 175. **Assets:** $70.3 bil.

Federal govt. Fed. civ. employees (Mar. 2002): 24,352. **Avg. salary:** $56,557. **Notable fed. facilities:** Thomas P. O'Neill Jr. Fed. Bldg., J.W. McCormack Bldg., JFK Fed. Bldg., Natick Army Soldier Systems Ctr.

Energy. Electricity production (est. 2002, kWh, by source): Coal: 1.1 bil; Petroleum: 55 mil; Gas: 233 mil; Hydroelectric: 133 mil.

State data. Motto: Ense Petit Placidam Sub Libertate Quietem (By the sword we seek peace, but peace only under liberty). **Flower:** Mayflower. **Bird:** Chickadee. **Tree:** American elm. **Song:** All Hail to Massachusetts. **Sixth** of the original 13 states to ratify Constitution, Feb. 6, 1788. **State Fair** at Topsfield, early Oct.

History. Early inhabitants were the Algonquian, Nauset, Wampanoag, Massachuset, Pennacook, Nipmuc, and Pocumtuc peoples. Pilgrims settled in Plymouth, 1620, giving thanks for their survival with the first Thanksgiving Day, 1621. About 20,000 new settlers arrived, 1630-40. Native American relations with the colonists deteriorated leading to King Philip's War, 1675-76, which the colonists won, ending Native American resistance. Demonstrations against British restrictions set off the Boston Massacre, 1770, and the Boston Tea Party, 1773. The first bloodshed of American Revolution was at Lexington, 1775.

Tourist attractions. Provincetown artists' colony; Cape Cod; Plymouth Rock, Plimoth Plantation, *Mayflower II*, all Plymouth; Freedom Trail, Isabella Stewart Gardner Museum, Museum of Fine Arts, Children's Museum, Museum of Science, New England Aquarium, JFK Library, Boston Ballet, Boston Pops, Boston Symphony Orchestra, all Boston; Tanglewood, Jacob's Pillow Dance Festival, Hancock Shaker Village, Berkshire Scenic Railway Museum, Norman Rockwell Museum, Edith Wharton and Herman Melville homes, all in the Berkshires; Salem; Old Sturbridge Village; Deerfield Historic District; Walden Pond; Naismith Memorial Basketball Hall of Fame, Springfield.

Famous "Bay Staters." John Adams, John Quincy Adams, Samuel Adams, Louisa May Alcott, Horatio Alger, Susan B. Anthony, Crispus Attucks, Clara Barton, Alexander Graham Bell, Stephen Breyer, George H. W. Bush, John Cheever, E. E. Cummings, Emily Dickinson, Charles Eliot, Ralph Waldo Emerson, William Lloyd Garrison, Edward Everett Hale, John Hancock, Nathaniel Hawthorne, Oliver Wendell Holmes, Winslow Homer, Elias Howe, John F. Kennedy, Jack Lemmon, James Russell Lowell, Cotton Mather, Samuel F. B. Morse, Edgar Allan Poe, Paul Revere, Norman Rockwell, Dr. Seuss (Theodore Seuss Geisel), Henry David Thoreau, Barbara Walters, James McNeil Whistler, John Greenleaf Whittier.

Tourist information. Massachusetts Office of Travel & Tourism, 100 Cambridge St., 13th Floor, Boston, MA 02202; 1-800-227-MASS. **Website.** www.massvacation.com **Website.** www.mass.gov

Michigan
Great Lakes State, Wolverine State

People. Population (2002 est.): 10,050,446; rank: 8; **net change** (2001-2002): 0.4%. **Pop. density:** 176.9 per sq mi. **Racial distribution** (2000): 80.2% white; 14.2% black; 1.8% Asian; 0.6% Native American/Nat. AK; <0.1% Hawaiian/Pacific Islander; 1.3% other race; 2 or more races, 1.9%. **Hispanic pop.** (any race): 3.3%.

Geography. Total area: 96,716 sq mi; rank: 11. **Land area:** 56,804 sq mi; rank: 22. **Acres forested:** 19.3 mil. **Location:** East North Central state bordering on 4 of the 5 Great Lakes, divided into an Upper and Lower Peninsula by the Straits of Mackinac, which link lakes Michigan and Huron. **Climate:** well-defined seasons tempered by the Great Lakes. **Topography:** low rolling hills give way to northern tableland of hilly belts in Lower Peninsula; Upper Peninsula is level in the east, with swampy areas; western region is higher and more rugged. **Capital:** Lansing.

Economy. Chief industries: manufacturing, services, tourism, agriculture, forestry/lumber. **Chief manuf. goods:** automobiles, transportation equipment, machinery, fabricated metals, food products, plastics, office furniture. **Chief crops:** corn, wheat, soybeans, dry beans, hay, potatoes, sweet corn, apples, cherries, sugar beets, blueberries, cucumbers, Niagra grapes. **Livestock:** (Jan. 2003) 990,000 cattle/calves; 75,000 sheep/lambs; (Dec. 2002) 860,000 hogs/pigs; 8.1 mil chickens (excl. broilers). **Timber/lumber** (est. 2002): 744 mil bd. ft.; maple, oak, aspen; 681 mil bd. ft. **Nonfuel minerals** (est. 2002): $1.6 bil.; cement (portland), iron ore (usable), sand and gravel (construction), stone (crushed), magnesium compounds. **Commercial fishing** (2001): $9.2 mil. Chief ports: Detroit, Saginaw River, Escanaba, Muskegon, Sault Ste. Marie, Port Huron, Marine City. **Principal internat. airports at:** Detroit, Flint, Grand Rapids, Kalamazoo, Lansing, Saginaw. **New private housing** (2002): 49,968 units/$6.4 bil. **Gross state product** (2001): $320.5 bil. **Employment distrib.** (May 2003): 15.9% govt.; 18.6% trade/trans./util.; 16.5% mfg.; 12.1% ed./health serv.; 13% prof./bus. serv.; 8.9% leisure/hosp.; 4.9% finance; 4.5% constr.; 1.7% info. **Per cap. pers. income** (2002): $30,296. **Sales tax** (2003): 6%. **Unemployment** (2002): 6.2%. **Tourism expends.** (2000): $12.8 bil. **Lottery** (2002): total sales: $1.7 bil; net income: $645.9 mil.

Finance. FDIC-insured commercial banks (2002): 160. **Deposits:** $97.1 bil. **FDIC-insured savings institutions** (2002): 20. **Assets:** $13.3 bil.

Federal govt. Fed. civ. employees (Mar. 2002): 21,427. **Avg. salary:** $57,064. **Notable fed. facilities:** Isle Royal, Sleeping Bear Dunes national parks.

Energy. Electricity production (est. 2002, kWh, by source): Coal: 65.6 bil; Petroleum: 955 mil; Gas: 2.1 bil; Hydroelectric: 524 mil; Nuclear: 31.1 bil; Other: 26 mil.

State data. Motto: Si Quaeris Peninsulam Amoenam, Circumspice (If you seek a pleasant peninsula, look about you). **Flower:** Apple blossom. **Bird:** Robin. **Tree:** White pine. **Song:** Michigan, My Michigan. **Entered union** Jan. 26, 1837; rank, 26th. **State fair** at Detroit, late Aug.–early Sept.; Upper Peninsula (Escanaba), mid-Aug.

History. Early inhabitants were the Ojibwa, Ottawa, Miami, Potawatomi, and Huron. French fur traders and missionaries visited the region, 1616, set up a mission at Sault Ste. Marie, 1641, and a settlement there, 1668. French settlements were taken over, 1763, by the British, who crushed a Native American uprising led by Ottawa chieftain Pontiac that same year. Treaty of Paris ceded territory to U.S., 1783, but British remained until 1796. The British seized Ft. Mackinac and Detroit, 1812. After Oliver H. Perry's Lake Erie victory and William H. Harrison's victory near the Thames River, 1813, the British retreated to Canada. The opening of the Erie Canal, 1825, and new land laws and Native American cessions led the way for a flood of settlers.

Tourist attractions. Henry Ford Museum, Greenfield Village, both in Dearborn; Michigan Space Center, Jackson; Tahquamenon (Hiawatha) Falls; DeZwaan windmill and Tulip Festival, Holland; "Soo Locks," St. Mary's Falls Ship Canal, Sault Ste. Marie, Kalamazoo Aviation History Museum; Mackinac Island; Kellogg's Cereal City USA, Battle Creek; Museum of African-American History, Motown Historical Museum, both Detroit.

Famous Michiganders. Ralph Bunche, Paul de Kruif, Thomas Edison, Edna Ferber, Gerald R. Ford, Henry Ford, Aretha Franklin, Edgar Guest, Lee Iacocca, Robert Ingersoll, Magic Johnson, Casey Kasem, Will Kellogg, Ring Lardner, Elmore Leonard, Charles Lindbergh, Joe Louis, Madonna, Malcolm X, Terry McMillan, Jack Paar, Pontiac, Diana Ross, Glenn Seaborg, Tom Selleck, Sinbad (David Adkins), John Smoltz, Lily Tomlin, Stewart Edward White, Serena Williams.

State Chamber of Commerce. 600 S. Walnut, Lansing, MI 48933. Phone: 517-371-2100; 1-888-78GREAT. **Website.** travel.michigan.org

Website. www.michigan.gov

Minnesota
North Star State, Gopher State

People. Population (2002 est.): 5,019,720; rank: 21; **net change** (2001-2002): 0.7%. **Pop. density:** 63.1 per sq mi. **Racial distribution** (2000): 89.4% white; 3.5% black; 2.9% Asian; 1.1% Native American/Nat. AK; <0.1% Hawaiian/Pacific Islander; 1.3% other race; 2 or more races, 1.7%. **Hispanic pop.** (any race): 2.9%.

Geography. Total area: 86,939 sq mi; rank: 12. **Land area:** 79,610 sq mi; rank: 14. **Acres forested:** 16.7 mil. **Location:** West North Central state bounded on the E by Wisconsin and Lake Superior, on the N by Canada, on the W by the Dakotas,

and on the S by Iowa. **Climate:** northern part of state lies in the moist Great Lakes storm belt; the western border lies at the edge of the semi-arid Great Plains. **Topography:** central hill and lake region covering approx. half the state; to the NE, rocky ridges and deep lakes; to the NW, flat plain; to the S, rolling plains and deep river valleys. **Capital:** St. Paul.

Economy. Chief industries: agribusiness, forest products, mining, manufacturing, tourism. **Chief manuf. goods:** food, chemical and paper products, industrial machinery, electric and electronic equipment, computers, printing & publishing, scientific and medical instruments, fabricated metal products, forest products. **Chief crops:** corn, soybeans, wheat, sugar beets, hay, barley, potatoes, sunflowers. **Livestock:** (Jan. 2003) 2.6 mil cattle/calves; 145,000 sheep/lambs; (Dec. 2002) 5.9 mil hogs/pigs; 14.7 mil chickens (excl. broilers); 44.2 mil broilers. **Timber/lumber** (est. 2002): 272 mil bd. ft.; needle-leaves and hardwoods. **Nonfuel minerals** (est. 2002): $1.1 bil.; iron ore (usable), sand and gravel (construction), stone (crushed), sand and gravel (industrial), stone (dimension). **Commercial fishing** (2001): $202,000. **Chief ports:** Duluth, St. Paul, Minneapolis. **Principal internat. airport at:** Minneapolis-St. Paul. **New private housing** (2002): 38,977 units/$5.4 bil. **Gross state product** (2001): $188.1 bil. **Employment distrib.** (May 2003): 15.6% govt.; 19.7% trade/trans./util.; 13% mfg.; 13.8% ed./health serv.; 10.9% prof./bus. serv.; 8.8% leisure/hosp.; 6.3% finance; 4.8% constr.; 2.5% info. **Per cap. pers. income** (2002): $34,071. **Sales tax** (2003): 6.5%. **Unemployment** (2002): 4.4%. **Tourism expends.** (2000): $8.4 bil. **Lottery** (2002): total sales: $377.1 mil; net income: $81.7 mil.

Finance. FDIC-insured commercial banks (2002): 465. **Deposits:** $81.6 bil. **FDIC-insured savings institutions** (2002): 22. **Assets:** $3.3 bil.

Federal govt. Fed. civ. employees (Mar. 2002): 13,146. **Avg. salary:** $54,931.

Energy. Electricity production (est. 2002, kWh, by source): Coal: 36.0 bil; Petroleum: 637 mil; Gas: 594 mil; Hydroelectric: 734 mil; Nuclear: 13.7 bil; Other: 411 mil.

State data. Motto: L'Etoile du Nord (The star of the north). **Flower:** Pink and white lady's-slipper. **Bird:** Common loon. **Tree:** Red pine. **Song:** Hail! Minnesota. **Entered union** May 11, 1858; rank, 32nd. **State fair** at St. Paul/Minneapolis; late Aug.-early Sept.

History. Dakota Sioux were early inhabitants of the area, and in the 16th cent., the Ojibwa began moving in from the east. French fur traders Médard Chouart and Pierre Esprit Radisson entered the region in the mid-17th cent. In 1679, French explorer Daniel Greysolon, sieur Duluth, claimed the entire region in the name of France. Britain took the area east of the Mississippi, 1763. The U.S. took over that portion after the American Revolution and in 1803, gained the western area in the Louisiana Purchase. The U.S. built Ft. St. Anthony (now Ft. Snelling), 1819, and in 1837, bought Native American lands, spurring an influx of settlers from the east. In 1849, the Territory of Minnesota was created. Sioux Indians staged a bloody uprising, the Battle of Woods Lake, 1862, and were driven from the state.

Tourist attractions. Minneapolis Institute of Arts, Walker Art Center, Minneapolis Sculpture Garden, Minnehaha Falls (inspiration for Longfellow's Hiawatha), Guthrie Theater, Minneapolis; Ordway Theater, St. Paul; Voyageurs Natl. Park; Mayo Clinic, Rochester; St. Paul Winter Carnival; North Shore (of Lake Superior).

Famous Minnesotans. Warren Burger, Ethan and Joel Coen, William O. Douglas, Bob Dylan, F. Scott Fitzgerald, Al Franken, Judy Garland, Cass Gilbert, Hubert Humphrey, Garrison Keillor, Sister Elizabeth Kenny, Jessica Lange, Sinclair Lewis, Paul Manship, Roger Maris, E. G. Marshall, William and Charles Mayo, Eugene McCarthy, Walter F. Mondale, Prince (Rodgers Nelson), Charles Schulz, Harold Stassen, Thorstein Veblen, Jesse Ventura.

Chamber of Commerce. 30 East 7th St., Suite 1700, St. Paul, MN 55101-4901; 1-800-657-3700. **Website:** www.explore minnesota.com

Website. www.state.mn.us

Mississippi
Magnolia State

People. Population (2002 est.): 2,871,782; rank: 31; **net change** (2001-2002): 0.4%. **Pop. density:** 61.2 per sq mi. **Racial distribution** (2000): 61.4% white; 36.3% black; 0.7% Asian; 0.4% Native American/Nat. AK; <0.1% Hawaiian/Pacific Islander; 0.5% other race; 2 or more races, 0.7%. **Hispanic pop.** (any race): 1.4%.

Geography. Total area: 48,430 sq mi; rank: 32. **Land area:** 46,907 sq mi; rank: 31. **Acres forested:** 18.6 mil. **Location:** East South Central state bordered on the W by the Mississippi R. and on the S by the Gulf of Mexico. **Climate:** semi-tropical, with abundant rainfall, long growing season, and extreme temperatures unusual. **Topography:** low, fertile delta between the Yazoo and Mississippi rivers; loess bluffs stretching around delta border; sandy gulf coastal terraces followed by piney woods and prairie; rugged, high sandy hills in extreme NE followed by Black Prairie Belt, Pontotoc Ridge, and flatwoods into the north central highlands. **Capital:** Jackson.

Economy. Chief industries: warehousing & distribution, services, manufacturing, government, wholesale and retail trade. **Chief manuf. goods:** chemicals & plastics, food & kindred products, furniture, lumber & wood products, electrical machinery, transportation equipment. **Chief crops:** cotton, rice, soybeans. **Livestock:** (Jan. 2003) 1.1 mil cattle/calves; (Dec. 2002) 275,000 hogs/pigs; 10.8 mil chickens (excl. broilers); 769.5 mil broilers. **Timber/lumber** (est. 2002): 2.5 bil bd. ft.; pine, oak, hardwoods. **Nonfuel minerals** (est. 2002): $176 mil.; sand and gravel (construction), clays (fuller's earth), cement (portland), stone (crushed), clays (bentonite). **Commercial fishing** (2001): $50.6 mil. **Chief ports:** Pascagoula, Vicksburg, Gulfport, Natchez, Greenville. **Principal internat. airport at:** Jackson. **New private housing** (2002): 11,276 units/$1.1 bil. **Gross state product** (2001): $67.1 bil. **Employment distrib.** (May 2003): 21.4% govt.; 19.9% trade/trans./util.; 16.1% mfg.; 9.9% ed./health serv.; 6.9% prof./bus. serv.; 10.9% leisure/hosp.; 4.1% finance; 4.9% constr.; 1.5% info. **Per cap. pers. income** (2002): $22,372. **Sales tax** (2003): 7%. **Unemployment** (2002): 6.8%. **Tourism expends.** (2000): $5 bil.

Finance. FDIC-insured commercial banks (2002): 97. **Deposits:** $29.7 bil. **FDIC-insured savings institutions** (2002): 8. **Assets:** $1.0 bil.

Federal govt. Fed. civ. employees (Mar. 2002): 16,655. **Avg. salary:** $48,877. **Notable fed. facilities:** Columbus AFB; Keesler AFB; Meridian NAS; NASA Stennis Space Ctr.; Army Corps of Engineers Waterways Experiment Sta.; Naval Constr. Battalion Ctr., Gulfport.

Energy. Electricity production (est. 2002, kWh, by source): Coal: 18.2 bil; Petroleum: 30 mil; Gas: 17.7 bil; Nuclear: 10.1 bil.

State data. Motto: Virtute et Armis (By valor and arms). **Flower:** Magnolia. **Bird:** Mockingbird. **Tree:** Magnolia. **Song:** Go, Mississippi! **Entered union** Dec. 10, 1817; rank, 20th. **State fair** at Jackson; early Oct.

History. Early inhabitants of the region were Choctaw, Chickasaw, and Natchez peoples. Hernando de Soto explored the area, 1540, and sighted the Mississippi River, 1541. Robert La Salle traced the river from Illinois to its mouth and claimed the entire valley for France, 1682. The first settlement was the French Ft. Maurepas, near Ocean Springs, 1699. The area was ceded to Britain, 1763; American settlers followed. During the American Revolution, Spain seized part of the area, remaining even after the U.S. acquired title at the end of the conflict; Spain finally moved out, 1798. The Territory of Mississippi was formed, 1798. Mississippi seceded, 1861. Union forces captured Corinth and Vicksburg and destroyed Jackson and much of Meridian. Mississippi was readmitted to the Union in 1870.

Tourist attractions. Vicksburg Natl. Military Park and Cemetery, other Civil War sites; Hattiesburg; Natchez Trace; Indian mounds; Antebellum homes; pilgrimages in Natchez and some 25 other cities; The Elvis Presley Birthplace & Museum, Tupelo; Smith Robertson Museum, Mynelle Gardens, both Jackson; Mardi Gras and Shrimp Festival, both in Biloxi; Gulf Islands Natl. Seashore; Casinos on the Mississippi River; the Mississippi Coast.

Famous Mississippians. Margaret Walker Alexander, Dana Andrews, Jimmy Buffett, Hodding Carter III, Bo Diddley, William Faulkner, Brett Favre, Shelby Foote, Morgan Freeman, John Grisham, Fannie Lou Hamer, Jim Henson, Faith Hill, John Lee Hooker, Robert Johnson, James Earl Jones, B. B. King, L. Q. C. Lamar, Trent Lott, Gerald McRaney, Willie Morris, Walter Payton, Elvis Presley, Leontyne Price, Charley Pride, LeAnn Rimes, Muddy Waters, Eudora Welty, Tennessee Williams, Oprah Winfrey, Johnny Winter, Richard Wright, Tammy Wynette.

Tourist information. Dept. of Economic & Community Development. PO Box 849, Jackson, MS 39205-0849; 1-800-927-6378. **Website:** www.visitmississippi.org

Website. www.ms.gov

Missouri
Show Me State

People. Population (2002 est.): 5,672,579; rank: 17; **net change** (2001-2002): 0.6%. **Pop. density:** 82.3 per sq mi. **Racial distribution** (2000): 84.9% white; 11.2% black; 1.1% Asian; 0.4% Native American/Nat. AK; 0.1% Hawaiian/Pacific Islander; 0.8% other race; 2 or more races, 1.5%. **Hispanic pop.** (any race): 2.1%.

Geography. Total area: 69,704 sq mi; rank: 21. **Land area:** 68,886 sq mi; rank: 18. **Acres forested:** 14.0 mil. **Location:** West North Central state near the geographic center of the conterminous U.S.; bordered on the E by the Mississippi R., on the NW by the Missouri R. **Climate:** continental, susceptible to cold Canadian air, moist, warm gulf air, and drier SW air. **Topography:** rolling hills, open, fertile plains, and well-watered prairie N of the Missouri R.; south of the river land is rough and hilly with deep, narrow valleys; alluvial plain in the SE; low elevation in the west. **Capital:** Jefferson City.

Economy. Chief industries: agriculture, manufacturing, aerospace, tourism. **Chief manuf. goods:** transportation equipment, food and related products, electrical and electronic equipment, chemicals. **Chief crops:** soybeans, corn, wheat, hay. **Livestock:** (Jan. 2003) 4.4 mil cattle/calves; 67,000 sheep/lambs; (Dec. 2002) 3.0 mil hogs/pigs; 8.6 mil chickens (excl. broilers). **Timber/lumber** (est. 2002): 616 mil bd. ft.; oak, hickory. **Nonfuel minerals** (est. 2002): $1.3 bil.; stone (crushed), cement (portland), lead, lime, sand and gravel (construction). **Chief ports:** St. Louis, Kansas City. **Principal internat. airports at:** Kansas City, St. Louis. **New private housing** (2002): 28,255 units/$3.2 bil. **Gross state product** (2001): $181.5 bil. **Employment distrib.** (May 2003): 16.2% govt.; 19.9% trade/trans./util.; 11.7% mfg.; 13.2% ed./health serv.; 11% prof./bus. serv.; 9.9% leisure/hosp.; 5.9% finance; 4.9% constr.; 2% info. **Per cap. pers. income** (2002): $28,936. **Sales tax** (2003): 4.225%. **Unemployment** (2002): 5.5%. **Tourism expends.** (2000) $9.8 bil. **Lottery** (2002): total sales: $585.2 mil; net income: $160 mil.

Finance. FDIC-insured commercial banks (2002): 349. **Deposits:** $59.1 bil. **FDIC-insured savings institutions** (2002): 33. **Assets:** $5.6 bil.

Federal govt. Fed. civ. employees (Mar. 2002): 32,356. **Avg. salary:** $49,010. **Notable fed. facilities:** Federal Reserve banks; Ft. Leonard Wood; Jefferson Barracks Natl. Cem.; Whiteman AFB.

Energy. Electricity production (est. 2002, kWh, by source): Coal: 67.2 bil; Petroleum: 528 mil; Gas: 3.3 bil; Hydroelectric: 1.2 bil; Nuclear: 8.4 bil; Other: 55 mil.

State data. Motto: Salus Populi Suprema Lex Esto (The welfare of the people shall be the supreme law). **Flower:** Hawthorn. **Bird:** Bluebird. **Tree:** Dogwood. **Song:** Missouri Waltz. **Entered union** Aug. 10, 1821; rank, 24th. **State fair** at Sedalia; 3rd week in Aug.

History. Early inhabitants of the region were Algonquian Sauk, Fox, and Illinois and Siouan Osage, Missouri, Iowa, and Kansa peoples. Hernando de Soto visited 1541. French hunters and lead miners made the first settlement c 1735, at Ste. Genevieve. The territory was ceded to Spain by the French, 1763, then returned to France, 1800. The U.S. acquired Missouri as part of the Louisiana Purchase, 1803. The influx of white settlers drove Native American tribes to the Kansas and Oklahoma territories; most were gone by 1836. The fur trade and the Santa Fe Trail provided prosperity; St. Louis became the gateway for pioneers heading West. Missouri entered the Union as a slave state, 1821. Though it remained with the Union, pro- and anti-slavery forces battled there during the Civil War.

Tourist attractions. Silver Dollar City, Branson; Mark Twain Area, Hannibal; Pony Express Museum, St. Joseph; Harry S. Truman Library, Independence; Gateway Arch, St. Louis; Worlds of Fun, Kansas City; Lake of the Ozarks; Churchill Mem., Fulton; State Capitol, Jefferson City.

Famous Missourians. Maya Angelou, Robert Altman, Burt Bacharach, Josephine Baker, Scott Bakula, Thomas Hart Benton, Tom Berenger, Yogi Berra, Chuck Berry, George Caleb Bingham, Daniel Boone, Omar Bradley, William Burroughs, Kate Capshaw, Dale Carnegie, George Washington Carver, Bob Costas, Walter Cronkite, Walt Disney, T. S. Eliot, Richard Gephardt, John Goodman, Betty Grable, Edwin Hubble, Jesse James, Rush Limbaugh, Marianne Moore, Reinhold Niebuhr, J. C. Penney, John J. Pershing, Brad Pitt, Joseph Pulitzer, Ginger Rogers, Bess Truman, Harry S. Truman, Kathleen Turner, Tina Turner, Mark Twain, Dick Van Dyke, Tennessee Williams, Lanford Wilson, Shelley Winters, Jane Wyman.

Chamber of Commerce. 428 E. Capitol, Jefferson City, MO 65101; 1-888-877-1234, ext. 124. **Website:** www.missouri tourism.com

Website. www.state.mo.us

Montana
Treasure State

People. Population (2002 est.): 909,453; rank: 44; **net change** (2001-2002): 0.4%. **Pop. density:** 6.2 per sq mi. **Racial distribution** (2000): 90.6% white; 0.3% black; 0.5% Asian; 6.2% Native American/Nat. AK; 0.1% Hawaiian/Pacific Islander; 0.6% other race; 2 or more races, 1.7%. **Hispanic pop.** (any race): 2.0%.

Geography. Total area: 147,042 sq mi; rank: 4. **Land area:** 145,552 sq mi; rank: 4. **Acres forested:** 23.3 mil. **Location:** Mountain state bounded on the E by the Dakotas, on the S by Wyoming, on the SSW by Idaho, and on the N by Canada. **Climate:** colder, continental climate with low humidity. **Topography:** Rocky Mts. in western third of the state; eastern two-thirds gently rolling northern Great Plains. **Capital:** Helena.

Economy. Chief industries: agriculture, timber, mining, tourism, oil and gas. **Chief manuf. goods:** food products, wood & paper products, primary metals, printing & publishing, petroleum and coal products. **Chief crops:** wheat, barley, sugar beets, hay, oats. **Livestock:** (Jan. 2003) 2.5 mil cattle/calves; 300,000 sheep/lambs; (Dec. 2002) 185,000 hogs/pigs; 480,000 chickens (excl. broilers). **Timber/lumber** (est. 2002): 1.2 bil bd. ft.; Douglas fir, pines, larch. **Nonfuel minerals** (est. 2002): $442 mil.; palladium metal, sand and gravel (construction), platinum metal, cement (portland), gold. **Principal internat. airports at:** Billings, Missoula. **New private housing** (2002): 3,574 units/$339 mil. **Gross state product** (2001): $22.6 bil. **Employment distrib.** (May 2003): 21.8% govt.; 21% trade/trans./util.; 4.7% mfg.; 13.3% ed./health serv.; 8.2% prof./bus. serv.; 12.8% leisure/hosp.; 4.9% finance; 5.6% constr.; 2% info. **Per cap. pers. income** (2002): $25,020. **Sales tax:** (2003): none. **Unemployment** (2002): 4.6%. **Tourism expends.** (2000): $2.1 bil. **Lottery** (2002): total sales: $33.6 mil; net income: $7.5 mil.

Finance. FDIC-insured commercial banks (2002): 80. **Deposits:** $11.0 bil. **FDIC-insured savings institutions** (2002): 4. **Assets:** $489 mil.

Federal govt. Fed. civ. employees (Mar. 2002): 8,384. **Avg. salary:** $48,176. **Notable fed. facilities:** Malmstrom AFB; Ft. Peck, Hungry Horse, Libby, Yellowtail dams; numerous missile silos.

Energy. Electricity production (est. 2002, kWh, by source): Coal: 286 mil; Petroleum: 1 mil; Gas: 7 mil; Hydroelectric: 6.4 bil.

State data. Motto: Oro y Plata (Gold and silver). **Flower:** Bitterroot. **Bird:** Western meadowlark. **Tree:** Ponderosa pine. **Song:** Montana. **Entered union** Nov. 8, 1889; rank, 41st. **State fair** at Great Falls; late July-early Aug.

History. Cheyenne, Blackfoot, Crow, Assiniboin, Salish (Flatheads), Kootenai, and Kalispel peoples were early inhabitants of the area. French explorers visited the region, 1742. The U.S. acquired the area partly through the Louisiana Purchase, 1803, partly through explorations of Lewis and Clark, 1805-6. Fur traders and missionaries established posts early 19th cent. Gold was discovered, 1863, and the Montana territory was established, 1864. Indian uprisings reached their peak with the Battle of Little Bighorn, 1876. Chief Joseph and the Nez Percé tribe surrendered here, 1877, after long trek across the state. Mining activity and the coming of the Northern Pacific Railway, 1883, brought population growth. Copper wealth from the Butte pits resulted in the turn of the century "War of Copper Kings" as factions fought for control of "the richest hill on earth."

Tourist attractions. Glacier Natl. Park; Yellowstone Natl. Park; Museum of the Rockies, Bozeman; Museum of the Plains Indian, Blackfeet Reservation, near Browning; Little Bighorn Battlefield Natl. Monument and Custer Natl. Cemetery; Flathead Lake; Helena; Lewis and Clark Caverns State Park, near Whitehall; Lewis and Clark Interpretive Center, Great Falls.

Famous Montanans. Dana Carvey, Gary Cooper, Marcus Daly, Chet Huntley, Will James, Myrna Loy, David Lynch, Mike Mansfield, Brent Musburger, Jeannette Rankin, Charles M. Russell, Lester Thurow.

Chamber of Commerce. 2030 11th Ave., PO Box 1730, Helena, MT 59624; 1-800-VISITMT. **Website:** www.visit mt.org

Website. www.state.mt.us

Nebraska
Cornhusker State

People. Population (2002 est.): 1,729,180; rank: 38; **net change** (2001-2002): 0.5%. **Pop. density:** 22.5 per sq mi. **Racial distribution** (2000): 89.6% white; 4.0% black; 1.3% Asian; 0.9% Native American/Nat. AK; 0.1% Hawaiian/Pacific Islander; 2.8% other race; 2 or more races, 1.4%. **Hispanic pop.** (any race): 5.5%.

Geography. Total area: 77,354 sq mi; rank: 16. **Land area:** 76,872 sq mi; rank: 15. **Acres forested:** 0.9 mil. **Location:** West North Central state with the Missouri R. for a NE and E border. **Climate:** continental semi-arid. **Topography:** till plains of the central lowland in the eastern third rising to the Great Plains and hill country of the north central and NW. **Capital:** Lincoln.

Economy. Chief industries: agriculture, manufacturing. **Chief manuf. goods:** processed foods, industrial machinery, printed materials, electric and electronic equipment, primary and fabricated metal products, transportation equipment. **Chief crops:** corn, sorghum, soybeans, hay, wheat, dry beans, oats, potatoes, sugar beets. **Livestock:** (Jan. 2003) 6.4 mil cattle/calves; 89,000 sheep/lambs; (Dec. 2002) 2.9 mil hogs/pigs; 13.7 mil chickens (excl. broilers); 3.7 mil broilers. **Timber/lumber** (est. 2002): 25 mil bd. ft.; oak, hickory, and elm. **Nonfuel minerals** (est. 2002): $88.6 mil.; cement (portland), stone (crushed), sand and gravel (construction), lime, cement (masonry). **Chief ports:** Omaha, Sioux City, Brownville, Blair, Plattsmouth, Nebraska City. **New private housing** (2002): 9,278 units/$1.0 bil. **Gross state product** (2001): $57.0 bil. **Employment distrib.** (May 2003): 17.7% govt.; 21.6% trade/trans./util.; 11.5% mfg.; 12.4% ed./health serv.; 9.8% prof./bus. serv.; 8.3% leisure/hosp.; 7% finance; 5% constr.; 2.7% info. **Per cap. pers. income** (2002): $29,771. **Sales tax** (2003): 5%. **Unemployment** (2002): 3.6%. **Tourism expends.** (2000): $2.7 bil. **Lottery** (2002): total sales: $74 mil; net income: $18.5 mil.

Finance. FDIC-insured commercial banks (2002): 268. **Deposits:** $25.2 bil. **FDIC-insured savings institutions** (2002): 13. **Assets:** $16.3 bil.

Federal govt. Fed. civ. employees (Mar. 2002): 7,965. **Avg. salary:** $49,643. **Notable fed. facilities:** Offutt AFB.

Energy. Electricity production (est. 2002, kWh, by source): Coal: 19.9 bil; Petroleum: 17 mil; Gas: 407 mil; Hydroelectric: 1.1 bil; Nuclear: 10.1 bil; Other: 3 mil.

State data. Motto: Equality before the law. **Flower:** Goldenrod. **Bird:** Western meadowlark. **Tree:** Cottonwood. **Song:** Beautiful Nebraska. **Entered union** Mar. 1, 1867; rank, 37th. **State fair** at Lincoln; Aug.- Sept.

History. When the Europeans first arrived, Pawnee, Ponca, Omaha, and Oto peoples lived in the region. Spanish and French explorers and fur traders visited the area prior to its acquisition in the Louisiana Purchase, 1803. Lewis and Clark passed through, 1804-6. The first permanent settlement was Bellevue, near Omaha, 1823. The region was gradually settled, despite the 1834 Indian Intercourse Act, which declared Nebraska Indian country and excluded white settlement. Conflicts with settlers eventually forced Native Americans to move to reservations. Many Civil War veterans settled under free land terms of the 1862 Homestead Act; as agriculture grew, struggles followed between homesteaders and ranchers.

Tourist attractions. State Museum (Elephant Hall), State Capitol, both Lincoln; Stuhr Museum of the Prairie Pioneer, Grand Island; Museum of the Fur Trade, Chadron; Henry Doorly Zoo, Joslyn Art Museum, both Omaha; Ashfall Fossil Beds, Strategic Air Command Museum, Ashland; Boys Town, west of Omaha; Arbor Lodge State Park, Nebraska City; Buffalo Bill Ranch State Hist. Park, North Platte; Pioneer Village, Minden; Oregon Trail landmarks; Scotts Bluff Natl. Monument; Chimney Rock Natl. Historic Site; Ft. Robinson; Hastings Museum, Hastings.

Famous Nebraskans. Grover Cleveland Alexander, Fred Astaire, Marlon Brando, Charles W. Bryan, William Jennings Bryan, Warren Buffett, Johnny Carson, Willa Cather, Dick Cavett, Dick Cheney, William F. "Buffalo Bill" Cody, Loren Eiseley, Rev. Edward J. Flanagan, Henry Fonda, Gerald R. Ford, Bob Gibson, Rollin Kirby, Harold Lloyd, Malcolm X, J. Sterling Morton, John Neihardt, Nick Nolte, George Norris, Tom Osborne, John J. Pershing, Roscoe Pound, Chief Red Cloud, Mari Sandoz, Robert Taylor, Darryl F. Zanuck.

Chamber of Commerce and Industry. 1320 Lincoln Mall, Ste. 201, Lincoln, NE 68508; 402-474-4422; 1-800-228-4307. **Website:** www.visitnebraska.org

Website. www.state.ne.us

IT'S A FACT: According to the U.S. Census Bureau, Nevada is the undisputed marriage capital of the U.S. In 2001, there were 75 marriages performed per every 1,000 residents in the Silver State. Hawaii ranked second, with 20 per 1,000, followed by Arkansas; with 15. The leading states in divorces per 1,000 residents were Nevada (6.8), Arkansas (6.6), and Wyoming (6.1).

Nevada
Sagebrush State, Battle Born State, Silver State

People. Population (2002 est.): 2,173,491; rank: 35; **net change** (2001-2002): 3.6%. **Pop. density:** 19.8 per sq mi. **Racial distribution** (2000): 75.2% white; 6.8% black; 4.5% Asian; 1.3% Native American/Nat. AK; 0.4% Hawaiian/Pacific Islander; 8.0% other race; 2 or more races, 3.8%. **Hispanic pop.** (any race): 19.7%.

Geography. Total area: 110,561 sq mi; rank: 7. **Land area:** 109,826 sq mi; rank: 7. **Acres forested:** 10.2 mil. **Location:** Mountain state bordered on N by Oregon and Idaho, on E by Utah and Arizona, on SE by Arizona, and on SW and W by California. **Climate:** semi-arid and arid. **Topography:** rugged N-S mountain ranges; highest elevation, Boundary Peak, 13,140 ft; southern area is within the Mojave Desert; lowest elevation, Colorado River at southern tip of state, 479 ft. **Capital:** Carson City.

Economy. Chief industries: gaming, tourism, mining, manufacturing, government, retailing, warehousing, trucking. **Chief manuf. goods:** food products, plastics, chemicals, aerospace products, lawn and garden irrigation equipment, seismic and machinery-monitoring devices. **Chief crops:** hay, alfalfa seed, potatoes, onions, garlic, barley, wheat. **Livestock:** (Jan. 2003) 500,000 cattle/calves; 95,000 sheep/lambs; (Dec. 2002) 6,500 hogs/pigs. **Timber/lumber** (est. 2002): <.5 mil bd. ft.; piñon, juniper, other pines. **Nonfuel minerals** (est. 2002): $2.9 bil.; gold, sand and gravel (construction), lime, silver, diatomite. **Principal internat. airports at:** Las Vegas, Reno. **New private housing** (2002): 35,615 units/$4.1 bil. **Gross state product** (2001): $79.2 bil. **Employment distrib.** (May 2003): 12.4% govt.; 17.8% trade/trans./util.; 4% mfg.; 7% ed./health serv.; 10.8% prof./bus. serv.; 28.1% leisure/hosp.; 5.3% finance; 8.9% constr.; 1.5% info. **Per cap. pers. income** (2002): $30,180. **Sales tax** (2003): 6.5%. **Unemployment** (2002): 5.5%. **Tourism expends.** (2000) $22.4 bil.

Finance. FDIC-insured commercial banks (2002): 33. **Deposits:** $21.3 bil. **FDIC-insured savings institutions** (2002): 3. **Assets:** $1.4 bil.

Federal govt. Fed. civ. employees (Mar. 2002): 7,674. **Avg. salary:** $53,806. **Notable fed. facilities:** Nevada Test Site; Hawthorne Army Depot; Nellis AFB and Range Complex; Fallon NAS; Natl. Wild Horse and Burro Ctr. at Palomino Valley.

Energy. Electricity production (est. 2002, kWh, by source): Coal: 16.4 bil; Petroleum: 25 mil; Gas: 6.2 bil; Hydroelectric: 2.3 bil.

State data. Motto: All for our country. **Flower:** Sagebrush. **Bird:** Mountain bluebird. **Trees:** Single-leaf piñon and bristlecone pine. **Song:** Home Means Nevada. **Entered union** Oct. 31, 1864; rank, 36th. **State fair** at Reno; late Aug.

History. Shoshone, Paiute, Bannock, and Washoe peoples lived in the area at the time of European contact. Nevada was first explored by Spaniards, 1776. Hudson's Bay Co. trappers explored the north and central region, 1825; trader Jedediah Smith crossed the state, 1826-27. The area was acquired by the U.S., 1848, at the end of the Mexican War. The first settlement, Mormon Station, now Genoa, was established, 1849. Discovery of the Comstock Lode, rich in gold and silver, 1859, spurred a population boom. In the early 20th cent., Nevada adopted progressive measures such as the initiative, referendum, recall, and woman suffrage.

Tourist attractions. Legalized gambling at: Lake Tahoe, Reno, Las Vegas, Laughlin, Elko County, and elsewhere. Hoover Dam; Lake Mead; Great Basin Natl. Park; Valley of Fire State Park; Virginia City; Red Rock Canyon Natl. Conservation Area; Liberace Museum, the Las Vegas Strip, Guinness World of Records Museum, Lost City Museum, Overton. Lamoille Canyon, Pyramid Lake, all Las Vegas. Skiing near Lake Tahoe.

Famous Nevadans. Andre Agassi, Walter Van Tilburg Clark, George Ferris, Sarah Winnemucca Hopkins, Paul Laxalt, Dat So La Lee, John William Mackay, Anne Martin, Pat McCarran, Key Pittman, William Morris Stewart.

Tourist information. Commission on Tourism, 5151 S. Carson St., Carson City, NV 89701; 1-800-NEVADA8. **Website:** www.travelnevada.com.

Website. www.nv.gov

New Hampshire
Granite State

People. Population (2002 est.): 1,275,056; rank: 41; **net change** (2001-2002): 1.2%. **Pop. density:** 142.2 per sq mi. **Racial distribution** (2000): 96.0% white; 0.7% black; 1.3% Asian; 0.2% Native American/Nat. AK; <0.1% Hawaiian/Pacific Islander; 0.6% other race; 2 or more races, 1.1%. **Hispanic pop.** (any race): 1.7%.

Geography. Total area: 9,350 sq mi; rank: 46. **Land area:** 8,968 sq mi; rank: 44. **Acres forested:** 4.8 mil. **Location:** New England state bounded on S by Massachusetts, on W by Vermont, on N and NW by Canada, on E by Maine and the Atlantic Ocean. **Climate:** highly varied, due to its nearness to high mountains and ocean. **Topography:** low, rolling coast followed by countless hills and mountains rising out of a central plateau. **Capital:** Concord.

Economy. Chief industries: tourism, manufacturing, agriculture, trade, mining. **Chief manuf. goods:** machinery, electrical and electronic products, plastics, fabricated metal products. **Chief crops:** dairy products, nursery & greenhouse products, hay, vegetables, fruit, maple syrup & sugar products. **Livestock:** (Jan. 2003) 41,000 cattle/calves; (Dec. 2002) 3,200 hogs/pigs; 229,000 chickens (excl. broilers). **Timber/lumber** (est. 2002): 287 mil bd. ft.; white pine, hemlock, oak, birch. **Nonfuel minerals** (est. 2002): $68 mil.; sand and gravel (construction), stone (crushed), stone (dimension), gemstones. **Commercial fishing** (2001): $17.9 mil. **Chief ports:** Portsmouth, Hampton, Rye. **New private housing** (2002): 8,708 units/$1.2 bil. **Gross state product** (2001): $47.2 bil. **Employment distrib.** (May 2003): 14% govt.; 22.3% trade/trans./util.; 13.3% mfg.; 15.2% ed./health serv.; 8.5% prof./bus. serv.; 10.1% leisure/hosp.; 6% finance; 4.4% constr.; 2% info. **Per cap. pers. income** (2002): $34,334. **Sales tax:** (2002): none. **Unemployment** (2002): 4.7%. **Tourism expends.** (2000): $2.6 bil. **Lottery** (2001): total sales: $212.8 mil; net income: $66.1 mil.

Finance. FDIC-insured commercial banks (2002): 15. **Deposits:** $13.8 bil. **FDIC-insured savings institutions** (2002): 17. **Assets:** $11.4 bil.

Federal govt. Fed. civ. employees (Mar. 2002): 3,034. **Avg. salary:** $63,554. **Notable fed. facilities:** U.S. Army Cold Regions Res. & Engineering Lab.

Energy. Electricity production (est. 2002, kWh, by source): Coal: 3.7 bil; Petroleum: 592 mil; Gas: 96 mil; Hydroelectric: 263 mil; Nuclear: 7.6 bil.

State data. Motto: Live free or die. **Flower:** Purple lilac. **Bird:** Purple finch. **Tree:** White birch. **Song:** Old New Hampshire. **Ninth** of the original 13 states to ratify the Constitution, June 21, 1788. **State Fair:** Many agricultural fairs statewide, July through Sept.; no State fair.

History. Algonquian-speaking peoples, including the Pennacook, lived in the region when the Europeans arrived. The first explorers to visit the area were England's Martin Pring, 1603, and France's Champlain, 1605. The first settlement was Odiorne's Point (now port of Rye), 1623. Native American conflicts were ended, 1759, by Robert Rogers' Rangers. Before the American Revolution, New Hampshire residents seized a British fort at Portsmouth, 1774, and drove the royal governor out, 1775. New Hampshire became the first colony to adopt its own constitution, 1776. Three regiments served in the Continental Army, and scores of privateers raided British shipping.

Tourist attractions. Mt. Washington, highest peak in Northeast; Lake Winnipesaukee; White Mt. National Forest; Crawford, Franconia—famous for the Old Man of the Mountain, described by Hawthorne as the Great Stone Face, Pinkham notches, all White Mt. region; the Flume, a spectacular gorge; the aerial tramway, Cannon Mt.; Strawbery Banke, Portsmouth; Shaker Village, Canterbury; Saint-Gaudens Natl. Historic Site, Cornish; Mt. Monadnock.

Famous New Hampshirites. Salmon P. Chase, Ralph Adams Cram, Mary Baker Eddy, Daniel Chester French, Robert Frost, Horace Greeley, Sarah Buell Hale, Franklin Pierce, Augustus Saint-Gaudens, Adam Sandler, Alan Shepard, David H. Souter, Daniel Webster.

Tourist information. Division of Travel & Tourism Development, PO Box 1856, Concord, NH 03302-1856; 1-800-FUNINNH, ext. 169. **Website:** www.visitnh.gov

Website. www.state.nh.us

New Jersey
Garden State

People. Population (2002 est.): 8,590,300; rank: 9; **net change** (2001-2002): 0.9%. **Pop. density:** 1,158.2 per sq mi. **Racial distribution** (2000): 72.6% white; 13.6% black; 5.7% Asian; 0.2% Native American/Nat. AK; <0.1% Hawaiian/Pacific Islander; 5.4% other race; 2 or more races, 2.5%. **Hispanic pop.** (any race): 13.3%.

Geography. Total area: 8,721 sq mi; rank: 47. **Land area:** 7,417 sq mi; rank: 46. **Acres forested:** 2.1 mil. **Location:** Middle Atlantic state bounded on N and E by New York and Atlantic Ocean, on S and W by Delaware and Pennsylvania. **Climate:** moderate, with marked difference bet. NW and SE extremities. **Topography:** Appalachian Valley in the NW also has highest elevation, High Pt., 1,801 ft; Appalachian Highlands, flat-topped NE-SW mountain ranges; Piedmont Plateau, low plains broken by high ridges (Palisades) rising 400-500 ft; Coastal Plain, covering three-fifths of state in SE, rises from sea level to gentle slopes. **Capital:** Trenton.

Economy. Chief industries: pharmaceuticals/drugs, telecommunications, biotechnology, printing & publishing. **Chief manuf. goods:** chemicals, electronic equipment, food. **Chief crops:** nursery/greenhouse, tomatoes, blueberries, peaches, peppers, cranberries, soybeans. **Livestock:** (Jan. 2003) 44,000 cattle/calves; (Dec. 2002) 15,000 hogs/pigs; 2.2 mil chickens (excl. broilers). **Timber/lumber** (est. 2002): 20 mil bd. ft.; pine, cedar, mixed hardwoods. **Nonfuel minerals** (est. 2002): $285 mil.; stone (crushed), sand and gravel (construction), sand and gravel (industrial), greensand marl, peat. **Commercial fishing** (2001): $110.2 mil. **Chief ports:** Newark, Elizabeth, Hoboken, Camden. **Principal internat. airports at:** Atlantic City, Newark. **New private housing** (2002): 30,441 units/$3.4 bil. **Gross state product** (2001): $365.4 bil. **Employment distrib.** (May 2003): 15.3% govt.; 21.8% trade/trans./util.; 8.9% mfg.; 13.5% ed./health serv.; 14.5% prof./bus. serv.; 7.9% leisure/hosp.; 6.9% finance; 4.1% constr.; 2.7% info. **Per cap. pers. income** (2002): $39,453. **Sales tax** (2003): 6%. **Unemployment** (2002): 5.8%. **Tourism expends.** (2000): $15.7 bil. **Lottery:** total sales: $2.1 bil; net income $754.6 mil.

Finance. FDIC-insured commercial banks (2002): 82. **Deposits:** $68.1 bil. **FDIC-insured savings institutions** (2002): 68. **Assets:** $53.0 bil.

Federal govt. Fed. civ. employees (Mar. 2002): 25,670. **Avg. salary:** $61,386. **Notable fed. facilities:** McGuire AFB; Ft. Dix; Ft. Monmouth; Picatinny Arsenal; Lakehurst Naval Air Engineering Ctr.; FAA William J.Hughes Technical Ctr.

Energy. Electricity production (est. 2002, kWh, by source): Coal 1.4 bil; Petroleum: 210 mil; Gas: 96 mil; Hydroelectric: -146 mil.

State data. Motto: Liberty and prosperity. **Flower:** Purple violet. **Bird:** Eastern goldfinch. **Tree:** Red oak. **Third** of the original 13 states to ratify the Constitution, Dec. 18, 1787. **State fair** at Cherry Hill; late July-early Aug.

History. The Lenni Lenape (Delaware) peoples lived in the region and had mostly peaceful relations with European colonists, who arrived after the explorers Verrazano, 1524, and Hudson, 1609. The first permanent European settlement was Dutch, at Bergen (now Jersey City), 1660. When the British took New Netherland, 1664, the area between the Delaware and Hudson Rivers was given to Lord John Berkeley and Sir George Carteret. During the American Revolution, New Jersey was the scene of nearly 100 battles, large and small, including Trenton, 1776; Princeton, 1777; Monmouth, 1778.

Tourist attractions. 127 mi of beaches; Miss America Pageant, Atlantic City; Grover Cleveland birthplace, Caldwell; Cape May Historic District; Edison Natl. Historic Site, W. Orange; Six Flags Great Adventure, Jackson; Liberty State Park, Jersey City; Meadowlands Sports Complex, E. Rutherford; Pine Barrens wilderness area; Princeton University; numerous Revolutionary War historical sites; State Aquarium, Camden.

Famous New Jerseyans. Jason Alexander, Count Basie, Judy Blume, Jon Bon Jovi, Bill Bradley, Aaron Burr, Grover Cleveland, James Fenimore Cooper, Stephen Crane, Danny DeVito, Thomas Edison, Albert Einstein, James Gandolfini, Allen Ginsberg, Alexander Hamilton, Ed Harris, Whitney Houston, Buster Keaton, Joyce Kilmer, Norman Mailer, Jack Nicholson, Thomas Paine, Dorothy Parker, Joe Pesci, Molly Pitcher, Paul Robeson, Philip Roth, Antonin Scalia, Wally Schirra, H. Norman Schwarzkopf, Frank Sinatra, Bruce Springsteen, Martha Stewart, Meryl Streep, Dave Thomas, John Travolta, Walt Whitman, William Carlos Williams, Woodrow Wilson.

Chamber of Commerce. 50 W. State St., Trenton, NJ 08608; 1-800-VISITNJ. **Website:** www.visitnj.org
Website. www.state.nj.us

New Mexico
Land of Enchantment

People. Population (2002 est.): 1,855,059; rank: 36; **net change** (2001-2002): 1.3%. **Pop. density:** 15.3 per sq mi. **Racial distribution** (2000): 66.8% white; 1.9% black; 1.1% Asian; 9.5% Native American/Nat. AK; 0.1% Hawaiian/Pacific Islander; 17.0% other race; 2 or more races, 3.6%. **Hispanic pop.** (any race): 42.1%.

Geography. Total area: 121,589 sq mi; rank: 5. **Land area:** 121,356 sq mi; rank: 5. **Acres forested:** 16.7 mil. **Location:** southwestern state bounded by Colorado on the N, Oklahoma, Texas, and Mexico on the E and S, and Arizona on the W. **Climate:** dry, with temperatures rising or falling 5x F with every 1,000 ft elevation. **Topography:** eastern third, Great Plains; central third, Rocky Mts. (85% of the state is over 4,000-ft elevation); western third, high plateau. **Capital:** Santa Fe.

Economy. Chief industries: government, services, trade. **Chief manuf. goods:** foods, machinery, apparel, lumber, printing, transportation equipment, electronics, semiconductors. **Chief crops:** hay, onions, chiles, greenhouse nursery, pecans, cotton. **Livestock:** (Jan. 2003) 1.6 mil cattle/calves; 215,000 sheep/lambs; (Dec. 2002) 3,000 hogs/pigs. **Timber/lumber** (est. 2002): 111 mil bd. ft.; ponderosa pine, Douglas fir. **Nonfuel minerals** (est. 2002): $571 mil.; potash, copper, sand and gravel (construction), stone (crushed), cement (portland). **Principal internat. airport at:** Albuquerque. **New private housing** (2002): 12,066 units/$1.4 bil. **Gross state product** (2001): $55.4 bil. **Employment distrib.** (May 2003): 24.8% govt.; 17.5% trade/trans./util.; 4.7% mfg.; 12.8% ed./health serv.; 11.6% prof./bus. serv.; 10.6% leisure/hosp.; 4.4% finance; 6% constr.; 2.2% info. **Per cap. pers. income** (2002): $23,941. **Sales tax** (2003): 5%. **Unemployment** (2002): 5.4%. **Tourism expends.** (2000): $3.9 bil. **Lottery** (2002): total sales: $134 mil; net income: $29.6 mil.

Finance. FDIC-insured commercial banks (2002): 51. **Deposits:** $12.7 bil. **FDIC-insured savings institutions** (2002): 9. **Assets:** $2.4 bil.

Federal govt. Fed. civ. employees (Mar. 2002): 21,262. **Avg. salary:** $50,238. **Notable fed. facilities:** Kirtland, Cannon, Holloman AF bases; Los Alamos Natl. Lab; White Sands Missile Range; Natl. Solar Observatory; Natl. Radio Astronomy Observatory; Sandia Natl. Labs.

Energy. Electricity production (est. 2002, kWh, by source): Coal: 1.7 bil; Petroleum: 7.4 bil; Gas: 10.7 bil; Hydroelectric: 19.8 bil; Nuclear: 3.8 bil.

State data. Motto: Crescit Eundo (It grows as it goes). **Flower:** Yucca. **Bird:** Roadrunner. **Tree:** Piñon. **Song:** O, Fair New Mexico; Asi Es Nuevo Mexico. **Entered union** Jan. 6, 1912; rank: 47th. **State fair** at Albuquerque; mid-Sept.

History. Early inhabitants were peoples of the Mogollon and Anasazi civilizations, followed by the Pueblo peoples, Anasazi descendants. The nomadic Navajo and Apache tribes arrived c 15th cent. Franciscan Marcos de Niza and a former black slave, Estevanico, explored the area, 1539, seeking gold. First settlements were at San Juan Pueblo, 1598, and Santa Fe, 1610. Settlers alternately traded and fought with the Apache, Comanche, and Navajo. Trade on the Santa Fe Trail to Missouri started, 1821. The Mexican War was declared in May 1846; Gen. Stephen Kearny took Santa Fe without firing a shot, Aug. 18, 1846, declaring New Mexico part of the U.S. All Hispanic New Mexicans and Pueblo became U.S. citizens by terms of the 1848 treaty ending the war, but Congress denied the area statehood and created the territory of New Mexico, 1850. Pancho Villa raided Columbus, 1916, and U.S. troops were sent to the area. The world's first atomic bomb was exploded near Alamogordo, south of Santa Fe, 1945.

Tourist attractions. Carlsbad Caverns Natl. Park, with the largest natural underground chamber in the world; Santa Fe, oldest capital in U.S.; White Sands Natl. Monument, the largest gypsum deposit in the world; Chaco Culture National Historical Park; Acoma Pueblo, the "sky city," built atop a 357-ft mesa; Taos; Taos Art Colony; Taos Ski Valley; Ute Lake State Park; Shiprock.

Famous New Mexicans. Ben Abruzzo, Maxie Anderson, Jeff Bezos, Billy (the Kid) Bonney, Kit Carson, Bob Foster, Peter Hurd, Tony Hillerman, Archbishop Jean Baptiste Lamy, Nancy Lopez, Bill Mauldin, Georgia O'Keeffe, Kim Stanley, Al Unser, Bobby Unser, Lew Wallace.

Tourist information. New Mexico Dept. of Tourism, PO Box 20002, Santa Fe, NM 87503; 1-800-733-6396, ext. 0643. **Website:** www.newmexico.org
Website. www.state.nm.us

New York
Empire State

People. Population (2002 est.): 19,157,532; rank: 3; **net change** (2001-2002): 0.4%. **Pop. density:** 405.8 per sq mi. **Racial distribution** (2000): 67.9% white; 15.9% black; 5.5% Asian; 0.4% Native American/Nat. AK; 0.1% Hawaiian/Pacific Islander; 7.1% other race; 2 or more races, 3.1%. **Hispanic pop.** (any race): 15.1%.

Geography. Total area: 54,556 sq mi; rank: 27. **Land area:** 47,214 sq mi; rank: 30. **Acres forested:** 18.4 mil. **Location:** Middle Atlantic state, bordered by the New England states, Atlantic Ocean, New Jersey and Pennsylvania, Lakes Ontario and Erie, and Canada. **Climate:** variable; the SE region moderated by the ocean. **Topography:** highest and most rugged mountains in the NE Adirondack upland; St. Lawrence-Champlain lowlands extend from Lake Ontario NE along the Canadian border; Hudson-Mohawk lowland follows the flows of the rivers N and W, 10-30 mi wide; Atlantic coastal plain in the SE; Appalachian Highlands, covering half the state westward from the Hudson Valley, include the Catskill Mts., Finger Lakes; plateau of Erie-Ontario lowlands. **Capital:** Albany.

Economy. Chief industries: manufacturing, finance, communications, tourism, transportation, services. **Principal manufactured goods:** books & periodicals, clothing & apparel, pharmaceuticals, machinery, instruments, toys & sporting goods, electronic equipment, automotive & aircraft components. **Chief crops:** apples, grapes, strawberries, cherries, pears, onions, potatoes, cabbage, sweet corn, green beans, cauliflower, field corn, hay, wheat, oats, dry beans. **Products:** milk, cheese, maple syrup, wine. **Livestock:** (Jan. 2003) 1.4 mil cattle/calves; 65,000 sheep/lambs; (Dec. 2002) 86,000 hogs/pigs; 4.9 mil chickens (excl. broilers); 2.4 mil broilers. **Timber/lumber** (est. 2002): 464 mil bd. ft.; birch, sugar and red maple, basswood, hemlock, pine, oak, ash. **Nonfuel minerals** (est. 2002): $1.0 bil.; stone (crushed), cement (portland), salt, sand and gravel (construction), wollastonite. **Commercial fishing** (2001): $55.2 mil. **Chief ports:** New York, Buffalo, Albany. **Principal internat. airports at:** Albany, Buffalo, New York, Newburgh, Rochester, Syracuse. **New private housing** (2002): 49,149 units/$5.9 bil. **Gross state product** (2001): $826.5 bil. **Employment distrib.** (May 2003): 17.9% govt.; 17.5% trade/trans./util.; 7.4% mfg.; 17.7% ed./health serv.; 12.3% prof./bus. serv.; 7.8% leisure/hosp.; 8.3% finance; 4% constr.; 3.3% info. **Per cap. pers. income** (2002): $36,043. **Sales tax** (2003): 4%. **Unemployment** (2002): 6.1%. **Tourism expends.** (2000): $39.3 bil. **Lottery** (2002): total sales: $4.8 bil; net income: $1.6 bil.

Finance. FDIC-insured commercial banks (2002): 136. **Deposits:** $877.4 bil. **FDIC-insured savings institutions** (2002): 75. **Assets:** $130.9 bil.

Federal govt. Fed. civ. employees (Mar. 2002): 57,002. **Avg. salary:** $54,531. **Notable fed. facilities:** West Point Military Academy; Merchant Marine Academy; Ft. Drum; Rome Labs.; Watervliet Arsenal; Brookhaven Natl. Lab.

Energy. Electricity production (est. 2002, kWh, by source): Coal: 26.9 bil; Petroleum: 31 mil; Gas: 2.8 bil; Hydroelectric: 260 mil.

State data. Motto: Excelsior (Ever upward). **Flower:** Rose. **Bird:** Bluebird. **Tree:** Sugar maple. **Song:** I Love New York. Eleventh of the original 13 states to ratify the Constitution, July 26, 1788. **State fair** at Syracuse; late Aug.-early Sept.

History. Algonquians including the Mahican, Wappinger, and Lenni Lenape inhabited the region, as did the Iroquoian Mohawk, Oneida, Onondaga, Cayuga, and Seneca tribes, who established the League of the Five Nations. In 1609, Henry Hudson visited the river named for him, and Champlain explored the lake named for him. The first permanent settlement was Dutch, near present-day Albany, 1624. New Amsterdam was settled, 1626, at the S tip of Manhattan Island. A British fleet seized New Netherland, 1664. Ninety-two of the 300 or more engagements of the American Revolution were fought in New York, including the Battle of Bemis Heights-Saratoga, 1777, a turning point of the war. Completion of Erie Canal, 1825, established the state as a gateway to the West. The first women's rights convention was held in Seneca Falls, 1848.

Tourist attractions. New York City; Adirondack and Catskill Mts.; Finger Lakes; Great Lakes; Thousand Islands; Niagara Falls; Saratoga Springs; Philipsburg Manor, Sunnyside (Washington Irving's home), the Dutch Church of Sleepy Hollow, all in Tarrytown area; Corning Glass Center and Steuben factory, Corning; Fenimore House, Natl. Baseball Hall of Fame and Museum, both in Cooperstown; Ft. Ticonderoga overlooking Lakes George and Champlain; Empire State Plaza, Albany; Lake Placid; Franklin D. Roosevelt Natl. Historic Site, including the Roosevelt Library, Hyde Park; Long Island beaches; Theodore Roosevelt estate, Sagamore Hill, Oyster Bay; Turning Stone Casino.

Famous New Yorkers. Woody Allen, Susan B. Anthony, James Baldwin, Lucille Ball, L. Frank Baum, Milton Berle, Humphrey Bogart, Barbara Boxer, Mel Brooks, Benjamin Cardozo, De Witt Clinton, Peter Cooper, Aaron Copland, George Eastman, Millard Fillmore, Lou Gehrig, George and Ira Gershwin, Ruth Bader Ginsburg, Rudolph Giuliani, Jackie Gleason, Stephen Jay Gould, Julia Ward Howe, Charles Evans Hughes, Sarah Hughes, Washington Irving, Henry and William James, John Jay, Michael Jordan, Edward Koch, Fiorello LaGuardia, Herman Melville, J. Pierpont Morgan Jr., Eddie Murphy, Joyce Carol Oates, Carroll O'Connor, Rosie O'Donnell, Eugene O'Neill, George Pataki, Colin Powell, Nancy Reagan, John D. Rockefeller, Nelson Rockefeller, Ray Romano, Eleanor Roosevelt, Franklin D. Roosevelt, Theodore Roosevelt, Tim Russert, J. D. Salinger, Jerry Seinfeld, Al Sharpton, Paul Simon, Alfred E. Smith, Elizabeth Cady Stanton, Barbra Streisand, Donald Trump, William (Boss) Tweed, Martin Van Buren, Gore Vidal, Denzel Washington, Edith Wharton, Walt Whitman.

Tourist information. Empire State Development, Travel Information Center, 1 Commerce Plaza, Albany, NY 12245; 1-800-CALLNYS from U.S. states and territories and Canada; 1-518-474-4116 from other areas. **Website:** www.iloveny.com

Website. www.state.ny.us

North Carolina
Tar Heel State, Old North State

People. Population (2002 est.): 8,320,146; rank: 11; **net change** (2001-2002): 1.4%. **Pop. density:** 170.8 per sq mi. **Racial distribution** (2000): 72.10% white; 21.6% black; 1.4% Asian; 1.2% Native American/Nat. AK; 0.1% Hawaiian/Pacific Islander; 2.3% other race; 2 or more races, 1.3%. **Hispanic pop.** (any race): 4.7%.

Geography. Total area: 53,819 sq mi; rank: 28. **Land area:** 48,711 sq mi; rank: 29. **Acres forested:** 19.3 mil. **Location:** South Atlantic state bounded by Virginia, South Carolina, Georgia, Tennessee, and the Atlantic Ocean. **Climate:** sub-tropical in SE, medium-continental in mountain region; tempered by the Gulf Stream and the mountains in W. **Topography:** coastal plain and tidewater, two-fifths of state, extending to the fall line of the rivers; piedmont plateau, another two-fifths, of gentle to rugged hills; southern Appalachian Mts. contains the Blue Ridge and Great Smoky Mts. **Capital:** Raleigh.

Economy. Chief industries: manufacturing, agriculture, tourism. **Chief manuf. goods:** food products, textiles, industrial machinery and equipment, electrical and electronic equipment, furniture, tobacco products, apparel. **Chief crops:** tobacco, cotton, soybeans, corn, food grains, wheat, peanuts, sweet potatoes. **Livestock:** (Jan. 2003) 950,000 cattle/calves; (Dec. 2002) 9.6 mil hogs/pigs; 17.0 mil chickens (excl. broilers); 735.2 mil broilers. **Timber/lumber** (est. 2002): 2.5 bil bd. ft.; yellow pine, oak, hickory, poplar, maple. **Principal internat. airports at:** Charlotte, Greensboro, Raleigh/Durham, Wilmington. **Nonfuel minerals** (est. 2002): $708 mil.; stone (crushed), phosphate rock, sand and gravel (construction), sand and gravel (industrial), feldspar. **Commercial fishing** (2001): $85.9 mil. **Chief ports:** Morehead City, Wilmington. **New private housing** (2002): 79,824 units/$9.9 bil. **Gross state product** (2001): $275.6 bil. **Employment distrib.** (May 2003): 16.8% govt.; 18.6% trade/trans./util.; 15.9% mfg.; 11.1% ed./health serv.; 10.9% prof./bus. serv.; 8.6% leisure/hosp.; 5% finance; 5.6% constr.; 2.1% info. **Per cap.**

pers. income (2002): $27,711. Sales tax (2003): 4.5%. Unemployment (2002): 6.7%. Tourism expends. (2000): $12.8 bil.

Finance. FDIC-insured commercial banks (2002): 70. Deposits: $673.5 bil. FDIC-insured savings institutions (2002): 38. Assets: $6.6 bil.

Federal govt. Fed. civ. employees (Mar. 2002): 30,562. Avg. salary: $48,874. Notable fed. facilities: Ft. Bragg; Camp LeJeune Marine Base; U.S. EPA R &D Labs, Cherry Point Marine Corps Air Station; Natl. Humanities Ctr.; Natl. Inst. of Environmental Health Science; Natl. Ctr. for Health Statistics Lab, Research Triangle Park.

Energy. Electricity production (est. 2002, kWh, by source): Coal: 71.2 bil; Petroleum: 348 mil; Gas: 1.9 bil; Hydroelectric: 2.4 bil; Nuclear: 39.6 bil.

State data. Motto: Esse Quam Videri (To be rather than to seem). Flower: Dogwood. Bird: Cardinal. Tree: Pine. Song: The Old North State. Twelfth of the original 13 states to ratify the Constitution, Nov. 21, 1789. State fair at Raleigh; mid-Oct.

History. Algonquian, Siouan, and Iroquoian peoples lived in the region at the time of European contact. The first English colony in America was the first of 2 established by Sir Walter Raleigh on Roanoke Island, 1585 and 1587. The first group returned to England; the second, the "Lost Colony," disappeared without a trace. Permanent settlers came from Virginia, c 1660. Roused by British repression, the colonists drove out the royal governor, 1775. The province's congress was the first to vote for independence; ten regiments were furnished to the Continental Army. Cornwallis's forces were defeated at Kings Mountain, 1780, and forced out after Guilford Courthouse, 1781. The state seceded in 1861, and provided more troops to the Confederacy than any other state; readmitted in 1868.

Tourist attractions. Cape Hatteras and Cape Lookout natl. seashores; Great Smoky Mts.; Guilford Courthouse and Moore's Creek parks; 66 American Revolution battle sites; Bennett Place, near Durham, where Gen. Joseph Johnston surrendered the last Confederate army to Gen. William Sherman; Ft. Raleigh, Roanoke Island, where Virginia Dare, first child of English parents in the New World, was born Aug. 18, 1587; Wright Brothers Natl. Memorial, Kitty Hawk; Battleship North Carolina, Wilmington; NC Zoo, Asheboro; NC Symphony, NC Museum, Raleigh; Carl Sandburg Home, Hendersonville, Biltmore House & Gardens, Asheville.

Famous North Carolinians. David Brinkley, Robert Byrd, Shirley Caesar, John Coltrane, Rick Dees, Elizabeth Hanford Dole, John Edwards, Ava Gardner, Richard J. Gatling, Billy Graham, Andy Griffith, O. Henry, Andrew Jackson, Andrew Johnson, Michael Jordan, Wm. Rufus King, Charles Kuralt, Meadowlark Lemon, Dolley Madison, Thelonious Monk, Edward R. Murrow, Arnold Palmer, Richard Petty, James K. Polk, Charlie Rose, Carl Sandburg, Enos Slaughter, Dean Smith, James Taylor, Thomas Wolfe.

Tourist information. North Carolina Division of Tourism, Film & Sports Development, 301 N. Wilmington St., Raleigh, NC 27601; 1-800-VISITNC. Website: www.visitnc.com Website. www.nc.gov

North Dakota
Peace Garden State

People. Population (2002 est.): 634,110; rank: 48; net change (2001-2002): −0.4%. Pop. density: 9.2 per sq mi. Racial distribution (2000): 92.4% white; 0.6% black; 0.6% Asian; 4.9% Native American/Nat. AK; <0.1% Hawaiian/Pacific Islander; 0.4% other race; 2 or more races, 1.2%. Hispanic pop. (any race): 1.2%.

Geography. Total area: 70,700 sq mi; rank: 19. Land area: 68,976 sq mi; rank: 17. Acres forested: 0.7 mil. Location: West North Central state, situated exactly in the middle of North America, bounded on the N by Canada, on the E by Minnesota, on the S by South Dakota, on the W by Montana. Climate: continental, with a wide range of temperature and moderate rainfall. Topography: Central Lowland in the E comprises the flat Red River Valley and the Rolling Drift Prairie; Missouri Plateau of the Great Plains on the W. Capital: Bismarck.

Economy. Chief industries: agriculture, mining, tourism, manufacturing, telecommunications, energy, food processing. Chief manuf. goods: farm equipment, processed foods, fabricated metal, high-tech. electronics. Chief crops: spring wheat, durum, barley, flaxseed, oats, potatoes, dry edible beans, honey, soybeans, sugar beets, sunflowers, rye. Livestock: (Jan. 2003) 2.0 mil cattle/calves; 125,000 sheep/lambs; (Dec. 2002) 154,000 hogs/pigs. Timber/lumber (est.

2002): 1 mil bd. ft.; oak, ash, cottonwood, aspen. Nonfuel minerals (est. 2002): $38.7 mil.; sand and gravel (construction), lime, stone (crushed), clays (common), sand and gravel (industrial). Principal internat. airport at: Fargo. New private housing (2002): 3,265 units/$310 mil. Gross state product (2001): $19.0 bil. Employment distrib. (May 2003): 22.8% govt.; 21.6% trade/trans./util.; 7% mfg.; 14.2% ed./ health serv.; 7.1% prof./bus. serv.; 9.1% leisure/hosp.; 5.4% finance; 4.6% constr.; 2.4% info. Per cap. pers. income (2002): $26,982. Sales tax (2003): 5%. Unemployment (2002): 4.0%. Tourism expends. (2000): $1.2 bil.

Finance. FDIC-insured commercial banks (2002): 104. Deposits: $13.7 bil. FDIC-insured savings institutions (2002): 3. Assets: $1.0 bil.

Federal govt. Fed. civ. employees (Mar. 2002): 5,047. Avg. salary: $47,068. Notable fed. facilities: Strategic Air Command Base; Northern Prairie Wildlife Res. Ctr.; Garrison Dam; Theodore Roosevelt Natl. Park; Grand Forks Energy Res. Ctr.; Ft. Union Natl. Historic Site.

Energy. Electricity production (est. 2002, kWh, by source): Coal: 29.5 bil; Petroleum: 36 mil; Hydroelectric: 1.6 bil.

State data. Motto: Liberty and union, now and forever, one and inseparable. Flower: Wild prairie rose. Bird: Western meadowlark. Tree: American elm. Song: North Dakota Hymn. Entered union Nov. 2, 1889; rank, 39th. State fair at Minot; July.

History. At the time of European contact, the Ojibwa, Yanktonai and Teton Sioux, Mandan, Arikara, and Hidatsa peoples lived in the region. Pierre de Varennes was the first French fur trader in the area, 1738, followed later by the English. The U.S. acquired half the territory in the Louisiana Purchase, 1803. Lewis and Clark built Ft. Mandan, near present-day Stanton, 1804-5, and wintered there. In 1818, American ownership of the other half was confirmed by agreement with Britain. The first permanent settlement was at Pembina, 1812. Missouri River steamboats reached the area, 1832, the first railroad, 1873, bringing many homesteaders. The "bonanza farm" craze of the 1870s-80s attracted many settlers. The state was first to hold a national Presidential primary, 1912.

Tourist attractions. North Dakota Heritage Center, Bismarck; Bonanzaville, Fargo; Ft. Union Trading Post Natl. Historic Site; Lake Sakakawea; Intl. Peace Garden; Theodore Roosevelt Natl. Park, including Elkhorn Ranch, Badlands; Ft. Abraham Lincoln State Park and Museum, near Mandan; Dakota Dinosaur Museum, Dickinson; Knife River Indian Villages-National Historic Site.

Famous North Dakotans. Maxwell Anderson, Angie Dickinson, John Bernard Flannagan, Phil Jackson, Louis L'Amour, Peggy Lee, Eric Sevareid, Vilhjalmur Stefansson, Lawrence Welk.

Greater North Dakota Association (Chamber of Commerce). PO Box 2639, 2000 Schafer St., Bismarck, ND 58501; 1-800-HELLO-ND. Website: www.ndtourism.com Website. www.discovernd.com

Ohio
Buckeye State

People. Population (2002 est.): 11,421,267; rank: 7; net change (2001-2002): 0.3%. Pop. density: 278.9 per sq mi. Racial distribution (2000): 85.0% white; 11.5% black; 1.2% Asian; 0.2% Native American/Nat. AK; <0.1% Hawaiian/Pacific Islander; 0.8% other race; 2 or more races, 1.4%. Hispanic pop. (any race): 1.9%.

Geography. Total area: 44,825 sq mi; rank: 34. Land area: 40,948 sq mi; rank: 35. Acres forested: 7.9 mil. Location: East North Central state bounded on the N by Michigan and Lake Erie, on the E and S by Pennsylvania, West Virginia, and Kentucky; on the W by Indiana. Climate: temperate but variable; weather subject to much precipitation. Topography: generally rolling plain; Allegheny plateau in E; Lake Erie plains extend southward; central plains in the W. Capital: Columbus.

Economy. Chief industries: manufacturing, trade, services. Chief manuf. goods: transportation equipment, machinery, primary and fabricated metal products. Chief crops: corn, hay, winter wheat, oats, soybeans. Livestock: (Jan. 2003) 1.3 mil cattle/calves; 150,000 sheep/lambs; (Dec. 2002) 1.4 mil hogs/pigs; 37.9 mil chickens (excl. broilers); 39 mil broilers. Timber/lumber (est. 2002): 381 mil bd. ft.; oak, ash, maple, walnut, beech. Nonfuel minerals (est. 2002): $1.1 bil.; stone (crushed), sand and gravel (construction), salt, lime, cement (portland). Commercial fishing (2001): $3.3 mil. Chief ports: Toledo, Conneaut, Cleveland, Ashtabula. Principal internat. airports at: Akron, Cincinnati, Cleveland, Columbus,

Dayton. **New private housing** (2002): 51,246 units/$6.8 bil. **Gross state product** (2001): $373.7 bil. **Employment distrib.** (May 2003): 15.1% govt.; 19.3% trade/trans./util.; 15.9% mfg.; 13.2% ed./health serv.; 11.3% prof./bus. serv.; 9.2% leisure/hosp.; 5.7% finance; 4.3% constr.; 1.8% info. **Per cap. pers. income** (2002): $29,405. **Sales tax** (2003): 5%. **Unemployment** (2002): 5.7%. **Tourism expends.** (2000): $13.6 bil. **Lottery** (2002): total sales: $2 bil; net income: $635.2 mil.

Finance. FDIC-insured commercial banks (2002): 199. **Deposits:** $341.0 bil. **FDIC-insured savings institutions** (2002): 116. **Assets:** $45.9 bil.

Federal govt. Fed. civ. employees (Mar. 2002): 41,642. **Avg. salary:** $57,497. **Notable fed. facilities:** Wright Patterson AFB; Defense Supply Ctr., Columbus; NASA John H. Glenn Res. Ctr.; Portsmouth Gaseous Diffusion Plant; Lima Army Tank Plant.

Energy. Electricity production (est. 2002, kWh, by source): Coal: 125.6 bil; Petroleum: 341 mil; Gas: 803 mil; Hydroelectric: 473 mil; Nuclear: 10.9 bil.

State data. Motto: With God, all things are possible. **Flower:** Scarlet carnation. **Bird:** Cardinal. **Tree:** Buckeye. **Song:** Beautiful Ohio. **Entered union** Mar. 1, 1803; rank, 17th. **State fair** at Columbus; Aug.

History. Wyandot, Delaware, Miami, and Shawnee peoples sparsely occupied the area when the first Europeans arrived. La Salle visited the region, 1669, and France claimed the area, 1682. Around 1730, traders from Pennsylvania and Virginia entered the area; the French and their Native American allies sought to drive them out. France ceded its claim, 1763, to Britain. During the American Revolution, George Rogers Clark seized British posts and held the region, until Britain gave up its claim, 1783, in the Treaty of Paris. The region became U.S. territory after the American Revolution. First organized settlement was at Marietta, 1788. Indian warfare ended with Anthony Wayne's victory at Fallen Timbers, 1794. In the War of 1812, Oliver Hazard Perry's victory on Lake Erie and William Henry Harrison's invasion of Canada, 1813, ended British incursions.

Tourist attractions. Mound City Group, a group of 24 prehistoric Indian burial mounds in Hopewell Culture Natl. Historical Park; Neil Armstrong Air and Space Museum, Wapakoneta; Air Force Museum, Dayton; Pro Football Hall of Fame, Canton; King's Island amusement park, Mason; Lake Erie Islands, Cedar Point amusement park, both Sandusky; birthplaces, homes of, and memorials to U.S. Pres. W. H. Harrison, Grant, Garfield, Hayes, McKinley, Harding, Taft, B. Harrison; Amish Region, Tuscarawas/Holmes counties; German Village, Columbus; Sea World, Aurora; Jack Nicklaus Sports Center, Mason; Bob Evans Farm, Rio Grande; Rock and Roll Hall of Fame and Museum, Cleveland.

Famous Ohioans. Sherwood Anderson, Neil Armstrong, George Bellows, Halle Berry, Ambrose Bierce, Erma Bombeck, Drew Carey, Hart Crane, George Custer, Clarence Darrow, Paul Laurence Dunbar, Thomas Edison, Clark Gable, John Glenn, Zane Grey, Bob Hope, William Dean Howells, Toni Morrison, Jack Nicklaus, Jesse Owens, Pontiac, Eddie Rickenbacker, John D. Rockefeller Sr. and Jr., Roy Rogers, Pete Rose, Arthur Schlesinger Jr., Gen. William Sherman, Steven Spielberg, Gloria Steinem, Harriet Beecher Stowe, Charles Taft, Robert A. Taft, William H. Taft, Tecumseh, James Thurber, Ted Turner, Orville and Wilbur Wright.

Chamber of Commerce. PO Box 15159. 230 E. Town St., Columbus, OH 43215-0159.; 1-800-BUCKEYE. **Website:** www.ohiotourism.com

Website. www.state.oh.us

Oklahoma

Sooner State

People. Population (2002 est.): 3,493,714; rank: 28; **net change** (2001-2002): 0.7%. **Pop. density:** 50.9 per sq mi. **Racial distribution** (2000): 76.2% white; 7.6% black; 1.4% Asian; 7.9% Native American/Nat. AK; 0.1% Hawaiian/Pacific Islander; 2.4% other race; 2 or more races, 4.5%. **Hispanic pop.** (any race): 5.2%.

Geography. Total area 69,898 sq mi; rank: 20. **Land area:** 68,667 sq mi; rank: 19. **Acres forested:** 7.7 mil. **Location:** West South Central state bounded on the N by Colorado and Kansas; on the E by Missouri and Arkansas; on the S and W by Texas and New Mexico. **Climate:** temperate; southern humid belt merging with colder northern continental; humid eastern and dry western zones. **Topography:** high plains predominate in the W, hills and small mountains in the E; the east central region is dominated by the Arkansas R. Basin, and the Red R. Plains, in the S. **Capital:** Oklahoma City.

Economy. Chief industries: manufacturing, mineral and energy exploration and production, agriculture, services. **Chief manuf. goods:** nonelectrical machinery, transportation equipment, food products, fabricated metal products. **Chief crops:** wheat, cotton, hay, peanuts, grain sorghum, soybeans, corn, pecans. **Livestock** (Jan. 2003) 5.2 mil cattle/calves; 65,000 sheep/lambs; (Dec. 2002) 2.5 mil hogs/pigs; 5.6 mil chickens (excl. broilers); 232.8 mil broilers. **Timber/lumber:** (est. 2002): (undisclosed); pine, oak, hickory; **Nonfuel minerals** (est. 2002): $462 mil.; stone (crushed), cement (portland), sand and gravel (construction), sand and gravel (industrial), gypsum (crude). **Chief ports:** Catoosa, Muskogee. **Principal internat. airports at:** Oklahoma City, Tulsa. **New private housing** (2002): 12,979 units/$1.6 bil. **Gross state product** (2001): $93.9 bil. **Employment distrib.** (May 2003): 20.6% govt.; 19.2% trade/trans./util.; 9.9% mfg.; 11.5% ed./health serv.; 10.7% prof./bus. serv.; 8.9% leisure/hosp.; 5.7% finance; 4.4% constr.; 2.3% info. **Per cap. pers. income** (2002): $25,575. **Sales tax** (2003): 4.5%. **Unemployment** (2002): 4.5%. **Tourism expends.** (2000): $3.9 bil.

Finance. FDIC-insured commercial banks (2002): 274. **Deposits:** $35.5 bil. **FDIC-insured savings institutions** (2002): 6. **Assets:** $8.9 bil.

Federal govt. Fed. civ. employees (Mar. 2002): 33,088. **Avg. salary:** $48,900. **Notable fed. facilities:** FAA Mike Monroney Aeronautical Ctr.; Altus AFB; Tinker AFB; Vance AFB; Ft. Sill; Natl. Inst. for Petroleum & Energy Res.; Natl. Severe Storms Lab.

Energy. Electricity production (est. 2002, kWh, by source): Coal: 33.4 bil; Petroleum: 9 mil; Gas: 15.0 bil; Hydroelectric: 1.8 bil.

State data. Motto: Labor Omnia Vincit (Labor conquers all things). **Flower:** Mistletoe. **Bird:** Scissor-tailed flycatcher. **Tree:** Redbud. **Song:** Oklahoma! **Entered union** Nov. 16, 1907; rank, 46th. **State fair** at Oklahoma City; last 2 full weeks of Sept.

History. The region was sparsely inhabited by Native American tribes when Coronado, the first European, arrived in 1541; in the 16th and 17th cent., French traders visited. Part of the Louisiana Purchase, 1803, Oklahoma was established as Indian Territory (but not given territorial government). It became home to the "Five Civilized Tribes"—Cherokee, Choctaw, Chickasaw, Creek, and Seminole—after the forced removal of Indians from the eastern U.S., 1828-46. The land was also used by Comanche, Osage, and other Plains Indians. As white settlers pressed west, land was opened for homesteading by runs and lottery, the first run on Apr. 22, 1889. The most famous run was to the Cherokee Outlet, 1893.

Tourist attractions. Cherokee Heritage Center, Tahlequah; Oklahoma City Natl. Memorial; White Water Bay and Frontier City theme pks., both Oklahoma City; Will Rogers Memorial, Claremore; Natl. Cowboy Hall of Fame and Remington Park Race Track, both Oklahoma City; Ft. Gibson Stockade, near Muskogee; Ouachita Natl. Forest; Tulsa's art deco district; Wichita Mts. Wildlife Refuge, Lawton; Woolaroc Museum & Wildlife Preserve, Bartlesville; Sequoyah's Home Site, near Sallisaw; Philbrook Museum of Art and Gilcrease Museum, both Tulsa.

Famous Oklahomans. Troy Aikman, Carl Albert, Gene Autry, Johnny Bench, William "Hopalong Cassidy" Boyd, Garth Brooks, Lon Chaney, L. Gordon Cooper, Walter Cronkite, Jerome "Dizzy" Dean, Ralph Ellison, John Hope Franklin, James Garner, Geronimo, Woody Guthrie, Paul Harvey, Ron Howard, Gen. Patrick J. Hurley, Ben Johnson, Jeane Kirkpatrick, Louis L'Amour, Shannon Lucid, Mickey Mantle, Reba McEntire, Wiley Post, Tony Randall, Oral Roberts, Will Rogers, Sam Snead, Barry Switzer, Maria Tallchief, Jim Thorpe, J.C. Watts Jr.

Chamber of Commerce. Chamber of Commerce, 330 NE 10th, Oklahoma City, OK 73104.

Tourism Dept. PO Box 60789, Oklahoma City, OK 73146-0789; 1-800-652-OKLA. **Website:** www.travelok.com

Website. www.state.ok.us

Oregon

Beaver State

People. Population (2002 est.): 3,521,515; rank: 27; **net change** (2001-2002): 1.4%. **Pop. density:** 36.7 per sq mi. **Racial distribution** (2000): 86.6% white; 1.6% black; 3.0% Asian; 1.3% Native American/Nat. AK; 0.2% Hawaiian/Pacific Islander; 4.2% other race; 2 or more races, 3.1%. **Hispanic pop.** (any race): 8.0%.

Geography. Total area 98,381 sq mi; rank: 9. **Land area:** 95,997 sq mi; rank: 10. **Acres forested:** 29.7 mil. **Location:** Pacific state, bounded on N by Washington; on E by Idaho; on

S by Nevada and California; on W by the Pacific. **Climate:** coastal mild and humid climate; continental dryness and extreme temperatures in the interior. **Topography:** Coast Range of rugged mountains; fertile Willamette R. Valley to E and S; Cascade Mt. Range of volcanic peaks E of the valley; plateau E of Cascades, remaining two-thirds of state. **Capital:** Salem.

Economy. Chief industries: manufacturing, services, trade, finance, insurance, real estate, government, construction. **Chief manuf. goods:** electronics & semiconductors, lumber & wood products, metals, transportation equipment, processed food, paper. **Chief crops:** greenhouse, hay, wheat, grass seed, potatoes, onions, Christmas trees, pears, mint. **Livestock:** (Jan. 2003) 1.4 mil cattle/calves; 235,000 sheep/lambs; (Dec. 2002) 31,000 hogs/pigs; 3.4 mil chickens (excl. broilers). **Timber/lumber** (est. 2002): 6.4 bil bd. ft. Douglas fir, hemlock, ponderosa pine. **Nonfuel minerals** (est. 2002): $320 mil.; stone (crushed), sand and gravel (construction), cement (portland), diatomite, pumice and pumicite. **Commercial fishing** (2001): $69.1 mil. **Chief ports:** Portland, Astoria, Coos Bay. **Principal internat. airports at:** Portland, Medford. **New private housing** (2002): 22,186 units/ $3.3 bil. **Gross state product** (2001): $120.1 bil. **Employment distrib.** (May 2003): 17.9% govt.; 19.8% trade/trans./ util.; 12.4% mfg.; 12.1% ed./health serv.; 11% prof./bus. serv.; 9.7% leisure/hosp.; 6% finance; 4.8% constr.; 2.3% info. **Per cap. pers. income** (2002): $28,731. **Sales tax:** (2003): none. **Unemployment** (2002): 7.5%. **Tourism expends.** (2000): $5.9 bil. **Lottery** (2002): total sales: $817.1 mil; net income: $340.6 mil.

Finance. FDIC-insured commercial banks (2002): 32. **Deposits:** $7.4 bil. **FDIC-insured savings institutions** (2002): 5. **Assets:** $2.9 bil.

Federal govt. Fed. civ. employees (Mar. 2002): 17,345. **Avg. salary:** $52,314. **Notable fed. facilities:** Bonneville Power Administration.

Energy. Electricity production (est. 2002, kWh, by source): Coal: 3.8 bil; Petroleum: 6 mil; Gas: 1.8 bil; Hydroelectric: 34.1 bil.

State data. Motto: She flies with her own wings. **Flower:** Oregon grape. **Bird:** Western meadowlark. **Tree:** Douglas fir. **Song:** Oregon, My Oregon. **Entered union** Feb. 14, 1859; rank, 33rd. **State fair** at Salem; 12 days ending with Labor Day.

History. More than 100 Native American tribes inhabited the area at the time of European contact, including the Chinook, Yakima, Cayuse, Modoc, and Nez Percé. Capt. Robert Gray sighted and sailed into the Columbia River, 1792; Lewis and Clark, traveling overland, wintered at its mouth, 1805-6; John Jacob Astor established a trading post in the Columbia River region, 1811. Settlers arrived in the Williamette Valley, 1834. In 1843, the first large wave of settlers arrived via the Oregon Trail. Early in the 20th cent., the "Oregon System"—political reforms that included the initiative, referendum, recall, direct primary, and woman suffrage—was adopted.

Tourist attractions. John Day Fossil Beds Natl. Monument; Columbia River Gorge; Timberline Lodge, Mt. Hood Natl. Forest; Crater Lake Natl. Park; Oregon Dunes Natl. Recreation Area; Ft. Clatsop Natl. Memorial; Oregon Caves Natl. Monument; Oregon Museum of Science and Industry, Portland; Shakespearean Festival, Ashland; High Desert Museum, Bend; Multnomah Falls; Diamond Lake; "Spruce Goose," Evergreen Aviation Museum, McMinnville.

Famous Oregonians. Ernest Bloch, Bill Bowerman, Ernest Haycox, Chief Joseph, Ken Kesey, Phil Knight, Ursula K. Le Guin, Edwin Markham, Tom McCall, Dr. John McLoughlin, Joaquin Miller, Bob Packwood, Linus Pauling, Steve Prefontaine, John Reed, Alberto Salazar, Mary Decker Slaney, William Simon U'Ren.

Tourist information. Economic Development Department, 775 Summer St. NE, Salem, OR 97310; 1-800-547-7842.
Website: www.traveloregon.com
     Website. www.oregon.gov

Pennsylvania
Keystone State

People. Population (2002 est.): 12,335,091; rank: 6; **net change** (2001-2002): 0.3%. **Pop. density:** 275.2 per sq mi. **Racial distribution** (2000): 85.4% white; 10.0% black; 1.8% Asian; 0.1% Native American/Nat. AK; <0.1% Hawaiian/Pacific Islander; 1.5% other race; 2 or more races, 1.2%. **Hispanic pop.** (any race): 3.2%.

Geography. Total area: 46,055 sq mi; rank: 33. **Land area:** 44,817 sq mi; rank: 32. **Acres forested:** 16.9 mil. **Location:** Middle Atlantic state, bordered on the E by the Delaware R.; on the S by the Mason-Dixon Line; on the W by West Virginia and

Ohio; on the N/NE by Lake Erie and New York. **Climate:** continental with wide fluctuations in seasonal temperatures. **Topography:** Allegheny Mts. run SW to NE, with Piedmont and Coast Plain in the SE triangle; Allegheny Front a diagonal spine across the state's center; N and W rugged plateau falls to Lake Erie Lowland. **Capital:** Harrisburg.

Economy. Chief industries: agribusiness, advanced manufacturing, health care, travel & tourism, depository institutions, biotechnology, printing & publishing, research & consulting, trucking & warehousing, transportation by air, engineering & management, legal services. **Chief manuf. goods:** fabricated metal products; industrial machinery & equipment, transportation equipment, rubber & plastics, electronic equipment, chemicals & pharmaceuticals, lumber & wood products, stone, clay, & glass products. **Chief crops:** corn, hay, mushrooms, apples, potatoes, winter wheat, oats, vegetables, tobacco, grapes, peaches. **Livestock:** (Jan. 2003) 1.6 mil cattle/calves; 83,000 sheep/ lambs; (Dec. 2002) 1.1 mil hogs/pigs; 29.3 mil chickens (excl. broilers); 133.2 mil broilers. **Timber/lumber** (est. 2002): 1.1 bil bd. ft.; pine, oak, maple. **Nonfuel minerals** (est. 2002): $1.3 bil.; stone (crushed), cement (portland), sand and gravel (construction), lime, cement (masonry). **Commercial fishing** (2001): $44,000. **Chief ports:** Philadelphia, Pittsburgh, Erie. **Principal internat. airports at:** Allentown, Harrisburg, Philadelphia, Pittsburgh, Wilkes-Barre/Scranton. **New private housing** (2002): 45,114 units/ $5.6 bil. **Gross state product** (2001): $408.4 bil. **Employment distrib.** (May 2003): 13.2% govt.; 19.3% trade/trans./ util.; 12.9% mfg.; 17.4% ed./health serv.; 10.6% prof./bus. serv.; 8.5% leisure/hosp.; 6% finance; 4.5% constr.; 2.3% info. **Per cap. pers. income** (2002): $31,727. **Sales tax** (2003): 6%. **Unemployment** (2002): 5.7%. **Tourism expends.** (2000): $16 bil. **Lottery** (2002): total sales: $1.9 bil; net income: $749.2 mil.

Finance. FDIC-insured commercial banks (2002): 173. **Deposits:** $129.1 bil. **FDIC-insured savings institutions** (2002): 110. **Assets:** $107.8 bil.

Federal govt. Fed. civ. employees (Mar. 2002): 61,295. **Avg. salary:** $50,696. **Notable fed. facilities:** Carlisle Barracks; Army War College; Naval Inventory Control Point, Phila. and Mechanicsbrg; Defense Personnel Supply Ctr., Phila.; Defense Distribution Ctr., New Cumberland; Tobyhanna Army Depot; Letterkenny Army Depot; NAS Willow Grove; 911th Air Wing, Pittsburgh; Naval Surface Warfare Ctr., Phila.; Charles E. Kelly Support Facility.

Energy. Electricity production (est. 2002, kWh, by source): Coal: 15.9 bil; Petroleum: 39 mil; Gas: 1 mil; Hydroelectric: 835 mil; Nuclear: 13.6 bil.

State data. Motto: Virtue, liberty and independence. **Flower:** Mountain laurel. **Bird:** Ruffed grouse. **Tree:** Hemlock. **Song:** Pennsylvania. **Second** of the original 13 states to ratify the Constitution, Dec. 12, 1787. **State fair** at Harrisburg; 2nd week in Jan. at State Farm Show Building.

History. At the time of European contact, Lenni Lenape (Delaware), Shawnee and Iroquoian Susquehannocks, Erie, and Seneca occupied the region. Swedish explorers established the first permanent settlement, 1643, on Tinicum Island. In 1655, the Dutch seized the settlement but lost it to the British, 1664. The region was given by Charles II to William Penn, 1681. Philadelphia ("brotherly love") was the capital of the colonies during most of the American Revolution, and of the U.S., 1790-1800. Philadelphia was taken by the British, 1777; Washington's troops encamped at Valley Forge in the bitter winter of 1777-78. The Declaration of Independence, 1776, and the Constitution, 1787, were signed in Philadelphia. The Civil War battle of Gettysburg, July 1-3, 1863, marked a turning point, favoring Union forces.

Tourist attractions. Independence Natl. Historic Park, Franklin Institute Science Museum, Philadelphia Museum of Art, all in Philadelphia; Valley Forge Natl. Historic Park; Gettysburg Natl. Military Park; Pennsylvania Dutch Country; Hershey; Duquesne Incline, Carnegie Institute, Heinz Hall, all in Pittsburgh; Pocono Mts.; Pennsylvania's Grand Canyon, Tioga County; Allegheny Natl. Forest; Laurel Highlands; Presque Isle State Park; Fallingwater, Mill Run; Johnstown; SteamTown U.S.A., Scranton; State Flagship Niagara, Erie; Oil Heritage Region, Northwest PA.

Famous Pennsylvanians. Marian Anderson, Maxwell Anderson, George Blanda, James Buchanan, Andrew Carnegie, Rachel Carson, Perry Como, Bill Cosby, Thomas Eakins, Stephen Foster, Benjamin Franklin, Robert Fulton, Martha Graham, Milton Hershey, Gene Kelly, Grace Kelly (Princess Grace of Monaco), Dan Marino, George C. Marshall, Chris Matthews, John J. McCloy, Margaret Mead, Andrew W. Mellon, Joe Montana, Stan Musial, Joe Namath,

John O'Hara, Arnold Palmer, Robert E. Peary, Mike Piazza, Tom Ridge, Mary Roberts Rinehart, Fred Rogers, Betsy Ross, Will Smith, Jimmy Stewart, Jim Thorpe, Johnny Unitas, John Updike, Honus Wagner, Andy Warhol, Benjamin West.

Chamber of Business and Industry. 417 Walnut St., Harrisburg, PA 17120; 1-800-VISITPA. **Website:** www.experiencepa.co

Website. www.state.pa.us

Rhode Island
Little Rhody, Ocean State

People. Population (2002 est.): 1,069,725; rank: 43; **net change** (2001-2002): 0.9%. **Pop. density:** 1,023.7 per sq mi. **Racial distribution** (2000): 85.0% white; 4.5% black; 2.3% Asian; 0.5% Native American/Nat. AK; 0.1% Hawaiian/Pacific Islander; 5.0% other race; 2 or more races, 2.7%. **Hispanic pop.** (any race): 8.7%.

Geography. Total area: 1,545 sq mi; rank: 50. **Land area:** 1,045 sq mi; rank: 50. **Acres forested:** 0.4 mil. **Location:** New England state. **Climate:** invigorating and changeable. **Topography:** eastern lowlands of Narragansett Basin; western uplands of flat and rolling hills. **Capital:** Providence.

Economy. Chief industries: services, manufacturing. **Chief manuf. goods:** costume jewelry, toys, machinery, textiles, electronics. **Chief crops:** nursery products, turf & vegetable production. **Livestock:** (Jan. 2003) 5,500 cattle/calves; (Dec. 2002) 2,900 hogs/pigs. **Timber/lumber** (est. 2002): 10 mil bd. ft.; **Nonfuel minerals** (est. 2002): $17.3 mil.; sand and gravel (construction), stone (crushed), sand and gravel (industrial), gemstones. **Commercial fishing** (2001): $65.5 mil. **Chief ports:** Providence, Quonset Point, Newport. **New private housing** (2002): 2,848 units/$344 mil. **Gross state product** (2001): $36.9 bil. **Employment distrib.** (May 2003): 13.7% govt.; 16.9% trade/trans./util.; 12.5% mfg.; 18.8% ed./health serv.; 9.9% prof./bus. serv.; 10.1% leisure/hosp.; 6.7% finance; 4.1% constr.; 2.3% info. **Per cap. pers. income** (2002): $31,319. **Sales tax** (2003): 7%. **Unemployment** (2002): 5.1%. **Tourism expends.** (2000): $1.5 bil. **Lottery** (2002): total sales: $1.2 bil; net income: $214.1 mil.

Finance. FDIC-insured commercial banks (2002): 7. **Deposits:** $139.3 bil. **FDIC-insured savings institutions** (2002): 7. **Assets:** $2.3 bil.

Federal govt. Fed. civ. employees (Mar. 2002): 5,820. **Avg. salary:** $61,772. **Notable fed. facilities:** Naval War College; Naval Underwater Warfare Ctr.; Natl. Marine Fisheries Lab; EPA Environmental Res. Lab.

Energy. Electricity production (est. 2002, kWh, by source): Petroleum: 8 mil.

State data. Motto: Hope. **Flower:** Violet. **Bird:** Rhode Island red. **Tree:** Red maple. **Song:** Rhode Island. **Thirteenth** of original 13 states to ratify the Constitution, May 29, 1790. **State fair** at Richmond; mid-Aug.

History. When the Europeans arrived Narragansett, Niantic, Nipmuc, and Wampanoag peoples lived in the region. Verrazano visited the area, 1524. The first permanent settlement was founded at Providence, 1636, by Roger Williams, who was exiled from the Massachusetts Bay Colony; Anne Hutchinson, also exiled, settled Portsmouth, 1638. Quaker and Jewish immigrants seeking freedom of worship began arriving, 1650s-60s. The colonists broke the power of the Narragansett in the Great Swamp Fight, 1675, the decisive battle in King Philip's War. British trade restrictions angered colonists, and they burned the British customs vessel *Gaspee*, 1772. The colony became the first to formally renounce all allegiance to King George III, May 4, 1776. Initially opposed to joining the Union, Rhode Island was the last of the 13 colonies to ratify the Constitution, 1790.

Tourist attractions. Newport mansions; yachting races including Newport to Bermuda; Block Island; Touro Synagogue, oldest in U.S.; Newport; first Baptist Church in America, Providence; Slater Mill Historic Site, Pawtucket; Gilbert Stuart birthplace, Saunderstown.

Famous Rhode Islanders. Ambrose Burnside, George M. Cohan, Nelson Eddy, Jabez Gorham, Nathanael Greene, Christopher and Oliver La Farge, John McLaughlin, Matthew C. and Oliver Hazard Perry, Gilbert Stuart.

Tourist Information. Rhode Island Economic Development Corporation, One W. Exchange St., Providence, RI 02903; 1-800-556-2484. **Website:** visitrhodeisland.com

Website. www.state.ri.us

South Carolina
Palmetto State

People. Population (2002 est.): 4,107,183; rank: 25; **net change** (2001-2002): 1.1%. **Pop. density:** 136.4 per sq mi. **Racial distribution** (2000): 67.2% white; 29.5% black; 0.9% Asian; 0.3% Native American/Nat. AK; <0.1% Hawaiian/Pacific Islander; 1.0% other race; 2 or more races, 1.0%. **Hispanic pop.** (any race): 2.4%.

Geography. Total area: 32,020 sq mi; rank: 40. **Land area:** 30,109 sq mi; rank: 40. **Acres forested:** 12.5 mil. **Location:** South Atlantic state, bordered by North Carolina on the N; Georgia on the SW and W; the Atlantic Ocean on the E, SE, and S. **Climate:** humid subtropical. **Topography:** Blue Ridge province in NW has highest peaks; piedmont lies between the mountains and the fall line; coastal plain covers two-thirds of the state. **Capital:** Columbia.

Economy. Chief industries: tourism, agriculture, manufacturing. **Chief manuf. goods:** textiles, chemicals and allied products, machinery and fabricated metal products, apparel and related products. **Chief crops:** tobacco, cotton, soybeans, corn, wheat, peaches, tomatoes. **Livestock:** (Jan. 2003) 430,000 cattle/calves; (Dec. 2002) 300,000 hogs/pigs; 6.6 mil chickens (excl. broilers); 192.9 mil broilers. **Timber/lumber** (est. 2002): 1.4 bil bd. ft.; pine, oak. **Nonfuel minerals** (est. 2002): $460 mil.; cement (portland), stone (crushed), cement (masonry), sand and gravel (construction), clays (kaolin). **Commercial fishing** (2001): $23.9 mil. **Gross state product** (2001): $115.2 bil. **Principal internat. airports at:** Charleston, Greenville/Spartanburg, Myrtle Beach. **New private housing** (2002): 34,104 units/$4.1 bil. **Employment distrib.** (May 2003): 17.7% govt.; 19.1% trade/trans./util.; 15.5% mfg.; 9.8% ed./health serv.; 9.8% prof./bus. serv.; 10.5% leisure/hosp.; 5% finance; 6% constr.; 1.5% info. **Per cap. pers. income** (2002): $25,400. **Sales tax** (2003): 5%. **Unemployment** (2002): 6.0%. **Tourism expends.** (2000): $7.4 bil. **Lottery** (2002): total sales: $335.5 mil; net income: $81.2 mil.

Finance. FDIC-insured commercial banks (2002): 77. **Deposits:** $21.5 bil. **FDIC-insured savings institutions** (2002): 25. **Assets:** $7.6 bil.

Federal govt. Fed. civ. employees (Mar. 2002): 15,887. **Avg. salary:** $49,506. **Notable fed. facilities:** Polaris Submarine Base; Barnwell Nuclear Power Plant; Ft. Jackson; Parris Island; Savannah River Plant.

Energy. Electricity production (est. 2002, kWh, by source): Coal: 36.5 bil; Petroleum: 178 mil; Gas: 3.5 bil; Hydroelectric: 185 mil; Nuclear: 53.3 bil; Other: 16 mil.

State data. Motto: Dum Spiro Spero (While I breathe, I hope). **Flower:** Yellow jessamine. **Bird:** Carolina wren. **Tree:** Palmetto. **Song:** Carolina. **Eighth** of the original 13 states to ratify the Constitution, May 23, 1788. **State fair** at Columbia; mid-Oct.

History. At the time of European settlement, Cherokee, Catawba, and Muskogean peoples lived in the area. The first English colonists settled near the Ashley River, 1670, and moved to the site of Charleston, 1680. The colonists seized the government, 1775, and the royal governor fled. The British took Charleston, 1780, but were defeated at Kings Mountain that same year, and at Cowpens and Eutaw Springs, 1781. In the 1830s, South Carolinians, angered by federal protective tariffs, adopted the Nullification Doctrine, holding that a state can void an act of Congress. The state was the first to secede from the Union, 1860, and Confederate troops fired on and forced the surrender of U.S. troops at Ft. Sumter, in Charleston Harbor, launching the Civil War. South Carolina was readmitted,1868.

Tourist attractions. Historic Charleston; Ft. Sumter Natl. Monument, in Charleston Harbor; Charleston Museum, est. 1773, oldest museum in U.S.; Middleton Place, Magnolia Plantation, Cypress Gardens, Drayton Hall, all near Charleston; other gardens at Brookgreen, Edisto, Glencairn; Myrtle Beach; Hilton Head Island; Revolutionary War battle sites; Andrew Jackson State Park & Museum; South Carolina State Museum, Columbia; Riverbanks Zoo, Columbia.

Famous South Carolinians. Charles Bolden, James F. Byrnes, John C. Calhoun, Joe Fraizer, DuBose Heyward, Ernest F. Hollings, Andrew Jackson, Jesse Jackson, "Shoeless" Joe Jackson, James Longstreet, Francis Marion, Andie McDowell, Ronald McNair, Charles Pinckney, John Rutledge, Thomas Sumter, Strom Thurmond, John B. Watson.

Tourist information. S. Carolina Dept. of Parks, Recreation, & Tourism; 803-734-0122; 1-800-346-3634. **Website:** www.discoversouthcarolina.com

Website. www.myscgov.com

South Dakota
Coyote State, Mount Rushmore State

People. Population (2002 est.): 761,063; rank: 46; **net change** (2001-2002): 0.4%. **Pop. density:** 10.0 per sq mi. **Racial distribution** (2000): 88.7% white; 0.6% black; 0.6% Asian; 8.3% Native American/Nat. AK; <0.1% Hawaiian/Pacific Islander; 0.5% other race; 2 or more races, 1.3%. **Hispanic pop.** (any race): 1.4%.

Geography. Total area: 77,116 sq mi; rank: 17. **Land area:** 75,885 sq mi; rank: 16. **Acres forested:** 1.6 mil. **Location:** West North Central state bounded on the N by North Dakota; on the E by Minnesota and Iowa; on the S by Nebraska; on the W by Wyoming and Montana. **Climate:** characterized by extremes of temperature, persistent winds, low precipitation and humidity. **Topography:** Prairie Plains in the E; rolling hills of the Great Plains in the W; the Black Hills, rising 3,500 ft, in the SW corner. **Capital:** Pierre.

Economy. Chief industries: agriculture, services, manufacturing. **Chief manuf. goods:** food and kindred products, machinery, electric and electronic equipment. **Chief crops:** corn, soybeans, oats, wheat, sunflowers, sorghum. **Livestock:** (Jan. 2003) 4.0 mil cattle/calves; 380,000 sheep/lambs; (Dec. 2002) 1.3 mil hogs/pigs; 2.7 mil chickens (excl. broilers). **Timber/lumber** (est. 2002): (undisclosed); ponderosa pine. **Nonfuel minerals** (est. 2002): $186 mil.; cement (portland), sand and gravel (construction), stone (crushed), gold, stone (dimension). **New private housing** (2002): 4,816 units/$464 mil. **Gross state product** (2001): $24.3 bil. **Employment distrib.** (May 2003): 20% govt.; 20.2% trade/trans./util.; 9.8% mfg.; 14.5% ed./health serv.; 6.3% prof./bus. serv.; 10.6% leisure/hosp.; 7.2% finance; 5.1% constr.; 1.8% info. **Per cap. pers. income** (2002): $26,894. **Sales tax** (2003): 4%. **Unemployment** (2002): 3.1%. **Tourism expends.** (2000): $1.4 bil. **Lottery** (2002): total sales: $629.9 mil; net income: $109.3 mil.

Finance. FDIC-insured commercial banks (2002): 93. **Deposits:** $14.3 bil. **FDIC-insured savings institutions** (2002): 4. **Assets:** $1.2 bil.

Federal govt. Fed. civ. employees (Mar. 2002): 6,973. **Avg. salary:** $45,782. **Notable fed. facilities:** Ellsworth AFB, Corp of Engineers, Nat'l Park Service.

Energy. Electricity production (est. 2002, kWh, by source): Coal: 3.3 bil; Petroleum: 4 mil; Gas: 86 mil; Hydroelectric: 4.4 bil; Other: 6 mil.

State data. Motto: Under God, the people rule. **Flower:** Pasqueflower. **Bird:** Chinese ring-necked pheasant. **Tree:** Black Hills spruce. **Song:** Hail, South Dakota. **Entered union** Nov. 2, 1889; rank, 40th. **State fair** at Huron; late July-early Aug.

History. At the time of first European contact, Mandan, Hidatsa, Arikara, and Sioux lived in the area. The French Verendrye brothers explored the region, 1742-43. The U.S. acquired the area, 1803, in the Louisiana Purchase. Lewis and Clark passed through the area, 1804-6. In 1817 a trading post was opened at Fort Pierre, which later became the site of the first European settlement in South Dakota. Gold was discovered, 1874, in the Black Hills on the great Sioux reservation; the "Great Dakota Boom" began in 1879. Conflicts with Native Americans led to the Great Sioux Agreement, 1889, which established reservations and opened up more land for white settlement. The massacre of Native American families at Wounded Knee, 1890, ended Sioux resistance.

Tourist attractions. Black Hills; Mt. Rushmore; Needles Highway; Harney Peak, tallest E. of Rockies; Deadwood, 1876 Gold Rush town; Custer State Park; Jewel Cave Natl. Monument; Badlands Natl. Park "moonscape"; "Great Lakes of S. Dakota"; Ft. Sisseton; Great Plains Zoo & Museum, Sioux Falls; Corn Palace, Mitchell; Wind Cave Natl. Park; Crazy Horse Memorial, mountain carving in progress.

Famous South Dakotans. Sparky Anderson, Black Elk, Bob Barker, Tom Brokaw, Crazy Horse, Thomas Daschle, Myron Floren, Mary Hart, Cheryl Ladd, Dr. Ernest O. Lawrence, George McGovern, Billy Mills, Allen Neuharth, Pat O'Brien, Sitting Bull.

Tourist information. Department of Tourism, Capitol Lake Plaza, 711 E. Wells Ave., c/o 500 E. Capitol Ave., Pierre, SD 57501-5070; 1-800-SDAKOTA. **Website:** www.travelsd.com **Website.** www.state.sd.us

Tennessee
Volunteer State

People. Population (2002 est.): 5,797,289; rank: 16; **net change** (2001-2002): 0.8%. **Pop. density:** 140.7 per sq mi. **Racial distribution** (2000): 80.2% white; 16.4% black; 1.0% Asian; 0.3% Native American/Nat. AK; <0.1% Hawaiian/Pacific Islander; 1.0% other race; 2 or more races, 1.1%. **Hispanic pop.** (any race): 2.2%.

Geography. Total area: 42,143 sq mi; rank: 36. **Land area:** 41,217 sq mi; rank: 34. **Acres forested:** 14.4 mil. **Location:** East South Central state bounded on the N by Kentucky and Virginia; on the E by North Carolina; on the S by Georgia, Alabama, and Mississippi; on the W by Arkansas and Missouri. **Climate:** humid continental to the N; humid subtropical to the S. **Topography:** rugged country in the E; the Great Smoky Mts. of the Unakas; low ridges of the Appalachian Valley; the flat Cumberland Plateau; slightly rolling terrain and knobs of the Interior Low Plateau, the largest region; Eastern Gulf Coastal Plain to the W, laced with streams; Mississippi Alluvial Plain, a narrow strip of swamp and flood plain in the extreme W. **Capital:** Nashville.

Economy. Chief industries: manufacturing, trade, services, tourism, finance, insurance, real estate. **Chief manuf. goods:** chemicals, food, transportation equipment, industrial machinery & equipment, fabricated metal products, rubber/ plastic products, paper & allied products, printing & publishing. **Chief crops:** tobacco, cotton, lint, soybeans, grain, corn. **Livestock:** (Jan. 2003) 2.2 mil cattle/calves; (Dec. 2002) 220,000 hogs/pigs; 2.2 mil chickens (excl. broilers); 186.4 mil broilers. **Timber/lumber** (est. 2002): 899 mil bd. ft.; red oak, white oak, yellow poplar, hickory. **Nonfuel minerals** (est. 2002): $629 mil.; stone (crushed), cement (portland), zinc, sand and gravel (construction), clays (ball). **Chief ports:** Memphis, Nashville, Chattanooga, Knoxville. **Principal internat. airports at:** Memphis, Nashville. **New private housing** (2002): 34,273 units/$4.0 bil. **Gross state product** (2001): $182.5 bil. **Employment distrib.** (May 2003): 15.3% govt.; 21.3% trade/trans./util.; 15.5% mfg.; 11.5% ed./health serv.; 11.7% prof./bus. serv.; 9.2% leisure/ hosp.; 5.2% finance; 4.1% constr.; 1.9% info. **Per cap. pers. income** (2002): $27,671. **Sales tax** (2003): 7%. **Unemployment** (2002): 5.1%. **Tourism expends.** (2000): $10.3 bil.

Finance. FDIC-insured commercial banks (2002): 192. **Deposits:** $79.0 bil. **FDIC-insured savings institutions** (2002): 21. **Assets:** $5.4 bil.

Federal govt. Fed. civ. employees (Mar. 2002): 33,991. **Avg. salary:** $50,777. **Notable fed. facilities:** Tennessee Valley Authority; Oak Ridge Nat'l. Lab; Arnold Engineering Development Ctr.; Ft. Campbell; Naval Support Activity, Mid-South.

Energy. Electricity production (est. 2002, kWh, by source): Coal: 58.1 bil; Petroleum: 196 mil; Gas: 40 mil; Hydroelectric: 6.6 bil; Nuclear: 27.6 bil.

State data. Motto: Agriculture and commerce. **Flower:** Iris. **Bird:** Mockingbird. **Tree:** Tulip poplar. **Songs:** My Homeland, Tennessee; When It's Iris Time in Tennessee; My Tennessee; Tennessee Waltz; Rocky Top. **Entered union** June 1, 1796; rank, 16th. **State fair** at Nashville; mid-Sept.

History. When the first European explorers arrived, Creek and Yuchi peoples lived in the area; the Cherokee moved into the region in the early 18th cent. Spanish explorers first visited the area, 1541. English traders crossed the Great Smokies from the east while France's Marquette and Jolliet sailed down the Mississippi on the west, 1673. The first permanent settlement was by Virginians on the Watauga River, 1769. During the American Revolution, the colonists helped win the Battle of Kings Mountain (NC), 1780, and joined other eastern campaigns. The state seceded from the Union, 1861, and saw many Civil War engagements, but 30,000 soldiers fought for the Union. Tennessee was readmitted in 1866, the only former Confederate state not to have a postwar military government.

Tourist attractions. Reelfoot Lake; Lookout Mountain, Chattanooga; Fall Creek Falls; Great Smoky Mountains Natl. Park; Lost Sea, Sweetwater; Cherokee Natl. Forest; Cumberland Gap Natl. Park; Andrew Jackson's home, the Hermitage, near Nashville; homes of Pres. Polk and Andrew Johnson; American Museum of Science and Energy, Oak Ridge; Parthenon, Grand Old Opry, Opryland USA, all Nashville; Dollywood theme park, Pigeon Forge; Tennessee Aquarium, Chattanooga; Graceland, home of Elvis Presley, Memphis; Alex Haley Home and Museum, Henning; Casey Jones Home and Museum, Jackson.

Famous Tennesseans. Roy Acuff, Davy Crockett, David Farragut, Ernie Ford, Aretha Franklin, Morgan Freeman, Bill Frist, Al Gore Jr., Alex Haley, William C. Handy, Sam Houston, Cordell Hull, Andrew Jackson, Andrew Johnson, Casey Jones, Estes Kefauver, Grace Moore, Dolly Parton, Minnie Pearl, James Polk, Elvis Presley, Dinah Shore, Bessie Smith, Fred Thompson, Hank Williams Jr., Alvin York.

Tourist information. Dept. of Tourist Development, 5th Floor, Rachel Jackson Bldg., 320 6th Ave. N., Nashville, TN 37202. **Website:** www.tennesseeanytime.org/travel/index.html

Website. www.tn.gov

Texas
Lone Star State

People. Population (2002 est.): 21,779,893; rank: 2; **net change** (2001-2002): 1.9%. **Pop. density:** 83.2 per sq mi. **Racial distribution** (2000): 71.0% white; 11.5% black; 2.7% Asian; 0.6% Native American/Nat. AK; 0.1% Hawaiian/Pacific Islander; 11.7% other race; 2 or more races, 2.5%. **Hispanic pop.** (any race): 32.0%.

Geography. Total area: 268,581 sq mi; rank: 2. **Land area:** 261,797 sq mi; rank: 2. **Acres forested:** 17.1 mil. **Location:** Southwestern state, bounded on the SE by the Gulf of Mexico; on the SW by Mexico, separated by the Rio Grande; surrounding states are Louisiana, Arkansas, Oklahoma, New Mexico. **Climate:** extremely varied; driest region is the Trans-Pecos; wettest is the NE. **Topography:** Gulf Coast Plain in the S and SE; North Central Plains slope upward with some hills; the Great Plains extend over the Panhandle, are broken by low mountains; the Trans-Pecos is the southern extension of the Rockies. **Capital:** Austin.

Economy. Chief industries: manufacturing, trade, oil and gas extraction, services. **Chief manuf. goods:** industrial machinery and equipment, foods, electrical and electronic products, chemicals and allied products, apparel. **Chief crops:** cotton, grains (wheat), sorghum grain, vegetables, citrus and other fruits, greenhouse/nursery, pecans, peanuts. **Chief farm products:** milk, eggs **Livestock:** (Jan. 2003) 13.6 mil cattle/calves; 1.1 mil sheep/lambs; (Dec. 2002) 930,000 hogs/pigs; 25.5 mil chickens (excl. broilers); 588.1 mil broilers. **Timber/lumber** (est. 2002): 1.6 bil bd. ft.; pine, cypress. **Nonfuel minerals** (est. 2002): $2.2 bil.; cement (portland), stone (crushed), sand and gravel (construction), salt, lime. **Commercial fishing** (2001): $218.0 mil. **Chief ports:** Houston, Galveston, Brownsville, Beaumont, Port Arthur, Corpus Christi. **Principal internat. airports at:** Amarillo, Austin, Corpus Christi, Dallas/Ft. Worth, El Paso, Harlingen, Houston, Lubbock, Odessa, San Antonio. **New private housing** (2002): 165,027 units/$17.6 bil. **Gross state product** (2001): $763.9 bil. **Employment distrib.** (May 2003): 17.3% govt.; 20.4% trade/trans./util.; 9.7% mfg.; 11.8% ed./health serv.; 11.1% prof./bus. serv.; 9.2% leisure/hosp.; 6.2% finance; 6.1% constr.; 2.5% info. **Per cap. pers. income** (2002): $28,551. **Sales tax** (2003): 6.25%. **Unemployment** (2002): 6.3%. **Tourism expends.** (2000): $36 bil. **Lottery** (2002): total sales: $3 bil; net income: $928.9 mil.

Finance. FDIC-insured commercial banks (2002): 669. **Deposits:** $129.1 bil. **FDIC-insured savings institutions** (2002): 46. **Assets:** $59.5 bil.

Federal govt. Fed. civ. employees (Mar. 2002): 101,612. **Avg. salary:** $51,438. **Notable fed. facilities:** Ft. Hood, Kelly AFB; Ft. Sam Houston; NASA Johnson Space Ctr.; Naval Air Training School; Corpus Christi NAS; Kingsville NAS; Ft. Worth Western Currency Facility.

Energy. Electricity production (est. 2002, kWh, by source): Coal: 90.5 bil; Petroleum: 29 mil; Gas: 39.4 bil; Hydroelectric: 921 mil; Nuclear: 19.1 bil.

State data. Motto: Friendship. **Flower:** Bluebonnet. **Bird:** Mockingbird. **Tree:** Pecan. **Song:** Texas, Our Texas. **Entered union** Dec. 29, 1845; rank, 28th. **State fair** at Dallas; mid-Oct.

History. At the time of European contact, Native American tribes in the region were numerous and diverse in culture. Coahuiltecan, Karankawa, Caddo, Jumano, and Tonkawa peoples lived in the area, and during the 19th cent., the Apache, Comanche, Cherokee, and Wichita arrived. Spanish explorer Pineda sailed along the Texas coast, 1519; Cabeza de Vaca and Coronado visited the interior, 1541. Spaniards made the first settlement at Ysleta, near El Paso, 1682. Americans moved into the land early in the 19th cent. Mexico, of which Texas was a part, won independence from Spain, 1821; Santa Anna became dictator in 1835; Texans rebelled. Santa Anna wiped out defenders of the Alamo, 1836; Sam Houston's Texans defeated Santa Anna at San Jacinto, and independence was proclaimed that same year. The Republic of Texas, with Sam Houston as its first president, functioned as a nation until 1845, when it was admitted to the Union.

Tourist attractions. Padre Island Natl. Seashore; Big Bend, Guadalupe Mts. natl. parks; The Alamo; Ft. Davis; Six Flags Amusement Park; Sea World and Fiesta Texas, both in San Antonio; San Antonio Missions Natl. Historical Park; Cowgirl Hall of Fame, Fort Worth; Lyndon B. Johnson Natl. Historical Park, marking his birthplace, boyhood home, and ranch, near Johnson City; Lyndon B. Johnson Library and Museum, Austin; Texas State Aquarium, Corpus Christi; Kimball Art Museum, Fort Worth; George Bush Library, College Station.

Famous Texans. Lance Armstrong, Stephen F. Austin, Lloyd Bentsen, James Bowie, Carol Burnett, George H. W. Bush, George W. Bush, Joan Crawford, J. Frank Dobie, Dwight D. Eisenhower, Morgan Fairchild, Farrah Fawcett, Sam Houston, Howard Hughes, Kay Bailey Hutchison, Molly Ivins, Lyndon B. Johnson, Tommy Lee Jones, Janis Joplin, Barbara Jordan, Mary Martin, Chester Nimitz, Sandra Day O'Connor, H. Ross Perot, Katherine Ann Porter, Dan Rather, Sam Rayburn, Ann Richards, Sissy Spacek, Kenneth Starr, George Strait.

Chamber of Commerce. 900 Congress, Suite 501, Austin, TX 78701; 1-800-8888TEX. **Website:** www.traveltex.com

Website. www.state.tx.us

Utah
Beehive State

People. Population (2002 est.): 2,316,256; rank: 34; **net change** (2001-2002): 1.6%. **Pop. density:** 28.2 per sq mi. **Racial distribution** (2000): 89.2% white; 0.8% black; 1.7% Asian; 1.3% Native American/Nat. AK; 0.7% Hawaiian/Pacific Islander; 4.2% other race; 2 or more races, 2.1%. **Hispanic pop.** (any race): 9.0%.

Geography. Total area: 84,899 sq mi; rank: 13. **Land area:** 82,144 sq mi; rank: 12. **Acres forested:** 15.7 mil. **Location:** Middle Rocky Mountain state; its southeastern corner touches Colorado, New Mexico, and Arizona, and is the only spot in the U.S. where 4 states join. **Climate:** arid; ranging from warm desert in SW to alpine in NE. **Topography:** high Colorado plateau is cut by brilliantly colored canyons of the SE; broad, flat, desert-like Great Basin of the W; the Great Salt Lake and Bonneville Salt Flats to the NW; Middle Rockies in the NE run E-W; valleys and plateaus of the Wasatch Front. **Capital:** Salt Lake City.

Economy. Chief industries: services, trade, manufacturing, government, transportation, utilities. **Chief manuf. goods:** medical instruments, electronic components, food products, fabricated metals, transportation equipment, steel and copper. **Chief crops:** hay, corn, wheat, barley, apples, potatoes, cherries, onions, peaches, pears. **Livestock:** (Jan. 2003) 920,000 cattle/calves; 320,000 sheep/lambs; (Dec. 2002) 670,000 hogs/pigs; 3.9 mil chickens (excl. broilers). **Timber/lumber** (est. 2002): 53 mil bd. ft.; aspen, spruce, pine. **Nonfuel minerals** (est. 2002): $1.2 bil.; copper, gold, sand and gravel (construction), cement (portland), salt. **Commercial fishing** (2001): $6.1 mil. **Principal internat. airport at:** Salt Lake City. **New private housing** (2002): 19,327 units/$2.5 bil. **Gross state product** (2001): $70.4 bil. **Employment distrib.** (May 2003): 18.4% govt.; 20% trade/trans./util.; 10.4% mfg.; 10.6% ed./health serv.; 12.2% prof./bus. serv.; 9.2% leisure/hosp.; 6% finance; 6.2% constr.; 2.9% info. **Per cap. pers. income** (2002): $24,306. **Sales tax** (2003): 4.75%. **Unemployment** (2002): 6.1%. **Tourism expends.** (2000): $4.2 bil.

Finance. FDIC-insured commercial banks (2002): 56. **Deposits:** $97.5 bil. **FDIC-insured savings institutions** (2002): 4. **Assets:** $1.7 bil.

Federal govt. Fed. civ. employees (Mar. 2002): 26,424. **Avg. salary:** $46,383. **Notable fed. facilities:** Hill AFB; Tooele Army Depot; Army Dugway Proving Ground.

Energy. Electricity production (est. 2002, kWh, by source): Coal: 34.1 bil; Petroleum: 47 mil; Gas: 911 mil; Hydroelectric: 476 mil; Other: 184 mil.

State data. Motto: Industry. **Flower:** Sego lily. **Bird:** Seagull. **Tree:** Blue spruce. **Song:** Utah, We Love Thee. **Entered union** Jan. 4, 1896; rank, 45th. **State fair** at Salt Lake City; Sept.

History. Ute, Gosiute, Southern Paiute, and Navajo peoples lived in the region at the time of European contact. Spanish Franciscans visited the area, 1776; American fur traders followed. Permanent settlement began with the arrival of the Mormons, 1847; they made the arid land bloom and created a prosperous economy. The State of Deseret was organized in 1849, and asked admission to the Union. In 1850, Congress established the region as the territory of Utah, and Brigham Young was appointed governor. The Union Pacific and Central Pacific railroads met near Promontory Point, May 10, 1869, creating the first transcontinental railroad. Statehood was not achieved until 1896, after a long period of controversy over the Mormon Church's doctrine of polygamy, which it discontinued in 1890.

Tourist attractions. Temple Square, Mormon Church headquarters, Salt Lake City; Great Salt Lake; Zion National Park, Canyonlands, Bryce Canyon, Arches, and Capitol Reef natl. parks; Dinosaur, Rainbow Bridge, Timpanogos Cave, and Natural Bridges natl. monuments; Lake Powell; Flaming Gorge Natl. Recreation Area.

> **IT'S A FACT:** Eight U.S. presidents were born in Virginia: George Washington, Thomas Jefferson, James Madison, James Monroe, William Harrison, John Tyler, Zachary Taylor, and Woodrow Wilson. Seven presidents are buried in the Old Dominion state: Washington, Jefferson, Madison, Monroe, Tyler, William Taft, and John F. Kennedy.

Famous Utahans. Maude Adams, Ezra Taft Benson, John Moses Browning, Mariner Eccles, Philo Farnsworth, James Fletcher, David M. Kennedy, J. Willard Marriott, Merlin Olsen, Osmond family, Ivy Baker Priest, George Romney, Roseanne, Wallace Stegner, Brigham Young, Loretta Young.

Tourist information. Utah Travel Council, Council Hall, Salt Lake City, UT 84114; 801-538-1030; 1-800-200-1160 or 1-800 UTAH-FUN. **Website:** www.utah.com
Website. www.utah.gov

Vermont
Green Mountain State

People. Population (2002 est.): 616,592; rank: 49; **net change** (2001-2002): 0.6%. **Pop. density:** 66.7 per sq mi. **Racial distribution** (2000): 96.8% white; 0.5% black; 0.9% Asian; 0.4% Native American/Nat. AK; <0.1% Hawaiian/Pacific Islander; 0.2% other race; 2 or more races, 1.2%. **Hispanic pop.** (any race): 0.9%.

Geography. Total area: 9,614 sq mi; rank: 45. **Land area:** 9,250 sq mi; rank: 43. **Acres forested:** 4.6 mil. **Location:** northern New England state. **Climate:** temperate, with considerable temperature extremes; heavy snowfall in mountains. **Topography:** Green Mts. N-S backbone 20-36 mi wide; avg. altitude 1,000 ft. **Capital:** Montpelier.

Economy. Chief industries: manufacturing, tourism, agriculture, trade, finance, insurance, real estate, government. **Chief manuf. goods:** machine tools, furniture, scales, books, computer components, speciality foods. **Chief crops:** dairy products, apples, maple syrup, greenhouse/nursery, vegetables and small fruits. **Livestock:** (Jan. 2003) 285,000 cattle/calves; (Dec. 2002) 2,500 hogs/pigs; 201,000 chickens (excl. broilers). **Timber/lumber** (est. 2002): 206 mil bd. ft.; pine, spruce, fir, hemlock. **Nonfuel minerals** (est. 2002): $70.7 mil.; stone (dimension), stone (crushed), sand and gravel (construction), talc (crude), gemstones. **Principal internat. airport at:** Burlington. **Employment distrib.** (May 2003): 17.3% govt.; 19.8% trade/trans./util.; 12.8% mfg.; 17.2% ed./health serv.; 6.9% prof./bus. serv.; 10.1% leisure/hosp.; 4.4% finance; 5% constr.; 2.2% info. **Per cap. pers. income** (2002): $29,567. **New private housing** (2002): 3,072 units/$451 mil. **Gross state product** (2001): $19.1 bil. **Sales tax** (2003): 5%. **Unemployment** (2002): 3.7%. **Tourism expends.** (2000): $1.5 bil. **Lottery** (2002): total sales: $82 mil; net income: $16.7 mil.

Finance. FDIC-insured commercial banks (2002): 15. **Deposits:** $5.2 bil. **FDIC-insured savings institutions** (2002): 5. **Assets:** $1.1 bil.

Federal govt. Fed. civ. employees (Mar. 2002): 2,993. **Avg. salary:** $48,792.

Energy. Electricity production (est. 2002, kWh, by source): Petroleum: 8 mil; Gas: 3 mil; Hydroelectric: 409 mil; Nuclear: 2.4 bil; Other: 187 mil.

State data. Motto: Freedom and unity. **Flower:** Red clover. **Bird:** Hermit thrush. **Tree:** Sugar maple. **Song:** These Green Mountains. **Entered union** Mar. 4, 1791; rank, 14th. **State fair** at Rutland; early Sept.

History. Before the arrival of the Europeans, Abnaki and Mahican peoples lived in the region. Champlain explored the lake that bears his name, 1609. The first American settlement was Ft. Dummer, 1724, near Brattleboro. During the American Revolution, Ethan Allen and the Green Mountain Boys captured Ft. Ticonderoga (NY), 1775; John Stark defeated part of Burgoyne's forces near Bennington, 1777. In the War of 1812, Thomas MacDonough defeated a British fleet on Lake Champlain off Plattsburgh (NY), 1814.

Tourist attractions. Shelburne Museum; Rock of Ages Quarry, Graniteville; Vermont Marble Exhibit, Proctor; Bennington Battle Monument; Pres. Calvin Coolidge homestead, Plymouth; Maple Grove Maple Museum, St. Johnsbury; Ben & Jerry's Factory, Waterbury.

Famous Vermonters. Ethan Allen, Chester A. Arthur, Calvin Coolidge, John Deere, George Dewey, John Dewey, Stephen A. Douglas, Dorothy Canfield Fisher, James Fisk, James Jeffords, Rudy Vallee.

Chamber of Commerce. PO Box 37, Montpelier, VT 05601.

Tourist information. Vermont Dept. of Tourism and Marketing, 6 Baldwin St., Drawer 33, Montpelier, VT 05633-1301; 1-800-VERMONT. **Website:** www.1-800-vermont.com
Website: www.vermont.gov

Virginia
Old Dominion

People. Population (2002 est.): 7,293,542; rank: 12; **net change** (2001-2002): 1.3%. **Pop. density:** 184.2 per sq mi. **Racial distribution** (2000): 72.3% white; 19.6% black; 3.7% Asian; 0.3% Native American/Nat. AK; 0.1% Hawaiian/Pacific Islander; 2.0% other race; 2 or more races, 2.0%. **Hispanic pop.** (any race): 4.7%.

Geography. Total area: 42,774 sq mi; rank: 35. **Land area:** 39,594 sq mi; rank: 37. **Acres forested:** 16.1 mil. **Location:** South Atlantic state bounded by the Atlantic Ocean on the E and surrounded by North Carolina, Tennessee, Kentucky, West Virginia, and Maryland. **Climate:** mild and equable. **Topography:** mountain and valley region in the W, including the Blue Ridge Mts.; rolling piedmont plateau; tidewater, or coastal plain, including the eastern shore. **Capital:** Richmond.

Economy. Chief industries: services, trade, government, manufacturing, tourism, agriculture. **Chief manuf. goods:** food processing, transportation equipment, printing, textiles, electronic & electrical equipment, industrial machinery & equipment, lumber & wood products, chemicals, rubber & plastics, furniture. **Chief crops:** tobacco, grain corn, soybeans, winter wheat, peanuts, lint & seed cotton. **Livestock:** (Jan. 2003) 1.7 mil cattle/calves; 62,000 sheep/lambs; (Dec. 2002) 400,000 hogs/pigs; 4.6 mil chickens (excl. broilers). **Timber/lumber** (est. 2002): 1.5 bil bd. ft.; pine and hardwoods. **Nonfuel minerals** (est. 2002): $697 mil.; stone (crushed), cement (portland), sand and gravel (construction), lime, clays (fuller's earth). **Commercial fishing** (2001): $119.4 mil. **Chief ports:** Hampton Roads, Richmond, Alexandria. **Principal internat. airports at:** Arlington, Norfolk, Loudon, Richmond, Newport News. **New private housing** (2002): 59,445 units/$6.6 bil. **Gross state product** (2001): $273.1 bil. **Employment distrib.** (May 2003): 18.2% govt.; 17.9% trade/trans./util.; 8.8% mfg.; 10.6% ed./health serv.; 15.7% prof./bus. serv.; 9.2% leisure/hosp.; 5.2% finance; 6% constr.; 2.9% info. **Per cap. pers. income** (2002): $32,922. **Sales tax** (2003): 4.5%. **Unemployment** (2002): 4.1%. **Tourism expends.** (2000): $13.7 bil. **Lottery** (2002): total sales: $1.1 bil; net income: $367.7 mil.

Finance. FDIC-insured commercial banks (2002): 130. **Deposits:** $60.2 bil. **FDIC-insured savings institutions** (2002): 16. **Assets:** $67.1 bil.

Federal govt. Fed. civ. employees (Mar. 2002): 112,682. **Avg. salary:** $61,189. **Notable fed. facilities:** Pentagon; Norfolk Naval Sta., Shipyard; Marine Corps Base; Langley AFB; NASA Langley Res. Ctr.; CIA George Bush Ctr. for Intelligence, Langley; Quantico USMC Base; FBI Academy (Quantico); Dahlgren Nav. Surface Warfare Ctr. & Lab; USDA Food and Nutrition Serv.; U.S. Geological Survey Natl. Ctr.

Energy. Electricity production (est. 2002, kWh, by source): Coal: 30.9 bil; Petroleum: 3.5 bil; Gas: 2.1 bil; Hydroelectric: −1.1 bil; Nuclear: 27.3 bil.

State data. Motto: Sic Semper Tyrannis (Thus always to tyrants). **Flower:** Dogwood. **Bird:** Cardinal. **Tree:** Dogwood. **Song Emeritus:** Carry Me Back to Old Virginia. **Tenth** of the original 13 states to ratify the Constitution, June 25, 1788. **State fair** at Richmond; late Sept.-early Oct.

History. Living in the area at the time of European contact were the Cherokee and Susquehanna and the Algonquians of the Powhatan Confederacy. English settlers founded Jamestown, 1607. Virginians took over much of the government from royal governor Dunmore, 1775, forcing him to flee. Virginians under George Rogers Clark freed the Ohio-Indiana-Illinois area of British forces. Benedict Arnold burned Richmond and Petersburg for the British, 1781. That same year, Britain's Cornwallis was trapped at Yorktown and surrendered, ending the American Revolution. Virginia seceded from the Union, 1861, and Richmond became the capital of the Confederacy. Hampton Roads, off the Virginia coast, was the site of the famous naval battle of the USS Monitor and CSS Virginia (Merrimac), 1862. Virginia was readmitted, 1870.

Tourist attractions. Colonial Williamsburg; Busch Gardens, Williamsburg; Wolf Trap Farm, near Falls Church; Arlington Natl. Cemetery; Mt. Vernon, home of George Washington; Jamestown Festival Park; Yorktown; Jefferson's Monticello, Charlottesville; Robert E. Lee's birthplace, Stratford Hall, and grave, Lexington; Appomattox; Shenandoah

Natl. Park; Blue Ridge Parkway; Virginia Beach; Paramount's King's Dominion, near Richmond.

Famous Virginians. Richard E. Byrd, James B. Cabell, Henry Clay, Jubal Early, Jerry Falwell, William Henry Harrison, Patrick Henry, A.P. Hill, Thomas Jefferson, Joseph E. Johnston, Robert E. Lee, Meriwether Lewis and William Clark, James Madison, John Marshall, George Mason, James Monroe, George Pickett, Pocahontas, Edgar Allan Poe, John Randolph, Walter Reed, Rev. Pat Robertson, John Smith, J.E.B. Stuart, William Styron, Zachary Taylor, John Tyler, Maggie Walker, Booker T. Washington, George Washington, L. Douglas Wilder, Woodrow Wilson.

Chamber of Commerce. 9 South Fifth St., Richmond, VA 23219; 1-800-321-3244. **Website:** www.virginia.org

Website. www.vipnet.org

Washington
Evergreen State

People. Population (2002 est.): 6,068,996; rank: 15; **net change** (2001-2002): 1.3%. **Pop. density:** 91.2 per sq mi. **Racial distribution** (2000): 81.8% white; 3.2% black; 5.5% Asian; 1.6% Native American/Nat. AK; 0.4% Hawaiian/Pacific Islander; 3.9% other race; 2 or more races, 3.6%. **Hispanic pop.** (any race): 7.5%.

Geography. Total area: 71,300 sq mi; rank: 18. **Land area:** 66,544 sq mi; rank: 20. **Acres forested:** 21.8 mil. **Location:** Pacific state bordered by Canada on the N; Idaho on the E; Oregon on the S; and the Pacific Ocean on the W. **Climate:** mild, dominated by the Pacific Ocean and protected by the Cascades. **Topography:** Olympic Mts. on NW peninsula; open land along coast to Columbia R.; flat terrain of Puget Sound Lowland; Cascade Mts. region's high peaks to the E; Columbia Basin in central portion; highlands to the NE; mountains to the SE. **Capital:** Olympia.

Economy. Chief industries: advanced technology, aerospace, biotechnology, intl. trade, forestry, tourism, recycling, agriculture & food processing. **Chief manuf. goods:** computer software, aircraft, pulp & paper, lumber and plywood, aluminum, processed fruits and vegetables, machinery, electronics. **Chief crops:** apples, potatoes, hay, farm forest products. **Livestock:** (Jan. 2003) 1.1 mil cattle/calves; 51,000 sheep/lambs; (Dec. 2002) 24,000 hogs/pigs; 6.5 mil chickens (excl. broilers); 265.5 mil broilers. **Timber/lumber** (est. 2002): 4.9 mil bd. ft.; Douglas fir, hemlock, cedar, pine. **Nonfuel minerals** (est. 2002): $450 mil.; sand and gravel (construction), stone (crushed), cement (portland), diatomite, gold. **Commercial fishing** (2001): $138.1 mil. **Chief ports:** Seattle, Tacoma, Vancouver, Kelso-Longview. **Principal internat. airports at:** Seattle/Tacoma, Spokane, Boeing Field. **New private housing** (2002): 40,200 units/$5.5 bil. **Gross state product** (2001): $223.0 bil. **Employment distrib.** (May 2003): 19.7% govt.; 18.9% trade/trans./util.; 10% mfg.; 11.8% ed./health serv.; 10.9% prof./bus. serv.; 9.3% leisure/hosp.; 5.6% finance; 5.8% constr.; 3.5% info. **Per cap. pers. income** (2002): $32,677. **Sales tax** (2003): 6.5%. **Unemployment** (2002): 7.3%. **Tourism expends.** (2000): $9 bil. **Lottery** (2002): total sales: $438.6 mil; net income: $93.9 mil.

Finance. FDIC-insured commercial banks (2002): 80. **Deposits:** $19.4 bil. **FDIC-insured savings institutions** (2002): 22. **Assets:** $47.7 bil.

Federal govt. Fed. civ. employees (Mar. 2002): 43,313. **Avg. salary:** $53,993. **Notable fed. facilities:** Bonneville Power Admin.; Ft. Lewis; McChord AFB; Hanford Nuclear Reservation; Bremerton Naval Shipyards; Naval Sub Base, Bangor; Naval Sta., Everett; Pacific Northwest Natl. Lab.

Energy. Electricity production (est. 2002, kWh, by source): Petroleum: 5 mil; Gas: 1.1 bil; Hydroelectric: 76.8 bil; Nuclear: 9.0 bil. Other: 299 mil.

State data. Motto: Alki (By and by). **Flower:** Western rhododendron. **Bird:** Willow goldfinch. **Tree:** Western hemlock. **Song:** Washington, My Home. **Entered union** Nov. 11, 1889; rank, 42nd. **State fairs:** 5 area fairs, in Aug. and Sept.; no state fair.

History. At the time of European contact, many Native American tribes lived in the area, including the Nez Percé, Spokan, Yakima, Cayuse, Okanogan, Walla Walla, and Colville peoples, who lived in the interior region, and the Nooksak, Chinook, Nisqually, Clallam, Makah, Quinault, and Puyallup peoples, who inhabited the coastal area. Spain's Bruno Hezeta sailed the coast, 1775. In 1792, British naval officer George Vancouver mapped Puget Sound area, and that same year, American Capt. Robert Gray sailed up the Columbia River. Canadian fur traders set up Spokane House, 1810. Americans under John Jacob Astor established a post at Ft.

Okanogan, 1811, and missionary Marcus Whitman settled near Walla Walla, 1836. Final agreement on the border of Washington and Canada was made with Britain, 1846, and Washington became part of the Oregon Territory, 1848. Gold was discovered, 1855.

Tourist attractions. Seattle Waterfront, Seattle Center and Space Needle, Museum of Flight, Underground Tour, all Seattle; Mt. Rainier, Olympic, and North Cascades natl. parks; Mt. St. Helens; Puget Sound; San Juan Islands; Grand Coulee Dam; Columbia R. Gorge Natl. Scenic Area; Spokane's Riverfront Park.

Famous Washingtonians. Raymond Carver, Kurt Cobain, Bing Crosby, William O. Douglas, Bill Gates, Jimi Hendrix, Henry M. Jackson, Gary Larson, Mary McCarthy, Robert Motherwell, Edward R. Murrow, Theodore Roethke, Ann Rule, Hilary Swank, Julia Sweeney, Adam West, Marcus Whitman, Minoru Yamasaki.

Tourist information. WA State Tourism Division, PO Box 42500, Olympia, WA 98504-2500; 360-725-5052. **Website:** www.tourism.wa.gov

Website. access.wa.gov

West Virginia
Mountain State

People. Population (2002 est.): 1,801,873; rank: 37; **net change** (2001-2002): 0.0%. **Pop. density:** 74.8 per sq mi. **Racial distribution** (2000): 95.0% white; 3.2% black; 0.5% Asian; 0.2% Native American/Nat. AK; <0.1% Hawaiian/Pacific Islander; 0.2% other race; 2 or more races, 0.9%. **Hispanic pop.** (any race): 0.7%.

Geography. Total area: 24,230 sq mi; rank: 41. **Land area:** 24,078 sq mi; rank: 41. **Acres forested:** 12.1 mil. **Location:** South Atlantic state bounded on the N by Ohio, Pennsylvania, Maryland; on the S and W by Virginia, Kentucky, Ohio; on the E by Maryland and Virginia. **Climate:** humid continental climate except for marine modification in the lower panhandle. **Topography:** ranging from hilly to mountainous; Allegheny Plateau in the W, covers two-thirds of the state; mountains here are the highest in the state, over 4,000 ft. **Capital:** Charleston.

Economy. Chief industries: manufacturing, services, mining, tourism. **Chief manuf. goods:** machinery, plastic & hardwood prods., fabricated metals, chemicals, aluminum, automotive parts, steel. **Chief crops:** apples, peaches, hay, tobacco, corn, wheat, oats. **Chief farm products:** dairy products, eggs. **Livestock:** (Jan. 2003) 415,000 cattle/calves; 34,000 sheep/lambs; (Dec. 2002) 11,000 hogs/pigs; 2.0 mil chickens (excl. broilers); 89.7 mil broilers. **Timber/lumber** (est. 2002): 724 mil bd. ft.; oak, yellow poplar, hickory, walnut, cherry. **Nonfuel minerals** (est. 2002): $173 mil.; stone (crushed), cement (portland), sand and gravel (industrial), lime, salt. **Chief port:** Huntington. **New private housing** (2002): 4,890 units/$560 mil. **Gross state product** (2001): $42.4 bil. **Employment distrib.** (May 2003): 19.3% govt.; 18.5% trade/trans./util.; 9% mfg.; 14.7% ed./health serv.; 8.1% prof./bus. serv.; 8.9% leisure/hosp.; 4.3% finance; 4.6% constr.; 1.8% info. **Per cap. pers. income** (2002): $23,688. **Sales tax** (2003): 6%. **Unemployment** (2002): 6.1%. **Tourism expends.** (2000): $1.7 bil. **Lottery** (2002): total sales: $848.6 mil; net income: $315.9 mil.

Finance. FDIC-insured commercial banks (2002): 69. **Deposits:** $15.0 bil. **FDIC-insured savings institutions** (2002): 7. **Assets:** $1.0 bil.

Federal govt. Fed. civ. employees (Mar. 2002): 12,283. **Avg. salary:** $50,627. **Notable fed. facilities:** Natl. Radio Astronomy Observatory; Bureau of Public Debt Bldg.; Harpers Ferry Natl. Park; Correctional Institution for Women; FBI Identification Ctr.

Energy. Electricity production (est. 2002, kWh, by source): Coal: 62.8 bil; Petroleum: 231 mil; Gas: 3 mil; Hydroelectric: 236 mil; Other: 22 mil.

State data. Motto: Montani Semper Liberi (Mountaineers are always free). **Flower:** Big rhododendron. **Bird:** Cardinal. **Tree:** Sugar maple. **Songs:** The West Virginia Hills; This Is My West Virginia; West Virginia, My Home, Sweet Home. **Entered union** June 20, 1863; rank, 35th. **State fair** at Lewisburg (Fairlea); late Aug.

History. Sparsely inhabited at the time of European contact, the area was primarily Native American hunting grounds. British explorers Thomas Batts and Robert Fallam reached the New River, 1671. Early American explorers included George Washington, 1753, and Daniel Boone. In the fall of 1774, frontiersmen defeated an allied Indian uprising at Point Pleasant. The area was part of Virginia and often objected to rule by the eastern part of the state. When Virginia seceded in

1861, the Wheeling Convention repudiated the act and created a new state, Kanawha, later renamed West Virginia. It was admitted to the Union 1863.

Tourist attractions. Harpers Ferry Natl. Historic Park; Science and Cultural Center, Charleston; White Sulphur (in Greenbrier) and Berkeley Springs mineral water spas; New River Gorge, Fayetteville; Winter Place, Exhibition Coal Mine, both Beckley; Monongahela Natl. Forest; Fenton Glass, Williamstown; Viking Glass, New Martinsville; Blenko Glass, Milton; Sternwheel Regatta, Charleston; Mountain State Forest Festival; Snowshoe Ski Resort, Slaty Fork; Canaan State Park, Davis; Mountain State Arts & Crafts Fair, Ripley; Ogle Bay, Wheeling; White water rafting, several locations.

Famous West Virginians. Newton D. Baker, Pearl Buck, John W. Davis, Thomas "Stonewall" Jackson, Don Knotts, Dwight Whitney Morrow, Michael Owens, Mary Lou Retton, Walter Reuther, Cyrus Vance, Jerry West, Charles "Chuck" Yeager.

Tourist information. Dept. of Commerce, West Virginia Division of Tourism, State Capitol, Charleston WV 25305; 1-800-CALLWVA. **Website:** www.callwva.com
Website. www.state.wv.us

Wisconsin
Badger State

People. Population (2002 est.): 5,441,196; rank: 20; **net change** (2001-2002): 0.7%. **Pop. density:** 100.2 per sq mi. **Racial distribution** (2000): 88.9% white; 5.7% black; 1.7% Asian; 0.9% Native American/Nat. AK; <0.1% Hawaiian/Pacific Islander; 1.6% other race; 2 or more races, 1.2%. **Hispanic pop.** (any race): 3.6%.

Geography. Total area: 65,498 sq mi; rank: 23. **Land area:** 54,310 sq mi; rank: 25. **Acres forested:** 16.0 mil. **Location:** East North Central state, bounded on the N by Lake Superior and Upper Michigan; on the E by Lake Michigan; on the S by Illinois; on the W by the St. Croix and Mississippi Rivers. **Climate:** long, cold winters and short, warm summers tempered by the Great Lakes. **Topography:** narrow Lake Superior Lowland plain met by Northern Highland, which slopes gently to the sandy crescent Central Plain; Western Upland in the SW; 3 broad parallel limestone ridges running N-S are separated by wide and shallow lowlands in the SE. **Capital:** Madison.

Economy. Chief industries: services, manufacturing, trade, government, agriculture, tourism. **Chief manuf. goods:** food products, motor vehicles & equip., paper products, medical instruments and supplies, printing, plastics. **Chief crops:** corn, hay, soybeans, potatoes, cranberries, sweet corn, peas, oats, snap beans. **Chief products:** milk, butter, cheese, canned and frozen vegetables. **Livestock** (Jan. 2003) 3.3 mil cattle/calves; 80,000 sheep/lambs; (Dec. 2002) 520,000 hogs/pigs; 5.6 mil chickens (excl. broilers); 33.8 mil broilers. **Timber/lumber** (est. 2002): 583 mil bd. ft.; maple, birch, oak, evergreens. ft. **Nonfuel minerals** (est. 2002): $340 mil.; sand and gravel (construction), stone (crushed), lime, sand and gravel (industrial), stone (dimension). **Commercial fishing** (2001): $4.9 mil. **Chief ports:** Superior, Ashland, Milwaukee, Green Bay, Kewaunee, Pt. Washington, Manitowoc, Sheboygan, Marinette, Kenosha. **Principal internat. airports at:** Green Bay, Milwaukee. **New private housing** (2002): 38,208 units/$4.8 bil. **Gross state product** (2001): $177.4 bil. **Employment distrib.** (May 2003): 15.3% govt.; 19.2% trade/trans./util.; 18.5% mfg.; 13% ed./health serv.; 8.6% prof./bus. serv.; 8.8% leisure/hosp.; 5.6% finance; 4.2% constr.; 1.8% info. **Per cap. pers. income** (2002): $29,923. **Sales tax** (2003): 5%. **Unemployment** (2002): 5.5%. **Tourism expends.** (2000): $7.1 bil. **Lottery** (2002): total sales: $427.6 mil; net income: $119 mil.

Finance. FDIC-insured commercial banks (2002): 273. **Deposits:** $59.8 bil. **FDIC-insured savings institutions** (2002): 41. **Assets:** $22.0 bil.

Federal govt. Fed. civ. employees (Mar. 2002): 11,176. **Avg. salary:** $49,257. **Notable fed. facilities:** Ft. McCoy.

Energy. Electricity production (est. 2002, kWh, by source): Coal: 38.6 bil; Petroleum: 161 mil; Gas: 975 mil; Hydroelectric: 2.3 bil; Nuclear: 12.4 bil. Other: 322 mil.

State data. Motto: Forward. **Flower:** Wood violet. **Bird:** Robin. **Tree:** Sugar maple. **Song:** On, Wisconsin! **Entered union** May 29, 1848; rank, 30th. **State fair** at State Fair Park, West Allis; July-Aug.

History. At the time of European contact, Ojibwa, Menominee, Winnebago, Kickapoo, Sauk, Fox, and Potawatomi peoples inhabited the region. Jean Nicolet was the first European to see the Wisconsin area, arriving in Green Bay, 1634; French missionaries and fur traders followed. The British took

over, 1763. The U.S. won the land after the American Revolution, but the British were not ousted until after the War of 1812. Lead miners came next, then farmers. In 1816, the U.S. government built a fort at Prairie du Chien on Wisconsin's border with Iowa. Native Americans in the area rebelled against the seizure of their tribal lands in the Black Hawk War of 1832, but treaties from 1829 to 1848, transferred all land titles in Wisconsin to the U.S. government. Railroads were started in 1851, serving growing wheat harvests and iron mines. Some 96,000 soldiers served the Union cause during the Civil War.

Tourist attractions. Old Wade House and Carriage Museum, Greenbush; Villa Louis, Prairie du Chien; Circus World Museum, Baraboo; Wisconsin Dells; Old World Wisconsin, Eagle; Door County peninsula; Chequamegon and Nicolet national forests; Lake Winnebago; House on the Rock, Dodgeville; Monona Terrace, Madison.

Famous Wisconsinites. Don Ameche, Carrie Chapman Catt, Willem Dafoe, Edna Ferber, King Camp Gillette, Harry Houdini, Robert La Follette, Alfred Lunt, Pat O'Brien, Georgia O'Keeffe, William H. Rehnquist, John Ringling, Donald K. "Deke" Slayton, Spencer Tracy, Thorstein Veblen, Orson Welles, Laura Ingalls Wilder, Thornton Wilder, Frank Lloyd Wright.

Tourist information. Wisconsin Dept. of Tourism, 201 W. Washington Ave., PO Box 7976, Madison, WI 53707-7976; 1-800-432-TRIP. **Website:** www.travelwisconsin.com
Website. www.wisconsin.gov

Wyoming
Equality State, Cowboy State

People. Population (2002 est.): 498,703; rank: 51; **net change** (2001-2002): 1.0%. **Pop. density:** 5.1 per sq mi. **Racial distribution** (2000): 92.1% white; 0.8% black; 0.6% Asian; 2.3% Native American/Nat. AK; 0.1% Hawaiian/Pacific Islander; 2.5% other race; 2 or more races, 1.8%. **Hispanic pop.** (any race): 6.4%.

Geography. Total area: 97,814 sq mi; rank: 10. **Land area:** 97,100 sq mi; rank: 9. **Acres forested:** 11.0 mil. **Location:** Mountain state lying in the high western plateaus of the Great Plains. **Climate:** semi-desert conditions throughout; true desert in the Big Horn and Great Divide basins. **Topography:** the eastern Great Plains rise to the foothills of the Rocky Mts.; the Continental Divide crosses the state from the NW to the SE. **Capital:** Cheyenne.

Economy. Chief industries: mineral extraction, oil, natural gas, tourism and recreation, agriculture. **Chief manuf. goods:** refined petroleum, wood, stone, clay products, foods, electronic devices, sporting apparel, and aircraft. **Chief crops:** wheat, beans, barley, oats, sugar beets, hay. **Livestock:** (Jan. 2003) 1.5 mil cattle/calves; 460,000 sheep/lambs; (Dec. 2002) 115,000 hogs/pigs; 17,000 chickens (excl. broilers). **Timber/lumber** (est. 2002): 230 mil bd. ft.; ponderosa & lodgepole pine, Douglas fir, Engelmann spruce. **Nonfuel minerals** (est. 2002): $1.0 bil.; soda ash, clays (bentonite), helium (Grade-A), cement (portland), sand and gravel (construction). **Principal internat. airport at:** Casper. **New private housing** (2002): 2,045 units/$304 mil. **Gross state product** (2001): $20.4 bil. **Employment distrib.** (May 2003): 25.5% govt.; 19.4% trade/trans./util.; 3.5% mfg.; 7.9% ed./health serv.; 6.3% prof./bus. serv.; 12% leisure/hosp.; 4.1% finance; 8.2% constr.; 1.7% info. **Per cap. pers. income** (2002): $30,578. **Sales tax** (2003): 4%. **Unemployment** (2002): 4.2%. **Tourism expends.** (2000): $1.6 bil.

Finance. FDIC-insured commercial banks (2002): 47. **Deposits:** $5.3 bil. **FDIC-insured savings institutions** (2002): 3. **Assets:** $362 mil.

Federal govt. Fed. civ. employees (Mar. 2002): 4,593. **Avg. salary:** $46,999. **Notable fed. facilities:** Warren AFB.

Energy. Electricity production (est. 2002, kWh, by source): Coal: 41.7 bil; Petroleum: 39 mil; Gas: 171 mil; Hydroelectric: 585 mil; Other: 19 mil.

State data. Motto: Equal Rights. **Flower:** Indian Paintbrush. **Bird:** Western Meadowlark. **Tree:** Plains Cottonwood. **Song:** Wyoming. **Entered union** July 10, 1890; rank, 44th. **State fair** at Douglas; late Aug.

History. Shoshone, Crow, Cheyenne, Oglala Sioux, and Arapaho peoples lived in the area at the time of European contact. France's François and Louis La Verendrye were the first Europeans to see the region, 1743. John Colter, an American, was first to traverse Yellowstone area, 1807-8. Trappers and fur traders followed in the 1820s. Forts Laramie and Bridger became important stops on the pioneer trails to the West Coast. Population grew after the Union Pacific crossed the state, 1868. Women won the vote, for the first time in the U.S., from the Territorial Legislature, 1869. Disputes between large land owners and small ranchers culminated in the Johnson County Cattle War, 1892; federal troops were called in to restore order.

Tourist attractions. Yellowstone Natl. Park, the first U.S. national park, est. 1872; Grand Teton Natl. Park; Natl. Elk Refuge; Devils Tower Natl. Monument; Fort Laramie Natl. Historic Site and nearby pioneer trail ruts; Buffalo Bill Historical Center, Cody; Cheyenne Frontier Days, Cheyenne.

Famous Wyomingites. James Bridger, William F. "Buffalo Bill" Cody, Curt Gowdy, Esther Hobart Morris, Nellie Tayloe Ross.

Tourist information. Division of Tourism & State Marketing, I-25 at College Dr., Cheyenne, WY 82002; 1-800-CALL-WYO. **Website:** www.wyomingtourism.org
    Website. www.state.wy.us

District of Columbia

People. Population (2002 est.): 570,898; rank: 50; **net change** (2001-2002): –0.5%. **Pop. density:** 9,359.0 per sq mi. **Racial distribution** (2000): 30.8% white; 60.0% black; 2.7% Asian; 0.3% Native American/Nat. AK; 0.1% Hawaiian/ Pacific Islander; 3.8% other race; 2 or more races, NA. **Hispanic pop.** (any race): 7.9%.

Geography. Total area: 68 sq mi; rank: 50. **Land area:** 61 sq mi; rank: 51. **Location:** at the confluence of the Potomac and Anacostia rivers, flanked by Maryland on the N, E, and SE and by Virginia on the SW. **Climate:** hot humid summers, mild winters. **Topography:** low hills rise toward the N away from the Potomac R. and slope to the S; highest elevation, 410 ft, lowest Potomac R., 1 ft.

Economy. Chief industries: government, service, tourism. **New private housing** (2002): 1,591 units/$121 mil. **Gross state product** (2001): $64.5 bil. **Employment distrib.** (May 2003): 33.3% govt.; 4.2% trade/trans./util.; 0.4% mfg.; 13.1% ed./health serv.; 21.3% prof./bus. serv.; 7.5% leisure/ hosp.; 4.7% finance; 1.8% constr.; 3.9% info. **Per cap. pers. income** (2002): $42,120. **Sales tax** (2003): 5.75%. **Unemployment** (2002): 6.4%. **Tourism expends.** (2000): $6.3 bil. **Lottery** (2002): total sales: $211.1 mil; net income: $63 mil.

Finance. FDIC-insured commercial banks & trust companies (2002): 4. **Deposits:** $400 mil. **FDIC-insured savings institutions** (2002): 1. **Assets:** $251 mil.il.

Federal govt. No. of federal employees (Mar. 2002): 149,300. **Avg. salary:** $72,246.

Energy. Electricity production (2000, kWh, by source): Petroleum: 95 mil; Other: 28 mil.

District data. Motto: Justitia omnibus (Justice for all). **Flower:** American beauty rose. **Tree:** Scarlet oak. **Bird:** Wood thrush.

History. The District of Columbia, coextensive with the city of Washington, is the seat of the U.S. federal government. It lies on the west central edge of Maryland on the Potomac River, opposite Virginia. Its area was originally 100 sq mi taken from the sovereignty of Maryland and Virginia. Virginia's portion south of the Potomac was given back to that state in 1846.

The 23rd Amendment (1961) granted residents the right to vote for president and vice president for the first time since 1800 and gave them 3 members in the Electoral College. The first such votes were cast in Nov. 1964.

Congress, which has legislative authority over the District under the Constitution, established in 1874 a government of 3 commissioners appointed by the president. The Reorganization Plan of 1967 substituted a single appointive commissioner (also called mayor), assistant, and 9-member City Council. Funds were still appropriated by Congress; residents had no vote in local government, except to elect school board members. In Sept. 1970, Congress approved legislation giving the District one delegate to the House of Representatives, who can vote in committee but not on the floor. The first delegate was elected 1971.

In May 1974, voters approved a congressionally drafted charter giving them the right to elect their own mayor and a 13-member city council; the first took office Jan. 2, 1975. The district won the right to levy taxes; Congress retained power to veto council actions and approve the city budget.

Proposals for a "federal town" for the deliberations of the Continental Congress were made in 1783, 4 years before the adoption of the Constitution. Rivalry between Northern and Southern delegates over the site appeared in the First Congress, 1789. John Adams, presiding officer of the Senate, cast the deciding vote of that body for Germantown, PA. In 1790 Congress compromised by making Philadelphia the temporary capital for 10 years. The Virginia members of the House wanted a permanent capital on the eastern bank of the Potomac, while the Southerners opposed having the nation assume the war debts of the 13 original states as provided under the Assumption Bill, fathered by Alexander Hamilton. Hamilton and Jefferson arranged a compromise: the Virginia men voted for the Assumption Bill, and the Northerners conceded the capital to the Potomac. Pres. Washington chose the site in Oct. 1790 and persuaded landowners to sell their holdings to the government. The capital was named Washington.

Washington appointed Pierre Charles L'Enfant, a Frenchman, to plan the capital on an area not more than 10 mi square. The L'Enfant plan, for streets 100 to 110 ft. wide and one avenue 400 ft. wide and a mile long, seemed grandiose and foolhardy, but Washington endorsed it. When L'Enfant ordered a wealthy landowner to remove his new manor house because it obstructed a vista, and demolished it when the owner refused, Washington stepped in and dismissed the architect. Andrew Ellicott, who was working on surveying the area, finished the official map and design of the city. Ellicott was assisted by Benjamin Banneker, a distinguished black architect and astronomer.

On Sept. 18, 1793, Pres. Washington laid the cornerstone of the north wing of the Capitol. On June 3, 1800, Pres. John Adams moved to Washington, and on June 10, Philadelphia ceased to be the temporary capital. The City of Washington was incorporated in 1802; the District of Columbia was created as a municipal corporation in 1874, embracing Washington, Georgetown, and Washington County.

Tourist attractions. *See* Washington, DC, Capital of the U.S.

Tourist information. Washington, DC Convention and Visitors Association, 1212 New York Ave. NW, #600, Washington, DC 20005; 202-789-7000. **Website:** www.washington. org
    Website. dc.gov

OUTLYING U.S. AREAS

American Samoa

People. Population (2003 est.): 70,260. **Population growth rate** (2003 est.): 2.2%. **Pop. density** (2003): 912.5 per sq mi. **Major ethnic groups:** Samoan (Polynesian), Caucasian, Tongan. **Languages:** Samoan, English.

Land area: 77 sq. mi. **Total area:** 90 sq mi. **Capital:** Pago Pago, Island of Tutuila. **Motto:** Samoa Muamua le Atua (In Samoa, God Is First). **Song:** Amerika Samoa. **Flower:** Paogo (Ula-fala). **Plant:** Ava.

Public education. Student-teacher ratio (1995): 20.

Boasting spectacular scenery and delightful South Seas climate, American Samoa is the most southerly of all lands under U.S. sovereignty. It is an unincorporated territory consisting of 7 small islands of the Samoan group: **Tutuila, Aunu'u, Manu'a Group (Ta'u, Olosega, Ofu), Rose,** and **Swains Island.** The islands are 2,300 mi SW of Honolulu.

Economy. Chief industries: tuna processing, trade, services, tourism. **Chief crops:** vegetables, nuts, melons and other fruits. **Livestock** (2001): 103 cattle; 10,700 hogs/pigs; 37,000 chickens. **Commercial fishing** (2000): $2 mil. **Principal airport at:** Pago Pago.

Finance. FDIC-insured commercial banks (2002): 1. **Deposits:** $67 mil.

Energy. Electricity production (2001): 130 mil. kWh.

A tripartite agreement between Great Britain, Germany, and the U.S. in 1899 gave the U.S. sovereignty over the eastern islands of the Samoan group; these islands became American Samoa. Local chiefs ceded Tutuila and Aunu'u to the U.S. in 1900, and the Manu'a group and Rose in 1904; Swains Island was annexed in 1925. Samoa (Western), comprising the larger islands of the Samoan group, was a New Zealand mandate and UN Trusteeship until it became independent Jan. 1, 1962 (now called Samoa).

Tutuila and Aunu'u have an area of 53 sq mi. Ta'u has an area of 17 sq mi, and the islets of Ofu and Olosega, 5 sq mi with a population of a few thousand. Swains Island has nearly 2 sq mi and a population of about 100.

About 70% of the land is bush and mountains. Chief exports are fish products. Taro, breadfruit, yams, coconuts, pineapples, oranges, and bananas are also produced.

From 1900 to 1951, American Samoa was under the jurisdiction of the U.S. Navy. Since 1951, it has been under the Interior Dept. On Jan. 3, 1978, the first popularly elected Samoan governor and lieutenant governor were inaugurated.

Previously, the governor was appointed by the Secretary of the Interior. American Samoa has a bicameral legislature and elects a delegate to the House of Representatives, with no vote except in committees.

The American Samoans are of Polynesian origin. They are nationals of the U.S.; approximately 20,000 live in Hawaii, 65,000 in California and Washington.
Website. www.samoanet.com
Tourism website: www.amsamoa.com

Guam
Where America's Day Begins

People. Population (2003 est.): 163,941. **Population growth rate** (2003 est.): 1.9%. **Pop. density** (2003): 780.1 per sq mi. **Major ethnic groups:** Chamorro, Filipino, Caucasian, Chinese, Japanese, Korean. (Native Guamanians, ethnically Chamorros, are basically of Indonesian stock, with a mixture of Spanish and Filipino; in addition to the official language, they speak the native Chamorro). **Languages:** English, Chamorro, Japanese. **Migration** (1990): About 52% of population were born elsewhere; of these, 48% in Asia, 40% in U.S.

Geography. Total area: 217 sq mi. **Land area:** 210 sq. mi. **Location:** largest and southernmost of the Mariana Islands in the West Pacific, 3,700 mi W of Hawaii. **Climate:** tropical, with temperatures from 70° to 90° F; avg. annual rainfall, about 70 in. **Topography:** coralline limestone plateau in the N; southern chain of low volcanic mountains sloping gently to the W, more steeply to coastal cliffs on the E; general elevation, 500 ft; highest point, Mt. Lamlam, 1,334 ft. **Capital:** Hagatna.

Economy. Chief industries: tourism, U.S. military, construction, banking, printing & publishing. **Chief manuf. goods:** textiles, foods. **Chief crops:** cabbages, eggplants, cucumber, long beans, tomatoes, bananas, coconuts, watermelon, yams, cantaloupe, papayas, maize, sweet potatoes. **Livestock** (2001): 100 cattle; 5,000 hogs/pigs; 20,000 chickens. **Commercial fishing** (2000): $1.3 mil. **Chief port:** Apra Harbor. **Principal internat. airport at:** Hagatna. **Construction sales** (1997): $506 mil. **Employment distrib.** (2000 est.): 26% govt.; 24% trade; 40% serv.; 10% indust. **Per capita income** (2000 est.): $21,000. **Unemployment** (2000 est.): 15%. **Tourism expends.** (1995): $4.9 bil.

Finance. FDIC-insured commercial banks (2002): 2. **Deposits:** $684 mil. **FDIC-insured savings institutions** (2002): 1. **Assets:** $83 mil.

Energy. Electricity production (2001): 30 mil. kWh
Federal govt. Federal employees (1990): 7,200. **Notable fed. facilities:** Anderson AFB; naval, air, and port bases.
Public education. Student-teacher ratio (1995): 18.3.
Misc. data. Flower: Puti Tai Nobio (Bougainvillea). **Bird:** Toto (Fruit dove). **Tree:** Ifit (Intsiabijuga). **Song:** Stand Ye Guamanians.

History. Guam was probably settled by voyagers from the Indonesian-Philippine archipelago by 3rd cent. BC. Pottery, rice cultivation, and megalithic technology show strong East Asian cultural influence. Centralized, village clan-based communities engaged in agriculture and offshore fishing. The estimated population by the early 16th cent. was 50,000-75,000. Magellan arrived in the Marianas Mar. 6, 1521. They were colonized in 1668 by Spanish missionaries, who named them the Mariana Islands in honor of Maria Anna, queen of Spain. When Spain ceded Guam to the U.S., it sold the other Marianas to Germany. Japan obtained a League of Nations mandate over the German islands in 1919; in Dec. 1941 it seized Guam, which was retaken by the U.S. in July-August 1944.

Guam is a self-governing organized unincorporated U.S. territory. The Organic Act of 1950 provided for a governor, elected to a 4-year term, and a 21-member unicameral legislature, elected biennially by the residents, who are American citizens. In 1970, the first governor was elected. In 1972, a U.S. law gave Guam one delegate to the U.S. House of Representatives who has a voice but no vote, except in committees.

Guam's quest to change its status to a U.S. Commonwealth began in the late 1970s. The Guam Commission on Self-Determination, created in 1984, developed a draft Commonwealth Act. In 1993, legislation proposing a change of status was submitted to the U.S. Congress. In 1994, the U.S. Congress passed legislation transferring 3,200 acres of land on Guam from federal to local control.

Tourist attractions. Tropical climate, oceanic marine environment; annual mid-Aug. Merizo Water Festival; Tarzan Falls; beaches; water sports; duty-free port shopping.
Website. www.gov.gu
Tourism website. www.gov.gu/visiting.html

Commonwealth of the Northern Mariana Islands

People. Population (2003 est.): 80,006. **Population growth rate** (2003 est.): 3.4%. **Pop. density** (2003): 447 per sq mi. **Major ethnic groups:** Chamorro, Carolinians and other Micronesians, Caucasian, Japanese, Chinese, Korean. **Languages:** English, Chamorro, Carolinian.

Total area: 189 sq. mi. **Land area:** 179 sq. mi. Located in the perpetually warm climes between Guam and the Tropic of Cancer, the 14 islands of the Northern Marianas form a 300-mi. long archipelago. The indigenous population in 1990 was concentrated on the 3 largest of the 6 inhabited islands: **Saipan**, the seat of government and commerce (38,896), **Rota** (2,295), and **Tinian** (2,118).

Economy. Chief industries: trade, services, and tourism. **Chief manuf. goods:** apparel, stone, clay and glass products. **Chief crops:** melons, vegetables, horticulture, fruits and nuts. **Livestock:** (1998): 1,789 cattle; 831 hogs/pigs; 29,409 chickens. **Commercial fishing** (2000): $938,365. **Construction sales** (1997): $88 mil. **Employment distrib.** (1999 est.): 35% manuf.; 18% managerial; 16% serv. **Unemployment** (1999): 4.3%. **Tourism expends.** (1997): $585 mil.

Education. Pupil-teacher ratio (2000): 18

The people of the Northern Marianas are predominantly of Chamorro cultural extraction, although Carolinians and immigrants from other areas of E. Asia and Micronesia have also settled in the islands. English is among the several languages commonly spoken. Pursuant to the Covenant of 1976, which established the Northern Marianas as a commonwealth in political union with the U.S., most of the indigenous population and many domiciliaries of these islands achieved U.S. citizenship on Nov. 3, 1986, when the U.S. terminated its administration of the UN trusteeship as it affected the Northern Marianas. From July 18, 1947, the U.S. had administered the Northern Marianas under a trusteeship agreement with the UN Security Council.

The Northern Mariana Islands has been self-governing since 1978, when a constitution drafted and adopted by the people became effective and a popularly elected bicameral legislature (2-year term), with offices of governor (4-year term) and lieut. governor, was inaugurated.

Website: www.mariana-islands.gov.mp
Tourism website: www.mariana-islands.gov.mp/tourism.htm

Commonwealth of Puerto Rico
(Estado Libre Asociado de Puerto Rico)

People. Population (2003 est): 3,885,877 (about 2.7 mil more Puerto Ricans reside in the mainland U.S.). **Population growth rate:** (2003 est.): 0.6%. **Net change** (1999-2000): 8.1%. **Pop. density** (2003): 1,134.6 per sq mi. **Urban** (1990): 66.8%. **Racial distribution** (2000): 80.5% white; 8% black; 0.2% Asian; 0.4% Native American/Nat. AK; 3.8% Other. **Hispanic pop.** (any race): 98.8%. **Languages:** Spanish and English are joint official languages.

Geography. Total area: 5,324 sq. mi. **Land area:** 3,425 sq mi. **Location:** island lying between the Atlantic to the N and the Caribbean to the S; it is easternmost of the West Indies group called the Greater Antilles, of which Cuba, Hispaniola, and Jamaica are the larger islands. **Climate:** mild, with a mean average temperature of 77° F. **Topography:** mountainous throughout three-fourths of its rectangular area, surrounded by a broken coastal plain; highest peak, Cerro de Punta, 4,390 ft. **Capital:** San Juan.

Economy. Chief industries: manufacturing, service. **Chief manuf. goods:** pharmaceuticals, apparel, electronics & other electric equipment, industrial machinery. **Gross domestic product:** (1999 est.) $38.1 bil. **Chief crops:** coffee, plantains, pineapples, tomatoes, sugarcane, bananas, mangos, ornamental plants. **Livestock** (2001): 390,000 cattle; 118,000 hogs/pigs; 12.5 mil. chickens. **Nonfuel minerals** (1996): $31.1 mil, mostly portland cement, crushed stone. **Commercial fishing** (2000): $6.4 mil. **Chief ports/river shipping:** San Juan, Ponce, Mayagüez. **Principal airports at:** San Juan, Ponce, Mayagüez, Aguadilla. **Construction sales** (1997): $4 bil. **Employment distrib.** (May 2003): 28.4% govt.; 17.4% trade/trans./util.; 12% mfg.; 9.1% ed./health serv.; 9.9% prof./bus. serv.; 6.5% leisure/hosp.; 4.5% finance; 6.6% constr.; 2.1% info. **Per capita income** (1999 est.): $9,800. **Unemployment** (2002): 12%. **Tourism expends.** (1999): $2.1 bil.

Finance. FDIC-insured commercial banks (2002): 11. **Deposits:** $33.7 bil.
Federal govt. Fed. civ. employees (1997): 13,874. **Notable fed. facilities:** U.S. Naval Station at Roosevelt Roads;

P.R. Natl. Guard Training Area at Camp Santiago, and at Ft. Allen, Juana Diaz; Sabana SECA Communications Ctr. (U.S. Navy); U.S. Army Station at Ft. Buchanan.

Energy. Electricity production (2001): 20.9 bil kWh

Public education. Student-teacher ratio (1995): 16. **Min. teachers' salary** (1997): $1,500 monthly.

Misc. data. Motto: Joannes Est Nomen Eius (John is his name). **Flower:** Maga. **Bird:** Reinita. **Tree:** Ceiba. **National anthem:** La Borinqueña.

History. Puerto Rico (or Borinquen, after the original Arawak Indian name, Boriquen) was visited by Columbus on his second voyage, Nov. 19, 1493. In 1508, the Spanish arrived.

Sugarcane was introduced, 1515, and slaves were imported 3 years later. Gold mining petered out, 1570. Spaniards fought off a series of British and Dutch attacks; slavery was abolished, 1873. Under the treaty of Paris, Puerto Rico was ceded to the U.S. after the Spanish-American War, 1898. In 1952 the people voted in favor of Commonwealth status.

The Commonwealth of Puerto Rico is a self-governing part of the U.S. with a primarily Hispanic culture. The island's citizens have virtually the same control over their internal affairs as do the 50 states of the U.S. However, they do not vote in national general elections, only in national primaries.

Puerto Rico is represented in the U.S. House of Representatives by a Resident Commissioner who has a voice but no vote, except in committees.

No federal income tax is collected from residents on income earned from local sources in Puerto Rico. Nevertheless, as part of the U.S. legal system, Puerto Rico is subject to the provisions of the U.S. Constitution; most federal laws apply as they do in the 50 states.

Puerto Rico's famous "Operation Bootstrap," begun in the late 1940s, succeeded in changing the island from "The Poorhouse of the Caribbean" to an area with the highest per capita income in Latin America. This program encouraged manufacturing and development of the tourist trade by selective tax exemption, low-interest loans, and other incentives. Despite the marked success of Puerto Rico's development efforts over an extended period of time, per capita income in Puerto Rico is low in comparison to that of the 50 states.

Tourist attractions. Ponce Museum of Art; Forts El Morro and San Cristobal; Old Walled City of San Juan; Arecibo Observatory; Cordillera Central and state parks; El Yunque Rain Forest; San Juan Cathedral; Porta Coeli Chapel and Museum of Religious Art, Interamerican Univ., San Germán; Condado Convention Center; Casa Blanca, Ponce de León family home, Puerto Rican Family Museum of 16th and 17th centuries, and Fine Arts Center all in San Juan.

Cultural facilities and events. Festival Casals classical music concerts, mid-June; Puerto Rico Symphony Orchestra at Music Conservatory; Botanical Garden and Museum of Anthropology, Art, and History at the University of Puerto Rico; Institute of Puerto Rican Culture, at the Dominican Convent; and many popular festivals.

Famous Puerto Ricans. Julia de Burgos, Marta Casals Istomin, Pablo Casals, José Celso Barbosa, Orlando Cepeda, Roberto Clemente, José de Diego, José Feliciano, Doña Felisa Rincón de Gautier, Luis A. Ferré, José Ferrer, Commodore Diégo E. Hernández, Miguel Hernández Agosto, Rafael Hernández (El Jibarito), Rafael Hernández Colón, Raúl Julía, René Marqués, Ricky Martin, Concha Meléndez, Rita Moreno, Luis Muñoz Marín, Luis Palés Matos, Adm. Horacio Rivero.

Chamber of Commerce. PO Box 9024033, San Juan, PR 00902. **Websites:** www.gobierno.pr (site is in Spanish); www.gotopuertorico.com

Website. www.welcome.topuertorico.org/government.shtml

Virgin Islands

St. John, St. Croix, St. Thomas

People. Population (2003 est.): 124,778. **Population growth rate** (2003 est.): 1.0%. **Pop. density** (2002): 931.2 per sq mi. **Major ethnic groups:** West Indian, French, Hispanic. **Languages:** English (official), Spanish, Creole.

Geography. Total area: 171 sq mi. **Land area:** 134 sq mi. **Location:** 3 larger and 50 smaller islands and cays in the S

and W of the V.I. group (British V.I. colony to the N and E), which is situated 70 mi E of Puerto Rico, located W of the Anegada Passage, a major channel connecting the Atlantic Ocean and the Caribbean Sea. **Climate:** subtropical; the sun tempered by gentle trade winds; humidity is low; average temperature, 78° F. **Topography:** St. Thomas is mainly a ridge of hills running E and W, and has little tillable land; St. Croix rises abruptly in the N but slopes to the S to flatlands and lagoons; St. John has steep, lofty hills and valleys with little level tillable land. **Capital:** Charlotte Amalie, St. Thomas.

Economy. Chief industries: tourism, rum, alumina, petroleum refining, watches, textiles, electronics, printing & publishing. **Chief manuf. goods:** rum, textiles, pharmaceuticals, perfumes, stone, glass & clay products. **Chief crops:** vegetables, horticulture, fruits and nuts. **Livestock** (2001): 8,000 cattle; 2,600 hogs/pigs; 35,000 chickens. **Minerals:** sand, gravel. **Chief ports:** Cruz Bay, St. John; Frederiksted and Christiansted, St. Croix; Charlotte Amalie, St. Thomas. **Principal internat. airports on:** St. Thomas, St. Croix. **Construction sales** (1997): $185 mil. **Employment distrib.** (1992): 50% trade; 43% serv. **Per capita income** (2001 est.): $19,000. **Unemployment** (1999): 4.9%. **Tourism expends.** (1995): $792 mil.

Finance. FDIC-insured **commercial banks** (2002): 2. **Deposits:** $112 mil.

Energy. Electricity production (2001): 1 bil kWh

Public education. Student-teacher ratio (1995): 14.

Misc. data. Flower: Yellow elder or yellow trumpet, local designation Ginger Thomas. **Bird:** Yellow breast. **Song:** Virgin Islands March.

History. The islands were visited by Columbus in 1493. Spanish forces, 1555, defeated the Caribes and claimed the territory; by 1596 the native population was annihilated. First permanent settlement in the U.S. territory, 1672, by the Danes; U.S. purchased the islands, 1917, for defense purposes.

The Virgin Islands has a republican form of government, headed by a governor and lieut. governor elected, since 1970, by popular vote for 4-year terms. There is a 15-member unicameral legislature, elected by popular vote for a 2-year term. Residents of the V.I. have been U.S. citizens since 1927. Since 1973 they have elected a delegate to the U.S. House of Representatives, who has a voice but no vote, except in committees.

Tourist attractions. Magens Bay, St. Thomas; duty-free shopping; Virgin Islands Natl. Park, beaches, Indian relics, and evidence of colonial Danes.

Tourist information. Dept. of Economic Development & Agriculture: St. Thomas, PO Box 6400, St. Thomas, VI 00801; St. Croix, PO Box 4535, Christiansted, St. Croix 00820. **Website:** www.usvitourism.vi

Website. www.usvi.net

Other Islands

Navassa lies between Jamaica and Haiti, 100 mi south of Guantanamo Bay, Cuba, in the Caribbean; it covers about 2 sq mi, is reserved by the U.S. for a lighthouse, and is uninhabited. It is administered by the U.S. Coast Guard.

Wake Atoll, and its neighboring atolls, **Wilkes** and **Peale,** lie in the Pacific Ocean on the direct route from Hawaii to Hong Kong, about 2,300 mi W of Honolulu and 1,290 mi E of Guam. The group is 4.5 mi long, 1.5 mi wide, and totals less than 3 sq mi in land area. The U.S. flag was hoisted over Wake Atoll, July 4, 1898; formal possession taken Jan. 17, 1899. Wake was administered by the U.S. Air Force, 1972-94. The population consists of about 200 persons.

Midway Atoll, acquired in 1867, consists of 2 atolls, **Sand** and **Eastern,** in N Pacific 1,150 mi. NW of Honolulu, with an area of about 2 sq mi, administered by the U.S. Navy. There is no indigenous population; total pop. is about 450. **Johnston Atoll,** 717 mi WSW of Honolulu, area 1 sq mi, is operated by the Defense Nuclear Agency, and the Fish and Wildlife Service, U.S. Dept. of the Interior; its population is about 1,200. **Kingman Reef,** 920 mi S of Hawaii, is under Navy control. **Howland, Jarvis,** and **Baker Islands,** 1,400-1,650 mi SW of Honolulu, uninhabited since World War II, are under the Interior Dept. **Palmyra** is an atoll about 1,000 mi S of Hawaii, 5 sq mi. Privately owned, it is under the Interior Dept.

WORLD ALMANAC QUICK QUIZ

Before the ratification of the 19th Amendment in 1920, a number of states had granted women the right to vote. Which was the first?

    (a) Massachusetts   (b) New York   (c) Wyoming   (d) New Jersey

For the answer look in this chapter, or see page 1008.

WASHINGTON, DC, CAPITAL OF THE U.S.

Most attractions are free. All times are subject to change. For more details call the Washington, DC, Convention and Visitors Association at 1-800-422-8644, or check out the website at: www.washington.org

Bureau of Engraving and Printing

The **Bureau of Engraving and Printing** of the U.S. Treasury Dept. is the headquarters for the making of U.S. paper money. Free 40-minute self-guided tours (tickets required) Mon.-Fri., 9 AM-2 PM year-round; extended hours, June-Aug., 5 PM-6:45 PM. Closed federal holidays. 14th and C Sts. SW. Phone: 202-874-3019.

Website. www.moneyfactory.com

Capitol

The **United States Capitol** was originally designed by Dr. William Thornton, an amateur architect, who submitted a plan in 1793 that won him $500 and a city lot. The south, or House, wing was completed in 1807 under the direction of Benjamin H. Latrobe. The present Senate and House wings and the iron dome were designed and constructed by Thomas U. Walter, 4th architect of the Capitol, between 1851 and 1863.

The present cast iron dome at its greatest exterior measures 135 ft 5 in., and it is topped by the bronze Statue of Freedom that stands 19½ ft and weighs 14,985 lb. On its base are the words E Pluribus Unum (Out of Many, One).

The Capitol is open from 9 AM to 8 PM, March-Aug., and 9 AM to 4:30 PM, Sept.-Feb., daily. It is closed Jan. 1, Thanksgiving Day, and Dec. 25. Tours (tickets required) through the Capitol, including the House and Senate galleries, are conducted Mon.-Sat. from 9 AM to 4:30 PM.

To observe debate in the House or Senate while Congress is in session, individuals living in the U.S. may obtain tickets to the visitor's galleries from their U.S. representative or senator. Visitors from other countries may obtain passes at the Capitol. Between Constitution & Independence Ave., at Pennsylvania Ave. Phone: 202-225-6827.

Website. www.aoc.gov

Federal Bureau of Investigation

The **Federal Bureau of Investigation** offers guided one-hour tours of its headquarters, beginning with a videotape presentation. Visitors learn about the history of the FBI and see such things as the weapons confiscated from famous gangsters, photos of the most-wanted fugitives, the DNA laboratory, goods forfeited and seized in narcotics operations, and a sharpshooting demonstration.

As of late 2003, tours were suspended for building renovation. J. Edgar Hoover Bldg., Pennsylvania Ave., between 9th and 10th Sts. NW. Phone: 202-324-3000.

Website. www.fbi.gov

Folger Shakespeare Library

The **Folger Shakespeare Library,** on Capitol Hill, is a research institution holding rare books and manuscripts of the Renaissance period and the largest collection of Shakespearean materials in the world, including 79 copies of the First Folio. The library's museum and performing arts programs are presented in the Elizabethan Theatre, which resembles an innyard theater of Shakespeare's day.

Exhibit may be visited Mon.-Sat., 10 AM-4 PM, 201 E. Capitol St., SE , Phone: 202-544-4600.

Website. www.folger.edu

Holocaust Memorial Museum

The **U.S. Holocaust Memorial Museum** opened on Apr. 21, 1993. The museum documents, through permanent and temporary displays, interactive videos, and special lectures, the events of the Holocaust beginning in 1933 and continuing through World War II. The permanent exhibition is not recommended for children under the age of 11.

The museum is open daily, 10 AM-5:30 PM, except Yom Kippur and Dec. 25, and extended hours Tuesdays (8 AM-10 PM) Apr.-Sept. A limited number of free tickets are available on day of visit; advance tickets may be ordered for a small fee. 100 Raoul Wallenberg Pl. SW. Phone: 202-488-0400.

Website. www.ushmm.org

Jefferson Memorial

Dedicated in 1943, the **Thomas Jefferson Memorial** stands on the south shore of the Tidal Basin in West Potomac Park. It is a circular stone structure, with Vermont marble on the exterior and Georgia white marble inside, and combines architectural elements of the dome of the Pantheon in Rome and the rotunda designed by Jefferson for the Univ. of Virginia.

The memorial, on the south edge of the Tidal Basin, is open daily, 8 AM-midnight. An elevator and curb ramps for the handicapped are in service. Phone: 202-426-6841.

Website. www.nps.gov/thje/home.htm

John F. Kennedy Center

The **John F. Kennedy Center for the Performing Arts,** designated by Congress as the National Cultural Center and the official memorial in Washington, DC, to Pres. John F. Kennedy, opened Sept. 8, 1971. Designed by Edward Durell Stone, the center includes an opera house, a concert hall, several theaters, 2 restaurants, and a library.

Free tours are available Monday-Friday, 10 AM-5 PM and Sat. & Sun., 10 AM-1 PM. 2700 F St. NW. Phone: 202-467-4600, or 1-800-444-1324.

Website. www.kennedy-center.org

Korean War Veterans Memorial

Dedicated on July 27, 1995, the **Korean War Veterans Memorial** honors all Americans who served in the Korean War. Situated at the west end of the Mall, across the reflecting pool from the Vietnam Memorial, the triangular-shaped stone and steel memorial features a multiservice formation of 19 troops clad in ponchos with the wind at their back, ready for combat. A granite wall, with images of the men and women who served, juts into a pool of water, the Pool of Remembrance, and is inscribed with the words Freedom Is Not Free.

The $18 mil memorial, which was funded by private donations, is open 8 AM-midnight. French Dr., SW across from Lincoln Memorial. Phone: 202-426-6841.

Website. www.nps.gov/kwvm

Library of Congress

Established by and for Congress in 1800, the **Library of Congress** has extended its services over the years to other government agencies and other libraries, to scholars, and to the general public, and it now serves as the national library. It contains more than 80 million items in 470 languages.

Exhibit halls are open to the public Mon.-Fri., 8:30 AM-9:30 PM; Sat., 8:30 AM-6:30 PM. The Library is closed Jan. 1 and Dec. 25. 101 Independence Ave., SE. Phone: 202-707-5000.

Website. www.loc.gov

Lincoln Memorial

Designed by Henry Bacon, the **Lincoln Memorial** in West Potomac Park, on the axis of the Capitol and the Washington Monument, is a large marble hall enclosing a heroic statue of Abraham Lincoln in meditation sitting on an armchair. The memorial was dedicated May 30, 1922. The statue was designed by Daniel Chester French and sculpted by French and the Piccirilli brothers. Murals and ornamentation on the ceiling beams are by Jules Guerin. The text of the Gettysburg Address is in the south chamber; that of Lincoln's Second Inaugural speech is in the north chamber. Each is engraved on a stone tablet.

The memorial is open daily 8 AM-midnight. An elevator for the handicapped is in service. W. Potomac Park at 23rd St. NW. Phone: 202-426-6841.

Website. www.nps.gov/linc/home.htm

National Archives and Records

Original copies of the Declaration of Independence, the Constitution, and the Bill of Rights are on permanent display in the **National Archives** Exhibition Hall. The National Archives also holds other valuable U.S. government records and historic maps, photographs, and manuscripts.

Central Research and Microfilm Research Rooms are also available to the public for genealogical research.

The Exhibition Hall, which had been closed for renovations, reopened in September 2003. 7th & Pennsylvania Ave. NW. Phone: 202-501-5000, or 1-866-325-7208.

Website. www.archives.gov

National Gallery of Art

The **National Gallery of Art,** situated on the north side of the Mall facing Constitution Avenue, was established by Congress, Mar. 24, 1937, and opened Mar. 17, 1941. The original West building was designed by John Russell Pope. The East building, opened in 1978, was designed by I. M. Pei. The National Gallery is separate from, but maintains a relationship with, the Smithsonian Institution.

Open daily, Mon.-Sat. 10 AM-5 PM, Sunday 11 AM-6 PM. Closed Jan. 1 and Dec. 25. 4th & Constitution Ave NW. Phone: 202-737-4215.

Website. www.nga.gov

WORLD ALMANAC EDITORS' PICKS
Top Sites to Visit in Washington, DC

The editors of *The World Almanac* have ranked the following as the top spots for adults to visit in Washington, DC.

1. White House (limited tours resumed Sept. 2003)
2. Capitol
3. Lincoln Memorial
4. National Museum of American History (part of the Smithsonian Institution)
5. Washington Monument
6. Vietnam Veterans Memorial
7. Holocaust Memorial Museum
8. National Air and Space Museum (part of the Smithsonian Institution)
9. National Gallery of Art
10. National Archives (reopened as of Sept. 2003)

Readers are invited to submit their own list for this and other Editors' Picks; see instructions on page 1007. Results will be published in *The World Almanac 2005.*

Franklin Delano Roosevelt Memorial

Opened May 2, 1997, by Pres. Bill Clinton, the **FDR Memorial** features 9 bronze sculptural ensembles depicting FDR, Eleanor Roosevelt (the first First Lady to be honored in a national memorial), and events from the Great Depression and World War II. This 7.5-acre memorial is located near the Tidal Basin in a park-like setting and includes waterfalls, quiet pools, and reddish Dakota granite upon which some of Pres. Roosevelt's well-known words are carved. The monument is wheelchair accessible.

Grounds, staffed daily, 8 AM-midnight, except Dec. 25. 1850 W. Basin Dr. SW. Phone: 202-426-6841.

Website. www.nps.gov/fdrm

Smithsonian Institution

The **Smithsonian Institution**, established in 1846, is the world's largest museum complex and consists of 14 museums and the National Zoo. It holds some 100 mil. artifacts and specimens in its trust. Nine museums are on the National Mall between the Washington Monument and the Capitol; 5 other museums and the zoo are elsewhere in Washington (the Cooper-Hewitt Museum and the National Museum of the American Indian, also administered by the Smithsonian, are in New York City). The **Smithsonian Information Center** is located in "the Castle" on the Mall. Also on the Mall are the **National Museum of American History**, the **National Museum of Natural History**, the **National Air and Space Museum**, the **Hirshhorn Museum and Sculpture Garden**, the **Arthur M. Sackler Gallery**, the **National Museum of African Art**, the **Freer Gallery of Art**, and the **Arts and Industries Building.** Near the Sackler Gallery is the **Enid A. Haupt Garden.** Located nearby are the **National Postal Museum**, the **National Museum of American Art**, the **National Portrait Gallery**, and the **Renwick Gallery.** Farther away, at 1901 Fort Place SE, is the **Anacostia Museum.**

Most museums are open daily, except Dec. 25, 10 AM-5:30 PM. Phone: 202-357-2700.

Website. www.si.edu

Vietnam Veterans Memorial

Originally dedicated on Nov. 13, 1982, the **Vietnam Veterans Memorial** is a recognition of the men and women who served in the armed forces in the Vietnam War. On a V-shaped black-granite wall, designed by Maya Ying Lin, are inscribed the names of the more than 58,000 Americans who lost their lives or remain missing.

Since 1982, 2 additions have been made to the Memorial. The 1st, dedicated on Nov. 11, 1984, is the Frederick Hart sculpture *Three Servicemen*. On Nov. 11, 1993, the Vietnam Women's Memorial was dedicated, honoring the more than 11,500 women who served in Vietnam. The bronze sculpture, portraying 3 women helping a wounded male soldier, was designed by Glenna Goodacre.

The memorial is open 8 AM-midnight daily. Constitution Ave. & Bacon Dr. NW. Phone: 202-426-6841.

Website. www.thevirtualwall.org

Washington Monument

The **Washington Monument**, dedicated in 1885, is a tapering shaft, or obelisk, of white marble, 555 ft, 5 $1/_8$ inches in height and 55 ft, 1 ½ in. square at base. Eight small windows, 2 on each side, are located at the 500-ft level, where points of interest are indicated.

Open daily (except Dec. 25), 9 AM-4:45 PM. Free timed passes are available; passes are available in advance for a small fee. 15th & Constitution Ave. NW. Phone: 202-426-6841.

Website. www.nps.gov/wash

White House

The **White House,** the President's residence, stands on 18 acres on the south side of Pennsylvania Ave., between the Treasury and the old Executive Office Building. The walls are of sandstone, quarried at Aquia Creek, VA. The exterior walls were painted, causing the building to be termed the "White House." On Aug. 24, 1814, during Madison's administration, the house was burned by the British. James Hoban rebuilt it by Oct. 1817.

The White House is normally open for free self-guided tours Tues.-Sat., 7:30 AM-10:30 AM. (Tour requests must be made at least one month in advance through your member of Congress.) Only the public rooms on the ground floor and state floor may be visited. 1600 Pennsylvania Ave. The White House Visitor Center at 1450 Pennsylvania Ave. is open daily 7:30 AM - 4 PM. Phone: 202-456-7041.

Website. www.whitehouse.gov

Attractions Near Washington, DC
Arlington National Cemetery

Arlington National Cemetery, on the former Custis-Lee estate in Arlington, VA, is the site of the **Tomb of the Unknowns** and is the final resting place of Pres. John Fitzgerald Kennedy, who was buried there on Nov. 25, 1963. His wife, Jacqueline Bouvier Kennedy Onassis, was buried at the same site on May 23, 1994. An eternal flame burns over the grave site. In an adjacent area is the grave of Pres. Kennedy's brother Sen. Robert F. Kennedy (NY), interred on June 8, 1968. Many other famous Americans are also buried at Arlington, as well as more than 200,000 American soldiers from every major war.

North of the National Cemetery stands the **U.S. Marine Corps War Memorial**, also known as Iwo Jima. The memorial is a bronze statue of the raising of the U.S. flag on Mt. Suribachi, Feb. 23, 1945, during World War II, executed by Felix de Weldon from the photograph by Joe Rosenthal.

On the southern side of the Memorial Bridge, near the cemetery entrance, a memorial honoring the women in the military was dedicated, Oct. 18, 1997. The **Women in Military Service for America Memorial** is a half-circle granite monument, 30 ft. high and 226 ft. in diameter, with the Great Seal of the United States in the center.

Open daily, 8 AM-5 PM (8 AM-7 PM., Apr.-Sept.), Arlington, VA. Phone: 703-607-8000.

Website. www.arlingtoncemetery.org

Mount Vernon

Mount Vernon, George Washington's estate, is on the south bank of the Potomac R., 16 mi below Washington, DC, in northern Virginia. The present house is an enlargement of one apparently built on the site by Augustine Washington, who lived there 1735-38. His son Lawrence came there in 1743, and renamed the plantation Mount Vernon in honor of Admiral Vernon, under whom he had served in the West Indies. Lawrence Washington died in 1752 and was succeeded as proprietor by his half-brother, George Washington. The estate has been restored to its 18th-century appearance and includes many original furnishings. Washington and his wife, Martha, are buried on the grounds.

Open 365 days, 8 AM-5 PM, Apr.-Aug., 9 AM-5 PM, Sept., Oct., Mar.; 9 AM-4 PM, Nov.-Feb. Phone: 703-780-2000, or 1-800-429-1520. Admission: adults $11, seniors (62+) $10, children (6-11) $5, age 5 and under free.

Website. www.mountvernon.org

The Pentagon

The **Pentagon**, headquarters of the Department of Defense, is one of the world's largest office buildings. Situated in Arlington, VA, it has housed more than 23,000 employees in offices occupying 3,707,745 sq ft. The building was, however, severely damaged when struck by a plane Sept. 11, 2001.

Tours available to schools, educational organizations, and other select groups by reservation only. Arlington, VA (I-395 South to Boundary Channel Drive exit). Pentagon tour office: 703-695-1776.

Website. www.defenselink.mil/pubs/pentagon

UNITED STATES POPULATION

Census Bureau Takes Pulse of Life in America

by Louis Kincannon, Director, U.S. Census Bureau

We at the Census Bureau pride ourselves on being "America's factfinder" when it comes to collecting data on U.S. people and businesses. Between our decennial population and housing census, numerous household surveys, and population estimates programs, we take the nation's demographic pulse on a constant basis. Our economic census and many business surveys permit us to do the same for the economy. Additionally, the new American Community Survey will provide a host of socioeconomic data for small geographic areas throughout the decade.

Our latest statistics show a nation that is becoming better educated and more racially and ethnically diverse, with increasingly complex living arrangements, growing equality between women and men, and a rapidly expanding online economy.

The Population Continues to Grow . . .

The nation's population increased by 1.1% (3.1 million people) between July 1, 2001, and July 1, 2002, reaching 288,368,698. For the 16th consecutive year, Nevada was the fastest-growing state, this time with a 3.6% population increase to 2.2 million. Not far behind were Arizona (2.8%), Florida (2.1%), Texas (1.9%), and Georgia (1.8%).

California remained the most populous state, with 35.1 million people in 2002, constituting 12.2% of the nation's total. The second and third most populous states were Texas (21.8 million) and New York (19.2 million).

From July 1, 2001, to July 1, 2002, Rockwall County, TX (a small, once-rural county now part of the Dallas metropolitan area) had the fastest growth rate among counties at 7.9%, 7 times as fast as the national rate. Two northern Virginia counties, Loudoun (2nd) and Stafford (9th), both in the Washington, DC, area, and 3 counties in the Atlanta vicinity, Henry (3rd), Forsyth (4th), and Newton (7th), were also among the 10 counties with the highest rates of growth during the 2001-2002 period. Of the 100 fastest-growing counties with 10,000 or more residents, 63 were in the South, 18 in the West, 17 in the Midwest, and 2 in the Northeast.

. . . and Becomes More Diverse

Official population estimates now indicate that the Hispanic community is the nation's largest minority community, increasing from 35.3 million on Apr. 1, 2000, to 38.8 million on July 1, 2002, representing 13.5% of the total population. The increase constitutes a 9.8% growth rate—far higher than the national rate of 2.5%. 53% of the growth can be attributed to international migration; the rest is the result of natural increase (births minus deaths).

For the first time, Census 2000 provided the option of selecting more than one race category to indicate racial identities. Projecting from the reported figures, as of July 1, 2002, an estimated 38.3 million residents, or 13.3% of the population, were African-American alone or African-American in combination with one or more other races.

Other minority groups were smaller, with 13.1 million (4.5%) classifying themselves as Asian alone or in combination with one or more other races, 4.3 million (1.5%) as American Indian and Alaska native alone or in combination with one or more other races, and 943,000 (0.3%) as native Hawaiian and other Pacific Islander alone or in combination with one or more other races. The population that was white alone or in combination with one or more other races—but non-Hispanic—totaled about 200 million, or 69.3%.

Education on the Rise

Judging from census statistics, the U.S. population is better educated than ever before: more than one-quarter (27%) of adults aged 25 and older had at least a bachelor's degree in 2002—a record high. The percentage increased by about one point from the previous year, the result of significant increases for women, non-Hispanic whites, and African-Americans.

Among race and ethnic groups, Asians and Pacific Islanders had by far the highest proportion of college graduates

(47%), followed by non-Hispanic whites (29%), African-Americans (17%), and Hispanics (11%).

Is it worth it to stay in school and earn a higher degree? Our data show the answer to be a resounding yes! Adults aged 18 and over with a bachelor's degree earned an average of $50,623 a year in 2001—while those with only a high school diploma earned an average of $26,795. Those without a high school diploma averaged $18,793. Advanced degree-holders made the most of all, an average of $72,869.

School districts in New York and New Jersey led all other states in the amount of money spent per student on public elementary and secondary education in 2001, at $10,922 and $10,893, respectively.

Living Arrangements Increasingly Complex

In 2000, there were about 105 million households in the United States, 60 million of which were "coupled." The vast majority—54.5 million of these households—were headed by married-couples, compared to 5.5 million headed by unmarried partners. Of the unmarried partners, about 600,000 were of the same sex. Opposite-sex, unmarried-partner households were almost as likely to have children as married-couple households—43% compared with 46%. One-third of female same-sex couples and one-fifth of male same-sex couples were living with their own children.

The majority of the nation's 72 million children under 15—50 million, or about 7 in 10—lived with both their parents in 2002. These children were nearly 60 times more likely to live with stay-at-home moms than dads (11 million compared with 189,000). Another 20 million children lived with only one parent—about 16.5 million with their mothers and 3.3 million with their fathers. The fathers were more likely to have partners than the mothers. Three in 10 children living with single fathers lived in a household with their father and his unmarried partner. The comparable figure for children and single mothers was 1 in 10.

In all, 5.6 million children lived in a household with at least one grandparent. Most of those (3.7 million) lived in their grandparents' home; of these, two-thirds had a parent present.

More Newcomers

The nation's foreign-born population in 2002 numbered 32.5 million—the highest total in U.S. history. Among these immigrants, 52% were born in Latin America (36% in Mexico or Central America), 26% in Asia, 14% in Europe, and the remaining 8% in other regions of the world, such as Africa and Oceania. More than 1 in 3 foreign-born people were naturalized U.S. citizens. Two out of three (67%) of foreign-born people aged 25 or more were high school graduates, compared to 87% of native-born Americans. In the year 2001, 31% of the foreign born with full-time jobs earned less than $20,000, compared to 17% of all native-born workers. The poverty rate among the foreign born was also higher than that of the native population—16% versus 11%.

Poverty Up, Income Down

The nation's poverty rate rose for a second consecutive year in 2002, increasing from 11.7% in 2001 to 12.1% in 2002. Median household income declined 1.1% from $42,900 in 2001 to $42,409 in 2002, a second straight annual decline.

Averaging 2000, 2001, and 2002 figures, real median household income in Maryland, though not significantly different from the figures for Alaska or Minnesota, was higher than the values for the remaining 47 states and the District of Columbia. At the other end of the scale, median household income for West Virginia was lower than the incomes of the remaining 49 states and the District of Columbia. Oklahoma was the only state which had a statistically significant increase in median household income. Ten states experienced significant declines.

Women Making Progress

Women have narrowed the gap with men in many areas, and surpassed them in some. In 2002, 34% of women age 16 and over worked in professional, executive, administrative, and managerial jobs, compared with 30% of men. Women who worked full time, year-round earned only 76 cents for every $1 their male counterparts earned in 2001. But this represented an all-time high.

When it comes to education, younger women have inched ahead of men. Breaking a 13-year statistical dead heat, women edged out men in 2002 in their high school graduation rate (84.4% compared with 83.8%). In the same year, 33% of women ages 25 to 34 had completed college, exceeding the 29% rate of their male counterparts. In fact, in each year since 1982, more American women than men have been awarded bachelor's degrees.

A Graying Nation

At the beginning of the 20th century, with life expectancy relatively low, there were a mere 3.1 million people aged 65 and over. By the dawn of this century, the older population had increased more than tenfold, with 35.6 million people aged 65 and over as of July 1, 2002. Beginning in 2011, the year those born in the first year (1946) of the "baby-boom" generation reach age 65, the older population will loom even larger on the nation's demographic landscape.

For many older Americans, age 65 is too soon to retire. Instead, it's a time to continue their careers. Nearly 1 in 8 seniors (4.5 million) were still on the job or looking for work in 2002.

The older population is notable for voter participation. In the last presidential election, more than 7 in 10 citizens aged 65 to 74 cast a ballot, the highest rate of any age group. The national rate was 55%.

Among people aged 65 to 84, 74% of men and 45% of women were married and living with their spouse. By age 85 and over, this was true for 58% of men, but only 12% of women.

In 2001, women 65 and over were more likely to be poor than men in this age group: 12.4% versus 7.0%.

Economic Patterns

Census Bureau figures show that in 2000 and early 2001, prior to the more recent downturn, the U.S. economy added about 25,000 business establishments, 1 million employees, and over $100 billion in payroll. The most consistent growth occurred in Orange and San Diego counties in California, the only counties among the nation's largest with gains in all three categories. Los Angeles County was the leader in busi-

ness growth; Santa Clara (CA) in employment gains, and New York County (Manhattan), NY, led in payroll growth.

Not all of these businesses were huge conglomerates. In fact, a large majority (70%) had no paid employees. These are "mom-and-pop" shops and other sole proprietorships. They include such businesses as barber and beauty shops, child-care providers, real estate agents, carpenters, plumbers, writers, and tax preparers. In terms of sales or receipts, nonemployers account for roughly 3% of business activity. The number of such businesses grew 2.3% between 1999 and 2000. Nevada led all states in the growth of nonemployer businesses, with an increase of 6.9%. Maryland was second, at 5.0%, followed by Delaware, at 4.9%.

One of the more telling signs of the Internet age is the emergence of e-commerce, as more and more Americans opt to shop online, rather than in person. Census Bureau retail sales statistics reflect this trend. Total e-commerce sales for 2002 were estimated at $45.6 billion, an increase of 27% from 2001, while retail sales as a whole rose 3.1% over the same period. Overall, e-commerce sales in 2002 accounted for 1.4% of total sales, up from 1.1% the previous year.

Proud to Serve

Throughout U.S. history, in times of peace and war, millions of Americans have put on a uniform to serve the nation in the military. This includes the 1.4 million men and women currently on active duty in the U.S. armed forces, and the 1.2 million ready reservists and National Guard members who were serving as of Feb. 28, 2003, just prior to the start of the war in Iraq. Women comprised 15% of active duty forces. As of Dec. 31, 2002, some 210,000 men and women on active duty were legal residents of Texas—the highest total for any state.

In addition to those currently serving, there were more than 26 million veterans across the country, according to Census 2000. Nearly 6 million served in World War II; about 4 million in the Korean War; more than 8 million during the Vietnam era; and over 2 million in the Gulf War.

About 1.6 million of these veterans (6%) were women, 2.6 million were African-American, and 1.1 million were Hispanic. California, Florida, and Texas had the highest veteran populations at 2.6 million, 1.9 million, and 1.8 million, respectively. Alaska boasted the highest percentage—17% of the state's civilian adult residents had served in the U.S. military.

The Census: Looking Back

The U.S. Census is conducted every 10 years as mandated by the U.S. Constitution, Article I, Section 2. The primary purpose is to apportion seats in the U.S. House of Representatives and determine state legislative district boundaries. The data are also critical for a vast array of government programs at every level, and for providing demographic information to individuals and businesses.

The first U.S. census, which counted 3.9 million people, was conducted in 1790, shortly after George Washington became president. It counted the number of free white males age 16 and over, and under 16 (to measure how many men might be available for military service), the number of free white females, all other free persons (including any American Indians who paid taxes), and slaves. It took 18 months to collect the data, often on unofficial sheets of paper supplied by U.S. marshals. In contrast to today's pledge of confidentiality, the 1790 census was displayed "at two of the most public places." The 1790 census resulted in an increase of 41 seats (65 to 106) in the House of Representatives.

As the nation expanded, so did the scope of the census data. The first inquiry on manufactures was made in 1810. Questions on agriculture, mining, and fisheries were added in 1840. In 1850, the census included inquiries on social issues—taxation, churches, pauperism, and crime.

The 1880 census had so many questions that it took the full 10 years between censuses to publish all the results. Because of this delay, Congress limited the 1900 census to questions on population, manufactures, agriculture, and mortality. (Many of the dropped topics reappeared in later censuses.)

For many years, the undertaking of each census had to be authorized by a specific act of Congress. In 1954, Congress specified the laws under which the Census Bureau operates in Title 13 of the U.S. Code. This title delineates the basic scope of the census, the requirements for the public to provide information as well as for the Bureau to keep information confidential, and the penalties for violating any of these obligations.

Today, the secretary of commerce (and through that individual, the Census Bureau) is directed by law to take censuses of population, housing, agriculture, irrigation, manufactures, mineral industries, other businesses (wholesale trade, retail trade, services), construction, transportation, and governments at stated intervals, and may take surveys related to any of these subjects.

U.S. marshals supervised their assistants' enumeration of the first 9 censuses and reported to the president (1790), the secretary of state (1800-1840), or the secretary of the interior (1850-1870). There was no continuity of personnel from one census to the next. However, in 1902, Congress authorized the president to set up a permanent Census Office in the Interior Dept. In 1903, the agency was transferred to the new Dept. of Commerce and Labor, and when the department split in 1913, the Bureau of the Census was placed in the Commerce Dept.

The Census Bureau began using statistical sampling techniques in the 1940s, computers in the 1950s, and mail enumeration in the 1960s, all as part of an effort to publish more data sooner and at a lower cost, and with less burden on the public.

U.S. Population by Official

STATE	1790[1]	1800[1]	1810[1]	1820[1]	1830[1]	1840	1850	1860	1870	1880	1890	1900
AL..		1	9	128	310	590,756	771,623	964,201	996,992	1,262,505	1,513,401	1,828,697
AK..										33,426	32,052	63,592
AZ..									9,658	40,440	88,243	122,931
AR..			1	14	30	97,574	209,897	435,450	484,471	802,525	1,128,211	1,311,564
CA..							92,597	379,994	560,247	864,694	1,213,398	1,485,053
CO..								34,277	39,864	194,327	413,249	539,700
CT..	238	251	262	275	298	309,978	370,792	460,147	537,454	622,700	746,258	908,420
DE..	59	64	73	73	77	78,085	91,532	112,216	125,015	146,608	168,493	184,735
DC..		8	16	23	30	33,745	51,687	75,080	131,700	177,624	230,392	278,718
FL..					35	54,477	87,445	140,424	187,748	269,493	391,422	528,542
GA..	83	163	252	341	517	691,392	906,185	1,057,286	1,184,109	1,542,180	1,837,353	2,216,331
HI..												154,001
ID..									14,999	32,610	88,548	161,772
IL..			12	55	157	476,183	851,470	1,711,951	2,539,891	3,077,871	3,826,352	4,821,550
IN..		6	25	147	343	685,866	988,416	1,350,428	1,680,637	1,978,301	2,192,404	2,516,462
IA..						43,112	192,214	674,913	1,194,020	1,624,615	1,912,297	2,231,853
KS..								107,206	364,399	996,096	1,428,108	1,470,495
KY..	74	221	407	564	688	779,828	982,405	1,155,684	1,321,011	1,648,690	1,858,635	2,147,174
LA..			77	153	216	352,411	517,762	708,002	726,915	939,946	1,118,588	1,381,625
ME..	97	152	229	298	399	501,793	583,169	628,279	626,915	648,936	661,086	694,466
MD..	320	342	381	407	447	470,019	583,034	687,049	780,894	934,943	1,042,390	1,188,044
MA..	379	423	472	523	610	737,699	994,514	1,231,066	1,457,351	1,783,085	2,238,947	2,805,346
MI..			5	9	32	212,267	397,654	749,113	1,184,059	1,636,937	2,093,890	2,420,982
MN..							6,077	172,023	439,706	780,773	1,310,283	1,751,394
MS..		8	31	75	137	375,651	606,526	791,305	827,922	1,131,597	1,289,600	1,551,270
MO..			20	67	140	383,702	682,044	1,182,012	1,721,295	2,168,380	2,679,185	3,106,665
MT..									20,595	39,159	142,924	243,329
NE..								28,841	122,993	452,402	1,062,656	1,066,300
NV..								6,857	42,491	62,266	47,355	42,335
NH..	142	184	214	244	269	284,574	317,976	326,073	318,300	346,991	376,530	411,588
NJ..	184	211	246	278	321	373,306	489,555	672,035	906,096	1,131,116	1,444,933	1,883,669
NM..							61,547	93,516	91,874	119,565	160,282	195,310
NY..	340	589	959	1,373	1,919	2,428,921	3,097,394	3,880,735	4,382,759	5,082,871	6,003,174	7,268,894
NC..	394	478	556	639	736	753,419	869,039	992,622	1,071,361	1,399,750	1,617,949	1,893,810
ND..									2,405[2]	36,909	190,983	319,146
OH..		45	231	581	938	1,519,467	1,980,329	2,339,511	2,665,260	3,198,062	3,672,329	4,157,545
OK..											258,657	790,391
OR..							12,093	52,465	90,923	174,768	317,704	413,536
PA..	434	602	810	1,049	1,348	1,724,033	2,311,786	2,906,215	3,521,951	4,282,891	5,258,113	6,302,115
RI..	69	69	77	83	97	108,830	147,545	174,620	217,353	276,531	345,506	428,556
SC..	249	346	415	503	581	594,398	668,507	703,708	705,606	995,577	1,151,149	1,340,316
SD..								4,837[2]	11,776[2]	98,268	348,600	401,570
TN..	36	106	262	423	682	829,210	1,002,717	1,109,801	1,258,520	1,542,359	1,767,518	2,020,616
TX..							212,592	604,215	818,579	1,591,749	2,235,527	3,048,710
UT..							11,380	40,273	86,786	143,963	210,779	276,749
VT..	85	154	218	236	281	291,948	314,120	315,098	330,551	332,286	332,422	343,641
VA..	692	808	878	938	1,044	1,025,227	1,119,348	1,219,630	1,225,163	1,512,565	1,655,980	1,854,184
WA..							1,201	11,594	23,955	75,116	357,232	518,103
WV..	56	79	105	137	177	224,537	302,313	376,688	442,014	618,457	762,794	958,800
WI..						30,945	305,391	775,881	1,054,670	1,315,497	1,693,330	2,069,042
WY..									9,118	20,789	62,555	92,531
U.S.	3,929	5,308	7,240	9,638	12,866[3]	17,068,953[3]	23,191,876[3]	31,443,321	38,558,371	50,189,209	62,979,766	76,212,168

Note: Where possible, population shown is that of the 2000 area of the state. Members of the Armed Forces overseas or other U.S. nationals abroad are not included. Totals revised to include corrections of initial tabulated counts. (1) Totals for 1790 through 1830 are in thousands. (2) 1860 figure is for Dakota Territory; 1870 figures are for parts of Dakota Territory. (3) Includes persons (5,318 in 1830 and 6,100 in 1840) on public ships in the service of the U.S. not credited to any region, division, or state.

Estimated Population of American Colonies, 1630-1780

Source: Bureau of the Census, U.S. Dept. of Commerce; in thousands

Colony	1630	1650	1670	1690	1700	1720	1740	1750	1770	1780
TOTAL	4.6	50.4	111.9	210.4	250.9	466.2	905.6	1,170.8	2,148.1	2,780.4
Maine (counties)[1]									31.3	49.1
New Hampshire[2]	0.5	1.3	1.8	4.2	5.0	9.4	23.3	27.5	62.4	87.8
Vermont[3]									10.0	47.6
Plymouth and Massachusetts[1,2,4]	0.9	15.6	35.3	56.9	55.9	91.0	151.6	188.0	235.3	268.6
Rhode Island[2]		0.8	2.2	4.2	5.9	11.7	25.3	33.2	58.2	52.9
Connecticut[2]		4.1	12.6	21.6	26.0	58.8	89.6	111.3	183.9	206.7
New York[2]	0.4	4.1	5.8	13.9	19.1	36.9	63.7	76.7	162.9	210.5
New Jersey[2]			1.0	8.0	14.0	29.8	51.4	71.4	117.4	139.6
Pennsylvania[2]				11.4	18.0	31.0	85.6	119.7	240.1	327.3
Delaware[2]		0.2	0.7	1.5	2.5	5.4	19.9	28.7	35.5	45.4
Maryland[2]		4.5	13.2	24.0	29.6	66.1	116.1	141.1	202.6	245.5
Virginia[2]	2.5	18.7	35.3	53.0	58.6	87.8	180.4	231.0	447.0	538.0
North Carolina[2]			3.8	7.6	10.7	21.3	51.8	73.0	197.2	270.1
South Carolina[2]			0.2	3.9	5.7	17.0	45.0	64.0	124.2	180.0
Georgia[2]							2.0	5.2	23.4	56.1
Kentucky[5]									15.7	45.0
Tennessee[6]									1.0	10.0

(1) For 1660-1750, Maine counties are included with Massachusetts. Maine was part of Massachusetts until it became a separate state in 1820. (2) One of the original 13 states. (3) Admitted to statehood in 1791. (4) Plymouth became a part of the Province of Massachusetts in 1691. (5) Admitted to statehood in 1792. (6) Admitted to statehood in 1796.

Census, 1790-2000

1910	1920	1930	1940	1950	1960	1970	1980	1990	2000
2,138,093	2,348,174	2,646,248	2,832,961	3,061,743	3,266,740	3,444,354	3,894,025	4,040,587	4,447,100
64,356	55,036	59,278	72,524	128,643	226,167	302,583	401,851	550,043	626,932
204,354	334,162	435,573	499,261	749,587	1,302,161	1,775,399	2,716,546	3,665,228	5,130,632
1,574,449	1,752,204	1,854,482	1,949,387	1,909,511	1,786,272	1,923,322	2,286,357	2,350,725	2,673,400
2,377,549	3,426,861	5,677,251	6,907,387	10,586,223	15,717,204	19,971,069	23,667,764	29,760,021	33,871,648
799,024	939,629	1,035,791	1,123,296	1,325,089	1,753,947	2,209,596	2,889,735	3,294,394	4,301,261
1,114,756	1,380,631	1,606,903	1,709,242	2,007,280	2,535,234	3,032,217	3,107,564	3,287,116	3,405,565
202,322	223,003	238,380	266,505	318,085	446,292	548,104	594,338	666,168	783,600
331,069	437,571	486,869	663,091	802,178	763,956	756,668	638,432	606,900	572,059
752,619	968,470	1,468,211	1,897,414	2,771,305	4,951,560	6,791,418	9,746,961	12,937,926	15,982,378
2,609,121	2,895,832	2,908,506	3,123,723	3,444,578	3,943,116	4,587,930	5,462,982	6,478,216	8,186,453
191,874	255,881	368,300	422,770	499,794	632,772	769,913	964,691	1,108,229	1,211,537
325,594	431,866	445,032	524,873	588,637	667,191	713,015	944,127	1,006,749	1,293,953
5,638,591	6,485,280	7,630,654	7,897,241	8,712,176	10,081,158	11,110,285	11,427,409	11,430,602	12,419,293
2,700,876	2,930,390	3,238,503	3,427,796	3,934,224	4,662,498	5,195,392	5,490,214	5,544,159	6,080,485
2,224,771	2,404,021	2,470,939	2,538,268	2,621,073	2,757,537	2,825,368	2,913,808	2,776,755	2,926,324
1,690,949	1,769,257	1,880,999	1,801,028	1,905,299	2,178,611	2,249,071	2,364,236	2,477,574	2,688,418
2,289,905	2,416,630	2,614,589	2,845,627	2,944,806	3,038,156	3,220,711	3,660,324	3,685,296	4,041,769
1,656,388	1,798,509	2,101,593	2,363,880	2,683,516	3,257,022	3,644,637	4,206,116	4,219,973	4,468,976
742,371	768,014	797,423	847,226	913,774	969,265	993,722	1,125,043	1,227,928	1,274,923
1,295,346	1,449,661	1,631,526	1,821,244	2,343,001	3,100,689	3,923,897	4,216,933	4,781,468	5,296,486
3,366,416	3,852,356	4,249,614	4,316,721	4,690,514	5,148,578	5,689,170	5,737,093	6,016,425	6,349,097
2,810,173	3,668,412	4,842,325	5,256,106	6,371,766	7,823,194	8,881,826	9,262,044	9,295,297	9,938,444
2,075,708	2,387,125	2,563,953	2,792,300	2,982,483	3,413,864	3,806,103	4,075,970	4,375,099	4,919,479
1,797,114	1,790,618	2,009,821	2,183,796	2,178,914	2,178,141	2,216,994	2,520,770	2,573,216	2,844,658
3,293,335	3,404,055	3,629,367	3,784,664	3,954,653	4,319,813	4,677,623	4,916,766	5,117,073	5,595,211
376,053	548,889	537,606	559,456	591,024	674,767	694,409	786,690	799,065	902,195
1,192,214	1,296,372	1,377,963	1,315,834	1,325,510	1,411,330	1,485,333	1,569,825	1,578,385	1,711,263
81,875	77,407	91,058	110,247	160,083	285,278	488,738	800,508	1,201,833	1,998,257
430,572	443,083	465,293	491,524	533,242	606,921	737,681	920,610	1,109,252	1,235,786
2,537,167	3,155,900	4,041,334	4,160,165	4,835,329	6,066,782	7,171,112	7,365,011	7,730,188	8,414,350
327,301	360,350	423,317	531,818	681,187	951,023	1,017,055	1,303,302	1,515,069	1,819,046
9,113,614	10,385,227	12,588,066	13,479,142	14,830,192	16,782,304	18,241,391	17,558,165	17,990,455	18,976,457
2,206,287	2,559,123	3,170,276	3,571,623	4,061,929	4,556,155	5,084,411	5,880,095	6,628,637	8,049,313
577,056	646,872	680,845	641,935	619,636	632,446	617,792	652,717	638,800	642,200
4,767,121	5,759,394	6,646,697	6,907,612	7,946,627	9,706,397	10,657,423	10,797,603	10,847,115	11,353,140
1,657,155	2,028,283	2,396,040	2,336,434	2,233,351	2,328,284	2,559,463	3,025,487	3,145,585	3,450,654
672,765	783,389	953,786	1,089,684	1,521,341	1,768,687	2,091,533	2,633,156	2,842,321	3,421,399
7,665,111	8,720,017	9,631,350	9,900,180	10,498,012	11,319,366	11,800,766	11,864,720	11,881,643	12,281,054
542,610	604,397	687,497	713,346	791,896	859,488	949,723	947,154	1,003,464	1,048,319
1,515,400	1,683,724	1,738,765	1,899,804	2,117,027	2,382,594	2,590,713	3,120,729	3,486,703	4,012,012
583,888	636,547	692,849	642,961	652,740	680,514	666,257	690,768	696,004	754,844
2,184,789	2,337,885	2,616,556	2,915,841	3,291,718	3,567,089	3,926,018	4,591,023	4,877,185	5,689,283
3,896,542	4,663,228	5,824,715	6,414,824	7,711,194	9,579,677	11,198,655	14,225,513	16,986,510	20,851,820
373,351	449,396	507,847	550,310	688,862	890,627	1,059,273	1,461,037	1,722,850	2,233,169
355,956	352,428	359,611	359,231	377,747	389,881	444,732	511,456	562,758	608,827
2,061,612	2,309,187	2,421,851	2,677,773	3,318,680	3,966,949	4,651,448	5,346,797	6,187,358	7,078,515
1,141,990	1,356,621	1,563,396	1,736,191	2,378,963	2,853,214	3,413,244	4,132,353	4,866,692	5,894,121
1,221,119	1,463,701	1,729,205	1,901,974	2,005,552	1,860,421	1,744,237	1,950,186	1,793,477	1,808,344
2,333,860	2,632,067	2,939,006	3,137,587	3,434,575	3,951,777	4,417,821	4,705,642	4,891,769	5,363,675
145,965	194,402	225,565	250,742	290,529	330,066	332,416	469,557	453,588	493,782
92,228,496	106,021,537	123,202,624	132,164,569	151,325,798	179,323,175	203,302,031	226,542,203	248,709,873	281,421,906

U.S. Center of Population, 1790-2000

Source: Bureau of the Census, U.S. Dept. of Commerce

The U.S. Center of Population is considered here as the center of population gravity, or that point upon which the U.S. would balance if it were a rigid plane without weight and the population distributed thereon, with each individual assumed to have equal weight and to exert an influence on a central point proportional to his or her distance from that point. The 2000 center is 12.1 miles south and 32.5 miles west of the 1990 center of population, and is more than 1,000 miles from the 1790 center.

YEAR	N Lat °	′	″	W Long °	′	″	APPROXIMATE LOCATION
1790	39	16	30	76	11	12	23 miles east of Baltimore, MD
1800	39	16	6	76	56	30	18 miles west of Baltimore, MD
1810	39	11	30	77	37	12	40 miles northwest by west of Washington, DC (in VA)
1820	39	5	42	78	33	0	16 miles east of Moorefield, WV[1]
1830	38	57	54	79	16	54	19 miles west-southwest of Moorefield, WV[1]
1840	39	2	0	80	18	0	16 miles south of Clarksburg, WV[1]
1850	38	59	0	81	19	0	23 miles southeast of Parkersburg, WV[1]
1860	39	0	24	82	48	48	20 miles south by east of Chillicothe, OH
1870	39	12	0	83	35	42	48 miles east by north of Cincinnati, OH
1880	39	4	8	84	39	40	8 miles west by south of Cincinnati, OH (in KY)
1890	39	11	56	85	32	53	20 miles east of Columbus, IN
1900	39	9	36	85	48	54	6 miles southeast of Columbus, IN
1910	39	10	12	86	32	20	In the city of Bloomington, IN
1920	39	10	21	86	43	15	8 miles south-southeast of Spencer, Owen Co., IN
1930	39	3	45	87	8	6	3 miles northeast of Linton, Greene Co., IN
1940	38	56	54	87	22	35	2 miles southeast by east of Carlisle, Haddon township, Sullivan Co., IN
1950 (incl. Alaska & Hawaii)	38	48	15	88	22	8	3 miles northeast of Louisville, Clay Co., IL
1960	38	35	58	89	12	35	6½ miles northwest of Centralia, Clinton Co., IL
1970	38	27	47	89	42	22	5 miles east southeast of Mascoutah, St. Clair Co., IL
1980	38	8	13	90	34	26	¼ mile west of De Soto, Jefferson Co., MO
1990	37	52	20	91	12	55	9.7 miles northwest of Steelville, MO
2000	37	41	49	91	48	34	2.8 miles east of Edgar Springs, MO

(1) West Virginia was set off from Virginia on Dec. 31, 1862, and was admitted as a state on June 20, 1863.

U.S. Area and Population, 1790-2000

Source: Bureau of the Census, U.S. Dept. of Commerce

Census date	AREA Gross Area	Land Area	Water Area	POPULATION Number	Per sq mi of land	Increase over preceding census Number	%
1790 (Aug. 2)	891,364	864,746	26,618	3,929,214	4.5	—	—
1800 (Aug. 4)	891,364	864,746	26,618	5,308,483	6.1	1,379,269	35.1
1810 (Aug. 6)	1,722,685	1,681,828	40,857	7,239,881	4.3	1,931,398	36.4
1820 (June 1)	1,792,552	1,749,462	43,090	9,638,453	5.5	2,398,572	33.1
1830 (June 1)	1,792,552	1,749,462	43,090	12,866,020[2]	7.4	3,227,567	33.5
1840 (June 1)	1,792,552	1,749,462	43,090	17,068,953[2]	9.8	4,203,433	32.7
1850 (June 1)	2,991,655	2,940,042	51,613	23,191,876	7.9	6,122,423	35.9
1860 (June 1)	3,021,295	2,969,640	51,655	31,443,321	10.6	8,251,445	35.6
1870 (June 1)	3,612,299	3,540,705	71,594	38,558,371	10.9	7,115,050	22.6
1880 (June 1)	3,612,299	3,540,705	71,594	50,189,209	14.2	11,630,838	30.2
1890 (June 1)	3,612,299	3,540,705	71,594	62,979,766	17.8	12,790,557	25.5
1900 (June 1)	3,618,770	3,547,314	71,456	76,212,168	21.5	13,232,402	21.0
1910 (Apr. 15)	3,618,770	3,547,045	71,725	92,228,496	26.0	16,016,328	21.0
1920 (Jan. 1)	3,618,770	3,546,931	71,839	106,021,537	29.9	13,793,041	15.0
1930 (Apr. 1)	3,618,770	3,551,608	67,162	123,202,624	34.7	17,181,087	16.2
1940 (Apr. 1)	3,618,770	3,554,608	64,162	132,164,569	37.2	8,961,945	7.3
1950 (Apr. 1)	3,618,770	3,552,206	66,564	151,325,798	42.6	19,161,229	14.5
1960 (Apr. 1)	3,618,770	3,540,911	77,859	179,323,175	50.6	27,997,377	18.5
1970 (Apr. 1)	3,618,770	3,536,855	81,915	203,302,031	57.5	23,978,856	13.4
1980 (Apr. 1)	3,618,770	3,539,289	79,481	226,542,203	64.0	23,240,172	11.4
1990 (Apr. 1)	3,717,796[1]	3,536,278	181,518[1]	248,709,873	70.3	22,167,670	9.8
2000 (Apr. 1)	3,794,085	3,537,440	256,648[1]	281,421,906	79.6	32,712,033	13.2

(1) Includes inland, coastal, and Great Lakes. Data before 1990 cover inland water only. (2) The U.S. total includes persons (5,318 in 1830 and 6,100 in 1840) on public ships in the service of the U.S. not credited to any region, division, or state. **NOTE:** Percent changes are computed on the basis of change in population since the preceding census date, so the period covered is not always exactly 10 years. Population density figures given for various years represent the area within the boundaries of the U.S. that was under the jurisdiction on the date in question—including, in some cases, considerable areas not organized or settled and not actually covered by the census. In 1870, for example, Alaska was not covered by the census. Population figures shown here may reflect corrections made to the initial tabulated census counts.

Congressional Apportionment

Source: Bureau of the Census, U.S. Dept. of Commerce; by census year

	2000	1990	1980	1970	1950	1900	1850
AL	7	7	7	7	9	9	7
AK	1	1	1	1	NA	NA	NA
AZ	8	6	5	4	2	NA	NA
AR	4	4	4	4	6	7	2
CA	53	52	45	43	30	8	2
CO	7	6	6	5	4	3	NA
CT	5	6	6	6	6	5	4
DE	1	1	1	1	1	1	1
FL	25	23	19	15	8	3	1
GA	13	11	10	10	10	11	8
HI	2	2	2	2	1	NA	NA
ID	2	2	2	2	2	1	NA
IL	19	20	22	24	25	25	9
IN	9	10	10	11	11	13	11
IA	5	5	6	6	8	11	2
KS	4	4	5	5	6	8	NA
KY	6	6	7	7	8	11	10
LA	7	7	8	8	8	7	4
ME	2	2	2	2	3	4	6
MD	8	8	8	8	7	6	6
MA	10	10	11	12	14	14	11
MI	15	16	18	19	18	12	4
MN	8	8	8	8	9	9	2
MS	4	5	5	5	6	8	5
MO	9	9	9	10	11	16	7
MT	1	1	2	2	2	1	NA
NE	3	3	3	3	4	6	NA
NV	3	2	2	1	1	1	NA
NH	2	2	2	2	2	2	3
NJ	13	13	14	15	14	10	5
NM	3	3	3	2	2	NA	NA
NY	29	31	34	39	43	37	33
NC	13	12	11	11	12	10	8
ND	1	1	1	1	2	2	NA
OH	18	19	21	23	23	21	21
OK	5	6	6	6	6	5	NA
OR	5	5	5	4	4	2	1
PA	19	21	23	25	30	32	25
RI	2	2	2	2	2	2	2
SC	6	6	6	6	7	7	6
SD	1	1	1	2	2	2	NA
TN	9	9	9	8	9	10	10
TX	32	30	27	24	22	16	2
UT	3	3	3	2	2	1	NA
VT	1	1	1	1	2	2	3
VA	11	11	10	10	10	10	13
WA	9	9	8	7	7	3	NA
WV	3	3	4	4	6	5	NA
WI	8	9	9	9	10	11	3
WY	1	1	1	1	1	1	NA
TOTAL	435	435	435	435	435	391	237

Note: NA = Not applicable.

The Constitution, in Article 1, Section 2, provided for a census of the population every 10 years to establish a basis for apportionment of representatives among the states. This apportionment largely determines the number of electoral votes allotted to each state.

The number of representatives of each state in Congress is determined by the state's population, but each state is entitled to one representative regardless of population. A congressional apportionment has been made after each decennial census except that of 1920. (The year given above is the year of the census on which apportionment for the next election year is based.) Prior to 1870, $3/5$ the number of slaves were added to the total free population. Indians "not taxed" were excluded until 1940.

Under provisions of a law that became effective Nov. 15, 1941, representatives are apportioned by the method of equal proportions. In the application of this method, the apportionment is made so that the average population per representative has the least possible variation between one state and any other.

The first House of Representatives, in 1789, had 65 members, as provided by the Constitution. Of these, the largest numbers were from Virginia (19), Massachusetts (14), and Pennsylvania (13).

As the population grew, the number of representatives was increased, but the total membership has been fixed at 435 since the apportionment based on the 1910 census.

IT'S A FACT: In 2002, Hispanics became the largest minority community in the U.S., at 13.5% of the total population. In 1980, this group only comprised 6.4% of the population.

Population, by Sex, Race, Residence, and Median Age, 1790-2002

Source: Bureau of the Census, U.S. Dept. of Commerce

(in thousands, except as indicated)

	SEX		RACE				RESIDENCE		MEDIAN AGE (years)		
	Male	Female	White	Black or Afr. Am. Number	Percent	Other[5]	Urban	Rural	All races	White	Black
Conterminous U.S.[1]											
1790 (Aug. 2)	NA	NA	3,172	757	19.3	NA	202	3,728	NA	NA	NA
1810 (Aug. 6)	NA	NA	5,862	1,378	19.0	NA	525	6,714	NA	16.0	NA
1820 (Aug. 7)	4,897	4,742	7,867	1,772	18.4	NA	693	8,945	16.7	16.6	17.2
1840 (June 1)	8,689	8,381	14,196	2,874	16.8	NA	1,845	15,224	17.8	17.9	17.6
1860 (June 1)	16,085	15,358	26,923	4,442	14.1	79	6,217	25,227	19.4	19.7	17.5
1870 (June 1)	19,494	19,065	33,589	4,880	12.7	89	9,902	28,656	20.2	20.4	18.5
1880 (June 1)	25,519	24,637	43,403	6,581	13.1	172	14,130	36,026	20.9	21.4	18.0
1890 (June 1)	32,237	30,711	55,101	7,489	11.9	358	22,106	40,841	22.0	22.5	17.8
1900 (June 1)	38,816	37,178	66,809	8,834	11.6	351	30,160	45,835	22.9	23.4	19.4
1920 (Jan. 1)	53,900	51,810	94,821	10,463	9.9	427	54,158	51,553	25.3	25.5	22.3
1930 (Apr. 1)	62,137	60,638	110,287	11,891	9.7	597	68,955	53,820	26.5	26.9	23.5
1940 (Apr. 1)	66,062	65,608	118,215	12,866	9.8	589	74,424	57,246	29.0	29.5	25.3
United States											
1950 (Apr. 1)	74,833	75,864	135,150	15,045	9.9	1,131	96,467	54,230	30.2	30.7	26.2
1960 (Apr. 1)	88,331	90,992	158,832	18,872	10.5	1,620	125,269	54,054	29.5	30.3	23.5
1970 (Apr. 1)[2]	98,912	104,300	177,749	22,580	11.1	2,883	149,647	53,565	28.1	28.9	22.4
1980 (Apr. 1)[3]	110,053	116,493	194,713	26,683	11.8	5,150	167,051	59,495	30.0	30.9	24.9
1985 (July 1, est.). . .	115,730	122,194	202,031	28,569	12.0	7,324	NA	NA	31.4	32.3	26.6
1990 (Apr. 1)	121,239	127,470	199,686	29,986	12.1	9,233	187,053	61,656	32.9	34.4	28.1
1991 (July 1, est.). . .	122,984	129,122	210,979	31,107	12.3	10,020	NA	NA	33.1	34.1	28.1
1992 (July 1, est.). . .	124,506	130,496	212,885	31,670	12.4	10,446	NA	NA	33.4	34.4	28.5
1993 (July 1, est.). . .	125,938	131,858	214,760	32,168	12.5	10,867	NA	NA	33.7	34.7	28.7
1994 (July 1, est.). . .	127,216	133,076	216,413	32,653	12.5	11,227	NA	NA	34.0	35.0	29.0
1995 (July 1, est.). . .	128,569	134,321	218,149	33,095	12.6	11,646	NA	NA	34.3	35.3	29.2
1996 (July 1, est.). . .	129,746	135,434	219,686	33,514	12.6	11,979	NA	NA	34.6	35.7	29.5
1997 (July 1, est.). . .	131,018	136,618	221,334	33,947	12.7	12,355	NA	NA	34.9	36.0	29.7
1998 (July 1, est.). . .	132,263	137,766	222,932	34,370	12.7	12,727	NA	NA	35.3	36.3	29.9
1999 (July 1, est.). . .	133,352	139,526	224,692	34,903	12.8	13,283	NA	NA	35.5	36.6	30.1
2000 (Apr. 1)[4]	138,054	143,368	228,105	35,816	12.7	13,716	222,361	59,061	35.3	NA	NA
2001 (July 1, est.)[4] . .	140,076	145,242	230,664	36,283	12.7	14,316	NA	NA	35.6	NA	NA
2002 (July 1, est.)[4] . .	141,661	146,708	232,647	36,746	12.7	14,795	NA	NA	35.7	NA	NA

NA = Not available. **NOTE:** Urban and rural definitions may change from census to census. Figures have been adjusted to be consistent with the 1990 urban and rural definitions. (1) Excludes Alaska and Hawaii. (2) The revised 1970 resident population count is 203,302,031, which incorporates changes due to errors found after tabulations were completed. The race and sex data shown here reflect the official 1970 census count; the residence data come from the tabulated count. (3) The race data shown for Apr. 1, 1980, have been modified. (4) Race data for 2000-2002 are for one race alone. (5) "Other" consists of American Indians, Alaska Natives, Asians, and Pacific Islanders.

U.S. Population by Race and Hispanic or Latino Origin, 1990-2000

	Census 2000		1990 Census		% increase, 1990 - 2000	
	One race only	One race or more[3]	Number	% of total pop.	Using one race only for 2000	Using one race only or in combination for 2000[4]
RACE[1]						
Total U.S. population[2]	281,421,906	281,421,906	248,709,873	100.0	13.2	13.2
White	211,460,626	216,930,975	199,686,070	80.3	5.9	8.6
Black or African American	34,658,190	36,419,434	29,986,060	12.1	15.6	21.5
American Indian and Alaska Native . . .	2,475,956	4,119,301	1,959,234	0.8	26.4	110.3
Asian	10,242,998	11,898,828	6,908,638	2.8	48.3	72.2
Native Hawaiian and other Pac. Isl. . . .	398,835	874,414	365,024	0.1	9.3	139.5
Some other race.	15,359,073	18,521,486	9,804,847	3.9	56.6	88.9
HISPANIC OR LATINO AND RACE						
Total U.S. population[2]	281,421,906	281,421,906	248,709,873	100.0	13.2	13.2
Hispanic or Latino (of any race)[2]	35,305,818	35,305,818	22,354,059	9.0	57.9	57.9
Not Hispanic or Latino[2]	246,116,088	246,116,088	226,355,814	91.0	8.7	8.7
White	195,575,485	198,177,900	188,128,296	75.6	3.4	5.3
Black or African American	34,313,007	35,383,751	29,216,293	11.7	16.2	21.1
American Indian and Alaska Native .	2,097,440	3,444,700	1,793,773	0.7	15.3	92.0
Asian	10,356,804	11,579,494	6,642,481	2.7	52.4	74.3
Native Hawaiian and other Pac. Isl. .	367,104	748,149	325,878	0.1	8.5	129.6
Some other race.	467,770	1,770,645	249,093	0.1	87.8	610.8

(1) Because individuals could report only one race in 1990 and could report more than one race in 2000, and because of other changes in the census questionnaire, the race data for 1990 and 2000 are not directly comparable. (2) The data for total U.S. population, Hispanic or Latino population, and total Not Hispanic or Latino population are not affected by the changes cited in (1). Hispanic or Latino persons may be of any race. (3) Alone or in combination with one or more of the other five races listed. (4) Columns 5 and 6 provide, respectively, a "minimum-maximum" range for the percent increase in population for each race between 1990 and 2000.

Population by State, 2000-2002

Source: Bureau of the Census, U.S. Dept. of Commerce

Rank	State	2002 population	2000 population	Percent change 2000-2002	Rank	State	2002 population	2000 population	Percent change 2000-2002
1.	California	35,116,033	33,871,648	3.7	27.	Oregon	3,521,515	3,421,399	2.9
2.	Texas	21,779,893	20,851,820	4.5	28.	Oklahoma	3,493,714	3,450,654	1.2
3.	New York	19,157,532	18,976,457	1.0	29.	Connecticut	3,460,503	3,405,565	1.6
4.	Florida	16,713,149	15,982,378	4.6	30.	Iowa	2,936,760	2,926,324	0.4
5.	Illinois	12,600,620	12,419,293	1.5	31.	Mississippi	2,871,782	2,844,658	1.0
6.	Pennsylvania	12,335,091	12,281,054	0.4	32.	Kansas	2,715,884	2,688,418	1.0
7.	Ohio	11,421,267	11,353,140	0.6	33.	Arkansas	2,710,079	2,673,400	1.4
8.	Michigan	10,050,446	9,938,444	1.1	34.	Utah	2,316,256	2,233,169	3.7
9.	New Jersey	8,590,300	8,414,350	2.1	35.	Nevada	2,173,491	1,998,257	8.8
10.	Georgia	8,560,310	8,186,453	4.6	36.	New Mexico	1,855,059	1,819,046	2.0
11.	North Carolina	8,320,146	8,049,313	3.4	37.	West Virginia	1,801,873	1,808,344	-0.4
12.	Virginia	7,293,542	7,078,515	3.0	38.	Nebraska	1,729,180	1,711,263	1.0
13.	Massachusetts	6,427,801	6,349,097	1.2	39.	Idaho	1,341,131	1,293,953	3.6
14.	Indiana	6,159,068	6,080,485	1.3	40.	Maine	1,294,464	1,274,923	1.5
15.	Washington	6,068,996	5,894,121	3.0	41.	New Hampshire	1,275,056	1,235,786	3.2
16.	Tennessee	5,797,289	5,689,283	1.9	42.	Hawaii	1,244,898	1,211,537	2.8
17.	Missouri	5,672,579	5,595,211	1.4	43.	Rhode Island	1,069,725	1,048,319	2.0
18.	Maryland	5,458,137	5,296,486	3.1	44.	Montana	909,453	902,195	0.8
19.	Arizona	5,456,453	5,130,632	6.4	45.	Delaware	807,385	783,600	3.0
20.	Wisconsin	5,441,196	5,363,675	1.4	46.	South Dakota	761,063	754,844	0.8
21.	Minnesota	5,019,720	4,919,479	2.0	47.	Alaska	643,786	626,932	2.7
22.	Colorado	4,506,542	4,301,261	4.8	48.	North Dakota	634,110	642,200	-1.3
23.	Alabama	4,486,508	4,447,100	0.9	49.	Vermont	616,592	608,827	1.3
24.	Louisiana	4,482,646	4,468,976	0.3	50.	District of Columbia	570,898	572,059	-0.2
25.	South Carolina	4,107,183	4,012,012	2.4	51.	Wyoming	498,703	493,782	1.0
26.	Kentucky	4,092,891	4,041,769	1.3		**Total Resident Pop.**	**288,368,698**	**281,421,906**	**13.2**

Density of Population by State, 1930-2000

Source: Bureau of the Census, U.S. Dept. of Commerce

(per square mile, land area only)

STATE	1930	1960	1980	1990	2000	STATE	1930	1960	1980	1990	2000
AL	51.8	64.2	76.6	79.6	87.6	MT	3.7	4.6	5.4	5.5	6.2
AK*	.1	0.4	0.7	1.0	1.1	NE	18.0	18.4	20.5	20.5	22.3
AZ	3.8	11.5	23.9	32.3	45.2	NV	.8	2.6	7.3	10.9	18.2
AR	35.2	34.2	43.9	45.1	51.3	NH	51.6	67.2	102.4	123.7	137.8
CA	36.2	100.4	151.4	190.8	217.2	NJ	537.3	805.5	986.2	1,042.0	1,134.5
CO	10.0	16.9	27.9	31.8	41.5	NM	3.5	7.8	10.7	12.5	15.0
CT	328.0	520.6	637.8	678.4	702.9	NY	262.6	350.6	370.6	381.0	401.9
DE	120.5	225.2	307.6	340.8	401.0	NC	64.5	93.2	120.4	136.1	165.2
DC	7,981.5	12,523.9	10,132.3	9,882.8	9,378.0	ND	9.7	9.1	9.4	9.3	9.3
FL	27.1	91.5	180.0	239.6	296.4	OH	161.6	236.6	263.3	264.9	277.3
GA	49.7	67.8	94.1	111.9	141.4	OK	34.6	33.8	44.1	45.8	50.3
HI*	57.5	98.5	150.1	172.5	188.6	OR	9.9	18.4	27.4	29.6	35.6
ID	5.4	8.1	11.5	12.2	15.6	PA	213.8	251.4	264.3	265.1	274.0
IL	136.4	180.4	205.3	205.6	223.4	RI	649.8	819.3	897.8	960.3	1,003.2
IN	89.4	128.8	152.8	154.6	169.5	SC	56.8	78.7	103.4	115.8	133.2
IA	44.1	49.2	52.1	49.7	52.4	SD	9.1	9.0	9.1	9.2	9.9
KS	22.9	26.6	28.9	30.3	32.9	TN	62.4	86.2	111.6	118.3	138.0
KY	65.2	76.2	92.3	92.8	101.7	TX	22.1	36.4	54.3	64.9	79.6
LA	46.5	72.2	94.5	96.9	102.6	UT	6.2	10.8	17.8	21.0	27.2
ME	25.7	31.3	36.3	39.8	41.3	VT	38.8	42.0	55.2	60.8	65.8
MD	165.0	313.5	428.7	489.2	541.9	VA	60.7	99.6	134.7	156.3	178.8
MA	537.4	657.3	733.3	767.6	809.8	WA	23.3	42.8	62.1	73.1	88.6
MI	84.9	137.7	162.6	163.6	175.0	WV	71.8	77.2	80.8	74.5	75.1
MN	32.0	43.1	51.2	55.0	61.8	WI	53.7	72.6	86.5	90.1	98.8
MS	42.4	46.0	53.4	54.9	60.6	WY	2.3	3.4	4.9	4.7	5.1
MO	52.4	62.6	71.3	74.3	81.2	U.S.	41.2	50.6	64.0	70.3	79.6

* For purposes of comparison, Alaska and Hawaii are included in above tabulation for 1930, even though not states then.

25 Largest Counties, by Population, 2000-2002

Source: Bureau of the Census, U.S. Dept of Commerce

County	2002 Population	2000 Population	Percent change	County	2002 Population	2000 Population	Percent change
Los Angeles, CA	9,806,577	9,519,330	2.9	Broward, FL	1,709,118	1,623,018	5.0
Cook, IL	5,377,507	5,376,741	0.0	Riverside, CA	1,699,112	1,545,387	9.0
Harris, TX	3,557,055	3,400,578	4.4	Santa Clara, CA	1,683,505	1,682,585	0.1
Maricopa, AZ	3,303,876	3,072,149	7.0	New York, NY	1,546,856	1,537,195	0.6
Orange, CA	2,938,507	2,846,289	3.1	Tarrant, TX	1,527,366	1,446,219	5.3
San Diego, CA	2,906,660	2,813,833	3.2	Clark, NV	1,522,164	1,375,738	9.6
Kings, NY	2,488,194	2,465,326	0.9	Philadelphia, PA	1,492,231	1,517,550	-1.7
Miami-Dade, FL	2,332,599	2,253,362	3.4	Middlesex, MA	1,474,160	1,465,396	0.6
Dallas, TX	2,283,953	2,218,899	2.8	Alameda, CA	1,472,310	1,443,741	1.9
Queens, NY	2,237,815	2,229,379	0.4	Suffolk, NY	1,458,655	1,419,369	2.7
Wayne, MI	2,045,540	2,061,162	-0.8	Bexar, TX	1,446,333	1,392,927	3.7
San Bernardino, CA	1,816,072	1,709,434	5.9	Cuyahoga, OH	1,379,049	1,393,845	-1.1
King, WA	1,759,604	1,737,032	1.3				

Note on least populated counties: The following are the ten smallest counties by 2002 population: Loving County, TX (64); Kalawao County, HI (132); King County, TX (333); Arthur County, NE (416); Kenedy County, TX (419); Petroleum County, MT (500); Blaine County, NE (529); McPherson County, NE (546); San Juan County, CO (552); and Thomas County, NE (699).

Metropolitan Areas, 1990-2000

Source: Bureau of the Census, U.S. Dept. of Commerce

(CMSAs and MSAs of more than 600,000 persons listed by Census 2000 population counts)

Metropolitan statistical areas (MSAs) are defined for federal statistical use by the Office of Management and Budget (OMB), with technical assistance from the Bureau of the Census. Most individual metropolitan areas with populations over 1 million may, under specified circumstances, be subdivided into component Primary Metropolitan Statistical Areas (PMSAs), in which case the area as a whole is designated a Consolidated Metropolitan Statistical Area (CMSA).

Effective June 30, 1999, the Office of Management and Budget designated 261 MSAs, 76 PMSAs, and 19 CMSAs for the U.S. and Puerto Rico.

CMSAs and MSAs	Population 2000	Population 1990	Percent Change 1990-2000
New York–Northern New Jersey–Long Island, NY–NJ–CT–PA CMSA	21,199,865	19,549,649	8.4
Los Angeles–Riverside–Orange County, CA CMSA	16,373,645	14,531,529	12.7
Chicago–Gary–Kenosha, IL–IN–WI CMSA	9,157,540	8,239,820	11.1
Washington–Baltimore, DC–MD–VA–WV CMSA	7,608,070	6,727,050	13.1
San Francisco–Oakland–San Jose, CA CMSA	7,039,362	6,253,311	12.6
Philadelphia–Wilmington–Atlantic City, PA–NJ–DE–MD CMSA	6,188,463	5,892,937	5.0
Boston–Worcester–Lawrence, MA–NH–ME–CT CMSA	5,819,100	5,455,403	6.7
Detroit–Ann Arbor–Flint, MI CMSA	5,456,428	5,187,171	5.2
Dallas–Fort Worth, TX CMSA	5,221,801	4,037,282	29.3
Houston–Galveston–Brazoria, TX CMSA	4,669,571	3,731,131	25.2
Atlanta, GA MSA	4,112,198	2,959,950	38.9
Miami–Fort Lauderdale, FL CMSA	3,876,380	3,192,582	21.4
Seattle–Tacoma–Bremerton, WA CMSA	3,554,760	2,970,328	19.7
Phoenix–Mesa, AZ MSA	3,251,876	2,238,480	45.3
Minneapolis–St. Paul, MN–WI MSA	2,968,806	2,538,834	16.9
Cleveland–Akron, OH CMSA	2,945,831	2,859,644	3.0
San Diego, CA MSA	2,813,833	2,498,016	12.6
St. Louis, MO–IL MSA	2,603,607	2,492,525	4.5
Denver–Boulder–Greeley, CO CMSA	2,581,506	1,980,140	30.4
San Juan–Caguas–Arecibo, PR CMSA	2,450,292	2,270,808	7.9
Tampa–St. Petersburg–Clearwater, FL MSA	2,395,997	2,067,959	15.9
Pittsburgh, PA MSA	2,358,695	2,394,811	−1.5
Portland–Salem, OR–WA CMSA	2,265,223	1,793,476	26.3
Cincinnati–Hamilton, OH–KY–IN CMSA	1,979,202	1,817,571	8.9
Sacramento–Yolo, CA CMSA	1,796,857	1,481,102	21.3
Kansas City, MO–KS MSA	1,776,062	1,582,875	12.2
Milwaukee–Racine, WI CMSA	1,689,572	1,607,183	5.1
Orlando, FL MSA	1,644,561	1,224,852	34.3
Indianapolis, IN MSA	1,607,486	1,380,491	16.4
San Antonio, TX MSA	1,592,383	1,324,749	20.2
Norfolk–Virginia Beach–Newport News, VA–NC MSA	1,569,541	1,443,244	8.8
Las Vegas, NV–AZ MSA	1,563,282	852,737	83.3
Columbus, OH MSA	1,540,157	1,345,450	14.5
Charlotte–Gastonia–Rock Hill, NC–SC MSA	1,499,293	1,162,093	29.0
New Orleans, LA MSA	1,337,726	1,285,270	4.1
Salt Lake City–Ogden, UT MSA	1,333,914	1,072,227	24.4
Greensboro–Winston-Salem–High Point, NC MSA	1,251,509	1,050,304	19.2
Austin–San Marcos, TX MSA	1,249,763	846,227	47.7
Nashville, TN MSA	1,231,311	985,026	25.0
Providence–Fall River–Warwick, RI–MA MSA	1,188,613	1,134,350	4.8
Raleigh–Durham–Chapel Hill, NC MSA	1,187,941	855,545	38.9
Hartford, CT MSA	1,183,110	1,157,585	2.2
Buffalo–Niagara Falls, NY MSA	1,170,111	1,189,288	−1.6
Memphis, TN–AR–MS MSA	1,135,614	1,007,306	12.7
West Palm Beach–Boca Raton, FL MSA	1,131,184	863,518	31.0
Jacksonville, FL MSA	1,100,491	906,727	21.4
Rochester, NY MSA	1,098,201	1,062,470	3.4
Grand Rapids–Muskegon–Holland, MI MSA	1,088,514	937,891	16.1
Oklahoma City, OK MSA	1,083,346	958,839	13.0
Louisville, KY–IN MSA	1,025,598	948,829	8.1
Richmond–Petersburg, VA MSA	996,512	865,640	15.1
Greenville–Spartanburg–Anderson, SC MSA	962,441	830,563	15.9
Dayton–Springfield, OH MSA	950,558	951,270	−0.1
Fresno, CA MSA	922,516	755,580	22.1
Birmingham, AL MSA	921,106	840,140	9.6
Honolulu, HI MSA	876,156	836,231	4.8
Albany–Schenectady–Troy, NY MSA	875,583	861,424	1.6
Tucson, AZ MSA	843,746	666,880	26.5
Tulsa, OK MSA	803,235	708,954	13.3
Syracuse, NY MSA	732,117	742,177	−1.4
Omaha, NE–IA MSA	716,998	639,580	12.1
Albuquerque, NM MSA	712,738	589,131	21.0
Knoxville, TN MSA	687,249	585,960	17.3
El Paso, TX MSA	679,622	591,610	14.9
Bakersfield, CA MSA	661,645	543,477	21.7
Allentown–Bethlehem–Easton, PA MSA	637,958	595,081	7.2
Harrisburg–Lebanon–Carlisle, PA MSA	629,401	587,986	7.0
Scranton–Wilkes-Barre–Hazleton, PA MSA	624,776	638,466	−2.1
Toledo, OH MSA	618,203	614,128	0.7
Baton Rouge, LA MSA	602,894	528,264	14.1

Final 2000 census figures showed that the nation in that year had 50 metropolitan areas of at least 1 mil people, including 9 that had reached that size since 1990. The 50 areas had 161.5 mil people, or 57.5% of the U.S. population, in 2000.

Almost 226 mil people resided in metropolitan areas in 2000, an increase of 27.6 mil (13.9%) since 1990. The population outside metropolitan areas totaled 55.4 mil in 2000, up 5.1 mil (10.2%) from 1990. The metropolitan population in 2000 was 80.3% of the U.S. total, compared with 79.8% in 1990 and 76.2% in 1980.

IT'S A FACT: Since 2000, 3 U.S. cities—Henderson, NV, Chandler, AZ, and Modesto, CA—were added to the Census Bureau's list of the 100 most populous cities. Three dropped off the list: Augusta, GA, Mobile, AL, and Irving, TX.

Population of 100 Largest U.S. Cities, 1850-2002

Source: Bureau of the Census, U.S. Dept. of Commerce; ranked by estimated 2002 population

Rank City	2002	2000	1990	1980	1970	1950	1900	1850
1. New York, NY	8,084,316	8,008,278	7,322,564	7,071,639	7,895,563	7,891,957	3,437,202	696,115
2. Los Angeles, CA	3,798,981	3,694,820	3,485,398	2,968,528	2,811,801	1,970,358	102,479	1,610
3. Chicago, IL	2,886,251	2,896,016	2,783,726	3,005,072	3,369,357	3,620,962	1,698,575	29,963
4. Houston, TX	2,009,834	1,953,631	1,630,553	1,595,138	1,233,535	596,163	44,633	2,396
5. Philadelphia, PA	1,492,231	1,517,550	1,585,577	1,688,210	1,949,996	2,071,605	1,293,697	121,376
6. Phoenix, AZ	1,371,960	1,321,045	983,403	789,704	584,303	106,818	5,544	...
7. San Diego, CA	1,259,532	1,223,400	1,110,549	875,538	697,471	334,387	17,700	...
8. Dallas, TX	1,211,467	1,188,580	1,006,877	904,599	844,401	434,462	42,638	...
9. San Antonio, TX	1,194,222	1,144,646	935,933	785,940	654,153	408,442	53,321	3,488
10. Detroit, MI	925,051	951,270	1,027,974	1,203,368	1,514,063	1,849,568	285,704	21,019
11. San Jose, CA	900,443	894,943	782,248	629,400	459,913	95,280	21,500	...
12. Indianapolis, IN[1]	783,612	791,926	741,952	700,807	736,856	427,173	169,164	8,091
13. San Francisco, CA	764,049	776,733	723,959	678,974	715,674	775,357	342,782	34,776
14. Jacksonville, FL[1]	762,461	735,617	635,230	540,920	504,265	204,517	28,429	1,045
15. Columbus, OH	725,228	711,470	632,910	565,021	540,025	375,901	125,560	17,882
16. Austin, TX	671,873	656,562	465,622	345,890	253,539	132,459	22,258	629
17. Memphis, TN	648,882	650,100	610,337	646,174	623,988	396,000	102,320	8,841
18. Baltimore, MD	638,614	651,154	736,014	786,741	905,787	949,708	508,957	169,054
19. Milwaukee, WI	590,895	596,974	628,088	636,297	717,372	637,392	285,315	20,061
20. Boston, MA	589,281	589,141	574,283	562,994	641,071	801,444	560,892	136,881
21. Charlotte, NC	580,597	540,828	395,934	315,474	241,420	134,042	18,091	1,065
22. El Paso, TX	577,415	563,662	515,342	425,259	322,261	130,485	15,906	...
23. Washington, DC	570,898	572,059	606,900	638,432	756,668	802,178	278,718	40,001
24. Seattle, WA	570,426	563,374	516,259	493,846	530,831	467,591	80,671	...
25. Fort Worth, TX	567,516	534,694	447,619	385,164	393,455	278,778	26,688	...
26. Denver, CO	560,415	554,636	467,610	492,686	514,678	415,786	133,859	...
27. Nashville, TN[1]	545,915	569,891	510,784	455,651	426,029	174,307	80,865	10,165
28. Portland, OR	539,438	529,121	437,319	368,148	379,967	373,628	90,426	...
29. Oklahoma City, OK	519,034	506,132	444,719	404,014	368,164	243,504	10,037	...
30. Las Vegas, NV	508,604	478,434	258,295	164,674	125,787	24,624	...	...
31. Tucson, AZ	503,151	486,699	405,390	330,537	262,933	45,454	7,531	...
32. New Orleans, LA	473,681	484,674	496,938	557,927	593,471	570,445	287,104	116,375
33. Long Beach, CA	472,412	461,522	429,433	361,498	358,879	250,767	2,252	...
34. Cleveland, OH	467,851	478,403	505,616	573,822	750,879	914,808	381,768	17,034
35. Albuquerque, NM	463,874	448,607	384,736	332,920	244,501	96,815	6,238	...
36. Fresno, CA	445,227	427,652	354,202	217,491	165,655	91,669	12,470	...
37. Kansas City, MO	443,471	441,545	435,146	448,028	507,330	456,622	163,752	...
38. Sacramento, CA	435,245	407,018	369,365	275,741	257,105	137,572	29,282	6,820
39. Virginia Beach, VA	433,934	425,257	393,069	262,199	172,106	5,390	...	...
40. Mesa, AZ	426,841	396,375	288,091	152,404	63,049	16,790	722	...
41. Atlanta, GA	424,868	416,474	394,017	425,022	495,039	331,314	89,872	2,572
42. Oakland, CA	402,777	399,484	372,242	339,337	361,561	384,575	66,960	...
43. Omaha, NE	399,357	390,007	335,795	313,939	346,929	251,117	102,555	...
44. Tulsa, OK	391,908	393,049	367,302	360,919	330,350	182,740	1,390	...
45. Honolulu, HI[2]	378,155	371,657	365,272	365,048	324,871	248,034	39,306	...
46. Minneapolis, MN	375,635	382,618	368,383	370,951	434,400	521,718	202,718	...
47. Miami, FL	374,791	362,470	358,548	346,681	334,859	249,276	1,681	...
48. Colorado Springs, CO	371,182	360,890	281,140	215,105	135,517	45,472	21,085	...
49. Wichita, KS	355,126	344,284	304,011	279,838	276,554	168,279	24,671	...
50. Arlington, TX	349,944	332,969	261,721	160,113	90,229	7,692	1,079	...
51. Santa Ana, CA	343,413	337,977	293,742	204,023	155,710	45,533	4,933	...
52. St. Louis, MO	338,353	348,189	396,685	452,801	622,236	856,796	575,238	77,860
53. Anaheim, CA	332,642	328,014	266,406	219,494	166,408	14,556	1,456	...
54. Pittsburgh, PA	327,898	334,563	369,879	423,959	520,089	676,806	321,616	46,601
55. Cincinnati, OH	323,885	331,285	364,040	385,409	453,514	503,998	325,902	115,435
56. Tampa, FL	315,140	303,447	280,015	271,577	277,714	124,681	15,839	...
57. Toledo, OH	309,106	313,619	332,943	354,635	383,062	303,616	131,822	3,829
58. Raleigh, NC	306,944	276,093	207,951	150,255	122,830	65,679	13,643	4,518
59. Buffalo, NY	287,698	292,648	328,123	357,870	462,768	580,132	352,387	42,261
60. Aurora, CO	286,028	276,393	222,103	158,588	74,974	11,421	202	...
61. St. Paul, MN	284,037	287,151	272,235	270,230	309,866	311,349	163,065	1,112
62. Corpus Christi, TX	278,520	277,454	257,453	232,134	204,525	108,287	4,703	...
63. Newark, NJ	277,000	273,546	275,221	329,248	381,930	438,776	246,070	38,894
64. Riverside, CA	274,226	255,166	226,505	170,591	140,089	46,764	7,973	...
65. Anchorage, AK	268,983	260,283	226,338	174,431	48,081	11,254	...	...
66. Lexington, KY	263,618	260,512	225,366	204,165	108,137	55,534	26,369	8,159
67. Stockton, CA	262,835	243,771	210,943	148,283	109,963	70,853	17,506	...
68. Bakersfield, CA	260,969	247,057	174,820	105,611	69,515	34,784	4,836	...
69. Louisville, KY	251,399	256,231	269,063	298,694	361,706	369,129	204,731	43,194
70. St. Petersburg, FL	248,546	248,232	238,629	238,647	216,159	96,738	1,575	...
71. Jersey City, NJ	240,100	240,055	228,537	223,532	260,350	299,017	206,433	6,856
72. Birmingham, AL	239,416	242,820	265,968	284,413	300,910	326,037	38,415	...
73. Norfolk, VA	239,036	234,403	261,229	266,979	307,951	213,513	46,624	14,326
74. Plano, TX	238,091	222,030	128,713	72,331	17,872	2,126	1,304	...
75. Lincoln, NE	232,362	225,581	191,972	171,932	149,518	98,884	40,169	...
76. Glendale, AZ	230,564	218,812	148,134	96,988	36,228	8,179	...	...
77. Greensboro, NC	228,217	223,891	183,521	155,642	144,076	74,389	10,035	...
78. Hialeah, FL	228,149	226,419	188,004	145,254	102,452	19,676	...	...
79. Baton Rouge, LA	225,702	227,818	219,531	220,394	165,921	125,629	11,269	3,905
80. Garland, TX	219,646	215,768	180,650	138,857	81,437	10,571	819	...
81. Rochester, NY	217,158	219,773	231,636	241,741	295,011	332,488	162,608	36,403
82. Scottsdale, AZ	215,779	202,705	130,069	88,364	67,823	2,032	...	...

Rank City	2002	2000	1990	1980	1970	1950	1900	1850
83. Madison, WI	215,211	208,054	191,262	170,616	171,809	96,056	19,164	1,525
84. Akron, OH	214,349	217,074	223,019	237,177	275,425	274,605	42,728	3,266
85. Fort Wayne, IN	210,070	205,727	173,072	172,391	178,269	133,607	45,115	4,282
86. Fremont, CA	206,856	203,413	173,339	131,945	100,869	...	...	...
87. Chesapeake, VA	206,665	199,184	151,976	114,486	89,580	...	...	...
88. Henderson, NV	206,153	175,381	64,942	23,376	16,400	5,717	...	...
89. Lubbock, TX	203,715	199,564	186,206	174,361	149,101	71,747	...	...
90. Modesto, CA	203,555	188,856	164,730	106,963	61,712	17,389	2,024[3]	...
91. Chandler, AZ	202,016	176,581	89,862	29,673	13,763	3,799	...	...
92. Montgomery, AL	201,425	201,568	187,106	177,857	133,386	106,525	30,346	8,728
93. Glendale, CA	199,430	194,973	180,038	139,060	133,000	96,000	...	...
94. Shreveport, LA	199,033	200,145	198,525	206,989	182,064	127,206	16,013	1,728
95. Des Moines, IA	198,076	198,682	193,187	191,003	201,404	177,965	62,139	...
96. Tacoma, WA	197,553	193,556	176,664	158,501	154,407	143,673	37,714	...
97. Richmond, VA	197,456	197,790	203,056	219,214	249,332	230,310	85,050	27,570
98. Yonkers, NY	197,234	196,086	188,082	195,351	204,297	152,798	47,931	...
99. Grand Rapids, MI	196,595	197,800	189,126	181,843	197,649	176,515	87,565	2,686
100. Spokane, WA	196,305	195,629	177,196	171,300	170,516	161,721	36,848	...

(1) Indianapolis, IN; Jacksonville, FL; and Nashville, TN, are parts of consolidated city-county governments. Populations of other incorporated places in the county have been excluded from the population totals shown here. For years that predate the establishment of a consolidated city-county government, city population is shown. (2) Locations in Hawaii are called "census designated places (CDPs)." Although these areas are not incorporated, they are recognized for census purposes as large urban places. Honolulu CDP is coextensive with Honolulu Judicial District within the city and county of Honolulu. (3) Estimated.

Mobility, by Selected Characteristics, 2000-2001
Source: Bureau of the Census, U.S. Dept. of Commerce
(numbers in thousands)

	Total no. of movers[1]	Same county	MOVED TO: Diff. county, same state	Diff. state	Abroad		Total no. of movers[1]	Same county	MOVED TO: Diff. county, same state	Diff. state	Abroad
Marital status						**Income[3]**					
Married, spouse present	11,957	6,241	2,457	1,175	586	Under $5,000	3,534	1,841	709	339	260
Married, spouse absent .	772	322	180	64	120	$5,000-$9,999	3,655	2,044	732	328	149
Widowed	881	519	149	103	27	$10,000-$19,999	6,321	3,785	1,121	648	153
Divorced	3,431	2,119	671	341	53	$20,000-$29,999	5,042	3,079	1,038	400	107
Separated	1,059	697	200	79	27	$30,000-$39,999	3,321	1,833	735	377	58
Never married	12,363	7,079	2,403	1,238	572	$40,000-$49,999	1,892	1,016	433	205	48
Educational attainment[2]						$50,000-$59,999	1,104	602	250	124	23
Less than 9th grade	1,368	759	205	102	200	$60,000-$74,999	1,057	537	237	112	37
Grades 9-12, no diploma	2,058	1,219	399	192	87	$75,000-$99,999	750	354	156	104	30
High school grad.	6,247	3,786	1,103	658	149	$100,000 and over	779	368	163	86	40
Some college or AA						**Ownership status**					
degree	5,573	3,108	1,182	551	141	Owner	15,008	8,407	3,374	1,287	411
Bachelor's degree	4,383	2,126	980	471	254	Renter	24,877	14,366	4,404	2,428	1,341
Prof. or graduate degree	1,859	795	392	221	151	**TOTAL[4]**	39,885	22,773	7,778	3,715	1,752

(1) People who moved to a new residence in 12-month period ending in Mar. 2001. (2) People 25 years and older. (3) People 15 years and older. (4) People 1 year and older.

U.S. Population, by Age, Sex, and Household, 2000
Source: Bureau of the Census, U.S. Dept. of Commerce; 2000 Census

	Number	%		Number	%
Total population	281,421,906	100	62 years and over	41,256,029	14.7
AGE			65 years and over	34,991,753	12.4
Under 5 years	19,175,798	6.8	**SEX**		
5 to 9 years	20,549,505	7.3	Male	138,053,563	49.1
10 to 14 years	20,528,072	7.3	Female	143,368,343	50.9
15 to 19 years	20,219,890	7.2	**HOUSEHOLDS BY TYPES**		
20 to 24 years	18,964,001	6.7	**Total Households**	105,480,101	100.0
25 to 34 years	39,891,724	14.2	Family households (families)	71,787,347	68.1
35 to 44 years	45,148,527	16.0	Married-couple families	54,493,232	51.7
45 to 54 years	37,677,952	13.4	Female householder, no husband		
55 to 59 years	13,469,237	4.8	present	12,900,103	12.2
60 to 64 years	10,805,447	3.8	Nonfamily households	33,692,754	31.9
65 to 74 years	18,390,986	6.5	Householder living alone	27,230,075	25.8
75 to 84 years	12,361,180	4.4	Householder 65 years and over	9,722,857	9.2
85 years and over	4,239,587	1.5	Persons living in households	273,643,273	97.2
18 years and over	209,128,094	74.3	Persons per household	2.59	NA
Male	100,994,367	35.9	Persons living in group quarters	7,778,633	2.8
Female	108,133,727	38.4	Institutionalized persons	4,059,039	1.4
21 years and over	196,899,193	70.0	Other persons in group quarters	3,719,594	1.3

NA = Not applicable.

Children by Relationship to Householder, 2000
Source: Bureau of the Census, U.S. Dept. of Commerce
(numbers in thousands)

	Total, all ages	Under 18 years Total	Under 6	6 to 11	12 to 14	15 to 17	18 years and over Total	18 to 24	25 and over
Children of householder	83,714	64,652	20,120	22,804	11,200	10,528	19,062	11,186	7,876
Adopted children	2,059	1,586	389	598	317	282	473	274	199
Stepchildren	4,385	3,292	328	1,271	847	846	1,092	778	314
Biological children	77,271	59,774	19,402	20,935	10,036	9,400	17,497	10,134	7,363
Percent of age group									
Adopted children	2.5	2.5	1.9	2.6	2.8	2.7	2.5	2.4	2.5
Stepchildren	5.2	5.1	1.6	5.6	7.6	8.0	5.7	7.0	4.0
Biological children	92.3	92.5	96.4	91.8	89.6	89.3	91.8	90.6	93.5

U.S. Foreign-Born Population

Source: Bureau of the Census, U.S. Dept. of Commerce; total population based on Mar. 2002 Current Population Survey

Percentage of Population That Is Foreign-Born, 1900-2002

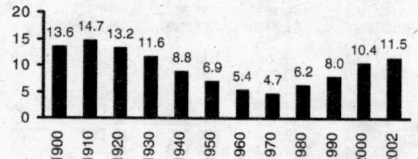

U.S. Foreign-Born Population by Regional Origin, 1995-2002

Region	2002 (thous.)	2000 (thous.)	1995 (thous.)
Europe.........	4,548	4,355	3,937
Under 18	296	250	232
Asia...........	8,281	7,246	6,121
Under 18	660	657	767
Latin America ...	16,943	14,477	11,777
Under 18	1,802	1,684	1,481
Other	2,680	2,301	2,658
Under 18	281	245	275
ALL REGIONS ..	32,453	28,379	24,493
Under 18.....	3,038	2,837	2,726

Foreign-Born Population: Top Countries of Origin, 1920, 1960, 2000

Source: Bureau of the Census, U.S. Dept. of Commerce
(totals in thousands; % is percent of all foreign-born)

1920 Country	Number	%	1960 Country	Number	%	2000 Country	Number	%
Germany	1,686	12.1	Italy..............	1,256	12.9	Mexico............	7,841	27.6
Italy.............	1,610	11.6	Germany..........	989	10.2	Philippines........	1,222	4.3
Soviet Union.......	1,400	10.1	Canada..........	953	9.8	China and Hong Kong	1,066	3.8
Poland	1,139	8.2	Great Britain	764	7.9	India	1,007	3.5
Canada..........	1,138	8.2	Poland...........	747	7.7	Cuba	952	3.4
Great Britain	1,135	8.2	Soviet Union	690	7.1	Vietnam..........	863	3.0
Ireland	1,037	7.5	Mexico	575	5.9	El Salvador	765	2.7
Sweden	625	4.5	Ireland...........	338	3.5	Korea	701	2.5
Austria	575	4.1	Austria...........	304	3.1	Dominican Republic .	692	2.4
Mexico	486	3.5	Hungary	245	2.5	Canada	678	2.4

Immigrants Admitted, by Top 50 Metropolitan Areas of Intended Residence, 2002

Source: Bureau of Citizenship and Immigration Services, U.S. Dept. of Homeland Security
(fiscal year 2002)

Metropolitan Statistical Area (MSA)	Number	Percentage	Metropolitan Statistical Area (MSA)	Number	Percentage
TOTAL immigrants admitted to U.S. ...	1,063,732	100.0	Sacramento, CA	8,970	0.9
Los Angeles-Long Beach, CA	100,397	9.9	Jersey City, NJ	8,204	0.8
New York, NY......................	86,898	8.6	Tampa-St. Petersburg-Clearwater, FL ...	7,947	0.8
Chicago, IL........................	41,616	4.1	Denver, CO	7,239	0.7
Miami, FL.........................	39,712	3.9	West Palm Beach-Boca Raton, FL	7,183	0.7
Washington, DC-MD-VA-WV	36,371	3.6	Las Vegas, NV-AZ.................	7,099	0.7
Houston, TX.......................	26,788	2.6	Baltimore, MD	6,340	0.6
San Jose, CA......................	25,640	2.5	Fresno, CA	5,855	0.6
Orange County, CA	24,039	2.4	Austin-San Marcos, TX	5,380	0.5
San Diego, CA	20,859	2.1	Fort Worth-Arlington, TX	5,319	0.5
Boston, MA-NH	20,769	2.0	Orlando, FL......................	5,317	0.5
Riverside-San Bernardino, CA........	18,767	1.9	St. Louis, MO-IL	5,086	0.5
Oakland, CA......................	18,608	1.8	McAllen-Edinburg-Mission, TX	5,013	0.5
Dallas, TX........................	17,027	1.7	San Antonio, TX	4,617	0.5
Atlanta, GA.......................	15,556	1.5	Ventura, CA......................	4,553	0.4
San Francisco, CA.................	14,685	1.4	Cleveland-Lorain-Elyria, OH	4,086	0.4
Seattle-Bellevue-Everett, WA.........	14,187	1.4	Honolulu, HI......................	3,970	0.4
Newark, NJ.......................	13,817	1.4	El Paso, TX	3,866	0.4
Fort Lauderdale, FL	13,717	1.4	Hartford, CT......................	3,532	0.3
Detroit, MI........................	13,487	1.3	Monmouth-Ocean, NJ..............	3,479	0.3
Philadelphia, PA-NJ................	12,925	1.3	Raleigh-Durham-Chapel Hill, NC	3,463	0.3
Nassau-Suffolk, NY	12,208	1.2	Salt Lake City-Ogden, UT	3,450	0.3
Bergen-Passaic, NJ................	12,192	1.2	Columbus, OH....................	3,369	0.3
Middlesex-Somerset-Hunterdon, NJ	12,068	1.2	Bakersfield, CA	3,297	0.3
Phoenix-Mesa, AZ	11,738	1.2	Other MSA.......................	180,146	17.8
Minneapolis-St. Paul, MN-WI	10,624	1.0	Unknown	62,359	6.2
Portland-Vancouver, OR-WA..........	9,895	1.0			

Immigrants Admitted, by State of Intended Residence, 2002

Source: Bureau of Citizenship and Immigration Services, U.S. Dept. of Homeland Security
(fiscal year 2002)

STATE	Immigrants	STATE	Immigrants	STATE	Immigrants	STATE	Immigrants
Alabama........	2,570	Iowa...........	5,591	New Jersey....	57,721	Vermont	1,007
Alaska	1,564	Kansas........	4,508	New Mexico....	3,399	Virginia	25,411
Arizona........	17,719	Kentucky	4,681	New York......	114,827	Washington.....	25,704
Arkansas	2,535	Louisiana	3,199	North Carolina..	12,910	West Virginia....	636
California......	291,216	Maine.........	1,269	North Dakota...	776	Wisconsin	6,498
Colorado.......	12,060	Maryland	23,751	Ohio..........	13,875	Wyoming........	281
Connecticut	11,243	Massachusetts..	31,615	Oklahoma	4,229	Guam	1,698
Delaware	1,862	Michigan	21,787	Oregon	12,125	Northern Mariana	
Dist. of Columbia	2,723	Minnesota	13,522	Pennsylvania...	19,473	Islands......	138
Florida	90,819	Mississippi	1,155	Rhode Island...	3,067	Puerto Rico.....	3,071
Georgia	20,555	Missouri	8,610	South Carolina..	2,966	U.S. Virgin Isls .	994
Hawaii	5,503	Montana	422	South Dakota...	902	Armed Services	
Idaho	2,236	Nebraska	3,657	Tennessee	5,694	Posts......	100
Illinois.........	47,235	Nevada	9,499	Texas.........	88,365	Other or unknown	8
Indiana........	6,853	New Hampshire .	3,009	Utah..........	4,889	Total..........	1,063,732

The Elderly U.S. Population, 1900-2025

Source: Bureau of the Census, U.S. Dept. of Commerce

Year[1]	65 AND OVER Number[2]	Percent	85 AND OVER Number[2]	Percent	Year[1]	65 AND OVER Number[2]	Percent	85 AND OVER Number[2]	Percent
1900	3,080	4.1	122	0.2	1980	25,550	11.3	2,240	1.0
1910	3,949	4.3	167	0.2	1990	31,079	12.5	3,021	1.2
1920	4,933	4.7	210	0.2	1995	33,619	12.8	3,685	1.4
1930	6,634	5.4	272	0.2	2000	34,992	12.4	4,240	1.5
1940	9,019	6.8	365	0.3	2001[3]	35,353	12.4	4,448	1.6
1950	12,269	8.1	577	0.4	2002[3]	35,602	12.3	4,593	1.6
1960	16,560	9.2	929	0.5	2010[4]	39,715	13.2	5,786	1.9
1970	19,980	9.8	1,409	0.7	2025[4]	62,641	18.5	7,441	2.2

NOTE: Figures for 1900 to 1950 exclude Alaska and Hawaii. (1) Date of Census. (2) Resident population, in thousands. (3) Estimate for July 1 of year indicated. (4) Projected.

Projections of Total U.S. Population, by Age, 2010-2100

Source: Bureau of the Census, U.S. Dept. of Commerce

Age	2010 Population[1]	2010 Percentage Distribution	2025 Population[1]	2025 Percentage Distribution	2050 Population[1]	2050 Percentage Distribution	2100 Population[1]	2100 Percentage Distribution
TOTAL	299,862	100.0	337,815	100.0	403,687	100.0	570,954	100.0
Under 5 years	20,099	6.7	22,551	6.7	26,914	6.7	36,068	6.3
5-14 years	39,346	13.1	44,486	13.2	52,869	13.1	71,807	12.6
15-24 years	42,819	14.3	43,614	12.9	52,769	13.1	72,620	12.7
25-34 years	38,851	13.0	42,872	12.7	50,458	12.5	68,775	12.0
35-44 years	39,443	13.2	43,234	12.8	49,588	12.3	67,912	11.9
45-54 years	44,161	14.7	38,291	11.3	45,445	11.3	63,787	11.2
55-64 years	35,429	11.8	40,125	11.9	43,644	10.8	58,822	10.3
65 years and over	39,715	13.2	62,641	18.5	81,999	20.3	131,163	23.0
85 years and over	5,786	1.9	7,441	2.2	19,352	4.8	37,030	6.5
100 years and over	129	0.0	313	0.1	1,095	0.3	5,323	0.9

NOTE: Assumptions were based on July 1 estimates of U.S. population consistent with the 1990 decennial census, as enumerated. All figures shown are for July 1 of the given year, exclude Armed Forces overseas, and are middle series population projections. For the series shown, different assumptions were made regarding fertility rates (lifetime births per woman), life expectancy, and immigration in the coming decades. Yearly net immigration was assumed to be 820,000. Percentage distribution may not equal 100, because of overlapping categories shown and rounding. (1) In thousands.

U.S. Households Headed by Couples, 1960-2002

Source: Bureau of the Census, U.S. Dept. of Commerce

(numbers in thousands)

YEAR	Total households	Married-couple households	% of Total	Unmarried-couple households[1]	% of Total	YEAR	Total households	Married-couple households	% of Total	Unmarried-couple households[1]	% of Total
1960	52,799	39,254	74	439	0.8	1991	94,312	52,147	55	3,039	3.2
1970	63,401	44,728	71	523	0.8	1992	95,669	52,457	55	3,308	3.5
1980	80,776	49,112	61	1,589	2.0	1993	96,426	53,090	55	3,510	3.6
1981	82,368	49,294	60	1,808	2.2	1994	97,107	53,171	55	3,661	3.8
1982	83,527	49,630	59	1,863	2.2	1995	98,990	53,858	54	3,668	3.7
1983	83,918	49,908	59	1,891	2.3	1996	99,627	53,567	54	3,958	4.0
1984	85,407	50,090	59	1,988	2.3	1997	101,018	53,604	53	4,130	4.1
1985	86,789	50,350	58	1,983	2.3	1998	102,528	54,317	53	4,236	4.1
1986	88,458	50,933	58	2,220	2.5	1999	103,874	54,770	53	4,486	4.3
1987	89,479	51,537	58	2,334	2.6	2000	104,705	55,311	53	4,736	4.5
1988	91,124	51,675	57	2,588	2.8	2001[2]	108,209	56,592	52	4,893	4.5
1989	92,830	52,100	56	2,764	3.0	2002[2]	109,297	56,747	52	4,898	4.5
1990	93,347	52,317	56	2,856	3.1						

(1) Does not include figures for same-sex couples. (2) Data for 2001 and 2002 are based on Census 2000 figures and an expanded sample of households.

Young Adults Living at Home in the U.S., 1960-2002

Source: Bureau of the Census, U.S. Dept. of Commerce

(numbers in thousands)

YEAR	18-24 Male Total	18-24 Male At home[1]	%	18-24 Female Total	18-24 Female At home[1]	%	YEAR	25-34 Male Total	25-34 Male At home[1]	%	25-34 Female Total	25-34 Female At home[1]	%
1960	6,842	3,583	52	7,876	2,750	35	1960	10,896	1,185	11	11,587	853	7
1970	10,398	5,641	54	11,959	4,941	41	1970	11,929	1,129	9	12,637	829	7
1980	14,278	7,755	54	14,844	6,336	43	1980	18,107	1,894	10	18,689	1,300	7
1985	13,695	8,172	60	14,149	6,758	48	1985	20,184	2,685	13	20,673	1,661	8
1990	12,450	7,232	58	12,860	6,135	48	1990	21,462	3,213	15	21,779	1,774	8
1991	12,275	7,385	60	12,627	6,163	49	1991	21,319	3,172	15	21,586	1,887	9
1992	12,083	7,296	60	12,351	5,929	48	1992	21,125	3,225	15	21,368	1,874	9
1993	12,049	7,145	59	12,260	5,746	47	1993	20,856	3,300	16	21,007	1,844	9
1994	12,683	7,547	60	12,792	5,924	46	1994	20,873	3,261	16	21,073	1,859	9
1995	12,545	7,328	58	12,613	5,896	47	1995	20,589	3,166	15	20,800	1,759	8
1996	12,402	7,327	59	12,441	5,955	48	1996	20,390	3,213	16	20,528	1,810	9
1997	12,534	7,501	60	12,452	6,006	48	1997	20,039	2,909	15	20,217	1,745	9
1998	12,633	7,399	59	12,568	5,974	48	1998	19,526	2,845	15	19,828	1,680	8
1999	12,936	7,440	58	13,031	6,389	49	1999	18,924	2,636	14	19,551	1,690	9
2000	13,291	7,593	57	13,242	6,232	47	2000	18,563	2,387	13	19,222	1,602	8
2001[2]	13,412	7,385	55	13,361	6,068	45	2001[2]	19,308	2,520	13	19,527	1,583	8
2002[2]	13,696	7,575	55	13,602	6,222	46	2002[2]	19,220	2,610	14	19,428	1,618	8

(1) Includes young adults living in their parent(s)' home and unmarried college students living in a dormitory. (2) Data for 2001 and later use population controls based on Census 2000 and an expanded sample of households.

Grandchildren Living in the Home of Their Grandparents, 1970-2002

Source: Bureau of the Census, U.S. Dept. of Commerce (numbers in thousands)

YEAR	Total children under 18	Grandchildren living with grandparents				
			WITH PARENT(S) PRESENT			
		Total	Both parents present	Mother only present	Father only present	Without parent(s) present
1970	69,276	2,214	363	817	78	957
1980	63,369	2,306	310	922	86	988
1990	64,137	3,155	467	1,563	191	935
1991	65,093	3,320	559	1,674	151	937
1992	65,965	3,253	502	1,740	144	867
1993	66,893	3,368	475	1,647	229	1,017
1994	69,508	3,735	436	1,764	175	1,359
1995	70,254	3,965	427	1,876	195	1,466
1996	70,908	4,060	467	1,943	220	1,431
1997	70,983	3,894	554	1,785	247	1,309
1998	71,377	3,989	503	1,827	241	1,417
1999	71,703	3,919	535	1,803	250	1,331
2000	72,012	3,842	531	1,732	220	1,359
2001[1]	72,006	3,844	510	1,755	231	1,348
2002[1]	72,321	3,681	477	1,658	275	1,274

(1) Data for 2001 and 2002 are based on Census 2000 figures and an expanded sample of households.

Living Arrangements of Children, 1970-2002

Source: Bureau of the Census, U.S. Dept. of Commerce
(excludes persons under 18 years of age who maintained households or resided in group quarters)

Race, Hispanic origin, and year	Number (1,000)	BOTH PARENTS	Percentage of children who live with—					FATHER ONLY	NEITHER PARENT
			MOTHER ONLY						
			Total	Divorced	Married Spouse absent	Single[1]	Widowed		
White									
1970	58,790	90	8	3	3	Z	2	1	2
1980	52,242	83	14	7	4	1	2	2	2
1990	51,390	79	16	8	4	3	1	3	2
1998	56,118	74	18	8	4	5	1	5	3
1999	56,265	74	18	NA	NA	NA	NA	4	3
2000	56,455	75	17	NA	NA	NA	NA	4	3
2001	56,135	75	18	8	1	5	1	4	3
2002	58,276	75	18	8	1	5	1	5	3
Black									
1970	9,422	59	30	5	16	4	4	2	10
1980	9,375	42	44	11	16	13	4	2	12
1990	10,018	38	51	10	12	27	2	4	8
1998	11,407	36	51	9	9	32	1	4	9
1999	11,425	35	51	NA	NA	NA	NA	4	10
2000	11,412	38	49	NA	NA	NA	NA	4	9
2001	11,578	38	48	8	2	30	2	5	10
2002	11,646	39	48	9	2	31	1	5	8
Hispanic[2]									
1970	4,006[3]	78	NA	NA	NA	NA	NA	NA	NA
1980	5,459	75	20	6	8	4	2	2	4
1990	7,174	67	27	7	10	8	2	3	3
1998	10,857	64	27	6	8	12	1	4	5
1999	11,236	63	27	NA	NA	NA	NA	5	5
2000	11,613	65	25	NA	NA	NA	NA	4	5
2001	12,446	65	25	6	2	11	1	5	6
2002	12,817	65	25	6	2	11	1	5	5

NA = Not available. Z = Less than 0.5%. (1) Never married. (2) Hispanic persons may be of any race. (3) All persons under 18 years old.

Block Grants for Welfare (Temporary Assistance for Needy Families), Fiscal Year 2002[1]

Source: Office of Family Assistance, Admin. for Children and Families, U.S. Dept. of Health and Human Services

State	Total Federal and State TANF Expenditures, 2002[1]	2002 Average Monthly Expenditure per		2002 Average Monthly Number of		
		Family	Recipient	Families	Recipients	Children
Alabama	$134,707	$622.22	$262.86	18,041	42,706	34,012
Alaska	92,820	1,282.00	438.92	6,034	17,623	11,927
Arizona	309,071	642.34	273.19	40,097	94,279	70,313
Arkansas	69,754	484.24	209.61	12,004	27,731	20,558
California	5,477,301	987.27	393.19	462,328	1,160,882	911,543
Colorado	233,235	1,608.21	617.20	12,086	31,491	23,343
Connecticut	435,751	1,532.69	683.83	23,692	53,102	37,733
Delaware	55,506	845.82	374.33	5,469	12,357	9,423
Dist. of Columbia	209,139	1,078.67	413.40	16,157	42,159	31,445
Florida	992,525	1,401.57	671.09	59,013	123,247	99,508
Georgia	510,737	792.90	332.05	53,678	128,177	99,537
Hawaii	136,649	1,023.40	373.78	11,127	30,466	21,306
Idaho	39,370	2,397.39	1,382.08	1,369	2,374	1,955
Illinois	971,266	1,683.05	605.34	48,091	133,708	106,858
Indiana	327,816	554.51	196.70	49,265	138,885	99,066

State	Total Federal and State TANF Expenditures, 2002[1]	2002 Average Monthly Expenditure per Family	2002 Average Monthly Expenditure per Recipient	2002 Average Monthly Number of Families	2002 Average Monthly Number of Recipients	Children
Iowa	$150,270	$621.34	$234.36	20,154	53,434	35,945
Kansas	137,125	818.65	319.12	13,958	35,808	25,320
Kentucky	206,644	493.37	221.75	34,904	77,658	57,413
Louisiana	240,184	844.53	329.72	23,700	60,704	48,476
Maine	104,047	894.58	332.99	9,692	26,039	17,764
Maryland	427,767	1,313.85	543.69	27,132	65,565	48,116
Massachusetts	670,371	1,181.97	516.93	47,264	108,068	76,545
Michigan	1,266,805	1,420.10	523.40	74,338	201,695	148,794
Minnesota	465,753	1,082.37	410.35	35,859	94,584	68,113
Mississippi	143,769	680.46	296.30	17,607	40,434	30,468
Missouri	326,273	604.20	228.96	45,001	118,753	84,401
Montana	60,667	867.47	307.52	5,828	16,440	10,785
Nebraska	76,757	618.92	250.84	10,335	25,500	18,508
Nevada	89,315	675.74	269.28	11,015	27,640	20,502
New Hampshire	72,197	993.53	414.94	6,056	14,499	9,915
New Jersey	952,208	1,889.93	769.48	41,986	103,123	77,614
New Mexico	123,106	602.93	216.71	17,015	47,338	33,731
New York	3,851,521	1,883.24	778.03	170,430	412,530	292,833
North Carolina	471,348	916.20	431.24	42,872	91,084	70,218
North Dakota	32,902	848.47	328.60	3,232	8,344	5,961
Ohio	901,112	893.64	393.16	84,031	190,998	141,951
Oklahoma	147,601	831.06	333.13	14,801	36,923	28,258
Oregon	258,235	1,199.15	525.94	17,946	40,916	30,154
Pennsylvania	1,062,999	1,098.72	420.63	80,624	210,595	155,064
Rhode Island	173,642	1,004.51	371.44	14,405	38,957	27,107
South Carolina	133,977	539.42	219.49	20,698	50,866	37,109
South Dakota	23,134	676.17	291.97	2,851	6,603	5,390
Tennessee	311,499	411.46	157.49	63,088	164,823	118,710
Texas	740,812	475.11	186.30	129,937	331,363	253,098
Utah	109,903	1,174.45	458.34	7,798	19,982	14,420
Vermont	68,723	1,119.98	427.16	5,113	13,407	8,611
Virginia	264,499	733.48	327.70	30,051	67,262	49,074
Washington	627,983	965.74	379.89	54,188	137,755	95,744
West Virginia	214,194	1,125.80	428.63	15,855	41,643	28,193
Wisconsin	489,416	2,151.61	901.69	18,955	45,231	36,689
Wyoming	21,975	4,042.52	2,216.58	453	826	691
2002 Totals	$25,414,383	$1,039.38	$418.01	2,037,618	5,066,574	3,790,207
2001 Totals	$25,667,381	$1,024.57	$400.86	2,087,646	5,335,891	3,968,499
2000 Totals	$24,780,711	$926.32	$353.72	2,229,315	5,838,043	4,303,943

NOTE: Under 1996 legislation, the Aid to Families with Dependent Children (AFDC) program was converted to this state block-grant program. (1) In thousands. FY 2002 covers period from October 2001 to September 2002.

Adults Receiving TANF[1] (Welfare) Funds, by Employment Status, Fiscal Year 2000

Source: Office of Family Assistance, Admin. for Children and Families, U.S. Dept. of Health and Human Services

STATE	Adults	Employed	STATE	Adults	Employed	STATE	Adults	Employed	STATE	Adults	Employed
AL	9,196	25.7%	IN	26,710	27.6%	NV	3,293	14.8%	SC	7,895	21.3%
AK	7,210	14.1	IA	13,606	26.4	NH	4,409	25.3	SD	1,305	20.6
AZ	20,824	4.1	KS	9,005	19.7	NJ	32,951	12.2	TN	37,179	26.4
AR	6,231	10.4	KY	24,988	16.6	NM	21,364	30.1	TX	92,372	15.2
CA	314,081	34.9	LA	17,147	19.4	NY	226,838	20.5	UT	6,175	32.2
CO	7,067	24.5	ME	8,963	33.3	NC	23,854	17.7	VT	5,880	27.7
CT	19,495	35.6	MD	23,532	6.7	ND	2,043	32.1	Virgin		
DE	3,224	37.1	MA	29,148	18.1	OH	65,164	31.2	Islands	1,077	2.2
DC	12,756	28.9	MI	54,788	41.5	OK	8,550	21.5	VA	19,183	33.5
FL	31,804	27.1	MN	35,916	35.5	OR	11,925	23.1	WA	47,700	37.7
GA	28,679	17.4	MS	6,085	14.1	PA	63,783	24.3	WV	10,262	18.2
Guam	NA	NA	MO	36,214	25.8	Puerto			WI	5,689	15.8
HI	13,007	39.3	MT	4,324	15.0	Rico	31,870	9.1	WY	229	14.3
ID	419	27.8	NE	6,572	12.4	RI	13,888	27.9	U.S.	1,578,598	26.4
IL	62,732	41.4									

NA = Not available. (1) TANF = the state block grant program known as Temporary Assistance for Needy Families.

Poverty Rate

Source: Bureau of the Census, U.S. Dept. of Commerce

The poverty rate is the proportion of the population whose income falls below the government's official poverty level, which is adjusted each year for inflation. The national poverty rate was 12.1% in 2002, an increase from the 2001 rate of 11.7%, but still below the 1990 rate of 13.5%. The 2002 data showed 16.7% of children lived in poverty; the poverty rate among people aged 65 and older was 10.4%.

Poverty Level by Family Size, 1980-2002

Source: Bureau of the Census, U.S. Dept. of Commerce

	2002	2000	1990	1980		2002	2000	1990	1980
1 person	$9,183[1]	$8,794	$6,652	$4,186	3 persons	$14,072	$13,783	$10,419	$6,570
Under 65 years	9,359	8,959	6,800	4,284	4 persons	18,556	17,603	13,359	8,415
65 years and over	8,628	8,259	6,268	3,950	5 persons	22,377	20,819	15,792	9,967
2 persons	11,756[1]	11,239	8,509	5,361	6 persons	25,738	23,528	17,839	11,272
Householder under 65 years	12,047	11,590	8,794	5,537	7 persons	29,615	26,754	20,241	12,761
					8 persons	33,121	29,701	22,582	14,199
Householder 65 years and over	10,874	10,419	7,905	4,982	9 persons or more	39,843	35,060	26,848	16,896

(1) Weighted average; not used for computing poverty data.

Persons Below Poverty Level, 1960-2002

Source: Bureau of the Census, U.S. Dept. of Commerce

YEAR	Number below poverty level (in millions)				Percentage below poverty level				Avg. income cutoffs for family of 4 at poverty level[3]
	All races[1]	White	Black	Hispanic origin[2]	All races[1]	White	Black	Hispanic origin[2]	
1960	39.9	28.3	NA	NA	22.2	17.8	NA	NA	$3,022
1970	25.4	17.5	7.5	NA	12.6	9.9	33.5	NA	3,968
1980	29.3	19.7	8.6	3.5	13.0	10.2	32.5	25.7	8,414
1990	33.6	22.3	9.8	6.0	13.5	10.7	31.9	28.1	13,359
1991	35.7	23.7	10.2	6.3	14.2	11.3	32.7	28.7	13,924
1992	38.0	25.3	10.8	7.6	14.8	11.9	33.4	29.6	14,335
1993	39.3	26.2	10.9	8.1	15.1	12.2	33.1	30.6	14,763
1994	38.1	25.4	10.2	8.4	14.5	11.7	30.6	30.7	15,141
1995	36.4	24.4	9.9	8.6	13.8	11.2	29.3	30.3	15,569
1996	36.5	24.7	9.7	8.7	13.7	11.2	28.4	29.4	16,036
1997	35.6	24.4	9.1	8.3	13.3	11.0	26.5	27.1	16,400
1998	34.5	23.5	9.1	8.1	12.7	10.5	26.1	25.6	16,660
1999	32.3	21.9	8.4	7.4	11.8	9.8	23.6	22.8	17,029
2000	31.1	21.2	7.9	7.2	11.3	9.4	22.2	21.2	17,063
2001	32.9	22.7	8.1	8.0	11.7	9.9	22.7	21.4	18,104
2002	34.6	23.5	8.6	8.6	12.1	10.2	24.1	21.8	18,556

NA = Not available. **NOTE:** Because of a change in the definition of poverty, data prior to 1980 are not directly comparable to data since 1980. (1) Includes other races not shown separately. (2) Persons of Hispanic origin may be of any race. (3) Figures for 1960-80 represent only nonfarm families.

Poverty by Family Status, Sex, and Race, 1986-2002

Source: Bureau of the Census, U.S. Dept. of Commerce
(No. in thousands)

	2002		2000		1995		1990		1986	
	No.	%[1]	No.	%[1]	No.	%[1]	No.	%[1]	No.	%[1]
TOTAL POOR	34,570	12.1	31,054	11.3	36,425	13.8	33,585	13.5	32,370	13.6
In families	24,534	10.4	22,015	9.6	27,501	12.3	25,232	12.0	24,754	12.0
Head of household	7,229	9.6	6,222	8.6	7,532	10.8	7,098	10.7	7,023	10.9
Related children	11,646	16.3	11,018	15.6	13,999	20.2	12,715	19.9	12,257	19.8
Unrelated individuals	9,618	20.4	8,503	18.9	8,247	20.9	7,446	20.7	6,846	21.6
In families, female householder, no husband present	11,657	28.8	10,425	27.9	14,205	36.5	12,578	37.2	11,944	38.3
Head of household	3,613	26.5	3,096	24.7	4,057	32.4	3,768	33.4	3,613	34.6
Related children	7,203	13.1	6,116	39.8	8,364	50.3	7,363	53.4	6,943	54.4
Unrelated female individuals	5,595	22.9	5,071	21.6	4,865	23.5	4,589	24.0	4,311	25.1
All other families	NA	NA	NA	NA	13,296	7.2	12,654	7.1	12,811	7.3
Head of household	NA	NA	NA	NA	3,475	6.1	3,330	6.0	3,410	6.3
Related children	NA	NA	NA	NA	5,635	10.7	5,352	10.7	5,313	10.8
Unrelated male individuals	4,023	17.7	3,548	16.0	3,382	18.0	2,857	16.9	2,536	17.5
TOTAL WHITE POOR[2]	23,466	10.2	21,242	9.4	24,423	11.2	22,326	10.7	22,183	11.0
In families	16,043	8.4	14,392	7.7	17,593	9.6	15,916	9.0	16,393	9.4
Head of household	NA	NA	4,151	6.9	4,994	8.5	4,622	8.1	4,811	8.6
Related children	3,570	32.1	6,838	12.3	8,474	15.5	7,696	15.1	7,714	15.3
Female householder, no spouse present	5,992	24.1	1,655	20	2,200	26.6	2,010	26.8	2,041	28.2
Unrelated individuals	7,105	18.4	6,402	17.2	6,336	19.0	5,739	18.6	5,198	19.2
TOTAL BLACK POOR[2]	8,602	24.1	7,862	22.0	9,872	29.3	9,837	31.9	8,983	31.1
In families	6,761	22.8	6,108	20.7	8,189	28.5	8,160	31.0	7,410	29.7
Head of household	NA	NA	1,685	19.1	2,127	26.4	2,193	29.3	1,987	28.0
Related children	3,570	32.1	3,417	30.4	4,644	41.5	4,412	44.2	4,039	42.7
Female householder, no spouse present	4,980	38.2	1,301	34.6	1,701	45.1	1,648	48.1	1,488	50.1
Unrelated individuals	1,800	30.7	1,708	28.0	1,551	32.6	1,131	34.3	1,431	38.5

NA = Not available. (1) Percentage of total U.S. population in each category who fell below poverty level and are enumerated here. For example, of all persons in families in 2002, 10.4%, or 24,534,000, were poor. (2) Data are for one race only. The Census Bureau revised race categories in 2002; figures are not directly comparable with previous years.

Persons in Poverty, by State, 2000-2002

Source: Bureau of the Census, U.S. Dept. of Commerce

	% 2001-02[1]	% 2000-01[1]		% 2001-02[1]	% 2000-01[1]		% 2001-02[1]	% 2000-01[1]
Alabama	15.2	14.6	Kentucky	13.4	12.6	North Dakota	12.7	12.1
Alaska	8.7	8.1	Louisiana	16.9	16.7	Ohio	10.1	10.3
Arizona	14.1	13.2	Maine	11.9	10.2	Oklahoma	14.6	15.0
Arkansas	18.8	17.1	Maryland	7.3	7.3	Oregon	11.3	11.3
California	12.8	12.6	Massachusetts	9.5	9.4	Pennsylvania	9.5	9.1
Colorado	9.2	9.2	Michigan	10.5	9.6	Rhode Island	10.3	9.9
Connecticut	7.8	7.5	Minnesota	6.9	6.5	South Carolina	14.7	13.1
Delaware	7.9	7.6	Mississippi	18.9	17.1	South Dakota	10.0	9.6
District of Columbia	17.6	16.7	Missouri	9.8	9.4	Tennessee	14.5	13.8
Florida	12.6	11.9	Montana	13.4	13.7	Texas	15.3	15.2
Georgia	12.1	12.5	Nebraska	10.0	9.0	Utah	10.2	9.1
Hawaii	11.4	10.2	Nevada	8.0	7.9	Vermont	9.8	9.9
Idaho	11.4	12.0	New Hampshire	6.1	5.5	Virginia	8.9	8.1
Illinois	11.5	10.4	New Jersey	8.0	7.7	Washington	10.8	10.8
Indiana	8.8	8.5	New Mexico	17.9	17.7	West Virginia	16.6	15.6
Iowa	8.3	7.8	New York	14.1	14.0	Wisconsin	8.2	8.6
Kansas	10.1	9.1	North Carolina	13.4	12.5	Wyoming	8.8	9.7
						U.S. Total	11.9	11.5

(1) 2-year average.

U.S. Places of 5,000 or More Population—With ZIP and Area Codes

Source: U.S. Bureau of the Census, Dept. of Commerce; NeuStar Inc.

The following is a list of places of 5,000 or more inhabitants recognized by the Bureau of the Census, U.S. Dept. of Commerce, based on 2002 Census Bureau estimates. Also given are 1990 census populations. This list includes **places that are incorporated** under the laws of their respective states as cities, boroughs, towns, and villages, as well as boroughs in Alaska and towns in the 6 New England states, New York, and Wisconsin. Townships are not included.

Places that the Census Bureau designates as **"census designated places" (CDPs)** are also included; these are marked (c). CDP boundaries can change from one census to another. Hawaii is the only state that has no incorporated places recognized by the Census Bureau; all places shown for Hawaii are CDPs.

Note: The Census Bureau does not calculate estimates for CDPs; for these places, the 2000 Census figure is given, in *italics*.

This list also includes, in *italics*, **minor civil divisions (MCDs)**, for Connecticut, Maine, Massachusetts, New Hampshire, Rhode Island, and Vermont. MCDs are not incorporated and not recognized as CDPs, but are often the primary political or administrative divisions of a county.

An **asterisk** (*) denotes that the ZIP code given is for general delivery; named streets and/or P.O. boxes within the community may differ; consult local postmaster. **Area codes** are given in parentheses. Some regions have 2 or more area codes intermixed; these are known as **overlays**. States where this occurs are noted. When 2 or more area codes are listed for one place, consult local operators for assistance. Area codes based on latest information as of Sept. 2003. For a listing in numerical order of all area codes in the U.S., Canada, and the Caribbean, see the Telecommunications chapter.

For some places listed, no area code and/or ZIP code is available. — = Not available.

Alabama

ZIP	Place	Area Code	2002	1990
35007	Alabaster	(205)	24,877	14,619
*35950	Albertville	(256)	17,602	14,507
*35010	Alexander City	(256)	14,832	14,917
36420	Andalusia	(334)	8,627	9,269
*36201	Anniston	(256)	23,792	26,638
35016	Arab	(251)	7,286	6,321
*35611	Athens	(256)	19,550	16,901
*36502	Atmore	(334)	7,557	8,046
35954	Attalla	(256)	6,443	6,859
*36830	Auburn	(251)	45,389	33,830
36507	Bay Minette	(251)	7,808	7,168
*35020	Bessemer	(205)	29,358	33,581
*35203	Birmingham	(205)	239,416	265,347
*35957	Boaz	(256)	7,641	6,928
*36426	Brewton	(251)	5,384	5,885
35243	Cahaba Heights (c)	(205)	*5,203*	4,778
35220	Center Point (c)	(205)	*22,784*	22,658
36671	Chickasaw	(251)	6,161	6,651
35044	Childersburg	(256)	5,038	4,756
*35045	Clanton	(205)	8,037	7,669
*35055	Cullman	(256)	14,058	13,367
36526	Daphne	(251)	17,230	11,291
*35601	Decatur	(256)	53,941	49,917
36732	Demopolis	(334)	7,435	7,512
*36302	Dothan	(334)	58,998	54,131
*36330	Enterprise	(334)	21,370	20,119
*36027	Eufaula	(334)	13,768	13,220
35064	Fairfield	(205)	12,068	12,200
*36532	Fairhope	(251)	13,477	9,189
*35630	Florence	(256)	35,814	36,426
*36535	Foley	(251)	8,791	4,937
35214	Forestdale (c)	(205)	*10,509*	10,395
*35967	Fort Payne	(256)	13,081	11,838
36362	Fort Rucker (c)	(334)	*6,052*	7,593
35068	Fultondale	(205)	6,643	6,400
*35901	Gadsden	(205)	37,966	42,523
35071	Gardendale	(205)	12,005	9,251
35905	Glencoe	(256)	5,078	4,687
35235	Grayson Valley (c)	(205)	*5,447*	—
36037	Greenville	(334)	7,131	7,847
36542	Gulf Shores	(251)	5,504	3,261
*35976	Guntersville	(256)	7,492	7,038
35570	Hamilton	(205)	6,575	6,171
35640	Hartselle	(256)	12,174	11,114
35080	Helena	(205)	11,402	4,303
35259	Homewood	(205)	24,782	23,644
*35244	Hoover	(205)	64,265	39,988
35023	Hueytown	(205)	15,413	15,280
*35801	Huntsville	(256)	162,536	159,880
35210	Irondale	(205)	9,733	9,458
36545	Jackson	(251)	5,297	5,819
36265	Jacksonville	(256)	8,532	10,283
*35501	Jasper	(205)	13,924	13,553
—	Lake Purdy (c)		*5,799*	1,840
36863	Lanett	(334)	7,738	8,985
35094	Leeds	(205)	10,792	10,009
*35758	Madison	(256)	32,335	14,792
35228	Midfield	(205)	5,508	5,559
36054	Millbrook	(334)	11,465	6,046
*36601	Mobile	(251)	194,862	199,973
*36460	Monroeville	(251)	6,809	6,993
*36104	Montgomery	(334)	201,425	190,350
35004	Moody	(205)	8,936	4,921
—	Moores Mill (c)	(256)	*5,178*	3,362
35253	Mountain Brook	(205)	20,151	19,810
*35661	Muscle Shoals	(256)	12,232	9,611
*35476	Northport	(205)	19,791	17,297
35121	Oneonta	(205)	5,873	4,844
*36801	Opelika	(334)	23,596	22,122
36467	Opp	(334)	6,433	7,011
36203	Oxford	(256)	15,212	9,537
*36360	Ozark	(334)	14,976	13,030
35124	Pelham	(205)	16,521	9,356
*35125	Pell City	(205)	10,098	7,945
*36867	Phenix City	(334)	28,503	25,311
35126	Pinson (c)	(205)	*5,033*	10,987
35127	Pleasant Grove	(205)	10,245	8,458
*36067	Prattville	(334)	25,867	19,816
36610	Prichard	(251)	28,200	34,320
35906	Rainbow City	(256)	8,749	7,667
36274	Roanoke	(334)	6,566	6,362
*35653	Russellville	(256)	8,806	7,812
36201	Saks (c)	(205)	*10,698*	11,138
36571	Saraland	(251)	12,415	11,784
36572	Satsuma	(334)	5,797	5,194
*35768	Scottsboro	(256)	14,811	13,786
*36701	Selma	(334)	19,991	23,755
35660	Sheffield	(256)	9,413	10,380
36877	Smiths (c)	(334)	*21,756*	3,456
35901	Southside	(256)	7,271	5,580
*36527	Spanish Fort	(251)	5,527	3,732
*35150	Sylacauga	(256)	12,645	12,520
*35160	Talladega	(256)	15,026	18,175
35217	Tarrant	(205)	6,893	8,046
*36582	Theodore (c)	(251)	*6,811*	6,509
36619	Tillman's Corner (c)	(251)	*15,685*	17,988
*36081	Troy	(334)	13,833	13,051
35173	Trussville	(205)	13,859	8,283
*35401	Tuscaloosa	(205)	79,149	77,866
*35674	Tuscumbia	(256)	7,949	8,413
36083	Tuskegee	(334)	11,836	12,257
*36854	Valley	(334)	9,028	9,556
*35266	Vestavia Hills	(205)	25,653	19,550
*36092	Wetumpka	(334)	6,287	4,670

Alaska (907)

ZIP	Place	2002	1990
*99501	Anchorage	268,983	226,338
99559	Bethel	5,903	4,674
*99708	College (c)	*11,402*	11,249
99702	Eielson AFB (c)	*5,400*	5,251
*99701	Fairbanks	30,780	30,843
*99801	Juneau	30,751	26,751
99611	Kenai	7,213	6,327
*99901	Ketchikan	7,589	8,263
—	Knik-Fairview (c)	*7,049*	272
*99615	Kodiak	6,441	6,365
—	Lakes (c)	*6,706*	—
99645	Palmer	5,388	2,901
*99835	Sitka	8,829	8,588
*99654	Wasilla	6,375	4,028

Arizona

ZIP	Place	Area Code	2002	1990
*85220	Apache Junction	(480)	33,988	18,092
85323	Avondale	(623)	48,738	17,595
85653	Avra Valley (c)	(520)	*5,038*	3,403
—	Big Park (c)	(928)	*5,245*	3,024
85603	Bisbee	(520)	5,985	6,288
85326	Buckeye	(623)	8,901	4,436
*86442	Bullhead City	(928)	35,460	21,951
86322	Camp Verde	(928)	9,783	6,243
*85222	Casa Grande	(520)	28,697	19,076
85740	Casas Adobes (c)	(520)	*54,011*	—
85738	Catalina (c)	(520)	*7,025*	4,864
—	Catalina Foothills (c)	(520)	*53,794*	—
*85225	Chandler	(480)	292,016	89,862
86503	Chinle (c)	(928)	*5,366*	5,059
86323	Chino Valley	(928)	8,648	4,837
85228	Coolidge	(520)	8,361	6,934
86326	Cottonwood	(928)	10,055	5,918
86326	Cottonwood-Verde Village (c)	(928)	*10,610*	7,037
86327	Dewey-Humboldt (c)	(928)	*6,295*	3,640
*85607	Douglas	(520)	16,441	13,908
—	Drexel Heights (c)		*23,849*	—
85335	El Mirage	(623)	13,255	5,001
85231	Eloy	(520)	10,752	7,211
*86004	Flagstaff	(928)	55,713	45,857
85232	Florence	(520)	15,404	7,321
*85726	Flowing Wells (c)	(520)	*15,050*	14,013

ZIP	Place	Area Code	2002	1990
—	Fortuna Foothills (c)	(928)	20,478	7,737
*85268	Fountain Hills	(480)	21,947	10,030
*85299	Gilbert.	(480)	135,005	29,149
*85301	Glendale.	(623)	230,564	147,070
*85501	Globe	(928)	7,335	6,062
—	Gold Camp (c)		6,029	—
85338	Goodyear.	(623)	27,735	6,258
*85622	Green Valley (c)	(520)	17,283	13,231
85283	Guadalupe	(480)	5,238	5,458
86025	Holbrook.	(520)	5,048	4,770
*86401	Kingman.	(928)	22,092	13,208
*86403	Lake Havasu City	(928)	46,407	24,363
85653	Marana.	(520)	18,083	2,565
*85201	Mesa	(480)	426,841	289,199
*86440	Mohave Valley (c).	(928)	13,694	6,962
—	New Kingman-Butler (c)	(928)	14,810	11,627
*85027	New River (c)	(602)	10,740	—
*85621	Nogales.	(520)	21,280	19,489
85737	Oro Valley.	(520)	33,669	9,024
86004	Page.	(928)	6,933	6,598
85253	Paradise Valley	(480)	14,102	11,903
*85541	Payson	(928)	14,136	8,377
*85345	Peoria.	(623)	123,239	51,080
*85034	Phoenix	(602)	1,371,960	988,015
—	Picture Rocks (c)	(520)	8,139	4,026
*86301	Prescott	(928)	36,300	26,592
86314	Prescott Valley .	(928)	26,151	8,904
85242	Queen Creek	(480)	5,449	2,639
85546	Safford	(928)	9,019	7,359
85349	San Luis	(928)	17,816	4,212
85251	Scottsdale	(480)	215,779	130,099
*86336	Sedona.	(928)	10,757	7,720
85901	Show Low.	(928)	8,378	5,020
*85635	Sierra Vista	(520)	38,999	32,983
85635	Sierra Vista Southeast (c).	(520)	14,348	9,237
85350	Somerton.	(928)	8,089	5,293
85713	South Tucson.	(520)	5,531	5,171
*85351	Sun City (c).	(623)	38,309	38,126
85351	Sun City West (c).	(623)	26,344	15,997
85248	Sun Lakes (c)	(480)	11,936	6,578
*85374	Surprise	(623)	44,659	7,122
—	Tanque Verde (c).	(520)	16,195	—
*85285	Tempe	(480)	159,508	141,993
—	Three Points (c)	(520)	5,273	2,175
85353	Tolleson	(623)	5,118	4,483
86045	Tuba City (c).	(928)	8,225	7,323
*85726	Tucson	(520)	503,151	415,444
—	Tucson Estates (c)	(520)	9,755	2,662
85941	Whiteriver (c)	(928)	5,220	3,775
*85390	Wickenburg	(928)	5,299	4,515
86047	Winslow	(928)	9,746	9,279
*85364	Yuma	(928)	80,358	56,966

Arkansas

ZIP	Place	Area Code	2002	1990
71923	Arkadelphia	(870)	11,043	10,014
*72501	Batesville	(870)	9,501	9,187
72012	Beebe.	(501)	5,286	4,809
72714	Bella Vista (c)	(479)	16,582	9,083
*72015	Benton	(501)	23,277	18,177
72712	Bentonville	(479)	24,086	11,257
*72315	Blytheville	(870)	17,555	22,523
72022	Bryant.	(501)	10,515	5,940
72023	Cabot	(501)	16,898	8,319
*71701	Camden	(870)	12,624	14,701
72830	Clarksville.	(479)	7,838	5,833
72032	Conway	(501)	45,915	26,481
71635	Crossett	(870)	6,007	6,282
71832	De Queen	(870)	5,741	4,633
71639	Dumas	(870)	5,034	5,520
72065	East End (c)	(501)	5,623	—
*71730	El Dorado	(870)	21,119	23,146
*72701	Fayetteville	(479)	60,732	42,247
*72335	Forrest City	(870)	14,498	13,364
*72901	Fort Smith.	(479)	81,519	72,798
72936	Greenwood.	(479)	7,415	3,984
*72601	Harrison	(870)	12,353	9,936
72543	Heber Springs	(501)	6,628	5,628
72342	Helena.	(870)	5,921	7,491
*71801	Hope.	(870)	10,482	9,768
*71901	Hot Springs.	(501)	36,356	33,095
*71909	Hot Springs Village (c)	(501)	8,397	6,361
72076	Jacksonville	(501)	30,383	29,101
*72401	Jonesboro	(870)	56,888	46,535
*72201	Little Rock.	(501)	184,055	175,727
72745	Lowell	(479)	5,954	1,224
*71753	Magnolia.	(870)	10,694	11,151
72104	Malvern.	(501)	8,967	9,236
72360	Marianna.	(870)	5,040	6,033
72364	Marion	(870)	9,105	4,405
72113	Maumelle	(501)	12,020	6,714
71953	Mena	(479)	5,596	5,475
*71655	Monticello.	(870)	9,186	8,119
72110	Morrilton.	(501)	6,521	6,551
*72653	Mountain Home.	(870)	11,143	9,027
72112	Newport	(870)	7,507	7,459
*72114	North Little Rock.	(501)	60,007	61,829
72370	Osceola.	(870)	8,577	9,165

ZIP	Place	Area Code	2002	1990
*72450	Paragould.	(870)	22,609	18,540
*71601	Pine Bluff.	(870)	54,169	57,140
72455	Pocahontas	(870)	6,524	6,151
*72756	Rogers.	(479)	41,545	24,692
*72801	Russellville.	(479)	24,693	21,260
*72143	Searcy.	(501)	19,542	15,180
72120	Sherwood.	(501)	21,919	18,890
72761	Siloam Springs.	(479)	11,593	8,151
*72764	Springdale.	(479)	50,941	29,945
72160	Stuttgart.	(870)	9,503	10,420
71854	Texarkana.	(870)	28,268	22,631
72472	Trumann.	(870)	6,848	6,346
*72956	Van Buren.	(479)	19,777	14,899
71671	Warren.	(870)	6,434	6,455
72390	West Helena.	(870)	8,187	10,137
*72301	West Memphis.	(870)	28,030	28,259
72396	Wynne.	(870)	8,532	8,187

California

ZIP	Place	Area Code	2002	1990
92301	Adelanto.	(760)	18,869	6,815
*91376	Agoura Hills	(818)	21,704	20,396
*94501	Alameda.	(510)	72,927	73,979
94507	Alamo (c)	(925)	15,626	12,277
94706	Albany.	(510)	16,628	16,327
*91802	Alhambra.	(323)/(626)	87,655	82,087
92656	Aliso Viejo	(949)	40,596	7,612
90249	Alondra Park (c).	(310)	8,622	12,215
*91901	Alpine (San Diego) (c)	(619)	13,143	9,695
*91003	Altadena (c)	(626)	42,610	42,658
95945	Alta Sierra (c).	(530)	6,522	5,709
95127	Alum Rock (c).	(408)	13,479	—
94589	American Canyon	(707)	12,152	7,734
*92803	Anaheim.	(909)	332,642	266,406
96007	Anderson	(530)	9,420	8,299
*94509	Antioch.	(925)	99,870	62,195
*92307	Apple Valley.	(760)	57,925	46,079
*95003	Aptos (c).	(831)	9,396	9,061
*91006	Arcadia.	(626)	54,904	48,284
*95521	Arcata.	(707)	16,663	15,211
95825	Arden-Arcade (c)	(916)	96,025	92,040
*93420	Arroyo Grande	(805)	16,290	14,432
*90701	Artesia.	(562)	16,755	15,464
93203	Arvin.	(661)	13,654	9,286
94577	Ashland (c).	(510)	20,793	16,590
*93422	Atascadero.	(805)	26,912	23,138
94027	Atherton.	(650)	7,096	7,163
95301	Atwater.	(209)	24,677	22,282
*95603	Auburn.	(530)	12,546	10,653
95201	August (c).	(209)	7,808	6,376
93204	Avenal.	(559)	15,333	9,770
91746	Avocado Heights (c).	(626)	15,148	14,232
91702	Azusa.	(626)	46,323	41,203
*93302	Bakersfield.	(661)	260,969	176,264
91706	Baldwin Park.	(626)	77,828	69,330
92220	Banning.	(909)	25,590	20,572
*92312	Barstow.	(760)	22,554	21,472
94565	Bay Point (c).	(925)	21,534	17,453
—	Bayview-Montalvin (c)	(510)	5,004	3,988
93402	Baywood-Los Osos (c).	(805)	14,351	14,377
95903	Beale AFB (c).	(530)	5,115	6,912
92223	Beaumont.	(909)	13,274	9,685
90201	Bell.	(323)	37,359	34,365
*90706	Bellflower.	(323)	74,525	61,815
90202	Bell Gardens	(213)/(323)/(562)	45,270	42,315
94002	Belmont.	(650)	24,816	24,165
94510	Benicia.	(707)	27,159	24,437
*94704	Berkeley.	(510)	103,640	102,724
92201	Bermuda Dunes (c)	(760)	6,229	4,571
*90210	Beverly Hills.	(213)/(310)/(323)	34,857	31,971
92314	Big Bear City (c).	(909)	5,779	4,920
92315	Big Bear Lake	(909)	5,752	5,351
94526	Blackhawk-Camino Tassajara (c)	(925)	10,048	6,199
92316	Bloomington (c)	(909)	19,318	15,116
*92225	Blythe	(760)	21,376	10,835
93637	Bonadelle Ranchos-Madera Ranchos (c)	(559)	7,300	5,705
*91902	Bonita (c)	(619)	12,401	12,542
92021	Bostonia (c)	(619)	15,169	13,670
95416	Boyes Hot Springs (c)	(707)	6,665	5,973
92227	Brawley	(760)	21,842	18,923
*92822	Brea	(562)/(714)	37,023	32,873
94513	Brentwood	(925)	31,527	7,563
—	Bret Harte (c)	(209)	5,161	—
*90622	Buena Park	(714)	79,015	68,784
*91510	Burbank (Los Angeles)	(818)	102,913	93,649
—	Burbank (Santa Clara) (c)	(408)	5,239	4,902
*94010	Burlingame.	(650)	27,773	26,666
*91372	Calabasas	(818)	20,689	16,577
*92231	Calexico.	(760)	30,746	18,633
93504	California City.	(760)	9,351	5,955
92320	Calimesa.	(909)	7,469	6,554
92233	Calipatria	(760)	7,513	2,701
94515	Calistoga	(707)	5,296	4,468
*93010	Camarillo.	(805)	59,444	52,297
93428	Cambria (c)	(805)	6,232	5,382
95682	Cameron Park (c).	(530)	14,549	11,897
*95008	Campbell	(408)	37,474	36,088

ZIP	Place	Area Code	2002	1990
92055	Camp Pendleton North (c)	(949)	8,197	10,373
92055	Camp Pendleton South (c)	(949)	8,854	11,299
92587	Canyon Lake	(909)	10,642	9,991
95010	Capitola	(831)	9,949	10,171
*92008	Carlsbad	(760)	86,639	63,292
*95608	Carmichael (c)	(916)	49,742	48,702
*93013	Carpinteria	(805)	14,234	13,747
*90745	Carson	(310)	92,929	83,995
92077	Casa de Oro-Mt. Helix (c)	(619)	18,874	30,727
*94546	Castro Valley (c)	(510)	57,292	48,619
95012	Castroville (c)	(831)	6,724	5,272
*92235	Cathedral City	(760)	46,295	30,085
95307	Ceres	(209)	36,707	26,413
90703	Cerritos	(562)	52,620	53,244
91724	Charter Oak (c)	(626)	9,027	8,858
94541	Cherryland (c)	(510)	13,837	11,088
92223	Cherry Valley (c)	(909)	5,891	5,945
*95926	Chico	(530)	65,904	39,970
*91708	Chino	(909)	69,961	59,682
91709	Chino Hills	(909)	72,295	37,868
93610	Chowchilla	(559)	14,310	5,930
*91910	Chula Vista	(619)	193,919	135,160
91702	Citrus (c)	(626)	10,581	9,481
*95621	Citrus Heights	(916)	88,567	107,439
91711	Claremont	(909)	34,831	32,610
94517	Clayton	(925)	11,037	7,317
95422	Clearlake	(707)	13,971	11,804
95425	Cloverdale	(707)	7,275	4,924
*93612	Clovis	(559)	74,503	50,323
92236	Coachella	(760)	27,178	16,896
93210	Coalinga	(559)	16,051	8,212
92324	Colton	(909)	49,833	40,213
95932	Colusa	(530)	5,553	4,934
90022	Commerce	(323)/(562)	13,118	12,135
*90221	Compton	(310)	95,559	90,454
94520	Concord	(925)	125,225	111,308
93212	Corcoran	(559)	20,929	13,360
96021	Corning	(530)	6,823	5,870
*91718	Corona	(909)	138,326	75,943
92138	Coronado	(619)	23,862	26,540
*94925	Corte Madera	(415)	9,306	8,272
*92628	Costa Mesa	(714)/(949)	110,126	96,357
94931	Cotati	(707)	6,706	5,714
92679	Coto de Caza (c)	(949)	13,057	2,853
94556	Country Club (c)	(209)	9,462	9,325
91722	Covina	(626)	48,019	43,332
95531	Crescent City	(707)	7,242	5,824
92325	Crestline (c)	(909)	10,218	8,594
90201	Cudahy	(323)	25,164	22,817
*90230	Culver City	(230)/(310)/(323)	39,698	38,793
*95014	Cupertino	(408)	50,005	39,967
90630	Cypress	(714)	47,249	42,655
*94015	Daly City	(415)/(650)	101,901	92,088
*92629	Dana Point	(949)	35,804	31,896
*94526	Danville	(925)	42,565	31,306
*95616	Davis	(530)	64,221	46,322
90250	Del Aire (c)	(310)	9,012	8,040
93215	Delano	(661)	42,092	22,762
95315	Delhi (c)	(209)	8,022	3,280
*92240	Desert Hot Springs	(760)	17,310	11,668
91765	Diamond Bar	(909)	57,919	53,672
93618	Dinuba	(559)	17,587	12,743
94514	Discovery Bay (c)	(925)	8,981	5,351
95620	Dixon	(707)	16,261	10,417
*90241	Downey	(562)	109,840	91,444
*91009	Duarte	(626)	22,072	20,716
94568	Dublin	(925)	34,345	23,229
95938	Durham (c)	(530)	5,220	4,784
93219	Earlimart (c)	(661)	6,583	5,881
90220	East Compton (c)	(310)	9,286	7,967
—	East Foothills (c)		8,133	14,898
92343	East Hemet (c)	(909)	14,823	17,611
90638	East La Mirada (c)	(562)	9,538	9,367
90022	East Los Angeles (c)	(323)/(562)	124,283	126,379
94303	East Palo Alto	(650)	31,709	23,451
91117	East Pasadena (c)		6,045	5,910
93257	East Porterville (c)	(559)	6,730	5,790
—	East San Gabriel (c)	(626)	14,512	12,736
95253	Edwards AFB (c)	(661)	5,909	7,423
*92020	El Cajon	(619)	95,555	88,918
*92244	El Centro	(760)	37,684	31,405
94530	El Cerrito	(510)	23,513	22,869
95762	El Dorado Hills (c)	(916)	18,016	6,395
94018	El Granada (c)	(650)	5,724	4,426
*95624	Elk Grove	(916)	75,175	17,483
*91734	El Monte	(626)	119,918	106,162
*93446	El Paso de Robles	(805)	26,358	18,583
93030	El Rio (c)	(805)	6,193	6,419
90245	El Segundo	(310)	16,385	15,223
*94802	El Sobrante (c)	(510)	12,260	9,852
*94617	Emeryville	(510)	7,427	5,740
*92024	Encinitas	(760)	59,796	55,406
95320	Escalon	(209)	6,572	4,437
*92025	Escondido	(760)	135,908	108,648
*95501	Eureka	(707)	25,866	27,025
93221	Exeter	(559)	9,504	7,276
*94930	Fairfax	(415)	7,263	6,931
94533	Fairfield	(707)	101,935	78,650
95628	Fair Oaks (Sacramento) (c)	(916)	28,008	26,867
—	Fairview		9,470	9,045
*92028	Fallbrook (c)	(760)	29,100	22,095
93223	Farmersville	(559)	9,033	6,235
*93015	Fillmore	(805)	14,919	11,992
93622	Firebaugh	(209)	5,993	4,429
90001	Florence-Graham (c)	(323)	60,197	57,147
95828	Florin (c)	(916)	27,653	24,330
*95630	Folsom	(916)	61,256	29,802
*92334	Fontana	(909)	143,607	87,535
95841	Foothill Farms (c)	(916)	17,426	17,135
92610	Foothill Ranch (c)	(949)	10,899	—
95437	Fort Bragg	(707)	7,029	6,078
95540	Fortuna	(707)	10,701	8,788
94404	Foster City	(650)	29,194	28,176
*92728	Fountain Valley	(714)	55,553	53,691
95019	Freedom(c)	(831)	6,000	8,361
*94537	Fremont	(510)	206,856	173,339
*93706	Fresno	(559)	445,227	354,091
*92834	Fullerton	(714)	128,842	114,144
95632	Galt	(209)	22,321	8,889
*90247	Gardena	(310)	59,657	51,481
95205	Garden Acres (c)	(209)	9,747	8,547
*92842	Garden Grove	(714)	167,429	142,965
*95020	Gilroy	(408)	43,145	31,487
92509	Glen Avon (c)	(909)	14,853	12,663
*91209	Glendale	(323)/(626)/(818)	199,430	180,038
*91741	Glendora	(626)	50,567	47,832
93561	Golden Hills (c)	(661)	7,434	5,423
95670	Gold River (c)	(916)	8,023	—
*93116	Goleta	(805)	28,626	—
93926	Gonzales	(831)	8,307	4,660
92324	Grand Terrace	(909)	12,067	10,946
95746	Granite Bay (c)	(916)	19,388	—
*95945	Grass Valley	(530)	11,131	9,048
93927	Greenfield (Monterey)	(831)	12,935	7,464
95948	Gridley	(530)	5,663	4,631
93433	Grover Beach	(805)	13,077	11,602
93434	Guadalupe	(805)	5,778	5,479
95322	Gustine	(209)	5,236	4,137
91745	Hacienda Heights (c)	(626)	53,122	52,354
94019	Half Moon Bay	(650)	11,982	8,886
*93230	Hanford	(559)	44,350	30,463
90716	Hawaiian Gardens	(323)	15,236	13,639
*90250	Hawthorne	(213)/(310)/(323)	85,934	71,349
*94544	Hayward	(510)	142,718	114,705
95448	Healdsburg	(707)	11,101	9,469
*92546	Hemet	(909)	63,367	43,366
94547	Hercules	(510)	20,232	16,829
90254	Hermosa Beach	(310)	19,281	18,219
*92340	Hesperia	(760)	67,021	50,418
92346	Highland	(909)	47,085	34,439
94010	Hillsborough	(650)	10,703	10,667
92250	Holtville	(760)	5,550	4,820
*95023	Hollister	(831)	36,449	19,318
91720	Home Gardens (c)	(909)	9,461	7,780
95326	Hughson	(209)	5,033	2,918
*92647	Huntington Beach	(714)	193,799	181,519
90255	Huntington Park	(323)	62,976	56,129
93234	Huron	(559)	6,917	4,766
92251	Imperial	(760)	8,093	4,113
*91932	Imperial Beach	(619)	27,235	26,512
*92201	Indio	(760)	54,221	36,850
*90301	Inglewood	(213)/(310)/(323)	114,959	109,602
—	Interlaken (c)	(831)	7,328	6,404
95640	Ione	(209)	7,450	6,516
*92619	Irvine	(714)/(949)	162,122	110,330
93117	Isla Vista (c)	(805)	18,344	20,395
91935	Jamul (c)	(619)	5,920	2,258
93630	Kerman	(559)	9,344	5,448
93930	King City	(831)	11,283	7,634
93631	Kingsburg	(559)	10,060	7,245
*91011	La Cañada Flintridge	(818)	20,857	19,378
*91024	La Crescenta-Montrose (c)	(818)	18,532	16,968
90045	Ladera Heights (c)	(310)	6,568	6,316
94549	Lafayette	(925)	24,546	23,366
—	Laguna (c)		34,309	9,828
*92652	Laguna Beach	(949)	24,169	23,170
*92654	Laguna Hills	(949)	33,627	22,719
*92607	Laguna Niguel	(949)	63,057	44,723
—	Laguna West-Lakeside (c)		8,414	—
*92654	Laguna Woods	(949)	16,514	—
*90631	La Habra	(562)/(949)	59,984	51,263
90631	La Habra Heights	(562)	5,916	6,226
92352	Lake Arrowhead (c)	(909)	8,934	6,539
92531	Lake Elsinore	(909)	31,866	19,733
92630	Lake Forest	(714)	76,942	56,036
92530	Lakeland Village (c)	(909)	5,626	5,159
93535	Lake Los Angeles (c)	(661)	11,523	7,977
95453	Lakeport	(707)	5,104	4,567
92040	Lakeside (c)	(619)	19,560	39,412
*90714	Lakewood	(562)	81,051	73,553
*91941	La Mesa	(619)	54,966	52,911
*90638	La Mirada	(562)/(714)	48,478	40,452
93241	Lamont (c)	(661)	13,296	11,517
*93539	Lancaster	(661)	124,592	97,300
90623	La Palma	(562)/(714)	15,774	15,392

ZIP	Place	Area Code	2002	1990
—	La Presa (c)		32,721	—
*91747	La Puente	(626)	42,007	36,955
92253	La Quinta	(760)	30,043	11,215
95401	La Riviera (c)	(916)	10,273	10,986
95403	Larkfield-Wikiup (c)	(707)	7,479	6,779
*94939	Larkspur	(415)	11,931	11,068
92688	Las Flores (c)	(949)	5,625	—
95330	Lathrop	(209)	11,753	6,841
91750	La Verne	(909)	32,711	30,843
*90260	Lawndale	(310)	32,388	27,331
*91945	Lemon Grove	(619)	25,057	23,984
93245	Lemoore	(559)	21,076	13,622
93245	Lemoore Station (c)	(559)	5,749	0
90304	Lennox (c)	(310)	22,950	22,757
95648	Lincoln	(916)	19,676	7,248
95901	Linda (c)	(530)	13,474	13,033
93247	Lindsay	(559)	10,524	8,338
95062	Live Oak (Santa Cruz) (c)	(831)	16,628	15,212
95953	Live Oak (Sutter)	(530)	6,405	4,320
95334	Livingston	(209)	11,246	7,317
*95240	Lodi	(209)	60,656	51,874
92354	Loma Linda	(909)	19,813	18,470
90717	Lomita	(213)	20,482	19,442
*93436	Lompoc	(805)	41,389	37,649
*90801	Long Beach	(310)/(562)	472,412	429,321
95650	Loomis	(916)	6,316	5,705
*90720	Los Alamitos	(562)/(949)	11,710	11,788
*94022	Los Altos	(650)	27,314	26,599
94022	Los Altos Hills	(650)	8,002	7,514
*90086	Los Angeles	(213)/(310)/(323)/(818)	3,798,981	3,485,557
93635	Los Banos	(209)	29,525	14,519
*95030	Los Gatos	(408)	28,209	27,357
94903	Lucas Valley-Marinwood (c)	(415)	6,357	5,982
90262	Lynwood	(213)/(310)/(323)	71,387	61,945
93250	Mc Farland	(661)	9,974	7,005
95521	McKinleyville (c)	(707)	13,599	10,749
*93638	Madera	(559)	46,214	29,283
93637	Madera Acres (c)	(559)	7,741	5,245
95954	Magalia (c)	(530)	10,569	8,987
*90265	Malibu	(310)	13,086	11,730
93546	Mammoth Lakes	(760)	7,404	4,785
*90266	Manhattan Beach	(310)	35,501	32,063
*95336	Manteca	(209)	56,904	40,773
93933	Marina	(831)	21,146	26,512
*90291	Marina del Rey (c)	(310)	8,176	7,431
94553	Martinez	(925)	36,707	31,800
95901	Marysville	(530)	12,520	12,324
—	Mayflower Village (c)		5,081	4,978
*90270	Maywood	(323)	28,710	27,893
92254	Mecca (c)	(619)	5,402	1,966
93640	Mendota	(559)	8,268	6,821
*94025	Menlo Park	(650)	30,277	28,403
92359	Mentone (c)	(909)	7,803	5,675
*95340	Merced	(209)	68,225	56,155
94030	Millbrae	(650)	20,317	20,414
*94941	Mill Valley	(415)	13,557	13,029
*95035	Milpitas	(408)	63,700	50,690
91752	Mira Loma (c)	(909)	17,617	15,786
93641	Mira Monte (c)	(805)	7,177	7,744
*92690	Mission Viejo	(949)	96,307	79,464
*95350	Modesto	(209)	203,555	164,746
*91017	Monrovia	(626)	37,848	35,733
91763	Montclair	(909)	34,377	28,434
90640	Montebello	(323)	63,607	59,564
*93940	Monterey	(831)	29,649	31,954
*91754	Monterey Park	(323)/(626)/(818)	61,822	60,738
*93021	Moorpark	(805)	34,577	25,494
*94556	Moraga	(925)	16,686	15,987
*92552	Moreno Valley	(909)	150,773	118,779
*95037	Morgan Hill	(408)	33,791	23,928
*93442	Morro Bay	(805)	10,504	9,664
*94041	Mountain View	(650)	70,046	67,365
*92564	Murrieta	(909)	54,100	18,557
92045	Muscoy (c)	(714)	8,919	7,541
*94558	Napa	(707)	75,032	61,865
*91950	National City	(619)	55,541	54,249
92363	Needles	(760)	5,193	5,475
94560	Newark	(510)	43,331	37,861
95360	Newman	(209)	7,516	4,158
*92658	Newport Beach	(949)	78,096	66,643
93444	Nipomo (c)	(805)	12,626	7,109
91760	Norco	(909)	25,838	23,302
95603	North Auburn (c)	(530)	11,847	10,301
94025	North Fair Oaks (c)	(650)	15,440	13,912
95660	North Highlands (c)	(916)	44,187	42,105
*90650	Norwalk	(562)	106,084	94,279
*94947	Novato	(415)	48,131	47,585
95361	Oakdale	(209)	16,895	11,978
94617	Oakland	(510)	402,777	372,242
94561	Oakley	(925)	26,206	18,374
93445	Oceano (c)	(805)	7,260	6,169
*92056	Oceanside	(760)	165,880	128,090
93308	Oildale (c)	(661)	27,885	26,553
*93023	Ojai	(805)	7,948	7,613
95961	Olivehurst (c)	(530)	11,061	9,738
*91761	Ontario	(909)	165,064	133,179
95060	Opal Cliffs (c)	(831)	6,458	5,940
*92863	Orange	(714)	131,606	110,658
93646	Orange Cove	(559)	8,678	5,604
95662	Orangevale (c)	(916)	26,705	26,266
93457	Orcutt (c)	(805)	28,830	—
94563	Orinda	(925)	18,069	16,642
95963	Orland	(530)	6,283	5,052
93647	Orosi (c)	(559)	7,318	5,486
*95965	Oroville	(530)	13,111	11,885
95965	Oroville East (c)	(530)	8,680	8,462
*93030	Oxnard	(805)	177,984	142,560
94044	Pacifica	(650)	37,771	37,670
93950	Pacific Grove	(831)	15,648	16,117
95968	Palermo (c)	(530)	5,720	5,260
*93590	Palmdale	(661)	124,346	73,314
*92260	Palm Desert	(760)	44,327	23,252
*92262	Palm Springs	(760)	44,526	40,144
*94303	Palo Alto	(650)	57,543	55,900
90274	Palos Verdes Estates	(310)	13,750	13,512
*95969	Paradise	(530)	26,743	25,401
90723	Paramount	(562)	56,489	47,669
95823	Parkway-So. Sacramento (c)	(916)	36,468	31,903
93648	Parlier	(559)	12,293	7,938
*91109	Pasadena	(323)/(626)/(818)	139,712	131,586
	Paso Robles. See El Paso de Robles			
95363	Patterson	(209)	13,521	8,626
92509	Pedley (c)	(909)	11,207	8,869
*92572	Perris	(909)	38,298	21,500
*94952	Petaluma	(707)	55,252	43,166
	Phoenix Lake-Cedar Ridge (c)		5,123	3,569
90660	Pico Rivera	(562)	64,859	59,177
94611	Piedmont	(510)	11,036	10,602
94564	Pinole	(510)	19,439	17,460
*93449	Pismo Beach	(805)	8,646	7,669
94565	Pittsburg	(925)	60,525	47,607
*92871	Placentia	(714)	47,798	41,259
95667	Placerville	(530)	10,124	8,286
94523	Pleasant Hill	(925)	33,537	31,583
94566	Pleasanton	(925)	66,151	50,570
*91769	Pomona	(909)	153,555	131,700
93257	Porterville	(559)	41,309	29,521
*93041	Port Hueneme	(805)	22,249	20,322
92679	Portola Hills (c)	(949)	6,391	2,677
*92064	Poway	(858)	49,115	43,396
93907	Prunedale (c)	(831)	16,432	7,393
*93551	Quartz Hill (c)	(661)	9,890	9,626
92065	Ramona (c)	(760)	15,691	13,040
*95670	Rancho Cordova (c)	(916)	55,060	48,731
91729	Rancho Cucamonga	(909)	143,711	101,409
92270	Rancho Mirage	(760)	14,614	9,778
90275	Rancho Palos Verdes	(310)	42,126	41,667
91941	Rancho San Diego (c)	(619)	20,155	6,977
92688	Rancho Santa Margarita	(949)	48,161	11,390
96080	Red Bluff	(530)	13,508	12,363
96049	Redding	(530)	85,660	66,176
*92373	Redlands	(909)	66,749	62,667
90277	Redondo Beach	(310)	65,793	60,167
*94063	Redwood City	(650)	74,453	66,072
93654	Reedley	(559)	21,231	15,791
92377	Rialto	(909)	96,616	72,395
*94802	Richmond	(510)	102,553	86,019
*93356	Ridgecrest	(760)	25,332	28,295
95003	Rio del Mar (c)	(831)	9,198	8,919
95673	Rio Linda (c)	(916)	10,466	9,481
94571	Rio Vista	(707)	5,684	3,488
95366	Ripon	(209)	11,470	7,455
95367	Riverbank	(209)	17,640	8,591
*92502	Riverside	(909)	274,226	226,546
*95677	Rocklin	(916)	43,263	18,806
94572	Rodeo (c)	(510)	8,717	7,589
*94928	Rohnert Park	(707)	42,342	36,326
90274	Rolling Hills Estates	(310)	7,922	7,789
93560	Rosamond (c)	(661)	14,349	7,430
—	Rosedale (c)	(805)	8,445	4,673
95401	Roseland (c)	(707)	6,369	8,779
91770	Rosemead	(626)	54,955	51,638
95826	Rosemont (c)	(916)	22,904	22,851
*95678	Roseville	(916)	91,761	44,685
90720	Rossmoor (c)	(714)	10,298	9,893
91748	Rowland Heights (c)	(818)	48,553	42,647
92519	Rubidoux (c)	(909)	29,180	24,367
92382	Running Springs (c)	(909)	5,125	4,195
*95814	Sacramento	(916)	435,245	369,365
94574	Saint Helena	(707)	6,069	4,990
95368	Salida (c)	(209)	12,560	4,499
*93907	Salinas	(831)	148,744	108,777
*94960	San Anselmo	(415)	12,252	11,735
*92401	San Bernardino	(909)	191,631	170,036
94066	San Bruno	(650)	39,366	38,961
93001	San Buenaventura (Ventura)	(805)	103,619	92,557
94070	San Carlos	(650)	27,165	26,382
92674	San Clemente	(949)	55,986	41,100
*92138	San Diego	(619)/(858)	1,259,532	1,110,623
92065	San Diego Country Estates (c)	(760)	9,262	6,874
91773	San Dimas	(909)	35,876	32,398
91341	San Fernando	(818)	24,175	22,580
*94142	San Francisco	(415)	764,049	723,959
*91778	San Gabriel	(626)	40,784	37,120
93657	Sanger	(559)	19,829	16,839

ZIP	Place	Area Code	2002	1990
*92581	San Jacinto	(909)	25,689	17,614
*95113	San Jose	(408)	900,443	782,224
*92690	San Juan Capistrano	(949)	34,637	26,183
*94577	San Leandro	(510)	80,609	68,223
94580	San Lorenzo (c)	(510)	21,898	19,987
*93401	San Luis Obispo	(805)	44,256	41,958
*92069	San Marcos	(760)	62,133	38,974
*91109	San Marino	(626)	13,217	12,959
*94402	San Mateo	(650)	91,935	85,619
94806	San Pablo	(510)	30,990	25,158
*94915	San Rafael	(415)	56,288	48,410
94583	San Ramon	(925)	46,217	35,303
*92711	Santa Ana	(714)/(949)	343,413	293,827
*93102	Santa Barbara	(805)	89,382	85,571
*95050	Santa Clara	(408)	101,867	93,613
*91380	Santa Clarita	(661)	160,554	120,500
*95060	Santa Cruz	(831)	53,836	49,711
90670	Santa Fe Springs	(562)	17,938	15,520
*93454	Santa Maria	(805)	80,006	61,552
*90401	Santa Monica	(310)	86,799	86,905
*93060	Santa Paula	(805)	28,835	25,062
*95402	Santa Rosa	(707)	153,489	113,261
*92071	Santee	(619)	53,230	52,902
*95070	Saratoga	(408)	29,496	28,061
*94965	Sausalito	(415)	7,294	7,152
*95066	Scotts Valley	(831)	11,438	8,667
90740	Seal Beach	(714)	24,527	25,098
93955	Seaside	(831)	32,327	38,826
*95472	Sebastopol	(707)	7,787	7,008
93662	Selma	(559)	20,538	14,757
—	Shackelford (c)		5,170	—
93263	Shafter	(661)	13,410	9,404
*96019	Shasta Lake	(916)	9,693	8,821
*91025	Sierra Madre	(626)	10,878	10,762
90806	Signal Hill	(562)	10,005	8,371
*93065	Simi Valley	(805)	116,562	100,218
92075	Solana Beach	(858)	13,068	12,956
93960	Soledad	(831)	23,440	13,426
*93463	Solvang	(805)	5,332	4,741
95476	Sonoma	(707)	9,354	8,168
95073	Soquel (c)	(831)	5,081	9,188
91733	South El Monte	(626)	21,675	20,850
90280	South Gate	(323)/(562)	98,791	86,284
*96151	South Lake Tahoe	(530)	23,973	21,586
95965	South Oroville (c)	(530)	7,695	7,463
*91030	South Pasadena	(213)/(323)/(626)/(818)	24,840	23,936
*94080	South San Francisco	(650)	59,955	54,312
91770	South San Gabriel (c)	(626)	7,595	7,700
91744	South San Jose Hills (c)	(626)	20,218	17,814
90605	South Whittier (c)	(562)	55,193	49,514
95991	South Yuba City (c)	(530)	12,651	8,816
*91977	Spring Valley (c)	(619)	26,663	55,331
94309	Stanford (c)	(650)	13,315	18,097
90680	Stanton	(714)	37,958	30,491
*95208	Stockton	(209)	262,835	210,943
95375	Strawberry (c)	(209)	5,302	4,377
94585	Suisun City	(707)	26,979	22,704
*92586	Sun City (c)	(909)	17,773	14,930
*94086	Sunnyvale	(408)	129,687	117,324
*96130	Susanville	(530)	17,711	12,130
93268	Taft	(661)	8,903	5,902
94941	Tamalpais-Homestead Valley (c)	(415)	10,691	9,601
94806	Tara Hills (c)	(510)	5,332	4,998
*93581	Tehachapi	(661)	11,042	6,182
*92589	Temecula	(909)	73,793	27,177
91780	Temple City	(626)	35,616	31,153
95965	Thermalito (c)	(530)	6,045	5,646
*91359	Thousand Oaks	(805)	122,700	104,381
92276	Thousand Palms (c)	(760)	5,120	4,122
94920	Tiburon	(415)	8,746	7,554
*90503	Torrance	(310)	141,615	133,107
95376	Tracy	(209)	68,018	33,558
*96161	Truckee	(916)	14,630	8,848
*93274	Tulare	(559)	45,979	33,249
*95380	Turlock	(209)	61,647	42,224
*92781	Tustin	(714)/(949)	68,637	50,689
92705	Tustin Foothills (c)	(714)	24,044	24,358
*92277	Twentynine Palms	(760)	29,186	11,821
92278	Twentynine Palms Base (c)	(760)	8,413	10,606
95060	Twin Lakes (c)	(831)	5,533	5,379
95482	Ukiah	(707)	15,544	14,632
94587	Union City	(510)	69,879	53,762
*91785	Upland	(909)	70,983	63,374
*95687	Vacaville	(707)	93,573	71,476
91744	Valinda (c)	(626)	21,776	18,735
*94590	Vallejo	(707)	119,798	109,199
*92343	Valle Vista (c)	(909)	10,488	8,751
92082	Valley Center (c)	(760)	7,323	1,711
93437	Vandenberg AFB (c)	(805)	6,151	9,846
93436	Vandenberg Village (c)	(805)	5,802	5,971
	Ventura. See San Buenaventura			
*92393	Victorville	(760)	70,828	50,103
90043	View Park-Windsor Hills (c)	(310)	10,958	11,769
92861	Villa Park	(714)	6,060	6,299
—	Vincent (c)		15,097	13,713
—	Vineyard (c)		10,109	—
*93291	Visalia	(559)	96,889	75,659
*92083	Vista	(760)	91,565	71,861
—	Waldon (c)		5,133	—
*91788	Walnut	(909)	30,773	29,105
*94596	Walnut Creek	(925)	65,345	60,569
90255	Walnut Park (c)	(213)	16,180	14,722
93280	Wasco	(661)	22,496	12,412
95386	Waterford	(209)	7,530	4,771
*95076	Watsonville	(831)	46,644	31,099
90044	West Athens (c)	(310)	9,101	8,859
90502	West Carson (c)	(323)	21,138	20,143
90247	West Compton (c)	(310)	5,435	5,451
*91790	West Covina	(626)	107,694	96,226
90069	West Hollywood	(310)/(323)	36,670	36,118
*91359	Westlake Village	(805)	8,550	7,455
*92685	Westminster	(714)	89,515	78,293
—	West Modesto (c)		6,096	—
90047	Westmont (c)	(323)	31,623	31,044
91746	West Puente Valley (c)	(626)	22,409	20,254
*95691	West Sacramento	(916)	36,544	28,898
90606	West Whittier-Los Nietos (c)	(562)	25,129	24,164
*90605	Whittier	(562)	85,446	77,671
92595	Wildomar (c)	(909)	14,064	10,411
95490	Willits	(707)	5,096	5,027
90222	Willowbrook (c)	(323)	34,138	32,772
95988	Willows	(530)	6,220	5,988
95492	Windsor	(707)	24,180	12,002
—	Winter Gardens (c)		19,771	—
95694	Winters	(530)	6,550	4,639
95388	Winton (c)	(209)	8,832	7,559
92502	Woodcrest (c)	(909)	8,342	7,796
93286	Woodlake (c)	(559)	6,829	5,678
*95695	Woodland	(530)	50,850	40,230
94062	Woodside	(650)	5,299	5,034
*92885	Yorba Linda	(714)	61,065	52,422
96097	Yreka	(530)	7,176	6,948
*95991	Yuba City	(530)	47,213	27,385
92399	Yucaipa	(909)	43,830	32,819
*92286	Yucca Valley	(760)	17,760	16,539

Colorado

Area code (720) overlays area code (303). See introductory note.

ZIP	Place	Area Code	2002	1990
*80840	Air Force Academy (c)	(719)	7,526	9,062
81101	Alamosa	(719)	8,422	7,579
80401	Applewood (c)	(303)	7,123	11,069
*80004	Arvada	(303)	102,190	89,261
*81611	Aspen	(970)	5,902	5,049
*80017	Aurora	(303)	286,028	222,103
81620	Avon	(970)	5,783	1,798
—	Berkley (c)		10,743	—
80513	Berthoud	(970)	5,176	3,087
80908	Black Forest (c)	(719)	13,247	8,143
*80302	Boulder	(303)	94,167	85,127
80601	Brighton	(303)	23,512	14,203
*80020	Broomfield	(303)	40,823	24,638
80723	Brush	(970)	5,159	4,165
*81212	Canon City	(719)	15,691	12,687
81623	Carbondale	(970)	5,577	3,004
—	Castle Pines (c)	(303)	5,958	—
80104	Castle Rock	(303)	25,826	8,710
80120	Castlewood (c)	(303)	25,567	24,392
*80015	Centennial	(303)	99,447	—
80110	Cherry Hills Village	(303)	6,078	5,245
81220	Cimarron Hills (c)	(719)	15,194	11,160
81520	Clifton (c)	(970)	17,345	12,671
*80903	Colorado Springs	(719)	371,182	280,430
80120	Columbine (c)	(303)	24,095	23,969
*80022	Commerce City	(303)	23,927	16,466
81321	Cortez	(970)	8,137	7,284
81212	Craig	(970)	9,208	8,091
81416	Delta	(970)	7,702	3,789
*80022	Denver	(303)	560,415	467,610
80022	Derby (c)	(303)	6,423	6,043
*81301	Durango	(970)	14,630	12,439
80214	Edgewater	(303)	5,449	4,613
81632	Edwards (c)	(970)	8,257	—
*80110	Englewood	(303)	32,963	29,396
80516	Erie	(303)	8,425	1,258
*80517	Estes Park	(970)	5,640	3,184
80620	Evans	(970)	13,293	5,876
80439	Evergreen (c)	(303)	9,216	7,582
80221	Federal Heights	(303)	12,109	9,342
80913	Fort Carson (c)	(719)	10,566	11,309
*80525	Fort Collins	(970)	124,665	87,491
80621	Fort Lupton	(303)	7,150	5,159
80701	Fort Morgan	(970)	11,022	9,068
80817	Fountain	(719)	15,697	10,754
81521	Fruita	(970)	6,686	4,045
81504	Fruitvale (c)	(303)	6,936	5,222
*81601	Glenwood Springs	(970)	8,306	6,561
*80401	Golden	(303)	17,366	13,127
*81501	Grand Junction	(970)	43,170	32,893
*80631	Greeley	(970)	82,115	60,454
*80111	Greenwood Village	(303)	12,703	7,589
80501	Gunbarrel (c)	(303)	9,435	9,388

ZIP	Place	Area Code	2002	1990
*81230	Gunnison	(970)	5,348	4,636
80163	Highlands Ranch (c)	(303)	70,931	10,181
80127	Ken Caryl (c)	(303)	30,887	24,391
80026	Lafayette	(303)	23,809	14,708
81050	La Junta	(719)	7,397	7,678
*80226	Lakewood	(303)	143,754	126,475
81052	Lamar	(719)	8,677	8,343
*81126	Littleton	(303)	40,376	33,711
80124	Lone Tree	(303)	7,479	1,261
*80501	Longmont	(303)	78,694	51,976
80027	Louisville	(303)	18,715	12,363
80538	Loveland	(970)	55,273	37,357
80829	Manitou Springs	(719)	5,062	4,540
*81401	Montrose	(970)	13,784	8,854
80233	Northglenn	(303)	33,652	27,195
80649	Orchard Mesa (c)	(303)	6,456	5,977
*80134	Parker	(303)	32,347	5,450
*81003	Pueblo	(719)	103,411	98,640
81007	Pueblo West (c)	(719)	16,899	4,386
81503	Redlands (c)	(970)	8,043	9,355
81650	Rifle	(970)	7,387	4,858
81201	Salida	(719)	5,557	4,737
80911	Security-Widefield (c)	(719)	29,845	23,822
80110	Sheridan	(303)	5,573	4,976
80221	Sherrelwood (c)	(303)	17,657	16,636
80122	Southglenn (c)	(303)	43,520	43,087
*80477	Steamboat Springs	(970)	9,337	6,695
80751	Sterling	(970)	12,904	10,362
—	Stonegate (c)	...	6,284	—
80906	Stratmoor (c)	(719)	6,650	5,854
80027	Superior	(303)	10,116	255
—	The Pinery (c)	(303)	7,253	4,885
80229	Thornton	(303)	93,623	55,031
81082	Trinidad	(719)	9,163	8,580
81251	Twin Lakes (c)	(719)	6,301	—
80229	Welby (c)	(303)	12,973	10,218
80030	Westminster	(303)	103,599	74,619
*80033	Wheat Ridge	(303)	32,279	29,419
80550	Windsor	(970)	12,514	5,062
*80863	Woodland Park	(719)	6,734	4,610
80132	Woodmoor (c)	(719)	7,177	3,858

Connecticut

See introductory note.

ZIP	Place	Area Code	2002	1990
06401	Ansonia	(203)	18,739	18,403
06001	Avon	(860)	16,346	13,937
06403	Beacon Falls	(203)	5,475	5,083
06037	Berlin	(860)	19,116	16,787
06524	Bethany	(203)	5,202	—
06801	Bethel	(203)	18,449	17,541
06002	Bloomfield	(860)	19,794	19,483
06043	Bolton	(860)	5,154	—
06405	Branford	(203)	28,951	27,603
06405	Branford Center (c)	(203)	5,735	5,688
*06602	Bridgeport	(203)	140,104	141,686
*06010	Bristol	(860)	60,541	60,640
06804	Brookfield	(203)	15,923	14,113
06234	Brooklyn	(860)	7,361	6,681
06013	Burlington	(860)	8,640	7,026
06019	Canton	(860)	9,061	8,268
06040	Central Manchester (c)	(860)	30,595	30,934
06410	Cheshire	(203)	29,096	25,684
06410	Cheshire Village (c)	(203)	5,789	5,759
06413	Clinton	(860)	13,406	12,767
06415	Colchester	(860)	14,998	10,980
06237	Columbia	(860)	5,150	4,510
06340	Conning Towers-Nautilus Park (c)	(860)	10,241	10,013
06238	Coventry	(860)	11,974	10,063
06416	Cromwell	(860)	13,370	12,286
*06810	Danbury	(203)	76,917	65,585
06820	Darien	(203)	19,887	18,196
06418	Derby	(203)	12,520	12,199
06422	Durham	(860)	6,982	5,732
06423	East Haddam	(860)	8,638	6,676
06424	East Hampton	(860)	13,831	10,428
*06101	East Hartford	(860)	49,650	50,452
06512	East Haven	(203)	28,563	26,144
06333	East Lyme	(860)	17,983	15,340
06612	Easton	(203)	7,483	6,303
06088	East Windsor	(860)	10,095	10,081
06029	Ellington	(860)	13,571	11,197
*06082	Enfield	(860)	45,379	45,532
06426	Essex	(860)	6,730	5,904
*06430	Fairfield	(203)	57,715	53,418
*06032	Farmington	(860)	24,189	20,608
06033	Glastonbury	(860)	32,575	27,901
06033	Glastonbury Center (c)	(860)	7,157	7,082
06035	Granby	(860)	10,696	9,369
*06830	Greenwich	(203)	61,784	58,441
06351	Griswold	(860)	10,988	10,384
06340	Groton	(860)	10,078	9,837
06340	Groton	(860)	40,270	45,144
06437	Guilford	(203)	21,868	19,848
06438	Haddam	(860)	7,360	6,769
*06514	Hamden	(203)	57,927	52,434
*06101	Hartford	(860)	124,558	139,739

ZIP	Place	Area Code	2002	1990
06791	Harwinton	(860)	5,429	5,228
06248	Hebron	(860)	8,907	7,079
06037	Kensington (c)	(860)	8,541	8,306
06239	Killingly	(860)	16,740	15,889
06419	Killingworth	(860)	6,280	4,814
06249	Lebanon	(860)	7,076	6,041
06339	Ledyard	(860)	14,882	14,913
06759	Litchfield	(860)	8,446	8,365
06443	Madison	(203)	18,546	15,485
*06040	Manchester	(860)	55,084	51,618
06250	Mansfield	(860)	21,458	21,103
06447	Marlborough	(860)	5,979	5,535
*06450	Meriden	(203)	58,675	59,479
06762	Middlebury	(203)	6,648	6,145
06457	Middletown	(860)	44,156	42,762
06460	Milford	(203)	53,472	48,168
06468	Monroe	(203)	19,551	16,896
06353	Montville	(860)	19,606	16,673
06770	Naugatuck	(203)	31,429	30,625
*06050	New Britain	(860)	71,589	75,491
06840	New Canaan	(203)	19,734	17,864
06812	New Fairfield	(203)	14,149	12,911
06057	New Hartford	(860)	6,413	5,769
*06511	New Haven	(203)	124,176	130,474
*06101	Newington	(860)	29,623	29,208
06320	New London	(860)	26,068	28,540
06776	New Milford	(860)	27,959	23,629
06470	Newtown	(203)	25,866	20,779
06471	North Branford	(203)	14,095	12,996
06473	North Haven	(203)	23,460	22,247
06359	North Stonington	(860)	5,096	4,907
*06856	Norwalk	(203)	84,127	78,331
06360	Norwich	(860)	36,003	37,391
06779	Oakville (c)	(860)	8,618	8,741
06371	Old Lyme	(860)	7,442	6,535
06475	Old Saybrook	(860)	10,485	9,552
06477	Orange	(203)	13,383	12,830
06478	Oxford	(203)	10,430	8,685
06379	Pawcatuck (c)	(860)	5,474	5,289
06374	Plainfield	(860)	15,017	14,363
06062	Plainville	(860)	17,407	17,392
06782	Plymouth	(860)	11,976	11,822
06480	Portland	(860)	9,125	8,418
06712	Prospect	(203)	9,052	7,775
06260	Putnam	(860)	9,060	9,031
06260	Putnam District (c)	(860)	6,746	6,835
06896	Redding	(203)	8,504	7,927
06877	Ridgefield (c)	(203)	7,212	6,363
06877	Ridgefield	(203)	24,054	20,919
06066	Rockville (c)	(860)	7,708	—
06067	Rocky Hill	(860)	18,305	16,554
06483	Seymour	(203)	15,727	14,288
06484	Shelton	(203)	38,845	35,418
06082	Sherwood Manor (c)	(860)	5,689	6,357
06070	Simsbury	(860)	23,421	22,023
06070	Simsbury Center (c)	(860)	5,603	5,577
06071	Somers	(860)	10,608	9,108
06488	Southbury	(203)	18,953	15,818
06489	Southington	(860)	40,943	38,518
06074	South Windsor	(860)	24,846	22,090
06082	Southwood Acres (c)	(860)	8,067	8,963
06075	Stafford	(860)	11,592	11,091
*06904	Stamford	(203)	119,850	108,056
06378	Stonington	(860)	18,084	16,919
06268	Storrs (c)	(860)	10,996	12,198
*06602	Stratford	(203)	50,171	49,389
06078	Suffield	(860)	14,021	11,427
06786	Terryville (c)	(860)	5,360	5,426
06787	Thomaston	(860)	7,766	6,947
06277	Thompson	(860)	9,064	8,668
06082	Thompsonville (c)	(860)	8,125	8,458
06084	Tolland	(860)	14,005	11,001
06790	Torrington	(860)	35,655	33,687
06611	Trumbull	(203)	34,857	32,016
06066	Vernon	(860)	28,718	29,841
06492	Wallingford	(203)	43,826	40,822
06492	Wallingford Center (c)	(203)	17,509	17,827
*06702	Waterbury	(203)	107,883	108,961
06385	Waterford	(860)	19,439	17,930
06795	Watertown	(860)	22,100	20,456
06498	Westbrook	(860)	6,507	5,414
*06101	West Hartford	(860)	61,365	60,110
06516	West Haven	(203)	52,733	54,021
06883	Weston	(203)	10,229	8,648
*06880	Westport	(203)	26,171	24,410
*06101	Wethersfield	(860)	26,390	25,651
06226	Willimantic (c)	(860)	15,823	14,746
06279	Willington	(860)	6,116	5,979
06897	Wilton	(203)	17,860	15,989
06094	Winchester	(860)	10,755	11,524
06280	Windham	(860)	22,976	22,039
06095	Windsor	(860)	28,519	27,817
06096	Windsor Locks	(860)	12,237	12,358
06098	Winsted (c)	(860)	7,321	8,254
06716	Wolcott	(203)	15,682	13,700
06525	Woodbridge	(203)	9,146	7,924
06798	Woodbury	(860)	9,466	8,131
06281	Woodstock	(860)	7,518	6,008

IT'S A FACT: Area codes were introduced in 1947, back in the days of rotary phones. The easier-to-dial, lower numbers were assigned to places with large populations (such as 212 in New York City and 213 in Los Angeles). The higher-numbered (i.e., harder-to-dial) area codes were given to places with the fewest people (808 in Hawaii and 907 in Alaska).

Delaware (302)

ZIP	Place	2002	1990
19701	Bear (c)	17,593	—
19713	Brookside (c)	14,806	15,307
19703	Claymont (c)	9,220	9,800
*19901	Dover	32,581	27,630
19809	Edgemoor (c)	5,992	5,853
19805	Elsmere	5,798	5,935
19702	Glasgow (c)	12,840	—
19707	Hockessin (c)	12,902	—
19709	Middletown	6,333	3,834
19963	Milford	6,909	6,032
*19711	Newark	29,798	26,463
—	North Star (c)	8,277	—
19800	Pike Creek (c)	19,751	10,163
19973	Seaford	6,857	5,689
19977	Smyrna	5,913	5,231
*19899	Wilmington	72,503	71,529
19720	Wilmington Manor (c)	8,262	8,568

District of Columbia (202)

ZIP	Place	2002	1990
*20090	Washington	572,059	606,900

Florida

Area code (321) overlays area code (407). Area code (754) overlays (954). Area code (786) overlays (305). See introductory note.

ZIP	Place	Area Code	2002	1990
*32615	Alachua	(386)	6,489	4,667
*32714	Altamonte Springs	(407)	40,976	35,167
—	Andover (c)	(305)	8,489	6,251
33572	Apollo Beach (c)	(813)	7,444	6,025
*32712	Apopka	(407)	29,664	13,611
*34266	Arcadia	(863)	6,798	6,488
32233	Atlantic Beach	(904)	13,551	11,636
33823	Auburndale	(863)	11,683	8,846
*33160	Aventura	(305)	26,499	14,914
*33825	Avon Park	(863)	8,632	8,078
32857	Azalea Park (c)	(407)	11,073	8,926
*33830	Bartow	(863)	15,455	14,716
33154	Bay Harbor Islands	(305)	5,243	4,703
—	Bay Hill (c)	(407)	5,177	5,346
34667	Bayonet Point (c)	(727)	23,577	21,860
33505	Bayshore Gardens (c)	(941)	17,350	17,062
33589	Beacon Square (c)	(727)	7,263	6,265
34233	Bee Ridge (c)	(941)	8,744	6,406
32073	Bellair-Meadowbrook Terrace (c)	(904)	16,539	15,606
33430	Belle Glade	(561)	15,205	16,177
*32802	Belle Isle	(407)	6,198	5,272
*34420	Belleview (c)	(352)	21,201	19,386
*34461	Beverly Hills (c)	(352)	8,317	6,163
33043	Big Pine Key (c)	(305)	5,032	4,206
*33509	Bloomingdale (c)	(813)	19,839	13,912
33433	Boca Del Mar (c)	(561)	21,832	17,754
*33431	Boca Raton	(561)	77,411	61,486
*34135	Bonita Springs	(239)	32,585	13,600
33547	Boyette (c)	(813)	5,895	—
*33436	Boynton Beach	(561)	63,683	46,284
*34206	Bradenton	(941)	51,364	43,769
*33509	Brandon (c)	(813)	77,895	57,985
32503	Brent (c)	(850)	22,257	21,624
33317	Broadview Park (c)	(954)	6,798	6,109
33313	Broadview-Pompano Park (c)	(954)	5,314	5,230
*34601	Brooksville	(352)	7,353	7,589
33142	Brownsville (c)	(305)	14,393	15,607
32404	Callaway	(850)	14,473	12,253
32920	Cape Canaveral	(321)	9,156	8,014
*33909	Cape Coral	(239)	112,899	74,991
33055	Carol City (c)	(305)	59,443	53,331
*32707	Casselberry	(407)	23,682	20,736
—	Cedar Grove	(850)	5,438	1,479
33401	Century Village (c)	(305)	7,616	8,363
—	Cheval (c)	(813)	7,602	—
33624	Citrus Park (c)	(813)	20,226	—
*32966	Citrus Ridge (c)	(772)	12,015	—
*33758	Clearwater	(727)	108,313	98,669
*34711	Clermont	(352)	10,139	6,910
33440	Clewiston	(863)	6,680	6,085
*32922	Cocoa	(321)	16,403	17,710
*32931	Cocoa Beach	(321)	12,509	12,123
32922	Cocoa West (c)	(321)	5,921	6,160
*33097	Coconut Creek	(954)	47,713	27,269
33064	Collier Manor-Cresthaven (c)	(954)	7,741	7,322
33801	Combee Settlement (c)	(863)	5,436	5,463
32809	Conway (c)	(407)	14,394	13,159
33328	Cooper City	(954)	28,872	21,335
*33114	Coral Gables	(305)	42,631	40,091
*33075	Coral Springs	(954)	125,674	78,864
33157	Coral Terrace (c)	(305)	24,380	23,255
33015	Country Club (c)	(305)	36,310	3,408
—	Country Walk (c)	(305)	10,653	—
*32536	Crestview	(850)	15,353	9,886
33803	Crystal Lake (c)	(863)	5,341	5,300
33157	Cutler (c)	(305)	17,390	16,201
33157	Cutler Ridge (c)	(305)	24,781	21,268
33884	Cypress Gardens (c)	(863)	8,844	9,188
33919	Cypress Lake (c)	(239)	12,072	10,491
*33525	Dade City	(352)	6,363	5,633
33004	Dania Beach	(954)	28,066	—
33329	Davie	(954)	79,853	47,143
*32114	Daytona Beach	(386)	64,605	61,991
32713	De Bary	(386)	15,908	9,327
*33441	Deerfield Beach	(954)	65,635	46,997
*32433	DeFuniak Springs	(850)	5,151	5,200
32720	De Land	(386)	21,437	16,622
*33444	Delray Beach	(561)	62,272	47,184
32738	Deltona	(407)	73,788	49,429
32541	Destin	(850)	11,651	8,090
32819	Doctor Phillips (c)	(407)	9,548	7,963
33178	Doral (c)	(305)	20,438	3,126
*34698	Dunedin	(727)	36,664	34,427
33610	East Lake (c)	(813)	29,394	—
33610	East Lake-Orient Park (c)	(813)	5,703	6,171
—	East Perrine (c)	(305)	7,079	—
*32132	Edgewater	(386)	19,737	15,351
32542	Eglin AFB (c)	(850)	8,082	8,347
—	Egypt Lake-Leto (c)	(813)	32,782	—
34680	Elfers (c)	(727)	13,161	12,356
*34295	Englewood (c)	(941)	16,196	15,025
32534	Ensley (c)	(850)	18,752	16,362
33928	Estero (c)	(239)	9,503	3,177
32726	Eustis	(352)	15,891	12,856
32804	Fairview Shores (c)	(305)	13,898	13,192
32034	Fernandina Beach	(904)	11,021	8,765
32730	Fern Park (c)	(407)	8,318	8,294
32514	Ferry Pass (c)	(850)	27,176	26,301
32136	Flagler Beach	(386)	5,257	3,851
33034	Florida City	(305)	7,888	5,978
32960	Florida Ridge (c)	(772)	15,217	12,218
32714	Forest City (c)	(407)	12,612	10,638
*33310	Fort Lauderdale	(954)	158,194	149,238
33841	Fort Meade	(863)	5,693	5,151
*33902	Fort Myers	(239)	49,960	44,947
*33931	Fort Myers Beach	(239)	6,756	9,284
33922	Fort Myers Shores (c)	(239)	5,793	5,460
34981	Fort Pierce	(772)	37,989	36,830
33452	Fort Pierce North (c)	(772)	7,386	5,833
34982	Fort Pierce South (c)	(772)	5,672	5,320
*32548	Fort Walton Beach	(850)	20,098	21,407
—	Fountainbleau (c)	(305)	59,549	—
*32043	Fruit Cove (c)	(904)	16,077	5,904
34230	Fruitville (c)	(941)	12,741	9,808
33823	Fussels Corner (c)	(863)	5,313	3,840
*32602	Gainesville	(352)	95,117	91,482
33534	Gibsonton (c)	(813)	8,752	7,706
32960	Gifford (c)	(772)	7,599	6,278
33138	Gladeview (c)	(954)	14,468	15,637
33143	Glenvar Heights (c)	(305)	16,243	14,823
34116	Golden Gate (c)	(239)	20,951	14,148
33055	Golden Glades (c)	(305)	32,623	25,474
33411	Golden Lakes (c)	(561)	6,694	3,867
32733	Goldenrod (c)	(407)	12,871	12,362
32560	Gonzalez (c)	(850)	11,365	7,669
33170	Goulds (c)	(305)	7,453	7,284
—	Greater Carrollwood (c)	(813)	33,519	—
33624	Greater Northdale (c)	(813)	20,461	16,318
—	Greater Sun Center (c)	(813)	16,321	—
33454	Greenacres	(561)	30,439	18,683
32043	Green Cove Springs	(904)	5,547	4,497
*32561	Gulf Breeze	(850)	5,967	5,530
33581	Gulf Gate Estates (c)	(941)	11,647	11,622
33737	Gulfport	(727)	12,568	11,709
*33844	Haines City	(863)	13,708	11,683
*33009	Hallandale Beach	(305)/(954)	35,295	30,997
33434	Hamptons at Boca Raton (c)	(561)	11,306	11,686
34442	Hernando (c)	(352)	8,253	2,103
*33010	Hialeah	(305)	228,149	188,008
33016	Hialeah Gardens	(305)	19,877	7,727
*33455	Hobe Sound (c)	(772)	11,376	11,507
*34689	Holiday (c)	(727)	21,904	19,360
32125	Holly Hill	(386)	12,562	11,141
*33022	Hollywood	(954)	143,213	121,720
34218	Holmes Beach	(941)	5,008	4,826
*33030	Homestead	(305)	33,727	26,694
34447	Homosassa Springs (c)	(352)	12,458	6,271
*34668	Hudson (c)	(727)	12,765	7,344
—	Hunters Creek (c)	(407)	9,369	—
*34142	Immokalee (c)	(239)	19,763	14,120
32937	Indian Harbour Beach	(321)	8,444	6,933
32963	Indian River Estates (c)	(772)	5,793	4,858
33785	Indian Rocks Beach	(727)	5,169	3,963

ZIP	Place	Area Code	2002	1990
34956	Indiantown (c)	(772)	5,588	4,794
*34450	Inverness	(352)	7,101	5,797
—	Inverness Highlands South (c)	(352)	5,781	—
33880	Inwood (c)	(863)	6,925	6,824
33908	Iona (c)	(239)	11,756	9,565
33036	Islamorada, Village of Islands	(305)	6,819	1,220
33162	Ives Estates (c)	(305)	17,586	13,531
*32203	Jacksonville	(904)	762,461	635,230
*32250	Jacksonville Beach	(904)	21,247	17,839
33880	Jan Phyl Village (c)	(863)	5,633	5,308
33568	Jasmine Estates (c)	(727)	18,213	17,136
*34957	Jensen Beach (c)	(772)	11,100	9,884
*33458	Jupiter	(561)	43,385	26,753
33183	Kendale Lakes (c)	(305)	56,901	48,524
33256	Kendall (c)	(305)	75,226	87,271
—	Kendall West (c)	(305)	38,034	—
33149	Key Biscayne (c)	(305)	10,471	8,854
33037	Key Largo (c)	(305)	11,886	11,336
—	Keystone (c)	(813)	14,627	—
*33040	Key West	(305)	25,273	24,832
*33573	Kings Point (c)	(305)	12,207	12,422
*34744	Kissimmee	(407)	48,932	30,337
*32159	Lady Lake	(352)	12,536	8,071
—	Lake Butler (c)		7,062	—
*32055	Lake City	(386)	10,178	9,626
*33804	Lakeland	(863)	86,175	70,576
33801	Lakeland Highlands (c)	(863)	12,557	9,972
32569	Lake Lorraine (c)	(850)	7,106	6,779
33054	Lake Lucerne (c)	(305)	9,132	9,478
33612	Lake Magdalene (c)	(813)	28,755	15,973
*32746	Lake Mary	(407)	12,646	5,929
33403	Lake Park	(561)	8,883	6,704
—	Lakes by the Bay (c)	(305)	9,055	5,615
32073	Lakeside (c)	(904)	30,927	29,137
*33853	Lake Wales	(863)	10,386	9,670
34951	Lakewood Park (c)	(772)	10,458	7,211
*33461	Lake Worth	(561)	35,575	28,564
—	Lake Worth Corridor (c)		18,663	—
34639	Land O'Lakes (c)	(813)	20,971	7,892
33465	Lantana	(561)	9,591	8,392
*33770	Largo	(727)	70,650	65,910
33062	Lauderdale-by-the-Sea	(954)	5,247	4,014
33313	Lauderdale Lakes	(954)	31,665	27,341
33313	Lauderhill	(954)	58,821	49,015
34272	Laurel (c)	(941)	8,393	8,245
*34461	Lecanto (c)	(352)	5,161	1,243
*34748	Leesburg	(352)	16,477	14,783
*33936	Lehigh Acres (c)	(239)	33,430	13,611
33033	Leisure City (c)	(305)	22,152	19,379
33074	Lighthouse Point	(954)	11,084	10,378
*32060	Live Oak	(386)	6,618	6,332
32860	Lockhart (c)	(407)	12,944	11,636
34228	Longboat Key	(941)	7,557	5,937
*32750	Longwood	(407)	13,695	13,316
*33549	Lutz (c)	(813)	17,081	10,552
32444	Lynn Haven	(850)	13,265	9,270
33919	McGregor (c)	(239)	7,136	6,504
*32751	Maitland	(407)	12,002	8,932
33550	Mango (c)	(813)	8,842	8,700
33050	Marathon	(305)	10,199	8,857
*34145	Marco Island	(239)	15,191	—
33093	Margate	(954)	54,786	42,985
*32446	Marianna	(850)	6,170	6,292
32824	Meadow Woods (c)	(407)	11,286	4,876
33811	Medulla (c)	(863)	6,637	3,977
*32901	Melbourne	(321)	73,804	60,034
32666	Melrose Park (c)	(954)	7,114	6,477
33561	Memphis (c)	(941)	7,264	6,760
*32953	Merritt Island (c)	(321)	36,090	32,886
*33101	Miami	(305)	374,791	358,648
*33152	Miami Beach	(305)	89,575	92,639
33014	Miami Lakes	(305)	22,868	12,750
33153	Miami Shores	(305)	10,364	10,084
33266	Miami Springs	(305)	13,743	13,268
32976	Micco (c)	(772)	9,498	8,757
*32068	Middleburg (c)	(904)	10,338	6,223
32570	Milton	(850)	7,470	7,216
32754	Mims (c)	(321)	9,147	9,412
34755	Minneola	(352)	5,887	1,515
33023	Miramar	(954)	90,359	40,663
32757	Mount Dora	(352)	9,955	7,294
32526	Myrtle Grove (c)	(850)	17,211	17,402
*34102	Naples	(239)	21,162	19,505
34113	Naples Manor (c)	(239)	5,186	4,574
34102	Naples Park (c)	(239)	6,741	8,002
32266	Neptune Beach	(904)	7,230	6,816
34653	New Port Richey	(727)	16,465	14,044
33552	New Port Richey East (c)	(727)	9,916	9,683
32168	New Smyrna Beach	(386)	20,475	16,549
*32578	Niceville	(850)	12,071	10,509
33269	Norland (c)	(305)	22,995	22,109
33308	North Andrews Gardens (c)	(954)	9,656	9,002
33141	North Bay Village	(305)	6,741	5,383
33918	North Fort Myers (c)	(239)	40,214	30,027
33068	North Lauderdale	(954)	33,228	26,473
33261	North Miami	(305)	60,034	50,001
33160	North Miami Beach	(305)	40,848	35,361
33408	North Palm Beach	(561)	12,525	11,538
*34287	North Port	(941)	27,572	11,973
34234	North Sarasota (c)	(941)	6,738	6,702
33307	Oakland Park	(305)	31,487	26,326
33860	Oak Ridge (c)	(407)	22,349	15,388
34478	Ocala	(352)	46,931	42,045
32848	Ocean City (c)	(850)	5,594	5,422
34761	Ocoee	(407)	26,179	12,778
33163	Ojus (c)	(305)	16,642	15,519
*34972	Okeechobee	(863)	5,497	4,943
34677	Oldsmar	(813)	12,725	8,361
33265	Olympia Heights (c)	(305)	13,452	37,792
*33054	Opa-Locka	(305)	14,964	15,283
33054	Opa-Locka North (c)	(305)	6,224	6,568
*32763	Orange City	(386)	6,667	5,372
*32073	Orange Park	(904)	9,182	9,488
*32802	Orlando	(407)	193,722	164,674
32861	Orlo Vista (c)	(407)	6,047	5,990
*32174	Ormond Beach	(386)	37,202	29,721
32074	Ormond By-The-Sea (c)	(386)	8,430	8,157
*32765	Oviedo	(407)	27,597	11,114
32571	Pace (c)	(850)	7,393	6,277
33476	Pahokee	(561)	6,175	6,822
32177	Palatka	(386)	10,307	10,447
*32905	Palm Bay	(321)	83,038	62,543
33480	Palm Beach	(561)	9,766	9,814
33408	Palm Beach Gardens	(561)	38,127	24,139
*34990	Palm City (c)	(772)	20,097	3,925
32135	Palm Coast	(386)	35,027	14,287
*34221	Palmetto	(941)	12,815	9,268
33157	Palmetto Estates (c)	(305)	13,675	12,293
*34683	Palm Harbor (c)	(727)	59,248	50,256
*33601	Palm River-Clair Mel (c)	(813)	17,589	13,691
33460	Palm Springs	(561)	13,163	9,763
33012	Palm Springs North (c)	(305)	5,460	5,300
32082	Palm Valley (c)	(904)	19,860	9,960
*32401	Panama City	(850)	36,721	34,396
32417	Panama City Beach	(850)	7,874	4,051
33060	Parkland	(954)	17,577	3,773
34108	Pelican Bay (c)		5,686	—
33021	Pembroke Park (c)	(954)	5,666	4,933
33029	Pembroke Pines	(954)	146,637	65,566
*32502	Pensacola	(850)	55,240	59,198
32347	Perry	(850)	6,742	7,151
32859	Pine Castle (c)	(407)	8,803	8,276
33156	Pinecrest	(305)	19,428	—
32858	Pine Hills (c)	(407)	41,764	35,322
33324	Pine Island Ridge (c)	(954)	5,199	5,244
*33781	Pinellas Park	(727)	46,382	43,571
—	Pine Ridge (c)	(352)	5,490	—
33168	Pinewood (c)	(305)	16,523	15,518
33318	Plantation	(954)	84,818	66,814
*33566	Plant City	(813)	30,975	22,754
*34758	Poinciana (c)	(407)	13,647	—
*33060	Pompano Beach	(954)	87,153	72,411
33064	Pompano Beach Highlands (c)	(954)	6,504	17,915
*33952	Port Charlotte (c)	(941)	46,451	41,535
32129	Port Orange	(904)	49,322	35,399
32927	Port St. John (c)	(321)	12,112	8,933
*34981	Port St. Lucie	(772)	98,538	55,761
34983	Port St. Lucie-River Park (c)	(772)	5,175	4,874
34992	Port Salerno (c)	(772)	10,141	7,786
*33032	Princeton (c)	(305)	10,090	7,073
*33950	Punta Gorda	(941)	16,010	10,637
*32351	Quincy	(850)	6,910	7,452
33156	Richmond Heights (c)	(305)	8,479	8,583
—	Richmond West (c)	(305)	28,082	—
34231	Ridge Wood Heights (c)	(941)	5,028	4,851
*33569	Riverview (c)	(813)	12,035	6,478
33419	Riviera Beach	(561)	30,456	27,646
*32955	Rockledge	(321)	21,673	16,023
33947	Rotonda (c)	(941)	6,574	3,576
33411	Royal Palm Beach	(561)	25,490	15,532
33570	Ruskin (c)	(813)	8,321	6,046
34695	Safety Harbor	(727)	17,372	15,120
*32084	Saint Augustine	(904)	11,795	11,695
32084	Saint Augustine Beach	(904)	5,050	3,830
32086	Saint Augustine South (c)	(904)	5,035	4,218
*34769	Saint Cloud	(407)	20,602	12,684
*33736	Saint Pete Beach	(727)	9,988	9,200
*33733	Saint Petersburg	(727)	248,546	240,318
33912	San Carlos Park (c)	(239)	16,317	11,785
33432	Sandalfoot Cove (c)	(305)	16,582	14,214
*32771	Sanford	(407)	43,445	32,387
33957	Sanibel	(239)	6,135	5,468
*34230	Sarasota	(941)	53,321	50,897
33577	Sarasota Springs (c)	(941)	15,875	16,088
32937	Satellite Beach	(321)	10,238	9,889
33055	Scott Lake (c)	(305)	14,401	14,588
*32958	Sebastian	(772)	17,153	10,248
*33870	Sebring	(863)	9,791	8,841
*33584	Seffner (c)	(813)	5,467	5,371
*33770	Seminole	(813)	16,664	9,251
34610	Shady Hills (c)	(727)	7,798	—
*34242	Siesta Key (c)	(941)	7,150	7,772

ZIP	Place	Area Code	2002	1990
34472	Silver Springs Shores (c)	(352)	6,690	6,421
32809	Sky Lake (c)	(407)	5,651	6,202
32703	South Apopka (c)	(407)	5,800	6,360
33505	South Bradenton (c)	(941)	21,587	20,398
32121	South Daytona	(386)	13,251	12,488
34266	Southeast Arcadia (c)	(863)	6,064	4,145
34277	Southgate (c)	(941)	7,455	7,324
34233	South Gate Ridge (c)	(941)	5,655	5,924
—	South Highpoint (c)	(727)	8,839	—
33243	South Miami	(305)	10,788	10,404
33157	South Miami Heights (c)	(305)	33,522	30,030
33707	South Pasadena	(727)	5,772	5,644
32937	South Patrick Shores (c)	(321)	8,913	10,249
34230	South Sarasota (c)	(941)	5,314	5,298
33595	South Venice (c)	(941)	13,539	11,951
*33331	Southwest Ranches	(954)	7,291	—
32401	Springfield	(850)	8,936	8,719
*34601	Spring Hill (c)	(352)	69,078	31,117
32091	Starke	(904)	5,631	5,226
*34994	Stuart	(772)	14,759	11,936
34446	Sugarmill Woods (c)	(352)	6,409	4,073
33160	Sunny Isles Beach	(305)	15,467	—
33345	Sunrise	(954)	88,478	65,683
33283	Sunset (c)	(305)	17,150	15,810
33144	Sweetwater	(305)	14,302	13,909
*32301	Tallahassee	(850)	155,171	124,773
33320	Tamarac	(954)	57,469	44,822
33144	Tamiami (c)	(305)	54,788	33,845
*33601	Tampa	(813)	315,140	280,015
34689	Tarpon Springs	(727)	21,936	17,874
32778	Tavares	(352)	10,391	7,488
33687	Temple Terrace	(813)	21,935	16,444
33469	Tequesta	(561)	5,405	4,499
33186	The Crossings (c)	(305)	23,557	—
—	The Hammocks (c)	(305)	47,379	—
32159	The Villages (c)	(352)	8,333	—
33592	Thonotosassa (c)	(813)	6,091	—
—	Three Lakes (c)	(305)	6,955	—
33025	Timber Pines (c)	(352)	5,840	3,182
*32780	Titusville	(321)	41,126	39,394
32685	Town 'n' Country (c)	(813)	72,523	60,946
33706	Treasure Island	(727)	7,493	7,266
32867	Union Park (c)	(407)	10,191	6,890
33024	University (c)	(813)	30,736	—
—	University Park (c)	(305)	26,538	—
32401	Upper Grand Lagoon (c)	(850)	10,889	7,855
32580	Valparaiso	(850)	6,400	6,316
*33594	Valrico (c)	(813)	6,582	—
34231	Varno (c)	(941)	5,285	3,325
*34285	Venice	(941)	18,601	17,052
33595	Venice Gardens (c)	(941)	7,466	7,701
*32960	Vero Beach	(772)	17,343	17,350
32960	Vero Beach South (c)	(772)	20,362	16,973
33901	Villas (c)	(239)	11,346	9,898
32507	Warrington (c)	(850)	15,207	16,040
32791	Wekiva Springs (c)	(407)	23,169	23,026
33414	Wellington	(561)	43,552	20,670
33543	Wesley Chapel (c)	(813)	5,691	—
—	West and East Lealman (c)	(727)	21,753	—
33626	Westchase (c)	(813)	11,116	—
33155	Westchester (c)	(305)	30,271	29,883
33409	Westgate-Belvedere Homes (c)	(561)	8,134	6,880
33138	West Little River (c)	(305)	32,498	33,575
32912	West Melbourne	(321)	11,501	8,398
33144	West Miami	(305)	6,018	5,727
33326	Weston	(954)	61,557	—
*33416	West Palm Beach	(561)	86,517	67,764
32505	West Pensacola (c)	(850)	21,939	22,107
33157	West Perrine (c)	(305)	8,600	—
34208	West Samoset (c)	(941)	5,507	3,819
—	West Vero Corridor (c)	(772)	7,695	—
33168	Westview (c)	(305)	9,692	9,668
33165	Westwood Lakes (c)	(305)	12,005	11,522
33496	Whisper Walk (c)	(561)	5,135	3,037
32821	Williamsburg (c)	(407)	6,736	3,093
33305	Wilton Manors	(954)	12,880	11,804
33803	Winston (c)	(813)	9,024	9,118
*34787	Winter Garden	(407)	18,257	9,863
*33880	Winter Haven	(863)	26,422	24,725
*32789	Winter Park	(407)	25,260	24,260
*32707	Winter Springs	(407)	31,280	22,151
32547	Wright (c)	(850)	21,697	18,945
34972	Yeehaw Junction (c)	(407)	21,778	—
*32097	Yulee (c)	(904)	8,392	6,915
*33540	Zephyrhills	(813)	11,265	8,220
33541	Zephyrhills West (c)	(813)	5,242	4,249

Georgia

Area code (678) overlays (770). See introductory note.

ZIP	Place	Area Code	2002	1990
*30101	Acworth	(770)	16,605	4,519
31620	Adel	(229)	5,346	5,093
*31706	Albany	(229)	76,325	78,804
30004	Alpharetta	(770)	35,739	13,002
31709	Americus	(229)	16,918	16,516
*30603	Athens-Clarke County[1]	(706)	102,663	86,522
*30301	Atlanta	(404)	424,868	393,929
30011	Auburn	(770)	6,905	3,139
*30903	Augusta-Richmond County[2]	(706)	193,101	186,616
30168	Austell	(770)	6,281	4,173
*31717	Bainbridge	(229)	11,898	10,803
30204	Barnesville	(770)	6,153	4,747
30032	Belvedere Park (c)	(404)	18,945	18,089
31723	Blakely	(229)	5,580	5,595
*31520	Brunswick	(912)	15,598	16,433
30518	Buford	(404)	10,823	8,771
31728	Cairo	(229)	9,231	9,035
*30701	Calhoun	(706)	11,715	7,135
31730	Camilla	(229)	5,672	5,124
30032	Candler-McAfee (c)	(404)	28,294	29,491
30114	Canton	(770)	11,338	4,817
30117	Carrollton	(770)	20,154	16,029
30120	Cartersville	(770)	17,169	12,037
30125	Cedartown	(770)	9,483	7,976
31028	Centerville	(770)	5,059	3,509
30366	Chamblee	(404)	9,494	7,668
30021	Clarkston	(404)	7,214	5,385
30337	College Park	(404)	19,529	20,645
*31908	Columbus	(706)	185,948	178,683
30529	Commerce	(770)	5,347	4,108
30288	Conley (c)	(404)	6,188	5,528
*30013	Conyers	(404)	11,790	7,380
*31015	Cordele	(229)	11,551	10,833
—	Country Club Estates (c)		7,594	7,500
*30014	Covington	(770)	12,511	9,860
*30132	Dallas	(770)	6,414	2,810
*30720	Dalton	(706)	29,895	22,218
31742	Dawson	(229)	5,060	5,295
*30030	Decatur (DeKalb)	(404)	18,172	17,304
31520	Dock Junction (c)	(912)	6,951	7,094
30362	Doraville	(404)	10,058	7,626
31533	Douglas	(912)	10,660	10,464
*30134	Douglasville	(404)	21,759	11,635
30333	Druid Hills (c)	(404)	12,741	12,174
*31021	Dublin	(478)	16,067	16,312
*30096	Duluth	(404)	22,788	9,821
30356	Dunwoody (c)	(404)	32,808	26,302
31023	Eastman	(478)	5,345	5,153
30364	East Point	(404)	37,867	34,595
31024	Eatonton	(706)	6,910	6,479
30809	Evans (c)	(706)	17,727	13,713
30213	Fairburn	(770)	5,971	4,013
*30060	Fair Oaks (c)	(404)	8,443	6,996
30535	Fairview (c)	(706)	6,601	6,444
*30214	Fayetteville	(404)	12,930	5,827
31750	Fitzgerald	(229)	8,637	8,901
*30297	Forest Park	(404)	21,315	16,958
31905	Fort Benning South (c)	(706)	11,737	14,617
30742	Fort Oglethorpe	(706)	7,582	5,880
*31313	Fort Stewart (c)	(912)	11,205	13,774
31030	Fort Valley	(478)	7,965	8,198
*30501	Gainesville	(770)	27,968	17,885
31418	Garden City	(912)	11,084	7,410
31754	Georgetown (c)	(912)	10,599	5,554
30316	Gresham Park (c)	(404)	9,215	9,000
*30223	Griffin	(770)	23,226	21,325
30813	Grovetown	(706)	6,510	3,596
30354	Hapeville	(404)	5,913	5,483
*31313	Hinesville	(912)	30,541	21,596
—	Irondale (c)		7,727	3,352
*31546	Jesup	(912)	9,309	8,958
*30144	Kennesaw	(404)	24,822	8,936
31548	Kingsland	(912)	10,990	6,089
30728	La Fayette	(706)	6,676	6,655
*30240	LaGrange	(706)	26,424	25,574
*30045	Lawrenceville	(404)	25,576	17,250
*30047	Lilburn	(404)	11,406	9,295
30052	Loganville	(770)	7,294	3,180
30126	Mableton (c)	(404)	29,733	25,725
30253	McDonough	(770)	9,997	2,929
*31201	Macon	(478)	95,862	107,365
*30060	Marietta	(404)	62,020	44,129
30917	Martinez (c)	(706)	27,749	33,731
—	Midway-Hardwick (c)		5,135	4,910
*31061	Milledgeville	(478)	18,762	17,727
*30655	Monroe	(770)	11,764	9,759
*31768	Moultrie	(229)	14,377	14,865
30087	Mountain Park (c)	(404)	11,753	11,025
*30263	Newnan	(770)	19,365	12,497
*30071	Norcross	(404)	9,173	5,947
30319	North Atlanta (c)	(404)	38,579	27,812
30033	North Decatur (c)	(404)	15,270	13,936
30033	North Druid Hills (c)	(404)	18,852	14,170
30032	Panthersville (c)	(404)	11,791	9,874
30269	Peachtree City	(404)	32,406	19,027
31069	Perry	(478)	10,149	9,452
31322	Pooler	(912)	7,481	4,649
30127	Powder Springs	(404)	13,399	6,862
30074	Redan (c)	(404)	33,841	24,376
31324	Richmond Hill	(912)	7,685	2,934
31326	Rincon	(912)	5,185	2,992
*30274	Riverdale	(404)	14,508	9,495
*30161	Rome	(706)	35,237	30,425

ZIP	Place	Area Code	2002	1990
*30077	Roswell.................	(404)	79,031	47,986
31558	Saint Marys...............	(912)	15,103	8,204
31522	Saint Simons (c)...........	(912)	13,381	12,026
31082	Sandersville..............	(478)	5,983	6,290
30358	Sandy Springs (c)..........	(404)	85,781	67,842
*31402	Savannah.................	(912)	127,691	137,812
30079	Scottdale (c)...............	(404)	9,803	8,636
—	Skidaway Island (c)........	(912)	6,914	4,495
*30080	Smyrna..................	(404)	45,678	32,453
*30078	Snellville................	(404)	17,543	12,084
*30458	Statesboro...............	(912)	23,324	20,770
30281	Stockbridge..............	(404)	10,777	3,359
*30086	Stone Mountain...........	(404)	7,171	6,544
30518	Sugar Hill...............	(404)	13,254	4,519
30024	Suwanee................	(770)	10,441	2,412
30401	Swainsboro..............	(478)	7,155	7,361
31791	Sylvester................	(229)	5,876	6,023
30286	Thomaston...............	(706)	9,288	9,127
*31792	Thomasville..............	(229)	17,964	17,554
30824	Thomson................	(706)	6,790	6,862
*31794	Tifton..................	(229)	15,873	14,215
*30577	Toccoa.................	(706)	9,488	8,720
*30084	Tucker (c)...............	(404)	26,532	25,781
30291	Union City...............	(404)	12,458	9,347
*31603	Valdosta................	(229)	44,707	40,038
*30474	Vidalia.................	(912)	10,524	11,118
30180	Villa Rica...............	(770)	6,985	3,916
30339	Vinings (c)...............	(404)	9,677	7,417
*31088	Warner Robins............	(478)	52,565	43,861
*31501	Waycross................	(912)	15,166	16,410
30830	Waynesboro..............	(706)	5,844	5,669
—	Whitemarsh Island (c).......		5,824	2,824
*31410	Wilmington Island (c).......	(912)	14,213	11,230
30680	Winder.................	(770)	11,158	7,373
*30188	Woodstock...............	(770)	13,192	4,361

(1) Athens merged with Clarke County in 1991. The 2002 and 1990 populations are for all of Clarke County except for Winterville and Bogart, which are part of the county but are also separate incorporated places. (2) Augusta merged with Richmond County in 1996. The 2002 and 1990 populations are for all of Richmond County except for Blythe and Hephzibah, which are part of the county but are also separate incorporated places.

Hawaii (808)

ZIP	Place	2002	1990
—	Ahuimanu (c)...............	8,506	8,387
96701	Aiea (c)...................	9,019	8,906
96706	Ewa Beach (c).............	14,650	14,315
—	Haiku-Pauwela (c)..........	6,578	4,509
—	Halawa (c)................	13,891	13,408
96778	Hawaiian Paradise Park (c)....	7,051	3,389
96853	Hickam Housing (c).........	5,471	6,553
*96720	Hilo (c)..................	40,759	37,808
96725	Holualoa (c)..............	6,107	3,834
*96820	Honolulu (c)..............	378,155	377,059
*96732	Kahului (c)...............	20,146	16,889
96734	Kailua (Hawaii) (c)..........	9,870	9,126
96863	Kailua (Honolulu) (c)........	36,513	36,818
96740	Kalaoa (c)................	6,794	4,490
96744	Kaneohe (c)..............	34,970	35,448
—	Kaneohe Station (c)........	11,827	11,662
96746	Kapaa (c)................	9,472	8,149
96753	Kihei (c).................	16,749	11,107
*96761	Lahaina (c)...............	9,118	9,073
96766	Lihue (c).................	5,674	5,536
96792	Maili (c).................	5,943	6,059
96792	Makaha (c)...............	7,753	7,990
96706	Makakilo (c)..............	13,156	9,828
96768	Makawao (c)..............	6,327	5,405
96789	Mililani Town (c)...........	28,608	29,359
96792	Nanakuli (c)..............	10,814	9,575
96761	Napili-Honokowai (c)........	6,788	4,332
96782	Pearl City (c).............	30,976	30,993
96788	Pukalani (c)..............	7,380	5,879
96786	Schofield Barracks (c).......	14,428	19,597
—	Village Park (c)............	9,625	7,407
96786	Wahiawa (c)..............	16,151	17,386
96792	Waianae (c)..............	10,506	8,758
—	Waihee-Waiehu (c)..........	7,310	4,004
96753	Wailea-Makena (c)..........	5,671	3,799
96793	Wailuku (c)..............	12,296	10,688
—	Waimalu (c)..............	29,371	29,967
96796	Waimea (c)...............	7,028	5,972
96797	Waipahu (c)..............	33,108	31,435
96797	Waipio (c)...............	11,672	11,812
96786	Waipio Acres (c)...........	5,298	5,304

Idaho (208)

ZIP	Place	2002	1990
83401	Ammon..................	7,756	5,002
83221	Blackfoot................	10,552	9,646
*83707	Boise..................	189,847	126,685
83318	Burley..................	9,375	8,702
*83605	Caldwell.................	29,466	18,586
83202	Chubbuck................	10,002	7,794
*83814	Coeur d'Alene.............	36,259	24,561

ZIP	Place	2002	1990
83616	Eagle...................	13,659	3,327
83617	Emmett.................	5,752	4,601
83714	Garden City..............	10,985	6,369
83333	Hailey..................	7,084	3,575
83835	Hayden.................	9,885	4,888
*83402	Idaho Falls...............	51,096	43,973
83338	Jerome.................	7,866	6,529
*83654	Kuna...................	7,773	1,955
83501	Lewiston................	30,487	28,082
*83642	Meridian................	39,067	9,596
83843	Moscow.................	21,674	18,398
83647	Mountain Home............	11,531	7,913
83648	Mountain Home AFB (c)......	8,894	5,936
*83653	Nampa..................	60,259	28,365
83661	Payette.................	7,148	5,672
*83201	Pocatello................	51,242	46,117
*83854	Post Falls...............	18,738	7,349
83858	Rathdrum................	5,081	2,014
83440	Rexburg................	17,558	14,298
83350	Rupert.................	5,402	5,455
83864	Sandpoint...............	7,167	5,561
*83301	Twin Falls...............	35,633	27,634
83672	Weiser.................	5,367	4,571

Illinois

Area code (224) overlays area code (847). See introductory note.

ZIP	Place	Area Code	2002	1990
60101	Addison.................	(630)	36,378	32,053
60102	Algonquin................	(847)	26,362	11,764
60803	Alsip..................	(708)	19,635	18,227
62002	Alton..................	(618)	30,190	33,060
62906	Anna..................	(618)	5,084	4,805
60002	Antioch.................	(847)	9,867	6,105
*60005	Arlington Heights..........	(847)	76,422	75,463
60505	Aurora.................	(630)	156,974	99,672
*60010	Barrington...............	(847)	10,271	9,504
60103	Bartlett.................	(630)	37,304	19,395
61607	Bartonville..............	(309)	6,212	6,555
60510	Batavia.................	(630)	25,281	17,076
60085	Beach Park...............	(847)	10,310	9,492
62618	Beardstown..............	(217)	5,714	5,270
*62220	Belleville................	(618)	41,325	42,806
60104	Bellwood................	(708)	20,355	20,241
61008	Belvidere...............	(815)	22,084	16,059
60106	Bensenville..............	(630)	20,832	17,767
62812	Benton.................	(618)	6,847	7,216
60163	Berkeley................	(708)	5,199	5,137
60402	Berwyn.................	(708)	53,309	45,426
62010	Bethalto................	(618)	9,601	9,507
60108	Bloomingdale.............	(630)	21,908	16,614
*61701	Bloomington..............	(309)	67,411	51,889
60406	Blue Island..............	(708)	23,343	21,203
*60440	Bolingbrook..............	(630)	62,797	40,843
60538	Boulder Hill (c)...........	(630)	8,169	8,894
60914	Bourbonnais..............	(815)	15,385	13,929
60915	Bradley.................	(815)	13,176	10,954
60408	Braidwood...............	(815)	5,588	3,584
60455	Bridgeview...............	(708)	15,397	14,402
60153	Broadview...............	(708)	8,187	8,538
60513	Brookfield...............	(708)	18,899	18,876
60089	Buffalo Grove.............	(847)	43,307	36,417
60459	Burbank.................	(708)	28,095	27,600
60521	Burr Ridge...............	(630)	10,743	8,247
62206	Cahokia................	(618)	16,199	17,550
60409	Calumet City..............	(708)	38,849	37,840
60643	Calumet Park.............	(708)	8,446	8,418
61520	Canton.................	(309)	15,046	13,959
*62901	Carbondale..............	(618)	25,168	27,033
62626	Carlinville...............	(217)	5,647	5,416
62821	Carmi..................	(618)	5,332	5,735
*60188	Carol Stream.............	(630)	40,352	31,759
60110	Carpentersville...........	(847)	34,235	23,049
60013	Cary...................	(847)	16,950	10,025
62801	Centralia................	(618)	13,895	14,476
62206	Centreville..............	(618)	5,890	7,489
*61821	Champaign..............	(217)	69,443	63,502
60410	Channahon..............	(815)	9,218	4,266
61920	Charleston..............	(217)	20,975	20,398
62629	Chatham................	(217)	9,092	6,074
62233	Chester................	(618)	8,330	8,204
*60607	Chicago................	(312)/(773)	2,886,251	2,783,726
60411	Chicago Heights...........	(708)	32,610	32,966
60415	Chicago Ridge............	(708)	14,038	13,643
61523	Chillicothe...............	(309)	5,837	5,959
60804	Cicero..................	(708)	84,254	67,436
60514	Clarendon Hills...........	(630)	8,047	6,994
61727	Clinton.................	(217)	7,318	7,437
62234	Collinsville..............	(618)	25,091	22,424
61241	Colona.................	(309)	5,187	2,237
62236	Columbia................	(618)	8,349	5,524
60478	Country Club Hills..........	(708)	16,368	15,431
60525	Countryside..............	(708)	5,989	5,961
60435	Crest Hill...............	(815)	14,823	10,999
60445	Crestwood...............	(708)	11,363	10,823
60417	Crete..................	(708)	7,669	6,773
61610	Creve Coeur.............	(309)	5,348	5,938
*60014	Crystal Lake.............	(815)	39,594	24,692
*61832	Danville................	(217)	33,365	33,828
60561	Darien.................	(630)	23,076	20,556

ZIP	Place	Area Code	2002	1990
*62525	Decatur	(217)	79,842	83,900
60015	Deerfield	(847)	19,086	17,327
60115	DeKalb	(815)	40,103	35,076
*60018	Des Plaines	(847)	58,732	53,414
61021	Dixon	(815)	15,827	15,134
60419	Dolton	(708)	25,438	23,956
*60515	Downers Grove	(630)	48,869	47,464
62832	Du Quoin	(618)	6,383	6,697
62024	East Alton	(618)	6,775	7,063
61244	East Moline	(309)	21,279	20,147
61611	East Peoria	(309)	22,434	21,378
*62201	East St. Louis	(618)	30,995	40,944
62025	Edwardsville	(618)	23,119	14,582
62401	Effingham	(217)	12,406	11,927
*60120	Elgin	(847)	96,539	77,014
*60009	Elk Grove Village	(847)	35,028	33,429
60126	Elmhurst	(630)	43,419	42,029
60707	Elmwood Park	(708)	25,180	23,206
*60201	Evanston	(847)	73,421	73,233
60805	Evergreen Park	(708)	20,665	20,874
62837	Fairfield	(618)	5,382	5,439
62208	Fairview Heights	(618)	15,226	14,768
60422	Flossmoor	(708)	9,445	8,651
60130	Forest Park	(708)	15,552	14,918
60020	Fox Lake	(847)	9,649	7,539
60021	Fox River Grove	(847)	5,051	3,629
60423	Frankfort	(815)	12,390	7,180
—	Frankfort Square (c)	(815)	7,766	6,227
60131	Franklin Park	(847)	19,275	18,485
61032	Freeport	(815)	25,929	25,840
60030	Gages Lake (c)	(847)	10,415	8,349
*61401	Galesburg	(309)	33,237	33,530
61254	Geneseo	(309)	6,448	5,990
60134	Geneva	(630)	21,502	12,625
62034	Glen Carbon	(618)	10,945	7,774
60022	Glencoe	(847)	8,892	8,499
60139	Glendale Heights	(630)	32,953	27,915
*60137	Glen Ellyn	(630)	27,187	24,919
60025	Glenview	(847)	44,042	38,436
60425	Glenwood	(708)	8,934	9,289
62035	Godfrey	(618)	16,556	15,675
—	Goodings Grove (c)	(815)	17,084	14,054
62040	Granite City	(618)	31,622	32,766
60030	Grayslake	(847)	20,865	7,388
62246	Greenville	(618)	7,077	5,108
60031	Gurnee	(847)	30,115	13,715
60103	Hanover Park	(630)	38,037	32,918
62946	Harrisburg	(618)	9,616	9,318
60033	Harvard	(815)	8,413	5,975
60426	Harvey	(708)	29,714	29,771
60656	Harwood Heights	(708)	8,367	7,680
60047	Hawthorn Woods	(847)	6,658	4,423
60429	Hazel Crest	(708)	14,863	13,334
62948	Herrin	(618)	11,364	10,857
60457	Hickory Hills	(708)	13,848	13,021
62249	Highland	(618)	8,674	7,546
60035	Highland Park	(847)	30,568	30,575
60040	Highwood	(708)	5,498	5,358
60162	Hillside	(708)	8,091	7,672
*60521	Hinsdale	(630)	17,855	16,029
*60195	Hoffman Estates	(847)	49,795	46,363
60491	Homer Glen	(708)	22,899	—
60430	Homewood	(708)	19,540	19,278
60942	Hoopeston	(217)	5,873	5,871
60142	Huntley	(847)	9,797	2453
60067	Inverness	(847)	6,918	6,516
60042	Island Lake	(847)	8,399	4,449
60143	Itasca	(630)	8,408	6,947
*62650	Jacksonville	(217)	19,619	19,327
62052	Jerseyville	(618)	7,953	7,382
60050	Johnsburg	(815)	5,763	
*60436	Joliet	(815)	118,423	77,217
60458	Justice	(708)	12,297	11,137
60901	Kankakee	(815)	27,168	27,541
61443	Kewanee	(309)	12,797	12,969
60525	La Grange	(708)	15,584	15,362
60526	La Grange Park	(708)	13,208	12,861
60044	Lake Bluff	(847)	6,162	5,486
60045	Lake Forest	(847)	20,723	17,836
60102	Lake in the Hills	(847)	26,125	5,862
60046	Lake Villa	(847)	7,701	2,857
60047	Lake Zurich	(847)	18,742	14,927
60438	Lansing	(708)	28,156	28,131
61301	La Salle	(815)	9,646	9,717
60439	Lemont	(630)	14,057	7,359
*60048	Libertyville	(847)	21,094	19,174
62656	Lincoln	(217)	15,070	15,418
60069	Lincolnshire	(847)	6,360	4,928
60645	Lincolnwood	(847)	12,329	11,365
60046	Lindenhurst	(847)	14,037	8,044
60532	Lisle	(630)	21,779	19,584
62056	Litchfield	(217)	6,769	6,883
60441	Lockport	(815)	17,923	9,401
60148	Lombard	(630)	43,251	39,408
60047	Long Grove	(847)	7,363	4,747
*61130	Loves Park	(815)	21,205	15,457
60411	Lynwood	(708)	7,560	6,535
60534	Lyons (Cook)	(708)	10,434	9,828
*60050	McHenry	(815)	22,618	16,343

ZIP	Place	Area Code	2002	1990
61115	Machesney Park	(815)	21,049	19,042
61455	Macomb	(309)	18,588	19,952
61853	Mahomet	(217)	5,242	3,499
60950	Manteno	(815)	6,766	3,709
60152	Marengo	(815)	6,567	4,768
62959	Marion	(618)	16,168	14,597
60426	Markham (Cook)	(708)	12,626	13,136
62258	Mascoutah	(618)	5,670	5,511
60443	Matteson	(708)	13,807	11,378
61938	Mattoon	(217)	17,844	18,441
60153	Maywood	(708)	26,728	27,139
*60160	Melrose Park	(708)	23,029	20,859
61342	Mendota	(815)	7,203	7,017
62960	Metropolis	(618)	6,362	6,734
60445	Midlothian	(708)	14,347	14,372
61264	Milan	(309)	5,325	5,753
60448	Mokena	(708)	16,174	6,128
*61265	Moline	(309)	43,221	43,080
61462	Monmouth	(309)	9,525	9,489
60538	Montgomery	(630)	6,932	4,487
61856	Monticello	(217)	5,149	4,775
60450	Morris	(815)	12,257	10,274
61550	Morton	(309)	15,281	13,799
60053	Morton Grove	(847)	22,502	22,373
62863	Mount Carmel	(618)	7,748	8,287
60056	Mount Prospect	(847)	56,096	53,168
62864	Mount Vernon	(618)	16,492	17,082
60060	Mundelein	(847)	31,972	21,224
62966	Murphysboro	(618)	8,814	9,176
*60540	Naperville	(630)	135,389	85,806
60451	New Lenox	(815)	20,228	9,698
60714	Niles	(847)	30,076	28,375
61761	Normal	(309)	47,078	40,023
60634	Norridge	(708)	14,490	14,459
60542	North Aurora	(630)	12,648	6,010
*60062	Northbrook	(708)	33,956	32,565
60064	North Chicago	(847)	36,097	34,978
60093	Northfield	(847)	5,449	4,924
60164	Northlake	(708)	11,802	12,505
60546	North Riverside	(708)	6,635	6,180
60521	Oak Brook	(630)	8,857	9,087
60452	Oak Forest	(708)	28,370	26,202
*60303	Oak Lawn	(708)	55,406	56,182
*60303	Oak Park	(708)	51,601	53,648
62269	O'Fallon	(618)	23,068	16,064
62450	Olney	(618)	8,555	8,873
60477	Orland Hills	(708)	7,034	5,510
*60462	Orland Park	(708)	53,325	35,720
60543	Oswego	(630)	17,313	3,949
61350	Ottawa	(815)	18,453	17,574
*60067	Palatine	(847)	66,431	41,554
60463	Palos Heights	(708)	11,996	11,478
60465	Palos Hills	(708)	17,704	17,803
62557	Pana	(217)	5,535	5,796
61944	Paris	(217)	8,943	9,105
60085	Park City	(847)	6,818	4,677
60466	Park Forest	(708)	23,710	24,656
60068	Park Ridge	(847)	37,771	37,075
61554	Pekin	(309)	33,428	32,254
*61601	Peoria	(309)	112,670	113,508
61603	Peoria Heights	(309)	6,428	6,930
61354	Peru	(815)	9,794	9,302
62274	Pinckneyville	(618)	5,446	3,372
60544	Plainfield	(815)	17,193	4,557
60545	Plano	(630)	5,702	5,104
61764	Pontiac	(815)	11,832	11,428
62040	Pontoon Beach	(618)	5,881	4,013
61356	Princeton	(815)	7,528	7,197
60070	Prospect Heights	(847)	16,975	15,236
*62301	Quincy	(217)	39,916	39,682
61866	Rantoul	(217)	13,005	17,212
60471	Richton Park	(708)	12,831	10,523
60827	Riverdale	(708)	14,923	13,671
60305	River Forest	(708)	11,673	11,669
60171	River Grove	(708)	10,574	9,961
60546	Riverside	(708)	8,755	8,774
60472	Robbins	(708)	6,610	7,498
62454	Robinson	(618)	6,641	6,740
61068	Rochelle	(815)	9,465	8,769
61071	Rock Falls	(815)	9,468	9,669
*61125	Rockford	(815)	151,068	142,815
*61201	Rock Island	(309)	39,045	40,630
61072	Rockton	(815)	5,441	2,928
60008	Rolling Meadows	(847)	24,582	22,598
60446	Romeoville	(815)	28,765	14,101
61072	Roscoe	(815)	6,332	2,079
60172	Roselle	(630)	23,383	20,803
60073	Round Lake	(847)	7,563	3,550
60073	Round Lake Beach	(847)	27,966	16,406
60073	Round Lake Park	(847)	6,178	4,045
*60174	Saint Charles	(630)	30,963	22,636
62881	Salem	(618)	7,768	7,470
60548	Sandwich	(815)	6,687	5,607
62481	Sauk Village	(708)	10,544	10,734
*60194	Schaumburg	(847)	74,919	68,586
*60176	Schiller Park	(847)	11,782	11,189
*62269	Shiloh	(618)	8,692	2,655
60436	Shorewood	(815)	8,772	6,264
61282	Silvis	(309)	7,267	6,926
*60077	Skokie	(847)	63,126	59,432

ZIP	Place	Area Code	2002	1990
61080	South Beloit	(815)	5,432	4,072
60177	South Elgin	(847)	19,651	7,474
60473	South Holland	(708)	22,197	22,105
*62703	Springfield	(217)	111,834	105,412
61362	Spring Valley	(815)	5,378	5,246
62088	Staunton	(618)	5,023	4,806
60475	Steger	(708)	9,971	9,251
61081	Sterling	(815)	15,332	15,142
60402	Stickney	(708)	6,101	5,678
60165	Stone Park	(708)	5,105	4,383
60107	Streamwood	(630)	37,654	31,197
61364	Streator	(815)	14,091	14,121
60554	Sugar Grove	(630)	5,418	2,123
60501	Summit	(708)	10,569	9,971
62221	Swansea	(618)	11,376	8,201
60178	Sycamore	(815)	12,747	9,896
62568	Taylorville	(217)	11,349	11,133
60477	Tinley Park	(708)	52,142	37,115
62294	Troy	(618)	8,871	6,194
60466	University Park	(708)	6,993	6,204
*61801	Urbana	(217)	38,241	36,383
62471	Vandalia	(618)	6,865	6,114
60061	Vernon Hills	(847)	21,839	15,319
60181	Villa Park	(630)	23,120	22,279
60555	Warrenville	(630)	13,375	11,389
61571	Washington	(309)	11,907	10,136
62204	Washington Park	(618)	5,283	7,431
62298	Waterloo	(618)	8,468	5,030
60970	Watseka	(815)	5,610	5,424
60084	Wauconda	(847)	9,891	6,294
*60085	Waukegan	(847)	91,323	69,481
60154	Westchester	(708)	16,862	17,301
*60185	West Chicago	(630)	25,133	14,808
60118	West Dundee	(847)	6,697	3,728
60558	Western Springs	(708)	12,575	11,956
62896	West Frankfort	(618)	8,253	8,526
60559	Westmont	(630)	24,747	21,402
*60187	Wheaton	(630)	55,352	51,441
60090	Wheeling	(847)	35,483	29,911
60514	Willowbrook	(630)	9,031	8,651
60480	Willow Springs	(708)	5,862	4,509
60091	Wilmette	(847)	27,531	26,694
60481	Wilmington	(815)	5,326	4,743
60190	Winfield	(630)	9,202	7,096
60093	Winnetka	(847)	12,468	12,210
60097	Winthrop Harbor	(847)	6,827	6,240
60097	Wonder Lake (c)	(815)	7,463	6,664
60191	Wood Dale	(630)	13,560	12,394
60517	Woodridge	(630)	33,734	26,359
62095	Wood River	(618)	11,208	11,490
60098	Woodstock	(815)	20,772	14,368
60482	Worth	(708)	11,018	11,208
60560	Yorkville	(630)	7,371	3,974
60099	Zion	(847)	23,601	19,783

Indiana

ZIP	Place	Area Code	2002	1990
46001	Alexandria	(765)	6,142	5,709
*46011	Anderson	(765)	58,853	59,518
46703	Angola	(260)	7,612	5,851
46706	Auburn	(260)	12,277	9,386
46123	Avon	(317)	6,904	—
47006	Batesville	(812)	6,340	4,720
47421	Bedford	(812)	13,549	13,817
46107	Beech Grove	(317)	14,626	13,383
*47408	Bloomington	(812)	69,987	62,735
46714	Bluffton	(260)	9,512	9,104
47601	Boonville	(812)	6,856	6,686
47834	Brazil	(812)	8,026	7,640
47025	Bright (c)	(812)	5,405	3,945
46112	Brownsburg	(317)	16,273	7,751
*46032	Carmel	(317)	40,878	25,380
46303	Cedar Lake	(219)	9,412	8,885
47111	Charlestown	(812)	5,912	5,889
46304	Chesterton	(219)	10,916	9,118
47129	Clarksville (Clark)	(812)	21,307	19,838
46725	Columbia City	(260)	7,523	5,883
*47201	Columbus	(812)	38,770	33,948
47331	Connersville	(765)	15,078	15,550
47933	Crawfordsville	(765)	15,330	13,584
46307	Crown Point	(219)	20,491	17,728
46229	Cumberland	(317)	5,433	4,557
46122	Danville	(317)	6,930	4,345
46733	Decatur	(260)	9,446	8,642
46514	Dunlap (c)	(574)	5,887	5,705
46311	Dyer	(219)	14,461	10,923
46312	East Chicago	(219)	31,731	33,892
*46515	Elkhart	(574)	51,782	44,661
47429	Ellettsville	(812)	5,121	3,275
46036	Elwood	(765)	9,476	9,494
*47708	Evansville	(812)	119,081	126,272
46038	Fishers	(317)	44,441	7,189
*46802	Fort Wayne	(260)	210,070	195,680
46041	Frankfort	(765)	16,593	14,754
46131	Franklin	(317)	20,513	12,932
46738	Garrett	(260)	5,722	5,349
*46401	Gary	(219)	100,945	116,646
46933	Gas City	(765)	5,804	6,311
*46526	Goshen	(574)	29,683	23,794

ZIP	Place	Area Code	2002	1990
46530	Granger (c)	(574)	28,284	20,241
46135	Greencastle	(765)	9,915	8,984
46140	Greenfield	(317)	15,554	11,657
47240	Greensburg	(812)	10,161	9,286
*46142	Greenwood	(317)	38,949	26,507
46319	Griffith	(219)	17,109	17,914
*46320	Hammond	(219)	81,413	84,236
47348	Hartford City	(765)	6,714	6,960
46322	Highland	(219)	23,589	23,696
46342	Hobart	(219)	26,464	24,440
47542	Huntingburg	(812)	5,811	5,236
46750	Huntington	(260)	17,305	16,389
*46206	Indianapolis	(317)	783,612	731,278
*47546	Jasper	(812)	12,686	10,030
*47130	Jeffersonville	(812)	27,822	24,016
46755	Kendallville	(260)	9,762	7,984
*46902	Kokomo	(765)	45,956	44,996
*47901	Lafayette	(765)	60,594	45,933
—	Lakes of the Four Seasons (c)	(219)	7,291	6,556
46405	Lake Station	(219)	13,918	13,899
*46350	La Porte	(219)	21,293	21,507
46226	Lawrence	(317)	40,456	26,849
46052	Lebanon	(765)	14,231	12,059
47441	Linton	(812)	5,765	5,814
46947	Logansport	(574)	19,466	16,865
46356	Lowell	(219)	7,711	6,430
47250	Madison	(812)	12,126	12,006
*46952	Marion	(765)	30,653	32,607
46151	Martinsville	(765)	11,577	11,677
*46401	Merrillville	(219)	30,943	27,257
*46360	Michigan City	(219)	32,564	33,822
46544	Mishawaka	(574)	48,264	42,635
47960	Monticello	(574)	5,586	5,237
46158	Mooresville	(317)	10,235	5,779
47620	Mount Vernon	(812)	7,387	7,217
*47302	Muncie	(765)	67,195	71,170
46321	Munster	(219)	21,874	19,949
46550	Nappanee	(574)	6,741	5,474
*47150	New Albany	(812)	37,529	36,322
47362	New Castle	(765)	18,994	17,753
46774	New Haven	(260)	13,490	11,234
*46060	Noblesville	(317)	31,869	17,655
46962	North Manchester	(260)	6,152	6,383
47265	North Vernon	(812)	6,421	5,129
47130	Oak Park (c)	(812)	5,379	5,630
46970	Peru	(765)	12,915	12,843
46168	Plainfield	(317)	20,719	14,953
46563	Plymouth	(574)	10,438	8,291
46368	Portage	(219)	34,498	29,062
46304	Porter	(219)	5,058	3,242
47371	Portland	(260)	6,300	6,483
47670	Princeton	(812)	8,433	8,127
47978	Rensselaer	(219)	6,133	5,045
*47374	Richmond	(765)	38,470	38,705
46975	Rochester	(574)	6,490	5,969
46173	Rushville	(765)	5,802	5,533
46373	Saint John	(219)	9,119	4,921
47167	Salem	(812)	6,333	5,619
46375	Schererville	(219)	25,576	20,155
47170	Scottsburg	(812)	6,014	5,334
47712	Sellersburg	(812)	6,124	5,936
47274	Seymour	(812)	18,397	15,605
46176	Shelbyville	(765)	17,870	15,347
*46624	South Bend	(574)	106,558	105,511
46383	South Haven (c)	(219)	5,619	6,112
46224	Speedway	(317)	12,903	13,092
47586	Tell City	(812)	7,755	8,088
*47808	Terre Haute	(812)	58,642	57,475
46072	Tipton	(765)	5,272	4,751
*46383	Valparaiso	(219)	28,185	24,414
47591	Vincennes	(812)	18,246	19,867
46992	Wabash	(260)	11,519	12,127
*46580	Warsaw	(574)	12,436	10,968
47501	Washington	(812)	11,283	10,864
46074	Westfield	(317)	10,511	3,304
*46580	West Lafayette	(765)	29,081	26,144
46391	Westville	(219)	5,274	5,234
46077	Zionsville	(317)	10,062	6,207

Iowa

ZIP	Place	Area Code	2002	1990
50511	Algona	(515)	5,641	6,015
50009	Altoona	(515)	10,953	7,242
*50010	Ames	(515)	50,913	47,198
50021	Ankeny	(515)	29,866	18,482
52205	Anamosa	(319)	5,620	5,100
50022	Atlantic	(712)	7,058	7,432
52722	Bettendorf	(563)	31,547	28,139
*50036	Boone	(515)	12,802	12,392
52601	Burlington	(319)	26,048	27,208
51401	Carroll	(712)	9,994	9,579
50613	Cedar Falls	(319)	36,660	34,298
*52401	Cedar Rapids	(319)	122,514	108,772
52544	Centerville	(641)	5,743	5,936
50616	Charles City	(641)	7,667	7,878
51012	Cherokee	(712)	5,271	6,026
51632	Clarinda	(712)	5,655	5,104
50428	Clear Lake	(641)	8,198	8,183
*52732	Clinton	(563)	27,443	29,201

ZIP	Place	Area Code	2002	1990
50325	Clive	(515)	13,557	7,446
52241	Coralville	(319)	16,490	10,347
*51501	Council Bluffs	(712)	58,640	54,315
50801	Creston	(641)	7,448	7,911
*52802	Davenport	(563)	97,777	95,333
52101	Decorah	(563)	8,189	8,063
51442	Denison	(712)	7,414	6,604
*50318	Des Moines	(515)	198,076	193,189
*50274	De Witt	(563)	5,027	4,514
*52001	Dubuque	(563)	57,031	57,538
51334	Estherville	(712)	6,481	6,720
52556	Fairfield	(641)	9,486	9,955
50501	Fort Dodge	(515)	24,897	26,057
52627	Fort Madison	(319)	11,006	11,614
51534	Glenwood	(712)	5,393	4,960
50111	Grimes	(515)	5,399	2,653
50112	Grinnell	(641)	9,141	8,902
*51537	Harlan	(712)	5,282	5,148
52233	Hiawatha	(319)	6,521	5,354
50644	Independence	(319)	5,956	5,972
50125	Indianola	(515)	13,114	11,340
*52240	Iowa City	(319)	63,816	59,735
50126	Iowa Falls	(641)	5,144	5,435
50131	Johnston	(515)	10,011	4,702
52632	Keokuk	(319)	11,029	12,451
50138	Knoxville	(641)	7,718	8,232
51031	Le Mars	(712)	9,226	8,454
52057	Manchester	(563)	5,213	5,137
52060	Maquoketa	(563)	6,087	6,130
52302	Marion	(319)	27,611	20,422
50158	Marshalltown	(641)	26,102	25,178
*50401	Mason City	(641)	28,464	29,040
52641	Mount Pleasant	(319)	8,611	7,959
52761	Muscatine	(563)	22,650	22,881
50201	Nevada	(515)	6,686	6,009
50208	Newton	(641)	15,621	14,799
52317	North Liberty	(319)	6,081	2,926
50211	Norwalk	(515)	7,605	5,726
50662	Oelwein	(319)	6,559	6,691
51041	Orange City	(712)	5,671	4,940
52577	Oskaloosa	(641)	10,991	10,600
52501	Ottumwa	(641)	24,695	24,488
50219	Pella	(641)	10,219	9,270
50220	Perry	(515)	7,913	6,652
*50317	Pleasant Hill	(515)	5,557	3,671
*51566	Red Oak	(712)	6,025	6,264
51601	Shenandoah	(712)	5,338	5,572
51250	Sioux Center	(712)	6,274	5,074
*51101	Sioux City	(712)	84,131	80,505
51301	Spencer	(712)	11,196	11,066
50588	Storm Lake	(712)	10,084	8,769
*50318	Urbandale	(515)	31,152	23,775
52349	Vinton	(319)	5,228	5,103
52353	Washington	(319)	7,189	7,074
*50701	Waterloo	(319)	67,742	66,467
50263	Waukee	(515)	6,579	2,512
50677	Waverly	(319)	9,070	8,539
50595	Webster City	(515)	8,061	7,894
*50265	West Des Moines	(515)	49,961	31,702

Kansas

ZIP	Place	Area Code	2002	1990
67410	Abilene	(785)	6,438	6,242
67002	Andover	(316)	7,750	4,204
67005	Arkansas City	(620)	12,043	12,762
66002	Atchison	(913)	10,106	10,656
67010	Augusta	(316)	8,493	7,848
66952	Bel Aire	(316)	6,424	3,695
66012	Bonner Springs	(913)	6,815	6,413
66720	Chanute	(620)	9,128	9,488
67337	Coffeyville	(620)	10,606	12,917
67701	Colby	(785)	5,364	5,510
66901	Concordia	(785)	5,512	6,152
67037	Derby	(316)	18,908	14,691
67801	Dodge City	(620)	25,345	21,129
67042	El Dorado	(316)	12,669	11,495
66801	Emporia	(620)	26,739	25,512
66442	Fort Riley North (c)	(785)	8,114	12,848
66701	Fort Scott	(620)	8,113	8,362
67846	Garden City	(620)	27,678	24,097
66030	Gardner	(913)	10,701	4,277
67530	Great Bend	(620)	15,066	15,427
67601	Hays	(785)	19,908	18,632
67060	Haysville	(316)	9,379	8,364
*67501	Hutchinson	(620)	40,741	39,308
67301	Independence	(620)	9,521	10,030
66749	Iola	(620)	6,186	6,351
66441	Junction City	(785)	17,753	20,642
*66102	Kansas City	(913)	146,978	151,521
66043	Lansing	(913)	9,526	7,120
*66044	Lawrence	(785)	81,604	65,608
66048	Leavenworth	(913)	35,410	38,495
66209	Leawood	(913)	28,270	19,693
66214	Lenexa	(913)	41,249	34,110
*67901	Liberal	(620)	20,082	16,573
67460	McPherson	(620)	13,774	12,422
*66502	Manhattan	(785)	43,794	43,081
66202	Merriam	(913)	10,844	11,819
66203	Mission	(913)	9,578	9,504
67110	Mulvane	(316)	5,488	4,683

ZIP	Place	Area Code	2002	1990
67114	Newton	(316)	17,913	16,700
*66061	Olathe	(913)	101,413	63,402
66067	Ottawa	(785)	11,978	10,667
66204	Overland Park	(913)	158,430	111,790
66671	Paola	(913)	5,048	4,698
67219	Park City	(316)	6,405	5,081
67357	Parsons	(620)	11,289	11,919
66762	Pittsburg	(620)	19,086	17,789
66208	Prairie Village	(913)	21,764	23,186
67124	Pratt	(620)	6,497	6,687
66205	Roeland Park	(913)	6,705	7,706
*67401	Salina	(785)	45,969	42,299
66203	Shawnee	(913)	52,715	37,962
*66601	Topeka	(785)	122,103	119,883
67880	Ulysses	(620)	5,918	5,474
67147	Valley Center	(316)	5,008	4,272
67152	Wellington	(620)	8,421	8,517
*67202	Wichita	(316)	355,126	304,011
67156	Winfield	(620)	12,214	11,931

Kentucky

ZIP	Place	Area Code	2002	1990
41001	Alexandria	(859)	8,274	5,592
*41101	Ashland	(606)	21,601	23,622
40004	Bardstown	(502)	10,400	6,712
41073	Bellevue	(859)	6,267	6,997
40403	Berea	(859)	10,838	9,129
*42101	Bowling Green	(270)	50,226	41,688
40261	Buechel (c)	(502)	7,272	7,081
41005	Burlington (c)	(859)	10,779	6,070
*42718	Campbellsville	(270)	10,614	9,592
42330	Central City	(270)	5,801	4,979
*40701	Corbin	(606)	7,855	7,644
*41011	Covington	(859)	42,983	43,646
41031	Cynthiana	(859)	6,196	6,497
*40422	Danville	(859)	15,388	14,454
41074	Dayton	(859)	5,790	6,576
40243	Douglass Hills	(502)	5,770	5,431
41017	Edgewood	(859)	9,276	8,143
*42701	Elizabethtown	(270)	23,080	18,167
41018	Elsmere	(859)	8,140	6,447
41018	Erlanger	(859)	16,792	15,979
40118	Fairdale (c)	(502)	7,658	6,563
42091	Fern Creek (c)	(502)	17,870	16,406
41139	Flatwoods	(606)	7,550	7,799
*41042	Florence	(859)	24,308	18,586
42223	Fort Campbell North (c)	(270)	14,338	18,861
40121	Fort Knox (c)	(270)	12,377	21,495
41017	Fort Mitchell	(859)	7,928	7,438
41075	Fort Thomas	(859)	16,238	16,032
41011	Fort Wright	(859)	5,622	6,404
*40601	Frankfort	(502)	27,660	26,535
*42134	Franklin	(270)	8,081	7,607
40324	Georgetown	(502)	19,013	11,414
*42141	Glasgow	(270)	13,434	12,777
40330	Harrodsburg	(859)	7,993	7,335
*42420	Henderson	(270)	27,426	25,945
41076	Highland Heights	(859)	6,534	4,223
40228	Highview (c)	(502)	15,161	14,814
40229	Hillview	(502)	7,143	6,119
*42240	Hopkinsville	(270)	29,279	29,809
41051	Independence	(859)	16,309	10,444
40269	Jeffersontown	(502)	26,156	23,223
40031	La Grange	(502)	5,808	3,901
40342	Lawrenceburg	(502)	9,145	5,911
40033	Lebanon	(270)	5,802	5,695
*42754	Leitchfield	(270)	6,214	4,965
*40507	Lexington	(859)	263,618	225,366
40741	London	(606)	7,528	5,757
40232	Louisville	(502)	251,399	269,555
40252	Lyndon	(502)	10,261	8,037
42431	Madisonville	(270)	19,240	18,693
42066	Mayfield	(270)	10,259	9,935
41056	Maysville	(606)	8,998	8,113
40965	Middlesborough	(606)	10,342	11,328
40253	Middletown	(502)	5,902	5,016
42633	Monticello	(606)	6,000	5,357
40351	Morehead	(606)	7,596	8,357
40353	Mount Sterling	(859)	5,992	5,362
40047	Mount Washington	(502)	8,569	5,256
42071	Murray	(270)	15,099	14,442
40218	Newburg (c)	(502)	20,636	21,647
*41071	Newport	(859)	16,560	18,871
*40356	Nicholasville	(859)	21,343	13,603
—	Oakbrook (c)		7,726	4,113
42262	Oak Grove	(502)	7,813	2,863
40259	Okolona (c)	(502)	17,807	18,902
*42301	Owensboro	(270)	54,176	53,577
*42003	Paducah	(270)	25,577	27,256
*40361	Paris	(859)	9,231	8,730
*41501	Pikeville	(606)	6,196	6,324
40268	Pleasure Ridge Park (c)	(502)	25,776	25,131
42445	Princeton	(502)	6,455	6,940
*40160	Radcliff	(502)	21,978	19,778
*40475	Richmond	(859)	28,093	21,183
42276	Russellville	(270)	7,197	7,454
40216	Saint Dennis (c)	(502)	9,177	10,326
*40206	Saint Matthews	(502)	17,414	15,691
*40066	Shelbyville	(502)	10,316	6,155

ZIP	Place	Area Code	2002	1990
40165	Shepherdsville	(502)	8,494	4,805
40256	Shively	(502)	15,297	15,535
*42501	Somerset	(606)	11,558	10,735
41015	Taylor Mill	(859)	6,905	5,530
40272	Valley Station (c)	(502)	22,946	22,840
40383	Versailles	(859)	7,447	7,269
41016	Villa Hills	(859)	7,945	7,370
40769	Williamsburg	(606)	5,167	5,493
40390	Wilmore	(859)	5,841	4,215
*40391	Winchester	(859)	16,446	15,799

Louisiana

ZIP	Place	Area Code	2002	1990
*70510	Abbeville	(337)	11,778	11,769
*71301	Alexandria	(318)	45,856	49,049
70032	Arabi (c)	(504)	8,093	8,787
70094	Avondale (c)	(504)	5,441	5,813
*70714	Baker	(225)	13,648	13,087
*71220	Bastrop	(318)	12,717	13,916
*70821	Baton Rouge	(225)	225,702	219,531
70360	Bayou Cane (c)	(985)	17,046	15,876
70037	Belle Chasse (c)	(504)	9,848	8,512
*70427	Bogalusa	(985)	13,064	14,280
*71111	Bossier City	(318)	57,156	52,721
70517	Breaux Bridge	(337)	7,394	6,694
70094	Bridge City (c)	(504)	8,323	8,327
70518	Broussard	(337)	6,236	3,213
70811	Brownfields (c)	(225)	5,222	5,229
71291	Brownsville-Bawcomville (c)	(318)	7,616	7,397
70520	Carencro	(337)	6,093	5,518
*70043	Chalmette (c)	(504)	32,069	31,860
71291	Claiborne (c)	(318)	9,830	8,300
*70433	Covington	(985)	8,582	7,691
*70526	Crowley	(337)	13,988	13,983
70345	Cut Off (c)	(985)	5,635	5,325
*70726	Denham Springs	(225)	9,134	8,381
70634	De Ridder	(337)	9,742	10,475
70047	Destrehan (c)	(985)	11,260	8,031
70346	Donaldsonville	(225)	7,563	7,949
—	Eden Isle (c)		6,261	3,768
70072	Estelle (c)	(504)	15,880	14,091
70535	Eunice	(337)	11,409	11,162
71459	Fort Polk South (c)	(337)	11,000	10,911
70538	Franklin	(337)	8,121	9,004
70354	Galliano (c)	(985)	7,356	4,294
70820	Gardere (c)	(225)	8,992	7,209
*70737	Gonzales	(225)	8,240	7,208
*70053	Gretna	(504)	17,170	17,208
*70401	Hammond	(985)	17,624	15,871
70123	Harahan	(504)	9,812	9,927
*70058	Harvey (c)	(504)	22,226	21,222
*70360	Houma	(985)	32,130	30,495
70544	Jeanerette	(337)	5,969	6,205
70502	Jefferson (c)	(504)	11,843	14,521
70546	Jennings	(337)	10,785	11,305
70548	Kaplan	(337)	5,129	4,535
*70062	Kenner	(504)	70,502	72,033
70445	Lacombe (c)	(985)	7,518	6,523
*70501	Lafayette	(337)	111,272	101,865
*70601	Lake Charles	(337)	70,726	70,580
71254	Lake Providence (c)	(318)	5,104	5,380
*70068	Laplace (c)	(985)	27,684	24,194
70373	Larose (c)	(985)	7,306	5,772
*71446	Leesville	(337)	6,451	7,638
70070	Luling (c)	(985)	11,512	2,803
*70471	Mandeville	(985)	11,360	7,474
71052	Mansfield	(318)	5,520	5,389
71351	Marksville	(318)	5,568	5,526
*70072	Marrero (c)	(504)	36,165	36,671
70075	Meraux (c)	(504)	10,192	8,849
70812	Merrydale (c)	(225)	10,427	10,395
*70009	Metairie (c)	(504)	146,136	149,428
*71055	Minden	(318)	13,246	13,661
*71207	Monroe	(318)	52,360	54,909
*70380	Morgan City	(985)	12,256	14,531
70612	Moss Bluff (c)	(337)	10,535	8,039
*71457	Natchitoches	(318)	17,714	16,609
*70560	New Iberia	(337)	32,506	31,828
*70140	New Orleans	(504)	473,681	496,938
71463	Oakdale	(318)	8,157	6,837
70808	Oak Hills Place (c)	(225)	7,996	5,479
—	Old Jefferson (c)		5,631	4,531
*70570	Opelousas	(337)	22,688	19,091
70392	Patterson	(985)	5,130	5,166
*71360	Pineville	(318)	13,875	15,308
*70764	Plaquemine	(225)	6,958	7,101
70454	Ponchatoula	(985)	5,400	5,499
70767	Port Allen	(225)	5,160	6,277
70601	Prien (c)	(337)	7,215	6,448
70394	Raceland (c)	(985)	10,224	5,564
70578	Rayne	(337)	8,553	8,502
71037	Red Chute (c)	(318)	5,984	5,431
*70084	Reserve (c)	(985)	9,111	8,847
70123	River Ridge (c)	(504)	14,588	14,800
*71270	Ruston	(318)	20,592	20,071
70776	Saint Gabriel	(225)	5,529	3,854
70582	Saint Martinville	(337)	7,012	7,226

ZIP	Place	Area Code	2002	1990
70087	Saint Rose (c)	(504)	6,540	6,259
70395	Schriever (c)	(985)	5,880	4,958
70583	Scott	(337)	7,896	4,912
70817	Shenandoah (c)		17,070	13,429
*71102	Shreveport	(318)	199,033	198,518
*70458	Slidell	(985)	26,466	24,124
71075	Springhill	(318)	5,307	5,668
*70663	Sulphur	(337)	20,042	20,125
*71282	Tallulah	(318)	8,903	8,526
70056	Terrytown (c)	(504)	25,430	23,787
*70301	Thibodaux	(985)	14,514	14,125
70053	Timberlane (c)	(504)	11,405	12,614
70809	Village Saint George (c)	(225)	6,993	6,242
70586	Ville Platte	(337)	8,438	9,037
70092	Violet (c)	(504)	8,555	8,574
70094	Waggaman (c)	(504)	9,435	9,405
70785	Walker	(225)	5,137	3,846
*71291	West Monroe	(318)	13,049	14,096
*70094	Westwego	(504)	10,583	11,218
71483	Winnfield	(318)	5,563	6,138
71295	Winnsboro	(318)	5,171	5,755
—	Woodmere (c)		13,058	—
70791	Zachary	(225)	11,642	9,036

Maine (207)

See introductory note.

ZIP	Place		2002	1990
*04210	Auburn		23,142	24,309
*04330	Augusta		18,551	21,325
*04401	Bangor		31,541	33,181
04530	Bath		9,284	9,799
04915	Belfast		6,693	6,355
03901	Berwick		6,853	5,995
*04005	Biddeford		21,685	20,710
*04412	Brewer		9,028	9,021
04011	Brunswick (c)		14,816	14,683
04011	Brunswick		21,364	20,906
04093	Buxton		7,831	6,494
04843	Camden		5,353	5,060
04107	Cape Elizabeth		8,999	8,854
04736	Caribou		8,262	9,415
04021	Cumberland		7,405	5,836
03903	Eliot		6,245	5,329
04605	Ellsworth		6,620	5,975
04937	Fairfield		6,576	6,718
04105	Falmouth		10,508	7,610
04938	Farmington		7,424	7,436
04032	Freeport		7,924	6,905
04345	Gardiner		6,172	6,746
04038	Gorham		14,620	11,856
04039	Gray		7,073	5,904
04444	Hampden		6,454	5,974
04079	Harpswell		5,157	5,012
04730	Houlton (c)		5,270	5,627
04730	Houlton		6,613	6,613
04043	Kennebunk		11,143	8,004
03904	Kittery		9,895	9,372
04027	Lebanon		5,296	—
*04240	Lewiston		35,648	39,757
04457	Lincoln		5,209	5,587
04250	Lisbon		9,127	9,457
04462	Millinocket (c)		5,153	6,956
04462	Millinocket (c)		5,190	6,922
04260	New Gloucester		5,018	3,878
04963	Oakland		6,021	5,595
04064	Old Orchard Beach		9,143	7,789
04064	Old Orchard Beach (c)		8,856	7,789
04468	Old Town		8,110	8,317
04473	Orono		9,113	10,573
04473	Orono (c)		8,253	9,789
*04101	Portland		63,882	64,157
04769	Presque Isle		9,397	10,550
04841	Rockland		7,688	7,972
04276	Rumford		6,446	7,078
04072	Saco		17,634	15,181
04073	Sanford (c)		10,133	10,296
04073	Sanford		21,550	20,463
*04074	Scarborough		18,262	12,518
04976	Skowhegan (c)		6,696	6,990
04976	Skowhegan		8,788	8,725
03908	South Berwick		7,083	5,877
*04101	South Portland		23,255	23,163
04084	Standish		9,625	7,678
04086	Topsham (c)		6,147	6,147
04086	Topsham		9,464	8,746
04282	Turner		5,110	4,293
04087	Waterboro		6,785	4,510
*04901	Waterville		15,629	17,173
04090	Wells		9,804	7,778
*04092	Westbrook		16,103	16,121
04062	Windham		15,194	13,020
04901	Winslow (c)		7,743	5,436
04901	Winslow		7,792	7,997
04364	Winthrop		6,313	5,968
04096	Yarmouth		8,313	7,862
03909	York		13,315	9,818

IT'S A FACT: According to Rand McNally, the most popular names for cities, towns, and places on U.S. maps are Union (234), Washington (222), Jackson (188), and Liberty (188).

Maryland

Area code (240) overlays area code (301). Area code (443) overlays (410). See introductory note.

ZIP	Place	Area Code	2002	1990
21001	Aberdeen	(410)	14,018	13,087
20607	Accokeek (c)	(301)	7,349	4,477
20783	Adelphi (c)	(301)	14,998	13,524
20762	Andrews AFB (c)	(410)	7,925	10,228
*21401	Annapolis	(410)	36,196	33,195
21227	Arbutus (c)	(410)	20,116	19,750
21012	Arnold (c)	(410)	23,422	20,261
20916	Aspen Hill (c)	(301)	50,228	45,494
21220	Ballenger Creek (c)	(410)	13,518	5,546
*21203	Baltimore	(410)	638,614	736,014
*21014	Bel Air	(410)	10,317	8,942
21050	Bel Air North (c)	(410)	25,798	14,880
21014	Bel Air South (c)	(410)	39,711	26,421
*20705	Beltsville (c)	(301)	15,690	14,476
—	Bennsville (c)		7,325	—
*20814	Bethesda (c)	(301)	55,277	62,936
20710	Bladensburg (c)	(301)	7,882	8,064
*20715	Bowie	(301)	52,123	37,642
21220	Bowleys Quarters (c)	(410)	6,314	5,595
21225	Brooklyn Park (c)	(410)	10,938	10,987
21716	Brunswick	(301)	5,049	5,091
20866	Burtonsville (c)	(301)	7,305	5,853
20619	California (c)	(410)	9,307	7,626
20705	Calverton (c)	(301)	12,610	12,046
21613	Cambridge	(410)	10,792	11,514
20748	Camp Springs (c)	(301)	17,968	16,392
21401	Cape St. Clair (c)	(410)	8,022	7,878
21234	Carney (c)	(410)	28,264	25,578
21228	Catonsville (c)	(410)	39,820	35,233
	Chesapeake Ranch Estates-			
20657	Drum Point (c)	(301)	11,503	5,423
20784	Cheverly (c)	(301)	6,621	6,023
*20814	Chevy Chase (c)	(301)	9,381	8,559
20783	Chillum (c)	(301)	34,252	31,309
20735	Clinton (c)	(301)	26,064	19,987
20904	Cloverly (c)	(301)	7,835	7,904
21030	Cockeysville (c)	(410)	19,388	18,668
20914	Colesville (c)	(301)	19,810	18,819
*20740	College Park	(301)	25,320	23,714
*21045	Columbia (c)	(410)/(301)	88,254	75,883
20743	Coral Hills (c)	(410)	10,720	11,032
—	Cresaptown-Bel Air (c)		5,884	4,586
21114	Crofton (c)	(410)	20,091	12,781
*21502	Cumberland	(301)	21,082	23,712
20872	Damascus (c)	(301)	11,430	9,817
20874	Darnestown (c)		6,378	—
*20747	District Heights (c)	(301)	6,142	6,711
21222	Dundalk (c)	(410)	62,306	65,800
21601	Easton	(410)	12,180	9,372
20737	East Riverdale (c)	(301)	14,961	14,187
21219	Edgemere (c)	(410)	9,248	9,226
21040	Edgewood (c)	(410)	23,378	23,903
21784	Eldersburg (c)	(410)	27,741	9,720
21227	Elkridge (c)	(410)	22,042	12,953
*21921	Elkton	(410)	13,094	9,073
*21043	Ellicott City (c)	(410)	56,397	41,396
21221	Essex (c)	(410)	39,078	40,872
20904	Fairland (c)	(301)	21,738	19,828
21047	Fallston (c)	(410)	8,427	5,730
21061	Ferndale (c)	(410)	16,056	16,355
—	Forest Glen (c)		7,344	—
20747	Forestville (c)	(301)	12,707	16,731
20755	Fort Meade (c)	(301)	9,882	12,509
*20744	Fort Washington (c)	(301)	23,845	24,032
*21701	Frederick	(301)	56,063	40,186
20744	Friendly (c)	(301)	10,938	9,028
21532	Frostburg	(301)	8,098	8,069
*20877	Gaithersburg	(301)	56,300	39,676
21055	Garrison (c)	(410)	7,969	5,045
*20874	Germantown (c)	(301)	55,419	41,145
20706	Glenarden (c)	(301)	6,526	5,025
*21061	Glen Burnie (c)	(410)	38,922	37,305
20769	Glenn Dale (c)	(301)	12,609	9,689
—	Goddard (c)		5,554	4,576
—	Greater Landover (c)		22,900	—
20772	Greater Upper Marlboro (c)		18,720	11,528
*20770	Greenbelt (c)	(301)	22,006	20,561
21122	Green Haven (c)	(410)	17,415	14,416
21771	Green Valley (c)		12,262	9,424
*21740	Hagerstown	(301)	36,659	35,306
21740	Halfway (c)	(301)	10,065	8,873
21074	Hampstead (c)	(410)	5,261	2,608
21211	Hampton (c)		5,004	4,926
21078	Havre de Grace	(410)	11,318	8,952
20748	Hillcrest Heights (c)	(301)	16,359	17,136
*20780	Hyattsville	(301)	15,121	13,864
20794	Jessup (c)	(410)	7,865	6,537
21085	Joppatowne (c)	(410)	11,391	11,084
—	Kemp Mill (c)		9,956	—
20772	Kettering (c)	(301)	11,008	9,901
—	Lake Arbor (c)		8,533	—
21122	Lake Shore (c)	(410)	13,065	13,269
21787	Langley Park (c)	(301)	16,214	17,474
20706	Lanham-Seabrook (c)	(301)	18,190	16,792
21227	Lansdowne-Baltimore Highlands (c)		15,724	15,509
20646	La Plata	(301)	7,265	5,841
20772	Largo (c)	(301)	8,408	9,475
*20707	Laurel	(301)	20,590	19,086
20653	Lexington Park (c)	(410)	11,021	9,943
—	Linganore-Bartonsville (c)		12,529	4,079
21090	Linthicum (c)	(410)	7,539	7,547
21207	Lochearn (c)	(410)	25,269	25,240
21037	Londontowne (c)	(301)	7,595	6,992
*21093	Lutherville-Timonium (c)	(410)	15,814	16,442
20748	Marlow Heights (c)	(301)	6,059	5,885
20772	Marlton (c)	(301)	7,798	5,523
20707	Maryland City (c)	(301)	6,814	6,813
21093	Mays Chapel (c)	(410)	11,427	10,132
21220	Middle River (c)	(410)	23,958	24,616
21207	Milford Mill (c)	(301)	26,527	22,547
20717	Mitchellville (c)	(301)	9,611	12,593
20886	Montgomery Village (c)	(301)	38,051	32,315
21771	Mount Airy	(301)/(410)	7,647	3,730
20712	Mount Rainier	(301)	8,713	7,954
20784	New Carrollton	(301)	12,983	12,002
20815	North Bethesda (c)	(301)	38,610	29,656
20895	North Kensington (c)	(301)	8,940	8,607
20707	North Laurel (c)	(301)	20,468	15,008
20878	North Potomac (c)	(301)	23,044	18,456
*21842	Ocean City	(410)	7,182	5,146
21811	Ocean Pines (c)	(410)	10,496	4,251
21113	Odenton (c)	(410)	20,534	12,833
*20832	Olney (c)	(301)	31,438	23,019
21206	Overlea (c)	(410)	12,148	12,137
21117	Owings Mills (c)	(410)	20,193	9,474
*20750	Oxon Hill-Glassmanor (c)	(301)	35,355	35,794
21234	Parkville (c)	(410)	31,118	31,617
21401	Parole (c)	(410)	14,031	10,054
*21122	Pasadena (c)	(410)	12,093	10,012
21128	Perry Hall (c)	(410)	28,705	22,723
21282	Pikesville (c)	(410)	29,123	24,815
20837	Poolesville (c)	(301)	5,374	3,796
*20850	Potomac (c)	(301)	44,822	45,634
21227	Pumphrey (c)		5,317	5,483
21133	Randallstown (c)	(301)	30,870	26,277
—	Redland (c)		16,998	16,145
21136	Reisterstown (c)	(410)	22,438	19,314
20737	Riverdale Park (c)	(301)	6,528	4,843
21017	Riverside (c)		6,128	—
21122	Riviera Beach (c)	(410)	12,695	11,376
*20850	Rockville	(301)	52,573	44,830
20772	Rosaryville (c)	(301)	12,322	8,976
21237	Rosedale (c)	(410)	19,199	18,703
—	Rossmoor (c)		7,569	6,182
21221	Rossville (c)	(410)	11,515	9,492
20602	Saint Charles (c)	(301)	33,379	28,717
*21801	Salisbury	(410)	24,645	20,592
20763	Savage-Guilford (c)	(410)	12,918	9,669
20743	Seat Pleasant	(301)	5,027	5,354
21144	Severn (c)	(410)	35,076	24,499
21146	Severna Park (c)	(410)	28,507	25,879
20764	Shady Side (c)	(301)	5,559	4,107
*20907	Silver Spring (c)	(301)	76,540	76,046
21061	South Gate (c)	(410)	28,672	27,564
20895	South Kensington (c)	(301)	7,887	8,777
20707	South Laurel (c)	(301)	20,479	18,591
21666	Stevensville (c)	(410)	5,880	1,862
*20752	Suitland-Silver Hills (c)	(301)	33,515	35,111
*20913	Takoma Park	(301)	17,687	16,724
21787	Taneytown	(410)	5,264	3,695
*20748	Temple Hills (c)	(301)	7,792	6,865
21788	Thurmont	(301)	5,797	3,398
*21202	Towson (c)	(410)	51,793	49,445
—	Travilah (c)		7,442	—
*20602	Waldorf (c)	(301)	22,312	15,058
20743	Walker Mill (c)	(301)	11,104	10,920
21793	Walkersville (c)	(301)	5,417	4,145
*21157	Westminster	(410)	17,128	13,060
20902	Wheaton-Glenmont (c)	(301)	57,694	53,720
21162	White Marsh (c)	(410)	8,485	8,183
20903	White Oak (c)	(301)	20,973	18,671
21207	Woodlawn (c) (Baltimore)	(301)	36,079	32,907
21284	Woodlawn (c) (Prince George's)	(410)	6,251	5,329
—	Woodmore (c)	(240)/(301)	6,077	2,874

Massachusetts

Area code (339) overlays area code (781). Area code (351) overlays (978). Area code (774) overlays (508). Area code (857) overlays (617). See introductory note.

ZIP	Place	Area Code	2002	1990
02351	Abington	(781)	15,255	13,817
01720	Acton	(978)	20,832	17,872
02743	Acushnet	(508)	10,477	9,554
01220	Adams	(413)	8,636	9,445
01220	Adams (c)	(413)	5,784	6,356
01001	Agawam	(413)	28,391	27,323
01913	Amesbury	(978)	16,680	14,997
01913	Amesbury (c)	(978)	12,327	12,109
*01002	Amherst	(413)	34,417	35,228
*01002	Amherst Center (c)	(413)	17,050	17,824
01810	Andover	(978)	7,900	8,242
01810	Andover	(978)	31,818	29,151
*02205	Arlington	(781)	42,140	44,630
01430	Ashburnham	(978)	5,732	5,433
01721	Ashland	(508)	15,392	12,066
01331	Athol	(978)	11,468	11,451
01331	Athol (c)	(978)	8,370	8,732
02703	Attleboro	(508)	43,164	38,383
01501	Auburn	(508)	16,287	15,005
01432	Ayer	(978)	7,304	6,871
02630	Barnstable Town	(508)	48,854	40,949
01005	Barre	(978)	5,295	1,094
01730	Bedford	(781)	12,647	12,996
01007	Belchertown	(413)	13,512	10,579
02019	Bellingham	(508)	15,592	14,877
02478	Belmont	(781)	24,045	24,720
02779	Berkley	(508)	6,133	4,237
01915	Beverly	(978)	40,235	38,195
*01821	Billerica	(978)	39,453	37,609
01504	Blackstone	(508)	9,007	8,023
—	Bliss Corner (c)		5,466	4,908
*02205	Boston	(617)	589,281	574,283
02532	Bourne	(508)	19,372	16,064
01921	Boxford	(978)	8,179	6,266
*02205	Braintree	(781)	33,917	33,836
02631	Brewster	(508)	10,363	8,440
*02324	Bridgewater (c)	(508)	6,664	7,242
02324	Bridgewater	(508)	25,620	21,249
*02303	Brockton	(508)	95,437	92,788
02446	Brookline	(617)	57,032	54,718
01803	Burlington	(781)	22,923	23,302
*02139	Cambridge	(617)	101,807	95,802
02021	Canton	(781)	21,341	18,530
02330	Carver	(508)	11,467	10,590
01507	Charlton	(508)	11,868	9,576
02633	Chatham	(508)	6,806	6,579
01824	Chelmsford	(978)	33,997	32,383
02150	Chelsea	(617)	34,913	28,710
*01020	Chicopee	(413)	54,833	56,632
01510	Clinton	(978)	13,733	13,222
01510	Clinton (c)	(978)	7,884	7,943
01778	Cochituate (c)	(508)	6,768	6,046
02025	Cohasset	(781)	7,307	7,075
01742	Concord	(978)	17,028	17,076
*01226	Dalton	(413)	6,792	7,155
01923	Danvers	(978)	25,446	24,174
02714	Dartmouth	(508)	30,767	27,244
*02026	Dedham	(781)	23,378	23,782
02638	Dennis	(508)	16,194	13,864
02715	Dighton	(508)	6,448	5,631
01516	Douglas	(508)	7,505	5,438
02030	Dover	(508)	5,669	4,915
01826	Dracut	(978)	28,828	25,594
01571	Dudley	(508)	10,509	9,540
*02332	Duxbury	(781)	14,578	13,895
02333	East Bridgewater	(508)	13,501	11,104
02536	East Falmouth (c)	(508)	6,615	5,577
02642	Eastham	(508)	5,618	4,462
01027	Easthampton	(413)	16,180	15,537
01028	East Longmeadow	(413)	14,505	13,367
02334	Easton	(508)	22,698	19,807
02149	Everett	(617)	37,772	35,701
02719	Fairhaven	(508)	16,349	16,132
*02722	Fall River	(508)	92,660	92,703
*02540	Falmouth	(508)	33,628	27,960
01420	Fitchburg	(978)	39,727	41,194
02035	Foxborough	(508)	16,401	14,637
02035	Foxborough (c)	(508)	5,509	5,706
*01701	Framingham	(508)	66,827	64,989
02038	Franklin	(508)	29,958	22,095
02702	Freetown	(508)	8,728	8,522
01440	Gardner	(978)	20,991	20,125
01833	Georgetown	(978)	7,717	6,384
*01930	Gloucester	(978)	30,664	28,716
01519	Grafton	(508)	15,739	13,035
01033	Granby	(413)	6,271	5,565
01230	Great Barrington	(413)	7,476	7,725
01301	Greenfield	(413)	18,005	18,666
01301	Greenfield (c)	(413)	13,716	14,016
01450	Groton	(978)	10,015	7,511
01834	Groveland	(978)	6,220	5,214
02338	Halifax	(781)	7,733	6,526
01936	Hamilton	(978)	8,420	7,280
01036	Hampden	(413)	5,252	—
02339	Hanover	(781)	13,596	11,912
02341	Hanson	(781)	9,827	9,028
01451	Harvard	(978)	6,093	12,329
02645	Harwich	(508)	12,801	10,275
*01830	Haverhill	(978)	59,634	51,418
*02018	Hingham (c)	(781)	5,352	5,454
02043	Hingham	(781)	20,221	19,821
02343	Holbrook	(781)	10,877	11,041
01520	Holden	(508)	16,137	14,628
01746	Holliston	(508)	13,989	12,926
*01040	Holyoke	(413)	39,869	43,704
01747	Hopedale	(508)	6,102	5,666
01748	Hopkinton	(508)	13,930	9,191
01749	Hudson	(978)	18,336	17,233
01749	Hudson (c)	(978)	14,388	14,267
02045	Hull	(781)	11,347	10,466
02601	Hyannis (c)	(508)	11,050	14,120
01938	Ipswich	(978)	13,270	11,873
02364	Kingston	(781)	5,380	4,774
02364	Kingston	(781)	12,156	9,045
02347	Lakeville	(508)	10,359	7,785
01523	Lancaster	(978)	7,501	6,661
*01842	Lawrence	(978)	72,451	70,207
01238	Lee	(413)	5,902	5,849
01524	Leicester	(508)	10,757	10,191
01240	Lenox	(413)	5,158	5,069
01453	Leominster	(978)	41,895	38,145
*02205	Lexington	(781)	30,663	28,974
01773	Lincoln	(781)	8,111	7,666
01460	Littleton	(978)	8,523	7,051
*01028	Longmeadow	(413)	15,652	15,467
*01853	Lowell	(978)	104,901	103,439
01056	Ludlow	(413)	21,678	18,820
01462	Lunenburg	(978)	9,783	9,117
*01901	Lynn	(781)	89,590	81,245
01940	Lynnfield	(781)	11,660	11,049
02148	Malden	(781)	56,155	53,884
01944	Manchester-by-the-Sea	(978)	5,307	5,286
*02048	Mansfield	(508)	22,827	16,568
02048	Mansfield Center (c)	(508)	7,320	7,170
01945	Marblehead	(781)	20,482	19,971
02738	Marion	(508)	5,280	4,496
01752	Marlborough	(508)	38,144	31,813
02050	Marshfield	(781)	24,815	21,531
02649	Mashpee	(508)	13,983	7,884
02739	Mattapoisett	(508)	6,409	5,850
01754	Maynard	(978)	10,446	10,325
02052	Medfield (c)	(508)	6,670	5,985
02052	Medfield	(508)	12,447	10,531
*02155	Medford	(781)	55,137	57,407
02053	Medway	(508)	12,888	9,931
02176	Melrose	(781)	26,963	28,150
01756	Mendon	(508)	5,581	—
01860	Merrimac	(978)	6,289	5,166
01844	Methuen	(978)	44,638	39,990
02346	Middleborough	(508)	20,722	17,867
02346	Middleborough Center (c)	(508)	6,913	6,837
01949	Middleton	(978)	8,781	4,921
01757	Milford	(508)	27,309	25,355
01757	Milford (c)	(508)	24,230	23,339
01527	Millbury	(508)	13,168	12,228
02054	Millis	(508)	8,015	7,613
02186	Milton	(617)	26,010	25,725
01057	Monson	(413)	8,534	7,776
01351	Montague	(413)	8,456	8,316
*02584	Nantucket	(508)	10,416	6,012
01760	Natick	(508)	32,384	30,510
*02205	Needham	(781)	29,197	27,557
*02740	New Bedford	(508)	94,088	99,922
01951	Newbury	(978)	6,852	5,623
01950	Newburyport	(978)	17,504	16,317
*02205	Newton	(617)	83,880	82,585
02056	Norfolk	(508)	10,500	9,259
01247	North Adams	(413)	14,430	16,797
01059	North Amherst (c)	(413)	6,019	6,239
*01060	Northampton	(413)	28,979	11,929
01845	North Andover	(978)	27,837	29,289
*02760	North Attleborough	(508)	27,826	22,792
02760	North Attleborough Center (c)	(508)	16,796	16,178
01532	Northborough (c)	(508)	6,257	5,761
01532	Northborough	(508)	14,246	13,371
01534	Northbridge	(508)	13,521	12,002
01864	North Reading	(978)	13,999	25,038
02060	North Scituate (c)	(781)	5,065	4,891
02766	Norton	(508)	18,567	14,265
02061	Norwell	(781)	10,166	9,279
02062	Norwood	(781)	28,844	28,700
02065	Ocean Bluff-Brant Rock (c)	(781)	5,100	4,541
01364	Orange	(978)	7,530	7,312
02653	Orleans	(508)	6,470	5,838

ZIP	Place	Area Code	2002	1990
01540	Oxford (c)	(508)	5,899	5,969
01540	Oxford	(508)	13,700	12,588
01069	Palmer	(413)	12,708	12,054
*01960	Peabody	(978)	49,668	47,264
02359	Pembroke	(781)	17,541	14,544
01463	Pepperell	(978)	11,418	10,098
01866	Pinehurst (c)	(978)	6,941	6,614
*01201	Pittsfield	(413)	45,023	48,622
02762	Plainville	(508)	7,914	6,871
*02360	Plymouth (c)	(508)	7,658	7,258
*02360	Plymouth	(508)	53,789	45,608
*02205	Quincy	(617)	89,187	84,985
02368	Randolph	(781)	31,044	30,093
02767	Raynham	(508)	12,276	9,867
01867	Reading	(781)	23,680	22,539
02769	Rehoboth	(508)	10,721	8,656
02151	Revere	(781)	47,496	42,786
02370	Rockland	(781)	18,026	16,123
01966	Rockport (c)	(978)	5,606	5,448
01966	Rockport	(978)	7,816	7,482
01969	Rowley	(978)	5,574	4,452
01543	Rutland	(508)	6,808	4,936
*01970	Salem	(978)	42,149	38,091
01952	Salisbury	(978)	7,955	6,882
02563	Sandwich	(508)	20,792	15,489
01906	Saugus	(781)	26,415	25,549
02066	Scituate (c)	(781)	5,069	5,180
02066	Scituate	(781)	18,152	16,786
02771	Seekonk	(508)	13,670	13,046
02067	Sharon	(781)	17,536	15,517
02067	Sharon (c)	(781)	5,941	5,893
01464	Shirley	(978)	6,540	6,118
01545	Shrewsbury	(508)	32,751	24,146
*02722	Somerset	(508)	18,654	17,655
*02205	Somerville	(617)	76,922	76,210
01002	South Amherst (c)	(413)	5,039	5,053
01073	Southampton	(413)	5,595	—
01772	Southborough	(508)	9,202	6,628
01550	Southbridge	(508)	17,398	17,816
01550	Southbridge (c)	(508)	12,878	13,631
01075	South Hadley	(413)	17,248	16,685
01077	Southwick	(413)	9,123	7,667
02664	South Yarmouth (c)	(508)	11,603	10,358
01562	Spencer (c)	(508)	6,032	6,306
01562	Spencer	(508)	11,930	11,645
*01101	Springfield	(413)	151,915	156.983
01564	Sterling	(978)	7,569	6,481
02180	Stoneham	(781)	22,165	22,203
02072	Stoughton	(781)	27,227	26,777
01775	Stow	(978)	6,084	5,328
01566	Sturbridge	(508)	8,247	7,775
01776	Sudbury	(978)	17,259	14,358
01590	Sutton	(508)	8,705	6,824
01907	Swampscott	(781)	14,461	13,650
02777	Swansea	(508)	16,178	15,411
02780	Taunton	(508)	56,647	49,832
01468	Templeton	(978)	7,143	6,438
01876	Tewksbury	(978)	29,355	27,266
01983	Topsfield	(978)	6,234	5,754
01469	Townsend	(978)	9,317	8,496
01879	Tyngsborough	(978)	11,330	8,642
01568	Upton	(508)	6,006	4,677
01569	Uxbridge	(508)	11,764	10,415
01880	Wakefield	(781)	24,817	24,825
*02081	Walpole (c)	(508)	5,867	5,495
02081	Walpole	(508)	23,199	20,223
*02205	Waltham	(781)	59,073	57,878
01082	Ware (c)	(413)	6,174	6,533
01082	Ware	(413)	9,823	9,808
02571	Wareham	(508)	20,935	19,232
*02205	Watertown	(781)	32,857	33,284
01778	Wayland	(508)	13,239	11,874
01570	Webster	(508)	16,736	16,196
01570	Webster (c)	(508)	11,600	11,849
*02205	Wellesley	(781)	26,671	26,615
01581	Westborough	(508)	18,543	14,133
01583	West Boylston	(508)	7,609	6,611
02379	West Bridgewater	(508)	6,835	6,389
01742	West Concord (c)	(978)	5,632	5,761
*01085	Westfield	(413)	40,314	38,372
01886	Westford	(978)	21,249	16,392
01473	Westminster	(978)	7,149	6,191
02493	Weston	(781)	11,652	10,200
02790	Westport	(508)	14,556	13,852
*01089	West Springfield	(413)	27,984	27,537
02090	Westwood	(781)	14,181	12,557
02673	West Yarmouth (c)	(508)	6,460	5,409
*02205	Weymouth	(781)	54,754	54.063
01588	Whitinsville (c)	(508)	6,340	5,639
02382	Whitman	(781)	14,341	13,240
01095	Wilbraham	(413)	13,726	12,635
01267	Williamstown	(413)	8,333	8,220
01887	Wilmington	(978)	21,629	17,651
01475	Winchendon	(978)	9,909	8,805
01890	Winchester	(781)	21,093	20,267
02152	Winthrop	(617)	18,235	18,127
*01801	Woburn	(781)	38,003	35,943

ZIP	Place	Area Code	2002	1990
*01613	Worcester	(508)	174,962	169,759
02093	Wrentham	(508)	10,951	9,006
02675	Yarmouth	(508)	25,236	21,174
02675	Yarmouth Port (c)	(508)	5,395	4,271

Michigan

Area code (947) overlays area code (248). See introductory note.

ZIP	Place	Area Code	2002	1990
49221	Adrian	(517)	21,359	22,097
49224	Albion	(517)	9,086	10,066
49401	Allendale(c)	(616)	11,555	6,950
48101	Allen Park	(313)	29,147	31,092
48801	Alma	(989)	9,296	9,034
49707	Alpena	(989)	11,071	11,354
*48106	Ann Arbor	(734)	115,213	109,608
*48321	Auburn Hills	(248)	20,328	17,076
*49016	Battle Creek	(269)	53,650	53,516
48707	Bay City	(989)	35,844	38,936
48505	Beecher (c)	(810)	12,793	14,465
48809	Belding	(616)	5,801	5,969
*49022	Benton Harbor	(269)	11,052	12,818
49022	Benton Heights(c)	(269)	5,458	5,465
48072	Berkley	(248)	15,369	16,960
48025	Beverly Hills	(248)	10,311	10,610
49307	Big Rapids	(231)	10,321	12,603
48012	Birmingham	(248)	19,280	19,997
48301	Bloomfield (c)	(248)	43,021	42,137
48722	Bridgeport (c)	(989)	7,849	8,569
*48116	Brighton	(810)	6,991	5,686
49601	Buena Vista (c)	(989)	7,845	8,196
48501	Burton	(810)	30,385	27,437
49601	Cadillac	(231)	10,034	10,104
48185	Canton (c)	(734)	76,366	57,047
48724	Carrollton (c)	(989)	6,602	6,521
48015	Center Line	(586)	8,480	9,026
48813	Charlotte	(517)	8,817	8,083
49721	Cheboygan	(231)	5,276	4,997
48017	Clawson	(248)	12,568	13,874
*48046	Clinton (c)	(517)	95,648	85,866
49036	Coldwater	(517)	10,697	9,607
49321	Comstock Park (c)	(616)	10,674	6,530
49508	Cutlerville (c)	(616)	15,114	11,228
48423	Davison	(810)	5,482	5,693
*48120	Dearborn	(313)	97,833	89,286
*48127	Dearborn Heights	(313)	58,047	60,838
*48231	Detroit	(313)	925,051	1,027,974
49047	Dowagiac	(269)	6,034	6,418
49506	East Grand Rapids	(616)	10,677	10,807
*48826	East Lansing	(517)	46,272	50,677
48021	Eastpointe	(586)	33,866	35,283
49001	Eastwood (c)	(269)	6,265	6,340
48827	Eaton Rapids	(517)	5,329	4,695
48229	Ecorse	(313)	11,248	12,180
49829	Escanaba	(906)	12,814	13,659
49022	Fair Plain (c)	(269)	7,828	8,051
*48333	Farmington	(248)	10,267	10,170
48333	Farmington Hills	(248)	81,427	74,614
48430	Fenton	(810)	11,832	8,434
48220	Ferndale	(248)	21,858	25,084
48134	Flat Rock	(734)	8,726	7,290
*48501	Flint	(810)	121,763	140,925
48433	Flushing	(810)	8,240	8,542
49506	Forest Hills (c)	(616)	20,942	16,690
48026	Fraser	(586)	15,309	13,899
48623	Freeland (c)	(989)	5,147	1,421
*48135	Garden City	(734)	29,880	31,846
49837	Gladstone	(906)	5,272	4,565
48439	Grand Blanc	(810)	8,088	7,760
49417	Grand Haven	(616)	10,930	11,951
48837	Grand Ledge	(517)	7,841	7,562
*49501	Grand Rapids	(616)	196.595	189,126
*49418	Grandville	(616)	16,598	15,624
48838	Greenville	(616)	8,142	8,101
48138	Grosse Ile (c)	(734)	10,894	9,781
*48231	Grosse Pointe	(313)	5,634	5,681
48230	Grosse Pointe Farms	(313)	9,682	10,092
48230	Grosse Pointe Park	(313)	12,352	12,857
48230	Grosse Pointe Woods	(313)	16,935	17.715
48212	Hamtramck	(313)	22,752	18,372
48225	Harper Woods	(313)	14,133	14,903
48625	Harrison (c)	(989)	24.461	24,685
48840	Haslett (c)	(517)	11,283	10,230
49058	Hastings	(269)	7,091	6,549
48030	Hazel Park	(248)	18,690	20,051
48203	Highland Park	(313)	16,281	20,121
49242	Hillsdale	(517)	8,059	8,175
*49423	Holland	(616)	34,688	30,745
48842	Holly	(248)	6,134	5,595
48842	Holt (c)	(517)	11,315	11,744
49931	Houghton	(906)	7,005	7,498
*48844	Howell	(517)	9,463	8,147
49426	Hudsonville	(616)	7,161	6,170
48070	Huntington Woods	(248)	6,066	6,419
48141	Inkster	(313)/(734)	29,895	30,772
48846	Ionia	(616)	11,029	10,349
49801	Iron Mountain	(906)	8,038	8,525
49938	Ironwood	(906)	6,021	6,849
49849	Ishpeming	(906)	6,556	7,200
*49204	Jackson	(517)	35,514	37,425

ZIP	Place	Area Code	2002	1990
*49428	Jenison (c)	(616)	17,211	17,882
*49001	Kalamazoo	(269)	75,858	80,277
49518	Kentwood	(616)	46,317	37,826
49802	Kingsford	(906)	5,474	5,480
48144	Lambertville (c)	(734)	9,299	7,860
*48901	Lansing	(517)	118,588	127,321
48446	Lapeer	(810)	9,395	7,759
48146	Lincoln Park	(313)	39,659	41,832
*48150	Livonia	(734)	100,341	100,850
49431	Ludington	(231)	8,434	8,507
48071	Madison Heights	(248)	30,698	32,196
49660	Manistee	(231)	6,379	6,734
49855	Marquette	(906)	20,547	21,977
49068	Marshall	(269)	7,315	6,941
48040	Marysville	(810)	9,831	8,515
48854	Mason	(517)	7,016	6,768
48122	Melvindale	(313)	10,656	11,216
49858	Menominee	(906)	8,902	9,398
*48640	Midland	(989)	42,080	38,053
*48381	Milford	(248)	6,270	5,500
*48161	Monroe	(734)	22,029	22,902
*48046	Mount Clemens	(586)	17,360	18,405
*48804	Mount Pleasant	(989)	26,018	23,299
*49440	Muskegon	(231)	39,431	39,809
49444	Muskegon Heights	(231)	11,857	13,176
*48047	New Baltimore	(586)	9,014	5,798
49120	Niles	(269)	11,974	12,458
49505	Northview (c)	(616)	14,730	13,712
48167	Northville	(248)	6,487	6,226
49441	Norton Shores	(231)	23,084	21,755
*48376	Novi	(248)	49,114	32,998
48237	Oak Park	(248)	29,427	30,468
*48805	Okemos (c)	(517)	22,805	20,216
48867	Owosso	(989)	15,479	16,322
49770	Petoskey	(231)	6,169	6,056
48170	Plymouth	(734)	8,984	9,560
48170	Plymouth Township (c)	(734)	27,798	23,646
*48343	Pontiac	(248)	66,137	71,136
*49081	Portage	(269)	44,994	41,042
*48061	Port Huron	(810)	32,304	33,694
*48231	Redford (c)	(313)	51,622	54,387
48062	Richmond	(586)	5,230	4,028
48218	River Rouge	(313)	9,737	11,314
48192	Riverview	(734)	13,201	13,894
*48308	Rochester	(248)	10,770	7,130
48306	Rochester Hills	(248)	68,601	61,766
48174	Romulus	(313)/(734)	23,596	22,897
48066	Roseville	(586)	48,336	51,412
*48068	Royal Oak	(248)	59,220	65,410
*48605	Saginaw	(989)	60,096	69,512
48604	Saginaw Township North (c)	(989)	24,994	23,018
48603	Saginaw Township South (c)	(989)	13,801	13,987
48079	Saint Clair	(810)	5,860	5,116
*48080	Saint Clair Shores	(313)	62,737	68,107
48879	Saint Johns	(989)	7,642	7,392
49085	Saint Joseph	(269)	8,660	9,214
48176	Saline	(734)	8,523	6,663
49783	Sault Sainte Marie	(906)	14,264	14,689
49455	Shelby (c)	(231)	65,159	48,655
48609	Shields (c)	(989)	6,590	6,634
*48037	Southfield	(248)	77,859	75,727
48195	Southgate	(734)	30,399	30,771
48178	South Lyon	(248)	10,664	6,479
48161	South Monroe (c)	(734)	6,370	5,266
49015	Springfield	(269)	5,230	5,582
*48311	Sterling Heights	(586)	126,146	117,810
49091	Sturgis	(269)	11,120	10,130
48473	Swartz Creek	(810)	5,203	4,851
48180	Taylor	(313)/(734)	65,893	70,811
49286	Tecumseh	(517)	8,704	7,462
48182	Temperance (c)	(734)	7,757	6,542
49093	Three Rivers	(269)	7,167	7,464
*49684	Traverse City	(231)	14,468	15,155
48183	Trenton	(734)	19,615	20,586
*48099	Troy	(248)	80,912	72,884
49504	Walker	(616)	23,040	17,279
*48390	Walled Lake	(248)	6,653	6,278
*48090	Warren	(586)	137,672	144,864
*48329	Waterford (c)	(248)	73,150	66,692
48917	Waverly (c)	(517)	16,194	15,614
48184	Wayne	(734)	19,021	19,899
*48325	West Bloomfield Township (c)	(248)	64,862	54,843
*48185	Westland	(313)/(734)	86,282	84,724
49019	Westwood (c)	(269)	9,122	8,957
48189	Whitmore Lake (c)	(734)	6,574	3,251
48393	Wixom	(248)	13,529	8,550
48183	Woodhaven	(734)	12,764	11,631
48192	Wyandotte	(734)	27,845	30,938
49509	Wyoming	(616)	70,328	63,891
*48197	Ypsilanti	(734)	22,816	24,846
49464	Zeeland	(616)	5,702	5,417

Minnesota

ZIP	Place	Area Code	2002	1990
56007	Albert Lea	(507)	18,013	18,310
56308	Alexandria	(320)	9,456	8,029
55304	Andover	(763)	28,544	15,216
*55303	Anoka	(612)/(763)	17,939	17,192
55124	Apple Valley	(952)	48,480	34,598
55112	Arden Hills	(651)	9,910	9,199

ZIP	Place	Area Code	2002	1990
55912	Austin	(507)	23,501	21,926
56425	Baxter	(218)	6,227	3,695
*56601	Bemidji	(218)	12,374	11,165
55309	Big Lake	(763)	7,385	3,113
55014	Blaine	(651)/(763)	48,535	38,975
*55420	Bloomington	(952)	84,092	86,335
56401	Brainerd	(218)	13,312	12,353
55429	Brooklyn Center	(763)	28,753	28,887
55443	Brooklyn Park	(763)	68,128	56,381
55313	Buffalo	(763)	11,655	7,302
*55337	Burnsville	(651)/(952)	60,033	51,288
55008	Cambridge	(763)	5,879	5,094
55316	Champlin	(763)	22,925	16,849
55317	Chanhassen	(952)	21,410	11,736
55318	Chaska	(952)	19,416	11,339
55720	Cloquet	(218)	11,322	10,885
55421	Columbia Heights	(612)/(763)	18,572	18,910
55433	Coon Rapids	(763)	62,329	52,978
55340	Corcoran	(763)	5,747	5,199
55016	Cottage Grove	(651)	31,090	22,935
56716	Crookston	(218)	8,050	8,119
*54028	Crystal	(763)	22,524	23,788
*56501	Detroit Lakes	(218)	7,557	7,141
*55806	Duluth	(218)	86,419	85,493
55121	Eagan	(651)/(952)	64,047	47,409
55005	East Bethel	(763)	11,488	8,050
56721	East Grand Forks	(218)	7,538	8,658
*55344	Eden Prairie	(612)/(952)	57,341	39,311
55424	Edina	(952)	47,114	46,075
55330	Elk River	(763)	18,055	11,143
56031	Fairmont	(507)	10,679	11,265
55113	Falcon Heights	(651)	5,523	5,380
55021	Faribault	(507)	21,340	17,085
55024	Farmington	(651)/(952)	14,721	5,940
56537	Fergus Falls	(218)	13,820	12,362
55025	Forest Lake	(651)	15,098	5,833
55432	Fridley	(763)	27,388	28,335
55336	Glencoe	(320)	5,462	4,648
55427	Golden Valley	(763)	20,721	20,971
*55744	Grand Rapids	(218)	7,778	7,976
55304	Ham Lake	(763)	13,750	8,924
55033	Hastings	(651)	19,093	15,478
55810	Hermantown	(218)	8,173	6,761
*55746	Hibbing	(218)	16,975	18,046
55343	Hopkins	(952)	17,106	16,529
55038	Hugo	(651)	8,343	4,417
55350	Hutchinson	(320)	13,243	11,459
56649	International Falls	(218)	6,467	8,325
*55076	Inver Grove Heights	(651)	30,745	22,477
55041	Lake City	(651)	5,115	4,490
55042	Lake Elmo	(651)	7,495	5,900
55044	Lakeville	(952)	46,402	24,854
55014	Lino Lakes	(651)	18,270	8,807
55355	Litchfield	(320)	6,582	6,041
55117	Little Canada	(651)	9,847	8,971
56345	Little Falls	(320)	7,848	7,371
55115	Mahtomedi	(651)	8,066	5,633
56001	Mankato	(507)	33,158	31,459
55311	Maple Grove	(763)	56,709	38,736
55109	Maplewood	(651)	35,712	30,954
56258	Marshall	(507)	12,686	12,023
55118	Mendota Heights	(651)	11,474	9,388
*55440	Minneapolis	(612)/(763)/(952)	375,635	368,383
55345	Minnetonka	(952)	51,120	48,370
56265	Montevideo	(320)	5,425	5,499
55362	Monticello	(763)	9,117	5,045
*56560	Moorhead	(218)	32,582	32,295
56267	Morris	(320)	5,133	5,613
55364	Mound	(952)	9,371	9,634
55112	Mounds View	(763)	12,722	12,541
55112	New Brighton	(651)	22,057	22,207
54427	New Hope	(763)	20,599	21,853
56071	New Prague	(952)	5,073	3,575
56073	New Ulm	(507)	13,465	13,132
55056	North Branch	(651)/(763)	9,064	4,267
55057	Northfield	(507)	17,820	14,684
56001	North Mankato	(507)	12,053	10,662
55109	North Saint Paul	(651)	11,838	12,376
55128	Oakdale	(651)	27,584	18,377
55011	Oak Grove	(763)	7,218	5,488
55323	Orono	(952)	7,636	7,285
55330	Otsego	(763)	6,683	5,219
55060	Owatonna	(507)	23,004	19,386
55446	Plymouth	(763)	67,304	50,889
55372	Prior Lake	(952)	18,123	11,482
55303	Ramsey	(763)	19,078	12,408
55066	Red Wing	(651)	16,035	15,134
56283	Redwood Falls	(507)	5,348	4,859
55423	Richfield	(612)	34,697	35,710
55422	Robbinsdale	(763)	13,879	14,396
*55901	Rochester	(507)	90,515	70,729
55374	Rogers	(763)	5,471	722
55068	Rosemount	(651)/(952)	16,262	8,622
55113	Roseville	(651)	33,449	33,485
55418	Saint Anthony	(612)	7,974	7,727
*56301	Saint Cloud	(320)	59,752	48,812
55070	Saint Francis	(763)	5,925	2,479
55426	Saint Louis Park	(952)	44,123	43,787
*55334	Saint Michael	(763)	11,615	2,506
*55101	Saint Paul	(651)	284,037	272,235

ZIP	Place	Area Code	2002	1990
55071	Saint Paul Park	(651)	5,042	4,965
56082	Saint Peter	(507)	9,873	9,481
56377	Sartell	(320)	11,036	5,409
56379	Sauk Rapids	(320)	11,395	7,823
56378	Savage	(952)	24,811	9,906
55379	Shakopee	(612)	25,316	11,739
55126	Shoreview	(651)	26,935	24,587
55331	Shorewood	(952)	7,611	5,913
55075	South Saint Paul	(651)	19,906	20,197
55432	Spring Lake Park	(763)	6,803	6,532
55976	Stewartville	(507)	5,488	4,520
*55082	Stillwater	(651)	16,192	13,882
56701	Thief River Falls	(218)	8,373	8,010
55127	Vadnais Heights	(651)	13,223	11,041
*55792	Virginia	(218)	8,989	9,432
55387	Waconia	(952)	7,610	3,498
56387	Waite Park	(320)	6,802	5,020
56093	Waseca	(507)	9,602	8,385
55118	West Saint Paul	(651)	19,740	19,248
*55110	White Bear Lake	(651)	24,465	24,622
56201	Willmar	(320)	18,081	17,531
55987	Winona	(507)	26,537	25,435
55125	Woodbury	(651)	49,163	20,075
56187	Worthington	(507)	11,091	9,977

Mississippi

ZIP	Place	Area Code	2002	1990
39730	Aberdeen	(662)	6,288	6,837
38821	Amory	(662)	6,804	7,093
38606	Batesville	(662)	7,496	6,403
*39520	Bay Saint Louis	(228)	8,143	8,063
*39530	Biloxi	(228)	49,800	46,319
38829	Booneville	(662)	8,619	7,955
*39042	Brandon	(601)	17,494	11,089
*39601	Brookhaven	(601)	9,807	10,243
39272	Byram (c)	(601)	7,386	—
39046	Canton	(601)	12,955	11,723
38614	Clarksdale	(662)	20,290	21,180
*38732	Cleveland	(662)	13,398	15,384
*39056	Clinton	(601)	24,082	21,847
39429	Columbia	(601)	6,425	6,815
*39701	Columbus	(662)	25,252	23,799
*38834	Corinth	(662)	14,019	11,820
39059	Crystal Springs	(601)	5,827	5,643
39525	Diamondhead (c)	(228)	5,912	2,661
39532	D'Iberville	(228)	7,622	6,566
39232	Flowood	(601)	6,188	2,770
39074	Forest	(601)	5,929	5,062
39553	Gautier	(228)	11,734	10,088
*38701	Greenville	(662)	40,286	45,226
*38930	Greenwood	(662)	17,773	18,906
*38901	Grenada	(662)	14,704	10,864
39564	Gulf Hills(c)	(228)	5,900	5,004
*39501	Gulfport	(228)	72,511	64,045
*39401	Hattiesburg	(601)	45,773	45,325
38632	Hernando		7,788	3,125
*38635	Holly Springs	(662)	7,977	7,261
38637	Horn Lake	(662)	14,664	9,069
38751	Indianola	(662)	11,775	11,809
*39205	Jackson	(601)	180,881	202,062
39090	Kosciusko	(662)	7,391	6,986
*39440	Laurel	(601)	18,076	18,827
38756	Leland	(662)	5,319	6,366
39560	Long Beach	(228)	17,003	15,804
39339	Louisville	(662)	6,896	7,165
*39648	McComb	(601)	13,182	11,797
*39110	Madison	(601)	15,418	7,471
*39302	Meridian	(601)	39,518	41,036
*39563	Moss Point	(228)	15,476	17,837
*39120	Natchez	(601)	17,864	19,460
38652	New Albany	(662)	7,797	6,775
*39564	Ocean Springs	(228)	17,306	15,221
38654	Olive Branch	(662)	23,371	3,567
38655	Oxford	(662)	12,487	10,026
*39567	Pascagoula	(228)	25,990	25,899
39571	Pass Christian	(228)	6,655	5,557
39288	Pearl	(601)	22,642	19,588
39465	Petal	(601)	7,636	7,883
39350	Philadelphia	(601)	7,285	6,758
39466	Picayune	(601)	10,651	10,633
38863	Pontotoc	(662)	5,558	4,570
39218	Richland	(601)	6,279	4,014
*39157	Ridgeland	(601)	20,693	11,714
38663	Ripley	(662)	5,531	5,371
39533	Saint Martin(c)	(228)	6,676	6,349
38668	Senatobia	(601)	6,704	4,772
38671	Southaven	(662)	33,161	18,705
*39759	Starkville	(662)	22,204	18,458
*38801	Tupelo	(662)	34,975	30,685
*39180	Vicksburg	(601)	26,226	26,886
39576	Waveland	(228)	6,737	5,369
39367	Waynesboro	(601)	5,146	5,143
—	West Hattiesburg(c)	(601)	6,305	5,450
39773	West Point	(662)	11,990	8,489
38967	Winona	(662)	5,127	5,965
39194	Yazoo City	(662)	12,076	12,427

Missouri

ZIP	Place	Area Code	2002	1990
63123	Affton(c)	(314)	20,535	21,106
63010	Arnold	(636)	19,962	18,828
65605	Aurora	(417)	7,097	6,459
*63011	Ballwin	(636)	31,265	27,054
63012	Barnhart (c)	(314)	6,108	4,911
63137	Bellefontaine Neighbors	(314)	10,987	10,918
64012	Belton	(816)	23,214	18,145
63134	Berkeley	(314)	9,960	12,250
63031	Black Jack	(314)	6,945	6,131
*64015	Blue Springs	(816)	49,451	40,103
65613	Bolivar	(417)	9,455	6,845
65233	Boonville	(660)	8,438	7,095
63334	Bowling Green	(573)	5,203	3,046
*65615	Branson	(417)	5,999	3,706
63144	Brentwood	(314)	7,594	8,150
63044	Bridgeton	(314)	15,563	17,732
64429	Cameron	(816)	8,326	6,782
*63701	Cape Girardeau	(573)	35,665	34,475
64834	Carl Junction	(417)	5,673	4,123
64836	Carthage	(417)	12,810	10,747
63830	Caruthersville	(573)	6,636	7,389
63834	Charleston	(573)	5,465	5,131
*63017	Chesterfield	(636)	47,126	42,325
64601	Chillicothe	(660)	8,732	8,799
63105	Clayton	(314)	16,049	13,926
64735	Clinton	(660)	9,287	8,703
*65201	Columbia	(573)	86,981	69,133
63128	Concord(c)	(314)	16,689	19,859
63126	Crestwood	(314)	11,874	11,229
63141	Creve Coeur	(314)	16,763	12,289
*63135	Dellwood	(314)	5,195	5,245
63020	De Soto	(636)	6,522	5,993
63131	Des Peres	(314)	8,659	8,395
63841	Dexter	(573)	7,429	7,506
63011	Ellisville	(636)	9,203	7,183
63025	Eureka	(636)	8,378	4,683
64024	Excelsior Springs	(816)	11,138	10,373
63640	Farmington	(573)	14,085	11,596
63135	Ferguson	(314)	22,132	22,290
63028	Festus	(636)	9,757	8,105
*63033	Florissant	(314)	49,976	51,038
65473	Fort Leonard Wood(c)	(573)	13,656	15,863
65251	Fulton	(573)	12,767	10,033
64118	Gladstone	(816)	26,778	26,243
65254	Glasgow Village(c)	(573)	5,234	5,199
63122	Glendale	(314)	5,708	5,945
64029	Grain Valley	(816)	6,250	1,898
64030	Grandview	(816)	25,542	24,973
63401	Hannibal	(573)	17,517	18,004
64701	Harrisonville	(816)	9,264	7,696
63042	Hazelwood	(314)	26,042	15,512
*64050	Independence	(816)	113,027	112,301
63755	Jackson	(573)	12,304	9,256
*65101	Jefferson City	(573)	39,079	35,517
63136	Jennings	(314)	15,318	15,841
*64801	Joplin	(417)	46,187	41,175
64108	Kansas City	(816)	443,471	434,829
64060	Kearney	(816)	6,313	1,790
63857	Kennett	(573)	11,156	10,941
63501	Kirksville	(660)	17,282	17,152
63122	Kirkwood	(314)	27,425	28,318
63124	Ladue (St. Louis Co.)	(314)	8,626	8,795
63367	Lake Saint Louis	(636)	10,982	7,536
65536	Lebanon	(417)	12,386	9,983
*64063	Lee's Summit	(816)	74,948	46,418
63125	Lemay(c)	(314)	17,215	18,005
64068	Liberty	(816)	27,532	20,459
63552	Macon	(660)	5,427	5,571
63011	Manchester	(636)	19,186	6,506
63143	Maplewood	(314)	9,081	9,962
65340	Marshall	(660)	12,089	12,711
65706	Marshfield	(417)	6,131	4,374
63043	Maryland Heights	(314)	25,782	25,440
64468	Maryville	(816)	10,565	10,663
63129	Mehlville(c)	(314)	28,822	27,557
65265	Mexico	(573)	11,011	11,290
65270	Moberly	(660)	13,612	12,839
65708	Monett	(417)	7,586	6,529
63026	Murphy(c)	(636)	9,048	9,342
64850	Neosho	(417)	10,597	9,254
64772	Nevada	(417)	8,451	8,597
65714	Nixa	(417)	13,671	4,893
63121	Normandy	(314)	5,095	4,480
64075	Oak Grove	(816)	6,486	4,565
63129	Oakville(c)	(314)	35,309	31,750
63366	O'Fallon	(636)	59,678	17,427
63132	Olivette	(314)	7,552	7,573
63114	Overland	(314)	16,606	17,987
65721	Ozark	(417)	11,651	4,401
63069	Pacific	(636)	5,643	4,350
63601	Park Hills	(573)	8,252	7,866
63775	Perryville	(573)	7,743	6,933
64080	Pleasant Hill	(816)	6,019	3,827
*63901	Poplar Bluff	(573)	16,595	16,841
64083	Raymore	(816)	12,612	5,592
64133	Raytown	(816)	30,060	30,601
65738	Republic	(417)	9,378	6,290
64085	Richmond	(816)	6,099	5,738

ZIP	Place	Area Code	2002	1990
63117	Richmond Heights	(314)	9,500	10,448
*65401	Rolla	(573)	16,962	14,090
63074	Saint Ann	(314)	13,532	14,449
*63301	Saint Charles	(636)	60,755	50,634
63114	Saint John	(314)	6,778	7,502
*64501	Saint Joseph	(816)	73,148	71,852
*63166	Saint Louis	(314)	338,353	396,685
63376	Saint Peters	(636)	53,596	40,660
63126	Sappington(c)	(314)	7,287	10,917
*65301	Sedalia	(660)	20,225	19,800
63119	Shrewsbury	(314)	6,571	6,416
63801	Sikeston	(573)	16,865	17,641
64089	Smithville	(816)	5,990	2,525
63138	Spanish Lake(c)	(314)	21,337	20,322
*65801	Springfield	(417)	151,010	140,494
63080	Sullivan	(573)	6,414	5,661
63127	Sunset Hills	(314)	8,363	4,915
63006	Town and Country	(314)	10,951	10,944
64683	Trenton	(660)	6,076	6,129
63379	Troy	(314)	7,668	3,811
63084	Union	(636)	8,193	6,196
63130	University City	(314)	37,851	40,087
63088	Valley Park	(636)	6,443	4,165
64093	Warrensburg	(660)	16,938	15,244
63383	Warrenton	(636)	5,792	3,564
63090	Washington	(636)	13,461	11,367
64870	Webb City	(417)	10,151	7,538
63119	Webster Groves	(314)	23,414	22,992
63304	Weldon Spring	(636)	5,289	1,470
63385	Wentzville	(636)	9,992	4,640
65775	West Plains	(417)	10,835	9,214
*63011	Wildwood	(314)	33,870	16,742

Montana (406)

ZIP	Place		2002	1990
59711	Anaconda		9,069	10,356
59714	Belgrade		6,588	3,422
*59101	Billings		92,008	81,125
*59718	Bozeman		29,459	22,660
*59701	Butte		32,716	33,336
59901	Evergreen (c)		6,215	4,109
*59401	Great Falls		56,046	55,125
59501	Havre		9,454	10,201
*59601	Helena		26,353	24,609
—	Helena Valley Southeast (c)		7,141	4,601
—	Helena Valley West Central(c)		6,983	6,327
*59901	Kalispell		15,463	11,917
59044	Laurel		6,268	5,686
59457	Lewistown		5,899	6,097
59047	Livingston		7,018	6,701
59301	Miles City		8,224	8,461
*59801	Missoula		59,518	42,918
59801	Orchard Homes(c)		5,199	10,317
59937	Whitefish		5,489	4,368

Nebraska

ZIP	Place	Area Code	2002	1990
69301	Alliance	(308)	8,727	9,765
68310	Beatrice	(402)	12,805	12,352
*68108	Bellevue	(402)	46,217	39,240
*68008	Blair	(402)	7,689	6,860
69337	Chadron	(308)	5,592	5,588
68108	Chalco(c)	(402)	10,736	7,337
68601	Columbus	(402)	20,877	19,480
68333	Crete	(402)	6,195	4,841
68022	Elkhorn	(402)	7,779	1,398
*68025	Fremont	(402)	25,188	23,680
69341	Gering	(308)	7,767	7,946
*68802	Grand Island	(308)	43,010	39,487
*68901	Hastings	(402)	23,908	22,837
68949	Holdrege	(308)	5,513	5,671
*68847	Kearney	(308)	27,910	24,396
68128	La Vista	(402)	12,960	9,992
68850	Lexington	(308)	10,118	6,600
*68501	Lincoln	(402)	232,362	191,972
69001	McCook	(308)	7,939	8,112
68410	Nebraska City	(402)	7,122	6,547
*68701	Norfolk	(402)	24,183	21,476
*69101	North Platte	(308)	23,674	22,605
68113	Offutt AFB (c)	(402)	8,901	
*68005	Omaha	(402)	399,357	344,463
*68046	Papillion	(402)	17,318	13,892
68048	Plattsmouth	(402)	6,941	6,415
68127	Ralston	(402)	6,264	6,236
68661	Schuyler	(402)	5,419	4,052
*69361	Scottsbluff	(308)	14,689	13,711
68434	Seward	(402)	6,561	5,641
69162	Sidney	(308)	6,468	5,959
68776	South Sioux City	(402)	11,969	9,677
68787	Wayne	(402)	5,413	5,142
68467	York	(402)	7,890	7,940

Nevada

ZIP	Place	Area Code	2002	1990
*89005	Boulder City	(702)	15,364	12,567
*89701	Carson City	(775)	54,311	40,443
89403	Dayton (c)	(775)	5,907	2,217
*89801	Elko	(775)	16,278	14,836
—	Enterprise (c)		14,676	6,412
*89406	Fallon	(775)	7,496	6,430
89408	Fernley	(775)	8,959	5,164

ZIP	Place	Area Code	2002	1990
89410	Gardnerville Ranchos (c)	(775)	11,054	7,455
*89015	Henderson	(702)	206,153	64,948
89450	Incline Village-Crystal Bay (c)	(775)	9,952	7,119
*89125	Las Vegas	(702)	508,604	258,877
89028	Laughlin (c)	(702)	7,076	4,791
89506	Lemmon Valley-Golden Valley (c)	(702)	6,855	
*89024	Mesquite	(702)	11,264	1,871
89040	Moapa Valley (c)	(702)	5,784	3,444
89191	Nellis AFB (c)	(702)	8,896	8,377
*89030	North Las Vegas	(702)	135,902	47,849
*89041	Pahrump (c)	(775)	24,631	7,424
89109	Paradise (c)	(775)	186,070	124,682
*89501	Reno	(775)	190,248	134,230
89434	Spanish Springs (c)	(775)	9,018	
*89431	Sparks	(775)	73,730	53,367
89815	Spring Creek (c)	(702)	10,548	5,866
—	Spring Valley (c)	(702)	117,390	51,726
89110	Sunrise Manor (c)	(702)	156,120	95,362
89433	Sun Valley (c)	(775)	19,461	11,391
*89161	Winchester (c)	(702)	26,958	23,365
*89445	Winnemucca	(775)	6,709	6,473

New Hampshire (603)
See introductory note.

ZIP	Place	2002	1990
03031	Amherst	11,305	9,068
03811	Atkinson	6,606	5,188
03825	Barrington	7,913	6,164
03110	Bedford	19,842	12,563
03220	Belmont	7,090	5,796
03570	Berlin	10,209	11,824
03304	Bow	7,401	5,500
03743	Claremont	13,195	13,902
*03301	Concord	41,404	36,006
03818	Conway	8,884	7,940
03038	Derry (c)	22,661	20,446
03038	Derry	34,535	29,603
*03820	Dover	27,784	25,042
03824	Durham (c)	9,024	9,236
03824	Durham	12,845	11,818
03042	Epping	5,936	5,162
03833	Exeter (c)	9,759	9,556
03833	Exeter	14,326	12,481
03835	Farmington	6,045	5,739
03235	Franklin	8,553	8,304
03246	Gilford	7,187	5,867
03045	Goffstown	17,244	14,621
03841	Hampstead	8,465	6,732
*03842	Hampton (c)	9,126	7,989
*03842	Hampton	15,157	12,278
03755	Hanover Compact (c)	8,162	6,538
03755	Hanover	11,123	9,212
03244	Hillsborough	5,076	4,698
03049	Hollis	7,416	5,705
03106	Hooksett	12,433	9,002
03229	Hopkinton	5,536	4,806
03051	Hudson (c)	7,814	7,626
03051	Hudson	23,476	19,530
03452	Jaffrey	5,564	5,361
03431	Keene	22,714	22,430
03848	Kingston	6,133	5,591
*03246	Laconia	16,949	15,743
*03766	Lebanon	12,788	12,183
03052	Litchfield	7,846	5,516
03561	Littleton	5,948	5,827
03053	Londonderry (c)	11,417	10,114
03053	Londonderry	24,219	19,781
*03103	Manchester	108,398	99,332
03253	Meredith	6,238	4,837
03054	Merrimack	26,448	22,156
03055	Milford (c)	8,293	8,015
03055	Milford	14,021	11,795
*03060	Nashua	87,705	79,662
03857	Newmarket (c)	5,124	4,917
03857	Newmarket	8,449	7,157
03773	Newport	6,342	6,110
03076	Pelham	11,672	9,408
03275	Pembroke	7,138	6,561
03458	Peterborough	5,956	5,239
03102	Pinardville (c)	5,779	4,654
03865	Plaistow	7,851	7,316
03264	Plymouth	6,156	5,811
*03801	Portsmouth	21,048	25,925
03077	Raymond	9,842	8,713
03461	Rindge	5,727	4,941
*03867	Rochester	29,350	26,630
03870	Rye	5,286	—
03079	Salem	28,980	25,746
03873	Sandown	5,410	—
03874	Seabrook	8,334	6,503
03878	Somersworth	11,758	11,249
03106	South Hooksett (c)	5,282	3,638
03885	Stratham	6,624	4,955
03275	Suncook (c)	5,362	5,214
03446	Swanzey	6,914	6,236
03281	Weare	8,217	6,193
03087	Windham	11,852	9,000
03894	Wolfeboro	6,354	4,807

New Jersey

Area code (551) overlays area code (201). Area code (848) overlays (732). Area code (862) overlays (973). See introductory note.

ZIP	Place	Area Code	2002	1990
08201	Absecon	(609)	7,700	7,298
07401	Allendale	(201)	6,788	5,900
07712	Asbury Park	(732)	16,795	16,799
08034	Ashland (c)		*8,375*	—
*08401	Atlantic City	(609)	40,172	37,986
08106	Audubon	(856)	9,139	9,205
07001	Avenel(c)	(732)	*17,552*	15,504
—	Barclay-Kingston (c)		*10,728*	—
08007	Barrington	(856)	7,077	6,792
07002	Bayonne	(201)	61,605	61,464
08722	Beachwood	(732)	10,628	9,324
07109	Belleville (c)	(973)	*35,928*	34,213
*08031	Bellmawr	(856)	11,265	12,603
07719	Belmar	(732)	6,005	5,877
07621	Bergenfield	(201)	26,215	24,458
07922	Berkeley Heights (c)	(908)	*13,407*	11,980
08009	Berlin	(856)	6,759	5,672
07924	Bernardsville	(908)	7,558	6,597
07003	Bloomfield (c)	(973)	*47,683*	45,061
07403	Bloomingdale	(973)	7,688	7,530
07603	Bogota	(201)	8,210	7,824
07005	Boonton	(973)	8,424	8,343
08805	Bound Brook	(732)	10,195	9,487
08302	Bridgeton	(856)	22,653	18,942
08203	Brigantine	(609)	12,604	11,354
08015	Browns Mills (c)	(609)	*11,257*	11,429
07828	Budd Lake (c)	(973)	*8,100*	7,272
08016	Burlington	(609)	9,783	9,835
07405	Butler	(973)	8,102	7,392
*07006	Caldwell	(973)	7,667	7,542
*08101	Camden	(856)	79,685	87,492
07072	Carlstadt	(201)	5,973	5,510
08069	Carney's Point (c)	(856)	*6,914*	8,443
07008	Carteret	(732)	21,640	19,025
07009	Cedar Grove (c) (Essex)	(973)	*12,300*	12,053
07928	Chatham	(973)	8,436	8,007
08002	Cherry Hill Mall (c)	(856)	*13,238*	—
07066	Clark (c)	(732)/(908)	*14,597*	14,629
08312	Clayton	(856)	7,141	6,155
07010	Cliffside Park	(201)	22,954	20,393
*07015	Clifton	(973)	79,626	71,984
07624	Closter	(201)	8,484	8,094
08108	Collingswood	(856)	14,261	15,289
07067	Colonia (c)	(732)	*17,811*	18,238
07016	Cranford (c)	(908)	*22,578*	22,633
07626	Cresskill	(201)	7,861	7,558
08759	Crestwood Village (c)	(732)	*8,392*	8,030
08810	Dayton (c)	(732)	*6,235*	4,321
*07801	Dover	(973)	18,108	15,115
07628	Dumont	(201)	17,533	17,187
08812	Dunellen	(732)	6,947	6,528
08816	East Brunswick (c)	(732)	*46,756*	43,548
*07019	East Orange	(973)	69,750	73,552
07073	East Rutherford	(201)/(973)	8,713	7,902
*07724	Eatontown	(732)	14,086	13,800
08043	Echelon (c)	(856)	*10,440*	—
07020	Edgewater	(201)	9,220	5,001
*08818	Edison (c)	(732)/(908)	*97,687*	88,680
*07207	Elizabeth	(908)	123,279	110,002
07407	Elmwood Park	(201)	18,961	17,623
07630	Emerson	(201)	7,265	6,930
07631	Englewood	(201)	26,159	24,850
07632	Englewood Cliffs	(201)	5,475	5,634
08002	Erlton-Ellisburg (c)		*8,168*	—
08618	Ewing (c)	(609)	*35,707*	34,185
07004	Fairfield (Essex) (c)	(973)	*7,063*	7,615
07704	Fair Haven	(732)	5,963	5,270
07410	Fair Lawn	(201)/(973)	31,631	30,548
07022	Fairview (Bergen)	(201)	13,363	10,733
07023	Fanwood	(908)	7,283	7,115
08518	Florence-Roebling (c)	(609)	*8,200*	8,564
07932	Florham Park	(973)	12,247	8,521
08863	Fords (c)	(732)	*15,032*	14,392
08640	Fort Dix (c)	(609)	*7,464*	10,205
07024	Fort Lee	(201)	36,963	31,997
07416	Franklin (Sussex)	(973)	5,207	4,977
07417	Franklin Lakes	(201)	11,055	9,873
07728	Freehold	(732)	11,507	10,742
07026	Garfield	(201)	29,765	26,727
08028	Glassboro	(856)	19,050	15,614
07028	Glen Ridge	(973)	7,230	7,076
07452	Glen Rock	(201)	11,527	10,883
08030	Gloucester City	(856)	11,457	12,649
—	Greentree (c)		*11,536*	—
07093	Guttenberg	(201)	11,075	8,268
*07602	Hackensack	(201)	43,525	37,049
07840	Hackettstown	(908)	10,760	8,120
08033	Haddonfield	(856)	11,640	11,633
08035	Haddon Heights	(856)	7,513	7,860
*07508	Haledon	(973)	8,377	6,951
08037	Hammonton	(609)	12,840	12,208
07029	Harrison	(973)	14,378	13,425
07604	Hasbrouck Heights	(201)	11,647	11,488
*07506	Hawthorne	(973)	18,349	17,084
07422	Highland Lake (c)	(973)	*5,051*	4,550
08904	Highland Park (Middlesex)	(732)	14,225	13,279
07732	Highlands	(732)	5,167	4,849
08520	Hightstown	(609)	5,299	5,126
07642	Hillsdale	(201)	10,099	9,750
07205	Hillside (c)	(908)/(973)	*21,747*	21,044
07030	Hoboken	(201)	39,507	33,397
08753	Holiday City-Berkeley (c)	(732)	*13,884*	14,293
07843	Hopatcong	(973)	15,980	15,586
07111	Irvington (c)	(973)	*60,695*	59,774
08830	Iselin (c)	(732)	*16,698*	16,141
08831	Jamesburg	(732)	6,391	5,294
*07303	Jersey City	(201)	240,100	228,517
07734	Keansburg	(732)	10,812	11,069
07032	Kearny	(201)/(973)	40,300	34,874
08824	Kendall Park (c)	(908)	*9,006*	7,127
07033	Kenilworth	(908)	7,769	7,574
07735	Keyport	(732)	7,519	7,586
07405	Kinnelon	(973)	9,447	8,470
07871	Lake Mohawk (c)	(973)	*9,755*	8,930
08701	Lakewood (c)	(732)	*36,065*	26,095
08879	Laurence Harbor (c)	(732)	*6,227*	6,361
*08733	Leisure Village West-Pine Lake Park (c)	(732)	*11,085*	10,139
07605	Leonia	(201)	8,888	8,365
07035	Lincoln Park	(973)	10,867	10,978
07738	Lincroft (c)	(732)	*6,255*	6,193
07036	Linden	(732)/(908)	40,002	36,701
08021	Lindenwold	(856)	17,394	18,734
08221	Linwood	(609)	7,306	6,866
07424	Little Falls (c)	(973)	*10,855*	11,294
07643	Little Ferry	(201)	10,805	9,989
07739	Little Silver	(732)	6,153	5,721
07039	Livingston (c)	(973)	*27,391*	26,609
07644	Lodi	(201)/(973)	24,141	22,355
07740	Long Branch	(732)	31,571	28,658
07071	Lyndhurst (c)	(201)	*19,383*	18,262
08641	McGuire AFB (c)	(609)	*6,478*	7,580
07940	Madison	(973)	15,536	15,850
08859	Madison Park (c)	(732)	*6,929*	7,490
08736	Manasquan	(732)	6,364	5,369
08835	Manville	(908)	10,449	10,567
07040	Maplewood (c)	(973)	*23,868*	21,756
08402	Margate City	(609)	8,273	8,431
08053	Marlton (c)	(856)	*10,260*	10,228
07747	Matawan	(732)	8,912	9,239
07607	Maywood	(201)	9,511	9,536
07945	Mendham	(973)	5,111	4,890
08619	Mercerville-Hamilton Sq. (c)	(609)	*26,419*	26,873
08840	Metuchen	(732)	13,242	12,804
08846	Middlesex	(732)	13,974	13,055
07432	Midland Park	(201)	6,932	7,047
07041	Millburn (c)	(973)	*19,765*	18,630
08850	Milltown (Middlesex)	(732)	7,172	6,968
08332	Millville	(856)	26,917	25,992
*07042	Montclair (c)	(973)	*38,977*	37,729
07645	Montvale	(201)	7,277	6,946
08057	Moorestown-Lenola (c)	(856)	*13,860*	13,242
07751	Morganville (c)	(732)	*11,255*	—
07950	Morris Plains	(973)	5,221	5,219
*07960	Morristown	(973)	18,831	16,189
07092	Mountainside	(908)	6,687	6,657
08087	Mystic Island (c)	(609)	*8,694*	7,400
07753	Neptune City	(732)	5,205	4,997
*07102	Newark	(973)	277,000	275,221
*08901	New Brunswick	(732)	49,397	41,711
07646	New Milford	(201)	16,386	15,990
07974	New Providence	(908)	12,045	11,439
07860	Newton	(973)	8,338	7,521
07031	North Arlington	(201)	15,220	13,790
08902	North Brunswick Twp. (c)	(732)	*36,287*	31,287
07006	North Caldwell	(973)	7,403	6,706
08225	Northfield	(609)	7,868	7,305
07508	North Haledon	(973)	8,033	7,987
07060	North Plainfield	(908)	21,189	18,820
07648	Norwood	(201)	6,131	4,858
07110	Nutley (c)	(973)	*27,362*	27,099
07436	Oakland	(201)	13,282	11,997
*08050	Ocean Acres (c)	(609)	*13,155*	5,587
08226	Ocean City	(609)	15,516	15,512
07757	Oceanport	(732)	5,931	6,146
08857	Old Bridge (c)	(732)	*22,833*	22,151
07675	Old Tappan	(201)	5,694	4,254
07649	Oradell	(201)	8,044	8,024
*07051	Orange (c)	(973)	*32,868*	29,925
07650	Palisades Park	(201)	17,801	14,536
08065	Palmyra	(856)	7,604	7,056
*07652	Paramus	(201)	26,275	25,004
07656	Park Ridge	(201)	8,808	8,102
07055	Passaic	(973)	68,445	58,041
*07510	Paterson	(973)	150,750	140,891
08066	Paulsboro	(856)	6,121	6,577
08110	Pennsauken (c)	(856)	*35,737*	34,738
08070	Pennsville (c)	(856)	*11,657*	12,218
*08861	Perth Amboy	(732)	48,143	41,967
08865	Phillipsburg	(908)	15,245	15,757
08021	Pine Hill	(856)	10,947	9,854
08071	Pitman	(856)	9,266	9,365
*07061	Plainfield	(908)	48,273	46,577
08232	Pleasantville	(609)	19,008	16,027
08742	Point Pleasant	(732)	19,668	18,177

ZIP	Place	Area Code	2002	1990
08742	Point Pleasant Beach	(732)	5,379	5,112
07442	Pompton Lakes	(973)	10,897	10,539
*08540	Princeton	(609)	14,235	12,016
—	Princeton Meadows (c)	(609)	13,436	—
07508	Prospect Park	(973)	5,800	5,053
07065	Rahway	(732)	26,909	25,325
08057	Ramblewood (c)	(856)	6,003	6,181
07446	Ramsey	(201)	14,498	13,228
—	Ramtown (c)	(732)	5,932	—
08869	Raritan	(908)	6,379	5,798
07701	Red Bank	(732)	11,839	10,636
07657	Ridgefield	(201)	10,929	9,996
07660	Ridgefield Park	(201)	12,823	12,454
*07451	Ridgewood	(201)/(973)	24,877	24,152
07456	Ringwood	(973)	12,625	12,623
07661	River Edge	(201)	10,988	10,603
07675	River Vale(c)	(201)	9,449	9,410
07662	Rochelle Park (c)	(201)	5,528	5,587
07866	Rockaway	(973)	6,431	6,243
07068	Roseland	(973)	5,317	4,847
07203	Roselle	(908)	21,539	20,314
07204	Roselle Park	(908)	13,388	12,805
07760	Rumson	(732)	7,268	6,701
08078	Runnemede	(856)	8,538	9,042
07070	Rutherford	(201)	18,047	17,790
07663	Saddle Brook (c)	(201)/(973)	13,155	13,296
08079	Salem	(856)	5,776	6,883
*08872	Sayreville	(732)	41,768	34,998
07076	Scotch Plains (c)	(732)/(908)	22,732	21,150
*07094	Secaucus	(201)	15,882	14,061
08083	Somerdale	(856)	5,192	5,440
*08873	Somerset (c)	(732)	23,040	22,070
08244	Somers Point	(609)	11,535	11,216
08876	Somerville	(908)	12,460	11,632
08879	South Amboy	(732)	8,032	7,851
07079	South Orange (c)	(973)	16,964	16,390
07080	South Plainfield	(732)/(908)	22,899	20,489
08882	South River	(732)	15,829	13,692
08884	Spotswood	(732)	8,145	7,983
—	Springdale (c)	(856)	14,409	—
07081	Springfield (c)	(908)/(973)	14,429	13,420
07762	Spring Lake Heights	(732)	5,252	5,341
08084	Stratford	(856)	7,258	7,614
07747	Strathmore (c)	(732)	6,740	7,060
07876	Succasunna-Kenvil (c)	(201)	12,569	11,781
*07901	Summit	(908)	21,335	19,757
07666	Teaneck (c)	(201)	39,260	37,825
07670	Tenafly	(201)	13,951	13,326
07724	Tinton Falls	(732)	15,709	12,361
*08753	Toms River (c)	(732)	86,327	7,524
*07512	Totowa	(973)	10,010	10,177
*08650	Trenton	(609)	85,650	88,675
08520	Twin Rivers (c)	(609)	7,422	7,715
07083	Union (Union) (c)	(908)	54,405	50,024
07735	Union Beach	(732)	6,773	6,156
07087	Union City	(201)	66,902	58,012
07458	Upper Saddle River	(201)	8,096	7,198
08406	Ventnor City	(609)	12,826	11,005
07044	Verona (c)	(973)	13,533	13,597
08251	Villas (c)	(609)	9,064	8,136
*07360	Vineland	(856)	56,340	54,780
07463	Waldwick	(201)	9,608	9,757
07057	Wallington	(201)/(973)	11,553	10,828
07465	Wanaque	(201)/(973)	10,368	9,711
07882	Washington	(908)	6,777	6,474
07675	Washington Twp. (Bergen) (c)	(201)	8,938	9,245
07060	Watchung	(908)	5,913	5,110
*07470	Wayne (c)	(973)	54,069	47,025
*07006	West Caldwell (c)	(973)	11,233	10,422
*07091	Westfield	(732)/(908)	30,028	28,870
07728	West Freehold (c)	(732)	12,498	11,166
07764	West Long Branch	(732)	8,248	7,690
07480	West Milford (c)	(973)	26,410	25,430
07093	West New York	(201)	46,884	38,125
07052	West Orange (c)	(973)	44,943	39,103
07424	West Paterson	(973)	11,200	10,982
07675	Westwood (c)	(201)	11,016	10,446
07885	Wharton	(973)	6,325	5,405
08610	White Horse (c)	(609)	9,373	9,397
07886	White Meadow Lake (c)	(973)	9,052	8,002
08260	Wildwood	(609)	5,279	4,484
08094	Williamstown (c)	(856)	11,812	10,891
07095	Woodbridge (c)	(732)	18,309	17,434
08096	Woodbury	(856)	10,439	10,904
07675	Woodcliff Lake	(201)	5,840	5,303
07075	Wood-Ridge	(201)/(973)	7,638	7,506
07481	Wyckoff (c)	(201)	16,508	15,372
08620	Yardville-Groveville (c)	(609)	9,208	9,248
07726	Yorketown(c)	(609)	6,712	6,313

New Mexico (505)

ZIP	Place	2002	1990
*86310	Alamogordo	35,107	27,596
*87101	Albuquerque	463,874	384,915
88021	Anthony(c)	7,904	5,160
*88210	Artesia	10,478	10,610
87410	Aztec	6,749	5,480
87002	Belen	6,991	6,547
87004	Bernalillo	6,923	5,864
87413	Bloomfield	7,118	5,214

ZIP	Place		2002	1990
*88220	Carlsbad		25,196	24,952
88021	Chaparral (c)		6,117	2,962
*88101	Clovis		32,511	30,954
87048	Corrales		7,510	5,453
*88030	Deming		14,126	11,422
—	El Cerro-Monterey Park (c)		5,483	—
—	Eldorado at Santa Fe (c)		5,799	2,260
*87532	Espanola		9,791	8,389
*87401	Farmington		40,563	33,997
*87301	Gallup		20,177	19,157
87020	Grants		8,921	8,626
*88240	Hobbs		28,479	29,121
87417	Kirtland (c)		6,190	3,552
*88001	Las Cruces		75,015	62,360
88701	Las Vegas		14,223	14,753
87544	Los Alamos (c)		11,909	11,455
87002	Los Chaves (c)		5,033	3,872
87031	Los Lunas		10,883	6,013
87107	Los Ranchos de Albuquerque (c)		5,155	5,075
88260	Lovington		9,484	9,322
87107	North Valley(c)		11,923	12,507
88130	Portales		11,098	10,690
87740	Raton		7,262	7,372
*87124	Rio Rancho		56,614	32,512
*88201	Roswell		44,058	44,260
*88345	Ruidoso		8,004	4,600
*87501	Santa Fe		65,127	56,537
87420	Shiprock(c)		8,156	7,687
*88061	Silver City		10,213	10,683
87801	Socorro		8,700	8,159
87105	South Valley(c)		39,060	35,701
88063	Sunland Park		13,595	8,179
87901	Truth or Consequences		7,068	6,221
88401	Tucumcari		5,711	6,827
87544	White Rock(c)		6,045	6,192
87327	Zuni Pueblo(c)		6,367	5,857

New York

Area code (347) overlays area code (718). Area codes (646) and (917) overlay (212). See introductory note.

ZIP	Place	Area Code	2002	1990
10901	Airmont	(845)	8,319	7,674
*12201	Albany	(518)	93,779	100,031
11507	Albertson(c)	(516)	5,200	5,166
14411	Albion	(585)	5,886	5,863
*11701	Amityville	(516)/(631)	9,559	9,286
12010	Amsterdam	(518)	18,065	20,714
12603	Arlington (c)	(845)	12,481	11,948
13021	Auburn	(315)	28,186	31,258
11702	Babylon	(631)	12,713	12,249
11510	Baldwin (c)	(516)	23,455	22,719
11510	Baldwin Harbor (c)	(516)	8,147	7,899
13027	Baldwinsville	(315)	7,189	6,591
12020	Ballston Spa	(518)	5,579	5,194
*14020	Batavia	(585)	15,940	16,310
14810	Bath	(607)	5,616	5,801
11705	Bayport (c)	(631)	8,662	7,702
11706	Bay Shore (c)	(631)	23,852	21,279
11709	Bayville	(516)	7,172	7,193
11751	Baywood (c)	(631)	7,571	7,351
12508	Beacon	(845)	13,954	13,243
11710	Bellmore (c)	(516)	16,441	16,438
11714	Bethpage (c)	(516)	16,543	15,761
*13902	Binghamton	(607)	46,736	53,008
10913	Blauvelt (c)	(845)	5,207	4,838
11716	Bohemia (c)	(631)	9,871	9,556
11717	Brentwood (c)	(631)	53,917	45,218
10510	Briarcliff Manor	(914)	7,814	7,070
14610	Brighton (c)	(585)	35,584	34,455
14420	Brockport	(585)	8,243	8,749
10708	Bronxville	(914)	6,546	6,028
*14240	Buffalo	(716)	287,698	328,175
11933	Calverton (c)	(631)	5,704	4,759
14424	Canandaigua	(585)	11,256	10,725
13617	Canton	(315)	5,811	6,379
11514	Carle Place (c)	(516)	5,247	5,107
10512	Carmel Hamlet (c)	(845)	5,650	4,800
11516	Cedarhurst	(516)	6,165	5,716
11720	Centereach (c)	(631)	27,285	26,720
11934	Center Moriches (c)	(631)	6,655	5,987
11721	Centerport (Suffolk) (c)	(631)	5,446	5,333
11722	Central Islip (c)	(516)	31,950	26,028
10514	Chappaqua (c)	(914)	9,468	—
14225	Cheektowaga (c)	(716)	79,988	84,387
10977	Chestnut Ridge	(845)	7,883	7,517
12047	Cohoes	(518)	15,333	16,825
12205	Colonie	(518)	7,987	8,019
11725	Commack (c)	(631)	36,367	36,124
10920	Congers (c)	(845)	8,303	8,003
11726	Copiague (c)	(631)	21,922	20,769
11727	Coram (c)	(631)	34,923	30,111
14830	Corning	(607)	10,716	11,938
13045	Cortland	(607)	18,799	19,801
10520	Croton-on-Hudson	(914)	7,696	7,018
11729	Deer Park (c)	(631)	28,316	28,840
12054	Delmar (c)	(518)	8,292	8,360
14043	Depew	(716)	16,346	17,673
11746	Dix Hills (c)	(631)	26,024	25,849
10522	Dobbs Ferry	(914)	10,956	9,940
14048	Dunkirk	(716)	12,841	13,989

ZIP	Place	Area Code	2002	1990
14052	East Aurora	(585)/(716)	6,556	6,647
10709	Eastchester (c)	(914)	18,564	18,537
12302	East Glenville (c)	(518)	6,064	6,518
11576	East Hills	(516)	6,860	6,746
11730	East Islip (c)	(631)	14,078	14,325
11758	East Massapequa (c)	(516)	19,565	19,550
11554	East Meadow (c)	(516)	37,461	36,909
11731	East Northport (c)	(631)	20,845	20,411
11772	East Patchogue (c)	(631)	20,824	20,195
14445	East Rochester	(585)	6,569	6,932
11518	East Rockaway	(516)	10,397	10,152
11786	East Shoreham (c)	(631)	5,809	5,461
*14901	Elmira	(607)	30,417	33,724
11003	Elmont (c)	(516)	32,657	28,612
11731	Elwood (c)	(631)	10,916	10,916
*13760	Endicott	(607)	12,886	13,531
13762	Endwell (c)	(607)	11,706	12,602
13219	Fairmount (c)	(315)	10,795	12,266
14450	Fairport	(585)	5,679	5,943
—	Fairview (c)	(845)	5,421	4,811
11735	Farmingdale	(516)	8,531	8,022
11738	Farmingville(c)	(631)	16,458	14,842
11001	Floral Park	(516)	15,974	15,947
13603	Fort Drum(c)	(315)	12,123	11,578
11768	Fort Salonga (c)	(631)	9,634	9,176
11010	Franklin Square (Nassau) (c)	(516)	29,342	28,205
14063	Fredonia	(716)	10,650	10,436
11520	Freeport	(516)	43,978	39,894
13069	Fulton	(315)	11,681	12,929
*11530	Garden City	(516)	21,700	21,675
11040	Garden City Park (c)	(516)	7,554	7,437
14624	Gates-North Gates (c)	(585)	15,138	14,995
14454	Geneseo	(585)	7,847	7,187
14456	Geneva	(315)	13,557	14,143
11542	Glen Cove	(516)	26,886	24,149
12801	Glens Falls	(518)	14,194	15,023
12801	Glens Falls North (c)	(518)	8,061	7,978
12078	Gloversville	(518)	15,254	16,656
10924	Goshen	(845)	5,801	5,255
*11021	Great Neck	(516)	9,640	8,745
11020	Great Neck Plaza	(516)	6,787	5,897
14616	Greece (c)	(585)	14,614	15,632
11740	Greenlawn (c)	(631)	13,286	13,208
*10583	Greenville (Westchester) (c)	(914)	8,648	9,528
14075	Hamburg	(716)	9,935	10,442
11946	Hampton Bays (c)	(631)	12,236	7,893
10528	Harrison	(914)	24,951	23,308
10530	Hartsdale (c)	(914)	9,830	9,587
10706	Hastings-on-Hudson	(914)	7,735	8,000
*11788	Hauppauge (c)	(631)	20,100	19,750
10927	Haverstraw	(845)	10,153	9,438
10532	Hawthorne (c)	(914)	5,083	4,764
*11551	Hempstead	(516)	53,474	45,982
13350	Herkimer	(315)	7,334	7,945
11557	Hewlett (c)	(516)	7,060	6,620
*11802	Hicksville (c)	(516)	41,260	40,174
12528	Highland (c)	(845)	5,060	4,492
10977	Hillcrest (c)	(845)	7,106	6,447
14468	Hilton (c)	(585)	5,929	5,216
11741	Holbrook (c)	(631)	27,512	25,273
11742	Holtsville (c)	(631)	17,006	14,972
14843	Hornell	(607)	8,897	9,877
*14845	Horseheads (c)	(607)	6,392	6,802
12534	Hudson	(518)	7,452	8,034
12839	Hudson Falls	(518)	6,843	7,651
11743	Huntington (c)	(631)	18,403	18,243
11746	Huntington Station (c)	(631)	29,910	28,247
13357	Ilion	(315)	9,418	8,888
11096	Inwood (c)	(516)	9,325	7,767
14617	Irondequoit (c)	(585)	52,354	52,322
10533	Irvington	(914)	6,675	6,348
11751	Islip (c)	(631)	20,575	18,924
11752	Islip Terrace (c)	(631)	5,641	5,530
*14850	Ithaca	(607)	29,974	29,541
*14702	Jamestown	(716)	31,033	34,681
10535	Jefferson Valley-Yorktown (c)	(914)	14,891	14,118
11753	Jericho (Nassau) (c)	(516)	13,045	13,141
13790	Johnson City	(607)	15,347	16,578
12095	Johnstown	(518)	8,385	9,058
14217	Kenmore	(716)	16,100	17,180
11754	Kings Park (c)	(631)	16,146	17,773
11024	Kings Point	(516)	5,169	4,843
*12401	Kingston	(845)	23,347	23,095
10950	Kiryas Joel	(845)	14,904	7,437
14218	Lackawanna	(716)	18,792	20,585
10512	Lake Carmel (c)	(845)	8,663	8,489
11755	Lake Grove	(631)	10,591	9,612
10547	Lake Mohegan (c)	(914)	5,979	—
11779	Lake Ronkonkoma (c)	(631)	19,701	18,997
11552	Lakeview (c)	(516)	5,607	5,476
14086	Lancaster	(716)	10,983	11,940
10538	Larchmont	(914)	6,488	6,181
11559	Lawrence	(516)	6,555	6,513
11756	Levittown (c)	(516)	53,067	53,286
11757	Lindenhurst	(631)	28,048	26,879
13365	Little Falls	(315)	5,075	5,829
*14094	Lockport	(716)	21,775	24,426
11561	Long Beach	(516)	35,593	33,510
11563	Lynbrook	(516)	19,933	19,208
10541	Mahopac (c)	(845)	8,478	7,755
12953	Malone	(518)	5,983	6,777
11565	Malverne	(516)	8,942	9,054
10543	Mamaroneck	(914)	18,833	17,325
11030	Manhasset (c)	(516)	8,362	7,718
11050	Manorhaven (c)	(516)	6,253	5,672
11949	Manorville (c)	(631)	11,131	6,198
11758	Massapequa (c)	(516)	22,652	22,018
11762	Massapequa Park	(516)	17,555	18,044
13662	Massena	(315)	10,992	11,716
11950	Mastic (c)	(631)	15,436	13,778
11951	Mastic Beach (c)	(631)	11,543	10,293
13211	Mattydale (c)	(315)	6,367	6,418
—	Mechanicstown (c)	(845)	6,061	—
12118	Mechanicville	(518)	5,020	5,249
11763	Medford (c)	(631)	21,985	21,274
14103	Medina	(585)/(716)	6,355	6,686
11747	Melville (c)	(631)	14,533	12,586
11566	Merrick (c)	(516)	22,764	23,042
11953	Middle Island (c)	(631)	9,702	7,848
*10940	Middletown	(845)	25,775	24,160
11764	Miller Place(c)	(631)	10,580	9,315
11501	Mineola	(516)	19,283	19,005
10950	Monroe	(845)	8,033	6,672
10952	Monsey(c)	(845)	14,504	13,986
12701	Monticello	(845)	6,455	6,597
10970	Mount Ivy(c)	(845)	6,536	6,013
10549	Mount Kisco	(914)	10,064	9,108
11766	Mount Sinai (c)	(631)	8,734	8,023
*10551	Mount Vernon	(914)	68,615	67,153
12590	Myers Corner(c)	(845)	5,546	5,599
10954	Nanuet(c)	(845)	16,707	14,065
11767	Nesconset(c)	(631)	11,992	10,712
14513	Newark	(315)	9,587	9,849
*12550	Newburgh	(845)	28,382	26,454
11590	New Cassel(c)	(516)	13,298	10,257
10956	New City(c)	(845)	34,038	33,673
*11040	New Hyde Park	(516)	9,563	9,728
12561	New Paltz	(845)	6,419	5,470
*10802	New Rochelle	(914)	72,472	67,265
10977	New Square	(845)	5,305	2,623
*12550	New Windsor (c)	(845)	9,077	8,898
*10001	New York	(212)/(718)	8,084,316	7,322,564
*14302	Niagara Falls	(716)	54,358	61,840
11701	North Amityville(c)	(631)	16,552	13,849
11703	North Babylon(c)	(631)	17,877	18,081
11706	North Bay Shore(c)	(631)	14,992	12,799
11710	North Bellmore(c)	(516)	20,079	19,707
11713	North Bellport(c)	(631)	9,007	8,182
11757	North Lindenhurst(c)	(631)	11,767	10,563
11758	North Massapequa(c)	(516)	19,152	19,365
11566	North Merrick(c)	(516)	11,844	12,113
11040	North New Hyde Park(c)	(516)	14,542	14,359
11772	North Patchogue(c)	(631)	7,825	7,374
11768	Northport (c)	(631)	7,685	7,572
13212	North Syracuse	(315)	6,915	7,363
14120	North Tonawanda	(716)	32,587	34,989
11580	North Valley Stream(c)	(516)	15,789	14,574
11793	North Wantagh(c)	(516)	12,156	12,276
13815	Norwich	(607)	7,237	7,613
10960	Nyack	(845)	6,768	6,558
11769	Oakdale(c)	(631)	8,075	7,875
11572	Oceanside(c)	(516)	32,733	32,423
13669	Ogdensburg	(315)	12,040	13,521
11804	Old Bethpage(c)	(516)	5,400	5,610
14760	Olean	(585)/(716)	15,024	16,946
13421	Oneida	(315)	10,948	10,850
13820	Oneonta	(607)	13,117	13,954
12550	Orange Lake(c)	(845)	6,085	5,196
10562	Ossining	(914)	24,138	22,582
13126	Oswego	(315)	18,027	19,195
11771	Oyster Bay(c)	(516)	6,826	6,687
11772	Patchogue	(631)	12,026	11,060
10965	Pearl River(c)	(845)	15,553	15,314
10566	Peekskill	(914)	23,077	19,536
10803	Pelham	(914)	6,421	5,443
10803	Pelham Manor	(914)	5,475	6,413
14527	Penn Yan	(315)	5,108	5,248
11714	Plainedge(c)	(516)	9,195	8,739
11803	Plainview(c)	(516)	25,637	26,207
*12901	Plattsburgh	(518)	19,156	21,255
10570	Pleasantville	(914)	7,202	6,592
10573	Port Chester	(914)	27,949	24,728
11777	Port Jefferson	(631)	7,964	7,455
11776	Port Jefferson Station(c)	(631)	7,527	7,232
12771	Port Jervis	(845)	9,100	9,060
11050	Port Washington (c)	(516)	15,215	15,387
13676	Potsdam	(315)	9,471	10,251
*12601	Poughkeepsie	(845)	30,073	28,844
12144	Rensselaer	(518)	7,679	8,255
11961	Ridge(c)	(631)	13,380	11,734
11901	Riverhead(c)	(631)	10,513	8,814
*14692	Rochester	(585)	217,158	230,356
*11571	Rockville Centre	(516)	24,573	24,727
11778	Rocky Point(c)	(631)	10,185	8,596
*13440	Rome	(315)	34,709	44,350
11779	Ronkonkoma(c)	(631)	20,029	20,391
11575	Roosevelt(c)	(516)	15,854	15,030
11577	Roslyn Heights(c)	(516)	6,295	6,405
12303	Rotterdam(c)	(518)	20,536	21,228

ZIP	Place	Area Code	2002	1990
10580	Rye	(914)	15,092	14,936
10573	Rye Brook	(914)	9,043	7,765
11780	Saint James(c)	(631)	13,268	12,703
14779	Salamanca	(716)	5,973	6,566
13454	Salisbury (c)	(315)	12,341	12,226
12866	Saratoga Springs	(518)	27,014	25,001
11782	Sayville (c)	(631)	16,735	16,550
10583	Scarsdale	(914)	17,958	16,987
*12301	Schenectady	(518)	61,420	65,566
10940	Scotchtown(c)	(845)	8,954	8,765
12302	Scotia	(518)	7,912	7,359
11579	Sea Cliff	(516)	5,073	5,054
11783	Seaford(c)	(516)	15,791	15,597
11507	Searingtown(c)	(516)	5,034	5,020
11784	Selden(c)	(631)	21,861	20,608
13148	Seneca Falls	(315)	6,877	7,370
11733	Setauket-East Setauket(c)	(516)	15,931	13,634
11967	Shirley (Suffolk)(c)	(631)	25,395	22,936
10591	Sleepy Hollow[1]	(914)	9,283	8,152
11787	Smithtown(c)	(631)	26,901	25,638
13209	Solvay	(315)	6,794	6,717
11789	Sound Beach(c)	(631)	9,807	9,102
11735	South Farmingdale(c)	(516)	15,061	15,377
14850	South Hill(c)	(607)	6,003	5,423
11746	South Huntington(c)	(631)	9,465	9,624
14094	South Lockport(c)	(716)	8,552	7,112
11971	Southold(c)	(631)	5,465	5,192
14904	Southport(c)	(607)	7,396	7,753
11581	South Valley Stream(c)	(516)	5,638	5,328
10977	Spring Valley	(845)	25,574	21,802
*11790	Stony Brook(c)	(631)	13,727	13,726
10980	Stony Point(c) (Rockland)	(845)	11,744	10,587
10901	Suffern	(845)	11,046	11,055
11791	Syosset(c)	(516)	18,544	18,967
*13220	Syracuse	(315)	145,164	163,860
10983	Tappan(c)	(845)	6,757	6,867
10591	Tarrytown	(914)	11,447	10,739
11776	Terryville(c)	(631)	10,589	10,275
10594	Thornwood (c)	(914)	5,980	7,025
*14150	Tonawanda	(716)	15,848	17,284
*14150	Tonawanda(c)	(716)	61,729	65,284
*12180	Troy	(518)	48,818	54,269
10707	Tuckahoe	(914)	6,235	6,302
11553	Uniondale(c)	(516)	23,011	20,328
*13504	Utica	(315)	59,947	68,637
10595	Valhalla (c)	(914)	5,379	—
10989	Valley Cottage(c)	(845)	9,269	9,007
*11582	Valley Stream	(516)	36,433	33,946
—	Viola (c)		5,931	4,504
11792	Wading River(c)	(631)	6,668	5,317
12586	Walden	(845)	6,528	5,836
11793	Wantagh(c)	(516)	18,971	18,567
10990	Warwick	(845)	6,531	5,984
10992	Washingtonville	(845)	6,226	4,906
13165	Waterloo	(315)	5,117	5,116
*13601	Watertown	(315)	25,581	29,429
12189	Watervliet	(518)	10,074	11,061
14580	Webster	(585)	5,175	5,464
10952	Wesley Hills	(845)	5,000	4,308
*11704	West Babylon(c)	(631)	43,452	42,410
11590	Westbury (Nassau)	(516)	14,370	13,060
14905	West Elmira(c)	(607)	5,136	5,218
12801	West Glens Falls(c)	(518)	6,721	5,964
10993	West Haverstraw	(845)	10,318	9,183
11552	West Hempstead (c)	(516)	18,713	17,689
11743	West Hills(c)	(631)	5,607	5,849
11795	West Islip(c)	(631)	28,907	28,419
12203	Westmere(c)	(518)	7,188	6,750
*10996	West Point(c)	(845)	7,138	8,024
11796	West Sayville (c)	(631)	5,003	4,680
14224	West Seneca(c)	(716)	45,943	47,866
13219	Westvale(c)	(315)	5,166	5,952
11798	Wheatley Heights(c)	(631)	5,013	5,027
*10602	White Plains	(914)	55,394	48,718
14231	Williamsville	(716)	5,475	5,583
11596	Williston Park	(516)	7,260	7,516
11797	Woodbury(c)	(516)	9,010	8,008
11598	Woodmere(c)	(516)	16,447	15,578
11798	Wyandach(c)	(631)	10,546	8,950
11980	Yaphank(c)	(631)	5,025	4,637
*10702	Yonkers	(914)	197,234	188,082
10598	Yorktown Heights(c)	(914)	7,972	7,690

(1) North Tarrytown changed its name to Sleepy Hollow on Dec. 12, 1996.

North Carolina

Area code (980) overlays area code (704). See introductory note.

ZIP	Place	Area Code	2002	1990
*28001	Albemarle	(704)	15,452	14,940
27502	Apex	(919)	24,682	4,789
27263	Archdale	(336)	9,178	6,975
*27203	Asheboro	(336)	22,607	16,362
*28802	Asheville	(828)	69,193	63,379
28012	Belmont	(704)	8,997	8,434
28016	Bessemer City	(704)	5,133	4,698
28711	Black Mountain	(828)	7,507	7,156
28607	Boone	(828)	13,229	12,949
28712	Brevard	(828)	6,741	5,452
*27215	Burlington	(336)	46,016	39,498
27509	Butner (c)	(919)	5,792	4,679

ZIP	Place	Area Code	2002	1990
28428	Carolina Beach	(910)	5,112	4,002
27510	Carrboro	(919)	16,898	12,134
*27511	Cary	(919)	98,041	44,394
27514	Chapel Hill	(919)	51,636	38,719
*28204	Charlotte	(704)	580,597	419,558
28021	Cherryville	(704)	5,482	4,756
27520	Clayton	(919)	10,706	4,756
27012	Clemmons	(336)	16,192	5,982
*28328	Clinton	(910)	8,571	8,385
*28025	Concord	(704)	58,490	29,591
28613	Conover	(828)	6,744	5,311
28031	Cornelius	(704)	14,084	2,581
28036	Davidson	(704)	7,465	4,046
*28334	Dunn	(910)	9,567	9,258
*27701	Durham	(919)	195,914	138,894
*27288	Eden	(336)	15,723	15,238
27932	Edenton	(252)	5,282	5,268
*27909	Elizabeth City	(252)	17,255	16,087
27244	Elon	(336)	6,964	4,394
*28302	Fayetteville	(910)	124,286	75,850
28043	Forest City	(828)	7,410	7,475
28307	Fort Bragg (c)	(910)	29,183	34,744
27526	Fuquay-Varina	(919)	9,060	4,447
27529	Garner	(919)	19,953	14,716
*28052	Gastonia	(704)	61,820	54,725
*27530	Goldsboro	(919)	38,478	40,736
27253	Graham	(336)	13,241	10,368
*27420	Greensboro	(336)	228,217	185,125
*27834	Greenville	(252)	65,497	46,274
28540	Half Moon (c)	(910)	6,645	6,306
28345	Hamlet	(910)	5,931	6,722
28532	Havelock	(252)	22,973	20,300
27536	Henderson	(252)	16,295	15,655
*28739	Hendersonville	(828)	10,685	7,284
28603	Hickory	(828)	39,310	28,474
*27260	High Point	(336)	90,639	69,428
27278	Hillsborough	(919)	5,406	4,263
27540	Holly Springs	(919)	11,820	1,203
28348	Hope Mills	(910)	11,797	8,272
*28070	Huntersville	(704)	28,017	3,014
28079	Indian Trail	(704)	13,876	1,942
*28540	Jacksonville	(910)	66,913	78,031
—	James City (c)	(252)	5,420	4,279
*28081	Kannapolis	(704)	38,027	31,592
*27284	Kernersville	(336)	19,659	11,860
27948	Kill Devil Hills	(252)	6,182	4,238
27021	King	(336)	6,125	4,059
—	Kings Grant (c)		7,738	—
28086	Kings Mountain	(704)	10,526	8,768
*28502	Kinston	(252)	23,238	25,295
27545	Knightdale	(919)	6,003	1,884
*28352	Laurinburg	(910)	15,762	16,131
28645	Lenoir	(828)	18,078	16,337
27023	Lewisville	(336)	9,278	6,433
*27292	Lexington	(336)	20,143	16,583
28092	Lincolnton	(704)	9,966	6,955
*28358	Lumberton	(910)	21,042	18,656
28403	Masonboro (c)	(910)	11,812	7,010
*28105	Matthews	(704)	23,606	13,756
27302	Mebane	(919)	7,858	4,754
28227	Mint Hill	(704)	17,307	13,637
28110	Monroe	(704)	27,532	18,623
*28115	Mooresville	(704)	19,307	9,563
28557	Morehead City	(252)	7,844	6,473
*28655	Morganton	(828)	17,311	15,085
27560	Morrisville	(919)	6,679	1,022
27030	Mount Airy	(336)	8,428	7,156
28120	Mount Holly	(704)	9,671	7,710
—	Murraysville (c)		7,279	—
—	Myrtle Grove (c)		7,125	4,275
*28560	New Bern	(252)	23,098	20,728
28658	Newton	(828)	12,641	11,134
*28465	Oak Island	(910)	6,770	—
—	Ogden (c)		5,481	3,228
27565	Oxford	(919)	8,440	7,965
*28374	Pinehurst	(910)	10,439	5,825
28399	Piney Green (c)	(910)	11,658	8,999
*27611	Raleigh	(919)	306,944	218,859
*27320	Reidsville	(336)	14,871	14,085
27870	Roanoke Rapids	(252)	16,597	15,722
*28379	Rockingham	(910)	9,431	9,399
*27801	Rocky Mount	(252)	56,015	53,078
27573	Roxboro	(336)	8,792	7,332
28704	Royal Pines (c)		5,334	4,418
28601	Saint Stephens(c)	(828)	9,439	8,734
*28144	Salisbury	(704)	26,444	23,626
*27330	Sanford	(919)	23,338	18,881
27576	Selma	(919)	6,273	4,600
28150	Shelby	(704)	19,598	15,460
27344	Siler City	(919)	7,505	4,808
—	Silver Lake (c)		5,788	4,071
27577	Smithfield	(919)	11,931	10,180
*28387	Southern Pines	(910)	11,419	9,213
28052	South Gastonia(c)	(704)	5,433	5,487
28390	Spring Lake	(910)	8,188	7,552
*28677	Statesville	(704)	23,846	20,647
27358	Summerfield	(336)	7,075	2,051
*27886	Tarboro	(252)	10,633	11,037
*27360	Thomasville	(336)	21,569	15,915

ZIP	Place	Area Code	2002	1990
27370	Trinity	(336)	6,768	5,469
28110	Unionville	(704)	5,397	—
*27587	Wake Forest	(919)	14,634	5,832
27889	Washington	(252)	9,718	9,160
28786	Waynesville	(828)	9,255	7,282
28104	Weddington	(704)	7,402	3,803
28472	Whiteville	(910)	5,128	5,340
27892	Williamston	(252)	5,649	5,870
*28402	Wilmington	(910)	90,644	55,530
27893	Wilson	(252)	45,562	38,400
*27102	Winston-Salem	(336)	188,934	162,292

North Dakota (701)

ZIP	Place		2002	1990
*58501	Bismarck		56,234	49,272
58301	Devils Lake		7,042	7,782
58601	Dickinson		15,679	16,097
*58102	Fargo		91,204	74,084
*58201	Grand Forks		48,546	49,417
58401	Jamestown		15,115	15,571
58554	Mandan		16,769	15,177
*58701	Minot		35,617	34,544
*58701	Minot AFB(c)		7,599	9,095
58072	Valley City		6,526	7,163
*58075	Wahpeton		8,440	8,751
58078	West Fargo		15,801	12,287
*58801	Williston		12,376	13,136

Ohio

Area code (234) overlays area code (330). Area code (567) overlays (419). See introductory note.

ZIP	Place	Area Code	2002	1990
45810	Ada	(419)	5,546	5,428
*44309	Akron	(330)	214,349	223,019
44601	Alliance	(330)	22,982	23,376
44001	Amherst	(440)	11,718	10,332
44805	Ashland	(419)	21,132	20,079
*44004	Ashtabula	(440)	20,482	21,633
45701	Athens	(740)	21,545	21,265
44202	Aurora	(330)	14,245	9,192
44515	Austintown(c)	(330)	31,627	32,371
44011	Avon	(440)	13,009	7,337
44012	Avon Lake	(440)	19,131	15,066
44203	Barberton	(330)	27,663	27,623
44140	Bay Village	(440)	15,874	17,000
44122	Beachwood	(216)	12,036	10,644
45434	Beavercreek	(937)	38,046	33,626
—	Beckett Ridge (c)		8,663	4,505
44146	Bedford	(216)/(440)	13,974	14,822
44146	Bedford Heights	(216)/(440)	11,293	12,131
45305	Bellbrook	(937)	7,008	6,511
43311	Bellefontaine	(937)	12,969	12,126
44811	Bellevue	(419)	8,153	8,157
45714	Belpre	(740)	6,556	6,796
44017	Berea	(440)	18,746	19,051
43209	Bexley	(614)	12,850	13,088
43004	Blacklick Estates(c)	(614)	9,518	10,080
45242	Blue Ash	(513)	12,353	11,923
44513	Boardman(c)	(419)	37,215	38,596
43402	Bowling Green	(419)	29,482	28,303
44141	Brecksville	(440)	13,548	11,818
45211	Bridgetown North(c)	(513)	12,569	11,748
44147	Broadview Heights	(440)	16,343	12,219
44144	Brooklyn	(216)	11,414	11,706
44142	Brook Park	(216)/(440)	20,940	22,865
45309	Brookville	(937)	5,249	4,621
44212	Brunswick	(330)	35,200	28,218
43506	Bryan	(419)	8,317	8,348
44820	Bucyrus	(419)	13,026	13,496
43725	Cambridge	(740)	11,503	11,748
44405	Campbell	(330)	9,149	10,038
44614	Canal Fulton	(330)	5,033	4,157
43110	Canal Winchester	(614)	5,049	2,652
44406	Canfield	(330)	7,242	5,409
*44711	Canton	(330)	79,772	84,161
45005	Carlisle	(937)	5,321	4,872
45822	Celina	(419)	10,246	9,945
*45441	Centerville (Montgomery)	(937)	23,072	21,082
44024	Chardon	(440)	5,183	4,446
45211	Cheviot	(513)	8,765	9,616
45601	Chillicothe	(740)	22,145	21,923
*45202	Cincinnati	(513)	323,885	364,114
43113	Circleville	(740)	13,520	11,666
45315	Clayton	(937)	13,362	713
*44101	Cleveland	(216)	467,851	505,616
44118	Cleveland Heights	(216)	49,734	54,052
43410	Clyde	(419)	6,034	6,087
44408	Columbiana	(330)	5,730	4,961
*43216	Columbus	(614)	725,228	632,945
44030	Conneaut	(440)	12,322	13,241
44410	Cortland	(330)	6,761	5,652
43812	Coshocton	(740)	11,544	12,193
45238	Covedale(c)	(513)	6,360	6,669
44827	Crestline	(419)	5,011	4,934
*44222	Cuyahoga Falls	(330)	49,236	48,950
*45401	Dayton	(937)	162,669	182,011
45236	Deer Park	(513)	5,939	6,181
43512	Defiance	(419)	16,274	16,787
43015	Delaware	(740)	26,469	19,966
45833	Delphos	(419)	6,888	7,093

ZIP	Place	Area Code	2002	1990
45247	Dent(c)	(513)	7,612	6,416
44622	Dover (Tuscarawas)	(330)	12,264	11,329
45663	Dry Run(c)	(614)	6,553	5,389
*43016	Dublin	(614)/(740)	32,806	16,366
44112	East Cleveland	(216)	26,652	33,096
44094	Eastlake	(440)	20,127	21,161
43920	East Liverpool	(330)	12,862	13,654
45320	Eaton	(937)	8,248	7,396
*44035	Elyria	(440)	56,283	56,746
45322	Englewood	(937)	12,390	11,402
*44117	Euclid	(216)	51,911	54,875
45324	Fairborn	(937)	32,459	31,300
*45011	Fairfield	(513)	42,095	39,709
44334	Fairlawn	(330)	7,333	5,779
44126	Fairview Park	(440)	17,306	18,028
*45839	Findlay	(419)	39,446	35,703
45224	Finneytown(c)	(513)	13,492	13,096
45405	Forest Park	(513)	19,160	18,621
45230	Forestville(c)	(513)	10,978	9,185
44830	Fostoria	(419)	13,683	14,971
45005	Franklin	(513)	11,748	11,026
43420	Fremont	(419)	17,081	17,619
43230	Gahanna	(614)	33,502	23,898
44833	Galion	(419)	11,582	11,859
44125	Garfield Heights	(216)	30,262	31,739
44041	Geneva	(440)	6,521	6,597
44420	Girard	(330)	10,766	11,304
43212	Grandview Heights	(614)	6,488	7,010
44232	Green	(330)	23,047	19,179
45331	Greenville	(937)	13,146	12,863
45253	Groesbeck(c)	(513)	7,202	6,684
43123	Grove City	(614)	28,979	19,661
*45011	Hamilton	(513)	60,091	61,438
45030	Harrison	(513)	7,457	7,520
43056	Heath	(740)	8,671	7,231
44134	Highland Heights	(440)	8,446	6,249
43026	Hilliard	(614)/(740)	25,352	11,794
45133	Hillsboro	(937)	6,551	6,235
44484	Howland Center(c)	(330)	6,481	6,732
44425	Hubbard	(330)	8,181	8,248
45424	Huber Heights	(937)	38,055	38,696
*44236	Hudson	(330)	22,959	5,159
44839	Huron	(419)	7,830	7,067
44131	Independence (Cuyahoga)	(216)/(440)	7,149	6,500
45638	Ironton	(740)	11,205	12,751
45640	Jackson	(740)	6,142	6,167
*44240	Kent	(330)	27,742	28,835
43326	Kenton	(419)	8,231	8,356
43606	Kenwood(c)	(513)	7,423	7,469
45429	Kettering	(937)	56,680	60,569
44094	Kirtland	(440)	6,908	5,881
44107	Lakewood	(216)	55,286	59,718
43130	Lancaster	(740)	36,081	34,507
45039	Landen(c)	(513)	12,766	9,263
45036	Lebanon (Warren)	(513)	17,896	10,461
*45802	Lima	(419)	40,820	45,553
43228	Lincoln Village(c)	(614)	9,482	9,958
43138	Logan	(740)	6,806	6,725
43140	London	(614)/(740)	8,875	7,807
*44052	Lorain	(440)	67,704	71,245
44641	Louisville	(330)	9,107	8,087
45140	Loveland	(513)	11,511	10,122
44124	Lyndhurst	(216)/(440)	15,055	15,982
44056	Macedonia	(330)	9,859	7,509
—	Mack South(c)		5,837	5,767
45243	Madeira	(513)	8,775	9,141
*44901	Mansfield	(419)	50,747	50,627
44137	Maple Heights	(216)	25,794	27,089
45750	Marietta	(740)	14,119	15,026
*43302	Marion	(740)	37,108	34,075
43935	Martins Ferry	(740)	7,081	8,003
43040	Marysville	(937)	16,246	10,362
45040	Mason	(513)	25,656	11,450
*44646	Massillon	(330)	31,561	30,969
43537	Maumee	(419)	14,844	15,561
44124	Mayfield Heights	(440)	19,121	19,847
44256	Medina	(330)	26,082	19,231
*44060	Mentor	(440)	50,176	47,410
44060	Mentor-on-the-Lake	(216)	8,248	8,271
*45343	Miamisburg	(937)	19,789	17,834
44130	Middleburg Heights	(216)/(440)	15,710	14,702
*45042	Middletown	(513)	51,185	46,758
45150	Milford	(513)	6,341	5,660
45050	Monroe	(513)	6,372	5,380
45242	Montgomery	(513)	10,011	9,733
—	Montrose-Ghent (c)		5,261	4,906
45439	Moraine	(937)	6,859	5,989
45231	Mount Healthy	(513)	6,997	7,580
43050	Mount Vernon	(740)	14,845	14,550
44262	Munroe Falls	(330)	5,320	5,359
43545	Napoleon	(419)	9,341	8,884
45764	Nelsonville	(740)	5,412	4,563
*43055	Newark	(740)	46,444	44,396
45344	New Carlisle	(937)	5,680	6,049
44663	New Philadelphia	(330)	17,321	15,698
44446	Niles	(330)	20,580	21,128
45239	Northbrook(c)	(513)	11,076	11,471
44720	North Canton	(330)	16,576	14,904
45239	North College Hill	(513)	9,881	11,002
45251	Northgate(c)	(513)	8,016	7,864

ZIP	Place	Area Code	2002	1990
44057	North Madison(c)	(440)	8,451	8,699
44070	North Olmsted	(440)	33,786	34,204
45502	Northridge(c) (Clark)	(937)	6,853	5,939
45414	Northridge(c) (Montgomery)	(937)	8,487	9,448
44039	North Ridgeville	(440)	23,397	21,564
44133	North Royalton	(440)	30,596	23,197
43619	Northwood	(419)	5,475	5,506
44203	Norton	(330)	11,589	11,477
44857	Norwalk	(419)	16,312	14,731
45212	Norwood	(513)	20,985	23,674
45873	Oakwood	(973)	8,984	8,957
44074	Oberlin	(440)	8,138	8,191
44138	Olmsted Falls	(440)	8,326	6,741
44862	Ontario	(419)	5,261	4,026
*45054	Oregon	(419)	19,438	18,334
44667	Orrville	(330)	8,547	7,955
45056	Oxford	(513)	23,888	19,013
44077	Painesville	(440)	17,544	15,769
44129	Parma	(216)/(440)	84,534	87,876
44130	Parma Heights	(216)/(440)	21,383	21,448
43062	Pataskala	(740)	10,555	3,046
44124	Pepper Pike	(216)/(440)	5,988	6,185
44646	Perry Heights(c)	(330)	8,900	9,055
*43551	Perrysburg	(419)	16,866	12,551
43147	Pickerington	(614)/(740)	11,146	5,668
45356	Piqua	(937)	20,700	20,612
—	Pleasant Run (c)		5,267	4,964
44419	Portage Lakes(c)	(330)	9,870	13,373
43452	Port Clinton	(419)	6,321	7,106
45662	Portsmouth	(740)	20,439	22,676
43065	Powell	(614)	6,783	2,154
44266	Ravenna	(330)	11,592	12,069
45215	Reading	(513)	11,012	12,038
43068	Reynoldsburg	(614)/(740)	32,796	25,748
44143	Richmond Heights	(216)/(440)	10,933	9,611
44270	Rittman	(330)	6,280	6,147
45431	Riverside	(937)	23,449	1,471
44116	Rocky River	(440)	20,429	20,410
43460	Rossford	(419)	6,381	5,861
43950	Saint Clairsville	(740)	5,037	5,136
45885	Saint Marys	(419)	8,242	8,441
44460	Salem	(330)	12,318	12,233
*44870	Sandusky	(419)	27,356	29,764
44870	Sandusky South(c)	(419)	6,599	6,336
44131	Seven Hills	(216)/(440)	12,139	12,339
44122	Shaker Heights	(216)	28,854	30,955
*45241	Sharonville	(513)	13,667	13,121
44054	Sheffield Lake	(440)	9,248	9,825
44875	Shelby	(419)	9,592	9,610
44878	Shiloh(c)	(419)	11,272	11,607
45365	Sidney	(937)	20,327	18,710
45236	Silverton	(513)	5,054	5,859
44139	Solon	(440)	22,189	18,548
44121	South Euclid	(216)	23,152	23,866
45066	Springboro	(513)	14,170	6,574
45246	Springdale	(513)	10,343	10,621
*45501	Springfield	(937)	64,132	70,487
*43952	Steubenville	(740)	19,688	22,125
44224	Stow	(330)	33,913	27,998
44241	Streetsboro	(330)	12,566	9,932
44136	Strongsville	(440)	44,511	35,308
44471	Struthers	(330)	11,454	12,284
—	Summerside (c)		5,523	4,573
43560	Sylvania	(419)	18,980	17,489
44278	Tallmadge	(330)	17,028	14,870
45243	The Village of Indian Hill	(513)	6,077	5,383
44883	Tiffin	(419)	17,772	18,604
45371	Tipp City	(937)	9,233	6,483
*43601	Toledo	(419)	309,106	332,943
43964	Toronto	(740)	5,496	6,127
45067	Trenton	(513)	9,383	6,189
45426	Trotwood	(937)	27,138	29,358
45373	Troy	(937)	22,029	19,478
44087	Twinsburg	(330)	17,261	9,606
44683	Uhrichsville	(740)	5,671	5,604
45322	Union	(937)	5,838	5,531
44122	University Heights	(216)	13,933	14,787
43221	Upper Arlington	(614)	32,944	34,128
43351	Upper Sandusky	(419)	6,476	5,906
43078	Urbana	(937)	11,523	11,353
45377	Vandalia	(937)	14,463	13,872
45891	Van Wert	(419)	10,644	10,922
44089	Vermilion	(440)	10,867	11,127
*44281	Wadsworth	(330)	19,071	15,718
45895	Wapakoneta	(419)	9,497	9,214
*44481	Warren	(330)	47,225	50,793
44122	Warrensville Heights	(216)	14,897	15,884
43160	Washington	(740)	13,258	13,080
43566	Waterville	(419)	5,125	4,594
43557	Wauseon	(419)	7,195	6,322
45692	Wellston	(740)	5,979	6,049
45449	West Carrollton City	(937)	13,562	14,403
*43081	Westerville	(614)	35,520	30,269
44145	Westlake	(440)	32,160	27,018
45694	Wheelersburg(c)	(740)	6,471	5,113
43213	Whitehall	(614)	18,851	20,572
45239	White Oak(c)	(513)	13,277	12,430
44092	Wickliffe	(440)	13,343	14,558
44890	Willard	(419)	6,852	6,210
*44094	Willoughby	(440)	22,582	20,510
44094	Willoughby Hills	(440)	8,523	8,427
*44095	Willowick	(440)	14,188	15,269
45177	Wilmington	(937)	12,139	11,199
45459	Woodbourne-Hyde Park(c)	(937)	7,910	7,837
44691	Wooster	(330)	25,069	22,427
43085	Worthington	(614)	13,842	14,869
45433	Wright-Patterson AFB(c)	(937)	6,656	8,579
45215	Wyoming	(513)	8,109	8,128
45385	Xenia	(937)	24,160	24,836
*44501	Youngstown	(330)	80,026	95,732
*43701	Zanesville	(740)	25,447	26,778

Oklahoma

ZIP	Place	Area Code	2002	1990
*74820	Ada	(580)	15,852	15,765
*73521	Altus	(580)	20,569	21,910
73717	Alva	(580)	5,084	5,495
73005	Anadarko	(405)	6,555	6,586
*73401	Ardmore	(580)	23,939	23,079
*74003	Bartlesville	(918)	34,765	34,256
73008	Bethany	(405)	20,241	20,075
74008	Bixby	(918)	15,573	9,502
74631	Blackwell	(580)	7,518	7,538
*74012	Broken Arrow	(918)	83,088	58,082
74015	Catoosa	(918)	5,798	2,954
*73018	Chickasha	(405)	16,064	14,988
73020	Choctaw	(405)	10,026	8,545
74017	Claremore	(918)	16,579	13,280
73601	Clinton	(580)	8,422	9,298
74429	Coweta	(918)	7,353	6,159
74023	Cushing	(918)	8,390	7,218
73115	Del City	(405)	22,181	23,928
*73533	Duncan	(580)	22,125	21,732
*74701	Durant	(580)	13,827	12,929
*73034	Edmond	(405)	70,540	52,310
*73644	Elk City	(580)	10,492	10,428
73036	El Reno	(405)	16,146	15,414
*73701	Enid	(580)	46,531	45,309
74033	Glenpool	(918)	8,213	6,688
*74344	Grove	(918)	5,401	4,020
73044	Guthrie	(405)	9,987	10,440
73942	Guymon	(580)	10,667	7,803
74437	Henryetta	(918)	6,060	5,872
74848	Holdenville	(405)	5,629	4,893
74743	Hugo	(580)	5,473	5,978
74745	Idabel	(580)	6,984	6,957
74037	Jenks	(918)	10,955	7,484
*73501	Lawton	(580)	91,333	80,561
*74501	McAlester	(918)	17,652	16,739
*74354	Miami	(918)	13,562	13,142
73140	Midwest City	(405)	54,503	52,267
73153	Moore	(405)	43,739	40,318
*74401	Muskogee	(918)	38,600	37,708
73064	Mustang	(405)	13,993	10,434
73065	Newcastle	(405)	5,686	4,214
73068	Noble	(405)	5,342	4,710
73069	Norman	(405)	97,831	80,071
*73125	Oklahoma City	(405)	519,034	444,724
74447	Okmulgee	(918)	12,872	13,441
74055	Owasso	(918)	20,555	11,151
73075	Pauls Valley	(405)	6,181	6,150
73077	Perry	(580)	5,170	4,978
*74601	Ponca City	(580)	25,796	26,359
74953	Poteau	(918)	7,928	7,210
74361	Pryor Creek	(918)	9,115	8,327
73080	Purcell	(405)	5,574	4,784
74955	Sallisaw	(918)	8,314	7,122
74063	Sand Springs	(918)	17,644	15,339
74066	Sapulpa	(918)	19,802	18,074
74868	Seminole	(405)	6,836	7,071
*74801	Shawnee	(405)	29,313	26,017
74070	Skiatook	(918)	5,663	4,910
*74074	Stillwater	(405)	40,586	36,676
74464	Tahlequah	(918)	15,012	10,586
74873	Tecumseh	(405)	6,208	5,750
73156	The Village	(405)	10,117	10,353
*74103	Tulsa	(918)	391,908	367,302
74301	Vinita	(918)	5,894	5,804
*74467	Wagoner	(918)	7,806	6,894
73123	Warr Acres	(405)	9,694	9,288
73096	Weatherford	(580)	9,649	10,124
*73801	Woodward	(580)	11,796	12,340
*73099	Yukon	(405)	21,121	20,935

Oregon

Area code (971) overlays area code (503). See introductory note.

ZIP	Place	Area Code	2002	1990
97321	Albany	(541)	42,190	33,523
*97006	Aloha(c)	(503)	41,741	34,284
97601	Altamont(c)	(541)	19,603	18,591
97520	Ashland	(541)	20,215	16,252
97103	Astoria	(503)	9,730	10,069
97814	Baker City	(541)	9,739	9,140
*97005	Beaverton	(503)	79,768	53,307
*97701	Bend	(541)	57,010	23,740
97415	Brookings	(541)	5,684	4,400
97013	Canby	(503)	13,577	8,990
97225	Cedar Hills(c)	(503)	8,949	9,294
97291	Cedar Mill(c)	(503)	12,597	9,697
97502	Central Point	(541)	13,818	7,512

ZIP	Place	Area Code	2002	1990
97058	City of the Dalles	(541)	12,006	11,021
97015	Clackamas (c)	(503)	5,177	2,578
97420	Coos Bay	(541)	15,281	15,076
97113	Cornelius	(503)	9,940	6,148
*97333	Corvallis	(541)	49,781	44,757
97424	Cottage Grove	(541)	8,451	7,403
97338	Dallas	(503)	12,865	9,422
97524	Eagle Point	(541)	5,822	3,026
*97440	Eugene	(541)	140,395	112,733
97024	Fairview	(503)	8,532	2,588
97439	Florence	(541)	7,439	5,171
97116	Forest Grove	(503)	18,724	13,559
97301	Four Corners(c)	(541)	13,922	12,156
97223	Garden Home-Whitford(c)	(503)	6,931	6,652
97027	Gladstone	(503)	11,876	10,152
*97526	Grants Pass	(541)	24,843	17,503
97470	Green(c)	(541)	6,174	5,076
*97030	Gresham	(503)	94,706	68,285
97015	Happy Valley	(503)	5,913	1,552
97303	Hayesville(c)	(503)	18,222	14,318
97838	Hermiston	(541)	13,572	10,047
*97123	Hillsboro	(503)	75,945	37,598
97031	Hood River	(541)	6,075	4,632
97351	Independence	(503)	6,782	4,425
97222	Jennings Lodge(c)	(503)	7,036	6,530
97448	Junction City	(541)	5,153	3,961
97307	Keizer	(503)	33,503	21,884
*97601	Klamath Falls	(541)	19,315	17,737
97850	La Grande	(541)	12,259	11,766
*97034	Lake Oswego	(503)	35,839	30,576
97739	La Pine (c)	(541)	5,799	—
97355	Lebanon	(541)	13,156	10,950
97367	Lincoln City	(541)	7,400	5,903
97128	McMinnville	(503)	27,999	17,894
97741	Madras	(541)	5,178	3,443
*97501	Medford	(541)	64,653	47,021
97862	Milton-Freewater	(541)	6,472	5,533
97269	Milwaukie	(503)	20,563	18,670
97038	Molalla	(503)	5,943	3,651
97361	Monmouth	(503)	7,924	6,288
97132	Newberg	(503)	19,261	13,086
97365	Newport	(541)	9,588	8,437
97459	North Bend	(541)	9,509	9,614
97268	Oak Grove(c)	(503)	12,808	12,576
—	Oak Hills(c)		9,050	6,450
—	Oatfield(c)		15,750	15,348
97914	Ontario	(541)	10,947	9,394
97045	Oregon City	(503)	27,775	14,698
97801	Pendleton	(541)	16,407	15,142
*97208	Portland	(503)	539,438	485,975
97754	Prineville	(541)	7,871	5,355
97225	Raleigh Hills(c)	(503)	5,865	6,066
97756	Redmond	(541)	16,023	7,165
—	Redwood (c)		5,844	3,702
—	Rockcreek(c)		9,404	8,282
97470	Roseburg	(541)	19,957	18,389
97470	Roseburg North(c)	(541)	5,439	6,831
97051	Saint Helens	(503)	10,767	7,535
*97309	Salem	(503)	140,977	107,793
97055	Sandy	(503)	6,688	4,154
97056	Scappoose	(503)	5,326	3,550
97138	Seaside	(503)	5,888	5,359
97378	Sheridan	(503)	5,534	3,950
97140	Sherwood	(503)	13,506	3,093
97381	Silverton	(503)	7,690	5,635
*97477	Springfield	(541)	54,035	44,664
97383	Stayton	(503)	6,980	5,011
—	Sunnyside (c)	(503)	6,791	4,423
97479	Sutherlin	(541)	6,962	5,020
97386	Sweet Home	(541)	8,145	6,850
97540	Talent	(541)	5,525	3,274
97281	Tigard	(503)	45,152	29,435
97060	Troutdale	(503)	14,892	7,852
97062	Tualatin	(503)	23,877	14,664
97882	Umatilla	(541)	5,127	3,058
97225	West Haven-Sylvan(c)	(503)	7,147	6,009
97068	West Linn	(503)	24,172	16,389
*97225	West Slope(c)	(503)	6,442	7,959
97503	White City(c)	(541)	5,466	5,891
97070	Wilsonville	(503)	14,782	7,510
97071	Woodburn	(503)	21,209	13,404

Pennsylvania

Area code (267) overlays area code (215). Area code (484) overlays (610). Area code (878) overlays (412). See introductory note.

ZIP	Place	Area Code	2002	1990
15001	Aliquippa	(724)	11,429	13,374
*18105	Allentown (Lehigh)	(610)	106,105	105,301
*16603	Altoona	(814)	48,490	51,881
19002	Ambler	(215)	6,420	6,609
15003	Ambridge	(724)	7,541	8,133
18403	Archbald	(570)	6,220	6,291
19003	Ardmore(c)	(610)	12,616	12,646
15210	Arlington Heights (c)	(412)	5,132	4,768
15068	Arnold	(724)	5,536	6,113
19407	Audubon (c)	(610)	6,549	6,328
15202	Avalon	(412)	5,183	5,784
—	Back Mountain (c)		26,690	
15234	Baldwin	(412)	19,648	21,923

ZIP	Place	Area Code	2002	1990
18013	Bangor	(610)	5,273	5,383
15010	Beaver Falls	(724)	9,662	10,687
16823	Bellefonte	(814)	6,372	6,358
15202	Bellevue	(412)	8,595	9,126
18603	Berwick	(570)	10,536	10,976
15102	Bethel Park	(412)	33,135	33,823
*18016	Bethlehem	(610)	71,749	71,427
18015	Birdsboro	(610)	5,188	4,222
18447	Blakely	(570)	6,900	7,222
17815	Bloomsburg	(570)	12,438	12,439
19422	Blue Bell(c)	(215)/(610)	6,395	6,091
19061	Boothwyn(c)	(610)	5,206	5,069
16701	Bradford	(814)	8,880	9,625
15227	Brentwood	(412)	10,249	10,823
15017	Bridgeville	(412)	5,229	5,445
19007	Bristol	(215)	10,031	10,405
19015	Brookhaven	(610)	7,922	8,570
19008	Broomall(c)	(610)	11,046	10,930
*16001	Butler	(724)	14,841	15,714
15419	California	(724)	5,452	5,748
*17011	Camp Hill	(717)	7,580	7,831
15317	Canonsburg	(724)	8,693	9,200
18407	Carbondale	(570)	9,559	10,664
17013	Carlisle	(717)	18,036	18,419
15106	Carnegie	(412)	8,288	9,278
15108	Carnot-Moon (c)	(412)	10,637	10,187
15234	Castle Shannon	(412)	8,399	9,135
18032	Catasauqua	(610)	6,523	6,662
17201	Chambersburg	(717)	17,839	16,647
*19013	Chester	(610)	37,058	41,856
15025	Clairton	(412)	8,301	9,656
16214	Clarion	(814)	6,031	6,457
18411	Clarks Summit	(570)	5,062	5,433
16830	Clearfield	(814)	6,493	6,633
19018	Clifton Heights	(610)	6,708	7,111
19320	Coatesville	(610)	11,115	11,038
19023	Collingdale	(610)	8,568	9,175
17109	Colonial Park(c) (Dauphin)	(717)	13,259	13,777
17512	Columbia	(717)	10,235	10,701
15425	Connellsville	(724)	8,831	9,229
19428	Conshohocken	(610)	7,702	8,064
15108	Coraopolis	(412)	5,998	6,747
16407	Corry	(814)	6,739	7,216
15205	Crafton	(412)	6,561	7,188
19021	Croydon(c)	(215)	9,993	9,967
19023	Darby	(610)	10,186	11,140
19036	Darby Twp.(c)	(610)	9,622	10,955
19333	Devon-Berwyn(c)	(610)	5,067	5,019
18519	Dickson City	(570)	6,063	6,276
15033	Donora	(724)	5,530	5,928
15216	Dormont	(412)	9,087	9,772
19335	Downingtown	(610)	7,751	7,749
18901	Doylestown	(215)	8,196	8,575
19026	Drexel Hill (c)	(610)	29,364	29,744
15801	Du Bois	(814)	7,962	8,286
18512	Dunmore	(570)	13,754	15,403
15110	Duquesne	(412)	7,201	8,525
19401	East Norriton(c)	(610)	13,211	13,324
*18042	Easton	(610)	26,139	26,276
18301	East Stroudsburg	(570)	10,110	8,781
17402	East York(c)	(717)	8,782	8,487
15005	Economy	(724)	9,308	9,305
16412	Edinboro	(814)	7,086	7,736
17022	Elizabethtown	(717)	11,905	9,952
16117	Ellwood City	(724)	8,513	8,894
18049	Emmaus	(610)	11,250	11,157
17025	Enola(c)	(717)	5,627	5,961
17522	Ephrata	(717)	13,117	12,133
*16501	Erie	(814)	102,122	108,718
18643	Exeter	(570)	6,037	5,691
19030	Fairless Hills(c)	(215)	8,365	9,026
16121	Farrell	(724)	5,880	6,835
19053	Feasterville-Trevose(c)	(215)	6,525	6,696
16063	Fernway(c)	(724)	12,188	9,072
19032	Folcroft	(610)	6,945	7,506
19033	Folsom(c)	(610)	8,072	8,173
15221	Forest Hills	(412)	6,695	7,335
15238	Fox Chapel	(412)	5,385	5,319
16323	Franklin	(814)	7,051	7,329
15143	Franklin Park	(412)	11,526	10,109
18052	Fullerton(c)	(610)	14,268	13,127
17325	Gettysburg	(717)	7,653	7,025
19036	Glenolden	(610)	7,404	7,260
19038	Glenside(c)	(215)	7,914	8,704
15601	Greensburg	(724)	15,617	16,318
16125	Greenville	(724)	6,381	6,734
16127	Grove City	(412)	7,873	8,240
15101	Hampton Twp.(c) (Allegheny)	(412)	17,526	15,568
17331	Hanover	(717)	14,712	14,399
19438	Harleysville(c)	(215)	8,795	7,405
*17105	Harrisburg	(717)	48,540	52,376
15065	Harrison Twp.(c) (Allegheny)	(412)	10,934	11,763
19040	Hatboro	(570)	7,390	7,382
18201	Hazleton	(570)	22,752	24,730
18055	Hellertown	(610)	5,575	5,662
16148	Hermitage	(724)	16,362	15,260
17033	Hershey(c)	(814)	12,771	11,860
16648	Hollidaysburg	(814)	5,339	5,624
16001	Homeacre-Lyndora(c)	(724)	6,685	7,511
19044	Horsham(c)	(215)	14,779	15,051

ZIP	Place	Area Code	2002	1990
16652	Huntingdon	(814)	6,841	6,843
15701	Indiana	(724)	14,823	15,174
15644	Jeannette	(724)	10,456	11,221
15025	Jefferson Hills	(412)	9,672	—
*15907	Johnstown	(814)	23,231	28,124
15108	Kennedy Twp.(c)	(412)	7,504	7,152
19348	Kennett Square	(610)	5,263	5,218
19406	King of Prussia(c)	(610)	18,511	18,406
18704	Kingston	(570)	13,512	14,507
19443	Kulpsville(c)	(215)	8,005	5,183
19530	Kutztown	(610)	5,082	4,704
*17604	Lancaster	(717)	55,628	55,551
19446	Lansdale	(215)	16,129	16,362
19050	Lansdowne	(610)	10,916	11,712
15650	Latrobe	(724)	8,817	9,265
17540	Leacock-Leola-Bareville(c)	(717)	6,625	5,685
*17042	Lebanon	(717)	24,013	24,800
18235	Lehighton	(610)	5,529	5,914
*19055	Levittown(c)	(215)	53,966	55,362
17837	Lewisburg	(570)	5,506	5,785
17044	Lewistown (Mifflin)	(717)	8,837	9,341
17112	Linglestown(c)	(717)	6,414	5,862
19353	Lionville-Marchwood (c)	(610)	6,298	6,468
17543	Lititz	(717)	8,979	8,280
17745	Lock Haven	(570)	9,072	9,230
17011	Lower Allen(c)	(717)	6,619	6,329
15068	Lower Burrell	(724)	12,554	12,251
15237	McCandless Twp.(c)	(412)	29,022	28,781
*15134	McKeesport	(412)	23,583	26,016
15136	McKees Rocks	(412)	6,473	7,691
19002	Maple Glen(c)	(215)	7,042	5,881
16335	Meadville	(814)	13,497	14,318
17055	Mechanicsburg	(717)	8,953	9,452
*19063	Media	(610)	5,487	5,957
17057	Middletown (Dauphin)	(717)	9,158	9,254
18017	Middletown (c) (Northampton)	(610)	7,378	6,866
17551	Millersville	(717)	7,585	8,099
17847	Milton	(570)	6,548	6,746
15061	Monaca	(724)	6,128	6,739
15062	Monessen	(724)	8,527	9,901
18936	Montgomeryville(c)	(215)	12,031	9,114
18507	Moosic	(570)	5,622	5,397
19067	Morrisville (Bucks)	(215)	10,026	9,765
18707	Mountain Top (c)	(570)	15,269	—
17851	Mount Carmel	(570)	6,216	7,196
17552	Mount Joy	(717)	6,831	6,398
15228	Mount Lebanon(c)	(412)	33,017	34,414
15120	Munhall	(412)	12,011	13,158
15146	Municipality of Monroeville	(412)	28,952	29,169
15668	Municipality of Murrysville	(724)	19,042	17,240
18634	Nanticoke	(570)	10,660	12,267
18064	Nazareth	(610)	5,986	5,713
19086	Nether Providence Twp.(c)	(610)	13,456	12,730
15066	New Brighton	(724)	6,451	6,854
*16108	New Castle	(724)	25,708	28,334
17070	New Cumberland	(717)	7,277	7,665
17557	New Holland	(717)	5,175	4,484
15068	New Kensington	(724)	14,385	15,894
*19403	Norristown	(610)	31,311	30,754
18067	Northampton	(610)	9,496	8,717
15104	North Braddock	(412)	6,264	7,036
15137	North Versailles(c)	(412)	11,125	13,294
16421	Northwest Harborcreek(c)	(814)	8,658	7,485
19074	Norwood (Delaware)	(610)	5,926	6,162
15139	Oakmont (Allegheny)	(412)	6,802	6,961
15238	O'Hara Twp.(c)	(412)	8,856	9,096
16301	Oil City	(814)	11,252	11,949
18518	Old Forge	(570)	8,627	8,834
19075	Oreland(c)	(215)	5,509	5,695
18071	Palmerton	(610)	5,253	5,394
17078	Palmyra	(717)	7,003	6,910
19301	Paoli(c)	(610)	5,425	5,277
16801	Park Forest Village(c)	(814)	8,830	6,703
17331	Parkville(c)	(717)	6,593	5,009
17112	Paxtonia (c)	(717)	5,254	4,862
15235	Penn Hills(c)	(412)	46,809	57,632
19096	Penn Wynne(c)	(610)	5,382	5,807
18944	Perkasie	(215)	8,867	7,878
*19104	Philadelphia	(215)	1,492,231	1,585,577
19460	Phoenixville	(610)	14,785	15,066
*15233	Pittsburgh	(412)	327,898	369,879
*18640	Pittston	(570)	7,897	9,389
15236	Pleasant Hills	(412)	8,260	8,884
15239	Plum	(412)	26,985	25,609
18651	Plymouth	(570)	6,328	7,134
19462	Plymouth Meeting(c)	(610)	5,593	6,241
*19464	Pottstown	(610)	21,824	21,831
17901	Pottsville	(570)	15,167	16,603
17109	Progress(c)	(717)	9,647	9,654
19076	Prospect Park	(610)	6,525	6,764
15767	Punxsutawney	(814)	6,169	6,782
18951	Quakertown	(215)	8,890	8,982
19087	Radnor Twp.(c)	(610)	30,878	27,676
*19612	Reading	(610)	80,494	78,380
17356	Red Lion	(717)	6,113	6,130
18954	Richboro(c)	(215)	6,678	5,141
19078	Ridley Park	(610)	7,125	7,592
15136	Robinson Twp. (Allegheny)(c)	(412)	12,289	10,830
15237	Ross Twp.(c)	(412)	32,551	35,102
15857	Saint Marys	(814)	14,236	14,020

ZIP	Place	Area Code	2002	1990
19464	Sanatoga(c)	(610)	7,734	3,723
18840	Sayre	(570)	5,711	5,791
17972	Schuylkill Haven	(570)	5,427	5,610
15106	Scott Twp.(c)	(412)	17,288	20,413
*18505	Scranton	(570)	74,712	81,805
17870	Selinsgrove	(570)	5,465	5,384
15116	Shaler Twp.(c)	(412)	29,757	33,694
17872	Shamokin	(570)	7,798	9,184
16146	Sharon	(724)	15,861	17,533
19079	Sharon Hill	(610)	5,412	5,771
17976	Shenandoah	(570)	5,462	6,221
19607	Shillington	(610)	5,023	5,062
17404	Shiloh(c)	(717)	10,192	5,315
17257	Shippensburg	(717)	5,622	5,331
15501	Somerset	(814)	6,673	6,454
18964	Souderton	(215)	6,770	5,957
15129	South Park Twp.(c)	(814)	14,340	14,292
17701	South Williamsport	(570)	6,277	6,496
19064	Springfield (c) (Delaware)	(610)	23,677	25,326
*16804	State College	(814)	38,098	38,981
17113	Steelton	(717)	5,796	5,152
—	Stonybrook-Wilshire(c)		5,414	4,887
15136	Stowe Twp.(c)	(412)	6,706	9,202
18360	Stroudsburg	(570)	5,963	5,312
16323	Sugarcreek	(814)	5,255	5,532
17801	Sunbury	(570)	10,356	11,591
19081	Swarthmore	(610)	6,164	6,157
15218	Swissvale	(412)	9,443	10,637
18704	Swoyersville	(570)	5,057	5,630
18252	Tamaqua	(570)	6,972	7,943
18517	Taylor	(570)	6,345	6,941
16354	Titusville	(814)	5,958	6,434
19401	Trooper(c)	(610)	6,061	7,370
15145	Turtle Creek	(412)	5,947	6,556
16686	Tyrone	(814)	5,445	5,743
15401	Uniontown (Fayette)	(724)	12,212	12,034
19063	Upper Providence Twp.(c)	(610)	10,039	9,477
15241	Upper Saint Clair(c)	(412)	20,053	19,023
15690	Vandergrift	(724)	5,320	5,904
19013	Village Green-Green Ridge(c)	(610)	8,279	9,026
16365	Warren	(814)	9,965	11,122
15301	Washington (Washington)	(724)	14,941	15,864
17268	Waynesboro	(717)	9,600	9,578
17715	Weigelstown(c)	(717)	10,117	8,665
*19380	West Chester	(610)	17,831	18,041
19380	West Goshen(c)	(610)	8,472	8,948
15122	West Mifflin	(412)	22,133	23,644
15905	Westmont	(814)	5,386	5,789
19401	West Norriton(c)	(610)	14,901	15,209
15229	West View	(412)	7,137	7,734
15227	Whitehall (Allegheny)	(412)	14,236	14,451
15131	White Oak	(412)	8,471	8,761
18703	Wilkes-Barre	(570)	42,021	47,523
15221	Wilkinsburg	(412)	18,774	21,080
15145	Wilkins Twp.(c)	(412)	6,917	7,487
*17701	Williamsport	(570)	30,084	31,933
19090	Willow Grove(c) (Montgomery)	(215)	16,234	16,325
17584	Willow Street(c)	(717)	7,258	5,817
15025	Wilson	(412)	7,620	7,830
19094	Woodlyn(c)	(610)	10,036	10,151
19038	Wyndmoor(c)	(215)	5,601	5,682
19610	Wyomissing	(610)	8,563	7,332
19050	Yeadon	(610)	11,640	11,980
*17405	York	(717)	40,296	42,192

Rhode Island (401)
See introductory note.

ZIP	Place	2002	1990
02806	Barrington	16,985	15,849
02809	Bristol	22,815	21,625
02830	Burrillville	16,279	16,230
02863	Central Falls	19,168	17,637
02813	Charlestown	8,141	6,478
02816	Coventry	34,664	31,083
*02904	Cranston	81,113	76,060
02864	Cumberland	33,104	29,038
02864	Cumberland Hill(c)	7,738	6,379
02818	East Greenwich	13,347	11,865
02914	East Providence	49,658	50,380
02822	Exeter	6,274	5,461
02814	Glocester	10,283	9,227
02828	Greenville(c)	8,626	8,303
02833	Hopkinton	8,064	6,873
02835	Jamestown	5,680	4,999
02919	Johnston	29,023	26,542
02881	Kingston(c)	5,446	6,504
02865	Lincoln	21,971	18,045
02842	Middletown	17,398	19,460
02882	Narragansett	16,809	15,004
02840	Newport	26,312	28,227
02843	Newport East(c)	11,463	11,080
02852	North Kingstown	26,985	23,786
02908	North Providence	33,238	32,090
02896	North Smithfield	10,919	10,497
*02860	Pawtucket	74,033	72,644
02871	Portsmouth	17,460	16,857
*02904	Providence	175,901	160,728
02812	Richmond	7,580	5,351
02857	Scituate	10,696	9,796

ZIP	Place	2002	1990
02917	Smithfield	21,138	19,163
02879	South Kingstown	28,617	24,612
02878	Tiverton (c)	7,282	7,259
02878	Tiverton	15,505	14,312
02864	Valley Falls (c)	11,599	11,175
*02879	Wakefield-Peacedale (c)	8,468	7,134
02885	Warren	11,487	11,385
*02886	Warwick	87,039	85,427
02891	Westerly (c)	17,682	16,477
02891	Westerly	23,623	21,605
02817	West Greenwich	5,508	—
02893	West Warwick	29,941	29,268
02895	Woonsocket	43,879	43,877

South Carolina

ZIP	Place	Area Code	2002	1990
29620	Abbeville	(864)	5,833	5,778
*29801	Aiken	(803)	26,047	20,386
*29621	Anderson	(864)	25,690	26,385
—	Batesburg-Leesville	(803)	5,520	6,107
*29902	Beaufort	(843)	12,480	9,576
29841	Belvedere(c)	(803)	5,631	6,133
29512	Bennettsville	(843)	9,290	10,095
29611	Berea(c)	(864)	14,158	13,535
29902	Burton(c)	(843)	7,180	6,917
29020	Camden	(803)	6,825	6,696
29033	Cayce	(803)	12,388	10,824
—	Centerville (c)	(573)	5,181	4,866
*29402	Charleston	(843)	98,795	88,256
29520	Cheraw	(843)	5,436	5,553
29706	Chester	(803)	6,409	7,158
*29631	Clemson	(864)	11,967	11,145
29325	Clinton	(864)	8,645	9,603
*29201	Columbia	(803)	117,394	110,734
29526	Conway	(843)	12,020	9,819
*29532	Darlington	(843)	6,625	7,310
29204	Dentsville(c)	(803)	13,009	11 839
29536	Dillon	(843)	6,295	6,829
*29640	Easley	(864)	18,379	15,179
—	Five Forks (c)		8,064	—
*29501	Florence	(843)	30,019	29,913
29206	Forest Acres	(803)	10,411	7,181
*29715	Fort Mill	(803)	7,666	4,930
29644	Fountain Inn	(864)	6,346	4,388
*29341	Gaffney	(864)	12,923	13,149
29605	Gantt(c)	(864)	13,962	13,891
29576	Garden City(c)	(843)	9,357	6,305
*29442	Georgetown	(843)	8,954	9,517
29445	Goose Creek	(843)	30,179	24,692
*29602	Greenville	(864)	56,181	58,256
*29646	Greenwood	(864)	22,181	20,807
*29650	Greer	(864)	18,742	10,322
29406	Hanahan	(843)	12,843	13,176
*29550	Hartsville	(843)	7,467	8,372
*29928	Hilton Head Island	(843)	34,601	23,694
29621	Homeland Park(c)	(864)	6,337	6,569
29063	Irmo	(803)	11,066	11,284
29456	Ladson(c)	(843)	13,264	13,540
29560	Lake City	(843)	6,535	7,153
*29720	Lancaster	(803)	8,395	8,914
29902	Laurel Bay (c)	(843)	6,625	4,972
29360	Laurens	(864)	9,866	9,694
29072	Lexington	(803)	10,357	4,046
29566	Little River (c)	(843)	7,027	3,470
29078	Lugoff (c)	(803)	6,278	3,211
29571	Marion	(843)	7,009	7,658
29662	Mauldin	(864)	16,826	11,662
29461	Moncks Corner	(843)	6,057	5,599
*29465	Mount Pleasant	(843)	53,096	30,108
29576	Murrells Inlet (c)	(843)	5,519	3,334
29575	Myrtle Beach	(803)	24,525	24,848
29108	Newberry	(803)	10,686	10,543
*29841	North Augusta	(803)	18,071	15,684
*29410	North Charleston	(843)	80,691	70,304
29582	North Myrtle Beach	(843)	12,018	8,731
29565	Oak Grove(c)	(803)	8,183	7,173
*29115	Orangeburg	(803)	12,584	13,772
—	Parker(c)		10,760	11,072
—	Powderville (c)		5,362	—
29072	Red Bank(c)	(803)	8,811	5,950
29020	Red Hill(c)	(843)	10,509	6,112
*29730	Rock Hill	(803)	54,606	42,112
29417	Saint Andrews(c)	(843)	21,814	25,692
29609	Sans Souci(c)	(864)	7,836	7,612
29678	Seneca	(864)	7,793	7,726
29210	Seven Oaks(c)	(803)	15,755	15,722
29681	Simpsonville	(864)	14,700	11,744
29577	Socastee(c)	(843)	14,295	10,426
29306	Spartanburg	(864)	39,068	43,479
*29483	Summerville	(843)	29,999	22,519
29150	Sumter	(803)	39,382	40,977
29687	Taylors(c)	(864)	20,125	19,619
29379	Union	(864)	8,570	9,840
29607	Wade Hampton(c)	(864)	20,458	20,014
29488	Walterboro	(843)	5,123	5,595
29611	Welcome(c)	(864)	6,390	6,560
29169	West Columbia	(803)	12,947	10,974
29206	Woodfield(c)	(803)	9,238	8,862
29745	York	(803)	7,035	6,709

South Dakota (605)

ZIP	Place	2002	1990
*57401	Aberdeen	24,312	24,995
57005	Brandon	6,212	3,545
57006	Brookings	18,703	16,270
57350	Huron	11,569	12,448
57042	Madison	6,505	6,257
57301	Mitchell	14,626	13,798
57501	Pierre	14,012	12,906
*57701	Rapid City	60,262	54,523
57701	Rapid Valley(c)	7,043	5,968
*57101	Sioux Falls	130,491	100,836
57783	Spearfish	8,650	6,966
57785	Sturgis	6,404	5,537
57069	Vermillion	10,065	10,034
57201	Watertown	20,191	17,623
57078	Yankton	13,440	12,703

Tennessee

ZIP	Place	Area Code	2002	1990
37701	Alcoa	(865)	8,118	6,400
*37303	Athens	(423)	13,464	12,054
38184	Bartlett	(901)	41,869	27,038
*37660	Bloomingdale(c)	(423)	10,350	10,953
38008	Bolivar	(731)	5,747	5,969
*37027	Brentwood	(615)	27,756	16,392
*37621	Bristol	(423)	24,889	23,421
38012	Brownsville	(731)	10,017	10,017
*37401	Chattanooga	(423)	155,404	152,393
37642	Church Hill	(423)	6,073	5,208
*37040	Clarksville	(931)	105,898	75,542
*37311	Cleveland	(423)	37,380	32,236
37716	Clinton	(865)	9,350	8,960
37315	Collegedale	(423)	6,996	5,048
38017	Collierville	(901)	34,168	14,501
37663	Colonial Heights(c)	(423)	7,067	6,716
38401	Columbia	(931)	33,067	28,583
*38501	Cookeville	(931)	25,901	21,744
38019	Covington	(901)	8,577	7,487
*38555	Crossville	(931)	9,537	6,930
37321	Dayton	(423)	6,324	5,671
*37055	Dickson	(615)	12,325	10,487
38024	Dyersburg	(731)	17,228	16,321
37411	East Brainerd(c)	(423)	14,132	11,594
37412	East Ridge	(423)	20,215	21,101
*37643	Elizabethton	(423)	13,132	13,087
37650	Erwin	(423)	5,560	5,318
37062	Fairview	(615)	6,376	4,210
37922	Farragut	(865)	18,370	12,802
37334	Fayetteville	(931)	6,979	7,158
*37064	Franklin	(615)	45,175	20,098
37066	Gallatin	(615)	24,644	18,794
*38138	Germantown	(901)	37,648	33,159
37072	Goodlettsville	(615)	14,096	11,219
37073	Greenbrier	(615)	5,583	3,062
*37743	Greeneville	(423)	15,168	13,532
37215	Green Hill(c)	(615)	7,068	6,763
37748	Harriman	(865)	6,680	7,119
37341	Harrison(c)	(423)	7,630	7,191
37074	Hartsville-Trousdale	(615)	7,354	2,222
38340	Henderson	(731)	6,142	4,760
37075	Hendersonville	(615)	42,216	32,188
38343	Humboldt	(731)	9,425	9,651
*38301	Jackson	(731)	60,635	49,145
37760	Jefferson City	(865)	7,742	5,875
*37601	Johnson City	(423)	56,767	50,354
*37662	Kingsport	(423)	44,362	40,457
37763	Kingston	(423)	5,306	4,552
*37950	Knoxville	(865)	173,661	169,761
37766	La Follette	(423)	7,970	7,201
38002	Lakeland	(901)	7,139	1,204
37086	La Vergne	(615)	21,506	7,496
38464	Lawrenceburg	(931)	10,801	10,393
*37087	Lebanon	(615)	20,853	15,208
*37771	Lenoir City	(865)	7,097	6,147
37091	Lewisburg	(931)	10,745	9,879
38351	Lexington	(731)	7,410	5,810
37352	Lynchburg	(931)	5,928	4,721
38201	McKenzie	(731)	5,338	5,168
*37110	McMinnville	(931)	12,941	11,194
*37355	Manchester	(931)	8,830	7,709
38237	Martin	(731)	10,199	8,588
*37804	Maryville	(865)	24,106	19,208
*38101	Memphis	(901)	648,882	618,652
37343	Middle Valley(c)	(423)	11,854	12,255
38358	Milan	(731)	7,803	7,512
37357	Millersville	(615)	5,876	2,575
*38053	Millington	(901)	10,382	17,866
37813	Morristown	(423)	25,137	22,513
37645	Mount Carmel	(423)	5,044	4,268
*37122	Mount Juliet	(615)	15,465	5,389
38058	Munford	(901)	5,108	2,944
*37130	Murfreesboro	(615)	74,894	44,922
*37202	Nashville	(615)	545,915	488,366
*37821	Newport	(423)	7,206	7,123
*37830	Oak Ridge	(865)	27,228	27,310
37363	Ooltewah (c)	(423)	5,681	4,903
38242	Paris	(731)	9,676	9,332
*37862	Pigeon Forge	(865)	5,325	3,027
37148	Portland	(615)	9,419	5,539

ZIP	Place	Area Code	2002	1990
38478	Pulaski	(931)	7,965	7,916
37415	Red Bank	(423)	12,146	12,320
38063	Ripley	(731)	7,715	6,634
37854	Rockwood	(865)	5,726	5,348
38372	Savannah	(731)	6,997	6,547
*37862	Sevierville	(865)	13,438	7,178
37865	Seymour(c)	(865)	8,850	7,026
*37160	Shelbyville	(931)	17,184	14,042
37377	Signal Mountain	(423)	7,331	7,034
37167	Smyrna	(615)	28,826	14,720
*37379	Soddy-Daisy	(423)	11,881	8,240
37311	South Cleveland(c)	(423)	6,216	5,372
37172	Springfield	(615)	14,982	11,227
37174	Spring Hill	(931)	10,283	1,464
37874	Sweetwater	(423)	5,663	5,066
37388	Tullahoma	(931)	18,304	16,761
*38261	Union City	(731)	10,770	10,513
37188	White House	(615)	7,958	2,987
38075	Whiteville	(731)	5,975	1,229
37398	Winchester	(931)	7,512	6,305

Texas

Area codes (281) and (832) overlay area code (713). Area code (430) overlays (903). Area code (682) overlays (817). Area codes (972) and (469) overlay (214). See introductory note.

ZIP	Place	Area Code	2002	1990
*79604	Abilene	(325)	115,225	106,707
—	Abram-Perezville (c)		5,444	3,999
75001	Addison	(214)	14,117	8,783
78516	Alamo	(956)	15,518	8,352
78209	Alamo Heights	(210)	7,262	6,502
77039	Aldine(c)	(713)	13,979	11,133
*78332	Alice	(361)	19,104	19,788
*75002	Allen	(214)	57,216	19,315
*79830	Alpine	(432)	5,934	5,622
—	Alton North (c)		5,051	—
*77511	Alvin	(713)	22,025	19,220
*79105	Amarillo	(806)	177,010	157,571
78750	Anderson Mill(c)		8,953	9,468
79714	Andrews	(432)	9,576	10,678
*77515	Angleton	(979)	18,538	17,140
*78336	Aransas Pass	(361)	8,276	7,180
*76004	Arlington	(817)	349,944	261,717
77346	Atascocita (c)	(281)	35,757	—
75751	Athens	(903)	11,716	10,982
75551	Atlanta	(214)	5,640	6,118
78712	Austin	(512)	671,873	472,020
*76020	Azle	(817)	9,968	8,868
75518	Balcliff(c)	(409)	6,962	5,549
75180	Balch Springs	(214)	19,480	17,406
78602	Bastrop	(512)	6,233	4,044
*77414	Bay City	(979)	18,450	18,170
*77520	Baytown	(713)	67,360	63,843
77707	Beaumont	(409)	112,871	114,323
76021	Bedford	(817)	48,378	43,762
*78102	Beeville	(361)	12,962	13,547
*77401	Bellaire	(713)	16,739	13,844
76715	Bellmead	(254)	9,480	8,336
76513	Belton	(254)	14,621	12,463
76126	Benbrook	(817)	20,652	19,564
*79720	Big Spring	(432)	24,798	23,093
*78006	Boerne	(830)	6,566	4,361
75418	Bonham	(903)	10,045	6,688
*79007	Borger	(806)	13,709	15,675
76230	Bowie	(940)	5,231	4,990
76825	Brady	(325)	5,289	5,946
76424	Breckenridge	(254)	5,690	5,665
*77833	Brenham	(979)	13,568	11,952
—	Briar (c)		5,350	3,899
77611	Bridge City	(409)	8,629	8,010
79316	Brownfield	(806)	9,438	9,560
*78520	Brownsville	(956)	150,425	107,027
*76801	Brownwood	(325)	19,093	18,387
78717	Brushy Creek(c)	(903)	15,371	5,833
*77801	Bryan	(979)	66,669	55,002
76354	Burkburnett	(940)	10,778	10,145
*76028	Burleson	(817)	23,825	16,113
76520	Cameron	(254)	5,757	5,635
—	Cameron Park (c)		5,961	3,802
79835	Canutillo (c)	(915)	5,129	4,442
79015	Canyon	(806)	12,980	11,365
78130	Canyon Lake(c)	(830)	16,870	9,975
78834	Carrizo Springs	(830)	5,584	5,745
*75006	Carrollton	(214)	115,107	82,169
75633	Carthage	(903)	6,544	6,496
*75104	Cedar Hill	(214)	37,269	19,988
*78613	Cedar Park	(512)	37,764	5,161
75935	Center	(936)	5,635	4,950
77530	Channelview(c)	(713)	29,685	25,564
79201	Childress	(940)	6,650	5,055
—	Cinco Ranch (c)	(281)	11,196	—
*76031	Cleburne	(817)	27,492	22,205
*77327	Cleveland	(713)	7,830	7,124
77015	Cloverleaf(c)	(713)	23,508	18,230
77531	Clute	(979)	10,698	9,467
76834	Coleman	(325)	5,010	5,410
*77840	College Station	(979)	70,550	52,443
76034	Colleyville	(817)	21,085	12,724
*75428	Commerce	(903)	8,243	6,825

ZIP	Place	Area Code	2002	1990
*77301	Conroe	(936)	39,065	27,675
78109	Converse	(210)	11,939	8,887
75019	Coppell	(214)	39,460	16,881
76522	Copperas Cove	(254)	29,599	24,079
76205	Corinth	(940)	14,925	3,944
*78469	Corpus Christi	(361)	278,520	257,428
*75110	Corsicana	(903)	25,187	22,911
75835	Crockett	(936)	7,084	7,024
76036	Crowley	(817)	8,174	6,974
78839	Crystal City	(830)	7,114	8,263
77954	Cuero	(361)	6,654	6,700
79022	Dalhart	(806)	7,164	6,246
*75221	Dallas	(214)	1,211,467	1,007,618
77535	Dayton	(936)	6,038	5,042
76234	Decatur	(214)	5,584	4,245
77536	Deer Park	(713)	28,992	27,424
*75840	Del Rio	(830)	34,611	30,705
*75020	Denison	(903)	23,169	21,505
*76201	Denton	(940)	90,349	66,270
*75115	De Soto	(214)	39,440	30,544
75941	Diboll	(936)	5,439	4,341
77539	Dickinson	(281)	17,668	11,692
78537	Donna	(956)	15,478	12,652
79029	Dumas	(806)	13,808	12,871
*75138	Duncanville	(214)	36,203	35,008
76135	Eagle Mountain(c)	(817)	6,599	5,847
*78852	Eagle Pass	(830)	23,506	20,651
*78539	Edinburg	(956)	52,764	31,091
77957	Edna	(361)	5,871	5,436
—	Eidson Road (c)		9,348	—
77437	El Campo	(979)	10,889	10,511
78621	Elgin	(512)	6,313	4,846
*79910	El Paso	(915)	577,415	515,342
78543	Elsa	(956)	5,934	5,242
75119	Ennis	(214)	17,883	13,869
*76039	Euless	(817)	48,464	38,149
76140	Everman	(817)	5,880	5,672
79838	Fabens(c)	(915)	8,043	5,599
78015	Fair Oaks Ranch	(210)	5,186	1,886
78355	Falfurrias	(361)	5,134	5,788
75381	Farmers Branch	(214)	27,454	24,250
78114	Floresville	(830)	6,329	5,247
75067	Flower Mound	(214)	58,642	15,527
76119	Forest Hill	(817)	13,223	11,482
75126	Forney	(214)	6,378	4,070
79906	Fort Bliss(c)	(915)	8,264	13,915
76544	Fort Hood(c)	(254)	33,711	35,580
79735	Fort Stockton	(432)	7,588	8,524
*76161	Fort Worth	(817)	567,516	447,619
78624	Fredericksburg	(830)	9,346	6,934
*77541	Freeport	(979)	12,802	11,389
*77546	Friendswood	(281)	31,497	22,814
75034	Frisco	(214)	47,652	6,138
76240	Gainesville	(940)	15,930	14,256
77547	Galena Park	(713)	10,588	10,033
*77550	Galveston	(409)	56,685	59,067
*75040	Garland	(214)	219,646	180,635
76528	Gatesville	(254)	15,195	11,492
*78626	Georgetown	(512)	33,246	14,840
78942	Giddings	(979)	5,269	4,093
75647	Gladewater	(903)	6,161	6,027
75115	Glenn Heights	(214)	7,946	4,564
78629	Gonzales	(830)	7,244	6,527
76450	Graham	(940)	8,581	8,986
*76048	Granbury	(817)	6,162	4,045
*75051	Grand Prairie	(214)	135,303	99,606
*76051	Grapevine	(817)	45,830	29,407
—	Greatwood (c)		6,640	—
*75401	Greenville	(903)	24,504	23,071
77619	Groves	(409)	15,414	16,744
75147	Gun Barrel City	(903)	5,411	3,526
76117	Haltom City	(817)	39,889	32,856
76548	Harker Heights	(254)	18,055	12,923
78550	Harlingen	(956)	59,384	48,746
75032	Heath	(214)	5,455	2,128
77445	Hempstead	(979)	5,692	3,598
*77652	Henderson	(903)	11,150	11,139
79045	Hereford	(806)	14,423	14,745
76643	Hewitt	(254)	11,944	8,983
78557	Hidalgo	(956)	8,599	3,292
75205	Highland Park	(214)	8,920	8,739
77562	Highlands(c)	(713)	7,089	6,632
75067	Highland Village	(214)	13,527	7,027
76645	Hillsboro	(254)	8,590	7,072
77563	Hitchcock	(409)	7,107	5,868
—	Homestead Meadows South (c)		6,807	—
78861	Hondo	(830)	8,117	6,018
79927	Horizon City	(915)	6,707	2,308
*77052	Houston	(281)/(713)/(832)	2,009,834	1,654,348
77338	Humble	(713)	14,847	12,060
*77340	Huntsville	(936)	35,730	30,628
76053	Hurst	(817)	36,809	33,574
78362	Ingleside	(361)	8,796	5,696
76367	Iowa Park	(940)	6,323	6,072
*75015	Irving	(214)	196,119	155,037
77029	Jacinto City	(713)	10,382	9,343
75766	Jacksonville	(214)	14,034	12,765
75951	Jasper	(409)	7,634	7,160
77040	Jersey Village	(713)	7,181	4,826
78729	Jollyville(c)	(512)	15,813	15,206

ZIP	Place	Area Code	2002	1990
76058	Joshua	(817)	5,004	3,634
*77449	Katy	(713)	12,430	8,004
75142	Kaufman	(214)	7,204	5,251
76059	Keene	(817)	5,396	3,944
*76248	Keller	(817)	32,921	13,683
76060	Kennedale	(817)	6,320	4,096
79745	Kermit	(432)	5,466	6,875
*78028	Kerrville	(830)	21,090	17,384
75662	Kilgore	(903)	11,477	11,066
76540	Killeen	(254)	92,707	63,535
78363	Kingsville	(361)	25,175	25,276
78219	Kirby	(210)	8,707	8,326
78640	Kyle	(512)	8,540	2,225
78236	Lackland AFB(c)	(210)	7,123	9,352
76705	Lacy-Lakeview	(254)	5,778	3,617
78559	La Feria	(956)	6,361	4,360
—	La Homa (c)		10,433	1,403
75065	Lake Dallas	(940)	6,647	3,656
77566	Lake Jackson	(979)	26,954	22,771
78734	Lakeway	(512)	8,236	4,044
77568	La Marque	(409)	13,729	14,120
79331	Lamesa	(806)	9,657	10,809
76550	Lampasas	(512)	7,207	6,382
*75146	Lancaster	(214)	27,082	22,117
*77571	La Porte	(713)	33,214	27,923
*78041	Laredo	(956)	191,538	122,893
*77573	League City	(281)	51,397	30,159
*78641	Leander	(512)	11,661	3,354
78268	Leon Valley	(210)	9,338	9,581
*79336	Levelland	(806)	12,932	13,986
*75067	Lewisville	(214)	83,960	46,521
77575	Liberty	(936)	8,263	7,690
75068	Little Elm	(214)	9,147	1,242
79339	Littlefield	(806)	6,456	6,489
78233	Live Oak	(210)	9,567	10,023
77351	Livingston	(936)	6,172	5,019
78644	Lockhart	(512)	12,769	9,205
*75606	Longview	(903)	74,330	70,311
*79408	Lubbock	(806)	203,715	186,206
*75901	Lufkin	(936)	32,748	30,210
78648	Luling	(830)	5,281	4,661
77657	Lumberton	(409)	8,905	6,640
*78501	McAllen	(956)	113,877	84,021
75070	McKinney	(214)	73,081	21,283
76063	Mansfield	(817)	31,630	15,615
78654	Marble Falls	(830)	5,276	4,017
76661	Marlin	(254)	6,428	6,386
*75670	Marshall	(903)	23,977	23,682
78368	Mathis	(361)	5,198	5,423
77477	Meadows Place	(281)/(713)	5,176	4,663
78570	Mercedes	(956)	14,150	12,694
75149	Mesquite	(214)	128,776	101,484
76667	Mexia	(254)	6,583	6,933
*79701	Midland	(432)	95,829	89,343
76065	Midlothian	(214)	9,815	5,040
76067	Mineral Wells	(940)	16,968	14,935
*78572	Mission	(956)	51,432	28,653
—	Mission Bend(c)		30,831	24,945
*77489	Missouri City	(713)	59,186	36,143
79756	Monahans	(432)	6,541	8,101
*75455	Mount Pleasant	(903)	14,174	12,291
75094	Murphy	(214)	6,675	1,603
*75961	Nacogdoches	(936)	30,289	30,872
77868	Navasota	(936)	7,154	6,296
77627	Nederland	(409)	17,035	16,192
78130	New Braunfels	(830)	41,239	27,334
—	New Territory (c)	(281)	13,861	—
*76161	North Richland Hills	(817)	59,186	45,895
—	Nurillo (c)		5,056	—
*79761	Odessa	(432)	90,961	89,699
*79630	Orange	(409)	18,198	19,370
77465	Palacios	(361)	5,238	4,418
*75801	Palestine	(903)	17,731	18,042
—	Palmview South (c)		6,219	
*79065	Pampa	(806)	17,312	19,959
*75460	Paris	(903)	26,212	24,799
*77501	Pasadena	(713)	145,034	119,604
*77581	Pearland	(713)	44,540	18,927
78061	Pearsall	(830)	7,105	6,924
78721	Pecan Grove(c)		13,551	9,502
79772	Pecos	(432)	8,945	12,069
79070	Perryton	(806)	7,827	7,619
*78660	Pflugerville	(512)	23,072	4,444
78577	Pharr	(956)	51,278	32,921
*79072	Plainview	(806)	21,916	21,698
*75074	Plano	(214)	238,091	127,885
78064	Pleasanton	(830)	8,732	7,678
*77640	Port Arthur	(409)	56,885	58,551
78578	Port Isabel	(956)	5,174	4,740
78374	Portland	(361)	15,422	12,224
77979	Port Lavaca	(361)	11,939	10,886
77651	Port Neches	(409)	13,338	12,908
78579	Progreso	(956)	5,053	2,808
78580	Raymondville	(956)	9,630	8,880
75154	Red Oak	(214)	5,458	3,660
76028	Rendon(c)	(817)	9,022	7,658
*75080	Richardson	(214)	96,956	74,840
76118	Richland Hills	(817)	8,204	7,978
*77469	Richmond	(713)	11,863	10,042
78043	Rio Bravo		5,657	

ZIP	Place	Area Code	2002	1990
78582	Rio Grande City	(956)	12,603	10,725
76219	River Oaks	(817)	7,049	6,580
76701	Robinson	(254)	8,220	7,111
78380	Robstown	(361)	12,608	12,849
76567	Rockdale	(512)	5,439	5,235
*78382	Rockport	(361)	8,192	5,619
75087	Rockwall	(214)	22,334	10,486
78584	Roma	(956)	10,135	8,059
77471	Rosenberg	(713)	27,136	20,183
*78681	Round Rock	(512)	73,858	30,923
75088	Rowlett	(214)	49,908	23,260
75785	Rusk	(903)	5,228	4,366
75048	Sachse	(214)	13,015	5,346
76179	Saginaw	(817)	15,389	8,551
*76902	San Angelo	(325)	87,423	84,462
*78265	San Antonio	(210)	1,194,222	976,514
78586	San Benito	(956)	24,068	20,125
79849	San Elizario (c)	(915)	11,046	4,385
76266	Sanger	(940)	5,006	3,602
78589	San Juan	(956)	28,182	12,561
78666	San Marcos	(512)	41,602	28,738
*77510	Santa Fe	(409)	10,019	8,429
78154	Schertz	(210)	20,762	10,597
77586	Seabrook	(281)	10,177	6,685
75159	Seagoville	(214)	11,094	8,969
77474	Sealy	(979)	5,563	4,541
78155	Seguin	(830)	22,741	18,692
79360	Seminole	(432)	5,803	6,342
—	Shady Hollow (c)		5,140	—
*75090	Sherman	(903)	35,788	31,584
77656	Silsbee	(409)	6,451	6,368
78387	Sinton	(361)	5,590	5,549
79364	Slaton	(806)	6,047	6,078
*79549	Snyder	(325)	10,415	12,195
79910	Socorro	(915)	27,964	22,995
77587	South Houston	(713)	16,102	14,207
76092	Southlake	(817)	23,767	7,082
*77373	Spring(c)	(713)	36,385	33,111
77477	Stafford	(713)	17,935	8,395
76401	Stephenville	(254)	14,894	13,502
77478	Sugar Land	(713)	68,599	33,712
*75482	Sulphur Springs	(903)	14,612	14,062
79556	Sweetwater	(325)	10,937	11,967
76574	Taylor	(512)	14,062	11,472
*76501	Temple	(254)	54,447	46,150
*75160	Terrell	(214)	15,147	12,490
78209	Terrell Hills	(210)	5,044	4,592
*75501	Texarkana	(903)	35,205	32,294
*77590	Texas City	(409)	43,063	40,822
75056	The Colony	(214)	32,257	22,113
77387	The Woodlands(c)	(713)	55,649	29,205
—	Timberwood Park (c)	(210)	5,889	2,578
*77375	Tomball	(713)	9,725	6,370
76262	Trophy Club	(817)	7,027	3,922
75702	Tyler	(903)	87,030	75,450
*78148	Universal City	(830)	15,073	13,057
76308	University Park	(214)	23,817	22,259
78801	Uvalde	(830)	15,179	14,729
76384	Vernon	(940)	11,044	12,001
*77901	Victoria	(361)	61,031	55,076
*77662	Vidor	(409)	11,302	10,935
76702	Waco	(254)	115,749	103,590
75501	Wake Village	(903)	5,175	4,761
76148	Watauga	(817)	23,376	20,009
*75165	Waxahachie	(214)	23,059	17,984
*76086	Weatherford	(817)	20,619	14,804
77598	Webster	(281)	9,158	4,678
78728	Wells Branch(c)		11,271	7,094
*78596	Weslaco	(956)	29,094	22,739
—	West Livingston (c)		6,612	—
*79764	West Odessa(c)	(432)	17,799	16,568
77005	West University Place	(713)	14,908	12,920
77488	Wharton	(979)	9,386	9,011
75791	Whitehouse	(903)	6,235	4,018
75693	White Oak	(903)	5,786	5,136
76108	White Settlement	(817)	15,154	15,472
*76307	Wichita Falls	(940)	102,926	96,259
78239	Windcrest	(210)	5,110	5,331
—	Windemere (c)		6,868	3,207
76712	Woodway	(254)	8,721	8,695
75098	Wylie	(214)	18,380	8,716
77995	Yoakum	(361)	5,715	5,611

Utah

Area code (385) goes into effect Mar. 30, 2005. Before then use (801).

ZIP	Place	Area Code	2002	1990
84004	Alpine	(385)	7,738	3,492
84003	American Fork	(385)	22,501	15,722
*84010	Bountiful	(385)	41,270	37,544
84302	Brigham City	(435)	17,389	15,644
84109	Canyon Rim(c)	(435)	10,428	10,527
84720	Cedar City	(435)	21,427	13,443
84014	Centerville	(385)	14,690	11,500
*84015	Clearfield	(385)	26,309	21,435
84015	Clinton	(385)	14,353	7,945
84121	Cottonwood Heights(c)	(801)	27,569	28,766
84121	Cottonwood West(c)	(801)	18,727	17,476
84020	Draper	(801)	29,268	7,143
84043	Eagle Mountain	(801)	6,093	30
84109	East Millcreek(c)	(801)	21,385	21,184

ZIP	Place	Area Code	2002	1990
84025	Farmington	(385)	12,954	9,049
84029	Grantsville	(435)	6,636	4,500
84032	Heber	(801)	8,470	4,782
84003	Highland	(385)	9,724	5,007
84117	Holladay	(801)	13,524	14,095
84737	Hurricane	(435)	9,138	3,915
84319	Hyrum	(435)	6,303	4,829
84738	Ivins	(435)	5,554	1,639
84037	Kaysville	(385)	20,959	13,961
84118	Kearns(c)	(801)	33,659	28,374
*84041	Layton	(385)	60,064	41,784
84043	Lehi	(385)	21,841	8,475
84042	Lindon	(385)	8,647	3,818
—	Little Cottonwood Creek Valley(c)	(801)	7,221	5,042
*84321	Logan	(435)	42,922	32,771
84044	Magna (c)	(801)	22,770	17,829
84664	Mapleton	(801)	6,053	3,572
84047	Midvale	(801)	27,318	11,886
84109	Millcreek(c)	(801)	30,377	32,230
84117	Mount Olympus(c)	(801)	7,103	7,413
84157	Murray	(801)	35,055	31,274
84341	North Logan	(435)	6,745	3,775
84404	North Ogden	(385)	15,815	11,593
84054	North Salt Lake	(801)	9,176	6,464
*84401	Ogden	(385)	78,641	63,943
—	Oquirrh(c)	(801)	10,390	7,593
*84057	Orem	(801)	83,662	67,561
*84060	Park City	(801)	7,715	4,468
84651	Payson	(385)	14,335	9,510
84062	Pleasant Grove	(385)	23,597	13,476
84404	Pleasant View	(385)	5,898	3,597
84501	Price	(435)	8,330	8,712
*84601	Provo	(385)	105,170	86,835
84701	Richfield	(435)	6,873	5,593
84403	Riverdale	(385)	7,805	6,419
84065	Riverton	(801)	28,297	11,261
84067	Roy	(385)	34,997	24,560
*84770	Saint George	(435)	54,049	28,572
*84101	Salt Lake City	(801)	181,266	159,928
*84070	Sandy	(801)	89,244	75,240
84765	Santa Clara	(435)	5,096	2,323
84655	Santaquin	(801)	5,422	2,522
84335	Smithfield	(435)	7,604	5,566
84095	South Jordan	(801)	31,816	12,215
84403	South Ogden	(385)	14,700	12,105
84165	South Salt Lake	(801)	21,901	10,129
*84403	South Weber	(801)	5,176	2,853
84660	Spanish Fork	(385)	22,413	11,272
84663	Springville	(385)	21,544	13,950
84098	Summit Park (c)		6,597	—
84015	Sunset	(385)	5,101	5,128
84075	Syracuse	(385)	12,423	4,658
84107	Taylorsville	(801)	59,115	51,550
84074	Tooele	(435)	25,959	13,887
84337	Tremonton	(435)	5,996	4,262
*84078	Vernal	(435)	7,879	6,640
84780	Washington	(435)	9,683	4,198
84403	Washington Terrace	(385)	8,530	8,189
*84084	West Jordan	(801)	73,355	42,915
84015	West Point	(385)	6,251	4,258
84170	West Valley City	(801)	111,254	86,969
84070	White City(c)	(801)	5,988	6,506
84087	Woods Cross	(385)	7,020	5,384

Vermont (802)
See introductory note.

ZIP	Place		2002	1990
05641	Barre		9,245	9,482
05641	Barre		7,770	7,411
05201	Bennington(c)		9,168	9,532
05201	Bennington		15,675	16,451
*05301	Brattleboro		11,986	12,241
*05301	Brattleboro (c).		8,289	8,612
*05401	Burlington		39,466	39,127
*05446	Colchester		17,167	14,731
05451	Essex		18,896	16,498
05452	Essex Junction		8,641	8,396
05047	Hartford		10,459	9,404
05465	Jericho		5,063	1,405
05849	Lyndon		5,504	5,371
05753	Middlebury (c).		6,252	6,007
*05753	Middlebury		8,188	8,034
05468	Milton		9,906	8,404
*05602	Montpelier		8,026	8,247
05661	Morristown		5,346	4,733
05855	Newport		5,045	4,434
05663	Northfield		5,826	5,610
05101	Rockingham		5,248	5,484
*05701	Rutland		17,098	18,230
05478	Saint Albans		7,653	7,339
05478	Saint Albans		5,320	4,606
05819	Saint Johnsbury (c)		6,319	6,424
05819	Saint Johnsbury		7,540	7,608
05482	Shelburne		6,953	5,071
*05401	South Burlington		15,870	12,809
05156	Springfield		9,056	9,579
05488	Swanton		6,351	5,636
05676	Waterbury		5,086	4,614
05495	Williston		8,178	4,887
05404	Winooski		6,469	6,649

Virginia
Area code (571) overlays area code (703). See introductory note.

ZIP	Place	Area Code	2002	1990
*24210	Abingdon	(276)	7,619	7,003
*22313	Alexandria	(703)	130,804	111,182
22003	Annandale(c)	(703)	54,994	50,975
22554	Aquia Harbour(c)	(703)	7,856	6,308
*22210	Arlington(c)	(703)	189,453	170,897
23005	Ashland	(804)	6,840	5,864
*22041	Bailey's Crossroads(c)	(703)	23,166	19,507
24523	Bedford	(540)	6,225	6,177
22306	Belle Haven(c)	(757)	6,269	6,427
23234	Bellwood(c)	(804)	5,974	6,178
23234	Bensley(c)	(804)	5,435	5,093
24219	Big Stone Gap	(276)	5,823	4,847
24060	Blacksburg	(540)	40,108	34,590
23235	Bon Air(c)	(804)	16,213	16,413
22812	Bridgewater	(540)	5,167	3,918
*24203	Bristol	(276)	17,118	18,426
24416	BuenaVista	(540)	6,300	6,406
—	Bull Run(c)	(703)	11,337	5,525
*22150	Burke(c)	(703)	57,737	57,734
24018	Cave Spring(c)	(540)	24,941	24,053
20120	Centreville(c)	(703)	48,661	26,585
*20151	Chantilly(c)	(703)	41,041	29,337
22906	Charlottesville	(434)	43,833	40,475
*23320	Chesapeake	(757)	206,665	151,982
23831	Chester(c)	(804)	17,890	14,986
*24073	Christiansburg	(540)	17,545	15,004
24078	Collinsville(c)	(276)	7,777	7,280
23834	Colonial Heights	(804)	17,063	16,064
24426	Covington	(540)	6,361	7,198
22701	Culpeper	(540)	10,138	8,581
22193	Dale City(c)	(540)	55,971	47,170
*24541	Danville	(434)	47,596	53,056
23228	Dumbarton(c)	(804)	6,674	8,526
22026	Dumfries	(703)	5,007	4,280
22027	Dunn Loring(c)	(703)	7,861	6,509
23222	East Highland Park(c)	(804)	12,488	11,850
23847	Emporia	(434)	5,734	5,479
23803	Ettrick(c)	(804)	5,627	5,290
*22030	Fairfax	(703)	22,055	19,894
*22046	Falls Church	(703)	10,659	9,522
23901	Farmville	(434)	6,788	6,505
24551	Forest(c)	(434)	8,006	5,624
22060	Fort Belvoir(c)	(703)	7,176	8,590
22308	Fort Hunt(c)	(703)	12,923	12,989
23801	Fort Lee(c)	(804)	7,269	6,895
22310	Franconia(c)	(703)	31,907	19,882
23851	Franklin	(757)	8,170	7,864
*22404	Fredericksburg	(540)	20,076	19,027
22630	Front Royal	(540)	13,894	11,880
24333	Galax	(276)	6,590	6,699
*23060	Glen Allen(c)	(804)	12,562	9,010
23062	Gloucester Point(c)	(804)	9,429	8,509
22066	Great Falls(c)	(703)	8,549	6,945
22306	Groveton(c)	(703)	21,296	19,997
*23670	Hampton	(757)	145,921	133,811
22801	Harrisonburg	(540)	40,909	30,707
23075	Highland Springs(c)	(804)	15,137	13,823
24019	Hollins(c)	(540)	14,309	13,305
23860	Hopewell	(804)	22,525	23,101
22303	Huntington(c)	(703)	8,325	7,489
22306	Hybla Valley(c)	(703)	16,721	15,491
22043	Idylwood(c)	(703)	16,005	14,710
22042	Jefferson(c)	(703)	27,422	25,782
22041	Lake Barcroft(c)	(703)	8,906	8,686
22963	Lake Monticello (c)	(434)	6,852	2,331
22191	Lake Ridge(c)	(540)	30,404	23,862
23228	Lakeside(c)	(804)	11,157	12,081
23060	Laurel(c)	(804)	14,875	13,011
*20175	Leesburg	(703)	31,584	16,202
24450	Lexington	(540)	6,910	6,959
22312	Lincolnia(c)	(703)	15,788	13,041
—	Linton Hall (c)		8,620	—
*22079	Lorton(c)	(703)	17,786	15,385
*24506	Lynchburg	(434)	64,616	66,049
*22101	McLean(c)	(703)	38,929	-38,168
24572	Madison Heights(c)	(434)	11,584	11,700
*20110	Manassas	(703)	37,288	27,957
20113	Manassas Park	(703)	10,909	6,734
22030	Mantua(c)	(703)	7,485	6,804
24354	Marion	(276)	6,231	6,630
*24112	Martinsville	(276)	15,263	16,162
*23111	Mechanicsville(c)	(804)	30,464	22,027
*22116	Merrifield(c)	(703)	11,170	8,399
—	Montclair(c)		15,728	11,399
23231	Montrose(c)	(804)	7,018	6,405
22121	Mount Vernon(c)	(703)	28,582	27,485
22122	Newington(c)	(703)	19,784	17,965
*23607	Newport News	(757)	180,272	171,439
*23501	Norfolk	(757)	239,036	261,250
22151	North Springfield(c)	(703)	9,173	8,996
22124	Oakton(c)	(703)	29,348	24,610
*23804	Petersburg	(804)	33,115	37,027
22043	Pimmit Hills(c)	(703)	6,152	6,019
23662	Poquoson	(757)	11,686	11,005
*23707	Portsmouth	(757)	99,790	103,910
24301	Pulaski	(540)	9,232	9,985

ZIP	Place	Area Code	2002	1990
22134	Quantico Station(c)	(703)	6,571	7,425
*24141	Radford	(540)	15,670	15,940
*20190	Reston(c)	(703)	56,407	48,556
*23232	Richmond	(804)	197,456	202,798
*24022	Roanoke	(540)	93,873	96,509
24281	Rose Hill(c)	(276)	15,058	12,675
24153	Salem	(540)	24,836	23,797
22044	Seven Corners(c)	(703)	8,701	7,280
*23430	Smithfield	(757)	6,594	4,686
24592	South Boston	(434)	8,323	6,997
22150	Springfield(c)	(703)	30,417	23,706
*24402	Staunton	(540)	23,635	24,461
24477	Stuarts Draft(c)	(540)	8,367	5,087
23162	Sudley(c)	(540)	7,719	7,321
*23434	Suffolk	(757)	69,966	52,143
24502	Timberlake(c)	(434)	10,683	10,314
22172	Triangle	(703)	5,500	4,740
23229	Tuckahoe(c)	(804)	43,242	42,629
22101	Tysons Corner(c)	(703)	18,540	13,124
*22180	Vienna	(703)	14,855	14,852
24179	Vinton	(540)	7,669	7,643
*23450	Virginia Beach	(757)	433,934	393,089
*20186	Warrenton	(540)	7,413	4,882
22980	Waynesboro	(540)	20,134	18,549
22110	West Gate(c)	(703)	7,493	6,565
22152	West Springfield(c)	(703)	28,378	28,126
*23185	Williamsburg	(757)	11,693	11,409
*22601	Winchester	(540)	24,228	21,947
24592	Wolf Trap(c)	(703)	14,001	13,133
*22191	Woodbridge(c)	(540)	31,941	26,401
—	Wyndham (c)		6,176	—
24382	Wytheville	(276)	7,816	8,036
22110	Yorkshire(c)	(703)	6,732	5,699

Washington

ZIP	Place	Area Code	2002	1990
98520	Aberdeen	(360)	16,271	16,565
98036	Alderwood Manor(c)	(425)	15,329	22,945
98221	Anacortes	(360)	15,203	11,451
98223	Arlington	(360)	13,366	4,037
98335	Artondale(c)	(253)	8,630	7,141
*98002	Auburn	(253)	44,132	33,650
98110	Bainbridge Island	(206)	21,303	—
98315	Bangor Trident Base (c)	(360)	7,253	3,702
98604	Battle Ground	(360)	9,900	3,758
*98009	Bellevue	(425)	112,894	95,213
*98225	Bellingham	(360)	70,480	52,179
98390	Bonney Lake	(360)	12,396	7,494
*98011	Bothell	(425)	30,706	12,575
*98337	Bremerton	(360)	36,306	38,142
98036	Brier	(425)	6,391	5,633
98178	Bryn Mawr-Skyway(c)	(206)	13,977	12,514
98166	Burien	(206)	31,448	27,507
98233	Burlington	(360)	7,464	4,349
—	Camano (c)		13,347	—
98607	Camas	(360)	13,957	6,762
98055	Cascade-Fairwood(c)	(425)	34,580	30,107
98531	Centralia	(360)	14,912	12,101
98532	Chehalis	(360)	7,071	6,527
99004	Cheney	(509)	9,497	7,723
99403	Clarkston	(509)	7,192	6,753
—	Clarkston Heights-Vineland (c)		6,117	2,832
99324	College Place	(509)	8,264	6,308
98072	Cottage Lake (c)	(206)	24,330	—
99218	Country Homes(c)	(509)	5,203	5,126
98042	Covington	(253)	14,407	—
98198	Des Moines	(206)	29,328	20,830
99213	Dishman(c)	(509)	10,031	9,671
98019	Duvall	(425)	5,420	2,640
—	East Hill-Meridian(c)		29,308	42,696
98386	East Port Orchard(c)	(360)	5,116	5,409
98056	East Renton Highlands(c)	(425)	13,264	13,218
98802	East Wenatchee	(509)	8,506	3,886
98801	East Wenatchee Bench(c)	(509)	13,658	12,539
98371	Edgewood	(253)	9,450	8,702
*98020	Edmonds	(425)	40,014	30,743
98387	Elk Plain(c)		15,697	12,197
99926	Ellensburg	(509)	15,767	12,360
98022	Enumclaw	(360)	11,013	7,243
98823	Ephrata	(509)	7,028	5,349
*98201	Everett	(425)	97,088	70,937
99218	Fairwood(c)	(509)	6,764	5,807
*98002	Federal Way	(253)	82,174	67,535
98685	Felida (c)	(360)	5,683	3,109
98248	Ferndale	(360)	9,392	5,398
99336	Finley (c)	(509)	5,770	4,897
98466	Fircrest	(253)	5,992	5,270
98597	Five Corners(c)		12,207	6,776
98433	Fort Lewis(c)	(253)	19,089	22,224
98373	Frederickson (c)	(206)	5,758	3,502
*98329	Gig Harbor	(253)	6,581	3,236
98338	Graham (c)	(253)	8,739	—
98930	Grandview	(509)	8,457	7,169
99016	Green Acres (c)	(509)	5,158	4,626
98660	Hazel Dell North(c)	(360)	9,261	6,924
98665	Hazel Dell South(c)	(360)	6,605	5,796
98025	Hobart (c)		6,251	—
—	Hockinson (c)	(360)	5,136	—
98550	Hoquiam	(360)	8,960	8,972

ZIP	Place	Area Code	2002	1990
98011	Inglewood-Finn Hill(c)	(425)	22,661	29,132
*98027	Issaquah	(425)	13,169	7,786
98626	Kelso	(360)	11,787	11,767
98028	Kenmore	(425)	19,008	8,917
*99336	Kennewick	(509)	57,949	42,148
*98031	Kent	(253)/(425)	81,724	37,960
98033	Kingsgate(c)	(425)	12,222	14,259
*98033	Kirkland	(425)	45,534	40,059
98509	Lacey	(360)	32,418	19,279
98155	Lake Forest Park	(206)	12,702	4,031
98002	Lakeland North(c)	(253)	15,085	14,402
98002	Lakeland South(c)	(253)	11,436	9,027
—	Lake Morton-Berrydale (c)		9,659	—
98665	Lake Shore(c)	(360)	6,670	6,268
98258	Lake Stevens	(425)	6,839	3,435
98259	Lakewood	(253)	58,768	55,937
—	Lea Hill(c)		10,871	6,876
98632	Longview	(360)	35,464	31,499
98264	Lynden	(360)	9,581	5,709
*98046	Lynnwood	(425)	33,908	28,637
98290	Maltby (c)	(360)	8,267	—
98038	Maple Valley	(425)	14,112	1,211
98012	Martha Lake(c)	(425)	12,633	10,155
*98270	Marysville	(360)	27,759	12,248
98040	Mercer Island	(206)	22,313	20,816
98444	Midland(c)	(253)	7,414	5,587
98802	Mill Creek	(425)	12,554	7,180
—	Mill Plain (c)	(360)	7,400	—
98354	Milton	(253)	6,099	4,995
98661	Minnehaha(c)	(360)	7,689	9,661
98272	Monroe	(360)	14,532	4,275
98837	Moses Lake	(509)	15,976	11,235
98043	Mountlake Terrace	(425)	20,814	19,320
*98273	Mount Vernon	(360)	27,208	17,647
—	Mount Vista (c)		5,770	—
98275	Mukilteo	(425)	18,951	11,575
98059	Newcastle	(425)	8,599	4,649
98166	Normandy Park	(206)	6,310	6,794
—	North Creek(c)		25,742	23,236
98270	North Marysville(c)	(425)	21,161	18,711
98277	Oak Harbor	(360)	20,573	17,176
*98501	Olympia	(360)	43,519	33,729
99214	Opportunity(c)	(509)	25,065	22,326
98662	Orchards (c)	(360)	17,852	—
*99327	Othello	(509)	5,897	4,638
99027	Otis Orchards-East Farms(c)	(509)	6,318	5,811
98047	Pacific	(253)	5,489	4,622
—	Paine Field-Lake Stickney(c)		24,383	18,670
98444	Parkland(c)	(253)	24,053	20,882
98366	Parkwood(c)	(360)	7,213	6,853
*99301	Pasco	(509)	35,420	20,337
—	Picnic Point-North Lynnwood (c)		22,953	—
*98362	Port Angeles	(360)	18,425	17,710
98366	Port Orchard	(360)	7,660	4,984
98368	Port Townsend	(360)	8,521	7,001
98370	Poulsbo	(360)	7,185	4,848
98390	Prairie Ridge(c)		11,688	8,278
99350	Prosser	(509)	5,015	4,492
*99163	Pullman	(509)	24,929	23,478
*98371	Puyallup	(253)	35,401	23,878
98848	Quincy	(509)	5,341	3,738
*98052	Redmond	(425)	45,929	35,800
*98058	Renton	(425)	53,176	41,688
99352	Richland	(509)	41,496	32,315
98188	Riverton-Boulevard Park(c)	(206)	11,188	15,337
98686	Salmon Creek(c)	(360)	16,767	11,989
*98074	Sammamish	(425)	33,888	—
*98148	SeaTac	(206)	25,233	22,760
*98101	Seattle	(206)/(425)	570,426	516,259
—	Seattle Hill-Silver Firs (c)		35,311	—
98284	Sedro-Woolley	(360)	9,119	6,333
98942	Selah	(509)	6,508	5,113
98584	Shelton	(360)	8,661	7,241
*98133	Shoreline	(206)	52,791	46,979
*98315	Silverdale(c)	(360)	15,816	7,660
*98290	Snohomish	(360)	8,535	6,499
98373	South Hill(c)		31,623	12,963
98387	Spanaway(c)	(253)	21,588	15,001
*99210	Spokane	(509)	196,305	177,165
98388	Steilacoom	(253)	6,188	5,728
*98371	Summit(c)	(253)	8,041	6,312
98390	Sumner	(253)	8,882	7,535
98944	Sunnyside	(509)	14,022	11,238
*98402	Tacoma	(253)	197,553	176,664
98501	Tanglewilde-Thompson Place(c)	(360)	5,670	6,061
—	Terrace Heights (c)		6,447	4,223
98948	Toppenish	(509)	9,081	7,419
98138	Tukwila	(206)	17,157	14,506
98501	Tumwater	(360)	13,104	9,976
*98901	Union Gap	(509)	5,697	3,120
—	Union Hill-Novelty Hill (c)		11,265	—
98467	University Place	(253)	30,608	26,724
*98661	Vancouver	(360)	149,811	62,065
*98013	Vashon(c)	(206)	10,123	—
99037	Veradale(c)	(509)	9,387	7,836
99362	Walla Walla	(509)	29,818	26,482
—	Waller(c)		9,200	6,415
—	Walnut Grove (c)		7,164	3,906
98671	Washougal	(360)	9,197	4,764

ZIP	Place	Area Code	2002	1990
*98801	Wenatchee	(509)	28,268	21,746
—	West Lake Sammamish(c)		5,937	6,087
98258	West Lake Stevens(c)	(425)	18,071	12,453
99353	West Richland	(509)	9,071	3,962
99181	West Valley(c)		10,433	6,594
98166	White Center(c)	(206)	20,975	20,531
98072	Woodinville	(425)	9,150	7,628
*98903	Yakima	(509)	73,298	58,427

West Virginia (304)

ZIP	Place		2002	1990
*25801	Beckley		17,006	18,274
24701	Bluefield		11,190	12,756
26330	Bridgeport		7,403	6,837
26201	Buckhannon		5,724	5,909
*25301	Charleston		51,702	57,287
*26507	Cheat Lake (c)		6,396	3,992
*26301	Clarksburg		16,498	17,970
25301	Cross Lanes(c)		10,353	10,878
25064	Dunbar		7,913	8,697
26241	Elkins		6,990	7,494
*26554	Fairmont		19,026	20,210
26354	Grafton		5,369	5,524
*25704	Huntington		49,910	54,844
25526	Hurricane		5,478	4,461
26726	Keyser		5,562	5,870
*25401	Martinsburg		15,119	14,073
*26505	Morgantown		27,342	25,879
26041	Moundsville		9,764	10,753
26155	New Martinsville		5,872	6,705
25143	Nitro		6,714	6,851
25901	Oak Hill		7,443	6,812
*26101	Parkersburg		32,299	33,862
—	Pea Ridge(c)		6,363	6,535
24740	Princeton		6,233	7,043
25177	Saint Albans		11,223	12,241
25303	South Charleston		12,992	13,645
25569	Teays Valley(c)		12,704	8,436
26105	Vienna		10,855	10,862
26062	Weirton		20,027	22,124
26003	Wheeling		30,367	34,882

Wisconsin

ZIP	Place	Area Code	2002	1990
54301	Ailouez	(920)	15,292	14,431
54720	Altoona	(715)	6,640	5,889
54409	Antigo	(715)	8,390	8,284
*54911	Appleton	(920)	70,633	65,695
54806	Ashland	(715)	8,519	8,695
54304	Ashwaubenon	(920)	17,357	16,376
53913	Baraboo	(608)	10,654	9,203
53916	Beaver Dam	(920)	14,972	14,196
54311	Bellevue Town(c)	(920)	11,828	7,541
*53511	Beloit	(608)	35,678	35,571
54923	Berlin	(920)	5,260	5,371
*53045	Brookfield	(262)	39,510	35,184
53209	Brown Deer	(414)	12,098	12,236
53105	Burlington	(262)	10,540	8,851
53012	Cedarburg	(262)	11,130	10,086
54729	Chippewa Falls	(715)	12,734	12,749
53110	Cudahy	(414)	18,442	18,659
53532	De Forest	(608)	7,852	4,882
53018	Delafield	(262)	6,713	5,347
53115	Delavan	(262)	8,187	6,073
54115	De Pere	(920)	21,635	16,594
*54703	Eau Claire	(715)	62,361	56,806
53121	Elkhorn	(262)	7,819	5,337
53122	Elm Grove	(262)	6,299	6,261
53714	Fitchburg	(608)	21,319	15,648
*54935	Fond du Lac	(920)	42,295	37,755
53538	Fort Atkinson	(920)	11,819	10,213
53217	Fox Point	(414)	6,966	7,238
53132	Franklin	(414)	31,567	21,855
53022	Germantown	(262)	18,739	13,658
53209	Glendale	(414)	13,315	14,088
53024	Grafton	(262)	11,158	9,340
*54303	Green Bay	(920)	101,515	96,466
53129	Greendale	(414)	14,291	15,128
53220	Greenfield	(414)	35,885	33,403
53130	Hales Corners	(414)	7,740	7,623
53027	Hartford	(262)	11,508	8,188
53029	Hartland	(262)	8,530	6,906
54636	Holmen	(608)	6,740	3,220
54303	Howard	(920)	14,794	9,874
54016	Hudson	(715)	9,736	6,378
53037	Jackson	(262)	5,453	2,603
*53545	Janesville	(608)	60,921	52,210
53549	Jefferson	(920)	7,318	6,078
54130	Kaukauna	(920)	13,808	11,982
*53140	Kenosha	(262)	92,513	80,426
54136	Kimberly	(920)	6,185	5,406
*54601	La Crosse	(608)	51,209	51,140
53147	Lake Geneva	(262)	7,249	5,979
54140	Little Chute	(920)	10,833	9,207
53558	McFarland	(608)	6,886	5,232

ZIP	Place	Area Code	2002	1990
*53714	Madison	(608)	215,211	190,766
*54220	Manitowoc	(920)	34,188	32,521
54143	Marinette	(715)	11,559	11,843
54449	Marshfield	(715)	18,606	19,293
53050	Mayville	(920)	5,020	4,416
54952	Menasha	(920)	16,412	14,711
*53051	Menomonee Falls	(262)	33,309	26,840
54751	Menomonie	(715)	15,017	13,547
53097	Mequon	(262)	23,261	18,885
54452	Merrill	(715)	10,143	9,860
53562	Middleton	(608)	16,223	13,785
53563	Milton	(608)	5,130	4,574
*53201	Milwaukee	(414)	590,895	628,088
53716	Monona	(608)	8,032	8,637
53566	Monroe	(608)	10,691	10,241
53572	Mount Horeb	(608)	6,043	4,182
53149	Mukwonago	(262)	6,444	4,495
53150	Muskego	(414)	22,054	16,813
*54956	Neenah	(920)	24,475	23,219
53186	New Berlin	(262)	38,649	33,592
54961	New London	(920)	7,060	6,658
54017	New Richmond	(715)	6,733	5,106
53154	Oak Creek	(414)	30,556	19,513
53066	Oconomowoc	(262)	12,868	10,993
54650	Onalaska	(608)	15,252	12,201
53575	Oregon	(608)	7,873	4,519
*54901	Oshkosh	(920)	63,464	55,006
53072	Pewaukee (city)	(262)	12,492	—
53072	Pewaukee (village)	(262)	8,566	5,287
53818	Platteville	(608)	9,858	9,862
53158	Pleasant Prairie	(262)	17,433	12,037
54467	Plover	(715)	10,786	8,176
53073	Plymouth	(920)	8,056	6,769
53901	Portage	(608)	9,892	8,640
53074	Port Washington	(262)	10,518	9,338
53821	Prairie du Chien	(608)	5,832	5,657
*53401	Racine	(262)	80,712	84,298
53959	Reedsburg	(608)	8,013	5,834
54501	Rhinelander	(715)	7,795	7,382
54401	Rib Mountain (c).	(715)	6,059	4,634
54868	Rice Lake	(715)	8,308	7,998
53581	Richland Center	(608)	5,148	5,018
54971	Ripon	(920)	6,714	7,241
54022	River Falls	(715)	12,637	10,610
53235	Saint Francis	(414)	8,881	9,245
54166	Shawano	(715)	8,249	7,598
*53081	Sheboygan	(920)	49,446	49,587
53085	Sheboygan Falls	(920)	6,825	5,823
53211	Shorewood	(414)	13,543	14,116
53172	South Milwaukee	(414)	21,438	20,958
54656	Sparta	(608)	8,752	7,788
54481	Stevens Point	(715)	24,368	23,002
53589	Stoughton	(608)	12,577	8,786
54235	Sturgeon Bay	(920)	9,480	9,176
53177	Sturtevant	(262)	5,280	3,803
53590	Sun Prairie	(608)	22,531	15,352
54880	Superior	(715)	27,212	27,134
53089	Sussex	(262)	9,248	5,039
54660	Tomah	(608)	8,501	7,572
53181	Twin Lakes	(262)	5,227	3,989
54241	Two Rivers	(920)	12,357	13,030
53593	Verona	(608)	8,965	5,374
*53094	Watertown	(920)	22,367	19,142
53186	Waukesha	(262)	66,186	56,894
53597	Waunakee	(608)	9,536	5,897
54981	Waupaca	(715)	5,864	4,946
53963	Waupun	(920)	10,365	8,844
*54403	Wausau	(715)	37,732	37,060
53213	Wauwatosa	(414)	46,713	49,366
53214	West Allis	(414)	60,638	63,221
*53095	West Bend	(262)	28,670	24,470
54476	Weston	(715)	12,421	9,714
53217	Whitefish Bay	(414)	13,980	14,272
53190	Whitewater	(262)	13,909	12,636
53185	Wind Lake (c)	(262)	5,202	3,748
*54494	Wisconsin Rapids	(715)	18,214	18,245

Wyoming (307)

ZIP	Place		2002	1990
*82609	Casper		50,024	46,765
*82009	Cheyenne		53,658	50,008
82414	Cody		8,832	7,897
82633	Douglas		5,443	5,076
*82930	Evanston		11,448	10,904
*82716	Gillette		21,130	17,545
82935	Green River		11,628	12,711
*83002	Jackson		8,765	4,708
82520	Lander		6,883	7,023
*82072	Laramie		26,885	26,687
82435	Powell		5,255	5,292
82301	Rawlins		8,689	9,380
82501	Riverton		9,443	9,202
*82901	Rock Springs		18,464	19,050
82801	Sheridan		15,946	13,904
82240	Torrington		5,620	5,651
82401	Worland		5,068	5,742

Populations and Areas of Counties and States

Source: U.S. Bureau of the Census, Dept. of Commerce; World Almanac research

Counties are the primary legal divisions of most states and generally are functioning governmental units. In Alaska, however, the chief units of local government are boroughs; outside the boroughs there are "census areas," delineated for statistical purposes. In Louisiana, the primary legal divisions are known as parishes.

State population figures are estimates for July 1, 2002. For counties, July 1, 2002, population estimates and Apr. 1, 1990, decennial census figures are given. Land areas are from the 2000 census. County areas may not add to state areas because of rounding.

Alabama
(67 counties, 50,744 sq. mi. land; pop. 4,486,508)

County	County seat or courthouse	2002 pop.	1990 pop.	Land area sq. mi.
Autauga	Prattville	45,604	34,222	596
Baldwin	Bay Minette	147,932	98,280	1,596
Barbour	Clayton	28,826	25,417	885
Bibb	Centreville	21,838	16,598	623
Blount	Oneonta	52,968	39,248	646
Bullock	Union Springs	11,367	11,042	625
Butler	Greenville	20,911	21,892	777
Calhoun	Anniston	111,616	116,032	608
Chambers	Lafayette	36,251	36,876	597
Cherokee	Centre	24,315	19,543	553
Chilton	Clanton	40,516	32,458	694
Choctaw	Butler	15,418	16,018	914
Clarke	Grove Hill	27,557	27,240	1,238
Clay	Ashland	14,163	13,252	605
Cleburne	Heflin	14,578	12,730	553
Coffee	Elba	43,878	40,240	679
Colbert	Tuscumbia	54,850	51,666	595
Conecuh	Evergreen	13,687	14,054	851
Coosa	Rockford	11,871	11,063	652
Covington	Andalusia	36,956	36,478	1,034
Crenshaw	Luverne	13,663	13,635	610
Cullman	Cullman	77,973	67,613	738
Dale	Ozark	49,186	49,633	561
Dallas	Selma	45,653	48,130	981
De Kalb	Fort Payne	65,605	54,651	778
Elmore	Wetumpka	68,771	49,210	621
Escambia	Brewton	38,347	35,518	947
Etowah	Gadsden	103,105	99,840	535
Fayette	Fayette	18,256	17,962	628
Franklin	Russellville	30,851	27,814	636
Geneva	Geneva	25,346	23,647	576
Greene	Eutaw	10,035	10,153	646
Hale	Greensboro	17,067	15,498	644
Henry	Abbeville	16,292	15,374	562
Houston	Dothan	89,966	81,331	580
Jackson	Scottsboro	54,035	47,796	1,079
Jefferson	Birmingham	661,153	651,520	1,113
Lamar	Vernon	15,499	15,715	605
Lauderdale	Florence	87,116	79,661	669
Lawrence	Moulton	34,655	31,513	693
Lee	Opelika	118,123	87,146	609
Limestone	Athens	67,842	54,135	568
Lowndes	Hayneville	13,508	12,658	718
Macon	Tuskegee	23,788	24,928	611
Madison	Huntsville	285,900	238,912	805
Marengo	Linden	22,475	23,084	977
Marion	Hamilton	30,369	29,830	741
Marshall	Guntersville	83,548	70,832	567
Mobile	Mobile	400,163	378,643	1,233
Monroe	Monroeville	24,043	23,968	1,026
Montgomery	Montgomery	223,346	209,085	790
Morgan	Decatur	111,725	100,043	582
Perry	Marion	11,637	12,759	719
Pickens	Carrollton	20,852	20,699	881
Pike	Troy	29,588	27,595	671
Randolph	Wedowee	22,527	19,881	581
Russell	Phenix City	49,415	46,860	641
Saint Clair	Ashville & Pell City	67,215	49,811	634
Shelby	Columbiana	153,832	99,363	795
Sumter	Livingston	14,376	16,174	905
Talladega	Talladega	80,638	74,109	740
Tallapoosa	Dadeville	40,946	38,826	718
Tuscaloosa	Tuscaloosa	166,512	150,500	1,324
Walker	Jasper	70,655	67,670	794
Washington	Chatom	17,927	16,694	1,081
Wilcox	Camden	13,137	13,568	889
Winston	Double Springs	24,745	22,053	614

Alaska
(27 divisions, 571,951 sq. mi. land; pop. 643,786)

Census Division	2002 Pop.	1990 Pop.	Land area sq. mi.
Aleutians East Borough	2,525	2,464	6,988
Aleutians West Census Area	5,720	9,478	4,397
Anchorage Municipality	268,983	226,338	1,697
Bethel Census Area	16,905	13,660	40,633
Bristol Bay Borough	1,155	1,410	505
Denali Borough	1,882	1,682	12,750
Dillingham Census Area	5,043	4,010	18,675
Fairbanks North Star Borough	85,051	77,720	7,366
Haines Borough	2,323	2,117	2,344
Juneau Borough	30,751	26,752	2,717
Kenai Peninsula Borough	50,835	40,802	16,013
Ketchikan Gateway Borough	13,668	13,828	1,233
Kodiak Island Borough	13,822	13,309	6,560
Lake and Peninsula Borough	1,622	1,666	23,782
Matanuska-Susitna Borough	65,141	39,683	24,682
Nome Census Area	9,232	8,288	23,001
North Slope Borough	7,263	5,986	88,817
Northwest Arctic Borough	7,321	6,106	35,898
Prince of Wales-Outer Ketchikan Census Area	5,771	6,278	7,411
Sitka Borough	8,829	8,588	2,874
Skagway-Hoonah-Angoon Census Area	3,300	3,679	7,896
Southeast Fairbanks Census Area	5,631	5,925	24,815
Valdez-Cordova Census Area	10,126	9,920	34,319
Wade Hampton Census Area	7,257	5,789	17,194
Wrangell-Petersburg Census Area	6,501	7,042	5,835
Yakutat Borough	754	725	7,650
Yukon-Koyukuk Census Area	6,375	6,798	145,900

Arizona
(15 counties, 113,635 sq. mi. land; pop. 5,456,453)

County	County seat or courthouse	2002 Pop.	1990 Pop.	Land area sq. mi.
Apache	Saint Johns	68,002	61,591	11,205
Cochise	Bisbee	120,439	97,624	6,169
Coconino	Flagstaff	120,295	96,591	18,617
Gila	Globe	51,565	40,216	4,768
Graham	Safford	33,141	26,554	4,629
Greenlee	Clifton	7,828	8,008	1,847
La Paz	Parker	19,517	13,844	4,500
Maricopa	Phoenix	3,303,876	2,122,101	9,203
Mohave	Kingman	165,593	93,497	13,312
Navajo	Holbrook	102,202	77,674	9,953
Pima	Tucson	881,221	666,957	9,186
Pinal	Florence	196,275	116,397	5,370
Santa Cruz	Nogales	40,035	29,676	1,238
Yavapai	Prescott	179,057	107,714	8,123
Yuma	Yuma	167,407	106,895	5,514

Arkansas
(75 counties, 52,068 sq. mi. land; pop. 2,710,079)

County	County seat or courthouse	2002 Pop.	1990 Pop.	Land area sq.mi.
Arkansas	DeWitt & Stuttgart	20,355	21,653	988
Ashley	Hamburg	23,875	24,319	921
Baxter	Mountain Home	38,672	31,186	554
Benton	Bentonville	165,500	97,530	846
Boone	Harrison	34,713	28,297	591
Bradley	Warren	12,531	11,793	651
Calhoun	Hampton	5,681	5,826	628
Carroll	Berryville & Eureka Springs	26,166	18,623	630
Chicot	Lake Village	13,623	15,713	644
Clark	Arkadelphia	23,535	21,437	865
Clay	Corning & Piggott	17,127	18,107	639
Cleburne	Heber Springs	24,570	19,411	553
Cleveland	Rison	8,541	7,781	595
Columbia	Magnolia	25,343	25,691	766
Conway	Morrilton	20,411	19,151	556
Craighead	Jonesboro & Lake City	84,074	68,956	711
Crawford	Van Buren	54,973	42,493	595
Crittenden	Marion	51,291	49,939	610
Cross	Wynne	19,343	19,225	616
Dallas	Fordyce	8,785	9,614	667
Desha	Arkansas City	14,805	16,798	765
Drew	Monticello	18,639	17,369	828
Faulkner	Conway	89,590	60,006	647
Franklin	Charleston & Ozark	17,868	14,897	610
Fulton	Salem	11,527	10,037	618
Garland	Hot Springs	90,059	73,397	677
Grant	Sheridan	16,848	13,948	632
Greene	Paragould	38,038	31,804	578
Hempstead	Hope	23,492	21,621	729
Hot Spring	Malvern	30,558	26,115	615
Howard	Nashville	14,251	13,569	587
Independence	Batesville	34,431	31,192	764
Izard	Melbourne	13,192	11,364	581
Jackson	Newport	17,802	18,944	634
Jefferson	Pine Bluff	83,374	85,487	885
Johnson	Clarksville	23,148	18,221	662
Lafayette	Lewisville	8,382	9,643	527
Lawrence	Walnut Ridge	17,587	17,455	587

County	County seat or courthouse	2002 Pop.	1990 Pop.	Land area sq.mi.
Lee	Marianna	12,217	13,053	602
Lincoln	Star City	14,247	13,690	561
Little River	Ashdown	13,474	13,966	532
Logan	Booneville & Paris	22,394	20,557	710
Lonoke	Lonoke	55,302	39,268	766
Madison	Huntsville	14,345	11,618	837
Marion	Yellville	16,259	12,001	598
Miller	Texarkana	41,133	38,467	624
Mississippi	Blytheville & Osceola	50,380	57,525	898
Monroe	Clarendon	9,589	11,333	607
Montgomery	Mount Ida	9,243	7,841	781
Nevada	Prescott	9,742	10,101	620
Newton	Jasper	8,506	7,666	823
Ouachita	Camden	27,868	30,574	732
Perry	Perryville	10,436	7,969	551
Phillips	Helena	25,001	28,830	693
Pike	Murfreesboro	11,137	10,086	603
Poinsett	Harrisburg	25,401	24,664	758
Polk	Mena	20,200	17,347	859
Pope	Russellville	55,223	45,883	812
Prairie	Des Arc & De Valls Bluff	9,440	9,518	646
Pulaski	Little Rock	364,381	349,773	771
Randolph	Pocahontas	18,102	16,558	652
Saint Francis	Forrest City	28,773	28,497	634
Saline	Benton	86,290	64,183	723
Scott	Waldron	11,004	10,205	894
Searcy	Marshall	8,039	7,841	667
Sebastian	Fort Smith & Greenwood	117,220	99,590	536
Sevier	De Queen	15,811	13,637	564
Sharp	Ash Flat	17,270	14,109	604
Stone	Mountain View	11,518	9,775	607
Union	El Dorado	45,279	46,719	1,039
Van Buren	Clinton	16,314	14,008	712
Washington	Fayetteville	166,511	113,409	950
White	Searcy	69,354	54,676	1,034
Woodruff	Augusta	8,466	9,520	587
Yell	Danville & Dardanelle	21,410	17,759	928

California
(58 counties, 155,959 sq. mi. land; pop. 35,116,033)

County	County seat or courthouse	2002 Pop.	1990 Pop.	Land area sq.mi.
Alameda	Oakland	1,472,310	1,304,347	738
Alpine	Markleeville	1,200	1,113	739
Amador	Jackson	36,657	30,039	593
Butte	Oroville	209,203	182,120	1,639
Calaveras	San Andreas	42,978	31,998	1,020
Colusa	Colusa	19,312	16,275	1,151
Contra Costa	Martinez	992,358	803,731	720
Del Norte	Crescent City	27,482	23,460	1,008
El Dorado	Placerville	165,744	125,995	1,711
Fresno	Fresno	834,632	667,479	5,963
Glenn	Willows	26,623	24,798	1,315
Humboldt	Eureka	127,159	119,118	3,572
Imperial	El Centro	146,248	109,303	4,175
Inyo	Independence	18,214	18,281	10,203
Kern	Bakersfield	694,059	544,981	8,141
Kings	Hanford	135,043	101,469	1,391
Lake	Lakeport	61,970	50,631	1,258
Lassen	Susanville	34,007	27,598	4,557
Los Angeles	Los Angeles	9,806,577	8,863,052	4,061
Madera	Madera	130,265	88,090	2,136
Marin	San Rafael	247,581	230,096	520
Mariposa	Mariposa	17,195	14,302	1,451
Mendocino	Ukiah	87,240	80,345	3,509
Merced	Merced	225,398	178,403	1,929
Modoc	Alturas	9,289	9,678	3,944
Mono	Bridgeport	13,117	9,956	3,044
Monterey	Salinas	413,408	355,660	3,322
Napa	Napa	130,268	110,765	754
Nevada	Nevada City	95,047	78,510	958
Orange	Santa Ana	2,938,507	2,410,668	789
Placer	Auburn	278,509	172,796	1,404
Plumas	Quincy	20,890	19,739	2,554
Riverside	Riverside	1,699,112	1,170,413	7,207
Sacramento	Sacramento	1,305,082	1,066,789	966
San Benito	Hollister	55,938	36,697	1,389
San Bernardino	San Bernardino	1,816,072	1,418,380	20,053
San Diego	San Diego	2,906,660	2,498,016	4,200
San Francisco	San Francisco	764,049	723,959	47
San Joaquin	Stockton	614,302	480,628	1,399
San Luis Obispo	San Luis Obispo	253,408	217,162	3,304
San Mateo	Redwood City	703,202	649,623	449
Santa Barbara	Santa Barbara	403,084	369,608	2,737
Santa Clara	San Jose	1,683,505	1,497,577	1,291
Santa Cruz	Santa Cruz	253,814	229,734	445
Shasta	Redding	171,799	147,036	3,785
Sierra	Downieville	3,552	3,318	953
Siskiyou	Yreka	44,103	43,531	6,287
Solano	Fairfield	411,072	339,469	829
Sonoma	Santa Rosa	468,386	388,222	1,576
Stanislaus	Modesto	482,440	370,522	1,494
Sutter	Yuba City	82,580	64,409	603
Tehama	Red Bluff	57,472	49,625	2,951
Trinity	Weaverville	13,174	13,063	3,179
Tulare	Visalia	381,772	311,932	4,824
Tuolumne	Sonora	55,850	48,456	2,235
Ventura	Ventura	783,920	669,016	1,845
Yolo	Woodland	180,856	141,212	1,013
Yuba	Marysville	62,339	58,234	631

Colorado
(64 counties, 103,718 sq. mi. land; pop. 4,506,542)

County	County seat or courthouse	2002 Pop.	1990 Pop.	Land area sq. mi.
Adams[1]	Brighton	374,099	265,038	1,192
Alamosa	Alamosa	15,130	13,617	723
Arapahoe	Littleton	510,136	391,572	803
Archuleta	Pagosa Springs	11,012	5,345	1,350
Baca	Springfield	4,392	4,556	2,556
Bent	Las Animas	5,717	5,048	1,514
Boulder[1]	Boulder	279,197	225,339	742
Broomfield[2]	Broomfield	40,823	NA	27
Chaffee	Salida	16,833	12,684	1,013
Cheyenne	Cheyenne Wells	2,162	2,397	1,781
Clear Creek	Georgetown	9,447	7,619	395
Conejos	Conejos	8,423	7,453	1,287
Costilla	San Luis	3,590	3,190	1,227
Crowley	Ordway	5,449	3,946	789
Custer	Westcliffe	3,648	1,926	739
Delta	Delta	28,916	20,980	1,142
Denver	Denver	560,415	467,549	153
Dolores	Dove Creek	1,865	1,504	1,067
Douglas	Castle Rock	211,091	60,391	840
Eagle	Eagle	45,091	21,928	1,688
Elbert	Kiowa	21,959	9,646	1,851
El Paso	Colorado Springs	543,818	397,014	2,126
Fremont	Canon City	47,423	32,273	1,533
Garfield	GlenwoodSprings	47,249	29,974	2,947
Gilpin	Central City	4,893	3,070	150
Grand	Hot Sulphur Springs	12,984	7,966	1,847
Gunnison	Gunnison	14,148	10,273	3,239
Hinsdale	Lake City	778	467	1,118
Huerfano	Walsenburg	7,831	6,009	1,591
Jackson	Walden	1,530	1,605	1,613
Jefferson[1]	Golden	531,723	438,430	772
Kiowa	Eads	1,492	1,688	1,771
Kit Carson	Burlington	7,948	7,140	2,161
Lake	Leadville	7,796	6,007	377
La Plata	Durango	45,668	32,284	1,692
Larimer	Fort Collins	264,605	186,136	2,601
Las Animas	Trinidad	15,455	13,765	4,772
Lincoln	Hugo	5,905	4,529	2,586
Logan	Sterling	21,084	17,567	1,839
Mesa	Grand Junction	121,419	93,145	3,328
Mineral	Creede	860	558	876
Moffat	Craig	13,370	11,357	4,742
Montezuma	Cortez	24,157	18,672	2,037
Montrose	Montrose	35,314	24,423	2,241
Morgan	Fort Morgan	27,709	21,939	1,285
Otero	La Junta	19,794	20,185	1,263
Ouray	Ouray	3,921	2,295	540
Park	Fairplay	15,993	7,174	2,201
Phillips	Holyoke	4,531	4,189	688
Pitkin	Aspen	14,994	12,661	970
Prowers	Lamar	14,209	13,347	1,640
Pueblo	Pueblo	146,880	123,051	2,389
Rio Blanco	Meeker	6,042	6,051	3,221
Rio Grande	Del Norte	12,273	10,770	912
Routt	Steamboat Springs	20,405	14,088	2,362
Saguache	Saguache	6,439	4,619	3,168
San Juan	Silverton	552	745	387
San Miguel	Telluride	7,165	3,653	1,287
Sedgwick	Julesburg	2,681	2,690	548
Summit	Breckenridge	24,869	12,881	608
Teller	Cripple Creek	21,586	12,468	557
Washington	Akron	4,889	4,812	2,521
Weld[1]	Greeley	205,014	131,821	3,992
Yuma	Wray	9,751	8,954	2,366

NA = Not available. (1) Part of this county was taken to create Broomfield county in 2001. Because the Census Bureau will not be retabulating land areas until after Census 2010, the Land area shown here is from Census 2000. (2) Created in 2001.

Connecticut
(8 counties, 4,845 sq. mi. land; pop. 3,460,503)

County	County seat or courthouse	2002 Pop.	1990 Pop.	Land area sq. mi.
Fairfield	Bridgeport	896,202	827,645	626
Hartford	Hartford	867,332	851,783	735
Litchfield	Litchfield	186,515	174,092	920
Middlesex	Middletown	159,679	143,196	369
New Haven	New Haven	835,657	804,219	606
New London	New London	262,689	254,957	666
Tolland	Rockville	141,089	128,699	410
Windham	Putnam	111,340	102,525	513

Delaware
(3 counties, 1,954 sq. mi. land; pop. 807,385)

County	County seat or courthouse	2002 Pop.	1990 Pop.	Land area sq. mi.
Kent	Dover	131,069	110,993	590
New Castle	Wilmington	512,370	441,946	426
Sussex	Georgetown	163,946	113,229	938

District of Columbia
(61 sq. mi. land; pop. 570,898)
Has no counties; coextensive with city of Washington.

Florida
(67 counties, 53,927 sq. mi. land; pop. 16,713,149)

County	County seat or courthouse	2002 Pop.	1990 Pop.	Land area sq. mi.
Alachua	Gainesville	222,254	181,596	874
Baker	Macclenny	22,793	18,486	585
Bay	Panama City	151,901	126,994	764
Bradford	Starke	26,297	22,515	293
Brevard	Titusville	495,576	398,978	1,018
Broward	Fort Lauderdale	1,709,118	1,255,531	1,205
Calhoun	Blountstown	12,567	11,011	567
Charlotte	Punta Gorda	148,678	110,975	694
Citrus	Inverness	123,685	93,513	584
Clay	Green Cove Springs	152,093	105,986	601
Collier	Naples	276,691	152,099	2,025
Columbia	Lake City	58,028	42,613	797
De Soto	Arcadia	32,819	23,865	637
Dixie	Cross City	14,063	10,585	704
Duval	Jacksonville	806,120	672,971	774
Escambia	Pensacola	297,272	262,445	662
Flagler	Bunnell	57,377	28,701	485
Franklin	Apalachicola	10,069	8,967	544
Gadsden	Quincy	45,279	41,116	516
Gilchrist	Trenton	14,720	9,667	349
Glades	Moore Haven	10,786	7,591	774
Gulf	Port Saint Joe	14,789	11,504	555
Hamilton	Jasper	13,710	10,930	515
Hardee	Wauchula	27,333	19,499	637
Hendry	La Belle	36,891	25,773	1,153
Hernando	Brooksville	138,470	101,115	478
Highlands	Sebring	89,952	68,432	1,028
Hillsborough	Tampa	1,053,864	834,054	1,051
Holmes	Bonifay	18,628	15,778	482
Indian River	Vero Beach	118,007	90,208	503
Jackson	Marianna	46,408	41,375	916
Jefferson	Monticello	13,695	11,296	598
Lafayette	Mayo	7,009	5,578	543
Lake	Tavares	233,835	152,104	953
Lee	Fort Myers	475,639	335,113	804
Leon	Tallahassee	243,995	192,493	667
Levy	Bronson	35,953	25,912	1,118
Liberty	Bristol	6,902	5,569	836
Madison	Madison	18,309	16,569	692
Manatee	Bradenton	280,511	211,707	741
Marion	Ocala	272,553	194,835	1,579
Martin	Stuart	132,218	100,900	556
Miami-Dade	Miami	2,332,599	1,937,194	1,946
Monroe	Key West	79,330	78,024	997
Nassau	Fernandina Beach	60,558	43,941	652
Okaloosa	Crestview	175,708	143,777	936
Okeechobee	Okeechobee	36,906	29,627	774
Orange	Orlando	946,484	677,491	907
Osceola	Kissimmee	190,187	107,728	1,322
Palm Beach	West Palm Beach	1,190,390	863,503	1,974
Pasco	Dade City	371,245	281,131	745
Pinellas	Clearwater	926,716	851,659	280
Polk	Bartow	498,721	405,382	1,874
Putnam	Palatka	71,016	65,070	722
Saint Johns	Saint Augustine	136,038	83,829	609
Saint Lucie	Fort Pierce	205,420	150,171	572
Santa Rosa	Milton	127,212	81,961	1,017
Sarasota	Sarasota	339,625	277,776	572
Seminole	Sanford	381,686	287,521	308
Sumter	Bushnell	57,517	31,577	546
Suwannee	Live Oak	36,121	26,780	688
Taylor	Perry	19,339	17,111	1,042
Union	Lake Butler	13,877	10,252	240
Volusia	De Land	459,435	370,737	1,103
Wakulla	Crawfordville	24,900	14,202	607
Walton	De Funiak Springs	43,843	27,759	1,058
Washington	Chipley	21,419	16,919	580

Georgia
(159 counties, 57,906 sq. mi. land; pop. 8,560,310)

County	County seat or courthouse	2002 Pop.	1990 Pop.	Land area sq. mi.
Appling	Baxley	17,650	15,744	509
Atkinson	Pearson	7,712	6,213	338
Bacon	Alma	10,055	9,566	285
Baker	Newton	4,025	3,615	343
Baldwin	Milledgeville	44,787	39,530	258
Banks	Homer	15,123	10,308	234
Barrow	Winder	51,016	29,721	162
Bartow	Cartersville	82,607	55,915	459
Ben Hill	Fitzgerald	17,450	16,245	252
Berrien	Nashville	16,285	14,153	452
Bibb	Macon	154,824	150,137	250
Bleckley	Cochran	11,855	10,430	217
Brantley	Nahunta	15,060	11,077	444
Brooks	Quitman	16,428	15,398	494
Bryan	Pembroke	25,256	15,438	442
Bulloch	Statesboro	57,307	43,125	682
Burke	Waynesboro	22,794	20,579	830
Butts	Jackson	21,346	15,326	187
Calhoun	Morgan	6,395	5,013	280
Camden	Woodbine	44,702	30,167	630
Candler	Metter	9,764	7,744	247
Carroll	Carrollton	94,907	71,422	499
Catoosa	Ringgold	56,341	42,464	162
Charlton	Folkston	10,533	8,496	781
Chatham	Savannah	233,702	216,774	438
Chattahoochee	Cusseta	15,440	16,934	249
Chattooga	Summerville	26,161	22,236	313
Cherokee	Canton	159,295	90,204	424
Clarke	Athens	103,881	87,594	121
Clay	Fort Gaines	3,392	3,364	195
Clayton	Jonesboro	252,733	181,436	143
Clinch	Homerville	6,904	6,160	809
Cobb	Marietta	651,485	447,745	340
Coffee	Douglas	38,298	29,592	599
Colquitt	Moultrie	42,802	36,645	552
Columbia	Appling	94,958	66,031	290
Cook	Adel	16,122	13,456	229
Coweta	Newnan	97,771	53,853	443
Crawford	Knoxville	12,509	8,991	325
Crisp	Cordele	22,018	20,011	274
Dade	Trenton	15,615	13,183	174
Dawson	Dawsonville	17,538	9,429	211
Decatur	Bainbridge	28,243	25,517	597
DeKalb	Decatur	676,996	546,174	268
Dodge	Eastman	19,047	17,607	500
Dooly	Vienna	11,505	9,901	393
Dougherty	Albany	95,875	96,321	330
Douglas	Douglasville	98,650	71,120	199
Early	Blakely	12,172	11,854	511
Echols	Statenville	3,842	2,334	404
Effingham	Springfield	40,832	25,687	479
Elbert	Elberton	20,667	18,949	369
Emanuel	Swainsboro	22,099	20,546	686
Evans	Claxton	11,095	8,724	185
Fannin	Blue Ridge	20,986	15,992	386
Fayette	Fayetteville	96,611	62,415	197
Floyd	Rome	92,606	81,251	513
Forsyth	Cumming	116,924	44,083	226
Franklin	Carnesville	20,778	16,650	263
Fulton	Atlanta	825,431	648,776	529
Gilmer	Ellijay	25,203	13,368	427
Glascock	Gibson	2,598	2,357	144
Glynn	Brunswick	69,036	62,496	422
Gordon	Calhoun	46,531	35,067	356
Grady	Cairo	23,838	20,279	458
Greene	Greensboro	15,101	11,793	388
Gwinnett	Lawrenceville	650,771	352,910	433
Habersham	Clarkesville	37,979	27,622	278
Hall	Gainesville	152,235	95,434	394
Hancock	Sparta	10,026	8,908	473
Haralson	Buchanan	26,755	21,966	282
Harris	Hamilton	25,092	17,788	464
Hart	Hartwell	23,249	19,712	232
Heard	Franklin	11,340	8,628	296
Henry	McDonough	139,699	58,741	323
Houston	Perry	116,768	89,208	377
Irwin	Ocilla	9,945	8,649	357
Jackson	Jefferson	45,374	30,005	342
Jasper	Monticello	12,283	8,453	370
Jeff Davis	Hazlehurst	12,910	12,032	333
Jefferson	Louisville	17,138	17,408	528
Jenkins	Millen	8,647	8,247	350
Johnson	Wrightsville	8,676	8,329	304
Jones	Gray	24,492	20,739	394
Lamar	Barnesville	16,442	13,038	185
Lanier	Lakeland	7,216	5,531	187
Laurens	Dublin	45,890	39,988	812
Lee	Leesburg	27,382	16,250	356
Liberty	Hinesville	61,749	52,745	519
Lincoln	Lincolnton	8,459	7,442	211
Long	Ludowici	10,761	6,202	401
Lowndes	Valdosta	93,658	75,981	504
Lumpkin	Dahlonega	22,665	14,573	284
McDuffie	Thomson	21,438	20,119	260
McIntosh	Darien	11,150	8,634	433
Macon	Oglethorpe	14,062	13,114	403
Madison	Danielsville	26,717	21,050	284
Marion	Buena Vista	7,238	5,590	367
Meriwether	Greenville	22,623	22,411	503
Miller	Colquitt	6,400	6,280	283
Mitchell	Camilla	23,974	20,275	512
Monroe	Forsyth	22,675	17,113	396
Montgomery	Mount Vernon	8,397	7,379	245

County	County seat or courthouse	2002 Pop.	1990 Pop.	Land area sq. mi.
Morgan	Madison	16,301	12,883	350
Murray	Chatsworth	38,544	26,147	344
Muscogee	Columbus	185,948	179,280	216
Newton	Covington	71,594	41,808	276
Oconee	Watkinsville	27,264	17,618	186
Oglethorpe	Lexington	13,176	9,763	441
Paulding	Dallas	94,184	41,611	313
Peach	Fort Valley	24,224	21,189	151
Pickens	Jasper	25,619	14,432	232
Pierce	Blackshear	15,982	13,328	343
Pike	Zebulon	14,599	10,224	218
Polk	Cedartown	39,444	33,815	311
Pulaski	Hawkinsville	9,716	8,108	247
Putnam	Eatonton	19,390	14,137	345
Quitman	Georgetown	2,621	2,210	152
Rabun	Clayton	15,521	11,648	371
Randolph	Cuthbert	7,451	8,023	429
Richmond	Augusta	197,842	189,719	324
Rockdale	Conyers	73,558	54,091	131
Schley	Ellaville	3,975	3,590	168
Screven	Sylvania	15,201	13,842	648
Seminole	Donalsonville	9,310	9,010	238
Spalding	Griffin	59,410	54,457	198
Stephens	Toccoa	25,712	23,436	179
Stewart	Lumpkin	5,040	5,654	459
Sumter	Americus	33,247	30,232	485
Talbot	Talbotton	6,713	6,524	393
Taliaferro	Crawfordville	1,977	1,915	195
Tattnall	Reidsville	22,560	17,722	484
Taylor	Butler	8,913	7,642	377
Telfair	McRae	11,780	11,000	441
Terrell	Dawson	10,871	10,653	335
Thomas	Thomasville	42,976	38,943	548
Tift	Tifton	39,338	34,998	265
Toombs	Lyons	26,388	24,072	367
Towns	Hiawassee	9,768	6,754	167
Treutlen	Soperton	6,837	5,994	201
Troup	La Grange	59,767	55,532	414
Turner	Ashburn	9,691	8,703	286
Twiggs	Jeffersonville	10,545	9,806	360
Union	Blairsville	18,275	11,993	323
Upson	Thomaston	27,773	26,300	325
Walker	La Fayette	61,949	58,310	447
Walton	Monroe	67,069	38,586	329
Ware	Waycross	35,558	35,471	902
Warren	Warrenton	6,211	6,078	286
Washington	Sandersville	20,803	19,112	680
Wayne	Jesup	27,062	22,356	645
Webster	Preston	2,315	2,263	210
Wheeler	Alamo	6,183	4,903	298
White	Cleveland	21,904	13,006	242
Whitfield	Dalton	87,037	72,462	290
Wilcox	Abbeville	8,529	7,008	380
Wilkes	Washington	10,734	10,597	471
Wilkinson	Irwinton	10,357	10,228	447
Worth	Sylvester	21,767	19,744	570

Hawaii
(5 counties, 6,423 sq. mi. land; pop. 1,244,898)

County	County seat or courthouse	2002 Pop.	1990 Pop.	Land area sq. mi.
Hawaii	Hilo	154,794	120,317	4,028
Honolulu	Honolulu	896,019	836,231	600
Kalawao[1]		132	130	13
Kauai	Lihue	59,946	51,177	622
Maui	Wailuku	134,007	100,374	1,159

(1) Administered by state government.

Idaho
(44 counties, 82,747 sq. mi. land; pop. 1,341,131)

County	County seat or courthouse	2002 Pop.	1990 Pop.	Land area sq. mi.
Ada	Boise	319,687	205,775	1,055
Adams	Council	3,448	3,254	1,365
Bannock	Pocatello	75,804	66,026	1,113
Bear Lake	Paris	6,360	6,084	971
Benewah	Saint Maries	8,993	7,937	776
Bingham	Blackfoot	42,458	37,583	2,095
Blaine	Hailey	20,378	13,552	2,645
Boise	Idaho City	7,067	3,509	1,902
Bonner	Sandpoint	38,205	26,622	1,738
Bonneville	Idaho Falls	85,180	72,207	1,868
Boundary	Bonners Ferry	10,085	8,332	1,269
Butte	Arco	2,890	2,918	2,233
Camas	Fairfield	1,037	727	1,075
Canyon	Caldwell	144,983	90,076	590
Caribou	Soda Springs	7,319	6,963	1,766
Cassia	Burley	21,720	19,532	2,566
Clark	Dubois	997	762	1,765
Clearwater	Orofino	8,446	8,505	2,461
Custer	Challis	4,185	4,133	4,925
Elmore	Mountain Home	29,481	21,205	3,078
Franklin	Preston	11,699	9,232	665
Fremont	Saint Anthony	11,859	10,937	1,867

County	County seat or courthouse	2002 Pop.	1990 Pop.	Land area sq. mi.
Gem	Emmett	15,495	11,844	563
Gooding	Gooding	14,307	11,633	731
Idaho	Grangeville	15,308	13,768	8,485
Jefferson	Rigby	19,781	16,543	1,095
Jerome	Jerome	18,703	15,138	600
Kootenai	Coeur d'Alene	113,954	69,795	1,245
Latah	Moscow	35,218	30,617	1,077
Lemhi	Salmon	7,649	6,899	4,564
Lewis	Nez Perce	3,721	3,516	479
Lincoln	Shoshone	4,207	3,308	1,206
Madison	Rexburg	27,686	23,674	472
Minidoka	Rupert	19,465	19,361	760
Nez Perce	Lewiston	37,106	33,754	849
Oneida	Malad City	4,131	3,492	1,200
Owyhee	Murphy	10,862	8,392	7,678
Payette	Payette	21,007	16,434	408
Power	American Falls	7,379	7,086	1,406
Shoshone	Wallace	13,090	13,931	2,634
Teton	Driggs	6,859	3,439	450
Twin Falls	Twin Falls	65,472	53,580	1,925
Valley	Cascade	7,526	6,109	3,678
Washington	Weiser	9,924	8,550	1,456

Illinois
(102 counties, 55,584 sq. mi. land; pop. 12,600,620)

County	County seat or courthouse	2002 Pop.	1990 Pop.	Land area sq. mi.
Adams	Quincy	67,631	66,090	857
Alexander	Cairo	9,469	10,626	236
Bond	Greenville	17,929	14,991	380
Boone	Belvidere	44,620	30,806	281
Brown	Mount Sterling	6,871	5,836	306
Bureau	Princeton	35,239	35,688	869
Calhoun	Hardin	5,052	5,322	254
Carroll	Mount Carroll	16,348	16,805	444
Cass	Virginia	13,665	13,437	376
Champaign	Urbana	183,159	173,025	997
Christian	Taylorville	35,215	34,418	709
Clark	Marshall	16,942	15,921	502
Clay	Louisville	14,168	14,460	469
Clinton	Carlyle	35,855	33,944	474
Coles	Charleston	52,538	51,644	508
Cook	Chicago	5,377,507	5,105,044	946
Crawford	Robinson	20,151	19,464	444
Cumberland	Toledo	11,084	10,670	346
DeKalb	Sycamore	91,561	77,932	634
De Witt	Clinton	16,547	16,516	398
Douglas	Tuscola	19,996	19,464	417
DuPage	Wheaton	924,589	781,689	334
Edgar	Paris	19,264	19,595	624
Edwards	Albion	6,781	7,440	222
Effingham	Effingham	34,275	31,704	479
Fayette	Vandalia	21,629	20,893	716
Ford	Paxton	14,192	14,275	486
Franklin	Benton	39,134	40,319	412
Fulton	Lewiston	37,772	38,080	866
Gallatin	Shawneetown	6,191	6,909	324
Greene	Carrollton	14,511	15,317	543
Grundy	Morris	38,839	32,337	420
Hamilton	McLeansboro	8,422	8,499	435
Hancock	Carthage	19,726	21,373	795
Hardin	Elizabethtown	4,775	5,189	178
Henderson	Oquawka	8,147	8,096	379
Henry	Cambridge	50,614	51,159	823
Iroquois	Watseka	30,944	30,787	1,116
Jackson	Murphysboro	59,631	61,067	588
Jasper	Newton	10,011	10,609	494
Jefferson	Mount Vernon	40,286	37,020	571
Jersey	Jerseyville	21,858	20,539	369
Jo Daviess	Galena	22,390	21,821	601
Johnson	Vienna	13,130	11,347	345
Kane	Geneva	443,041	317,471	520
Kankakee	Kankakee	104,657	96,255	677
Kendall	Yorkville	61,222	39,413	321
Knox	Galesburg	55,056	56,393	716
Lake	Waukegan	674,850	516,418	448
La Salle	Ottawa	111,975	106,913	1,135
Lawrence	Lawrenceville	15,207	15,972	372
Lee	Dixon	36,027	34,392	725
Livingston	Pontiac	39,596	39,301	1,044
Logan	Lincoln	30,692	30,798	618
McDonough	Macomb	32,653	35,244	589
McHenry	Woodstock	277,710	183,241	604
McLean	Bloomington	154,453	129,180	1,184
Macon	Decatur	112,013	117,206	581
Macoupin	Carlinville	48,636	47,679	864
Madison	Edwardsville	261,409	249,238	725
Marion	Salem	41,036	41,561	572
Marshall	Lacon	13,031	12,846	386
Mason	Havana	15,924	16,269	539
Massac	Metropolis	15,021	14,752	239
Menard	Petersburg	12,571	11,164	314
Mercer	Aledo	16,910	17,290	561
Monroe	Waterloo	29,058	22,422	388
Montgomery	Hillsboro	30,528	30,728	704

County	County seat or courthouse	2002 Pop.	1990 Pop.	Land area sq. mi.
Morgan	Jacksonville	36,173	36,397	569
Moultrie	Sullivan	14,310	13,930	336
Ogle	Oregon	52,129	45,957	759
Peoria	Peoria	182,362	182,827	620
Perry	Pinckneyville	22,869	21,412	441
Piatt	Monticello	16,295	15,548	440
Pike	Pittsfield	17,079	17,577	830
Pope	Golconda	4,284	4,373	371
Pulaski	Mound City	7,159	7,523	201
Putnam	Hennepin	6,132	5,730	160
Randolph	Chester	33,641	34,583	578
Richland	Olney	15,934	16,545	360
Rock Island	Rock Island	148,171	148,723	427
Saint Clair	Belleville	257,904	262,852	664
Saline	Harrisburg	26,080	26,551	383
Sangamon	Springfield	190,630	178,386	868
Schuyler	Rushville	7,028	7,498	437
Scott	Winchester	5,477	5,644	251
Shelby	Shelbyville	22,558	22,261	759
Stark	Toulon	6,226	6,534	288
Stephenson	Freeport	48,092	48,052	564
Tazewell	Pekin	128,167	123,692	649
Union	Jonesboro	18,157	17,619	416
Vermilion	Danville	83,142	88,257	899
Wabash	Mount Carmel	12,605	13,111	223
Warren	Monmouth	18,235	19,181	543
Washington	Nashville	15,159	14,965	563
Wayne	Fairfield	16,997	17,241	714
White	Carmi	15,096	16,522	495
Whiteside	Morrison	60,354	60,186	685
Will	Joliet	559,861	357,313	837
Williamson	Marion	61,713	57,733	423
Winnebago	Rockford	282,627	252,913	514
Woodford	Eureka	36,100	32,653	528

Indiana
(92 counties, 35,867 sq. mi. land; pop. 6,159,068)

County	County seat or courthouse	2002 Pop.	1990 Pop.	Land area sq. mi.
Adams	Decatur	33,500	31,095	339
Allen	Fort Wayne	337,512	300,836	657
Bartholomew	Columbus	71,636	63,657	407
Benton	Fowler	9,207	9,441	406
Blackford	Hartford City	13,804	14,067	165
Boone	Lebanon	48,277	38,147	423
Brown	Nashville	15,211	14,080	312
Carroll	Delphi	20,226	18,809	372
Cass	Logansport	40,752	38,413	413
Clark	Jeffersonville	98,198	87,774	375
Clay	Brazil	26,357	24,705	358
Clinton	Frankfort	33,972	30,974	405
Crawford	English	11,076	9,914	306
Daviess	Washington	29,851	27,533	431
Dearborn	Lawrenceburg	47,333	38,835	305
Decatur	Greensburg	24,515	23,645	373
De Kalb	Auburn	40,525	35,324	363
Delaware	Muncie	118,197	119,659	393
Dubois	Jasper	40,015	36,616	430
Elkhart	Goshen	186,465	156,198	464
Fayette	Connersville	25,249	26,015	215
Floyd	New Albany	71,633	64,404	148
Fountain	Covington	17,700	17,808	396
Franklin	Brookville	22,585	19,580	386
Fulton	Rochester	20,728	18,840	369
Gibson	Princeton	32,590	31,913	489
Grant	Marion	72,189	74,169	414
Greene	Bloomfield	33,155	30,410	542
Hamilton	Noblesville	205,610	108,936	398
Hancock	Greenfield	58,343	45,527	306
Harrison	Corydon	35,244	29,890	485
Hendricks	Danville	114,301	75,717	408
Henry	New Castle	47,983	48,139	393
Howard	Kokomo	84,838	80,827	293
Huntington	Huntington	38,243	35,427	383
Jackson	Brownstown	41,557	37,730	509
Jasper	Rensselaer	30,815	24,823	560
Jay	Portland	21,631	21,512	384
Jefferson	Madison	32,113	29,797	361
Jennings	Vernon	28,192	23,661	377
Johnson	Franklin	121,604	88,109	320
Knox	Vincennes	38,531	39,884	516
Kosciusko	Warsaw	74,794	65,294	538
Lagrange	Lagrange	35,410	29,477	380
Lake	Crown Point	487,016	475,594	497
La Porte	La Porte	110,384	107,066	598
Lawrence	Bedford	46,097	42,836	449
Madison	Anderson	132,068	130,669	452
Marion	Indianapolis	863,429	797,159	396
Marshall	Plymouth	45,735	42,182	444
Martin	Shoals	10,370	10,369	336
Miami	Peru	36,199	36,897	376
Monroe	Bloomington	121,229	108,978	394
Montgomery	Crawfordsville	37,957	34,436	505
Morgan	Martinsville	67,791	55,920	406
Newton	Kentland	14,360	13,551	402

County	County seat or courthouse	2002 Pop.	1990 Pop.	Land area sq. mi.
Noble	Albion	47,209	37,877	411
Ohio	Rising Sun	5,804	5,315	87
Orange	Paoli	19,433	18,409	400
Owen	Spencer	22,541	17,281	385
Parke	Rockville	17,262	15,410	445
Perry	Tell City	18,827	19,107	381
Pike	Petersburg	12,908	12,509	336
Porter	Valparaiso	150,403	128,932	418
Posey	Mount Vernon	26,990	25,968	409
Pulaski	Winamac	13,731	12,780	434
Putnam	Greencastle	36,440	30,315	480
Randolph	Winchester	27,191	27,148	453
Ripley	Versailles	27,525	24,616	446
Rush	Rushville	17,918	18,129	408
Saint Joseph	South Bend	267,120	247,052	457
Scott	Scottsburg	23,334	20,991	190
Shelby	Shelbyville	43,674	40,307	413
Spencer	Rockport	20,353	19,490	399
Starke	Knox	22,832	22,747	309
Steuben	Angola	33,429	27,446	309
Sullivan	Sullivan	21,825	18,993	447
Switzerland	Vevay	9,410	7,738	221
Tippecanoe	Lafayette	152,001	130,598	500
Tipton	Tipton	16,534	16,119	260
Union	Liberty	7,440	6,976	162
Vanderburgh	Evansville	171,744	165,058	235
Vermillion	Newport	16,499	16,773	257
Vigo	Terre Haute	105,078	106,107	403
Wabash	Wabash	34,655	35,069	413
Warren	Williamsport	8,747	8,176	365
Warrick	Boonville	53,624	44,920	384
Washington	Salem	27,618	23,717	514
Wayne	Richmond	70,547	71,951	404
Wells	Bluffton	27,796	25,948	370
White	Monticello	24,985	23,265	505
Whitley	Columbia City	31,339	27,651	336

Iowa
(99 counties, 55,869 sq. mi. land; pop. 2,936,760)

County	County seat or courthouse	2002 Pop.	1990 Pop.	Land area sq. mi.
Adair	Greenfield	7,987	8,409	569
Adams	Corning	4,384	4,866	424
Allamakee	Waukon	14,591	13,855	640
Appanoose	Centerville	13,404	13,743	496
Audubon	Audubon	6,647	7,334	443
Benton	Vinton	26,096	22,429	716
Black Hawk	Waterloo	127,394	123,798	567
Boone	Boone	26,167	25,186	571
Bremer	Waverly	23,275	22,813	438
Buchanan	Independence	20,886	20,844	571
Buena Vista	Storm Lake	20,360	19,965	575
Butler	Allison	15,062	15,731	580
Calhoun	Rockwell City	10,818	11,508	570
Carroll	Carroll	21,113	21,423	569
Cass	Atlantic	14,234	15,128	564
Cedar	Tipton	18,357	17,444	580
Cerro Gordo	Mason City	45,339	46,733	568
Cherokee	Cherokee	12,764	14,098	577
Chickasaw	New Hampton	12,890	13,295	505
Clarke	Osceola	9,058	8,287	431
Clay	Spencer	17,066	17,585	569
Clayton	Elkader	18,374	19,054	779
Clinton	Clinton	49,650	51,040	695
Crawford	Denison	16,959	16,775	714
Dallas	Adel	44,222	29,755	586
Davis	Bloomfield	8,592	8,312	503
Decatur	Leon	8,623	8,338	532
Delaware	Manchester	18,325	18,035	578
Des Moines	Burlington	41,458	42,614	416
Dickinson	Spirit Lake	16,524	14,909	381
Dubuque	Dubuque	89,387	86,403	608
Emmet	Estherville	10,728	11,569	396
Fayette	West Union	21,696	21,843	731
Floyd	Charles City	16,552	17,058	501
Franklin	Hampton	10,714	11,364	582
Fremont	Sidney	7,748	8,226	511
Greene	Jefferson	10,149	10,045	568
Grundy	Grundy Center	12,421	12,029	503
Guthrie	Guthrie Center	11,318	10,935	591
Hamilton	Webster City	16,231	16,071	577
Hancock	Garner	11,833	12,638	571
Hardin	Eldora	18,385	19,094	569
Harrison	Logan	15,585	14,730	697
Henry	Mount Pleasant	20,122	19,226	434
Howard	Cresco	9,806	9,809	473
Humboldt	Dakota City	10,160	10,756	434
Ida	Ida Grove	7,656	8,365	432
Iowa	Marengo	15,809	14,630	586
Jackson	Maquoketa	20,208	19,950	636
Jasper	Newton	37,375	34,795	730
Jefferson	Fairfield	15,947	16,310	435
Johnson	Iowa City	114,300	96,119	614
Jones	Anamosa	20,419	19,444	575
Keokuk	Sigourney	11,418	11,624	579

County	County seat or courthouse	2002 Pop.	1990 Pop.	Land area sq. mi.
Kossuth	Algona	16,673	18,591	973
Lee	Fort Madison & Keokuk	36,902	38,687	517
Linn	Cedar Rapids	194,970	168,767	717
Louisa	Wapello	12,245	11,592	402
Lucas	Chariton	9,443	9,070	431
Lyon	Rock Rapids	11,699	11,952	588
Madison	Winterset	14,499	12,483	561
Mahaska	Oskaloosa	22,222	21,532	571
Marion	Knoxville	32,674	30,001	554
Marshall	Marshalltown	39,482	38,276	572
Mills	Glenwood	14,714	13,202	437
Mitchell	Osage	10,688	10,928	469
Monona	Onawa	9,827	10,034	693
Monroe	Albia	7,838	8,114	433
Montgomery	Red Oak	11,434	12,076	424
Muscatine	Muscatine	42,040	39,907	439
O'Brien	Primghar	14,837	15,444	573
Osceola	Sibley	6,821	7,267	399
Page	Clarinda	16,533	16,870	535
Palo Alto	Emmetsburg	9,886	10,669	564
Plymouth	Le Mars	24,626	23,388	864
Pocahontas	Pocahontas	8,331	9,525	578
Polk	Des Moines	385,691	327,140	569
Pottawattamie	Council Bluffs	88,157	82,628	954
Poweshiek	Montezuma	18,901	19,033	585
Ringgold	Mount Ayr	5,297	5,420	538
Sac	Sac City	11,098	12,324	576
Scott	Davenport	159,445	150,973	458
Shelby	Harlan	12,972	13,230	591
Sioux	Orange City	31,829	29,903	768
Story	Nevada	80,649	74,252	573
Tama	Toledo	17,946	17,419	721
Taylor	Bedford	6,900	7,114	534
Union	Creston	12,117	12,750	424
Van Buren	Keosauqua	7,800	7,676	485
Wapello	Ottumwa	35,787	35,696	432
Warren	Indianola	41,523	36,033	572
Washington	Washington	21,106	19,612	569
Wayne	Corydon	6,651	7,067	526
Webster	Fort Dodge	39,821	40,342	715
Winnebago	Forest City	11,580	12,122	400
Winneshiek	Decorah	21,416	20,847	690
Woodbury	Sioux City	103,331	98,276	873
Worth	Northwood	7,766	7,991	400
Wright	Clarion	13,986	14,269	581

Kansas
(105 counties, 81,815 sq. mi. land; pop. 2,715,884)

County	County seat or courthouse	2002 Pop.	1990 Pop.	Land area sq. mi.
Allen	Iola	14,234	14,638	503
Anderson	Garnett	8,147	7,803	583
Atchison	Atchison	16,683	16,932	432
Barber	Medicine Lodge	5,085	5,874	1,134
Barton	Great Bend	27,743	29,382	894
Bourbon	Fort Scott	15,171	14,966	637
Brown	Hiawatha	10,501	11,128	571
Butler	El Dorado	60,534	50,580	1,428
Chase	Cottonwood Falls	2,930	3,021	776
Chautauqua	Sedan	4,210	4,407	642
Cherokee	Columbus	21,953	21,374	587
Cheyenne	Saint Francis	3,123	3,243	1,020
Clark	Ashland	2,382	2,418	975
Clay	Clay Center	8,704	9,158	644
Cloud	Concordia	9,932	11,023	716
Coffey	Burlington	8,902	8,404	630
Comanche	Coldwater	1,985	2,313	788
Cowley	Winfield	36,427	36,915	1,126
Crawford	Girard	38,052	35,582	593
Decatur	Oberlin	3,407	4,021	894
Dickinson	Abilene	19,144	18,958	848
Doniphan	Troy	8,215	8,134	392
Douglas	Lawrence	102,316	81,798	457
Edwards	Kinsley	3,337	3,787	622
Elk	Howard	3,138	3,327	647
Ellis	Hays	27,274	26,004	900
Ellsworth	Ellsworth	6,418	6,586	716
Finney	Garden City	39,732	33,070	1,302
Ford	Dodge City	32,662	27,463	1,099
Franklin	Ottawa	25,322	21,994	574
Geary	Junction City	26,410	30,453	385
Gove	Gove	2,992	3,231	1,071
Graham	Hill City	2,847	3,543	898
Grant	Ulysses	7,895	7,159	575
Gray	Cimarron	6,045	5,396	869
Greeley	Tribune	1,472	1,774	778
Greenwood	Eureka	7,653	7,847	1,140
Hamilton	Syracuse	2,658	2,388	996
Harper	Anthony	6,278	7,124	801
Harvey	Newton	33,375	31,028	539
Haskell	Sublette	4,291	3,886	577
Hodgeman	Jetmore	2,149	2,177	860
Jackson	Holton	12,741	11,525	656
Jefferson	Oskaloosa	18,664	15,905	536
Jewell	Mankato	3,495	4,251	909
Johnson	Olathe	476,536	355,021	477
Kearny	Lakin	4,543	4,027	871
Kingman	Kingman	8,426	8,292	863
Kiowa	Greensburg	3,107	3,660	722
Labette	Oswego	22,281	23,693	649
Lane	Dighton	2,000	2,375	717
Leavenworth	Leavenworth	70,789	64,371	463
Lincoln	Lincoln	3,542	3,653	719
Linn	Mound City	9,674	8,254	599
Logan	Oakley	2,998	3,081	1,073
Lyon	Emporia	35,904	34,732	851
McPherson	McPherson	29,413	27,268	900
Marion	Marion	13,248	12,888	943
Marshall	Marysville	10,583	11,705	903
Meade	Meade	4,620	4,247	978
Miami	Paola	28,904	23,466	577
Mitchell	Beloit	6,693	7,203	700
Montgomery	Independence	35,307	38,816	645
Morris	Council Grove	6,082	6,198	697
Morton	Elkhart	3,360	3,480	730
Nemaha	Seneca	10,463	10,446	718
Neosho	Erie	16,638	17,035	572
Ness	Ness City	3,316	4,033	1,075
Norton	Norton	5,879	5,947	878
Osage	Lyndon	16,928	15,248	704
Osborne	Osborne	4,236	4,867	892
Ottawa	Minneapolis	6,289	5,634	721
Pawnee	Larned	6,946	7,555	754
Phillips	Phillipsburg	5,871	6,590	886
Pottawatomie	Westmoreland	18,489	16,128	844
Pratt	Pratt	9,541	9,702	735
Rawlins	Atwood	2,887	3,404	1,070
Reno	Hutchinson	63,790	62,389	1,254
Republic	Belleville	5,468	6,482	716
Rice	Lyons	10,501	10,610	727
Riley	Manhattan	61,480	67,139	610
Rooks	Stockton	5,492	6,039	888
Rush	LaCrosse	3,492	3,842	718
Russell	Russell	7,055	7,835	885
Saline	Salina	53,910	49,301	720
Scott	Scott City	4,923	5,289	718
Sedgwick	Wichita	461,937	403,662	999
Seward	Liberal	23,072	18,743	640
Shawnee	Topeka	170,748	160,976	550
Sheridan	Hoxie	2,641	3,043	895
Sherman	Goodland	6,398	6,926	1,056
Smith	Smith Center	4,365	5,078	895
Stafford	Saint John	4,662	5,365	792
Stanton	Johnson	2,410	2,333	680
Stevens	Hugoton	5,332	5,048	728
Sumner	Wellington	25,533	25,841	1,182
Thomas	Colby	8,092	8,258	1,075
Trego	WaKeeney	3,140	3,694	888
Wabaunsee	Alma	6,715	6,603	797
Wallace	Sharon Springs	1,692	1,821	914
Washington	Washington	6,271	7,073	898
Wichita	Leoti	2,502	2,758	719
Wilson	Fredonia	10,143	10,289	574
Woodson	Yates Center	3,668	4,116	501
Wyandotte	Kansas City	158,331	162,026	151

Kentucky
(120 counties, 39,728 sq. mi. land; pop. 4,092,891)

County	County seat or courthouse	2002 Pop.	1990 Pop.	Land area sq. mi.
Adair	Columbia	17,348	15,360	407
Allen	Scottsville	18,170	14,628	346
Anderson	Lawrenceburg	19,561	14,571	203
Ballard	Wickliffe	8,163	7,902	251
Barren	Glasgow	38,749	34,001	491
Bath	Owingsville	11,407	9,692	279
Bell	Pineville	30,114	31,506	361
Boone	Burlington	93,290	57,589	246
Bourbon	Paris	19,576	19,236	291
Boyd	Catlettsburg	49,603	51,096	160
Boyle	Danville	27,865	25,590	182
Bracken	Brooksville	8,482	7,766	203
Breathitt	Jackson	15,886	15,703	495
Breckinridge	Hardinsburg	18,952	16,312	572
Bullitt	Shepherdsville	63,800	47,567	299
Butler	Morgantown	13,158	11,245	428
Caldwell	Princeton	12,913	13,232	347
Calloway	Murray	34,392	30,735	386
Campbell	Newport	88,604	83,866	152
Carlisle	Bardwell	5,323	5,238	192
Carroll	Carrollton	10,223	9,292	130
Carter	Grayson	27,055	24,340	411
Casey	Liberty	15,773	14,211	446
Christian	Hopkinsville	71,267	68,941	721
Clark	Winchester	33,726	29,496	254
Clay	Manchester	24,264	21,746	471
Clinton	Albany	9,667	9,135	197

County	County seat or courthouse	2002 Pop.	1990 Pop.	Land area sq. mi.
Crittenden	Marion	9,223	9,196	362
Cumberland	Burkesville	7,179	6,784	306
Daviess	Owensboro	91,694	87,189	462
Edmonson	Brownsville	11,841	10,357	303
Elliott	Sandy Hook	6,752	6,455	234
Estill	Irvine	15,341	14,614	254
Fayette	Lexington	263,618	225,366	285
Fleming	Flemingsburg	14,095	12,292	351
Floyd	Prestonsburg	42,226	43,586	394
Franklin	Frankfort	48,201	44,143	210
Fulton	Hickman	7,551	8,271	209
Gallatin	Warsaw	7,836	5,393	99
Garrard	Lancaster	15,618	11,579	231
Grant	Williamstown	23,620	15,737	260
Graves	Mayfield	37,225	33,550	556
Grayson	Leitchfield	24,410	21,050	504
Green	Greensburg	11,733	10,371	289
Greenup	Greenup	36,761	36,796	346
Hancock	Hawesville	8,573	7,864	189
Hardin	Elizabethtown	95,724	89,240	628
Harlan	Harlan	32,585	36,574	467
Harrison	Cynthiana	18,079	16,248	310
Hart	Munfordville	17,667	14,890	416
Henderson	Henderson	44,995	43,044	440
Henry	New Castle	15,367	12,823	289
Hickman	Clinton	5,200	5,566	244
Hopkins	Madisonville	46,588	46,126	551
Jackson	McKee	13,778	11,955	346
Jefferson	Louisville	698,080	665,123	385
Jessamine	Nicholasville	40,740	30,508	173
Johnson	Paintsville	23,356	23,248	262
Kenton	Covington	152,164	142,005	162
Knott	Hindman	17,729	17,906	352
Knox	Barbourville	31,841	29,676	388
Larue	Hodgenville	13,372	11,679	263
Laurel	London	54,313	43,438	436
Lawrence	Louisa	15,784	13,998	419
Lee	Beattyville	7,949	7,422	210
Leslie	Hyden	12,281	13,642	404
Letcher	Whitesburg	24,934	27,000	339
Lewis	Vanceburg	13,944	13,029	484
Lincoln	Stanford	24,055	20,096	336
Livingston	Smithland	9,846	9,062	316
Logan	Russellville	26,800	24,416	556
Lyon	Eddyville	8,163	6,624	216
McCracken	Paducah	64,534	62,879	251
McCreary	Whitley City	16,993	15,603	428
McLean	Calhoun	10,047	9,628	254
Madison	Richmond	73,334	57,508	441
Magoffin	Salyersville	13,358	13,077	309
Marion	Lebanon	18,427	16,499	346
Marshall	Benton	30,261	27,205	305
Martin	Inez	12,529	12,526	231
Mason	Maysville	16,916	16,666	241
Meade	Brandenburg	27,439	24,170	309
Menifee	Frenchburg	6,708	5,092	204
Mercer	Harrodsburg	21,047	19,148	251
Metcalfe	Edmonton	10,046	8,963	291
Monroe	Tompkinsville	11,783	11,401	331
Montgomery	Mount Sterling	23,262	19,561	199
Morgan	West Liberty	14,204	11,648	381
Muhlenberg	Greenville	31,702	31,318	475
Nelson	Bardstown	38,823	29,710	423
Nicholas	Carlisle	6,934	6,725	197
Ohio	Hartford	23,272	21,105	594
Oldham	La Grange	49,310	33,263	189
Owen	Owenton	10,936	9,035	352
Owsley	Booneville	4,761	5,036	198
Pendleton	Falmouth	14,815	12,062	281
Perry	Hazard	29,371	30,283	342
Pike	Pikeville	67,803	72,584	788
Powell	Stanton	13,205	11,686	180
Pulaski	Somerset	57,160	49,489	662
Robertson	Mount Olivet	2,359	2,124	100
Rockcastle	Mount Vernon	16,783	14,803	318
Rowan	Morehead	22,265	20,353	281
Russell	Jamestown	16,628	14,716	254
Scott	Georgetown	35,320	23,867	285
Shelby	Shelbyville	35,125	24,824	384
Simpson	Franklin	16,666	15,145	236
Spencer	Taylorsville	13,523	6,801	186
Taylor	Campbellsville	23,202	21,146	270
Todd	Elkton	11,987	10,940	376
Trigg	Cadiz	12,681	10,361	443
Trimble	Bedford	8,672	6,090	149
Union	Morganfield	15,562	16,557	345
Warren	Bowling Green	94,730	77,720	545
Washington	Springfield	11,103	10,441	301
Wayne	Monticello	20,089	17,468	459
Webster	Dixon	14,079	13,955	335
Whitley	Williamsburg	36,636	33,326	440
Wolfe	Campton	6,936	6,503	223
Woodford	Versailles	23,403	19,955	191

Louisiana
(64 parishes, 43,562 sq. mi. land; pop. 4,482,646)

Parish	Parish seat or courthouse	2002 Pop.	1990 Pop.	Land area sq. mi.
Acadia	Crowley	58,920	55,882	655
Allen	Oberlin	25,290	21,226	765
Ascension	Donaldsonville	81,792	58,214	292
Assumption	Napoleonville	23,217	22,753	339
Avoyelles	Marksville	41,467	39,159	832
Beauregard	De Ridder	33,328	30,083	1,160
Bienville	Arcadia	15,445	16,232	811
Bossier	Benton	100,736	86,088	839
Caddo	Shreveport	251,145	248,253	882
Calcasieu	Lake Charles	183,344	168,134	1,071
Caldwell	Columbia	10,682	9,806	529
Cameron	Cameron	9,644	9,260	1,313
Catahoula	Harrisonburg	10,890	11,065	704
Claiborne	Homer	16,452	17,405	755
Concordia	Vidalia	20,019	20,828	696
De Soto	Mansfield	26,004	25,668	877
East Baton Rouge	Baton Rouge	412,008	380,105	455
East Carroll	Lake Providence	9,101	9,709	421
East Feliciana	Clinton	21,119	19,211	453
Evangeline	Ville Platte	35,442	33,274	664
Franklin	Winnsboro	20,851	22,387	624
Grant	Colfax	18,732	17,526	645
Iberia	New Iberia	73,850	68,297	575
Iberville	Plaquemine	33,095	31,049	619
Jackson	Jonesboro	15,377	15,859	570
Jefferson	Gretna	452,789	448,306	307
Jefferson Davis	Jennings	31,184	30,722	652
Lafayette	Lafayette	192,896	164,762	270
Lafourche	Thibodaux	91,222	85,860	1,085
La Salle	Jena	14,216	13,662	624
Lincoln	Ruston	42,351	41,745	471
Livingston	Livingston	99,066	70,523	648
Madison	Tallulah	13,317	12,463	624
Morehouse	Bastrop	30,443	31,938	794
Natchitoches	Natchitoches	38,663	37,254	1,255
Orleans	New Orleans	473,681	496,938	181
Ouachita	Monroe	147,342	142,191	611
Plaquemines	Pointe a la Hache	27,332	25,575	845
Pointe Coupee	New Roads	22,569	22,540	557
Rapides	Alexandria	126,881	131,556	1,323
Red River	Coushatta	9,592	9,526	389
Richland	Rayville	20,696	20,629	558
Sabine	Many	23,598	22,646	865
Saint Bernard	Chalmette	66,219	66,631	465
Saint Charles	Hahnville	49,250	42,437	284
Saint Helena	Greensburg	10,403	9,874	408
Saint James	Convent	21,349	20,879	246
Saint John the Baptist	Edgard	44,521	39,996	219
Saint Landry	Opelousas	88,199	80,312	929
Saint Martin	Saint Martinville	49,657	44,097	740
Saint Mary	Franklin	52,425	58,086	613
Saint Tammany	Covington	201,462	144,500	854
Tangipahoa	Amite	102,593	85,709	790
Tensas	Saint Joseph	6,493	7,103	602
Terrebonne	Houma	105,638	96,982	1,255
Union	Farmerville	22,771	20,796	878
Vermilion	Abbeville	54,114	50,055	1,174
Vernon	Leesville	51,008	61,961	1,328
Washington	Franklinton	43,882	43,185	670
Webster	Minden	41,509	41,989	595
West Baton Rouge	Port Allen	21,625	19,419	191
West Carroll	Oak Grove	12,103	12,093	359
West Feliciana	Saint Francisville	15,140	12,915	406
Winn	Winnfield	16,497	16,498	950

Maine
(16 counties, 30,862 sq. mi. land; pop. 1,294,464)

County	County seat or courthouse	2002 Pop.	1990 Pop.	Land area sq. mi.
Androscoggin	Auburn	104,805	105,259	470
Aroostook	Houlton	73,122	86,936	6,672
Cumberland	Portland	269,083	243,135	836
Franklin	Farmington	29,683	29,008	1,698
Hancock	Ellsworth	52,359	46,948	1,588
Kennebec	Augusta	118,244	115,904	868
Knox	Rockland	40,477	36,310	366
Lincoln	Wiscasset	34,407	30,357	456
Oxford	South Paris	55,604	52,602	2,078
Penobscot	Bangor	146,015	146,601	3,396
Piscataquis	Dover-Foxcroft	17,203	18,653	3,966
Sagadahoc	Bath	35,983	33,535	254
Somerset	Skowhegan	50,963	49,767	3,927
Waldo	Belfast	37,628	33,018	730
Washington	Machias	33,401	35,308	2,568
York	Alfred	195,487	164,587	991

Maryland
(23 counties, 1 ind. city, 9,774 sq. mi. land; pop. 5,458,137)

County	County seat or courthouse	2002 Pop.	1990 Pop.	Land area sq. mi.
Allegany	Cumberland	74,203	74,946	425
Anne Arundel	Annapolis	503,388	427,239	416
Baltimore	Towson	770,298	692,134	599
Calvert	Prince Frederick	80,906	51,372	215
Caroline	Denton	30,300	27,035	320
Carroll	Westminster	159,025	123,372	449
Cecil	Elkton	90,335	71,347	348
Charles	La Plata	129,040	101,154	461
Dorchester	Cambridge	30,451	30,236	558
Frederick	Frederick	209,125	150,208	663
Garrett	Oakland	29,878	28,138	648
Harford	Bel Air	227,713	182,132	440
Howard	Ellicott City	260,117	187,328	252
Kent	Chestertown	19,613	17,842	279
Montgomery	Rockville	910,156	762,875	496
Prince George's	Upper Marlboro	833,084	722,705	485
Queen Anne's	Centreville	42,835	33,953	372
Saint Mary's	Leonardtown	90,044	75,974	361
Somerset	Princess Anne	25,555	23,440	327
Talbot	Easton	34,263	30,549	269
Washington	Hagerstown	134,246	121,393	458
Wicomico	Salisbury	86,318	74,339	377
Worcester	Snow Hill	48,630	35,028	473
Independent City				
Baltimore		638,614	736,014	81

Massachusetts
(14 counties, 7,840 sq. mi. land; pop. 6,427,801)

County	County seat or courthouse	2002 Pop.	1990 Pop.	Land area sq. mi.
Barnstable	Barnstable	228,577	186,605	396
Berkshire	Pittsfield	133,462	139,352	931
Bristol	Taunton	543,434	506,325	556
Dukes	Edgartown	15,431	11,639	104
Essex	Salem	735,606	670,080	501
Franklin	Greenfield	71,721	70,086	702
Hampden	Springfield	459,116	456,310	618
Hampshire	Northampton	153,399	146,568	529
Middlesex	East Cambridge	1,474,160	1,398,468	823
Nantucket	Nantucket	10,416	6,012	48
Norfolk	Dedham	656,486	616,087	400
Plymouth	Plymouth	485,747	435,276	661
Suffolk	Boston	689,925	663,906	59
Worcester	Worcester	770,321	709,711	1,513

Michigan
(83 counties, 56,804 sq. mi. land; pop. 10,050,446)

County	County seat or courthouse	2002 Pop.	1990 Pop.	Land area sq. mi.
Alcona	Harrisville	11,455	10,145	674
Alger	Munising	9,796	8,972	918
Allegan	Allegan	109,336	90,509	827
Alpena	Alpena	31,026	30,605	574
Antrim	Bellaire	23,809	18,185	477
Arenac	Standish	17,185	14,906	360
Baraga	L'Anse	8,694	7,954	904
Barry	Hastings	57,943	50,057	556
Bay	Bay City	109,672	111,723	444
Benzie	Beulah	16,818	12,200	321
Berrien	Saint Joseph	162,285	161,378	571
Branch	Coldwater	46,189	41,502	507
Calhoun	Marshall	138,375	135,982	709
Cass	Cassopolis	51,284	49,477	492
Charlevoix	Charlevoix	26,386	21,468	417
Cheboygan	Cheboygan	27,072	21,398	716
Chippewa	Sault Sainte Marie	38,898	34,604	1,561
Clare	Harrison	31,686	24,952	567
Clinton	Saint Johns	66,668	57,893	571
Crawford	Grayling	14,734	12,260	558
Delta	Escanaba	38,336	37,780	1,170
Dickinson	Iron Mountain	27,325	26,831	766
Eaton	Charlotte	105,590	92,879	576
Emmet	Petoskey	32,329	25,040	468
Genesee	Flint	441,423	430,459	640
Gladwin	Gladwin	26,745	21,896	507
Gogebic	Bessemer	17,407	18,052	1,102
Grand Traverse	Traverse City	81,263	64,273	465
Gratiot	Ithaca	42,365	38,982	570
Hillsdale	Hillsdale	46,980	43,431	599
Houghton	Houghton	35,883	35,446	1,012
Huron	Bad Axe	35,422	34,951	837
Ingham	Mason	281,362	281,912	559
Ionia	Ionia	62,941	57,024	573
Iosco	Tawas City	26,979	30,209	549
Iron	Crystal Falls	12,736	13,175	1,166
Isabella	Mount Pleasant	64,523	54,624	574
Jackson	Jackson	160,972	149,756	707
Kalamazoo	Kalamazoo	241,471	223,411	562
Kalkaska	Kalkaska	17,043	13,497	561
Kent	Grand Rapids	587,951	500,631	856
Keweenaw	Eagle River	2,204	1,701	541
Lake	Baldwin	11,623	8,583	567
Lapeer	Lapeer	90,776	74,768	654
Leelanau	Leland	21,722	16,527	348
Lenawee	Adrian	100,145	91,476	751
Livingston	Howell	168,862	115,645	568
Luce	Newberry	7,027	5,763	903
Mackinac	Saint Ignace	11,505	10,674	1,022
Macomb	Mount Clemens	808,529	717,400	480
Manistee	Manistee	25,082	21,265	544
Marquette	Marquette	64,342	70,887	1,821
Mason	Ludington	28,879	25,537	495
Mecosta	Big Rapids	41,465	37,308	556
Menominee	Menominee	25,109	24,920	1,044
Midland	Midland	84,119	75,651	521
Missaukee	Lake City	14,950	12,147	567
Monroe	Monroe	149,253	133,600	551
Montcalm	Stanton	62,420	53,059	708
Montmorency	Atlanta	10,560	8,936	548
Muskegon	Muskegon	171,765	158,983	509
Newaygo	White Cloud	49,013	38,206	842
Oakland	Pontiac	1,202,721	1,083,592	873
Oceana	Hart	27,650	22,455	540
Ogemaw	West Branch	21,758	18,681	564
Ontonagon	Ontonagon	7,703	8,854	1,312
Osceola	Reed City	23,500	20,146	566
Oscoda	Mio	9,449	7,842	565
Otsego	Gaylord	24,155	17,957	515
Ottawa	Grand Haven	245,913	187,768	566
Presque Isle	Rogers City	14,320	13,743	660
Roscommon	Roscommon	25,818	19,776	521
Saginaw	Saginaw	210,087	211,946	809
Saint Clair	Port Huron	167,712	145,607	724
Saint Joseph	Centreville	62,366	58,913	504
Sanilac	Sandusky	44,535	39,928	964
Schoolcraft	Manistique	8,778	8,302	1,178
Shiawassee	Corunna	72,122	69,770	539
Tuscola	Caro	58,249	55,498	812
Van Buren	Paw Paw	77,235	70,060	611
Washtenaw	Ann Arbor	334,351	282,937	710
Wayne	Detroit	2,045,540	2,111,687	614
Wexford	Cadillac	30,777	26,360	565

Minnesota
(87 counties, 79,610 sq. mi. land; pop. 5,019,720)

County	County seat or courthouse	2002 Pop.	1990 Pop.	Land area sq. mi.
Aitkin	Aitkin	15,494	12,425	1,819
Anoka	Anoka	309,790	243,641	424
Becker	Detroit Lakes	30,787	27,881	1,310
Beltrami	Bemidji	41,026	34,384	2,505
Benton	Foley	36,316	30,185	408
Big Stone	Ortonville	5,677	6,285	497
Blue Earth	Mankato	56,704	54,044	752
Brown	New Ulm	26,673	26,984	611
Carlton	Carlton	32,577	29,259	860
Carver	Chaska	75,620	47,915	357
Cass	Walker	27,833	21,791	2,018
Chippewa	Montevideo	12,930	13,228	583
Chisago	Center City	44,580	30,521	418
Clay	Moorhead	51,947	50,422	1,045
Clearwater	Bagley	8,400	8,309	995
Cook	Grand Marais	5,194	3,868	1,451
Cottonwood	Windom	12,043	12,694	640
Crow Wing	Brainerd	56,903	44,249	997
Dakota	Hastings	368,972	275,210	570
Dodge	Mantorville	18,551	15,731	440
Douglas	Alexandria	33,520	28,674	634
Faribault	Blue Earth	15,925	16,937	714
Fillmore	Preston	21,418	20,777	861
Freeborn	Albert Lea	32,092	33,060	708
Goodhue	Red Wing	44,769	40,690	758
Grant	Elbow Lake	6,256	6,246	546
Hennepin	Minneapolis	1,122,259	1,032,431	557
Houston	Caledonia	19,846	18,497	558
Hubbard	Park Rapids	18,425	14,939	922
Isanti	Cambridge	33,799	25,921	439
Itasca	Grand Rapids	44,144	40,863	2,665
Jackson	Jackson	11,281	11,677	702
Kanabec	Mora	15,455	12,802	525
Kandiyohi	Willmar	40,832	38,761	796
Kittson	Hallock	5,059	5,767	1,097
Koochiching	International Falls	13,978	16,299	3,102
Lac qui Parle	Madison	7,932	8,924	765
Lake	Two Harbors	11,094	10,415	2,099
Lake of the Woods	Baudette	4,385	4,076	1,297
Le Sueur	Le Center	26,005	23,239	449
Lincoln	Ivanhoe	6,232	6,890	537
Lyon	Marshall	25,118	24,789	714
McLeod	Glencoe	35,403	32,030	492
Mahnomen	Mahnomen	5,150	5,044	556
Marshall	Warren	9,909	10,993	1,772
Martin	Fairmont	21,237	22,914	709
Meeker	Litchfield	22,878	20,846	609
Mille Lacs	Milaca	23,628	18,670	574
Morrison	Little Falls	32,360	29,604	1,125
Mower	Austin	38,785	37,385	712

County	County seat or courthouse	2002 Pop.	1990 Pop.	Land area sq. mi.
Murray	Slayton	9,008	9,660	704
Nicollet	Saint Peter	30,267	28,076	452
Nobles	Worthington	20,449	20,098	715
Norman	Ada	7,315	7,975	876
Olmsted	Rochester	128,961	106,470	653
Otter Tail	Fergus Falls	58,039	50,714	1,980
Pennington	Thief River Falls	13,514	13,306	617
Pine	Pine City	27,340	21,264	1,411
Pipestone	Pipestone	9,761	10,491	466
Polk	Crookston	31,115	32,589	1,970
Pope	Glenwood	11,190	10,745	670
Ramsey	Saint Paul	510,568	485,760	156
Red Lake	Red Lake Falls	4,313	4,525	432
Redwood	Redwood Falls	16,275	17,254	880
Renville	Olivia	17,052	17,673	983
Rice	Faribault	58,581	49,183	498
Rock	Luverne	9,794	9,806	483
Roseau	Roseau	16,229	15,026	1,663
Saint Louis	Duluth	199,983	198,232	6,225
Scott	Shakopee	103,681	57,846	357
Sherburne	Elk River	71,471	41,945	436
Sibley	Gaylord	15,384	14,366	589
Stearns	Saint Cloud	135,867	119,324	1,345
Steele	Owatonna	34,391	30,729	430
Stevens	Morris	9,886	10,634	562
Swift	Benson	11,602	10,724	744
Todd	Long Prairie	24,463	23,363	942
Traverse	Wheaton	3,952	4,463	574
Wabasha	Wabasha	21,903	19,744	525
Wadena	Wadena	13,584	13,154	535
Waseca	Waseca	19,436	18,079	423
Washington	Stillwater	210,270	145,860	392
Watonwan	Saint James	11,665	11,682	435
Wilkin	Beckenridge	6,969	7,516	751
Winona	Winona	49,362	47,828	626
Wright	Buffalo	98,083	68,710	661
Yellow Medicine	Granite Falls	10,806	11,684	758

Mississippi

(82 counties, 46,907 sq. mi. land; pop. 2,871,782)

County	County seat or courthouse	2002 Pop.	1990 Pop.	Land area sq. mi.
Adams	Natchez	33,573	35,356	460
Alcorn	Corinth	34,733	31,722	400
Amite	Liberty	13,451	13,328	730
Attala	Kosciusko	19,748	18,481	735
Benton	Ashland	7,935	8,046	407
Bolivar	Cleveland & Rosedale	39,839	41,875	876
Calhoun	Pittsboro	14,900	14,908	587
Carroll	Carrollton & Vaiden	10,628	9,237	628
Chickasaw	Houston & Okolona	19,524	18,085	502
Choctaw	Ackerman	9,652	9,071	419
Claiborne	Port Gibson	11,755	11,370	487
Clarke	Quitman	17,968	17,313	691
Clay	West Point	21,857	21,120	409
Coahoma	Clarksdale	30,158	31,665	554
Copiah	Hazlehurst	28,808	27,592	777
Covington	Collins	19,728	16,527	414
De Soto	Hernando	118,458	67,910	478
Forrest	Hattiesburg	73,465	68,314	467
Franklin	Meadville	8,349	8,377	565
George	Lucedale	19,797	16,673	478
Greene	Leakesville	13,095	10,220	713
Grenada	Grenada	22,915	21,555	422
Hancock	Bay Saint Louis	44,673	31,760	477
Harrison	Gulfport	190,936	165,365	581
Hinds	Jackson & Raymond	249,579	254,441	869
Holmes	Lexington	21,651	21,604	756
Humphreys	Belzoni	10,750	12,134	418
Issaquena	Mayersville	2,194	1,909	413
Itawamba	Fulton	22,975	20,017	532
Jackson	Pascagoula	133,259	115,243	727
Jasper	Bay Springs & Paulding	18,286	17,114	676
Jefferson	Fayette	9,661	8,653	519
Jefferson Davis	Prentiss	13,521	14,051	408
Jones	Ellisville & Laurel	65,053	62,031	694
Kemper	De Kalb	10,595	10,356	766
Lafayette	Oxford	39,524	31,826	631
Lamar	Purvis	41,167	30,424	497
Lauderdale	Meridian	77,600	75,555	704
Lawrence	Monticello	13,448	12,458	431
Leake	Carthage	21,540	18,436	583
Lee	Tupelo	77,220	65,579	450
Leflore	Greenwood	37,099	37,341	592
Lincoln	Brookhaven	33,448	30,278	586
Lowndes	Columbus	60,978	59,308	502
Madison	Canton	77,872	53,794	717
Marion	Columbia	25,319	25,544	542
Marshall	Holly Springs	35,163	30,361	706
Monroe	Aberdeen	37,746	36,582	764
Montgomery	Winona	11,863	12,387	407
Neshoba	Philadelphia	29,027	24,800	570
Newton	Decatur	21,967	20,291	578
Noxubee	Macon	12,438	12,604	695
Oktibbeha	Starkville	42,751	38,375	458
Panola	Batesville & Sardis	34,913	29,996	684
Pearl River	Poplarville	50,473	38,714	811
Perry	New Augusta	12,200	10,865	647
Pike	Magnolia	38,987	36,882	409
Pontotoc	Pontotoc	27,032	22,237	497
Prentiss	Booneville	25,746	23,278	415
Quitman	Marks	9,806	10,490	405
Rankin	Brandon	121,577	87,161	775
Scott	Forest	28,338	24,137	609
Sharkey	Rolling Fork	6,252	7,066	428
Simpson	Mendenhall	27,672	23,953	589
Smith	Raleigh	15,893	14,798	636
Stone	Wiggins	14,280	10,750	445
Sunflower	Indianola	33,889	35,129	694
Tallahatchie	Charleston & Sumner	14,411	15,210	644
Tate	Senatobia	25,751	21,432	404
Tippah	Ripley	21,044	19,523	458
Tishomingo	Iuka	19,050	17,683	424
Tunica	Tunica	9,575	8,164	455
Union	New Albany	26,099	22,085	415
Walthall	Tylertown	15,141	14,352	404
Warren	Vicksburg	49,443	47,880	587
Washington	Greenville	61,315	67,935	724
Wayne	Waynesboro	21,219	19,517	810
Webster	Walthall	10,317	10,222	422
Wilkinson	Woodville	10,228	9,678	677
Winston	Louisville	20,001	19,433	607
Yalobusha	Coffeeville & Water Valley	13,312	12,033	467
Yazoo	Yazoo City	28,199	25,506	919

Missouri

(114 counties, 1 ind. city, 68,886 sq. mi. land; pop. 5,672,579)

County	County seat or courthouse	2002 Pop.	1990 Pop.	Land area sq. mi.
Adair	Kirksville	24,946	24,577	567
Andrew	Savannah	16,751	14,632	435
Atchison	Rockport	6,323	7,457	545
Audrain	Mexico	25,639	23,599	693
Barry	Cassville	34,527	27,547	779
Barton	Lamar	12,862	11,312	594
Bates	Butler	16,976	15,025	848
Benton	Warsaw	17,583	13,859	706
Bollinger	Marble Hill	12,248	10,619	621
Boone	Columbia	139,492	112,379	685
Buchanan	Saint Joseph	85,313	83,083	410
Butler	Poplar Buff	40,764	38,765	698
Caldwell	Kingston	9,096	8,380	429
Callaway	Fulton	42,210	32,809	839
Camden	Camdenton	37,857	27,495	655
Cape Girardeau	Jackson	69,511	61,633	579
Carroll	Carrollton	10,263	10,748	695
Carter	Van Buren	5,860	5,515	508
Cass	Harrisonville	87,310	63,808	699
Cedar	Stockton	13,825	12,093	476
Chariton	Keytesville	8,197	9,202	756
Christian	Ozark	59,117	32,644	563
Clark	Kahoka	7,432	7,547	507
Clay	Liberty	191,381	153,411	396
Clinton	Plattsburg	19,632	16,595	419
Cole	Jefferson City	71,894	63,579	391
Cooper	Boonville	17,007	14,835	565
Crawford	Steelville	23,173	19,173	743
Dade	Greenfield	7,877	7,449	490
Dallas	Buffalo	15,874	12,646	542
Daviess	Gallatin	8,030	7,865	567
De Kalb	Maysville	11,553	9,967	424
Dent	Salem	14,922	13,702	754
Douglas	Ava	13,330	11,876	815
Dunklin	Kennett	32,805	33,112	546
Franklin	Union	95,890	80,603	923
Gasconade	Hermann	15,461	14,006	521
Gentry	Albany	6,607	6,854	492
Greene	Springfield	243,355	207,949	675
Grundy	Trenton	10,213	10,536	436
Harrison	Bethany	8,785	8,469	725
Henry	Clinton	22,250	20,044	702
Hickory	Hermitage	8,909	7,335	399
Holt	Oregon	5,136	6,034	462
Howard	Fayette	10,004	9,631	466
Howell	West Plains	37,280	31,447	928
Iron	Ironton	10,381	10,726	551
Jackson	Independence	660,773	633,234	605
Jasper	Carthage	107,073	90,465	640
Jefferson	Hillsboro	203,993	171,380	657
Johnson	Warrensburg	49,779	42,514	830
Knox	Edina	4,285	4,482	506
Laclede	Lebanon	32,757	27,158	766
Lafayette	Lexington	33,125	31,107	629
Lawrence	Mount Vernon	36,082	30,236	613
Lewis	Monticello	10,384	10,233	505
Lincoln	Troy	42,280	28,892	630

County	County seat or courthouse	2002 Pop.	1990 Pop.	Land area sq. mi.
Linn	Linneus	13,515	13,885	620
Livingston	Chillicothe	14,283	14,592	535
McDonald	Pineville	21,687	16,938	540
Macon	Macon	15,497	15,345	804
Madison	Fredericktown	11,807	11,127	497
Maries	Vienna	8,700	7,976	528
Marion	Palmyra	28,079	27,682	438
Mercer	Princeton	3,669	3,723	454
Miller	Tuscumbia	24,176	20,700	592
Mississippi	Charleston	13,966	14,442	413
Moniteau	California	15,023	12,298	417
Monroe	Paris	9,262	9,104	646
Montgomery	Montgomery City	12,063	11,355	537
Morgan	Versailles	19,593	15,574	597
New Madrid	New Madrid	19,138	20,928	678
Newton	Neosho	53,130	44,445	626
Nodaway	Maryville	21,651	21,709	877
Oregon	Alton	10,265	9,470	791
Osage	Linn	13,040	12,018	606
Ozark	Gainesville	9,397	8,598	742
Pemiscot	Caruthersville	19,849	21,921	493
Perry	Perryville	18,274	16,648	475
Pettis	Sedalia	39,542	35,437	685
Phelps	Rolla	40,932	35,248	673
Pike	Bowling Green	18,389	15,969	673
Platte	Platte City	77,655	57,867	420
Polk	Bolivar	27,710	21,826	637
Pulaski	Waynesville	43,263	41,307	547
Putnam	Unionville	5,208	5,079	518
Ralls	New London	9,584	8,476	471
Randolph	Huntsville	24,699	24,370	482
Ray	Richmond	23,811	21,968	569
Reynolds	Centerville	6,629	6,661	811
Ripley	Doniphan	13,399	12,303	629
Saint Charles	Saint Charles	309,030	212,751	560
Saint Clair	Osceola	9,663	8,457	677
Sainte Genevieve	Sainte Genevieve	18,104	16,037	502
Saint Francois	Farmington	56,775	48,904	449
Saint Louis	Clayton	1,018,102	993,508	508
Saline	Marshall	23,018	23,523	756
Schuyler	Lancaster	4,211	4,236	308
Scotland	Memphis	4,868	4,822	438
Scott	Benton	40,279	39,376	421
Shannon	Eminence	8,382	7,613	1,004
Shelby	Shelbyville	6,681	6,942	501
Stoddard	Bloomfield	29,828	28,895	827
Stone	Galena	29,381	19,078	463
Sullivan	Milan	7,315	6,326	651
Taney	Forsyth	40,601	25,561	632
Texas	Houston	24,625	21,476	1,179
Vernon	Nevada	20,274	19,041	834
Warren	Warrenton	26,193	19,534	431
Washington	Potosi	23,503	20,380	760
Wayne	Greenville	13,122	11,543	761
Webster	Marshfield	32,671	23,753	593
Worth	Grant City	2,298	2,440	267
Wright	Hartville	18,035	16,758	682
Independent City				
Saint Louis		338,353	396,685	62

Montana
(56 counties, 145,552 sq. mi. land; pop. 909,453)

County	County seat or courthouse	2002 Pop.	1990 Pop.	Land area sq. mi.
Beaverhead	Dillon	9,009	8,424	5,542
Big Horn	Hardin	12,886	11,337	4,995
Blaine	Chinook	6,895	6,728	4,226
Broadwater	Townsend	4,366	3,318	1,191
Carbon	Red Lodge	9,675	8,080	2,048
Carter	Ekalaka	1,343	1,503	3,340
Cascade	Great Falls	79,389	77,691	2,698
Chouteau	Fort Benton	5,566	5,452	3,973
Custer	Miles City	11,341	11,697	3,783
Daniels	Scobey	1,967	2,266	1,426
Dawson	Glendive	8,713	9,505	2,373
Deer Lodge	Anaconda	9,069	10,356	737
Fallon	Baker	2,715	3,103	1,620
Fergus	Lewistown	11,678	12,083	4,339
Flathead	Kalispell	77,240	59,218	5,098
Gallatin	Bozeman	71,206	50,484	2,606
Garfield	Jordan	1,230	1,589	4,668
Glacier	Cut Bank	13,106	12,121	2,995
Golden Valley	Ryegate	1,063	912	1,175
Granite	Philipsburg	2,863	2,548	1,727
Hill	Havre	16,372	17,654	2,896
Jefferson	Boulder	10,424	7,939	1,657
Judith Basin	Stanford	2,273	2,282	1,870
Lake	Polson	26,908	21,041	1,494
Lewis & Clark	Helena	56,554	47,495	3,461
Liberty	Chester	2,037	2,295	1,430
Lincoln	Libby	18,665	17,481	3,613
McCone	Circle	1,827	2,276	2,643
Madison	Virginia City	7,005	5,989	3,587
Meagher	White Sulphur Springs	1,941	1,819	2,392
Mineral	Superior	3,803	3,315	1,220
Missoula	Missoula	98,102	78,687	2,598
Musselshell	Roundup	4,410	4,106	1,867
Park	Livingston	15,767	14,515	2,802
Petroleum	Winnett	500	519	1,654
Phillips	Malta	4,321	5,163	5,140
Pondera	Conrad	6,232	6,433	1,625
Powder River	Broadus	1,829	2,090	3,297
Powell	Deer Lodge	7,045	6,620	2,326
Prairie	Terry	1,190	1,383	1,737
Ravalli	Hamilton	37,868	25,010	2,394
Richland	Sidney	9,265	10,716	2,084
Roosevelt	Wolf Point	10,494	10,999	2,356
Rosebud	Forsyth	9,273	10,505	5,012
Sanders	Thompson Falls	10,367	8,669	2,762
Sheridan	Plentywood	3,798	4,732	1,677
Silver Bow	Butte	33,403	33,941	718
Stillwater	Columbus	8,420	6,536	1,795
Sweet Grass	Big Timber	3,623	3,154	1,855
Teton	Choteau	6,315	6,271	2,273
Toole	Shelby	5,103	5,046	1,911
Treasure	Hysham	785	874	979
Valley	Glasgow	7,382	8,239	4,921
Wheatland	Harlowton	2,164	2,246	1,423
Wibaux	Wibaux	1,046	1,191	889
Yellowstone	Billings	131,622	113,419	2,635

Nebraska
(93 counties, 76,872 sq. mi. land; pop. 1,729,180)

County	County seat or courthouse	2002 Pop.	1990 Pop.	Land area sq. mi.
Adams	Hastings	31,222	29,625	563
Antelope	Neligh	7,307	7,965	857
Arthur	Arthur	416	462	715
Banner	Harrisburg	765	852	746
Blaine	Brewster	529	675	711
Boone	Albion	6,080	6,667	687
Box Butte	Alliance	11,868	13,130	1,075
Boyd	Butte	2,317	2,835	540
Brown	Ainsworth	3,518	3,657	1,221
Buffalo	Kearney	42,765	37,447	968
Burt	Tekamah	7,610	7,868	493
Butler	David City	8,854	8,601	584
Cass	Plattsmouth	24,839	21,318	559
Cedar	Hartington	9,264	10,131	740
Chase	Imperial	3,991	4,381	895
Cherry	Valentine	6,167	6,307	5,961
Cheyenne	Sidney	9,964	9,494	1,196
Clay	Clay Center	6,921	7,123	573
Colfax	Schuyler	10,555	9,139	413
Cuming	West Point	10,005	10,117	572
Custer	Broken Bow	11,501	12,270	2,576
Dakota	Dakota City	20,339	16,742	264
Dawes	Chadron	8,996	9,021	1,396
Dawson	Lexington	24,613	19,940	1,013
Deuel	Chappell	2,065	2,237	440
Dixon	Ponca	6,246	6,143	476
Dodge	Fremont	35,989	34,500	534
Douglas	Omaha	472,744	416,444	331
Dundy	Benkelman	2,222	2,582	920
Fillmore	Geneva	6,530	7,103	576
Franklin	Franklin	3,464	3,938	575
Frontier	Stockville	2,963	3,101	975
Furnas	Beaver City	5,242	5,553	718
Gage	Beatrice	23,121	22,794	855
Garden	Oshkosh	2,194	2,460	1,704
Garfield	Burwell	1,879	2,141	570
Gosper	Elwood	2,057	1,928	458
Grant	Hyannis	706	769	776
Greeley	Greeley	2,653	3,006	569
Hall	Grand Island	53,613	48,925	546
Hamilton	Aurora	9,371	8,862	544
Harlan	Alma	3,635	3,810	553
Hayes	Hayes Center	1,109	1,222	713
Hitchcock	Trenton	3,023	3,750	710
Holt	O'Neill	11,191	12,599	2,413
Hooker	Mullen	745	793	721
Howard	Saint Paul	6,479	6,057	569
Jefferson	Fairbury	8,250	8,759	573
Johnson	Tecumseh	4,449	4,673	376
Kearney	Minden	6,853	6,629	516
Keith	Ogallala	8,729	8,584	1,061
Keya Paha	Springview	962	1,029	773
Kimball	Kimball	3,957	4,108	952
Knox	Center	9,082	9,564	1,108
Lancaster	Lincoln	257,513	213,641	839
Lincoln	North Platte	34,390	32,508	2,564
Logan	Stapleton	743	878	571
Loup	Taylor	739	683	570
McPherson	Tryon	546	546	859
Madison	Madison	36,035	32,655	573
Merrick	Central City	8,033	8,062	485
Morrill	Bridgeport	5,291	5,423	1,424
Nance	Fullerton	3,911	4,275	441
Nemaha	Auburn	7,306	7,980	409

County	County seat or courthouse	2002 Pop.	1990 Pop.	Land area sq. mi.
Nuckolls	Nelson	4,843	5,786	575
Otoe	Nebraska City	15,458	14,252	616
Pawnee	Pawnee City	3,030	3,317	432
Perkins	Grant	3,065	3,367	883
Phelps	Holdrege	9,593	9,715	540
Pierce	Pierce	7,846	7,827	574
Platte	Columbus	31,215	29,820	678
Polk	Osceola	5,518	5,655	439
Red Willow	McCook	11,372	11,705	717
Richardson	Falls City	9,094	9,937	553
Rock	Bassett	1,714	2,019	1,008
Saline	Wilber	14,121	12,715	575
Sarpy	Papillion	129,319	102,583	241
Saunders	Wahoo	19,894	18,285	754
Scotts Bluff	Gering	36,764	36,025	739
Seward	Seward	16,665	15,450	575
Sheridan	Rushville	6,064	6,750	2,441
Sherman	Loup City	3,173	3,718	566
Sioux	Harrison	1,426	1,549	2,067
Stanton	Stanton	6,536	6,244	430
Thayer	Hebron	5,692	6,635	575
Thomas	Thedford	699	851	713
Thurston	Pender	7,199	6,936	394
Valley	Ord	4,542	5,169	568
Washington	Blair	19,211	16,607	390
Wayne	Wayne	9,497	9,364	443
Webster	Red Cloud	3,973	4,279	575
Wheeler	Bartlett	876	948	575
York	York	14,345	14,428	576

Nevada
(16 counties, 1 ind. city, 109,826 sq. mi. land; pop. 2,173,491)

County	County seat or courthouse	2002 Pop.	1990 Pop.	Land area sq. mi.
Churchill	Fallon	24,022	17,938	4,929
Clark	Las Vegas	1,522,164	741,368	7,910
Douglas	Minden	43,189	27,637	710
Elko	Elko	44,549	33,463	17,179
Esmeralda	Goldfield	884	1,344	3,589
Eureka	Eureka	1,585	1,547	4,176
Humboldt	Winnemucca	15,004	12,844	9,648
Lander	Battle Mountain	5,253	6,266	5,494
Lincoln	Pioche	4,243	3,775	10,634
Lyon	Yerington	37,879	20,001	1,994
Mineral	Hawthorne	4,834	6,475	3,756
Nye	Tonopah	34,499	17,781	18,147
Pershing	Lovelock	6,638	4,336	6,037
Storey	Virginia City	3,423	2,526	263
Washoe	Reno	362,325	254,667	6,342
White Pine	Ely	8,689	9,264	8,876

Independent City

Carson City		54,311	40,443	143

New Hampshire
(10 counties, 8,968 sq. mi. land; pop. 1,275,056)

County	County seat or courthouse	2002 Pop.	1990 Pop.	Land area sq. mi.
Belknap	Laconia	59,112	49,216	401
Carroll	Ossipee	45,344	35,410	934
Cheshire	Keene	75,206	70,121	707
Coos	Lancaster	33,100	34,828	1,800
Grafton	Woodsville	83,411	74,929	1,713
Hillsborough	Nashua	392,410	335,838	876
Merrimack	Concord	141,245	120,240	934
Rockingham	Brentwood	287,869	245,845	695
Strafford	Dover	116,106	104,233	369
Sullivan	Newport	41,253	38,592	537

New Jersey
(21 counties, 7,417 sq. mi. land; pop. 8,590,300)

County	County seat or courthouse	2002 Pop.	1990 Pop.	Land area sq. mi.
Atlantic	Mays Landing	259,423	224,327	561
Bergen	Hackensack	895,091	825,380	234
Burlington	Mount Holly	437,871	395,066	805
Camden	Camden	511,957	502,824	222
Cape May	Cape May Court House	102,013	95,089	255
Cumberland	Bridgeton	147,768	138,053	489
Essex	Newark	798,301	777,964	126
Gloucester	Woodbury	262,049	230,082	325
Hudson	Jersey City	611,439	553,099	47
Hunterdon	Flemington	125,795	107,852	430
Mercer	Trenton	359,463	325,759	226
Middlesex	New Brunswick	775,549	671,712	310
Monmouth	Freehold	629,836	553,192	472
Morris	Morristown	478,730	421,330	469
Ocean	Toms River	537,065	433,203	636
Passaic	Paterson	496,646	470,872	185
Salem	Salem	64,438	65,294	338
Somerset	Somerville	309,886	240,222	305
Sussex	Newton	148,680	130,936	521
Union	Elizabeth	530,763	493,819	103
Warren	Belvidere	107,537	91,675	358

New Mexico
(33 counties, 121,356 sq. mi. land; pop. 1,855,059)

County	County seat or courthouse	2002 Pop.	1990 Pop.	Land area sq. mi.
Bernalillo	Albuquerque	573,675	480,577	1,166
Catron	Reserve	3,523	2,563	6,928
Chaves	Roswell	60,177	57,849	6,071
Cibola	Grants	26,221	23,794	4,539
Colfax	Raton	14,189	12,925	3,757
Curry	Clovis	45,022	42,207	1,406
DeBaca	Fort Sumner	2,132	2,252	2,325
Dona Ana	Las Cruces	178,664	135,510	3,807
Eddy	Carlsbad	51,139	48,605	4,182
Grant	Silver City	30,237	27,676	3,966
Guadalupe	Santa Rosa	4,545	4,156	3,030
Harding	Mosquero	751	987	2,125
Hidalgo	Lordsburg	5,343	5,958	3,446
Lea	Lovington	55,655	55,765	4,393
Lincoln	Carrizozo	19,814	12,219	4,831
Los Alamos	Los Alamos	18,305	18,115	109
Luna	Deming	25,238	18,110	2,965
McKinley	Gallup	73,973	60,686	5,449
Mora	Mora	5,269	4,264	1,931
Otero	Alamogordo	61,577	51,928	6,627
Quay	Tucumcari	9,811	10,823	2,875
Rio Arriba	Tierra Amarilla	41,049	34,365	5,858
Roosevelt	Portales	18,121	16,702	2,449
Sandoval	Bernalillo	96,071	63,319	3,709
San Juan	Aztec	120,367	91,605	5,514
San Miguel	Las Vegas	29,674	25,743	4,717
Santa Fe	Santa Fe	134,525	98,928	1,909
Sierra	Truth or Consequences	12,988	9,912	4,180
Socorro	Socorro	18,043	14,764	6,646
Taos	Taos	30,785	23,118	2,203
Torrance	Estancia	16,664	10,285	3,345
Union	Clayton	3,934	4,124	3,830
Valencia	Los Lunas	67,578	45,235	1,068

New York
(62 counties, 47,214 sq. mi. land; pop. 19,157,532)

County	County seat or courthouse	2002 Pop.	1990 Pop.	Land area sq. mi.
Albany	Albany	296,173	292,812	523
Allegany	Belmont	50,181	50,470	1,030
Bronx[1]	Bronx	1,354,068	1,203,789	42
Broome	Binghamton	200,324	212,160	707
Cattaraugus	Little Valley	83,269	84,234	1,310
Cayuga	Auburn	81,562	82,313	693
Chautauqua	Mayville	138,332	141,895	1,062
Chemung	Elmira	90,614	95,195	408
Chenango	Norwich	51,324	51,768	894
Clinton	Plattsburgh	81,069	85,969	1,039
Columbia	Hudson	63,532	62,982	636
Cortland	Cortland	48,814	48,963	500
Delaware	Delhi	47,302	47,352	1,446
Dutchess	Poughkeepsie	287,752	259,462	802
Erie	Buffalo	945,049	968,584	1,044
Essex	Elizabethtown	38,935	37,152	1,797
Franklin	Malone	50,964	46,540	1,631
Fulton	Johnstown	55,049	54,191	496
Genesee	Batavia	59,799	60,060	494
Greene	Catskill	48,538	44,739	648
Hamilton	Lake Pleasant	5,295	5,279	1,720
Herkimer	Herkimer	63,741	65,809	1,411
Jefferson	Watertown	108,160	110,943	1,272
Kings[1]	Brooklyn	2,488,194	2,300,664	71
Lewis	Lowville	26,673	26,796	1,275
Livingston	Geneseo	64,824	62,372	632
Madison	Wampsville	69,789	69,166	656
Monroe	Rochester	738,422	713,968	659
Montgomery	Fonda	49,387	51,981	405
Nassau	Mineola	1,344,892	1,287,873	287
New York[1]	New York	1,546,856	1,487,536	23
Niagara	Lockport	218,099	220,756	523
Oneida	Utica	234,966	250,836	1,213
Onondaga	Syracuse	460,776	468,973	780
Ontario	Canandaigua	101,567	95,101	644
Orange	Goshen	356,773	307,571	816
Orleans	Albion	43,891	41,846	391
Oswego	Oswego	122,932	121,785	953
Otsego	Cooperstown	62,070	60,390	1,003
Putnam	Carmel	98,257	83,941	231
Queens[1]	Jamaica	2,237,815	1,951,598	109
Rensselaer	Troy	153,299	154,429	654
Richmond[1]	Saint George	457,383	378,977	58
Rockland	New City	291,835	265,475	174
Saint Lawrence	Canton	111,173	111,974	2,686
Saratoga	Ballston Spa	207,135	181,276	812
Schenectady	Schenectady	147,120	149,285	206
Schoharie	Schoharie	31,855	31,840	622
Schuyler	Watkins Glen	19,375	18,662	329
Seneca	Waterloo	34,976	33,683	325
Steuben	Bath	99,313	99,088	1,393
Suffolk	Riverhead	1,458,655	1,321,339	912
Sullivan	Monticello	74,273	69,277	970

County	County seat or courthouse	2002 Pop.	1990 Pop.	Land area sq. mi.
Tioga	Owego	51,772	52,337	519
Tompkins	Ithaca	99,207	94,097	476
Ulster	Kingston	179,986	165,380	1,126
Warren	Lake George	63,906	59,209	869
Washington	Hudson Falls	61,195	59,330	835
Wayne	Lyons	94,078	89,123	604
Westchester	White Plains	937,279	874,866	433
Wyoming	Warsaw	43,165	42,507	593
Yates	Penn Yan	24,523	22,810	338

(1) New York City is comprised of 5 counties: Bronx, Kings (Brooklyn), New York (Manhattan), Queens, and Richmond (Staten Island).

North Carolina
(100 counties, 48,711 sq. mi. land; pop. 8,320,146)

County	County seat or courthouse	2002 Pop.	1990 Pop.	Land area sq. mi.
Alamance	Graham	135,893	108,213	430
Alexander	Taylorsville	34,400	27,544	260
Alleghany	Sparta	10,837	9,590	235
Anson	Wadesboro	25,351	23,474	532
Ashe	Jefferson	24,796	22,209	426
Avery	Newland	17,610	14,867	247
Beaufort	Washington	45,571	42,283	828
Bertie	Windsor	19,697	20,388	699
Bladen	Elizabethtown	32,509	28,663	875
Brunswick	Bolivia	78,567	50,985	855
Buncombe	Asheville	211,201	174,357	656
Burke	Morganton	89,638	75,740	507
Cabarrus	Concord	140,182	98,935	364
Caldwell	Lenoir	78,513	70,709	472
Camden	Camden	7,465	5,904	241
Carteret	Beaufort	60,232	52,407	520
Caswell	Yanceyville	23,555	20,662	425
Catawba	Newton	146,690	118,412	400
Chatham	Pittsboro	53,893	38,979	683
Cherokee	Murphy	24,869	20,170	455
Chowan	Edenton	14,525	13,506	173
Clay	Hayesville	9,186	7,155	215
Cleveland	Shelby	97,960	84,958	465
Columbus	Whiteville	54,930	49,587	935
Craven	New Bern	91,926	81,812	708
Cumberland	Fayetteville	303,328	274,713	653
Currituck	Currituck	19,623	13,736	262
Dare	Manteo	32,106	22,746	384
Davidson	Lexington	151,238	126,688	552
Davie	Mocksville	36,734	27,859	265
Duplin	Kenansville	50,800	39,995	818
Durham	Durham	234,199	181,844	290
Edgecombe	Tarboro	55,007	56,692	505
Forsyth	Winston-Salem	314,933	265,855	410
Franklin	Louisburg	50,449	36,414	492
Gaston	Gastonia	193,443	174,769	356
Gates	Gatesville	10,635	9,305	341
Graham	Robbinsville	8,045	7,196	292
Granville	Oxford	50,946	38,341	531
Greene	Snow Hill	19,416	15,384	265
Guilford	Greensboro	430,937	347,431	649
Halifax	Halifax	56,606	55,516	725
Harnett	Lillington	97,045	67,833	595
Haywood	Waynesville	54,831	46,948	554
Henderson	Hendersonville	92,526	69,747	374
Hertford	Winton	22,037	22,317	353
Hoke	Raeford	36,032	22,856	391
Hyde	Swan Quarter	5,702	5,411	613
Iredell	Statesville	130,178	93,205	576
Jackson	Sylva	33,763	26,835	491
Johnston	Smithfield	133,159	81,306	792
Jones	Trenton	10,259	9,361	472
Lee	Sanford	49,521	41,370	257
Lenoir	Kinston	59,073	57,274	400
Lincoln	Lincolnton	66,598	50,319	299
McDowell	Marion	42,880	35,681	442
Macon	Franklin	30,752	23,504	516
Madison	Marshall	20,004	16,953	449
Martin	Williamston	25,062	25,078	461
Mecklenburg	Charlotte	737,950	511,211	526
Mitchell	Bakersville	15,844	14,433	221
Montgomery	Troy	27,288	23,359	492
Moore	Carthage	78,191	59,000	698
Nash	Nashville	89,286	76,677	540
New Hanover	Wilmington	165,712	120,284	199
Northampton	Jackson	21,803	21,004	536
Onslow	Jacksonville	149,003	149,838	767
Orange	Hillsborough	120,458	93,662	400
Pamlico	Bayboro	12,882	11,368	337
Pasquotank	Elizabeth City	35,445	31,298	227
Pender	Burgaw	42,734	28,855	871
Perquimans	Hertford	11,486	10,447	247
Person	Roxboro	36,610	30,180	392
Pitt	Greenville	137,240	108,480	652
Polk	Columbus	18,845	14,458	238
Randolph	Asheboro	134,217	106,546	787
Richmond	Rockingham	46,841	44,511	474
Robeson	Lumberton	125,351	105,170	949
Rockingham	Wentworth	92,778	86,064	566
Rowan	Salisbury	133,359	110,605	511
Rutherford	Rutherfordton	63,287	56,956	564
Sampson	Clinton	61,256	47,297	945
Scotland	Laurinburg	36,109	33,763	319
Stanly	Albemarle	58,553	51,765	395
Stokes	Danbury	44,984	37,224	452
Surry	Dobson	72,211	61,704	537
Swain	Bryson City	13,137	11,268	528
Transylvania	Brevard	29,499	25,520	378
Tyrrell	Columbia	4,193	3,856	390
Union	Monroe	139,611	84,210	637
Vance	Henderson	44,348	38,892	254
Wake	Raleigh	675,518	426,311	832
Warren	Warrenton	19,914	17,265	429
Washington	Plymouth	13,526	13,997	348
Watauga	Boone	42,857	36,952	313
Wayne	Goldsboro	112,954	104,666	553
Wilkes	Wilkesboro	66,773	59,393	757
Wilson	Wilson	74,942	66,061	371
Yadkin	Yadkinville	37,329	30,488	336
Yancey	Burnsville	17,959	15,419	312

North Dakota
(53 counties, 68,976 sq. mi. land; pop. 634,110)

County	County seat or courthouse	2002 Pop.	1990 Pop.	Land area sq. mi.
Adams	Hettinger	2,476	3,174	988
Barnes	Valley City	11,245	12,545	1,492
Benson	Minnewaukan	6,899	7,198	1,381
Billings	Medora	842	1,108	1,151
Bottineau	Bottineau	6,880	8,011	1,669
Bowman	Bowman	3,130	3,596	1,162
Burke	Bowbells	2,143	3,002	1,104
Burleigh	Bismarck	71,080	60,131	1,633
Cass	Fargo	125,117	102,874	1,765
Cavalier	Langdon	4,559	6,064	1,488
Dickey	Ellendale	5,515	6,107	1,131
Divide	Crosby	2,183	2,899	1,260
Dunn	Manning	3,542	4,005	2,010
Eddy	New Rockford	2,629	2,951	630
Emmons	Linton	4,105	4,830	1,510
Foster	Carrington	3,604	3,983	635
Golden Valley	Beach	1,834	2,108	1,002
Grand Forks	Grand Forks	64,920	70,683	1,438
Grant	Carson	2,695	3,549	1,659
Griggs	Cooperstown	2,601	3,303	709
Hettinger	Mott	2,600	3,445	1,132
Kidder	Steele	2,579	3,332	1,351
La Moure	La Moure	4,511	5,383	1,147
Logan	Napoleon	2,181	2,847	993
McHenry	Towner	5,694	6,528	1,874
McIntosh	Ashley	3,258	4,021	975
McKenzie	Watford City	5,708	6,383	2,742
McLean	Washburn	9,007	10,457	2,110
Mercer	Stanton	8,542	9,808	1,045
Morton	Mandan	25,269	23,700	1,926
Mountrail	Stanley	6,522	7,021	1,824
Nelson	Lakota	3,399	4,410	982
Oliver	Center	1,911	2,381	724
Pembina	Cavalier	8,270	9,238	1,119
Pierce	Rugby	4,531	5,052	1,018
Ramsey	Devils Lake	11,754	12,681	1,185
Ransom	Lisbon	5,794	5,921	863
Renville	Mohall	2,546	3,160	875
Richland	Wahpeton	17,569	18,148	1,437
Rolette	Rolla	13,802	12,772	902
Sargent	Forman	4,250	4,549	859
Sheridan	McClusky	1,561	2,148	972
Sioux	Fort Yates	4,152	3,761	1,094
Slope	Amidon	747	907	1,218
Stark	Dickinson	22,147	22,832	1,338
Steele	Finley	2,093	2,420	712
Stutsman	Jamestown	21,249	22,241	2,221
Towner	Cando	2,728	3,627	1,025
Traill	Hillsboro	8,259	8,752	862
Walsh	Grafton	11,979	13,840	1,282
Ward	Minot	57,128	57,921	2,013
Wells	Fessenden	4,826	5,864	1,271
Williams	Williston	19,545	21,129	2,070

IT'S A FACT: The most popular name for a county is Washington; 31 states have a Washington county. Runners up: Jefferson (27 states), Franklin (25 states).

Ohio

(88 counties, 40,048 sq. mi. land; pop. 11,421,267)

County	County seat or courthouse	2002 Pop.	1990 Pop.	Land area sq. mi.
Adams	West Union	27,804	25,371	584
Allen	Lima	108,120	109,755	404
Ashland	Ashland	52,900	47,507	424
Ashtabula	Jefferson	102,515	99,880	702
Athens	Athens	63,256	59,549	507
Auglaize	Wapakoneta	46,464	44,585	401
Belmont	Saint Clairsville	69,448	71,074	537
Brown	Georgetown	43,464	34,966	492
Butler	Hamilton	340,543	291,479	467
Carroll	Carrollton	29,166	26,521	395
Champaign	Urbana	39,121	36,019	429
Clark	Springfield	143,416	147,548	400
Clermont	Batavia	183,352	150,094	452
Clinton	Wilmington	41,090	35,444	411
Columbiana	Lisbon	111,806	108,276	532
Coshocton	Coshocton	36,836	35,427	564
Crawford	Bucyrus	46,420	47,870	402
Cuyahoga	Cleveland	1,379,049	1,412,140	458
Darke	Greenville	52,966	53,617	600
Defiance	Defiance	39,334	39,350	411
Delaware	Delaware	125,399	66,929	442
Erie	Sandusky	79,207	76,781	255
Fairfield	Lancaster	129,161	103,468	505
Fayette	Washington Court House	28,176	27,466	407
Franklin	Columbus	1,086,814	961,437	540
Fulton	Wauseon	42,573	38,498	407
Gallia	Gallipolis	31,301	30,954	469
Geauga	Chardon	92,980	81,087	404
Greene	Xenia	149,964	136,731	415
Guernsey	Cambridge	40,987	39,024	522
Hamilton	Cincinnati	833,721	866,228	407
Hancock	Findlay	72,286	65,536	531
Hardin	Kenton	31,731	31,111	470
Harrison	Cadiz	15,890	16,085	404
Henry	Napoleon	29,478	29,108	417
Highland	Hillsboro	41,851	35,728	553
Hocking	Logan	28,481	25,533	423
Holmes	Millersburg	40,375	32,849	423
Huron	Norwalk	60,020	56,238	493
Jackson	Jackson	32,854	30,230	420
Jefferson	Steubenville	72,402	80,298	410
Knox	Mount Vernon	56,037	47,473	527
Lake	Painesville	229,004	215,500	228
Lawrence	Ironton	62,172	61,834	455
Licking	Newark	148,731	128,300	687
Logan	Bellefontaine	46,262	42,310	458
Lorain	Elyria	288,360	271,126	493
Lucas	Toledo	453,506	462,361	340
Madison	London	40,365	37,078	465
Mahoning	Youngstown	253,308	264,806	415
Marion	Marion	66,028	64,274	404
Medina	Medina	158,439	122,354	422
Meigs	Pomeroy	23,111	22,987	429
Mercer	Celina	40,815	39,443	463
Miami	Troy	99,596	93,184	407
Monroe	Woodsfield	14,973	15,497	456
Montgomery	Dayton	554,470	573,809	462
Morgan	McConnelsville	14,749	14,194	418
Morrow	Mount Gilead	32,976	27,749	406
Muskingum	Zanesville	85,349	82,068	665
Noble	Caldwell	14,088	11,336	399
Ottawa	Port Clinton	41,049	40,029	255
Paulding	Paulding	19,841	20,488	416
Perry	New Lexington	34,408	31,557	410
Pickaway	Circleville	53,437	48,248	502
Pike	Waverly	27,921	24,249	441
Portage	Ravenna	153,886	142,585	492
Preble	Eaton	42,680	40,113	425
Putnam	Ottawa	34,736	33,819	484
Richland	Mansfield	128,004	126,137	497
Ross	Chillicothe	74,469	69,330	688
Sandusky	Fremont	61,698	61,963	409
Scioto	Portsmouth	78,041	80,327	612
Seneca	Tiffin	58,077	59,733	551
Shelby	Sidney	48,516	44,915	409
Stark	Canton	377,940	367,585	576
Summit	Akron	546,381	514,990	413
Trumbull	Warren	223,518	227,795	616
Tuscarawas	New Philadelphia	91,490	84,090	568
Union	Marysville	43,010	31,969	437
Van Wert	Van Wert	29,399	30,464	410
Vinton	McArthur	13,128	11,098	414
Warren	Lebanon	175,133	113,973	400
Washington	Marietta	62,561	62,254	635
Wayne	Wooster	112,704	101,461	555
Williams	Bryan	39,020	36,956	422
Wood	Bowling Green	122,387	113,269	617
Wyandot	Upper Sandusky	22,773	22,254	406

Oklahoma

(77 counties, 68,667 sq. mi. land; pop. 3,493,714)

County	County seat or courthouse	2002 Pop.	1990 Pop.	Land area sq. mi.
Adair	Stillwell	21,361	18,421	576
Alfalfa	Cherokee	5,898	6,416	867
Atoka	Atoka	13,990	12,778	978
Beaver	Beaver	5,575	6,023	1,814
Beckham	Sayre	19,868	18,812	902
Blaine	Watonga	12,082	11,470	928
Bryan	Durant	37,037	32,089	909
Caddo	Anadarko	30,000	29,550	1,278
Canadian	El Reno	91,441	74,409	900
Carter	Ardmore	46,199	42,919	824
Cherokee	Tahlequah	43,419	34,049	751
Choctaw	Hugo	15,155	15,302	774
Cimarron	Boise City	3,004	3,301	1,835
Cleveland	Norman	215,652	174,253	536
Coal	Coalgate	5,913	5,780	518
Comanche	Lawton	113,414	111,486	1,069
Cotton	Walters	6,465	6,651	637
Craig	Vinita	14,603	14,104	761
Creek	Sapulpa	68,836	60,915	956
Custer	Arapaho	25,188	26,897	967
Delaware	Jay	37,813	28,070	741
Dewey	Taloga	4,609	5,551	1,000
Ellis	Arnett	3,967	4,497	1,229
Garfield	Enid	57,246	56,735	1,058
Garvin	Pauls Valley	27,176	26,605	807
Grady	Chickasha	46,664	41,747	1,101
Grant	Medford	5,030	5,689	1,001
Greer	Mangum	5,787	6,559	639
Harmon	Hollis	3,078	3,793	538
Harper	Buffalo	3,461	4,063	1,039
Haskell	Stigler	11,726	10,940	577
Hughes	Holdenville	14,009	13,014	807
Jackson	Altus	27,333	28,764	803
Jefferson	Waurika	6,579	7,010	759
Johnston	Tishomingo	10,454	10,032	645
Kay	Newkirk	47,680	48,056	919
Kingfisher	Kingfisher	13,731	13,212	903
Kiowa	Hobart	9,927	11,347	1,015
Latimer	Wilburton	10,537	10,333	722
Le Flore	Poteau	48,432	43,270	1,586
Lincoln	Chandler	32,264	29,216	958
Logan	Guthrie	34,527	29,011	744
Love	Marietta	8,911	7,788	515
McClain	Purcell	28,236	22,795	570
McCurtain	Idabel	34,187	33,433	1,852
McIntosh	Eufaula	19,736	16,779	620
Major	Fairview	7,498	8,055	957
Marshall	Madill	13,547	10,829	371
Mayes	Pryor	38,858	33,366	656
Murray	Sulphur	12,631	12,042	418
Muskogee	Muskogee	69,979	68,078	814
Noble	Perry	11,310	11,045	732
Nowata	Nowata	10,747	9,992	565
Okfuskee	Okemah	11,668	11,551	625
Oklahoma	Oklahoma City	672,487	599,611	709
Okmulgee	Okmulgee	39,822	36,490	697
Osage	Pawhuska	45,166	41,645	2,251
Ottawa	Miami	33,040	30,561	471
Pawnee	Pawnee	16,831	15,575	569
Payne	Stillwater	69,915	61,507	686
Pittsburg	McAlester	44,006	40,950	1,306
Pontotoc	Ada	34,869	34,119	720
Pottawatomie	Shawnee	66,740	58,760	788
Pushmataha	Antlers	11,704	10,997	1,397
Roger Mills	Cheyenne	3,203	4,147	1,142
Rogers	Claremore	75,567	55,170	675
Seminole	Wewoka	24,735	25,412	633
Sequoyah	Sallisaw	39,852	33,828	674
Stephens	Duncan	42,637	42,299	874
Texas	Guymon	20,171	16,419	2,037
Tillman	Frederick	8,984	10,384	872
Tulsa	Tulsa	571,348	503,341	570
Wagoner	Wagoner	60,339	47,883	563
Washington	Bartlesville	49,189	48,066	417
Washita	Cordell	11,454	11,441	1,003
Woods	Alva	8,758	9,103	1,287
Woodward	Woodward	18,459	18,976	1,242

Oregon

(36 counties, 95,997 sq. mi. land; pop. 3,521,515)

County	County seat or courthouse	2002 Pop.	1990 Pop.	Land area sq. mi.
Baker	Baker City	16,496	15,317	3,068
Benton	Corvallis	78,618	70,811	676
Clackamas	Oregon City	351,815	278,850	1,868
Clatsop	Astoria	35,791	33,301	827
Columbia	Saint Helens	45,313	37,557	657
Coos	Coquille	62,670	60,273	1,600
Crook	Prineville	19,999	14,111	2,979
Curry	Gold Beach	21,294	19,327	1,627
Deschutes	Bend	125,258	74,976	3,018
Douglas	Roseburg	100,921	94,649	5,037

County	County seat or courthouse	2002 Pop.	1990 Pop.	Land area sq. mi.
Gilliam	Condon	1,842	1,717	1,204
Grant	Canyon City	7,480	7,853	4,529
Harney	Burns	7,339	7,060	10,134
Hood River	Hood River	20,805	16,903	522
Jackson	Medford	186,430	146,387	2,785
Jefferson	Madras	19,768	13,676	1,781
Josephine	Grants Pass	77,496	62,649	1,640
Klamath	Klamath Falls	64,363	57,702	5,944
Lake	Lakeview	7,444	7,186	8,136
Lane	Eugene	326,666	282,912	4,554
Lincoln	Newport	44,644	38,889	960
Linn	Albany	104,941	91,227	2,292
Malheur	Vale	31,248	26,038	9,887
Marion	Salem	293,155	228,483	1,184
Morrow	Heppner	11,585	7,625	2,032
Multnomah	Portland	677,626	583,887	435
Polk	Dallas	64,657	49,541	741
Sherman	Moro	1,784	1,918	823
Tillamook	Tillamook	24,613	21,570	1,102
Umatilla	Pendleton	71,428	59,249	3,215
Union	La Grande	24,484	23,598	2,037
Wallowa	Enterprise	7,025	6,911	3,145
Wasco	The Dalles	23,667	21,683	2,381
Washington	Hillsboro	473,263	311,554	724
Wheeler	Fossil	1,532	1,396	1,715
Yamhill	McMinnville	88,055	65,551	716

Pennsylvania
(67 counties, 44,817 sq. mi. land; pop. 12,335,091)

County	County seat or courthouse	2002 Pop.	1990 Pop.	Land area sq. mi.
Adams	Gettysburg	94,437	78,274	520
Allegheny	Pittsburgh	1,269,904	1,336,449	730
Armstrong	Kittanning	71,673	73,478	654
Beaver	Beaver	179,351	186,093	434
Bedford	Bedford	49,944	47,919	1,015
Berks	Reading	382,108	336,523	859
Blair	Hollidaysburg	127,840	130,542	526
Bradford	Towanda	62,810	60,967	1,151
Bucks	Doylestown	610,440	541,174	607
Butler	Butler	178,078	152,013	789
Cambria	Ebensburg	150,452	163,062	688
Cameron	Emporium	5,843	5,913	397
Carbon	Jim Thorpe	59,688	56,803	381
Centre	Bellefonte	138,524	124,121	1,108
Chester	West Chester	450,160	376,389	756
Clarion	Clarion	41,316	41,699	602
Clearfield	Clearfield	83,203	78,097	1,147
Clinton	Lock Haven	37,680	37,182	891
Columbia	Bloomsburg	64,134	63,202	486
Crawford	Meadville	89,856	86,154	1,013
Cumberland	Carlisle	217,743	195,257	550
Dauphin	Harrisburg	252,933	237,813	525
Delaware	Media	553,435	547,658	184
Elk	Ridgway	34,454	34,878	829
Erie	Erie	280,370	275,575	802
Fayette	Uniontown	146,654	145,351	790
Forest	Tionesta	4,888	4,802	428
Franklin	Chambersburg	131,598	121,082	772
Fulton	McConnellsburg	14,365	13,837	438
Greene	Waynesburg	40,520	39,550	576
Huntingdon	Huntingdon	45,707	44,164	874
Indiana	Indiana	88,780	89,994	829
Jefferson	Brookville	45,818	46,083	655
Juniata	Mifflintown	22,760	20,625	392
Lackawanna	Scranton	210,711	219,039	459
Lancaster	Lancaster	478,561	422,822	949
Lawrence	New Castle	94,104	96,246	360
Lebanon	Lebanon	121,199	113,744	362
Lehigh	Allentown	317,533	291,130	347
Luzerne	Wilkes-Barre	314,643	328,149	891
Lycoming	Williamsport	119,000	118,710	1,235
McKean	Smethport	44,884	47,131	982
Mercer	Mercer	119,514	121,003	672
Mifflin	Lewistown	46,435	46,197	412
Monroe	Stroudsburg	148,839	95,681	609
Montgomery	Norristown	766,517	678,193	483
Montour	Danville	18,214	17,735	131
Northampton	Easton	273,324	247,110	374
Northumberland	Sunbury	93,371	96,771	460
Perry	New Bloomfield	43,602	41,172	554
Philadelphia	Philadelphia	1,492,231	1,585,577	135
Pike	Milford	50,095	28,032	547
Potter	Coudersport	18,217	16,717	1,081
Schuylkill	Pottsville	148,505	152,585	778
Snyder	Middleburg	37,828	36,680	331
Somerset	Somerset	79,456	78,218	1,075
Sullivan	Laporte	6,482	6,104	450
Susquehanna	Montrose	42,082	40,380	823
Tioga	Wellsboro	41,461	41,126	1,134
Union	Lewisburg	42,006	36,176	317
Venango	Franklin	56,810	59,381	675
Warren	Warren	43,290	45,050	883
Washington	Washington	204,110	204,584	857
Wayne	Honesdale	48,889	39,944	729
Westmoreland	Greensburg	368,428	370,321	1,025
Wyoming	Tunkhannock	27,801	28,076	397
York	York	389,209	339,574	904

Rhode Island
(5 counties, 1,045 sq. mi. land; pop. 1,069,725)

County	County seat or courthouse	2002 Pop.	1990 Pop.	Land area sq. mi.
Bristol	Bristol	51,287	48,859	25
Kent	East Greenwich	170,499	161,143	170
Newport	Newport	85,986	87,194	104
Providence	Providence	634,827	596,270	413
Washington	West Kingston	127,126	109,998	333

South Carolina
(46 counties, 30,110 sq. mi. land; pop. 4,107,183)

County	County seat or courthouse	2002 Pop.	1990 Pop.	Land area sq. mi.
Abbeville	Abbeville	26,422	23,862	508
Aiken	Aiken	145,276	120,991	1,073
Allendale	Allendale	10,949	11,727	408
Anderson	Anderson	170,578	145,177	718
Bamberg	Bamberg	16,314	16,902	393
Barnwell	Barnwell	23,407	20,293	548
Beaufort	Beaufort	127,977	86,425	587
Berkeley	Moncks Corner	145,274	128,658	1,098
Calhoun	Saint Matthews	15,366	12,753	380
Charleston	Charleston	316,559	295,159	919
Cherokee	Gaffney	53,524	44,506	393
Chester	Chester	34,212	32,170	581
Chesterfield	Chesterfield	43,206	38,575	799
Clarendon	Manning	32,895	28,450	607
Colleton	Walterboro	38,804	34,377	1,056
Darlington	Darlington	67,931	61,851	561
Dillon	Dillon	30,914	29,114	405
Dorchester	Saint George	100,833	83,060	575
Edgefield	Edgefield	24,868	18,360	502
Fairfield	Winnsboro	24,003	22,295	687
Florence	Florence	127,237	114,344	800
Georgetown	Georgetown	58,263	46,302	815
Greenville	Greenville	391,334	320,127	790
Greenwood	Greenwood	67,461	59,567	456
Hampton	Hampton	21,316	18,186	560
Horry	Conway	206,039	144,053	1,134
Jasper	Ridgeland	20,969	15,487	656
Kershaw	Camden	53,630	43,599	726
Lancaster	Lancaster	62,220	54,516	549
Laurens	Laurens	70,508	58,132	715
Lee	Bishopville	20,450	18,437	410
Lexington	Lexington	222,897	167,526	699
McCormick	McCormick	10,218	8,868	360
Marion	Marion	34,964	33,899	489
Marlboro	Bennettsville	28,682	29,716	480
Newberry	Newberry	36,897	33,172	631
Oconee	Walhalla	67,918	57,494	625
Orangeburg	Orangeburg	91,190	84,804	1,106
Pickens	Pickens	113,097	93,896	497
Richland	Columbia	329,086	286,321	756
Saluda	Saluda	19,247	16,441	452
Spartanburg	Spartanburg	259,322	226,793	811
Sumter	Sumter	105,198	101,276	665
Union	Union	29,482	30,337	514
Williamsburg	Kingstree	36,491	36,815	934
York	York	173,755	131,497	682

South Dakota
(66 counties, 75,885 sq. mi. land; pop. 761,063)

County	County seat or courthouse	2002 Pop.	1990 Pop.	Land area sq. mi.
Aurora	Plankinton	2,961	3,135	708
Beadle	Huron	16,568	18,253	1,259
Bennett	Martin	3,535	3,206	1,185
Bon Homme	Tyndall	7,148	7,089	563
Brookings	Brookings	28,392	25,207	794
Brown	Aberdeen	34,999	35,580	1,713
Brule	Chamberlain	5,146	5,485	819
Buffalo	Gannvalley	1,989	1,759	471
Butte	Belle Fourche	9,015	7,914	2,249
Campbell	Mound City	1,739	1,965	736
Charles Mix	Lake Andes	9,207	9,131	1,098
Clark	Clark	4,004	4,403	958
Clay	Vermillion	13,199	13,186	412
Codington	Watertown	25,888	22,698	688
Corson	McIntosh	4,356	4,195	2,473
Custer	Custer	7,467	6,179	1,558
Davison	Mitchell	18,768	17,503	435
Day	Webster	6,073	6,978	1,029
Deuel	Clear Lake	4,407	4,522	624
Dewey	Timber Lake	6,039	5,523	2,303

County	County seat or courthouse	2002 Pop.	1990 Pop.	Land area sq. mi.
Douglas	Armour	3,378	3,746	434
Edmunds	Ipswich	4,251	4,356	1,146
Fall River	Hot Springs	7,305	7,353	1,740
Faulk	Faulkton	2,492	2,744	1,000
Grant	Milbank	7,675	8,372	683
Gregory	Burke	4,489	5,359	1,016
Haakon	Philip	2,052	2,624	1,813
Hamlin	Hayti	5,544	4,974	507
Hand	Miller	3,542	4,272	1,437
Hanson	Alexandria	3,366	2,994	435
Harding	Buffalo	1,275	1,669	2,671
Hughes	Pierre	16,738	14,817	741
Hutchinson	Olivet	7,949	8,262	813
Hyde	Highmore	1,574	1,696	861
Jackson	Kadoka	2,873	2,811	1,869
Jerauld	Wessington Springs	2,221	2,425	530
Jones	Murdo	1,089	1,324	971
Kingsbury	De Smet	5,662	5,925	838
Lake	Madison	11,236	10,550	563
Lawrence	Deadwood	21,616	20,655	800
Lincoln	Canton	27,655	15,427	578
Lyman	Kennebec	3,977	3,638	1,640
McCook	Salem	5,776	5,688	575
McPherson	Leola	2,829	3,228	1,137
Marshall	Britton	4,404	4,844	838
Meade	Sturgis	24,472	21,878	3,471
Mellette	White River	1,939	2,137	1,306
Miner	Howard	2,807	3,272	570
Minnehaha	Sioux Falls	152,545	123,809	810
Moody	Flandreau	6,520	6,507	520
Pennington	Rapid City	90,856	81,343	2,776
Perkins	Bison	3,268	3,932	2,872
Potter	Gettysburg	2,511	3,190	866
Roberts	Sisseton	10,013	9,914	1,101
Sanborn	Woonsocket	2,589	2,833	569
Shannon	(Attached to Fall River)	13,228	9,902	2,094
Spink	Redfield	7,123	7,981	1,504
Stanley	Fort Pierre	2,763	2,453	1,443
Sully	Onida	1,505	1,589	1,007
Todd	(Attached to Tripp)	9,452	8,352	1,388
Tripp	Winner	6,296	6,924	1,614
Turner	Parker	8,678	8,576	617
Union	Elk Point	12,886	10,189	460
Walworth	Selby	5,688	6,087	708
Yankton	Yankton	21,450	19,252	522
Ziebach	Dupree	2,606	2,220	1,962

Tennessee

(95 counties, 41,217 sq. mi. land; pop. 5,797,289)

County	County seat or courthouse	2002 Pop.	1990 Pop.	Land area sq. mi.
Anderson	Clinton	71,627	68,250	338
Bedford	Shelbyville	39,408	30,411	474
Benton	Camden	16,483	14,524	395
Bledsoe	Pikeville	12,478	9,669	406
Blount	Maryville	109,849	85,962	559
Bradley	Cleveland	89,677	73,712	329
Campbell	Jacksboro	40,013	35,079	480
Cannon	Woodbury	13,060	10,467	266
Carroll	Huntingdon	29,320	27,514	599
Carter	Elizabethton	56,746	51,505	341
Cheatham	Ashland City	36,986	27,140	303
Chester	Henderson	15,923	12,819	289
Claiborne	Tazewell	30,163	26,137	434
Clay	Celina	8,021	7,238	236
Cocke	Newport	34,115	29,141	434
Coffee	Manchester	49,408	40,343	429
Crockett	Alamo	14,522	13,378	265
Cumberland	Crossville	48,604	34,736	682
Davidson	Nashville	570,785	510,786	502
Decatur	Decaturville	11,529	10,472	334
De Kalb	Smithville	17,700	14,360	305
Dickson	Charlotte	44,231	35,061	490
Dyer	Dyersburg	36,984	34,854	511
Fayette	Somerville	31,202	25,559	705
Fentress	Jamestown	16,868	14,669	499
Franklin	Winchester	39,998	34,923	555
Gibson	Trenton	48,274	46,315	603
Giles	Pulaski	29,355	25,741	611
Grainger	Rutledge	21,109	17,095	280
Greene	Greeneville	63,763	55,832	622
Grundy	Altamont	14,335	13,362	361
Hamblen	Morristown	58,623	50,480	161
Hamilton	Chattanooga	309,321	285,536	542
Hancock	Sneedville	6,793	6,739	222
Hardeman	Bolivar	29,812	23,377	668
Hardin	Savannah	25,825	22,633	578
Hawkins	Rogersville	54,793	44,565	487
Haywood	Brownsville	19,655	19,437	533
Henderson	Lexington	25,733	21,844	520
Henry	Paris	31,192	27,888	562
Hickman	Centerville	23,125	16,754	613
Houston	Erin	7,948	7,018	200
Humphreys	Waverly	18,081	15,813	532
Jackson	Gainesboro	11,138	9,297	309
Jefferson	Dandridge	45,801	33,016	274
Johnson	Mountain City	17,925	13,766	298
Knox	Knoxville	389,327	335,749	508
Lake	Tiptonville	7,793	7,129	163
Lauderdale	Ripley	28,007	23,491	470
Lawrence	Lawrenceburg	40,463	35,303	617
Lewis	Hohenwald	11,463	9,247	282
Lincoln	Fayetteville	31,777	28,157	570
Loudon	Loudon	40,631	31,255	229
McMinn	Athens	50,051	42,383	430
McNairy	Selmer	24,716	22,422	560
Macon	Lafayette	20,860	15,906	307
Madison	Jackson	93,367	77,982	557
Marion	Jasper	27,654	24,683	498
Marshall	Lewisburg	27,370	21,539	375
Maury	Columbia	71,600	54,812	613
Meigs	Decatur	11,310	8,033	195
Monroe	Madisonville	40,159	30,541	635
Montgomery	Clarksville	138,241	100,498	539
Moore	Lynchburg	5,928	4,696	129
Morgan	Wartburg	19,847	17,300	522
Obion	Union City	32,394	31,717	545
Overton	Livingston	20,276	17,636	433
Perry	Linden	7,548	6,612	415
Pickett	Byrdstown	4,999	4,548	163
Polk	Benton	16,142	13,643	435
Putnam	Cookeville	64,300	51,373	401
Rhea	Dayton	28,939	24,344	316
Roane	Kingston	52,316	47,227	361
Robertson	Springfield	57,446	41,492	476
Rutherford	Murfreesboro	194,934	118,570	619
Scott	Huntsville	21,558	18,358	532
Sequatchie	Dunlap	11,787	8,863	266
Sevier	Sevierville	74,456	51,050	592
Shelby	Memphis	905,678	826,330	755
Smith	Carthage	18,177	14,143	314
Stewart	Dover	12,704	9,479	458
Sullivan	Blountville	153,051	143,596	413
Sumner	Gallatin	136,170	103,281	529
Tipton	Covington	53,436	37,568	459
Trousdale	Hartsville	7,354	5,920	114
Unicoi	Erwin	17,740	16,549	186
Union	Maynardville	18,541	13,694	224
Van Buren	Spencer	5,541	4,846	273
Warren	McMinnville	38,896	32,992	433
Washington	Jonesborough	109,019	92,336	326
Wayne	Waynesboro	17,312	13,995	734
Weakley	Dresden	34,208	31,972	580
White	Sparta	23,434	20,090	377
Williamson	Franklin	136,889	81,021	583
Wilson	Lebanon	93,079	67,675	571

Texas

(254 counties, 261,797 sq. mi. land; pop. 21,779,893)

County	County seat or courthouse	2002 Pop.	1990 Pop.	Land area sq. mi.
Anderson	Palestine	54,585	48,024	1,071
Andrews	Andrews	12,951	14,338	1,501
Angelina	Lufkin	80,582	69,884	802
Aransas	Rockport	22,928	17,892	252
Archer	Archer City	8,996	7,973	910
Armstrong	Claude	2,145	2,021	914
Atascosa	Jourdanton	40,948	30,533	1,232
Austin	Bellville	24,596	19,832	653
Bailey	Muleshoe	6,480	7,064	827
Bandera	Bandera	19,153	10,562	792
Bastrop	Bastrop	63,934	38,263	888
Baylor	Seymour	3,929	4,385	871
Bee	Beeville	32,277	25,135	880
Bell	Belton	244,668	191,073	1,060
Bexar	San Antonio	1,446,333	1,185,394	1,247
Blanco	Johnson City	8,866	5,972	711
Borden	Gail	701	799	899
Bosque	Meridian	17,535	15,125	989
Bowie	Boston	89,894	81,665	888
Brazoria	Angleton	257,256	191,707	1,386
Brazos	Bryan	156,099	121,862	586
Brewster	Alpine	9,009	8,653	6,193
Briscoe	Silverton	1,716	1,971	900
Brooks	Falfurrias	7,766	8,204	943
Brown	Brownwood	37,957	34,371	944
Burleson	Caldwell	16,874	13,625	666
Burnet	Burnet	36,889	22,677	996
Caldwell	Lockhart	35,050	26,392	546
Calhoun	Port Lavaca	20,595	19,053	512
Callahan	Baird	12,762	11,859	899
Cameron	Brownsville	353,561	260,120	906
Camp	Pittsburg	11,643	9,904	198
Carson	Panhandle	6,582	6,576	923
Cass	Linden	30,133	29,982	937
Castro	Dimmitt	8,075	9,070	898
Chambers	Anahuac	27,244	20,088	599
Cherokee	Rusk	47,450	41,049	1,052
Childress	Childress	7,571	5,953	710

County	County seat or courthouse	2002 Pop.	1990 Pop.	Land area sq. mi.	County	County seat or courthouse	2002 Pop.	1990 Pop.	Land area sq. mi.
Clay	Henrietta	11,396	10,024	1,098	Kerr	Kerrville	44,857	36,304	1,106
Cochran	Morton	3,482	4,377	775	Kimble	Junction	4,502	4,122	1,251
Coke	Robert Lee	3,844	3,424	899	King	Guthrie	333	354	912
Coleman	Coleman	8,906	9,710	1,260	Kinney	Brackettville	3,447	3,119	1,363
Collin	McKinney	566,798	264,036	848	Kleberg	Kingsville	31,145	30,274	871
Collingsworth	Wellington	3,103	3,573	919	Knox	Benjamin	4,061	4,837	849
Colorado	Columbus	20,384	18,383	963	Lamar	Paris	49,079	43,949	917
Comal	New Braunfels	85,109	51,832	561	Lamb	Littlefield	14,662	15,072	1,016
Comanche	Comanche	13,565	13,381	938	Lampasas	Lampasas	18,846	13,521	712
Concho	Paint Rock	3,854	3,044	991	La Salle	Cotulla	5,876	5,254	1,489
Cooke	Gainesville	37,634	30,777	874	Lavaca	Hallettsville	18,935	18,690	970
Coryell	Gatesville	74,495	64,226	1,052	Lee	Giddings	16,329	12,854	629
Cottle	Paducah	1,797	2,247	901	Leon	Centerville	15,885	12,665	1,072
Crane	Crane	3,874	4,652	786	Liberty	Liberty	73,739	52,726	1,160
Crockett	Ozona	3,807	4,078	2,807	Limestone	Groesbeck	22,263	20,946	909
Crosby	Crosbyton	6,865	7,304	900	Lipscomb	Lipscomb	3,103	3,143	932
Culberson	Van Horn	2,839	3,407	3,812	Live Oak	George West	12,014	9,556	1,036
Dallam	Dalhart	6,184	5,461	1,505	Llano	Llano	17,758	11,631	935
Dallas	Dallas	2,283,953	1,852,691	880	Loving	Mentone	64	107	673
Dawson	Lamesa	14,712	14,349	902	Lubbock	Lubbock	247,574	222,636	899
Deaf Smith	Hereford	18,396	19,153	1,497	Lynn	Tahoka	6,325	6,758	892
Delta	Cooper	5,362	4,857	277	McCulloch	Brady	7,885	8,778	1,069
Denton	Denton	488,481	273,644	889	McLennan	Waco	217,713	189,123	1,042
DeWitt	Cuero	20,067	18,840	909	McMullen	Tilden	856	817	1,113
Dickens	Dickens	2,702	2,571	904	Madison	Madisonville	13,105	10,931	470
Dimmit	Carrizo Springs	10,200	10,433	1,331	Marion	Jefferson	11,081	9,984	381
Donley	Clarendon	3,887	3,696	930	Martin	Stanton	4,673	4,956	915
Duval	San Diego	12,811	12,918	1,793	Mason	Mason	3,771	3,423	932
Eastland	Eastland	18,210	18,488	926	Matagorda	Bay City	37,954	36,928	1,114
Ector	Odessa	122,312	118,934	901	Maverick	Eagle Pass	48,651	36,378	1,280
Edwards	Rocksprings	2,081	2,266	2,120	Medina	Hondo	40,924	27,312	1,328
Ellis	Waxahachie	120,052	85,167	940	Menard	Menard	2,329	2,252	902
El Paso	El Paso	697,562	591,610	1,013	Midland	Midland	117,669	106,611	900
Erath	Stephenville	33,077	27,991	1,086	Milam	Cameron	24,880	22,946	1,017
Falls	Marlin	18,091	17,712	769	Mills	Goldthwaite	5,133	4,531	748
Fannin	Bonham	31,672	24,804	891	Mitchell	Colorado City	9,348	8,016	910
Fayette	La Grange	22,304	20,095	950	Montague	Montague	19,237	17,274	931
Fisher	Roby	4,246	4,842	901	Montgomery	Conroe	328,449	182,201	1,044
Floyd	Floydada	7,455	8,497	992	Moore	Dumas	20,350	17,865	900
Foard	Crowell	1,545	1,794	707	Morris	Daingerfield	13,240	13,200	255
Fort Bend	Richmond	399,537	225,421	875	Motley	Matador	1,336	1,532	989
Franklin	Mount Vernon	9,699	7,802	286	Nacogdoches	Nacogdoches	59,514	54,753	947
Freestone	Fairfield	18,595	15,818	877	Navarro	Corsicana	46,792	39,926	1,008
Frio	Pearsall	16,249	13,472	1,133	Newton	Newton	14,946	13,569	933
Gaines	Seminole	14,312	14,123	1,502	Nolan	Sweetwater	15,172	16,594	912
Galveston	Galveston	261,219	217,396	398	Nueces	Corpus Christi	314,696	291,145	836
Garza	Post	4,976	5,143	896	Ochiltree	Perryton	9,048	9,128	918
Gillespie	Fredericksburg	21,607	17,204	1,061	Oldham	Vega	2,156	2,278	1,501
Glasscock	Garden City	1,369	1,447	901	Orange	Orange	84,384	80,509	356
Goliad	Goliad	7,075	5,980	854	Palo Pinto	Palo Pinto	27,306	25,055	953
Gonzales	Gonzales	18,884	17,205	1,068	Panola	Carthage	22,734	22,035	801
Gray	Pampa	22,088	23,967	928	Parker	Weatherford	94,618	64,785	904
Grayson	Sherman	113,860	95,019	934	Parmer	Farwell	9,877	9,863	882
Gregg	Longview	113,255	104,948	274	Pecos	Fort Stockton	16,421	14,675	4,764
Grimes	Anderson	24,740	18,843	794	Polk	Livingston	44,449	30,687	1,057
Guadalupe	Seguin	94,215	64,873	711	Potter	Amarillo	116,093	97,841	909
Hale	Plainview	35,900	34,671	1,005	Presidio	Marfa	7,681	6,637	3,856
Hall	Memphis	3,662	3,905	903	Rains	Emory	10,236	6,715	232
Hamilton	Hamilton	8,079	7,733	836	Randall	Canyon	106,822	89,673	914
Hansford	Spearman	5,288	5,848	920	Reagan	Big Lake	3,182	4,514	1,175
Hardeman	Quanah	4,490	5,283	695	Real	Leakey	2,999	2,412	700
Hardin	Kountze	48,988	41,320	894	Red River	Clarksville	13,941	14,317	1,050
Harris	Houston	3,557,055	2,818,101	1,729	Reeves	Pecos	12,478	15,852	2,636
Harrison	Marshall	62,534	57,483	899	Refugio	Refugio	7,724	7,976	770
Hartley	Channing	5,464	3,634	1,462	Roberts	Miami	857	1,025	924
Haskell	Haskell	5,909	6,820	903	Robertson	Franklin	16,044	15,511	855
Hays	San Marcos	109,570	65,614	678	Rockwall	Rockwall	50,858	25,604	129
Hemphill	Canadian	3,332	3,720	910	Runnels	Ballinger	11,123	11,294	1,051
Henderson	Athens	75,797	58,543	874	Rusk	Henderson	47,541	43,735	924
Hidalgo	Edinburg	614,474	383,545	1,570	Sabine	Hemphill	10,370	9,586	490
Hill	Hillsboro	33,701	27,146	962	San Augustine	San Augustine	8,922	7,999	528
Hockley	Levelland	22,838	24,199	908	San Jacinto	Coldspring	23,247	16,372	571
Hood	Granbury	44,149	28,981	422	San Patricio	Sinton	67,492	58,749	692
Hopkins	Sulphur Springs	32,299	28,833	782	San Saba	San Saba	6,148	5,401	1,134
Houston	Crockett	23,225	21,375	1,231	Schleicher	Eldorado	2,944	2,990	1,311
Howard	Big Spring	33,215	32,343	903	Scurry	Snyder	15,877	18,634	903
Hudspeth	Sierra Blanca	3,341	2,915	4,571	Shackelford	Albany	3,338	3,316	914
Hunt	Greenville	79,361	64,343	841	Shelby	Center	25,439	22,034	794
Hutchinson	Stinnett	23,061	25,689	887	Sherman	Stratford	3,285	2,858	923
Irion	Mertzon	1,757	1,629	1,051	Smith	Tyler	181,437	151,309	928
Jack	Jacksboro	8,965	6,981	917	Somervell	Glen Rose	7,224	5,360	187
Jackson	Edna	14,364	13,039	829	Starr	Rio Grande City	56,686	40,518	1,223
Jasper	Jasper	35,776	31,102	937	Stephens	Breckenridge	9,453	9,010	895
Jeff Davis	Fort Davis	2,211	1,946	2,264	Sterling	Sterling City	1,346	1,438	923
Jefferson	Beaumont	248,890	239,389	904	Stonewall	Aspermont	1,493	2,013	919
Jim Hogg	Hebbronville	5,173	5,109	1,136	Sutton	Sonora	4,117	4,135	1,454
Jim Wells	Alice	39,945	37,679	865	Swisher	Tulia	8,082	8,133	900
Johnson	Cleburne	136,332	97,165	729	Tarrant	Fort Worth	1,527,366	1,170,103	863
Jones	Anson	20,284	16,490	931	Taylor	Abilene	125,647	119,655	916
Karnes	Karnes City	15,411	12,455	750	Terrell	Sanderson	998	1,410	2,358
Kaufman	Kaufman	77,954	52,220	786	Terry	Brownfield	12,723	13,218	890
Kendall	Boerne	25,390	14,589	662	Throckmorton	Throckmorton	1,711	1,880	912
Kenedy	Sarita	419	460	1,457	Titus	Mount Pleasant	28,405	24,009	411
Kent	Jayton	807	1,010	902	Tom Green	San Angelo	103,018	98,458	1,522
					Travis	Austin	850,813	576,407	989

County	County seat or courthouse	2002 Pop.	1990 Pop.	Land area sq. mi.
Trinity	Groveton	14,088	11,445	693
Tyler	Woodville	20,743	16,646	923
Upshur	Gilmer	36,499	31,370	588
Upton	Rankin	3,287	4,447	1,242
Uvalde	Uvalde	26,508	23,340	1,557
Val Verde	Del Rio	45,903	38,721	3,170
Van Zandt	Canton	50,124	37,944	849
Victoria	Victoria	84,932	74,361	883
Walker	Huntsville	62,388	50,917	787
Waller	Hempstead	34,057	23,374	514
Ward	Monahans	10,507	13,115	835
Washington	Brenham	30,626	26,154	609
Webb	Laredo	207,611	133,239	3,357
Wharton	Wharton	41,329	39,955	1,090
Wheeler	Wheeler	5,022	5,879	914
Wichita	Wichita Falls	129,964	122,378	628
Wilbarger	Vernon	14,027	15,121	971
Willacy	Raymondville	19,990	17,705	597
Williamson	Georgetown	289,924	139,551	1,123
Wilson	Floresville	34,548	22,650	807
Winkler	Kermit	6,892	8,626	841
Wise	Decatur	52,926	34,679	905
Wood	Quitman	38,053	29,380	650
Yoakum	Plains	7,305	8,786	800
Young	Graham	17,725	18,126	922
Zapata	Zapata	12,788	9,279	997
Zavala	Crystal City	11,556	12,162	1,298

Utah
(29 counties, 82,144 sq. mi. land; pop. 2,316,256)

County	County seat or courthouse	2002 Pop.	1990 Pop.	Land area sq. mi.
Beaver	Beaver	6,099	4,765	2,590
Box Elder	Brigham City	44,032	36,485	5,723
Cache	Logan	93,695	70,183	1,165
Carbon	Price	19,879	20,228	1,478
Daggett	Manila	886	690	698
Davis	Farmington	249,224	187,941	304
Duchesne	Duchesne	14,844	12,645	3,238
Emery	Castle Dale	10,626	10,332	4,452
Garfield	Panguitch	4,584	3,980	5,174
Grand	Moab	8,735	6,620	3,682
Iron	Parowan	35,204	20,789	3,298
Juab	Nephi	8,569	5,817	3,392
Kane	Kanab	6,121	5,169	3,992
Millard	Fillmore	12,446	11,333	6,589
Morgan	Morgan	7,380	5,528	609
Piute	Junction	1,361	1,277	758
Rich	Randolph	1,966	1,725	1,029
Salt Lake	Salt Lake City	919,308	725,956	737
San Juan	Monticello	13,781	12,621	7,820
Sanpete	Manti	23,392	16,259	1,588
Sevier	Richfield	19,091	15,431	1,910
Summit	Coalville	31,857	15,518	1,871
Tooele	Tooele	46,032	26,601	6,930
Uintah	Vernal	26,155	22,211	4,477
Utah	Provo	387,817	263,590	1,998
Wasatch	Heber City	16,996	10,089	1,177
Washington	Saint George	99,442	48,560	2,427
Wayne	Loa	2,567	2,177	2,460
Weber	Ogden	204,167	158,330	576

Vermont
(14 counties, 9,250 sq. mi. land; pop. 616,592)

County	County seat or courthouse	2002 Pop.	1990 Pop.	Land area sq. mi.
Addison	Middlebury	36,544	32,953	770
Bennington	Bennington	37,153	35,845	676
Caledonia	Saint Johnsbury	30,055	27,846	651
Chittenden	Burlington	148,916	131,761	539
Essex	Guildhall	6,542	6,405	665
Franklin	Saint Albans	46,694	39,980	637
Grand Isle	North Hero	7,333	5,318	83
Lamoille	Hyde Park	23,914	19,735	461
Orange	Chelsea	28,681	26,149	689
Orleans	Newport	26,622	24,053	698
Rutland	Rutland	63,250	62,142	933
Washington	Montpelier	58,837	54,928	689
Windham	Newfane	44,231	41,588	789
Windsor	Woodstock	57,820	54,055	971

Virginia
(95 counties, 39 ind. cities, 39,594 sq. mi. land; pop. 7,293,542)

County	County seat or courthouse	2002 Pop.	1990 Pop.	Land area sq. mi.
Accomack	Accomac	39,007	31,703	455
Albemarle	Charlottesville	81,888	68,177	723
Alleghany[1]	Covington	16,960	12,815	445
Amelia	Amelia Court House	11,714	8,787	357
Amherst	Amherst	31,976	28,578	475
Appomattox	Appomattox	13,696	12,300	334
Arlington	Arlington	189,927	170,895	26
Augusta	Staunton	67,046	54,557	970
Bath	Warm Springs	5,063	4,799	532
Bedford	Bedford	61,875	45,553	755
Bland	Bland	6,916	6,514	359
Botetourt	Fincastle	31,272	24,992	543
Brunswick	Lawrenceville	18,250	15,987	566
Buchanan	Grundy	25,994	31,333	504
Buckingham	Buckingham	15,767	12,873	581
Campbell	Rustburg	51,471	47,499	504
Caroline	Bowling Green	22,622	19,217	533
Carroll	Hillsville	29,109	26,519	476
Charles City	Charles City	7,239	6,282	183
Charlotte	Charlotte Court House	12,209	11,688	475
Chesterfield	Chesterfield	271,142	209,599	426
Clarke	Berryville	13,290	12,101	177
Craig	New Castle	5,118	4,372	331
Culpeper	Culpeper	36,893	27,791	381
Cumberland	Cumberland	8,899	7,825	298
Dickenson	Clintwood	16,216	17,620	332
Dinwiddie	Dinwiddie	24,747	22,279	504
Essex	Tappahannock	9,993	8,689	258
Fairfax	Fairfax	997,580	818,310	395
Fauquier	Warrenton	59,245	48,700	650
Floyd	Floyd	14,248	11,965	381
Fluvanna	Palmyra	22,207	12,429	287
Franklin	Rocky Mount	48,462	39,549	692
Frederick	Winchester	62,971	45,723	415
Giles	Pearisburg	17,083	16,366	357
Gloucester	Gloucester	35,755	30,131	217
Goochland	Goochland	17,523	14,163	284
Grayson	Independence	16,612	16,278	443
Greene	Stanardsville	16,269	10,297	157
Greensville	Emporia	11,572	8,553	295
Halifax	Halifax	36,973	36,030	819
Hanover	Hanover	92,050	63,306	473
Henrico	Richmond	268,270	217,878	238
Henry	Collinsville	57,395	56,942	382
Highland	Monterey	2,415	2,635	416
Isle of Wight	Isle of Wight	31,085	25,053	316
James City	Williamsburg	51,418	34,779	143
King and Queen	King and Queen Court House	6,558	6,289	316
King George	King George	17,657	13,527	180
King William	King William	13,822	10,913	275
Lancaster	Lancaster	11,463	10,896	133
Lee	Jonesville	23,396	24,496	437
Loudoun	Leesburg	204,054	86,185	520
Louisa	Louisa	27,007	20,325	497
Lunenburg	Lunenburg	13,318	11,419	432
Madison	Madison	12,947	11,949	321
Mathews	Mathews	9,258	8,348	86
Mecklenburg	Boydton	32,274	29,241	624
Middlesex	Saluda	10,178	8,653	130
Montgomery	Christiansburg	85,368	73,913	388
Nelson	Lovingston	14,727	12,778	472
New Kent	New Kent	14,157	10,466	210
Northampton	Eastville	12,929	13,061	207
Northumberland	Heathsville	12,431	10,524	192
Nottoway	Nottoway	15,861	14,993	315
Orange	Orange	27,298	21,421	342
Page	Luray	23,310	21,690	311
Patrick	Stuart	19,455	17,473	483
Pittsylvania	Chatham	61,745	55,672	971
Powhatan	Powhatan	23,997	15,328	261
Prince Edward	Farmville	19,985	17,320	353
Prince George	Prince George	34,135	27,390	266
Prince William	Manassas	311,892	214,954	338
Pulaski	Pulaski	35,028	34,496	321
Rappahannock	Washington	7,206	6,622	267
Richmond	Warsaw	8,837	7,273	191
Roanoke	Salem	85,937	79,278	251
Rockbridge	Lexington	20,777	18,350	600
Rockingham	Harrisonburg	68,648	57,482	851
Russell	Lebanon	28,974	28,667	475
Scott	Gate City	23,136	23,204	537
Shenandoah	Woodstock	36,315	31,636	512
Smyth	Marion	32,827	32,370	452
Southampton	Courtland	17,448	17,022	600
Spotsylvania	Spotsylvania	102,570	57,397	401
Stafford	Stafford	104,823	62,255	270
Surry	Surry	7,107	6,145	279
Sussex	Sussex	12,221	10,248	491
Tazewell	Tazewell	44,011	45,960	520
Warren	Front Royal	32,910	26,142	214
Washington	Abingdon	51,331	45,887	563
Westmoreland	Montross	16,676	15,480	229
Wise	Wise	41,710	39,573	404
Wythe	Wytheville	27,790	25,471	463
York	Yorktown	59,720	42,434	106
Independent Cities				
Alexandria		130,804	111,183	15
Bedford		6,225	6,176	7
Bristol		17,118	18,426	13
Buena Vista		6,300	6,406	7
Charlottesville		43,833	40,470	10
Chesapeake		206,665	151,982	341
Colonial Heights		17,063	16,064	7

Independent Cities	2002 Pop.	1990 Pop.	Land area sq. mi.
Covington	6,361	7,352	6
Danville	47,596	53,056	43
Emporia	5,734	5,556	7
Fairfax	22,055	19,945	6
Falls Church	10,659	9,464	2
Franklin	8,170	8,392	8
Fredericksburg	20,076	19,033	11
Galax	6,590	6,745	8
Hampton	145,921	133,773	52
Harrisonburg	40,909	30,707	18
Hopewell	22,525	23,101	10
Lexington	6,910	6,959	2
Lynchburg	64,616	66,120	49
Manassas	37,288	27,757	10
Manassas Park	10,909	6,798	2
Martinsville	15,263	16,162	11
Newport News	180,272	171,477	68
Norfolk	239,036	261,250	54
Norton	3,972	4,247	8
Petersburg	33,115	37,071	23
Poquoson	11,686	11,005	16
Portsmouth	99,790	103,910	33
Radford	15,670	15,940	10
Richmond	197,456	202,713	60
Roanoke	93,873	96,487	43
Salem	24,836	23,835	15
Staunton	23,635	24,581	20
Suffolk	69,966	52,143	400
Virginia Beach	433,934	393,089	248
Waynesboro	20,134	18,549	15
Williamsburg	11,693	11,600	9
Winchester	24,228	21,947	9

(1) The independent city of Clifton Forge became part of Alleghany County in 2001.

Washington
(39 counties, 66,544 sq. mi. land; pop. 6,068,996)

County	County seat or courthouse	2002 Pop.	1990 Pop.	Land area sq. mi.
Adams	Ritzville	16,434	13,603	1,925
Asotin	Asotin	20,453	17,605	635
Benton	Prosser	150,366	112,560	1,703
Chelan	Wenatchee	67,050	52,250	2,921
Clallam	Port Angeles	66,302	56,210	1,739
Clark	Vancouver	370,236	238,053	628
Columbia	Dayton	4,103	4,024	869
Cowlitz	Kelso	94,514	82,119	1,139
Douglas	Waterville	33,409	26,205	1,821
Ferry	Republic	7,268	6,295	2,204
Franklin	Pasco	52,745	37,473	1,242
Garfield	Pomeroy	2,327	2,248	711
Grant	Ephrata	77,983	54,798	2,681
Grays Harbor	Montesano	68,470	64,175	1,917
Island	Coupeville	75,050	60,195	208
Jefferson	Port Townsend	26,761	20,406	1,814
King	Seattle	1,759,604	1,507,305	2,126
Kitsap	Port Orchard	236,174	189,731	396
Kittitas	Ellensburg	34,370	26,725	2,297
Klickitat	Goldendale	19,381	16,616	1,872
Lewis	Chehalis	69,710	59,358	2,408
Lincoln	Davenport	10,096	8,864	2,311
Mason	Shelton	51,008	38,341	961
Okanogan	Okanogan	39,186	33,350	5,268
Pacific	South Bend	20,778	18,882	933
Pend Oreille	Newport	12,008	8,915	1,400
Pierce	Tacoma	732,282	586,203	1,679
San Juan	Friday Harbor	14,565	10,035	175
Skagit	Mount Vernon	106,906	79,545	1,735
Skamania	Stevenson	10,049	8,289	1,656
Snohomish	Everett	633,947	465,628	2,089
Spokane	Spokane	427,506	361,333	1,764
Stevens	Colville	40,556	30,948	2,478
Thurston	Olympia	217,641	161,238	727
Wahkiakum	Cathlamet	3,793	3,327	264
Walla Walla	Walla Walla	56,149	48,439	1,271
Whatcom	Bellingham	174,362	127,780	2,120
Whitman	Colfax	40,631	38,775	2,159
Yakima	Yakima	224,823	188,823	4,296

West Virginia
(55 counties, 24,078 sq. mi. land; pop. 1,801,873)

County	County seat or courthouse	2002 Pop.	1990 Pop.	Land area sq. mi.
Barbour	Philippi	15,507	15,699	341
Berkeley	Martinsburg	81,262	59,253	321
Boone	Madison	25,554	25,870	503
Braxton	Sutton	14,800	12,998	513
Brooke	Wellsburg	25,179	26,992	89
Cabell	Huntington	95,266	96,827	282
Calhoun	Grantsville	7,451	7,885	281
Clay	Clay	10,357	9,983	342
Doddridge	West Union	7,425	6,994	320
Fayette	Fayetteville	47,129	47,952	664
Gilmer	Glenville	6,986	7,669	340

County	County seat or courthouse	2002 Pop.	1990 Pop.	Land area sq. mi.
Grant	Petersburg	11,368	10,428	477
Greenbrier	Lewisburg	34,453	34,693	1,021
Hampshire	Romney	21,035	16,498	642
Hancock	New Cumberland	32,082	35,233	83
Hardy	Moorefield	12,795	10,977	583
Harrison	Clarksburg	67,856	69,371	416
Jackson	Ripley	28,204	25,938	466
Jefferson	Charles Town	44,926	35,926	210
Kanawha	Charleston	195,790	207,619	903
Lewis	Weston	16,690	17,223	382
Lincoln	Hamlin	22,256	21,382	437
Logan	Logan	37,004	43,032	454
McDowell	Welch	26,137	35,233	535
Marion	Fairmont	56,433	57,249	310
Marshall	Moundsville	34,898	37,356	307
Mason	Point Pleasant	26,004	25,178	432
Mercer	Princeton	62,207	64,980	420
Mineral	Keyser	27,087	26,697	328
Mingo	Williamson	27,561	33,739	423
Monongalia	Morgantown	82,895	75,509	361
Monroe	Union	14,613	12,406	473
Morgan	Berkeley Springs	15,263	12,128	229
Nicholas	Summersville	26,404	26,775	649
Ohio	Wheeling	46,126	50,871	106
Pendleton	Franklin	7,911	8,054	698
Pleasants	St. Marys	7,579	7,546	131
Pocahontas	Marlinton	8,957	9,008	940
Preston	Kingwood	29,460	29,037	648
Putnam	Winfield	52,230	42,835	346
Raleigh	Beckley	78,899	76,819	607
Randolph	Elkins	28,267	27,803	1,040
Ritchie	Harrisville	10,278	10,233	454
Roane	Spencer	15,267	15,120	484
Summers	Hinton	12,526	14,204	361
Taylor	Grafton	16,059	15,144	173
Tucker	Parsons	7,168	7,728	419
Tyler	Middlebourne	9,399	9,796	258
Upshur	Buckhannon	23,318	22,867	355
Wayne	Wayne	42,382	41,636	506
Webster	Webster Springs	9,697	10,729	556
Wetzel	New Martinsville	17,363	19,258	359
Wirt	Elizabeth	5,935	5,192	233
Wood	Parkersburg	87,306	86,915	367
Wyoming	Pineville	24,869	28,990	501

Wisconsin
(72 counties, 54,310 sq. mi. land; pop. 5,441,196)

County	County seat or courthouse	2002 Pop.	1990 Pop.	Land area sq. mi.
Adams	Friendship	20,515	15,682	648
Ashland	Ashland	16,827	16,307	1,044
Barron	Barron	45,436	40,750	863
Bayfield	Washburn	15,161	14,008	1,476
Brown	Green Bay	232,185	194,594	529
Buffalo	Alma	13,726	13,584	684
Burnett	Siren	15,999	13,084	822
Calumet	Chilton	42,365	34,291	320
Chippewa	Chippewa Falls	56,076	52,360	1,010
Clark	Neillsville	33,826	31,647	1,216
Columbia	Portage	53,374	45,088	774
Crawford	Prairie du Chien	16,897	15,940	573
Dane	Madison	443,110	367,085	1,202
Dodge	Juneau	86,820	76,559	882
Door	Sturgeon Bay	28,101	25,690	483
Douglas	Superior	43,738	41,758	1,309
Dunn	Menomonie	40,695	35,909	852
Eau Claire	Eau Claire	94,219	85,183	638
Florence	Florence	5,032	4,590	488
Fond du Lac	Fond du Lac	97,809	90,083	723
Forest	Crandon	10,011	8,776	1,014
Grant	Lancaster	49,320	49,266	1,148
Green	Monroe	34,081	30,339	584
Green Lake	Green Lake	19,062	18,651	354
Iowa	Dodgeville	23,119	20,150	763
Iron	Hurley	6,828	6,153	757
Jackson	Black River Falls	19,400	16,588	987
Jefferson	Jefferson	75,179	67,783	557
Juneau	Mauston	24,832	21,650	768
Kenosha	Kenosha	154,433	128,181	273
Kewaunee	Kewaunee	20,422	18,878	343
La Crosse	La Crosse	108,148	97,904	453
Lafayette	Darlington	16,243	16,074	634
Langlade	Antigo	20,717	19,505	873
Lincoln	Merrill	29,871	26,993	883
Manitowoc	Manitowoc	82,481	80,421	592
Marathon	Wausau	126,728	115,400	1,545
Marinette	Marinette	43,494	40,548	1,402
Marquette	Montello	14,694	12,321	455
Menominee	Keshena	4,679	4,075	358
Milwaukee	Milwaukee	937,136	959,212	242
Monroe	Sparta	41,609	36,633	901
Oconto	Oconto	36,629	30,226	998
Oneida	Rhinelander	36,860	31,679	1,125
Outagamie	Appleton	166,148	140,510	640
Ozaukee	Port Washington	83,915	72,894	232

County	County seat or courthouse	2002 Pop.	1990 Pop.	Land area sq. mi.
Pepin	Durand	7,291	7,107	232
Pierce	Ellsworth	37,422	32,765	576
Polk	Balsam Lake	42,698	34,773	917
Portage	Stevens Point	67,321	61,405	806
Price	Phillips	15,402	15,600	1,253
Racine	Racine	191,012	175,034	333
Richland	Richland Center	18,026	17,521	586
Rock	Janesville	154,092	139,510	720
Rusk	Ladysmith	15,311	15,079	913
Saint Croix	Hudson	68,122	50,251	722
Sauk	Baraboo	55,632	46,975	838
Sawyer	Hayward	16,563	14,181	1,256
Shawano	Shawano	40,928	37,157	893
Sheboygan	Sheboygan	112,480	103,877	514
Taylor	Medford	19,650	18,901	975
Trempealeau	Whitehall	27,215	25,263	734
Vernon	Viroqua	28,346	25,617	795
Vilas	Eagle River	21,636	17,707	874
Walworth	Elkhorn	97,003	75,000	555
Washburn	Shell Lake	16,448	13,772	810
Washington	West Bend	120,899	95,328	431
Waukesha	Waukesha	370,554	304,715	556
Waupaca	Waupaca	52,321	46,104	751
Waushara	Wautoma	23,299	19,385	626
Winnebago	Oshkosh	158,401	140,320	439
Wood	Wisconsin Rapids	75,174	73,605	793

Wyoming
(23 counties, 97,100 sq. mi. land; pop. 498,703)

County	County seat or courthouse	2002 Pop.	1990 Pop.	Land area sq. mi.
Albany	Laramie	31,742	30,797	4,273
Big Horn	Basin	11,212	10,525	3,137
Campbell	Gillette	36,110	29,370	4,797
Carbon	Rawlins	15,346	16,659	7,896
Converse	Douglas	12,433	11,128	4,255
Crook	Sundance	5,929	5,294	2,859
Fremont	Lander	36,113	33,662	9,182
Goshen	Torrington	12,244	12,373	2,225
Hot Springs	Thermopolis	4,701	4,809	2,004
Johnson	Buffalo	7,374	6,145	4,166
Laramie	Cheyenne	82,894	73,142	2,686
Lincoln	Kemmerer	14,890	12,625	4,069
Natrona	Casper	67,336	61,226	5,340
Niobrara	Lusk	2,302	2,499	2,626
Park	Cody	25,894	23,178	6,942
Platte	Wheatland	8,725	8,145	2,085
Sheridan	Sheridan	26,908	23,562	2,523
Sublette	Pinedale	6,240	4,843	4,883
Sweetwater	Green River	37,194	38,823	10,425
Teton	Jackson	18,586	11,173	4,008
Unita	Evanston	19,792	18,705	2,082
Washakie	Worland	8,044	8,388	2,240
Weston	Newcastle	6,694	6,518	2,398

Population of Outlying Areas

Source: Bureau of the Census, U.S. Dept. of Commerce; World Almanac research

Population estimates for July 1, 2002, are given for Puerto Rican municipios (a municipio is the governmental unit that is the primary legal subdivision of Puerto Rico; the Census Bureau treats the municipio as the statistical equivalent of a county). All other population counts and all Land area figures are from the 2000 census. Because only selected areas are shown, the population and Land area figures may not equal the total reported. ZIP codes with an asterisk (*) are general delivery ZIP codes. Consult the local postmaster for more specific delivery information. Wake Atoll, Johnston Atoll, and Midway Atoll receive mail through APO and FPO addresses.

Commonwealth of Puerto Rico

ZIP code	Municipio	2002 Pop.	Land area sq. mi.
00601	Adjuntas	19,056	67
00602	Aguada	43,143	31
*00605	Aguadilla	65,607	37
00703	Aguas Buenas	29,671	31
00705	Aibonito	26,751	31
00610	Añasco	28,894	39
*00613	Arecibo	101,283	126
00714	Arroyo	19,151	15
00617	Barceloneta	22,556	19
00794	Barranquitas	29,490	34
*00958	Bayamón	224,670	44
00623	Cabo Rojo	48,453	70
00726	Caguas	141,693	59
00627	Camuy	36,407	46
00729	Canóvanas	44,510	33
*00984	Carolina	187,468	45
*00963	Cataño	28,888	5
*00737	Cayey	47,505	52
00735	Ceiba	18,149	29
00638	Ciales	20,110	67
00739	Cidra	44,057	36
00769	Coamo	38,252	78
00782	Comerio	19,927	28
00783	Corozal	37,525	43
00775	Culebra	1,928	12
00646	Dorado	34,583	23
*00738	Fajardo	41,377	30
00650	Florida	13,105	15
00653	Guánica	22,217	37
*00785	Guayama	44,762	65
00656	Guayanilla	23,326	42
*00970	Guaynabo	101,280	27
00778	Gurabo	38,256	28
00659	Hatillo	40,053	42
00660	Hormigueros	16,856	11
*00791	Humacao	59,688	45
00662	Isabela	45,379	55
00664	Jayuya	17,631	45
00795	Juana Díaz	51,464	60
00777	Juncos	37,511	27
00667	Lajas	26,787	60
00669	Lares	35,392	61
00670	Las Marías	11,379	46
00771	Las Piedras	35,706	34
00772	Loíza	33,100	19
00773	Luquillo	20,114	26
00674	Manatí	46,617	45
00606	Maricao	6,490	37
00707	Maunabo	12,807	21
*00681	Mayagüez	97,886	78
00676	Moca	40,934	50
00687	Morovis	30,811	39
00718	Naguabo	23,944	52
00719	Naranjito	30,014	27
00720	Orocovis	24,316	63
00723	Patillas	20,238	47
00624	Peñuelas	27,480	44
*00732	Ponce	186,112	115
00678	Quebradillas	26,179	23
00677	Rincón	15,234	14
00745	Río Grande	53,554	61
00637	Sabana Grande	26,481	36
00751	Salinas	31,594	69
00683	San Germán	37,469	55
*00936	San Juan	433,412	48
00754	San Lorenzo	42,042	53
00685	San Sebastián	45,160	70
00757	Santa Isabel	22,076	34
*00954	Toa Alta	67,950	27
*00950	Toa Baja	94,867	23
*00976	Trujillo Alto	78,439	21
00641	Utuado	35,395	113
00692	Vega Alta	38,490	28
*00694	Vega Baja	62,960	46
00765	Vieques	9,191	51
00766	Villalba	28,700	35
00767	Yabucoa	39,719	55
00698	Yauco	47,135	68
TOTAL		**3,858,806**	**3,425**

Commonwealth of the Northern Mariana Islands

ZIP code	Municipality	2000 Pop.	Land area sq. mi.
96950	Northern Islands	6	60
96951	Rota	3,283	33
96950	Saipan	62,392	45
96952	Tinian	3,540	42
TOTAL		**69,221**	**179**

Other U.S. External Territories

ZIP code	Location	2000 Pop.	Land area sq. mi.
American Samoa			
96799	American Samoa	57,291	77
Guam			
96919	Agaña Hts.	3,940	1
96928	Agat	5,656	10
96910	Asan	2,090	6
*96913	Barrigada	8,652	8
96924	Chalan-Pago-Ordot	5,923	6
96912	Dededo	42,980	31
*96913	Hagåtña	1,100	1
96917	Inarajan	3,052	19
96923	Mangilao	13,313	10
96916	Merizo	2,163	6
96910	Mongmong-Toto-Maite	5,845	2
96925	Piti	1,666	7
96915	Santa Rita	7,500	16
96926	Sinajana	2,853	1
96915	Talofofo	3,215	18
*96913	Tamuning	18,012	6
96915	Umatac	887	6
96929	Yigo	19,474	35
96914	Yona	6,484	20
TOTAL		**154,805**	**210**
Virgin Islands			
00820	Saint Croix	53,234	83
*00820	Christiansted	2,637	
*00841	Frederiksted	732	
*00830	Saint John	4,197	20
*00804	Saint Thomas	51,181	31
*00802	Charlotte Amalie	11,004	
TOTAL		**108,612**	**134**

BUILDINGS, BRIDGES, AND TUNNELS

50 Tallest Buildings in the World

Source: Council on Tall Buildings and Urban Habitat. Lehigh Univ., www.ctbuh.com

Structures under construction are denoted by asterisk *. Year in parentheses is date of completion or projected completion.

Building	Ht. (ft.)	Stories	Building	Ht. (ft.)	Stories
*Taipei 101, Taipei, Taiwan (2004)	1,667	101	Baiyoke Tower II, Bangkok, Thailand (1998)	997	85
Petronas Tower I. Kuala Lumpur, Malaysia (1998)	1,483	88	Kingdom Centre, Riyadh, Saudi Arabia (2001)	992	72
Petronas Tower II, Kuala Lumpur, Malaysia (1998)	1,483	88	Two Prudential Plaza, Chicago, IL, U.S. (1990)	995	64
Sears Tower, Chicago, IL, U.S. (1974)	1,450	110	First Canadian Place, Toronto, Canada (1975)	978	72
Jin Mao Bldg., Shanghai, China (1999)	1,381	88	Wells Fargo Plaza, Houston, TX, U.S. (1983)	972	71
*Two International Finance Centre, Hong Kong, China (2003)	1,352	88	Landmark Tower, Yokohama, Japan (1993)	971	70
CITIC Plaza, Guangzhou, China (1996)	1,283	80	Bank of America Tower, Seattle, WA, U.S. (1984)	967	76
Shun Hing Square, Shenzhen, China (1996)	1,260	69	311 S. Wacker Drive, Chicago, IL, U.S. (1990)	961	65
Empire State Building, New York, U.S. (1931)	1,250	102	SEG Plaza, Shenzhen, China (2000)	957	72
Central Plaza, Hong Kong. China. (1992)	1,227	78	American International Bldg., New York, U.S. (1932)	952	67
Bank of China, Hong Kong, China (1989)	1,209	70	Cheung Kong Centre, Hong Kong, China (1999)	951	70
Emirates Tower One, Dubai, U.A.E. (1999)	1,165	55	Key Tower, Cleveland, OH, U.S. (1991)	947	57
The Centre, Hong Kong, China (1998)	1,148	79	Plaza 66, Shanghai, China (2001)	945	62
Tuntex & Chein-Tai Tower, Kaohsiung, Taiwan (1998)	1,140	85	One Liberty Place, Philadelphia, PA, U.S. (1987)	945	61
Aon Center, Chicago, IL, U.S. (1973)	1,136	83	Sunjoy Tomorrow Square, Shanghai, China (1999)	934	59
John Hancock Center, Chicago, IL, U.S. (1969)	1,127	100	The Trump Bldg., New York, U.S. (1930)	927	72
Pyongyang Hotel, Pyongyang, North Korea (1992)	1,083	105	Bank of America Plaza, Dallas, TX, U.S. (1985)	921	72
Burj al Arab Hotel, Dubai, U.A.E. (1999)	1,053	60	Overseas Union Bank Centre, Singapore (1986)	919	66
Chrysler Bldg., New York, U.S. (1930)	1,046	77	United Overseas Bank Plaza One, Singapore (1992)	919	66
Bank of America Plaza, Atlanta, GA, U.S. (1992)	1,023	55	Republic Plaza, Singapore (1995)	919	66
Library Tower, Los Angeles, CA, U.S. (1990)	1,018	73	Citigroup Center, New York, U.S. (1977)	915	59
Telekom Malaysia Headquarters, Kuala Lumpur, Malaysia (1999)	1,017	55	Hong Kong New World Building, Shanghai, China (2001)	913	58
Emirates Towers Two, Dubai, U.A.E. (2000)	1,014	54	Scotia Plaza, Toronto, Canada (1989)	902	68
AT&T Corporate Center, Chicago, IL, U.S. (1989)	1,007	60	Williams Tower, Houston, TX, U.S. (1983)	901	64
JP Morgan Chase Tower, Houston, TX, U.S. (1982)	1,002	75	Wuhan World Trade Tower, Wuhan, China (1998)	896	60
			Renaissance Tower, Dallas, TX, U.S. (1975)	886	56

> ▶ **IT'S A FACT:** At 1,667 feet, Taipei 101, named for its 101 floors and also known as the Taipei Financial Center, became the world's tallest building when it was topped off in July 2003. Once open and occupied, Taipei 101 will also hold world records for the highest-up occupied floor and, at 38 miles per hour, the fastest elevators.

World's 10 Tallest Free-Standing Towers

Name	City	Country	Ht. (ft.)	Year	Name	City	Country	Ht. (ft.)	Year
CN Tower	Toronto	Canada	1,815	1976	Tehran Tele- communications Tower.	Tehran	Iran	1,427	2001
Ostankino Tower	Moscow	Russia	1,772	1967	Manara Kuala Lumpur	Kuala Lumpur	Malaysia	1,379	1996
*Xi'an Broadcasting, Telephone and Tele-vision Tower.	Xi'an	China	1,542	NA	Beijing Radio & T.V. Tower.	Beijing	China	1,369	1992
					Tianjin Radio & T.V. Tower.	Tianjin	China	1,362	1991
Oriental Pearl Tele-vision Tower	Shanghai	China	1,535	1995	T.V. Tower	Kiev	Ukraine	1,246	1974
					Tashkent Tower	Tashkent	Uzbekistan	1,230	1985

*Under construction. NA = Not available.

Tall Buildings in Selected North American Cities

Source: Marshall Gerometta and Rick Bronson, Skyscrapers.com, www.skyscrapers.com; Council on Tall Buildings and Urban Habitat, Lehigh Univ., www.ctbuh.org

Lists include freestanding towers and other structures that do not have stories and are not technically considered "buildings." Also included are some structures still under construction (denoted by asterisk *). Year in parentheses is date of completion or projected completion. Height is generally measured from sidewalk to roof, including penthouse and tower if enclosed as integral part of structure; stories generally counted from street level. NA = not available or not applicable.

Atlanta, GA

Building	Ht. (ft.)	Stories
Bank of America Plaza, 600 Peachtree NE (1992)	1,023	55
SunTrust Bank Tower, 303 Peachtree NE (1992)	871	60
One Atlantic Center, 1201 W. Peachtree (1987)	820	50
191 Peachtree Tower (1991)	770	50
Westin Peachtree Plaza, 210 Peachtree NW (1976)	723	73
Georgia Pacific Tower, 133 Peachtree St. NE (1981)	697	51
Promenade II/A.T.& T., 1203 Peachtree St. NE (1989)	691	40
Bellsouth, 675 Peachtree W (1980)	677	47
GLG Grand/Four Seasons Hotel, 75 14th St. (1992)	609	53
Wachovia Bank of Georgia, 2 Peachtree St. NW (1967)	556	44
Marriott Marquis, 265 Peachtree Center Ave. NE (1985)	554	52
Park Avenue Condominiums, 750 Park Ave. NE (2000)	486	44
Centennial Tower, 101 Marietta St. (1976)	459	36
Equitable Bldg., 100 Peachtree St. (1967)	453	34
*Regent at Tower Place	451	40
One Park Tower, 34 Peachtree St. NE (1961)	439	32
Bell South Enterprises, 1100 Peachtree St. (1990)	428	34
Atlanta Plaza I, 950 E. Paces Ferry Rd. (1986)	425	32
Park Place, 2660 Peachtree Rd. NW (1986)	420	40
2828 Peachtree Luxury Condominiums (2002)	420	33
Oakwood Apts., 1280 W. Peachtree St. NW (1989)	410	38
Peachtree Summit No. 1, 401 Peachtree NE (1975)	406	31
One Coca-Cola Plaza, 310 North Ave. (1979)	403	29
Tower Place, 3340 Peachtree Rd. NE (1974)	401	29

Baltimore, MD

Building	Ht. (ft.)	Stories
Legg Mason Building, 100 Light St. (1973)	529	40
Bank of America Building, 10 Light St. (1924)	509	37
William Donald Schaefer Tower, 6 St. Paul Pl. (1992)	493	29
Commerce Place, 1 South St. (1992)	454	31

Building	Ht. (ft.)	Stories
Marriott Baltimore Inner Harbor East, 700 Aliceanna St. (2001)	430	32
World Trade Center 401 E. Pratt St. (1977)	405	32

Bellevue, WA

Building	Ht. (ft.)	Stories
*One Lincoln Tower, 604 Bellevue Way (2003)	450	42
*Lincoln Square, 770 Bellevue Way NE (2003)	412	28

Birmingham, AL

Building	Ht. (ft.)	Stories
Southtrust Tower, 420 N. 20th St. (1986)	454	34
AmSouth/Harbert Plaza, 1901 6th Ave. N (1989)	437	32

Boston, MA

Building	Ht. (ft.)	Stories
John Hancock Tower, 200 Clarendon St. (1976)	790	60
Prudential Tower, 800 Boylston St. (1964)	750	52
Federal Reserve Bldg., 600 Atlantic Ave. (1978)	604	32
Boston Company Bldg., 1 Boston Place (1970)	601	41
One International Place, 100 Oliver St. (1987)	600	46
First National Bank of Boston, 100 Federal St. (1971)	591	37
One Financial Center, 10 Dewey Sq. (1984)	590	46
111 Huntington Ave. (2001)	564	36
Two International Place (1993)	538	35
One Post Office Square (1981)	525	40
1 Federal St. (1975)	520	38
Exchange Place, 53 State St. (1984)	510	39
Sixty State St. (1977)	509	38
1 Beacon St. (1972)	507	36
1 Lincoln Place (2003)	503	36
28 State Street (1969)	500	40
Mariott's Custom House, 3 McKinley Sq. (1915)	496	32
John Hancock Bldg., 175 Berkeley St. (1949)	495	26
*33 Arch St. (2003)	489	31
State St. Bank, 225 Franklin St., (1966)	477	33
Millennium Place I, Ritz Carlton Hotel (2001)	475	38

Building	Ht. (ft.)	Stories
125 High St. (1990)	452	30
100 Summer St. (1975)	450	33
Millennium Place 2, 3 Avery St. (2001)	445	36
McCormack Bldg., 1 Ashburton Pl. (1975)	401	22
Harbor Towers I, 85 E. India (1971)	400	40
Keystone Building (1971)	400	32

Calgary, Alberta

Building	Ht. (ft.)	Stories
Petro Canada Centre, 150 6th Ave. SW (1984)	705	53
Bankers Hall East Tower, 855 2nd St. SW (1989)	645	50
Bankers Hall West Tower, 888 3rd St. SW (2000)	645	50
Calgary Tower, 101 9th Ave. SW (1967)	626	NA
TransCanada Tower, 450 1st St. SW (2000)	608	37
Canterra Tower, 400 3rd Ave. SW (1988)	580	46
First Canadian Centre, 350 7th Ave. SW (1983)	530	43
Canada Trust, Calgary Eatons Centre, 421 7th Ave. SW (1991)	530	40
Scotia Square, 700 2nd St. SW (1975)	525	42
Western Canadian Place–N. Tower, 700 6th St. SW (1983)	507	41
Nexen Bldg., 801 7th Ave. SW (1982)	500	37
Petro-Canada Tower, E. Tower, 111 5th Ave. SW (1983)	469	33
Two Bow Valley Square, 205 5th Ave. SW (1974)	468	39
Dome Tower, 333 7th Ave. (1976)	463	34
5th & 5th Bldg., 605 5th Ave. SW (1980)	460	35
Shell Centre, 400 4th Ave. SW (1977)	460	34
T.D. Square North, 324 8th Ave. (1976)	449	33
Four Bow Valley Square, 250 6th Ave. SW (1982)	441	37
Fifth Avenue Place, 425 1st St. SW (1981)	435	34
Esso Plaza West Tower (1981)	435	34
Western Canadian Place–S. Tower, 801 6th Ave. SW (1983)	420	32
Family Life Bldg.	410	33
Pan Canadian Bldg., 150 9th Ave. SW (1982)	410	28
Serval Tower, 715 5th Ave. SW (1976)	408	33
Alberta Stock Exchange, 300 5th Ave. (1979)	407	33

Charlotte, NC

Building	Ht. (ft.)	Stories
Bank of America Corporate Center, N. Tryon St. (1992)	871	60
Hearst Tower, 214 N. Tryon St. (2002)	659	50
One Wachovia Center, 301 S. College St. (1988)	588	42
Bank of America Plaza, 101 S. Tryon St. (1974)	503	40
Interstate Tower, 121 W. Trade St. (1990)	462	32
IJL Financial Center, 201 N. Tryon St. (1997)	447	30
Three Wachovia Center, 401 S. Tryon St. (2000)	440	29
Two Wachovia Plaza, 301 S. Tryon St. (1971)	433	32
Wachovia Center, 400 S. Tryon St. (1974)	420	32

Chicago, IL

Building	Ht. (ft.)	Stories
Sears Tower, 233 S. Wacker Dr. (1974)	1,450	110
Aon Center, 200 E. Randolph St. (1973)	1,136	83
John Hancock Center, 875 N. Michigan Ave. (1969)	1,127	100
AT&T Corporate Center, 227 W. Monroe St. (1989)	1,007	60
Two Prudential Plaza, 180 N. Stetson Ave. (1990)	995	64
311 S. Wacker Drive (1990)	961	65
900 N. Michigan Ave. (1989)	871	66
Water Tower Place, 845 N. Michigan Ave. (1976)	859	74
Bank One Plaza (1969)	850	60
Park Tower, 800 N. Michigan Ave. (2000)	844	67
3 First National Plaza, 70 W. Madison St. (1981)	767	57
Chicago Title & Trust Center, 161 N. Clark St. (1991)	756	50
Olympia Centre, 737 N. Michigan Ave. (1986)	725	63
*111 S. Wacker Drive (2005)	702	52
IBM Bldg., 330 N. Wabash Ave. (1973)	695	52
Paine Webber Bldg., 181 W. Madison (1990)	680	50
*Hyatt Center, 71 S. Wacker Drive (2005)	679	48
One Magnificent Mile, 980 N. Michigan Ave. (1983)	673	58
R.R. Donnelley Center, 77 W. Wacker Dr. (1992)	668	49
UBS Tower, 1 N. Wacker Dr. (2001)	652	50
Daley Center, 55 W. Washington St. (1965)	648	31
*55 E. Erie St. (2003)	647	56
Lake Point Tower, 505 N. Lake Shore Dr. (1968)	645	70
River East Center 1, 350 E. Illinois St. (2001)	644	58
Grand Plaza 1, 540 N. State St. (2003)	641	57
Leo Burnett Bldg., 35 W. Wacker Dr. (1989)	635	50
NBC Tower, 445 N. Cityfront Plaza Dr. (1989)	627	34
*The Heritage at Millennium Park, 130 N. Garland Ct. (2004)	621	57
*Millennium Centre, 33 W. Ontario St. (2003)	596	59
Chicago Place, 700 N. Michigan Ave. (1991)	610	49
Board of Trade (incl. statue), 141 W. Jackson Blvd. (1930)	605	44
CNA Plaza, 325 S. Wabash St. (1972)	601	45
Prudential Bldg., 130 E. Randolph St. (1955)	601	41
Heller International Tower, 500 W. Monroe St. (1992)	600	45
One Madison Plaza, 200 W. Madison St. (1982)	599	45
1000 Lake Shore Plaza Apts. (1964)	590	55
Marina City Apts. 1, 300 N. State St. (1964)	588	61
Marina City Apts. 2, 300 N. State St. (1964)	588	61
Citicorp Center, 500 W. Madison St. (1985)	588	41
Mid Continental Plaza, 55 E. Monroe St. (1972)	582	50
North Pier Apt. Tower, 474 N. Lake Shore Dr. (1990)	581	61
Bank One Corporate Center, 131 S. Dearborn St. (2003)	580	39
Smurfit-Stone Bldg., 150 N. Michigan Ave. (1983)	575	41
The Fordham, 25 E. Superior St. (2003)	574	52
190 S. LaSalle St. (1986)	573	42
Onterie Center, 446 E. Ontario St. (1985)	570	57
Chicago Temple, 77 W. Washington St. (1923)	568	21
Palmolive Bldg., 919 N. Michigan Ave. (incl. beacon) (1929)	565	37
Huron Plaza Apts., 30 E. Huron St. (1983)	560	56
Boeing Int'l Headquarters, 100 N. Riverside Plaza (1990)	560	36
The Parkshore, 195 N. Harbor Dr. (1991)	556	56
North Harbor Tower, 175 N. Harbor Dr. (1991)	556	55
Civic Opera Bldg., 20 N. Wacker Dr. (1929)	555	45
Newberry Plaza, 1000 N. State St. (1974)	553	53
Michigan Plaza South, 205 N. Michigan Ave. (1985)	553	44
30 N. LaSalle St. (1975)	553	43
Pittsfield, 55 E. Washington St. (1927)	551	38
Harbor Point, 155 N. Harbor Dr. (1975)	550	54
One S. Wacker Dr. (1983)	550	42
Park Millennium, 222 N. Columbus Dr. (2002)	544	53
USG Building, 125 S. Franklin St. (1992)	538	35
LaSalle National Bank, 135 S. LaSalle St. (1934)	535	44
Park Place Tower, 655 W. Irving Park Rd. (1973)	531	56
*The Pinnacle, 21 E. Huron St. (2004)	535	48
One N. LaSalle St. (1930)	530	49
The Elysees, 111 E. Chestnut St. (1972)	529	56
River Plaza, 405 N. Wabash St. (1977)	524	56
35 E. Wacker Dr. (1926)	523	40
Unitrin Bldg., 1 E. Wacker Dr. (1962)	522	41
Chicago Mercantile Exchange, 10 S. Wacker Dr. (1987)	520	40
Mather Tower, 75 E. Wacker Dr. (1928)	521	41
Chicago Merc. Exchange, 10 S. Wacker Dr. (1987)	520	40
Kluczynski Federal Bldg., 230 S. Dearborn St. (1976)	520	40
191 N. Wacker Dr. (2002)	516	37
401 E. Ontario Dr. (1990)	515	51
One Financial Place, 440 S. LaSalle St. (1985)	515	40
Park Tower Condos, 5415 N. Sheridan Rd. (1973)	513	54
LaSalle-Wacker, 221 N. LaSalle St. (1930)	512	41
321 N. Clark St. (1987)	510	35
Harris Bank III, 115 S. LaSalle St. (1977)	510	35
400 E. Ohio St. (1982)	505	50
Carbide & Carbon, 230 N. Michigan Ave. (1929)	503	37
1 Superior Place, 1 W. Superior St. (1999)	502	52
120 N. LaSalle St. (1991)	501	41
Chase Plaza, 10 S. LaSalle St. (1986)	501	37
200 S. Wacker Dr. (1981)	500	38
Ontario Place, 10 E. Ontario St. (1983)	495	49
Xerox Centre, 55 W. Monroe St. (1980)	495	40
1 N. Franklin St. (1990)	494	34
The Bristol, 57E. Delaware Pl. (2000)	488	42
333 W. Wacker Dr. (1983)	487	36
AT&T, 10 S. Canal St. (1971)	485	32
Plaza 440, 440 N. Wabash Ave. (1991)	480	49
American National Bank, 33 N. LaSalle St. (1930)	479	40
Bankers Bldg., 106 W. Adams St. (1927)	476	41
Britannica Center, 310 S. Michigan Ave. (1924)	475	37
Brunswick Bldg., 69 W. Washington St. (1965)	475	37
American Furniture Mart, 680 N. Lake Shore Dr. (1926)	474	30
Intercontinental Hotel, 505 N. Michigan Ave. (1929)	471	42
City Place, 676 N. Michigan Ave. (1990)	470	40
Columbus Plaza, 233 E. Wacker Dr. (1980)	468	49
The Sterling, 345 N. LaSalle St. (2001)	466	50
Randolph Tower, 188 W. Randolph St. (1925)	465	45
The Bristol, 57 E. Delaware Pl. (2000)	465	42
200 N. Dearborn St. (1989)	463	47
Tribune Tower, 435 N. Michigan Ave. (1925)	463	36
The New York, 3660 N. Lake Shore Dr. (1986)	461	50
Presidential Towers, 555 W. Madison St. (1985)	461	49
Presidential Towers, 575 W. Madison St. (1985)	461	49
Presidential Towers, 605 W. Madison St. (1985)	461	49
Presidential Towers, 625 W. Madison St. (1985)	461	49
Chicago Marriott, 540 N. Michigan Ave. (1978)	460	45
Swissotel, 323 E. Wacker Dr. (1989)	457	43
Equitable Bldg., 401 N. Michigan Ave. (1964)	457	35
*400 N. LaSalle St. (2003)	454	45
*ABN-AMRO Plaza I, 550 W. Madison St. (2003)	453	37
Roanoke Bldg., 11 S. LaSalle St. (1925)	452	37
River Bend, 323 N. Canal St. (2001)	451	32
Eugenie Terrace on the Park, 1730 N. Clark St. (1987)	450	44
Gateway Center III, 222 S. Riverside Plaza (1972)	450	35

Cincinnati, OH

Building	Ht. (ft.)	Stories
Carew Tower, 441 Vine St. (1931)	574	49
PNC Tower , 1 W. 4th St. (1913)	495	31
Scripps Center, 312 Walnut St. (1990)	468	36
Fifth Third Center, 511 Walnut St. (1969)	423	32
Chemed Center, 255 5th St. (1990)	410	32
Convergys Center, 600 Vine St. (1984)	402	29

Cleveland, OH

Building	Ht. (ft.)	Stories
Key Tower, 127 Public Square (1991)	947	57
Terminal Tower, 50 Public Square (1930)	708	52
BP America, 200 Public Square (1985)	658	46
100 Erieview, 1801 E. 9th St. (1964)	529	40
One Cleveland Center, 1375 E. 9th St. (1983)	450	31
Bank One Center, 600 Superior Ave. (1991)	446	28
Federal Courthouse, 801 W. Superior Ave. (2002).	430	24
Justice Center, 1250 Ontario St. (1976)	420	26
Federal Building, 240 E. 9th St. (1967)	419	32
National City Center, 1900 E. 9th St. (1980)	410	35

Columbus, OH

Building	Ht. (ft.)	Stories
James A. Rhodes State Office Tower, 30 E. Broad (1973)	624	41
Leveque-Lincoln Tower, 50 W. Broad St. (1927)	555	37
William Green Building, 30 W. Spring St. (1990)	530	33
Huntington Center, 41 S. High St. (1983)	512	37
Vern Riffe State Office Tower, 77 S. High St. (1988).	503	33
One Nationwide Plaza (1976)	485	40
Franklin County Courthouse, 373 S. High St. (1991)	464	27
AEP Building, One Riverside Plaza (1983)	456	31
Borden Bldg., 180 E. Broad St. (1974)	438	34
Three Nationwide Plaza (1989)	408	27

Dallas, TX

Building	Ht. (ft.)	Stories
Bank of America Plaza, 901 Main St. (1985)	921	72
Renaissance Tower, 1201 Elm St. (1974)	886	56
Bank One Center, 1717 Main St. (1987)	787	60
Chase Texas Plaza, 2200 Ross Ave. (1987)	738	55
Fountain Place, 1445 Ross Ave. (1986)	720	58
Trammel Crow Center, 2001 Ross Ave. (1984)	686	50
1700 Pacific Ave. (1983)	655	50
Thanksgiving Tower, 1600 Pacific Ave. (1982)	645	50
Energy Plaza, 1601 Bryan St. (1983)	629	49
Elm Place, 1401 Elm St. (1965)	625	52
Republic Center Tower I, 300 N. Ervay (incl. spire) (1954)	602	36
Republic Center Tower II, 325 N. St. Paul (1964).	598	50
One Bell Plaza, 208 S. Akard St. (1984)	580	37
One Lincoln Plaza, 500 Akard St. (1984)	579	45
Cityplace Center East, 2711 N.Haskell Ave. (1989)	560	42
Reunion Tower, 300 Reunion Blvd. (1976)	560	NA
Adams Mark Hotel Center Tower, 400 Olive St. (1959)	550	42
Mercantile Bldg., 1700 Main St. (1943)	523	31
2001 Bryan St. (1973)	512	40
Harwood Center, 1999 Bryan St. (1982)	483	36
KMPG Centre. 717 N. Harwood St. (1980)	481	34
San Jacinto Tower, 2121 San Jacinto St. (1982)	456	33
Renaissance Hotel, 2222 Stemmons Fwy. (1983)	451	29
Adam's Mark Hotel North Tower (1980)	448	31
One Dallas Centre, 350 N. Paul St. (1979)	448	30
One Main Place, 1201 Main St. (1968)	445	34
1600 Pacific Bldg. (1964)	434	31
Magnolia Bldg., 108 Akard St. (1923)	430	27
Fidelity Union Tower, 1507 Pacific Ave. (1959)	400	33

Denver, CO

Building	Ht. (ft.)	Stories
Republic Plaza, 330 17th St. (1984)	714	56
Marriott City Center, 1801 California St. (1982)	709	52
Wells Fargo Center, 1700 Lincoln Ave.(1983)	698	50
1999 Broadway (1985)	544	43
MCI Plaza, 707 17th St. (1981)	522	42
Qwest Tower, 555 17th St. (1978)	507	40
*Colorado Convention Center Hotel (2005)	489	38
Amoco Bldg., 1670 Broadway (1980)	448	36
17th St. Plaza, 1225 17th St. (1982)	438	32
First Interstate Tower North, 633 17th St. (1974)	434	32
Brooks Towers, 1020 15th St. (1968)	420	42
Denver Place South Tower, 999 18th St. (1981)	416	34
One Tabor Center, 1200 17th St. (1984)	408	32
Manville Plaza, 717 17th St. (1989)	404	29

Des Moines, IA

Building	Ht. (ft.)	Stories
801 Grand, 801 Grand Ave. (1991)	630	44
Ruan Center, 666 Grand Ave. (1974)	457	36

Detroit, MI

Building	Ht. (ft.)	Stories
Marriott Hotel, Renaissance Center I (1977)	713	73
Comerica Tower, 500 Woodward (1991)	619	45
Penobscot Bldg., 633 Griswold Ave. (1928)	566	46
Renaissance Center 100 Tower (1976)	508	39
Renaissance Center 200 Tower(1976)	508	39
Renaissance Center 300 Tower(1976)	508	39
Renaissance Center 400 Tower (1976)	508	39
Guardian Bldg., 500 Griswold Ave. (1928)	485	40
Book Tower, 1249 Washington Blvd. (1925)	472	35
Madden Bldg., 150 W. Jefferson Ave. (1988)	470	29
Fisher Bldg., 301 W. Grand Blvd. (1928)	447	28
Cadillac Tower, 65 Cadillac Sq. (1928)	437	40
David Stott Bldg., 1150 Griswold (1928)	436	38
ANR Bldg., 1 Woodward Ave. (1962)	430	40

Edmonton, Alberta

Building	Ht. (ft.)	Stories
Manulife Place, 10170-101 St. (1983)	480	36
Telus Plaza South, 10020-100 St. (1971)	441	34
Bell Tower, 10104-103 Ave. (1982)	426	34
Commerce Place, 10155-102 St. (1990)	404	27

Fort Worth, TX

Building	Ht. (ft.)	Stories
Burnett Plaza, 801 Cherry St. (1983)	567	40
City Center Tower II, 301 Commerce St. (1984)	547	38
Carter Burgess Plaza, 777 Main St. (1982)	525	40
Landmark Tower, 200 W. 7th St. (1957)	481	32
Chase Texas Tower, 201 Main St. (1982)	477	33
Block 82 Tower, 400 Throckmorton St. (1974)	454	36

Hartford, CT

Building	Ht. (ft.)	Stories
City Place 1, 185 Asylum St. (1980)	535	38
Travelers Tower (CitiGroup Building) 26 Grove St. (1919)	527	34
Goodwin Square, 225 Asylum St. (1990)	522	30
Hartford Plaza, 690 Asylum Ave. (1967)	420	22

Honolulu, HI

Building	Ht. (ft.)	Stories
First Hawaiian Bank Bldg., 999 Bishop St. (1996)	429	30
Nauru Tower, 1330 Ala Moana Blvd. (1991)	418	45
Hawaiki Tower, 88 Pii Koi St. (1999)	400	45
One Waterfront Tower, Makai, 425 S. King St. (1990)	400	45
One Archer Lane, 801 S. King St.(1998)	400	41
Imperial Plaza, 725 Kapiolani Blvd. (1992)	400	40

Houston, TX

Building	Ht. (ft.)	Stories
JPMorgan Chase Tower, 600 Travis St. (1982)	1.002	75
Wells Fargo Plaza, 1000 Louisiana St. (1983)	972	71
Williams Tower, 2800 Post Oak Blvd. (1983)	901	64
Bank of America Center, 700 Louisiana St. (1983)	780	56
Texaco Heritage Plaza, 1111 Bagby (1987)	762	53
1100 Louisiana Bldg. (1980)	748	55
Houston Industries Plaza, 1111 Louisiana St. (1974)	741	53
Continental Airlines Center, 1600 Smith St. (1984)	732	55
Chevron Tower, 1301 McKinney St. (1982)	725	52
One Shell Plaza, 900 Louisiana St. (1970)	714	50
1400 Smith St. (1983)	691	50
Allen Center, 333 Clay St. (1980)	685	50
One Houston Center, 1221 McKinney St. (1978)	678	47
First City Tower, 1001 Fannin St. (1984)	662	47
San Felipe Plaza, 5847 San Felipe Blvd. (1984)	625	45
Exxon Bldg., 800 Bell Ave. (1962)	606	44
1500 Louisiana St. (2002)	600	40
America Tower, 2929 Allen Parkway (1983)	590	42
Two Houston Center, 909 Fannin St. (1974)	579	40
San Jacinto Column (monument) (1983)	570	NA
Marathon Oil Tower, 5555 San Felipe Blvd. (1983)	562	41
Wedge International Tower, 1415 Louisiana St. (1983)	550	44
Kellogg Tower, 601 Jefferson St. (1973)	550	40
Pennzoil Place 1, 700 Milam St. (1976)	523	36
Pennzoil Place 2, 700 Louisiana St. (1976)	523	36
Devon Energy Center, 1200 Smith St. (1978)	521	36
*1000 Main Street (2003)	518	36
Louisiana Place, 1201 Louisiana Bldg. (1971)	518	35
The Huntington, 2121 Kirby Dr. (1982)	503	34
El Paso Energy Bldg., 1010 Milam St. (1962)	502	33
5 Greenway Plaza (1973)	465	31
*Calpine Center, 717 Texas Ave. (2003)	453	34
One Allen Center, 500 Dallas (1974)	452	34
Four Leafs Towers I, 5100 San Felipe Blvd. (1982)	444	40
Four Leafs Towers II, 5110 San Felipe Blvd. (1982)	444	40
9 Greenway Plaza (1978)	441	31
11 Greenway Plaza (1979)	441	31
Phoenix Tower, 3200 Southwest Fwy. (1984)	434	34
Chase Bank Bldg., 712 Main St. (1929)	428	37
The Spires, 2001 Halcomb Blvd. (1984)	426	41
AON Tower, 4 Oaks Place, 1, 1330 Post Oak Blvd. (1983)	420	30
One City Center, 1001 Main St. (1960)	410	32
Bob Lanier Public Works Bldg., 611 Walker Ave. (1968)	410	27
Neils Esperson Bldg., 802 Travis St. (1927)	410	31
Hyatt Regency, 1200 Lousiana St. (1972)	401	30
The Mercer West Tower, 3288 Sage Rd. (2003)	401	30

Indianapolis, IN

Building	Ht. (ft.)	Stories
Bank One Tower, 111 Monument Circle (1990)	811	49
American United Life Ins., 1 America Sq. (1981)	533	37
One Indiana Square (1970)	504	36
Market Tower, 10 W. Market St. (1988)	421	32
300 N. Meridian Bldg. (1988)	408	28
First Indiana Plaza. 135 N. Pennsylvania St.(1988)	401	31

Jacksonville, FL

Building	Ht. (ft.)	Stories
Bank of America Tower, 50 N. Laura St. (1990)	617	42
Modis Tower, 1 Independent Dr. (1975)	535	37
BellSouth Tower 424 N. Pearl St. (1983)	435	27
Riverplace Tower, 1301 Riverplace Blvd. (1967)	433	28

Jersey City, NJ

Building	Ht. (ft.)	Stories
*30 Hudson St. (2003)	781	42
Merrill Lynch Building, 101 Hudson St. (1992)	548	42
Newport Tower, 525 Washington Blvd. (1990)	528	37
Exchange Place Centre, 10 Exchange Place (1990)	516	32
*Colgate Center, 77 Hudson St. (2003)	491	32
Harborside Financial Plaza 5 (2002)	480	34

Kansas City, MO

Building	Ht. (ft.)	Stories
KCTV Tower (1956)	1,042	NA
One Kansas City Place, 1200 Main St. (1988)	632	42
Transamerica Tower, 1111 Main St. (1986)	591	38
Hyatt Regency, 2345 McGee St. (1980)	504	45
Power & Light Bldg., 1330 Baltimore Ave. (1931)	476	32
City Hall, 414 E. 12th St. (1937)	443	29
Federal Office Bldg., 911 Walnut St. (1931)	433	35
1201 Walnut St. (1991)	427	30
Commerce Tower, 911 Main St. (1965)	407	32
City Center Square, 1100 Main St. (1977)	404	30

Las Vegas, NV

Building	Ht. (ft.)	Stories
Stratosphere Tower, 2000 S. Las Vegas Blvd. (1996)	1,149	NA
Eiffel Tower, Paris Hotel and Casino, 3645 S. Las Vegas Blvd. (1998)	540	NA
New York, New York Hotel and Casino, 3790 S. Las Vegas Blvd. (1997)	525	48
*Le Reve (2005)	514	42
Bellagio Hotel and Casino, 3600 S. Las Vegas Blvd. (1998)	508	36
Mandalay Bay Hotel and Casino, 3950 S. Las Vegas Blvd. (1999)	480	43
Turnberry Place I 2777 Paradise Road (2001)	477	38
Turnberry Place II 2777 Paradise Road (2002)	477	38
*Turnberry Place III 2777 Paradise Road (2003)	477	38
Venetian Resort-Hotel and Casino, 3355 S. Las Vegas Blvd. (1999)	475	35
Caesars Palace Hotel Tower, 3570 S. Las Vegas Blvd. (1998)	470	29
Treasure Island Hotel and Casino, 3300 S. Las Vegas Blvd. (1993)	456	38
Paris Hotel and Casino, 3645 S. Las Vegas Blvd. (1999)	440	34
Rio Masquerade Tower, 3700 W. Flamingo Blvd. (1996)	422	42
Palms Casino Hotel, 4321 W. Flamingo Rd. (2001)	413	42
Aladdin Resort and Casino, 3667 S. Las Vegas Blvd. (2000)	408	39
The Mirage, 3400 S. Las Vegas Blvd. (1989)	400	36
Harrahs Carnaval Tower, 3475 S. Las Vegas Blvd. (1997)	400	35
Fitzgeralds Hotel & Casino, 301 Fremont St. (1980)	400	33

Little Rock, AR

Building	Ht. (ft.)	Stories
TCBY Tower, 425 W. Capitol Ave. (1986)	546	40
Regions Center, 400 W. Capitol Ave. (1975)	454	30

Los Angeles, CA

Building	Ht. (ft.)	Stories
US Bank Tower (Library Tower), 633 W. 5th St. (1990)	1,018	73
Aon Center, 707 Wilshire Blvd. (1974)	858	62
Two California Plaza, 350 S. Grand Ave. (1992)	750	52
Gas Company Tower, 555 W. 5th St. (1991)	749	52
BP Plaza, 333 South Hope St. (1975)	735	55
777 Tower, 777 S. Figueroa St. (1990)	725	53
Wells Fargo Center, 333 S. Grand Ave. (1983)	723	54
Figueroa at Wiltshire, 601 S. Figueroa St. (1989)	717	52
Atlantic Richfield Tower, 515 S. Flower St. (1971)	699	52
Bank of America Tower, 555 S. Flower St. (1971)	699	52
Citibank Center, 444 S. Flower St. (1979)	625	48
611 Place, 611 W. 6th St. (1969)	620	42
One California Plaza, 300 S. Grand Ave. (1985)	578	42
Century Plaza Tower 1, 2029 Cent. Park E. (1973)	571	44
Century Plaza Tower 2, 2049 Cent. Park E. (1973)	571	44
KPMG Tower, 355 S. Grand Ave. (1984)	560	45
Ernst & Young, LLP Plaza, 725 S. Figueroa St. (1986)	534	41
SunAmerica Tower, 1999 Ave. of the Stars (1989)	533	39
TCW Tower, 865 S. Figueroa St. (1990)	517	37
Union Bank Plaza, 445 S. Figueroa St. (1968)	516	40
10 Universal City Plaza (1984)	506	36
1100 Wilshire (1987)	496	36
Fox Plaza, 2121 Ave. of the Stars (1987)	492	34
*Constellation Place, 10250 Constellation Blvd. (2003)	491	35
ARCO Tower 1055 W. 7th St. (1989)	462	33
Equitable Life, 3435 Wilshire Blvd. (1969)	454	34
City Hall, 200 N. Spring St. (1927)	454	28
Transamerica Center, 1150 Olive St. (1965)	452	32
Madison Complex/Pacific Bell Switching Station, 420 S. Grand Ave. (1961)	448	17
Mutual Life Benefit Bldg., 5900 Wilshire Blvd. (1971)	435	32

Building	Ht. (ft.)	Stories
550 S. Hope St. (1991)	423	28
Warner Center Plaza III, 21650 Oxnard St., Woodland Hills (1991)	415	25
MCI Center, 700 S. Flower St. (1973)	414	33

Louisville, KY

Building	Ht. (ft.)	Stories
AEGON Center, 400 W. Market St. (1992)	549	35
National City Tower, 101 S. 5th St. (1972)	512	40
PNC Bank Bldg., 500 W. Jefferson St. (1971)	420	30
Humana Center, 500 W. Main St. (1985)	417	27

Mexico City, Mexico

Building	Ht. (ft.)	Stories
Torre Mayor (2003)	738	55
Torre Pemex (1984)	702	52
Torre Altus (1999)	640	42
Torre Latino Americana (1956)	597	45
World Trade Center, Montecito 38 Col. Napoles (1972)	565	50
Los Arcos Bosques I (1997)	529	34
*Los Arcos Bosques II (2004)	529	34
Torre Las Lomas (1993)	453	36
Hotel Nikko Mexico, Campos Eliseos 24	446	38
Torre del Caballito	443	34
Torre Mural, Insurgentes Sur 1605 (1995)	440	33
Edificio Mexicana de Avincion (1984)	433	30
Presidente Inter-Continental Hotel, Campos Eliseos 218 (1976)	427	42
Torre Dahnos I, Reforma 222 (2003)	427	31
Nonoalco Tlatelolco Tower (1962)	417	25
Torre Reforma, Andres Bello 45	410	28
JW Marriott Hotel, Andres Bello 29	400	27

Miami, FL

Building	Ht. (ft.)	Stories
*Four Seasons Hotel and Tower, 1441 Brickell Ave. (2003)	784	64
Wachovia Financial Center, 200 S. Biscayne Blvd. (1983)	764	55
Bank of America Tower, 100 S. E. 2nd St (1987)	625	47
Santa Maria, 1643 Brickell Ave. (1997)	520	51
Stephen P. Clark Center, 111 NW 1st St. (1985)	510	28
*Jade at Brickell Bay, 1295 Brickell Bay Dr. (2004)	500	48
*Espirito Santo Plaza, 1301 Brickell Ave. (2003)	487	36
Citicorp Tower, 201 S. Biscayne Blvd. (1986)	484	35
Three Tequesta Point, 848 Brickell Key Dr. (2001)	480	46
One Biscayne Tower, 2 S. Biscayne Blvd. (1974)	456	30
701 Brickell Ave. (1986)	450	33
Mellon Financial Center, 1111 Brickell Ave.(2001)	435	31
*Summit Brickell View Condominums, 1200 S. Miami Ave. (2004)	423	37
Mark on Bricknell, 1155 Brickell Bay Dr. (2001)	420	36
Two Tequesta Point, 808 Brickell Key Dr. (1999)	410	40
Courthouse Center, 175 NW First Ave. (1986)	405	30
The Palace, 1541 Brickell Ave. (1982)	400	42

Miami Beach, FL

Building	Ht. (ft.)	Stories
Blue Diamond Tower, 4779 Collins Ave. (2000)	559	44
Green Diamond Tower, 4775 Collins Ave. (2000)	559	44
*Akoya Condominiums, 6365 Collins Ave. (2004)	492	47
PortofinoTower, 1 S. Pointe Dr. (1997)	484	44
The Continuum on South Beach, South Tower (2002)	474	43
Murano Grande at Portofino (2003)	407	37
Murano at Portofino, 1000 S. Pointe Dr. (2001)	402	38

Milwaukee, WI

Building	Ht. (ft.)	Stories
U.S. Bank Center, 777 E. Wisconsin Ave. (1973)	601	42
100 E. Wisconsin Ave (1989)	549	37
Milwaukee Center, 111 E. Kilbourn Ave. (1987)	426	29
411 Bldg., 411 E. Wisconsin Ave. (1983)	408	30

Minneapolis, MN

Building	Ht. (ft.)	Stories
225 South Sixth, 601 2nd Ave. South (1992)	776	56
IDS Center, 80 S. 8th St. (1973)	775	57
Wells Fargo Center, 90 S. 7th St. (1988)	774	57
33 S. 6th St. (1983)	668	52
Campbell Mithun Tower, 222 S. 9th St. (1984)	579	42
Pillsbury Center 1, 200 S. 6th St. (1981)	561	41
Dain Rauscher Plaza, 60 S. 6th St. (1992)	539	40
Fifth Street Towers II, 150 S. 5th St. (1988)	503	36
American Express Tower, 707 2nd Ave. South (2000)	498	31
Target Plaza South, 1000 Nicollet Mall (2001)	492	33
Plaza VII, 45 S. 7th St. (1987)	475	36
US Bancorp Center, 800 Nicollet Mall (2000)	468	32
AT&T Tower, 901 Marquette Ave. (1991)	464	34
Accenture Tower, 333 S. 7th St. (1987)	455	32
Foshay Tower, 821 Marquette Ave. (1929)	447	32
Qwest, 224 S. 5th St. (1931)	416	26
Hennepin Co. Government Center, 300 S. 6th St. (1977)	403	24
Dorsey & Whitney Tower, 50 S. Sixth St. (2001)	401	30

Montreal, Quebec

Building	Ht. (ft.)	Stories
Marathon (IBM), 1250 Blvd. René Lévesque (1992).	743	47
1000 Rue de la Gauchetière (1992)	673	51
Tour de la Bourse, 800 Place Victoria (1963)	624	47
1 Place Villa Marie (1962)	616	42
La Tour CIBC, 1155 Blvd. René Lévesque (1962)	604	43
Montreal Tower (1987)	574	NA
Tour McGill College, 1501 Ave. McGill College (1992)	519	38
Le Complexe Desjardins Sud (1975)	498	40
Les Cooperants, 600 Maisonneuve (1987)	479	34
Place Montreal Trust, 1800 Ave. McGill College (1988)	440	30
Tour TELUS, 630 Blvd. Réné Lévesque (1962)	429	32
Le Complexe Desjardins Est (1975)	428	32
Port Royal Apts., 1455 Sherbrooke Quest (1964)	424	33
Marriott Hotel, 1 Place du Canada (1967)	420	38
Tour de la Banque Nationale, 600 Rue de la Gauchetiere (1983)	420	29
Tour Bell, 700 Rue de la Gauchetiere (1983)	420	28
Centre Mount Royal, 1000 Sherbrooke Quest (1976).	420	28
Tour Terminal, 800 Rene Lévesque Blvd. Quest (1966)	400	30

Nashville, TN

Building	Ht. (ft.)	Stories
BellSouth Tower, 333 Commerce St. (1994)	617	33
Sun Trust Bank, 424 Church St. (1986)	490	31
William R. Snodgrass Tennessee Tower, 311 7th Avenue North (1970)	452	31
Nashville Life & Casualty Tower, 401 Church St. (1957)	409	30
City Center, 511 Union St. (1987)	402	27

Newark, NJ

Building	Ht. (ft.)	Stories
Midatlantic National Bank, 744 Broad St. (1931)	465	36
1180 Raymond Blvd. (1930)	448	34

New Orleans, LA

Building	Ht. (ft.)	Stories
One Shell Square, 701 Poydras St. (1972)	697	51
Bank One Center, 201 St. Charles Ave. (1985)	645	53
Plaza Tower, 1001 Howard Ave. (1969)	531	45
Energy Centre, 1100 Poydras St. (1984)	530	39
LL&E Tower, 901 Poydras St. (1987)	481	36
Sheraton Hotel, 500 Canal St. (1985)	478	47
Marriott Hotel, 555 Canal St. (1972)	450	42
Texaco Bldg., 400 Poydras St. (1983)	442	33
Canal Place One, 365 Canal St. (1979)	439	32
Bank of New Orleans, 1010 Common St. (1971)	438	31
World Trade Center, 2 Canal St. (1965)	407	33
CNG Tower, 1450 Poydras St. (1989)	406	26

New York, NY

Building	Ht. (ft.)	Stories
Empire State Bldg., 350 5th Ave. (1931)	1,250	102
Chrysler Bldg., 405 Lexington Ave. (1930)	1,046	77
American International Bldg., 70 Pine St. (1932)	952	67
The Trump Bldg., 40 Wall St. (1930)	927	71
Citigroup Center, 153 E. 53rd St. (1977)	915	59
Trump World Tower, 845 UN Plaza (2001)	861	72
*Bloomberg Tower, 731 Lexington Ave. (2004)	856	54
G. E. Bldg., 30 Rockefeller Center (1933)	850	70
Cityspire, 150 W. 56th St. (1989)	814	75
One Chase Manhattan Plaza (1960)	813	60
Condé Nast Bldg., 4 Times Square (1999)	809	48
MetLife Bldg., 200 Park Ave. (1963)	808	59
Woolworth Bldg., 233 Broadway (1913)	792	57
1 Worldwide Plaza, 935 8th Ave. (1989)	778	47
Carnegie Hall Tower, 152 W. 57th St. (1991)	757	60
Bear Stearns World Headquarters, 383 Madison Ave. (2001)	757	47
AXA Center West, 787 7th Ave. (1985)	752	51
One Penn Plaza, 250 W. 34th St. (1972)	750	57
*Time Warner Center North Tower (2003)	750	55
*Time Warner Center South Tower (2003)	750	55
1251 Ave. of Americas (1971)	750	54
*7 World Trade Center (2005)	750	52
J.P. Morgan Headquarters, 60 Wall St. (1989)	745	55
1 Liberty Plaza, 165 Broadway (1973)	743	54
20 Exchange Place (1931)	741	57
American Express Tower, Three World Financial Center, 200 Vesey St. (1986)	739	51
One Astor Plaza, 1515 Broadway (1969)	730	54
*Times Square Tower (2003)	696	49
Metropolitan Tower, 142 W. 57th St. (1985)	716	68
J.P. Morgan Chase World Headquarters, 270 Park Ave. (1960)	707	52
General Motors Bldg., 767 5th Ave. (1968)	705	50
Metropolitan Life Tower, 1 Madison Ave. (1909)	700	50
500 5th Ave. (1931)	697	60
Americas Tower, 1177 Ave. of the Amer. (1992)	692	48
Solow Bldg., 9 W. 57th St. (1974)	689	49
HSBC Bank Bldg., 140 Broadway (1966)	688	52
55 Water St. (1972)	687	53
277 Park Ave. (1963)	687	50
1585 Broadway (1989)	685	42
Random House Park Imperial, 1739 Broadway (2003)	684	52
Four Seasons Hotel, 57 E. 57th St. (1993)	682	52
Bertelsmann Bldg., 1540 Broadway (1990)	676	42
McGraw Hill Bldg., 1221 Ave. of Amer. (1972)	674	51
Lincoln Bldg., 60 E. 42nd St. (1930)	673	53
Paramount Plaza, 1633 Broadway (1970)	670	48
Trump Tower, 725 5th Ave. (1982)	664	58
Citicorp, Queens (1990)	658	50
Bank of New York Bldg., 1 Wall St. (1932)	654	50
599 Lexington Ave. (1986)	653	51
712 5th Ave. (1990)	650	53
Chanin Bldg., 122 E. 42nd St. (1929)	649	56
245 Park Ave. (1967)	648	47
Sony Bldg., 550 Madison Ave. (1983)	647	37
Merrill Lynch, Two World Financial Center, 225 Liberty St. (1986)	645	44
RCA Victor Bldg., 570 Lexington Ave. (1930)	642	50
One New York Plaza, 1 Water St. (1969)	640	50
1 Dag Hammarskjold Plaza, 885 2nd Ave. (1972)	637	48
345 Park Ave. (1968)	634	44
Grace Plaza, 1114 Ave. of the Amer. (1972)	630	50
Home Insurance Co., 59 Maiden Lane (1966)	630	44
Verizon Tower, 1095 Ave. of the Amer. (1970)	630	40
101 Park Ave. (1982)	629	49
Central Park Place, 301 W. 57th St. (1988)	628	56
888 7th Ave. (1971)	628	45
Alliance Capital Bldg., 1345 Ave. of the Amer. (1969)	625	50
Waldorf-Astoria, 301 Park Ave. (1931)	625	47
Trump Palace, 200 E. 69th St. (1991)	623	55
Olympic Tower, 645 5th Ave. (1976)	620	51
Mercantile Bldg., 10 E. 40th St. (1929)	620	48
*425 Fifth Avenue (2003)	618	55
919 Third Ave. (1970)	615	47
750 7th Ave. (1989)	615	35
New York Life, 51 Madison Ave. (1928)	615	33
Tower 49, 12 E. 49th St. (1985)	614	44
Credit Lyonnais Bldg., 1301 Ave. of the Amer. (1964)	609	46
IBM, 590 Madison Ave. (1983)	603	41
*Hearst Tower, 959 8th Avenue, (2006)	596	42
3 Lincoln Center, 160 W. 66th St. (1993)	595	60
Celanese Bldg., 1211 Ave. of the Amer. (1973)	592	45
Rihga Royal Hotel, 151 W. 54th St. (1990)	590	54
U.S. Court House, 505 Pearl St. (1927)	590	37
Millenium Hilton Hotel, 55 Church St. (1992)	588	58
Museum Tower Apts., 21 W. 53rd St. (1985)	588	52
Time-Life, 1271 Ave. of the Amer. (1959)	587	48
Jacob K. Javits Federal Bldg., 26 Federal Plaza (1967)	587	41
W Times Square, 1567 Broadway (2000)	584	53
Stevens Tower, 1185 Ave. of Amer. (1971)	580	42
Municipal Bldg., 1 Centre St. (1914)	580	34
Trump International Hotel & Tower (1970)	579	44
100 UN Plaza, 327 E. 48th St. (1986)	557	52
520 Madison Ave. (1981)	577	43
Oppenheimer & Co., 1 World Financial Ctr., 200 Liberty St. (1985)	577	37
Merchandise Mart, 41 Madison Ave. (1973)	576	42
Park Ave. Plaza, 55 E. 52nd St. (1981)	575	44
Lehman Building, 745 7th Ave., (2001)	575	38
One Financial Square, 33 Old Slip (1987)	575	37
Ernst & Young Tower, 5 Times Sq., 580 7th Ave. (2002)	574	40
Marriott Marquis Times Square, 1531 Broadway (1985)	574	50
Westavco Bldg., 299 Park Ave. (1967)	574	42
1166 Ave. of the Americas (1974)	572	44
Socony Mobil, 150 E. 42nd Street (1956)	572	42
Wang Bldg., 780 3rd Ave. (1983)	570	49
AXA Finance Center, 1290 Ave. of the Amer. (1963)	570	43
600 3rd Ave. (1971)	570	42
450 Lexington Ave. (1991)	568	38
Paramount Tower, 240 E. 39th St. (1998)	567	51
Deutsche Bank, 130 Liberty St. (1974)	565	40
Helmsley Bldg., 230 Park Ave. (1928)	565	35
New York Palace Hotel, 455 Madison Ave. (1980)	563	51
30 Broad St. (1932)	562	48
Park Ave. Tower, 65 E. 55th St. (1986)	561	36
Nelson Tower, 450 7th Ave. (1931)	560	46
Sherry-Netherland, 781 5th Ave. (1927)	560	40
Swiss Bank Tower, 10 E. 50th St. (1990)	560	36
Continental Can, 633 3rd Ave. (1962)	557	39
3 Park Ave. (1975)	556	42
Continental Corp., 180 Maiden Lane (1983)	555	41
Sperry & Hutchinson, 330 Madison Ave. (1964)	555	41
Reuters Bldg., 3 Times Square (2001)	555	30
Madison Belvedere, 14 E. 29th St. (1999)	554	48
Inmont Bldg., 1133 Ave. of the Amer. (1970)	552	45
Equitable Trust Co. Bldg., 15 Broad St. (1927)	551	42
Biltmore Tower, 267 W. 45th St. (2003)	550	51
Burroughs Bldg., 605 3rd Ave. (1963)	550	44
Bell Atlantic, 33 Thomas St. (1974)	550	29
Two Grand Central Tower, 140 E. 45th St. (1982)	550	44

Oklahoma City, OK

Building	Ht. (ft.)	Stories
Bank One Center, 100 N. Broadway Ave. (1971)	500	36
First National Center, 120 N. Robinson St. (1931)	493	33
City Place Tower, 204 N. Robinson St. (1931)	440	32
Oklahoma Tower, 210 Park Ave. (1982)	434	31

Omaha, NE

Building	Ht. (ft.)	Stories
The Tower at First National Center, 1601 Dodge St. (2002)	634	45
Woodmen Tower, 1700 Farnam St. (1969)	478	30

Orlando, FL

Building	Ht. (ft.)	Stories
SunTrust Center Tower, 200 S. Orange Ave. (1988)	441	31
Orange County Courthouse, 425 N. Orange Ave. (1997)	416	24
Bank of America Center, 390 N. Orange Ave. (1988)	409	28

Philadelphia, PA

Building	Ht. (ft.)	Stories
One Liberty Place, 1650 Market St. (1987)	945	61
Two Liberty Place, 1601 Chestnut St. (1989)	848	58
Mellon Bank Center, 1735 Market St. (1990)	792	54
Bell Atlantic Tower, 1717 Arch St. (1991)	725	53
Blue Cross Tower, 1901 Market St. (1990)	625	45
Commerce Square #1, 2005 Market St. (1990)	572	40
Commerce Square #2, 2001 Market St. (1992)	572	40
City Hall (incl. statue) (1901)	548	7
*The St. James, 700 Walnut St. (2004)	501	47
1818 Market St. (1974)	500	40
Lowes Philadelphia Hotel, 12 S. 12th St. (1932)	492	39
PNC, 1600 Market St. (1983)	491	40
Centre Square II, 1542 Market St. (1973)	490	38
5 Penn Center (1970)	488	36
1700 Market St. (1969)	482	32
Philadelphia National Bank, 1 S. Broad St. (1930)	475	34
Two Logan Square, 100 N. 18th St. (1988)	435	34
2000 Market St. (1973)	435	29
11 Penn Center, 1835 Market St. (1985)	430	29
Aramark Tower, 1101 Market St. (1984)	417	31
Centre Square, 1500 Market St. (1973)	416	32
First Union Bank, 123 S. Broad St. (1927)	405	30
Ritz-Carlton Hotel, 28 S. Broad St. (1930)	404	30
Lewis Tower, 1419 Locust St. (1929)	400	33
One Logan Square, 130 N. 18th St. (1982)	400	32

Phoenix, AZ

Building	Ht. (ft.)	Stories
Bank One Center, 201 N. Central (1972)	486	40
101 N. Second Ave. (1976)	407	31

Pittsburgh, PA

Building	Ht. (ft.)	Stories
USX Tower, 600 Grant St. (1970)	841	64
One Mellon Bank Center, 500 Grant St. (1983)	725	54
One PPG Place, 120 5th Avenue (1984)	635	40
Fifth Ave. Place, 120 5th Ave. (1987)	616	32
One Oxford Centre, 301 Grant St. (1982)	615	46
Gulf Tower, 707 Grant St. (1932)	582	44
Univ. of Pittsburgh Cath. of Learning, 4200 5th Ave. (1936)	535	42
3 Mellon Bank Center, 525 Wm. Penn Way (1951)	520	41
Freemarket Center, 210 6th Ave. (1968)	511	40
Grant Bldg., 330 Grant St. (1928)	485	40
Koppers Bldg., 436 7th Ave. (1929)	475	34
2 PNC Plaza, 620 Liberty Ave. (1976)	445	34
Dominion Tower, 625 Liberty Ave. (1987)	430	32
One PNC Plaza, 249 5th Avenue (1972)	424	30
Regional Enterprise Tower, 425 6th Ave. (1953)	410	30

Portland, OR

Building	Ht. (ft.)	Stories
Wells Fargo Tower, 1300 SW 5th Ave. (1973)	546	40
U.S. Bancorp Tower, 111 SW 5th Ave. (1983)	536	42
Koin Tower Plaza, 2225 W. Columbia St. (1984)	509	31
Pacwest Center, 1211 SW 5th Ave. (1984)	418	30

Providence, RI

Building	Ht. (ft.)	Stories
Fleet Bank Bldg., 55 Exchange Pl. (1927)	428	26
Fleet Boston Tower, Kennedy Plaza (1973)	410	28

Richmond, VA

Building	Ht. (ft.)	Stories
James Monroe Bldg., 101 N. Virginia St. (1981)	449	29
SunTrust Plaza, 919 E. Main St. (1984)	400	24

Rochester, NY

Building	Ht. (ft.)	Stories
Xerox Tower (1968)	443	30
Bausch & Lomb Place (1995)	401	20

St. Louis, MO

Building	Ht. (ft.)	Stories
Gateway Arch (1965)	630	NA
Metropolitan Square Tower, 211 N. Broadway (1988)	593	42
One Bell Center, 900 Pine St. (1984)	588	44
Thomas F. Eagleton Fed. Courthouse, 111 S. 10th St. (2000)	557	29
U.S. Bank Plaza, 505 N. 7th St. (1976)	484	35
Laclede Gas Bldg., 720 Olive St. (1969)	400	31

St. Paul, MN

Building	Ht. (ft.)	Stories
Minnesota World Trade Center, 30 E. 7th St. (1987)	471	36
Galtier Plaza Jackson Tower, 168 E. 6th St. (1986)	453	46
First National Bank, 332 Minnesota St. (1930)	417	32

Salt Lake City, UT

Building	Ht. (ft.)	Stories
Wells Fargo Center, 299 S. Main St. (1998)	422	24
L.D.S. Church Office Bldg., 50 E. North Temple St. (1972)	420	28

San Antonio, TX

Building	Ht. (ft.)	Stories
Tower of the Americas, 600 Hemisphere Way (1968)	622	NA
Marriott Rivercenter, 101 Bowie St. (1988)	546	38
Weston Centre, 112 Pecan St. (1988)	444	32
Tower Life, 310 S. St. Mary's St. (1929)	404	30

San Diego, CA

Building	Ht. (ft.)	Stories
One American Plaza, 600 W. Broadway (1991)	500	34
Symphony Towers, 759 B St. (1989)	499	34
Manchester Grand Hyatt, One Market Pl. (1992)	497	40
Emerald Plaza, 400 W. Broadway (1990)	450	30
One and Two Harbor Drive (2 bldgs.), 100 Harbor Dr. (1992)	424	41

Sandy Springs, GA

Building	Ht. (ft.)	Stories
Concourse Tower V, 5 Concourse Pkwy. (1988)	570	34
Concourse Tower VI, 6 Concourse Pkwy. (1991)	553	34

San Francisco, CA

Building	Ht. (ft.)	Stories
Transamerica Pyramid, 600 Montgomery St. (1972)	853	48
Bank of America, 555 California St. (1969)	779	52
345 California Center (1986)	695	48
101 California St. (1986)	600	48
50 Fremont Center (1983)	600	43
Chevron Tower, 575 Market St. (1975)	573	40
Four Embarcadero Center, 55 Clay St. (1984)	570	45
One Embarcadero Center, 355 Clay St. (1970)	569	45
Spear Tower, 1 Market St. (1976)	565	42
Wells Fargo, 44 Montgomery St. (1967)	565	43
Citicorp Center, 1 Sansome St. (1984)	550	39
Shaklee Terrace Bldg., 444 Market St. (1979)	537	38
One Post Plaza, 1 Post St. (1969)	529	38
525 Market St. (1972)	529	38
One Metro Plaza, 425 Market St. (1973)	524	38
Pacific Telesis Center, 1 Montgomery St. (1982)	500	38
333 Bush St. (1986)	495	43
Hilton Hotel, 201 Mason St. (1971)	493	46
Pacific Gas & Electric, 77 Beale St. (1970)	492	34
50 California St. (1972)	487	37
*St. Regis Museum Tower (2003)	484	42
100 Pine Center (1972)	476	34
Bechtel Bldg., 45 Fremont St. (1979)	475	34
333 Market Bldg. (1979)	474	33
Hartford Bldg., 650 California St. (1965)	465	33
100 First Plaza (1988)	447	37
One California St. (1969)	438	32
Marriott Hotel, 777 Market St. (1989)	436	39
Russ Bldg., 235 Montgomery St. (1927)	435	32
Pacific Bell Headquarters, 140 Montgomery St. (1925)	435	26
J.P. Morgan Chase Bldg. (2002)	420	31
Paramount, 680 Mission St. (2002)	418	41
Providian Financial Bldg., 201 Mission St. (1983)	416	30
Two Embarcadero Center, 255 Clay St.(1974)	413	30
Three Embarcadero Center, 155 Clay St. (1976)	413	31
595 Market Bldg. (1977)	410	31
123 Mission Bldg. (1986)	406	28
Embarcadero Center West, 275 Battery St. (1988)	405	33
101 Montgomery St. (1983)	405	29

Seattle, WA

Building	Ht. (ft.)	Stories
Bank of America Tower, 701 5th Ave. (1985)	967	76
Two Union Square, 600 Union St. (1989)	740	56
Washington Mutual Tower, 1201 3rd Ave. (1988)	735	55
Key Tower, 700 5th Ave. (1990)	722	49
1001 Fourth Avenue Plaza (1969)	609	50
Space Needle, 203 6th Ave. (1962)	605	NA
U.S. Bank Centre, 1420 5th Ave. (1989)	580	44
Wells Fargo Center, 999 3rd Ave. (1983)	574	47
800 Fifth Avenue Plaza (1981)	543	42
Security Pacific Bank, 900 4th Ave. (1973)	536	41
Rainier Tower, 1301 5th Ave. (1977)	514	31
IDX Tower, 915 4th Ave. (2003)	512	40
1000 2nd Ave. (1986)	493	40
Henry M. Jackson Bldg., 915 2nd Ave. (1974)	487	37
Qwest Plaza, 1600 7th Ave. (1976)	466	36
Smith Tower, 506 2nd Ave. (1914)	465	38
One Union Square, 600 University Ave. (1981)	456	36
1111 3rd Ave. (1980)	454	34
Westin Hotel North Tower, 1900 5th Ave. (1982)	448	44
Westin Bldg., 2001 6th Ave. (1981)	409	34

Southfield, MI

Building	Ht. (ft.)	Stories
Prudential, 3000 Town Center (1975)	448	32
1000 Town Center (1988)	405	32

Sunny Isles Beach, FL

Building	Ht. (ft.)	Stories
*Trump Palace, 18101 Collins Ave. (2005)	551	43
*Aqualina, 17875 Collins Ave. (2004)	550	51
The Pinnacle, 17555 Collins Ave. (1999)	476	40
Ocean Two, 19111 Collins Ave. (2001)	426	40
*Ocean Three, 18925 Collins Ave. (2004)	405	37

Tampa, FL

Building	Ht. (ft.)	Stories
AmSouth Bldg., 100 N. Tampa St. (1992)	579	42
Bank of America Plaza, 101 E. Kennedy Blvd. (1986)	577	42
One Tampa City Center, 201 N. Franklin St. (1981)	537	39
Suntrust Financial Center, 401 E. Jackson St. (1992)	525	36
First Financial Tower, 400 N. Tampa St. (1973)	458	36
400 N. Ashley Plaza. 400 N. Ashley Dr. (1988)	454	33

Toledo, OH

Building	Ht. (ft.)	Stories
One SeaGate (1982)	411	32
HyTower, 200 N. St. Clair St. (1970)	400	30

Toronto, Ontario

Building	Ht. (ft.)	Stories
CN Tower, 301 Front St. W (1976)	1,815	NA
First Canadian Place, 100 King St. West (1975)	978	72
Scotia Plaza, 40 King St. West (1989)	902	68
BCE Place, Canada Trust Tower, 161 Bay St. (1990)	856	53
Commerce Court West, 199 Bay St. (1973)	784	57
TD Tower—Toronto Dominion Bank Tower. 66 Wellington St. West (1967)	730	56
BCE Place, Bay-Wellington Tower, 181 Bay St. (1991)	679	49
Royal Trust Tower, 77 King St. W. (1969)	600	46
*1 King West (2004)	578	51
Royal Bank Plaza–South Tower, 200 Bay St. (1976)	567	41
Manulife Centre, 44 Charles St. West (1974)	545	51
TD Centre–79 Wellington St. West (1985)	504	39
The 250, 250 Yonge St. (1991)	494	35
Two Bloor West (1974)	488	34
Simcoe Place, 200 Front St. (1995)	486	33
Exchange Tower, 130 King St. West (1983)	480	30
CIBC-Commerce Court North. 25 King St. West (1931)	477	34
Simpson Tower, 401 Bay St. (1968)	473	33
Cadillac-Fairview Tower, 20 Queen St. West (1982)	465	36

Building	Ht. (ft.)	Stories
Pantages Tower (2003)	458	45
One Palace Pier Court, Etobicoke (1991)	424	31
Palace Pier, 2405 Lakeshore Blvd. West (1978)	453	46
Continental Bank, 130 Adelaide St. West (1980)	453	35
Sheraton Centre, 123 Queen St. West (1972)	443	43
Two Bloor St. East (1974)	439	35
Royal York Hotel. 200 Front Street (1929)	439	26
Ernst & Young Tower, 222 Bay St. (1990)	424	31
One Financial Place (1991)	450	32
Leaside Towers (2 bldgs.), 95 Thorncliffe Park Dr. (1970)	423	44
Canadian Pacific Tower, 100 Wellington St. West (1974)	420	32
Metro Hall West, 55 John St. (1991)	420	27
Marriott Hotel/Plaza 2 Apts., 90 Bloor St. East (1973)	415	41
Sun Life Financial Center East Tower, 150 King St. West (1981)	410	27
Young-Eglington Centre–Triathlon Tower, 2300 Younge St. (1975)	408	30

Tulsa, OK

Building	Ht. (ft.)	Stories
Williams Center, 1 W. 2nd St. (1975)	667	52
Cityplex Central Tower, 2448 E. 81st St. (1981)	648	60
First National Bank, 15 E. 5th St. (1973)	516	41
Mid-Continent Tower, 401 S. Boston St. (1984)	513	36
Fourth National Bank, 15 W. 6th St. (1966)	412	33
National Bank of Tulsa, 320 S. Boston St. (1918)	400	24

Vancouver, British Columbia

Building	Ht. (ft.)	Stories
One Wall Centre, 1000 Burrard St. (2001)	491	45
*Shaw Tower, 298 Thurlow St. (2004)	489	40
200 Granville Square (1973)	466	32
Royal Bank Tower, 1055 W. Georgia St. (1973)	461	37
Park Place, 666 Burrard St. (1984)	459	35
Bentall IV Canada Trust, 1055 Dunsmir (1981)	454	36
Scotia Tower, 650 W. Georgia St. (1977)	452	36
Harbour Centre, 555 W. Hastings (1977)	426	28
Toronto Dominion Bank Tower, 700 W. Georgia St. (1970)	417	30
Bentall III, Bank of Montreal, 595 Burrard St. (1974)	400	31

Winnipeg, Manitoba

Building	Ht. (ft.)	Stories
Toronto Dominion Centre, 201 Portage Ave. (1990)	420	33
Richardson Bldg., 1 Lombard Place (1969)	406	34

Winston-Salem, NC

Building	Ht. (ft.)	Stories
Wachovia Center, 100 N. Main St. (1995)	460	34
301 N. Main St. (1965)	410	27

> **IT'S A FACT:** After the 164-foot-high Cairo apartment building was erected on Q Street in 1894, towering well above neighboring buildings in Washington, DC, Congress passed the 1899 Height of Buildings Act, stipulating that no private building in the city could ever be higher than the Capitol. The law has been modified over the years, and 4 public buildings are actually higher—2 cathedrals, the Old Post Office, and (highest of all, at 555 feet) the Washington Monument. Still, at 288 feet, the Capitol is a lofty and imposing sight in a city of not very tall buildings.

Other Tall Buildings in North American Cities

Building		Ht. (ft.)	Stories
Erastus Corning II Tower (1973)	Albany, NY	589	44
San Jacinto Monument (1936)	La Porte, TX	570	NA
Washington Monument (1884)	Washington, DC	555	NA
Dataflux Tower (2000)	Monterrey, Mexico.	549	43
One HSBC Center (1970)	Buffalo, NY	529	40
Vehicle Assembly Bldg. (1965)	Cape Canaveral, FL	525	40
*Frost Bank Tower (2004)	Austin, TX	516	33
Mohegan Sun Hotel (2002)	Uncasville, CT	487	34
Borgata Hotel and Casino (2003)	Atlantic City, NJ.	480	40
State Capitol (1932)	Baton Rouge, LA.	460	34
Burbank Tower, 2900 W. Burbank (1988)	Burbank, CA	460	32
*Los Olas River House 1 (2004)	Ft. Lauderdale, FL.	452	42
*One Lincoln Tower (2003)	Bellevue, WA	450	42
The Diplomat (2001)	Hollywood, FL	444	39
Ravinia #3 (1991)	Dunwoody, GA	444	34
One Summit Square (1981)	Fort Wayne, IN	442	27
Anadarko Tower (2002)	The Woodlands, TX	439	32
AmSouth/Harbert Plaza (1989).	Birmingham, AL.	437	32
The Palisades (2001)	Fort Lee, NJ	434	42
BBT/Two Hanover Square (1991).	Raleigh, NC.	431	29
Union Planters Bank, 100 N. Main (1965)	Memphis, TN.	430	38
Taj Mahal, 1000 Boardwalk (1990)	Atlantic City, NJ.	429	43
Torre Commercial America (1994).	Monterrey, Mexico.	427	35
AmSouth Bank Bldg. (1969)	Mobile, AL	424	33
Wells Fargo Center (1991)	Sacramento, CA	423	30
Plaza Tower (1986)	Knoxville, TN.	422	30
Century 21	Hamilton, Ont.	418	43

Building		Ht. (ft.)	Stories
Oakbrook Terrace Tower (1985)	Oakbrook, IL	418	31
Hidden Bay 1 (2000)	Aventura, FL	417	40
Galaxie Apts. (3 bldgs.) (1976)	Guttenberg, NJ	415	44
Complexe G (1972)	Quebec City, Que.	415	33
AmSouth Bank Bldg. (1996)	Montgomery, AL.	415	24
*Lincoln Square (2003)	Bellevue, WA	412	28
One Shoreline Plaza, South Tower (1988)	Corpus Christi, TX.	411	28
Silver Legacy Hotel & Casino, 407 N. Virginia St. (1995)	Reno, NV	410	38
AutoNation Tower (1988)	Ft. Lauderdale, FL.	410	30
Financial Center (1986)	Lexington, KY	410	30
Clark Tower (1972)	Memphis, TN.	410	33
Plaza in Clayton (2002)	Clayton, MO	409	30
Kettering Tower (1970)	Dayton, OH	408	30
Wells Fargo Center (1991)	Sacramento, CA	404	30
Ordway Bldg. (1985)	Oakland, CA	404	28
Three Lakeway Center (1987)	Metairie, LA.	403	34
Monarch Place (1987)	Springfield, MA	400	26
Bank of America (1990)	St. Petersburg, FL.	400	26

IT'S A FACT: The total length of wire used in the two main cables that support the Golden Gate Bridge is equal to approximately 80,000 miles.

Notable Bridges in North America

Source: Federal Highway Administration, Bridge Division, U.S. Dept. of Transportation; World Almanac research

Asterisk (*) designates railroad bridge. Year is date of completion. Span of a bridge is the distance between its supports.

Suspension

Year	Bridge	Location	Main span (ft.)
1964	Verrazano-Narrows	New York, NY	4,260
1937	Golden Gate	San Fran. Bay, CA	4,200
1957	Mackinac Straits	Sts. of Mackinac, MI	3,800
1931	Geo. Washington	Hudson R., NY–NJ	3,500
1940	Tacoma Narrows	Tacoma, WA	2,800
1950	Tacoma Narrows II	Tacoma, WA	2,800
1936	San. Fran.-Oakland Bay[1]	San Fran. Bay, CA	2,310
1939	Bronx-Whitestone	East R., NY	2,300
1970	Pierre Laporte	Quebec, Canada	2,190
1951	Del. Memorial	Wilmington, DE	2,150
1957	Walt Whitman	Philadelphia, PA	2,000
1929	Ambassador	Detroit, MI–Can.	1,850
1961	Throgs Neck	Long Is. Sound, NY	1,800
1926	Benjamin Franklin	Philadelphia, PA	1,750
1924	Bear Mt.	Hudson R., NY	1,632
1903	Williamsburg	East R., NY	1,600
1952	Wm. Preston La. Mem.[2]	Sandy Point, MD	1,600
1969	Newport	Narragansett Bay, RI	1,600
1883	Brooklyn	East R., NY	1,595
1939	Lion's Gate	Burrard Inlet, BC	1,550
1930	Mid-Hudson	Poughkeepsie, NY	1,500
1963	Vincent Thomas	L. A. Harbor, CA	1,500
1909	Manhattan	East R., NY	1,470
1955	MacDonald Bridge	Halifax, Nova Scotia	1,447
1970	A. Murray Mackay	Halifax, Nova Scotia	1,400
1936	Triborough Br.,QB Mainline	East R., NY	1,380
1931	St. Johns	Portland, OR	1,207
1929	Mount Hope	RI	1,200
1960	Ogdensburg	St. Lawrence R., NY	1,150
1965	Bidwell Bar Bridge	Oroville, CA	1,108
1964	Middle Fork Feather	CA	1,105
1939	Deer Isle	ME	1,080
1931	Simon Kenton Memorial	Ohio R., Maysville, KY	1,060
1936	Ile d'Orleans	St. Lawrence R., Quebec	1,059
1867	John A. Roebling	Ohio R., KY	1,057
1971	Dent	Clearwater Co., ID	1,050
1900	Miampimi	Mexico	1,030
1849	Wheeling	Ohio R., WV	1,010
1949	Rte. 55	Mississippi R., AR–TN	790
1910	*P&LE RR Bridge	Ohio R., PA	750
1930	Coal Grove Bridge	Ashland-Coal Grove Bridge, OH	739
1922	Ohio River, N&W RR	Ironton-Russell Bridge, OH.	725
1932	Bi-State Vietnam Gold Star	Henderson, KY	720
1979	I-275	Ohio R., Fort Thomas, KY.	720
1926	Columbia R.	Cascade Locks, OR	706
1964	John F. Kennedy (I-65)	Ohio R., Louisville, KY	700
1928	Ohio River, B&O RR, HV RR.	Pomeroy-Mason, OH	657
1943	*Pit River	Redding, CA	620
1941	Columbia R.	Kettle Falls, WA	600
1954	Columbia R.	Umatilla, OR	600
1965	Bi-State Vietnam Gold Star	Henderson , KY	600
1954	Columbia R.	The Dalles, OR	576
1968	W. 17th St.	Huntington, WV	562

Cantilever

Year	Bridge	Location	Main span (ft.)
1917	Québec Bridge	St. Lawrence R., Quebec	1,800
1988	Greater New Orleans Bridge	Mississippi R., New Orleans, LA	1,575
1995	Gramercy Bridge	Mississippi R., Gramercy, LA	1,460
1936	Transbay	San Fran. Bay, CA	1,400
1968	Baton Rouge Bridge	Mississippi R., Baton Rouge, LA	1,235
1955	Tappan Zee	Hudson R., NY	1,212
1930	Lewis and Clark	Longview, WA–OR	1,200
1909	Queensboro	East R., NY	1,182
1927	Carquinez Strait	CA	1,100
1958	Parallel Span	CA	1,100
1930	Jacques Cartier	Montreal, Quebec	1,097
1968	Isaiah D. Hart	Jacksonville, FL	1,088
1956	Richmond[3]	San Fran. Bay, CA	1,070
1929	Grace Memorial	Charleston, SC	1,050
1980	Newburgh-Beacon	Hudson R., NY	1,000
1949	Martin Luther King	St. Louis, MO.	963
1975	Caruthersville	Mississippi R., MO–TN	920
1969	Silver Memorial	Pt. Pleasant, WV–OH	900
1977	Saint Marys	Saint Marys, WV–OH	900
1981	Ravenswood	WV	900
1987	Carl Perkins	Ohio R., KY	900
1941	Mississippi R.	Natchez, MS	875
1988	Mississippi R.	Natchez, MS	875
1938	Blue Water	Pt. Huron, MI	871
1972	Mississippi R.	Vicksburg, MS	870
1972	N. Fork American R.	Auburn, CA	862
1940	*Baton Rouge	Mississippi R., LA	848
1899	*Cornwall	St. Lawrence R.	843
1940	Rte. 82	Mississippi R., AR.	840
1961	Mississippi R.	Greenville, MS	840
1963	Brent Spence	KY–OH	830
1940	Mississippi R.	Vicksburg, MS	825
1963	Mississippi R.	Donaldsonville, LA.	825
1931	Mississippi R.	Vicksburg, MS	824
1929	Clark Memorial	Ohio R., KY	820
1961	Campbellton-Cross Pt.	New Brunswick, Can.	815
1932	Washington Mem.	Seattle, WA	800
1935	Rip Van Winkle	Catskill, NY	800
1938	Cairo	Ohio R., IL–KY	800
1936	McCullough	Coos Bay, OR	793
1949	Memphis	Mississippi R., TN	790
1935	Huey P. Long[4]	New Orleans, LA	790

Simple Truss

Year	Bridge	Location	Main span (ft.)
1976	Chester	Chester, WV	745
1929	Irvin S. Cobb	Ohio R., IL–KY	716
1922	*Tanana R.	Nenana, AK	700
1967	I-77, Ohio R.	Williamstown, WV	650
1917	MacArthur[4]	St. Louis, IL–MO	647
1992	St. Charles	Missouri R, MO	625
1933	Atchafalaya	Morgan City, LA	608
1924	*Castleton	Hudson R., NY	598
1937	Delaware R.	Easton, PA.	550
1930	Swindell Bridge	Pittsburgh, PA	545
1952	Allegheny R. Tpk.	Pittsburgh, PA	534
1951	Rankin	Pittsburgh, PA	525
1914	Old Brownsville	Brownsville, PA	520
1906	Donora-Webster	Donora-Webster, PA	515
1909	Hulton	Pittsburgh, PA	505
1967	Tanana R.	AK	500

Steel Truss

Year	Bridge	Location	Main span (ft.)
1988	Glade Creek	Raleigh Co., WV	784
1973	Atchafalaya R.	Krotz Springs, LA	780
1972	Piscataqua R.	NH–ME	756
1972	Atchafalaya R.	Simmesport, LA	720
1957	SR-3, Rappahannock R.	Middlesex Co., VA	648
1978	Atchafalaya R.	Morgan City, LA	607
1959	Summit	Summit, DE	600
1969	Reedy Point.	Delaware City, DE	600
1937	US-22	Delaware R., NJ	550
1955	Interstate (I-5)	Columbia R., OR–WA	531
1910	McKinley, St. Louis[4]	Mississippi R., MO	517
1972	Mississippi R.	Muscatine, IA	512
1896	Newport	Ohio R., KY	511
1989	US 190, Atchafalaya R.	Krotz Springs, LA	506
1900	Norfolk Southern RR	Cincinnati, OH.	500
1931	Lucy Jefferson Lewis	Cumberland, KY	500
1958	Lake Oahe	Gettysburg, SD	500
1958	Lake Oahe	Mobridge, SD	500
1970	Lake Koocanusa	Lincoln Co., MT	500

Continuous Truss

Year	Bridge	Location	Main span (ft.)
1966	Columbia R. (Astoria)	OR–WA	1,232
1976	Francis Scott Key	Baltimore, MD	1,200
1981	Ravenswood/Ohio R.	Ravenswood, WV	902
1995	Central	Ohio R., KY–OH	850
1943	Dubuque	Mississippi R., IA	845
1966	Charles Braga	Fall River, MA	840
1956	Earl C. Clements[5]	Ohio R., IL–KY	825
1929	U.S. 31	Ohio R., IN–KY	820
1953	John E. Mathews	Jacksonville, FL	810
1950	Maurice J. Tobin	Boston, MA.	801
1940	Gov. Nice Memorial	Potomac River, MD	800
1957	Kingston-Rhinecliff	Hudson R., NY	800
1992	Mark Clark Expy. I-526	Cooper R., Charleston, SC.	800
1986	Rochester-Monaca	Rochester-Monaca, PA.	780
1940	U.S. 231	Ohio R., IN	750
1974	Carroll L. Cropper (I-275)	Ohio R., IN–KY	750
1981	Sewickley	Sewickley, PA	750
1984	13th St. Bridge, Ohio R.	Ashland, KY	740
1959	Monaca-E. Rochester	Monaca-E. Rochester, PA.	730
1976	Betsy Ross	Philadelphia, PA	729
1929	U.S. 421	Ohio R., IN–KY	727
1967	Matthew E. Welsh (SR135)	Mauckport, IN	725
1962	U.S. 41	Ohio R., IN–KY	720
1994	6th St.	Huntington, WV	720
1970	Vanport	Vanport, PA	715
1962	Champlain	Montreal, Que.	707
1962	John F. Kennedy (I-65)	Ohio R., IN–KY	701
1973	Girard Point	Philadelphia, PA	700

Year	Bridge	Location	Main span (ft.)
1954	PA Tpk., Delaware R.	Philadelphia, PA.	682
1938	Rainbow Br., Neches R.	Port Arthur-Orange, TX	680
1949	George Platt	Philadelphia, PA.	680
1926	Cape Girardeau	Mississippi R., MO.	677
1946	Chester	Mississippi R, IL	670
1994	Williamstown-Marietta	Williamstown, WV	650
1955	Jefferson City.	Missouri R., MO.	640
1930	Quincy Memorial Bridge	Mississippi R., IL.	628
1959	US 181. over harbor	Corpus Christi, TX	620
1961	Shippingport	Shippingport, PA	620
1935	Bourne-Sagamore	Cape Cod Canal, MA	616
1965	Clarion R. (i-80).	Clarion, PA.	612
1975	Donora-Monessen	Donora-Monessen, PA.	608
1957	Blatnik	Duluth, MN	600
1965	Rio Grande Gorge	Taos, NM	600
1991	Hoffstadt Creek	Mt. St. Helens, WA	600
1991	Jefferson City.	Missouri R., MO.	596
1962	W. Branch Feather R.	Oroville, CA	576
1967	Glenwood	Pittsburgh, PA	567
1936	Mark Twain Mem.	Hannibal, MO	562
1932	Pulaski Skyway	Passaic R.-Hackensack R., NJ	550
1966	Emlenton	Emlenton, PA.	540
1973	Gold Star Memorial	New London, CT	540
1936	Homestead High Level	Pittsburgh, PA	534
1959	Martinez.	Benicia-Martinez, CA.	528
1960	Brownsville High Level.	Brownsville, PA	518
1971	Grandad.	Elk River, ID.	504
1945	Mansfield-Dravosburg	Pittsburgh, PA	500

Continuous Box and Plate Girder

Year	Bridge	Location	Main span (ft.)
1967	San Mateo-Hayward #2.	San Fran. Bay, CA	750
1976	Intracoastal Canal	Forked Is., LA	750
1977	Intracoastal Canal	Gibbstown, LA	750
1969	San Diego-Coronado[8]	San Diego Bay, CA	660
1987	Umatilla, Columbia R.	OR–WA	660
1994	Acosta	Jacksonville, FL	630
1981	Douglas	Juneau, AK	620
1976	Wax L. Outlet.	Calumet, LA.	618
1963	Poplar St.	St. Louis, MO.	600
1981	Glenn Jackson (I-205)	Columbia R., OR–WA	600
1976	Stanislaus River.	Sonora, CA	580
1982	Illinois R.	Pekin, IL.	550
1982	I-440	Arkansas R., AR	540
1980	US-64, Tennessee R.	Savannah, TN	525
1965	McDonald-Cartier	Ottawa, Ont.	520
1988	Mon City	Monongahela, PA	520
1984	Columbia R.	Richland, WA	450
1986	Veterans	Pittsburgh, PA	440
1987	SR 76, Cumberland R.	Dover, TN	440
1987	SR 20, Tennessee R.	Perryville, TN	440
1970	Willamette R., I-205.	West Linn, OR	430
1974	I-430	Arkansas R., AR	430
1965	I-24, Tennessee R.	Marion Co., TN	420
1974	Dunbar-S. Charleston	S. Charleston, WV	420
1975	36th St.	Charleston, WV	420
1978	Snake R.	Clarkston, WA	420
1984	FAU 3456, TN R.	Chattanooga, TN	420

Continuous Plate

Year	Bridge	Location	Main span (ft.)
1973	Sidney Sherman Bridge, I-610	Houston, TX	630
1971	W. Atchafalaya	Henderson, LA	573
1992	State Route 76.	Paris, TN.	525
1997	SR 114, Clifton	Tennessee R., TN	525
1981	Illinois 23	Illinois R., IL.	510
1968	IH-45 over Trinity R.	Dallas, TX	480
1978	San Joaquin R.	Antioch, CA	460
1977	Thomas Johnson Mem.	Solomons, MD.	451
1967	Mississippi R.	La Crosse, WI	450
1975	I-129	Missouri R., IA–NE	450
1979	Lewis	St. Louis, MO.	450
1992	Cuba Landing Bridge.	Tennessee R., TN	450
1966	I-480.	Missouri R., IA–NE	425
1972	Whiskey Bay Pilot	Ramah, LA	425
1972	I-80.	Missouri R., IA–NE	425
1972	I-635, Kansas City	Missouri R., KS–MO	425
1983	US-36	Missouri R., KS–MO.	425
1987	I-435.	Missouri R., KS–MO.	425
1978	I-24	Cumberland R., KY	420
1993	Bob Michel Bridge	Peoria, IL.	360
1999	SR 53, Clear Fork River	Fentress/Morgan Co., TN	350

Cable-Stayed

Year	Bridge	Location	Main span (ft.)
1986	Annacis (Alex Fraser)	Vancouver, BC.	1,526
1993	Quetzalapa Bridge.	Quetzalapa, Mexico.	1,391
1988	Dames Point	Jacksonville, FL	1,300
1995	Fred Hartlan Bridge, Houston Ship Channel	Baytown,TX	1,250
1983	Hale Boggs Memorial	Luling, LA	1,222
1987	Sunshine Skyway	Tampa Bay, FL.	1,200
1988	Tampico/Panuco R.	Mexico	1,181
1988	ALRT Fraser River Bridge	Vancouver, BC.	1,115
1990	Talmadge Mem.	Savannah, GA.	1,100

Year	Bridge	Location	Main span (ft.)
1993	Mezcala.	Mex. City/Acapulco Hwy.	1,024
1978	Pasco-Kennewick	Columbia R., WA.	981
1984	Coatzacoalcos R.	Mexico	919
1985	E. Huntington	E. Huntington, WV.	900
1987	Bayview Bridge	Quincy, IL.	900
1970	Burton Bridge	New Brunswick, Canada	850
1990	Weirton-Steubenville	WV–OH	820
1969	Papineau-Leblanc	Montreal, Que.	790
1991	Cochrane.	Mobile, AL	780
1994	Clark Bridge	Alton, IL.	756
1995	Chesapeake & Delaware Canal Bridge	Dover-Wilmington, DE.	750
2002	Leonard Zakim	Bunker Hill, Boston, MA	745
1966	Longs Creek	New Brunswick, Canada	713
1967	Hawkshaw	New Brunswick, Canada	713
1993	Quetzalapa Bridge	Quetzalapa, Mexico.	699
1993	Burlington Bridge.	Burlington, IA.	660
1991	Veterans Memorial Br., Neches R.	Port Arthur-Orange,TX	640
1989	James River Bridge.	Richmond, VA.	630

I-Beam Girder

Year	Bridge	Location	Main span (ft.)
1980	Interstate 20	Shreveport, LA	438
200?	Moore Haven Bridge	Lake Okeechobee, FL.	320
1988	Route 18	Weston's Mill Pond, NJ	276

Steel Arch

Year	Bridge	Location	Main span (ft.)
1977	New River Gorge.	Fayetteville, WV.	1,700
1931	Bayonne (Kill Van Kull)	Bayonne, NJ	1,675
1973	Fremont.	Portland, OR	1,255
1964	Port Mann	Vancouver, BC.	1,200
1967	Lavioleete	Three Rivers, Canada	1,100
1967	Trois-Rivieres	St. Lawrence R., Que.	1,100
1992	Roosevelt Lake	Roosevelt Lake, AZ	1,080
1959	Glen Canyon	Page, AZ.	1,028
1962	Lewiston-Queenston	Niagara R., Ont.	1,000
1976	Perrine.	Twin Falls, ID.	993
1941	Rainbow Bridge	Niagara Falls, NY	984
1917	*Hell Gate	East R., N.Y	977
1977	Moundsville	Ohio R., WV	912
1992	I-255, Miss. R.	St. Louis, MO.	909
1972	I-40, Miss. R.[9]	AR–TN	900
1936	Henry Hudson	Harlem R., NY	840
1967	Lincoln Trail Bridge	Ohio R., IN–KY	825
1978	I-57, Miss. R.	Cairo , IL.	821
1961	Sherman-Minton Bridge, I-64	IN.	800
1980	I-65, Mobile R.	Mobile, AL	800
1930	West End.	Pittsburgh, PA	780
1470	I-470 Bridge, Ohio R.	Wheeling, WV	780
1996	Navajo Bridge	Glen Canyon, AZ.	726
1917	Cuyohoga River.	Cleveland, OH.	591

Concrete Arch

Year	Bridge	Location	Main span (ft.)
1995	Natchez Trace Pkwy.	Franklin, TN.	582
1993	Lake Street Bridge	St. Paul, MN	556
1971	Selah Creek (twin)	Selah, WA.	549
1968	Cowlitz R.	Mossyrock, WA	520
1931	Westinghouse	Pittsburgh, PA	460
1923	Cappelen.	Minneapolis, MN	435
2000	Crooked River Gorge	Madras, OR.	410
1930	Jack's Run.	Pittsburgh, PA	400
1931	Rogue River	Gold Beach, OR	230

Segmental Concrete

Year	Bridge	Location	Main span (ft.)
1997	Confederation Bridge	Prince Edward Isl., NB	820
1978	Shubenacadie River	S. Maitland, Nova Scotia.	790
1982	Jesse H, Jones Memorial	Houston, TX	750
1992	Narragansett Bay Crossing	Jamestown, RI.	674
2002	SR-895, James R. & I-95	Richmond, VA.	672
1986	WB I-82 (Columbia R.)	Umatilla, OR.	660
1976	Stanislaus River	Parrets Ferry, CA	640
1992	Jamestown-Verrazano.	Jamestown, RI.	636
1981	Gastineau Channel Br.	Juneau, AK	620
1991	Veterans Memorial Centennial Bridge	Coeur d'Alene, ID.	520
2001	Smart Highway	Blacksburg, VA	472
1974	Pine Valley Creek	Pine Valley, CA.	450
1988	Zilwaukee Bridge (twin).	Zilwaukee, MI	392
1985	Red River Bridge	Boyce, LA	370

Twin Concrete Trestle[10]

Year	Bridge	Location	Main span (ft.)
1979	I-55/I-10.	Manchac, LA.	181,157
1969	L. Pontchartrain Cswy.	Mandeville, LA.	126,720
1972	Atchafalaya Flwy.	Baton Rouge, LA.	93,984
1963	L. Pontchartrain	Slidell, LA.	28,547
1983	*Interstate 310.	Kenner, LA.	25.925

Concrete Slab Dam[10]

Year	Bridge	Location	Main span (ft.)
1927	Conowingo Dam	MD.	4,611
1952	SR-4, Roanoke R.	Mecklenburg Co., VA.	2,785
1936	Hoover Dam	Lake Mead, NV.	1,324

Miscellaneous Bridges

Year	Bridge	Type	Location	Main span (ft.)
1962	International	Arch Truss	Sault Ste. Marie, MI	430
1997	Second Blue Water	Continuous Tied Arch	Pt. Huron, MI	922
1982	SR 193	Seg. Box Girder	Dauphin Is., AL	400
1958	Castleton	Through Truss	Hudson R., NY	598
1939	US 43, Tenn. R.	Through Truss	Florence, AL	420
1958	SR 117, Tenn. R.	Through Truss	Stevenson, AL	500
1936	Yaquina Bay	Steel Braced and Concrete Tied Arches	Newport, OR	600
1958	Tombigbee R.	Steel Girder	Choctow Co., AL	400
1916	C&O RR	Steel Girder	Portsmouth, OH	775
1987	Powder Point[10]	Tropical Hardwood	Duxbury, MA	2,200
2002	Croatan Sound[10]	Continuous Postension Girder	Manteo, NC	5.2 mi

Drawbridges
Vertical Lift

Year	Bridge	Location	Main span (ft.)
1959	*Arthur Kill	NY–NJ	558
1965	Pennsylvania Railroad	Kirkwood-Mt. Pleas., DE	548
1935	*Cape Cod Canal	Cape Cod, MA	544
1961	*Delair	Delaware R., NJ	542
1931	Burlington-Bristol	Delaware R., NJ–PA	540
1937	Marine Parkway	Jamaica Bay, NY	540
1908	*Willamette R.	Portland, OR	521
1968	Second Narrows	Vancouver, B.C.	493
1912	*A-S-B Fratt	Kansas City, MO	428
1945	*Harry S Truman	Kansas City, MO	427
1955	Roosevelt Island	East R., NY	418
1980	US-17, James R.	Isle of Wight, Co., VA	415
1932	*M-K-T R.R.	Missouri R., MO	414
1969	Cape Fear Mem.	Wilmington, NC	408
1930	Aerial	Duluth, MN	386
1962	Burlington	Ontario, Can.	370
1941	Main Street	Jacksonville, FL	365
1967	SR-156, James R.	Prince George Co., VA	364

Year	Bridge	Location	Main span (ft.)
1950	Red R.	Moncla, LA	360
1957	Industrial Canal	New Orleans, LA	360
1936	Triborough	Harlem R., NY	344
1939	U.S. 1&9, Passaic R.	Newark, NJ	333
1930	*Martinez	Martinez, CA	328
1960	St. Andrews Bay	Panama City, FL	327
1929	*Penn-Lehigh	Newark Bay, PA	322
1987	Industrial Canal	New Orleans, LA	320
1920	*Chattanooga	Tennessee R., TN	310
1910	Willamette R. Hawthorne	Portland, OR	244

Steel Suspension

1931	Maumee R.	Toledo, OH	785

Bascule

1917	SR-8, Tennessee R.	Chattanooga, TN	306
2003	*SW 2nd Avenue Br.	Miami, FL	302
1956	Duwamish R.	Seattle, WA	300
1955	Chehalis R.	Aberdeen, WA	288
1968	Elizabeth R.	Chesapeake, VA	280
1913	Broadway	Portland, OR	278
1936	Siuslaw River	Florence, OR	154

Swing Bridges

1927	Fort Madison[4]	Mississippi R., IA	545
1991	SW. Spokane St.	Seattle, WA	480
1930	Rigolets Pass	New Orleans, LA	400
1950	Douglass Memorial	Washington, DC	386
1945	Lord Delaware	Mattaponi R., VA	252

Swing Span

1897	*Duluth	St. Louis Bay, MN	486
1899	*C.M.&N.R.R.	Chicago, IL	474
1913	Rt. 82, Conn-R.	E. Haddam, CT	465
1914	*Coos Bay RR Xing	OR	458
1936	Umpqua River	Reedsport. OR	430

Floating Pontoon

1963	Evergreen Pt.	Seattle, WA	7,578
1961	Hood Canal	Pt. Gamble, WA	6,521
1993	Lacey V. Murrow[11]	Seattle, WA	6,620
1989	Third Lake Washington	Seattle, WA	5,811

(1) Swing span bridge with 2 spans of 2,310 ft. each. (2) A second bridge in parallel was completed in 1978. (3) The Richmond Bridge has twin spans 1,070 ft. each. (4) Railroad and vehicular bridge. (5) Two spans each 825 ft. (6) Two spans each 707 ft. (7) Two spans each 700 ft. (8) Two spans each 660 ft. (9) Two spans each 900 ft. (10) Length listed is total length of bridge. (11) Replaces the original Lacey V. Murrow bridge, which opened in 1940 and sank in 1990.

Oldest U.S. Bridges in Continuous Use

Built in 1697, the stone-arch Frankford Ave. Bridge crosses Pennypack Creek in Philadelphia. PA. A 3-span bridge with a total length of 75 ft., it was constructed as part of the King's Road, which eventually connected Philadelphia to New York.

The oldest covered bridge, completed in 1827, is the double-span, 278-ft, Haverhill Bath Bridge, which spans the Ammonoosuc River, between the towns of Bath and Haverhill, NH.

Some Notable International Bridges

Span of bridge is the distance between its supports. Asterisk (*) designates under construction.

Suspension

Year	Bridge	Location	Main span (ft.)
1998	Akashi Kaikyo	Japan	6,570
2003	*Izmit Bay	Turkey	5,538
1998	Storebælt (East Bridge)	Denmark	5,328
1981	Humber	England	4,626
1999	Jiangyin Yangtze	China	4,544
1997	Tsing Ma[1]	China	4,518
1997	Hoga Kusten	Sweden	3,970
1988	Minami Bisan-Seto	Japan	3,609
1988	Bosphorus II	Turkey	3,576
1973	Bosphorus I	Turkey	3,524
1999	Kurushima III	Japan	3,379
1999	Kurushima II	Japan	3,346
1966	Tagus River[2]	Portugal	3,323
1964	Forth Road	Scotland	3,300
1988	Kita Bisan-Seto.	Japan	3,248
1966	Severn	England	3,241
1988	Shimotsui Strait	Japan	3,084

Steel Arch

1932	Sydney Harbour	Australia	1,650
1967	Zdakov	Czech Republic	1,244
1962	Thatcher	Panama Canal Zone.	1,128
1961	Runcorn-Widnes.	England	1,082
1935	Birchenough	Zimbabwe	1,080

Concrete Arch

1980	Krk I	Croatia	1,280
1964	Gladesville	Australia	1,000
1964	Amizade	Brazil	951

Year	Bridge	Location	Main span (ft.)
1963	Arrabida	Portugal	886
1943	Sando	Sweden	866

Cantilever

1890	Forth[3] (rail)	Scotland	1,710
1974	Nanko	Japan	1,673

Steel Plate and Box Girder

1974	President Costa e Silva	Brazil	984
1956	Sava I	Serbia & Montenegro	856
1966	Zoobrüke	Germany	850

Cable-Stayed

1999	Tatara	Japan	2,920
1995	Pont de Normandie	France	2,808
1996	Quingzhou Minjang	China	1,985
1993	Yangpu	China	1,975
1993	Xupu	China	1,936
1998	Meiko Chuo	Japan	1,936
1991	Skarnsundet	Norway	1,739
1999	Queshi	China	1,700
1995	Tsurumi Tsubasa	Japan	1,673
2000	Oresund	Denmark/Sweden.	1,614
1991	Ikuchi	Japan	1,608
1994	Higashi Kobe	Japan	1,591
1998	Zhanjiang	China	1,575
1997	Ting Kau	China	1,558
1999	Seo Hae Grand	South Korea	1,542
1989	Yokohama Bay	Japan	1,509
1993	Second Hooghly River	India	1,499
1995	Second Severn Crossing	England/Wales	1,496

(1) Double-decked road and rail bridge. (2) Railroad and highway bridge. (3) Two spans of 1,710 ft. each.

Underwater Vehicular Tunnels in North America

(more than 5,000 ft. in length; year in parentheses is year of completion)

Name	Location	Waterway	Feet
Brooklyn-Battery (1950) (twin)	New York, NY	East River	9,117
Holland Tunnel (1927) (twin)	New York, NY	Hudson River	8,557
Ted Williams Tunnel (1995)	Boston, MA	Boston Harbor	8,448
Lincoln Tunnel (1937, 1945, 1957) (3 tubes)	New York, NY	Hudson River	8,216
Thimble Shoal Channel (1964)	Northampton Co., VA	Chesapeake Bay	8,187
Chesapeake Channel (1964)	Northampton Co., VA	Chesapeake Bay	7,941
Fort McHenry Tunnel (1985) (twin)	Baltimore, MD	Baltimore Harbor	7,920
Hampton Roads (1957) (twin)	Hampton, VA	Hampton Roads	7,479
Baltimore Harbor Tunnel (1957) (twin)	Baltimore, MD	Patapsco River	7,392
Queens Midtown (1940) (twin)	New York, NY	East River	6,414
Sumner Tunnel (1934)	Boston, MA	Boston Harbor	5,653
Louis-Hippolyte Lafontaine Tunnel	Montreal, Que.	St. Lawrence River	5,280
Detroit-Windsor (1930)	Detroit, MI	Detroit River	5,160
Callahan Tunnel (1961)	Boston, MA	Boston Harbor	5,070

Land Vehicular Tunnels in the U.S.

Source: Federal Highway Administration

(more than 3,000 ft. in length)

Name	Location	Feet	Name	Location	Feet
Anton Anderson Mem. Tunnel[1]	Whittier, AK	13,300	Blue Mountain (twin)	PA Turnpike	4,435
E. Johnson Memorial	I-70, CO	8,959	Lehigh (twin)	PA Turnpike	4,379
Eisenhower Memorial	I-70, CO	8,941	Wawona	Yosemite Natl. Pk., CA.	4,233
Allegheny (twin)	PA Turnpike	6,072	Big Walker Mt. (twin)	Bland Co., VA.	4,229
Liberty Tubes	Pittsburgh, PA	5,920	Squirrel Hill	Pittsburgh, PA	4,225
Zion Natl. Park	Rte. 9, UT.	5,766	Hanging Lake (twin)	Glenwood Canyon, CO.	4,000
East River Mt.	Mercer Co., WV/ Bland Co., VA.	5,654	Caldecott (3 tubes)	Oakland, CA	3,616
East River Mt. (twin)	VA–WV	5,412	Fort Pitt (twin)	Pittsburgh, PA	3,560
Tuscarora (twin)	PA Turnpike	5,400	Mount Baker Ridge	Seattle, WA	3,456
Tetsuo Harano (twin)	H-3, HI	5,165	Devil's Side Tunnel	U.S. 101 CA.	3,400
Kittatinny (twin)	PA Turnpike	4,660	Dingess Tunnel	Mingo Co., WV.	3,400
Cumberland Gap (twin)	KY–TN	4,600	Mall Tunnel	Dist. of Columbia	3,400
			Cody No. 1	U.S. 14, 16, 20, WY	3,202

(1) Tunnel is used for vehicular and railroad traffic.

World's Longest Railway Tunnels

Source: Railway Directory & Year Book

Tunnel	Date	Miles	Operating railway	Country
Seikan	1985	33.50	Japanese Railway	Japan
English Channel Tunnel	1994	31.04	Eurotunnel	United Kingdom-France
Dai-shimizu	1979	14.00	Japanese Railway	Japan
Simplon No. 1 and 2	1906, 1922	12.00	Swiss Fed. & Italian St.	Switzerland-Italy
Kanmon	1975	12.00	Japanese Railway	Japan
Apennine	1934	11.00	Italian State	Italy
Rokko	1972	10.00	Japanese Railway	Japan
Mt. MacDonald	1989	9.10	Canadian Pacific	Canada
Gotthard	1882	9.00	Swiss Federal	Switzerland
Lotschberg	1913	9.00	Bern-Lotschberg-Simplon	Switzerland
Hokuriku	1962	9.00	Japanese Railway	Japan
Mont Cenis (Frejus)	1871	8.00	Italian State	France-Italy
Cascade	1929	8.00	Burlington Northern	United States
Shin-Shimizu	1961	8.00	Japanese Railway	Japan
Flathead	1970	8.00	Burlington Northern	United States
Aki	1975	8.00	Japanese Railway	Japan

World's Largest-Capacity Hydro Plants

Source: U.S. Committee on Large Dams of the Intl. Commission on Large Dams

Rank[1]	Name	Country	Rated capacity now (MW)	Rated capacity planned (MW)	Rank[1]	Name	Country	Rated capacity now (MW)	Rated capacity planned (MW)
1.	Turukhansk (Lower Tungu-ska)*	Russia	—	20,000	12.	Xingo	Brazil	3,012	5,020
2.	Three Gorges Dam*	China	—	18,200	13.	Tarbela	Pakistan	1,750	4,678
3.	Itaipu	Brazil/Paraguay	7,400	13,320	14.	Bratsk	Russia	4,500	4,500
4.	Grand Coulee	U.S.	6,495	10,830	14.	Ust-Ilim	Russia	3,675	4,500
5.	Guri (Raúl Leoni)	Venezuela	10,300	10,300	16.	Cabora Bassa	Mozambique	2,425	4,150
6.	Tucuruí	Brazil	2,640	7,260	17.	Boguchany*	Russia	—	4,000
7.	Sayano-Shushensk*	Russia	—	6,400	18.	Oak Creek	U.S.	3,600	3,600
8.	Corpus Posadas	Argentina / Paraguay	4,700	6,000	19.	Paulo Afonso I	Brazil	1,524	3,409
					20.	Pati*	Argentina	—	3,300
8.	Krasnoyarsk	Russia	6,000	6,000	21.	Ilha Solteira	Brazil	3,200	3,200
10.	La Grande 2	Canada	5,328	5,328	22.	Chapetón*	Argentina	—	3,000
11.	Churchill Falls	Canada	5,225	5,225	23.	Gezhouba	China	2,715	2,715

(1) Ranked by rated capacity planned. *Planned or under construction.

WORLD ALMANAC QUICK QUIZ

Can you rank these from tallest to shortest?
(a) CN Tower, Toronto
(b) Sears Tower, Chicago
(c) Petronas Tower, Malaysia
(d) Empire State Building, New York

For the answer look in this chapter, or see page 1008.

World's Largest-Capacity Reservoirs

Source: U.S. Committee on Large Dams of the Intl. Commission on Large Dams, 2002

Rank order	Name	Country	Capacity cubic meters x 1,000,000	Rank order	Name	Country	Capacity cubic meters x 1,000,000
1.	Kariba	Zimbabwe/Zambia	180,600	9.	Krasnoyarsk	Russia	73,300
2.	Bratsk	Russia	169,000	10.	Zeya	Russia	68,400
3.	High Aswan	Egypt	162,000	11.	La Grande 2	Canada	61,715
4.	Akosombo	Ghana	147,960	12.	La Grande 3	Canada	60,020
5.	Daniel Johnson	Canada	141,851	13.	Ust-Ilim	Russia	59,300
6.	Xinfeng	China	138,960	14.	Kuibyshev	Russia	58,000
7.	Guri	Venezuela	135,000	15.	Serra da Mesa	Brazil	54,400
8.	W A C Bennett	Canada	74,300				

Major Dams of the World

Source: U.S. Committee on Large Dams of the Intl. Commission on Large Dams

World's Highest Dams

Rank order	Name	Country	Height above lowest formation (m)
1.	Nurek	Tajikistan	300
2.	Grand Dixence	Switzerland	285
3.	Inguri	Georgia	272
4.	Vajont	Italy	262
5.	Manuel M. Torres	Mexico	261
6.	Alvaro Obregon	Mexico	260
7.	Mauvoisin	Switzerland	250
8.	Mica	Canada	243
9.	Alberto Lleras C.	Colombia	243
10.	Sayano-Shushensk	Russia	242
11.	Ertan	China	240
12.	La Esmeralda	Colombia	237
13.	Oroville	U.S.	235
14.	El Cajón	Honduras	234
15.	Chirkey	Russia	233
16.	Bhakra	India	226
17.	Luzzone	Switzerland	225
18.	Hoover	U.S.	223
19.	Contra	Switzerland	220
20.	Mratinje	Serbia & Montenegro	220

World's Largest-Volume Embankment Dams

Rank order	Name	Country	Volume cubic meters x 1000
1.	Tarbela	Pakistan	148,500
2.	Fort Peck	U.S.	96,050
3.	Tucurui	Brazil	85,200
4.	Ataturk*	Turkey	85,000
5.	Yacireta*	Argentina	81,000
6.	Rogun*	Tajikistan	75,500
7.	Oahe	U.S.	70,339
8.	Guri	Venezuela	70,000
9.	Parambikulam	India	69,165
10.	High Island West	China	67,000
11.	Gardiner	Canada	65,000
12.	Afsluitdijk	Netherlands	63,400
13.	Mangla	Pakistan	63,379
14.	Oroville	U.S.	59,635
15.	San Luis	U.S.	59,559
16.	Nurek	Tajikistan	58,000
17.	Tanda	Pakistan	57,250
18.	Garrison	U.S.	50,843
19.	Cochiti	U.S.	50,228
20.	Oosterschelde	Netherlands	50,000

*Under construction.

Major U.S. Dams and Reservoirs

Source: Committee on Register of Dams, Corps of Engineers, U.S. Army, Sept. 2002

Highest U.S. Dams

Rank Order	Dam name	River	State	Type	Height Feet	Height Meters	Year completed
1.	Oroville	Feather	California	E	754	230	1968
2.	Hoover	Colorado	Nevada-Arizona	A	725	221	1936
3.	Dworshak	N. Fork Clearwater	Idaho	G	718	219	1973
4.	Glen Canyon	Colorado	Arizona	A	708	216	1966
5.	New Bullards Bar	North Yuba	California	A	636	194	1970
6.	Seven Oaks	Santa Ana	California	E	632	193	1999
7.	New Melones	Stanislaus	California	R	626	191	1979
8.	Swift	Lewis	Washington	E	610	186	1958
9.	Mossyrock	Cowlitz	Washington	A	607	185	1968
10.	Shasta	Sacramento	California	G	600	183	1945

E = Embankment, Earthfill; R = Embankment, Rockfill; G = Gravity; A = Arch.

Largest U.S. Embankment Dams

Rank Order	Dam name	River	State	Type	Volume Cubic yards x 1000	Cubic meters x 1000	Year completed
1.	Fort Peck	Missouri	Montana	E	125,624	96,050	1957
2.	Oahe	Missouri	South Dakota	E	91,996	70,339	1958
3.	Oroville	Feather	California	E	77,997	59,635	1968
4.	San Luis	San Luis Creek	California	E	77,897	59,559	1967
5.	Garrison	Missouri	North Dakota	E	66,498	50,843	1953
6.	Cochiti	Rio Grande	New Mexico	E	65,693	50,228	1975
7.	Fort Randall	Missouri	South Dakota	E	49,962	38,200	1952
8.	Castaic	Castaic Creek	California	E	43,998	33,640	1973
9.	Ludington P/S	Lake Michigan	Michigan	E	37,699	28,824	1973
10.	Kingsley	N. Platte	Nebraska	E	31,999	24,466	1941

E = Earthfill.

Largest U.S. Reservoirs

Rank Order	Dam name	Reservoir name	State	Reservoir capacity Acre-Feet	Cubic meters x 1000	Year completed
1.	Hoover	Lake Mead	AZ/NV	28,255,000	34,850,000	1936
2.	Glen Canyon	Lake Powell	AZ/UT	27,000,000	33,300,000	1964
3.	Oahe	Lake Oahe	ND/SD	19,300,000	27,430,000	1966
4.	Garrison	Lake Sakakawea	ND	18,500,000	27,920,000	1953
5.	Fort Peck	Fort Peck Lake	MT	15,400,000	22,120,000	1957
6.	Grand Coulee	F. D. Roosevelt Lake	WA	9,562,000	11,790,000	1942
7.	Libby	Lake Koocanusa	MT	5,809,000	7,170,000	1973
8.	Shasta	Lake Shasta	CA	4,552,000	5,610,000	1945
9.	Toledo Bend	Toledo Bend Lake	LA/TX	4,477,000	5,520,000	1966
10.	Fort Randall	Lake Francis Case	SD	3,800,000	5,700,000	1954

1 acre-foot = 1 acre of water, 1 foot deep

HISTORICAL FIGURES

Ancient Greeks and Romans

Greeks

Aeschines, orator, 389-314 BC
Aeschylus, dramatist, 525-456 BC
Aesop, fableist, c620-c560 BC
Alcibiades, politician, 450-404 BC
Anacreon, poet, c582-c485 BC
Anaxagoras, philosopher, c500-428 BC
Anaximander, philosopher, 611-546 BC
Anaximenes, philosopher, c570-500 BC
Antiphon, speechwriter, c480-411 BC
Apollonius, mathematician, c265-170 BC
Archimedes, math., 287-212 BC
Aristophanes, dramatist, c448-380 BC
Aristotle, philosopher, 384-322 BC
Athenaeus, scholar, fl. c200
Callicrates, architect, fl. 5th cent. BC
Callimachus, poet, c305-240 BC
Cratinus, comic dramatist, 520-421 BC
Democritus, philosopher, c460-370 BC
Demosthenes, orator, 384-322 BC
Diodorus, historian, fl. 20 BC

Diogenes, philosopher, 372-c287 BC
Dionysius, historian, d. c7 BC
Empedocles, philosopher, c490-430 BC
Epicharmus, dramatist, c530-440 BC
Epictetus, philosopher, c55-c135
Epicurus, philosopher, 341-270 BC
Eratosthenes, scientist, 276-194 BC
Euclid, mathematician, fl. c300 BC
Euripides, dramatist, c484-406 BC
Galen, physician, 130-200
Heraclitus, philosopher, c540-c475 BC
Herodotus, historian, c484-420 BC
Hesiod, poet, 8th cent. BC
Hippocrates, physician, c460-377 BC
Homer, poet, fl. c700 BC(?)
Isocrates, orator, 436-338 BC
Menander, dramatist, 342-292 BC
Parmenides, philosopher, b. c515 BC
Pericles, statesman, c495-429 BC
Phidias, sculptor, c500-435 BC

Pindar, poet, c518-c438 BC
Plato, philosopher, c428-347 BC
Plutarch, biographer, c46-120
Polybius, historian, c200-c118 BC
Praxiteles, sculptor, 400-330 BC
Pythagoras, phil., math., c580-c500 BC
Sappho, poet, c610-c580 BC
Simonides, poet, 556-c468 BC
Socrates, philosopher, 469-399 BC
Solon, statesman, 640-560 BC
Sophocles, dramatist, c496-406 BC
Strabo, geographer, c63 BC-AD 24
Thales, philosopher, c634-546 BC
Themistocles, politician, c524-c460 BC
Theocritus, poet, c310-250 BC
Theophrastus, phil., c372-c287 BC
Thucydides, historian, fl. 5th cent. BC
Timon, philosopher, c320-c230 BC
Xenophon, historian, c434-c355 BC
Zeno, philosopher, c335-c263 BC

Romans

Ammianus, historian, c330-395
Apuleius, satirist, c124-c170
Boethius, scholar, c480-524
Caesar, Julius, leader, 100-44 BC
Catiline, politician, c108-62 BC
Cato (Elder), statesman, 234-49 BC
Catullus, poet, c84-54 BC
Cicero, orator, 106-43 BC
Claudian, poet, c370-c404
Ennius, poet, 239-170 BC
Gellius, author, c130-c165
Horace, poet, 65-8 BC

Juvenal, satirist, 60-127
Livy, historian, 59 BC-AD 17
Lucan, poet, 39-65
Lucilius, poet, c180-c102 BC
Lucretius, poet, c99-c55 BC
Martial, epigrammatist, c38-c103
Nepos, historian, c100-c25 BC
Ovid, poet, 43 BC-AD 17
Persius, satirist, 34-62
Plautus, dramatist, c254-c184 BC
Pliny the Elder, scholar, 23-79
Pliny the Younger, author, 62-113

Quintilian, rhetorician, c35-c97
Sallust, historian, 86-34 BC
Seneca, philosopher, 4 BC-AD 65
Silius, poet, c25-101
Statius, poet, c45-c96
Suetonius, biographer, c69-c122
Tacitus, historian, 56-120
Terence, dramatist, 185-c159 BC
Tibullus, poet, c55-c19 BC
Vergil, poet, 70-19 BC
Vitruvius, architect, fl. 1st cent. BC

Rulers of England and Great Britain

Name	ENGLAND	Reign Began	Died	Death Age	Years Reigned
Saxons and Danes					
Egbert	King of Wessex, won allegiance of all English	829	839	—	10
Ethelwulf	Son, King of Wessex, Sussex, Kent, Essex	839	858	—	19
Ethelbald	Son of Ethelwulf, displaced father in Wessex	858	860	—	2
Ethelbert	2nd son of Ethelwulf, united Kent and Wessex	860	866	—	6
Ethelred I	3rd son, King of Wessex, fought Danes	866	871	—	5
Alfred	The Great, 4th son, defeated Danes, fortified London	871	899	52	28
Edward	The Elder, Alfred's son, united English, claimed Scotland	899	924	55	25
Athelstan	The Glorious, Edward's son, King of Mercia, Wessex	924	940	45	16
Edmund	3rd son of Edward, King of Wessex, Mercia	940	946	25	6
Edred	4th son of Edward	946	955	32	9
Edwy	The Fair, eldest son of Edmund, King of Wessex	955	959	18	3
Edgar	The Peaceful, 2nd son of Edmund, ruled all English	959	975	32	17
Edward	The Martyr, eldest son of Edgar, murdered by stepmother	975	978	17	4
Ethelred II	The Unready, 2nd son of Edgar, married Emma of Normandy	978	1016	48	37
Edmund II	Ironside, son of Ethelred II, King of London	1016	1016	27	0
Canute	The Dane, gave Wessex to Edmund, married Emma	1016	1035	40	19
Harold I	Harefoot, natural son of Canute	1035	1040	—	5
Hardecanute	Son of Canute by Emma, Danish King	1040	1042	24	2
Edward	The Confessor, son of Ethelred II (canonized 1161)	1042	1066	62	24
Harold II	Edward's brother-in-law, last Saxon King	1066	1066	44	0
House of Normandy					
William I	The Conqueror, defeated Harold at Hastings	1066	1087	60	21
William II	Rufus, 3rd son of William I, killed by arrow	1087	1100	43	13
Henry I	Beauclerc, youngest son of William I	1100	1135	67	35
House of Blois					
Stephen	Son of Adela, daughter of William I, and Count of Blois	1135	1154	50	19
House of Plantagenet					
Henry II	Son of Geoffrey Plantagenet (Angevin) by Matilda, daughter of Henry I	1154	1189	56	35
Richard I	Coeur de Lion, son of Henry II, crusader	1189	1199	42	10
John	Lackland, son of Henry II, approved Magna Carta, 1215	1199	1216	50	17
Henry III	Son of John, acceded at 9, under regency until 1227	1216	1272	65	56
Edward I	Son of Henry III	1272	1307	68	35
Edward II	Son of Edward I, deposed by Parliament, 1327	1307	1327	43	20
Edward III	Of Windsor, son of Edward II	1327	1377	65	50
Richard II	Grandson of Edward III, minor until 1389, deposed 1399	1377	1400	33	22

Name	House of Lancaster	Reign Began	Died	Death Age	Years Reigned
Henry IV......	Son of John of Gaunt, Duke of Lancaster, son of Edward III	1399	1413	47	13
Henry V......	Son of Henry IV, victor of Agincourt	1413	1422	34	9
Henry VI......	Son of Henry V, deposed 1461, died in Tower	1422	1471	49	39
	House of York				
Edward IV	Great-great-grandson of Edward III, son of Duke of York....................	1461	1483	40	22
Edward V.....	Son of Edward IV, murdered in Tower of London	1483	1483	13	0
Richard III	Brother of Edward IV, fell at Bosworth Field	1483	1485	32	2
	House of Tudor				
Henry VII	Son of Edmund Tudor, Earl of Richmond, whose father had married the widow of Henry V; descended from Edward III through his mother, Margaret Beaufort, via John of Gaunt. By marrying daughter of Edward IV united Lancaster and York ..	1485	1509	53	24
Henry VIII......	Son of Henry VII, by Elizabeth, daughter of Edward IV	1509	1547	56	38
Edward VI	Son of Henry VIII, by Jane Seymour, his 3rd queen. Ruled under regents. Was forced to name Lady Jane Grey his successor. Council of State proclaimed her queen July 10, 1553. Mary Tudor won Council, was proclaimed queen July 19, 1553. Mary had Lady Jane Grey beheaded for treason, Feb. 1554	1547	1553	16	6
Mary I.........	Daughter of Henry VIII, by Catherine of Aragon...........................	1553	1558	43	5
Elizabeth I	Daughter of Henry VIII, by Anne Boleyn..................................	1558	1603	69	44

GREAT BRITAIN

	House of Stuart				
James I	James VI of Scotland, son of Mary, Queen of Scots. *First to call himself King of Great Britain. This became official with the Act of Union, 1707*	1603	1625	59	22
Charles I	Only surviving son of James I; beheaded Jan. 30, 1649	1625	1649	48	24

	Commonwealth, 1649–1660 Council of State, 1649; Protectorate, 1653[1]				
The Cromwells	Oliver Cromwell, Lord Protector	1653	1658	59	5
	Richard Cromwell, son, Lord Protector, resigned May 25, 1659	1658	1712	86	1

	House of Stuart (Restored)				
Charles II......	Eldest son of Charles I, died without issue...............................	1660	1685	55	25
James II.......	2nd son of Charles I. Deposed 1688. Interregnum 1688-1689	1685	1701	68	3
William III.....	Son of William, Prince of Orange, by Mary, daughter of Charles I	1689	1702	51	13
and Mary II	Eldest daughter of James II and wife of William III........................	1689	1694	33	6
Anne	2nd daughter of James II	1702	1714	49	12
	House of Hanover				
George I......	Son of Elector of Hanover, by Sophia, granddaughter of James I	1714	1727	67	13
George II......	Only son of George I, married Caroline of Brandenburg	1727	1760	77	33
George III.....	Grandson of George II, married Charlotte of Mecklenburg	1760	1820	81	59
George IV	Eldest son of George III, Prince Regent, from Feb. 1811..................	1820	1830	67	10
William IV	3rd son of George III, married Adelaide of Saxe-Meiningen	1830	1837	71	7
Victoria	Daughter of Edward, 4th son of George III; married (1840) Prince Albert of Saxe-Coburg and Gotha, who became Prince Consort	1837	1901	81	63
	House of Saxe-Coburg and Gotha				
Edward VII	Eldest son of Victoria, married Alexandra, Princess of Denmark............	1901	1910	68	9
	House of Windsor[2]				
George V	2nd son of Edward VII, married Princess Mary of Teck	1910	1936	70	25
Edward VIII	Eldest son of George V; acceded Jan. 20, 1936, abdicated Dec. 11, 1936......	1936	1972	77	1
George VI	2nd son of George V; married Lady Elizabeth Bowes-Lyon................	1936	1952	56	15
Elizabeth II	Elder daughter of George VI, acceded Feb. 6, 1952	1952			

— = age/birth date not certain. (1) The Cromwells ruled Britain following overthow of the monarchy in 1649. (2) Name adopted by proclamation of George V, July 17, 1917.

Rulers of Scotland

Kenneth I MacAlpin was the first Scot to rule both Scots and Picts, AD 846.

Duncan I was the first general ruler, 1034. Macbeth seized the kingdom 1040, was slain by Duncan's son, Malcolm III MacDuncan (Canmore), 1057.

Malcolm married Margaret, Saxon princess who had fled from the Normans. Queen Margaret introduced English language and monastic customs. She was canonized, 1250. Her son Edgar, 1097, moved the court to Edinburgh. His brothers Alexander I and David I succeeded. Malcolm IV, the Maiden, 1153, grandson of David I, was followed by his brother, William the Lion, 1165, whose son was Alexander II, 1214. The latter's son, Alexander III, 1249, defeated the Norse and regained the Hebrides. When he died, 1286, his granddaughter, Margaret, child of Eric of Norway and grandniece of Edward I of England, known as the Maid of Norway, was chosen ruler, but died 1290, aged 8.

John Baliol, 1292-1296. (Interregnum, 10 years.)

Robert Bruce (The Bruce), 1306-1329, victor at Bannockburn, 1314. David II, his only son, 1329-1371.

Robert II, 1371-1390, grandson of Robert Bruce, son of Walter, the Steward of Scotland, was called The Steward, first of the so-called Stuart line.

Robert III, son of Robert II, 1390-1406.

James I, son of Robert III, 1406-1437.

James II, son of James I, 1437-1460.

James III, eldest son of James II, 1460-1488.

James IV, eldest son of James III, 1488-1513.

James V, eldest son of James IV, 1513-1542.

Mary, daughter of James V, b. 1542, became queen at 1 week old; crowned 1543. Married, 1558, Francis, son of Henry II of France, who became king 1559, d. 1560. Mary ruled Scots 1561 until abdication, 1567. She also married Henry Stewart, Lord Darnley (1565), and James, Earl of Bothwell (1567). Imprisoned by Elizabeth I; beheaded 1587.

James VI, 1566-1625, son of Mary and Lord Darnley, became King of England on death of Elizabeth in 1603. Although the thrones were thus united, the legislative union of Scotland and England was not effected until the Act of Union, May 1, 1707.

▶ **IT'S A FACT:** King George III of England was notorious for his "mad" behavior. This was the result of an inherited disease called porphyria, which inhibits the body's production of heme, an essential component of hemoglobin. Acute forms of the disease can cause severe neurological damage, resulting in erratic, psychotic behavior.

Prime Ministers of Great Britain

Designations in parentheses describe each government:
W=Whig; T=Tory; Cl=Coalition; P=Peelite; Li=Liberal; C=Conservative[1]; La=Labour.

Sir Robert Walpole (W)[2]	1721-1742	Benjamin Disraeli (C)	1868
Earl of Wilmington (W)	1742-1743	William E. Gladstone (Li)	1868-1874
Henry Pelham (W)	1743-1754	Benjamin Disraeli (C)	1874-1880
Duke of Newcastle (W)	1754-1756	William E. Gladstone (Li)	1880-1885
Duke of Devonshire (W)	1756-1757	Marquess of Salisbury (C)	1885-1886
Duke of Newcastle (W)	1757-1762	William E. Gladstone (Li)	1886
Earl of Bute (T)	1762-1763	Marquess of Salisbury (C)	1886-1892
George Grenville (W)	1763-1765	William E. Gladstone (Li)	1892-1894
Marquess of Rockingham (W)	1765-1766	Earl of Rosebery (Li)	1894-1895
William Pitt the Elder (Earl of Chatham) (W)	1766-1768	Marquess of Salisbury (C)	1895-1902
Duke of Grafton (W)	1768-1770	Arthur J. Balfour (C)	1902-1905
Frederick North (Lord North) (T)	1770-1782	Sir Henry Campbell Bannerman (Li)	1905-1908
Marquess of Rockingham (W)	1782	Herbert H. Asquith (Li)	1908-1915
Earl of Shelburne (W)	1782-1783	Herbert H. Asquith (Cl)	1915-1916
Duke of Portland (Cl)	1783	David Lloyd George (Cl)	1916-1922
William Pitt the Younger (T)	1783-1801	Andrew Bonar Law (C)	1922-1923
Henry Addington (T)	1801-1804	Stanley Baldwin (C)	1923-1924
William Pitt the Younger (T)	1804-1806	James Ramsay MacDonald (La)	1924
William Wyndham Grenville, Baron Grenville (W)	1806-1807	Stanley Baldwin (C)	1924-1929
Duke of Portland (T)	1807-1809	James Ramsay MacDonald (La)	1929-1931
Spencer Perceval (T)	1809-1812	James Ramsay MacDonald (Cl)	1931-1935
Earl of Liverpool (T)	1812-1827	Stanley Baldwin (Cl)	1935-1937
George Canning (T)	1827	Neville Chamberlain (Cl)	1937-1940
Viscount Goderich (T)	1827-1828	Winston Churchill (Cl)	1940-1945
Duke of Wellington (T)	1828-1830	Winston Churchill (C)	1945
Earl Grey (W)	1830-1834	Clement Attlee (La)	1945-1951
Viscount Melbourne (W)	1834	Sir Winston Churchill (C)	1951-1955
Sir Robert Peel (C)	1834-1835	Sir Anthony Eden (C)	1955-1957
Viscount Melbourne (W)	1835-1841	Harold Macmillan (C)	1957-1963
Sir Robert Peel (C)	1841-1846	Sir Alec Douglas-Home (C)	1963-1964
Lord (later Earl) John Russell (W)	1846-1852	Harold Wilson (La)	1964-1970
Earl of Derby (C)	1852	Edward Heath (C)	1970-1974
Earl of Aberdeen (P)	1852-1855	Harold Wilson (La)	1974-1976
Viscount Palmerston (Li)	1855-1858	James Callaghan (La)	1976-1979
Earl of Derby (C)	1858-1859	Margaret Thatcher (C)	1979-1990
Viscount Palmerston (Li)	1859-1865	John Major (C)	1990-1997
Earl Russell (Li)	1865-1866	Tony Blair (La)	1997-
Earl of Derby (C)	1866-1868		

(1) The Conservative Party was formed in 1834, an outgrowth of the Tory party. (2) Walpole is commonly regarded as the first prime minister of Britain, though the title was not commonly used then and did not become official until 1905.

▶ **IT'S A FACT:** Benjamin Disraeli, one of England's most influential prime ministers, was also an accomplished writer. Besides his many political works, such as "Vindication of the English Constitution," he authored ten novels. Disraeli wrote his first novel, *Vivian Grey,* in 1826 in order to pay off large debts he incurred in the stock market.

Historical Periods of Japan

Yamato	c. 300-592	Conquest of Yamato plain c. AD 300.	Muromachi	1392-1573	Unification of Southern and Northern Courts, 1392.
Asuka	592-710	Accession of Empress Suiko, 592.			
Nara	710-794	Completion of Heijo (Nara), 710; the capital moves to Nagaoka, 784.	Sengoku	1467-1600	Beginning of the Onin war, 1467.
			Momoyama	1573-1603	Oda Nobunaga enters Kyoto, 1568;
Heian	794-1185	Completion of Heian (Kyoto), 794.			Nobunaga deposes last Ashikaga
Fujiwara	858-1160	Fujiwara-no-Yoshifusa becomes regent, 858.			shogun, 1573; Tokugawa Ieyasu victor at Sekigahara, 1600.
Taira	1160-1185	Taira-no-Kiyomori assumes control, 1160; Minamoto-no-Yoritomo victor over Taira, 1185.	Edo	1603-1867	Ieyasu becomes shogun, 1603.
			Meiji	1868-1912	Enthronement of Emperor Mutsuhito (Meiji), 1867; Meiji Restoration and Charter Oath, 1868.
Kamakura	1192-1333	Yoritomo becomes shogun, 1192.			
Namboku	1334-1392	Restoration of Emperor Godaigo, 1334; Southern Court established by Godaigo at Yoshino, 1336.	Taisho	1912-1926	Accession of Emperor Yoshihito, 1912.
			Showa	1926-1989	Accession of Emperor Hirohito, 1926.
Ashikaga	1338-1573	Ashikaga Takauji becomes shogun, 1338.	Heisei	1989-	Accession of Emperor Akihito, 1989.

Rulers of France: Kings, Queens, Presidents

Caesar to Charlemagne

Julius Caesar subdued the Gauls, native tribes of Gaul (France), 58 to 51 BC. The Romans ruled 500 years. The Franks, a Teutonic tribe, reached the Somme from the East c. AD 250. By the 5th century the Merovingian Franks ousted the Romans. In 451, with the help of Visigoths, Burgundians, and others, they defeated Attila and the Huns at Chalons-sur-Marne.

Childeric I became leader of the Merovingians 458. His son Clovis I (Chlodwig, Ludwig, Louis), crowned 481, founded the dynasty. After defeating the Alemanni (Germans) 496, he was baptized a Christian and made Paris his capital. His line ruled until Childeric III was deposed, 751.

The West Merovingians were called Neustrians, the eastern Austrasians. Pepin of Herstal (687-714), major domus,

or head of the palace, of Austrasia, took over Neustria as dux (leader) of the Franks. Pepin's son, Charles, called Martel (the Hammer), defeated the Saracens at Tours-Poitiers, 732; was succeeded by his son, Pepin the Short, 741, who deposed Childeric III and ruled as king until 768.

His son, Charlemagne, or Charles the Great (742-814), became king of the Franks, 768, with his brother Carloman, who died 771. Charlemagne ruled France, Germany, parts of Italy, Spain, and Austria, and enforced Christianity. Crowned Emperor of the Romans by Pope Leo III in St. Peter's, Rome, Dec. 25, 800. Succeeded by son, Louis I the Pious, 814. At death, 840, Louis left empire to sons, Lothair (Roman emperor); Pepin I (king of Aquitaine); Louis II (of Germany); Charles the Bald (France). They quarreled and, by the peace of Verdun, 843, divided the empire.

The date preceding each entry is year of accession.

The Carolingians

843 Charles I (the Bald); Roman Emperor, 875
877 Louis II (the Stammerer), son
879 Louis III (died 882) and Carloman, brothers
885 Charles II (the Fat); Roman Emperor, 881
888 Eudes (Odo), elected by nobles
898 Charles III (the Simple), son of Louis II, defeated by
922 Robert, brother of Eudes, killed in war
923 Rudolph (Raoul), Duke of Burgundy
936 Louis IV, son of Charles III
954 Lothair, son, aged 13, defeated by Capet
986 Louis V (the Sluggard), left no heirs

The Capets

987 Hugh Capet, son of Hugh the Great
996 Robert II (the Wise), his son
1031 Henry I, son
1060 Philip I (the Fair), son
1108 Louis VI (the Fat), son
1137 Louis VII (the Younger), son
1180 Philip II (Augustus), son, crowned at Reims
1223 Louis VIII (the Lion), son
1226 Louis IX, son, crusader; Louis IX (1214-1270) reigned 44 years, arbitrated disputes with English King Henry III; led crusades, 1248 (captured in Egypt 1250) and 1270, when he died of plague in Tunis. Canonized 1297 as St. Louis.
1270 Philip III (the Hardy), son
1285 Philip IV (the Fair), son, king at 17
1314 Louis X (the Headstrong), son. His posthumous son, John I, lived only 7 days
1316 Philip V (the Tall), brother of Louis X
1322 Charles IV (the Fair), brother of Louis X

House of Valois

1328 Philip VI (of Valois), grandson of Philip III
1350 John II (the Good), his son, retired to England
1364 Charles V (the Wise), son
1380 Charles VI (the Beloved), son
1422 Charles VII (the Victorious), son. In 1429 Joan of Arc (Jeanne d'Arc) promised Charles to oust the English who occupied northern France. Joan won at Orleans and Patay and had Charles crowned at Reims, July 17, 1429. Joan was captured May 24, 1430, and executed May 30, 1431, at Rouen for heresy. Charles ordered her rehabilitation, effected 1455.
1461 Louis XI (the Cruel), son, civil reformer
1483 Charles VIII (the Affable), son
1498 Louis XII, great-grandson of Charles V
1515 Francis I, of Angouleme, nephew, son-in-law. Francis I (1494-1547) reigned 32 years, fought 4 big wars, was patron of the arts, aided Cellini, del Sarto, Leonardo da Vinci, Rabelais, embellished Fontainebleau.
1547 Henry II, son, killed at a joust in a tournament. He was the husband of Catherine de Medicis (1519-1589) and the lover of Diane de Poitiers (1499-1566). Catherine was born in Florence, daughter of Lorenzo de Medici. By her marriage to Henry II she became the mother of Francis II, Charles IX, Henry III, and Queen Margaret (Reine Margot), wife of Henry IV. She persuaded Charles IX to order the massacre of Huguenots on the Feast of St. Bartholomew, Aug. 24, 1572, six days after her daughter was married to Henry of Navarre.
1559 Francis II, son. In 1548, Mary, Queen of Scots since infancy, was betrothed when 6 to Francis, aged 4. They were married 1558. Francis died 1560, aged 16; Mary ruled Scotland, abdicated 1567.
1560 Charles IX, brother
1574 Henry III, brother, assassinated

House of Bourbon

1589 Henry IV, of Navarre, assassinated. Henry IV made enemies when he gave tolerance to Protestants by Edict of Nantes, 1598. He was grandson of Queen Margaret of Navarre, literary patron. He married Margaret of Valois, daughter of Henry II and Catherine de Medicis; was divorced; in 1600 married Marie de Medicis, who became Regent of France, 1610-1617, for her son, Louis XIII, but was exiled by Richelieu, 1631.
1610 Louis XIII (the Just), son. Louis XIII (1601-1643) married Anne of Austria. He came to be dominated by his chief minister (1622-42), Cardinal Richelieu.

1643 Louis XIV ("the Sun King"), son. Louis XIV was king 72 years. Until 1661, Anne of Austria was regent, with Cardinal Mazarin as chief minister; after that, Louis ruled absolutely. Known for his lavish court and patronage of the arts, he exhausted a prosperous country in wars for thrones and territory.
1715 Louis XV, great-grandson. Louis XV married a Polish princess; lost Canada to the English. His favorites, Mme. Pompadour and Mme. Du Barry, influenced policies. Noted for saying "After me, the deluge."
1774 Louis XVI, grandson; married Marie Antoinette, daughter of Empress Maria Therese of Austria. King and queen beheaded by Revolution, 1793. Their son, called Louis XVII, died in prison, never ruled.

First Republic

1792 National Convention of the French Revolution
1795 Directory, under Barras and others
1799 Consulate, Napoleon Bonaparte, first consul. Elected consul for life, 1802.

First Empire

1804 Napoleon I (Napoleon Bonaparte), emperor. Josephine (de Beauharnais), empress, 1804-1809; Marie Louise, empress, 1810-1814. Her son, Francois (1811-1832), titular King of Rome, later Duke de Reichstadt and "Napoleon II," never ruled. Napoleon abdicated 1814, died 1821.

Bourbons Restored

1814 Louis XVIII, king; brother of Louis XVI
1824 Charles X, brother; reactionary; deposed by the July Revolution, 1830

House of Orleans

1830 Louis-Philippe, the "citizen king"

Second Republic

1848 Louis Napoleon Bonaparte, president, nephew of Napoleon I.

Second Empire

1852 Napoleon III (Louis Napoleon Bonaparte), emperor; Eugenie (de Montijo), empress. Lost Franco-Prussian war, deposed 1870. Son, Prince Imperial (1856-1879), died in Zulu War. Eugenie died 1920.

Third Republic—Presidents

1871 Thiers, Louis Adolphe (1797-1877)
1873 MacMahon, Marshal Patrice M. de (1808-1893)
1879 Grevy, Paul J. (1807-1891)
1887 Sadi-Carnot, M. (1837-1894), assassinated
1894 Casimir-Perier, Jean P. P. (1847-1907)
1895 Faure, François Felix (1841-1899)
1899 Loubet, Emile (1838-1929)
1906 Fallieres, C. Armand (1841-1931)
1913 Poincare, Raymond (1860-1934)
1920 Deschanel, Paul (1856-1922)
1920 Millerand, Alexandre (1859-1943)
1924 Doumergue, Gaston (1863-1937)
1931 Doumer, Paul (1857-1932), assassinated
1932 Lebrun, Albert (1871-1950), resigned 1940
1940 Vichy govt. under German armistice: Henri Philippe Petain (1856-1951), Chief of State, 1940-1944.

Provisional govt. after liberation: Charles de Gaulle (1890-1970), Oct. 1944-Jan. 21, 1946; Felix Gouin (1884-1977), Jan. 23, 1946; Georges Bidault (1899-1983), June 24, 1946.

Fourth Republic—Presidents

1947 Auriol, Vincent (1884-1966)
1954 Coty, Rene (1882-1962)

Fifth Republic—Presidents

1959 De Gaulle, Charles Andre J. M. (1890-1970)
1969 Pompidou, Georges (1911-1974)
1974 Giscard d'Estaing, Valery (1926-   )
1981 Mitterrand, François (1916-1996)
1995 Chirac, Jacques (1932-   )

Rulers of Middle Europe; Rise and Fall of Dynasties; Rulers of Germany

Carolingian Dynasty

Charles the Great, or Charlemagne, ruled France, Italy, and Middle Europe; established Ostmark (later Austria); crowned Roman emperor by pope in Rome, AD 800; died 814.

Louis I (Ludwig) the Pious, son; crowned by Charlemagne 814; died 840.

Louis II, the German, son; succeeded to East Francia (Germany) 843-876.

Charles the Fat, son; inherited East Francia and West Francia (France) 876, reunited empire, crowned emperor by pope 881, deposed 887.

Arnulf, nephew, 887-899. Partition of empire.

Louis the Child, 899-911, last direct descendant of Charlemagne.

Conrad I, duke of Franconia, first elected German king, 911-918, founded House of Franconia.

Saxon Dynasty; First Reich

Henry I, the Fowler, duke of Saxony, 919-936.

Otto I, the Great, 936-973, son; crowned Holy Roman Emperor by pope, 962.

Otto II, 973-983, son; failed to oust Greeks and Arabs from Sicily.

Otto III, 983-1002, son; crowned emperor at 16.

Henry II, the Saint, duke of Bavaria, 1002-1024, great-grandson of Otto the Great.

House of Franconia

Conrad II, 1024-1039, elected king of Germany.

Henry III, the Black, 1039-1056, son; deposed 3 popes; annexed Burgundy.

Henry IV, 1056-1106, son; regency by his mother, Agnes of Poitou. Banned by Pope Gregory VII, he did penance at Canossa.

Henry V, 1106-1125, son; last of Salic House.

Lothair, duke of Saxony, 1125-1137. Crowned emperor in Rome, 1134.

House of Hohenstaufen

Conrad III, duke of Swabia, 1138-1152. In 2nd Crusade.

Frederick I, Barbarossa, 1152-1190; Conrad's nephew.

Henry VI, 1190-1196, took lower Italy from Normans. Son became king of Sicily.

Philip of Swabia, 1197-1208, brother.

Otto IV, of House of Welf, 1198-1215; deposed.

Frederick II, 1215-1250, son of Henry VI; king of Sicily; crowned king of Jerusalem in 5th Crusade.

Conrad IV, 1250-1254, son; lost lower Italy to Charles of Anjou.

Conradin, 1252-1268, son, king of Jerusalem and Sicily, beheaded. Last Hohenstaufen.

Interregnum, 1254-1273, Rise of the Electors.

Transition

Rudolph I of Hapsburg, 1273-1291, defeated King Ottocar II of Bohemia. Bequeathed duchy of Austria to eldest son, Albert.

Adolph of Nassau, 1292-1298, killed in war with Albert of Austria.

Albert I, king of Germany, 1298-1308, son of Rudolph.

Henry VII, of Luxemburg, 1308-1313, crowned emperor in Rome. Seized Bohemia, 1310.

Louis IV of Bavaria (Wittelsbach), 1314-1347. Also elected was Frederick of Austria, 1314-1330 (Hapsburg). Abolition of papal sanction for election of Holy Roman Emperor.

Charles IV, of Luxemburg, 1347-1378, grandson of Henry VII, German emperor and king of Bohemia, Lombardy, Burgundy; took Mark of Brandenburg.

Wenceslaus, 1378-1400, deposed.

Rupert, Duke of Palatine, 1400-1410.

Sigismund, 1411-1437.

Hungary

Stephen I, house of Arpad, 997-1038. Crowned king 1000; converted Magyars; canonized 1083. After several centuries of feuds Charles Robert of Anjou became Charles I, 1308-1342.

Louis I, the Great, son, 1342-1382; joint ruler of Poland with Casimir III, 1370. Defeated Turks.

Mary, daughter. 1382-1395, ruled with husband. Sigismund of Luxemburg, 1387-1437, also king of Bohemia. As brother of Wenceslaus he succeeded Rupert as Holy Roman Emperor, 1410.

Albert, 1438-1439, son-in-law of Sigismund; also Roman emperor as Albert II (see under Hapsburg).

Ulaszlo I of Poland, 1440-1444.

Ladislaus V, posthumous son of Albert II, 1444-1457. John Hunyadi (Hunyadi Janos), governor (1446-1452), fought Turks, Czechs; died 1456.

Matthias I (Corvinus), son of Hunyadi, 1458-1490. Shared rule of Bohemia, captured Vienna, 1485, annexed Austria, Styria, Carinthia.

Ulaszlo II (king of Bohemia), 1490-1516.

Louis II, son, aged 10, 1516-1526. Wars with Suleiman, Turk.

In 1527 Hungary split between Ferdinand I, Archduke of Austria, bro.-in-law of Louis II, and John Zapolya of Transylvania. After Turkish invasion, 1547, Hungary split between Ferdinand, Prince John Sigismund (Transylvania), and the Turks.

House of Hapsburg

Albert V of Austria, Hapsburg, crowned king of Hungary, Jan. 1438, Roman emperor, March 1438, as Albert II; died 1439.

Frederick III, cousin, 1440-1493. Fought Turks.

Maximilian I, son, 1493-1519. Assumed title of Holy Roman Emperor (German), 1493.

Charles V, grandson, 1519-1556. King of Spain with mother co-regent; crowned Roman emperor at Aix, 1520. Confronted Luther at Worms; attempted church reform and religious conciliation; abdicated 1556.

Ferdinand I, son of Bohemia, 1526, of Hungary, 1527; disputed German king, 1531. Crowned Roman emperor on abdication of brother Charles V, 1556.

Maximilian II, son, 1564-1576.

Rudolph II, son, 1576-1612.

Matthias, brother, 1612-1619, king of Bohemia and Hungary.

Ferdinand II of Styria, king of Bohemia, 1617, of Hungary, 1618, Roman emperor, 1619. Bohemian Protestants deposed him, elected Frederick V of Palatine, starting Thirty Years War.

Ferdinand III, son, king of Hungary, 1625, Bohemia, 1627, Roman emperor, 1637. Peace of Westphalia, 1648, ended war. Leopold I, 1658-1705; Joseph I, 1705-1711; Charles VI, 1711-1740.

Maria Theresa, daughter, 1740-1780, Archduchess of Austria, queen of Hungary; ousted pretender, Charles VII, crowned 1742; in 1745 obtained election of her husband Francis I as Roman emperor and co-regent (d. 1765). Fought Seven Years' War with Frederick II of Prussia. Mother of Marie Antoinette.

Joseph II, son, 1765-1790, Roman emperor, reformer; powers restricted by Empress Maria Theresa until her death, 1780. First partition of Poland. Leopold II, 1790-1792.

Francis II, son, 1792-1835. Fought Napoleon. Proclaimed first hereditary emperor of Austria, 1804. Forced to abdicate as Roman emperor 1806; last use of title. Ferdinand I, son, 1835-1848, abdicated during revolution.

Austro-Hungarian Monarchy

Francis Joseph I, nephew, 1848-1916, emperor of Austria, king of Hungary. Dual monarchy of Austria-Hungary formed, 1867. After assassination of heir, Archduke Francis Ferdinand, June 28, 1914, Austrian diplomacy precipitated World War I.

Charles I, grand-nephew, 1916-1918, last emperor of Austria and king of Hungary. Abdicated Nov. 11-13, 1918, died 1922.

Rulers of Prussia

Nucleus of Prussia was the Mark of Brandenburg. First margrave Albert the Bear (Albrecht), 1134-1170. First Hohenzollern margrave was Frederick, burgrave of Nuremberg, 1417-1470.

Frederick William, 1640-1688, the Great Elector. Son, Frederick III, 1688-1713, crowned King Frederick of Prussia, 1701.

Frederick William I, son, 1713-1740.

Frederick II, the Great, son, 1740-1786, annexed Silesia, part of Austria.

Frederick William II, nephew, 1786-1797.

Frederick William III, son, 1797-1840. Napoleonic wars.

Frederick William IV, son, 1840-1861. Uprising of 1848 and first parliament and constitution.

Second and Third Reich

William I, 1861-1888, brother. Annexation of Schleswig and Hanover; Franco-Prussian war, 1870-1871, proclamation of German Reich, Jan. 18, 1871, at Versailles; William, German emperor (Deutscher Kaiser), Bismarck, chancellor.

Frederick III, son, 1888.

William II, son, 1888-1918. Led Germany in World War I, abdicated as German emperor and king of Prussia, Nov. 9, 1918. Died in exile in Netherlands, June 4, 1941. Minor rulers of Bavaria, Saxony, Wurttemberg also abdicated.

Germany proclaimed republic at Weimar, July 1, 1919. Presidents included: Frederick Ebert, 1919-1925; Paul von Hindenburg-Beneckendorff, 1925, reelected 1932, d. Aug. 2, 1934. Adolf Hitler, chancellor, chosen successor as Leader-Chancellor (Fuehrer-Reichskanzler) of Third Reich. Annexed Austria, Mar. 1938. Precipitated World War II, 1939-1945. Suicide Apr. 30, 1945.

Germany After 1945

Following World War II, Germany was split between democratic West and Soviet-dominated East. West German chancellors: Konrad Adenauer, 1949-1963; Ludwig Erhard, 1963-1966; Kurt Georg Kiesinger, 1966-1969; Willy Brandt, 1969-1974; Helmut Schmidt, 1974-1982; Helmut Kohl, 1982-1990. East German Communist party leaders: Walter Ulbricht, 1946-1971; Erich Honecker, 1971-1989; Egon Krenz, 1989-1990.

Germany reunited Oct. 3, 1990. Post-reunification chancellors: Helmut Kohl, 1990-1998; Gerhard Schröder, 1998- .

Rulers of Poland

House of Piasts

Miesko I, 962?-992; Poland Christianized 966. Expansion under 3 Boleslavs: I, 992-1025, son, crowned king 1024; II, 1058-1079, great-grandson, exiled after killing bishop Stanislav who became chief patron saint of Poland; III, 1106-1138, nephew, divided Poland among 4 sons, eldest suzerain.

1138-1306, feudal division. 1226 founding in Prussia of military order Teutonic Knights. 1226 invasion by Tartars/Mongols.

Vladislav I, 1306-1333, reunited most Polish territories, crowned king 1320. Casimir III the Great, 1333-1370, son, developed economic, cultural life, foreign policy.

House of Anjou

Louis I, 1370-1382, nephew/was also Louis I of Hungary.
Jadwiga, 1384-1399, daughter, married 1386 Jagiello, Grand Duke of Lithuania.

House of Jagiellonians

Vladislav II, 1386-1434, Christianized Lithuania, founded personal union between Poland and Lithuania. Defeated 1410 Teutonic Knights at Grunwald.

Vladislav III, 1434-1444, son, simultaneously king of Hungary. Fought Turks, killed 1444 in battle of Varna.

Casimir IV, 1446-1492, brother, competed with Hapsburgs, put son Vladislav on throne of Bohemia, later also of Hungary (Ulaszlo II).

Sigismund I, 1506-1548, son, patronized science and arts, his and son's reign "Golden Age."

Sigismund II, 1548-1572, son, established 1569 real union of Poland and Lithuania (lasted until 1795).

Elective Kings

Polish nobles in 1572 proclaimed Poland a republic headed by king to be elected by whole nobility.

Stephen Batory, 1576-1586, duke of Transylvania, married Ann, sister of Sigismund II August. Fought Russians.

Sigismund III Vasa, 1587-1632, nephew of Sigismund II. 1592-1598 also king of Sweden. His generals fought Russians, Turks.

Vladislav II Vasa, 1632-1648, son. Fought Russians.

John II Casimir Vasa, 1648-1668, brother. Fought Cossacks, Swedes, Russians, Turks, Tatars (the "Deluge"). Abdicated 1668.

John III Sobieski, 1674-1696. Won Vienna from besieging Turks, 1683.

Stanislav II, 1764-1795, last king. Encouraged reforms; 1791 1st modern Constitution in Europe. 1772, 1793, 1795 Poland partitioned among Russia, Prussia, Austria. Unsuccessful insurrection against foreign invasion 1794 under Kosciusko, American-Polish general.

1795-1918: Poland Under Foreign Rule

1807-1815 Grand Duchy of Warsaw created by Napoleon I, Frederick August of Saxony grand duke.

1815 Congress of Vienna proclaimed part of Poland "Kingdom" in personal union with Russia.

Polish uprisings: 1830 against Russia; 1846, 1848 against Austria; 1863 against Russia—all repressed.

1918-1939: Second Republic

1918-1922 Head of State Jozef Pilsudski. Presidents: Gabriel Narutowicz 1922, assassinated; Stanislav Wojciechowski 1922-1926, had to abdicate after Pilsudski's coup d'état; Ignacy Moscicki, 1926-1939, ruled (with Pilsudski until his death, 1935) as virtual dictator.

1939-1945: Poland Under Foreign Occupation

Nazi and Soviet invasion Sept. 1939. Polish government-in-exile, first in France, then in England. Vladislav Raczkiewicz president; Gen. Vladislav Sikorski, then Stanislav Mikolajczyk, prime ministers. Soviet-sponsored Polish Committee of National Liberation proclaimed at Lublin July 1944, transformed into government Jan. 1, 1945.

Poland After 1945

In the late 1940s, Poland came increasingly under Soviet control. Communist party ruled in Poland until Aug. 1989, when democratic Solidarity party, led by Lech Walesa, gained control of government. Walesa was elected president in 1990, but lost the office to former communist Aleksander Kwasniewski in 1995. The government remained democratic, and Kwasniewski was re-elected in Oct. 2000.

Rulers of Denmark, Sweden, Norway

Denmark

Earliest rulers invaded Britain; King Canute, who ruled in London 1016-1035, was most famous. The Valdemars furnished kings until the 15th century. In 1282 the Danes won the first national assembly, Danehof, from King Erik V.

Most redoubtable medieval character was Margaret, daughter of Valdemar IV, born 1353, married at 10 to King Haakon VI of Norway. In 1376 she had her first infant-son Olaf made king of Denmark. After his death, 1387, she was regent of Denmark and Norway. In 1388 Sweden accepted her as sovereign. In 1389 she made her grand-nephew, Duke Erik of Pomerania, titular king of Denmark, Sweden, and Norway, with herself as regent. In 1397 she effected the Union of Kalmar of the three kingdoms and had Erik VII crowned. In 1439 the three kingdoms deposed him and elected, 1440, Christopher of Bavaria king (Christopher III). On his death, 1448, the union broke up.

Succeeding rulers were unable to enforce their claims as rulers of Sweden until 1520, when Christian II conquered Sweden. He was thrown out 1522, and in 1523 Gustavus Vasa united Sweden. Denmark continued to dominate Norway until the Napoleonic wars, when Frederick VI, 1808-1839, joined the Napoleonic cause after Britain had destroyed the Danish fleet, 1807. In 1814 he was forced to cede Norway to Sweden and Helgoland to Britain, receiving Lauenburg. Successors Christian VIII, 1839; Frederick VII, 1848; Christian IX, 1863; Frederick VIII, 1906; Christian X, 1912; Frederick IX, 1947; Margrethe II, 1972.

Sweden

Early kings ruled at Uppsala, but did not dominate the country. Sverker, c1130-c1156, united the Swedes and Goths. In 1435 Sweden obtained the Riksdag, or parliament. After the Union of Kalmar, 1397, the Danes either ruled or harried the country until Christian II of Denmark conquered it anew, 1520. This led to a rising under Gustavus Vasa, who ruled Sweden 1523-1560, and established an independent kingdom. Charles IX, 1599-1611, crowned 1604, conquered Moscow. Gustavus II Adolphus, 1611-1632, was called the Lion of the North. Later rulers: Christina, 1632; Charles X Gustavus, 1654; Charles XI, 1660; Charles XII (invader of Russia and Poland, defeated at Poltava, June 28, 1709), 1697; Ulrika Eleanora, sister, elected queen 1718; Frederick I (of Hesse), her husband, 1720; Adolphus Frederick, 1751; Gustavus III, 1771; Gustavus IV Adolphus, 1792; Charles XIII, 1809. (Union with Norway began 1814.) Charles XIV John, 1818 (he was Jean Bernadotte, Napoleon's Prince of Ponte Corvo, elected 1810 to succeed Charles XIII); he founded the present dynasty: Oscar I, 1844; Charles XV, 1859; Oscar II, 1872; Gustavus V, 1907; Gustav VI Adolf, 1950; Carl XVI Gustaf, 1973.

Norway

Overcoming many rivals, Harald Haarfager, 872-930, conquered Norway, Orkneys, and Shetlands; Olaf I, great-grandson, 995-1000, brought Christianity into Norway, Iceland, and Greenland. In 1035 Magnus the Good also became king of Denmark. Haakon V, 1299-1319, had married his daughter to Erik of Sweden. Their son, Magnus, became ruler of Norway and Sweden at 6. His son, Haakon VI, married Margaret of Denmark; their son Olaf IV became king of Norway and Denmark, followed by Margaret's regency and the Union of Kalmar, 1397.

In 1450 Norway became subservient to Denmark. Christian IV, 1588-1648, founded Christiania, now Oslo. After Napoleonic wars, when Denmark ceded Norway to Sweden, a strong nationalist movement forced recognition of Norway as an independent kingdom united with Sweden under the Swedish kings, 1814-1905. In 1905 the union was dissolved and Prince Charles of Denmark became Haakon VII. He died Sept. 21, 1957; succeeded by son, Olav V. Olav V died Jan. 17, 1991; succeeded by son, Harald V.

Rulers of the Netherlands and Belgium

The Netherlands (Holland)

William Frederick, Prince of Orange, led a revolt against French rule, 1813; crowned king, 1815. Belgium seceded Oct. 4, 1830, after a revolt. The secession was ratified by the two kingdoms by treaty, Apr. 19, 1839.

Succession: William II, son, 1840; William III, son, 1849; Wilhelmina, daughter of William III and his 2nd wife Princess Emma of Waldeck, 1890; Wilhelmina abdicated, Sept. 4, 1948, in favor of daughter, Juliana. Juliana abdicated, Apr. 30, 1980, in favor of daughter, Beatrix.

Belgium

A national congress elected Prince Leopold of Saxe-Coburg as king; he took the throne July 21, 1831, as Leopold I.

Succession: Leopold II, son, 1865; Albert I, nephew of Leopold II, 1909; Leopold III, son of Albert, 1934; Prince Charles, Regent 1944; Leopold returned 1950, yielded powers to son Baudouin, Prince Royal, Aug. 6, 1950, abdicated July 16, 1951. Baudouin I took throne July 17, 1951, died July 31, 1993; succeeded by brother, Albert II.

Roman Rulers

From Romulus to the end of the Empire in the West. Rulers in the East sat in Constantinople and, for a brief period, in Nicaea, until the capture of Constantinople by the Turks in 1453, when Byzantium was succeeded by the Ottoman Empire.

The Kingdom

BC
753 Romulus (Quirinus)
716 Numa Pompilius
673 Tullus Hostilius
640 Ancus Marcius
616 L. Tarquinius Priscus
578 Servius Tullius
534 L. Tarquinius Superbus

The Republic

509 Consulate established
509 Quaestorship instituted
498 Dictatorship introduced
494 Plebeian Tribunate created
494 Plebeian Aedileship created
444 Consular Tribunate organized
435 Censorship instituted
366 Praetorship established
366 Curule Aedileship created
362 Military Tribunate elected
326 Proconsulate introduced
311 Naval Duumvirate elected
217 Dictatorship of Fabius Maximus
133 Tribunate of Tiberius Gracchus
123 Tribunate of Gaius Gracchus
82 Dictatorship of Sulla
60 First Triumvirate formed (Caesar, Pompeius, Crassus)
46 Dictatorship of Caesar
43 Second Triumvirate formed (Octavianus, Antonius, Lepidus)

The Empire

27 Augustus (Octavian)

AD
14 Tiberius I
37 Caligula
41 Claudius I
54 Nero
68 Galba
69 Galba; Otho, Vitellius
69 Vespasianus
79 Titus

81 Domitianus
96 Nerva
98 Trajanus
117 Hadrianus
138 Antoninus Pius
161 Marcus Aurelius and Lucius Verus
169 Marcus Aurelius (alone)
180 Commodus
193 Pertinax; Julianus I
193 Septimius Severus
211 Caracalla and Geta
212 Caracalla (alone)
217 Macrinus
218 Elagabalus (Heliogabalus)
222 Alexander Severus
235 Maximinus I (the Thracian)
238 Gordianus I and Gordianus II; Pupienus and Balbinus
238 Gordianus III
244 Philippus (the Arabian)
249 Decius
251 Gallus and Volusianus
253 Aemilianus
253 Valerianus and Gallienus
258 Gallienus (alone)
268 Claudius Gothicus
270 Quintillus
270 Aurelianus
275 Tacitus
276 Florianus
276 Probus
282 Carus
283 Carinus and Numerianus
286 Diocletianus and Maximianus
305 Galerius and Constantius I
306 Galerius, Maximinus II, Severus I
307 Galerius, Maximinus II, Constantinus I, Licinius, Maxentius
311 Maximinus II, Constantinus I, Licinius, Maxentius
314 Maximinus II, Constantinus I, Licinius
314 Constantinus I and Licinius

324 Constantinus I (the Great)
337 Constantinus II, Constans I, Constantius II
340 Constantius II and Constans I
350 Constantius II
361 Julianus II (the Apostate)
363 Jovianus

West (Rome) and East (Constantinople)

364 Valentinianus I (West) and Valens (East)
367 Valentinianus I with Gratianus (West) and Valens (East)
375 Gratianus with Valentinianus II (West) and Valens (East)
378 Gratianus with Valentinianus II (West), Theodosius I (East)
383 Valentinianus II (West) and Theodosius I (East)
394 Theodosius I (the Great)
395 Honorius (West) and Arcadius (East)
408 Honorius (West) and Theodosius II (East)
423 Valentinianus III (West) and Theodosius II (East)
450 Valentinianus III (West) and Marcianus (East)
455 Maximus (West), Avitus (West); Marcianus (East)
456 Avitus (West), Marcianus (East)
457 Majorianus (West), Leo I (East)
461 Severus II (West), Leo I (East)
467 Anthemius (West), Leo I (East)
472 Olybrius (West), Leo I (East)
473 Glycerius (West), Leo I (East)
474 Julius Nepos (West), Leo II (East)
475 Romulus Augustulus (West) and Zeno (East)
476 End of Empire in West; Odovacar, King, drops title of Emperor; murdered by King Theodoric of Ostrogoths, 493

Rulers of Modern Italy

After the fall of Napoleon in 1814, the Congress of Vienna, 1815, restored Italy as a political patchwork, comprising the Kingdom of Naples and Sicily, the Papal States, and smaller units. Piedmont and Genoa were awarded to Sardinia, ruled by King Victor Emmanuel I of Savoy.

United Italy emerged under the leadership of Camillo, Count di Cavour (1810-1861), Sardinian prime minister. Agitation was led by Giuseppe Mazzini (1805-1872) and Giuseppe Garibaldi (1807-1882), soldier; Victor Emmanuel I abdicated 1821. After a brief regency for a brother, Charles Albert was king 1831-1849, abdicating when defeated by the Austrians at Novara. Succeeded by Victor Emmanuel II, 1849-1861.

In 1859 France forced Austria to cede Lombardy to Sardinia, which gave rights to Savoy and Nice to France. In 1860 Garibaldi led 1,000 volunteers in a spectacular campaign, took Sicily and expelled the King of Naples. In 1860 the House of Savoy annexed Tuscany, Parma, Modena, Romagna, the Two Sicilys, the Marches, and Umbria. Victor Emmanuel assumed the title of King of Italy at Turin Mar. 17, 1861.

In 1866, Victor Emmanuel allied with Prussia in the Austro-Prussian War, and with Prussia's victory received Venetia. On Sept. 20, 1870, his troops under Gen. Raffaele Cadorna entered Rome and took over the Papal States, ending the temporal power of the Roman Catholic Church.

Succession: Umberto I, 1878, assassinated 1900; Victor Emmanuel III, 1900, abdicated 1946, died 1947; Humbert II, 1946, ruled a month. In 1921 Benito Mussolini (1883-1945) formed the Fascist party; he became prime minister Oct. 31, 1922. He entered World War II as an ally of Hitler. He was deposed July 25, 1943.

At a plebiscite June 2, 1946, Italy voted for a republic; Premier Alcide de Gasperi became chief of state June 13, 1946. On June 28, 1946, the Constituent Assembly elected Enrico de Nicola, Liberal, provisional president. Successive presidents: Luigi Einaudi, elected May 11, 1948; Giovanni Gronchi, Apr. 29, 1955; Antonio Segni, May 6, 1962; Giuseppe Saragat, Dec. 28, 1964; Giovanni Leone, Dec. 29, 1971; Alessandro Pertini, July 9, 1978; Francesco Cossiga, July 9, 1985; Oscar Luigi Scalfaro, May 28, 1992; Carlo Azeglio Ciampi, May 18, 1999.

Rulers of Spain

From 8th to 11th centuries Spain was dominated by the Moors (Arabs and Berbers). The Christian reconquest established small kingdoms (Asturias, Aragon, Castile, Catalonia, Leon, Navarre, and Valencia). In 1474 Isabella. b. 1451, became Queen of Castile & Leon. Her husband, Ferdinand, b. 1452, inherited Aragon 1479, with Catalonia, Valencia, and the Balearic Islands, became Ferdinand V of Castile. By Isabella's request Pope Sixtus IV established the Inquisition, 1478. Last Moorish kingdom, Granada, fell 1492. Columbus opened New World of colonies, 1492. Isabella died 1504, succeeded by her daughter, Juana "the Mad," but Ferdinand ruled until his death 1516.

Charles I, b. 1500, son of Juana, grandson of Ferdinand and Isabella, and of Maximilian I of Hapsburg; succeeded later as Holy Roman Emperor, Charles V, 1520; abdicated 1556. Philip II. son, 1556-1598, inherited only Spanish throne: conquered Portugal, fought Turks, sent Armada vs. England. Married to Mary I of England, 1554-1558. Succession: Philip III, 1598-1621; Philip IV, 1621-1665; Charles II, 1665-1700, left Spain to Philip of Anjou, grandson of Louis XIV, who as Philip V, 1700-1746, founded Bourbon dynasty; Ferdinand VI, 1746-1759; Charles III, 1759-1788; Charles IV, 1788-1808, abdicated.

Napoleon now dominated politics and made his brother Joseph King of Spain 1808, but the Spanish ousted him in 1813. Ferdinand VII, 1808, 1814-1833, lost American colonies; succeeded by daughter Isabella II, aged 3, with wife Maria Christina of Naples regent until 1843. Isabella deposed by revolution 1868. Elected king by the Cortes, Amadeo of Savoy, 1870; abdicated 1873. First republic, 1873-74. Alfonso XII, son of Isabella, 1875-85. His posthumous son was Alfonso XIII, with his mother. Queen Maria Christina regent; Spanish-American war, Spain lost Cuba, gave up Puerto Rico, Philippines, Sulu Is., Marianas. Alfonso took throne 1902. aged 16, married British Princess Victoria Eugenia of Battenberg. Dictatorship of Primo de Rivera, 1923-30, precipitated revolution of 1931. Alfonso agreed to leave without formal abdication. Monarchy abolished; the second republic established, with socialist backing. Niceto Alcala Zamora was president until 1936, when Manuel Azaña was chosen.

In July 1936, the army in Morocco revolted against the government and General Francisco Franco led the troops into Spain. The revolution succeeded by Feb. 1939, when Azaña resigned. Franco became chief of state, with provisions that if he was incapacitated, the Regency Council by two-thirds vote could propose a king to the Cortes, which needed to have a two-thirds majority to elect him.

Alfonso XIII died in Rome Feb. 28, 1941, aged 54. His property and citizenship had been restored.

A law restoring the monarchy was approved in a 1947 referendum. Prince Juan Carlos, b. 1938, grandson of Alfonso XIII, was designated by Franco and the Cortes (Parliament) in 1969 as future king and chief of state. Franco died in office, Nov. 20, 1975; Juan Carlos proclaimed king, Nov. 22.

Leaders in the South American Wars of Liberation

Simon Bolivar (1783-1830), Jose Francisco de San Martin (1778-1850), and Francisco Antonio Gabriel Miranda (1750-1816) are among the heroes of the early 19th-century struggles of South American nations to free themselves from Spain. All three, and their contemporaries, operated in periods of factional strife, during which soldiers and civilians suffered.

Miranda, a Venezuelan, who had served with the French in the American Revolution and commanded parts of the French Revolutionary armies in the Netherlands, attempted to start a revolt in Venezuela in 1806 and failed. In 1810, with British and American backing, he returned and briefly a dictator, until the British withdrew their support. In 1812 he was overcome by the royalists in Venezuela and taken prisoner, dying in a Spanish prison in 1816.

San Martin was born in Argentina and during 1789-1811 served in campaigns of the Spanish armies in Europe and Africa. He first joined the independence movement in Argentina in 1812 and in 1817 invaded Chile with 4,000 men over the mountain passes. Here he and Gen. Bernardo O'Higgins (1778-1842) defeated the Spaniards at Chacabuco, 1817; O'Higgins was named Liberator and became first director of Chile, 1817-23. In 1821 San Martin occupied Lima and Callao, Peru, and became protector of Peru.

Bolivar, the greatest leader of South American liberation from Spain, was born in Venezuela, the son of an aristocratic family. He first served under Miranda in 1812 and in 1813 captured Caracas, where he was named Liberator. Forced out next year by civil strife, he led a campaign that captured Bogota in 1814. In 1817 he was again in control of Venezuela and was named dictator. He organized Nueva Granada with the help of General Francisco de Paula Santander (1792-1840). By joining Nueva Granada, Venezuela, and the area that is now Panama and Ecuador, the republic of Colombia was formed, with Bolivar president. After numerous setbacks he decisively defeated the Spaniards in the second battle of Carabobo, Venezuela, June 24, 1821.

In May 1822, Gen. Antonio Jose de Sucre, Bolivar's lieutenant, took Quito. Bolivar went to Guayaquil to confer with San Martin, who resigned as protector of Peru and withdrew from politics. With a new army of Colombians and Peruvians Bolivar defeated the Spaniards in a battle at Junin in 1824 and cleared Peru.

De Sucre organized Charcas (Upper Peru) as Republica Bolivar (now Bolivia) and acted as president in place of Bolivar, who wrote its constitution. De Sucre defeated the Spanish faction of Peru at Ayacucho, Dec. 19, 1824.

Continued civil strife finally caused the Colombian federation to break apart. Santander turned against Bolivar, but the latter defeated him and banished him. In 1828 Bolivar gave up the presidency he had held precariously for 14 years. He became ill from tuberculosis and died Dec. 17, 1830. He is buried in the national pantheon in Caracas.

Rulers of Russia; Leaders of the USSR and Russian Federation

First ruler to consolidate Slavic tribes was Rurik, leader of the Russians who established himself at Novgorod, AD 862. He and his immediate successors had Scandinavian affiliations. They moved to Kiev after 972 and ruled as Dukes of Kiev. In 988 Vladimir was converted and adopted the Byzantine Greek Orthodox service, later modified by Slav influences. Important as organizer and lawgiver was Yaroslav, 1019-1054, whose daughters married kings of Norway, Hungary, and France. His grandson, Vladimir II (Monomakh), 1113-1125, was progenitor of several rulers, but in 1169 Andrew Bogolubski overthrew Kiev and began the line known as Grand Dukes of Vladimir.

Of the Grand Dukes of Vladimir, Alexander Nevsky, 1246-1263, had a son, Daniel, first to be called Duke of Muscovy (Moscow), who ruled 1263-1303. His successors became Grand Dukes of Muscovy. After Dmitri III Donskoi defeated the Tatars in 1380, they also became Grand Dukes of all Russia. Tatar independence and considerable territorial expansion were achieved under Ivan III, 1462-1505.

Tsars of Muscovy—Ivan III was referred to in church ritual as Tsar. He married Sofia, niece of the last Byzantine emperor. His successor, Basil III, died in 1533 when Basil's son Ivan was only 3. He became Ivan IV, "the Terrible": crowned 1547 as Tsar of all the Russias, ruled until 1584. Under the weak rule of his son, Feodor I, 1584-1598, Boris Godunov had control. The dynasty died, and after years of tribal strife and intervention by Polish and Swedish armies, the Russians united under 17-year-old Michael Romanov, distantly related to the first wife of Ivan IV. He ruled 1613-1645 and established the Romanov line. Fourth ruler after Michael was Peter I.

Tsars, or Emperors, of Russia (Romanovs)—Peter I, 1682-1725, known as Peter the Great, took title of Emperor in 1721. His successors and dates of accession were: Catherine, his widow, 1725; Peter II, his grandson, 1727; Anne, Duchess of Courland, 1730, daughter of Peter the Great's brother, Tsar Ivan V; Ivan VI, 1740, great-grandson of Ivan V, child, kept in prison and murdered 1764; Elizabeth, daughter of Peter I, 1741; Peter III, grandson of Peter I, 1761, deposed 1762 for his consort, Catherine II, former princess of Anhalt Zerbst (Germany) who is known as Catherine the Great; Paul I, her son, 1796, killed 1801; Alexander I, son of Paul, 1801, defeated Napoleon; Nicholas I, his brother, 1825; Alexander II, son of Nicholas, 1855, assassinated 1881 by terrorists; Alexander III, son, 1881. Nicholas II, son, 1894-1917, last Tsar of Russia, was forced to abdicate by the Revolution that followed losses to Germany in WWI. The Tsar, the Empress, the Tsarevich (Crown Prince), and the Tsar's 4 daughters were murdered by the Bolsheviks in Yekaterinburg, July 16, 1918.

Provisional Government—Prince Georgi Lvov and Alexander Kerensky, premiers, 1917.

Union of Soviet Socialist Republics

Bolshevik Revolution, Nov. 7, 1917, removed Kerensky from power; council of People's Commissars formed, Lenin (Vladimir Ilyich Ulyanov) became premier. Lenin died Jan. 21, 1924. Aleksei Rykov (executed 1938) and V. M. Molotov held the office, but actual ruler was Joseph Stalin (Joseph Vissarionovich Djugashvili), general secretary of the Central Committee of the Communist Party. Stalin became president of the Council of Ministers (premier) May 7, 1941, died Mar. 5, 1953. Succeeded by Georgi M. Malenkov, as head of the Council and premier, and Nikita S. Khrushchev, first secretary of the Central Committee. Malenkov resigned Feb. 8, 1955, became deputy premier, was dropped July 3, 1957. Marshal Nikolai A. Bulganin became premier Feb. 8, 1955; was demoted and Khrushchev became premier Mar. 27, 1958.

Khrushchev was ousted Oct. 14-15, 1964, replaced by Leonid I. Brezhnev as first secretary of the party and by Aleksei N. Kosygin as premier. On June 16, 1977, Brezhnev also took office as president. He died Nov. 10, 1982; 2 days later the Central Committee elected former KGB head Yuri V. Andropov president. Andropov died Feb. 9, 1984; on Feb. 13, Konstantin U. Chernenko chosen by Central Committee as its general secretary. Chernenko died Mar. 10, 1985; on Mar. 11, he was succeeded as general secretary by Mikhail Gorbachev, who replaced Andrei Gromyko as president on Oct. 1, 1988. Gorbachev resigned Dec. 25, 1991, and the Soviet Union officially disbanded the next day. Each of the 15 former Soviet constituent republics became independent.

Post-Soviet Russia

After adopting a degree of sovereignty, the Russian Republic had held elections in June 1991. Boris Yeltsin was sworn in July 10, 1991, as Russia's first elected president. With the Dec. 1991 dissolution of the Soviet Union, Russia (officially Russian Federation) became a founding member of the Commonwealth of Independent States. On Dec. 31, 1999, Yeltsin stepped down as president; he named Vladimir Putin his interim successor. Putin won a presidential election Mar. 26, 2000, and was sworn in May 7.

> **IT'S A FACT:** Stalin's real name was Iosif (Joesph) Vissarionovich Dzhugashvili. In 1910, while still a young revolutionary, he adopted the name Stalin, which means "man of steel."

Governments of China

(Until 221 BC and frequently thereafter, China was not a unified state. Where dynastic dates overlap, the rulers or events referred to appeared in different areas of China.)

Hsia	1994 BC – c1523 BC
Shang	c1523 BC – c1028 BC
Western Chou	c1027 BC – 770 BC
Eastern Chou	770 – 256 BC
Warring States	403 BC – 222 BC
Ch'in (first unified empire)	221 BC – 206 BC
Han	202 BC – AD 220
Western Han (expanded Chinese state beyond the Yellow and Yangtze River valleys)	202 BC – AD 9
Hsin (Wang Mang, usurper)	AD 9 – 23
Eastern Han (expanded Chinese state into Indochina and Turkestan)	25 – 220
Three Kingdoms (Wei, Shu, Wu)	220 – 265
Chin (western)	265 – 317
(eastern)	317 – 420
Northern Dynasties (followed several short-lived governments by Turks, Mongols, etc.)	386 – 581
Southern Dynasties (capital: Nanjing)	420 – 589
Sui (reunified China)	581 – 618

Tang (a golden age of Chinese culture; capital: Xian)	618 – 906
Five Dynasties (Yellow River basin)	902 – 960
Ten Kingdoms (southern China)	907 – 979
Liao (Khitan Mongols; capital at site of Beijing)	947 – 1125
Sung	960 – 1279
Northern Sung (reunified central and southern China)	960 – 1126
Western Hsai (non-Chinese rulers in northwest)	990 – 1227
Chin (Tatars; drove Sung out of central China)	1115 – 1234
Yuan (Mongols; Kublai Khan est. capital at site of Beijing, c. 1264)	1271 – 1368
Ming (China reunified under Chinese rule; capital: Nanjing, then Beijing in 1420)	1368 – 1644
Ch'ing (Manchus, descendents of Tatars)	1644 – 1911
Republic (disunity; provincial rulers, warlords)	1912 – 1949
People's Republic of China	1949 –

Leaders of China Since 1949

Mao Zedong	Chairman, Central People's Administrative Council, Communist Party (CPC), 1949-1976
Zhou Enlai	Premier, foreign minister, 1949-1976
Deng Xiaoping	Vice Premier, 1952-1966, 1973-1976, 1977-1980; "paramount leader," 1978-1997
Liu Shaoqi	President, 1959-1969
Hua Guofeng	Premier, 1976-1980; CPC Chairman, 1976-1981
Zhao Ziyang	Premier, 1980-1988; CPC General Secretary, 1987-1989
Hu Yaobang	CPC Chairman, 1981-1982; CPC General Secretary, 1982-1987
Li Xiannian	President, 1983-1988
Yang Shangkun	President, 1988-1993
Li Peng	Premier, 1988-98
Jiang Zemin	CPC General Secretary, 1989-2002; President, 1993-2003
Zhu Rongji	Premier, 1998-2003
Hu Jintao	CPC General Secretary, 2002-; President, 2003-
Wen Jiabao	Premier, 2003-

WORLD HISTORY

Chronology of World History

Prehistory: Our Ancestors Emerge

Revised by Susan Skomal, Ph.D., American Anthropological Association

Evidence of the origins of *Homo sapiens sapiens*, the species to which all humans belong, comes from a small, but increasing, number of fossils, from genetic and anatomical studies, and from interpretation of the geological record. Most scientists agree that humans evolved from apelike primate ancestors in a process that began millions of years ago. Although all humans living today are members of a single subspecies, the fossil record confirms that our ancestors coexisted with a number of similar species throughout evolution. Current theories trace the first hominid (upright walking, humanlike primate) to Africa, where several distinct species appeared 5-7 mil years ago (MYA). These species lived in a variety of environments throughout the continent including swampy forests, woodlands, and open savannas. In addition to Australopithecus—best known from "Lucy," an Ethiopian specimen found in 1974—these early hominid species include such recent discoveries as Sahelanthropus, Ardipithecus, Kenyanthropus, and Orrorin.

Our own human ancestry arose 2-3 MYA, when hominid species began to produce elaborate stone tools. The oldest tools are dated to 2.5-2.6 MYA from Ethiopia, and were made by systematically removing sharp flakes from a core. This produced tools for scraping meat and sinew, as well as a sharp chopping implement useful for obtaining marrow from long bones. Although we cannot determine whether these early hominids had the ability to speak, they were social animals, lived in semi-permanent camps, and had a food-gathering economy. A closer ancestor, *Homo erectus*, appeared in Africa 1.8 MYA and was the first to leave the continent, spreading into Asia by 1.3 MYA, and Europe by 800,000 years before the present (BP). It had a skeletal structure similar to modern humans, hunted, learned to control fire, and may have had primitive language skills.

Europe may have provided a particularly rich set of fossil evidence. Human-like in many important respects, Neanderthal appeared c. 200,000 BP, had sophisticated tools and developed social culture, and was well adapted to the harsh climate that prevailed in Ice Age Europe. Recent genetic evidence supports the theory that Neanderthal was a distinct species that in some places coexisted with, but did not interbreed with, early modern humans (also called Cro-Magnons). A similar situation may have occurred in Asia, where more primitive species of *Homo* coexisted with early modern humans 100,000-150,000 BP. Further study of *Homo antecessor*, a new species identified in Spain, may clarify the relationship between anatomically modern *Homo sapiens* and Neanderthals in Europe.

The 1st *Homo sapiens sapiens* originated in E Africa 100,000-200,000 BP. The oldest modern human fossils are dated to 160,000 BP, and were found at the Ethiopian site of Herto in 2003. Our species quickly spread. Humans were

living in Israel by 100,000 BP, and in Romania by 35,000 BP. Migration from Asia to Australia via the Timor Straits took place as early as 100,000 BP. First confirmation for the crossing from Asia to the Americas by land bridge dates to the end of the last Ice Age, at 11,000 BP. Growing evidence in N and S America, however, suggests that humans sailed from Asia to the New World earlier (before 13,000 BP), along coastal routes or directly across the Pacific.

A variety of cultural modes—in toolmaking, diet, shelter, social arrangements, and artistic expression—arose as humans adapted to different geographic and climatic zones and the knowledge base grew. Sites from all over the world show seasonal migration patterns and efficient exploitation of a wide range of plant and animal foods.

Fire was used for heating and cooking by 465,000 BP in W France. Fire-hardened wooden spears, weighted and set with small stone blades, were fashioned by big-game hunters 400,000 BP in Germany. Scraping tools, dated 30,000-200,000 BP in Europe, N Africa, the Middle East, and Cent. Asia, suggest the treatment of skins for clothing. By the time Australia was settled, human ancestors had learned to navigate in boats over open water. The earliest bone tools found so far are developed 80,000 BP in the Congo basin by fishermen, who created sophisticated fishing tackle to catch giant catfish.

About 60,000 BP the earliest immigrants to Australia carved and painted designs on rocks. Painting and decoration flourished, along with stone and ivory sculpture, from 30,000 BP in Europe, where more than 200 caves show remarkable examples of naturalistic wall painting. A variety of musical instruments, including bone flutes with precisely bored holes, have been found in sites dated to 40,000-80,000 BP.

Some time after 10,000 BC, among widely separated communities, a series of dramatic technological and social changes occurred, marking the Neolithic, or New Stone, Age. As the world climate became drier and warmer, humans learned to cultivate plants and domesticate animals. This encouraged growth of permanent settlements. Manufacture of pottery and cloth began at this time. These techniques permitted a dramatic increase in world population and social complexity.

Sites in the Americas, SE Europe, and the Middle East show roughly contemporaneous (8000-10,000 BC) evidence of Neolithic traits. Dates near 3000-6000 BC have been given for E and S Asian, W European, and sub-Saharan African Neolithic remains. Farming spread rapidly throughout the Mediterranean, perhaps in 100-200 years. The variety of crops—field grains, rice, maize, squash, and roots—and a mix of other characteristics suggest that this adaptation occurred independently in each region.

History Begins: 4000-1000 BC

Near Eastern cradle. If history began with writing, the first chapter opened in Mesopotamia, the Tigris-Euphrates river valley. The Sumerians used clay tablets with pictographs to keep records after 4000 BC. A **cuneiform** (wedge-shaped) script evolved by 3000 BC as a full syllabic alphabet. Neighboring peoples adapted the script for their own use.

Sumerian life centered, from 4000 BC, on large cities (Eridu, Ur, Uruk, Nippur, Kish, and Lagash) organized around temples and priestly bureaucracies, with surrounding plains watered by vast irrigation works and worked with traction plows. Sailboats, wheeled vehicles, potter's wheels, and kilns were used. Copper was smelted and tempered from c 4000 BC; bronze was produced not long after. Ores, as well as precious stones and metals, were obtained through long-distance ship and caravan trade. Iron was used from c 2000 BC. Improved ironworking, developed partly by the Hittites, became widespread by 1200 BC.

Sumerian political primacy passed among cities and their kingly dynasties. Semitic-speaking peoples, with cultures derived from the Sumerian, founded a succession of dynasties that ruled in Mesopotamia and neighboring areas for

most of 1,800 years; among them were the **Akkadians** (first under Sargon I, c 2350 BC), the Amorites (whose laws, codified by **Hammurabi**, c 1792-1750 BC, have biblical parallels), and the Assyrians, with interludes of rule by the Hittites, Kassites, and Mitanni.

Mesopotamian learning, maintained by scribes and preserved in vast libraries, was practically oriented. Advances in mathematics related mostly to construction, commerce, and administration. Lists of astronomical phenomena, plants, animals, and stones were maintained; medical texts listed ailments and herbal cures. The Sumerians worshiped anthropomorphic gods representing natural forces. Sacrifices were made at **ziggurats**—huge stepped temples.

The Syria-Palestine area, site of some of the earliest urban remains (Jericho, 7000 BC), and of the recently uncovered **Ebla** civilization (fl 2500 BC), experienced Egyptian cultural and political influence along with Mesopotamian. The **Phoenician** coast was an active commercial center. A phonetic alphabet was invented here before 1600 BC. It became the ancestor of many other alphabets.

Major Gods & Goddesses of Ancient Egypt			
Name	**Relations**	**Sphere or Position**	**Emblem/Attribute**
Ra (Re)/Atum/Amon	Self-created	The sun, creation	Hawk
Thoth (Djeheuty)	Son of Ra	The moon, wisdom, writing	Ibis/baboon
Ptah	Creator of Atum	Creation, craftsmen	----
Osiris	Brother of Set(h) & Isis	The underworld (dead), fertility, resurrection, vegetation	Bull
Isis	Sister/consort of Osiris	The underworld (dead)	----
Set(h)	Brother of Osiris	Evil, trickery, chaos	Boar, pig
Horus	Son of Osiris & Isis/ Ra & Hathor	The earth	Falcon
Hathor	Consort of Ra	Motherhood, love	Cow
Anubis	Son of Osiris	Embalmer & judge of the dead	Jackal/dog

Egypt. Agricultural villages along the Nile River were united by around 3300 BC into 2 kingdoms, Upper and Lower Egypt, unified (c 3100 BC) under the pharaoh Menes. A bureaucracy supervised construction of canals and monuments (**pyramids** starting 2700 BC). Control over Nubia to the S was asserted from 2600 BC. Brilliant Old Kingdom Period achievements in architecture, sculpture, and painting reached their height during the 3rd and 4th Dynasties. **Hieroglyphic writing** appeared by 3200 BC, recording a sophisticated literature that included religious writings, philosophy, history, and science. An ordered hierarchy of gods, including totemistic animal elements, was served by a powerful priesthood in Memphis. The pharaoh was identified with the falcon god Horus. Other trends included belief in an afterlife and short-lived quasi-monotheistic reforms introduced by the pharaoh **Akhenaton** (c 1379-1362 BC).

After a period of dominance by Semitic Hyksos from Asia (c 1700-1550 BC), the New Kingdom established an empire in Syria. Egypt became increasingly embroiled in Asiatic wars and diplomacy. Conquered by Persia in 525 BC, it eventually faded away as an independent culture.

India. An urban civilization with a so-far-undeciphered writing system stretched across the Indus Valley and along the Arabian Sea c 3000-1500 BC. Major sites are Harappa and **Mohenjo-Daro** in Pakistan, well-planned geometric cities with underground sewers and vast granaries. The entire region may have been ruled as a single state. Bronze was used, and arts and crafts were well developed. Religious life apparently took the form of fertility cults. Indus civilization was probably in decline when it was destroyed by **Aryans who arrived** from the NW, speaking an Indo-European language from which most languages of Pakistan, N India, and

Bangladesh descend. Led by a warrior aristocracy whose legendary deeds are in the **Rig Veda**, the Aryans spread E and S, bringing their sky gods, priestly (Brahman) ritual, and the beginnings of the caste system; local customs and beliefs were assimilated by the conquerors.

Europe. On Crete, the Bronze Age **Minoan civilization** emerged c 2500 BC. A prosperous economy and richly decorative art was supported by seaborne commerce. Mycenae and other cities in mainland Greece and Asia Minor (e.g., **Troy**) preserved elements of the culture until c 1200 BC. Cretan Linear A script (c 2000-1700 BC) remains undeciphered; Linear B script (c 1300-1200 BC) records an early Greek dialect. Unclear is the possible connection between Mycenaean monumental stonework and the megalithic monuments of W Europe, Iberia, and Malta (c 4000-1500 BC).

China. Proto-Chinese neolithic cultures had long covered N and SE China when the first large political state was organized in the N by the **Shang dynasty** (c 1523 BC). Shang kings called themselves Sons of Heaven, and they presided over a cgalult of human and animal sacrifice to ancestors and nature gods. The Chou dynasty, starting c 1027 BC, expanded the area of the Son of Heaven's dominion, but feudal states exercised most temporal power. A writing system with 2,000 characters was already in use under the Shang, with **pictographs** later supplemented by phonetic characters. Many of its principles and symbols, despite changes in spoken Chinese, were preserved in later writing systems. Technical advances allowed urban specialists to create fine ceramic and jade products, and bronze casting after 1500 BC was the most advanced in the world. Bronze artifacts have recently been discovered in N Thailand dating from 3600 BC, hundreds of years before similar Middle Eastern finds.

Americas. **Olmecs** settled (1500 BC) on the Gulf coast of Mexico and developed the first known civilization in the western hemisphere. Temple cities and huge stone sculpture date from 1200 BC. A rudimentary calendar and writing system existed. Olmec religion, centering on a jaguar god, and Olmec art forms influenced later Meso-American cultures.

Classical Era of Old World Civilizations: 1000 BC-400 BC

Greece. After a period of decline during the Dorian Greek invasions (1200-1000 BC), the Aegean area developed a unique civilization. Drawing on Mycenaean traditions, Mesopotamian learning (weights and measures, lunisolar calendar, astronomy, musical scales), the Phoenician alphabet (modified for Greek), and Egyptian art, **Greek city-states** saw a rich elaboration of intellectual life. The two great epic poems attributed to Homer, the *Iliad* and the *Odyssey*, were probably composed around the 8th cent. BC. Long-range commerce was aided by metal coinage (introduced by the Lydians in Asia Minor before 700 BC); colonies were founded around the Mediterranean (Cumae in Italy in 760 BC; Massalia in France c 600 BC) and Black Sea shores.

Parthenon

Philosophy, starting with Ionian speculation on the nature of matter (Thales, c 634-546 BC), continued by other "Pre-

Socratics" (e.g., Heraclitus, c 535-415 BC; Parmenides, b. c 515 BC), reached a high point in Athens in the rationalist idealism of **Plato** (c 428-347 BC), a disciple of **Socrates** (c 469-399 BC; executed for alleged impiety), and in **Aristotle** (384-322 BC), a pioneer in many fields, from natural sciences to logic, ethics, and metaphysics. The **arts** were highly valued. Architecture culminated in the **Parthenon** (438 BC) by Phidias (fl 490-430 BC). Poetry (Sappho, c 610-580 BC; Pindar, c 518-438 BC) and **drama** (Aeschylus, 525-456 BC; Sophocles, c 496-406 BC; Euripides, c 484-406 BC) thrived. Male beauty and strength, a chief artistic theme, were celebrated at the national games at Olympia.

Ruled by local tyrants or **oligarchies**, the Greeks were not politically united, but managed to resist inclusion in the Persian Empire—Persian king Darius was defeated at Marathon (490 BC), his son Xerxes at Salamis (480 BC), and the Persian army at Plataea (479 BC). Local warfare was common; the **Peloponnesian Wars** (431-404 BC) ended in Sparta's victory over Athens. Greek political power subsequently waned, but Greek cultural forms spread far and wide.

The Seven Wonders of the Ancient World

These ancient works of art and architecture were considered awe-inspiring by the Greek and Roman world of the first few centuries BC. Later classical writers disagreed as to which works belonged, but the following were usually included:

The Pyramids of Egypt: The only surviving ancient Wonder, these monumental structures of masonry, located at Giza on the W bank of the Nile R above Cairo, were built from c 2700 to 2500 BC as royal tombs. Three—Khufu (Cheops), Khafra (Chephren), and Menkaura (Mycerimus)—were often grouped as the first Wonder of the World. The largest, the Great Pyramid of Khufu, is a solid mass of limestone blocks covering 13 acres. It is estimated to contain 2.3 million blocks of stone, the stones themselves averaging 2½ tons and some weighing 30 tons. Its construction reputedly took 100,000 laborers 20 years.

The Hanging Gardens of Babylon: These gardens were laid out on a brick terrace 400 ft square and 75 ft above the ground. To irrigate the plants, screws were turned to lift water from the Euphrates R. The gardens were probably built by King Nebuchadnezzar II about 600 BC. The Walls of Babylon, long, thick, and made of colorfully glazed brick, were also considered by some among the Seven Wonders.

The Pharos (Lighthouse) of Alexandria: This structure was designed about 270 BC, during the reign of Ptolemy II, by the Greek architect Sostratos. Estimates of its height range from 200 to 600 ft.

The Colossus of Rhodes: A bronze statue of the sun god Helios, the Colossus was worked on for 12 years in the third cent. BC by the sculptor Chares. It was probably 120 ft high. A symbol of the city of Rhodes at its height, the statue stood on a promontory overlooking the harbor.

The Temple of Artemis (Diana) at Ephesus: This largest and most complex temple of ancient times was built about 550 BC and was made of marble except for its tile-covered wooden roof. It was begun in honor of a non-Hellenic goddess who later became identified with the Greek goddess of the same name. Ephesus was one of the greatest of the Ionian cities.

The Mausoleum at Halicarnassus: The source of our word *mausoleum*, this marble tomb was built in what is now SE Turkey by Artemisia for her husband Mausolus, king of Caria in Asia Minor, who died in 353 BC. About 135 ft high, the tomb was adorned with the works of 4 sculptors.

The Statue of Zeus (Jupiter) at Olympia: This statue of the king of the gods showed him seated on a throne. His flesh was made of ivory, his robe and ornaments of gold. Reputedly 40 ft high, the statue was made by Phidias and was placed in the great temple of Zeus in the sacred grove of Olympia about 457 BC.

Hebrews. Nomadic Hebrew tribes entered Canaan before 1200 BC, settling among other Semitic peoples speaking the same language. They brought from the desert a **monotheistic** faith said to have been revealed to Abraham in Canaan c 1800 BC and Moses at Mt. Sinai c 1250 BC, after the Hebrews' escape from bondage in Egypt. David (r 1000-961 BC) and Solomon (r 961-922 BC) united them in a kingdom that briefly dominated the area. **Phoenicians** to the N founded Mediterranean colonies (Carthage, c 814 BC) and sailed into the Atlantic.

A temple in Jerusalem became the national religious center, with sacrifices performed by a hereditary priesthood. Polytheistic influences, especially of the fertility cult of Baal, were opposed by **prophets** (Elijah, Amos, Isaiah).

Divided into **two kingdoms** after Solomon, the Hebrews were unable to resist the revived Assyrian empire, which conquered Israel, the N kingdom, in 722 BC. Judah, the S kingdom, was conquered in 586 BC by the Babylonians under Nebuchadnezzar II. With the fixing of most of the biblical canon by the mid-4th cent. BC and the emergence of rabbis, Judaism successfully survived the loss of Hebrew autonomy. A Jewish kingdom was revived under the Hasmoneans (168-42 BC).

China. During the **Eastern Chou** dynasty (770-256 BC), Chinese culture spread E to the sea and S to the Yangtze R. Large feudal states on the periphery of the empire contended for preeminence, but continued to recognize the Son of Heaven (king), who retained a purely ritual role enriched with courtly music and dance. In the Age of Warring States (403-221 BC), when the first sections of the **Great Wall** were built, the Ch'in state in the W gained supremacy and finally united all of China.

Iron tools entered China c 500 BC, and casting techniques were advanced, aiding agriculture. Peasants owned their land and owed civil and military service to nobles. China's cities grew in number and size; barter remained the chief trade medium.

Intellectual ferment among noble scribes and officials produced the Classical Age of Chinese literature and philosophy. **Confucius** (551-479 BC) urged a restoration of a supposedly harmonious social order of the past through proper conduct in accordance with one's station and through filial and ceremonial piety. The *Analects* attributed to him are revered throughout E Asia.

Among other thinkers of this period, Mencius (d 289 BC) added the view that the Mandate of Heaven can be removed from an unjust dynasty. The Legalists sought to curb the supposed natural wickedness of people through new institutions and harsh laws; they aided the Ch'in rise to power. The Naturalists emphasized the balance of opposites—yin, yang—in the world. **Taoists** sought mystical knowledge through meditation and disengagement.

India. The political and cultural center of India shifted from the Indus to the Ganges River Valley. Buddhism, Jainism, and mystical revisions of orthodox Vedism all developed c 500-300 BC. The *Upanishads*, last part of the *Veda*, urged escape from the physical world. Vedism remained the preserve of the Brahman caste.

In contrast, **Buddhism**, founded by Siddarta Gautama (c 563-c 483 BC)—Buddha ("Enlightened One")—appealed to merchants in the urban centers and took hold at first (and most lastingly) on the geographic fringes of Indian civilization. The classic Indian epics were composed in this era: the **Ramayana** perhaps c 300 BC, the **Mahabharata** over a period starting around 400 BC.

N India was divided into a large number of monarchies and aristocratic republics, probably derived from tribal groupings, when the Magadha kingdom was formed in Bihar c 542 BC. It soon became the dominant power. The **Maurya dynasty**, founded by Chandragupta c 321 BC, expanded the kingdom, uniting most of N India in a centralized bureaucratic empire. The third Mauryan king, **Asoka** (reigned c 274-236 BC), conquered most of the subcontinent. He converted to Buddhism and inscribed its tenets on pillars throughout India. He downplayed the caste system.

Before its final decline in India, Buddhism developed into a popular worship of heavenly Bodhisattvas ("enlightened beings"), and it produced a refined architecture (the Great Stupa [shrine] at Sanchi, AD 100) and sculpture (Gandhara reliefs, AD 1-400).

Persia. Aryan peoples (Persians, Medes) dominated the area of present Iran by the beginning of the 1st millennium BC. The prophet **Zoroaster** (born c 628 BC) introduced a dualistic religion in which the forces of good (Ahura Mazda, "Lord of Wisdom") and evil (Ahriam) battle for dominance; individuals are judged by their actions and earn damnation or salvation. Zoroaster's hymns (*Gathas*) are included in the *Avesta*, the Zoroastrian scriptures. A version of this faith became the established religion of the Persian Empire.

Africa. Nubia, periodically occupied by Egypt since about 2600 BC, ruled Egypt c 750-661 BC and survived as an independent Egyptianized kingdom (**Kush**; capital Meroe) for 1,000 years. The Iron Age Nok culture flourished c 500 BC- AD 200 on the Benue Plateau of **Nigeria.**

Americas. The Chavin culture controlled N Peru c 900 BC to 200 BC. Its ceremonial centers, featuring the jaguar god, survived long after. Its architecture, ceramics, and textiles had influenced other Peruvian cultures. **Mayan civilization** began to develop in Central America as early as 1500 BC.

Mayan temple

Great Empires Unite the Civilized World: 400 BC-AD 400

Persia and Alexander the Great. Cyrus, ruler of a small kingdom in Persia from 559 BC, united the Persians and Medes within 10 years and conquered Asia Minor and Babylonia in another 10. His son Cambyses, followed by **Darius** (r 522-486 BC), added vast lands to the E and N as far as the Indus Valley and Central Asia, as well as Egypt and Thrace. The whole empire was ruled by an international bureaucracy and army, with Persians holding the chief positions. The resources and styles of all the subject civilizations were exploited to create a rich syncretic art.

The kingdom of Macedon, which under Philip II dominated the Greek world and Egypt, was passed on to his son **Alexander** in 336 BC. Within 13 years, Alexander had conquered all the Persian dominions. Imbued with his tutor Aristotle with Greek ideals, Alexander encouraged Greek colonization, and Greek-style cities were founded. After his death in 323 BC, wars of succession divided the empire into 3 parts—**Macedon,** Egypt (ruled by the **Ptolemies**), and the **Seleucid** Empire. In the ensuing 300 years (the **Hellenistic Era**), a cosmopolitan Greek-oriented culture permeated the ancient world from W Europe to the borders of India, absorbing native elites everywhere.

Hellenistic philosophy stressed the private individual's search for happiness. The Cynics followed Diogenes (c 372-287 BC), who stressed self-sufficiency and restriction of desires and expressed contempt for luxury and social convention. Zeno (c 335-c 263 BC) and the **Stoics** exalted reason, identified it with virtue, and counseled an ascetic disregard for misfortune. The **Epicureans** tried to build lives of moderate pleasure without political or emotional involvement. Hellenistic arts imitated life realistically, especially in sculpture and literature (comedies of Menander, 342-292 BC).

The sciences thrived, especially at Alexandria, where the Ptolemies financed a great library and museum. Fields of study included mathematics (**Euclid's** geometry, c 300 BC); astronomy (heliocentric theory of Aristarchus, 310-230 BC; Julian calendar, 45 BC; **Ptolemy**'s *Almagest*, c AD 150); geography (world map of Eratosthenes, 276-194 BC); hydraulics (**Archimedes,** 287-212 BC); medicine (Galen, AD 130-200); and chemistry. Inventors refined uses for siphons, valves, gears, springs, screws, levers, cams, and pulleys.

A restored Persian empire under the **Parthians** (northern Iranian tribesmen) controlled the eastern Hellenistic world from 250 BC to AD 229. The Parthians and the succeeding Sassanian dynasty (c AD 224-651) fought with Rome periodically. The **Sassanians** revived Zoroastrianism as a state religion and patronized a nationalistic artistic and scholarly renaissance.

Rome. The city of Rome was founded, according to legend, by Romulus in 753 BC. Through military expansion and colonization, and by granting citizenship to conquered tribes, the city annexed all of Italy S of the Po in the 100-year period before 268 BC. The Latin and other Italic tribes were annexed first, followed by the **Etruscans** (founders of a great civilization, N of Rome) and the Greek colonies in

the S. With a large standing army and reserve forces of several hundred thousand, Rome was able to defeat **Carthage** in the 3 **Punic Wars** (264-241, 218-201, 149-146 BC), despite the invasion of Italy (218 BC) by **Hannibal,** thus gaining Sicily and territory in Spain and N Africa.

Rome exploited local disputes to conquer Greece and Asia Minor in the 2nd cent. BC, and Egypt in the 1st (after the defeat and suicide of **Antony and Cleopatra,** 30 BC). All the Mediterranean civilized world up to the disputed Parthian border was now Roman and remained so for 500 years. Less civilized regions were added to the Empire: Gaul (conquered by **Julius Caesar,** 58-51 BC), Britain (AD 43), and Dacia NE of the Danube (AD 107).

The original aristocratic republican government, with democratic features added in the 5th and 4th cent. BC, deteriorated under the pressures of empire and class conflict (**Gracchus** brothers, social reformers, murdered in 133 BC and 121 BC; slave revolts in 135 BC and 73 BC). After a series of civil wars (Marius vs. Sulla 88-82 BC, Caesar vs. **Pompey** 49-45 BC, triumvirate vs. Caesar's assassins 44-43 BC, Antony vs. Octavian 32-30 BC), the empire came under the rule of a deified monarch (first emperor, **Augustus,** 27 BC-AD 14).

Julius Caesar

Provincials (nearly all granted citizenship by Caracalla, AD 212) came to dominate the army and civil service. Traditional **Roman law,** systematized and interpreted by independent jurists, and local self-rule in provincial cities were supplanted by a vast tax-collecting bureaucracy in the 3rd and 4th cent. The legal rights of women, children, and slaves were strengthened.

Roman innovations in **civil engineering** included water mills, windmills, and rotary mills and use of cement that hardened under water. Monumental architecture (baths, theaters, temples) relied on the arch and the dome. The network of roads (some still standing) stretched 53,000 mi, passing through mountain tunnels as long as 3.5 mi. Aqueducts brought water to cities; underground sewers removed waste.

Roman art and literature were to a large extent derivative of Greek models. Innovations were made in sculpture (naturalistic busts, equestrian statues), decorative wall painting (as at Pompeii), satire (**Juvenal,** AD 60-127), history (**Tacitus,** AD 56-120), prose romance (Petronius, d AD 66). Gladiatorial contests dominated public amusements, which were supported by the state.

India. The **Gupta** monarchs reunited N India c AD 320. Their peaceful and prosperous reign saw a revival of Hindu religious thought and Brahman power. The old Vedic traditions were combined with devotion to many indigenous deities (who were seen as manifestations of Vedic gods). **Caste**

Major Gods & Goddesses of the Classical World

Greek	Roman	Relations	Sphere or Position
Aphrodite	Venus	Daughter of Zeus & Dione	Love
Apollo	——	Son of Zeus & Leto	Healing, poetry, light
Ares	Mars	Son of Zeus & Hera	War
Artemis	Diana	Daughter of Zeus & Leto	Hunting, chastity
Athena	Minerva	Daughter of Zeus & Metis	Wisdom, crafts, war
Cronus	Saturn	Father of Zeus	Titans' ruler
Demeter	Ceres	Sister of Zeus	Agriculture, fertility
Dionysus	Bacchus	Son of Zeus & Semele	Wine, fertility, ecstasy
Eros	Cupid	Son of Ares & Aphrodite	Love
Hades	Pluto	Brother of Zeus	The underworld, death
Hephaestus	Vulcan	Son of Zeus & Hera	Fire
Hera	Juno	Wife & sister of Zeus	Earth
Hermes	Mercury	Son of Zeus & Maia	Travel, commerce, gods' messenger
Hestia	Vesta	Sister of Zeus	The hearth
Pan		Son of Hermes & a wood nymph	Forests, flocks, shepherds
Persephone	Proserpina	Daughter of Zeus & Demeter	Grain
Poseidon	Neptune	Brother of Zeus	The sea
Rhea	Ops	Mother of Zeus	The earth
Uranus	Uranus	Father of Titans (elder gods)	The heavens
Zeus	Jupiter	Son of Cronus & Rhea	Ruler of the gods

lines were reinforced, and Buddhism gradually disappeared. The art (often erotic), architecture, and literature of the period, patronized by the Gupta court, are considered among India's finest achievements (Kalidasa, poet and dramatist, fl. c AD 400). Mathematical innovations included use of the zero and decimal numbers. Invasions by White Huns from the NW destroyed the empire c 550.

Rich cultures also developed in S India during this period. Emotional Tamil religious poetry contributed to the Hindu revival. The Pallava kingdom controlled much of S India c 350-880 and helped to spread Indian civilization to SE Asia.

China. The Ch'in ruler Shih Huang Ti (r 221-210 BC), known as the First Emperor, centralized political authority, standardized the written language, laws, weights, measures, and coinage, and conducted a census, but tried to destroy most philosophical texts. The **Han dynasty** (202 BC-AD 220) instituted the Mandarin bureaucracy, which lasted 2,000 years. Local officials were selected by examination in Confucian classics and trained at the imperial university and provincial schools.

The invention of **paper** facilitated this bureaucratic system. Agriculture was promoted, but peasants bore most of the tax burden. Irrigation was improved, water clocks and sundials were used, astronomy and mathematics thrived, and landscape painting was perfected.

With the expansion S and W (to nearly the present borders of today's China), trade was opened with India, SE Asia, and the Middle East, over sea and caravan routes. Indian missionaries brought Mahayana Buddhism to China by the 1st cent. AD and spawned a variety of sects. Taoism was revived and merged with popular superstitions. Taoist and Buddhist monasteries and convents multiplied in the turbulent centuries after the collapse of the Han dynasty.

Monotheism Spreads: AD 1-750

Roman Empire. Polytheism was practiced in the Roman Empire, and religions indigenous to particular Middle Eastern nations became international. Roman citizens worshiped **Isis** of Egypt, **Mithras** of Persia, **Demeter** of Greece, and the great mother **Cybele** of Phrygia. Their cults centered on mysteries (secret ceremonies) and the promise of an afterlife, symbolized by the death and rebirth of the god. The Jews of the empire preserved their monotheistic religion, Judaism, the world's oldest (c 1300 BC) continuous religion. Its teachings are contained in the Bible (the Old Testament). First-cent. Judaism embraced several sects, including the **Sadducees**, mostly drawn from the Temple priesthood, who were culturally Hellenized; the **Pharisees**, who upheld the full range of traditional customs and practices of equal weight to literal scriptural law and elaborated synagogue worship; and the **Essenes**, an ascetic, millennarian sect. Messianic fervor led to repeated, unsuccessful rebellions against Rome (66-70, 135). As a result, the Temple in Jerusalem was destroyed and the population decimated; this event marked the beginning of the Diaspora (living in exile). To preserve the faith, a program of codification of law was begun at the academy of Yavneh. The work continued for some 500 years in Palestine and in Babylonia, ending in the final redaction (c 600) of the **Talmud**, a huge collection of legal and moral debates, rulings, liturgy, biblical exegesis, and legendary materials.

Christianity, which emerged as a distinct sect by the 2nd half of the 1st cent., is based on the teachings of **Jesus**, whom believers considered the Savior (Messiah or Christ) and son of God. Missionary activities of the Apostles and such early leaders as **Paul of Tarsus** spread the faith. Intermittent persecution, as in Rome under Nero in AD 64, on grounds of suspected disloyalty, failed to disrupt the Christian communities. Each congregation, generally urban and of plebeian character, was tightly organized under a leader (bishop), elders (presbyters or priests), and assistants (deacons). The four **Gospels** (accounts of the life and teachings of Jesus) and the Acts of the Apostles were written down in the late 1st and early 2nd cent. and circulated along with letters of Paul and other Christian leaders. An authoritative canon of these writings was not fixed until the 4th cent.

A school for priests was established at Alexandria in the 2nd cent. Its teachers (**Origen** c 182-251) helped define doctrine and promote the faith in Greek-style philosophical works. Neoplatonism underwent Christian coloration in the writings of Church Fathers such as **Augustine** (354-430). Christian hermits began to associate in monasteries, first in Egypt (St. Pachomius c 290-345), then in other eastern lands, then in the W (**St. Benedict's rule**, 529). Devotion to saints, especially Mary, mother of Jesus, spread. Under **Constantine** (r 306-37), Christianity became in effect the established religion of the Empire. Pagan temples were expropriated, state funds were used to build churches and support the hierarchy, and laws were adjusted in accordance with Christian ideas. Pagan worship was banned by the end of the 4th cent., and severe restrictions were placed on Judaism.

The newly established church was rocked by doctrinal disputes, often exacerbated by regional rivalries. Chief heresies (as defined by church councils, backed by imperial authority) were **Arianism**, which denied the divinity of Jesus; **Monophysitism**, denying the human nature of Christ; **Donatism**, which regarded as invalid any sacraments administered by sinful clergy; and **Pelagianism**, which denied the necessity of unmerited divine aid (grace) for salvation.

Islam. The earliest Arab civilization emerged by the end of the 2nd millennium BC in the watered highlands of Yemen. Seaborne and caravan trade in frankincense and myrrh connected the area with the Nile and Fertile Crescent. The Minaean, Sabean (Sheba), and Himyarite states successively held sway. By Muhammad's time (7th cent. AD), the region was a province of Sassanian Persia. In the N, the Nabataean kingdom at Petra and the kingdom of Palmyra were Aramaicized, Romanized, and finally absorbed, as neighboring Judea had been, into the Roman Empire. Nomads shared the central region with a few trading towns and oases. Wars between tribes and raids on communities were common and were celebrated in a poetic tradition that by the 6th cent. helped establish a classic literary Arabic.

About 610, **Muhammad**, a 40-year-old Arab of Mecca, emerged as a prophet. He proclaimed a revelation from the one true God, calling on contemporaries to abandon idolatry and restore the faith of Abraham. He introduced his religion as "Islam," meaning "submission" to the one God, Allah, as a continuation of the biblical faith of Abraham, Moses, and Jesus, all respected as prophets in this system. His teachings, recorded in the **Koran** (al-Qur'an in Arabic), in many ways were inclusive of Abrahamic monotheistic ideas known to the Jews and Christians in Arabia. A key aspect of the Abrahamic connection was insistence on justice in society, which led to severe opposition among the aristocrats in Mecca. As conditions worsened for Muhammad and his followers, he decided in 622 to make a *hijra* (emigration) to Medina, 200 mi to the N. This event marks the beginning of the Muslim lunar calendar. Hostilities between Mecca and Medina increased, and in 629 Muhammad conquered Mecca. By the time he died in 632, nearly all the Arabian peninsula accepted his political and religious leadership.

After his death the majority of Muslims recognized the leadership of the **caliph** ("successor") Abu Bakr (632-34), followed by Umar (634-44), Uthman (644-56), and Ali (656-60). A minority, the **Shiites**, insisted instead on the leadership of Ali, Muhammad's cousin and son-in-law. By 644, **Muslim rule** over Arabia was confirmed. Muslim armies had threatened the Byzantine and Persian empires, which were weakened by wars and disaffection among subject peoples (including Coptic and Syriac Christians opposed to the Byzantine Orthodox establishment). Syria, Palestine, Egypt, Iraq, and Persia fell to Muslim armies. The new administration assimilated existing systems in the region; hence the conquered peoples participated in running of the empire. The Koran recognized the so-called Peoples of the Book, i.e., Christians, Jews, and Zoroastrians, as tolerated monotheists, and Muslim policy was relatively tolerant to minorities living as "protected" peoples. An expanded tax system, based on conquests of the Persian and Byzantine empires, provided revenue to organize campaigns against neighboring non-Muslim regions.

Under the **Umayyads** (661-750) and **Abbasids** (750-1256), territorial expansion led Muslim armies across N Africa and into Spain (711). Muslim armies in the W were stopped at Tours (France) in 732 by the Frankish ruler **Charles Martel**. Asia Minor, the Indus Valley, and Transoxiana were conquered in the E. The conversion of conquered peoples to Islam was gradual. In many places the

official Arabic language supplanted the local tongues. But in the eastern regions the Arab rulers and their armies adopted Persian cultures and language as part of their Muslim identity.

Disputes over succession, and pious opposition to injustices in society, led to a number of oppositional movements, which also led to the factionalization of Muslim community. The **Shiites** supported leadership candidates descended from Muhammad, believing them to be carriers of some kind of divine authority. The **Kharijites** supported an egalitarian system derived from the Koran, opposing and even engaging in battle against those who did not agree with them.

Major Norse Gods & Goddesses

Name	Relations	Sphere or Position	Emblem/Attribute
Odin	Father of the Aesir (gods)	War and death, poetry, wisdom, magic	Spear, mead, ring/One-eyed
Thor	Son of Odin	Thunder, lightning, rain; champion of the gods	Hammer, belt
Njord	Father of Freyja & Freyr	Wind and sea, wealth and prosperity	----
Frigg	Wife of Odin	Marriage and motherhood, home	----
Freyja (Freya)	Daughter of Njord	Fertility, birth, crops	Necklace
Freyr	Son of Njord	Agriculture, sun, rain	Magic ship, golden boar
Tyr	Son of Odin ?	Justice, war	Spear/One-handed
Heimdall	Son of nine giantesses	Watchman of the gods; keen sight & hearing	Horn
Balder (Baldur)	Son of Odin	Light, purity	----
Loki	Son of giants; father of Hel (goddess of death), Jormungand (serpent encompassing the world), Fenrir (the wolf).	Malicious trickster	----

New Peoples Enter World History: 400-900

Barbarian invasions. Germanic tribes infiltrated S and E from their Baltic homeland during the 1st millennium BC, reaching S Germany by 100 BC and the Black Sea by AD 214. Organized into large federated tribes under elected kings, most resisted Roman domination and raided the empire in time of civil war (Goths took Dacia in 214, raided Thrace in 251-69). Germanic troops and commanders dominated the Roman armies by the end of the 4th cent. **Huns**, invaders from Asia, entered Europe in 372, driving more Germans into the W empire. Emperor Valens allowed Visigoths to cross the Danube in 376. Huns under Attila (d 453) raided Gaul, Italy, and the Balkans.

The W empire, weakened by overtaxation and social stagnation, was overrun in the 5th cent. Gaul was effectively lost in 406-7, Spain in 409, Britain in 410, Africa in 429-39. Rome was sacked in 410 by Visigoths under Alaric and in 455 by Vandals. The last western emperor, Romulus Augustulus, was deposed in 476 by the Germanic chief Odovacar.

Celts. Celtic cultures, which in pre-Roman times covered most of W Europe, were confined almost entirely to the British Isles after the Germanic invasions. St. Patrick completed (c 457-92) the conversion of Ireland. A strong monastic tradition took hold. Irish monastic missionaries in Scotland, England, and the continent (Columba c 521-97; Columban c 543-615) helped restore Christianity after the Germanic invasions. Monasteries became centers of classic and Christian learning and presided over the recording of a Christianized Celtic mythology, elaborated by secular writers and bards. An intricate decorative art style developed, especially in book illumination (Lindisfarne Gospels, c 700; Book of Kells, 8th cent.).

Successor states. The Visigothic kingdom in Spain (from 419) and much of France (to 507) saw continuation of Roman administration, language, and law (Breviary of Alaric, 506) until its destruction by the Muslims (711). The Vandal kingdom in Africa (from 429) was conquered by the Byzantines in 533. Italy was ruled successively by an Ostrogothic kingdom under Byzantine suzerainty (489-554), direct Byzantine government, and German Lombards (568-774). The Lombards divided the peninsula with the Byzantines and papacy under the dynamic reformer **Pope Gregory the Great** (590-604) and successors.

King Clovis (r 481-511) united the Franks on both sides of the Rhine and, after his conversion to Christianity, defeated the Arian heretics, Burgundians (after 500), and Visigoths (507) with the support of native clergy and the papacy. Under the **Merovingian** kings, a feudal system emerged: Power was fragmented among hierarchies of military landowners. Social stratification, which in late Roman times had acquired legal, hereditary sanction, was reinforced. The Carolingians (747-987) expanded the kingdom and restored central power. **Charlemagne** (r 768-814) conquered nearly all the Germanic lands, including Lombard Italy, and was crowned Emperor by Pope Leo III in Rome in 800. A centuries-long decline in commerce and arts was reversed under Charlemagne's patronage. He welcomed Jews to his kingdom, which became a center of Jewish learning (Rashi, 1040-1105). He sponsored the Carolingian Renaissance of learning under the Anglo-Latin scholar Alcuin (c 732-804), who reformed church liturgy.

Byzantine Empire. Under **Diocletian** (r 284-305) the empire had been divided into 2 parts to facilitate administration and defense. **Constantine** founded (330) **Constantinople** (at old Byzantium) as a fully Christian city. Commerce and taxation financed a sumptuous, orientalized court, a class of hereditary bureaucratic families, and magnificent urban construction (Hagia Sophia, 532-37). The city's fortifications and naval innovations repelled assaults by Goths, Huns, Slavs, Bulgars, Avars, Arabs, and Scandinavians. Greek replaced Latin as the official language by c 700. Byzantine art, a solemn, sacral, and stylized variation of late classical styles (mosaics at the Church of San Vitale, Ravenna, Italy 526-48), was a starting point for medieval art in E and W Europe.

Justinian (r 527-65) reconquered parts of Spain, N Africa, and Italy, codified Roman law (Codex Justinianus [529] was medieval Europe's chief legal text), closed the Platonic Academy at Athens, and ordered all pagans to convert. Lombards and Arabs in Africa retook most of his conquests. The Isaurian dynasty from Anatolia (from 717) and the Macedonian dynasty (867-1054) restored military and commercial power. The Iconoclast controversy (726-843) over the permissibility of images helped alienate the Eastern Church from the papacy.

Abbasid Empire. Baghdad (est. 762), became seat of the **Abbasid dynasty** (est 750), while Ummayads continued to rule in Spain. A brilliant cosmopolitan civilization emerged, inaugurating a Muslim-Arab golden age. Arabic was the lingua franca of the empire; intellectual sources from Persian, Sanskrit, Greek, and Syriac were rendered into Arabic. Christians and Jews equally participated in this translation movement, which also involved interaction between Jewish legal thought and Islamic law, as much as between Christian theology and Muslim scholasticism. Persian-style court life, with art and music, flourished at the court of **Harun al-Rashid** (786-809), celebrated in the masterpiece known to English readers as *The Arabian Nights*. The sciences, medicine, and mathematics were pursued at Baghdad, Cordova, and Cairo (est. 969). The culmination of this intellectual synthesis in Islamic civilization came with the scientific and philosophical works of **Avicenna** (Ibn Sina, 980-1037), **Averroes** (Ibn Rushd, 1126-98), and **Maimonides** (1135-1204), a Jew who wrote in Arabic. This intellectual tradition was translated into Latin and opened a new period in Christian thought.

The decentralization of the **Abbasid** empire, from 874, led to establishment of various Muslim dynasties under different ethnic groups. Persians, Berbers, and Turks ruled different regions, retaining connection with the Abbasid caliph at the religious level. The Abbasid period also saw various religious movements against the orthodox position held by governing authorities. This situation in Muslim religion led to the establishment of different legal, theological, and mystical schools of thought. The most influential mass movement was **Sufism**, which aimed at the reaching out of the average individual in quest of a spiritual path. Al-Ghazali (1058-1111) is credited with reconciling personal Sufism with orthodox Sunni tradition.

Africa. Immigrants from Saba in S Arabia helped set up the **Axum** kingdom in Ethiopia in the 1st cent. (their language, Ge'ez, is preserved by the Ethiopian Church). In the 3rd cent., when the kingdom became Christianized, it defeated Kushite Meroe and expanded its influence into Yemen. Axum was the center of a vast ivory trade and controlled the Red Sea coast until c 1100. Arab conquest in Egypt cut Axum's political and economic ties with Byzantium.

The Iron Age entered W Africa by the end of the 1st millennium BC. **Ghana**, the first known sub-Saharan state, ruled in the upper Senegal-Niger region c 400-1240, controlling the trade of gold from mines in the S to trans-Sahara caravan routes to the N. The **Bantu** peoples, probably of W African origin, began to spread E and S perhaps 2,000 years ago, displacing the Pygmies and Bushmen of central and S Africa during a 1,500-year period.

Japan. The advanced Neolithic Yayoi period, when irrigation, rice farming, and iron and bronze casting techniques were introduced from China or Korea, persisted to c AD 400. The myriad Japanese states were then united by the **Yamato** clan, under an emperor who acted as chief priest of the animistic Shinto cult. Japanese political and military intervention by the 6th cent. in Korea, then under strong Chinese influence, quickened a Chinese cultural invasion of Japan, bringing Buddhism, the Chinese language (which long remained a literary and governmental medium), Chinese ideographs, and Buddhist styles in painting, sculpture, literature, and architecture (7th cent., Horyu-ji temple at Nara). The Taika Reforms (646) tried unsuccessfully to centralize Japan according to Chinese bureaucratic and Buddhist philosophical values.

A nativist reaction against the Buddhist **Nara period** (710-94) ushered in the **Heian period** (794-1185) centered at the new capital, Kyoto. Japanese elegance and simplicity modified Chinese styles in architecture, scroll painting, and literature; the writing system was also simplified. The courtly novel *Tale of Genji* (1010-20) testifies to the enhanced role of women.

Southeast Asia. The historic peoples of SE Asia began arriving some 2,500 years ago from China and Tibet, displacing scattered aborigines. Their agriculture relied on rice and yams. Indian cultural influences were strongest; literacy and Hindu and Buddhist ideas followed the S India-China trade route. From the S tip of Indochina, the kingdom of **Funan** (1st-7th cent.) traded as far W as Persia. It was absorbed by Chenla, itself conquered by the **Khmer Empire** (600-1300). The Khmers, under Hindu god-kings (Suryavarman II, 1113-c 1150), built the monumental Angkor Wat temple center for the royal phallic cult. The **Nam-Viet** kingdom in Annam, dominated by China and Chinese culture for 1,000 years, emerged in the 10th cent., growing at the expense of the Khmers, who also lost ground in the NW to the new, highly organized **Thai** kingdom. On Sumatra, the **Srivijaya** Empire controlled vital sea lanes (7th to 10th cent.). A Buddhist dynasty, the Sailendras, ruled central **Java** (8th-9th cent.), building at Borobudur one of the largest stupas in the world.

China. The Sui dynasty (581-618) ushered in a period of commercial, artistic, and scientific achievement in China, continuing under the **Tang** dynasty (618-906). Inventions like the magnetic compass, gunpowder, the abacus, and printing were introduced or perfected. Medical innovations included cataract surgery. The state, from its cosmopolitan capital, Chang-an, supervised foreign trade, which exchanged Chinese silks, porcelains, and art for spices, ivory, etc., over Central Asian caravan routes and sea routes reaching Africa. A golden age of poetry bequeathed valuable works to later generations (Tu Fu, 712-70; Li Po, 701-62). Landscape painting flourished.

Commercial and industrial expansion continued under the **Northern Sung** dynasty (960-1126), facilitated by paper money and credit notes. But commerce never achieved respectability; government monopolies expropriated successful merchants. The population, long stable at 50 million, doubled in 200 years with the introduction of early-ripening rice and the double harvest. In art, native Chinese styles were revived.

Americas. From 300 to 600 a Native American empire stretched from the Valley of Mexico to Guatemala, centering on the huge city **Teotihuacán** (founded 100 BC). To the S, in Guatemala, a high **Mayan** civilization developed (150-900) around hundreds of rural ceremonial centers. The Mayans improved on Olmec writing and the calendar and pursued astronomy and mathematics. In South America, a widespread pre-Inca culture grew from **Tiahuanacu**, Bolivia, near Lake Titicaca (Gateway of the Sun, c 700).

Christian Europe Regroups and Expands: 900-1300

Scandinavians. Pagan Danish and Norse (Viking) adventurers, traders, and pirates raided the coasts of the British Isles (Dublin, est. c 831), France, and even the Mediterranean for over 200 years beginning in the late 8th cent. Inland settlement in the W was limited to Great Britain (King Canute, 994-1035) and Normandy, settled (911) under Rollo, as a fief of France. Vikings also reached Iceland (874), Greenland (c 986), and North America (**Leif Ericson** and others, c 1000). Norse traders (**Varangians**) developed Russian river commerce from the 8th to the 11th cent. and helped set up a state at Kiev in the late 9th cent. Conversion to Christianity occurred in the 10th cent., reaching Sweden 100 years later. In the 11th cent. Norman bands conquered S Italy and Sicily, and Duke **William of Normandy** conquered (1066) England, bringing feudalism and the French language, essential elements in later English civilization.

Central and East Europe. Slavs began to expand from about AD 150 in all directions in Europe, and by the 7th cent. they reached as far S as the Adriatic and Aegean seas. In the Balkan Peninsula they dislocated Romanized local populations or assimilated newcomers (Bulgarians, a Turkic people). The first Slavic states were Moravia (628) in Central Europe and the Bulgarian state (680) in the Balkans. Missions of St. Methodius and Cyril (whose Greek-based cyrillic alphabet is still used by some S and E Slavs) converted (863) Moravia.

The Eastern Slavs, part-civilized under the overlordship of the Turkish-Jewish **Khazar** trading empire (7th-10th cent.), gravitated toward Constantinople by the 9th cent. The **Kievan state** adopted (989) Eastern Christianity under Prince Vladimir. King Boleslav I (992-1025) began **Poland's** long history of eastern conquest. The Magyars (**Hungarians**), in present-day Hungary since 896, accepted (1001) Latin Christianity.

Germany. The German kingdom that emerged after the breakup of Charlemagne's W Empire remained a confederation of largely autonomous states. Otto I, a Saxon who was king from 936, established the **Holy Roman Empire**—a union of Germany and N Italy—in alliance with Pope John XII, who crowned (962) him emperor; he defeated (955) the Magyars. Imperial power was greatest under the **Hohenstaufens** (1138-1254), despite the growing opposition of the papacy, which ruled central Italy, and the Lombard League cities. Frederick II (1194-1250) improved administration and patronized the arts; after his death, German influence was removed from Italy.

Christian Spain. From its N mountain redoubts, Christian rule slowly migrated S through the 11th cent., when Muslim unity collapsed. After the capture (1085) of **Toledo**, the kingdoms of Portugal, Castile, and Aragon undertook repeated crusades of reconquest, finally completed in 1492. Elements of Islamic civilization persisted in recaptured areas, influencing all Western Europe.

Crusades. Pope Urban II called (1095) for a crusade to restore Asia Minor to Byzantium and to regain the Holy Land from the Turks. Some ten crusades (lasting until 1291) succeeded only in founding four temporary Frankish states in the Levant. The 4th crusade sacked (1204) Constantinople. In Rhineland (1096), England (1290), and France (1306), Jews were massacred or expelled, and wars were launched against Christian heretics (**Albigensian** crusade in France, 1229). Trade in eastern luxuries expanded, led by the Venetian naval empire.

Economy. The agricultural base of European life benefited from improvements in **plow design** (c 1000) and by draining of lowlands and clearing of forests, leading to a rural population increase. Towns grew in N Italy, Flanders, and N Germany (Hanseatic League). Improvements in **loom design** permitted factory textile production. **Guilds** dominated urban trades from the 12th cent. Banking (cen-

tered in Italy, 12th-15th cent.) facilitated long-distance trade.

The Church. The split between the Eastern and Western churches was formalized in 1054. Western and Central Europe was divided into 500 bishoprics under one united hierarchy, but conflicts between secular and church authorities were frequent (German **Investiture Controversy**, 1075-1122). Clerical power was first strengthened through the international monastic reform begun at Cluny in 910. Popular religious enthusiasm often expressed itself in heretical movements (Waldensians from 1173), but was channeled by the **Dominican** (1215) and **Franciscan** (1223) friars into the religious mainstream.

Chartres Cathedral

Arts. Romanesque architecture (11th-12th cent.) expanded on late Roman models, using the rounded arch and massed stone to support enlarged basilicas. Painting and sculpture followed Byzantine models. The literature of **chivalry** was exemplified by the epic (*Chanson de Roland*, c 1100) and by courtly love poems of the troubadours of Provence and minnesingers of Germany. **Gothic** architecture emerged in France (choir of St. Denis, c 1040) and spread along with French cultural influence. Rib vaulting and pointed arches were used to combine soaring heights with delicacy, and they freed walls for display of stained glass. Exteriors were covered with painted relief sculpture and embellished with elaborate architectural detail.

Learning. Law, medicine, and philosophy were advanced at independent **universities** (Bologna, late 11th cent.), originally corporations of students and masters. Twelfth-cent. translations of Greek classics, especially Aristotle, encouraged an analytic approach. Scholastic philosophy, from Anselm (1033-1109) to **Aquinas** (1225-74), attempted to understand revelation through reason.

Apogee of Central Asian Power; Islam Grows: 1250-1500

Turks. Turkic peoples, of Central Asian ancestry, were a military threat to the Byzantine and Persian Empires from the 6th cent. After several waves of invasions, during which most of the Turks adopted Islam, the **Seljuk Turks** took (1055) Baghdad. They ruled Persia, Iraq and, after 1071, Asia Minor, where massive numbers of Turks settled. The empire was divided in the 12th cent. into smaller states ruled by Seljuks, Kurds (**Saladin**, c 1137-93), and Mamluks (a military caste of former Turk, Kurd, and Circassian slaves), which governed Egypt and the Middle East until the Ottoman era (c 1290-1922).

Osman I (r c 1290-1326) and succeeding sultans united Anatolian Turkish warriors in a militaristic state that waged holy war against Byzantium and Balkan Christians. Most of the Balkans had been subdued, and Anatolia united, when Constantinople fell (1453). By the mid-16th cent., Hungary, the Middle East, and N Africa had been conquered. The Turkish advance was stopped at Vienna (1529) and at the naval battle of Lepanto (1571) by Spain, Venice, and the papacy.

The Ottoman state was governed in accordance with orthodox Muslim law. Greek, Armenian, and Jewish communities were segregated and were ruled by religious leaders responsible for taxation; they dominated trade. State offices and most army ranks were filled by slaves through a system of child conscription among Christians.

India. Mahmud of Ghazni (971-1030) led repeated Turkish raids into N India. Turkish power was consolidated in 1206 with the start of the **Sultanate at Delhi**. Centralization of state power under the early Delhi sultans went far beyond traditional Indian practice. Muslim rule of most of the subcontinent lasted until the British conquest 600 years later.

Mongols. Genghis Khan (c 1167-1227) first united the feuding Mongol tribes, and built their armies into an effective offensive force around a core of highly mobile cavalry. He and his immediate successors created the largest land empire in history; by 1279 it stretched from the E coast of Asia to the Danube, from the Siberian steppes to the Arabian Sea. East-West trade and contacts were facilitated (Marco Polo, c 1254-1324). The W Mongols were Islamized by 1295; successor states soon lost their Mongol character by assimilation. They were briefly reunited under the Turk Tamerlane (1336-1405).

Kublai Khan ruled China from his new capital Beijing (est. c 1264). Naval campaigns against Japan (1274, 1281) and Java (1293) were defeated, the latter by the Hindu-Buddhist maritime kingdom of Majapahit. The **Yuan** dynasty used Mongols and other foreigners (including Europeans) in official posts and tolerated the return of Nestorian Christianity (suppressed 841-45) and the spread of Islam in the S and W. A native reaction expelled the Mongols in 1367-68.

Russia. The Kievan state in Russia, weakened by the decline of Byzantium and the rise of the Catholic Polish-Lithuanian state, was overrun (1238-40) by the Mongols. Only the northern trading republic of Novgorod remained independent. The grand dukes of Moscow emerged as leaders of a coalition of princes that eventually (by 1481) defeated the Mongols. After the fall of Constantinople in 1453, the **Tsars** (Caesars) at Moscow (from Ivan III, r 1462-1505) set up an independent Russian Orthodox Church. Commerce failed to revive. The isolated Russian state remained agrarian, with the peasant class falling into serfdom.

Persia. A revival of Persian literature, making use of the Arab alphabet and literary forms, began in the 10th cent. (epic

---

> **IT'S A FACT:** Geneticists studying the Y chromosome have concluded that 8% of the males living in the region of the vast former Mongol empire, or about 16 million males, carry nearly identical Y chromosomes. The researchers, writing in the *American Journal of Human Genetics* in Jan. 2003, theorize that these men all could be descendants of the 13th-century warrior Genghis Khan and his relatives, who held sway over much of Eurasia for hundreds of years, in societies where harems and concubines were common and males often had many children. It will never be known for sure unless Genghis's grave is found and his DNA can be analyzed.

---

of Firdausi, 935-1020). An art revival, influenced by Chinese styles introduced after the Mongols came to power in Iran, began in the 13th cent. Persian cultural and political forms, and often the Persian language, were used for centuries by Turkish and Mongol elites from the Balkans to India. Persian mystics from Rumi (1207-73) to Jami (1414-92) promoted **Sufism** in their poetry.

Africa. Two militant Islamic Berber dynasties emerged from the Sahara to carve out empires from the Sahel to central Spain—the **Almoravids** (c 1050-1140) and the fanatical **Almohads** (c 1125-1269). The Ghanaian empire was replaced in the upper Niger by Mali (c 1230-1340), whose Muslim rulers imported Egyptians to help make **Timbuktu** a center of commerce (in gold, leather, and slaves) and learning. The Songhay empire (to 1590) replaced Mali. To the S, forest kingdoms produced refined artworks (Ife terra cotta, **Benin** bronzes). Other Muslim states in Nigeria (Hausas) and Chad originated in the 11th cent. and continued in some form until the 19th-cent. European conquest. Less-developed Bantu kingdoms existed across central Africa.

Some 40 Muslim Arab-Persian trading colonies and city-states were established all along the E African coast from the 10th cent. (Kilwa, Mogadishu). The interchange with Bantu peoples produced the **Swahili** language and culture. Gold, palm oil, and slaves were brought from the interior, stimulating the growth of the Monamatapa kingdom of the Zambezi (15th cent.). The Christian Ethiopian empire (from 13th cent.) continued the traditions of Axum.

Southeast Asia. Islam was introduced into Malaya and the Indonesian islands by Arab, Persian, and Indian traders. Coastal Muslim cities and states (starting before 1300) soon dominated the interior. Chief among these was the **Malacca** state (c 1400-1511), on the Malay peninsula.

Arts and Statecraft Thrive in Europe: 1350-1600

Italian Renaissance and Humanism. Distinctive Italian achievements in the arts in the late Middle Ages (**Dante**, 1265-1321; Giotto, 1276-1337) led to the vigorous new styles of the Renaissance (14th-16th cent.). Patronized by the rulers of the quarreling petty states of Italy (**Medicis** in Florence and the papacy, c 1400-1737), the plastic arts perfected realistic techniques, including **perspective** (Masaccio, 1401-28, **Leonardo**, 1452-1519). Classical motifs were used in architecture, and increased talent and expense were put into secular buildings. The Florentine dialect was refined as a national literary language (**Petrarch**, 1304-74). Greek refugees from the E strengthened the respect of humanist scholars for the classic sources. Soon an international movement aided by the spread of **printing** (Gutenberg, c 1397(?)-1468), **humanism** was optimistic about the power of human reason (Erasmus of Rotterdam, 1466-1536, **More's** *Utopia*, 1516) and valued individual effort in the arts and in politics (**Machiavelli**, 1469-1527).

France. The French monarchy, strengthened in its repeated struggles with powerful nobles (Burgundy, Flanders, Aquitaine) by alliances with the growing commercial towns, consolidated bureaucratic control under Philip IV (r 1285-1314) and extended French influence into Germany and Italy (popes at Avignon, France, 1309-1417). The **Hundred Years War** (1337-1453) ended English dynastic claims in France (battles of Crécy, 1346, and Poitiers, 1356; Joan of Arc executed, 1431). A French Renaissance, dating from royal invasions (1494, 1499) of Italy, was encouraged at the court of Francis I (r 1515-47), who centralized taxation and law. French vernacular literature consciously asserted its independence (La Pléiade, 1549).

England. The evolution of England's unique political institutions began with the **Magna Carta** (1215), by which King John guaranteed the privileges of nobles and church against the monarchy and assured jury trial. After the **Wars of the Roses** (1455-85), the **Tudor dynasty** reasserted royal prerogatives (Henry VIII, r 1509-47), but the trend toward independent departments and ministerial government also continued. English trade (wool exports from c 1340) was protected by the nation's growing maritime power (**Spanish Armada** destroyed, 1588).

English replaced French and Latin in the late 14th cent. in law and literature (**Chaucer**, c 1340-1400) and English translation of the Bible began (Wycliffe, 1380s). **Elizabeth I** (r 1558-1603) presided over a confident flowering of poetry (Spenser, 1552-99), drama (**Shakespeare**, 1564-1616), and music.

German Empire. From among a welter of minor feudal states, church lands, and independent cities, the **Habsburgs** assembled a far-flung territorial domain, based in Austria from 1276. Family members held the title of Holy Roman Emperor from 1438 to the Empire's dissolution in 1806, but failed to centralize its domains, leaving Germany disunited for centuries. Resistance to Turkish expansion brought Hungary under Austrian control from the 16th cent. The Netherlands, Luxembourg, and Burgundy were added in 1477, curbing French expansion.

The Flemish painting tradition of naturalism, technical proficiency, and bourgeois subject matter began in the 15th cent. (**Jan Van Eyck,** c 1390-1441), the earliest northern manifestation of the Renaissance. Albrecht **Dürer** (1471-1528) typified the merging of late Gothic and Italian trends in 16th-cent. German art. Imposing civic architecture flourished in the prosperous commercial cities.

Spain. Despite the unification of Castile and Aragon in 1479, the 2 countries retained separate governments, and the nobility, especially in Aragon and Catalonia, retained many privileges. Spanish lands in Italy (Naples, Sicily) and the Netherlands entangled the country in European wars through the mid-17th cent., while explorers, traders, and conquerors built up a Spanish empire in the Americas and the Philippines. From the late 15th cent., a **golden age** of literature and art produced works of social satire (plays of Lope de Vega, 1562-1635; **Cervantes,** 1547-1616), as well as spiritual intensity (**El Greco,** 1541-1614; **Velazquez,** 1599-1660).

Black Death. The bubonic plague reached Europe from the E in 1348, killing up to half the population by 1350. Labor scarcity forced wages to rise and brought greater freedom to the peasantry, making possible **peasant uprisings** (Jacquerie in France, 1358; Wat Tyler's rebellion in England, 1381).

Explorations. Organized European maritime exploration began, seeking to evade the Venice-Ottoman monopoly of E trade and to promote Christianity. Beginning in 1418, expeditions from Portugal explored the W coast of Africa, until Vasco da Gama rounded the Cape of Good Hope in 1497

and reached India. A Portuguese trading empire was consolidated by the seizure of Goa (1510) and Malacca (1551). Japan was reached in 1542. The voyages of Christopher **Columbus** (1492-1504) uncovered a world new to Europeans, which Spain hastened to subdue. Navigation schools in Spain and Portugal, the development of large sailing ships (carracks), and the invention (c 1475) of the rifle aided European penetration.

Christopher Columbus

Mughals and Safavids. E. of the Ottoman Empire, 2 Muslim dynasties ruled unchallenged in the 16th and 17th cent. The Mughal dynasty of India, founded by Persianized Turkish invaders from the NW under Babur, dates from their 1526 conquest of the Delhi Sultanate. The dynasty ruled most of India for more than 200 years, surviving nominally until 1857. **Akbar** (r 1556-1605) consolidated administration at his glorious court, where the Urdu language (Persian-influenced Hindi) developed. Trade relations with Europe increased. Under Shah Jahan (1629-58), a secularized art fusing Hindu and Muslim elements flourished in miniature painting and in architecture (**Taj Mahal**). **Sikhism** (founded c 1519) combined elements of both faiths. Suppression of Hindus and Shi'ite Muslims in S India in the late 17th cent. weakened the empire.

Taj Mahal

Fanatical devotion to the Shi'ite sect characterized the Safavids (1502-1736) of Persia and led to hostilities with the Sunni Ottomans for more than a century. The prosperity and the strength of the empire are evidenced by the mosques at its capital city, **Isfahan**. The Safavids enhanced Iranian national consciousness.

China. The **Ming** emperors (1368-1644), the last native dynasty in China, wielded unprecedented personal power, while the Confucian bureaucracy began to suffer from inertia. European trade (Portuguese monopoly through **Macao** from 1557) was strictly controlled. Jesuit scholars and scientists (Matteo Ricci, 1552-1610) introduced some Western science; their writings familiarized the West with China. Chinese technological inventiveness declined from this era, but the arts thrived, especially in the areas of painting and ceramics.

Japan. After the decline of the first hereditary shogunate (chief generalship) at **Kamakura** (1185-1333), fragmentation of power accelerated, as did the consequent social mobility. Under Kamakura and the Ashikaga shogunate (1338-1573), the daimyos (lords) and samurai (warriors) grew more powerful and promoted a martial ideology. Japanese pirates and traders plied the China coast. Popular Buddhist movements included the nationalist Nichiren sect (from c 1250) and **Zen** (brought from China, 1191), which stressed meditation and a disciplined esthetic (tea ceremony, gardening, martial arts, No drama).

Reformed Europe Expands Overseas: 1500-1700

Reformation begun. Theological debate and protests against real and perceived clerical corruption existed in the medieval Christian world, expressed by such dissenters as John **Wycliffe** (c 1320-84) and his followers, the Lollards, in England, and **Huss** (burned as a heretic, 1415) in Bohemia.

Martin **Luther** (1483-1546) preached that faith alone leads to salvation, without the mediation of clergy or good works. He attacked the authority of the pope, rejected priestly celibacy, and recommended individual study of the Bible (which he translated c 1525). His 95 Theses (1517) led to his excommunication (1521). John **Calvin** (1509-64) said that God's elect were predestined for salvation and that good conduct and success were signs of election. Calvin in Geneva and John **Knox** (1505-72) in Scotland established theocratic states.

Henry VIII asserted English national authority and secular power by breaking away (1534) from the Catholic Church. Monastic property was confiscated, and some Protestant doctrines given official sanction.

Religious wars. A century and a half of religious wars began with a S German peasant uprising (1524), repressed with Luther's support. Radical sects—democratic, pacifist, millennarian—arose (Anabaptists ruled Münster in 1534-35) and were suppressed violently. Civil war in France from 1562 between **Huguenots** (Protestant nobles and merchants) and Catholics ended with the 1598 **Edict of Nantes,** tolerating Protestants (revoked 1685). Habsburg attempts to restore Catholicism in Germany were resisted in 25 years of fighting; the 1555 Peace of Augsburg guarantee of religious independence to local princes and cities was confirmed only after the **Thirty Years War** (1618-48), when much of Germany was devastated by local and foreign armies (Sweden, France).

A Catholic Reformation, or **Counter Reformation,** met the Protestant challenge, defining an official theology at the Council of Trent (1545-63). The **Jesuit** order (Society of Jesus), founded in 1534 by Ignatius Loyola (1491-1556), helped reconvert large areas of Poland, Hungary, and S Germany and sent missionaries to the New World, India, and China, while the **Inquisition** suppressed heresy in Catholic countries. A revival of religious fervor appeared in the devotional literature (Teresa of Avila, 1515-82) and in grandiose **Baroque** art (Bernini, 1598-1680).

Scientific Revolution. The late nominalist thinkers (Ockham, c 1300-49) of Paris and Oxford challenged Aristotelian orthodoxy, allowing for a freer scientific approach. At the same time, metaphysical values, such as the Neoplatonic faith in an orderly, mathematical cosmos, still motivated and directed inquiry. Nicolaus **Copernicus** (1473-1543) promoted the heliocentric theory, which was confirmed when

Johannes **Kepler** (1571-1630) discovered the mathematical laws describing the orbits of the planets. The traditional Christian-Aristotelian belief that the heavens and the earth were fundamentally different collapsed when **Galileo** (1564-1642) discovered moving sunspots, irregular moon topography, and moons around Jupiter. He and Sir Isaac **Newton** (1642-1727) developed a mechanics that unified cosmic and earthly phenomena. Newton and Gottfried

Galileo

von **Leibniz** (1646-1716) invented calculus. René **Descartes** (1596-1650), best known for his influential philosophy, also invented analytic geometry.

An explosion of **observational science** included the discovery of blood circulation (Harvey, 1578-1657) and microscopic life (Leeuwenhoek, 1632-1723) and advances in anatomy (Vesalius, 1514-64, dissected corpses) and chemistry (Boyle, 1627-91). Scientific research institutes were founded: Florence (1657), London (**Royal Society**, 1660), Paris (1666). Inventions proliferated (Savery's steam engine, 1696).

Arts. Mannerist trends of the High Renaissance (**Michelangelo,** 1475-1564) exploited virtuosity, grace, novelty, and exotic subjects and poses. The notion of artistic genius was promoted. Private connoisseurs entered the art market. These trends were elaborated in the 17th cent. **Baroque** era on a grander scale. Dynamic movement in painting and sculpture was emphasized by sharp lighting effects, rich materials (colored marble, gilt), and realistic details. Curved facades, broken lines, rich detail, and ceiling decoration characterized Baroque architecture. Monarchs, princes, and prelates, usually Catholic, used Baroque art to enhance and embellish their authority, as in royal portraits (Velazquez, 1599-1660; Van Dyck, 1599-1641).

National styles emerged. In France, a taste for rectilinear order and serenity (Poussin, 1594-1665), linked to the new rational philosophy, was expressed in classical forms. The influence of **classical values** in French literature (tragedies of **Racine,** 1639-99) gave rise to the "battle of the Ancients and Moderns." New forms included the essay (**Montaigne,** 1533-92) and novel (*Princesse de Cleves*, La Fayette, 1678).

Dutch painting of the 17th cent. was unique in its wide social distribution. The Flemish tradition of undemonstrative realism reached its peak in **Rembrandt** (1606-69) and Jan Vermeer (1632-75).

Economy. European economic expansion was stimulated by the new trade with the East, by New World gold and silver, and by a doubling of population (50 million in 1450, 100 million in 1600). New business and financial techniques were developed and refined, such as joint-stock companies, insurance, and letters of credit and exchange. The Bank of Amsterdam (1609) and the Bank of England (1694) broke the old monopoly of private banking families. The rise of a business mentality was typified by the spread of clock towers in cities in the 14th cent. By the mid-15th cent., portable clocks were available; the first watch was invented in 1502.

By 1650, most governments had adopted the **mercantile system**, in which they sought to amass metallic wealth by protecting their merchants' foreign and colonial trade monopolies. The rise in prices and the new coin-based economy undermined the craft guild and feudal manorial systems. Expanding industries (clothweaving, mining) benefited from technical advances. Coal replaced disappearing wood as the chief fuel; it was used to fuel new 16th-cent. blast furnaces making cast iron.

Aztec ruins

New World. The **Aztecs** united much of the Meso-American culture area in a militarist empire by 1519, from their capital, Tenochtitlán (pop. 300,000), which was the center of a cult requiring ritual human sacrifice. Most of the civilized areas of South America were ruled by the centralized Inca Empire (1476-1534), stretching 2,000 mi from Ecuador to NW Argentina. Lavish and sophisticated traditions in pottery, weaving, sculpture, and architecture were maintained in both regions.

These empires, beset by revolts, fell in 2 short campaigns to gold-seeking Spanish forces based in the Antilles and Panama. Hernan **Cortes** took Mexico (1519-21); Francisco **Pizarro,** Peru (1532-35). From these centers, land and sea expeditions claimed most of North and South America for Spain. The Indian high cultures did not survive the impact of Christian missionaries and the new upper class of whites and mestizos. In turn, New World silver and such Indian products as potatoes, tobacco, corn, peanuts, chocolate, and rubber exercised a major economic influence on Europe. Although the Spanish administration intermittently concerned itself with the welfare of Indians, the population remained impoverished at most levels. European diseases reduced the native population.

Brazil, which the Portuguese reached in 1500 and settled after 1530, and the Caribbean colonies of several European nations developed a plantation economy where sugarcane, tobacco, cotton, coffee, rice, indigo, and lumber were grown by slaves. From the early 16th to late 19th cent., 10 million Africans were transported to **slavery** in the New World.

Netherlands. The urban, Calvinist N provinces of the Netherlands rebelled (1568) against Habsburg Spain and founded an oligarchic mercantile republic. Their control of the Baltic grain market enabled them to exploit Mediterranean food shortages. Religious refugees—French and Belgian Protestants, Iberian Jews—added to the commercial talent pool. After Spain absorbed Portugal (1580), the Dutch seized Portuguese possessions and created a vast but short-lived commercial empire in Brazil, the Antilles, Africa, India, Ceylon, Malacca, Indonesia, and Taiwan. The Dutch

also challenged or supplanted Portuguese traders in China and Japan. Revolution in 1640 restored Portuguese independence.

England. Anglicanism became firmly established under **Elizabeth I** after a brief Catholic interlude under "Bloody Mary" (1553-58). But religious and political conflicts led to a rebellion (1642) by Parliament. Forces of the Roundheads (Puritans) defeated the Cavaliers (Royalists);

Elizabeth I

Charles I was beheaded (1649). The new Commonwealth was ruled as a military dictatorship by Oliver **Cromwell,** who also brutally crushed (1649-51) an Irish rebellion. Conflicts within the Puritan camp (democratic Levelers defeated, 1649) aided the Stuart restoration (1660), but Parliament was strengthened and the peaceful "**Glorious Revolution**" (1688) advanced political and religious liberties (writings of **Locke,** 1632-1704). British privateers (Drake, 1540-96) challenged Spanish control of the New World and penetrated Asian trade routes (Madras taken, 1639). North American colonies (Jamestown, 1607; Plymouth, 1620) provided an outlet for religious dissenters from Europe.

France. Emerging from the religious civil wars in 1628, France regained military and commercial great power status (under the ministries of **Richelieu,** Mazarin, and Colbert). Under **Louis XIV** (reigned 1643-1715), royal absolutism triumphed over nobles and local *parlements* (defeat of Fronde, 1648-53). Permanent colonies were founded in Canada (1608), the Caribbean (1626), and India (1674).

Sweden. Sweden seceded from the Scandinavian Union in 1523. The thinly populated agrarian state (with copper, iron, and timber exports) was united by the Vasa kings, whose conquests by the mid-17th cent. made Sweden the dominant Baltic power. The empire collapsed in the Great Northern War (1700-21).

Poland. After the union with Lithuania in 1447, Poland ruled vast territories from the Baltic to the Black Sea, resisting German and Turkish incursions. Catholic nobles failed to gain the loyalty of their Orthodox Christian subjects in the E; commerce and trades were practiced by German and Jewish immigrants. The bloody 1648-49 Cossack uprising began the kingdom's dismemberment.

China. A new dynasty, the **Manchus,** invaded from the NE, seized power in 1644, and expanded Chinese control to its greatest extent in Central and SE Asia. Trade and diplomatic contact with Europe grew, carefully controlled by China. New crops (sweet potato, maize, peanut) allowed an economic and population growth (pop. 300 million, in 1800). Traditional arts and literature were pursued with increased sophistication (*Dream of the Red Chamber,* novel, mid-18th cent.).

Japan. Tokugawa Ieyasu, shogun from 1603, finally unified and pacified feudal Japan. Hereditary daimyos and samurai monopolized government office and the professions. An urban merchant class grew, literacy spread, and a cultural renaissance occurred (**haiku,** a verse innovation of the poet Basho, 1644-94). Fear of European domination led to persecution of Christian converts from 1597 and to stringent isolation from outside contact from 1640.

Philosophy, Industry, and Revolution: 1700-1800

Science and Reason. Greater faith in reason and empirical observation, espoused since the Renaissance (Francis Bacon, 1561-1626), was bolstered by scientific discoveries despite theological opposition (Galileo's retraction, 1633). René **Descartes** (1596-1650) used a rationalistic approach modeled on geometry and introspection to discover "self-evident" truths as a foundation of knowledge. Sir Isaac **Newton** emphasized induction from experimental observation. Baruch de **Spinoza** (1632-77), who called for political and

intellectual freedom, developed a systematic rationalistic philosophy in his classic work *Ethics*.

French philosophers assumed leadership of the **Enlightenment** in the 18th cent. Montesquieu (1689-1755) used British history to support his notions of limited government. **Voltaire's** (1694-1778) diaries and novels of exotic travel illustrated the intellectual trends toward secular ethics and relativism. Jean-Jacques **Rousseau's** (1712-1778) radical concepts of the **social contract** and of the inherent goodness of the common man gave impetus to antimonarchical republicanism. The *Encyclopedia* (1751-72, edited by Diderot and d'Alembert), designed as a monument to reason, was largely devoted to practical technology.

In England, ideals of liberty were connected with empiricist philosophy and science in the followers of John **Locke**. But British empiricism, especially as developed by the skeptical David **Hume** (1711-76), radically reduced the role of reason in philosophy, as did the evolutionary approach to law and politics of Edmund Burke (1729-97) and the utilitarian ethics of Jeremy Bentham (1748-1832). Adam Smith (1723-90) and other **physiocrats** called for a rationalization of economic activity by removing artificial barriers to a supposedly natural free exchange of goods.

German writers participated in the new philosophical trends popularized by Christian von Wolff (1679-1754). Immanuel **Kant's** (1724-1804) transcendental idealism, unifying an empirical epistemology with a priori moral and logical concepts, directed German thought away from skepticism. Italian contributions included work on electricity (Galvani, 1737-98; Volta, 1745-1827), the pioneer historiography of Vico (1668-1744), and writings on penal reform (Beccaria, 1738-94). Benjamin Franklin (1706-90) was celebrated in Europe for his varied achievements.

The growth of the **press** (*Spectator*, 1711-12) and the wide distribution of realistic but sentimental **novels** attested to the increase of a large bourgeois public.

Arts. Rococo art, characterized by extravagant decorative effects, asymmetries copied from organic models, and artificial pastoral subjects, was favored by the continental aristocracy for most of the cent. (Watteau, 1684-1721) and had musical analogies in the ornamentalized polyphony of late Baroque. The **Neoclassical** art after 1750, associated with the new scientific archaeology, was more streamlined and was infused with the supposed moral and geometric rectitude of the Roman Republic (David, 1748-1825). In England, **town planning** on a grand scale began.

Industrial Revolution in England. Agricultural improvements, such as the sowing drill (1701) and livestock breeding, were implemented on the large fields provided by enclosure of common lands by private owners. Profits from agriculture and from colonial and foreign trade (1800 volume, £54 million) were channeled through hundreds of banks and the **Stock Exchange** (est 1773) into new industrial processes.

The Newcomen steam pump (1712) aided coal mining. Coal fueled the new efficient steam engines patented by James Watt in 1769, and coke-smelting produced cheap, sturdy iron for machinery by the 1730s. The **flying shuttle** (1733) and **spinning jenny** (c 1764) were used in the large new cotton textile factories, where women and children were much of the work force. Goods were transported cheaply over **canals** (2,000 mi; built 1760-1800).

American Revolution. The British colonies in North America attracted a mass immigration of religious dissenters and poor people throughout the 17th and 18th cent., coming from the British Isles, Germany, the Netherlands, and other countries. The population reached 3 million non-natives by the 1770s. The small native population was greatly reduced by European diseases and by wars with and between the various colonies. British attempts to control colonial trade and to tax the colonists to pay for the costs of colonial administration and defense clashed with traditions of local self-government and eventually provoked the colonies to rebellion.

Central and East Europe. The monarchs of the three states that dominated E Europe—Austria, Prussia, and Russia—accepted the advice and legitimation of philosophes in creating modern, centralized institutions in their kingdoms, which were enlarged by the division (1772-95) of Poland.

Under **Frederick II** (called the Great) (r 1740-86) Prussia, with its efficient modern army, doubled in size. State monopolies and tariff protection fostered industry, and some legal reforms were introduced. Austria's heterogeneous realms were unified under **Maria Theresa** (r 1740-80) and **Joseph II** (r 1780-90). Reforms in education, law, and religion were enacted, and the Austrian serfs were freed (1781). With its defeat in the Seven Years' War in 1763, Austria failed to regain Silesia, which had been seized by Prussia, but it was compensated by expansion to the E and S (Hungary, Slavonia, 1699; Galicia, 1772).

Russia, whose borders continued to expand, adopted some Western bureaucratic and economic policies under **Peter I** (r 1682-1725) and **Catherine II** (r 1762-96). Trade and cultural contacts with the West multiplied from the new Baltic Sea capital, **St. Petersburg** (est 1703).

French Revolution. The growing French middle class lacked political power and resented aristocratic tax privileges, especially in light of the successful American Revolution. Peasants lacked adequate land and were burdened with feudal obligations to nobles. War with Britain led to the loss of French Canada and drained the treasury, finally forcing the king to call the **Estates-General** in 1789 (first time since 1614), in an atmosphere of food riots (poor crop in 1788).

Aristocratic resistance to absolutism was soon overshadowed by the reformist Third Estate (middle class), which proclaimed itself the **National Constituent Assembly** June 17 and took the "Tennis Court oath" on June 20 to secure a constitution. The storming of the **Bastille** on July 14, 1789, by Parisian artisans was followed by looting and seizure of aristocratic property throughout France. Assembly reforms included abolition of class and regional privileges, a Declaration of Rights, suffrage by taxpayers (75% of males), and the **Civil Constitution of the Clergy** providing for election and loyalty oaths for priests. A republic was declared Sept. 22, 1792, in spite of royalist pressure from Austria and Prussia, which had declared war in April (joined by Britain the next year). Louis XVI was beheaded Jan. 21, 1793, and Queen Marie Antoinette was beheaded Oct. 16, 1793.

Napoleon Bonaparte

Royalist uprisings in La Vendée and military reverses led to institution of a **reign of terror** in which tens of thousands of opponents of the Revolution and criminals were executed. Radical reforms in the **Convention** period (Sept. 1793-Oct. 1795) included the abolition of colonial slavery, economic measures to aid the poor, support of public education, and a short-lived de-Christianization.

Division among radicals (execution of Hebert, Danton, and Robespierre, 1794) aided the ascendancy of a moderate **Directory**, which consolidated military victories. **Napoleon Bonaparte** (1769-1821), a popular young general, exploited political divisions and participated in a coup Nov. 9, 1799, making himself first consul (dictator).

India. Sikh and Hindu rebels (Rajputs, Marathas) and Afghans destroyed the power of the Mughals during the 18th cent. After France's defeat (1763) in the Seven Years' War, Britain was the primary European trade power in India. Its control of inland **Bengal and Bihar** was recognized (1765) by the Mughal shah, who granted the **British East India Co.** (under Clive, 1725-74) the right to collect land revenue there. Despite objections from Parliament (1784 India Act), the company's involvement in local wars and politics led to repeated acquisitions of new territory. The company exported Indian textiles, sugar, and indigo.

Change Gathers Steam: 1800-40

French ideals and empire spread. Inspired by the ideals of the French Revolution, and supported by the expanding French armies, new republican regimes arose near France: the **Batavian** Republic in the Netherlands (1795-1806), the **Helvetic** Republic in Switzerland (1798-1803), the **Cisal-** pine Republic in N Italy (1797-1805), the **Ligurian** Republic in Genoa (1797-1805), and the **Parthenopean** Republic in S Italy (1799). A Roman Republic existed briefly in 1798 after Pope Pius VI was arrested by French troops. In Italy and Germany, new nationalist sentiments were stimulated both in imitation of and in reaction to developments in France (anti-French and anti-Jacobin peasant uprisings in Italy, 1796-99).

From 1804, when Napoleon declared himself emperor, to 1812, a succession of military victories (Austerlitz, 1805; Jena, 1806) extended his control over most of Europe, through puppet states (**Confederation of the Rhine** united W German states for the first time and **Grand Duchy of Warsaw** revived Polish national hopes), expansion of the empire, and alliances.

Among the lasting reforms initiated under Napoleon's absolutist reign were: establishment of the Bank of France, centralization of tax collection, codification of law along Roman models (Code Napoléon), and reform and extension of secondary and university education. In an 1801 concordat, the papacy recognized the effective autonomy of the French Catholic Church.

Napoleon's continental successes were offset by British victory under Adm. Horatio Nelson in the **Battle of Trafalgar** (1805).

In all, some 400,000 French soldiers were killed in the Napoleonic Wars, along with about 600,000 foreign troops.

Last gasp of old regime. The disastrous 1812 invasion of Russia exposed Napoleon's overextension. After Napoleon's 1814 exile at Elba, his armies were defeated (1815) at **Waterloo**, by British and Prussian troops.

At the **Congress of Vienna**, the monarchs and princes of Europe redrew their boundaries, to the advantage of Prussia (in Saxony and the Ruhr), Austria (in Illyria and Venetia), and Russia (in Poland and Finland). British conquest of Dutch and French colonies (S Africa, Ceylon, Mauritius) was recognized, and France, under the restored Bourbons, retained its expanded 1792 borders. The settlement brought 50 years of international peace to Europe.

But the Congress was unable to check the advance of liberal ideals and of nationalism among the smaller European nations. The 1825 **Decembrist uprising** by liberal officers in Russia was easily suppressed. But an independence movement in Greece, stirred by commercial prosperity and a cultural revival, succeeded in expelling Ottoman rule by 1831, with the aid of Britain, France, and Russia.

A constitutional monarchy was secured in France by the **1830 Revolution**; Louis Philippe became king. The revolutionary contagion spread to **Belgium**, which gained its independence (1830) from the Dutch monarchy, to **Poland**, whose rebellion was defeated (1830-31) by Russia, and to Germany.

Romanticism. A new style in intellectual and artistic life began to replace Neoclassicism and Rococo after the mid-18th cent. By the early 19th cent., this style, Romanticism, had prevailed in the European world.

Rousseau had begun the reaction against rationalism: in education (*Émile*, 1762) he stressed subjective spontaneity over regularized instruction. German writers (Lessing,

1729-81; Herder, 1744-1803) favorably compared the German folk song to classical forms and began a cult of Shakespeare, whose passion and "natural" wisdom was a model for the romantic *Sturm und Drang* (Storm and Stress) movement. **Goethe's** *Sorrows of Young Werther* (1774) set the model for the tragic, passionate genius.

A new interest in **Gothic architecture** in England after 1760 (Walpole, 1717-97) spread through Europe, associated with an aesthetic Christian and mystic revival (**Blake**, 1757-1827). Celtic, Norse, and German mythology and folk tales were revived or imitated (Macpherson's Ossian translation, 1762; Grimm's Fairy Tales, 1812-22). The medieval revival (Scott's *Ivanhoe*, 1819) led to a new interest in history, stressing national differences and organic growth (**Carlyle**, 1795-1881; Michelet, 1798-1874), corresponding to theories of natural evolution (Lamarck's *Philosophie Zoologique*, 1809; Lyell's *Geology*, 1830-33). A reaction against classicism characterized the English **romantic poets** (beginning with Wordsworth, 1770-1850). Revolution and war fed an emphasis on freedom and conflict, expressed by both poets (**Byron**, 1788-1824; **Hugo**, 1802-85) and philosophers (**Hegel**, 1770-1831).

Wild gardens replaced the formal French variety, and painters favored rural, stormy, and mountainous landscapes (**Turner**, 1775-1851; **Constable**, 1776-1837). Clothing became freer, with wigs, hoops, and ruffles discarded. Originality and genius were expected in the life as well as the work of inspired artists (Murger's *Scenes from Bohemian Life*, 1847-49). Exotic locales and themes (as in Gothic horror stories) were used in art and literature (Delacroix, 1798-1863; **Poe**, 1809-49).

Music exhibited the new dramatic style and a breakdown of classical forms (**Beethoven**, 1770-1827). The use of folk melodies and modes aided the growth of distinct national traditions (Glinka in Russia, 1804-57).

Latin America. Francois **Toussaint L'Ouverture** led a successful slave revolt in Haiti, which subsequently became the first Latin American state to achieve independence (1804). The mainland Spanish colonies won their independence (1810-24), under such leaders as Simon **Bolivar** (1783-1830). Brazil became an independent empire (1822) under the Portuguese prince regent. A new class of military officers divided power with large landholders and the church.

United States. Heavy immigration and exploitation of ample natural resources fueled rapid economic growth. The spread of the franchise, public education, and antislavery sentiment were signs of a widespread democratic ethic.

China. Failure to keep pace with Western arms technology exposed China to greater European influence and hampered efforts to bar imports of opium, which had damaged Chinese society and drained wealth overseas. In the **Opium War** (1839-42), Britain forced China to expand trade opportunities and to cede Hong Kong.

Triumph of Progress: 1840-80

Idea of Progress. As a result of the cumulative scientific, economic, and political changes of the preceding eras, the idea took hold among literate people in the West that continuing growth and improvement was the usual state of human and natural life.

Charles **Darwin's** statement of the theory of evolution and survival of the fittest (*Origin of Species*, 1859), defended by intellectuals and scientists against theological objections, was taken as confirmation that progress was the natural direction of life. The controversy helped define popular ideas of the dedicated scientist

Charles Darwin

and of science's increasing control over the world (Foucault's demonstration of earth's rotation, 1851; **Pasteur's** germ theory, 1861).

Liberals following Ricardo (1772-1823) in their faith that unrestrained competition would bring continuous economic expansion sought to adjust political life to the new social realities and believed that unregulated competition of ideas would yield truth (**Mill**, 1806-73). In England, successive reform bills (1832, 1867, 1884) gave representation to the new industrial towns and extended the franchise to the middle and lower classes and to Catholics, Dissenters, and Jews. On both sides of the Atlantic, reformists tried to improve conditions for the mentally ill (**Dix**, 1802-87), women (Anthony, 1820-1906), and prisoners. Slavery was barred in the British Empire (1833), the U.S. (1865), and Brazil (1888).

Socialist theories based on ideas of human perfectibility or progress were widely disseminated. Utopian socialists such as Saint-Simon (1760-1825) envisaged an orderly, just society directed by a technocratic elite. A model factory town, New Lanark, Scotland, was set up by utopian Robert Owen (1771-1858), and communal experiments were tried in the U.S. (most notably, Brook Farm, Mass., 1841-47). Bakunin's (1814-76) anarchism represented the opposite utopian extreme of total freedom. Karl **Marx** (1818-83) posited the inevitable triumph of socialism in industrial countries through a dialectical process of class conflict.

Spread of industry. The technical processes and managerial innovations of the English industrial revolution spread to Europe (especially Germany) and the U.S., causing an explosion of industrial production, demand for raw materials, and competition for markets. Inventors, both trained and self-educated, provided the means for larger-scale production (Bessemer steel, 1856; sewing machine, 1846). Many inventions were shown at the 1851 London Great Exhibition at the **Crystal Palace**, the theme of which was universal prosperity.

Local specialization and long-distance trade were aided by a revolution in transportation and communication. Railroads were first introduced in the 1820s in England and the U.S. More than 150,000 mi of track had been laid worldwide by 1880, with another 100,000 mi laid in the next decade. Steamships were improved (*Savannah* crossed Atlantic, 1819). The **telegraph**, perfected by 1844 (Morse), connected the Old and New Worlds by cable in 1866 and quickened the pace of international commerce and politics. The first commercial **telephone** exchange went into operation in the U.S. in 1878.

The new class of industrial workers, uprooted from their rural homes, lacked job security and suffered from dangerous overcrowded conditions at work and at home. Many responded by organizing **trade unions** (legalized in England, 1824; France, 1884). The U.S. Knights of Labor had 700,000 members by 1886. The First International (1864-76) tried to unite workers internationally around a Marxist program. The quasi-Socialist Paris Commune uprising (1871) was violently suppressed. Factory Acts to reduce child labor and regulate conditions were passed (1833-50 in England). Social security measures were introduced by the Bismarck regime (1883-89) in Germany.

Revolutions of 1848. Among the causes of the continent-wide revolutions were an international collapse of credit and resulting unemployment, bad harvests in 1845-47, and a cholera epidemic. The new urban proletariat and expanding bourgeoisie demanded a greater political role. Republics were proclaimed in France, Rome, and Venice. Nationalist feelings reached fever pitch in the Habsburg empire, as Hungary declared independence under Kossuth, as a Slav Congress demanded equality, and as Piedmont tried to drive Austria from Lombardy. A national liberal assembly at Frankfurt called for German unification.

But riots fueled bourgeois fears of socialism (**Marx and Engels**, *Communist Manifesto*, 1848), and peasants remained conservative. The old establishment—the Papacy, the Habsburgs with the help of the Czarist Russian army — was able to rout the revolutionaries by 1849. The French Republic succumbed to a renewed monarchy by 1852 (Emperor Napoleon III).

Great nations unified. Using the "blood and iron" tactics of Bismarck from 1862, Prussia controlled N Germany by 1867 (war with Denmark, 1864; Austria, 1866). After defeating France in 1870 (annexation of Alsace-Lorraine), it won the allegiance of S German states. A new **German Em-**

pire was proclaimed (1871). **Italy**, inspired by Giuseppe Mazzini (1805-72) and Giuseppe Garibaldi (1807-82), was unified by the reformed Piedmont kingdom through uprisings, plebiscites, and war.

The **U.S.**, its area expanded after the 1846-48 Mexican War, defeated (1861-65) a secession attempt by slave states. in the **Civil War.** Canadian provinces were united in an autonomous **Dominion of Canada** (1867). Control in **India** was removed from the East India Co. and centralized under British administration after the 1857-58 Sepoy rebellion, laying the groundwork for the modern Indian State. Queen Victoria was named Empress of India (1876).

Europe dominates Asia. The Ottoman Empire began to collapse in the face of Balkan nationalisms and European imperial incursions in N Africa (**Suez Canal**, 1869). The Turks had lost control of most of both regions by 1882. Russia completed its expansion S by 1884 (despite the temporary setback of the **Crimean War** with Turkey, Britain, and France, 1853-56), taking Turkestan, all the Caucasus, and Chinese areas in the E and sponsoring Balkan Slavs against the Turks. A succession of reformist and reactionary regimes presided over a slow modernization (serfs freed, 1861). Persian independence suffered as Russia and British India competed for influence.

China was forced to sign a series of unequal treaties with European powers and Japan. Overpopulation and an inefficient dynasty brought misery and caused rebellions (Taiping, Muslims) leaving tens of millions dead. **Japan** was forced by the U.S. (Commodore Perry's visits, 1853-54) and Europe to end its isolation. The Meiji restoration (1868) gave power to a Westernizing oligarchy. Intensified empire-building gave Burma to Britain (1824-85) and Indochina to France (1862-95). Christian missionary activity followed imperial and trade expansion in Asia.

Respectability. The fine arts were expected to reflect and encourage the good morals and manners among the Victorians. Prudery, exaggerated delicacy, and familial piety were heralded by **Bowdler's** expurgated edition (1818) of Shakespeare. Government-supported mass education sought to inculcate a work ethic as a means to escape poverty (**Horatio Alger**, 1832-99).

The official **Beaux Arts** school in Paris set an international style of imposing public buildings (Paris Opera, 1861-74; Vienna Opera, 1861-69) and uplifting statuary (Bartholdi's Statue of Liberty, 1884). Realist painting, influenced by photography (Daguerre, 1837), appealed to a new mass audience with social or historical narrative (Wilkie, 1785-1841; Poynter, 1836-1919) or with serious religious, moral, or social messages (pre-Raphaelites, Millet's *Angelus*, 1858) often drawn from ordinary life. The **Impressionists** (Monet, 1840-1926; Pissarro, 1830-1903; Renoir, 1841-1919) rejected the formalism, sentimentality, and precise techniques of academic art in favor of a spontaneous, undetailed rendering of the world through careful representation of the effect of natural light on objects.

Realistic **novelists** presented the full panorama of social classes and personalities, but retained sentimentality and moral judgment (**Dickens**, 1812-70; **Eliot**, 1819-80; **Tolstoy**, 1828-1910; **Balzac**, 1799-1850).

Veneer of Stability: 1880-1900

Imperialism triumphant. The vast **African** interior, visited by European explorers (Barth, 1821-65; Livingstone, 1813-73), was conquered by the European powers in rapid, competitive thrusts from their coastal bases after 1880, mostly for domestic political and international strategic reasons. W African Muslim kingdoms (Fulani), Arab slave traders (Zanzibar), and Bantu military confederations (Zulu) were alike subdued. Only Christian Ethiopia (defeat of Italy, 1896) and Liberia resisted successfully. France (W Africa) and Britain ("Cape to Cairo," **Boer War**, 1899-1902) were the major beneficiaries. The ideology of "the white man's burden" (Kipling, *Barrack Room Ballads*, 1892) or of a "civilizing mission" (France) justified the conquests.

W European foreign capital investment soared to nearly $40 billion by 1914, but most was in E Europe (France, Ger-

many), the Americas (Britain), and the Europeans' colonies. The foundation of the modern interdependent world economy was laid, with cartels dominating raw material trade.

An industrious world. Industrial and technological proficiency characterized the 2 new great powers—Germany and the U.S. Coal and iron deposits enabled Germany to reach 2nd or 3rd place status in iron, steel, and shipbuilding by the 1900s. German electrical and chemical industries were world leaders. The U.S. post-Civil War boom (interrupted by "panics"—1884, 1893, 1896) was shaped by massive immigration from S and E Europe from 1880, government subsidy of railroads, and huge private monopolies (Standard Oil, 1870; U.S. Steel, 1901). The **Spanish-American War**, 1898 (Philippine Insurrection, 1899-1902), and the **Open Door policy** in China (1899) made the U.S. a world power.

Hyde Park, London

England led in **urbanization**, with **London** the world capital of finance, insurance, and shipping. Sewer systems (Paris, 1850s), electric subways (London, 1890), parks, and bargain department stores helped improve living standards for most of the urban population of the industrial world.

Westernization of Asia. Asian reaction to European economic, military, and religious incursions took the form of imitation of Western techniques and adoption of Western ideas of progress and freedom. The Chinese "self-strengthening" movement of the 1860s and 1870s included rail, port, and arsenal improvements and metal and textile mills. Reformers such as **K'ang Yu-wei** (1858-1927) won liberalizing reforms in 1898, right after the European and Japanese "scramble for concessions."

A universal education system in Japan and importation of foreign industrial, scientific, and military experts aided Japan's unprecedented rapid modernization after 1868, under the authoritarian Meiji regime. Japan's victory in the **Sino-Japanese War** (1894-95) put Formosa and Korea in its power.

In India, the British alliance with the remaining princely states masked reform sentiment among the Westernized urban elite; higher education had been conducted largely in English for 50 years. The **Indian National Congress**, founded in 1885, demanded a larger government role for Indians.

Fin-de-siècle **sophistication. Naturalist** writers pushed realism to its extreme limits, adopting a quasi-scientific attitude and writing about formerly taboo subjects such as sex, crime, extreme poverty, and corruption (Flaubert, 1821-80; Zola, 1840-1902; Hardy, 1840-1928). Unseen or repressed psychological motivations were explored in the clinical and theoretical works of Sigmund **Freud** (1856-1939) and in works of fiction (**Dostoyevsky**, 1821-81; James, 1843-1916; Schnitzler, 1862-1931; others).

A contempt for bourgeois life or a desire to shock a complacent audience was shared by the French **symbolist** poets (Verlaine, 1844-96; Rimbaud, 1854-91), by neopagan English writers (Swinburne, 1837-1909), by continental dramatists (**Ibsen**, 1828-1906), and by satirists (**Wilde**, 1854-1900). The German philosopher Friedrich **Nietzsche** (1844-1900) was influential in his elitism and pessimism.

Postimpressionist art neglected long-cherished conventions of representation (Cézanne, 1839-1906) and showed a willingness to learn from primitive and non-European art (Gauguin, 1848-1903; Japanese prints).

Racism. Gobineau (1816-82) gave a pseudobiological foundation to modern racist theories, which spread in Europe in the latter 19th cent., along with **Social Darwinism**, the belief that societies are and should be organized as a struggle for survival of the fittest. The medieval period was interpreted as an era of natural Germanic rule (Chamberlain, 1855-1927), and notions of racial superiority were associated with German national aspirations (Treitschke, 1834-96). **Anti-Semitism**, with a new racist rationale, became a significant political force in Germany (Anti-Semitic Petition, 1880), Austria (Lueger, 1844-1910), and France (**Dreyfus case**, 1894-1906).

Last Respite: 1900-9

Alliances. While the peace of Europe (and its dependencies) continued to hold (1907 **Hague Conference** extended the rules of war and international arbitration procedures), imperial rivalries, protectionist trade practices (in Germany and France), and the escalating arms race (British *Dreadnought* battleship launched; Germany widens Kiel canal, 1906) exacerbated minor disputes (German-French Moroccan "crises," 1905, 1911).

Security was sought through alliances: **Triple Alliance** (Germany, Austria-Hungary, Italy; renewed in 1902 and 1907); Anglo-Japanese Alliance (1902), Franco-Russian Alliance (1899), **Entente Cordiale** (Britain, France, 1904), Anglo-Russian Treaty (1907), German-Ottoman friendship.

Ottomans decline. The inefficient, corrupt Ottoman government was unable to resist further loss of territory. Nearly all European lands were lost in 1912 to Serbia, Greece, Montenegro, and Bulgaria. Italy took Libya and the Dodecanese islands the same year, and Britain took Kuwait (1899) and the Sinai (1906). The **Young Turk** revolution in 1908 forced the sultan to restore a constitution, and it introduced some social reform, industrialization, and secularization.

British Empire. British trade and cultural influence remained dominant in the empire, but constitutional reforms presaged its eventual dissolution: The colonies of **Australia** were united in 1901 under a self-governing commonwealth. **New Zealand** acquired dominion status in 1907. The old Boer republics joined Cape Colony and Natal in the self-governing **Union of South Africa** in 1910.

The 1909 Indian Councils Act enhanced the role of elected province legislatures in **India**. The Muslim League (founded 1906) sought separate communal representation.

East Asia. Japan exploited its growing industrial power to expand its empire. Victory in the 1904-5 war against Russia (naval battle of Tsushima, 1905) assured Japan's domination of **Korea** (annexed 1910) and Manchuria (Port Arthur taken, 1905).

In China, central authority began to crumble (empress died, 1908). Reforms (Confucian exam system ended 1905, modernization of the army, building of railroads) were inadequate, and secret societies of reformers and nationalists, inspired by the Westernized **Sun Yat-sen** (1866-1925) fomented periodic uprisings in the S.

Siam, whose independence had been guaranteed by Britain and France in 1896, was split into spheres of influence by those countries in 1907.

Russia. The population of the Russian Empire approached 150 million in 1900. Reforms in education, in law, and in local institutions (*zemstvos*) and an industrial boom starting in the 1880s (oil, railroads) created the beginnings of a modern state, despite the autocratic tsarist regime. Liberals (1903 Union of Liberation), Socialists (Social Democrats founded 1898, Bolsheviks split off 1903), and populists (Social Revolutionaries founded 1901) were periodically repressed, and national minorities were persecuted (anti-Jewish pogroms, 1903, 1905-6).

An industrial crisis after 1900 and harvest failures aggravated poverty among urban workers, and the 1904-5 defeat by Japan (which checked Russia's Asian expansion) sparked **the Revolution of 1905-6.** A **Duma** (parliament) was created, and an agricultural reform (under Stolypin, prime minister 1906-11) created a large class of land-owning peasants (kulaks).

1903 Wright Flyer

The world shrinks. Developments in transportation and communication and mass population movements helped create an awareness of an interdependent world. Early **automobiles** (Daimler, Benz, 1885) were experimental or were designed as luxuries. Assembly-line mass production (Ford Motor Co., 1903) made the invention practicable, and by 1910 nearly 500,000 motor vehicles were registered in the U.S. alone. **Heavier-than-air flights** began in 1903 in the U.S. (Wright brothers' *Flyer*), preceded by glider, balloon, and model plane advances in several countries. Trade was advanced by improvements in **ship design** (gyrocompass, 1910), speed (*Lusitania* crossed Atlantic in 5 days, 1907), and reach (Panama Canal begun, 1904).

The first transatlantic **radio** telegraphic transmission occurred in 1901, 6 years after Marconi discovered radio. Radio transmission of human speech had been made in 1900. Telegraphic transmission of photos was achieved in 1904, lending immediacy to news reports. **Phonographs**, popularized by Caruso's recordings (starting 1902), made for quick international spread of musical styles (ragtime). **Motion pictures**, perfected in the 1890s (Dickson, Lumière brothers), became a popular and artistic medium after 1900; newsreels appeared in 1909.

Emigration from crowded European centers soared in the decade: 9 million migrated to the U.S., and millions more went to Siberia, Canada, Argentina, Australia, South Africa, and Algeria. Some 70 million Europeans emigrated in the cent. before 1914. Several million Chinese, Indians, and Japanese migrated to SE Asia, where their urban skills often enabled them to take a predominant economic role.

Social reform. The social and economic problems of the poor were kept in the public eye by realist fiction writers (Dreiser's *Sister Carrie*, 1900; Gorky's *Lower Depths*, 1902; Sinclair's *The Jungle*, 1906), journalists (U.S. **muckrakers**—Steffens, Tarbell), and artists (Ashcan school). Frequent labor strikes and occasional assassinations by anarchists or radicals (Empress Elizabeth of Austria, 1898; King Umberto I of Italy, 1900; U.S. Pres. McKinley, 1901; Russian Interior Minister Plehve, 1904; Portugal's King Carlos, 1908) added to social tension and fear of revolution.

But democratic reformism prevailed. In Germany, Bernstein's (1850-1932) **revisionist Marxism**, downgrading rev-olution, was accepted by the powerful Social Democrats and trade unions. The British Fabian Society (the Webbs, Shaw) and the Labour Party (founded 1906) worked for reforms such as Social Security and union rights (1906), while woman suffragists grew more militant. U.S. **progressives** fought big business (Pure Food and Drug Act, 1906). In France, the 10-hour work day (1904) and separation of church and state (1905) were reform victories, as was universal suffrage in Austria (1907).

Arts. An unprecedented period of experimentation, centered in France, produced several new **painting** styles: Fauvism exploited bold color areas (Matisse, *Woman With Hat*, 1905); expressionism reflected powerful inner emotions (the Brücke group, 1905); cubism combined several views of an object on one flat surface (Picasso's *Demoiselles*, 1906-7); futurism tried to depict speed and motion (Italian Futurist Manifesto, 1910). **Architects** explored new uses of steel structures, with facades either neoclassical (Adler and Sullivan in U.S.); curvilinear Art Nouveau (Gaudi's Casa Mila, 1905-10); or functionally streamlined (Wright's Robie House, 1909).

Music and dance shared the experimental spirit. Ruth St. Denis (1877-1968) and Isadora Duncan (1878-1927) pioneered modern dance, while Sergei Diaghilev in Paris revitalized classic ballet from 1909. Composers explored atonal music (Debussy, 1862-1918) and dissonance (Schoenberg, 1874-1951) or revolutionized classical forms (Stravinsky, 1882-1971), often showing jazz or folk music influences.

War and Revolution: 1910-19

War threatens. Germany under Wilhelm II sought a political and imperial role consonant with its industrial strength, challenging Britain's world supremacy and threatening France, which was still resenting the loss (1871) of Alsace-Lorraine. Austria wanted to curb an expanded Serbia (after 1912) and the threat it posed to its own Slav lands. Russia feared Austrian and German political and economic aims in the Balkans and Turkey.

An accelerated arms race resulted from these circumstances. The German standing army rose to more than 2 million men by 1914. Russia and France had more than a million each, and Austria and the British Empire nearly a million each. Dozens of enormous battleships were built by the powers after 1906.

The **assassination of Austrian Archduke Franz Ferdinand** by a Serbian, June 28, 1914, was the pretext for war. The system of alliances made the conflict Europe-wide; Germany's invasion of Belgium to outflank France forced Britain to enter the war. Patriotic fervor was nearly unanimous among all classes in most countries.

World War I. German forces were stopped in France in one month. The rival armies dug **trench networks**. Artillery and improved machine guns prevented either side from any lasting advance despite repeated assaults (600,000 dead at **Verdun**, Feb.-July 1916). Poison gas, used by Germany in 1915, proved ineffective. The entrance of more than 1 million U.S. troops tipped the balance after mid-1917, forcing Germany to sue for peace the next year. The formal armistice was signed on Nov. 11, 1918.

In the E, the Russian armies were thrown back (battle of **Tannenberg**, Aug. 20, 1914), and the war grew unpopular in Russia. An allied attempt to relieve Russia through Turkey failed (**Gallipoli**, 1915). The **Russian Revolution** (1917) abolished the monarchy. The new Bolshevik regime signed the capitulatory Brest-Litovsk peace in March 1918. Italy entered the war on the allied side in May 1915 but was pushed back by Oct. 1917. A renewed offensive with Allied aid in Oct.-Nov. 1918 forced Austria to surrender.

The British Navy successfully blockaded Germany, which responded with submarine U-boat attacks; **unrestricted submarine warfare** against neutrals after Jan. 1917 helped bring the U.S. into the war. Other battlefields included Palestine and Mesopotamia, both of which Britain wrested from the Turks in 1917, and the African and Pacific colonies of Germany, most of which fell to Britain, France, Australia, Japan, and South Africa.

Settlement. At the **Paris Peace Conference** (Jan.-June 1919), concluded by the **Treaty of Versailles**, and in subsequent negotiations and local wars (Russian-Polish War, 1920), the map of Europe was redrawn with a nod to U.S. Pres. Woodrow Wilson's principle of self-determination. Austria and Hungary were separated, and much of their land was given to Yugoslavia (formerly Serbia), Romania, Italy, and the newly independent Poland and Czechoslovakia. Germany lost territory in the W, N, and E, while Finland and the Baltic states were detached from Russia. Turkey lost nearly all its Arab lands to British-sponsored Arab states or to direct French and British rule. Belgium's sovereignty was recognized.

From 1916, the civilian populations and economies of both sides were mobilized to an unprecedented degree. Hardships intensified among fighting nations in 1917 (French mutiny crushed in May). More than 10 million soldiers died in the war.

A huge **reparations** burden and partial demilitarization were imposed on Germany. Pres. Wilson obtained approval for a League of Nations, but the U.S. Senate refused to allow the U.S. to join.

Russian revolution. Military defeats and high casualties caused a contagious lack of confidence in Tsar Nicholas, who was forced to abdicate Mar. 1917. A liberal provisional government lasted to end the war, and massive desertions, riots, and fighting between factions followed. A moderate socialist government under Aleksandr Kerensky was overthrown (Nov. 1917) in a violent coup by the **Bolsheviks** in Petrograd under **Lenin**, who later disbanded the elected Constituent Assembly.

The Bolsheviks brutally suppressed all opposition and ended the war with Germany in Mar. 1918. **Civil war** broke out in the summer between the Red Army, including the Bolsheviks and their supporters, and monarchists, anarchists, nationalities (Ukrainians, Georgians, Poles), and others. Small U.S.,

Vladimir Lenin

> **IT'S A FACT:** World War I pitted three first cousins, King George V of Great Britain, Kaiser Wilhelm II of Germany, and Tsar Nicholas II of Russia (all grandchildren of England's Queen Victoria), against one another. The conflict prompted George V in 1917 to change the British royal family's surname from Saxe-Coburg-Gotha to the name of his castle, Windsor, thereby renouncing all the German titles belonging to his relations.

British, French, and Japanese units also opposed the Bolsheviks (1918-19; Japan in Vladivostok to 1922). The civil war, anarchy, and pogroms devastated the country until the 1920 Red Army victory. The wartime total monopoly of political, economic, and police power by the Communist Party leadership was retained.

Other European revolutions. An unpopular monarchy in Portugal was overthrown in 1910. The new republic took severe anticlerical measures in 1911.

After a century of Home Rule agitation, during which **Ireland** was devastated by famine (1 million dead, 1846-47) and emigration, republican militants staged an unsuccessful uprising in Dublin during Easter 1916. The execution of the leaders and mass arrests by the British won popular support for the rebels. The Irish Free State, comprising all but the 6 N counties, achieved dominion status in 1922.

In the aftermath of the world war, radical revolutions were attempted in Germany (**Spartacist** uprising, Jan. 1919), Hungary (Kun regime, 1919), and elsewhere. All were suppressed or failed for lack of support.

Chinese revolution. The Manchu Dynasty was overthrown and a republic proclaimed in Oct. 1911. First Pres. Sun Yat-sen resigned in favor of strongman Yuan Shih-k'ai. Sun organized the parliamentarian **Kuomintang** party.

Students launched protests on May 4, 1919, against League of Nations concessions in China to Japan. National-

ist, liberal, and socialist ideas and political groups spread. The **Communist Party** was founded in 1921. A Communist regime took power in Mongolia with Soviet support in 1921.

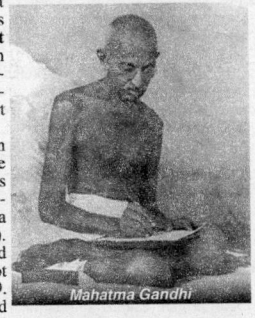
Mahatma Gandhi

India restive. Indian objections to British rule erupted in nationalist riots as well as in the nonviolent tactics of Mahatma **Gandhi** (1869-1948). Nearly 400 unarmed demonstrators were shot at **Amritsar** in Apr. 1919. Britain approved limited self-rule that year.

Mexican revolution. Under the long Diaz dictatorship (1877-1911) the economy advanced, but Indian and mestizo lands were confiscated, and concessions to foreigners (mostly U.S.) damaged the middle class. A **revolution in 1910** led to civil wars and U.S. intervention (1914, 1916-17). Land reform and a more democratic constitution (1917) were achieved.

The Aftermath of War: 1920-29

U.S. Easy credit, technological ingenuity, and war-related industrial decline in Europe caused a long economic boom, in which ownership of the new products—**autos, phones, radios**—became democratized. Prosperity, an increase in women workers, woman suffrage (1920), and drastic change in fashion (flappers, mannish bob for women, clean-shaven men) created a wide perception of social change, despite prohibition of alcoholic beverages (1919-33). Union membership and strikes increased. Fear of radicals led to Palmer raids (1919-20) and the Sacco/Vanzetti case (1921-27).

Europe sorts itself out. Germany's liberal **Weimar constitution** (1919) could not guarantee a stable government in the face of rightist violence (Rathenau assassinated, 1922) and Communist refusal to cooperate with Socialists. Reparations and Allied occupation of the Rhineland caused staggering inflation that destroyed middle-class savings, but economic expansion resumed at mid-decade, aided by U.S. loans. A sophisticated, **innovative culture** developed in architecture and design (Bauhaus, 1919-28), film (Lang, *M*, 1931), painting (Grosz), music (Weill, *Threepenny Opera*, 1928), theater (Brecht, *A Man's a Man*, 1926), criticism (Benjamin), philosophy (Jung), and fashion. This culture was considered decadent and socially disruptive by rightists.

England elected its first Labour governments (Jan. 1924, June 1929). A 10-day general strike in support of coal miners failed in May 1926. In **Italy**, strikes, political chaos, and violence by small Fascist bands culminated in the Oct. 1922 Fascist March on Rome, which established **Mussolini's** dictatorship. Strikes were outlawed (1926), and Italian influence was pressed in the Balkans (Albania a protectorate, 1926). A conservative dictatorship was also established in **Portugal** in a 1926 military coup.

Czechoslovakia, the only stable democracy to emerge from the war in Central or East Europe, faced opposition from Germans (in the Sudetenland), Ruthenians, and some Slovaks. As the industrial heartland of the old Habsburg empire, it remained fairly prosperous. With French backing, it formed the Little Entente with Yugoslavia (1920) and Romania (1921) to block Austrian or Hungarian irredentism. Hungary remained dominated by the landholding classes and expansionist feeling. Croats and Slovenes in Yugosla-

via demanded a federal state until King Alexander I proclaimed (1929) a royal dictatorship. Poland faced nationality problems as well (Germans, Ukrainians, Jews); Pilsudski ruled as dictator from 1926. The Baltic states were threatened by traditionally dominant ethnic Germans and by Soviet-supported Communists.

An economic collapse and famine in **Russia** (1921-22) claimed 5 million lives. The New Economic Policy (1921) allowed land ownership by peasants and some private commerce and industry. Stalin was absolute ruler within 4 years of Lenin's death (1924). He inaugurated a brutal collectivization program (1929-32) and used foreign Communist parties for Soviet state advantage.

Internationalism. Revulsion against World War I led to pacifist agitation, to the Kellogg-Briand Pact renouncing aggressive war (1928), and to **naval disarmament** pacts (Washington, 1922; London, 1930). But the League of Nations was able to arbitrate only minor disputes (Greece-Bulgaria, 1925).

Middle East. Mustafa Kemal (**Ataturk**) led **Turkish** nationalists in resisting Italian, French, and Greek military advances (1919-23). The sultanate was abolished (1922), and elaborate reforms were passed, including secularization of law and adoption of the Latin alphabet. Ethnic conflict led to persecution of **Armenians** (more than 1 million dead in 1915, 1 million expelled), Greeks (forced Greek-Turk population exchange, 1923), and Kurds (1925 uprising).

With evacuation of the Turks from **Arab** lands, the puritanical Wahabi dynasty of E Arabia conquered (1919-25) what is now Saudi Arabia. British, French, and Arab dynastic and nationalist maneuvering resulted in the creation of 2 more Arab monarchies in 1921—Iraq and Transjordan (both under British control)—and 2 French mandates—Syria and Lebanon. Jewish immigration into British-mandated **Palestine**, inspired by the Zionist movement, was resisted by Arabs, at times violently (1921, 1929 massacres).

Reza Khan ruled **Persia** after his 1921 coup (shah from 1925), centralized control, and created the trappings of a modern secular state.

China. The Kuomintang under **Chiang Kai-shek** (1887-1975) subdued the warlords by 1928. The Communists were brutally suppressed after their alliance with the Kuomintang was broken in 1927. Relative peace thereafter allowed for industrial and financial improvements, with some Russian, British, and U.S. cooperation.

Arts. Nearly all bounds of subject matter, style, and attitude were broken in the arts of the period. **Abstract** art first took inspiration from natural forms or narrative themes (Kandinsky from 1911) and then worked free of any representational aims (Malevich's suprematism, 1915-19; Mondrian's geometric style from 1917). The **Dada** movement (from 1916) mocked artistic pretension with absurd collages and constructions (Arp, Tzara, from 1916). Paradox, illusion, and psychological taboos were exploited by **surrealists** by the latter 1920s (Dali, Magritte). Architectural schools celebrated industrial values, whether vigorous abstract constructivism (Tatlin, *Monument to 3rd International*, 1919) or the machined, streamlined **Bauhaus** style,

which was extended to many design fields (Helvetica typeface).

Prose writers explored revolutionary narrative modes related to dreams (Kafka's *Trial*, 1925), internal monologue (Joyce's **Ulysses**, 1922), and word play (Stein's *Making of Americans*, 1925). Poets and novelists wrote of modern alienation (Eliot's *Waste Land*, 1922) and aimlessness (Lost Generation).

Sciences. Scientific specialization prevailed by the 20th cent. Advances in knowledge and technological aptitude increased with the geometric rise in the number of practitioners. Physicists challenged common-sense views of causality, observation, and a mechanistic universe, putting science further beyond popular grasp (**Einstein's** general theory of relativity, 1916; Bohr's quantum mechanics, 1913; Heisenberg's uncertainty principle, 1927).

Rise of Totalitarians: 1930-39

Depression. A worldwide financial panic and economic depression began with the Oct. 1929 U.S. stock market crash and the May 1931 failure of the Austrian Credit-Anstalt. A credit crunch caused international bankruptcies and **unemployment**: 12 million jobless by 1932 in the U.S., 5.6 million in Germany, 2.7 million in England. Governments responded with **tariff restrictions** (Smoot-Hawley Act, 1930; Ottawa Imperial Conference, 1932), which dried up world trade. Government public works programs were vitiated by deflationary budget balancing.

Germany. Years of agitation by violent extremists were brought to a head by the Depression. Nazi leader Adolf Hit-

Mussolini & Hitler

ler was named chancellor in Jan. 1933 and given dictatorial power by the Reichstag in March. Opposition parties were disbanded, strikes banned, and all aspects of economic, cultural, and religious life were brought under central government and Nazi party control and manipulated by sophisticated propaganda. Severe persecution of Jews began (**Nuremberg Laws**, Sept. 1935). Many Jews, political opponents, and others were sent to concentration camps (Dachau, 1933), where thousands died or were killed. Public works, renewed conscription (1935), arms production, and a 4-year plan (1936) all but ended unemployment.

Hitler's expansionism started with reincorporation of the Saar (1935), occupation of the **Rhineland** (Mar. 1936), and annexation of Austria (Mar. 1938). At **Munich** (Sept. 1938) an indecisive Britain and France sanctioned German dismemberment of Czechoslovakia.

Russia. Urbanization and education advanced. Rapid industrialization was achieved through successive **5-year plans** starting in 1928, using severe labor discipline and mass forced labor. Industry was financed by a decline in living standards and exploitation of agriculture, which was almost totally collectivized by the early 1930s (*kolkhoz*, collective farm; *sovkhoz*, state farm, often in newly worked lands). Successive **purges** increased the role of professionals and management at the expense of workers. Millions perished in a series of manufactured disasters: extermination (1929-34) of kulaks (peasant landowners), severe famine (1932-33), party purges and show trials (Great Purge, 1936-38), suppression of nationalities, and poor conditions in labor camps.

Spain. An industrial revolution during World War I created an urban proletariat, which was attracted to socialism and anarchism; Catalan nationalists challenged central authority. The 5 years after King Alfonso left Spain in Apr. 1931 were dominated by tension between intermittent leftist and anticlerical governments and clericals, monarchists, and other rightists. Anarchist and Communist rebellions were

crushed, but a July 1936 extreme right rebellion led by Gen. Francisco **Franco** and aided by Nazi Germany and Fascist Italy succeeded, after a 3-year **civil war** (more than 1 million dead in battles and atrocities). The war polarized international public opinion.

Italy. Despite propaganda for the ideal of the Corporate State, few domestic reforms were attempted. An entente with Hungary and Austria (Mar. 1934), a pact with Germany and Japan (Nov. 1937), and intervention by 50,000-75,000 troops in Spain (1936-39) sealed Italy's identification with the fascist bloc (anti-Semitic laws after Mar. 1938). Ethiopia was conquered (1935-36) and Albania annexed (Jan. 1939) in conscious imitation of ancient Rome.

East Europe. Repressive regimes fought for power against an active opposition (liberals, socialists, Communists, peasants, Nazis). Minority groups and Jews were restricted within national boundaries that did not coincide with ethnic population patterns. In the destruction of **Czechoslovakia**, Hungary occupied S Slovakia (Nov. 1938) and Ruthenia (Mar. 1939), and a pro-Nazi regime took power in the rest of Slovakia. Other boundary disputes (e.g., Poland-Lithuania, Yugoslavia-Bulgaria, and Romania-Hungary) doomed attempts to build joint fronts against Germany or Russia. Economic depression was severe.

East Asia. After a period of liberalism in **Japan**, nativist militarists dominated the government with peasant support. Manchuria was seized (Sept. 1931-Feb. 1932), and a puppet state was set up (Manchukuo). Adjacent Jehol (Inner Mongolia) was occupied in 1933. China proper was invaded in July 1937; large areas were conquered by Oct. 1938. Hundreds of thousands of rapes, murders, and other atrocities were attributed to the Japanese.

In **China** Communist forces left Kuomintang-besieged strongholds in the S in a Long March (1934-35) to the N. The Kuomintang-Communist civil war was suspended in Jan. 1937 in the face of threatening Japan.

The democracies. The Roosevelt Administration, in office Mar. 1933, embarked on an extensive program of **New Deal** social reform and economic stimulation, including protection for labor unions (heavy industries organized), Social Security, public works, wage-and-hour laws, and assistance to farmers. Isolationist sentiment (1937 Neutrality Act) prevented U.S. intervention in Europe, but military expenditures were increased in 1939.

French political instability and polarization prevented resolution of economic and international security questions. The **Popular Front** government under Leon Blum (June 1936-Apr. 1938) passed social reforms (40-hr week) and raised arms spending. National coalition governments, which ruled Britain from Aug. 1931, brought economic recovery but failed to define a consistent international policy until Chamberlain's government (from May 1937), which practiced **appeasement** of Germany and Italy.

India. Twenty years of agitation for autonomy and then for independence (Gandhi's **salt march**, 1930) achieved some constitutional reform (extended provincial powers, 1935) despite Muslim-Hindu strife. Social issues assumed prominence with peasant uprisings (1921), strikes (1928),

> **IT'S A FACT:** The Maginot Line, built in the 1930s and named after its chief creator, French war minister Andre Maginot, was an elaborate network of bunkers stretching 150 miles along the French-German border. Buried 100 feet or more beneath hills and ridges, armed with heavy artillery and buttressed with thick concrete, containing storehouses, living quarters, even underground rail lines between key points, it was considered an impregnable fortress with the conveniences of a modern city. But the line did not extend to the French-Belgian order, so in World War II the Germans outflanked the line, invading with tanks and planes through Belgium.

Gandhi's efforts for untouchables (1932 "fast unto death"), and social and agrarian reform by the provinces after 1937.

Arts. The streamlined, geometric design motifs of Art Deco (from 1925) prevailed through the 1930s. **Abstract art** flourished (Moore sculptures from 1931) alongside a new **realism** related to social and political concerns (Socialist Realism, the official Soviet style from 1934; Mexican muralist Rivera, 1886-1957; and Orozco, 1883-1949), which

were also expressed in fiction and poetry (Steinbeck's *Grapes of Wrath*, 1939; Sandburg's *The People, Yes*, 1936). Modern architecture (International Style, 1932) was unchallenged in its use of artificial materials (concrete, glass), lack of decoration, and monumentality (Rockefeller Center, 1929-40). U.S.-made films captured a worldwide audience with their larger-than-life fantasies (*Gone With the Wind*, *The Wizard of Oz*, both 1939).

War, Hot and Cold: 1940-49

War in Europe. The Nazi-Soviet nonaggression pact (Aug. 1939) freed Germany to attack Poland (Sept.). Britain and France, which had guaranteed Polish independence, declared war on Germany. Russia seized E Poland (Sept.), attacked Finland (Nov.), and took the Baltic states (July 1940). Mobile German forces staged *blitzkrieg* attacks during Apr.-June 1940, conquering neutral Denmark, Norway, and the Low Countries and defeating France; 350,000 British and French troops were evacuated at **Dunkirk** (May). The **Battle of Britain** (June-Dec. 1940) denied Germany air superiority. German-Italian campaigns won the Balkans by Apr. 1941. Three million Axis troops **invaded Russia** in June 1941, marching through Ukraine to the Caucasus, and through White Russia and the Baltic republics to Moscow and Leningrad.

Russian winter counterthrusts (1941-42 and 1942-43) stopped the German advance (**Stalingrad**, Sept. 1942-Feb. 1943). With British and U.S. Lend-Lease aid and sustaining great casualties, the Russians drove the Axis from all E Europe and the Balkans in the next 2 years. Invasions of N Africa (Nov. 1942), Italy (Sept. 1943), and **Normandy** (launched on D-Day, June 6, 1944) brought U.S., British, Free French, and allied troops to Germany by spring 1945. In Feb. 1945, the 3 Allied leaders, Winston **Churchill** (Britain), Joseph **Stalin** (USSR), and Franklin D. Roosevelt (U.S.), met in Yalta to discuss strategy and resolve political issues, including the postwar Allied occupation of Germany. Germany surrendered May 7, 1945.

War in Asia-Pacific. Japan occupied Indochina in Sept. 1940, dominated Thailand in Dec. 1941, and attacked Hawaii (**Pearl Harbor**), the Philippines, Hong Kong, and Malaya on Dec. 7, 1941 (precipitating U.S. entrance into the war). Indonesia was attacked in Jan. 1942, and Burma was conquered in Mar. 1942. The Battle of **Midway** (June 1942) turned back the Japanese advance. "Island-hopping" battles (**Guadalcanal**, Aug. 1942-Jan. 1943; **Leyte Gulf**, Oct. 1944; **Iwo Jima**, Feb.-Mar. 1945; **Okinawa**, Apr. 1945) and

massive bombing raids on Japan from June 1944 wore out Japanese defenses. U.S. atom bombs, dropped Aug. 6 and 9 on **Hiroshima** and Nagasaki, forced Japan to agree, on Aug. 14, to surrender; formal surrender was on Sept. 2, 1945.

Pearl Harbor

Atrocities. The war brought 20th-cent. cruelty to its peak. The Nazi regime systematically killed an estimated 5-6 million Jews, including some 3 million who died in death camps (e.g., **Auschwitz**). Gypsies, political opponents, sick and retarded people, and others deemed undesirable were also murdered by the Nazis, as were vast numbers of Slavs, especially leaders.

Civilian deaths. German bombs killed 70,000 British civilians. More than 100,000 Chinese civilians were killed by

Japanese forces in the capture and occupation of Nanking. Severe retaliation by the Soviet army, E European partisans, Free French, and others took a heavy toll. U.S. and British bombing of Germany killed hundreds of thousands, as did U.S. bombing of Japan (80,000-200,000 at Hiroshima alone). Some 45 million people lost their lives in the war.

Settlement. The **United Nations** charter was signed in San Francisco on June 26, 1945, by 50 nations. The International Tribunal at **Nuremberg** convicted 22 German leaders for war crimes in Sept. 1946; 23 Japanese leaders were convicted in Nov. 1948. Postwar border changes included large gains in territory for the USSR, losses for Germany, a shift to the W in Polish borders, and minor losses for Italy. Communist regimes, supported by Soviet troops, took power in most of E Europe, including Soviet-occupied Germany (GDR proclaimed Oct. 1949). Japan lost all overseas lands.

Recovery. Basic political and social changes were imposed on Japan and W Germany by the western allies (Japan constitution adopted, Nov. 1946; W German basic law, May 1949). U.S. **Marshall Plan** aid ($12 billion, 1947-51) spurred W European economic recovery after a period of severe inflation and strikes in Europe and the U.S. The British Labour Party introduced a national health service and nationalized basic industries in 1946.

Cold War. Western fears of further Soviet advances (Cominform formed in Oct. 1947; Czechoslovakia coup, Feb. 1948; Berlin blockade, Apr. 1948-Sept. 1949) led to the formation of **NATO**. Civil War in Greece and Soviet pressure on Turkey led to U.S. aid under the **Truman Doctrine** (Mar. 1947). Other anti-Communist security pacts were the Organization of American States (Apr. 1948) and the SE Asia Treaty Organization (Sept. 1954). A new wave of **Soviet purges** and repression intensified in the last years of Stalin's rule, extending to E Europe (Slansky trial in Czechoslovakia, 1951). Only Yugoslavia resisted Soviet control (expelled by Cominform, June 1948; U.S. aid, June 1949).

China, Korea. Communist forces emerged from World War II strengthened by the Soviet takeover of industrial Manchuria. In 4 years of fighting, the Kuomintang was driven from the mainland; the People's Republic was proclaimed Oct. 1, 1949. Korea was divided by USSR and U.S. occupation forces. Separate republics were proclaimed in the 2 zones in Aug.-Sept. 1948.

India. India and Pakistan became independent dominions on Aug. 15, 1947. Millions of Hindu and Muslim refugees were created by the partition; riots (1946-47) took hundreds of thousands of lives; Mahatma **Gandhi** was assassinated in Jan. 1948. Burma became completely independent in Jan. 1948; Ceylon took dominion status in Feb.

Middle East. The UN approved partition of Palestine into Jewish and Arab states. **Israel** was proclaimed a state, May 14, 1948. Arabs rejected partition, but failed to defeat Israel in war (May 1948-July 1949). Immigration from Europe and the Middle East swelled Israel's Jewish population. British and French forces left Lebanon and Syria in 1946. Transjordan occupied most of Arab Palestine.

Southeast Asia. Communists and others fought against restoration of French rule in Indochina from 1946; a non-Communist government was recognized by France in Mar.

1949, but fighting continued. Both Indonesia and the Philippines became independent; the former in 1949 after 4 years of war with Netherlands, the latter in 1946. Philippine economic and military ties with the U.S. remained strong; a Communist-led peasant rising was checked in 1948.

Arts. New York became the center of the world art market; **abstract expressionism** was the chief mode (Pollock

from 1943, de Kooning from 1947). Literature and philosophy explored **existentialism** (Camus's *The Stranger,* 1942; Sartre's *Being and Nothingness,* 1943). Non-Western attempts to revive or create regional styles (Senghor's Négritude, Mishima's novels) only confirmed the emergence of a universal culture. Radio and phonograph records spread American popular music (swing, bebop) around the world.

The American Decade: 1950-59

Polite decolonization. The peaceful decline of European political and military power in Asia and Africa accelerated in the 1950s. Nearly all of **N Africa** was freed by 1956, but France fought a bitter war to retain Algeria, with its large European minority, until 1962. **Ghana**, independent in 1957, led a parade of new black African nations (more than 2 dozen by 1962), which altered the political character of the UN. Ethnic disputes often exploded in the new nations after decolonization (UN troops in Cyprus, 1964; **Nigerian civil war**, 1967-70). Leaders of the new states, mostly sharing socialist ideologies, tried to create an Afro-Asian bloc (Bandung Conference, 1955), but Western economic influence and U.S. political ties remained strong (Baghdad Pact, 1955).

Trade. World trade volume soared, in an atmosphere of monetary stability assured by international accords (**Bretton Woods,** 1944). In Europe, economic integration advanced (**European Economic Community,** 1957; European Free Trade Association, 1960). Comecon (1949) coordinated the economies of Soviet-bloc countries.

U.S. Economic growth produced an abundance of consumer goods (9.3 million motor vehicles sold, 1955). Suburban housing tracts changed life patterns for middle and working classes (Levittown, 1947-51). Pres. Dwight **Eisenhower's** landslide election victories (1952, 1956) reflected consensus politics. Senate condemnation of Senator Joseph **McCarthy** (Dec. 1954) curbed the political abuse of anti-Communism. A system of alliances and military bases bolstered U.S. influence on all continents. Trade and payments surpluses were balanced by overseas investments and foreign aid ($50 billion, 1950-59).

USSR. In the "thaw" after Stalin's death in 1953, relations with the West improved (evacuation of Vienna, Geneva summit conference, both 1955). Repression of scientific and cultural life eased, and many prisoners were freed or rehabilitated culminating in **de-Stalinization** (1956). **Nikita Khrushchev's** leadership aimed at consumer sector growth, but farm production lagged, despite the virgin lands program (from 1954). Soviet crushing of the 1956 Hungarian revolution, the 1960 U-2 spy plane episode, and other incidents renewed East-West tension and domestic curbs.

East Europe. Resentment of Russian domination and Stalinist repression combined with nationalist, economic, and religious factors to produce periodic violence. E Berlin workers rioted (1953), Polish workers rioted in Poznan (June 1956), and a broad-based **revolution** broke out in **Hungary** (Oct. 1956). All were suppressed by Soviet force or threats (at least 7,000 dead in Hungary). But Poland was allowed to restore private ownership of farms, and a degree of personal and economic freedom returned to Hungary. Yugoslavia experimented with worker self-management and a market economy.

Korea. The 1945 division of Korea along the 38th parallel left industry in the N, which was organized into a militant regime and armed by the USSR. The S was politically disunited. More than 60,000 N Korean troops invaded the S on June 25, 1950. The U.S., backed by the UN Security Council, sent troops. UN troops reached the Chinese border in Nov. Some 200,000 Chinese troops crossed the Yalu R. and

drove back UN forces. By spring 1951 battle lines had become stabilized near the original 38th parallel border, but heavy fighting continued. Finally, an armistice was signed on July 27, 1953. U.S. troops remained in the S, and U.S. economic and military aid continued. The war stimulated rapid economic recovery in Japan.

China. Starting in 1952, industry, agriculture, and social institutions were forcibly collectivized. In a massive purge, as many as several million people were executed as Kuomintang supporters or as class and political enemies. The **Great Leap Forward** (1958-60) unsuccessfully tried to force the pace of development by substituting labor for investment.

Indochina. Ho Chi Minh's forces, aided by the USSR and the new Chinese Communist government, fought French and pro-French Vietnamese forces to a standstill and captured the strategic **Dienbienphu** camp in May 1954. The Geneva Agreements divided Vietnam in half pending elections (never held) and recognized Laos and Cambodia as independent. The U.S. aided the anti-Communist Republic of Vietnam in the S.

Middle East. Arab revolutions placed leftist, militantly nationalist regimes in power in Egypt (1952) and Iraq (1958). But Arab unity attempts failed (United Arab Republic joined Egypt, Syria, Yemen, 1958-61). Arab refusal to recognize Israel (Arab League economic blockade began Sept. 1951) led to a permanent state of war, with repeated incidents (Gaza, 1955). Israel occupied Sinai, and Britain and France took (Oct. 1956) the Suez Canal, but were replaced by the UN Emergency Force. The Mossadegh government in Iran nationalized (May 1951) the British-owned oil industry in May, but was overthrown (Aug. 1953) in a U.S.-aided coup.

Latin America. Argentinian dictator Juan **Perón,** in office 1946, enforced land reform, some nationalization, welfare state measures, and curbs on the Roman Catholic Church, and crushed opposition. A Sept. 1955 coup deposed Perón. The 1952 revolution in Bolivia brought land reform, nationalization of tin mines, and improvement in the status of Indians, who nevertheless remained poor. The Batista regime in Cuba was overthrown (Jan. 1959) by Fidel **Castro,** who imposed a Communist dictatorship, aligned Cuba with the USSR, but improved education and health care. A U.S.-backed anti-Castro invasion (**Bay of Pigs,** Apr. 1961) was crushed. Self-government advanced in the British Caribbean.

Technology. Large outlays on research and development in the U.S. and the USSR focused on military applications (H-bomb in U.S., 1952; USSR, 1953; Britain, 1957; intercontinental missiles, late 1950s). Soviet launching of the **Sputnik** satellite (Oct. 4, 1957) spurred increases in U.S. science education funds (National Defense Education Act).

Literature and film. Alienation from social and literary conventions reached an extreme in the theater of the absurd (Beckett's *Waiting for Godot,* 1952), the "new novel" (Robbe-Grillet's *Voyeur,* 1955), and avant-garde film (Antonioni's *L'Avventura,* 1960). U.S. beatniks (Kerouac's *On the Road,* 1957) and others rejected the supposed conformism of Americans (Riesman's *The Lonely Crowd,* 1950).

Rising Expectations: 1960-69

Economic boom. The longest sustained economic boom on record spanned almost the entire decade in the capitalist world; the closely watched GNP figure doubled (1960-70) in the U.S., fueled by Vietnam War–related budget deficits. The **General Agreement on Tariffs and Trade** (1967)

stimulated W European prosperity, which spread to peripheral areas (Spain, Italy, E Germany). Japan became a top economic power. Foreign investment aided the industrialization of Brazil. There were limited Soviet economic reform attempts.

Reform and radicalization. Pres. John F. **Kennedy**, inaugurated 1961, emphasized youthful idealism and vigor; his assassination Nov. 22, 1963, was a national trauma. A series of political and social reform movements took root in the U.S., later spreading to other countries. Blacks demonstrated nonviolently and with partial success against segregation and poverty (1963 March on Washington; 1964 **Civil Rights Act**), but some urban ghettos erupted in extensive riots (Watts, 1965; Detroit, 1967; **Martin Luther King** assassination, Apr. 4, 1968). New concern for the poor (Harrington's *Other America*, 1963) helped lead to Pres. Lyndon Johnson's **"Great Society"** programs (Medicare, Water Quality Act, Higher Education Act, all 1965). Concern with the **environment** surged (Carson's *Silent Spring*, 1962).

Feminism revived as a cultural and political movement (Friedan's *Feminine Mystique*, 1963; National Organization for Women founded 1966), and a movement for homosexual rights emerged (Stonewall riot in NYC, 1969). Pope John XXIII called the **Second Vatican Council** (1962-65), which liberalized Roman Catholic liturgy and some other aspects of Catholicism.

Opposition to U.S. involvement in Vietnam, especially among university students (**Moratorium** protest, Nov. 1969), turned violent (Weatherman Chicago riots, Oct. 1969). **New Left** and Marxist theories became popular, and membership in radical groups (Students for a Democratic Society, Black Panthers) increased. Maoist groups, especially in Europe, called for total transformation of society. In France, students sparked a nationwide strike affecting 10 million workers in May-June 1968, but an electoral reaction barred revolutionary change.

China. China's revolutionary militancy under **Mao Zedong** caused disputes with the USSR under "revisionist" Khrushchev, starting in 1960. The 2 powers exchanged fire in 1969 border disputes. China used force to capture (1962) areas disputed with India. The **"Great Proletarian Cultural Revolution"** tried to impose a utopian egalitarian program in China and spread revolution abroad; political struggle, often violent, convulsed China in 1965-68.

Indochina. Communist-led guerrillas aided by N Vietnam fought from 1960 against the S Vietnam government of Ngo Dinh Diem (killed 1963). The U.S. military role increased after the 1964 **Tonkin Gulf** incident. U.S. forces peaked at 543,400 in Apr. 1969. Massive numbers of N Vietnamese troops also fought. Laotian and Cambodian neutrality were threatened by Communist insurgencies, with N Vietnamese aid, and U.S. intrigues.

Third World. A bloc of authoritarian leftist regimes among the newly independent nations emerged in political opposition to the U.S.-led Western alliance and came to dominate the conference of nonaligned nations (Belgrade, 1961; Cairo, 1964; Lusaka, 1970). Soviet political ties and military bases were established in Cuba, Egypt, Algeria, Guinea, and other countries whose leaders were regarded as revolutionary heroes by opposition groups in pro-Western or colonial countries. Some leaders were ousted in coups by pro-Western groups—Zaire's Patrice Lumumba (killed 1961), Ghana's Kwame Nkrumah (exiled 1966), and Indonesia's Sukarno (effectively ousted in 1965 after a Communist coup failed).

Middle East. Arab-Israeli tension erupted into a brief war June 1967. Israel emerged from the war as a major regional power. Military shipments before and after the war brought much of the Arab world into the Soviet political sphere. Most Arab states broke U.S. diplomatic ties, while Communist countries cut their ties to Israel. Intra-Arab disputes continued: Egypt and Saudi Arabia supported rival factions in a bloody Yemen civil war 1962-70; Lebanese troops fought Palestinian commandos 1969.

East Europe. To stop the large-scale exodus of citizens, E German authorities built (Aug. 1961) a **fortified wall across Berlin.** Soviet sway in the Balkans was weakened by Albania's support of China (USSR broke ties in Dec. 1961) and Romania's assertion (1964) of industrial and foreign policy autonomy. Liberalization (spring 1968) in Czechoslovakia was crushed with massive force by troops of 5 Warsaw Pact countries. W German treaties (1970) with the USSR and Poland facilitated the transfer of German technology and confirmed postwar boundaries.

Arts and styles. The boundary between fine and popular arts was blurred to some extent by Pop Art (Warhol) and rock musicals (*Hair*, 1968). Informality and exaggeration prevailed in fashion (beards, miniskirts). A nonpolitical "counterculture" developed, rejecting traditional bourgeois life goals and personal habits, and use of marijuana and hallucinogens spread (**Woodstock** festival, Aug. 1969). Indian influence was felt in religion (Ram Dass) and fashion, and The **Beatles,** who brought unprecedented sophistication to rock music, became for many a symbol of the decade.

Science. Achievements in space (**humans on the moon,** July 1969) and electronics (lasers, integrated circuits) encouraged a faith in scientific solutions to problems in agriculture ("green revolution"), medicine (heart transplants, 1967), and other areas. Harmful technology, it was believed, could be controlled (1963 nuclear weapon test ban treaty, 1968 nonproliferation treaty).

Mao Zedong

Buzz Aldrin on Moon, 1969

Disillusionment: 1970-79

U.S.: Caution and neoconservatism. A relatively sluggish economy, energy shortages, and environmental problems contributed to a **"limits of growth"** philosophy. Suspicion of science and technology killed or delayed major projects (supersonic transport dropped, 1971; Seabrook nuclear power plant protests, 1977-78) and was fed by the Three Mile Island nuclear reactor accident (Mar. 1979).

There were signs of growing mistrust of big government and less support for new social policies. School busing and racial quotas were opposed (Bakke decision, June 1978); the proposed Equal Rights Amendment for women languished; civil rights legislation aimed at protecting homosexuals was opposed (Dade County referendum, June 1977).

Completion of Communist forces' takeover of **South Vietnam** (evacuation of U.S. civilians, Apr. 1975), revelations of Central Intelligence Agency misdeeds (Rockefeller Commission report, June 1975), and **Watergate** scandals (Nixon resigned in Aug. 1974) reduced faith in U.S. moral and material capacity to influence world affairs. Revelations of Soviet crimes (Solzhenitsyn's *Gulag Archipelago*, 1974) and Soviet intervention in Africa helped foster a revival of anti-Communist sentiment.

Economy sluggish. The 1960s boom faltered in the 1970s; a severe recession in the U.S. and Europe (1974-75) followed a huge oil price hike (Dec. 1973). Monetary instability (U.S. cut ties to gold in Aug. 1971), the decline of the dollar, and protectionist moves by industrial countries (1977-78) threatened trade. Business investment and spending for research declined. Severe inflation plagued many countries (25% in Britain, 1975; 18% in U.S., 1979).

China picks up pieces. After the 1976 deaths of Mao Zedong and Zhou Enlai, struggle for the leadership succession was won by pragmatists. A nationwide purge of orthodox Maoists was carried out, and the **Gang of Four,** led by Mao's widow, Chiang Ching, arrested. The new leaders freed more than 100,000 political prisoners and reduced public adulation of Mao. Political and trade ties were expanded with Japan, Europe, and the U.S. in the late 1970s, as relations worsened with the USSR, Cuba, and Vietnam (4-week invasion by China, 1979). Ideological guidelines in industry, science, education, and the armed forces, which the ruling faction said had caused chaos and decline, were reversed (bonuses to workers, Dec. 1977; exams for college entrance, Oct. 1977). Severe restrictions on cultural expression were eased.

Europe. European unity moves (EEC-EFTA trade accord, 1972) faltered as economic problems appeared (Britain floated pound, 1972; France floated franc, 1974). Germany and Switzerland curbed guest workers from southern Europe. Greece and Turkey quarreled over Cyprus and Aegean oil rights.

All non-Communist Europe was under democratic rule after free elections were held (June 1976) in **Spain** 7 months after the death of Franco. The conservative, colonialist regime in **Portugal** was overthrown in Apr. 1974. In **Greece** the 7-year-old military dictatorship yielded power in 1974. Northern Europe, though ruled mostly by Socialists (**Swedish** Socialists unseated in 1976 after 44 years in power), turned more conservative. The **British** Labour government imposed (1975) wage curbs and suspended nationalization schemes. Terrorism in **Germany** (1972 Munich Olympics killings) led to laws curbing some civil liberties. French "new philosophers" rejected leftist ideologies, and the shaky Socialist-Communist coalition lost a 1978 election bid.

Religion and politics. The improvement in **Muslim** countries' political fortunes by the 1950s (with the exception of Central Asia under Soviet and Chinese rule) and the growth of Arab oil wealth were followed by a resurgence of traditional religious fervor. Libyan dictator Muammar al-Qaddafi mixed Islamic laws with socialism and called for Muslim return to Spain and Sicily. The illegal Muslim Brotherhood in **Egypt** was accused of violence, while extreme groups bombed (1977) theaters to protest Western and secular values.

In **Turkey**, the National Salvation Party was the first Islamic group to share (1974) power since secularization in the 1920s. In **Iran, Ayatollah Ruhollah Khomeini,** led a revolution that deposed the secular shah (Jan. 1979) and created an Islamic republic there. Religiously motivated Muslims took part in an insurrection in Saudi Arabia that briefly seized (1979) the Grand Mosque in Mecca. Muslim puritan opposition to **Pakistan** Pres. Zulfikar Ali-Bhutto helped lead to his overthrow in July 1977. Muslim solidarity, however, could not prevent Pakistan's eastern province (**Bangladesh**) from declaring (Dec. 1971) independence after a bloody civil war.

Muslim and Hindu resentment of coerced sterilization in **India** helped defeat the Gandhi government, which was replaced (Mar. 1977) by a coalition including religious Hindu parties. Muslims in the **S Philippines**, aided by Libya, rebelled against central rule from 1973.

The Buddhist Soka Gakkai movement launched (1964) the Komeito party in **Japan**, which became a major opposition party in 1972 and 1976 elections.

Evangelical Protestant groups grew in the U.S. A revival of interest in Orthodox Christianity occurred among **Russian** intellectuals (Solzhenitsyn). The secularist **Israeli** Labor party, after decades of rule, was ousted in 1977 by conservatives led by Menachem Begin; religious militants founded settlements on the disputed West Bank, part of biblically promised Israel. U.S. Reform Judaism revived many previously discarded traditional practices.

Old-fashioned religious wars raged intermittently in **Northern Ireland** (Catholic vs. Protestant, 1969-   ) and **Lebanon** (Christian vs. Muslim, 1975-   ), while religious militancy complicated the Israel-Arab dispute (1973 Israel-Arab war). Despite a 1979 **peace treaty between Egypt and Israel,** increased militancy on the West Bank impeded further progress.

Latin America. Repressive conservative regimes strengthened their hold on most of the continent, with a violent coup against the elected (Sept. 1973) Allende government in **Chile,** a 1976 military coup in **Argentina,** and coups against reformist regimes in **Bolivia** (1971, 1979) and **Peru** (1976). In Central America increasing liberal and leftist militancy led to the ouster (1979) of the Somoza regime of **Nicaragua** and to civil conflict in **El Salvador.**

Indochina. Communist victories in Vietnam, Cambodia, and Laos by May 1975 led to new turmoil. The **Pol Pot regime** ordered millions of city-dwellers to resettle in rural areas, in a program of forced labor, combined with terrorism, that cost more than 1 million lives (1975-79) and caused hundreds of thousands of ethnic Chinese and others to flee Vietnam ("boat people," 1979). The Vietnamese invasion of Cambodia swelled the refugee population and contributed to widespread starvation in that devastated country.

Russian expansion. Soviet influence, checked in some countries (troops ousted by Egypt, 1972), was projected farther afield, often with the use of Cuban troops (Angola, 1975-89; Ethiopia, 1977-88) and aided by a growing navy, a merchant fleet, and international banking ability. **Détente** with the West—1972 Berlin pact, 1972 strategic arms pact (**SALT**)—gave way to a more antagonistic relationship in the late 1970s, exacerbated by the Soviet invasion (1979) of **Afghanistan.**

Africa. The last remaining European colonies were granted independence (**Spanish Sahara**, 1976; **Djibouti**, 1977) and, after 10 years of civil war and many negotiation sessions, a black government took over (1979) in Zimbabwe (Rhodesia); white domination remained in **South Africa**. Great power involvement in local wars (Russia in **Angola, Ethiopia**; France in **Chad, Zaire, Mauritania**) and the use of tens of thousands of Cuban troops were denounced by some African leaders. Ethnic or tribal clashes made Africa a locus of sustained warfare during the late 1970s.

Arts. Traditional modes of painting, architecture, and music received increased popular and critical attention in the 1970s. These more conservative styles coexisted with modernist works in an atmosphere of increased variety and tolerance.

Revitalization of Capitalism, Demand for Democracy: 1980-89

USSR, Eastern Europe. A troublesome 1980-85 for the USSR was followed by 5 years of astonishing change: the surrender of the Communist monopoly, the remaking of the Soviet state, and the beginning of the disintegration of the Soviet empire. After the deaths of Leonid **Brezhnev** (1982) and 2 successors (Andropov in 1984 and Chernenko in 1985), the harsh treatment of dissent and restriction of emigration, and the Soviet invasion (Dec. 1979) of Afghanistan, Gen. Sec. Mikhail **Gorbachev** (in office 1985-1991) promoted *glasnost* and *perestroika*—economic, political, and social reform. Supported by the Communist Party (July 1988), he signed (Dec. 1987) the INF disarmament treaty, and he pledged (1988) to cut the military budget. Military withdrawal from Afghanistan was completed in Feb. 1989, the process of democratization went ahead unhindered in Poland and Hungary, and the Soviet people chose (Mar. 1989) part of the new Congress of People's Deputies from competing candidates. By decade's end the **Cold War** appeared to be fading away.

In **Poland, Solidarity**, the labor union founded (1980) by Lech **Walesa**, was outlawed in 1982 and then legalized in 1988, after years of unrest. Poland's first free election since the Communist takeover brought Solidarity victory (June 1989); Tadeusz Mazowiecki, a Walesa adviser, became (Aug. 1989) prime minister in a government with the Communists. In the fall of 1989 the failure of Marxist economies in **Hungary, East Germany, Czechoslovakia, Bulgaria,** and **Romania** brought the collapse of the Communist monopoly and a demand for democracy. In a historic step, the **Berlin Wall** was opened in Nov. 1989.

U.S. "The Reagan Years" (1981-88) brought the **longest economic boom** yet in U.S. history via budget and tax cuts, deregulation, "junk bond" financing, leveraged buyouts, and mergers and takeovers. However, there was a stock market crash (Oct. 1987), and federal budget deficits and the trade deficit increased. Foreign policy showed a **strong anti-Communist stance**, via increased defense spending, aid to anti-Communists in Central America, invasion of Cuba-threatened Grenada, and championing of the MX missile system and "Star Wars" missile defense program. Four Reagan-Gorbachev summits (1985-88) climaxed in the INF treaty (1987), as the Cold War began to wind down. The Iran-contra affair (North's TV testimony, July 1987) was a major political scandal. Homelessness and drug abuse (especially "crack" cocaine) were growing social problems. In 1988, Vice Pres. George Bush was elected to succeed Ronald Reagan as president.

Middle East. The Middle East remained militarily unstable, with sharp divisions along economic, political, racial, and religious lines. In **Iran**, the Islamic revolution of 1979 created a strong anti-U.S. stance (hostage crisis, Nov. 1979-Jan. 1981). In Sept. 1980, **Iraq** repudiated its border agreement with Iran and began major hostilities that led to an 8-year war in which millions were killed.

Libya's support for international terrorism induced the U.S. to close (May 1981) its diplomatic mission there and embargo (Mar. 1982) Libyan oil. The U.S. accused Libyan leader Muammar al-Qaddafi of aiding (Dec. 1985) terrorists in Rome and of Vienna airport attacks, and retaliated by bombing Libya (Apr. 1986).

Israel affirmed (July 1980) all Jerusalem as its capital, destroyed (1981) an Iraqi atomic reactor, and invaded (1982) Lebanon, forcing the PLO to agree to withdraw. A **Palestinian uprising**, including women and children hurling rocks and bottles at troops, began (Dec. 1987) in Israeli-occupied Gaza and spread to the West Bank; troops responded with force, killing 300 by the end of 1988, with 6,000 more in detention camps.

Israeli withdrawal from **Lebanon** began in Feb. 1985 and ended in June 1985, as Lebanon continued torn by military and political conflict. Artillery duels (Mar.-Apr. 1989) between Christian East Beirut and Muslim West Beirut left 200 dead and 700 wounded. At decade's end, violence still dominated.

Latin America. In **Nicaragua**, the leftist Sandinista National Liberation Front, in power after the 1979 civil war, faced problems as a result of Nicaragua's military aid to leftist guerrillas in El Salvador and U.S. backing of antigovernment contras. The U.S. CIA admitted (1984) having directed the mining of Nicaraguan ports, and the U.S. sent humanitarian (1985) and military (1986) aid. Profits from secret arms sales to Iran were found (1987) diverted to contras. Cease-fire talks between the Sandinista government and contras came in 1988, and elections were held in Nicaragua in Feb. 1990.

In **El Salvador**, a military coup (Oct. 1979) failed to halt extreme right-wing violence and left-wing terrorism. Archbishop Oscar Romero was assassinated in Mar. 1980; from Jan. to June some 4,000 civilians reportedly were killed in the civil unrest. In 1984, newly elected Pres. José Napoleon Duarte worked to stem human rights abuses, but violence continued.

In **Chile**, Gen. Augusto Pinochet yielded the presidency after a democratic election (Dec. 1989), but remained as head of the army. He had ruled the country since 1973, imposing harsh measures against leftists and dissidents; at the same time he introduced economic programs that restored prosperity to Chile.

Africa. 1980-85 marked a rapid decline in the economies of virtually all African countries, a result of accelerating desertification, the world economic recession, heavy indebtedness to overseas creditors, rapid population growth, and political instability. Some 60 million Africans faced prolonged hunger in 1981; much of Africa had one of the worst droughts ever in 1983, and by year's end **150 million faced near-famine**. "Live Aid," a marathon rock concert, was presented in July 1985, and the U.S. and Western nations sent aid in Sept. 1985. Economic hardship fueled political unrest and coups. Wars in Ethiopia and Sudan and military strife in several other nations continued. AIDS took a heavy toll.

South Africa. Anti-apartheid sentiment gathered force in South Africa as demonstrations and violent police response grew. White voters approved (Nov. 1983) the first constitution to give Coloureds and Asians a voice, while still excluding blacks (70% of the population). The U.S. imposed economic sanctions in Aug. 1985, and 11 Western nations followed in September. P. W. **Botha**, 1980s president, was succeeded by F. W. **de Klerk**, in Sept. 1989, who promised "evolutionary" change via negotiation with the black population.

China. During the 1980s the Communist government and paramount leader **Deng Xiaoping** pursued **far-reaching changes**, expanding commercial and technical ties to the industrialized world and increasing the role of market forces in stimulating urban development. Apr. 1989 brought new demands for political reforms; student demonstrators camped out in Tiananmen Square, Beijing, in a massive peaceful protest. Some 100,000 students and workers marched, and at least 20 other cities saw protests. In response, martial law was imposed; army troops crushed the demonstration in and around Tiananmen Square on June 3-4, with death toll estimates at 500-7,000, up to 10,000 dissidents arrested, 31 people tried and executed. The conciliatory Communist Party chief was ousted; the Politburo adopted (July) reforms against official corruption.

Japan. Japan's relations with other nations, especially the U.S., were dominated by **trade imbalances favoring Japan**. In 1985 the U.S. trade deficit with Japan was $49.7 billion, one-third of the total U.S. trade deficit. After Japan was found (Apr. 1986) to sell semiconductors and computer memory chips below cost, the U.S. was assured a "fair share" of the market, but charged (Mar. 1987) Japan with failing to live up to the agreement.

European Community. With the addition of Greece, Portugal, and Spain, the EC became a common market of more than **300 million people**, the West's largest trading entity. Margaret **Thatcher** became the first British prime minister in the 20th century to win a 3rd consecutive term (1987). France elected (1981) its first socialist president, François **Mitterrand**, who was reelected in 1988. Italy elected (1983) its first socialist premier, Bettino **Craxi**.

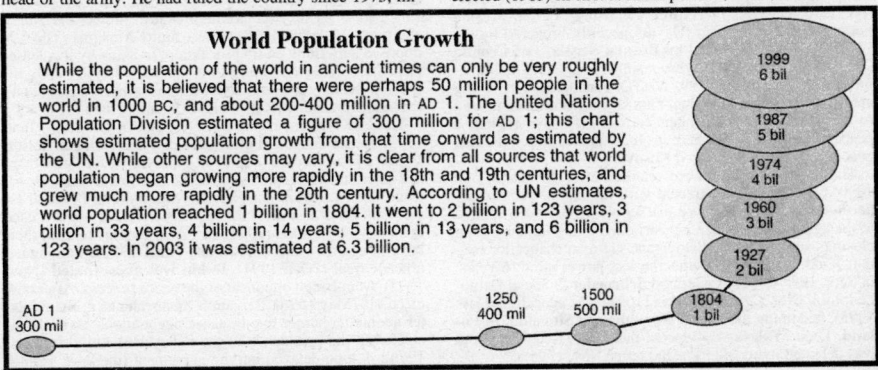

World Population Growth

While the population of the world in ancient times can only be very roughly estimated, it is believed that there were perhaps 50 million people in the world in 1000 BC, and about 200-400 million in AD 1. The United Nations Population Division estimated a figure of 300 million for AD 1; this chart shows estimated population growth from that time onward as estimated by the UN. While other sources may vary, it is clear from all sources that world population began growing more rapidly in the 18th and 19th centuries, and grew much more rapidly in the 20th century. According to UN estimates, world population reached 1 billion in 1804. It went to 2 billion in 123 years, 3 billion in 33 years, 4 billion in 14 years, 5 billion in 13 years, and 6 billion in 123 years. In 2003 it was estimated at 6.3 billion.

1999 6 bil
1987 5 bil
1974 4 bil
1960 3 bil
1927 2 bil

AD 1 300 mil   1250 400 mil   1500 500 mil   1804 1 bil

International terrorism. With the 1979 overthrow of the shah of Iran, terrorism became a prominent tactic. It increased through the 1980s, but with fewer high-profile attacks after 1985. In 1979-81, Iranian militants held 52 U.S. hostages in Iran for 444 days; in 1983 a TNT-laden suicide terrorist blew up U.S. Marine headquarters in Beirut, killing 241 Americans, and a truck bomb blew up a French para-troop barracks, killing 58. The *Achille Lauro* cruise ship was hijacked in 1986, and an American passenger killed; the U.S. subsequently intercepted the Egyptian plane flying the terrorists to safety. Incidents rose to 700 in 1985, and to 1,000 in 1988. **Assassinated leaders** included Egypt's Pres. Anwar al-**Sadat** (1981), India's Prime Min. Indira **Gandhi** (1984), and Lebanese Premier Rashid **Karami** (1987).

Post–Cold War World: 1990-99

Soviet Empire breakup. The world community witnessed the extraordinary spectacle of a superpower's disintegration when the **Soviet Union** broke apart into 15 independent states. The 1980s had already seen internal reforms and a decline of Communist power both within the Soviet Union and in Eastern Europe. The Soviet breakup began in earnest with the declarations of independence adopted by the Baltic republics of **Lithuania, Latvia,** and **Estonia** during an abortive coup against reformist leader Mikhail **Gorbachev** (Aug. 1991). The other republics soon took the same step. In Dec. 1991, **Russia, Ukraine,** and **Belarus** declared the Soviet Union dead; Gorbachev resigned, and the Soviet Parliament went out of existence. The Warsaw Pact and the Council for Mutual Economic Assistance (Comecon) were disbanded. Most of the former republics joined in a loose confederation called the **Commonwealth of Independent States. Russia** remained the predominant country after the breakup, but its people soon suffered severe economic hardship as the nation, under Pres. Boris **Yeltsin,** moved to revamp the economy and to adopt a free market system. In Oct. 1993, **anti-Yeltsin forces** occupied the Parliament building and were ousted by the army; about 140 people died in the fighting.

The Muslim republic of **Chechnya** declared independence from the rest of Russia, but this was met with an invasion by Russian troops (Dec. 1994). After almost 21 months of vicious fighting, a cease-fire took hold in 1996, and the Russians withdrew. In 1999 Russia forcibly suppressed Muslim insurgents in Dagestan and entered neighboring Chechnya, again fighting to gain control over separatist rebels there. Yeltsin resigned office Dec. 31, 1999, to be replaced by Vladimir **Putin** (elected in his own right, Mar. 2000).

Europe. Yugoslavia broke apart, and hostilities ensued among the republics along ethnic and religious lines. **Croatia, Slovenia,** and **Macedonia** declared independence (1991), followed by **Bosnia-Herzegovina** (1992). **Serbia** and **Montenegro** remained as the republic of Yugoslavia. Bitter fighting followed, especially in Bosnia, where Serbs reportedly engaged in **"ethnic cleansing"** of the Muslim population; a peace plan (Dayton accord), brokered by the United States, was signed by **Bosnia, Serbia,** and **Croatia** (Dec. 1995), with **NATO** responsible for policing its implementation. In spring 1999, NATO conducted a bombing campaign aimed at stopping Yugoslavia from its campaign to drive out ethnic Albanians from the Kosovo region; a peace accord was reached in June under which NATO peacekeeping troops entered Kosovo.

The two **Germanys** were reunited after 45 years (Oct. 1990). The union was greeted with jubilation, but stresses became apparent when free market principles were applied to the aging East German industries, resulting in many plant closings and rising unemployment. German chancellor Helmut **Kohl,** a Christian Democrat, lost power after 16 years, in Sept. 1998 elections; Gerhard **Schroeder,** a Social Democrat, took over. Czechoslovakia broke apart peacefully (Jan. 1993), becoming the **Czech Republic** and **Slovakia.** In **Poland,** Lech **Walesa** was elected president (Dec. 1991) but was defeated in his bid for a 2nd term (Nov. 1995).

NATO approved the **Partnership for Peace** Program (Jan. 1994) coordinating the defense of **Eastern** and **Central European** countries; Russia joined the program later that year. NATO signed a pact with **Russia** (1997) providing for NATO expansion into the former Soviet-bloc countries; a similar treaty was set up with **Ukraine.** The **Czech Republic, Hungary,** and **Poland** became members in Jan. 1999; in that year **NATO** celebrated its 50th anniversary. Efforts toward European unity continued with adoption of a single market (Jan. 1993) and conversion of the European Community to the **European Union** as the Maastricht Treaty took effect (Nov. 1993). Agreement was reached for 11 EU members to participate in Economic and Monetary Union, adopting a common currency (**euro**) for some purposes in Jan. 1999.

An intraparty revolt forced Margaret **Thatcher** out as prime minister of **Great Britain,** to be succeeded by John **Major** (Nov. 1990); 7 years later, Major suffered an overwhelming defeat at the hands of the new Labour Party leader, Tony **Blair** (May 1997). The divorce of Prince **Charles** and Princess **Diana,** followed by the death of Diana in a car accident (Aug. 1997), made headlines around the world. Talks on **peace** in **Northern Ireland** that included participation of Sinn Fein, political arm of the IRA, led to a ground-breaking peace plan, approved in an all-Ireland vote (May 1998). In Dec. 1999, Northern Ireland was granted home rule under a power-sharing cabinet. In **Scotland** voters overwhelmingly approved establishment of a regional legislature (1997), and in **Wales** voters narrowly approved establishment of a local assembly (1997). In a historic innovation, the Church of England **ordained 32 women** as priests (Mar. 1994).

Middle East. In Aug. 1990, **Iraq's Saddam Hussein** ordered his troops to invade **Kuwait.** The UN approved military action in response (Nov. 1990), and U.S. Pres. George **Bush** put together an international military force. Allied planes bombed Iraq (Jan. 1991) and launched a land attack, crushing the invasion (Feb. 1991). After Iraq accepted a cease-fire (Apr. 1991), U.S. troops withdrew, but "no-fly" zones were set up over northern Iraq to protect the Kurds and over southern Iraq to protect Shiite Muslims. The **UN** imposed **sanctions** on Iraq for failure to abide by the cease-fire. Iraq's reported failure to cooperate with UN arms inspectors seeking to eliminate "weapons of mass destruction" led to repeated air strikes by the U.S. and Britain.

The last Western hostages were freed in **Lebanon,** June 1992. **Israel** and the **Palestine Liberation Organization** signed a peace accord (Sept. 1993) providing for Palestinian self-government in the West Bank and Gaza Strip. Prime Min. Yitzhak **Rabin** and Foreign Min. Shimon **Peres** of Israel and Yasir **Arafat** of the PLO received the Nobel Peace Prize for their efforts (1994). Six Arab nations relaxed their boycott against Israel (1994), and Israel and **Jordan** signed a peace treaty (Oct. 1994). **Rabin was assassinated** (Nov. 1995) by an Israeli opponent of the peace process. After new elections (May 1996), Benjamin Netanyahu as prime minister adopted a harder line in peace negotiations. **Arafat** was elected to the presidency of the Palestinian Authority (Jan. 1996). A long-delayed interim agreement (the Wye Memorandum) on Israel military withdrawal from part of the West Bank was reached Oct. 1998. A Labour government under Ehud **Barak** took power after May 1999 elections, but further progress in peace negotiations proved elusive.

King **Hussein** of Jordan died (Feb. 1999), to be succeeded by his son Abdullah.

Asia and the Pacific. Hong Kong was returned to **China** (July 1997) after being a British colony for 156 years. China, which emerged in the decade as a major developing economic power, had agreed to follow a policy of "one country, two systems" in Hong Kong. The territory of **Macao** reverted to Chinese sovereignty (Dec. 1999) after over 400 years of Portuguese rule; it retained its capitalist economic system. **Jiang Zemin**, general secretary of the Chinese Communist Party, assumed the additional post of president of China (Mar. 1993) and emerged as the key leader after the death of paramount leader **Deng Xiaoping** (Feb. 1997). China released from prison—and exiled—some well-known dissidents but continued to be criticized for detentions and other alleged widespread **human rights abuses**. In Nov. 1999 the U.S. and China signed a landmark pact normalizing trade relations.

After years of prosperity, **Thailand, Indonesia,** and **South Korea** in 1997 began to suffer economic reverses that had a worldwide ripple effect. These countries received billion-dollar IMF bailout packages. In **Indonesia,** protests over mismanagement led to the resignation of Pres. **Suharto** (May 1998) after 32 years of nearly autocratic rule. Abdurraham Wahid was elected (Oct. 1999) in the country's first fully democratic elections. In a referendum (Aug. 1999), **East Timor** voted overwhelmingly for independence from Indonesia; pro-Indonesian militias then rampaged through the territory, but a multinational peacekeeping force was allowed in (Sept. 1999) to help restore order. In **South Korea,** former dissident **Kim Dae Jung** was elected president (Dec. 1997). Two previous presidents, Roh Tae Woo and Chun Doo Hwan, were convicted of crimes committed in office but were given amnesty by the new president.

In **Japan** members of a religious cult, released the nerve gas sarin on 5 Tokyo subway cars, killing 12 people and injuring more than 5,500 (Mar. 1995). Tamil rebels continued their armed conflict in **Sri Lanka.** In **Afghanistan** the **Taliban,** an extreme Islamic fundamentalist group, gained control of Kabul (Sept. 1996) and, eventually, most of the country. In **North Korea,** longtime dictator **Kim Il Sung** died (July 1994), to be succeeded by his son, **Kim Jong Il.** In the same year the country signed an agreement with the U.S. setting a timetable for North Korea to eliminate its nuclear program. The country also suffered a severe drought, and widespread starvation was feared.

India was beset by riots following destruction of a mosque by Hindu militants (Dec. 1992); Indian army troops repeatedly clashed with pro-independence demonstrators in the disputed Muslim region of **Kashmir,** exacerbating relations with **Pakistan.** Uneasy relations between India and Pakistan reached a new level when both nations conducted nuclear tests in 1998. Conflict in Pakistan between government and the military led to a bloodless coup (Oct. 1999).

Africa. South Africa was transformed as the white-dominated government abandoned **apartheid** and the country made the transition to a nonracial democratic government. Pres. F. W. **de Klerk** released Nelson **Mandela** from prison (Feb. 1990), after he had been held by the government for 27 years, and lifted a ban on the African National Congress. The white government repealed its apartheid laws (1990, 1991). **Mandela** was elected **president** (Apr. 1994), and a new constitution became law (Dec. 1996). Thabo **Mbeki**, the ANC's candidate to succeed Mandela, was overwhelmingly elected president in June 1999. In **Nigeria,** Gen. Olusegun **Obasanjo** was elected president (Feb. 1999), to become the country's first civilian leader in 15 years.

The decades-long rule of **Mobutu** Sese Seko in **Zaire** came to an end (May 1997) at the hands of rebel forces led by Laurent **Kabila;** an ailing Mobutu fled the country and soon after died. Kabila changed the country's name back to **Democratic Republic of the Congo;** conditions remained unstable. After the presidents of **Burundi** and **Rwanda** were

killed in an airplane crash (Apr. 1994), violence erupted in Rwanda between Hutu and Tutsi factions; tens of thousands were slain. The conflict spread to refugee camps in neighboring Zaire and Burundi. Factional fighting also erupted in **Somalia** after Pres. Muhammad Siad Barre was ousted (Jan. 1991). The UN sent a U.S.-led **peacekeeping force,** but it was unsuccessful in restoring order. Some soldiers of the peacekeeping force were killed, including 23 Pakistanis (June 1993) and 18 U.S. Rangers (Oct. 1993). The UN ended its mission (Mar. 1995) with no durable government in place. **Liberia** endured factional fighting that lasted almost 5 years and claimed over 150,000 lives; a cease-fire was concluded in Aug. 1995. The World Health Organization reported (1995) that Africa accounted for 70% of **AIDS** cases worldwide.

A 16-year civil war appeared to end in **Angola** (May 1991) when the government signed a peace accord with the rebel UNITA faction. But despite the inauguration of a national unity government (Apr. 1997), insurgents continued to fight and gain territory. **Namibia** officially became independent in Mar. 1990. Claimed by South Africa since 1919 and placed under UN authority in 1971, it had long been a focus of colonial rivalries. In **Algeria,** the army cancelled a 2nd round of parliamentary elections (Jan. 1992) after the Islamic party won a first round. Islamic fundamentalists then began a terrorist campaign that, along with killings by pro-government squads, eventually claimed thousands of lives. A peace plan was worked out with the militants in 1999.

North America. The North American Free Trade Agreement (NAFTA), liberalizing trade between the United States, Canada, and Mexico, went into effect Jan. 1, 1994. In Canada, the Progressive Conservative Party suffered a crushing defeat in general elections (Oct. 1993), and liberal Jean **Chrétien** became prime minister. The map of Canada was altered in Apr. 1999 to create a new territory, **Nunavut,** out of an area that had been part of Northwest Territories.

In the **United States,** in the 1992 presidential election, Democrat Bill **Clinton** defeated Pres. George Bush, but in 1994 congressional elections Republicans gained control of Congress. Congress passed legislation under which federal protection for welfare recipients was ended and funds turned over to the states for their programs. Clinton reached agreement with Congress on measures to eliminate the federal budget deficit. Clinton won reelection in 1996; the new administration was plagued by scandals but remained popular amid continued economic prosperity. In Dec. 1998 **Clinton** was **impeached** by the U.S. House on charges related to the Monica Lewinsky scandal; he was **acquitted** by the Senate in Feb. 1999.

The U.S. Army and Navy were torn by sexual scandals involving abuse of women personnel. The **United States** suffered embarrassment with the discovery of espionage by CIA agents (Aldrich Ames, Harold Nicholson).

In **Mexico,** Ernesto **Zedillo** of the ruling PRI party was elected president (July 1994) after the party's first candidate was assassinated. The country soon faced a crisis affecting the value of the peso, but recovered with the help of a bailout package from the U.S. A peasant revolt spearheaded by the **Zapatista National Liberation Army** erupted in the state of Chiapas (Jan. 1994) and was suppressed.

Central America. In **Haiti,** Jean-Bertrand **Aristide** was elected president (Dec. 1990) but was ousted in a military coup after 9 months in office. The UN approved a U.S.-led invasion to restore the elected leader; shortly before troops arrived, a delegation headed by former U.S. Pres. Jimmy Carter arranged (Sept. 1994) for the junta to step aside for Aristide. In **Nicaragua,** Violetta Chamorro defeated Daniel **Ortega** in the presidential election (Feb. 1990), thus ousting the Sandinistas. In **Panama,** U.S. troops invaded and overthrew the government of Manuel **Noriega** (Dec. 1989), who was wanted on drug charges; Noriega was captured Jan. 1990. On Dec. 31, 1999, Panama assumed full control of the **Panama Canal,** in accord with a treaty with the U.S. In **El Salvador** (1992) and **Guatemala** (1996) the governments signed agreements with rebel factions aimed at ending long-running civil conflicts.

South America. Alberto **Fujimori** was elected president of **Peru** in June 1990 and, despite his suppression of the constitution (1992), was reelected in 1995. Peru succeeded in capturing (Sept. 1992) the leader of the **Shining Path** guerrilla movement. Leftist guerrillas took hostages at an ambassador's residence in Lima (Dec. 1996); one hostage was killed during a government assault rescuing the rest (Apr. 1997). Peronist Pres. Carlos Saúl **Menem** served as **Argentina**'s president for much of the decade (elected 1989, reelected 1995), imposing stringent economic measures; he was succeeded in 1999 by Fernando de la **Rúa**.

Former Chilean Pres. Gen. Augusto **Pinochet** continued to head the army until Mar. 1998; he was arrested in London (Oct. 1998) on human rights charges but was judged medically unfit for trial and returned to Chile (Mar. 2000).

In **Brazil**, Fernando Henrique **Cardoso** was elected president (Oct. 1994) and reelected in 1998 amid a growing economic slump; the IMF announced a $42 billion aid package (Nov. 1998). The first UN Conference on Environment and Development, or **Earth Summit**, was held (June 1992) in **Rio de Janeiro**, with delegates from 178 nations.

Terrorism and Crime. Terrorism, often linked to Mideastern sources and with the U.S. as object, continued. A terrorist bomb exploded in a garage beneath New York City's **World Trade Center**, killing 6 people (Feb. 1993). Bombings of a U.S. military training center (Nov. 1995) and a barracks holding U.S. airmen (June 1996), both in **Saudi Arabia**, killed 7 and 19, respectively. Bombs exploded outside **U.S. embassies** in Kenya and Tanzania, Aug. 1998, killing over 220 people; the U.S. retaliated with missiles fired at alleged terrorist-linked sites in Afghanistan and Sudan. The Alfred P. Murrah Federal Building in **Oklahoma City**, OK, was destroyed by a bomb that killed 168 people (Apr. 1995).

Science. The powerful **Hubble Space Telescope** was launched in Apr. 1990; flaws in its mirrors and solar panels e repaired by space-walking astronauts (Dec. 1993). U.S. space shuttle *Atlantis* docked with the orbiting Russian space station *Mir* (June 1995) in first of several joint missions in a spirit of post-Cold-War cooperation. In Nov. 1998 first component for a new **International Space Station** was launched into space from Kazakhstan. But space prospects were subsequently dimmed by disaster when **U.S. space shuttle *Columbia* exploded** on reentry (Feb. 2003), killing the 7 astronauts aboard.

Scottish scientist Ian Wilmut announced (Feb. 1997) the **cloning** of a sheep, nicknamed Dolly—the first mammal successfully cloned from a cell from an adult animal.

Opening a New Century: 2000-2002

Middle East. Violence between Israelis and Palestinians escalated, with **suicide bombings** by Palestinians and retaliation by Israeli armed forces, the peace process languished. Likud leader Ariel **Sharon** was **elected** prime minister of Israel (Feb. 2001). Syrian Pres. Hafez al-**Assad died** (June 2000); succeeded by his son.

Europe. In Oct. 2000, Yugoslav strongman Slobodan **Milosevic yielded** power to Vojislav Kostunica, who had declared himself president in the face of anti-Milosevic protests after a disputed election. Milosevic surrendered to Serbian authorities; in Feb. 2002 went on trial for **war crimes** allegedly committed during 1990s ethnic conflicts in the Balkans. The first-ever **Concorde jet crash**, near Paris, killed 113 people (July 2000). The Russian nuclear sub *Kursk* sank in the Barents Sea (Aug. 2000) killing 118 crew members. By early 2002 the **euro** was the common currency in 12 European Union nations.

Asia. South Korean Pres. Kim Dae **Jung** and **North Korean** ruler Kim **Jong Il** held a **summit** meeting and agreed to seek peace and reunification (June 2000), but tensions rose after North Korea admitted conducting a covert **nuclear weapons** development program (Oct. 2002). Nepal's King **Birendra** and other Nepal royals were shot to death inside the palace, apparently by Crown Prince Dipendra, who then killed himself (June 2001). **Chinese** Pres. Jiang Zemin and **Russian** Pres. Vladimir Putin signed a **friendship treaty** (July 2001).

Africa. The 13th International **AIDS Conference**, held in Durban, South Africa (July 2000), focused on ways of controlling surging AIDS rates in developing countries. **Ethiopia and Eritrea** signed a **peace treaty** (Dec. 2000). Laurent **Kabila**, president of the Democratic Republic of the **Congo**, was **shot to death** by a bodyguard (Jan. 2001).

North and South America. Vicente **Fox** of the center-right National Action Party (PAN) was **elected president of Mexico** (July 2000), in a historic defeat for the long-supreme Institutional Revolutionary Party (PRI). Peruvian Pres. Alberto **Fujimori stepped down** in the midst of his 3rd term (Nov. 2000), amid scandal, and did not run for reelection. In Jan. 2001, George W. **Bush** was inaugurated as U.S. president, after one of the tightest and most controversial elections in U.S. history. **Venezuelan** Pres. Hugo **Chavez** regained power after 48-hr. coup (Dec. 2002).

Terrorism and Crime. In Oct. 2000, 17 American sailors were killed aboard the **USS *Cole*** in Aden, **Yemen**, when a small boat exploded alongside it in a terrorist attack. On **Sept. 11, 2001**, hijackers crashed 2 jetliners into the twin towers of the **World Trade Center** in New York City and another into the **Pentagon** outside Washington, DC; a 4th crashed in a field in **Pennsylvania**. The attacks, which destroyed both towers and damaged the Pentagon, killed an estimated 3,000 people, including all 265 aboard the planes. Pres. Bush launched a U.S.-led military campaign to root out terrorist infrastructure in **Afghanistan;** a transitional govt. was installed; instability persisted. Bush also promoted action to depose the regime of **Saddam Hussein** in **Iraq,** though direct links to terrorism were not clear. (A U.S.-British war was launched in Mar. 2003, **Hussein** ousted.) A terrorist **bomb** on the Indonesian island of Bali (Oct. 2002) killed 202. **Chechen** guerrillas seized a **Moscow movie theater** (Oct. 2002); more than 100 hostages were killed.

International. Negotiators from 178 countries agreed to adopt the **Kyoto Protocol**, calling for a reduction of greenhouse gases in developed nations (July 2001).

WORLD EXPLORATION AND GEOGRAPHY
Early Explorers of the Western Hemisphere
Reviewed by Susan Skomal, PhD, American Anthropological Assn., and Paul B. Frederic, PhD, prof. of geography, Univ. of Maine.

In the light of recent discoveries, theories about how the first people arrived in the western hemisphere are being reconsidered. It was once thought that humans came across a "land bridge" from Siberia to Alaska, spreading through the Americas 12,000 to 14,000 years ago. Whereas the preponderance of genetic, skeletal, and linguistic evidence indicate that current Native Americans are descended from peoples from N Asia, skeletal remains of Kennewick Man found in Washington state (dated to 9,200-9,600 BP, or before present) and "Luzia" from Brazil (11,500 BP) attest to an earlier arrival of a people with markedly different physical characteristics and uncertain origin.

Archaeologists have confirmed evidence of habitation at least 12,900 BP at sites located on the shores of ancient lakes 2 miles high in the Atacama Desert of Monte Verde Chile. (There is also growing evidence that humans had settled the lowland jungles of Chile at least 2,000 years earlier.) Because a glacier covered most of N America from 20,000 to 13,000 years ago, those who settled in S America may have traveled in vessels along the west coast, sailed directly from Australia or Asia, or spread from N to S America before the ice came. There is even recent evidence from a burial site at Santana do Riacho 1 in Brazil (8,000-11,000 BP) to suggest that some of the early immigrants who crossed to the New World via the land bridge from Siberia may have originated in Africa.

Norsemen (Norwegian Vikings sailing out of Iceland and Greenland), led by Leif Ericson, are credited with having been the first Europeans to reach America, with at least 5 voyages occurring about AD 1000 to areas they called Hellu-

land, Markland, and Vinland—possibly what are known today as Labrador, Nova Scotia or Newfoundland, and New England. L'Anse aux Meadows, on the N tip of Newfoundland, is the only documented settlement.

Sustained contact between the hemispheres began with the first voyage of Christopher Columbus (born Cristoforo Colombo, c 1451, near Genoa, Italy). Columbus made trips to the New World while sailing for the Spanish.

He left Palos, Spain, Aug. 3, 1492, with 88 men and landed at San Salvador (Watling Islands, Bahamas), Oct. 12, 1492. His fleet included 3 vessels, the Niña, Pinta, and Santa María. Stops also were made on Cuba and Hispaniola. A 2nd expedition left Cadiz, Spain, Sept. 25, 1493, with 17 ships and 1,500 men, reaching the Lesser Antilles Nov. 3. His 3rd voyage brought him from Sanlucar, Spain (May 30, 1498, with 6 ships), to the N coast of S America. A 4th voyage reached the mainland of Central America, after leaving Cadiz, Spain, May 9, 1502. Columbus died in 1506 convinced he had reached Asia by sailing west.

In N America, John Cabot and Sebastian Cabot, Italian explorers sailing for the English, reached Newfoundland and possibly Nova Scotia in 1497. John's 2nd voyage (1498), seeking a new trade route to Asia, resulted in the loss of his entire fleet. During this period exploration was dominated by Spain and Portugal. In 1497 and 1499 Amerigo Vespucci (for whom the Americas are named), an Italian explorer sailing for Spain, passed along the N and E coasts of S America. He was the first to argue that the newly discovered lands were a continent other than Asia.

Year	Explorer	Nationality (sponsor, if different)	Area reached or explored
c1000	Leif Ericson	Norse	Newfoundland
1492-1502	Christopher Columbus	Italian (Spanish)	West Indies, S. and C. America
1497	John and Sebastian Cabot	Italian (English)	Atlantic Canada
1497-98	Vasco de Gama	Portuguese	Cape of Good Hope (Africa), India
1497-99	Amerigo Vespucci	Italian (Spanish)	E and N Coast of S. America
1499	Alonso de Ojeda	Spanish	N South American coast, Venezuela
1500, Feb.	Vicente Yañez Pinzon	Spanish	S. American coast, Amazon R.
1500, Apr.	Pedro Álvarez Cabral	Portuguese	Brazil
1500-02	Gaspar Corte-Real	Portuguese	Labrador
1501	Rodrigo de Bastidas	Spanish	Central America
1513	Vasco Núñez de Balboa	Spanish	Panama, Pacific Ocean
1513	Juan Ponce de León	Spanish	Florida, Yucatán Peninsula
1515	Juan de Solis	Spanish	Río de la Plata
1519	Alonso de Pineda	Spanish	Mouth of Mississippi R.
1519	Hernando Cortes	Spanish	Mexico
1519-20	Ferdinand Magellan	Portuguese (Spanish)	Straits of Magellan, Tierra del Fuego
1524	Giovanni da Verrazano	Italian (French)	Atlantic coast, incl. New York harbor
1528	Cabeza de Vaca	Spanish	Texas coast and interior
1532	Francisco Pizarro	Spanish	Peru
1534	Jacques Cartier	French	Canada, Gulf of St. Lawrence
1536	Pedro de Mendoza	Spanish	Buenos Aires
1539	Francisco de Ulloa	Spanish	California coast
1539-41	Hernando de Soto	Spanish	Mississippi R., near Memphis
1539	Marcos de Niza	Italian (Spanish)	SW United States
1540	Francisco de Coronado	Spanish	SW United States
1540	Hernando Alarcon	Spanish	Colorado R.
1540	Garcia de Lopez Cardenas	Spanish	Colorado, Grand Canyon
1541	Francisco de Orellana	Spanish	Amazon R.
1542	Juan Rodriguez Cabrillo	Portuguese (Spanish)	W Mexico, San Diego harbor
1565	Pedro Menéndez de Aviles	Spanish	St. Augustine, FL
1576	Sir Martin Frobisher	English	Frobisher Bay, Canada
1577-80	Sir Francis Drake	English	California coast
1582	Antonio de Espejo	Spanish	Southwest U.S. (New Mexico)
1584	Amadas & Barlow (for Raleigh)	English	Virginia
1585-87	Sir Walter Raleigh's men	English	Roanoke Isl., NC
1595	Sir Walter Raleigh	English	Orinoco R.
1603-09	Samuel de Champlain	French	Canadian interior, Lake Champlain
1607	Capt. John Smith	English	Atlantic coast
1609-10	Henry Hudson	English (Dutch)	Hudson R., Hudson Bay
1634	Jean Nicolet	French	Lake Michigan, Wisconsin
1673	Jacques Marquette, Louis Jolliet	French	Mississippi R., S to Arkansas
1682	Robert Cavelier, sieur de La Salle	French	Mississippi R., S to Gulf of Mexico
1727-29	Vitus Bering	Danish (Russian)	Bering Strait and Alaska
1789	Sir Alexander Mackenzie	Canadian	NW Canada
1804-06	Meriwether Lewis and William Clark	American	Missouri R., Rocky Mts., Columbia R.

Arctic Exploration

Early Explorers

1587 — John Davis (Eng.). Davis Strait to Sanderson's Hope, 72°12′N.

1596 — Willem Barents and Jacob van Heemskerck (Holland). Discovered Bear Isl., touched NW tip of Spitsbergen, 79°49′ N, rounded Novaya Zemlya, wintered at Ice Haven.

1607 — Henry Hudson (Eng.). North along Greenland's E coast to Cape Hold-with-Hope, 73°30′, then N of Spitsbergen to 80°23′. Explored Hudson's Touches (Jan Mayen).

1616 — William Baffin and Robert Bylot (Eng.). Baffin Bay to Smith Sound.

1728 — Vitus Bering (Russ.). Sailed through strait (Bering) proving Asia and America are separate.

1733-40 — Great Northern Expedition (Russ.). Surveyed Siberian Arctic coast.

1741 — Vitus Bering (Russ.). Sighted Alaska, named Mount St. Elias. His lieutenant, Chirikof, explored coast.

1771 — Samuel Hearne (Hudson's Bay Co.). Overland from Prince of Wales Fort (Churchill) on Hudson Bay to mouth of Coppermine R.

1778 — James Cook (Brit.). Through Bering Strait to Icy Cape, AK, and North Cape, Siberia.

1789 — Alexander Mackenzie (North West Co., Brit.). Montreal to mouth of Mackenzie River.

1806 — William Scoresby (Brit.). N of Spitsbergen to 8°30′.

1820-23 — Ferdinand von Wrangel (Russ.). Surveyed Siberian Arctic coast. His exploration joined James Cook's at North Cape, confirming separation of the continents.

1878-79 — (Nils) Adolf Erik Nordenskjöld (Swed.). The 1st to navigate the Northeast Passage—an ocean route connecting Europe's North Sea, along the Arctic coast of Asia and through the Bering Sea, to the Pacific Ocean.

1881 — The U.S. steamer *Jeannette*, led by Lt. Cmdr. George W. DeLong, was trapped in ice and crushed, June 1881. DeLong and 11 others died; 12 survived.

1888 — Fridtjof Nansen (Nor.) crossed Greenland icecap.

1893-96 — Nansen in *Fram* drifted from New Siberian Isls. to Spitsbergen; tried polar dash in 1895, reached Franz Josef Land, 86°14′N.

1897 — Salomon A. Andrée (Sweden) and 2 others started in balloon from Spitsbergen, July 11, to drift across pole to U.S., and disappeared. Aug. 6, 1930, their bodies were found on White Isl., 82°57′N, 29°52′E.

1903-6 — Roald Amundsen (Nor.) 1st sailed the Northwest Passage—an ocean route linking the Atlantic Ocean to the Pacific via Canada's marine waterways.

North Pole Exploration

Robert E. Peary explored Greenland's coast, 1891-92; tried for North Pole, 1893. In 1900 he reached N limit of Greenland and 83°36′N; in 1902 he reached 84°17′N; in 1906 he went from Ellesmere Isl. to 87° 06′N. He sailed in the *Roosevelt*, July 1908, to winter off Cape Sheridan, Grant Land. The dash for the North Pole began Mar. 1 from Cape Columbia, Ellesmere Isl. Peary reportedly reached the pole, 90°N, Apr. 6, 1909; however, later research suggests that he may have fallen short of his goal by c. 30-60 mi. Peary had several support groups carrying supplies until the last group turned back at 87°47′ N. Peary, Matthew Henson, and 4 Eskimos proceeded with dog teams and sleds. They were said to have crossed the pole several times, then built an igloo there and remained 36 hours. Started south, Apr. 7 at 4 PM, for Cape Columbia.

1914 — Donald MacMillan (U.S.). Northwest, 200 mi, from Axel Heiberg Isl. to seek Peary's Crocker Land.

1915-17 — Vihjalmur Stefansson (Can.). Discovered Borden, Brock, Meighen, and Lougheed Isls.

1918-20 — Amundsen sailed the Northeast Passage.

1925 — Amundsen and Lincoln Ellsworth (U.S.) reached 87°44′N in attempt to fly to N Pole from Spitsbergen.

1926 — Richard E. Byrd and Floyd Bennett (U.S.) reputedly flew over North Pole, May 9. (Claim to have reached the pole is in dispute, however.)

1926 — Amundsen, Ellsworth, and Umberto Nobile (It.) flew from Spitsbergen over N Pole May 12, to Teller, AK, in dirigible *Norge*.

1928 — Nobile crossed N Pole in airship, May 24; crashed, May 25. Amundsen died attempting a rescue.

North Pole Exploration Records

On Aug. 3, 1958, submarine *Nautilus*, under Comdr. William R. Anderson, crossed the N Pole beneath the ice.

In Aug. 1960, the nuclear-powered U.S. submarine *Seadragon* (Comdr. George P. Steele 2nd) made the 1st E-W underwater transit through the Northwest Passage. Traveling submerged for the most part, it took 6 days to make the 850-mi trek from Baffin Bay to the Beaufort Sea.

On Aug. 16, 1977, the Soviet nuclear icebreaker *Arktika* became the 1st surface ship to reach the N Pole.

On Apr. 30, 1978, Naomi Uemura (Jap.) became the 1st person to reach the N Pole alone, traveling by dog sled in a 54-day, 600-mi trek over the frozen Arctic.

In Apr. 1982, Sir Ranulph Fiennes and Charles Burton, Brit. explorers, reached the N Pole and became the 1st to circle the earth from pole to pole. They had reached the S Pole 16 months earlier. The 52,000-mi trek took 3 years, involved 23 people, and cost an estimated $18 mil.

On May 2, 1986, 6 explorers reached the N Pole assisted only by dogs. They became the 1st to reach the pole without aerial logistics support since at least 1909. The explorers, Amer. Will Steger, Paul Schurke, Ann Bancroft, and Geoff Carroll, and Can. Brent Boddy and Richard Weber, completed the 500-mi journey in 56 days.

On June 15, 1995, Weber and Russ. Mikhail Malakhov became the 1st pair to make it to the pole and back without any mechanical assistance. The 940-mi trip, made entirely on skis, took 121 days.

On May 20, 2003, Pen Hadow (U.K.) became the 1st to reach the pole from Canada unaided. The 377-mile journey across the ice took 64 days.

Antarctic Exploration

Antarctica has been approached since 1773-75, when Capt. James Cook (Brit.) reached 71°10′S. Many sea and landmarks bear names of early explorers. Fabian von Bellingshausen (Russ.) discovered Peter I and Alexander I Isls., 1819-21. Nathaniel Palmer (U.S.) traveled throughout Palmer Peninsula, 60°W, 1820, without realizing that this was a continent. Capt. John Davis (U.S.) made the 1st known landing on the continent on Feb. 7, 1821. Later, in 1823, James Weddell (Brit.) found Weddell Sea, 74°15′S, the southernmost point that had been reached.

First to announce existence of the continent of Antarctica was Charles Wilkes (U.S.), who followed the coast for 1,500 mi, 1840. Adelie Coast, 140°E, was found by Dumont d'Urville (Fr.), 1840. Ross Ice Shelf was found by James Clark Ross (Brit.), 1841-42.

1895 — Leonard Kristensen (Nor.) landed a party on the coast of Victoria Land. They were the 1st ashore on the main continental mass. C. E. Borchgrevink, a member of that party, returned in 1899 with a Brit. expedition, 1st to winter on Antarctica.

1902-4 — Robert Falcon Scott (Brit.) explored Edward VII Peninsula to 82°17′S, 146°33′E from McMurdo Sound.

1908-9 — Ernest Shackleton (Brit.) 1st to use Manchurian ponies in Antarctic sledging. He reached 88°23′S, discovering a route on to the plateau by way of the Beardmore Glacier and pioneering the way to the pole.

1911 — Roald Amundsen (Nor.) with 4 men and dog teams reached the S Pole, Dec. 14.

1912 — Scott reached the pole from Ross Isl., Jan. 18, with 4 companions. None of Scott's party survived. Their bodies and expedition notes were found, Nov. 12.

1928 — 1st person to use an airplane over Antarctica was Sir George Hubert Wilkins (Austral.).

1929 — Richard E. Byrd (U.S.) established Little America on Bay of Whales. On 1,600-mi airplane flight begun Nov. 28, he crossed S Pole, Nov. 29, with 3 others.

1934-35 — Byrd led 2nd expedition to Little America, explored 450,000 sq mi, wintered alone at 80°08´S.

1934-37 — John Rymill led British Graham Land expedition; discovered Palmer Penin. is part of mainland.

1935 — Lincoln Ellsworth (U.S.) flew S along E Coast of Palmer Penin., then crossed continent to Little America, making 4 landings.

1939-41 — U.S. Navy plane flights discovered about 150,000 sq mi of new land.

1940 — Byrd charted most of coast between Ross Sea and Palmer Penin.

1946-47 — U.S. Navy undertook Operation Highjump, commanded by Byrd, included 13 ships and 4,000 men. Airplanes photomapped coastline and penetrated beyond pole.

1946-48 — Ronne Antarctic Research Expedition Comdr., Finn Ronne, USNR, determined the Antarctic to be only one continent with no strait between Weddell Sea and Ross Sea; explored 250,000 sq mi of land by flights to 79°S.

1955-57 — U.S. Navy's Operation Deep Freeze led by Adm. Byrd. Supporting U.S. scientific efforts for the International Geophysical Year (IGY), the operation established 5 coastal stations fronting the Indian, Pacific, and Atlantic oceans and also 3 interior stations; explored more than 1,000,000 sq mi in Wilkes Land.

1957-58 — During the IGY, July 1957 through Dec. 1958, scientists from 12 countries conducted Antarctic research at a network of some 60 stations on Antarctica.

Dr. Vivian E. Fuchs led a 12-person Trans-Antarctic Expedition on the 1st land crossing of Antarctica. Starting from the Weddell Sea, they reached Scott Station, Mar. 2, 1958, after traveling 2,158 mi in 98 days.

1958 — A group of 5 U.S. scientists led by Edward C. Thiel, seismologist, moving by tractor from Ellsworth Station on Weddell Sea, identified a huge mountain range,

5,000 ft above the ice sheet and 9,000 ft above sea level. The range, originally seen by a Navy plane, was named the Dufek Massif, for Rear Adm. George Dufek.

1959 — Argentina, Australia, Belgium, Chile, France, Japan, New Zealand, Norway, South Africa, USSR, U.K., and U.S. signed a treaty suspending territorial claims for 30 yrs. and reserving the continent, S of 60°S, for research.

1961-62 — Scientists discovered the Bentley Trench, running from Ross Ice Shelf into Marie Byrd Land, near the end of the Ellsworth Mts., toward the Weddell Sea.

1962 — Nuclear power plant online at McMurdo Sound.

1963 — On Feb. 22, a U.S. plane made the region's longest nonstop flight: from McMurdo Station S past the pole to Shackleton Mts., SE to the "Area of Inaccessibility," and back to McMurdo Station covering 3,600 mi in 10 hrs.

1964 — New Zealanders mapped the mountain area from from Cape Adare W some 400 mi to Pennell Glacier.

1985 — Igor A. Zotikov, a Russian researcher, discovered sediments in the Ross Ice Shelf that seem to support the continental drift theory. Ocean Drilling Project finds that the ice sheets of E Antarctica are 37 million yrs. old.

1989 — Victoria Murden and Shirley Metz became both the 1st women and the 1st Americans to reach the S Pole overland when they arrived with 9 others on Jan. 17, 1989.

1991 — 24 nations approved a protocol to the 1959 Antarctica Treaty, Oct. 4. New conservation provisions, including banning oil and other mineral exploration for 50 yrs.

1994 — On Dec. 25, after 50-day trek, Liv Arnesen (Nor.) became 1st woman to ski alone and unaided to the S Pole.

1995 — On Dec. 22, a Norwegian, Borge Ousland, reached the S Pole in the fastest time on skis: 44 days.

1996-97 — Ousland became 1st person to traverse Antarctica alone; reached S Pole Dec. 19, 1996; traveled 1,675 mi in 64 days, ending Jan. 18, 1997.

2000-2001 — On Feb. 11, Ann Bancroft and Liv Arnesen (Nor.) became 1st women to ski unaided across Antarctica. The 1,717-mile journey took 94 days.

Volcanoes

Sources: *Volcanoes of the World*, Geoscience Press; Global Volcanism Network, Smithsonian Institution

Roughly 540 volcanoes are known to have erupted during historical times. Nearly 75% of these historically active volcanoes lie along the so-called Ring of Fire, running along the W coast of the Americas from the southern tip of Chile to Alaska, down the E coast of Asia from Kamchatka to Indonesia, and continuing from New Guinea to New Zealand. The Ring of Fire marks the boundary between the mobile tectonic plates underlying the Pacific Ocean and those of the surrounding continents. Other active regions occur along rift zones, where plates pull apart, as in Iceland, or where molten material moves up from the mantle over local "hot spots," as in Hawaii. The vast majority of the earth's volcanism occurs at submarine rift zones. For more information on volcanoes, see the website at www.volcano.si.edu/gvp

Notable Volcanic Eruptions

Approximately 7,000 years ago, Mazama, a 9,900-ft volcano in southern Oregon, erupted violently, ejecting large amounts of ash and pumice and voluminous pyroclastic flows. The ash spread over the entire northwestern U.S. and as far away as Saskatchewan, Can. During the eruption, the top of the mountain collapsed, leaving a caldera 6 mi across and about a half mile deep, which filled with rainwater to form what is now called Crater Lake.

In AD 79, Vesuvio, or Vesuvius, a 4,190-ft volcano overlooking Naples Bay, became active after several centuries of apparent inactivity. On Aug. 24 of that year, a heated mud and ash flow swept down the mountain, engulfing the cities of Pompeii, Herculaneum, and Stabiae with debris more than 60 ft deep. About 10% of the population of the 3 towns were killed.

In 1883, an eruption similar to the Mazama eruption occurred on the island of Krakatau. At least 2,000 people died in pyroclastic flows on Aug. 26. The next day, the 2,640-ft peak of the volcano collapsed to 1,000 ft below sea level, sinking most of the island and killing over 3,000. A tsunami (tidal wave) generated by the collapse killed more than 31,000 people in Java and Sumatra, and eventually reached England. Ash from the eruption colored sunsets around the world for 2 years. A similar, even more powerful eruption had taken place 68 years earlier at Mt. Tambora on the Indonesian island of Sumbawa.

Date	Volcano	Deaths (est.)	Date	Volcano	Deaths (est.)
Aug. 24, AD 79	Mt. Vesuvius, Italy	16,000	May 8, 1902	Mt. Pelée, Martinique	28,000
1586	Kelut, Java, Indon.	10,000	Jan. 30, 1911	Mt. Taal, Phil.	1,400
Dec. 15, 1631	Mt. Vesuvius, Italy	4,000	May 19, 1919	Mt. Kelut, Java, Indon.	5,000
Aug. 12, 1772	Mt. Papandayan, Java, Indon.	3,000	Jan. 17-21, 1951	Mt. Lamington, New Guinea	3,000
June 8, 1783	Laki, Iceland	9,350	May 18, 1980	Mt. St. Helens, U.S.	57
May 21, 1792	Mt. Unzen, Japan	14,500	Mar. 28, 1982	El Chichon, Mex.	1,880
Apr. 10-12, 1815	Mt. Tambora, Sumbawa, Indon	92,000[1]	Nov. 13, 1985	Nevado del Ruiz, Colombia	23,000
Aug. 26-28, 1883	Krakatau, Indon.	36,000	Aug. 21, 1986	Lake Nyos, Cameroon	1,700
Apr. 24, 1902	Santa María, Guatemala	1,000[2]	June 15, 1991	Mt. Pinatubo, Luzon, Phil.	800

(1) Of these, 10,000 were directly related to the eruption; an additional 82,000 were the result of starvation and disease brought on by the event. (2) An additional 3,000 deaths due to a malaria outbreak are sometimes attributed to the eruption.

Notable Active Volcanoes

Active volcanoes display a wide range of activity. In this table, years are given for last display of eruptive activity, as of mid-2003; the list does not include submarine volcanoes. An eruption may involve explosive ejection of new or old fragmental material, escape of liquid lava, or both. Volcanoes are listed by height, which does not reflect eruptive magnitude.

Africa

Name (latest eruption)	Location	Height (ft)
Mt. Cameroon (2000)	Cameroon	13,435
Nyiragongo (2002)	Congo	11,384
Nyamuragira (2002)	Congo	10,033
Mt. Oku [Lake Nyos] (1986)	Cameroon	9,878
Ol Doinyo Lengai (2003)	Tanzania	9,482
Fogo (1995)	Cape Verde Isls.	9,281
Piton de la Fournaise (2002)	Réunion Isl., Indian O.	8,632
Karthala (1991)	Comoros.	7,746
Erta-Ale (2003)	Ethiopia	2,011

Antarctica

Name (latest eruption)	Location	Height (ft)
Erebus (2003)	Ross Isl	12,447
Deception Island (1970)	S. Shetland Isl.	1,890

Asia-Oceania

Name (latest eruption)	Location	Height (ft)
Kliuchevskoi (2003)	Kamchatka, Russia	15,863
Kerinci (2002)	Sumatra, Indon.	12,467
Fuji (1708)	Honshu, Japan	12,388
Tolbachik (1976)	Kamchatka, Russia	12,080
Semeru (2003)	Java, Indon.	12,060
Slamet (1999)	Java, Indon.	11,260
Raung (2002)	Java, Indon.	10,932
Shiveluch (2003)	Kamchatka, Russia	10,771
On-take (1980)	Honshu, Japan	10,049
Merapi (2002)	Java, Indon.	9,737
Bezymianny (2003)	Kamchatka, Russia	9,455
Peuet Sague (2000)	Sumatra, Indon.	9,190
Ruapehu (1997)	New Zealand	9,176
Heard (2001)	Indian Ocean	9,006
Baitoushan (1702)	China/Korea	9,003
Asama (1990)	Honshu, Japan	8,425
Mayon (2002)	Luzon, Phil.	8,077
Canlaon (2002)	Negros Isls., Phil.	7,989
Niigata Yake-yama (1989)	Honshu, Japan	7,874
Alaid (1996)	Kuril Isl., Russia	7,674
Ulawun (2002)	Papua New Guinea	7,657
Ngauruhoe (1977)	New Zealand	7,515
Chokai (1974)	Honshu, Japan	7,326
Galunggung (1984)	Java, Indon.	7,113
Azuma (1977)	Honshu, Japan	6,640
Sangeang Api (1988)	Lesser Sunda Isl., Indon.	6,394
Nasu (1963)	Honshu, Japan	6,283
Karkar (1979)	Papua New Guinea	6,033
Tiatia (1981)	Kuril Isl., Russia	5,968
Bandai (1888)	Honshu, Japan	5,968
Manam (2002)	Papua New Guinea	5,928
Kuju (1996)	Kyushu, Japan	5,876
Karangetang-Api Siau (2003)	Sangihe, Indon.	5,853
Soputan (2000)	Sulawesi, Indon.	5,853
Bagana (2000)	Papua New Guinea	5,741
Kelut (1990)	Java, Indon.	5,679
Adatara (1996)	Honshu, Japan	5,636
Gamalama (1994)	Halmahera, Indon.	5,627
Kirishima (1992)	Kyushu, Japan	5,577
Gamkonora (1987)	Halmahera, Indon.	5,364
Aso (1995)	Kyushu, Japan	5,223
Lokon-Empung (2002)	Sulawesi, Indon.	5,184
Bulusan (1995)	Luzon, Phil.	5,134
Karymsky (2003)	Kamchatka, Russia	5,039
Unzen (1996)	Kyushu, Japan	4,921
Akan (1998)	Hokkaido, Japan	4,918
Sarychev Peak (1989)	Kuril Isl., Russia	4,908
Pinatubo (1993)	Luzon, Phil.	4,875
Lopevi (2001)	Vanuatu	4,636
Akita-Yake-yama (1997)	Honshu, Japan	4,482
Ambrym (2003)	Vanuatu	4,377
Langila (2003)	Papua New Guinea	4,363
Awu (1992)	Sangihe Isl., Indon.	4,331
Dukono (2003)	Halmahera, Indonesia	3,888
Akademia Nauk (1996)	Kamchatka, Russia	3,871
Komaga-take (2000)	Hokkaido, Japan	3,740
Sakura-jima (2003)	Kyushu, Japan	3,665
Miyake-jima (2002)	Izu Isls., Japan	2,674
Krakatau (2001)	Indonesia	2,667
Suwanose-jima (2003)	Kyushu, Japan	2,621
Gaua (1982)	Vanuatu	2,615
Oshima (1990)	Izu Isls., Japan	2,507
Usu (2001)	Hokkaido, Japan	2,418
Rabaul (2003)	Papua New Guinea	2,257
Pagan (1993)	N. Mariana Isl.	1,870
Taal (1977)	Luzon, Phil.	1,312
Yasur (2003)	Tanna Island, Vanuatu	1,184
White Island (2001)	Bay of Plenty, New Zealand	1,053
McDonald Islands (2000)	Indian Ocn., Australia	755

Central America—Caribbean

Name (latest eruption)	Location	Height (ft)
Tacaná (1986)	Guatemala	13,320
Acatenango (1972)	Guatemala	13,044
Santa María (2003)	Guatemala	12,375
Fuego (2003)	Guatemala	12,346
Irazú (1994)	Costa Rica	11,260
Turrialba (1866)	Costa Rica	10,958
Póas (1996)	Costa Rica	8,884
Pacaya (2002)	Guatemala	8,373
San Miguel (2002)	El Salvador	6,998
Rincón de la Vieja (1999)	Costa Rica	6,286
San Cristobal (2002)	Nicaragua	5,725
Concepción (1999)	Nicaragua	5,577
Arenal (2003)	Costa Rica	5,436
Soufrière Guadeloupe (1977)	Guadeloupe	4,813
Pelée (1932)	Martinique	4,583
Momotombo (1905)	Nicaragua	4,255
Soufrière St. Vincent (1979)	St. Vincent	4,003
Soufrière Hills (2003)	Montserrat	3,002
Masaya (2001)	Nicaragua	2,083

South America

Name (latest eruption)	Location	Height (ft)
Llullaillaco (1877)	Argentina-Chile	22,109
Guallatiri (1960)	Chile	19,918
Tupungatito (1986)	Chile	19,685
Cotopaxi (1940)	Ecuador	19,393
El Misti (1870?)	Peru	19,101
Láscar (2002)	Chile	18,346
Nevado del Ruiz (1991)	Colombia	17,457
Sangay (2003)	Ecuador	17,159
Irruputuncu (1995)	Chile	16,939
Guagua Pichincha (2001)	Ecuador	15,695
Puracé (1977)	Colombia	15,256
Tungurahua (2003)	Ecuador	14,479
Galeras (2002)	Colombia	14,029
Llaima (1998)	Chile	10,253
Villarrica (2002)	Chile	9,340
Cerro Hudson (1991)	Chile	6,250
Fernandina (1995)	Galapagos Isls., Ecuad.	4,842

Mid-Pacific

Name (latest eruption)	Location	Height (ft)
Mauna Loa (1984)	Hawaii, HI	13,681
Kilauea (2003)	Hawaii, HI	4,009

Mid-Atlantic Ridge

Name (latest eruption)	Location	Height (ft)
Jan Mayen (1985)	N. Atlantic Ocn., Norway	7,470
Grímsvötn (1998)	Iceland	5,659
Hekla (2000)	Iceland	4,892
Krafla (1984)	Iceland	2,133

Europe

Name (latest eruption)	Location	Height (ft)
Etna (2003)	Italy	10,991
Vesuvius (1944)	Italy	4,203
Stromboli (2003)	Italy	3,038
Santorini (1950)	Greece	1,204

North America

Name (latest eruption)	Location	Height (ft)
Pico de Orizaba (1846)	Mexico	18,619
Popocatépetl (2003)	Mexico	17,802
Rainier (1894?)	Washington	14,409
Wrangell (1902)	Alaska	14,163
Shasta (1786)	California	14,163
Colima (2003)	Mexico	12,631
Lassen Peak (1917)	California	10,456
Redoubt (1990)	Alaska	10,197
Iliamna (1876)	Alaska	10,016
Shishaldin (1999)	Aleutian Isl., AK	9,373
St. Helens (1991)	Washington	8,363
Pavlof (1997)	Alaska	8,264
Veniaminof (2002)	Alaska	8,225
Katmai [Novarupta] (1912)	Alaska	6,716
Makushin (1995)	Aleutian Isl., AK	5,905
Great Sitkin (1974)	Aleutian Isl., AK	5,709
Cleveland (2001)	Aleutian Isl., AK	5,676
Gareloi (1989)	Aleutian Isl., AK	5,161
Korovin [Atka complex] (1998)	Indian Isl., AK	5,029
Akutan (1992)	Aleutian Isl., AK	4,275
Augustine (1986)	Alaska	4,108
Kiska (1990)	Aleutian Isl., AK	4,003
El Chichón (1982)	Mexico	3,773
Okmok (1997)	Aleutian Isl., AK	3,520
Seguam (1993)	Aleutian Isl., AK	3,458

IT'S A FACT: First known to westerners as Peak XV, the world's tallest peak was named in 1865 in honor of British Surveyor General Sir George Everest. In Nepal it is called Sagarmatha, "goddess of the sky." Tibetans call it Chomolungma, "goddess mother of the world."

Mountains
Height of Mount Everest

Mt. Everest, the world's highest mountain, was considered 29,002 ft when Edmund Hillary and Tenzing Norgay became the 1st climbers to scale it, in 1953. This triangulation figure had been accepted since 1850. In 1954 the Surveyor General of the Republic of India set the height at 29,028 ft, plus or minus 10 ft because of snow; this figure was also accepted by the National Geographic Society.

In 1999, a team of climbers sponsored by Boston's Museum of Science and the National Geographic Society measured the height at the summit using sophisticated satellite-based technology. This new measurement, of 29,035 ft, was accepted by the National Geographic Society and other authorities, including the U.S. National Imagery and Mapping Agency.

By May 29, 2003, 50 years after the 1st climbers had reached the summit, some 1,300 more had followed, and about 175 had died in the attempt.

United States, Canada, Mexico

Name	Place	Height (ft)	Name	Place	Height (ft)	Name	Place	Height (ft)
McKinley	AK	20,320	Alverstone	AK-Yukon	14,565	Shavano	CO	14,229
Logan	Yukon	19,551	Browne Tower	AK	14,530	Belford	CO	14,197
Pico de Orizaba	Mexico	18,555	Whitney	CA	14,494	Princeton	CO	14,197
St. Elias	AK-Yukon	18,008	Elbert	CO	14,433	Crestone Needle	CO	14,197
Popocatépetl	Mexico	17,930	Massive	CO	14,421	Yale	CO	14,196
Foraker	AK	17,400	Harvard	CO	14,420	Bross	CO	14,172
Iztaccihuatl	Mexico	17,343	Rainier	WA	14,410	Kit Carson	CO	14,165
Lucania	Yukon	17,147	University Peak	AK	14,410	Wrangell	AK	14,163
King	Yukon	16,971	Williamson	CA	14,375	Shasta	CA	14,162
Steele	Yukon	16,644	La Plata Peak	CO	14,361	El Diente Peak	CO	14,159
Bona	AK	16,550	Blanca Peak	CO	14,345	Point Success	WA	14,158
Blackburn	AK	16,390	Uncompahgre Peak	CO	14,309	Maroon Peak	CO	14,156
Kennedy	AK	16,286	Crestone Peak	CO	14,294	Tabeguache	CO	14,155
Sanford	AK	16,237	Lincoln	CO	14,286	Oxford	CO	14,153
Vancouver	AK-Yukon	15,979	Grays Peak	CO	14,270	Sill	CA	14,153
South Buttress	AK	15,885	Antero	CO	14,269	Sneffels	CO	14,150
Wood	Yukon	15,885	Torreys Peak	CO	14,267	Democrat	CO	14,148
Churchill	AK	15,638	Castle Peak	CO	14,265	Capitol Peak	CO	14,130
Fairweather	AK-BC	15,300	Quandary Peak	CO	14,265	Liberty Cap	WA	14,112
Zinantecatl (Toluca)	Mexico	15,016	Evans	CO	14,264	Pikes Peak	CO	14,110
Hubbard	AK-Yukon	15,015	Longs Peak	CO	14,255	Snowmass	CO	14,092
Bear	AK	14,831	McArthur	Yukon	14,253	Russell	CA	14,088
Walsh	Yukon	14,780	Wilson	CO	14,246	Eolus	CO	14,083
East Buttress	AK	14,730	White Mt. Peak	CA	14,246	Windom	CO	14,082
Matlalcueyetl	Mexico	14,636	North Palisade	CA	14,242	Columbia	CO	14,073
Hunter	AK	14,573	Cameron	CO	14,238	Augusta	AK	14,070

South America

Peak, country	Height (ft)	Peak, country	Height (ft)	Peak, country	Height (ft)
Aconcagua, Argentina	22,834	Coropuna, Peru	21,083	Solo, Argentina	20,492
Ojos del Salado, Arg.-Chile	22,572	Laudo, Argentina	20,997	Polleras, Argentina	20,456
Bonete, Argentina	22,546	Ancohuma, Bolivia	20,958	Pular, Chile	20,423
Tupungato, Argentina-Chile	22,310	Ausangate, Peru	20,945	Chani, Argentina	20,341
Pissis, Argentina	22,241	Toro, Argentina-Chile	20,932	Aucanquilcha, Chile	20,295
Mercedario, Argentina	22,211	Illampu, Bolivia	20,873	Juncal, Argentina-Chile	20,276
Huascaran, Peru	22,205	Tres Cruces, Argentina-Chile	20,853	Negro, Argentina	20,184
Llullaillaco, Argentina-Chile	22,109	Huandoy, Peru	20,852	Quela, Argentina	20,128
El Libertador, Argentina	22,047	Parinacota, Bolivia-Chile	20,768	Condoriri, Bolivia	20,095
Cachi, Argentina	22,047	Tortolas, Argentina-Chile	20,745	Palermo, Argentina	20,079
Incahuasi, Argentina-Chile	21,720	Ampato, Peru	20,702	Solimana, Peru	20,068
Yerupaja, Peru	21,709	El Condor, Argentina	20,669	San Juan, Argentina-Chile	20,049
Galan, Argentina	21,654	Salcantay, Peru	20,574	Sierra Nevada, Arg.-Chile	20,023
El Muerto, Argentina-Chile	21,457	Chimborazo, Ecuador	20,561	Antofalla, Argentina	20,013
Sajama, Bolivia	21,391	Huancarhuas, Peru	20,531	Marmolejo, Argentina-Chile	20,013
Nacimiento, Argentina	21,302	Famatina, Argentina	20,505	Chachani, Peru	19,931
Illimani, Bolivia	21,201	Pumasillo, Peru	20,492		

The highest point in the West Indies is in the Dominican Republic, Pico Duarte (10,417 ft).

Africa

Peak, country	Height (ft)	Peak, country	Height (ft)	Peak, country	Height (ft)
Kilimanjaro, Tanzania	19,340	Meru, Tanzania	14,979	Guna, Ethiopia	13,881
Kenya, Kenya	17,058	Karisimbi, Congo-Rwanda	14,787	Gughe, Ethiopia	13,780
Margherita Pk., Uganda-Congo	16,763	Elgon, Kenya-Uganda	14,178	Toubkal, Morocco	13,661
Ras Dashan, Ethiopia	15,158	Batu, Ethiopia	14,131	Cameroon, Cameroon	13,435

Australia, New Zealand, SE Asian Islands

Peak, country/island	Height (ft)	Peak, country/island	Height (ft)	Peak, country/island	Height (ft)
Jaya, New Guinea	16,500	Wilhelm, New Guinea	14,793	Cook, New Zealand	12,349
Trikora, New Guinea	15,585	Kinabalu, Malaysia	13,455	Semeru, Java, Indon.	12,060
Mandala, New Guinea	15,420	Kerinci, Sumatra, Indon.	12,467	Kosciusko, Australia	7,310

Europe

Peak, country	Height (ft)	Peak, country	Height (ft)	Peak, country	Height (ft)
Alps		Dent D'Herens, Switz.	13,686	Gletscherhorn, Switz.	13,068
Mont Blanc, Fr.-It.	15,771	Breithorn, It., Switz.	13,665	Schalihorn, Switz.	13,040
Monte Rosa (highest peak		Bishorn, Switz.	13,645	Scerscen, Switz.	13,028
of group), Switz.	15,203	Jungfrau, Switz.	13,642	Eiger, Switz.	13,025
Dom, Switz.	14,911	Ecrins, Fr.	13,461	Jagerhorn, Switz.	13,024
Liskamm, It., Switz.	14,852	Monch, Switz.	13,448	Rottalhorn, Switz.	13,022
Weisshorn, Switz.	14,780	Pollux, Switz.	13,422		
Taschhorn, Switz.	14,733	Schreckhorn, Switz.	13,379	**Pyrenees**	
Matterhorn, It., Switz.	14,690	Ober Gabelhorn, Switz.	13,330	Aneto, Sp.	11,168
Dent Blanche, Switz.	14,293	Gran Paradiso, It.	13,323	Posets, Sp.	11,073
Nadelhorn, Switz.	14,196	Bernina, It., Switz.	13,284	Perdido, Sp.	11,007
Grand Combin, Switz.	14,154	Fiescherhorn, Switz.	13,283	Vignemale, Fr.-Sp.	10,820
Lenzpitze, Switz.	14,088	Grunhorn, Switz.	13,266	Long, Sp.	10,479
Finsteraarhorn, Switz.	14,022	Lauteraarhorn, Switz.	13,261	Estats, Sp.	10,304
Castor, Switz.	13,865	Durrenhorn, Switz.	13,238	Montcalm, Sp.	10,105
Zinalrothorn, Switz.	13,849	Allalinhorn, Switz.	13,213		
Hohberghorn, Switz.	13,842	Weissmies, Switz.	13,199	**Caucasus (Europe-Asia)**	
Alphubel, Switz.	13,799	Lagginhorn, Switz.	13,156	Elbrus, Russia	18,510
Rimpfischhorn, Switz.	13,776	Zupo, Switz.	13,120	Shkhara, Georgia	17,064
Aletschorn, Switz.	13,763	Fletschhorn, Switz.	13,110	Dykh Tau, Russia	17,054
Strahlhorn, Switz.	13,747	Adlerhorn, Switz.	13,081	Kashtan Tau, Russia	16,877
				Janqi, Georgia	16,565
				Kazbek, Georgia	16,558

Asia (Mainland)

Peak	Place	Height (ft)	Peak	Place	Height (ft)	Peak	Place	Height (ft)
Everest	Nepal-Tibet	29,035	Tirich Mir	Pakistan	25,230	Gauri Sankar	Nepal-Tibet	23,440
K2 (Godwin Austen)	Kashmir	28,250	Makalu II	Nepal-Tibet	25,120	Badrinath	India	23,420
Kanchenjunga	India-Nepal	28,208	Minya Konka	China	24,900	Nunkun	Kashmir	23,410
Lhotse I (Everest)	Nepal-Tibet	27,923	Kula Gangri	Bhutan-Tibet	24,784	Lenin Peak	Tajikistan	23,405
Makalu I	Nepal-Tibet	27,824	Changtzu (Everest)	Nepal-Tibet	24,780	Pyramid	India-Nepal	23,400
Lhotse II (Everest)	Nepal-Tibet	27,560	Muz Tagh Ata	Xinjiang	24,757	Api	Nepal	23,399
Dhaulagiri	Nepal	26,810	Skyang Kangri	Kashmir	24,750	Pauhunri	India-Tibet	23,385
Manaslu I	Nepal	26,760	Ismail Semani			Trisul	India	23,360
Cho Oyu	Nepal-Tibet	26,750	Peak	Tajikistan	24,590	Kangto	India-Tibet	23,260
Nanga Parbat	Kashmir	26,660	Jongsang Peak	India-Nepal	24,472	Nyenchhe		
Annapurna I	Nepal	26,504	Jengish Chokusu	Xinjiang-Kyrgyzstan	24,406	Thanglha	Tibet	23,255
Gasherbrum	Kashmir	26,470	Sia Kangri	Kashmir	24,350	Trisuli	India	23,210
Broad	Kashmir	26,400	Haramosh Peak	Pakistan	24,270	Pumori	Nepal-Tibet	23,190
Gosainthan	Tibet	26,287	Istoro Nal	Pakistan	24,240	Dunagiri	India	23,184
Annapurna II	Nepal	26,041	Tent Peak	India-Nepal	24,165	Lombo Kangra	Tibet	23,165
Gyachung Kang	Nepal-Tibet	25,910	Chomo Lhari	Bhutan-Tibet	24,040	Saipal	Nepal	23,100
Disteghil Sar	Kashmir	25,868	Chamlang	Nepal	24,012	Macha Pucchare	Nepal	22,958
Himalchuli	Nepal	25,801	Kabru	India-Nepal	24,002	Numbar	Nepal	22,817
Nuptse (Everest)	Nepal-Tibet	25,726	Alung Gangri	Tibet	24,000	Kanjiroba	Nepal	22,580
Masherbrum	Kashmir	25,660	Baltoro Kangri	Kashmir	23,990	Ama Dablam	Nepal	22,350
Nanda Devi	India	25,645	Mussu Shan	Xinjiang	23,890	Cho Polu	Nepal	22,093
Rakaposhi	Kashmir	25,550	Mana	India	23,860	Lingtren	Nepal-Tibet	21,972
Kamet	India-Tibet	25,447	Baruntse	Nepal	23,688	Khumbutse	Nepal-Tibet	21,785
Namcha Barwa	Tibet	25,445	Nepal Peak	India-Nepal	23,500	Hlako Gangri	Tibet	21,266
Gurla Mandhata	Tibet	25,355	Amne Machin	China	23,490	Mt. Grosvenor	China	21,190
Ulugh Muz Tagh	Xinjiang-Tibet	25,340				Thagchhab Gangri	Tibet	20,970
Kungur	Xinjiang	25,325				Damavand	Iran	18,606
						Ararat	Turkey	16,804

Antarctica

Peak	Height (ft)	Peak	Height (ft)	Peak	Height (ft)
Vinson Massif	16,864	Miller	13,650	Falla	12,549
Tyree	16,290	Long Gables	13,620	Rucker	12,520
Shinn	15,750	Dickerson	13,517	Goldthwait	12,510
Gardner	15,375	Giovinetto	13,412	Morris	12,500
Epperly	15,100	Wade	13,400	Erebus	12,450
Kirkpatrick	14,855	Fisher	13,386	Campbell	12,434
Elizabeth	14,698	Fridtjof Nansen	13,350	Don Pedro Christophersen	12,355
Markham	14,290	Wexler	13,202	Lysaght	12,326
Bell	14,117	Lister	13,200	Huggins	12,247
Mackellar	14,098	Shear	13,100	Sabine	12,200
Anderson	13,957	Odishaw	13,008	Astor	12,175
Bentley	13,934	Donaldson	12,894	Mohl	12,172
Kaplan	13,878	Ray	12,808	Frankes	12,064
Andrew Jackson	13,750	Sellery	12,779	Jones	12,040
Sidley	13,720	Waterman	12,730	Gjelsvik	12,008
Ostenso	13,710	Anne	12,703	Coman	12,000
Minto	13,668	Press	12,566		

Some Notable U.S. Mountains

Name	Place	Height (ft)	Name	Place	Height (ft)	Name	Place	Height (ft)
Gannett Peak	WY	13,804	Adams	WA	12,277	Clingmans Dome	NC-TN	6,643
Grand Teton	WY	13,766	San Gorgonio	CA	11,502	Washington	NH	6,288
Kings	UT	13,528	Hood	OR	11,239	Rogers	VA	5,729
Cloud	WY	13,175	Lassen	CA	10,457	Marcy	NY	5,344
Wheeler	NM	13,161	Granite	CA	10,321	Katahdin	ME	5,268
Boundary	NV	13,140	Guadalupe	TX	8,749	Spruce Knob	WV	4,861
Granite	MT	12,799	Olympus	WA	7,965	Mansfield	VT	4,393
Borah	ID	12,662	Harney	SD	7,242	Black Mountain	KY	4,145
Humphreys	AZ	12,633	Mitchell	NC	6,684			

Important Islands and Their Areas

Reviewed by Laurel Duda, Marine Biological Laboratory/Woods Hole Oceanographic Inst. Library.

Figures are for total areas in square miles. Figure in parentheses shows rank among the world's 10 largest individual islands. Because some islands have not been surveyed accurately, some areas shown are estimates. Some "islands" listed are island groups. Only the largest islands in a group are listed individually. Only islands over 10 sq. miles in area are listed.

Antarctica

Adelaide	1,400
Alexander	16,700
Berkner	18,500
Roosevelt	2,900

Arctic Ocean

Akimiski, Nunavut	1,159
Amund Ringnes, Nun.	2,029
Axel Heiberg, Nun.	16,671
Baffin, Nun. (5)	195,928
Banks, Northwest Territories	27,038
Bathurst, Nun.	6,194
Bolshevik, Russia	4,368
Bolshoy Lyakhovsky, Russia	1,776
Borden, NWT., Nun.	1,079
Bylot, Nun.	4,273
Coats, Nun.	2,123
Cornwallis, Nun.	2,701
Devon, Nun.	21,331
Disko, Greenland	3,312
Ellef Ringnes, Nun.	4,361
Ellesmere, Nun. (10)	75,767
Faddayevskiy, Russia	1,930
Franz Josef Land, Russia	8,000
Iturup (Etorofu), Russia	2,596
King William, Nun.	5,062
Komsomolets, Russia	3,477
Mackenzie King, NWT	1,949
Mansel, Nun.	1,228
Melville, NWT., Nun.	16,274
Milne Land, Greenland	1,400
New Siberian Islands, Russia	14,500
Kotelnyy, Russia	4,504
Novaya Zemlya, Russia (2 isls.)	31,730
Oktyabrskoy, Russia	5,471
Prince Charles, NWT	3,676
Prince of Wales, Nun.	12,872
Prince Patrick, NWT.	6,119
Somerset, Nun.	9,570
Southampton, Nun.	15,913
Svalbard (tot. group)	23,957
Nordaustlandet	5,410
Spitsbergen	15,060
Traill, Greenland	1,300
Victoria, NWT., Nun. (9)	83,897
Wrangel, Russia	2,800

Atlantic Ocean

Anticosti, Canada	3,068
Ascension, UK	34
Azores, Portugal (tot. group)	868
Faial	67
San Miguel	291
Bahama Isls., Bahama (tot. group)	5,382
Andros, Bahamas	2,300
Bermuda Islands, UK	20
Bioko Isl., Equatorial Guinea	785
Block Islands, RI, US	21
Canary Islands, Spain (tot. group)	2,807
Fuerteventura	688
Gran Canaria	592
Tenerife	795
Cape Breton, Canada	3,981
Cape Verde Islands	1,557
Caviana, Para, Brazil	1,918
Channel Islands, UK (tot. group)	75
Guernsey	24
Jersey	45
Faroe Islands, Denmark	540
Falkland Islands, UK (tot. group)	4,700
East Falkland	2,550
West Falkland	1,750
Great Britain, UK (8)	84,200
Greenland, Denmark (1)	840,000
Gurupa, Para, Brazil	1,878
Hebrides, Scotland	2,744
Iceland	39,699
Ireland (tot. group)	32,589
Irish Republic	27,137
Northern Ireland (UK)	5,452
Isle of Man, UK.	227
Isle of Wight, England	147
Long Island, NY, US.	1,320

Atlantic Ocean

Madeira Islands, Portugal	306
Marajo, Brazil	15,444
Martha's Vineyard, MA, US	89
Mount Desert, ME, US.	104
Nantucket, MA, US	45
Newfoundland, Canada	42,031
Orkney Islands, Scotland	390
Prince Edward, Canada	2,185
St. Helena, UK.	47
Shetland Islands, Scotland	587
Skye, Scotland	670
South Georgia, UK	1,450
Tierra del Fuego, Chile, Arg.	18,800
Tristan da Cunha, UK	40

Baltic Sea

Aland Islands, Finland	590
Bornholm, Denmark	227
Gotland, Sweden	1,159

Caribbean Sea

Antigua	108
Aruba, Netherlands	75
Barbados	166
Cuba	42,804
Isle of Youth.	926
Cayman Islands	100
Curacao, Netherlands	171
Dominica	290
Guadeloupe, France	687
Hispaniola (Haiti and Dominican Rep).	29,389
Jamaica	4,244
Martinique, France.	436
Puerto Rico, US.	3,339
Tobago	116
Trinidad	1,864
Virgin Islands, UK	59
Virgin Islands, US	134

East Indies

Bali, Indonesia	2,171
Bangka, Indonesia.	4,375
Borneo, Indonesia-Malaysia-Brunei (3).	280,100
Bougainville, Papua New Guinea	3,880
Buru, Indonesia	3,670
Celebes, Indonesia	69,000
Flores, Indonesia	5,500
Halmahera, Indonesia	6,865
Java (Jawa), Indonesia	48,900
Madura, Indonesia.	2,113
Moluccas, Indonesia	32,307
New Britain, Papua New Guinea	14,093
New Guinea, Indon.-PNG (2)	306,000
New Ireland, PNG	3,707
Seram, Indonesia	6,621
Sumba, Indonesia	4,306
Sumbawa, Indonesia	5,965
Sumatra, Indonesia (6)	165,000
Timor, Indonesia	13,094
Yos Sudarsa, Indonesia	4,500

Indian Ocean

Andaman Isls., India	2,500
Kerguelen	2,247
Madagascar (4)	226,658
Mauritius	720
Pemba, Tanzania	380
Reunion, France	970
Seychelles	176
Sri Lanka	25,332
Zanzibar, Tanzania	640

Mediterranean Sea

Balearic Isls., Spain	1,927
Corfu, Greece	229
Corsica, France	3,369
Crete, Greece	3,189
Cyprus	3,572
Elba, Italy	86
Euboea, Greece	1,411
Malta	95
Rhodes, Greece	540
Sardinia, Italy.	9,301
Sicily, Italy	9,926

Pacific Ocean

Admiralty, AK, US	1,709
Aleutian Isls., AK, US (tot. group)	6,912
Adak	275
Amchitka	116
Attu	350
Kanaga	142
Kiska	106
Tanaga	195
Umnak	686
Unalaska	1,051
Unimak	1,571
Baranof, AK, US	1,636
Chichagof, AK, US	2,062
Chiloe, Chile	3,241
Christmas, Kiribati	94
Diomede, Big, Russia	11
Easter Isl., Chile	69
Fiji (tot. group)	7,056
Vanua Levu	2,242
Viti Levu	4,109
Galapagos Isls., Ecuador	3,043
Graham Isl., British Columbia	2,456
Guadalcanal, Solomon Isls.	2,180
Guam, US	210
Hainan, China	13,000
Hawaiian Isls., HI, US (tot. group)	6,428
Hawaii	4,028
Oahu	600
Hong Kong, China.	31
Hoste, Chile.	1,590
Japan (tot. group)	145,850
Hokkaido	30,144
Honshu (7).	87,805
Kyushu	14,114
Okinawa	459
Shikoku	7,049
Kangaroo, South Australia	1,680
Kodiak, AK, US	3,485
Kupreanof, AK, US	1,084
Marquesas Isls., France	492
Marshall Isls.	70
Melville, Northern Territory, Aus..	2,240
Micronesia	271
New Caledonia, France.	6,530
New Zealand (tot. group)	104,454
Chatham Isls.	372
North	44,204
South	58,384
Stewart	674
North Mariana Isls., US	179
Nunivak, AK, US	1,600
Palau	188
Philippines (tot. group)	115,860
Leyte	2,787
Luzon.	40,680
Mindanao.	36,775
Mindoro	3,690
Negros.	4,907
Palawan.	4,554
Panay	4,446
Samar	5,050
Prince of Wales, AK, US.	2,770
Revillagigedo, AK, US.	1,134
Riesco, Chile	1,973
St. Lawrence, AK, US	1,780
Sakhalin, Russia	29,500
Samoa Isls. (tot. group).	1,177
American Samoa, US	77
Tutuila, US.	55
Savaii, Samoa	659
Upolu, Samoa	432
Santa Catalina, CA, US.	75
Santa Ines, Chile.	1,407
Tahiti, France	402
Taiwan, China (tot. group).	13,969
Jinmen Dao (Quemoy)	56
Tasmania, Australia	26,178
Tonga Isls.	290
Vancouver Isl., Brit. Columbia.	12,079
Vanuatu.	4,707
Wellington, Chile	2,549

Persian Gulf

Bahrain	217

IT'S A FACT: Lake Huron's Manitoulin Island (1,068 square miles) is the largest freshwater-lake island in the world.

Areas and Average Depths of Oceans, Seas, and Gulfs[1]

Geographers and mapmakers recognize 4 major bodies of water: the Pacific, the Atlantic, the Indian, and the Arctic oceans. The Atlantic and Pacific oceans are considered divided at the equator into the N and S Atlantic and the N and S Pacific. The Arctic Ocean is the name for waters N of the continental landmasses in the region of the Arctic Circle.

	Area (sq mi)	Avg. depth (ft)		Area (sq mi)	Avg. depth (ft)
Pacific Ocean	64,186,300	12,925	Hudson Bay	281,900	305
Atlantic Ocean	33,420,000	11,730	East China Sea	256,600	620
Indian Ocean	28,350,500	12,598	Andaman Sea	218,100	3,667
Arctic Ocean	5,105,700	3,407	Black Sea	196,100	3,906
South China Sea	1,148,500	4,802	Red Sea	174,900	1,764
Caribbean Sea	971,400	8,448	North Sea	164,900	308
Mediterranean Sea	969,100	4,926	Baltic Sea	147,500	180
Bering Sea	873,000	4,893	Yellow Sea	113,500	121
Gulf of Mexico	582,100	5,297	Persian Gulf	88,800	328
Sea of Okhotsk	537,500	3,192	Gulf of California	59,100	2,375
Sea of Japan	391,100	5,468			

(1) The International Hydrographic Organization delimited a fifth world ocean in 2000. The Southern Ocean as defined extends from the coast of Antarctica north to 60° south latitude, covering portions of the Atlantic, Indian, and Pacific oceans, an area of 7,848,400 square miles.

Principal Ocean Depths

Source: National Imagery and Mapping Agency, U.S. Dept. of Defense

Name of area	Location (lat.)	(long.)	Depth (meters)	(fathoms)	(ft)
Pacific Ocean					
Marianas Trench	11°22′ N	142°36′ E	10,924	5,973	35,840
Tonga Trench	23°16′ S	174°44′ W	10,800	5,906	35,433
Philippine Trench	10°38′ N	126°36′ E	10,057	5,499	32,995
Kermadec Trench	31°53′ S	177°21′ W	10,047	5,494	32,963
Bonin Trench	24°30′ N	143°24′ E	9,994	5,464	32,788
Kuril Trench	44°15′ N	150°34′ E	9,750	5,331	31,988
Izu Trench	31°05′ N	142°10′ E	9,695	5,301	31,808
New Britain Trench	06°19′ S	153°45′ E	8,940	4,888	29,331
Yap Trench	08°33′ N	138°02′ E	8,527	4,663	27,976
Japan Trench	36°08′ N	142°43′ E	8,412	4,600	27,599
Peru-Chile Trench	23°18′ S	71°14′ W	8,064	4,409	26,457
Palau Trench	07°52′ N	134°56′ E	8,054	4,404	26,424
Aleutian Trench	50°51′ N	177°11′ E	7,679	4,199	25,194
New Hebrides Trench	20°36′ S	168°37′ E	7,570	4,139	24,836
North Ryukyu Trench	24°00′ N	126°48′ E	7,181	3,927	23,560
Mid. America Trench	14°02′ N	93°39′ W	6,662	3,643	21,857
Atlantic Ocean					
Puerto Rico Trench	19°55′ N	65°27′ W	8,605	4,705	28,232
S Sandwich Trench	55°42′ S	25°56′ W	8,325	4,552	27,313
Romanche Gap	0°13′ S	18°26′ W	7,728	4,226	25,354
Cayman Trench	19°12′ N	80°00′ W	7,535	4,120	24,721
Brazil Basin	09°10′ S	23°02′ W	6,119	3,346	20,076
Indian Ocean					
Java Trench	10°19′ S	109°58′ E	7,125	3,896	23,376
Ob' Trench	09°45′ S	67°18′ E	6,874	3,759	22,553
Diamantina Trench	35°50′ S	105°14′ E	6,602	3,610	21,660
Vema Trench	09°08′ S	67°15′ E	6,402	3,501	21,004
Agulhas Basin	45°20′ S	26°50′ E	6,195	3,387	20,325
Arctic Ocean					
Eurasia Basin	82°23′ N	19°31′ E	5,450	2,980	17,881
Mediterranean Sea					
Ionian Basin	36°32′ N	21°06′ E	5,150	2,816	16,896

Note: Greater depths have been reported in some areas but are not officially confirmed by research vessels.

Latitude and Longitude of World Cities

Source: National Imagery Mapping Agency, U.S. Dept. of Defense

City	Lat. ° ′	Long. ° ′	City	Lat. ° ′	Long. ° ′
Athens, Greece	37 59 N	23 44 E	Mexico City, Mexico	19 24 N	99 09 W
Bangkok, Thailand	13 45 N	100 31 E	Moscow, Russia	55 45 N	37 35 E
Beijing, China	39 56 N	116 24 E	New Delhi, India	28 36 N	77 12 E
Berlin, Germany	52 31 N	13 25 E	Panama City, Panama	08 58 N	79 32 W
Bogotá, Colombia	04 36 N	74 05 W	Paris, France	48 52 N	02 20 E
Bombay (Mumbai), India	18 58 N	72 50 E	Quito, Ecuador	00 13 S	78 30 W
Buenos Aires, Argentina	34 36 S	58 28 W	Rio de Janeiro, Brazil	22 43 S	43 13 W
Cairo, Egypt	30 03 N	31 15 E	Rome, Italy	41 53 N	12 30 E
Jakarta, Indonesia	06 10 S	106 48 E	Santiago, Chile	33 27 S	70 40 W
Jerusalem, Israel	31 46 N	35 14 E	Seoul, South Korea	37 34 N	127 00 E
Johannesburg, South Africa	26 12 S	28 05 E	Sydney, Australia	33 53 S	151 12 E
Kathmandu, Nepal	27 43 N	85 19 E	Tehran, Iran	35 40 N	51 26 E
Kiev, Ukraine	50 26 N	30 31 E	Tokyo, Japan	35 42 N	139 46 E
London, UK (Greenwich)	51 30 N	00 00	Warsaw, Poland	52 15 N	21 00 E
Manila, Philippines	14 35 N	121 00 E	Wellington, New Zealand	41 18 S	174 47 E

Latitude, Longitude, and Altitude of U.S. and Canadian Cities

Source: U.S. geographic positions, U.S. altitudes provided by Geological Survey, U.S. Dept. of the Interior. Canadian geographic positions and altitudes provided by Natural Resources Canada.

City	Lat. N °	'	''	Long. W °	'	''	Elev. (ft)
Abilene, TX	32	26	55	99	43	58	1,718
Akron, OH	41	4	53	81	31	9	1,050
Albany, NY	42	39	9	73	45	24	20
Albuquerque, NM	35	5	4	106	39	2	4,955
Alert, N.W.T.	82	30	0	62	22	0	100
Allentown, PA	40	36	30	75	29	26	350
Amarillo, TX	35	13	19	101	49	51	3,685
Anchorage, AK	61	13	5	149	54	1	101
Ann Arbor, MI	42	16	15	83	43	35	880
Asheville, NC	35	36	3	82	33	15	2,134
Ashland, KY	38	28	42	82	38	17	558
Atlanta, GA	33	44	56	84	23	17	1,050
Atlantic City, NJ	39	21	51	74	25	24	8
Augusta, GA	33	28	15	81	58	30	414
Augusta, ME	44	18	38	69	46	48	45
Austin, TX	30	16	1	97	44	34	501
Bakersfield, CA	35	22	24	119	1	4	408
Baltimore, MD	39	17	25	76	36	45	100
Bangor, ME	44	48	4	68	46	42	158
Baton Rouge, LA	30	27	2	91	9	16	53
Battle Creek, MI	42	19	16	85	10	47	820
Bay City, MI	43	35	40	83	53	20	595
Beaumont, TX	30	5	9	94	6	6	20
Belleville, Ont.	44	14	0	77	21	0	320
Bellingham, WA	48	45	35	122	29	13	100
Berkeley, CA	37	52	18	122	16	18	150
Billings, MT	45	47	0	108	30	0	3,124
Biloxi, MS	30	23	45	88	53	7	25
Binghamton, NY	42	5	55	75	55	6	865
Birmingham, AL	33	31	14	86	48	9	600
Bismarck, ND	46	48	30	100	47	0	1,700
Bloomington, IL	40	29	3	88	59	37	829
Boise, ID	43	36	49	116	12	9	2,730
Boston, MA	42	21	30	71	3	37	20
Bowling Green, KY	36	59	25	86	26	37	510
Brandon, Man.	49	54	35	99	57	03	1,343
Brantford, Ont.	43	08	0	80	16	0	815
Brattleboro, VT	42	51	3	72	33	30	240
Bridgeport, CT	41	10	1	73	12	19	10
Brockton, MA	42	5	0	71	1	8	112
Buffalo, NY	42	53	11	78	52	43	585
Burlington, Ont.	43	23	10	79	50	15	640
Burlington, VT	44	28	33	73	12	45	113
Butte, MT	46	0	14	112	32	2	5,549
Calgary, Alta.	51	03	0	114	05	0	3,557
Cambridge, MA	42	22	30	71	6	22	30
Canton, OH	40	47	56	81	22	43	1,100
Carson City, NV	39	9	50	119	45	59	4,730
Cedar Rapids, IA	42	0	30	91	38	38	730
Central Islip, NY	40	47	26	73	12	8	88
Champaign, IL	40	6	59	88	14	36	740
Charleston, SC	32	46	35	79	55	52	118
Charleston, WV	38	20	59	81	37	58	606
Charlotte, NC	35	13	37	80	50	36	850
Charlottetown, P.E.I.	46	14	25	63	08	05	160
Chattanooga, TN	35	2	44	85	18	35	685
Cheyenne, WY	41	8	24	104	49	11	6,067
Chicago, IL	41	51	0	87	39	0	596
Churchill, Man.	58	43	30	94	07	0	94
Cincinnati, OH	39	9	43	84	27	25	683
Cleveland, OH	41	29	58	81	41	44	690
Colorado Springs, CO	38	50	2	104	49	15	6,008
Columbia, MO	38	57	6	92	20	2	758
Columbia, SC	34	0	2	81	2	6	314
Columbus, GA	32	27	39	84	59	16	300
Columbus, OH	39	57	40	82	59	56	800
Concord, NH	43	12	29	71	32	17	288
Corpus Christi, TX	27	48	1	97	23	46	35
Dallas, TX	32	47	0	96	48	0	463
Dawson, Yukon	64	03	45	139	25	50	1,214
Dayton, OH	39	45	32	84	11	30	750
Daytona Beach, FL	29	12	38	81	1	23	10
Decatur, IL	39	50	25	88	57	17	670
Denver, CO	39	44	21	104	59	3	5,260
Des Moines, IA	41	36	2	93	36	32	803
Detroit, MI	42	19	53	83	2	45	585
Dodge City, KS	37	45	10	100	1	0	2,550
Dubuque, IA	42	30	2	90	39	52	620
Duluth, MN	46	47	0	92	6	23	610
Durham, NC	35	59	38	78	53	56	394
Eau Claire, WI	44	48	41	91	29	54	850
Edmonton, Alta.	53	33	0	113	28	0	2,200
Elizabeth, NJ	40	39	50	74	12	40	38
El Paso, TX	31	45	31	106	29	11	3,695
Enid, OK	36	23	44	97	52	41	1,246
Erie, PA	42	7	45	80	5	7	650
Eugene, OR	44	3	8	123	5	8	419
Eureka, CA	40	48	8	124	9	45	44
Evansville, IN	37	58	29	87	33	21	388
Fairbanks, AK	64	50	16	147	42	59	440
Fall River, MA	41	42	5	71	9	20	200
Fargo, ND	46	52	38	96	47	22	900
Flagstaff, AZ	35	11	53	111	39	2	6,900
Flint, MI	43	0	45	83	41	15	750
Ft. Smith, AR	35	23	9	94	23	54	446
Ft. Wayne, IN	41	7	50	85	7	44	781
Ft. Worth, TX	32	43	31	97	19	14	670
Fredericton, N.B.	45	56	43	66	40	0	67
Fresno, CA	36	44	52	119	46	17	296
Gadsden, AL	34	0	51	86	0	24	554
Gainesville, FL	29	39	5	82	19	30	183
Gallup, NM	35	31	41	108	44	31	6,508
Galveston, TX	29	18	4	94	47	51	10
Gary, IN	41	35	36	87	20	47	600
Grand Junction, CO	39	3	50	108	33	0	4,597
Grand Rapids, MI	42	57	48	85	40	5	610
Great Falls, MT	47	30	1	111	18	0	3,334
Green Bay, WI	44	31	9	88	1	11	594
Greensboro, NC	36	4	21	79	47	32	770
Greenville, SC	34	51	9	82	23	39	966
Guelph, Ont.	43	33	0	80	15	0	1,100
Gulfport, MS	30	22	2	89	5	34	25
Halifax, N.S.	44	52	0	63	43	0	477
Hamilton, OH	39	23	58	84	33	41	600
Hamilton, Ont.	43	14	0	79	57	0	780
Harrisburg, PA	40	16	25	76	53	5	320
Hartford, CT	41	45	49	72	41	8	40
Helena, MT	46	35	34	112	2	7	4,090
Hilo, HI	19	43	47	155	5	24	38
Honolulu, HI	21	18	25	157	51	30	18
Houston, TX	29	45	47	95	21	47	40
Huntsville, AL	34	43	49	86	35	10	641
Indianapolis, IN	39	46	6	86	9	29	717
Iowa City, IA	41	39	40	91	31	48	685
Jackson, MI	42	14	45	84	24	5	940
Jackson, MS	32	17	55	90	11	5	294
Jacksonville, FL	30	19	55	81	39	21	12
Jersey City, NJ	40	43	41	74	4	41	83
Johnstown, PA	40	19	36	78	55	20	1200
Joplin, MO	37	5	3	94	30	47	990
Juneau, AK	58	18	7	134	25	11	50
Kalamazoo, MI	42	17	30	85	35	14	755
Kansas City, KS	39	6	51	94	37	38	750
Kansas City, MO	39	5	59	94	34	42	740
Kenosha, WI	42	35	5	87	49	16	610
Key West, FL	24	33	19	81	46	58	8
Kingston, Ont.	44	18	0	76	28	0	305
Kitchener, Ont.	43	27	0	80	29	0	1,040
Knoxville, TN	35	57	38	83	55	15	889
Lafayette, IN	40	25	0	86	52	31	567
Lancaster, PA	40	2	16	76	18	21	368
Lansing, MI	42	43	57	84	33	20	830
Laredo, TX	27	30	22	99	30	26	414
Las Vegas, NV	36	10	30	115	8	11	2,000
Lawrence, MA	42	42	25	71	9	49	50
Lethbridge, Alta.	49	42	0	112	49	0	3,047
Lexington, KY	37	59	19	84	28	40	955
Lihue, HI	21	58	52	159	22	16	206
Lima, OH	40	44	33	84	6	19	875
Lincoln, NE	40	48	0	96	40	0	1,150
Little Rock, AR	34	44	47	92	17	22	350
London, Ont.	42	59	0	81	14	0	875

City	Lat. N °	'	"	Long. W °	'	"	Elev. (ft)
Los Angeles, CA	34	3	8	118	14	34	330
Louisville, KY	38	15	15	85	45	34	462
Lowell, MA	42	38	0	71	19	0	102
Lubbock, TX	33	34	40	101	51	17	3,195
Macon, GA	32	50	26	83	37	57	400
Madison, WI	43	4	23	89	24	4	863
Manchester, NH	42	59	44	71	27	19	175
Marshall, TX	32	32	41	94	22	2	410
Medicine Hat, Alta.	50	03	0	110	40	0	2,352
Memphis, TN	35	8	58	90	2	56	254
Meriden, CT	41	32	17	72	48	27	190
Miami, FL	25	46	26	80	11	38	11
Milwaukee, WI	43	2	20	87	54	23	634
Minneapolis, MN	44	58	48	93	15	49	815
Minot, ND	48	13	57	101	17	45	1,555
Mobile, AL	30	41	39	88	2	35	16
Moncton, N.B.	46	06	57	64	48	11	232
Montgomery, AL	32	22	0	86	18	0	250
Montpelier, VT	44	15	36	72	34	33	525
Montréal, Que.	45	31	0	73	39	0	221
Moose Jaw, Sask.	50	24	0	105	32	0	1,892
Muncie, IN	40	11	36	85	23	11	952
Nashville, TN	36	9	57	86	47	4	440
Natchez, MS	31	33	37	91	24	11	230
Newark, NJ	40	44	8	74	10	22	95
New Britain, CT	41	39	40	72	46	48	200
New Haven, CT	41	18	29	72	55	43	40
New Orleans, LA	29	57	16	90	4	30	11
New York, NY	40	42	51	74	0	23	55
Niagara Falls, Ont.	43	06	0	79	04	0	589
Nome, AK	64	30	4	165	24	23	25
Norfolk, VA	36	50	48	76	17	8	10
North Bay, Ont.	46	19	0	79	28	0	1,200
Oakland, CA	37	48	16	122	16	11	42
Ogden, UT	41	13	23	111	58	23	4,299
Oklahoma City, OK	35	28	3	97	30	58	1,195
Omaha, NE	41	15	31	95	56	15	1,040
Orlando, FL	28	32	17	81	22	46	106
Ottawa, Ont.	45	16	0	75	45	0	382
Paducah, KY	37	5	0	88	36	0	345
Pasadena, CA	34	8	52	118	8	37	865
Paterson, NJ	40	55	0	74	10	20	70
Pensacola, FL	30	25	16	87	13	1	32
Peoria, IL	40	41	37	89	35	20	470
Peterborough, Ont.	44	18	0	78	19	0	628
Philadelphia, PA.	39	57	8	75	9	51	40
Phoenix, AZ	33	26	54	112	4	24	1,090
Pierre, SD	44	22	6	100	21	2	1,484
Pittsburgh, PA	40	26	26	79	59	46	770
Pittsfield, MA	42	27	0	73	14	45	1,039
Pocatello, ID.	42	52	17	112	26	41	4,464
Pt. Arthur, TX	29	53	55	93	55	43	10
Portland, ME	43	39	41	70	15	21	25
Portland, OR	45	31	25	122	40	30	50
Portsmouth, NH	43	4	18	70	45	47	21
Portsmouth, VA	36	50	7	76	17	55	10
Prince Rupert, B.C.	54	19	0	130	19	0	116
Providence, RI	41	49	26	71	24	48	80
Provo, UT	40	14	2	111	39	28	4,549
Pueblo, CO	38	15	16	104	36	31	4,662
Québec City, Que.	46	49	0	71	13	0	244
Racine, WI	42	43	34	87	46	58	630
Raleigh, NC	35	46	19	78	38	20	350
Rapid City, SD	44	4	50	103	13	50	3,247
Reading, PA.	40	20	8	75	55	38	266
Regina, Sask.	50	27	0	104	37	0	1,894
Reno, NV	39	31	47	119	48	46	4,498
Richmond, VA	37	33	13	77	27	38	190
Roanoke, VA	37	16	15	79	56	30	940
Rochester, MN	44	1	18	92	28	11	990
Rochester, NY	43	9	17	77	36	57	515
Rockford, IL	42	16	16	89	5	38	715
Sacramento, CA.	38	34	54	121	29	36	20
Saginaw, MI	43	25	10	83	57	3	595
St. Catharines, Ont.	43	10	0	79	15	0	321
St. Cloud, MN	45	33	39	94	9	44	1,040
St. John, N.B.	45	15	33	66	02	20	357
St. John's, Nfld.	47	34	0	52	44	0	461
St. Joseph, MO	39	46	7	94	50	47	850
St. Louis, MO	38	37	38	90	11	52	455

City	Lat. N °	'	"	Long. W °	'	"	Elev. (ft)
St. Paul, MN	44	56	40	93	5	35	780
St. Petersburg, FL	27	46	14	82	40	46	44
Salem, OR	44	56	35	123	2	2	154
Salina, KS	38	50	25	97	36	40	1,225
Salt Lake City, UT	40	45	39	111	53	25	4,266
San Antonio, TX	29	25	26	98	29	36	650
San Bernardino, CA	34	6	30	117	17	20	1,200
San Diego, CA	32	42	55	117	9	23	40
San Francisco, CA	37	46	30	122	25	6	63
San Jose, CA	37	20	22	121	53	38	87
San Juan, P.R.	18	28	6	66	6	22	8
Santa Barbara, CA	34	25	15	119	41	50	50
Santa Cruz, CA	36	58	27	122	1	47	20
Santa Fe, NM	35	41	13	105	56	14	6,989
Sarasota, FL	27	20	10	82	31	51	27
Saskatoon, Sask.	52	07	0	106	38	0	1,653
Sault Ste. Marie, Ont.	46	31	0	84	20	0	630
Savannah, GA	32	5	0	81	6	0	42
Schenectady, NY	42	48	51	73	56	24	245
Seattle, WA	47	36	23	122	19	51	350
Sheboygan, WI	43	45	3	87	42	52	630
Sherbrooke, Que.	45	24	0	71	54	0	792
Sheridan, WY	44	47	50	106	57	20	3,742
Shreveport, LA	32	31	30	93	45	0	209
Sioux City, IA	42	30	0	96	24	0	1,117
Sioux Falls, SD	43	32	48	96	43	48	1,442
South Bend, IN	41	41	0	86	15	0	725
Spartanburg, SC	34	56	58	81	55	56	816
Spokane, WA	47	39	32	117	25	30	2,000
Springfield, IL	39	48	6	89	38	37	610
Springfield, MA	42	6	5	72	35	25	70
Springfield, MO	37	12	55	93	17	53	1,300
Springfield, OH	39	55	27	83	48	32	1,000
Stamford, CT	41	3	12	73	32	21	35
Steubenville, OH	40	22	11	80	38	3	1,060
Stockton, CA	37	57	28	121	17	23	15
Sudbury, Ont.	46	31	0	80	54	0	1,140
Superior, WI	46	43	15	92	6	14	642
Sydney, N.S.	46	09	0	60	11	0	203
Syracuse, NY	43	2	53	76	8	52	400
Tacoma, WA	47	15	11	122	26	35	380
Tallahassee, FL	30	26	17	84	16	51	188
Tampa, FL	27	56	50	82	27	31	48
Terre Haute, IN	39	28	0	87	24	50	501
Texarkana, TX	33	25	30	94	2	51	324
Thunder Bay, Ont.	48	24	0	89	19	0	653
Timmins, Ont.	48	28	0	81	20	0	967
Toledo, OH	41	39	50	83	33	19	615
Topeka, KS	39	2	54	95	40	40	1,000
Toronto, Ont.	43	37	39	79	23	46	251
Trenton, NJ	40	13	1	74	44	36	54
Trois-Rivières, Que.	46	21	0	72	33	0	198
Troy, NY	42	43	42	73	41	32	35
Tucson, AZ	32	13	18	110	55	33	2,390
Tulsa, OK	36	9	14	95	59	33	804
Urbana, IL	40	6	38	88	12	26	725
Utica, NY	43	6	3	75	13	59	415
Vancouver, B.C.	49	15	0	123	07	0	14
Victoria, B.C.	48	26	0	123	22	0	63
Waco, TX	31	32	57	97	8	47	405
Walla Walla, WA	46	3	53	118	20	31	1,000
Washington, DC	38	53	42	77	2	12	25
Waterloo, IA	42	29	34	92	20	34	850
West Palm Beach, FL	26	42	54	80	3	13	21
Wheeling, WV	40	3	50	80	43	16	672
Whitehorse, Yukon	60	43	0	135	03	0	2,305
White Plains, NY	41	2	2	73	45	48	220
Wichita, KS	37	41	32	97	20	14	1,305
Wilkes-Barre, PA.	41	14	45	75	52	54	550
Wilmington, DE	39	44	45	75	32	49	100
Wilmington, NC	34	13	32	77	56	42	50
Windsor, Ont.	42	18	0	83	01	0	622
Winnipeg, Man.	49	54	39	97	14	36	783
Winston-Salem, NC.	36	5	59	80	14	40	912
Worcester, MA.	42	15	45	71	48	10	480
Yakima, WA.	46	36	8	120	30	17	1,066
Yellowknife, N.W.T.	62	27	20	114	21	0	675
Youngstown, OH	41	5	59	80	38	59	861
Yuma, AZ	32	43	31	114	37	25	160
Zanesville, OH	39	56	25	82	0	48	710

Principal World Rivers

Reviewed by Laurel Duda, Marine Biological Laboratory, Woods Hole Oceanogr. Inst. Library. For N American rivers, see separate table.

River	Outflow	Length (mi)
Africa		
Chari	Lake Chad	500
Congo	Atlantic Ocean	2,900
Gambia	Atlantic Ocean	700
Kasai	Congo River	1,000
Limpopo	Indian Ocean	1,100
Lualaba	Congo River	1,100
Niger	Gulf of Guinea	2,590
Nile	Mediterranean	4,160
Okavango	Okavango Delta	1,000
Orange	Atlantic Ocean	1,300
Senegal	Atlantic Ocean	1,020
Ubangi	Congo River	660
Zambezi	Indian Ocean	1,700
Asia		
Amu Darya	Aral Sea	1,550
Amur	Tatar Strait	1,780
Angara	Yenisey River	1,151
Brahmaputra	Bay of Bengal	1,800
Chang	East China Sea	3,964
Euphrates	Shatt al-Arab	1,700
Ganges	Bay of Bengal	1,560
Godavari	Bay of Bengal	900
Hsi (see Xi)		
Huang	Yellow Sea	3,395
Indus	Arabian Sea	1,800
Irrawaddy	Andaman Sea	1,337
Jordan	Dead Sea	200
Kolyma	Arctic Ocean	1,323
Krishna	Bay of Bengal	800
Kura	Caspian Sea	848
Lena	Laptev Sea	2,734
Mekong	South China Sea	2,700
Narbada (see Narmada)		
Narmada	Arabian Sea	800
Ob	Gulf of Ob	2,268
Ob-Irtysh	Gulf of Ob	3,362
Salween	Gulf of Martaban	1,500
Songhua	Amur River	1,150
Sungari	Amur River	1,197
Sutlej	Indus River	900
Syr	Aral Sea	1,370
Tarim	Lop Nor Basin	1,261
Tigris	Shatt al-Arab	1,180
Xi	South China Sea	1,200
Yamuna	Ganges River	855
Yangtze (see Chang)		
Yellow (see Huang)		
Yenisey	Kara Seav	2,543
Australia		
Murray-Darling	Indian Ocean	2,310
Murrumbidgee	Murray River	981
Europe		
Bug, Northern	Wisla	481
Bug, Southern	Dnieper River	532
Danube	Black Sea	1,776
Don	Sea of Azov	1,224
Dnieper	Black Sea	1,420
Dniester	Black Sea	877
Drava	Danube River	447
Dvina, North	White Sea	824
Dvina, West	Gulf of Riga	634
Ebro	Mediterranean	565
Elbe	North Sea	724
Garonne	Bay of Biscay	357
Kama	Volga River	1,122
Loire	Bay of Biscay	634
Mame	Seine River	326
Meuse	North Sea	580
Oder	Baltic Sea	567
Oka	Volga River	932
Pechora	Barents Sea	1,124
Po	Adriatic Sea	405
Rhine	North Sea	820
Rhone	Gulf of Lions	505
Seine	English Channel	496
Shannon	Atlantic Ocean	230
Tagus	Atlantic Ocean	626
Thames	North Sea	210
Tiber	Tyrrhenian Sea	252
Tisza	Danube River	600
Ural	Caspian Sea	1,575
Volga	Caspian Sea	2,290
Weser	North Sea	454
Wisla	Gulf of Gdansk	675
South America		
Amazon	Atlantic Ocean	4,000
Araguaia	Tocantins River	1,100
Iça (see Putumayo)		
Iguaça	Parana River	808
Japura	Amazon River	1,750
Madeira	Amazon River	2,013
Magdalena	Caribbean Sea	956
Negro	Amazon River	1,400
Orinoco	Atlantic Ocean	1,600
Paraguay	Parana River	1,584
Parana	Rio de la Plata	2,485
Pilcomayo	Paraguay River	1,000
Purus	Amazon River	2,100
Putumayo	Amazon River	1,000
Rio de la Plata	Atlantic Ocean	150
Rio Roosevelt	Aripuana	400
Sao Francisco	Atlantic Ocean	1,988
Tocantins	Para River	1,677
Ucayali	Marañón River	910
Uruguay	Rio de la Plata	1,000
Xingu	Amazon River	1,300

Major Rivers in North America

Reviewed by Laurel Duda, Marine Biological Laboratory, Woods Hole Oceanographic Inst. Library.

River	Source or upper limit of length	Outflow	Length (mi)
Alabama	Gilmer County, GA	Mobile River	729
Albany	Lake St. Joseph, Ontario	James Bay	610
Allegheny	Potter County, PA.	Ohio River	325
Altamaha-Ocmulgee	Junction of Yellow and South Rivers, Newton County, GA	Atlantic Ocean	392
Apalachicola-Chattahoochee	Towns County, GA	Gulf of Mexico	524
Arkansas	Lake County, CO	Mississippi River	1,459
Assiniboine	Eastern Saskatchewan	Red River	450
Attawapiskat	Attawapiskat, Ontario	James Bay	465
Back (NWT)	Contwoyto Lake	Chantrey Inlet, Arctic Ocean	605
Big Black (MS)	Webster County, MS	Mississippi River	330
Brazos	Junction of Salt and Double Mountain Forks, Stonewall County, TX	Gulf of Mexico	950
Canadian	Las Animas County, CO	Arkansas River	906
Cedar (IA)	Dodge County, MN	Iowa River	329
Cheyenne	Junction of Antelope Creek and Dry Fork, Converse County, WY	Missouri River	290
Churchill, Lab.	Lake Ashuanipi, Labrador	Atlantic Ocean	532
Churchill, Man.	Methy Lake, Saskatchewan	Hudson Bay	1,000
Cimarron	Colfax County, NM	Arkansas River	600
Colorado (AZ)	Rocky Mountain Natl. Park, CO (90 mi in Mexico)	Gulf of California	1,450
Colorado (TX)	West Texas	Matagorda Bay	862
Columbia	Columbia Lake, British Columbia	Pacific Ocean, bet. OR and WA	1,243
Columbia, Upper	Columbia Lake, British Columbia	To mouth of Snake River	890
Connecticut	Third Connecticut Lake, NH	Long Island Sound, CT	407
Coppermine (NWT)	Lac de Gras	Coronation Gulf, Arctic Ocean	525
Cumberland	Letcher County, KY	Ohio River	720
Delaware	Schoharie County, NY	Liston Point, Delaware Bay	390
Fraser	Near Mount Robson (on Continental Divide)	Strait of Georgia	850
Gila	Catron County, NM.	Colorado River	649
Green (UT-WY)	Junction of Wells and Trail Creeks, Sublette County, WY	Colorado River	730
Hudson	Henderson Lake, Essex County, NY	Upper NY Bay	306
Illinois	St. Joseph County, IN	Mississippi River	420
James (ND-SD)	Wells County, ND	Missouri River	710
James (VA)	Junction of Jackson and Cowpasture Rivers, Botetourt County, VA	Hampton Roads	340
Kanawha-New	Junction of North and South Forks of New River, NC	Ohio River	352
Kentucky	Junction of North and Middle Forks, Lee County, KY	Ohio River	259
Klamath	Lake Ewauna, Klamath Falls, OR	Pacific Ocean	250
Kootenay	Kootenay Lake, British Columbia	Columbia River	485
Koyukuk	Endicott Mountains, AK	Yukon River	470
Kuskokwim	Alaska Range	Kuskokwim Bay	724
Liard	Southern Yukon, AK	Mackenzie River	693
Little Missouri	Crook County, WY	Missouri River	560
Mackenzie	Great Slave Lake, N.W.T.	Arctic Ocean	1,060
Milk	Junction of North and South Forks, Alberta	Missouri River	625

River	Source or upper limit of length	Outflow	Length (mi)
Minnesota	Big Stone Lake, MN	Mississippi River	332
Mississippi	Lake Itasca, MN	Gulf of Mexico	2,340
Mississippi-Missouri-Red Rock	Source of Red Rock, Beaverhead Co., MT	Gulf of Mexico	3,710
Missouri	Junction of Jefferson, Madison, and Gallatin Rivers, Gallatin County, MT	Mississippi River	2,315
Missouri-Red Rock	Source of Red Rock, Beaverhead Co., MT	Mississippi River	2,540
Mobile-Alabama-Coosa	Gilmer County, GA	Mobile Bay	774
Nelson (Man.)	Lake Winnipeg	Hudson Bay	410
Neosho	Morris County, KS	Arkansas River, OK	460
Niobrara	Niobrara County, WY	Missouri River, NE	431
North Canadian	Union County, NM	Canadian River, OK	800
North Platte	Junction of Grizzly and Little Grizzly Creeks, Jackson County, CO	Platte River, NE	618
Ohio	Junction of Allegheny and Monongahela Rivers, Pittsburgh, PA	Mississippi River	981
Ohio-Allegheny	Potter County, PA.	Mississippi River	1,310
Osage	East-central Kansas	Missouri River	500
Ottawa	Lake Capimitchigama	St. Lawrence River	790
Ouachita	Polk County, AR	Black River	605
Peace	Stikine Mountains, B.C.	Slave River	1,210
Pearl	Neshoba County, MS	Gulf of Mexico	411
Pecos	Mora County, NM	Rio Grande	926
Pee Dee-Yadkin	Watauga County, NC	Winyah Bay	435
Pend Oreille-Clark Fork	Near Butte, MT.	Columbia River	531
Platte	Junction of North and South Platte Rivers, NE	Missouri River	310
Porcupine	Ogilvie Mountains, AK	Yukon River, AK	569
Potomac	Garrett County, MD	Chesapeake Bay	383
Powder	Junction of South and Middle Forks, WY	Yellowstone River	375
Red (OK-TX-LA)	Curry County, NM.	Mississippi River	1,290
Red River of the North	Junction of Otter Tail and Bois de Sioux Rivers, Wilkin County, MN	Lake Winnipeg	545
Republican	Junction of North Fork and Arikaree River, NE	Kansas River	445
Rio Grande	San Juan County, CO	Gulf of Mexico	1,900
Roanoke	Junction of N and S Forks, Montgomery Co., VA.	Albemarle Sound	380
Rock (IL-WI)	Dodge County, WI	Mississippi River	300
Sabine	Junction of S and Caddo Forks, Hunt County, TX	Sabine Lake	380
Sacramento	Siskiyou County, CA.	Suisun Bay	377
St. Francis	Iron County, MO	Mississippi River	425
St. John	Northwestern Maine	Bay of Fundy	418
St. Lawrence	Lake Ontario	Gulf of St. Lawrence, Atlantic Ocean	800
Saguenay	Lake St. John, Quebec	St. Lawrence River	434
Salmon (ID)	Custer County, ID.	Snake River	420
San Joaquin	Junction of S and Middle Forks, Madera Co., CA	Suisun Bay	350
San Juan	Silver Lake, Archuleta County, CO.	Colorado River	360
Santee-Wateree-Catawba	McDowell County, NC	Atlantic Ocean	538
Saskatchewan, North	Rocky Mountains	Saskatchewan R.	800
Saskatchewan, South	Rocky Mountains	Saskatchewan R.	865
Savannah	Junction of Seneca and Tugaloo Rivers, Anderson County, SC	Atlantic Ocean, GA-SC	314
Severn (Ont.)	Sandy Lake	Hudson Bay	610
Smoky Hill	Cheyenne County, CO	Kansas River, KS	540
Snake	Teton County, WY	Columbia River, WA	1,038
South Platte	Junction of S and Middle Forks, Park County, CO.	Platte River	424
Susitna	Alaska Range	Cook Inlet	313
Susquehanna	Huyden Creek, Otsego County, NY	Chesapeake Bay	447
Tallahatchie	Tippah County, MS.	Yazoo River	301
Tanana	Wrangell Mountains, AK.	Yukon River	659
Tennessee	Junction of French Broad and Holston Rivers	Ohio River	652
Tennessee-French Broad	Courthouse Creek, Transylvania County, NC	Ohio River	886
Tombigbee	Prentiss County, MS.	Mobile River	525
Trinity	North of Dallas, TX	Galveston Bay	360
Wabash	Darke County, OH	Ohio River	512
Washita	Hemphill County, TX	Red River, OK	500
White (AR-MO)	Madison County, AR	Mississippi River	722
Willamette	Douglas County, OR	Columbia River	309
Wind-Bighorn	Junction of Wind and Little Wind Rivers, Fremont Co., WY (Source of Wind R. is Togwotee Pass, Teton Co., WY)	Yellowstone River	338
Wisconsin	Lac Vieux Desert, Vilas County, WI	Mississippi River	430
Yellowstone	Park County, WY	Missouri River	682
Yukon	McNeil R., Yukon Territory	Bering Sea	1,979

Highest and Lowest Continental Altitudes

Source: National Geographic Society

Continent	Highest point	Elev. (ft)	Lowest point	ft below sea level
Asia	Mount Everest, Nepal-Tibet	29,035	Dead Sea, Israel-Jordan	1,348
South America	Mount Aconcagua, Argentina	22,834	Valdes Peninsula, Argentina	131
North America	Mount McKinley, Alaska	20,320	Death Valley, California	282
Africa	Kilimanjaro, Tanzania	19,340	Lake Assal, Djibouti	512
Europe	Mount Elbrus, Russia	18,510	Caspian Sea, Russia, Azerbaijan	92
Antarctica	Vinson Massif	16,864	Bentley Subglacial Trench	8,327[1]
Australia	Mount Kosciusko, New South Wales	7,310	Lake Eyre, South Australia	52

(1) Estimated level of the continental floor. Lower points that have yet to be discovered may exist further beneath the ice.

> **IT'S A FACT:** A stream on Nevado Mismi, an 18,363-foot peak in Southern Peru, is the source of the Amazon River. A National Geographic team using satellite navigation equipment solved the 300-year-old mystery in 2000.

Major Natural Lakes of the World

Source: Geological Survey, U.S. Dept. of the Interior

A lake is generally defined as a body of water surrounded by land. By this definition some bodies of water that are called seas, such as the Caspian Sea and the Aral Sea, are really lakes. In the following table, the word *lake* is omitted when it is part of the name.

Name	Continent	Area (sq mi)	Length (mi)	Maximum depth (ft)	Elevation (ft)
Caspian Sea[1]	Asia-Europe	143,244	760	3,363	-92
Superior	North America	31,700	350	1,330	600
Victoria	Africa	26,828	250	270	3,720
Huron	North America	23,000	206	750	579
Michigan	North America	22,300	307	923	579
Aral Sea[1]	Asia	13,000[2]	260	220	125
Tanganyika	Africa	12,700	420	4,823	2,534
Baykal	Asia	12,162	395	5,315	1,493
Great Bear	North America	12,096	192	1,463	512
Nyasa (Malawi)	Africa	11,150	360	2,280	1,550
Great Slave	North America	11,031	298	2,015	513
Erie	North America	9,910	241	210	570
Winnipeg	North America	9,417	266	60	713
Ontario	North America	7,340	193	802	245
Balkhash[1]	Asia	7,115	376	85	1,115
Ladoga	Europe	6,835	124	738	13
Maracaibo	South America	5,217	133	115	sea level
Onega	Europe	3,710	145	328	108
Eyre[1]	Australia	3,600[3]	90	4	-52
Titicaca	South America	3,200	122	922	12,500
Nicaragua	North America	3,100	102	230	102
Athabasca	North America	3,064	208	407	700
Reindeer	North America	2,568	143	720	1,106
Tonle Sap	Asia	2,500[3]	...	45	...
Turkana (Rudolf)	Africa	2,473	154	240	1,230
Issyk Kul[1]	Asia	2,355	115	2,303	5,279
Torrens[1]	Australia	2,230[3]	130	...	92
Vanern	Europe	2,156	91	328	144
Nettilling	North America	2,140	67	...	95
Winnipegosis	North America	2,075	141	38	830
Albert	Africa	2,075	100	168	2,030
Nipigon	North America	1,872	72	540	1,050
Gairdner[1]	Australia	1,840[3]	90	...	112
Urmia[1]	Asia	1,815	90	49	4,180
Manitoba	North America	1,799	140	12	813
Chad	Africa	839[4]	175	24	787

(1) Salt lake. (2) Approximate figure, could be less. The diversion of feeder rivers since the 1960s has devastated the Aral—once the world's 4th-largest lake (26,000 sq. miles). By 2000, the Aral had effectively become three lakes, with the total area shown. (3) Approximate figure, subject to great seasonal variation. (4) Once 4th-largest lake in Africa (about 10,000 sq. miles in the 1960s), Chad had shrunk more than 90% by 2001 due to irrigation and long-term drought.

The Great Lakes

Source: National Ocean Service, U.S. Dept. of Commerce

The Great Lakes form the world's largest body of fresh water (in surface area), and with their connecting waterways are the largest inland water transportation unit. Draining the great North Central basin of the U.S., they enable shipping to reach the Atlantic via their outlet, the St. Lawrence R., and to reach the Gulf of Mexico via the Illinois Waterway, from Lake Michigan to the Mississippi R. A 3rd outlet connects with the Hudson R. and then the Atlantic via the New York State Barge Canal System. Traffic on the Illinois Waterway and the N.Y. State Barge Canal System is limited to recreational boating and small shipping vessels.

Only one of the lakes, Lake Michigan, is wholly in the U.S.; the others are shared with Canada. Ships move from the shores of Lake Superior to Whitefish Bay at the E end of the lake, then through the Soo (Sault Ste. Marie) locks, through the St. Mary's R. and into Lake Huron. To reach Gary and the Port of Indiana and South Chicago, IL, ships move W from Lake Huron to Lake Michigan through the Straits of Mackinac. Lake Superior is 601 ft above low water datum at Rimouski, Quebec, on the International Great Lakes Datum (1985). From Duluth, MN, to the E end of Lake Ontario is 1,156 mi.

	Superior	Michigan	Huron	Erie	Ontario
Length in mi	350	307	206	241	193
Breadth in mi	160	118	183	57	53
Deepest soundings in ft	1,333	923	750	210	802
Volume of water in cu mi	2,935	1,180	850	116	393
Area (sq mi) water surface—U.S.	20,600	22,300	9,100	4,980	3,460
Canada	11,100	.....	13,900	4,930	3,880
Area (sq mi) entire drainage basin—U.S.	16,900	45,600	16,200	18,000	15,200
Canada	32,400	.....	35,500	4,720	12,100
TOTAL AREA (sq mi) U.S. and Canada	**81,000**	**67,900**	**74,700**	**32,630**	**34,850**
Low water datum above mean water level at Rimouski, Quebec, avg. level in ft (1985)	601.10	577.50	577.50	569.20	243.30
Latitude, N	46° 25'	41° 37'	43° 00'	41° 23'	43° 11'
	49° 00'	46° 06'	46° 17'	42° 52'	44° 15'
Longitude, W	84° 22'	84° 45'	79° 43'	78° 51'	76° 03'
	92° 06'	88° 02'	84° 45'	83° 29'	79° 53'
National boundary line in mi	282.8	None	260.8	251.5	174.6
United States shoreline (mainland only) mi	863	1,400	580	431	300

> **IT'S A FACT:** While the Great Lakes Michigan and Huron are widely considered to be 2 separate lakes, in hydrological terms they are one lake joined by a 120-foot-deep channel known as the Straits of Mackinac.

Famous Waterfalls

Source: National Geographic Society

The earth has thousands of waterfalls, some of considerable magnitude. Their relative importance is determined not only by height but also by volume of flow, steadiness of flow, crest width, whether the water drops sheerly or over a sloping surface, and whether it descends in one leap or in a succession of leaps. A series of low falls flowing over a considerable distance is known as a **cascade.**

Estimated mean annual flow, in cubic feet per second, of major waterfalls are as follows: Niagara, 212,200; Paulo Afonso, 100,000; Urubupunga, 97,000; Iguazu, 61,000; Patos-Maribondo, 53,000; Victoria, 35,400; and Kaieteur, 23,400.

Height = total drop in feet in one or more leaps. #=falls of more than one leap; *= falls that diminish greatly seasonally; **= falls that reeduce to a trickle or are dry for part of each year. If the river names are not shown, they are same as the falls. R. = river; (C) = cascade type.

Name and location	Height (ft)
Africa	
Angola	
Ruacana, Cuene R.	406
Ethiopia	
Fincha	508
Lesotho	
Maletsunyane*	630
Zimbabwe-Zambia	
Victoria, Zambezi R.*	343
South Africa	
Augrabies, Orange R.*	480
Tugela#	2,014
Tanzania-Zambia	
Kalambo*	726
Asia	
India	
Cauvery*	330
Jog (Gersoppa),	
Sharavathi R.*	830
Japan	
Kegon, Daiya R.*	330
Australia	
New South Wales	
Wentworth	614
Wollomombi	1,100
Queensland	
Tully	885
Wallaman, Stony Cr.#	1,137
New Zealand	
Helena	890
Sutherland, Arthur R.#	1,904
Europe	
Austria	
Gastein#	492
Krimml#	1,312
France	
Gavarnie*	1,385
Great Britain	
Scotland	
Glomach	370
Wales	
Rhaiadr	240
Italy	
Frua, Toce R. (C).	470

Name and location	Height (ft)
Norway	
Mardalsfossen (Northern)	1,535
Mardalsfossen (Southern)#	2,149
Skjeggedal, Nybuai R.#**	1,378
Skykje**	984
Vetti, Morka-Koldedola R.	900
Sweden	
Handol#	427
Switzerland	
Giessbach (C)	984
Reichenbach#	656
Simmen#	459
Staubbach	984
Trummelbach#	1,312
North America	
Canada	
Alberta	
Panthver, Nigel Cr.	600
British Columbia	
Della#	1,443
Takakkaw, Daly Glacier#	1,200
Quebec	
Montmorency	274
Canada—United States	
Niagara: American	182
Horseshoe.	173
United States	
California	
Feather, Fall R.*	640
Yosemite National Park	
Bridalveil*	620
Illilouette*.	370
Nevada, Merced R.*	594
Ribbon**	1,612
Silver Strand, Meadow Br.**	1,170
Vernal, Merced R. *	317
Yosemite#**	2,425
Colorado	
Seven, South	
Cheyenne Cr.#	300
Hawaii	
Akaka, Kolekole Str.	442
Idaho	
Shoshone, Snake R.**	212
Kentucky	
Cumberland.	68

Name and location	Height (ft)
Maryland	
Great, Potomac R. (C) *	71
Minnesota	
Minnehaha**	53
New Jersey	
Passaic	70
New York	
Taughannock*	215
Oregon	
Multnomah#	620
Tennessee	
Fall Creek	256
Washington	
Mt. Rainier Natl. Park	
Sluiskin, Paradise R.	300
Snoquvalmie**	268
Wisconsin	
Big Manitou, Black R. (C)*	165
Wyoming	
Yellowstone Natl. Pk. Tower.	132
Yellowstone (upper)*	109
Yellowstone (lower)*	308
Mexico	
El Salo	218
South America	
Argentina-Brazil	
Iguazu	230
Brazil	
Glass	1,325
Patos-Maribondo, Grande R.	115
Paulo Afonso,	
Sao Francisco R.	275
Urubupunga, Parana R.	39
Colombia	
Catarvata de Candelas,	
Cusiana R.	984
Tequendama, Bogota R.*	427
Ecuador	
Agoyan, Pastaza R.*	200
Guyana	
Kaieteur, Potaro R.	741
Great, Kamarang R.	1,600
Marina, Ipobe R.#.	500
Venezuela	
Angel#*	3,212
Cuquenan.	2,000

Notable Deserts of the World

Arabian (Eastern), 70,000 sq mi in Egypt between the Nile R. and Red Sea, extending southward into Sudan

Atacama, 600-mi-long area rich in nitrate and copper deposits in N Chile

Chihuahuan, 140,000 sq mi in TX, NM, AZ, and Mexico

Dasht-e Kauir, approx. 300 mi long by approx. 100 mi wide in N central Iran

Dasht-e Lut, 20,000 sq mi in E Iran

Death Valley, 3,300 sq mi in CA and NV

Gibson, 120,000 sq mi in the interior of W Australia

Gobi, 500,000 sq mi in Mongolia and China

Great Sandy, 150,000 sq mi in W Australia

Great Victoria, 150,000 sq mi in SW Australia

Kalahari, 225,000 sq mi in S Africa

Kara Kum, 120,000 sq mi in Turkmenistan

Kyzyl Kum, 100,000 sq mi in Kazakhstan and Uzbekistan

Libyan, 450,000 sq mi in the Sahara, extending from Libya through SW Egypt into Sudan

Mojave, 15,000 sq mi in southern CA

Namib, long narrow area (varies from 30-100 mi wide) extending 800 mi along SW coast of Africa

Nubian, 100,000 sq mi in the Sahara in NE Sudan

Painted Desert, section of high plateau in northern AZ extending 150 mi

Patagonia, 300,000 sq mi in S Argentina

Rub al-Khali (Empty Quarter), 250,000 sq mi in the S Arabian Peninsula

Sahara, 3,500,000 sq mi in N Africa, extending westward to the Atlantic. Largest desert in the world

Sonoran, 70,000 sq mi in southwestern AZ and southeastern CA extending into NW Mexico

Syrian, 100,000-sq-mi arid wasteland extending over much of N Saudi Arabia, E Jordan, S Syria, and W Iraq

Taklimakan, 140,000 sq mi in Xinjiang Prov., China

Thar (Great Indian), 100,000-sq-mi arid area extending 400 mi along India-Pakistan border

AFGHANISTAN · ALBANIA · ALGERIA · ANDORRA · ANGOLA

ANTIGUA AND BARBUDA · ARGENTINA · ARMENIA · AUSTRALIA · AUSTRIA

AZERBAIJAN · THE BAHAMAS · BAHRAIN · BANGLADESH · BARBADOS

BELARUS · BELGIUM · BELIZE · BENIN · BHUTAN

BOLIVIA · BOSNIA AND HERZEGOVINA · BOTSWANA · BRAZIL · BRUNEI

BULGARIA · BURKINA FASO · BURUNDI · CAMBODIA · CAMEROON

CANADA · CAPE VERDE · CENTRAL AFRICAN REPUBLIC · CHAD · CHILE

CHINA · COLOMBIA · COMOROS · CONGO, DEM. REP. OF THE · CONGO REPUBLIC

COSTA RICA · CÔTE D'IVOIRE · CROATIA · CUBA · CYPRUS

CZECH REPUBLIC · DENMARK · DJIBOUTI · DOMINICA · DOMINICAN REPUBLIC

EAST TIMOR · ECUADOR · EGYPT · EL SALVADOR · EQUATORIAL GUINEA

ERITREA

ESTONIA

ETHIOPIA

FIJI

FINLAND

FRANCE

GABON

THE GAMBIA

GEORGIA

GERMANY

GHANA

GREECE

GRENADA

GUATEMALA

GUINEA

GUINEA-BISSAU

GUYANA

HAITI

HONDURAS

HUNGARY

ICELAND

INDIA

INDONESIA

IRAN

IRAQ

IRELAND

ISRAEL

ITALY

JAMAICA

JAPAN

JORDAN

KAZAKHSTAN

KENYA

KIRIBATI

NORTH KOREA

SOUTH KOREA

KUWAIT

KYRGYZSTAN

LAOS

LATVIA

LEBANON

LESOTHO

LIBERIA

LIBYA

LIECHTENSTEIN

LITHUANIA

LUXEMBOURG

MACEDONIA

MADAGASCAR

MALAWI

MALAYSIA

MALDIVES

MALI

MALTA

MARSHALL ISLANDS

MAURITANIA   MAURITIUS   MEXICO   MICRONESIA   MOLDOVA

MONACO   MONGOLIA   MOROCCO   MOZAMBIQUE   MYANMAR (BURMA)

NAMIBIA   NAURU   NEPAL   NETHERLANDS   NEW ZEALAND

NICARAGUA   NIGER   NIGERIA   NORWAY   OMAN

PAKISTAN   PALAU   PANAMA   PAPUA NEW GUINEA   PARAGUAY

PERU   PHILIPPINES   POLAND   PORTUGAL   QATAR

ROMANIA   RUSSIA   RWANDA   ST. KITTS AND NEVIS   ST. LUCIA

ST. VINCENT AND THE GRENADINES   SAMOA   SAN MARINO   SÃO TOMÉ AND PRÍNCIPE   SAUDI ARABIA

SENEGAL   SERBIA & MONTENEGRO   SEYCHELLES   SIERRA LEONE   SINGAPORE

SLOVAKIA   SLOVENIA   SOLOMON ISLANDS   SOMALIA   SOUTH AFRICA

SPAIN   SRI LANKA   SUDAN   SURINAME   SWAZILAND

500

SWEDEN

SWITZERLAND

SYRIA

TAIWAN

TAJIKISTAN

TANZANIA

THAILAND

TOGO

TONGA

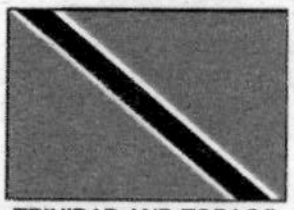

TRINIDAD AND TOBAGO

TUNISIA

TURKEY

TURKMENISTAN

TUVALU

UGANDA

UKRAINE

UNITED ARAB EMIRATES

UNITED KINGDOM

UNITED STATES

URUGUAY

UZBEKISTAN

VANUATU

VATICAN CITY

VENEZUELA

VIETNAM

YEMEN

ZAMBIA

ZIMBABWE

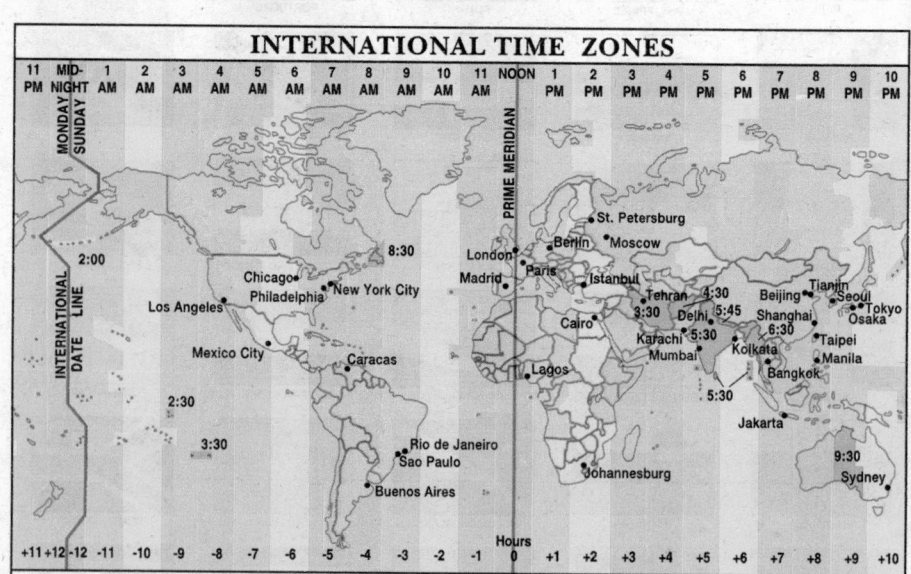

INTERNATIONAL TIME ZONES

The world is divided into 24 time zones, each 15° longitude wide. The longitudinal meridian passing through Greenwich, England, is the starting point, and is called the *prime meridian.* The 12th zone is divided by the 180th meridian (International Date Line). When the line is crossed going west, the date is advanced one day; when crossed going east, the date becomes a day earlier.

© MAPQUEST

UNITED STATES

ATLANTIC OCEAN

CANADA

MEXICO

PACIFIC OCEAN

Gulf of Mexico

BAHAMAS

CUBA

Tropic of Cancer

GREAT PLAINS

ROCKY MOUNTAINS

COLORADO PLATEAU

GREAT BASIN

SIERRA NEVADA

CASCADE RANGES

COAST RANGES

APPALACHIAN MOUNTAINS

EDWARDS PLATEAU

COASTAL PLAIN

Lake Superior • Lake Huron • Lake Michigan • Lake Erie • Lake Ontario

Lake of the Woods

Chesapeake Bay

Cape Cod • Long I. • Cape Hatteras • Cape Canaveral • Cape Sable • Key West • Cape Flattery

Rio Grande • Mississippi R. • Missouri R. • Columbia R. • Snake R. • Colorado R.

Washington: Seattle, Tacoma, Olympia, Spokane, Yakima, Bellingham, Vancouver, Kennewick, Mt. Rainier 14,410, Mt. Olympus 7,965

Oregon: Portland, Salem, Eugene, Medford, Bend, Coos Bay, Klamath Falls, Mt. Hood 11,235, Mt. Shasta 14,162

California: Sacramento, San Francisco, Oakland, San Jose, Fresno, Bakersfield, Los Angeles, Long Beach, San Bernardino, Riverside, San Diego, Santa Barbara, Monterey, Eureka, Redding, Mt. Whitney 14,494, Death Valley -282 Lowest point in the U.S., Channel Islands

Nevada: Carson City, Reno, Las Vegas, Elko, Winnemucca, Ely, Hawthorne, Boundary Pk. 13,143

Idaho: Boise, Idaho Falls, Twin Falls, Pocatello, Lewiston, Salmon, Borah Pk. 12,662

Montana: Helena, Billings, Great Falls, Butte, Missoula, Kalispell, Bozeman, Havre, Glasgow, Miles City, Granite Pk. 12,799

Wyoming: Cheyenne, Casper, Laramie, Rock Springs, Sheridan, Cody, Jackson, Lander, Gannett Pk. 13,804

Utah: Salt Lake City, Provo, Ogden, Logan, Cedar City, St. George, Richfield, Kings Pk. 13,528

Colorado: Denver, Colorado Springs, Pueblo, Boulder, Fort Collins, Grand Junction, Durango, Alamosa, La Junta, Sterling, Montrose, Mt. Elbert 14,433

Arizona: Phoenix, Tucson, Flagstaff, Yuma, Prescott, Kingman, Nogales, Casa Grande, Humphreys Pk. 12,633, GRAND CANYON

New Mexico: Santa Fe, Albuquerque, Las Cruces, Roswell, Clovis, Carlsbad, Gallup, Socorro, Silver City, Tucumcari, Raton, Farmington, Wheeler Pk. 13,161

North Dakota: Bismarck, Fargo, Grand Forks, Minot, Williston, Dickinson, Jamestown

South Dakota: Pierre, Rapid City, Sioux Falls, Aberdeen, Watertown, Mobridge, Huron, BLACK HILLS, Harney Pk. 7,242

Nebraska: Lincoln, Omaha, Grand Island, North Platte, Scottsbluff, Chadron, Broken Bow

Kansas: Topeka, Wichita, Kansas City, Salina, Dodge City, Goodland, Hutchinson, Lawrence, Parsons

Oklahoma: Oklahoma City, Tulsa, Lawton, Enid, Muskogee, Clinton, Durant, Bartlesville

Texas: Austin, Houston, Dallas, Fort Worth, San Antonio, El Paso, Amarillo, Lubbock, Abilene, Midland, Odessa, Waco, Corpus Christi, Brownsville, Laredo, McAllen, Del Rio, Galveston, Beaumont, Victoria, San Angelo, Wichita Falls, Bryan, Fort Stockton, Tyler

Minnesota: St. Paul, Minneapolis, Duluth, Rochester, St. Cloud, Bemidji, Mankato, International Falls, Virginia, Hibbing

Iowa: Des Moines, Davenport, Cedar Rapids, Waterloo, Sioux City, Dubuque, Mason City, Ottumwa, Council Bluffs

Missouri: Jefferson City, St. Louis, Kansas City, Springfield, Columbia, St. Joseph, Cape Girardeau, Rolla, Hannibal, Poplar Bluff

Wisconsin: Madison, Milwaukee, Green Bay, Eau Claire, La Crosse, Wausau, Appleton, Superior, Marquette

Illinois: Springfield, Chicago, Rockford, Peoria, Champaign, Rock Island, Bloomington, Carbondale

Indiana: Indianapolis, Fort Wayne, Gary, South Bend, Muncie, Evansville

Michigan: Lansing, Detroit, Grand Rapids, Flint, Saginaw, Kalamazoo, Traverse City, Sault Ste. Marie, Escanaba, Houghton, Alpena

Ohio: Columbus, Cleveland, Cincinnati, Toledo, Akron, Dayton, Youngstown, Canton, Mansfield

Kentucky: Frankfort, Louisville, Lexington, Bowling Green, Paducah, Owensboro

Tennessee: Nashville, Memphis, Knoxville, Chattanooga, Johnson City

Arkansas: Little Rock, Fort Smith, Fayetteville, Pine Bluff, El Dorado, Jonesboro, Texarkana

Louisiana: Baton Rouge, New Orleans, Shreveport, Lafayette, Monroe, Alexandria, Lake Charles

Mississippi: Jackson, Biloxi, Meridian, Hattiesburg, Greenville, Natchez, Columbus, Tupelo

Alabama: Montgomery, Birmingham, Mobile, Huntsville, Tuscaloosa, Dothan, Gadsden

Georgia: Atlanta, Augusta, Columbus, Macon, Savannah, Albany, Valdosta, Athens, Brunswick

Florida: Tallahassee, Orlando, Tampa, Miami, Jacksonville, St. Petersburg, Sarasota, Fort Myers, Pensacola, Panama City, Gainesville, Daytona Beach, West Palm Beach, Fort Lauderdale, Melbourne, St. Augustine

South Carolina: Columbia, Charleston, Greenville, Spartanburg, Florence

North Carolina: Raleigh, Charlotte, Greensboro, Durham, Winston-Salem, Asheville, Fayetteville, Wilmington, New Bern, Salisbury, Mt. Mitchell 6,684

Virginia: Richmond, Norfolk, Roanoke, Lynchburg, Newport News, Charlottesville

West Virginia: Charleston, Huntington, Parkersburg, Wheeling, Morgantown

Pennsylvania: Harrisburg, Philadelphia, Pittsburgh, Erie, Scranton, Allentown, Altoona

New York: Albany, New York, Buffalo, Rochester, Syracuse, Binghamton, Utica

Maine: Augusta, Portland, Bangor, Bar Harbor, Calais, Houlton, Caribou, Mt. Katahdin 5,268, Mt. Washington

New Hampshire: Concord, Manchester, Portsmouth, Berlin

Vermont: Montpelier, Burlington, Rutland

Massachusetts: Boston, Springfield, Worcester, New Bedford, Mass.

Connecticut: Hartford, New Haven, Bridgeport

New Jersey: Trenton, Newark

Maryland: Baltimore, Annapolis

Washington, D.C.

ADIRONDACK MOUNTAINS

GREEN MTS., WHITE MTS.

ALASKA....See page 502

Hawaii: Honolulu, Hilo, Waialua, Lihue, Niihau, Kauai, Oahu, Molokai, Lanai, Maui, Kahoolawe, Kahului, Mauna Kea 13,796, Mauna Loa 13,680, Kailua, Kailua

0 100 Miles / 0 150 Kilometers

0 250 500 750 Kilometers
0 250 500 Miles

MAPQUEST

20° 30°
80° 90° 100° 120° 155° 160°

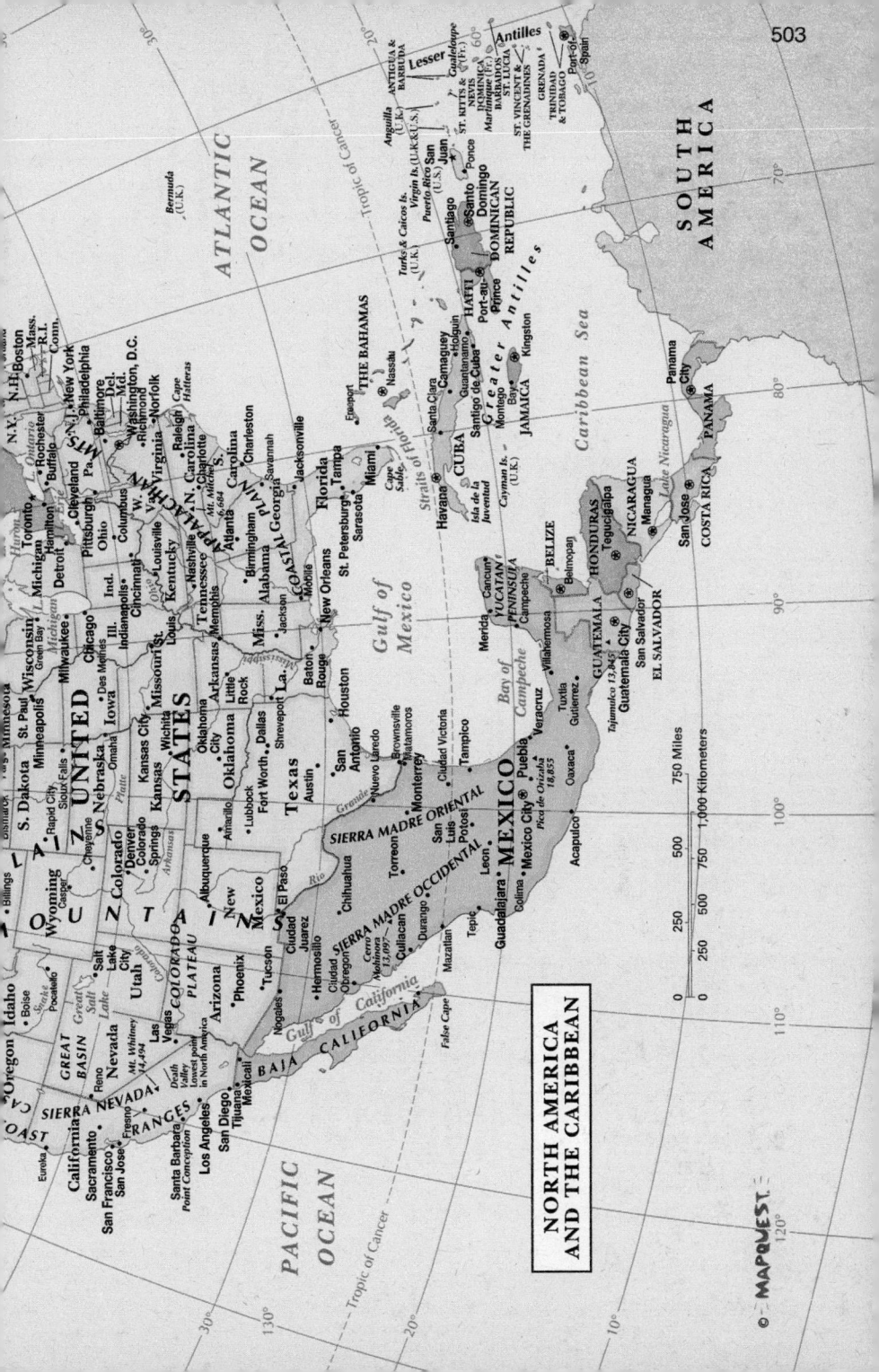

NORTH AMERICA AND THE CARIBBEAN

ATLANTIC OCEAN

PACIFIC OCEAN

SOUTH AMERICA

Caribbean Sea

Gulf of Mexico

UNITED STATES

MEXICO

Bermuda (U.K.)

THE BAHAMAS

CUBA

JAMAICA

HAITI

DOMINICAN REPUBLIC

Puerto Rico (U.S.)

Virgin Is. (U.K. & U.S.)

Lesser Antilles

Greater Antilles

ANTIGUA & BARBUDA

ST. KITTS & NEVIS

DOMINICA

ST. LUCIA

ST. VINCENT & THE GRENADINES

BARBADOS

GRENADA

TRINIDAD & TOBAGO

Guadeloupe (Fr.)

Martinique (Fr.)

GUATEMALA

BELIZE

HONDURAS

EL SALVADOR

NICARAGUA

COSTA RICA

PANAMA

Anguilla (U.K.)

Turks & Caicos Is. (U.K.)

Cayman Is. (U.K.)

Bay of Campeche

Gulf of California

Great Salt Lake

Lake Nicaragua

Straits of Florida

YUCATAN PENINSULA

SIERRA MADRE ORIENTAL

SIERRA MADRE OCCIDENTAL

BAJA CALIFORNIA

GREAT BASIN

COLORADO PLATEAU

SIERRA NEVADA

COAST RANGES

ROCKY MOUNTAINS

GREAT PLAINS

APPALACHIAN MTS.

COASTAL PLAIN

Tropic of Cancer

Cuba — Oregon, Idaho, California, Nevada, Utah, Arizona, New Mexico, Colorado, Wyoming, S. Dakota, Minnesota, Wisconsin, Michigan, Iowa, Nebraska, Kansas, Missouri, Illinois, Ind., Ohio, Kentucky, Tennessee, Mississippi, Alabama, Georgia, Florida, N. Carolina, S. Carolina, Virginia, W. Va., Md., Del., N.J., N.Y., Conn., R.I., Mass., N.H., Vermont, Maine, Texas, Oklahoma, Arkansas, La.

Seattle, Portland, Eureka, Sacramento, San Francisco, San Jose, Fresno, Santa Barbara, Los Angeles, San Diego, Reno, Las Vegas, Boise, Pocatello, Casper, Billings, Rapid City, Cheyenne, Denver, Colorado Springs, Pueblo, Salt Lake City, Phoenix, Tucson, Albuquerque, El Paso, Amarillo, Lubbock, Fort Worth, Dallas, Austin, San Antonio, Houston, Oklahoma City, Wichita, Kansas City, Omaha, Des Moines, Sioux Falls, St. Paul, Minneapolis, Duluth, Bismarck, Green Bay, Milwaukee, Chicago, St. Louis, Indianapolis, Louisville, Cincinnati, Detroit, Cleveland, Pittsburgh, Columbus, Buffalo, Rochester, Toronto, Hamilton, Nashville, Memphis, Little Rock, Shreveport, Baton Rouge, New Orleans, Mobile, Jackson, Birmingham, Atlanta, Charlotte, Raleigh, Charleston, Savannah, Jacksonville, Tampa, St. Petersburg, Sarasota, Miami, Richmond, Norfolk, Washington D.C., Baltimore, Philadelphia, New York, Boston

Mexicali, Tijuana, Ensenada, Nogales, Ciudad Obregon, Hermosillo, Ciudad Juarez, Chihuahua, Culiacan, Durango, Torreon, Monterrey, Nuevo Laredo, Matamoros, Brownsville, Tampico, Ciudad Victoria, San Luis Potosi, Leon, Guadalajara, Mazatlan, Tepic, Mexico City, Puebla, Veracruz, Villahermosa, Tuxtla Gutierrez, Campeche, Merida, Cancun, Oaxaca, Acapulco

Belmopan, Guatemala City, San Salvador, Tegucigalpa, Managua, San Jose, Panama City

Havana, Isla de la Juventud, Santa Clara, Camaguey, Holguin, Santiago de Cuba, Guantanamo Bay, Montego Bay, Kingston, Port-au-Prince, Santo Domingo, Santiago, San Juan, Ponce, Nassau, Freeport

Point Conception, Point Loma, Cape Hatteras, Cape Canaveral, Cape Sable, False Cape

Mt. Whitney 14,494

Mt. Mitchell 6,684

Cerro Las Tres Virgenes 12,093

Pico de Orizaba 18,855

Tajamulco 13,845

Death Valley lowest point in North America

Columbia, Snake, Platte, Arkansas, Rio Grande

Lakes Superior, Michigan, Huron, Erie, Ontario

0   250   500   750 Miles
0   250   500   750   1,000 Kilometers

© MAPQUEST

ATLANTIC OCEAN

Caribbean Sea

CENTRAL AMERICA

PACIFIC OCEAN

Galapagos Islands (Ecuador)

Equator

BRAZIL

COLOMBIA

VENEZUELA

GUYANA

SURINAME

French Guiana (Fr.)

BOLIVIA

PERU

ECUADOR

A M A Z O N   B A S I N

S E L V A S

GUIANA HIGHLANDS

LLANOS

BRAZILIAN HIGHLANDS

MATO GROSSO PLATEAU

ALTIPLANO

LA MONTAÑA

A N D E S

Pico da Neblina 9,885

Pico Bolívar 16,342

Pico Cristóbal 18,947

Nevada del Huila 18,865

Cotopaxi 19,347

Chimborazo 20,561

Nev. Huascarán 22,205

Cerro de Pasco

Nev. Yerupajá 21,709

Pico da Bandeira 9,482

Aruba (Neth.)
Bonaire (Neth.)
Curaçao (Neth.)
Margarita I.

Santa Marta
Barranquilla
Cartagena
Sincelejo
Montería
Coro
Maracaibo
Cabimas
Valledupar
Cúcuta
Bucaramanga
San Cristóbal
Mérida
Valera
Maracay
Valencia
Barquisimeto
Caracas
Barcelona
Cumaná
Maturín
El Tigre
Ciudad Bolívar
Ciudad Guayana
Boa Vista
Georgetown
New Amsterdam
Paramaribo
Cayenne
Kourou

Medellín
Barrancabermeja
Manizales
Pereira
Armenia
Tunja
Bogotá
Villavicencio
Palmira
Cali
Ibagué
Neiva
Popayán
Florencia
Pasto
Tumaco
Buenaventura

San Fernando de Apure
Puerto Ayacucho

Esmeraldas
Quito
Portoviejo
Ambato
Riobamba
Guayaquil
Machala
Cuenca
Loja
Tumbes
Talara
Sullana
Aguja Point
Piura
Chiclayo
Trujillo
Chimbote
Cajamarca

Iquitos
Leticia
Benjamín Constant
Crucero do Sul
Yurimaguas
Pucallpa
Huánuco
Huancayo
Ayacucho
Ica
Callao
Lima
Cuzco
Puno
Juliaca
Tacna
Arica
Iquique
Arequipa
Puerto Maldonado

Manaus
Santarém
Itaituba
Altamira
Maraba
Atuaína
Imperatriz
Belém
Macapá
Marajó Island
São Luís
Parnaíba
Floriano
Teresina
Caxias

Natal
João Pessoa
Recife
Maceió
Aracaju
Alagoinhas
Salvador
Ilhéus
Jequié
Itabuna
Vitória da Conquista
Otoni
Montes Claros
Teófilo Otoni
Governador Valadares
Juiz de Fora
Vitória
Ribeirão Preto
Belo Horizonte
Uberlândia
Uberaba
Anápolis
Goiânia
Brasília
Gurupi
Bauru
Presidente Prudente
São José do Rio Preto
Campo Grande
Corumbá
Rondonópolis
Cuiabá
Jataí

Mossoró
Campina Grande
Fortaleza
Juazeiro do Norte
Juazeiro
Petrolina
Feira de Santana

Pôrto Velho
Ji-Paraná
Guajará-Mirim
Ribeira
Riberalta
Cobija
Trinidad
Santa Cruz
Cochabamba
Sucre
La Paz
Oruro
Potosí
Camiri
Tarija

Río Branco

DESERT

Orinoco
Amazon
Negro
Juruá
Purus
Madeira
Tapajós
Xingu
Tocantins
São Francisco
Paraguay
Paraná

ACRE
PÓ

10°
0°
40°
50°
60°
70°
80°
90°

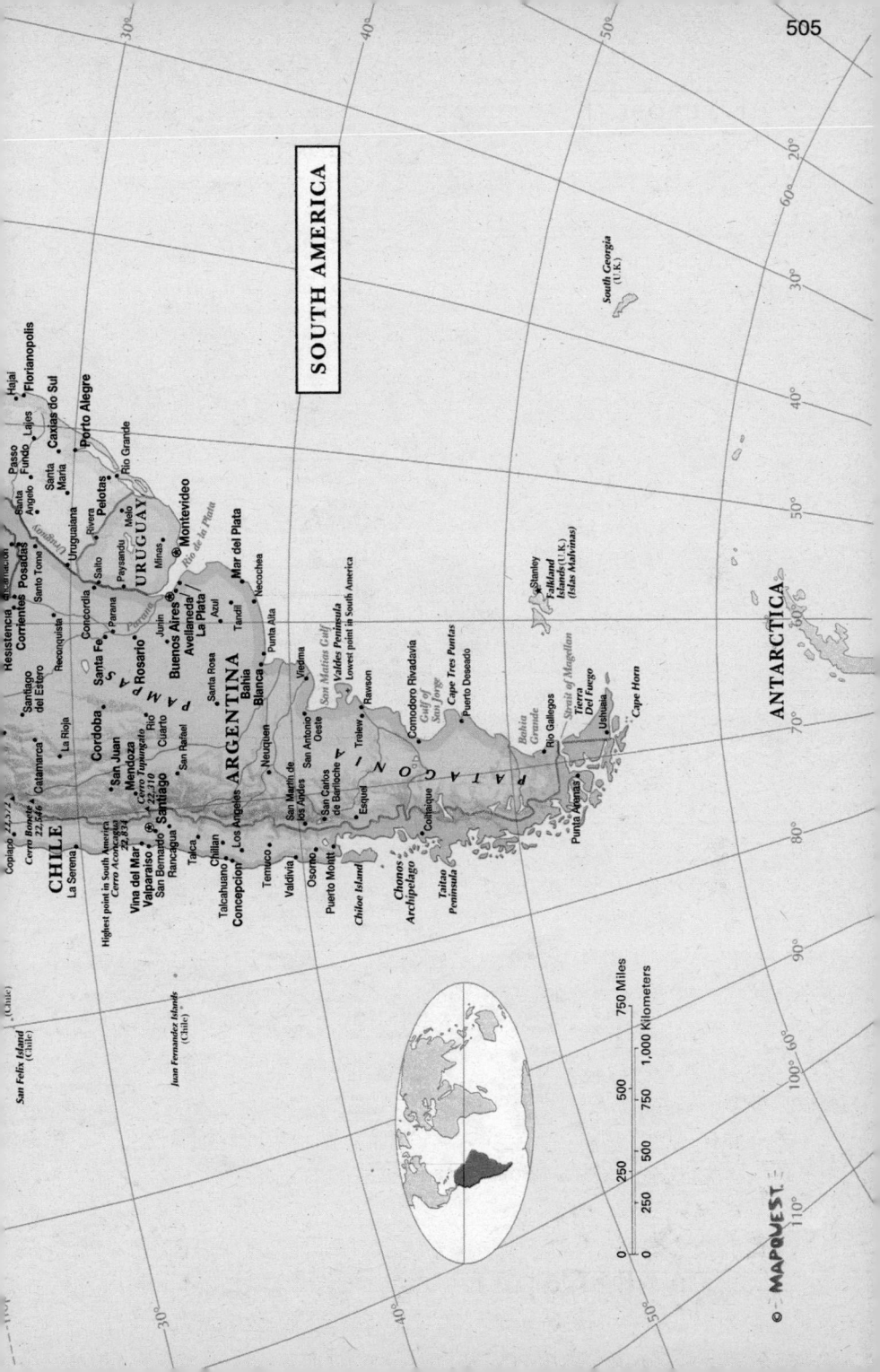

505

SOUTH AMERICA

CHILE
La Serena
Highest point in South America
Cerro Aconcagua 22,834
Viña del Mar
Valparaíso
San Bernardo Santiago
Rancagua
Talca
Chillán
Talcahuano
Concepción
Los Angeles
Temuco
Valdivia
Osorno
Puerto Montt
Chiloe Island
Chonos
Archipelago
Taitao
Peninsula

Copiapó 22,572
Cerro Bonete 22,546
Catamarca
La Rioja
Córdoba
San Juan
Cerro Tupungato 22,310
Mendoza
Rio Cuarto
San Rafael

ARGENTINA
Santiago
del Estero
Santa Fe
Rosario
Junín
Buenos Aires
Avellaneda
La Plata
Santa Rosa
Azul
Tandil
Punta Alta
Bahía
Blanca
Neuquén
San Antonio
Oeste
Viedma
San Martin de
los Andes
San Carlos
de Bariloche
Esquel
Trelew
Rawson

PAMPAS

PATAGONIA

Coihaique

Comodoro Rivadavia
Puerto Deseado
Cape Tres Puntas
Gulf of
San Jorge
Bahía
Grande
Río Gallegos
Tierra
Del Fuego
Punta Arenas
Ushuaia
Cape Horn
Strait of Magellan

San Matias Gulf
Valdez Peninsula
Lowest point in South America

Hajaí
Florianópolis
Lajes
Caxias do Sul
Porto Alegre
Passo
Fundo
Santa
Maria
Rio Grande
Santo Angelo
Uruguaiana

URUGUAY
Rivera
Pelotas
Melo
Minas
Montevideo
Mar del Plata
Necochea

Concordia
Paraná
Santa Fe
Resistencia
Corrientes
Posadas
Santo Tomé
Reconquista
Encarnación

Río de la Plata

Salto
Payandú
Paysandú
Asunción

South Georgia
(U.K.)

Stanley
Falkland
Islands (U.K.)
(Islas Malvinas)

ANTARCTICA

San Félix Island
(Chile)

Juan Fernandez Islands
(Chile)

750 Miles
1,000 Kilometers
500
750
250
500
0
250
0

© MAPQUEST

506

EUROPE

GREENLAND
(KALAALLIT NUNAAT)
(Denmark)

Isafjordhur

Akureyri

Keflavik   ICELAND
Reykjavik

Seydhisfjordhur

Arctic Circle

Bodo

Norwegian Sea

Namsos

Torshavn   Faroe
Islands
(Den.)

Molde

Trondheim

Alesund

NORWAY   SWED

Shetland
Islands
(U.K.)

Bergen

Os

Sur

Orkney
Islands

Haugesund   Oslo

Stavanger

Drammen   Karlstad

Skien

Upp

Thurso

Hebrides

Inverness

B

Stockh

ATLANTIC
OCEAN

Scotland

Glasgow

Aberdeen

Dundee

Ayr   Edinburgh

Kristiansand

Vattern

Orebro

Narrkoping

Jonkop

Vattern

Goteborg

North

Alborg

Vaxjo

Halmstad

Londonderry
Northern
Ireland   Belfast

Galway   IRELAND   Dublin

Limerick

Cork

Waterford

UNITED
KINGDOM

Liverpool

Manchester

Newcastle

Leeds

Kingston upon Hull

Sheffield

Sea

Jutland

Arhus

Esbjerg   Copenhagen

Odense

DENMARK

Helsingborg

Malmo

Borr
(Der

Wales   Swansea

Cardiff

Bristol

Birmingham

Coventry

England

Norwich

Groningen

Kiel

Lubeck   Rostock

Hamburg

NORTHE

Szczec

Bydg

Amsterdam

NETHERLANDS

Bremen

Plymouth

Land's End

Portsmouth

London

Dover

Thames

The Hague
Rotterdam
Antwerp   Essen

Hannover
Bielefeld

Madgeburg

Berlin

Oder

Channel Is.
(U.K.)

English Channel

Le Havre

Brest

Caen

Rouen

Lille

Brussels

BELGIUM   Liege

Bonn

Cologne

GERMANY

Wiesbaden

Kassel   Erfurt

Leipzig

Chemnitz   Dresden

Liberec

PO

W

LUXEMBOURG
Luxembourg

Frankfurt

Mannheim

Pizen

Prague

O

Rennes

Paris

Le Mans

Seine

Orleans

Saarbrucken

CZECH RE

Brno

Nancy

Strasbourg

Stuttgart

Nurnberg

Regensburg

Dijon

Nantes

Loire

Tours

Limoges

FRANCE

Augsburg

Munich

Linz

Donau

Salzburg

Innsbruck

Vienna

Basel

Zurich

Bern

SWITZERLAND   LIECHTENSTEIN

A

L

P

AUSTRIA

Graz

Clermont-Ferrand   Lyon

Geneva

Mt. Blanc
15,771

Matterhorn
14,690

Bergamo

Udine

SLOVENIA

Klagenfurt

Bay
of
Biscay

A Coruña

Vigo

Gijon

Santander

Donostia-
San Sebastian

Bordeaux

Saint-Etienne

Grenoble

Milan

Verona

Trieste   Ljubljana

Rijeka

CRO.

DINARI

Toring

Braga   Leon

Porto

Bilbao

Pamplona

Valladolid

PYRENEES

Picu de
Aneto
11,168

Toulouse

Montpellier

Marseille

Avignon

Nice

Genoa

Parma

Venice

Bologna

Adriatic

Coimbra

IBERIAN

Salamanca

Duero

ANDORRA

Toulon

MONACO

Florence

Pisa

San
Marino

Ancona

Split

Dubr

PORTUGAL

Lisbon

Madrid

Tagus

Zaragoza

Corsica
(Fr.)

Elba

Perugia

APENNINES

Setubal

Badajoz

Toledo

Barcelona

Tarragona

Ajaccio

VATICAN CITY

Rome

ITALY

Foggia

Cape
St. Vincent

SPAIN

PENINSULA

Cordoba

Seville

Valencia

Castellon de la Plana

Majorca

Palma de
Mallorca

Minorca

Balearic
Is.
(Sp.)

Sassari

Sardinia
(It.)

Naples

Vesuvius
202

Salerno

Cadiz

Malaga

Granada

Murcia

Alicante

Cartagena

Almeria

Strait of
Gibraltar

Gibraltar
(U.K.)

Cagliari

Tyrrhenian

Sea

Palermo

Messina

Etna
11,053
Sicily
(It.)

Reggio di
Calabria

Catania

Mediterranean

S

AFRICA

0   250   500 Miles

0   250   500   750 Kilometers

MALTA   Valletta

Barents Sea

Novaya Zemlya

North Cape

Vardo

ASIA

Naryan-Mar

•Murmansk

Apatity **KOLA PENINSULA**

Pechora

Ukhta.

R U S S I A

Ivalo

LAPLAND

•Rovaniemi

White Sea

Arkhangelsk

Belomorsk

Dvina

Syktyvkar

Berezniki

URAL

Kotlas

Perm

Oulu

FINLAND

Kuopio

Jyvaskyla

Vaasa

Lake Onega

Petrozavodsk

Kirov•

Izhevsk•

Ufa•

Sterlitzmak•

Orsk

Tampere

Lahti

Kotka

Lake Ladoga

Cherepovets•

•Vologda

Naberezhnye Chelny

M O U N T A I N S

Helsinki

St. Petersburg

Rybinsk•

Yaroslavl•

Kostroma

Yoshkar Ola

Kazan

Cheboksary

Kama

Tallinn

Velikiy Novgorod

Ivanovo•

Nizhniy Novgorod

ESTONIA

Tartu•

Pskov•

Tver•

Vladimir

Ulyanovsk•

Tolyatti

Orenburg

Riga

LATVIA

Moscow

Kaluga

Ryazan•

Saransk•

Penza

Samara

Ural

Liepaja

Daugavpils

Klaipeda

LITHUANIA

Kaunas Vilnius

(RUSSIA)

aliningrad

Vitsyebsk•

Smolensk•

Orsha

P L A I N

Mahilyow•

Tula•

Tambov

Saratov•

KAZAKHSTAN

ROPEAN

Hrodna

Minsk•

Lipetsk•

Volga

Bialystok•

Babruysk•

Bryansk•

Voronezh•

Warsaw

Brest

Pinsk

Homyel•

Kursk

Belgorod

Volgograd•

Astrakhan•

Radom

BELARUS

Chernihiv

Sumy•

Kielce

Lublin

Kharkiv•

Poltava

vice

Kiev (Kyiv)

Cherkasy

Luhansk•

Don

ow

Zhytomyr

UKRAINE

Vinnytsia

Dnieper

Donetsk•

Horlivka

Caspian

Lviv•

Dnipropetrovsk

ATHIA Chernivtsi

Kryvyi Rih

Zaporizhzhia

Mariupol•

Rostov-na-Donu•

Kosice MOUNTAINS

Miskolc

MOLDOVA

Chisinau

Mykolaiv•

Sea of Azov

Stavropol•

Makhachkala

cen Y

Oradea

Iasi

Odesa

Krasnodar

Mt. Elbrus Nalchik

Grozny

Sea

Cluj-Napoca

CRIMEA PENINSULA

Simferopol•

18,510 Highest point in Europe

Vladikavkaz

skemet

ROMANIA

Galati

Brasov

Sevastopol•

CAUCASUS MTS.

Timisoara

Ploiesti

S Sad

Bucharest

Constanta

Belgrade•

Craiova

Danube

RBIA & TENEGRO

Ruse

Black Sea

Nis•

Pleven

Varna

BULGARIA

Stara Zagora

Burgas

Sofia

ca

BALKAN

Skopje

Plovdiv

der

F.Y.R. MAC.

Istanbul•

PENINSULA

Kavala

TURKEY

BANIA

Thessaloniki

Olympus 9,570

Dardanelles

ASIA

Larisa

Aegean Sea

Ioannina

Volos

GREECE

Patras

Athens

Corinth

Peloponnese

Kalamata

Sparta

Cyclades

Rhodes (Gr.)

Sea of Crete

Hania Crete (Gr.) Iraklion

© MAPQUEST

ARCTIC OCEAN

EUROPE

RUSSIA As

WEST
SIBERIAN
PLAIN

KAZAKHSTAN

TURKEY

GEORGIA

ARMENIA
AZERBAIJAN

SYRIA

LEBANON
ISRAEL
JORDAN

IRAQ

Baghdad

AFRICA

IRAN

AFGHANISTAN

PAKISTAN

SAUDI
ARABIA

BAHRAIN
QATAR
UNITED ARAB
EMIRATES

OMAN

RUB AL KHALI

YEMEN

HIMALAYAS

NEPAL

INDIA

DECCAN
PLATEAU

Arabian
Sea

Bay of
Bengal

SRI LANKA

MALDIVES

Equator

INDIAN
OCEAN

TURKEY

CYPRUS

SYRIA

LEBANON

ISRAEL

JORDAN

SAUDI
ARABIA

IRAQ

EGYPT

The West Bank
and Gaza currently
occupied by Israel.
Permanent status
to be determined.

0   250 Miles

0   250 Kilometers

© MapQuest

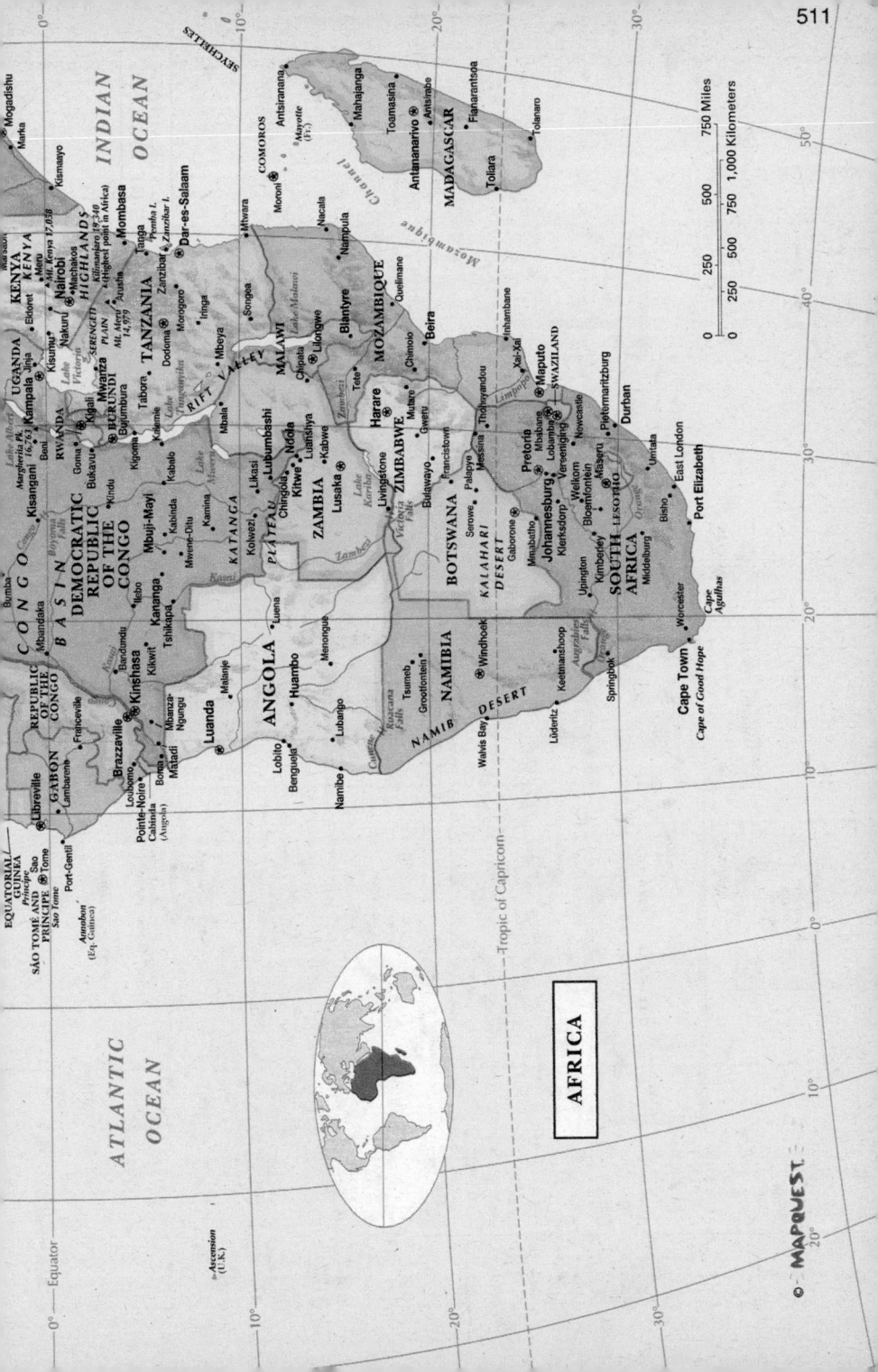

AFRICA

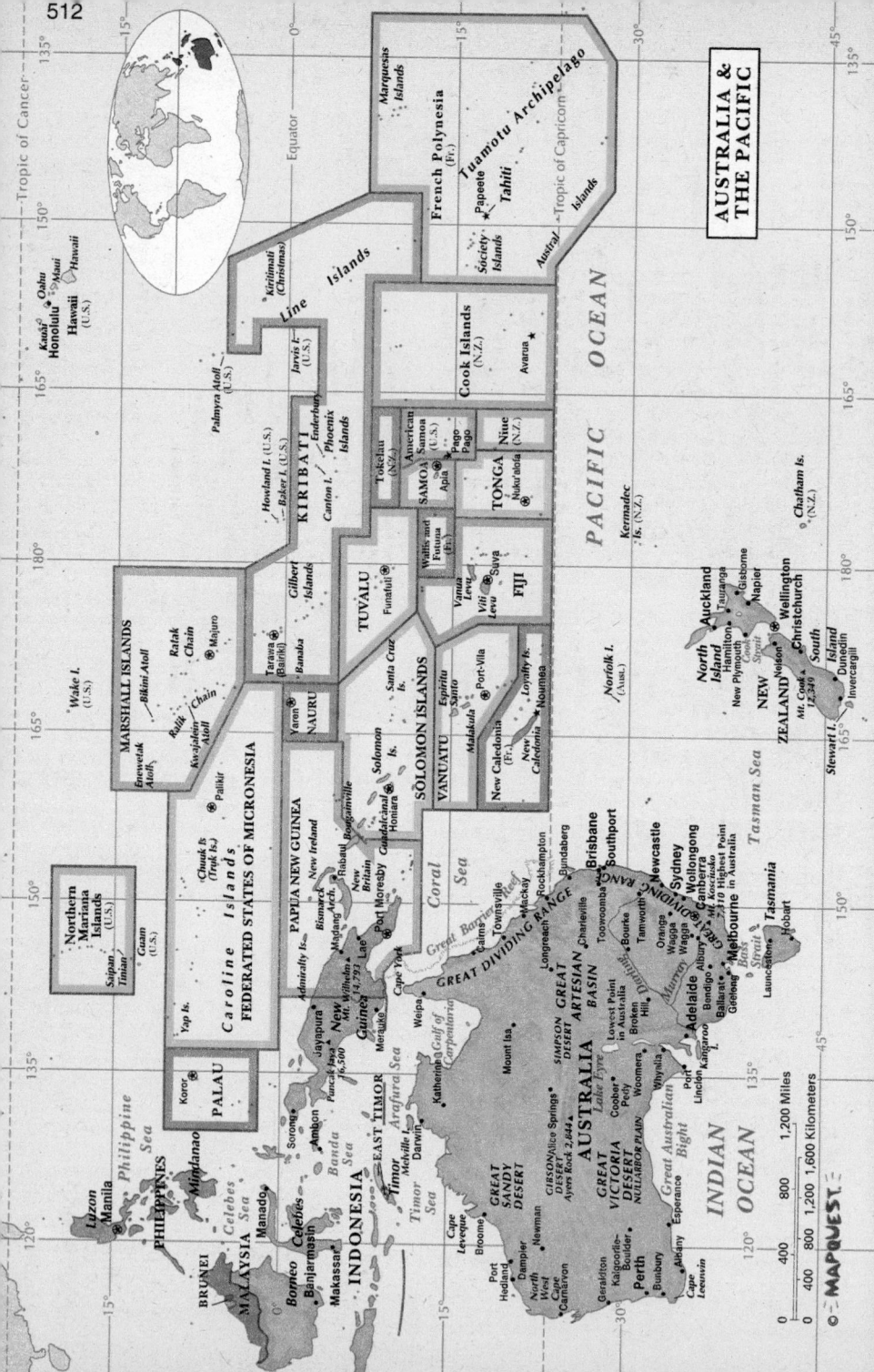

AUSTRALIA &
THE PACIFIC

UNITED STATES FACTS

Superlative U.S. Statistics[1]

Source: U.S. Geological Survey, Dept. of the Interior; U.S. Bureau of the Census, Dept. of Commerce; World Almanac research

Area for 50 states and Washington, DC . **TOTAL**		3,794,085 sq mi[4]
	Land, 3,537,440 sq mi; Water, 256,648 sq mi	
Largest state	Alaska	663,267 sq mi[1]
Smallest state	Rhode Island	1,545 sq mi
Largest county (excluding Alaska)	San Bernardino County, CA	20,105 sq mi
Smallest county	Arlington County, VA	26 sq mi
Largest incorporated city	Sitka, AK	4,812 sq mi
Northernmost city	Barrow, AK	71° 17′ N
Northernmost point	Point Barrow, AK	71° 23′ N
Southernmost city	Hilo, HI	19° 44′ N
Southernmost settlement	Naalehu, HI	19° 03′ N
Southernmost point	Ka Lae (South Cape), Island of Hawaii	18° 55′ N (155°41′ W)
Easternmost city	Eastport, ME	66° 59′05′′ W
Easternmost settlement[2]	Amchitka Isl., AK	179° 15′ E
Easternmost point[2]	Pochnoi Point, on Semisopochnoi Isl., AK	179° 46′ E
Westernmost city	Atka, AK	174° 12′ W
Westernmost settlement	Adak Station, AK	176° 39′ W
Westernmost point	Amatignak Isl., AK	179° 06′ W
Highest settlement	Climax, CO	11,360 ft
Lowest settlement	Calipatria, CA	−184 ft
Highest point on Atlantic coast	Cadillac Mountain, Mount Desert Isl., ME	1,530 ft
Oldest national park	Yellowstone National Park (1872), WY, MT, ID	2,219,791 acres
Largest national park	Wrangell-St. Elias, AK	8,323,148 acres
Highest waterfall	Yosemite Falls—Total in 3 sections	2,425 ft
	(consisting of Upper Yosemite Fall, 1,430 ft; Cascades, 675 ft; Lower Yosemite Fall, 320 ft)	
Longest river system	Mississippi-Missouri-Red Rock	3,710 mi
Highest mountain	Mount McKinley, AK	20,320 ft
Lowest point	Death Valley, CA	−282 ft
Deepest lake	Crater Lake, OR	1,932 ft
Rainiest spot	Mount Waialeale, HI	Annual avg rainfall 460 in
Largest canyon	Grand Canyon, Colorado River, AZ	277 mi long, 600 ft to 18 mi wide, 1 mi deep
Deepest gorge	Hells Canyon, Snake River, OR-ID	7,900 ft
Largest dam	New Cornelia Tailings, Ten Mile Wash, AZ[3]	274,026,000 cu yds material used
Tallest building	Sears Tower, Chicago, IL	1,450 ft
Largest building	Boeing Manufacturing Plant, Everett, WA	472,000,000 cu ft; covers 98 acres
Largest Office Building	Pentagon, Arlington, VA	77,025,000 cu ft; covers 29 acres
Tallest structure	TV tower, Blanchard, ND	2,063 ft
Longest bridge span	Verrazano-Narrows, NY	4,260 ft
Highest bridge	Royal Gorge, CO	1,053 ft above water
Deepest well	Gas well, Washita County, OK	31,441 ft

The 48 Contiguous States

Area for 48 states and Washington, DC	**TOTAL**	3,119,887 sq mi[4]
	Land, 2,959,066 sq mi; Water, 160,824 sq mi	
Largest state	Texas	268,581 sq mi
Northernmost city	Bellingham, WA	48°46′ N
Northernmost settlement	Angle Inlet, MN	49°21′ N
Northernmost point	Northwest Angle, MN	49°23′ N
Southernmost city	Key West, FL	24°33′ N
Southernmost mainland city	Florida City, FL	25°27′ N
Southernmost point	Key West, FL	24°33′ N
Easternmost settlement	Lubec, ME	66°58′49 W
Easternmost point	West Quoddy Head, ME	66°57′W
Westernmost town	La Push, WA	124°38′ W
Westernmost point	Cape Alava, WA	124°44′ W
Highest mountain	Mount Whitney, CA	14,494 ft

(1) All areas are total area, including water, unless otherwise noted. (2) Alaska's Aleutian Islands extend into the eastern hemisphere and thus technically contain the easternmost point and settlement in the U.S. (3) The New Cornelia Tailings Dam is a privately owned industrial dam composed of tailings, remnants of a mining process. (4) Does not add, because of rounding.

Geodetic Datum of North America

In July 1986, the National Oceanic and Atmospheric Administration's National Geodetic Survey (NGS), in cooperation with Canada and Mexico, completed readjustment and redefinition of the system of latitudes and longitudes. The resulting North American Datum of 1983 (NAD 83) replaces the North American Datum of 1927, as well as local reference systems for Hawaii and for Puerto Rico and the Virgin Islands. The change was prompted by Hawaii's increased need for accurate coordinate information. To facilitate use of satellite surveying and navigation systems, such as the Global Positioning System (GPS), the new datum was redefined using the Geodetic Reference System 1980 as the reference ellipsoid because this model more closely approximates the true size and shape of the earth. In addition, the origin of the coordinate system is referenced to the mass center of the earth to coincide with the orbital orientation of the GPS satellites. Positional changes resulting from the datum redefinition can reach 330 ft in the continental U.S., Canada, and Mexico. Changes that exceed 660 ft can be expected in Alaska, Puerto Rico, and the Virgin Islands. Hawaii's coordinates changed about 1,300 ft.

Additional Statistical Information About the U.S.

The annual *Statistical Abstract of the United States*, published by U.S. Dept. of Commerce, contains additional data. For information, write Supt. of Documents, Government Printing Office, PO Box 371954, Pittsburgh, PA 15250-7954, or call (202) 512-1800. For electronic products, write U.S. Dept. of Commerce, U.S. Census Bureau, PO Box 277943, Atlanta, GA 30384-7943, or call (301) 763-INFO (4636). Parts of *The Statistical Abstract* can be viewed on the Internet at www.census.gov/statab/www

► **IT'S A FACT:** At 4.2 million square feet, the Mall of America in Bloomington, MN, is the largest entertainment and retail complex in the U.S. With over 500 stores and 50 restaurants, the mall attracts 600,000-900,000 people a week. Because of the huge number of visitors and miles of lights, there is no need to heat the mall—even in the cold Minnesota winter!

Highest and Lowest Altitudes in U.S. States and Territories

Source: U.S. Geological Survey, Dept. of the Interior

(Minus sign means below sea level.)

	HIGHEST POINT			LOWEST POINT		
	Name	County	Elev. (ft)	Name	County	Elev. (ft)
Alabama	Cheaha Mountain	Cleburne	2,405	Gulf of Mexico		Sea level
Alaska	Mount McKinley	Denali	20,320	Pacific Ocean		Sea level
Arizona	Humphreys Peak	Coconino	12,633	Colorado R	Yuma	70
Arkansas	Magazine Mountain	Logan	2,753	Ouachita R	Ashley-Union	55
California	Mount Whitney	Inyo-Tulare	14,494	Death Valley	Inyo	−282
Colorado	Mount Elbert	Lake	14,433	Arikaree R	Yuma	3,315
Connecticut	Mount Frissell	Litchfield	2,380	Long Island Sound		Sea level
Delaware	On Ebright Road	New Castle	448	Atlantic Ocean		Sea level
Dist. of Columbia	Tenleytown	N W part	410	Potomac R		1
Florida	Sec. 30, T6N, R20W[1]	Walton	345	Atlantic Ocean		Sea level
Georgia	Brasstown Bald	Towns-Union	4,784	Atlantic Ocean		Sea level
Guam	Mount Lamlam	Agat District	1,332	Pacific Ocean		Sea level
Hawaii	Mauna Kea	Hawaii	13,796	Pacific Ocean		Sea level
Idaho	Borah Peak	Custer	12,662	Snake R	Nez Perce	710
Illinois	Charles Mound	Jo Daviess	1,235	Mississippi R	Alexander	279
Indiana	Franklin Township	Wayne	1,257	Ohio R	Posey	320
Iowa	Sec. 29, T100N, R41W[1]	Osceola	1,670	Mississippi R	Lee	480
Kansas	Mount Sunflower	Wallace	4,039	Verdigris R	Montgomery	679
Kentucky	Black Mountain	Harlan	4,145	Mississippi R	Fulton	257
Louisiana	Driskill Mountain	Bienville	535	New Orleans	Orleans	−8
Maine	Mount Katahdin	Piscataquis	5,267	Atlantic Ocean		Sea level
Maryland	Backbone Mountain[2]	Garrett	3,360	Atlantic Ocean		Sea level
Massachusetts	Mount Greylock	Berkshire	3,487	Atlantic Ocean		Sea level
Michigan	Mount Arvon	Baraga	1,979	Lake Erie	Monroe	571
Minnesota	Eagle Mountain	Cook	2,301	Lake Superior		602
Mississippi	Woodall Mountain	Tishomingo	806	Gulf of Mexico		Sea level
Missouri	Taum Sauk Mt.	Iron	1,772	St. Francis R	Dunklin	230
Montana	Granite Peak	Park	12,799	Kootenai R	Lincoln	1,800
Nebraska	Johnson Township	Kimball	5,424	Missouri R	Richardson	840
Nevada	Boundary Peak	Esmeralda	13,143	Colorado R	Clark	479
New Hampshire	Mt. Washington	Coos	6,288	Atlantic Ocean		Sea level
New Jersey	High Point	Sussex	1,803	Atlantic Ocean		Sea level
New Mexico	Wheeler Peak	Taos	13,161	Red Bluff Res.	Eddy	2,842
New York	Mount Marcy	Essex	5,344	Atlantic Ocean		Sea level
North Carolina	Mount Mitchell	Yancey	6,684	Atlantic Ocean		Sea level
North Dakota	White Butte	Slope	3,506	Red R	Pembina	750
Ohio	Campbell Hill	Logan	1,549	Ohio R	Hamilton	455
Oklahoma	Black Mesa	Cimarron	4,973	Little R	McCurtain	289
Oregon	Mount Hood	Clackamas-Hood R.	11,239	Pacific Ocean		Sea level
Pennsylvania	Mt. Davis	Somerset	3,213	Delaware R	Delaware	Sea level
Puerto Rico	Cerro de Punta	Ponce District	4,390	Atlantic Ocean		Sea level
Rhode Island	Jerimoth Hill	Providence	812	Atlantic Ocean		Sea level
Samoa	Lata Mountain	Tau Island	3,160	Pacific Ocean		Sea level
South Carolina	Sassafras Mountain	Pickens	3,560	Atlantic Ocean		Sea level
South Dakota	Harney Peak	Pennington	7,242	Big Stone Lake	Roberts	966
Tennessee	Clingmans Dome	Sevier	6,643	Mississippi R	Shelby	178
Texas	Guadalupe Peak	Culberson	8,749	Gulf of Mexico		Sea level
Utah	Kings Peak	Duchesne	13,528	Beaver Dam Wash	Washington	2,000
Vermont	Mount Mansfield	Lamoille	4,393	Lake Champlain		95
Virginia	Mount Rogers	Grayson-Smyth	5,729	Atlantic Ocean		Sea level
Virgin Islands	Crown Mountain	St. Thomas Island	1,556	Atlantic Ocean		Sea level
Washington	Mount Rainier West	Pierce	14,410	Pacific Ocean		Sea level
West Virginia	Spruce Knob	Pendleton	4,861	Potomac R	Jefferson	240
Wisconsin	Timms Hill	Price	1,951	Lake Michigan		579
Wyoming	Gannett Peak	Fremont	13,804	Belle Fourche R	Crook	3,099

(1) Sec.=section; T=township; R=range; N=north; W=west. (2) At the MD-WV border.

U.S. Coastline by States

Source: National Oceanic and Atmospheric Administration, U.S. Dept. of Commerce

(in statute miles)

	Coastline[1]	Shoreline[2]		Coastline[1]	Shoreline[2]
ATLANTIC COAST	2,069	28,673	**GULF COAST**	1,631	17,141
Connecticut	0	618	Alabama	53	607
Delaware	28	381	Florida	770	5,095
Florida	580	3,331	Louisiana	397	7,721
Georgia	100	2,344	Mississippi	44	359
Maine	228	3,478	Texas	367	3,359
Maryland	31	3,190			
Massachusetts	192	1,519	**PACIFIC COAST**	7,623	40,298
New Hampshire	13	131	Alaska	5,580	31,383
New Jersey	130	1,792	California	840	3,427
New York	127	1,850	Hawaii	750	1,052
North Carolina	301	3,375	Oregon	296	1,410
Pennsylvania	0	89	Washington	157	3,026
Rhode Island	40	384			
South Carolina	187	2,876	**ARCTIC COAST**	1,060	2,521
Virginia	112	3,315	**UNITED STATES**	12,383	88,633

(1) Figures are lengths of general outline of seacoast. Measurements were made with a unit measure of 30 minutes of latitude on charts as near the scale of 1:1,200,000 as possible. Coastline of sounds and bays is included to a point where they narrow to width of unit measure, and includes the distance across at such point. (2) Figures obtained in 1939-40 with a recording instrument on the largest-scale charts and maps then available. Shoreline of outer coast, offshore islands, sounds, bays, rivers, and creeks is included to the head of tidewater or to a point where tidal waters narrow to a width of 100 ft.

Key Data for the 50 States

The 13 colonies that declared independence from Great Britain and fought the War of Independence (American Revolution) became the 13 original states. They were (in the order in which they ratified the Constitution): Delaware, Pennsylvania, New Jersey, Georgia, Connecticut, Massachusetts, Maryland, South Carolina, New Hampshire, Virginia, New York, North Carolina, and Rhode Island.

State	Settled[1]	Capital	Entered Union Date	Entered Union Order	Extent in miles (approx. mean) Long	Extent in miles (approx. mean) Wide	Area in sq mi Land	Area in sq mi Water	Area in sq mi Total	Rank in area[2]
AL	1702	Montgomery	Dec. 14, 1819	22	330	190	50,744	1,675	52,419	30
AK	1784	Juneau	Jan. 3, 1959	49	1,480[3]	810	571,951	91,316	663,267	1
AZ	1776	Phoenix	Feb. 14, 1912	48	400	310	113,635	364	113,998	6
AR	1686	Little Rock	June 15, 1836	25	260	240	52,068	1,110	53,179	29
CA	1769	Sacramento	Sept. 9, 1850	31	770	250	155,959	7,736	163,696	3
CO	1858	Denver	Aug. 1, 1876	38	380	280	103,718	376	104,094	8
CT	1634	Hartford	Jan. 9, 1788	5	110	70	4,845	699	5,543	48
DE	1638	Dover	Dec. 7, 1787	1	100	30	1,954	536	2,489	49
DC	NA	NA	NA	NA	. . .	. . .	61	7	68	51
FL	1565	Tallahassee	Mar. 3, 1845	27	500	160	53,927	11,828	65,755	22
GA	1733	Atlanta	Jan. 2, 1788	4	300	230	57,906	1,519	59,425	24
HI	1820	Honolulu	Aug. 21, 1959	50	. . .	. . .	6,423	4,508	10,931	43
ID	1842	Boise	July 3, 1890	43	570	300	82,747	823	83,570	14
IL	1720	Springfield	Dec. 3, 1818	21	390	210	55,584	2,331	57,914	25
IN	1733	Indianapolis	Dec. 11, 1816	19	270	140	35,867	551	36,418	38
IA	1788	Des Moines	Dec. 28, 1846	29	310	200	55,869	402	56,272	26
KS	1727	Topeka	Jan. 29, 1861	34	400	210	81,815	462	82,277	15
KY	1774	Frankfort	June 1, 1792	15	380	140	39,728	681	40,409	37
LA	1699	Baton Rouge	Apr. 30, 1812	18	380	130	43,562	8,278	51,840	31
ME	1624	Augusta	Mar. 15, 1820	23	320	190	30,862	4,523	35,385	39
MD	1634	Annapolis	Apr. 28, 1788	7	250	90	9,774	2,633	12,407	42
MA	1620	Boston	Feb. 6, 1788	6	190	50	7,840	2,715	10,555	44
MI	1668	Lansing	Jan. 26, 1837	26	490	240	56,804	39,912	96,716	11
MN	1805	St. Paul	May 11, 1858	32	400	250	79,610	7,329	86,939	12
MS	1699	Jackson	Dec. 10, 1817	20	340	170	46,907	1,523	48,430	32
MO	1735	Jefferson City	Aug. 10, 1821	24	300	240	68,886	818	69,704	21
MT	1809	Helena	Nov. 8, 1889	41	630	280	145,552	1,490	147,042	4
NE	1823	Lincoln	Mar. 1, 1867	37	430	210	76,872	481	77,354	16
NV	1849	Carson City	Oct. 31, 1864	36	490	320	109,826	735	110,561	7
NH	1623	Concord	June 21, 1788	9	190	70	8,968	382	9,350	46
NJ	1660	Trenton	Dec. 18, 1787	3	150	70	7,417	1,304	8,721	47
NM	1610	Santa Fe	Jan. 6, 1912	47	370	343	121,356	234	121,589	5
NY	1614	Albany	July 26, 1788	11	330	283	47,214	7,342	54,556	27
NC	1660	Raleigh	Nov. 21, 1789	12	500	150	48,711	5,108	53,819	28
ND	1812	Bismarck	Nov. 2, 1889	39	340	211	68,976	1,724	70,700	19
OH	1788	Columbus	Mar. 1, 1803	17	220	220	40,948	3,877	44,825	34
OK	1889	Oklahoma City	Nov. 16, 1907	46	400	220	68,667	1,231	69,898	20
OR	1811	Salem	Feb. 14, 1859	33	360	261	95,997	2,384	98,381	9
PA	1682	Harrisburg	Dec. 12, 1787	2	283	160	44,817	1,239	46,055	33
RI	1636	Providence	May 29, 1790	13	40	30	1,045	500	1,545	50
SC	1670	Columbia	May 23, 1788	8	260	200	30,109	911	32,020	40
SD	1859	Pierre	Nov. 2, 1889	40	380	210	75,885	1,232	77,116	17
TN	1769	Nashville	June 1, 1796	16	440	120	41,217	926	42,143	36
TX	1682	Austin	Dec. 29, 1845	28	790	660	261,797	6,784	268,581	2
UT	1847	Salt Lake City	Jan. 4, 1896	45	350	270	82,144	2,755	84,899	13
VT	1724	Montpelier	Mar. 4, 1791	14	160	80	9,250	365	9,614	45
VA	1607	Richmond	June 25, 1788	10	430	200	39,594	3,180	42,774	35
WA	1811	Olympia	Nov. 11, 1889	42	360	240	66,544	4,756	71,300	18
WV	1727	Charleston	June 20, 1863	35	240	130	24,078	152	24,230	41
WI	1766	Madison	May 29, 1848	30	310	260	54,310	11,188	65,498	23
WY	1834	Cheyenne	July 10, 1890	44	360	280	97,100	713	97,814	10

Note: Land and water areas may not add to totals because of rounding. NA = Not applicable. (1) First permanent settlement by Europeans. (2) Rank is based on total area as shown. (3) Aleutian Islands and Alexander Archipelago not included.

The Continental Divide of the U.S.

The Continental Divide of the U.S., also known as the Great Divide, is located at the watershed created by the mountain ranges, or tablelands, of the Rocky Mountains. This watershed separates the waters that drain easterly into the Atlantic Ocean and its marginal seas, such as the Gulf of Mexico, from those waters that drain westerly into the Pacific Ocean. The majority of easterly flowing water in the U.S. drains into the Gulf of Mexico before reaching the Atlantic Ocean. The majority of westerly flowing water, before reaching the Pacific Ocean, drains either through the Columbia River or through the Colorado River, which flows into the Gulf of California before reaching the Pacific Ocean.

The location and route of the Continental Divide across the U.S. can briefly be described as follows:

Beginning at point of crossing the U.S.-Mexican boundary, near long. 108° 45´ W, the Divide, in a northerly direction, crosses New Mexico along the W edge of the Rio Grande drainage basin, entering Colorado near long. 106° 41´ W.

From there by a very irregular route north across Colorado along the W summits of the Rio Grande and of the Ar-

kansas, the South Platte, and the North Platte river basins, and across Rocky Mountain National Park, entering Wyoming near long. 106° 52´ W.

From there in a northwesterly direction, forming the W rims of the North Platte, the Big Horn, and the Yellowstone river basins, crossing the SW portion of Yellowstone National Park.

From there in a westerly and then a northerly direction forming the common boundary of Idaho and Montana, to a point on said boundary near long. 114° 00´ W.

From there northeasterly and northwesterly through Montana and the Glacier National Park, entering Canada near long. 114° 04´ W.

WORLD ALMANAC QUICK QUIZ

Which of the following states was named for an imaginary place?

(a) California   (b) Colorado
(c) Alaska   (d) Nevada

For the answer look in this chapter, or see page 1008.

Chronological List of Territories, With State Admissions to Union

Source: National Archives and Records Service

Name of territory	Date of act creating territory	When act took effect	Admission as state	Yrs. terr.
Northwest Territory[1]	July 13, 1787	No fixed date	Mar. 1, 1803[2]	16
Territory southwest of River Ohio	May 26, 1790	No fixed date	June 1, 1796[3]	6
Mississippi	Apr. 7, 1798	When president acted	Dec. 10, 1817	19
Indiana	May 7, 1800	July 4, 1800	Dec. 11, 1816	16
Orleans	Mar. 26, 1804	Oct. 1, 1804	Apr. 30, 1812[4]	7
Michigan	Jan. 11, 1805	June 30, 1805	Jan. 26, 1837	31
Louisiana-Missouri[5]	Mar. 3, 1805	July 4, 1805	Aug. 10, 1821	16
Illinois	Feb. 3, 1809	Mar. 1, 1809	Dec. 3, 1818	9
Alabama	Mar. 3, 1817	When MS became a state	Dec. 14, 1819	2
Arkansas	Mar. 2, 1819	July 4, 1819	June 15, 1836	17
Florida	Mar. 30, 1822	No fixed date	Mar. 3, 1845	23
Wisconsin	Apr. 20, 1836	July 3, 1836	May 29, 1848	12
Iowa	June 12, 1838	July 3, 1838	Dec. 28, 1846	8
Oregon	Aug. 14, 1848	Date of act	Feb. 14, 1859	10
Minnesota	Mar. 3, 1849	Date of act	May 11, 1858	9
New Mexico	Sept. 9, 1850	On president's proclamation	Jan. 6, 1912	61
Utah	Sept. 9, 1850	Date of act	Jan. 4, 1896	46
Washington	Mar. 2, 1853	Date of act	Nov. 11, 1889	36
Nebraska	May 30, 1854	Date of act	Mar. 1, 1867	12
Kansas	May 30, 1854	Date of act	Jan. 29, 1861	6
Colorado	Feb. 28, 1861	Date of act	Aug. 1, 1876	15
Nevada	Mar. 2, 1861	Date of act	Oct. 31, 1864	3
Dakota	Mar. 2, 1861	Date of act	Nov. 2, 1889	28
Arizona	Feb. 24, 1863	Date of act	Feb. 14, 1912	49
Idaho	Mar. 3, 1863	Date of act	July 3, 1890	27
Montana	May 26, 1864	Date of act	Nov. 8, 1889	25
Wyoming	July 25, 1868	When officers were qualified	July 10, 1890	22
Alaska[6]	May 17, 1884	No fixed date	Jan. 3, 1959	75
Oklahoma	May 2, 1890	Date of act	Nov. 16, 1907	17
Hawaii	Apr. 30, 1900	June 14, 1900	Aug. 21, 1959	59

(1) Included what is now Ohio, Indiana, Illinois, Michigan, Wisconsin, E Minnesota. (2) Whole territory admitted as the state of Ohio. (3) Admitted as the state of Tennessee. (4) Admitted as the state of Louisiana. (5) The act creating Missouri Territory (June 4, 1812) became effective Dec. 7, 1812. (6) Although the May 17, 1884, act actually constituted Alaska as a district, it was often referred to as a territory, and administered as such. The Territory of Alaska was formally organized by an act of Aug. 24, 1912.

Geographic Centers, U.S. and Each State

Source: U.S. Geological Survey, Dept. of the Interior

There is no generally accepted definition of geographic center and no uniform method for determining it. Following the U.S. Geological Survey, the geographic center of an area is defined here as the center of gravity of the surface, or that point on which the surface would balance if it were a plane of uniform thickness. All locations in the following list are approximate.

No marked or monumented point has been officially established by any government agency as the geographic center of the 50 states, the conterminous U.S. (48 states), or the North American continent. A group of private citizens erected a monument in Lebanon, KS, marking it as geographic center of the conterminous U.S., and a cairn erected in Rugby, ND, asserts that location as the center of the North American continent.

Geographic centers as reported by the U.S. Geological Survey are indicated below:

United States, including Alaska and Hawaii—W of Castle Rock, Butte County, SD; lat. 44° 58′ N, long. 103° 46′ W
Conterminous U.S. (48 states)—Near Lebanon, Smith Co., Kansas, lat. 39° 50′ N, long. 98° 35′ W
North American continent—6 mi W of Balta, Pierce County, North Dakota; lat. 48° 10′ N, long. 100° 10′ W
Alabama—Chilton, 12 mi SW of Clanton
Alaska—lat. 63° 50′ N, long. 152° W; approx. 60 mi NW of Mt. McKinley
Arizona—Yavapai, 55 mi E-SE of Prescott
Arkansas—Pulaski, 12 mi NW of Little Rock
California—Madera, 38 mi E of Madera
Colorado—Park, 30 mi NW of Pikes Peak
Connecticut—Hartford, at East Berlin
Delaware—Kent, 11 mi S of Dover
District of Columbia—Near 4th and L Sts. NW
Florida—Hernando, 12 mi N-NW of Brooksville
Georgia—Twiggs, 18 mi SE of Macon
Hawaii—lat. 20° 15′ N, long. 156° 20′ W, off Maui Is.
Idaho—Custer, SW of Challis
Illinois—Logan, 28 mi NE of Springfield
Indiana—Boone, 14 mi N-NW of Indianapolis
Iowa—Story, 5 mi NE of Ames
Kansas—Barton, 15 mi NE of Great Bend
Kentucky—Marion, 3 mi N-NW of Lebanon
Louisiana—Avoyelles, 3 mi SE of Marksville
Maine—Piscataquis, 18 mi N of Dover
Maryland—Prince George's, 4.5 mi NW of Davidsonville
Massachusetts—Worcester, N part of city
Michigan—Wexford, 5 mi N-NW of Cadillac
Minnesota—Crow Wing, 10 mi SW of Brainerd
Mississippi—Leake, 9 mi W-NW of Carthage
Missouri—Miller, 20 mi SW of Jefferson City
Montana—Fergus, 11 mi W of Lewistown
Nebraska—Custer, 10 mi NW of Broken Bow
Nevada—Lander, 26 mi SE of Austin
New Hampshire—Belknap, 3 mi E of Ashland
New Jersey—Mercer, 5 mi SE of Trenton
New Mexico—Torrance, 12 mi S-SW of Willard
New York—Madison, 12 mi S of Oneida and 26 mi SW of Utica
North Carolina—Chatham, 10 mi NW of Sanford
North Dakota—Sheridan, 5 mi SW of McClusky
Ohio—Delaware, 25 mi N-NE of Columbus
Oklahoma—Oklahoma, 8 mi N of Oklahoma City
Oregon—Crook, 25 mi S-SE of Prineville
Pennsylvania—Centre, 2.5 mi SW of Bellefonte
Rhode Island—Kent, 1 mi S-SW of Crompton
South Carolina—Richland, 13 mi SE of Columbia
South Dakota—Hughes, 8 mi NE of Pierre
Tennessee—Rutherford, 5 mi NE of Murfreesboro
Texas—McCulloch, 15 mi NE of Brady
Utah—Sanpete, 3 mi N of Manti
Vermont—Washington, 3 mi E of Roxbury
Virginia—Buckingham, 5 mi SW of Buckingham
Washington—Chelan, 10 mi W-SW of Wenatchee
West Virginia—Braxton, 4 mi E of Sutton
Wisconsin—Wood, 9 mi SE of Marshfield
Wyoming—Fremont, 58 mi E-NE of Lander

International Boundary Lines of the U.S.

The length of the N boundary of the conterminous U.S.—the U.S.-Canadian border, excluding Alaska—is 3,987 mi according to the U.S. Geological Survey, Dept. of the Interior. The length of the Alaskan-Canadian border is 1,538 mi. The U.S.-Mexican border, from the Gulf of Mexico to the Pacific Ocean, is about 1,933 mi (1963 boundary agreement).

Origins of the Names of U.S. States

Source: State officials, Smithsonian Institution, and Topographic Division, U.S. Geological Survey, Dept. of the Interior

Alabama—Indian for tribal town, later a tribe (Alabamas or Alibamons) of the Creek confederacy.

Alaska—Russian version of Aleutian (Eskimo) word, *alakshak*, for "peninsula," "great lands," or "land that is not an island."

Arizona—Spanish version of Pima Indian word for "little spring place," or Aztec *arizuma*, meaning "silver-bearing."

Arkansas—Algonquin name for the Quapaw Indians, meaning "south wind."

California—Bestowed by the Spanish conquistadors (possibly by Cortez). It was the name of an imaginary island, an earthly paradise, in *Las Serges de Esplandian*, a Spanish romance written by Montalvo in 1510. *Baja California* (Lower California, in Mexico) was first visited by Cortez in 1533. The present U.S. state was called *Alta* (Upper) *California*.

Colorado—From Spanish for "red," first applied to Colorado River.

Connecticut—From Mohican and other Algonquin words meaning "long river place."

Delaware—Named for Lord De La Warr, early governor of Virginia; first applied to river, then to Indian tribe (Lenni-Lenape), and the state.

District of Columbia—For Christopher Columbus, 1791.

Florida—Named by Ponce de Leon *Pascua Florida*, "Flowery Easter," on Easter Sunday, 1513.

Georgia—For King George II of England, by James Oglethorpe, colonial administrator, 1732.

Hawaii—Possibly derived from native word for homeland, *Hawaiki* or *Owhyhee*.

Idaho—Said to be a coined name with an invented meaning: "gem of the mountains"; originally suggested for the Pikes Peak mining territory (Colorado), then applied to the new mining territory of the Pacific Northwest. Another theory suggests *Idaho* may be a Kiowa Apache term for the Comanche.

Illinois—French for *Illini* or "land of *Illini*," Algonquin word meaning "men" or "warriors."

Indiana—Means "land of the Indians."

Iowa—Indian word variously translated as "here I rest" or "beautiful land." Named for the Iowa R., which was named for the Iowa Indians.

Kansas—Sioux word for "south wind people."

Kentucky—Indian word that is variously translated as "dark and bloody ground," "meadowland," and "land of tomorrow."

Louisiana—Part of territory called Louisiana by Sieur de La Salle for French King Louis XIV.

Maine—From Maine, ancient French province. Also: descriptive, referring to the mainland as distinct from the many coastal islands.

Maryland—For Queen Henrietta Maria, wife of Charles I of England.

Massachusetts—From Indian tribe named after "large hill place" identified by Capt. John Smith as being near Milton, MA.

Michigan—From Chippewa words, *mici gama*, meaning "great water," after the lake of the same name.

Minnesota—From Dakota Sioux word meaning "cloudy water" or "sky-tinted water" of the Minnesota River.

Mississippi—Probably Chippewa; *mici zibi*, "great river" or "gathering-in of all the waters." Also: Algonquin word, *messipi*.

Missouri—An Algonquin Indian term meaning "river of the big canoes."

Montana—Latin or Spanish for "mountainous."

Nebraska—From Omaha or Otos Indian word meaning "broad water" or "flat river," describing the Platte River.

Nevada—Spanish, meaning "snow-clad."

New Hampshire—Named, 1629, by Capt. John Mason of Plymouth Council for his home county in England.

New Jersey—The Duke of York, 1664, gave a patent to John Berkeley and Sir George Carteret to be called Nova Caesaria, or New Jersey, after England's Isle of Jersey.

New Mexico—Spaniards in Mexico applied term to land north and west of Rio Grande in the 16th century.

New York—For Duke of York and Albany, who received patent to New Netherland from his brother Charles II and sent an expedition to capture it, 1664.

North Carolina—In 1619 Charles I gave a large patent to Sir Robert Heath to be called Province of Carolana, from *Carolus*, Latin name for Charles. A new patent was granted by Charles II to Earl of Clarendon and others. Divided into North and South Carolina, 1710.

North Dakota—*Dakota* is Sioux for "friend" or "ally."

Ohio—Iroquois word for "fine or good river."

Oklahoma—Choctaw word meaning "red man," proposed by Rev. Allen Wright, Choctaw-speaking Indian.

Oregon—Origin unknown. One theory holds that the name may have been derived from that of the Wisconsin River, shown on a 1715 French map as "Ouaricon-sint."

Pennsylvania—William Penn, the Quaker who was made full proprietor of this area by King Charles II in 1681, suggested "Sylvania," or "woodland," for his tract. The king's government owed Penn's father, Admiral William Penn, 16,000 pounds, and the land was granted as partial settlement. Charles II added the "Penn" to Sylvania, against the desires of the modest proprietor, in honor of the admiral.

Puerto Rico—Spanish for "rich port."

Rhode Island—Exact origin is unknown. One theory notes that Giovanni de Verrazano recorded an island about the size of Rhodes in the Mediterranean in 1524, but others believe the state was named *Roode Eylandt* by Adriaen Block, Dutch explorer, because of its red clay.

South Carolina—See North Carolina.

South Dakota—See North Dakota.

Tennessee—*Tanasi* was the name of Cherokee villages on the Little Tennessee River. From 1784 to 1788 this was the State of Franklin, or Frankland.

Texas—Variant of word used by Caddo and other Indians meaning "friends" or "allies," and applied to them by the Spanish in eastern Texas. Also written *Texias, Tejas, Teysas*.

Utah—From a Navajo word meaning "upper," or "higher up," as applied to a Shoshone tribe called Ute. Spanish form is *Yutta*. The English is *Uta* or *Utah*. Proposed name *Deseret*, "land of honeybees," from Book of Mormon, was rejected by Congress.

Vermont—From French words *vert* (green) and *mont* (mountain). The Green Mountains were said to have been named by Samuel de Champlain. When the state was formed, 1777, Dr. Thomas Young suggested combining *vert* and *mont* into Vermont.

Virginia—Named by Sir Walter Raleigh, who fitted out the expedition of 1584, in honor of Queen Elizabeth, the Virgin Queen of England.

Washington—Named after George Washington. When the bill creating the Territory of Columbia was introduced in the 32nd Congress, the name was changed to Washington because of the existence of the District of Columbia.

West Virginia—So named when western counties of Virginia refused to secede from the U.S. in 1863.

Wisconsin—An Indian name, spelled *Ouisconsin* and *Mesconsing* by early chroniclers. Believed to mean "grassy place" in Chippewa. Congress made it *Wisconsin*.

Wyoming—From the Algonquin words for "large prairie place," "at the big plains," or "on the great plain."

Territorial Sea of the U.S.

According to a Dec. 27, 1988, proclamation by Pres. Ronald Reagan: "The territorial sea of the United States henceforth extends to 12 nautical miles from the baselines of the United States determined in accordance with international law. In accordance with international law, as reflected in the applicable provisions of the 1982 United Nations Convention on the Law of the Sea, within the territorial sea of the United States, the ships of all countries enjoy the right of innocent passage and the ships and aircraft of all countries enjoy the right of transit passage through international straits."

Major Accessions of Territory by the U.S.

Source: U.S. Dept. of the Interior; Bureau of the Census, U.S. Dept. of Commerce

Not including territories such as Panama Canal Zone and the Philippines which are no longer under U.S. jurisdiction; area figures may differ from figures for current areas given elsewhere.

	Acquisition date	Gross area (sq mi)		Acquisition date	Gross area (sq mi)		Acquisition date	Gross area (sq mi)
Territory in 1790[1]	NA	888,685	Texas	1845	390,143	Puerto Rico[2]	1899	3,435
Louisiana			Oregon Territory	1846	285,580	Guam[3]	1899	212
Purchase	1803	827,192	Mexican Cession	1848	529,017	American Samoa[4]	1900	76
Purchase of Florida	1819	58,560	Gadsden Purchase	1853	29,640	U.S. Virgin Islands	1917	133
Other areas from			Alaska	1867	586,412	Northern Mariana		
Spain	1819	13,443	Hawaii	1898	6,450	Islands[5]	1986	179

NA = Not applicable. (1) Includes that part of a drainage basin of Red River of the North, S of 49th parallel, sometimes considered part of Louisiana Purchase. (2) Ceded by Spain in 1898, ratified in 1899, and became the Commonwealth of Puerto Rico by Act of Congress on July 25, 1952. (3) Acquired in 1898; ratified 1899. (4) Acquired in 1899; ratified 1900. (5) Formerly a part of the U.S. administered Trust Territory of the Pacific Islands; became a U.S. commonwealth, Nov. 3, 1986.

Federally Owned Land, by State

Source: Office of Governmentwide Policy, General Services Administration; as of Sept. 30, 2002

State	Federal acreage[1]	Total acreage of state[2]	Percentage of federally owned acreage[1]	State	Federal acreage[1]	Total acreage of state[2]	Percentage of federally owned acreage[1]
AL	1,206,418.50	32,678,400	3.70	MT	29,238,455.40	93,271,040	31.30
AK	247,306,685.50	365,481,600	67.70	NE	1,459,511.40	49,031,680	3.00
AZ	36,408,099.50	72,688,000	50.10	NV	64,455,657.00	70,264,320	91.70
AR	4,019,495.90	33,599,360	12.00	NH	830,899.90	5,768,960	14.40
CA	47,075,073.40	100,206,720	47.00	NJ	181,685.30	4,813,440	3.80
CO	23,172,405.50	66,485,760	34.90	NM	26,518,225.90	77,766,400	34.10
CT	15,374.20	3,135,360	0.50	NY	319,932.50	30,680,960	1.00
DE	29,494.00	1,265,920	2.30	NC	3,497,642.20	31,402,880	11.10
DC	11,200.20	39,040	28.70	ND	1,342,703.70	44,452,480	3.00
FL	4,614,638.30	34,721,280	13.30	OH	458,445.50	26,222,080	1.70
GA	2,308,447.40	37,295,360	6.20	OK	1,331,301.90	44,087,680	3.00
HI	672,805.60	4,105,600	16.40	OR	30,640,289.50	61,598,720	49.70
ID	34,383,354.40	52,933,120	65.00	PA	719,800.90	28,804,480	2.50
IL	648,539.50	35,795,200	1.80	RI	5,231.80	677,120	0.80
IN	534,183.40	23,158,400	2.30	SC	1,234,523.40	19,374,080	6.40
IA	303,850.60	35,860,480	0.80	SD	2,366,754.10	48,881,920	4.80
KS	641,129.50	52,510,720	1.20	TN	1,954,235.50	26,727,680	7.30
KY	1,671,352.90	25,512,320	6.60	TX	3,215,460.40	168,217,600	1.90
LA	1,494,314.50	28,867,840	5.20	UT	35,025,327.80	52,696,960	66.50
ME	163,105.80	19,847,680	0.80	VT	450,169.50	5,936,640	7.60
MD	205,686.20	6,319,360	3.30	VA	2,549,105.20	25,496,320	10.00
MA	104,831.80	5,034,880	2.10	WA	13,156,214.50	42,693,760	30.80
MI	3,639,439.80	36,492,160	10.00	WV	1,233,548.80	15,410,560	8.00
MN	3,545,687.40	51,205,760	6.90	WI	1,986,456.50	35,011,200	5.70
MS	1,981,420.10	30,222,720	6.60	WY	31,530,863.10	62,343,040	50.60
MO	2,240,325.70	44,248,320	5.10	**TOTAL**	**674,099,756.30**	**2,271,343,360**	**29.70**

Note: Totals do not include inland water. (1) Excludes trust properties. (2) Bureau of the Census, U.S. Dept. of Commerce figures.

Special Recreation Areas Administered by the U.S. Forest Service, 2002

Source: U.S. Forest Service, Dept. of Agriculture

NHL=National Historic Landmark; NHS=National Historic Scenic Area; NM=National Monument; NP=National Preserve; NRA=National Recreation Area; NSA=National Scenic Area; NVM=National Volcanic Monument; SRA=Scenic Recreation Area

Area name	Location	Estab.	Acres	Area name	Location	Estab.	Acres
Admiralty Island NM	AK	1980	978,881	Mount Pleasant NSA	VA	1994	7,580
Allegheny NRA	PA	1984	23,063	Mount Rogers NRA	VA	1966	114,520
Arapaho NRA	CO	1978	30,690	Mount St. Helens NVM	WA	1989	112,593
Beech Creek NS & Botanic Area	OK	1988	7,500	Newberry NVM	OR	1990	54,822
Cascade Head NS (-Research)				North Cascades NSA	WA	1984	87,600
Area	OR	1974	6,630	Opal Creek SRA	OR	1996	13,000
Columbia River Gorge NSA	OR-WA	1986	63,150	Oregon Dunes NRA	OR	1972	27,212
Coosa Bald NSA	GA	1991	7,100	Pine Ridge NRA	NE	1986	6,600
Ed Jenkins NRA	GA	1991	23,166	Rattlesnake NRA	MT	1980	59,119
Flaming Gorge NRA	WY-UT	1968	189,825	Santa Rosa and San Jacinto			
Giant Sequoia NM	CA	2000	327,769	Mts. NM	CA	2000	272,000
Grand Island NRA	MI	1990	12,961	Sawtooth NRA	ID	1972	729,322
Grey Towers NHL	PA	1963	102	Smith River NRA	CA	1990	305,169
Hells Canyon NRA	ID-OR	1975	536,648	Spring Mt. NRA	NV	1993	316,000
Indian Nations NS & Wildlife Area	OK	1988	40,051	Spruce Knob-Seneca Rocks NRA	WV	1965	57,237
Jemez NRA	NM	1993	57,000	Valles Caldera NP	NM	2000	88,900
Land Between the Lakes NRA	KY-TN	1998	170,000	Whiskeytown-Shasta-			
Misty Fiords NM	AK	1980	2,293,428	Trinity NRA	CA	1965	176,367
Mono Basin NSA	CA	1984	115,600	White Rocks NRA	VT	1984	36,400
Mount Baker NRA	WA	1984	8,473	Winding Stair Mt. NRA	OK	1988	25,890

> **IT'S A FACT:** Congress established Hot Springs Reservation on Apr. 20, 1832, to protect the hot springs flowing from the southwestern slope of Arkansas' Hot Springs Mt. This makes it the oldest park in the National Park System—40 years older than Yellowstone—though it did not become a national park until 1921. The 47 springs produce a daily flow of about 1 million gallons at an average temperature of 143°F.

National Parks, Other Areas Administered by National Park Service

Dates when sites were authorized for initial protection by Congress or by presidential proclamation are given in parentheses. If different, the date the area got its current designation, or was transferred to the National Park Service, follows. Gross area in acres, as of Dec. 31, 2002, follows date(s). Over 84 mil acres of federal land are now administered by the National Park Service.

NATIONAL PARKS

Acadia, ME (1916/1929) 47,549. Includes Mount Desert Isl., half of Isle au Haut, Schoodic Peninsula on mainland. Highest elevation on Eastern seaboard.

American Samoa, AS (1988) 9,000. Features a paleotropical rain forest and a coral reef. No federal facilities.

Arches, UT (1929/1971) 76,519. Contains giant red sandstone arches and other products of erosion.

Badlands, SD (1929/1978) 242,756. Prairie with bison, bighorn, and antelope. Animal fossils 26-37 mil years old.

Big Bend, TX (1935) 801,163. Rio Grande, Chisos Mts.

Biscayne, FL (1968/1980) 172,924. Aquatic park encompassing chain of islands south of Miami.

Black Canyon of the Gunnison, CO (1933/1999) 30,045. Has a canyon 2,900 ft deep and 40 ft wide at its narrowest part.

Bryce Canyon, UT (1923/1928) 35,835. Spectacularly colorful and unusual display of erosion effects.

Canyonlands, UT (1964) 337,598. At junction of Colorado and Green rivers; extensive evidence of prehistoric Indians.

Capitol Reef, UT (1937/1971) 241,904. A 70-mi uplift of sandstone cliffs dissected by high-walled gorges.

Carlsbad Caverns, NM (1923/1930) 46,766. Largest known caverns; not yet fully explored.

Channel Islands, CA (1938/1980) 249,561. Sea lion breeding place, nesting sea birds, unique plants.

Crater Lake, OR (1902) 183,224. Extraordinary blue lake in the crater of Mt. Mazama, a volcano that erupted about 7,700 years ago; deepest U.S. lake.

Cuyahoga Valley, OH (1974/2000) 32,860. Rural landscape along Ohio and Erie Canal system between Akron and Cleveland.

Death Valley, CA-NV (1933/1994) 3,340,410. Large desert area. Includes the lowest point in the Western Hemisphere; also includes Scottys Castle.

Denali, AK (1917/1980) 4,740,912. Name changed from Mt. McKinley NP. Contains highest mountain in U.S.; wildlife.

Dry Tortugas, FL (1935/1992) 64,701. Formerly Ft. Jefferson National Monument.

Everglades, FL (1934) 1,508,492. Largest remaining subtropical wilderness in continental U.S.

Gates of the Arctic, AK (1978/1984) 7,523,898. Vast wilderness in north central region. Limited federal facilities.

Glacier, MT (1910) 1,013,572. Superb Rocky Mt. scenery, numerous glaciers and glacial lakes. Part of Waterton-Glacier Intl. Peace Park established by U.S. and Canada in 1932.

Glacier Bay, AK (1925/1986) 3,224,840. Great tidewater glaciers that move down mountainsides and break up into the sea; much wildlife.

Grand Canyon, AZ (1893/1919) 1,217,403. Most spectacular part of Colorado River's greatest canyon.

Grand Teton, WY (1929) 309,994. Most impressive part of the Teton Mts., winter feeding ground of largest American elk herd.

Great Basin, NV (1922/1986) 77,180. Includes Wheeler Pk., Lexington Arch, and Lehman Caves.

Great Smoky Mountains, NC-TN (1926/1934) 521,495. Largest Eastern mountain range, magnificent forests.

Guadalupe Mountains, TX (1966) 86,416. Extensive Permian limestone fossil reef; tremendous earth fault.

Haleakala, HI (1916/1960) 29,830. Dormant volcano on Maui with large colorful craters.

Hawaii Volcanoes, HI (1916/1961) 209,695. Contains Kilauea and Mauna Loa, active volcanoes.

Hot Springs, AR (1832/1921) 5,550. Bathhouses are furnished with thermal waters from the park's 47 hot springs; these waters are used for bathing and drinking.

Isle Royale, MI (1931) 571,790. Largest island in Lake Superior, noted for its wilderness area and wildlife.

Joshua Tree, CA (1936/1994) 784,162. Desert region includes Joshua trees, other plant and animal life.

Katmai, AK (1918/1980) 3,674,530. "Valley of Ten Thousand Smokes," scene of 1912 volcanic eruption.

Kenai Fjords, AK (1978/1980) 669,983. Abundant marine mammals, birdlife; the Harding Icefield, one of the 4 major icecaps in U.S.

Kings Canyon, CA (1890/1940) 461,901. Mountain wilderness, dominated by Kings River Canyons and High Sierra; contains giant sequoias.

Kobuk Valley, AK (1978/1980) 1,750,737. Contains geological and recreational sites. Limited federal facilities.

Lake Clark, AK (1978/1980) 2,619,733. Across Cook Inlet from Anchorage. A scenic wilderness rich in fish and wildlife. Limited federal facilities.

Lassen Volcanic, CA (1907/1916) 106,372. Contains Lassen Peak, recently active volcano, and other volcanic phenomena.

Mammoth Cave, KY (1926/1941) 52,830. 144 mi of surveyed underground passages, beautiful natural formations, river 300 ft below surface.

Mesa Verde, CO (1906) 52,122. Most notable and best preserved prehistoric cliff dwellings in the U.S.

Mount Rainier, WA (1899) 235,625. Greatest single-peak glacial system in the U.S.

North Cascades, WA (1968) 504,781. Spectacular mountainous region with many glaciers, lakes.

Olympic, WA (1909/1938) 922,651. Mountain wilderness containing finest remnant of Pacific Northwest rain forest, active glaciers, Pacific shoreline, rare elk.

Petrified Forest, AZ (1906/1962) 93,533. Extensive petrified wood and Indian artifacts. Contains part of Painted Desert.

Redwood, CA (1968) 112,513. 40 mi of Pacific coastline, groves of ancient redwoods and world's tallest trees.

Rocky Mountain, CO (1915) 265,765. On the Continental Divide; includes peaks over 14,000 ft.

Saguaro, AZ (1933/1994) 91,445. Part of the Sonoran Desert; includes the giant saguaro cacti, unique to the region.

Sequoia, CA (1890) 402,051. Groves of giant sequoias, highest mountain in conterminous U.S.—Mt. Whitney (14,494 ft). World's largest tree.

Shenandoah, VA (1926) 199,038. Portion of the Blue Ridge Mts.; overlooks Shenandoah Valley; Skyline Drive.

Theodore Roosevelt, ND (1947/1978) 70,447. Contains part of T.R.'s ranch and scenic badlands.

Virgin Islands, VI (1956) 14,689. Authorized to cover 75% of St. John Isl. and Hassel Isl.; lush growth, lovely beaches, Carib Indian petroglyphs, evidence of colonial Danes.

Voyageurs, MN (1971) 218,200. Abundant lakes, forests, wildlife, canoeing, boating.

Wind Cave, SD (1903) 28,295. Limestone caverns in Black Hills. Extensive wildlife includes a herd of bison.

Wrangell-St. Elias, AK (1978/1980) 8,323,148. Largest area in park system, most peaks over 16,000 ft, abundant wildlife; day's drive east of Anchorage. Limited federal facilities.

Yellowstone, ID-MT-WY (1872) 2,219,791. World's first national park. World's greatest geyser area has about 10,000 geysers and hot springs; spectacular falls and impressive canyons of the Yellowstone River; grizzly bear, moose, and bison.

Yosemite, CA (1890) 761,266. Yosemite Valley, the nation's highest waterfall, grove of sequoias, and mountains.

Zion, UT (1909/1919) 146,598. Unusual shapes and landscapes resulting from erosion and faulting; evidence of past volcanic activity; Zion Canyon has sheer walls ranging up to 2,640 ft.

NATIONAL HISTORICAL PARKS

Adams, MA (1946/1998) 24. Home of Pres. John Adams, John Quincy Adams, and celebrated descendants.

Appomattox Court House, VA (1930/1954) 1,772. Where Lee surrendered to Grant.

Boston, MA (1974) 43. Includes Faneuil Hall, Old North Church, Bunker Hill, Paul Revere House.

Cane River Creole (and heritage area), LA (1994) 207. Preserves the Creole culture as it developed along the Cane R.

Cedar Creek and Belle Grove, VA (2002) 3,567. Preserves a Civil War battle site and an antebellum plantation in the Shenandoah Valley.

Chaco Culture, NM (1907/1980) 33,960. Ruins of pueblos built by prehistoric Indians.

Chesapeake and Ohio Canal, MD-DC-WV (1938/1971) 19,575. 184-mi historic canal; DC to Cumberland, MD.

Colonial, VA (1930/1936) 9,452. Includes most of Jamestown Isl., site of first successful English colony; Yorktown, site of Cornwallis's surrender to George Washington; and the Colonial Parkway.

Cumberland Gap, KY-TN-VA (1940) 20,463. Mountain pass of the Wilderness Road, which carried the first great migration of pioneers into America's interior.

Dayton Aviation Heritage, OH (1992) 86. Commemorates the area's aviation heritage.

George Rogers Clark, Vincennes, IN (1966) 26. Commemorates American defeat of British in West during Revolution.

Harpers Ferry, MD-VA-WV (1944/1963) 2,502. At the confluence of the Shenandoah and Potomac rivers, the site of John Brown's 1859 raid on the Army arsenal.

WORLD ALMANAC QUICK QUIZ

Can you rank these states from smallest to largest in area?

    (a) Illinois   (b) Oklahoma
    (c) Alabama   (d) Ohio

For the answer look in this chapter, or see page 1008.

Hopewell Culture, OH (1923/1992) 1,170. Formerly Mound City Group National Monument.

Independence, PA (1948) 45. Contains several properties associated with the American Revolution and the founding of the U.S. Includes Independence Hall.

Jean Laffite (and preserve), LA (1907/1978) 20,005. Includes Chalmette, site of 1815 Battle of New Orleans; French Quarter.

Kalaupapa, HI (1980) 10,779. Molokai's former leper colony site and other historic areas.

Kaloko-Honokohau, HI (1978) 1,161. Preserves the native culture of Hawaii. No federal facilities.

Keweenaw, MI (1992) 1,869. Site of first significant copper mine in U.S. Federal facilities are under development.

Klondike Gold Rush, AK-WA (1976) 13,191. Alaskan Trails in 1898 Gold Rush. Museum in Seattle.

Lowell, MA (1978) 141. Textile mills, canal, 19th-cent. structures; park shows planned city of Industrial Revolution.

Lyndon B. Johnson, TX (1969/1980) 1,570. President's birthplace, boyhood home, ranch.

Marsh-Billings-Rockefeller, VT (1992) 643. Boyhood home of conservationist George Perkins Marsh. No federal facilities.

Minute Man, MA (1959) 971. Where the Minute Men battled the British, Apr. 19, 1775. Also contains Hawthorne's home.

Morristown, NJ (1933) 1,711. Sites of important military encampments during the American Revolution; Washington's headquarters, 1777, 1779-80.

Natchez, MS (1988) 105. Mansions, townhouses, and villas related to history of Natchez.

New Bedford Whaling, MA (1996) 34. Preserves structures and relics associated with the city's 19th-cent. whaling industry.

New Orleans Jazz, LA (1994) 5. Preserves, educates, and interprets jazz as it has evolved in New Orleans.

Nez Perce, ID (1965) 2,495. Illustrates the history and culture of the Nez Perce Indian country (38 separate sites).

Pecos, NM (1965/1990) 6,670. Ruins of ancient Pueblo of Pecos, archaeological sites, and 2 associated Spanish colonial missions from the 17th and 18th centuries.

Pu'uhonua o Honaunau, HI (1955/1978) 182. Until 1819, a sanctuary for Hawaiians vanquished in battle and for those guilty of crimes or breaking taboos.

Rosie the Riveter WWII Home Front, CA (2000) 145. Built on site that was a shipyard employing thousands of women in WWII; commemorates women who worked in war-time industries.

Salt River Bay (and ecological preserve), St. Croix, VI (1992) 948. The only site known where, 500 years ago, members of a Columbus party landed on what is now territory of the U.S.

San Antonio Missions, TX (1978) 826. Four of finest Spanish missions in U.S., 18th-cent. irrigation system.

San Francisco Maritime, CA (1988) 50. Artifacts, photographs, and historic vessels related to the development of the Pacific Coast.

San Juan Island, WA (1966) 1,752. Commemorates peaceful relations between the U.S., Canada, and Great Britain since the 1872 boundary disputes.

Saratoga, NY (1938) 3,392. Scene of a major 1777 battle that became a turning point in the American Revolution.

Sitka, AK (1910/1972) 113. Scene of last major resistance of the Tlingit Indians to the Russians, 1804.

Tumacacori, AZ (1908/1990) 46. Historic Spanish mission building stands near site first visited by Father Kino in 1691.

Valley Forge, PA (1976) 3,464. Continental Army campsite in 1777-78 winter.

War in the Pacific, GU (1978) 2,037. Seven distinct units illustrating the Pacific theater of WWII. Limited federal facilities.

Women's Rights, NY (1980) 7. Seneca Falls site where Lucretia Mott, Elizabeth Cady Stanton began rights movement in 1848.

NATIONAL BATTLEFIELDS

Antietam, MD (1890/1978) 3,244. Battle here ended first Confederate invasion of North, Sept. 17, 1862.

Big Hole, MT (1910/1963) 1,011. Site of major battle with Nez Perce Indians.

Cowpens, SC (1929/1972) 842. American Revolution battlefield.

Fort Donelson, TN-KY (1928/1985) 552. Site of first major Union victory.

Fort Necessity, PA (1931/1961) 903. Site of first battle of French and Indian War.

Monocacy, MD (1934/1976) 1,647. Civil War battle in defense of Washington, DC, fought here, July 9, 1864.

Moores Creek, NC (1926/1980) 88. 1776 battle between Patriots and Loyalists commemorated here.

Petersburg, VA (1926/1962) 2,659. Scene of 10-month Union campaigns, 1864-65.

Stones River, TN (1927/1960) 709. Scene of battle that began federal offensive to trisect the Confederacy.

Tupelo, MS (1929/1961) 1. Site of crucial battle over Sherman's supply line, 1865.

Wilson's Creek, MO (1960/1970) 1,750. Scene of Civil War battle for control of Missouri.

NATIONAL BATTLEFIELD PARKS

Kennesaw Mountain, GA (1917/1935) 2,884. Site of two major battles of Atlanta campaign in Civil War.

Manassas, VA (1940) 5,067. Scene of two battles in Civil War, 1861 and 1862.

Richmond, VA (1936) 2,152. Site of battles defending Confederate capital.

NATIONAL BATTLEFIELD SITE

Brices Cross Roads, MS (1929) 1. Civil War battlefield.

NATIONAL MILITARY PARKS

Chickamauga and Chattanooga, GA-TN (1890) 8,266. Site of major Confederate victory, 1863.

Fredericksburg and Spotsylvania County, VA (1927/1933) 8,362. Sites of several major Civil War battles and campaigns.

Gettysburg, PA (1895/1933) 5,990. Site of decisive Confederate defeat in North and of Gettysburg Address.

Guilford Courthouse, NC (1917/1933) 228. American Revolution battle site.

Horseshoe Bend, AL (1956) 2,040. On Tallapoosa River, where Gen. Andrew Jackson's forces broke the power of the Upper Creek Indian Confederacy.

Kings Mountain, SC (1931/1933) 3,945. Site of American Revolution battle.

Pea Ridge, AR (1956) 4,300. Scene of Civil War battle.

Shiloh, TN (1894/1933) 4,025. Major Civil War battlesite; includes some well-preserved Indian burial mounds.

Vicksburg, MS (1899/1933) 1,753. Union victory gave North control of the Mississippi and split the Confederate forces.

NATIONAL MEMORIALS

Arkansas Post, AR (1960) 747. First permanent French settlement in the lower Mississippi River valley.

Arlington House, the Robert E. Lee Memorial, VA (1925/1972) 28. Lee's home overlooking the Potomac.

Chamizal, El Paso, TX (1966/1974) 55. Commemorates 1963 settlement of 99-year border dispute with Mexico.

Coronado, AZ (1941/1952) 4,750. Commemorates first European exploration of the Southwest.

DeSoto, FL (1948) 27. Commemorates 16th-cent. Spanish explorations.

Federal Hall, NY (1939/1955) 0.45. First seat of U.S. government under the Constitution.

Fort Caroline, FL (1950) 138. On St. Johns River, overlooks site of a French Huguenot colony.

Fort Clatsop, OR (1958) 125. Lewis and Clark encampment, 1805-6.

Franklin Delano Roosevelt, DC (1982) 8. Statues of Pres. Roosevelt and Eleanor Roosevelt; waterfalls and gardens.

General Grant, NY (1958) 0.76. Tomb of Grant and wife.

Hamilton Grange, NY (1962) 1. Home of Alexander Hamilton.

Jefferson National Expansion Memorial, St. Louis, MO (1935) 193. Commemorates westward expansion.

Johnstown Flood, PA (1964) 164. Commemorates tragic flood of 1889.

Korean War Veterans, DC (1986) 2. Dedicated in 1995; honors those who served in the Korean War.

Lincoln Boyhood, IN (1962) 200. Lincoln grew up here.

Lincoln Memorial, DC (1911/1933) 107. Marble statue of the 16th U.S. president.

Lyndon B. Johnson Memorial Grove on the Potomac, DC (1973) 17. Overlooks the Potomac R.; vista of the Capitol.

Mount Rushmore, SD (1925) 1,278. World-famous sculpture of 4 presidents.

Oklahoma City, OK (1997) 6. Commemorates site of April 19, 1995, bombing which killed 168.

Perry's Victory and International Peace Memorial, Put-in-Bay, OH (1936/1972) 25. The world's most massive Doric column, constructed 1912-15, promotes pursuit of peace through arbitration and disarmament.

Roger Williams, Providence, RI (1965) 5. Memorial to founder of Rhode Island.

Thaddeus Kosciuszko, PA (1972) 0.02. Memorial to Polish hero of American Revolution.

Theodore Roosevelt Island, DC (1932/1933) 89. Statue of Roosevelt in wooded island sanctuary.

Thomas Jefferson Memorial, DC (1934) 18. Statue of Jefferson in an inscribed circular, colonnaded structure.

USS Arizona, HI (1980) 11. Memorializes American losses at Pearl Harbor.

Vietnam Veterans, DC (1980) 2. Black granite wall inscribed with names of those missing or killed in action in Vietnam War.

Washington Monument, DC (1848/1933) 106. Obelisk honoring the first U.S. president.

Wright Brothers, NC (1927/1953) 428. Site of first powered flight.

NATIONAL HISTORIC SITES

Abraham Lincoln Birthplace, Hodgenville, KY (1916/1959) 345. Early 17th-cent. cabin.

Allegheny Portage Railroad, PA (1964) 1,249. Linked the Pennsylvania Canal system and the West.

Andersonville, Andersonville, GA (1970) 495. Noted Civil War prisoner-of-war camp.

Andrew Johnson, Greeneville, TN (1935/1963) 17. Two homes and the tailor shop of the 17th U.S. president.

Bent's Old Fort, CO (1960) 799. Reconstruction of S Plains outpost.

Boston African-American, MA (1980) 0.59. Pre-Civil War black history structures.

Brown v. Board of Education, KS (1992) 2. Commemorates the landmark 1954 U.S. Supreme Court decision.

Carl Sandburg Home, Flat Rock, NC (1968) 264. Poet's home.

Charles Pinckney, SC (1988) 28. Statesman's farm.

Christiansted, St. Croix, VI (1952/1961) 27. Commemorates Danish colony.

Clara Barton, MD (1974) 9. Home of founder of American Red Cross.

Edgar Allan Poe, PA (1978/1980) 0.52. Writer's home.

Edison, West Orange, NJ (1955/1962) 21. Inventor's home and laboratory.

Eisenhower, Gettysburg, PA (1967) 690. Home of 34th president.

Eleanor Roosevelt, Hyde Park, NY (1977) 181. The former first lady's personal retreat.

Eugene O'Neill, Danville, CA (1976) 13. Playwright's home.

First Ladies, Canton, OH (2000) 0.33. Library devoted to America's first ladies.

Ford's Theatre, DC (1866/1970) 0.29. Includes theater, now restored, where Lincoln was assassinated, house where he died, and Lincoln Museum.

Fort Bowie, AZ (1964) 999. Focal point of operations against Geronimo and the Apaches.

Fort Davis, TX (1961) 474. Frontier outpost in West Texas.

Fort Laramie, WY (1938/1960) 833. Military post on Oregon Trail.

Fort Larned, KS (1964/1966) 718. Military post on Santa Fe Trail.

Fort Point, San Francisco, CA (1970) 29. West Coast fortification.

Fort Raleigh, NC (1941) 513. First attempted English settlement in North America.

Fort Scott, KS (1965/1978) 17. Commemorates U.S. frontier of 1840s and '50s.

Fort Smith, AR-OK (1961) 75. Active post during 1817-90.

Fort Union Trading Post, MT-ND (1966) 444. Principal fur-trading post on upper Missouri, 1829-67.

Fort Vancouver, WA (1948/1961) 209. Headquarters for Hudson's Bay Company in 1825. Early political seat.

Frederick Douglass, DC (1962/1988) 9. Home of famous black abolitionist, writer, and orator.

Frederick Law Olmsted, MA (1979) 7. Home of famous city planner.

Friendship Hill, PA (1978) 675. Home of Albert Gallatin, Jefferson's and Madison's secretary of treasury.

Golden Spike, UT (1957) 2,735. Commemorates completion of first transcontinental railroad in 1869.

Grant-Kohrs Ranch, MT (1972) 1,618. Ranch house and part of 19th-cent. ranch.

Hampton, MD (1948) 62. 18th-cent. Georgian mansion.

Harry S. Truman, MO (1983) 7. Home of Pres. Truman after 1919.

Herbert Hoover, West Branch, IA (1965) 187. Birthplace and boyhood home of 31st president.

Home of Franklin D. Roosevelt, Hyde Park, NY (1944) 800. FDR's birthplace, home, and "summer White House."

Hopewell Furnace, PA (1938/1985) 848. 19th-cent. iron-making village.

Hubbell Trading Post, AZ (1965) 160. Still active today.

James A. Garfield, Mentor, OH (1980) 8. Home of 20th president.

Jimmy Carter, GA (1987) 71. Birthplace and home of 39th president.

John Fitzgerald Kennedy, Brookline, MA (1967) 0.09. Birthplace and childhood home of 35th president.

John Muir, Martinez, CA (1964) 345. Home of early conservationist and writer.

Knife River Indian Villages, ND (1974) 1,758. Remnants of villages last occupied by Hidatsa and Mandan Indians.

Lincoln Home, Springfield, IL (1971) 12. Lincoln's residence at the time he was elected 16th president, 1860.

Little Rock Central High School, AR (1998) 27. Commemorates 1957 desegregation during which federal troops had to be called in to protect 9 black students.

Longfellow, Cambridge, MA (1972) 2. Poet's home, 1837-82; Washington's headquarters during Boston siege, 1775-76.

Maggie L. Walker, VA (1978) 1. Richmond home of black leader and bank president, daughter of an ex-slave.

Manzanar, Lone Pine, CA (1992) 814. Commemorates Manzanar War Relocation Ctr., a Japanese-American internment camp during WWII. No federal facilities.

Martin Luther King Jr., Atlanta, GA (1980) 39. Birthplace, grave, church of the civil rights leader. Limited federal facilities.

Martin Van Buren, NY (1974) 40. Lindenwald, home of 8th president, near Kinderhook.

Mary McLeod Bethune Council House, DC (1982/1991) 0.07. Commemorates Bethune's leadership in the black women's movement.

Minuteman Missile, SD (1999) 15. Missile launch facilities dating back to the Cold War era.

Nicodemus, KS (1996) 161. Only remaining western town established by African-Americans during Reconstruction.

Ninety Six, SC (1976) 989. Colonial trading village.

Palo Alto Battlefield, TX (1978) 3,407. Scene of first battle of the Mexican War.

Pennsylvania Avenue, DC (1965) Acreage undetermined. Also includes area next to the road between Capitol and White House, encompassing Ford's Theatre and other structures.

Puukohola Heiau, HI (1972) 86. Ruins of temple built by King Kamehameha.

Sagamore Hill, Oyster Bay, NY (1962) 83. Home of Pres. Theodore Roosevelt from 1885 until his death in 1919.

Saint-Gaudens, Cornish, NH (1964) 148. Home, studio, and gardens of American sculptor Augustus Saint-Gaudens.

Saint Paul's Church, NY, NY (1943) 6. Site associated with John Peter Zenger's "freedom of press" trial.

Salem Maritime, MA (1938) 9. Only port never seized from the patriots by the British. Major fishing and whaling port.

Sand Creek Massacre, Sand Creek, CO (2000) 12,583. Site where over 100 Cheyenne and Arapaho Indians were killed by U.S. soldiers in 1864.

San Juan, PR (1949) 75. 16th-cent. Span. fortifications.

Saugus Iron Works, MA (1974) 9. Reconstructed 17th-cent. colonial ironworks.

Springfield Armory, MA (1974) 55. Small-arms manufacturing center for nearly 200 years.

Steamtown, PA (1986) 62. Railyard, roadhouse, repair shops of former Delaware, Lackawanna & Western Railroad.

Theodore Roosevelt Birthplace, New York, NY (1962) 0.11. Reconstructed brownstone.

Theodore Roosevelt Inaugural, Buffalo, NY (1966) 1. Wilcox House where he took oath of office, 1901.

Thomas Stone, MD (1978) 328. Home of signer of Declaration of Independence, built in 1771.

Tuskegee Airmen, AL (1998) 90. Airfield where pilots of all-black air corps unit of WWII received flight training.

Tuskegee Institute, AL (1974) 58. College founded by Booker T. Washington in 1881 for blacks.

Ulysses S. Grant, St. Louis Co., MO (1989) 10. Home of Grant during pre-Civil War years.

Vanderbilt Mansion, Hyde Park, NY (1940) 212. Mansion of 19th-cent. financier.

Washita Battlefield, OK (1996) 315. Scene of Nov. 27, 1868, battle between Plains tribes and the U.S. army.

Weir Farm, Wilton, CT (1990) 74. Home and studio of American impressionist painter J. Alden Weir.

Whitman Mission, WA (1936/1963) 99. Site where Dr. and Mrs. Marcus Whitman ministered to the Indians until slain by them in 1847.

William Howard Taft, Cincinnati, OH (1969) 3. Birthplace and early home of the 27th president.

NATIONAL MONUMENTS

Name	State	Year[1]	Acreage
Agate Fossil Beds	NE	1965	3,055
Alibates Flint Quarries	TX	1965	1,371
Aniakchak[2]	AK	1978	137,176
Aztec Ruins	NM	1923	318
Bandelier	NM	1916	33,677
Booker T. Washington	VA	1956	224
Buck Island Reef	VI	1961	19,015
Cabrillo	CA	1913	160
Canyon de Chelly	AZ	1931	83,840
Cape Krusenstern[3]	AK	1978	649,085
Capulin Volcano	NM	1916	793
Casa Grande Ruins	AZ	1889	473
Castillo de San Marcos	FL	1924	20
Castle Clinton	NY	1946	1
Cedar Breaks	UT	1933	6,155
Chiricahua	AZ	1924	11,985
Colorado	CO	1911	20,534
Congaree Swamp	SC	1976	21,889
Craters of the Moon National Monument and Preserve	ID	1924	714,727
Devils Postpile	CA	1911	798

Name	State	Year[1]	Acreage
Devils Tower	WY	1906	1,347
Dinosaur	CO-UT	1915	210,278
Effigy Mounds	IA	1949	2,526
El Malpais	NM	1987	114,277
El Morro	NM	1906	1,279
Florissant Fossil Beds	CO	1969	5,998
Fort Frederica	GA	1936	241
Fort Matanzas	FL	1924	300
Fort McHenry National Monument and Historic Shrine	MD	1925	43
Fort Pulaski	GA	1924	5,623
Fort Stanwix	NY	1935	16
Fort Sumter	SC	1948	200
Fort Union	NM	1954	721
Fossil Butte	WY	1972	8,198
George Washington Birthplace	VA	1930	550
George Washington Carver	MO	1943	210
Gila Cliff Dwellings	NM	1907	533
Governors Island	NY	2001	23
Grand Portage	MN	1951	710
Great Sand Dunes National Monument and Preserve	CO	2000	83,958
Hagerman Fossil Beds[3]	ID	1988	4,351
Hohokam Pima[4]	AZ	1972	1,690
Homestead National Monument of America	NE	1936	195
Hovenweep	CO-UT	1923	785
Jewel Cave	SD	1908	1,274
John Day Fossil Beds	OR	1974	14,057
Lava Beds	CA	1925	46,560
Little Big Horn Battlefield	MT	1879	765
Minidoka Internment[2]	ID	2001	73
Montezuma Castle	AZ	1906	858
Muir Woods	CA	1908	554
Natural Bridges	UT	1908	7,636
Navajo	AZ	1909	360
Ocmulgee	GA	1934	702
Oregon Caves	OR	1909	488
Organ Pipe Cactus	AZ	1937	330,689
Petroglyph	NM	1990	7,232
Pinnacles	CA	1908	17,614
Pipe Spring	AZ	1923	40
Pipestone	MN	1937	282
Poverty Point[2]	LA	1988	911
Rainbow Bridge[3]	UT	1910	160
Russell Cave	AL	1961	310
Salinas Pueblo Missions	NM	1909	1,071
Scotts Bluff	NE	1919	3,003
Statue of Liberty	NJ-NY	1924	58
Sunset Crater Volcano	AZ	1930	3,040
Timpanogos Cave	UT	1922	250
Tonto	AZ	1907	1,120
Tuzigoot	AZ	1939	801
Virgin Islands Coral Reef	VI	2001	13,893
Walnut Canyon	AZ	1915	3,579
White Sands	NM	1933	143,733
Wupatki	AZ	1924	35,422
Yucca House[4]	CO	1919	34

NATIONAL PRESERVES

Name	State	Year	Acreage
Aniakchak	AK	1978	465,603
Bering Land Bridge	AK	1978	2,697,393
Big Cypress	FL	1974	720,565
Big Thicket	TX	1974	97,168
Denali	AK	1917	1,334,118
Gates of the Arctic	AK	1978	948,608
Glacier Bay	AK	1925	58,406
Katmai	AK	1918	418,699
Lake Clark	AK	1978	1,410,292
Little River Canyon[2]	AL	1992	13,633
Mojave	CA	1994	1,531,832
Noatak	AK	1978	6,569,904
Tallgrass Prairie	KS	1996	10,894
Timucuan Ecological & Historic Preserve[3]	FL	1988	46,289
Wrangell-St. Elias	AK	1978	4,852,753
Yukon-Charley Rivers[3]	AK	1978	2,526,512

NATIONAL SEASHORES

Name	State	Year	Acreage
Assateague Island	MD-VA	1965	39,733
Canaveral	FL	1975	57,662
Cape Cod	MA	1961	43,604
Cape Hatteras	NC	1937	30,321
Cape Lookout	NC	1966	28,243
Cumberland Island	GA	1972	36,415
Fire Island	NY	1964	19,580
Gulf Islands	FL-MS	1971	137,792
Padre Island	TX	1962	130,434
Point Reyes	CA	1962	71,068

NATIONAL PARKWAYS

Name	State	Year	Acreage
Blue Ridge	NC-VA	1933	91,813
George Washington Memorial	VA-MD-DC	1930	7,342
John D. Rockefeller Jr. Mem.	WY	1972	23,777
Natchez Trace	MS-AL-TN	1938	51,980

NATIONAL LAKESHORES

Name	State	Year	Acreage
Apostle Islands	WI	1970	69,372
Indiana Dunes	IN	1966	15,044
Pictured Rocks	MI	1966	73,236
Sleeping Bear Dunes	MI	1970	71,194

NATIONAL RESERVES

Name	State	Year	Acreage
City of Rocks[3]	ID	1988	14,107
Ebey's Landing[3]	WA	1978	19,323

NATIONAL RIVERS

Name	State	Year	Acreage
Big South Fork Natl. R and Recreation Area	KY-TN	1976	125,310
Buffalo	AR	1972	94,294
Mississippi Natl. R and Recreation Area	MN	1988	53,775
New River Gorge	WV	1978	70,465
Niobrara	NE-SD	1991	5,992
Ozark	MO	1964	80,785

NATIONAL WILD AND SCENIC RIVERS

Name	State	Year	Acreage
Alagnak	AK	1980	30,665
Bluestone[2]	WV	1978	4,310
Delaware	NY-NJ-PA	1978	1,973
Great Egg Harbor	NJ	1992	43,311
Missouri	NE-SD	1991	45,350
Obed	TN	1976	5,174
Rio Grande[2]	TX	1978	9,600
Saint Croix	MN-WI	1968	92,739
Upper Delaware	NY-PA	1978	75,000

NATIONAL RECREATION AREAS

Name	State	Year	Acreage
Amistad	TX	1965	58,500
Bighorn Canyon	MT-WY	1966	120,296
Boston Harbor Islands	MA	1996	1,482
Chattahoochee R.	GA	1978	9,164
Chickasaw	OK	1902	9,889
Curecanti	CO	1965	41,972
Delaware Water Gap	NJ-PA	1965	66,740
Gateway	NJ-NY	1972	26,607
Gauley R.[3]	WV	1988	11,505
Glen Canyon	AZ-UT	1958	1,254,306
Golden Gate	CA	1972	74,816
Lake Chelan	WA	1968	61,946
Lake Mead	AZ-NV	1936	1,495,664
Lake Meredith	TX	1965	44,978
Lake Roosevelt[5]	WA	1946	100,390
Ross Lake	WA	1968	117,575
Santa Monica Mts.[3]	CA	1978	153,673
Whiskeytown-Shasta-Trinity	CA	1965	42,503

NATIONAL SCENIC TRAIL

Name	State	Year	Acreage
Appalachian	ME to GA	1968	222,613
Natchez Trace	MS-TN	1983	10,995
Potomac Heritage	MD-DC-VA-PA	1983	NA

PARKS (no other classification)

Name	State	Year	Acreage
Catoctin Mountain	MD	1954	5,810
Constitution Gardens	DC	1974	52
Fort Washington	MD	1930	341
Greenbelt	MD	1950	1,176
National Capital	DC	1933	6,629
National Mall	DC	1933	146
Piscataway	MD	1961	4,625
Prince William Forest	VA	1948	18,856
Rock Creek	DC	1890	1,755
White House	DC	1933	18
Wolf Trap Farm Park for the Performing Arts	VA	1966	130

INTERNATIONAL HISTORIC SITE

Name	State	Year	Acreage
Saint Croix Island[3]	ME	1949	45

NA=Not available. (1) Year first designated. (2) No federal facilities. (3) Limited federal facilities. (4) Not open to the public. (5) Formerly Coulee Dam National Recreation Area.

20 Most-Visited Sites in the National Park System, 2002

Source: National Park Service, Dept. of the Interior

Attendance at all areas administered by the National Park Service in 2002 totaled 277,299,880 recreation visits.

Site (location)	Recreation visits	Site (location)	Recreation visits
Blue Ridge Parkway (NC-VA)	21,538,760	Grand Canyon National Park (AZ)	4,001,974
Golden Gate National Recreation Area (CA)	13,961,267	Olympic National Park (WA)	3,691,310
Great Smoky Mountains National Park (NC-TN)	9,316,420	San Francisco Maritime National Historical Park (CA)	3,558,544
Gateway National Recreation Area (NJ-NY)	9,014,438	Lincoln Memorial (DC)	3,551,973
Lake Mead National Recreation Area (AZ-NV)	7,550,284	Statue of Liberty National Monument (NJ-NY)	3,408,560
George Washington Memorial Pkwy (VA-MD-DC)	7,419,375	Yosemite National Park (CA)	3,361,867
Natchez Trace Parkway (MS-AL-TN)	5,643,170	Jefferson National Expansion Memorial (MO)	3,333,454
Delaware Water Gap National Recreation Area (NJ-PA)	5,165,415	Colonial National Historical Park ((VA)	3,324,188
Gulf Islands National Seashore (FL-MS)	4,561,862	Vietnam Veterans Memorial (DC)	3,296,596
Cape Cod National Seashore (MA)	4,455,931	Cuyahoga Valley National Park (OH)	3,217,935

U.S. States Ranked by American Indian and Alaska Native Population, 2000

Source: Bureau of the Census, U.S. Dept. of Commerce

Rank	State	One race only[1]	More than one race[2]	Rank	State	One race only[1]	More than one race[2]
1	California	333,346	294,216	27	Georgia	21,737	31,460
2	Oklahoma	273,230	118,719	28	Virginia	21,172	31,692
3	Arizona	255,879	36,673	29	New Jersey	19,492	29,612
4	New Mexico	173,483	17,992	30	Pennsylvania	18,348	34,302
5	Texas	118,362	97,237	31	Arkansas	17,808	19,194
6	North Carolina	99,551	32,185	32	Idaho	17,645	9,592
7	Alaska	98,043	21,198	33	Indiana	15,815	23,448
8	Washington	93,301	65,639	34	Maryland	15,423	24,014
9	New York	82,461	89,120	35	Tennessee	15,152	24, 036
10	South Dakota	62,283	5,998	36	Massachusetts	15,015	23,035
11	Michigan	58,479	65,933	37	Nebraska	14,896	7,308
12	Montana	56,068	10,252	38	South Carolina	13,718	13,738
13	Minnesota	54,967	26,107	39	Mississippi	11,652	7,903
14	Florida	53,541	64,339	40	Wyoming	11,133	3,879
15	Wisconsin	47,228	22,158	41	Connecticut	9,639	14,849
16	Oregon	45,211	40,456	42	Iowa	8,989	9,257
17	Colorado	44,241	35,448	43	Kentucky	8,616	15,936
18	North Dakota	31,329	3,899	44	Maine	7,098	6,058
19	Illinois	31,006	42,155	45	Rhode Island	5,121	5,604
20	Utah	29,684	10,761	46	West Virginia	3,606	7,038
21	Nevada	26,420	15,802	47	Hawaii	3,535	21,347
22	Louisiana	25,477	17,401	48	New Hampshire	2,964	4,921
23	Missouri	25,076	35,023	49	Delaware	2,731	3,338
24	Kansas	24,936	22,247	50	Vermont	2,420	3,976
25	Ohio	24,486	51,589	51	Washington, DC	1,713	3,062
26	Alabama	22,430	22,019		UNITED STATES	2,475,956	1,643,345

(1) Respondents classified themselves only under the category "American Indian and Alaska Native" on Census 2000. (2) Respondents classified themselves as "American Indian and Alaska Native" in combination with one or more other races.

Largest American Indian and Alaska Native Tribes in the U.S., 2000

Source: Bureau of the Census, U.S. Dept. of Commerce

Based on self-identification in Census 2000. Some respondents reported themselves as members of two or more tribes and/or as American Indian or Alaska Native in combination with one or more races. The last column is the sum of preceding columns.

Tribe[1]	American Indian and Alaska Native alone		American Indian and Alaska Native in combination with one or more races		American Indian and Alaska Native tribe alone or in any combination
	One tribe reported	Two or more tribes reported	One tribe reported	Two or more tribes reported	
ALL AMERICAN INDIANS	2,416,410	59,546	1,582,860	60,485	4,119,301
Cherokee	281,069	18,793	390,902	38,769	729,533
Navajo	269,202	6,789	19,491	2,715	298,197
Canadian and Latin American	108,802	2,236	79,499	2,233	192,770
Sioux	108,272	4,794	35,179	5,115	153,360
Chippewa	105,907	2,730	38,635	2,397	149,669
Choctaw	87,349	9,552	50,123	11,750	158,774
Pueblo	59,533	3,527	9,943	1,082	74,085
Apache	57,060	7,917	24,947	6,909	96,833
Lumbee	51,913	642	4,934	379	57,868
Iroquois	45,212	2,318	29,763	3,529	80,822
Creek	40,223	5,495	21,652	3,940	71,310
Blackfeet	27,104	4,358	41,389	12,899	85,750
Yup'ik	21,212	895	1,996	134	24,237
Chickasaw	20,887	3,014	12,025	2,425	38,351
Tohono O'Odham	17,466	714	1,748	159	20,087
Inupiat Eskimo	16,047	845	2,282	191	19,365
Potawatomi	15,817	592	8,602	584	25,595
Yaqui	15,224	1,245	5,184	759	22,412
Tlingit-Haida	14,825	1,059	6,047	434	22,365
Alaskan Athabascan	14,520	815	3,218	285	18,838
Seminole	12,431	2,982	9,505	2,513	27,431
Cheyenne	11,191	1,365	4,655	993	18,204
Puget Sound Salish	11,034	226	3,212	159	14,631
Comanche	10,120	1,568	6,120	1,568	19,376
Paiute	9,705	1,163	2,315	349	13,532

(1) Ranked by totals shown in first column.

UNITED STATES HISTORY

This chapter includes the following sections:

Chronology of Events

1492
Christopher Columbus and crew sighted land Oct. 12 in present-day Bahamas.

1497
John Cabot explored northeast coast to Delaware.

1513
Juan Ponce de León explored Florida coast.

1524
Giovanni da Verrazano led French expedition along coast from Carolina north to Nova Scotia; entered New York harbor.

1526
San Miguel de Guadalupe, **first European settlement** in what became U.S. territory, was established in the summer off S. Carolina coast; abandoned in Oct.

1539
Hernando de Soto landed in Florida May 28; crossed Mississippi River, **1541.**

1540
Francisco Vásquez de Coronado explored Southwest north of Rio Grande. Hernando de Alarcón reached Colorado River; Don Garcia Lopez de Cardenas reached Grand Canyon. Others explored California coast.

1562
First French colony in what became U.S. territory was founded on Paris Island off S. Carolina coast; abandoned **1564.**

1565
St. Augustine, FL, founded Sept. 8 by Pedro Menéndez. Razed by Francis Drake **1586.**

1579
Francis Drake entered San Francisco Bay and claimed region for Britain.

1585
"Lost colony" sponsored by **Sir Walter Raleigh** was founded on **Roanoke Island,** off N. Carolina coast; settlers found to have vanished, **1590.**

1587
Virginia Dare (on Roanoke Island) became first infant born in the Thirteen Colonies of English parents.

1607
Capt. John Smith and 105 cavaliers in 3 ships landed on Virginia coast, started first permanent English settlement in New World at **Jamestown** in May.

1609
Henry Hudson, English explorer of Northwest Passage, employed by Dutch, sailed into New York harbor in Sept., and up Hudson to Albany. **Samuel de Champlain** explored Lake Champlain, to the north.

Spaniards settled **Santa Fe, NM.**

1619
House of Burgesses, first representative assembly in New World, elected July 30 at Jamestown, VA.

First black laborers—indentured servants—in English N. American colonies, landed by Dutch at Jamestown in Aug. Chattel slavery legally recognized, **1650.**

1620
Plymouth Pilgrims, Puritan separatists, left Plymouth, England, Sept. 16 on *Mayflower.* They reached Cape Cod

Nov. 19, explored coast; 103 passengers landed Dec. 26 at Plymouth. **Mayflower Compact,** signed Nov. 11, was agreement to form a self-government. Half of colony died during harsh winter.

1624
Dutch colonies started in Albany and in New York area, where **New Netherland** was established in May.

1626
Peter Minuit bought **Manhattan** for Dutch West India Co. from Man-a-hat-a Indians during summer for goods valued at $24; named island **New Amsterdam.**

1630
Settlement of **Boston** established by Massachusetts colonists led by **John Winthrop.**

William Bradford began his chronicle *History of the Plymouth Plantation*; in the Mass. Bay Colony **John Winthrop** began *The History of New England.*

1634
Maryland was founded as a Catholic colony under a charter granted to Lord Baltimore. Religious toleration granted **1649.**

1636
Roger Williams founded Providence, RI, in June, as a democratically ruled colony with separation of church and state. Charter granted, **1644.**

Harvard College founded Oct. 28, now oldest in U.S.; grammar school, compulsory education established at Boston.

1640
First book was printed in America, the so-called Bay Psalm Book.

1647
Liberal constitution drafted in Rhode Island.

First law in America providing for **free compulsory basic education** enacted in Massachusetts.

1660
British Parliament passed First **Navigation Act** Dec. 1, regulating colonial commerce to suit English needs.

1661
A version of the New Testament translated into Algonquian became the **first Bible** printed in the colonies; an Old Testament translation was printed 2 years later.

1664
British troops **Sept. 8 seized New Netherland** from Dutch. Charles II granted New Netherland and city of New Amsterdam to brother, Duke of York; both renamed **New York.** Dutch recaptured colony **1673,** but ceded it to Britain Nov. 10, **1674.**

1670
Charles Town, South Carolina, was founded by English colonists in Apr.

1673
Jacques **Marquette** and Louis **Jolliet** reached the upper **Mississippi** and traveled down it.

Regular **mail service** on horseback was instituted Jan. 1 between New York and Boston.

1674
Future **Salem witch trial** judge Samuel Sewall began a renowned diary covering events through 1729.

1676
Nathaniel Bacon led planters against autocratic British Gov. Sir William Berkeley, burned Jamestown, VA, Sept. 19. Rebellion collapsed when Bacon died; 23 followers executed.
Bloody Indian war in New England ended Aug. 12. King Philip, Wampanoag chief, and Narragansett Indians killed.

1678
A book of poetry by Anne Bradstreet was published posthumously in Massachusetts.

1679
A fire destroyed 150 houses in Boston.

1681
John Bunyan's The Pilgrim's Progress published in America; became a best-seller.

1682
Robert Cavelier, Sieur de La Salle, claimed lower Mississippi River country for France, called it Louisiana Apr. 9. Had French outposts built in Illinois and Texas, 1684. Killed during mutiny Mar. 19, 1687.
William Penn arrived in Pennsylvania.
Spanish colonists became the first Europeans to settle in Texas, at the site of present-day El Paso.

1683
William Penn signed treaty with Delaware Indians Apr. 23, and made payment for Pennsylvania lands. The first German colonists in America settled near Philadelphia.

1689
New York's English colonial governor, Sir Edmund Andros, resigned after an armed uprising in Boston on Apr. 18.

1690
The New England Primer came into use in elementary schools.
The first colonial newspaper, *Publick Occurrences*, was published by Benjamin Harris, but promptly shut down for lack of official permission.
Whaling began large-scale operations in Nantucket.

1692
Witchcraft delusion at Salem, MA; 20 alleged witches executed by special court.

1696
Capt. William Kidd arrested and sent to England; hanged for piracy 1701.

1697
The Essays of Sir Francis Bacon, published in England in 1597, was published in America; it became a best-seller.

1699
French settlements made in Mississippi, Louisiana.

1702
Legislation was enacted making the Church of England the established church in Maryland.

1704
Indians attacked Deerfield, MA, Feb. 28-29; killed 40, carried off 100.
Boston News Letter, first regular newspaper, started by John Campbell, postmaster.

1709
British-colonial troops captured French fort, Port Royal, Nova Scotia, in Queen Anne's War 1701-13. France yielded Nova Scotia by treaty 1713.

1712
Slaves revolted in New York Apr. 6; 21 were executed. Second rising, 1741; 13 slaves hanged, 13 burned, 71 deported.

1716
First theater in colonies opened in Williamsburg, VA.

1726
Poor people rioted in Philadelphia.
Great Awakening religious revival began.

1731
America's first circulating library founded in Philadelphia by Benjamin Franklin.

1732
Benjamin Franklin published the first *Poor Richard's Almanack;* published annually to 1757.
Last of the 13 colonies, Georgia, chartered.

1733
Influenza epidemic swept through New York City and Philadelphia.

1735
Editor John Peter Zenger acquitted Aug. 5 in New York of libeling British governor by criticizing his conduct in office.

1739
A series of slave uprisings put down in South Carolina.

1741
Famous sermon "Sinners in the Hands of an Angry God," delivered at Enfield, MA July 8, by Jonathan Edwards, a major figure in the revivalist Great Awakening.
Capt. Vitus Bering reached Alaska.

1744
King George's War pitted British and colonials vs. French. Colonials captured Louisburg, Cape Breton Is., June 17, 1745. Returned to France 1748 by Treaty of Aix-la-Chapelle.

1752
Benjamin Franklin, flying kite in thunderstorm, proved lightning is electricity June 15; invented lightning rod.
Liberty Bell, cast in England, was delivered to Pennsylvania.

1754
Delegates from 7 colonies to Albany, NY, Congress, July 19, approved a "Plan of Union" by Benjamin Franklin; but plan was rejected by the colonies.
French and Indian War began when French occupied Ft. Duquesne (Pittsburgh). British moved Acadian French from Nova Scotia to Louisiana Oct. 8, 1755. British captured Québec Sept. 18, 1759, in battles in which French Gen. Joseph de Montcalm and British Gen. James Wolfe were killed. Peace pact signed Feb. 10, 1763. French lost Canada and Midwest.

1757
The first street lights appeared in Philadelphia.

1764
Sugar Act, Apr. 5, placed duties on lumber, foodstuffs, molasses, and rum in colonies, to pay French and Indian War debts.

1765
Stamp Act, enacted by Parliament Mar. 22, required revenue stamps to help fund royal troops. Nine colonies, at Stamp Act Congress in New York Oct. 7-25, adopted Declaration of Rights. Stamp Act repealed Mar. 17, 1766.
Quartering Act, requiring colonists to house British troops, went into effect Mar. 24.

1767
Townshend Acts levied taxes on glass, painter's lead, paper, and tea. In 1770 all duties except on tea were repealed.

1770
British troops fired Mar. 5 into Boston mob, killed 5 including Crispus Attucks, a black man, reportedly leader of group; later called Boston Massacre.

1773
East India Co. tea ships turned back at Boston, New York, and Philadelphia in May. Cargo ship burned at Annapolis Oct. 14; cargo thrown overboard at Boston Tea Party Dec. 16, to protest the tea tax.
First museum in the colonies was officially established in Charleston, SC; later named the Charleston Museum.

1774
"Intolerable Acts" of Parliament curtailed Massachusetts self-rule; barred use of Boston harbor till tea was paid for.
First Continental Congress held in Philadelphia Sept. 5-Oct. 26; called for civil disobedience against British.
Rhode Island abolished slavery.

1775
Patrick Henry addressed Virginia convention, Mar. 23, said, "Give me liberty or give me death."

Paul Revere and William Dawes Apr. 18 rode to alert Patriots that British were on their way to Concord to destroy arms. At **Lexington**, MA, Apr. 19, Minutemen lost 8. On return from **Concord**, British took 273 casualties.

Col. Ethan Allen (joined by Col. Benedict Arnold) captured **Ft. Ticonderoga, NY,** May 10; also Crown Point. Colonials headed for **Bunker Hill,** fortified Breed's Hill, Charlestown, MA. Repulsed British under Gen. William Howe twice before retreating June 17.

Continental Congress June 15 named **George Washington** commander in chief. Established a postal system, July 26; **Benjamin Franklin** became the first postmaster general.

1776

Common Sense, famous pro-independence pamphlet by Thomas Paine, was published Jan. 10; quickly sold some 100,000 copies.

France and Spain each agreed May 2 to provide arms.

In Continental Congress June 7, Richard Henry Lee (VA) moved "that these united colonies are and of right ought to be free and independent states." Resolution adopted July 2. **Declaration of Independence** approved July 4.

Col. William Moultrie's batteries at **Charleston, SC,** repulsed British sea attack June 28. Washington lost **Battle of Long Island** Aug. 27; evacuated New York.

Nathan Hale executed as spy by British Sept. 22.

Brig. Gen. Arnold's **Lake Champlain** fleet was defeated at Valcour Oct. 11, but British returned to Canada. Howe failed to destroy Washington's army at White Plains Oct. 28. Hessians captured Ft. Washington, Manhattan, and 3,000 men Nov. 16; captured Ft. Lee, NJ, Nov. 18.

Washington, in Pennsylvania, recrossed **Delaware River** Dec. 25-26, defeated Hessians at Trenton, NJ, Dec. 26.

1777

Washington defeated Lord Cornwallis at **Princeton** Jan. 3.

Continental Congress, June 14, authorized an **American flag,** the Stars and Stripes.

Maj. Gen. John Burgoyne's force of 8,000 from Canada, captured **Ft. Ticonderoga** July 6. Americans beat back Burgoyne at Bemis Heights Oct. 7, cut off British escape route. Burgoyne surrendered 5,000 men at **Saratoga,** NY, Oct. 17.

Articles of Confederation adopted by Continental Congress Nov. 15.

1778

France signed treaty of aid with U.S. Feb. 6. Sent fleet; British evacuated Philadelphia in consequence, June 18.

1779

George Rogers Clark took Vincennes in **Feb.**

John Paul Jones on the *Bonhomme Richard* defeated *Serapis* in British North Sea waters, Sept. 23.

1780

Charleston, SC, fell to the British May 12, but a British force was defeated near **Kings Mountain, NC,** Oct. 7 by militiamen.

Benedict Arnold found to be a traitor Sept. 23. Arnold escaped, made brigadier general in British army.

1781

Articles of Confederation took effect Mar. 1.

Bank of North America incorporated May 26.

Cornwallis retired to **Yorktown, VA.** Adm. Francois Joseph de Grasse landed 3,000 French and stopped British fleet in **Hampton Roads.** Washington and Jean Baptiste de Rochambeau joined forces, arrived near Williamsburg Sept. 26. Siege of Cornwallis began Oct. 6; **Cornwallis surrendered** Oct. 19.

1782

New **British** cabinet agreed in March to **recognize U.S.** independence. Preliminary agreement signed in Paris Nov. 30.

Use of the **scarlet letter A,** sewn on clothing or branded on skin of adulterers, was **discontinued** in New England.

1783

Massachusetts Supreme Court declared **slavery** illegal in that state.

Britain, U.S. signed **Paris peace treaty** Sept. 3 recognizing American independence (Congress ratified it Jan. 14, **1784).**

Washington ordered army disbanded Nov. 3, bade farewell to his officers at **Fraunces Tavern,** New York City, Dec. 4.

First regular daily newspaper, *Pennsylvania Evening Post,* went on sale in Philadelphia, May 30.

Noah Webster published *American Spelling Book.*

1784

Thomas Jefferson's proposal to **ban slavery** in new territory after 1802 was narrowly defeated Mar. 1.

First successful daily newspaper, *Pennsylvania Packet & General Advertiser,* published Sept. 21.

1785

Regular **stagecoach routes** established between Albany, New York City, and Philadelphia.

1786

Delegates from 5 states at **Annapolis, MD,** Sept. 11-14 asked Congress to call a constitutional convention.

1787

Shays's Rebellion of debt-ridden farmers in Massachusetts failed Jan. 25.

Northwest Ordinance adopted July 13 by Continental Congress for Northwest Territory, N of Ohio River, W of New York; made rules for statehood. Guaranteed freedom of religion, support for schools, no slavery.

Constitutional convention opened at Philadelphia May 25, with Washington presiding. Constitution accepted by delegates Sept. 17; Delaware became 1st state to ratify it, Dec. 7; ratification by 9th state, New Hampshire, June 21, **1788,** meant adoption; declared in effect Mar. 4, **1789.**

Federalist Papers ran in *NY Independent Journal.*

1789

George Washington chosen president by all electors voting (73 eligible, 69 voting, 4 absent); **John Adams, vice president,** got 34 votes. **First Congress** met at Federal Hall, New York City, Mar. 4; Washington **inaugurated** there Apr. 30; first inaugural ball held May 7.

Tammany Hall founded as benevolent organization, May 12.

U.S. **State Dept.** established by Congress July 27. (Thomas **Jefferson** installed as first secretary of state Feb. 1790.) **War Dept.** created, Aug. 7, with Henry **Knox** to be secretary; **Treasury Dept.** created Sept. 2, with Alexander **Hamilton** to be secretary.

Supreme Court created by Federal Judiciary Act, Sept. 24; **John Jay** confirmed by Congress as first Supreme Court **chief justice,** Sept. 26. Congress submitted **Bill of Rights** to states, Sept. 25.

1790

Congress, Mar. 1, authorized decennial **U.S. census; Naturalization Act** (2-year residency) passed Mar. 26.

John Carroll consecrated as **1st American Catholic bishop,** Aug. 15.

Congress met in **Philadelphia,** new temporary capital, Dec. 6.

1791

Bill of Rights went into effect Dec. 15.

1792

Coinage Act established **U.S. Mint** in Philadelphia Apr. 2.

Gen. **"Mad" Anthony Wayne** made commander in Ohio-Indiana area, trained "American Legion," established string of forts. Routed Indians at Fallen Timbers on Maumee River Aug. 20, **1794,** checked British at Fort Miami, OH.

White House cornerstone laid Oct. 13.

1793

Washington inaugurated for 2nd term, Mar. 4, having received 132 electoral votes; John **Adams** again became vice president, having received the 2nd highest total, 77.

Washington declared **U.S. neutrality,** Apr. 22, in war between Britain and France.

Eli Whitney invented **cotton gin,** reviving Southern slavery.

1794

Whiskey Rebellion, W Pennsylvania farmers protesting liquor tax of **1791,** suppressed by federal militia in Sept.

Jay's controversial **treaty** with Britain signed Nov. 19, ratified June 24, **1795.**

1795

U.S. bought peace from **Algerian pirates** by paying $1 mil ransom for 115 seamen Sept. 5, followed by annual tributes.

Gen. Wayne signed peace with Indians at Fort Greenville.

University of North Carolina became first operating state university.

1796

Washington's Farewell Address as president delivered Sept. 17. Warned against permanent alliances with foreign powers, big public debt, large military establishment, and devices of "small, artful, enterprising minority."

1797

U.S. **frigate** *United States* launched at Philadelphia July 10; *Constellation* at Baltimore Sept. 7; *Constitution* (Old Ironsides) at Boston Sept. 20.

John Adams inaugurated as 2nd president Mar. 4, after having received 71 electoral votes; **Thomas Jefferson** became vice president having received 68.

1798

Alien & Sedition Acts passed by Federalists June-July; intended to silence political opposition.

War with France threatened over French raids on U.S. shipping and rejection of U.S. diplomats. Navy (45 ships) and 365 privateers captured 84 French ships. USS *Constellation* took French warship *Insurgente* **1799.** Napoleon stopped French raids after becoming First Consul.

1799

Washington died at Mount Vernon Dec. 17.

1800

Federal government moved to **Washington, DC.**

1801

John Marshall named Supreme Court chief justice, Jan. 20.

Thomas Jefferson, who had received same number of electoral votes as Aaron Burr in 1800 election, **won** out over Burr **in House** vote reached Feb. 17; Burr named vice president.

Tripoli declared war June 10 against U.S., which refused added tribute to commerce-raiding Arab corsairs. Land and naval campaigns forced Tripoli to negotiate **peace** June 4, **1805.**

Oldest U.S. art institution, Pennsylvania Academy of Fine Arts, founded.

1802

Congress established the U.S. Military Academy at **West Point,** N.Y.

1803

Supreme Court, in **Marbury *v* Madison** case, for the first time overturned a U.S. law Feb. 24.

Napoleon sold all of **Louisiana,** stretching to Canadian border, to U.S., for $11,250,000 in bonds, plus $3,750,000 indemnities to American citizens with claims against France. U.S. took title Dec. 20. Purchase doubled U.S. area.

1804

Lewis and Clark expedition ordered by Pres. Thomas Jefferson to explore what is now northwest U.S. Started from St. Louis May 14; ended Sept. 23, **1806.**

Vice Pres. **Aaron Burr shot Alexander Hamilton** in a duel July 11 in Weehawken, NJ; Hamilton died next day.

1805

U.S. Marines aided by Arab mercenaries, Apr. 27, captured Tripolitan port of Derna, major victory in war against **Barbary pirates;** inspiration for "to the **shores of Tripoli**" in Marines Corps song.

1807

Robert Fulton made first practical steamboat trip; left New York City Aug. 17, reached Albany, 150 mi, in 32 hr.

Embargo Act banned all trade with foreign countries, forbidding ships to set sail for foreign ports Dec. 22.

1808

Slave importation outlawed. Some 250,000 slaves were illegally imported **1808-60.**

1810

Third U.S. Census found a population of 7,239,881. The black population was put at 1,378,110, of whom 186,746 were free citizens.

1811

William Henry Harrison, governor of Indiana, defeated Indians under the Prophet, in battle of **Tippecanoe** Nov. 7.

Cumberland Road begun at Cumberland, MD; became important route to West.

About 400 **slaves revolted** in Louisiana, killing the son of a plantation owner and marching on **New Orleans.** The insurrection was suppressed; some 75 slaves killed.

1812

War of 1812 had 3 main causes: Britain seized U.S. ships trading with France; Britain seized 4,000 naturalized U.S. sailors by **1810;** Britain armed Indians who raided western border. U.S. stopped trade with Europe **1807** and **1809.** Trade with Britain only was stopped **1810.**

Unaware that Britain had raised the blockade against France 2 days before, **Congress declared war** June 18.

USS *Essex* captured *Alert* Aug. 13; USS *Constitution* destroyed *Guerriere* Aug. 19; USS *Wasp* took *Frolic* Oct. 18; USS *United States* defeated *Macedonian* off Azores Oct. 25; USS *Constitution* beat *Java* Dec. 29. British took Detroit Aug. 16.

1813

Oliver H. Perry defeated British fleet at **Battle of Lake Erie,** Sept. 10. U.S. won Battle of the Thames, Ontario, Oct. 5, but failed in Canadian invasion attempts. York (Toronto) and Buffalo were burned.

1814

British landed in Maryland in Aug., defeated U.S. force Aug. 24, **burned Capitol and White House.** Maryland militia stopped British advance Sept. 12. Bombardment of Ft. McHenry, Baltimore, for 25 hours, Sept. 13-14, by British fleet failed; Francis Scott Key wrote words to **"The Star Spangled Banner."**

Troops under Andrew Jackson defeated Creek Indians led by Chief Weatherford at **Battle of Horshoe Bend in Alabama,** Mar. 29, ending Creek Indian War (1813-14).

U.S. won naval **Battle of Lake Champlain** Sept. 11. Peace treaty signed at Ghent Dec. 24.

1815

Some 5,300 British, unaware of peace treaty, attacked U.S. entrenchments near **New Orleans,** Jan. 8. British had more than 2,000 casualties; Americans lost 71.

U.S. flotilla finally ended piracy by **Algiers, Tunis, Tripoli** by Aug. 6.

1816

Second **Bank of the U.S.** chartered Apr. 10.

The **American Colonization Society,** which sought to address slavery issue by transporting freed blacks to Africa, formed in Washington, DC., Dec. **1816**-Jan. **1817.**

1817

Rush-Bagot treaty signed Apr. 28-29; limited U.S., British armaments on the Great Lakes.

William Cullen Bryant's poem **"Thanatopsis"** published.

Thomas Hopkins Gallaudet established the **first free public school for the deaf** in Hartford, CT.

1818

Connecticut **expanded suffrage among white male voters.** Massachusetts followed suit in 1820, and New York in 1821, reducing or eliminating property qualifications.

1819

Spain ceded **Florida** to U.S. Feb. 22.

American steamship *Savannah* made first part-steampowered, part-sail-powered crossing of Atlantic: Savannah, GA, to Liverpool, England, 29 days.

Washington Irving's *Sketch Book* became a best-seller.

1820

First organized **immigration of blacks to Africa** from U.S. began with 86 free blacks sailing Feb. to Sierra Leone.

Henry Clay's **Missouri Compromise** bill passed by Congress Mar. 3. Slavery was allowed in Missouri, but not elsewhere west of the Mississippi River north of 36°30′ latitude (the southern line of Missouri). Repealed **1854.**

WORLD ALMANAC QUICK QUIZ

Can you put these events in chronological order?

    (a) first Model Ts manufactured
    (b) Brooklyn Bridge opened
    (c) Prohibition takes effect
    (d) first powered air flight

For the answer look in this chapter, or see page 1008.

1821

Emma Willard founded Troy Female Seminary, first U.S. women's college.

Stephen Austin established the **first American community in Texas**, San Felipe de Austin.

The Spy, a novel by James Fenimore Cooper set during the American Revolution, was published and became a best-seller.

1822

Tension between sports and academics surfaced when Yale College Pres. Timothy Dwight **banned a primitive form of football,** setting fines for violators.

1823

Monroe Doctrine, opposing European intervention in the Americas, enunciated by Pres. James Monroe Dec. 2. The **Hudson River School,** painters who focused on the beauties of nature, began to come to public attention.

1824

Pawtucket, RI, **weavers strike,** first such action by women.

Slavery abolished in the state of Illinois Aug. 2.

1825

After a deadlocked election, **John Quincy Adams** was elected president by the U.S. House, Feb. 9.

Erie Canal opened; first boat left Buffalo Oct. 26, reached New York City Nov. 4.

John Stevens, of Hoboken, NJ, built and operated first experimental **steam locomotive** in U.S.

1826

Thomas **Jefferson** and John **Adams** both died July 4.

James Fenimore Cooper's *The Last of the Mohicans* published.

1827

Massachusetts passed a law providing for **tax-supported public high schools,** the first state to do so.

1828

South Carolina Dec. 19 declared the right of state **nullification of federal laws,** opposing the "Tariff of Abominations."

Noah Webster published his *American Dictionary of the English Language.*

Baltimore & Ohio, the first U.S. passenger railroad, begun July 4.

1829

Andrew Jackson inaugurated as president, Mar. 4.

1830

Famous **debate** Jan. 27 between Sen. **Daniel Webster** (MA) and Robert Hayne (SC), on state right to nullify federal law.

Mormon church organized by Joseph Smith in Fayette, NY, Apr. 6.

Pres. Jackson, May 28, signed **Indian Removal Act** providing land and some pay to Indians agreeing to resettle in west.

1831

William Lloyd Garrison began **abolitionist newspaper** *The Liberator* Jan. 1.

Nat Turner, black slave in Virginia, led local **slave rebellion,** starting Aug. 21; 57 whites killed. Troops called in, 100 slaves killed. Turner captured, tried, hanged Nov. 11.

1832

Black Hawk War (IL-WI) Apr.-Sept. pushed Sauk and Fox Indians west across Mississippi.

South Carolina convention passed **Ordinance of Nullification** Nov. 24 against permanent tariff, threatening to withdraw from Union. Congress Feb. **1833** passed compromise tariff act, whereupon South Carolina repealed its act.

1833

American Anti-Slavery Society founded in Philadelphia, Dec. 4.

Oberlin College became first in U.S. to adopt coeducation.

1835

Liberty Bell cracked July 8, tolling death of Chief Justice John Marshall.

Seminole Indians in Florida under Osceola began attacks Nov. 1, protesting forced removal. The unpopular war ended Aug. 14, **1842;** most of the Indians were sent to Oklahoma.

Texas proclaimed right to secede from Mexico; Sam Houston put in command of Texas army, Nov. 2-4.

Gold discovered on **Cherokee land** in Georgia. Indians forced to cede lands, Dec. 20, and to cross Mississippi.

1836

Texans besieged at Alamo in San Antonio by Mexicans under Santa Anna, Feb. 23-Mar. 6; entire garrison killed. Texas independence declared, Mar. 2. At San Jacinto Apr. 21, Sam Houston and Texans defeated Mexicans.

Ralph Waldo Emerson published his first work, *Nature,* espousing his philosophy of **transcendentalism.**

Marcus Whitman, H. H. Spaulding, and wives reached Fort Walla Walla on Columbia River, OR. **First white women to cross plains.**

1838

Cherokee Indians made **"Trail of Tears,"** as they were removed from Georgia to Oklahoma starting Oct.

1841

First emigrant **wagon train for California,** 47 persons, left Independence, MO, May 1, reached California Nov. 4.

Edgar Allen Poe published one of the first American detective stories, *The Murders in the Rue Morgue.*

Brook Farm commune set up by New England Transcendentalist intellectuals. Lasted to **1846.**

1842

Webster-Ashburton Treaty signed Aug. 9, fixing the U.S.-Canada border in Maine and Minnesota.

First use of **anesthetic** (sulfuric ether gas).

Settlement of Oregon began via **Oregon Trail.**

1843

More than 1,000 settlers left Independence, MO, for **Oregon** May 22, arrived Oct.

1844

First message over first **telegraph line** sent May 24 by inventor Samuel F.B. Morse from Washington to Baltimore: "What hath God wrought!"

1845

Texas Congress voted for annexation by U.S., July 4. U.S. Congress admitted Texas to Union, Dec. 29.

Edgar Allen Poe's poem "The Raven" published.

1846

Mexican War began after Pres. James K. Polk ordered Gen. Zachary Taylor to seize disputed Texan land settled by Mexicans. After border clash, U.S. declared war May 13; Mexico May 23.

Bear flag of **Republic of California** raised by American settlers at Sonoma June 14.

About 12,000 U.S. troops took Vera Cruz Mar. 27, **1847,** and Mexico City Sept. 14, **1847.** By **treaty,** signed Feb. 2, **1848,** war was ended, and Mexico ceded claims to Texas, California, and other territory.

Treaty with Britain June 15 set **boundary in Oregon** territory at 49th parallel (extension of existing line). Expansionists had used slogan "54° 40′ or fight." The term **"manifest destiny,"** coined by a journalist in 1845, also came into play.

Mormons, after violent clashes with settlers over polygamy, left Nauvoo, IL, for West under Brigham Young; settled July **1847** at Salt Lake City, UT.

Elias Howe invented **sewing machine.**

1847

First **adhesive U.S. postage stamps** on sale July 1; Benjamin Franklin 5¢, Washington 10¢.

Ralph Waldo Emerson published first book of poems; Henry Wadsworth Longfellow published *Evangeline*.

1848

Gold discovered Jan. 24 in California; 80,000 prospectors emigrated in 1849.

Lucretia Mott and Elizabeth Cady Stanton led Seneca Falls, NY, Women's Rights Convention July 19-20.

1850

Sen. Henry Clay's Compromise of 1850 admitted California as 31st state Sept. 9, with slavery forbidden; made Utah and New Mexico territories; made Fugitive Slave Law more harsh; ended District of Columbia slave trade.

1851

Herman Melville's *Moby-Dick* published.

1852

Uncle Tom's Cabin, by Harriet Beecher Stowe, published as a book.

1853

Comm. Matthew C. Perry, U.S.N., received by Japan, July 14; negotiated treaty to open Japan to U.S. ships.

New York City hosted first World's Fair in the U.S., beginning July 14.

Stephen Foster published "My Old Kentucky Home."

1854

Republican Party formed at Ripon, WI, Feb. 28. Opposed Kansas-Nebraska Act (became law May 30), which left issue of slavery to vote of settlers.

Henry David Thoreau published *Walden*.

Treaty ratified with Mexico Apr. 25, providing for purchase of a strip of land (Gadsden Purchase).

1855

Walt Whitman published *Leaves of Grass*.

First railroad train crossed Mississippi River on the river's first bridge, Rock Island, IL, Davenport, IA, Apr. 21.

Castle Garden opened on island off Lower Manhattan, to process immigrants; closed 1892.

1856

Republican Party's first nominee for president, John C. Fremont, defeated. Abraham Lincoln made 50 speeches for him.

Lawrence, KS, sacked May 21 by proslavery group; abolitionist John Brown led antislavery men against Missourians at Osawatomie, KS, Aug. 30.

The first U.S. kindergarten was opened, in Watertown, WI.

1857

Dred Scott decision by Supreme Court Mar. 6 held that slaves did not become free in a free state, Congress could not bar slavery from a territory, and blacks could not be citizens.

Currier & Ives issued their first print.

1858

First Atlantic cable completed, by Cyrus W. Field Aug. 5.

Lincoln-Douglas debates in Illinois, Aug. 21-Oct. 15.

1859

First commercially productive oil well, drilled near Titusville, PA, by Edwin L. Drake Aug. 27.

Abolitionist John Brown, with 21 men, seized U.S. Armory at Harpers Ferry Oct. 16. U.S. Marines captured raiders, killing several. Brown hanged for treason Dec. 2.

1860

Approximately 20,000 New England shoe workers went on strike Feb. 22 and won higher wages.

Abraham Lincoln, Republican, elected president Nov. 6 in 4-way race.

First Pony Express between Sacramento, CA, and St. Joseph, MO, started Apr. 3.

1861

Seven southern states set up Confederate States of America Feb. 8, with Jefferson Davis as president, captured federal arsenals and forts. Civil War began as Confederates fired on Ft. Sumter in Charleston, SC, Apr. 12, capturing it Apr. 14.

Pres. Lincoln called for 75,000 volunteers Apr. 15. By May, 11 states had seceded. Lincoln blockaded Southern ports Apr. 19, cutting off vital exports, aid.

Confederates repelled Union forces at first Battle of Bull Run, July 21.

First transcontinental telegraph line was put in operation.

1862

Union forces were victorious in Western campaigns, took New Orleans May 1. Battles in East were largely inconclusive despite heavy casualties. The Battle of Antietam, in western Maryland Sept. 17, was the bloodiest one-day battle of the war; each side lost over 2,000 men.

Homestead Act approved May 20; it granted free farms to settlers.

Land Grant Act approved July 7, providing for public land sale to benefit agricultural education; eventually led to establishment of state university systems.

1863

Pres. Lincoln issued Emancipation Proclamation Jan. 1, freeing "all slaves in areas still in rebellion."

Entire Mississippi River was in Union hands by July 4. Union forces won a major victory at Gettysburg, PA, July 1-3. Lincoln gave his Gettysburg Address Nov. 19.

Confederate forces under siege surrendered Vicksburg to Union forces under Gen. Ulysses S. Grant, July 4.

In draft riots in New York City about 1,000 were killed or wounded; some blacks were hanged by mobs July 13-16.

Pres. Lincoln declared Thanksgiving to be a national holiday.

1864

Gen. William Tecumseh Sherman marched through Georgia, taking Atlanta Sept. 1, Savannah Dec. 22.

Sand Creek massacre of Cheyenne and Arapaho Indians Nov. 29. Soldiers drove Indians out of village; about 150 killed.

1865

Gen. Robert E. Lee surrendered 27,800 Confederate troops to Gen. Grant at Appomattox Court House, VA, Apr. 9. J. E. Johnston surrendered 31,200 to Sherman at Durham Station, NC, Apr. 18. Last rebel troops surrendered May 26.

Pres. Lincoln was shot Apr. 14 by John Wilkes Booth in Ford's Theater, Washington, DC; died the following morning. Vice Pres. Andrew Johnson was sworn in as president. Booth was hunted down; fatally wounded, perhaps by his own hand, Apr. 26. Four co-conspirators hanged July 7.

13th Amendment, abolishing slavery, ratified Dec. 6.

1866

Ku Klux Klan formed secretly in South to terrorize blacks who voted. Disbanded 1869-71. A 2nd Klan organized 1915.

Congress took control of Southern Reconstruction, backed freedmen's rights in legislation vetoed by Johnson; veto overridden by Congress (for first time ever), Apr. 9.

1867

Alaska sold to U.S. by Russia for $7.2 mil Mar. 30, through efforts of Sec. of State William H. Seward.

The Grange was organized Dec. 4, to protect farmer interests.

Horatio Alger published first book, *Ragged Dick*.

1868

Pres. Johnson tried to remove Edwin M. Stanton, secretary of war; was impeached by House Feb. 24 for violation of Tenure of Office Act; acquitted by Senate Mar.-May.

14th Amendment, providing for citizenship of all persons born or naturalized in U.S., ratified July 9.

Louisa May Alcott published *Little Women*.

The World Almanac, a publication of the *New York World*, appeared for the first time.

1869

Financial "Black Friday" in New York Sept. 24; caused by attempt to "corner" gold.

Transcontinental railroad completed; golden spike driven at Promontory, UT, May 10, marking the junction of Central Pacific and Union Pacific.

Knights of Labor formed in Philadelphia. By 1886, this labor union had 700,000 members nationally.

Woman suffrage law passed in Wyoming Territory Dec. 10.

1870

15th Amendment, making race no bar to voting rights, ratified Feb. 8.
First U.S. boardwalk completed, in Atlantic City, NJ.
U.S. Weather Bureau founded.

1871

Great fire destroyed **Chicago** Oct. 8-11.
National Rifle Association founded.

1872

Amnesty Act restored civil rights to citizens of the South May 22, except for 500 Confederate leaders.
Congress established first national park—**Yellowstone.**
James McNeill Whistler painted famous portrait known informally as **"Whistler's Mother."**

1873

First U.S. **postal card** issued May 1.
Jesse James and his gang robbed their first passenger train July 21.
Banks failed, panic began in Sept. Depression lasted 5 years.
"Boss" William Tweed of New York City convicted Nov. 19 of stealing public funds. He died in jail in **1878.**
New York's Bellevue Hospital started **first nursing school.**

1874

Women's Christian Temperance Union established in Cleveland.
The **first** U.S. public **zoo** was established in Philadelphia.

1875

Congress passed **Civil Rights Act** Mar. 1, giving equal rights to blacks in public accommodations and jury duty. Act invalidated in **1883** by Supreme Court.
First **Jim Crow** segregation law enacted, in Tennessee.
First **Kentucky Derby** held May 17.

1876

Samuel J. Tilden, Democrat, received majority of popular votes for president over **Rutherford B. Hayes,** Republican, but 22 electoral votes were in dispute; issue left to Congress. Congress agreed to certify Hayes as winner in Feb. **1877** after Republicans agreed to end federal Reconstruction of South.
Alexander Graham Bell patented the telephone Mar. 7
Col. **George A. Custer** and 264 soldiers of the 7th Cavalry killed June 25 in "last stand," Battle of the **Little Big Horn,** MT, in Sioux Indian War.

1877

Molly Maguires, Irish terrorist society in Scranton, PA, mining areas, was broken up by the hanging, June 21, of 11 leaders for murders of mine officials and police.
Pres. Rutherford B. Hayes sent troops in violent national **railroad strike.**

1878

First commercial **telephone** exchange opened, New Haven, CT, Jan. 28.
Thomas A. Edison founded **Edison Electric Light Co.** on Oct. 15.

1879

F. W. Woolworth opened his first five-and-ten store, in Utica, NY, Feb. 22.
Henry George published *Progress & Poverty,* advocating single tax on land.
French actress **Sarah Bernhardt** made her U.S. debut Nov. 8 at New York City's Booth Theater.

1880

Chinese Exclusion Treaty signed with China, Nov. 17, providing for restitution of Chinese naturals entering U.S.
Lew Wallace's *Ben Hur* published.

1881

Clara Barton May 21 founded the **American Red Cross.**
Pres. **James A. Garfield shot** in Washington, DC, July 2; died Sept. 19.

Famous gun battle between the Earp brothers and outlaw rustlers, Oct. 26 near the **OK Corral,** Tombstone, AZ.
Booker T. Washington founded Tuskegee Institute for blacks.
Helen Hunt Jackson published *A Century of Dishonor,* about mistreatment of Indians.

1882

Chinese Exclusion Act, barring Chinese immigration, passed by Congress May 6.

1883

Pendleton Act passed Jan. 16, reformed civil service.
Northern Pacific Railroad completed, Sept. 8.
Brooklyn Bridge opened May 24.
Buffalo Bill Cody's Wild West Show began its 30-year touring run.

1884

First **long-distance** telephone call completed, Mar. 27, between Boston and New York.
First roller coaster in the U.S. opened at Coney Island in New York City.
Mark Twain's masterpiece, *The Adventures of Huckleberry Finn,* appeared.

1885

Washington Monument dedicated Feb. 21
Postal rates lowered to 2 cents an ounce.

1886

Haymarket riot and bombing, May 4, followed bitter labor battles for 8-hour day in Chicago; 7 police and 4 workers died. Eight anarchists found guilty Aug. 20; 4 hanged Nov. 11.
Coca-Cola first sold, May 8 at Jacob's Pharmacy in Atlanta.
Geronimo, Apache Indian, surrendered Sept. 4, ending last major Indian war.
Statue of Liberty dedicated Oct. 28.
American Federation of Labor (AFL) formed Dec. 8 by 25 craft unions.

1887

Interstate Commerce Act enacted Feb. 4.
Pres. Grover Cleveland signed the **Hatch Act,** Mar. 2.
Eugene Field published poem **"Little Boy Blue."**

1888

Great blizzard struck eastern U.S. Mar. 11-14, causing about 400 deaths.
Ernest Thayer's poem **Casey at the Bat** was recited for the first time in public, at a New York City theater in May.

1889

U.S. opened Oklahoma to white settlement Apr. 22; within 24 hours **claims for 2 mil acres** were staked by 50,000 "sooner" settlers.
Johnstown, PA, flood May 31; 2,200 lives lost.
Electric lights installed at the White House.

1890

Battle of **Wounded Knee,** SD, Dec. 29, the last major conflict between Indians and U.S. troops. About 200 Indian men, women, and children and 29 soldiers were killed.
Sherman Antitrust Act passed July 2, began federal effort to curb monopolies.
Jacob Riis published *How the Other Half Lives,* about city slums.
Poems of **Emily Dickinson** published, 4 years after her death.

1891

Forest Reserve Act, Mar. 3, let president close public forest land to settlement for establishment of national parks.
Carnegie Hall, in New York City, opened May 5.

1892

Ellis Island, in New York Bay, opened Jan. 1 to receive immigrants.
Homestead, PA, strike at Carnegie steel mills; 7 guards and 11 strikers and spectators shot to death July 6.
Heavyweight **James J. Corbett** KO'd John L. Sullivan Sept. 7, in first title bout to use padded gloves.

1893
Columbian Exposition, blockbuster world's fair, held May-Oct. in Chicago.
Financial panic began, led to 4-year depression.
Mormon Temple dedicated in Salt Lake City, UT.

1894
Thomas A. Edison's kinetoscope, for motion pictures (invented **1887**), given first public showing Apr. 14.
Jacob S. Coxey led army of unemployed from the Midwest, reaching Washington, DC, Apr. 30. Coxey arrested May 1 for trespassing on Capitol grounds; his army disbanded.
Pullman strike began May 11 at a railroad car plant in Chicago.
Milton Hershey started **Hershey Chocolate Company**.

1895
"America the Beautiful" appeared for 1st time, in church publication, July 4.
Stephen Crane's *The Red Badge of Courage* published.

1896
William Jennings Bryan delivered "Cross of Gold" speech July 8; won Democratic Party nomination.
Supreme Court, in **Plessy v. Ferguson**, May 18, approved racial segregation under the "separate but equal" doctrine.
John Philip Sousa composed "Stars and Stripes Forever" on Dec. 25.

1897
Olney-Pauncefote Treaty signed with **Britain**, Jan. 11, giving wide scope to arbitration in settling disputes; never ratified by U.S.
John J. McDermott won **first Boston Marathon** Apr. 19.
First Klondike **gold** arrived in San Francisco July 14.
Coal miners **strike** settled Sept. 11, after more than 20 miners fired on and killed by lawmen.

1898
U.S. **battleship** *Maine* blown up Feb. 15 at Havana; 260 killed.
U.S. **blockaded Cuba** Apr. 22 in aid of independence forces. U.S. declared **war on Spain** Apr. 24; destroyed Spanish fleet in **Philippines** May 1; took **Guam** June 20.
Puerto Rico taken by U.S. July 25-Aug. 12. Spain agreed Dec. 10 to cede Philippines, Puerto Rico, and Guam, and approved independence for Cuba.
Annexation of **Hawaii** signed by Pres. William McKinley, July 7.

1899
Filipino insurgents, unable to get recognition of independence from U.S., started guerrilla war Feb. 4. Their leader, Emilio Aguinaldo, captured May 23, **1901**. Philippine Insurrection ended **1902**. 20,000 Filipino troops killed, and some 200,000 civilian deaths, mostly from disease and starvation.
Pres. McKinley signed **treaty** officially ending Spanish-America War, Feb. 10.
U.S. declared **Open Door Policy** Sept. 6, to make China an open international market.
John Dewey published *The School and Society,* advocating "progressive education."
Pianist Scott Joplin's "Maple Leaf Rag" was published, popularizing **ragtime**.

1900
Carry Nation, Kansas antisaloon agitator, began raiding with hatchet.
U.S. helped suppress **"Boxer Rebellion"** in Beijing.
International Ladies' Garment Workers Union was founded in New York City June 3.
Eastman Kodak Co. introduced the **Brownie camera,** popularizing picture-taking.

1901
Texas had first significant **oil strike**, Jan. 10.
Pres. **McKinley was shot** Sept. 6 in Buffalo, NY, by an anarchist, Leon Czolgosz; died Sept. 14. Vice-Pres. Theodore **Roosevelt** sworn in as youngest-ever president, age 42 years, 11 months.
Booker T. Washington published **Up From Slavery.**

1902
Permanent Bureau of the **Census** established Mar. 6.
U.S. withdrew troops from **Cuba** May 20, and Cuba became independent.
Helen Keller autobiography appeared in serial form.

1903
Treaty between U.S. and Colombia to have U.S. dig **Panama Canal** signed Jan. 22, rejected by Colombia. Panama declared independence from Colombia with U.S. support Nov. 3; recognized by Pres. Theodore Roosevelt Nov. 6. U.S., Panama signed **canal treaty** Nov. 18.
Wisconsin set first **direct primary** voting system, May 23.
Henry Ford founded Ford Motor Co., June 16.
Boston defeated Pittsburgh, 5 games to 3, Oct. 13 in the **first modern World Series**.
First successful flight in heavier-than-air mechanically propelled airplane by **Orville Wright** Dec. 17 near Kitty Hawk, NC, 120 ft. in 12 secs. Later flight same day by **Wilbur Wright**, 852 ft. in 59 secs. Improved plane patented, **1906**.
Fire in Iroquois Theater, Chicago, killed about 600, Dec. 30
Great Train Robbery, pioneering film, produced.

1904
St. Louis hosted **first Olympics** in U.S., July 1-Nov. 23.
First section of New York **subway** system opened, Oct. 27.
Ida Tarbell published muckraking *The History of the Standard Oil Company.*
Henry James's last great novel, *The Golden Bowl,* appeared.

1905
International Workers of the World (Wobblies) founded by radicals in Chicago, June 27.
First **Rotary Club** founded in Chicago.

1906
Upton Sinclair published *The Jungle*.
San Francisco earthquake and fire, Apr. 18-19, left 503 dead, $350 mil damages.
Pure Food and Drug Act and Meat Inspection Act both passed June 30.

1907
Financial panic and depression started Mar. 13.
First round-world cruise of U.S. **"Great White Fleet":** 16 battleships, 12,000 men.

1908
Springfield, IL, torn by anti-black **rioting**, Aug. 14-15.
Henry Ford introduced **Model T** car, priced at $850, Oct. 1.

1909
Adm. Robert E. Peary claimed to have reached **North Pole** Apr. 6 on 6th attempt, accompanied by Matthew Henson, a black man, and 4 Eskimos; may have fallen short.
National Conference on the Negro convened May 30, leading to founding of National Association for the Advancement of Colored People.

1910
Boy Scouts of America founded Feb. 8.
In a famous speech in Kansas, Aug. 10, former Pres. Roosevelt called for a **"new nationalism."**

1911
Supreme Court dissolved **Standard Oil** Co. May 15.
Building holding New York City's **Triangle Shirtwaist** Co. factory caught fire Mar. 25; 146 died.
First **transcontinental airplane flight** (with numerous stops) by C. P. Rodgers, New York to Pasadena, CA, Sept. 17-Nov. 5; time in air 82 hr., 4 min.

1912
American Girl Guides founded Mar. 12; name changed in **1913** to **Girl Scouts.**
U.S. sent Marines Aug. 14 to **Nicaragua**, which was in default of loans to U.S. and Europe.

1913
16th Amendment, authorizing federal income tax, ratified Feb. 3.
NY Armory Show brought modern art to U.S. Feb. 17.
17th Amendment, providing for direct popular election of U.S. senators, ratified Apr. 8.

Federal Reserve System was authorized Dec. 23, in a major reform of U.S. banking and finance.

U.S. blockaded Mexico in support of revolutionaries.

Charles Beard published his *Economic Interpretation of the Constitution.*

1914

Ford Motor Co. raised basic wage rates from $2.40 for 9-hr. day to $5 for 8-hr. day, Jan. 5.

When U.S. sailors were arrested at Tampico, Mexico, Apr. 9, Atlantic fleet was sent to **Veracruz**, occupied city.

Pres. Woodrow Wilson proclaimed **U.S. neutrality** in the European war, Aug. 4.

Panama Canal was officially opened Aug. 15.

The **Clayton Antitrust Act** was passed Oct. 15, strengthening federal antimonopoly powers.

1915

First transcontinental **telephone call,** New York to San Francisco, was completed Jan. 25, by Alexander Graham Bell and Thomas A. Watson.

British ship *Lusitania* sunk May 7 by German submarine; 128 American passengers lost (Germany had warned passengers in advance). As a result of U.S. campaign, Germany issued apology and promise of payments, Oct. 5. Pres. Wilson asked for a military fund increase, Dec. 7.

U.S. troops landed in **Haiti,** July 28. Haiti became a virtual U.S. protectorate under Sept. 16 treaty.

D.W. Griffith's film *The Birth of a Nation* released.

1916

Gen. John J. **Pershing entered Mexico** to pursue Francisco (Pancho) Villa, who had raided U.S. border areas. Forces withdrawn Feb. 5, **1917.**

Rural Credits Act passed July 17, followed by Warehouse Act Aug. 11; both provided financial aid to farmers.

Bomb exploded during **San Francisco** Preparedness Day parade July 22, killed 10. Thomas J. Mooney, labor organizer, and Warren K. Billings, shoe worker, were convicted **1917;** both later pardoned.

U.S. bought **Virgin Islands** from Denmark Aug. 4.

Jeannette Rankin (R, MT) elected as **first-ever female** member of U.S. **House.**

U.S. established military government in the **Dominican Republic** Nov. 29.

Trade and loans to **European allies** soared during the year.

1917

Germany, suffering from British blockade, declared almost unrestricted **submarine warfare** Jan. 31. U.S. cut diplomatic ties with Germany Feb. 3, and formally **declared war** Apr. 6.

Jones Act, passed Mar. 2, made **Puerto Rico U.S. territory,** its inhabitants U.S. citizens.

Conscription law was passed May 18. First U.S. troops arrived in Europe June 26.

18th Amendment to the Constitution, providing for **prohibition** of manufacture, sale, or transportation of alcoholic beverages, was submitted to the states by Congress Dec. 18.

1918

Pres. Wilson set out his **14 Points** as basis for peace, Jan. 8. More than 1 mil **American troops** were in Europe by July. Allied counteroffensive launched at Château-Thierry July 18. War ended with signing of **armistice** Nov. 11.

Influenza epidemic killed an estimated 20 mil worldwide, 548,000 in U.S.

1919

18th **(prohibition)** Amendment, ratified Jan. 16, to take effect in 1 year.

First **transatlantic flight,** by U.S. Navy seaplane, left Rockaway, NY, May 8, stopped at Newfoundland, Azores, Lisbon May 27.

Boston police strike Sept. 9; National Guard breaks strike. About 250 **alien radicals** were deported Dec. 22.

Sherwood Anderson published *Winesburg, Ohio.*

1920

In national **Red Scare,** some 2,700 Communists, anarchists, and other radicals were arrested Jan.-May.

League of Women Voters founded Feb. 14.

Senate refused Mar. 19 to ratify the **League of Nations Covenant.**

Radicals Nicola **Sacco** and Bartolomeo **Vanzetti** accused of killing 2 men in Massachusetts payroll holdup Apr. 15. Found guilty **1921.** A 6-year campaign for their release failed, and both were executed Aug. 23, **1927.** Verdict repudiated **1977,** by proclamation of Massachusetts Gov. Michael Dukakis.

19th Amendment ratified Aug. 18, giving women the vote.

First regular licensed **radio broadcasting** begun Aug. 20.

Wall St., New York City, **bomb** explosion killed 30, injured 100, did $2 mil damage, Sept. 16.

Sinclair Lewis's *Main Street,* **F. Scott Fitzgerald's** *This Side of Paradise,* **Edith Wharton's** *The Age of Innocence* published.

1921

Congress sharply **curbed immigration,** set national quota system May 19.

Joint congressional resolution declaring **peace with Germany, Austria,** and **Hungary** signed July 2 by Pres. Warren G. Harding; treaties were signed in Aug.

In so-called **Black Sox** scandal, 8 Chicago **White Sox** players were banned from baseball Aug. 4 for conspiring with gamblers to throw the **1919** World Series.

Limitation of Armaments Conference met in Washington, DC, Nov. 12-Feb. 6, **1922.** Major powers agreed to curtail naval construction, outlaw poison gas, restrict submarine attacks on merchant vessels, respect integrity of China.

Ku Klux Klan began revival with violence against Catholics in North, South, and Midwest.

1922

Violence during **coal-mine strike** at Herrin, IL, June 22-23 cost 36 lives, including those of 21 nonunion miners.

Reader's Digest founded.

T. S. Eliot's *The Waste Land* published in London.

1923

First **sound-on-film motion picture,** *Phonofilm,* shown at Rivoli Theater, New York City, beginning in April.

Pres. Calvin Coolidge addressed Congress, Dec. 6; **first** official **broadcast** of a presidential speech.

1924

Law approved by Congress June 15 making all **Indians citizens.**

Nellie Tayloe Ross elected governor of Wyoming Nov. 9; inaugurated as nation's first woman governor Jan. 5, **1925.** **Miriam (Ma) Ferguson** elected governor of Texas Nov. 9; installed Jan. 20, **1925.**

George Gershwin wrote *Rhapsody in Blue.*

1925

John T. Scopes found guilty of having taught **evolution** in Dayton, TN, high school, fined $100 and costs, July 24.

F. Scott Fitzgerald's *The Great Gatsby* appeared.

1926

Dr. Robert H. Goddard demonstrated practicality of rockets, Mar. 16 at Auburn, MA, with first liquid-fuel rocket; rocket traveled 184 ft. in 2.5 sec.

Congress established **Army Air Corps** July 2.

Air Commerce Act passed Nov. 2, providing federal aid for airlines and airports.

Ernest Hemingway's *The Sun Also Rises* published.

1927

About 1,000 **marines landed in China** Mar. 5 to protect property in civil war.

Capt. **Charles A. Lindbergh** left Roosevelt Field, NY, May 20 alone in plane *Spirit of St. Louis* on first New York-Paris nonstop flight. Reached Le Bourget airfield May 21, 3,610 mi in 33½ hours.

The Jazz Singer, with **Al Jolson,** demonstrated part-talking pictures in New York City Oct. 6.

Show Boat opened in New York Dec. 27.

O. E. Rolvaag published *Giants in the Earth.*

1928

Amelia Earhart became first woman to fly across the Atlantic, June 17.

Herbert Hoover elected president Nov. 6, defeating New York Gov. **Alfred E. Smith,** a Catholic.

1929

"St. Valentine's Day massacre" in Chicago Feb. 14; gangsters killed 7 rivals.

Farm price stability aided by **Agricultural Marketing Act,** passed June 15.

Albert B. Fall, former secretary of the interior, was convicted of accepting bribe of $100,000 in the leasing of the **Elk Hills (Teapot Dome)** naval oil reserve; sentenced Nov. 1 to a year in prison and fined $100,000.

Stock market crash Oct. 29 marked end of past prosperity as stock prices plummeted. Stock losses for **1929-31** estimated at $50 bil; worst American depression began.

Thomas Wolfe published *Look Homeward, Angel.* **William Faulkner** published *The Sound and the Fury.*

1930

London **Naval Reduction Treaty** signed by U.S., Britain, Italy, France, and Japan Apr. 22; in effect Jan. 1, **1931;** expired Dec. 31, **1936.**

Hawley-Smoot Tariff signed; rate hikes slash world trade.

Sinclair Lewis became the first American to win a **Nobel Prize in literature.**

1931

Empire State Building opened in New York City May 1.

Al Capone was convicted of tax evasion Oct. 17.

Pearl Buck published *The Good Earth.*

1932

Reconstruction Finance Corp. established Jan. 22 to stimulate banking and business. Unemployment at 12 mil.

19-month-old **Charles Lindbergh Jr. was kidnapped** Mar. 1; found dead May 12. Bruno Hauptmann found guilty in trial Jan.-Feb. **1935;** executed Apr. 3, **1936.**

Bonus March on Washington, DC, launched May 29 by World War I veterans demanding Congress pay their bonus in full.

Franklin D. Roosevelt elected president for the first time in Democratic landslide, Nov. 8.

Chicago Bears won **first NFL title game** Dec. 18, defeating the Portsmouth (OH) Spartans, 9–0

1933

Pres. Roosevelt named **Frances Perkins** U.S. secretary of labor; first woman in U.S. cabinet.

All **banks in the U.S. ordered closed** by Pres. Roosevelt Mar. 6.

In a "100 days" special session, Mar. 9-June 16, Congress passed **New Deal** social and economic measures, including measures to regulate banks, distribute funds to the jobless, create jobs, raise agricultural prices, and set wage and production standards for industry.

Tennessee Valley Authority created by act of Congress, May 18.

Gold standard dropped by U.S.; announced by Pres. Roosevelt Apr. 19, ratified by Congress June 5.

Prohibition ended in the U.S. as 36th state ratified 21st Amendment Dec. 5.

Pres. Roosevelt foreswore armed intervention in **western hemisphere** nations Dec. 26.

1934

Pres. Roosevelt signed law creating the **Securities and Exchange Commission,** June 6.

U.S. troops pulled out of **Haiti** Aug. 6.

1935

Boulder Dam (later renamed Hoover Dam) completed, May 29.

Works Progress Administration **(WPA)** instituted May 6. Rural Electrification Administration created May 11. National Industrial Recovery Act struck down by Supreme Court May 27.

Comedian **Will Rogers** and aviator Wiley Post killed Aug. 15 in Alaska plane crash.

Social Security Act passed by Congress Aug. 14.

Huey Long, senator from Louisiana and national political leader, **assassinated** Sept. 8.

George Gershwin's *Porgy and Bess* opened Oct. 10 in New York.

Committee for Industrial Organization (CIO; later Congress of Industrial Organizations) formed to expand industrial unionism Nov. 9.

1936

Jesse Owens won 4 gold medals a the Berlin **Olympics** in August.

Baseball Hall of Fame founded in Cooperstown, NY.

Margaret Mitchell published *Gone With the Wind.*

1937

Hindenburg exploded May 6 landing at Lakehurst, NJ.

Golden Gate Bridge opened, May 27.

Joe Louis knocked out James J. Braddock, became world heavyweight champ June 22.

Amelia Earhart, aviator, and copilot Fred Noonan lost July 2 near Howland Island, in the Pacific.

Pres. Roosevelt asked for 6 additional Supreme Court justices; **"packing" plan** defeated.

Auto, steel labor unions won first big contracts.

1938

Naval Expansion Act passed May 17.

National minimum wage enacted June 25.

Orson Welles radio dramatization of **Martian invasion,** *War of the Worlds,* Oct. 30, caused scare.

Seabiscuit beat *War Admiral* in match race of the century, at Pimlico track, MD, Nov. 1.

"Grandma Moses" discovered.

Thornton Wilder's *Our Town* produced on Broadway.

1939

Pres. Roosevelt asked for **defense budget hike** in Jan.

New York World's Fair opened Apr. 30, closed Oct. 31; reopened May 11, **1940,** ended Oct. 21.

Lou Gehrig, seriously ill, said farewell to fans at Yankee Stadium, July 4.

Albert Einstein alerted Pres. Roosevelt to **A-bomb** possibilities in Aug. 2 letter.

U.S. declared its neutrality in European war Sept. 5.

Roosevelt proclaimed a limited national emergency Sept. 8, an unlimited emergency May 27, **1941.** Both ended by Pres. Harry Truman, Apr. 28, **1952.**

John Steinbeck published *Grapes of Wrath.*

Pocket books appeared in U.S.

Gone With the Wind and *The Wizard of Oz* films released.

1940

U.S. okayed sale of **surplus war materiel** to Britain June 3; announced transfer of 50 overaged destroyers Sept. 3.

First **peacetime military draft** in U.S. history approved Sept. 14.

40-hour work week went into effect, Oct. 24.

Roosevelt elected Nov. 5 to 3rd term as president.

Richard Wright published *Native Son.*

1941

Four Freedoms termed essential by Pres. Roosevelt in speech to Congress Jan. 6: freedom of speech and religion, freedom from want and fear.

Lend-Lease Act signed Mar. 11 provided $7 bil in military credits for Britain. Lend-Lease for USSR approved in Nov.

The **Atlantic Charter,** 8-point declaration of principles, issued by Roosevelt and British Prime Min. Winston Churchill, Aug. 14.

U.S. occupied **Iceland** July 7.

Japan attacked **Pearl Harbor,** Hawaii, 7:55 am Hawaiian time, Dec. 7; called by Roosevelt "a date that will live in infamy"; 19 ships sunk or damaged, 2,300 dead. U.S. declared war on Japan Dec. 8, on Germany and Italy Dec. 11.

Japanese invaded Philippines, Dec. 22; Wake Island fell Dec. 23.

1942

Japanese troops took **Bataan** peninsula Apr. 8, **Corregidor** May 6.

Federal government forcibly moved 110,000 **Japanese-Americans** from West Coast to detention camps. Exclusion lasted 3 years.

Battle of **Midway** June 4-7 was Japan's first major defeat.
Marines landed on **Guadalcanal** Aug. 7; last Japanese not expelled until Feb. 9, **1943.**

U.S., Britain invaded **North Africa** Nov. 8.

First **nuclear chain reaction** (fission of uranium isotope U-235) produced at Univ. of Chicago, under physicists Arthur Compton, Enrico Fermi, others, Dec. 2.

1943

Oklahoma! opened Mar. 31 on Broadway.

War contractors barred from **racial discrimination,** May 27.

Pres. Roosevelt signed June 10 pay-as-you-go income tax bill. Starting July 1, wage and salary earners were subject to a **paycheck withholding** tax.

Race riot in Detroit June 21; 34 dead, 700 injured. Riot in Harlem section of New York City Aug. 2; 6 killed.

U.S., Britain invaded **Sicily** July 9, Italian **mainland** Sept. 3.

Marines in Nov. recaptured the **Gilbert Islands,** captured by Japan in **1941** and **1942.**

1944

U.S., Allied forces invaded Europe at **Normandy** on "D Day," June 6, in greatest amphibious landing in history. **Battle of the Bulge**, failed Nazi counter offensive, waged Dec. 16, 1944, to Jan. 28, 1945; 500,000 Americans fought.

GI Bill of Rights signed by Pres. Roosevelt June 22, providing benefits for veterans.

Representatives of the U.S. and other major powers met at **Dunbarton Oaks**, Washington, DC, Aug. 21-Oct. 7, to work out formation of postwar world organziation that became the **United Nations.**

U.S. forces landed on **Leyte**, Philippines, Oct. 20.

Roosevelt elected to 4th term as president, Nov. 7.

Federal Highway Act passed by Congress, Nov. 29, creating national system of **interstate highways.**

1945

Yalta Conference met in the Crimea, USSR, Feb. 4-11. Roosevelt, Churchill, and Soviet leader Joseph Stalin agreed that their 3 countries, plus France, would occupy Germany and that the Soviet Union would enter war against Japan.

Marines landed on **Iwo Jima** Feb. 19, won control Mar. 16 after heavy casualties. U.S. forces invaded **Okinawa** Apr. 1, captured Okinawa June 21.

Pres. Roosevelt died in Warm Springs, GA, Apr. 12; Vice Pres. **Harry S. Truman** became president.

Germany surrendered May 7; May 8 proclaimed V-E Day.

First **atomic bomb**, produced at Los Alamos, NM, exploded at Alamogordo, NM, July 16. Bomb dropped on **Hiroshima** Aug. 6, with about 75,000 people killed; bomb dropped on **Nagasaki** Aug. 9, killing about 40,000. Japan agreed to surrender Aug. 14; formally surrendered Sept. 2.

Empire State Building struck by Army B-25 bomber, July 28, killing 13.

At **Potsdam Conference,** July 17-Aug. 2, leaders of U.S., USSR, and Britain agreed on disarmament of Germany, occupation zones, war crimes trials.

U.S. forces entered **Korea** south of 38th parallel to displace Japanese Sept. 8.

Gen. Douglas MacArthur took over supervision of Japan Sept. 9.

1946

Steel strike by 750,000 started Jan. 21, settled in 4 weeks. Strike by 400,000 **mine workers** began Apr. 1 (settled May 29); other industries followed.

At a speech at a Fulton, MO college, Mar. 5, Winston Churchill employed the phrase **"iron curtain."**

Atomic bomb tested off Bikini Atoll in Pacific, July 1.

Philippines given independence by U.S. July 4.

Mother Frances Xavier Cabrini 1st American to be canonized, July 7.

Dr. Benjamin Spock's *Baby and Child Care* published as 1946-64 **baby boom** began.

1947

Pres. Truman asked Congress for financial and military aid for Greece and Turkey to help combat Communist subversion (**Truman Doctrine),** Mar. 12. Approved May 15.

UN Security Council voted Apr. 2 to place under **U.S. trusteeship** the Pacific islands formerly mandated to Japan.

Jackie Robinson joined the Brooklyn Dodgers Apr. 11, breaking the color barrier in major league baseball.

The **Marshall Plan,** for U.S. aid to European countries, was proposed by Sec. of State George C. Marshall June 5. Congress authorized some $12 bil in next 4 years.

Taft-Hartley Labor Act restricting labor union power was vetoed by Truman June 20; Congress overrode the veto.

Air Force Capt. **Chuck Yeager** broke the sound barrier, Oct. 14, in X-1 rocket plane.

1948

USSR halted all surface traffic into **W. Berlin,** June 23; in response, U.S. and British troops launched an **airlift.** Soviet blockade halted May 12, **1949;** airlift ended Sept. 30.

Organization of American States founded Apr. 30.

Alger Hiss indicted Dec. 15 for perjury, after denying he had passed secret documents to Whittaker Chambers for transmission to a **Communist spy ring.** Convicted Jan. 21, **1950.**

Pres. Truman, elected Nov. 2, defeating Gov. Thomas E. Dewey in a historic upset.

Kinsey Report on sexuality in the human male published.

1949

NATO established Aug. 24 by U.S., Canada, and 10 Western European nations, agreeing that an armed attack against one would be considered an attack against all.

Mrs. I. Toguri D'Aquino (**Tokyo Rose** of Japanese wartime broadcasts) was sentenced Oct. 7 to 10 years in prison for treason. Paroled **1956,** pardoned **1977.**

Eleven leaders of **U.S. Communist Party** convicted Oct. 14 of advocating violent overthrow of U.S. government; sentenced to prison. Supreme Court upheld convictions **1951.**

Pres. Truman Oct. 26 signed legislation raising federal **minimum wage** from 40¢ an hour to 75¢.

Arthur Miller's *Death of a Salesman* opened on Broadway.

1950

Masked bandits robbed **Brink's, Inc.,** Boston express office, Jan. 17 of $2.8 mil. Case solved **1956;** 8 sentenced to life.

Pres. Truman authorized production of the **H-bomb** Jan. 31.

North Korean forces invaded **South Korea** June 25. UN asked for troops to restore peace.

Truman ordered Air Force and Navy to Korea June 27. Truman approved ground forces, air strikes against **North Korea** June 30.

U.S. sent 35 military advisers to **South Vietnam** June 27, and agreed to aid anti-Communist government.

Army seized all railroads Aug. 27 on Truman's order to prevent a general strike; returned to owners in **1952.**

U.S. forces landed at Inchon Sept. 15; UN force took Pyongyang Oct. 20, reached China border Nov. 20; China sent troops across border Nov. 26.

Two members of **Puerto Rican nationalist** movement tried to kill Pres. Truman Nov. 1.

U.S. banned shipments Dec. 8 to Communist **China** and to Asiatic ports trading with it.

Your Show of Shows debuted on TV.

Peanuts comic strip appeared.

David Riesman's *The Lonely Crowd* published.

1951

Sen. **Estes Kefauver** led Senate probe into organized crime.

22nd Amendment, limiting **presidential term of office,** ratified Feb. 27.

Julius Rosenberg, his wife, **Ethel**, and Morton Sobell found guilty Mar. 29 of conspiracy to commit wartime **espionage.** Rosenbergs received death penalty. Sobell sentenced to 30 years; released **1969.**

Gen. Douglas MacArthur removed from Korea command Apr. 11 by Pres. Truman, for unauthorized policy statements.

Korea cease-fire talks began in July; lasted 2 years. Fighting ended July 27, **1953**.

Tariff concessions by the U.S. to the Soviet Union, China, and all Communist-dominated lands were suspended Aug. 1.

The U.S., Australia, and New Zealand signed **Anzus** mutual security pact Sept. 1.

Transcontinental TV begun Sept. 4 with Pres. Truman's address at Japanese Peace Treaty Conference in San Francisco.

Japanese peace treaty signed in San Francisco Sept. 8 by U.S., Japan, and 47 other nations.

J. D. Salinger published *Catcher in the Rye*.

1952

Seizure of nation's steel mills was ordered by Pres. Truman Apr. 8 to avert a strike. Ruled illegal by Supreme Court June 2.

Peace contract between West Germany, U.S., Great Britain, and France was signed May 26.

The last racial and ethnic barriers to naturalization removed, June 26-27, with passage of **Immigration and Naturalization Act of 1952.**

Richard Nixon, as vice-pres. candidate, gave **"Checkers" speech,** Sept. 23

Puerto Rico proclaimed commonwealth July 25, after referendum Mar. 3.

First **hydrogen device** explosion Nov. 1 in Pacific.

1953

Federal jury in New York convicted 13 **Communist** leaders on conspracy charges, Jan. 20.

Pres. Dwight D. Eisenhower announced May 8 that U.S. had given France $60 mil for **Indochina War.** More aid was announced in Sept.

Julius and Ethel Rosenberg executed in the Sing Sing Prison electric chair, Ossining, NY, June 19, for betraying nuclear secrets to Soviet Union.

Korean War armistice signed July 27.

California Gov. **Earl Warren** was sworn in Oct. 5 as 14th **chief justice** of U.S. Supreme Court.

1954

Nautilus, first atomic-powered submarine, was launched at Groton, CT, Jan. 21.

Five members of Congress were **wounded** in the House Mar. 1 by 4 **Puerto Rican independence supporters** who fired at random from a spectators' gallery.

At televised **Army-McCarthy hearings,** Apr. 22-June 17, before a Senate subcommittee, Army officials accused Sen. Joseph McCarthy (R, WI) of seeking preferential treatment for a draftee, and McCarthy accused the Army of hindering probe of Communist infiltration into the Army.

Racial segregation in public schools unanimously ruled unconstitutional by Supreme Court May 17, in *Brown* v. *Board of Education of Topeka.*

Southeast Asia Treaty Organization (**SEATO**) formed by defense pact signed in Manila Sept. 8 by U.S., Britain, France, Australia, New Zealand, Philippines, Pakistan, and Thailand.

Condemnation of **Sen. McCarthy** voted by Senate, 67-22, Dec. 2, for abuse of the Senate during hearings and debates.

Ernest Hemingway won Nobel Prize.

1955

U.S. agreed Feb. 12 to help train **South Vietnamese** army.

Supreme Court ordered **"all deliberate speed"** in integration of public schools May 31.

A **summit meeting** of leaders of U.S., Britain, France, and USSR took place July 18-23 in Geneva, Switzerland.

Rosa Parks refused Dec. 1 to give her seat to a white man on a **bus in Montgomery, AL.** Bus segregation ordinance declared unconstitutional by a federal court following **boycott** organized by **Rev. Martin Luther King Jr.**

America's 2 largest labor organizations merged Dec. 5, creating the **AFL-CIO.**

1956

Massive resistance to Supreme Court desegregation rulings was called for Mar. 12 by 101 Southern congressmen.

U.S. Supreme Court, Apr. 23, unanimously ruled against **racial segregation** on intrastate buses.

Federal-Aid **Highway Act** signed June 29, inaugurating interstate highway system.

First transatlantic **telephone cable** activated Sept. 25.

On Oct. 8, in Game 5, Yankee right-hander Don Larsen pitched the only **World Series perfect game.**

My Fair Lady opened on Broadway in Mar., Eugene O'Neill's **Long Day's Journey Into Night** opened in Nov.

1957

Congress approved first **civil rights bill** for blacks since Reconstruction, Apr. 29, to protect voting rights.

The U.S. surgeon general July 12 said studies showed a "direct link" between cigarette **smoking and lung cancer**.

National Guardsmen, called out by Arkansas Gov. Orval Faubus Sept. 4, barred 9 black students from entering all-white high school in **Little Rock.** Faubus complied Sept. 21 with federal court order to remove Guardsmen, but the blacks were ordered to withdraw by local authorities. Pres. Eisenhower sent troops Sept. 24 to enforce court order.

Jack Kerouac published *On the Road.*

1958

First U.S. **earth satellite** to go into orbit, **Explorer I,** launched by Army Jan. 31 at Cape Canaveral, FL; discovered Van Allen radiation belt.

U.S. Marines sent to **Lebanon** to protect elected government from threatened overthrow July-Oct.

Nuclear sub **Nautilus** made first undersea crossing of the **North Pole** Aug. 5.

Presidential aide **Sherman Adams resigned** Sept. 22 over a scandal involving alleged improper gifts.

First domestic **jet airline** passenger service in U.S. opened by National Airlines Dec. 10 between New York and Miami.

1959

Alaska admitted as 49th state Jan. 3; **Hawaii** admitted as 50th Aug. 21.

St. Lawrence Seaway opened Apr. 25.

Vice Pres. **Richard Nixon,** on tour of U.S.S.R, held so-called kitchen debate, July 24, with Soviet Prem. **Nikita Khrushchev** at U.S. exhibit in Moscow.

Prem. **Khrushchev** paid unprecedented visit to U.S. Sept. 15-27; made transcontinental tour.

Pres. Eisenhower issued an injunction Oct. 12, upheld and made effective by the Supreme Court Nov. 7, ending a record 116-day **steel strike.**

In an emerging **quiz show scandal,** Columbia Univ. Prof. Charles Van Doren admitted to a U.S. House subcommittee Nov. 2 that he had been coached before appearances on NBC-TV's *21* in 1956; he had won $129,000.

1960

Sit-ins began Feb. 1 when 4 black college students in Greensboro, NC, refused to move from a Woolworth lunch counter when denied service. By Sept. **1961** over 70,000 students, whites and blacks, had participated in sit-ins.

Congress approved a strong **voting rights act** Apr. 21.

A U.S. **U-2 reconnaissance plane** was shot down in the Soviet Union May 1; pilot Gary Powers captured. The incident led to cancellation of a Paris summit conference.

Vice Pres. Richard Nixon and Sen. John F. Kennedy faced each other Sept. 26 in the first in a series of televised **debates. Kennedy defeated Nixon** to win presidency, Nov. 8.

U.S. announced Dec. 15 it backed rightist group in **Laos,** which took power the next day.

1961

U.S. severed diplomatic and consular relations with **Cuba** Jan. 3, after disputes over nationalizations of U.S. firms, U.S. military presence at Guantanamo base.

Invasion of Cuba's **Bay of Pigs** Apr. 17 by Cuban exiles trained, armed, and directed by U.S. unsuccessfully attempted to overthrow the regime of Prem. Fidel Castro.

Peace Corps created by executive order, Mar. 1.

23rd Amendment, giving **District of Columbia** citizens the right to vote in presidential elections, ratified Mar. 29.

Commander Alan B. Shepard Jr. was rocketed from Cape Canaveral, FL, 116.5 mi above the earth in a Mercury capsule May 5, in first U.S.-crewed suborbital space flight.

"Freedom Rides" from Washington, DC, across deep South were launched May 20 to **protest segregation** in interstate transportation.

Pres. Kennedy, May 27, signed bill creating **Alliance for Progress**, for Latin America.

In *Mapp v. Ohio*, June 19, Supreme Court ruled that **illegally obtained evidence** is inadmissible in state as well as federal trials.

1962

Lt. Col. **John H. Glenn Jr.** became first American in orbit Feb. 20 when he circled the earth 3 times in the Mercury capsule *Friendship 7.*

Pres. John F. Kennedy said Feb. 14 that U.S. military advisers in **Vietnam** would fire if fired upon.

In *Baker v. Carr*, Mar. 26, Supreme Court backed **"one-man one-vote"** apportionment of seats in state legislatures.

James Meredith became first black student at University of Mississippi Oct. 1 after 3,000 troops put down riots.

A Soviet **offensive missile buildup in Cuba** was revealed Oct. 22 by Pres. Kennedy, who ordered a naval and air quarantine on shipment of offensive military equipment to the island. He and Soviet Prem. Khrushchev agreed Oct. 28 on formula to end the crisis. Kennedy announced Nov. 2 that Soviet missile bases in Cuba were being dismantled.

Rachel Carson's *Silent Spring* launched environmentalist movement.

1963

In *Gideon v. Wainwright*, Mar. 18, Supreme Court ruled that all **criminal defendants** must have counsel.

University of Alabama **desegregated** after Gov. **George Wallace** stepped aside when confronted by federally deployed National Guard troops June 11.

Civil rights leader **Medgar Evers** was assassinated June 12.

Supreme Court ruled, 8-1, June 17 that laws requiring **recitation of the Lord's Prayer** or Bible verses in public schools were unconstitutional.

President **Kennedy**, on Europe trip, addressed huge crowd in **West Berlin**, June 23.

A limited **nuclear test-ban treaty** was agreed upon July 25 by the U.S., the Soviet Union, and Britain.

Birmingham, AL, rocked in Apr. and May by civil rights **demonstrations**, led by **Rev. Martin Luther King Jr.**; 200,000 joined in. **March on Washington** Aug. 28 in support of **black demands** for equal rights. Highlight was "I have a dream" speech by **King**.

16th St. Baptist Church in Birmingham, AL, bombed Sept. 15 in racial violence; 4 black girls killed.

South Vietnam Pres. **Ngo Dinh Diem assassinated** Nov. 2; U.S. had earlier withdrawn support.

Pres. Kennedy shot and fatally wounded Nov. 22 as he rode in a motorcade through downtown Dallas, TX. Vice Pres. **Lyndon B. Johnson sworn in** as president. **Lee Harvey Oswald arrested** and charged with the murder; he was shot and fatally wounded Nov. 24. **Jack Ruby**, a nightclub owner, was convicted of Oswald's murder; he died in **1967**, while awaiting retrial following reversal of his conviction.

Betty Friedan's *Feminine Mystique* was published.

1964

Panama suspended relations with U.S. Jan. 9 after riots. U.S. offered Dec. 18 to negotiate a new canal treaty.

The **Beatles** arrived in U.S. for first time, appeared Feb. 9 on CBS-TV's *Ed Sullivan Show.*

Supreme Court ordered Feb. 17 that **congressional districts** have equal populations.

U.S. reported May 27 it was sending military planes to **Laos.**

Omnibus **civil rights bill** cleared by Congress July 2, signed same day by Pres. Johnson, banning discrimination in voting, jobs, public accommodations.

Three **civil rights workers** were reported missing in Mississippi June 22; found buried Aug. 4. Twenty-one white men were arrested. On Oct. 20, **1967**, an all-white federal jury convicted 7 of conspiracy in the slayings.

Congress Aug. 7 passed the **Tonkin Gulf Resolution**, authorizing presidential action in Vietnam, after N Vietnamese boats reportedly attacked 2 U.S. destroyers Aug. 2.

Congress approved **War on Poverty** bill Aug. 11, providing for a domestic Peace Corps (**VISTA**), a **Job Corps**, and antipoverty funding.

The **Warren Commission** released Sept. 27 a report concluding that Lee Harvey Oswald was solely responsible for the Kennedy assassination.

Pres. Johnson was elected to a full term, Nov. 3, defeating Republican **Sen. Barry Goldwater** (AZ) in a landslide.

Verrazano-Narrows Bridge opened in New York City Nov. 21.

1965

In State of the Union address Jan. 4, Pres. Johnson outlined plans for his **"Great Society."**

Pres. Johnson in Feb. ordered continuous **bombing of North Vietnam** below 20th parallel.

Malcolm X assassinated Feb. 21 at New York City rally.

Some 14,000 U.S. troops sent to **Dominican Republic** during civil war Apr. 28. All troops withdrawn by next year.

March from Selma to Montgomery, AL, begun Mar. 21 by Rev. Martin Luther King Jr. to demand federal protection of **blacks' voting rights**. New **Voting Rights Act** signed Aug. 6.

Bill establishing **Medicare**, government health insurance program for persons over 65, signed by Pres. Johnson July 30.

Los Angeles riot by blacks living in **Watts** area resulted in 34 deaths and $200 mil in property damage Aug. 11-16.

National **immigration** quota system abolished Oct. 3.

Electric power failure blacked out most of northeastern U.S., parts of 2 Canadian provinces the night of Nov. 9-10.

1966

U.S. forces began firing into **Cambodia** May 1.

Bombing of Hanoi area of N Vietnam by U.S. planes began June 29. By Dec. 31, 385,300 U.S. troops were stationed in S Vietnam, plus 60,000 offshore and 33,000 in Thailand.

U.S. Supreme Court ruled June 13, in *Miranda v. Arizona,* that suspects must be read their rights before police questioning.

Medicare began July 1.

Charles Whitman, 25, **killed 13 students** from a tower at the **Univ. of Texas**, Austin, Aug. 1, before being shot dead by police.

U.S. **Dept. of Transportation** created, Oct. 15.

Edward Brooke (R, MA) elected Nov. 8 as first black U.S. senator in 85 years.

Robert C. Weaver named secretary of newly created Dept. of Housing and Urban Development (**HUD**), becoming **1st black cabinet member**

1967

Green Bay Packers beat Kansas City Chiefs, 35-10, in **first Super Bowl**, Jan. 15 in Los Angeles.

Black U.S. Rep. **Adam Clayton Powell** (D, NY) was denied his seat Mar. 1 because of charges he misused government funds. Reelected in **1968**, he was seated, but fined $25,000 and stripped of his seniority.

Pres. Johnson and Soviet Prem. Aleksei Kosygin met June 23 and 25 at Glassboro State College in NJ; agreed not to let any crisis push them into war.

25th Amendment, providing for **presidential succession**, was ratified Feb. 10.

USS *Liberty*, an intelligence ship, was torpedoed by Israel in the Mediterranean, apparently by accident, June 8; 34 killed.

Riots by blacks in **Newark, NJ**, July 12-17 killed 26, injured 1,500; more than 1,000 arrested. In **Detroit, MI,** July 23-30, 43 died; 2,000 injured, 5,000 left homeless by rioting, looting, burning in city's black ghetto.

An **antiwar march** on Washington, Oct. 21-22, drew 50,000 participants.

Thurgood Marshall was sworn in Oct. 2 as first black U.S. Supreme Court Justice. **Carl B. Stokes** (D, Cleveland) and **Richard G. Hatcher** (D, Gary, IN) were elected first black mayors of major U.S. cities Nov. 7.

1968

USS *Pueblo* and 83-man crew seized in Sea of Japan Jan. 23 by North Koreans; 82 men released Dec. 22.

"Tet offensive": Communist troops attacked Saigon, 30 province capitals Jan. 30, suffered heavy casualties.

Pres. Johnson **curbed bombing** of North Vietnam Mar. 31. Peace talks began in Paris May 10. All bombing of North halted Oct. 31.

Martin Luther King Jr., 39, assassinated Apr. 4 in Memphis, TN. **James Earl Ray,** an escaped convict, pleaded guilty to the slaying, was sentenced to 99 years.

Students at **Columbia** Univ., Apr. 23-24, seized school buildings in protest demonstrations.

Sen. Robert F. Kennedy (D, NY), 42, **shot** June 5 in Los Angeles, after celebrating presidential primary victories. Died June 6. Sirhan Bishara Sirhan, convicted of murder, **1969;** death sentence commuted to life in prison, **1972.**

Vice Pres. **Hubert Humphrey nominated** for president by Democrats **at national convention in Chicago,** marked by clash between police and **antiwar protesters,** Aug. 26-29. The Republican nominee, **Richard Nixon, won** the **presidency,** defeating Hubert Humphrey in a close race Nov. 5.

Apollo 8 **orbited moon** in 5-day mission, Dec. 21-27.

1969

Expanded 4-party **Vietnam peace talks** began Jan. 18. U.S. force peaked at 543,400 in April. Withdrawal started July 8. Pres. Nixon set Vietnamization policy Nov. 3.

Earl Warren retired and swearing in **Warren Burger,** June 23, as Supreme Court chief justice.

U.S. astronaut **Neil Armstrong,** commander of the *Apollo 11* mission, became the first person to **set foot on the moon,** July 20; followed by astronaut **Edwin Aldrin;** astronaut **Michael Collins** remained aboard command module.

Woodstock music **festival** near Bethel, NY, drew 300,000-500,000 people, Aug. 15-18.

Anti-Vietnam War **demonstrations** increased in U.S.; some 250,000 marched in Washington, DC, Nov. 15.

Massacre of hundreds of civilians at **My Lai, South Vietnam,** in **1968** incident reported Nov. 16.

Sesame Street launched on public TV.

1970

United Mine Workers official **Joseph A. Yablonski,** his wife, and their daughter found shot to death Jan. 5; UMW chief W. A. (Tony) Boyle later convicted of the killing.

A federal jury Feb. 18 found the **"Chicago 7"** antiwar activists innocent of conspiring to incite riots during the 1968 **Democratic National Convention.** However, 5 were convicted of crossing state lines with intent to incite riots.

Millions of Americans participated in antipollution demonstrations Apr. 22 to mark the **first Earth Day.**

U.S. and South Vietnamese forces crossed **Cambodian** borders Apr. 30 to get at enemy bases.

Four students were killed May 4 at **Kent State** Univ. in Ohio by National Guardsmen during a protest against the war. In protest at **Jackson State** Univ. in Mississippi police fired on protesters; 2 killed.

Two **women generals,** the first in U.S. history, were named by Pres. Nixon May 15.

A **postal reform** measure was signed Aug. 12, creating an independent U.S. Postal Service.

Pres. Nixon, Dec. 31, signed **clean air bill** calling for development of a cleaner auto engine and national air quality standards for 10 major pollutants.

Doonesbury comic strip launched in 30 papers.

1971

Charles Manson and 3 of his cult followers were found guilty Jan. 25 of first-degree murder in **1969** slaying of actress Sharon Tate and 6 others.

Pres. Nixon, Apr. 14, relaxed 20-year trade embargo with **China**.

The 26th Amendment, lowering the **voting age to 18** in all elections, was ratified June 30.

A court-martial jury Mar. 29 convicted **Lt. William L. Calley Jr.** in murder of 22 South Vietnamese at **My Lai** on Mar. 16, **1968.** He was sentenced to life imprisonment Mar. 31. Sentence was reduced to 20 years Aug. 20.

Publication of classified **Pentagon papers** on U.S. involvement in Vietnam was begun June 13 by the *New York Times.* Supreme Court June 30 upheld, 6-3, the right of the *Times* and *Washington Post* to publish the documents.

Pres. Nixon, Aug. 15, instituted a 90-day **wage and price** freeze.

U.S. bombers struck massively in North Vietnam for 5 days starting Dec. 26 in retaliation for alleged violations of agreements reached prior to the 1968 bombing halt.

1972

Pres. Nixon arrived in **Beijing** Feb. 21 for an 8-day visit to China, in a "journey for peace;" a joint communiqué released Feb. 27 called for increased Sino-U.S. contracts.

By a vote of 84 to 8, the Senate, Mar. 22, approved **Equal Rights Amendment** banning **discrimination** on the basis of sex, and sent the measure to the states for ratification.

North Vietnamese forces launched the biggest attacks in 4 years across the demilitarized zone Mar. 30. The U.S. responded Apr. 15 by resumption of bombing of Hanoi and Haiphong after a 4-year lull.

Pres. Nixon announced May 8 the mining of **North Vietnam ports.** Last U.S. combat troops left Aug. 11.

Gov. George C. Wallace (AL), campaigning for president at a Laurel, MD, shopping center May 15, **was shot** and seriously wounded. Arthur Bremer **convicted** Aug. 4, sentenced to 63 years for shooting Wallace and 3 others.

In **first visit of a U.S. president to Moscow,** Pres. Nixon arrived May 22 for a week of summit talks with Kremlin leaders that culminated in a landmark strategic arms pact (SALT I).

Five men were arrested June 17 for breaking into the offices of the Democratic National Committee in the **Watergate** office complex in Washington, DC.

Mark Spitz won 7 gold medals in world record times, at the Munich Olympics in Sept.

Pres. **Nixon reelected** Nov. 7 in a landslide, carrying 49 states to defeat Democratic Sen. George McGovern (SD).

The **Dow Jones** Industrial Average closed above 1,000 for the first time, Nov. 14.

Full-scale **bombing of North Vietnam** resumed after Paris peace negotiations reached an impasse Dec. 18.

1973

Five of 7 defendants in **Watergate** break-in trial pleaded guilty Jan. 11 and 15; the other 2 were convicted Jan. 30.

In *Roe v. Wade,* Supreme Court ruled, 7-2, Jan. 22, that states may not ban **abortions** during **first 3 months of pregnancy** and may regulate, but may not ban, abortions during 2nd trimester.

Wounded Knee, SD, occupied in protest by activists in American Indian Movement, Feb. 27.

Four-party **Vietnam peace pacts** were signed in Paris Jan. 27, and North Vietnam released some 590 U.S. prisoners by Apr. 1. Last U.S. troops left Mar. 29.

End of the military **draft** announced Jan. 27.

Top **Nixon aides** H. R. Haldeman, John D. Ehrlichman, and John Dean and Attorney Gen. Richard Kleindienst **resigned** Apr. 30, amid charges of White House efforts to obstruct justice in the Watergate case.

Skylab, 1st U.S. space station, launched May 14 by Saturn rocket.

John Dean, former Nixon counsel, told Senate hearings June 25 that Nixon, his staff and campaign aides, and the Justice Dept. had conspired to cover up **Watergate** facts.

The U.S. officially ceased bombing in **Cambodia** at midnight Aug. 14 in accord with a June congressional action.

Vice Pres. Spiro Agnew, Oct. 10, **resigned** and pleaded no contest to a charge of tax evasion on payments made to him by contractors when he was governor of Maryland. **Gerald R. Ford,** Oct. 12, became **first appointed vice president** under the 25th Amendment; sworn in Dec. 6.

A total ban on **oil exports** to the U.S. was imposed by Arab oil-producing nations Oct. 19-21 after the outbreak of an Arab-Israeli war. The ban was lifted Mar. 18, **1974.**

Attorney Gen. Elliot Richardson resigned, and his deputy William D. Ruckelshaus and **Watergate special prosecutor Archibald Cox** were **fired** by Pres. Nixon, Oct. 20, when Cox threatened to secure a judicial ruling that Nixon was violating a court order to give tapes to Judge John Sirica. **Leon Jaworski** named Nov. 1 by the Nixon administration to succeed Cox.

Congress overrode Nov. 7 Pres. Nixon's veto of the **war powers** bill, which curbed president's power to commit forces to hostilities abroad without congressional approval.

1974

On Apr. 18, **Hank Aaron** of the Atlanta Braves hit his 715th career **home run** to break **Babe Ruth's** record.

Impeachment hearings opened May 9 against Pres. Nixon by the House Judiciary Committee

John D. Ehrlichman and 3 **White House "plumbers"** found guilty July 12 of conspiring to violate the civil rights of Pentagon Papers leaker Daniel Ellsberg's psychiatrist by breaking into his office.

Supreme Court ruled, 8-0, July 24 that Nixon had to turn over **64 tapes** of White House conversations.

House Judiciary Committee, in televised hearings July 24-30, recommended 3 **articles of impeachment** against Pres. Nixon. The first, voted 27-11, charged conspiracy to obstruct justice in the Watergate cover-up. The 2nd, voted 28-10, charged abuses of power. The 3rd, voted 21-17, charged defiance of committee subpoenas. (The House voted Aug. 20, 412-3, to accept the committee report, which included the impeachment articles.)

Pres. Nixon announced his resignation, Aug. 8, and **resigned** Aug. 9; his support in Congress had begun to collapse Aug. 5, after release of tapes appearing to implicate him in Watergate cover-up. **Vice Pres. Ford** was **sworn in** Aug. 9 as 38th U.S. president.

Ford, Aug. 20, nominated Nelson **Rockefeller** to be **vice-president**; he was sworn in Dec. 10.

A **pardon** to ex-Pres. Nixon for any federal crimes he committed while president issued by Pres. Ford Sept. 8.

1975

Found guilty of Watergate cover-up charges Jan. 1 were ex-Atty. Gen. John Mitchell and ex-presidential advisers H. R. Haldeman and John Ehrlichman.

U.S. launched **evacuation** of Americans and some South Vietnamese **from Saigon** Apr. 29 as Communist forces completed takeover of South Vietnam; **South Vietnamese** government officially **surrendered** Apr. 30.

U.S. merchant ship *Mayaguez* and its crew of 39 were seized by Cambodian forces in Gulf of Siam May 12. In rescue operation, U.S. Marines attacked Tang Island, planes bombed air base; Cambodia surrendered ship and crew.

Congress voted $405 mil for **South Vietnam refugees** May 16; 140,000 were flown to the U.S.

Illegal CIA operations described by panel headed by Vice Pres. **Rockefeller** June 10.

Publishing heiress **Patricia (Patty) Hearst,** kidnapped Feb. 5, **1974,** by "Symbionese Liberation Army" militants, captured in San Francisco Sept. 18 with others. She was convicted Mar. 20, **1976,** of bank robbery.

1976

Nationwide **swine flu vaccination** program launched Mar. 24, discontinued Oct. 12 after several deaths reported.

In **"right to die"** case, New Jersey Supreme Court Mar. 31 allowed deeply comatose **Karen Ann Quinlan** to be removed from respirator; she survived, dying in a nursing home in **1985.**

Supreme Court **reinstated death penalty,** July 2, subject to conditions.

U.S. celebrated **200th anniversary of independence** July 4, with festivals, parades, and New York City's Operation Sail, a gathering of tall ships from around the world.

"Legionnaire's disease" killed 29 persons who attended an American Legion convention July 21-24 in Philadelphia.

Viking II set down on **Mars'** Utopia Plains Sept. 3, following the successful landing by *Viking I* July 20.

Two U.S. officers on routine mission near DMZ slain by **North Korean soldiers,** Aug. 18; North Korea stated "regret," Aug. 21.

1977

Pres. Jimmy Carter Jan. 21 pardoned most Vietnam War **draft evaders**.

Convicted murderer **Gary Gilmore executed** by a Utah firing squad Jan. 17, in the first exercise of capital punishment in the U.S. since **1967.**

Natural gas shortage, caused by severe winter weather, led Congress Feb. 2 to approve emergency federal allocation program.

Pres. Carter signed an act Aug. 4 creating a new cabinet-level **Energy Department.**

Elvis Presley died Aug. 16.

FBI Dec. 7 released 40,000 pages of previously secret files relating to Kennedy assassination.

Steven Spielberg's first **Star Wars** film produced.

1978

Crippling 110-day coal miners **strike** ended Mar. 25 with ratification of new contract.

Senate voted, 68-32, Apr. 18 to turn over **Panama Canal** to Panama on Dec. 31, **1999**; a Mar. 16 vote had given approval to a treaty guaranteeing the area's neutrality after the year 2000.

Californians, June 6, approved **Proposition 13,** a state constitutional amendment slashing property taxes.

Supreme Court, June 28, ruled against **racial quotas** in *Bakke* v. *University of California.*

Egyptian Pres. Anwar al-**Sadat** and Israeli Prem. Menachem **Begin** reached accord on "framework for peace," Sept. 17, after Carter-mediated talks at **Camp David.**

New York's Chemical Bank Dec. 20 led move to raise **prime interest rate** to near-record 11.75%.

1979

Former Atty. Gen. John Mitchell, last of 25 persons still jailed for crimes relating to **Watergate scandal,** released Jan. 19.

Partial meltdown released radioactive material Mar. 28, at nuclear reactor on **Three Mile Island** near Middletown, PA.

American Airlines DC-10 **jetliner crashed** May 25 after takeoff from Chicago, killing 275 persons.

In a July 15, Pres. Carter spoke of a national **"malaise"** and outlined a proposed 10-year $140 bil program to **reduce U.S. dependence on foreign oil.**

Federal government announced, Nov. 1, a $1.5 bil loan-guarantee plan to aid the ailing **Chrysler Corp.**

Some 90 people, including 63 Americans, **taken hostage,** Nov. 4, at **American embassy in Tehran,** Iran, by militant followers of **Ayatollah Khomeini.** He demanded return of former Shah Muhammad Reza Pahlavi, who was undergoing medical treatment in New York City.

1980

Pres. Carter announced, Jan. 4, economic sanctions against the USSR, in retaliation for Soviet invasion of Afghanistan. At Carter's request, **U.S. Olympic Committee** voted, Apr. 12, against U.S. participation in Moscow Summer Olympics.

Lake Placid, NY, hosted the **Winter Olympics** for the 2nd time. The U.S. hockey team defeated the heavily-favored Russian team Feb. 22 en route to winning the gold medal.

An 11-day New York City **transit strike** ended, Apr. 11, after union leaders approved a tentative agreement on a new contract.

Eight Americans killed and 5 wounded, Apr. 24, **in ill-fated** attempt to **rescue hostages** held by Iranian militants.

Mt. St. Helens, in Washington state, **erupted** May 18. The blast, with others May 25 and June 12, left 57 dead.

In a sweeping victory, Nov. 4, **Ronald Reagan** (R) was elected 40th president, defeating incumbent Pres. Carter. Republicans gained control of the Senate.

Former Beatle **John Lennon** was shot and **killed,** Dec. 8, in New York City.

1981

Minutes after Reagan's inauguration Jan. 20, the **52 Americans** held **hostage in Iran** for 444 days were **freed.**

Pres. Reagan was **shot and seriously wounded,** Mar. 30, in Washington, DC; also seriously wounded were a Secret Service agent, a policeman, and Press Sec. **James Brady. John W. Hinckley Jr.** arrested, found not guilty by reason of insanity in **1982,** committed to mental institution.

World's first reusable spacecraft, the **space shuttle** *Columbia,* was sent into space, Apr. 12.

Congress, July 29, passed Pres. Reagan's **tax-cut legislation,** expected to save taxpayers $750 bil over 5 years.

Federal air traffic controllers, Aug. 3, began an illegal **nationwide strike.** Most defied a back-to-work order and were dismissed by Pres. Reagan Aug. 5.

In a 99-0 vote, the Senate confirmed, Sept. 21, appointment of **Sandra Day O'Connor** as **first woman justice** of U.S. Supreme Court.

1982

The 13-year-old lawsuit against **AT&T** by the **Justice Dept.** was settled Jan. 8. AT&T agreed to give up the 22 Bell System companies and was allowed to expand.

The Equal Rights Amendment was **defeated** after a 10-year struggle, when the deadline for ratification expired June 30.

Centers for Disease Control, July 16, reported evidence of growing **AIDS epidemic,** responsible for 184 U.S. deaths since 1st reported in U.S. in June **1981.**

The economy showed signs of recovery from the **recession** that began in mid-**1981,** as the **Dow Jones** Industrials Average Oct. 13 hit 1016.93, its highest level in 18 months, amid falling interest rates.

The most expensive **strike** in sports history ended, Nov. 16, when players for **NFL** teams reached a settlement with owners.

Space shuttle *Columbia* completed its first operational flight, Nov. 16.

A retired dentist, **Dr. Barney B. Clark,** 61, became first recipient of a **permanent artificial heart,** Dec. 2; he died Mar. 23, **1983,** after 112 days.

EPA administrator Anne Gorsuch was **cited for contempt** by the House Dec. 16, after refusing to produce certain documents concerning the Superfund.

1983

Pres. Reagan, Jan. 3, declared Times Beach, MO, a federal disaster area because of the threat posed by toxic **dioxin** in the soil.

The Commerce Dept. Jan 19 reported that average real **GNP** in the recessionary year **1982** fell 1.8% from **1981** levels, the **worst decline** since 1946.

Harold Washington was elected Apr. 12 as the first African American **mayor of Chicago.**

On Apr. 20, **Pres. Reagan** signed a compromise bipartisan bill designed to save **Social Security** from bankruptcy.

Sally Ride became the first American **woman** to travel in **space,** June 18, when the **space shuttle** *Challenger* was launched from Cape Canaveral, FL.

On Sept. 1, a **South Korean passenger jet** infringing on Soviet air space and apparently misidentified as a surveillance plane was **shot down;** 269 people, including 61 Americans, were killed.

On Oct. 23, 241 **U.S. Marines and sailors** were killed in Lebanon when a TNT-laden suicide bomb blew up Marine headquarters at **Beirut** International Airport.

U.S. troops, with a small force from 6 **Caribbean** nations, invaded **Grenada** Oct. 25. In a few days, Grenadian militia and Cuban "construction workers" were overcome, U.S. citizens evacuated, and the **Marxist regime deposed.**

1984

Seven regional companies took over local telephone service from AT&T, Jan. 1.

The space shuttle *Challenger* was launched on its 4th trip into space, Feb. 3. On Feb. 7, Navy Capt. Bruce McCandless, followed by Army Lt. Colonel Robert Stewart, became **first humans to fly free of a spacecraft.**

On May 7, American **Vietnam war** veterans reached an out-of-court **settlement with 7 chemical companies** in a class-action suit over the herbicide **Agent Orange.**

Former Vice Pres. **Walter Mondale** won the Democratic **presidential nomination,** June 6; he chose **Rep. Geraldine Ferraro** (D, NY), as candidate for **vice president.**

Pres. Reagan signed a bill July 17 cutting federal transportation aid to states that keep their **drinking age** under 21.

Pres. **Reagan** was **reelected** Nov. 6 in a Republican **landslide,** carrying 49 states for a record 525 electoral votes.

Bernhard Goetz shot and wounded 4 allegedly menacing teen-age boys, on a NYC subway train, Dec. 22; later was acquitted of major charges but was successfully sued.

1985

Visiting Germany, Pres. Reagan, May 5, laid wreath at concentration camp site and also at a **Bitburg** cemetery, where some Nazis lay.

Philadelphia police bombed a rowhouse occupied by **MOVE anarchists,** May 13; 11 were killed, and fire damaged 2 blocks of houses.

On June 14 a **TWA jet was seized** by terrorists after take-off from Athens; 153 passengers and crew held hostage for 17 days; 1 U.S. serviceman killed.

Reversing an earlier decision to market "new" coke, the **Coca-Cola Co.** said, July 10, it would resume marketing soda made under its original "Classic" formula.

"Live Aid," a rock concert broadcast around the world July 13, raised $70 mil for starving peoples of Africa.

On Oct. 7, **4 Palestinian hijackers seized** Italian cruise ship *Achille Lauro* in the Mediterranean and held it hostage for 2 days; one American, Leon Klinghoffer, was killed.

For first time in 6 years U.S. and Soviet leaders met at **summit in Geneva,** Nov.19-20.

General Electric agreed Dec. 11 to buy RCA Corp. for $6.28 bil.

1986

On Jan. 20, for the first time, the U.S. officially observed **Martin Luther King Jr. Day.**

The space shuttle **Challenger exploded** 73 seconds after liftoff, Jan. 28, **killing 6 astronauts and Christa McAuliffe,** a New Hampshire teacher, on board.

In a 4-day extravaganza in July, the U.S. celebrated the 100th birthday of the **Statue of Liberty.**

Congress completed action Oct. 2 overriding Pres. Reagan's veto and imposing economic **sanctions on South Africa.**

The Senate confirmed, Sept. 17, Reagan's nomination of **William Rehnquist** as chief justice and **Antonin Scalia** as associate justice of the Supreme Court.

Press reports in early Nov. broke first news of the **Iran-contra scandal,** involving secret U.S. sale of arms to Iran.

Ivan Boesky, accused of insider trading, agreed, Nov. 14, to plead guilty to an unspecified criminal count.

Robert Penn Warren named by the Library of Congress as America's **first poet laureate.**

1987

Pres. Reagan produced the nation's first **trillion-dollar budget,** Jan. 5.

Dow Jones closed above 2,000 for first time, Jan. 8.

The U.S. government, Mar. 20, approved for the first time the use of a drug in the fight against AIDS (AZT).

Nearly **1.4 mil illegal aliens** met May 4 deadline for applying for **amnesty** under a new federal policy.

An **Iraqi missile killed 37 sailors** on the frigate USS *Stark* in the Persian Gulf, May 17. Iraq called it an accident.

Public hearings by Senate and House committees investigating the **Iran-contra affair** were held May-Aug. Lt. Col. **Oliver North** said he had believed all his activities were authorized by his superiors. Pres. Reagan, Aug. 12, denied knowing of a diversion of funds to the contras.

The 200th anniversary of the signing of the **U.S. Constitution** was observed, Sept. 17, in Philadelphia and around the U.S.

Wall Street crashed, Oct. 19, with the Dow Jones plummeting a record 508 points to 1738, ending a bull market that began in mid-**1982.**

Pres. Reagan and Soviet leader **Mikhail Gorbachev,** Dec. 8, signed a **pact to dismantle** all 1,752 U.S. and 859 Soviet **missiles** with a 300- to 3,400-mi. range.

1988

In a report issued May 16, Surgeon Gen. C. Everett Koop declared that **cigarettes** and other tobacco products were addictive.

Congress approved, in June, the greatest expansion yet of **Medicare** benefits, to protect the **elderly and disabled** against "catastrophic" medical costs.

Much of the U.S. suffered worst **drought** in over 50 years; by late June half the nation's agricultural counties had been declared disaster areas.

A missile, fired from **U.S. Navy warship** *Vincennes,* in the Persian Gulf, mistakenly struck a commercial **Iranian airliner,** July 3, killing all 290.

George H. W. Bush was **elected** 41st U.S. **president,** Nov. 8, decisively defeating Gov. **Michael Dukakis** (MA).

Pan Am Flight 103 exploded and crashed into the town of **Lockerbie, Scotland,** Dec. 21, killing all 259 people aboard and 11 on the ground.

Drexel Burnham Lambert agreed, Dec. 21, **to plead guilty** to insider trading and other violations, and **pay penalties of $650 mil,** the largest such settlement ever.

1989

Major oil spill occurred when the *Exxon Valdez* struck Bligh Reef in Alaska's Prince William Sound, Mar. 24.

Former National Security Council staff member **Oliver North** was convicted, May 4, on charges related to **Iran-contra** scandal. Conviction thrown out on appeal in **1991** because of his immunized testimony.

A measure to **rescue the savings and loan industry** was signed into law, Aug. 9, by Pres. Bush.

Army Gen. Colin Powell was nominated Aug. 10 by Pres. Bush, as **chairman of the Joint Chiefs of Staff;** he became the first black to hold the post.

Pete Rose, a baseball legend, was **banned** from the game for life Aug. 24, for involvement with gamblers.

Hurricane Hugo swept through the Caribbean and the Carolinas Sept. 10-22, causing at least 40 deaths and $6 bil in damage in the Carolinas alone.

Just before a World Series game, Oct. 17, an **earthquake** struck the **San Francisco Bay area,** causing 62 deaths.

L. Douglas Wilder (D) elected governor of Virginia, the **first U.S. black governor** since Reconstruction.

U.S. troops invaded Panama, Dec. 20, overthrowing the government of **Manuel Noriega.** Noriega, wanted by U.S. authorities on drug charges, surrendered Jan. 3, **1990.**

1990

Junk bond financier Michael Milkin pleaded guilty to fraud related charges, Apr. 14; agreed to pay $500 mil in restitution; sentenced Nov. 21 to 10 years in prison.

Justice William Brennan announced, July 20, his resignation from the U.S. Supreme Court; his replacement, **Judge David Souter,** was confirmed Sept. 27.

Pres. Bush signed **Americans With Disabilities Act** on July 26, barring discrimination against handicapped.

Operation Desert Shield forces left for **Saudi Arabia,** Aug. 7, to defend that country following the **invasion** of its neighbor **Kuwait by Iraq,** Aug. 2.

Pres. Bush signed, Nov. 5, a bill to **reduce budget deficits** $500 bil over 5 years, by spending curbs and tax hikes.

Pres. Bush Nov. 15 signed into law a strengthened version of the 1970 **Clean Air Act.**

1991

The **U.S. and its allies defeated Iraq** in the **Persian Gulf War** and liberated Kuwait, which Iraq had overrun in Aug. **1990.** On Jan. 17, the allies launched a devastating **air at-**

tack. In a **rapid ground war** starting Feb. 24, which lasted just 100 hours, the U.S.-led forces killed or captured thousands of Iraqi soldiers and sent the rest into retreat before Pres. Bush ordered a cease-fire Feb. 27.

An 8-month **recession** showed signs of having ended in Mar.

Dow-Jones Industrials Average closed above **3000** for first time, Apr. 17.

Justice **Thurgood Marshall,** first black to sit on U.S. Supreme Court, June 17, announced plans **to retire.**

U.S. **House bank** ordered closed Oct. 3 after revelations that House members had written 8,331 bad checks.

The **Senate approved,** Oct. 15, nomination of **Clarence Thomas** to the Supreme Court, despite allegations of sexual harassment against him by **Anita Hill,** a former aide. He became the 2nd African-American to serve on the Court, replacing retiring Justice **Thurgood Marshall,** the 1st black.

Charles Keating convicted of securities fraud Dec. 4. The prosecution asserted that as chairman of an S&L he had induced investors to buy $250 mil in uninsured bonds.

1992

Retail giant **R.H. Macy & Co.** filed for bankruptcy, Jan. 27. **Trans World Airlines,** Jan. 31, became the latest major U.S. carrier to file for bankruptcy.

Riots swept South-Central **Los Angeles** Apr. 29, after **jury acquitted 4 white policemen** on all but one count in videotaped 1991 beating of black motorist **Rodney King.** Death toll in the L.A. violence was put at 52.

The **27th Amendment,** regarding congressional pay raises, became part of the Constitution May 7 when it was ratified by the 38th state, Michigan.

Comedian **Johnny Carson** retired May 22 after 29 years as host of *The Tonight Show* on NBC.

Hurricane Andrew ravaged South Florida and Louisiana Aug. 24-26, killing 23 people.

White supremacist and fugitive Randall Weaver surrendered Aug. 31 after an 11-day FBI **siege** at his **Ruby Ridge,** ID, cabin, during which his wife and son and a deputy sheriff were killed in exchanges of gunfire.

Bill Clinton (D) was **elected** 42nd president, Nov. 3, defeating **Pres. Bush** (R) and independent **Ross Perot.**

A UN-sanctioned military force, led by U.S. troops, arrived in **Somalia** Dec. 9.

Presidents of U.S., Canada, and Mexico Dec. 17 signed North American Free Trade Agreement **(NAFTA),** to establish a free trade zone.

More than 1.1 million votes were cast in an election to choose a portrait of the late **Elvis Presley** (died 1977) for a **U.S. postage stamp.**

1993

A bomb exploded in a parking garage beneath the **World Trade Center** in New York City, Feb. 26, killing 6 people. Two Islamic militants were convicted in the bombing, Nov. 12, **1997.** Four men were found guilty, Mar. 4, **1994.**

Janet Reno became the first woman U.S. attorney general Mar. 12.

Four federal agents were killed, Feb. 28, during an unsuccessful raid on the **Branch Davidian compound near Waco, TX.** A 51-day siege by federal agents ended Apr. 19, when the compound **burned down,** leaving more than 70 cult members dead. 11 **cult** members were acquitted Feb. 26, **1994,** of charges in the deaths of the federal agents.

A federal jury, Apr. 17, found **2 Los Angeles police officers guilty** and 2 not guilty of violating the civil rights of motorist Rodney King in 1991 beating incident.

Defense Sec. Les Aspin, Apr. 28, removed restrictions on aerial **combat roles by women** in the armed forces.

In a May 14 **plebiscite** voters in **Puerto Rico** supported continuing commonwealth status with U.S.

A **"motor-voter"** bill was signed by Pres. Clinton, May 20, allowing citizens to register to vote by mail when applying for a driver's license or certain benefits.

"The Great Flood of 1993" inundated 8 mil acres in 9 Midwestern states in summer, leaving 50 dead.

Pres. Clinton July 2 approved recommendations that 33 major U.S. **military bases** be **closed.** On July 19 he announced a **"don't ask, don't tell, don't pursue"** policy for homosexuals in the U.S. military.

Vincent Foster, deputy White House counsel, found shot to death July 20 in a N Virginia park, an apparent suicide.

Judge Ruth Bader Ginsburg was sworn in, Aug. 10, as 107th justice of the Supreme Court.

Pres. Clinton, Aug. 10, signed a measure designed to **cut federal budget deficits** $496 bil over 5 years, through spending cuts and new taxes.

The **"Brady Bill,"** a major gun-control measure, was signed into law by Pres. Clinton Nov. 30.

1994

North American Free Trade Agreement took effect Jan. 1.

A predawn **earthquake** struck the Los Angeles area, Jan. 17, claiming 61 lives and causing widespread devastation.

Pres. Clinton Feb. 3 lifted 19-year ban on U.S. **trade with Vietnam.**

Kenneth Starr named Aug. 5 as independent counsel to probe **Whitewater affair;** congressional committees, late July, began Whitewater hearings.

Byron De La Beckwith convicted Feb. 5 of the **1963** murder of civil rights leader **Medgar Evers.**

Longtime CIA officer **Aldrich Ames** and his wife were **charged** Feb. 21 **with spying.** Under a plea bargain, he received life in prison, while she drew 63 months.

U.S. troops Mar. 25 officially ended peacekeeping and humanitarian aid mission in **Somalia** begun in **1992.**

Major league **baseball players went on strike,** following Aug. 11 games; World Series cancelled; strike ended Apr. 25, **1995.**

Senate Majority Leader George Mitchell (D, ME), Sept. 26, dropped efforts to pass Clinton's **health-care reform** package.

1995

When the 104th Congress opened, Jan. 4, **Sen. Bob Dole** (R, KS) became **Senate majority leader** and **Rep. Newt Gingrich** (R, GA) was elected **House Speaker.** A bill to end Congress's exemption from federal labor laws, first in a series of measures in Republicans' **"Contract With America,"** cleared Congress Jan. 17; signed into law Jan. 23.

Clinton invoked emergency powers, Jan. 31, to extend a **$20 bil loan** to help **Mexico** avert financial collapse.

The last UN peacekeeping troops withdrew from **Somalia** Feb. 28-Mar. 3, with the aid of U.S. Marines. In **Haiti,** peacekeeping responsibilities were transferred from U.S. to UN forces Mar. 31, with the U.S. providing 2,400 soldiers.

A truck **bomb** exploded outside **a federal office building in Oklahoma City** Apr. 19, **killing 168** people in all, in deadliest terrorist attack yet on U.S. soil; **Timothy McVeigh** was 1st and key suspect arrested, Apr. 21.

The U.S. space shuttle *Atlantis* made the first in a series of **dockings with** Russian space station *Mir*, June 29-July 4.

A U.S. **F-16 fighter jet** piloted by Air Force Capt. **Scott O'Grady** was **shot down** over Bosnia and Herzegovina June 2; O'Grady was **rescued** by U.S. Marines 6 days later.

The U.S. announced on July 11 that it was reestablishing diplomatic **relations with Vietnam.**

Former football star **O. J. Simpson** found **not guilty** Oct. 3 of the **June 1994** murders of his former wife, Nicole Brown Simpson, and her friend Ronald Goldman.

Ten **Muslim militants** convicted in New York, Oct. 1, in a **failed plot** to blow up **UN Headquarters** and other buildings and assassinate political leaders.

Shannon Faulkner won a legal fight to gain admission to the previously all-male cadet corps of **The Citadel,** Aug. 11, though she dropped out after a few days of training.

Hundreds of thousands of African-American men participated in **"Million Man March"** and rally in Washington, DC, Oct. 16, organized by Rev. Louis Farrakhan.

The federal **55-mile-per-hour speed limit** was **repealed** by a measure signed Nov. 28.

After talks outside Dayton, OH, **warring parties in Bosnia and Herzegovina reached agreement** Nov. 21 to end their conflict; treaty was signed Dec. 14, after which first of some 20,000 **U.S. peacekeeping troops** arrived in Bosnia.

Five Americans were among 7 **killed,** Nov. 13, in bombing of a U.S. military post in **Riyadh, Saudi Arabia.**

A budget impasse between Congress and Pres. Clinton led to a partial **government shutdown** beginning Nov. 14. Operations resumed Nov. 20 under continuing resolutions.

1996

Long-sought records released by White House Jan. 5 showed **Hillary Rodham Clinton** did 60 hours of work for an S&L linked to **Whitewater** scandal. Responding to a subpoena, she testified Jan. 26 before a grand jury.

Senate, Jan. 26, approved, 87-4, the Second Strategic Arms Reduction Treaty (**START II**).

On Feb. 24 **Cuban jets shot down** 2 civilian planes owned by a Cuban exile organization; 4 persons killed. Cuba claimed its territory was violated; U.S., Feb. 26, tightened embargo.

John Salvi found guilty, Mar. 18, in the **1994 murder** of receptionists at 2 **abortion clinics** in Brookline, MA.

Congress, in Mar., approved a **"line item veto"** bill, but it was struck down by the Supreme Court, June 25, **1998.**

U.S. Commerce Sec. **Ron Brown** was killed Apr. 3 in a plane crash in Croatia.

An auction, Apr. 23-26, of items owned by former First Lady **Jacqueline Kennedy Onassis** brought in $34 mil.

James and Susan McDougal were convicted May 28 of fraud and conspiracy. Arkansas Gov. **Jim Guy Tucker** was convicted of similar charges by the same jury.

The antitax **Freemen** surrendered to federal authorities June 13 after an 81-day standoff near Jordan, MT; 4 were convicted, July 8, **1998,** of conspiring to defraud banks.

Republicans June 12 chose Sen. **Trent Lott** (MS) as new majority leader to replace Sen. **Robert Dole,** who resigned, June 11, to focus on his presidential campaign.

A **bomb** exploded at a military complex near Dhahran, **Saudi Arabia,** June 25, killing 19 American servicemen.

On July 27 **a bomb exploded** in Atlanta, GA, near the **Olympics;** one person was directly killed.

Major **welfare reform bill** was signed into law Aug. 22.

Shannon Lucid, Sept. 26, completed a space voyage of 188 days, a record for women and for U.S. astronauts.

Archer Daniels Midland Co. announced, Oct. 14, it had agreed to pay a fine of $100 mil for price fixing.

Pres. Clinton was reelected to 2nd term, Nov. 5.

1997

Bombs were detonated at **abortion clinics** in Tulsa, OK, Jan. 1, in Atlanta on Jan. 16, and again at the first site in Tulsa on Jan. 19; 6 people were injured.

Newt Gingrich (R, GA) was reelected Speaker of the U.S. House, Jan. 7 but was fined and reprimanded by colleagues for alleged misuse of tax-exempt donations.

Madeleine Albright was sworn in as secretary of state Jan. 23, becoming the first woman to head State Dept.

Harold Nicholson, a former CIA official, pleaded guilty, Mar. 3, to spying for Russia.

39 members of the **Heaven's Gate religious cult** found dead in a house in Rancho Santa Fe, CA, Mar. 26, in an apparent mass suicide.

James McDougal, former partner in Whitewater, sentenced Apr. 14 to 3 years in prison for seeking to profit from fraudulent loans. He died in prison, Mar. 8, **1998.**

Timothy McVeigh convicted of conspiracy and murder, June 2, in 1995 Oklahoma City bombing.

On **Oct. 27,** the **Dow Jones** fell 554.26 points, largest 1-day point decline yet. On Oct. 28, the Dow rebounded, surging 337.17 points, largest-yet single-day point advance.

Islamic militants **Ramzi Ahmed Yousef** and **Eyad Ismoil Yousef** convicted, Nov. 12, in the **1993** bombing of the World Trade Center in New York City.

On Nov. 19, **Bobbi McCaughey,** 29, delivered the first set of live septuplets to survive more than a month.

Terry Nichols convicted Dec. 23 on charges related to the 1995 Oklahoma City bombing.

1998

It was reported Jan. 21 that Whitewater independent counsel Kenneth Starr, had evidence of a **sexual relationship** between **Pres. Clinton** and onetime White House intern Monica Lewinsky. Clinton denied it.

Theodore Kaczynski, the "Unabomber," arrested in Montana in 1993, pleaded guilty Jan. 22 in California and New Jersey bombings that killed 3 people and injured 2.

The state of Texas, Feb. 3, executed its first female convict in 135 years—**Karla Faye Tucker.**

2 youths aged 11 and 13 were arrested, Mar. 24, in the killing of 4 schoolgirls and a teacher outside a **Jonesboro, AR,** school; later committed to a juvenile detention center.

On Apr. 25, First Lady **Hillary Rodham Clinton** provided videotaped testimony at the White House for the Little Rock, AR, grand jury in the **Whitewater** case.

Monica Lewinsky, Aug. 6, testified to having had a sexual relationship with **Pres. Clinton,** but said she was never asked to lie. In grand jury testimony and an address to the nation, Aug. 17, **Clinton** acknowledged an inappropriate relationship with Lewinsky. On Sept. 9, independent counsel **Kenneth Starr** sent the House what he called "credible information that may constitute grounds" for impeachment.

Mark McGwire, Sept. 8, hit his 62nd **home run** of the season, breaking **Roger Maris's** season record.

On Sept. 30, Pres. Clinton announced a **budget surplus** of $70 billion for fiscal year 1998, the first since 1969.

Terrorist **bombs** in **U.S. embassies** in Nairobi, Kenya, and Dar es Salaam, Tanzania, killed at least 257, Aug. 7. The U.S. launched **retaliatory strikes,** Aug. 20, against alleged terrorist-related targets in Afghanistan and Sudan.

The House Judiciary Committee, Oct. 5, voted 21-16 along party lines to recommend that the Clinton **impeachment** investigation proceed. The House concurred Oct. 8, voting 258-176; 31 Democrats voted yes.

Dr. Barnett Slepian, an obstetrician who performed abortions, was killed by a sniper near Buffalo, NY, Oct. 23.

John Glenn, first U.S. astronaut to orbit Earth, returned to space Oct. 29-Nov. 7, aboard the shuttle *Discovery.*

Pres. Clinton, Nov. 13, settled a suit by agreeing to pay $850,000 to **Paula Corbin Jones.** She alleged that he had made an unwanted sexual advance to her in 1991.

The country's 4 largest **tobacco** companies, in a settlement, Nov. 23, with 46 states, the District of Columbia, and 4 territories, agreed to pay $206 bil over 25 years to cover public health costs related to smoking.

The U.S. House, Dec. 19, approved 2 articles of **impeachment** charging **Pres. Clinton** with grand jury perjury (228-206) and obstruction of justice (221-212) in a cover-up of his sexual relationship with **Monica Lewinsky;** 2 other impeachment articles failed.

1999

J. Dennis Hastert (IL) was elected Speaker of the House for the 106th Congress, Jan. 6.

Pres. Clinton's impeachment trial—the 2nd such trial in U.S. history—began in the GOP-controlled Senate Jan. 7. He was acquitted, Feb. 12. The perjury article failed, with 45 votes; the obstruction of justice article drew a 50-50 vote, with a two-thirds vote needed for conviction.

Dr. Jack Kevorkian, who claimed he had helped 130 people kill themselves, convicted of 2nd-degree murder Mar. 26 in one death. On Apr. 13, sentenced to 10 to 25 years in prison.

Two men were convicted in the **1998** beating death of **Matthew Shepard,** an openly homosexual student at the Univ. of Wyoming.

Eric Harris, 18, and Dylan Klebold, 17, killed 12 fellow students and a teacher Apr. 20 at **Columbine** High School in Littleton, CO, then shot themselves fatally. More than 30 people were wounded, some critically.

One NYC police officer pleaded guilty to 6 charges, May 25, and another was convicted on an assault charge, June 8, in connection with the **1997** torture and sodomizing of Haitian immigrant **Abner Louima** in a police station.

John F. Kennedy Jr., son of the former president, died in a plane crash July 16 along with his wife, Carolyn Bessette Kennedy, and his sister-in-law, Lauren Bessette.

On July 23, with the launch of the space shuttle *Columbia,* Air Force Col. **Eileen M. Collins** became the first woman to command a shuttle flight.

The **Dow Jones** Industrial Average closed the year at a **record** level of 11,497.12—25.2% above the **1998** close.

2000

Across the U.S., midnight **celebrations** marked the changeover to the **year 2000** on Jan. 1; the feared **Y2K** computer glitch caused only minor problems.

America Online Inc. announced Jan. 10 that it would buy **Time Warner Inc.,** in the largest merger to date. The FTC approved it Dec. 14.

Teams of scientists from the U.S. and Britain announced jointly, June 26, that they had determined the structure of the **human genome.**

Following a bitter legal controversy, 6-year-old Cuban **Elián González** returned to Cuba June 28, 7 months after he was rescued from a boat wreck off the coast of Florida.

The Justice Dept., July 21, cleared U.S. agents of any wrongdoing in a **1993** assault on the compound of the Branch Davidian religious sect in **Waco,** TX.

Tiger Woods, 24, became the youngest to win all 4 of golf's majors, winning the British Open July 23 in a record 19 under par.

17 U.S. sailors were killed Oct. 12 in terrorist bombing of the USS *Cole,* refueling in Aden, Yemen.

The U.S. Food and Drug Administration announced, Sept. 28, approval of **RU-486,** a pill that induces abortions.

On **election night,** Nov. 7, the winner of Florida's 25 deciding electoral votes remained uncertain. The Florida Supreme Court, Dec. 8, ordered a manual recount of all ballots that did not have a vote for president recorded by machine. On Dec. 12, the U.S. Supreme Court reversed that decision. Vice Pres. Gore conceded the presidential election to Gov. **George W. Bush** (TX) in a televised address, Dec. 13.

2001

Congress, Jan. 6, certified **George W. Bush** as winner of the presidency by an electoral vote of 271 to 266, with 1 Gore elector abstaining.

AOL-Time Warner merger completed, Jan. 11.

Outgoing Pres. Clinton issued 176 pardons and commutations, Jan. 20, including that of **Marc Rich,** a fugitive commodities trader whose ex-wife was a financial backer.

George Walker Bush, was sworn in as 43rd president Jan. 20.

FBI agent **Robert Hanssen** arrested Feb. 20 and charged 2 days later with spying for the Soviet Union and Russia.

A **U.S. Navy spy plane** collided with a Chinese fighter plane over the South China Sea Apr. 1, killing the fighter pilot. The 24 U.S. crew members were detained in Hainan until U.S. officials expressed apology, Apr. 12.

Sen. James Jeffords (R, VT) announced May 24 he was leaving his party, giving Democrats control of the Senate.

Congress approved, May 26, a $1.35 trillion **tax cut** spread over 10 years.

Oklahoma City bomber **Timothy McVeigh** was executed June 11 by lethal injection in Terre Haute, IN.

Rep. **Gary Condit** (D, CA) in a TV interview Aug. 23 denied involvement in the Apr. 30 disappearance of 24-year-old intern **Chandra Levy,** with whom he had an affair. Levy's remains were found in a DC park May 22, **2002.**

Bush announced Aug. 9 he would allow federal funding of limited **stem-cell research** using human embryos.

On the morning of **Sept. 11,** 2 hijacked commercial airliners struck and destroyed the twin towers of the **World Trade Center** in New York City, in the worst-ever **terrorist attack** on American soil. A 3rd hijacked plane destroyed a portion of the **Pentagon** and a 4th crashed in **Pennsylvania.** Some 3,000 people were killed, including about 2,800 at the World Trade Center. U.S. observed a national day of mourning, Sept. 14.

Congress, Sept. 21, approved a $15 bil bailout package for the **airline industry.**

The **U.S.** and **Britain** Oct. 7 launched a sustained air strike campaign against Afghan-based terrorist organization **al-Qaeda** and the country's ruling Taliban militia.

On Oct. 7, San Francisco Giant outfielder **Barry Bonds** hit his **73rd** home run for a single season record.

Pres. Bush created a new **Office of Homeland Security,** Oct. 8, and signed a federal **antiterrorism bill** Oct. 26.

5 people died and 14 took ill from exposure to **anthrax** traveling through the U.S. mail, Oct. 5-Nov. 21.

The **Taliban** surrendered Kabul, the Afghan capital, Nov. 13, and fled from Kandahar, their stronghold, Dec. 7.

Leading energy-trading company **Enron** became the largest firm thus far to file for bankruptcy, Dec. 2.

The U.S. government, Dec. 11, indicted **Zacarias Moussaoui** as an alleged conspirator in the Sept. 11 attacks.

Pres. Bush announced Dec. 13 that the U.S. would withdraw from the 1972 **Antiballistic Missile Treaty**.

Pres. Bush, Dec. 28, formally granted permanent normal trade status to **China**, as of Jan. 1, 2002.

Taliban member **John Walker Lindh**, a U.S. citizen, was captured Dec. 2 by U.S. forces in Afghanistan.

2002

A 15-year-old pilot, flying alone, crashed a single-engine Cessna into the 28th floor of the **Bank of America building** in Tampa, FL, Jan. 5; he was the only casualty.

Taliban and al-Qaeda fighters captured in Afghanistan were flown to a U.S. **naval base at Guantanamo Bay** in Cuba, with the first 20 arriving Jan. 11.

A House committee Jan. 14 released parts of an Aug. 2001 letter from Sherron Watkins, an **Enron** employee, to CEO Kenneth Lay, warning him the company could "implode" in scandal. Lay resigned as CEO Jan. 23.

Committees in Congress Jan. 24 began public hearings into the **Enron** bankruptcy. Lay and other top executives took the Fifth Amendment when testifying.

In his first State of the Union address, Jan. 29, Pres. Bush called Iran, Iraq, and North Korea part of an **"axis of evil."**

Eight U.S. troops were killed Mar. 2-4 in an assault against Taliban and al-Qaeda forces in eastern Afghanistan. By Mar. 6, 1,200 U.S. troops were involved in the mission, **Operation Anaconda**, which ended Mar. 12.

Andrea Yates, who confessed to drowning her 5 children, was convicted by a Houston, TX, jury, Mar. 12.

A final independent prosecutor's report Mar. 20 found **insufficient evidence** that Pres. Clinton or Hillary Rodham Clinton had committed any crime in connection with **Whitewater**.

Pres. Bush Mar. 27 signed into law a major **campaign-finance** reform bill.

Former Pres. Jimmy **Carter** arrived in **Cuba** May 12 and met with Pres. Fidel Castro.

A ceremonial last girder was removed May 30 from the site of the **World Trade Center** towers in New York, signaling the end of a massive clean-up and recovery operation.

Wildfires in June consumed large acreages in Colorado, Arizona, California, and other western states.

Coleen Rowley testified before a congressional committee June 6 that Washington FBI agents had stymied investigative efforts in Minneapolis.

U.S. **Roman Catholic bishops**, meeting in Dallas, TX, June 13-15, approved stringent policies dealing with priests who sexually abuse minors; revised rules formulated with Vatican approval were adopted by the bishops Nov. 13.

The **Arthur Andersen** accounting firm was convicted of obstruction of justice by a federal jury, June 15; the firm ended U.S. operations Aug. 31.

WorldCom announced June 25 that it had overstated its cash flow by billions; on July 21, it displaced Enron Corp. as the largest U.S. company to declare bankruptcy.

On July 4, an Egyptian-born gunman killed 2 people near an **El Al ticket counter** at the L.A. international airport; he was shot dead by an El Al guard.

The U.S. House July 24 expelled **James Traficant** (D, OH), convicted of racketeering and corruption by a Cleveland jury Apr. 11.

A dramatic **rescue** operation July 28 saved the lives of 9 miners who had been trapped for days 240 feet underground in a southwest Pennsylvania **coal mine**.

Pres. Bush July 30 signed a bill revising **corporate fraud**, accounting, and security laws.

Pres. Bush Aug. 6 signed a **fast-track trade** bill.

US Airways filed for bankruptcy protection Aug. 11.

Major League Baseball owners and players agreed to a new **contract**, Aug. 30, averting a strike.

Serena Williams defeated sister, Venus, for 3rd straight time in a Grand Slam final, winning the U.S. Open Sept. 7; also defeated Venus in French Open and Wimbledon.

The 1st **anniversary** of the Sept. 11, **2001**, terrorist attacks was observed at sites where hijacked airplanes had crashed.

Ramzi bin al-Shibh, a Yemeni implicated in Sept. 11 **terrorist attacks**, was **arrested** in Pakistan Sept. 10-11 and, with 4 others, handed over to the U.S. On Sept. 13-14 the FBI arrested 5 U.S. citizens of Yemeni descent in Lackawanna, NY, charged with giving "material support" to terrorists. A 6th arrested in Bahrain Sept. 15 and extradited.

Pres. Bush told the **UN General Assembly** Sept. 12 that he would work with the Security Council to deal with the threat posed by **Iraqi weapons** of mass destruction.

An American soldier and a Filipino were killed Oct. 2 in the **Philippines**, when a **bomb** exploded outside a karaoke bar. A U.S. Marine was killed and a 2nd wounded Oct. 8, in an attack by 2 **gunmen** on a **Kuwaiti** island.

Richard Reid pleaded guilty Oct. 4 to all charges stemming from an incident aboard a Paris-to-Miami flight in Dec. 2001, when he tried to ignite **explosives in his shoes**.

Four men arrested in **Portland, OR**, Oct. 4, charged with plotting to join **al-Qaeda** and Taliban forces; a 5th suspect later arrested in Malaysia. On Oct. 9, the head of an Islamic charity, the Benevolence International Foundation, was charged with funneling money to al-Qaeda.

Pres. Bush Oct. 8 invoked the Taft-Hartley Act to get West Coast **longshoremen** back to work.

Former Pres. **Carter** was named Oct. 10 as winner of the 2002 **Nobel Peace Prize**.

After bouncing up from a low in late July, **stock** averages slid again, reaching a **5-year low** of 7286, Oct. 9.

On Oct. 10-11 the House, 296-133, and Senate, 77-23, gave Bush **backing** for using **military force** against Iraq.

The Bush administration revealed Oct. 16 that **North Korea** had acknowledged it was developing nuclear arms.

John Allen Williams, 41, aka John Allen Muhammad, and John Lee Malvo, 17, were arrested Oct. 24 in connection with a series of random **sniper shootings** in the Washington, DC, area that left 10 dead.

Sen. **Paul Wellstone** (D, MN) died in a plane crash near Eveleth, MN, Oct. 25, with his wife, daughter, and 5 others.

Pres Bush, Oct. 29, signed a measure providing $3.9 bil to the states to fix shortcomings in their **election** process.

An antitrust settlement between **Microsoft** Corp. and U.S. Justice Dept. was approved Nov. 1 by a federal judge.

Republicans emerged from elections, Nov. 5, with a majority in the Senate and an increased margin in the House.

Rep. **Nancy Pelosi** (CA) was elected by House Democrats Nov. 14 to head their caucus in the new Congress, the **first woman** to lead either party in the House.

Pres. **Bush** Nov. 25 signed legislation creating a cabinet-Dept. of **Homeland Security**.

UAL Corp., the parent of **United Airlines**, filed for bankruptcy in Chicago Dec. 9.

Pres. **Bush** Dec. 13 announced a plan for **smallpox** vaccination of vital personnel.

Cardinal Bernard Law, Dec. 13, resigned under pressure as archbishop of Boston.

Former Vice Pres. **Al Gore** announced Dec. 15 that he would not seek his party's 2004 nomination for president.

On Dec. 16, Pres. Bush named former NJ Gov. Thomas Kean (R) to chair a national **commission** investigating the Sept. 11, 2001, **attacks**.

Bush Dec. 17 ordered the Pentagon to proceed with construction of a limited **missile defense shield**.

Trent Lott (R, MS), just chosen as majority leader in the new Senate, **bowed** out Dec. 20, amid furor over a comment apparently supporting the 1948 segregationist presidential campaign of Sen. Strom Thurmond (R, SC). Sen. **Bill Frist** (R, TN) was elected as leader Dec. 23.

A gunman linked to **Islamic Jihad** killed 3 Americans at a Baptist missionary hospital in Jibla, Yemen, Dec. 30.

The Mayflower Compact

The threat of James I to "harry them out of the land" sent a band of religious dissenters from England to Holland in 1608. They were known as Separatists because they wished to cut all ties with the established church. In 1620, some of them, known now as the Pilgrims, joined with a larger group in England to set sail on the *Mayflower* for the New World. A joint stock company financed their venture.

In November, they sighted Cape Cod and decided to land an exploring party at Plymouth Harbor. A rebellious group picked up at Southampton and London troubled the Pilgrim leaders, however, and to control their actions 41 Pilgrims drew up the Mayflower Compact and signed it before going ashore. The voluntary agreement to govern themselves was America's first written constitution. It reads as follows:

In the name of God, Amen. We, whose names are underwritten, the Loyal Subjects of our dread Sovereign Lord, King *James*, by the Grace of God, of *Great Britain, France and Ireland*, King, *Defender of the Faith*, etc.

Having undertaken for the Glory of God, and Advancement of the Christian Faith, and the Honour of our King and Country, a voyage to plant the first colony in the northern Parts of Virginia; do by these Presents, solemnly and mutually in the Presence of God and one of another, covenant and combine ourselves together into a civil Body Politick, for our better Ordering and Preservation, and Furtherance of the Ends aforesaid; And by Virtue hereof to enact, constitute, and frame, such just and equal Laws, Ordinances, Acts, Constitutions and Offices, from time to time, as shall be thought most meet and convenient for the General good of the Colony; unto which we promise all due Submission and Obedience.

In Witness whereof we have hereunto subscribed our names at *Cape Cod* the eleventh of *November*, in the Reign of our Sovereign Lord, King *James* of *England, France* and *Ireland*, the eighteenth, and of *Scotland* the fifty-fourth. *Anno Domini, 1620.*

The Continental Congress: Meetings, Presidents

Meeting places	Dates of meetings	Congress presidents	Date elected
Philadelphia, PA	Sept. 5 to Oct. 26, 1774	Peyton Randolph, VA (1)	Sept. 5, 1774
		Henry Middleton, SC	Oct. 22, 1774
Philadelphia, PA	May 10, 1775 to Dec. 12, 1776	Peyton Randolph, VA	May 10, 1775
		John Hancock, MA	May 24, 1775
Baltimore, MD	Dec. 20, 1776 to Mar. 4, 1777		
Philadelphia, PA	Mar. 5 to Sept. 18, 1777		
Lancaster, PA	Sept. 27, 1777 (one day)		
York, PA	Sept. 30, 1777 to June 27, 1778	Henry Laurens, SC	Nov. 1, 1777 (4)
Philadelphia, PA	July 2, 1778 to June 21, 1783	John Jay, NY	Dec. 10, 1778
"	"	Samuel Huntington, CT	Sept. 28, 1779
"	"	Thomas McKean, DE	July 10, 1781
"	"	John Hanson, MD (2)	Nov. 5, 1781
"	"	Elias Boudinot, NJ	Nov. 4, 1782
Princeton, NJ	June 30 to Nov. 4, 1783	Thomas Mifflin, PA	Nov. 3, 1783
Annapolis, MD	Nov. 26, 1783 to June 3, 1784		
Trenton, NJ	Nov. 1 to Dec. 24, 1784	Richard Henry Lee, VA	Nov. 30, 1784
New York City, NY	Jan. 11 to Nov. 4, 1785		
"	Nov. 7, 1785 to Nov. 3, 1786	John Hancock, MA (3)	Nov. 23, 1785
"		Nathaniel Gorham, MA	June 6, 1786
"	Nov. 6, 1786 to Oct. 30, 1787	Arthur St. Clair, PA	Feb. 2, 1787
"	Nov. 5, 1787 to Oct. 21, 1788	Cyrus Griffin, VA	Jan. 22, 1788
"	Nov. 3, 1788 to Mar. 2, 1789		

(1) Resigned Oct. 22, 1774. (2) Titled "President of the United States in Congress Assembled," John Hanson is considered by some the first U.S. president because he was the first to serve under the Articles of Confederation. He was, however, little more than presiding officer of the Congress, which retained full executive power. He could be considered the head of government, but not head of state. (3) Elected Nov. 1785, meetings held Nov. 1785-Nov. 1786; resigned May 29, 1786, without having served, because of illness. (4) Articles of Confederation agreed upon, Nov. 15, 1777; last ratification from Maryland, Mar. 1, 1781.

Patrick Henry's Speech to the Virginia Convention

The following is an excerpt from Patrick Henry's speech to the Virginia Convention on Mar. 23, 1775:

Gentlemen may cry, peace, peace—but there is no peace. The war is actually begun! The next gale that sweeps from the north will bring to our ears the clash of resounding arms! Our brethren are already in the field! Why stand we here idle? What is it that gentlemen wish? What would they have? Is life so dear, or peace so sweet, as to be purchased at the price of chains and slavery? Forbid it, Almighty God! I know not what course others may take; but as for me, give me liberty, or give me death!

How the Declaration of Independence Was Adopted

On June 7, 1776, Richard Henry Lee, who had issued the first call for a congress of the colonies, introduced in the Continental Congress at Philadelphia a resolution declaring "that these United Colonies are, and of right ought to be, free and independent states, that they are absolved from all allegiance to the British Crown, and that all political connection between them and the state of Great Britain is, and ought to be, totally dissolved."

The resolution, seconded by John Adams on behalf of the Massachusetts delegation, came up again on June 10 when a committee of 5, headed by Thomas Jefferson, was appointed to express the purpose of the resolution in a declaration of independence. The others on the committee were John Adams, Benjamin Franklin, Robert R. Livingston, and Roger Sherman.

Drafting the Declaration was assigned to Jefferson, who worked on a portable desk of his own construction in a room at Market and 7th Sts. The committee reported the result on June 28, 1776. The members of the Congress suggested a number of changes, which Jefferson called "deplorable." They didn't approve Jefferson's arraignment of the British people and King George III for encouraging and fostering the slave trade, which Jefferson called "an execrable commerce." They made 86 changes, eliminating 480 words and leaving 1,337. In the final form, capitalization was erratic. Jefferson had written that men were endowed with "inalienable" rights; in the final copy it came out as "unalienable" and has been thus ever since.

The Lee-Adams resolution of independence was adopted by 12 yeas on July 2—the actual date of the act of independence. The Declaration, which explains the act, was adopted July 4, in the evening.

After the Declaration was adopted, July 4, 1776, it was turned over to John Dunlap, printer, to be printed on broadsides. The original copy was lost and one of his broadsides was attached to a page in the journal of the Congress. It was read aloud July 8 in Philadelphia, PA, Easton, PA, and Trenton, NJ. On July 9 at 6 PM it was read by order of Gen. George Washington to the troops assembled on the Common in New York City (City Hall Park).

The Continental Congress of July 19, 1776, adopted the following resolution:

"Resolved, That the Declaration passed on the 4th, be fairly engrossed on parchment with the title and stile of 'The Unanimous Declaration of the thirteen United States of America' and that the same, when engrossed, be signed by every member of Congress."

Not all delegates who signed the engrossed Declaration were present on July 4. Robert Morris (PA), William Williams (CT), and Samuel Chase (MD) signed on Aug. 2; Oliver Wolcott (CT), George Wythe (VA), Richard Henry Lee (VA), and Elbridge Gerry (MA) signed in August and September; Matthew Thornton (NH) joined the Congress Nov. 4 and signed later. Thomas McKean (DE) rejoined Washington's army before signing and said later that he signed in 1781.

Charles Carroll of Carrollton was appointed a delegate by Maryland on July 4, 1776, presented his credentials July 18, and signed the engrossed Declaration on Aug. 2. Born Sept. 19, 1737, he was 95 years old and the last surviving signer when he died on Nov. 14, 1832.

Two Pennsylvania delegates who did not support the Declaration on July 4 were replaced.

The 4 New York delegates did not have authority from their state to vote on July 4. On July 9, the New York state convention authorized its delegates to approve the Declaration, and the Congress was so notified on July 15, 1776. The 4 signed the Declaration on Aug. 2.

The original engrossed Declaration is preserved in the National Archives Building in Washington, DC.

Declaration of Independence

The Declaration of Independence was adopted by the Continental Congress in Philadelphia on July 4, 1776. John Hancock was president of the Congress, and Charles Thomson was secretary. A copy of the Declaration, engrossed on parchment, was signed by members of Congress on and after Aug. 2, 1776. On Jan. 18, 1777, Congress ordered that "an authenticated copy, with the names of the members of Congress subscribing the same, be sent to each of the United States, and that they be desired to have the same put upon record." Authenticated copies were printed in broadside form in Baltimore, where the Continental Congress was then in session. The following text is that of the original printed by John Dunlap at Philadelphia for the Continental Congress. The original is on display at the National Archives in Washington, DC.

IN CONGRESS, July 4, 1776.
A DECLARATION
By the REPRESENTATIVES of the
UNITED STATES OF AMERICA,
In GENERAL CONGRESS assembled

When in the Course of human Events, it becomes necessary for one People to dissolve the Political Bands which have connected them with another, and to assume among the Powers of the Earth, the separate and equal Station to which the Laws of Nature and of Nature's God entitle them, a decent Respect to the Opinions of Mankind requires that they should declare the causes which impel them to the Separation.

We hold these Truths to be self-evident, that all Men are created equal, that they are endowed by their Creator with certain unalienable Rights, that among these are Life, Liberty, and the Pursuit of Happiness—That to secure these Rights, Governments are instituted among Men, deriving their just Powers from the Consent of the Governed, that whenever any Form of Government becomes destructive of these Ends, it is the Right of the People to alter or to abolish it, and to institute new Government, laying its Foundation on such Principles, and organizing its Powers in such Form, as to them shall seem most likely to effect their Safety and Happiness. Prudence, indeed, will dictate that Governments long established should not be changed for light and transient Causes; and accordingly all Experience hath shewn, that Mankind are more disposed to suffer, while Evils are sufferable, than to right themselves by abolishing the Forms to which they are accustomed. But when a long Train of Abuses and Usurpations, pursuing invariably the same Object, evinces a Design to reduce them under absolute Despotism, it is their Right, it is their Duty, to throw off such Government, and to provide new Guards for their future Security. Such has been the patient Sufferance of these Colonies; and such is now the Necessity which constrains them to alter their former Systems of Government. The History of the present King of Great-Britain is a History of repeated Injuries and Usurpations, all having in direct Object the Establishment of an absolute Tyranny over these States. To prove this, let Facts be submitted to a candid World.

He has refused his Assent to Laws, the most wholesome and necessary for the public Good.

He has forbidden his Governors to pass Laws of immediate and pressing Importance, unless suspended in their Operation till his Assent should be obtained; and when so suspended, he has utterly neglected to attend to them.

He has refused to pass other Laws for the Accommodation of large Districts of People, unless those People would relinquish the Right of Representation in the Legislature, a Right inestimable to them, and formidable to Tyrants only.

He has called together Legislative Bodies at Places unusual, uncomfortable, and distant from the Depository of their Public Records, for the sole Purpose of fatiguing them into Compliance with his Measures.

He has dissolved Representative Houses repeatedly, for opposing with manly Firmness his Invasions on the Rights of the People.

He has refused for a long Time, after such Dissolutions, to cause others to be elected; whereby the Legislative Powers, incapable of Annihilation, have returned to the People at large for their exercise; the State remaining in the mean time exposed to all the Dangers of Invasion from without, and Convulsions within.

He has endeavoured to prevent the Population of these States; for that Purpose obstructing the Laws for Naturalization of Foreigners; refusing to pass others to encourage their Migrations hither, and raising the Conditions of new Appropriations of Lands.

He has obstructed the Administration of Justice, by refusing his Assent to Laws for establishing Judiciary Powers.

He has made Judges dependent on his Will alone, for the Tenure of their Offices, and the Amount and payment of their Salaries.

He has erected a Multitude of new Offices, and sent hither Swarms of Officers to harrass our People, and eat out their Substance.

He has kept among us, in Times of Peace, Standing Armies, without the consent of our Legislatures.

He has affected to render the Military independent of, and superior to the Civil Power.

He has combined with others to subject us to a Jurisdiction foreign to our Constitution, and unacknowledged by our Laws; giving his Assent to their Acts of pretended Legislation:

For quartering large Bodies of Armed Troops among us:

For protecting them, by a mock Trial, from Punishment for any Murders which they should commit on the Inhabitants of these States:

For cutting off our Trade with all Parts of the World:

For imposing Taxes on us without our Consent:

For depriving us, in many Cases, of the Benefits of Trial by Jury:

For transporting us beyond Seas to be tried for pretended Offences:

For abolishing the free System of English Laws in a neighbouring Province, establishing therein an arbitrary Government, and enlarging its Boundaries, so as to render it at once an Example and fit Instrument for introducing the same absolute Rule into these Colonies:

For taking away our Charters, abolishing our most valuable Laws, and altering fundamentally the Forms of our Governments:

For suspending our own Legislatures, and declaring themselves invested with Power to legislate for us in all Cases whatsoever.

He has abdicated Government here, by declaring us out of his Protection and waging War against us.

He has plundered our Seas, ravaged our Coasts, burnt our towns, and destroyed the Lives of our People.

He is, at this Time, transporting large Armies of foreign Mercenaries to complete the works of Death, Desolation, and Tyranny, already begun with circumstances of Cruelty and Perfidy, scarcely paralleled in the most barbarous Ages, and totally unworthy the Head of a civilized Nation.

He has constrained our fellow Citizens taken Captive on the high Seas to bear Arms against their Country, to become the Executioners of their Friends and Brethren, or to fall themselves by their Hands.

He has excited domestic Insurrections amongst us, and has endeavoured to bring on the Inhabitants of our Frontiers, the merciless Indian Savages, whose known Rule of Warfare, is an undistinguished Destruction, of all Ages, Sexes and Conditions.

In every stage of these Oppressions we have Petitioned for Redress in the most humble Terms: Our repeated Petitions have been answered only by repeated Injury. A Prince, whose Character is thus marked by every act which may define a Tyrant, is unfit to be the Ruler of a free People.

Nor have we been wanting in Attentions to our British Brethren. We have warned them from Time to Time of Attempts by their Legislature to extend an unwarrantable Jurisdiction over us. We have reminded them of the Circumstances of our Emigration and Settlement here. We have appealed to their native Justice and Magnanimity, and we have conjured them by the Ties of our common Kindred to disavow these Usurpations, which, would inevitably interrupt our Connections and Correspondence. They too have been deaf to the Voice of Justice and of Consanguinity. We must, therefore, acquiesce in the Necessity, which denounces our Separation, and hold them, as we hold the rest of Mankind, Enemies in War, in Peace, Friends.

We, therefore, the Representatives of the UNITED STATES OF AMERICA, in General Congress, Assembled, appealing to the Supreme Judge of the World for the Rectitude of our Intentions, do, in the Name, and by Authority of the good People of these Colonies, solemnly Publish and Declare, That these United Colonies are, and of Right ought to be, Free and Independent States; that they are absolved from all Allegiance to the British Crown, and that all political Connection between them and the State of Great-Britain, is and ought to be totally dissolved; and that as Free and Independent States, they have full Power to levy War, conclude Peace, contract Alliances, establish Commerce, and to do all other Acts and Things which Independent States may of right do. And for the support of this declaration, with a firm Reliance on the Protection of Divine Providence, we mutually pledge to each other our lives, our Fortunes, and our sacred Honor.

JOHN HANCOCK, President

Attest.

CHARLES THOMSON, Secretary.

Signers of the Declaration of Independence

Delegate (state)	Occupation	Birthplace	Born	Died
Adams, John (MA)	Lawyer	Braintree (Quincy), MA	Oct. 30, 1735	July 4, 1826
Adams, Samuel (MA)	Political leader	Boston, MA	Sept. 27, 1722	Oct. 2, 1803
Bartlett, Josiah (NH)	Physician, judge	Amesbury, MA	Nov. 21, 1729	May 19, 1795
Braxton, Carter (VA)	Farmer	Newington Plantation, VA	Sept. 10, 1736	Oct. 10, 1797
Carroll, Chas. of Carrollton (MD)	Lawyer	Annapolis, MD	Sept. 19, 1737	Nov. 14, 1832
Chase, Samuel (MD)	Judge	Princess Anne, MD	Apr. 17, 1741	June 19, 1811
Clark, Abraham (NJ)	Surveyor	Roselle, NJ	Feb. 15, 1726	Sept. 15, 1794
Clymer, George (PA)	Merchant	Philadelphia, PA	Mar. 16, 1739	Jan. 23, 1813
Ellery, William (RI)	Lawyer	Newport, RI	Dec. 22, 1727	Feb. 15, 1820
Floyd, William (NY)	Soldier	Brookhaven, NY	Dec. 17, 1734	Aug. 4, 1821
Franklin, Benjamin (PA)	Printer, publisher	Boston, MA	Jan. 17, 1706	Apr. 17, 1790
Gerry, Elbridge (MA)	Merchant	Marblehead, MA	July 17, 1744	Nov. 23, 1814
Gwinnett, Button (GA)	Merchant	Down Hatherly, England	c. 1735	May 19, 1777
Hall, Lyman (GA)	Physician	Wallingford, CT	Apr. 12, 1724	Oct. 19, 1790
Hancock, John (MA)	Merchant	Braintree (Quincy), MA	Jan. 12, 1737	Oct. 8, 1793
Harrison, Benjamin (VA)	Farmer	Berkeley, VA	Apr. 5, 1726	Apr. 24, 1791
Hart, John (NJ)	Farmer	Stonington, CT	c. 1711	May 11, 1779
Hewes, Joseph (NC)	Merchant	Princeton, NJ	Jan. 23, 1730	Nov. 10, 1779
Heyward, Thos. Jr. (SC)	Lawyer, farmer	St. Luke's Parish, SC	July 28, 1746	Mar. 6, 1809
Hooper, William (NC)	Lawyer	Boston, MA	June 28, 1742	Oct. 14, 1790
Hopkins, Stephen (RI)	Judge, educator	Providence, RI	Mar. 7, 1707	July 13, 1785
Hopkinson, Francis (NJ)	Judge, author	Philadelphia, PA	Sept. 21, 1737	May 9, 1791
Huntington, Samuel (CT)	Judge	Windham County, CT	July 3, 1731	Jan. 5, 1796
Jefferson, Thomas (VA)	Lawyer	Shadwell, VA	Apr. 13, 1743	July 4, 1826
Lee, Francis Lightfoot (VA)	Farmer	Westmoreland County, VA	Oct. 14, 1734	Jan. 11, 1797
Lee, Richard Henry (VA)	Farmer	Westmoreland County, VA	Jan. 20, 1732	June 19, 1794
Lewis, Francis (NY)	Merchant	Llandaff, Wales	Mar., 1713	Dec. 31, 1802
Livingston, Philip (NY)	Merchant	Albany, NY	Jan. 15, 1716	June 12, 1778
Lynch, Thomas Jr. (SC)	Farmer	Winyah, SC	Aug. 5, 1749	(at sea) 1779
McKean, Thomas (DE)	Lawyer	New London, PA	Mar. 19, 1734	June 24, 1817
Middleton, Arthur (SC)	Farmer	Charleston, SC	June 26, 1742	Jan. 1, 1787
Morris, Lewis (NY)	Farmer	Morrisania (Bronx County), NY	Apr. 8, 1726	Jan. 22, 1798
Morris, Robert (PA)	Merchant	Liverpool, England	Jan. 20, 1734	May 9, 1806
Morton, John (PA)	Judge	Ridley, PA	1724	Apr., 1777
Nelson, Thos. Jr. (VA)	Farmer	Yorktown, VA	Dec. 26, 1738	Jan. 4, 1789
Paca, William (MD)	Judge	Abingdon, MD	Oct. 31, 1740	Oct. 23, 1799
Paine, Robert Treat (MA)	Judge	Boston, MA	Mar. 11, 1731	May 12, 1814
Penn, John (NC)	Lawyer	Near Port Royal, VA	May 17, 1741	Sept. 14, 1788
Read, George (DE)	Judge	Near North East, MD	Sept. 18, 1733	Sept. 21, 1798
Rodney, Caesar (DE)	Judge	Dover, DE	Oct. 7, 1728	June 29, 1784
Ross, George (PA)	Judge	New Castle, DE	May 10, 1730	July 14, 1779

Delegate (state)	Occupation	Birthplace	Born	Died
Rush, Benjamin (PA)	Physician	Byberry, PA (Philadelphia)	Dec. 24, 1745	Apr. 19, 1813
Rutledge, Edward (SC)	Lawyer	Charleston, SC	Nov. 23, 1749	Jan. 23, 1800
Sherman, Roger (CT)	Lawyer	Newton, MA	Apr. 19, 1721	July 23, 1793
Smith, James (PA)	Lawyer	Dublin, Ireland	c. 1719	July 11, 1806
Stockton, Richard (NJ)	Lawyer	Near Princeton, NJ	Oct. 1, 1730	Feb. 28, 1781
Stone, Thomas (MD)	Lawyer	Charles County, MD	1743	Oct. 5, 1787
Taylor, George (PA)	Ironmaster	Ireland	1716	Feb. 23, 1781
Thornton, Matthew (NH)	Physician	Ireland	1714	June 24, 1803
Walton, George (GA)	Judge	Prince Edward County, VA	1741	Feb. 2, 1804
Whipple, William (NH)	Merchant, judge	Kittery, ME	Jan. 14, 1730	Nov. 28, 1785
Williams, William (CT)	Merchant	Lebanon, CT	Apr. 23, 1731	Aug. 2, 1811
Wilson, James (PA)	Judge	Carskerdo, Scotland	Sept. 14, 1742	Aug. 28, 1798
Witherspoon, John (NJ)	Clergyman, educator	Gifford, Scotland	Feb. 5, 1723	Nov. 15, 1794
Wolcott, Oliver (CT)	Judge	Windsor, CT	Dec. 1, 1726	Dec. 1, 1797
Wythe, George (VA)	Lawyer	Elizabeth City Co. (Hampton), VA	1726	June 8, 1806

Origin of the Constitution

The War of Independence was conducted by delegates from the original 13 states, called the Congress of the United States of America and known as the Continental Congress. In 1777 the Congress submitted to the legislatures of the states the Articles of Confederation and Perpetual Union, which were ratified by New Hampshire, Massachusetts, Rhode Island, Connecticut, New York, New Jersey, Pennsylvania, Delaware, Virginia, North Carolina, South Carolina, and Georgia and finally, in 1781, by Maryland.

The first article read: "The stile of this confederacy shall be the United States of America." This did not signify a sovereign nation, because the states delegated only those powers they could not handle individually, such as to wage war, make treaties, and contract debts for general expenses (e.g. paying the army). Taxes for payment of such debts were levied by the individual states. The president signed himself "President of the United States in Congress assembled," but here the United States were considered in the plural, a cooperating group.

When the war was won, it became evident that a stronger federal union was needed. The Congress left the initiative to the legislatures. Virginia in Jan. 1786 appointed commissioners to meet with representatives of other states; delegates from Virginia, Delaware, New York, New Jersey, and Pennsylvania met at Annapolis. Alexander Hamilton prepared their call asking delegates from all states to meet in Philadelphia in May 1787 "to render the Constitution of the federal government adequate to the exigencies of the union." Congress endorsed the plan on Feb. 21, 1787. Delegates were appointed by all states except Rhode Island.

The convention met on May 14, 1787. George Washington was chosen president (presiding officer). The states certified 65 delegates, but 10 did not attend. The work was done by 55, not all of whom were present at all sessions. Of the 55 attending delegates, 16 failed to sign, and 39 actually signed Sept. 17, 1787, some with reservations. Some historians have said 74 delegates (9 more than the 65 actually certified) were named and 19 failed to attend. These 9 additional persons refused the appointment, were never delegates, and were never counted as absentees. Washington sent the Constitution to Congress, and that body, Sept. 28, 1787, ordered it sent to the legislatures, "in order to be submitted to a convention of delegates chosen in each state by the people thereof."

The Constitution was ratified by votes of state conventions as follows: Delaware, Dec. 7, 1787, unanimous; Pennsylvania, Dec. 12, 1787, 43 to 23; New Jersey, Dec. 18, 1787, unanimous; Georgia, Jan. 2, 1788, unanimous; Connecticut, Jan. 9, 1788, 128 to 40; Massachusetts, Feb. 6, 1788, 187 to 168; Maryland, Apr. 28, 1788, 63 to 11; South Carolina, May 23, 1788, 149 to 73; New Hampshire, June 21, 1788, 57 to 46; Virginia, June 25, 1788, 89 to 79; New York, July 26, 1788, 30 to 27. Nine states were needed to establish the operation of the Constitution "between the states so ratifying the same," and New Hampshire was the 9th state. The government did not declare the Constitution in effect until the first Wednesday in Mar. 1789, which was Mar. 4. After that, North Carolina ratified it on Nov. 21, 1789, 194 to 77; and Rhode Island, May 29, 1790, 34 to 32. Vermont in convention ratified it on Jan. 10, 1791, and by act of Congress approved on Feb. 18, 1791, was admitted into the Union as the 14th state, Mar. 4, 1791.

Constitution of the United States

The Original 7 Articles

The text of the Constitution given here (exception for Amendment XXVII) is taken from the pocket-size edition of the Constitution published by the U.S. Government Printing Office as a result of a U.S. House and Senate resolution to print the Constitution in its original form as amended through July 5, 1971. *Text in brackets* indicates that an item has been superseded or amended, or provides background information. **Boldface text preceding** each article, section, or amendment is a brief summary, added by *The World Almanac*.

PREAMBLE

We, the People of the United States, in Order to form a more perfect Union, establish Justice, insure domestic Tranquility, provide for the common defence, promote the general Welfare, and secure the Blessings of Liberty to ourselves and our Posterity, do ordain and establish this Constitution for the United States of America.

ARTICLE I.

Section 1—Legislative powers; in whom vested:

All legislative Powers herein granted shall be vested in a Congress of the United States, which shall consist of a Senate and House of Representatives.

Section 2—House of Representatives, how and by whom chosen. Qualifications of a Representative. Representatives and direct taxes, how apportioned. Enumeration. Vacancies to be filled. Power of choosing officers, and of impeachment.

The House of Representatives shall be composed of Members chosen every second Year by the People of the several States, and the Electors in each State shall have the Qualifications requisite for Electors of the most numerous Branch of the State Legislature.

No person shall be a Representative who shall not have attained to the Age of twenty-five Years, and been seven Years a Citizen of the United States, and who shall not, when elected, be an Inhabitant of that State in which he shall be chosen.

[Representatives and direct taxes shall be apportioned among the several States which may be included within this Union, according to their respective Numbers, which shall be determined by adding to the whole Number of free Persons, including those bound to Service for a Term of Years, and excluding Indians not taxed, three-fifths of all other persons.] *[The previous sentence was superseded by Amendment XIV, section 2.]* The actual Enumeration shall be made within three Years after the first Meeting of the Congress of the United States, and within every subsequent Term of ten Years, in such Manner as they shall by Law direct. The Number of Representatives shall not exceed one for every thirty Thousand, but each State shall have at Least one Representative; and until such enumeration shall be made, the State of New Hampshire shall be entitled to chuse three, Massachusetts eight, Rhode-Island and Providence Plantations one, Connecticut five, New-York six, New Jersey four, Pennsylvania eight, Delaware one, Maryland six, Virginia ten, North Carolina five, South Carolina five, and Georgia three.

When vacancies happen in the Representation from any State, the Executive Authority thereof shall issue Writs of Election to fill such Vacancies.

The House of Representatives shall chuse their Speaker and other Officers; and shall have the sole Power of Impeachment.

Section 3—Senators, how and by whom chosen. How classified. Qualifications of a Senator. President of the Senate, his right to vote. President pro tem., and other officers of the Senate, how chosen. Power to try impeachments. When President is tried, Chief Justice to preside. Sentence.

The Senate of the United States shall be composed of two Senators from each State, *[chosen by the Legislature thereof] [the preceding five words were superseded by Amendment XVII, section 1]* for six Years; and each Senator shall have one Vote.

Immediately after they shall be assembled in Consequence of the first Election, they shall be divided as equally as may be into three Classes. The Seats of the Senators of the first Class shall be vacated at the Expiration of the second Year, of the second Class at the Expiration of the fourth Year, and of the third Class at the Expiration of the Sixth year, so that one-third may be chosen every second Year; *[and if Vacancies happen by Resignation, or otherwise, during the Recess of the Legislature of any State, the Executive thereof may make temporary Appointments until the next Meeting of the Legislature, which shall then fill such Vacancies.] [The words in parentheses were superseded by Amendment XVII, section 2.]*

No person shall be a Senator who shall not have attained to the Age of thirty Years, and been nine Years a Citizen of the United States, and who shall not, when elected, be an Inhabitant of that State for which he shall be chosen.

The Vice President of the United States shall be President of the Senate, but shall have no Vote, unless they be equally divided.

The Senate shall chuse their other Officers, and also a President pro tempore, in the absence of the Vice President, or when he shall exercise the Office of President of the United States.

The Senate shall have the sole Power to try all Impeachments. When sitting for that Purpose, they shall be on Oath or Affirmation. When the President of the United States is tried, the Chief Justice shall preside: And no Person shall be convicted without the Concurrence of two thirds of the Members present.

Judgment in Cases of Impeachment shall not extend further than to removal from Office, and disqualification to hold and enjoy any Office of honor, Trust or Profit under the United States: but the Party convicted shall nevertheless be liable and subject to Indictment, Trial, Judgment and Punishment, according to Law.

Section 4—Times, etc., of holding elections, how prescribed. One session each year.

The Times, Places and Manner of holding Elections for Senators and Representatives, shall be prescribed in each State by the Legislature thereof; but the Congress may at any time by Law make or alter such Regulations, except as to the Place of Chusing Senators.

The Congress shall assemble at least once in every Year, and such Meeting shall *[be on the first Monday in December,] [The words in parentheses were superseded by Amendment XX, section 2.]* unless they shall by Law appoint a different Day.

Section 5—Membership, quorum, adjournments, rules. Power to punish or expel. Journal. Time of adjournments, how limited, etc.

Each House shall be the Judge of the Elections, Returns and Qualifications of its own Members, and a Majority of each shall constitute a Quorum to do Business; but a smaller number may adjourn from day to day, and may be authorized to compel the Attendance of absent Members, in such manner, and under such Penalties as each House may provide.

Each House may determine the Rules of its Proceedings, punish its members for disorderly Behavior, and, with the Concurrence of two thirds, expel a Member.

Each House shall keep a Journal of its Proceedings, and from time to time publish the same, excepting such Parts as may in their Judgment require Secrecy; and the Yeas and Nays of the Members of either House on any question shall, at the Desire of one fifth of those Present, be entered on the Journal.

Neither House, during the Session of Congress, shall, without the Consent of the other, adjourn for more than three days, nor to any other Place than that in which the two Houses shall be sitting.

Section 6—Compensation, privileges, disqualifications in certain cases.

The Senators and Representatives shall receive a Compensation for their Services, to be ascertained by Law, and paid out of the Treasury of the United States. They shall in all Cases, except Treason, Felony and Breach of the Peace, be privileged from Arrest during their Attendance at the Session of their respective Houses, and in going to and returning from the same; and for any Speech or Debate in either House, they shall not be questioned in any other Place.

No Senator or Representative shall, during the Time for which he was elected, be appointed to any civil Office under the Authority of the United States, which shall have been created, or the Emoluments whereof shall have been encreased during such time; and no Person holding any Office under the United States, shall be a Member of either House during his Continuance in Office.

Section 7—House to originate all revenue bills. Veto. Bill may be passed by two-thirds of each House, notwithstanding, etc. Bill, not returned in ten days, to become a law. Provisions as to orders, concurrent resolutions, etc.

All bills for raising Revenue shall originate in the House of Representatives; but the Senate may propose or concur with Amendments as on other Bills.

Every Bill which shall have passed the House of Representatives and the Senate, shall, before it become a Law, be presented to the President of the United States: If he approve he shall sign it, but if not he shall return it, with his Objections to that House in which it shall have originated, who shall enter the Objections at large on their Journal, and proceed to reconsider it. If after such Reconsideration two thirds of that House shall agree to pass the Bill, it shall be sent, together with the Objections, to the other House, by which it shall likewise be reconsidered, and if approved by two thirds of that House, it shall become a Law. But in all such Cases the Votes of both Houses shall be determined by Yeas and Nays, and the Names of the Persons voting for and against the Bill shall be entered on the Journal of each House respectively. If any Bill shall not be returned by the President within ten Days (Sundays excepted) after it shall have been presented to him, the Same shall be a Law, in like Manner as if he had signed it, unless the Congress by their Adjournment prevent its Return, in which Case it shall not be a Law.

Every order, Resolution, or Vote to which the Concurrence of the Senate and House of Representatives may be necessary (except on a question of Adjournment) shall be presented to the President of the United States; and before the Same shall take Effect, shall be approved by him, or being disapproved by him, shall be repassed by two thirds of the Senate and House of Representatives, according to the Rules and Limitations prescribed in the Case of a Bill.

Section 8—Powers of Congress.

The Congress shall have Power To lay and collect Taxes, Duties, Imposts and Excises, to pay the Debts and provide for the common Defence and general Welfare of the United States; but all Duties, Imposts and Excises shall be uniform throughout the United States;

To borrow money on the credit of the United States;

To regulate Commerce with foreign Nations, and among the several States, and with the Indian Tribes;

To establish an uniform Rule of Naturalization, and uniform Laws on the subject of Bankruptcies throughout the United States;

To coin Money, regulate the Value thereof, and of foreign Coin, and fix the Standard of Weights and Measures;

To provide for the Punishment of counterfeiting the Securities and current Coin of the United States;

To establish Post Offices and post Roads;

To promote the Progress of Science and useful Arts, by securing for limited Times to Authors and Inventors the exclusive Right to their respective Writings and Discoveries;

To constitute Tribunals inferior to the supreme Court;

To define and punish Piracies and Felonies committed on the high Seas, and Offenses against the Law of Nations;

To declare War, grant Letters of Marque and Reprisal, and make Rules concerning Captures on Land and Water;

To raise and support Armies, but no Appropriation of Money to that Use shall be for a longer Term than two Years;

To provide and maintain a Navy;

To make Rules for the Government and Regulation of the land and naval Forces;

To provide for calling forth the Militia to execute the Laws of the Union, suppress Insurrections and repel Invasions;

To provide for organizing, arming, and disciplining the Militia, and for governing such Part of them as may be employed in the Service of the United States, reserving to the States respectively, the Appointment of the Officers, and the Authority of training the Militia according to the discipline prescribed by Congress;

To exercise exclusive Legislation in all Cases whatsoever, over such District (not exceeding ten Miles square) as may, by Cession of particular States, and the acceptance of Congress, become the Seat of the Government of the United States, and to exercise like Authority over all Places purchased by the Consent of the Legislature of the State in which the Same shall be, for the Erection of Forts, Magazines, Arsenals, dock-Yards, and other needful Buildings;—And

To make all Laws which shall be necessary and proper for carrying into Execution the foregoing Powers, and all other Powers vested by this Constitution in the Government of the United States, or in any Department or Officer thereof.

Section 9—Provision as to migration or importation of certain persons. Habeas corpus, bills of attainder, etc. Taxes, how apportioned. No export duty. No commercial preference. Money, how drawn from Treasury, etc. No titular nobility. Officers not to receive presents, etc.

The Migration or Importation of such Persons as any of the States now existing shall think proper to admit, shall not be prohibited by the Congress prior to the Year one thousand eight hundred and eight, but a tax or duty may be imposed on such Importation, not exceeding ten dollars for each Person.

The privilege of the Writ of Habeas Corpus shall not be suspended, unless when in Cases of Rebellion or Invasion the public Safety may require it.

No Bill of Attainder or ex post facto Law shall be passed.

No capitation, or other direct, Tax shall be laid, unless in Proportion to the Census or Enumeration herein before directed to be taken. *[Modified by Amendment XVI.]*

No Tax or Duty shall be laid on Articles exported from any State.

No Preference shall be given by any Regulation of Commerce or Revenue to the Ports of one State over those of another: nor shall Vessels bound to, or from, one State, be obliged to enter, clear, or pay Duties in another.

No Money shall be drawn from the Treasury, but in Consequence of Appropriations made by Law; and a regular Statement and Account of the Receipts and Expenditures of all public Money shall be published from time to time.

No Title of Nobility shall be granted by the United States: and no Person holding any Office of Profit or Trust under them, shall, without the Consent of the Congress, accept of any present, Emolument, Office, or Title, of any kind whatever, from any King, Prince, or foreign State.

Section 10—States prohibited from the exercise of certain powers.

No State shall enter into any Treaty, Alliance, or Confederation; grant Letters of Marque and Reprisal; coin Money; emit Bills of Credit; make any Thing but gold and silver Coin a Tender in Payment of Debts; pass any Bill of Attainder, ex post facto Law, or Law impairing the Obligation of Contracts, or grant any Title of Nobility.

No State shall, without the Consent of the Congress, lay any Imposts or Duties on Imports or Exports, except what may be absolutely necessary for executing its inspection Laws: and the net Produce of all Duties and Imposts, laid by any State on Imports or Exports, shall be for the Use of the Treasury of the United States; and all such Laws shall be subject to the Revision and Control of the Congress.

No State shall, without the Consent of Congress, lay any duty of Tonnage, keep Troops, or Ships of War in time of Peace, enter into any Agreement or Compact with another State, or with a foreign Power, or engage in War, unless actually invaded, or in such imminent Danger as will not admit of delay.

ARTICLE II.

Section 1—President: his term of office. Electors of President; number and how appointed. Electors to vote on same day. Qualification of President. On whom his duties devolve in case of his removal, death, etc. President's compensation. His oath of office.

The executive Power shall be vested in a President of the United States of America. He shall hold his Office during the Term of four Years, and, together with the Vice President, chosen for the same Term, be elected, as follows.

Each State shall appoint, in such Manner as the Legislature thereof may direct, a Number of Electors, equal to the whole Number of Senators and Representatives to which the State may be entitled in the Congress: but no Senator or Representative, or Person holding an Office of Trust or Profit under the United States, shall be appointed an Elector.

[The Electors shall meet in their respective States, and vote by Ballot for two persons, of whom one at least shall not be an Inhabitant of the same State with themselves. And they shall make a List of all the Persons voted for, and of the Number of Votes for each; which List they shall sign and certify, and transmit sealed to the Seat of the Government of the United States, directed to the President of the Senate. The President of the Senate shall, in the Presence of the Senate and House of Representatives, open all the Certificates, and the Votes shall then be counted. The Person having the greatest Number of Votes shall be the President, if such Number be a Majority of the whole Number of Electors appointed; and if there be more than one who have such Majority, and have an equal Number of Votes, then the House of Representatives shall immediately chuse by Ballot one of them for President; and if no Person have a Majority, then from the five highest on the List the said House shall in like Manner chuse the President. But in chusing the President, the Votes shall be taken by States, the Representation from each State having one Vote; a quorum for this Purpose shall consist of a Member or Members from two thirds of the States, and a Majority of all the States shall be necessary to a Choice. In every Case, after the Choice of the President, the Person having the greatest Number of Votes of the Electors shall be the Vice President. But if there should remain two or more who have equal Votes, the Senate shall chuse from them by Ballot the Vice-President.]

[This clause was superseded by Amendment XII.]

The Congress may detemine the Time of chusing the Electors, and the Day on which they shall give their Votes; which Day shall be the same throughout the United States.

No person except a natural born Citizen, or a Citizen of the United States, at the time of the Adoption of this Constitution, shall be eligible to the Office of President; neither shall any Person be eligible to that Office who shall not have attained to the Age of thirty-five Years, and been fourteen Years a Resident within the United States.

[For qualification of the Vice President, see Amendment XII.]

In Case of the Removal of the President from Office, or of his Death, Resignation, or Inability to discharge the Powers and Duties of the said Office, the same shall devolve on the Vice President, and the Congress may by Law, provide for the Case of Removal, Death, Resignation or Inability, both of the President and Vice President, declaring what Officer shall then act as President, and such Officer shall act accordingly, until the Disability be removed, or a President shall be elected.

[This clause has been modified by Amendments XX and XXV.]

The President shall, at stated Times, receive for his Services, a Compensation, which shall neither be encreased nor diminished during the Period for which he shall have been elected, and he shall not receive within that Period any other Emolument from the United States, or any of them.

Before he enter on the Execution of his Office, he shall take the following Oath or Affirmation:–"I do solemnly swear (or affirm) that I will faithfully execute the Office of President of the United States, and will to the best of my Ability, preserve, protect and defend the Constitution of the United States."

Section 2—President to be Commander-in-Chief. He may require opinions of cabinet officers, etc., may pardon. Treaty-making power. Nomination of certain officers. When President may fill vacancies.

The President shall be Commander in Chief of the Army and Navy of the United States, and of the Militia of the several States, when called into the actual Service of the United States; he may require the Opinion, in writing, of the principal Officer in each of the executive Departments, upon any subject relating to the Duties of their respective Offices, and he shall have Power to Grant Reprieves and Pardons for Offenses against the United States, except in Cases of Impeachment.

He shall have Power, by and with the Advice and Consent of the Senate, to make Treaties, provided two-thirds of the Senators present concur; and he shall nominate, and by and with the Advice and Consent of the Senate, shall appoint Ambassadors, other public Ministers and Consuls, Judges of the supreme Court, and all other Officers of the United States, whose Appointments are not herein otherwise provided for,

and which shall be established by Law: but the Congress may by Law vest the Appointment of such inferior Officers, as they think proper, in the President alone, in the Courts of Law, or in the Heads of Departments.

The President shall have Power to fill up all Vacancies that may happen during the Recess of the Senate, by granting Commissions which shall expire at the End of their next Session.

Section 3—President shall communicate to Congress. He may convene and adjourn Congress, in case of disagreement, etc. Shall receive ambassadors, execute laws, and commission officers.

He shall from time to time give to the Congress Information of the State of the Union, and recommend to their Consideration such Measures as he shall judge necessary and expedient; he may, on extraordinary Occasions, convene both Houses, or either of them, and in Case of Disagreement between them, with Respect to the Time of Adjournment, he may adjourn them to such Time as he shall think proper; he shall receive Ambassadors and other public Ministers; he shall take Care that the Laws be faithfully executed, and shall Commission all the Officers of the United States.

Section 4—All civil offices forfeited for certain crimes.

The President, Vice President and all civil Officers of the United States, shall be removed from Office on Impeachment for, and Conviction of, Treason, Bribery, or other high Crimes and Misdemeanors.

ARTICLE III.

Section 1—Judicial powers, Tenure. Compensation.

The judicial Power of the United States, shall be vested in one supreme Court, and in such inferior Courts as the Congress may from time to time ordain and establish. The Judges, both of the supreme and inferior Courts, shall hold their Offices during good Behaviour, and shall, at stated Times, receive for their Services, a Compensation, which shall not be diminished during their Continuance in Office.

Section 2—Judicial power; to what cases it extends. Original jurisdiction of Supreme Court; appellate jurisdiction. Trial by jury, etc. Trial, where.

The judicial Power shall extend to all Cases, in Law and Equity, arising under this Constitution, the Laws of the United States, and Treaties made, or which shall be made, under their Authority;–to all Cases affecting Ambassadors, other public Ministers and Consuls;–to all Cases of admiralty and maritime Jurisdiction;–to Controversies to which the United States shall be a Party;–to Controversies between two or more States;–between a State and Citizens of another State;–between Citizens of different States;–between Citizens of the same State claiming Lands under Grants of different States, and between a State, or the Citizens thereof, and foreign States, Citizens or Subjects.

[This section is modified by Amendment XI.]

In all Cases affecting Ambassadors, other public Ministers and Consuls, and those in which a State shall be Party, the supreme Court shall have original Jurisdiction. In all the other Cases before mentioned, the supreme Court shall have appellate Jurisdiction, both as to Law and Fact, with such Exceptions, and under such Regulations as the Congress shall make.

The trial of all Crimes, except in Cases of Impeachment, shall be by Jury; and such Trial shall be held in the State where the said Crimes shall have been committed; but when not committed within any State, the Trial shall be at such Place or Places as the Congress may by Law have directed.

Section 3—Treason Defined, Proof of, Punishment of.

Treason against the United States, shall consist only in levying War against them, or in adhering to their Enemies, giving them Aid and Comfort. No Person shall be convicted of Treason unless on the Testimony of Two Witnesses to the same overt Act, or on Confession in open Court.

The Congress shall have Power to declare the Punishment of Treason, but no Attainder of Treason shall work Corruption of Blood, or Forfeiture except during the Life of the Person attainted.

ARTICLE IV.

Section 1—Each State to give cr edit to the public acts, etc., of every other State.

Full Faith and Credit shall be given in each State to the public Acts, Records, and judicial Proceedings of every other State. And the Congress may by general Laws prescribe the Manner in which such Acts, Records and Proceedings shall be proved, and the Effect thereof.

Section 2—Privileges of citizens of each State. Fugitives from justice to be delivered up. Persons held to service having escaped, to be delivered up.

The Citizens of each State shall be entitled to all Privileges and Immunities of Citizens in the several States.

A Person charged in any State with Treason, Felony, or other Crime, who shall flee from Justice, and be found in another State, shall on demand of the executive Authority of State from which he fled, be delivered up, to be removed to the State having Jurisdiction of the Crime.

[No Person held to Service or Labour in one State, under the Laws thereof, escaping into another, shall, in Consequence of any Law or Regulation therein, be discharged from such Service or Labour, but shall be delivered up on Claim of the Party to whom such Service or Labour may be due.] [This clause was superseded by Amendment XIII.]

Section 3—Admission of new States. Power of Congress over territory and other property.

New States may be admitted by the Congress into this Union; but no new State shall be formed or erected within the Jurisdiction of any other State; nor any State be formed by the Junction of two or more States, or parts of States, without the Consent of the Legislatures of the States concerned as well as of the Congress.

The Congress shall have Power to dispose of and make all needful Rules and Regulations respecting the Territory or other Property belonging to the United States; and nothing in this Constitution shall be so construed as to Prejudice any Claims of the United States, or of any particular State.

Section 4—Republican form of government guaranteed. Each state to be protected.

The United States shall guarantee to every State in this Union a Republican Form of Government, and shall protect each of them against Invasion; and on Application of the Legislature, or of the Executive (when the Legislature cannot be convened) against domestic Violence.

ARTICLE V.

Constitution: how amended; proviso.

The Congress, whenever two-thirds of both Houses shall deem it necessary, shall propose Amendments to this Constitution, or, on the Application of the Legislatures of two-thirds of the several States, shall call a Convention for proposing Amendments, which, in either Case, shall be valid to all Intents and Purposes, as part of this Constitution, when ratified by the Legislatures of three-fourths of the several States, or by Conventions in three-fourths thereof, as the one or the other Mode of Ratification may be proposed by the Congress: Provided that no Amendment which may be made prior to the Year One thousand eight hundred and eight shall in any Manner affect the first and fourth Clauses in the Ninth Section of the first Article; and that no State, without its Consent, shall be deprived of its equal Suffrage in the Senate.

ARTICLE VI.

Certain debts, etc., declared valid. Supremacy of Constitution, treaties, and laws of the United States. Oath to support Constitution, by whom taken. No religious test.

All Debts contracted and Engagements entered into, before the Adoption of this Constitution, shall be as valid against the United States under this Constitution, as under the Confederation.

This Constitution, and the Laws of the United States which shall be made in Pursuance thereof; and all Treaties made, or which shall be made, under the Authority of the United States, shall be the supreme Law of the Land; and the Judges in every State shall be bound thereby, any Thing in the Constitution or Laws of any State to the Contrary notwithstanding.

The Senators and Representatives before mentioned, and the Members of the several State Legislatures, and all executive and judicial Officers, both of the United States and of the several States, shall be bound by Oath or Affirmation, to support this Constitution; but no religious Test shall ever be required as a Qualification to any Office or public Trust under the United States.

ARTICLE VII.

What ratification shall establish Constitution.

The Ratification of the Conventions of nine States shall be sufficient for the Establishment of this Constitution between the States so ratifying the Same.

Done in Convention by the Unanimous Consent of the States present the Seventeenth Day of September in the Year of our Lord one thousand seven hundred and Eighty seven and of the Independence of the United States of America the Twelfth.

In Witness whereof We have hereunto subscribed our Names.

Go WASHINGTON, Presidt and deputy from Virginia

New Hampshire—John Langdon, Nicholas Gilman

Massachusetts—Nathaniel Gorham, Rufus King

Connecticut—Wm. Saml. Johnson, Roger Sherman

New York—Alexander Hamilton

New Jersey—Wil: Livingston, David Brearley, Wm. Paterson, Jona: Dayton

Pennsylvania—B Franklin, Thomas Mifflin, Robt Morris, Geo. Clymer, Thos. FitzSimons, Jared Ingersoll, James Wilson, Gouv Morris

Delaware—Geo: Read, Gunning Bedford jun, John Dickinson, Richard Bassett, Jaco: Broom

Maryland—James McHenry, Dan of St Thos. Jenifer, Danl Carroll

Virginia—John Blair, James Madison Jr.

North Carolina—Wm. Blount, Rich'd Dobbs Spaight, Hu Williamson

South Carolina—J. Rutledge, Charles Cotesworth Pinckney, Charles Pinckney, Pierce Butler

Georgia—William Few, Abr Baldwin

Attest: William Jackson, Secretary.

Ten Original Amendments: The Bill of Rights

In force Dec. 15, 1791

[The First Congress, at its first session in the City of New York, Sept. 25, 1789, submitted to the states 12 amendments to clarify certain individual and state rights not named in the Constitution. They are generally called the Bill of Rights.

Influential in framing these amendments was the Declaration of Rights of Virginia, written by George Mason (1725-1792) in 1776. Mason, a Virginia delegate to the Constitutional Convention, did not sign the Constitution and opposed its ratification on the ground that it did not sufficiently oppose slavery or safeguard individual rights.

In the preamble to the resolution offering the proposed amendments, Congress said: "The conventions of a number of the States having at the time of their adopting the Constitution, expressed a desire, in order to prevent misconstruction or abuse of its powers, that further declaratory and restrictive clauses should be added, and as extending the ground of public confidence in the government will best insure the beneficent ends of its institution, be it resolved," etc.

Ten of these amendments, now commonly known as one to 10 inclusive, but originally 3 to 12 inclusive, were ratified by the states as follows: New Jersey, Nov. 20, 1789; Maryland, Dec. 19, 1789; North Carolina, Dec. 22, 1789; South Carolina, Jan. 19, 1790; New Hampshire, Jan. 25, 1790; Delaware, Jan. 28, 1790; New York, Feb. 27, 1790; Pennsylvania, Mar. 10, 1790; Rhode Island, June 7, 1790; Vermont, Nov. 3, 1791; Virginia, Dec. 15, 1791; Massachusetts, Mar. 2, 1939; Georgia, Mar. 18, 1939; Connecticut, Apr. 19, 1939. These original 10 ratified amendments follow as Amendments I to X inclusive.

Of the two original proposed amendments that were not ratified promptly by the necessary number of states, the first related to apportionment of Representatives; the second, relating to compensation of members of Congress, was ratified in 1992 and became Amendment 27.]

AMENDMENT I.

Religious establishment prohibited. Freedom of speech, of press, right to assemble and to petition.

Congress shall make no law respecting an establishment of religion, or prohibiting the free exercise thereof; or abridging the freedom of speech, or of the press; or the right of the people peaceably to assemble, and to petition the Government for a redress of grievances.

AMENDMENT II.

Right to keep and bear arms.

A well regulated Militia, being necessary to the security of a free State, the right of the people to keep and bear Arms, shall not be infringed.

AMENDMENT III.

Conditions for quarters for soldiers.

No Soldier shall, in time of peace be quartered" in any house, without the consent of the Owner, nor in time of war, but in a manner to be prescribed by law.

AMENDMENT IV.

Protection from unreasonable search and seizure.

The right of the people to be secure in their persons, houses, papers, and effects, against unreasonable searches and seizures, shall not be violated, and no Warrants shall issue, but upon probable cause, supported by Oath or affirmation, and particularly describing the place to be searched, and the persons or things to be seized.

AMENDMENT V.

Provisions concerning prosecution and due process of law. Double jeopardy restriction. Private property not to be taken without compensation.

No person shall be held to answer for a capital, or otherwise infamous crime, unless on a presentment or indictment of a Grand Jury, except in cases arising in the land or naval forces, or in the Militia, when in actual service in time of War or public danger; nor shall any person be subject for the same offence to be twice put in jeopardy of life or limb; nor shall be compelled in any criminal case to be a witness against himself, nor be deprived of life, liberty, or property, without due process of law; nor shall private property be taken for public use, without just compensation.

AMENDMENT VI.

Right to speedy trial, witnesses, etc.

In all criminal prosecutions, the accused shall enjoy the right to a speedy and public trial, by an impartial jury of the State and district wherein the crime shall have been committed, which district shall have been previously ascertained by law, and to be informed of the nature and cause of the accusation; to be confronted with the witnesses against him; to have compulsory process for obtaining witnesses in his favor, and to have the Assistance of Counsel for his defence.

AMENDMENT VII.

Right of trial by jury.

In suits at common law, where the value in controversy shall exceed twenty dollars, the right of trial by jury shall be preserved, and no fact tried by a jury, shall be otherwise reexamined in any Court of the United States, than according to the rules of the common law.

AMENDMENT VIII.

Excessive bail or fines; cruel and unusual punishment.

Excessive bail shall not be required, nor excessive fines imposed, nor cruel and unusual punishments inflicted.

AMENDMENT IX.

Rule of construction of Constitution.

The enumeration in the Constitution, of certain rights, shall not be construed to deny or disparage others retained by the people.

AMENDMENT X.

Rights of States under Constitution.

The powers not delegated to the United States by the Constitution, nor prohibited by it to the States, are reserved to the States respectively, or to the people.

Amendments Since the Bill of Rights

AMENDMENT XI.
Judicial powers construed.

The Judicial power of the United States shall not be construed to extend to any suit in law or equity, commenced or prosecuted against one of the United States by Citizens of another State, or by Citizens or Subjects of any Foreign State.

[This amendment was proposed to the Legislatures of the several States by the Third Congress on March. 4, 1794, and was declared to have been ratified in a message from the President to Congress, dated Jan. 8, 1798.

[It was on Jan. 5, 1798, that Secretary of State Pickering received from 12 of the States authenticated ratifications, and informed President John Adams of that fact.

[As a result of later research in the Department of State, it is now established that Amendment XI became part of the Constitution on Feb. 7, 1795, for on that date it had been ratified by 12 States as follows:

[1. New York, Mar. 27, 1794. 2. Rhode Island, Mar. 31, 1794. 3. Connecticut, May 8, 1794. 4. New Hampshire, June 16, 1794. 5. Massachusetts, June 26, 1794. 6. Vermont, between Oct. 9, 1794, and Nov. 9, 1794. 7. Virginia, Nov. 18, 1794. 8. Georgia, Nov. 29, 1794. 9. Kentucky, Dec. 7, 1794. 10. Maryland, Dec. 26, 1794. 11. Delaware, Jan. 23, 1795. 12. North Carolina, Feb. 7, 1795.

[On June 1, 1796, more than a year after Amendment XI had become a part of the Constitution—but before anyone was officially aware of this—Tennessee had been admitted as a State; but not until Oct. 16, 1797, was a certified copy of the resolution of Congress proposing the amendment sent to the Governor of Tennessee, John Sevier, by Secretary of State Pickering, whose office was then at Trenton, New Jersey, because of the epidemic of yellow fever at Philadelphia; it seems, however, that the Legislature of Tennessee took no action on Amendment XI, owing doubtless to the fact that public announcement of its adoption was made soon thereafter.

[Besides the necessary 12 States, one other, South Carolina, ratified Amendment XI, but this action was not taken until Dec. 4, 1797; the two remaining States, New Jersey and Pennsylvania, failed to ratify.]

AMENDMENT XII.

Manner of choosing President and Vice-President.

[Proposed by Congress Dec. 9, 1803; ratified June 15, 1804.]

The Electors shall meet in their respective states and vote by ballot for President and Vice-President, one of whom, at least, shall not be an inhabitant of the same state with themselves; they shall name in their ballots the person voted for as President, and in distinct ballots the person voted for as Vice-President, and they shall make distinct lists of all persons voted for as President, and of all persons voted for as Vice-President, and of the number of votes for each, which lists they shall sign and certify, and transmit sealed to the seat of the government of the United States, directed to the President of the Senate;–The President of the Senate shall, in presence of the Senate and House of Representatives, open all the certificates and the votes shall then be counted;—The person having the greatest number of votes for President, shall be the President, if such number be a majority of the whole number of Electors appointed; and if no person have such majority, then from the persons having the highest numbers not exceeding three on the list of those voted for as President, the House of Representatives shall choose immediately, by ballot, the President. But in choosing the President, the votes shall be taken by states, the representation from each state having one vote; a quorum for this purpose shall consist of a member or members from two-thirds of the states, and a majority of all the states shall be necessary to a choice. *[And if the House of Representatives shall not choose a President whenever the right of choice shall devolve upon them, before the fourth day of March next following, then the Vice-President shall act as President, as in the case of the death or other constitutional disability of the President.] [The words in parentheses were superseded by Amendment XX, section 3.]* The person having the greatest number of votes as Vice-President, shall be the Vice-President, if such number be a majority of the whole number of Electors appointed, and if no person have a majority, then from the two highest numbers on the list, the Senate shall choose the Vice-President; a quorum for the purpose shall consist of two-thirds of the whole number of Senators, and a majority of the whole number shall be necessary to a choice. But no person constitutionally ineligible to the office of President shall be eligible to that of Vice-President of the United States.

THE RECONSTRUCTION AMENDMENTS

[Amendments XIII, XIV, and XV are commonly known as the Reconstruction Amendments, inasmuch as they followed the Civil War, and were drafted by Republicans who were bent on imposing their own policy of reconstruction on the South. Post-bellum legislatures there—Mississippi, South Carolina, Georgia, for example—had set up laws which, it was charged, were contrived to perpetuate Negro slavery under other names.]

AMENDMENT XIII.
Slavery abolished.

[Proposed by Congress Jan. 31, 1865; ratified Dec. 6, 1865. The amendment, when first proposed by a resolution in Congress, was passed by the Senate, 38 to 6, on Apr. 8, 1864, but was defeated in the House, 95 to 66 on June 15, 1864. On reconsideration by the House, on Jan. 31, 1865, the resolution passed, 119 to 56. It was approved by President Lincoln on Feb. 1, 1865, although the Supreme Court had decided in 1798 that the President has nothing to do with the proposing of amendments to the Constitution, or their adoption.]

1. Neither slavery nor involuntary servitude, except as a punishment for crime whereof the party shall have been duly convicted, shall exist within the United States, or any place subject to their jurisdiction.

2. Congress shall have power to enforce this article by appropriate legislation.

AMENDMENT XIV.
Citizenship rights not to be abridged.

[The following amendment was proposed to the Legislatures of the several states by the 39th Congress, June 13, 1866, ratified July 9, 1868, and declared to have been ratified in a proclamation by the Secretary of State, July 28, 1868.]

[The 14th amendment was adopted only by virtue of ratification subsequent to earlier rejections. Newly constituted legislatures in both North Carolina and South Carolina (respectively July 4 and 9, 1868), ratified the proposed amendment, although earlier legislatures had rejected the proposal. The Secretary of State issued a proclamation, which, though doubtful as to the effect of attempted withdrawals by Ohio and New Jersey, entertained no doubt as to the validity of the ratification by North and South Carolina. The following day (July 21, 1868), Congress passed a resolution which declared the 14th Amendment to be a part of the Constitution and directed the Secretary of State so to promulgate it. The Secretary waited, however, until the newly constituted Legislature of Georgia had ratified the amendment, subsequent to an earlier rejection, before the promulgation of the ratification of the new amendment.]

1. All persons born or naturalized in the United States, and subject to the jurisdiction thereof, are citizens of the United States and of the State wherein they reside. No State shall make or enforce any law which shall abridge the privileges and immunities of citizens of the United States; nor shall any State deprive any person of life, liberty, or property, without due process of law; nor deny to any person within its jurisdiction the equal protection of the laws.

2. Representatives shall be apportioned among the several States according to their respective numbers, counting the whole number of persons in each State, excluding Indians not taxed. But when the right to vote at any election for the choice of electors for President and Vice-President of the United States, Representatives in Congress, the Executive and Judicial officers of a State, or the members of the Legislature thereof, is denied to any of the male inhabitants of such State, being twenty-one years of age, and citizens of the United States, or in any way abridged, except for participation in rebellion, or other crime, the basis of representation therein shall be reduced in the proportion which the number of such male citizens shall bear to the whole number of male citizens twenty-one years of age in such State.

3. No person shall be a Senator or Representative in Congress, or elector of President and Vice-President, or hold any office, civil or military, under the United States, or under any State, who, having previously taken an oath, as a member of Congress, or as an officer of the United States, or as a member of any State legislature, or as an executive or judicial officer of any State, to support the Constitution of the United States, shall have engaged in insurrection or rebellion against the same, or given aid or comfort to the enemies thereof. But Congress may by a vote of two-thirds of each House, remove such disability.

4. The validity of the public debt of the United States, authorized by law, including debts incurred for payment of pensions and bounties for services in suppressing insurrection or rebellion, shall not be questioned. But neither the United States nor any State shall assume or pay any debt or obligation incurred in aid of insurrection or rebellion against the United States, or any claim for the loss or emancipation of any slave; but all such debts, obligations and claims shall be held illegal and void.

The Congress shall have power to enforce, by appropriate legislation, the provisions of this article.

AMENDMENT XV.
Race no bar to voting rights.

[The following amendment was proposed to the legislatures of the several States by the 40th Congress, Feb. 26, 1869, and ratified Feb. 8, 1870.]

1. The right of citizens of the United States to vote shall not be denied or abridged by the United States or by any State on account of race, color, or previous condition of servitude–

2. The Congress shall have power to enforce this article by appropriate legislation.

AMENDMENT XVI.
Income taxes authorized.

[Proposed by Congress July 12, 1909; ratified Feb. 3, 1913.]

The Congress shall have power to lay and collect taxes on incomes, from whatever source derived, without apportionment among the several States, and without regard to any census or enumeration.

AMENDMENT XVII.
United States Senators to be elected by direct popular vote.

[Proposed by Congress May 13, 1912; ratified Apr. 8, 1913.]

The Senate of the United States shall be composed of two Senators from each State, elected by the people thereof, for six years; and each Senator shall have one vote. The electors in each State shall have the qualifications requisite for electors of the most numerous branch of the State legislatures.

When vacancies happen in the representation of any State in the Senate, the executive authority of such State shall issue writs of election to fill such vacancies: *Provided*, That the legislature of any State may empower the executive thereof to make temporary appointments until the people fill the vacancies by election as the legislature may direct.

This amendment shall not be so construed as to affect the election or term of any Senator chosen before it becomes valid as part of the Constitution.

AMENDMENT XVIII.
Liquor prohibition amendment.
[Proposed by Congress Dec. 18, 1917; ratified Jan. 16, 1919. Repealed by Amendment XXI, effective Dec. 5, 1933.]

1. After one year from the ratification of this article the manufacture, sale, or transportation of intoxicating liquors within, the importation thereof into, or the exportation thereof from the United States and all territory subject to the jurisdiction thereof for beverage purposes is hereby prohibited.

2. The Congress and the several States shall have concurrent power to enforce this article by appropriate legislation.

3. This article shall be inoperative unless it shall have been ratified as an amendment to the Constitution by the legislatures of the several States as provided in the Constitution, within seven years from the date of the submission hereof to the States by the Congress.

[The total vote in the Senates of the various States was 1,310 for, 237 against—84.6% dry. In the lower houses of the States the vote was 3,782 for, 1,035 against—78.5% dry.

[The amendment ultimately was adopted by all the States except Connecticut and Rhode Island.]

AMENDMENT XIX.
Giving nationwide suffrage to women.
[Proposed by Congress June 4, 1919; ratified Aug. 18, 1920.]

The right of citizens of the United States to vote shall not be denied or abridged by the United States or by any State on account of sex.

Congress shall have power to enforce this Article by appropriate legislation.

AMENDMENT XX.
Terms of President and Vice President to begin on Jan. 20; those of Senators, Representatives, Jan. 3.
[Proposed by Congress Mar. 2, 1932; ratified Jan. 23, 1933.]

1. The terms of the President and Vice President shall end at noon on the 20th day of January, and the terms of Senators and Representatives at noon on the 3d day of January, of the years in which such terms would have ended if this article had not been ratified; and the terms of their successors shall then begin.

2. The Congress shall assemble at least once in every year, and such meeting shall begin at noon on the 3d day of January, unless they shall by law appoint a different day.

3. If, at the time fixed for the beginning of the term of the President, the President elect shall have died, the Vice President elect shall become President. If a President shall not have been chosen before the time fixed for the beginning of his term, or if the President elect shall have failed to qualify, then the Vice President elect shall act as President until a President shall have qualified; and the Congress may by law provide for the case wherein neither a President elect nor a Vice President elect shall have qualified, declaring who shall then act as President, or the manner in which one who is to act shall be selected, and such person shall act accordingly until a President or Vice President shall have qualified.

4. The Congress may by law provide for the case of the death of any of the persons from whom the House of Representatives may choose a President whenever the right of choice shall have devolved upon them, and for the case of the death of any of the persons from whom the Senate may choose a Vice President whenever the right of choice shall have devolved upon them.

5. Sections 1 and 2 shall take effect on the 15th day of October following the ratification of this article (Oct. 1933).

6. This article shall be inoperative unless it shall have been ratified as an amendment to the Constitution by the legislatures of three-fourths of the several States within seven years from the date of its submission.

AMENDMENT XXI.
Repeal of Amendment XVIII.
[Proposed by Congress Feb. 20, 1933; ratified Dec. 5, 1933.]

1. The eighteenth article of amendment to the Constitution of the United States is hereby repealed.

2. The transportation or importation into any State, Territory, or possession of the United States for delivery or use therein of intoxicating liquors, in violation of the laws thereof, is hereby prohibited.

3. This article shall be inoperative unless it shall have been ratified as an amendment to the Constitution by conventions in the several States, as provided in the Constitution, within seven years from the date of the submission hereof to the States by the Congress.

AMENDMENT XXII.
Limiting Presidential terms of office.
[Proposed by Congress Mar. 24, 1947; ratified Feb. 27, 1951.]

1. No person shall be elected to the office of the President more than twice, and no person who has held the office of President, or acted as President, for more than two years of a term to which some other person was elected President shall be elected to the office of the President more than once. But this Article shall not apply to any person holding the office of President when this Article was proposed by the Congress, and shall not prevent any person who may be holding the office of President, or acting as President, during the term within which this Article becomes operative from holding the office of President or acting as President during the remainder of such term.

2. This article shall be inoperative unless it shall have been ratified as an amendment to the Constitution by the legislatures of three-fourths of the several States within seven years from the date of its submission to the States by the Congress.

AMENDMENT XXIII.
Presidential vote for District of Columbia.
[Proposed by Congress June 16, 1960; ratified Mar. 29, 1961.]

1. The District constituting the seat of Government of the United States shall appoint in such manner as the Congress may direct:

A number of electors of President and Vice President equal to the whole number of Senators and Representatives in Congress to which the District would be entitled if it were a State, but in no event more than the least populous State; they shall be in addition to those appointed by the States, but they shall be considered, for the purposes of the election of President and Vice President, to be electors appointed by a State; and they shall meet in the District and perform such duties as provided by the twelfth article of amendment.

2. The Congress shall have power to enforce this article by appropriate legislation.

AMENDMENT XXIV.
Barring poll tax in federal elections.
[Proposed by Congress Aug. 27, 1962; ratified Jan. 23, 1964.]

1. The right of citizens of the United States to vote in any primary or other election for President or Vice President, for electors for President or Vice President, or for Senator or Representative in Congress, shall not be denied or abridged by the United States or any State by reason of failure to pay any poll tax or other tax.

2. The Congress shall have power to enforce this article by appropriate legislation.

AMENDMENT XXV.
Presidential disability and succession.
[Proposed by Congress July 6, 1965; ratified Feb. 10, 1967.]

1. In case of the removal of the President from office or of his death or resignation, the Vice President shall become President.

2. Whenever there is a vacancy in the office of the Vice President, the President shall nominate a Vice President who shall take office upon confirmation by a majority vote of both houses of Congress.

3. Whenever the President transmits to the President pro tempore of the Senate and the Speaker of the House of Representatives his written declaration that he is unable to discharge the powers and duties of his office, and until he transmits to them a written declaration to the contrary, such powers and duties shall be discharged by the Vice President as Acting President.

4. Whenever the Vice President and a majority of either the principal officers of the executive departments or of such other body as Congress may by law provide, transmit to the President pro tempore of the Senate and the Speaker of the House of Representatives their written declaration that the President is unable to discharge the powers and duties of his

office, the Vice President shall immediately assume the powers and duties of the office as Acting President.

Thereafter, when the President transmits to the President pro tempore of the Senate and the Speaker of the House of Representatives his written declaration that no inability exists, he shall resume the powers and duties of his office unless the Vice President and a majority of either the principal officers of the executive department or of such other body as Congress may by law provide, transmit within four days to the President pro tempore of the Senate and the Speaker of the House of Representatives their written declaration that the President is unable to discharge the powers and duties of his office. Thereupon Congress shall decide the issue, assembling within forty-eight hours for that purpose if not in session. If the Congress, within twenty-one days after receipt of the latter written declaration, or, if Congress is not in session, within twenty-one days after Congress is required to assemble, determines by two-thirds vote of both Houses that the President is unable to discharge the powers and duties of his office, the Vice President shall continue to discharge the same as Acting President;

otherwise, the President shall resume the powers and duties of his office.

AMENDMENT XXVI.
Lowering voting age to 18 years.
[Proposed by Congress Mar. 23, 1971; ratified June 30, 1971.]
1. The right of citizens of the United States, who are eighteen years of age or older, to vote shall not be denied or abridged by the United States or by any State on account of age.
2. The Congress shall have the power to enforce this article by appropriate legislation.

AMENDMENT XXVII.
Congressional pay.
[Proposed by Congress Sept. 25, 1789; ratified May 7, 1992.]
No law, varying the compensation for the services of the Senators and Representatives, shall take effect, until an election of Representatives shall have intervened.

How a Bill Becomes a Law

A senator or representative introduces a bill in Congress by sending it to the clerk of the House or the Senate, who assigns it a number and title. This procedure is termed the first reading. The clerk then refers the bill to the appropriate committee of the Senate or House.

If the committee opposes the bill, it will table, or kill, it. Otherwise, the committee holds hearings to listen to opinions and facts offered by members and other interested people. The committee then debates the bill and possibly offers amendments. A vote is taken, and if favorable, the bill is sent back to the clerk of the House or Senate.

The clerk reads the bill to the house—the second reading. Members may then debate the bill and suggest amendments.

After debate and possibly amendment, the bill is given a third reading, simply of the title, and put to a voice or roll-call vote.

If passed, the bill goes to the other house, where it may be defeated or passed, with or without amendments. If defeated, the bill dies. If passed with amendments, a conference committee made up of members of both houses works out the differences and arrives at a compromise.

After passage of the final version by both houses, the bill is sent to the president. If the president signs it, the bill becomes a law. The president may, however, veto the bill by refusing to sign it and sending it back to the house where it originated, with reasons for the veto.

The president's objections are then read and debated, and a roll-call vote is taken. If the bill receives less than a two-thirds majority, it is defeated. If it receives at least two-thirds, it is sent to the other house. If that house also passes it by at least a two-thirds majority, the veto is overridden, and the bill becomes a law.

The Capitol

If the president neither signs nor vetoes the bill within 10 days—not including Sundays—it automatically becomes a law even without the president's signature. However, if Congress has adjourned within those 10 days, the bill is automatically killed; this indirect rejection is termed a pocket veto.

Note: Under "line-item veto" legislation effective Jan. 1, 1997, the president was authorized, under certain circumstances, to veto a bill in part, but the legislation was found unconstitutional by the Supreme Court, June 25, 1998.

Confederate States and Secession

The American Civil War (1861-65) grew out of sectional disputes over the continued existence of slavery in the South and the contention of Southern legislators that the states retained many rights, including the right to secede.

The war was not fought by state against state but by one federal regime against another, the Confederate government in Richmond assuming control over the economic, political, and military life of the South, under protest from Georgia and South Carolina.

South Carolina voted an ordinance of secession from the Union, repealing its 1788 ratification of the U.S. Constitution on Dec. 20, 1860, to take effect on Dec. 24. Other states seceded in 1861. Their votes in conventions were: Mississippi, Jan. 9, 84-15; Florida, Jan. 10, 62-7; Alabama, Jan. 11, 61-39; Georgia, Jan. 19, 208-89; Louisiana, Jan. 26, 113-17; Texas, Feb. 1, 166-7, ratified by popular vote on Feb. 23 (for 34,794, against 11,325); Virginia, Apr. 17, 88-55, ratified by popular vote on May 23 (for 128,884; against 32,134); Arkansas, May

6, 69-1; Tennessee, May 7, ratified by popular vote on June 8 (for 104,019, against 47,238); North Carolina, May 21.

Missouri Unionists stopped secession in conventions Feb. 28 and Mar. 9. The legislature condemned secession Mar. 7. Under the protection of Confederate troops, secessionist members of the legislature adopted a resolution of secession at Neosho, Oct. 31. The Confederate Congress seated the secessionists' representatives.

Kentucky did not secede, and its government remained Unionist. In a part of the state occupied by Confederate troops, Kentuckians approved secession, and the Confederate Congress admitted their representatives.

The Maryland legislature voted against secession Apr. 27, 53-13. Delaware did not secede. Western Virginia held conventions at Wheeling, named a pro-Union governor on June 11, 1861, and was admitted to the Union as West Virginia on June 20, 1863. Its constitution provided for gradual abolition of slavery.

Confederate Government

Forty-two delegates from South Carolina, Georgia, Alabama, Mississippi, Louisiana, and Florida met in convention at Montgomery, AL, on Feb. 4, 1861. They adopted a provisional constitution of the Confederate States of America and elected Jefferson Davis (MS) as provisional president and Alexander H. Stephens (GA) as provisional vice president.

A permanent constitution was adopted Mar. 11. It abolished the African slave trade, but it did not bar interstate commerce

in slaves. On July 20 the Congress moved to Richmond, VA. Davis was elected president in October and was inaugurated on Feb. 22, 1862.

The Congress adopted a flag, consisting of a red field with a white stripe, and a blue jack with a circle of white stars. Later the more popular flag was the red field with blue diagonal crossbars that held 13 white stars, for the 11 states in the Confederacy plus Kentucky and Missouri.

> **IT'S A FACT:** The Battle of Gettysburg (PA) on July 1-3, 1863, repelled the Confederates' 2nd and last major invasion of the North and is often considered the turning point of the Civil War. But there were heavy losses, with close to 50,000 troops on the two sides left dead, wounded, or missing. Lincoln's famous Gettysburg Address, delivered at the battlefield Nov. 19, 1863, for the dedication of the Gettysburg National Cemetery, followed a two-hour oration by one of the most famous orators of the day, Edward Everett Horton. Many listeners were thus too fatigued to appreciate Lincoln's brief speech. But contrary to later myths, some newspapers of the time did recognize its merits, as did Horton himself. Also contrary to myth, Lincoln did not compose the speech on an old brown envelope while riding on the train to Gettysburg; he basically finished it in Washington before he left. He did make some revisions after that and made other changes as he spoke, including the addition of the phrase "under God."

Lincoln's Address at Gettysburg, 1863

Fourscore and seven years ago our fathers brought forth on this continent a new nation, conceived in liberty and dedicated to the proposition that all men are created equal.

Now we are engaged in a great civil war, testing whether that nation or any nation so conceived and so dedicated can long endure. We are met on a great battle field of that war. We have come to dedicate a portion of that field, as a final resting-place for those who here gave their lives that that nation might live. It is altogether fitting and proper that we should do this.

But, in a larger sense, we can not dedicate—we can not consecrate—we can not hallow—this ground. The brave men, living and dead, who struggled here, have consecrated it, far above our poor power to add or detract. The world will little note, nor long remember, what we say here, but it can never forget what they did here. It is for us the living, rather, to be dedicated here to the unfinished work which they who fought here have thus far so nobly advanced. It is rather for us to be here dedicated to the great task remaining before us—that from these honored dead we take increased devotion to that cause for which they gave the last full measure of devotion—that we here highly resolve that these dead shall not have died in vain—that this nation, under God, shall have a new birth of freedom—and that government of the people, by the people, for the people, shall not perish from the earth.

Selected Landmark Decisions of the U.S. Supreme Court, 1803-2002

1803: Marbury v. Madison. The Court ruled that Congress exceeded its power in the Judiciary Act of 1789; the Court thus established its power to review acts of Congress and declare invalid those it found in conflict with the Constitution.

1819: McCulloch v. Maryland. The Court ruled that Congress had the authority to charter a national bank, under the Constitution's granting of the power to enact all laws "necessary and proper" to responsibilities of government.

1819: Trustees of Dartmouth College v. Woodward. The Court ruled that a state could not arbitrarily alter the terms of a college's contract. (The Court later used a similar principle to limit the states' ability to interfere with business contracts.)

1857: Dred Scott v. Sanford. The Court declared unconstitutional the already-repealed Missouri Compromise of 1820 because it deprived a person of his or her property—a slave—without due process of law. The Court also ruled that slaves were not citizens of any state nor of the U.S. (The latter part of the decision was overturned by ratification of the 14th Amendment in 1868.)

1896: Plessy v. Ferguson. The Court ruled that a state law requiring federal railroad trains to provide separate but equal facilities for black and white passengers neither infringed upon federal authority to regulate interstate commerce nor violated the 13th and 14th Amendments. (The "separate but equal" doctrine remained effective until the 1954 **Brown v. Board of Education** decision.)

1904: Northern Securities Co. v. U.S. The Court ruled that a holding company formed solely to eliminate competition between two railroad lines was a combination in restraint of trade, violating the federal antitrust act.

1908: Muller v. Oregon. The Court upheld a state law limiting the working hours of women. (Louis D. Brandeis, counsel for the state, cited evidence from social workers, physicians, and factory inspectors that the number of hours women worked affected their health and morals.)

1911: Standard Oil Co. of New Jersey et al. v. U.S. The Court ruled that the Standard Oil Trust must be dissolved because of its unreasonable restraint of trade.

1919: Schenck v. U.S. The Court sustained the Espionage Act of 1917, maintaining that freedom of speech and press could be constrained if "the words used . . . create a clear and present danger. . ."

1925: Gitlow v. New York. The Court ruled that the First Amendment prohibition against government abridgment of the freedom of speech applied to the states as well as to the federal government. The decision was the first of a number of rulings holding that the 14th Amendment extended the guarantees of the Bill of Rights to state action.

1935: Schechter Poultry Corp. v. U.S. The Court ruled that Congress exceeded its authority to delegate legislative powers and to regulate interstate commerce when it enacted the National Industrial Recovery Act, which afforded the U.S. president too much discretionary power.

1951: Dennis et al. v. U.S. The Court upheld convictions under the Smith Act of 1940 for invoking Communist theory that advocated the forcible overthrow of the government. (In the 1957 **Yates v. U.S.** decision, the Court moderated this ruling by allowing such advocacy in the abstract, if not connected to action to achieve the goal.)

1954: Brown v. Board of Education of Topeka. The Court ruled that separate public schools for black and white students were inherently unequal, so that state-sanctioned segregation in public schools violated the equal protection guarantee of the 14th Amendment. And in **Bolling v. Sharpe** the Court ruled that the congressionally mandated segregated public school system in the District of Columbia violated the 5th Amendment's due process guarantee of personal liberty. (The Brown ruling also led to abolition of state-sponsored segregation in other public facilities.)

1957: Roth v. U.S., Alberts v. California. The Court ruled obscene material was not protected by First Amendment guarantees of freedom of speech and press, defining obscene as "utterly without redeeming social value" and appealing to "prurient interests" in the view of the average person. This definition was modified in later decisions, and the "average person" standard was replaced by the "local community" standard in **Miller v. California (1973).**

1961: Mapp v. Ohio. The Court ruled that evidence obtained in violation of the 4th Amendment guarantee against unreasonable search and seizure must be excluded from use at state as well as federal trials.

1962: Engel v. Vitale. The Court held that public schools could not require pupils to recite a state-composed prayer, even if nondenominational and voluntary, because this would be an unconstitutional attempt to establish religion.

1962: Baker v. Carr. The Court held that the constitutional challenges to the unequal distribution of voters among legislative districts could be resolved by federal courts.

1963: Gideon v. Wainwright. The Court ruled that state and federal defendants charged with serious crimes must have access to an attorney, at state expense if necessary.

1964: New York Times Co. v. Sullivan. The Court ruled that the First Amendment protected the press from libel suits for defamatory reports about public officials unless an injured party could prove that a defamatory report was made out of malice or "reckless disregard" for the truth.

1965: Griswold v. Conn. The Court ruled that a state unconstitutionally interfered with personal privacy in the marriage relationship when it prohibited anyone, including married couples, from using contraceptives.

1966: Miranda v. Arizona. The Court ruled that, under the guarantee of due process, suspects in custody, before being questioned, must be informed that they have the right to remain silent, that anything they say may be used against them, and that they have the right to counsel.

1973: Roe v. Wade, Doe v. Bolton. The Court ruled that the fetus was not a "person" with constitutional rights and that a right to privacy inherent in the 14th Amendment's due process guarantee of personal liberty protected a woman's decision to have an abortion. During the first trimester of pregnancy, the Court maintained, the decision should be left entirely to a woman and her physician. Some regulation of abortion procedures was allowed in the 2nd trimester, and some restriction of abortion in the 3rd.

1974: U.S. v. Nixon. The Court ruled that neither the separation of powers nor the need to preserve the confidentiality of presidential communications could alone justify an absolute executive privilege of immunity from judicial demands for evidence to be used in a criminal trial.

1976: Gregg v. Georgia, Profitt v. Fla., Jurek v. Texas. The Court held that death, as a punishment for persons convicted of first degree murder, was not in and of itself cruel and unusual punishment in violation of the 8th Amendment. But the Court ruled that the sentencing judge and jury must consider the individual character of the offender and the circumstances of the particular crime.

1978: Regents of Univ. of Calif. v. Bakke. The Court ruled that a special admissions program for a state medical school, under which a set number of places were reserved for minorities, violated the 1964 Civil Rights Act, which forbids excluding anyone, because of race, from a federally funded program. However, the Court ruled that race could be considered as one of a complex of factors.

1986: Bowers v. Hardwick. The Court refused to extend any constitutional right of privacy to homosexual activity, upholding a Georgia law that in effect made such activity a crime. (Although the Georgia law made no distinction between heterosexual or homosexual sodomy, enforcement had been confined to homosexuals; the statute was invalidated by the state supreme court in 1998.) In **Romer v. Evans (1996),** the Court struck down a Colorado constitutional provision that barred legislation protecting homosexuals from discrimination.

1990: Cruzan v. Missouri. The Court ruled that a person had the right to refuse life-sustaining medical treatment. However, the Court also ruled that, before treatment could be withheld from a comatose patient, a state could require "clear and convincing evidence" that the patient would not have wanted to live. And in 2 **1997** rulings, **Washington v. Glucksberg** and **Vacco v. Quill,** the Court ruled that states could ban doctor-assisted suicide.

1995: Adarand Constructors v. Peña. The Court held that federal programs that classify people by race, unless "narrowly tailored" to accomplish a "compelling governmental interest," may violate the right to equal protection.

1995: U.S. Term Limits Inc. v. Thornton. The Court ruled that neither states nor Congress could limit terms of members of Congress, since the Constitution reserves to the people the right to choose federal lawmakers.

1997: Clinton v. Jones. Rejecting an appeal by Pres. Clinton in a sexual harassment suit, the Court ruled that a sitting president did not have temporary immunity from a lawsuit for actions outside the realm of official duties.

1997: City of Boerne v. Flores. The Court overturned a 1993 law that banned enforcement of laws that "substantially burden" religious practice unless there is a "compelling need" to do so. The Court held that the act was an unwarranted intrusion by Congress on states' prerogatives and an infringement of the judiciary's role.

1997: Reno v. ACLU. Citing the right to free expression, the Court overturned a provision making it a crime to display or distribute "indecent" or "patently offensive" material on the Internet. In **1998,** however, the Court ruled in **NEA v. Finley** that "general standards of decency" may be used as a criterion in federal arts funding.

1998: Clinton v. City of New York. The Court struck down the Line-Item Veto Act (1996), holding that it unconstitutionally gave the president "the unilateral power to change the text of duly enacted statutes."

1998: Faragher v. City of Boca Raton, Burlington Industries, Inc. v. Ellerth. The Court issued new guidelines for workplace sexual harassment suits, holding employers responsible for misconduct by supervisory employees. And in **Oncale v. Sundowner Offshore Services,** the Court ruled that the law against sexual harassment applies regardless of whether harasser and victim are the same sex.

1999: Dept. of Commerce v. U.S. House. Upholding a challenge to plans for the 2000 census, the Court required an actual head count for apportioning the U.S. House of Representatives, but allowed statistical sampling for other purposes, such as the allocation of federal funds.

1999: Alden v. Maine, Florida Prepaid v. College Savings Bank, College Savings Bank v. Florida. In a series of rulings, the Court applied the principle of "sovereign immunity" to shield states in large part from being sued under federal law.

2000: Troxel v. Granville. The justices found that a Washington state law allowing grandparents visitation rights, as broadly applied, interfered with parents' right to determine the best care for their children.

2000: Boy Scouts of America v. Dale. The Court ruled that the Boy Scouts could dismiss a troop leader after learning he was gay, holding that the right to freedom of association outweighed a New Jersey anti-discrimination statute.

2000: Stenberg v. Carhart. The Court struck down a Nebraska law that banned so-called partial-birth abortion. It argued that the law could be interpreted as banning other abortion procedures and that it should have made exception for reasons of health. (See 1973: *Roe* v. *Wade.*)

2000: Bush v. Gore. The Court ruled that manual recounts of presidential ballots in the Nov. 2000 election could not proceed because inconsistent evaluation standards in different counties violated the equal protection clause. In effect, the ruling meant existing official results leaving George W. Bush as narrow winner of the election would prevail.

2001: Easley v. Cromartie. The Court ruled that North Carolina's 12th Congressional District, whose irregular shape had been challenged as an unconstitutional racial gerrymander, was the permissible result of attempts to create a majority-Democrat district.

2001: Good News Club v. Milford Central School. The justices found that religious and secular organizations were entitled to equal access to public elementary school grounds for after-school meetings.

2002: Atkins v. Virginia. The Court ruled that the execution of mentally retarded felons violated the Eighth Amendment ban on "cruel and unusual punishment."

2002: Ring v. Arizona. The Court found that only a jury, not a judge, could decide to impose the death penalty.

2002: Zelman v. Simmons-Harris. The Court ruled that publicly funded tuition vouchers could be used at religious schools without violating the separation of church and state.

2002: Federal Maritime Commission v. South Carolina State Ports Authority. The Court ruled that the 11th Amendment gave states immunity from private lawsuits involving federal agencies.

Presidential Oath of Office

The Constitution (Article II) directs that the president-elect shall take the following oath or affirmation to be inaugurated as president: "I do solemnly swear [affirm] that I will faithfully execute the office of President of the United States, and will, to the best of my ability, preserve, protect, and defend the Constitution of the United States." (Custom decrees the addition of the words "So help me God" at the end of the oath when taken by the president-elect, with the left hand on the Bible for the duration of the oath, and the right hand slightly raised.)

WORLD ALMANAC QUICK QUIZ

Which of the following people did not sign the Constitution?
(a) George Washington   (b) Thomas Jefferson   (c) Alexander Hamilton   (d) James Madison
For the answer look in this chapter, or see page 1008.

Law on Succession to the Presidency

If by reason of death, resignation, removal from office, inability, or failure to qualify there is neither a president nor vice president to discharge the powers and duties of the office of president, then the speaker of the House of Representatives shall upon his resignation as speaker and as representative, act as president. The same rule shall apply in the case of the death, resignation, removal from office, or inability of an individual acting as president.

If at the time when a speaker is to begin the discharge of the powers and duties of the office of president there is no speaker, or the speaker fails to qualify as acting president, then the president pro tempore of the Senate, upon his resignation as president pro tempore and as senator, shall act as president.

An individual acting as president shall continue to act until the expiration of the then current presidential term, except that (1) if his discharge of the powers and duties of the office is founded in whole or in part in the failure of both the president-

elect and the vice president-elect to qualify, then he shall act only until a president or vice president qualifies, and (2) if his discharge of the powers and duties of the office is founded in whole or in part on the inability of the president or vice president, then he shall act only until the removal of the disability of one of such individuals.

If, by reason of death, resignation, removal from office, or failure to qualify, there is no president pro tempore to act as president, then the officer of the United States who is highest on the following list, and who is not under any disability to discharge the powers and duties of president shall act as president; the secretaries of state, treasury, defense, attorney general; secretaries of interior, agriculture, commerce, labor, health and human services, housing and urban development, transportation, energy, education, veterans affairs.

(*Legislation approved July 18, 1947; amended Sept. 9, 1965, Oct. 15, 1966, Aug. 4, 1977, and Sept. 27, 1979. See also Constitutional Amendment XXV.*)

Origin of the United States National Motto

In God We Trust, designated as the U.S. National Motto by Congress in 1956, originated during the Civil War as an inscription for U. S. coins, although it was used by Francis Scott Key in a slightly different form when he wrote "The Star-Spangled Banner" in 1814. On Nov. 13, 1861, when Union morale had been shaken by battlefield defeats, the Rev. M. R. Watkinson, of Ridleyville, PA, wrote to Secy. of the Treasury Salmon P. Chase. "From my heart I have felt our national

shame in disowning God as not the least of our present national disasters," the minister wrote, suggesting "recognition of the Almighty God in some form on our coins." Secy. Chase ordered designs prepared with the inscription *In God We Trust* and backed coinage legislation that authorized use of this slogan. The motto first appeared on some U.S. coins in 1864, and disappeared and reappeared on various coins until 1955, when Congress ordered it placed on all paper money and all coins.

The American's Creed

William Tyler Page, Clerk of the U.S. House of Representatives, wrote "The American's Creed" in 1917.
It was accepted by the House on behalf of the American people on April 3, 1918.

"I believe in the United States of America as a government of the people, by the people, for the people; whose just powers are derived from the consent of the governed; a democracy in a republic; a sovereign Nation of many sovereign States; a perfect union, one and inseparable; established upon those

principles of freedom, equality, justice, and humanity for which American patriots sacrificed their lives and fortunes.

"I therefore believe it is my duty to my country to love it, to support its Constitution, to obey its laws, to respect its flag, and to defend it against all enemies."

The Great Seal of the U.S.

On July 4, 1776, the Continental Congress appointed a committee consisting of Benjamin Franklin, John Adams, and Thomas Jefferson "to bring in a device for a seal of the United States of America." The designs submitted by this and a subsequent committee were considered unacceptable. After many delays, a third committee, appointed early in 1782, presented a design prepared by William Barton. Charles Thomson, the

secretary of Congress, suggested certain changes, and Congress finally approved the design on June 20, 1782. The obverse side of the seal shows an American bald eagle. In its mouth is a ribbon bearing the motto *e pluribus unum* (one out of many). In the eagle's talons are the arrows of war and an olive branch of peace. The reverse side shows an unfinished pyramid with an eye (the eye of Providence) above it.

The Flag of the U.S.—The Stars and Stripes

The 50-star flag of the United States was raised for the first time officially at 12:01 AM on July 4, 1960, at Fort McHenry National Monument in Baltimore, MD. The 50th star had been added for Hawaii; a year earlier the 49th, for Alaska. Before that, no star had been added since 1912, when New Mexico and Arizona were admitted to the Union.

The true history of the Stars and Stripes has become so cluttered by myth and tradition that the facts are difficult, and in some cases impossible, to establish. For example, it is not certain who designed the Stars and Stripes, who made the first such flag, or even whether it ever flew in any sea fight or land battle of the American Revolution.

All agree, however, that the Stars and Stripes originated as the result of a resolution offered by the Marine Committee of

the Second Continental Congress at Philadelphia and adopted on June 14, 1777. It read:

Resolved: that the flag of the United States be thirteen stripes, alternate red and white; that the union be thirteen stars, white in a blue field, representing a new constellation.

Congress gave no hint as to the designer of the flag, no instructions as to the arrangement of the stars, and no information on its appropriate uses. Historians have been unable to find the original flag law.

The resolution establishing the flag was not even published until Sept. 2, 1777. Despite repeated requests, Washington did not get the flags until 1783, after the American Revolution was over. And there is no certainty that they were the Stars and Stripes.

Early Flags

Many historians consider the first flag of the U.S. to have been the Grand Union (sometimes called Great Union) flag, although the Continental Congress never officially adopted it. This flag was a modification of the British Meteor flag, which had the red cross of St. George and the white cross of St. Andrew combined in the blue canton. For the Grand Union flag, 6 horizontal stripes were imposed on the red field, dividing it into 13 alternating red and white stripes. On Jan. 1, 1776, when the Continental Army came into formal existence, this flag was unfurled on Prospect Hill, Somerville, MA. Washington wrote that "we hoisted the Union Flag in compliment to the United Colonies."

One of several flags about which controversy has raged for years is at Easton, PA. Containing the devices of the national flag in reversed order, this flag has been in the public library at Easton for more than 150 years. Some contend that this flag was actually the first Stars and Stripes, first displayed on July 8, 1776. This flag has 13 red and white stripes in the canton, 13 white stars centered in a blue field.

A flag was hastily improvised from garments by the defenders of Fort Schuyler at Rome, NY, Aug. 3-22, 1777. Historians believe it was the Grand Union Flag.

The Sons of Liberty had a flag of 9 red and white stripes, to signify 9 colonies, when they met in New York in 1765 to oppose the Stamp Tax. By 1775, the flag had grown to 13 red and white stripes, with a rattlesnake on it.

At Concord, Apr. 19, 1775, the minutemen from Bedford, MA, are said to have carried a flag having a silver arm with sword on a red field. At Cambridge, MA, the Sons of Liberty used a plain red flag with a green pine tree on it.

In June 1775, Washington went from Philadelphia to Boston to take command of the army, escorted to New York by the Philadelphia Light Horse Troop. It carried a yellow flag that had an elaborate coat of arms—the shield charged with 13 knots, the motto "For These We Strive"—and a canton of 13 blue and silver stripes.

In Feb. 1776, Col. Christopher Gadsden, a member of the Continental Congress, gave the South Carolina Provincial Congress a flag "such as is to be used by the commander-in-chief of the American Navy." It had a yellow field, with a rattlesnake about to strike and the words "Don't Tread on Me."

At the Battle of Bennington, Aug. 16, 1777, patriots used a flag of 7 white and 6 red stripes with a blue canton extending down 9 stripes and showing an arch of 11 white stars over the figure 76 and a star in each of the upper corners. The stars are 7-pointed. This flag is preserved in the Historical Museum at Bennington, VT.

At the Battle of Cowpens, Jan. 17, 1781, the 3d Maryland Regiment is said to have carried a flag of 13 red and white stripes, with a blue canton containing 12 stars in a circle around one star.

Who Designed the Flag? No one knows for certain. Francis Hopkinson, designer of a naval flag, declared he also had designed the flag and in 1781 asked Congress to reimburse him for his services. Congress did not do so. Dumas Malone of Columbia University wrote: "This talented man . . . designed the American flag."

Who Called the Flag "Old Glory"? The flag is said to have been named Old Glory by William Driver, a sea captain of Salem, MA. One legend has it that when he raised the flag on his brig, the *Charles Doggett*, in 1824, he said: "I name thee Old Glory." But his daughter, who presented the flag to the Smithsonian Institution, said he named it at his 21st birthday celebration on Mar. 17, 1824, when his mother presented the homemade flag to him.

The Betsy Ross Legend. The widely publicized legend that Mrs. Betsy Ross made the first Stars and Stripes in June 1776, at the request of a committee composed of George Washington, Robert Morris, and George Ross, an uncle, was first made public in 1870, by a grandson of Mrs. Ross. Historians have been unable to find a historical record of such a meeting or committee.

Adding New Stars

The flag of 1777 was used until 1795. Then, on the admission of Vermont and Kentucky to the Union, Congress passed and Pres. Washington signed an act that after May 1, 1795, the flag should have 15 stripes, alternating red and white, and 15 white stars on a blue field.

When new states were admitted, it became evident that the flag would become burdened with stripes. Congress thereupon ordered that after July 4, 1818, the flag should have 13 stripes, symbolizing the 13 original states; that the union have 20 stars, and that whenever a new state was admitted a new star should be added on the July 4 following admission.

No law designates the permanent arrangement of the stars. However, since 1912, when a new state has been admitted, the new design has been announced by executive order. No star is specifically identified with any state.

Code of Etiquette for Display and Use of the U.S. Flag

Reviewed by National Flag Foundation

Although the Stars and Stripes originated in 1777, it was not until 146 years later that there was a serious attempt to establish a uniform code of etiquette for the U.S. flag. On Feb. 15, 1923, the War Department issued a circular on the rules of flag usage. These rules were adopted almost in their entirety June 14, 1923, by a conference of 68 patriotic organizations in Washington, D.C. Finally, on June 22, 1942, a joint resolution of Congress, amended by Public Law 94-344, July 7, 1976, codified "existing rules and customs pertaining to the display and use of the flag . . ."

When to Display the Flag—The flag should be displayed on all days, especially on legal holidays and other special occasions, on official buildings when in use, in or near polling places on election days, and in or near schools when in session. Citizens may fly the flag at any time. It is customary to display it only from sunrise to sunset on buildings and on stationary flagstaffs in the open. It may be displayed at night, however, on special occasions, properly lighted. The flag now flies over the White House both day and night. It flies over the Senate wing of the Capitol when the Senate is in session and over the House wing when that body is in session. It flies day and night over the east and west fronts of the Capitol, without floodlights at night but receiving illumination from the Capitol Dome. It flies 24 hours a day at several other places, including the Fort McHenry National Monument in Baltimore, where it inspired Francis Scott Key to write "The Star Spangled Banner." The flag also flies 24 hours a day, properly illuminated, at U.S. Customs ports of entry.

Flying the Flag at Half-Staff—Flying the flag at half-staff, that is, halfway up the staff, is a signal of mourning. The flag should be hoisted to the top of the staff for an instant before being lowered to half-staff. It should be hoisted to the peak again before being lowered for the day or night.

As provided by presidential proclamation, the flag should fly at half-staff for 30 days from the day of death of a president or former president; for 10 days from the day of death of a vice president, chief justice or retired chief justice of the U.S., or speaker of the House of Representatives; from day of death until burial of an associate justice of the Supreme Court, cabinet member, former vice president, Senate president pro tempore, or majority or minority Senate or House leader; for a U.S. senator, representative, territorial delegate, or the resident commissioner of Puerto Rico, on day of death and the following day within the metropolitan area of the District of Columbia and from day of death until burial within the decedent's state, congressional district, territory or commonwealth; and for the death of the governor of a state, territory, or possession of the U.S., from day of death until burial.

On Memorial Day, the flag should fly at half-staff until noon and then be raised to the peak. The flag should also fly at half-staff on Korean War Veterans Armistice Day (July 27), National Pearl Harbor Remembrance Day (Dec. 7), and Peace Officers Memorial Day (May 15).

How to Fly the Flag—The flag should be hoisted briskly and lowered ceremoniously and should never be allowed to touch the ground or the floor. When the flag is hung over a sidewalk from a rope extending from a building to a pole, the union should be away from the building. When the flag is hung over the center of a street the union should be to the north in an east-west street and to the east in a north-south street. No other flag may be flown above or, if on the same level, to the right of the U.S. flag, except that at the United Nations Headquarters the UN flag may be placed above flags of all member nations and other national flags may be flown with equal prominence or honor with the flag of the U.S. At services by Navy chaplains at sea, the church pennant may be flown above the flag.

When 2 flags are placed against a wall with crossed staffs, the U.S. flag should be at right—its own right, and its staff should be in front of the staff of the other flag; when a number of flags are grouped and displayed from staffs, it should be at the center and highest point of the group.

Church and Platform Use—In an auditorium, the flag may be displayed flat, above and behind the speaker. When displayed from a staff in a church or in a public auditorium, the flag should hold the position of superior prominence, in advance of the audience, and in the position of honor at the speaker's right as she or he faces the audience. Any other flag so displayed should be placed on the left of the speaker or to the right of the audience.

When the flag is displayed horizontally or vertically against a wall, the stars should be uppermost and at the observer's left.

When used to cover a casket, the flag should be placed so that the union is at the head and over the left shoulder. It should not be lowered into the grave nor touch the ground.

How to Dispose of Worn Flags—When the flag is in such condition that it is no longer a fitting emblem for display, it should be destroyed in a dignified way, preferably by burning.

When to Salute the Flag—All persons present should face the flag, stand at attention, and salute on the following occasions: (1) when the flag is passing in a parade or in a review, (2) during the ceremony of hoisting or lowering, (3) when the national anthem is played, and (4) during the Pledge of Allegiance. Those present in uniform should render the military salute. Those not in uniform should place the right hand over the heart. A man wearing a hat should remove it with his right hand and hold it to his left shoulder during the salute.

Prohibited Uses of the Flag—The flag should not be dipped to any person or thing. (An exception—customarily, ships salute by dipping their colors.) It should never be displayed with the union down save as a distress signal. It should never be carried flat or horizontally, but always aloft and free.

It should not be displayed on a float, an automobile, or a boat except from a staff. It should never be used as a covering for a ceiling, nor have placed on it any word, design, or drawing. It should never be used as a receptacle for carrying anything. It should not be used to cover a statue or a monument.

The flag should never be used for advertising purposes, nor be embroidered on such articles as cushions or handkerchiefs, printed or otherwise impressed on boxes or anything that is designed for temporary use and discard; or used as a costume or athletic uniform. Advertising signs should not be fastened to its staff or halyard.

The flag should never be used as drapery of any sort, never festooned, drawn back, nor up, in folds, but always allowed to fall free. Bunting of blue, white, and red, always arranged with the blue above and the white in the middle, should be used for covering a speaker's desk, draping the front of a platform, and for decoration in general.

An act of Congress approved on Feb. 8, 1917, provided certain penalties for the desecration, mutilation, or improper use of the flag within the District of Columbia. A 1968 federal law provided penalties of as much as a year's imprisonment or a $1,000 fine or both for publicly burning or otherwise desecrating any U.S. flag. In addition, many states have laws against flag desecration. In 1989, the Supreme Court ruled that no laws could prohibit political protesters from burning the flag. The decision had the effect of declaring unconstitutional the flag desecration laws of 48 states, as well as a similar federal statute, in cases of peaceful political expression.

The Supreme Court, in June 1990, declared that a new federal law making it a crime to burn or deface the American flag violated the free-speech guarantee of the First Amendment. The 5-4 Court decision led to renewed calls in Congress for a constitutional amendment to make it possible to prosecute flag burners.

Pledge of Allegiance to the Flag

I pledge allegiance to the flag of the United States of America and to the republic for which it stands, one nation under God, indivisible, with liberty and justice for all.

This, the current official version of the Pledge of Allegiance, has developed from the original pledge, which was first published in the Sept. 8, 1892, issue of *Youth's Companion*, a weekly magazine then published in Boston. The original pledge contained the phrase "my flag," which was changed more than 30 years later to "flag of the United States of America." A 1954 act of Congress added the words "under God." (In June 2002 a 3-judge panel of the 9th Circuit U.S. Court of Appeals ruled, 2-1, that recitation of the pledge in public schools could not include that phrase; the decision was being appealed.)

The authorship of the pledge was in dispute for many years. The *Youth's Companion* stated in 1917 that the original draft was written by James B. Upham, an executive of the magazine who died in 1910. A leaflet circulated by the magazine later named Upham as the originator of the draft "afterwards condensed and perfected by him and his associates of the Companion force."

Francis Bellamy, a former member of *Youth's Companion* editorial staff, publicly claimed authorship of the pledge in 1923. In 1939, the United States Flag Association, acting on the advice of a committee named to study the controversy, upheld the claim of Bellamy, who had died 8 years earlier. In 1957 the Library of Congress issued a report attributing the authorship to Bellamy.

The History of the National Anthem

"The Star-Spangled Banner" was ordered played by the military and naval services by Pres. Woodrow Wilson in 1916. It was designated the national anthem by Act of Congress, Mar. 3, 1931. The words were written by Francis Scott Key, of Georgetown, MD, during the bombardment of Fort McHenry, Baltimore, Sept. 13-14, 1814. Key was a lawyer, a graduate of St. John's College, Annapolis, and a volunteer in a light artillery company. When a friend, Dr. Beanes, a Maryland physician, was taken aboard Admiral Cockburn's British squadron for interfering with ground troops, Key and J. S. Skinner, carrying a note from Pres. Madison, went to the fleet under a flag of truce on a cartel ship to ask Beanes's release. Cockburn consented, but as the fleet was about to sail up the Patapsco to bombard Fort McHenry, he detained them, first on HMS *Surprise* and then on a supply ship.

Key witnessed the bombardment from his own vessel. It began at 7 AM, Sept. 13, 1814, and lasted, with intermissions, for 25 hr. The British fired more than 1,500 shells, each weighing as much as 220 lb. They were unable to approach closely because the U.S. had sunk 22 vessels. Only 4 Americans were killed and 24 wounded. A British bomb-ship was disabled.

During the event, Key wrote a stanza on the back of an envelope. Next day at Indian Queen Inn, Baltimore, he wrote out the poem and gave it to his brother-in-law, Judge J. H. Nicholson. Nicholson suggested as one of the tune, "Anacreon in Heaven" (attributed to a British composer named John Stafford Smith), and had the poem printed on broadsides, of which 2 survive. On Sept. 20 it appeared in the *Baltimore American*. Later Key made 3 copies: one is in the Library of Congress, and one in the Pennsylvania Historical Society. The copy Key wrote on Sept. 14 remained in the Nicholson family for 93 years. In 1907 it was sold to Henry Walters of Baltimore. In 1934 it was bought at auction by the Walters Art Gallery, Baltimore, for $26,400. In 1953 it was sold to the Maryland Historical Society for the same price.

The flag that Key saw during the bombardment is preserved in the Smithsonian Institution, Washington, DC. It measures 30 by 42 ft and has 15 alternating red and white stripes and 15 stars, for the original 13 states plus Kentucky and Vermont. It was made by Mary Young Pickersgill. The Baltimore Flag House, a museum, occupies her premises, which were restored in 1953.

The Star-Spangled Banner

I

Oh, say can you see by the dawn's early light
What so proudly we hailed at the twilight's last gleaming?
Whose broad stripes and bright stars thru the perilous fight,
O'er the ramparts we watched were so gallantly streaming?
And the rocket's red glare, the bombs bursting in air,
Gave proof through the night that our flag was still there.
Oh, say does that star-spangled banner yet wave
O'er the land of the free and the home of the brave?

II

On the shore, dimly seen through the mists of the deep,
Where the foe's haughty host in dread silence reposes,
What is that which the breeze, o'er the towering steep,
As it fitfully blows, half conceals, half discloses?
Now it catches the gleam of the morning's first beam,
In full glory reflected now shines in the stream:
'Tis the star-spangled banner! Oh long may it wave
O'er the land of the free and the home of the brave!

III

And where is that band who so vauntingly swore
That the havoc of war and the battle's confusion,
A home and a country should leave us no more!
Their blood has washed out their foul footsteps' pollution.
No refuge could save the hireling and slave
From the terror of flight, or the gloom of the grave:
And the star-spangled banner in triumph doth wave
O'er the land of the free and the home of the brave!

IV

Oh! thus be it ever, when freemen shall stand
Between their loved home and the war's desolation!
Blest with victory and peace, may the heav'n rescued land
Praise the Power that hath made and preserved us a nation.
Then conquer we must, when our cause it is just,
And this be our motto: "In God is our trust."
And the star-spangled banner in triumph shall wave
O'er the land of the free and the home of the brave!

America (My Country 'Tis of Thee)

First sung in public on July 4, 1831, at a service in the Park Street Church, Boston, the words were written by Rev. Samuel Francis Smith, a Baptist clergyman, who set them to a melody he found in a German songbook, unaware that it was the tune for the British anthem, "God Save the King/Queen."

My country, 'tis of thee,
Sweet land of liberty,
Of thee I sing.
Land where my fathers died!
Land of the Pilgrims' pride!
From ev'ry mountainside,
Let freedom ring!

My native country, thee,
Land of the noble free,
Thy name I love.
I love thy rocks and rills,
Thy woods and templed hills;
My heart with rapture thrills
Like that above.

Let music swell the breeze,
And ring from all the trees
Sweet freedom's song.
Let mortal tongues awake;
Let all that breathe partake;
Let rocks their silence break,
The sound prolong.

Our fathers' God, to Thee,
Author of liberty,
To Thee we sing.
Long may our land be bright
With freedom's holy light;
Protect us by Thy might,
Great God, our King!

America, the Beautiful

Words composed by Katharine Lee Bates, a Massachusetts educator and author, in 1893, inspired by the view she experienced atop Pikes Peak. The final form was established in 1911, and it is set to the music of Samuel A. Ward's "Materna."

O beautiful for spacious skies.
For amber waves of grain,
For purple mountain majesties
Above the fruited plain.
America! America!
God shed His grace on thee,
And crown thy good with
brotherhood
From sea to shining sea.

O beautiful for pilgrim feet
Whose stern impassion'd stress
A thorough-fare for freedom
beat
Across the wilderness.
America! America!
God mend thine ev'ry flaw,
Confirm thy soul in self control,
Thy liberty in law.

O beautiful for heroes prov'd
In liberating strife,
Who more than self their
country lov'd
And mercy more than life.
America! America!
May God thy gold refine
Till all success be nobleness,
And ev'ry gain divine.

O beautiful for patriot dream
That sees beyond the years,
Thine alabaster cities gleam,
Undimmed by human tears.
America! America!
God shed His grace on thee,
And crown thy good with
brotherhood
From sea to shining sea.

The Liberty Bell: Its History and Significance

The Liberty Bell is housed in Independence National Historical Park, Philadelphia.

The original bell was ordered by Assembly Speaker and Chairman of the State House Superintendents Isaac Norris and was ordered from Thomas Lester, Whitechapel Foundry, London. It reached Philadelphia at the end of August 1752. It bore an inscription from Leviticus 25:10: "PROCLAIM LIBERTY THROUGHOUT ALL THE LAND UNTO ALL THE INHABITANTS THEREOF."

The bell was cracked by a stroke of its clapper in Sept. 1752 while it hung on a truss in the State House yard for testing. Pass & Stow, Philadelphia founders, recast the bell, adding 1½ ounces of copper to a pound of the original "Whitechapel" metal to reduce its high tone and brittleness. It was found that the bell contained too much copper, injuring its tone, so Pass & Stow recast it again, this time successfully.

In June 1753 the bell was hung in the old wooden steeple of the State House. In use while the Continental Congress was in session in the State House, it rang out in defiance of British tax and trade restrictions, and it proclaimed the Boston Tea Party and the first public reading of the Declaration of Independence.

On Sept. 18, 1777, when the British Army was about to occupy Philadelphia, the Liberty Bell was moved in a baggage train of the American Army to Allentown, PA, where it was hidden until June 27, 1778. The bell was moved back to Philadelphia after the British left the city.

In July 1781 the wooden steeple became insecure and had to be taken down. The bell was lowered into the brick section of the tower, where it remained until 1828. Between 1828 and 1844 the old State House bell continued to ring during special occasions. It rang for the last time on Feb. 23, 1846. In 1852 it was placed on exhibition in the Declaration Chamber of Independence Hall.

In 1876, when many thousands of Americans visited Philadelphia for the Centennial Exposition, the bell was placed in its old wooden support in the tower hallway. In 1877 it was hung from the ceiling of the tower by a chain of 13 links. It was returned again to the Declaration Chamber and in 1896 taken back to the tower hall, where it occupied a glass case. In 1915 the case was removed so that the public might touch it. On Jan. 1, 1976, just after midnight to mark the opening of the Bicentennial Year, the bell was moved to a new glass and steel pavilion behind Independence Hall for easier viewing.

The measurements of the bell are: circumference around the lip, 12 ft ½ in; circumference around the crown, 6 ft 11 ¼ in; lip to the crown, 3 ft; height over the crown, 2 ft 3 in; thickness at lip, 3 in; thickness at crown, 1¼ in; weight, 2,080 lb; length of clapper, 3 ft 2 in.

The specific source of the crack in the bell is unknown.

Statue of Liberty National Monument

Since 1886, the Statue of Liberty, formally known as "Liberty Enlightening the World," has stood as a symbol of freedom in New York harbor. It also commemorates French-American friendship, for it was given by the people of France and designed by French sculptor Frederic Auguste Bartholdi (1834-1904).

Edouard de Laboulaye, French historian, suggested the French present a monument to the U.S., the latter to provide pedestal and site. Bartholdi visualized a colossal statue at the entrance of New York harbor, welcoming the peoples of the world with the torch of liberty.

On Washington's Birthday, Feb. 22, 1877, Congress approved the use of a site on Bedloe's Island suggested by Bartholdi. This island of 12 acres had been owned in the 17th century by a Walloon named Isaac Bedloe. It was called Bedloe's until Aug. 3, 1956, when Pres. Eisenhower approved a resolution of Congress changing the name to Liberty Island.

The statue was finished on May 21, 1884, and formally presented to the U.S. minister to France, Levi Parsons Morton, July 4, 1884, by Ferdinand de Lesseps, head of the Franco-American Union, promoter of the Panama Canal, and builder of the Suez Canal.

On Aug. 5, 1884, the Americans laid the cornerstone for the pedestal. This was to be built on the foundations of Fort Wood, which had been erected by the government in 1811. The American committee had raised $125,000, but this was found to be inadequate. Joseph Pulitzer, owner of the *New York World*, appealed on Mar. 16, 1885, for general donations. By Aug. 11, 1885, he had raised $100,000.

The statue arrived dismantled, in 214 packing cases, from Rouen, France, in June 1885. The last rivet of the statue was driven on Oct. 28, 1886, when Pres. Grover Cleveland dedicated the monument.

The Statue of Liberty National Monument was designated as such in 1924. It is administered by the National Park Service. A $2.5 million building housing the American Museum of Immigration was opened by Pres. Richard Nixon on Sept. 26, 1972, at the base of the statue. It houses a permanent exhibition of photos, posters, and artifacts tracing the history of American immigration.

Four years of restoration work funded and led by The Statue of Liberty-Ellis Island Foundation, Inc., were completed before the statue's centennial celebration on July 4, 1986. Among other repairs, the $87 million project included replacing the 1,600 wrought iron bands that hold the statue's copper skin to its frame, replacing its torch, and installing an elevator.

A 4-day "Liberty Weekend" extravaganza of concerts, tall ships, ethnic festivals, and fireworks, July 3-6, 1986, celebrated the 100th anniversary. The festivities included Chief Justice Warren E. Burger's swearing-in of 5,000 new citizens on Ellis Island, while 20,000 others across the country were simultaneously sworn in through a satellite telecast.

The ceremonies were followed by others on Oct. 28, 1986, to mark the statue's exact 100th birthday.

As a security precaution following the terrorist attacks on Sept. 11, 2001, the pedestal and statue were closed indefinitely. Only the park on Liberty Island was accessbile as of Sept 2003.

Statue Statistics

The statue weighs 450,000 lb, or 225 tons. The copper sheeting weighs 200,000 lb. There are 167 steps from the land level to the top of the pedestal, 168 steps inside the statue to the head, and 54 rungs on the ladder leading to the arm that holds the torch.

	Ft.	In.		Ft.	In.
Height from base to torch (45.3 meters)	151	1	Length of nose	4	6
Foundation of pedestal to torch (91.5 meters)	305	1	Right arm, length	42	0
Heel to top of head	111	1	Right arm, greatest thickness	12	0
Length of hand	16	5	Thickness of waist	35	0
Index finger	8	0	Width of mouth	3	0
Size of finger nail, 13x10 in.			Tablet, length	23	7
Head from chin to cranium	17	3	Tablet, width	13	7
Head thickness from ear to ear	10	0	Tablet, thickness	2	0

Emma Lazarus's Famous Poem

Engraved on pedestal below the statue.

The New Colossus

Not like the brazen giant of Greek fame,
With conquering limbs astride from land to land;
Here at our sea-washed, sunset gates shall stand
A mighty woman with a torch, whose flame
Is the imprisoned lightning, and her name
Mother of Exiles. From her beacon-hand
Glows world-wide welcome; her mild eyes command
The air-bridged harbor that twin cities frame.
"Keep ancient lands, your storied pomp!" cries she
With silent lips. "Give me your tired, your poor,
Your huddled masses yearning to breathe free,
The wretched refuse of your teeming shore.
Send these, the homeless, tempest-tost to me,
I lift my lamp beside the golden door!"

Ellis Island

Ellis Island was the gateway to America for more than 12 million immigrants between 1892 and 1924. In the late 18th century, Samuel Ellis, a New York City merchant, purchased the island and gave it his name. From Ellis, it passed to New York State, and the U.S. government bought it in 1808. On Jan. 1, 1892, the government opened the first federal immigration center in the U.S. on the island. The 27½-acre site eventually supported more than 35 buildings, including the Main Building with its Great Hall, in which as many as 5,000 people a day were processed.

Closed as an immigration station in 1954, Ellis Island was proclaimed part of the Statue of Liberty National Monument in 1965 by Pres. Lyndon B. Johnson. After a 6-year, $170 million restoration project funded by The Statue of Liberty-Ellis Island Foundation, Inc., Ellis Island was reopened as a museum in 1990. Artifacts, historic photographs and documents, oral histories, and ethnic music depicting 400 years of American immigration are housed in the museum. The museum also includes The American Immigrant Wall of Honor® (www.wallofhonor.com), which is inscribed with more than 600,000 names that have been placed in tribute. Registrations are still being accepted for inclusion in the memorial.

The American Family Immigration History Center® opened in April 2001. It contains an electronic database of ship passenger arrival information through the Port of New York and Ellis Island from 1892 to 1924. Data on over 25 million individuals are available, as well as an interactive database which features a Living Family Archive, multimedia presentations on various immigration groups and patterns, reproductions of original ships' passenger manifests, and pictures of over 800 immigrant ships (www.ellisisland.org).

In 1998, the Supreme Court ruled that nearly 90% of the island (the 24.2 acres which are landfill) lies in New Jersey, while the original 3.3 acres, on which the museum is located, are in New York.

PRESIDENTS OF THE UNITED STATES

U.S. Presidents

No.	Name	Politics	Born	In	Inaug.	at age	Died	at age
1.	George Washington	Fed.	1732, Feb. 22	VA	1789	57	1799, Dec. 14	67
2.	John Adams	Fed.	1735, Oct. 30	MA	1797	61	1826, July 4	90
3.	Thomas Jefferson	Dem.-Rep.	1743, Apr. 13	VA	1801	57	1826, July 4	83
4.	James Madison	Dem.-Rep.	1751, Mar. 16	VA	1809	57	1836, June 28	85
5.	James Monroe	Dem.-Rep.	1758, Apr. 28	VA	1817	58	1831, July 4	73
6.	John Quincy Adams	Dem.-Rep.	1767, July 11	MA	1825	57	1848, Feb. 23	80
7.	Andrew Jackson	Dem.	1767, Mar. 15	SC	1829	61	1845, June 8	78
8.	Martin Van Buren	Dem.	1782, Dec. 5	NY	1837	54	1862, July 24	79
9.	William Henry Harrison	Whig	1773, Feb. 9	VA	1841	68	1841, Apr. 4	68
10.	John Tyler	Whig	1790, Mar. 29	VA	1841	51	1862, Jan. 18	71
11.	James Knox Polk	Dem.	1795, Nov. 2	NC	1845	49	1849, June 15	53
12.	Zachary Taylor	Whig	1784, Nov. 24	VA	1849	64	1850, July 9	65
13.	Millard Fillmore	Whig	1800, Jan. 7	NY	1850	50	1874, Mar. 8	74
14.	Franklin Pierce	Dem.	1804, Nov. 23	NH	1853	48	1869, Oct. 8	64
15.	James Buchanan	Dem.	1791, Apr. 23	PA	1857	65	1868, June 1	77
16.	Abraham Lincoln	Rep.	1809, Feb. 12	KY	1861	52	1865, Apr. 15	56
17.	Andrew Johnson	(1)	1808, Dec. 29	NC	1865	56	1875, July 31	66
18.	Ulysses Simpson Grant	Rep.	1822, Apr. 27	OH	1869	46	1885, July 23	63
19.	Rutherford Birchard Hayes	Rep.	1822, Oct. 4	OH	1877	54	1893, Jan. 17	70
20.	James Abram Garfield	Rep.	1831, Nov. 19	OH	1881	49	1881, Sept. 19	49
21.	Chester Alan Arthur	Rep.	1829, Oct. 5	VT	1881	50	1886, Nov. 18	57
22.	Grover Cleveland	Dem.	1837, Mar. 18	NJ	1885	47	1908, June 24	71
23.	Benjamin Harrison	Rep.	1833, Aug. 20	OH	1889	55	1901, Mar. 13	67
24.	Grover Cleveland	Dem.	1837, Mar. 18	NJ	1893	55	1908, June 24	71
25.	William McKinley	Rep.	1843, Jan. 29	OH	1897	54	1901, Sept. 14	58
26.	Theodore Roosevelt	Rep.	1858, Oct. 27	NY	1901	42	1919, Jan. 6	60
27.	William Howard Taft	Rep.	1857, Sept. 15	OH	1909	51	1930, Mar. 8	72
28.	Woodrow Wilson	Dem.	1856, Dec. 28	VA	1913	56	1924, Feb. 3	67
29.	Warren Gamaliel Harding	Rep.	1865, Nov. 2	OH	1921	55	1923, Aug. 2	57
30.	Calvin Coolidge	Rep.	1872, July 4	VT	1923	51	1933, Jan. 5	60
31.	Herbert Clark Hoover	Rep.	1874, Aug. 10	IA	1929	54	1964, Oct. 20	90
32.	Franklin Delano Roosevelt	Dem.	1882, Jan. 30	NY	1933	51	1945, Apr. 12	63
33.	Harry S. Truman	Dem.	1884, May 8	MO	1945	60	1972, Dec. 26	88
34.	Dwight David Eisenhower	Rep.	1890, Oct. 14	TX	1953	62	1969, Mar. 28	78
35.	John Fitzgerald Kennedy	Dem.	1917, May 29	MA	1961	43	1963, Nov. 22	46
36.	Lyndon Baines Johnson	Dem.	1908, Aug. 27	TX	1963	55	1973, Jan. 22	64
37.	Richard Milhous Nixon (2)	Rep.	1913, Jan. 9	CA	1969	56	1994, Apr. 22	81
38.	Gerald Rudolph Ford	Rep.	1913, July 14	NE	1974	61		
39.	Jimmy (James Earl) Carter	Dem.	1924, Oct. 1	GA	1977	52		
40.	Ronald Reagan	Rep.	1911, Feb. 6	IL	1981	69		
41.	George H. W. Bush	Rep.	1924, June 12	MA	1989	64		
42.	Bill (Wm. Jefferson) Clinton	Dem.	1946, Aug. 19	AR	1993	46		
43.	George W. Bush	Rep.	1946, July 6	CT	2001	54		

(1) Andrew Johnson was a Democrat, nominated vice president by Republicans, and elected with Lincoln on National Union ticket.
(2) Resigned Aug. 9, 1974.

U.S. Presidents, Vice Presidents, Congresses

President	Service	Vice President	Congresses
1. George Washington	Apr. 30, 1789—Mar. 3, 1797	1. John Adams	1, 2, 3, 4
2. John Adams	Mar. 4, 1797—Mar. 3, 1801	2. Thomas Jefferson	5, 6
3. Thomas Jefferson	Mar. 4, 1801—Mar. 3, 1805	3. Aaron Burr	7, 8
	Mar. 4, 1805—Mar. 3, 1809	4. George Clinton	9, 10
4. James Madison	Mar. 4, 1809—Mar. 3, 1813	(1)	11, 12
	Mar. 4, 1813—Mar. 3, 1817	5. Elbridge Gerry (2)	13, 14
5. James Monroe	Mar. 4, 1817—Mar. 3, 1825	6. Daniel D. Tompkins	15, 16, 17, 18
6. John Quincy Adams	Mar. 4, 1825—Mar. 3, 1829	7. John C. Calhoun	19, 20
7. Andrew Jackson	Mar. 4, 1829—Mar. 3, 1833	(3)	21, 22
	Mar. 4, 1833—Mar. 3, 1837	8. Martin Van Buren	23, 24
8. Martin Van Buren	Mar. 4, 1837—Mar. 3, 1841	9. Richard M. Johnson	25, 26
9. William Henry Harrison (4)	Apr. 6, 1841—Apr. 4, 1841	10. John Tyler	27
10. John Tyler	Apr. 6, 1841—Mar. 3, 1845		27, 28
11. James K. Polk	Mar. 4, 1845—Mar. 3, 1849	11. George M. Dallas	29, 30
12. Zachary Taylor (4)	Mar. 5, 1849—July 9, 1850	12. Millard Fillmore	31
13. Millard Fillmore	July 10, 1850—Mar. 3, 1853		31, 32
14. Franklin Pierce	Mar. 4, 1853—Mar. 3, 1857	13. William R. King (5)	33, 34
15. James Buchanan	Mar. 4, 1857—Mar. 3, 1861	14. John C. Breckinridge	35, 36
16. Abraham Lincoln	Mar. 4, 1861—Mar. 3, 1865	15. Hannibal Hamlin	37, 38
(4)	Mar. 4, 1865—Apr. 15, 1865	16. Andrew Johnson	39
17. Andrew Johnson	Apr. 15, 1865—Mar. 3, 1869		39, 40
18. Ulysses S. Grant	Mar. 4, 1869—Mar. 3, 1873	17. Schuyler Colfax	41, 42
	Mar. 4, 1873—Mar. 3, 1877	18. Henry Wilson (6)	43, 44
19. Rutherford B. Hayes	Mar. 4, 1877—Mar. 3, 1881	19. William A. Wheeler	45, 46
20. James A. Garfield (4)	Mar. 4, 1881—Sept. 19, 1881	20. Chester A. Arthur	47
21. Chester A. Arthur	Sept. 20, 1881—Mar. 3, 1885		47, 48
22. Grover Cleveland (7)	Mar. 4, 1885—Mar. 3, 1889	21. Thomas A. Hendricks (8)	49, 50
23. Benjamin Harrison	Mar. 4, 1889—Mar. 3, 1893	22. Levi P. Morton	51, 52
24. Grover Cleveland (7)	Mar. 4, 1893—Mar. 3, 1897	23. Adlai E. Stevenson	53, 54
25. William McKinley	Mar. 4, 1897—Mar. 3, 1901	24. Garret A. Hobart (9)	55, 56
(4)	Mar. 4, 1901—Sept. 14, 1901	25. Theodore Roosevelt	57
26. Theodore Roosevelt	Sept. 14, 1901—Mar. 3, 1905		57, 58
	Mar. 4, 1905—Mar. 3, 1909	26. Charles W. Fairbanks	59, 60
27. William H. Taft	Mar. 4, 1909—Mar. 3, 1913	27. James S. Sherman (10)	61, 62
28. Woodrow Wilson	Mar. 4, 1913—Mar. 3, 1921	28. Thomas R. Marshall	63, 64, 65, 66
29. Warren G. Harding (4)	Mar. 4, 1921—Aug. 2, 1923	29. Calvin Coolidge	67

President	Service	Vice President	Congresses
30. Calvin Coolidge	Aug. 3, 1923—Mar. 3, 1925		68
	Mar. 4, 1925—Mar. 3, 1929	30. Charles G. Dawes	69, 70
31. Herbert C. Hoover	Mar. 4, 1929—Mar. 3, 1933	31. Charles Curtis	71, 72
32. Franklin D. Roosevelt (11)	Mar. 4, 1933—Jan. 20, 1941	32. John N. Garner	73, 74, 75, 76
	Jan. 20, 1941—Jan. 20, 1945	33. Henry A. Wallace	77, 78
(4)	Jan. 20, 1945—Apr. 12, 1945	34. Harry S. Truman	79
33. Harry S. Truman	Apr. 12, 1945—Jan. 20, 1949		79, 80
	Jan. 20, 1949—Jan. 20, 1953	35. Alben W. Barkley	81, 82
34. Dwight D. Eisenhower	Jan. 20, 1953—Jan. 20, 1961	36. Richard M. Nixon	83, 84, 85, 86
35. John F. Kennedy (4)	Jan. 20, 1961—Nov. 22, 1963	37. Lyndon B. Johnson	87, 88
36. Lyndon B. Johnson	Nov. 22, 1963—Jan. 20, 1965		88
	Jan. 20, 1965—Jan. 20, 1969	38. Hubert H. Humphrey	89, 90
37. Richard M. Nixon	Jan. 20, 1969—Jan. 20, 1973	39. Spiro T. Agnew (12)	91, 92, 93
(13)	Jan. 20, 1973—Aug. 9, 1974	40. Gerald R. Ford (14)	93
38. Gerald R. Ford (15)	Aug. 9, 1974—Jan. 20, 1977	41. Nelson A. Rockefeller (16)	93, 94
39. Jimmy (James Earl) Carter	Jan. 20, 1977—Jan. 20, 1981	42. Walter F. Mondale	95, 96
40. Ronald Reagan	Jan. 20, 1981—Jan. 20, 1989	43. George H. W. Bush	97, 98, 99, 100
41. George H. W. Bush	Jan. 20, 1989—Jan. 20, 1993	44. Dan Quayle	101, 102
42. Bill (Wm. Jefferson) Clinton	Jan. 20, 1993—Jan. 20, 2001	45. Al Gore	103, 104, 105, 106
43. George W. Bush	Jan. 20, 2001—	46. Richard Cheney	107, 108

(1) Died Apr. 20, 1812. (2) Died Nov. 23, 1814. (3) Resigned Dec. 28, 1832, to become U.S. senator. (4) Died in office. (5) Died Apr. 18, 1853. (6) Died Nov. 22, 1875. (7) Terms not consecutive. (8) Died Nov. 25, 1885. (9) Died Nov. 21, 1899. (10) Died Oct. 30, 1912. (11) First president to be inaugurated under 20th Amendment, Jan. 20, 1937. (12) Resigned Oct. 10, 1973. (13) Resigned Aug. 9, 1974. (14) First nonelected vice president, chosen under 25th Amendment procedure. (15) First president never elected president or vice president. (16) Second nonelected vice president, chosen under 25th Amendment.

Vice Presidents of the U.S.

The numerals given vice presidents do not coincide with those given presidents, because some presidents had none and some had more than one.

#	Name	Birthplace	Year	Home	Inaug.	Politics	Place of death	Year	Age
1.	John Adams	Quincy, MA	1735	MA	1789	Fed.	Quincy, MA	1826	90
2.	Thomas Jefferson	Shadwell, VA	1743	VA	1797	Dem.-Rep.	Monticello, VA	1826	83
3.	Aaron Burr	Newark, NJ	1756	NY	1801	Dem.-Rep.	Staten Island, NY	1836	80
4.	George Clinton	Ulster Co., NY	1739	NY	1805	Dem.-Rep.	Washington, DC	1812	73
5.	Elbridge Gerry	Marblehead, MA	1744	MA	1813	Dem.-Rep.	Washington, DC	1814	70
6.	Daniel D. Tompkins	Scarsdale, NY	1774	NY	1817	Dem.-Rep.	Staten Island, NY	1825	51
7.	John C. Calhoun (1)	Abbeville, SC	1782	SC	1825	Dem.-Rep.	Washington, DC	1850	68
8.	Martin Van Buren	Kinderhook, NY	1782	NY	1833	Dem.	Kinderhook, NY	1862	79
9.	Richard M. Johnson (2)	Louisville, KY	1780	KY	1837	Dem.	Frankfort, KY	1850	70
10.	John Tyler	Greenway, VA	1790	VA	1841	Whig	Richmond, VA	1862	71
11.	George M. Dallas	Philadelphia, PA	1792	PA	1845	Dem.	Philadelphia, PA	1864	72
12.	Millard Fillmore	Summerhill, NY	1800	NY	1849	Whig	Buffalo, NY	1874	74
13.	William R. King	Sampson Co., NC	1786	AL	1853	Dem.	Dallas Co., AL	1853	67
14.	John C. Breckinridge	Lexington, KY	1821	KY	1857	Dem.	Lexington, KY	1875	54
15.	Hannibal Hamlin	Paris, ME	1809	ME	1861	Rep.	Bangor, ME	1891	81
16.	Andrew Johnson	Raleigh, NC	1808	TN	1865	(3)	Carter Co., TN	1875	66
17.	Schuyler Colfax	New York, NY	1823	IN	1869	Rep.	Mankato, MN	1885	62
18.	Henry Wilson	Farmington, NH	1812	MA	1873	Rep.	Washington, DC	1875	63
19.	William A. Wheeler	Malone, NY	1819	NY	1877	Rep.	Malone, NY	1887	68
20.	Chester A. Arthur	Fairfield, VT	1829	NY	1881	Rep.	New York, NY	1886	57
21.	Thomas A. Hendricks	Muskingum Co., OH	1819	IN	1885	Dem.	Indianapolis, IN	1885	66
22.	Levi P. Morton	Shoreham, VT	1824	NY	1889	Rep.	Rhinebeck, NY	1920	96
23.	Adlai E. Stevenson (4)	Christian Co., KY	1835	IL	1893	Dem.	Chicago, IL	1914	78
24.	Garret A. Hobart	Long Branch, NJ	1844	NJ	1897	Rep.	Paterson, NJ	1899	55
25.	Theodore Roosevelt	New York, NY	1858	NY	1901	Rep.	Oyster Bay, NY	1919	60
26.	Charles W. Fairbanks	Unionville Centre, OH	1852	IN	1905	Rep.	Indianapolis, IN	1918	66
27.	James S. Sherman	Utica, NY	1855	NY	1909	Rep.	Utica, NY	1912	57
28.	Thomas R. Marshall	N. Manchester, IN	1854	IN	1913	Dem.	Washington, DC	1925	71
29.	Calvin Coolidge	Plymouth, VT	1872	MA	1921	Rep.	Northampton, MA	1933	60
30.	Charles G. Dawes	Marietta, OH	1865	IL	1925	Rep.	Evanston, IL	1951	85
31.	Charles Curtis	Topeka, KS	1860	KS	1929	Rep.	Washington, DC	1936	76
32.	John Nance Garner	Red River Co., TX	1868	TX	1933	Dem.	Uvalde, TX	1967	98
33.	Henry Agard Wallace	Adair County, IA	1888	IA	1941	Dem.	Danbury, CT	1965	77
34.	Harry S. Truman	Lamar, MO	1884	MO	1945	Dem.	Kansas City, MO	1972	88
35.	Alben W. Barkley	Graves County, KY	1877	KY	1949	Dem.	Lexington, VA	1956	78
36.	Richard M. Nixon	Yorba Linda, CA	1913	CA	1953	Rep.	New York, NY	1994	81
37.	Lyndon B. Johnson	Johnson City, TX	1908	TX	1961	Dem.	San Antonio, TX	1973	64
38.	Hubert H. Humphrey	Wallace, SD	1911	MN	1965	Dem.	Waverly, MN	1978	66
39.	Spiro T. Agnew (5)	Baltimore, MD	1918	MD	1969	Rep.	Berlin, MD	1996	77
40.	Gerald R. Ford (6)	Omaha, NE	1913	MI	1973	Rep.			
41.	Nelson A. Rockefeller (7)	Bar Harbor, ME	1908	NY	1974	Rep.	New York, NY	1979	70
42.	Walter F. Mondale	Ceylon, MN	1928	MN	1977	Dem.			
43.	George H. W. Bush	Milton, MA	1924	TX	1981	Rep.			
44.	Dan Quayle	Indianapolis, IN	1947	IN	1989	Rep.			
45.	Al Gore	Washington, DC	1948	TN	1993	Dem.			
46.	Richard Cheney	Lincoln, NE	1941	WY	2001	Rep.			

(1) John C. Calhoun resigned Dec. 28, 1832, having been elected to the Senate to fill a vacancy. (2) Richard M. Johnson was the only vice president to be chosen by the Senate because of a tied vote in the Electoral College. (3) Andrew Johnson was a Democrat, nominated vice president by Republicans, and elected with Lincoln on the National Union Ticket. (4) Adlai E. Stevenson, 23rd vice president, was grandfather of Democratic candidate for president in 1952 and 1956. (5) Resigned Oct. 10, 1973. (6) First nonelected vice president, chosen under 25th Amendment procedure. (7) Second nonelected vice president, chosen under 25th Amendment procedure.

▶ **IT'S A FACT:** 14 of the 46 U.S. vice presidents went on to the White House. Of these, 9 assumed the office upon the death or resignation of the president. The other 5 were elected to their initial terms as president; all but one—Richard Nixon—succeeded the presidents under whom they served.

Biographies of the Presidents

GEORGE WASHINGTON (1789-97), 1st president, Federalist, was born on Feb. 22, 1732, in Wakefield on Pope's Creek, Westmoreland Co., VA, the son of Augustine and Mary Ball Washington. He spent his early childhood on a farm near Fredericksburg. His father died when George was 11. He studied mathematics and surveying, and at 16, he went to live with his elder half brother, Lawrence, who built and named Mount Vernon. George surveyed the lands of Thomas Fairfax in the Shenandoah Valley, keeping a diary. He accompanied Lawrence to Barbados, West Indies, where he contracted smallpox and was deeply scarred. Lawrence died in 1752, and George inherited his property. He valued land, and when he died, he owned 70,000 acres in Virginia and 40,000 acres in what is now West Virginia. Washington's military service began in 1753, when Lt. Gov. Robert Dinwiddie of Virginia sent him on missions deep into Ohio country. He clashed with the French and had to surrender Fort Necessity on July 3, 1754. He was an aide to the British general Edward Braddock and was at his side when the army was ambushed and defeated (July 9, 1755) on a march to Fort Duquesne. He helped take Fort Duquesne from the French in 1758.

After Washington's marriage to Martha Dandridge Custis, a widow, in 1759, he managed his family estate at Mount Vernon. Although not at first for independence, he opposed the repressive measures of the British crown and took charge of the Virginia troops before war broke out. He was made commander of the newly created Continental Army by the Continental Congress on June 15, 1775.

The American victory was due largely to Washington's leadership. He was resourceful, a stern disciplinarian, and the one strong, dependable force for unity. Washington favored a federal government. He became chairman of the Constitutional Convention of 1787 and helped get the Constitution ratified. Unanimously elected president by the Electoral College, he was inaugurated Apr. 30, 1789, on the balcony of New York's Federal Hall. He was reelected in 1792. Washington made an effort to avoid partisan politics as president.

Refusing to consider a 3rd term, Washington retired to Mount Vernon in March 1797. He suffered acute laryngitis after a ride in snow and rain around his estate, was bled profusely, and died Dec. 14, 1799.

JOHN ADAMS (1797-1801), 2nd president, Federalist, was born on Oct. 30, 1735, in Braintree (now Quincy), MA, the son of John and Susanna Boylston Adams. He was a great-grandson of Henry Adams, who came from England in 1636. He graduated from Harvard in 1755 and then taught school and studied law. He married Abigail Smith in 1764. In 1765 he argued against taxation without representation before the royal governor. In 1770 he successfully defended in court the British soldiers who fired on civilians in the Boston Massacre. He was a delegate to the Continental Congress and a signer of the Declaration of Independence. In 1778, Congress sent Adams and John Jay to join Benjamin Franklin as diplomatic representatives in Europe. Because he ran second to Washington in Electoral College balloting in February 1789, Adams became the nation's first vice president, a post he characterized as highly insignificant; he was reelected in 1792.

In 1796 Adams was chosen president by the electors. His administration was marked by growing conflict with fellow Federalist Alexander Hamilton and with others in his own cabinet who supported Hamilton's strongly anti-French position. Adams avoided full-scale war with France, but became unpopular, especially after securing passage of the Alien and Sedition Acts in 1798. His foreign policy contributed significantly to the election of Thomas Jefferson in 1800.

Adams lived for a quarter century after he left office, during which time he wrote extensively. He died July 4, 1826, on the same day as Jefferson (the 50th anniversary of the Declaration of Independence).

THOMAS JEFFERSON (1801-9), 3rd president, Democratic-Republican, was born on Apr. 13, 1743, in Shadwell in Goochland (now Albemarle) Co., VA, the son of Peter and Jane Randolph Jefferson. Peter died when Thomas was 14, leaving him 2,750 acres and his slaves. Jefferson attended (1760-62) the College of William and Mary, read Greek and Latin classics, and played the violin. In 1769 he was elected to the Virginia House of Burgesses. In 1770 he began building his home, Monticello, and in 1772 he married Martha Wayles Skelton, a wealthy widow. Jefferson helped establish the Virginia Committee of Correspondence. As a member of the Second Continental Congress he drafted the Declaration of Independence. He also was a member of the Virginia House of Delegates (1776-79) and was elected governor of Virginia in 1779, succeeding Patrick Henry. He was reelected in 1780 but resigned in 1781 after British troops invaded Virginia. During his term he wrote the statute on religious freedom. After his wife's death in 1782, Jefferson again became a delegate to the Congress, and in 1784 he drafted the report that was the basis for the Ordinances of 1784, 1785, and 1787. He was minister to France from 1785 to 1789, when George Washington appointed him secretary of state.

Jefferson's strong faith in the consent of the governed conflicted with the emphasis on executive control, favored by Alexander Hamilton, secretary of the Treasury, and Jefferson resigned on Dec. 31, 1793. In the 1796 election Jefferson was the Democratic-Republican candidate for president; John Adams won the election, and Jefferson became vice president. In 1800, Jefferson and Aaron Burr received equal Electoral College votes; the House of Representatives elected Jefferson president. Jefferson was a strong advocate of westward expansion, major events of his first term were the Louisiana Purchase (1803) and the Lewis and Clark Expedition. An important development during his second term was passage of the Embargo Act, barring U.S. ships from setting sail to foreign ports. Jefferson established the University of Virginia and designed its buildings. He died July 4, 1826, on the same day as John Adams (the 50th anniversary of the Declaration of Independence).

Following analysis of DNA taken from descendants of Jefferson and Sally Hemings, one of his slaves, it has been widely acknowledged that Jefferson fathered at least one, perhaps all, of her six known children.

JAMES MADISON (1809-17), 4th president Democratic-Republican, was born on Mar. 16, 1751, in Port Conway, King George Co., VA, the son of James and Eleanor Rose Conway Madison. Madison graduated from Princeton in 1771. He served in the Virginia Constitutional Convention (1776), and, in 1780, became a delegate to the Second Continental Congress. He was chief recorder at the Constitutional Convention in 1787 and supported ratification in the *Federalist Papers*, written with Alexander Hamilton and John Jay. In 1789, Madison was elected to the House of Representatives, where he helped frame the Bill of Rights and support passage of the Alien and Sedition Acts. In the 1790s, he helped found the Democratic-Republican Party, which ultimately became the Democratic Party. He became Jefferson's secretary of state in 1801.

Madison was elected president in 1808. His first term was marked by tensions with Great Britain, and his conduct of foreign policy was criticized by the Federalists and by his own party. Nevertheless, he was reelected in 1812, the year war was declared on Great Britain. The war that many considered a second American revolution ended with a treaty that settled none of the issues. Madison's most important action after the war was demilitarizing the U.S.-Canadian border.

In 1817, Madison retired to his estate, Montpelier, where he served as an elder statesman. He edited his famous papers on the Constitutional Convention and helped found the University of Virginia, of which he became rector in 1826. He died June 28, 1836.

JAMES MONROE (1817-25), 5th president, Democratic-Republican, was born on Apr. 28, 1758, in Westmoreland Co., VA, the son of Spence and Eliza Jones Monroe. He entered the College of William and Mary in 1774 but left to serve in the 3d Virginia Regiment during the American Revolution. After the war, he studied law with Thomas Jefferson. In 1782 he was elected to the Virginia House of Delegates, and he served (1783-86) as a delegate to the Confederation Congress. He opposed ratification of the Constitution because it lacked a bill of rights. Monroe was elected to the U.S. Senate in 1790. In 1794 President George Washington appointed Monroe minister to France. He served twice as governor of Virginia (1799-1802, 1811). President Jefferson also sent him to France as minister (1803), and from 1803 to 1807 he served as minister to Great Britain.

In 1816 Monroe was reelected president; he was reelected in 1820 with all but one Electoral College vote. His administration became known as the Era of Good Feeling. He obtained Florida from Spain, settled boundary disputes with Britain over Canada, and eliminated border forts. He supported the antislavery position that led to the Missouri Compromise. His most significant contribution was the Monroe Doctrine, which opposed European intervention in the Western Hemisphere and became a cornerstone of U.S. foreign policy.

Although Monroe retired to Oak Hill, VA, financial problems forced him to sell his property and move to New York City. He died there on July 4, 1831.

JOHN QUINCY ADAMS (1825-29), 6th president, independent Federalist, later Democratic-Republican, was born on July 11, 1767, in Braintree (now Quincy), MA, the son of John and Abigail Adams. His father was the 2nd president. He studied abroad and at Harvard University, from which he graduated in 1787. In 1803, he was elected to the U.S. Senate. President Monroe chose him as his secretary of state in 1817. In this capacity he negotiated the cession of Florida from Spain, supported exclusion of slavery in the Missouri Compromise, and helped formulate the Monroe Doctrine. In 1824 Adams was elected president by the House of Representatives after he failed to win an Electoral College majority. His expansion of executive powers was strongly opposed, and in the 1828 election he lost to Andrew Jackson. In 1831 he entered the House of Representatives and served 17 years with distinction. He opposed slavery, the annexation of Texas, and the Mexican War. He helped establish the Smithsonian Institution.

Adams suffered a stroke in the House and died in the Speaker's Room on Feb. 23, 1848.

ANDREW JACKSON (1829-37), 7th president, Democratic-Republican, later a Democrat, was born on Mar. 15, 1767, in the Waxhaw district, on the border of North Carolina and South Carolina, the son of Andrew and Elizabeth Hutchinson Jackson. At the age of 13, he joined the militia to fight in the American Revolution and was captured. Orphaned at the age of 14, Jackson was brought up by a well-to-do uncle. By age 20, he was practicing law, and he later served as prosecuting attorney in Nashville, TN. In 1796 he helped draft the constitution of Tennessee, and for a year he occupied its one seat in the House of Representatives. The next year he served in the U.S. Senate.

In the War of 1812, Jackson crushed (1814) the Creek Indians at Horseshoe Bend, AL, and, with an army consisting chiefly of backwoodsmen, defeated (1815) General Edward Pakenham's British troops at the Battle of New Orleans. In 1818 he briefly invaded Spanish Florida to quell Seminoles and outlaws who harassed frontier settlements. In 1824 he ran for president against John Quincy Adams. Although he won the most popular and electoral votes, he did not have a majority. The House of Representatives decided the election and chose Adams, carrying the West and the South.

As president, Jackson introduced what became known as the spoils system—rewarding party members with government posts. Perhaps his most controversial act, however, was depositing federal funds in so-called pet banks, those directed by Democratic bankers, rather than in the Bank of the United States. "Let the people rule" was his slogan. In 1832, Jackson killed the congressional caucus for nominating presidential candidates and substituted the national convention. When South Carolina refused to collect imports under his protective tariff, he ordered army and naval forces to Charleston. After leaving office in 1837, he retired to the Hermitage, outside Nashville, where he died on June 8, 1845.

MARTIN VAN BUREN (1837-41), 8th president, Democrat, was born on Dec. 5, 1782, in Kinderhook, NY, the son of Abraham and Maria Hoes Van Buren. After attending local schools, he studied law and became a lawyer at the age of 20. A consummate politician, Van Buren began his career in the New York state senate and then served as state attorney general from 1816 to 1819. He was elected to the U.S. Senate in 1821. He helped swing eastern support to Andrew Jackson in the 1828 election and then served as Jackson's secretary of state from 1829 to 1831. In 1832 he was elected vice president. Known as the Little Magician, Van Buren was extremely influential in Jackson's administration.

In 1836, Van Buren defeated William Henry Harrison for president and took office as the financial panic of 1837 initiated a nationwide depression. Although he instituted the independent treasury system, his refusal to spend land revenues led to his defeat by William Henry Harrison in 1840. In 1844 he lost the Democratic nomination to James Knox Polk. In 1848 he again ran for president on the Free Soil ticket but lost. He died in Kinderhook on July 24, 1862.

WILLIAM HENRY HARRISON (1841), 9th president, Whig, who served only 31 days, was born on Feb. 9, 1773, in Berkeley, Charles City Co., VA, the son of Benjamin Harrison, a signer of the Declaration of Independence, and of Elizabeth Bassett Harrison. He attended Hampden-Sydney College. Harrison served as secretary of the Northwest Territory in 1798 and was its delegate to the House of Representatives in 1799. He was the first governor of the Indiana Territory and served as superintendent of Indian affairs. With 900 men he put down a Shawnee uprising at Tippecanoe, IN, on Nov. 7, 1811. A generation later, in 1840, he waged a rousing presidential campaign, using the slogan "Tippecanoe and Tyler too." The Tyler of the slogan was his running mate, John Tyler.

Although born to one of the wealthiest, most prestigious, and most influential families in Virginia, Harrison was elected president with a "log cabin and hard cider" slogan. He caught pneumonia during the inauguration and died Apr. 4, 1841, after only one month in office.

JOHN TYLER (1841-45), 10th president, independent Whig, was born on Mar. 29, 1790, in Greenway, Charles City Co., VA, the son of John and Mary Armistead Tyler. His father was governor of Virginia (1808-11). Tyler graduated from the College of William and Mary in 1807 and in 1811 was elected to the Virginia legislature. In 1816 he was chosen for the U.S. House of Representatives. He served in the Virginia legislature again from 1823 to 1825, when he was elected governor of Virginia. After a stint in the U.S. Senate (1827-36), he was elected vice president (1840).

When William Henry Harrison died only a month after taking office, Tyler succeeded him. Because he was the first person to occupy the presidency without having been elected to that office, he was referred to as "His Accidency." He gained passage of the Preemption Act of 1841, which gave squatters on government land the right to buy 160 acres at the minimum auction price. His last act as president was to sign a resolution annexing Texas. Tyler accepted renomination in 1844 from some Democrats but withdrew in favor of the official party candidate, James K. Polk. He died in Richmond, VA, on Jan. 18, 1862.

IT'S A FACT: John Tyler is the only president who served in the Confederate government. After leaving the White House in 1845, he returned to his native Virginia. In the months leading up to the Civil War he presided over the Washington Peace Convention, held to devise a compromise that could avert war. When the convention failed, he became a member of the Confederate House of Representatives, serving until his death in 1862.

JAMES KNOX POLK (1845-49), 11th president, Democrat, was born on Nov. 2, 1795, in Mecklenburg Co., NC, the son of Samuel and Jane Knox Polk. He graduated from the University of North Carolina in 1818 and served in the Tennessee state legislature from 1823 to 1825. He served in the U.S. House of Representatives from 1825 to 1839, the last 4 years as Speaker. He was governor of Tennessee from 1839 to 1841. In 1844, after the Democratic National Convention became deadlocked, it nominated Polk, who became the first "dark horse" candidate for president. He was nominated primarily because he favored annexation of Texas.

As president, Polk reestablished the independent treasury system originated by Van Buren. He was so intent on acquiring California from Mexico that he sent troops to the Mexican border and, when Mexicans attacked, declared that a state of war existed. The Mexican War ended with the annexation of California and much of the Southwest as part of America's "manifest destiny." Polk compromised on the Oregon boundary ("54-40 or fight!") by accepting the 49th parallel and yielding Vancouver Island to the British. A few weeks after leaving office, Polk died in Nashville, TN, on June 15, 1849.

ZACHARY TAYLOR (1849-50), 12th president, Whig, who served only 16 months, was born on Nov. 24, 1784, in Orange Co., VA, the son of Richard and Sarah Strother Taylor. He grew up on his father's plantation near Louisville, KY, where he was educated by private tutors. In 1808 Taylor joined the regular army and was commissioned first lieutenant. He fought in the War of 1812, the Black Hawk War (1832), and the second Seminole War (beginning in 1837). He was called "Old Rough and Ready." In 1846 President Polk sent him with an army to the Rio Grande. When the Mexicans attacked him, Polk declared war. Outnumbered 4-1, Taylor defeated (1847) Santa Anna at Buena Vista.

A national hero, Taylor received the Whig nomination in 1848 and was elected president, even though he had never bothered to vote. He resumed the spoils system and, though a slaveholder, worked to admit California as a free state. He fell ill and died in office on July 9, 1850.

MILLARD FILLMORE (1850-53), 13th president, Whig, was born on Jan. 7, 1800, in Cayuga Co., NY, the son of Nathaniel and Phoebe Millard Fillmore. Although he had little schooling, he became a law clerk at the age of 22 and a year later was admitted to the bar. He was elected to the New York state assembly in 1828 and served until 1831. From 1833 until 1835 and again from 1837 to 1843, he represented his district in the U.S. House of Representatives. He opposed the entrance of Texas as a slave state and voted for a protective tariff. In 1844 he was defeated for governor of New York.

In 1848 he was elected vice president, and he succeeded as president after Taylor's death. Fillmore favored the Compromise of 1850 and signed the Fugitive Slave Law. His policies pleased neither expansionists nor slaveholders, and he was not renominated in 1852. In 1856 he was nominated by the American (Know-Nothing) Party, but despite the support of the Whigs, he was defeated by James Buchanan. He died in Buffalo, NY, on Mar. 8, 1874.

FRANKLIN PIERCE (1853-57), 14th president, Democrat, was born on Nov. 23, 1804, in Hillsboro, NH, the son of Benjamin Pierce, Revolutionary War general and governor of New Hampshire, and Anna Kendrick. He graduated from Bowdoin College in 1824 and was admitted to the bar in 1827. He was elected to the New Hampshire state legislature in 1829 and was chosen Speaker in 1831. He went to the U.S. House in 1833 and was elected a U.S. senator in 1837. He enlisted in the Mexican War and became brigadier general under Gen. Winfield Scott.

In 1852 Pierce was nominated as the Democratic presidential candidate on the 49th ballot. He decisively defeated Gen. Scott, his Whig opponent, in the election. Although against slavery, Pierce was influenced by pro-slavery Southerners. He supported the controversial Kansas-Nebraska Act, which left the question of slavery in the new territories of Kansas and Nebraska to popular vote. Pierce signed a reciprocity treaty with Canada and approved the Gadsden Purchase of a border area on a proposed railroad route, from Mexico. Denied renomination, he spent most of his remaining years in Concord, NH, where he died on Oct. 8, 1869.

JAMES BUCHANAN (1857-61), 15th president, Federalist, later Democrat, was born on Apr. 23, 1791, near Mercersburg, PA, the son of James and Elizabeth Speer Buchanan. He graduated from Dickinson College in 1809 and was admitted to the bar in 1812. He fought in the War of 1812 as a volunteer. He was twice elected to the Pennsylvania general assembly, and in 1821 he entered the U.S. House of Representatives. After briefly serving (1832-33) as minister to Russia, he was elected U.S. senator from Pennsylvania. As Polk's secretary of state (1845-49), he ended the Oregon dispute with Britain and supported the Mexican War and annexation of Texas. As minister to Great Britain, he signed the Ostend Manifesto (1854), declaring a U.S. right to take Cuba by force should efforts to purchase it fail.

Nominated by Democrats, Buchanan was elected president in 1856. On slavery he favored popular sovereignty and choice by state constitutions but did not consistently uphold this position. He denied the right of states to secede but opposed coercion and attempted to keep peace by not provoking secessionists. Buchanan left office having failed to deal decisively with the situation. He died at Wheatland, his estate, near Lancaster, PA, on June 1, 1868.

ABRAHAM LINCOLN (1861-65), 16th president, Republican, was born on Feb. 12, 1809, in a log cabin on a farm then in Hardin Co., KY, now in Larue, the son of Thomas and Nancy Hanks Lincoln. The Lincolns moved to Spencer Co., IN, near Gentryville, when Abe was 7. After Abe's mother died, his father married (1819) Mrs. Sarah Bush Johnston. In 1830 the family moved to Macon Co., IL.

Defeated in 1832 in a race for the state legislature, Lincoln was elected on the Whig ticket 2 years later and served in the lower house from 1834 to 1842. In 1837 Lincoln was admitted to the bar and became partner in a Springfield, IL, law office. He soon won recognition as an effective and resourceful attorney. In 1846, he was elected to the House of Representatives, where he attracted attention during a single term for his opposition to the Mexican War and his position on slavery. In 1856 he campaigned for the newly founded Republican Party, and in 1858 he became its senatorial candidate against Stephen A. Douglas. Although he lost the election, Lincoln gained national recognition from his debates with Douglas.

In 1860, Lincoln was nominated for president by the Republican Party on a platform of restricting slavery. He ran against Douglas, a northern Democrat; John C. Breckinridge, a Southern proslavery Democrat; and John Bell, of the Constitutional Union Party. As a result of Lincoln's winning the election, South Carolina seceded from the Union on Dec. 20, 1860, followed in 1861 by 10 other Southern states.

The Civil War erupted when Fort Sumter, which Lincoln decided to resupply, was attacked by Confederate forces on Apr. 12, 1861. Lincoln called successfully for recruits from the North. On Sept. 22, 1862, 5 days after the Battle of Antietam, Lincoln announced that slaves in territory then in rebellion would be free Jan. 1, 1863, the date of the Emancipation Proclamation. His speeches, including his Gettysburg and Inaugural addresses, are remembered for their eloquence.

Lincoln was reelected, in 1864, over Gen. George B. McClellan, Democrat. Lee surrendered on Apr. 9, 1865. On Apr. 14, Lincoln was shot by actor John Wilkes Booth in Ford's Theater, in Washington, DC. He died the next day.

ANDREW JOHNSON (1865-69), 17th president, Democrat, was born on Dec. 29, 1808, in Raleigh, NC, the son of Jacob and Mary McDonough Johnson. He was apprenticed to a tailor as a youth, but ran away after two years and eventually settled in Greeneville, TN. He became popular with the townspeople and in 1829 was elected councilman and later mayor. In 1835 he was sent to the state general assembly. In 1843 he was elected to the U.S. House of Representatives, where he served for 10 years. Johnson was governor of Tennessee from 1853 to 1857, when he was elected to the U.S. Senate. He supported John C. Breckinridge against Lincoln in the 1860 election. Although Johnson had held slaves, he opposed secession and tried to prevent Tennessee from seceding. In Mar. 1862, Lincoln appointed him military governor of occupied Tennessee.

In 1864, in order to balance Lincoln's ticket with a Southern Democrat, the Republicans nominated Johnson for vice president. He was elected vice president with Lincoln and then succeeded to the presidency upon Lincoln's death. Soon afterward, in a controversy with Congress over the president's power over the South, he proclaimed an amnesty to all Confederates, except certain leaders, if they would ratify the 13th Amendment abolishing slavery. States doing so added anti-Negro provisions that enraged Congress, which restored military control over the South. When Johnson removed Edwin M. Stanton, secretary of war, without notifying the Senate, the House, in Feb. 1868, impeached him. Charging him with thereby having violated the Tenure of Office Act, the House was actually responding to his opposition to harsh congressional Reconstruction, expressed in repeated vetoes. He was tried by the Senate, and in May, in two separate votes on different counts, was acquitted, both times by only one vote.

Johnson was denied renomination but remained politically active. He was reelected to the Senate in 1874. Johnson died July 31, 1875, at Carter Station, TN.

ULYSSES SIMPSON GRANT (1869-77), 18th president, Republican, was born on Apr. 27, 1822, in Point Pleasant, OH, the son of Jesse R. and Hannah Simpson Grant. The next year the family moved to Georgetown, OH. Grant was named Hiram Ulysses, but on entering West Point in 1839, his name was put down as Ulysses Simpson, and he adopted it. He graduated in 1843. During the Mexican War, Grant served under both Gen. Zachary Taylor and Gen. Winfield Scott. In 1854, he resigned his commission because of loneliness and drinking problems, and in the following years he engaged in generally unsuccessful farming and business ventures. With the start of the Civil War, he was named colonel and then brigadier general of the Illinois Volunteers. He took Forts Henry and Donelson and fought at Shiloh. His brilliant campaign against Vicksburg and his victory at Chattanooga made him so prominent that Lincoln placed him in command of all Union armies. Grant accepted Lee's surrender at Appomattox Court House on Apr. 9, 1865. President Johnson appointed Grant secretary of war when he suspended Stanton, but Grant was not confirmed.

Grant was nominated for president by the Republicans in 1868 and elected over Horatio Seymour, Democrat. The 15th Amendment, the amnesty bill, and peaceful settlement of disputes with Great Britain were events of his administration. The Liberal Republicans and Democrats opposed him with Horace Greeley in the 1872 election, but Grant was reelected. His second administration was marked by scandals, including widespread corruption in the Treasury Department and the Indian Service. An attempt by the Stalwarts (Old Guard Republicans) to nominate him in 1880 failed. In 1884 the collapse of an investment firm in which he was a partner left him penniless. He wrote his personal memoirs while ill with cancer and completed them shortly before his death at Mt. McGregor, NY, on July 23, 1885.

RUTHERFORD BIRCHARD HAYES (1877-81), 19th president, Republican, was born on Oct. 4, 1822, in Delaware, OH, the son of Rutherford and Sophia Birchard Hayes. He was reared by his uncle, Sardis Birchard. Hayes graduated from Kenyon College in 1842 and from Harvard Law School in 1845. He practiced law in Lower Sandusky (now Fremont), OH, and was city solicitor of Cincinnati from 1858 to 1861. During the Civil War, he was major of the 23rd Ohio Volunteers. He was wounded several times, and by the end of the war he had risen to the rank of brevet major general. While serving (1865-67) in the U.S. House of Representatives, Hayes supported Reconstruction and Johnson's impeachment. He was twice elected governor of Ohio (1867, 1869). After losing a race for the U.S. House in 1872, he was reelected governor of Ohio in 1875.

In 1876, Hayes was nominated for president and believed he had lost the election to Samuel J. Tilden, Democrat. But a few Southern states submitted 2 sets of electoral votes, and the result was in dispute. An electoral commission, consisting of 8 Republicans and 7 Democrats, awarded all disputed votes to Hayes, allowing him to become president by one electoral vote. Hayes, keeping a promise to southerners, withdrew troops from areas still occupied in the South, ending the era of Reconstruction. He proposed civil service reforms, alienating those favoring the spoils system, and advocated repeal of the Tenure of Office Act restricting presidential power to dismiss officials. He supported sound money and specie payments.

Hayes died in Fremont, OH, on Jan. 17, 1893.

JAMES ABRAM GARFIELD (1881), 20th president, Republican, was born on Nov. 19, 1831, in Orange, Cuyahoga Co., OH, the son of Abram and Eliza Ballou Garfield. His father died in 1833, and he was reared in poverty by his mother. He worked as a canal bargeman, a farmer, and a carpenter and managed to secure a college education. He taught at Hiram College and later became principal. In 1859 he was elected to the Ohio legislature. Antislavery and antisecession, he volunteered for military service in the Civil War, becoming colonel of the 42nd Ohio Infantry and brigadier in 1862. He fought at Shiloh, was chief of staff for Gen. William Starke Rosecrans, and was made major general for gallantry at Chickamauga. He entered Congress as a radical Republican in 1863, calling for execution or exile of Confederate leaders, but he moderated his views after the Civil War. On the electoral commission in 1877 he voted for Hayes against Tilden on strict party lines.

Garfield was a senator-elect in 1880 when he became the Republican nominee for president. He was chosen as a compromise over Gen. Grant, James G. Blaine, and John Sherman, and won election despite some bitterness among Grant's supporters. Much of his brief tenure as president was concerned with a fight with New York Sen. Roscoe Conkling, who opposed two major appointments made by Garfield. On July 2, 1881, Garfield was shot and seriously wounded by a mentally disturbed office-seeker, Charles J. Guiteau, while entering a railroad station in Washington, DC. He died on Sept. 19, 1881, in Elberon, NJ.

CHESTER ALAN ARTHUR (1881-85), 21st president, Republican, was born on Oct. 5, 1829, in Fairfield, VT, to William and Malvina Stone Arthur. He graduated from Union College in 1848, taught school in Vermont, then studied law and practiced in New York City. In 1853 he argued in a fugitive slave case that slaves transported through New York state were thereby freed. In 1871, he was appointed collector of the Port of New York. President Hayes, an opponent of the spoils system, forced him to resign in 1878. This made the New York machine enemies of Hayes. Arthur and the Stalwarts (Old Guard Republicans) tried to nominate Grant for a 3rd term as president in 1880. When Garfield was nominated, Arthur was nominated for vice president in the interests of harmony.

Upon Garfield's assassination, Arthur became president. Despite his past connections, he signed major civil service reform legislation. Arthur tried to dissuade Congress from enacting the high protective tariff of 1883. He was defeated for renomination in 1884 by James G. Blaine. He died in New York City on Nov. 18, 1886.

GROVER CLEVELAND (1885-89; 1893-97) *(According to a ruling of the State Dept., Grover Cleveland should be counted as both the 22nd and the 24th president, because his 2 terms were not consecutive.)*
Grover Cleveland, Democrat, was born Stephen Grover Cleveland on Mar. 18, 1837, in Caldwell, NJ, the son of Richard F. and Ann Neal Cleveland. When he was a small boy, his family moved to New York. Prevented by his father's death from attending college, he studied by himself and was admitted to the bar in Buffalo, NY, in 1859. In succession he became assistant district attorney (1863), sheriff (1871), mayor (1881), and governor of New York (1882). He was an independent, honest administrator who hated corruption. Cleveland was nominated for president over Tammany Hall opposition in 1884 and defeated Republican James G. Blaine.

As president, he enlarged the civil service and vetoed many pension raids on the Treasury. In the 1888 election he was defeated by Benjamin Harrison, although his popular vote was larger. Reelected over Harrison in 1892, he faced a money crisis brought about by a lowered gold reserve, circulation of paper, and exorbitant silver purchases under the Sherman Silver Purchase Act. He obtained a repeal of the Sherman Act, but was unable to secure effective tariff reform. A severe economic depression and labor troubles racked his administration, but he refused to interfere in business matters and rejected Jacob Coxey's demand for unemployment relief. In 1894, he broke the Pullman strike. Cleveland was not renominated in 1896. He died in Princeton, NJ, on June 24, 1908.

BENJAMIN HARRISON (1889-93), 23rd president, Republican, was born on Aug. 20, 1833, in North Bend, OH, the son of John Scott and Elizabeth Irwin Harrison. His great-grandfather, Benjamin Harrison, was a signer of the Declaration of Independence; his grandfather, William Henry Harrison, was 9th president; his father was a member of Congress. He attended school on his father's farm and graduated from Miami University in Oxford, OH, in 1852. He was admitted to the bar in 1854 and practiced in Indianapolis. During the Civil War, he rose to the rank of brevet brigadier general and fought at Kennesaw Mountain, at Peachtree Creek, at Nashville, and in the Atlanta campaign. He lost the 1876 gubernatorial election in Indiana but succeeded in becoming a U.S. senator in 1881.

In 1888 he defeated Cleveland for president despite receiving fewer popular votes. As president, he expanded the pension list and signed the McKinley high tariff bill, the Sherman Antitrust Act, and the Sherman Silver Purchase Act. During his administration, 6 states were admitted to the Union. He was defeated for reelection in 1892. He died in Indianapolis on Mar. 13, 1901.

WILLIAM McKINLEY (1897-1901), 25th president, Republican, was born on Jan. 29, 1843, in Niles, OH, the son of William and Nancy Allison McKinley. McKinley briefly attended Allegheny College. When the Civil War broke out in 1861, he enlisted and served for the duration. He rose to captain and in 1865 was made brevet major. After studying law in Albany, NY, he opened (1867) a law office in Canton, OH. He served twice in the U.S. House (1877-83; 1885-91) and led the fight there for the McKinley Tariff, passed in 1890; he was not reelected to the House as a result. He served two terms (1892-96) as governor of Ohio.

In 1896 he was elected president as a proponent of a protective tariff and sound money (gold standard), over William Jennings Bryan, the Democrat and a proponent of free silver. McKinley was reluctant to intervene in Cuba, but the loss of the battleship *Maine* at Havana crystallized opinion. He demanded Spain's withdrawal from Cuba; Spain made some

concessions, but Congress announced a state of war as of Apr. 21, 1898. He was reelected in the 1900 campaign, defeating Bryan's anti-imperialist arguments with the promise of a "full dinner pail." McKinley was respected for his conciliatory nature and for his conservative stance on business issues. On Sept. 6, 1901, while welcoming citizens at the Pan-American Exposition, in Buffalo, NY, he was shot by Leon Czolgosz, an anarchist. He died Sept. 14.

THEODORE ROOSEVELT (1901-9), 26th president, Republican, was born on Oct. 27, 1858, in New York City, the son of Theodore and Martha Bulloch Roosevelt. He was a 5th cousin of Franklin D. Roosevelt and an uncle of Eleanor Roosevelt. Roosevelt graduated from Harvard University in 1880. He attended Columbia Law School briefly but abandoned law to enter politics. He was elected to the New York state assembly in 1881 and served until 1884. He spent the next 2 years ranching and hunting in the Dakota Territory. In 1886, he ran unsuccessfully for mayor of New York City. He was Civil Service commissioner in Washington, DC, from 1889 to 1895. From 1895 to 1897, he served as New York City's police commissioner. He was assistant secretary of the navy under McKinley. The Spanish-American War made him nationally known. He organized the 1st U.S. Volunteer Cavalry (Rough Riders) and, as lieutenant colonel, led the charge up Kettle Hill in San Juan. Elected New York governor in 1898, he fought the spoils system and achieved taxation of corporation franchises.

Nominated for vice president in 1900, he became the nation's youngest president when McKinley was assassinated. He was reelected in 1904. As president he fought corruption of politics by big business, dissolved the Northern Securities Co. and others for violating antitrust laws, intervened in the 1902 coal strike on behalf of the public, obtained the Elkins Law (1903) forbidding rebates to favored corporations, and helped pass the Hepburn Railway Rate Act of 1906 (extending jurisdiction of the Interstate Commerce Commission). He helped obtain passage of the Pure Food and Drug Act (1906), and of employers' liability laws. Roosevelt vigorously organized conservation efforts. He mediated (1905) the peace between Japan and Russia, for which he won the Nobel Peace Prize. He abetted the 1903 revolution in Panama that led to U.S. acquisition of territory for the Panama Canal.

In 1908 Roosevelt obtained the nomination of William H. Taft, who was elected. Feeling that Taft had abandoned his policies, he unsuccessfully sought the nomination in 1912. He then ran on the Progressive "Bull Moose" ticket against Taft and Woodrow Wilson, splitting the Republicans and ensuring Wilson's election. He was shot during the campaign but recovered. In 1916, after unsuccessfully seeking the presidential nomination, he supported the Republican candidate, Charles E. Hughes. A strong friend of Britain, he fought for U.S. intervention in World War I. He wrote some 40 books, of which *The Winning of the West* is perhaps best known. He died Jan. 6, 1919, at Sagamore Hill, Oyster Bay, NY.

WILLIAM HOWARD TAFT (1909-13), 27th president, Republican, and 10th chief justice of the U.S., was born on Sept. 15, 1857, in Cincinnati, OH, the son of Alphonso and Louisa Maria Torrey Taft. His father was secretary of war and attorney general in Grant's cabinet and minister to Austria and Russia under Arthur. Taft graduated from Yale in 1878 and from Cincinnati Law School in 1880. After working as a law reporter for Cincinnati newspapers, he served as assistant prosecuting attorney (1881-82), assistant county solicitor (1885), judge, superior court (1887), U.S. solicitor-general (1890), and federal circuit judge (1892). In 1900 he became head of the U.S. Philippines Commission and was the first civil governor of the Philippines (1901-4). In 1904 he served as secretary of war, and in 1906 he was sent to Cuba to help avert a threatened revolution.

Taft was groomed for the presidency by Theodore Roosevelt and elected over William Jennings Bryan in 1908. Taft vigorously continued Roosevelt's trust-busting, instituted the Department of Labor, and drafted the amendments calling for direct election of senators and the income tax. His tariff and conservation policies angered progressives. Although renominated in 1912, he was opposed by Roosevelt, who ran on the Progressive Party ticket; the result was Democrat Woodrow Wilson's election.

Taft, with some reservations, supported the League of Nations. After leaving office, he was professor of constitutional law at Yale (1913-21) and chief justice of the U.S. (1921-30). Taft was the only person in U.S. history to have been both president and chief justice. He died in Washington, DC, on Mar. 8, 1930.

(THOMAS) WOODROW WILSON (1913-21), 28th president, Democrat, was born on Dec. 28, 1856, in Staunton, VA, the son of Joseph Ruggles and Janet (Jessie) Woodrow Wilson. He grew up in Georgia and South Carolina. He attended Davidson College in North Carolina before graduating from Princeton University in 1879. He studied law at the University of Virginia and political science at Johns Hopkins University, where he received his PhD in 1886. He taught at Bryn Mawr (1885-88) and then at Wesleyan (1888-90) before joining the faculty at Princeton. He was president of Princeton from 1902 until 1910, when he was elected governor of New Jersey. In 1912 he was nominated for president with the aid of William Jennings Bryan, who sought to block James "Champ" Clark and Tammany Hall. Wilson won because the Republican vote for Taft was split by the Progressives.

As president, Wilson protected American interests in revolutionary Mexico and fought for American rights on the high seas. He oversaw the creation of the Federal Reserve system, cut the tariff, and developed a reputation as a reformer. His sharp warnings to Germany led to the resignation of his secretary of state, Bryan, a pacifist. In 1916 he was reelected by a slim margin with the slogan, "He kept us out of war," although his attempts to mediate in the war failed. After several American ships had been sunk by the Germans, he secured a declaration of war against Germany on Apr. 6, 1917.

Wilson outlined his peace program on Jan. 8, 1918, in the Fourteen Points, a state paper that had worldwide influence. He enunciated a doctrine of self-determination for the settlement of territorial disputes. The Germans accepted his terms and an armistice on Nov. 11, 1918.

Wilson went to Paris to help negotiate the peace treaty, the crux of which he considered the League of Nations. The Senate demanded reservations that would not make the U.S. subordinate to the votes of other nations in case of war. Wilson refused and toured the country to get support. He suffered a stroke in Oct. 1919. An invalid, he clung to his office while his wife and doctors effectively functioned as president.

Wilson was awarded the 1919 Nobel Peace Prize, but the treaty embodying the League of Nations was ultimately rejected by the Senate in 1920. He left the White House in Mar. 1921. He died in Washington, DC, on Feb. 3, 1924.

WARREN GAMALIEL HARDING (1921-23), 29th president, Republican, was born on Nov. 2, 1865, near Corsica (now Blooming Grove), OH, the son of George Tyron and Phoebe Elizabeth Dickerson Harding. He attended Ohio Central College, studied law, and became editor and publisher of a county newspaper. He entered the political arena as state senator (1901-4) and then served as lieutenant governor (1904-6). In 1910 he ran unsuccessfully for governor of Ohio; then in 1914 he was elected to the U.S. Senate. In the Senate he voted for antistrike legislation, woman suffrage, and the Volstead Prohibition Enforcement Act over President Wilson's veto. He opposed the League of Nations. In 1920 he was nominated for president and defeated James M. Cox in the election. The Republicans capitalized on war weariness and fear that Wilson's League of Nations would curtail U.S. sovereignty.

Harding stressed a return to "normalcy" and worked for tariff revision and the repeal of excess profits law and high income taxes. His secretary of interior, Albert B. Fall, became involved in the Teapot Dome scandal. As rumors began to circulate about the corruption in his administration, Harding be-

came ill while returning from a trip to Alaska, and he died in San Francisco on Aug. 2, 1923.

(JOHN) CALVIN COOLIDGE (1923-29), 30th president, Republican, was born on July 4, 1872, in Plymouth, VT, the son of John Calvin and Victoria J. Moor Coolidge. Coolidge graduated from Amherst College in 1895. He entered Republican state politics and served as mayor of Northampton, MA, as state senator, as lieutenant governor, and, in 1919, as governor. In Sept. 1919, Coolidge attained national prominence by calling out the state guard in the Boston police strike. He declared: "There is no right to strike against the public safety by anybody, anywhere, anytime." This brought his name before the Republican convention of 1920, where he was nominated for vice president.

Coolige succeeded to the presidency on Harding's death. As president, he opposed the League of Nations and the soldiers' bonus bill, which was passed over his veto. In 1924 he was elected to the presidency by a huge majority. He substantially reduced the national debt. He twice vetoed the McNary-Haugen farm bill, which would have provided relief to financially hard-pressed farmers.

With Republicans eager to renominate him, Coolidge simply announced, Aug. 2, 1927: "I do not choose to run for president in 1928." He died in Northampton, MA, on Jan. 5, 1933.

HERBERT CLARK HOOVER (1929-33), 31st president, Republican, was born on Aug. 10, 1874, in West Branch, IA, the son of Jesse Clark and Hulda Randall Minthorn Hoover. Hoover grew up in Indian Territory (now Oklahoma) and Oregon and graduated from Stanford University with a degree in geology in 1895. He worked briefly with the U.S. Geological Survey and then managed mines in Australia, Asia, Europe, and Africa. While chief engineer of imperial mines in China, he directed food relief for victims of the Boxer Rebellion. He gained a reputation not only as an engineer but as a humanitarian as he directed the American Relief Committee, London (1914-15) and the U.S. Commission for Relief in Belgium (1915-19). He was U.S. Food Administrator (1917-19), American Relief Administrator (1918-23), and in charge of Russian Relief (1918-23). He served as secretary of commerce under both Harding and Coolidge. Some historians believe that he was the most effective secretary of commerce ever to hold that office.

In 1928 Hoover was elected president over Alfred E. Smith. In 1929 the stock market crashed, and the economy collapsed. During the Great Depression, Hoover inaugurated some government assistance programs, but he was opposed to administration of aid through a federal bureaucracy. As the effects of the depression continued, he was defeated in the 1932 election by Franklin D. Roosevelt. Hoover remained active after leaving office. President Truman named him coordinator of the European Food Program (1946) and chairman of the Commission on Organization of the Executive Branch (1947-49; 1953-55). Hoover died in New York City on Oct. 20, 1964.

FRANKLIN DELANO ROOSEVELT (1933-45), 32nd president, Democrat, was born on Jan. 30, 1882, near Hyde Park, NY, the son of James and Sara Delano Roosevelt. He graduated from Harvard University in 1904. He attended Columbia University Law School without taking a degree and was admitted to the New York state bar in 1907. His political career began when he was elected to the New York state senate in 1910. In 1913 President Wilson appointed him assistant secretary of the navy, a post he held during World War I.

In 1920 Roosevelt ran for vice president with James Cox and was defeated. From 1921 to 1928 he worked in his New York law office and was also vice president of a bank. In Aug. 1921, he was stricken with poliomyelitis, which left his legs paralyzed. As a result of therapy he was able to stand, or walk a few steps, with the aid of leg braces.

▶ **IT'S A FACT:** Three presidents have won the Nobel Peace Prize: Theodore Roosevelt, in 1906, while president, for brokering the peace that ended the Russo-Japanese War; Woodrow Wilson, in 1919, while president, for planning the League of Nations; and Jimmy Carter, in 2002, largely for his peace efforts while in the White House and afterward.

Roosevelt served 2 terms as governor of New York (1929-33). In 1932, W. G. McAdoo, pledged to John N. Garner, threw his votes to Roosevelt, who was nominated for president. The Depression and the promise to repeal Prohibition ensured his election. He asked for emergency powers, proclaimed the New Deal, and put into effect a vast number of administrative changes. Foremost was the use of public funds for relief and public works, resulting in deficit financing. He greatly expanded the federal government's regulation of business and by an excess profits tax and progressive income taxes produced a redistribution of earnings on an unprecedented scale. He also promoted legislation establishing the Social Security system. He was the last president inaugurated on Mar. 4 (1933) and the first inaugurated on Jan. 20 (1937).

Roosevelt was the first president to use radio for "fireside chats." When the Supreme Court nullified some New Deal laws, he sought power to "pack" the Court with additional justices, but Congress refused to give him the authority. He was the first president to break the "no 3rd term" tradition (1940) and was elected to a 4th term in 1944, despite failing health. Roosevelt was openly hostile to fascist governments before World War II and launched a lend-lease program on behalf of the Allies. With British Prime Min. Winston Churchill he wrote a declaration of principles to be followed after Nazi defeat (the Atlantic Charter of Aug. 14, 1941) and urged the Four Freedoms (freedom of speech, of worship, from want, from fear) Jan. 6, 1941. When Japan attacked Pearl Harbor on Dec. 7, 1941, the U.S. entered the war. Roosevelt conferred with allied heads of state at Casablanca (Jan. 1943), Quebec (Aug. 1943), Tehran (Nov.-Dec. 1943), Cairo (Nov. and Dec, 1943), and Yalta (Feb. 1945).

Roosevelt did not, however, live to see the end of the war. He died of a cerebral hemorrhage in Warm Springs, GA, on Apr. 12, 1945.

HARRY S. TRUMAN (1945-53), 33rd president, Democrat, was born on May 8, 1884, in Lamar, MO, the son of John Anderson and Martha Ellen Young Truman. A family disagreement on whether his middle name should be Shippe or Solomon, after names of 2 grandfathers, resulted in his using only the middle initial S. After graduating from high school in Independence, MO, he worked (1901) for the *Kansas City Star*, as a railroad timekeeper, and as a clerk in Kansas City banks until about 1905. He ran his family's farm from 1906 to 1917. He served in France during World War I. After the war he opened a haberdashery shop, was a judge on the Jackson Co. Court (1922-24), and attended Kansas City School of Law (1923-25).

Truman was elected to the U.S. Senate in 1934 and reelected in 1940. In 1944, with Roosevelt's backing, he was nominated for vice president and elected. On Roosevelt's death in 1945, Truman became president. In 1948, in a famous upset victory, he defeated Republican Thomas E. Dewey to win election to a new term.

Truman authorized the first uses of the atomic bomb (Hiroshima and Nagasaki, Aug. 6 and 9, 1945), bringing World War II to a rapid end. He was responsible for what came to be called the Truman Doctrine (to aid nations such as Greece and Turkey, threatened by Communist takeover), and his strong commitment to NATO and to the Marshall Plan helped bring them about. In 1948-49, he broke a Soviet blockade of West Berlin with a massive airlift. When Communist North Korea invaded South Korea (June 1950), he won UN approval for a "police action" and sent in forces under Gen. Douglas MacArthur. When MacArthur opposed his policy of limited objectives, Truman removed him.

He died in Kansas City, MO, on Dec. 26, 1972.

DWIGHT DAVID EISENHOWER (1953-61), 34th president, Republican, was born on Oct. 14, 1890, in Denison, TX, the son of David Jacob and Ida Elizabeth Stover Eisenhower. He grew up on a small farm in Abilene, KS, and graduated from West Point in 1915. He was on the staff of Gen. Douglas MacArthur in the Philippines from 1935 to 1939. In 1942, he was made commander of Allied forces landing in North Africa; the next year he was made full general. He became supreme Allied commander in Europe that same year and as such led the Normandy invasion (June 6, 1944). He was given the rank of general of the army on Dec. 20, 1944, which was made permanent in 1946. On May 7, 1945, Eisenhower received the surrender of Germany at Rheims. He returned to the U.S. to serve as chief of staff (1945-48). His war memoir, *Crusade in Europe* (1948), was a best-seller. In 1948 he became president of Columbia University; in 1950 he became Commander of NATO forces.

Eisenhower resigned from the army and was nominated for president by the Republicans in 1952. He defeated Adlai E. Stevenson in the 1952 election and again in 1956. Eisenhower called himself a moderate, favored the "free market system" vs. government price and wage controls, kept government out of labor disputes, reorganized the defense establishment, and promoted missile programs. He continued foreign aid, sped the end of the Korean War, endorsed Taiwan and SE Asia defense treaties, backed the UN in condemning the Anglo-French raid on Egypt, and advocated the "open skies" policy of mutual inspection with the USSR. He sent U.S. troops into Little Rock, AR, in Sept. 1957, during the segregation crisis.

Eisenhower died on Mar. 28, 1969, in Washington, DC.

JOHN FITZGERALD KENNEDY (1961-63), 35th president, Democrat, was born on May 29, 1917, in Brookline, MA, the son of Joseph P. and Rose Fitzgerald Kennedy. He graduated from Harvard University in 1940. While serving in the navy (1941-45), he commanded a PT boat in the Solomons and won the Navy and Marine Corps Medal. In 1956, while recovering from spinal surgery, he wrote *Profiles in Courage*, which won a Pulitzer Prize in 1957. He served in the House of Representatives from 1947 to 1953 and was elected to the Senate in 1952 and 1958. In 1960, he won the Democratic nomination for president and narrowly defeated Republican Vice Pres. Richard M. Nixon. Kennedy was the youngest president ever elected to the office and the first Catholic.

Despite the image of youth and vigor he conveyed to the public, Kennedy suffered from serious medical problems, including Addison's disease and severe chronic back pain that required him to wear a back brace. The public was not aware of the extent of these problems, or of his extensive womanizing, including an affair with a young White House press aide that only became known in 2003. However, scholars have not generally claimed that these aspects of his life affected his performance in office.

In Apr. 1961, the new Kennedy administration suffered a severe setback when an invasion force of anti-Castro Cubans, trained and directed by the CIA, failed to establish a beachhead at the Bay of Pigs in Cuba. By the same token, one of Kennedy's most important acts as president was his successful demand on Oct. 22, 1962, that the Soviet Union dismantle its missile bases in Cuba. Kennedy also defied Soviet attempts to force the Allies out of Berlin. He started the Peace Corps, and he backed civil rights and expanded medical care for the aged. Space exploration was greatly developed during his administration.

On Nov. 22, 1963, President Kennedy was assassinated while riding in a motorcade in Dallas, TX. A commission chaired by Chief Justice Earl Warren concluded in Sept. 1964 that the sole assassin had been Lee Harvey Oswald, who was captured two days after the assassination but was then shot dead by nightclub owner Jack Ruby while being moved to a county jail.

LYNDON BAINES JOHNSON (1963-69), 36th president, Democrat, was born on Aug. 27, 1908, near Stonewall, TX, the son of Sam Ealy and Rebekah Baines Johnson. He graduated from Southwest Texas State Teachers College in 1930 and attended Georgetown University Law School. He taught public speaking in Houston (1930-31) and then served as secretary to Rep. R. M. Kleberg (1931-35). In 1937 Johnson won an election to fill the vacancy caused by the death of a U.S. representative and in 1938 was elected to the full term, after which he returned for 4 terms. During 1941 and 1942 he also served in the Navy in the Pacific, earning a Silver Star for bravery. He was elected U.S. senator in 1948 and reelected in 1954. He became Democratic leader of the Senate in 1953. Johnson had strong support for the Democratic presidential nomination at the 1960 convention, where the nominee, John F. Kennedy, asked him to run for vice president. His campaigning helped overcome religious bias against Kennedy in the South.

Johnson became president when Kennedy was assassinated. He was elected to a full term in 1964. Johnson's domestic program was of considerable importance. He won passage of major civil rights, anti-poverty, aid to education, and health-care (Medicare, Medicaid) legislation—the "Great Society" program. However, his escalation of the war in Vietnam came to overshadow the achievements of his administration. In the face of increasing division in the nation and in his own party over his handling of the war, Johnson declined to seek another term.

Johnson died on Jan. 22, 1973, in San Antonio, TX.

RICHARD MILHOUS NIXON (1969-74), 37th president, Republican, was born on Jan. 9, 1913, in Yorba Linda, CA, the son of Francis Anthony and Hannah Milhous Nixon. He graduated from Whittier College in 1934 and from Duke University Law School in 1937. After practicing law in Whittier and serving briefly in the Office of Price Administration in 1942, he entered the Navy and served in the South Pacific. Nixon was elected to the House of Representatives in 1946 and 1948. He achieved prominence as the House Un-American Activities Committee member who forced the showdown leading to the Alger Hiss perjury conviction. In 1950 he was elected to the Senate.

Nixon was elected vice president in the Eisenhower landslides of 1952 and 1956. He won the Republican nomination for president in 1960 but was narrowly defeated by John F. Kennedy. He ran unsuccessfully for governor of California in 1962. In 1968 he again won the GOP presidential nomination, then defeated Hubert Humphrey for the presidency.

Nixon's 2nd term was cut short by scandal, after disclosures relating to a June 1972 burglary of Democratic Party headquarters in the Watergate office complex. The courts and Congress sought tapes of Nixon's office conversations and calls for criminal proceedings against former White House aides and for a House inquiry into possible impeachment. Nixon claimed executive privilege, but the Supreme Court ruled against him. In July the House Judiciary Committee recommended adoption of 3 impeachment articles charging him with obstruction of justice, abuse of power, and contempt of Congress. On Aug. 5, he released transcripts of conversations that linked him to cover-up activities. He resigned on Aug. 9, becoming the first president ever to do so. In later years, Nixon emerged as an elder statesman.

As president, Nixon appointed 4 Supreme Court justices, including the chief justice, moving the court to the right, and as a "new federalist" sought to shift responsibility to state and local governments. He dramatically altered relations with China, which he visited in 1972—the first president to do so. With foreign affairs adviser Henry Kissinger he pursued détente with the Soviet Union. He began a gradual withdrawal from Vietnam, but U.S. troops remained there through his first term. He ordered an incursion into Cambodia (1970) and the bombing of Hanoi and mining of Haiphong Harbor (1972). Reelected by a large majority in Nov. 1972, he secured a Vietnam cease-fire in Jan. 1973.

Nixon died Apr. 22, 1994, in New York City.

GERALD RUDOLPH FORD (1974-77), 38th president, Republican, was born on July 14, 1913, in Omaha, NE, the son of Leslie and Dorothy Gardner King, and was named Leslie Jr. When he was 2, his parents were divorced, and his mother moved with the boy to Grand Rapids, MI. There she met and married Gerald R. Ford, who formally adopted him and gave him his own name. Ford graduated from the University of Michigan in 1935 and from Yale Law School in 1941. He began practicing law in Grand Rapids, but in 1942 joined the navy and served in the Pacific, leaving the service in 1946 as a lieutenant commander. He entered the House of Representatives in 1949 and spent 25 years in the House, 8 of them as Republican leader.

On Oct. 12, 1973, after Vice President Spiro T. Agnew resigned, Ford was nominated by President Nixon to replace him. It was the first use of the procedures set out in the 25th Amendment. When Nixon resigned, Aug. 9, 1974, because of the Watergate scandal, Ford became president; he was the only president who was never elected either to the presidency or to the vice presidency.

President Ford was widely credited with having contributed to rebuilding morale after the Nixon presidency. But he was also criticized by many when, in a controversial move, he pardoned Nixon for any federal crimes he might have committed as president. Ford vetoed 48 bills in his first 21 months in office, mostly in the interest of fighting high inflation; he was less successful in curbing high unemployment. In foreign policy, Ford continued to pursue détente.

Ford was narrowly defeated in the 1976 election.

JIMMY (JAMES EARL) CARTER (1977-81), 39th president, Democrat, was the first president from the Deep South since before the Civil War. He was born on Oct. 1, 1924, in Plains, GA, the son of James and Lillian Gordy Carter. Carter graduated from the U.S. Naval Academy in 1946 and in 1952 entered the navy's nuclear submarine program as an aide to Capt. (later Adm.) Hyman Rickover. He studied nuclear physics at Union College. Carter's father died in 1953, and he left the navy to take over the family peanut farming businesses. He served in the Georgia state senate (1963-67) and as governor of Georgia (1971-75). In 1976, Carter won the Democratic nomination and defeated President Gerald R. Ford.

On his first full day in office, Carter pardoned all Vietnam draft evaders. He played a major role in the negotiations leading to the 1979 peace treaty between Israel and Egypt, and he won passage of new treaties with Panama providing for U.S. control of the Panama Canal to end in 2000. However, Carter was widely criticized for the poor state of the economy and was viewed by some as weak in his handling of foreign policy. In Nov. 1979, Iranian student militants attacked the U.S. embassy in Tehran and held members of the embassy staff hostage. Efforts to obtain release of the hostages were a major preoccupation during the rest of his term. He reacted to the Soviet invasion of Afghanistan by imposing a grain embargo and boycotting the Moscow Olympic Games.

Carter was defeated by Ronald Reagan in the 1980 election. The American hostages were finally released on Inauguration Day, 1981, just after Reagan officially became president. After leaving office, Carter was active in humanitarian efforts and in seeking to mediate international disputes. In large part for his diplomatic efforts in office and subsequently, he was awarded the Nobel Peace Prize in 2002.

RONALD WILSON REAGAN (1981-89), 40th president, Republican, was born on Feb. 6, 1911, in Tampico, IL, the son of John Edward and Nellie Wilson Reagan. Reagan graduated from Eureka College in 1932, after which he worked as a sports announcer in Des Moines, IA. He began a successful career as an actor in 1937, starring in numerous movies, and later in television, until the 1960s. He served as president of the Screen Actors Guild from 1947 to 1952 and in 1959-60. Reagan was elected governor of California in 1966 and reelected in 1970.

In 1980, Reagan gained the Republican presidential nomination and won a landslide victory over Jimmy Carter. He was easily reelected in 1984. Reagan successfully forged a bipartisan coalition in Congress, which led to enactment of his program of large-scale tax cuts, cutbacks in many government programs, and a major defense buildup. He signed a Social Security reform bill designed to provide for the long-term solvency of the system. In 1986, he signed into law a major tax-reform bill. He was shot and wounded in an assassination attempt in 1981.

 IT'S A FACT: Gerald Ford was the only person to serve as both vice president and president without having been elected to either office. In accordance with the 25th Amendment (ratified 1967), Pres. Nixon appointed Ford, then House minority leader, as vice president in Oct. 1973 after the resignation of Spiro Agnew; when Nixon resigned, in Aug. 1974, Ford succeeded him.

In 1982, the U.S. joined France and Italy in maintaining a peacekeeping force in Beirut, Lebanon, and the next year Reagan sent a task force to invade the island of Grenada after 2 Marxist coups there. Reagan's opposition to international terrorism led to the U.S. bombing of Libyan military installations in 1986. He strongly supported El Salvador, the Nicaraguan contras, and other anti-communist governments and forces throughout the world. He also held 4 summit meetings with Soviet leader Mikhail Gorbachev. At the 1987 meeting in Washington, DC, a historic treaty eliminating short- and medium-range missiles from Europe was signed.

Reagan faced a crisis in 1986-87, when it was revealed that the U.S. had sold weapons through Israeli brokers to Iran in exchange for release of U.S. hostages being held in Lebanon and that subsequently some of the money was diverted to the Nicaraguan contras (Congress had barred U.S. aid to the contras). The scandal led to the resignation of leading White House aides. As Reagan left office in Jan. 1989, the nation was experiencing its 6th consecutive year of economic prosperity. Over the same period, however, the federal government recorded large budget deficits. In 1994, in a letter to the American people, Reagan revealed that he was suffering from Alzheimer's disease.

GEORGE HERBERT WALKER BUSH (1989-93), 41st president, Republican, was born on June 12, 1924, in Milton, MA, the son of Prescott and Dorothy Walker Bush. He served as a U.S. Navy pilot in World War II. After graduating from Yale University in 1948, he settled in Texas, where, in 1953, he helped found an oil company. After losing a bid for a U.S. Senate seat in Texas in 1964, he was elected to the House of Representatives in 1966 and 1968. He lost a 2nd U.S. Senate race in 1970. Subsequently he served as U.S. ambassador to the United Nations (1971-73), headed the U.S. Liaison Office in Beijing (1974-75), and was director of central intelligence (1976-77).

Following an unsuccessful bid for the 1980 Republican presidential nomination, Bush was chosen by Ronald Reagan as his vice presidential running mate. He served as U.S. vice president from 1981 to 1989.

In 1988, Bush gained the GOP presidential nomination and defeated Michael Dukakis in the November election. Bush took office faced with U.S. budget and trade deficits as well as the rescue of insolvent U.S. savings and loan institutions. He faced a severe budget deficit annually, struggled with military cutbacks in light of reduced cold war tensions, and vetoed abortion-rights legislation. In 1990 he agreed to a budget deficit-reduction plan that included tax hikes.

Bush supported Soviet reforms, Eastern Europe democratization, and good relations with Beijing. In Dec. 1989, Bush sent troops to Panama; they overthrew the government and captured strongman Gen. Manuel Noriega.

Bush reacted to Iraq's Aug. 1990 invasion of Kuwait by sending U.S. forces to the Persian Gulf area and assembling a UN-backed coalition, including NATO and Arab League members. After a month-long air war, in Feb. 1991, Allied forces retook Kuwait in a 4-day ground assault. The quick victory, with extremely light casualties on the U.S. side, gave Bush at the time one of the highest presidential approval ratings in history. His popularity plummeted by the end of 1991, however, as the economy slipped into recession. He was defeated by Bill Clinton in the 1992 election.

BILL (WILLIAM JEFFERSON) CLINTON (1993-2001), 42nd president, Democrat, was born on Aug. 19, 1946, in Hope, AR, son of William Blythe and Virginia Cassidy Blythe, and was named William Jefferson Blythe IV. Blythe died in an automobile accident before his son was born. His widow married Roger Clinton, and at the age of 16, William Jefferson Blythe IV changed his last name to Clinton.

Clinton became interested in politics in high school and went on to Georgetown University in Washington, DC, where he graduated with high honors in 1968. He then attended Oxford University for 2 years as a Rhodes scholar. During that time he legally avoided the draft and possible service in Vietnam, according to some critics by misleading his draft board. He went on to earn a degree from Yale Law School in 1973.

Clinton worked on George McGovern's 1972 presidential campaign. He taught at the University of Arkansas from 1973 to 1976, when he was elected state attorney general. In 1978, he was elected governor, becoming the nation's youngest. Defeated for reelection in 1980, he was returned to office several times thereafter. He married Hillary Rodham in 1975.

Despite some issues raised about his character, Clinton won most of the 1992 presidential primaries, moving his party toward the center as he tried to broaden his appeal; as the party's presidential nominee he defeated Pres. George H.W. Bush and Reform Party candidate Ross Perot in the November election. In 1993, Clinton won passage of a measure to reduce the federal budget deficit and won congressional approval of the North American Free Trade Agreement. His administration's plan for major health-care reform legislation died in Congress. After 1994 midterm elections, Clinton faced Republican majorities in both houses of Congress. He followed a centrist course at home, sent troops to Bosnia to help implement a peace settlement, and cultivated relations with Russia and China.

Though accused of improprieties in his involvement in an Arkansas real estate venture (Whitewater), Clinton easily won reelection in 1996, and an independent prosecutor found insufficient evidence of any criminality by Clinton or his wife. In 1997 he reached agreement with Congress on legislation to balance the federal budget by 2002. In 1998, Clinton became the 2nd U.S. president ever to be impeached by the House of Representatives. Charged with perjury and obstruction of justice in connection with an attempted cover-up of a sexual relationship with a former White House intern, Monica Lewinsky, he was acquitted by the Senate in 1999. He retained wide popularity, aided by a strong economy.

In 1999, the United States, under Clinton, joined other NATO nations in an aerial bombing campaign that induced Serbia to withdraw troops from the Kosovo region, where they had been terrorizing ethnic Albanians. In 2000 he became the 1st president since the Vietnam war to visit Vietnam.

After leaving office, Clinton remained active in political affairs and encouraged the career of his wife, who was elected in 2000 to the U.S. Senate from New York.

GEORGE WALKER BUSH (2001-), 43rd president, Republican, was born on July 6, 1946, in New Haven, CT. He was the first of six children born to George Herbert Walker Bush and his wife, the former Barbara Pierce, a descendant of Pres. Franklin Pierce. (His brother Jeb won the Florida governorship in 1998.) Bush was the first son of a former president to win the White House since John Quincy Adams.

Fun-loving, athletic, and popular, the young George Bush grew up in Midland and Houston, TX. In 1961 he was sent to the Phillips Academy in Andover, MA, the same prep school his father had attended. In 1964 he entered Yale University, his father's alma mater, where he majored in history. Eligible for the draft upon graduation, he signed on with the Texas Air National Guard. After earning a master's degree from the Harvard Business School, he returned to Midland in 1975 and went into the oil business. Two years later he married Laura Welch, a schoolteacher and librarian; in 1981 she gave birth to twin daughters.

Bush, who had lost a race for Congress in 1978, returned to the oil business, but success proved elusive. Realizing that he had a drinking problem, he swore off alcohol and renewed commitment to Christian faith. After aiding in his father's successful 1988 presidential campaign, he put together a group of investors to buy the Texas Rangers baseball club and took a hands-on role as managing partner. Bush ran for governor in 1994, defeating a popular incumbent, Ann Richards. He won reelection by a landslide in 1998. As governor, he concentrated on building personal bonds with Democratic leaders and backed education reforms.

After defeating Sen. John McCain of Arizona and other rivals in the Republican party primaries, Bush chose Dick Cheney, a former U.S. representative and defense secretary, as his running mate. The Nov. 2000 presidential election was one of the closest in history. While Bush came out behind in the popular vote, by about 540,000 out of more than 100 million cast, the electoral vote total hinged on the outcome in Florida, where official totals, challenged by Democrats, gave him a razor-thin lead. In December the Supreme Court in effect ended a controversial attempt to recount the vote there, and Florida's 25 electoral votes decided the election in Bush's favor.

Among the issues Bush had campaigned on was that of lowering federal taxes, and in May 2001 he won approval from Congress for a large tax cut package.

On Sept. 11, 2001, Bush was faced with a crisis that would redefine his presidency. In a terrorist attack, 2 hijacked jetliners crashed into the twin towers of the World Trade Center in New York City, which were destroyed; another jet struck the Pentagon near Washington, DC, with a 4th crashing in rural Pennsylvania. Some 3,000 people were killed in the attack. The president vowed to punish those responsible, and in a "war against terrorism," the U.S. military attacked and deposed the Taliban regime in Afghanistan's capital, which was sheltering elements of the al-Qaeda terrorist network, held responsible for the attacks. However, Taliban and al-Qaeda continued to function in parts of Afghanistan, and al-Qaeda was blamed for continuing terrorist acts in a number of countries. In 2002 Bush won congressional approval to create a cabinet-level department for homeland security.

Bush met in May 2002 with Russian Pres. Vladimir Putin in Moscow, where they signed a pact cutting nuclear armaments in each country. In July, with corporate scandals and a slumping stock market fueling demands for tighter regulation of business, Bush signed legislation aimed at curbing abuses.

In March 2003, the United States, aided mainly by forces from Great Britain, launched an air and ground war against Iraq and successfully deposed the dictatorial regime of Pres. Saddam Hussein, with relatively few casualties on the U.S. side. The regime was accused of harboring weapons of mass destruction and other violations of UN resolutions; critics of the U.S. action disputed that Iraq represented an imminent threat and accused the administration of deception. After the war, Bush sought to promote a "road map" for peace in the Middle East. North Korea's nuclear weapons program also represented a major foreign policy challenge.

On the domestic front, the administration won passage of new tax cuts which Bush maintained would provide a strong stimulus to the economy. As of mid-2003, Bush was considered a strong candidate for reelection in 2004.

Wives and Children of the Presidents

Name (Born–died; married)	State	Sons/ Daughters	Name (Born–died; married)	State	Sons/ Daughters
Martha Dandridge Custis Washington (1731-1802; 1759)	VA	None	Caroline Lavinia Scott Harrison (1832-92; 1853)	OH	1/1
Abigail Smith Adams (1744-1818; 1764)	MA	3/2	Mary Scott Lord Dimmick Harrison (1858-1948; 1896)	PA	0/1
Martha Wayles Skelton Jefferson (1748-82; 1772)	VA	1/5	Ida Saxton McKinley (1847-1907; 1871)	OH	0/2
Dorothea "Dolley" Payne Todd Madison (1768-1849; 1794)	NC	None	Alice Hathaway Lee Roosevelt (1861-84; 1880)	MA	0/1
Elizabeth Kortright Monroe (1768-1830; 1786)	NY	0/2 (A)	Edith Kermit Carow Roosevelt (1861-1948; 1886)	CT	4/1
Louisa Catherine Johnson Adams (1775-1852; 1797)	MD (B)	3/1	Helen Herron Taft (1861-1943; 1886)	OH	2/1
Rachel Donelson Robards Jackson (1767-1828; 1791)	VA	None	Ellen Louise Axson Wilson (1860-1914; 1885)	GA	0/3
Hannah Hoes Van Buren (1783-1819; 1807)	NY	4/0	Edith Bolling Galt Wilson (1872-1961; 1915)	VA	None
Anna Tuthill Symmes Harrison (1775-1864; 1795)	NJ	6/4	Florence Kling De Wolfe Harding (1860-1924; 1891)	OH	None
Letitia Christian Tyler (1790-1842; 1813)	VA	3/4(A)	Grace Anna Goodhue Coolidge (1879-1957; 1905)	VT	2/0
Julia Gardiner Tyler (1820-89; 1844)	NY	5/2	Lou Henry Hoover (1875-1944; 1899)	IA	2/0
Sarah Childress Polk (1803-91; 1824)	TN	None	Anna Eleanor Roosevelt Roosevelt (1884-1962; 1905)	NY	4/1(A)
Margaret Mackall Smith Taylor (1788-1852; 1810)	MD	1/5	Elizabeth Virginia "Bess" Wallace Truman (1885-1982; 1919)	MO	0/1
Abigail Powers Fillmore (1798-1853; 1826)	NY	1/1	Mamie Geneva Doud Eisenhower (1896-1979; 1916)	IA	1/0(A)
Caroline Carmichael McIntosh Fillmore (1813-81; 1858)	NJ	None	Jacqueline Lee Bouvier Kennedy (1929-94; 1953)	NY	1/1(A)
Jane Means Appleton Pierce (1806-63; 1834)	NH	3/0	Claudia "Lady Bird" Alta Taylor Johnson (1912; 1934)	TX	0/2
Mary Todd Lincoln (1818-82; 1842)	KY	4/0	Thelma Catherine Patricia Ryan Nixon (1912-1993; 1940)	NV	0/2
Eliza McCardle Johnson (1810-76; 1827)	TN	3/2	Elizabeth Bloomer Warren Ford (1918; 1948)	IL	3/1
Julia Boggs Dent Grant (1826-1902; 1848)	MO	3/1	Rosalynn Smith Carter (1927; 1946)	GA	3/1
Lucy Ware Webb Hayes (1831-89; 1852)	OH	7/1	Anne Frances "Nancy" Robbins Davis Reagan (1921; 1952)	NY	1/1(C)
Lucretia Randolph Garfield (1832-1918; 1858)	OH	4/1	Barbara Pierce Bush (1925; 1945)	NY	4/2
Ellen Lewis Herndon Arthur (1837-80; 1859)	VA	2/1	Hillary Rodham Clinton (1947; 1975)	IL	0/1
Frances Folsom Cleveland (1864-1947; 1886)	NY	2/3	Laura Welch Bush (1946; 1977)	TX	0/2

NOTE: Pres. Buchanan was unmarried. (A) plus 1 infant, deceased. (B) Born in London, father a MD citizen. (C) Pres. Reagan married and divorced Jane Wyman; they had a daughter who died in infancy, and a son and daughter who lived past infancy.

First Lady Laura Welch Bush

Laura Welch Bush was born in Midland, TX, Nov. 4, 1946. She graduated from Southern Methodist University, earned a master's in library science at the Univ. of Texas at Austin, and became a librarian and teacher in Texas public schools. She and George W. Bush were married in 1977; in 1981, their twin daughters, Jenna and Barbara, were born.

As First Lady of Texas from 1995 to 2001, Laura Bush stressed advocacy of educational reform and literacy programs. She launched an early childhood development initiative and also worked to promote breast cancer awareness.

Laura Bush's first solo appearance as First Lady came at the launch of D.C. Teaching Fellows, a program encouraging professionals to become teachers. In Nov. 2001 she became the first First Lady to give a speech of her own in place of the president's weekly radio address. Laura Bush planned a poetry symposium for Feb. 2003, but it was postponed indefinitely for fear it would be politicized by opponents of the Iraq war. During 2003 the First Lady made fund-raising appearances, and she accompanied the president on a tour of Africa in July.

Burial Places of the Presidents

President	Burial Place	President	Burial Place	President	Burial Place
Washington	Mt. Vernon, VA	Fillmore	Buffalo, NY	T. Roosevelt	Oyster Bay, NY
J. Adams	Quincy, MA	Pierce	Concord, NH	Taft	Arlington Natl. Cemetery
Jefferson	Charlottesville, VA	Buchanan	Lancaster, PA	Wilson	Wash. Natl. Cathedral
Madison	Montpelier Station, VA	Lincoln	Springfield, IL	Harding	Marion, OH
Monroe	Richmond, VA	A. Johnson	Greeneville, TN	Coolidge	Plymouth, VT
J. Q. Adams	Quincy, MA	Grant	New York, NY	Hoover	West Branch, IA
Jackson	Nashville, TN	Hayes	Fremont, OH	F. Roosevelt	Hyde Park, NY
Van Buren	Kinderhook, NY	Garfield	Cleveland, OH	Truman	Independence, MO
W. H. Harrison	North Bend, OH	Arthur	Albany, NY	Eisenhower	Abilene, KS
Tyler	Richmond, VA	Cleveland	Princeton, NJ	Kennedy	Arlington Natl. Cemetery
Polk	Nashville, TN	B. Harrison	Indianapolis, IN	L. B. Johnson	Johnson City, TX
Taylor	Louisville, KY	McKinley	Canton, OH	Nixon	Yorba Linda, CA

Presidential Facts

First president to live in the White House: John Adams, who moved there in 1800

First president inaugurated in Washington, DC: Thomas Jefferson, in 1801

First president born a U.S. citizen: Martin Van Buren, in Kinderhook, NY; 1782

First president born outside the original colonies: Abraham Lincoln, in Kentucky, 1809

First president born west of the Mississippi River: Herbert Hoover, in 1874

First president of all 50 states: Dwight D. Eisenhower, first inaugurated in 1953

First president to be photographed while in office: James K. Polk, in 1849

First president to use electricity in the White House: Benjamin Harrison, in 1891; but he and his wife were afraid to touch the switches for fear of getting a shock

First president to leave the continental U.S. while in office: Theodore Roosevelt, in 1906, on a visit to inspect construction work on the Panama Canal

First president to ride in an airplane: Theodore Roosevelt, in 1910, a year after leaving office, when he took a 4-minute ride in a Wright brothers' plane

First president to address the nation on radio: Warren G. Harding, in 1922

First president to appear on TV: Franklin D. Roosevelt, at opening ceremonies for the 1939 World's Fair

First president to speak from the White House on TV: Harry S. Truman, in 1947

First president to give a live, televised news conference: John F. Kennedy, in 1961

Only president elected unanimously: George Washington, by 63 electoral votes

Only presidents who lost the popular vote while winning election: Rutherford B. Hayes, in 1876; Benjamin Harrison, in 1888; George W. Bush, in 2000

Only presidents chosen by the House of Representatives: Thomas Jefferson (1st term) and John Quincy Adams

Only presidents to graduate from West Point: Ulysses S. Grant and Dwight D. Eisenhower

Only president with a Ph.D.: Woodrow Wilson; received a doctorate in political science from Johns Hopkins Univ. in 1886

Only president to serve in the Senate after leaving office: Andrew Johnson

Only president to serve in the House of Representatives after leaving office: John Quincy Adams

Only president to also serve as chief justice of the U.S.: William Howard Taft

Presidents who died on July 4: John Adams and Thomas Jefferson (both 1826) and James Monroe (1831)

Presidents who died in office: Eight presidents have died in office. Of these, 4 were assassinated: Abraham Lincoln, James Garfield, William McKinley, and John F. Kennedy. The other 4 were William Henry Harrison, Zachary Taylor, Warren G. Harding, and Franklin D. Roosevelt

Presidential Libraries

The libraries listed here, except for that of Richard Nixon (which is private), are coordinated by the National Archives and Records Administration (Website: www.archives.gov/presidential_libraries/index.html). NARA also has custody of the Nixon presidential historical materials and those of Bill Clinton. The William J. Clinton Library was under construction in 2003. NARA will release Clinton presidential records to the public at the Clinton Library beginning Jan. 20, 2006. Materials for presidents before Herbert Hoover are held by private institutions.

Herbert Hoover Library
210 Parkside Dr., Box 488
West Branch, IA 52358-9685
PHONE: 319-643-5301
E-MAIL: hoover.library@nara.gov
WEBSITE: www.hoover.archives.gov

Franklin D. Roosevelt Library
4079 Albany Post Rd.
Hyde Park, NY 12538-1990
PHONE: 845-486-7770; 1-800-FDR-VISIT
E-MAIL: roosevelt.library@nara.gov
WEBSITE: www.fdrlibrary.marist.edu

Harry S. Truman Library
500 West U.S. Hwy. 24
Independence, MO 64050-2481
PHONE: 816-833-1400; 1-800-833-1225
E-MAIL: truman.library@nara.gov
WEBSITE: www.trumanlibrary.org

Dwight D. Eisenhower Library
200 S.E. 4th St.
Abilene, KS 67410-2900
PHONE: 785-263-4751; 1-800-RING-IKE
E-MAIL: eisenhower.library@nara.gov
WEBSITE: www.eisenhower.archives.gov

John Fitzgerald Kennedy Library
Columbia Pt.
Boston, MA 02125-3398
PHONE: 617-514-1600; 1-866-JFK-1960
E-MAIL: kennedy.library@nara.gov
WEBSITE: www.jfklibrary.org

Lyndon Baines Johnson Library
2313 Red River St.
Austin, TX 78705-5702
PHONE: 512-721-0200
E-MAIL: johnson.library@nara.gov
WEBSITE: www.lbjlib.utexas.edu

Richard Nixon Library & Birthplace
18001 Yorba Linda Blvd.
Yorba Linda, CA 92886
PHONE: 714-993-5075
E-MAIL: archives@nixonlibrary.org
WEBSITE: www.nixonfoundation.org

Gerald R. Ford Library
1000 Beal Ave.
Ann Arbor, MI 48109-2114
PHONE: 734-205-0555
E-MAIL: ford.library@nara.gov
WEBSITE: www.ford.utexas.edu

Jimmy Carter Library
441 Freedom Pkwy.
Atlanta, GA 30307-1496
PHONE: 404-331-3942
E-MAIL: carter.library@nara.gov
WEBSITE: www.jimmycarterlibrary.org

Ronald Reagan Library
40 Presidential Dr.
Simi Valley, CA 93065-0600
PHONE: 800-410-8354
E-MAIL: reagan.library@nara.gov
WEBSITE: www.reagan.utexas.edu

George H. W. Bush Library
1000 George Bush Dr. West
College Station, TX 77845
PHONE: 979-691-4000
E-MAIL: library.bush@nara.gov
WEBSITE: bushlibrary.tamu.edu

William J. Clinton Library
1000 La Harpe Blvd.
Little Rock, AR 72201
PHONE: 501-244-9756
E-MAIL: clinton.library@nara.gov
WEBSITE: www.clinton.archives.gov

Impeachment in U.S. History

The U.S. Constitution provides for impeachment and removal from office of federal officials on grounds of "Treason, Bribery, or other high Crimes and Misdemeanors" (Article II, Sect. 4). Impeachment is the bringing of charges by the House of Representatives. It is followed by a Senate trial; a two-thirds Senate vote is needed for conviction and removal from office.

In 1868, Andrew Johnson became the first president impeached by the House; he was tried but not convicted by the Senate. In 1974, impeachment articles against Pres. Richard Nixon, in connection with the Watergate scandal, were voted by the House Judiciary Committee; he resigned Aug. 9, before the full House could vote on impeaching him. In 1998, Pres. Bill Clinton was impeached by the House in connection with covering up a relationship with a former White House intern; he was tried in the Senate in 1999 and acquitted.

PRESIDENTIAL ELECTIONS

Popular and Electoral Vote, 1996 and 2000

Source: Voter News Service; Federal Election Commission; totals are official.

	2000								1996					
	Electoral Vote				Democrat	Republican	Green[1]	Reform[2]	Electoral Vote			Democrat	Republican	Reform[2]
State	Gore	Bush	Nader	Buchanan	Gore	Bush	Nader	Buchanan	Clinton	Dole	Perot	Clinton	Dole	Perot
AL	0	9	0	0	692,611	941,173	18,323	6,351	0	9	0	662,165	769,044	92,149
AK	0	3	0	0	79,004	167,398	28,747	5,192	0	3	0	80,380	122,746	26,333
AZ	0	8	0	0	685,341	781,652	45,645	12,373	8	0	0	653,288	622,073	112,072
AR	0	6	0	0	422,768	472,940	13,421	7,358	6	0	0	475,171	325,416	69,884
CA	54	0	0	0	5,861,203	4,567,429	418,707	44,987	54	0	0	5,119,835	3,828,380	697,847
CO	0	8	0	0	738,227	883,748	91,434	10,465	0	8	0	671,152	691,848	99,629
CT	8	0	0	0	816,015	561,094	64,452	4,731	8	0	0	735,740	483,109	139,523
DE	3	0	0	0	180,068	137,288	8,307	777	3	0	0	140,355	99,062	28,719
DC	2[3]	0	0	—	171,923	18,073	10,576		3	0	0	158,220	17,339	3,611
FL	0	25	0	0	2,912,253	2,912,790	97,488	17,484	25	0	0	2,545,968	2,243,324	483,776
GA	0	13	—	0	1,116,230	1,419,720	—	10,926	0	13	0	1,053,849	1,080,843	146,337
HI	4	0	0	0	205,286	137,845	21,623	1,071	4	0	0	205,012	113,943	27,358
ID	0	4	—	0	138,637	336,937		7,615	0	4	0	165,443	256,595	62,518
IL	22	0	0	0	2,589,026	2,019,421	103,759	16,106	22	0	0	2,341,744	1,587,021	346,408
IN	0	12	0	0	901,980	1,245,836	—	16,959	0	12	0	887,424	1,006,693	224,299
IA	7	0	0	0	638,517	634,373	29,374	5,731	7	0	0	620,258	492,644	105,159
KS	0	6	0	0	399,276	622,332	36,086	7,370	0	6	0	387,659	583,245	92,639
KY	0	8	0	0	638,923	872,520	23,118	4,152	8	0	0	636,614	623,283	120,396
LA	0	9	0	0	792,344	927,871	20,473	14,356	9	0	0	927,837	712,586	123,293
ME	4	0	0	0	319,951	286,616	37,127	4,443	4	0	0	312,788	186,378	85,970
MD	10	0	0	0	1,144,008	813,827	53,768	4,248	10	0	0	966,207	681,530	115,812
MA	12	0	0	0	1,616,487	878,502	173,564	11,149	12	0	0	1,571,509	718,058	227,206
MI	18	0	0	—	2,170,418	1,953,139	84,165	—	18	0	0	1,989,653	1,481,212	336,670
MN	10	0	0	0	1,168,266	1,109,659	126,696	22,166	10	0	0	1,120,438	766,476	257,704
MS	0	7	0	0	404,614	572,844	8,122	2,265	0	7	0	394,022	439,838	52,222
MO	0	11	0	0	1,111,138	1,189,924	38,515	9,818	11	0	0	1,025,935	890,016	217,188
MT	0	3	0	0	137,126	240,178	24,437	5,697	0	3	0	167,922	179,652	55,229
NE	0	5	0	0	231,780	433,862	24,540	3,646	0	5	0	236,761	363,467	71,278
NV	0	4	0	0	279,978	301,575	15,008	4,747	4	0	0	203,974	199,244	43,986
NH	0	4	0	0	266,348	273,559	22,198	2,615	4	0	0	246,166	196,486	48,387
NJ	15	0	0	0	1,788,850	1,284,173	94,554	6,989	15	0	0	1,652,361	1,103,099	262,134
NM	5	0	0	0	286,783	286,417	21,251	1,392	5	0	0	273,495	232,751	32,257
NY	33	0	0	0	4,112,965	2,405,570	244,360	31,554	33	0	0	3,756,177	1,933,492	503,458
NC	0	14	—	0	1,257,692	1,631,163	—	8,874	0	14	0	1,107,849	1,225,938	168,059
ND	0	3	0	0	95,284	174,852	9,486	7,288	0	3	0	106,905	125,050	32,515
OH	0	21	0	0	2,186,190	2,351,209	117,857	26,724	21	0	0	2,148,222	1,859,883	483,207
OK	0	8	—	0	474,276	744,337	—	9,014	0	8	0	488,105	582,315	130,788
OR	7	0	0	0	720,342	713,577	77,357	7,063	7	0	0	649,641	538,152	121,221
PA	23	0	0	0	2,485,967	2,281,127	103,392	16,023	23	0	0	2,215,819	1,801,169	430,984
RI	4	0	0	0	249,508	130,555	25,052	2,273	4	0	0	233,050	104,683	43,723
SC	0	8	0	0	566,039	786,892	20,279	3,309	0	8	0	506,283	573,458	64,386
SD	0	3	—	0	118,804	190,700	—	3,322	0	3	0	139,333	150,543	31,250
TN	0	11	0	0	981,720	1,061,949	19,781	4,250	11	0	0	909,146	863,530	105,918
TX	0	32	0	0	2,433,746	3,799,639	137,994	12,394	0	32	0	2,459,683	2,736,167	378,537
UT	0	5	0	0	203,053	515,096	35,850	9,319	0	5	0	221,633	361,911	66,461
VT	3	0	0	0	149,022	119,775	20,374	2,192	3	0	0	137,894	80,352	31,024
VA	0	13	0	0	1,217,290	1,437,490	59,398	5,455	0	13	0	1,091,060	1,138,350	159,861
WA	11	0	0	0	1,247,652	1,108,864	103,002	7,171	11	0	0	1,123,323	840,712	201,003
WV	0	5	0	0	295,497	336,475	10,680	3,169	5	0	0	327,812	233,946	71,639
WI	11	0	0	0	1,242,987	1,237,279	94,070	11,446	11	0	0	1,071,971	845,029	227,339
WY	0	3	0	0	60,481	147,947	—	2,724	0	3	0	77,934	105,388	25,928
Total	266[3]	271	0	0	51,003,894	50,459,211	2,834,410	446,743	379	159	0	47,401,185	39,197,469	8,085,294

(—) = Not listed on state's ballot. (1) Listed on the ballot in some states as party other than Green. (2) Listed on the ballot in some states as party other than Reform. (3) One Washington, DC, elector abstained.

2000 Official Presidential General Election Results

Source: Voter News Service; Federal Election Commission

Candidate (Party)	Popular Vote	Percent of Popular Vote	Candidate (Party)	Popular Vote	Percent of Popular Vote
Al Gore (Democrat)	51,003,894	48.41	Monica Moorehead (Workers World)	4,795	0.00
George W. Bush (Republican)	50,459,211	47.89	David McReynolds (Socialist)	4,194	0.00
Ralph Nader (Green)	2,834,410	2.69	Cathy Gordon Brown (Independent)	1,606	0.00
Patrick J. Buchanan (Reform)	446,743	0.42	Denny Lane (Vermont Grassroots)	1,044	0.00
Harry Browne (Libertarian)	386,041	0.37	Randall Venson (Independent)	535	0.00
Howard Phillips (Constitution)	96,919	0.09	Earl F. Dodge (Prohibition)	208	0.00
John S. Hagelin (Natural Law)	83,117	0.08	Louie G. Youngkeit (Unaffiliated)	161	0.00
James E. Harris Jr. (Socialist Workers)	7,354	0.01	Write-in	20,938	0.02
L. Neil Smith (Libertarian)	5,775	0.01	None of These Candidates (Nevada)	3,315	0.00
			Total	105,360,260	100.00

Note: Party designations may vary from one state to another

PRESIDENTIAL ELECTION RETURNS BY COUNTIES

All results official. Results for New England states are for selected cities or towns. All totals statewide. D-Democrat; R-Republican; RF-Reform; I-Independent. (In 1996, Ross Perot was listed on the ballot in some states as "Independent.")

Source: Voter News Service; Federal Election Commission; Alaska Division of Elections

Alabama

County	2000 Gore (D)	2000 Bush (R)	1996 Clinton (D)	1996 Dole (R)	1996 Perot (RF)
Autauga	4,942	11,993	5,015	9,509	813
Baldwin	13,997	40,872	12,776	29,487	4,520
Barbour	2,197	1,860	4,787	3,627	515
Bibb	2,710	4,273	2,775	3,037	455
Blount	4,977	12,667	5,061	9,056	985
Bullock	3,395	1,433	3,078	1,154	111
Butler	3,606	4,127	3,828	3,352	538
Calhoun	15,781	22,306	15,725	18,088	2,613
Chambers	5,616	6,037	5,515	4,707	812
Cherokee	3,497	4,154	4,399	3,048	899
Chilton	4,806	10,066	5,354	7,910	929
Choctaw	3,707	3,600	4,074	2,623	413
Clarke	4,679	5,988	4,831	4,785	478
Clay	2,045	3,719	2,306	2,694	538
Cleburne	1,664	3,333	1,737	2,063	385
Coffee	5,220	9,938	5,168	7,805	1,042
Colbert	10,543	10,518	10,226	8,305	1,696
Conecuh	2,783	2,699	2,903	2,093	445
Coosa	2,104	2,382	2,121	1,721	262
Covington	4,440	8,961	4,543	6,035	1,098
Crenshaw	1,934	2,793	2,172	1,939	317
Cullman	9,758	19,157	9,544	14,308	2,440
Dale	4,906	10,593	4,732	8,288	1,216
Dallas	10,967	7,360	10,507	6,612	477
DeKalb	7,056	12,827	6,544	9,823	1,609
Elmore	6,652	16,777	6,530	12,937	1,368
Escambia	4,523	6,975	4,651	5,214	867
Etowah	17,433	21,087	17,976	16,835	2,529
Fayette	3,064	4,582	3,381	3,191	590
Franklin	4,793	6,119	5,028	4,449	966
Geneva	2,769	6,588	3,174	4,725	857
Greene	3,504	850	3,526	796	55
Hale	4,652	2,984	3,372	1,893	190
Henry	2,782	4,054	3,019	3,082	515
Houston	9,412	22,150	8,791	17,476	1,653
Jackson	9,066	8,475	8,204	5,650	1,573
Jefferson	129,889	138,491	120,208	130,980	7,997
Lamar	2,653	4,470	2,843	2,955	597
Lauderdale	13,875	17,478	13,619	14,058	2,574
Lawrence	6,296	5,671	5,254	3,893	964
Lee	14,574	22,433	12,919	17,985	1,949
Limestone	8,992	14,204	8,045	10,862	1,659
Lowndes	4,557	1,638	3,970	1,369	72
Macon	7,665	1,091	7,018	987	150
Madison	48,199	62,151	42,259	50,390	7,437
Marengo	4,841	4,690	4,899	4,013	337
Marion	4,600	6,910	5,049	4,742	979
Marshall	10,381	17,084	8,722	12,323	2,150
Mobile	58,640	78,162	54,749	66,775	7,555
Monroe	3,741	5,153	3,815	4,382	486
Montgomery	40,371	38,827	38,382	37,784	2,036
Morgan	16,060	25,774	14,616	21,765	3,348
Perry	4,020	1,732	4,053	1,703	119
Pickens	4,143	4,306	4,018	3,322	403
Pike	4,357	6,058	4,514	5,281	503
Randolph	3,094	4,666	3,023	3,304	603
Russell	8,396	6,198	7,834	5,025	792
St. Clair	6,485	17,117	6,187	12,762	1,417
Shelby	13,183	47,651	11,280	37,090	2,035
Sumter	4,415	1,629	4,706	1,561	172
Talladega	11,264	13,807	10,385	10,931	1,335
Tallapoosa	6,183	9,805	6,071	7,627	1,038
Tuscaloosa	24,614	34,003	23,067	27,939	3,048
Walker	11,621	13,486	12,929	9,837	2,012
Washington	3,386	4,117	3,935	2,900	819
Wilcox	3,444	1,661	3,303	1,454	71
Winston	2,692	6,413	3,120	4,728	723
Totals	**692,611**	**941,173**	**662,165**	**769,044**	**92,149**

Alabama Vote Since 1952

1952, Eisenhower, Rep., 149,231; Stevenson, Dem., 275,075; Hamblen, Proh., 1,814.

1956, Stevenson, Dem., 290,844; Eisenhower, Rep., 195,694; Independent electors, 20,323.

1960, Kennedy, Dem., 324,050; Nixon, Rep., 237,981; Faubus, States' Rights, 4,367; Decker, Proh., 2,106; King, Afro-Americans, 1,485; scattering, 236.

1964, Dem. (electors unpledged), 209,848; Goldwater, Rep., 479,085; scattering, 105.

1968, Nixon, Rep., 146,923; Humphrey, Dem., 196,579; Wallace, 3d Party 691,425; Munn, Proh., 4,022.

1972, Nixon, Rep., 728,701; McGovern, Dem., 219,108 plus 37,815 Natl. Dem. Party of Alabama; Schmitz, Conservative, 11,918; Munn., Proh., 8,551.

1976, Carter, Dem., 659,170; Ford, Rep., 504,070; Maddox, Amer. Ind., 9,198; Bubar, Proh., 6,669; Hall, Com., 1,954; MacBride, Libertarian, 1,481.

1980, Reagan, Rep., 654,192; Carter, Dem., 636,730; Anderson, Independent, 16,481; Rarick, Amer. Ind., 15,010; Clark, Libertarian, 13,318; Bubar, Statesman, 1,743; Hall, Com., 1,629; DeBerry, Soc. Workers, 1,303; McReynolds, Socialist, 1,006; Commoner, Citizens, 517.

1984, Reagan, Rep., 872,849; Mondale, Dem., 551,899; Bergland, Libertarian, 9,504.

1988, Bush, Rep., 815,576; Dukakis, Dem., 549,506; Paul, Lib., 8,460; Fulani, Ind., 3,311.

1992, Bush, Rep., 804,283; Clinton, Dem., 690,080; Perot, Ind., 183,109; Marrou, Libertarian, 5,737; Fulani, New Alliance, 2,161.

1996, Dole, Rep., 769,044; Clinton, Dem., 662,165; Perot, Ind. (Ref.), 92,149; Browne, Libertarian, 5,290; Phillips, Ind., 2,365; Hagelin, Natural Law, 1,697; Harris, Ind., 516.

2000, Bush, Rep., 941,173; Gore, Dem., 692,611; Nader, Ind., 18,323; Buchanan, Ind., 6,351; Browne, Libertarian, 5,893; Phillips, Ind., 775 Hagelin, Ind., 447.

Alaska

Election District	2000 Gore (D)	2000 Bush (R)	1996 Clinton (D)	1996 Dole (R)	1996 Perot (RF)
No. 1	1,284	4,681	1,480	4,209	696
No. 2	2,081	4,235	2,563	3,247	912
No. 3	3,693	3,135	3,724	2,671	654
No. 4	2,715	4,127	3,037	3,336	694
No. 5	1,931	3,545	2,148	2,564	826
No. 6	1,542	3,862	1,576	2,707	557
No. 7	1,893	4,868	2,177	3,517	907
No. 8	1,498	5,371	1,643	3,624	826
No. 9	1,203	4,789	1,334	3,459	727
No. 10	2,194	5,673	2,203	4,184	642
No. 11	2,043	3,960	1,946	3,073	603
No. 12	2,051	4,626	1,825	3,568	543
No. 13	2,661	3,853	2,780	3,270	608
No. 14	1,626	3,750	1,471	3,005	458
No. 15	2,106	2,453	2,178	1,974	552
No. 16	1,969	1,980	1,629	1,328	414
No. 17	2,230	4,564	1,868	3,284	633
No. 18	2,739	5,421	2,708	4,245	694
No. 19	2,350	4,619	2,014	3,159	636
No. 20	2,259	3,648	2,144	3,025	545
No. 21	2,309	3,263	2,228	2,553	557
No. 22	2,656	4,910	2,511	3,887	624
No. 23	1,282	2,961	1,071	2,127	388
No. 24	1,985	5,063	1,914	3,653	548
No. 25	1,697	5,489	1,629	4,099	691
No. 26	1,608	5,869	1,519	3,913	883
No. 27	2,199	6,714	1,887	4,384	1,122
No. 28	2,116	7,113	1,645	4,202	1,333
No. 29	2,806	4,054	3,023	3,012	658
No. 30	1,698	3,622	1,794	2,785	601
No. 31	1,831	3,326	1,903	2,721	684
No. 32	1,389	4,178	1,275	2,736	675
No. 33	1,765	5,804	1,852	4,089	759
No. 34	1,300	5,243	1,388	3,677	734
No. 35	1,208	4,278	1,447	3,016	875
No. 36	1,945	3,007	2,321	1,992	453
No. 37	1,821	2,725	2,134	1,835	456
No. 38	2,015	2,467	2,436	1,716	393
No. 39	2,282	2,321	2,692	1,618	404
No. 40	1,024	1,831	1,260	1,280	368
Totals	**79,004**	**167,398**	**80,377**	**122,744**	**26,333**

Alaska Vote Since 1960

1960, Kennedy, Dem., 29,809; Nixon, Rep., 30,953.

1964, Johnson, Dem., 44,329; Goldwater, Rep., 22,930.

1968, Nixon, Rep., 37,600; Humphrey, Dem., 35,411; Wallace, 3d Party, 10,024.

1972, Nixon, Rep., 55,349; McGovern, Dem., 32,967; Schmitz, Amer., 6,903.

1976, Carter, Dem., 44,058; Ford, Rep., 71,555; MacBride, Libertarian, 6,785.

1980, Reagan, Rep., 86,112; Carter, Dem., 41,842; Clark, Libertarian, 18,479; Anderson, Ind., 11,155; write-in, 857.

1984, Reagan, Rep., 138,377; Mondale, Dem., 62,007; Bergland, Libertarian, 6,378.

1988, Bush, Rep., 119,251; Dukakis, Dem., 72,584; Paul, Lib., 5,484; Fulani, New Alliance, 1,024.

1992, Bush, Rep., 102,000; Clinton, Dem., 78,294; Perot, Ind., 73,481; Gritz, Populist/America First, 1,379; Marrou, Libertarian, 1,378.

1996, Dole, Rep., 122,746; Clinton, Dem., 80,380; Perot, Ref., 26,333; Nader, Green, 7,597; Browne, Libertarian, 2,276; Phillips, Taxpayers, 925; Hagelin, Natural Law, 729.

2000, Bush, Rep., 167,398; Gore, Dem., 79,004; Nader, Green, 28,747; Buchanan, Reform, 5,192; Browne, Libertarian, 2,636; Hagelin, Natural Law, 919; Phillips, Constitution, 596.

Arizona

	2000		1996		
County	Gore (D)	Bush (R)	Clinton (D)	Dole (R)	Perot (RF)
Apache	13,025	5,947	12,394	4,761	1,296
Cochise	13,360	18,180	13,782	14,365	3,346
Coconino	20,280	17,562	20,475	13,638	3,666
Gila	7,700	9,158	8,577	6,407	2,211
Graham	3,355	6,007	3,938	4,222	1,034
Greenlee	1,216	1,619	1,755	1,159	426
La Paz	1,769	2,543	1,964	1,902	597
Maricopa	386,683	479,967	363,991	386,015	58,479
Mohave	17,470	24,386	16,629	17,997	6,369
Navajo	11,794	12,386	12,912	9,262	2,461
Pima	147,688	124,579	137,983	104,121	18,809
Pinal	19,650	20,122	19,579	13,034	3,972
Santa Cruz	5,233	3,344	5,241	2,256	600
Yavapai	24,063	40,144	21,801	29,921	6,649
Yuma	12,055	15,708	12,267	13,013	2,157
Totals	**685,341**	**781,652**	**653,288**	**622,073**	**112,072**

Arizona Vote Since 1952

1952, Eisenhower, Rep., 152,042; Stevenson, Dem., 108,528.

1956, Eisenhower, Rep., 176,990; Stevenson, Dem., 112,880; Andrews, Ind. 303.

1960, Kennedy, Dem., 176,781; Nixon, Rep., 221,241; Hass, Soc. Labor, 469.

1964, Johnson, Dem., 237,753; Goldwater, Rep., 242,535; Hass, Soc. Labor, 482.

1968, Nixon, Rep., 266,721; Humphrey, Dem., 170,514; Wallace, 3d Party, 46,573; McCarthy, New Party, 2,751; Halstead, Soc. Workers, 85; Cleaver, Peace and Freedom, 217; Blomen, Soc. Labor, 75.

1972, Nixon, Rep., 402,812; McGovern, Dem., 198,540; Schmitz, Amer., 21,208; Soc. Workers, 30,945. Because of ballot peculiarities in 3 counties (particularly Pima), thousands of voters cast ballots for the Soc. Workers Party and one of the major candidates. Court ordered both votes counted as official.

1976, Carter, Dem., 295,602; Ford, Rep., 418,642; McCarthy, Ind., 19,229; MacBride, Libertarian, 7,647; Camejo, Soc. Workers, 928; Anderson, Amer., 564; Maddox, Amer. Ind., 85.

1980, Reagan, Rep., 529,688; Carter, Dem., 246,843; Anderson, Ind., 76,952; Clark, Libertarian, 18,784; De Berry, Soc. Workers, 1,100; Commoner, Citizens, 551; Hall, Com., 25; Griswold, Workers World, 2.

1984, Reagan, Rep., 681,416; Mondale, Dem., 333,854; Bergland, Libertarian, 10,585.

1988, Bush, Rep., 702,541; Dukakis, Dem., 454,029; Paul, Lib., 13,351; Fulani, New Alliance, 1,662.

1992, Bush, Rep., 572,086; Clinton, Dem., 543,050; Perot, Ind., 353,741; Gritz, Populist/America First, 8,141; Marrou, Libertarian, 6,759; Hagelin, Natural Law, 2,267.

1996, Clinton, Dem., 653,288; Dole, Rep., 622,073; Perot, Ref., 112,072; Browne, Libertarian, 14,358.

2000, Bush, Rep., 781,652; Gore, Dem., 685,341; Nader, Green, 45,645; Buchanan, Reform, 12,373; Smith, Libertarian, 5,775; Hagelin, Natural Law, 1,120.

Arkansas

	2000		1996		
County	Gore (D)	Bush (R)	Clinton (D)	Dole (R)	Perot (RF)
Arkansas	2,877	3,353	4,220	1,910	463
Ashley	4,253	3,876	5,011	2,428	704
Baxter	6,516	9,538	6,703	6,877	1,572
Benton	17,277	34,838	17,205	23,748	4,147
Boone	4,493	8,569	5,745	6,093	1,132
Bradley	2,122	1,793	2,566	1,146	221
Calhoun	1,017	1,128	1,306	727	237
Carroll	3,595	5,556	3,689	3,957	986
Chicot	2,820	1,564	3,090	1,056	233
Clark	4,661	3,776	5,281	2,112	567
Clay	3,527	2,254	3,848	1,512	464
Cleburne	4,120	5,730	4,475	3,807	1,021
Cleveland	1,414	1,678	1,741	990	268

	2000		1996		
County	Gore (D)	Bush (R)	Clinton (D)	Dole (R)	Perot (RF)
Columbia	4,003	5,018	4,730	3,376	678
Conway	3,496	3,545	4,055	2,307	746
Craighead	12,376	12,158	13,284	9,210	1,778
Crawford	6,288	10,804	6,749	7,182	1,683
Crittenden	7,224	5,857	8,415	4,673	554
Cross	3,096	3,033	3,631	2,000	466
Dallas	1,710	1,571	2,118	1,041	236
Desha	2,776	1,603	3,230	978	247
Drew	3,060	2,756	3,570	1,657	395
Faulkner	11,950	16,055	12,032	10,178	1,528
Franklin	2,674	3,277	3,269	2,246	626
Fulton	1,976	2,036	2,361	1,351	455
Garland	15,840	19,098	19,211	13,662	2,769
Grant	2,535	3,285	2,948	1,925	557
Greene	6,319	5,831	6,622	3,757	1,014
Hempstead	3,937	3,257	4,983	2,021	501
Hot Spring	5,527	5,042	6,002	2,864	1,123
Howard	2,063	2,326	2,741	1,478	369
Independence	5,146	6,145	6,240	4,021	1,126
Izard	2,587	2,301	2,818	1,678	541
Jackson	3,651	2,280	4,304	1,525	611
Jefferson	17,716	8,765	19,701	6,330	1,284
Johnson	3,270	3,657	3,585	2,367	757
Lafayette	1,806	1,538	2,466	971	374
Lawrence	3,255	2,626	3,652	1,823	609
Lee	2,727	1,351	3,267	1,013	257
Lincoln	1,957	1,526	2,517	907	221
Little River	2,883	2,283	3,183	1,409	480
Logan	3,283	4,487	3,832	2,966	1,048
Lonoke	6,851	10,606	8,049	6,414	1,369
Madison	2,055	3,387	2,504	2,303	461
Marion	2,233	3,402	2,735	2,312	764
Miller	6,278	7,276	6,469	4,874	1,043
Mississippi	7,107	5,199	8,301	3,919	1,016
Monroe	1,910	1,329	2,247	973	202
Montgomery	1,438	2,128	1,830	1,137	427
Nevada	1,867	1,796	2,279	976	345
Newton	1,205	2,529	1,631	1,927	498
Ouachita	5,464	4,739	6,635	3,136	733
Perry	1,648	2,114	1,873	1,143	395
Phillips	6,018	3,154	5,715	2,205	461
Pike	1,604	2,275	2,362	1,401	441
Poinsett	4,102	2,988	4,686	2,034	647
Polk	2,315	4,600	2,824	2,852	876
Pope	6,669	11,244	8,433	8,243	1,891
Prairie	1,563	1,862	2,211	1,025	305
Pulaski	68,320	55,866	75,084	44,780	6,014
Randolph	3,019	2,673	3,213	1,789	561
St. Francis	4,986	3,414	5,562	2,523	506
Saline	12,700	18,617	14,027	11,695	2,612
Scott	1,444	2,399	2,259	1,426	513
Searcy	1,229	2,610	1,669	1,786	381
Sebastian	15,555	23,483	15,514	16,482	2,899
Sevier	2,095	2,111	2,553	1,379	446
Sharp	3,236	3,698	3,573	2,635	687
Stone	2,043	2,623	2,227	1,526	579
Union	6,261	8,647	8,373	6,053	1,073
Van Buren	3,202	3,485	3,521	2,345	830
Washington	21,425	28,231	20,419	19,476	3,133
White	8,342	13,170	10,204	8,659	1,828
Woodruff	1,699	898	2,044	598	186
Yell	3,062	3,223	3,794	2,111	714
Totals	**422,768**	**472,940**	**475,171**	**325,416**	**69,884**

Arkansas Vote Since 1952

1952, Eisenhower, Rep., 177,155; Stevenson, Dem., 226,300; Hamblen, Proh., 886; MacArthur, Christian Nationalist, 458; Hass, Soc. Labor, 1.

1956, Stevenson, Dem., 213,277; Eisenhower, Rep., 186,287; Andrews, Ind., 7,008.

1960, Kennedy, Dem., 215,049; Nixon, Rep., 184,508; Natl. States' Rights, 28,952.

1964, Johnson, Dem., 314,197; Goldwater, Rep., 243,264; Kasper, Natl. States' Rights, 2,965.

1968, Nixon, Rep., 189,062; Humphrey, Dem., 184,901; Wallace, 3d Party, 235,627.

1972, Nixon, Rep., 445,751; McGovern, Dem., 198,899; Schmitz, Amer., 3,016.

1976, Carter, Dem., 498,604; Ford, Rep., 267,903; McCarthy, Ind., 639; Anderson, Amer., 389.

1980, Reagan, Rep., 403,164; Carter, Dem., 398,041; Anderson, Ind., 22,468; Clark, Libertarian, 8,970; Commoner, Citizens, 2,345; Bubar, Statesman, 1,350; Hall, Com., 1,244.

1984, Reagan, Rep., 534,774; Mondale, Dem., 338,646; Bergland, Libertarian, 2,220.

1988, Bush, Rep., 466,578; Dukakis, Dem., 349,237; Duke, Chr. Pop., 5,146; Paul, Lib., 3,297.

1992, Clinton, Dem., 505,823; Bush, Rep., 337,324; Perot, Ind., 99,132; Phillips, U.S. Taxpayers, 1,437; Marrou, Libertarian, 1,261; Fulani, New Alliance, 1,022.

1996, Clinton, Dem., 475,171; Dole, Rep., 325,416; Perot, Ref., 69,884; Nader, Ind., 3,649; Browne, Ind., 3,076; Phillips, Ind., 2,065; Forbes, Ind., 932; Collins, Ind., 823; Masters, Ind., 749; Hagelin, Ind., 729; Moorehead, Ind., 747; Hollis, Ind., 538; Dodge, Ind., 483.

2000, Bush, Rep., 472,940; Gore, Dem., 422,768; Nader, Green, 13,421; Buchanan, Reform, 7,358; Browne, Libertarian, 2,781; Phillips, Constitution, 1,415; Hagelin, Natural Law, 1,098.

California

County	2000 Gore (D)	Bush (R)	1996 Clinton (D)	Dole (R)	Perot (RF)
Alameda ...	342,889	119,279	303,903	106,581	24,270
Alpine	265	281	258	264	63
Amador	5,906	8,766	5,868	6,870	1,267
Butte	31,338	45,584	30,651	38,961	6,393
Calaveras ..	7,093	10,599	6,646	8,279	1,612
Colusa	1,745	3,629	2,054	3,047	404
Contra Costa	224,338	141,373	196,512	123,954	20,416
Del Norte...	3,117	4,526	3,652	3,670	1,225
El Dorado ..	26,220	42,045	22,957	32,759	5,077
Fresno	95,059	117,342	94,448	98,813	10,962
Glenn	2,498	5,795	2,841	5,041	788
Humboldt. ..	24,851	23,219	24,628	19,803	5,811
Imperial	15,489	12,524	14,591	9,705	1,778
Inyo	2,652	4,713	2,601	3,924	811
Kern.......	66,003	110,663	62,658	92,151	13,452
Kings	11,041	16,377	11,254	12,368	1,745
Lake	10,717	8,699	10,432	7,458	2,539
Lassen	2,982	7,080	3,318	5,194	1,080
Los Angeles	1,710,505	871,930	1,430,629	746,544	157,752
Madera	11,650	20,283	11,254	16,510	2,192
Marin	79,135	34,872	67,406	32,714	6,559
Mariposa ...	2,816	4,727	2,920	3,976	729
Mendocino..	16,634	12,272	14,952	9,765	3,685
Merced	22,726	26,102	21,786	20,847	3,427
Modoc	945	2,969	1,368	2,285	528
Mono......	1,788	2,296	1,580	1,882	447
Monterey ...	67,618	43,761	57,700	39,794	7,240
Napa	28,097	20,633	24,588	17,439	4,254
Nevada	17,670	25,998	15,369	21,784	3,330
Orange	391,819	541,299	327,485	446,717	66,195
Placer	42,449	69,835	34,981	49,808	6,542
Plumas	3,458	6,343	3,540	4,905	919
Riverside ...	202,576	231,955	168,579	178,611	35,481
Sacramento .	212,792	195,619	203,019	166,049	23,856
San Benito..	9,131	7,015	7,030	5,384	1,044
San Bernardino	214,749	221,757	183,372	180,135	39,330
San Diego ..	437,666	475,736	389,964	402,876	63,037
San Francisco .	241,578	51,496	209,777	45,479	9,659
San Joaquin	79,776	81,773	67,253	65,131	9,692
San Luis Obispo	44,526	56,859	40,395	46,733	8,204
San Mateo .	166,757	80,296	152,304	73,508	15,047
Santa Barbara ..	73,411	71,493	70,650	63,915	9,457
Santa Clara	332,490	188,750	297,639	168,291	34,908
Santa Cruz .	66,618	29,627	58,250	27,766	6,555
Shasta	20,127	43,278	20,848	34,736	5,875
Sierra	540	1,172	573	877	170
Siskiyou...	6,323	12,198	7,022	8,653	1,879
Solano	75,116	51,604	64,644	40,742	8,682
Sonoma	117,295	63,529	100,738	53,555	13,862
Stanislaus ..	56,448	67,188	53,738	52,403	8,360
Sutter......	8,416	17,350	8,504	14,264	1,533
Tehama	6,507	13,270	7,290	10,292	2,325
Trinity......	1,932	3,340	2,203	2,530	856
Tulare	33,006	54,070	32,669	46,272	5,106
Tuolumne...	9,359	13,172	8,950	10,386	1,925
Ventura	133,258	136,173	110,772	109,202	23,054
Yolo	33,747	23,057	33,033	18,807	3,150
Yuba	5,546	9,838	5,789	7,971	1,308
Totals	5,861,203	4,567,429	5,119,835	3,828,380	697,847

California Vote Since 1952

1952, Eisenhower, Rep., 2,897,310; Stevenson, Dem., 2,197,548; Hallinan, Prog., 24,106; Hamblen, Proh., 15,653; MacArthur, (Tenny Ticket), 3,326; (Kellems Ticket) 178; Hass, Soc. Labor, 273; Hoopes, Soc., 206; scattered, 3,249.

1956, Eisenhower, Rep., 3,027,668; Stevenson, Dem., 2,420,136; Holtwick, Proh., 11,119; Andrews, Constitution, 6,087; Hass, Soc. Labor, 300; Hoopes, Soc., 123; Dobbs, Soc. Workers, 96; Smith, Christian Natl., 8.

1960, Kennedy, Dem., 3,224,099; Nixon, Rep., 3,259,722; Decker, Proh., 21,706; Hass, Soc. Labor, 1,051.

1964, Johnson, Dem., 4,171,877; Goldwater, Rep., 2,879,108; Hass, Soc. Labor, 489; DeBerry, Soc. Workers, 378; Munn, Proh., 305; Hensley, Universal, 19.

1968, Nixon, Rep., 3,467,664; Humphrey, Dem., 3,244,318; Wallace, 3d Party, 487,270; Peace and Freedom, 27,707; McCarthy, Alternative, 20,721; Gregory, write-in, 3,230; Mitchell, Com., 260; Munn, Proh., 59; Blomen, Soc. Labor, 341; Soeters, Defense, 17.

1972, Nixon, Rep., 4,602,096; McGovern, Dem., 3,475,847; Schmitz, Amer., 232,554; Spock, Peace and Freedom, 55,167; Hall, Com., 373; Hospers, Libertarian, 980; Munn, Proh., 53; Fisher, Soc. Labor, 197; Jenness, Soc. Workers, 574; Green, Universal, 21.

1976, Carter, Dem., 3,742,284; Ford, Rep., 3,882,244; MacBride, Libertarian, 56,388; Maddox, Amer. Ind., 51,098; Wright, People's, 41,731; Camejo, Soc. Workers, 17,259; Hall, Com., 12,766; write-in, McCarthy, 58,412; other write-in, 4,935.

1980, Reagan, Rep. 4,524,858; Carter, Dem., 3,083,661; Anderson, Ind., 739,833; Clark, Libertarian, 148,434; Commoner, Ind., 61,063; Smith, Peace and Freedom, 18,116; Rarick, Amer. Ind., 9,856.

1984, Reagan, Rep. 5,305,410; Mondale, Dem., 3,815,947; Bergland, Libertarian, 48,400.

1988, Bush, Rep., 5,054,917; Dukakis, Dem., 4,702,233; Paul, Lib., 70,105; Fulani, Ind., 31,181.

1992, Clinton, Dem., 5,121,325; Bush, Rep., 3,630,575; Perot, Ind., 2,296,006; Marrou, Libertarian, 48,139; Daniels, Ind., 18,597; Phillips, U.S. Taxpayers, 12,711.

1996, Clinton, Dem., 5,119,835; Dole, Rep., 3,828,380; Perot, Ref., 697,847; Nader, Green, 237,016; Browne, Libertarian, 73,600; Feinland, Peace & Freedom, 25,332; Phillips, Amer. Ind., 21,202; Hagelin, Natural Law, 15,403.

2000, Gore, Dem., 5,861,203; Bush, Rep., 4,567,429; Nader, Green, 418,707; Browne, Libertarian, 45,520; Buchanan, Reform, 44,987; Phillips, Amer. Ind., 17,042; Hagelin, Natural Law, 10,934.

Colorado

County	2000 Gore (D)	Bush (R)	1996 Clinton (D)	Dole (R)	Perot (RF)
Adams	54,132	47,561	48,314	36,666	7,206
Alamosa	2,455	2,857	2,330	2,038	437
Arapahoe	82,614	97,768	68,306	82,778	8,476
Archuleta	1,432	2,988	997	1,963	360
Baca	531	1,663	659	1,321	203
Bent	783	1,096	1,046	917	209
Boulder	69,983	50,873	63,316	41,922	6,840
Chaffee.....	2,768	4,300	2,768	3,052	538
Cheyenne	209	957	328	739	91
Clear Creek ..	2,188	2,247	1,863	1,746	365
Conejos	1,749	1,772	1,726	1,149	245
Costilla	1,054	504	1,168	333	112
Crowley	511	855	559	680	114
Custer.......	507	1,451	412	920	164
Delta	3,264	8,372	3,584	6,047	1,060
Denver	122,693	61,224	120,312	58,529	8,777
Dolores	293	741	276	417	95
Douglas	27,076	56,007	16,232	32,120	2,662
Eagle	6,772	7,165	5,094	4,637	1,193
Elbert	2,326	6,151	1,894	4,125	507
El Paso	61,799	128,294	55,822	102,403	11,175
Fremont	5,293	9,914	5,344	7,437	1,438
Garfield	6,087	9,103	5,722	6,281	1,562
Gilpin	1,099	1,006	799	682	184
Grand	2,308	3,570	2,012	2,264	473
Gunnison	3,059	3,128	2,812	2,230	570
Hinsdale	188	316	185	289	56
Huerfano	1,495	1,466	1,483	996	210
Jackson	173	682	222	486	107
Jefferson	100,970	120,138	89,494	101,517	12,967
Kiowa	211	728	246	549	74
Kit Carson	809	2,542	1,073	2,068	235
Lake	1,296	1,056	1,338	728	274
La Plata	7,864	9,993	6,509	8,057	1,403
Larimer	46,055	62,429	40,965	45,935	6,823
Las Animas ...	3,243	2,569	3,611	1,905	427
Lincoln	510	1,630	729	1,272	164
Logan	2,296	5,531	2,765	4,032	609
Mesa	15,465	32,396	17,114	24,761	3,707
Mineral	168	294	192	179	69
Moffat	1,223	3,840	1,635	2,466	649
Montezuma ...	2,556	6,158	2,578	4,175	827
Montrose	4,041	9,266	4,019	6,730	1,187
Morgan	2,885	5,722	3,347	4,557	687
Otero	2,963	4,082	3,386	3,356	581
Ouray	705	1,279	569	984	167

County	2000 Gore (D)	Bush (R)	1996 Clinton (D)	Dole (R)	Perot (RF)
Park	2,393	3,677	1,844	2,661	534
Philips	564	1,576	706	1,284	156
Pitkin	4,137	2,565	3,949	1,969	535
Prowers	1,361	3,026	1,745	2,504	342
Pueblo	28,888	22,827	28,791	17,402	3,374
Rio Blanco	543	2,185	731	1,697	243
Rio Grande	1,707	3,111	1,720	2,129	379
Routt	4,208	4,472	3,660	3,019	859
Saguache	1,145	1,078	969	712	160
San Juan	149	210	133	153	50
San Miguel	1,598	1,043	1,535	773	231
Sedgwick	384	877	519	715	101
Summit	5,304	4,497	3,970	3,261	823
Teller	2,750	6,477	2,312	4,458	707
Washington	477	1,878	649	1,566	190
Weld	23,436	37,409	21,325	26,518	4,347
Yuma	1,082	3,156	1,439	2,589	319
Totals	**738,227**	**883,748**	**671,152**	**691,848**	**99,629**

Colorado Vote Since 1952

1952, Eisenhower, Rep., 379,782; Stevenson, Dem., 245,504; MacArthur, Constitution, 2,181; Hallinan, Prog., 1,919; Hoopes, Soc., 365; Hass, Soc. Labor, 352.

1956, Eisenhower, Rep., 394,479; Stevenson, Dem., 263,997; Hass, Soc. Lab., 3,308; Andrews, Ind., 759; Hoopes, Soc., 531.

1960, Kennedy, Dem., 330,629; Nixon, Rep., 402,242; Hass, Soc. Labor, 2,803; Dobbs, Soc. Workers, 572.

1964, Johnson, Dem., 476,024; Goldwater, Rep., 296,767; Hass, Soc. Labor, 302; DeBerry, Soc. Workers, 2,537; Munn, Proh., 1,356.

1968, Nixon, Rep., 409,345; Humphrey, Dem., 335,174; Wallace, 3d Party, 60,813; Blomen, Soc. Labor, 3,016; Gregory, New-party, 1,393; Munn, Proh., 275; Halstead, Soc. Workers, 235.

1972, Nixon, Rep., 597,189; McGovern, Dem., 329,980; Fisher, Soc. Labor, 4,361; Hospers, Libertarian, 1,111; Hall, Com., 432; Jenness, Soc. Workers, 555; Munn, Proh., 467; Schmitz, Amer., 17,269; Spock, Peoples, 2,403.

1976, Carter, Dem., 460,353; Ford, Rep., 584,367; McCarthy, Ind., 26,107; MacBride, Libertarian, 5,330; Bubar, Proh., 2,882.

1980, Reagan, Rep., 652,264; Carter, Dem., 367,973; Anderson, Ind., 130,633; Clark, Libertarian, 25,744; Commoner, Citizens, 5,614; Bubar, Statesman, 1,180; Pulley, Socialist, 520; Hall, Com., 487.

1984, Reagan, Rep., 821,817; Mondale, Dem., 454,975; Bergland, Libertarian, 11,257.

1988, Bush, Rep., 728,177; Dukakis, Dem., 621,453; Paul, Lib., 15,482; Dodge, Proh., 4,604.

1992, Clinton, Dem., 629,681; Bush, Rep., 562,850; Perot, Ind., 366,010; Marrou, Libertarian, 8,669; Fulani, New Alliance, 1,608.

1996, Dole, Rep., 691,848; Clinton, Dem., 671,152; Perot, Ref., 99,629; Nader, Green, 25,070; Browne, Libertarian, 12,392; Collins, Ind., 2,809; Phillips, Amer. Constitution, 2,813; Hagelin, Natural Law, 2,547; Hollis, Soc., 669; Moorehead, Workers World, 599; Templin, Amer., 557; Dodge, Proh., 375; Harris, Soc. Workers, 244.

2000, Bush, Rep., 883,748; Gore, Dem, 738,227; Nader, Green, 91,434; Browne, Libertarian, 12,799; Buchanan, Reform, 10,465; Hagelin, Reform, 2,240; Phillips, Amer. Constitution, 1,319; McReynolds, Soc., 712; Harris, Soc. Workers, 216; Dodge, Proh., 208.

Connecticut

City	2000 Gore (D)	Bush (R)	1996 Clinton (D)	Dole (R)	Perot (RF)
Bridgeport	24,303	7,406	22,883	6,785	2,367
Bristol	14,665	7,948	13,616	6,560	3,049
Danbury	12,987	9,371	12,102	7,965	2,158
Fairfield	14,210	13,042	12,639	12,314	2,092
Greenwich	12,780	14,905	11,622	14,308	1,437
Hartford	21,445	3,095	22,929	3,082	1,010
New Britain	13,913	5,059	14,322	4,911	1,717
New Haven	28,145	5,160	26,161	4,822	1,555
Norwalk	19,293	11,519	17,354	10,800	2,237
Stamford	27,430	15,159	25,005	14,696	2,595
Waterbury	18,069	12,415	18,901	12,075	3,169
West Hartford	21,069	10,447	19,037	10,781	1,890
Other	587,706	445,568	519,169	374,010	114,247
Totals	**816,015**	**561,094**	**735,740**	**483,109**	**139,523**

Connecticut Vote Since 1952

1952, Eisenhower, Rep., 611,012; Stevenson, Dem., 481,649; Hoopes, Soc., 2,244; Hallinan, Peoples, 1,466; Hass, Soc. Labor, 535; write-in, 5.

1956, Eisenhower, Rep., 711,837; Stevenson, Dem., 405,079; scattered, 205.

1960, Kennedy, Dem., 657,055; Nixon, Rep., 565,813.

1964, Johnson, Dem., 826,269; Goldwater, Rep., 390,996; scattered, 1,313.

1968, Nixon, Rep., 556,721; Humphrey, Dem., 621,561; Wallace, 3d Party, 76,650; scattered, 1,300.

1972, Nixon, Rep., 810,763; McGovern, Dem., 555,498; Schmitz, Amer., 17,239; scattered, 777.

1976, Carter, Dem., 647,895; Ford, Rep., 719,261; Maddox, George Wallace Party, 7,101; LaRouche, U.S. Labor, 1,789.

1980, Reagan, Rep., 677,210; Carter, Dem., 541,732; Anderson, Ind., 171,807; Clark, Libertarian, 8,570; Commoner, Citizens, 6,130; scattered, 836.

1984, Reagan, Rep., 890,877; Mondale, Dem., 569,597.

1988, Bush, Rep., 750,241; Dukakis, Dem., 676,584; Paul, Lib., 14,071; Fulani, New Alliance, 2,491.

1992, Clinton, Dem., 682,318; Bush, Rep., 578,313; Perot, Ind., 348,771; Marrou, Libertarian, 5,391; Fulani, New Alliance, 1,363.

1996, Clinton, Dem., 735,740; Dole, Rep., 483,109; Perot, Ref., 139,523; Nader, Green, 24,321; Browne, Libertarian, 5,788; Phillips, Concerned Citizens, 2,425; Hagelin, Natural Law, 1,703.

2000, Gore, Dem., 816,015; Bush, Rep., 561,094; Nader, Green, 64,452; Phillips, Concerned Citizens, 9,695; Buchanan, Reform, 4,731; Browne, Libertarian, 3,484.

Delaware

County	2000 Gore (D)	Bush (R)	1996 Clinton (D)	Dole (R)	Perot (RF)
Kent	22,790	24,081	18,327	15,932	4,705
New Castle	127,539	78,587	98,837	60,943	17,748
Sussex	29,739	34,620	23,191	22,187	6,266
Totals	**180,068**	**137,288**	**140,355**	**99,062**	**28,719**

Delaware Vote Since 1952

1952, Eisenhower, Rep., 90,059; Stevenson, Dem., 83,315; Hass, Soc. Labor, 242; Hamblen, Proh., 234; Hallinan, Prog., 155; Hoopes, Soc., 20.

1956, Eisenhower, Rep., 98.057; Stevenson, Dem., 79,421; Oltwick, Proh., 400; Hass, Soc. Labor, 110.

1960, Kennedy, Dem., 99,590; Nixon, Rep., 96,373; Faubus, States' Rights, 354; Decker, Proh., 284; Hass, Soc. Labor, 82.

1964, Johnson, Dem., 122,704; Goldwater, Rep., 78,078; Hass, Soc. Labor, 113; Munn, Proh., 425.

1968, Nixon, Rep., 96,714; Humphrey, Dem., 89,194; Wallace, 3d Party, 28,459.

1972, Nixon, Rep., 140,357; McGovern, Dem., 92,283; Schmitz, Amer., 2,638; Munn, Proh., 238.

1976, Carter, Dem., 122,596; Ford, Rep., 109,831; McCarthy, non-partisan, 2,437; Anderson, Amer., 645; LaRouche, U.S. Labor, 136; Bubar, Proh., 103; Levin, Soc. Labor, 86.

1980, Reagan, Rep., 111,252; Carter, Dem., 105,754; Anderson, Ind., 16,288; Clark, Libertarian, 1,974; Greaves, Amer., 400.

1984, Reagan, Rep., 152,190; Mondale, Dem., 101,656; Bergland, Libertarian, 268.

1988, Bush, Rep., 139,639; Dukakis, Dem., 108,647; Paul, Lib., 1,162; Fulani, New Alliance, 443.

1992, Clinton, Dem., 126,054; Bush, Rep., 102,313; Perot, Ind., 59,213; Fulani, New Alliance, 1,105.

1996, Clinton, Dem., 140,355; Dole, Rep., 99,062; Perot, Ind. (Ref.), 28,719; Browne, Libertarian, 2,052; Phillips, Taxpayers, 348; Hagelin, Natural Law, 274.

2000, Gore, Dem., 180,068; Bush, Rep., 137,288; Nader, Green, 8,307; Buchanan, Reform, 777; Browne, Libertarian, 774; Phillips, Constitution, 208; Hagelin, Natural Law, 107.

District of Columbia

	2000 Gore (D)	Bush (R)	1996 Clinton (D)	Dole (R)	Perot (RF)
Totals	**171,923**	**18,073**	**158,220**	**17,339**	**3,611**

District of Columbia Vote Since 1964

1964, Johnson, Dem., 169,796; Goldwater, Rep., 28,801.

1968, Nixon, Rep., 31,012; Humphrey, Dem., 139, 566.

1972, Nixon, Rep., 35,226; McGovern, Dem., 127,627; Reed, Soc. Workers, 316; Hall, Com., 252.

1976, Carter, Dem., 137,818; Ford, Rep., 27,873; Camejo, Soc. Workers, 545; MacBride, Libertarian, 274; Hall, Com., 219; LaRouche, U.S. Labor, 157.

1980, Reagan, Rep., 23,313; Carter, Dem., 130,231; Anderson, Ind., 16,131; Commoner, Citizens, 1,826; Clark, Libertarian, 1,104; Hall, Com., 369; DeBerry, Soc. Workers, 173; Griswold, Workers World, 52; write-ins, 690.

1984, Mondale, Dem., 180,408; Reagan, Rep., 29,009; Bergland, Libertarian, 279.

1988, Bush, Rep., 27,590; Dukakis, Dem., 159,407; Fulani, New Alliance, 2,901; Paul, Lib., 554.
1992, Clinton, Dem., 192,619; Bush, Rep., 20,698; Perot, Ind., 9,681; Fulani, New Alliance, 1,459; Daniels, Ind., 1,186.
1996, Clinton, Dem., 158,220; Dole, Rep., 17,339; Perot, Ref., 3,611; Nader, Green, 4,780; Browne, Libertarian, 588; Hagelin, Natural Law, 283; Harris, Soc. Workers, 257.
2000, Gore, Dem., 171,923; Bush, Rep., 18,073; Nader, Green, 10,576; Browne, Libertarian, 669; Harris, Soc. Workers, 114.

1968, Nixon, Rep., 886,804; Humphrey, Dem., 676,794; Wallace, 3d Party, 624,207.
1972, Nixon, Rep., 1,857,759; McGovern, Dem., 718,117; scattered, 7,407.
1976, Carter, Dem., 1,636,000; Ford, Rep., 1,469,531; McCarthy, Ind., 23,643; Anderson, Amer., 21,325.
1980, Reagan, Rep., 2,046,951; Carter, Dem., 1,419,475; Anderson, Ind., 189,692; Clark, Libertarian, 30,524; write-ins, 285.
1984, Reagan, Rep., 2,728,775; Mondale, Dem., 1,448,344.
1988, Bush, Rep., 2,616,597; Dukakis, Dem., 1,655,851; Paul, Lib., 19,796, Fulani, New Alliance, 6,655.
1992, Bush, Rep., 2,171,781; Clinton, Dem., 2,071,651; Perot, Ind., 1,052,481; Marrou, Libertarian, 15,068.
1996, Clinton, Dem., 2,545,968; Dole, Rep., 2,243,324; Perot, Ref., 483,776; Browne, Libertarian, 23,312.
2000, Bush, Rep., 2,912,790; Gore, Dem., 2,912,253; Nader, Green, 97,488; Buchanan, Reform, 17,484; Browne, Libertarian, 16,415; Hagelin, Natural Law, 2,281; Moorehead, Workers World, 1,804; Phillips, Constitution, 1,371; McReynolds, Soc., 622; Harris, Soc. Workers, 562.

Florida

	2000		1996		
County	Gore (D)	Bush (R)	Clinton (D)	Dole (R)	Perot (RF)
Alachua	47,380	34,135	40,144	25,303	8,072
Baker	2,392	5,611	2,273	3,684	667
Bay	18,873	38,682	17,020	28,290	5,922
Bradford	3,075	5,416	3,356	4,038	819
Brevard	97,341	115,253	80,416	87,980	25,249
Broward	387,760	177,939	320,736	142,834	38,964
Calhoun	2,156	2,873	1,794	1,717	630
Charlotte	29,646	35,428	27,121	27,836	7,783
Citrus	25,531	29,801	22,042	20,114	7,244
Clay	14,668	41,903	13,246	30,332	3,281
Collier	29,939	60,467	23,182	42,590	6,320
Columbia	7,049	10,968	6,691	7,588	1,970
Dade[1]	328,867	289,574	317,378	209,634	24,722
De Soto	3,321	4,256	3,219	3,272	965
Dixie	1,827	2,697	1,731	1,398	652
Duval	108,039	152,460	112,258	126,857	13,844
Escambia	40,990	73,171	37,768	60,839	8,587
Flagler	13,897	12,618	9,583	8,232	2,185
Franklin	2,047	2,454	2,095	1,563	878
Gadsden	9,736	4,770	9,405	3,813	938
Gilchrist	1,910	3,300	1,985	1,939	841
Glades	1,442	1,841	1,530	1,361	521
Gulf	2,398	3,553	2,480	2,424	1,054
Hamilton	1,723	2,147	1,734	1,518	406
Hardee	2,342	3,765	2,417	2,926	851
Hendry	3,240	4,747	3,882	3,855	1,135
Hernando	32,648	30,658	28,520	22,039	7,272
Highlands	14,169	20,207	14,244	15,608	3,739
Hillsborough	169,576	180,794	144,223	136,621	25,154
Holmes	2,177	5,012	2,310	3,248	1,208
Indian River	19,769	28,639	16,373	22,709	4,635
Jackson	6,870	9,139	6,665	7,187	1,602
Jefferson	3,041	2,478	2,543	1,851	393
Lafayette	789	1,670	829	1,166	316
Lake	36,571	50,010	29,750	35,089	8,813
Lee	73,571	106,151	65,692	80,882	18,389
Leon	61,444	39,073	50,058	33,914	6,672
Levy	5,398	6,863	4,938	4,299	1,774
Liberty	1,017	1,317	868	913	376
Madison	3,015	3,038	2,791	2,195	578
Manatee	49,226	58,023	41,835	44,059	10,360
Marion	44,674	55,146	37,033	41,397	11,340
Martin	26,621	33,972	20,851	28,516	5,005
Monroe	16,487	16,063	15,219	12,021	4,817
Nassau	6,955	16,408	7,276	12,134	1,657
Okaloosa	16,989	52,186	16,434	40,631	5,432
Okeechobee	4,589	5,057	4,824	3,415	1,666
Orange	140,236	134,531	105,513	106,026	18,191
Osceola	28,187	26,237	21,870	18,335	6,091
Palm Beach	269,754	152,964	230,621	133,762	30,739
Pasco	69,576	68,607	66,472	48,346	18,011
Pinellas	200,657	184,849	184,728	152,125	36,990
Polk	75,207	90,310	66,735	67,943	14,991
Putnam	12,107	13,457	12,008	9,781	3,272
St. Johns	19,509	39,564	16,713	27,311	4,205
St. Lucie	41,560	34,705	36,168	28,892	8,482
Santa Rosa	12,818	36,339	10,923	26,244	4,957
Sarasota	72,869	83,117	63,648	69,198	14,939
Seminole	59,227	75,790	45,051	59,778	9,357
Sumter	9,637	12,127	7,014	5,960	2,375
Suwannee	4,076	8,009	4,479	5,742	1,874
Taylor	2,649	4,058	3,583	3,188	1,140
Union	1,407	2,332	1,388	1,636	425
Volusia	97,313	82,368	78,905	63,067	17,319
Wakulla	3,838	4,512	3,054	2,931	1,091
Walton	5,643	12,186	5,341	7,706	2,342
Washington	2,798	4,995	2,992	3,522	1,287
Totals	2,912,253	2,912,790	2,545,968	2,243,324	483,776

(1) In 1997, Dade County changed its name to Miami-Dade County.

Florida Vote Since 1952

1952, Eisenhower, Rep., 544,036; Stevenson, Dem., 444,950; scattered, 351.
1956, Eisenhower, Rep., 643,849; Stevenson, Dem., 480,371.
1960, Kennedy, Dem., 748,700; Nixon, Rep., 795,476.
1964, Johnson, Dem., 948,540; Goldwater, Rep., 905,941.

Georgia

	2000		1996		
County	Gore (D)	Bush (R)	Clinton (D)	Dole (R)	Perot (RF)
Appling	2,093	3,940	2,070	2,572	446
Atkinson	821	1,228	823	784	215
Bacon	956	1,210	1,360	1,580	402
Baker	893	615	955	408	105
Baldwin	5,893	6,041	5,740	4,570	849
Banks	1,220	3,202	1,536	1,925	595
Barrow	3,657	7,925	3,928	5,342	942
Bartow	7,508	14,720	6,853	9,250	1,770
Ben Hill	2,234	2,381	2,198	1,516	358
Berrien	1,640	2,718	2,066	1,950	525
Bibb	24,996	24,071	26,727	20,778	2,268
Bleckley	1,273	2,436	1,365	1,632	300
Brantley	1,372	3,118	1,494	1,738	386
Brooks	2,096	2,406	1,977	1,738	314
Bryan	2,172	4,835	2,152	3,577	513
Bulloch	5,561	8,990	5,396	6,646	939
Burke	3,720	3,381	3,915	2,590	389
Butts	2,281	3,198	2,271	2,027	416
Calhoun	1,107	768	1,217	541	106
Camden	3,636	6,371	3,644	4,222	572
Candler	1,053	1,643	1,097	1,131	264
Carroll	8,752	16,326	8,438	11,157	2,002
Catoosa	5,470	12,033	5,185	8,237	1,257
Charlton	1,015	1,770	1,368	1,374	280
Chatham	37,590	37,847	35,781	31,987	3,028
Chattahoo-chee	600	590	565	398	115
Chattooga	2,729	3,640	3,003	2,513	796
Cherokee	12,295	38,033	10,802	24,527	2,872
Clarke	15,167	11,850	15,206	10,504	1,201
Clay	821	448	787	293	62
Clayton	40,042	19,966	30,687	20,625	3,494
Clinch	816	1,091	973	789	182
Cobb	86,676	140,494	73,750	114,188	10,438
Coffee	3,593	5,756	3,407	3,934	711
Colquitt	3,297	6,589	4,135	4,847	977
Columbia	8,969	26,660	8,601	21,291	1,709
Cook	1,639	2,279	1,780	1,354	267
Coweta	9,056	21,327	7,794	13,058	1,949
Crawford	1,513	1,987	1,534	1,290	270
Crisp	2,268	3,285	2,504	2,321	445
Dade	1,628	3,333	1,737	2,295	618
Dawson	1,458	4,210	1,434	2,343	473
Decatur	3,398	4,187	3,245	3,035	497
DeKalb	154,509	58,807	137,903	60,255	6,742
Dodge	2,326	3,472	2,696	2,478	587
Dooly	1,901	1,588	1,951	990	207
Dougherty	16,650	12,248	15,600	11,144	1,072
Douglas	11,162	18,893	9,631	14,495	2,109
Early	1,622	1,938	1,648	1,374	246
Echols	272	614	308	335	97
Effingham	3,232	7,326	3,031	5,022	769
Elbert	2,527	3,262	2,900	2,393	552
Emanuel	2,835	3,343	2,947	2,451	450
Evans	1,217	1,841	1,117	1,206	204
Fannin	2,736	5,463	2,741	3,373	782
Fayette	11,912	29,338	9,875	21,005	2,016
Floyd	10,282	16,194	10,464	12,426	2,345
Forsyth	6,694	27,769	5,957	15,013	1,889
Franklin	2,040	3,659	2,338	2,364	665
Fulton	152,039	104,870	143,306	89,809	7,720
Gilmer	2,230	4,941	2,464	3,121	725
Glascock	249	763	348	532	128
Glynn	7,778	14,346	8,058	12,305	1,137
Gordon	4,032	7,944	4,239	5,232	1,284
Grady	2,721	3,894	2,862	2,674	633

County	2000 Gore (D)	Bush (R)	1996 Clinton (D)	Dole (R)	Perot (RF)
Greene ...	2,137	2,980	2,115	1,702	173
Gwinnett ..	61,434	121,756	53,819	96,610	10,236
Habersham	2,530	6,964	3,170	4,730	1,149
Hall	10,259	26,841	10,362	19,280	2,321
Hancock ..	2,414	662	2,135	438	71
Haralson ..	2,869	5,153	2,850	3,260	808
Harris	2,912	5,554	2,779	3,829	489
Hart	3,192	4,242	3,486	2,884	767
Heard	1,178	1,947	1,248	1,170	406
Henry	11,971	25,815	9,498	16,968	2,320
Houston...	13,301	23,174	12,760	17,050	2,730
Irwin.....	1,105	1,720	1,225	1,085	224
Jackson...	3,420	7,878	3,746	4,782	899
Jasper	1,558	2,298	1,553	1,423	243
Jeff Davis .	1,379	2,797	1,576	1,796	428
Jefferson..	2,973	2,559	3,404	2,077	298
Jenkins ...	1,250	1,317	1,336	955	166
Johnson...	1,065	1,797	1,194	815	242
Jones.....	3,102	4,850	3,195	3,272	497
Lamar	2,194	2,912	2,125	1,988	409
Lanier	832	1,048	818	519	160
Laurens ...	5,724	8,133	5,792	6,118	818
Lee	1,936	5,872	2,005	3,983	506
Liberty ...	5,347	4,455	4,462	3,042	580
Lincoln...	1,275	1,807	1,334	1,391	208
Long	975	1,320	936	791	236
Lowndes ..	10,616	14,462	9,470	10,578	1,518
Lumpkin...	2,121	4,427	1,949	2,576	588
McDuffie ..	2,580	3,926	2,725	3,254	395
McIntosh ..	2,047	1,766	1,927	1,219	293
Macon	2,757	1,566	2,618	1,006	159
Madison...	2,285	5,529	2,571	3,992	868
Marion	982	1,187	977	678	159
Meriwether	3,441	3,162	3,492	2,259	480
Miller	783	1,349	909	847	235
Mitchell ...	2,971	2,790	3,165	2,033	372
Monroe ...	2,839	4,561	2,768	3,054	488
Montgomery	1,013	1,465	1,233	1,163	284
Morgan ...	2,238	3,524	2,111	2,118	364
Murray ...	2,684	5,539	2,861	3,289	938
Muscogee .	28,193	23,479	24,867	19,360	1,891
Newton ...	6,703	11,127	6,759	7,274	1,258
Oconee ...	3,184	7,611	2,992	5,116	615
Oglethorpe	1,519	2,706	1,570	1,826	369
Paulding ..	6,743	16,881	5,699	10,152	1,603
Peach	3,540	3,525	3,582	2,676	471
Pickens ...	2,489	5,488	2,693	3,041	783
Pierce	1,300	3,348	1,420	2,319	333
Pike......	1,413	3,358	1,474	2,054	357
Polk......	4,112	5,841	4,298	4,130	1,076
Pulaski....	1,390	1,922	1,554	1,196	268
Putnam ...	2,612	3,596	2,340	2,306	474
Quitman...	542	348	514	224	59
Rabun	1,776	3,451	1,943	2,213	585
Randolph..	1,381	1,174	1,438	816	126
Richmond..	31,413	25,485	30,738	23,670	2,310
Rockdale ..	8,295	15,440	7,656	13,006	1,750
Schley	460	706	576	470	123
Screven ...	2,233	2,461	2,087	1,862	263
Seminole ..	1,313	1,537	1,265	1,003	250
Spalding ..	5,831	9,271	6,017	7,376	1,059
Stephens ..	2,869	5,370	3,072	3,890	979
Stewart ...	1,267	675	1,537	525	152
Sumter....	4,748	4,847	4,239	3,358	451
Talbot....	1,662	844	1,579	652	111
Taliaferro ..	556	271	615	235	36
Tattnall....	1,963	3,597	2,369	2,518	541
Taylor....	1,340	1,412	1,450	1,002	195
Telfair....	1,777	1,693	1,856	1,143	322
Terrell	1,584	1,504	1,509	1,111	129
Thomas ...	4,862	7,093	5,183	5,649	667
Tift.......	3,547	6,678	4,198	5,613	728
Toombs ...	2,643	4,487	2,763	3,646	602
Towns	1,495	2,902	1,664	2,030	459
Treutlen ...	879	1,062	912	723	122
Troup	6,379	11,198	5,940	8,716	1,090
Turner	1,169	1,258	1,272	924	246
Twiggs....	1,977	1,570	1,927	958	210
Union	2,230	4,567	2,175	2,685	622
Upson	3,158	5,019	3,491	3,783	731
Walker	6,341	12,326	6,743	8,817	1,969
Walton	5,484	12,966	5,618	7,934	1,323
Ware	3,480	6,099	4,171	4,746	636
Warren ...	1,196	933	1,230	735	83
Washington	3,476	3,162	4,057	2,348	488
Wayne	2,736	5,219	2,734	3,709	665
Webster...	541	359	529	235	59
Wheeler...	752	813	751	460	141
White.....	2,014	4,857	1,864	2,959	556
Whitfield ..	7,034	15,852	7,720	12,368	1,637

County	2000 Gore (D)	Bush (R)	1996 Clinton (D)	Dole (R)	Perot (RF)
Wilcox....	962	1,381	1,067	882	171
Wilkes.....	1,940	2,044	1,971	1,417	184
Wilkinson ..	1,884	1,800	2,278	1,332	287
Worth	2,214	3,792	2,300	2,752	521
Totals.....	**1,116,230**	**1,419,720**	**1,053,849**	**1,080,843**	**146,337**

Georgia Vote Since 1952

1952, Eisenhower, Rep., 198,979; Stevenson, Dem., 456,823; Liberty Party, 1.

1956, Stevenson, Dem., 444,388; Eisenhower, Rep., 222,778; Andrews, Ind., write-in, 1,754.

1960, Kennedy, Dem., 458,638; Nixon, Rep., 274,472; write-in, 239.

1964, Johnson, Dem., 522,557; Goldwater, Rep., 616,600.

1968, Nixon, Rep., 380,111; Humphrey, Dem., 334,440; Wallace, 3d Party 535,550; write-in, 162.

1972, Nixon, Rep., 881,496; McGovern, Dem., 289,529; scattered, 2,935; Schmitz, Amer., 812.

1976, Carter, Dem., 979,409; Ford, Rep., 483,743; write-in, 4,306.

1980, Reagan, Rep., 654,168; Carter, Dem., 890,955; Anderson, Ind., 36,055; Clark, Libertarian, 15,627.

1984, Reagan, Rep., 1,068,722; Mondale, Dem., 706,628.

1988, Bush, Rep., 1,081,331; Dukakis, Dem., 714,792; Paul, Lib., 8,435; Fulani, New Alliance, 5,099.

1992, Clinton, Dem., 1,008,966; Bush, Rep., 995,252; Perot, Ind., 309,657; Marrou, Libertarian, 7,110.

1996, Dole, Rep., 1,080,843; Clinton, Dem., 1,053,849; Perot, Ref., 146,337; Browne, Libertarian, 17,870.

2000, Bush, Rep., 1,419,720; Gore, Dem., 1,116,230; Browne, Libertarian, 36,332; Buchanan, Independent, 10,926.

Hawaii

County	2000 Gore (D)	Bush (R)	1996 Clinton (D)	Dole (R)	Perot (RF)
Hawaii	28,670	17,050	27,262	13,516	5,137
Honolulu.....	139,662	101,336	143,793	85,779	17,389
Kauai	13,470	6,583	13,357	5,325	1,568
Maui	23,484	12,876	20,600	9,323	3,264
Totals........	**205,286**	**137,845**	**205,012**	**113,943**	**27,358**

Hawaii Vote Since 1960

1960, Kennedy, Dem., 92,410; Nixon, Rep., 92,295.

1964, Johnson, Dem., 163,249; Goldwater, Rep., 44,022.

1968, Nixon, Rep., 91,425; Humphrey, Dem., 141,324; Wallace, 3d Party, 3,469.

1972, Nixon, Rep., 168,865; McGovern, Dem., 101,409.

1976, Carter, Dem., 147,375; Ford, Rep., 140,003; MacBride, Libertarian, 3,923.

1980, Reagan, Rep., 130,112; Carter, Dem., 135,879; Anderson, Ind., 32,021; Clark, Libertarian, 3,269; Commoner, Citizens, 1,548; Hall, Com., 458.

1984, Reagan, Rep., 184,934; Mondale, Dem., 147,098; Bergland, Libertarian, 2,167.

1988, Bush, Rep., 158,625; Dukakis, Dem., 192,364; Paul, Lib., 1,999; Fulani, New Alliance, 1,003.

1992, Clinton, Dem., 179,310; Bush, Rep., 136,822; Perot, Ind., 53,003; Gritz, Populist/America First, 1,452; Marrou, Libertarian, 1,119.

1996, Clinton, Dem., 205,012; Dole, Rep., 113,943; Perot, Ref., 27,358; Nader, Green, 10,386; Browne, Libertarian, 2,493; Hagelin, Natural Law, 570; Phillips, Taxpayers, 358.

2000, Gore, Dem., 205,286; Bush, Rep., 137,845; Nader, Green, 21,623; Browne, Libertarian, 1,477; Buchanan, Reform, 1,071; Phillips, Constitution, 343; Hagelin, Natural Law, 306.

Idaho

County	2000 Gore (D)	Bush (R)	1996 Clinton (D)	Dole (R)	Perot (RF)
Ada.........	40,650	75,050	43,040	61,811	11,171
Adams	336	1,476	537	1,053	311
Bannock.....	10,892	18,223	12,806	14,058	4,158
Bear Lake....	517	2,296	805	1,583	396
Benewah	895	2,606	1,488	1,667	701
Bingham.....	3,310	10,628	4,304	8,391	2,021
Blaine	3,748	3,528	3,840	3,003	1,193
Boise	745	2,019	879	1,576	440
Bonner	4,318	8,945	5,294	6,207	2,669
Bonneville...	7,235	24,988	9,013	19,977	3,921
Boundary ...	832	2,797	1,194	1,937	626
Butte.......	354	1,054	507	741	233
Camas	113	359	156	283	95
Canyon	10,588	30,560	11,800	23,988	3,956
Caribou	475	2,601	841	1,740	501
Cassia	1,087	5,983	1,596	4,663	976
Clark........	63	311	117	266	45
Clearwater ...	841	2,885	1,507	1,658	650

County	2000 Gore (D)	2000 Bush (R)	1996 Clinton (D)	1996 Dole (R)	Perot (RF)
Custer	416	1,794	635	1,249	400
Elmore	1,840	4,891	2,324	3,668	845
Franklin	513	3,594	807	2,435	589
Fremont	699	4,242	1,114	3,042	630
Gem	1,346	4,376	1,968	3,362	833
Gooding	1,282	3,502	1,503	2,637	980
Idaho	1,187	5,806	1,979	3,871	1,083
Jefferson	1,100	6,480	1,427	4,925	994
Jerome	1,360	4,418	1,679	3,358	1,014
Kootenai	13,488	28,162	13,627	18,740	6,083
Latah	5,661	8,161	7,741	6,311	1,828
Lemhi	660	2,859	1,015	2,334	461
Lewis	335	1,295	674	861	316
Lincoln	437	1,049	478	744	319
Madison	816	7,941	1,216	5,706	744
Minidoka	1,344	4,907	1,977	4,008	977
Nez Perce	4,995	10,577	7,491	6,675	2,385
Oneida	307	1,426	429	993	285
Owyhee	623	2,450	895	2,033	354
Payette	1,643	4,961	2,119	3,901	906
Power	755	1,872	1,070	1,501	344
Shoshone	2,225	2,879	2,981	1,588	1,283
Teton	720	1,745	866	1,251	326
Twin Falls	5,777	15,794	6,826	12,393	3,383
Valley	1,129	2,548	1,564	2,089	568
Washington	980	2,899	1,314	2,318	525
Totals	**138,637**	**336,937**	**164,443**	**256,595**	**62,518**

Idaho Vote Since 1952

1952, Eisenhower, Rep., 180,707; Stevenson, Dem., 95,081; Hallinan, Prog., 443; write-in, 23.
1956, Eisenhower, Rep., 166,979; Stevenson, Dem., 105,868; Andrews, Ind., 126; write-in, 16.
1960, Kennedy, Dem., 138,853; Nixon, Rep., 161,597.
1964, Johnson, Dem., 148,920; Goldwater, Rep., 143,557.
1968, Nixon, Rep., 165,369; Humphrey, Dem., 89,273; Wallace, 3d Party, 36,541.
1972, Nixon, Rep., 199,384; McGovern, Dem., 80,826; Schmitz, Amer., 28,869; Spock, Peoples, 903.
1976, Carter, Dem., 126,549; Ford, Rep., 204,151; Maddox, Amer., 5,935; MacBride, Libertarian, 3,558; LaRouche, U.S. Labor, 739.
1980, Reagan, Rep., 290,699; Carter, Dem., 110,192; Anderson, Ind., 27,058; Clark, Libertarian, 8,425; Rarick, Amer., 1,057.
1984, Reagan, Rep., 297,523; Mondale, Dem., 108,510; Bergland, Libertarian, 2,823.
1988, Bush, Rep., 253,881; Dukakis, Dem., 147,272; Paul, Lib., 5,313; Fulani, Ind., 2,502.
1992, Clinton, Dem., 137,013; Bush, Rep., 202,645; Perot, Ind., 130,395; Gritz, Populist/America First, 10,281; Marrou, Libertarian, 1,167.
1996, Dole, Rep., 256,595; Clinton, Dem., 165,443; Perot, Ref., 62,518; Browne, Libertarian, 3,325; Phillips, Taxpayers, 2,230; Hagelin, Natural Law, 1,600.
2000, Bush, Rep., 336,937; Gore, Dem., 138,637; Buchanan, Reform, 7,615; Browne, Libertarian, 3,488; Phillips, Constitution, 1,469; Hagelin, Natural Law, 1,177.

Illinois

County	2000 Gore (D)	2000 Bush (R)	1996 Clinton (D)	1996 Dole (R)	Perot (RF)
Adams	12,197	17,331	11,336	13,836	3,069
Alexander	2,357	1,588	2,753	1,212	321
Bond	3,060	3,804	3,213	3,018	685
Boone	6,481	8,617	5,345	6,181	1,377
Brown	1,077	1,529	997	1,053	237
Bureau	7,754	8,526	7,651	6,528	1,798
Calhoun	1,310	1,229	1,676	941	363
Carroll	3,113	3,835	2,926	3,029	792
Cass	2,789	2,968	2,834	2,214	589
Champaign	35,515	34,645	32,454	28,232	4,806
Christian	6,799	7,537	7,431	5,563	1,727
Clark	2,932	4,398	2,995	3,409	781
Clay	2,212	3,789	2,750	2,703	719
Clinton	6,436	8,588	6,104	6,065	1,580
Coles	8,904	10,495	8,950	8,038	2,137
Cook	1,280,547	534,542	1,153,289	461,557	96,633
Crawford	3,333	4,974	3,627	3,965	1,057
Cumberland	1,872	2,964	1,776	2,002	657
DeKalb	14,798	17,139	12,715	12,380	3,009
DeWitt	2,870	3,968	2,878	2,978	694
Douglas	3,215	4,734	2,955	3,272	740
DuPage	152,550	201,037	129,709	164,630	27,419
Edgar	3,216	4,833	3,552	3,746	935
Edwards	978	2,212	1,089	1,613	384
Effingham	4,225	9,855	4,825	7,696	1,555
Fayette	3,886	5,200	3,887	3,881	964

County	2000 Gore (D)	2000 Bush (R)	1996 Clinton (D)	1996 Dole (R)	Perot (RF)
Ford	2,090	3,889	2,065	3,077	590
Franklin	10,201	8,490	9,814	5,354	2,096
Fulton	8,940	6,936	8,857	5,155	1,610
Gallatin	1,878	1,591	2,113	856	527
Greene	2,490	3,129	2,734	2,245	903
Grundy	7,516	8,709	6,759	6,177	1,860
Hamilton	1,943	2,519	2,242	1,677	560
Hancock	4,256	5,134	4,001	3,961	1,148
Hardin	1,184	1,366	1,323	790	485
Henderson	2,030	1,708	1,953	1,233	408
Henry	11,921	10,896	11,201	8,393	2,194
Iroquois	4,397	8,685	4,559	6,564	1,522
Jackson	11,773	9,823	12,214	7,422	2,082
Jasper	1,815	3,119	2,038	2,234	641
Jefferson	6,685	8,362	7,263	5,937	1,647
Jersey	4,355	4,699	4,275	3,211	1,186
Jo Daviess	4,585	5,304	4,171	3,915	1,131
Johnson	1,928	3,285	2,009	2,241	640
Kane	60,127	76,996	47,902	54,375	11,270
Kankakee	19,180	20,049	16,820	14,595	3,574
Kendall	8,444	13,688	6,499	8,958	2,055
Knox	12,572	9,912	12,487	7,822	2,096
Lake	115,058	120,988	93,315	93,149	16,640
LaSalle	23,355	21,276	21,643	15,299	5,259
Lawrence	2,822	3,594	2,871	2,568	916
Lee	6,111	8,069	5,895	6,677	1,520
Livingston	5,829	9,187	5,641	7,653	1,409
Logan	4,600	8,141	4,618	6,518	1,141
McDonough	6,080	6,465	5,632	5,049	1,217
McHenry	40,698	62,112	31,240	41,136	10,082
McLean	24,936	34,008	22,708	26,428	3,816
Macon	24,262	23,830	24,256	18,161	4,540
Macoupin	11,015	9,749	11,107	7,235	2,532
Madison	59,077	48,821	53,568	35,758	10,121
Marion	8,068	8,240	7,792	5,999	1,825
Marshall	2,570	3,145	2,640	2,453	586
Mason	3,192	3,411	3,385	2,430	600
Massac	2,912	3,676	2,841	2,507	675
Menard	2,164	3,862	2,204	3,106	534
Mercer	4,400	3,688	4,278	2,688	889
Monroe	5,797	7,632	4,798	5,350	1,276
Montgomery	6,542	6,226	6,338	4,770	1,436
Morgan	5,899	8,058	6,150	6,352	1,633
Moultrie	2,529	3,058	2,629	2,199	596
Ogle	7,673	12,325	6,769	9,558	1,876
Peoria	38,604	36,398	37,383	30,990	5,220
Perry	4,862	4,802	5,347	3,237	1,262
Piatt	3,488	4,619	3,274	3,265	818
Pike	3,198	4,706	3,604	3,225	1,039
Pope	927	1,346	915	850	277
Pulaski	1,518	1,430	1,524	1,036	235
Putnam	1,657	1,437	1,425	987	322
Randolph	6,794	7,127	7,419	5,422	1,698
Richland	2,491	4,718	2,679	3,137	927
Rock Island	37,957	25,194	34,822	20,626	5,135
St. Clair	55,961	42,299	53,405	33,066	7,027
Saline	5,427	5,933	6,156	3,693	1,752
Sangamon	38,414	50,374	38,902	42,174	6,446
Schuyler	1,587	2,077	1,636	1,597	483
Scott	954	1,458	1,012	1,112	396
Shelby	4,018	5,851	4,249	4,215	1,262
Stark	1,211	1,694	1,262	1,278	312
Stephenson	8,062	10,715	7,145	8,871	1,940
Tazewell	25,379	31,537	24,139	24,395	4,814
Union	3,982	4,397	4,252	3,147	832
Vermilion	15,406	15,783	15,525	12,015	3,577
Wabash	1,987	3,406	2,177	2,381	683
Warren	3,524	3,899	3,500	2,974	742
Washington	2,638	4,353	2,744	3,339	790
Wayne	2,209	5,347	3,054	4,029	999
White	2,958	4,521	3,553	2,878	888
Whiteside	12,886	11,252	11,913	8,859	2,436
Will	90,902	95,828	69,354	62,506	15,485
Williamson	12,192	14,012	12,510	9,734	2,877
Winnebago	51,981	53,816	46,264	44,479	8,192
Woodford	5,529	10,905	5,270	8,527	1,170
Totals	**2,589,026**	**2,019,421**	**2,341,744**	**1,587,021**	**346,408**

Illinois Vote Since 1952

1952, Eisenhower, Rep., 2,457,327; Stevenson, Dem., 2,013,920; Hass, Soc. Labor, 9,363; write-in, 448.
1956, Eisenhower, Rep., 2,623,327; Stevenson, Dem., 1,775,682; Hass, Soc. Labor, 8,342; write-in, 56.
1960, Kennedy, Dem., 2,377,846; Nixon, Rep., 2,368,988; Hass, Soc. Labor, 10,560; write-in, 15.
1964, Johnson, Dem., 2,796,833; Goldwater, Rep., 1,905,946; write-in, 62.
1968, Nixon, Rep., 2,174,774; Humphrey, Dem., 2,039,814; Wallace, 3d Party, 390,958; Blomen, Soc. Labor, 13,878; write-in, 325.

1972, Nixon, Rep. 2,788,179; McGovern, Dem., 1,913,472; Fisher, Soc. Labor, 12,344; Schmitz, Amer., 2,471; Hall, Com., 4,541; others, 2,229.

1976, Carter, Dem., 2,271,295; Ford, Rep., 2,364,269; McCarthy, Ind., 55,939; Hall, Com., 9,250; MacBride, Libertarian, 8,057; Camejo, Soc. Workers, 3,615; Levin, Soc. Labor, 2,422; LaRouche, U.S. Labor, 2,018; write-in, 1,968.

1980, Reagan, Rep., 2,358,049; Carter, Dem., 1,981,413; Anderson, Ind., 346,754; Clark, Libertarian, 38,939; Commoner, Citizens, 10,692; Hall, Com., 9,711; Griswold, Workers World, 2,257; DeBerry, Soc. Workers, 1,302; write-ins, 604.

1984, Reagan, Rep., 2,707,103; Mondale, Dem., 2,086,499; Bergland, Libertarian, 10,086.

1988, Bush, Rep., 2,310,939; Dukakis, Dem., 2,215,940; Paul, Lib., 14,944; Fulani, Solid., 10,276.

1992, Clinton, Dem., 2,453,350; Bush, Rep., 1,734,096; Perot, Ind., 840,515; Marrou, Libertarian, 9,218; Fulani, New Alliance, 5,267; Gritz, Populist/America First, 3,577; Hagelin, Natural Law, 2,751; Warren, Soc. Workers, 1,361.

1996, Clinton, Dem., 2,341,744; Dole, Rep., 1,587,021; Perot, Ref., 346,408; Browne, Libertarian, 22,548; Phillips, Taxpayers, 7,606; Hagelin, Natural Law, 4,606.

2000, Gore, Dem., 2,589,026; Bush, Rep., 2,019,421; Nader, Green, 103,759; Buchanan, Ind., 16,106; Browne, Libertarian, 11,623; Hagelin, Reform, 2,127.

Indiana

County	2000 Gore (D)	Bush (R)	1996 Clinton (D)	Dole (R)	Perot (RF)
Adams	3,775	8,555	4,247	6,960	1,346
Allen	41,636	70,426	41,450	59,255	8,808
Bartholomew	9,015	16,200	9,301	13,188	2,815
Benton	1,328	2,441	1,311	1,947	609
Blackford	2,103	2,699	2,335	2,070	681
Boone	4,763	13,161	4,625	11,338	1,498
Brown	2,608	3,871	2,413	2,988	802
Carroll	2,965	5,102	2,747	4,062	1,171
Cass	5,412	9,305	5,419	8,020	2,029
Clark	17,360	19,417	17,799	14,396	3,578
Clay	3,605	6,393	3,605	4,858	1,406
Clinton	3,643	7,141	3,949	6,156	1,355
Crawford	1,817	2,327	2,324	1,759	700
Daviess	2,697	6,872	3,230	5,531	994
Dearborn	6,020	11,452	6,269	8,318	1,731
Decatur	2,889	6,115	3,190	4,782	1,389
Dekalb	4,776	8,701	4,840	6,851	1,534
Delaware	20,876	22,105	20,385	18,126	6,042
Dubois	5,090	10,134	6,499	6,840	1,777
Elkhart	16,402	36,756	16,598	28,770	5,133
Fayette	3,415	5,060	3,822	4,091	1,137
Floyd	13,209	16,486	13,814	12,473	2,609
Fountain	2,717	4,408	2,327	3,984	1,033
Franklin	2,591	5,587	2,808	4,167	943
Fulton	2,960	5,218	2,956	3,934	1,143
Gibson	5,802	7,734	6,488	5,392	1,585
Grant	9,712	16,153	9,818	13,443	3,008
Greene	4,898	7,452	5,277	5,746	1,690
Hamilton	18,002	56,372	14,153	42,792	4,234
Hancock	6,503	15,943	6,123	12,907	2,258
Harrison	5,870	8,711	5,900	6,073	1,839
Hendricks	10,786	28,651	9,392	22,293	3,405
Henry	7,647	10,321	7,667	8,537	2,381
Howard	12,899	20,331	11,999	16,771	4,172
Huntington	4,119	10,113	4,287	8,275	1,400
Jackson	5,330	9,054	5,150	5,883	1,590
Jasper	3,744	7,212	3,554	5,173	1,271
Jay	3,167	4,687	3,356	3,584	1,022
Jefferson	5,117	6,582	5,441	4,827	1,438
Jennings	3,549	5,732	4,223	4,461	1,629
Johnson	11,952	29,404	11,278	23,733	3,975
Knox	6,300	8,485	7,003	6,395	2,022
Kosciusko	5,785	19,040	6,166	15,084	2,531
LaGrange	2,733	5,437	2,704	4,033	949
Lake	109,078	63,389	100,198	47,873	15,051
LaPorte	19,736	18,994	19,879	14,106	5,133
Lawrence	5,071	10,677	5,703	8,107	2,063
Madison	23,403	27,956	23,772	23,151	6,447
Marion	134,189	137,810	124,448	133,329	21,358
Marshall	5,541	10,266	5,486	8,158	1,698
Martin	1,518	3,008	1,848	2,281	485
Miami	4,155	8,401	4,260	6,719	1,657
Monroe	17,523	19,147	18,531	16,744	3,179
Montgomery	3,899	8,891	3,825	7,705	1,766
Morgan	6,228	15,286	5,812	12,872	2,755
Newton	2,101	3,250	1,897	2,075	801
Noble	4,822	9,103	5,101	6,782	1,521
Ohio	951	1,515	1,083	1,098	281
Orange	2,601	4,687	3,016	3,355	938
Owen	2,253	4,019	2,244	3,056	874
Parke	2,481	3,841	2,453	3,151	981
Perry	3,823	3,461	4,427	2,554	913
Pike	2,605	3,566	2,780	2,174	884
Porter	26,790	31,157	24,044	22,931	7,169
Posey	4,430	6,498	4,965	4,638	1,304
Pulaski	1,919	3,497	2,010	2,693	634
Putnam	4,123	7,352	3,962	5,958	1,619
Randolph	3,906	6,020	4,087	4,708	1,557
Ripley	3,498	6,988	4,097	5,303	1,216
Rush	2,370	4,749	2,578	3,827	973
St. Joseph	47,703	47,581	45,704	38,281	8,379
Scott	3,915	3,761	3,798	2,620	760
Shelby	5,374	9,590	5,374	7,778	1,874
Spencer	3,752	5,096	4,058	3,770	739
Starke	4,136	4,349	3,854	3,108	1,096
Steuben	4,103	6,953	4,124	5,513	1,390
Sullivan	3,833	4,319	4,076	3,207	1,178
Switzerland	1,336	1,831	1,496	1,266	403
Tippecanoe	18,220	26,106	17,232	22,556	5,394
Tipton	2,392	4,784	2,478	3,980	861
Union	927	1,838	1,019	1,334	364
Vanderburgh	29,222	35,846	30,934	28,509	6,132
Vermillion	3,370	3,130	3,251	2,334	1,029
Vigo	17,570	18,021	17,974	15,751	4,508
Wabash	4,277	8,321	4,577	6,990	1,294
Warren	1,471	2,218	1,394	1,678	560
Warrick	8,749	13,205	9,285	9,221	2,471
Washington	3,675	5,868	3,819	4,066	1,264
Wayne	10,273	14,273	10,905	12,188	2,525
Wells	3,319	7,755	3,752	6,322	1,157
White	3,655	6,037	3,396	4,642	1,610
Whitley	4,107	8,080	4,176	5,965	1,392
Totals	901,980	1,245,836	887,424	1,006,693	224,299

Indiana Vote Since 1952

1952, Eisenhower, Rep., 1,136,259; Stevenson, Dem., 801,530; Hamblen, Proh., 15,335; Hallinan, Prog., 1,222; Hass, Soc. Labor, 979.

1956, Eisenhower, Rep., 1,182,811; Stevenson, Dem., 783,908; Holtwick, Proh., 6,554; Hass, Soc. Labor, 1,334.

1960, Kennedy, Dem., 952,358; Nixon, Rep., 1,175,120; Decker, Proh., 6,746; Hass, Soc. Labor, 1,136.

1964, Johnson, Dem., 1,170,848; Goldwater, Rep., 911,118; Munn, Proh., 8,266; Hass, Soc. Labor, 1,374.

1968, Nixon, Rep., 1,067,885; Humphrey, Dem., 806,659; Wallace, 3d Party, 243,108; Munn, Proh., 4,616; Halstead, Soc. Workers, 1,293; Gregory, write-in, 36.

1972, Nixon, Rep., 1,405,154; McGovern, Dem., 708,568; Reed, Soc. Workers, 5,575; Fisher, Soc. Labor, 1,688; Spock, Peace and Freedom, 4,544.

1976, Carter, Dem., 1,014,714; Ford, Rep., 1,185,958; Anderson, Amer., 14,048; Camejo, Soc. Workers, 5,695; LaRouche, U.S. Labor, 1,947.

1980, Reagan, Rep., 1,255,656; Carter, Dem., 844,197; Anderson, Ind., 111,639; Clark, Libertarian, 19,627; Commoner, Citizens, 4,852; Greaves, Amer., 4,750; Hall, Com., 702; DeBerry, Soc., 610.

1984, Reagan, Rep., 1,377,230; Mondale, Dem., 841,481; Bergland, Libertarian, 6,741.

1988, Bush, Rep., 1,297,763; Dukakis, Dem., 860,643; Fulani, New Alliance, 10,215.

1992, Bush, Rep., 989,375; Clinton, Dem., 848,420; Perot, Ind., 455,934; Marrou, Libertarian, 7,936; Fulani, New Alliance, 2,583.

1996, Dole, Rep., 1,006,693; Clinton, Dem., 887,424; Perot, Ref., 224,299; Browne, Libertarian, 15,632.

2000, Bush, Rep., 1,245,836; Gore, Dem., 901,980; Buchanan, Ind., 16,959; Browne, Libertarian, 15,530.

Iowa

County	2000 Gore (D)	Bush (R)	1996 Clinton (D)	Dole (R)	Perot (RF)
Adair	1,753	2,275	1,802	1,655	458
Adams	897	1,170	1,070	920	320
Allamakee	2,883	3,277	2,551	2,457	680
Appanoose	2,560	2,992	2,747	2,233	554
Audubon	1,780	1,909	1,827	1,314	314
Benton	5,915	5,468	5,546	3,835	846
Black Hawk	30,112	23,468	29,651	19,322	3,623
Boone	6,270	5,625	6,446	4,293	987
Bremer	5,169	5,675	5,023	4,213	862
Buchanan	5,045	4,092	4,997	3,043	836
Buena Vista	3,297	4,354	3,420	3,636	831
Butler	2,735	3,837	3,061	3,036	489
Calhoun	2,132	2,776	2,193	2,077	462
Carroll	4,463	4,879	4,333	3,392	998
Cass	2,481	4,206	2,616	3,384	809

County	2000 Gore (D)	Bush (R)	1996 Clinton (D)	Dole (R)	Perot (RF)
Cedar	4,033	4,031	3,856	2,966	756
Cerro Gordo	12,185	9,397	11,943	7,427	1,689
Cherokee	2,845	3,463	2,853	2,629	834
Chickasaw	3,435	2,936	3,355	2,191	759
Clarke	2,081	1,984	2,053	1,401	440
Clay	3,294	3,992	3,659	3,129	802
Clayton	4,238	4,034	4,284	2,944	912
Clinton	12,276	9,229	11,481	7,624	2,300
Crawford	2,838	3,482	3,140	2,686	847
Dallas	8,561	10,306	8,017	6,647	1,198
Davis	1,691	1,956	1,894	1,445	382
Decatur	1,674	1,903	1,846	1,287	452
Delaware	3,808	4,273	3,704	3,065	679
Des Moines	11,351	7,385	10,761	5,778	1,792
Dickinson	3,660	4,225	3,562	3,129	901
Dubuque	22,341	16,462	20,839	13,391	3,304
Emmet	2,165	2,331	2,270	1,641	470
Fayette	4,640	4,747	4,832	3,848	890
Floyd	3,830	3,191	3,769	2,379	689
Franklin	2,122	2,657	2,232	2,054	417
Fremont	1,459	2,069	1,481	1,576	480
Greene	2,301	2,282	2,519	1,861	396
Grundy	2,139	3,851	2,322	2,928	401
Guthrie	2,493	2,840	2,552	2,034	515
Hamilton	3,407	3,968	3,455	3,109	661
Hancock	2,281	2,988	2,399	2,353	529
Hardin	3,734	4,486	4,053	3,505	713
Harrison	2,551	3,802	2,576	3,070	820
Henry	3,907	4,476	3,798	3,478	914
Howard	2,426	1,922	2,303	1,528	555
Humboldt	1,949	2,846	2,080	2,236	590
Ida	1,411	1,968	1,589	1,684	436
Iowa	3,230	3,894	3,354	3,042	575
Jackson	4,945	3,769	4,609	2,827	936
Jasper	8,699	8,729	8,776	6,414	1,263
Jefferson	2,863	3,248	2,597	2,541	571
Johnson	31,174	17,899	27,888	13,402	2,313
Jones	4,690	4,201	4,668	3,083	765
Keokuk	2,181	2,571	2,545	2,080	432
Kossuth	3,960	4,612	4,031	3,477	932
Lee	9,632	6,339	8,831	4,932	1,734
Linn	48,897	40,417	45,497	30,958	5,607
Louisa	2,294	2,207	2,081	1,565	590
Lucas	1,934	2,262	2,168	1,586	433
Lyon	1,313	3,918	1,489	3,396	422
Madison	3,093	3,662	3,070	2,550	654
Mahaska	3,370	5,971	3,737	4,473	656
Marion	5,741	8,358	5,978	6,100	871
Marshall	8,322	8,785	8,669	7,017	1,455
Mills	2,039	3,684	2,068	2,958	683
Mitchell	2,650	2,388	2,596	1,877	563
Monona	2,086	2,304	1,952	1,674	580
Monroe	1,699	1,858	1,884	1,272	329
Montgomery	1,838	3,417	1,912	2,583	663
Muscatine	8,058	7,483	7,674	5,858	1,705
O'Brien	2,170	4,674	2,236	3,877	578
Osceola	913	2,064	1,010	1,736	274
Page	2,293	4,588	2,220	4,032	753
Palo Alto	2,326	2,341	2,371	1,817	477
Plymouth	3,499	6,189	3,745	5,117	997
Pocahontas	1,736	2,242	1,981	1,707	478
Polk	89,715	79,927	83,877	60,884	9,516
Pottawattamie	14,726	18,783	13,276	15,648	3,534
Poweshiek	4,222	4,396	4,183	3,221	681
Ringgold	1,246	1,369	1,439	967	310
Sac	2,099	2,776	2,170	2,209	579
Scott	35,857	32,801	32,694	26,751	4,991
Shelby	2,179	3,655	2,176	3,056	652
Sioux	2,148	12,241	2,392	10,864	718
Story	17,478	16,228	17,234	12,468	2,091
Tama	4,045	4,034	3,994	2,986	713
Taylor	1,247	1,770	1,458	1,419	379
Union	2,540	3,003	2,787	2,156	660
Van Buren	1,440	2,016	1,536	1,460	347
Wapello	8,355	6,313	8,437	4,828	1,376
Warren	9,521	9,621	9,120	6,905	1,267
Washington	3,932	4,827	3,828	3,600	636
Wayne	1,300	1,666	1,650	1,295	310
Webster	8,479	8,172	8,380	6,275	1,580
Winnebago	2,691	2,662	2,679	2,211	590
Winneshiek	4,349	4,647	4,122	3,532	973
Woodbury	17,691	18,864	17,224	16,368	3,436
Worth	2,208	1,659	2,293	1,284	403
Wright	2,796	3,384	2,912	2,473	536
Totals	**638,517**	**634,373**	**620,258**	**492,644**	**105,159**

Iowa Vote Since 1952

1952, Eisenhower, Rep., 808,906; Stevenson, Dem., 451,513; Hallinan, Prog., 5,085; Hamblen, Proh., 2,882; Hoopes, Soc., 219; Hass, Soc. Labor, 139; scattering, 29.

1956, Eisenhower, Rep., 729,187; Stevenson, Dem., 501,858; Andrews (A.C.P. of Iowa), 3,202; Hoopes, Soc., 192; Hass, Soc. Labor, 125.

1960, Kennedy, Dem., 550,565; Nixon, Rep., 722,381; Hass, Soc. Labor, 230; write-in, 634.

1964, Johnson, Dem., 733,030; Goldwater, Rep., 449,148; Hass, Soc. Labor, 182; DeBerry, Soc. Workers, 159; Munn, Proh., 1,902.

1968, Nixon, Rep., 619,106; Humphrey, Dem., 476,699; Wallace, 3d Party, 66,422; Munn, Proh., 362; Halstead, Soc. Workers, 3,377; Cleaver, Peace and Freedom, 1,332; Blomen, Soc. Labor, 241.

1972, Nixon, Rep., 706,207; McGovern, Dem., 496,206; Schmitz, Amer., 22,056; Jenness, Soc. Workers, 488; Fisher, Soc. Labor, 195; Hall, Com., 272; Green, Universal, 199; scattered, 321.

1976, Carter, Dem., 619,931; Ford, Rep., 632,863; McCarthy, Ind., 20,051; Anderson, Amer., 3,040; MacBride, Libertarian, 1,452.

1980, Reagan, Rep., 676,026; Carter, Dem., 508,672; Anderson, Ind., 115,633; Clark, Libertarian, 13,123; Commoner, Citizens, 2,273; McReynolds, Socialist, 534; Hall, Com., 298; DeBerry, Soc. Workers, 244; Greaves, Amer., 189; Bubar, Statesman, 150; scattering, 519.

1984, Reagan, Rep., 703,088; Mondale, Dem., 605,620; Bergland, Libertarian, 1,844.

1988, Bush, Rep., 545,355; Dukakis, Dem., 670,557; LaRouche, Ind., 3,526; Paul, Lib., 2,494.

1992, Clinton, Dem., 586,353; Bush, Rep., 504,891; Perot, Ind., 253,468; Hagelin, Natural Law, 3,079; Gritz, Populist/America First, 1,177; Marrou, Libertarian, 1,076.

1996, Clinton, Dem., 620,258; Dole, Rep., 492,644; Perot, Ref., 105,159; Nader, Green, 6,550; Hagelin, Natural Law, 3,349; Browne, Libertarian, 2,315; Phillips, Taxpayers, 2,229; Harris, Soc. Workers, 331.

2000, Gore, Dem., 638,517; Bush, Rep., 634,373; Nader, Green, 29,374; Buchanan, Reform, 5,731; Browne, Libertarian, 3,209; Hagelin, Ind., 2,281; Phillips, Constitution, 613; Harris, Soc. Workers, 190; McReynolds, Soc., 107.

Kansas

County	2000 Gore (D)	Bush (R)	1996 Clinton (D)	Dole (R)	Perot (RF)
Allen	2,132	3,379	2,299	2,797	554
Anderson	1,327	1,984	1,367	1,636	449
Atchison	3,171	3,378	2,926	2,828	727
Barber	637	1,755	730	1,696	279
Barton	3,238	7,302	3,121	7,855	1,004
Bourbon	2,211	3,852	2,491	3,318	760
Brown	1,512	2,985	1,529	2,688	497
Butler	6,755	13,377	7,294	13,979	2,274
Chase	391	848	496	778	259
Chautauqua	443	1,347	568	1,142	222
Cherokee	3,783	5,014	3,771	4,138	1,072
Cheyenne	350	1,312	422	1,211	174
Clark	292	926	334	855	109
Clay	951	2,998	963	2,793	389
Cloud	1,314	2,918	1,615	2,743	609
Coffey	1,196	2,700	1,118	2,369	572
Comanche	211	760	298	691	133
Cowley	5,535	8,080	5,588	7,872	1,904
Crawford	7,076	7,160	7,504	6,447	1,785
Decatur	424	1,255	417	1,255	156
Dickinson	2,413	5,243	2,423	5,174	888
Doniphan	1,134	2,350	1,050	1,962	0
Douglas	18,249	17,062	18,116	16,116	2,630
Edwards	447	1,062	539	1,088	180
Elk	402	1,080	488	933	206
Ellis	3,926	6,516	4,142	6,809	894
Ellsworth	825	1,845	899	2,078	245
Finney	2,431	6,442	2,420	6,188	805
Ford	2,566	6,050	2,628	5,681	914
Franklin	3,321	5,925	3,552	5,007	1,184
Geary	2,660	3,977	2,444	3,686	618
Gove	296	1,122	351	1,123	141
Graham	346	1,058	432	1,031	152
Grant	683	2,126	633	1,772	250
Gray	482	1,631	404	1,457	164
Greeley	143	628	161	567	47
Greenwood	1,027	2,392	1,108	1,932	552
Hamilton	264	901	342	811	84
Harper	869	2,076	836	1,941	355
Harvey	4,591	8,271	4,918	8,382	1,023
Haskell	263	1,323	304	1,143	96
Hodgeman	217	835	251	808	99
Jackson	1,990	3,001	1,983	2,682	735

County	2000 Gore (D)	Bush (R)	1996 Clinton (D)	Dole (R)	Perot (RF)
Jefferson	3,000	4,423	2,757	3,781	1,030
Jewell	380	1,400	417	1,374	188
Johnson	79,118	129,965	68,129	110,368	10,425
Kearny	320	1,084	335	1,041	106
Kingman	991	2,672	1,006	2,659	409
Kiowa	294	1,262	331	1,264	170
Labette	3,745	4,475	3,931	4,283	1,091
Lane	252	846	271	865	86
Leavenworth	9,733	12,583	9,098	10,778	2,419
Lincoln	469	1,295	528	1,372	212
Linn	1,587	2,513	1,590	2,077	535
Logan	231	1,088	296	1,155	112
Lyon	5,190	6,652	4,884	6,612	1,584
McPherson	3,272	8,501	3,536	8,142	1,115
Marion	1,475	4,156	1,673	4,173	492
Marshall	1,831	3,066	1,932	2,811	713
Meade	400	1,604	426	1,443	173
Miami	4,554	6,611	4,237	5,256	1,339
Mitchell	751	2,350	833	2,435	246
Montgomery	4,770	8,496	5,269	7,428	1,528
Morris	882	1,599	965	1,553	451
Morton	321	1,203	376	1,073	124
Nemaha	1,494	3,578	1,648	3,014	676
Neosho	2,588	4,014	2,527	3,409	907
Ness	383	1,420	428	1,336	186
Norton	598	1,744	640	1,814	265
Osage	2,530	3,770	2,502	3,487	1,101
Osborne	484	1,432	608	1,582	191
Ottawa	631	1,977	752	1,846	261
Pawnee	968	1,850	932	1,927	275
Phillips	611	2,057	758	2,005	242
Pottawatomie	2,037	4,985	1,997	4,504	1,035
Pratt	1,314	2,885	1,367	2,591	408
Rawlins	306	1,349	335	1,393	146
Reno	9,025	15,179	9,108	14,275	2,661
Republic	604	2,239	688	2,283	268
Rice	1,422	2,903	1,434	2,842	482
Riley	6,188	10,672	6,746	11,113	1,478
Rooks	597	2,016	650	1,864	251
Rush	505	1,235	547	1,239	185
Russell	886	2,434	705	3,347	164
Saline	7,487	12,412	7,728	12,475	2,192
Scott	418	1,811	458	1,750	160
Sedgwick	62,561	93,724	59,643	93,397	11,875
Seward	1,126	3,869	1,309	3,812	396
Shawnee	34,818	35,894	32,803	34,845	7,304
Sheridan	281	1,132	264	1,053	95
Sherman	681	1,894	736	2,110	220
Smith	534	1,534	638	1,628	213
Stafford	567	1,546	651	1,604	276
Stanton	215	785	189	628	60
Stevens	345	1,714	405	1,548	213
Sumner	3,549	6,176	3,638	5,952	1,260
Thomas	807	2,822	866	2,725	295
Trego	516	1,220	548	1,205	209
Wabaunsee	1,025	2,182	966	1,884	479
Wallace	103	737	160	738	65
Washington	687	2,446	804	2,397	326
Wichita	207	859	239	796	80
Wilson	1,186	2,748	1,297	2,458	562
Woodson	521	974	598	953	269
Wyandotte	32,411	14,024	31,252	14,011	3,931
Totals	**399,276**	**622,332**	**387,659**	**583,245**	**92,639**

Kansas Vote Since 1952

1952, Eisenhower, Rep., 616,302; Stevenson, Dem., 273,296; Hamblen, Proh., 6,038; Hoopes, Soc., 530.

1956, Eisenhower, Rep., 566,878; Stevenson, Dem., 296,317; Holtwick, Proh., 3,048.

1960, Kennedy, Dem., 363,213; Nixon, Rep., 561,474; Decker, Proh., 4,138.

1964, Johnson, Dem., 464,028; Goldwater, Rep., 386,579; Munn, Proh., 5,393; Hass, Soc. Labor, 1,901.

1968, Nixon, Rep., 478,674; Humphrey, Dem., 302,996; Wallace, 3d Party, 88,921; Munn, Proh., 2,192.

1972, Nixon, Rep., 619,812; McGovern, Dem., 270,287; Schmitz, Conservative, 21,808; Munn, Proh., 4,188.

1976, Carter, Dem., 430,421; Ford, Rep., 502,752; McCarthy, Ind., 13,185; Anderson, Amer., 4,724; MacBride, Libertarian, 3,242; Maddox, Conservative, 2,118; Bubar, Proh., 1,403.

1980, Reagan, Rep., 566,812; Carter, Dem., 326,150; Anderson, Ind., 68,231; Clark, Libertarian, 14,470; Shelton, Amer., 1,555; Hall, Com., 967; Bubar, Statesman, 821; Rarick, Conservative, 789.

1984, Reagan, Rep., 674,646; Mondale, Dem., 332,471; Bergland, Libertarian, 3,585.

1988, Bush, Rep., 554,049; Dukakis, Dem., 422,636; Paul, Ind., 12,553; Fulani, Ind., 3,806.

1992, Clinton, Dem., 390,434; Bush, Rep., 449,951; Perot, Ind., 312,358; Marrou, Libertarian, 4,314.

1996, Dole, Rep., 583,245; Clinton, Dem., 387,659; Perot, Ref., 92,639; Browne, Libertarian, 4,557; Phillips, Ind., 3,519; Hagelin, Ind., 1,655.

2000, Bush, Rep., 622,332; Gore, Dem., 399,276; Nader, Ind., 36,086; Buchanan, Reform, 7,370; Browne, Libertarian, 4,525; Hagelin, Ind., 1,373; Phillips, Constitution, 1,254.

Kentucky

County	2000 Gore (D)	Bush (R)	1996 Clinton (D)	Dole (R)	Perot (RF)
Adair	1,779	5,460	1,821	3,876	790
Allen	1,950	4,415	1,781	3,032	393
Anderson	2,902	4,909	2,898	2,972	751
Ballard	1,880	1,824	2,255	1,064	411
Barren	4,930	8,741	5,044	5,700	1,065
Bath	2,087	2,303	1,886	1,229	428
Bell	4,787	5,585	5,058	3,917	940
Boone	9,248	22,016	8,379	15,085	1,900
Bourbon	3,048	3,881	3,030	2,592	603
Boyd	9,541	9,247	9,668	7,054	2,070
Boyle	3,963	6,126	3,877	4,157	709
Bracken	888	2,065	1,055	1,371	271
Breathitt	2,902	2,084	3,106	1,058	397
Breckinridge	2,595	4,763	2,956	3,151	670
Bullitt	8,195	14,054	7,651	8,697	1,973
Butler	1,299	3,654	1,260	2,531	348
Caldwell	2,223	3,161	2,434	2,067	637
Calloway	5,635	7,705	5,281	4,989	1,223
Campbell	12,040	20,789	11,957	16,640	2,312
Carlisle	1,149	1,405	1,355	816	245
Carroll	1,601	1,818	1,689	1,170	351
Carter	4,182	4,617	3,728	3,240	781
Casey	1,122	4,284	1,106	3,187	525
Christian	6,778	10,787	6,843	8,285	1,064
Clark	4,918	7,297	4,987	4,739	1,095
Clay	1,723	4,926	2,135	3,716	478
Clinton	1,032	3,224	1,072	2,521	350
Crittenden	1,610	2,469	1,480	1,509	400
Cumberland	736	2,220	753	1,654	227
Daviess	14,126	21,361	15,366	15,844	3,344
Edmonson	1,710	3,250	1,595	2,619	298
Elliott	1,525	827	1,298	421	284
Estill	1,591	3,033	1,724	2,220	479
Fayette	47,277	54,495	43,632	42,930	5,345
Fleming	1,813	3,282	1,913	2,313	522
Floyd	10,088	5,068	9,655	3,139	1,518
Franklin	10,853	10,209	11,251	7,132	1,873
Fulton	1,452	1,293	1,614	863	223
Gallatin	1,049	1,345	1,189	838	299
Garrard	1,713	4,043	1,486	2,540	337
Grant	2,568	4,405	2,541	2,697	661
Graves	6,097	7,849	6,991	5,130	1,596
Grayson	2,604	5,843	2,716	4,249	677
Green	1,085	3,615	1,285	2,763	475
Greenup	7,164	7,233	6,883	5,370	1,627
Hancock	1,508	2,032	1,547	1,356	418
Hardin	11,095	18,964	11,031	12,642	2,815
Harlan	5,365	4,980	5,874	3,337	884
Harrison	2,658	3,793	2,934	2,433	801
Hart	2,201	3,725	2,527	2,701	501
Henderson	8,054	7,698	8,051	5,092	1,556
Henry	2,117	3,244	2,324	2,110	564
Hickman	940	1,151	1,220	695	247
Hopkins	6,734	9,490	7,239	6,363	1,512
Jackson	701	4,079	960	3,045	299
Jefferson	149,901	145,052	144,207	114,860	19,413
Jessamine	4,633	10,074	4,428	6,686	1,040
Johnson	2,374	4,811	3,348	3,262	1,010
Kenton	19,100	35,363	19,407	28,579	3,680
Knott	4,349	2,029	4,842	1,201	517
Knox	3,690	6,058	3,736	4,502	811
Larue	1,727	3,384	2,040	2,140	469
Laurel	4,856	13,029	4,306	9,454	1,211
Lawrence	2,258	2,969	2,195	1,812	481
Lee	836	1,893	1,023	1,302	181
Leslie	1,210	3,159	1,466	2,296	304
Letcher	4,698	4,092	4,160	2,222	782
Lewis	1,293	3,217	1,415	2,365	561
Lincoln	2,678	4,795	2,550	3,006	526
Livingston	2,022	2,118	2,228	1,258	449
Logan	3,885	5,344	4,181	3,888	704
Lyon	1,680	1,688	1,641	999	284
McCracken	11,412	14,745	12,670	10,221	2,268
McCreary	1,418	3,321	1,710	2,527	488
McLean	1,747	2,219	1,834	1,368	385
Madison	9,309	13,682	8,142	9,212	1,613
Magoffin	2,603	2,785	2,249	1,434	337

County	2000 Gore (D)	Bush (R)	1996 Clinton (D)	Dole (R)	Perot (RF)
Marion	2,778	3,259	2,922	2,013	757
Marshall	6,203	7,294	6,054	4,579	1,391
Martin	1,714	2,667	1,807	1,612	401
Mason	2,178	3,572	2,444	2,588	484
Meade	3,596	5,319	3,653	2,855	912
Menifee	1,038	1,170	979	608	179
Mercer	3,092	5,362	3,179	3,264	738
Metcalfe	1,318	2,476	1,349	1,651	355
Monroe	1,158	4,377	1,114	3,300	415
Montgomery	3,833	4,534	3,372	2,681	705
Morgan	1,875	2,295	1,843	1,439	380
Muhlenberg	6,295	5,518	6,564	3,569	1,218
Nelson	5,481	7,714	5,392	4,645	1,067
Nicholas	994	1,613	1,092	950	265
Ohio	3,303	5,413	3,487	3,475	1,076
Oldham	6,236	13,580	6,202	10,477	1,521
Owen	1,394	2,582	1,603	1,709	454
Owsley	339	1,466	647	920	153
Pendleton	1,670	3,044	1,926	2,177	462
Perry	5,514	5,300	6,015	3,382	894
Pike	13,611	11,005	14,126	7,160	2,148
Powell	2,008	2,258	2,156	1,526	523
Pulaski	5,415	15,845	5,340	11,945	1,420
Robertson	341	630	360	368	117
Rockcastle	1,174	3,992	1,160	3,106	338
Rowan	3,505	3,546	3,215	2,309	724
Russell	1,710	5,268	1,582	4,017	837
Scott	5,472	7,952	4,258	4,349	977
Shelby	4,435	8,068	4,629	5,307	780
Simpson	2,583	3,169	2,749	2,186	401
Spencer	1,554	3,150	1,404	1,614	341
Taylor	2,790	6,151	2,897	4,573	829
Todd	1,496	2,646	1,744	1,912	424
Trigg	2,110	3,130	2,087	1,975	394
Trimble	1,181	1,837	1,245	999	308
Union	2,547	2,749	2,913	1,554	598
Warren	12,180	20,235	11,642	15,784	1,835
Washington	1,458	3,044	1,639	2,116	383
Wayne	2,312	4,069	2,422	3,122	481
Webster	2,388	2,599	2,852	1,568	660
Whitley	4,101	7,502	4,174	5,402	1,027
Wolfe	1,136	1,267	1,297	772	202
Woodford	3,995	5,890	3,910	4,270	746
Totals	**638,923**	**872,520**	**636,614**	**623,283**	**120,396**

Kentucky Vote Since 1952

1952, Eisenhower, Rep., 495,029; Stevenson, Dem., 495,729; Hamblen, Proh., 1,161; Hass, Soc. Labor, 893; Hallinan, Proh., 336.

1956, Eisenhower, Rep., 572,192; Stevenson, Dem., 476,453; Byrd, States' Rights, 2,657; Holtwick, Proh., 2,145; Hass, Soc. Labor, 358.

1960, Kennedy, Dem., 521,855; Nixon, Rep., 602,607.

1964, Johnson, Dem., 669,659; Goldwater, Rep., 372,977; Kasper, Natl. States Rights, 3,469.

1968, Nixon, Rep., 462,411; Humphrey, Dem., 397,547; Wallace, 3d Party, 193,098; Halstead, Soc. Workers, 2,843.

1972, Nixon, Rep., 676,446; McGovern, Dem., 371,159; Schmitz, Amer., 17,627; Spock, Peoples, 1,118; Jenness, Soc. Workers, 685; Hall, Com., 464.

1976, Carter, Dem., 615,717; Ford, Rep., 531,852; Anderson, Amer., 8,308; McCarthy, Ind., 6,837; Maddox, Amer. Ind., 2,328; MacBride, Libertarian, 814.

1980, Reagan, Rep., 635,274; Carter, Dem., 616,417; Anderson, Ind., 31,127; Clark, Libertarian, 5,531; McCormack, Respect For Life, 4,233; Commoner, Citizens, 1,304; Pulley, Socialist, 393; Hall, Com., 348.

1984, Reagan, Rep., 815,345; Mondale, Dem., 536,756.

1988, Bush, Rep., 734,281; Dukakis, Dem., 580,368; Duke, Pop., 4,494; Paul, Lib., 2,118.

1992, Clinton, Dem., 665,104; Bush, Rep., 617,178; Perot, Ind., 203,944; Marrou, Libertarian, 4,513.

1996, Clinton, Dem., 636,614; Dole, Rep., 623,283; Perot, Ref., 120,396; Browne, Libertarian, 4,009; Phillips, Taxpayers, 2,204; Hagelin, Natural Law, 1,493.

2000, Bush, Rep., 872,520; Gore, Dem., 638,923; Nader, Green, 23,118; Buchanan, Reform, 4,152; Browne, Libertarian, 2,885; Hagelin, Natural Law, 1,513; Phillips, Constitution, 915.

Louisiana

Parish	2000 Gore (D)	Bush (R)	1996 Clinton (D)	Dole (R)	Perot (RF)
Acadia	8,892	13,814	12,300	9,246	2,234
Allen	3,914	4,035	4,930	2,589	1,187
Ascension	13,385	16,818	15,263	10,885	3,027
Assumption	5,222	4,388	6,416	2,698	904
Avoyelles	6,701	7,329	9,689	4,433	1,937
Beauregard	3,958	7,862	4,925	5,526	1,834
Bienville	3,413	3,269	4,335	2,402	457
Bossier	11,933	23,224	15,504	16,852	2,660
Caddo	47,530	46,807	55,543	38,445	4,821
Calcasieu	33,919	38,086	38,238	26,494	8,281
Caldwell	1,359	2,817	2,117	1,842	514
Cameron	1,435	2,593	2,103	1,365	594
Catahoula	1,718	2,912	2,692	1,770	615
Claiborne	2,721	3,384	3,609	2,500	530
Concordia	3,569	4,627	4,565	3,134	855
DeSoto	5,036	5,260	6,221	3,526	646
E. Baton Rouge	76,516	89,128	83,493	77,811	7,990
East Carroll	1,876	1,280	2,149	1,008	186
East Feliciana	3,870	4,051	4,714	2,949	660
Evangeline	5,763	7,290	7,847	5,278	1,447
Franklin	2,792	5,363	4,076	3,961	814
Grant	2,099	4,784	2,980	3,117	1,055
Iberia	11,762	17,236	15,087	12,014	2,448
Iberville	8,355	5,573	9,553	4,031	1,076
Jackson	2,582	4,347	3,368	3,030	571
Jefferson	70,411	105,003	80,407	92,820	9,667
Jefferson Davis	5,162	6,946	6,897	4,311	1,543
Lafayette	27,190	48,491	32,504	36,419	4,631
Lafourche	14,627	18,575	18,810	12,105	2,984
LaSalle	1,397	4,564	2,543	2,925	947
Lincoln	6,851	9,246	7,903	6,973	761
Livingston	11,008	24,889	13,276	16,159	4,150
Madison	2,489	2,127	3,085	1,591	315
Morehouse	5,289	6,641	6,160	5,193	963
Natchitoches	6,924	7,332	8,296	5,471	1,053
Orleans	137,630	39,404	144,720	39,576	3,805
Ouachita	21,457	35,107	24,525	28,559	3,586
Plaquemines	4,425	6,302	5,348	4,493	856
Pointe Coupee	5,813	4,710	6,835	3,545	845
Rapides	18,898	28,831	23,004	21,548	4,670
Red River	2,177	2,200	2,641	1,344	268
Richland	3,282	4,895	4,143	3,765	645
Sabine	2,846	5,754	4,263	3,543	1,043
St. Bernard	11,682	16,255	14,312	13,549	2,664
St. Charles	8,918	11,981	10,612	9,316	1,307
St. Helena	3,059	1,965	3,692	1,455	417
St. James	6,523	3,813	7,247	2,832	608
St. John the Baptist	9,745	7,423	9,937	6,025	966
St. Landry	18,067	15,449	20,636	12,273	2,311
St. Martin	9,853	9,961	12,492	6,296	1,607
St. Mary	9,851	11,325	12,402	8,018	1,850
St. Tammany	22,722	59,193	24,281	44,761	4,741
Tangipahoa	15,843	20,421	18,617	15,517	3,144
Tensas	1,580	1,330	1,882	1,000	176
Terrebonne	14,414	21,314	18,550	13,944	3,359
Union	3,205	5,772	4,260	4,418	696
Vermilion	8,704	12,495	12,609	7,653	1,954
Vernon	4,655	8,794	6,195	5,449	2,068
Washington	7,399	8,983	9,603	6,642	1,643
Webster	7,197	9,420	9,688	6,153	1,324
W. Baton Rouge	5,058	4,924	5,697	3,254	799
West Carroll	1,319	3,220	1,853	2,366	461
W. Feliciana	2,187	2,512	2,416	1,616	388
Winn	2,187	4,028	3,779	2,803	735
Totals	**792,344**	**927,871**	**927,837**	**712,586**	**123,293**

Louisiana Vote Since 1952

1952, Eisenhower, Rep., 306,925; Stevenson, Dem., 345,027.

1956, Eisenhower, Rep., 329,047; Stevenson, Dem., 243,977; Andrews, States' Rights, 44,520.

1960, Kennedy, Dem., 407,339; Nixon, Rep., 230,890; States' Rights (unpledged), 169,572.

1964, Johnson, Dem., 387,068; Goldwater, Rep., 509,225.

1968, Nixon, Rep., 257,535; Humphrey, Dem., 309,615; Wallace, 3d Party, 530,300.

1972, Nixon, Rep., 686,852; McGovern, Dem., 298,142; Schmitz, Amer., 52,099; Jenness, Soc. Workers, 14,398.

1976, Carter, Dem., 661,365; Ford, Rep., 587,446; Maddox, Amer., 10,058; Hall, Com., 7,417; McCarthy, Ind., 6,588; MacBride, Libertarian, 3,325.

1980, Reagan, Rep., 792,853; Carter, Dem., 708,453; Anderson, Ind., 26,345; Rarick, Amer. Ind., 10,333; Clark, Libertarian, 8,240; Commoner, Citizens, 1,584; DeBerry, Soc. Work., 783.

1984, Reagan, Rep., 1,037,299; Mondale, Dem., 651,586; Bergland, Libertarian, 1,876.

1988, Bush, Rep., 883,702; Dukakis, Dem., 717,460; Duke, Pop., 18,612; Paul, Lib., 4,115.

1992, Clinton, Dem., 815,971; Bush, Rep., 733,386; Perot, Ind., 211,478; Gritz, Populist/America First, 18,545; Marrou, Libertarian, 3,155; Daniels, Ind., 1,663; Phillips, U.S. Taxpayers, 1,552; Fulani, New Alliance, 1,434; LaRouche, Ind., 1,136.

1996, Clinton, Dem., 927,837; Dole, Rep., 712,586; Perot, Ref., 123,293; Browne, Libertarian, 7,499; Nader, Liberty, Ecology, Community, 4,719; Phillips, Taxpayers, 3,366; Hagelin, Natural Law, 2,981; Moorehead, Workers World, 1,678.
2000, Bush, Rep., 927,871; Gore, Dem., 792,344; Nader, Green, 20,473; Buchanan, Reform, 14,356; Phillips, Constitution, 5,483; Browne, Libertarian, 2,951; Harris, Soc. Workers, 1,103; Hagelin, Natural Law, 1,075.

Maine

City	2000 Gore (D)	Bush (R)	1996 Clinton (D)	Dole (R)	Perot (RF)
Auburn	6,014	4,568	5,750	3,060	1,484
Augusta	5,116	3,344	5,307	2,353	1,100
Bangor	7,311	6,131	7,609	4,476	1,399
Biddeford	5,383	3,126	5,653	1,768	1,019
Brunswick	5,547	3,767	5,258	2,850	841
Gorham	3,394	3,353	2,990	2,269	710
Lewiston	9,663	5,255	10,275	3,182	2,113
Orono	2,701	1,506	2,748	1,106	369
Portland	20,506	8,838	19,755	7,178	2,255
Presque Isle	2,004	2,231	2,015	1,491	594
Saco	4,783	3,402	4,506	2,140	834
Sanford	4,653	3,871	4,368	2,239	1,524
Scarborough	4,278	4,964	3,906	3,214	805
S. Portland	7,267	4,390	6,777	3,241	906
Waterville	4,279	2,115	4,219	1,478	750
Westbrook	4,316	3,258	4,373	2,186	864
Windham	3,550	3,754	3,251	2,396	898
York	3,708	3,462	2,970	2,525	649
Other	215,478	215,281	211,058	137,226	66,856
Totals	319,951	286,616	312,788	186,378	85,970

Maine Vote Since 1952

1952, Eisenhower, Rep., 232,353; Stevenson, Dem., 118,806; Hallinan, Prog., 332; Hass, Soc. Labor, 156; Hoopes, Soc., 138; scattered, 1.
1956, Eisenhower, Rep., 249,238; Stevenson, Dem., 102,468.
1960, Kennedy, Dem., 181,159; Nixon, Rep., 240,608.
1964, Johnson, Dem., 262,264; Goldwater, Rep., 118,701.
1968, Nixon, Rep., 169,254; Humphrey, Dem., 217,312; Wallace, 3d Party, 6,370.
1972, Nixon, Rep., 256,458; McGovern, Dem., 160,584; scattered, 229.
1976, Carter, Dem., 232,279; Ford, Rep., 236,320; McCarthy, Ind., 10,874; Bubar, Proh., 3,495.
1980, Reagan, Rep., 238,522; Carter, Dem., 220,974; Anderson, Ind., 53,327; Clark, Libertarian, 5,119; Commoner, Citizens, 4,394; Hall, Com., 591; write-ins, 84.
1984, Reagan, Rep., 336,500; Mondale, Dem., 214,515.
1988, Bush, Rep., 307,131; Dukakis, Dem., 243,569; Paul, Lib., 2,700; Fulani, New Alliance, 1,405.
1992, Clinton, Dem., 263,420; Perot, Ind., 206,820; Bush, Rep., 206,504; Marrou, Libertarian, 1,681.
1996, Clinton, Dem., 312,788; Dole, Rep., 186,378; Perot, Ref., 85,970; Nader, Green, 15,279; Browne, Libertarian, 2,996; Phillips, Taxpayers, 1,517; Hagelin, Natural Law, 825.
2000, Gore, Dem., 319,951; Bush, Rep., 286,616; Nader, Green, 37,127; Buchanan, Reform, 4,443; Browne, Libertarian, 3,074; Phillips, Constitution, 579.

Maryland

County	2000 Gore (D)	Bush (R)	1996 Clinton (D)	Dole (R)	Perot (RF)
Allegany	10,894	14,656	11,025	12,136	2,652
Anne Arundel	89,624	104,209	72,147	83,574	14,287
Baltimore	160,635	133,033	132,599	114,449	20,393
Calvert	12,986	16,004	10,008	11,509	1,932
Caroline	3,396	5,300	3,251	3,874	947
Carroll	20,146	41,742	17,122	30,316	4,873
Cecil	12,327	15,444	10,144	10,885	3,124
Charles	21,873	21,768	15,890	17,432	2,333
Dorchester	5,232	5,847	4,613	4,337	1,008
Frederick	30,725	45,350	25,081	34,494	4,989
Garrett	2,872	7,514	3,121	5,400	1,200
Harford	35,665	52,862	29,779	39,686	7,939
Howard	58,556	49,809	47,569	40,849	6,011
Kent	3,627	4,155	3,207	3,055	676
Montgomery	232,453	124,580	198,807	117,730	14,450
Prince George's	214,345	50,017	176,612	52,697	9,153
Queen Anne's	6,257	9,970	5,054	7,147	1,312
St. Mary's	11,912	16,856	9,988	11,835	1,827
Somerset	3,785	3,609	3,557	2,919	613
Talbot	5,854	8,874	4,821	6,997	914
Washington	18,221	27,948	16,481	21,434	3,934
Wicomico	14,469	16,338	12,303	12,687	2,160
Worcester	9,389	10,742	7,587	7,621	1,612
City					
Baltimore	158,765	27,150	145,441	28,467	7,473
Totals	1,144,008	813,827	966,207	681,530	115,812

Maryland Vote Since 1952

1952, Eisenhower, Rep., 499,424; Stevenson, Dem., 395,337; Hallinan, Prog., 7,313.
1956, Eisenhower, Rep., 559,738; Stevenson, Dem., 372,613.
1960, Kennedy, Dem., 565,800; Nixon, Rep., 489,538.
1964, Johnson, Dem., 730,912; Goldwater, Rep., 385,495; write-in, 50.
1968, Nixon, Rep., 517,995; Humphrey, Dem., 538,310; Wallace, 3d Party, 178,734.
1972, Nixon, Rep., 829,305; McGovern, Dem., 505,781; Schmitz, Amer., 18,726.
1976, Carter, Dem., 759,612; Ford, Rep., 672,661.
1980, Reagan, Rep., 680,606; Carter, Dem., 726,161; Anderson, Ind., 119,537; Clark, Libertarian, 14,192.
1984, Reagan, Rep., 879,918; Mondale, Dem., 787,935; Bergland, Libertarian, 5,721.
1988, Bush, Rep., 876,167; Dukakis, Dem., 826,304; Paul, Lib., 6,748; Fulani, New Alliance, 5,115.
1992, Clinton, Dem., 988,571; Bush, Rep., 707,094; Perot, Ind., 281,414; Marrou, Libertarian, 4,715; Fulani, New Alliance, 2,768.
1996, Clinton, Dem., 966,207; Dole, Rep., 681,530; Perot, Ref., 115,812; Browne, Libertarian, 8,765; Phillips, Taxpayers, 3,402; Hagelin, Natural Law, 2,517.
2000, Gore, Dem., 1,144,008; Bush, Rep., 813,827; Nader, Green, 53,768; Browne, Libertarian, 5,310; Buchanan, Reform, 4,248; Phillips, Constitution, 918.

Massachusetts

City	2000 Gore (D)	Bush (R)	1996 Clinton (D)	Dole (R)	Perot (RF)
Boston	132,393	36,389	125,529	33,366	8,428
Brockton	18,563	8,288	16,361	6,972	2,738
Brookline	19,384	4,350	18,812	4,579	799
Cambridge	28,846	5,166	29,913	4,976	1,415
Chicopee	13,236	6,512	14,203	5,188	2,495
Fall River	22,051	5,621	22,796	4,287	2,612
Framingham	17,308	7,347	16,836	6,669	1,700
Lawrence	10,048	3,700	8,615	2,804	1,096
Lowell	17,554	7,790	16,912	5,896	2,911
Lynn	18,836	6,776	18,370	5,634	2,726
Medford	16,776	6,353	16,639	5,844	1,741
New Bedford	23,880	5,473	23,620	4,151	2,547
Newton	29,918	8,132	30,005	8,499	1,674
Quincy	23,117	11,282	23,182	9,824	3,066
Somerville	19,984	4,468	20,206	3,983	1,455
Springfield	29,728	10,288	31,266	9,110	3,407
Waltham	13,736	6,700	13,607	5,830	1,663
Weymouth	15,570	8,884	13,536	6,904	2,181
Worcester	35,231	14,042	35,607	12,879	3,925
Other	1,110,328	710,581	1,075,494	570,663	178,627
Totals	1,616,487	878,502	1,571,509	718,058	227,206

Massachusetts Vote Since 1952

1952, Eisenhower, Rep., 1,292,325; Stevenson, Dem., 1,083,525; Hallinan, Prog., 4,636; Hass, Soc. Labor, 1,957; Hamblen, Proh., 886; scattered, 69; blanks, 41,150.
1956, Eisenhower, Rep., 1,393,197; Stevenson, Dem., 948,190; Hass, Soc. Labor, 5,573; Holtwick, Proh., 1,205; others, 341.
1960, Kennedy, Dem., 1,487,174; Nixon, Rep., 976,750; Hass, Soc. Labor, 3,892; Decker, Proh., 1,633; others, 31; blank and void, 26,024.
1964, Johnson, Dem., 1,786,422; Goldwater, Rep., 549,727; Hass, Soc. Labor, 4,755; Munn, Proh., 3,735; scattered, 159; blank, 48,104.
1968, Nixon, Rep., 766,844; Humphrey, Dem., 1,469,218; Wallace, 3d Party, 87,088; Blomen, Soc. Labor, 6,180; Munn, Proh., 2,369; scattered, 53; blanks, 25,394.
1972, Nixon, Rep., 1,112,078; McGovern, Dem., 1,332,540; Jenness, Soc. Workers, 10,600; Fisher, Soc. Labor, 129; Schmitz, Amer., 2,877; Spock, Peoples, 101; Hall, Com., 46; Hospers, Libertarian, 43; scattered, 342.
1976, Carter, Dem., 1,429,475; Ford, Rep., 1,030,276; McCarthy, Ind., 65,637; Camejo, Soc. Workers, 8,138; Anderson, Amer., 7,555; La Rouche, U.S. Labor, 4,922; MacBride, Libertarian, 135.
1980, Reagan, Rep., 1,057,631; Carter, Dem., 1,053,802; Anderson, Ind., 382,539; Clark, Libertarian, 22,038; DeBerry, Soc. Workers, 3,735; Commoner, Citizens, 2,056; McReynolds, Soc., 62; Bubar, Statesman, 34; Griswold, Workers World, 19; scattered, 2,382.
1984, Reagan, Rep., 1,310,936; Mondale, Dem., 1,239,606.
1988, Bush, Rep., 1,194,635; Dukakis, Dem., 1,401,415; Paul, Lib., 24,251; Fulani, New Alliance, 9,561.
1992, Clinton, Dem., 1,318,639; Bush, Rep., 805,039; Perot, Ind., 630,731; Marrou, Libertarian, 9,021; Fulani, New Alliance, 3,172; Phillips, U.S. Taxpayers, 2,218; Hagelin, Natural Law, 1,812; LaRouche, Ind., 1,027.
1996, Clinton, Dem., 1,571,509; Dole, Rep., 718,058; Perot, Ref., 227,206; Browne, Libertarian, 20,424; Hagelin, Natural Law, 5,183; Moorehead, Workers World, 3,276.

2000, Gore, Dem., 1,616,487; Bush, Rep., 878,502; Nader, Green, 173,564; Browne, Libertarian, 16,366; Buchanan, Reform, 11,149; Hagelin, Natural Law, 2,884.

Michigan

County	2000 Gore (D)	2000 Bush (R)	1996 Clinton (D)	1996 Dole (R)	1996 Perot (RF)
Alcona	2,696	3,152	2,619	2,227	669
Alger	2,071	2,142	2,229	1,429	537
Allegan	15,495	28,197	14,361	20,859	3,269
Alpena	7,053	6,769	7,114	4,525	1,730
Antrim	4,329	6,780	4,226	4,630	1,129
Arenac	3,685	3,421	3,472	2,247	844
Baraga	1,400	1,836	1,601	1,209	460
Barry	9,769	15,716	9,467	11,139	2,282
Bay	28,251	22,150	27,835	16,038	5,410
Benzie	3,546	4,172	3,081	2,856	763
Berrien	28,152	35,689	24,614	28,254	5,958
Branch	6,691	8,743	6,567	6,321	1,779
Calhoun	27,312	26,291	26,287	20,953	4,765
Cass	8,808	10,545	8,207	7,373	2,241
Charlevoix	4,958	7,018	4,689	4,864	1,303
Cheboygan	5,484	6,815	5,018	4,244	1,462
Chippewa	6,370	7,526	6,532	5,137	1,453
Clare	6,287	5,937	6,311	3,742	1,531
Clinton	13,394	18,054	11,945	13,694	2,698
Crawford	2,790	3,345	2,666	2,157	840
Delta	7,970	8,871	8,561	5,925	1,543
Dickinson	5,533	6,932	5,614	4,408	1,478
Eaton	23,211	24,803	19,781	20,092	4,378
Emmet	5,451	8,602	4,892	6,002	1,512
Genesee	119,833	66,641	106,065	49,332	17,671
Gladwin	5,573	5,743	5,494	3,670	1,466
Gogebic	4,066	3,929	4,436	2,769	917
Grand Traverse	14,371	22,358	12,987	16,355	3,527
Gratiot	6,538	8,312	6,793	6,214	1,762
Hillsdale	6,495	10,483	5,955	7,947	2,262
Houghton	5,688	7,895	5,957	5,941	1,584
Huron	6,899	8,911	6,827	6,126	1,811
Ingham	69,231	47,314	63,584	43,096	8,640
Ionia	9,481	13,915	9,261	9,574	2,354
Iosco	6,505	6,345	6,240	4,410	1,710
Iron	3,014	2,967	3,232	2,014	755
Isabella	10,228	10,053	9,635	7,460	2,069
Jackson	28,160	32,066	24,633	24,987	5,968
Kalamazoo	48,807	48,254	45,644	40,703	5,867
Kalkaska	2,774	3,842	2,666	2,455	922
Kent	95,442	148,602	85,912	121,335	14,120
Keweenaw	540	740	572	491	169
Lake	2,584	1,961	2,606	1,213	552
Lapeer	15,749	20,351	14,308	13,369	4,793
Leelanau	4,635	6,840	4,019	5,155	924
Lenawee	18,365	20,681	16,924	14,168	4,167
Livingston	28,780	44,637	22,517	30,598	6,337
Luce	956	1,480	1,107	964	366
Mackinac	2,533	3,272	2,700	2,281	742
Macomb	172,625	164,265	151,430	120,616	29,859
Manistee	5,639	5,401	5,383	3,807	1,230
Marquette	15,503	12,577	15,168	8,805	2,492
Mason	5,579	7,066	5,597	5,066	1,525
Mecosta	6,300	8,072	6,370	5,289	1,373
Menominee	4,597	5,529	4,880	4,038	1,205
Midland	15,959	21,887	15,177	16,547	3,964
Missaukee	2,062	4,274	2,256	3,012	719
Monroe	31,555	28,940	26,072	19,678	6,315
Montcalm	9,627	12,696	10,053	8,679	2,530
Montmorency	2,139	2,750	2,120	1,760	682
Muskegon	37,865	30,028	35,328	21,873	5,794
Newaygo	7,677	11,399	7,614	7,868	2,047
Oakland	281,201	274,319	241,884	219,855	36,709
Oceana	4,597	5,913	4,419	3,947	1,286
Ogemaw	4,896	4,706	4,725	2,904	1,369
Ontonagon	1,514	2,472	2,080	1,523	604
Osceola	4,006	5,680	4,085	3,855	1,068
Oscoda	1,677	2,207	1,652	1,545	503
Otsego	4,034	6,108	3,351	3,638	1,280
Ottawa	29,600	78,703	27,024	61,436	6,275
Presque Isle	3,242	3,660	3,449	2,463	932
Roscommon	6,433	6,190	6,092	4,135	1,539
Saginaw	50,825	41,152	47,579	31,577	8,081
St. Clair	33,002	33,571	28,881	22,495	8,134
St. Joseph	8,574	12,906	8,529	9,764	2,319
Sanilac	7,153	10,966	7,092	7,821	2,265
Schoolcraft	2,036	2,088	2,187	1,200	460
Shiawassee	15,520	15,816	14,662	11,714	3,703
Tuscola	10,845	13,213	10,314	9,154	3,013
Van Buren	13,796	14,792	13,355	11,347	2,946
Washtenaw	86,647	52,459	73,106	40,097	8,020
Wayne	530,414	223,021	504,466	175,886	43,554
Wexford	5,326	7,215	5,510	4,866	1,386
Totals	2,170,418	1,953,139	1,989,653	1,481,212	336,670

Michigan Vote Since 1952

1952, Eisenhower, Rep., 1,551,529; Stevenson, Dem., 1,230,657; Hamblen, Proh., 10,331; Hallinan, Prog., 3,922; Hass, Soc. Labor, 1,495; Dobbs, Soc. Workers, 655; scattered, 3.

1956, Eisenhower, Rep., 1,713,647; Stevenson, Dem., 1,359,898; Holtwick, Proh., 6,923.

1960, Kennedy, Dem., 1,687,269; Nixon, Rep., 1,620,428; Dobbs, Soc. Workers, 4,347; Decker, Proh., 2,029; Daly, Tax Cut, 1,767; Hass, Soc. Labor, 1,718; Ind. Amer., 539.

1964, Johnson, Dem., 2,136,615; Goldwater, Rep., 1,060,152; DeBerry, Soc. Workers, 3,817; Hass, Soc. Labor, 1,704; Proh. (no candidate listed), 699; scattering, 145.

1968, Nixon, Rep., 1,370,665; Humphrey, Dem., 1,593,082; Wallace, 3d Party, 331,968; Halstead, Soc. Workers, 4,099; Blomen, Soc. Labor, 1,762; Cleaver, New Politics, 4,585; Munn, Proh., 60; scattering, 29.

1972, Nixon, Rep., 1,961,721; McGovern, Dem., 1,459,435; Schmitz, Amer., 63,321; Fisher, Soc. Labor, 2,437; Jenness, Soc. Workers, 1,603; Hall, Com., 1,210.

1976, Carter, Dem., 1,696,714; Ford, Rep., 1,893,742; McCarthy, Ind., 47,905; MacBride, Libertarian, 5,406; Wright, People's, 3,504; Camejo, Soc. Workers, 1,804; LaRouche, U.S. Labor, 1,366; Levin, Soc. Labor, 1,148; scattering, 2,160.

1980, Reagan, Rep., 1,915,225; Carter, Dem., 1,661,532; Anderson, Ind., 275,223; Clark, Libertarian, 41,597; Commoner, Citizens, 11,930; Hall, Com., 3,262; Griswold, Workers World, 30; Greaves, Amer., 21; Bubar, Statesman, 9.

1984, Reagan, Rep., 2,251,571; Mondale, Dem., 1,529,638; Bergland, Libertarian, 10,055.

1988, Bush, Rep., 1,965,486; Dukakis, Dem., 1,675,783; Paul, Lib., 18,336; Fulani, Ind., 2,513.

1992, Clinton, Dem., 1,871,182; Bush, Rep., 1,554,940; Perot, Ind., 824,813; Marrou, Libertarian, 10,175; Phillips, U.S. Taxpayers, 8,263; Hagelin, Natural Law, 2,954.

1996, Clinton, Dem., 1,989,653; Dole, Rep., 1,481,212; Perot, Ref., 336,670; Browne, Libertarian, 27,670; Hagelin, Natural Law, 4,254; Moorehead, Workers World, 3,153; White, Soc. Equality, 1,554.

2000, Gore, Dem., 2,170,418; Bush, Rep., 1,953,139; Nader, Green, 84,165; Browne, Libertarian, 16,711; Phillips, U.S. Taxpayers, 3,791; Hagelin, Natural Law, 2,426.

Minnesota

County	2000 Gore (D)	2000 Bush (R)	1996 Clinton (D)	1996 Dole (R)	1996 Perot (RF)
Aitkin	3,830	3,755	3,810	2,327	1,155
Anoka	68,008	69,256	63,756	41,745	16,448
Becker	5,253	8,152	5,911	5,461	1,813
Beltrami	7,301	8,346	8,006	5,806	1,635
Benton	6,009	7,663	6,006	4,835	2,133
Big Stone	1,430	1,370	1,619	990	368
Blue Earth	12,329	12,942	12,420	9,082	3,324
Brown	4,650	7,370	4,864	5,580	1,786
Carlton	8,620	5,578	8,052	4,034	1,591
Carver	12,462	20,790	11,554	12,380	3,781
Cass	5,534	7,134	5,437	4,791	1,620
Chippewa	2,952	2,977	3,178	2,119	782
Chisago	9,593	10,937	8,611	5,984	2,812
Clay	10,128	11,712	10,476	8,764	1,733
Clearwater	1,466	2,137	1,578	1,423	471
Cook	1,171	1,295	1,169	1,010	246
Cottonwood	2,503	3,369	2,737	2,633	741
Crow Wing	11,255	15,035	11,156	10,095	3,423
Dakota	85,446	87,250	77,297	57,244	17,095
Dodge	3,370	4,213	3,233	2,888	1,223
Douglas	6,352	9,811	6,450	6,747	2,093
Faribault	3,624	4,336	3,817	3,272	1,103
Fillmore	5,020	4,646	4,732	3,466	1,575
Freeborn	8,514	6,843	8,458	5,166	2,226
Goodhue	9,981	10,852	9,931	7,293	2,806
Grant	1,507	1,804	1,806	1,284	434
Hennepin	307,599	225,657	285,126	173,887	47,663
Houston	4,502	5,077	4,153	3,674	1,439
Hubbard	3,632	5,307	3,802	3,593	1,141
Isanti	6,247	7,668	6,041	4,450	2,242
Itasca	10,583	9,545	10,706	6,506	2,889
Jackson	2,364	2,773	2,727	2,153	908
Kanabec	2,831	3,480	2,927	1,924	996
Kandiyohi	8,220	10,026	9,009	7,119	2,229
Kittson	1,107	1,353	1,394	1,055	270
Koochiching	2,903	3,523	3,472	2,080	1,098
LacQuiParle	2,244	1,941	2,420	1,447	561
Lake	3,579	2,465	3,388	1,684	752

County	2000 Gore (D)	Bush (R)	1996 Clinton (D)	Dole (R)	Perot (RF)
Lake of the Woods...	848	1,216	888	814	287
Le Sueur....	5,361	6,138	5,457	3,902	1,699
Lincoln.....	1,590	1,513	1,641	1,199	504
Lyon......	4,737	6,087	5,062	4,932	1,351
McLeod....	5,609	8,782	6,027	5,474	2,402
Mahnomen .	921	1,122	1,026	877	270
Marshall...	1,910	2,912	2,333	2,068	710
Martin	4,166	5,686	4,718	4,303	1,405
Meeker	4,402	5,520	4,531	3,428	1,571
Mille Lacs ..	4,376	5,223	4,336	2,948	1,467
Morrison ...	5,274	8,197	5,728	5,054	2,310
Mower.....	10,693	6,873	10,413	4,994	2,464
Murray.....	2,093	2,407	2,173	1,907	753
Nicollet	7,041	7,221	6,772	5,057	1,737
Nobles.....	3,760	4,766	4,106	3,769	1,132
Norman	1,575	1,808	1,875	1,392	425
Olmsted....	25,822	30,641	22,857	22,860	5,640
Otter Tail ..	9,844	16,963	10,519	11,808	3,191
Pennington .	2,458	3,380	2,814	2,129	910
Pine......	6,148	5,854	5,432	3,080	1,597
Pipestone ..	1,970	2,693	1,999	2,096	599
Polk......	5,764	7,609	6,369	5,563	1,502
Pope	2,771	2,808	2,803	1,992	665
Ramsey....	138,470	87,669	133,878	66,954	20,351
Red Lake...	830	1,090	1,053	695	334
Redwood....	2,681	4,589	2,997	3,700	1,053
Renville	3,533	4,036	3,956	2,887	1,311
Rice.......	13,140	10,876	12,821	7,016	2,872
Rock	2,081	2,772	2,142	2,169	554
Roseau	2,128	4,695	2,759	2,988	1,081
St. Louis ...	64,237	35,420	60,736	25,553	11,308
Scott	17,503	23,954	14,657	12,734	4,886
Sherburne ..	12,109	16,813	10,551	8,699	3,665
Sibley	2,687	4,087	2,769	2,590	1,226
Stearns	24,800	32,402	24,238	21,474	8,150
Steele	6,900	8,223	6,974	5,617	2,197
Stevens	2,434	2,831	2,741	2,141	467
Swift	2,698	2,376	3,054	1,541	690
Todd	4,132	6,031	4,520	4,078	1,958
Traverse....	884	1,074	1,135	775	295
Wabasha ...	4,522	5,245	4,523	3,452	1,474
Wadena	2,251	3,733	2,480	2,696	801
Waseca	3,694	4,408	3,819	3,171	1,385
Washington .	49,637	51,502	45,119	31,219	10,106
Watonwan ..	2,258	2,562	2,534	1,997	711
Wilkin......	1,046	2,032	1,319	1,508	358
Winona	11,069	10,773	10,272	7,955	2,907
Wright	16,762	23,861	15,542	13,224	5,550
Yellow Medicine .	2,528	2,598	2,741	2,006	818
Totals	**1,168,266**	**1,109,659**	**1,120,438**	**766,476**	**257,704**

Minnesota Vote Since 1952

1952, Eisenhower, Rep., 763,211; Stevenson, Dem., 608,458; Hallinan, Prog., 2,666; Hass, Soc. Labor, 2,383; Hamblen, Proh., 2,147; Dobbs, Soc. Workers, 618.

1956, Eisenhower, Rep., 719,302; Stevenson, Dem., 617,525; Hass, Soc. Labor (Ind. Gov.), 2,080; Dobbs, Soc. Workers, 1,098.

1960, Kennedy, Dem., 779,933; Nixon, Rep., 757,915; Dobbs, Soc. Workers, 3,077; Industrial Gov., 962.

1964, Johnson, Dem., 991,117; Goldwater, Rep., 559,624; DeBerry, Soc. Workers, 1,177; Hass, Industrial Gov., 2,544.

1968, Nixon, Rep., 658,643; Humphrey, Dem., 857,738; Wallace, 3d Party, 68,931; scattered, 2,443; Halstead, Soc. Workers, 808; Blomen, Ind. Gov't., 285; Mitchell, Com., 415; Cleaver, Peace, 935; McCarthy, write-in, 585; scattered, 170.

1972, Nixon, Rep., 898,269; McGovern, Dem., 802,346; Schmitz, Amer., 31,407; Spock, Peoples, 2,805; Fisher, Soc. Labor, 4,261; Jenness, Soc. Workers, 940; Hall, Com., 662; scattered, 962.

1976, Carter, Dem., 1,070,440; Ford, Rep., 819,395; McCarthy, Ind., 35,490; Anderson, Amer., 13,592; Camejo, Soc. Workers, 4,149; MacBride, Libertarian, 3,529; Hall, Com., 1,092.

1980, Reagan, Rep., 873,268; Carter, Dem., 954,173; Anderson, Ind., 174,997; Clark, Libertarian, 31,593; Commoner, Citizens, 8,406; Hall, Com., 1,117; DeBerry, Soc. Workers, 711; Griswold, Workers World, 698; McReynolds, Soc., 536; write-ins, 281.

1984, Reagan, Rep., 1,032,603; Mondale, Dem., 1,036,364; Bergland, Libertarian, 2,996.

1988, Bush, Rep., 962,337; Dukakis, Dem., 1,109,471; McCarthy, Minn. Prog., 5,403; Paul, Lib., 5,109.

1992, Clinton, Dem., 1,020,997; Bush, Rep., 747,841; Perot, Ind., 562,506; Marrou, Libertarian, 3,373; Gritz, Populist/America First, 3,363; Hagelin, Natural Law, 1,406.

1996, Clinton, Dem., 1,120,438; Dole, Rep., 766,476; Perot, Ref., 257,704; Nader, Green, 24,908; Browne, Libertarian,

8,271; Peron, Grass Roots, 4,898; Phillips, Taxpayers, 3,416; Hagelin, Natural Law, 1,808; Birrenbach, Ind. Grass Roots, 787; Harris, Soc. Workers, 684; White, Soc. Equality, 347.

2000, Gore, Dem., 1,168,266; Bush, Rep., 1,109,659; Nader, Green, 126,696; Buchanan, Reform Minnesota, 22,166; Browne, Libertarian, 5,282; Phillips, Constitution, 3,272; Hagelin, Reform, 2,294; Harris, Soc. Workers, 1,022.

Mississippi

County	2000 Gore (D)	Bush (R)	1996 Clinton (D)	Dole (R)	Perot (RF)
Adams	8,065	6,691	8,218	5,378	779
Alcorn........	5,059	7,254	4,964	4,960	929
Amite	2,673	3,677	2,824	2,521	351
Attala	2,922	4,206	3,092	3,130	383
Benton	1,886	1,561	1,944	993	209
Bolivar	8,436	4,847	8,670	4,027	320
Calhoun	2,251	3,448	2,178	2,470	351
Carroll........	1,726	3,165	2,041	2,629	245
Chickasaw	3,519	3,549	2,971	2,535	401
Choctaw......	1,278	2,398	1,247	1,715	247
Claiborne.....	3,670	883	3,739	784	103
Clarke........	2,368	4,503	2,337	3,470	366
Clay	4,515	3,570	4,267	2,948	337
Coahoma	5,662	3,695	5,776	3,441	256
Copiah	4,845	5,643	4,415	4,138	375
Covington.....	2,623	4,180	2,628	3,219	417
DeSoto.......	9,586	24,879	10,282	18,135	2,399
Forrest	8,500	13,281	7,965	11,278	1,094
Franklin	1,486	2,427	1,381	1,586	329
George.......	1,977	5,143	1,888	3,311	710
Greene	1,317	3,082	1,347	1,947	322
Grenada	3,813	4,743	4,402	4,527	470
Hancock	4,801	9,326	4,303	5,820	1,143
Harrison	19,142	32,256	18,775	25,486	3,726
Hinds	46,789	37,753	45,410	35,653	2,929
Holmes.......	5,447	1,937	4,720	1,536	140
Humphreys....	2,288	1,628	2,305	1,382	110
Issaquena	555	366	546	269	42
Itawamba	2,994	5,424	2,987	3,490	732
Jackson	14,193	30,068	13,598	24,918	2,947
Jasper	3,104	3,294	3,170	2,615	353
Jefferson	2,786	600	2,531	489	89
Jefferson Davis .	2,835	2,437	2,663	1,890	264
Jones	7,713	16,341	7,360	13,020	1,362
Kemper.......	2,311	1,915	2,048	1,439	188
Lafayette......	5,139	7,081	4,646	4,753	580
Lamar........	3,478	12,795	3,169	8,609	925
Lauderdale....	8,412	17,315	8,668	15,055	1,036
Lawrence	2,841	3,674	2,481	2,392	471
Leake	2,793	4,114	2,902	3,017	406
Lee	9,142	15,551	8,438	11,815	1,361
Leflore	6,401	4,626	6,853	4,456	240
Lincoln	4,358	8,540	4,294	5,960	778
Lowndes......	7,537	11,404	6,220	9,169	750
Madison	10,416	19,109	9,354	14,467	759
Marion	4,114	6,796	4,334	5,023	585
Marshall......	7,735	4,723	7,521	3,272	482
Monroe.......	5,783	7,397	5,184	5,206	889
Montgomery...	2,187	2,630	1,970	1,943	197
Neshoba......	2,563	6,409	2,646	4,545	560
Newton.......	2,147	5,540	2,163	4,223	464
Noxubee......	3,383	1,530	2,801	1,287	119
Oktibbeha.....	6,443	7,959	5,923	6,142	395
Panola	5,880	5,424	5,408	3,701	513
Pearl River....	4,611	11,575	4,892	8,212	1,190
Perry.........	1,285	3,026	1,413	2,178	450
Pike	6,544	7,464	6,302	5,403	683
Pontotoc	2,771	6,601	2,597	4,289	774
Prentiss	3,287	5,101	3,053	3,473	574
Quitman	2,103	1,280	2,186	1,121	126
Rankin	8,050	32,983	8,614	24,585	2,093
Scott.........	3,548	5,601	3,163	4,018	466
Sharkey	1,706	1,074	1,566	906	70
Simpson	3,227	6,254	2,851	4,455	525
Smith	1,620	4,838	1,858	3,371	522
Stone	1,677	3,702	1,551	2,288	417
Sunflower.....	4,981	3,369	4,960	2,926	290
Tallahatchie ...	3,041	2,428	2,990	1,676	251
Tate	3,441	5,148	3,195	3,694	406
Tippah	2,908	5,381	2,992	3,249	661
Tishomingo....	2,747	4,122	2,709	2,766	609
Tunica........	1,539	792	1,263	557	55
Union	3,094	6,087	3,316	4,375	788
Walthall	2,356	3,476	2,240	2,239	444
Warren	7,485	10,892	8,774	9,261	1,259
Washington ...	10,405	7,367	10,053	6,762	437
Wayne	2,981	4,635	2,652	3,219	595
Webster	1,426	3,069	1,379	2,254	255
Wilkinson	2,551	1,423	2,807	1,016	226
Winston	3,672	4,645	3,488	3,498	434
Yalobusha.....	2,674	2,470	2,437	1,711	332
Yazoo	4,997	5,254	4,754	4,152	362
Totals.........	**404,614**	**572,844**	**394,022**	**439,838**	**52,222**

Mississippi Vote Since 1952

1952, Eisenhower, Ind. vote pledged to Rep. candidate, 112,966; Stevenson, Dem., 172,566.

1956, Eisenhower, Rep., 56,372; Stevenson, Dem., 144,498; Black and Tan Grand Old Party, 4,313; total, 60,685; Byrd, Ind., 42,966.

1960, Kennedy, Dem., 108,362; Democratic unpledged electors, 116,248; Nixon, Rep., 73,561. Mississippi's victorious slate of 8 unpledged Democratic electors cast their votes for Sen. Harry F. Byrd (D, VA).

1964, Johnson, Dem., 52,618; Goldwater, Rep., 356,528.

1968, Nixon, Rep., 88,516; Humphrey, Dem., 150,644; Wallace, 3d Party, 415,349.

1972, Nixon, Rep., 505,125; McGovern, Dem., 126,782; Schmitz, Amer., 11,598; Jenness, Soc. Workers, 2,458.

1976, Carter, Dem., 381,309; Ford, Rep., 366,846; Anderson, Amer., 6,678; McCarthy, Ind., 4,074; Maddox, Ind., 4,049; Camejo, Soc. Workers, 2,805; MacBride, Libertarian, 2,609.

1980, Reagan, Rep., 441,089; Carter, Dem., 429,281; Anderson, Ind., 12,036; Clark, Libertarian, 5,465; Griswold, Workers World, 2,402; Pulley, Soc. Workers, 2,347.

1984, Reagan, Rep., 582,377; Mondale, Dem., 352,192; Bergland, Libertarian, 2,336.

1988, Bush, Rep., 557,890; Dukakis, Dem., 363,921; Duke, Ind., 4,232; Paul, Lib., 3,329.

1992, Bush, Rep., 487,793; Clinton, Dem., 400,258; Perot, Ind., 85,626; Fulani, New Alliance, 2,625; Marrou, Libertarian, 2,154; Phillips, U.S. Taxpayers, 1,652; Hagelin, Natural Law, 1,140.

1996, Dole, Rep., 439,838; Clinton, Dem., 394,022; Perot, Ind. (Ref.), 52,222; Browne, Libertarian, 2,809; Phillips, Taxpayers, 2,314; Hagelin, Natural Law, 1,447; Collins, Ind., 1,205.

2000, Bush, Rep., 572,844; Gore, Dem., 404,614; Nader, Ind., 8,122; Phillips, Constitution, 3,267; Buchanan, Reform, 2,265; Browne, Libertarian, 2,009; Harris, Ind., 613; Hagelin, Natural Law, 450.

Missouri

County	2000 Gore (D)	Bush (R)	1996 Clinton (D)	Dole (R)	Perot (RF)
Adair	4,101	6,050	4,441	4,656	1,170
Andrew	2,795	4,257	2,807	3,281	964
Atchison	1,013	1,798	1,266	1,327	367
Audrain	4,551	5,256	4,690	3,955	1,046
Barry	4,135	7,885	4,352	5,855	1,494
Barton	1,424	3,836	1,625	2,812	563
Bates	3,386	4,245	3,224	2,904	949
Benton	3,150	4,218	2,996	2,895	764
Bollinger	1,692	3,487	2,044	2,420	506
Boone	28,811	28,426	24,984	22,047	4,083
Buchanan	17,085	16,423	15,848	12,610	4,248
Butler	4,996	9,111	5,780	6,996	1,414
Caldwell	1,488	2,220	1,487	1,464	468
Callaway	6,708	8,238	5,880	5,567	1,530
Camden	6,323	10,358	5,566	7,190	1,809
Cape Girardeau	9,334	19,832	9,957	15,557	1,861
Carroll	1,620	2,880	2,080	1,839	580
Carter	997	1,730	1,172	1,180	301
Cass	14,921	20,113	11,743	13,495	3,474
Cedar	1,979	3,530	2,027	2,484	658
Chariton	1,792	2,300	2,072	1,508	423
Christian	7,896	14,824	6,627	9,477	2,301
Clark	1,812	1,899	1,749	1,081	458
Clay	39,084	39,083	32,603	26,935	7,048
Clinton	3,994	4,323	3,445	2,780	848
Cole	12,056	20,167	10,857	16,140	2,121
Cooper	2,567	4,072	2,753	2,900	891
Crawford	3,350	4,754	3,349	2,990	1,223
Dade	1,193	2,468	1,243	1,822	447
Dallas	2,311	3,723	2,277	2,554	787
Daviess	1,367	2,011	1,534	1,321	466
DeKalb	1,562	2,363	1,679	1,627	492
Dent	1,839	3,996	2,234	2,542	693
Douglas	1,546	3,599	1,744	2,601	775
Dunklin	4,947	5,426	5,428	3,766	934
Franklin	16,172	21,863	13,908	13,715	5,517
Gasconade	2,257	4,190	2,104	2,997	820
Gentry	1,271	1,771	1,493	1,361	416
Greene	41,091	59,178	39,300	48,193	8,569
Grundy	1,563	2,976	2,073	1,883	631
Harrison	1,328	2,552	1,628	1,737	484
Henry	4,459	5,120	4,579	3,260	1,231
Hickory	1,961	2,172	1,858	1,491	531
Holt	871	1,738	1,144	1,323	314
Howard	1,944	2,414	2,014	1,545	568
Howell	4,641	9,018	5,261	5,991	2,066
Iron	2,044	2,237	2,221	1,328	568
Jackson	160,419	104,418	140,317	85,534	21,047
Jasper	11,737	24,899	11,462	18,361	3,545
Jefferson	38,616	36,766	32,073	23,877	8,893
Johnson	6,926	9,339	6,220	6,276	1,911
Knox	787	1,226	891	862	254
Laclede	4,183	8,556	4,047	5,887	1,459
Lafayette	6,343	7,849	6,118	5,489	1,516
Lawrence	4,235	8,305	4,465	6,099	1,613
Lewis	2,023	2,388	2,050	1,453	644
Lincoln	6,961	8,549	5,644	4,897	1,881
Linn	2,646	3,246	2,967	2,097	781
Livingston	2,425	3,709	2,913	2,384	777
McDonald	1,866	4,460	1,980	3,008	923
Macon	2,817	4,232	2,937	2,634	848
Madison	1,828	2,460	2,351	1,595	625
Maries	1,554	2,216	1,540	1,560	516
Marion	4,993	6,550	4,924	4,653	1,082
Mercer	555	1,250	700	660	208
Miller	3,217	5,945	3,110	4,387	1,185
Mississippi	2,756	2,395	3,235	1,595	380
Moniteau	2,176	3,764	2,129	2,603	693
Monroe	1,860	2,175	1,938	1,333	532
Montgomery	2,092	3,106	2,277	2,124	772
Morgan	3,235	4,460	3,006	3,059	1,006
New Madrid	3,738	3,416	4,451	2,417	663
Newton	6,447	14,232	5,840	10,067	1,995
Nodaway	3,553	5,161	3,966	3,362	1,043
Oregon	1,568	2,521	1,795	1,502	475
Osage	1,938	4,154	2,045	2,890	608
Ozark	1,432	2,663	1,445	1,882	595
Pemiscot	3,245	2,750	3,371	1,820	458
Perry	2,085	4,667	2,517	3,427	777
Pettis	5,855	9,533	6,057	7,336	1,716
Phelps	6,262	9,444	6,405	6,990	1,703
Pike	3,557	3,648	3,495	2,209	916
Platte	15,325	17,785	12,705	13,332	3,035
Polk	3,606	6,430	3,307	4,521	1,169
Pulaski	3,800	6,531	3,783	4,089	1,141
Putnam	708	1,593	857	1,091	276
Ralls	2,033	2,446	1,998	1,513	520
Randolph	4,116	4,844	4,502	3,274	1,130
Ray	4,970	4,517	4,714	2,884	1,113
Reynolds	1,298	1,762	1,631	903	386
Ripley	1,820	3,121	2,081	1,988	530
St. Charles	53,806	72,114	41,369	47,705	11,591
St. Clair	1,866	2,731	1,974	1,815	650
St. Francois	9,075	9,327	9,034	6,200	2,266
St. Louis	250,631	224,689	225,524	196,096	34,850
Ste. Genevieve	3,600	3,505	3,597	2,078	942
Saline	4,585	4,572	4,765	2,931	1,090
Schuyler	808	1,159	857	777	287
Scotland	790	1,335	990	773	326
Scott	6,452	8,999	7,011	6,641	1,483
Shannon	1,430	2,245	1,882	1,339	524
Shelby	1,262	1,936	1,410	1,213	413
Stoddard	4,476	7,727	4,883	5,020	1,185
Stone	4,055	7,793	3,497	5,223	1,353
Sullivan	1,127	1,877	1,402	1,275	340
Taney	5,092	9,647	4,623	6,844	1,580
Texas	3,486	6,136	3,897	4,065	1,335
Vernon	3,156	4,985	3,363	3,123	1,135
Warren	4,524	5,979	3,443	3,768	1,254
Washington	4,047	4,020	4,315	2,259	1,169
Wayne	2,387	3,346	2,754	2,172	674
Webster	4,174	7,350	3,855	4,958	1,214
Worth	469	651	572	540	150
Wright	2,250	5,391	2,280	3,754	890
City					
St. Louis	96,557	24,799	91,233	22,121	7,276
Totals	**1,111,138**	**1,189,924**	**1,025,935**	**890,016**	**217,188**

Missouri Vote Since 1952

1952, Eisenhower, Rep., 959,429; Stevenson, Dem., 929,830; Hallinan, Prog., 987; Hamblen, Proh., 885; MacArthur, Christian Nationalist, 302; America First, 233; Hoopes, Soc., 227; Hass, Soc. Labor, 169.

1956, Stevenson, Dem., 918,273; Eisenhower, Rep., 914,299.

1960, Kennedy, Dem., 972,201; Nixon, Rep., 962,221.

1964, Johnson, Dem., 1,164.344; Goldwater, Rep., 653,535.

1968, Nixon, Rep., 811,932; Humphrey, Dem., 791,444; Wallace, 3d Party, 206,126.

1972, Nixon, Rep., 1,154,058; McGovern, Dem., 698,531.

1976, Carter, Dem., 999,163; Ford, Rep., 928,808; McCarthy, Ind., 24,329.

1980, Reagan, Rep., 1,074,181; Carter, Dem., 931,182; Anderson, Ind., 77,920; Clark, Libertarian, 14,422; DeBerry, Soc. Workers, 1,515; Commoner, Citizens, 573; write-ins, 31.

1984, Reagan, Rep., 1,274,188; Mondale, Dem., 848,583.

1988, Bush, Rep., 1,084,953; Dukakis, Dem., 1,001,619; Fulani, New Alliance, 6,656; Paul, write-in, 434.

1992, Clinton, Dem., 1,053,873; Bush, Rep., 811,159; Perot, Ind., 518,741; Marrou, Libertarian, 7,497.

1996, Clinton, Dem., 1,025,935; Dole, Rep., 890,016; Perot, Ref., 217,188; Phillips, Taxpayers, 11,521; Browne, Libertarian, 10,522; Hagelin, Natural Law, 2,287.

2000, Bush, Rep., 1,189,924; Gore, Dem., 1,111,138; Nader, Green, 38,515; Buchanan, Reform, 9,818; Browne, Libertarian, 7,436; Phillips, Constitution, 1,957; Hagelin, Natural Law, 1,104.

Montana

County	2000 Gore (D)	2000 Bush (R)	1996 Clinton (D)	1996 Dole (R)	1996 Perot (RF)
Beaverhead	799	3,113	1,164	2,414	412
Big Horn	2,345	1,651	2,453	1,336	424
Blaine	1,246	1,410	1,316	1,127	435
Broadwater	462	1,488	603	1,029	318
Carbon	1,434	3,008	1,854	2,147	713
Carter	53	573	150	522	89
Cascade	13,137	18,164	15,707	14,291	4,749
Chouteau	686	2,039	1,039	1,660	434
Custer	1,501	3,156	2,115	2,467	695
Daniels	303	750	510	558	240
Dawson	1,364	2,723	1,903	1,890	842
Deer Lodge	2,672	1,493	3,331	883	772
Fallon	256	1,061	452	778	276
Fergus	1,352	4,353	1,866	3,671	605
Flathead	8,329	22,519	10,452	16,542	4,786
Gallatin	10,009	18,833	10,972	14,559	3,146
Garfield	61	651	107	562	69
Glacier	2,211	1,709	2,292	1,270	491
Golden Valley	88	405	128	284	73
Granite	295	1,181	429	733	228
Hill	2,760	3,392	3,517	2,601	950
Jefferson	1,513	3,308	1,775	2,248	729
Judith Basin	278	1,057	452	753	126
Lake	3,884	6,441	4,195	4,723	1,804
Lewis & Clark	9,982	15,091	11,535	11,665	3,140
Liberty	243	752	379	634	144
Lincoln	1,629	5,578	2,705	3,552	1,425
McCone	267	827	390	615	244
Madison	758	2,656	955	1,984	516
Meagher	176	698	281	505	142
Mineral	382	1,078	658	549	383
Missoula	17,241	21,474	21,874	16,034	5,586
Musselshell	512	1,582	652	1,121	291
Park	2,154	4,523	2,564	3,837	959
Petroleum	36	254	62	186	36
Phillips	423	1,727	705	1,392	401
Pondera	792	1,948	1,123	1,438	383
Powder River	115	860	236	663	137
Powell	638	1,971	952	1,274	531
Prairie	164	541	259	417	99
Ravalli	4,451	11,241	5,200	8,138	2,731
Richland	1,018	2,858	1,614	2,021	906
Roosevelt	2,059	1,605	2,118	1,209	645
Rosebud	1,394	1,826	1,681	1,413	547
Sanders	1,165	3,144	1,573	2,043	990
Sheridan	702	1,176	1,187	832	408
Silver Bow	8,967	6,299	11,199	3,909	2,447
Stillwater	925	2,765	1,282	1,871	618
Sweet Grass	305	1,450	469	1,109	186
Teton	847	2,294	1,188	1,701	416
Toole	630	1,639	874	1,203	386
Treasure	106	344	171	237	87
Valley	1,273	2,500	1,674	1,838	645
Wheatland	243	708	391	563	127
Wibaux	121	369	197	284	128
Yellowstone	20,370	33,922	22,992	26,367	6,139
Totals	137,126	240,178	167,922	179,652	55,229

Montana Vote Since 1952

1952, Eisenhower, Rep., 157,394; Stevenson, Dem., 106,213; Hallinan, Prog., 723; Hamblen, Proh., 548; Hoopes, Soc., 159.

1956, Eisenhower, Rep., 154,933; Stevenson, Dem., 116,238.

1960, Kennedy, Dem., 134,891; Nixon, Rep., 141,841; Decker, Proh., 456; Dobbs, Soc. Workers, 391.

1964, Johnson, Dem., 164,246; Goldwater, Rep., 113,032; Kasper, Natl. States' Rights, 519; Munn, Proh., 499; DeBerry, Soc. Workers, 332.

1968, Nixon, Rep., 138,835; Humphrey, Dem., 114,117; Wallace, 3d Party, 20,015; Halstead, Soc. Workers, 457; Munn, Proh., 510; Caton, New Reform, 470.

1972, Nixon, Rep., 183,976; McGovern, Dem., 120,197; Schmitz, Amer., 13,430.

1976, Carter, Dem., 149,259; Ford, Rep., 173,703; Anderson, Amer., 5,772.

1980, Reagan, Rep., 206,814; Carter, Dem., 118,032; Anderson, Ind., 29,281; Clark, Libertarian, 9,825.

1984, Reagan, Rep., 232,450; Mondale, Dem., 146,742; Bergland, Libertarian, 5,185.

1988, Bush, Rep., 190,412; Dukakis, Dem., 168,936; Paul, Lib., 5,047; Fulani, New Alliance, 1,279.

1992, Clinton, Dem., 154,507; Bush, Rep., 144,207; Perot, Ind., 107,225; Gritz, Populist/America First, 3,658.

1996, Dole, Rep., 179,652; Clinton, Dem., 167,922; Perot, Ref., 55,229; Browne, Libertarian, 2,526; Hagelin, Natural Law, 1,754.

2000, Bush, Rep. 240,178; Gore, Dem., 137,126; Nader, Green, 24,437; Buchanan, Reform, 5,697; Browne, Libertarian, 1,718; Phillips, Constitution, 1,155; Hagelin, Natural Law, 675.

Nebraska

County	2000 Gore (D)	2000 Bush (R)	1996 Clinton (D)	1996 Dole (R)	1996 Perot (RF)
Adams	3,686	8,162	3,935	6,924	1,513
Antelope	678	2,562	884	2,005	457
Arthur	26	235	25	187	46
Banner	65	390	62	309	30
Blaine	43	299	53	284	39
Boone	575	2,196	806	1,695	424
Box Butte	1,614	3,208	1,782	2,458	695
Boyd	265	931	372	778	181
Brown	250	1,375	359	1,105	289
Buffalo	3,927	11,931	4,277	10,004	1,484
Burt	1,223	2,056	1,237	1,707	497
Butler	1,028	2,638	1,099	2,042	512
Cass	3,656	6,144	3,477	4,878	1,239
Cedar	1,062	2,989	1,218	2,171	739
Chase	306	1,505	365	1,277	197
Cherry	446	2,322	551	1,905	332
Cheyenne	844	3,207	1,059	2,571	287
Clay	774	2,326	880	1,982	425
Colfax	863	2,338	1,065	1,954	492
Cuming	857	3,232	1,033	2,520	503
Custer	976	4,245	1,293	3,453	615
Dakota	2,695	3,119	2,632	2,592	721
Dawes	823	2,549	1,108	1,991	442
Dawson	1,740	5,511	2,180	4,794	1,044
Deuel	213	783	245	629	111
Dixon	820	1,834	931	1,478	414
Dodge	5,021	8,871	5,181	7,484	1,894
Douglas	73,347	101,025	70,708	92,334	14,863
Dundy	179	801	224	752	112
Fillmore	848	2,024	1,058	1,696	321
Franklin	420	1,196	483	1,013	215
Frontier	244	1,102	310	901	169
Furnas	534	1,849	663	1,475	207
Gage	3,516	5,538	4,008	4,413	1,346
Garden	203	963	279	851	155
Garfield	202	718	249	625	111
Gosper	228	757	275	609	150
Grant	49	324	84	258	55
Greeley	416	839	472	642	155
Hall	5,952	11,803	6,708	10,183	2,403
Hamilton	1,066	3,251	1,172	2,623	457
Harlan	438	1,358	520	1,120	203
Hayes	66	486	87	439	39
Hitchcock	312	1,126	409	977	173
Holt	846	3,954	1,107	3,436	677
Hooker	74	317	115	308	83
Howard	955	1,760	853	1,294	417
Jefferson	1,361	2,351	1,520	1,979	495
Johnson	794	1,210	770	1,009	309
Kearney	680	2,333	782	1,953	296
Keith	778	2,953	830	2,504	460
Keya Paha	78	422	94	385	47
Kimball	379	1,379	527	1,011	212
Knox	1,037	2,784	1,266	2,123	531
Lancaster	44,650	55,514	43,339	44,812	8,595
Lincoln	5,205	9,220	5,165	7,482	2,043
Logan	60	336	79	294	72
Loup	84	284	74	229	28
McPherson	48	244	50	233	33
Madison	2,772	9,636	3,047	7,965	1,554
Merrick	848	2,380	997	2,084	449
Morrill	460	1,597	620	1,296	262
Nance	497	1,105	585	892	238
Nemaha	1,063	2,177	1,232	1,888	485
Nuckolls	644	1,701	757	1,383	306
Otoe	2,208	4,178	2,279	3,290	877
Pawnee	522	937	580	766	207
Perkins	243	1,170	352	1,018	163
Phelps	934	3,575	1,071	3,015	465
Pierce	570	2,534	697	1,923	446
Platte	2,612	9,861	3,010	7,948	1,353
Polk	610	1,925	750	1,504	268
Red Willow	1,188	3,680	1,365	3,112	499
Richardson	1,382	2,623	1,517	2,089	633
Rock	141	725	180	564	135
Saline	2,321	2,581	2,523	1,945	689
Sarpy	14,637	28,979	12,806	23,023	3,722
Saunders	2,852	5,688	2,777	4,514	1,223
Scotts Bluff	3,937	9,397	4,547	7,641	1,251
Seward	2,250	4,457	2,432	3,479	745
Sheridan	392	2,105	573	1,834	289
Sherman	564	1,072	567	822	266
Sioux	98	629	138	551	75
Stanton	500	1,895	577	1,457	386
Thayer	821	2,096	933	1,698	334
Thomas	55	329	64	303	62
Thurston	924	1,040	962	835	293
Valley	583	1,610	758	1,346	274
Washington	2,550	5,758	2,248	4,391	971
Wayne	1,001	2,774	1,048	2,150	440

County	2000 Gore (D)	Bush (R)	1996 Clinton (D)	Dole (R)	Perot (RF)
Webster......	584	1,302	621	1,094	236
Wheeler.....	85	351	106	241	69
York........	1,407	4,816	1,653	4,266	559
Totals	231,780	433,862	236,761	363,467	71,278

Nebraska Vote Since 1952

1952, Eisenhower, Rep., 421,603; Stevenson, Dem., 188,057.

1956, Eisenhower, Rep., 378,108; Stevenson, Dem., 199,029.

1960, Kennedy, Dem., 232,542; Nixon, Rep., 380,553.

1964, Johnson, Dem., 307,307; Goldwater, Rep., 276,847.

1968, Nixon, Rep., 321,163; Humphrey, Dem., 170,784; Wallace, 3d Party, 44,904.

1972, Nixon, Rep., 406,298; McGovern, Dem., 169,991; scattered, 817.

1976, Carter, Dem., 233,287; Ford, Rep., 359,219; McCarthy, Ind., 9,383; Maddox, Amer. Ind., 3,378; MacBride, Libertarian, 1,476.

1980, Reagan, Rep., 419,214; Carter, Dem., 166,424; Anderson, Ind., 44,854; Clark, Libertarian, 9,041.

1984, Reagan, Rep., 459,135; Mondale, Dem., 187,475; Bergland, Libertarian, 2,075.

1988, Bush, Rep., 397,956; Dukakis, Dem., 259,235; Paul, Lib., 2,534; Fulani, New Alliance, 1,740.

1992, Bush, Rep., 343,678; Clinton, Dem., 216,864; Perot, Ind., 174,104; Marrou, Libertarian, 1,340.

1996, Dole, Rep., 363,467; Clinton, Dem., 236,761; Perot, Ref., 71,278; Browne, Libertarian, 2,792; Phillips, Ind., 1,928; Hagelin, Natural Law, 1,189.

2000, Bush, Rep., 433,862; Gore, Dem., 231,780; Nader, Green, 24,540; Buchanan, Ind., 3,646; Browne, Libertarian, 2,245; Hagelin, Natural Law, 478; Phillips, Ind., 468.

Nevada

County	2000 Gore (D)	Bush (R)	1996 Clinton (D)	Dole (R)	Perot (RF)
Churchill ...	2,191	6,237	2,282	4,369	821
Clark	196,100	170,932	127,963	103,431	23,177
Douglas....	5,837	11,193	5,109	8,828	1,486
Elko.......	2,542	11,025	3,149	6,512	1,539
Esmeralda..	116	333	140	277	91
Eureka.....	150	632	158	412	90
Humboldt...	1,128	3,638	1,467	2,334	603
Lander.....	395	1,619	660	1,107	361
Lincoln.....	461	1,372	499	936	255
Lyon.......	3,955	7,270	3,419	4,753	1,104
Mineral	916	1,227	1,068	814	361
Nye	4,525	6,904	3,300	3,979	1,544
Pershing ...	476	1,221	565	743	203
Storey	666	1,014	614	705	244
Washoe....	52,097	63,640	44,915	49,477	9,970
White Pine..	1,069	2,234	1,397	1,399	546
City					
Carson City.	7,354	11,084	7,269	9,168	1,591
Totals	279,978	301,575	203,974	199,244	43,986

Nevada Vote Since 1952

1952, Eisenhower, Rep., 50,502; Stevenson, Dem., 31,688.

1956, Eisenhower, Rep., 56,049; Stevenson, Dem., 40,640.

1960, Kennedy, Dem., 54,880; Nixon, Rep., 52,387.

1964, Johnson, Dem., 79,339; Goldwater, Rep., 56,094.

1968, Nixon, Rep., 73,188; Humphrey, Dem., 60,598; Wallace, 3d Party, 20,432.

1972, Nixon, Rep., 115,750; McGovern, Dem., 66,016.

1976, Carter, Dem., 92,479; Ford, Rep., 101,273; MacBride, Libertarian, 1,519; Maddox, Amer. Ind., 1,497; scattered, 5,108.

1980, Reagan, Rep., 155,017; Carter, Dem., 66,666; Anderson, Ind., 17,651; Clark, Libertarian, 4,358.

1984, Reagan, Rep., 188,770; Mondale, Dem., 91,655; Bergland, Libertarian, 2,292.

1988, Bush, Rep., 206,040; Dukakis, Dem., 132,738; Paul, Lib., 3,520; Fulani, New Alliance, 835.

1992, Clinton, Dem., 189,148; Bush, Rep., 175,828; Perot, Ind., 132,580; Gritz, Populist/America First, 2,892; Marrou, Libertarian, 1,835.

1996, Clinton, Dem., 203,974; Dole, Rep., 199,244; Perot, Ref., 43,986; "None of These Candidates," 5,608; Nader, Green, 4,730; Browne, Libertarian, 4,460; Phillips, Ind. Amer., 1,732; Hagelin, Natural Law, 545.

2000, Bush, Rep., 301,575; Gore, Dem., 279,978; Nader, Green, 15,008; Buchanan, Citizens First, 4,747; "None of these candidates," 3,315; Browne, Libertarian, 3,311; Phillips, Ind. Amer., 621; Hagelin, Natural Law, 415.

New Hampshire

City	2000 Gore (D)	Bush (R)	1996 Clinton (D)	Dole (R)	Perot (RF)
Concord........	10,025	6,981	9,719	5,082	1,164
Derry.........	5,530	6,093	4,814	4,503	1,083
Dover........	6,812	5,008	6,332	3,752	930
Hudson......	4,573	4,527	3,841	3,167	976
Keene........	5,856	3,704	5,401	2,910	621
Laconia	3,015	3,814	2,865	2,842	508
Londonderry ...	4,348	5,463	3,466	4,076	838
Manchester ...	19,991	19,152	20,185	14,704	3,053
Merrimack	5,571	6,239	4,934	4,499	949
Nashua	18,398	14,803	16,584	11,479	2,858
Portsmouth....	6,862	3,896	6,343	3,014	661
Rochester....	5,401	5,522	5,489	3,650	1,108
Salem.......	5,711	5,713	5,164	4,257	1,241
Other	164,255	182,644	150,829	128,551	32,397
Totals........	266,318	273,559	246,166	196,486	48,387

New Hampshire Vote Since 1952

1952, Eisenhower, Rep., 166,287; Stevenson, Dem., 106,663.

1956, Eisenhower, Rep., 176,519; Stevenson, Dem., 90,364; Andrews, Const., 111.

1960, Kennedy, Dem., 137,772; Nixon, Rep., 157,989.

1964, Johnson, Dem., 182,065; Goldwater, Rep., 104,029.

1968, Nixon, Rep., 154,903; Humphrey, Dem., 130,589; Wallace, 3d Party, 11,173; New Party, 421; Halstead, Soc. Workers, 104.

1972, Nixon, Rep., 213,724; McGovern, Dem., 116,435; Schmitz, Amer., 3,386; Jenness, Soc. Workers, 368; scattered, 142.

1976, Carter, Dem., 147,645; Ford, Rep., 185,935; McCarthy, Ind., 4,095; MacBride, Libertarian, 936; Reagan, write-in, 388; La Rouche, U.S. Labor, 186; Camejo, Soc. Workers, 161; Levin, Soc. Labor, 66; scattered, 215.

1980, Reagan, Rep., 221,705; Carter, Dem., 108,864; Anderson, Ind., 49,693; Clark, Libertarian, 2,067; Commoner, Citizens, 1,325; Hall, Com., 129; Griswold, Workers World, 76; DeBerry, Soc. Workers, 72; scattered, 68.

1984, Reagan, Rep., 267,051; Mondale, Dem., 120,377; Bergland, Libertarian, 735.

1988, Bush, Rep., 281,537; Dukakis, Dem., 163,696; Paul, Lib., 4,502; Fulani, New Alliance, 790.

1992, Clinton, Dem., 209,040; Bush, Rep., 202,484; Perot, Ind., 121,337; Marrou, Libertarian, 3,548.

1996, Clinton, Dem., 246,166; Dole, Rep., 196,486; Perot, Ref., 48,387; Browne, Libertarian, 4,214; Phillips, Taxpayers, 1,344.

2000, Bush, Rep., 273,559; Gore, Dem., 266,348; Nader, Green, 22,198; Browne, Libertarian, 2,757; Buchanan, Independence, 2,615; Phillips, Constitution, 328.

New Jersey

County	2000 Gore (D)	Bush (R)	1996 Clinton (D)	Dole (R)	Perot (RF)
Atlantic....	52,880	35,593	44,434	29,538	8,261
Bergen....	202,682	152,731	191,085	141,164	25,512
Burlington...	99,506	72,254	85,086	57,337	18,407
Camden....	127,166	62,464	114,962	52,791	17,433
Cape May..	22,189	23,794	19,849	19,357	4,978
Cumberland	28,188	18,882	25,444	14,744	5,348
Essex.....	185,505	66,842	175,387	65,172	9,513
Gloucester .	61,095	42,315	51,928	32,138	14,361
Hudson....	118,206	43,804	116,121	38,288	8,965
Hunterdon ..	21,387	32,210	18,446	26,379	5,686
Mercer	83,256	46,670	77,641	40,559	10,536
Middlesex..	154,998	93,545	145,201	82,433	24,643
Monmouth ..	131,476	119,291	120,414	99,975	22,754
Morris	88,039	111,066	81,092	95,830	15,299
Ocean	102,104	105,684	94,243	82,830	22,864
Passaic....	90,324	61,043	85,879	53,584	10,944
Salem.....	13,718	12,257	12,044	9,294	4,124
Somerset ..	56,232	59,725	50,673	51,868	8,377
Sussex	21,353	33,277	19,525	26,746	6,705
Union	112,003	68,554	108,102	65,912	12,432
Warren	22,172	22,172	14,805	17,160	4,992
Totals.....	1,788,850	1,284,173	1,652,361	1,103,099	262,134

New Jersey Vote Since 1952

1952, Eisenhower, Rep., 1,373,613; Stevenson, Dem., 1,015,902; Hoopes, Soc., 8,593; Hass, Soc. Labor, 5,815; Hallinan, Prog., 5,589; Krajewski, Poor Man's, 4,203; Dobbs, Soc. Workers, 3,850; Hamblen, Proh., 989.

1956, Eisenhower, Rep., 1,606,942; Stevenson Dem., 850,337; Holtwick, Proh., 9,147; Hass, Soc. Labor, 6,736; Andrews, Cons., 5,317; Dobbs, Soc. Workers, 4,004; Krajewski, Amer. Third Party, 1,829.

1960, Kennedy, Dem., 1,385,415; Nixon, Rep., 1,363,324; Dobbs, Soc. Workers, 11,402; Lee, Cons., 8,708; Hass, Soc. Labor, 4,262.

1964, Johnson, Dem., 1,867,671; Goldwater, Rep., 963,843; DeBerry, Soc. Workers, 8,181; Hass, Soc. Labor, 7,075.

1968, Nixon, Rep., 1,325,467; Humphrey, Dem., 1,264,206; Wallace, 3d Party, 262,187; Halstead, Soc. Workers, 8,667; Gregory, Peace and Freedom, 8,084; Blomen, Soc. Labor, 6,784.

1972, Nixon, Rep., 1,845,502; McGovern, Dem., 1,102,211; Schmitz, Amer., 34,378; Spock, Peoples, 5,355; Fisher, Soc. Labor, 4,544; Jenness, Soc. Workers, 2,233; Mahalchik, Amer. First, 1,743; Hall, Com., 1,263.

1976, Carter, Dem., 1,444,653; Ford, Rep., 1,509,688; McCarthy, Ind., 32,717; MacBride, Libertarian, 9,449; Maddox, Amer., 7,716; Levin, Soc. Labor, 3,686; Hall, Com., 1,662; LaRouche, U.S. Labor, 1,650; Camejo, Soc. Workers, 1,184; Wright, People's, 1,044; Bubar, Proh., 554; Zeidler, Soc., 469.

1980, Reagan, Rep., 1,546,557; Carter, Dem., 1,147,364; Anderson, Ind., 234,632; Clark, Libertarian, 20,652; Commoner, Citizens, 8,203; McCormack, Right to Life, 3,927; Lynen, Middle Class, 3,694; Hall, Com., 2,555; Pulley, Soc. Workers, 2,198; McReynolds, Soc., 1,973; Gahres, Down With Lawyers, 1,718; Griswold, Workers World, 1,288; Wendelken, Ind., 923.

1984, Reagan, Rep., 1,933,630; Mondale, Dem., 1,261,323; Bergland, Libertarian, 6,416.

1988, Bush, Rep., 1,740,604; Dukakis, Dem., 1,317,541; Lewin, Peace and Freedom, 9,953; Paul, Lib., 8,421.

1992, Clinton, Dem., 1,436,206; Bush, Rep., 1,356,865; Perot, Ind., 521,829; Marrou, Libertarian, 6,822; Fulani, New Alliance, 3,513; Phillips, U.S. Taxpayers, 2,670; LaRouche, Ind., 2,095; Warren, Soc. Workers, 2,011; Daniels, Ind., 1,996; Gritz, Populist/America First, 1,867; Hagelin, Natural Law, 1,353.

1996, Clinton, Dem., 1,652,361; Dole, Rep., 1,103,099; Perot, Ref., 262,134; Nader, Green, 32,465; Browne, Libertarian, 14,763; Hagelin, Natural Law, 3,887; Phillips, Taxpayers, 3,440; Harris, Soc. Workers, 1,837; Moorehead, Workers World, 1,337; White, Soc. Equality, 537.

2000, Gore, Dem., 1,788,850; Bush, Rep., 1,284,173; Nader, Ind., 94,554; Buchanan, Ind., 6,989; Browne, Ind., 6,312; Hagelin, Ind., 2,215; McReynolds, Ind., 1,880; Phillips, Ind., 1,409; Harris, Ind., 844.

New Mexico

County	2000 Gore (D)	2000 Bush (R)	1996 Clinton (D)	1996 Dole (R)	1996 Perot (RF)
Bernalillo	99,461	95,249	88,140	78,832	8,708
Catron	353	1,273	423	923	114
Chaves	6,340	11,378	7,014	9,991	1,271
Cibola	4,127	2,752	4,030	2,245	488
Colfax	2,653	2,600	2,659	1,975	411
Curry	3,471	8,301	4,116	7,378	842
De Baca	349	612	509	489	86
Dona Ana ...	23,912	21,263	22,766	17,541	2,269
Eddy	7,108	10,335	8,959	8,534	1,297
Grant	5,673	4,961	5,860	3,993	778
Guadalupe...	1,076	548	1,208	436	79
Harding	214	366	264	321	28
Hidalgo	839	954	943	789	209
Lea	3,855	10,157	5,393	7,661	1,465
Lincoln......	2,027	4,458	2,209	3,396	666
Los Alamos ..	4,149	5,623	3,983	4,999	560
Luna	2,975	3,395	3,001	2,616	598
McKinley	10,281	5,070	10,124	4,470	650
Mora	1,456	668	1,646	561	131
Otero	5,465	10,258	5,938	9,065	1,096
Quay	1,471	2,292	1,830	1,943	377
Rio Arriba ...	8,169	3,495	7,965	2,551	469
Roosevelt ...	1,762	3,762	2,097	3,245	467
Sandoval ...	14,899	15,423	13,081	11,015	1,482
San Juan....	11,980	21,434	12,070	17,478	2,355
San Miguel ..	6,540	2,215	6,995	1,938	405
Santa Fe ...	32,017	13,974	26,349	10,857	1,846
Sierra.......	1,689	2,721	2,154	2,140	431
Socorro	3,294	3,173	3,374	2,315	455
Taos........	7,039	2,744	6,635	2,126	545
Torrance	1,868	2,891	2,072	2,154	332
Union.......	452	1,269	519	995	125
Valencia.....	9,819	10,803	9,169	7,779	1,222
Totals	**286,783**	**286,417**	**273,495**	**232,751**	**32,257**

New Mexico Vote Since 1952

1952, Eisenhower, Rep., 132,170; Stevenson, Dem., 105,661; Hamblen, Proh., 297; Hallinan, Ind. Prog., 225; MacArthur, Christian National, 220; Hass, Soc. Labor, 35.

1956, Eisenhower, Rep., 146,788; Stevenson, Dem., 106,098; Holtwick, Proh., 607; Andrews, Ind., 364; Hass, Soc. Labor, 69.

1960, Kennedy, Dem., 156,027; Nixon, Rep., 153,733; Decker, Proh., 777; Hass, Soc. Labor, 570.

1964, Johnson, Dem., 194,017; Goldwater, Rep., 131,838; Hass, Soc. Labor, 1,217; Munn, Proh., 543.

1968, Nixon, Rep., 169,692; Humphrey, Dem., 130,081; Wallace, 3d Party, 25,737; Chavez, 1,519; Halstead, Soc. Workers, 252.

1972, Nixon, Rep., 235,606; McGovern, Dem., 141,084; Schmitz, Amer., 8,767; Jenness, Soc. Workers, 474.

1976, Carter, Dem., 201,148; Ford, Rep., 211,419; Camejo, Soc. Workers, 2,462; MacBride, Libertarian, 1,110; Zeidler, Soc., 240; Bubar, Proh., 211.

1980, Reagan, Rep., 250,779; Carter, Dem., 167,826; Anderson, Ind., 29,459; Clark, Libertarian, 4,365; Commoner, Citizens, 2,202; Bubar, Statesman, 1,281; Pulley, Soc. Workers, 325.

1984, Reagan, Rep., 307,101; Mondale, Dem., 201,769; Bergland, Libertarian, 4,459.

1988, Bush, Rep., 270,341; Dukakis, Dem., 244,497; Paul, Lib., 3,268; Fulani, New Alliance, 2,237.

1992, Clinton, Dem., 261,617; Bush, Rep., 212,824; Perot, Ind., 91,895; Marrou, Libertarian, 1,615.

1996, Clinton, Dem., 273,495; Dole, Rep., 232,751; Perot, Ref., 32,257; Nader, Green, 13,218; Browne, Libertarian, 2,996; Phillips, Taxpayers, 713; Hagelin, Natural Law, 644.

2000, Gore, Dem., 286,783; Bush, Rep., 286,417; Nader, Green, 21,251; Browne, Libertarian, 2,058; Buchanan, Reform, 1,392; Hagelin, Natural Law, 361; Phillips, Constitution, 343.

New York

County	2000 Gore (D)	2000 Bush (R)	1996 Clinton (D)	1996 Dole (R)	1996 Perot (RF)
Albany	85,617	47,624	85,993	39,785	11,957
Allegany ...	6,336	11,436	6,621	8,107	2,730
Bronx	265,801	36,245	248,276	30,435	7,186
Broome	45,381	36,946	44,407	31,327	9,114
Cattaraugus	13,697	18,382	13,029	12,971	5,151
Cayuga	17,031	14,988	15,879	11,093	4,420
Chautauqua	27,016	29,064	26,831	21,261	7,484
Chemung ...	17,424	18,779	16,977	14,287	3,967
Chenango ..	9,112	10,033	8,797	7,319	2,822
Clinton	15,542	13,274	15,386	9,759	3,488
Columbia ...	13,489	13,153	12,910	10,324	3,466
Cortland ...	9,691	9,857	9,130	7,606	2,398
Delaware ...	8,450	10,662	8,724	7,684	2,601
Dutchess ...	52,390	52,669	47,339	41,929	12,294
Erie.......	240,174	160,176	224,554	132,343	45,679
Essex	7,927	8,822	7,893	6,379	2,363
Franklin	8,870	7,643	8,494	5,072	2,499
Fulton	9,314	11,434	9,779	7,881	3,214
Genesee ...	10,191	14,459	10,074	10,821	2,996
Greene.....	8,480	11,332	8,251	8,712	2,790
Hamilton ...	1,114	2,388	1,228	1,841	492
Herkimer ...	12,224	14,147	11,910	10,085	4,235
Jefferson ...	16,799	18,192	16,783	12,362	4,561
Kings	497,513	96,609	432,232	81,406	15,031
Lewis	4,333	6,103	4,402	3,965	1,669
Livingston ..	10,476	15,244	10,868	10,981	2,889
Madison ...	12,017	14,879	11,832	11,324	3,379
Monroe.....	161,743	141,266	164,858	115,694	23,936
Montgomery	10,249	9,765	10,485	7,172	3,253
Nassau	341,610	226,954	303,587	196,820	36,122
New York ..	454,523	82,113	394,131	67,839	11,144
Niagara....	47,781	40,952	44,203	31,438	12,564
Oneida	43,933	47,603	44,399	37,996	11,296
Onondaga ..	109,896	83,678	100,190	73,771	17,602
Ontario	19,761	23,885	19,156	17,237	4,391
Orange	58,170	62,852	54,995	45,956	11,778
Orleans	5,991	9,202	6,233	6,865	1,986
Oswego	22,857	23,249	20,440	17,159	7,499
Otsego	11,460	12,219	11,470	8,774	3,217
Putnam	18,525	21,853	16,173	17,452	4,032
Queens	416,967	122,052	372,925	107,650	22,288
Rensselaer.	34,808	29,562	34,273	23,482	8,405
Richmond...	73,828	63,903	64,684	52,207	8,968
Rockland ..	69,530	48,441	63,127	40,395	6,798
St. Lawrence	21,386	16,449	21,798	10,827	5,309
Saratoga ...	43,359	46,623	39,832	34,337	10,141
Schenectady	35,534	27,961	35,404	22,106	7,865
Schoharie ..	5,390	7,459	5,902	5,353	1,796
Schuyler....	3,301	4,381	3,303	3,134	1,037
Seneca	6,841	6,734	6,825	5,004	1,889
Steuben	14,600	24,200	14,481	17,710	5,496
Suffolk	306,306	240,992	261,828	182,510	52,209
Sullivan.....	14,348	12,703	15,052	9,321	3,453
Tioga	9,170	12,239	8,769	9,416	2,721
Tompkins ...	21,807	13,351	20,772	11,532	2,623
Ulster	38,162	33,447	35,852	26,212	9,246
Warren	12,193	14,993	11,603	11,152	3,623
Washington .	9,641	12,596	9,572	8,954	3,648
Wayne	14,977	21,701	15,145	15,837	4,619
Westchester .	218,010	139,278	196,310	123,719	18,028
Wyoming ...	5,935	10,809	5,735	7,477	2,411
Yates	3,962	5,565	4,066	3,925	1,190
Totals	**4,112,963**	**2,405,570**	**3,756,177**	**1,933,492**	**503,458**

New York Vote Since 1952

1952, Eisenhower, Rep., 3,952,815; Stevenson, Dem., 2,687,890; Liberal, 416,711; total, 3,104,601; Hallinan, Amer. Lab., 64,211; Hoopes, Soc., 2,664; Dobbs, Soc. Workers, 2,212; Hass, Ind. Gov't., 1,560; scattering, 178; blank and void, 87,813.

1956, Eisenhower, Rep., 4,340,340; Stevenson, Dem., 2,458,212; Liberal, 292,557; total, 2,750,769; write-in votes for Andrews, 1,027; Werdel, 492; Hass, 150; Hoopes, 82; others, 476.

1960, Kennedy, Dem., 3,423,909; Liberal, 406,176; total, 3,830,085; Nixon, Rep., 3,446,419; Dobbs, Soc. Workers, 14,319; scattering, 256; blank and void, 88,896.
1964, Johnson, Dem., 4,913,156; Goldwater, Rep., 2,243,559; Hass, Soc. Labor, 6,085; DeBerry, Soc. Workers, 3,215; scattering, 188; blank and void, 151,383.
1968, Nixon, Rep., 3,007,932; Humphrey, Dem., 3,378,470; Wallace, 3d Party, 358,864; Blomen, Soc. Labor, 8,432; Halstead, Soc. Workers, 11,851; Gregory, Freedom and Peace, 24,517; blank, void, and scattering, 171,624.
1972, Nixon, Rep., 3,824,642; Cons., 368,136; McGovern, Dem., 2,767,956; Liberal, 183,128; Reed, Soc. Workers, 7,797; Fisher, Soc. Labor, 4,530; Hall, Com., 5,641; blank, void, or scattered, 161,641.
1976, Carter, Dem., 3,389,558; Ford, Rep., 3,100,791; MacBride, Libertarian, 12,197; Hall, Com., 10,270; Camejo, Soc. Workers, 6,996; LaRouche, U.S. Labor, 5,413; blank, void, or scattered, 143,037.
1980, Reagan, Rep., 2,893,831; Carter, Dem., 2,728,372; Anderson, Ind., 467,801; Clark, Libertarian, 52,648; McCormack, Right To Life, 24,159; Commoner, Citizens, 23,186; Hall, Com., 7,414; DeBerry, Soc. Workers, 2,068; Griswold, Workers World, 1,416; scattering, 1,064.
1984, Reagan, Rep., 3,664,763; Mondale, Dem., 3,119,609; Bergland, Libertarian, 11,949.
1988, Bush, Rep., 3,081,871; Dukakis, Dem., 3,347,882; Marra, Right to Life, 20,497; Fulani, New Alliance, 15,845.
1992, Clinton, Dem., 3,444,450; Bush, Rep., 2,346,649; Perot, Ind., 1,090,721; Warren, Soc. Workers, 15,472; Marrou, Libertarian, 13,451; Fulani, New Alliance, 11,318; Hagelin, Natural Law, 4,420.
1996, Clinton, Dem., 3,756,177; Dole, Rep., 1,933,492; Perot, Ind. (Ref.), 503,458; Nader, Green, 75,956; Phillips, Right to Life, 23,580; Browne, Libertarian, 12,220; Hagelin, Natural Law, 5,011; Harris, Soc. Workers, 2,762; Moorehead, Workers World, 3,473.
2000, Gore, Dem., 4,112,965; Bush, Rep., 2,405,570; Nader, Green, 244,360; Buchanan, Reform, 31,554; Hagelin, Independence, 24,369; Browne, Libertarian, 7,664; Harris, Soc. Workers, 1,790; Phillips, Constitution, 1,503.

North Carolina

County	2000 Gore (D)	2000 Bush (R)	1996 Clinton (D)	1996 Dole (R)	1996 Perot (RF)
Alamance ..	17,459	29,305	15,814	22,461	3,395
Alexander ..	4,166	9,242	3,955	6,748	1,004
Alleghany ..	1,715	2,531	1,801	1,936	458
Anson	4,792	3,161	4,890	2,193	512
Ashe	4,011	6,226	3,825	5,203	865
Avery	1,686	4,956	1,586	3,870	655
Beaufort ..	6,634	10,531	6,172	8,154	834
Bertie.....	4,660	2,488	4,202	1,745	316
Bladen....	5,889	4,977	4,952	3,335	655
Brunswick .	13,118	15,427	10,041	10,065	1,815
Buncombe..	38,545	46,101	31,658	30,518	6,254
Burke.....	11,924	18,466	11,678	13,853	2,654
Cabarrus ..	16,284	32,704	14,447	23,035	3,626
Caldwell...	8,588	17,337	8,050	12,653	2,099
Camden....	1,187	1,628	1,186	1,074	293
Carteret...	8,839	17,361	7,566	11,721	1,467
Caswell ...	4,091	4,270	4,312	3,310	510
Catawba ...	16,246	34,244	15,601	26,898	3,629
Chatham...	10,461	10,248	9,353	7,731	1,113
Cherokee...	3,239	6,305	3,129	3,883	785
Chowan....	2,430	2,415	2,239	1,659	359
Clay......	1,361	2,416	1,462	1,769	387
Cleveland .	13,455	19,064	12,728	13,474	1,931
Columbus ..	9,986	8,342	9,019	6,017	1,170
Craven.....	12,213	19,494	10,317	13,264	1,528
Cumberland	38,626	38,129	32,739	29,804	3,776
Currituck ..	2,595	4,095	2,277	2,569	770
Dare	5,589	7,301	4,522	4,977	1,258
Davidson ..	16,199	35,387	13,593	24,797	3,698
Davie	3,651	10,184	3,525	8,141	915
Duplin	6,475	7,840	6,179	5,432	766
Durham	53,907	30,150	49,186	27,825	3,122
Edgecombe.	11,315	6,836	10,568	6,010	660
Forsyth ...	52,457	67,700	46,543	59,160	5,747
Franklin ...	7,454	8,501	6,448	5,648	891
Gaston.....	19,281	39,453	19,458	33,149	3,921
Gates......	1,944	1,480	2,155	1,072	307
Graham	1,006	2,304	1,210	1,801	270
Granville ...	7,733	7,364	6,747	5,498	432
Greene	2,478	3,353	2,224	2,689	280
Guilford ...	80,787	84,394	69,208	67,727	9,739
Halifax....	10,222	6,698	9,551	5,700	816
Harnett	9,155	14,762	8,767	11,596	1,287
Haywood...	9,793	12,118	9,350	7,995	2,594
Henderson .	12,562	25,688	10,626	19,182	2,679
Hertford...	5,484	2,382	4,856	1,823	356
Hoke	5,017	3,439	3,510	1,914	481
Hyde	1,088	1,132	1,109	782	143

County	2000 Gore (D)	2000 Bush (R)	1996 Clinton (D)	1996 Dole (R)	1996 Perot (RF)
Iredell	15,434	29,853	13,102	21,163	2,970
Jackson ...	5,722	6,237	5,211	4,244	970
Johnston ..	13,704	27,212	11,175	18,704	2,163
Jones	1,822	2,114	1,829	1,682	197
Lee.......	6,785	9,406	6,290	7,321	980
Lenoir	9,527	11,512	8,635	9,433	822
Lincoln ...	8,412	15,951	7,721	11,439	1,619
McDowell .	4,747	9,109	4,553	6,407	1,275
Macon	4,683	8,406	4,209	5,267	1,121
Madison ...	3,505	4,676	3,333	3,110	538
Martin	4,929	4,420	4,500	3,590	445
Mecklenburg	126,911	134,068	103,429	97,719	10,473
Mitchell ...	1,535	4,984	1,496	3,874	549
Montgomery	3,979	4,946	3,856	3,379	587
Moore.....	11,232	19,882	9,847	14,760	1,761
Nash......	12,376	17,995	11,142	15,309	1,751
New Hanover .	29,292	36,503	22,839	27,889	3,615
Northampton..	5,513	2,667	5,207	1,881	402
Onslow	10,269	19,657	8,685	13,396	1,857
Orange ...	30,921	17,930	28,674	15,053	1,534
Pamlico ...	2,188	2,999	2,204	2,270	297
Pasquotank	5,874	4,943	4,233	2,999	565
Pender ...	6,415	7,661	5,409	5,538	945
Perquimans	2,033	2,230	2,069	1,561	369
Person	5,042	6,722	4,540	4,883	591
Pitt	19,685	23,192	17,555	18,227	2,037
Polk	3,114	5,074	2,704	3,516	493
Randolph ..	11,366	30,959	10,783	23,030	3,593
Richmond..	7,935	6,263	7,564	3,973	1,230
Robeson...	17,834	11,721	17,361	8,146	2,105
Rockingham	13,260	18,979	12,096	14,255	2,528
Rowan	14,891	28,922	13,461	22,754	2,902
Rutherford .	7,697	13,755	7,162	9,792	1,585
Sampson ..	8,768	10,410	8,150	8,241	825
Scotland ..	5,627	3,740	4,870	2,858	548
Stanly	7,066	15,548	7,131	11,446	1,690
Stokes	5,030	12,028	4,769	9,471	1,025
Surry	7,757	15,401	7,303	11,117	1,538
Swain	2,097	2,224	1,869	1,444	401
Transylvania	5,044	9,011	4,842	6,734	1,183
Tyrrell	849	706	908	488	112
Union	14,890	31,876	11,525	18,802	2,477
Vance	7,092	5,564	6,385	4,651	575
Wake	123,446	142,494	103,574	108,780	11,811
Warren ...	4,576	2,202	4,141	1,861	319
Washington	2,704	2,169	2,790	1,562	171
Watauga ...	7,959	10,438	7,349	8,146	1,415
Wayne	13,005	20,758	11,580	16,588	1,178
Wilkes....	7,226	16,826	6,793	12,395	1,967
Wilson ...	11,266	13,466	9,779	10,518	1,100
Yadkin....	3,127	10,435	2,927	8,439	913
Yancey	3,714	4,970	3,956	3,973	720
Totals ...	**1,257,692**	**1,631,163**	**1,107,849**	**1,225,938**	**168,059**

North Carolina Vote Since 1952

1952, Eisenhower, Rep., 558,107; Stevenson, Dem., 652,803.
1956, Eisenhower, Rep., 575,062; Stevenson, Dem., 590,530.
1960, Kennedy, Dem., 713,136; Nixon, Rep., 655,420.
1964, Johnson, Dem., 800,139; Goldwater, Rep., 624,844.
1968, Nixon, Rep., 627,192; Humphrey, Dem., 464,113; Wallace, 3d Party, 496,188.
1972, Nixon, Rep., 1,054,889; McGovern, Dem., 438,705; Schmitz, Amer., 25,018.
1976, Carter, Dem., 927,365; Ford, Rep., 741,960; Anderson, Amer., 5,607; MacBride, Libertarian, 2,219; LaRouche, U.S. Labor, 755.
1980, Reagan, Rep., 915,018; Carter, Dem., 875,635; Anderson, Ind., 52,800; Clark, Libertarian, 9,677; Commoner, Citizens, 2,287; DeBerry, Soc. Workers, 416.
1984, Reagan, Rep., 1,346,481; Mondale, Dem., 824,287; Bergland, Libertarian, 3,794.
1988, Bush, Rep., 1,237,258; Dukakis, Dem., 890,167; Fulani, New Alliance, 5,682; Paul, write-in, 1,263.
1992, Clinton, Dem., 1,114,042; Bush, Rep., 1,134,661; Perot, Ind., 357,864; Marrou, Libertarian, 5,171.
1996, Dole, Rep., 1,225,938; Clinton, Dem., 1,107,849; Perot, Ref., 168,059; Browne, Libertarian, 8,740; Hagelin, Natural Law, 2,771.
2000, Bush, Rep., 1,631,163; Gore, Dem., 1,257,692; Browne, Libertarian, 13,891; Buchanan, Reform, 8,874.

North Dakota

County	2000 Gore (D)	2000 Bush (R)	1996 Clinton (D)	1996 Dole (R)	1996 Perot (RF)
Adams	286	826	366	575	200
Barnes	1,933	3,452	2,317	2,449	666
Benson	952	1,055	1,059	850	252
Billings	82	394	116	281	107

County	2000 Gore (D)	Bush (R)	1996 Clinton (D)	Dole (R)	Perot (RF)
Bottineau	1,173	2,349	1,280	1,682	536
Bowman	330	1,080	489	710	261
Burke	296	698	416	483	176
Burleigh	9,842	22,467	10,679	15,464	3,535
Cass	21,451	33,536	21,693	24,238	4,116
Cavalier	618	1,513	941	1,188	326
Dickey	806	1,853	953	1,418	276
Divide	306	443	637	488	209
Dunn	474	1,124	587	830	304
Eddy	458	703	553	517	201
Emmons	405	1,430	544	1,148	441
Foster	474	1,172	664	801	265
Golden Valley	156	611	235	520	163
Grand Forks	10,593	15,875	11,376	11,606	2,663
Grant	235	1,077	300	760	295
Griggs	484	920	670	731	162
Hettinger	353	1,057	418	765	238
Kidder	283	837	434	691	242
La Moure	689	1,590	880	1,220	276
Logan	223	812	360	705	254
McHenry	888	1,682	1,096	1,187	453
McIntosh	350	1,178	470	1,005	295
McKenzie	653	1,634	928	1,338	428
McLean	1,465	2,891	1,759	1,988	618
Mercer	1,011	2,984	1,300	1,953	764
Morton	3,439	6,993	3,745	4,699	1,566
Mountrail	1,256	1,466	1,277	965	360
Nelson	687	1,031	827	745	206
Oliver	244	709	333	499	183
Pembina	1,093	2,430	1,191	1,678	400
Pierce	500	1,348	671	1,017	270
Ramsey	1,658	3,005	2,123	2,077	549
Ransom	1,080	1,488	1,199	920	303
Renville	443	820	562	576	210
Richland	2,490	4,999	2,890	3,345	782
Rolette	2,681	1,416	2,299	823	448
Sargent	959	1,103	1,003	814	241
Sheridan	161	707	252	566	121
Sioux	724	269	393	207	82
Slope	85	316	123	260	60
Stark	2,784	6,387	3,095	4,086	1,456
Steele	475	655	620	486	115
Stutsman	3,067	5,488	3,589	3,784	1,141
Towner	410	694	649	542	187
Traill	1,512	2,392	1,822	1,820	380
Walsh	1,743	3,099	2,082	2,222	599
Ward	7,533	13,997	8,660	10,546	2,587
Wells	661	1,610	962	1,192	373
Williams	2,330	5,187	3,018	3,590	1,174
Totals	**95,284**	**174,852**	**106,905**	**125,050**	**32,515**

North Dakota Vote Since 1952

1952, Eisenhower, Rep., 191,712; Stevenson, Dem., 76,694; MacArthur, Christian Nationalist, 1,075; Hallinan, Prog., 344; Hamblen, Proh., 302.

1956, Eisenhower, Rep., 156,766; Stevenson, Dem., 96,742; Andrews, Amer., 483.

1960, Kennedy, Dem., 123,963; Nixon, Rep., 154,310; Dobbs, Soc. Workers, 158.

1964, Johnson, Dem., 149,784; Goldwater, Rep., 108,207; DeBerry, Soc. Workers, 224; Munn, Proh., 174.

1968, Nixon, Rep., 138,669; Humphrey, Dem., 94,769; Wallace, 3d Party, 14,244; Halstead, Soc. Workers, 128; Munn, Prohibition, 38; Troxell, Ind., 34.

1972, Nixon, Rep., 174,109; McGovern, Dem., 100,384; Jenness, Soc. Workers, 288; Hall, Com., 87; Schmitz, Amer., 5,646.

1976, Carter, Dem., 136,078; Ford, Rep., 153,470; Anderson, Amer., 3,698; McCarthy, Ind., 2,952; Maddox, Amer. Ind., 269; MacBride, Libertarian, 256; scattering, 371.

1980, Reagan, Rep., 193,695; Carter, Dem., 79,189; Anderson, Ind., 23,640; Clark, Libertarian, 3,743; Commoner, Libertarian, 429; McLain, Natl. People's League, 296; Greaves, Amer., 235; Hall, Com., 93; DeBerry, Soc. Workers, 89; McReynolds, Soc., 82; Bubar, Statesman, 54.

1984, Reagan, Rep., 200,336; Mondale, Dem., 104,429; Bergland, Libertarian, 703.

1988, Bush, Rep., 166,559; Dukakis, Dem., 127,739; Paul, Lib., 1,315; LaRouche, Natl. Econ. Recovery, 905.

1992, Clinton, Dem., 99,168; Bush, Rep., 136,244; Perot, Ind., 71,084.

1996, Dole, Rep., 125,050; Clinton, Dem., 106,905; Perot, Ref., 32,515; Browne, Libertarian, 847; Phillips, Ind., 745; Hagelin, Natural Law, 349.

2000, Bush, Rep., 174,852; Gore, Dem., 95,284; Nader, Ind., 9,486; Buchanan, Reform, 7,288; Browne, Ind., 660; Phillips, Constitution, 373; Hagelin, Ind., 313.

Ohio

County	2000 Gore (D)	Bush (R)	1996 Clinton (D)	Dole (R)	Perot (RF)
Adams	3,581	6,380	4,317	4,763	1,223
Allen	13,996	28,647	15,529	24,325	3,799
Ashland	6,685	13,533	6,573	10,402	2,630
Ashtabula	19,831	17,940	19,341	13,287	5,700
Athens	13,158	9,703	13,418	7,154	2,777
Auglaize	5,564	13,770	6,652	10,169	2,641
Belmont	15,980	12,625	17,705	8,213	4,452
Brown	5,972	10,027	6,318	6,970	1,941
Butler	46,390	86,587	43,690	67,023	10,540
Carroll	4,960	6,732	4,792	4,449	2,445
Champaign	5,955	9,220	5,990	6,568	2,219
Clark	27,984	27,660	27,890	22,297	7,083
Clermont	20,927	47,129	21,329	36,457	5,795
Clinton	4,791	9,824	5,303	7,504	1,588
Columbiana	20,657	21,804	20,716	15,386	7,127
Coshocton	5,594	8,243	6,005	6,018	2,183
Crawford	6,721	11,666	7,449	8,730	3,072
Cuyahoga	359,913	192,099	341,357	163,770	50,691
Darke	7,741	14,817	8,871	10,798	3,168
Defiance	6,175	9,540	6,343	7,469	1,929
Delaware	17,134	36,639	13,463	24,123	3,471
Erie	17,732	16,105	16,730	12,204	4,225
Fairfield	19,065	33,523	18,821	26,850	4,660
Fayette	3,363	5,685	3,665	4,831	1,047
Franklin	202,018	197,962	192,795	178,412	25,400
Fulton	6,805	11,546	6,662	8,703	2,412
Gallia	4,872	7,511	5,386	5,135	1,839
Geauga	15,327	25,417	14,143	19,662	4,848
Greene	25,059	37,946	25,082	30,677	5,246
Guernsey	6,643	8,181	6,731	5,970	2,251
Hamilton	161,578	204,175	160,458	186,493	21,335
Hancock	8,798	20,985	9,334	17,252	2,904
Hardin	4,557	7,124	4,930	5,506	1,365
Harrison	3,351	3,417	3,721	2,310	1,302
Henry	4,367	8,530	4,762	6,385	1,550
Highland	5,328	9,728	5,837	7,102	1,629
Hocking	4,474	5,702	4,646	4,017	1,564
Holmes	2,066	6,754	2,531	5,213	1,276
Huron	8,183	12,286	8,858	8,750	3,338
Jackson	5,131	6,958	5,538	4,922	1,529
Jefferson	17,488	15,038	19,402	10,212	4,748
Knox	7,133	13,393	7,562	10,159	2,138
Lake	46,497	51,747	43,186	40,974	12,507
Lawrence	11,307	12,531	11,595	8,832	3,232
Licking	23,196	37,180	22,624	28,276	6,516
Logan	5,945	11,849	6,397	8,325	2,264
Lorain	59,809	47,957	55,744	34,937	14,889
Lucas	108,344	73,342	104,911	58,120	17,282
Madison	5,287	8,892	5,072	6,871	1,386
Mahoning	69,212	40,460	72,716	31,397	13,213
Marion	10,370	13,617	10,482	11,112	2,897
Medina	26,635	37,349	23,727	26,120	8,700
Meigs	3,674	5,750	4,275	3,622	1,453
Mercer	5,212	12,485	6,300	8,832	2,361
Miami	15,584	26,037	15,540	19,509	4,599
Monroe	3,605	3,145	3,914	1,856	1,128
Montgomery	114,597	109,792	115,416	95,391	18,298
Morgan	2,261	3,451	2,385	2,566	922
Morrow	4,529	7,842	4,627	5,655	1,745
Muskingum	13,415	17,995	13,813	13,861	4,880
Noble	2,296	3,435	2,366	2,183	899
Ottawa	9,485	9,917	9,321	6,991	2,438
Paulding	3,384	5,210	3,449	3,760	1,292
Perry	5,895	6,440	5,819	4,606	1,854
Pickaway	6,598	10,717	7,042	8,666	1,702
Pike	4,923	5,333	5,542	3,759	1,402
Portage	31,446	28,271	29,441	18,939	9,118
Preble	6,375	11,176	6,611	8,139	2,235
Putnam	4,063	12,837	4,972	9,294	1,767
Richland	20,572	30,138	20,832	23,697	6,613
Ross	11,662	13,706	12,649	10,286	2,648
Sandusky	11,146	13,699	11,547	10,033	3,617
Scioto	13,997	15,022	15,041	11,679	4,418
Seneca	9,512	13,863	10,044	9,713	3,498
Shelby	6,593	12,476	6,729	8,773	2,686
Stark	75,308	78,153	73,437	60,212	23,004
Summit	119,759	96,721	112,050	73,555	27,723
Trumbull	57,643	34,654	55,604	24,811	13,563
Tuscarawas	15,879	19,549	15,244	13,388	5,682
Union	5,040	11,502	4,989	8,290	1,596
Van Wert	4,209	8,679	4,453	6,999	1,487
Vinton	2,037	2,720	2,350	1,673	728
Warren	19,142	48,318	17,089	33,210	4,689
Washington	10,383	15,342	10,945	11,965	2,832
Wayne	14,779	25,901	14,850	19,628	5,771
Williams	5,454	9,941	5,524	7,747	2,121
Wood	22,687	27,504	23,183	20,518	5,065
Wyandot	3,397	6,113	3,677	4,473	1,347
Totals	**2,186,190**	**2,351,209**	**2,148,222**	**1,859,883**	**483,207**

Ohio Vote Since 1952

1952, Eisenhower, Rep., 2,100,391; Stevenson, Dem., 1,600,367.
1956, Eisenhower, Rep., 2,262,610; Stevenson, Dem., 1,439,655.
1960, Kennedy, Dem., 1,944,248; Nixon, Rep., 2,217,611.
1964, Johnson, Dem., 2,498,331; Goldwater, Rep., 1,470,865.
1968, Nixon, Rep., 1,791,014; Humphrey, Dem., 1,700,586; Wallace, 3d Party, 467,495; Gregory, 372; Munn, Proh., 19; Blomen, Soc. Labor, 120; Halstead, Soc. Workers, 69; Mitchell, Com., 23.
1972, Nixon, Rep., 2,441,827; McGovern, Dem., 1,558,889; Fisher, Soc. Labor, 7,107; Hall, Com., 6,437; Schmitz, Amer., 80,067; Wallace, Ind., 460.
1976, Carter, Dem., 2,011,621; Ford, Rep., 2,000,505; McCarthy, Ind., 58,258; Maddox, Amer. Ind., 15,529; MacBride, Libertarian, 8,961; Hall, Com., 7,817; Camejo, Soc. Workers, 4,717; LaRouche, U.S. Labor, 4,335; scattered, 130.
1980, Reagan, Rep., 2,206,545; Carter, Dem., 1,752,414; Anderson, Ind., 254,472; Clark, Libertarian, 49,033; Commoner, Citizens, 8,564; Hall, Com., 4,729; Congress, Ind., 4,029; Griswold, Workers World, 3,790; Bubar, Statesman, 27.
1984, Reagan, Rep., 2,678,559; Mondale, Dem., 1,825,440; Bergland, Libertarian, 5,886.
1988, Bush, Rep., 2,416,549; Dukakis, Dem., 1,939,629; Fulani, Ind., 12,017; Paul, Ind., 11,926.
1992, Clinton, Dem., 1,984,942; Bush, Rep., 1,894,310; Perot, Ind., 1,036,426; Marrou, Libertarian, 7,252; Fulani, New Alliance, 6,413; Gritz, Populist/America First, 4,699; Hagelin, Natural Law, 3,437; LaRouche, Ind., 2,446.
1996, Clinton, Dem., 2,148,222; Dole, Rep., 1,859,883; Perot, Ref., 483,207; Browne, Ind., 12,851; Moorehead, Ind., 10,813; Hagelin, Natural Law, 9,120; Phillips, Ind., 7,361.
2000, Bush, Rep., 2,351,209; Gore, Dem., 2,186,190; Nader, Ind., 117,857; Buchanan, Ind., 26,724; Browne, Libertarian, 13,475; Hagelin, Natural Law, 6,169; Phillips, Ind., 3,823.

Oklahoma

| | 2000 | | 1996 | | |
County	Gore (D)	Bush (R)	Clinton (D)	Dole (R)	Perot (RF)
Adair	2,361	3,503	2,792	2,956	751
Alfalfa	583	1,886	796	1,504	348
Atoka	1,906	2,375	2,281	1,542	532
Beaver	339	2,092	515	1,893	199
Beckham	2,408	4,067	2,797	2,912	817
Blaine	1,402	2,633	1,832	2,127	563
Bryan	5,554	6,084	5,962	3,943	1,396
Caddo	4,272	4,835	4,844	3,422	1,358
Canadian	8,367	22,679	8,977	18,139	3,297
Carter	6,659	9,667	6,979	6,769	1,997
Cherokee	7,256	6,918	6,817	5,046	1,777
Choctaw	2,799	2,461	3,198	1,580	589
Cimarron	227	1,230	361	986	102
Cleveland	27,792	47,393	26,038	36,457	6,785
Coal	1,148	1,196	1,205	734	323
Comanche	11,971	17,103	12,841	14,461	2,819
Cotton	1,068	1,388	1,258	1,042	381
Craig	2,568	2,815	2,649	2,058	758
Creek	9,753	13,580	9,674	9,861	2,837
Custer	3,115	6,527	4,027	4,723	1,101
Delaware	5,514	7,618	5,094	5,230	1,573
Dewey	599	1,607	816	1,179	292
Ellis	468	1,513	619	1,090	279
Garfield	6,543	14,902	7,504	11,712	2,523
Garvin	4,189	5,536	4,639	3,745	1,345
Grady	6,037	10,040	6,256	7,228	2,048
Grant	709	1,762	867	1,382	384
Greer	839	1,287	1,240	905	361
Harmon	507	692	729	448	143
Harper	374	1,296	511	1,036	219
Haskell	2,510	2,039	2,762	1,442	590
Hughes	2,334	2,196	2,748	1,510	730
Jackson	2,515	5,591	3,245	4,422	892
Jefferson	1,245	1,320	1,430	865	337
Johnston	1,809	2,072	1,998	1,229	532
Kay	6,122	11,768	6,882	9,741	2,785
Kingfisher	1,304	4,693	1,626	3,423	621
Kiowa	1,544	2,173	1,973	1,638	510
Latimer	1,865	1,739	2,222	1,189	578
Le Flore	6,536	8,215	6,831	5,689	1,721
Lincoln	4,140	7,387	4,332	5,243	1,500
Logan	4,510	8,187	4,854	5,949	1,410
Love	1,530	1,807	1,675	1,224	385
McClain	3,679	6,750	3,753	4,363	1,289
McCurtain	3,752	6,601	4,350	3,892	1,483
McIntosh	4,206	3,444	4,219	2,400	1,044
Major	635	2,672	900	2,188	410
Marshall	2,210	2,641	2,624	1,605	663
Mayes	6,618	7,132	6,377	5,268	1,617
Murray	2,263	2,609	2,620	1,712	723
Muskogee	12,520	11,820	12,963	8,974	3,163
Noble	1,416	3,230	1,756	2,318	694
Nowata	1,703	2,069	1,788	1,457	586
Okfuskee	1,814	1,910	2,074	1,380	536
Oklahoma	81,590	139,078	80,438	120,429	18,411
Okmulgee	7,186	5,797	7,555	4,246	1,487
Osage	7,540	8,138	7,342	5,827	1,938
Ottawa	5,647	5,625	5,844	4,127	1,496
Pawnee	2,435	3,386	2,663	2,560	756
Payne	9,319	15,256	9,985	11,686	2,472
Pittsburg	7,627	8,514	8,475	5,966	2,217
Pontotoc	5,387	7,299	6,470	5,366	1,712
Pottawatomie	8,763	13,235	9,141	9,802	2,724
Pushmataha	1,969	2,331	2,270	1,458	588
Roger Mills	441	1,234	733	959	233
Rogers	10,813	17,713	9,544	12,883	3,022
Seminole	3,783	4,011	4,225	2,935	1,041
Sequoyah	5,425	6,614	5,665	4,733	1,673
Stephens	6,467	10,860	7,248	8,144	2,312
Texas	1,084	4,964	1,408	4,139	518
Tillman	1,400	1,920	1,827	1,346	471
Tulsa	81,656	134,152	76,924	111,243	18,201
Wagoner	8,244	12,981	7,749	9,392	2,357
Washington	6,644	13,788	6,732	11,605	2,255
Washita	1,564	2,850	1,913	1,994	748
Woods	1,235	2,774	1,431	2,151	497
Woodward	1,950	5,067	2,403	4,093	963
Totals	474,276	744,337	488,105	582,315	130,788

Oklahoma Vote Since 1952

1952, Eisenhower, Rep., 518,045; Stevenson, Dem., 430,939.
1956, Eisenhower, Rep., 473,769; Stevenson, Dem., 385,581.
1960, Kennedy, Dem., 370,111; Nixon, Rep., 533,039.
1964, Johnson, Dem., 519,834; Goldwater, Rep., 412,665.
1968, Nixon, Rep., 449,697; Humphrey, Dem., 301,658; Wallace, 3d Party, 191,731.
1972, Nixon, Rep., 759,025; McGovern, Dem., 247,147; Schmitz, Amer., 23,728.
1976, Carter, Dem., 532,442; Ford, Rep., 545,708; McCarthy, Ind., 14,101.
1980, Reagan, Rep., 695,570; Carter, Dem., 402,026; Anderson, Ind., 38,284; Clark, Libertarian, 13,828.
1984, Reagan, Rep., 861,530; Mondale, Dem., 385,080; Bergland, Libertarian, 9,066.
1988, Bush, Rep., 678,367; Dukakis, Dem., 483,423; Paul, Lib., 6,261; Fulani, New Alliance, 2,985.
1992, Clinton, Dem., 473,066; Bush, Rep., 592,929; Perot, Ind., 319,878; Marrou, Libertarian, 4,486.
1996, Dole, Rep., 582,315; Clinton, Dem., 488,105; Perot, Ref., 130,788; Browne, Libertarian, 5,505.
2000, Bush, Rep., 744,337; Gore, Dem., 474,276; Buchanan, Reform, 9,014; Browne, Libertarian, 6,602.

Oregon

| | 2000 | | 1996 | | |
County	Gore (D)	Bush (R)	Clinton (D)	Dole (R)	Perot (RF)
Baker	2,195	5,618	2,547	3,975	900
Benton	19,444	15,825	17,211	12,450	2,445
Clackamas	76,421	77,539	67,709	59,443	12,304
Clatsop	8,296	6,950	7,732	5,334	1,582
Columbia	10,331	9,369	9,275	6,205	2,330
Coos	11,610	15,626	12,171	10,886	3,460
Crook	2,474	5,363	2,607	3,250	948
Curry	4,090	6,551	4,202	4,790	1,560
Deschutes	22,061	32,132	17,151	21,135	5,306
Douglas	14,193	30,294	15,250	21,855	4,465
Gilliam	359	679	485	398	143
Grant	589	3,078	1,180	2,110	432
Harney	766	2,799	980	1,948	506
Hood River	4,072	3,721	3,654	2,794	721
Jackson	33,153	46,052	29,230	33,771	7,470
Jefferson	2,681	3,838	2,555	2,634	813
Josephine	11,864	22,186	11,113	16,048	3,546
Klamath	7,541	18,855	7,207	12,116	2,538
Lake	707	2,830	962	2,239	385
Lane	78,583	61,578	69,461	48,253	11,498
Lincoln	10,861	8,446	10,552	6,717	2,269
Linn	16,682	25,359	17,041	18,331	4,773
Malheur	2,336	7,624	2,827	6,045	844
Marion	49,430	57,443	48,637	46,415	8,802
Morrow	1,197	2,224	1,426	1,381	455
Multnomah	188,441	83,677	159,878	71,094	17,536
Polk	11,921	14,988	10,942	11,478	2,093
Sherman	326	679	444	476	126
Tillamook	5,762	5,775	5,775	3,884	1,263
Umatilla	7,809	14,140	8,774	9,703	2,500
Union	3,577	7,836	4,379	5,414	1,241
Wallowa	836	3,279	1,321	2,379	483
Wasco	4,616	5,356	4,967	3,662	1,004
Washington	90,662	86,091	76,619	65,221	11,446
Wheeler	202	584	299	418	121
Yamhill	14,254	19,193	13,078	13,900	2,913
Totals	720,342	713,577	649,641	538,152	121,221

Oregon Vote Since 1952

1952, Eisenhower, Rep., 420,815; Stevenson, Dem., 270,579; Hallinan, Ind., 3,665.

1956, Eisenhower, Rep., 406,393; Stevenson, Dem., 329,204.

1960, Kennedy, Dem., 367,402; Nixon, Rep., 408,060.

1964, Johnson, Dem., 501,017; Goldwater, Rep., 282,779; write-in, 2,509.

1968, Nixon, Rep., 408,433; Humphrey, Dem., 358,866; Wallace, 3d Party, 49,683; write-in McCarthy, 1,496; N. Rockefeller, 69; others, 1,075.

1972, Nixon, Rep., 486,686; McGovern, Dem., 392,760; Schmitz, Amer., 46,211; write-in, 2,289.

1976, Carter, Dem., 490,407; Ford, Rep., 492,120; McCarthy, Ind., 40,207; write-in, 7,142.

1980, Reagan, Rep., 571,044; Carter, Dem., 456,890; Anderson, Ind., 112,389; Clark, Libertarian, 25,838; Commoner, Citizens, 13,642; scattered, 1,713.

1984, Reagan, Rep., 658,700; Mondale, Dem., 536,479.

1988, Bush, Rep., 560,126; Dukakis, Dem., 616,206; Paul, Lib., 14,811; Fulani, Ind., 6,487.

1992, Clinton, Dem., 621,314; Bush, Rep., 475,757; Perot, Ind., 354,091; Marrou, Libertarian, 4,277; Fulani, New Alliance, 3,030.

1996, Clinton, Dem., 649,641; Dole, Rep., 538,152; Perot, Ref., 121,221; Nader, Pacific, 49,415; Browne, Libertarian, 8,903; Phillips, Taxpayers, 3,379; Hagelin, Natural Law, 2,798; Hollis, Soc., 1,922.

2000, Gore, Dem., 720,342; Bush, Rep., 713,577; Nader, Green, 77,357; Browne, Libertarian, 7,447; Buchanan, Ind., 7,063; Hagelin, Reform, 2,574; Phillips, Constitution, 2,189.

Pennsylvania

County	2000 Gore (D)	2000 Bush (R)	1996 Clinton (D)	1996 Dole (R)	1996 Perot (RF)
Adams	11,682	20,848	10,774	15,338	3,186
Allegheny	329,963	235,361	284,480	204,067	42,309
Armstrong	11,127	15,508	11,130	11,052	3,452
Beaver	38,925	32,491	39,578	26,048	8,276
Bedford	5,474	13,598	5,954	10,064	2,041
Berks	59,150	71,273	49,887	56,289	13,788
Blair	15,774	28,376	15,036	21,282	4,014
Bradford	7,911	14,660	7,736	10,393	2,712
Bucks	132,914	121,927	103,313	94,899	24,544
Butler	25,037	44,009	21,990	32,038	6,145
Cambria	30,308	28,001	30,391	20,341	7,837
Cameron	779	1,383	822	1,113	283
Carbon	10,668	9,717	9,457	7,193	2,992
Centre	21,409	26,172	21,145	20,935	4,173
Chester	82,047	100,080	64,783	77,029	14,067
Clarion	5,605	9,796	5,954	6,916	2,064
Clearfield	11,718	18,019	11,991	12,987	3,758
Clinton	5,521	6,064	5,658	4,293	1,424
Columbia	8,975	12,095	8,379	8,234	3,654
Crawford	13,250	18,858	12,943	14,659	3,519
Cumberland	31,053	54,802	28,749	43,943	5,669
Dauphin	44,390	53,631	40,936	44,417	6,967
Delaware	134,861	105,836	115,946	92,628	21,883
Elk	5,754	7,347	5,749	4,889	2,293
Erie	59,399	49,027	57,508	39,884	10,386
Fayette	28,152	20,013	26,359	14,019	5,722
Forest	843	1,371	964	944	325
Franklin	14,922	33,042	14,980	25,392	4,127
Fulton	1,425	3,753	1,620	2,665	554
Greene	7,230	5,890	7,620	4,002	2,052
Huntingdon	5,073	10,408	5,285	7,324	1,813
Indiana	13,667	16,799	13,868	12,874	3,674
Jefferson	5,566	11,473	5,846	8,156	2,322
Juniata	2,656	5,795	2,896	4,128	911
Lackawanna	57,471	35,096	46,377	26,930	8,189
Lancaster	54,968	115,900	49,120	92,875	11,601
Lawrence	20,593	18,060	18,993	13,088	4,002
Lebanon	16,093	28,534	14,187	21,885	4,235
Lehigh	56,667	55,492	48,568	45,103	10,947
Luzerne	62,199	52,328	60,174	43,577	12,424
Lycoming	14,663	27,137	13,516	21,535	3,855
McKean	5,510	9,661	5,509	6,838	2,350
Mercer	23,817	23,132	23,003	17,213	5,108
Mifflin	4,835	9,400	5,327	6,888	1,392
Monroe	21,939	23,265	16,547	17,326	4,650
Montgomery	177,990	145,623	143,664	121,047	24,392
Montour	2,356	3,960	2,183	2,785	784
Northampton	53,097	47,396	43,959	35,726	9,848
Northumberland	13,670	18,142	13,418	13,551	5,173
Perry	4,459	11,184	4,611	8,156	1,609
Philadelphia	449,182	100,959	412,988	85,345	29,329
Pike	7,330	9,339	5,509	6,697	1,873
Potter	2,037	4,858	2,146	3,714	925
Schuylkill	26,215	29,841	24,860	22,920	8,471
Snyder	3,536	8,963	3,405	6,742	1,451
Somerset	12,028	20,218	12,719	14,735	3,968
Sullivan	1,066	1,928	1,071	1,352	418
Susquehanna	6,481	10,226	5,912	7,354	2,266
Tioga	4,617	9,635	4,961	7,382	1,993
Union	4,209	8,523	3,658	6,570	1,431
Venango	8,196	11,642	8,205	8,398	2,777
Warren	7,537	9,290	7,291	7,056	2,504
Washington	44,961	37,339	40,952	27,777	8,661
Wayne	6,904	11,201	5,928	8,077	2,126
Westmoreland	71,792	80,858	63,686	62,058	16,230
Wyoming	4,363	6,922	4,049	4,888	1,414
York	51,958	87,652	49,596	65,188	11,652
Totals	2,485,967	2,281,127	2,215,819	1,801,169	430,984

Pennsylvania Vote Since 1952

1952, Eisenhower, Rep., 2,415,789; Stevenson, Dem., 2,146,269; Hamblen, Proh., 8,771; Hallinan, Prog., 4,200; Hoopes, Soc., 2,684; Dobbs, Militant Workers, 1,502; Hass, Ind. Gov., 1,347; scattered, 155.

1956, Eisenhower, Rep., 2,585,252; Stevenson, Dem., 1,981,769; Hass, Soc. Labor, 7,447; Dobbs, Militant Workers, 2,035.

1960, Kennedy, Dem., 2,556,282; Nixon, Rep., 2,439,956; Hass, Soc. Labor, 7,185; Dobbs, Soc. Workers, 2,678; scattering, 440.

1964, Johnson, Dem., 3,130,954; Goldwater, Rep., 1,673,657; DeBerry, Soc. Workers, 10,456; Hass, Soc. Labor, 5,092; scattering, 2,531.

1968, Nixon, Rep., 2,090,017; Humphrey, Dem., 2,259,405; Wallace, 3d Party, 378,582; Blomen, Soc. Labor, 4,977; Halstead, Soc. Workers, 4,862; Gregory, Peace and Freedom, 7,821; others, 2,264.

1972, Nixon, Rep., 2,714,521; McGovern, Dem., 1,796,951; Schmitz, Amer., 70,593; Jenness, Soc. Workers, 4,639; Hall, Com., 2,686; others, 2,715.

1976, Carter, Dem., 2,328,677; Ford, Rep., 2,205,604; McCarthy, Ind., 50,584; Maddox, Constitution, 25,344; Camejo, Soc. Workers, 3,009; LaRouche, U.S. Labor, 2,744; Hall, Com., 1,891; others, 2,934.

1980, Reagan, Rep., 2,261,872; Carter, Dem., 1,937,540; Anderson, Ind., 292,921; Clark, Libertarian, 33,263; DeBerry, Soc. Workers, 20,291; Commoner, Consumer, 10,430; Hall, Com., 5,184.

1984, Reagan, Rep., 2,584,323; Mondale, Dem., 2,228,131; Bergland, Libertarian, 6,982.

1988, Bush, Rep., 2,300,087; Dukakis, Dem., 2,194,944; McCarthy, Consumer, 19,158; Paul, Lib., 12,051.

1992, Clinton, Dem., 2,239,164; Bush, Rep., 1,791,841; Perot, Ind., 902,667; Marrou, Libertarian, 21,477; Fulani, New Alliance, 4,661.

1996, Clinton, Dem., 2,215,819; Dole, Rep., 1,801,169; Perot, Ref., 430,984; Browne, Libertarian, 28,000; Phillips, Constitutional, 19,552; Hagelin, Natural Law, 5,783.

2000, Gore, Dem., 2,485,967; Bush, Rep., 2,281,127; Nader, Green, 103,392; Buchanan, Reform, 16,023; Phillips, Constitution, 14,428; Browne, Libertarian, 11,248.

Rhode Island

City	2000 Gore (D)	2000 Bush (R)	1996 Clinton (D)	1996 Dole (R)	1996 Perot (RF)
Cranston	21,204	10,420	20,901	9,098	3,457
East Providence	13,033	5,072	12,846	4,199	1,971
Pawtucket	15,429	4,598	14,719	3,877	2,508
Providence	31,979	7,669	29,450	7,068	2,733
Warwick	23,948	12,741	23,152	10,414	4,541
Other	143,915	90,055	131,982	70,027	28,513
Totals	249,508	130,555	233,050	104,683	43,723

Rhode Island Vote Since 1952

1952, Eisenhower, Rep., 210,935; Stevenson, Dem., 203,293; Hallinan, Prog., 187; Hass, Soc. Labor, 83.

1956, Eisenhower, Rep., 225,819; Stevenson, Dem., 161,790.

1960, Kennedy, Dem., 258,032; Nixon, Rep., 147,502.

1964, Johnson, Dem., 315,463; Goldwater, Rep., 74,615.

1968, Nixon, Rep., 122,359; Humphrey, Dem., 246,518; Wallace, 3d Party, 15,678; Halstead, Soc. Workers, 383.

1972, Nixon, Rep., 220,383; McGovern, Dem., 194,645; Jenness, Soc. Workers, 729.

1976, Carter, Dem., 227,636; Ford, Rep., 181,249; MacBride, Libertarian, 715; Camejo, Soc. Workers, 462; Hall, Com., 334; Levin, Soc. Labor, 188.

1980, Reagan, Rep., 154,793; Carter, Dem., 198,342; Anderson, Ind., 59,819; Clark, Libertarian, 2,458; Hall, Com., 218; McReynolds, Soc., 170; DeBerry, Soc. Workers, 90; Griswold, Workers World, 77.

1984, Reagan, Rep., 212,080; Mondale, Dem., 197,106; Bergland, Libertarian, 277.

1988, Bush, Rep., 177,761; Dukakis, Dem., 225,123; Paul, Lib., 825; Fulani, New Alliance, 280.

1992, Clinton, Dem., 213,299; Bush, Rep., 131,601; Perot, Ind., 105,045; Fulani, New Alliance, 1,878.

1996, Clinton, Dem., 233,050; Dole, Rep., 104,683; Perot, Ref., 43,723; Nader, Green, 6,040; Browne, Libertarian, 1,109; Phillips, Taxpayers, 1,021; Hagelin, Natural Law, 435; Moorehead, Workers World, 186.
2000, Gore, Dem., 249,508; Bush, Rep., 130,555; Nader, Ind., 25,052; Buchanan, Reform, 2,273; Browne, Ind., 742; Hagelin, Ind., 271; Moorehead, Ind., 199; Phillips, Ind., 97; McReynolds, Ind., 52; Harris, Ind., 34.

South Carolina

County	2000 Gore (D)	2000 Bush (R)	1996 Clinton (D)	1996 Dole (R)	1996 Perot (RF)
Abbeville	3,766	4,450	3,493	3,054	537
Aiken	16,409	33,203	14,314	26,539	1,984
Allendale	2,338	967	2,222	941	87
Anderson	19,606	35,827	17,460	24,137	3,896
Bamberg	3,451	2,047	3,380	1,715	192
Barnwell	3,661	4,521	3,620	3,808	310
Beaufort	17,487	25,561	15,764	17,575	1,838
Berkeley	17,707	24,796	13,358	17,691	1,922
Calhoun	3,063	3,216	2,716	2,520	316
Charleston	49,520	58,229	43,571	48,675	3,514
Cherokee	6,138	9,900	5,821	6,689	1,064
Chester	5,242	4,986	5,108	3,157	758
Chesterfield	6,111	6,266	5,734	4,028	768
Clarendon	5,999	5,186	5,930	3,841	395
Colleton	6,449	6,767	5,329	4,462	550
Darlington	10,253	11,290	8,943	8,220	898
Dillon	4,930	3,975	3,992	2,774	275
Dorchester	12,168	20,734	9,931	15,283	1,591
Edgefield	3,950	4,760	3,576	3,640	244
Fairfield	5,263	3,011	4,719	2,414	284
Florence	17,157	23,678	15,804	18,490	1,563
Georgetown	9,445	10,535	8,298	7,023	950
Greenville	43,810	92,714	41,605	71,210	6,761
Greenwood	8,139	12,193	8,193	8,865	985
Hampton	4,896	2,798	4,828	2,111	344
Horry	29,113	40,300	23,722	26,159	4,446
Jasper	3,646	2,414	4,053	2,024	348
Kershaw	7,428	11,911	6,764	8,513	996
Lancaster	8,782	11,676	8,752	7,544	1,598
Laurens	7,920	12,102	7,055	8,057	1,341
Lee	3,899	2,675	3,588	1,973	320
Lexington	22,830	58,095	18,907	39,658	3,703
McCormick	1,896	1,704	1,858	1,104	148
Marion	7,358	4,687	6,359	3,595	356
Marlboro	5,060	2,699	5,348	2,148	494
Newberry	4,428	7,492	4,804	5,670	682
Oconee	7,571	15,364	7,398	10,503	1,961
Orangeburg	19,802	12,657	18,610	10,494	1,112
Pickens	8,927	24,681	8,369	17,151	2,211
Richland	63,179	50,164	52,222	39,092	3,158
Saluda	2,682	4,098	2,486	2,825	371
Spartanburg	29,559	52,114	26,814	35,972	3,885
Sumter	14,365	15,915	12,198	12,080	933
Union	4,662	6,234	5,407	3,855	749
Williamsburg	6,723	4,524	6,987	3,957	375
York	19,251	33,776	16,873	22,222	3,173
Totals	566,039	786,892	506,283	573,458	64,386

South Carolina Vote Since 1952

1952, Eisenhower ran on two tickets. Under state law votes cast for two Eisenhower slates of electors could not be combined. Eisenhower, Rep., 158,289; Rep., 9,793; total, 168,082; Stevenson, Dem., 173,004; Hamblen, Proh., 1.
1956, Eisenhower, Rep., 75,700; Stevenson, Dem., 136,372; Byrd, Ind., 88,509; Andrews, Ind., 2.
1960, Kennedy, Dem., 198,129; Nixon, Rep., 188,558; write-in, 1.
1964, Johnson, Dem., 215,700; Goldwater, Rep., 309,048; write-ins: Nixon, 1, Wallace, 5; Powell, 1; Thurmond, 1.
1968, Nixon, Rep., 254,062; Humphrey, Dem., 197,486; Wallace, 3d Party, 215,430.
1972, Nixon, Rep., 477,044; McGovern, Dem., 184,559; United Citizens, 2,265; Schmitz, Amer., 10,075; write-in, 17.
1976, Carter, Dem., 450,807; Ford, Rep., 346,149; Anderson, Amer., 2,996; Maddox, Amer. Ind., 1,950; write-in, 681.
1980, Reagan, Rep., 439,277; Carter, Dem., 428,220; Anderson, Ind., 13,868; Clark, Libertarian, 4,807; Rarick, Amer. Ind., 2,086.
1984, Reagan, Rep., 615,539; Mondale, Dem., 344,459; Bergland, Libertarian, 4,359.
1988, Bush, Rep., 606,443; Dukakis, Dem., 370,554; Paul, Lib., 4,935; Fulani, United Citizens, 4,077.
1992, Clinton, Dem., 479,514; Bush, Rep., 577,507; Perot, Ind., 138,872; Marrou, Libertarian, 2,719; Phillips, U.S. Taxpayers, 2,680; Fulani, New Alliance, 1,235.
1996, Dole, Rep., 573,458; Clinton, Dem., 506,283; Perot, Ref./Patriot, 64,386; Browne, Libertarian, 4,271; Phillips, Taxpayers, 2,043; Hagelin, Natural Law, 1,248.
2000, Bush, Rep., 786,892; Gore, Dem., 566,039; Nader, United Citizens, 20,279; Browne, Libertarian, 4,898; Buchanan, Reform, 3,309; Phillips, Constitution, 1,682; Hagelin, Natural Law, 943.

South Dakota

County	2000 Gore (D)	2000 Bush (R)	1996 Clinton (D)	1996 Dole (R)	1996 Perot (RF)
Aurora	513	847	664	709	199
Beadle	3,216	4,347	3,984	3,670	842
Bennett	377	712	507	539	93
Bon Homme	1,162	1,901	1,569	1,428	391
Brookings	4,546	6,212	5,105	5,112	979
Brown	7,173	9,060	7,913	6,801	1,622
Brule	818	1,268	1,091	981	281
Buffalo	256	140	465	134	35
Butte	840	2,760	1,132	1,947	541
Campbell	147	739	202	623	140
Charles Mix	1,300	2,205	1,913	1,711	390
Clark	791	1,272	956	998	272
Clay	2,638	2,363	2,980	2,008	505
Codington	4,192	6,718	4,722	4,995	1,239
Corson	549	629	539	533	216
Custer	955	2,495	1,122	1,740	418
Davison	2,936	4,445	3,364	3,371	737
Day	1,492	1,623	1,840	1,282	395
Deuel	926	1,245	1,090	955	275
Dewey	880	761	1,114	657	195
Douglas	363	1,311	524	1,210	161
Edmunds	676	1,257	973	1,055	263
Fall River	1,133	2,185	1,357	1,636	417
Faulk	388	904	493	726	165
Grant	1,475	2,235	1,805	1,782	471
Gregory	718	1,487	923	1,208	286
Haakon	164	938	284	887	110
Hamlin	923	1,731	1,101	1,352	285
Hand	565	1,419	803	1,187	250
Hanson	457	944	541	801	170
Harding	64	650	151	537	90
Hughes	2,212	5,188	2,788	4,469	531
Hutchinson	1,052	2,497	1,285	2,177	409
Hyde	218	592	309	493	95
Jackson/Washabaugh	319	687	423	646	88
Jerauld	468	624	656	530	151
Jones	137	509	184	463	75
Kingsbury	1,049	1,612	1,357	1,297	320
Lake	2,331	2,724	2,526	1,966	593
Lawrence	2,797	6,327	3,568	4,430	1,308
Lincoln	3,844	6,546	3,643	4,201	682
Lyman	482	875	646	726	130
McCook	965	1,610	1,166	1,292	245
McPherson	295	1,073	463	1,080	182
Marshall	939	1,097	1,185	861	189
Meade	2,267	6,870	2,960	4,984	1,133
Mellette	222	495	302	417	67
Miner	523	724	739	571	170
Minnehaha	27,042	33,428	29,790	27,432	4,425
Moody	1,318	1,361	1,443	1,024	284
Pennington	11,123	24,696	12,784	19,293	3,149
Perkins	297	1,237	460	983	225
Potter	356	1,112	534	979	181
Roberts	1,700	2,237	2,186	1,646	474
Sanborn	468	767	647	630	151
Shannon	1,667	252	1,926	253	87
Spink	1,274	1,957	1,636	1,651	360
Stanley	402	955	454	795	121
Sully	209	633	321	592	106
Todd	993	478	1,380	482	108
Tripp	799	1,909	1,088	1,680	337
Turner	1,414	2,514	1,682	1,970	385
Union	2,358	3,265	2,378	2,234	555
Walworth	721	1,758	939	1,461	366
Yankton	3,596	4,904	3,775	3,885	1,073
Ziebach	314	384	483	375	62
Totals	118,804	190,700	139,333	150,543	31,250

South Dakota Vote Since 1952

1952, Eisenhower, Rep., 203,857; Stevenson, Dem., 90,426.
1956, Eisenhower, Rep., 171,569; Stevenson, Dem., 122,288.
1960, Kennedy, Dem., 128,070; Nixon, Rep., 178,417.
1964, Johnson, Dem., 163,010; Goldwater, Rep., 130,108.
1968, Nixon, Rep., 149,841; Humphrey, Dem., 118,023; Wallace, 3d Party, 13,400.
1972, Nixon, Rep., 166,476; McGovern, Dem., 139,945; Jenness, Soc. Workers, 994.
1976, Carter, Dem., 147,068; Ford, Rep., 151,505; MacBride, Libertarian, 1,619; Hall, Com., 318; Camejo, Soc. Workers, 168.
1980, Reagan, Rep., 198,343; Carter, Dem., 103,855; Anderson, Ind., 21,431; Clark, Libertarian, 3,824; Pulley, Soc. Workers, 250.
1984, Reagan, Rep., 200,267; Mondale, Dem., 116,113.
1988, Bush, Rep., 165,415; Dukakis, Dem., 145,560; Paul, Lib., 1,060; Fulani, New Alliance, 730.
1992, Clinton, Dem., 124,888; Bush, Rep., 136,718; Perot, Ind., 73,295.

1996, Dole, Rep., 150,543; Clinton, Dem., 139,333; Perot, Ref., 31,250; Browne, Libertarian, 1,472; Phillips, Taxpayers, 912; Hagelin, Natural Law, 316.
2000, Bush, Rep., 190,700; Gore, Dem., 118,804; Buchanan, Reform, 3,322; Phillips, Ind., 1,781; Browne, Libertarian, 1,662.

Tennessee

County	2000 Gore (D)	2000 Bush (R)	1996 Clinton (D)	1996 Dole (R)	1996 Perot (RF)
Anderson	13,556	14,688	13,457	11,943	1,817
Bedford	6,136	5,911	5,735	4,634	823
Benton	3,700	2,484	4,341	2,395	663
Bledsoe	1,756	2,380	1,621	1,626	251
Blount	14,688	25,273	14,687	19,304	2,556
Bradley	8,768	20,167	9,095	15,478	1,856
Campbell	6,492	5,784	6,122	4,393	785
Cannon	2,697	1,924	2,318	1,468	361
Carroll	5,239	5,465	4,912	4,206	697
Carter	6,724	12,111	6,218	10,540	1,383
Cheatham	6,062	6,356	4,883	4,283	705
Chester	2,192	3,487	1,922	2,746	203
Claiborne	3,841	5,023	3,861	4,023	727
Clay	1,931	1,468	1,559	1,108	316
Cocke	3,872	6,185	3,326	4,481	798
Coffee	8,741	8,788	7,951	7,038	1,205
Crockett	2,705	2,676	2,256	1,872	201
Cumberland	7,644	10,994	6,676	8,096	1,399
Davidson	120,508	84,117	110,805	78,453	9,018
Decatur	2,278	2,046	2,262	1,712	229
De Kalb	3,765	2,411	3,213	1,696	342
Dickson	8,332	7,016	7,458	5,283	996
Dyer	5,425	6,282	5,602	5,059	676
Fayette	5,037	6,402	4,655	4,406	416
Fentress	2,529	3,417	2,332	2,307	386
Franklin	7,828	6,560	6,929	5,296	1,057
Gibson	8,663	8,286	8,851	6,614	891
Giles	5,527	4,377	4,948	3,269	733
Grainger	2,361	3,746	2,162	2,875	382
Greene	7,909	12,540	6,885	9,779	1,604
Grundy	2,970	1,553	2,596	1,094	326
Hamblen	7,564	11,824	7,006	9,797	1,106
Hamilton	51,708	66,605	48,006	55,205	6,699
Hancock	690	1,343	760	1,259	116
Hardeman	4,953	3,729	4,859	2,961	346
Hardin	3,735	4,951	3,508	3,980	594
Hawkins	6,753	10,071	6,367	8,164	1,282
Haywood	3,887	2,554	3,565	2,293	154
Henderson	3,166	5,153	2,841	4,002	408
Henry	6,093	5,944	6,153	4,272	992
Hickman	4,239	2,914	3,917	2,002	460
Houston	2,081	993	1,868	742	182
Humphreys	4,205	2,387	3,675	1,892	423
Jackson	3,304	1,384	2,889	944	289
Jefferson	5,226	8,657	4,688	6,446	882
Johnson	1,813	3,740	1,698	3,137	489
Knox	60,969	86,851	61,158	70,761	6,402
Lake	1,419	781	1,273	589	110
Lauderdale	4,224	3,329	4,349	2,481	308
Lawrence	6,643	7,613	6,188	6,115	973
Lewis	2,281	2,037	1,971	1,298	316
Lincoln	5,060	5,435	4,361	4,551	761
Loudon	5,905	10,266	5,552	7,097	889
McMinn	6,142	10,155	5,987	7,655	1,033
McNairy	4,003	4,897	4,050	3,960	519
Macon	3,059	3,366	2,240	2,481	421
Madison	15,781	17,862	13,577	14,908	968
Marion	5,441	4,651	5,194	3,166	768
Marshall	5,107	4,105	4,447	2,781	603
Maury	11,127	11,930	10,367	8,737	1,366
Meigs	1,555	1,797	1,476	1,228	245
Monroe	5,327	7,514	4,872	5,257	713
Montgomery	18,818	19,644	16,498	15,133	1,781
Moore	1,107	1,145	935	846	177
Morgan	2,921	3,144	2,767	2,070	446
Obion	6,056	6,168	6,226	4,310	932
Overton	4,507	2,875	3,800	1,756	431
Perry	1,650	1,165	1,444	747	178
Pickett	939	1,281	901	1,046	116
Polk	2,574	2,907	2,450	1,910	377
Putnam	10,785	11,248	10,047	9,093	1,487
Rhea	3,722	5,900	3,969	4,476	694
Roane	9,575	11,345	9,744	9,044	1,438
Robertson	10,249	9,675	8,465	6,685	993
Rutherford	27,360	33,445	22,815	24,565	3,787
Scott	2,967	3,579	2,506	2,646	431
Sequatchie	1,648	2,169	1,598	1,391	288
Sevier	8,208	16,734	7,136	11,847	1,650
Shelby	190,404	141,756	179,663	136,315	8,307
Smith	4,884	2,384	3,812	1,857	346
Stewart	2,870	1,826	2,962	1,306	386
Sullivan	21,354	33,482	20,571	29,296	3,555
Sumner	22,118	27,601	19,205	20,863	2,783
Tipton	6,300	10,070	6,596	7,585	799
Trousdale	1,966	950	1,615	683	190

County	2000 Gore (D)	2000 Bush (R)	1996 Clinton (D)	1996 Dole (R)	1996 Perot (RF)
Unicoi	2,566	3,780	2,131	3,122	447
Union	2,564	3,199	2,421	2,253	385
Van Buren	1,255	845	1,010	504	128
Warren	7,378	5,552	6,389	4,226	917
Washington	14,769	22,579	13,259	18,960	2,237
Wayne	1,859	3,370	1,574	2,715	323
Weakley	5,570	6,106	5,657	4,622	873
White	4,135	3,525	3,592	2,498	505
Williamson	18,745	38,901	15,231	27,699	2,071
Wilson	16,561	18,844	13,655	13,817	1,841
Totals	**981,720**	**1,061,949**	**909,146**	**863,530**	**105,918**

Tennessee Vote Since 1952

1952, Eisenhower, Rep., 446,147; Stevenson, Dem., 443,710; Hamblen, Proh., 1,432; Hallinan, Prog., 885; MacArthur, Christian Nationalist, 379.
1956, Eisenhower, Rep., 462,288; Stevenson, Dem., 456,507; Andrews, Ind., 19,820; Holtwick, Proh., 789.
1960, Kennedy, Dem., 481,453; Nixon, Rep., 556,577; Faubus, States' Rights, 11,304; Decker, Proh., 2,458.
1964, Johnson, Dem., 635,047; Goldwater, Rep., 508,965; write-in, 34.
1968, Nixon, Rep. 472,592; Humphrey, Dem., 351,233; Wallace, 3d Party, 424,792.
1972, Nixon, Rep., 813,147; McGovern, Dem., 357,293; Schmitz, Amer., 30,373; write-in, 369.
1976, Carter, Dem., 825,879; Ford, Rep., 633,969; Anderson, Amer., 5,769; McCarthy, Ind., 5,004; Maddox, Amer. Ind., 2,303; MacBride, Libertarian, 1,375; Hall, Com., 547; LaRouche, U.S. Labor, 512; Bubar, Proh., 442; Miller, Ind., 316; write-in, 230.
1980, Reagan, Rep., 787,761; Carter, Dem., 783,051; Anderson, Ind., 35,991; Clark, Libertarian, 7,116; Commoner, Citizens, 1,112; Bubar, Statesman, 521; McReynolds, Soc., 519; Hall, Com., 503; DeBerry, Soc. Workers, 490; Griswold, Workers World, 400; write-ins, 152.
1984, Reagan, Rep., 990,212; Mondale, Dem., 711,714; Bergland, Libertarian, 3,072.
1988, Bush, Rep., 947,233; Dukakis, Dem., 679,794; Paul, Ind., 2,041; Duke, Ind., 1,807.
1992, Clinton, Dem., 933,521; Bush, Rep., 841,300; Perot, Ind., 199,968; Marrou, Libertarian, 1,847.
1996, Clinton, Dem., 909,146; Dole, Rep., 863,530; Perot, Ind. (Ref.), 105,918; Nader, Ind., 6,427; Browne, Ind., 5,020; Phillips, Ind., 1,818; Collins, Ind., 688; Hagelin, Ind., 636; Michael, Ind., 408; Dodge, Ind., 324.
2000, Bush, Rep., 1,061,949; Gore, Dem., 981,720; Nader, Green, 19,781; Browne, Libertarian, 4,284; Buchanan, Reform, 4,250; Brown, Ind., 1,606; Phillips, Ind., 1,015; Hagelin, Reform, 613; Venson, Ind., 535.

Texas

County	2000 Gore (D)	2000 Bush (R)	1996 Clinton (D)	1996 Dole (R)	1996 Perot (RF)
Anderson	5,041	9,835	5,693	6,458	1,170
Andrews	876	3,091	1,181	2,360	431
Angelina	9,957	16,648	11,346	11,789	2,160
Aransas	2,637	5,390	2,964	3,769	655
Archer	993	2,951	1,235	1,974	437
Armstrong	150	772	272	582	75
Atascosa	4,322	6,231	4,259	4,102	813
Austin	2,407	6,661	2,719	4,669	577
Bailey	488	1,589	706	1,246	109
Bandera	1,426	5,613	1,383	3,700	520
Bastrop	6,973	10,310	6,773	6,323	1,342
Baylor	663	1,285	955	860	262
Bee	3,795	4,429	4,561	3,611	539
Bell	21,011	41,208	22,638	30,348	3,666
Bexar	185,158	215,613	180,308	161,619	17,822
Blanco	811	2,777	1,028	1,919	330
Borden	62	283	93	194	45
Bosque	1,930	4,745	2,427	2,840	739
Bowie	11,662	18,325	13,657	12,750	2,760
Brazoria	24,883	53,445	22,959	36,392	5,869
Brazos	12,359	32,864	13,968	22,082	2,215
Brewster	1,349	1,867	1,643	1,438	299
Briscoe	224	544	408	416	65
Brooks	1,854	556	2,945	413	108
Brown	3,138	9,609	4,138	6,524	1,081
Burleson	2,235	3,542	2,419	2,174	347
Burnet	3,557	9,286	4,123	5,744	1,108
Caldwell	3,872	5,216	3,961	3,239	545
Calhoun	2,766	3,724	2,753	2,832	507
Callahan	1,174	3,465	1,666	2,480	534
Cameron	33,214	27,800	34,891	18,434	2,760
Camp	1,625	2,121	1,912	1,488	252
Carson	480	2,216	742	1,742	227
Cass	4,618	6,295	5,691	4,066	1,038
Castro	727	1,607	1,107	1,231	144

County	2000 Gore (D)	2000 Bush (R)	1996 Clinton (D)	1996 Dole (R)	1996 Perot (RF)
Chambers	2,888	6,769	2,876	4,101	818
Cherokee	4,755	9,599	5,185	6,483	971
Childress	602	1,506	719	1,072	165
Clay	1,460	3,112	1,690	1,997	465
Cochran	344	807	541	667	127
Coke	355	1,137	595	790	157
Coleman	853	2,687	1,488	1,793	349
Collin	42,884	128,179	37,854	83,750	10,443
Collingsworth	429	974	581	729	118
Colorado	2,229	4,913	2,795	3,381	574
Comal	7,131	24,599	7,132	16,763	1,903
Comanche	1,636	3,334	2,138	2,123	511
Concho	268	818	434	488	107
Cooke	3,153	10,128	3,782	7,320	1,150
Coryell	4,493	10,321	5,300	7,143	1,443
Cottle	241	502	404	331	77
Crane	387	1,246	616	984	201
Crockett	467	924	684	714	147
Crosby	705	1,270	1,122	968	189
Culberson	577	413	804	329	99
Dallam	341	1,385	483	970	170
Dallas	275,308	322,345	255,766	260,058	36,759
Dawson	1,463	3,337	1,612	2,319	232
Deaf Smith	1,240	3,687	1,655	3,051	310
Delta	726	1,143	849	744	146
Denton	40,144	102,171	36,138	65,313	9,294
DeWitt	1,570	4,541	2,074	3,577	483
Dickens	284	589	509	421	117
Dimmit	2,678	1,032	2,242	604	128
Donley	360	1,333	495	988	97
Duval	3,990	1,010	3,958	543	136
Eastland	1,774	4,531	2,594	3,272	705
Ector	9,425	22,900	12,017	17,746	2,511
Edwards	261	663	437	511	60
Ellis	10,629	26,091	10,832	16,046	2,750
El Paso	83,848	57,574	83,964	43,255	6,300
Erath	2,804	8,126	3,664	4,750	1,134
Falls	2,417	3,239	3,256	2,260	479
Fannin	4,102	6,074	4,276	3,495	980
Fayette	2,542	6,658	3,119	4,195	708
Fisher	884	968	1,142	537	170
Floyd	580	1,830	986	1,530	126
Foard	263	286	355	166	52
Fort Bend	47,569	73,567	38,163	49,945	4,363
Franklin	1,018	2,420	1,484	1,575	386
Freestone	2,316	4,247	2,630	2,888	568
Frio	2,317	1,774	2,593	1,225	253
Gaines	723	2,691	1,012	1,812	353
Galveston	40,020	50,397	38,458	35,251	5,897
Garza	454	1,302	703	946	103
Gillespie	1,511	8,096	1,655	5,867	542
Glasscock	39	528	70	382	30
Goliad	1,233	2,108	1,135	1,335	148
Gonzales	1,877	4,092	2,110	2,687	354
Gray	1,376	6,732	2,114	6,102	548
Grayson	13,647	25,596	14,338	17,169	3,745
Gregg	11,244	26,739	13,659	21,611	2,079
Grimes	2,450	4,197	2,584	2,564	538
Guadalupe	8,311	21,499	8,079	14,254	1,811
Hale	2,158	6,868	3,204	5,905	605
Hall	472	966	750	626	94
Hamilton	878	2,447	1,200	1,493	323
Hansford	198	1,874	343	1,493	105
Hardeman	566	976	750	610	168
Hardin	5,595	11,962	7,179	8,529	2,112
Harris	418,267	529,159	386,726	421,462	42,364
Harrison	8,878	13,834	10,307	9,835	1,427
Hartley	359	1,645	463	1,242	101
Haskell	1,401	1,488	1,374	966	225
Hays	11,387	20,170	11,580	12,865	1,990
Hemphill	251	1,203	344	986	104
Henderson	8,704	16,607	10,085	10,345	2,274
Hidalgo	61,390	38,301	56,335	24,437	3,536
Hill	3,524	7,054	3,988	4,401	1,052
Hockley	1,419	5,250	2,170	4,230	519
Hood	4,704	12,429	5,459	7,575	1,445
Hopkins	3,692	7,076	4,522	4,341	1,034
Houston	2,833	5,308	3,383	3,443	585
Howard	2,744	6,668	3,732	5,007	1,037
Hudspeth	380	514	427	367	92
Hunt	7,857	16,177	8,801	10,746	2,225
Hutchinson	1,796	7,443	2,553	6,350	864
Irion	162	624	213	386	86
Jack	822	2,107	1,019	1,162	301
Jackson	1,446	3,365	1,785	2,533	309
Jasper	4,533	7,071	5,039	4,523	1,041
Jeff Davis	283	708	370	482	99
Jefferson	45,409	40,320	45,854	32,821	5,314
Jim Hogg	1,512	623	1,437	307	64
Jim Wells	7,418	4,498	7,116	2,989	430
Johnson	11,778	26,202	12,817	16,246	3,250
Jones	1,899	4,080	2,422	2,351	614
Karnes	1,617	2,638	2,154	1,869	291
Kaufman	7,455	15,290	7,383	8,697	1,831
Kendall	1,901	8,788	2,092	5,940	620
Kenedy	119	106	133	71	4
Kent	185	346	260	187	67
Kerr	4,002	14,637	4,192	11,173	1,236
Kimble	328	1,313	521	898	131
King	14	120	46	97	29
Kinney	486	932	503	650	97
Kleberg	4,481	4,526	5,136	3,391	431
Knox	617	947	785	599	149
Lamar	5,553	9,775	6,075	6,393	1,198
Lamb	1,114	3,451	1,683	2,593	283
Lampasas	1,569	4,526	1,819	3,008	509
LaSalle	1,266	731	1,522	570	85
Lavaca	2,171	5,288	2,575	3,697	551
Lee	1,733	3,699	2,008	2,354	421
Leon	1,893	4,362	2,217	2,839	499
Liberty	7,311	12,458	6,877	7,784	2,011
Limestone	2,768	4,212	3,236	2,691	693
Lipscomb	206	1,072	357	869	115
Live Oak	1,114	2,828	1,372	1,929	292
Llano	2,143	6,295	2,633	4,290	762
Loving	29	124	14	48	15
Lubbock	18,469	56,054	22,786	47,304	3,996
Lynn	562	1,507	903	1,151	136
McCulloch	794	2,084	1,231	1,465	296
McLennan	23,462	43,955	27,050	30,666	5,131
McMullen	77	358	117	274	35
Madison	1,241	2,333	1,470	1,576	293
Marion	1,852	2,039	2,028	1,260	353
Martin	415	1,520	643	973	140
Mason	417	1,352	618	949	151
Matagorda	4,696	7,584	5,374	5,876	1,190
Maverick	5,995	3,143	5,307	1,050	202
Medina	4,025	8,590	3,880	5,710	715
Menard	334	642	490	443	102
Midland	7,534	31,514	9,513	25,382	2,079
Milam	3,429	4,706	3,869	3,019	657
Mills	548	1,738	748	1,044	230
Mitchell	837	1,708	1,213	949	232
Montague	2,256	4,951	2,718	3,209	842
Montgomery	23,286	80,600	20,722	51,011	6,065
Moore	1,040	4,201	1,358	3,353	359
Morris	2,455	2,381	2,973	1,449	402
Motley	118	514	164	380	56
Nacogdoches	6,204	13,145	7,641	10,361	1,352
Navarro	5,366	8,358	6,078	5,236	1,140
Newton	2,503	2,423	2,554	1,409	474
Nolan	1,874	3,337	2,582	2,166	613
Nueces	45,349	49,906	50,009	37,470	5,103
Ochiltree	251	2,687	467	2,448	167
Oldham	108	659	213	583	77
Orange	11,887	17,325	13,741	12,560	2,836
Palo Pinto	3,263	5,690	3,938	3,666	1,011
Panola	3,011	5,975	4,168	4,008	777
Parker	8,878	23,651	9,447	14,580	2,703
Parmer	447	2,274	676	2,042	160
Pecos	1,539	2,700	1,816	1,730	369
Polk	6,877	11,746	6,360	6,473	1,347
Potter	7,242	17,629	9,273	14,995	1,799
Presidio	1,064	618	1,205	383	111
Rains	1,225	2,049	1,265	1,123	335
Randall	7,209	33,921	9,177	28,266	1,985
Reagan	282	959	407	645	101
Real	316	1,146	414	845	178
Red River	2,219	2,941	2,339	1,783	433
Reeves	1,872	1,273	2,279	1,007	245
Refugio	1,172	1,721	1,635	1,376	222
Roberts	72	472	122	421	40
Robertson	3,283	3,007	2,912	1,944	315
Rockwall	3,642	13,666	3,289	8,319	1,121
Runnels	969	3,020	1,417	1,941	396
Rusk	4,841	11,611	5,988	8,423	1,072
Sabine	1,753	2,764	1,913	1,660	334
San Augustine	1,636	2,116	1,924	1,296	324
San Jacinto	2,946	4,623	2,771	2,878	810
San Patricio	7,840	10,599	8,132	7,678	1,085
San Saba	618	1,691	726	991	194
Schleicher	338	826	505	587	111
Scurry	1,193	4,060	2,099	2,929	813
Shackelford	264	1,066	502	792	169
Shelby	3,227	5,692	3,720	3,482	815
Sherman	144	998	243	809	89
Smith	16,470	43,320	18,265	32,171	2,933
Somervell	752	2,120	993	1,099	273
Starr	6,505	1,911	6,312	756	157
Stephens	811	2,425	1,218	1,714	336
Sterling	132	520	186	394	86
Stonewall	294	496	487	323	105
Sutton	468	1,063	508	688	102

	2000		1996		
	Gore	Bush	Clinton	Dole	Perot
County	(D)	(R)	(D)	(R)	(RF)
Swisher...	856	1,612	1,224	1,159	195
Tarrant....	173,758	286,921	170,431	208,312	28,715
Taylor.....	10,504	31,701	13,213	23,682	2,912
Terrell	219	243	278	185	47
Terry	1,108	2,910	1,272	2,013	269
Throckmorton	228	608	285	360	90
Titus	3,008	4,995	3,725	3,438	744
Tom Green	9,288	24,733	11,782	18,112	2,757
Travis.....	125,526	141,235	128,970	98,454	14,008
Trinity.....	2,142	3,093	2,774	2,058	460
Tyler......	2,775	4,236	3,340	2,804	645
Upshur. ...	4,180	8,448	5,032	5,174	1,086
Upton.....	266	982	424	685	88
Uvalde....	3,436	4,855	3,397	3,494	403
Val Verde..	5,056	6,223	5,623	4,357	548
Van Zandt..	5,245	12,383	5,752	7,453	1,756
Victoria ...	8,176	18,787	8,238	14,457	1,197
Walker	4,943	9,076	6,088	7,177	1,186
Waller	5,046	5,686	4,535	3,559	499
Ward	1,256	2,534	1,644	1,620	446
Washington	2,996	8,645	3,460	6,319	601
Webb......	18,120	13,076	18,997	4,712	936
Wharton ...	4,838	8,455	5,176	6,163	871
Wheeler...	579	1,787	750	1,355	174
Wichita ...	14,108	27,802	15,775	20,495	3,371
Wilbarger..	1,356	3,138	1,730	2,037	465
Willacy....	3,218	1,789	3,789	1,332	241
Williamson..	26,591	65,041	24,175	36,836	4,931
Wilson	3,997	7,509	3,713	4,530	760
Winkler ...	556	1,468	872	1,009	218
Wise	4,830	11,234	5,056	6,330	1,516
Wood.....	3,893	9,810	4,711	6,228	1,184
Yoakum ...	531	1,911	738	1,485	218
Young	1,843	5,022	2,394	3,647	639
Zapata....	1,638	953	1,786	521	131
Zavala	2,616	751	2,629	463	91
Totals	**2,433,746**	**3,799,639**	**2,459,683**	**2,736,167**	**378,537**

Texas Vote Since 1952

1952, Eisenhower, Rep., 1,102,878; Stevenson, Dem., 969,228; Hamblen, Proh., 1,983; MacArthur, Christian Nationalist, 833; MacArthur, Constitution, 730; Hallinan, Prog., 294.

1956, Eisenhower, Rep., 1,080,619; Stevenson, Dem., 859,958; Andrews, Ind., 14,591.

1960, Kennedy, Dem., 1,167,932; Nixon, Rep., 1,121,699; Sullivan, Constitution, 18,169; Decker, Proh., 3,870; write-in, 15.

1964, Johnson, Dem., 1,663,185; Goldwater, Rep., 958,566; Lightburn, Constitution, 5,060.

1968, Nixon, Rep., 1,227,844; Humphrey, Dem., 1,266,804; Wallace, 3d Party, 584,269; write-in, 489.

1972, Nixon, Rep., 2,298,896; McGovern, Dem., 1,154,289; Schmitz, Amer., 6,039; Jenness, Soc. Workers, 8,664; others, 3,393.

1976, Carter, Dem., 2,082,319; Ford, Rep., 1,953,300; McCarthy, Ind., 20,118; Anderson, Amer., 11,442; Camejo, Soc. Workers, 1,723; write-in, 2,982.

1980, Reagan, Rep., 2,510,705; Carter, Dem., 1,881,147; Anderson, Ind., 111,613; Clark, Libertarian, 37,643; write-in, 528.

1984, Reagan, Rep., 3,433,428; Mondale, Dem., 1,949,276.

1988, Bush, Rep., 3,036,829; Dukakis, Dem., 2,352,748; Paul, Lib., 30,355; Fulani, New Alliance, 7,208.

1992, Clinton, Dem., 2,281,815; Bush, Rep., 2,496,071; Perot, Ind., 1,354,781; Marrou, Libertarian, 19,699.

1996, Dole, Rep., 2,736,167; Clinton, Dem., 2,459,683; Perot, Ind. (Ref.), 378,537; Browne, Libertarian, 20,256; Phillips, Taxpayers, 7,472; Hagelin, Natural Law, 4,422.

2000, Bush, Rep., 3,799,639; Gore, Dem., 2,433,746; Nader, Green, 137,994; Browne, Libertarian, 23,160; Buchanan, Ind., 12,394.

Utah

	2000		1996		
	Gore	Bush	Clinton	Dole	Perot
County	(D)	(R)	(D)	(R)	(RF)
Beaver.........	541	1,653	687	1,164	217
Box Elder.......	2,555	12,288	3,170	8,373	1,578
Cache	5,170	25,920	6,595	16,832	2,399
Carbon	3,298	3,758	4,172	2,343	952
Daggett	104	317	131	237	55
Davis	18,845	64,375	19,301	42,768	7,495
Duchesne	779	3,622	892	2,648	566
Emery	958	3,243	1,371	2,033	663
Garfield	178	1,719	283	1,330	222
Grand	1,158	1,822	1,199	1,384	432
Iron	1,789	10,106	1,887	6,550	716
Juab	619	2,023	928	1,290	353
Kane	387	2,254	304	1,682	290
Millard	696	3,850	945	2,681	505
Morgan	553	2,464	859	1,659	337
Piute	133	626	176	475	59
Rich...........	152	736	179	523	88
Salt Lake	107,576	171,585	117,951	127,951	27,620

	2000		1996		
	Gore	Bush	Clinton	Dole	Perot
County	(D)	(R)	(D)	(R)	(RF)
San Juan	1,838	2,721	1,675	2,139	271
Sanpete	1,211	5,781	1,568	3,631	801
Sevier..........	1,046	5,763	1,327	4,031	670
Summit.........	4,601	6,168	4,177	3,867	971
Tooele..........	4,001	7,807	3,992	3,881	1,244
Uintah	1,387	6,733	1,714	4,743	899
Utah	16,445	98,255	18,291	69,653	8,106
Wasatch	1,476	3,819	1,374	2,222	558
Washington	5,465	25,481	4,816	17,637	2,069
Wayne	202	953	265	741	121
Weber..........	19,890	39,254	21,404	27,443	6,204
Totals........	**203,053**	**515,096**	**221,633**	**361,911**	**66,461**

Utah Vote Since 1952

1952, Eisenhower, Rep., 194,190; Stevenson, Dem., 135,364.

1956, Eisenhower, Rep., 215,631; Stevenson, Dem., 118,364.

1960, Kennedy, Dem., 169,248; Nixon, Rep., 205,361; Dobbs, Soc. Workers, 100.

1964, Johnson, Dem., 219,628; Goldwater, Rep., 181,785.

1968, Nixon, Rep., 238,728; Humphrey, Dem., 156,665; Wallace, 3d Party, 26,906; Halstead, Soc. Workers, 89; Peace and Freedom, 180.

1972, Nixon, Rep., 323,643; McGovern, Dem., 126,284; Schmitz, Amer., 28,549.

1976, Carter, Dem., 182,110; Ford, Rep., 337,908; Anderson, Amer., 13,304; McCarthy, Ind., 3,907; MacBride, Libertarian, 2,438; Maddox, Amer. Ind., 1,162; Camejo, Soc. Workers, 268; Hall, Com., 121.

1980, Reagan, Rep., 439,687; Carter, Dem., 124,266; Anderson, Ind., 30,284; Clark, Libertarian, 7,226; Commoner, Citizens, 1,009; Greaves, Amer., 965; Rarick, Amer. Ind., 522; Hall, Com., 139; DeBerry, Soc. Workers, 124.

1984, Reagan, Rep., 469,105; Mondale, Dem., 155,369; Bergland, Libertarian, 2,447.

1988, Bush, Rep., 428,442; Dukakis, Dem., 207,352; Paul, Lib., 7,473; Dennis, Amer., 2,158.

1992, Clinton, Dem., 183,429; Bush, Rep., 322,632; Perot, Ind., 203,400; Gritz, Populist/America First, 28,602; Marrou, Libertarian, 1,900; Hagelin, Natural Law, 1,319; LaRouche, Ind., 1,089.

1996, Dole, Rep., 361,911; Clinton, Dem., 221,633; Perot, Ref., 66,461; Nader, Green, 4,615; Browne, Libertarian, 4,129; Phillips, Taxpayers, 2,601; Templin, Ind. Amer., 1,290; Crane, Ind., 1,101; Hagelin, Natural Law, 1,085; Moorehead, Workers World, 298; Harris, Soc. Workers, 235; Dodge, Proh., 111.

2000, Bush, Rep., 515,096; Gore, Dem., 203,053; Nader, Green, 35,850; Buchanan, Reform, 9,319; Browne, Libertarian, 3,616; Phillips, Ind. Amer., 2,709; Hagelin, Natural Law, 763; Harris, Soc. Workers, 186; Youngkeit, Ind., 161.

Vermont

	2000		1996		
	Gore	Bush	Clinton	Dole	Perot
City	(D)	(R)	(D)	(R)	(RF)
Barre City	1,895	1,676	1,890	1,107	376
Bennington......	3,745	2,384	3,454	1,654	960
Brattleboro......	3,128	1,486	3,016	1,195	395
Burlington.......	10,961	4,273	11,600	3,762	1,309
Colchester......	3,876	2,989	3,314	2,035	769
Essex..........	4,632	4,344	4,063	2,944	796
Hartford........	2,462	1,957	2,106	1,290	400
Montpelier	2,576	1,265	2,458	1,118	269
Rutland City	3,916	3,003	3,817	2,320	741
S. Burlington.....	4,393	2,995	3,929	2,274	548
Springfield	2,386	1,720	2,267	1,189	561
Other	105,052	191,683	95,980	59,464	23,900
Totals..........	**149,022**	**119,775**	**137,894**	**80,352**	**31,024**

Vermont Vote Since 1952

1952, Eisenhower, Rep., 109,717; Stevenson, Dem., 43,355; Hallinan, Prog., 282; Hoopes, Soc., 185.

1956, Eisenhower, Rep., 110,390; Stevenson, Dem., 42,549; scattered, 39.

1960, Kennedy, Dem., 69,186; Nixon, Rep., 98,131.

1964, Johnson, Dem., 107,674; Goldwater, Rep., 54,868.

1968, Nixon, Rep., 85,142; Humphrey, Dem., 70,255; Wallace, 3d Party, 5,104; Halstead, Soc. Workers, 295; Gregory, New Party, 579.

1972, Nixon, Rep., 117,149; McGovern, Dem., 68,174; Spock, Liberty Union, 1,010; Jenness, Soc. Workers, 296; scattered, 318.

1976, Carter, Dem., 77,798; Carter, Ind. Vermonter, 991; Ford, Rep., 100,387; McCarthy, Ind., 4,001; Camejo, Soc. Workers, 430; LaRouche, U.S. Labor, 196; scattered, 99.

1980, Reagan, Rep., 94,598; Carter, Dem., 81,891; Anderson, Ind., 31,760; Commoner, Citizens, 2,316; Clark, Libertarian, 1,900; McReynolds, Liberty Union, 136; Hall, Com., 118; DeBerry, Soc. Workers, 75; scattering, 413.

1984, Reagan, Rep., 135,865; Mondale, Dem., 95,730; Bergland, Libertarian, 1,002.

1988, Bush, Rep., 124,331; Dukakis, Dem., 115,775; Paul, Lib., 1,000; LaRouche, Ind., 275.

1992, Clinton, Dem., 133,590; Bush, Rep., 88,122; Perot, Ind., 65,985.
1996, Clinton, Dem., 137,894; Dole, Rep., 80,352; Perot, Ref., 31,024; Nader, Green, 5,585; Browne, Libertarian, 1,183; Hagelin, Natural Law, 498; Peron, Grass Roots, 480; Phillips, Taxpayers, 382; Hollis, Liberty Union, 292; Harris, Soc. Workers, 199.
2000, Gore, Dem., 149,022; Bush, Rep., 119,775; Nader, Green, 20,374; Buchanan, Reform, 2,192; Lane, Grass Roots, 1,044; Browne, Libertarian, 784; Hagelin, Natural Law, 219; McReynolds, Liberty Union, 161; Phillips, Constitution, 153; Harris, Soc. Workers, 70.

Virginia

| | 2000 | | 1996 | | |
County	Gore (D)	Bush (R)	Clinton (D)	Dole (R)	Perot (RF)
Accomack	5,092	6,352	5,220	5,013	1,218
Albemarle	16,255	18,291	14,089	15,243	1,533
Alleghany	2,214	2,808	2,398	2,015	607
Amelia	1,754	2,947	1,625	2,119	323
Amherst	4,812	6,660	4,864	5,094	835
Appomattox	2,132	3,654	2,239	2,625	510
Arlington	50,260	28,555	45,573	26,106	2,782
Augusta	6,643	17,744	5,965	13,458	1,916
Bath	822	1,311	922	847	247
Bedford	8,160	17,224	7,786	11,955	1,976
Bland	851	1,759	939	1,167	385
Botetourt	4,627	8,867	4,576	6,404	1,138
Brunswick	3,387	2,561	3,442	2,059	340
Buchanan	5,745	3,867	6,551	2,785	858
Buckingham	2,561	2,738	2,374	1,974	392
Campbell	6,659	13,162	6,788	10,273	1,505
Caroline	4,314	3,873	3,897	2,816	521
Carroll	3,638	7,142	3,611	5,088	1,158
Charles City	1,981	1,023	1,842	729	178
Charlotte	2,017	2,855	2,007	2,103	431
Chesterfield	38,638	69,924	30,220	56,650	6,004
Clarke	2,166	2,883	1,906	2,201	379
Craig	851	1,580	895	979	262
Culpeper	4,364	7,440	3,907	5,688	787
Cumberland	1,405	1,974	1,303	1,544	275
Dickenson	3,951	3,122	3,913	2,229	660
Dinwiddie	4,001	4,959	3,871	3,503	666
Essex	1,750	1,995	1,668	1,627	188
Fairfax	196,501	202,181	170,150	176,033	16,134
Fauquier	8,296	14,456	6,759	11,063	1,287
Floyd	1,957	3,423	1,909	2,374	545
Fluvanna	3,431	4,962	2,676	3,442	457
Franklin	7,145	11,225	7,300	7,382	2,015
Frederick	7,158	14,574	5,976	10,608	1,599
Giles	3,004	3,574	3,196	2,566	841
Gloucester	4,553	8,718	4,710	6,447	1,266
Goochland	3,197	5,378	2,784	4,119	424
Grayson	2,467	4,236	2,661	3,004	675
Greene	1,774	3,375	1,440	2,351	346
Greensville	2,314	1,565	2,381	1,176	263
Halifax	5,963	7,732	5,599	6,490	876
Hanover	12,044	28,614	9,880	22,086	2,447
Henrico	48,645	62,887	41,121	54,430	5,920
Henry	8,898	11,870	9,061	9,110	2,370
Highland	453	942	446	631	134
Isle of Wight	5,162	7,587	4,952	5,416	893
James City	9,090	14,628	7,247	10,120	1,116
King and Queen	1,387	1,423	1,393	1,073	213
King George	2,070	3,590	1,875	2,597	341
King William	2,125	3,547	1,765	2,346	339
Lancaster	1,937	3,411	1,844	2,709	324
Lee	4,031	4,551	4,444	3,225	822
Loudoun	30,938	42,453	19,942	25,715	3,082
Louisa	4,309	5,461	3,761	3,768	693
Lunenburg	2,026	2,510	1,995	2,063	299
Madison	1,844	2,940	1,734	2,296	360
Mathews	1,499	2,951	1,602	2,206	403
Mecklenburg	4,797	6,600	4,408	4,933	789
Middlesex	1,671	2,844	1,704	2,141	350
Montgomery	11,720	13,991	10,867	10,517	2,594
Nelson	2,907	2,913	2,782	1,988	411
New Kent	2,055	3,934	1,859	2,852	520
Northampton	2,340	2,299	2,569	1,763	522
Northumberland	2,118	3,362	1,957	2,605	375
Nottoway	2,460	2,870	2,327	2,416	346
Orange	4,126	5,991	3,590	4,435	750
Page	2,726	5,089	2,868	3,876	640
Patrick	2,254	4,901	2,301	3,547	719
Pittsylvania	7,834	15,760	7,681	12,127	1,469
Powhatan	2,708	6,820	2,254	4,679	626
Prince Edward	2,922	3,214	2,678	2,530	403
Prince George	4,182	6,579	3,498	5,216	698
Prince William	44,745	52,788	33,462	39,292	4,881
Pulaski	5,255	7,089	5,333	5,387	1,399
Rappahannock	1,462	1,850	1,405	1,505	213
Richmond	1,076	1,784	1,101	1,424	201
Roanoke	16,141	25,740	15,387	20,700	2,934
Rockbridge	2,953	4,522	3,116	3,274	760
Rockingham	5,834	17,482	5,867	14,035	1,318
Russell	5,442	5,065	5,437	3,706	862
Scott	3,552	5,535	3,449	4,086	798
Shenandoah	4,420	9,636	4,224	7,440	1,353
Smyth	4,836	6,580	4,990	4,966	1,407
Southampton	3,359	3,293	3,454	2,275	564
Spotsylvania	13,545	20,739	10,342	13,786	1,860
Stafford	12,596	20,731	9,902	14,098	1,856
Surry	1,845	1,313	1,753	947	181
Sussex	2,006	1,745	2,089	1,378	256
Tazewell	7,227	8,655	7,500	6,131	1,554
Warren	4,313	6,335	3,814	4,657	904
Washington	7,549	12,064	6,939	9,098	1,654
Wesmoreland	2,922	2,932	2,949	2,333	427
Wise	6,412	6,504	6,712	4,660	1,478
Wythe	3,462	6,539	3,275	4,274	955
York	8,622	15,312	7,731	11,396	1,469
Cities					
Alexandria	33,633	19,043	27,968	15,554	1,472
Bedford	1,078	1,269	1,065	990	212
Bristol	2,646	3,495	2,586	2,983	429
Buena Vista	941	980	1,090	713	216
Charlottesville	7,762	4,034	7,916	4,091	565
Chesapeake	33,578	39,684	28,713	29,251	4,456
Clifton Forge	868	613	974	486	147
Colonial Heights	2,100	5,519	1,782	4,632	518
Covington	1,168	966	1,394	763	255
Danville	8,221	9,427	8,168	9,254	762
Emporia	1,116	938	1,103	835	98
Fairfax	4,361	4,762	3,909	4,319	422
Falls Church	3,109	2,131	2,375	1,644	202
Franklin	1,763	1,393	1,962	1,200	201
Fredericksburg	3,360	2,935	3,215	2,579	300
Galax	996	1,160	1,033	910	221
Hampton	27,490	19,561	24,493	16,596	2,783
Harrisonburg	3,482	5,741	3,346	4,945	434
Hopewell	3,024	3,749	2,868	3,493	550
Lexington	1,048	957	1,059	850	112
Lynchburg	10,374	12,518	10,281	11,441	1,155
Manassas	5,262	6,752	4,378	5,799	670
Manassas Park	1,048	1,460	748	916	151
Martinsville	3,048	2,560	2,941	2,446	387
Newport News	29,779	27,006	27,678	23,072	3,090
Norfolk	38,221	21,920	37,655	18,693	3,435
Norton	867	639	802	416	138
Petersburg	8,751	2,109	8,105	2,261	423
Poquoson	1,448	4,271	1,409	3,422	400
Portsmouth	22,286	12,628	22,150	10,686	2,238
Radford	2,063	2,190	2,113	1,742	381
Richmond	42,717	20,265	42,273	20,993	2,762
Roanoke	17,920	14,630	17,282	12,283	2,169
Salem	4,348	6,188	4,282	4,936	796
Staunton	3,324	4,878	3,162	4,526	605
Suffolk	12,471	11,836	10,827	8,572	1,266
Virginia Beach	62,268	83,674	52,142	63,741	9,328
Waynesboro	2,737	4,084	2,398	3,466	462
Williamsburg	1,724	1,777	1,820	1,560	162
Winchester	3,318	4,314	3,027	3,681	434
Totals	1,217,290	1,437,490	1,091,060	1,138,350	159,861

Virginia Vote Since 1952

1952, Eisenhower, Rep., 349,037; Stevenson, Dem., 268,677; Hass, Soc. Labor, 1,160; Hoopes, Soc. Dem., 504; Hallinan, Prog., 311.
1956, Eisenhower, Rep., 386,459; Stevenson, Dem., 267,760; Andrews, States' Rights, 42,964; Hoopes, Soc. Dem., 444; Hass, Soc. Labor, 351.
1960, Kennedy, Dem., 362,327; Nixon, Rep., 404,521; Coiner, Cons., 4,204; Hass, Soc. Labor, 397.
1964, Johnson, Dem., 558,038; Goldwater, Rep., 481,334; Hass, Soc. Labor, 2,895.
1968, Nixon, Rep., 590,319; Humphrey, Dem., 442,387; Wallace, 3d Party, *320,272; Blomen, Soc. Labor, 4,671; Munn, Proh., 601; Gregory, Peace and Freedom, 1,680.
*10,561 votes for Wallace were omitted in the count.
1972, Nixon, Rep., 988,493; McGovern, Dem., 438,887; Schmitz, Amer., 19,721; Fisher, Soc. Labor, 9,918.
1976, Carter, Dem., 813,896; Ford, Rep., 836,554; Camejo, Soc. Workers, 17,802; Anderson, Amer., 16,686; LaRouche, U.S. Labor, 7,508; MacBride, Libertarian, 4,648.
1980, Reagan, Rep., 989,609; Carter, Dem., 752,174; Anderson, Ind., 95,418; Commoner, Citizens, 14,024; Clark, Libertarian, 12,821; DeBerry, Soc. Workers, 1,986.
1984, Reagan, Rep., 1,337,078; Mondale, Dem., 796,250.
1988, Bush, Rep., 1,309,162; Dukakis, Dem., 859,799; Fulani, Ind., 14,312; Paul, Lib., 8,336.

1992, Clinton, Dem., 1,038,650; Bush, Rep., 1,150,517; Perot, Ind., 348,639; LaRouche, Ind., 11,937; Marrou, Libertarian, 5,730; Fulani, New Alliance, 3,192.

1996, Dole, Rep., 1,138,350; Clinton, Dem., 1,091,060; Perot, Ref., 159,861; Phillips, Taxpayers, 13,687; Browne, Libertarian, 9,174; Hagelin, Natural Law, 4,510.

2000, Bush, Rep., 1,437,490; Gore, Dem., 1,217,290; Nader, Green, 59,398; Browne, Libertarian, 15,198; Buchanan, Reform, 5,455; Phillips, Constitution, 1,809.

Washington

County	2000 Gore (D)	2000 Bush (R)	1996 Clinton (D)	1996 Dole (R)	1996 Perot (RF)
Adams....	1,406	3,440	1,740	2,356	448
Asotin	2,736	4,909	3,349	2,860	936
Benton.....	19,512	38,367	20,783	26,664	5,311
Chelan....	8,412	16,980	8,595	12,363	2,332
Clallam....	13,779	16,251	12,585	12,432	3,187
Clark	61,767	67,219	52,254	46,794	9,663
Columbia...	515	1,523	743	948	228
Cowlitz....	18,233	16,873	18,054	11,221	3,441
Douglas..	3,822	8,512	3,913	5,682	1,132
Ferry	932	1,896	1,197	1,091	408
Franklin ...	4,653	8,594	4,961	5,946	992
Garfield	300	982	497	623	117
Grant.....	7,073	15,830	8,065	10,895	2,496
Grays Harbor	13,304	11,225	14,082	7,635	3,757
Island....	14,778	16,408	12,157	12,387	2,787
Jefferson ...	8,281	6,095	7,145	4,607	1,385
King......	476,700	273,171	417,846	232,811	51,309
Kitsap	50,302	46,427	44,167	35,304	8,769
Kittitas ...	5,516	7,727	5,707	5,224	1,214
Klickitat ...	3,062	4,557	3,214	2,662	875
Lewis.....	9,891	18,565	10,331	13,238	3,373
Lincoln....	1,417	3,546	1,806	2,587	518
Mason	10,876	10,257	10,088	7,149	2,816
Okanogan ..	4,335	9,384	4,810	5,890	1,797
Pacific	4,895	4,042	5,095	2,598	1,131
Pend Oreille.	1,973	3,076	2,126	2,012	709
Pierce.....	138,249	118,431	120,893	89,295	22,051
San Juan...	4,426	3,005	3,663	2,523	508
Skagit	20,432	22,163	18,295	16,397	4,818
Skamania ..	1,753	2,151	1,724	1,387	450
Snohomish .	129,612	109,615	109,624	81,885	22,731
Spokane ...	74,604	89,299	71,727	66,628	16,532
Stevens	5,560	11,299	5,591	7,524	2,158
Thurston ...	50,467	39,924	45,522	29,835	7,622
Wahkiakum..	803	1,033	924	619	215
Walla Walla	7,188	13,304	8,038	9,085	1,894
Whatcom...	34,033	34,287	29,074	27,153	4,854
Whitman ...	6,509	9,003	7,262	6,734	1,315
Yakima....	25,676	39,494	25,676	27,668	4,724
Totals	**1,247,652**	**1,108,864**	**1,123,323**	**840,712**	**201,003**

Washington Vote Since 1952

1952, Eisenhower, Rep., 599,107; Stevenson, Dem., 492,845; MacArthur, Christian Nationalist, 7,290; Hallinan, Prog., 2,460; Hass, Soc. Labor, 633; Hoopes, Soc., 254; Dobbs, Soc. Workers, 119.

1956, Eisenhower, Rep., 620,430; Stevenson, Dem., 523,002; Hass, Soc. Labor, 7,457.

1960, Kennedy, Dem., 599,298; Nixon, Rep., 629,273; Hass, Soc. Labor, 10,895; Curtis, Constitution, 1,401; Dobbs, Soc. Workers, 705.

1964, Johnson, Dem., 779,699; Goldwater, Rep., 470,366; Hass, Soc. Labor, 7,772; DeBerry, Freedom Soc., 537.

1968, Nixon, Rep., 588,510; Humphrey, Dem., 616,037; Wallace, 3d Party, 96,990; Blomen, Soc. Labor, 488; Cleaver, Peace and Freedom, 1,609; Halstead, Soc. Workers, 270; Mitchell, Free Ballot, 377.

1972, Nixon, Rep., 837,135; McGovern, Dem., 568,334; Schmitz, Amer., 58,906; Spock, Ind., 2,644; Fisher, Soc. Labor, 1,102; Jenness, Soc. Workers, 623; Hall, Com., 566; Hospers, Libertarian, 1,537.

1976, Carter, Dem., 717,323; Ford, Rep., 777,732; McCarthy, Ind., 36,986; Maddox, Amer. Ind., 8,585; Anderson, Amer., 5,046; MacBride, Libertarian, 5,042; Wright, People's, 1,124; Camejo, Soc. Workers, 905; LaRouche, U.S. Labor, 903; Hall, Com., 817; Levin, Soc. Labor, 713; Zeidler, Soc., 358.

1980, Reagan, Rep., 865,244; Carter, Dem., 650,193; Anderson, Ind., 185,073; Clark, Libertarian, 29,213; Commoner, Citizens, 9,403; DeBerry, Soc. Workers, 1,137; McReynolds, Soc., 956; Hall, Com., 834; Griswold, Workers World, 341.

1984, Reagan, Rep., 1,051,670; Mondale, Dem., 798,352; Bergland, Libertarian, 8,844.

1988, Bush, Rep., 903,835; Dukakis, Dem., 933,516; Paul, Lib., 17,240; LaRouche, Ind., 4,412.

1992, Clinton, Dem., 993,037; Bush, Rep., 731,234; Perot, Ind., 541,780; Marrou, Libertarian, 7,533; Gritz, Populist/America

First, 4,854; Hagelin, Natural Law, 2,456; Phillips, U.S. Taxpayers, 2,354; Fulani, New Alliance, 1,776; Daniels, Ind., 1,171.

1996, Clinton, Dem., 1,123,323; Dole, Rep., 840,712; Perot, Ref., 201,003; Nader, Ind., 60,322; Browne, Libertarian, 12,522; Hagelin, Natural Law, 6,076; Phillips, Taxpayers, 4,578; Collins, Ind., 2,374; Moorehead, Workers World, 2,189; Harris, Soc. Workers, 738.

2000, Gore, Dem., 1,247,652; Bush, Rep., 1,108,864; Nader, Green, 103,002; Browne, Libertarian, 13,135; Buchanan, Freedom, 7,171; Hagelin, Natural Law, 2,927; ; Phillips, Constitution, 1,989; Moorehead, Workers World, 1,729; McReynolds, Soc., 660; Harris, Soc. Workers, 304.

West Virginia

County	2000 Gore (D)	2000 Bush (R)	1996 Clinton (D)	1996 Dole (R)	1996 Perot (RF)
Barbour	2,503	3,411	3,076	2,155	784
Berkeley	8,797	13,619	8,321	9,859	2,291
Boone	5,656	3,353	6,048	1,917	927
Braxton........	2,719	2,529	3,001	1,441	527
Brooke	4,678	4,195	5,338	2,741	1,375
Cabell........	14,896	16,440	16,277	13,179	2,968
Calhoun	1,112	1,425	1,402	1,000	307
Clay	1,617	1,887	2,074	1,137	355
Doddridge	773	1,955	865	1,335	382
Fayette	8,371	5,897	9,471	3,669	1,552
Gilmer........	1,092	1,560	1,390	933	316
Grant	891	3,571	1,206	2,599	481
Greenbrier	5,627	6,866	6,286	4,434	1,418
Hampshire	2,069	3,879	2,335	2,814	605
Hancock	6,249	6,458	7,521	4,268	2,158
Hardy	1,621	2,816	1,911	1,895	438
Harrison	13,009	12,948	14,746	8,857	3,135
Jackson	4,937	6,341	4,882	4,235	1,295
Jefferson	6,860	7,045	6,361	5,287	1,307
Kanawha	38,524	36,809	40,357	29,311	6,412
Lewis	2,355	3,606	2,868	2,285	974
Lincoln	3,939	3,389	4,994	2,530	696
Logan	8,927	5,334	10,840	2,627	1,532
McDowell	4,845	2,348	5,989	1,550	655
Marion	12,315	9,972	12,994	6,160	2,881
Marshall	6,000	6,859	7,045	4,460	2,202
Mason	4,963	5,972	5,284	3,581	1,533
Mercer	8,347	10,206	8,721	7,768	2,141
Mineral	3,341	6,180	3,487	4,380	1,170
Mingo	6,049	3,866	7,584	2,229	1,020
Monongalia ...	12,603	13,595	13,406	10,189	3,040
Monroe	2,094	2,940	2,382	2,131	559
Morgan........	1,939	3,639	1,929	2,599	513
Nicholas	4,059	4,359	4,769	2,649	1,071
Ohio	7,653	9,607	8,781	7,267	2,065
Pendleton	1,172	1,996	1,591	1,431	276
Pleasants	1,267	1,884	1,478	1,265	416
Pocahontas ...	1,392	1,970	1,796	1,242	426
Preston	3,515	6,607	4,237	4,257	1,760
Putnam	7,891	12,173	8,029	8,803	1,901
Raleigh	11,047	12,587	12,547	8,628	2,355
Randolph	4,028	5,248	5,469	3,348	1,184
Ritchie	1,024	2,717	1,385	1,906	522
Roane	2,332	3,172	2,572	2,069	622
Summers	2,299	2,304	2,397	1,505	438
Taylor	2,473	3,124	2,692	1,977	844
Tucker	1,319	1,935	1,649	1,217	424
Tyler	1,214	2,582	1,459	734	563
Upshur	2,770	5,165	3,052	3,325	1,031
Wayne	7,940	7,993	8,300	5,492	1,633
Webster	1,764	1,484	2,292	654	369
Wetzel	2,849	3,239	3,209	2,037	1,004
Wirt..........	818	1,518	906	928	280
Wood	12,664	20,428	13,261	15,502	3,694
Wyoming	4,289	3,473	5,550	2,155	812
Totals.........	**295,497**	**336,475**	**327,812**	**233,946**	**71,639**

West Virginia Vote Since 1952

1952, Eisenhower, Rep., 419,970; Stevenson, Dem., 453,578.

1956, Eisenhower, Rep., 449,297; Stevenson, Dem., 381,534.

1960, Kennedy, Dem., 441,786; Nixon, Rep., 395,995.

1964, Johnson, Dem., 538,087; Goldwater, Rep., 253,953.

1968, Nixon, Rep., 307,555; Humphrey, Dem., 374,091; Wallace, 3d Party, 72,560.

1972, Nixon, Rep., 484,964; McGovern, Dem., 277,435.

1976, Carter, Dem., 435,864; Ford, Rep., 314,726.

1980, Carter, Dem., 334,206; Carter, Dem., 367,462; Anderson, Ind., 31,691; Clark, Libertarian, 4,356.

1984, Reagan, Rep., 405,483; Mondale, Dem., 328,125.

1988, Bush, Rep., 310,065; Dukakis, Dem., 341,016; Fulani, New Alliance, 2,230.

1992, Clinton, Dem., 331,001; Bush, Rep., 241,974; Perot, Ind., 108,829; Marrou, Libertarian, 1,873.

1996, Clinton, Dem., 327,812; Dole, Rep., 233,946; Perot, Ref., 71,639; Browne, Libertarian, 3,062.
2000, Bush, Rep., 336,475; Gore, Dem., 295,497; Nader, Green, 10,680; Buchanan, Reform, 3,169; Browne, Libertarian, 1,912; Hagelin, Natural Law, 367.

Wisconsin

County	2000 Gore (D)	Bush (R)	1996 Clinton (D)	Dole (R)	Perot (RF)
Adams	4,826	3,920	4,119	2,450	1,122
Ashland	4,356	3,038	3,808	1,863	861
Barron	8,928	9,848	8,025	6,158	2,692
Bayfield	4,427	3,266	3,895	2,250	899
Brown	49,096	54,258	42,823	38,563	8,036
Buffalo	3,237	3,038	2,681	1,800	972
Burnett	3,626	3,967	3,625	2,452	962
Calumet	8,202	10,837	6,940	7,049	2,112
Chippewa	12,102	12,835	9,647	7,520	3,567
Clark	5,931	7,461	5,540	4,622	2,486
Columbia	12,636	11,987	10,336	8,377	2,377
Crawford	4,005	3,024	3,658	2,149	1,060
Dane	142,317	75,790	109,347	59,487	12,436
Dodge	14,580	21,684	12,625	12,890	3,322
Door	6,560	7,810	5,590	4,948	1,475
Douglas	13,593	6,930	10,976	5,167	2,001
Dunn	9,172	8,911	7,536	4,917	2,555
Eau Claire	24,078	20,921	20,298	13,900	5,160
Florence	816	1,528	869	927	316
Fond du Lac	18,181	26,548	15,542	16,488	4,204
Forest	2,158	2,404	2,092	1,166	678
Grant	10,691	10,240	9,203	7,021	2,648
Green	7,863	6,790	6,136	4,697	1,534
Green Lake	3,301	5,451	3,152	3,565	1,025
Iowa	5,842	4,221	4,690	2,866	1,071
Iron	1,620	1,734	1,725	1,260	469
Jackson	3,813	3,670	3,705	2,262	1,163
Jefferson	15,203	19,204	13,188	12,681	3,177
Juneau	4,813	4,910	4,331	3,226	1,393
Kenosha	32,429	28,891	27,964	18,296	6,507
Kewaunee	4,670	4,883	4,311	3,431	1,161
La Crosse	28,455	24,327	23,647	16,482	4,844
La Fayette	3,710	3,336	3,261	2,172	944
Langlade	4,199	5,125	4,074	3,206	1,249
Lincoln	6,664	6,727	6,166	4,076	1,800
Manitowoc	17,667	19,358	16,750	13,239	3,941
Marathon	26,546	28,883	24,012	19,874	6,749
Marinette	8,676	10,535	8,413	7,231	2,367
Marquette	3,437	3,522	2,859	2,208	915
Menominee	949	225	992	230	107
Milwaukee	252,329	163,491	216,620	119,407	26,027
Monroe	7,460	8,217	6,924	5,299	2,081
Oconto	7,260	8,706	6,723	5,389	1,655
Oneida	8,339	9,512	7,619	6,339	2,604
Outagamie	32,735	39,460	28,815	27,758	7,235
Ozaukee	15,030	31,155	13,269	22,078	2,774
Pepin	1,854	1,631	1,585	1,007	456
Pierce	8,559	8,169	7,970	4,599	2,074
Polk	8,961	9,557	8,334	5,387	2,369
Portage	17,942	13,214	15,901	9,631	3,410
Price	3,413	4,136	3,523	2,545	1,218
Racine	41,563	44,014	38,567	30,107	7,611
Richland	3,837	3,994	3,502	2,642	901
Rock	40,472	27,467	32,450	20,096	6,800
Rusk	3,161	3,758	2,941	2,219	1,331
St. Croix	13,077	15,240	11,384	8,253	3,180
Sauk	13,035	11,586	9,889	7,448	2,448
Sawyer	3,333	3,972	2,773	2,603	962
Shawano	7,335	9,548	6,850	6,396	2,071
Sheboygan	23,569	29,648	22,022	20,067	4,157
Taylor	3,254	5,278	3,253	3,108	1,457
Trempealeau	6,678	5,002	5,848	3,035	1,688
Vernon	6,577	5,684	5,572	3,796	1,523
Vilas	4,706	6,958	4,226	4,496	1,548
Walworth	15,492	22,982	13,283	15,099	3,729
Washburn	3,695	3,912	3,231	2,703	920
Washington	18,115	41,162	17,154	25,829	4,786
Waukesha	64,319	133,105	57,354	91,729	13,109
Waupaca	8,787	12,980	7,800	8,679	2,464
Waushara	4,239	5,571	3,824	3,573	1,264
Winnebago	33,983	38,330	29,564	27,880	6,531
Wood	15,936	17,803	14,650	12,666	4,599
Totals	1,242,987	1,237,279	1,071,971	845,029	227,339

Wisconsin Vote Since 1952

1952, Eisenhower, Rep., 979,744; Stevenson, Dem., 622,175; Hallinan, Ind., 2,174; Dobbs, Ind., 1,350; Hoopes, Ind., 1,157; Hass, Ind., 770.
1956, Eisenhower, Rep., 954,844; Stevenson, Dem., 586,768; Andrews, Ind., 6,918; Hoopes, Soc., 754; Hass, Soc. Labor, 710; Dobbs, Soc. Workers, 564.
1960, Kennedy, Dem., 830,805; Nixon, Rep., 895,175; Dobbs, Soc. Workers, 1,792; Hass, Soc. Labor, 1,310.
1964, Johnson, Dem., 1,050,424; Goldwater, Rep., 638,495; DeBerry, Soc. Workers, 1,692; Hass, Soc. Labor, 1,204.

1968, Nixon, Rep., 809,997; Humphrey, Dem., 748,804; Wallace, 3d Party, 127,835; Blomen, Soc. Labor, 1,338; Halstead, Soc. Workers, 1,222; scattered, 2,342.
1972, Nixon, Rep., 989,430; McGovern, Dem., 810,174; Schmitz, Amer., 47,525; Spock, Ind., 2,701; Fisher, Soc. Labor, 998; Hall, Com., 663; Reed, Ind., 506; scattered, 893.
1976, Carter, Dem., 1,040,232; Ford, Rep., 1,004,987; McCarthy, Ind., 34,943; Maddox, Amer. Ind., 8,552; Zeidler, Soc., 4,298; MacBride, Libertarian, 3,814; Camejo, Soc. Workers, 1,691; Wright, People's, 943; Hall, Com., 749; LaRouche, U.S. Lab., 738; Levin, Soc. Labor, 389; scattered, 2,839.
1980, Reagan, Rep., 1,088,845; Carter, Dem., 981,584; Anderson, Ind., 160,657; Clark, Libertarian, 29,135; Commoner, Citizens, 7,767; Rarick, Constitution, 1,519; McReynolds, Soc., 808; Hall, Com., 772; Griswold, Workers World, 414; DeBerry, Soc. Workers, 383; scattering, 1,337.
1984, Reagan, Rep., 1,198,584; Mondale, Dem., 995,740; Bergland, Libertarian, 4,883.
1988, Bush, Rep., 1,047,499; Dukakis, Dem., 1,126,794; Paul, Lib., 5,157; Duke, Pop., 3,056.
1992, Clinton, Dem., 1,041,066; Bush, Rep., 930,855; Perot, Ind., 544,479; Marrou, Libertarian, 2,877; Gritz, Populist/America First, 2,311; Daniels, Ind., 1,883; Phillips, U.S. Taxpayers, 1,772; Hagelin, Natural Law, 1,070.
1996, Clinton, Dem., 1,071,971; Dole, Rep., 845,029; Perot, Ref., 227,339; Nader, Green, 28,723; Phillips, Taxpayers, 8,811; Browne, Libertarian, 7,929; Hagelin, Natural Law, 1,379; Moorehead, Workers World, 1,333; Hollis, Soc., 848; Harris, Soc. Workers, 483.
2000, Gore, Dem., 1,242,987; Bush, Rep., 1,237,279; Nader, Green, 94,070; Buchanan, Reform, 11,446; Browne, Libertarian, 6,640; Phillips, Constitution, 2,042; Moorehead, Workers World, 1,063; Hagelin, Reform, 878; Harris, Soc. Workers, 306.

Wyoming

County	2000 Gore (D)	Bush (R)	1996 Clinton (D)	Dole (R)	Perot (RF)
Albany	5,069	7,814	6,399	5,967	1,333
Big Horn	1,004	3,720	1,438	2,821	545
Campbell	1,967	10,203	3,468	6,382	1,954
Carbon	2,206	4,498	2,690	2,930	855
Converse	1,076	3,919	1,520	2,702	639
Crook	361	2,289	651	1,698	394
Fremont	4,172	10,560	5,445	7,554	1,840
Goshen	1,439	3,922	1,923	2,989	547
Hot Springs	544	1,733	779	1,348	287
Johnson	555	2,886	815	2,071	378
Laramie	12,162	21,797	13,676	16,924	2,958
Lincoln	1,184	5,415	1,803	3,764	906
Natrona	8,646	18,439	11,240	13,182	3,524
Niobrara	190	888	325	757	209
Park	2,424	9,884	3,240	7,430	1,318
Platte	1,249	2,925	1,631	2,155	579
Sheridan	3,330	8,424	4,594	5,892	1,414
Sublette	458	2,624	677	1,829	401
Sweetwater	5,521	9,425	7,088	5,591	2,792
Teton	4,019	5,454	4,042	3,918	839
Uinta	1,650	5,469	2,414	3,471	1,242
Washakie	806	3,138	1,205	2,250	470
Weston	449	2,521	871	1,763	504
Totals	60,481	147,947	77,934	105,388	25,928

Wyoming Vote Since 1952

1952, Eisenhower, Rep., 81,047; Stevenson, Dem., 47,934; Hamblen, Proh., 194; Hoopes, Soc., 40; Haas, Soc. Labor, 36.
1956, Eisenhower, Rep., 74,573; Stevenson, Dem., 49,554.
1960, Kennedy, Dem., 63,331; Nixon, Rep., 77,451.
1964, Johnson, Dem., 80,718; Goldwater, Rep., 61,998.
1968, Nixon, Rep., 70,927; Humphrey, Dem., 45,173; Wallace, 3d Party, 11,105.
1972, Nixon, Rep., 100,464; McGovern, Dem., 44,358; Schmitz, Amer., 748.
1976, Carter, Dem., 62,239; Ford, Rep., 92,717; McCarthy, Ind., 624; Reagan, Ind., 307; Anderson, Amer., 290; MacBride, Libertarian, 89; Brown, Ind., 47; Maddox, Amer. Ind., 30.
1980, Reagan, Rep., 110,700; Carter, Dem., 49,427; Anderson, Ind., 12,072; Clark, Libertarian, 4,514.
1984, Reagan, Rep., 133,241; Mondale, Dem., 53,370; Bergland, Libertarian, 2,357.
1988, Bush, Rep., 106,867; Dukakis, Dem., 67,113; Paul, Lib., 2,026; Fulani, New Alliance, 545.
1992, Clinton, Dem., 68,160; Bush, Rep., 79,347; Perot, Ind., 51,263.
1996, Dole, Rep., 105,388; Clinton, Dem., 77,934; Perot, Ind. (Ref.), 25,928; Browne, Libertarian, 1,739; Hagelin, Natural Law, 582.
2000, Bush, Rep., 147,947; Gore, Dem., 60,481; Buchanan, Reform, 2,724; Browne, Libertarian, 1,443; Phillips, Ind., 720; Hagelin, Natural Law, 411.

Voter Turnout in Presidential Elections, 1932-2000

Source: Federal Election Commission; Commission for Study of American Electorate; *Congressional Quarterly*

Candidates	Voter Participation (% of voting-age population)	Candidates	Voter Participation (% of voting-age population)
1932 Roosevelt-Hoover	52.4	1968 Nixon-Humphrey	60.9
1936 Roosevelt-Landon	56.0	1972 Nixon-McGovern	55.2[1]
1940 Roosevelt-Willkie	58.9	1976 Carter-Ford	53.5
1944 Roosevelt-Dewey	56.0	1980 Reagan-Carter	54.0
1948 Truman-Dewey	51.1	1984 Reagan-Mondale	53.1
1952 Eisenhower-Stevenson	61.6	1988 Bush-Dukakis	50.2
1956 Eisenhower-Stevenson	59.3	1992 Clinton-Bush-Perot	55.9
1960 Kennedy-Nixon	62.8	1996 Clinton-Dole-Perot	49.0
1964 Johnson-Goldwater	61.9	2000 Bush-Gore	51.3

(1) The sharp drop in 1972 followed the expansion of eligibility with the enfranchisement of 18- to 20-year-olds.

Electoral Votes for President

(Figures in **boldface**, based on 1990 census, were in force for 1992, 1996, and 2000 elections; where figures for 2004 election will be different, based on 2000 census, these are given in parentheses.)

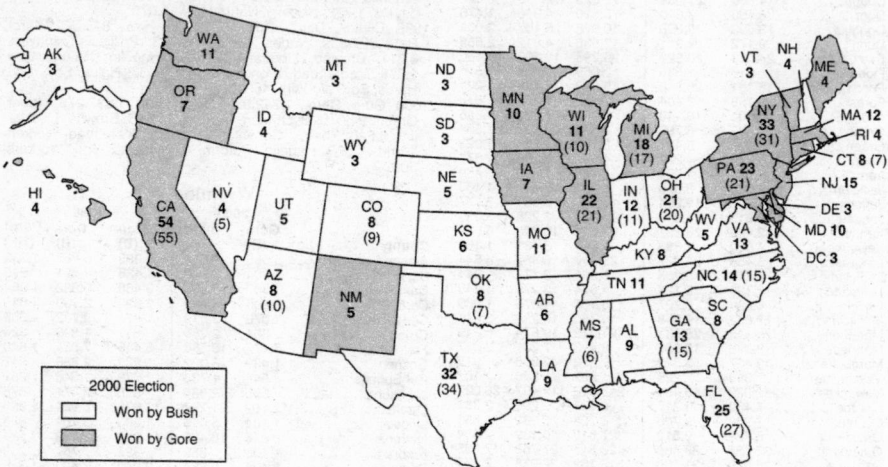

The Electoral College

The president and the vice president are the only elective federal officials not chosen by direct vote of the people. They are elected by the members of the Electoral College, an institution provided for in the U.S. Constitution.

On presidential election day, the first Tuesday after the first Monday in November of every 4th year, each state chooses as many electors as it has senators and representatives in Congress. In 1964, for the first time, as provided by the 23rd Amendment to the Constitution, the District of Columbia voted for 3 electors. Thus, with 100 senators and 435 representatives, there are 538 members of the Electoral College, with a majority of 270 electoral votes needed to elect the president and vice president.

Although political parties were not part of the original plan created by the Founding Fathers, today political parties customarily nominate their lists of electors at their respective state conventions. Some states print names of the candidates for president and vice president at the top of the Nov. ballot; others list only the electors' names. In either case, the electors of the party receiving the highest vote are elected. Two states, Maine and Nebraska, allow for proportional allocation.

The electors meet on the first Monday after the 2nd Wednesday in December in their respective state capitals or in some other place prescribed by state legislatures. By long-established custom, they vote for their party nominees, although this is not required by federal law; some states do require it.

The Constitution requires electors to cast a ballot for at least one person who is not an inhabitant of that elector's home state. This ensures that presidential and vice presidential candidates from the same party will not be from the same state. (In 2000, Republican vice presidential nominee Dick Cheney changed his voter registration to Wyoming from Gov. George W. Bush's home state of Texas.) Also, an elector cannot be a member of Congress or hold federal office.

Certified and sealed lists of the votes of the electors in each state are sent to the president of the U.S. Senate, who then opens them in the presence of the members of the Senate and House of Representatives in a joint session held in early Jan., and the electoral votes of all the states are then officially counted.

If no candidate for president has a majority, the House of Representatives chooses a president from the top 3 candidates, with all representatives from each state combining to cast one vote for that state. The House decided the outcome of the 1800 and 1824 presidential elections. If no candidate for vice president has a majority, the Senate chooses from the top 2, with the senators voting as individuals. The Senate chose the vice president following the 1836 election.

Under the electoral college system, a candidate who fails to be the top vote getter in the popular vote still may win a majority of electoral votes. This happened in the elections of 1876, 1888, and 2000.

Third-Party and Independent Presidential Candidates

Although many "third party" candidates or independents have pursued the presidency, only 10 of these have polled more than a million votes. In most elections since 1860, fewer than one vote in 20 has been cast for a third-party candidate. In only 5 presidential elections since then have all non-major-party candidates combined polled more than 10% of the vote. The major vote getters in those elections were James B. Weaver (People's Party), 1892; former President Theodore Roosevelt (Progressive Party), 1912; Robert M. La Follette (Progressive Party), 1924; George C. Wallace (American Independent Party), 1968; and H. Ross Perot, as an independent in 1992 and with the Reform Party in 1996.

Roosevelt outpolled the Republican candidate, William Howard Taft, in 1912, capturing 28% of the popular vote

and 88 electoral votes. In 1948, Strom Thurmond was able to capture 39 electoral votes (from 5 Southern states); however, all third parties received only 5.75% of the popular vote in the election. Twenty years later, George Wallace's popularity in the same region allowed him to get 46 electoral votes and 13.5% of the popular vote.

In 1992 Perot captured 19% of the popular vote; however, he did not win a single state. In 1996, Perot won 8% of the popular vote; all third-party candidates combined won about 10%. Ralph Nader won about 3% of the vote in 2000.

Despite the difficulty in winning the presidency, independent and third-party candidates sometimes succeed in winning other offices and often bring to the attention of the nation their most prominent issues.

Notable Third Party and Independent Campaigns by Year

Party	Presidential nominee	Year	Issues	Strength in . . .
Anti-Masonic	William Wirt	1832	Against secret societies and oaths	PA, VT
Liberty	James G. Birney	1844	Anti-slavery	North
Free Soil	Martin Van Buren	1848	Anti-slavery	NY, OH
American (Know-Nothing)	Millard Fillmore	1856	Anti-immigrant	Northeast, South
Greenback	Peter Cooper	1876	For "cheap money," labor rights	National
Greenback	James B. Weaver	1880	For "cheap money," labor rights	National
Prohibition	John P. St. John	1884	Anti-liquor	National
People's (Populists)	James B. Weaver	1892	For "cheap money," end of national banks	South, West
Socialist	Eugene V. Debs	1900-12; 1920.	For public ownership	National
Progressive (Bull Moose)	Theodore Roosevelt	1912	Against high tariffs	Midwest, West
Progressive	Robert M. La Follette	1924	Farmer and labor rights	Midwest, West
Socialist	Norman Thomas	1928-48	Liberal reforms	National
Union	William Lemke	1936	Anti-New Deal	National
States' Rights (Dixiecrats)	Strom Thurmond	1948	For states' rights	South
Progressive	Henry A. Wallace	1948	Anti-cold war	NY, CA
American Independent	George C. Wallace	1968	For states' rights	South
American	John G. Schmitz	1972	For "law and order"	Far West, OH, LA
None (Independent)	John B. Anderson	1980	A 3rd choice	National
None (Independent)	H. Ross Perot	1992	Federal budget deficit	National
Reform	H. Ross Perot	1996	Deficit; campaign finance	National
Green	Ralph Nader	2000	Corporate power	National

Major-Party Nominees for President and Vice President

Asterisk (*) denotes winning ticket

	Democratic			Republican	
Year	President	Vice President	Year	President	Vice President
1856	James Buchanan*	John Breckinridge	1856	John Frémont	William Dayton
1860	Stephen A. Douglas (1)	Herschel V. Johnson	1860	Abraham Lincoln*	Hannibal Hamlin
1864	George McClellan	G.H. Pendleton	1864	Abraham Lincoln*	Andrew Johnson
1868	Horatio Seymour	Francis Blair	1868	Ulysses S. Grant*	Schuyler Colfax
1872	Horace Greeley	B. Gratz Brown	1872	Ulysses S. Grant*	Henry Wilson
1876	Samuel J. Tilden	Thomas Hendricks	1876	Rutherford B. Hayes*	William Wheeler
1880	Winfield Hancock	William English	1880	James A. Garfield*	Chester A. Arthur
1884	Grover Cleveland*	Thomas Hendricks	1884	James Blaine	John Logan
1888	Grover Cleveland	A.G. Thurman	1888	Benjamin Harrison*	Levi Morton
1892	Grover Cleveland*	Adlai Stevenson	1892	Benjamin Harrison	Whitelaw Reid
1896	William J. Bryan	Arthur Sewall	1896	William McKinley*	Garret Hobart
1900	William J. Bryan	Adlai Stevenson	1900	William McKinley*	Theodore Roosevelt
1904	Alton Parker	Henry Davis	1904	Theodore Roosevelt*	Charles Fairbanks
1908	William J. Bryan	John Kern	1908	William H. Taft*	James Sherman
1912	Woodrow Wilson*	Thomas Marshall	1912	William H. Taft	James Sherman (2)
1916	Woodrow Wilson*	Thomas Marshall	1916	Charles Hughes	Charles Fairbanks
1920	James M. Cox	Franklin D. Roosevelt	1920	Warren G. Harding*	Calvin Coolidge
1924	John W. Davis	Charles W. Bryan	1924	Calvin Coolidge*	Charles G. Dawes
1928	Alfred E. Smith	Joseph T. Robinson	1928	Herbert Hoover*	Charles Curtis
1932	Franklin D. Roosevelt*	John N. Garner	1932	Herbert Hoover	Charles Curtis
1936	Franklin D. Roosevelt*	John N. Garner	1936	Alfred M. Landon	Frank Knox
1940	Franklin D. Roosevelt*	Henry A. Wallace	1940	Wendell L. Willkie	Charles McNary
1944	Franklin D. Roosevelt*	Harry S. Truman	1944	Thomas E. Dewey	John W. Bricker
1948	Harry S. Truman*	Alben W. Barkley	1948	Thomas E. Dewey	Earl Warren
1952	Adlai E. Stevenson	John J. Sparkman	1952	Dwight D. Eisenhower*	Richard M. Nixon
1956	Adlai E. Stevenson	Estes Kefauver	1956	Dwight D. Eisenhower*	Richard M. Nixon
1960	John F. Kennedy*	Lyndon B. Johnson	1960	Richard M. Nixon	Henry Cabot Lodge
1964	Lyndon B. Johnson*	Hubert H. Humphrey	1964	Barry M. Goldwater	William E. Miller
1968	Hubert H. Humphrey	Edmund S. Muskie	1968	Richard M. Nixon*	Spiro T. Agnew
1972	George S. McGovern	R. Sargent Shriver Jr. (3)	1972	Richard M. Nixon*	Spiro T. Agnew
1976	Jimmy Carter*	Walter F. Mondale	1976	Gerald R. Ford	Bob Dole
1980	Jimmy Carter	Walter F. Mondale	1980	Ronald Reagan*	George H. W. Bush
1984	Walter F. Mondale	Geraldine Ferraro	1984	Ronald Reagan*	George H. W. Bush
1988	Michael S. Dukakis	Lloyd Bentsen	1988	George H.W. Bush*	Dan Quayle
1992	Bill Clinton*	Al Gore	1992	George H.W. Bush	Dan Quayle
1996	Bill Clinton*	Al Gore	1996	Bob Dole	Jack Kemp
2000	Al Gore	Joseph Lieberman	2000	George W. Bush*	Richard Cheney

(1) Douglas and Johnson were nominated at the Baltimore convention. An earlier convention in Charleston, SC, failed to reach a consensus and resulted in a split in the party. The Southern faction of the Democrats nominated John Breckinridge for president and Joseph Lane for vice president. (2) Died Oct. 30; replaced on ballot by Nicholas Butler. (3) Chosen by Democratic National Committee after Thomas Eagleton withdrew because of controversy over past treatments for depression.

Popular and Electoral Vote for President, 1789-2000

(D) Democrat; (DR) Democratic Republican; (F) Federalist; (LR) Liberal Republican; (NR) National Republican; (P) People's; (PR) Progressive; (R) Republican; (RF) Reform; (SR) States' Rights; (W) Whig; Asterisk (*)–See notes at bottom.

Year	President elected	Popular	Elec.	Major losing candidate(s)	Popular	Elec.
1789	George Washington (F)	Unknown	69	No opposition	—	—
1792	George Washington (F)	Unknown	132	No opposition	—	—
1796	John Adams (F)	Unknown	71	Thomas Jefferson (DR)	Unknown	68
1800*	Thomas Jefferson (DR)	Unknown	73	Aaron Burr (DR)	Unknown	73
1804	Thomas Jefferson (DR)	Unknown	162	Charles Pinckney (F)	Unknown	14
1808	James Madison (DR)	Unknown	122	Charles Pinckney (F)	Unknown	47
1812	James Madison (DR)	Unknown	128	DeWitt Clinton (F)	Unknown	89
1816	James Monroe (DR)	Unknown	183	Rufus King (F)	Unknown	34
1820	James Monroe (DR)	Unknown	231	John Quincy Adams (DR)	Unknown	1
1824*	John Quincy Adams (DR)	105,321	84	Andrew Jackson (DR)	155,872	99
				Henry Clay (DR)	46,587	37
				William H. Crawford (DR)	44,282	41
1828	Andrew Jackson (D)	647,231	178	John Quincy Adams (NR)	509,097	83
1832	Andrew Jackson (D)	687,502	219	Henry Clay (NR)	530,189	49
1836	Martin Van Buren (D)	762,678	170	William H. Harrison (W)	548,007	73
1840	William H. Harrison (W)	1,275,017	234	Martin Van Buren (D)	1,128,702	60
1844	James K. Polk (D)	1,337,243	170	Henry Clay (W)	1,299,068	105
1848	Zachary Taylor (W)	1,360,101	163	Lewis Cass (D)	1,220,544	127
				Martin Van Buren (Free Soil)	291,501	—
1852	Franklin Pierce (D)	1,601,474	254	Winfield Scott (W)	1,386,578	42
1856	James Buchanan (D)	1,927,995	174	John C. Fremont (R)	1,391,555	114
				Millard Fillmore (American)	873,053	8
1860	Abraham Lincoln (R)	1,866,352	180	Stephen A. Douglas (D)	1,375,157	12
				John C. Breckinridge (D)	845,763	72
				John Bell (Const. Union)	589,581	39
1864	Abraham Lincoln (R)	2,216,067	212	George McClellan (D)	1,808,725	21
1868	Ulysses S. Grant (R)	3,015,071	214	Horatio Seymour (D)	2,709,615	80
1872*	Ulysses S. Grant (R)	3,597,070	286	Horace Greeley (D-LR)*	2,834,079	—
1876*	Rutherford B. Hayes (R)	4,033,950	185	Samuel J. Tilden (D)	4,284,757	184
1880	James A. Garfield (R)	4,449,053	214	Winfield S. Hancock (D)	4,442,030	155
1884	Grover Cleveland (D)	4,911,017	219	James G. Blaine (R)	4,848,334	182
1888*	Benjamin Harrison (R)	5,444,337	233	Grover Cleveland (D)	5,540,050	168
1892	Grover Cleveland (D)	5,554,414	277	Benjamin Harrison (R)	5,190,802	145
				James Weaver (P)	1,027,329	22
1896	William McKinley (R)	7,035,638	271	William J. Bryan (D-P)	6,467,946	176
1900	William McKinley (R)	7,219,530	292	William J. Bryan (D)	6,358,071	155
1904	Theodore Roosevelt (R)	7,628,834	336	Alton B. Parker (D)	5,084,491	140
1908	William H. Taft (R)	7,679,006	321	William J. Bryan (D)	6,409,106	162
1912	Woodrow Wilson (D)	6,286,214	435	Theodore Roosevelt (PR)	4,216,020	88
				William H. Taft (R)	3,483,922	8
1916	Woodrow Wilson (D)	9,129,606	277	Charles E. Hughes (R)	8,538,221	254
1920	Warren G. Harding (R)	16,152,200	404	James M. Cox (D)	9,147,353	127
1924	Calvin Coolidge (R)	15,725,016	382	John W. Davis (D)	8,385,586	136
				Robert M. La Follette (PR)	4,822,856	13
1928	Herbert Hoover (R)	21,392,190	444	Alfred E. Smith (D)	15,016,443	87
1932	Franklin D. Roosevelt (D)	22,821,857	472	Herbert Hoover (R)	15,761,841	59
1936	Franklin D. Roosevelt (D)	27,751,597	523	Alfred Landon (R)	16,679,583	8
1940	Franklin D. Roosevelt (D)	27,243,466	449	Wendell Willkie (R)	22,304,755	82
1944	Franklin D. Roosevelt (D)	25,602,505	432	Thomas E. Dewey (R)	22,006,278	99
1948	Harry S. Truman (D)	24,105,812	303	Thomas E. Dewey (R)	21,970,065	189
				Strom Thurmond (SR)	1,169,021	39
				Henry A. Wallace (PR)	1,157,172	—
1952	Dwight D. Eisenhower (R)	33,936,252	442	Adlai E. Stevenson (D)	27,314,992	89
1956*	Dwight D. Eisenhower (R)	35,585,316	457	Adlai E. Stevenson (D)	26,031,322	73
1960*	John F. Kennedy (D)	34,227,096	303	Richard M. Nixon (R)	34,108,546	219
1964	Lyndon B. Johnson (D)	43,126,506	486	Barry M. Goldwater (R)	27,176,799	52
1968	Richard M. Nixon (R)	31,785,480	301	Hubert H. Humphrey (D)	31,275,166	191
				George C. Wallace (3rd party)	9,906,473	46
1972*	Richard M. Nixon (R)	47,165,234	520	George S. McGovern (D)	29,170,774	17
1976*	Jimmy Carter (D)	40,828,929	297	Gerald R. Ford (R)	39,148,940	240
1980	Ronald Reagan (R)	43,899,248	489	Jimmy Carter (D)	35,481,435	49
				John B. Anderson (independent)	5,719,437	—
1984	Ronald Reagan (R)	54,281,858	525	Walter F. Mondale (D)	37,457,215	13
1988*	George H. W. Bush (R)	48,881,221	426	Michael S. Dukakis (D)	41,805,422	111
1992	Bill Clinton (D)	44,908,254	370	George H. W. Bush (R)	39,102,343	168
				H. Ross Perot (independent)	19,741,065	—
1996	Bill Clinton (D)	47,401,185	379	Bob Dole (R)	39,197,469	159
				H. Ross Perot (RF)	8,085,294	—
2000*	George W. Bush (R)	50,459,211	271	Al Gore (D)	51,003,894	266
				Ralph Nader (Green)	2,834,410	—

*1800—Elected by House of Representatives because of tied electoral vote. 1824—Elected by House of Representatives because no candidate had polled a majority. By 1824, the Democratic Republicans had become a loose coalition of competing political groups. By 1828, the supporters of Jackson were known as Democrats, and the John Q. Adams and Henry Clay supporters as National Republicans. 1872—Greeley died Nov. 29, 1872. His electoral votes were split among 4 individuals. 1876—FL, LA, OR, and SC election returns were disputed. Congress in joint session (Mar. 2, 1877) declared Hayes and Wheeler elected president and vice president. 1888—Cleveland had more popular votes than Harrison, but since Harrison won 233 electoral votes against 168 for Cleveland, Harrison won the presidency. 1956—Democrats elected 74 electors, but one from Alabama refused to vote for Stevenson. 1960—Sen. Harry F. Byrd (D, VA) received 15 electoral votes. 1972—John Hospers of California received one vote from an elector of Virginia. 1976—Ronald Reagan of CA received one vote from an elector of Washington. 1988—Sen. Lloyd Bentsen (D, TX) received 1 vote from an elector of West Virginia. 2000—One Gore elector from Washington, DC, abstained. Nader was listed as "Independent" on the ballot in some states, and was not on the ballot in all states.

RELIGION

Membership of Religious Groups in the U.S.

Sources: *2003 Yearbook of American & Canadian Churches*, © National Council of the Churches of Christ in the USA; *World Almanac* research

These membership figures are the latest available and generally are based on reports made by officials of each group, and not on any religious census. Figures from other sources may vary. Many groups keep careful records; others only estimate. Not all groups report annually. Church membership figures reported in this table are generally inclusive and do not refer simply to full communicants or confirmed members. Specific definitions of "member" vary from one denomination to another.

The number of houses of worship appears in parentheses. * Indicates that the group declines to make membership figures public. Groups reporting fewer than 5,000 members are not included; where membership numbers are not available, only those groups with 50 or more houses of worship are listed.

Religious Group	Members
Adventist churches:	
Advent Christian Ch. (303)	26,264
Seventh-day Adventist Ch. (4,594)	900,985
American Catholic Church (100)	**25,000**
Apostolic Christian Churches of America (91)	**12,890**
Apostolic Episcopal Church (250)	**18,000**
Bahá'í Faith (1,183 assemblies; 6,994 localities)	**149,222**
Baptist churches:	
American Baptist Assn. (1,760)	275,000
American Baptist Chs. in the U.S.A. (5,786)	1,442,824
Baptist Bible Fellowship Intl. (4,500)	1,200,000
Baptist General Conference (880)	143,200
Baptist Missionary Assn. of America (1,334)	234,732
Conservative Baptist Assn. of America (1,200)	200,000
Free Will Baptists, Natl. Assn. of (2,470)	197,919
General Assn. of General Baptists (715)	66,296
General Assn. of Regular Baptist Chs. (1,417)	132,522
Natl. Baptist Convention, U.S.A., Inc. (9,000)	5,000,000
Natl. Missionary Baptist Convention of America	2,500,000
North American Baptist Conference (276)	49,017
Progressive National Baptist Convention (2,000)	2,500,000
Separate Baptists in Christ (100)	8,000
Southern Baptist Convention (42,334)	16,052,920
Brethren in Christ (232)	**20,739**
Brethren (German Baptists):	
Brethren Ch. (Ashland, OH) (119)	10,381
Church of the Brethren (1,070)	134,828
Grace Brethren Chs., Fellowship of (260)	30,371
Old German Baptist Brethren (55)	6,205
Buddhists	**c. 2,000,000-3,000,000[1]**
Christian Brethren (Plymouth Brethren) (1,125)	**95,000**
Christian Church (Disciples of Christ) (3,717)	**804,842**
Christian Ch. of N. America, Gen. Council (96)	**7,200**
Christian Congregation, Inc. (1,439)	**119,391**
Christian and Missionary Alliance	**381,677**
Christian Union, Churches of Christ in (216)	**10,104**
Church of Christ (Holiness) U.S.A. (163)	**10,475**
Church of Christ, Scientist (2,200)	*
Church of the United Brethren in Christ (228)	**23,585**
Churches of Christ (15,000)	**1,500,000**
Churches of God:	
Chs. of God, General Conference (339)	32,429
Chs. of God, General Conference (Oregon, IL and Morrow, GA) (91)	5,396
Ch. of God (Anderson, IN) (2,353)	234,311
Ch. of God (Seventh Day), Denver, CO (200)	11,000
Ch. of God by Faith, Inc. (148)	30,000
Ch. of God, Mountain Assembly (118)	6,140
Church of the Nazarene (5,070)	**636,564**
Community Churches, Intl. Council of (192)	**115,812**
Congreg. Christian Chs., Nat'l Assoc. of (432)	**65,392**
Conservative Congregational Christian Conference (256)	**40,857**
Eastern Orthodox churches:	
American Carpatho-Russian Orthodox Greek Catholic Ch. (80)	13,210
Antiochian Orthodox Christian Archdiocese of N.A. (225)	360,000
Apostolic Catholic Assyrian Ch. of the East, N.A. Dioceses (22)	120,000
Armenian Apostolic Ch. of America (34)	360,000
Armenian Apostolic Church, Dioceses of America (72)	414,000
Coptic Orthodox Ch. (100)	300,000
Greek Orthodox Archdiocese of America (510)	1,500,000
Mar Thoma Syrian Church of India (68)	32,000
Orthodox Ch. in America (721)	1,000,000
Patriarchal Parishes of the Russian Orthodox Ch. in the USA (31)	7,000
Russian Orthodox Church Outside of Russia (177)	*
Serbian Orthodox Ch. of the U.S. and Can. (68)	67,000
Syrian Orthodox Ch. of Antioch (22)	32,500
Ukrainian Orthodox Ch. of the USA (115)	13,000

Religious Group	Members
Episcopal Church (7,364)	**2,333,327**
Evangelical Church (133)	**12,475**
Evangelical Congregational Church (149)	**21,463**
Evangelical Covenant Church (800)	**101,003**
Evangelical Free Church of America (1,224)	**242,619**
Friends:	
Evangelical Friends Intl.-N.A. Region (278)	27,057
Friends General Conference (650)	34,000
Friends United Meeting (436)	41,297
Religious Society of Friends (Conservative) (1,200)	104,000
Full Gospel Fellowship of Churches and Ministers Intl. (902)	**326,900**
General Church of the New Jerusalem (34)	**6,364**
Grace Gospel Fellowship (128)	**60,000**
Hindus (678)	**c. 1,285,000[1]**
Independent Fundamental Churches of America Int'l., Inc. (IFCA) (659)	**61,655**
Jehovah's Witnesses (11,706)	**989,403**
Jews	**6,150,000[2]**
Jewish organizations:[3]	
Union of American Hebrew Congregations (Reform) (896)	1,500,000
Union of Orthodox Jewish Congregations of America (1,000)	1,075,000
United Synagogue of Conservative Judaism, The (762)	1,500,000
Jewish Reconstructionist Federation (100)	65,000
Latter-day Saints:	
Ch. of Jesus Christ of Latter-day Saints (Mormon) (11,731)	5,310,598
Reorganized Ch. of Jesus Christ of Latter-day Saints (1,236)	137,038
Liberal Catholic Church—Province of the U.S.A. (24)	**6,500**
Lutheran churches:	
Apostolic Lutheran Ch. of America (58)	*
Ch. of the Lutheran Brethren of America (108)	13,702
Ch. of the Lutheran Confession (76)	8,643
Evangelical Lutheran Ch. in America (10,766)	5,099,877
Evangelical Lutheran Synod (141)	21,333
Free Lutheran Congregations, Assn. of (245)	36,400
Latvian Evangelical Lutheran Church in America (68)	13,845
Lutheran Ch.—Missouri Synod (6,187)	2,540,045
Lutheran Chs., American Assn. of (101)	18,252
Wisconsin Evangelical Lutheran Synod (1,228)	401,615
Mennonite churches:	
Beachy Amish Mennonite Ch. (153)	9,205
Church of God in Christ (Mennonite) (111)	12,754
Hutterian Brethren (444)	43,000
Mennonite Brethren Chs., Gen. Conf. (368)	82,130
Mennonite Church (994)	118,070
Old Order Amish Ch. (898)	80,820
Methodist churches:	
African Methodist Episcopal Ch.	2,311,398
African Methodist Episcopal Zion Ch. (3,226)	1,447,934
Evangelical Methodist Ch. (123)	8,615
Free Methodist Ch. of North America (978)	69,342
Southern Methodist Ch. (117)	7,686
United Methodist Ch. (35,275)	8,298,145
The Wesleyan Church (1,614)	123,274
Metropolitan Community Churches, Universal Fellowship of (300)	**44,000**
Missionary Church (375)	**41,328**
Moravian Ch. in America, Northern Province (93)	**25,872**
Muslims	**c. 5,000,000-6,000,000[1]**
Natl. Organization of the New Apostolic Ch. of North America (380)	**36,438**
Pentecostal churches:	
Apostolic Faith Mission Ch. of God (21)	10,350
Assemblies of God (12,082)	2,627,029
Bible Church of Christ, Inc. (6)	6,850
Bible Fellowship Church (55)	7,197

Religious Group	Members
Church of God (Cleveland, TN) (6,605)	932,024
Church of God in Christ (15,300)	5,499,875
Church of God of Prophecy (1,876)	77,609
Elim Fellowship (100)	*
Intl. Ch. of the Foursquare Gospel (1,834)	319,349
Intl. Pentecostal Church of Christ (67)	5,610
Intl. Pentecostal Holiness Church (1,911)	209,922
Open Bible Standard Chs. (317)	37,000
Pentecostal Assemblies of the World Inc. (1,750)	1,500,000
Pentecostal Church of God (1,186)	102,000
Pentecostal Free Will Baptist Ch. (150)	28,000
United Pentecostal Ch. Intl. (3,790)	*
Presbyterian churches:	
Associate Reformed Presbyterian Ch.	
(General Synod) (257)	40,861
Cumberland Presbyterian Ch. (784)	85,427
Cumberland Presbyterian Ch. in America (152). .	15,142
Evangelical Presbyterian Ch. (193)	67,808
Genl. Assembly of the Korean Presbyterian	
Church in America (305)	54,000

Religious Group	Members
Orthodox Presbyterian Ch. (224).	26,090
Presbyterian Ch. in America (1,498)	306,784
Presbyterian Ch. (U.S.A.) (11,142)	3,445,952
Reformed Presbyterian Ch. of N. America (86). .	6,105
Reformed churches:	
Christian Reformed Ch. in N. America (242).	82,453
Hungarian Reformed Ch. in America (27).	6,000
Netherlands Reformed Congregations (26).	9,395
Protestant Reformed Churches in	
America (27)	6,825
Reformed Ch. in America (901).	285,453
United Church of Christ (5,888).	1,359,105
Reformed Episcopal Church (125).	**6,400**
Roman Catholic Church (19,496).	**65,270,444**
Salvation Army (1,369).	**454,982**
Sikhs (216).	**c. 250,000[1]**
Unitarian Universalist Assn. of	
Congregations (1,051).	**220,000**

(1) Estimate; figures from other sources may vary. (2) From
American Jewish Committee. (3) As reported by organizations.

Headquarters of Selected Religious Groups in the U.S.

Sources: *2003 Yearbook of American & Canadian Churches*, © National Council of the Churches of Christ in the USA; *World Almanac* research
(Year organized in parentheses)

African Methodist Episcopal Church (1787), 3801 Market St., Suite 300, Philadelphia, PA 29204; Senior Bishop, Bishop John Hurst Adams

African Methodist Episcopal Zion Church (1796), 3225 West Sugar Creek Rd., Charlotte, NC 28269; Pres. Keith Thompson (Note: Presidency rotates every 6 mos. according to seniority.)

American Baptist Churches in the U.S.A. (1907), PO Box 851, Valley Forge, PA 19482; www.abc-usa.org; Pres., David Hunt

American Hebrew Congregations, Union of, 633 3rd Ave., New York, NY 10017; www.uahc.org; Pres., Rabbi Eric Yoffie

American Rescue Workers (1890), 25 Ross St., Williamsport, PA 17701; www.arwus.com; Commander-in-Chief & Pres., Gen. Claude S. Astin Jr., Rev.

Antiochian Orthodox Christian Archdiocese of North America (1895), 358 Mountain Rd., Englewood, NJ 07631; www.antiochian.org; Primate, Metropolitan Philip Saliba

Armenian Apostolic Church of America (1887), **Eastern Prelacy:** 138 E. 39th St., New York, NY 10016; www.armprelacy.org; Prelate, Archbishop Oshagan Choloyan; **Western Prelacy:** 4401 Russel Ave., Los Angeles, CA 90027; Prelate, Bishop Moushegh Mardirossian

Assemblies of God (1914), 1445 N. Boonville Ave., Springfield, MO 65802; www.ag.org; Gen. Supt., Thomas E. Trask

Bahá'í Faith, National Spiritual Assembly of the Bahá'í's of the U.S., 1233 Central St., Evanston, IL 60201; www.bahai.org; Secy. Gen., Dr. Robert C. Henderson

Baptist Bible Fellowship Intl. (1950), Baptist Bible Fellowship Missions Bldg., 720 E. Kearney St., Springfield, MO 65803; www.bbfi.org; Pres., Rev. Bill Monroe

Baptist Convention, Southern (1845), 901 Commerce St., Ste. 750, Nashville, TN 37203; www.sbc.net; Pres., Morris H. Chapman

Baptist Convention, U.S.A., Inc., National 1700 Baptist World Center Dr., Nashville, TN 37207; www.nationalbaptist.com; Pres., Dr. William J. Shaw

Baptist Convention of America, National (1880), 777 S. R.L. Thornton Freeway, Ste. 205, Dallas, TX 75203; members.aol.com/nbyc1/nbca.html; Pres., Dr. E. Edward Jones

Baptist Convention of America, Natl. Missionary (1988), 1404 E. Firestone, Los Angeles, CA 90001; www.natlmissionarybaptist.com; Pres., Dr. W. T. Snead Sr.

Baptist General Conference (1852), 2002 S. Arlington Heights Rd., Arlington Heights, IL 60005; www.bgcworld.org; Pres., Dr. Robert S. Ricker

Brethren in Christ Church (1778), PO Box A, Grantham, PA 17027; www.bic-church.org/index.htm; Moderator, Dr. Warren L. Hoffman

Buddhist Churches of America (1899), 1710 Octavia St., San Francisco, CA 94109; Presiding Bishop, Hakubun Watanabe

Christian and Missionary Alliance (1897), PO Box 35000, Colorado Springs, CO 80935; www.cmalliance.org; Pres., Rev. Peter N. Nanfelt, D.D.

Christian Church (Disciples of Christ) (1832), 130 E. Washington St., PO Box 1986, Indianapolis, IN 46206; www.disciples.org; Gen. Minister and Pres., Richard L. Hamm

Christian Churches and Churches of Christ, 4210 Bridgetown Rd., Box 11326, Cincinnati, OH 45211

Christian Congregation, Inc., The (1887), 812 W. Hemlock St., LaFollette, TN 37766; www.netministries.org/see/churches.exe/ch10619; Gen. Supt., Rev. Ora W. Eads, D.D.

Christian Methodist Episcopal Church (1870), 4466 Elvis Presley Blvd., Memphis, TN 38116; Executive Secretary, Attorney Juanita Bryant

Christian Reformed Church in North America (1857), 2850 Kalamazoo Ave. SE, Grand Rapids, MI 49560; www.crcna.org; Gen. Secy., Dr. David H. Engelhard

Church of the Brethren (1708), 1451 Dundee Ave., Elgin, IL 60120; www.brethren.org; Moderator, Harriet W. Finney

Church of Christ (1830), PO Box 472, Independence, MO 64051; www.church-of-christ.com; Council of Apostles, Secy., Apostle Smith N. Brickhouse

Church of God (Anderson, IN) (1881), Box 2420, Anderson, IN 46018; www.chog.org; Comm. Coord., Don Taylor

Church of God (Cleveland, TN) (1886), 2490 Keith St. NW, Cleveland, TN 37320; www.churchofgod.cc/default_nav40.asp; Gen. Overseer, R. Lamar Vest

Church of God in Christ (1907), Mason Temple, 938 Mason St., Memphis, TN 38126; www.netministries.org/see/churches/ch00833; Presiding Bishop, Bishop Chandler D. Owens

Church of Jesus Christ (Bickertonites) (1862), 6th & Lincoln Sts., Monongahela, PA 15063; Pres., Dominic Thomas

Church of Jesus Christ of Latter-day Saints (Mormon), The (1830), 47 E. South Temple St., Salt Lake City, UT 84150; www.lds.org; Pres., Gordon B. Hinckley

Church of the Nazarene (1907), 6401 The Paseo, Kansas City, MO 64131; www.nazarene.org; Gen. Secy., Jack Stone

Community Churches, International Council of (1950), 21116 Washington Pkwy., Frankfort, IL 60423; Pres., Rev. Abraham Wright

Conservative Judaism, United Synagogue of, 155 5th Ave., New York, NY 10010; www.uscj.org; Exec. Vice Pres., Rabbi Jerome M. Epstein

Coptic Orthodox Church, 5 Woodstone Dr., Cedar Grove, NJ 07009; www.coptic.org; Fr. Abraam D. Sleman

Cumberland Presbyterian Church (1810), 1978 Union Ave., Memphis, TN 38104; www.cumberland.org; Moderator, Rev. Bert Owen

Episcopal Church (1789), 815 Second Ave., New York, NY 10017; www.ecusa.anglican.org; Presiding Bishop and Primate, Most Rev. Frank Tracy Griswold III

Evangelical Free Church of America (1884), 901 E. 78th St., Minneapolis, MN 55420; www.efca.org; Acting Pres., Rev. William Hamel

Evangelical Lutheran Church in America (1987), 8765 W. Higgins Rd., Chicago, IL 60631; www.elca.org; Presiding Bishop, Rev. Mark Hanson

Fellowship of Grace Brethren Churches (1882), PO Box 386, Winona Lake, IN 46590; www.fgbc.org; Moderator, Dr. Galen Wiley

First Church of Christ, Scientist, The (1879), 175 Huntington Ave., Boston, MA 02115; www.tfccs.com; Pres., Christiane West Little

Free Methodist Church of North America (1860), World Ministries Center, 770 N. High School Rd., Indianapolis, IN 46214; www.freemethodistchurch.org

Friends General Conference (1900), 1216 Arch St. 2B, Philadelphia, PA 19107; www.fgcquaker.org; Gen. Secy., Bruce Birchard

Greek Orthodox Archdiocese of America (1922), 8-10 E. 79th St., New York, NY 10021; www.goarch.org; Primate, Archbishop Demetrios

International Church of the Foursquare Gospel (1927), 1910 W. Sunset Blvd., Ste. 200, PO Box 26902, Los Angeles, CA 90026; www.foursquare.org; Pres., Dr. Paul C. Risser

Islamic Society of North America, P.O. Box 38, Plainfield, IN 46168; www.isna.net; Genl. Secy., Dr. Sayyid M. Syeed

Jehovah's Witnesses, 25 Columbia Heights, Brooklyn, NY 11201; www.watchtower.org; Pres., Don Adams

Jewish Reconstructionist Federation (1922), Beit Devora, 7804 Montgomery Ave., Suite 9, Elkins Park, PA 19027; www.jrf.org; Dir., Lani Moss

Lutheran Church—Missouri Synod (1847), 1333 S. Kirkwood Rd., St. Louis, MO 63122; www.lcms.org; Pres., Dr. Gerald B. Kieschnick

Mennonite Brethren Churches, General Conference of (1860), 4812 E. Butler Ave., Fresno CA 93727; Moderator, Ed Boschman

Mennonite Church USA (2001), 722 Main St., PO Box 347, Newton, KS 67114. ; www.MennoniteChurchUSA.org; Moderator, Ervin Stutzman

Mennonite Church, The General Conference (1860), 722 Main, P.O. Box 347, Newton, KS 67114; http://www2.southwind.net/~gcmc; Moderator, Lee Snyder

Moravian Church in America (1735), **Northern Prov.:** 1021 Center St., PO Box 1245, Bethlehem, PA 18016; www.moravian.org; Pres., David L. Wickmann; **Southern Prov.:** 459 S. Church St., Winston-Salem, NC 27101; Pres., Rev. Dr. Robert E. Sawyer; **Alaska Prov.:** PO Box 545, 361 3rd Ave., Bethel, AK 99559; Pres., Rev. Isaac Amik

Orthodox Church in America (1794), PO Box 675, Syosset, NY 11791; www.oca.org; Primate, Most Blessed Herman

Orthodox Jewish Congregations in America, Union of, 11 Broadway, New York, NY 10004; www.ou.org; Exec. Vice Pres., Rabbi Dr. Tzvi Hersh Weinreb

Pentecostal Assemblies of the World, Inc., 3939 Meadows Dr., Indianapolis, IN 46205; Presiding Bishop, Norman L. Wagner

Presbyterian Church (U.S.A.), (1983), 100 Witherspoon St., Louisville, KY 40202; www.pcusa.org; Moderator, Fahed Abu-Akei

Presbyterian Church in America (1973), 1700 N. Brown Rd., Lawrenceville, GA 30043 www.pcanet.org; Moderator, Mr. Skip Ryan

Salvation Army (1865), 615 Slaters Lane, Alexandria, VA 22313; www.salvationarmy.org; National Comdr., Commissioner W. Todd Bassett

Progressive National Baptist Convention, Inc. (1961), 601 50th St., NE, Washington, DC 20019; www.pribc.org; Pres., Dr. Bennett W. Smith Sr.

Reformed Church in America (1628), 475 Riverside Dr., New York, NY 10115; www.rca.org; Pres., Rev. John Chang

Roman Catholic Church (1634), National Conference of Catholic Bishops, 3211 Fourth St., Washington, DC 20017; www.nccbuscc.org; Pres., Bishop Joseph A. Fiorenza

Romanian Orthodox Episcopate of America (1929), PO Box 309, Grass Lake, MI 49240; www.roea.org; Ruling Bishop, His Eminence Archbishop Nathaniel Popp

Seventh-day Adventist Church (1863), 12501 Old Columbia Pike, Silver Spring, MD 20904; Pres., Jan Paulsen

Swedenborgian Church (1792), 11 Highland Ave., Newtonville, MA 02460; www.swedenborg.org; Pres., Rev. Ronald P. Brugler

Unitarian Universalist Association of Congregations (1961), 25 Beacon St., Boston, MA 02108; www.uua.org; Pres., The Rev. William Sinkford

United Church of Christ (1957), 700 Prospect Ave., Cleveland, OH 44115; www.ucc.org; Pres., Rev. John H. Thomas

United Methodist Church (1968), 1204 Freedom Rd., Cranberry Twp., PA 16066; www.umc.org; Pres. Council of Bishops, Bishop Sharon Brown Christopher

United Pentecostal Church Intl. (1925), 8855 Dunn Rd., Hazelwood, MO 63042; www.upci.org; Gen. Superintendent, Rev. Kenneth F. Haney

Volunteers of America (1896), 1660 Duke St., Alexandria, VA 22314; www.voa.org; Chairperson, Frances Hesselbein

Wesleyan Church (1968), PO Box 50434, Indianapolis, IN 46250; www.wesleyan.org; Gen. Supts., Dr. Earle L. Wilson, Dr. David H. Holdren, Dr. Thomas E. Armiger

Membership of Religious Groups in Canada

Sources: *2003 Yearbook of American & Canadian Churches,* © National Council of the Churches of Christ in the USA; Statistics Canada

Figures are generally based on reports by officials of each group. The numbers are generally inclusive and not restricted to full communicants or the like. Specific definitions of "member" may vary, however. Some groups keep careful records; others only estimate. Not all groups report annually. The number of houses of worship appears in parentheses. *Indicates membership figures were not reported. Groups reporting fewer than 5,000 members are not included. Where membership numbers are not available, only groups with 50 or more houses of worship are listed.

Religious Group	Members
Anglican Church of Canada (2,836)	686,362
Antiochian Orthodox Christian Archdiocese of North America (15)	70,000
Apostolic Church of Pentecost of Canada, Inc. (152)	24,000
Armenian Holy Apostolic Church (Canadian Diocese) (15)	85,000
Associated Gospel Churches (135)	10,439
Bahá'í Faith (1,480)	18,020
Baptist Conference, North American (124)	17,486
Baptist Convention of Ontario and Quebec (372)	55,585
Baptist General Conf. of Canada (92)	7,045
Baptist Ministries, Canadian (1,133)	129,055
Baptist Union of Western Canada (155)	20,427
Buddhists	300,345[1]
Canadian Yearly Meeting of the Religious Society of Friends (24)	17,333
Christian Brethren (also known as Plymouth Brethren) (600)	50,000
Christian and Missionary Alliance in Canada (413)	116,960
Christian Reformed Church in North America (242)	82,572
Church of God (Cleveland, TN) (128)	11,360
Church of Jesus Christ of Latter-day Saints in Canada	157,000
Church of the Nazarene Canada (165)	12,199
Churches of Christ in Canada (140)	8,000
Community of Christ (94)	11,264
Congreg. Christian Chs. in Canada (95)	7,500
The Coptic Orthodox Ch. in Canada (24)	45,000
Estonian Evangelical Lutheran Church (31)	6,959
Evangelical Baptist Churches in Canada, Fellowship of (493)	71,073
Evangelical Free Church of Canada (143)	7,800
Evangelical Lutheran Church in Canada (623)	199,236
Evangelical Mennonite Conference of Canada (50)	7,000

Religious Group	Members
Evangelical Missionary Church of Canada (145)	12,217
Free Methodist Church in Canada (136)	6,930
Greek Orthodox Metropolis of Toronto (Canada) (76)	350,000
Hindus	297,200[1]
Independent Assemblies of God Intl. (Canada) (310)	
Jehovah's Witnesses (1,383)	184,787
Jews (270+)	329,995
Lutheran Church–Canada (328)	79,178
Mennonite Brethren Churches, Canadian Conference of (232)	34,864
Mennonite Church (Canada) (223)	35,995
Muslims	579,640[1]
North American Baptist Conference (124)	17,486
Open Bible Faith Fellowship of Canada (90)	10,000
Orthodox Church in America (Canada Section) (606)	1,000,000
Pentecostal Assemblies of Canada (1,108)	232,000
Pentecostal Assemblies of Newfoundland (126)	25,431
Presbyterian Church in Canada (968)	198,693
Reformed Church in Canada (41)	5,845
Reformed Churches, Canadian and American (55)	15,736
Reorganized Church of Jesus Christ of Latter Day Saints (75)	11,264
Roman Catholic Church in Canada (5,496)	12,793,125[1]
Salvation Army in Canada (356)	75,732
Serbian Orthodox Church in the U.S.A. and Canada, Diocese of Canada (23)	230,000
Seventh-Day Adventist Church in Canada (330)	50,620
Sikhs	278,410[1]
Southern Baptists, Canadian Convention of (152)	9,626
United Baptist Convention of the Atlantic Provinces (555)	62,276
United Church of Canada (3,677)	1,537,479
United Pentecostal Church in Canada (199)	
The Wesleyan Church of Canada (89)	6,173

(1) According to 2001 Canadian census

Headquarters of Selected Religious Groups in Canada

Sources: *2003 Yearbook of American & Canadian Churches*, © National Council of the Churches of Christ in the USA; *World Almanac* research

(Year organized in parentheses)

Anglican Church of Canada (1700), Church House, 600 Jarvis St., Toronto, ON M4Y 2J6; www.anglican.ca; Primate, Most Rev. Michael G. Peers

Bahá'í National Centre of Canada, 7200 Leslie St., Thornhill, ON L3T 6L8; Gen'l.-Secy., Judy Filson

Baptist Ministries, Canadian, 7185 Millcreek Dr., Mississauga, ON L5N 5R4; www.cbmin.org; Pres., Doug Coomas

Christian and Missionary Alliance in Canada (1887), 30 Carrier Dr, Suite 100, Toronto, ON M9W 5T7; www.cmacan.org; Pres., Dr. Franklin Pyles

Church of Jesus Christ of Latter-day Saints (Mormon), The (1830), 50 E. North Temple St., Salt Lake City, UT 84150

Church of the Nazarene in Canada (1902), 20 Regan Rd. Unit 9, Brampton, ON L7A 1C3; web.1-888.com.nazarene/national/; Natl. Dir., Dr. William E. Stewart

Evangelical Baptist Churches in Canada, Fellowship of (1953), 679 Southgate Dr., Guelph, ON N1G 4S2; Pres., Rev. Terry D. Cuthbert

Evangelical Lutheran Church in Canada (1985), 302-393 Portage Ave., Winnipeg, MB R3B 3H6; www.elcic.ca; Bishop, Rev. Raymond L. Schultz

Evangelical Missionary Church in Canada (1993), 4031 Brentwood Rd., NW, Calgary, AB T2L 1L1; Pres., Rev. Mark Bolender

Greek Orthodox Metropolis of Toronto, 86 Overlea Blvd., Toronto, ON M4H 1C6; www.gocanada.org; His Eminence Metropolitan Archbishop Sotirios

Jehovah's Witnesses (1879), Canadian office: Box 4100, Halton Hills, ON L7G 4Y4; Pres., Don Adams

Jewish Congress, Canadian (1919), 100 Sparks St., Ste. 650, Ottawa, Ont. K1P 5B7; www.cjc.ca; Pres., Keith M. Landy (Nonreligious umbrella organization of Jewish groups)

Lutheran Church—Canada (1959), 3074 Portage Ave., Winnipeg, MB R3K OY2; www.lutheranchurch-canada.ca; Pres., Rev. Ralph Mayan

Mennonite Church in Canada (1902), 600 Shaftesbury Blvd., Winnipeg, MB R3P 0M4; www.mennonitechurch.ca; Chairperson, Ron Sawatsky

Muslim Communities in Canada, Council of, 1250 Ramsey View Court, Suite. 504, Sudbury, ON P3E 2E7; Director, Mir Iqbal Ali

North American Shi'a Muslim Communities Organization (NASIMCO), 300 John St., PO Box 87629, Dawnhill, ON L3T 7R3; www.nasimco.org; Pres. Ghulamabbas Sajan

Pentecostal Assemblies of Canada (1919), 2450 Milltower Ct., Mississauga, ON L5N 5Z6; www.paoc.org; Gen. Supt., Rev. William D. Morrow

Presbyterian Church in Canada (1925), 50 Wynford Dr., Toronto, ON M3C 1J7; www.presbyterian.ca; Principal Clerk: Rev. Stephen Kendall

Roman Catholic Church (1618), Canadian Conference of Catholic Bishops, 90 Parent Ave., Ottawa, ON K1N 7B1; www.cccb.ca; Pres., Most Rev. Jacques Barthelet, CSV

Salvation Army (1909), 2 Overlea Blvd., Toronto, ON M4H 1P4; www.salvationarmy.ca; Territorial Cmdr., Commissioner Bill Lutrell

Seventh-Day Adventist Church (1901), 1148 King St. E., Oshawa, ON L1H 1H8; Pres., Orville Parchment

Ukrainian Orthodox Church (1918), Office of the Consistory, 9 St. John's Ave., Winnipeg, MB R2W 1G8; www.uocc.ca; Primate, Most Rev. Metropolitan Wasyly Fedak

United Brethren Church (1767) 302 Lake St., Huntington, IN 46750; Pres., Rev. Brian Magnus

United Church of Canada (1925), The United Church House, 3250 Bloor St. W., Ste. 300, Etobicoke, ON M8X 2Y4; www.ucan.org; Mod., Marion Pardy

Wesleyan Church (1968), The Wesleyan Church Intl. Center, PO Box 50434, Indianapolis, IN 46250; Dist. Supt., Rev. Donald E. Hodgins

Adherents of All Religions by Six Continental Areas[1], Mid-2002

Source: *2003 Encyclopædia Britannica Book of the Year*

	Africa	Asia	Europe	Latin America	Northern America	Oceania	World
Baha'is	1,826,000	3,603,000	134,000	914,000	813,000	116,000	7,406,000
Buddhists	143,000	358,437,000	1,593,000	674,000	2,855,000	312,000	364,014,000
Chinese folk religionists	33,800	388,123,000	262,000	199,000	861,000	65,000	389,543,000
Christians	376,453,000	322,753,000	559,083,000	492,148,000	262,884,000	25,580,000	2,038,905,000
Roman Catholics	126,631,000	113,718,000	285,133,000	471,291,000	71,749,000	8,427,000	1,076,951,000
Protestants	93,028,000	51,480,000	77,466,000	49,901,000	70,350,000	7,566,000	349,792,000
Orthodox	36,790,000	14,326,000	158,648,000	571,000	6,458,000	730,000	217,522,000
Anglicans	44,531,000	742,000	26,619,000	1,106,000	3,217,000	5,447,000	81,663,000
Independents	87,150,000	160,535,000	25,978,000	41,020,000	81,834,000	1,567,000	398,085,000
Confucianists	260	6,291,000	10,900	450	0	24,200	6,327,000
Ethnic religionists	98,734,000	129,718,000	1,253,000	1,287,000	448,000	267,000	231,708,000
Hindus	2,417,000	821,759,000	1,435,000	782,000	1,373,000	364,000	828,130,000
Jains	67,800	4,270,000	0	0	7,000	0	4,345,000
Jews	215,000	4,523,000	2,485,000	1,148,000	6,065,000	98,200	14,535,000
Muslims	329,869,000	858,018,000	31,883,000	1,732,000	4,587,000	313,000	1,226,403,000
New-Religionists	29,300	101,494,000	162,00	645,000	851,000	67,300	103,249,000
Shintoists	0	2,639,000	0	7,000	57,200	0	2,703,000
Sikhs	55,800	22,961,000	242,000	0	543,000	18,900	23,821,000
Spiritists	2,600	2,000	135,000	12,300,000	154,000	7,100	12,601,000
Taoists	0	2,673,000	0	0	11,300	0	2,685,000
Zoroastrians	930	2,575,000	680	0	80,600	1,400	2,659,000
Other religionists	69,000	64,100	240,000	101,000	613,000	9,500	1,096,000
Nonreligious	5,320,000	615,192,000	104,669,000	16,507,000	29,526,000	3,401,000	774,615,000
Atheists	445,000	122,877,000	22,201,000	2,817,000	1,720,000	374,000	150,434,000

(1) **Continental Areas.** Following current UN demographic terminology, which divides the world into the six major areas shown above. Note that "Asia" includes the former Soviet Central Asian states and "Europe" includes all of Russia extending eastward to Vladivostok, the Sea of Japan, and the Bering Strait.

Adherents. As defined in the 1948 Universal Declaration of Human Rights, a person's religion is what he or she says it is. Totals are enumerated following the methodology of the *World Christian Encyclopedia*, 2nd ed. (2001), and *World Christian Trends* (2001), using recent censuses, polls, literature, and other data. As a result of the varieties of sources used, totals may differ from standard estimates for total populations.

Buddhists. 56% Mahayana, 38% Theravada (Hinayana), 6% Tantrayana (Lamaism).

Chinese folk religionists. Followers of traditional Chinese religion (local deities, ancestor veneration, Confucian ethics, universism, divination, some Buddhist elements).

Christians. Total Christians include those affiliated with churches not shown, plus other persons professing in censuses or polls to be Christians but not affiliated with any church. Figures for the subgroups of Christians do not add up to the totals because all subgroups are not shown and some Christians adhere to more than one denomination.

Confucianists. Non-Chinese followers of Confucius and Confucianism, mostly Koreans in Korea.

Ethnic religionists. Followers of local, tribal, animistic, or shamanistic religions, with members restricted to one ethnic group.

Hindus. 70% Vaishnavites, 25% Shaivites, 2% neo-Hindus and reform Hindus.

Independents. Members of churches and networks that regard themselves as postdenominationalist and neo-apostolic and thus independent of historic, organized, institutionalized denominationalist Christianity.

Jews. Adherents of Judaism.

Muslims. 83% Sunni Muslims, 16% Shia Muslims (Shi'ites), 1% other schools.

New-Religionists. Followers of Asian 20th-cent. New Religions, New Religious movements, radical new crisis religions, and non-Christian syncretistic mass religions, all founded since 1800 and most since 1945.
Other religionists. Including a handful of religions, quasi-religions, pseudo religions, parareligions, religious or mystic systems, and religious and semireligious brotherhoods of numerous varieties.
Nonreligious. Persons professing no religion, nonbelievers, agnostics, freethinkers, uninterested, dereligionized secularists indifferent to all religion.
Atheists. Persons professing atheism, skepticism, disbelief, or irreligion, including antireligious (opposed to all religion).

Episcopal Church Liturgical Colors and Calendar

Source: The Rt. Reverend Barry E. Yingling, Editor, the *Churchman's Ordo Kalendar*

The liturgical colors in the Episcopal Church are as follows: **White**—from Christmas Day through the First Sunday after Epiphany; Maundy Thursday (as an alternative to crimson at the Eucharist); from the Vigil of Easter to the Day of Pentecost (Whitsunday); Trinity Sunday; Feasts of the Lord (except Holy Cross Day); the Confession of St. Peter; the Conversion of St. Paul; St. Joseph; St. Mary Magdalene; St. Mary the Virgin; St. Michael and All Angels; All Saints' Day; St. John the Evangelist; memorials of other saints who were not martyred; Independence Day and Thanksgiving Day; weddings and funerals. **Red**—the Day of Pentecost; Holy Cross Day; feasts of apostles and evangelists (except those listed above); feasts and memorials of martyrs (including Holy Innocents' Day). **Violet**—Advent and Lent. **Crimson** or oxblood (dark red)—Holy Week. **Green**—the seasons after Epiphany and after Pentecost. **Black**—optional alternative for funerals and Good Friday. Alternative colors used in some churches: **Blue**—Advent; **Lenten White (unbleached linen)**—Ash Wednesday to Palm Sunday.

In the Episcopal Church the days of fasting are Ash Wednesday and Good Friday. Other days of special devotion (penitence) are the 40 days of Lent and all Fridays of the year, except those in Christmas and Easter seasons and any Feasts of the Lord that occur on a Friday or during Lent. Ember Days (optional) are days of prayer for the church's ministry. They fall on the Wednesday, Friday, and Saturday after the first Sunday in Lent, the Day of Pentecost, Holy Cross Day, and December 13. Rogation Days (also optional), the 3 days before Ascension Day, are days of prayer for God's blessing on the crops, on commerce and industry, and for conservation of the earth's resources.

Days, etc.	2003	2004	2005	2006	2007
Golden Number	9	10	11	12	13
Sunday Letter	E	D & C	B	A	G
Sundays after Epiphany	8	7	5	8	7
Ash Wednesday	Mar. 5	Feb. 25	Feb. 9	Mar. 1	Feb. 21
First Sunday in Lent	Mar. 9	Feb. 29	Feb. 13	Mar. 5	Feb. 25
Passion/Palm Sunday	Apr. 13	Apr. 4	Mar. 20	Apr. 9	Apr. 1
Good Friday	Apr. 18	Apr. 9	Mar. 25	Apr. 14	Apr. 6
Easter Day	Apr. 20	Apr. 11	Mar. 27	Apr. 16	Apr. 8
Ascension Day	May 29	May 20	May 5	May 25	May 17
The Day of Pentecost	June 8	May 30	May 15	June 4	May 27
Trinity Sunday	June 15	June 6	May 22	June 11	June 3
Numbered Proper of 2 Pentecost	#7	#6	#4	#6	#5
First Sunday of Advent	Nov. 30	Nov. 28	Nov. 27	Dec. 3	Dec. 2

Greek Orthodox Movable Ecclesiastical Dates, 2003-2007

This 5-year chart has the dates of feast days and fasting days, which are determined annually on the basis of the date of Holy Pascha (Easter). This ecclesiastical cycle begins with the first day of the Triodion and ends with the Sunday of All Saints, a total of 18 weeks.

	2003	2004	2005	2006	2007
Triodion begins	Feb. 16	Feb. 1	Feb. 20	Feb. 12	Jan. 28
1st Sat. of Souls	Mar. 1	Feb. 14	Mar. 5	Feb. 25	Feb. 10
Meat Fare	Mar. 2	Feb. 15	Mar. 6	Feb. 26	Feb. 11
2nd Sat. of Souls	Mar. 8	Feb. 21	Mar. 12	Mar. 4	Feb. 17
Lent Begins	Mar. 10	Feb. 23	Mar. 14	Mar. 6	Feb. 19
St. Theodore—3rd Sat. of Souls	Mar. 15	Feb. 28	Mar. 19	Mar. 11	Feb. 24
Sunday of Orthodoxy	Mar. 16	Feb. 29	Mar. 20	Mar. 12	Feb. 25
Sat. of Lazarus	Apr. 19	Apr. 3	Apr. 23	Apr. 15	Mar. 31
Palm Sunday	Apr. 20	Apr. 4	Apr. 24	Apr. 16	Apr. 1
Holy (Good) Friday	Apr. 25	Apr. 9	Apr. 29	Apr. 21	Apr. 6
Western Easter	Apr. 20	Apr. 11	Mar. 27	Apr. 16	Apr. 8
Orthodox Easter	Apr. 27	Apr. 11	May 1	Apr. 23	Apr. 8
Ascension	June 5	May 20	June 9	June 1	May 17
Sat. of Souls	June 14	May 29	June 18	June 10	May 26
Pentecost	June 15	May 30	June 19	June 11	May 27
All Saints	June 22	June 7	June 26	June 18	June 3

Important Islamic Dates, 1424-1428 (2003-2007)

Source: Imad-ad-Dean, Inc., Bethesda, MD 20814

The Islamic calendar is a strict lunar calendar reckoned from the year of the Hijra—Muhammad's flight from Mecca to Medina in 622 CE. Each year consists of 12 lunar months of 29 or 30 days beginning and ending with each new moon's visible crescent. Common years have 354 days; leap years have 355 days. Some Muslim countries employ a conventionalized calendar with the leap day added to the last month, Dhûl Hijah, but for religious purposes the leap date is taken into account by tracking each new moon sighting. The dates given below are based on the convention that the first new moon must be seen before the following dawn on the East Coast of the Americas. Actual (local) Western Hemisphere sightings may occur a day later, but never a day earlier, than these dates reflect. Holy days begin at sunset on the previous day.

	(1424) 2003-04	(1425) 2004-05	(1426) 2005-06	(1427) 2006	(1428) 2007
New Year's Day (Muharram 1)	Mar. 4, 2003	Feb. 21, 2004	Feb. 10, 2005	Jan. 30, 2006	Jan. 20, 2007
Ashura (Muharram 10)	Mar. 13, 2003	Mar. 1, 2004	Feb. 19, 2005	Feb. 8, 2006	Jan. 29, 2007
Mawlid (Rabi'l 12)	May 13, 2003	May 1, 2004	April 21, 2005	Apr. 10, 2006	Mar. 31, 2007
Ramadan 1	Oct. 26, 2003	Oct. 15, 2004	Oct. 4, 2005	Sept. 23, 2006	Sept. 12, 2007
Eid al-Fitr (Shawwal)	Nov. 25, 2003	Nov. 13, 2004	Nov. 3, 2005	Oct. 23, 2006	Oct. 12, 2007
Eid al-Adha (Dhûl-Hijjah 10)	Feb. 1, 2004	Jan. 20, 2005	Jan. 10, 2006	Dec. 30, 2006	Dec. 20, 2007

▶ *IT'S A FACT:* Members of the Church of Jesus Christ of Latter-day Saints are commonly referred to as Mormons, named after the Book of Mormon. Joseph Smith Jr., published the book in 1830, which he purportedly translated from golden plates found near his family's farm in Palmyra, NY. It is an account of the emigration of ancient Israelites to North America, and their history in the New World.

Jewish Holy Days, Festivals, and Fasts, 5764-5768 (2003-2008)

The Jewish Calendar consists of 12 lunar months, alternating between 29 and 30 days. It is *lunisolar*, and adjusts for the solar cycle by inserting an extra, intercalary month (Adar II) in the 3rd, 6th, 8th, 11th, 14th, 17th, and 19th years within a 19-year cycle. The calendar started on the day of Creation, calculated in the 2nd and 3rd centuries BC as Tishrei 1, 3,761 years before the common era. The months are 1) Tishrei; 2) Cheshvan (also Marcheshvan); 3) Kislev; 4) Tevet (also Tebeth); 5) Shevat (also Shebhat); 6) Adar; 6a) Adar Sheni (II) added in leap years; 7) Nisan; 8) Iyar; 9) Sivan; 10) Tammuz; 11) Av (also Abh); 12) Elul. The names are Aramaic versions of the Babylonian months, adopted during the Jews' exile in Babylon in the 4th century BC. Rosh Hashanah, the New Year, begins on Tishrei 1 (Sept.-Oct.). Yom Kippur is the holiest day of the year. All holidays listed below begin at sunset on the previous day.

Holiday	Date on Jewish Cal.	(5764) 2003-04	(5765) 2004-05	(5766) 2005-06	(5767) 2006-07	(5768) 2007-08
Rosh Hashanah (New Year)	Tishrei 1-2	Sept. 27 Sat.	Sept. 16 Thu.	Oct. 4 Tue.	Sept. 23 Sat.	Sept. 13 Thu.
		Sept. 28 Sun.	Sept. 17 Fri.	Oct. 5 Wed.	Sept. 24 Sun	Sept. 14 Fri.
Fast of Gedalya	Tishrei 3	Sept. 29 Mon.	Sept. 19 Sun.*	Oct. 6 Thu.	Sept. 25 Mon.	Sept. 16 Sun.
Yom Kippur (Day of Atonement)	Tishrei 10	Oct. 6 Mon.	Sept. 25 Sat.	Oct. 13 Thu.	Oct. 2 Mon.	Sept. 22 Sat.
Sukkot	Tishrei 15-20	Oct. 11 Sat.	Sept. 30 Thu.	Oct. 18 Tue.	Oct. 7 Sat.	Sept. 27 Thu.
		Oct. 17 Fri.	Oct. 6 Wed.	Oct. 24 Mon.	Oct. 13 Fri.	Oct. 2 Wed.
Shmeini Atzeret	Tishrei 22	Oct. 18 Sat.	Oct. 7 Thu.	Oct. 25 Tue.	Oct. 14 Sat.	Oct. 4 Thu.
Simchat Torah	Tishrei 23	Oct. 19 Sun.	Oct. 8 Fri.	Oct. 26 Wed.	Oct. 15 Sun.	Oct. 5 Fri.
Hanukkah	Kislev 25-Tevet 3	Dec. 20 Sat.	Dec. 8 Wed.	Dec. 26 Mon.	Dec. 16 Sat.	Dec. 5 Wed.
		Dec. 27 Sat.	Dec. 15 Wed.	Jan. 2, 2006 Mon.	Dec. 23 Sat.	Dec. 12 Wed.
Fast of the 10th of Tevet	Tevet 10	Jan. 4, 2004 Sun.	Dec. 22 Wed.	Jan. 10, Tue.	Dec. 31 Sun.	Dec. 19 Wed.
Tu B'Shevat	Shevat 15	Jan. 18 Sat.	Feb. 7, 2005 Sat.	Jan. 25 Tue.	Feb. 13, 2007 Mon.	Jan. 22, 2008 Tue.
Ta'anis Esther (Fast of Esther)	Adar 13	Mar. 17 Mon.	Mar. 4 Thu.*	Mar. 24 Thu.	Mar. 13 Mon.	Mar. 20 Thu.
Purim	Adar 14	Mar. 18 Tue.	Mar. 7 Sun.	Mar. 25 Fri.	Mar. 14 Tue.	Mar. 21 Fri.
Pesach (Passover)	Nisan 15-22	Apr. 17 Thu.	Apr. 6 Tue.	Apr. 24 Sun.	Apr. 13 Thu.	Apr. 20 Sun.
		Apr. 24 Thu.	Apr. 13 Tue.	May 1 Sun.	Apr. 20 Thu.	Apr. 27 Sun.
Lag B'Omer	Iyar 18	May. 20 Tue.	May 9 Sun.	May 27 Fri.	May 16 Tue.	May 23 Fri.
Shavuot (Pentecost)	Sivan 6-7	June 6 Fri.	May 26 Wed.	June 13 Mon.	June 2 Fri.	June 9 Mon.
		June 7 Sat.	May 27 Thu.	June 14 Tue.	June 3 Sat.	June 10 Tue.
Fast of the 17th Day of Tammuz	Tammuz 17	July 17 Thu.	July 6 Tue.	July 24 Sun.	July 13 Thu.	July 20 Sun.
Fast of the 9th Day of Av	Av 9	Aug. 7 Thu.	July 27 Tue.	Aug. 14 Sun.	Aug. 3 Thu.	Aug.10 Sun.

*Date changed to avoid Sabbath.

Ash Wednesday and Easter Sunday (Western churches), 1901-2100

Year	Ash Wed.	Easter Sunday	Year	Ash Wed.	Easter Sunday	Year	Ash Wed.	Easter Sunday	Year	Ash Wed.	Easter Sunday	Year	Ash Wed.	Easter Sunday
1901	Feb. 20	Apr. 7	1941	Feb. 26	Apr. 13	1981	Mar. 4	Apr. 19	2021	Feb. 17	Apr. 4	2061	Feb. 23	Apr. 10
1902	Feb. 12	Mar. 30	1942	Feb. 18	Apr. 5	1982	Feb. 24	Apr. 11	2022	Mar. 2	Apr. 17	2062	Feb. 8	Mar. 26
1903	Feb. 25	Apr. 12	1943	Mar. 10	Apr. 25	1983	Feb. 16	Apr. 3	2023	Feb. 22	Apr. 9	2063	Feb. 28	Apr. 15
1904	Feb. 17	Apr. 3	1944	Feb. 23	Apr. 9	1984	Mar. 7	Apr. 22	2024	Feb. 14	Mar. 31	2064	Feb. 20	Apr. 6
1905	Mar. 8	Apr. 23	1945	Feb. 14	Apr. 1	1985	Feb. 20	Apr. 7	2025	Mar. 5	Apr. 20	2065	Feb. 11	Mar. 29
1906	Feb. 28	Apr. 15	1946	Mar. 6	Apr. 21	1986	Feb. 12	Mar. 30	2026	Feb. 18	Apr. 5	2066	Feb. 24	Apr. 11
1907	Feb. 13	Mar. 31	1947	Feb. 19	Apr. 6	1987	Mar. 4	Apr. 19	2027	Feb. 10	Mar. 28	2067	Feb. 16	Apr. 3
1908	Mar. 4	Apr. 19	1948	Feb. 11	Mar. 28	1988	Feb. 17	Apr. 3	2028	Mar. 1	Apr. 16	2068	Mar. 7	Apr. 22
1909	Feb. 24	Apr. 11	1949	Mar. 2	Apr. 17	1989	Feb. 8	Mar. 26	2029	Feb. 14	Apr. 1	2069	Feb. 27	Apr. 14
1910	Feb. 9	Mar. 27	1950	Feb. 22	Apr. 9	1990	Feb. 28	Apr. 15	2030	Mar. 6	Apr. 21	2070	Feb. 12	Mar. 30
1911	Mar. 1	Apr. 16	1951	Feb. 7	Mar. 25	1991	Feb. 13	Mar. 31	2031	Feb. 26	Apr. 13	2071	Mar. 4	Apr. 19
1912	Feb. 21	Apr. 7	1952	Feb. 27	Apr. 13	1992	Mar. 4	Apr. 19	2032	Feb. 11	Mar. 28	2072	Feb. 24	Apr. 10
1913	Feb. 5	Mar. 23	1953	Feb. 18	Apr. 5	1993	Feb. 24	Apr. 11	2033	Mar. 2	Apr. 17	2073	Feb. 8	Mar. 26
1914	Feb. 25	Apr. 12	1954	Mar. 3	Apr. 18	1994	Feb. 16	Apr. 3	2034	Feb. 22	Apr. 9	2074	Feb. 28	Apr. 15
1915	Feb. 17	Apr. 4	1955	Feb. 23	Apr. 10	1995	Mar. 1	Apr. 16	2035	Feb. 7	Mar. 25	2075	Feb. 20	Apr. 7
1916	Mar. 8	Apr. 23	1956	Feb. 15	Apr. 1	1996	Feb. 21	Apr. 7	2036	Feb. 27	Apr. 13	2076	Mar. 4	Apr. 19
1917	Feb. 21	Apr. 8	1957	Mar. 6	Apr. 21	1997	Feb. 12	Mar. 30	2037	Feb. 18	Apr. 5	2077	Feb. 24	Apr. 11
1918	Feb. 13	Mar. 31	1958	Feb. 19	Apr. 6	1998	Feb. 25	Apr. 12	2038	Mar. 10	Apr. 25	2078	Feb. 16	Apr. 3
1919	Mar. 5	Apr. 20	1959	Feb. 11	Mar. 29	1999	Feb. 17	Apr. 4	2039	Feb. 23	Apr. 10	2079	Mar. 8	Apr. 23
1920	Feb. 18	Apr. 4	1960	Mar. 2	Apr. 17	2000	Mar. 8	Apr. 23	2040	Feb. 15	Apr. 1	2080	Feb. 21	Apr. 7
1921	Feb. 9	Mar. 27	1961	Feb. 15	Apr. 2	2001	Feb. 28	Apr. 15	2041	Mar. 6	Apr. 21	2081	Feb. 12	Mar. 30
1922	Mar. 1	Apr. 16	1962	Mar. 7	Apr. 22	2002	Feb. 13	Mar. 31	2042	Feb. 19	Apr. 6	2082	Mar. 4	Apr. 19
1923	Feb. 14	Apr. 1	1963	Feb. 27	Apr. 14	2003	Mar. 5	Apr. 20	2043	Feb. 11	Mar. 29	2083	Feb. 17	Apr. 4
1924	Mar. 5	Apr. 20	1964	Feb. 12	Mar. 29	2004	Feb. 25	Apr. 11	2044	Mar. 2	Apr. 17	2084	Feb. 9	Mar. 26
1925	Feb. 25	Apr. 12	1965	Mar. 3	Apr. 18	2005	Feb. 9	Mar. 27	2045	Feb. 22	Apr. 9	2085	Feb. 28	Apr. 15
1926	Feb. 17	Apr. 4	1966	Feb. 23	Apr. 10	2006	Mar. 1	Apr. 16	2046	Feb. 7	Mar. 25	2086	Feb. 13	Mar. 31
1927	Mar. 2	Apr. 17	1967	Feb. 8	Mar. 26	2007	Feb. 21	Apr. 8	2047	Feb. 27	Apr. 14	2087	Mar. 5	Apr. 20
1928	Feb. 22	Apr. 8	1968	Feb. 28	Apr. 14	2008	Feb. 6	Mar. 23	2048	Feb. 19	Apr. 5	2088	Feb. 25	Apr. 11
1929	Feb. 13	Mar. 31	1969	Feb. 19	Apr. 6	2009	Feb. 25	Apr. 12	2049	Mar. 3	Apr. 18	2089	Feb. 16	Apr. 3
1930	Mar. 5	Apr. 20	1970	Feb. 11	Mar. 29	2010	Feb. 17	Apr. 4	2050	Feb. 23	Apr. 10	2090	Mar. 1	Apr. 16
1931	Feb. 18	Apr. 5	1971	Feb. 24	Apr. 11	2011	Mar. 9	Apr. 24	2051	Feb. 15	Apr. 2	2091	Feb. 21	Apr. 8
1932	Feb. 10	Mar. 27	1972	Feb. 16	Apr. 2	2012	Feb. 22	Apr. 8	2052	Mar. 6	Apr. 21	2092	Feb. 13	Mar. 30
1933	Mar. 1	Apr. 16	1973	Mar. 7	Apr. 22	2013	Feb. 13	Mar. 31	2053	Feb. 19	Apr. 6	2093	Feb. 25	Apr. 12
1934	Feb. 14	Apr. 1	1974	Feb. 27	Apr. 14	2014	Mar. 5	Apr. 20	2054	Feb. 11	Mar. 29	2094	Feb. 17	Apr. 4
1935	Mar. 6	Apr. 21	1975	Feb. 12	Mar. 30	2015	Feb. 18	Apr. 5	2055	Mar. 3	Apr. 18	2095	Mar. 9	Apr. 24
1936	Feb. 26	Apr. 12	1976	Mar. 3	Apr. 18	2016	Feb. 10	Mar. 27	2056	Feb. 16	Apr. 2	2096	Feb. 29	Apr. 15
1937	Feb. 10	Mar. 28	1977	Feb. 23	Apr. 10	2017	Mar. 1	Apr. 16	2057	Mar. 7	Apr. 22	2097	Feb. 13	Mar. 31
1938	Mar. 2	Apr. 17	1978	Feb. 8	Mar. 26	2018	Feb. 14	Apr. 1	2058	Feb. 27	Apr. 14	2098	Mar. 5	Apr. 20
1939	Feb. 22	Apr. 9	1979	Feb. 28	Apr. 15	2019	Mar. 6	Apr. 21	2059	Feb. 12	Mar. 30	2099	Feb. 25	Apr. 12
1940	Feb. 7	Mar. 24	1980	Feb. 20	Apr. 6	2020	Feb. 26	Apr. 12	2060	Mar. 3	Apr. 18	2100	Feb. 10	Mar. 28

The Ten Commandments

According to Judeo-Christian tradition, as related in the Bible, the Ten Commandments were revealed by God to Moses and form the basic moral component of God's covenant with Israel. The Ten Commandments appear in 2 places in the Old Testament—Exodus 20:1-17 and Deuteronomy 5:6-21.

Following is the text of the Ten Commandments as it appears in Exodus 20:1-17, in the King James version of the Bible [Roman numerals added; some wording omitted].

I. I am the LORD thy God, which have brought thee out of the land of Egypt, out of the house of bondage. Thou shalt have no other gods before me.

II. Thou shalt not make unto thee any graven image, or any likeness of any thing that is in heaven above, or that is in the earth beneath, or that is in the water under the earth. Thou shalt not bow down thyself to them, nor serve them: for I the LORD thy God am a jealous God, visiting the iniquity of the fathers upon the children unto the third and fourth generation of them that hate me; . . .

III. Thou shalt not take the name of the LORD thy God in vain; for the LORD will not hold him guiltless that taketh his name in vain.

IV. Remember the sabbath day, to keep it holy. . .

V. Honour thy father and thy mother: that thy days may be long upon the land which the LORD thy God giveth thee.

VI. Thou shalt not kill.

VII. Thou shalt not commit adultery.

VIII. Thou shalt not steal.

IX. Thou shalt not bear false witness against thy neighbour.

X. Thou shalt not covet thy neighbour's house, thou shalt not covet thy neighbour's wife, nor his manservant, nor his maidservant, nor his ox, nor his ass, nor any thing that is thy neighbour's.

Most Protestant, Anglican, and Orthodox Christians follow Jewish tradition, which considers the introduction ("I am the Lord . . .") the first commandment and makes the prohibition against idolatry the second. Roman Catholic and Lutheran traditions combine I and II and split the last commandment into 2 that separately prohibit coveting of a neighbor's wife and a neighbor's goods. This arrangement alters the numbering of the other commandments by one.

Books of the Bible

Old Testament—Standard Protestant List

Genesis	I Kings	Ecclesiastes	Obadiah
Exodus	II Kings	Song of Solomon	Jonah
Leviticus	I Chronicles	Isaiah	Micah
Numbers	II Chronicles	Jeremiah	Nahum
Deuteronomy	Ezra	Lamentations	Habakkuk
Joshua	Nehemiah	Ezekiel	Zephaniah
Judges	Esther	Daniel	Haggai
Ruth	Job	Hosea	Zechariah
I Samuel	Psalms	Joel	Malachi
II Samuel	Proverbs	Amos	

New Testament List

Matthew	Ephesians	Hebrews
Mark	Phillippians	James
Luke	Colossians	I Peter
John	I Thessalonians	II Peter
Acts	II Thessalonians	I John
Romans	I Timothy	II John
I Corinthians	II Timothy	III John
II Corinthians	Titus	Jude
Galatians	Philemon	Revelation

The standard Protestant Old Testament consists of the same 39 books as in the Bible of Judaism, but the latter is organized differently. The Old Testament used by Roman Catholics has 7 additional "deuterocanonical" books, plus some additional parts of books. The 7 are: **Tobit, Judith, Wisdom, Sirach (Ecclesiasticus), Baruch, I Maccabees,** and **II Maccabees**. Both Catholic and Protestant versions of the New Testament have 27 books, with the same names.

Roman Catholic Hierarchy

Sources: U.S. Catholic Conference; Holy See Press Office

Supreme Pontiff

At the head of the Roman Catholic Church is the supreme pontiff, Pope John Paul II, Karol Wojtyla, born at Wadowice (Kraków), Poland, May 18, 1920; ordained priest Nov. 1, 1946; appointed bishop July 4, 1958; named archbishop of Kraków Jan. 13, 1964; proclaimed cardinal June 26, 1967; elected pope Oct. 16, 1978; installed Oct. 22, 1978.

Chronological List of Popes

Source: Annuario Pontificio. Table lists year of accession of each pope.

The Roman Catholic Church named the Apostle Peter as founder of the church in Rome and the first pope. He arrived there c 42, was martyred there c 67, and was ultimately canonized as a saint. **The pope's temporal title is:** Sovereign of the State of Vatican City. **The pope's spiritual titles are:** Bishop of Rome, Vicar of Jesus Christ, Successor of St. Peter, Prince of the Apostles, Supreme Pontiff of the Universal Church, Patriarch of the West, Primate of Italy, Archbishop and Metropolitan of the Roman Province.

The names of antipopes are *in italics* and followed by an *. Antipopes were illegitimate claimants to the papal throne.

Year	Pope	Year	Pope	Year	Pope	Year	Pope	Year	Pope
	St. Peter	251	St. Cornelius	401	St. Innocent I	536	St. Silverius,	676	Donus
67	St. Linus	251	*Novatian**	417	St. Zosimus		Martyr	678	St. Agatho
76	St. Anacletus	253	St. Lucius I	418	St. Boniface I	537	Vigilius	682	St. Leo II
	or Cletus	254	St. Stephen I	418	*Eulalius**	556	Pelagius I	684	St. Benedict II
88	St. Clement I	257	St. Sixtus II	422	St. Celestine I	561	John III	685	John V
97	St. Evaristus	259	St. Dionysius	432	St. Sixtus III	575	Benedict I	686	Conon
105	St. Alexander I	269	St. Felix I	440	St. Leo I	579	Pelagius II	687	*Theodore**
115	St. Sixtus I	275	St. Eutychian	461	St. Hilary	590	St. Gregory I	687	*Paschal**
125	St. Telesphorus	283	St. Caius	468	St. Simplicius	604	Sabinian	687	St. Sergius I
136	St. Hyginus	296	St. Marcellinus	483	St. Felix III (II)	607	Boniface III	701	John VI
140	St. Pius I	308	St. Marcellus I	492	St. Gelasius I	608	St. Boniface IV	705	John VII
155	St. Anicetus	309	St. Eusebius	496	Anastasius II	615	St. Deusdedit or	708	Sisinnius
166	St. Soter	311	St. Melchiades	498	St. Symmachus		Adeodatus	708	Constantine
175	St. Eleutherius	314	St. Sylvester I	498	*Lawrence**	619	Boniface V	715	St. Gregory II
189	St. Victor I	336	St. Marcus		(501-505)	625	Honorius I	731	St. Gregory III
199	St. Zephyrinus	337	St. Julius I	514	St. Hormisdas	640	Severinus	741	St. Zachary
217	St. Callistus I	352	Liberius	523	St. John I, Martyr	640	John IV	752	Stephen II (III)[1]
217	*St. Hippolytus**	355	*Felix II**	526	St. Felix IV (III)	642	Theodore I	757	St. Paul I
222	St. Urban I	366	St. Damasus I	530	Boniface II	649	St. Martin I, Martyr	767	*Constantine**
230	St. Pontian	366	*Ursinus**	530	*Dioscorus**	654	St. Eugene I	768	*Philip**
235	St. Anterus	384	St. Siricius	533	John II	657	St. Vitalian	768	Stephen III (IV)
236	St. Fabian	399	St. Anastasius I	535	St. Agapitus I	672	Adeodatus II	772	Adrian I

Year	Pope	Year	Pope	Year	Pope	Year	Pope	Year	Pope
795	St. Leo III	964	Benedict V	1118	Gregory VIII*	1294	Boniface VIII	1572	Gregory XIII
816	Stephen IV (V)	965	John XIII	1119	Callistus II	1303	Bl. Benedict XI	1585	Sixtus V
817	St. Paschal I	973	Benedict VI	1124	Honorius II	1305	Clement V	1590	Urban VII
824	Eugene II	974	Boniface VII*	1124	Celestine II*	1316	John XXII	1590	Gregory XIV
827	Valentine	974	Benedict VII	1130	Innocent II	1328	Nicholas V*	1591	Innocent IX
827	Gregory IV	983	John XIV	1130	Anacletus II*	1334	Benedict XII	1592	Clement VIII
844	John*	985	John XV	1138	Victor IV*	1342	Clement VI	1605	Leo XI
844	Sergius II	996	Gregory V	1143	Celestine II	1352	Innocent VI	1605	Paul V
847	St. Leo IV	997	John XVI*	1144	Lucius II	1362	Bl. Urban V	1621	Gregory XV
855	Benedict III	999	Sylvester II	1145	Bl. Eugene III	1370	Gregory XI	1623	Urban VIII
855	Anastasius*	1003	John XVII	1153	Anastasius IV	1378	Urban VI	1644	Innocent X
858	St. Nicholas I	1004	John XVIII	1154	Adrian IV	1378	Clement VII*	1655	Alexander VII
867	Adrian II	1009	Sergius IV	1159	Alexander III	1389	Boniface IX	1667	Clement IX
872	John VIII	1012	Benedict VIII	1159	Victor IV*	1394	Benedict XIII*	1670	Clement X
882	Marinus I	1012	Gregory*	1164	Paschal III*	1404	Innocent VII	1676	Bl. Innocent XI
884	St. Adrian III	1024	John XIX	1168	Callistus III*	1406	Gregory XII	1689	Alexander VIII
885	Stephen V (VI)	1032	Benedict IX	1179	Innocent III*	1409	Alexander V*	1691	Innocent XII
891	Formosus	1045	Sylvester III	1181	Lucius III	1410	John XXIII*	1700	Clement XI
896	Boniface VI	1045	Benedict IX	1185	Urban III	1417	Martin V	1721	Innocent XIII
896	Stephen VI (VII)	1045	Gregory VI	1187	Clement III	1431	Eugene IV	1724	Benedict XIII
897	Romanus	1046	Clement II	1187	Gregory VIII	1439	Felix V*	1730	Clement XII
897	Theodore II	1047	Benedict IX	1191	Celestine III	1447	Nicholas V	1740	Benedict XIV
898	John IX	1048	Damasus II	1198	Innocent III	1455	Callistus III	1758	Clement XIII
900	Benedict IV	1049	St. Leo IX	1216	Honorius III	1458	Pius II	1769	Clement XIV
903	Leo V	1055	Victor II	1227	Gregory IX	1464	Paul II	1775	Pius VI
903	Christopher*	1057	Stephen IX (X)	1241	Celestine IV	1471	Sixtus IV	1800	Pius VII
904	Sergius III	1058	Benedict X*	1243	Innocent IV	1484	Innocent VIII	1823	Leo XII
911	Anastasius III	1059	Nicholas II	1254	Alexander IV	1492	Alexander VI	1829	Pius VIII
913	Landus	1061	Alexander II	1261	Urban IV	1503	Pius III	1831	Gregory XVI
914	John X	1061	Honorius II*	1265	Clement IV	1503	Julius II	1846	Pius IX
928	Leo VI	1073	St. Gregory VII	1271	Bl. Gregory X	1513	Leo X	1878	Leo XIII
928	Stephen VII(VIII)	1080	Clement III*	1276	Bl. Innocent V	1522	Adrian VI	1903	St. Pius X
931	John XI	1086	Bl. Victor III	1276	Adrian V	1523	Clement VII	1914	Benedict XV
936	Leo VII	1088	Bl. Urban II	1276	John XXI	1534	Paul III	1922	Pius XI
939	Stephen VIII(IX)	1099	Paschal II	1277	Nicholas III	1550	Julius III	1939	Pius XII
942	Marinus II	1100	Theodoric*	1281	Martin IV	1555	Marcellus II	1958	John XXIII
946	Agapitus II	1102	Albert*	1285	Honorius IV	1555	Paul IV	1963	Paul VI
955	John XII	1105	Sylvester IV*	1288	Nicholas IV	1559	Pius IV	1978	John Paul I
963	Leo VIII	1118	Gelasius II	1294	St. Celestine V	1566	St. Pius V	1978	John Paul II

(1) After St. Zachary, a Roman priest named Stephen was elected, but died before assuming the papacy. Another Stephen was then elected to succeed Zachary as Stephen II. The ordinal III appears after Stephen II because the deceased priest was included in some lists.

College of Cardinals

Members of the Sacred College of Cardinals are chosen by the pope to be his chief assistants and advisers in the administration of the church. Among their duties is the election of the pope when the Holy See becomes vacant.

In its present form, the College of Cardinals dates from the 12th century. The first cardinals, from about the 6th century, were deacons and priests of the leading churches of Rome and were bishops of neighboring dioceses. The title of cardinal was limited to members of the college in 1567. The number of cardinals was set at 70 in 1586 by Pope Sixtus V. From 1959 Pope John XXIII began to increase the number; however, the number eligible to participate in papal elections was limited to 120. Previous limitations were set aside by Pope John Paul II in 1998, and again in 2001 when he created 44 new cardinals. As of July 2003, there were 166 members of the College, of whom 109 remained eligible to vote. In 1918 the Code of Canon Law specified that all cardinals must be priests. Pope John XXIII in 1962 established that all cardinals must be bishops, but this can be dispensed with, as in the case of Cardinal Avery Dulles. In 1971, Pope Paul VI decreed that at age 80 cardinals must retire from curial departments and offices and from participation in papal elections.

North American Cardinals

Name	Office	Born	Named Cardinal
Aloysius M. Ambrozic	Archbishop of Toronto	1930	1998
William W. Baum	Archbishop emeritus of Washington, DC	1926	1976
Anthony J. Bevilacqua	Archbishop emeritus of Philadelphia	1923	1991
Ernesto Corripio Ahumada[1]	Archbishop emeritus of Mexico	1919	1979
Avery Robert Dulles[1]	Professor, Fordham University, NYC	1918	2001
Edward M. Egan	Archbishop of New York	1932	2001
Edouard Gagnon[1]	Pres. Emeritus of the Commission of Intl. Eucharistic Congresses	1918	1985
Francis E. George	Archbishop of Chicago	1937	1998
James A. Hickey[1]	Archbishop emeritus of Washington, DC	1920	1988
William Henry Keeler	Archbishop of Baltimore	1931	1994
Bernard F. Law	Archbishop emeritus of Boston	1931	1985
Roger Mahony	Archbishop of Los Angeles	1936	1991
Adam Joseph Maida	Archbishop of Detroit	1930	1994
Luis Aponte Martinez[1]	Archibishop emeritus of San Juan	1922	1973
Theodore E. McCarrick	Archbishop of Washington, DC	1930	2001
Norberto Rivera Carrera	Archbishop of Mexico City	1942	1998
Juan Sandoval Iniguez	Archbishop of Guadalajara	1933	1994
James F. Stafford	President of the Pontifical Council for the Laity	1932	1998
Adolfo Antonio Suarez Rivera	Archbishop of Monterrey	1927	1994
Edmund C. Szoka	Pres. of Prefecture of Economic Affairs of Holy See, the Vatican	1927	1988
Jean-Claude Turcotte	Archbishop of Montreal	1936	1994
Louis-Albert Vachon[1]	Archbishop emeritus of Quebec	1912	1985

(1) Ineligible to take part in papal elections (as of Sept. 2003).

Major Non-Christian World Religions

Sources: Reviewed by Anthony Padovano, PhD, STD, prof. of literature & relig. studies, Ramapo College, NJ, adj. prof. of theol., Fordham U., NYC; Islam reviewed by Abdulaziz Sachedina, PhD, prof. of Islamic studies, Univ. of Virginia

Buddhism

Founded: About 525 BC, reportedly near Benares, India.

Founder: Gautama Siddhartha (c 563-483 BC), the Buddha, who achieved enlightenment through intense meditation.

Sacred Texts: The *Tripitaka*, a collection of the Buddha's teachings, rules of monastic life, and philosophical commentaries on the teachings; also a vast body of Buddhist teachings and commentaries, many of which are called *sutras*.

Organization: The basic institution is the *sangha*, or monastic order, through which the traditions are passed to from generation to generation. Monastic life tends to be democratic and anti-authoritarian. Large lay organizations have developed in some sects.

Practice: Varies widely according to the sect, and ranges from austere meditation to magical chanting and elaborate temple rites. Many practices, such as exorcism of devils, reflect pre-Buddhist beliefs.

Divisions: A variety of sects grouped into 3 primary branches: Theravada (sole survivor of the ancient Hinayana schools), which emphasizes the importance of pure thought and deed; Mahayana (includes Zen and Soka-gakkai), which ranges from philosophical schools to belief in the saving grace of higher beings or ritual practices and to practical meditative disciplines; and Tantrism, a combination of belief in ritual magic and sophisticated philosophy.

Location: Throughout Asia, from Sri Lanka to Japan. Zen and Soka-gakkai have some 15,000 adherents in the U.S.

Beliefs: Life is misery and decay, and there is no ultimate reality in it or behind it. The cycle of endless birth and rebirth continues because of desire and attachment to the unreal "self." Right meditation and deeds will end the cycle and achieve Nirvana, the Void, nothingness.

Hinduism

Founded: About 1500 BC by Aryans who migrated to India, where their Vedic religion intermixed with the practices and beliefs of the natives.

Sacred texts: The *Veda*, including the *Upanishads*, a collection of rituals and mythological and philosophical commentaries; a vast number of epic stories about gods, heroes, and saints, including the *Bhagavadgita*, a part of the *Mahabharata*, and the *Ramayana;* and a great variety of other literature.

Organization: None, strictly speaking. Generally, rituals should be performed or assisted by Brahmins, the priestly caste, but in practice, simpler rituals can be performed by anyone. Brahmins are the final judges of ritual purity, the vital element in Hindu life. Temples and religious organizations are usually presided over by Brahmins.

Practice: A variety of private rituals, primarily passage rites (e.g., initiation, marriage, death, etc.) and daily devotions, and a similar variety of public rites in temples. Of the public rites, the *puja*, a ceremonial dinner for a god, is the most common.

Divisions: There is no concept of orthodoxy in Hinduism, which presents a variety of sects, most of them devoted to the worship of one of the many gods. The 3 major living traditions are those devoted to the gods Vishnu and Shiva and to the goddess Shakti; each is divided into further subsects. Numerous folk beliefs and practices, often in amalgamation with the above groups, exist side by side with sophisticated philosophical schools and exotic cults.

Location: Mainly India, Nepal, Malaysia, Guyana, Suriname, and Sri Lanka.

Beliefs: There is only one divine principle; the many gods are only aspects of that unity. Life in all its forms is an aspect of the divine, but it appears as a separation from the divine, a meaningless cycle of birth and rebirth (*samsara*) determined by the purity or impurity of past deeds (*karma*). To improve one's *karma* or escape *samsara* by pure acts, thought, and/or devotion is the aim of every Hindu.

Islam

Founded: About AD 622 in Mecca, Arabian Peninsula.

Founder: Muhammad (c 570-632), the Prophet.

Sacred texts: The *Koran* (al-Qur'an), the Word of God; *Sunna*, collections of *Hadith*, describing what Muhammad said or did.

Organization: Since the founder was both a prophet and a statesman, Muslim leadership has combined the civil and moral function of a state. Within the larger community, there are cultural and national groups, held together by a common religious law, the *Shari'a*, enforced uniformly in matters of religion only. In social transactions the community has often departed from traditional formulations. Although Islam is basically egalitarian and suspicious of authoritarianism, Muslim culture tends to be dominated by the conservative spirit of its religious establishment, the *ulema*.

Practice: Besides the general moral guidance that determines everyday life, there are "Five Pillars of Islam": profession of faith (oneness of God and prophethood of Muhammad); prayer 5 times a day; alms *(zakat)* from one's savings and estate; dawn-to-dusk fasting in the month of Ramadan; and once in a lifetime, pilgrimage to Mecca, if possible.

Divisions: There are 2 major groups: the majority known as Sunni and the minority Shiites. Shiites believe in Twelve Imams (perfect teachers) after the Prophet, of whom the last Imam has lived an invisible existence since 874, continuing to guide his community. Sunni Muslims believe in God's overpowering will over their affairs and tend to be predestinarian; Shiites believe in free will and give a substantial role to human reason in daily life. Sufism (mystical dimension of Islam) is prevalent among both Sunni and Shiites. Sufis emphasize personal relation to God and obedience informed by love of God.

Location: W Africa to Philippines, across band including E Africa, Central Asia and W China, India, Malaysia, Indonesia. Islam has several million adherents in North America.

Beliefs: Strictly monotheistic. God is creator of the universe, omnipotent, omniscient, just, forgiving, and merciful. The human is God's highest creation, but weak and egocentric, prone to forget the goal of life, constantly tempted by the Satan, an evil being. God revealed the Koran to Muhammad to guide humanity to truth and justice. Those who repent and sincerely "submit" (literal meaning of "islam") to God attain salvation. The forgiven enter the Paradise, and the wicked burn in Hell.

Judaism

Founded: About 2000 BC.

Founder: Abraham is regarded as the founding patriarch, but the Torah of Moses is the basic source of the teachings.

Sacred Texts: The 5 books of Moses constitute the written Torah. Special sanctity is also assigned other writings of the Hebrew Bible—the teachings of oral Torah are recorded in the Talmud, in the Midrash, and in various commentaries.

Organization: Originally theocratic, Judaism has evolved a congregational polity. The basic institution is the local synagogue, operated by the congregation and led by a rabbi of their choice. Chief rabbis in France and Great Britain have authority only over those who accept it; in Israel, the 2 chief rabbis have civil authority in family law.

Practice: Among traditional practicioners, almost all areas of life are governed by strict religious discipline. Sabbath and holidays are marked by special observances, and attendance at public worship is considered especially important then. Chief annual observances are Passover, celebrating liberation of the Israelites from Egypt and marked by the Seder meal in homes, and the 10 days from Rosh Hashanah (New Year) to Yom Kippur (Day of Atonement), a period of fasting and penitence.

Divisions: Judaism is an unbroken spectrum from ultraconservative to ultraliberal, largely reflecting different points of view regarding the binding character of the prohibitions and duties—particularly the dietary and Sabbath observations—traditionally prescribed for the daily life of the Jew.

Location: Almost worldwide, with concentrations in Israel and the U.S.

Beliefs: Strictly monotheistic. God is the creator and absolute ruler of the universe. Men and women are free to choose to rebel against God's rule. God established a particular relationship with the Hebrew people: by obeying a divine law God gave them, they would be a special witness to God's mercy and justice. Judaism stresses ethical behavior (and, among the traditional, careful ritual obedience) as true worship of God.

Major Christian Denominations:

Brackets indicate some features that tend to

Denomination	Origins	Organization	Authority	Special rites
Baptists	In radical Reformation, objections to infant baptism, demands for church and state separation; John Smyth, English Separatist, in 1609; Roger Williams, 1638, Providence, RI.	Congregational; each local church is autonomous.	Scripture; some Baptists, particularly in the South, interpret the Bible literally.	[Baptism, usually early teen years and after, by total immersion;] Lord's Supper.
Church of Christ (Disciples)	Among evangelical Presbyterians in KY (1804) and PA (1809), in distress over Protestant factionalism and decline of fervor; organized in 1832.	Congregational.	["Where the Scriptures speak, we speak; where the Scriptures are silent, we are silent."]	Adult baptism; Lord's Supper (weekly).
Episcopalians	Henry VIII separated English Catholic Church from Rome, 1534, for political reasons; Protestant Episcopal Church in U.S. founded in 1789.	[Diocesan bishops, in apostolic succession, are elected by parish representatives; the national Church is headed by General Convention and Presiding Bishop; part of the Anglican Communion.]	Scripture as interpreted by tradition, especially 39 Articles (1563); tri-annual convention of bishops, priests, and lay people.	Infant baptism, Eucharist, and other sacraments; sacrament taken to be symbolic, but as having real spiritual effect.
Jehovah's Witnesses	Founded in 1870 in PA by Charles Taze Russell; incorporated as Watch Tower Bible and Tract Society of PA, 1884; name Jehovah's Witnesses adopted in 1931.	A governing body located in NY coordinates worldwide activities; each congregation cared for by a body of elders; each Witness considered a minister.	The Bible.	Baptism by immersion; annual Lord's Meal ceremony.
Latter-day Saints (Mormons)	In a vision of the Father and the Son reported by Joseph Smith (1820s) in NY. Smith also reported receiving new scripture on golden tablets: The Book of Mormon.	Theocratic; 1st Presidency (church president, 2 counselors), 12 Apostles preside over international church. Local congregations headed by lay priesthood leaders.	Revelation to living prophet (church president). The Bible, Book of Mormon, and other revelations to Smith and his successors.	Baptism, at age 8; laying on of hands (which confers the gift of the Holy Ghost); Lord's Supper; temple rites: baptism for the dead, marriage for eternity, others.
Lutherans	Begun by Martin Luther in Wittenberg, Germany, in 1517; objection to Catholic doctrine of salvation and sale of indulgences; break complete, 1519.	Varies from congregational to episcopal; in U.S., a combination of regional synods and congregational polities is most common.	Scripture alone. The Book of Concord (1580), which includes the three Ecumenical Creeds, is subscribed to as a correct exposition of Scripture.	Infant baptism; Lord's Supper; Christ's true body and blood present "in, with, and under the bread and wine."
Methodists	Rev. John Wesley began movement in 1738, within Church of England; first U.S. denomination, Baltimore (1784).	Conference and superintendent system; [in United Methodist Church, general superintendents are bishops—not a priestly order, only an office—who are elected for life.]	Scripture as interpreted by tradition, reason, and experience.	Baptism of infants or adults; Lord's Supper commanded; other rites: marriage, ordination, solemnization of personal commitments.
Orthodox	Developed in original Christian proselytizing; broke with Rome in 1054, after centuries of doctrinal disputes and diverging traditions.	Synods of bishops in autonomous, usually national, churches elect a patriarch, archbishop, or metropolitan; these men, as a group, are the heads of the church.	Scripture, tradition, and the first 7 church councils up to Nicaea II in 787; bishops in council have authority in doctrine and policy.	Seven sacraments: infant baptism and anointing, Eucharist, ordination, penance, marriage, and anointing of the sick.
Pentecostal	In Topeka, KS (1901) and Los Angeles (1906), in reaction to perceived evangelical fervor among Methodists and others.	Originally a movement, not a formal organization, Pentecostalism now has a variety of organized forms and continues also as a movement.	Scripture; individual charismatic leaders, the teachings of the Holy Spirit.	[Spirit baptism, especially as shown in "speaking in tongues"; healing and sometimes exorcism;] adult baptism; Lord's Supper.
Presbyterians	In 16th-cent. Calvinist reformation; differed with Lutherans over sacraments, church government; John Knox founded Scotch Presbyterian church about 1560.	[Highly structured representational system of ministers and lay persons (presbyters) in local, regional, and national bodies (synods).]	Scripture.	Infant baptism; Lord's Supper; bread and wine symbolize Christ's spiritual presence.
Roman Catholics	Traditionally, founded by Jesus who named St. Peter the 1st vicar; developed in early Christian proselytizing, especially after the conversion of imperial Rome in the 4th cent.	[Hierarchy with supreme power vested in pope elected by cardinals;] councils of bishops advise on matters of doctrine and policy.	[The pope, when speaking for the whole church in matters of faith and morals; and tradition (which is expressed in church councils and in part contained in Scripture).]	Mass; 7 sacraments: baptism, reconciliation, Eucharist, confirmation, marriage, ordination, and anointing of the sick (unction).
United Church of Christ	[By ecumenical union, in 1957, of Congregationalists and Evangelical & Reformed, representing both Calvinist and Lutheran traditions.]	Congregational; a General Synod, representative of all congregations, sets general policy.	Scripture.	Infant baptism; Lord's Supper.

How Do They Differ?

distinguish a denomination sharply from others.

Practice	Ethics	Doctrine	Other	Denomination
Worship style varies from staid to evangelistic; extensive missionary activity.	Usually opposed to alcohol and tobacco; some tendency toward a perfectionist ethical standard.	[No creed; true church is of believers only, who are all equal.]	Believing no authority can stand between the believer and God, the Baptists are strong supporters of church and state separation.	**Baptists**
Tries to avoid any rite not considered part of the 1st-century church; some congregations may reject instrumental music.	Some tendency toward perfectionism; increasing interest in social action programs.	Simple New Testament faith; avoids any elaboration not firmly based on Scripture.	Highly tolerant in doctrinal and religious matters; strongly supportive of scholarly education.	**Church of Christ (Disciples)**
Formal, based on "Book of Common Prayer," updated 1979; services range from austerely simple to highly liturgical.	Tolerant, sometimes permissive; some social action programs.	Scripture; the "historic creeds," which include the Apostles, Nicene, and Athanasian, and the "Book of Common Prayer"; ranges from Anglo-Catholic to low church, with Calvinist influences.	Strongly ecumenical, holding talks with many branches of Christendom.	**Episcopalians**
Meetings are held in Kingdom Halls and members' homes for study and worship; [extensive door-to-door visitations.]	High moral code; stress on marital fidelity and family values; avoidance of tobacco and blood transfusions.	[God, by his first creation, Christ, will soon destroy all wickedness; 144,000 faithful ones will rule in heaven with Christ over others on a paradise earth.]	Total allegiance proclaimed only to God's kingdom or heavenly government by Christ; main periodical, The Watchtower, is printed in 115 languages.	**Jehovah's Witnesses**
Simple service with prayers, hymns, sermon; private temple ceremonies may be more elaborate.	Temperance; strict moral code; [tithing]; a strong work ethic with communal self-reliance; [strong missionary activity]; family emphasis.	Jesus Christ is the Son of God, the Eternal Father. Jesus' atonement saves all humans; those who are obedient to God's laws may become joint-heirs with Christ in God's kingdom.	Mormons believe theirs is the true church of Jesus Christ, restored by God through Joseph Smith. Official name: The Church of Jesus Christ of Latter-day Saints.	**Latter-day Saints (Mormons)**
Relatively simple, formal liturgy with emphasis on the sermon.	Generally conservative in personal and social ethics; doctrine of "2 kingdoms" (worldly and holy) supports conservatism in secular affairs.	Salvation by grace alone through faith; Lutheranism has made major contributions to Protestant theology.	Though still somewhat divided along ethnic lines (German, Swedish, etc.), main divisions are between fundamentalists and liberals.	**Lutherans**
Worship style varies widely by denomination, local church, geography.	Originally pietist and perfectionist; always strong social activist elements.	No distinctive theological development; 25 Articles abridged from Church of England's 39, not binding.	In 1968, The United Methodist Church was formed by the union of The Methodist Church and The Evangelical United Brethren Church.	**Methodists**
[Elaborate liturgy, usually in the vernacular, though extremely traditional; the liturgy is the essence of Orthodoxy; veneration of icons.]	Tolerant; little stress on social action; divorce, remarriage permitted in some cases; bishops are celibate; priests need not be.	Emphasis on Christ's resurrection, rather than crucifixion; the Holy Spirit proceeds from God the Father only.	Orthodox Church in America originally under Patriarch of Moscow, was granted autonomy in 1970; Greek Orthodox do not recognize this autonomy.	**Orthodox**
Loosely structured service with rousing hymns and sermons, culminating in spirit baptism.	Usually, emphasis on perfectionism, with varying degrees of tolerance.	Simple traditional beliefs, usually Protestant, with emphasis on the immediate presence of God in the Holy Spirit.	Once confined to lower-class "holy rollers," Pentecostalism now appears in mainline churches and has established middle-class congregations.	**Pentecostal**
A simple, sober service in which the sermon is central.	Traditionally, a tendency toward strictness, with firm church- and self-discipline; otherwise tolerant.	Emphasizes the sovereignty and justice of God; no longer dogmatic.	Although traces of belief in predestination (that God has foreordained salvation for the "elect") remain, this idea is no longer a central element in Presbyterianism.	**Presbyterians**
Relatively elaborate ritual centered on the Mass; also rosary recitation, novenas, etc.	Traditionally strict, but increasingly tolerant in practice; divorce and remarriage not accepted, but annulments sometimes granted; celibate clergy, except in Eastern rite.	Highly elaborated; salvation by merit gained through grace; dogmatic; special veneration of Mary, the mother of Jesus.	Relatively rapid change followed Vatican Council II; Mass now in vernacular; more stress on social action, tolerance, ecumenism.	**Roman Catholics**
Usually simple services with emphasis on the sermon.	Tolerant; some social action emphasis.	Standard Protestant; "Statement of Faith" (1959) is not binding.	The 2 main churches in the 1957 union represented earlier unions with small groups of almost every Protestant denomination.	**United Church of Christ**

LANGUAGE

New Words in English

The following words and definitions were provided by Merriam-Webster Inc., publishers of *Merriam-Webster's Collegiate Dictionary, Eleventh Edition*, released in 2003. The words or meanings are among those that the Merriam-Webster editors decided had achieved enough currency in English to be added to this latest revision of the dictionary. (See also the glossary in the Science and Technology and Computers and the Internet chapters for some other new words.)

agita a feeling of agitation or anxiety

air rage an airline passenger's uncontrolled anger that is usually expressed in aggressive or violent behavior

bioterrorism terrorism involving the use of biological weapons

brick-and-mortar relating to or being a traditional business serving customers in a building as contrasted to an online business

comb-over an arrangement of hair on a balding man in which hair from the side of the head is combed over the bald spot

dead-cat bounce a brief and insignificant recovery (as of stock prices) after a steep decline

earbud a small earphone inserted into the ear

four-peat a fourth consecutive championship

Frankenfood genetically engineered food

funplex an entertainment complex that includes facilities for various sports and games and often restaurants

gaydar *slang*: the ability to recognize homosexuals through observation and intuition

hoodie a hooded sweatshirt

identity theft the illegal use of someone else's personal information (as a Social Security number) in order to obtain money or credit

LASIK a surgical operation to reshape the cornea for correction of myopia, farsightedness, or astigmatism

lip-lock a long, amorous kiss

McJob a low-paying job that requires little skill and provides little opportunity for advancement

narcoterrorism terrorism financed by profits from illegal drug trafficking

neuroimaging a clinical specialty concerned with producing images of the brain by noninvasive techniques (as computed tomography and magnetic resonance imaging)

new jack swing pop music usually performed by black musicians that combines elements of jazz, funk, rap, and rhythm and blues

paintball a game in which two teams try to capture each other's flag while defending their own using compressed-air guns that shoot paint-filled pellets

phallocratic relating to, resulting from, or advocating masculine power and dominance

piercing a piece of jewelry (as a ring or stud) that is attached to pierced flesh

pumped filled with energetic excitement and enthusiasm

punditocracy a group of powerful and influential political commentators

shock jock a radio personality noted for provocative or inflammatory commentary

smashmouth characterized by brute force without finesse

s'more a dessert consisting usually of toasted marshmallow and pieces of chocolate bar sandwiched between two graham crackers

strip mall a long, usually one-story building or group of buildings housing several adjacent retail stores or service establishments

tiki bar a restaurant or bar decorated in a simulated Polynesian theme that usually serves exotic cocktails

unplugged of, relating to, or being a musical instrument whose sound is not electronically modified

Eponyms
(words named for people)

Bloody Mary—a vodka and tomato juice drink; after the nickname of Mary I, Queen of England (1553-58), notorious for persecution of Protestants

bloomers—full, loose trousers that are gathered at the knee; after Amelia Bloomer, an American social reformer who advocated (1851) such clothing

bobbies—in Great Britain, police officers; after Sir Robert Peel, who organized the London police force in 1850

bowdlerize—to delete written matter considered indelicate; after Thomas Bowdler, English editor of an expurgated Shakespeare (1825)

boycott—to avoid trade or dealings with, as a protest; after Charles C. Boycott, an English land agent in County Mayo, Ireland, ostracized in 1880 for refusing to reduce rents

Braille—a system of writing for the blind; after Louis Braille, the French teacher of the blind who invented it (1853)

Casanova—a man who is a promiscuous and unscrupulous lover; after Giovanni Giacomo Casanova (1725-98), an Italian adventurer

chauvinist—excessively patriotic; after Nicolas Chauvin, a character in a 19th-cent. play who is devoted to Napoleon

derby—a stiff felt hat with a dome-shaped crown and rather narrow rolled brim; after Edward Stanley, 12th earl of Derby, who in 1780 founded the Derby horse race, to which these hats are worn

diesel—a type of internal combustion engine; after Rudolf Diesel (1858-1913), who built the first successful diesel engine

gerrymander—to draw an election district in such a way as to favor a political party; after Elbridge Gerry, who created (1812) just such an election district (shaped like a salamander) during his governorship of Massachusetts

guillotine—a machine for beheading; after Joseph Guillotin, a French physician who proposed its use in 1789 as more humane than hanging

leotard—a close-fitting garment, worn by dancers, acrobats, and the like; after Julius Leotard, a 19th-cent. French aerial gymnast

sandwich—2 or more slices of bread with a filling in between; after John Montagu, 4th earl of Sandwich (1718-92), who supposedly ate these at the gaming table

silhouette—an outline image; from Étienne de Silhouette (1709-67), a close-fisted French finance minister

National Spelling Bee

The Scripps Howard National Spelling Bee, conducted by Scripps Howard Newspapers and other leading newspapers since 1939, was instituted by the Louisville (KY) *Courier-Journal* in 1925. Children under 16 years old and not beyond 8th grade are eligible to compete for cash prizes at the finals, held annually in Washington, DC. (*Spellbound*, a film chronicling the experiences of 8 contestants in the 1999 spelling bee, was released in late 2002.) The 2003 winners were: 1st place, Sai Gunturi, Dallas, TX; 2nd place, Evelyn Blacklock, Middletown, NY.

Here are the last words given, and spelled correctly, in each of the years 1980-2003 at the national spelling bee.

1980	elucubrate	1985	milieu	1990	fibranne	1995	xanthosis	2000	demarche
1981	sarcophagus	1986	odontalgia	1991	antipyretic	1996	vivisepulture	2001	succedaneum
1982	psoriasis	1987	staphylococci	1992	lyceum	1997	euonym	2002	prospicience
1983	purim	1988	elegiacal	1993	kamikaze	1998	chiaroscurist	2003	pococurante
1984	luge	1989	spoliator	1994	antediluvian	1999	logorrhea		

Names of the Days

ENGLISH	RUSSIAN	HEBREW	FRENCH	ITALIAN	SPANISH	GERMAN	JAPANESE
Sunday	voskresenye	yom rishon	dimanche	domenica	domingo	Sonntag	nichiyoubi
Monday	ponedelnik	yom sheni	lundi	lunedì	lunes	Montag	getsuyoubi
Tuesday	vtornik	yom shlishi	mardi	martedì	martes	Dienstag	kayoubi
Wednesday	sreda	yom ravii	mercredi	mercoledì	miércoles	Mittwoch	suiyoubi
Thursday	chetverg	yom hamishi	jeudi	giovedì	jueves	Donnerstag	mokuyoubi
Friday	pyatnitsa	yom shishi	vendredi	venerdì	viernes	Freitag	kinyoubi
Saturday	subbota	shabbat	samedi	sabato	sábado	Samstag	doyoubi

Foreign Words and Phrases

(F=French; Ger=German; Gk=Greek; I=Italian; L=Latin; S=Spanish; Y=Yiddish)

ad absurdum (L; ad ahb-SUR-dum): to the point of absurdity

ad hoc (L; ad HOK): for the end or purpose at hand; impromptu.

ad hominem (L; ad HOH-mee-nem): emotional rather than intellectual; in a dispute, using slander to obscure issues.

adios (S; ah-di-OHS): goodbye

antebellum (L; AHN-teh-BEL-lum): pre-war

apercu(s) (F; ah-per-SOO): first perception or insight; outline

auf Wiedersehen (Ger; owf-VEE-duh-zehn): Good-bye

belles lettres (F; bel-LET-truh): writing valued for artistic merit

bête noire (F; BET NWAHR): a thing or person viewed with particular dislike or fear

Bildungsroman (Ger; BIL-doongs-roh-mahn): novel with coming-of-age story

bourgeois (F; boo-ZHWAH): middle-class; conventional; materialistic

carte blanche (F; kahrt BLANSH): full discretionary power

cause célèbre (F; kawz suh-LEB-ruh): a notorious incident

cognoscenti (I; koh-nyoh-SHEN-tee): experts; connoissuers

contretemps (F; kon-truh-TAHM): awkward situation

coup de grâce (F; kooh duh GRAHS): the final blow

cum laude/magna cum laude/summa cum laude (L; kuhm LOUD-ay; MAGN-a ...; SOO-ma ...): with praise or honor/with great praise or honor/with the highest praise or honor

de facto (L; day FAK-toh): in fact, if not by law

de jure (L; dee JOOR-ee, day YOOR-ay): in accordance with right or law; officially

de rigueur (F; duh ree-GUR): necessary according to convention or etiquette

détente (F; day-TAHNT): an easing of strained relations

double entendre (F; DOO-blahn-TAHN-druh): expression with with double meaning, one meaning of which is often risqué

éminence grise (F; ay-meh-nahns-GREEZ): one who wields power behind the scenes

enfant terrible (F; ahn-FAHN te-REE-bluh): one who is noteworthy for embarrassing or unconventional behavior

ennui (F; ah-NOOEE): boredom; world-weariness; annoyance

e pluribus unum (L; eh-PLOO-ree-boos-OO-noom): out of many, one (U.S. motto)

ersatz (Ger; EHR-zats): artificial, inferior

esprit de corps (F; es-PREE duh KAWR): group spirit; feeling of camaraderie

eureka (Gk; yoor-EE-kuh): I have found it!; hurrah!

ex post facto (L; eks pohst FAK-toh): retroactive(ly)

fait accompli (F; fayt uh-kom-PLEE): an accomplished fact

habeas corpus (L; HAY-bee-ahs KOR-pus): an order for an accused person to be brought to court

hasta la vista (S; asta-la-VIS-ta): goobye

hoi polloi (Gk; hoy puh-LOY): the masses

in loco parentis (L; in LOH-koh puh-REN-tis): in place of parent

in omnibus (L; in OHM-nee-bus): in all things; in all ways

je ne sais quoi (F; zhuh nuh say KWAH): I don't know what; the little something that eludes description

joie de vivre (F; zhwah duh VEEV-ruh): zest for life

mano a mano (S; MAH-noh ah MAH-noh): hand to hand; in direct combat

mea culpa (L; MAY-uh CUL-puh): through my fault

mensch (Y; mensh): an upright, noble, admirable person

modus operandi (L; MOH-duhs op-uh-RAN-dee): method of operation

noblesse oblige (F; noh-BLES oh-BLEEZH): the obligation of nobility to help the less fortunate

nolo contendere (L; NOH-loh-kohn-TEN-deh-reh): "I will not contest," a plea of no defense, equivalent to a plea of guilty.

non compos mentis (L; non KOM-puhs MEN-tis): not of sound mind

nouveau riche (F; noo-voh REESH): a person newly rich, perhaps one who spends money conspicuously

par excellence (F; par ek-seh-LANS): best of all; incomparable.

parvenu (F; par-vuh-NOO): upstart

persona non grata (L; per-SOH-nah non GRAH-tah): unwelcome person

pro bono (L; proh BOH-noh): (legal work) donated for the public good

qué será será (S; keh sair-AH sair-AH): what will be will be

quid pro quo (L; kwid proh KWOH): something given or received for something else

raison d'être (F; RAY-zohnn DET-ruh): reason for being

sans souci (F; SAHNN sooh-SEE): without worry

savoir faire (F; sav-wahr-FAIR): dexterity in social affairs

Schadenfreude (Ger; SHAH-d'n-froy-deh): joy at another's misfortune

schlemiel (Y; shleh-MEEL): an unlucky, bungling person

schlepp (Y; shlep): move slowly, tediously, drag oneself along

semper fidelis (L; SEM-puhr fee-DAY-lis): always faithful

sobriquet (F; soh-bree-KAY): nickname

terra firma (L; TER-uh FUR-muh): solid ground

tour de force (F; TOOR duh FAWRS): feat accomplished through great skill

vis-à-vis (F; vee-zuh-VEE): compared with; with regard to

zeitgeist (Ger; ZITE-gyste): the general intellectual, moral, and cultural climate of an era

Names for Animal Young

bunny: rabbit
calf: cattle, elephant, antelope, rhino, hippo, whale, others
cheeper: grouse, partridge, quail
chick, chicken: fowl
cockerel: rooster
codling, sprag: codfish
colt: horse (male)
cub: lion, bear, shark, fox, others
cygnet: swan

duckling: duck
eaglet: eagle
elver: eel
eyas: hawk, others
fawn: deer
filly: horse (female)
fingerling: fish generally
flapper: wild fowl
fledgling: birds generally
foal: horse, zebra, others
fry: fish generally
gosling: goose
heifer: cow

joey: kangaroo, others
kid: goat
kit: fox, beaver, rabbit, cat
kitten, kitty, catling: cats, other small mammals
lamb, lambkin, cosset, hog: sheep
leveret: hare
nestling: birds generally
owlet: owl
parr, smolt, grilse: salmon
piglet, shoat, farrow, suckling: pig

polliwog, tadpole: frog
poult: turkey
pullet: hen
pup: dog, seal, sea lion, fox
puss, pussy: cat
spike, blinker, tinker: mackerel
squab: pigeon
squeaker: pigeon, others
whelp: dog, tiger, beasts of prey
yearling: cattle, sheep, horse, others

Names for Animal Collectives

alligators: congregation
ants: army or colony
apes: shrewdness
badgers: cete
bats: colony
bears: sleuth
bees: grist or swarm
birds: flight or volery
boars/swine: sounder
butterflies: flutter
buzzards: wake
camels: train or caravan
cats: clowder or clutter
cattle: drove
chicks: brood or clutch
clams/oysters: bed
cockroaches: intrusion
cormorants: gulp

cranes: sedge or siege
crocodiles: bask
crows: murder
doves: dule or pitying
ducks: brace or team
eagles: convocation
elephants: herd
elks: gang
finches: charm
fish: school or shoal
flamingos: stand
foxes: skulk
frogs: army
geese: flock, gaggle, or skein
gnats: cloud or horde
goats: tribe or trip
gorillas: band
grasshoppers: cloud

hares: down or husk
hawks: cast
horses: pair or team
hounds: cry, mute, or pack
jellyfish: smack
kangaroos: mob or troop
kittens: kindle or kendle
larks: exaltation
leopards: leap
lions: pride
monkeys: troop
mules: span
nightingales: watch
oxen: yoke
partridge/quail: covey
peacocks: muster
pheasants: nest or nide
pigs: litter

ravens: unkindness
rhinoceroses: crash
seals: pod
sharks: shiver
sheep: flock, drove
snakes: nest
squirrels: dray or scurry
swans: bevy
swine: drift
tigers: streak
toads: knot
turkeys: gang or rafter
turtles: bale
vultures: committee
whales: gam
wolves: pack
woodchuck: fall
woodpeckers: descent

Some Common Abbreviations and Acronyms

Acronyms are pronounceable words formed from first letters (or syllables) of other words. Some **abbreviations** below (e.g., AIDS, NATO) are thus acronyms. Some acronyms are words coined as abbreviations and written in lower case (e.g., "radar," "yuppie"). Acronyms do not have periods: usage for other abbreviations varies, but periods have become less common. Capitalization usage may vary from what is shown here. Italicized words preceding parenthetical definitions below are Latin unless otherwise noted. See also other chapters, including Computers and the Internet; Weights and Measures.

AA=Alcoholics Anonymous; Associate in Arts; administrative assistant
AAA=American Automobile Association
AARP=American Association of Retired Persons
ABA=American Bar Association
AC=alternating current
AD=*anno Domini* (in the year of the Lord)
AFL-CIO=American Federation of Labor and Congress of Industrial Organizations
AI=artificial intelligence
AIDS=acquired immune deficiency syndrome
AM=*ante meridiem* (before noon)
AMA=American Medical Association
anon=anonymous
APO=army post office
APR=annual percentage rate
ASCAP=American Society of Composers, Authors, and Publishers
ASPCA=American Society for Prevention of Cruelty to Animals
ATM=automated teller machine
AWOL=absent without leave
BA=Bachelor of Arts
bbl=barrel(s)
BC=before Christ
BCE=before Common Era
bpd=barrels per day
BS=Bachelor of Science
Btu=British thermal unit(s)
bu=bushel(s)
BYOB=bring your own bottle
C= Celsius, centigrade
c=*circa* (about), copyright
CAT=computerized axial tomography
CDC=Centers for Disease Control and Prevention
CE=Common Era
CEO=chief executive officer
cf.=*confer* (compare)
CFO=chief financial officer
CIA=Central Intelligence Agency
CIF=cost, insurance, and freight
CIO=chief information officer
COD=cash (or collect) on delivery
Col.=Colonel
COO=chief operating officer
CPA=certified public accountant
CPI=Consumer Price Index
Cpl.=Corporal
CPR=cardiopulmonary resuscitation
CPU=central processing unit
CST=Central Standard time
DA=district attorney
DC=direct current
DD=Doctor of Divinity
DDS=Doctor of Dental Science (or Surgery)
DMD=Doctor of Dental Medicine
DMZ=demilitarized zone
DNA=deoxyribonucleic acid
DNR=do not resuscitate
DOA=dead on arrival
DOB=date of birth
dpi=dots per inch
DUI=driving under the influence
DVD=digital video disc
DVM=Doctor of Veterinary Medicine
DWI=driving while intoxicated
ed.=edited, edition, editor
EEG=electroencephalogram
e.g.=*exempli gratia* (for example)
EKG=electrocardiogram
EOE=equal opportunity employer
EPA=Environmental Protection Agency

ERA=Equal Rights Amendment; earned run average
ESP=extrasensory perception
EST=Eastern Standard time
et al.=*et alii* (and others)
etc.=*et cetera* (and so forth)
EU=European Union
EVA=extravehicular activity
F=Fahrenheit
FBI=Federal Bureau of Investigation
FDA=Food and Drug Administration
FDIC=Federal Deposit Insurance Corp.
FEMA=Federal Emergency Management Agency
ff.=and those following
FICA=Federal Insurance Contributions Act (Social Security)
fl.=*floruit* (flourished), used for historical figures when dates of birth and death uncertain
FOB=free on board
FTE=full-time equivalent
FY=fiscal year
FYI=for your information
GB=gigabyte(s)
GDP=gross domestic product
GED=general equivalency diploma (for high school)
GMT=Greenwich mean time
GNP=gross national product
GOP=Grand Old Party (Republican Party)
Hazmat=hazardous material
Hon.=the Honorable
HOV=high-occupancy vehicle
HRH=her (his) royal highness
HVAC=heating, ventilating, and air-conditioning
Hz=hertz
ibid=*ibidem* (in the same place)
i.e.=*id est* (that is)
IMF=International Monetary Fund
IOC=International Olympic Committee
IQ=intelligence quotient
IRA=individual retirement account; Irish Republican Army
IRS=Internal Revenue Service
ISBN=International Standard Book Number
JD=*Juris Doctor* (doctor of laws)
K=Kelvin
k=karat
K of C=Knights of Columbus
kWh=kilowatt-hour(s)
laser=Light Amplification by Stimulated Emission of Radiation
Lieut. or Lt.=Lieutenant
LLB=*Legum Baccalaurens* (Bachelor of Laws)
LLP=limited licensed partners
loc. cit.=*loco citato* (in the place cited)
MA=Master of Arts
MBA=Master of Business Administration
MV=megabyte(s)
MD=*Medicinae Doctor* (doctor of medicine)
MFN=most favored nation
MIA=missing in action
modem=MOdulator-DEModulator
mph=miles per hour
MRI=magnetic resonance imaging
MS=Master of Science; manuscript; multiple sclerosis
MSG=monosodium glutamate
MVP=most valuable player
NA=not applicable; not available
NAACP=National Association for the Advancement of Colored People

NAFTA=North American Free Trade Agreement
NASA=National Aeronautics and Space Administration
NATO=North Atlantic Treaty Org.
NB=*nota bene* (note carefully)
NCAA=National Collegiate Athletic Assn.
NIH=National Institutes of Health
NOW=National Organization for Women
NRA=National Rifle Association
OE=Old English
op=*opus* (work)
OPEC=Organization of Petroleum Exporting Countries
OTC=over the counter
p, pp=page(s)
PAC=political action committee
Ph.D.=*Philosophiae Doctor* (doctor of philosophy)
PIN=Personal Identification Number
PM=*post meridiem* (afternoon)
PS=*post scriptum* (postscript)
PST=Pacific Standard time
pt=part(s), pint(s), point(s)
Pvt.=Private
q.v.=*quod vide* (which see)
radar=radio detecting and ranging
REM=rapid eye movement
Rev.=Reverend
rev.=revised
RFD=rural free delivery
RIP=*requiescat in pace* (May he/she rest in peace)
RN=registered nurse
RNA=ribonucleic acid
ROTC=Reserve Officers' Training Corps
rpm=revolutions per minute
RSVP=*répondez s'il vous plaît* (Fr.) (Please reply)
SARS=severe acute respiratory syndrome
SASE=self-addressed stamped envelope
Sgt.=Sergeant
SIDS=suddent infant death syndrome
S.J.=Society of Jesus (Jesuits)
sonar=sound navigation and ranging
SRO=standing room only
SSI=Supplementary Security Income
SUV=sport utility vehicle
TBA=to be announced
TBD=to be determined
TGIF=thank God it's Friday
UFO=unidentified flying object
UPC=Universal Product Code
USS=United States ship
UTC=coordinated univeral time
v (or vs)=*versus* (against)
VCR=videocassette recorder
W=watt(s)
WHO=World Health Organization
WMD=weapons of mass destruction
WPM=words per minute
YTD=year to date
yuppie=young urban professional
ZIP=zone improvement plan (U.S. Postal Service)

Top 10 First Names of Americans by Decade of Birth

Source: Compiled by Dr. Cleveland Kent Evans, Bellevue University, Bellevue, NE; based on Social Security Administration records

BOYS:

1880-1889	John, William, Charles, George, James, Frank, Joseph, Harry, Henry, Edward
1890-1899	John, William, George, James, Charles, Joseph, Frank, Robert, Harry, Henry
1900-1909	John, William, James, George, Joseph, Charles, Robert, Frank, Edward, Henry
1910-1919	John, William, James, Robert, Joseph, Charles, George, Edward, Frank, Walter
1920-1929	John, Robert, James, William, Charles, George, Joseph, Richard, Edward, Donald
1930-1939	Robert, James, John, William, Richard, Charles, Donald, George, Thomas, Joseph
1940-1949	James, Robert, John, William, Richard, David, Charles, Thomas, Michael, Ronald
1950-1959	Michael, James, Robert, John, David, William, Steven, Richard, Thomas, Mark
1960-1969	Michael, John, David, James, Robert, Mark, Steven, William, Jeffrey, Richard
1970-1979	Michael, Christopher, Jason, David, James, John, Brian, Robert, Steven, William
1980-1989	Michael, Christopher, Matthew, Joshua, David, Daniel, James, John, Robert, Brian
1990-1999	Michael, Christopher, Matthew, Joshua, Nicholas, Jacob, Andrew, Daniel, Brandon, Tyler

GIRLS:

1880-1889	Mary, Anna, Elizabeth, Catherine, Margaret, Emma, Bertha, Minnie, Florence, Clara
1890-1899	Mary, Anna, Margaret, Helen, Catherine, Elizabeth, Florence, Ruth, Rose, Ethel
1900-1909	Mary, Helen, Margaret, Anna, Ruth, Catherine, Elizabeth, Dorothy, Marie, Mildred
1910-1919	Mary, Helen, Dorothy, Margaret, Ruth, Catherine, Mildred, Anna, Elizabeth, Frances
1920-1929	Mary, Dorothy, Betty, Helen, Margaret, Ruth, Virginia, Catherine, Doris, Frances
1930-1939	Mary, Betty, Barbara, Shirley, Patricia, Dorothy, Joan, Margaret, Carol, Nancy
1940-1949	Mary, Linda, Barbara, Patricia, Carol, Sandra, Nancy, Sharon, Judith, Susan
1950-1959	Deborah, Mary, Linda, Patricia, Susan, Barbara, Karen, Nancy, Donna, Catherine
1960-1969	Lisa, Deborah, Mary, Karen, Michelle, Susan, Kimberly, Lori, Teresa, Linda
1970-1979	Jennifer, Michelle, Amy, Melissa, Kimberly, Lisa, Angela, Heather, Kelly, Sarah
1980-1989	Jessica, Jennifer, Ashley, Sarah, Amanda, Stephanie, Nicole, Melissa, Katherine, Megan
1990-1999	Ashley, Jessica, Sarah, Brittany, Emily, Kaitlyn, Samantha, Megan, Brianna, Katherine

> ▶ **IT'S A FACT:** The top ten baby names in 2002, according to the Social Security Administration, were: **boys,** Jacob, Michael, Joshua, Matthew, Ethan, Joseph, Andrew, Christopher, Daniel, Nicholas; **girls,** Emily, Madison, Hannah, Emma, Alexis, Ashley, Abigail, Sarah, Samantha, Olivia.

Origins of Popular American Given Names

Source: Dr. Cleveland Kent Evans, Bellevue University, Bellevue, NE

Boys

Andrew: Gr. *andreios*, "man, manly"
Brandon: Eng. place name, "gorse-covered hill"
Brian: Irish, perhaps Celtic Brigonos, "high, noble"
Charles: Ger. *ceorl*, "free man"
Christopher: Gr. *Khristophoros*, "bearing Christ [in one's heart]"
Daniel: Heb. "God is my judge"
David: Heb. *Dodavehu*, perhaps "darling"
Donald: Scots Gaelic *Domhnall*, "world rule"
Edward: Old Eng. *Eadweard*, "wealth-guard"
Ethan: Heb. "solid," "firm"

Frank: Ger. "Frenchman"
George: Gr. *georgos*, "soil tiller, farmer"
Harry: Middle Eng. form of Henry
Henry: Ger. *Haimric*, "home-power"
Jacob: Heb. *Yaakov*, "God protects" or "supplanter"
James: Late Lat. *Iacomus*, form of Jacob
Jason: Gr. *Iason*, "healer"
Jeffrey: Norman Fr., from Ger. *Gaufrid*, "land-peace," or *Gisfrid*, "pledge-peace"
John: Heb. *Yohanan*, "God is gracious"
Joseph: Heb. *Yosef*, "[God] shall add"
Joshua: Heb. *Yoshua*, "God saves"
Mark: Lat. *Marcus*, perhaps "of Mars, the war god"

Matthew: Heb. *Mattathia*, "gift of God"
Michael: Heb. "Who could ever be like God?"
Nicholas: Gr. *Nikolaos*, "victory-people"
Patrick: Lat. *Patricius*, "belonging to the noble class"
Richard: Ger. "power-hardy"
Robert: Ger. *Hrodberht*, "fame-bright"
Sean: Gaelic form of John
Steven: Gr. *stephanos*, "crown, garland"
Theodore: Gr. *Theodoros*, "gift of God"
Thomas: Aramaic "twin"
Tyler: Old Eng. *tigeler*, "tile layer"
Walter: Ger. *Waldheri*, "rule-army"
William: Ger. *Wilhelm*, "will-helmet"

Girls

Abigail: Heb. "My father is joy"
Alexis: Gr. "helper" or "defender"
Amanda: 17th-cent. invention from Lat., "lovable"
Amy: Old Fr. *Amee*, "beloved"
Angela: Gr. *angelos*, "messenger [of God]"
Ann (Eng. form), **Anne** (Eng., Fr., Ger. form) of Hannah
Anna: Lat. and Gr. form of Hannah
Ashley: Eng. place name, "ash grove"
Barbara: Gr. *barbarus*, "foreign"
Bertha: Ger. *behrt*, "bright"
Betty: 18th-cent. pet form of Elizabeth
Brianna: modern fem. form of Brian
Brittany: place name, Fr. province settled by Britons
Carol: form of Charles
Clara: Lat. *clarus*, "famous"
Deborah: Heb. "bee"
Donna: Ital. "lady"
Doris: Gr. "woman of the Dorian tribe," name of a sea nymph
Dorothy: Gr. *Dorothea*, "gift of God"
Elizabeth: Heb. *Elisheba*, perhaps "God is my oath" or "God is good fortune"
Emily: Roman *Aemilia*, possibly from Lat. *aemulus*, "rival"
Emma: Ger. *ermen*, "whole, entire"
Ethel: Old Eng. *aethel*, "noble"
Florence: Lat. *florens*, "flourishing"
Frances: fem. form of Francis, "a Frenchman"

Haley: Eng. place name, "hay clearing"
Hannah: Heb. "He has favored me"
Heather: Middle Eng. *hathir*, "heather"
Helen: Gr. *Helene*, possibly "sunbeam"
Jennifer: Cornish form of Welsh *Gwenhwyfar*, "fair-smooth"
Jessica: Shakespearean invention, probably fem. form of Jesse, Heb. "God exists"
Joan: Middle Eng. fem. form of John
Judith: Hebrew "Jewish woman"
Kaitlyn: American spelling of Caitlin, the Irish form of Katherine
Karen: Danish form of Katherine
Katherine: from *Aikaterine*, Egyptian name later modified to resemble Gr. *katharos*, "pure"
Kelly: Irish Gaelic *Ceallagh*, perhaps "churchgoer" or "bright-headed"
Kimberly: Eng. place name, "Cyneburgh's clearing"
Linda: Sp. "pretty" or Ger. "tender"
Lisa: pet form of Elizabeth
Lori: pet form of either Lorraine (French "land of Lothar's people") or Laura (Latin "laurel")
Madison: Middle Eng. surname, "son of Madeline or Maud"
Margaret: Gr. *margaron*, "pearl"
Maria: Lat. form of Mary
Marie: Fr. form of Mary
Mary: Eng. form of Heb. *Maryam*, perhaps "seeress" or "wished-for child"

Megan: Welsh form of Margaret
Melissa: Gr. "bee"
Michelle: Fr. fem. form of Michael
Mildred: Old Eng. *Mildthryth*, "mild-strength"
Minnie: Pet form of Wilhelminia, fem. form of William
Nancy: medieval Eng. pet form of Agnes, Gr. *hagnos*, "holy"; later also used as pet form for Ann
Nicole: Fr. fem. form of Nicholas
Patricia: Lat. fem. form of Patrick
Rose: Ger. *hros*, "horse," or Lat. *rosa*, "rose"
Ruth: Heb., perhaps "companion"
Samantha: colonial American invention, probably combining Sam from Samuel [Heb. "name of God"] with -antha from Gr. *anthos*, "flower"
Sandra: short form of Alessandra, Ital. fem. of Alexander, Gr. "defend-man"
Sarah: Heb., "princess"
Sharon: Biblical place name, Hebrew "plain"
Shirley: Eng. place name, "bright clearing" or "shire meadow"
Stephanie: Fr. fem. form of Steven
Susan: Eng. form of Heb. *Shoshana*, "lily"
Teresa: Spanish, perhaps "woman from Therasia"
Virginia: Lat., "virgin-like"

PALINDROMES

DID HANNAH SAY AS HANNAH DID? is a palindrome. A palindrome, from Greek words for "run back again," reads the same backward as forward. Famous palindromes range from Adam's possible introduction to his wife ("Madam, I'm Adam.") to a slogan that could have applied to Theodore Roosevelt ("A man, a plan, a canal, Panama!"). Some are one word only (e.g., "deified," "kayak," "radar") or simple phrases (e.g. "senile felines," "war, sir, is raw"). Some are more involved (e.g., "Deer flee freedom in Oregon? No, Geronimo, deer feel freed.")

Forms of Address

	Address	Salutation
GOVERNMENT		
President of the U.S.	The President, The White House, Washington, DC 20500; also, The President and Mrs. ____ or The President and Mr.	Dear Sir or Madam; Mr. President or Madam President; Dear Mr. President or Dear Madam President
U.S. Vice President	The Vice President, The White House, Washington, DC 20500; also, The Vice President and Mrs. ____ or The Vice President and Mr. ____	Dear Sir or Madam; Mr. Vice President or Madam Vice President; Dear Mr. Vice President or Dear Madam Vice President
Chief Justice	The Hon. *Firstname Surname*, Chief Justice of the U.S., The Supreme Court, Washington, DC 20543	Dear Sir or Madam; Dear Mr. or Madam Chief Justice
Associate Justice	The Hon. Justice *Firstname Surname*, The Supreme Court, Washington, DC 20543	Dear Sir or Madam; Dear Justice *Surname*
Judge	The Hon. *Firstname Surname*, Associate Judge, U.S. District Court	Dear Judge *Surname*
Attorney General	The Hon. *Firstname Surname*, Attorney General, Dept. of Justice, Constitution Ave. & 10th St. NW, Washington, DC 20530	Dear Sir or Madam; Dear Mr. or Ms. Attorney General
Cabinet Officer	The Hon. *Firstname Surname*, Secretary of ____	Dear Mr. or Madam Secretary; or Dear Mr. or Ms. *Surname*
Senator	The Hon. or Sen. *Firstname Surname*, U.S. Senate, Washington, DC 20510	Dear Mr. or Madam Senator, or Dear Mr. or Ms. *Surname*
Representative	The Hon. or Rep. *Firstname Surname*, House of Representatives, Washington, DC 20515	Dear Mr. or Madam *Surname*
Speaker of the House	The Hon. Speaker of the House of Representatives, House of Representatives, Washington, DC 20515	Dear Mr. or Madam Speaker
Ambassador, U.S.	The Hon. *Firstname Surname*, American Ambassador[1]	Sir or Madam; Dear Mr. or Madam Ambassador
Ambassador, Foreign	His or Her Excellency[2] *Firstname Surname*, Ambassador of ____	Excellency[2] ; Dear Mr. or Madam Ambassador
Governor	The Hon. *Firstname Surname*, Governor of *State*; or in some states, His or Her Excellency, the Governor of *State*	Sir or Madam; Dear Governor *Surname*
Mayor	The Hon. *Firstname Surname*, Mayor of *City*	Sir or Madam; Dear Mayor *Surname*
MILITARY PERSONNEL		
All Titles	Full or abbreviated rank + full name + comma + abbreviation for branch of service. *Example*: Adm. John Smith, USN	Dear *Rank Surname*
RELIGIOUS		
Clergy, Protestant	The Reverend *Firstname Surname*[3]	Dear Ms. or Mr. *Surname*
Pope	His Holiness Pope *Name* or His Holiness the Pope	Your Holiness or Most Holy Father
Priest	The Reverend *Firstname Surname* or The Reverend Father *Surname*	Reverend Father, Dear Father *Surname*, or Dear Father
Rabbi	Rabbi *Firstname Surname*	Dear Rabbi *Surname*
ROYALTY AND NOBILITY		
King/Queen	His or Her Majesty, King or Queen of *Country*	Sir or Madam, or May it please Your Majesty

(1) If in Canada or Latin America, The Ambassador of the United States of America. (2) An American ambassador is not properly addressed as His or Her Excellency. (3) A member of the Protestant clergy who has a doctorate may be so addressed; for example, The Reverend Firstname Surname, DD, and Dear Dr. Surname.

Commonly Misspelled English Words

accidentally	Cincinnati	existence	irresistible	mysterious	receipt
accommodate	collectible	fascinating	judgment	necessary	restaurant
acknowledgment	commitment	feasible	laboratory	noticeable	rhythm
acquainted	committee	February	leisure	occasionally	ridiculous
acquire	connoisseur	fluorine	library	occurrence	separate
across	conscientious	foreign	license	opportunity	seize
all right	conscious	forty	lieutenant	optimistic	sincerely
already	convenience	gauge	lightning	parallel	stubbornness
amateur	deceive	government	liquefy	performance	supersede
appearance	defendant	grammar	maintenance	permanent	tangible
appropriate	definite	grateful	marriage	permissible	temperament
bureau	desirable	harass	medieval	perseverance	temperature
business	despair	humorous	millennium	personnel	transferred
calendar	desperate	hurrying	miniature	possess	truly
Caribbean	eligible	incidentally	miscellaneous	privilege	twelfth
cemetery	eliminate	independent	Mississippi	propaganda	Wednesday
changeable	embarrass	indispensable	misspelled	questionnaire	weird
chrysanthemum	environment	inoculate	mnemonic	receive	wholly

Commonly Confused English Words

adverse: unfavorable
averse: opposed

affect: to influence
effect: to bring about

allusion: an indirect reference
illusion: an unreal impression

appraise: to set a value on
apprise: to inform

biannual: occurring twice a year
biennial: occurring every two years

capital: the seat of government
capitol: building where a legislature meets

complement: to make complete; something that completes
compliment: to praise; praise

counselor: one who gives advice or counsel
councilor: a member of a council

denote: to mean
connote: to suggest beyond the explicit meaning

discreet: prudent
discrete: separate, distinct

disinterested: impartial
uninterested: without interest

elicit: to draw or bring out
illicit: illegal

emigrate: to leave for another place
immigrate: to come to another place

ensure: to make certain
insure: to protect against
assure: to inform postively or confidently

exalt: to glorify
exult: to rejoice

farther: at a greater distance
further: to a greater extent or degree

fewer: a smaller number (of things)
less: a smaller amount (of something)

grisly: inspiring horror or great fear
grizzly: sprinkled or streaked with gray

historic: important in history
historical: relating to history

hoard: a supply stored up and often hidden
horde: a teeming croud or throng

I: nominative case
me: objective case

immanent: inherent; residing within
imminent: ready to take place
eminent: standing out

imply: to suggest but not explicitly
infer: to assume or understand information not relayed explicitly

include: used when the items following are part of a whole
comprise: used when the items following are all of a whole

ingenious: clever
ingenuous: innocent

it's: it is
its: a possessive adjective

lay: to put or place
lie: (intransitive) to recline or rest

oral: spoken, as opposed to written
verbal: relating to language

principal: n., business owner, head of school; adj., most important
principle: a basic law or truth; a moral or ethical standard

their: belonging to them
there: in that place
they're: they are

who: nominative case
whom: objective case

your: belonging to you
you're: you are

► **IT'S A FACT:** In February 1863, after writing under such names as "Sergeant Fathom," "Thomas Jefferson Snodgrass," and "W. Epaminandos Adrastus Blab," Samuel Langhorne Clemens adopted the pseudonym Mark Twain, a phrase used by riverboat pilots on the Mississippi that means "2 fathoms deep," that is, safe clearance for the riverboat.

Pen Names

Shalom Aleichem	Solomon J. Rabinowitz
Woody Allen	Allen Stewart Konigsberg
Currer, Ellis, and Acton Bell	Charlotte, Emily, and Anne Brontë
John le Carré	David John Moore Cornwell
Lewis Carroll	Charles Lutwidge Dodgson
Colette	Sidonie Gabrielle Colette
Amanda Cross	Carolyn Heilbrun
Isak Dinesen	Karen Blixen
Elia	Charles Lamb
George Eliot	Mary Ann or Marian Evans
Maksim Gorky	Aleksey Maksimovich Peshkov
O. Henry	William Sydney Porter
James Herriot	James Alfred Wight
P. D. James	Phyllis Dorothy James White

[John] Ross Macdonald	Kenneth Millar
André Maurois	Émile Herzog
Molière	Jean Baptiste Poquelin
Toni Morrison	Chloe Anthony Wofford
Frank O'Connor	Michael Donovan
George Orwell	Eric Arthur Blair
Mary Renault	Mary Challans
Ellery Queen	Frederic Dannay and Manfred B. Lee
Françoise Sagan	Françoise Quoirez
Saki	Hector Hugh Munro
George Sand	Amandine Lucie Aurore Dupin
Dr. Seuss	Theodor Seuss Geisel
Stendhal	Marie Henri Beyle
Mark Twain	Samuel Clemens
Voltaire	François Marie Arouet

WORLD ALMANAC EDITORS' PICKS
Favorite First Lines From Novels

The editors of *The World Almanac* have ranked the following as their 10 favorite familiar first lines from novels. (The definition of novel was slightly stretched, to include *The Metamorphosis*, which is generally considered to be a long short story, or novelette.)

1. "It was the best of times, it was the worst of times, it was the age of wisdom, it was the age of foolishness, it was the epoch of belief, it was the epoch of incredulity, it was the season of Light, it was the season of Darkness, it was the spring of hope, it was the winter of despair, we had everything before us, we had nothing before us, we were all going direct to Heaven, we were all going direct the other way—in short, the period was so far like the present period, that some of its noisiest authorities insisted on its being received, for good or for evil, in the superlative degree of comparison only." — *A Tale of Two Cities*, Charles Dickens

2. "Call me Ishmael." — *Moby Dick,* Herman Melville

3. "Happy families are all alike, but every unhappy family is unhappy in its own way."— *Anna Karenina*, Leo Tolstoy

4. "It is a truth universally acknowledged, that a single man in possession of a good fortune, must be in want of a wife." — *Pride and Prejudice*, Jane Austen

5. "Many years later, as he faced the firing squad, Colonel Aureliano Buendia was to remember that distant afternoon when his father took him to discover ice." — *One Hundred Years of Solitude*, Gabriel Garcia Marquez

6. "When Gregor Samsa woke up one morning from unsettling dreams, he found himself changed into a monstrous vermin." — *The Metamorphosis*, Franz Kafka

7. "Last night I dreamt I went to Manderley again." — *Rebecca*, Daphne Du Maurier

8. "It was a bright cold day in April, and the clocks were striking thirteen." — *1984*, George Orwell

9. "Whether I shall turn out to be the hero of my own life, or whether that station will be held by anybody else, these pages must show." — *David Copperfield*, Charles Dickens

10. "If you really want to hear about it, the first thing you'll probably want to know is where I was born, and what my lousy childhood was like, and how my parents were occupied and all before they had me, and all that David Copperfield kind of crap, but I don't feel like going into it, if you want to know the truth." — *The Catcher in the Rye*, J. D. Salinger

Readers are invited to submit their own list for this and other Editors' Picks; see instructions on page 1007. Results will be published in *The World Almanac 2005*.

American Manual Alphabet

In the American Manual Alphabet, each letter of the alphabet is represented by a position of the fingers. This system was originally developed in France by Abbe Charles Michel De l'Epee in the late 1700s. It was brought to the United States by Laurent Clerce (1785-1869), a Frenchman who taught deaf or hearing-impaired people.

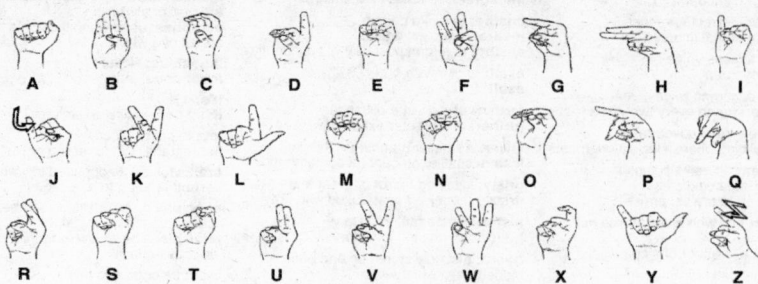

The Principal Languages of the World

Source: From Ethnologue Volume 1, Languages of the World, 14th edition,
Edited by Barbara F. Grimes. © 2000 by SIL International. Used by permission.
The following tables count only "first language" speakers. All figures are estimates, as of 2000.

Languages Spoken by the Most People

Speakers (millions)		Speakers (millions)		Speakers (millions)		Speakers (millions)	
Chinese, Mandarin	874	Bengali	207	German, Standard	100	Javanese	75
Hindi	366	Portuguese	176	Korean	78	Chinese, Yue	71
English	341	Russian	167	French	77	Telugu	69
Spanish	322	Japanese	125	Chinese, Wu	77		

Languages Spoken by at Least 2 Million People

A "Hub" country is the country of origin, not necessarily the country where the most speakers reside (e.g., Portugal is the "hub" country of Portuguese, although more Portuguese speakers live in Brazil).

Language	Hub	Countries	Speakers (millions)	Language	Hub	Countries	Speakers (millions)
Chinese, Mandarin	China	16	874	Farsi, Western	Iran	26	24
Hindi	India	17	366	Hausa	Nigeria	13	24
English	United Kingdom	104	341	Maithili	India	2	24
Spanish	Spain	43	322-358	Arabic, Algerian, spoken	Algeria	6	22
Bengali	Bangladesh	9	207	Serbo-Croatian	Serbia & Montenegro	7	21
Portuguese	Portugal	33	176	Thai	Thailand	5	20-25
Russian	Russia	30	167	Yoruba	Nigeria	5	20
Japanese	Japan	26	125	Dutch	Netherlands	14	20
German, standard	Germany	40	100	Awadhi	India	2	20
Korean	Korea, South	31	78	Chinese, Gan	China	1	20
French	France	53	77	Sindhi	Pakistan	7	19
Chinese, Wu	China	1	77	Arabic, Moroccan, spoken	Morocco	8	19
Javanese	Indonesia	4	75	Arabic, Saidi, spoken	Egypt	1	18
Chinese, Yue	China	20	71	Igbo	Nigeria	1	18
Telugu	India	7	69	Uzbek, Northern	Uzbekistan	12	18
Marathi	India	3	68	Malay	Malaysia	8	18
Vietnamese	Vietnam	20	68	Indonesian	Indonesia	6	17-30
Tamil	India	15	66	Tagalog	Philippines	8	17
Italian	Italy	29	62	Amharic	Ethiopia	4	17
Turkish	Turkey	35	61	Nepali	Nepal	4	16
Urdu	Pakistan	21	60	Arabic, Sudanese, spoken	Sudan	5	16-19
Ukrainian	Ukraine	25	47	Arabic, N. Levantine, spoken	Syria	15	15
Gujarati	India	17	46	Saraiki	Pakistan	3	15-30
Arabic, Egyptian, spoken	Egypt	9	46	Cebuano	Philippines	2	15
Chinese, Jinyu	China	1	45	Assamese	India	3	15
Chinese, Min Nan	China	9	45	Thai, Northeastern	Thailand	1	15-23
Polish	Poland	21	44	Hungarian	Hungary	11	14
Chinese, Xiang	China	1	36	Chittagonian	Bangladesh	2	14
Malayalam	India	9	35	Haryanvi	India	1	13
Kannada	India	1	35	Sinhala	Sri Lanka	7	13
Chinese, Hakka	China	16	33	Madura	Indonesia	2	13
Oriya	India	2	32	Arabic, Mesop., spoken	Iraq	5	13
Burmese	Myanmar	5	32	Greek	Greece	35	12
Panjabi, Western	Pakistan	7	30-45	Marwari	India	2	12
Sunda	Indonesia	1	27	Czech	Czech Republic	9	12
Panjabi, Eastern	India	11	27	Magahi	India	1	11
Romanian	Romania	17	26	Chhattisgarhi	India	1	11
Bhojpuri	India	3	26				
Azerbaijani, South	Iran	8	24				

Language	Hub	Countries	Speakers (millions)
Zhuang, Northern	China	1	10
Belarusan	Belarus	16	10
Deccan	India	1	10
Chinese, Min Bei	China	2	10
Arabic, Najdi, spoken	Saudi Arabia	7	9
Zulu	South Africa	6	9
Pashto, Southern	Afghanistan	6	9
Somali	Somalia	12	9-10
Arabic, Tunisian, spoken	Tunisia	5	9
Swedish	Sweden	7	9
Malagasy	Madagascar	3	9
Bulgarian	Bulgaria	11	9
Pashto, Northern	Pakistan	5	9
Lombard	Italy	3	8
Ilocano	Philippines	2	8
Oromo, West-Central	Ethiopia	2	8
Kazakh	Kazakhstan	13	8
Tatar	Russia	19	7
Haitian-Creole French	Haiti	8	7
Fulfulde, Nigerian	Nigeria	3	7
Hiligaynon	Philippines	2	7
Uyghur	China	16	7
Shona	Zimbabwe	4	7
Khmer, Central	Cambodia	6	7
Kurmanji	Turkey	25	7-8
Akan	Ghana	1	7
Azerbaijani, North	Azerbaijan	9	7
Arabic, Sanaani, spoken	Yemen	1	7
Napoletano-Calabrese	Italy	1	7
Farsi, Eastern	Afghanistan	2	7
Rwanda	Rwanda	5	7
Arabic, Hijazi spoken	Saudi Arabia	2	6
Luba-Kasai	Dem. Rep. of Congo	1	6
Thai, Northern	Thailand	2	6
Finnish	Finland	7	6
Arabic, N. Mesopotamian, spoken	Iraq	4	6
Afrikaans	South Africa	10	6
Arabic, S. Levantine, spoken	Jordan	8	6
Armenian	Armenia	29	6
Rundi	Burundi	4	6
Santali	India	4	6
Alemannisch	Switzerland	5	6
Catalan-Valencian-Balear	Spain	18	6
Turkmen	Turkmenistan	13	6
Xhosa	South Africa	3	6
Kanauji	India	1	6
Arabic, Taizzi-Adeni, spoken	Yemen	5	6
Minangkabau	Indonesia	1	6
Kurdi	Iraq	3	6
Sylhetti	Bangladesh	2	5
Slovak	Slovakia	8	5
Swahili	Tanzania	12	5
Thai, Southern	Thailand	1	5
Tigrigna	Ethiopia	3	5
Hebrew	Israel	8	5
Nyanja	Malawi	6	5
Danish	Denmark	8	5
Guarani, Paraguayan	Paraguay	2	5
Gikuyu	Kenya	1	5
Moore	Burkina Faso	6	5
Sukuma	Tanzania	1	5
Norwegian, Bokmaal	Norway	6	5
Lithuanian	Lithuania	19	4
Oromo, Eastern	Ethiopia	1	4
Tswana	Botswana	4	4
Arabic, Libyan, spoken	Libya	3	4
Sotho, Southern	Lesotho	3	4
Umbundu	Angola	2	4
Kashmiri	India	3	4
Konkani	India	1	4
Galician	Spain	2	4
Georgian	Georgia	13	4
Luri	Iran	3	4
Tajiki	Tajikistan	7	4
Sicilian	Italy	1	4

Language	Hub	Countries	Speakers (millions)
Kituba	Dem. Rep. of Congo	1	4
Zhuang, Southern	China	1	4
Bali	Indonesia	1	3
Kabyle	Algeria	3	3
Gilaki	Iran	1	3
Aceh	Indonesia	1	3
Kanuri, Central	Nigeria	6	3
Emiliano-Romagnolo	Italy	2	3
Mazanderani	Iran	1	3
Wolof	Senegal	7	3
Yiddish, Eastern	Israel	20	3
Shan	Myanmar	3	3
Luo	Kenya	2	3
Luyia	Kenya	2	3
Tachelhit	Morocco	3	3
Malay, Pattani	Thailand	1	3
Tamazight, Central Atlas	Morocco	3	3
Quechua, South Bolivian	Bolivia	2	3
Balochi, Southern	Pakistan	4	3
Ganda	Uganda	2	3
Albanian, Tosk	Albania	9	3
Kongo	Dem. Rep. of Congo	3	3
Oromo, Borana-Arsi-Guji	Ethiopia	3	3
Bugis	Indonesia	2	3
Lao	Laos	5	3
Banjar	Indonesia	2	3
Mbundu, Loanda	Angola	1	3
Piedmontese	Italy	3	3
Tsonga	South Africa	4	3
Mongolian, Peripheral	China	2	3
Sotho, Northern	South Africa	2	3
Kamba	Kenya	1	2
Garhwali	India	1	2
Dogri-Kangri	India	1	2
Mundari	India	3	2
Venetian	Italy	3	2
Lambadi	India	1	2
Bemba	Zambia	5	2
Sasak	Indonesia	1	2
Aymara, Central	Bolivia	4	2
Karen, Sgaw	Myanmar	2	2
Albanian, Gheg	Serbia & Montenegro	7	2
Kirghiz	Kyrgyzstan	7	2
SW-Caribbean-Creole English	Jamaica	7	2
Betawi	Indonesia	1	2
Macedonian	Macedonia	7	2
Tumbuka	Malawi	3	2
Rajbangsi	India	3	2
Batak Toba	Indonesia	1	2
Arabic, Gulf, spoken	Iraq	9	2
Waray-Waray	Philippines	1	2
Mongolian, Halh	Mongolia	4	2
Malagasy, Southern	Madagascar	1	2
Konkani, Goanese	India	3	2
Kalenjin	Kenya	1	2
Bicolano, Central	Philippines	1	2
Bagri	India	2	2
Zarma	Niger	5	2
Baoule	Côte d'Ivoire	1	2
Kumauni	India	2	2
Lomwe	Mozambique	2	2
Tarifit	Morocco	4	2
Saxon, Upper	Germany	1	2
Kurux	India	2	2
Makhuwa	Mozambique	2	2
Maninka, Kankan	Guinea	3	2
Tiv	Nigeria	2	2
Bamanankan	Mali	7	2
Ewe	Ghana	2	2
Pulaar	Senegal	6	2
Hassaniyya	Mauritania	6	2
Arakanese	Myanmar	3	2
Slovenian	Slovenia	10	2
Jula	Burkina Faso	3	2
Bouyei	China	2	2
Brahui	Pakistan	4	2
Fuuta Jalon	Guinea	6	2

> **IT'S A FACT:** When counting things in Japanese, suffixes called "counters" are attached to each number. Over 500 different "counters" are used in the language, depending on the object being counted. For example, *go* is the basic word for "five," but when counting flat things you must add *mai (gomai)*, when counting people you (usually) add *nin (gonin)*, when counting books you add *satsu (gosatsu)*, and so forth.

ASSOCIATIONS AND SOCIETIES

Source: World Almanac questionnaire; World Almanac research

Selected list, by first distinctive key word in each title. (Listed by acronym when that is the official name.) Founding year in parentheses; figure after ZIP code = membership as reported. Information, especially website addresses, subject to change. For other organizations, see Directory of Sports Organizations; Where to Get Help directory in Health chapter; Labor Union Directory in Employment chapter; Membership of Religious Groups in the U.S.; Major International Organizations in Nations chapter.

AACSB-The Intl. Assoc. for Management Education (1916), 600 Emerson Rd., Ste. 300, St. Louis, MO 63141; 941 institutions; www.aacsb.edu

Abortion Federation, National (1977), 1755 Massachusetts Ave. NW, Ste. 600, Wash., DC 20036; 440 institutions; www.prochoice.org

Academies, Natl. (1863), 500 Fifth St. NW, Wash., DC 20001; approx. 6,000; www.nationalacademies.org

Accountants, American Institute of Certified Public (1887), 1211 Ave. of the Americas, New York, NY 10036; 328,000+; www.aicpa.org

Acoustical Society of America (1929), 2 Huntington Quad., Ste. 1NO1, Melville, NY 11747; 7,000; asa.aip.org

Actuaries, Society of (1949), 475 N. Martingale Rd., Ste. 600, Schaumburg, IL 60173; 17,000; www.soa.org

Administrative Professionals, Intl. Assn. of (1942), 10502 NW Ambassador Dr., PO Box 20404, Kansas City, MO 64195-0404; 40,000; www.iaap-hq.org

Advancement and Support of Education, Council for (1974); 1307 New York Ave. NW, Ste. 1000, Wash., DC 20005; 23,500 members, 3000 schools; www.case.org

Aeronautic Assn., Natl. (1922), 1815 N. Fort Myer Dr., Ste. 500, Arlington, VA 22209; 3,000; www.naa-usa.org

Aerospace Industries Assn. of America Inc. (1919), 1000 Wilson Blvd., Ste. 1700, Arlington, VA 22209; 63 cos.; www.aia-aerospace.org

Aerospace Medical Assn. (1929), 320 S. Henry St., Alexandria, VA 22314; 3,300; www.asma.org

AFCEA (Armed Forces Communications and Electronics Assn.) (1946), 4400 Fair Lakes Ct., Fairfax, VA 22033; 20,000 indiv., 10,000 corp.; www.afcea.org

African-American Life and History, Assn. for the Study of (1915), 7961 Eastern Ave., Ste. 301, Silver Spring, MD 20910; 1,200; www.asalh.org

African Violet Soc. of America Inc. (1946), 2375 North St., Beaumont, TX 77702; 9,000; www.avsa.org

AFS Intercultural Programs USA (1947), 198 Madison Ave., 8th Fl., New York, NY 10016; www.afs.org/usa

Agricultural Economics Assn., American (1910), 415 S. Duff Ave., Ste. C, Ames, IA 50010; 3,500; www.aaea.org

Agricultural Engineers, American Soc. of (ASAE) (1907), 2950 Niles Road, St. Joseph, MI 49085; 9,000; www.asae.org

Air & Waste Management Assn. (1907), One Gateway Center, 3rd Fl., 420 Fort Duquesne Blvd., Pittsburgh, PA 15222; 8,000+; www.awma.org

Aircraft Owners and Pilots Assn. (1939), 421 Aviation Way, Frederick, MD 21701; 390,000+; www.aopa.org

Air Force Assn. (1946), 1501 Lee Hwy., Arlington, VA 22209; 142,000+; www.afa.org

Al-Anon Family Group Headquarters, Inc. (1951), 1600 Corporate Landing Pkwy., Virginia Beach, VA 23454; 350,000+ worldwide; www.al-anon.alateen.org

Alcoholics Anonymous (1935), 475 Riverside Dr., New York, NY 10115; 2,215,293; www.aa.org

Alcoholism and Drug Dependence, Inc., Natl. Council on (1944), 20 Exchange Pl., Ste. 2902, New York, NY 10005; 100 affil.; www.ncadd.org

Alexander Graham Bell Assn. for the Deaf & Hard of Hearing (1890), 3417 Volta Pl. NW, Wash., DC 20007; 5,000; www.agbell.org

Allergy, Asthma, and Immunology, American Academy of (1943), 611 E. Wells St., Milwaukee, WI 53202; 6,000+; www.aaaai.org

Alpha Delta Kappa Sorority Inc. (1947), 1615 West 92nd St., Kansas City, MO 64114; 48,756; www.alphadeltakappa.org

Alpha Lambda Delta, Natl. (1924), P.O. Box 4403, Macon, GA 31208-4403;700,000; www.mercer.edu/ald

Alpine Club, American (1902), 710 Tenth St., Ste. 100, Golden, CO 80401; 7,000; www.americanalpineclub.org

Alzheimer's Assn. (1980), 225 N. Michigan Ave., 17th Fl., Chicago, IL 60611; www.alz.org

Amateur Chamber Music Players, Inc. (1969), 1123 Broadway, Rm. 304, New York, NY 10010-2007; 5,4300; www.acmp.net

Amateur Radio Union, Intl. (IARU) (1925), P.O. Box 310905, Newington, CT 06131; 150 org.; www.iaru.org

AMBUCS, Inc., Natl. (1922), 3315 N Main St., High Point, NC 27262; 5,400; www.ambucs.com

American Indians, Natl. Congress of (1944), 1301 Connecticut Ave. NW, Ste. 200, Wash., DC 20036; 250+ member tribes; www.ncai.org

American-Islamic Relations, Council on, 453 New Jersey Ave. SE, Wash., DC 20003; www.cair-net.org

American Legion (1919), P.O. Box 1055, 700 N. Pennsylvania St., Indianapolis, IN 46206; 3 mil.+; www.legion.org

American Legion Auxiliary (1919), 777 N. Meridian St., 3rd Floor, Indianapolis, IN 46204; 910,000+; www.legion-aux.org

Americares Foundation (1982), 161 Cherry St., New Canaan, CT 06840; www.americares.org

AMIDEAST (formerly American Mideast Educational & Training Services) (1951), 1730 M St. NW, Ste. 1100, Wash., DC 20036; www.amideast.org

Amnesty Intl. USA (1961), 322 8th Ave., New York, NY 10001; 320,000+; www.amnestyusa.org

Amputation Foundation, Inc., Natl. (1919), 40 Church St., Malverne, NY 11565; 750; www.nationalamputation.org

AMVETS (American Veterans) (1943); **AMVETS Natl. Auxiliary** (1946), 4647 Forbes Blvd., Lanham, MD 20706; 250,000; www.amvets.org

Amusement Parks and Attractions, Intl. Assn. of (IAAPA) (1918), 1448 Duke St., Alexandria, VA 22314; 4,000; www.iaapa.org

Animals, American Society for Prevention of Cruelty to (ASPCA) (1866), 424 E. 92nd St., New York, NY 10128; 687,267; www.aspca.org

Animal Protection Institute (1968), 1122 S St., Sacramento, CA 95814; 85,000; www.api4animals.org

Animal Welfare Institute (1951), P.O. Box 3650, Wash., DC 20027; 23,000 www.awionline.org

Anthropological Assn., American (1902), 2200 Wilson Blvd., Ste. 600, Arlington, VA 22201; 11,500; www.aaanet.org

Antiquarian Society, American (1812), 185 Salisbury St., Worcester, MA 01609; 675; www.americanantiquarian.org

Anti-Vivisection Society, American (AAVS), (1883), 801 Old York Road, #204, Jenkintown, PA 19046; 12,000; www.aavs.org

APICS (1957), 5301 Shawnee Rd., Alexandria, VA 22312-2317; 70,000; www.apics.org

Appalachian Mountain Club (1876), 5 Joy St., Boston, MA 02108; 90,000+; www.outdoors.org

Appalachian Trail Conference (1925), 799 Washington St., P.O. Box 807, Harpers Ferry, WV 25425; 125,000; www.appalachiantrail.org

Arbitration Assn., American (1926), 335 Madison Ave., Fl. 10, New York, NY 10017; 7,000; www.adr.org

Arc of the United States, The (1950), 1010 Wayne Avenue, Ste. 650, Silver Spring, MD 20910; 140,000+; www.thearc.org

Archaeological Institute of America (1879), 656 Beacon St., 4th Fl., Boston, MA 02215; 10,000; www.archaeological.org

Archery Assn. of the United States, Natl. (1879), One Olympic Plaza, Colorado Springs, CO 80909; 6,000; www.USArchery.org

Architects, American Institute of (1857), 1735 New York Ave. NW, Wash., DC 20006; 63,000; www.aia.org

ARMA Intl. (formerly Assn. of Records Managers & Administrators) (1955), 13725 W. 109th St., Lenexa, KS 66218; 10,000; www.arma.org

Army, Assn. of the United States (1950), 2425 Wilson Blvd., Arlington, VA 22201; 117,000; www.ausa.org

Arthritis Foundation (1948), 1330 W. Peachtree St., Atlanta, GA 30309; www.arthritis.org

Arts, Americans for the (1996), 1000 Vermont Ave. NW, 6th Fl., Wash., D.C. 20005; 1,500; www.artsusa.org

Arts and Sciences, American Academy of (1780), Norton's Woods, 136 Irving St., Cambridge, MA 02138; 4,300 fellows; www.amacad.org

ASPRS, The Imaging and Geospatial Information Society (1934), 5410 Grosvenor Ln., Ste. 210, Bethesda, MD 20814; 7,000; www.asprs.org

Associated Press (1848), 50 Rockefeller Plaza, New York, NY 10020; 1,500+ newspapers, 5,000+ U.S. broadcast stations; www.ap.org

Astrologers, Inc., American Federation of (AFA, Inc.) (1938), 6535 South Rural Road, Tempe, AZ 85283; 3,500; www.astrologers.com

Astronautical Society, American (1954), 6352 Rolling Mill Pl., # 102, Springfield, VA 22152; 1,500; www.astronautical.org

Astronomical Society, American (1899), 2000 Florida Ave. NW, #400, Wash., DC 20009; 7,500; www.aas.org

Ataxia Foundation, Natl. (1957), 2600 Fernbrook Ln., Ste. 119, Minneapolis, MN 55447-4752; 10,000; www.ataxia.org

Atheists, American (1963), P.O. Box 5733, Parsippany, NJ 07054; 2,300; www.atheists.org

Audubon Soc., Natl. (1905), 700 Broadway, New York, NY 10003; 600,000; www.audubon.org

Authors Guild, The (1912), 31 E. 28th St., New York, NY 10016; 8,200; www.authorsguild.org

> **IT'S A FACT:** The Bald-Headed Men of America, which is actually open to "all Men, Women, and Children around the world who believe 'Bald is Beautiful,'" says it is the only organization in the world that grows because of a lack of growth.

Authors Registry, The (1995), 31 E. 28th St., New York, NY 10016; 30,000; www.authorsregistry.org

Autism Soc. of America (1965), 7910 Woodmont Ave., Ste. 300, Bethesda, MD 20814; 24,000; www.autism-society.org

Autograph Collectors Club, Universal (1965), P.O. Box 6181, Wash., DC 20044-6181; 1,450; www.uacc.org

Automobile Club of America, Antique (1935), 501 W. Governor Road, P.O. Box 417, Hershey, PA 17033; 60,000; www.aaca.org

Automobile License Plate Collectors Assn. (1953), 7365 Main. St., #214, Stratford, CT 06614; 3,200; www.alpca.org

Automotive Hall of Fame (1939), 21400 Oakwood Blvd., Dearborn, MI 48124; 200; www.automotivehalloffame.org

Badminton, USA (1938), One Olympic Plaza, Colorado Springs, CO 80909; 4,000; www.usabadminton.org

Bald-Headed Men of America (1973), 102 Bald Dr., Morehead City, NC 28557; approx. 22,000; members.aol.com/baldusa

Bar Assn., American (1878), 541 N. Fairbanks Ct., Chicago, IL 60611; 400,000+; www.abanet.org

Bar Assn., Federal (1920), 2215 M Street NW, Wash., DC 20037; 16,000; www.fedbar.org

Barber Shop Quartet Singing in America, Inc., Soc. for the Preservation & Encouragement of (1938), 7930 Sheridan Rd., Kenosha, WI 53143; 33,000+; www.spebsqsa.org

Baseball Congress, American Amateur (1935), 118-119 Redfield Plaza, P.O. Box 467, Marshall, MI 49068; 14,500 teams; www.aabc.us

Baseball Congress, Natl. (1935), 300 S. Sycamore, P.O. Box 1420, Wichita, KS 67201; 35,000; www.nbcbaseball.com

Baseball Research, Inc., Society for American (1971), 812 Huron Road E #719, Cleveland, OH 44115; 6,500; www.sabr.org

Battleship Assn., American (1964), P.O. Box 711247, San Diego, CA 92171; 1,109

Beer Can Collectors of America (1970), 747 Merus Ct., Fenton, MO 63026; 4,000; www.bcca.com

Beta Gamma Sigma, Inc. (1913), 125 Weldon Parkway, Maryland Heights, MO 63043; 470,000; www.betagamasigma.org

Beta Sigma Phi (1931), 1800 W. 91st Pl., Kansas City, MO 64114; 165,00; www.betasigmaphi.org

Better Business Bureaus, Council of (1970), 4200 Wilson Blvd., Suite 800, Arlington, VA 22203; 150 bureaus; www.bbb.org

Bible Society, American (1816), 1865 Broadway, New York, NY 10023; 650,000; www.americanbible.org

Biblical Literature, Society of (1947), 825 Houston Mill Rd., Ste. 350, Atlanta, GA 30329; 2,700; www.sbl-site.org

Bibliographical Society of America (1904), P.O. Box 1537, Lenox Hill Station, New York, NY 10021; 1,200; www.bibsoc amer.org

Big Brothers/Big Sisters of America (1904), 230 N. 13th St., Philadelphia, PA 19107; 494 agencies; bbbsa.org

Biochemistry and Molecular Biology, American Society for (1905), 9650 Rockville Pike, Bethesda, MD 20814; 11,250; www.asbmb.org

Biological Sciences, American Institute of (1947), 1444 I St. NW, Ste. 200, Wash., DC 20005; 6,000; www.aibs.org

Blind, American Council of the (1961), 1155 15th St. NW, Ste. 1004, Wash., DC 20005; 25,000; www.acb.org

Blind, Natl. Federation of the (1940), 1800 Johnson St., Baltimore, MD 21230; 50,000; www.nfb.org

Blinded Veterans Assn. (1958), 477 H St. NW, Wash., DC 20001; 9,970; www.bva.org

Blindness America, Prevent (1908), 500 E. Remington Rd., Ste. 200, Schaumburg, IL 60173; 50,000; www.prevent blindness.com

B'nai B'rith Intl. (1843), 2020 K St. NW, 7th Fl., Wash., DC 20006; 250,000; www.bbinet.org

Boat Owners Assn. of the U.S. (1966), 880 S. Pickett St., Alexandria. VA 22304; 540,000; www.boatUS.com

Bookplate Collectors and Designers, American Soc. of (1922), P.O. Box 380340, Cambridge, MA 02238-0340; 250; www.bookplate.org

Boy Scouts of America (1910), 1325 Walnut Hill Lane, Irving, TX 75015; 8 mil+; www.bsa.scouting.org

Boys & Girls Clubs of America (1906), 1230 W. Peachtree St. NW, Atlanta, GA 30309; 3.3 mil; www.bgca.org

Bread for the World (1974), 50 F St. NW, Ste. 500, Washington, DC 20001; 47,000; www.bread.org

Brewing Chemists, American Society for (1934), 3340 Pilot Knob Road, St. Paul, MN 55121-2097; approx. 1,000; www.asbcnet.org

Broadcasters, Natl. Assn. of (1923), 1771 N St. NW, Wash., DC 20036; www.nab.org

Burroughs Bibliophiles, The (1960), 454 Elaine Dr., Pittsburgh, PA 15236-2417; 852

Business Communicators, Intl. Assn. of (1970), 1 Hallidie Plaza, Ste. 600, San Francisco, CA 94102; 13,700; www.iabc.com

Business Women's Assn., American (1949), 9100 Ward Pkwy., P.O. Box 8728, Kansas City, MO 64114; 55,000; www.abwa.org

Button Society, Natl. (1938), c/o Lois Pool, 2733 Juno Pl., Akron, OH 44333-4137; 4,000

Camp Fire USA (formerly Camp Fire Boys & Girls) (1910), 4601 Madison Ave., Kansas City, MO 64112; 650,000; www.campfireusa.org

Camping Assn., American (1910), 5000 State Rd. 67 N., Martinsville, IN 46151; 6,700; www.acacamps.org

Cancer Society, American (1913), 2200 Lake Blvd., Atlanta, GA 30319; 3400 local offices; www.cancer.org

Cartoonists Society, Natl. (1948), 1133 West Morse Blvd., Ste. 201, Winter Park, FL 32789; 600; www.reuben.org

Cat Fanciers' Assn., The (1906), 1805 Atlantic Ave., P.O. Box 1005, Manasquan, NJ 08736-0805; www.cfainc.org

Catholic Bishops, United States Conference of (1966), 3211 4th St. NE, Wash., DC 20017; 402 members, 350 staff; www.nccbuscc.org

Catholic Church Extension Society of the USA (1905), 150 S. Wacker Dr., Chicago, IL 60606; 54 staff; www.catholic-extension.org/Home.cfm

Catholic Daughters of the Americas (1903), 10 West 71st Street, New York, NY 10023; 100,000; www.catholic daughters.org

Catholic Educational Assn., Natl. (1904), 1077 30th St. NW, Ste. 100, Wash., DC 20007; 200,000; www.ncea.org

Catholic Historical Soc., American (1884), 263 S. Fourth St., Philadelphia, PA 19106-3819; 425; www.AMCHS.org

Catholic Library Association (1921), 100 North St., Ste. 224, Pittsfield, MA 01201-5109; 1,000; www.cathla.org

Catholic War Veterans, USA Inc. (1935), 441 N. Lee St., Alexandria, VA 22314-2301; 20,000; cwv.org

Cemetery and Funeral Assn., Intl. (1887), 1895 Preston White Dr., #220, Reston, VA 22091; 6,000; www.icfa.org

Ceramic Society, The American (1899), 735 Ceramic Pl., Westerville, OH 43081; 8,000; www.ceramics.org

Cereal Chemists, American Society of (1915), 3340 Pilot Knob Road, St. Paul, MN 55121-2097; 3,020; www.aacc net.org

Cerebral Palsy Assns., Inc., United (1949), 1660 L St. NW, Ste. 700, Wash., DC 20036; 150; www.ucpa.org

Certification of Computing Professionals, Institute for (1973), 2350 E. Devon Ave., Ste. 115, Des Plaines, IL 60018-4610; 50,000; www.iccp.org

Chamber of Commerce of the U.S.A. (1912), 1615 H St. NW, Wash., DC 20062; 215,000; www.uschamber.com

Chamber Music Players, Inc., Amateur (1947), 1123 Broadway, Rm. 304, New York, NY 10010; 5,400; www.acmp.net

Checker Federation, American (1949), 5304 Barton Vale Ct., Nashville, TN 37211; 500; www.acfcheckers.com

Chemical Society, American (1876), 1155 16th St. NW, Wash., DC 20036; 163,000; www.chemistry.org

Chemistry Council, American (1872), 1300 Wilson Blvd., Arlington, VA 22209; 170; www.americanchemistry.com

Chess Federation, U.S. (1939), 3054 US Rt. 9W, New Windsor, NY 12553; 90,000+; www.uschess.org

Chiefs of Police, Intl. Assn. of (1893), 515 N. Washington St., Alexandria, VA 22314; 19,000; www.theiacp.org

Childhood Education Intl., Assn. for (1892), 17904 Georgia Ave., Ste. 215, Olney, MD 20832; 10,000; www.acei.org

Children's Aid Society (1912), 181 West Valley Ave., Ste. 300, Homewood, AL 35209; www.childrensaid.org

Children's Book Council, The (1945), 12 W. 37th St., 2nd Fl., New York, NY 10018; 78 publishers; www.cbcbooks.org

Child Welfare League of America (1920), 440 First St. NW, Third Fl., Wash., DC 20001; 1,100 agencies; www.cwla.org

Chiropractic Assn., American (1963), 1701 Clarendon Blvd., Arlington, VA 22209; 19,000; www.amerchiro.org

Chris-Craft Antique Boat Club (1973), 217 S. Adams St., Tallahassee, FL 32301-1708; 3,000; www.chris-craft.org

Christian Children's Fund (1938), 2821 Emerywood Pkwy., Richmond, VA 23294; 161; www.christianchildrensfund.org

Cities, Natl. League of (1924), 1301 Pennsylvania Ave. NW, Ste. 550, Wash., DC 20004; 1,780; www.nlc.org

Citizen Information Center, Federal (1970), Pueblo, CO 81009; www.pueblo.gsa.gov

Civil Air Patrol (1941), 105 S. Hansell St., Maxwell AFB, AL 36112; 60,000; www.capnhq.gov

Civil Engineers, American Society of (1852), 1801 Alexander Bell Dr., Reston, VA 20191; 123,000+; www.asce.org

Civil Liberties Union, American (ACLU) (1920), 125 Broad St., 18th Fl., New York, NY 10004; 380,000; www.aclu.org

Clean Energy Research Inst. (1973), Univ. of Miami, Coral Gables, FL 33124; 500; www.miami.edu

Coaster Enthusiasts, American (1978), 7700 Shawnee Mission Pkwy, Ste. 201, Overland Park, KS 66202; 8,420; www.aceonline.org

Coast Guard Combat Veterans Assn. (1985), 295 Shalimar Dr., Shalimar, FL 32579; 1,800; www.aug.edu/~libwrw/cgcva/cgcva.htm

Co-dependents Anonymous (1986), PO Box 33577; Phoenix, AZ 85067; www.codependents.org

College Admission Counseling, Natl. Assn. for (1937), 1631 Prince Street, Alexandria, VA 22314; 8,000; www.nacac.com

College Board, The (1900), 45 Columbus Ave., New York, NY 10023; 4,300+ institutions; www.collegeboard.org

College Music Society, The (1958), 312 East Pine St., Missoula, MT 59802; 8,800; www.music.org

Colleges and Employers, Natl. Assn. of (1956), 62 Highland Ave., Bethlehem, PA 18017; 3,700; www.jobweb.org

Colleges and Universities, Assn. of American (1915), 1818 R St. NW, Wash., DC 20009; 850+ institutions; www.aacu.org

Colonial Dames XVII Century, Natl. Soc. (1915), 1300 New Hampshire Ave. NW, Wash., DC 20036; 13,240; www.execpc.com/~sril/ilcd17.html

Commercial Collectors, Inc., Int'l. Assn. of (1970), 4040 W. 70th Street, Minneapolis, MN 55435; 450; www.commercial collector.com

Commercial Law League of America (1895), 150 N. Michigan Avenue, # 600, Chicago, IL 60601; 3,400; www.clla.org

Common Cause (1970), 1250 Connecticut Ave. NW, Ste. 600, Wash., DC 20036; 200,000+; www.commoncause.org

Communication Assn., Natl. (1914), 1765 N St. NW, Wash., DC, 20036; 5,600; www.natcom.org

Community and Justice, National Conference for (1927), 475 Park Ave. S.; New York, NY 10016; 3,500; www.nccj.org

Community Colleges, American Assn. of (1920), One Dupont Circle NW, Ste. 410, Wash., DC 20036; 1,113 inst; www.aacc.nche.edu

Composers, Authors & Publishers, American Soc. of (ASCAP) (1914), One Lincoln Plaza, New York, NY 10023; 160,000+; www.ascap.com

Composers/USA, Natl. Assn. of (1932), P.O. Box 49256, Barrington Station, Los Angeles, CA 90049; 600; www.music-usa.org/nacusa

Computing Machinery, Assn. for (1947), 1515 Broadway, 17th Fl., New York, NY 10036; 75,000+; www.acm.org

Concerned Women for America (1979), 1015 Fifteenth St. NW, Ste. 1100, Wash., DC 20005; 500,000; www.cwfa.org

Congress of Racial Equality (CORE) (1942), 817 Broadway, 3rd Floor, New York, NY 10003; 100,000; www.core-online.org

Conscientious Objectors, Central Committee for (1948), 630 20th St., #302, Oakland, CA 94612; 5,000-6,000; www.objector.org

Construction Inspectors, Assn. of (1974), 1224 N. Nokomis NE, Alexandria, MN 56308; 1,000; www.iami.org/aci

Construction Specifications Institute (1948); 99 Canal Center Plaza, Ste. 300, Alexandria, VA 22301; 17,500; www.csinet.org

Consumer Federation of America (1968), 1424 16th St. NW, Ste. 604, Wash., DC 20036; 300 member organizations; www.consumerfed.org

Consumer Interests, American Council on (ACCI) (1953), 415 S Duff Ave. Ste. C, Ames, IA 50010; 750; www.consumerinterests.org

Consumers Union of the U.S (1936), 101 Truman Ave., Yonkers, NY 10703; 405,990; www.consumersunion.org

Contract Bridge League, American (1937), 2990 Airways Blvd., Memphis, TN 38116; 170,000; www.acbl.org

Co-op America (1982), 1612 K St. NW, Ste. 600, Wash., DC 20006; 50,000 individuals, 2,000 businesses; www.coopamerica.org

Correctional Assn., American (1870), 4380 Forbes Blvd., Lanham, MD 20706; 20,000; www.aca.org

Cosmetology Assn., Natl. (1921); 401 N. Michigan Ave., Chicago, IL 60611; 30,000; www.salonprofessionals.org

Counseling Assn., American (1952), 5999 Stevenson Ave., Alexandria, VA 22304; 55,000; www.counseling.org

Country Music Assn. (1958), One Music Circle S, Nashville, TN 37203; 6,700; www.CMAworld.com

Crafts & Creative Industries, Assn. of (ACCI) (1976), 1100-H Brandywine Blvd., P.O. Box 3388, Zanesville, OH 43702; 6,327; www.accicrafts.org

Crime and Delinquency, Natl. Council on (1907), 1970 Broadway, Ste. 500, Oakland, CA 94612; 300+; www.nccd-crc.org

Croplife America (1933), 1156 15th St. NW, Ste. 400, Wash., DC 20005; 80 cos.; www.croplifeamerica.org

Cryogenic Soc. of America, Inc. (1967), 1033 South Blvd., Ste. 13, Oak Park, IL 60302; 3829; www.cryogenicsociety.org

Customs Brokers and Forwarders Assn. of America, Inc., Natl. (1897), 1200 18th St. NW, Ste. 901, Wash., DC 20036; 800; www.ncbfaa.org

Cystic Fibrosis Foundation (1955), 6931 Arlington Rd., Bethesda, MD 20814; 30,000; www.cff.org

Dark-Sky Association, Intl.(1988), 3225 N. First Ave., Tucson, AZ 85719-2103; 10,179; www.darksky.org

Daughters of the American Revolution, Natl. Society (1890), 1776 D Street NW, Wash., DC 20006; 170,000; www.dar.org

Daughters of the Confederacy, United (1894), 328 North Blvd., Richmond, VA 23220; 25,000; www.hqudc.org

Deaf, Natl. Assn. of the (1880), 814 Thayer Ave., Ste. 250, Silver Spring, MD 20910; 16,500; www.nad.org

Defenders of Wildlife (1947), 1130 17th St. NW, Wash., DC 20036; 430,000; www.defenders.org

Delta Kappa Gamma Society Intl. (1929), P.O. Box 1589., Austin, TX 78767; 136,000; deltakappagamma.org

Delta Mu Delta Honor Soc. (1913), 2 Slt Creek Ln., Hinsdale, IL 60521; 90,000; www.deltamudelta.org

Democratic Natl. Committee (1848), 430 S. Capitol Street SE, Wash., DC 20003; 440 elected members; www.democrats.org

DeMolay International (1919), 10200 NW Ambassador Dr., Kansas City, MO 64153; 30,000; www.demolay.org

Dental Assn., American (1859), 211 E. Chicago Ave., Chicago, IL 60611; 147,000; www.ada.org

Diabetes Assn., American (1940), 1701 North Beauregard St., Alexandria, VA 22311; 416,967; www.diabetes.org

Dialect Society, American (1889), c/o Allan Metcalf, English Dept., MacMurray College, Jacksonville, IL 62650; 500; www.americandialect.org

Directors Guild of America (1936), 7920 Sunset Blvd., Los Angeles, CA 90046; 12,700+; dga.org

Disabled American Veterans (1920), P.O. Box 14301, Cincinnati, OH 45250; 1,050,000; www.dav.org

Disabled Sports USA (1967), 451 Hungerford Dr., Ste. 100, Rockville, MD 20850; 60,000+; www.dsusa.org

Dogs on Stamps Study Unit (1979), 202A Newport Rd., Monroe Twp., NJ 08531-3920; 350; www.dossu.org

Down Syndrome Society, Natl. (1979), 666 Broadway, New York, NY 10012; 50,000; www.ndss.org

Dozenal Society of America (1944), Six Brancatelli, West Islip LI, NY 11795; 144; www.dozens.org

Ducks Unlimited (1937), One Waterfowl Way, Memphis, TN 38120; 620,000; www.ducks.org

Eagles, Fraternal Order of (1898), 1623 Gateway Circle South, Grove City, OH 43123; 1.1 mil; www.foe.com

Easter Seals (1919), 230 W. Monroe St., Ste. 1800, Chicago, IL 60606; www.easter-seals.org

Eastern Star, General Grand Chapter, Order of the (1876), 1618 New Hampshire Ave. NW, Wash., DC 20009; 1 mil.+; www.easternstar.org

Edsel Club (1967), 19296 Tuckaway Ct., N. Fort Myers, FL 33903; 300; www.edselworld.com

Education, American Council on (1918), One Dupont Circle NW, Wash., DC 20036; 1,700 org.; www.acenet.edu

Education, Council for Advancement & Support of (1974), 1307 New York Ave. NW, Ste 1000, Wash., DC 20005; 3,000+ schools; www.case.org

Education of Young Children, Natl. Assn. for the (1926), 2021 21st Ave. S., Ste. 108, Nashville, TN 37212; 103,000; www.naeyc.org

Educators for World Peace, Intl. Assn. of (1969), P.O. Box 3282, Mastin Lake Station, Huntsville, AL 35810; 50,000; www.earthportals.com/portal_messenger/mercieca.html

Egalitarian Communities, Federation of (1978), HC-3 Box 3370-BF, Tecumseh, MO, 65760; 250; www.thefec.org

8th Air Force Historical Society (1975), P.O. Box 3556, Hollywood, FL 33083; home.fuse.net/ghilliard/8th.htm

88th Infantry Division Assn. (1946), 11 Lovett Ave., Brockton, MA 02301-1750; 4,200; www.88infdiv.org

84th Infantry Div. Railsplitters Soc., The (1945), P.O. Box 827, Sioux Falls, SD 57101-0827; 2,300

82nd Airborne Division Assn., Inc. (1946), P.O. Box 9308, Fayetteville, NC 28311-9308; 27,400+; www.fayettevillenc.com/airborne82dassn

Electrical and Electronics Engineers, Institute of (1963), 445 Hoes Lane, Piscataway, NJ 08854; 380,000; www.ieee.org

Electrical Manufacturers Assn., Natl. (1926), 1300 N. 17th St., Ste. 1847, Rosslyn, VA 22209; 560 cos.; www.nema.org

Electrochemical Society, Inc.,The (ECS, Inc.) (1902), 65 South Main St., Bldg. D, Pennington, NJ 08534-2839; 8,000+; www.electrochem.org

Electronics Service Dealers Assciation, Natl. (NESDA) (1963), 3608 Pershing Ave., Ft. Worth, TX 76107; 734; www.nesda.com

▶ **IT'S A FACT:** The 4 'H's in "4-H Clubs" stand for Head, Heart, Hands, and Health. There are over 60 million alumni of 4-H Clubs and programs; the original focus on education in agriculture and home economics has broadened over the years to include science and technology, expressive arts, citizenship, and other areas.

Electronics Technicians, Intl. Society of Certified (1965), 3608 Pershing Ave., Ft. Worth, TX 76107; 1,380; www.iscet.org

Elks of the U.S.A., Benevolent and Protective Order of (1868), 2750 N. Lakeview Ave., Chicago, IL 60614; 1.1 mil+; www.elks.org

Energy Engineers, Assn. of (1977), 4025 Pleasantdale Rd., Ste. 420, Atlanta, GA 30340; 9,000; www.aeecenter.org

Engineers, Natl. Society of Professional (1934), 1420 King St., Alexandria, VA 22314; 54,000; www.nspe.org

English Inc., U.S. (1983), 1747 Pennsylvania Ave. NW, Ste. 1050, Wash., DC 20006; 1.7 mil; www.us-english.org

English-Speaking Union of the U.S. (1920), 144 E. 39th St., New York, NY 10036; 18,000; www.english-speakingunion.org

Entomological Society of America (1889), 9301 Annapolis Rd., Ste. 300, Lanham, MD 20706-3115; 6,000; www.ent.soc.org

Environmental Assessment Association (1972), 1224 North Nokomis NE, Alexandria, MN 56308; 3,000; www.iami.org/eaa

Environmental Health Assn., Natl. (1937), 720 S. Colorado Blvd., Ste. 970-S, Denver, CO 80246-1925; 4,900; www.neha.org

Environmental Medicine, American Academy of (1965), 7701 E. Kellogg, Ste. 625, Wichita, KS 67207; 397; www.aaem.com

Equipment Manufacturers, Assn. of (2002), 111 E. Wisconsin Ave., Ste. 1000, Milwaukee, WI 53202; 550+ cos.; www.aem.org

Esperanto League for North America Inc. (1952), P.O. Box 1129, El Cerrito, CA 94530; 750; www.esperanto-usa.org

Evangelism Crusades, Inc., Intl. (1959) 14617 Victory Blvd., Van Nuys, CA 91411; 300

Experimental Aircraft Assn. (1953), P.O. Box 3086, Oshkosh, WI 54903; 170,000+; www.eaa.org

Ex-Prisoners of War, American (1942), 3201 E. Pioneer Pkwy., #40, Arlington, TX 76010; 30,000; www.axpow.org

Fairs & Expositions, Intl. Assn. of (1885), P.O. Box 985, Springfield, MO 65809; 2,900; www.fairsandexpos.com

Family, Career and Community Leaders of America (1945), 1910 Association Dr., Reston, VA 20791; 227,000; www.fcclainc.org

Family Physicians, American Academy of (1947), PO Box 11210, Leawood, KS 66211; 94,300; www.aafp.org

Family Relations, Natl. Council on (1938), 3989 Central Avenue NE, Suite 550, Minneapolis, MN 55421; 4,000; www.ncfr.org

Farm Bureau Federation, American (1919), 600 Maryland Ave. SW, Wash., DC 20024; 5 mil+ families; www.fb.com

Farmers of America Org., Natl. Future (1928), P.O. Box 68960, 6060 FFA Drive, Indianapolis, IN 4626; 452,000; www.ffa.org

Farmers Union, Natl. (1902), 11900 E. Cornell Ave., Aurora, CO 80014; 300,000; www.nfu.org

Fat Acceptance, Inc., Natl. Assn. to Advance (NAAFA) (1969), P.O. Box 188620, Sacramento, CA 95818; 2,500; www.naafa.org

Fellowship of Reconciliation, The (1915), 521 N Broadway, Nyack, NY 10960; 30,000; www.forusa.org

Feminists for Life of America (1972), 733 15th St. NW, Ste. 1100, Wash., DC 20005; c. 5,000; www.feministsforlife.org

Financial Professionals, Assn. for (formerly Treasury Management Assn.) (1979), 7315 Wisconsin Ave., Ste. 600W, Bethesda, MD 20814; 14,000; www.AFPonline.org

Financial Service Professionals, Soc. of (formerly American Society of CLU & ChFC) (1928), 270 S. Bryn Mawr Ave., Bryn Mawr, PA 19010; 25,000; www.financialpro.org

Financial Women Intl. (1921 as Natl. Assoc. of Bank Women), 200 N. Glebe Rd., Ste. 820, Arlington, VA 22203; 2,000+; www.fwi.org

Fire Chiefs, Intl. Assn. of (1873), 4025 Fair Ridge Dr., Ste. 300, Fairfax, VA 22033; 12,000; www.iafc.org

Fire Protection Assn., Natl. (NFPA) (1896), 1 Batterymarch Park, Quincy, MA 02169; 75,000; www.nfpa.org

Fire Protection Engineers, Soc. of (1950), 7315 Wisconsin Avenue, Ste. 1225W, Bethesda, MD 20814; 3,500; www.sfpe.org

First Amendment Studies, Inc., Institute for (1984), P.O. Box 589, Great Barrington, MA 01230; 10,000; www.ifas.org

Fisheries Soc., American (1870), 5410 Grosvenor Ln., Ste. 110, Bethesda, MD 20814; 9,000; www.fisheries.org

Food Industry Suppliers, Intl. Assn. of (1911), 1451 Dolley Madison Blvd., McLean, VA 22101; 700 cos.; www.iafis.org

Food Technologists, Institute of (1939), 525 W. Van Buren, Ste. 1000, Chicago, IL 60607; 28,000; www.ift.org

Foreign Study, American Institute for, The (1964), River Plaza, 9 W. Broad St., Stamford, CT 06902; 1 mil+; www.aifs.com

Foreign Trade Council, Inc., Natl. (1914), 1625 K St. NW, Wash., DC 20006; 300 companies.; www.nftc.org

Forensic Sciences, American Academy of (1948), P.O. Box 669, Colorado Springs, CO 80904; 5,300; www.aafs.org

Foresters, Society of American (1900), 5400 Grosvenor La., Bethesda, MD 20814; 17,500; www.safnet.org

Forest History Society (1946), 701 Wm. Vickers Ave., Durham, NC 27701-3162; 1,000; www.foresthistory.org

Forests, American (1875), P.O. Box 2000, Wash., DC 20013; 12,000; www.americanforests.org

4-H Clubs (1914), CSREES/USDA, 1400 Independence Ave. SW, Wash., DC 20250; 6.8 mil; www.4h-usa.org

Frederick A. Cook Society, (1940), 207 Grandview Dr. South, Pittsburgh, PA 15215; 254; www.cookpolar.org

Freedom From Religion Foundation (1978), P.O. Box 750, Madison, WI 53701; 5,000; www.ffrf.org

Freedom of Information Center (1958), Missouri School of Journalism, 133 Neff Annex, Ninth & Elm, Columbia, MO 65211-0012; foi.missouri.edu

Freemasonry, Supreme Council Ancient and Accepted Scottish Rite of, Northern Masonic Jurisdiction (1872), P.O. Box 519, Lexington, MA 02420; 270,000; www.supremecouncil.org

Free Men, Natl. Coalition of (1977), P.O. Box 582023, Minneapolis, MN 55458; 2,000; www.ncfm.org

Free Press Readership Council, American (2001), 1433 Pennsylvania Ave., S.E., Wash., DC 20003; 4,500; www.americanfreepress.net

French Institute/Alliance Française (1971), 22 E. 60th St., New York, NY 10022; 6,500; www.fiaf.org

Frozen Food Institute, American (1942), 2000 Corporate Ridge, Suite 1000, McLean, VA 22102; 505; www.affi.com

Funeral Consumers Alliance (FAMSA) (1963), 33 Patchen Rd., South Burlington, VT 05403; 280,000; www.funerals.org/famsa

Gamblers Anonymous (1957), P.O. Box 17173, Los Angeles, CA 90017; approx. 30,000; www.gamblersanonymous.org

Garden Club of America (1913), 14 E. 60th St., 3rd Floor, New York, NY 10022; 195 clubs; www.gcamerica.org

Garden Clubs, Inc., National Council of State (1929), 4401 Magnolia Ave., St. Louis, MO 63110; 235,316; www.gardenclub.org

Gay and Lesbian Task Force, Natl. (1973), 1325 Massachusetts Ave. NW, Ste. 600, Wash., DC 20005; 30,000; www. ngltf.org

Genealogical Society, Natl. (1903), 4527 17th St. N, Arlington, VA 22207; 17,000; www.ngsgenealogy.org

General Contractors of America, The Associated (1918), 333 John Carlyle St., Ste. 200, Alexandria, VA 22314; 33,000+ cos.; www.agc.org

Genetic Association, American (1903), P.O. Box 257, Buckeystown, MD 21717; lsvl.la.asu.edu/aga

Geographers, Assn. of American (1904), 1710 16th St. NW, Wash., DC 20009; 7,500+; www.aag.org

Geographic Education, Natl. Council for (1915), 206A Martin Hall, Jacksonville State University, 700 Pelham Rd. N, Jacksonville, AL 36265; 2,700; www.ncge.org

Geographic Society, Natl. (1888), 1145 17th St. NW, Wash., DC 20036; 10 mil.; www.nationalgeographic.com

Geographical Society, The American (1851), 120 Wall St., Ste. 100, New York, NY 10005; 1,000; www.amergeog.org

Geological Society of America (1888), 3300 Penrose Pl., P.O. Box 9140, Boulder, CO 80301; 17,000; www.geosociety.org

Geriatrics Society, American (1942), 350 5th Ave., Ste. 801, New York, NY 10118; 6,000; www.americangeriatrics.org

Gideons Intl. (1899), 2900 Lebanon Rd., Nashville, TN 37214; 236,000; www.gideons.org

Gifted Children, Natl. Assn. for (1954), 1707 L Street NW, Suite 550, Washington, DC 20036; 8,000; www.nagc.org

Girl Scouts of the U.S.A. (1912), 420 5th Ave., New York, NY 10018; 3.7 mil; www.girlscouts.org

Golden Key National Honor Society (1977), 1189 Ponce de Leon Ave., Atlanta, GA 30306; 335 chapters; goldenkey.gsu.edu

Gold Star Mothers of America, Inc. (1929), 2128 Leroy Place NW, Wash., DC 20008; 1,200; www.goldstarmoms.com.

Golf Assn., U.S. (1894), Golf House, P.O. Box 708, Far Hills, NJ 07931; 800,000; www.usga.org
Gospel Music Assn. (1964), 1205 Division St., Nashville, TN 37203; 5,000+; www.gospelmusic.org
Governors' Assn., Natl. (1908), Hall of the States, 444 N. Capitol, Wash., DC 20001; 55 govs.; www.nga.org
Grange Patrons of Husbandry, Natl. (1867), 1616 H Street NW, Wash., DC 20006; 300,000; www.nationalgrange.org
Graphic Arts, American Institute of (1914), 164 5th Ave., New York, NY 10010; 16,000; www.aiga.org
Gray Panthers (1970), 733 15th St. NW, Ste 437, Wash., DC 20005; approx. 17,000; www.graypanthers.org
Green Mountain Club, The (1910), 4711 Waterbury-Stowe Rd., Waterbury Ctr., VT 05677; 7,500+; www.greenmountainclub.org
Green Party (1984), P.O. Box 1406, Chicago, IL 60690; 1,500+; www.greenparty.org
Greenpeace U.S.A. (1971), 702 H St. NW, Suite 300, Wash., DC 20001; 250,000; www.greenpeaceusa.org.
Ground Water Assn., Natl. (1948), 601 Dempsey Rd., Westerville, OH 43081; 16,500; www.ngwa.org
Group Against Smokers' Pollution, Inc. (GASP) (1971), P.O. Box 632, College Park, MD 20741; 10,000+
Guide Dog Foundation for the Blind, Inc. (1946), 371 E. Jericho Turnpike, Smithtown, NY 11787; 162,500; www.guidedog.org

Hadassah, the Women's Zionist Organization of America (1912), 50 W. 58th St., New York, NY 10019; 300,000+; www.hadassah.org
Handball Assn., U.S. (1951), 2333 N. Tucson Blvd., Tucson, AZ 85716; 8,000; www.ushandball.org
Health Council, Natl. (1920), 1730 M St. NW, Ste. 500, Wash., DC 20036; 115 org.; www.nationalhealthcouncil.org
Hearing Society, Intl. (1951), 16880 Middlebelt Rd., Ste. 4, Livonia, MI 48154; 3,000; www.ihsinfo.org
Heart Assn., American (1924), 7272 Greenville Ave., Dallas, TX 75231; 22.5 mil.; www.americanheart.org
Heating, Refrigerating & Air-Conditioning Engineers, Inc., American Soc. of (1894), 1791 Tullie Cir. NE, Atlanta, GA 30329; 55,000; www.ashrae.org
Hebrew Immigrant Aid Society (HIAS) (1881), 333 Seventh Ave., 17th Fl., New York, NY 10001; 20,000; www.hias.org
Helicopter Society, American (1944), 217 N. Washington St., Alexandria, VA 22314; 6,140; www.vtol.org
Future Business Leaders of America/Phi Beta Lambda, Inc. (1942), 1912 Association Drive, Reston, VA 20191; 240,000+; www.fbla-pbl.org
Hemispheric Affairs, Council on (1975), 1730 M St., Ste. 1010, NW, Wash., DC 20036; 1,875; www.coha.org
Hibernians in America, Ancient Order of (1836), 1301 S.W. 26th Avenue, Ft. Lauderdale, FL 33312; 200,000; www.aoh.com
Highpointers Club (1986), P.O. Box 1496, Golden, CO 80402; 2,600; www.highpointers.org
High School Band Directors Hall of Fame, Natl. (1985), 519 N. Halifax Ave., Daytona Beach, FL 32118; 1,500-3,000; www.banddirectorshalloffame.homestead.com
Hiking Society, American (1976), 1422 Fenwick Lane, Silver Spring, MD 20910; 5,000; www.americanhiking.org
Historic Preservation, Natl. Trust for (1949), 1785 Massachusetts Avenue NW, Wash., DC 20036; 250,000; www. nationaltrust.org
Historical Assn., American (1884), 400 A St. SE, Wash., DC 20003; 15,000; www.theaha.org
Historical Society Doll Collection, United States (1971), 1st and Main Sts., Richmond, VA 23219; 250,000; www.ushsdolls.org
Hockey, U.S.A. (1936), 1775 Bob Johnson Dr., Colorado Springs, CO 80906; 585,000; www.usahockey.com
Home Builders, Natl. Assn. of (1942), 1201 15th St. NW, Wash., DC 20005; 203,000; www.nahb.com
Homeless, Natl. Coalition for the (1984), 1012 14th St., Ste. 600, Wash., DC 20005; 10,000; www.nationalhomeless.org
Honor Society, Natl. (1921), 1904 Association Dr., Reston, VA 20191; appr. 1 mil; dsa.principals.org
Horatio Alger Soc. (1965), P.O. Box 70361, Richmond, VA 23255; 250; www.ihot.com/~has
Horse Council, American (1969), 1616 H St., NW, 7th Fl., Wash., DC 20006; 175 org.,1,800 ind.; www.horsecouncil.org
Hospital Assn., American (1898), 1 N. Franklin, Chicago, IL 60606; 5,000 hospitals, 37,000 individual members; www.aha.org

Hostelling Intl. USA (1934), 8401 Colesville Rd, Ste. 600, Silver Spring, MD 20910; 120,000; www.hiayh.org
Hotel & Motel Assn., American (1910), 1201 New York Ave. NW, #600, Wash., DC 20005; 11,000+; www.ahma.com
Hot Rod Assn., Natl. (1951), 2035 Financial Way, Glendora, CA 91741; 80,000; www.nhra.com
Housing Inspection Foundation (1979), 1224 N. Nokomis NE, Alexandria, MN 56308; 1,800; www.iami.org/hif
Huguenot Society, Natl. (1951), 3 Free Ferry Heights, Fort Smith, AR 72903; 3,800; www.huguenot.netnation.com
Humane Society of the U.S. (1954), 2100 L St. NW, Wash., DC 20037; 650,000; www.hsus.org
Human Resource Management, Society for (SHRM) (1948), 1800 Duke St., Alexandria, VA 22314; 175,000; www.shrm.org
Hydrogen Energy, Intl. Assn. for (1974), P.O. Box 248266, Coral Gables, FL 33124; 2,500; www.iahe.org

Illustrators, Inc., Society of (1901), 128 E. 63rd St., New York, NY 10021-7303; 1,000; www.societyillustrators.org
Independent Community Bankers of America (1930), One Thomas Circle NW, Ste. 400, Wash., DC 20005; 5,000; www.icba.org
Industrial and Applied Mathematics, Society for (1952), 3600 Univ. City Science Ctr., Philadelphia, PA 19104; 9,000; www.siam.org
Industrial Designers Society of America (1965), 45195 Business Ct., Ste. 250, Dulles, VA 20166; 3,200; www.idsa.org
Industrial Security, American Soc. for (1955), 1625 Prince St., Alexandria, VA 22314; 33,000; www.asisonline.org
Insurance Assn., American (1964), 1130 Connecticut Avenue NW, Suite 1000, Wash., DC 20036; 5,000 institutions; www.icba.org
Intellectual Property Owners Assoc. (1972), 1255 23rd St. NW, Ste. 200, Wash., DC 20037; 350; www.ipo.org
Intelligence Officers, Assoc. of Former (1975), 6723 Whittier Ave., Ste. 303A, McLean, VA 22101-4533; 3,100+; www.afio.com
Intercollegiate Athletics, Natl. Assn. of (1937), 23500 W. 105th St., P.O. Box 1325, Olathe, KS 66051-1325; 360 member colleges/universities; www.naia.org
Interior Designers, American Society of (1975), 608 Massachusetts Avenue NE, Wash., DC 20008; 30,000; www.asid.org
Intl. Education, Institute of (1919), 809 United Nations Plaza, New York, NY 10017; 650 U.S. colleges and universities; www.iie.org
Intl. Educational Exchange, Council on (1947), 7 Custom House St., 3rd Fl., Portland, ME 04101; 240 organizations; www.ciee.org
Intl. Educators, Assn. of (NAFSA) (1948), 1307 New York Ave. NW, 8th Fl.,Wash., DC 20005; 7,500; www.nafsa.org
Intl. Law, American Society of (1906), 2223 Massachusetts Ave. NW, Wash., DC 20008; 4,000; www.asil.org
Inventors, American Soc. of (1953), P.O. Box 58426, Philadelphia, PA 19102; 150; www.asoi.org
Investigative Pathology, American Soc. for (1900), 9650 Rockville Pike, Bethesda, MD 20814; 1,718; www.asip.org
Investment Management and Research, Assn. for (AIMR) (1990), 560 Ray C. Hunt Dr., Charlottesville, VA 22903-0668; 65,000; www.aimr.org
Investors Corp., Natl. Assn. of (1951), P.O. Box 220, Royal Oak, MI 48068; 400,000; www.better-investing.org
Irish American Cultural Inst. (1962), 1 Lackawanna Pl., Morristown, NJ 07960; 4,500; www.irishaci.org
Irish Historical Society, American (1897), 991 5th Ave., New York, NY 10028; about 600; www.aihs.org

Jail Assn., American (1981), 1135 Professional Ct., Hagerstown, MD 21740; 4,500; www.aja.com
Japanese-American Citizens League (1929), 1765 Sutter St., San Francisco, CA 94115; 21,000; www.jacl.org
Jewish Committee, American (1906), P.O. Box 705, New York, NY 10150; 110,000; www.ajc.org
Jewish Community Centers Assn. of North America (1917), 15 E. 26th St., New York, NY 10010; 1,000,000+; www.jcca.org
Jewish Congress, American (1918), 15 E. 84th St., New York, NY 10028; 50,000; www.ajcongress.org
Jewish Historical Society, American (1892), 15 West 16th St. New York, NY 10011; 9,000; www.ajhs.org
Jewish War Veterans of the U.S.A. (1896), 1811 R St. NW, Wash., DC 20009; 37,000; jwv.org

Jewish Women, Natl. Council of (1893), 53 W. 23rd St., 6th Fl., New York, NY 10010; 90,000; www.ncjw.org

John Birch Society (1958), P.O. Box 8040, Appleton, WI 54912; www.jbs.org

Joint Action in Community Service (JACS) (1967), 5225 Wisconsin Ave. NW, Ste. 404, Wash., DC 20015; www.jac inc.org

Joseph Diseases Foundation, Inc., Intl. (1977), P.O. Box 994268, Redding CA 96099; 1,550; www.ijdf.net

Journalists, Society of Professional (1909), 3909 N. Meridian St., Indianapolis, IN 46208; 10,000+; spj.org

Journalists and Authors, American Society of (1948), 1501 Broadway, Ste. 302, New York, NY 10036; 1,000+; www. asja.org

Judicature Society, American (1913), 2700 University Ave., Des Moines, IA 50311; 6,000; www.ajs.org

Jugglers Assn., Intl. (1947), 2811 E. Avalon Dr., Phoenix, AZ 85016; 2,500; www.juggle.org

Junior Achievement, Inc. (1919), One Education Way, Colorado Springs, CO 80906; www.ja.org

Junior Auxiliaries, Natl. Assn. of (1941), 845 South Main St., Greenville, MS 38701; 12,876; www.najanet.org

Junior Chamber of Commerce, U.S. (1920), P.O. Box 7, Tulsa, OK 74102; 200,000; www.usjaycees.org

Junior College Athletic Assn., Natl. (1937), P.O. Box 7305, Colorado Springs, CO 80933; 520; www.njcaa.org

Junior Honor Society, Natl. (1929), 1904 Association Dr., Reston, VA 20191; approx. 250,000; dsa.principals.org

Junior Leagues, Assn. of (1901), 132 West 31st St., New York, NY 10016; 193,000; www.ajli.org

Kidney Fund, The American (1971), 6110 Executive Blvd., Ste. 1010, Rockville, MD 20852; www.kidneyfund.org

Kiwanis International (1915), 3636 Woodview Trace, Indianapolis, IN 46268; 500,000+; www.kiwanis.org

Knights of Columbus (1882), One Columbus Plaza, New Haven, CT 06510-4000; 1,660,197; www.kofc.org

Knights of Pythias, (1864), 59 Coddington Street, #202, Quincy, MA 02169; approx. 70,000; www.pythias.org

Krishna Consciousness, Intl. Soc. for (ISKON, Inc.)(1966), 3764 Watseka Ave., Los Angeles, CA 90034; approx. 250,000; www.krishna.com

La Leche League Intl. (1956), 1400 N. Meacham Rd., P.O. Box 4079, Schaumburg, IL 60168; 3,000 local grps.; www.laleche league.org

Lady Bird Johnson Wildflower Center (1982), 4801 La Crosse Avenue, Austin, TX 78739; 22,000; www.wild flower.org

Landscape Architects, American Society of (1899), 636 I St. NW, Wash., DC 20001-3736; 12,500; www.asla.org

Law Libraries, American Assn. of (1906), 53 W. Jackson Blvd., #940, Chicago, IL 60604; 5,150; www.aallnet.org

Learned Societies, American Council of (1919), 633 Third Ave., New York, NY 10017; 64 societies; www.acls.org

Legal Administrators, Assn. of (1971), 175 E. Hawthorn Parkway, Suite 325, Vernon Hills, IL 60061-1428; 9,000; www.alanet.org

Legal Secretaries, Natl. Assn. of (NALS) (1929), 314 E 3rd St., Ste. 210, Tulsa, OK 74120; 8,500; www.nals.org

Legion of Valor of the U.S.A., Inc. (1890), c/o Legion of Valor Museum, 2425 Fresno St., Ste. 103, Fresno, CA 93721; 811; www.legionofvalor.com

Leprosy Missions, Inc., American (1906), One Alm Way, Greenville, SC 29601; www.leprosy.org

Leukemia and Lymphoma Society (1949), 1311 Mamaroneck Ave., White Plains, NY 10605; 58 chapters nationwide; www. leukemia-lymphoma.org

Lewis and Clark Trail Heritage Foundation. (1969), P.O. Box 3434, Great Falls, MT 59403; 3,600; www.lewisandclark.org

Libertarian Party (1971), 2600 Virginia Ave. NW, Ste. 100, Wash., DC 20037; 224,000; www.lp.org

Liberty Lobby (1955), 300 Independence Ave. SE, Wash., DC 20003; 90,000; www.spotlight.org

Libraries Assn., Special (1909), 1700 18th St. NW, Wash., DC 20009; 12,000; www.sla.org

Library Assn., American (1876), 50 E. Huron St., Chicago, IL 60611; 64,000+; www.ala.org

Lifesaving Assn., U.S. (1964), PO Box 366, Huntington Beach, CA 92648; 100+ chapters; www.usla.org

Lighter-Than-Air Society (1952), 526 S. Main St., Akron, OH 44306; 850; www.blimpinfo.com

Linguistic Society of America (1924), 1325 18th St. NW, Ste. 211, Wash., DC 20036-6501; 6,000 indiv., 2,200 inst.; www. lsadc.org

Lions Clubs, Intl., Assn. of (1917), 300 W. 22nd St., Oak Brook, IL 60523; 1,400,000; www.lionsclubs.org

Little League Baseball, Inc. (1939), P.O. Box 3485, S. Williamsport, PA 17701; approx. 3 mil, 7,300 leagues; www.littleleague.org

Little People of America, Inc. (1961), Box 65030, Lubbock, TX 79464; 8,000+; www.lpaonline.org

Logistics, International Society of (SOLE) (1966), 8100 Professional Place, Ste. 111, Hyattsville, MD 20785; 3,500; www.sole.org

London Club (1975), 214 North 2100 Rd., Lecompton, KS 66050; 100+.

Lung Assn., American (1904), 61 Broadway, 6th Fl., New York, NY 10006; www.lungusa.org

Magazine Publishers of America (1919), 919 Third Ave., 22 Fl., New York, NY 10022; 1,200 titles; www.magazine.org

Magicians, Intl. Brotherhood of (1922), 11155 S. Towne Sq., Ste. B, St. Louis, MO 63123-7813; 13,253; www.magician.org

Management Accountants, Institute of (1919), 10 Paragon Dr., Montvale, NJ 07645; 75,000; www.imanet.org

Management Assn., American (1923), 1601 Broadway, New York, NY 10019; 70,000+; www.amanet.org

Manufacturing Engineers, Soc. of (1932), One SME Dr., Dearborn, MI 48121-0930; 40,000; www.sme.org

Manufacturers, Natl. Assn. of (1895), 1331 Pennsylvania Ave. NW, Wash., DC 20004; 14,000 cos.; www.nam.org

March of Dimes Birth Defects Foundation (1938), 1275 Mamaroneck Avenue, White Plains, NY 10605; 3 mil; www. modimes.org

Marine Corps League (1923), P.O. Box 3070, Merrifield, VA 22116; 56,000; www.mcleague.org

Marketing Assn., Am. (1915), 311 S. Wacker Dr., Ste. 5800, Chicago, IL 60606; 38,000; www.marketingpower.com

Master Brewers Association of the Americas (1887), 3340 Pilot Knob Rd., St. Paul, MN 55121-2097; 2,500; www. mbaa.org

Materials and Process Engineering, Soc. for the Advancement of (1944), 1161 Parkview Drive, Covina, CA 91724-3748; 5,000; www.sampe.org

Mathematical Society, American (1888), 201 Charles St., Providence, RI 02904; 30,000; www.ams.org

Mayflower Descendants, General Society of (1897), 4 Winslow St., Plymouth, MA 02361; 26,000; www.may flower.org

Mayors, U.S. Conference of (1932), 1620 Eye St. NW, Wash., DC 20006; 1,183; www.usmayors.org

Mechanical Engineers, American Soc. of (1880), 3 Park Ave., New York, NY 10016; 125,000; www.asme.org

Medical Assn., American (1847), 515 N. State St., Chicago, IL 60610; 300,000; www.ama-assn.org

Medical Library Assn. (1898), 65 E. Wacker Pl., Ste. 1900, Chicago, IL 60602; 5,000; www.mlanet.org

Medieval Academy of America (1925), 104 Mt. Auburn St., Cambridge, MA 02138; 4,500; www.medievalacademy.org

Meeting Planners, Intl. Society of (1981) 1224 N. Nokomis NE, Alexandria, MN 56308; 500; www.iami.org/ismp

MENC: The Natl. Assn. for Music Education (formerly Music Educators Natl. Conference) (1907), 1806 Robert Fulton Dr., Reston, VA 20191; 90,000; www.menc.org

Mended Hearts, Inc. (1950), 7272 Greenville Ave., Dallas, TX 75231; 24,000; www.mendedhearts.org

Mensa, Ltd., American (1960), 1229 Corporate Dr. W, Arlington, TX 76006; 100,000; www.us.mensa.org

Mental Health Assn., Natl. (1909), 2001 N. Beauregard St., 12th fl., Alexandria, VA 22311; www.nmha.org

Mentally Ill, Natl. Alliance for the (1979), Colonial Place Three, 2107 Wilson Blvd. Ste. 300, Arlington, VA 22201; 220,000; www.nami.org

Merrill's Marauders Assn. (1947), 11244 N. 33rd St., Phoenix, AZ 85028-2723; 1,698; www.marauder.org

Meteorological Society, American (1919), 45 Beacon St., Boston, MA 02108; 11,000+; www.ametsoc.org

Metric Assn., Inc., U.S. (1916), 10245 Andasol Ave., Northridge, CA 91325-1504; 1,200; www.metric.org

Microbiology, American Society for (1899), 1752 N. St. NW, Wash., DC 20036; 42,000; www.asmusa.org

Military Officers Assn. (1940), 201 N. Washington St., Alexandria, VA 22314; 391,000; www.moaa.org

Military Order of the Purple Heart of the USA (1958), 5413-B Backlick Road, Springfield, VA 22151; 36,765; www.purple heart.org

Military Order of the World Wars (1919), 435 N. Lee St., Alexandria, VA 22314; 11,250; www.militaryorder.org

Military Surgeons of the U.S., Assn. of (1898), 9320 Old Georgetown Road, Bethesda, MD 20814; 10,000+; www. amsus.org

Missing and Exploited Children, Natl. Center for (1984), The Charles B. Wang International Children's Building, 699 Prince St., Alexandria, VA 22314; www.missingkids.com

Model A Ford Club of America, Inc. (1955), 250 S Cypress St., La Habra, CA 90631; 15,500; www.mafca.com

Model Railroad Assn., Natl. (1935), 4121 Cromwell Rd., Chattanooga, TN 37421-2119; 20,500; www.nmra.org

Modern Language Assn. of America (1883), 26 Broadway, 3rd Fl., New York, NY 10014; 30,000+; www.mla.org

Molecular Plant-Microbe Interactions, Intl. Soc. for (1990), 3340 Pilot Knob Rd., St. Paul, MN 55121-2097; 500; www.ismpinet.org

Moose Intl., inc. (1888), 155 S. International Dr., Mooseheart, IL 60539; 1.5 mil; www.mooseintl.org

Mothers, Inc.®, American (1938), 15 DuPont Circle N.W., Wash., DC 20036; 3,700; www.americanmothers.org

Mothers of Twins Clubs, Natl. Organization of (1963), P.O. Box 438, Thompson Station, TN 37179-0438; 24,000; www.nomotc.org

Motion Picture Arts & Sciences, Academy of (1927), 8949 Wilshire Blvd., Beverly Hills, CA 90211; 6,300; www.oscars.org

Motion Picture & Television Engineers, Soc. of (1916), 595 W. Hartsdale Ave., White Plains, NY 10607; 10,000; www.smpte.org

Motorcyclist Assn., American (1924), 13515 Yarmouth Dr., Pickerington, OH 43147; 250,000+; www.amadirectlink.com

Motorists Association, Natl. (1982), 402 W. 2nd St., Waunakee, WI 53597; 7,000; www.motorists.org

Multiple Sclerosis Society, Natl. (1946), 733 Third Ave. 6th Fl., New York, NY 10017; 616,305; www.nationalmssociety.org

Muscular Dystrophy Assn., Inc. (1950), 3300 E. Sunrise Dr., Tucson, AZ 85718; 2 mil. volunteers; www.mdausa.org

Museums, American Assn. of (1906), 1575 Eye St. NW, Ste. 400, Wash., DC 20005; 16,000; www.aam-us.org

Music Center, American (1939), 30 W. 26th St., #1001, New York, NY 10010; 2,500; www.amc.net

Music Teachers Natl. Assn. (1876), 441 Vine St., Ste. 505, Cincinnati, OH 45202; 24,000; www.mtna.org

Musicological Society, American (1934), 201 S. 34th St., Philadelphia, PA 19104-6313; 4,600; www.ams-net.org

Muzzle Loading Rifle Assn., Natl. (1933), P.O. Box 67, Friendship, IN 47021; 19,699; www.nmlra.org

Myasthenia Gravis Foundation of America (1952), 5841 Cedar Lake Rd., Ste. 204, Minneapolis, MN 55416; 45,000; www.myasthenia.org

Mystery Writers of America, Inc. (1945), 17 E. 47th St., 6th Fl., New York, NY 10017; 2,235; www.mysterywriters.org

NA'AMAT USA (1921), 350 Fifth Ave., Ste. 4700, New York, NY 10118; 50,000, U.S.; 900,000 worldwide; www.naamat.org

Name Society, American (1951), Couper Admin. Building, SUNY Binghamton, Binghamton, NY 13902; 325; www.wtsn.binghamton.edu/ANS

Narcotics Anonymous World Services (1953), P.O Box 9999, Van Nuys, CA 94109; 250,000; www.na.org

Natl. Assn. for the Advancement of Colored People (NAACP) (1909), 4805 Mt. Hope Dr., Baltimore, MD 21215; www.naacp.org

National Guard Assn. of the U.S. (1878), One Massachusetts Ave. NW, Wash., DC 20001; 56,000; www.ngaus.org

National Press Club (1908), 529 14th St., 13th Fl., NW, Wash., DC 20045; 4,000+; www.press.org

Nature Conservancy, The (1951), 4245 N. Fairfax Drive, Ste. 100, Arlington, VA 22203; 1 mil+; nature.org

Naturist Society LLC (1980), P.O. Box 132, Oshkosh, WI 54903; 27,000; www.naturistsociety.com

Naval Institute, U.S. (1873), 291 Wood Rd., Annapolis, MD 21402; 70,000; www.usni.org

Naval Reserve Assn. (1954), 1619 King St., Alexandria, VA 22314; 23,000; www.navy-reserve.org

Navy League of the United States (1902), 2300 Wilson Blvd., Arlington,VA 22201-3308; 75,000; www.navyleague.org

Negro College Fund, United (1944), 8260 Willow Oaks Corporate Drive, P.O. Box 10444, Fairfax, VA 22031; 39 institutions; www.uncf.org

Neurofibromatosis Foundation, Natl. (1978), 95 Pine St., 16th Fl., New York, NY 10005; 9,433; 30,000; www.nf.org

Newspaper Assn. of America (NAA) (1992), 1921 Gallows Rd., Ste. 600, Vienna, VA 22182-3900; 2,000+; www.naa.org

Ninety-Nines (Intl. Organization of Women Pilots) (1929), 4300 Amelia Earhart Rd., Oklahoma City, OK 73159; 6,000; www.ninety-nines.org

Non-Commissioned Officers Assn. (1960), 10635 IH 35 North, San Antonio, TX 78233; 160,000; www.ncoausa.org

Northern Cross Society (1983), 214 N. 2100 Rd., Lecompton, KS 66050; 40

NOT-SAFE: Nat'l Organization Taunting Safety and Fairness Everywhere (1985), P.O. Box 5743-WA, Montecito, CA 93150; 1,995; www.notsafe.org

Notaries, American Society of (1965), P.O. Box 5707, Tallahassee, FL 32314; approx. 20,000; www.notaries.org

Nuclear Society, American (1954), 555 N. Kensington Ave., La Grange Park, IL 60526; 11,000; www.ans.org

Nude Recreation Inc., American Assn. for (1931), 1703 N. Main St., Ste. E, Kissimmee, FL 34744; 50,000; www.aanr.com

Numismatic Assn., American (1891), 818 N. Cascade Ave., Colorado Springs, CO 80903; 28,000; www.money.org

Numismatic Society, The American (1858), 140 William St., New York, NY 10038; 2,000+; www.amnumsoc.org

Nursing, Natl. League fo (1952), 61 Broadway, New York, NY 10006; 5,000; www.nln.org

Nutritional Sciences, American Society for (1928), 9650 Rockville Pike, Ste. 4500, Bethesda, MD 20814; 3,500+; www.asns.org

Ocean Conservancy (1972), 1725 DeSales St. NW, #600, Wash.,DC 20036; 900,000; www.oceanconservancy.org

Odd Fellows, Independent Order of (1819), 422 Trade St., Winston-Salem, NC 27101; 295,077; www.ioof.org

Old Crows, Assn. of (1964), 1000 N. Payne St., Alexandria, VA 22314; 14,00; www.crows.org

Optimist Intl. (1919), 4494 Lindell Blvd., St. Louis, MO 63108; 114,000; www.optimist.org

Optometric Assn., American (1918), 243 N. Lindbergh Blvd., St. Louis, MO 63141; 32,904; www.aoa.org

Organ Sharing, United Network for (1984), P.O. Box 2484, Richmond, VA 23218; 434; www.unos.org

Organists, American Guild of (1896), 475 Riverside Dr., Ste. 1260, New York, NY 10115; 20,000; www.agohq.org

Oriental Society, American (1842), Univ. of Michigan, Hatcher Graduate Library, 110D, Ann Arbor, MI 48109; 1,350; www.umich.edu/~aos

ORT Inc., American (Org. for Rehabilitation Through Training) (1922), 817 Broadway, 10th Fl., New York, NY 10003; 8,000; www.aort.org

Ornithologists' Union, American (1883), 10th St. and Constitution, Wash., DC 20001; 4,200; www.aou.org

Outlaw and Lawman History, Inc., Natl. Assn. for (NOLA) (1974), 1917 Sutton Place Trail., Harker Heights, TX 76548-6043; 480; www.outlawlawman.com

Overeaters Anonymous (1960) P.O. Box 44020, Rio Rancho, NM 87124-4020; www.oa.org

Oxfam America (1970) 26 West St., Boston, MA 02111; 100,000; www.oxfamamerica.org

Paralyzed Veterans of America (1946), 801 18th St. NW, Wash., DC 20006; 18,000; www.pva.org

Parapsychology Institute of America (1972), P.O. Box 5442, Babylon, NY, 11707; 110

Parents Without Partners, Inc. (1957), 1650 South Dixie Highway, Suite 510, Boca Raton, FL 33432; 50,000; www.parentswithoutpartners.org

Parkinson's Disease Foundation, Inc. (1957), 710 W. 168th St., New York, NY 10032; 100,000; www.pdf.org

Parliamentarians, Natl. Assn. of (1930), 213 S. Main St., Independence, MO 64050; 4,000; www.parliamentarians.org

Patton, George S. Jr. Society (1970), 3116 Thorn St., San Diego, CA 92104; 350; www.pattonhq.com/homeghq.html

PBY Catalina International Association (1987), 1510 Kabel Dr., New Orleans, LA 70131; 700; www.pbycia.org

Peace Corps (1961), 1111 20th St., NW, Wash., DC 20526; 6,700; www.peacecorps.gov

Pearl Harbor History Associates, Inc. (1985), P.O. Box 1007, Stratford, CT 06615; approx. 275; www.pearlharborhistory.org

PEN American Center, Inc. (1921), 568 Broadway, 4th Fl., New York, NY 10012; 2,700; www.pen.org

Pen Friends, Intl. (1967), 500 University Ave., #2415, Honolulu, HI 96826; 300,000; www.pen-pals.net

Pension Plan, Committee For a National (1979) P.O. Box 27851, Las Vegas, NV 89126; 360

Pen Women, Natl. League of American (1897), 1300 17th St. NW, Wash., DC 20036-1973; 4,000; www.americanpenwomen.com

People for the Ethical Treatment of Animals (PETA) (1981), 501 Front St., Norfolk, VA 23510; 750,000; www.teachkind.org

Performance Improvement, Intl. Society for (1962), 1400 Spring St., Ste. 260, Silver Spring, MD 20910; 6,000; www.ispi.org

Petroleum Institute, American (1919), 1220 L St. NW, Wash., DC 20005; 400 companies; www.api.org

Pharmaceutical Assn., American (1852), 2215 Constitution Ave. NW, Wash., DC 20037; 50,000; www.aphanet.org

Phi Beta Kappa Society (1776), 1606 New Hampshire Ave. NW, Wash., DC 20009; approx. 500,000; www.pbk.org

Phi Delta Kappa Intl., Inc. (1906), 408 N. Union St., P.O. Box 789, Bloomington, IN 47402; 95,223; www.pdkintl.org

Phi Kappa Phi (1897), P.O. Box 16000, LSU Baton Rouge, Baton Rouge, LA 70893; 1,000,000; www.phikappaphi.org

Phi Theta Kappa Int'l. Honor Society (1918), 1625 Eastover Drive, Jackson, MS 39211; 800,000; www.ptk.org

Philatelic Society, American (1886), 100 Oakwood Ave., State College, PA 16803; 48,327; www.stamps.org

Philological Association, American (1869), Univ. of Penn., 292 Logan Hall, 249 S. 36th St., Philadelphia, PA, 19104-6304; 3,100; www.apaclassics.org

Philosophical Assn., American (1900), 31 Amstel Ave., Univ. of Delaware, Newark, DE 19716; 11,097; www.apaonline.org

Photographers of America, Inc., Professional (1880) 229 Peachtree St. NE, Ste. 2200, Atlanta, GA 30303; 14,000; www.ppa.com

Physical Therapy Assn., American (1921), 1111 N. Fairfax St., Alexandria, VA 22314; 65,000; www.apta.org

Physically Handicapped, Inc., Natl. Assn. of the (1958), Scarlet Oaks, 440 Lafayette Ave., #GA4, Cincinnati, OH 45220-1022; approx. 400; www.naph.net

Physics, American Inst. of (1931), One Physics Ellipse, College Park, MD 20740; 123,500; www.aip.org

Physiological Society, American (1887), 9650 Rockville Pike, Bethesda, MD 20814-3991; 10,500; www.the-aps.org

Phytopathological Society, American (1908), 3340 Pilot Knob Rd., St. Paul, MN 55121; 4,800; www.apsnet.org

Pilgrims Natl. Soc., Sons and Daughters of (1909), 3917 Heritage Dr., #104, Bloomington, MN 55437-2633; 2,000; www. nssdp.org

Pilot Intl. & Pilot Intl. Foundation (1921), P.O. Box 4844, Macon, GA 31208; 14,557; www.pilotinternational.org

Planetary Society (1979), 65 N. Catalina Ave., Pasadena, CA 91106; approx. 70,000; www.planetary.org

Planned Parenthood Federation of America, Inc. (1916), 434 West 33rd Street, New York, NY 10001; www.planned parenthood.org

Plastics Engineers, Society of (1942), 14 Fairfield Dr., P.O. Box 403, Brookfield, CT 06804; 25,000+; www.4spe.org

Poetry Society of America (1910), 15 Gramercy Park, New York, NY 10003; approx. 3,000; www.poetrysociety.org

Poets, The Academy of American (1934), 588 Broadway, Ste. 1203, New York, NY 10012; 8,000; www.poets.org

Police Assn., Intl. (1950 in UK, 1962 in U.S.), 100 Chase Ave., Yonkers, NY 10703; 291,000+; www.ipa-usa.org

Political Items Collectors, American (1945), P.O. Box 1149, Cibolo, TX 78108; 2,500; apic.ws

Political Science Assn., American (1903), 1527 New Hampshire Ave. NW, Wash., DC 20036; 14,500; www. apsanet.org

Political Science Assn., Southern (1928), PO Box 8101, Georgia Southern Univ., Statesboro, GA 30460; www2. gasou.edu/spsa

Political Science, Academy of (1880), 475 Riverside Drive, Ste. 1274, New York, NY 10115; 6,000; www.psqonline.org

Political & Social Science, American Academy of (1889), 3814 Walnut St., Univ. of Penn., Philadelphia, PA 19104; 400; www.aapss.org

Polo Assn., U.S. (1890), 771 Corporate Dr., Ste. 505, Lexington, KY 40503; 3,545; www.uspolo.org

Population Assn. of America (1931), 8630 Fenton St., Ste. 722, Silver Spring, MD 20910; 3,000; www.popassoc.org

Population Connection (formerly Zero Population Growth) (1968), 1400 16th St. NW, Ste 320, Washington, DC 20036; www.populationconnection.org

Portuguese Continental Union of the U.S.A. (1925), 30 Cummings Park, Woburn, MA 01801; 5,488; members.aol. com/upceua

Postal Stationery Society, United (1945) P.O. Box 1792, Norfolk, VA 23501-1792; 1,100; www.upss.org

Postcard Dealers, Inc., International Federation of (1979), P.O. Box 1765, Manassas, VA 20108; 297; www.members. tripod.com/~IFPD

Postmasters of the U.S., Natl. League of (1887), 1023 N. Royal St., Alexandria, VA 22314; 27,000; www.post masters.org

Postmasters of the U.S., Natl. Assn. of (1898), 8 Herbert St., Arlington, VA 22305; 43,000, www.napus.org

Power Boat Assn., American (1903), 17640 Nine Mile Rd., Eastpointe, MI 48021; 6,000; www.apba-racing.com

Printing Industries of America, Inc. (1887), 100 Daingerfield Rd., Alexandria, VA 22314; 14,000; www.gain.net

Procrastinators Club of America (1956), P.O. Box 712, Bryn Athyn, PA 19006; 3,800; www.geocities.com/ PROCRASTINATORS_CLUB_OF_AMERICA

Professional Ball Players of America, Assn. of (1924), 1820 W. Orangewood Ave., Ste. 206, Orange, CA 92868; 11,000; www.apbpa.org

ProLiteracy Worldwide (2002), 1320 Jamesville Ave., Syracuse, NY 13210; 1400 affiliates; www.proliteracy.org

Protection of Old Fishes, Soc. for the (1967), NOAA HAZMAT, 7600 Sand Point Way, N.E., Seattle, WA 98115; 150.

Psoriasis Foundation, Natl. (1968), 6600 SW 92nd Ave., Ste. 300, Portland, OR 97223; 52,000; www.psoriasis.org

Psychiatric Assn., American (1844), 1000 Wilson Blvd., Suite 1825, Arlington, VA 22209-3901; 37,000; www.psych.org

Psychical Research, American Society for (1885), 5 W. 73rd St., New York, NY 10023; www.aspr.com

Psychoanalytic Assn., American (1911), 309 E. 49th St., New York, NY 10017; 3,500; apsa.org

Psychological Assn., American (1892), 750 1st St. NE, Wash., DC 20002; 159,000; www.apa.org

PTA, Natl. (1897), 330 N. Wabash Ave., Ste. 2100, Chicago, IL 60611; approx. 6.5 mil; www.pta.org

Public Administration, American Soc. for (1939), 1120 G St. NW, Wash., DC 20005; 9,000+; www.aspanet.org

Public Health Assn., American (1872), 800 I St. NW, Wash., DC 20001; 50,000+; www.apha.org

Publishers, Assn. of American (1970), 71 5th Ave., New York, NY 10003; 300; www.publishers.org

Quill and Scroll Society (1926), School of Journalism, The University of Iowa, Iowa City, IA 52242; www.uiowa.edu/ ~quill-sc

Quota International, Inc. (1919), 1420 21st St. NW, Wash., DC 20036; 11,000+; www.quota.org

Rabbis, Central Conference of American (1889), 355 Lexington Ave., New York, NY 10017; 1,800; ccarnet.org

Racquetball Assn., U.S. (1968), 1685 W. Uintah, Colorado Springs, CO 80904; 20,000; www.usra.org

Radio Relay League, American (1914), 225 Main St., Newington, CT 06111; 160,000; www.arrl.org

Radio and Television Society Foundation, Intl. (1939), 420 Lexington Ave., Ste. 1601, New York, NY 10170; 1,787; www.irts.org

Railway Historical Society, Natl. (1936), P.O. Box 58547, Philadelphia, PA 19102; app. 15,000; www.nrhs.com

Range Management, Society for (1948), 445 Union Blvd., Ste. 230, Lakewood, CO 80228; 3,700; www.rangelands.org/ srm.shtml

Reading Assn., Intl. (1956), 800 Barksdale Rd., P.O. Box 8139, Newark, DE 19714; 300,000; www.reading.org

Real Estate Institute, Intl. (1975), 1224 N. Nokomis, Alexandria, MN 56308; 700; www.iami.org/irei

Real Estate Appraisers, Natl. Assn. of (1966) 1224 N. Nokomis NE, Alexandria, MN 56308; 3,000; www.iami.org/ narea

Rebekah Assemblies, Intl. Assn. of (1922), 422 Trade St., Winston-Salem, NC 27101; 84,247

Recreation and Park Assn., Natl. (1965), 22377 Belmont Ridge Road, Ashburn, VA 20148; 23,425; www.nrpa.org

Recycling Coalition, Natl. (1978), 1325 G St., NW, Wash., DC, 20005; 3,500; www.nrc-recycle.org

Red Cross, American (1881), 2025 E St. NW, Wash., DC 20006; 1.3 mil volunteers; www.redcross.org

Reform Party of the U.S.A (1996),18935 Atasca Oaks Dr., Kingwood, TX 77346; 500,000; www.reformparty.org

Refugee Committee, American (1978), 430 Oak Grove St., Ste. 204, Minneapolis, MN 55403; www.archq.org

Rehabilitation Assn., Natl. (1925), 633 S. Washington St., Alexandria, VA 22310-4109; approx. 11,000; www.national rehab.org

Religion, American Academy of (1909), 825 Houston Mill Rd., Suite 300, Atlanta, GA 30329; 8,000+; www.aarweb.org

Renaissance Society of America (1954), 365 5th. Ave., Rm. 5400, New York, NY 10016; 2,700; www.r-s-a.org

Republican National Committee (1856), 310 1st St. SE, Wash., DC 20003; www.rnc.org

Reserve Officers Assn. of the U.S. (1922), One Constitution Ave. NE, Wash., DC 20002; 95,000; www.roa.org

Retail Federation, Natl. (1908), 325 7th St. NW, Ste. 1100, Wash., DC 20004; 50,000; www.nrf.com

Retired Persons, American Assn. of (1958), 601 E St. NW, Wash., DC 20049; 35 mil+; www.aarp.org

Reye's Syndrome Foundation, Natl. (1974), 426 N. Lewis, Bryan, OH 43506-0829; 4,760; www.reyessyndrome.org

Richard III Society, Inc. (1961),P.O. Box 13786, New Orleans, LA 70185; 750; www.r3.org

Rifle Assn., Natl. (1871). 11250 Waples Mill Rd., Fairfax, VA 22030; approx 3 mil; www.nra.org

Road & Transportation Builders Assn., American (1902), The ARTBA Building, 1010 Massachusetts Ave. NW, Wash., DC 20001; 5,000+; www.artba.org

Roller Sports, U.S.A. (1937), 4730 South St., Lincoln, NE 68506; 30,000; www.usarollersports.org

Rose Society, American (1892), 8877 Jefferson Page Rd, Shreveport, LA 71119; 20,000; www.ars.org

Rotary Intl. (1905), One Rotary Center, 1560 Sherman Ave., Evanston, IL 60201; 1,220,543; www.rotary.org

Running and Fitness Assn., American (1968), 4405 East West Highway, Ste. 405, Bethesda, MD 20814; 16,500+; www.americanrunning.org

Ruritan Natl., Inc. (1928), P.O. Box 487, Dublin, VA 24084; 33,447; www.ruritan.org

Safety Council, Natl. (1913), 1121 Spring Lake Dr., Itasca, IL 60143; 37,000 member facilities; www.nsc.org

Safety Engineers, American Soc. of (1911), 1800 E. Oakton St., Des Plaines, IL 60018; 32,000; www.asse.org

Salt Institute (1914), 700 N. Fairfax St., Ste. 600, Alexandria, VA, 22314; 7 U.S., 37 Int'l.; www.saltinstitute.org

Save-the-Redwoods League (1918), 114 Sansome St., Ste. 1200, San Francisco, CA 94104; 40,000; www.savethe redwoods.org

School Administrators, American Assn. of (1865), 801 N. Quincy St., Ste 700, Arlington, VA 22203; 14,000+; www. aasa.org

Science, American Assn. for the Advancement of (1848), 1200 New York Ave. NW, Wash., DC 20005; 138,000+; www. aaas.org

Science Fiction Society, World (1939), P.O. Box 426159, Kendall Square Station, Cambridge, MA 02142; 10,000; www.wsfs.org

Sciences, Natl. Academy of (1863), 500 5th St. NW, Wash., DC 20001; 2,000+; www.nas.edu

Science Teachers Assn., Natl. (1944), 1840 Wilson Blvd., Arlington, VA 22201; 55,000; www.nsta.org

Science Writers, Natl. Assn. of (1934), P.O. Box 890, Hedgeville, WV 25427; 2,210; www.nasw.org

Scrabble® Assn., Natl. (1980), P.O. Box 700, 403 Front St., Greenport, NY 11944; 10,000+; www.scrabble-assoc.com

Screen Actors Guild (1933), 5757 Wilshire Blvd., Los Angeles, CA 90036; 90,000; www.sag.com

Screenprinting & Graphic Imaging Assn., Intl. (1958), 10015 Main St., Fairfax, VA 22031; 4,000 ; www.sgia.org

2nd Air Division Assn. of the 8th Air Force (1948), P.O. Box 484, Elkhorn, WI 53121-0484; 4,500.

Secular Humanism, Council for (1980), P.O. Box 664, Amherst, NY 14226; 24,000; www.secularhumanism.org

Separation of Church & State, Americans United for (1947), 518 C St. NE, Wash., DC 20002; 75,000; www.au.org

Sertoma International (1912), 1912 E. Meyer Blvd., Kansas City, MO 64132; 20,000; www.sertoma.org

Sharkhunters Intl. (1983), P.O. Box 1539, Hernando, FL 34442; 7,000; www.sharkhunters.com

Shipbuilders Council of America (1920), 1455 F St., NW, Ste. 225, Wahington, DC 20005; 37 member cos; www.ship builders.org

Ships in Bottles Assn. of America (1983), P.O. Box 180550, Coronado, CA 92178; 250; www.shipsinbottles.org

Shrine of North America, The (1872), 2900 N. Rocky Point Dr., Tampa, FL 33607; approx 500,000+; shrinershq.org

Sierra Club (1892), 85 2nd St., 2nd Fl., San Francisco, CA 94105; 700,000+; www.sierraclub.org

Sigma Beta Delta (1994) P.O. Box 210570, St. Louis, MO 63121-0570; 20,000; www.sigmabetadelta.org

Skeet Shooting Assn., Natl. (1946), 5931 Roft Rd., San Antonio, TX 78253; 30,000; www.mynsca.com

Small Business United, Natl. (1937), 1156 15th St. NW, Ste. 1100, Wash., DC 20005; 65,000+; www.nsba.biz

Social Work Education, Council on (1952), 1725 Duke St., Ste. 500, Alexandria, VA 22314; 2,501; www.cswe.org

Sociological Assn., American (1905), 1307 New York Avenue NW, Suite 700, Wash., DC 20005; 13,000; www.asanet.org

Softball Assn., Amateur (1933), 2801 NE 50th St., Oklahoma City, OK 73111; 250,000+ teams; www. softball.org

Software and Information Industry Assn. (formerly Information Industry Assn.) (1999), 1090 Vermont Ave. NW, 6th Fl., Wash. DC 20005; 1,200 companies; www.siia.net

Soldiers', Sailors', Marines' and Airmen's Club (1919), 283 Lexington Ave., New York, NY 10016; 190; www.ssmaclub.org

Songwriters Guild of America (1931), 1222 16th Ave S., Ste. 25, Nashville, TN 37212; 5,000+; www.songwriters.org

Sons of the American Colonists, Natl. Society of (1970) 5611 N. 15th St., Arlington, VA 22205-0482; 250

Sons of the American Legion (1932), Box 1055, Indianapolis, IN 46206; 240,000; www.sal.legion.org

Sons of the American Revolution, Natl. Society of (1889), 1000 S. Fourth St., Louisville, KY 40203; 26,000; www.sar.org

Sons of Confederate Veterans (1896), 740 Mooresville Pike, Columbia, TN 3840; 35,000; www.scv.org

Sons of the Desert Laurel & Hardy Appreciation Society (1965), P.O. Box 8341, Universal City, CA 91608; 10,000; www.wayoutwest.org.

Sons of Italy in America, Order (1905), 219 E St. NE, Wash., DC 20002; 600,000; www.osia.org

Sons of Norway (1895), 1455 W. Lake St., Minneapolis, MN 55408; 65,000; www.sofn.com

Soroptimist Intl. of the Americas (1921), Two Penn Center Plaza, Ste. 1000, Philadelphia, PA 19102; 45,000; www. soroptimist.org

Southern Christian Leadership Conference (1957), P.O. Box 89128, Atlanta, GA 30312; 1 mil.; www.sclcnational.org

Space Society, Natl. (1974), 600 Pennsylvania Ave SE, Ste. 201, Wash., DC 20003; 22,000+; www.nss.org

Speech-Language-Hearing Assn., American (1925), 10801 Rockville Pike, Rockville, MD 20852; 99,000+; www.asha.org

Speedskating, U.S. (1966), P.O. Box 450639, Westlake, OH 44145; www.usspeedskating.org

Speleological Society, Natl. (1941), 2813 Cave Ave., Huntsville, AL 35810; 12,238; www.caves.org

Sports Car Club of America (1944), P.O. Box 19400, Topeka, KS 66619; 50,000+; www.scca.org

Sportscasters Assn., The American (1979), 225 Broadway, Ste. 2030, New York, NY 10007; 500+; www.american sportscasters.com

State & Local History, American Assn. for (1940), 1717 Church St., Nashville, TN 37203; 6,000; www.aaslh.org

State Governments, Council of (1933), 2760 Research Park Drive, P.O. Box 11910, Lexington, KY 40578; 50 states, 4 territories; www.csg.org

Statistical Assn., American (1839), 1429 Duke St., Alexandria, VA 22314; 16,000; www.amstat.org

Steamship Historical Society of America, Inc. (1935), P.O. Box 2394, Providence, RI 02906; 3,000; www.sshsa.org

Stock Exchange, American (1911), 86 Trinity Pl., New York, NY 10006; www.amex.com

Stock Exchange, New York (1792), 11 Wall St., New York, NY 10005; www.nyse.com

Stock Exchange, Philadelphia (1790), 1900 Market St., Philadelphia, PA 19103; www.phlx.com

Student Councils, Natl. Society of (1931) 1904 Association Dr., Reston, VA 20191; approx. 1.5 mil; dsa.principals.org

Stuttering Project, Natl. (1977), 4071 E. LaPalma Ave., Ste. A, Anaheim Hills, CA 92807; 2,800; www.nsastutter.org

Sudden Infant Death Syndrome Alliance (1987), 1314 Bedford Avenue, Suite 210, Baltimore, MD 21208; www.sids alliance.org

Supreme Council, 33°, Scottish Rite of Freemasonry, Southern Jurisdiction (1801), 1733 16th St. NW, Wash., DC 20009-3103; 413,793; www.srmason-sj.org

Surgeons, American College of (1913), 633 N. Saint Clair St., Chicago, IL 60611; 65,000; www.facs.org

Symphony Orchestra League, American (1942), 33 W. 60th St., 5th Fl., New York, NY 10023; 850; www.symphony.org

Table Tennis Assn., U.S. (1933), OneOlympic Plaza, Colorado Springs, CO 80903; 8,000; www.usatt.org

Tailhook Assn. (1956), 9696 Businesspark Ave., San Diego, CA 92131; 10,850; www.tailhook.org

Tall Buildings and Urban Habitat, Council on (1969), Illinois Inst. of Tech., S.R. Crown Hall, 3360 S. State St., Chicago, IL 60616; 1200; www.ctbuh.org

Tau Beta Pi Association (1885), 508 Daugherty, Engineering Hall, Univ of Tenn., Knoxville, TN 37901-2697; 400,000; www.tbp.org

Tax Administrators, Federation of (1932), 444 N. Capitol St. NW, Ste. 348, Wash., DC 20001; www.taxadmin.org

Tax Foundation (1937), 1900 M St. NW, Ste. 550, Wash., DC 20036; 50 U.S. states; www.taxfoundation.org

Taxpayers Union, Natl. (1969), 108 N. Alfred St., Alexandria, VA 22314; 335,000; www.ntu.org

Tea Assn. of the U.S.A., Inc. (1899), 420 Lexington Ave., New York, NY 10170; 300 corps; www.teausa.com

Teachers of English, Natl. Council of (1911), 1111 W. Kenyon Rd., Urbana, IL 61801; 77,000; www.ncte.org

Teachers of English to Speakers of Other Languages (1966), 700 S. Washington St., Ste. 200, Alexandria, VA 22314; 16,000; www.tesol.edu

Teachers of French, American Assn. of (1936), Southern Illinois University, Mailcode 4510, Carbondale, IL 62901-4510; 9,500; www.frenchteachers.org

Teachers of German, Inc., American Assn. of (AATG) (1926), 112 Haddontowne Ct. #104, Cherry Hill, NJ 08034-3668; 6,000; www.aatg.org

Teachers of Mathematics, Natl. Council of (1920), 1906 Association Drive, Reston, VA 20191-1502; 100,000; www. nctm.org

Teachers of Singing, Natl. Assn. of (1944), 4745 Sutton Park Ct. Ste. 201, Jacksonville, FL 32224; 5,443; www.nats.org

Teachers of Spanish & Portuguese, American Assn. of (1917), 423 Exton Commons, Exton, PA, 19341-2451; 11,522; www.aatsp.org

Telecommunications Pioneer Assn., Independent (1911), 1401 H St. NW, Ste. 600, Wash., DC 20005; 750,000+; www.telecom-pioneers.org

Television Arts & Sciences, Natl. Academy of (1957), 111 W. 57th St., Ste. 600, New York, NY 10019; 11,000; www.emmyonline.org

Theodore Roosevelt Assn. (1919), Nassau Hall, 1864 Muttontown Road, Muttontown, NY 11791; 2,239; www. theodoreroosevelt.org

Theological Library Assn., American (1946), 250 S. Wacker Dr., Ste. 1600, Chicago, IL 60606; 933; www.atla.com

Theological Schools in the U.S. and Canada, The Assn. of (1918), 10 Summit Park Dr., Pittsburgh, PA 15275-1103; 243; www.ats.edu

Theological Seminary of California, Intl. (1985) 14617 Victory Blvd., Suite 4, Van Nuys, CA 94411; 500+

Theosophical Society in America (1875), 1926 N. Main St., Wheaton, IL 60187; 5,000; www.theosophical.org

Therapy Dogs Intl., Inc (1976), 88 Bartley Rd., Flanders, NJ 07836; 12,000; www.tdi-dog.org

Thoreau Society (1941), 44 Baker Farm, Lincoln, MA 01773; 1,700+; www.walden.org

Thoroughbred Racing Assns. (1942), 420 Fair Hill Dr., Ste. 1, Elkton, MD 21921; 49 racing assoc.; www.tra-online.com

318th Service Group Assn. 9th AF (1991), 2114 West 29th St., Erie, PA 16508-1066; 306

Tin Can Sailors (1976), P.O. Box 100, Somerset, MA 02726; 24,000; www.destroyers.org

Titanic Historical Society, Inc. & Museum (1963), 208 Main St., Indian Orchard, MA 01151-0053; 4,387; www.titanic historicalsociety.org

Toastmasters Intl. (1924), P.O. Box 9052, Mission Viejo, CA 92690; 180,000+; www.toastmasters.org

Topical Assn., American (1949), P.O. Box 57, Arlington, TX, 76004-0057; 6,000; home.prcn.org/~pauld/ata

Totally Useless Skills, Institute of (1986), P.O. Box 181, Temple, NH 03084; 1250; www.jlc.net/~useless

Toy Industry Assn., Inc. (1916), 1115 Broadway, Suite 400, New York, NY 10010; 300+ cos; www.toy-tma.com

Transportation Alternatives (1973), 115 W. 30th St., #1207, New York, NY 10001; 5,000; www.transalt.org

Transportation Engineers, Inst. of (1930), 1099 14th St. NW, Suite 300 West, Wash., DC 20005-3438; 15,000; www.ite.org

Trapshooting Assn. of America, Amateur (1923), 601 W. National Road, Vandalia, OH 45377; 54,000; www.shoot ata.com

Travel Agents, American Soc. of (1931), 1101 King St., Ste. 200, Alexandria, VA 22314; 20,000+; www.astanet. com

Travelers Protective Assn. of America (1890), 3755 Lindell Blvd., St. Louis, MO 63108; 155,000; www.mindspring.com/~tpatxdiv/fraternal.htm

Trilateral Commission (1973), 1156 15th St., NW, Wash., DC 20005; 350; www.trilateral.org

Truck Historical Soc., American (1971), 10380 N. Ambassador Dr., Kansas City, MO 64153; 22,679; www.aths.org

Tuberous Sclerosis Alliance (1974), 801 Roeder Rd., Ste. 750, Silver Spring, MD 20910; aprox. 2000; www.tsalliance.org

UFOs, Natl. Investigations Committee on (1967) 14617 Victory Blvd., Ste. 4, Van Nuys, CA 91411; 250; www.tje.net/para/organizations/nicufo.htm

Underwriters (CPCU), Soc. of Chartered Property and Casualty (1944), 720 Providence Rd., P.O. Box 3009, Malvern, PA 19355; 28,500; www.cpcusociety.org

UNICEF, U.S. Fund for (1947), 333 E. 38th St., New York, NY 10016; www.unicefusa.org

Uniformed Services, Natl. Assn. for (1968), 5535 Hempstead Way, Springfield, VA 22151; 160,000+; www.naus.org

United Nations Assn. of the U.S.A. (1943), 801 2nd Ave., 2nd Fl., New York, NY 10017; 20,000+; www.unusa.org

United Order True Sisters, Inc. (1846), 100 State St., Ste. 1020, Albany, NY 12207; approx. 2,000; uots.org

United Press Intl. (1907), 1510 H St. NW, Wash., DC 20005; www.upi.com

United Service Organizations (USO) (1941), Washington Navy Yard, 1008 Eberle Place SE, Ste. 301, Wash., DC 20374; 12,000+; www.uso.org

United Way of America (1918), 701 N. Fairfax St., Alexandria, VA 22314; 1,353 org.; national.unitedway.org

Universities, Assn. of American (1900), 1200 New York Ave., NW, Ste. 550, Wash., DC 20005; 61 institutions; www. aau.edu

University Women, American Assn. of (1881), 1111 16th St. NW, Wash., DC 20036; 100,000+; www.aauw.org

Urban League, Natl. (1910), 120 Wall St., New York, NY 10005; 50,000; www.nul.org

U.S. Term Limits (1992), 10 G St.; Ste. 410, Wash., DC 20002; www.termlimits.org

USO World Headquarters (1941), 1008 Eberle Place SE, Ste. 301, Wash., DC 20374-5096; www.uso.org

USS Forrestal CVA/CV/AVT-59 Assn., Inc. (1990), 300 Cassady Avenue, Virginia Beach, VA 23452; 2,170; www. uss-forrestal.com

USS Idaho Assn. (1957), P.O. Box 711247, San Diego, CA 92171; 394

USS Los Angeles CA-135 (1978) 1240 Hendrick Dr. #K4, Carbondale, CO, 81623-2852; 748; www.uss-la-ca135.org

USS Missouri (BB-63) Assn., Inc. (1974), 24 Clark St., Plainview, NY 11803-5114; 1,520; www.ussmissouri.org

Ventriloquists, North American Assn. of (1944), P.O. Box 420, Littleton, CO 80160; 1,450; www.maherstudios.com/naav.htm

Veterans of Foreign Wars of the U.S. (1899), 406 W. 34th St., Kansas City, MO 64111; 1.8 mil+.; www.vfw.org

Veterans of Foreign Wars of the U.S., Ladies Auxiliary to the (1914), 406 W. 34th St., Kansas City, MO 64111; 671,501; www.ladiesauxvfw.com

Veterans of the Vietnam War, Inc. (1980), 805 S. Township Blvd., Pittston, PA 18640-3327; 15,000; www.vvnw.org

Veterinary Medical Assn., American (1863), 1931 N. Meacham Rd., Ste. 100, Schaumburg, IL 60173; 64,000; www.avma.org

Victorian Society in America (1966), 205 S Camac St., Philadelphia, PA 19107; 1,600; www.victoriansociety.org

Volleyball, USA (1928), 715 S. Circle Dr., Colorado Springs, CO 80910; 150,000; www.usavolleyball.org

Volunteers of America (1896), 1660 Duke St., Alexandria, VA 22314-3421; 11,000 staff; www.voa.org

War Mothers, American (1917), 5415 Connecticut Ave., NW, Ste. L-30, Wash., DC 20015; 500

Watch & Clock Collectors, Inc., Natl. Assn. of (NAWCC) (1943), 514 Poplar St., Columbia, PA 17512; 28,645; www. nawcc.org

Watercolor Society, American (1866), 47 5th Ave., New York, NY 10003; 480; www.americanwatercolorsociety.com

Water Environment Federation (1928), 601 Wythe St., Alexandria, VA 22314; 40,000; www.wef.org

Water Works Assn., American (1881), 6666 W. Quincy Ave., Denver, CO 80235; 57,000; www.awwa.org

Wheelchair Sports, USA (1957), 3595 E. Fountain Blvd., Ste. L-1, Colorado Springs, CO 80910; 4,000; www.wsusa.org

Wildlife Federation, Natl. (1936),11100 Wildlife Center Dr., Reston, VA, 20190; 4 mil.; www.nwf.org

Wildlife Management Institute (1911), 1146 19th St. NW, 7th Fl., Wash., DC 20036; 300; www.wildlifemanagement institute.org

Wizard of Oz Club, Intl. (1957), P.O. Box 26249, San Francisco, CA 94126-6249; app.1,300; www.ozclub.org

Women, Natl. Organization for (NOW) (1966), 733 15th St. NW, 2nd Fl., Wash., DC 20005; 500,000; www.now.org

Women and Families, Natl. Partnership for (1971), 1875 Connecticut Ave. NW, Ste. 650, Wash., DC 20009; 2,000; www.nationalpartnership.org

Women Artists, Inc., Natl. Assn. of (1889), 80 5th Ave., Ste. 1405, New York, NY 10001; 700; www.nawanet.org

Women in Communications, The Association for (1909 as Theta Sigma Phi), 780 Ritchie Hwy., Ste. 5-28, Severna Park, MD 21146; 7,500; www.womcom.org

Women in Radio and Television Inc., Amer. (1951), 8405 Greensboro Dr., Ste. 800, McLean, VA 22102; www.awrt.org

Women Engineers, Society of (1950), 230 E. Ohio St., Ste. 400, Chicago, IL 60611; 17,000; www.swe.org

Women Voters of the U.S., League of (1920), 1730 M St. NW, Ste. 1000, Wash., DC 20036; 130,000; www.lwv.org

Women's Army Corps Veterans Assn. (1942), P.O. Box 5577, Ft. McClellan, AL 36205; 4,000; www.armywomen.org

Women's Christian Temperance Union, Natl. (1874), 1730 Chicago Ave., Evanston, IL 60201-4585; www.wctu.org

Women's Clubs, General Federation of (1890), 1734 N St. NW, Wash., DC, 20036; 180,000 U.S.; www.gfwc.org

Woodmen of America, Modern (1883), 1701 1st Ave., Rock Island, IL 61204; 750,000; www.modern-woodmen.org

Workmen's Circle (1900), 45 E. 33rd St., New York, NY 10016; 35,000; www.circle.org

World Council of Churches, U.S. Office (1948), 475 Riverside Drive, Rm. 915, New York, NY 10115; 330+ denominations.

World Federalist Assn. (1947), 418 7th St. SE, Wash., DC 20003; 11,000; www.wfa.org

World Future Society (1966), 7910 Woodmont Ave., Ste. 450, Bethesda, MD 20814; 25,000; www.wfs.org

World Learning (1932), Kipling Rd., P.O. Box 676, Brattleboro, VT 05302-0676; 100,000; www.worldlearning.org

World Wildlife Fund (1961), 1250 24th St. NW, P.O. Box 97180, Wash., DC 20037; 1 mil+; www.worldwildlife.org

World's Fair Collectors Soc., Inc. (1968), P.O. Box 20806, Sarasota, FL 34276-3806; 350; members.aol.com/bbqprod/wfcs.html

Writers Guild of America, West (1933), 7000 W. Third St., Los Angeles, CA 90048; 10,500; www.wga.org

YMCA (Young Men's Christian Assns.) of the U.S.A. (1851) 101 N. Wacker Dr., Chicago, IL 60606; 17.9 mil.; www. ymca.net

YWCA (Young Women's Christian Assn.) of the U.S.A. (1907), 1015 18th St. NW, Ste. 1100, Wash., DC 20036; approx. 2 mil; www.ywca.org

Zionist Organization of America (1897), 4 E. 34th St., New York, NY 10016; 55,000; www.zoa.org

Zoo and Aquarium Assn., American (1924), 8403 Colesville Road, Suite 710, Silver Spring, MD 20910; 212 institutions, 5,500 individuals; www.aza.org

CALENDAR

Julian and Gregorian Calendars; Leap Year; Century

The **Julian calendar**, under which all Western nations measured time until AD 1582, was authorized by Julius Caesar in 46 BC. It called for a year of 365¼ days, starting in January, with every 4th year being a **leap year** of 366 days. St. Bede the Venerable, an Anglo-Saxon monk, announced in AD 730 that the Julian year was 11 min, 14 sec too long, a cumulative error of about a day every 128 years, but nothing was done about this for centuries.

By 1582 the accumulated error was estimated at 10 days. In that year Pope Gregory XIII decreed that the day following Oct. 4, 1582, should be called Oct. 15, thus dropping 10 days and initiating the **Gregorian calendar**.

The Gregorian calendar continued a system devised by the monk Dionysius Exiguus (6th century), starting from the first year following the birth of Jesus Christ, which was inaccurately taken to be year 753 in the Roman calendar. Leap years were continued but, to prevent further displacements, centesimal years (years ending in 00) were made common years, not leap years, unless divisible by 400. Under this plan, **1600** and **2000** are leap years (as is **2004**); 1700, 1800, and 1900 are not.

The Gregorian calendar was adopted at once by France, Italy, Spain, Portugal, and Luxembourg. Within 2 years most German Catholic states, Belgium, and parts of Switzerland and the Netherlands were brought under the new calendar, and Hungary followed in 1587. The rest of the Netherlands, along with Denmark and the German Protestant states, made the change in 1699-1700.

The British government adopted the Gregorian calendar and imposed it on all its possessions, including the American colonies, in 1752, decreeing that the day following Sept. 2, 1752, should be called Sept. 14, a loss of 11 days. All dates preceding were marked OS, for Old Style. In addition, New Year's Day was moved to Jan. 1 from Mar. 25

(under the old reckoning, for example, Mar. 24, 1700, had been followed by Mar. 25, 1701). Thus George Washington's birthdate, which was Feb. 11, 1731, OS, became Feb. 22, 1732, NS (New Style). In 1753 Sweden also went Gregorian.

In 1793 the French revolutionary government adopted a calendar of 12 months of 30 days with 5 extra days in September of each common year and a 6th every 4th year. Napoleon reinstated the Gregorian calendar in 1806.

The Gregorian system later spread to non-European regions, replacing traditional calendars at least for official purposes. Japan in 1873, Egypt in 1875, China in 1912, and Turkey in 1925 made the change, usually in conjunction with political upheaval. In China, the republican government began reckoning years from its 1911 founding. After 1949, the People's Republic adopted the Common, or Christian Era, year count, even for the traditional lunar calendar, which is also retained. In 1918 the Soviet Union decreed that the day after Jan. 31, 1918, OS, would be Feb. 14, 1918, NS. Greece changed over in 1923. For the first time in history, all major nations had one calendar. The Russian Orthodox church and some other Christian sects retained the Julian calendar.

To convert from the Julian to the Gregorian calendar, add 10 days to dates Oct. 5, 1582, through Feb. 28, 1700; after that date add 11 days through Feb. 28, 1800; 12 days through Feb. 28, 1900; and 13 days through Feb. 28, 2100.

A **century** consists of 100 consecutive years. The 1st century AD may be said to have run from the years 1 through 100. The 20th century by this reckoning consisted of the years 1901 through 2000 and technically ended Dec. 31, 2000, as did the 2nd millennium AD. The 21st century thus technically began Jan. 1, 2001.

For a **Perpetual Calendar,** see pages 640-641.

Julian Calendar

To find which of the 14 calendars of the Perpetual Calendar (pages 640-641) applies to any year under the Julian system, find the century for the desired year in the 3 leftmost columns below. Read across and find the year in the 4 top rows. Then read down. The number in the intersection is the calendar designation for that year. For some years and countries the Julian new year did not start Jan. 1; to find the correct Perpetual Calendar for Britain and its possessions, you can generally add one year for dates from Jan. 1-Mar. 24. For example, to look up Feb. 2, 1705, Old Style, use the year 1706.

Year (last 2 figures of desired year)

Century			00	01 29 57 85	02 30 58 86	03 31 59 87	04 32 60 88	05 33 61 89	06 34 62 90	07 35 63 91	08 36 64 92	09 37 65 93	10 38 66 94	11 39 67 95	12 40 68 96	13 41 69 97	14 42 70 98	15 43 71 99	16 44 72	17 45 73	18 46 74	19 47 75	20 48 76	21 49 77	22 50 78	23 51 79	24 52 80	25 53 81	26 54 82	27 55 83	28 56 84
0	700	1400	12	7	1	2	10	5	6	14	2	3	4	12	7	1	9	4	5	6	14	2	3	4	12
100	800	1500	11	6	7	1	9	4	5	6	14	2	3	4	12	7	1	2	10	5	6	7	8	3	4	5	13	1	2	3	11
200	900	1600	10	5	6	7	8	3	4	5	13	1	2	3	11	6	7	1	9	4	5	6	14	2	3	4	12
300	1000	1700	9	4	5	6	14	2	3	4	12	7	1	2	10	5	6	7	8	3	4	5	13	1	2	3	11	6	7	1	9
400	1100	1800	8	3	4	5	13	1	2	3	11	6	7	1	9	4	5	6	14	2	3	4	12	7	1	2	10	5	6	7	8
500	1200	1900	14	2	3	4	12	7	1	2	10	5	6	7	8	3	4	5	13	1	2	3	11	6	7	1	9	4	5	6	14
600	1300	2000	13	1	2	3	11	6	7	1	9	4	5	6	14	2	3	4	12	7	1	2	10	5	6	7	8	3	4	5	13

Gregorian Calendar

Choose the desired year from the table below or from the Perpetual Calendar (for years 1803 to 2080). The number after each year designates which calendar to use for that year, as shown in the Perpetual Calendar—see pages 640-641. (The Gregorian calendar was inaugurated Oct. 15, 1582. From that date to Dec. 31, 1582, use calendar 6.)

1583-1802

1583	7	1603	4	1623	1	1643	5	1663	2	1683	6	1703	2	1723	6	1743	3	1763	7	1783	4
1584	8	1604	12	1624	9	1644	13	1664	10	1684	14	1704	10	1724	14	1744	11	1764	8	1784	12
1585	3	1605	7	1625	4	1645	1	1665	5	1685	2	1705	5	1725	2	1745	6	1765	3	1785	7
1586	4	1606	1	1626	5	1646	2	1666	6	1686	3	1706	6	1726	3	1746	7	1766	4	1786	1
1587	5	1607	2	1627	6	1647	3	1667	7	1687	4	1707	7	1727	4	1747	1	1767	5	1787	2
1588	13	1608	10	1628	14	1648	11	1668	8	1688	12	1708	8	1728	12	1748	9	1768	13	1788	10
1589	1	1609	5	1629	2	1649	6	1669	3	1689	7	1709	3	1729	7	1749	4	1769	1	1789	5
1590	2	1610	6	1630	3	1650	7	1670	4	1690	1	1710	4	1730	1	1750	5	1770	2	1790	6
1591	3	1611	7	1631	4	1651	1	1671	5	1691	2	1711	5	1731	2	1751	6	1771	3	1791	7
1592	11	1612	8	1632	12	1652	9	1672	13	1692	10	1712	13	1732	10	1752	14	1772	11	1792	8
1593	6	1613	3	1633	7	1653	4	1673	1	1693	5	1713	1	1733	5	1753	2	1773	6	1793	3
1594	7	1614	4	1634	1	1654	5	1674	2	1694	6	1714	2	1734	6	1754	3	1774	7	1794	4
1595	1	1615	5	1635	2	1655	6	1675	3	1695	7	1715	3	1735	7	1755	4	1775	1	1795	5
1596	9	1616	13	1636	10	1656	14	1676	11	1696	8	1716	11	1736	8	1756	12	1776	9	1796	13
1597	4	1617	1	1637	5	1657	2	1677	6	1697	3	1717	6	1737	3	1757	7	1777	4	1797	1
1598	5	1618	2	1638	6	1658	3	1678	7	1698	4	1718	7	1738	4	1758	1	1778	5	1798	2
1599	6	1619	3	1639	7	1659	4	1679	1	1699	5	1719	1	1739	5	1759	2	1779	6	1799	3
1600	14	1620	11	1640	8	1660	12	1680	9	1700	6	1720	9	1740	13	1760	10	1780	14	1800	4
1601	2	1621	6	1641	3	1661	7	1681	4	1701	1	1721	4	1741	1	1761	5	1781	2	1801	5
1602	3	1622	7	1642	4	1662	1	1682	5	1702	2	1722	5	1742	2	1762	6	1782	3	1802	6

Chronological Eras

Era	Year	Begins in 2004	Era	Year	Begins in 2004
Byzantine	7513	Sept. 14	Grecian (Seleucidae)	2316	Sept. 14 or Oct. 14
Jewish	5765	Sept. 15[1]	Diocletian	1721	Sept. 11
Roman (Ab Urbe Condita)	2757	Jan. 14	Indian (Saka)	1926	Mar. 21
Nabonassar (Babylonian)	2753	Apr. 24	Islamic/Muslim (Hijra)	1425	Feb. 20[1]
Japanese	2664	Jan. 1	Chinese	4702	Jan. 22

(1) Year begins at sunset.

Chronological Cycles, 2004

Dominical Letter..........D and C   Roman Indiction...............12   Solar Cycle 25
Golden Number (Lunar Cycle).... 10   Epact.....................VIII   Julian Period (year of)........6717

How Far Apart Are Two Dates?

This table covers a period of 2 years. To use, find the **number** for each date and subtract the smaller from the larger. Example—for days from Feb. 10, 2002, to Dec. 15, 2003, subtract 41 from 714; the result is 673. For leap years, such as 2004, one day must be added; thus Feb. 4, 2003, and Mar. 13, 2004, are 403 days apart.

First Year

Date	Jan.	Feb.	Mar.	April	May	June	July	Aug.	Sept.	Oct.	Nov.	Dec.
1	1	32	60	91	121	152	182	213	244	274	305	335
2	2	33	61	92	122	153	183	214	245	275	306	336
3	3	34	62	93	123	154	184	215	246	276	307	337
4	4	35	63	94	124	155	185	216	247	277	308	338
5	5	36	64	95	125	156	186	217	248	278	309	339
6	6	37	65	96	126	157	187	218	249	279	310	340
7	7	38	66	97	127	158	188	219	250	280	311	341
8	8	39	67	98	128	159	189	220	251	281	312	342
9	9	40	68	99	129	160	190	221	252	282	313	343
10	10	41	69	100	130	161	191	222	253	283	314	344
11	11	42	70	101	131	162	192	223	254	284	315	345
12	12	43	71	102	132	163	193	224	255	285	316	346
13	13	44	72	103	133	164	194	225	256	286	317	347
14	14	45	73	104	134	165	195	226	257	287	318	348
15	15	46	74	105	135	166	196	227	258	288	319	349
16	16	47	75	106	136	167	197	228	259	289	320	350
17	17	48	76	107	137	168	198	229	260	290	321	351
18	18	49	77	108	138	169	199	230	261	291	322	352
19	19	50	78	109	139	170	200	231	262	292	323	353
20	20	51	79	110	140	171	201	232	263	293	324	354
21	21	52	80	111	141	172	202	233	264	294	325	355
22	22	53	81	112	142	173	203	234	265	295	326	356
23	23	54	82	113	143	174	204	235	266	296	327	357
24	24	55	83	114	144	175	205	236	267	297	328	358
25	25	56	84	115	145	176	206	237	268	298	329	359
26	26	57	85	116	146	177	207	238	269	299	330	360
27	27	58	86	117	147	178	208	239	270	300	331	361
28	28	59	87	118	148	179	209	240	271	301	332	362
29	29	—	88	119	149	180	210	241	272	302	333	363
30	30	—	89	120	150	181	211	242	273	303	334	364
31	31	—	90	—	151	—	212	243	—	304	—	365

Second Year

Date	Jan.	Feb.	Mar.	April	May	June	July	Aug.	Sept.	Oct.	Nov.	Dec.
1	366	397	425	456	486	517	547	578	609	639	670	700
2	367	398	426	457	487	518	548	579	610	640	671	701
3	368	399	427	458	488	519	549	580	611	641	672	702
4	369	400	428	459	489	520	550	581	612	642	673	703
5	370	401	429	460	490	521	551	582	613	643	674	704
6	371	402	430	461	491	522	552	583	614	644	675	705
7	372	403	431	462	492	523	553	584	615	645	676	706
8	373	404	432	463	493	524	554	585	616	646	677	707
9	374	405	433	464	494	525	555	586	617	647	678	708
10	375	406	434	465	495	526	556	587	618	648	679	709
11	376	407	435	466	496	527	557	588	619	649	680	710
12	377	408	436	467	497	528	558	589	620	650	681	711
13	378	409	437	468	498	529	559	590	621	651	682	712
14	379	410	438	469	499	530	560	591	622	652	683	713
15	380	411	439	470	500	531	561	592	623	653	684	714
16	381	412	440	471	501	532	562	593	624	654	685	715
17	382	413	441	472	502	533	563	594	625	655	686	716
18	383	414	442	473	503	534	564	595	626	656	687	717
19	384	415	443	474	504	535	565	596	627	657	688	718
20	385	416	444	475	505	536	566	597	628	658	689	719
21	386	417	445	476	506	537	567	598	629	659	690	720
22	387	418	446	477	507	538	568	599	630	660	691	721
23	388	419	447	478	508	539	569	600	631	661	692	722
24	389	420	448	479	509	540	570	601	632	662	693	723
25	390	421	449	480	510	541	571	602	633	663	694	724
26	391	422	450	481	511	542	572	603	634	664	695	725
27	392	423	451	482	512	543	573	604	635	665	696	726
28	393	424	452	483	513	544	574	605	636	666	697	727
29	394	—	453	484	514	545	575	606	637	667	698	728
30	395	—	454	485	515	546	576	607	638	668	699	729
31	396	—	455	—	516	—	577	608	—	669	—	730

Chinese Calendar, Asian Festivals

Source: Chinese Information and Culture Center, New York, NY

The Chinese calendar (like the Jewish and Islamic calendars; see the Religion chapter) is a lunar calendar. It is divided into 12 months of 29 or 30 days (compensating for the lunar month's mean duration of 29 days, 12 hr, 44.05 min). This calendar is synchronized with the solar year by the addition of extra months at fixed intervals.

The Chinese calendar runs on a 60-year cycle. The cycles 1876-1935 and 1936-95, with the years grouped under their 12 animal designations, are printed below, along with the first 24 years of the current cycle. This cycle began in 1996 and will last until 2055. Jan. 22, 2004, marks the beginning of the year 4702 in the Chinese calendar, and is designated the Year of the Monkey. Readers can find the animal name for the year of their birth in the chart below. (Note: The first 3-7 weeks of each Western year belong to the previous Chinese year and animal designation.)

Both the Western (Gregorian) and traditional lunar calendars are used publicly in China and in North and South Korea, and 2 New Year's celebrations are held. In Taiwan, in overseas Chinese communities, and in Vietnam, the lunar calendar is used only to set the dates for traditional festivals, with the Gregorian system in general use.

The 4-day Chinese New Year, Hsin Nien, the 3-day Vietnamese New Year festival, Tet, and the 3-to-4-day Korean festival, Suhl, begin at the 2nd new moon after the winter solstice. The new moon in the Far East, which is west of the International Date Line, may be a day later than the new moon in the U.S. The festivals may start, therefore, anywhere between Jan. 21 and Feb. 19 of the Gregorian calendar.

Rat	Ox	Tiger	Hare (Rabbit)	Dragon	Snake	Horse	Sheep (Goat)	Monkey	Rooster	Dog	Pig
1876	1877	1878	1879	1880	1881	1882	1883	1884	1885	1886	1887
1888	1889	1890	1891	1892	1893	1894	1895	1896	1897	1898	1899
1900	1901	1902	1903	1904	1905	1906	1907	1908	1909	1910	1911
1912	1913	1914	1915	1916	1917	1918	1919	1920	1921	1922	1923
1924	1925	1926	1927	1928	1929	1930	1931	1932	1933	1934	1935
1936	1937	1938	1939	1940	1941	1942	1943	1944	1945	1946	1947
1948	1949	1950	1951	1952	1953	1954	1955	1956	1957	1958	1959
1960	1961	1962	1963	1964	1965	1966	1967	1968	1969	1970	1971
1972	1973	1974	1975	1976	1977	1978	1979	1980	1981	1982	1983
1984	1985	1986	1987	1988	1989	1990	1991	1992	1993	1994	1995
1996	1997	1998	1999	2000	2001	2002	2003	2004	2005	2006	2007
2008	2009	2010	2011	2012	2013	2014	2015	2016	2017	2018	2019

Perpetual Calendar

The number shown for each year indicates which Gregorian calendar to use. For 1583-1802, see "Gregorian Calendar" on page 638. For 1803-20, use numbers for 1983-2000, respectively. For Julian Calendar, see "Julian Calendar" on page 638.

1821....2	1847....6	1873....4	1899....1	1925....5	1951....2	1977....7	2003....4	2029....2	2055....6
1822....3	1848...14	1874....5	1900....2	1926....6	1952...10	1978....1	2004...12	2030....3	2056...14
1823....4	1849....2	1875....6	1901....3	1927....7	1953....5	1979....2	2005....7	2031....4	2057....2
1824...12	1850....3	1876...14	1902....4	1928....8	1954....6	1980...10	2006....1	2032...12	2058....3
1825....7	1851....4	1877....2	1903....5	1929....3	1955....7	1981....5	2007....2	2033....7	2059....4
1826....1	1852...12	1878....3	1904...13	1930....4	1956....8	1982....6	2008...10	2034....1	2060...12
1827....2	1853....7	1879....4	1905....1	1931....5	1957....3	1983....7	2009....5	2035....2	2061....7
1828...10	1854....1	1880...12	1906....2	1932...13	1958....4	1984....8	2010....6	2036...10	2062....1
1829....5	1855....2	1881....7	1907....3	1933....1	1959....5	1985....3	2011....7	2037....5	2063....2
1830....6	1856...10	1882....1	1908...11	1934....2	1960...13	1986....4	2012....8	2038....6	2064...10
1831....7	1857....5	1883....2	1909....6	1935....3	1961....1	1987....5	2013....3	2039....7	2065....5
1832....8	1858....6	1884...10	1910....7	1936...11	1962....2	1988...13	2014....4	2040....8	2066....6
1833....3	1859....7	1885....5	1911....1	1937....6	1963....3	1989....1	2015....5	2041....3	2067....7
1834....4	1860....8	1886....6	1912....9	1938....7	1964...11	1990....2	2016...13	2042....4	2068....8
1835....5	1861....3	1887....7	1913....4	1939....1	1965....6	1991....3	2017....1	2043....5	2069....3
1836...13	1862....4	1888....8	1914....5	1940....9	1966....7	1992...11	2018....2	2044...13	2070....4
1837....1	1863....5	1889....3	1915....6	1941....4	1967....1	1993....6	2019....3	2045....1	2071....5
1838....2	1864...13	1890....4	1916...14	1942....5	1968....9	1994....7	2020...11	2046....2	2072...13
1839....3	1865....1	1891....5	1917....2	1943....6	1969....4	1995....1	2021....6	2047....3	2073....1
1840...11	1866....2	1892...13	1918....3	1944...14	1970....5	1996....9	2022....7	2048...11	2074....2
1841....6	1867....3	1893....1	1919....4	1945....2	1971....6	1997....4	2023....1	2049....6	2075....3
1842....7	1868...11	1894....2	1920...12	1946....3	1972...14	1998....5	2024....9	2050....7	2076...11
1843....1	1869....6	1895....3	1921....7	1947....4	1973....2	1999....6	2025....4	2051....1	2077....6
1844....9	1870....7	1896...11	1922....1	1948...12	1974....3	2000...14	2026....5	2052....9	2078....7
1845....4	1871....1	1897....6	1923....2	1949....7	1975....4	2001....2	2027....6	2053....4	2079....1
1846....5	1872....9	1898....7	1924...10	1950....1	1976...12	2002....3	2028...14	2054....5	2080....9

1 2006

JANUARY

S	M	T	W	T	F	S
1	2	3	4	5	6	7
8	9	10	11	12	13	14
15	16	17	18	19	20	21
22	23	24	25	26	27	28
29	30	31				

MAY

S	M	T	W	T	F	S
	1	2	3	4	5	6
7	8	9	10	11	12	13
14	15	16	17	18	19	20
21	22	23	24	25	26	27
28	29	30	31			

SEPTEMBER

S	M	T	W	T	F	S
					1	2
3	4	5	6	7	8	9
10	11	12	13	14	15	16
17	18	19	20	21	22	23
24	25	26	27	28	29	30

FEBRUARY

S	M	T	W	T	F	S
			1	2	3	4
5	6	7	8	9	10	11
12	13	14	15	16	17	18
19	20	21	22	23	24	25
26	27	28				

JUNE

S	M	T	W	T	F	S
				1	2	3
4	5	6	7	8	9	10
11	12	13	14	15	16	17
18	19	20	21	22	23	24
25	26	27	28	29	30	

OCTOBER

S	M	T	W	T	F	S
1	2	3	4	5	6	7
8	9	10	11	12	13	14
15	16	17	18	19	20	21
22	23	24	25	26	27	28
29	30	31				

MARCH

S	M	T	W	T	F	S
			1	2	3	4
5	6	7	8	9	10	11
12	13	14	15	16	17	18
19	20	21	22	23	24	25
26	27	28	29	30	31	

JULY

S	M	T	W	T	F	S
						1
2	3	4	5	6	7	8
9	10	11	12	13	14	15
16	17	18	19	20	21	22
23	24	25	26	27	28	29
30	31					

NOVEMBER

S	M	T	W	T	F	S
			1	2	3	4
5	6	7	8	9	10	11
12	13	14	15	16	17	18
19	20	21	22	23	24	25
26	27	28	29	30		

APRIL

S	M	T	W	T	F	S
						1
2	3	4	5	6	7	8
9	10	11	12	13	14	15
16	17	18	19	20	21	22
23	24	25	26	27	28	29
30						

AUGUST

S	M	T	W	T	F	S
		1	2	3	4	5
6	7	8	9	10	11	12
13	14	15	16	17	18	19
20	21	22	23	24	25	26
27	28	29	30	31		

DECEMBER

S	M	T	W	T	F	S
					1	2
3	4	5	6	7	8	9
10	11	12	13	14	15	16
17	18	19	20	21	22	23
24	25	26	27	28	29	30
31						

2 2001/2007

JANUARY

S	M	T	W	T	F	S
	1	2	3	4	5	6
7	8	9	10	11	12	13
14	15	16	17	18	19	20
21	22	23	24	25	26	27
28	29	30	31			

MAY

S	M	T	W	T	F	S
		1	2	3	4	5
6	7	8	9	10	11	12
13	14	15	16	17	18	19
20	21	22	23	24	25	26
27	28	29	30	31		

SEPTEMBER

S	M	T	W	T	F	S
						1
2	3	4	5	6	7	8
9	10	11	12	13	14	15
16	17	18	19	20	21	22
23	24	25	26	27	28	29
30						

FEBRUARY

S	M	T	W	T	F	S
				1	2	3
4	5	6	7	8	9	10
11	12	13	14	15	16	17
18	19	20	21	22	23	24
25	26	27	28			

JUNE

S	M	T	W	T	F	S
					1	2
3	4	5	6	7	8	9
10	11	12	13	14	15	16
17	18	19	20	21	22	23
24	25	26	27	28	29	30

OCTOBER

S	M	T	W	T	F	S
	1	2	3	4	5	6
7	8	9	10	11	12	13
14	15	16	17	18	19	20
21	22	23	24	25	26	27
28	29	30	31			

MARCH

S	M	T	W	T	F	S
				1	2	3
4	5	6	7	8	9	10
11	12	13	14	15	16	17
18	19	20	21	22	23	24
25	26	27	28	29	30	31

JULY

S	M	T	W	T	F	S
1	2	3	4	5	6	7
8	9	10	11	12	13	14
15	16	17	18	19	20	21
22	23	24	25	26	27	28
29	30	31				

NOVEMBER

S	M	T	W	T	F	S
				1	2	3
4	5	6	7	8	9	10
11	12	13	14	15	16	17
18	19	20	21	22	23	24
25	26	27	28	29	30	

APRIL

S	M	T	W	T	F	S
1	2	3	4	5	6	7
8	9	10	11	12	13	14
15	16	17	18	19	20	21
22	23	24	25	26	27	28
29	30					

AUGUST

S	M	T	W	T	F	S
			1	2	3	4
5	6	7	8	9	10	11
12	13	14	15	16	17	18
19	20	21	22	23	24	25
26	27	28	29	30	31	

DECEMBER

S	M	T	W	T	F	S
						1
2	3	4	5	6	7	8
9	10	11	12	13	14	15
16	17	18	19	20	21	22
23	24	25	26	27	28	29
30	31					

3 2002

JANUARY

S	M	T	W	T	F	S
		1	2	3	4	5
6	7	8	9	10	11	12
13	14	15	16	17	18	19
20	21	22	23	24	25	26
27	28	29	30	31		

MAY

S	M	T	W	T	F	S
			1	2	3	4
5	6	7	8	9	10	11
12	13	14	15	16	17	18
19	20	21	22	23	24	25
26	27	28	29	30	31	

SEPTEMBER

S	M	T	W	T	F	S
1	2	3	4	5	6	7
8	9	10	11	12	13	14
15	16	17	18	19	20	21
22	23	24	25	26	27	28
29	30					

FEBRUARY

S	M	T	W	T	F	S
					1	2
3	4	5	6	7	8	9
10	11	12	13	14	15	16
17	18	19	20	21	22	23
24	25	26	27	28		

JUNE

S	M	T	W	T	F	S
						1
2	3	4	5	6	7	8
9	10	11	12	13	14	15
16	17	18	19	20	21	22
23	24	25	26	27	28	29
30						

OCTOBER

S	M	T	W	T	F	S
		1	2	3	4	5
6	7	8	9	10	11	12
13	14	15	16	17	18	19
20	21	22	23	24	25	26
27	28	29	30	31		

MARCH

S	M	T	W	T	F	S
					1	2
3	4	5	6	7	8	9
10	11	12	13	14	15	16
17	18	19	20	21	22	23
24	25	26	27	28	29	30
31						

JULY

S	M	T	W	T	F	S
	1	2	3	4	5	6
7	8	9	10	11	12	13
14	15	16	17	18	19	20
21	22	23	24	25	26	27
28	29	30	31			

NOVEMBER

S	M	T	W	T	F	S
					1	2
3	4	5	6	7	8	9
10	11	12	13	14	15	16
17	18	19	20	21	22	23
24	25	26	27	28	29	30

APRIL

S	M	T	W	T	F	S
	1	2	3	4	5	6
7	8	9	10	11	12	13
14	15	16	17	18	19	20
21	22	23	24	25	26	27
28	29	30				

AUGUST

S	M	T	W	T	F	S
				1	2	3
4	5	6	7	8	9	10
11	12	13	14	15	16	17
18	19	20	21	22	23	24
25	26	27	28	29	30	31

DECEMBER

S	M	T	W	T	F	S
1	2	3	4	5	6	7
8	9	10	11	12	13	14
15	16	17	18	19	20	21
22	23	24	25	26	27	28
29	30	31				

4 2003

JANUARY

S	M	T	W	T	F	S
			1	2	3	4
5	6	7	8	9	10	11
12	13	14	15	16	17	18
19	20	21	22	23	24	25
26	27	28	29	30	31	

MAY

S	M	T	W	T	F	S
				1	2	3
4	5	6	7	8	9	10
11	12	13	14	15	16	17
18	19	20	21	22	23	24
25	26	27	28	29	30	31

SEPTEMBER

S	M	T	W	T	F	S
	1	2	3	4	5	6
7	8	9	10	11	12	13
14	15	16	17	18	19	20
21	22	23	24	25	26	27
28	29	30				

FEBRUARY

S	M	T	W	T	F	S
						1
2	3	4	5	6	7	8
9	10	11	12	13	14	15
16	17	18	19	20	21	22
23	24	25	26	27	28	

JUNE

S	M	T	W	T	F	S
1	2	3	4	5	6	7
8	9	10	11	12	13	14
15	16	17	18	19	20	21
22	23	24	25	26	27	28
29	30					

OCTOBER

S	M	T	W	T	F	S
			1	2	3	4
5	6	7	8	9	10	11
12	13	14	15	16	17	18
19	20	21	22	23	24	25
26	27	28	29	30	31	

MARCH

S	M	T	W	T	F	S
						1
2	3	4	5	6	7	8
9	10	11	12	13	14	15
16	17	18	19	20	21	22
23	24	25	26	27	28	29
30	31					

JULY

S	M	T	W	T	F	S
		1	2	3	4	5
6	7	8	9	10	11	12
13	14	15	16	17	18	19
20	21	22	23	24	25	26
27	28	29	30	31		

NOVEMBER

S	M	T	W	T	F	S
						1
2	3	4	5	6	7	8
9	10	11	12	13	14	15
16	17	18	19	20	21	22
23	24	25	26	27	28	29
30						

APRIL

S	M	T	W	T	F	S
		1	2	3	4	5
6	7	8	9	10	11	12
13	14	15	16	17	18	19
20	21	22	23	24	25	26
27	28	29	30			

AUGUST

S	M	T	W	T	F	S
					1	2
3	4	5	6	7	8	9
10	11	12	13	14	15	16
17	18	19	20	21	22	23
24	25	26	27	28	29	30
31						

DECEMBER

S	M	T	W	T	F	S
	1	2	3	4	5	6
7	8	9	10	11	12	13
14	15	16	17	18	19	20
21	22	23	24	25	26	27
28	29	30	31			

5 2009

JANUARY

S	M	T	W	T	F	S
				1	2	3
4	5	6	7	8	9	10
11	12	13	14	15	16	17
18	19	20	21	22	23	24
25	26	27	28	29	30	31

MAY

S	M	T	W	T	F	S
					1	2
3	4	5	6	7	8	9
10	11	12	13	14	15	16
17	18	19	20	21	22	23
24	25	26	27	28	29	30
31						

SEPTEMBER

S	M	T	W	T	F	S
		1	2	3	4	5
6	7	8	9	10	11	12
13	14	15	16	17	18	19
20	21	22	23	24	25	26
27	28	29	30			

FEBRUARY

S	M	T	W	T	F	S
1	2	3	4	5	6	7
8	9	10	11	12	13	14
15	16	17	18	19	20	21
22	23	24	25	26	27	28

JUNE

S	M	T	W	T	F	S
	1	2	3	4	5	6
7	8	9	10	11	12	13
14	15	16	17	18	19	20
21	22	23	24	25	26	27
28	29	30				

OCTOBER

S	M	T	W	T	F	S
				1	2	3
4	5	6	7	8	9	10
11	12	13	14	15	16	17
18	19	20	21	22	23	24
25	26	27	28	29	30	31

MARCH

S	M	T	W	T	F	S
1	2	3	4	5	6	7
8	9	10	11	12	13	14
15	16	17	18	19	20	21
22	23	24	25	26	27	28
29	30	31				

JULY

S	M	T	W	T	F	S
			1	2	3	4
5	6	7	8	9	10	11
12	13	14	15	16	17	18
19	20	21	22	23	24	25
26	27	28	29	30	31	

NOVEMBER

S	M	T	W	T	F	S
1	2	3	4	5	6	7
8	9	10	11	12	13	14
15	16	17	18	19	20	21
22	23	24	25	26	27	28
29	30					

APRIL

S	M	T	W	T	F	S
			1	2	3	4
5	6	7	8	9	10	11
12	13	14	15	16	17	18
19	20	21	22	23	24	25
26	27	28	29	30		

AUGUST

S	M	T	W	T	F	S
						1
2	3	4	5	6	7	8
9	10	11	12	13	14	15
16	17	18	19	20	21	22
23	24	25	26	27	28	29
30	31					

DECEMBER

S	M	T	W	T	F	S
		1	2	3	4	5
6	7	8	9	10	11	12
13	14	15	16	17	18	19
20	21	22	23	24	25	26
27	28	29	30	31		

6 2010

JANUARY

S	M	T	W	T	F	S
					1	2
3	4	5	6	7	8	9
10	11	12	13	14	15	16
17	18	19	20	21	22	23
24	25	26	27	28	29	30
31						

MAY

S	M	T	W	T	F	S
						1
2	3	4	5	6	7	8
9	10	11	12	13	14	15
16	17	18	19	20	21	22
23	24	25	26	27	28	29
30	31					

SEPTEMBER

S	M	T	W	T	F	S
			1	2	3	4
5	6	7	8	9	10	11
12	13	14	15	16	17	18
19	20	21	22	23	24	25
26	27	28	29	30		

FEBRUARY

S	M	T	W	T	F	S
	1	2	3	4	5	6
7	8	9	10	11	12	13
14	15	16	17	18	19	20
21	22	23	24	25	26	27
28						

JUNE

S	M	T	W	T	F	S
		1	2	3	4	5
6	7	8	9	10	11	12
13	14	15	16	17	18	19
20	21	22	23	24	25	26
27	28	29	30			

OCTOBER

S	M	T	W	T	F	S
					1	2
3	4	5	6	7	8	9
10	11	12	13	14	15	16
17	18	19	20	21	22	23
24	25	26	27	28	29	30
31						

MARCH

S	M	T	W	T	F	S
	1	2	3	4	5	6
7	8	9	10	11	12	13
14	15	16	17	18	19	20
21	22	23	24	25	26	27
28	29	30	31			

JULY

S	M	T	W	T	F	S
				1	2	3
4	5	6	7	8	9	10
11	12	13	14	15	16	17
18	19	20	21	22	23	24
25	26	27	28	29	30	31

NOVEMBER

S	M	T	W	T	F	S
	1	2	3	4	5	6
7	8	9	10	11	12	13
14	15	16	17	18	19	20
21	22	23	24	25	26	27
28	29	30				

APRIL

S	M	T	W	T	F	S
				1	2	3
4	5	6	7	8	9	10
11	12	13	14	15	16	17
18	19	20	21	22	23	24
25	26	27	28	29	30	

AUGUST

S	M	T	W	T	F	S
1	2	3	4	5	6	7
8	9	10	11	12	13	14
15	16	17	18	19	20	21
22	23	24	25	26	27	28
29	30	31				

DECEMBER

S	M	T	W	T	F	S
			1	2	3	4
5	6	7	8	9	10	11
12	13	14	15	16	17	18
19	20	21	22	23	24	25
26	27	28	29	30	31	

7 — 2005

JANUARY

S	M	T	W	T	F	S
						1
2	3	4	5	6	7	8
9	10	11	12	13	14	15
16	17	18	19	20	21	22
23	24	25	26	27	28	29
30	31					

FEBRUARY

S	M	T	W	T	F	S
		1	2	3	4	5
6	7	8	9	10	11	12
13	14	15	16	17	18	19
20	21	22	23	24	25	26
27	28					

MARCH

S	M	T	W	T	F	S
		1	2	3	4	5
6	7	8	9	10	11	12
13	14	15	16	17	18	19
20	21	22	23	24	25	26
27	28	29	30	31		

APRIL

S	M	T	W	T	F	S
					1	2
3	4	5	6	7	8	9
10	11	12	13	14	15	16
17	18	19	20	21	22	23
24	25	26	27	28	29	30

MAY

S	M	T	W	T	F	S
1	2	3	4	5	6	7
8	9	10	11	12	13	14
15	16	17	18	19	20	21
22	23	24	25	26	27	28
29	30	31				

JUNE

S	M	T	W	T	F	S
			1	2	3	4
5	6	7	8	9	10	11
12	13	14	15	16	17	18
19	20	21	22	23	24	25
26	27	28	29	30		

JULY

S	M	T	W	T	F	S
					1	2
3	4	5	6	7	8	9
10	11	12	13	14	15	16
17	18	19	20	21	22	23
24	25	26	27	28	29	30
31						

AUGUST

S	M	T	W	T	F	S
	1	2	3	4	5	6
7	8	9	10	11	12	13
14	15	16	17	18	19	20
21	22	23	24	25	26	27
28	29	30	31			

SEPTEMBER

S	M	T	W	T	F	S
				1	2	3
4	5	6	7	8	9	10
11	12	13	14	15	16	17
18	19	20	21	22	23	24
25	26	27	28	29	30	

OCTOBER

S	M	T	W	T	F	S
						1
2	3	4	5	6	7	8
9	10	11	12	13	14	15
16	17	18	19	20	21	22
23	24	25	26	27	28	29
30	31					

NOVEMBER

S	M	T	W	T	F	S
		1	2	3	4	5
6	7	8	9	10	11	12
13	14	15	16	17	18	19
20	21	22	23	24	25	26
27	28	29	30			

DECEMBER

S	M	T	W	T	F	S
				1	2	3
4	5	6	7	8	9	10
11	12	13	14	15	16	17
18	19	20	21	22	23	24
25	26	27	28	29	30	31

8

JANUARY

S	M	T	W	T	F	S
1	2	3	4	5	6	7
8	9	10	11	12	13	14
15	16	17	18	19	20	21
22	23	24	25	26	27	28
29	30	31				

FEBRUARY

S	M	T	W	T	F	S
			1	2	3	4
5	6	7	8	9	10	11
12	13	14	15	16	17	18
19	20	21	22	23	24	25
26	27	28	29			

MARCH

S	M	T	W	T	F	S
				1	2	3
4	5	6	7	8	9	10
11	12	13	14	15	16	17
18	19	20	21	22	23	24
25	26	27	28	29	30	31

APRIL

S	M	T	W	T	F	S
1	2	3	4	5	6	7
8	9	10	11	12	13	14
15	16	17	18	19	20	21
22	23	24	25	26	27	28
29	30					

MAY

S	M	T	W	T	F	S
		1	2	3	4	5
6	7	8	9	10	11	12
13	14	15	16	17	18	19
20	21	22	23	24	25	26
27	28	29	30	31		

JUNE

S	M	T	W	T	F	S
					1	2
3	4	5	6	7	8	9
10	11	12	13	14	15	16
17	18	19	20	21	22	23
24	25	26	27	28	29	30

JULY

S	M	T	W	T	F	S
1	2	3	4	5	6	7
8	9	10	11	12	13	14
15	16	17	18	19	20	21
22	23	24	25	26	27	28
29	30	31				

AUGUST

S	M	T	W	T	F	S
			1	2	3	4
5	6	7	8	9	10	11
12	13	14	15	16	17	18
19	20	21	22	23	24	25
26	27	28	29	30	31	

SEPTEMBER

S	M	T	W	T	F	S
						1
2	3	4	5	6	7	8
9	10	11	12	13	14	15
16	17	18	19	20	21	22
23	24	25	26	27	28	29
30						

OCTOBER

S	M	T	W	T	F	S
	1	2	3	4	5	6
7	8	9	10	11	12	13
14	15	16	17	18	19	20
21	22	23	24	25	26	27
28	29	30	31			

NOVEMBER

S	M	T	W	T	F	S
				1	2	3
4	5	6	7	8	9	10
11	12	13	14	15	16	17
18	19	20	21	22	23	24
25	26	27	28	29	30	

DECEMBER

S	M	T	W	T	F	S
						1
2	3	4	5	6	7	8
9	10	11	12	13	14	15
16	17	18	19	20	21	22
23	24	25	26	27	28	29
30	31					

9

JANUARY

S	M	T	W	T	F	S
	1	2	3	4	5	6
7	8	9	10	11	12	13
14	15	16	17	18	19	20
21	22	23	24	25	26	27
28	29	30	31			

FEBRUARY

S	M	T	W	T	F	S
				1	2	3
4	5	6	7	8	9	10
11	12	13	14	15	16	17
18	19	20	21	22	23	24
25	26	27	28	29		

MARCH

S	M	T	W	T	F	S
					1	2
3	4	5	6	7	8	9
10	11	12	13	14	15	16
17	18	19	20	21	22	23
24	25	26	27	28	29	30
31						

APRIL

S	M	T	W	T	F	S
	1	2	3	4	5	6
7	8	9	10	11	12	13
14	15	16	17	18	19	20
21	22	23	24	25	26	27
28	29	30				

MAY

S	M	T	W	T	F	S
			1	2	3	4
5	6	7	8	9	10	11
12	13	14	15	16	17	18
19	20	21	22	23	24	25
26	27	28	29	30	31	

JUNE

S	M	T	W	T	F	S
						1
2	3	4	5	6	7	8
9	10	11	12	13	14	15
16	17	18	19	20	21	22
23	24	25	26	27	28	29
30						

JULY

S	M	T	W	T	F	S
	1	2	3	4	5	6
7	8	9	10	11	12	13
14	15	16	17	18	19	20
21	22	23	24	25	26	27
28	29	30	31			

AUGUST

S	M	T	W	T	F	S
				1	2	3
4	5	6	7	8	9	10
11	12	13	14	15	16	17
18	19	20	21	22	23	24
25	26	27	28	29	30	31

SEPTEMBER

S	M	T	W	T	F	S
1	2	3	4	5	6	7
8	9	10	11	12	13	14
15	16	17	18	19	20	21
22	23	24	25	26	27	28
29	30					

OCTOBER

S	M	T	W	T	F	S
		1	2	3	4	5
6	7	8	9	10	11	12
13	14	15	16	17	18	19
20	21	22	23	24	25	26
27	28	29	30	31		

NOVEMBER

S	M	T	W	T	F	S
					1	2
3	4	5	6	7	8	9
10	11	12	13	14	15	16
17	18	19	20	21	22	23
24	25	26	27	28	29	30

DECEMBER

S	M	T	W	T	F	S
1	2	3	4	5	6	7
8	9	10	11	12	13	14
15	16	17	18	19	20	21
22	23	24	25	26	27	28
29	30	31				

10 — 2008

JANUARY

S	M	T	W	T	F	S
		1	2	3	4	5
6	7	8	9	10	11	12
13	14	15	16	17	18	19
20	21	22	23	24	25	26
27	28	29	30	31		

FEBRUARY

S	M	T	W	T	F	S
					1	2
3	4	5	6	7	8	9
10	11	12	13	14	15	16
17	18	19	20	21	22	23
24	25	26	27	28	29	

MARCH

S	M	T	W	T	F	S
						1
2	3	4	5	6	7	8
9	10	11	12	13	14	15
16	17	18	19	20	21	22
23	24	25	26	27	28	29
30	31					

APRIL

S	M	T	W	T	F	S
		1	2	3	4	5
6	7	8	9	10	11	12
13	14	15	16	17	18	19
20	21	22	23	24	25	26
27	28	29	30			

MAY

S	M	T	W	T	F	S
				1	2	3
4	5	6	7	8	9	10
11	12	13	14	15	16	17
18	19	20	21	22	23	24
25	26	27	28	29	30	31

JUNE

S	M	T	W	T	F	S
1	2	3	4	5	6	7
8	9	10	11	12	13	14
15	16	17	18	19	20	21
22	23	24	25	26	27	28
29	30					

JULY

S	M	T	W	T	F	S
		1	2	3	4	5
6	7	8	9	10	11	12
13	14	15	16	17	18	19
20	21	22	23	24	25	26
27	28	29	30	31		

AUGUST

S	M	T	W	T	F	S
					1	2
3	4	5	6	7	8	9
10	11	12	13	14	15	16
17	18	19	20	21	22	23
24	25	26	27	28	29	30
31						

SEPTEMBER

S	M	T	W	T	F	S
	1	2	3	4	5	6
7	8	9	10	11	12	13
14	15	16	17	18	19	20
21	22	23	24	25	26	27
28	29	30				

OCTOBER

S	M	T	W	T	F	S
			1	2	3	4
5	6	7	8	9	10	11
12	13	14	15	16	17	18
19	20	21	22	23	24	25
26	27	28	29	30	31	

NOVEMBER

S	M	T	W	T	F	S
						1
2	3	4	5	6	7	8
9	10	11	12	13	14	15
16	17	18	19	20	21	22
23	24	25	26	27	28	29
30						

DECEMBER

S	M	T	W	T	F	S
	1	2	3	4	5	6
7	8	9	10	11	12	13
14	15	16	17	18	19	20
21	22	23	24	25	26	27
28	29	30	31			

11

JANUARY

S	M	T	W	T	F	S
			1	2	3	4
5	6	7	8	9	10	11
12	13	14	15	16	17	18
19	20	21	22	23	24	25
26	27	28	29	30	31	

FEBRUARY

S	M	T	W	T	F	S
						1
2	3	4	5	6	7	8
9	10	11	12	13	14	15
16	17	18	19	20	21	22
23	24	25	26	27	28	29

MARCH

S	M	T	W	T	F	S
1	2	3	4	5	6	7
8	9	10	11	12	13	14
15	16	17	18	19	20	21
22	23	24	25	26	27	28
29	30	31				

APRIL

S	M	T	W	T	F	S
			1	2	3	4
5	6	7	8	9	10	11
12	13	14	15	16	17	18
19	20	21	22	23	24	25
26	27	28	29	30		

MAY

S	M	T	W	T	F	S
					1	2
3	4	5	6	7	8	9
10	11	12	13	14	15	16
17	18	19	20	21	22	23
24	25	26	27	28	29	30
31						

JUNE

S	M	T	W	T	F	S
	1	2	3	4	5	6
7	8	9	10	11	12	13
14	15	16	17	18	19	20
21	22	23	24	25	26	27
28	29	30				

JULY

S	M	T	W	T	F	S
			1	2	3	4
5	6	7	8	9	10	11
12	13	14	15	16	17	18
19	20	21	22	23	24	25
26	27	28	29	30	31	

AUGUST

S	M	T	W	T	F	S
						1
2	3	4	5	6	7	8
9	10	11	12	13	14	15
16	17	18	19	20	21	22
23	24	25	26	27	28	29
30	31					

SEPTEMBER

S	M	T	W	T	F	S
		1	2	3	4	5
6	7	8	9	10	11	12
13	14	15	16	17	18	19
20	21	22	23	24	25	26
27	28	29	30			

OCTOBER

S	M	T	W	T	F	S
				1	2	3
4	5	6	7	8	9	10
11	12	13	14	15	16	17
18	19	20	21	22	23	24
25	26	27	28	29	30	31

NOVEMBER

S	M	T	W	T	F	S
1	2	3	4	5	6	7
8	9	10	11	12	13	14
15	16	17	18	19	20	21
22	23	24	25	26	27	28
29	30					

DECEMBER

S	M	T	W	T	F	S
		1	2	3	4	5
6	7	8	9	10	11	12
13	14	15	16	17	18	19
20	21	22	23	24	25	26
27	28	29	30	31		

12 — 2004

JANUARY

S	M	T	W	T	F	S
				1	2	3
4	5	6	7	8	9	10
11	12	13	14	15	16	17
18	19	20	21	22	23	24
25	26	27	28	29	30	31

FEBRUARY

S	M	T	W	T	F	S
1	2	3	4	5	6	7
8	9	10	11	12	13	14
15	16	17	18	19	20	21
22	23	24	25	26	27	28
29						

MARCH

S	M	T	W	T	F	S
	1	2	3	4	5	6
7	8	9	10	11	12	13
14	15	16	17	18	19	20
21	22	23	24	25	26	27
28	29	30	31			

APRIL

S	M	T	W	T	F	S
				1	2	3
4	5	6	7	8	9	10
11	12	13	14	15	16	17
18	19	20	21	22	23	24
25	26	27	28	29	30	

MAY

S	M	T	W	T	F	S
						1
2	3	4	5	6	7	8
9	10	11	12	13	14	15
16	17	18	19	20	21	22
23	24	25	26	27	28	29
30	31					

JUNE

S	M	T	W	T	F	S
		1	2	3	4	5
6	7	8	9	10	11	12
13	14	15	16	17	18	19
20	21	22	23	24	25	26
27	28	29	30			

JULY

S	M	T	W	T	F	S
				1	2	3
4	5	6	7	8	9	10
11	12	13	14	15	16	17
18	19	20	21	22	23	24
25	26	27	28	29	30	31

AUGUST

S	M	T	W	T	F	S
1	2	3	4	5	6	7
8	9	10	11	12	13	14
15	16	17	18	19	20	21
22	23	24	25	26	27	28
29	30	31				

SEPTEMBER

S	M	T	W	T	F	S
			1	2	3	4
5	6	7	8	9	10	11
12	13	14	15	16	17	18
19	20	21	22	23	24	25
26	27	28	29	30		

OCTOBER

S	M	T	W	T	F	S
					1	2
3	4	5	6	7	8	9
10	11	12	13	14	15	16
17	18	19	20	21	22	23
24	25	26	27	28	29	30
31						

NOVEMBER

S	M	T	W	T	F	S
	1	2	3	4	5	6
7	8	9	10	11	12	13
14	15	16	17	18	19	20
21	22	23	24	25	26	27
28	29	30				

DECEMBER

S	M	T	W	T	F	S
			1	2	3	4
5	6	7	8	9	10	11
12	13	14	15	16	17	18
19	20	21	22	23	24	25
26	27	28	29	30	31	

13

JANUARY

S	M	T	W	T	F	S
					1	2
3	4	5	6	7	8	9
10	11	12	13	14	15	16
17	18	19	20	21	22	23
24	25	26	27	28	29	30
31						

FEBRUARY

S	M	T	W	T	F	S
	1	2	3	4	5	6
7	8	9	10	11	12	13
14	15	16	17	18	19	20
21	22	23	24	25	26	27
28	29					

MARCH

S	M	T	W	T	F	S
		1	2	3	4	5
6	7	8	9	10	11	12
13	14	15	16	17	18	19
20	21	22	23	24	25	26
27	28	29	30	31		

APRIL

S	M	T	W	T	F	S
					1	2
3	4	5	6	7	8	9
10	11	12	13	14	15	16
17	18	19	20	21	22	23
24	25	26	27	28	29	30

MAY

S	M	T	W	T	F	S
1	2	3	4	5	6	7
8	9	10	11	12	13	14
15	16	17	18	19	20	21
22	23	24	25	26	27	28
29	30	31				

JUNE

S	M	T	W	T	F	S
			1	2	3	4
5	6	7	8	9	10	11
12	13	14	15	16	17	18
19	20	21	22	23	24	25
26	27	28	29	30		

JULY

S	M	T	W	T	F	S
					1	2
3	4	5	6	7	8	9
10	11	12	13	14	15	16
17	18	19	20	21	22	23
24	25	26	27	28	29	30
31						

AUGUST

S	M	T	W	T	F	S
	1	2	3	4	5	6
7	8	9	10	11	12	13
14	15	16	17	18	19	20
21	22	23	24	25	26	27
28	29	30	31			

SEPTEMBER

S	M	T	W	T	F	S
				1	2	3
4	5	6	7	8	9	10
11	12	13	14	15	16	17
18	19	20	21	22	23	24
25	26	27	28	29	30	

OCTOBER

S	M	T	W	T	F	S
						1
2	3	4	5	6	7	8
9	10	11	12	13	14	15
16	17	18	19	20	21	22
23	24	25	26	27	28	29
30	31					

NOVEMBER

S	M	T	W	T	F	S
		1	2	3	4	5
6	7	8	9	10	11	12
13	14	15	16	17	18	19
20	21	22	23	24	25	26
27	28	29	30			

DECEMBER

S	M	T	W	T	F	S
				1	2	3
4	5	6	7	8	9	10
11	12	13	14	15	16	17
18	19	20	21	22	23	24
25	26	27	28	29	30	31

14 — 2000

JANUARY

S	M	T	W	T	F	S
						1
2	3	4	5	6	7	8
9	10	11	12	13	14	15
16	17	18	19	20	21	22
23	24	25	26	27	28	29
30	31					

FEBRUARY

S	M	T	W	T	F	S
		1	2	3	4	5
6	7	8	9	10	11	12
13	14	15	16	17	18	19
20	21	22	23	24	25	26
27	28	29				

MARCH

S	M	T	W	T	F	S
			1	2	3	4
5	6	7	8	9	10	11
12	13	14	15	16	17	18
19	20	21	22	23	24	25
26	27	28	29	30	31	

APRIL

S	M	T	W	T	F	S
						1
2	3	4	5	6	7	8
9	10	11	12	13	14	15
16	17	18	19	20	21	22
23	24	25	26	27	28	29
30						

MAY

S	M	T	W	T	F	S
	1	2	3	4	5	6
7	8	9	10	11	12	13
14	15	16	17	18	19	20
21	22	23	24	25	26	27
28	29	30	31			

JUNE

S	M	T	W	T	F	S
				1	2	3
4	5	6	7	8	9	10
11	12	13	14	15	16	17
18	19	20	21	22	23	24
25	26	27	28	29	30	

JULY

S	M	T	W	T	F	S
						1
2	3	4	5	6	7	8
9	10	11	12	13	14	15
16	17	18	19	20	21	22
23	24	25	26	27	28	29
30	31					

AUGUST

S	M	T	W	T	F	S
		1	2	3	4	5
6	7	8	9	10	11	12
13	14	15	16	17	18	19
20	21	22	23	24	25	26
27	28	29	30	31		

SEPTEMBER

S	M	T	W	T	F	S
					1	2
3	4	5	6	7	8	9
10	11	12	13	14	15	16
17	18	19	20	21	22	23
24	25	26	27	28	29	30

OCTOBER

S	M	T	W	T	F	S
1	2	3	4	5	6	7
8	9	10	11	12	13	14
15	16	17	18	19	20	21
22	23	24	25	26	27	28
29	30	31				

NOVEMBER

S	M	T	W	T	F	S
			1	2	3	4
5	6	7	8	9	10	11
12	13	14	15	16	17	18
19	20	21	22	23	24	25
26	27	28	29	30		

DECEMBER

S	M	T	W	T	F	S
					1	2
3	4	5	6	7	8	9
10	11	12	13	14	15	16
17	18	19	20	21	22	23
24	25	26	27	28	29	30
31						

Calendar for the Year 2004

JANUARY							FEBRUARY							MARCH							APRIL						
S	M	T	W	T	F	S	S	M	T	W	T	F	S	S	M	T	W	T	F	S	S	M	T	W	T	F	S
				1	2	3	1	2	3	4	5	6	7		1	2	3	4	5	6					1	2	3
4	5	6	7	8	9	10	8	9	10	11	12	13	14	7	8	9	10	11	12	13	4	5	6	7	8	9	10
11	12	13	14	15	16	17	15	16	17	18	19	20	21	14	15	16	17	18	19	20	11	12	13	14	15	16	17
18	*19*	20	21	22	23	24	22	23	24	25	26	27	28	21	22	23	24	25	26	27	18	19	20	21	22	23	24
25	26	27	28	29	30	31	29							28	29	30	31				25	26	27	28	29	30	

MAY							JUNE							JULY							AUGUST						
S	M	T	W	T	F	S	S	M	T	W	T	F	S	S	M	T	W	T	F	S	S	M	T	W	T	F	S
						1			1	2	3	4	5					1	2	3	1	2	3	4	5	6	7
2	3	4	5	6	7	8	6	7	8	9	10	11	12	*4*	5	6	7	8	9	10	8	9	10	11	12	13	14
9	10	11	12	13	14	15	13	14	15	16	17	18	19	11	12	13	14	15	16	17	15	16	17	18	19	20	21
16	17	18	19	20	21	22	20	21	22	23	24	25	26	18	19	20	21	22	23	24	22	23	24	25	26	27	28
23	24	25	26	27	28	29	27	28	29	30				25	26	27	28	29	30	31	29	30	31				
30	*31*																										

SEPTEMBER							OCTOBER							NOVEMBER							DECEMBER						
S	M	T	W	T	F	S	S	M	T	W	T	F	S	S	M	T	W	T	F	S	S	M	T	W	T	F	S
			1	2	3	4						1	2		1	2	3	4	5	6				1	2	3	4
5	*6*	7	8	9	10	11	3	4	5	6	7	8	9	7	8	9	10	*11*	12	13	5	6	7	8	9	10	11
12	13	14	15	16	17	18	10	*11*	12	13	14	15	16	14	15	16	17	18	19	20	12	13	14	15	16	17	18
19	20	21	22	23	24	25	17	18	19	20	21	22	23	21	22	23	24	*25*	26	27	19	20	21	22	23	24	*25*
26	27	28	29	30			24	25	26	27	28	29	30	28	29	30					26	27	28	29	30	31	
							31																				

Federal Holidays and Other Notable Dates, 2004

Some dates may be subject to change. Some events omitted where date not scheduled as of Sept. 2003.

The days marked on the calendar above and shown below *in italics* are U.S. federal holidays, designated by the president or Congress and applicable to federal employees and the District of Columbia. Most U.S. states also observe these holidays, and many states observe others; practices vary from state to state. In most states the secretary of states's office can provide details.

January

1 *New Year's Day*; Orange and Rose Bowls
2 Cotton and Fiesta Bowls
4 Sugar Bowl
19 *Martin Luther King Jr. Day* (3rd Mon. in Jan.)
19-Feb. 1 Australian Open tennis tournament
22 Chinese New Year
26 Australia Day, Australia

February

1 Super Bowl XXXVIII (Houston)
2 Groundhog Day
5 Constitution Day, Mexico
8 NFL Pro Bowl
9-10 Westminster Dog Show
12 Lincoln's Birthday
14 Valentine's Day
15 Daytona 500; NBA All-Star Game
16 *Washington's Birthday (observed), or Presidents' Day, or Washington-Lincoln Day* (3rd Mon. in Feb.)
20-24 Carnival, Brazil
24 Mardi Gras
25 Ash Wednesday
29 Academy Awards

March

3 Iditarod Trail Sled Dog Race begins
8 Commonwealth Day, Canada
17 St. Patrick's Day
20 First Day of Spring (Northern Hemisphere)
21 Benito Juarez's Birthday, Mexico

April

1 April Fool's Day
4 Daylight Saving Time begins in U.S.
5 NCAA men's basketball championship
6 Passover (1st full day); NCAA women's basketball championship
8-11 Masters golf tournament
9 Good Friday

11 Easter; Orthodox Easter
19 Patriots' Day; Boston Marathon
21 Administrative Professionals Day
22 Earth Day
29 Take Our Daughters and Sons to Work Day
30 Arbor Day, U.S.

May

1 May Day; Kentucky Derby
4 National Teacher Day, U.S.
5 Cinco de Mayo (Battle of Puebla Day), Mexico
9 Mother's Day
15 Armed Forces Day; Preakness Stakes
24 Victoria Day, Canada
24-June 6 French Open tennis tournament
26 Buddha's Birthday, Korea, Hong Kong
31 *Memorial Day or Decoration Day* (last Mon. in May)

June

4 Dragon Boat Festival, China
5 Belmont Stakes
14 Flag Day, U.S.
17-20 U.S. Open golf tournament
20 Father's Day; First Day of Summer (Northern Hemisphere)
21-July 4 Wimbledon tennis tournament

July

1 Canada Day
4 *Independence Day*
7-14 Running of the Bulls (Pamplona, Spain)
14 Bastille Day, France
15-18 British Open golf tournament

August

12-15 PGA Championship
29-Sept. 7 U.S. Open tennis tournament
30 St. Rose of Lima, Peru

September

6 *Labor Day*, U.S. (1st Monday in Sept.); Labor Day, Canada
12 Grandparents' Day, U.S.
16 Rosh Hashanah (1st full day); Independence Day, Mexico
17 Citizenship Day, U.S.
19 St. Gennaro, Italy
22 First day of Autumn (Northern Hemisphere)
25 Yom Kippur

October

3 German Unification Day, Germany
4 U.S. Supreme Court session begins
11 *Columbus Day* (2nd Mon. in Oct.); Thanksgiving Day, Canada
12 Día de la Raza, Mexico
15 Ramadan (1st full day)
24 United Nations Day
31 Daylight Saving Time ends in U.S.; Halloween

November

1 All Saints' Day
2 Election Day (1st Tues. after 1st Mon. in Nov.); Day of the Dead, Mexico
5 Guy Fawkes Day, UK
7 New York City Marathon
11 *Veterans Day*; Remembrance Day, Canada, UK
15 Shichi-Go-San (Seven-Five-Three), Japan
25 *Thanksgiving Day*, U.S. (4th Thurs. in Nov.)

December

8 Hanukkah (1st full day)
10 Nobel Prizes awarded (announced in Oct.)
12 Virgin of Guadalupe Day, Mexico
21 First day of Winter (Northern Hemisphere)
25 *Christmas Day*
26 Kwanzaa begins; Boxing Day, Australia, Canada, New Zealand, UK

> ▶ **IT'S A FACT:** Although January 1 started the new year in the imperial Roman calendar (begun in 46 BC), most European countries did not adopt this starting date until centuries later. For hundreds of years the German states considered Christmas Day as the beginning of the year, while France and the Low Countries used Easter. Until switching to the Gregorian calendar in 1582, England and its colonies started the new year on March 25, the feast of the Annunciation in the Christian calendar (marking the conception of Christ, 9 months before Christmas).

Special Months

Every year there are many thousands of special months, days, and weeks as a result of anniversaries, official proclamations, and promotional events, both trivial and serious. Here are a few of the special months:

January: National High-Tech Month, National Hot Tea Month, National Mentoring Month
February: Black History Month, American Heart Month, Library Lovers Month, National Hot Breakfast Month
March: Irish-American Heritage Month, Women's History Month, American Red Cross Month, National Umbrella Month
April: Alcohol Awareness Month, National Child Abuse Prevention Month, National Poetry Month, National Smile Month
May: National Book Month, Older Americans Month, Asian Pacific American Heritage Month, National Barbecue Month
June: Children's Awareness Month, Gay and Lesbian Pride Month, National Rivers Month, National Safety Month
July: Cell Phone Courtesy Month, National Culinary Arts Month, National Hot Dog Month, Anti-Boredom Month
August: National Back to School Month, National Inventors' Month, Admit You're Happy Month, Women's Small Business Month
September: Baby Safety Month, Hispanic Heritage Month (Sept. 15-Oct. 15), Be Kind to Editors and Writers Month
October: National Domestic Violence Awareness Month, National Breast Cancer Awareness Month, Diversity Awareness Month
November: National American Indian Heritage Month, National Adoption Month, American Diabetes Month
December: Universal Human Rights Month, National Drunk and Drugged Driving Prevention Month, National Tie Month

Signs of the Zodiac

The **zodiac** is the apparent yearly path of the sun among the stars as viewed from earth, and was divided by the ancients into 12 equal sections or signs, each named for the constellation situated within its limits in ancient times. Astrologers claim that the temperament and destiny of each individual depend on the zodiac sign under which the person was born and the relationships between the planets at that time and throughout life.

Below are the 12 traditional signs and the traditional range of dates pertaining to each:

Aries (Ram), March 21– April 19

Taurus (Bull), April 20– May 20

Gemini (Twins), May 21– June 21

Cancer (Crab), June 22– July 22

Leo (Lion), July 23– August 22

Virgo (Maiden), August 23– September 22

Libra (Balance), September 23– October 23

Scorpio (Scorpion), October 24– November 21

Sagittarius (Archer), November 22– December 21

Capricorn (Goat), December 22– January 19

Aquarius (Water Bearer), January 20 – February 18

Pisces (Fishes), February 19 – March 20

The Julian Period

How many days have you lived? To determine this, multiply your age by 365, add the number of days since your last birthday, and account for all leap years. Chances are your calculations will go wrong somewhere. Astronomers, however, find it convenient to express dates and time intervals in days rather than in years, months, and days. This is done by placing events within the Julian period.

The Julian period was devised in 1582 by the French classical scholar Joseph Scaliger (1540-1609), and it was named after his father, Julius Caesar Scaliger, not after the Julian calendar as might be supposed.

Scaliger began Julian Day (JD) #1 at noon, Jan. 1, 4713 BC, the most recent time that 3 major chronological cycles began on the same day: (1) the 28-year solar cycle, after which dates in the Julian calendar (e.g., Feb. 11) return to the same days of the week (e.g., Monday); (2) the 19-year lunar cycle, after which the phases of the moon return to the same dates of the year; and (3) the 15-year indiction cycle, used in ancient Rome to regulate taxes. It will take 7,980 years to complete the period, the product of 28, 19, and 15.

Noon of Dec. 31, 2003, marks the beginning of JD 2,453,005; that many days will have passed since the start of the Julian period. The JD at noon of any date in 2004 may be found by adding to this figure the day of the year for that date, which can be obtained from the left half of the "How Far Apart Are Two Dates?" chart on page 639.

IT'S A FACT: Days in the Roman calendar were classified according to celestial favor and governed daily life. If a day was *fastus*—favorable or lucky—government and private business were allowed. If the day was *nefastus*, or unlucky, government and businesses were closed. (These designations were subject to manipulation; politicians could sometimes get a day declared *nefastus* so as to prevent a popular assembly from meeting.) Anniversaries of disasters, and the days following the Kalends (1st), Nones (7th or 9th), and Ides (13th or 15th) of each month, were considered highly unfavorable, and even religious ceremonies were not permitted on those days.

Wedding Anniversaries

The traditional names for wedding anniversaries go back many years in social usage and have been used to suggest types of appropriate anniversary gifts. Traditional products for gifts are listed here in capital letters, with a few allowable revisions in parentheses, followed by common modern gifts in each category.

1st	PAPER, clocks	9th	POTTERY (CHINA), leather goods	25th	SILVER, sterling silver
2nd	COTTON, china	10th	TIN, ALUMINUM, diamond	30th	PEARL, diamond
3rd	LEATHER, crystal, glass	11th	STEEL, fashion jewelry	35th	CORAL (JADE), jade
4th	LINEN (SILK), appliances	12th	SILK, pearls, colored gems	40th	RUBY, ruby
5th	WOOD, silverware	13th	LACE, textiles, furs	45th	SAPPHIRE, sapphire
6th	IRON, wood objects	14th	IVORY, gold jewelry	50th	GOLD, gold
7th	WOOL (COPPER), desk sets	15th	CRYSTAL, watches	55th	EMERALD, emerald
8th	BRONZE, linens, lace	20th	CHINA, platinum	60th	DIAMOND, diamond

Birthstones

Source: Jewelry Industry Council

MONTH	Ancient	Modern	MONTH	Ancient	Modern
January	Garnet	Garnet	July	Onyx	Ruby
February	Amethyst	Amethyst	August	Carnelian	Sardonyx or Peridot
March	Jasper	Bloodstone or Aquamarine	September	Chrysolite	Sapphire
April	Sapphire	Diamond	October	Aquamarine	Opal or Tourmaline
May	Agate	Emerald	November	Topaz	Topaz
June	Emerald	Pearl, Moonstone, or Alexandrite	December	Ruby	Turquoise or Zircon

Standard Time, Daylight Saving Time, and Others

Source: National Imagery and Mapping Agency; U.S. Dept. of Transportation
See also Time Zone map, page 500.

Standard Time

Standard Time is reckoned from the Prime Meridian of Longitude in Greenwich, England. The world is divided into 24 zones, each 15 deg of arc, or one hour in time apart. The Greenwich meridian (0 deg) extends through the center of the initial zone, and the zones to the east are numbered from 1 to 12, with the prefix "minus" indicating the number of hours to be subtracted to obtain Greenwich Time. Each zone extends 7.5 deg on either side of its central meridian.

Westward zones are similarly numbered, but prefixed "plus," showing the number of hours that must be added to get Greenwich Time. Although these zones apply generally to sea areas, the Standard Time maintained in many countries does not coincide with zone time. A graphical representation of the zones is shown on the Standard Time Zone Chart of the World (WOBZC76) published by the National Imagery and Mapping Agency. This chart is available from the Federal Aviation Administration (FAA), 6501 Lafayette Avenue, Riverdale, MD 20737-1199; telephone: (800) 638-8972.

The U.S. and possessions are divided into 10 Standard Time zones. Each zone is approximately 15 deg of longitude in width. All places in each zone use, instead of their own local time, the time counted from the transit of the "mean sun" across the Standard Time meridian that passes near the middle of that zone. These time zones are designated as Atlantic, Eastern, Central, Mountain, Pacific, Alaska, Hawaii-Aleutian, Samoa, Wake Island, and Guam; the time in these zones is reckoned from the 60th, 75th, 90th, 105th, 120th, 135th, 150th, and 165th meridians west of Greenwich and the 165th and 150th meridians east of Greenwich. The time zone line wanders to conform to local geographical regions. The time in the various zones in the U.S. and U.S. territories west of Greenwich is earlier than Greenwich Time by 4, 5, 6, 7, 8, 9, 10, and 11 hours, respectively. However, Wake Island and Guam cross the International Date Line and are 12 and 10 hours later than Greenwich Time, respectively.

24-Hour Time

Twenty-four-hour time is widely used in scientific work throughout the world. In the U.S. it is also used in operations of the armed forces. In Europe it is frequently used by the transportation networks in preference to the 12-hour AM and PM system. With the 24-hour system the day begins at midnight, and times are designated 00:00 through 23:59.

International Date Line

The Date Line, approximately coinciding with the 180th meridian, separates the calendar dates. The date must be advanced one day when crossing in a westerly direction and set back one day when crossing in an easterly direction. The Date Line frequently deviates from the 180th meridian because of decisions made by individual nations affected. The line is deflected eastward through the Bering Strait and westward of the Aleutians to prevent separating these areas by date. The line is deflected eastward of the Tonga and New Zealand Islands in the South Pacific for the same reason. More recently it was deflected much farther eastward to include all of Kiribati. The line is established by international custom; there is no international authority prescribing its exact course.

Daylight Saving Time

Daylight Saving Time is achieved by advancing the clock one hour. Daylight Saving Time in the U.S. begins each year at 2 AM on the first Sunday in Apr. and ends at 2 AM on the last Sunday in Oct.

Daylight Saving Time was first observed in the U.S. during World War I, and then again during World War II. In the intervening years, some states and communities observed Daylight Saving Time, using whatever beginning and ending dates they chose. In 1966, Congress passed the Uniform Time Act, which provided that any state or territory that chooses to observe Daylight Saving Time must begin and end on the federal dates. Any state could, by law, exempt itself; a 1972 amendment to the act authorized states split by time zones to observe Daylight Saving Time in one time zone and standard time in the other time zone. Currently, Arizona, Hawaii, the eastern time zone portion of Indiana, Puerto Rico, the U.S. Virgin Islands, and American Samoa do not observe Daylight Saving Time.

Congress and the secretary of transportation both have authority to change time zone boundaries. Since 1966 there have been a number of changes to U.S. time zone boundaries. In addition, efforts to conserve energy have prompted various changes in the times that Daylight Saving Time is observed.

International Usage

Adjusting clock time so as to gain the added daylight on summer evenings is common throughout the world.

Canada, which extends over 6 time zones, generally observes Daylight Saving Time from the first Sunday of Apr. until the last Sunday of Oct. Saskatchewan remains on standard time all year. Communities elsewhere in Canada also may exempt themselves from Daylight Saving Time. Mexico, which occupies 3 time zones, observes Daylight Saving Time during the same period as most of Canada.

Member nations of the European Union (EU) observe a "summer-time period," the EU's version of Daylight Saving Time, from the last Sunday of Mar. until the last Sunday in Oct.

Russia, which extends over 11 time zones, maintains its Standard Time 1 hour fast for its zone designation. Additionally, it proclaims Daylight Saving Time from the last Sunday in Mar. until the 4th Sunday in Oct.

China, which extends across 5 time zones, has decreed that the entire country be placed on Greenwich Time plus 8 hours. Daylight Saving Time is not observed. Japan, which lies within one time zone, also does not modify its legal time during the summer months.

Many countries in the Southern Hemisphere maintain Daylight Saving Time, generally from Oct. to Mar.; however, most countries near the equator do not deviate from Standard Time.

Standard Time Differences—World Cities

The time indicated in the table is fixed by law and is called the legal time or, more generally, Standard Time. Use of Daylight Saving Time varies widely. * Indicates morning of the following day. At 12:00 noon, Eastern Standard Time, the Standard Time (in 24-hour time) in selected cities is as follows:

City	Time	City	Time	City	Time	City	Time
Addis Ababa	20 00	Caracas	13 00	Lima	12 00	St. Petersburg	20 00
Amsterdam	18 00	Casablanca	17 00	Lisbon	17 00	Santiago	13 00
Ankara	19 00	Copenhagen	18 00	London	17 00	Sarajevo	18 00
Athens	19 00	Dhaka	23 00	Madrid	18 00	Seoul	2 00*
Auckland	5 00*	Dublin	17 00	Manila	1 00*	Shanghai	1 00*
Baghdad	20 00	Edinburgh	17 00	Mecca	20 00	Singapore	1 00*
Bangkok	0 00*	Geneva	18 00	Melbourne	3 00*	Stockholm	18 00
Beijing	1 00*	Helsinki	19 00	Montevideo	14 00	Sydney	3 00*
Belfast	17 00	Ho Chi Minh City	0 00*	Moscow	20 00	Taipei	1 00*
Belgrade	18 00	Hong Kong	1 00*	Munich	18 00	Tashkent	22 00
Berlin	18 00	Islamabad	22 00	Nagasaki	2 00*	Tehran	20 30
Bogotá	12 00	Istanbul	19 00	Nairobi	20 00	Tel Aviv	19 00
Bombay (Mumbai)	22 30	Jakarta	0 00*	New Delhi	22 30	Tokyo	2 00*
Brussels	18 00	Jerusalem	19 00	Oslo	18 00	Vladivostok	3 00*
Bucharest	19 00	Johannesburg	19 00	Paris	18 00	Vienna	18 00
Budapest	18 00	Kabul	21 50	Prague	18 00	Warsaw	18 00
Buenos Aires	14 00	Karachi	22 00	Quito	12 00	Wellington	5 00*
Cairo	19 00	Kathmandu	22 45	Rio de Janeiro	14 00	Yangon (Rangoon)	23 30
Calcutta (Kolkata)	22 30	Kiev	19 00	Riyadh	20 00	Yokohama	2 00*
Cape Town	19 00	Lagos	18 00	Rome	18 00	Zurich	18 00

Standard Time Differences—North American Cities

At 12:00 noon, Eastern Standard Time, the Standard Time in selected North American cities is as follows:

City	Time	City	Time	City	Time
Akron, OH	12 00 Noon	*Fort Wayne, IN	12 00 Noon	Peoria, IL	11 00 AM
Albuquerque, NM	10 00 AM	Frankfort, KY	12 00 Noon	*Phoenix, AZ	10 00 AM
Anchorage, AK	8 00 am	Havana, Cuba	12 00 Noon	Pierre, SD	11 00 AM
Atlanta, GA	12 00 Noon	Helena, MT	10 00 AM	Pittsburgh, PA	12 00 Noon
Austin, TX	11 00 AM	*Honolulu, HI	7 00 AM	*Regina, Sask.	11 00 AM
Baltimore, MD	12 00 Noon	Houston, TX	11 00 AM	Reno, NV	9 00 AM
Birmingham, AL	11 00 AM	*Indianapolis, IN	12 00 Noon	Richmond, VA	12 00 Noon
Bismarck, ND	11 00 AM	Jacksonville, FL	12 00 Noon	Rochester, NY	12 00 Noon
Boise, ID	10 00 AM	Juneau, AK	8 00 AM	Sacramento, CA	9 00 AM
Boston, MA	12 00 Noon	Kansas City, MO	11 00 AM	St. John's, Nfld.	1 30 PM
Buffalo, NY	12 00 Noon	*Kingston, Jamaica	12 00 Noon	St. Louis, MO	11 00 AM
Butte, MT	10 00 AM	Knoxville, TN	12 00 Noon	St. Paul, MN	11 00 AM
Calgary, Alta.	10 00 AM	Las Vegas, NV	9 00 AM	Salt Lake City, UT	10 00 AM
Charleston, SC	12 00 Noon	Lexington, KY	12 00 Noon	San Antonio, TX	11 00 AM
Charleston, WV	12 00 Noon	Lincoln, NE	11 00 AM	San Diego, CA	9 00 AM
Charlotte, NC	12 00 Noon	Little Rock, AR	11 00 AM	San Francisco, CA	9 00 AM
Charlottetown, PEI	1 00 PM	Los Angeles, CA	9 00 AM	San Jose, CA	9 00 AM
Chattanooga, TN	12 00 Noon	Louisville, KY	12 00 Noon	*San Juan, PR	1 00 PM
Cheyenne, WY	10 00 AM	Mexico City, Mexico	11 00 AM	Santa Fe, NM	10 00 AM
Chicago, IL	11 00 AM	Memphis, TN	11 00 AM	Savannah, GA	12 00 Noon
Cleveland, OH	12 00 Noon	Miami, FL	12 00 Noon	Seattle, WA	9 00 AM
Colorado Spr., CO	10 00 AM	Milwaukee, WI	11 00 AM	Shreveport, LA	11 00 AM
Columbus, OH	12 00 Noon	Minneapolis, MN	11 00 AM	Sioux Falls, SD	11 00 AM
Dallas, TX	11 00 AM	Mobile, AL	11 00 AM	Spokane, WA	9 00 AM
*Dawson, Yuk.	9 00 AM	Montreal, Que.	12 00 Noon	Tampa, FL	12 00 Noon
Dayton, OH	12 00 Noon	Nashville, TN	11 00 AM	Toledo, OH	12 00 Noon
Denver, CO	10 00 AM	Nassau, Bahamas	12 00 Noon	Topeka, KS	11 00 AM
Des Moines, IA	11 00 AM	New Haven, CT	12 00 Noon	Toronto, Ont.	12 00 Noon
Detroit, MI	12 00 Noon	New Orleans, LA	11 00 AM	*Tucson, AZ	10 00 AM
Duluth, MN	11 00 AM	New York, NY	12 00 Noon	Tulsa, OK	11 00 AM
Edmonton, Alta.	10 00 AM	Nome, AK	8 00 AM	Vancouver, BC	9 00 AM
El Paso, TX	10 00 AM	Norfolk, VA	12 00 Noon	Washington, DC	12 00 Noon
Erie, PA	12 00 Noon	Oklahoma City, OK	11 00 AM	Wichita, KS	11 00 AM
Evansville, IN	11 00 AM	Omaha, NE	11 00 AM	Wilmington, DE	12 00 Noon
Fairbanks, AK	8 00 AM	Ottawa, Ont.	12 00 Noon	Winnipeg, Man.	11 00 AM
Flint, MI	12 00 Noon	*Panama City, Panama	12 00 Noon		

Note: This same table can be used for Daylight Saving Time when it is in effect, but allowance must be made for cities that do not observe it; they are marked with an asterisk (*). Daylight Saving Time is one hour later than Standard Time.

► **IT'S A FACT:** The Indian National Calendar is dated from 78 BC, the beginning of the Saka Era. This calendar was not made official until 1957, at which time about 30 different calendars were used throughout the country.

ASTRONOMY

Edited by Lee T. Shapiro, Ph. D., Head of Education and Public Outreach, National Radio Astronomy Observatory

Celestial Events Summary, 2004

There are 4 **eclipses** in 2004, 2 partial solar and 2 total lunar. The eclipse path of the April partial solar eclipse reaches parts of Antarctica, South Africa, and Madagascar. The eclipse path of the October partial solar eclipse reaches Japan, Korea, and parts of Russia, China, and Alaska. The total lunar eclipse in May is seen best in Africa, Europe, and Antarctica; Australia, New Zealand, Indonesia, South America, and Asia will see portions of it. The total lunar eclipse in October is best seen in North America, Central America, South America, Greenland, and Europe; Africa and Asia will see portions of it. In June there is also a rare transit of the Sun by Venus. The entire transit will be visible over most of Asia, across Africa, Europe, and Greenland. Much of North America and South America will see the end of the transit, while Australia and Indonesia will see the beginning. The most likely viewing successes for meteor showers will be the Quadrantids in January, the Lyrids in April, the Perseids in August, the Orionids in October, the Leonids in November, and the Geminids in December.

As for the **planets**, at the start of the year Saturn is up most of the night while Jupiter is up after midnight; Mars is up the first half of the night, and Venus is prominent in the early evening. By March all 4 of these planets are up after sunset, and in April, Mercury also appears, making it possible to see all 5 planets at the same time. In May, Venus, Mars, and Saturn are close together in the sky, while the lunar eclipse is visible in much of the E hemisphere. In June the planets are getting set to leave the evening sky, but there is the rare transit of the Sun by Venus. Summer is again scarce for planets, with Saturn and Venus hidden during June, while Jupiter and Mars are gone during August. By July, Venus is in the morning sky, joined by Saturn in August, with Jupiter and Mars in October, just in time for the total lunar eclipse for the W hemisphere. Mercury is best seen in the evening sky in early April and viewable in the morning sky in mid-September and late December.

The crescent **Moon**, with its light not overpowering, makes pretty pairings with the 2 brightest planets, Venus and Jupiter. Waxing crescent **pairings** are visible in the early evening soon after sunset, while waning crescent pairings are visible in the early morning rising shortly before sunrise. The waxing crescent Moon pairs with Venus in the late part of each month January through May, while pairing with Jupiter in late June, late July, and mid-August. The waning crescent Moon pairs with Venus in mid-July and mid-August, and early in September, October, November, and December. Of special interest are the close pairing of Venus and Uranus in mid-January as a means of seeing the faint 6th planet, the waxing crescent Moon above Mercury in late March with the other 4 planets stretched across the sky, and the triple groups of the 3 brightest objects—the Moon, Venus, and Jupiter—in the morning sky in early October and early November. In early December, there is also the triple grouping of Venus, Mars, and Antares, sometimes called the "rival" of Mars.

Astronomical Positions Defined

Two celestial bodies are in **conjunction** when they are due N and S of each other, either in **right ascension** (with respect to the N celestial pole) or in **celestial longitude** (with respect to the N ecliptic pole). If the bodies are seen near each other, they will rise and set at nearly the same time. For the inner planets—Mercury and Venus—**inferior conjunction** occurs when either planet passes between Earth and the Sun, while **superior conjunction** occurs when either Mercury or Venus is on the far side of the Sun. Celestial bodies are in **opposition** when their Right Ascensions differ by exactly 12 hours, or when their Celestial Longitudes differ by 180°. One of the 2 objects in opposition will rise while the other is setting. **Quadrature** refers to the arrangement where the coordinates of 2 bodies differ by exactly 90°. These terms may refer to the relative positions of any 2 bodies as seen from Earth, but one of the bodies is so frequently the Sun that mention of the Sun is omitted in that case; otherwise, both bodies are named.

When objects are in conjunction, the alignment is not perfect, and one is usually passing above or below the other. The geocentric angular separation between the Sun and an object is termed **elongation**. Elongation is limited only for Mercury and Venus; the greatest elongation for each of these bodies is noted in the appropriate table and is approximately the time for longest observation. **Perihelion** is the point in an orbit that is nearest to the Sun, and **aphelion**, the point farthest from the Sun. **Perigee** is the point in an orbit that is nearest Earth, and **apogee** the point that is farthest from Earth. An **occultation** of a planet or a star is an **eclipse** of it by some other body, usually the Moon. A **transit** of the Sun occurs when Mercury or Venus passes directly between Earth and the Sun, appearing to cross the disk of the Sun.

Astronomical Constants; Speed of Light

The following were adopted as part of the International Astronomical Union System of Astronomical Constants (1976): **Speed of light**, 299,792.458 km per sec., or about 186,282 statute mi per sec.; **solar parallax**, 8".794148; **Astronomical Unit**, 149,597,870 km, or 92,955,807 mi; **constant of nutation**, 9".2025; and **constant of aberration**, 20".49552.

Celestial Events Highlights, 2004

(in Coordinated Universal Time, or UTC—the standard time of the prime meridian)

January

Mercury emerges in the morning sky after the first week and remains visible very low in the SE for the rest of the month.

Venus, low in the SW after sunset, passes very close to Uranus on the 15th—use binoculars to view.

Mars, high in the S at sunset, sets about midnight.

Jupiter, rising shortly before midnight, is prominent in the morning sky.

Saturn, just past opposition, is up most of the night, setting a couple of hours before sunrise.

Moon passes Saturn on the 6th, Jupiter on the 12th, Mercury on the 20th, Uranus on the 23rd, Venus on the 24th, and Mars on the 28th. Watch for the thin waxing crescent Moon with Venus low in the SW on the 24th.

Jan. 1—Pluto in Serpens Cauda, the only divided constellation, all year. Neptune in Capricornus, Uranus in Aquarius, and Saturn in Gemini stay there all year. Jupiter in Leo. Mars in Pisces. Venus in Capricornus. Sun in Sagittarius.

Jan. 3—Quadrantid meteor shower late at night into the next morning.

Jan. 4—Jupiter stationary, begins retrograde motion. Earth at perihelion, closest approach to Sun.

Jan. 6—Mercury stationary, resumes direct motion. Moon passes 5° north of Saturn.

Jan. 12—Moon passes 3° north of Jupiter. Venus enters Aquarius.

Jan. 15—Venus passes 0.9° south of Uranus.

Jan. 17—Mercury at greatest western elongation of 24° (W of the Sun, rises before the Sun).

Jan. 20—Moon passes 5° south of Mercury. Sun enters Capricornus.

Jan. 23—Moon passes 4° south of Uranus.

Jan. 24—Moon passes 4° south of Venus.

Jan. 28—Moon passes 3° south of Mars.

February

Mercury, very low in the SE in the early morning, disappears into the glare of the Sun about mid-month, while passing Neptune on the 15th.

Venus, low in the SW after sunset, gets slowly higher during the month and gradually shifts to the W.

Mars, high in the S at sunset, sets before midnight.

Jupiter, rising a couple of hours before midnight, is prominent for the remainder of the night.

Saturn, in the E at sunset, sets a couple of hours after midnight.

Moon passes Saturn on the 4th, Jupiter on the 8th, Neptune on the 19th, Venus on the 23rd, and Mars on the 26th. Watch for the thin waxing crescent Moon with Venus low in the SW on the 23rd.

Feb. 1—Mars enters Aries.

Feb. 2—Neptune at conjunction.

Feb. 3—Moon passes 4° north of Saturn. Venus enters Pisces.

Feb. 6—Mercury at aphelion.

Feb. 8—Moon passes 3° north of Jupiter.

Feb. 14—Venus enters constellation of Cetus for part of day and then reenters Pisces.

Feb. 15—Mercury passes 2° south of Neptune.

Feb. 16—Sun enters Aquarius.

Feb. 19—Moon passes 5° south of Neptune.

Feb. 22—Uranus at conjunction.

Feb. 23—Moon passes 3° south of Venus.

Feb. 26—Moon passes 0.9° south of Mars.

March

Mercury reappears in the early evening sky, very low in the W during the second half of the month.

Venus, higher in the W, pairs with the Moon on the 24th with Mars above the pair.

Mars is now in the W after sunset, setting in a few hours.

Jupiter, in the E after sunset, is prominent for most of the night.

Saturn is very high in the E after sunset.

Moon passes Saturn on the 1st and 28th, Jupiter on the 6th, Neptune on the 17th, Uranus on the 18th, Mercury on the 22nd, Venus on the 24th, and Mars on the 26th. Watch for the waxing crescent Moon above Mercury on the 22nd, with the other four planets visible with the naked eye stretching across the sky above the Moon.

Mar. 1—Moon passes 5° north of Saturn.

Mar. 4—Mercury at superior conjunction, behind the Sun. Jupiter at opposition.

Mar. 5—Venus enters Aries.

Mar. 6—Moon passes 3° north of Jupiter.

Mar. 7—Saturn stationary, resumes direct motion.

Mar. 11—Sun enters Pisces.

Mar. 13—Mars enters Taurus.

Mar. 17—Moon passes 5° south of Neptune.

Mar. 18—Moon passes 4° south of Uranus.

Mar. 20—Vernal Equinox at 1:49 A.M. EST (6:49 UTC); spring begins in the northern hemisphere, autumn in the southern hemisphere.

Mar. 21—Mercury at perihelion. Venus at perihelion.

Mar. 22—Moon passes 4° south of Mercury.

Mar. 24—Moon passes 2° south of Venus. Pluto stationary, begins retrograde motion.

Mar. 26—Moon passes 0.8° north of Mars.

Mar. 27—Sun barely touches constellation of Cetus.

Mar. 28—Moon passes 5° north of Saturn.

Mar. 29—Mercury at greatest eastern elongation of 19° (E of the Sun and setting after the Sun). Venus at greatest eastern elongation of 46°. Venus enters Taurus.

April

Mercury is low in the W after sunset during the first part of the month, before lost in the glare of the Sun.

Venus, prominent in the W after sunset, passes Aldebaran on the 16th and is closer to Mars.

Mars, lower in the west after sunset, passes Aldebaran on the 7th.

Jupiter, in the E after sunset, is still prominent for most of the night.

Saturn is getting lower in the W after sunset.

Moon passes Jupiter on the 1st and 30th, Neptune on the 13th, Uranus on the 15th, Venus and Mars on the 23rd, and Saturn on the 25th. Watch for the waning crescent Moon paired with Venus and Mars on the 22nd and 23rd.

Apr. 1—Moon passes 3° north of Jupiter.

Apr. 6—Mercury stationary, begins retrograde motion.

Apr. 7—Mars passes 7° north of the star Aldebaran in Taurus.

Apr. 13—Moon passes 5° south of Neptune.

Apr. 15—Moon passes 4° south of Uranus.

Apr. 16—Venus passes 10° north of Aldebaran.

Apr. 17—Mercury at inferior conjunction, between Earth and the Sun.

Apr. 18—Sun enters Aries.

Apr. 19—Partial solar eclipse; see details under Eclipses.

Apr. 22—Lyrid meteor shower, starting early in the morning just after midnight.

Apr. 23—Moon passes 1.5° south of Venus and 2° north of Mars.

Apr. 25—Moon passes 5° north of Saturn.

Apr. 29—Mercury stationary, resumes direct motion.

Apr. 30—Moon passes 4° north of Jupiter.

May

Mercury is visible very low in the E during the month.

Venus is getting very low in the WNW after sunset.

Mars, getting lower in the W after sunset, passes Saturn on the 24th.

Jupiter is high in the S after sunset.

Saturn is getting low in the W after sunset.

Moon passes Neptune on the 10th, Uranus on the 12th, Mercury on the 16th, Venus on the 21st, Mars and Saturn on the 22nd, and Jupiter on the 27th. Thin, waxing crescent Moon low in the W pairs with Venus on the 21st and triples with Mars and Saturn the next night. Total lunar eclipse on the 4th commences at 2:48 P.M. EDT, thus not visible in North America.

May 4—Total lunar eclipse; see details under Eclipses. Mercury at aphelion.

May 5—Jupiter stationary, resumes direct motion.

May 7—Mars enters Gemini.

May 10—Moon passes 5° south of Neptune.

May 12—Moon passes 4° south of Uranus.

May 13—Sun enters Taurus.

May 14—Mercury at greatest western elongation of 26°.

May 16—Moon passes 3° north of Mercury.

May 17—Neptune stationary, begins retrograde motion. Venus stationary, begins retrograde motion.

May 21—Moon passes 0.3° north of Venus.

May 22—Moon passes 3° north of Mars and 5° north of Saturn.

May 24—Mars passes 1.6° north of Saturn.

May 27—Moon passes 4° north of Jupiter.

June

Mercury switches from the morning sky to the evening sky and thus is gone from view for much of the month.

Venus leaves the evening sky, transits the Sun on the 8th, and reappears in the morning sky at the end of the month, passing Aldebaran on the 24th.

Mars is very low in the WNW after sunset, passing Pollux on the 14th.

Jupiter is getting lower in the WSW after sunset.

Saturn disappears into the glare of sunset early in the month.

Moon passes Neptune on the 7th, Uranus on the 8th, Saturn on the 19th, Mars on the 20th, and Jupiter on the 23rd. Watch for waxing crescent Moon paired with Jupiter on the 23rd.

June 7—Moon passes 5° south of Neptune.

June 8—Venus transits the Sun; see details under Eclipses. Venus at inferior conjunction, passing between Earth and Sun. Moon passes 4° south of Uranus.

June 10—Uranus stationary, begins retrograde motion.

June 11—Pluto at opposition.

June 14—Mars passes 6° south of star Pollux in Gemini.

June 17—Mercury at perihelion.

June 18—Mercury at superior conjunction.

June 19—Moon passes 5° north of Saturn.

June 20—Moon passes 4° north of Mars. Northern solstice at 8:57 P.M. EDT (00:57 June 21 UTC); summer begins in the northern hemisphere, winter in the southern hemisphere. Mars enters Cancer.

June 21—Sun enters Gemini.

June 23—Moon passes 3° north of Jupiter.

June 24—Venus passes 2° north of Aldebaran.

June 27—Mercury at greatest eastern elongation of 27°.

June 29—Venus stationary, resumes direct motion.

July

Mercury, very low in the W after sunset, passes Pollux on the 1st and Regulus on the 25th.

Venus is low in the east before sunrise, passing Aldebaran on the 4th.

Mars is very low in the W, disappearing into the sunset at the end of the month.

Jupiter is very low in the W at sunset.

Saturn reappears in the morning sky, very low in the E during the 2nd half of the month.

Moon passes Neptune on the 4th and 31st, Uranus on the 6th, Venus on the 14th, Mars and Mercury on the 19th, and Jupiter on 21st. Watch for the thin waning crescent Moon paired with Venus in the early morning of the 14th and the thin waxing crescent Moon paired with Jupiter on the evening of the 21st.

July 1—Mercury passes 5° south of Pollux.

July 4—Venus passes 1.1° north of Aldebaran. Moon passes 5° south of Neptune.

July 5—Earth at aphelion, greatest distance from the Sun.

July 6—Moon passes 4° south of Uranus.

July 8—Saturn at conjunction.

July 10—Mercury passes 0.2° north of Mars.

July 12—Venus at aphelion.

July 14—Moon passes 8° north of Venus.

July 19—Moon passes 4° north of Mars and 5° north of Mercury.

July 20—Sun enters Cancer.

July 21—Moon passes 3° north of Jupiter. Mars enters Leo.

July 25—Mercury passes 1.5° south of star Regulus in Leo.

July 27—Mercury at greatest eastern elongation of 27°.

July 31—Mercury at aphelion. Moon passes 5° south of Neptune.

August

Mercury departs the early evening sky early in the month.

Venus in the morning sky is getting higher.

Mars hidden in close directional proximity to the Sun.

Jupiter disappears from the early evening sky into the glow of sunset at the end of the month, leaving the early evening sky devoid of bright planets.

Saturn is in the E before sunrise, gradually getting higher.

Moon passes Uranus on the 2nd and 29th, Venus on the 11th, Saturn on the 13th, Jupiter on the 18th, and Neptune on the 28th. Watch for the thin waning crescent Moon tripled with Venus and Saturn on the 12th.

Aug. 2—Moon passes 4° south of Uranus.

Aug. 4—Venus enters Orion.

Aug. 6—Neptune at opposition.

Aug. 7—Mars at aphelion.

Aug. 9—Mercury stationary, begins retrograde motion.

Aug. 10—Sun enters Leo.

Aug. 11—Moon passes 8° north of Venus.

Aug. 12—Perseid meteor shower, starting early in the morning just after midnight. Venus enters Gemini.

Aug. 13—Moon passes 5° north of Saturn.

Aug. 17—Mercury passes 6° south of Mars. Venus at greatest western elongation of 46° (W of the Sun and rising before the Sun).

Aug. 18—Moon passes 3° north of Jupiter.

Aug. 23—Mercury at inferior conjunction.

Aug. 25—Jupiter enters Virgo.

Aug. 27—Uranus at opposition.

Aug. 28—Moon passes 5° south of Neptune.

Aug. 29—Moon passes 4° south of Uranus.

Aug. 31—Pluto stationary, resumes direct motion.

September

Mercury is low in the E before sunrise, passing close to Regulus on the morning of the 10th.

Venus, prominent in the morning sky before sunset, passes Saturn on the 1st and Pollux on the 2nd.

Mars remains hidden in close directional proximity to the Sun.

Jupiter is also hidden in close proximity to the Sun.

Saturn, getting higher in the E before sunrise, passes Pollux on the 12th.

Moon passes Saturn on the 9th, Venus on the 10th, Mercury on the 13th, Neptune on the 24th, and Uranus on the 26th. Watch for the waning crescent Moon tripled with Venus and Saturn on the 10th.

Sept. 1—Venus passes 1.9° south of Saturn. Mercury stationary, resumes direct motion.

Sept. 2—Venus passes 9° south of Pollux.

Sept. 4—Venus enters Cancer.

Sept. 9—Mercury at greatest western elongation of 18°. Moon passes 5° north of Saturn.

Sept. 10—Mercury passes 0.06° south of Regulus. Moon passes 7° north of Venus.

Sept. 12—Saturn passes 7° south of Pollux.

Sept. 13—Moon passes 4° north of Mercury. Mercury at perihelion.

Sept. 15—Mars at conjunction.

Sept. 16—Sun and Mars enter Virgo.

Sept. 21—Jupiter at conjunction.

Sept. 22—Autumnal Equinox at 12:30 P.M. EDT (16:30 UTC); autumn begins in the northern hemisphere; spring begins in the southern hemisphere.

Sept. 23—Venus enters Leo.

Sept. 24—Moon passes 5° south of Neptune.

Sept. 26—Moon passes 4° south of Uranus.

October

Mercury reappears in the early evening sky at the end of the month.

Venus, prominent in the E before sunrise, passes Regulus on the 2nd.

Mars reappears very low in the ESE before sunrise, passing Spica on the 31st.

Jupiter reappears low in the ESE before sunrise.

Saturn, rising about midnight, is high in the S before sunrise.

Moon passes Saturn on the 7th, Venus on the 10th, Jupiter on the 12th, Neptune on the 21st, and Uranus on the 23rd. Watch for the waning crescent Moon paired with Venus on the 10th, then Jupiter on the 12th. Total lunar eclipse on the 27th commences at 9:14 P.M. EDT.

Oct. 2—Venus passes 0.2° south of Regulus.

Oct. 5—Mercury at superior conjunction.

Oct. 7—Moon passes 5° north of Saturn.

Oct. 10—Moon passes 4° north of Venus.

Oct. 12—Moon passes 1.6° north of Jupiter.

Oct. 14—Partial solar eclipse; see details under Eclipses.

Oct. 21—Moon passes 5° south of Neptune. Orionid meteor shower, starting early in the morning just after midnight.

Oct. 23—Moon passes 4° south of Uranus. Venus enters Virgo.

Oct. 24—Neptune stationary, resumes direct motion.

Oct. 27—Mercury at aphelion.

Oct. 27/28—Total lunar eclipse; see details under Eclipses.

Oct. 30—Sun enters Libra.

Oct. 31—Mars passes 3° north of star Spica in Virgo.

November

Mercury is very low in the SW after sunset, passes Aldebaran on the 11th.

Venus, getting lower in the SE before sunrise, passes Jupiter on the 4th and Spica on the 16th.

Mars is low in the SE before sunrise.

Jupiter, getting higher, is in the SSE at sunrise.

Saturn rises a few hours before midnight in the ENE and is in the W by sunrise.

Moon passes Saturn on the 3rd, Jupiter on the 9th, Venus on the 10th, Mars on the 11th, Mercury on the 14th, Neptune on the 18th, and Uranus on the 19th. Watch for the Moon in a small, straight line grouping with Jupiter, Venus, and Mars on the 10th as it passes all those three planets in three days.

Nov. 1—Venus at perihelion.

Nov. 3—Moon passes 5° north of Saturn.

Nov. 4—Venus passes 0.6° north of Jupiter.

Nov. 8—Saturn stationary, begins retrograde motion.

Nov. 9—Moon passes 1.0° north of Jupiter, occults Jupiter.

Nov. 10—Moon passes 0.2° south of Venus.

Nov. 11—Moon passes 0.5° south of Mars. Mercury passes 2° north of Aldebaran.

Nov. 12—Uranus stationary, resumes direct motion.

Nov. 14—Moon passes 0.9° south of Mercury.

Nov. 16—Venus passes 4° north of Spica.

Nov. 17—Leonid meteor shower, starting early in the morning just after midnight.

Nov. 18—Moon passes 5° south of Neptune.

Nov. 19—Moon passes 4° south of Uranus.

Nov. 21—Mercury at greatest eastern elongation of 22°.

Nov. 22—Mars enters Libra.

Nov. 23—Sun enters Scorpius.

Nov. 28—Venus enters Libra.

Nov. 29—Sun enters Ophiuchus.

Nov. 30—Mercury stationary, begins retrograde motion.

December

Mercury leaves the evening sky to appear in the morning sky during the second half of the month, passing Venus on the 29th—use Venus to help find Mercury this morning.

Venus, still getting lower in the SE, passes Mars on the 5th and Antares, the star sometimes labeled "the Rival of Mars" on the 23rd.

Mars is low in SE before sunrise in Scorpius, not far from its "rival," the star Antares; both objects have an orange-reddish appearance.

Jupiter, rising about midnight, is high in the S at sunrise.

Saturn, approaching opposition, is up all night long.

Moon passes Saturn on the 1st and 28th, Jupiter on the 7th, Mars and Venus on the 10th, Neptune on the 15th, and Uranus on the 16th. Watch for waxing crescent Moon tripled with Venus and Mars on the 10th.

Dec. 1—Moon passes 5° north of Saturn.

Dec. 5—Venus passes 1.3° north of Mars.

Dec. 7—Moon passes 0.3° north of Jupiter, occults Jupiter.

Dec. 10—Moon passes 2° south of Mars and 4° south of Venus. Mercury at inferior conjunction and at perihelion.

Dec. 13—Pluto at conjunction. Geminid meteor shower, starting about 7 P.M. until a couple of hours before sunrise the next morning.

Dec. 15—Moon passes 5° south of Neptune.

Dec. 16—Moon passes 4° south of Uranus.

Dec. 17—Sun enters Sagittarius.

Dec. 18—Venus enters Scorpius.

Dec. 20—Mercury stationary, resumes direct motion.

Dec. 21—Southern Solstice at 7:42 A.M. EST (12:42 UTC); winter begins in the northern hemisphere, summer begins in the southern hemisphere.

Dec. 22—Venus enters Ophiuchus.

Dec. 23—Venus passes 6° north of Antares in Scorpius.

Dec. 28—Moon passes 5° north of Saturn. Mars enters Scorpius.

Dec. 29—Mercury passes 1.2° north of Venus. Mercury at greatest western elongation of 22°.

Meteorites and Meteor Showers

When a chunk of material, ice or rock, plunges into Earth's atmosphere and burns up in a fiery display, the event is a **meteor**. While the chunk of material is still in space, it is a **meteoroid**. If a portion of the material survives passage through the atmosphere and reaches the ground, the remnant on the ground is a **meteorite**.

Meteorites found on Earth are classified into types, depending on their composition: **irons**, those composed chiefly of iron, a small percentage of nickel, and traces of other metals such as cobalt; **stones**, stony meteors consisting of silicates; and **stony irons**, containing varying proportions of both iron and stone.

Serious study of meteorites as non-earth objects began in the 20th century. Scientists now use sophisticated chemical analysis, X rays, and mass spectrography in determining their origin and composition. In 1996, the results of a study of a Mars rock recovered in 1984 from the Allan Hills region of Antarctica suggested that life once existed on Mars. Although most meteorites are now believed to be fragments of asteroids or comets, geochemical studies have shown that a few Antarctic stones came from the moon or from Mars, from which they presumably were ejected by the explosive impact of asteroids.

The **largest known meteorite**, estimated to weigh about 55 metric tons, is situated at Hoba West near Grootfontein, Namibia. The Manicouagan impact crater in Quebec, Canada, with an estimated diameter of 60 mi, is one of the largest crater structures still visible on the surface of the Earth. Other large impact craters include the Vredefort crater in South Africa at 185 mi across; the Sudbury crater in Ontario, Canada, estimated at 125 mi across; the Chicxulub crater in Yucatan, Mexico, at 105 mi across; the Woodleigh crater in Australia, at 75 mi across; and the Popigai crater in Russia, at 60 mi across.

Sporadic meteors, which enter the atmosphere throughout the year, seem to originate from the asteroid belt. Other meteors that come in groups and tend to occur at the same time each year create what are called **meteor showers**; these are the meteors associated with comets. As a comet orbits the Sun, the Sun slowly boils away some of the comet's material, and the comet leaves a trail of tiny particles which are dispersed along the comet's path. If Earth's orbit and this path intersect, then once a year, as Earth reaches that particular point in its orbit, there will be a meteor shower.

Meteor showers vary in strength, but usually the 3 best meteor showers of the year are the **Perseids**, around Aug. 12, the **Orionids**, around Oct. 21, and the **Geminids**, around Dec. 13. These showers feature meteors at the rate of about 60 per hour. Best observing conditions occur with the absence of moonlight, usually when the Moon's phase is between waning crescent Moon and waxing quarter Moon. Meteor showers are also usually seen better after the middle of the night.

For most meteor showers the cometary debris is relatively uniformly scattered along the comet's orbit. However, in the case of the **Leonid** meteor shower, which occurs every year around Nov. 17-18, the cometary debris, from Comet Temple-Tuttle, seems to be bunched up in one stretch. Hence, most years when Earth crosses the orbit of this comet, the meteor shower produced is relatively weak. However, approximately every 33 years Earth encounters the bunched-up debris. Sometimes the storm is a disappointment, as it was in 1899 and 1933; at other times it is a roaring success, as in 1833 and 1866. In 2001, the Leonids stormed again producing rates between 1,000-3,000 meteors per hour in the United States and across the Pacific to China; and in 2002, though hindered by a nearly full Moon, meteor rates reaching 800 per hour were recorded. Although the current cycle of Leonid storms is past, the shower may still be enhanced for a few years. In **2004** look for meteor-observing success with the Quadrantids, the Lyrids, the Perseids, the Orionids, the Leonids, and the Geminids. Typically, meteor showers are best observed after midnight, when one views debris hitting the Earth on the side facing its orbital direction, but the Geminids approach at such an angle that they can be seen well before midnight as well as after.

Rising and Setting of Planets, 2004

In Coordinated Universal Time (0 in the *h* col. designates midnight)

Venus, 2004

Date	20° N Latitude Rise h m	Set h m	30° N Latitude Rise h m	Set h m	40° N Latitude Rise h m	Set h m	50° N Latitude Rise h m	Set h m	60° N Latitude Rise h m	Set h m
Jan. 1	8 51	20 01	9 07	19 45	9 27	19 25	9 55	18 57	10 41	18 11
11	8 53	20 16	9 06	20 03	9 21	19 48	9 42	19 28	10 15	18 55
21	8 53	20 29	9 01	20 21	9 11	20 11	9 25	19 58	9 46	19 37
31	8 50	20 41	8 54	20 38	8 59	20 33	9 05	20 27	9 14	20 18
Feb. 10	8 46	20 52	8 45	20 53	8 45	20 54	8 43	20 56	8 42	20 58
20	8 41	21 02	8 36	21 08	8 30	21 14	8 21	21 23	8 08	21 37
Mar. 1	8 35	21 12	8 26	21 22	8 14	21 34	7 58	21 50	7 33	22 16
11	8 30	21 21	8 17	21 35	8 00	21 53	7 36	22 17	6 58	22 56
21	8 26	21 30	8 08	21 48	7 46	22 10	7 15	22 42	6 22	23 35
31	8 21	21 37	8 00	21 58	7 33	22 25	6 55	23 04	5 47	0 10
Apr. 10	8 16	21 41	7 52	22 05	7 22	22 35	6 37	23 20	5 11	0 45
20	8 09	21 40	7 43	22 05	7 10	22 39	6 21	23 28	4 38	1 11
30	7 57	21 30	7 31	21 57	6 56	22 32	6 04	23 24	4 10	1 20
May 10	7 37	21 09	7 10	21 36	6 36	22 11	5 44	23 02	3 49	1 00
20	7 04	20 32	6 38	20 58	6 05	21 31	5 16	22 19	3 32	0 08
30	6 15	19 36	5 51	19 59	5 21	20 29	4 37	21 13	3 11	22 37
June 9	5 16	18 27	4 55	18 48	4 29	19 14	3 51	19 51	2 44	20 57
19	4 20	17 21	4 02	17 39	3 39	18 02	3 07	18 33	2 13	19 27
29	3 34	16 32	3 18	16 48	2 58	17 08	2 29	17 37	1 42	18 24
July 9	3 02	15 59	2 47	16 15	2 27	16 35	1 59	17 03	1 13	17 48
19	2 41	15 40	2 25	15 56	2 05	16 17	1 36	16 46	0 48	17 33
29	2 29	15 30	2 11	15 48	1 50	16 09	1 20	16 39	0 29	17 30
Aug. 8	2 22	15 27	2 04	15 45	1 42	16 07	1 10	16 39	0 17	17 33
18	2 21	15 27	2 03	15 45	1 40	16 08	1 08	16 41	0 13	17 36
28	2 25	15 30	2 07	15 48	1 44	16 10	1 13	16 42	0 19	17 35
Sept. 7	2 31	15 33	2 15	15 50	1 53	16 11	1 24	16 40	0 34	17 29
17	2 40	15 35	2 25	15 50	2 07	16 09	1 40	16 35	0 58	17 17
27	2 51	15 37	2 38	15 50	2 23	16 05	2 01	16 26	1 27	17 00
Oct. 7	3 02	15 38	2 52	15 47	2 41	15 58	2 25	16 14	1 59	16 39
17	3 13	15 37	3 07	15 43	3 00	15 50	2 50	16 00	2 34	16 15
27	3 25	15 36	3 23	15 38	3 20	15 41	3 16	15 44	3 11	15 49
Nov. 6	3 37	15 35	3 39	15 33	3 41	15 31	3 44	15 28	3 48	15 23
16	3 50	15 34	3 56	15 29	4 03	15 21	4 12	15 12	4 26	14 57
26	4 04	15 35	4 13	15 25	4 25	15 13	4 41	14 57	5 06	14 32
Dec. 6	4 19	15 38	4 32	15 25	4 48	15 08	5 11	14 45	5 47	14 09
16	4 35	15 44	4 51	15 27	5 12	15 06	5 40	14 38	6 27	13 51
26	4 52	15 52	5 11	15 33	5 35	15 09	6 08	14 36	7 05	13 39

Mars, 2004

Date	20° N Latitude Rise h m	Set h m	30° N Latitude Rise h m	Set h m	40° N Latitude Rise h m	Set h m	50° N Latitude Rise h m	Set h m	60° N Latitude Rise h m	Set h m
Jan. 1	11 45	0 01	11 41	0 05	11 37	0 09	11 31	0 15	11 22	0 24
11	11 24	23 47	11 18	23 53	11 11	0.01	11 01	0 10	10 46	0 25
21	11 04	23 34	10 56	23 42	10 46	23 52	10 33	0 06	10 11	0 27
31	10 44	23 22	10 34	23 32	10 22	23 45	10 04	0 03	9 37	0 30
Feb. 10	10 25	23 11	10 13	23 23	9 58	23 38	9 37	24 00	9 03	0 33
20	10 07	23 00	9 53	23 14	9 35	23 32	9 11	23 57	8 30	0 37
Mar. 1	9 50	22 49	9 34	23 05	9 14	23 26	8 45	23 54	7 58	0 41
11	9 34	22 38	9 16	22 56	8 53	23 19	8 21	23 51	7 27	0 46
21	9 18	22 28	8 59	22 48	8 34	23 13	7 59	23 48	6 58	0 49
31	9 04	22 18	8 43	22 39	8 16	23 06	7 39	23 44	6 31	0 52
Apr. 10	8 50	22 08	8 28	22 30	8 00	22 58	7 20	23 38	6 06	0 52
20	8 37	21 57	8 14	22 20	7 45	22 49	7 03	23 31	5 45	0 50
30	8 25	21 46	8 02	22 10	7 32	22 39	6 49	23 22	5 28	0 44
May 10	8 13	21 35	7 50	21 58	7 20	22 28	6 37	23 11	5 15	0 34
20	8 02	21 23	7 39	21 46	7 10	22 15	6 27	22 58	5 07	0 19
30	7 51	21 10	7 29	21 32	7 00	22 01	6 19	22 42	5 03	23 58
June 9	7 41	20 56	7 19	21 18	6 52	21 45	6 13	22 24	5 01	23 35
19	7 30	20 42	7 10	21 02	6 44	21 28	6 07	22 04	5 02	23 08
29	7 19	20 26	7 00	20 45	6 37	21 09	6 03	21 42	5 05	22 40
July 9	7 08	20 10	6 51	20 27	6 29	20 49	5 59	21 19	5 07	22 10
19	6 57	19 53	6 42	20 09	6 22	20 28	5 55	20 55	5 11	21 39
29	6 46	19 35	6 32	19 49	6 16	20 06	5 52	20 29	5 14	21 07
Aug. 8	6 35	19 17	6 23	19 29	6 09	19 43	5 49	20 02	5 17	20 34
18	6 23	18 58	6 13	19 08	6 02	19 19	5 45	19 35	5 20	20 00
28	6 11	18 39	6 04	18 46	5 54	18 55	5 42	19 08	5 22	19 27
Sept. 7	5 59	18 20	5 54	18 25	5 47	18 31	5 38	18 40	5 25	18 53
17	5 47	18 00	5 44	18 03	5 40	18 06	5 35	18 11	5 27	18 19
27	5 35	17 40	5 34	17 41	5 33	17 42	5 32	17 43	5 29	17 45
Oct. 7	5 23	17 21	5 24	17 19	5 26	17 17	5 28	17 15	5 32	17 11
17	5 11	17 02	5 15	16 58	5 19	16 53	5 25	16 47	5 34	16 38
27	5 00	16 43	5 06	16 37	5 13	16 29	5 23	16 19	5 37	16 04
Nov. 6	4 49	16 24	4 57	16 16	5 07	16 06	5 20	15 52	5 41	15 32
16	4 38	16 07	4 48	15 56	5 01	15 43	5 18	15 26	5 45	14 59
26	4 28	15 50	4 40	15 37	4 56	15 22	5 16	15 01	5 49	14 28
Dec. 6	4 19	15 33	4 33	15 19	4 51	15 01	5 15	14 37	5 54	13 58
16	4 09	15 18	4 26	15 02	4 46	14 42	5 13	14 14	5 59	13 29
26	4 01	15 04	4 19	14 47	4 41	14 24	5 12	13 53	6 03	13 02

Jupiter, 2004

Date	20° N Latitude Rise h m	Set h m	30° N Latitude Rise h m	Set h m	40° N Latitude Rise h m	Set h m	50° N Latitude Rise h m	Set h m	60° N Latitude Rise h m	Set h m
Jan. 1	22 27	10 50	22 22	10 55	22 16	11 01	22 07	11 09	21 54	11 22
11	21 47	10 10	21 42	10 15	21 36	10 22	21 27	10 30	21 14	10 43
21	21 06	9 30	21 01	9 35	20 55	9 42	20 46	9 50	20 32	10 04
31	20 24	8 49	20 18	8 54	20 12	9 01	20 02	9 10	19 48	9 24
Feb. 10	19 40	8 06	19 35	8 12	19 27	8 19	19 18	8 29	19 02	8 45
20	18 56	7 24	18 50	7 30	18 42	7 37	18 32	7 48	18 15	8 04
Mar. 1	18 11	6 40	18 05	6 47	17 56	6 55	17 45	7 06	17 27	7 24
11	17 26	5 57	17 19	6 04	17 11	6 13	16 59	6 25	16 40	6 44
21	16 42	5 14	16 34	5 21	16 25	5 31	16 12	5 43	15 52	6 03
31	15 58	4 31	15 50	4 39	15 40	4 49	15 27	5 02	15 06	5 23
Apr. 10	15 15	3 49	15 07	3 57	14 57	4 07	14 43	4 21	14 21	4 43
20	14 33	3 08	14 25	3 16	14 14	3 26	14 00	3 40	13 38	4 02
30	13 52	2 27	13 44	2 36	13 34	2 46	13 19	3 00	12 57	3 23
May 10	13 13	1 48	13 05	1 56	12 55	2 06	12 40	2 21	12 18	2 43
20	12 35	1 09	12 27	1 17	12 17	1 28	12 03	1 42	11 41	2 04
30	11 58	0 32	11 50	0 40	11 41	0 50	11 27	1 03	11 06	1 25
June 9	11 23	23 51	11 15	0 03	11 06	0 12	10 53	0 25	10 32	0 46
19	10 48	23 15	10 41	23 23	10 32	23 32	10 19	23 44	10 00	0 07
29	10 15	22 40	10 08	22 47	9 59	22 55	9 48	23 07	9 29	23 25
July 9	9 42	22 06	9 35	22 12	9 27	22 20	9 17	22 30	9 00	22 47
19	9 09	21 31	9 04	21 37	8 56	21 44	8 47	21 54	8 31	22 09
29	8 38	20 58	8 33	21 03	8 26	21 09	8 17	21 18	8 04	21 31
Aug. 8	8 06	20 24	8 02	20 29	7 56	20 34	7 49	20 42	7 37	20 54
18	7 36	19 51	7 32	19 55	7 27	19 59	7 21	20 06	7 10	20 16
28	7 05	19 18	7 02	19 21	6 58	19 25	6 53	19 30	6 44	19 38
Sept. 7	6 35	18 45	6 32	18 48	6 29	18 51	6 25	18 55	6 19	19 01
17	6 05	18 13	6 03	18 14	6 01	18 16	5 58	18 19	5 53	18 24
27	5 34	17 40	5 33	17 41	5 32	17 42	5 31	17 44	5 28	17 46
Oct. 7	5 04	17 07	5 04	17 07	5 04	17 08	5 03	17 08	5 02	17 09
17	4 34	16 34	4 34	16 34	4 35	16 33	4 36	16 33	4 36	16 32
27	4 03	16 02	4 04	16 00	4 06	15 59	4 08	15 57	4 10	15 54
Nov. 6	3 32	15 28	3 34	15 27	3 36	15 24	3 39	15 21	3 44	15 17
16	3 01	14 55	3 04	14 53	3 07	14 50	3 10	14 46	3 16	14 40
26	2 29	14 21	2 32	14 18	2 36	14 14	2 41	14 10	2 48	14 02
Dec. 6	1 57	13 47	2 00	13 43	2 05	13 39	2 10	13 33	2 19	13 25
16	1 24	13 12	1 28	13 08	1 32	13 03	1 39	12 57	1 49	12 47
26	0 49	12 37	0 54	12 32	0 59	12 27	1 06	12 20	1 17	12 09

Saturn, 2004

Date	20° N Latitude Rise h m	Set h m	30° N Latitude Rise h m	Set h m	40° N Latitude Rise h m	Set h m	50° N Latitude Rise h m	Set h m	60° N Latitude Rise h m	Set h m
Jan. 1	17 22	6 38	17 01	6 59	16 35	7 25	15 57	8 03	14 50	9 10
11	16 39	5 56	16 18	6 16	15 52	6 43	15 14	7 21	14 06	8 28
21	15 56	5 13	15 35	5 34	15 09	6 01	14 31	6 39	13 23	7 46
31	15 14	4 31	14 53	4 52	14 26	5 19	13 48	5 57	12 40	7 05
Feb. 10	14 32	3 49	14 11	4 10	13 44	4 37	13 06	5 15	11 58	6 24
20	13 51	3 08	13 30	3 30	13 03	3 56	12 25	4 35	11 16	5 44
Mar. 1	13 11	2 28	12 50	2 49	12 23	3 16	11 45	3 55	10 35	5 04
11	12 31	1 49	12 10	2 10	11 43	2 37	11 05	3 15	9 56	4 25
21	11 53	1 10	11 32	1 32	11 05	1 58	10 26	2 37	9 17	3 46
31	11 15	0 32	10 54	0 54	10 27	1 21	9 48	1 59	8 39	3 09
Apr. 10	10 38	23 52	10 17	0 17	9 50	0 43	9 11	1 22	8 02	2 31
20	10 02	23 15	9 40	23 36	9 13	0 07	8 35	0 45	7 26	1 55
30	9 26	22 39	9 05	23 01	8 38	23 27	7 59	0 09	6 50	1 19
May 10	8 51	22 04	8 29	22 25	8 03	22 52	7 24	23 30	6 15	0 43
20	8 16	21 29	7 55	21 50	7 28	22 17	6 50	22 55	5 41	0 07
30	7 41	20 55	7 21	21 16	6 54	21 42	6 16	22 20	5 08	23 28
June 9	7 07	20 20	6 47	20 41	6 20	21 07	5 42	21 45	4 35	22 53
19	6 34	19 46	6 13	20 07	5 47	20 33	5 09	21 11	4 02	22 18
29	6 00	19 12	5 39	19 33	5 13	19 59	4 36	20 36	3 30	21 42
July 9	5 27	18 38	5 06	18 58	4 40	19 24	4 03	20 01	2 58	21 07
19	4 53	18 04	4 33	18 24	4 07	18 50	3 30	19 26	2 26	20 31
29	4 19	17 30	3 59	17 50	3 34	18 15	2 57	18 52	1 54	19 55
Aug. 8	3 46	16 55	3 26	17 15	3 00	17 41	2 25	18 16	1 21	19 19
18	3 12	16 21	2 52	16 41	2 27	17 06	1 51	17 41	0 49	18 43
28	2 37	15 46	2 18	16 05	1 53	16 30	1 18	17 05	0 16	18 07
Sept. 7	2 03	15 11	1 43	15 30	1 19	15 55	0 44	16 29	23 40	17 30
17	1 27	14 35	1 08	14 54	0 44	15 18	0 09	15 53	23 06	16 53
27	0 52	13 59	0 33	14 18	0 08	14 42	23 31	15 16	22 31	16 15
Oct. 7	0 15	13 22	23 53	13 41	23 29	14 05	22 55	14 39	21 56	15 37
17	23 34	12 44	23 15	13 03	22 52	13 27	22 18	14 01	21 19	14 59
27	22 56	12 06	22 38	12 25	22 14	12 49	21 40	13 23	20 42	14 21
Nov. 6	22 18	11 28	21 59	11 46	21 35	12 10	21 01	12 44	20 03	13 42
16	21 38	10 48	21 19	11 07	20 55	11 31	20 21	12 04	19 23	13 03
26	20 58	10 08	20 39	10 27	20 15	10 51	19 41	11 25	18 42	12 23
Dec. 6	20 16	9 27	19 57	9 46	19 33	10 10	18 59	10 44	18 00	11 43
16	19 34	8 45	19 15	9 05	18 51	9 29	18 17	10 03	17 17	11 03
26	18 52	8 03	18 33	8 23	18 08	8 47	17 33	9 22	16 33	10 22

Brightest Stars

This table lists stars of **greatest visual magnitude** as seen in the night sky (the lower the number, the brighter the star). The common name of the star is in parentheses. Stars of variable magnitude are designated by *v*. Coordinates are for mid-2004. Greek letters in the star names indicate perceived degree of brightness within the constellation, alpha being the brightest, though there are exceptions to this rule, such as Rigel (β Orionis), which is brighter than Betelgeuse (α Orionis).

To find the time when the star is on the meridian, subtract Right Ascension of Mean Sun (see the table Greenwich Sidereal Time for 0ʰ UTC) from the star's Right Ascension, first adding 24h to the latter if necessary. Mark this result P.M. if less than 12h; if greater than 12h, subtract 12h and mark the remainder A.M.

Star	Magni-tude	Paral-lax "	Light-yrs	Right ascen. h	Right ascen. m	Decli-nation °	Decli-nation '
α Canis Majoris (Sirius)	−1.44v	0.379	8.6	6	45.3	−16	43
α Carinae (Canopus)	−0.62v	0.010	313	6	24.0	−52	42
α Bootis (Arcturus)	−0.05v	0.089	37	14	15.9	+19	10
α Centauri (Rigel Kentaurus)	−0.01	0.742	4.4	14	39.9	−60	51
α Lyrae (Vega)	0.03v	0.129	25.3	18	37.1	+38	47
α Aurigae (Capella)	0.08v	0.077	42	5	17.0	+46	00
β Orionis (Rigel)	0.18v	0.004	773	5	14.7	−8	12
α Canis Minoris (Procyon)	0.40	0.286	11.4	7	39.5	+5	13
α Eridani (Achernar)	0.45v	0.023	144	1	37.9	−57	13
α Orionis (Betelgeuse)	0.45v	0.008	427	5	55.4	+7	25
β Centauri (Hadar)	0.61v	0.006	525	14	04.1	−60	24
α Aquilae (Altair)	0.76v	0.194	16.8	19	51.0	+8	53
α Crucis (Acrux)	0.77	0.010	321	12	26.8	−63	08
α Tauri (Aldebaran)	0.87v	0.050	65	4	36.1	+16	31
α Virginis (Spica)	0.98v	0.012	262	13	25.4	−11	11
α Scorpii (Antares)	1.06v	0.005	604	16	29.7	−26	27
β Geminorum (Pollux)	1.16v	0.097	33.7	7	45.6	+28	01
α Piscis Austrinis (Fomalhaut)	1.17	0.130	25.1	22	57.9	−29	36
β Crucis (Becrux)	1.25v	0.009	352	12	48.0	−59	43
α Cygni (Deneb)	1.25v	0.001	3230	20	41.6	+45	18
α Leonis (Regulus)	1.36	0.042	77	10	08.6	+11	57
ε Canis Majoris (Adhara)	1.50v	0.008	431	6	58.8	−28	59
α Geminorum (Castor)	1.58	0.063	52	7	34.9	+31	53
γ Crucis (Gacrux)	1.59v	0.037	88	12	31.4	−57	09
λ Scorpii (Shaula)	1.62v	0.005	703	17	33.9	−37	07
γ Orionis (Bellatrix)	1.64v	0.013	243	5	25.3	+6	21
β Tauri (Elnath)	1.65	0.025	131	5	26.5	+28	37
β Carinae (Miaplacidus)	1.67v	0.029	111	9	13.2	−69	44
ε Orionis (Alnilam)	1.69v	0.002	1340	5	36.4	−1	12
α Gruis (Al Nair)	1.73v	0.032	101	22	08.5	−46	56
ζ Orionis (Alnitak)	1.74	0.004	817	5	41.0	−1	56
γ Velorum (Al Suhail)	1.75v	0.004	840	8	09.6	−47	21
ε Ursae Majoris (Alioth)	1.76v	0.040	81	12	54.2	+55	56
ε Sagittarii (Kaus Australis)	1.79	0.023	145	18	24.5	−34	23
α Persei (Mirfak)	1.79v	0.006	592	3	24.6	+49	52
α Ursae Majoris (Dubhe)	1.81	0.026	124	11	04.0	+61	44
δ Canis Majoris (Wezen)	1.83v	0.002	1790	7	08.5	−26	24
η Ursae Majoris (Alkaid)	1.85v	0.032	101	13	47.7	+49	18
θ Scorpii	1.86	0.012	272	17	37.7	−43	00
ε Carinae (Avior)	1.86v	0.005	632	8	22.6	−59	31
β Aurigae (Menkalinan)	1.90v	0.040	82	5	59.8	+44	57
α Trianguli Australis (Atria)	1.91v	0.008	415	16	49.2	−69	02
γ Geminorum (Alhena)	1.93	0.031	105	6	37.9	+16	24
δ Velorum	1.93	0.041	80	8	44.8	−54	43
α Pavonis (Peacock)	1.94v	0.018	183	20	26.0	−56	43
α Ursae Minoris (Polaris)	1.97v	0.008	431	2	34.4	+89	17
β Canis Majoris (Mirzam)	1.98v	0.007	499	6	22.9	−17	57
α Hydrae (Alphard)	1.99v	0.018	177	9	27.8	−8	41
α Arietis (Hamal)	2.01	0.049	66	2	07.4	+23	29
γ Leonis (Algieba)	2.01v	0.026	126	10	20.2	+19	49
β Ceti (Deneb Kaitos)	2.04v	0.034	96	0	43.8	−17	58
σ Sagittarii (Nunki)	2.05v	0.015	224	18	55.6	−26	18
θ Centauri (Menkent)	2.06	0.054	61	14	06.9	−36	24
α Andromedae (Alpheratz)	2.07v	0.034	97	0	08.6	+29	07
β Andromedae (Mirach)	2.07v	0.016	199	1	10.0	+35	38
β Gruis	2.07v	0.019	170	22	42.9	−46	52
κ Orionis (Saiph)	2.07v	0.005	721	5	47.9	−9	40
β Ursae Minoris (Kochab)	2.07v	0.026	126	14	50.8	+74	08
α Ophiuchi (Rasalhague)	2.08	0.070	47	17	35.2	+12	33
β Persei (Algol)	2.09v	0.035	93	3	08.4	+40	58
γ Andromedae (Almaak)	2.10	0.009	355	2	04.1	+42	21
β Leonis (Denebola)	2.14	0.090	36.2	11	49.3	+14	33
γ Cassiopeiae	2.15v	0.005	613	0	57.0	+60	44
γ Centauri	2.20	0.025	130	12	41.8	−48	59
ι Carinae (Tureis)	2.21	0.005	692	9	17.2	−59	18
ζ Puppis (Naos)	2.21v	0.002	1400	8	03.7	−40	01
α Coronae Borealis (Alphecca)	2.22v	0.044	75	15	34.9	+26	42
ζ Ursae Majoris (Mizar)	2.23	0.042	78	13	24.1	+54	54
γ Cygni (Sadr)	2.23v	0.002	1520	20	22.4	+40	16
λ Velorum (Suhail)	2.23v	0.006	573	9	08.1	−43	27
γ Draconis (Eltanin)	2.24v	0.022	148	17	56.7	+51	29
δ Orionis (Mintaka)	2.25v	0.004	916	5	32.2	−0	18
β Cassiopeiae (Caph)	2.28v	0.060	54	0	09.4	+59	10
ε Scorpii	2.29	0.050	65	16	50.5	−34	18
γ Centauri	2.29v	0.009	386	13	40.2	−53	30
δ Scorpii (Dschubba)	2.29v	0.008	401	16	00.6	−22	38
α Lupi	2.30v	0.006	548	14	42.2	−47	25
η Centauri	2.33v	0.011	308	14	35.8	−42	11
β Ursae Majoris (Merak)	2.34	0.041	79	11	02.1	+56	22
ε Bootis (Izar)	2.35	0.016	210	14	45.2	+27	03
κ Scorpii	2.39v	0.007	464	17	42.8	−39	02

Morning and Evening Stars, 2004

(in Coordinated Universal Time)

	Morning	Evening		Morning	Evening
Jan.	Mercury Jupiter Pluto	Venus Mars Saturn Uranus Neptune	**Apr.**	Pluto	Jupiter Saturn
Feb.	Mercury Jupiter Uranus from Feb. 22 Neptune from Feb. 2 Pluto	Venus Mars Saturn Uranus to Feb. 22 Neptune to Feb. 2	**May**	Mercury Uranus Neptune Pluto	Venus Mars Jupiter Saturn
Mar.	Mercury to Mar. 4 Jupiter to Mar. 4 Uranus Neptune Pluto	Mercury from Mar. 4 Venus Mars Jupiter from Mar. 4 Saturn	**June**	Mercury to June 18 Venus from June 8 Uranus Neptune Pluto to June 11	Mercury from June 18 Venus to June 8 Mars Jupiter Saturn Pluto from June 11
Apr.	Mercury from Apr. 17 Uranus Neptune	Mercury to Apr. 17 Venus Mars	**July**	Venus Saturn from July 8 Uranus Neptune	Mercury Mars Jupiter Saturn to July 8 Pluto

	Morning	Evening		Morning	Evening
Aug.	Mercury from Aug. 23	Mercury to Aug. 23		Mars	Neptune
	Venus	Mars		Jupiter	Pluto
	Saturn	Jupiter		Saturn	
	Uranus to Aug. 27	Uranus from Aug. 27	Nov.	Venus	Mercury
	Neptune to Aug. 6	Neptune from Aug. 6		Mars	Uranus
		Pluto		Jupiter	Neptune
Sept.	Mercury	Mars to Sept. 15		Saturn	Pluto
	Venus	Jupiter to Sept. 22	Dec.	Mercury from Dec. 10	Mercury to Dec. 10
	Mars from Sept. 15	Uranus		Venus	Uranus
	Jupiter from Sept. 22	Neptune		Mars	Neptune
	Saturn	Pluto		Jupiter	Pluto to Dec. 12
Oct.	Mercury to Oct. 5	Mercury from Oct. 5		Saturn	
	Venus	Uranus		Pluto from Dec. 13	

Greenwich Sidereal Time for 0ʰ UTC, 2004

(Add 12 hours to obtain Right Ascension of Mean Sun)

Date	d	h	m	Date	d	h	m	Date	d	h	m
Jan. . .	1	6	40.0	May . .	10	15	12.5	Sept. . .	7	23	05.6
	11	7	19.4		20	15	52.0		17	23	45.1
	21	7	58.8		30	16	31.4		27	0	24.5
	31	8	38.3	June .	9	17	10.8	Oct. . . .	7	1	03.9
Feb. . .	10	9	17.7		19	17	50.2		17	1	43.3
	20	9	57.1		29	18	29.7		27	2	22.8
Mar. . .	1	10	36.5	July . .	9	19	09.1	Nov. . . .	6	3	02.2
	11	11	16.0		19	19	48.5		16	3	41.6
	21	11	55.4		29	20	27.9		26	4	21.0
	31	12	34.8	Aug. . .	8	21	07.4	Dec. . . .	6	5	00.5
Apr. . .	10	13	14.3		18	21	46.8		16	5	39.9
	20	13	53.7		28	22	26.2		26	6	19.3
	30	14	33.1								

Aurora Borealis and Aurora Australis

The **Aurora Borealis**, also called the **Northern Lights**, is a broad display of rather faint light in the northern skies at night. The **Aurora Australis**, a similar phenomenon, appears at the same time in southern skies. The aurora appears in a wide variety of forms. Sometimes it is seen as a quiet glow, almost foglike in character; sometimes as vertical streamers in which there may be considerable motion; sometimes as a series of luminous expanding arcs. There are many colors, with white, yellow, and red predominating.

The auroras are most vivid and most frequently seen at about 20° from the magnetic poles, along the northern coast of the N American continent and the eastern part of the northern coast of Europe. The Aurora Borealis has been seen as far S as Key West, and the Aurora Australis has been seen as far N as Australia and New Zealand. Such occurrences are rare, however.

The Sun produces a stream of charged particles, called the **solar wind**. These particles, mainly electrons and protons, approach Earth at speeds on the order of 300 mi per second. Coronal mass ejections are large-scale, high-speed releases of as much as 10 billion tons of coronal material. Some of these particles are trapped by Earth's magnetic field, forming the **Van Allen belts**—2 donut-shaped radiation bands

around Earth. Excess amounts of these charged particles, often produced by solar flares, follow Earth's magnetic lines of force toward Earth's magnetic poles. High in the atmosphere, collisions between solar and terrestrial atoms result in the glow in the upper atmosphere called the **aurora**. The glow may be vivid where the lines of magnetic force converge near the magnetic poles.

The auroral displays appear at heights ranging from 50 to about 600 mi and have given us a means of estimating the extent of Earth's atmosphere.

The auroras are often accompanied by **magnetic storms** whose forces, also guided by the lines of force of Earth's magnetic field, disrupt electrical communication. In February 2001, the Sun's magnetic field reversed, a marker that the Sun had reached its peak of the current solar cycle (#23). Sunspot activity, as expected, has declined over the past couple of years with the next minimum expected around 2007. Strong coronal mass ejections can still occur as witnessed by the double coronal mass ejections that swept past the Earth on May 29, 2003, triggering 9 hours of severe geomagnetic storms and producing displays of the northern lights as far south as Virginia.

Largest Telescopes

Astronomers indicate the size of telescopes not by length or magnification, but by the diameter of the primary light-gathering component of the system—such as the lens or mirror. This measurement is a direct indication of the telescope's light-gathering power. The bigger the diameter, the fainter the objects you are enabled to see. For larger telescopes, the Earth's atmosphere limits the resolution of what you see. That is why the Hubble Space Telescope, which is outside the atmosphere, can have better resolution than larger telescopes on the Earth. **Refracting (lens) telescopes** are currently not made with lens diameters of more than 40 in. Mirror telescopes can be made less expensively than lens telescopes, so all modern large optical telescopes are made with mirrors. **Radio telescopes**, also reflecting telescopes, view at wavelengths not visible to optical telescopes or to the human eye. Radio telescopes are made larger than optical telescopes because larger diameters are required at longer wavelengths to obtain equivalent resolution. Arrays of telescopes are used to achieve even better resolution.

Largest Refracting (lens) Optical Telescope: Yerkes Observatory—1 m (40 in), at Williams Bay, WI
Largest Reflecting (mirror) Optical/Infrared Telescope: Keck—10 m (33 ft), on Mauna Kea in Hawaii (segmented mirror; 2 equal-size telescopes)
Largest Infrared Interferometer: Four 8.2-m (27-ft) telescopes of the Very Large Telescope Interferometer (VLTI) with a 200-m (656-ft) baseline on Cerro Paranal in Chile
Largest Space Telescope: Hubble Space Telescope—2.4 m (94 in), in orbit around Earth
Largest Fully Steerable Radio Dish: Robert C. Byrd Green Bank Telescope—100 m x 110 m (328 ft x 361 ft), in West Virginia
Largest Single Radio Dish: Arecibo Observatory—305 m (1,000 ft), in Puerto Rico
Largest Radio Interferometer: Ten 25-m (82-ft) diameter telescopes of the Very Long Baseline Array (VLBA), dispersed from Hawaii to the Virgin Islands with a resolution equal to a radio dish of 8,600 km (5,000 mi)
Largest Millimeter Wavelength Interferometer: Sixty-four 12-m (39-ft) diameter telescopes of the Atacama Large Millimeter Array (ALMA), being built at 5,000 m (16,400 ft), will be the highest-altitude ground-based observatory

Constellations

Culturally, constellations are imagined patterns among the stars that, in some cases, have been recognized through millennia. Knowledge of constellations was once necessary in order to function as an astronomer. For today's astronomers, constellations are simply areas on the entire sky in which interesting objects await observation and interpretation.

Because Western culture has prevailed in establishing modern science, equally viable and interesting constellations and celestial traditions of other cultures are not well known outside their regions of origin. Even the patterns with which we are most familiar today have undergone considerable change over the centuries.

Today, **88 constellations** are officially recognized. Although many have ancient origins, some are "modern," devised out of unclaimed stars by astronomers a few centuries ago. Unclaimed stars were those too faint or inconveniently placed to be included in the more prominent constellations. Stars in a constellation are not necessarily near each other; they are just located in the same direction on the celestial sphere.

When astronomers began to travel to S Africa in the 16th and 17th centuries, they found an unfamiliar sky that showed numerous brilliant stars. Thus, we find constellations in the southern hemisphere that depict technological marvels of the time, as well as some arguably traditional forms, such as the "fly."

Many of the commonly recognized constellations had their **origins** in ancient Asia Minor. These were adopted by the Greeks and Romans, who translated their names and stories into their own languages, modifying some details in the process. After the declines of these cultures, most such knowledge entered oral tradition or remained hidden in monastic libraries. From the 8th century, the Muslim explosion spread through the Mediterranean world. Wherever possible, everything was translated into Arabic to be taught in the universities the Muslims established all over their new-found world.

In the 13th century, Alfonso X of Castile, an avid student of astronomy, had Ptolemy's *Almagest* translated into Latin. It thus became widely available to European scholars. In the process, the constellation names were translated, but the star names were retained in their Arabic forms. Thus the names of many stars—e.g., Altair, Alnitak, Mirfak—have Arabic roots, although linguistic adaptation and the inaccuracies of transliteration have wrought changes.

Until the 1920s, astronomers used curved boundaries for the constellation areas. As these were rather arbitrary at best, the International Astronomical Union adopted new constellation boundaries that ran due north-south and east-west, filling the sky much as the contiguous states fill up the area of the "lower 48" United States.

Common names of stars often referred to parts of the traditional figures they represented: Deneb, the tail of the swan; Betelgeuse, the armpit of the giant. Avoiding traditional names, astronomers may label stars by using Greek letters, generally to denote order of brightness. Thus, the "alpha star" would generally be the brightest star of that constellation. The "of" implies possession, so the genitive (possessive) form of the constellation name is used, as in Alpha Orionis, the first star of Orion (Betelgeuse). Astronomers usually use a 3-letter abbreviation for the constellation name, as indicated here.

Within these boundaries, and occasionally crossing them, popular "asterisms" are recognized: the so-called Big Dipper is a small part of the constellation Ursa Major, the big bear; the Sickle is the traditional head and mane of Leo, the lion; the three stars of the Summer Triangle are each in a different constellation, with Vega in Lyra the lyre, Deneb in Cynus the swan, and Altair in Aquila the eagle; the northeast star of the Great Square of Pegasus is Alpha Andromedae.

Name	Genitive Case	Abbr.	Meaning
Andromeda	Andromedae	And	Chained Maiden
Antlia	Antliae	Ant	Air Pump
Apus	Apodis	Aps	Bird of Paradise
Aquarius	Aquarii	Aqr	Water Bearer
Aquila	Aquilae	Aql	Eagle
Ara	Arae	Ara	Altar
Aries	Arietis	Ari	Ram
Auriga	Aurigae	Aur	Charioteer
Boötes	Boötis	Boo	Herdsmen
Caelum	Caeli	Cae	Chisel
Camelopardalis	Camelopardalis	Cam	Giraffe
Cancer	Cancri	Cnc	Crab
Canes Venatici	Canum Venaticorum	CVn	Hunting Dogs
Canis Major	Canis Majoris	CMa	Greater Dog
Canis Minor	Canis Minoris	CMi	Littler Dog
Capricornus	Capricorni	Cap	Sea-goat
Carina	Carinae	Car	Keel
Cassiopeia	Cassiopeiae	Cas	Queen
Centaurus	Centauri	Cen	Centaur
Cepheus	Cephei	Cep	King
Cetus	Ceti	Cet	Whale
Chamaeleon	Chamaeleontis	Cha	Chameleon
Circinus	Circini	Cir	Compasses (art)
Columba	Columbae	Col	Dove
Coma Berenices	Comae Berenices	Com	Berenice's Hair
Corona Australis	Coronae Australis	CrA	Southern Crown
Corona Borealis	Coronae Borealis	CrB	Northern Crown
Corvus	Corvi	Crv	Crow
Crater	Crateris	Crt	Cup
Crux	Crucis	Cru	Cross (southern)
Cygnus	Cygni	Cyg	Swan
Delphinus	Delphini	Del	Dolphin
Dorado	Doradus	Dor	Goldfish
Draco	Draconis	Dra	Dragon
Equuleus	Equulei	Equ	Little Horse
Eridanus	Eridani	Eri	River
Fornax	Fornacis	For	Furnace
Gemini	Geminorum	Gem	Twins
Grus	Gruis	Gru	Crane (bird)
Hercules	Herculis	Her	Hercules
Horologium	Horologii	Hor	Clock
Hydra	Hydrae	Hya	Water Snake (female)
Hydrus	Hydri	Hyi	Water Snake (male)
Indus	Indi	Ind	Indian
Lacerta	Lacertae	Lac	Lizard
Leo	Leonis	Leo	Lion
Leo Minor	Leonis Minoris	LMi	Littler Lion
Lepus	Leporis	Lep	Hare
Libra	Librae	Lib	Balance
Lupus	Lupi	Lup	Wolf
Lynx	Lyncis	Lyn	Lynx
Lyra	Lyrae	Lyr	Lyre
Mensa	Mensae	Men	Table Mountain
Microscopium	Microscopii	Mic	Microscope
Monoceros	Monocerotis	Mon	Unicorn
Musca	Muscae	Mus	Fly
Norma	Normae	Nor	Square (rule)
Octans	Octantis	Oct	Octant
Ophiuchus	Ophiuchi	Oph	Serpent Bearer
Orion	Orionis	Ori	Hunter
Pavo	Pavonis	Pav	Peacock
Pegasus	Pegasi	Peg	Flying Horse
Perseus	Persei	Per	Hero
Phoenix	Phoenicis	Phe	Phoenix
Pictor	Pictoris	Pic	Painter
Pisces	Piscium	Psc	Fishes
Piscis Austrinus	Piscis Austrini	PsA	Southern Fish
Puppis	Puppis	Pup	Stern (deck)
Pyxis	Pyxidis	Pyx	Compass (sea)
Reticulum	Reticuli	Ret	Reticle
Sagitta	Sagittae	Sge	Arrow
Sagittarius	Sagittarii	Sgr	Archer
Scorpius	Scorpii	Sco	Scorpion
Sculptor	Sculptoris	Scl	Sculptor
Scutum	Scuti	Sct	Shield
Serpens	Serpentis	Ser	Serpent
Sextans	Sextantis	Sex	Sextant
Taurus	Tauri	Tau	Bull
Telescopium	Telescopii	Tel	Telescope
Triangulum	Trianguli	Tri	Triangle
Triangulum Australe	Trianguli Australis	TrA	Southern Triangle
Tucana	Tucanae	Tuc	Toucan
Ursa Major	Ursae Majoris	UMa	Greater Bear
Ursa Minor	Ursae Minoris	UMi	Littler Bear
Vela	Velorum	Vel	Sail
Virgo	Virginis	Vir	Maiden
Volans	Volantis	Vol	Flying Fish
Vulpecula	Vulpeculae	Vul	Fox

Eclipses, 2004

(in Coordinated Universal Time, standard time of the prime meridian)

There are 4 eclipses in 2004, 2 partial eclipses of the Sun, and 2 total eclipses of the Moon. There is also a rare transit of the Sun by Venus.

I. Partial eclipse of the Sun, April 19

This partial solar eclipse is visible from the S Atlantic Ocean, southern part of Africa, Madagascar, SW Indian Ocean, and part of Antarctica.

Circumstances of the Eclipse

Event	Date	h	m
Partial eclipse begins	Apr. 19	11	29.9
Middle of eclipse	19	13	33.9
Partial eclipse ends	19	15	38.5

II. Total eclipse of the Moon, May 4

The beginning of the eclipse will be visible in Asia, eastern Europe, the Middle East, Indian Ocean, Antarctica, Australia, New Zealand, Indonesia, the SW Pacific Ocean, and all but western Africa. The end of the eclipse will be visible in India, the Middle East, Africa, Europe, western China, the Indian Ocean, the Atlantic Ocean, S America, Antarctica, and the SE Pacific Ocean.

Circumstances of the Eclipse

Event	Date	h	m
Partial eclipse begins	May 4	18	48.2
Total eclipse begins	4	19	52.0
Middle eclipse at midday	4	20	30.1
Total eclipse ends	4	21	8.3
Partial eclipse ends	4	22	12.1

III. Partial eclipse of the Sun, October 14

This partial solar eclipse is visible from the N Pacific Ocean, Alaska, Japan, Korea, most of Russia, and eastern portions of Mongolia and China.

Circumstances of the Eclipse

Event	Date	h	m
Partial eclipse begins	Oct. 14	0	54.5
Middle of eclipse	14	2	59.2
Partial eclipse ends	14	5	4.2

IV. Total eclipse of the Moon, October 28

The beginning of the eclipse will be visible in India, western China, Europe, Africa, the Atlantic Ocean, Greenland, the Arctic region, S America, eastern N America, Central America, and the SE Pacific Ocean. The end of the eclipse will be visible in western Africa, western Europe, Greenland, the Arctic region, all but the SE Atlantic Ocean, S America, N America, and most of the Pacific Ocean.

Circumstances of the Eclipse

Event	Date	h	m
Partial eclipse begins	Oct. 28	1	14.3
Total eclipse begins	28	2	23.4
Greatest eclipse	28	3	4.0
Total eclipse ends	28	3	44.6
Partial eclipse ends	28	4	53.7

V. Transit of the Sun by Venus, June 8

Since Venus does not block the Sun, it is dangerous to observe this event directly or with optical aids. The transit is visible in all of Europe except the southern part of Portugal, most of Africa except for western regions, a large portion of the Indian Ocean, and much of Asia except eastern regions including Japan, the Koreas, and portions of southeast Asia.

Circumstances of the Transit

Event	Date	h	m
Ingress begins	June 8	5	13.5
Least angular distance	8	8	19.7
Egress ends	8	11	25.9

Total Solar Eclipses in the U.S. in the 21st Century

During the 21st century Halley's Comet will return (2061-62), and there will be 8 total solar eclipses that are visible somewhere in the continental United States. The first comes after a long gap; the last one to be seen there was on Feb. 26, 1979, in the northwestern U.S.

Date	Path of Totality	Date	Path of Totality
Aug. 21, 2017	Oregon to South Carolina	Mar. 30, 2052	Florida to Georgia
Apr. 8, 2024	Mexico to Texas and up through Maine	May 11, 2078	Louisiana to North Carolina
Aug. 23, 2044	Montana to North Dakota	May 1, 2079	New Jersey to the lower edge of New England
Aug. 12, 2045	N California to Florida	Sept. 14, 2099	North Dakota to Virginia

Total Solar Eclipses, 1961-2025

Total solar eclipses actually take place nearly as often as total lunar eclipses; they occur at a rate of about 3 every 4 years, while total lunar eclipses come at a rate of about 5 every 6 years. However, total lunar eclipses are visible over at least half of the Earth, while total solar eclipses can be seen only along a very narrow path up to a few hundred miles wide and a few thousand miles long. Observing a total solar eclipse is thus a rarity for most people. Unlike lunar eclipses, solar eclipses can be dangerous to observe. This is not because the Sun emits more potent rays during a solar eclipse, but because the Sun is always dangerous to observe directly and people are particularly likely to stare at it during a solar eclipse.

Date	Duration[1] m	s	Width (mi)	Path of Totality
1961, Feb. 15	2	45	160	Europe, Soviet Union
1962, Feb. 5	4	8	91	Borneo, New Guinea, Pacific Ocean
1963, July 20	1	39	63	Pacific Ocean, Alaska, Canada, Maine
1965, May 30	5	15	123	New Zealand, Pacific Ocean
1966, Nov. 12	1	57	52	Pacific Ocean, S America, Atlantic Ocean
1968, Sept. 22	0	39	64	Soviet Union, China
1970, Mar. 7	3	27	95	Pacific Ocean, Mexico, Eastern U.S., Canada
1972, July 10	2	35	109	Siberia, Alaska, Canada
1973, June 30	7	3	159	Atlantic Ocean, Central Africa, Indian Ocean
1974, June 20	5	8	214	Indian Ocean, Australia
1976, Oct. 23	4	46	123	Africa, Indian Ocean, Australia
1977, Oct. 12	2	37	61	Pacific Ocean, Colombia, Venezuela
1979, Feb. 26	2	49	185	NW U.S., Canada, Greenland
1980, Feb. 16	4	8	92	Africa, Indian Ocean, India, Burma, China
1981, July 31	2	2	67	Soviet Union, Pacific Ocean
1983, June 11	5	10	123	Indian Ocean, Indonesia, New Guinea
1984, Nov. 22	1	59	53	New Guinea, Pacific Ocean
1985, Nov. 12	1	58	430	Antarctica
1986, Oct. 3[h]	0	1	1	N Atlantic Ocean
1987, Mar. 29[h]	0	7	3	S Atlantic Ocean, Africa
1988, Mar. 18	3	46	104	Sumatra, Borneo, Philippines, Pacific Ocean
1990, July 22	2	32	125	Finland, Soviet Union, Aleutian Islands
1991, July 11	6	53	160	Hawaii, Mexico, Central America, Colombia, Brazil

Date	Duration[1] m	s	Width (mi)	Path of Totality
1992, June 30	5	20	182	S Atlantic Ocean
1994, Nov. 3	4	23	117	Peru, Bolivia, Paraguay, Brazil
1995, Oct. 24	2	9	48	Iran, India, SE Asia
1997, Mar. 9	2	50	221	Mongolia, Siberia
1998, Feb. 26	4	8	94	Galapagos Islands, Panama, Colombia, Venezuela
1999, Aug. 11	2	22	69	Europe, Middle East, India
2001, June 21	4	56	125	Atlantic Ocean, Africa, Madagascar
2002, Dec. 4	2	4	54	S Africa, Indian Ocean, Australia
2003, Nov. 23	1	57	338	Antarctica
2005, Apr. 8[h]	0	42	17	Pacific Ocean, northwestern S America
2006, Mar. 29	4	7	118	Atlantic Ocean, Africa, Asia
2008, Aug. 1	2	27	157	Arctic Ocean, Asia
2009, July 22	6	39	160	Asia, Pacific Ocean
2010, July 11	5	20	164	Pacific Ocean, southern S America
2012, Nov. 13	4	2	112	N Australia, Pacific Ocean
2013, Nov. 3[h]	1	40	36	Atlantic Ocean, Africa
2015, Mar. 20	2	47	304	N Atlantic Ocean, Arctic Ocean
2016, Mar. 9	4	10	96	Indonesia, Pacific Ocean
2017, Aug. 21	2	40	71	Pacific Ocean, U.S., Atlantic Ocean
2019, July 2	4	33	125	S Pacific Ocean, S America
2020, Dec. 14	2	10	56	S Pacific Ocean, S America, S Atlantic Ocean
2021, Dec. 4	1	55	282	Antarctica, S Atlantic Ocean
2023, Apr. 20[h]	1	16	31	Indian Ocean, New Guinea, Pacific Ocean
2024, Apr. 8	4	28	127	Pacific Ocean, Mexico, N America, Atlantic Ocean

h = indicates annular-total hybrid eclipse. (1) Duration refers to length of time at optimal viewing area.

Mercury and Venus Cross the Sun

Transits of Mercury across the face of the Sun happen about 13 or 14 times a century, in May or November. Transits of Venus occur only once or twice a century, but when it is twice, as in the 21st century, they are about 8 years apart. Since either planet covers only a minuscule part of the Sun's face, it is dangerous to observe such events directly.

Date	Event	Duration	Date	Event	Duration
May 7, 2003	Transit of Mercury	5.3 hours	May 7, 2049	Transit of Mercury	6.7 hours
June 8, 2004	Transit of Venus	6.2 hours	Nov. 9, 2052	Transit of Mercury	5.2 hours
Nov. 8, 2006	Transit of Mercury	5.0 hours	May 10, 2062	Transit of Mercury	6.7 hours
June 6, 2012	Transit of Venus	6.7 hours	Nov. 11, 2065	Transit of Mercury	5.4 hours
May 9, 2016	Transit of Mercury	7.5 hours	Nov. 14, 2078	Transit of Mercury	4.0 hours
Nov. 11, 2019	Transit of Mercury	5.5 hours	Nov. 7, 2085	Transit of Mercury	3.7 hours
Nov. 13, 2032	Transit of Mercury	4.4 hours	May 8, 2095	Transit of Mercury	7.5 hours
Nov. 7, 2039	Transit of Mercury	3.0 hours	Nov. 10, 2098	Transit of Mercury	5.4 hours

On June 8, 2004, for the first time since 1882, Venus will cross the face of the Sun (as seen from Earth.) Venus appears to make first contact with the Sun at 1:13 A.M. EDT, and will be completely inside the disk of the Sun at 1:33 A.M. EDT. As the time indicates, the beginning of the transit will not be directly visible in either N or S America, but the entire transit will be visible over much of Asia, Europe, and Africa.

Remember, Venus blocks only a small fraction of the Sun, and it is always dangerous to look at the Sun. It is essential to use proper solar filtration and take precautions to observe the transit; there will probably be real-time coverage of the transit on the Internet. Since Venus will take more than 5.5 hours to transit the disk of the Sun, the latter stages of the process will be visible in the eastern half of N and S America.

Beginnings of the Universe

One of the dominating astronomical discoveries of the 20th century was the realization that the galaxies of the universe all seem to be moving away from us. It turned out that they are moving away not just from us but from one another—that is, the universe seems to be expanding. Scientists conclude that the universe must once, very long ago, have been extremely compact and dense. The explosion of matter that gave birth to the universe is called the **Big Bang**.

On the subatomic level, according to this theory, there were vast changes of energy and matter and the way physical laws operated during the first 5 minutes. After those minutes the percentages of the basic matter of the universe—hydrogen, helium, and lithium—were set. Everything was so compact and so hot that radiation dominated the early universe and there were no stable, un-ionized atoms. At first, the universe was opaque, in the sense that any energy emitted was quickly absorbed and then re-emitted by free electrons. As the universe expanded, density and temperature continued to drop. A few hundred thousand years after the Big Bang, the temperature dropped far enough that electrons and nuclei could combine to form stable atoms as the universe became transparent. Once that occurred, the radiation which had been trapped was free to escape.

In the 1940s, George Gamov and others predicted that astronomers should be able to see remnants of this escaped radiation. Astronomers were starting to search for this background radiation when physicists Arno Penzias and Robert Wilson using a radio telescope inadvertently beat them to the punch (the 2 were later awarded a Nobel Prize).

In 2003, NASA's Wilkinson Microwave Anisotropy Probe (WMAP), using highly sensitive amplifiers developed by the National Radio Astronomy Observatory (NRAO), made measurements of the temperature of this **cosmic microwave background** radiation to within millionths of a degree. From these measurements, scientists were able to deduce that our universe is 13.7 billion years old and the first generation stars began to form a mere 200 million years after the **Big Bang**.

A related mystery is that evidence suggests there is hidden matter and hidden energy that cannot be directly observed. This **dark matter** may be composed of gas, large numbers of cool, small objects, or even sub-atomic particles. The presence of **dark matter** is indicated by the rotation curves of galaxies and the dynamics of clusters of galaxies. Evidence for **dark energy** is derived from studies of distant Type Ia supernovae in far galaxies indicating the expansion of the universe is accelerating. The visible matter we see seems to constitute only about 4% of the total mass of the universe, while the rest of the mass of the universe is in the form of **dark matter** (23%) and **dark energy** (73%).

The Solar System

The planets of the solar system, in order of mean distance from the Sun, are Mercury, Venus, Earth, Mars, Jupiter, Saturn, Uranus, Neptune, and Pluto (Pluto sometimes nearer than Neptune). Both Uranus and Neptune are visible through good binoculars, but Pluto is so distant and so small that only large telescopes or long-exposure photographs can make it visible. All the planets orbit or revolve counterclockwise around the Sun.

Because Mercury and Venus are nearer to the Sun than is Earth, their motions about the Sun are seen from Earth as wide swings first to one side of the Sun then to the other, though both planets move continuously around the Sun in almost circular orbits. When their passage takes them either between Earth and the Sun or beyond the Sun as seen from Earth, they are invisible to us. Because of the geometry of the planetary orbits, Mercury and Venus require much less time to pass between Earth and the Sun than around the far side of the Sun; so their periods of visibility and invisibility are unequal.

The planets that lie farther from the Sun than does Earth may be seen for longer periods and are invisible only when so located in our sky that they rise and set at about the same time as the Sun—and thus become overwhelmed by the Sun's great brilliance. Although several of the giant planets emit their own energy, they are observed from Earth as a result of sunlight reflecting from their surfaces or cloud layers. However, on occasion, radio emissions from Jupiter exceed even those emitted by the Sun in intensity. Mercury and Venus, because they are between Earth and the Sun, show phases very much as the Moon does. The planets farther from the Sun are always seen as full, although Mars does occasionally present a slightly gibbous phase—like the Moon when not quite full.

The planets appear to move rapidly among the stars because of being closer. The stars are also in motion, some at tremendous speeds, but they are so far away that their motion does not change their apparent positions in the heavens sufficiently to be perceived. The nearest star is about 9,000 times farther away than Neptune, the most distant giant planet in our solar system. The count for identified moons in the solar system stood at 128 in mid-2003, but the rush to discover new moons continued at a frenetic pace.

Planets and the Sun, by Selected Characteristics

Sun and Planets	Radius: at unit distance[1] "	Radius: at mean least distance[2] "	Radius: in mi mean radius	Volume[3]	Mass[3]	Density[3]	Sidereal period d	Sidereal period h	Sidereal period m	Sidereal period s	Gravity at surface[3]	Reflecting power Pct°	Daytime surface temp. °F
Sun........	959.5	976	432,600	1,304,000	333,000	0.26	25	9	7	12	28.0		+9,941
Mercury ...	3.36	6.5	1,516	0.0562	0.0553	0.98	58	15	36		0.38	0.11	846
Venus	8.34	33.0	3,761	0.857	0.815	0.95	243	12	R		0.90	0.65	867
Earth	8.78		3,960	1.000	1.000	1.00		23	56	4.2	1.00	0.37	59
Moon	2.40	986.2	1,080	0.0203	0.0123	0.61	27	7	43	41	0.17	0.12	261
Mars.......	4.67	12.8	2,107	0.151	0.107	0.71		24	37	22	0.38	0.15	−76
Jupiter	96.40	24.5	43,450	1,321	317.83	0.24		9	55	30	2.36	0.52	−162
Saturn.....	80.29	10.05	36,191	764	95.16	0.12		10	39	22	0.92	0.47	−218
Uranus	34.97	2.05	15,762	63.1	14.54	0.23		17	14	24R	0.89	0.51	−323
Neptune	33.95	1.2	15,304	57.7	17.15	0.30		16	6	36	1.12	0.41	−330
Pluto.......	1.65	0.08	743	0.007	0.002	0.32	6	9	17	34R	0.06	0.6	−369

(1) Angular radius, in seconds of arc, if object were seen at a distance of 1 astronomical unit. (2) Angular radius, in seconds of arc, when object is closest to Earth. (3) Earth = 1. R = Retrograde rotation.

Planet Superlatives

Largest, most massive planet.............	Jupiter	Most circular orbit	Venus
Fastest orbiting planet	Mercury	Slowest orbiting planet	Pluto
Fastest Sidereal rotation.................	Jupiter	Slowest sidereal rotation................	Venus
Longest (synodic) day...................	Mercury	Shortest (synodic) day..................	Jupiter
Rotational pole closest to ecliptic	Uranus	Hottest planet	Venus
Most moons	Jupiter	No moons	Mercury, Venus
Planet with largest moon	Jupiter	Planet with moon with most eccentric orbit ..	Neptune
Greatest average density	Earth	Lowest average density.................	Saturn
Tallest mountain	Mars	Deepest oceans.......................	Jupiter
Strongest magnetic fields	Jupiter	Greatest amount of liquid, surface water....	Earth

The Planets: Motion, Distance, and Brightness

Planet	Mean daily motion[1]	Orbital velocity mi per sec.[2]	Sidereal revolution days[3]	Synodic revolution days[4]	Distance from Sun in millions of mi Max.	Distance from Sun in millions of mi Min.	Distance from Earth in millions of mi Max.	Distance from Earth in millions of mi Min.	Light at[5] perihelion	Light at[5] aphelion
Mercury	14,732	29.75	87.97	115.9	43.4	28.6	137.9	48.0	10.56	4.59
Venus	5,768	21.76	224.7	583.9	67.7	66.8	162.2	23.7	1.94	1.89
Earth	3,548	18.50	365.256	—	94.5	91.4	—	—	1.03	0.97
Mars	1,887	15.00	686.98	779.9	154.9	128.4	249.4	33.9	0.52	0.36
Jupiter	299	8.12	4,332.6	398.9	507.5	460.2	602	366	0.041	0.034
Saturn	120	6.02	10,759.2	378.1	941.3	840.6	1,031	743	0.012	0.0098
Uranus	42	4.23	30,685.4	369.7	1,867	1,704	1,962	1,605	0.0030	0.0025
Neptune	22	3.37	60,189.0	367.5	2,825	2,762	2,913	2,676	0.0011	0.0011
Pluto	14	2.93	90,465.0	366.7	4,538	2,756	4,682	2,669	0.0011	0.00041

(1) Average angular motion measured in seconds of arc per day. (2) Speed of revolution around Sun. (3) Number of Earth days to orbit Sun with respect to background stars. (4) Number of Earth days to get back to the same position in its orbit around Sun, relative to Earth. (5) Light at perihelion and aphelion is solar illumination measured in units of mean illumination at Earth.

Planets of the Solar System

Note: AU = astronomical unit (92.96 mil mi, mean distance of Earth from the Sun); **d** = 1 Earth synodic (solar) day (24 hrs); **synodic day** = rotation period of a planet measured with respect to the Sun (the "true" day, i.e. the time from midday to midday, or from sunrise to sunrise); **sidereal day** = the rotation period of a planet with respect to the stars

Mercury

Distance from Sun	
Perihelion	28.6 mil mi
Semi-major axis	0.387 AU
Aphelion	43.4 mil mi
Period of revolution around Sun	87.97 d
Orbital eccentricity	0.2056
Orbital inclination	7.00°
Synodic day (midday to midday)	175.942 d
Sidereal day	58.65 d
Rotational inclination	0.01°
Mass (Earth = 1)	0.0553
Mean radius	1,516 mi
Mean density (Earth = 1)	0.984
Natural satellites	0
Average surface temperature	333°F

Mercury, the nearest planet to the Sun, is the 2nd-smallest of the 9 known planets. Its diameter is 3,032 mi; its mean distance from the Sun is 35,990,000 mi.

Mercury moves with great speed around the Sun, averaging about 30 mi per second to complete its circuit in about 88 Earth days. Mercury rotates upon its axis over a period of nearly 59 days, thus exposing all its surface periodically to the Sun. Because its orbital period is only about 50% longer than its sidereal rotation, the solar (synodic) day on Mercury, or the time from one sunrise to the next, is about 176 days, twice as long as a Mercunian year. It is believed that the surface passing before the Sun may reach a temperature of about 845° F, while the temperature on the nighttime side may fall as low as –300° F.

Uncertainty about conditions on Mercury and its motion arises from its short angular distance from the Sun as seen from Earth. Mercury is too much in line with the Sun to be observed against a dark sky, but is always seen during either morning or evening twilight.

Mariner 10 passed Mercury 3 times in 1974 and 1975. Less than half of the surface was photographed, revealing a degree of cratering similar to that of the Moon. The most imposing feature on Mercury, the Caloris Basin, is a huge impact crater more than 800 mi in diameter. Mercury also has a higher percentage of iron than any other planet. A very thin atmosphere of hydrogen and helium may be made up of gases of the solar wind temporarily concentrated by the presence of Mercury. The discovery of a weak but permanent magnetic field was a surprise to scientists. It has been held that both a fluid core and rapid rotation are necessary for the generation of a planetary magnetic field. Mercury may demonstrate the contrary; the field may reveal something about the history of Mercury. In 1991 and 1994, radar mapping of Mercury revealed evidence of possible water ice near its north and south poles.

Venus

Distance from Sun	
Perihelion	66.8 mil mi
Semi-major axis	0.723 AU
Aphelion	67.7 mil mi
Period of revolution around Sun	224.70 d
Orbital eccentricity	0.0067
Orbital inclination	3.39°
Synodic day (midday to midday)	116.75 d (retrograde)
Sidereal day	243.02 d (retrograde)
Rotational inclination	177.4°
Mass (Earth = 1)	0.815
Mean radius	3,761 mi
Mean density (Earth = 1)	0.951
Natural satellites	0
Average surface temperature	867°F

Venus, slightly smaller than Earth, moves about the Sun at a mean distance of 67,240,000 mi in 225 Earth days. Its synodical revolution—its return to the same relationship with Earth and the Sun, which is a result of the combination of its own motion with that of Earth—is 584 days. As a result, every 19 months Venus is nearer to Earth than any other planet.

Venus is covered with a dense, white, cloudy atmosphere that conceals whatever is below it. This same cloud reflects sunlight efficiently so that Venus is the 3rd-brightest object in the sky, exceeded only by the Sun and the Moon.

Spectral analysis of sunlight reflected from Venus's cloud tops has shown features that can best be explained by identifying material of the clouds as sulfuric acid. The *Mariner 2* space probe in 1962 confirmed a high surface temperature. *Mariner 2* was unable to detect the existence of a magnetic field even as weak as 1/100,000 of Earth's magnetic field.

In 1967, a Soviet space probe, *Venera 4*, and the American *Mariner 5* arrived at Venus within a few hours of each other. *Venera 4* was designed to allow an instrument package to land gently on the surface, but it ceased to transmit information when its temperature reading went above 500° F, when it was still about 20 mi above the surface. The orbiting *Mariner 5*'s radio signals passed to Earth through Venus's atmosphere twice (once on the night side and once on the day side). The results were startling. Venus's atmosphere is nearly all carbon dioxide (96.5%), with 3.5% nitrogen and trace amounts of sulfur dioxide, carbon monoxide, argon, water, helium, and neon. It exerts a pressure at the planet's surface more than 90 times Earth's normal sea-level pressure of one atmosphere.

Because Earth and Venus are about the same size and were presumably formed at the same time by the same general process and from the same mixture of chemical elements, one is faced with the question: Why the difference? Recent measurements indicate that Venus has a surface temperature of over 865° F as a result of an extreme greenhouse effect. Because of the thick atmosphere, the temperature is essentially the same both day and night.

Radio astronomers determined the rotation period of Venus to be 243 days clockwise—in other words, contrary to the spin of the other planets and contrary to its own motion around the Sun. If it were exactly 243.16 days, Venus would present the same face toward Earth at every inferior conjunction. This rate and sense of rotation allows a solar day (sunrise to sunrise) on Venus of 116.8 Earth days. Any part of Venus will receive sunlight on its clouds for more than 58 days and then return to darkness for 58 days.

Mariner 10 passed Venus before traveling on to Mercury in 1974. The carbon dioxide found in abundance in the atmosphere is rather opaque to certain ultraviolet wavelengths, enabling sensitive cameras to photograph the cloud cover. Soviet spacecraft discovered that the clouds are confined in a 12-mi layer 30 to 42 mi above the surface.

In 1978, two U.S. *Pioneer* probes confirmed expected high surface temperatures and high winds aloft. Winds of about 200 mi per hour there may account for the transfer of heat into the night side despite the low rotation speed of the planet. However, at the surface, the winds are very slow. Soviet scientists obtained, in 1975 and later in 1982, 4 photos of surface rocks. Sulfur seems to play a large role in the chemistry of Venus, and reactions involving sulfur may be responsible for the glow. The *Pioneer* orbiter confirmed the cloud pattern and its circulation shown by *Mariner 10*. Radar produced maps of the entire planet showing large craters, continent-size highlands, and extensive dry lowlands.

The Venus orbiter *Magellan* launched in 1989 used sophisticated radar techniques to observe Venus and map more than 99% of the surface. The spacecraft observed over 1,600 volcanoes and volcanic features, enabling creation of a 3-dimensional map. *Magellan* has shown that more than 85% of the surface is covered by volcanic flows. Additionally, there are highly deformed mountain belts.

Craters more than 20 mi wide are believed to have been caused by impacting bodies. Theia Mons, a huge shield volcano, has a diameter of over 600 mi and a height of over 3.5 mi. (The largest Hawaiian volcano is only about 125 mi in diameter, but rises nearly 5.5 mi from the ocean floor.)

Erosion is a very slow process on Venus due to the extreme lack of water, and features persist for long periods of time. There are indications of only restricted wind movement of dust and sand.

Tectonic actions on Venus are distinctly different from such actions on Earth. No activity has been found to be similar to Earth's moving tectonic plates, but a system of global rift zones and numerous broad, low dome-like structures, which are called coronae, may be produced by the upwelling and subsidence of magma from the mantle. Volcanic surface features, such as vast lava plains, fields of small lava domes, and large shield volcanoes, are common. The few impact craters on Venus suggest that the surface is generally geologically young—less than 800 million years old. A channel about 4,200 mi long, due to lava flows, has been mapped.

The orbit of *Magellan* was adjusted to a nearly circular shape about 300 mi from the planet's surface in 1993. In this mode, variation in *Magellan*'s orbital speed revealed information on irregularities in the gravitational field, presumably due to details in the internal structure of the planet. In 2001, the Arecibo radio telescope and the Green Bank radio telescope were partnered to produce even more detailed images of Maxwell Montes, a Venusian mountain taller than Mt. Everest. A number of spacecraft missions to other planets have flown by Venus en route to their final destinations, including *Galileo* to Jupiter in 1989 and *Cassini* to Saturn in 1997.

Mars

Distance from Sun	
Perihelion	128.4 mil mi
Semi-major axis	1.524 AU
Aphelion	154.9 mil mi
Period of revolution around Sun	686.98 d (1.88 y)
Orbital eccentricity	0.0935
Orbital inclination	1.85°
Synodic day (midday to midday)	24h 39m 35s
Sidereal day	24h 37m 22s
Rotational inclination	25.19°
Mass (Earth = 1)	0.106
Mean radius	2,107 mi
Mean density (Earth = 1)	0.713
Natural satellites	2
Average surface temperature	−81° F

Mars is the first planet beyond Earth, away from the Sun. Mars's diameter is about 4,213 mi. Although Mars's orbit is nearly circular, it is somewhat more eccentric than the orbits of many of the other planets, and Mars is more than 26 mil mi farther from the Sun at its most distant point compared to its closest approach. Mars takes 687 Earth days to make one circuit of the Sun, traveling at about 15 mi a second. The planet rotates upon its axis in almost the same period of time as Earth—24 hours and 37 minutes. Mars's mean distance from the Sun is 142 mil mi, so its temperature would be lower than that on Earth even if its atmosphere were not so thin. In 1965, *Mariner 4* became the first spacecraft to fly by Mars, reporting that atmospheric pressure on Mars is between 1% and 2% of Earth's atmospheric pressure. As is the case with Venus, the atmosphere is composed largely of carbon dioxide. The planet is exposed to an influx of cosmic radiation about 100 times as intense as that on Earth.

Mars's position in its orbit and its speed around that orbit in relation to Earth's position and speed bring it fairly close to Earth about every 2 years. Every 15-17 years the close approaches are especially favorable for observation. In 2003, Mars came within 34,646,418 miles, its closest such approach to Earth in nearly 60,000 years.

Although early telescopic observations led some to believe the colors they saw were indications of vegetation, this would only be possible if Mars had water and oxygen.

Mars's axis of rotation is inclined from a vertical to the plane of its orbit about the Sun by about 25°, and therefore Mars has seasons as does Earth. White caps form about the poles of Mars, growing in the winter and shrinking in the summer. These polar caps are now believed to be both water ice and carbon dioxide ice. It is the carbon dioxide that is seen to come and go with the seasons. The water ice is apparently in many layers with dust between them, indicating climatic cycles.

Mariners 6 and *7* in 1969 sent back many photographs of higher quality showing cratering similar to the earlier views, but also other types of terrain. Some regions seemed featureless over large areas; others were chaotic, showing high relief without apparent organization into mountain chains or craters. *Mariner 9*, the first spacecraft to orbit Mars (1971), transmitted photos and other data showing that Mars resembles no other planet we know, yet there were features clearly of volcanic origin. One of these is Olympus Mons, a shield volcano whose caldera is more than 40 mi wide and whose outer slopes are 300 mi in diameter; it stands 15 mi above the surrounding plain—the tallest known mountain in the solar system. Some features may have been produced by cracking (faulting) and stretching of the surface. Valles Marineris, extending nearly 2,500 mi, is an example on a colossal scale. Many craters seem to have been produced by impacting bodies that may have come from the nearby asteroid belt. Features near the S pole may have been produced by glaciers no longer present.

In 1976, the U.S. landed 2 *Viking* spacecraft on Mars. The landers had devices to perform chemical analyses of the soil in search of evidence of life; results were inconclusive. The orbiters returned pictures of topographic features that scientists believe can be explained only if Mars once had large quantities of flowing water.

Two U.S. spacecraft—the *Mars Pathfinder* and the *Mars Global Surveyor*—were launched toward Mars in 1996. On July 4, 1997, using a unique array of balloons, *Pathfinder*, with its small movable robot named Sojourner, bounced to a safe landing on Mars. It actually bounded about 40 feet high after striking the ground at 40 mph and bounced 15 more times before coming to a halt. Sojourner spent 3 months examining rocks near *Pathfinder*. Geological results from the *Pathfinder* indicate that in its beginning stages Mars melted to a sufficient extent to separate into dense and lighter layers. It also appears that there was an era when the planet had large amounts of flooding waters on its surface.

The *Surveyor* did extensive mapping of the planet and reported the presence of a very weak magnetic field that may have been stronger in the distant past. *Surveyor* results support a view of the southern hemisphere of Mars covered with ancient craters like Earth's Moon. Interestingly, there is a significant difference in the northern hemisphere, which consists mainly of plains that are much younger and lower in elevation. The *Surveyor* has produced a dramatic 3-D map that clearly shows this dramatic contrast.

Mars has 2 satellites, discovered in 1877 by Asaph Hall. The outer satellite, Deimos, revolves around the planet in about 31 hours. The inner satellite, Phobos, whips around Mars in a little more than 7 hours, making 3 trips around the planet each Martian day. Since it orbits Mars faster than the planet rotates, Phobos rises in the W and sets in the E, opposite to what other bodies appear to do in the Martian sky. *Mariner* and *Viking* photos show these satellites to be irregularly shaped and pitted with numerous craters. Phobos also exhibits a system of linear grooves, each about 1/3 mi across and roughly parallel. Phobos measures about 8 by 12 mi and Deimos about 5 by 7.5 mi.

Of the tens of thousands of meteorites found on Earth, about a dozen may have originated on Mars. In 1996, a NASA research team concluded that a meteorite found in 1984 on an Antarctic ice field not only might be a rock blasted from the surface of Mars but also might contain evidence of life on Mars 3.5 bil years ago. The meteorite has been age-dated to about 4.5 bil years. The scientists theorize that 3.5 bil years ago, Mars may have been warmer and wetter, and microscopic life may have formed and left evidence in the rock, including possible fossilized microscopic organisms. It is thought that 16 mil years ago a huge asteroid or comet struck Mars, blasting material, including this rock, into space. The rock may have entered Earth's atmosphere about 13,000 years ago, landing in Antarctica. The evidence is intriguing, but not conclusive, in suggesting that Mars may have had microscopic life, at least far in the past.

2004 NASA Mars Probes

Twin NASA spacecraft—*Spirit* and *Opportunity*—launched in mid-2003, were scheduled to make bouncing, airbag-wrapped landings on Mars on Jan. 4 and Jan. 25, 2004, respectively. The land rovers will be able to travel farther—1 kilometer over the mission lifetime—and faster than the earlier *Pathfinder* rover did in 1997. *Spirit* was targeted to explore Gusev Crater, thought to have perhaps been a lake in the past, and *Opportunity* was planned to explore Meridiani Planum, where there are outcroppings of gray hematite, a mineral that usually forms in the presence of liquid water.

Pictures from the *Mars Global Surveyor* showed evidence for the presence of liquid water on Mars in recent times. The *Mars Odyssey* spacecraft, launched in 2001, detected evidence for the presence of water ice in the upper 3 feet of soil in a large area around the south pole.

In June 2003, the European Space Agency (ESA) launched its *Mars Express* spacecraft, its first probe to another planet. It was scheduled to reach Mars in December and release its small lander, Beagle 2. The mission should last at least one Martian year (687 Earth days).

Jupiter

Distance from Sun	
Perihelion	460.2 mil mi
Semi-major axis	5.204 AU
Aphelion	507.5 mil mi
Period of revolution around Sun	11.862 y
Orbital eccentricity	0.0489
Orbital inclination	1.304°
Synodic day (midday to midday)	9h 55m 33s
Sidereal day	9h 55m 30s
Rotational inclination	3.13°
Mass (Earth = 1)	317.8
Mean radius	43,450 mi
Mean density (Earth = 1)	0.24
Natural satellites	61
Average temperature*	–162°F

*i.e., temperature where atmosphere pressure equals 1 Earth atmosphere.

Jupiter, largest of the planets, has an equatorial diameter of nearly 89,000 mi, 11 times the diameter of Earth. Its polar diameter is more than 5,700 mi shorter. This noticeable oblateness is a result of the liquidity of the planet and its extremely rapid rate of rotation; a day is less than 10 Earth hours long. For a planet this size, this rotational speed is amazing. A point on Jupiter's equator moves at a speed of 22,000 mph, as compared with 1,000 mph for a point on Earth's equator. Jupiter is at an average distance of 484 mil mi from the Sun and takes almost 12 Earth years to make one complete circuit of the Sun.

The major chemical constituents of Jupiter's atmosphere are molecular hydrogen (H_2—90%) and helium (He—10%). Minor constituents include methane (CH_4), ammonia (NH_3), hydrogen deuteride (HD), ethane (C_2H_6), and water (H_2O).

The temperature at the tops of clouds may be about –280° F. The gases become denser with depth, until they may turn into a slush or slurry. There is no sharp interface between the gaseous atmosphere and the hydrogen ocean that accounts for most of Jupiter's volume. *Pioneer 10* and *11*, passing Jupiter in 1973 and 1974, provided evidence for considering Jupiter almost entirely liquid hydrogen. Jupiter apparently has a liquid hydrogen ocean more than 35,000 mi deep. It likely has a rocky core about the size of Earth, but 13 times more massive.

Jupiter's magnetic field is by far the strongest of any planet. Electrical activity caused by this field is so strong that it discharges billions of watts into Earth's magnetic field daily. At lower layers, under enormous pressure, the liquid hydrogen takes on the properties of a metal. It is likely that this liquid metallic hydrogen is the source for both Jupiter's persistent radio noise and its improbably strong magnetic field. Radio astronomy and information from the spacecraft passing in Jupiter's vicinity have revealed details of the overall structure of the huge magnetosphere surrounding Jupiter.

21 of Jupiter's 61 known satellites were found in 2003 through Earth-based observations. Four of the moons (in order from Jupiter), Io, Europa, Ganymede, and Callisto—all discovered by Galileo in 1610—are large and bright, rivaling Earth's Moon and Mercury in diameter, and may be seen through binoculars. They move rapidly around Jupiter, and it is easy to observe their change of position from night to

night. The other satellites are much smaller, with 4 closer to Jupiter than Io, 5 between Ganymede and Callisto, and the rest farther out. None of them can be seen except through powerful telescopes. All but one of the 21 newly discovered moons appear to be in retrograde orbits. Indeed, 45 of the 46 outermost satellites revolve around Jupiter clockwise as seen from the north, contrary to the motions of most satellites in the solar system and to the direction of revolution of planets around the Sun. These moons may be captured asteroids. Jupiter's mass is more than twice the mass of all the other planets, moons, and asteroids put together.

Photographs from *Pioneer 10* and *11* were far surpassed by those of *Voyager 1* and *2*, both of which rendezvoused with Jupiter in 1979. The Great Red Spot exhibited internal counterclockwise rotation. Much turbulence was seen in adjacent material passing N or S of it. The satellites Amalthea, Io, Europa, Ganymede, and Callisto were photographed, some in great detail. Io has active volcanoes that probably have ejected material into a doughnut-shaped ring, or torus, enveloping its orbit about Jupiter. This is not to be confused with Jupiter's rings which were the surprise of the *Voyager 1* mission. Since then, ground-based telescopes have imaged Jupiter's rings in the infrared.

In 1994, 21 large fragments of Comet Shoemaker-Levy 9 collided with Jupiter. Moving at 134,000 mph, stretched out like a 21-car freight train, the fragments impacted one after another. Massive plumes of gas erupted from the impact sites, forming brilliant fireballs and leaving dark blotches and smears behind. One of the largest chunks impacted with a force 100,000 times the power of the largest nuclear bomb ever detonated. It produced a plume 1,200-1,600 mi high and 5,000 mi wide and left a dark discoloration larger than Earth.

The *Galileo* spacecraft went into orbit around Jupiter and released an atmospheric probe into the Jovian atmosphere in Dec. 1995. The probe, traveling at a speed of over 100,000 mph, plunged into Jupiter's atmosphere relaying information about it for 57.6 minutes. The probe revealed a relatively dry atmosphere, with the upper part warmer and denser than expected. It also gave evidence of wind speeds of more than 400 mph and a relative absence of lightning. The probe found the atmosphere to be quite turbulent, driven by Jupiter's own internal heat. *Galileo* continued an extended mission to study the 4 large moons. *Galileo* observations show extensive ongoing volcanic eruptions on Io. Europa may have a 30-mi-deep liquid ocean beneath its icy crust, perhaps a small metallic core, and a very tenuous atmosphere. Ganymede, with a magnetosphere and a thin oxygen atmosphere, seems to be differentiated into 3 levels—a small metallic core and a rocky silicate mantle topped by an icy shell. Callisto has the oldest, most heavily cratered surface in the solar system, a very thin atmosphere of carbon dioxide, and possibly also a subsurface liquid ocean.

Saturn

Saturn, last of the planets visible to the unaided eye, is almost twice as far from the Sun as Jupiter. It is 2nd in size to Jupiter, but its mass is much smaller. Saturn's specific gravity is less than that of water. Its diameter is almost 74,900 mi at the equator while its polar diameter is almost 7,300 mi shorter—even more extreme than Jupiter. This noticeable oblateness is a result of the liquidity of the planet and its extremely rapid rate of rotation; a day is little more than 10 Earth hours long. Saturn's atmosphere is much like that of Jupiter, except that the temperature at the top of its cloud layer is at least 50° F colder. At about 300° F below zero, the ammonia would be frozen out of Saturn's clouds. The theoretical construction of Saturn resembles that of Jupiter; it likely has a small dense center surrounded by a layer of liquid and a deep atmosphere.

Distance from Sun
Perihelion	840.61 mil mi
Semi-major axis	9.582 AU
Aphelion	941.26 mil mi
Period of revolution around Sun	29.457 y
Orbital eccentricity	0.0565
Orbital inclination	2.485°
Synodic day (midday to midday)	10h 39m 23s
Sidereal day	10h 39m 22s
Rotational inclination	26.73°
Mass (Earth = 1)	95.159
Mean radius	36,191 mi
Mean density (Earth = 1)	0.125
Natural satellites	.31
Average temperature*	−218° F

*i.e., temperature where atmosphere pressure equals 1
Earth atmosphere.

Until *Pioneer 11* passed Saturn in 1979, only 10 satellites of the planet were known from ground-based observations. *Pioneer 11* discovered 2 more, and 6 others were found in the *Voyager 1* and 2 flybys, which also yielded more information about Saturn's icy satellites. 12 more moons were reported in 2000, and another one in 2003. Like Jupiter, Saturn is composed mostly of hydrogen (75%) and helium (25%), with traces of water, ammonia, methane, and rock.

Saturn's ring system begins about 4,000 mi above the visible disk of Saturn, lying above its equator and extending about 260,000 mi into space. The diameter of the ring system visible from Earth is about 170,000 mi; the rings are estimated to be about 700 feet thick. In 1973, radar observation showed the ring particles to be large chunks of material averaging a meter on a side. Later, *Voyager 1* and 2 observations showed the rings to be considerably more complex than had been believed.

2004 Saturn Probes

Launched in Oct. 1997, the *Cassini* spacecraft, with its tagalong companion Huygens, is scheduled to reach Saturn on July 1, 2004. *Cassini* is intended to orbit Saturn for many years, hopefully unlocking many of its secrets, while the *Huygens* probe attempts to enter the atmosphere of Titan, Saturn's largest moon, and land on its surface. Previous Saturn probes—*Pioneer 11* and *Voyagers 1* and *2*—have all been flybys.

Before orbiting Saturn, *Cassini* is scheduled to fly within 1,300 miles of Saturn's moon Phoebe and transmit images back to Earth. Titan, the object of the *Huygens* probe, is the 2nd-largest moon in the solar system (after Jupiter's Ganymede); it is larger in diameter than Pluto or Mercury and more massive than Pluto. It is also the only moon in the solar system with a significant atmosphere. But it does not have Earth's abundance of oxygen, and the surface temperature probably approaches −300° F.

Uranus

Distance from Sun
Perihelion	1,703.7 mil mi
Semi-major axis	19.201 AU
Aphelion	1,866.7 mil mi
Period of revolution around Sun	84.01 y
Orbital eccentricity	0.0457
Orbital inclination	0.772°
Synodic day (midday to midday)	17h 14m 23s (retrograde)
Sidereal day	17h 14m 24s (retrograde)
Rotational inclination	97.77°
Mass (Earth = 1)	14.536
Mean radius	15,762mi
Mean density (Earth = 1)	0.230
Natural satellites	.21
Average temperature*	−323° F

*i.e., temperature where atmosphere pressure equals 1
Earth atmosphere.

Voyager 2, after passing Saturn in 1981, headed for a rendezvous with Uranus, culminating in a flyby in 1986.

Uranus, discovered by Sir William Herschel on Mar. 13, 1781, lies 1.8 bil mi from the Sun, taking 84 years to make its circuit around our star. Uranus has a diameter of over 31,000 mi and spins once in some 17.4 hours, according to flyby magnetic data. One of the most fascinating features of Uranus is how far over it is tipped. Its N pole lies 98° from being directly up and down to its orbit plane. Thus, its seasons are extreme. When the Sun rises at the N pole, it stays

up for 42 Earth years; then it sets, and the N pole is in darkness (and winter) for 42 Earth years.

Uranus has 21 known moons, which have orbits lying in the plane of the planet's equator. 5 moons are relatively large, while 16 are very small and were only discovered with the *Voyager 2* mission or in later observations. In the equatorial plane there is also a complex of 10 rings, 9 of which were discovered in 1978. Invisible from Earth, the 9 original rings were found by observers watching Uranus pass before a star. As they waited, they saw their photoelectric equipment register several short eclipses of the star; then the planet occulted the star as expected. After the star came out from behind Uranus, the star winked out several more times. Subsequent observations and analyses indicated the 9 narrow, nearly opaque rings circling Uranus. Evidence from the *Voyager 2* flyby showed the ring particles to be predominantly a yard or so in diameter.

In addition to photos of 10 new, very small satellites, *Voyager 2* returned detailed photos of the 5 large satellites. As in the case of other satellites newly observed in the *Voyager* program, these bodies proved to be quite different from one another and from any others. Miranda has grooved markings, reminiscent of Jupiter's Ganymede, but often arranged in a chevron pattern. Ariel shows rifts and channels. Umbriel is extremely dark, prompting some observers to regard its surface as among the oldest in the system. Titania has rifts and fractures, but not the evidence of flow found on Ariel. Oberon's main feature is its surface saturated with craters, unrelieved by other formations.

Uranus likely does not have a rocky core, but rather a mixture of rocks and assorted ices with about 15% hydrogen and a little helium.The atmosphere is about 83% hydrogen, 15% helium, and 2% methane. In addition to its rotational tilt, Uranus's magnetic axis is tipped an incredible 58.6° from its rotational axis and is displaced about 30% of its radius away from the planet's center.

Neptune

Distance from Sun
Perihelion	2,762.2 mil mi
Semi-major axis	30.047 AU
Aphelion	2,825.1 mil mi
Period of revolution around Sun	164.79 y
Orbital eccentricity	0.0113
Orbital inclination	1.769°
Synodic day (midday to midday)	16h 6m 37s
Sidereal day	16h 6m 36s
Rotational inclination	28.32°
Mass (Earth = 1)	17.147
Mean radius	15,301 mi
Mean density (Earth = 1)	0.297
Natural satellites	11
Average temperature*	−330° F

*i.e., temperature where atmosphere pressure equals 1
Earth atmosphere.

Neptune lies at an average distance of 2.8 bil mi from the Sun. It was the last planet visited in *Voyager 2*'s epic 12-year trek (1977-89) from Earth.

As with other giant planets, Neptune may have no solid surface, or exact diameter. However, a mean value of 30,600 mi may be assigned to a diameter between atmosphere levels where the pressure is about the same as sea level on Earth. Without a solid surface to view, it is challenging to determine a "true" rotation rate for a giant planet.

Astronomers use a determination of the rotation rate of the planet's magnetic field to indicate the internal rotation rate, which in the case of Neptune is 16.1 hours. Neptune orbits the Sun in 164.8 years in a nearly circular orbit. Neptune, discovered in 1846, will not have completed one full trip around the Sun since its discovery until 2010.

Voyager 2, which passed 3,000 mi from Neptune's N pole, found a magnetic field that is considerably asymmetric to the planet's structure, similar to, but not so extreme as, that found at Uranus. Neptune's magnetic field axis is tipped 46.9° from its rotational axis and is displaced more than 55% of its radius away from the planet's center. Neptune's atmosphere was seen to be quite blue, with quickly changing white clouds often suspended high above an apparent surface. There is a Great Dark Spot, reminiscent of the Great Red Spot of Jupiter. Observations with the Hubble Space Telescope have shown that the Great Dark Spot originally seen by *Voyager* has apparently dissipated, but a new dark spot has since appeared. Neptune's atmosphere is about 80% hydrogen, 19% helium, and 1% methane. Although lightning and auroras have been found on other giant planets, only the aurora phenomenon has been seen on Neptune.

Six new satellites were definitively discerned around Neptune by *Voyager 2*: 5 of them orbit Neptune in a half day or less. In 2003 astronomers who had used large telescopes in Chile and Hawaii announced the discovery of 3 more satellites. Of the 11 satellites of Neptune in all, the largest, Triton, is the only large moon in a retrograde orbit, suggesting that it was captured rather than having been there from the beginning. Triton's large size, sufficient to raise significant tides on the planet, may one day, billions of years from now, cause Triton to come close enough to Neptune for it to be torn apart. Nereid was found in 1949 and has the highest orbital eccentricity (0.75) of any moon. Its long looping orbit suggests that it, too, was captured.

Each of the satellites that has been photographed by the 2 *Voyagers* in the planetary encounters has been different from any of the other satellites, and certainly different from any of the planets. Only about half of Triton has been observed, but its terrain shows cratering and a strange regional feature described as resembling the skin of a cantaloupe. Triton has a tenuous atmosphere of nitrogen with a trace of hydrocarbons and evidence of active geysers injecting material into it. At −390° F, the wintertime parts of Triton are the coldest regions yet found in the solar system.

Voyager 2 also confirmed the existence of 6 rings composed of very fine particles. There may be some clumpiness in the rings' structure. It is not known whether Neptune's satellites influence the formation or maintenance of the rings.

As with the other giant planets, Neptune is emitting more energy than it receives from the Sun. *Voyager* found the excess to be 2.7 times the solar contribution. Cooling from internal heat sources and from the heat of formation of the planets is thought to be responsible.

Pluto

Distance from Sun	
Perihelion	2,756.3 mil mi
Semi-major axis	39.236 AU
Aphelion	4,539.6 mil mi
Period of revolution around Sun	247.68 y
Orbital eccentricity	0.2444
Orbital inclination	17.16°
Synodic day (midday to midday)	6d 9h 17m (retrograde)
Sidereal day	6d 9h 18m (retrograde)
Rotational inclination	122.53°
Mass (Earth = 1)	0.0021
Mean radius	742.7 mi
Mean density (Earth = 1)	0.317
Natural satellites	1
Average surface temperature	−369°

Although Pluto on the average stays about 3.6 bil mi from the Sun, its orbit is so eccentric that its minimum distance of 2.76 bil mi is less than Neptune's distance from the Sun.

Pluto is currently the most distant planet, but for about 20 years of its orbit, Pluto is closer to the Sun than Neptune. Pluto takes 247.7 years to circumnavigate the Sun, a 3/2 resonance with Neptune.

About a century ago, a hypothetical planet was believed to lie beyond Neptune and Uranus because neither planet followed paths predicted by astronomers when all known gravitational influences were considered. In little more than a guess, a mass of 1 Earth was assigned to the mysterious body, and mathematical searches were begun. Amid some controversy about the validity of the predictive process, Pluto was discovered nearly where it had been predicted to lie, by Clyde Tombaugh at the Lowell Observatory in Flagstaff, AZ, in 1930.

At the U.S. Naval Observatory in Flagstaff, in 1978, James Christy obtained a photograph of Pluto that was distinctly elongated. Repeated observations of this shape and its variation were convincing evidence of the discovery of a satellite of Pluto, now named Charon. Later observations showed its diameter to be 737 mi across; it orbited Pluto at a distance of 12,100 mi and took 6.4 days to move around the planet. In this same length of time, Pluto and Charon both rotate once around their axes. The Pluto-Charon system thus appears to rotate as virtually a rigid body. This information allows the mass of Pluto to be calculated as 0.0021 of Earth. This mass, together with a new diameter for Pluto of 1,485 mi, make the density about twice that of water. Theorists predict that Pluto has a rocky core, surrounded by a thick mantle of ice.

It is now clear that Pluto could not have influenced Neptune and Uranus to go astray. Besides being the smallest planet, Pluto is actually smaller than 7 of the Solar System's moons. Although a 10th planet might be out there somewhere, theorists no longer believe there are unexplained perturbations in the orbit of Uranus or Neptune that might be caused by it. Astronomers have found over 600 asteroid-size objects, somewhat beyond Pluto, in a region called the Kuiper Belt, where some comets are believed to originate.

Because the rotational axis of the system is tipped more than 120°, there is only an interval of a few years every 125 years when Pluto and Charon alternately eclipse each other. Both worlds are roughly spherical and have comparable densities. Large regions on Pluto are dark, others light; Pluto has spots and perhaps polar caps. Although extremely cold, Pluto appears to have a thin nitrogen–carbon dioxide–methane atmosphere, at least while it is closer to the Sun. When Pluto occulted a star, the star's light faded in such a way as to suggest it had passed through a haze layer lying above the planet's surface, indicating an inversion of temperatures and the possibility that Pluto has primitive weather.

A recent controversy raised the issue of Pluto's planet status. Pluto is clearly different from both the rocky terrestrial planets and the giant planets. Although some astronomers think Pluto most closely resembles the Kuiper Belt Objects and should be grouped with them, most still classify Pluto as a planet. By way of comparison, Mercury, the 2nd-smallest planet, is about 2 times the radius of Pluto. Pluto is about twice the radius of Quaoar, the largest-known Kuiper Belt Object (discovered in 2002). Closest in size to Pluto is Neptune's largest moon, Triton, which is 1.13 times the radius of Pluto.

The Sun

The Sun, the controlling body of Earth's solar system, is a star often described as average. Yet, the Sun's mass and luminosity are greater than that of 90% of the stars in our Milky Way galaxy. On the other hand, most of the stars that can be easily seen on any clear night are bigger and brighter than the Sun. It is the Sun's proximity to Earth that makes it appear tremendously large and bright. The Sun is 400,000 times as bright as the full moon and gives Earth 6 mil times as much light as do all the other stars put together. A series of nuclear fusion reactions where hydrogen nuclei are converted to helium nuclei produces the heat and light that make life possible on Earth.

The Sun has a diameter of 865,000 miles and, on average, is 92,976,000 miles from Earth. It is 1.408 times as dense as water. The light of the Sun reaches Earth in 499 seconds, or in slightly more than 8 minutes. The average solar surface temperature has been measured at a value of 5,778 K, or about 9,941°F. The interior temperature of the Sun is theorized to be about 28,300,000° F.

When sunlight is analyzed with a spectroscope, it is found to consist of a continuous spectrum composed of all the colors of the rainbow in order, crossed by many dark lines. The dark "absorption lines" are produced by gaseous materials in the outer layers of the Sun. More than 60 of the natural terrestrial elements have been identified in the Sun, all in gaseous form because of the Sun's intense heat.

Spheres and Corona

The radiating surface of the Sun is called the **photosphere**; just above it is the **chromosphere**. The chromosphere is visible to the naked eye only at total solar eclipses, appearing then to be a pinkish-violet layer with occasional great prominences projecting above its general level. With proper instruments, the chromosphere can be seen or photographed whenever the Sun is visible without waiting for a total eclipse. Above the chromosphere is the **corona**, also visible to the naked eye only at times of total eclipse. Instruments also permit the brighter portions of the corona to be studied whenever conditions are favorable. The pearly light of the corona surges mil of mi from the Sun. Iron, nickel, and calcium are believed to be principal contributors to the composition of the corona, all in a state of extreme attenuation and high ionization that indicates temperatures nearly 2 mil° Fahrenheit.

Sunspots

There is an intimate connection between sunspots and the corona. At times of low sunspot activity, the fine streamers of the corona are longer above the Sun's equator than over the polar regions of the Sun; during periods of high sunspot activity, the corona extends fairly evenly outward from all regions of the Sun, but to a much greater distance in space. Sunspots are dark, irregularly shaped regions whose diameters may reach tens of thousands of miles. The average life of a sunspot group is 2 months, but some have lasted for more than a year.

Sunspots reach a low point, on average, every 11.3 years, with a peak of activity occurring irregularly between 2 successive minima. Launched in December 1995, the SOHO spacecraft was designed to provide several years of study of the Sun from an orbit around the Sun. The most recent solar maximum occurred in 2001; SOHO provided extraordinary views of the Sun's activity. The number of sunspots is now declining, heading towards solar minimum which should occur about 2006/2007. Observations from SOHO show that magnetic arches, called prominences, extending tens of thousands of miles into the corona, may release enormous amounts of energy heating the corona. SOHO has also highlighted enormous releases of solar energy called coronal mass ejections. Coronal holes are regions where the corona appears dark in X rays. These are regions associated with open magnetic field lines, where the magnetic field lines project out into space instead of back towards the Sun, and it is in these

The Moon

Distance from Earth	
Perigee	225,744 mi
Semi-major axis	238,855 mi
Apogee	251,966 mi
Period of revolution	27.322 d
Synodic orbital period (period of phases)	29.53 d
Orbital eccentricity	0.0549
rbital inclination	5.145°
Sidereal day (rotation period)	27.322 d
Rotational inclination	6.68°
Mass (Earth = 1)	0.0123
Mean radius	1,080 mi
Mean density (Earth = 1)	0.605
Average surface temperature	−10° F

The Moon completes a circuit around Earth in a period whose mean or average duration is 27 days, 7 hours, 43.2 minutes. This is the Moon's **sidereal period.** Because of the motion of the Moon in common with Earth around the Sun, the mean duration of the lunar month—the period from one New Moon to the next New Moon—is 29 days, 12 hours, 44.05 minutes. This is the Moon's **synodic period.**

The mean distance of the Moon from Earth is 238,855 mi. Because the orbit of the Moon about Earth is not circular but elliptical, however, the actual distance varies considerably. The maximum distance from Earth that the Moon may reach is 251,966 mi and the least distance is 225,744 mi. (All distances given here are from the center of one body to the center of the other.)

The Moon rotates on its axis in a period of time that is exactly equal to its sidereal revolution about Earth: 27.322 days. Thus the backside or farside of the Moon always faces away from Earth. This does not mean that the backside is always dark, since the Sun is the main source of light in the Solar System. The farside of the Moon gets just as much direct sunlight as the nearside. At New Moon phase, the farside of the Moon is fully lit. With its long day and night, the daytime temperature can reach 260° F, while the coldest nighttime temperature may reach −280° F. This day-to-night contrast is exceeded only by that on Mercury.

The Moon's revolution about Earth is irregular because of its elliptical orbit. The Moon's rotation, however, is regular, and this, together with the irregular revolution, produces what is called "libration in longitude," which permits the observer on Earth to see first farther around the E side and then farther around the W side of the Moon. The Moon's variation N or S of the ecliptic permits one to see farther over first one pole and then the other of the Moon; this is called "libration in latitude." These two libration effects permit observers on Earth to see a total of about 60% of the Moon's surface over a period of time.

The hidden side of the Moon was first photographed in 1959 by the Soviet space vehicle *Lunik III.* The moon's farside does appear noticeably different from the nearside, in that the farside has practically none of the large lava plains, called maria, so prominent on the nearside.

From 1969 through 1972, 6 American spacecraft brought 12 astronauts to walk on the surface of the Moon. In 1998 NASA's *Lunar Prospector* spacecraft provided evidence for the presence of 300 million metric tons of water ice at the lunar poles. *Lunar Prospector* results also indicate that the Moon has a small core, supporting the idea that most of the mass of the Moon was ripped away from the early Earth when a Mars-size object collided with Earth.

Tides on Earth are caused mainly by the Moon, because of its proximity to Earth. The ratio of the tide-raising power of the Moon to that of the Sun is 11 to 5.

Harvest Moon and Hunter's Moon

The Harvest Moon, the full Moon nearest the autumnal equinox, ushers in a period of several successive days when the Moon rises soon after sunset. This phenomenon gives farmers in temperate latitudes extra hours of light in which to harvest their crops before frost and winter. The 2004 Harvest Moon falls on Sept. 28 UTC. Harvest Moon in the southern hemisphere temperate latitudes falls on Mar. 6.

The next full Moon after Harvest Moon is called the Hunter's Moon; it is accompanied by a similar but less marked phenomenon. In 2004, the Hunter's Moon occurs on Oct. 28 in the northern hemisphere and on Apr. 5 in the southern hemisphere.

Moon's Perigee and Apogee, 2004

(Coordinated Universal Time, standard time of the prime meridian)

Perigee				Apogee			
Date	Hour	Date	Hour	Date	Hour	Date	Hour
Jan. 19	19	Jul. 30	6	Jan. 3	20	July 14	21
Feb. 16	8	Aug. 27	6	Jan. 31	14	Aug. 11	10
Mar. 12	4	Sept. 22	21	Feb. 28	11	Sept. 8	3
Apr. 8	2	Oct. 18	00	Mar. 27	7	Oct. 5	22
May 6	5	Nov. 14	14	Apr. 24	00	Nov. 2	18
June 3	13	Dec. 12	21	May 21	12	Nov. 30	11
July 1	23			June 17	16	Dec. 27	19

Moon Phases, 2004

(Coordinated Universal Time, standard time of the prime meridian)

New Moon			Waxing Quarter			Full Moon			Waning Quarter		
Month	d	h	m	Month	d	h	m	Month	d	h	m	Month	d	h	m
Jan.	21	21	5	Jan.	29	6	3	Jan.	7	15	40	Jan.	15	4	46
Feb.	20	9	18	Feb.	28	3	24	Feb.	6	8	47	Feb.	13	13	40
Mar.	20	22	41	Mar.	28	23	48	Mar.	6	23	14	Mar.	13	21	1
Apr.	19	13	21	Apr.	27	17	32	Apr.	5	11	3	Apr.	12	3	46
May	19	4	52	May	27	7	57	May	4	20	33	May	11	11	4
June	17	20	27	June	25	19	8	June	3	4	20	June	9	20	2
July	17	11	24	July	25	3	37	July	2	11	9	July	9	7	34
Aug.	16	1	24	Aug.	23	10	12	July	31	18	5	Aug.	7	22	1
Sept.	14	14	29	Sept.	21	15	54	Aug.	30	2	22	Sept.	6	15	11
Oct.	14	2	48	Oct.	20	21	59	Sept.	28	13	9	Oct.	6	10	12
Nov.	12	14	27	Nov.	19	5	50	Oct.	28	3	7	Nov.	5	5	53
Dec.	12	1	29	Dec.	18	16	40	Nov.	26	20	7	Dec.	5	0	53
								Dec.	25	15	6				

Searching for Planets

People have known of the existence of the 5 planets closest to the Sun since ancient times because they could be seen with the naked eye. However, the 3 farthest were discovered only since the invention of the telescope. The first, Uranus, was discovered in 1781 by the English astronomer William Herschel. Next, Neptune's existence and location were predicted through its action upon Uranus, by both John Couch Adams of England and Urbain Jean Joseph Le Verrier of France in 1845, leading to its discovery the following year. Finally, Pluto was discovered in 1930 by the American astronomer Clyde Tombaugh.

During the last 10 years of the 20th century, astronomers began to detect the presence of planets orbiting stars other than the Sun. As of yet, they are not actually seeing those objects, but merely inferring their existence by their effect on their parent star. The Sun is a typical star in many respects. With over 200 billion stars in the Milky Way galaxy, it seems plausible that many other stars might also have planets.

Using the Doppler Effect to detect radial velocity changes in the motions of individual stars, astronomers are more likely to find high-mass planets in close and eccentric orbits around stars, because that situation produces larger and more noticeable changes. As of mid-2003, astronomers had found 116 planets in 101 star systems where the planets are less than 13 times the mass of Jupiter (which is 318 times the mass of Earth). About 30 star systems may have planets less massive than Jupiter. In 2 cases planets may have been detected in orbit around pulsars.

The star Upsilon Andromedae seems to have 3 planets, with masses 0.69, 1.19, and 3.75 times the mass of Jupiter, yet 2 of the planets are closer to their star than Earth is to the Sun. Astronomers are puzzled as to how planets the size of Jupiter or larger can exist so close to a star. In 2002, a planet with a mass approximately 10% that of Jupiter was detected (the smallest extra-solar planet yet detected).

Earth: Size, Computation of Time, Seasons

Distance from the Sun	
Perihelion	91.4 mil mi
Semi-major axis	1.0000 AU
Aphelion	94.5 mil mi
Period of revolution	365.256 d
Orbital eccentricity	0.0167
Orbital inclination	0.0°
Sidereal day (rotation period)	23h 56m 4.2s
Synodic day (midday to midday)	24h 0m 0s
Rotational inclination	23.45°
Mass (Earth = 1)	1.00
Mean radius	3,959.6 mi
Mean density (Earth = 1)	1.00
Natural satellites	1
Average surface temperature	59° F

Earth is the 5th-largest planet and the 3rd from the Sun. Its mass is 6,569,000,000,000,000,000,000 tons. Earth's equatorial diameter is 7,928 miles while its polar diameter is only 7,902 miles.

Size and Dimensions

Earth is considered a solid mass, yet it has a large, liquid iron, **magnetic core** with a radius of about 2,155 miles. Surprisingly, it has a solid **inner core** that may be a large iron crystal, with a radius of 760 miles. Around the core is a thick shell, or **mantle**, of dense rock. This mantle is composed of materials rich in iron and magnesium. It is somewhat plastic-like, and under slow steady pressure, it can flow like a liquid. The mantle, in turn, is covered by a thin **crust** forming the solid granite and basalt base of the continents and ocean basins. Over broad areas of Earth's surface, the crust has a thin cover of sedimentary rock such as sandstone, shale, and limestone formed by weathering and by deposits of sands, clays, and plant and animal remains.

The **temperature** inside the Earth increases about 1° F with every 100 to 200 feet in depth, in the upper 100 km of Earth, and reaches about 8,000-9,000° F at the center. The heat is believed to come from radioactivity in rocks, pressures within Earth, and the original heat of formation.

Atmosphere of Earth

Earth's atmosphere is a blanket composed of nitrogen, oxygen, and argon, in amounts of about 78%, 21%, and 1% by volume. Present in minute quantities are carbon dioxide, hydrogen, neon, helium, krypton, and xenon. Water vapor displaces other gases and varies from nearly zero to about 4% by volume. The atmosphere rests on Earth's surface with a weight equivalent to a layer of water 34 feet deep. For about 300,000 feet upward, the gases remain in the proportions stated. Gravity holds the gases to Earth. The weight of the air compresses it at the bottom so that the greatest density is at Earth's surface. Pressure and density decrease as height increases.

The lowest layer of the atmosphere extending up about 7.5 mi is the **troposphere**, which contains 90% of the air and the tallest mountains. This is also where most weather phenomena occur. The temperature drops with increasing height throughout this layer. The atmosphere for about 23 miles above the troposphere is the **stratosphere**, where the temperature generally increases with height. The stratosphere contains **ozone**, which prevents ultraviolet rays from reaching Earth's surface. Since there is very little convection in the stratosphere, jets regularly cruise in the lower parts to provide a smoother ride for passengers.

Above the stratosphere is the **mesosphere**, where the temperature again decreases with height for another 19 mi. Extending above the mesosphere is the **thermosphere**, a region where temperature once more increases with height to a value measured in thousands of degrees Fahrenheit. The lower portion of this region, extending from 50 to about 400 mi in altitude, is characterized by a high ion density and is thus called the **ionosphere**. Most meteors are in the lower thermosphere or the mesosphere at the time they are observed.

Longitude, Latitude

Position on the globe is measured by meridians and parallels. Meridians, which are imaginary lines drawn around Earth through the poles, determine **longitude**. The meridian running through Greenwich, England, is the **prime meridian** of longitude, and all others are either E or W. Parallels, which are imaginary circles parallel with the equator, determine **latitude**. The length of a degree of longitude varies as the cosine of the latitude. At the equator a degree of longitude is 69.171 statute mi; this is gradually reduced toward the poles. Value of a longitude degree at the poles is zero.

Latitude is reckoned by the number of degrees N or S of the **equator**, an imaginary circle on Earth's surface everywhere equidistant between the two poles. According to the International Astronomical Union ellipsoid of 1964, the length of a degree of latitude is 68.708 statute mi at the equator and varies slightly N and S because of the oblate form of the globe; at the poles it is 69.403 statute mi.

Definitions of Time

Earth rotates on its axis and follows an elliptical orbit around the Sun. The rotation makes the Sun appear to move across the sky from E to W. This rotation determines day and night, and the complete rotation, in relation to the Sun, is called the **apparent** or **true solar day**. A sundial thus measures **apparent solar time**. This length of time varies, but an average determines the mean solar day of 24 hours.

The mean solar day and **mean solar time** are in universal use for civil purposes. Mean solar time may be obtained from apparent solar time by correcting observations of the Sun for the **equation of time**. Mean solar time may be up to 16 minutes different from apparent solar time.

Sidereal time is the measure of time defined by the diurnal motion of the vernal equinox and is determined from observation of the meridian transits of stars. One complete rotation of Earth relative to the equinox is called the **sidereal day**. The **mean sidereal day** is 23 hours, 56 minutes, 4.091 seconds of mean solar time.

The interval required for Earth to make one absolute revolution around the Sun is a **sidereal** year; it consisted of 365 days, 6 hours, 9 minutes, and 9.5 seconds of mean solar time (approximately 24 hours per day) in 1900 and has been increasing at the rate of 0.0001 second annually.

The **tropical year**, upon which our calendar is based, is the interval between 2 consecutive returns of the Sun to the vernal equinox. The tropical year consisted of 365 days, 5 hours, 48 minutes, and 46 seconds in 1900. It has been decreasing at the rate of 0.530 second per century. The **calendar year** begins at 12 o'clock midnight precisely, local clock time, on the night of Dec. 31-Jan. 1. The day and the calendar month also begin at midnight by the clock.

On Jan. 1, 1972, the Bureau International des Poids et Mesures in Paris introduced **International Atomic Time** (TAI) as the most precisely determined time scale for astronomical usage. The fundamental unit of TAI in the international system of units is the second, defined as the duration of 9,192,631,770 periods of the radiation corresponding to the transition between 2 hyperfine levels of the ground state of the cesium 133 atom. **Coordinated Universal Time** (UTC), which serves as the basis for civil timekeeping and is the standard time of the prime meridian, is officially defined by a formula which relates UTC to mean sidereal time in Greenwich, England. (UTC has replaced GMT as the basis for standard time for the world.)

The Zones and Seasons

The 5 zones of Earth's surface are the Torrid, lying between the Tropics of Cancer and Capricorn; the N Temperate, between Cancer and the Arctic Circle; the S Temperate, between Capricorn and the Antarctic Circle; and the 2 Frigid Zones, between the Polar Circles and the Poles.

The inclination, or **tilt**, of Earth's axis, 23°27′ away from a perpendicular to Earth's orbit of the Sun, determines the seasons. These are commonly marked in the N Temperate Zone, where spring begins at the vernal equinox, summer at the summer solstice, autumn at the autumnal equinox, and winter at the winter solstice. In the S Temperate Zone, the seasons are reversed. Spring begins at the autumnal equinox, summer at the winter solstice, etc.

The points at which the Sun crosses the equator are the **equinoxes**, when day and night are most nearly equal. The points at which the Sun is at a maximum distance from the equator are the **solstices**. Days and nights are then most unequal. However, at the equator, day and night are equal throughout the year.

In June, the North Pole is tilted 23° 27′ toward the Sun, and the days in the northern hemisphere are longer than the

nights, while the days in the southern hemisphere are shorter than the nights. In Dec., the North Pole is tilted 23°27′ away from the Sun, and the situation is reversed.

The Seasons in 2004

In 2004 the 4 seasons begin in the northern hemisphere as shown. (Add one hour to Eastern Standard Time for Atlantic Time; subtract one hour for Central, 2 for Mountain, 3 for Pacific, 4 for Alaska, 5 for Hawaii-Aleutian. Also shown is Coordinated Universal Time.)

Seasons	Date	EST	UTC
Vernal Equinox (spring)	Mar. 20	1:49	6:49
Northern Solstice (summer)	June 21	20:57*	0:57
Autumnal Equinox (autumn)	Sept. 22	12:30	16:30
Southern Solstice (winter)	Dec. 21	7:42	12:42

* previous day

Poles of Earth

The geographic (rotation) poles, or points where Earth's axis of rotation cuts the surface, are not absolutely fixed in the body of Earth. The pole of rotation describes an irregular curve about its mean position.

Two periods have been detected in this motion: (1) an annual period due to seasonal changes in barometric pressure, to load of ice and snow on the surface, and to other seasonal phenomena; (2) a period of about 14 months due to the shape and constitution of Earth. In addition, there are small but as yet unpredictable irregularities. The whole motion is so small that the actual pole at any time remains within a circle of 30 or 40 feet in radius centered at the mean position of the pole.

The pole of rotation for the time being is of course the pole having a latitude of 90° and an indeterminate longitude.

Magnetic Poles

Although Earth's magnetic field resembles that of an ordinary bar magnet, this magnetic field is probably produced by electric currents in the liquid currents of the Earth's outer core. The **north magnetic pole** of Earth is that region where the magnetic force is vertically downward, and the **south magnetic pole** is that region where the magnetic force is vertically upward. A compass placed at the magnetic poles experiences no directive force in azimuth (i.e., direction).

There are slow changes in the distribution of Earth's magnetic field. This slow temporal change is referred to as the secular change of the main magnetic field, and the magnetic poles shift due to this. The location of the N magnetic pole was first measured in 1831 at Cape Adelaide on the west coast of Boothia Peninsula in Canada's Northwest Territories (about latitude 70° N and longitude 96° W). Since then it has moved over 500 miles. It is now estimated to be at 82° N and 113°W, northwest of Ellef Ringnes Island in N Canada. Measurement for several decades by Canadian scientists indicates the motion of the pole has accelerated, now averaging about 25 mi per year.

The direction of the horizontal components of the magnetic field at any point is known as magnetic N at that point, and the angle by which it deviates E or W of true N is known as the magnetic declination.

A compass without error points in the direction of magnetic north. (In general, this is not the direction of the true rotational north pole.) If you follow the direction indicated by the N end of the compass, you will go along an irregular curve that eventually reaches the north magnetic pole (though not usually by a great-circle route). However, the action of the compass should not be thought of as due to any influence of the distant pole, but simply as an indication of the distribution of Earth's magnetism at the place of observation.

Rotation of Earth

The speed of rotation of Earth about its axis is slightly variable. The variations may be classified as:

(A) **Secular**. Tidal friction acts as a brake on the rotation and causes a slow secular increase in the length of the day, about 1 millisecond per century.

(B) **Irregular**. The speed of rotation may increase for a number of years, about 5 to 10, and then start decreasing. The maximum difference from the mean in the length of the day during a century is about 5 milliseconds. The accumulated difference in time has amounted to approximately 44 seconds since 1900. The cause is probably motion in the interior of Earth.

(C) **Periodic.** Seasonal variations exist with periods of 1 year and 6 months. The cumulative effect is such that each year, Earth is late about 30 milliseconds near June 1 and is ahead about 30 milliseconds near Oct. 1. The maximum seasonal variation in the length of the day is about 0.5 millisecond. It is believed that the principal cause of the annual variation is the seasonal change in the wind patterns of the northern and southern hemispheres. The semiannual varia-

tion is due chiefly to tidal action of the Sun, which distorts the shape of Earth slightly.

The secular and irregular variations were discovered by comparing time based on the rotation of Earth with time based on the orbital motion of the Moon about Earth and of the planets about the Sun. The periodic variation was determined largely with the aid of quartz-crystal clocks. The introduction of the cesium-beam atomic clock in 1955 made it possible to determine in greater detail than before the nature of the irregular and periodic variations.

Calculation of Rise Times

The Daily Calendar on pages 667-678 contains rise and set times for the Sun and Moon for the Greenwich Meridian at N latitudes 20°, 30°, 40°, 50°, and 60°. From day to day, the values for the Sun at any particular latitude do not change very much. This means that whatever time the Sun rises or sets at the 0° meridian, it will rise or set at the same time at the Standard Time meridian of your time zone. Standard Time meridians occur every 15° of longitude (15°E and W, 30°E and W, etc.). The corrections necessary to observe that event from your location will be to account for your distance from the Standard Time meridian and for your latitude. Thus, if your latitude is about 45°, sunrise on Jan. 1, 2004, is roughly halfway between 7:22 and 7:59 A.M. on the Standard Time meridian for your time zone. If you are 7.5°west of your Standard Time meridian, sunrise will be about ½ hour later than this; if 7.5°east, about ½ hour earlier.

The Moon, however, moves its own diameter, about one-half degree, in an hour, or about 13.2°in one complete turn of Earth—one day. Most of this is eastward against the background stars of the sky, but some is also N or S movement. All this motion considerably affects the times of rise or set, as you can see from the adjacent entries in the table. Thus, it is necessary to take your longitude into account in addition to your latitude. If you have no need for total accuracy, simply note that the time will be between the 4 values (see example below) you find surrounding your location and the dates of interest.

The process of finding more accurate corrections is called interpolation. In the example, linear interpolation involving simple differences is used. In extreme cases, higher order interpolation should be used. If such cases are important to you, it is suggested that you plot the times, draw smooth curves through the plots, and interpolate by eye between the relevant curves. Some people find this exercise fun.

Let's find the times of the moonset for the May Waning Quarter Moon and sunrise the same day at Seattle, WA.

First, where is Seattle, WA? Find Seattle's latitude and longitude in *The World Almanac*, page 492. You must also know Seattle's time zone, which you can estimate from the map on page 500.

I.   Seattle, WA: 47° 36′ 23″ N
       122° 19′ 51″ W

IA.   Convert these values to decimals:
       23/60 = 0.38
       36 + 0.38 = 36.38
       36.38/60 = 0.61
       47 + 0.61 = 47.61 N
       51/60 = 0.85
       19 + 0.85 = 19.85
       19.85/60 = 0.33
       122 + 0.33 = 122.33 W

IB.   Fraction Seattle lies between 40° and 50°:
       47.61 − 40 = 7.61; 7.61/10 = 0.761

IC.   Fraction world must turn between Greenwich and Seattle:
       122.33/360 = 0.340

ID.   Seattle is in the Pacific Standard Time zone and the PST meridian is 120°; thus 122.33 is 122.33 − 120 = 2.33° W of the Pacific Standard Meridian. In 24 hours, there are 24 x 60 = 1,440 minutes; 1,440/360 = 4 minutes for every degree around Earth. So events happen 4 x 2.33 = 9.3 minutes later in Seattle than at the 120° meridian. (If the location is E of the Standard Meridian, events happen earlier.)

IE.   The values IB and IC are interpolates for Seattle; ID is the time correction from local to Standard time for Seattle. These values need never be calculated again for Seattle.

IIA.   To find the time of moonset we start from the table of Moon Phases, 2004. We see that May's Waning Quarter Moon occurs on May 11. We need the Greenwich times for moonset at latitudes 40° and 50°, and for May 11 and 12, the day of the Waning Quarter Moon and the next day. These values are found in the Astronomy Daily Calendar 2004; we then compute the difference between the two latitudes.

	40°	Diff.	50°
May 11	11:13	−0:32	10:41
May 12	12:24	−0:22	12:02

IIB.   We want IB and the May 11 time difference:
       0.761 x −32 = −24.4

Add this to the May 11, 40° rise time:
       11:13 + (−24.4) = 10:48.6
And for May 12:
       0.761 x −22 = −16.7
Add this to the May 12, 40° rise time:
       12:24 + (−16.7) = 12.07.3
These 2 times are for the latitude of Seattle, but for the Greenwich meridian.

IIC.   To get the time for Seattle meridian, take the difference between these 2 times just determined,
       12:07.3 − 10:48.6 = 78.7 minutes,
       and calculate what fraction of this 24-hour change took place while Earth turned between Greenwich and Seattle (See IC).
       78.7 x 0.340 = 26.8 minutes after 10:48.6
       Thus 10:48.6 + 26.8 = 11:15.4 is the time the Waxing Quarter Moon will set in the local time of Seattle.

IID.   But this happens 9.3 minutes (See ID) later by PST clock time at Seattle, thus
       11:15.4 + 9.3 = 11:24.7 PST
       But this is late spring, and daylight time is in effect;
       11:24.7 + 1:00 = 12:25 PDT is the set time for the Waxing Quarter Moon at Seattle the afternoon of May 11, 2004.

IIIA. To find the time of sunrise we need the Greenwich times for sunrise at latitudes 40° and 50°. These values are found in the Astronomy Daily Calendar 2004; we then compute the difference between the two latitudes.

	40°	Diff.	50°
May 11	4:48	−0:28	4:20

IIIB. We want IB and the May 11 time difference:
       0.761 x −28 = −21.3
       Add this to the May 11, 40° rise time:
       4:48 + (−21.3) = 4:26.7
       This is the local time for the latitude of Seattle.

IIIC. But this happens 9.3 minutes (See ID) later by PST clock time at Seattle, thus
       4:26.7 + 9.3 = 4:36
       But daylight time is in effect;
       4:36 + 1:00 = 5:36 is sunrise at Seattle on May 11, 2004.

JANUARY 2004

1st Month   **31 days**

Coordinated Universal Time (Greenwich Mean Time)

NOTE: For rising and setting each day, numbers on first line indicate Sun; numbers on second line indicate Moon.
Degrees are North Latitude.

Moon Phases: FM = Full Moon; LQ = Last (Waning) Quarter; NM = New Moon; FQ = First (Waxing) Quarter;
Sun's distance is in Astronomical Units

CAUTION: Must be converted to local time. For instructions see "Calculation of Rise Times," page 666.

Day of month, of week, of year	Sun on Meridian Moon Phase h m s	Sun's Declination °' Distance	20° Rise Sun/Moon h m	20° Set Sun/Moon h m	30° Rise Sun/Moon h m	30° Set Sun/Moon h m	40° Rise Sun/Moon h m	40° Set Sun/Moon h m	50° Rise Sun/Moon h m	50° Set Sun/Moon h m	60° Rise Sun/Moon h m	60° Set Sun/Moon h m
1 TH	12 03 18	−23 04	6 35	17 32	6 56	17 11	7 22	16 45	7 59	16 08	9 03	15 04
1		.9833	13 10	1 20	13 00	1 28	12 47	1 38	12 31	1 52	12 05	2 13
2 FR	12 03 46	−23 00	6 35	17 32	6 56	17 12	7 22	16 46	7 59	16 09	9 02	15 06
2		.9833	13 45	2 10	13 30	2 22	13 12	2 39	12 47	3 01	12 07	3 36
3 SA	12 04 14	−22 54	6 36	17 33	6 56	17 12	7 22	16 47	7 58	16 10	9 02	15 07
3		.9833	14 22	3 00	14 03	3 18	13 39	3 39	13 06	4 10	12 12	5 02
4 SU	12 04 42	−22 49	6 36	17 34	6 56	17 13	7 22	16 47	7 58	16 11	9 01	15 09
4		.9833	15 03	3 52	14 40	4 14	14 12	4 41	13 31	5 19	12 20	6 28
5 MO	12 05 09	−22 42	6 36	17 34	6 57	17 14	7 22	16 48	7 58	16 12	9 00	15 10
5		.9833	15 48	4 45	15 23	5 10	14 51	5 41	14 04	6 26	12 36	7 53
6 TU	12 05 35	−22 36	6 36	17 35	6 57	17 15	7 22	16 49	7 58	16 14	8 59	15 12
6		.9833	16 38	5 39	16 11	6 05	15 37	6 39	14 48	7 28	13 08	9 08
7 WE	12 06 02	−22 29	6 37	17 36	6 57	17 15	7 22	16 50	7 57	16 15	8 58	15 14
7	15 40 FM	.9833	17 31	6 31	17 05	6 58	16 31	7 32	15 42	8 21	14 04	10 00
8 TH	12 06 27	−22 21	6 37	17 36	6 57	17 16	7 22	16 51	7 57	16 16	8 58	15 16
8		.9833	18 26	7 21	18 02	7 46	17 32	8 18	16 47	9 03	15 24	10 29
9 FR	12 06 53	−22 13	6 37	17 37	6 57	17 17	7 22	16 52	7 57	16 17	8 56	15 18
9		.9833	19 22	8 08	19 02	8 30	18 36	8 57	17 59	9 36	16 54	10 43
10 SA	12 07 17	−22 05	6 37	17 37	6 57	17 18	7 22	16 53	7 56	16 19	8 55	15 20
10		.9834	20 18	8 51	20 02	9 08	19 42	9 31	19 14	10 01	18 28	10 51
11 SU	12 07 42	−21 56	6 37	17 38	6 57	17 19	7 21	16 54	7 56	16 20	8 54	15 22
11		.9834	21 13	9 30	21 02	9 43	20 48	9 59	20 30	10 21	20 00	10 56
12 MO	12 08 05	−21 47	6 38	17 39	6 57	17 19	7 21	16 55	7 55	16 21	8 53	15 24
12		.9834	22 07	10 07	22 02	10 15	21 55	10 25	21 46	10 38	21 31	10 58
13 TU	12 08 28	−21 37	6 38	17 39	6 57	17 20	7 21	16 56	7 55	16 23	8 52	15 26
13		.9834	23 02	10 43	23 02	10 46	23 02	10 49	23 02	10 53	23 03	11 00
14 WE	12 08 50	−21 27	6 38	17 40	6 57	17 21	7 21	16 57	7 54	16 24	8 50	15 28
14		.9835	23 58	11 19	none	11 16	none	11 13	none	11 08	none	11 01
15 TH	12 09 12	−21 17	6 38	17 41	6 57	17 22	7 20	16 58	7 53	16 26	8 49	15 30
.15	04 46 LQ	.9836	none	11 57	0 04	11 48	0 11	11 38	0 21	11 24	0 36	11 03
16 FR	12 09 33	−21 06	6 38	17 41	6 57	17 23	7 20	17 00	7 52	16 27	8 47	15 33
16		.9836	0 56	12 38	1 08	12 24	1 22	12 07	1 42	11 43	2 14	11 06
17 SA	12 09 54	−20 55	6 38	17 42	6 56	17 24	7 19	17 01	7 52	16 29	8 46	15 35
17		.9837	1 58	13 23	2 15	13 04	2 37	12 40	3 07	12 07	3 59	11 12
18 SU	12 10 14	−20 43	6 38	17 43	6 56	17 24	7 19	17 02	7 51	16 30	8 44	15 37
18		.9838	3 03	14 16	3 25	13 52	3 54	13 22	4 34	12 39	5 49	11 22
19 MO	12 10 33	−20 31	6 38	17 43	6 56	17 25	7 19	17 03	7 50	16 32	8 42	15 40
19		.9839	4 11	15 15	4 37	14 48	5 10	14 15	5 58	13 25	7 35	11 47
20 TU	12 10 51	−20 19	6 38	17 44	6 56	17 26	7 18	17 04	7 49	16 33	8 40	15 42
20		.9840	5 18	16 20	5 45	15 53	6 20	15 18	7 11	14 27	8 56	12 43
21 WE	12 11 09	−20 06	6 38	17 45	6 56	17 27	7 17	17 05	7 48	16 35	8 39	15 44
21	21 05 NM	.9840	6 21	17 27	6 47	17 02	7 19	16 31	8 07	15 45	9 38	14 15
22 TH	12 11 26	−19 52	6 38	17 45	6 55	17 28	7 17	17 06	7 47	16 36	8 37	15 47
22		.9841	7 17	18 33	7 39	18 13	8 07	17 47	8 47	17 09	9 56	16 03
23 FR	12 11 42	−19 39	6 38	17 46	6 55	17 29	7 16	17 08	7 46	16 38	8 35	15 49
23		.9842	8 06	19 36	8 24	19 21	8 45	19 01	9 15	18 34	10 04	17 49
24 SA	12 11 57	−19 25	6 37	17 47	6 55	17 30	7 16	17 09	7 45	16 40	8 33	15 52
24		.9843	8 49	20 35	9 01	20 25	9 16	20 12	9 36	19 56	10 08	19 29
25 SU	12 12 12	−19 10	6 37	17 47	6 54	17 31	7 15	17 10	7 44	16 41	8 31	15 54
25		.9844	9 27	21 29	9 34	21 25	9 42	21 20	9 53	21 12	10 10	21 01
26 MO	12 12 26	−18 56	6 37	17 48	6 54	17 31	7 14	17 11	7 42	16 43	8 29	15 57
26		.9845	10 02	22 22	10 03	22 23	10 05	22 24	10 08	22 26	10 12	22 28
27 TU	12 12 38	−18 41	6 37	17 48	6 53	17 32	7 13	17 12	7 41	16 45	8 27	15 59
27		.9846	10 35	23 12	10 32	23 18	10 27	23 26	10 22	23 37	10 13	23 53
28 WE	12 12 50	−18 26	6 37	17 49	6 53	17 33	7 13	17 13	7 40	16 46	8 24	16 02
28		.9847	11 08	none	11 00	none	10 50	none	10 36	none	10 14	none
29 TH	12 13 02	−18 10	6 37	17 50	6 52	17 34	7 12	17 15	7 39	16 48	8 22	16 05
29	06 03 FQ	.9849	11 43	0 02	11 29	0 14	11 13	0 28	10 51	0 47	10 16	1 18
30 FR	12 13 12	−17 54	6 36	17 50	6 52	17 35	7 11	17 16	7 37	16 50	8 20	16 07
30		.9850	12 19	0 53	12 01	1 09	11 39	1 29	11 09	1 57	10 20	2 43
31 SA	12 13 22	−17 37	6 36	17 51	6 51	17 36	7 10	17 17	7 36	16 51	8 18	16 10
31		.9851	12 59	1 45	12 37	2 05	12 10	2 30	11 32	3 07	10 26	4 10

FEBRUARY 2004

2nd Month   **29 days**

Coordinated Universal Time (Greenwich Mean Time)

NOTE: For rising and setting each day, numbers on first line indicate Sun; numbers on second line indicate Moon.

Degrees are North Latitude.

Moon Phases: FM = Full Moon; LQ = Last (Waning) Quarter; NM = New Moon; FQ = First (Waxing) Quarter; Sun's distance is in Astronomical Units

CAUTION: Must be converted to local time. For instructions see "Calculation of Rise Times," page 666.

Day of month, of week, of year	Sun on Meridian / Moon Phase — h m s	Sun's Declination ° / Distance	20° Rise Sun/Moon	20° Set Sun/Moon	30° Rise Sun/Moon	30° Set Sun/Moon	40° Rise Sun/Moon	40° Set Sun/Moon	50° Rise Sun/Moon	50° Set Sun/Moon	60° Rise Sun/Moon	60° Set Sun/Moon
1 SU	12 13 30	−17 21	6 36	17 52	6 51	17 37	7 09	17 18	7 35	16 53	8 15	16 12
32		.9852	13 42	2 38	13 18	3 01	12 47	3 31	12 02	4 15	10 38	5 36
2 MO	12 13 38	−17 04	6 35	17 52	6 50	17 37	7 08	17 19	7 33	16 55	8 13	16 15
33		.9854	14 30	3 31	14 04	3 57	13 30	4 30	12 41	5 19	11 03	6 56
3 TU	12 13 46	−16 47	6 35	17 53	6 50	17 38	7 07	17 21	7 32	16 56	8 11	16 18
34		.9855	15 22	4 24	14 56	4 51	14 22	5 25	13 32	6 15	11 50	7 57
4 WE	12 13 52	−16 29	6 35	17 53	6 49	17 39	7 06	17 22	7 30	16 58	8 08	16 20
35		.9856	16 17	5 15	15 52	5 41	15 21	6 14	14 34	7 01	13 04	8 33
5 TH	12 13 57	−16 11	6 34	17 54	6 48	17 40	7 05	17 23	7 29	17 00	8 06	16 23
36		.9858	17 14	6 03	16 52	6 26	16 25	6 56	15 45	7 37	14 33	8 51
6 FR	12 14 02 / 08 47 FM	−15 53	6 34	17 54	6 48	17 41	7 04	17 24	7 27	17 02	8 03	16 26
37		.9859	18 11	6 48	17 53	7 07	17 31	7 31	17 00	8 05	16 08	9 01
7 SA	12 14 06	−15 35	6 34	17 55	6 47	17 42	7 03	17 25	7 26	17 03	8 01	16 28
38		.9861	19 07	7 29	18 55	7 44	18 39	8 02	18 17	8 27	17 42	9 06
8 SU	12 14 09	−15 16	6 33	17 55	6 46	17 43	7 02	17 27	7 24	17 05	7 58	16 31
39		.9863	20 03	8 07	19 56	8 17	19 47	8 29	19 35	8 44	19 16	9 08
9 MO	12 14 11	−14 57	6 33	17 56	6 45	17 43	7 01	17 28	7 22	17 07	7 56	16 33
40		.9864	20 58	8 44	20 56	8 48	20 55	8 53	20 52	9 00	20 48	9 10
10 TU	12 14 12	−14 38	6 32	17 56	6 45	17 44	7 00	17 29	7 21	17 09	7 53	16 36
41		.9866	21 54	9 20	21 58	9 19	22 03	9 17	22 11	9 15	22 22	9 12
11 WE	12 14 13	−14 19	6 32	17 57	6 44	17 45	6 59	17 30	7 19	17 10	7 51	16 39
42		.9868	22 51	9 57	23 01	9 50	23 14	9 42	23 31	9 31	23 58	9 13
12 TH	12 14 13	−13 59	6 31	17 57	6 43	17 46	6 58	17 31	7 17	17 12	7 48	16 41
43		.9870	23 51	10 37	none	10 24	none	10 09	none	9 48	none	9 15
13 FR	12 14 12 / 13 40 LQ	−13 39	6 31	17 58	6 42	17 47	6 56	17 33	7 15	17 14	7 45	16 44
44		.9872	none	11 20	0 06	11 02	0 26	10 40	0 54	10 09	1 40	9 19
14 SA	12 14 11	−13 19	6 30	17 58	6 41	17 47	6 55	17 34	7 14	17 15	7 43	16 47
45		.9874	0 54	12 08	1 14	11 46	1 41	11 18	2 19	10 38	3 26	9 27
15 SU	12 14 09	−12 59	6 30	17 59	6 41	17 48	6 54	17 35	7 12	17 17	7 40	16 49
46		.9876	1 59	13 03	2 23	12 37	2 55	12 05	3 42	11 17	5 12	9 44
16 MO	12 14 06	−12 38	6 29	17 59	6 40	17 49	6 53	17 36	7 10	17 19	7 37	16 52
47		.9878	3 04	14 04	3 31	13 37	4 06	13 02	4 57	12 11	6 43	10 24
17 TU	12 14 02	−12 17	6 28	18 00	6 39	17 50	6 51	17 37	7 08	17 21	7 35	16 55
48		.9880	4 07	15 09	4 33	14 43	5 07	14 09	5 58	13 20	7 38	11 41
18 WE	12 13 58	−11 56	6 28	18 00	6 38	17 50	6 50	17 38	7 06	17 22	7 32	16 57
49		.9882	5 04	16 14	5 28	15 52	5 59	15 23	6 42	14 41	8 02	13 24
19 TH	12 13 53	−11 35	6 27	18 01	6 37	17 51	6 49	17 40	7 05	17 24	7 29	17 00
50		.9884	5 55	17 18	6 15	17 00	6 40	16 37	7 15	16 05	8 13	15 11
20 FR	12 13 47 / 09 18 NM	−11 14	6 27	18 01	6 36	17 52	6 47	17 41	7 03	17 26	7 26	17 02
51		.9886	6 40	18 18	6 55	18 06	7 13	17 50	7 38	17 29	8 18	16 53
21 SA	12 13 41	−10 53	6 26	18 02	6 35	17 53	6 46	17 42	7 01	17 27	7 23	17 05
52		.9888	7 20	19 15	7 30	19 08	7 41	19 00	7 57	18 48	8 20	18 29
22 SU	12 13 34	−10 31	6 25	18 02	6 34	17 54	6 45	17 43	6 59	17 29	7 21	17 08
53		.9891	7 57	20 09	8 01	20 08	8 05	20 06	8 12	20 04	8 22	20 00
23 MO	12 13 26	−10 09	6 25	18 02	6 33	17 54	6 43	17 44	6 57	17 31	7 18	17 10
54		.9893	8 31	21 01	8 30	21 05	8 28	21 10	8 26	21 17	8 23	21 28
24 TU	12 13 18	−9 47	6 24	18 03	6 32	17 55	6 42	17 45	6 55	17 33	7 15	17 13
55		.9895	9 05	21 52	8 58	22 02	8 50	22 13	8 40	22 29	8 24	22 54
25 WE	12 13 09	−9 25	6 23	18 03	6 31	17 56	6 40	17 47	6 53	17 34	7 12	17 15
56		.9897	9 39	22 44	9 28	22 58	9 14	23 16	8 55	23 40	8 25	none
26 TH	12 13 00	−9 03	6 23	18 04	6 30	17 56	6 39	17 48	6 51	17 36	7 09	17 18
57		.9899	10 15	23 36	9 59	23 54	9 39	none	9 12	none	8 28	0 21
27 FR	12 12 50	−8 40	6 22	18 04	6 29	17 57	6 37	17 49	6 49	17 38	7 06	17 20
58		.9902	10 53	none	10 33	none	10 08	0 18	9 32	0 51	8 32	1 49
28 SA	12 12 39 / 03 24 FQ	−8 18	6 21	18 04	6 28	17 58	6 36	17 50	6 47	17 39	7 03	17 23
59		.9904	11 36	0 28	11 12	0 51	10 42	1 20	9 59	2 01	8 41	3 17
29 SU	12 12 28	−7 55	6 20	18 05	6 27	17 59	6 35	17 51	6 45	17 41	7 01	17 26
60		.9906	12 22	1 22	11 56	1 47	11 22	2 20	10 34	3 07	8 59	4 41

MARCH 2004

3rd Month　　　　　　　　　　　　　　　　　　　　　　　　**31 days**

Coordinated Universal Time (Greenwich Mean Time)

NOTE: For rising and setting each day, numbers on first line indicate Sun; numbers on second line indicate Moon.

Degrees are North Latitude.

Moon Phases: FM = Full Moon; LQ = Last (Waning) Quarter; NM = New Moon; FQ = First (Waxing) Quarter

Sun's distance is in Astronomical Units

CAUTION: Must be converted to local time. For instructions see "Calculation of Rise Times," page 666.

Day of month, of week, of year	Sun on Meridian / Moon Phase (h m s)	Sun's Declination / Distance	20° Rise Sun/Moon	20° Set Sun/Moon	30° Rise Sun/Moon	30° Set Sun/Moon	40° Rise Sun/Moon	40° Set Sun/Moon	50° Rise Sun/Moon	50° Set Sun/Moon	60° Rise Sun/Moon	60° Set Sun/Moon
1 MO / 61	12 12 16	−7 32	6 20	18 05	6 26	17 59	6 33	17 52	6 43	17 43	6 58	17 28
		.9909	13 12	2 15	12 45	2 42	12 11	3 16	11 20	4 07	9 35	5 51
2 TU / 62	12 12 04	−7 09	6 19	18 06	6 25	18 00	6 32	17 53	6 41	17 44	6 55	17 31
		.9911	14 06	3 07	13 40	3 33	13 06	4 07	12 17	4 57	10 39	6 36
3 WE / 63	12 11 51	−6 47	6 18	18 06	6 24	18 01	6 30	17 54	6 39	17 46	6 52	17 33
		.9913	15 02	3 56	14 38	4 20	14 08	4 51	13 25	5 36	12 04	6 59
4 TH / 64	12 11 38	−6 23	6 18	18 06	6 22	18 01	6 29	17 55	6 37	17 48	6 49	17 36
		.9916	15 59	4 42	15 39	5 03	15 15	5 29	14 40	6 07	13 39	7 10
5 FR / 65	12 11 24	−6 00	6 17	18 07	6 21	18 02	6 27	17 56	6 35	17 49	6 46	17 38
		.9918	16 56	5 24	16 41	5 41	16 23	6 02	15 57	6 30	15 15	7 16
6 SA / 66	12 11 10 / 23 14 FM	−5 37	6 16	18 07	6 20	18 03	6 25	17 58	6 32	17 51	6 43	17 41
		.9921	17 53	6 04	17 43	6 16	17 32	6 30	17 16	6 49	16 51	7 19
7 SU / 67	12 10 56	−5 14	6 15	18 07	6 19	18 03	6 24	17 59	6 30	17 52	6 40	17 43
		.9923	18 49	6 42	18 46	6 48	18 41	6 56	18 35	7 06	18 26	7 21
8 MO / 68	12 10 41	−4 50	6 14	18 08	6 18	18 04	6 22	18 00	6 28	17 54	6 37	17 46
		.9926	19 46	7 19	19 48	7 19	19 51	7 20	19 55	7 21	20 02	7 22
9 TU / 69	12 10 26	−4 27	6 13	18 08	6 17	18 05	6 21	18 01	6 26	17 56	6 34	17 48
		.9929	20 44	7 56	20 53	7 51	21 03	7 45	21 17	7 36	21 40	7 24
10 WE / 70	12 10 10	−4 03	6 12	18 08	6 16	18 05	6 19	18 02	6 24	17 57	6 31	17 51
		.9931	21 45	8 35	21 59	8 25	22 16	8 11	22 41	7 53	23 22	7 25
11 TH / 71	12 09 55	−3 40	6 12	18 08	6 14	18 06	6 18	18 03	6 22	17 59	6 28	17 53
		.9934	22 47	9 18	23 07	9 02	23 32	8 41	none	8 13	none	7 28
12 FR / 72	12 09 39	−3 16	6 11	18 09	6 13	18 07	6 16	18 04	6 20	18 01	6 25	17 56
		.9937	23 52	10 05	none	9 44	none	9 17	0 07	8 39	1 09	7 34
13 SA / 73	12 09 22 / 21 01 LQ	−2 53	6 10	18 09	6 12	18 07	6 14	18 05	6 17	18 02	6 22	17 58
		.9940	none	10 58	0 16	10 33	0 47	10 01	1 32	9 14	2 58	7 47
14 SU / 74	12 09 06	−2 29	6 09	18 09	6 11	18 08	6 13	18 06	6 15	18 04	6 19	18 01
		.9942	0 57	11 57	1 24	11 30	1 58	10 55	2 49	10 03	4 36	8 16
15 MO / 75	12 08 49	−2 05	6 08	18 10	6 10	18 08	6 11	18 07	6 13	18 05	6 16	18 03
		.9945	2 00	12 59	2 27	12 32	3 02	11 58	3 54	11 07	5 41	9 20
16 TU / 76	12 08 32	−1 42	6 07	18 10	6 08	18 09	6 10	18 08	6 11	18 07	6 13	18 05
		.9948	2 58	14 03	3 23	13 39	3 56	13 08	4 42	12 23	6 11	10 56
17 WE / 77	12 08 14	−1 18	6 07	18 10	6 07	18 10	6 08	18 09	6 09	18 09	6 10	18 08
		.9951	3 50	15 06	4 11	14 46	4 39	14 21	5 17	13 45	6 23	12 42
18 TH / 78	12 07 57	−0 54	6 06	18 11	6 06	18 10	6 06	18 10	6 07	18 10	6 07	18 10
		.9954	4 36	16 06	4 52	15 52	5 13	15 33	5 42	15 07	6 29	14 24
19 FR / 79	12 07 40	−0 30	6 05	18 11	6 05	18 11	6 05	18 11	6 05	18 12	6 04	18 13
		.9956	5 16	17 03	5 28	16 54	5 42	16 43	6 02	16 27	6 32	16 01
20 SA / 80	12 07 22 / 22 41 NM	−0 07	6 04	18 11	6 04	18 12	6 03	18 12	6 02	18 13	6 01	18 15
		.9959	5 53	17 58	6 00	17 54	6 07	17 50	6 18	17 43	6 33	17 33
21 SU / 81	12 07 04	+0 17	6 03	18 11	6 02	18 12	6 02	18 13	6 00	18 15	5 58	18 18
		.9962	6 28	18 50	6 29	18 52	6 30	18 54	6 32	18 57	6 34	19 02
22 MO / 82	12 06 46	+0 41	6 02	18 12	6 01	18 13	6 00	18 14	5 58	18 17	5 55	18 20
		.9965	7 02	19 42	6 57	19 49	6 52	19 58	6 45	20 10	6 34	20 29
23 TU / 83	12 06 28	+1 04	6 01	18 12	6 00	18 13	5 58	18 15	5 56	18 18	5 52	18 23
		.9968	7 36	20 34	7 26	20 46	7 15	21 01	6 59	21 23	6 35	21 57
24 WE / 84	12 06 10	+1 28	6 00	18 12	5 59	18 14	5 57	18 16	5 54	18 20	5 49	18 25
		.9970	8 11	21 26	7 57	21 43	7 39	22 04	7 15	22 35	6 37	23 25
25 TH / 85	12 05 52	+1 52	6 00	18 12	5 58	18 15	5 55	18 17	5 51	18 21	5 46	18 27
		.9973	8 49	22 19	8 30	22 40	8 06	23 07	7 34	23 46	6 40	none
26 FR / 86	12 05 34	+2 15	5 59	18 13	5 56	18 15	5 53	18 18	5 49	18 23	5 43	18 30
		.9976	9 29	23 12	9 07	23 37	8 38	none	7 58	none	6 46	0 55
27 SA / 87	12 05 16	+2 39	5 58	18 13	5 55	18 16	5 52	18 19	5 47	18 24	5 40	18 32
		.9979	10 14	none	9 48	none	9 16	0 08	8 29	0 54	6 59	2 23
28 SU / 88	12 04 58 / 23 48 FQ	+3 02	5 57	18 13	5 54	18 16	5 50	18 20	5 45	18 26	5 37	18 35
		.9982	11 02	0 06	10 35	0 32	10 01	1 06	9 10	1 57	7 25	3 41
29 MO / 89	12 04 40	+3 26	5 56	18 14	5 53	18 17	5 49	18 21	5 43	18 28	5 34	18 37
		.9985	11 54	0 58	11 27	1 25	10 53	1 59	10 02	2 51	8 17	4 37
30 TU / 90	12 04 22	+3 49	5 55	18 14	5 52	18 18	5 47	18 22	5 41	18 29	5 31	18 40
		.9987	12 49	1 47	12 24	2 13	11 52	2 46	11 05	3 34	9 34	5 06
31 WE / 91	12 04 04	+4 12	5 54	18 14	5 50	18 18	5 45	18 23	5 38	18 31	5 28	18 42
		.9990	13 45	2 34	13 23	2 57	12 56	3 26	12 16	4 07	11 06	5 21

APRIL 2004

4th Month   **30 days**

Coordinated Universal Time (Greenwich Mean Time)

NOTE: For rising and setting each day, numbers on first line indicate Sun; numbers on second line indicate Moon.
Degrees are North Latitude.

Moon Phases: FM = Full Moon; LQ = Last (Waning) Quarter; NM = New Moon; FQ = First (Waxing) Quarter

Sun's distance is in Astronomical Units

CAUTION: Must be converted to local time. For instructions see "Calculation of Rise Times," page 666.

Day of month, of week, of year	Sun on Meridian / Moon Phase (h m s)	Sun's Declination / Distance	20° Rise Sun/Moon (h m)	20° Set Sun/Moon (h m)	30° Rise Sun/Moon (h m)	30° Set Sun/Moon (h m)	40° Rise Sun/Moon (h m)	40° Set Sun/Moon (h m)	50° Rise Sun/Moon (h m)	50° Set Sun/Moon (h m)	60° Rise Sun/Moon (h m)	60° Set Sun/Moon (h m)
1 TH	12 03 46	+4 35	5 53	18 14	5 49	18 19	5 44	18 25	5 36	18 32	5 25	18 45
92		.9993	14 41	3 17	14 24	3 36	14 03	4 00	13 32	4 33	12 41	5 28
2 FR	12 03 28	+4 58	5 53	18 15	5 48	18 19	5 42	18 26	5 34	18 34	5 21	18 47
93		.9996	15 38	3 58	15 26	4 12	15 11	4 30	14 50	4 54	14 17	5 31
3 SA	12 03 10	+5 21	5 52	18 15	5 47	18 20	5 41	18 27	5 32	18 35	5 18	18 49
94		.9999	16 35	4 36	16 28	4 45	16 20	4 56	16 10	5 11	15 53	5 33
4 SU	12 02 53	+5 44	5 51	18 15	5 46	18 21	5 39	18 28	5 30	18 37	5 15	18 52
95		1.0001	17 32	5 14	17 31	5 17	17 31	5 21	17 30	5 26	17 30	5 34
5 MO	12 02 36	+6 07	5 50	18 15	5 44	18 21	5 37	18 29	5 28	18 39	5 12	18 54
96	11 03 FM	1.0004	18 31	5 51	18 36	5 49	18 43	5 46	18 53	5 41	19 09	5 35
6 TU	12 02 18	+6 30	5 49	18 16	5 43	18 22	5 36	18 30	5 26	18 40	5 09	18 57
97		1.0007	19 32	6 30	19 43	6 22	19 58	6 11	20 19	5 57	20 52	5 36
7 WE	12 02 01	+6 52	5 48	18 16	5 42	18 22	5 34	18 31	5 23	18 42	5 06	18 59
98		1.0010	20 36	7 13	20 53	6 58	21 16	6 40	21 47	6 16	22 42	5 38
8 TH	12 01 45	+7 15	5 47	18 16	5 41	18 23	5 33	18 32	5 21	18 43	5 03	19 02
99		1.0013	21 42	7 59	22 05	7 40	22 34	7 15	23 16	6 40	none	5 42
9 FR	12 01 28	+7 37	5 47	18 17	5 40	18 24	5 31	18 33	5 19	18 45	5 00	19 04
100		1.0016	22 49	8 52	23 15	8 28	23 49	7 57	none	7 13	0 35	5 51
10 SA	12 01 12	+8 00	5 46	18 17	5 39	18 24	5 30	18 34	5 17	18 46	4 57	19 07
101		1.0019	23 54	9 50	none	9 23	none	8 48	0 39	7 57	2 22	6 13
11 SU	12 00 56	+8 22	5 45	18 17	5 37	18 25	5 28	18 35	5 15	18 48	4 55	19 09
102		1.0022	none	10 53	0 22	10 25	0 57	9 50	1 50	8 58	3 42	7 06
12 MO	12 00 41	+8 44	5 44	18 17	5 36	18 26	5 26	18 36	5 13	18 50	4 52	19 11
103	03 46 LQ	1.0025	0 54	11 57	1 21	11 31	1 54	10 59	2 43	10 11	4 20	8 36
13 TU	12 00 26	+9 05	5 43	18 18	5 35	18 26	5 25	18 37	5 11	18 51	4 49	19 14
104		1.0028	1 48	13 00	2 11	12 38	2 40	12 11	3 21	11 32	4 35	10 21
14 WE	12 00 11	+9 27	5 43	18 18	5 34	18 27	5 23	18 38	5 09	18 53	4 46	19 16
105		1.0030	2 35	14 00	2 53	13 44	3 17	13 23	3 49	12 53	4 42	12 04
15 TH	11 59 56	+9 49	5 42	18 18	5 33	18 27	5 22	18 39	5 07	18 54	4 43	19 19
106		1.0033	3 16	14 57	3 30	14 46	3 46	14 32	4 09	14 13	4 45	13 42
16 FR	11 59 42	+10 10	5 41	18 19	5 32	18 28	5 20	18 40	5 05	18 56	4 40	19 21
107		1.0036	3 54	15 51	4 02	15 46	4 12	15 39	4 25	15 29	4 46	15 14
17 SA	11 59 28	+10 31	5 40	18 19	5 31	18 29	5 19	18 41	5 03	18 57	4 37	19 24
108		1.0039	4 28	16 43	4 31	16 43	4 34	16 43	4 39	16 43	4 46	16 42
18 SU	11 59 15	+10 52	5 40	18 19	5 30	18 29	5 17	18 42	5 01	18 59	4 34	19 26
109		1.0042	5 02	17 35	4 59	17 40	4 56	17 46	4 52	17 55	4 47	18 08
19 MO	11 59 02	+11 13	5 39	18 20	5 29	18 30	5 16	18 43	4 59	19 00	4 31	19 29
110	13 21 NM	1.0045	5 35	18 26	5 27	18 36	5 18	18 49	5 06	19 07	4 47	19 35
20 TU	11 58 50	+11 34	5 38	18 20	5 28	18 30	5 15	18 44	4 57	19 02	4 28	19 31
111		1.0047	6 09	19 18	5 57	19 33	5 41	19 52	5 21	20 19	4 48	21 03
21 WE	11 58 38	+11 54	5 37	18 20	5 27	18 31	5 13	18 45	4 55	19 04	4 25	19 34
112		1.0050	6 46	20 10	6 29	20 30	6 07	20 55	5 38	21 31	4 50	22 33
22 TH	11 58 26	+12 14	5 37	18 21	5 26	18 32	5 12	18 46	4 53	19 05	4 22	19 36
113		1.0053	7 25	21 04	7 04	21 27	6 37	21 57	5 59	22 41	4 55	none
23 FR	11 58 15	+12 34	5 36	18 21	5 25	18 32	5 10	18 47	4 51	19 07	4 20	19 39
114		1.0056	8 08	21 57	7 44	22 24	7 12	22 57	6 27	23 46	5 04	0 03
24 SA	11 58 04	+12 54	5 35	18 21	5 24	18 33	5 09	18 48	4 49	19 08	4 17	19 41
115		1.0058	8 55	22 50	8 28	23 17	7 54	23 52	7 04	none	5 23	1 26
25 SU	11 57 54	+13 14	5 35	18 22	5 23	18 34	5 08	18 49	4 47	19 10	4 14	19 44
116		1.0061	9 46	23 40	9 18	none	8 43	none	7 52	0 44	6 03	2 32
26 MO	11 57 44	+13 33	5 34	18 22	5 22	18 34	5 06	18 50	4 45	19 11	4 11	19 46
117		1.0063	10 39	none	10 13	0 07	9 39	0 41	8 50	1 31	7 11	3 11
27 TU	11 57 35	+13 53	5 33	18 22	5 21	18 35	5 05	18 51	4 43	19 13	4 08	19 49
118	17 32 FQ	1.0066	11 33	0 28	11 10	0 52	10 41	1 23	9 58	2 07	8 38	3 29
28 WE	11 57 26	+14 11	5 33	18 23	5 20	18 36	5 04	18 52	4 41	19 15	4 05	19 51
119		1.0069	12 29	1 12	12 09	1 33	11 45	1 59	11 10	2 35	10 11	3 38
29 TH	11 57 18	+14 30	5 32	18 23	5 19	18 36	5 02	18 53	4 40	19 16	4 03	19 54
120		1.0071	13 24	1 52	13 09	2 09	12 51	2 29	12 26	2 57	11 45	3 43
30 FR	11 57 10	+14 49	5 31	18 23	5 18	18 37	5 01	18 54	4 38	19 18	4 00	19 56
121		1.0074	14 19	2 31	14 10	2 42	13 59	2 56	13 43	3 15	13 19	3 45

MAY 2004

5th Month   **31 days**

Coordinated Universal Time (Greenwich Mean Time)

NOTE: For rising and setting each day, numbers on first line indicate Sun; numbers on second line indicate Moon.

Degrees are North Latitude.

Moon Phases: FM = Full Moon; LQ = Last (Waning) Quarter; NM = New Moon; FQ = First (Waxing) Quarter

Sun's distance is in Astronomical Units

CAUTION: Must be converted to local time. For instructions see "Calculation of Rise Times," page 666.

Day of month, of week, of year	Sun on Meridian Moon Phase (h m s)	Sun's Decli-nation Distance (° ')	20° Rise Sun/Moon (h m)	20° Set Sun/Moon (h m)	30° Rise Sun/Moon (h m)	30° Set Sun/Moon (h m)	40° Rise Sun/Moon (h m)	40° Set Sun/Moon (h m)	50° Rise Sun/Moon (h m)	50° Set Sun/Moon (h m)	60° Rise Sun/Moon (h m)	60° Set Sun/Moon (h m)
1 SA	11 57 02	+ 15 07	5 31	18 24	5 17	18 38	5 00	18 55	4 36	19 19	3 57	19 59
122		1.0076	15 15	3 07	15 12	3 14	15 07	3 21	15 02	3 31	14 53	3 46
2 SU	11 56 56	+ 15 25	5 30	18 24	5 16	18 38	4 59	18 56	4 34	19 21	3 55	20 01
123		1.0079	16 13	3 44	16 15	3 45	16 18	3 45	16 23	3 46	16 30	3 47
3 MO	11 56 49	+ 15 43	5 30	18 24	5 15	18 39	4 57	18 57	4 32	19 22	3 52	20 04
124		1.0081	17 12	4 22	17 21	4 17	17 32	4 10	17 47	4 01	18 11	3 47
4 TU	11 56 44	+ 16 00	5 29	18 25	5 14	18 39	4 56	18 58	4 31	19 24	3 49	20 06
125	20 33 FM	1.0084	18 16	5 03	18 31	4 51	18 50	4 37	19 16	4 18	20 00	3 49
5 WE	11 56 39	+ 16 17	5 28	18 25	5 14	18 40	4 55	18 59	4 29	19 25	3 47	20 08
126		1.0086	19 23	5 48	19 44	5 31	20 10	5 09	20 48	4 40	21 55	3 52
6 TH	11 56 34	+ 16 34	5 28	18 25	5 13	18 41	4 54	19 00	4 27	19 27	3 44	20 11
127		1.0088	20 32	6 39	20 58	6 17	21 30	5 49	22 17	5 08	23 51	3 58
7 FR	11 56 30	+ 16 51	5 27	18 26	5 12	18 41	4 53	19 01	4 26	19 28	3 41	20 13
128		1.0091	21 41	7 37	22 09	7 11	22 44	6 38	23 37	5 49	none	4 13
8 SA	11 56 27	+ 17 07	5 27	18 26	5 11	18 42	4 52	19 02	4 24	19 30	3 39	20 16
129		1.0093	22 46	8 41	23 13	8 13	23 48	7 37	none	6 45	1 29	4 52
9 SU	11 56 24	+ 17 23	5 26	18 27	5 11	18 43	4 51	19 03	4 23	19 31	3 36	20 18
130		1.0096	23 43	9 47	none	9 20	none	8 47	0 39	7 56	2 23	6 13
10 MO	11 56 22	+ 17 39	5 26	18 27	5 10	18 43	4 49	19 04	4 21	19 33	3 34	20 21
131		1.0098	none	10 52	0 08	10 29	0 39	10 00	1 23	9 18	2 45	7 59
11 TU	11 56 20	+ 17 55	5 25	18 27	5 09	18 44	4 48	19 05	4 20	19 34	3 31	20 23
132	11 04 LQ	1.0100	0 34	11 55	0 54	11 36	1 19	11 13	1 54	10 41	2 53	9 45
12 WE	11 56 19	+ 18 10	5 25	18 28	5 08	18 45	4 47	19 06	4 18	19 36	3 29	20 25
133		1.0103	1 17	12 53	1 32	12 40	1 51	12 24	2 16	12 02	2 57	11 25
13 TH	11 56 18	+ 18 25	5 25	18 28	5 08	18 45	4 46	19 07	4 17	19 37	3 26	20 28
134		1.0105	1 55	13 48	2 05	13 40	2 17	13 31	2 33	13 19	2 58	12 59
14 FR	11 56 19	+ 18 39	5 24	18 29	5 07	18 46	4 46	19 08	4 15	19 38	3 24	20 30
135		1.0107	2 30	14 40	2 35	14 38	2 40	14 36	2 48	14 32	2 59	14 27
15 SA	11 56 19	+ 18 54	5 24	18 29	5 06	18 46	4 45	19 09	4 14	19 40	3 22	20 33
136		1.0110	3 04	15 31	3 03	15 34	3 02	15 39	3 01	15 44	2 59	15 53
16 SU	11 56 21	+ 19 08	5 23	18 29	5 06	18 47	4 44	19 10	4 12	19 41	3 19	20 35
137		1.0112	3 36	16 21	3 31	16 30	3 23	16 41	3 14	16 55	3 00	17 18
17 MO	11 56 22	+ 19 21	5 23	18 30	5 05	18 48	4 43	19 10	4 11	19 43	3 17	20 37
138		1.0114	4 10	17 12	3 59	17 26	3 46	17 43	3 28	18 07	3 00	18 45
18 TU	11 56 25	+ 19 35	5 23	18 30	5 04	18 48	4 42	19 11	4 10	19 44	3 15	20 40
139		1.0116	4 45	18 04	4 30	18 23	4 10	18 46	3 44	19 18	3 02	20 14
19 WE	11 56 28	+ 19 48	5 22	18 31	5 04	18 49	4 41	19 12	4 09	19 45	3 13	20 42
140	04 52 NM	1.0118	5 23	18 57	5 03	19 20	4 39	19 48	4 04	20 29	3 05	21 43
20 TH	11 56 31	+ 20 00	5 22	18 31	5 04	18 50	4 40	19 13	4 07	19 47	3 11	20 44
141		1.0120	6 05	19 51	5 42	20 16	5 12	20 49	4 29	21 36	3 13	23 10
21 FR	11 56 35	+ 20 13	5 22	18 31	5 03	18 50	4 40	19 14	4 06	19 48	3 09	20 46
142		1.0122	6 51	20 44	6 25	21 11	5 51	21 46	5 03	22 37	3 28	none
22 SA	11 56 40	+ 20 25	5 22	18 32	5 03	18 51	4 39	19 15	4 05	19 49	3 06	20 48
143		1.0124	7 40	21 35	7 13	22 02	6 38	22 37	5 46	23 28	3 59	0 24
23 SU	11 56 45	+ 20 36	5 21	18 32	5 02	18 52	4 38	19 16	4 04	19 50	3 04	20 51
144		1.0126	8 32	22 23	8 06	22 49	7 31	23 21	6 41	none	4 58	1 12
24 MO	11 56 51	+ 20 47	5 21	18 33	5 02	18 52	4 37	19 17	4 03	19 52	3 02	20 53
145		1.0128	9 26	23 08	9 02	23 30	8 30	23 58	7 45	0 08	6 18	1 36
25 TU	11 56 57	+ 20 58	5 21	18 33	5 01	18 53	4 37	19 18	4 02	19 53	3 01	20 55
146		1.0129	10 20	23 49	9 59	none	9 33	none	8 55	0 38	7 48	1 47
26 WE	11 57 03	+ 21 09	5 21	18 34	5 01	18 53	4 36	19 18	4 01	19 54	2 59	20 57
147		1.0131	11 14	none	10 58	0 07	10 37	0 30	10 09	1 01	9 20	1 53
27 TH	11 57 10	+ 21 19	5 21	18 34	5 01	18 54	4 36	19 19	4 00	19 55	2 57	20 59
148	07 57 FQ	1.0133	12 08	0 27	11 57	0 41	11 43	0 58	11 23	1 20	10 52	1 56
28 FR	11 57 18	+ 21 29	5 20	18 34	5 00	18 54	4 35	19 20	3 59	19 56	2 55	21 01
149		1.0134	13 02	1 04	12 56	1 12	12 49	1 22	12 39	1 36	12 23	1 57
29 SA	11 57 26	+ 21 38	5 20	18 35	5 00	18 55	4 35	19 21	3 58	19 57	2 54	21 03
150		1.0136	13 57	1 39	13 57	1 42	13 56	1 46	13 56	1 51	13 55	1 58
30 SU	11 57 34	+ 21 47	5 20	18 35	5 00	18 56	4 34	19 21	3 57	19 59	2 52	21 04
151		1.0138	14 54	2 15	15 00	2 13	15 07	2 09	15 16	2 05	15 32	1 59
31 MO	11 57 42	+ 21 56	5 20	18 35	5 00	18 56	4 34	19 22	3 56	20 00	2 50	21 06
152		1.0139	15 54	2 53	16 06	2 45	16 21	2 35	16 41	2 21	17 15	1 59

JUNE 2004

6th Month   **30 days**

Coordinated Universal Time (Greenwich Mean Time)

NOTE: For rising and setting each day, numbers on first line indicate Sun; numbers on second line indicate Moon.
Degrees are North Latitude.

Moon Phases: FM = Full Moon; LQ = Last (Waning) Quarter; NM = New Moon; FQ = First (Waxing) Quarter
Sun's distance is in Astronomical Units

CAUTION: Must be converted to local time. For instructions see "Calculation of Rise Times," page 666.

Day of month, of week, of year	Sun on Meridian Moon Phase h m s	Sun's Declination ° ' / Distance	20° Rise Sun / Moon h m	20° Set Sun / Moon h m	30° Rise Sun / Moon h m	30° Set Sun / Moon h m	40° Rise Sun / Moon h m	40° Set Sun / Moon h m	50° Rise Sun / Moon h m	50° Set Sun / Moon h m	60° Rise Sun / Moon h m	60° Set Sun / Moon h m
1 TU	11 57 52	+ 22 04	5 20	18 36	4 59	18 57	4 33	19 23	3 56	20 01	2 49	21 08
153		1.0141	16 59	3 36	17 17	3 21	17 39	3 04	18 11	2 40	19 06	2 01
2 WE	11 58 01	+ 22 12	5 20	18 36	4 59	18 57	4 33	19 24	3 55	20 02	2 47	21 10
154		1.0142	18 08	4 24	18 31	4 04	19 01	3 39	19 43	3 04	21 03	2 06
3 TH	11 58 11	+ 22 20	5 20	18 37	4 59	18 58	4 32	19 24	3 54	20 03	2 46	21 11
155	04 20 FM	1.0144	19 19	5 19	19 46	4 54	20 20	4 23	21 11	3 38	22 56	2 16
4 FR	11 58 21	+ 22 27	5 20	18 37	4 59	18 58	4 32	19 25	3 54	20 03	2 45	21 13
156		1.0145	20 28	6 21	20 56	5 54	21 31	5 19	22 24	4 27	none	2 41
5 SA	11 58 31	+ 22 34	5 20	18 37	4 59	18 59	4 32	19 26	3 53	20 04	2 44	21 14
157		1.0146	21 31	7 29	21 57	7 01	22 30	6 26	23 17	5 34	0 14	3 44
6 SU	11 58 42	+ 22 40	5 20	18 38	4 59	18 59	4 31	19 26	3 53	20 05	2 43	21 16
158		1.0148	22 26	8 37	22 48	8 13	23 16	7 41	23 54	6 55	0 49	5 26
7 MO	11 58 53	+ 22 46	5 20	18 38	4 58	19 00	4 31	19 27	3 52	20 06	2 41	21 17
159		1.0149	23 14	9 43	23 31	9 23	23 52	8 58	none	8 21	1 02	7 17
8 TU	11 59 05	+ 22 51	5 20	18 38	4 58	19 00	4 31	19 27	3 52	20 07	2 41	21 18
160		1.0150	23 55	10 45	none	10 30	none	10 12	0 20	9 46	1 07	9 03
9 WE	11 59 16	+ 22 57	5 20	18 39	4 58	19 00	4 31	19 28	3 51	20 07	2 40	21 20
161	20 02 LQ	1.0152	none	11 42	0 06	11 33	0 21	11 22	0 40	11 06	1 10	10 41
10 TH	11 59 28	+ 23 01	5 20	18 39	4 58	19 01	4 31	19 28	3 51	20 08	2 39	21 21
162		1.0153	0 32	12 36	0 38	12 33	0 45	12 28	0 55	12 22	1 11	12 13
11 FR	11 59 41	+ 23 06	5 20	18 39	4 58	19 01	4 31	19 29	3 51	20 09	2 38	21 22
163		1.0154	1 06	13 28	1 07	13 30	1 07	13 32	1 09	13 35	1 11	13 40
12 SA	11 59 53	+ 23 10	5 20	18 40	4 58	19 02	4 31	19 29	3 51	20 09	2 37	21 23
164		1.0155	1 39	14 18	1 34	14 25	1 29	14 34	1 22	14 46	1 11	15 05
13 SU	12 00 06	+ 23 13	5 20	18 40	4 58	19 02	4 31	19 30	3 50	20 10	2 37	21 24
165		1.0156	2 12	15 09	2 02	15 21	1 51	15 36	1 36	15 57	1 12	16 31
14 MO	12 00 18	+ 23 16	5 20	18 40	4 58	19 02	4 31	19 30	3 50	20 11	2 36	21 25
166		1.0157	2 46	16 00	2 32	16 17	2 15	16 38	1 51	17 08	1 13	17 58
15 TU	12 00 31	+ 23 19	5 20	18 41	4 58	19 03	4 31	19 31	3 50	20 11	2 36	21 25
167		1.0158	3 23	16 53	3 05	17 14	2 42	17 41	2 09	18 19	1 16	19 27
16 WE	12 00 44	+ 23 21	5 21	18 41	4 59	19 03	4 31	19 31	3 50	20 11	2 36	21 26
168		1.0159	4 04	17 46	3 41	18 11	3 13	18 42	2 33	19 28	1 22	20 55
17 TH	12 00 57	+ 23 23	5 21	18 41	4 59	19 03	4 31	19 31	3 50	20 12	2 36	21 27
169	20 27 NM	1.0160	4 48	18 39	4 23	19 06	3 50	19 40	3 03	20 31	1 34	22 14
18 FR	12 01 10	+ 23 25	5 21	18 41	4 59	19 03	4 31	19 32	3 50	20 12	2 36	21 27
170		1.0161	5 36	19 31	5 09	19 58	4 35	20 33	3 44	21 24	2 00	23 11
19 SA	12 01 24	+ 23 26	5 21	18 42	4 59	19 04	4 31	19 32	3 50	20 12	2 36	21 27
171		1.0162	6 28	20 21	6 01	20 47	5 26	21 20	4 35	22 08	2 50	23 41
20 SU	12 01 37	+ 23 26	5 21	18 42	4 59	19 04	4 31	19 32	3 51	20 13	2 36	21 28
172		1.0162	7 21	21 06	6 56	21 30	6 24	21 59	5 37	22 41	4 05	23 56
21 MO	12 01 50	+ 23 26	5 22	18 42	4 59	19 04	4 31	19 32	3 51	20 13	2 36	21 28
173		1.0163	8 15	21 48	7 53	22 08	7 25	22 32	6 45	23 06	5 33	none
22 TU	12 02 03	+ 23 26	5 22	18 42	5 00	19 04	4 32	19 32	3 51	20 13	2 36	21 28
174		1.0164	9 09	22 27	8 51	22 42	8 29	23 00	7 57	23 26	7 04	0 03
23 WE	12 02 16	+ 23 26	5 22	18 42	5 00	19 05	4 32	19 33	3 51	20 13	2 36	21 28
175		1.0164	10 02	23 03	9 49	23 13	9 33	23 26	9 11	23 42	8 34	0 06
24 TH	12 02 29	+ 23 25	5 22	18 43	5 00	19 05	4 32	19 33	3 52	20 13	2 37	21 28
176		1.0165	10 55	23 38	10 47	23 43	10 37	23 49	10 24	23 57	10 03	0 08
25 FR	12 02 42	+ 23 23	5 23	18 43	5 01	19 05	4 32	19 33	3 52	20 13	2 38	21 28
177	19 08 FQ	1.0165	11 48	none	11 45	none	11 42	none	11 39	none	11 33	0 09
26 SA	12 02 54	+ 23 21	5 23	18 43	5 01	19 05	4 33	19 33	3 52	20 13	2 38	21 27
178		1.0165	12 42	0 12	12 45	0 12	12 49	0 11	12 55	0 11	13 04	0 09
27 SU	12 03 07	+ 23 19	5 23	18 43	5 01	19 05	4 33	19 33	3 53	20 13	2 39	21 27
179		1.0166	13 39	0 48	13 48	0 42	13 59	0 35	14 15	0 25	14 40	0 10
28 MO	12 03 19	+ 23 16	5 23	18 43	5 01	19 05	4 34	19 33	3 53	20 13	2 40	21 27
180		1.0166	14 39	1 27	14 54	1 15	15 13	1 01	15 40	0 42	16 24	0 11
29 TU	12 03 31	+ 23 13	5 24	18 43	5 02	19 05	4 34	19 33	3 54	20 13	2 40	21 26
181		1.0166	15 45	2 11	16 05	1 53	16 31	1 32	17 09	1 02	18 16	0 14
30 WE	12 03 43	+ 23 10	5 24	18 43	5 02	19 05	4 34	19 33	3 55	20 13	2 41	21 25
182		1.0166	16 54	3 01	17 19	2 39	17 51	2 10	18 38	1 31	20 11	0 20

JULY 2004

7th Month   31 days

Coordinated Universal Time (Greenwich Mean Time)

NOTE: For rising and setting each day, numbers on first line indicate Sun; numbers on second line indicate Moon.

Degrees are North Latitude.

Moon Phases: FM = Full Moon; LQ = Last (Waning) Quarter; NM = New Moon; FQ = First (Waxing) Quarter

Sun's distance is in Astronomical Units

CAUTION: Must be converted to local time. For instructions see "Calculation of Rise Times," page 666.

Day of month, of week, of year	Sun on Meridian / Moon Phase (h m s)	Sun's Decli-nation (° ') / Distance	20° Rise Sun/Moon (h m)	20° Set Sun/Moon (h m)	30° Rise Sun/Moon (h m)	30° Set Sun/Moon (h m)	40° Rise Sun/Moon (h m)	40° Set Sun/Moon (h m)	50° Rise Sun/Moon (h m)	50° Set Sun/Moon (h m)	60° Rise Sun/Moon (h m)	60° Set Sun/Moon (h m)
1 TH	12 03 54	+23 06	5 24	18 43	5 03	19 05	4 35	19 33	3 55	20 12	2 42	21 25
183		1.0167	18 04	3 59	18 31	3 33	19 07	3 00	19 59	2 11	21 50	0 36
2 FR	12 04 05	+23 02	5 25	18 44	5 03	19 05	4 35	19 32	3 56	20 12	2 44	21 24
184	11 09 FM	1.0167	19 11	5 05	19 38	4 37	20 13	4 02	21 03	3 09	22 46	1 17
3 SA	12 04 16	+22 57	5 25	18 44	5 03	19 05	4 36	19 32	3 57	20 12	2 45	21 23
185		1.0167	20 11	6 14	20 35	5 48	21 06	5 14	21 49	4 25	23 07	2 44
4 SU	12 04 27	+22 52	5 25	18 44	5 04	19 05	4 37	19 32	3 57	20 11	2 46	21 22
186		1.0167	21 04	7 24	21 23	7 01	21 47	6 33	22 20	5 52	23 16	4 36
5 MO	12 04 37	+22 46	5 26	18 44	5 04	19 05	4 37	19 32	3 58	20 11	2 47	21 21
187		1.0167	21 49	8 29	22 03	8 12	22 20	7 51	22 43	7 21	23 19	6 29
6 TU	12 04 47	+22 41	5 26	18 44	5 05	19 05	4 38	19 32	3 59	20 10	2 49	21 20
188		1.0167	22 29	9 31	22 37	9 19	22 47	9 05	23 00	8 46	23 21	8 14
7 WE	12 04 57	+22 34	5 26	18 44	5 05	19 05	4 38	19 31	4 00	20 10	2 50	21 19
189		1.0167	23 05	10 28	23 07	10 22	23 11	10 15	23 15	10 06	23 22	9 51
8 TH	12 05 06	+22 28	5 27	18 43	5 06	19 04	4 39	19 31	4 01	20 09	2 52	21 17
190		1.0167	23 39	11 21	23 36	11 22	23 33	11 22	23 29	11 22	23 22	11 22
9 FR	12 05 15	+22 21	5 27	18 43	5 06	19 04	4 40	19 31	4 02	20 08	2 53	21 16
191	07 34 LQ	1.0167	none	12 13	none	12 19	23 55	12 26	23 42	12 35	23 23	12 49
10 SA	12 05 23	+22 13	5 27	18 43	5 07	19 04	4 40	19 30	4 03	20 08	2 55	21 15
192		1.0167	0 12	13 05	0 05	13 15	none	13 29	23 57	13 47	23 24	14 16
11 SU	12 05 31	+22 05	5 28	18 43	5 07	19 04	4 41	19 30	4 04	20 07	2 57	21 13
193		1.0166	0 47	13 56	0 34	14 12	0 18	14 31	none	14 58	23 26	15 43
12 MO	12 05 39	+21 57	5 28	18 43	5 08	19 03	4 42	19 29	4 05	20 06	2 59	21 11
194		1.0166	1 23	14 48	1 06	15 08	0 44	15 33	0 14	16 09	23 31	17 12
13 TU	12 05 46	+21 49	5 28	18 43	5 08	19 03	4 42	19 29	4 06	20 05	3 00	21 10
195		1.0166	2 02	15 41	1 41	16 05	1 14	16 35	0 36	17 19	23 40	18 41
14 WE	12 05 52	+21 40	5 29	18 43	5 09	19 03	4 43	19 28	4 07	20 04	3 02	21 08
196		1.0165	2 46	16 35	2 21	17 01	1 49	17 34	1 04	18 24	none	20 04
15 TH	12 05 59	+21 30	5 29	18 43	5 09	19 02	4 44	19 28	4 08	20 03	3 04	21 06
197		1.0165	3 33	17 27	3 06	17 54	2 32	18 29	1 42	19 21	0 01	21 08
16 FR	12 06 04	+21 21	5 30	18 42	5 10	19 02	4 45	19 27	4 09	20 03	3 06	21 05
198		1.0164	4 23	18 17	3 56	18 44	3 21	19 18	2 30	20 07	0 43	21 46
17 SA	12 06 10	+21 11	5 30	18 42	5 10	19 02	4 45	19 26	4 10	20 02	3 08	21 03
199	11 24 NM	1.0164	5 16	19 05	4 51	19 29	4 18	19 59	3 29	20 43	1 52	22 03
18 SU	12 06 14	+21 00	5 30	18 42	5 11	19 01	4 46	19 26	4 11	20 00	3 10	21 01
200		1.0163	6 11	19 48	5 48	20 08	5 19	20 34	4 36	21 11	3 18	22 12
19 MO	12 06 18	+20 49	5 31	18 42	5 11	19 01	4 47	19 25	4 12	19 59	3 12	20 59
201		1.0163	7 05	20 27	6 46	20 44	6 22	21 04	5 48	21 32	4 49	22 16
20 TU	12 06 22	+20 38	5 31	18 41	5 12	19 00	4 48	19 24	4 14	19 58	3 14	20 57
202		1.0162	7 59	21 04	7 44	21 16	7 26	21 30	7 01	21 49	6 20	22 18
21 WE	12 06 25	+20 27	5 31	18 41	5 13	19 00	4 49	19 24	4 15	19 57	3 16	20 55
203		1.0161	8 51	21 39	8 42	21 45	8 31	21 53	8 15	22 04	7 50	22 20
22 TH	12 06 27	+20 15	5 32	18 41	5 13	18 59	4 50	19 23	4 16	19 56	3 19	20 53
204		1.0160	9 44	22 13	9 40	22 14	9 35	22 16	9 28	22 17	9 18	22 20
23 FR	12 06 29	+20 03	5 32	18 41	5 14	18 59	4 50	19 22	4 17	19 55	3 21	20 51
205		1.0159	10 36	22 48	10 38	22 43	10 40	22 38	10 43	22 31	10 47	22 20
24 SA	12 06 30	+19 50	5 33	18 40	5 14	18 58	4 51	19 21	4 19	19 53	3 23	20 48
206		1.0158	11 31	23 24	11 38	23 14	11 47	23 02	12 00	22 46	12 19	22 21
25 SU	12 06 30	+19 38	5 33	18 40	5 15	18 58	4 52	19 20	4 20	19 52	3 25	20 46
207	03 37 FQ	1.0157	12 28	none	12 41	23 49	12 57	23 30	13 20	23 04	13 57	22 23
26 MO	12 06 30	+19 24	5 33	18 39	5 16	18 57	4 53	19 19	4 21	19 51	3 27	20 44
208		1.0156	13 29	0 05	13 48	none	14 11	none	14 45	23 28	15 42	22 27
27 TU	12 06 30	+19 11	5 34	18 39	5 16	18 56	4 54	19 18	4 23	19 49	3 30	20 42
209		1.0155	14 35	0 50	14 58	0 30	15 28	0 04	16 12	none	17 34	22 37
28 WE	12 06 28	+18 57	5 34	18 39	5 17	18 56	4 55	19 17	4 24	19 48	3 32	20 39
210		1.0154	15 43	1 43	16 09	1 18	16 44	0 47	17 35	0 01	19 21	23 02
29 TH	12 06 26	+18 43	5 34	18 38	5 17	18 55	4 56	19 17	4 25	19 47	3 34	20 37
211		1.0153	16 50	2 44	17 18	2 16	17 53	1 41	18 46	0 50	20 37	none
30 FR	12 06 24	+18 29	5 35	18 38	5 18	18 54	4 57	19 16	4 27	19 45	3 37	20 34
212		1.0152	17 53	3 51	18 19	3 23	18 52	2 48	19 39	1 56	21 10	0 06
31 SA	12 06 20	+18 14	5 35	18 37	5 19	18 54	4 58	19 14	4 28	19 44	3 39	20 32
213	18 05 FM	1.0150	18 50	5 00	19 11	4 35	19 39	4 04	20 17	3 18	21 23	1 49

AUGUST 2004

8th Month   **31 days**

Coordinated Universal Time (Greenwich Mean Time)

NOTE: For rising and setting each day, numbers on first line indicate Sun; numbers on second line indicate Moon.

Degrees are North Latitude.

Moon Phases: FM = Full Moon; LQ = Last (Waning) Quarter; NM = New Moon; FQ = First (Waxing) Quarter

Sun's distance is in Astronomical Units

CAUTION: Must be converted to local time. For instructions see "Calculation of Rise Times," page 666.

Day of month, of week, of year	Sun on Meridian Moon Phase h m s	Sun's Decli-nation ° ' Distance	20° Rise Sun Moon h m	20° Set Sun Moon h m	30° Rise Sun Moon h m	30° Set Sun Moon h m	40° Rise Sun Moon h m	40° Set Sun Moon h m	50° Rise Sun Moon h m	50° Set Sun Moon h m	60° Rise Sun Moon h m	60° Set Sun Moon h m
1 SU	12 06 17	+ 17 59	5 36	18 37	5 19	18 53	4 59	19 13	4 30	19 42	3 41	20 30
214		1.0149	19 39	6 08	19 55	5 48	20 15	5 23	20 43	4 48	21 29	3 45
2 MO	12 06 12	+ 17 44	5 36	18 36	5 20	18 52	4 59	19 12	4 31	19 40	3 44	20 27
215		1.0148	20 22	7 13	20 32	6 59	20 45	6 41	21 03	6 17	21 31	5 36
3 TU	12 06 07	+ 17 28	5 36	18 36	5 20	18 52	5 00	19 11	4 32	19 39	3 46	20 25
216		1.0147	21 00	8 13	21 05	8 05	21 11	7 55	21 19	7 41	21 32	7 19
4 WE	12 06 02	+ 17 12	5 37	18 35	5 21	18 51	5 01	19 10	4 34	19 37	3 48	20 22
217		1.0145	21 36	9 10	21 35	9 08	21 34	9 05	21 34	9 01	21 32	8 55
5 TH	12 05 56	+ 16 56	5 37	18 35	5 22	18 50	5 02	19 09	4 35	19 36	3 51	20 19
218		1.0144	22 10	10 04	22 04	10 07	21 57	10 12	21 47	10 17	21 33	10 26
6 FR	12 05 49	+ 16 40	5 37	18 34	5 22	18 49	5 03	19 08	4 37	19 34	3 53	20 17
219		1.0142	22 45	10 57	22 34	11 05	22 20	11 17	22 02	11 32	21 33	11 55
7 SA	12 05 42	+ 16 23	5 38	18 34	5 23	18 48	5 04	19 07	4 38	19 32	3 56	20 14
220	22 01 LQ	1.0141	23 21	11 49	23 05	12 03	22 45	12 20	22 18	12 45	21 35	13 24
8 SU	12 05 34	+ 16 06	5 38	18 33	5 23	18 47	5 05	19 05	4 40	19 30	3 58	20 11
221		1.0140	24 00	12 42	23 39	13 00	23 14	13 24	22 39	13 57	21 39	14 54
9 MO	12 05 25	+ 15 49	5 38	18 32	5 24	18 46	5 06	19 04	4 41	19 29	4 00	20 09
222		1.0138	none	13 35	none	13 58	23 48	14 27	23 04	15 08	21 46	16 25
10 TU	12 05 16	+ 15 32	5 39	18 32	5 25	18 46	5 07	19 03	4 43	19 27	4 03	20 06
223		1.0136	0 42	14 29	0 18	14 54	none	15 27	23 38	16 15	22 01	17 51
11 WE	12 05 07	+ 15 14	5 39	18 31	5 25	18 45	5 08	19 02	4 44	19 25	4 05	20 03
224		1.0135	1 28	15 22	1 01	15 49	0 28	16 24	none	17 15	22 34	19 04
12 TH	12 04 56	+ 14 56	5 39	18 30	5 26	18 44	5 09	19 00	4 46	19 23	4 08	20 01
225		1.0133	2 17	16 13	1 50	16 40	1 15	17 14	0 23	18 05	23 36	19 50
13 FR	12 04 46	+ 14 38	5 39	18 30	5 26	18 43	5 10	18 59	4 47	19 21	4 10	19 58
226		1.0131	3 10	17 01	2 43	17 26	2 09	17 58	1 19	18 45	none	20 12
14 SA	12 04 35	+ 14 19	5 40	18 29	5 27	18 42	5 11	18 58	4 49	19 20	4 12	19 55
227		1.0130	4 04	17 46	3 40	18 08	3 09	18 35	2 24	19 14	0 59	20 22
15 SU	12 04 23	+ 14 01	5 40	18 28	5 27	18 41	5 12	18 56	4 50	19 18	4 15	19 52
228		1.0128	4 59	18 27	4 39	18 45	4 13	19 07	3 36	19 37	2 31	20 27
16 MO	12 04 11	+ 13 42	5 40	18 28	5 28	18 40	5 13	18 55	4 51	19 16	4 17	19 49
229	01 24 NM	1.0126	5 54	19 05	5 38	19 18	5 18	19 34	4 50	19 56	4 03	20 30
17 TU	12 03 58	+ 13 23	5 41	18 27	5 29	18 39	5 14	18 54	4 53	19 14	4 20	19 47
230		1.0124	6 47	19 40	6 36	19 48	6 23	19 58	6 04	20 11	5 35	20 31
18 WE	12 03 45	+ 13 04	5 41	18 26	5 29	18 38	5 15	18 52	4 54	19 12	4 22	19 44
231		1.0122	7 40	20 15	7 35	20 17	7 28	20 21	7 19	20 25	7 04	20 31
19 TH	12 03 31	+ 12 44	5 41	18 26	5 30	18 37	5 16	18 51	4 56	19 10	4 24	19 41
232		1.0120	8 33	20 49	8 33	20 46	8 33	20 43	8 33	20 38	8 34	20 31
20 FR	12 03 16	+ 12 24	5 41	18 25	5 30	18 36	5 17	18 49	4 57	19 08	4 27	19 38
233		1.0118	9 27	21 25	9 33	21 17	9 40	21 06	9 50	20 53	10 05	20 31
21 SA	12 03 02	+ 12 04	5 42	18 24	5 31	18 35	5 18	18 48	4 59	19 06	4 29	19 35
234		1.0116	10 23	22 03	10 34	21 50	10 49	21 33	11 09	21 09	11 41	20 33
22 SU	12 02 47	+ 11 44	5 42	18 23	5 32	18 34	5 18	18 46	5 00	19 04	4 32	19 32
235		1.0114	11 22	22 46	11 39	22 27	12 01	22 04	12 31	21 30	13 22	20 35
23 MO	12 02 31	+ 11 24	5 42	18 22	5 32	18 32	5 19	18 45	5 02	19 02	4 34	19 29
236	10 12 FQ	1.0112	12 25	23 35	12 47	23 12	13 15	22 42	13 56	21 59	15 10	20 42
24 TU	12 02 15	+ 11 04	5 43	18 22	5 33	18 31	5 20	18 43	5 03	19 00	4 36	19 26
237		1.0110	13 30	none	13 56	none	14 29	23 30	15 18	22 40	16 58	20 58
25 WE	12 01 58	+ 10 43	5 43	18 21	5 33	18 30	5 21	18 42	5 05	18 58	4 39	19 23
238		1.0107	14 36	0 32	15 04	0 05	15 39	none	16 33	23 37	18 27	21 42
26 TH	12 01 41	+ 10 22	5 43	18 20	5 34	18 29	5 22	18 40	5 06	18 56	4 41	19 20
239		1.0105	15 39	1 34	16 06	1 06	16 40	0 30	17 31	none	19 14	23 10
27 FR	12 01 24	+ 10 01	5 43	18 19	5 34	18 28	5 23	18 39	5 08	18 54	4 44	19 18
240		1.0103	16 37	2 41	17 01	2 15	17 31	1 41	18 14	0 51	19 32	none
28 SA	12 01 06	+9 40	5 44	18 18	5 35	18 27	5 24	18 37	5 09	18 52	4 46	19 15
241		1.0101	17 28	3 48	17 47	3 26	18 11	2 58	18 44	2 17	19 39	1 02
29 SU	12 00 48	+9 19	5 44	18 18	5 35	18 26	5 25	18 36	5 11	18 50	4 48	19 12
242		1.0098	18 13	4 54	18 27	4 37	18 43	4 16	19 06	3 46	19 41	2 55
30 MO	12 00 29	+8 57	5 44	18 17	5 36	18 25	5 26	18 34	5 12	18 48	4 51	19 09
243	02 22 FM	1.0096	18 53	5 56	19 01	5 45	19 10	5 31	19 23	5 12	19 43	4 41
31 TU	12 00 11	+8 36	5 44	18 16	5 37	18 23	5 27	18 33	5 14	18 46	4 53	19 06
244		1.0094	19 30	6 54	19 32	6 50	19 35	6 43	19 38	6 35	19 43	6 21

SEPTEMBER 2004

9th Month   **30 days**

Coordinated Universal Time (Greenwich Mean Time)

NOTE: For rising and setting each day, numbers on first line indicate Sun; numbers on second line indicate Moon.

Degrees are North Latitude.

Moon Phases: FM = Full Moon; LQ = Last (Waning) Quarter; NM = New Moon; FQ = First (Waxing) Quarter

Sun's distance is in Astronomical Units

CAUTION: Must be converted to local time. For instructions see "Calculation of Rise Times," page 666.

Day of month, of week, of year	Sun on Meridian / Moon Phase (h m s)	Sun's Declination ° ' / Distance	20° Rise Sun/Moon (h m)	20° Set Sun/Moon (h m)	30° Rise Sun/Moon (h m)	30° Set Sun/Moon (h m)	40° Rise Sun/Moon (h m)	40° Set Sun/Moon (h m)	50° Rise Sun/Moon (h m)	50° Set Sun/Moon (h m)	60° Rise Sun/Moon (h m)	60° Set Sun/Moon (h m)
1 WE	11 59 52	+8 14	5 44	18 15	5 37	18 22	5 28	18 31	5 15	18 43	4 55	19 03
245		1.0091	20 06	7 50	20 02	7 51	19 58	7 52	19 52	7 54	19 43	7 56
2 TH	11 59 32	+7 52	5 45	18 14	5 38	18 21	5 29	18 30	5 17	18 41	4 58	19 00
246		1.0089	20 41	8 45	20 32	8 51	20 21	8 59	20 06	9 11	19 43	9 28
3 FR	11 59 13	+7 30	5 45	18 13	5 38	18 20	5 30	18 28	5 18	18 39	5 00	18 57
247		1.0086	21 17	9 38	21 03	9 50	20 45	10 05	20 22	10 26	19 44	10 59
4 SA	11 58 53	+7 08	5 45	18 12	5 39	18 19	5 31	18 26	5 20	18 37	5 03	18 54
248		1.0084	21 55	10 32	21 36	10 49	21 13	11 10	20 40	11 40	19 47	12 31
5 SU	11 58 33	+6 46	5 45	18 11	5 39	18 17	5 32	18 25	5 21	18 35	5 05	18 51
249		1.0082	22 36	11 26	22 13	11 47	21 45	12 15	21 04	12 54	19 51	14 03
6 MO	11 58 12	+6 24	5 46	18 11	5 40	18 16	5 33	18 23	5 23	18 33	5 07	18 48
250	15 11 LQ	1.0079	23 21	12 20	22 55	12 45	22 22	13 17	21 35	14 04	20 02	15 34
7 TU	11 57 52	+6 01	5 46	18 10	5 40	18 15	5 34	18 21	5 24	18 30	5 10	18 45
251		1.0077	none	13 14	23 42	13 41	23 07	14 16	22 15	15 07	20 27	16 55
8 WE	11 57 31	+5 39	5 46	18 09	5 41	18 14	5 35	18 20	5 26	18 28	5 12	18 42
252		1.0074	0 10	14 06	none	14 34	23 59	15 09	23 07	16 01	21 17	17 52
9 TH	11 57 11	+5 16	5 46	18 08	5 41	18 12	5 35	18 18	5 27	18 26	5 14	18 39
253		1.0072	1 01	14 55	0 34	15 22	none	15 55	none	16 44	22 35	18 20
10 FR	11 56 50	+4 54	5 46	18 07	5 42	18 11	5 36	18 17	5 29	18 24	5 17	18 35
254		1.0069	1 55	15 41	1 30	16 05	0 57	16 35	0 09	17 17	none	18 33
11 SA	11 56 29	+4 31	5 47	18 06	5 42	18 10	5 37	18 15	5 30	18 22	5 19	18 32
255		1.0067	2 50	16 24	2 28	16 43	2 00	17 08	1 19	17 42	0 05	18 39
12 SU	11 56 08	+4 08	5 47	18 05	5 43	18 09	5 38	18 13	5 32	18 20	5 21	18 29
256		1.0064	3 45	17 03	3 27	17 18	3 04	17 36	2 33	18 02	1 39	18 42
13 MO	11 55 46	+3 45	5 47	18 04	5 44	18 08	5 39	18 12	5 33	18 17	5 24	18 26
257		1.0061	4 39	17 39	4 26	17 49	4 10	18 01	3 48	18 18	3 12	18 43
14 TU	11 55 25	+3 22	5 47	18 03	5 44	18 06	5 40	18 10	5 35	18 15	5 26	18 23
258	14 29 NM	1.0059	5 33	18 15	5 25	18 19	5 16	18 25	5 04	18 32	4 44	18 43
15 WE	11 55 04	+2 59	5 47	18 02	5 45	18 05	5 41	18 08	5 36	18 13	5 28	18 20
259		1.0056	6 27	18 49	6 25	18 48	6 23	18 47	6 19	18 45	6 15	18 43
16 TH	11 54 43	+2 36	5 48	18 02	5 45	18 04	5 42	18 07	5 38	18 11	5 31	18 17
260		1.0053	7 21	19 25	7 25	19 18	7 30	19 10	7 37	18 59	7 47	18 43
17 FR	11 54 21	+2 13	5 48	18 01	5 46	18 03	5 43	18 05	5 39	18 09	5 33	18 14
261		1.0051	8 17	20 03	8 27	19 51	8 39	19 36	8 56	19 15	9 23	18 43
18 SA	11 54 00	+1 49	5 48	18 00	5 46	18 01	5 44	18 03	5 41	18 06	5 35	18 11
262		1.0048	9 16	20 45	9 32	20 27	9 52	20 05	10 19	19 35	11 05	18 45
19 SU	11 53 39	+1 26	5 48	17 59	5 47	18 00	5 45	18 02	5 42	18 04	5 38	18 08
263		1.0045	10 18	21 32	10 39	21 10	11 06	20 41	11 44	20 01	12 52	18 49
20 MO	11 53 17	+1 03	5 48	17 58	5 47	17 59	5 46	18 00	5 44	18 02	5 40	18 05
264		1.0042	11 23	22 26	11 48	22 00	12 21	21 26	13 08	20 37	14 42	19 01
21 TU	11 52 56	+0 39	5 49	17 57	5 48	17 58	5 47	17 58	5 45	18 00	5 42	18 02
265	15 54 FQ	1.0039	12 28	23 26	12 56	22 58	13 32	22 22	14 25	21 28	16 20	19 32
22 WE	11 52 35	+0 16	5 49	17 56	5 48	17 56	5 48	17 57	5 47	17 58	5 45	17 59
266		1.0037	13 31	none	13 59	none	14 35	23 28	15 27	22 36	17 19	20 45
23 TH	11 52 14	−0 07	5 49	17 55	5 49	17 55	5 49	17 55	5 48	17 55	5 47	17 56
267		1.0034	14 29	0 30	14 55	0 03	15 27	none	16 13	23 56	17 42	22 30
24 FR	11 51 53	−0 31	5 49	17 54	5 50	17 54	5 50	17 53	5 50	17 53	5 50	17 53
268		1.0031	15 21	1 35	15 42	1 11	16 09	0 41	16 46	none	17 50	none
25 SA	11 51 32	−0 54	5 50	17 53	5 50	17 53	5 51	17 52	5 51	17 51	5 52	17 50
269		1.0028	16 07	2 40	16 23	2 21	16 43	1 57	17 10	1 22	17 53	0 22
26 SU	11 51 12	−1 17	5 50	17 52	5 51	17 51	5 52	17 50	5 53	17 49	5 54	17 47
270		1.0025	16 48	3 42	16 59	3 28	17 11	3 11	17 28	2 48	17 55	2 09
27 MO	11 50 51	−1 41	5 50	17 51	5 51	17 50	5 53	17 49	5 54	17 47	5 57	17 44
271		1.0022	17 26	4 41	17 30	4 33	17 36	4 24	17 43	4 10	17 55	3 50
28 TU	11 50 31	−2 04	5 50	17 51	5 52	17 49	5 54	17 47	5 56	17 44	5 59	17 41
272	13 09 FM	1.0019	18 02	5 37	18 00	5 35	17 59	5 33	17 57	5 30	17 55	5 25
29 WE	11 50 11	−2 27	5 50	17 50	5 52	17 48	5 55	17 45	5 57	17 42	6 01	17 38
273		1.0016	18 37	6 32	18 30	6 36	18 22	6 41	18 11	6 48	17 55	6 58
30 TH	11 49 51	−2 51	5 51	17 49	5 53	17 46	5 55	17 44	5 59	17 40	6 04	17 35
274		1.0014	19 12	7 26	19 00	7 36	18 46	7 48	18 26	8 04	17 55	8 30

OCTOBER 2004

10th Month   **31 days**

Coordinated Universal Time (Greenwich Mean Time)

NOTE: For rising and setting each day, numbers on first line indicate Sun; numbers on second line indicate Moon.

Degrees are North Latitude.

Moon Phases: FM = Full Moon; LQ = Last (Waning) Quarter; NM = New Moon; FQ = First (Waxing) Quarter

Sun's distance is in Astronomical Units

CAUTION: Must be converted to local time. For instructions see "Calculation of Rise Times," page 666.

Day of month, of week, of year	Sun on Meridian Moon Phase h m s	Sun's Declination ° ' Distance	20° Rise Sun / Moon h m	20° Set Sun / Moon h m	30° Rise Sun / Moon h m	30° Set Sun / Moon h m	40° Rise Sun / Moon h m	40° Set Sun / Moon h m	50° Rise Sun / Moon h m	50° Set Sun / Moon h m	60° Rise Sun / Moon h m	60° Set Sun / Moon h m
1 FR	11 49 32	−3 14	5 51	17 48	5 53	17 45	5 56	17 42	6 00	17 38	6 06	17 32
275		1.0011	19 50	8 20	19 33	8 35	19 12	8 54	18 43	9 20	17 56	10 03
2 SA	11 49 13	−3 37	5 51	17 47	5 54	17 44	5 57	17 40	6 02	17 36	6 08	17 29
276		1.0008	20 30	9 15	20 09	9 34	19 42	9 59	19 04	10 35	17 59	11 37
3 SU	11 48 54	−4 00	5 51	17 46	5 55	17 43	5 58	17 39	6 03	17 34	6 11	17 26
277		1.0005	21 14	10 10	20 49	10 33	20 17	11 04	19 32	11 48	18 07	13 11
4 MO	11 48 36	−4 24	5 52	17 45	5 55	17 42	5 59	17 37	6 05	17 31	6 13	17 23
278		1.0002	22 01	11 04	21 34	11 31	20 59	12 05	20 08	12 55	18 23	14 39
5 TU	11 48 18	−4 47	5 52	17 44	5 56	17 40	6 00	17 36	6 06	17 29	6 16	17 20
279		1.0000	22 52	11 57	22 24	12 25	21 48	13 01	20 55	13 54	19 01	15 48
6 WE	11 48 00	−5 10	5 52	17 44	5 56	17 39	6 01	17 34	6 08	17 27	6 18	17 17
280	10 12 LQ	.9997	23 45	12 48	23 18	13 15	22 44	13 50	21 54	14 41	20 10	16 26
7 TH	11 47 43	−5 33	5 52	17 43	5 57	17 38	6 02	17 32	6 10	17 25	6 20	17 14
281		.9994	none	13 35	none	14 00	23 45	14 32	23 00	15 18	21 37	16 43
8 FR	11 47 26	−5 56	5 53	17 42	5 58	17 37	6 03	17 31	6 11	17 23	6 23	17 11
282		.9991	0 39	14 19	0 15	14 40	none	15 07	none	15 45	23 10	16 50
9 SA	11 47 10	−6 19	5 53	17 41	5 58	17 36	6 04	17 29	6 13	17 21	6 25	17 08
283		.9988	1 33	14 59	1 13	15 16	0 48	15 37	0 12	16 06	none	16 54
10 SU	11 46 54	−6 41	5 53	17 40	5 59	17 35	6 05	17 28	6 14	17 19	6 28	17 05
284		.9985	2 28	15 36	2 12	15 48	1 53	16 03	1 27	16 23	0 43	16 55
11 MO	11 46 38	−7 04	5 54	17 39	5 59	17 33	6 07	17 26	6 16	17 17	6 30	17 02
285		.9983	3 21	16 11	3 11	16 18	2 59	16 27	2 42	16 38	2 15	16 55
12 TU	11 46 24	−7 27	5 54	17 39	6 00	17 32	6 08	17 25	6 17	17 14	6 33	16 59
286		.9980	4 15	16 46	4 11	16 48	4 05	16 50	3 58	16 52	3 47	16 55
13 WE	11 46 09	−7 49	5 54	17 38	6 01	17 31	6 09	17 23	6 19	17 12	6 35	16 56
287		.9977	5 10	17 22	5 11	17 18	5 13	17 13	5 16	17 06	5 20	16 55
14 TH	11 45 56	−8 11	5 55	17 37	6 01	17 30	6 10	17 22	6 21	17 10	6 38	16 53
288	02 48 NM	.9974	6 06	18 00	6 14	17 50	6 23	17 37	6 36	17 21	6 56	16 55
15 FR	11 45 42	−8 34	5 55	17 36	6 02	17 29	6 11	17 20	6 22	17 08	6 40	16 50
289		.9971	7 06	18 41	7 19	18 25	7 36	18 06	7 59	17 39	8 38	16 56
16 SA	11 45 30	−8 56	5 55	17 36	6 03	17 28	6 12	17 19	6 24	17 06	6 42	16 47
290		.9968	8 08	19 28	8 28	19 06	8 52	18 40	9 26	18 03	10 27	16 59
17 SU	11 45 17	−9 18	5 56	17 35	6 03	17 27	6 13	17 17	6 25	17 04	6 45	16 44
291		.9966	9 14	20 20	9 38	19 55	10 09	19 22	10 54	18 36	12 20	17 07
18 MO	11 45 06	−9 40	5 56	17 34	6 04	17 26	6 14	17 16	6 27	17 02	6 47	16 42
292		.9963	10 21	21 19	10 48	20 51	11 23	20 15	12 16	19 22	14 07	17 30
19 TU	11 44 55	−10 01	5 56	17 33	6 05	17 25	6 15	17 14	6 29	17 00	6 50	16 39
293		.9960	11 26	22 23	11 54	21 55	12 30	21 19	13 24	20 26	15 21	18 29
20 WE	11 44 45	−10 23	5 57	17 33	6 05	17 24	6 16	17 13	6 30	16 58	6 52	16 36
294	21 59 FQ	.9957	12 25	23 28	12 52	23 03	13 26	22 31	14 15	21 43	15 51	20 09
21 TH	11 44 35	−10 44	5 57	17 32	6 06	17 23	6 17	17 12	6 32	16 56	6 55	16 33
295		.9954	13 19	none	13 42	none	14 10	23 45	14 50	23 07	16 02	21 59
22 FR	11 44 26	−11 06	5 57	17 31	6 07	17 22	6 18	17 10	6 34	16 55	6 57	16 30
296		.9951	14 06	0 33	14 23	0 12	14 45	none	15 16	none	16 06	23 46
23 SA	11 44 18	−11 27	5 58	17 31	6 07	17 21	6 19	17 09	6 35	16 53	7 00	16 28
297		.9948	14 47	1 34	14 59	1 19	15 15	0 59	15 35	0 32	16 07	none
24 SU	11 44 10	−11 48	5 58	17 30	6 08	17 20	6 20	17 07	6 37	16 51	7 03	16 25
298		.9946	15 25	2 33	15 31	2 23	15 40	2 11	15 51	1 54	16 07	1 27
25 MO	11 44 03	−12 08	5 59	17 29	6 09	17 19	6 21	17 06	6 39	16 49	7 05	16 22
299		.9943	16 00	3 28	16 01	3 24	16 02	3 19	16 04	3 13	16 07	3 02
26 TU	11 43 57	−12 29	5 59	17 29	6 10	17 18	6 23	17 05	6 40	16 47	7 08	16 19
300		.9940	16 35	4 22	16 30	4 24	16 25	4 26	16 18	4 29	16 07	4 34
27 WE	11 43 51	−12 49	5 59	17 28	6 10	17 17	6 24	17 03	6 42	16 45	7 10	16 17
301		.9937	17 09	5 16	17 00	5 23	16 48	5 32	16 31	5 45	16 07	6 04
28 TH	11 43 46	−13 10	6 00	17 28	6 11	17 16	6 25	17 02	6 43	16 43	7 13	16 14
302	03 07 FM	.9935	17 46	6 09	17 31	6 22	17 12	6 38	16 47	7 00	16 07	7 36
29 FR	11 43 42	−13 29	6 00	17 27	6 12	17 15	6 26	17 01	6 45	16 42	7 15	16 11
303		.9932	18 25	7 04	18 05	7 22	17 41	7 44	17 07	8 16	16 10	9 09
30 SA	11 43 39	−13 49	6 01	17 26	6 13	17 14	6 27	17 00	6 47	16 40	7 18	16 09
304		.9929	19 07	7 59	18 44	8 21	18 14	8 49	17 31	9 30	16 15	10 44
31 SU	11 43 37	−14 09	6 01	17 26	6 13	17 14	6 28	16 59	6 48	16 38	7 20	16 06
305		.9927	19 53	8 54	19 27	9 20	18 53	9 52	18 04	10 41	16 27	12 16

NOVEMBER 2004

11th Month   **30 days**

Coordinated Universal Time (Greenwich Mean Time)
NOTE: For rising and setting each day, numbers on first line indicate Sun; numbers on second line indicate Moon.
Degrees are North Latitude.
Moon Phases: FM = Full Moon; LQ = Last (Waning) Quarter; NM = New Moon; FQ = First (Waxing) Quarter
Sun's distance is in Astronomical Units
CAUTION: Must be converted to local time. For instructions see "Calculation of Rise Times," page 666.

Day of month, of week, of year	Sun on Meridian / Moon Phase (h m s)	Sun's Declination / Distance	20° Rise Sun/Moon	20° Set Sun/Moon	30° Rise Sun/Moon	30° Set Sun/Moon	40° Rise Sun/Moon	40° Set Sun/Moon	50° Rise Sun/Moon	50° Set Sun/Moon	60° Rise Sun/Moon	60° Set Sun/Moon
1 MO	11 43 35	−14 28	6 02	17 25	6 14	17 13	6 29	16 57	6 50	16 36	7 23	16 03
306		.9924	20 43	9 48	20 15	10 16	19 40	10 51	18 47	11 44	16 54	13 36
2 TU	11 43 34	−14 47	6 02	17 25	6 15	17 12	6 30	16 56	6 52	16 35	7 25	16 01
307		.9922	21 35	10 40	21 08	11 08	20 33	11 43	19 41	12 36	17 50	14 27
3 WE	11 43 34	−15 06	6 03	17 24	6 16	17 11	6 32	16 55	6 53	16 33	7 28	15 58
308		.9919	22 29	11 29	22 03	11 55	21 31	12 28	20 44	13 16	19 12	14 50
4 TH	11 43 35	−15 25	6 03	17 24	6 16	17 10	6 33	16 54	6 55	16 31	7 31	15 56
309		.9917	23 22	12 13	23 01	12 36	22 33	13 05	21 54	13 47	20 42	15 01
5 FR	11 43 37	−15 43	6 04	17 23	6 17	17 10	6 34	16 53	6 57	16 30	7 33	15 53
310	05 53 LQ	.9914	none	12 54	23 59	13 13	23 37	13 37	23 06	14 10	22 14	15 05
6 SA	11 43 39	−16 01	6 04	17 23	6 18	17 10	6 35	16 52	6 58	16 28	7 36	15 51
311		.9912	0 16	13 32	none	13 46	none	14 04	none	14 28	23 45	15 07
7 SU	11 43 43	−16 19	6 05	17 23	6 19	17 08	6 36	16 51	7 00	16 27	7 38	15 48
312		.9910	1 09	14 07	0 56	14 17	0 41	14 28	0 20	14 44	none	15 07
8 MO	11 43 47	−16 36	6 05	17 22	6 20	17 08	6 37	16 50	7 02	16 25	7 41	15 46
313		.9907	2 02	14 42	1 55	14 46	1 46	14 51	1 34	14 57	1 15	15 07
9 TU	11 43 52	−16 54	6 06	17 22	6 20	17 07	6 39	16 49	7 03	16 24	7 43	15 43
314		.9905	2 55	15 16	2 54	15 15	2 52	15 13	2 50	15 11	2 46	15 07
10 WE	11 43 58	−17 11	6 06	17 22	6 21	17 06	6 40	16 48	7 05	16 22	7 46	15 41
315		.9903	3 50	15 53	3 55	15 46	4 00	15 37	4 08	15 25	4 20	15 07
11 TH	11 44 05	−17 27	6 07	17 21	6 22	17 06	6 41	16 47	7 07	16 21	7 49	15 39
316		.9900	4 48	16 33	4 59	16 20	5 12	16 03	5 30	15 42	5 59	15 07
12 FR	11 44 12	−17 44	6 07	17 21	6 23	17 05	6 42	16 46	7 08	16 19	7 51	15 37
317		.9898	5 50	17 17	6 07	16 59	6 28	16 35	6 57	16 03	7 47	15 09
13 SA	11 44 21	−18 00	6 08	17 21	6 24	17 05	6 43	16 45	7 10	16 18	7 54	15 34
318		.9896	6 56	18 09	7 19	17 45	7 47	17 15	8 27	16 32	9 41	15 15
14 SU	11 44 30	−18 15	6 08	17 20	6 24	17 04	6 44	16 44	7 12	16 17	7 56	15 32
319		.9893	8 05	19 07	8 31	18 40	9 05	18 05	9 55	17 14	11 37	15 30
15 MO	11 44 40	−18 31	6 09	17 20	6 25	17 04	6 45	16 44	7 13	16 16	7 59	15 30
320		.9891	9 14	20 12	9 42	19 43	10 18	19 07	11 12	18 13	13 11	16 14
16 TU	11 44 52	−18 46	6 10	17 20	6 26	17 03	6 47	16 43	7 15	16 14	8 01	15 28
321		.9889	10 18	21 19	10 45	20 52	11 20	20 19	12 11	19 28	13 56	17 45
17 WE	11 45 03	−19 01	6 10	17 20	6 27	17 03	6 48	16 42	7 16	16 13	8 04	15 26
322		.9887	11 15	22 25	11 39	22 03	12 09	21 34	12 53	20 53	14 11	19 37
18 TH	11 45 16	−19 15	6 11	17 20	6 28	17 03	6 49	16 41	7 18	16 12	8 06	15 24
323		.9885	12 05	23 29	12 24	23 11	12 48	22 50	13 21	22 19	14 17	21 27
19 FR	11 45 30	−19 29	6 11	17 19	6 29	17 02	6 50	16 41	7 20	16 11	8 09	15 22
324	05 50 FQ	.9882	12 48	none	13 02	none	13 19	none	13 42	23 42	14 19	23 10
20 SA	11 45 44	−19 43	6 12	17 19	6 29	17 02	6 51	16 40	7 21	16 10	8 11	15 20
325		.9880	13 26	0 28	13 35	0 17	13 45	0 02	13 58	none	14 20	none
21 SU	11 45 59	−19 56	6 13	17 19	6 30	17 01	6 52	16 39	7 23	16 09	8 13	15 18
326		.9878	14 02	1 24	14 04	1 18	14 08	1 11	14 12	1 01	14 19	0 46
22 MO	11 46 15	−20 09	6 13	17 19	6 31	17 01	6 53	16 39	7 24	16 08	8 16	15 16
327		.9876	14 36	2 18	14 33	2 18	14 30	2 18	14 25	2 17	14 19	2 17
23 TU	11 46 31	−20 22	6 14	17 19	6 32	17 01	6 54	16 38	7 26	16 07	8 18	15 14
328		.9874	6 14	17 19	6 32	17 01	6 54	16 38	7 26	16 07	8 18	15 14
24 WE	11 46 49	−20 34	6 14	17 19	6 33	17 01	6 56	16 38	7 27	16 06	8 20	15 13
329		.9872	15 45	4 03	15 32	4 14	15 16	4 27	14 54	4 46	14 19	5 16
25 TH	11 47 07	−20 46	6 15	17 19	6 34	17 00	6 57	16 37	7 29	16 05	8 23	15 11
330		.9870	16 22	4 56	16 04	5 12	15 42	5 32	15 11	6 01	14 21	6 47
26 FR	11 47 26	−20 58	6 16	17 19	6 34	17 00	6 58	16 37	7 30	16 04	8 25	15 09
331	20 07 FM	.9869	17 03	5 50	16 41	6 11	16 13	6 37	15 34	7 15	14 25	8 21
27 SA	11 47 45	−21 09	6 16	17 19	6 35	17 00	6 59	16 36	7 32	16 04	8 27	15 08
332		.9867	17 48	6 45	17 22	7 10	16 50	7 41	16 03	8 27	14 34	9 54
28 SU	11 48 06	−21 20	6 17	17 19	6 36	17 00	7 00	16 36	7 33	16 03	8 29	15 06
333		.9865	18 36	7 40	18 09	8 07	17 34	8 42	16 42	9 33	14 54	11 19
29 MO	11 48 27	−21 30	6 18	17 19	6 37	17 00	7 01	16 36	7 34	16 02	8 31	15 05
334		.9863	19 28	8 33	19 00	9 01	18 25	9 36	17 32	10 29	15 40	12 22
30 TU	11 48 48	−21 40	6 18	17 19	6 38	17 00	7 02	16 36	7 36	16 02	8 34	15 04
335		.9862	20 21	9 23	19 55	9 50	19 21	10 24	18 32	11 14	16 53	12 54

DECEMBER 2004

12th Month   **31 days**

Coordinated Universal Time (Greenwich Mean Time)

NOTE: For rising and setting each day, numbers on first line indicate Sun; numbers on second line indicate Moon.
Degrees are North Latitude.

Moon Phases: FM = Full Moon; LQ = Last (Waning) Quarter; NM = New Moon; FQ = First (Waxing) Quarter
Sun's distance is in Astronomical Units

CAUTION: Must be converted to local time. For instructions see "Calculation of Rise Times," page 666.

Day of month, of week, of year	Sun on Meridian / Moon Phase (h m s)	Sun's Decl. / Distance (° ')	20° Rise Sun/Moon	20° Set Sun/Moon	30° Rise Sun/Moon	30° Set Sun/Moon	40° Rise Sun/Moon	40° Set Sun/Moon	50° Rise Sun/Moon	50° Set Sun/Moon	60° Rise Sun/Moon	60° Set Sun/Moon
1 WE 336	11 49 11	−21 49	6 19	17 19	6 38	17 00	7 03	16 35	7 37	16 01	8 36	15 02
	.9860		21 14	10 09	20 51	10 33	20 22	11 04	19 40	11 48	18 21	13 08
2 TH 337	11 49 34	−21 58	6 19	17 20	6 39	17 00	7 04	16 35	7 38	16 00	8 38	15 01
	.9859		22 07	10 51	21 48	11 11	21 24	11 37	20 50	12 13	19 52	13 15
3 FR 338	11 49 57	−22 07	6 20	17 20	6 40	17 00	7 05	16 35	7 40	16 00	8 39	15 00
	.9857		22 59	11 29	22 45	11 45	22 27	12 05	22 02	12 33	21 22	13 17
4 SA 339	11 50 22	−22 15	6 21	17 20	6 41	17 00	7 06	16 35	7 41	16 00	8 41	14 59
	.9856		23 51	12 04	23 42	12 16	23 30	12 30	23 14	12 49	22 49	13 18
5 SU 340	11 50 46 / 00 53 LQ	−22 23	6 21	17 20	6 42	17 00	7 07	16 35	7 42	15 59	8 43	14 58
	.9854		none	12 38	none	12 44	none	12 52	none	13 03	none	13 18
6 MO 341	11 51 12	−22 30	6 22	17 20	6 42	17 00	7 08	16 35	7 43	15 59	8 45	14 57
	.9853		0 42	13 11	0 38	13 13	0 34	13 14	0 27	13 16	0 17	13 18
7 TU 342	11 51 38	−22 37	6 23	17 21	6 43	17 00	7 09	16 35	7 44	15 59	8 47	14 56
	.9852		1 35	13 46	1 37	13 42	1 39	13 36	1 42	13 29	1 46	13 18
8 WE 343	11 52 04	−22 44	6 23	17 21	6 44	17 00	7 09	16 35	7 46	15 58	8 48	14 56
	.9850		2 30	14 23	2 38	14 13	2 47	14 01	3 00	13 44	3 20	13 18
9 TH 344	11 52 31	−22 50	6 24	17 21	6 44	17 00	7 10	16 35	7 47	15 58	8 50	14 55
	.9849		3 29	15 05	3 42	14 49	3 59	14 29	4 23	14 02	5 01	13 19
10 FR 345	11 52 58	−22 55	6 24	17 21	6 45	17 01	7 11	16 35	7 48	15 58	8 51	14 54
	.9848		4 33	15 52	4 52	15 31	5 16	15 04	5 51	14 27	6 51	13 23
11 SA 346	11 53 26	−23 00	6 25	17 22	6 46	17 01	7 12	16 35	7 49	15 58	8 53	14 54
	.9847		5 41	16 48	6 05	16 22	6 36	15 49	7 21	15 02	8 49	13 32
12 SU 347	11 53 54 / 01 29 NM	−23 05	6 26	17 22	6 47	17 01	7 13	16 35	7 50	15 58	8 54	14 54
	.9846		6 51	17 51	7 18	17 23	7 54	16 47	8 47	15 54	10 40	14 00
13 MO 348	11 54 22	−23 09	6 26	17 22	6 47	17 01	7 13	16 35	7 50	15 58	8 55	14 53
	.9845		8 00	19 00	8 28	18 32	9 03	17 57	9 57	17 04	11 50	15 12
14 TU 349	11 54 51	−23 13	6 27	17 23	6 48	17 02	7 14	16 35	7 51	15 58	8 56	14 53
	.9844		9 02	20 10	9 28	19 45	10 00	19 15	10 47	18 29	12 17	17 03
15 WE 350	11 55 20	−23 16	6 27	17 23	6 48	17 02	7 15	16 36	7 52	15 58	8 57	14 53
	.9843		9 57	21 17	10 18	20 58	10 45	20 34	11 22	19 59	12 26	18 59
16 TH 351	11 55 49	−23 19	6 28	17 24	6 49	17 03	7 16	16 36	7 53	15 59	8 59	14 53
	.9842		10 45	22 20	11 00	22 07	11 20	21 50	11 47	21 27	12 29	20 48
17 FR 352	11 56 19	−23 23	6 28	17 24	6 50	17 03	7 16	16 36	7 54	15 59	9 00	14 53
	.9841		11 26	23 19	11 36	23 11	11 48	23 02	12 05	22 49	12 31	22 29
18 SA 353	11 56 48 / 16 40 FQ	−23 24	6 29	17 25	6 50	17 03	7 17	16 37	7 54	15 59	9 00	14 53
	.9840		12 03	none	12 07	none	12 12	none	12 20	none	12 31	none
19 SU 354	11 57 18	−23 25	6 30	17 25	6 51	17 04	7 17	16 37	7 55	16 00	9 01	14 54
	.9839		12 37	0 14	12 36	0 12	12 35	0 10	12 33	0 07	12 30	0 03
20 MO 355	11 57 48	−23 26	6 30	17 26	6 51	17 04	7 18	16 38	7 56	16 00	9 02	14 54
	.9838		13 11	1 07	13 05	1 11	12 57	1 16	12 46	1 22	12 30	1 33
21 TU 356	11 58 18	−23 26	6 31	17 26	6 52	17 05	7 18	16 38	7 56	16 00	9 02	14 54
	.9837		13 46	1 59	13 34	2 09	13 20	2 20	13 01	2 36	12 31	3 02
22 WE 357	11 58 47	−23 26	6 31	17 27	6 52	17 05	7 19	16 39	7 57	16 01	9 03	14 55
	.9837		14 22	2 52	14 06	3 07	13 45	3 25	13 17	3 50	12 32	4 32
23 TH 358	11 59 17	−23 26	6 32	17 27	6 53	17 06	7 19	16 39	7 57	16 02	9 03	14 56
	.9836		15 02	3 45	14 41	4 05	14 15	4 29	13 38	5 04	12 35	6 04
24 FR 359	11 59 47	−23 25	6 32	17 28	6 53	17 06	7 20	16 40	7 57	16 02	9 03	14 56
	.9835		15 45	4 40	15 20	5 03	14 49	5 33	14 05	6 16	12 42	7 36
25 SA 360	12 00 16	−23 24	6 32	17 28	6 54	17 07	7 20	16 40	7 58	16 03	9 03	14 56
	.9835		16 32	5 34	16 05	6 00	15 31	6 34	14 40	7 24	12 58	9 04
26 SU 361	12 00 46 / 15 06 FM	−23 22	6 33	17 29	6 54	17 08	7 21	16 41	7 58	16 04	9 04	14 58
	.9834		17 22	6 28	16 55	6 55	16 19	7 31	15 27	8 23	13 34	10 15
27 MO 362	12 01 16	−23 19	6 33	17 29	6 54	17 08	7 21	16 42	7 58	16 04	9 04	14 59
	.9834		18 15	7 18	17 48	7 46	17 14	8 20	16 24	9 12	14 40	10 57
28 TU 363	12 01 45	−23 17	6 34	17 30	6 55	17 09	7 21	16 42	7 58	16 05	9 03	15 00
	.9834		19 09	8 06	18 45	8 31	18 14	9 03	17 29	9 49	16 05	11 15
29 WE 364	12 02 14	−23 13	6 34	17 30	6 55	17 09	7 21	16 43	7 59	16 06	9 03	15 01
	.9833		20 02	8 49	19 42	9 11	19 16	9 38	18 39	10 17	17 35	11 23
30 TH 365	12 02 43	−23 10	6 34	17 31	6 55	17 10	7 22	16 44	7 59	16 07	9 03	15 03
	.9833		20 54	9 28	20 38	9 46	20 18	10 08	19 51	10 38	19 05	11 27
31 FR 366	12 03 11	−23 05	6 35	17 32	6 56	17 11	7 22	16 45	7 59	16 08	9 03	15 04
	.9833		21 45	10 04	21 34	10 17	21 21	10 33	21 02	10 55	20 32	11 29

SCIENCE AND TECHNOLOGY

Science News of 2003

Life Sciences news and glossary entries reviewed by Prof. Maura C. Flannery, St. John's Univ., NYC; Physical Sciences news and glossary entries reviewed by Prof. F. Paul Esposito, Univ. of Cincinnati.

The following were some of the more newsworthy developments in Science in the past year. (See also the chapters on Astronomy and Computers and the Internet.)

Life Sciences

• Researchers led by David Page of the Whitehead Institute at the Massachusetts Institute of Technology completed a **detailed analysis of the human Y chromosome**—the chromosome that contains the information which causes a person to be male—and found that it had 78 genes, almost twice as many as previously suspected (although still far fewer than other chromosomes), according to a study published in the June 19 issue of *Nature*. The Y chromosome differs from other human chromosomes, in that it does not occur as one of a pair of (nearly identical) chromosomes. As a result, it can't repair itself as other chromosomes do—by obtaining good copies of genes from its partners; since the Y chromosome lacks this option, some researchers had speculated that it was headed for extinction (in perhaps 5-10 million years). The new study, however, concluded that the Y chromosome employs a different tactic for self-repair, incorporating "palindromic" sequences of chemical units (that is, sequences that read the same forward and backward) arranged on both strands of the DNA molecule. When the DNA divides during reproduction, the faulty genes can be discarded and replaced with functioning genes from elsewhere on the DNA. This capacity for self-repair means that the Y chromosome may not be doomed by evolution. Page said that the mechanism of self-repair might be implicated, however, in genetic disorders affecting some men, such as some forms of infertility.

• An international team of researchers found 3 fossilized skulls in the Middle Awash region of Ethiopia that represent a **key link between remains of earlier protohumans and the fully modern humans** that entered the fossil record about 100,000 years ago, according to a report in the June 12 issue of *Nature*. The skulls—two of adults and one of a child—were dated to about 160,000 years ago. The remains were in good condition and could also be dated with considerable precision; previous finds had not been as intact, or as easy to date with accuracy. The skulls did not exactly resemble those of modern humans: These skulls were somewhat larger and longer and the brow ridges were more accentuated. The researchers coined a new subspecies—*Homo sapiens idaltu* (in the local Afar language, "idaltu" signifies *elder*)—for their find. Other human bones were not discovered near the skulls, indicating they had not been buried; some features of the skulls, including the smooth, "polished" surface on the child's cranium, suggested, the researchers said, that they may have been used for ritual purposes. The researchers also saw the find as supporting the "out-of-Africa" theory that all humans are descended from ancestors who evolved in Africa. A competing theory contends that humans are the result of interbreeding between some ancestors from Africa and some (such as European Neanderthals) from elsewhere. "All the genetics have pointed to a geologically recent origin for humans in Africa—and now we have the fossils," commented Prof. Tim White, a leader of the group that discovered the fossils.

• A group of Chinese paleontologists found **fossils of 6 small feathered and 4-winged dinosaurs** that perhaps represent a step in the evolution of flight in birds, according to a report published in *Nature* Jan. 23. The researchers, led by Xing Xu of the Institute of Vertebrate Paleontology and Paleoanthropology in Beijing, believe that the creatures—called *Microraptor gui* by their finders—may have used their wings to glide from trees. The sternum of the animal did not have a keel to which large-flight muscles could be attached, supporting the gliding hypothesis. The theory that full flight evolved from gliding contrasts with an opposing theory, that flight developed from running animals using wings to give themselves extra impetus. The new fossils were dated to about 130 million years ago, making them more recent than the 150-million-year-old *Archaeopteryx*, considered by scientists to be the first known bird. The first *Archaeopteryx* fossil was found in 1861; some scientists say the Chinese fossils represented the most important discovery in bird evolution since then.

• Teams of scientists at Oregon Health & Science Univ. in Portland and Univ. of Washington in Seattle **used adult stem cells to repair damaged livers in mice,** according to reports published in *Nature* Apr. 24. While welcoming the therapeutic success, the researchers also said their findings cast doubt on what has been viewed as a key desirable trait of stem cells: the ability to differentiate, or transform themselves, into completely different types of cells. In fact, the researchers said, the experiments showed that the stem cells (which were derived from bone marrow) combined with the liver cells through a mechanism known as cell fusion. Markus Grompe, leader of the Oregon group, maintained that there was now "serious concern about whether [previous] data reflect reality." The process of cell fusion gives the resulting combined cells more chromosomes than in ordinary cells. The scientists believe the genetic material from the stem cells perhaps reprogrammed the host liver cells, allowing them to function normally again. The presence of extra genetic material, while perhaps responsible for the therapeutic result, was, however, also a cause of concern: it could lead to instability and tumor formation, according to David Russell, leader of the Seattle team.

• Scientists and public officials from around the world Apr. 14 hailed the **completion of the Human Genome Project,** a vast undertaking to "sequence" or determine the order of the 4 chemical bases that make up DNA and carry the genetic blueprint for our species. The project took 13 years to complete, 2 years fewer than had originally been estimated, and cost $2.7 billion. A "draft" sequence had been announced 3 years earlier, but the researchers now had data both more accurate and more comprehensive: an error rate of less than 1 in 10,000 pairs of nucleotide bases (compared with 1 in 1,000 for the draft sequence), and coverage of some 99% of the gene-carrying stretches, versus 90% with the draft. The April finish had been sought by researchers as a way of commemorating the 50th anniversary of the publication, in April 1953, of James Watson's and Francis Crick's discovery of DNA's basic structure. Molecular biologists believe the sequencing of the human genome would prove invaluable to researchers looking for genetic remedies to many serious diseases.

• Scientists at the Whitehead Institute/MIT Center for Genome Research in Massachusetts **sequenced the genomes of 3 species of yeast** and used their results to draw comparisons with the already-sequenced genome of baker's yeast (*Saccharomyces cerevisiae*), according to a report published in *Nature* May 15. The study led to a greatly improved understanding of the yeast genome originally sequenced, including the discovery of 43 new genes and a refined estimate of 5,726 for the total number of genes in the *S. cerevisiae* genome. The comparative approach—which lead author Manolis Kellis compared to a Rosetta Stone in its contribution to understanding—allowed the researchers to learn much more about regulatory sequences, which are portions of the genome that are not themselves genes but turn genes on and off. The genome, in addition to the genes and the regulatory elements, contains vast stretches of nucleotides with no known use; the researchers reasoned that the functional sequences (the genes and the regulatory units) would be conserved by evolution and thus probably be the same for closely allied species, while the nonfunctioning sequences were more likely to exhibit random variation. Thus, comparison of the genomes of allied species could lead to identification of genes and regulatory units by finding sequences that were alike among all compared species, and help in ruling out mistaken gene identifications. The research also highlighted the significance of the chromosome ends, or telomeres, which the study suggested undergo genetic change more rapidly than the rest of the chromosome. The study was seen as offering a model for other genetic research, including that of the human genome, emphasizing the value of comparison with similar genomes.

• **Dolly the cloned sheep was euthanized** Feb. 14 after developing an incurable lung infection. Dolly was the first mammal to be cloned from an adult cell. She was born on July 5, 1996, at the Roslin Institute in Edinburgh, Scotland, and so was only 6½ years old at death. (Sheep sometimes live 11 or 12 years.) A year earlier, in Jan. 2002, it was reported that Dolly had developed premature arthritis. Scientists are not sure whether her health problems were related to her origins as a clone.

• Scientists in Cremona, Italy, succeeded in **cloning a horse,** according to a report in *Nature* Aug. 7. The mare that donated one of two cells from which the clone was developed also served as host mother; the clone was implanted in her womb.

• The organization Clonaid, founded by the Raelian religious sect, claimed in Dec. 2002 that its researchers **had successfully cloned several humans.** But they failed to produce documentation or evidence, and other scientists remained highly skeptical of the claim.

• Research by scientists at Harvard Medical School in Massachusetts identified a particular gene—PNC1—as playing **an important role in increasing longevity in yeast,** according to a report in *Nature* May 8. The researchers, led by David Sinclair, found that certain kinds of environmental factors—such as heat, osmotic stress, or reduced food—triggered the activity of PNC1. PNC1 would then convert the chemical nicotinamide to nicotinic acid. Nicotinic acid did not inhibit activity by the previously discovered longevity protein Sir2, whereas nicotinamide did. Studies over many years had shown that reducing food as well as some other actions can extend longevity; the research by Sinclair's team is significant because it helps chart the molecular mechanisms by which this result might be achieved.

• A report in *Science* May 9 noted that Joel Brown of the Univ. of Illinois, Chicago, and other scientists had found that **conservation efforts aimed at preserving or managing endangered species** sometimes cause rapid evolutionary changes with unintended consequences. For example, the report noted many scientists believe that efforts to preserve commercial fish stocks by setting minimum size limits on fish that can be kept (smaller fish being thrown back, so they have a chance to breed) have had the effect of creating an evolutionary selective advantage for smaller fish. By enhancing the survival chances of small fish, those fish become more likely to pass on their genes, and thus the species gets smaller, which was certainly not the goal of the fisheries managers. Daniel Heath, a biologist at the Univ. of Windsor in Ontario, Canada, observed, "If you grab the last few animals and you put them in a zoo to make sure they don't die, you could potentially drive evolution of some trait that you don't expect…[subsequent release into the wild could reveal] a loss of fitness [that] might mean the difference of survival and extinction."

Physical Sciences

• Teams of physicists at Osaka Univ. in Japan and the Jefferson lab in Newport News, VA, **found evidence for the existence of a pentaquark,** or 5-quark, subatomic particle, according to research published in *Physical Review Letters* July 4. Quarks are the basic constituents of protons, neutrons, and other more exotic subatomic particles, but until this latest discovery had always been found to come in particles made up either of 2 quarks (such particles are called mesons and are very short-lived) or 3 (baryons, a category that includes protons and neutrons). The pentaquark is allowed by theory, however, and a group of Russian scientists had made a prediction of its mass in 1997 that appeared to be confirmed by the recent experiments. The pentaquark decayed in a tiny fraction of a second into a meson and a neutron. The reaction producing the new particle involved the collision of a gamma ray with a neutron inside a carbon nucleus. As with other experiments involving objects that could not be directly observed, the conclusion that the particle existed was based on a statistical analysis of the evidence collected. This evidence was the tracks left in particle detectors by various short-lived particles created in the collision events. This analysis strongly suggested that the unusual data recorded were the result of a pentaquark particle, and not merely a fluctuation in the normal number of background events.

• Scientists at the Sandia National Laboratories in New Mexico **produced neutrons through fusion reactions with their "Z" machine,** it was announced at an Apr. 7 meeting of the American Physical Society in Philadelphia. The achievement was seen as a key step on the long, arduous, and expensive road to developing fusion—the nuclear reaction powering the Sun, in which hydrogen atoms combine to make helium atoms—into a practical source of energy. Researchers had long employed 2 approaches to fusion: confining superheated gasses (plasmas) in magnetic fields (the tokamak approach) and imploding small pellets by firing laser beams at them from all directions. The aim of both these methods was to create the extreme conditions necessary for atomic nuclei to join together. The Z machine sought to attain those conditions by a different means, employing precisely timed mega-pulses of electricity to create magnetic fields that crush tungsten wires into a foam cylinder. This in turn produces X rays that compress deuterium, a form of hydrogen with one proton and one neutron in the nucleus, in a capsule. The compression causes some of the deuterium to fuse and release neutrons, the signature that fusion has taken place. Ray Leeper, an official at the Sandia lab, observed, "Pulsed power electrical systems [like the Z machine] have always been energy-rich but power-poor…That is, we can deliver a lot of energy, but it wasn't clear we could concentrate it on a small enough area to create fusion. Now it seems clear we can do that."

• Experimenters claimed to have **measured "the speed of gravity,"** that is, the speed at which the gravitational field of one body affects another body. The researchers, Sergei Kopeikin of the Univ. of Missouri and Ed Fomalont of the National Radio Astronomy Observatory in Charlottesville, VA, claimed at a meeting of the American Astronomical Society Jan. 7 that their measurements agreed, within experimental error, with the theoretical prediction that the speed of gravity would match the speed of light. However, some other astronomers said that the claim was unfounded, and that the experimenters had not in fact succeeded in measuring gravity. Clifford Will, a physicist at Washington Univ., disputed the arguments of Kopeikin and Fomalont but contended that they had nevertheless "measured something important, I believe, and that is the effect of 'gravitomagnetism,' a contribution to gravity contributed by moving matter, analogous to magnetic fields generated by electrical currents." The measurements conducted by Kopeikin and Fomalont took place in 2002, when the planet Jupiter passed near the light from a distant quasar on its way to Earth: the observed deflection of the light from the quasar would, the two scientists believed, offer a means of measuring the speed of gravity, the gravitational effect of Jupiter's mass taking a short but measurable time to exert its influence on the passing photons.

• Canadian and U.S. astronomers announced at a NASA news conference in Washington, DC, July 10 that they had discovered **a planet nearly as old as the estimated age of the universe.** The planet, named "Methuselah" by the astronomers, was believed to have about 2½ times the mass of Jupiter, and to be located 5,600 light-years away from the Sun (far more distant than any previously discovered extra-solar planet). The planet also was found in a dense collection of stars called a globular cluster; previously it had been thought that globular clusters were unlikely candidates for planet formation. These circumstances, astronomers said, meant that planets could be far more common in the universe than had previously been thought, and this in turn meant that the chance of life existing elsewhere could also be greater than had been thought. Methuselah was thought to be about 13 billion years old, nearly three times the estimated age of Earth and perhaps only about a billion years younger than the generally accepted age of the universe. "What we think we've found is an example of the first generation of planets formed in the universe," said Steinn Sigurdsson of Pennsylvania State Univ., one of the astronomers involved in the research.

• Teams of physicists at the Indiana Univ. Cyclotron Facility and at the TRIUMF cyclotron in British Columbia, Canada, announced April 5 at the American Physical Society meeting in Philadelphia that they had conducted difficult measurements showing up **small but vital differences between neutrons and protons.** At the TRIUMF machine, the physicists studied collisions between protons and neutrons; at the Indiana cyclotron, they looked at the results of smashing together nuclei of deuterium (a form of hydrogen with one proton and one neutron in the nucleus). In many nuclear reactions, protons and neutrons are essentially interchangeable, even though the proton has a positive charge and the neutron is neutral. This fact is recognized with the term "charge symmetry" (the symmetry being that protons and neutrons can take each other's place without affecting the outcome). However, this symmetry, unlike certain others recognized in physicists' theories, is not perfect: it can be departed from slightly, a fact referred to as "charge symmetry breaking." The **charge-symmetry violation**, while subtle, is held by physicists to have profound effects, including being responsible for the difference in mass between protons and neutrons, which in turn is related to the existence of hydrogen—vital for star formation—in the universe. The experiments described at the Apr. 5 meeting detected the release of a particle called a pion. The pions released by the reaction were not emitted totally randomly; there was a slight but measurable preference in direction, an indicator of charge-symmetry breaking. The results were seen as offering vital clues for the understanding of what goes on inside atomic nuclei.

• Scientists at the Univ. of Texas in Dallas and at Trinity College in Dublin, Ireland, developed threads composed of carbon nanotubes that were **tougher than any other natural or artificial materials**, according to a report in *Nature* June 12. The team of researchers, led by Ray Baughman, spun nanotube fibers that were 3 or 4 times tougher, or able to absorb energy without breaking than spider silk, the toughest natural fiber known. In terms of tensile strength—that is, the level of stress a material can handle before it stops being elastic— the

nanotubes matched spider silk. The fibers were 17 times tougher than Kevlar, used in bulletproof vests and other products. The scientists were able to produce 100-meter fibers, mixing nanotubes with water and a special soap, and then injecting the mixture in a pipe with polyvinyl alcohol. The alcohol bound the nanotubes together, producing a gelatinous mixture, and the fiber that could then be spun out of this substance was made up of 60% nanotubes. In addition to the exceptional strength of the thread, the nanotube material had special electrical properties, suggesting that eventually it might be possible to incorporate micro sensors into clothes. Baughman said that the fiber's toughness "probably results from structural changes during the stretching. This aligns the nanotubes in the fiber direction."

• An experiment conducted by Roderic Lakes of the Univ. of Wisconsin and reported in *Physical Review Letters* Mar. 2, offered apparent **confirmation** for the assumption by most physicists **that photons, or particles of light, have zero mass**. Experiments dating back about a quarter of a century involving observations of the magnetic field of Jupiter had set a maximum value for the size of a photon's mass. (No mass was detected, but the experiment would not have detected a mass below a certain size, which thus became the maximum possible mass of photons.) Lakes, using a different approach that did not involve astronomical observations but instead employed a Cavendish balance (a steel toroid—doughnut-shaped object—wrapped in current-carrying coils). Using this apparatus Lakes was able to cut by a factor of 10 the possible size of a photon's mass.

Science Glossary

This glossary covers some basic concepts, and others that come up frequently in the news, in biology, chemistry, geology, and physics. See also Astronomy, Computers and the Internet, Environment, Health, Meteorology, Weights and Measures.

Biology

For classification terms such as *kingdom, phylum*, etc., see Environment chapter.

Amino acid: one of about 20 similar small molecules that are the building blocks of proteins.

Antibiotic: a drug made from a substance produced by a bacterium, fungus, or other organism that battles bacterial infections and diseases, killing the bacteria or halting their growth.

Autoimmunity: a condition in which an individual's immune system reacts against his or her own tissues; leads to diseases such as lupus, diabetes, inflammatory bowel disease, rheumatoid arthritis.

Bacterium (plural, bacteria): one of a large, varied class of microscopic and simple, single-celled organisms; bacteria live almost everywhere—some forms cause disease, while others are useful in digestion and other natural processes.

Biodiversity: richness of variety of life forms—both plant and animal—in a given environment.

Cell: the smallest unit of life capable of living independently, or with other cells; usually bounded by a membrane; may include a nucleus and other specialized parts.

Cholesterol: a fatty substance in animal tissues; it is produced by the liver in humans, and is found in foods such as butter, eggs, and meat, and is an essential body constituent.

Chromosome: one of the rod-like structures in the nuclei of cells that carry genetic material (DNA); humans have 46 chromosomes.

Cloning: the process of copying a particular piece of DNA to allow it to be sequenced, studied, or used in some other way; can also refer to producing a genetic copy of an organism.

DNA (deoxyribonucleic acid): the chemical substance that carries genetic information, which determines the form and functioning of all living things.

Ecosystem: an interdependent community of living organisms and their climatic and geographical habitat.

Enzyme: a protein that promotes a particular chemical reaction in the body.

Estrogen: one of a group of hormones that promote development of female secondary sex characteristics and the growth and health of the female reproductive system; males also produce small amounts of estrogen.

Evolution: the process of gradual change that may occur as a species adapts to its environment; natural selection is the process by which evolution occurs.

Fight-or-flight response: the physical response that occurs in all animals when they encounter a threat; bodies release hormones, such as cortisol and epinephrine, that speed up the heart rate and increase blood flow to the muscles, allowing animals to fight enemies or run away.

Gene: a portion of a DNA molecule that provides the blueprint for the assembly of a protein.

Gene pool: the collection and total diversity of genes in an interbreeding population.

Gene therapy: a treatment in which scientists try to implant functioning genes into a person's cells so the genes can produce proteins that the person lacks or that help the person fight disease.

Genetic sequencing: the process of determining the order of subunits within a gene or even the order of all genes for an organism.

Genome: the complete set of an organism's genetic material.

Hormone: a substance secreted in one part of an organism that regulates the functioning of other tissues or organs.

Metabolism: the sum total of the body's chemical processes providing energy for vital functions, and enabling new material to be synthesized.

Neuron: a nerve cell, of the type found in the brain or spinal cord, that sends electrical and chemical messages to other cells.

Nucleus (plural: nuclei): the center of an atom; or the portion of a cell containing the chemical directions for functioning.

Organism: a living being.

Phenotype: the observable properties and characteristics of an organism arising at least in part from its genetic makeup.

Pheromone: a chemical secreted by an animal to influence the behavior of other members of its own species.

Placebo effect: a phenomenon in which patients show improvements even though they have taken a medically inactive substance, called a placebo.

Protein: a complex molecule made up of one or more chains of amino acids; essential to the structure and function of all cells.

▶ **IT'S A FACT:** The Greek mathematician Euclid, best known for his geometry, also proved a fundamental fact about prime numbers—there are an infinite number of them. Euclid reasoned by contradiction: Suppose there are only a finite number of primes. In that case, you could make a list of all primes. Now consider the number that is one larger than all these primes multiplied together—in other words, 2x3x5x7x11...x (the last prime) + 1. If divided by any of the primes used in making it, there will be a remainder of 1. So either the number is prime itself, or it's the product of primes not on the list. But the list was supposed to have all primes, so we have a contradiction, and therefore, the assumption that there are a finite number of primes is false.

RNA (ribonucleic acid): a complex molecule similar to the genetic material DNA, but usually single-stranded; several forms of RNA translate the genetic code of DNA and use that code to assemble proteins for structural and biological functions in the body.

Species: a population of organisms that breed with each other in nature and produce fertile offspring; other definitions of species exist to accommodate the diversity of life on Earth.

Stem cell: a cell that can give rise to other types of cells; for instance, bone marrow stem cells divide and produce different types of blood cells.

Steroid: type of hormone that freely enters cells (other hormones bind to cell surfaces); different varieties can suppress immune response or influence stress reaction, blood pressure, or sexual development; includes testosterone- and estrogen-related compounds.

Testosterone: a hormone that stimulates the development and maintenance of male sexual characteristics and the production of sperm; women also produce small amounts of testosterone.

Virus: a microscopic, often disease-causing, organism made of genetic material surrounded by a protein shell; can only reproduce inside a living cell.

Chemistry

Acid: a class of compound that contrasts with bases. Acids taste sour, turn litmus red/pink, and often produce hydrogen gas in contact with some metals. Acids donate protons (hydrogen atoms minus the electron) in chemical reactions.

Base: a substance that yields hydroxyl ions (OH-) when dissolved in water; any of a class of compounds whose aqueous solutions taste bitter, feel slippery, turn litmus blue, and react with acids to form salts; also known as **alkaline.**

Carbon fiber: an extremely strong, thin fiber made by pyrolyzing (decomposing by heat) synthetic fibers, such as rayon, until charred; used to make high-strength composites

Chlorofluorocarbon (CFC): one of a group of industrial chemicals that contain chlorine, fluorine, and carbon and have been found to damage Earth's ozone layer.

Element: a substance that cannot be chemically decomposed into simpler substances; the atoms of an element all have the same number of protons and electrons.

Isotope: an atom of a chemical element with the same number of protons in its nucleus as other atoms of that element, but with a different number of neutrons.

Molecule: the basic unit of a chemical compound, composed of two or more atoms bound together.

Osmosis: the transfer of a fluid from an area of higher concentration to an area of lower concentration, usually through a membrane.

Phase: any of the possible states of matter—solid, liquid, gas, or plasma—that change according to temperature and pressure.

Polymer: a huge molecule containing hundreds or thousands of smaller molecules arranged in repeating units.

Salt: a neutral compound produced by the reaction of an acid and a base.

Geology

Fault, tectonic: a crack or break in Earth's crust, often due to the slippage of tectonic plates past or over one another; usually geologically unstable.

Igneous: a type of rock formed by solidification from a molten state, especially from molten magma.

Magma: hot liquid rock material under Earth's crust, from which igneous rock is formed by cooling.

Metamorphic: in geology, the name given to sedimentary rocks or minerals that have recrystallized under the influence of heat and pressure since their original deposition.

Pangaea: a single super-continent that scientists believe broke apart about 170 million years ago to form the current continents.

Plate tectonics: theory that Earth's crust is made up of many separate rigid plates of rock that float on top of hot semi-liquid rock.

Sedimentary rock: rock formed by the buildup of material at the bottoms of bodies of water.

Physics

Absolute zero: the theoretical temperature at which all motion within a molecule stops, corresponding to −273.15° Celsius (−459.67° Fahrenheit).

Antimatter: matter that consists of antiparticles, such as antiprotons, that have an opposite charge from normal particles; when matter meets antimatter, both are destroyed and their combined mass is converted to energy. Antimatter is created in certain radioactive decay processes, but appears to be present in only small amounts in the universe.

Atom: the basic unit of a chemical element.

WORLD ALMANAC QUICK QUIZ

Put these medical discoveries in order, from earliest to latest:
    (a) insulin   (b) polio vaccine
    (c) smallpox vaccine   (d) penicillin
For the answer look in this chapter, or see page 1008.

Atomic mass: the total mass of an atom of a given element; atoms of the same element with different atomic masses (different numbers of neutrons, not protons) are called isotopes.

Atomic number: the number of protons in an atom of a given element of the periodic table; the characteristic that sets atoms of different elements apart.

Bose-Einstein condensate: a "super-atom" comprised of thousands of atoms super-cooled to within a few billionths of a degree of absolute zero and thus condensed into the lowest energy state; atoms bound in the BEC behave synchronously, giving the BEC wavelike properties.

Boson: force-carrying particles including photons, gluons, and the W and Z particles; one of the two primary categories of particles in the Standard Model, the other being fermions.

Dark energy: a mysterious, undefined energy leading to a repulsive force pervading all of space-time; proposed by cosmologists as counteracting gravity and accelerating the expansion of the universe; predicted to make up 65% of the universe's composition.

Dark matter: hypothetical, invisible matter that some scientists believe makes up 90% of the matter in the universe; its existence was proposed to account for otherwise inexplicable gravitational forces observed in space.

Doppler effect: a change in the frequency of sound, light, or radio waves caused by the motion of the source emitting the waves or the motion of the person or instrument perceiving the waves.

Electron: negatively charged particle that is the least massive electrically charged fundamental particle; the most common charged lepton in the Standard Model.

Energy: capacity to perform work. Energy can take various forms, such as potential energy, kinetic energy, chemical energy, etc.

Entropy: A measure of disorder in a system. According to the Second Law of Thermodynamics, disorder or entropy can only increase in a closed system.

Fermion: any one of a number of matter particles including electrons, protons, neutrons, and quarks; one of the two primary categories of particles in the Standard Model, the other being bosons.

Field: the effects of forces (gravitational, electric, etc.) are visualized and described mathematically by physicists in terms of fields, which show the strength and direction of a force at a given position.

Fission: a nuclear reaction that occurs when the nuclei of large, unstable atoms break apart, releasing large amounts of energy.

Force: In classical physics, a force is something that causes acceleration in a body, and can be thought of as a push or pull.

Fusion: a nuclear reaction occurring when atomic nuclei collide at high temperatures and combine to form one heavier atomic nucleus, releasing enormous energy in the process.

Gravity: an attractive force between any 2 objects or particles, proportional to the mass (or energy) of the objects; strength of the force decreases with greater distance; the only fundamental force still unaccounted for by the Standard Model.

Half-life: the time it takes for half of a given amount of a radioactive element to decay.

Hertz: a measure of frequency, or how many times a given event occurs per second; applied to sound waves, electrical current, microchip clock speeds; abbreviated as Hz.

Inertia: the tendency of an object to resist a change in its state of motion (i.e., to stay at rest if it is at rest, or to continue moving at a constant speed if it is moving at a constant speed). Inertia is proportional to mass, so a heavier object has more inertia.

Laser: light consisting of a cascade of photons all having the same wavelength; *laser* stands for Light Amplification by Stimulated Emission of Radiation.

Neutrino: a tiny fundamental particle with no electrical charge and very small mass that moves very quickly through the universe; in sum, predicted to make up about 5% of the mass of the universe; comes in three varieties, or flavors, called electron, muon, and tau.

Neutron: a neutral particle found in the nuclei of atoms.

Photon: the elementary unit, or quantum, of light or electromagnetic radiation, having no mass or electrical charge; one of the fundamental force-carrying particles, or bosons, described by the Standard Model.

Plasma: a high-energy state of matter different from solid, liquid or gas in which atomic nuclei and the electrons orbiting them separate from each other.

Proton: a positively charged subatomic particle found in the nuclei of atoms.

Quantum: a natural unit of some physically measurable property, such as energy or electrical charge.

Quark: a fermion and a fundamental matter particle that makes up neutrons and protons, forming atomic nuclei; there are 6 different "flavors" of quarks grouped in pairs; up and down, charm and strange, top and bottom.

Radiation: energy emitted as rays or particles; radiation includes heat, light, ultraviolet rays, gamma rays, X rays, cosmic rays, alpha particles, beta particles, and the protons, neutrons, and electrons of radioactive atoms.

Relativity, general theory of: a theory of space-time proposed by Albert Einstein in 1915; gravitational and other forces are transmitted through the effects of the curvature of space-time.

Relativity, special theory of: Einstein's theory of space and time: all laws of physics are valid in all uniformly moving frames of reference and the speed of light in a vacuum is always the same, so long as the source and the observer are moving uniformly (not accelerating).

Standard Model: prevailing theory of fundamental particles and forces of matter; matter particles are fermions: either leptons or quarks; force-carrying particles are bosons: either gluons, W or Z bosons or photons; gravity has not yet been worked into the model.

String theory: a theory that seeks to unify quantum mechanics and general relativity, positing that the basic constituents of matter can best be understood not as point objects but as tiny closed loops ("strings").

Subatomic particle: one of the small particles, such as electrons, neutrons, and protons, which make up an atom.

Superconductivity: the property of certain materials, usually metals and chemically complex ceramics, to conduct electricity without resistance, generally at very cold temperatures.

Thermodynamics: the branch of physics that describes how energy, heat, and temperature flow in physical systems.

Ultraviolet radiation: a form of light, invisible to the human eye, that has a shorter wavelength and greater energy than visible light but a longer wavelength and less energy than X rays.

Uncertainty principle: the theory that certain pairs of observable quantities—like energy and time, or position and momentum—cannot be measured with complete accuracy simultaneously; presented in 1927 by German physicist Werner Heisenberg; also known as indeterminacy principle.

Virtual particle: subatomic particles that rapidly pop into and out of existence and can exert real forces; usually occur in particle-antiparticle pairs and are rapidly annihilated.

Chemical Elements, Atomic Numbers, Year Discovered

Reviewed by Darleane C. Hoffman, Ph.D., Lawrence Berkeley National Laboratory and Department of Chemistry, Univ. of California, Berkeley.

See Periodic Table of the Elements on page 684 for atomic weights.

Element	Symbol	Atomic number	Year discov.	Element	Symbol	Atomic number	Year discov.	Element	Symbol	Atomic number	Year discov.
Actinium	Ac	89	1899	Gold	Au	79	BC	Praseodymium	Pr	59	1885
Aluminum	Al	13	1825	Hafnium	Hf	72	1923	Promethium	Pm	61	1945
Americium	Am	95	1944	Hassium	Hs	108	1984	Protactinium	Pa	91	1917
Antimony	Sb	51	1450	Helium	He	2	1868	Radium	Ra	88	1898
Argon	Ar	18	1894	Holmium	Ho	67	1878	Radon	Rn	86	1900
Arsenic	As	33	13th c.	Hydrogen	H	1	1766	Rhenium	Re	75	1925
Astatine	At	85	1940	Indium	In	49	1863	Rhodium	Rh	45	1803
Barium	Ba	56	1808	Iodine	I	53	1811	Rubidium	Rb	37	1861
Berkelium	Bk	97	1949	Iridium	Ir	77	1804	Ruthenium	Ru	44	1845
Beryllium	Be	4	1798	Iron	Fe	26	BC	Rutherfordium	Rf	104	1969
Bismuth	Bi	83	15th c.	Krypton	Kr	36	1898	Samarium	Sm	62	1879
Bohrium	Bh	107	1981	Lanthanum	La	57	1839	Scandium	Sc	21	1879
Boron	B	5	1808	Lawrencium	Lr	103	1961	Seaborgium	Sg	106	1974
Bromine	Br	35	1826	Lead	Pb	82	BC	Selenium	Se	34	1817
Cadmium	Cd	48	1817	Lithium	Li	3	1817	Silicon	Si	14	1823
Calcium	Ca	20	1808	Lutetium	Lu	71	1907	Silver	Ag	47	BC
Californium	Cf	985	1950	Magnesium	Mg	12	1829	Sodium	Na	11	1807
Carbon	C	6	BC	Manganese	Mn	25	1774	Strontium	Sr	38	1790
Cerium	Ce	58	1803	Meitnerium	Mt	109	1982	Sulfur	S	16	BC
Cesium	Cs	55	1860	Mendelevium	Md	101	1955	Tantalum	Ta	73	1802
Chlorine	Cl	17	1774	Mercury	Hg	80	BC	Technetium	Tc	43	1937
Chromium	Cr	24	1797	Molybdenum	Mo	42	1782	Tellurium	Te	52	1782
Cobalt	Co	27	1735	Neodymium	Nd	60	1885	Terbium	Tb	65	1843
Copper	Cu	29	BC	Neon	Ne	10	1898	Thallium	Tl	81	1861
Curium	Cm	96	1944	Neptunium	Np	93	1940	Thorium	Th	90	1828
Darmstadtium	Ds	110	1995	Nickel	Ni	28	1751	Thulium	Tm	69	1879
Dubnium (Hahnium)[1]	Db (Ha)	105	1970	Niobium[2]	Nb	41	1801	Tin	Sn	50	BC
Dysprosium	Dy	66	1886	Nitrogen	N	7	1772	Titanium	Ti	22	1791
Einsteinium	Es	99	1952	Nobelium	No	102	1958	Tungsten (Wolfram)	W	74	1783
Erbium	Er	68	1843	Osmium	Os	76	1804	Uranium	U	92	1789
Europium	Eu	63	1901	Oxygen	O	8	1774	Vanadium	V	23	1830
Fermium	Fm	100	1953	Palladium	Pd	46	1803	Xenon	Xe	54	1898
Fluorine	F	9	1771	Phosphorus	P	15	1669	Ytterbium	Yb	70	1878
Francium	Fr	87	1939	Platinum	Pt	78	1735	Yttrium	Y	39	1794
Gadolinium	Gd	64	1886	Plutonium	Pu	94	1941	Zinc	Zn	30	BC
Gallium	Ga	31	1875	Polonium	Po	84	1898	Zirconium	Zr	40	1789
Germanium	Ge	32	1886	Potassium	K	19	1807				

Note: 110 elements are listed here. The name Darmstadtium (Ds) for element 110 (discovery reported by S. Hoffman et al. 1995) was approved by the Internatl. Union of Pure & Applied Chemistry (IUPAC) in 2003. Their identification of the isotopes with mass numbers 269 and 271 has been confirmed, but no confirmation of the isotope of mass 267 reported by A. Ghiorso et al. at Lawrence Berkeley National Laboratory or of mass 273 reported by Yu. Lazarev et al. at Dubna, Russia, has been published. Discovery of elements 111 and 112 with mass numbers of 272 and 277, respectively, was reported by Hofmann et al. in 1995-1996. Discovery of element 111 has been confirmed and a name will be proposed soon; element 112 awaits confirmation. In July 1999, a multinational group working at Dubna, Russia, published evidence for observation of element 114 with mass number 287. A Dubna/Lawrence Livermore National Laboratory group published evidence in Oct. 1999 for element 114 with mass number 289 and reported observation of element 114 with mass number 288 in Sept. 2000 and element 116 with mass number 292 in Dec. 2000. These reports await confirmation. (1) The name Dubnium (Db) has been approved by IUPAC for element 105, but the name Hahnium (Ha) is used in most of the scientific literature before 1998 and is still sometimes used in the U.S. (2) Formerly Columbium.

Periodic Table of the Elements

Source: © 1996 Lawrence Berkeley National Laboratory

Parentheses indicate undiscovered elements.

Legend:
- atomic number / atomic weight
- 14 / 28.09 — **Si** — Silicon — name / symbol

alkali metals	alkaline earth metals	transitional metals													nonmetals					noble gases
1 1.01 **H** Hydrogen																				2 4.003 **He** Helium
3 6.94 **Li** Lithium	4 9.01 **Be** Beryllium											5 10.81 **B** Boron	6 12.01 **C** Carbon	7 14.01 **N** Nitrogen	8 15.999 **O** Oxygen	9 18.998 **F** Fluorine	10 20.18 **Ne** Neon			
11 22.99 **Na** Sodium	12 24.31 **Mg** Magnesium											13 26.98 **Al** Aluminum	14 28.09 **Si** Silicon	15 30.97 **P** Phosphorus	16 32.06 **S** Sulfur	17 35.45 **Cl** Chlorine	18 39.95 **Ar** Argon			
19 39.10 **K** Potassium	20 40.08 **Ca** Calcium	21 44.96 **Sc** Scandium	22 47.90 **Ti** Titanium	23 50.94 **V** Vanadium	24 51.996 **Cr** Chromium	25 54.94 **Mn** Manganese	26 55.85 **Fe** Iron	27 58.93 **Co** Cobalt	28 58.70 **Ni** Nickel	29 63.55 **Cu** Copper	30 65.37 **Zn** Zinc	31 69.72 **Ga** Gallium	32 72.59 **Ge** Germanium	33 74.92 **As** Arsenic	34 78.96 **Se** Selenium	35 79.90 **Br** Bromine	36 83.80 **Kr** Krypton
37 85.47 **Rb** Rubidium	38 87.62 **Sr** Strontium	39 88.91 **Y** Yttrium	40 91.22 **Zr** Zirconium	41 92.91 **Nb** Niobium	42 95.94 **Mo** Molybdenum	43 98 **Tc** Technetium	44 101.07 **Ru** Ruthenium	45 102.91 **Rh** Rhodium	46 106.40 **Pd** Palladium	47 107.87 **Ag** Silver	48 112.41 **Cd** Cadmium	49 114.82 **In** Indium	50 118.69 **Sn** Tin	51 121.75 **Sb** Antimony	52 127.60 **Te** Tellurium	53 126.90 **I** Iodine	54 131.30 **Xe** Xenon
55 132.91 **Cs** Cesium	56 137.33 **Ba** Barium	57 138.91 **La** Lanthanum	72 178.49 **Hf** Hafnium	73 180.95 **Ta** Tantalum	74 183.85 **W** Tungsten	75 186.21 **Re** Rhenium	76 190.20 **Os** Osmium	77 192.22 **Ir** Iridium	78 195.09 **Pt** Platinum	79 196.97 **Au** Gold	80 200.59 **Hg** Mercury	81 204.37 **Tl** Thallium	82 207.19 **Pb** Lead	83 208.98 **Bi** Bismuth	84 210 **Po** Polonium	85 210 **At** Astatine	86 222 **Rn** Radon
87 223 **Fr** Francium	88 226.03 **Ra** Radium	89 227.03 **Ac** Actinium	104 261 **Rf** Rutherfordium	105 262 **Db (Ha)** Dubnium (Hahnium)	106 266 **Sg** Seaborgium	107 267 **Bh** Bohrium	108 269 **Hs** Hassium	109 268 **Mt** Meitnerium	110 271 **Ds** Darmstadtium	111 272	112 277	(113)	(114)	(115)	(116)	(117)	(118)

other metals (labels right of the table)

Lanthanide series

| 58 140.12 **Ce** Cerium | 59 140.91 **Pr** Praseodymium | 60 144.24 **Nd** Neodymium | 61 145 **Pm** Promethium | 62 150.35 **Sm** Samarium | 63 151.96 **Eu** Europium | 64 157.25 **Gd** Gadolinium | 65 158.93 **Tb** Terbium | 66 162.50 **Dy** Dysprosium | 67 164.93 **Ho** Holmium | 68 167.26 **Er** Erbium | 69 168.93 **Tm** Thulium | 70 173.04 **Yb** Ytterbium | 71 174.97 **Lu** Lutetium |

Actinide series

| 90 232.04 **Th** Thorium | 91 231.04 **Pa** Protactinium | 92 238.03 **U** Uranium | 93 237.05 **Np** Neptunium | 94 244 **Pu** Plutonium | 95 243 **Am** Americium | 96 247 **Cm** Curium | 97 247 **Bk** Berkelium | 98 251 **Cf** Californium | 99 252 **Es** Einsteinium | 100 257 **Fm** Fermium | 101 258 **Md** Mendelevium | 102 259 **No** Nobelium | 103 262 **Lr** Lawrencium |

Discoveries and Innovations: Chemistry, Physics, Biology, Medicine

	Date	Discoverer	Nationality
Acetylene gas	1862	Berthelot	French
ACTH	1927	Evans, Long	U.S.
Adrenalin	1901	Takamine	Japan
Aluminum, electrolytic process	1886	Hall	U.S.
Aluminum, isolated	1825	Oersted	Danish
Anesthesia, ether	1842	Long	U.S.
Anesthesia, local	1885	Koller	Austrian
Anesthesia, spinal	1898	Bier	German
Aniline dye	1856	Perkin	English
Anti-rabies	1885	Pasteur	French
Antiseptic surgery	1867	Lister	English
Antitoxin, diphtheria	1891	Von Behring	German
Argyrol	1897	Bayer	German
Arsphenamine	1910	Ehrlich	German
Aspirin	1853	Gerhardt	French
Atabrine	1932	Mietzsch, et al.	German
Atomic numbers	1913	Moseley	English
Atomic theory	1803	Dalton	English
Atomic time clock	1948	Lyons	U.S.
Atomic time clock, cesium beam	1948	Essen	English
Atom-smashing theory	1919	Rutherford	English
Bacitracin	1943	Johnson, Meleneyl	U.S.
Bacteria, description	1676	Leeuwenhoek	Dutch
Bleaching powder	1798	Tennant	English
Blood, circulation	1628	Harvey	English
Blood plasma storage (blood banks)	1940	Drew	U.S.
Bordeaux mixture	1885	Millardet	French
Bromine from the sea	1826	Balard	French
Calcium carbide	1888	Wilson	U.S.
Calculus	1670	Newton	English
Camphor synthetic	1896	Haller	French
Canning (food)	1804	Appert	French
Carbon oxides	1925	Fisher	German
Chemotherapy	1909	Ehrlich	German
Chloramphenicol	1947	Burkholder	U.S.
Chlorine	1774	Scheele	Swedish
Chloroform	1831	Guthrie, S.	U.S.
Chlortetracycline	1948	Duggen	U.S.
Classification of plants and animals	1735	Linnaeus	Swedish
Cloning, DNA	1973	Boyer, Cohen	U.S.
Cloning, mammal	1996	Wilmut, et al.	Scottish
Cocaine	1860	Niermann	German
Combustion explained	1777	Lavoisier	French
Conditioned reflex	1914	Pavlov	Russian
Cortisone	1936	Kendall	U.S.
Cortisone, synthesis	1946	Sarett	U.S.
Cosmic rays	1910	Gockel	Swiss
Cyanamide	1905	Frank, Caro	German
Cyclotron	1930	Lawrence	U.S.
DDT (not applied as insecticide until 1939)	1874	Zeidler	German
Deuterium	1932	Urey, Brickwedde, Murphy	U.S.
DNA (structure)	1953	Crick	English
		Watson	U.S.
		Wilkins	English
Electric resistance, law of	1827	Ohm	German
Electric waves	1888	Hertz	German
Electrolysis	1852	Faraday	English
Electromagnetism	1819	Oersted	Danish
Electron	1897	Thomson, J.	English
Electron diffraction	1936	Thomson	English
		G.Davisson	U.S.
Electroshock treatment	1938	Cerletti, Bini	Italian
Erythromycin	1952	McGuire	U.S.
Evolution, natural selection	1858	Darwin	English
Falling bodies, law of	1590	Galileo	Italian
Gases, law of combining volumes	1808	Gay-Lussac	French
Geometry, analytic	1619	Descartes	French
Gold, cyanide process for extraction	1887	MacArthur, Forest	British
Gravitation, law	1687	Newton	English
HIV (human immuno-deficiency virus)	1984	Mortagnier	French
		Gallo	U.S.
Holograph	1948	Gabor	British
Human heart transplant	1967	Barnard	S. African
Indigo, synthesis of	1880	Baeyer	German
Induction, electric	1830	Henry	U.S.
Insulin	1922	Banting, Best, Macleod	Canadian, Scottish
Intelligence testing	1905	Binet, Simon	French
In vitro fertilization	1978	Steptoe, Edwards	English
Isoniazid	1952	Hoffmann-LaRoche	U.S.
		Domagk	German
Isotopes, theory	1912	Soddy	English
Laser	1957	Gould	U.S.

	Date	Discoverer	Nationality
Light, velocity	1675	Roemer	Danish
Light, wave theory	1690	Huygens	Dutch
Lithography	1796	Senefelder	Bohemian
Logarithms	1614	Napier	Scottish
LSD-25	1943	Hoffman	Swiss
Mendelian laws	1866	Mendel	Austrian
Mercator projection (map)	1568	Mercator (Kremer)	Flemish
Methanol	1661	Boyle	Irish
Milk condensation	1853	Borden	U.S.
Molecular hypothesis	1811	Avogadro	Italian
Motion, laws of	1687	Newton	English
Neomycin	1949	Waksman,Lechevalier	U.S.
Neutron	1932	Chadwick	English
Nitric acid	1648	Glauber	German
Nitric oxide	1772	Priestley	English
Nitroglycerin	1846	Sobrero	Italian
Oil cracking process	1891	Dewar	U.S.
Oxygen	1774	Priestley	English
Oxytetracycline	1950	Finlay, et al.	U.S.
Ozone	1840	Schonbein	German
Paper, sulfite process	1867	Tilghman	U.S.
Paper, wood pulp, sulfate process	1884	Dahl	German
Penicillin	1928	Fleming	Scottish
practical use	1941	Florey, Chain	English
Periodic law and table of elements	1869	Mendeleyev	Russian
Physostigmine synthesis	1935	Julian	U.S.
Pill, birth-control	1954	Pincus, Rock	U.S.
Planetary motion, laws	1609	Kepler	German
Plutonium fission	1940	Kennedy, Wahl, Seaborg, Segre	U.S.
Polymyxin	1947	Ainsworth	English
Positron	1932	Anderson	U.S.
Proton	1919	Rutherford	N. Zealand
Psychoanalysis	1900	Freud	Austrian
Quantum theory	1900	Planck	German
Quasars	1963	Matthews, Sandage	U.S.
Quinine synthetic	1946	Woodward, Doering	U.S.
Radioactivity	1896	Becquerel	French
Radiocarbon dating	1947	Libby	U.S.
Radium	1898	Curie, Pierre	French
		Curie, Marie	Pol.-Fr.
Relativity theory	1905	Einstein	German
Reserpine	1949	Jal Vaikl	Indian
Schick test	1913	Schick	U.S.
Silicon	1823	Berzelius	Swedish
Smallpox eradication	1979	World Health Org.	UN
Streptomycin	1944	Waksman, et al	U.S.
Sulfanilamide	1935	Bovet, Trefouel	French
Sulfanilamide theory	1908	Gelmo	German
Sulfapyridine	1938	Ewins, Phelps	English
Sulfathiazole	1939	Fosbinder, Walter	U.S.
Sulfuric acid	1831	Phillips	English
Sulfuric acid, lead	1746	Roebuck	English
Syphilis test	1906	Wassermann	German
Thiacetazone	1950	Belmisch, Mietzsch, Domagk	German
Tuberculin	1890	Koch	German
Uranium fission theory	1939	Hahn, Meitner, Strassmann	German
		Bohr	Danish
		Fermi	Italian
		Einstein, Pegram, Wheeler	U.S.
Uranium fission, atomic reactor	1942	Fermi, Szilard	U.S.
Vaccine, measles	1963	Enders	U.S.
Vaccine, meningitis (first conjugate)	1987	Gordon, et al., Connaught Lab.	U.S.
Vaccine, polio	1954	Salk	U.S.
Vaccine, polio, oral	1960	Sabin	U.S.
Vaccine, rabies	1885	Pasteur	French
Vaccine, smallpox	1796	Jenner	English
Vaccine, typhus	1909	Nicolle	French
Vaccine, varicella	1974	Takahashi	Japan
Van Allen belts, radiation	1958	Van Allen	U.S.
Vitamin A	1913	McCollum, Davis	U.S.
Vitamin B	1916	McCollum	U.S.
Vitamin C	1928	Szent-Gyorgyi, King	U.S.
Vitamin D	1922	McCollum	U.S.
Vitamin K	1935	Dam, Doisy	U.S.
Xerography	1938	Carlson	U.S.
X ray	1895	Roentgen	German

WORLD ALMANAC QUICK QUIZ

Which element was not discovered until the 1700s?

(a) nickel　(b) tin　(c) silver　(d) mercury

For the answer look in this chapter, or see page 1008.

WORLD ALMANAC EDITORS' PICKS
Most Helpful Household Inventions

The editors of *The World Almanac* have ranked the following as the most helpful household products and inventions that have come into widespread use in the U.S. since the end of World War II. The ranking excludes entertainment and computing devices.

1. Air conditioning
2. Disposable diapers
3. Dishwasher
4. Telephone answering machine
5. Microwave oven
6. Cordless telephone
7. Plastic (polyethylene) garbage bags
8. Automatic drip coffeemaker
9. Self-sealing plastic containers (Tupperware®)
10. Smoke detector

Readers are invited to submit their own list for this and other Editors' Picks; see instructions on page 1007. Results will be published in *The World Almanac 2005*.

Inventions

Invention	Date	Inventor	Nationality
Adding machine	1642	Pascal	French
Adding machine	1885	Burroughs	U.S.
Aerosol spray	1926	Rotheim	Norwegian
Airbag	1952	Hetrick	U.S.
Air brake	1868	Westinghouse	U.S.
Air conditioning	1902	Carrier	U.S.
Air pump	1654	Guericke	German
Airplane, automatic pilot	1912	Sperry	U.S.
Airplane, experimental	1896	Langley	U.S.
Airplane, hydro	1911	Curtiss	U.S.
Airplane jet engine	1939	Ohain	German
Airplane with motor	1903	Wright Bros.	U.S.
Airship	1852	Giffard	French
Arc welder	1919	Thomson	U.S.
Aspartame	1965	Schlatter	U.S.
Autogyro	1920	de la Cierva	Spanish
Automobile, differential gear	1885	Benz	German
Automobile, electric	1892	Morrison	U.S.
Automobile, exp'mtl	1864	Marcus	Austrian
Automobile, gasoline	1889	Daimler	German
Automobile, gasoline	1892	Duryea	U.S.
Automobile magneto	1897	Bosch	German
Automobile muffler	1904	Pope	U.S.
Automobile self-starter	1911	Kettering	U.S.
Bakelite	1907	Baekeland	Belgium, U.S.
Balloon	1783	Montgolfier	French
Barometer	1643	Torricelli	Italian
Bicycle, modern	1885	Starley	English
Bifocal lens	1780	Franklin	U.S.
Bottle machine	1895	Owens	U.S.
Braille printing	1829	Braille	French
Bubble gum	1928	Diemer	U.S.
Burner, gas	1855	Bunsen	German
Calculating machine	1833	Babbage	English
Calculator, electronic pocket	1972	Merryman, Van Tassel	U.S.
Camera, Kodak	1888	Eastman, Walker	U.S.
Camera, Polaroid Land	1948	Land	U.S.
Car coupler	1873	Janney	U.S.
Carburetor, gasoline	1893	Maybach	German
Carding machine	1797	Whittemore	U.S.
Carpet sweeper	1876	Bissell	U.S.
Cash register	1879	Ritty	U.S.
Cassette, audio	1963	Philips Co.	Dutch
Cassette, videotape	1969	Sony	Japanese
Cathode-ray tube	1897	Braun	German
CAT, or CT, scan	1973	Hounsfield	English
Cellophane	1908	Brandenberger	Swiss
Celluloid	1870	Hyatt	U.S.
Cement, Portland	1824	Aspdin	English
Chronometer	1735	Harrison	English
Circuit breaker	1925	Hilliard	U.S.
Circuit, integrated	1959	Kilby, Noyce, Texas Instr.	U.S.
Clock, pendulum	1657	Huygens	Dutch
Coaxial cable system	1929	Affel, Espensched	U.S.
Coffeemaker, automatic drip	1963	Bunn Corp.	U.S.
Compressed air rock drill	1871	Ingersoll	U.S.
Comptometer	1887	Felt	U.S.
Computer, automatic sequence	1944	Aiken, et al.	U.S.
Computer, electronic	1942	Atanasoff, Berry	U.S.
Computer, laptop	1987	Sinclair	English
Computer, mini	1960	Digital Corp.	U.S.
Condenser microphone (telephone)	1916	Wente	U.S.
Contact lens, corneal	1948	Tuohy	U.S.
Contraceptive, oral	1954	Pincus, Rock	U.S.
Corn, hybrid	1917	Jones	U.S.
Cotton gin	1793	Whitney	U.S.
Cream separator	1878	DeLaval	Swedish
Cultivator, disc	1878	Mallon	U.S.
Cystoscope	1878	Nitze	German
Diapers, disposable	1950	Donovan	U.S.
Diesel engine	1895	Diesel	German
Disc, compact	1972	RCA	U.S.
Disc player, compact	1979	Sony, Philips Co.	Japan, Dutch
Dishwasher	1893	Cochrane	U.S.
Disk, floppy	1970	IBM	U.S.
Disk, video	1972	Philips Co.	Dutch
Dynamite	1866	Nobel	Swedish
Dynamo, contin. current	1871	Gramme	Belgian
Electric battery	1800	Volta	Italian
Electric fan	1882	Wheeler	U.S.
Electrocardiograph	1903	Einthoven	Dutch
Electroencephalograph	1929	Berger	German
Electromagnet	1824	Sturgeon	English
Electron spectrometer	1944	Deutsch, Elliott, Evans	U.S.
Electron tube multigrid	1913	Langmuir	U.S.
Electroplating	1805	Brugnatelli	Italian
Electrostatic generator	1929	Van de Graaff	U.S.
Elevator brake	1852	Otis	U.S.
Elevator, push button	1922	Larson	U.S.
Engine, automatic transmission	1910	Fottinger	German
Engine, coal-gas 4-cycle	1876	Otto	German
Engine, compression ignition	1883	Daimler	German
Engine, electric ignition	1883	Benz	German
Engine, gas, compound	1926	Eickemeyer	U.S.
Engine, gasoline	1872	Brayton, Geo.	U.S.
Engine, gasoline	1889	Daimler	German
Engine, jet	1930	Whittle	English
Engine, steam, piston	1705	Newcomen	English
Engine, steam, piston	1769	Watt	Scottish
Engraving, half-tone	1852	Talbot	U.S.
Fiberglass	1938	Owens-Corning	U.S.
Fiber optics	1955	Kapany	English
Fiber optic wire	1970	Keck, Maurer Schulz	U.S.
Filament, tungsten	1913	Coolidge	U.S.
Flanged rail	1831	Stevens	U.S.
Flatiron, electric	1882	Seely	U.S.
Food, frozen	1923	Birdseye	U.S.
Freon	1930	Midgley, et al.	U.S.
Furnace (for steel)	1858	Siemens	German
Galvanometer	1820	Sweigger	German
Garbage bag, polyethylene	1950	Wasylyk	Canadian
Gas discharge tube	1922	Hull	U.S.
Gas lighting	1792	Murdoch	Scottish
Gas mantle	1885	Welsbach	Austrian
Gasoline (lead ethyl)	1922	Midgley	U.S.
Gasoline, cracked	1913	Burton	U.S.
Gasoline, high octane	1930	Ipatieff	Russian
Geiger counter	1913	Geiger	German
Glass, laminated safety	1909	Benedictus	French
Glider	1853	Cayley	English
Gun, breechloader	1811	Thornton	U.S.
Gun, Browning	1897	Browning	U.S.
Gun, magazine	1875	Hotchkiss	U.S.
Gun, silencer	1908	Maxim, H.P.	U.S.
Guncotton	1847	Schoenbein	German
Gyrocompass	1911	Sperry	U.S.
Gyroscope	1852	Foucault	French
Harvester-thresher	1818	Lane	U.S.
Heart, artificial	1982	Jarvik	U.S.
Helicopter	1939	Sikorsky	U.S.
Hydrometer	1768	Baume	French
Iron lung	1928	Drinker, Slaw	U.S.
Kaleidoscope	1817	Brewster	Scottish
Kevlar	1965	Kwolek, Blades	U.S.
Kinetoscope	1889	Edison	U.S.
Lamp, arc	1847	Staite	English
Lamp, fluorescent	1938	General Electric, Westinghouse	U.S.
Lamp, incandescent	1879	Edison	U.S.
Lamp, incand., gas	1913	Langmuir	U.S.
Lamp, klieg	1911	Kliegl, A. & J.	U.S.
Lamp, mercury vapor	1912	Hewitt	U.S.
Lamp, miner's safety	1816	Davy	English
Lamp, neon	1909	Claude	French
Lathe, turret	1845	Fitch	U.S.

Invention	Date	Inventor	Nationality
Launderette	1934	Cantrell	U.S.
Lens, achromatic	1758	Dollond	English
Lens, fused bifocal	1908	Borsch	U.S.
Leyden jar (condenser)	1745	von Kleist	German
Lightning rod	1752	Franklin	U.S.
Linoleum	1860	Walton	English
Linotype	1884	Mergenthaler	U.S.
Liquid Paper	c.1951	Graham	U.S.
Lock, cylinder	1851	Yale	U.S.
Locomotive, electric	1851	Vail	U.S.
Locomotive, exp'mtl.	1802	Trevithick	English
Locomotive, exp'mtl.	1812	Fenton, et al.	English
Locomotive, exp'mtl.	1814	Stephenson	English
Locomotive, practical	1829	Stephenson	English
Locomotive, 1st U.S.	1830	Cooper, P.	U.S.
Loom, power	1785	Cartwright	English
Loudspeaker, dynamic	1924	Rice, Kellogg	U.S.
Machine gun	1862	Gatling	U.S.
Machine gun, improved	1872	Hotchkiss	U.S.
Machine gun (Maxim)	1883	Maxim, H.S.	U.S., Eng.
Magnet, electro	1828	Henry	U.S.
Magnetic Resonance Imaging (MRI)	1971	Damadian	U.S.
Mantle, gas	1885	Welsbach	Austrian
Mason jar	1858	Mason, J.	U.S.
Match, friction	1827	Walker, J.	English
Mercerized textiles	1843	Mercer, J.	English
Meter, induction	1888	Shallenberger	U.S.
Metronome	1816	Malezel	German
Microcomputer	1973	Truong, et al.	French
Micrometer	1636	Gascoigne	English
Microphone	1877	Berliner	U.S.
Microprocessor	1971	Intel Corp.	U.S.
Microscope, compound	1590	Janssen	Dutch
Microscope, electronic	1931	Knoll, Ruska	German
Microscope, field ion	1951	Mueller	German
Microwave oven	1947	Spencer	U.S.
Minivan	1983	Chrysler	U.S.
Monitor, warship	1861	Ericsson	U.S.
Monotype	1887	Lanston	U.S.
Motor, AC	1892	Tesla	U.S.
Motor, DC	1837	Davenport	U.S.
Motor, induction	1887	Tesla	U.S.
Motorcycle	1885	Daimler	German
Movie machine	1894	Jenkins	U.S.
Movie, panoramic	1952	Waller	U.S.
Movie, talking	1927	Warner Bros.	U.S.
Mower, lawn	1831	Budding, Ferrabee	English
Mowing machine	1822	Bailey	U.S.
Neoprene	1930	Carothers	U.S.
Nylon	1937	Du Pont lab	U.S.
Nylon synthetic	1930	Carothers	U.S.
Oil cracking furnace	1891	Gavrilov	Russian
Oil filled power cable	1921	Emanueli	Italian
Oleomargarine	1869	Mege-Mouries	French
Ophthalmoscope	1851	Helmholtz	German
Pacemaker	1952	Zoll	U.S.
Paper	105	Ts'ai	Chinese
Paper clip	1900	Waaler	Norwegian
Paper machine	1809	Dickinson	U.S.
Parachute	1785	Blanchard	French
Pen, ballpoint	1888	Loud	U.S.
Pen, fountain	1884	Waterman	U.S.
Pen, steel	1780	Harrison	English
Pendulum	1583	Galileo	Italian
Percussion cap	1807	Forsythe	Scottish
Phonograph	1877	Edison	U.S.
Photo, color	1892	Ives	U.S.
Photo film, celluloid	1893	Reichenbach	U.S.
Photo film, transparent	1884	Eastman, Goodwin	U.S.
Photoelectric cell	1895	Elster	German
Photocopier	1938	Carlson	U.S.
Photographic paper	1835	Talbot	English
Photography	1816	Niepce	French
Photography	1835	Talbot	English
Photography	1835	Daguerre	French
Photophone	1880	Bell	U.S.-Scot.
Phototelegraphy	1925	Bell Labs	U.S.
Piano	1709	Cristofori	Italian
Piano, player	1863	Fourneaux	French
Pin, safety	1849	Hunt	U.S.
Pistol (revolver)	1836	Colt	U.S.
Plow, cast iron	1785	Ransome	English
Plow, disc	1896	Hardy	U.S.
Pneumatic hammer	1890	King	U.S.
Post-it note	1980	3M	U.S.
Powder, smokeless	1884	Vieille	French
Printing press, rotary	1845	Hoe	U.S.
Printing press, web	1865	Bullock	U.S.
Propeller, screw	1804	Stevens	U.S.
Propeller, screw	1837	Ericsson	Swedish
Pulsars	1967	Bell	English
Punch card accounting	1889	Hollerith	U.S.
Radar	1940	Watson-Watt	Scottish
Radio, magnetic detector	1902	Marconi	Italian
Radio, signals	1895	Marconi	Italian
Radio amplifier	1906	De Forest	U.S.
Radio beacon	1928	Donovan	U.S.
Radio crystal oscillator	1918	Nicolson	U.S.
Radio receiver, cascade tuning	1913	Alexanderson	U.S.
Radio receiver, heterodyne	1913	Fessenden	U.S.
Radio transmitter triode modulation	1914	Alexanderson	U.S.
Radio tube diode	1904	Fleming	English
Radio tube oscillator	1915	De Forest	U.S.
Radio tube triode	1906	De Forest	U.S.
Radio FM, 2-path	1933	Armstrong	U.S.
Rayon (acetate)	1895	Cross	English
Rayon (cuprammonium)	1890	Despeissis	French
Rayon (nitrocellulose)	1884	Chardonnet	French
Razor, electric	1917	Schick	U.S.
Razor, safety	1895	Gillette	U.S.
Reaper	1834	McCormick	U.S.
Record, cylinder	1887	Bell, Tainter	U.S.
Record, disc	1887	Berliner	U.S.
Record, long playing	1947	Goldmark	U.S.
Record, wax cylinder	1888	Edison	U.S.
Refrigerator car	1868	David	U.S.
Resin, synthetic	1931	Hill	English
Richter scale	1935	Richter	U.S.
Rifle, repeating	1860	Henry	U.S.
Rocket, liquid fuel	1926	Goddard	U.S.
Rollerblades	1980	Olson	U.S.
Rubber, vulcanized	1839	Goodyear	U.S.
Saccharin	1879	Remsen, Fahlberg	U.S.
Saw, circular	1777	Miller	English
Scotch tape	1930	Drew	U.S.
Seat belt	1959	Volvo	Swedish
Sewing machine	1846	Howe	U.S.
Shoe-lasting machine	1883	Matzeliger	U.S.
Shoe-sewing machine	1860	McKay	U.S.
Shrapnel shell	1784	Shrapnel	English
Shuttle, flying	1733	Kay	English
Sleeping-car	1865	Pullman	U.S.
Slide rule	1620	Oughtred	English
Smoke detector	1969	Smith, House	U.S.
Soap, hardwater	1928	Bertsch	German
Spectroscope	1859	Kirchoff, Bunsen.	German
Spectroscope (mass)	1918	Dempster	U.S.
Spinning jenny	c.1764	Hargreaves	English
Spinning mule	1779	Crompton	English
Steamboat, exp'mtl	1778	Jouffroy	French
Steamboat, exp'mtl	1785	Fitch	U.S.
Steamboat, exp'mtl	1787	Rumsey	U.S.
Steamboat, exp'mtl	1803	Fulton	U.S.
Steamboat, exp'mtl	1804	Stevens	U.S.
Steamboat, practical	1802	Symington	Scottish
Steamboat, practical	1807	Fulton	U.S.
Steam car	1770	Cugnot	French
Steam turbine	1884	Parsons	English
Steel (converter)	1856	Bessemer	English
Steel alloy	1891	Harvey	U.S.
Steel alloy, high-speed	1901	Taylor, White	U.S.
Steel, manganese	1884	Hadfield	English
Steel, stainless	1916	Brearley	English
Stereoscope	1838	Wheatstone	English
Stethoscope	1819	Laennec	French
Stethoscope, binaural	1840	Cammann	U.S.
Stock ticker	1870	Edison	U.S.
Storage battery, rechargeable	1859	Plante	French
Stove, electric	1896	Hadaway	U.S.
Submarine	1891	Holland	U.S.
Submarine, even keel	1894	Lake	U.S.
Submarine, torpedo	1776	Bushnell	U.S.
Superconductivity	1957	Bardeen, Cooper, Schreiffer	U.S.
Superconductivity in ceramics at high temp	1986	Bednorz	German
		Muller	Swiss
Synthesizer	1964	Moog	U.S.
Tank, military	1914	Swinton	English
Tape recorder, magnetic	1899	Poulsen	Danish
Teflon	1938	Du Pont	U.S.
Telegraph, magnetic	1837	Morse	U.S.
Telegraph, quadruplex	1864	Edison	U.S.
Telegraph, railroad	1887	Woods	U.S.
Telegraph, wireless high frequency	1895	Marconi	Italian
Telephone[1]	1871	Meucci	U.S.-Italian
Telephone[1]	1876	Bell	U.S.-Scot.
Telephone answering machine (1st practical)	1954	Hashimoto	Japanese
Telephone, automatic	1891	Strowger	U.S.
Telephone, cellular	1947	Bell Labs	U.S.
Telephone, cordless[2]	1950	Gross	U.S.

Invention	Date	Inventor	Nationality
Telephone, radio	1900	Poulsen, Fessenden	Danish
Telephone, radio	1906	De Forest	U.S.
Telephone, radio, long dist.	1915	AT&T	U.S.
Telephone, recording	1898	Poulsen	Danish
Telephone amplifier	1912	De Forest	U.S.
Telescope	1608	Lippershey	Neth.
Telescope	1609	Galileo	Italian
Telescope, astronomical	1611	Kepler	German
Teletype	1928	Morkrum, Kleinschmidt	U.S.
Television, color	1928	Baird	Scottish
Television, electronic	1927	Farnsworth	U.S.
Television, iconoscope	1923	Zworykin	U.S.
Television, mech. scanner	1923	Baird	Scottish
Thermometer	1593	Galileo	Italian
Thermometer	1730	Reaumur	French
Thermometer, mercury	1714	Fahrenheit	German
Time recorder	1890	Bundy	U.S.
Tire, double-tube	1845	Thomson	Scottish
Tire, pneumatic	1888	Dunlop	Scottish
Toaster, automatic	1918	Strite	U.S.
Toilet, flush	1589	Harington	English
Tool, pneumatic	1865	Law	English
Torpedo, marine	1804	Fulton	U.S.
Tractor, crawler	1904	Holt	U.S.
Transformer, AC.	1885	Stanley	U.S.
Transistor	1947	Shockley, Brattain, Bardeen	U.S.

Invention	Date	Inventor	Nationality
Trolley car, electric	1884-87	Van DePoele, Sprague	U.S.
Tungsten, ductile	1912	Coolidge	U.S.
Tupperware®	1945	Tupper	U.S.
Turbine, gas	1849	Bourdin	French
Turbine, hydraulic	1849	Francis	U.S.
Turbine, steam	1884	Parsons	English
Type, movable	1447	Gutenberg	German
Typewriter	1867	Sholes, Soule, Glidden	U.S.
Vacuum cleaner, electric	1907	Spangler	U.S.
Vacuum evaporating pan	1846	Rillieux	U.S.
Velcro	1948	de Mestral	Swiss
Video game ("Pong")	1972	Bushnell	U.S.
Video home system (VHS)	1975	Matsushita, JVC.	Japan
Washer, electric	1901	Fisher	U.S.
Welding, atomic hydrogen	1924	Langmuir, Palmer.	U.S.
Welding, electric	1877	Thomson	U.S.
Windshield wiper	1903	Anderson	U.S.
Wind tunnel	1912	Eiffel	French
Wire, barbed	1874	Glidden	U.S.
Wrench, double-acting	1913	Owen	U.S.
X-ray tube	1913	Coolidge	U.S.
Zeppelin	1900	Zeppelin	German
Zipper, early model	1893	Judson	U.S.
Zipper, improved	1913	Sundback	Canadian

(1) While Alexander Graham Bell has traditionally been credited with invention of the telephone, which he patented, Antonio Meucci developed a working model before Bell. (2) Al Gross held a number of important early patents in the field of wireless communication; other people were also involved in the development of practical cordless telephones.

Top 20 Corporations Receiving U.S. Patents in 2002

Source: , U.S. Patent and Trademark Office, U.S. Department of Commerce

Rank	Company	Number of patents	Rank	Company	Number of patents
1.	International Business Machines Corp.	3,288	11.	Fujitsu Ltd.	1,211
2.	Canon Kabushiki Kaisha.	1,893	12.	Advanced Micro Devices, Inc.	1,154
3.	Micron Technology, Inc.	1,833	13.	Toshiba Corp.	1,130
4.	NEC Corp.	1,821	14.	Intel Corp.	1,077
5.	Hitachi, Ltd	1,601	15.	Hewlett-Packard Co.	1,061
6.	Matsushita Electric Industrial Co., Ltd.	1,544	16.	Koninklijke Philips Electronics N.V.	842
7.	Sony Corp.	1,434	17.	Texas Instruments, Inc.	717
8.	General Electric Co.	1,416	18.	Motorola, Inc.	712
9.	Mitsubishi Denki Kabushiki Kaisha	1,373	19.	Eastman Kodak Co.	694
10.	Samsung Electronics Co., Ltd.	1,328	20.	Xerox Corp.	693

Breaking the Sound Barrier; Speed of Sound

The prefix **Mach** is used to describe supersonic speed. It was named for Ernst Mach (1838-1916), a Czech-born Austrian physicist. When a plane moves at the speed of sound, it is Mach 1. When the plane is moving at twice the speed of sound, it is Mach 2. Mach may be defined as the ratio of the velocity of a rocket or a jet to the velocity of sound in the medium being considered.

When a plane passes the sound barrier—flying faster than sound travels—listeners in the area hear thunderclaps, but the pilot of the plane does not hear them.

Sound is produced by vibrations of an object and is transmitted by alternate increase and decrease in pressures that radiate outward through a material media of molecules—somewhat like waves spreading out on a pond after a rock has been tossed into it.

The **frequency of sound** is determined by the number of times the vibrating waves undulate per second and is measured in cycles per second. The slower the cycle of waves, the lower the frequency. As frequencies increase, the sound is higher in pitch. The human ear is usually not sensitive to frequencies of fewer than 20 vibrations per second or greater than about 20,000 vibrations per second—although this range varies among individuals.

Intensity, or loudness, is the strength of the pressure of these radiating waves and is measured in decibels. (See Weights and Measures.)

The **speed of sound** is generally defined as 1,088 feet per second at sea level at 32° F. It varies in other temperatures and in different media. Sound travels faster in water than in air, and even faster in iron and steel.

Light; Colors of the Spectrum

Light, a form of electromagnetic radiation similar to radiant heat, radio waves, and X rays, is emitted from a source in straight lines and spreads out over larger areas as it travels; light per unit area diminishes as the square of the distance.

The English mathematician and physicist Sir Isaac Newton (1642-1727) described light as an **emission of particles**; the Dutch astronomer, mathematician, and physicist Christiaan Huygens (1629-95) developed the theory that light travels by a **wave motion**. It is now believed that these 2 theories are essentially complementary, and the development of quantum theory has led to results where light acts like a series of particles in some experiments and like a wave in others.

The **speed of light** was first measured in a laboratory experiment by the French physicist Armand Hippolyte Louis Fizeau (1819-96). Today the speed of light is known very precisely as 299,792.458 km per sec (or 186,282.396 mi per sec) in a vacuum; in water the speed of light is about 25% less, and in glass, 33% less.

Color sensations are produced through the excitation of the retina of the eye by light vibrating at different frequencies. The different colors of the spectrum may be produced by viewing a light beam that is refracted by passage through a prism, which breaks the light into its wavelengths.

Customarily, the **primary colors** are taken to be the 6 monochromatic colors that occupy relatively large areas of the spectrum: red, orange, yellow, green, blue, and violet. Scientists have differed, however, in how many and which primary colors they recognized. The color sensation of **black** is due to complete lack of stimulation of the retina, that of **white** to complete stimulation. The **infrared and ultraviolet rays**, below the red (long) end of the spectrum and above the violet (short) end respectively, are invisible to the naked eye. Heat is the principal effect of the infrared rays, and chemical action that of the ultraviolet rays.

WEIGHTS AND MEASURES

Source: National Institute of Standards and Technology, U.S. Dept. of Commerce

The International System of Units (SI)

Two systems of weights and measures coexist in the U.S. today: the **U.S. Customary System** and the **International System of Units** (SI, after the initials of Système International). SI, **commonly identified with the metric system,** is actually a more complete, coherent version of it. Throughout U.S. history, the Customary System (inherited from, but now different from, the British Imperial System) has been generally used; federal and state legislation has given it, through implication, standing as the primary weights and measures system. The metric system, however, is the only system that Congress has ever specifically sanctioned. An 1866 law reads:

It shall be lawful throughout the United States of America to employ the weights and measures of the metric system; and no contract or dealing, or pleading in any court, shall be deemed invalid or liable to objection because the weights or measures expressed or referred to therein are weights or measures of the metric system.

Since that time, use of the metric system in the U.S. has slowly and steadily increased, particularly in the scientific community, in the pharmaceutical industry, and in the manufacturing sector—the last motivated by the practice in international commerce, in which the metric system is now predominantly used.

On Feb. 10, 1964, the National Bureau of Standards (now known as the National Institute of Standards and Technology) issued the following statement:

Henceforth it shall be the policy of the National Bureau of Standards to use the units of the International System (SI), as adopted by the 11th General Conference on Weights and Measures (October 1960), except when the use of these units would obviously impair communication or reduce the usefulness of a report.

On Dec. 23, 1975, Pres. Gerald R. Ford signed the Metric Conversion Act of 1975. It defines the metric system as being the International System of Units as interpreted in the U.S. by the secretary of commerce. The Trade Act of 1988 and other legislation declare the metric system the preferred system of weights and measures for U.S. trade and commerce, call for the federal government to adopt metric specifications, and mandate the Commerce Dept. to oversee the program. However, the metric system has still not become the system of choice for most Americans' daily use.

The following 7 units serve as the base units for the system: **length**—meter; **mass**—kilogram; **time**—second; **electric current**—ampere; **thermodynamic temperature**—kelvin; **amount of substance**—mole; and **luminous intensity**—candela.

Frequently Used Conversions

Boldface indicates exact values. For greater accuracy, use the "multiply by" number in parentheses. For more detailed tables, see pages 691-694.

U.S. Customary to Metric

	If you have:	Multiply by:		To get:
Length	inches	**25.4**		millimeters
	inches	**2.54**		centimeters
	inches	**0.0254**		meters
	feet	0.3	**(0.3048)**	meters
	yards	0.9	**(0.9144)**	meters
	miles[1]	1.6	**(1.609344)**	kilometers
Area	sq. inches	6.5	**(6.4516)**	sq. cm.
	sq. feet	0.09	(0.09290341)	sq. meters
	sq. yards	0.84	(0.83612736)	sq. meters
	acres	0.4	(0.4046873)	hectares
	sq. miles	2.6	(2.58998811)	sq. kilometers
Weight	ounces (avdp.)	28	**(28.349523125)**	grams
	pounds (avdp.)	454	**(453.59237)**	grams
	pounds (avdp.)	0.45	**(0.45359237)**	kilograms
	short tons[2]	0.91	**(0.90718474)**	metric tons
	long tons[3]	1	**(1.0160469088)**	metric tons
Liquid meas.	ounces	0.03	(0.02957353)	liters
	cups	0.24	(0.23658824)	liters
	pints	0.47	(0.473176473)	liters
	quarts	0.95	(0.946352946)	liters
	gallons	3.79	(3.785411784)	liters

Metric to U.S. Customary

	If you have:	Multiply by:		To get:
Length	millimeters	0.04	(0.03937)	inches
	centimeters	0.4	(0.3937)	inches
	meters	39	(39.37)	inches
	meters	3.3	(3.280840)	feet
	meters	1.1	(1.093613)	yards
	kilometers	0.6	(0.621371)	miles
Area	sq. cm.	0.16	(0.15500)	sq. inches
	sq. meters	10.8	(10.76391)	sq. feet
	sq. meters	1.2	(1.195990)	sq. yards
	hectares	2.5	(2.471044)	acres
	sq. kilometers	0.39	(0.386102)	sq. miles
Weight	grams	0.035	(0.03527396)	ounces (avdp)
	grams	0.002	(0.00220462)	pounds (avdp)
	kilograms	2.2	(2.204623)	pounds (avdp)
	metric tons	1.1	(1.102311)	short tons[2]
	metric tons	0.98	(0.9842065)	long tons[3]
Liquid meas.	liters	33.8	(33.81402)	ounces
	liters	4.2	(4.226752)	cups
	liters	2.1	(2.113376)	pints
	liters	1.1	(1.056688)	quarts
	liters	0.26	(0.264172)	gallons

(1) Statute mile. (2) A short ton is 2,000 pounds. (3) A long ton is 2,240 pounds.

Temperature Conversions

The left-hand column below gives a temperature according to the **Celsius** scale, and the right-hand gives the same temperature according to the **Fahrenheit** scale. The lowest number for each scale refers to what scientists call absolute zero, the temperature at which all molecular motion would be at its lowest level.

For temperatures not shown: To convert Fahrenheit to Celsius by formula, subtract 32 degrees and divide by 1.8; to convert Celsius to Fahrenheit, multiply by 1.8 and add 32 degrees.

Note: Although the term *centigrade* is still frequently used, the International Committee on Weights and Measures and the National Institute of Standards and Technology have recommended since 1948 that this scale be called *Celsius*.

Celsius	Fahrenheit	Celsius	Fahrenheit	Celsius	Fahrenheit	Celsius	Fahrenheit	Celsius	Fahrenheit
−273.15	−459.67	−45.6	−50	−1.1	30	30	86	66	150
−250	−418	−40	−40	0	32	32.2	90	70	158
−200	−328	−34.4	−30	4.4	40	35	95	80	176
−184	−300	−30	−22	10	50	37	98.6	90	194
−157	−250	−28.9	−20	15.6	60	37.8	100	93	200
−150	−238	−23.3	−10	20	68	40	104	100	212
−129	−200	−20	−4	21.1	70	43	110	121	250
−101	−150	−17.8	0	23.9	75	49	120	149	300
−100	−148	−12.2	10	25	77	50	122	150	302
−73.3	−100	−10	14	26.7	80	54	130	200	392
−50	−58	−6.7	20	29.4	85	60	140	300	572

Boiling and Freezing Points

Water boils at 212° F (100° C) at sea level. For every 550 feet above sea level, boiling point of water is lower by about 1° F. Methyl alcohol boils at 148° F. Average human oral temperature, 98.6° F. **Water freezes** at 32° F (0° C).

Mathematical Formulas

Note: The value of π (the Greek letter pi) is approximately 3.14159265 (equal to the ratio of the circumference of a circle to the diameter). The equivalence is typically rounded further to 3.1416 or 3.14.

To find the CIRCUMFERENCE of a:
Circle — Multiply the diameter by π.

To find the AREA of a:
Circle — Multiply the square of the radius (equal to ½ the diameter) by π.
Rectangle — Multiply the length of the base by the height.
Sphere (surface) — Multiply the square of the radius by π and multiply by 4.
Square — Square the length of one side.
Trapezoid — Add the 2 parallel sides, multiply by the height, and divide by 2.
Triangle — Multiply the base by the height, divide by 2.

To find the VOLUME of a:
Cone — Multiply the square of the radius of the base by π, multiply by the height, and divide by 3.
Cube — Cube the length of one edge.
Cylinder — Multiply the square of the radius of the base by π and multiply by the height.
Pyramid — Multiply the area of the base by the height and divide by 3.
Rectangular Prism — Multiply the length by the width by the height.
Sphere — Multiply the cube of the radius by π, multiply by 4, and divide by 3.

Playing Cards and Dice Chances

5-Card Poker Hands

Hand	Number possible	Odds against
Royal flush	4	649,739 to 1
Other straight flush	36	72,192 to 1
Four of a kind	624	4,164 to 1
Full house	3,744	693 to 1
Flush	5,108	508 to 1
Straight	10,200	254 to 1
Three of a kind	54,912	46 to 1
Two pairs	123,552	20 to 1
One pair	1,098,240	4 to 3 (1.37 to 1)
Nothing	1,302,540	1 to 1
TOTAL	**2,598,960**	

Note: Although there are only 13 4-of-a-kind combinations, the above numbers take into account the total possibilities when a 5th card is figured in to make a 5-card hand.

Bridge

The odds—against suit distribution in a hand of 4-4-3-2 are about 4 to 1, against 5-4-2-2 about 8 to 1, against 6-4-2-1 about 20 to 1, against 7-4-1-1 about 254 to 1, against 8-4-1-0 about 2,211 to 1, and against 13-0-0-0 about 158,753,389,899 to 1.

Dice
(probabilities of consecutive winning plays)

No. consecutive wins	By 7, 11, or point	No. consecutive wins	By 7, 11, or point
1	244 in 495	6	1 in 70
2	6 in 25	7	1 in 141
3	3 in 25	8	1 in 287
4	1 in 17	9	1 in 582
5	1 in 34		

Dice
(probabilities on 2 dice)

Total	Odds against (single toss)	Total	Odds against (single toss)
2	35 to 1	8	31 to 5
3	17 to 1	9	8 to 1
4	11 to 1	10	11 to 1
5	8 to 1	11	17 to 1
6	31 to 5	12	35 to 1
7	5 to 1		

Large Numbers

U.S.	No. of zeros	British[1], French, German	U.S.	No. of zeros	British[1], French, German	U.S.	No. of zeros	British[1], French, German
million	6	million	nonillion	30	quintillion	septendecillion	54	nonillion
billion	9	milliard	decillion	33	1,000 quintillion	octodecillion	57	1,000 nonillion
trillion	12	billion	undecillion	36	sextillion	novemdecillion	60	decillion
quadrillion	15	1,000 billion	duodecillion	39	1,000 sextillion	vigintillion	63	1,000 decillion
quintillion	18	trillion	tredecillion	42	septillion	googol	100	googol
sextillion	21	1,000 trillion	quattuordecillion	45	1,000 septillion	centillion	303	—
septillion	24	quadrillion	quindecillion	48	octillion	—	600	centillion
octillion	27	1,000 quadrillion	sexdecillion	51	1,000 octillion	googolplex	googol	googolplex

(1) In recent years, it has become more common in Britain to use American terminology for large numbers.

Prime Numbers

A prime number is an integer other than zero or ±1 that is divisible only by ±1 and itself.

Prime Numbers Between 1 and 1,000

	2	3	5	7	11	13	17	19	23
29	31	37	41	43	47	53	59	61	67
71	73	79	83	89	97	101	103	107	109
113	127	131	137	139	149	151	157	163	167
173	179	181	191	193	197	199	211	223	227
229	233	239	241	251	257	263	269	271	277
281	283	293	307	311	313	317	331	337	347
349	353	359	367	373	379	383	389	397	401
409	419	421	431	433	439	443	449	457	461
463	467	479	487	491	499	503	509	521	523
541	547	557	563	569	571	577	587	593	599
601	607	613	617	619	631	641	643	647	653
659	661	673	677	683	691	701	709	719	727
733	739	743	751	757	761	769	773	787	797
809	811	821	823	827	829	839	853	857	859
863	877	881	883	887	907	911	919	929	937
941	947	953	967	971	977	983	991	997	(1,009)

Roman Numerals

I — 1	VI — 6	XI — 11	L — 50	CD — 400
II — 2	VII — 7	XIX — 19	LX — 60	D — 500
III — 3	VIII — 8	XX — 20	XC — 90	CM — 900
IV — 4	IX — 9	XXX — 30	C — 100	M — 1,000
V — 5	X — 10	XL — 40	CC — 200	

Note: The numerals V, X, L, C, D, or M shown with a horizontal line on top denote 1,000 times the original value.

Common Fractions Reduced to Decimals

8ths	16ths	32nds	64ths		8ths	16ths	32nds	64ths		8ths	16ths	32nds	64ths		8ths	16ths	32nds	64ths	
			1 = 0.015625					17 = 0.265625					33 = 0.515625					49 = 0.765625
		1	2 = 0.03125				9	18 = 0.28125				17	34 = 0.53125				25	50 = 0.78125
			3 = 0.046875					19 = 0.296875					35 = 0.546875					51 = 0.796875
	1	2	4 = 0.0625			5	10	20 = 0.3125				18	36 = 0.5625			13	26	52 = 0.8125
			5 = 0.078125					21 = 0.328125					37 = 0.578125					53 = 0.828125
		3	6 = 0.09375				11	22 = 0.34375				19	38 = 0.59375				27	54 = 0.84375
			7 = 0.109375					23 = 0.359375					39 = 0.609375					55 = 0.859375
1	2	4	8 = 0.125		3	6	12	24 = 0.375		5	10	20	40 = 0.625		7	14	28	56 = 0.875
			9 = 0.140625					25 = 0.390625					41 = 0.640625					57 = 0.890625
	5	10 = 0.15625				13	26 = 0.40625				21	42 = 0.65625				29	58 = 0.90625
			11 = 0.171875					27 = 0.421875					43 = 0.671875					59 = 0.921875
	3	6	12 = 0.1875			7	14	28 = 0.4375			11	22	44 = 0.6875			15	30	60 = 0.9375
			13 = 0.203125					29 = 0.453125					45 = 0.703125					61 = 0.953125
		7	14 = 0.21875				15	30 = 0.46875				23	46 = 0.71875				31	62 = 0.96875
			15 = 0.234375					31 = 0.484375					47 = 0.734375					63 = 0.984375
2	4	8	16 = 0.25		4	8	16	32 = 0.5		6	12	24	48 = 0.75		8	16	32	64 = 1.0

► **IT'S A FACT:** When the metric system was first conceived, the meter was intended to be 1 ten-millionth of the distance from the North Pole to the Equator, the liter was to be the volume of 1 cubic decimeter (1 decimeter = 1/10 of a meter), and the kilogram was supposed to be the weight of a liter of pure water. The units are not now defined in these terms, but their values are still close to what was originally proposed.

Metric System Prefixes

The following prefixes, in combination with the basic unit names, provide the multiples and submultiples in thes metric system. For example, the unit name *meter*, with the prefix *kilo* added, produces *kilometer*, meaning "1,000 meters."

Prefix	Symbol	Multiples	Equivalent	Prefix	Symbol	Multiples	Equivalent
yotta	Y	10^{24}	septillionfold	deci	d	10^{-1}	tenth part
zetta	Z	10^{21}	sextillionfold	centi	c	10^{-2}	hundredth part
exa	E	10^{18}	quintillionfold	milli	m	10^{-3}	thousandth part
peta	P	10^{15}	quadrillionfold	micro	μ	10^{-6}	millionth part
tera	T	10^{12}	trillionfold	nano	n	10^{-9}	billionth part
giga	G	10^{9}	billionfold	pico	p	10^{-12}	trillionth part
mega	M	10^{6}	millionfold	femto	f	10^{-15}	quadrillionth part
kilo	k	10^{3}	thousandfold	atto	a	10^{-18}	quintillionth part
hecto	h	10^{2}	hundredfold	zepto	z	10^{-21}	sextillionth part
deka	da	10	tenfold	yocto	y	10^{-24}	septillionth part

Tables of Metric Weights and Measures

(**Note:** The metric system generally uses the term *mass* instead of *weight*. Mass is a measure of an object's inertial property, or the amount of matter it contains. Weight is a measure of the force exerted on an object by gravity or the force needed to support it. Also, the metric system does not make a distinction between "dry volume" and "liquid volume.")

Length

10 millimeters (mm)	= 1 centimeter (cm)
10 centimeters	= 1 decimeter (dm)
	= 100 millimeters
10 decimeters	= 1 meter (m)
	= 1,000 millimeters
10 meters	= 1 dekameter (dam)
10 dekameters	= 1 hectometer (hm)
	= 100 meters
10 hectometers	= 1 kilometer (km)
	= 10,000 meters

Area

100 square millimeters (mm²)	= 1 square centimeter (cm²)
10,000 square centimeters	= 1 square meter (m²)
	= 1,000,000 square millimeters
100 square meters	= 1 are (a)
100 ares	= 1 hectare (ha)
	= 10,000 square meters
100 hectares	= 1 square kilometer (km²)
	= 1,000,000 square meters

Volume

10 milliliters (mL)	= 1 centiliter (cL)
10 centiliters	= 1 deciliter (dL)
	= 100 milliliters
10 deciliters	= 1 liter (L)
	= 1,000 milliliters
10 liters	= 1 dekaliter (daL)
10 dekaliters	= 1 hectoliter (hL)
	= 100 liters
10 hectoliters	= 1 kiloliter (kL)
	= 1,000 liters

Volume (Cubic Measure)

1,000 cubic millimeters (mm³)	= 1 cubic centimeter (cm³)
1,000 cubic centimeters	= 1 cubic decimeter (dm³)
	= 1,000,000 cubic millimeters
1,000 cubic decimeters	= 1 cubic meter (m³)
	= 1 stere
	= 1,000,000 cubic centimeters
	= 1,000,000,000 cubic millimeters

Weight (Mass)

10 milligrams (mg)	= 1 centigram (cg)
10 centigrams	= 1 decigram (dg)
	= 100 milligrams
10 decigrams	= 1 gram (g)
	= 1,000 milligrams
10 grams	= 1 dekagram (dag)
10 dekagrams	= 1 hectogram (hg)
	= 100 grams
10 hectograms	= 1 kilogram (kg)
	= 1,000 grams
1,000 kilograms	= 1 metric ton (t)

Table of U.S. Customary Weights and Measures

Length

12 inches (in)	= 1 foot (ft)
3 feet	= 1 yard (yd)
5½ yards	= 1 rod (rd), pole, or perch (16½ feet)
40 rods	= 1 furlong (fur)
	= 220 yards
	= 660 feet
8 furlongs	= 1 statute mile (mi)
	= 1,760 yards
	= 5,280 feet
3 miles	= 1 league
	= 5,280 yards
	= 15,840 feet
6076.11549 feet	= 1 international nautical mile

Volume (Liquid Measure)

When necessary to distinguish the liquid pint or quart from the dry pint or quart, the word *liquid* or the abbreviation *liq* is used in combination with the name or abbreviation of the liquid unit.

4 gills (gi)	= 1 pint (pt)
	= 28.875 cubic inches
2 pints	= 1 quart (qt)
	= 57.75 cubic inches
4 quarts	= 1 gallon (gal)
	= 231 cubic inches
	= 8 pints
	= 32 gills

Volume (Dry Measure)

When necessary to distinguish the dry pint or quart from the liquid pint or quart, the word *dry* is used in combination with the name or abbreviation of the dry unit.

2 pints (pt)	= 1 quart (qt)
	= 67.2006 cubic inches
8 quarts	= 1 peck (pk)
	= 537.605 cubic inches
	= 16 pints
4 pecks	= 1 bushel (bu)
	= 2,150.42 cubic inches
	= 32 quarts

Area

Squares and cubes of units are sometimes abbreviated by using superscripts. For example, ft^2 means square foot, and ft^3 means cubic foot.

144 square inches	= 1 square foot (ft^2)
9 square feet	= 1 square yard (yd^2)
	= 1,296 square inches
30 ¼ square yards	= 1 square rod (rd^2)
	= 272¼ square feet
160 square rods	= 1 acre
	= 4,840 square yards
	= 43,560 square feet

640 acres	= 1 square mile (mi^2)
1 mile square	= 1 section (of land)
6 miles square	= 1 township
	= 36 sections
	= 36 square miles

Cubic Measure

1 cubic foot (ft^3)	= 1,728 cubic inches (in^3)
27 cubic feet	= 1 cubic yard (yd^3)

Gunter's, or Surveyor's, Chain Measure

7.92 inches (in)	= 1 link
100 links	= 1 chain (ch)
	= 4 rods
	= 66 feet
80 chains	= 1 statute mile (mi)
	= 320 rods
	= 5,280 feet

Avoirdupois Weight

When necessary to distinguish the avoirdupois ounce or pound from the troy ounce or pound, the word *avoirdupois* or the abbreviation *avdp* is used in combination with the name or abbreviation of the avoirdupois unit. The *grain* is the same in avoirdupois and troy weight.

27 $^{11}/_{32}$ grains	= 1 dram (dr)
16 drams	= 1 ounce (oz)
	= 437 ½ grains
16 ounces	= 1 pound (lb)
	= 256 drams
	= 7,000 grains
100 pounds	= 1 hundredweight (cwt)*
20 hundredweights	= 1 ton
	= 2,000 pounds*

In *gross* or *long* measure, the following values are recognized.

112 pounds	= 1 gross or long hundredweight*
20 gross or long hundredweights	= 1 gross or long ton
	= 2,240 pounds*

*When the terms *hundredweight* and *ton* are used unmodified, they are commonly understood to mean the 100-pound hundredweight and the 2,000-pound ton, respectively; these units may be designated *net* or *short* when necessary to distinguish them from the corresponding units in gross or long measure.

Troy Weight

24 grains	= 1 pennyweight (dwt)
20 pennyweights	= 1 ounce troy (oz t)
	= 480 grains
12 ounces troy	= 1 pound troy (lb t)
	= 240 pennyweights
	= 5,760 grains

Tables of Equivalents

In this table it is necessary to distinguish between the *international* and the *survey* foot. The international foot, defined in 1959 as exactly equal to 0.3048 meter, is shorter than the old survey foot by exactly 2 parts in 1 million. The survey foot is still used in data expressed in feet in geodetic surveys within the U.S. In this table the survey foot is indicated with capital letters.

When the name of a unit is enclosed in brackets, e.g., [1 hand], either (1) the unit is not in general current use in the U.S. or (2) the unit is believed to be based on custom and usage rather than on formal definition.

Equivalents involving decimals are, in most instances, rounded to the 3rd decimal place; exact equivalents are so designated.

Lengths

1 angstrom (Å)	= 0.1 nanometer (exactly)
	= 0.000 1 micrometer (exactly)
	= 0.000 000 1 millimeter (exactly)
	= 0.000 000 004 inch
1 cable's length	= 120 fathoms (exactly)
	= 720 FEET (exactly)
	= 219 meters
1 centimeter (cm)	= 0.3937 inch
1 chain (ch) (Gunter's or surveyor's)	= 66 FEET (exactly)
	= 20.1168 meters
1 chain (engineer's)	= 30.48 meters (exactly)
	= 100 feet
1 decimeter (dm)	= 3.937 inches
1 degree (geographical)	= 364,566.929 feet
	= 69.047 miles (avg.)
	= 111.123 kilometers (avg.)
of latitude	= 68.708 miles at equator
	= 69.403 miles at poles
of longitude	= 69.171 miles at equator
1 dekameter (dam)	= 32.808 feet

1 fathom	= 6 FEET (exactly)
	= 1.8288 meters
1 foot (ft)	= 0.3048 meters (exactly)
	= 0.015 chains (surveyors))
1 furlong (fur)	= 660 FEET (exactly)
	= $^1/_8$ statute mile (exactly)
	= 201.168 meters
[1 hand] (height measure for horses from ground to top of shoulders)	= 4 inches
1 inch (in)	= 2.54 centimeters (exactly)
1 kilometer (km)	= 0.621371 mile
	= 3,280.8 feet
1 league (land)	= 3 statute miles (exactly)
	= 4.828 kilometers
1 link (Gunter's or surveyor's)	= 7.92 inches (exactly)
	= 0.201 meter
1 link (engineer's)	= 1 foot
	= 0.305 meter
1 meter (m)	= 39.37 inches
	= 1.09361 yards
1 micrometer (μm)	= 0.001 millimeter (exactly)
	= 0.00003937 inch

1 mil	= 0.001 inch (exactly)
	= 0.0254 millimeter (exactly)
1 mile (mi) (statute or land) . .	= 5,280 FEET (exactly)
	= 1.609344 kilometers (exactly)
1 international nautical mile	
(nmi).	= 1.852 kilometers (exactly)
	= 1.150779 statute miles
	= 6,076.11549 feet
1 millimeter (mm)	= 0.03937 inch
1 nanometer (nm)	= 0.001 micrometer (exactly)
	= 0.00000003937 inch
1 pica (typography)	= 12 points
1 point (typography)	= 0.013 837 inch (exactly)
	= 0.351 millimeter
1 rod (rd), pole, or perch	= 16½ FEET (exactly)
	= 5.029 meters
1 yard (yd)	= 0.9144 meter (exactly)

Areas or Surfaces

1 acre	= 43,560 square FEET (exactly)
	= 4,840 square yards
	= 0.405 hectare
1 are (a)	= 119.599 square yards
	= 0.025 acre
1 bolt (cloth measure):	
length	= 100 yards (on modern looms)
width	= 45 or 60 inches
1 hectare (ha)	= 2.471 acres
[1 square (building)]	= 100 square feet
1 square centimeter (cm²) . . .	= 0.155 square inch
1 square decimeter (dm²). . . .	= 15.500 square inches
1 square foot (ft²)	= 929.030 square centimeters
1 square inch (in²)	= 6.4516 square centimeters
	(exactly)
1 square kilometer (km²)	= 247.104 acres
	= 0.386102 square mile
1 square meter (m²)	= 1.196 square yards
	= 10.764 square feet
1 square mile (mi²)	= 258.999 hectares
1 square millimeter (mm²) . . .	= 0.002 square inch
1 square rod (rd²), sq. pole,	
or sq. perch	= 25.293 square meters
1 square yard (yd²)	= 0.836127 square meter

Capacities or Volumes

1 barrel (bbl), liquid . . . . = 31 to 42 gallons*
*There are a variety of "barrels" established by law or usage. For example: federal taxes on fermented liquors are based on a barrel of 31 gallons; many state laws fix the "barrel for liquids" as 31½ gallons; one state fixes a 36-gallon barrel for cistern measurement; federal law recognizes a 40-gallon barrel for "proof spirits"; by custom, 42 gallons constitute a barrel of crude oil or petroleum products for statistical purposes, and this equivalent is recognized "for liquids" by 4 states.

1 barrel (bbl), standard	
for fruits, vegetables, and	
other dry commodities	
except dry cranberries	= 7,056 cubic inches
	= 1 barrel (bbl), standard for fruits
1 barrel (bbl), standard,	
cranberry	= 86 ⁴⁵/₆₄ dry quarts
	= 2.709 bushels, struck measure
	= 5,826 cubic inches
1 board foot (lumber measure)	= a foot-square board 1 inch thick
1 bushel (bu) (U.S.)	
(struck measure)	= 2,150.42 cubic inches (exactly)
	= 35.239 liters
[1 bushel, heaped (U.S.)] . . .	= 2,747.715 cubic inches
	= 1.278 bushels, struck measure*

*Frequently recognized as 1¼ bushels, struck measure.

[1 bushel (bu) (British Imperial)	
(struck measure)]	= 1.032 U.S. bushels, struck measure
	= 2,219.36 cubic inches
1 cord (cd) firewood	= 128 cubic feet (exactly)
1 cubic centimeter (cm³)	= 0.061 cubic inch
1 cubic decimeter (dm³)	= 61.024 cubic inches
1 cubic inch (in³)	= 0.554 fluid ounce
	= 4.433 fluid drams
	= 16.387 cubic centimeters
1 cubic foot (ft³)	= 7.481 gallons
	= 28.317 cubic decimeters
1 cubic meter (m³)	= 1.308 cubic yards
1 cubic yard (yd³)	= 0.765 cubic meter
1 cup, measuring	= 8 fluid ounces (exactly)
	= ½ liquid pint (exactly)

[1 dram, fluid (fl dr) (British)] . .	= 0.961 U.S. fluid dram
	= 0.217 cubic inch
	= 3.552 milliliters
1 dekaliter (daL)	= 2.642 gallons
	= 1.135 pecks
1 gallon (gal) (U.S.)	= 231 cubic inches (exactly)
	= 3.785 liters
	= 0.833 British gallon
	= 128 U.S. fluid ounces (exactly)
[1 gallon (gal) British Imperial].	= 277.42 cubic inches
	= 1.201 U.S. gallons
	= 4.546 liters
	= 160 British fluid ounces (exactly)
1 gill (gi)	= 7.219 cubic inches
	= 4 fluid ounces (exactly)
	= 0.118 liter
1 hectoliter (hL)	= 26.418 gallons
	= 2.838 bushels
1 liter (L)	
(1 cubic decimeter exactly) .	= 1.057 liquid quarts
	= 0.908 dry quart
	= 61.024 cubic inches
1 milliliter (mL)	
(1 cu cm exactly)	= 0.271 fluid dram
	= 16.231 minims
	= 0.061 cubic inch
1 ounce, liquid (U.S.)	= 1.805 cubic inches
	= 29.574 milliliters
	= 1.041 British fluid ounces
[1 ounce, fluid (fl oz) (British)] .	= 0.961 U.S. fluid ounce
	= 1.734 cubic inches
	= 28.412 milliliters
1 peck (pk)	= 8.810 liters
1 pint (pt), dry	= 33.600 cubic inches
	= 0.551 liter
1 pint (pt), liquid	= 28.875 cubic inches (exactly)
	= 0.473 liter
1 quart (qt), dry (U.S.)	= 67.201 cubic inches
	= 1.101 liters
	= 0.969 British quart
1 quart (qt), liquid (U.S.)	= 57.75 cubic in (exactly)
	= 0.946 liter
	= 0.833 British quart
[1 quart (qt) (British)]	= 69.354 cubic inches
	= 1.032 U.S. dry quarts
	= 1.201 U.S. liquid quarts
1 tablespoon	= 3 teaspoons*(exactly)
	= 4 fluid drams
	= ½ fluid ounce (exactly)
1 teaspoon	= ⅓ tablespoon*(exactly)
	= 1⅓ fluid drams*

*The equivalent "1 teaspoon = 1⅓ fluid drams" has been found to correspond more closely with the actual capacities of teaspoons in use than the equivalent "1 teaspoon = 1 fluid dram" which is given by many dictionaries.

Weights or Masses

1 assay ton** (AT) . . . . = 29.167 grams
** Used in assaying. The assay ton bears the same relation to the milligram that a ton of 2,000 pounds avoirdupois bears to the ounce troy; hence, the weight in milligrams of precious metal obtained from one assay ton of ore gives directly the number of troy ounces to the net ton.

1 bale (cotton measure)	= 500 pounds in U.S.
	= 750 pounds in Egypt
1 carat (c)	= 200 milligrams (exactly)
	= 3.086 grains
1 dram avoirdupois (dr avdp). .	= 27 ¹¹/₃₂ (= 27.344) grains
	= 1.772 grams
1 gamma (g)	= 1 microgram (exactly), see below
1 grain	= 64.7989 milligrams
1 gram	= 15.432 grains
	= 0.035 ounce, avoirdupois
1 hundredweight, gross	
or long*** (gross cwt)	=112 pounds (exactly)
	= 50.802 kilograms
1 hundredweight, net or short	
(cwt or net cwt)	= 100 pounds (exactly)
	= 45.359 kilograms
1 kilogram (kg)	= 2.20462 pounds
1 microgram (μg)	= 0.000001 gram (exactly)
1 milligram (mg)	= 0.015 grain
1 ounce, avoirdupois (oz avdp)	= 437.5 grains (exactly)
	= 0.911 troy ounce
	= 28.3495 grams

1 ounce, troy (oz t)	= 480 grains (exactly)
	= 1.097 avoirdupois ounces
	= 31.103 grams
1 pennyweight (dwt)	= 1.555 grams
1 pound, avoirdupois (lb avdp)	= 7,000 grains (exactly)
	= 1.215 troy pounds
	= 453.59237 grams (exactly)
1 pound, troy (lb t)	= 5,760 grains (exactly)
	= 0.823 pound, avoirdupois
	= 373.242 grams
1 stone, (avdp)	= 14 pounds avdp (exactly)
	= 6.350 kilograms

1 ton, gross or long*** (gross ton)	= 2,240 pounds (exactly)
	= 1.12 net tons (exactly)
	= 1.016 metric tons

***The gross or long ton and hundredweight are used commercially in the U.S. to only a limited extent, usually in restricted industrial fields. These units are the same as the British ton and hundredweight.

1 ton, metric (t)	= 2,204.623 pounds
	= 0.984 gross ton
	= 1.102 net tons
1 ton, net or short (sh ton)	= 2,000 pounds (exactly)
	= 0.893 gross ton
	= 0.907 metric ton

Electrical Units

The **watt** is the unit of power (electrical, mechanical, thermal, etc.). Electrical power is given by the product of the voltage and the current.

Energy is sold by the **joule,** but in common practice the billing of electrical energy is expressed in terms of the **kilowatt-hour,** which is 3,600,000 joules or 3.6 megajoules.

The **horsepower** is a nonmetric unit sometimes used in mechanics. It is equal to 746 watts.

The **ohm** is the unit of electrical resistance and represents the physical property of a conductor that offers a resistance to the flow of electricity, permitting just 1 ampere to flow at 1 volt of pressure.

Measures of Force and Pressure

Dyne = force necessary to accelerate a 1-gram mass 1 centimeter per second squared = 0.000072 poundal
Poundal = force necessary to accelerate a 1-pound mass 1 foot per second squared = 13,825.5 dynes = 0.138255 newtons

Newton = force needed to accelerate a 1-kilogram mass 1 meter per second squared
Pascal (pressure) = 1 newton per square meter = 0.020885 pound per square foot

Atmosphere (air pressure at sea level) = 2,116.102 pounds per square foot = 14.6952 pounds per square inch = 1.0332 kilograms per square centimeter = 101,323 newtons per square meter

Spirits Measures

Pony	= 0.5 jigger
Shot	= 0.666 jigger
	= 1.0 ounce
Jigger	= 1.5 shots
Pint	= 16 shots
	= 0.625 fifth
Fifth	= 25.6 shots
	= 1.6 pints
	= 0.8 quart
	= 0.75706 liter

Quart	= 32 shots
	= 1.25 fifths
Magnum	= 2 quarts
	= 2.49797 bottles (wine)

For champagne and brandy only:
Jeroboam	= 6.4 pints
	= 1.6 magnum
	= 0.8 gallon

For champagne only:
Rehoboam	= 3 magnums
Methuselah	= 4 magnums
Salmanazar	= 6 magnums
Balthazar	= 8 magnums
Nebuchadnezzar	= 10 magnums

| Wine bottle (standard) | = 0.800633 quart |
| | = 0.7576778 liter |

Miscellaneous Modern Measures

Caliber—the diameter of a gun bore. In the U.S., caliber is traditionally expressed in hundredths of inches, e.g., .22. In Britain, caliber is often expressed in thousandths of inches, e.g., .270. Now it is commonly expressed in millimeters, e.g., the 5.56 mm M16 rifle. Heavier weapons' caliber has long been expressed in millimeters, e.g., the 155 mm howitzer. Naval guns' caliber refers to the barrel length as a multiple of the bore diameter. A 5-inch, 50-caliber naval gun has a 5-inch bore and a barrel length of 250 inches.

Decibel (dB)—a measure of the relative loudness or intensity of sound. A 20-decibel sound is 10 times louder than a 10-decibel sound; 30 decibels is 100 times louder; 40 decibels is 1,000 times louder, etc.

One decibel is the smallest difference between sounds detectable by the human ear. A 120-decibel sound is painful.

10 decibels	– a light whisper
20	– quiet conversation
30	– normal conversation
40	– light traffic
50	– typewriter, loud conversation
60	– noisy office
70	– normal traffic, quiet train
80	– rock music, subway
90	– heavy traffic, thunder
100	– jet plane at takeoff

Em—a printer's measure designating the square width of any given type size. Thus, an em of 10-point type is 10 points. An en is half an em.

Gauge—a measure of shotgun bore diameter. Gauge numbers originally referred to the number of lead balls just fitting the gun barrel diameter required to make a pound. Thus, a 16-gauge shotgun's bore was smaller than a 12-gauge shotgun's. Today, an international agreement assigns millimeter measures to each gauge, e.g.:

Gauge	Bore diameter (in mm)
6	23.34
10	19.67
12	18.52
14	17.60
16	16.81
20	15.90

Horsepower—the power needed to lift 550 pounds 1 foot in 1 second or to lift 33,000 pounds 1 foot in 1 minute. Equivalent to 746 watts or 2,546.0756 Btu/h.

Karat or carat—a measure of fineness for gold equal to $1/24$ part of pure gold in an alloy. Thus 24-karat gold is pure; 18-karat gold is ¼ alloy. The *carat* is also used as a unit of weight for precious stones; it is equal to 200 milligrams or 3.086 grains.

Knot—a measure of the speed of ships. A knot equals 1 nautical mile per hour.

Quire—25 sheets of paper
Ream—500 sheets of paper

Ancient Measures

Biblical
Cubit	= 21.8 inches
Omer	= 0.45 peck
	= 3.964 liters
Ephah	= 10 omers
Shekel	= 0.497 ounce
	= 14.1 grams

Greek
Cubit	= 18.3 inches
Stadion	= 607.2 or 622 feet
Obolos	= 715.38 milligrams
Drachma	= 4.2923 grams
Mina	= 0.9463 pound
Talent	= 60 mina

Roman
Cubit	= 17.5 inches
Stadium	= 202 yards
As, libra, pondus	= 325.971 grams
	= 0.71864 pound

METEOROLOGY

National Weather Service Watches and Warnings

Source: National Weather Service, NOAA, U.S. Dept. of Commerce; *Glossary of Meteorology*, American Meteorological Society

The **National Weather Service** issues watches, warnings, and advisories for specific geographic areas to alert people to the possibility or imminent arrival of various forms of **severe weather**. A *Severe Thunderstorm* or *Tornado Watch* is issued for a specific area when a severe convective storm that usually covers a relatively small geographic area or moves in a narrow path is sufficiently intense to threaten life and/or property. Examples include thunderstorms with large hail, damaging winds, and/or tornadoes. Excessive *localized convective rains* are not classified as severe storms but are often the product of severe local storms. Such rainfall may result in phenomena that threaten life and property, such as *flash floods. Lightning* occurs with all thunderstorms and, along with flash floods, is a leading cause of storm deaths and injuries.

Severe Thunderstorm—a thunderstorm that produces a tornado, winds of at least 50 knots (58 mph), and/or hail at least 3/4 inch in diameter. A thunderstorm with winds of at least 35 knots (39 mph) and/or hail at least ½ inch in diameter is defined as approaching severe. A *Severe Thunderstorm Watch* is issued for a specific area where such storms are most likely to develop. A *Severe Thunderstorm Warning* indicates that a severe thunderstorm has been sighted or indicated by radar.

Tornado—a violent rotating column of air, usually pendant to a cumulonimbus cloud, with circulation reaching the ground. A tornado nearly always starts as a funnel cloud and may be accompanied by a loud roaring noise. On a local scale, it is the most destructive of all atmospheric phenomena. Tornado paths have varied in length from a few feet to more than 100 miles (avg. 5 mi); in diameter from a few feet to more than a mile (avg. 220 yd); average forward speed, 30 mph. Tornado watches and warnings follow the same criteria as those for thunderstorms.

Cyclone—an atmospheric circulation of winds rotating counterclockwise in the northern hemisphere and clockwise in the southern hemisphere. Tornadoes, hurricanes, and the lows shown on weather maps are all examples of cyclones of various size and intensity. Cyclones are usually accompanied by precipitation or stormy weather.

Subtropical Storm—a cyclone that develops over subtropical waters (N of 20° lat.) with one-minute sustained surface winds of 34 knots (39 mph) or more. It may form over warm or cold water, and can develop into a tropical storm or a hurricane.

Tropical Storm—a cyclone that develops over tropical waters (23.5° N-23.5° S lat.), with one-minute sustained surface winds within a range of 34 to 63 knots (39 to 73 mph). A *Tropical Storm Watch* is issued when tropical storm conditions may pose a threat to specified coastal areas within 36 hours. A *Tropical Storm Warning* is issued when tropical storm conditions are expecd in a specified costal area within 24 hours or less.

Hurricane—a severe cyclone originating over tropical ocean waters and having one-minute sustained surface winds of 64 knots (74 mph) or higher. (West of the international date line, in the western Pacific, such storms are known as *typhoons*.) The area of hurricane-force winds forms a circle or an oval, sometimes as wide as 300 mi in diameter. In the lower latitudes, hurricanes usually move west or northwest at 10 to 15 mph. When the center approaches 25° to 30° North Latitude, the direction of motion often changes to northeast, with increased forward speed. In the W Atlantic and E Pacific, hurricane season is June 1-Nov. 30. Hurricane watches and warnings follow the same criteria as those for tropical storms, and may remain in effect if dangerously high water and/or waves continue.

Winter Storm and Blizzard—A *Winter Storm Watch* is issued when conditions are favorable for hazardous winter weather, such as heavy snow, sleet, or freezing rain. A *Winter Storm Warning* is issued when hazardous winter weather conditions are imminent, and are usually issued for up to a 12-hour duration, which may be extended to 24 hours if needed. A *Blizzard Warning* is issued for winter storm conditions with winds of 35 mph or higher and sufficient falling and/or blowing snow to frequently reduce visibility to less than ¼ mi. for at least 3 hours.

Flood—Flooding takes many forms. *River Flooding:* This natural process occurs when rains, sometimes coupled with melting snow, fill river basins with too much water too quickly; torrential rains from decaying hurricanes or tropical systems can also be a major cause of river flooding. *Coastal Flooding:* Winds from tropical storms and hurricanes or intense offshore low pressure systems can drive ocean water inland and cause significant flooding. Coastal floods can also be produced by sea waves called *tsunamis*, sometimes referred to as tidal waves; these waves are produced by earthquakes or volcanic activity. *Flash Flooding:* Usually due to copious amounts of rain falling in a short time, flash flooding typically occurs within 6 hours of the rain event. Flash floods account for the majority of flood deaths in the U.S. and are the leading cause of deaths associated with thunderstorms. *Urban Flooding:* Urbanization significantly increases runoff over what would occur on natural terrain, making flash flooding in these areas extremely dangerous. Streets can become swift-moving rivers, and basements can become death traps as they fill with water. *Ice Jam Flooding:* Ice can accumulate at natural or artificial obstructions and stop the flow of water. As the water flow is stopped, water builds up and flooding can occur upstream. If the jam suddenly gives way, the gush of ice and water can cause serious downstream flash flooding.

Flash Flood or Flood Watch: means that flash flooding or flooding is possible within a designated area.

Flash Flood or Flood Warning: means that flash flooding or flooding has been reported or is imminent; all necessary precautions should be taken immediately.

National Weather Service Marine Warnings and Advisories

Small Craft Advisory—alerts mariners to sustained (exceeding 2 hours) weather and/or sea conditions, either present or forecast, potentially hazardous to small boats. Although "small craft" is not defined, hazardous conditions generally include winds of 18 to 33 knots and/or dangerous wave conditions. The advisory is also issued for lower wind speeds that may affect small craft operations. Criteria vary depending on region and type of marine environment. Upon receiving word of a Small Craft Advisory, the mariner should immediately obtain the latest marine forecast to determine the reason for the advisory.

Gale Warning—indicates that winds within the range 34 to 47 knots, not directly associated with a tropical storm, are forecast for the area.

Tropical Storm Warning—indicates that winds within the range of 34 to 63 knots associated with a tropical storm are forecast to occur within 24 hours or less.

Storm Warning—indicates that winds 48 knots or above, not directly associated with a tropical storm, are forecast for the area.

Hurricane Warning—indicates that winds 64 knots or greater associated with a hurricane are forecast for the area within 24 hours.

Special Marine Warning—indicates potentially hazardous weather conditions, usually of short duration (2 hours or less) and producing wind speeds of 34 knots or more, not adequately covered by existing marine warnings.

Primary sources of dissemination are commercial radio, TV, U.S. Coast Guard radio stations, and NOAA VHF-FM broadcasts. These NOAA broadcasts on 162.40 to 162.55 MHz can usually be received 20-40 mi from the transmitting antenna site, depending on terrain and quality of the receiver used. Where transmitting antennas are on high ground, the range may be somewhat greater, reaching 60 mi or more.

Monthly Normal Temperatures, Precipitation

Source: National Climatic Data Center, NESDIS, NOAA, U.S. Dept. of Commerce

The temperatures given here are based on records for the 30-year period 1971-2000. For stations that did not have continuous records from the same site for the entire 30 years, the means have been adjusted to the record at the present site. Figures are for airport stations unless otherwise indicated. * = city station. T = temp. in Fahrenheit; P = precipitation in inches.

	Jan.		Feb.		Mar.		Apr.		May		June		July		Aug.		Sept.		Oct.		Nov.		Dec.	
Station	**T**	**P**	**T**	**P**	**T**	**P**	**T**	**P**	**T**	**P**	**T**	**P**	**T**	**P**	**T**	**P**	**T**	**P**	**T**	**P**	**T**	**P**	**T**	**P**
Albany, NY	22	2.7	25	2.3	35	3.2	47	3.3	58	3.7	66	3.7	71	3.5	69	3.7	61	3.3	49	3.2	39	3.3	28	2.8
Albuquerque, NM	36	0.5	41	0.4	48	0.6	56	0.5	65	0.6	75	0.7	79	1.3	76	1.7	69	1.1	57	1.0	44	0.6	36	0.5
Anchorage, AK	16	0.7	19	0.7	26	0.7	36	0.5	47	0.7	55	1.1	58	1.7	56	2.9	48	2.9	34	2.1	22	1.1	18	1.1
Asheville, NC	36	3.1	39	3.2	46	3.9	54	3.2	62	3.5	69	3.2	73	3.0	72	3.3	66	3.0	55	2.4	46	2.9	39	2.6
Atlanta, GA	43	5.0	47	4.7	54	5.4	62	3.6	70	4.0	77	3.6	80	5.1	79	3.7	73	4.1	63	3.1	53	4.1	45	3.8
Atlantic City, NJ	32	3.6	34	2.9	42	4.1	51	3.5	61	3.4	70	2.7	75	3.9	74	4.3	66	3.1	55	2.9	46	3.3	37	3.2
Baltimore, MD	32	3.5	36	3.0	44	3.9	53	3.0	63	3.9	72	3.4	77	3.9	75	3.7	67	4.0	55	3.2	46	3.1	37	3.4
Barrow, AK	–14	0.1	–16	0.1	–14	0.1	–1	0.1	20	0.1	35	0.3	40	0.9	39	1.0	31	0.7	15	0.4	–1	0.2	–11	0.1
Birmingham, AL	43	5.5	47	4.2	55	6.1	61	4.7	69	4.8	76	3.8	80	5.1	80	3.5	74	4.1	63	3.2	53	4.6	46	4.5
Bismarck, ND	10	0.5	18	0.5	30	0.9	43	1.5	56	2.2	65	2.6	70	2.6	69	2.2	58	1.6	45	1.3	28	0.7	15	0.4
Boise, ID	30	1.4	37	1.1	44	1.4	51	1.3	59	1.3	67	0.7	75	0.4	74	0.3	64	0.8	53	0.8	40	1.4	31	1.4
Boston, MA	29	3.9	32	3.3	39	3.9	48	3.6	59	3.2	68	3.2	74	3.1	72	3.4	65	3.5	54	3.8	45	4.0	35	3.7
Buffalo, NY	25	3.2	26	2.4	34	3.0	45	3.0	57	3.4	66	3.8	71	3.1	69	3.9	62	3.8	51	3.2	40	3.9	30	3.8
Burlington, VT	18	2.2	20	1.7	31	2.3	44	2.9	57	3.3	66	3.4	71	4.0	68	4.0	59	3.8	48	3.1	37	3.1	25	2.2
Caribou, ME	10	3.0	13	2.1	25	2.6	38	2.6	52	3.3	61	3.3	66	3.9	63	4.2	54	3.3	43	3.0	31	3.1	16	3.2
Charleston, SC	48	4.1	51	3.1	58	4.0	64	2.8	72	3.7	78	5.9	82	6.1	81	6.9	76	6.0	66	3.1	58	2.7	51	3.2
Charleston, WV	33	3.3	37	3.2	45	3.9	54	3.3	62	4.3	70	4.1	74	4.9	73	4.1	66	3.5	55	2.7	46	3.7	38	3.3
Chicago, IL	22	1.8	27	1.6	37	2.7	48	3.7	59	3.4	68	3.6	73	3.5	72	4.6	64	3.3	52	2.7	39	3.0	27	2.4
Cleveland, OH	26	2.5	28	2.3	38	2.9	48	3.4	59	3.5	68	3.9	72	3.5	70	3.7	63	3.8	52	2.7	42	3.4	31	3.1
Columbus, OH	28	2.5	32	2.2	42	2.9	52	3.3	63	3.9	71	4.1	75	4.6	74	3.7	67	2.9	55	2.3	44	3.2	34	2.9
Dallas–Ft. Worth, TX	44	1.9	49	2.4	57	3.1	65	3.2	73	5.2	81	3.2	85	2.1	84	2.0	78	2.4	67	4.1	55	2.6	47	2.6
Denver, CO	29	0.5	33	0.5	40	1.3	48	1.9	57	2.3	68	1.6	73	2.2	72	1.8	62	1.1	51	1.0	38	1.0	30	0.6
Des Moines, IA	20	1.0	27	1.2	38	2.2	51	3.6	62	4.3	71	4.6	76	4.2	74	4.5	65	3.2	53	2.6	38	2.1	25	1.3
Detroit, MI	25	1.9	27	1.9	37	2.5	48	3.1	60	3.1	69	3.6	74	3.2	72	3.1	64	3.3	52	2.2	41	2.7	30	2.5
Dodge City, KS	30	0.6	36	0.7	44	1.8	54	2.3	64	3.0	74	3.2	80	3.2	78	2.7	69	1.7	57	1.5	42	1.0	33	0.8
Duluth, MN	8	1.1	15	0.8	25	1.7	39	2.1	52	3.0	60	4.3	66	4.2	64	4.2	55	4.1	44	2.5	28	2.1	14	0.9
Fairbanks, AK	–10	0.6	–4	0.4	11	0.3	32	0.2	49	0.6	60	1.4	62	1.7	56	1.7	45	1.1	24	1.0	2	0.7	–6	0.7
Fresno, CA	46	2.2	51	2.1	56	2.2	61	0.8	69	0.4	76	0.2	81	0.0	80	0.0	75	0.3	65	0.7	53	1.1	45	1.3
Galveston, TX*	56	4.1	58	2.6	64	2.8	70	2.6	77	3.7	82	4.0	84	3.5	84	4.2	81	5.8	74	3.5	65	3.6	58	3.5
Grand Rapids, MI	22	2.0	25	1.5	35	2.6	46	3.5	58	3.4	67	3.7	71	3.6	69	3.8	61	4.3	50	2.8	38	3.4	28	2.7
Hartford, CT	26	3.8	29	3.0	38	3.9	49	3.9	60	4.4	69	3.9	74	3.7	72	4.0	63	4.1	52	3.9	42	4.1	31	3.6
Helena, MT	20	0.5	26	0.4	35	0.6	44	0.9	53	1.8	61	1.8	68	1.3	67	1.3	56	1.1	45	0.7	31	0.5	21	0.5
Honolulu, HI	73	2.7	73	2.4	74	1.9	76	1.1	77	0.8	80	0.4	81	0.5	82	0.5	82	0.7	80	2.2	78	2.3	75	2.9
Houston, TX	52	3.7	55	3.0	62	3.4	69	3.6	76	5.2	81	5.4	84	3.2	83	3.8	79	4.3	70	4.5	61	4.2	54	3.7
Huron, SD	14	0.5	21	0.6	33	1.7	46	2.3	58	3.0	68	3.3	73	2.9	72	2.1	61	1.8	48	1.6	31	0.9	19	0.4
Indianapolis, IN	27	2.5	31	2.4	42	3.4	52	3.6	63	4.4	72	4.1	75	4.4	74	3.8	66	2.9	55	2.8	43	3.6	32	3.0
Jackson, MS	45	5.7	49	4.5	57	5.7	63	6.0	72	4.9	79	3.8	81	4.7	81	3.7	76	3.2	64	3.4	55	5.0	48	5.3
Jacksonville, FL	53	3.7	56	3.2	62	3.9	67	3.1	73	3.5	79	5.4	82	6.0	81	6.9	78	7.9	69	3.9	62	2.3	55	2.6
Juneau, AK	26	4.8	29	4.0	34	3.5	41	3.0	48	3.5	54	3.4	57	4.1	56	5.4	50	7.6	42	8.3	33	5.4	29	5.4
Kansas City, MO	27	1.2	33	1.3	44	2.4	54	3.4	64	5.4	74	4.4	79	4.4	77	3.5	68	4.6	57	3.3	43	2.3	31	1.6
Knoxville, TN	38	4.6	42	4.0	50	5.2	58	4.0	66	4.7	74	4.0	78	4.7	77	2.9	71	3.0	59	2.7	49	4.0	41	4.5
Lander, WY	20	0.5	26	0.5	36	1.2	44	2.1	53	2.4	64	1.2	71	0.8	69	0.6	59	1.1	46	1.4	30	1.0	21	0.6
Lexington, KY	32	3.3	36	3.3	46	4.4	55	3.7	64	4.8	72	4.6	76	4.8	75	3.8	68	3.1	57	2.7	46	3.4	36	4.0
Little Rock, AR	40	3.6	45	3.3	53	4.9	61	5.5	70	5.1	78	4.0	82	3.3	81	2.9	74	3.7	63	4.3	52	5.7	43	4.7
Los Angeles, CA*	57	3.0	58	3.1	58	2.4	61	0.6	63	0.2	66	0.1	69	0.0	71	0.1	70	0.3	67	0.4	62	1.1	58	1.8
Louisville, KY	33	3.3	38	3.3	47	4.4	56	3.9	66	4.9	74	3.8	78	4.3	77	3.4	70	3.1	59	2.8	48	3.8	38	3.7
Marquette, MI*	12	2.6	15	1.9	24	3.1	36	2.8	50	3.1	59	3.2	64	3.0	62	3.6	54	3.7	43	3.7	29	3.3	17	2.4
Memphis, TN	40	4.2	45	4.3	54	5.6	62	5.8	71	5.2	79	4.3	83	4.2	81	3.0	75	3.3	64	3.3	52	5.8	43	5.7
Miami, FL	68	1.9	69	2.1	72	2.6	76	3.4	80	5.5	82	8.5	84	5.8	84	8.6	82	8.4	79	6.2	74	3.4	70	2.2
Milwaukee, WI	21	1.9	25	1.7	35	2.6	45	3.8	56	3.1	66	3.6	72	3.6	71	4.0	63	3.3	51	2.5	38	2.7	26	2.2
Minneapolis, MN	13	1.0	20	0.8	32	1.9	47	2.3	59	3.2	68	4.3	73	4.0	71	4.1	61	2.7	49	2.1	33	1.9	19	1.0
Mobile, AL	61	5.8	65	5.1	71	7.2	77	5.1	84	6.1	89	5.0	91	6.5	91	6.2	87	6.0	79	3.3	70	5.4	63	4.7
Moline, IL	21	1.6	27	1.5	39	2.9	51	3.8	62	4.3	71	4.6	75	4.0	73	4.4	65	3.2	53	2.8	39	2.7	26	2.2
Nashua, NH	23	3.9	26	3.1	35	4.1	46	3.9	57	3.7	66	3.9	71	3.7	69	3.8	61	3.6	49	3.9	39	4.2	28	3.7
Nashville, TN	37	4.0	41	3.7	50	4.9	59	3.9	67	5.1	75	4.1	79	3.8	78	3.3	71	3.6	60	2.9	49	4.5	41	4.5
Newark, NJ	31	4.0	34	3.0	42	4.2	52	3.9	63	4.5	72	3.4	77	4.7	76	4.0	68	4.0	56	3.2	46	3.9	36	3.6
New Orleans, LA	53	5.9	56	5.5	62	5.2	68	5.0	76	4.6	81	6.8	83	6.2	83	6.2	79	5.6	70	3.1	61	5.1	55	5.1
New York, NY*	33	3.6	35	2.8	42	3.9	52	3.7	62	4.2	72	3.6	77	4.4	76	4.1	69	3.8	58	3.3	48	3.7	38	3.5
Norfolk, VA	40	3.9	42	3.3	49	4.1	57	3.4	66	3.7	75	3.8	79	5.2	77	4.8	72	4.1	61	3.5	52	3.0	44	3.0
Oklahoma City, OK	37	1.3	42	1.6	51	2.9	60	3.0	68	5.4	77	4.6	82	2.9	81	2.5	73	4.0	62	3.6	49	2.1	40	1.9
Omaha, NE	22	0.8	28	0.8	39	2.1	51	2.9	62	4.4	72	4.0	77	3.9	75	3.2	65	3.2	53	2.2	38	1.8	26	0.9
Philadelphia, PA	32	3.5	35	2.7	43	3.8	53	3.5	64	3.9	72	3.3	78	4.4	76	3.8	69	3.9	57	2.8	47	3.2	37	3.3
Phoenix, AZ	54	0.8	58	0.8	63	1.1	70	0.3	79	0.2	89	0.1	93	1.0	91	0.9	86	0.8	75	0.8	62	0.7	54	0.9
Pittsburgh, PA	28	2.7	31	2.4	40	3.2	50	3.0	60	3.8	68	4.1	73	4.0	71	3.4	64	3.2	53	2.3	42	3.0	33	2.9
Portland, ME	22	4.1	25	3.1	34	4.1	44	4.3	54	3.8	63	3.3	69	3.3	67	3.1	59	3.4	48	4.4	38	4.7	28	4.2
Portland, OR	40	5.1	43	4.2	47	3.7	51	2.6	57	2.4	63	1.6	68	0.7	69	0.9	64	1.7	54	2.9	46	5.6	40	5.7
Providence, RI	29	4.4	31	3.5	39	4.4	49	4.2	59	3.7	68	3.4	73	3.2	72	3.9	64	3.7	53	3.7	44	4.4	34	4.1
Raleigh, NC	40	4.0	43	3.5	51	4.0	59	2.8	67	3.8	75	3.4	79	4.3	77	3.8	71	4.3	60	3.2	51	3.0	43	3.0
Rapid City, SD	22	0.4	27	0.5	35	1.0	45	1.9	55	3.0	65	2.8	72	2.0	71	1.6	61	1.1	48	1.4	33	0.6	25	0.4
Reno, NV	34	1.1	39	1.1	43	0.9	49	0.4	56	0.6	65	0.5	71	0.2	70	0.3	62	0.5	52	0.4	41	0.8	34	0.9
Richmond, VA	36	3.6	40	3.0	48	4.1	57	3.2	65	4.0	74	3.5	78	4.7	76	4.2	70	4.0	58	3.6	49	3.1	40	3.1
St. Louis, MO	30	2.1	35	2.3	46	3.6	57	3.7	67	4.1	77	3.8	80	3.9	78	3.0	70	3.0	58	2.8	45	3.7	34	2.9
Salt Lake City, UT	29	1.4	35	1.3	43	1.9	50	2.0	59	2.1	69	0.8	77	0.7	76	0.8	65	1.3	53	1.6	40	1.4	30	1.2
San Antonio, TX	51	1.7	55	1.8	63	1.9	69	2.6	76	4.7	81	4.3	84	2.0	84	2.6	79	3.0	71	3.9	60	2.6	53	2.0
San Diego, CA	58	2.3	59	2.0	60	2.3	63	0.8	65	0.2	67	0.1	71	0.0	73	0.1	72	0.2	68	0.4	62	1.1	58	1.3
San Francisco, CA	49	4.5	52	4.0	54	3.3	56	1.2	59	0.4	61	0.1	63	0.0	64	0.1	64	0.2	61	1.0	55	2.5	50	2.9
San Juan, PR	77	3.0	77	2.3	78	2.1	79	3.7	81	5.3	82	3.5	82	4.2	82	5.2	82	5.6	82	5.1	80	6.2	78	4.6
Santa Fe, NM	29	0.6	35	0.5	41	0.8	48	0.7	57	1.3	66	1.2	70	2.3	68	2.1	62	1.7	51	1.3	38	1.1	30	0.7
Savannah, GA	49	4.0	53	2.9	59	3.6	65	3.3	73	3.6	79	5.5	82	6.0	81	7.2	77	5.1	67	3.1	59	2.4	51	2.8
Seattle, WA	41	5.1	43	4.2	46	3.8	50	2.6	56	1.8	61	1.5	65	0.8	66	1.0	61	1.6	53	3.2	45	5.9	41	5.6
Spokane, WA	27	1.8	33	1.5	40	1.5	47	1.3	54	1.6	62	1.2	69	0.8	69	0.7	59	0.8	47	1.1	35	2.2	27	2.3
Springfield, MO	32	2.1	37	2.3	46	3.8	56	4.3	65	4.6	73	5.0	79	3.6	78	3.4	69	4.8	58	3.5	46	4.5	36	3.2
Syracuse, NY	23	2.6	25	2.1	34	3.0	45	3.3	57	3.4	66	3.7	71	4.0	69	3.6	61	4.1	50	3.2	40	3.8	29	3.1
Tampa, FL	61	2.3	63	2.7	67	2.9	72	1.8	78	2.9	82	5.5	83	6.5	83	7.6	82	6.5	76	2.3	69	1.6	63	2.3
Washington, DC	34	3.6	36	2.8	44	3.9	54	3.3	64	4.3	73	3.6	78	4.2	76	3.9	69	4.1	57	3.4	47	3.3	38	3.2
Wilmington, DE	32	3.4	34	2.8	43	4.0	52	3.4	63	4.1	72	4.0	77	4.3	75	3.5	68	4.0	56	3.0	46	3.2	36	3.4

Normal High and Low Temperatures, Precipitation

Source: National Climatic Data Center, NESDIS, NOAA, U.S. Dept. of Commerce

The normal temperatures and precipitation data given here are based on records for the period 1971-2000. The extreme temperatures are based on records from time of each station's installation.

Figures are for airport stations unless otherwise indicated. * = city station. Temperatures are Fahrenheit.

State	Station	NORMAL TEMPERATURE January Max.	Min.	July Max.	Min.	EXTREME TEMPERATURE Highest	Lowest	AVG. ANNUAL PRECIPITATION (inches)
Alabama	Mobile	61	40	91	72	105	3	66.29
Alaska	Anchorage	22	9	65	52	85	−34	16.08
Alaska	Barrow	−8	−20	47	34	79	−56	4.16
Alaska	Juneau	31	21	64	49	90	−22	58.33
Arizona	Phoenix	65	43	104	81	122	17	8.29
Arkansas	North Little Rock	49	31	94	73	111	−6	49.19
California	Los Angeles*	66	49	75	63	110	23	13.15
California	San Francisco	56	43	71	55	106	20	20.11
Colorado	Denver	43	15	88	59	101	−19	15.81
Connecticut	Hartford	34	17	85	62	102	−26	46.16
Delaware	Wilmington	39	24	86	67	102	−14	42.81
District of Columbia	Washington–National	43	27	89	67	105	−5	39.35
Florida	Jacksonville	64	42	91	72	105	7	52.34
Florida	Miami	77	60	91	77	98	30	58.53
Georgia	Atlanta	52	34	89	71	105	−8	50.20
Georgia	Savannah	60	38	92	72	105	3	49.58
Hawaii	Honolulu	80	66	88	74	95	53	18.29
Idaho	Boise	37	24	89	60	111	−25	12.19
Illinois	Chicago	30	14	84	63	104	−27	36.27
Indiana	Indianapolis	35	19	86	65	104	−27	40.95
Iowa	Des Moines	29	12	86	66	108	−26	34.72
Kansas	Dodge City	41	19	97	67	—	—	22.35
Kentucky	Lexington	40	24	86	66	103	−21	45.91
Kentucky	Louisville	41	25	87	70	106	−22	44.54
Louisiana	New Orleans	62	43	91	74	102	11	64.16
Maine	Caribou	19	0	76	55	96	−41	37.44
Maine	Portland	31	13	79	59	103	−39	45.83
Maryland	Baltimore	41	24	87	66	105	−7	41.94
Massachusetts	Boston	37	22	82	66	102	−12	42.53
Michigan	Detroit	31	18	83	64	104	−21	32.89
Michigan	Grand Rapids	29	16	82	61	100	−22	37.13
Michigan	Sault Ste. Marie*	22	5	76	52	98	−36	34.67
Minnesota	Duluth	18	−1	76	55	97	−39	31.00
Minnesota	Minneapolis-St. Paul	22	4	83	63	105	−34	29.41
Mississippi	Jackson	55	35	91	71	107	2	55.95
Missouri	Kansas City	36	18	89	68	109	−23	37.98
Missouri	St. Louis	38	21	90	71	107	−18	38.75
Montana	Helena	31	10	83	52	105	−42	11.32
Nebraska	Omaha	32	12	87	66	114	−23	30.22
Nevada	Reno	46	22	91	51	108	−16	7.48
New Hampshire	Nashua	33	12	83	59	—	—	45.43
New Jersey	Atlantic City	41	23	85	65	106	−11	40.59
New Mexico	Albuquerque	48	24	92	65	107	−17	9.47
New Mexico	Santa Fe	43	16	86	54	—	—	14.22
New York	Albany	31	13	82	60	100	−28	38.60
New York	Buffalo	31	18	80	62	99	−20	40.54
New York	New York–Central Park*	38	26	84	69	106	−15	49.69
North Carolina	Raleigh	50	30	89	69	105	−9	43.05
North Dakota	Bismarck	21	−1	85	56	111	−44	16.84
Ohio	Cleveland	33	19	81	62	104	−20	38.71
Ohio	Columbus	36	20	85	65	102	−22	38.52
Oklahoma	Oklahoma City	47	26	93	71	110	−8	35.85
Oregon	Portland	46	34	79	57	107	−3	37.07
Pennsylvania	Philadelphia	39	26	86	70	104	−7	42.05
Pennsylvania	Pittsburgh	35	20	83	62	103	−22	37.85
Puerto Rico	San Juan	82	71	87	77	98	46	50.76
Rhode Island	Providence	37	20	83	64	104	−13	46.45
South Carolina	Charleston	59	37	91	73	105	6	51.53
South Dakota	Huron	25	4	86	61	112	−41	20.90
South Dakota	Rapid City	34	11	86	58	110	−31	16.64
Tennessee	Memphis	49	31	92	73	108	−13	54.65
Tennessee	Nashville	46	28	89	70	107	−17	48.11
Texas	Galveston*	62	50	89	80	101	8	43.84
Texas	Houston	62	41	94	74	109	7	47.84
Utah	Salt Lake City	37	21	91	63	107	−30	16.50
Vermont	Burlington	27	9	81	60	101	−30	36.05
Virginia	Norfolk	48	32	87	71	104	−3	45.74
Virginia	Richmond	45	28	88	68	105	−12	43.91
Washington	Seattle-Tacoma	46	36	75	55	100	0	37.07
Washington	Spokane	33	22	83	55	108	−25	16.67
West Virginia	Charleston	43	24	85	63	—	—	44.05
Wisconsin	Milwaukee	28	13	81	63	103	−26	34.81
Wyoming	Lander	32	9	86	55	101	−37	13.42

Mean Annual Snowfall (inches) based on records through 2002: Boston, MA, 41.8; Sault Ste. Marie, MI, 132.6; Albany, NY, 62.7; Burlington, VT, 83.1; Lander, WY, 102.9; Anchorage, AK, 69.5.

Wettest Spot: Mount Waialeale, HI, on the island of Kauai, is the rainiest place in the world and in the U.S., according to the National Geographic Society; it has an average annual rainfall of 460 inches.

Temperature Extremes: A temperature of 136° F observed at El Azizia (Al Aziziyah), near Tripoli, Libya, on Sept. 13, 1922, is generally accepted as the world's highest temperature recorded under standard conditions. The record high in the U.S. was 134° F in Death Valley, CA, July 10, 1913.

A record low of −129° F was recorded at the Soviet Antarctica station of Vostok on July 21, 1983. The record low in the United States was −80° F at Prospect Creek, AK, Jan. 23, 1971.

Annual Climatological Data, 2002

Source: National Climatic Data Center, NESDIS, NOAA, U.S. Dept. of Commerce

Station	Elev. (ft.)	Temperature °F				Precipitation[1]			Sleet or snow			Fastest[2] wind		No. of Days	
		Highest	Date	Lowest	Date	Total (in.)	Greatest in 24 hours	Date	Total (in.)	Greatest in 24 hours	Date	MPH	Date	Prec. .01 in. or more	Snow, sleet 1 in. or more
Albany, NY	278	96	8/14	1	1/08	41.36	1.79	12/25	85.3	19.5	12/25	44	8/14	150	19
Albuquerque, NM	5,305	101	7/01	14	2/01	6.39	.95	9/10-9/11	—	—	—	48	6/20	45	0
Anchorage, AK	130	79	7/31	-11	1/26	18.79	1.57	10/01	72.0	22.0	3/17	36	11/26	125	16
Asheville, NC	2,171	92	8/05	14	3/01	44.47	4.33	6/26-6/27	5.6	4.0	12/04	39	2/04	118	1
Atlanta, GA	971	97	8/06	18	2/28	47.82	2.39	10/28-10/29	—	—	—	36	1/19	119	0
Atlantic City, NJ	114	98	7/29	13	12/07+	43.66	2.39	4/27-4/28	8.1	5.0	12/05	41	11/23	126	2
Baltimore, MD	193	100	7/04	6	12/07	39.60	2.35	8/28-8/29	12.0	7.4	12/05	40	7/09	105	4
Barrow, AK	35	69	7/15	-46	1/22	4.75	.50	8/14	41.8	2.4	11/16	51	4/26	74	10
Birmingham, AL	636	99	9/05	15	1/04	64.41	3.88	9/21-9/22	T	T	2/27+	35	7/19	131	0
Bismarck, ND	1,651	111	6/29	-19	3/10	11.30	.90	7/09	45.8	5.9	3/19-3/20	52	6/09	95	13
Boise, ID	2,858	110	7/13	12	1/29	6.96	.86	12/30	20.4	8.4	1/20	40	12/16	61	7
Boston, MA	19	101	8/14	12	12/09	41.07	2.02	12/13-12/14	24.8	3.5	11/27	41	5/03	131	8
Buffalo, NY	714	91	9/09	3	12/03	39.74	1.60	1/31	94.0	15.3	12/01-12/02	51	2/01	172	26
Burlington, VT	345	98	9/09	-4	12/09	37.02	2.19	6/11-6/12	69.8	9.1	11/18	39	6/26	159	23
Caribou, ME	627	91	8/15	-18	2/14	37.08	2.31	7/04-7/05	114.0	10.4	3/26-3/27	35	12/11	170	38
Charleston, SC	45	101	6/02	21	2/28	60.97	4.92	10/10-10/11	—	—	—	40	7/31	119	0
Chicago, IL	655	96	7/21	-7	3/04	33.92	4.45	8/22	42.2	7.2	1/31	39	3/09	109	11
Cleveland, OH	802	95	8/13	3	12/04	36.38	1.80	9/27	69.8	10.2	12/25	46	3/09	152	19
Columbus, OH	846	96	7/22+	7	3/04	40.21	3.06	7/23	16.6	3.9	1/06	47	3/09	131	5
Dallas-Ft. Worth, TX	559	100	7/25	14	1/03	44.42	4.39	3/09	—	—	—	51	6/15	79	0
Denver, CO	5,379	100	8/16	-8	2/26	7.48	.81	6/03-6/04	—	—	—	49	5/21	62	0
Des Moines, IA	968	97	7/20	-3	3/04+	24.53	2.26	7/10-7/11	19.7	6.0	1/31	48	3/08	95	6
Detroit, MI	628	97	7/03	3	12/04	30.50	2.44	8/04-8/05	43.3	5.8	12/02	45	3/09	123	14
Duluth, MN	1,426	91	6/30	-14	1/18	31.17	3.42	6/22-6/23	79.3	9.0	3/07	44	5/09	129	19
Fairbanks, AK	461	83	8/03	-43	1/26	13.33	1.06	4/25-4/26	60.9	4.4	4/26	31	7/18	112	23
Fresno, CA	372	109	7/12+	28	1/23	6.75	1.12	11/07-11/08	—	—	—	35	4/14	36	0
Grand Rapids, MI	785	94	6/21	-1	12/03	29.49	1.69	8/01-8/02	72.8	13.6	3/02	47	3/09	125	20
Hartford, CT	162	99	8/14	8	12/09+	41.54	2.09	10/11-10/12	—	—	—	39	12/01	128	0
Helena, MT	3,864	105	7/12	-13	2/26	12.54	1.47	9/09-9/10	—	—	—	52	7/14	83	0
Honolulu, HI	15	90	10/04	60	3/02	12.18	2.38	1/28-1/29	—	—	—	36	1/19	64	0
Houston, TX	118	100	8/03	22	3/04	59.71	8.04	10/28	—	—	—	46	12/30	101	0
Huron, SD	1,281	110	7/20	-7	12/05	14.88	1.27	3/14	42.6	19.0	3/14	53	8/03	76	10
Indianapolis, IN	794	96	8/04	4	3/04	39.73	2.30	5/12-5/13	21.3	7.8	12/24-12/25	45	3/09	112	7
Jackson, MS	293	98	9/05	16	1/04	68.48	4.67	9/25-9/26	—	—	—	44	4/08	133	0
Jacksonville, FL	31	99	6/03	25	2/28	54.72	4.68	9/24-9/25	—	—	—	36	12/31	116	0
Kansas City, MO	1,005	103	7/26	-4	3/04	24.77	2.18	5/05-5/06	8.9	2.8	3/02	46	5/08	90	4
Knoxville, TN	979	95	9/10+	14	1/01	58.10	4.89	3/17-3/18	—	—	—	43	7/02	124	0
Lander, WY	5,557	101	7/14	-9	12/25	8.09	.98	10/01-10/02	88.5	8.7	10/01	52	5/21	48	21
Lexington, KY	977	99	8/04	4	3/04	49.31	3.07	3/19-3/20	—	—	—	45	11/10	134	0
Los Angeles, CA	323	89	2/21	36	1/31	5.03	1.12	12/16-12/17	—	—	—	35	3/16	27	0
Louisville, KY	481	101	8/04	11	3/04	52.96	5.28	9/26-9/27	15.6	3.7	1/19	44	8/13	120	5
Marquette, MI	1,415	95	7/1	-12	3/04+	44.15	1.73	9/20	296.2	19.6	2/26-2/27	—	—	173	60
Memphis, TN	283	98	7/10	18	3/04	74.84	7.11	9/19-9/20	—	—	—	37	8/13	129	0
Miami, FL	26	95	8/01	42	1/04	63.29	4.20	9/25-9/26	—	—	—	30	7/11	139	0
Milwaukee, WI	697	98	7/21	-6	3/04	26.69	2.69	8/12-8/13	39.8	9.4	3/02	37	3/09	108	10
Minn.-St. Paul, MN	871	97	6/30	-3	3/03	38.41	2.96	6/20-6/21	—	—	—	45	6/19	115	0
Mobile, AL	209	96	7/19+	19	1/04	72.48	6.19	9/25	T	T	3/31	48	9/26	121	0
Moline, IL	604	95	7/04	-9	3/04	32.88	2.55	5/11-5/12	27.7	6.3	1/30	46	3/09	103	8
Nashville, TN	571	97	5/05	11	1/04	56.63	3.21	9/26-9/27	—	—	—	38	4/08	130	0
Newark, NJ	25	100	8/13	18	12/09+	43.37	3.04	10/11-10/12	14.4	6.5	12/05	55	4/19	113	3
New Orleans, LA	4	95	8/07	26	1/04	62.51	9.55	9/25-9/26	—	—	—	46	9/26	116	0
New York, NY	158	98	8/13	19	12/09+	45.2	3.25	10/11-10/12	14.5	6.0	12/05	33	4/19	123	3
Norfolk, VA	66	98	8/13	23	12/07	50.87	3.79	9/16	7.4	6.6	1/03	38	8/17	119	1
North Little Rock, AR	563	99	8/24	16	3/04	47.42	2.92	9/19-9/20	5.4	3.8	2/06	—	—	116	2
Oklahoma City, OK	1,281	99	8/23	6	3/03	34.15	2.47	4/06-4/07	6.2	2.3	2/05	53	5/06	88	3
Philadelphia, PA	59	99	8/14+	16	12/07	39.34	2.32	10/10-10/11	12.4	7.0	12/05	43	5/12	119	3
Phoenix, AZ	1,103	113	7/02	36	1/31+	2.82	.77	7/14	—	—	—	40	7/09	18	0
Pittsburgh, PA	1,172	95	8/04+	7	12/04	32.33	2.22	9/26-9/27	34.6	4.8	12/05	48	5/14	142	13
Portland, ME	69	95	7/03	-3	2/03	44.24	2.02	10/16-10/17	49.1	12.5	12/25	44	12/14	136	15
Portland, OR	220	102	8/13	26	1/15	31.25	1.52	12/30-12/31	—	—	—	43	10/30	137	0
Providence, RI	50	98	8/14	12	12/07	42.34	2.12	5/13-5/14	26.5	6.2	12/05	40	12/25	124	9
Raleigh, NC	427	103	8/23	13	1/04	47.34	5.78	10/10-10/11	13.1	6.5	1/03	41	5/13	108	3
Rapid City, SD	3,150	109	6/29	-14	3/09	10.27	1.24	4/26-4/27	—	—	—	69	7/20	74	0
Reno, NV	4,404	108	7/11+	2	1/30	7.08	1.29	12/16	—	—	—	67	12/14	44	0
Richmond, VA	164	101	8/23	14	3/05	37.77	1.59	8/27-28	13.7	7.7	1/03	39	2/01	107	4
St. Louis, MO	707	101	8/01	6	3/04	40.95	2.68	8/06	23.4	5.8	12/24	43	6/24	111	8
Salt Lake City, UT	4,221	107	7/13	-5	1/30	10.29	.76	3/17	38.4	8.4	3/17	53	4/15	67	11
San Antonio, TX	818	100	8/27+	17	2/27	46.27	9.79	7/01-7/02	T	T	12/30+	43	5/26	81	0
San Diego, CA	78	91	9/01	39	1/30	4.23	.82	12/21	—	—	—	31	11/28	30	0
San Francisco, CA	86	94	8/09	35	1/30	19.54	2.58	12/13-12/14	—	—	—	51	11/07	47	0
San Juan, PR	7	94	8/07+	59	12/30	46.69	3.22	8/30	—	—	—	31	8/30	205	0
Sault Ste. Marie, MI	724	90	8/09	-7	3/04	29.19	1.75	8/01	—	—	—	39	3/10	162	0
Savannah, GA	48	101	6/02	19	1/05	47.42	4.05	6/07-6/08	—	—	—	32	6/07	117	0
Scottsbluff, NE	3,946	105	7/31	-9	3/02	7.77	.94	8/05	14.5	6.0	10/30	47	5/21	55	5
Seattle, WA	447	94	6/13	25	1/29+	31.36	1.48	4/12-4/13	—	—	—	41	12/27	140	0
Spokane, WA	2,381	102	7/13+	7	10/31	13.83	1.18	8/21-8/22	40.2	4.2	3/20	43	4/14	101	15
Springfield, MO	1,277	96	8/02	-2	3/04	37.82	3.46	5/07-5/08	31.3	7.8	12/23	38	7/02	106	4
Syracuse, NY	414	101	8/14	0	12/03	40.26	3.08	6/14-6/15	108.6	10.2	12/25	46	2/01	185	38
Tampa, FL	8	96	7/17	34	2/28	62.07	4.10	12/09-12/10	—	—	—	29	11/17	119	0
Washington, DC[3]	10	100	8/13+	18	12/07	34.33	2.20	6/13-6/14	10.3	6.1	12/05	44	3/21	109	2
Wilmington, DE	92	98	8/13+	10	12/07	39.80	2.61	6/13-6/14	11.4	6.8	12/05	41	7/09	118	3

(T) Trace. (—) Data not available or incomplete. (1) Where one date is shown, it is the starting date of the storm. (2) Sustained for at least 2 minutes, not peak gust. (3) As measured at Reagan Intl. airport.

Record Temperatures by State

Source: National Climatic Data Center, NESDIS, NOAA; U.S. Dept. of Commerce, through Dec. 2000

	LOWEST TEMPERATURE				HIGHEST TEMPERATURE			
State	°F	Latest date	Station	Approx. elevation in feet	°F	Latest date	Station	Approx. elevation in feet
Alabama	−27	Jan. 30, 1966	New Market	760	112	Sept. 5, 1925	Centerville	345
Alaska	−80	Jan. 23, 1971	Prospect Creek Camp	1,100	100	June 27, 1915	Fort Yukon	c. 420
Arizona	−40	Jan. 7, 1971	Hawley Lake	8,180	128	June 29, 1994	Lake Havasu City	505
Arkansas	−29	Feb. 13, 1905	Pond	1,250	120	Aug. 10, 1936	Ozark	396
California	−45	Jan. 20, 1937	Boca	5,532	134	July 10, 1913	Greenland Ranch	−178
Colorado	−61	Feb. 1, 1985	Maybell	5,920	118	July 11, 1888	Bennett	5,484
Connecticut	−32	Jan. 22 1961	Coventry	480	106	July 15, 1995	Danbury	450
Delaware	−17	Jan. 17, 1893	Millsboro	20	110	July 21, 1930	Millsboro	20
Florida	−2	Feb. 13, 1899	Tallahassee	193	109	June 29, 1931	Monticello	207
Georgia	−17	Jan. 27, 1940	CCC Camp F-16	1,000	112	Aug. 20, 1983	Greenville	860
Hawaii	12	May 17, 1979	Mauna Kea Obs. 111.2	13,770	100	Apr. 27, 1931	Pahala	850
Idaho	−60	Jan. 18, 1943	Island Park Dam	6,285	118	July 28, 1934	Orofino	1,027
Illinois	−36	Jan. 5, 1999	Congerville	635	117	July 14, 1954	East St. Louis	410
Indiana	−36	Jan. 19, 1994	New Whiteland	785	116	July 14, 1936	Collegeville	672
Iowa	−47	Feb. 3, 1996[1]	Elkader	770	118	July 20, 1934	Keokuk	614
Kansas	−40	Feb. 13, 1905	Lebanon	1,812	121	July 24, 1936[1]	Alton (near)	1,651
Kentucky	−37	Jan. 19, 1994	Shelbyville	730	114	July 28, 1930	Greensburg	581
Louisiana	−16	Feb. 13, 1899	Minden	194	114	Aug. 10, 1936	Plain Dealing	268
Maine	−48	Jan. 19, 1925	Van Buren	510	105	July 10, 1911[1]	North Bridgton	450
Maryland	−40	Jan. 13, 1912	Oakland	2,461	109	July 10, 1936[1]	Cumberland	623
							Frederick	325
Massachusetts	−35	Jan. 12, 1981	Chester	640	107	Aug. 2, 1975	Chester	640
							New Bedford	120
Michigan	−51	Feb. 9, 1934	Vanderbilt	785	112	July 13, 1936	Mio	963
Minnesota	−60	Feb. 2, 1996	Tower	1,460	114	July 6, 1936[1]	Moorhead	904
Mississippi	−19	Jan. 30, 1966	Corinth	420	115	July 29, 1930	Holly Springs	600
Missouri	−40	Feb. 13, 1905	Warsaw	700	118	July 14, 1954[1]	Warsaw	705
							Union	560
Montana	−70	Jan. 20, 1954	Rogers Pass	5,470	117	July 5, 1937	Medicine Lake	1,950
Nebraska	−47	Dec. 22, 1989	Oshkosh	3,379	118	July 24, 1936[1]	Minden	2,169
Nevada	−50	Jan. 8, 1937	San Jacinto	5,200	125	June 29, 1994[1]	Laughlin	605
New Hampshire	−47	Jan. 29, 1934	Mt. Washington	6,262	106	July 4, 1911	Nashua	125
New Jersey	−34	Jan. 5, 1904	River Vale	70	110	July 10, 1936	Runyon	18
New Mexico	−50	Feb. 1, 1951	Gavilan	7,350	122	June 27, 1994	Waste Isolat. Pilot Plt.	3,418
New York	−52	Feb. 18, 1979[1]	Old Forge	1,720	108	July 22, 1926	Troy	35
North Carolina	−34	Jan. 21, 1985	Mt. Mitchell	6,525	110	Aug. 21, 1983	Fayetteville	213
North Dakota	−60	Feb. 15, 1936	Parshall	1,929	121	July 6, 1936	Steele	1,857
Ohio	−39	Feb. 10, 1899	Milligan	800	113	July 21, 1934[1]	Gallipolis (near)	673
Oklahoma	−27	Jan. 18, 1930	Watts	958	120	June 27, 1994[1]	Tipton	1,350
Oregon	−54	Feb. 10, 1933[1]	Seneca	4,700	119	Aug. 10, 1898[1]	Pendleton	1,074
Pennsylvania	−42	Jan. 5, 1904	Smethport	c. 1,500	111	July 10, 1936[1]	Phoenixville	100
Rhode Island	−25	Feb. 5, 1996	Greene	425	104	Aug. 2, 1975	Providence	51
South Carolina	−19	Jan. 21, 1985	Caesars Head	3,115	111	June 28, 1954[1]	Camden	170
South Dakota	−58	Feb. 17, 1936	McIntosh	2,277	120	July 5, 1936	Gannvalley	1,750
Tennessee	−32	Dec. 30, 1917	Mountain City	2,471	113	Aug. 9, 1930[1]	Perryville	377
Texas	−23	Feb. 8, 1933[1]	Seminole	3,275	120	June 28 1994	Monahans	2,660
Utah	−50	Dec. 30, 1933	Bloomfield	915	117	Jul. 5, 1985	Saint George	2,880
Vermont	−69	Feb. 1, 1985	Peter's Sink	8,092	105	July 4, 1911	Vernon	310
Virginia	−30	Jan. 22, 1985	Mountain Lake Bio. Station	3,870	110	July 15, 1954	Balcony Falls	725
Washington	−48	Dec. 30, 1968	Mazama	2,120	118	Aug. 5, 1961[1]	Ice Harbor Dam	475
			Winthrop	1,755				
West Virginia	−37	Dec. 30, 1917	Lewisburg	2,200	112	July 10, 1936[1]	Martinsburg	435
Wisconsin	−55	Feb. 4, 1996	Couderay	1,300	114	July 13, 1936	Wisconsin Dells	900
Wyoming	−66	Feb. 9, 1933	Riverside R.S.	6,500	115	Aug. 8, 1983	Basin	3,500

(1) Also on earlier dates at the same or other places.

Hurricane and Tornado Classifications

Source: National Weather Service, NOAA, U.S. Dept. of Commerce

The Saffir-Simpson Hurricane Scale is a 1-5 rating based on a hurricane's intensity. The scale is used to give an estimate of the potential property damage and flooding expected along the coast from a hurricane landfall. Wind speed is the determining factor in the scale. The Fujita (or F) Scale, created by T. Theodore Fujita, is used to classify tornadoes. The F Scale uses rating numbers from 0 to 5, based on the amount and type of wind damage.

Saffir-Simpson Scale (Hurricanes)				Fujita Scale (Tornadoes)			
Category	Wind Speed	Severity	Storm Surge[1]	Rank	Wind Speed	Damage	Strength
1	74-95 MPH	Weak	4-5 feet	F-0	40-72 MPH	Light	Weak
2	96-110 MPH	Moderate	6-8 feet	F-1	73-112 MPH	Moderate	Weak
3	111-130 MPH	Strong	9-12 feet	F-2	113-157 MPH	Considerable	Strong
4	131-155 MPH	Very Strong	13-18 feet	F-3	158-206 MPH	Severe	Strong
5	above 155 MPH	Devastating	above 18 feet	F-4	207-260 MPH	Devastating	Violent
				F-5	above 261 MPH	Incredible	Violent

(1) Above normal tides.

> ▶ **IT'S A FACT:** A U.S. record-size hailstone fell in Aurora, NE, on June 22, 2003. It had a circumference of 18.75 in. and was 7 in. in diameter. The previous (longtime) record-holder was found in 1970 in Coffeyville, KS, with a circumference of 17.5 in. and diameter of 5.7 in.

Hurricane Names in 2004
Source: National Weather Service, NOAA, U.S. Dept. of Commerce

Atlantic hurricanes — Alex, Bonnie, Charley, Danielle, Earl, Frances, Gaston, Hermine, Ivan, Jeanne, Karl, Lisa, Matthew, Nicole, Otto, Paula, Richard, Shary, Tomas, Virginie, Walter.

Eastern Pacific hurricanes — Agatha, Blas, Celia, Darby, Estelle, Frank, Georgette, Howard, Isis, Javier, Kay, Lester, Madeline, Newton, Orlene, Paine, Roslyn, Seymour, Tina, Virgil, Winifred, Xavier, Yolanda, Zeke.

World Temperature and Precipitation
Source: World Meteorological Organization

Average daily maximum and minimum temperatures and annual precipitation are based on records for the period 1961-90. The record of extreme temperatures includes all available years of data for a given location and is usually for a longer period; record temperatures may have been measured at a different location within the city. Surface elevations are supplied by the WMO and may differ from city elevation figures in other sections of *The World Almanac*. NA = Not available.

Station	Surface elevation (feet)	Temperature °F AVERAGE DAILY January Max.	January Min.	July Max.	July Min.	EXTREME Max.	EXTREME Min.	Average annual precipitation (inches)
Algiers, Algeria	82	61.7	42.6	87.1	65.3	NA	NA	27.0
Athens, Greece	49	56.1	44.6	88.9	73.0	NA	NA	14.6
Auckland, New Zealand	20	74.8	61.2	58.5	46.4	NA	NA	49.4
Bangkok, Thailand	66	89.6	69.8	90.9	77.0	104	51	59.0
Berlin, Germany	190	35.2	26.8	73.6	55.2	107	-4	23.3
Bogotá, Colombia	8,357	67.3	41.7	64.6	45.5	75	21	32.4
Bombay (Mumbai), India	36	85.3	66.7	86.2	77.5	110	46	85.4
Bucharest, Romania	298	34.7	22.1	83.8	60.1	105	-18	23.4
Budapest, Hungary	456	34.2	24.8	79.7	59.7	103	-10	20.3
Buenos Aires, Argentina	82	85.8	67.3	59.7	45.7	104	22	45.2
Cairo, Egypt	243	65.8	48.2	93.9	71.1	118	34	1.0
Cape Town, South Africa	138	79.0	60.3	63.3	44.6	105	28	20.5
Caracas, Venezuela	2,739	79.9	60.8	81.3	66.0	96	45	36.1
Casablanca, Morocco	203	62.8	47.1	77.7	66.7	NA	NA	16.8
Copenhagen, Denmark	16	35.6	28.4	68.9	55.0	NA	NA	NA
Damascus, Syria	2,004	54.3	32.9	97.2	61.9	NA	NA	5.6
Dublin, Ireland	279	45.7	36.5	66.0	52.5	86	8	28.8
Geneva, Switzerland	1,364	38.3	27.9	76.3	53.2	101	-3	35.6
Havana, Cuba	164	78.4	65.5	88.3	74.8	NA	NA	46.9
Hong Kong, China	203	65.5	56.5	88.7	79.9	97	32	87.2
Istanbul, Turkey	108	47.8	37.2	82.8	65.3	105	7	27.4
Jerusalem, Israel	2,483	53.4	39.4	83.8	63.0	107	26	23.2
Lagos, Nigeria	125	90.0	72.3	82.8	72.1	NA	NA	59.3
Lima, Peru	43	79.0	66.9	66.4	59.4	NA	NA	0.2
London, England	203	44.1	32.7	71.1	52.3	99	2	29.7
Manila, Philippines	79	85.8	74.8	89.1	76.8	NA	NA	49.6
Mexico City, Mexico	7,570	70.3	43.7	73.8	53.2	NA	NA	33.4
Montreal, Canada	118	21.6	5.2	79.2	59.7	100	-36	37.0
Nairobi, Kenya	5,897	77.9	50.9	71.6	48.6	NA	NA	41.9
Paris, France	213	42.8	33.6	75.2	55.2	105	-1	25.6
Prague, Czech Republic	1,197	32.7	22.5	73.9	53.2	98	-16	20.7
Reykjavik, Iceland	200	35.4	26.6	55.9	46.9	76	-3	31.5
Rome, Italy	79	53.8	35.4	88.2	62.1	NA	NA	33.0
San Salvador, El Salvador	2,037	86.5	61.3	86.2	66.4	105	45	68.3
São Paulo, Brazil	2,598	81.1	65.7	71.2	53.1	NA	NA	57.4
Shanghai, China	23	45.9	32.9	88.9	76.6	104	10	43.8
Singapore	52	85.8	73.6	87.4	75.6	NA	NA	84.6
Stockholm, Sweden	171	30.7	23.0	71.4	56.1	97	-26	21.2
Sydney, Australia	10	79.5	65.5	62.4	43.9	114	32	46.4
Tehran, Iran	3,906	45.0	30.0	98.2	75.2	109	-5	9.1
Tokyo, Japan	118	49.1	34.2	83.8	72.1	NA	NA	55.4
Toronto, Canada	567	27.5	12.0	80.2	57.6	105	-26	30.8

Speed of Winds in the U.S.
Source: National Climatic Data Center, NESDIS, NOAA, U.S. Dept. of Commerce
In miles per hour; through 2002. Max. values for highest one-minute average, except where noted.

Station	Avg.	Max.	Station	Avg.	Max.	Station	Avg.	Max.
Albuquerque, NM	8.9	52	Honolulu, HI	11.3	46	Mt. Washington, NH[1]	35.1	231
Anchorage, AK[1]	7.1	75	Houston, TX	7.6	51	New Orleans, LA	8.2	69
Atlanta, GA	9.1	60	Indianapolis, IN	9.6	49	New York, NY[4]	9.3	40
Baltimore, MD	8.8	80	Jacksonville, FL	7.8	57	Omaha, NE	10.5	58
Bismarck, ND	10.2	64	Kansas City, MO	10.6	58	Philadelphia, PA[2]	9.5	73
Boston, MA[2]	12.4	54	Las Vegas, NV	9.2	56	Phoenix, AZ	6.2	51
Buffalo, NY	11.8	91	Lexington, KY	9.1	47	Pittsburgh, PA	9.0	58
Cape Hatteras, NC	10.9	60	Little Rock, AR[2]	7.8	65	Portland, OR	7.9	88
Casper, WY	12.7	81	Los Angeles, CA[2]	5.7	49	St. Louis, MO	9.6	52
Chicago, IL	10.3	58	Louisville, KY	8.3	56	Salt Lake City, UT[2]	8.8	71
Denver, CO	8.6	46	Memphis, TN	8.8	51	San Diego, CA[2]	7.0	56
Des Moines, IA[2]	10.7	76	Miami, FL[3]	9.2	86	San Francisco, CA[2]	8.7	47
Detroit, MI	10.3	53	Milwaukee, WI	11.5	54	Seattle, WA[2]	8.8	66
Hartford, CT	8.4	46	Minn.-St. Paul, MN	10.5	51	Spokane, WA[2]	8.9	59
Helena, MT[2]	7.7	73	Mobile, AL	8.8	63	Washington, DC	9.4	49

(1) Short gust. (2) Calculated from minimum time during which one mile of wind passed station. (3) Highest velocity ever recorded in Miami area was 132 mph, at former station in Miami Beach in Sept. 1926. (4) Data for Central Park; Battery Place data through 1960, avg. 14.5, high 113.

Tides and Their Causes

Source: U.S. Dept. of Commerce, Natl. Oceanic & Atmospheric Admin. (NOAA), Natl. Ocean Service (NOS)

The tides are a natural phenomenon involving the alternating rise and fall in the large fluid bodies of the earth caused by the combined gravitational attraction of the sun and moon. The combination of these 2 variable influences produces the complex recurrent cycle of the tides. Tides may occur in both oceans and seas, to a limited extent in large lakes, in the atmosphere, and, to a very minute degree, in the earth itself. The length of time between succeeding tides varies as the result of many factors.

The tide-generating force represents the difference between (1) the centrifugal force produced by the revolution of the earth around the common center-of-gravity of the earth-moon system and (2) the gravitational attraction of the moon acting upon the earth's overlying waters. The moon is about 400 times closer than the sun; so despite its smaller mass, the moon's tide-raising force is 2.5 times greater.

The tide-generating forces of the moon and sun acting tangentially to the earth's surface tend to cause a maximum accumulation of waters at 2 diametrically opposite positions on the surface of the earth and to withdraw compensating amounts of water from all points 90° removed from these tidal bulges. As the earth rotates beneath the maxima and minima of these tide-generating forces, a sequence of 2 high tides, separated by 2 low tides, ideally is produced each day (semidiurnal tide).

Twice in each month, when the sun, moon, and earth are directly aligned, with the moon between the earth and sun (at new moon) or on the opposite side of the earth from the sun (at full moon), the sun and moon exert gravitational force in a mutual or additive fashion. The highest high tides and lowest low tides are produced at these times. These are called *spring* tides. At 2 positions 90° in between, the gravitational forces of the moon and sun—imposed at right angles—counteract each other to the greatest extent, and the range between high and low tides is reduced. These are called *neap* tides. This semi-monthly variation between spring and neap tides is called the *phase inequality*.

The inclination to the equator of the moon's monthly orbit and the inclination of the sun to the equator during the earth's yearly orbit produce a difference in the height of succeeding high tides and in the extent of depression of succeeding low tides that is known as the *diurnal inequality*. In most cases, this produces a so-called *mixed tide*. In extreme cases, these phenomena may result in only one high tide and one low tide each (*diurnal tide*). There are other monthly and yearly variations in the tide because of the elliptical shape of the orbits themselves.

U.S. convention distinguishes between Mean Higher High Water (MHHW), Mean High Water (MHW), Mean Tide Level (MTL), Mean Sea Level (MSL), Mean Low Water (MLW), and Mean Lower Low Water (MLLW). Diurnal range of tide is the difference in height between MHHW and MLLW. Mean range of tide is the difference between MHW and MLW.

The range of tide in the open ocean is less than in shoreline regions. However, as the ocean tide approaches shoal waters and its effects are augmented, the tidal range may be greatly increased.

In Nova Scotia along the narrow channel of the Bay of Fundy, the range of tides, or difference between high and low waters, may reach 43½ feet or more (under spring tide conditions).

In every case, actual high or low tide can vary considerably from the average, as a result of weather conditions such as strong winds, abrupt barometric pressure changes, or prolonged periods of extreme high or low pressure.

Average Rise and Fall of Tides[1]

Places	Ft.	In.	Places	Ft.	In.	Places	Ft.	In.
Baltimore, MD	1	8	Hampton Roads, VA.	2	10	St. John's, Nfld.	2	7[2]
Boston, MA	10	4	Key West, FL	1	10	St. Petersburg, FL	2	3
Charleston, SC	5	10	Mobile, AL.	1	6	San Diego, CA	5	9
Cristobal, Panama	1	1	New London, CT.	3	1	Sandy Hook, NJ	5	2
Eastport, ME	19	4	Newport, RI.	3	11	San Francisco, CA.	5	10
Ft. Pulaski, GA	7	6	New York, NY	5	1	Seattle, WA	11	4
Galveston, TX	1	5	Philadelphia, PA	6	9	Vancouver, B.C.	10	6
Halifax, N.S.	4	5[2]	Portland, ME	9	11	Washington, DC	3	2

(1) Diurnal range. (2) Mean range.

El Niño and La Niña

Source: National Weather Service, NOAA, U.S. Dept. of Commerce

El Niño is a climatically significant disruption of the ocean-atmosphere system characterized by large scale weakening of trade winds and warming of the surface layers in the central and E equatorial Pacific. The term *El Niño*, Spanish for "the Christ Child," was originally used by fishermen to refer to a warm ocean current appearing around Christmas off the W coasts of Ecuador and Peru and lasting several months. The term has come to be reserved for exceptionally strong, warm currents that bring heavy rains.

El Niño events generally occur at irregular intervals of 2 to 7 years, at an average of once every 3 to 4 years. They typically last 12 to 18 months. The intensity of El Niño events varies; some are strong such as the 1982-83 and 1997-98 events; others are considerably weaker, based on intensity and area encompassed by the abnormally warm ocean temperatures. The eastward extent of warmer than normal water varies from episode to episode.

El Niño influences weather around the globe, and its impacts are most clearly seen in the winter. During El Niño years, winter temperatures in the continental U.S. tend to be warmer than normal in the N and W coast states and cooler than normal in the SE. Conditions tend to be wetter than normal over central and southern California, the SW states and across much of the South, and drier than normal over the N portions of the Rocky Mountains and in the Ohio valley. Globally, El Niño brings wetter than normal conditions to Peru and Chile and dry conditions to Australia and Indonesia. It should be noted that El Niño is only one of a number of factors influencing seasonal variations of climate.

The opposite of El Niño is La Niña, with colder than normal sea surface temperatures in the equatorial Pacific. La Niña typically brings wetter, cooler conditions to the Pacific NW and drier, warmer conditions to much of the southern U.S. during winter.

El Niño and La Niña are oppposite phases of the El Nino-Southern Oscillation (ENSO) cycle, an interannual shift in tropical sea level pressure between the E and W hemispheres. The events are monitored by satellites, and by buoys in the Pacific Ocean. Highly sophisticated numerical computer models of the ocean and atmosphere use this data to predict the onset and evolution of El Niño and La Niña.

WORLD ALMANAC QUICK QUIZ

Which of these U.S. cities has the coldest average temperatures in January, based on records for 1971-2000?

(a) Duluth, MN   (b) Buffalo, NY   (c) Juneau, AK   (d) Burlington, VT

For the answer look in this chapter, or see page 1008.

Wind Chill Table

Source: National Weather Service, NOAA, U.S. Dept. of Commerce

Temperature and wind combine to cause heat loss from body surfaces. The following table shows that, for example, a temperature of 5° Fahrenheit, plus a wind of 10 miles per hour, causes a body heat loss equal to that in minus 10 degrees temperature with no wind. In other words, a 10-mph wind makes 5° feel like minus 10.

The National Weather Service issued new wind chill calculations in 2002. The top line of figures shows temperatures in degrees Fahrenheit. The column at far left shows wind speeds up to 45 mph. (Wind speeds greater than 45 mph have little additional chilling effect.) At wind chills in the shaded area, frostbite occurs in 15 minutes or less.

Calm	40	35	30	25	20	15	10	5	0	-5	-10	-15	-20	-25	-30	-35	-40	-45
5	36	31	25	19	13	7	1	-5	-11	-16	-22	-28	-34	-40	-46	-52	-57	-63
10	34	27	21	15	9	3	-4	-10	-16	-22	-28	-35	-41	-47	-53	-59	-66	-72
15	32	25	19	13	6	0	-7	-13	-19	-26	-32	-39	-45	-51	-58	-64	-71	-77
20	30	24	17	11	4	-2	-9	-15	-22	-29	-35	-42	-48	-55	-61	-68	-74	-81
25	29	23	16	9	3	-4	-11	-17	-24	-31	-37	-44	-51	-58	-64	-71	-78	-84
30	28	22	15	8	1	-5	-12	-19	-26	-33	-39	-46	-53	-60	-67	-73	-80	-87
35	28	21	14	7	0	-7	-14	-21	-27	-34	-41	-48	-55	-62	-69	-76	-82	-89
40	27	20	13	6	-1	-8	-15	-22	-29	-36	-43	-50	-57	-64	-71	-78	-84	-91

Heat Index

The heat index is a measure of the contribution high humidity makes, in combination with abnormally high temperatures, to reducing the body's ability to cool itself. For example, the index shows that an air temperature of 100° Fahrenheit with a relative humidity of 50% has the same effect on the human body as a temperature of 120°. Sunstroke and heat exhaustion are likely when the heat index reaches 105. This index is a measure of what hot weather "feels like" to the average person.

Relative Humidity	Air Temperature (°F)										
	70	75	80	85	90	95	100	105	110	115	120
	Apparent Temperature (°F)										
0%	64	69	73	78	83	87	91	95	99	103	107
10%	65	70	75	80	85	90	95	100	105	111	116
20%	66	72	77	82	87	93	99	105	112	120	130
30%	67	73	78	84	90	96	104	113	123	135	148
40%	68	74	79	86	93	101	110	123	137	151	
50%	69	75	81	88	96	107	120	135	150		
60%	70	76	82	90	100	114	132	149			
70%	70	77	85	93	106	124	144				
80%	71	78	86	97	113	136					
90%	71	79	88	102	122						
100%	72	80	91	108							

Ultraviolet (UV) Index Forecast

Source: National Weather Service, NOAA, U.S. Dept. of Commerce

The National Weather Service (NWS), Environmental Protection Agency (EPA), and Centers for Disease Control and Prevention (CDC) developed and began offering a UV index on June 28, 1994, in response to increasing incidence of skin cancer, cataracts, and other effects from exposure to the sun's harmful rays. The UV Index is now a regular element of NWS atmospheric forecasts.

UV Index number and forecast. The UV Index number, ranging from 0 to 10+, is an indication of the expected intensity of UV radiation reaching the earth's surface during the solar noon hour (11:30 AM-12:30 PM standard time). The lower the number, the less the radiation. The UV Index forecast is produced daily for 58 cities by the NWS Climate Prediction Center, and uses the following scale.

UV Index	Exposure	Minimum Precautions
0-2	Minimal	SPF 15 sun screen
3-4	Low	Sun screen and hat
5-6	Moderate	Sun screen, hat, UV sunglasses
7-9	High	Above; and avoid sun 10AM - 4PM
10+	Very High	Same

The index number is based on several factors: latitude, day of year, time of day, total atmospheric ozone, elevation, and predicted cloud conditions. The index is valid for a radius of about 30 miles around a listed city; however, adjustments should be made for a number of factors.

Ozone. Ozone, a form of oxygen, the molecules of which consist of three atoms rather than two, blocks UV radiation. The more ozone, the lower the UV radiation at the surface.

Cloudiness. Cloud conditions affect the Index number. Clear skies allow 100% UV transmission to the surface, broken clouds allow about 73%, and overcast conditions allow 32%.

Reflectivity. Reflective surfaces intensify UV exposure. As an example, grass reflects 2.5% to 3% of UV radiation reaching the surface; sand, 20% to 30%; snow and ice, 80% to 90%; water, up to 100% (depending on reflection angle).

Elevation. At higher elevations, UV radiation travels a shorter distance to reach the surface so there is less atmosphere to absorb the rays. For every 4,000 ft. one travels above sea level, the UV Index increases by 1 unit. Snow and lack of pollutants intensify UV exposure at higher altitudes.

Latitude. The closer to the equator, the higher the UV radiation level.

SPF number. The UV Index is not linked in any way to the SPF number on suntan lotions and sunscreens. For an explanation of the SPF factor, contact the product's manufacturer or the Food and Drug Administration.

Further information. For precautions to take after learning the UV Index number, call the U.S. EPA hotline (800-296-1996) or your doctor. For questions on scientific aspects, call the NWS at 301-713-0622.

WORLD ALMANAC QUICK QUIZ

On the average, which of these world cities has the highest average maximum daily temperature in July, based on records for 1961-90?

(a) Tehran, Iran　　(b) Mumbai (Bombay), India　　(c) Havana, Cuba　　(d) Mexico City, Mexico

For the answer look in this chapter, or see page 1008.

Lightning

Source: National Weather Service

There are an estimated 25 million cloud-to-ground lightning bolts in the U.S. each year, killing an annual average of 73 people. This is a small number compared to deaths from fire (about 4,000 a year) and motor vehicle accidents (about 40,000), but still significant. By way of comparison with other weather phenomena, tornadoes cause an average of 68 deaths a year, and hurricanes an average of 16. Documented injuries from lightning in the U.S. number about 300 a year.

Lightning is a result of ice in storm clouds. As ice particles rise and sink in the cloud, numerous collisions between them cause a separation of electrical charge. Positively charged crystals rise to the top, while negatively charged crystals drop to lower parts. As the storm travels, a pool of positive charges gathers in the ground below and follows along, traveling up objects like trees and telephone poles. In a common form of lightning, the negatively charged area in the storm sends charges downward; these are attracted to positively charged objects, and a channel develops, with an electrical transfer that you see as lightning. Lightning can travel as much as miles away from the area of a storm.

The transfer of charges in lightning generates a huge amount of heat, sending the temperature in the channel to 30,000 degrees Fahrenheit and causing the air within it to expand rapidly; the sound of that expansion is thunder. Sound travels more slowly than light, so you usually see lightning before you hear thunder.

To (very roughly) gauge one's danger, use the 30-30 rule. In good visibility, count the time between a lightning flash and the crack of thunder. If it's less than 30 seconds the storm is within 6 miles and dangerous. Find shelter immediately. The threat of more lightning does not stop right away; you need to wait about 30 minutes after the last flash of the storm to be sure.

Most lightning deaths and injuries occur in the summer months when people are outdoors; when a storm threatens people need to move to a safe place promptly. Even while indoors, people are advised to stay away from windows and avoid contact with anything conducting electricity.

For more information about lightning, try the website www.lightningsafety.noaa.gov/overview.htm

Global Measured Extremes of Temperature and Precipitation Records

Source: National Climatic Data Center; based on latest available records data

Highest Temperature Extremes

Continent	Highest Temp. (deg F)	Place	Elevation (feet)	Date
Africa	136	El Azizia, Libya	367	Sept. 13, 1922
North America	134	Death Valley, CA (Greenland Ranch)	−178	July 10, 1913
Asia	129	Tirat Tsvi, Israel	−722	June 21, 1942
Australia	128	Cloncurry, Queensland	622	Jan. 16, 1889
Europe	122	Seville, Spain	26	Aug. 4, 1881
South America	120	Rivadavia, Argentina	676	Dec. 11, 1905
Oceania	108	Tuguegarao, Philippines	72	Apr. 29, 1912
Antarctica	59	Vanda Station, Scott Coast	49	Jan. 5, 1974

Lowest Temperature Extremes

Continent	Lowest Temp. (deg F)	Place	Elevation (feet)	Date
Antarctica	−129.0	Vostok	11,220	July 21, 1983
Asia	−90.0	Oimekon, Russia	2,625	Feb. 6, 1933
Asia	−90.0	Verkhoyansk, Russia	350	Feb. 7, 1892
Greenland	−87.0	Northice	7,687	Jan. 9, 1954
North America	−81.4	Snag, Yukon, Canada	2,120	Feb. 3, 1947
Europe	−67.0	Ust'Shchugor, Russia	279	Jan.*
South America	−27.0	Sarmiento, Argentina	879	June 1, 1907
Africa	−11.0	Ifrane, Morocco	5,364	Feb. 11, 1935
Australia	−9.4	Charlotte Pass, NSW	5,758	June 29, 1994
Oceania	14.0	Haleakala Summit, Maui, HI	9,750	Jan. 2, 1961

* Exact day and year unknown.

Greatest Measured Average Annual Precipitation Extremes

Continent	Highest Avg. (inches)	Place	Elevation (feet)	Years of Data
South America	523.6[1,2]	Lloro, Colombia	520[3]	29
Asia	467.4[1]	Mawsynram, India	4,597	38
Oceania	460.0[1]	Mt. Waialeale, Kauai, HI	5,148	30
Africa	405.0	Debundscha, Cameroon	30	32
South America	354.0[2]	Quibdo, Colombia	120	16
Australia	340.0	Bellenden Ker, Queensland	5,102	9
North America	256.0	Henderson Lake, British Columbia	12	14
Europe	183.0	Crkvica, Bosnia-Herzegovina	3,337	22

(1) The value given is continent's highest and possibly the world's depending on measurement practices, procedures, and period of record variations. (2) The official greatest average annual precipitation for South America is 354 inches at Quibdo, Colombia. The 523.6 inches average at Lloro, Colombia (14 miles SE and at a higher elevation than Quibdo) is an estimated amount. (3) Approximate elevation.

Lowest Measured Average Annual Precipitation Extremes

Continent	Lowest Avg. (inches)	Place	Elevation (feet)	Years of Data
South America	0.03	Arica, Chile	95	59
Africa	<0.1	Wadi Halfa, Sudan	410	39
Antarctica	0.8[1]	Amundsen-Scott South Pole Station	9,186	10
North America	1.2	Batagues, Mexico	16	14
Asia	1.8	Aden, Yemen	22	50
Australia	4.05	Mulka (Troudaninna), South Australia	160[2]	42
Europe	6.4	Astrakhan, Russia	45	25
Oceania	8.93	Puako, Hawaii	5	13

(1) The value given is the average amount of solid snow accumulating in one year as indicated by snow markers. The amount of liquid content of the snow is undetermined. (2) Approximate elevation.

▶ **IT'S A FACT:** The highest temperature ever recorded in England was 38.1°C (about 100.6° F), reached Aug. 9, 2003, in Gravesend, Kent.

AEROSPACE

Memorable Moments in Human Spaceflight

Sources: National Aeronautics and Space Administration; Congressional Research Service; World Almanac research

Listed are selected notable U.S. missions by the National Aeronautics and Space Administration (NASA), plus non-U.S. missions (shown with an asterisk), sponsored by the USSR or, later, the Commonwealth of Independent States. Dates are Eastern standard time. EVA = extravehicular activity. ASTP = Apollo-Soyuz Test Project. STS = Space Transportation System, NASA's name for the overall Shuttle program. Number of total flights by each crew member is given in parentheses when flight listed is not the first.

Launch Date	Mission[1]	Crew (no. of flights)	Duration (hr:min)	Remarks
4/12/61	*Vostok 1	Yuri A. Gagarin	1:48	**1st human orbital flight**
5/5/61	Mercury-Redstone 3	Alan B. Shepard Jr.	0:15	**1st American in space**
7/21/61	Mercury-Redstone 4	Virgil I. Grissom	0:15	Spacecraft sank, Grissom rescued
8/6/61	*Vostok 2	Gherman S. Titov	25:18	1st spaceflight of more than 24 hrs
2/20/62	Mercury-Atlas 6	John H. Glenn Jr.	4:55	**1st American in orbit;** 3 orbits
5/24/62	Mercury-Atlas 7	M. Scott Carpenter	4:56	Manual retrofire error caused 250-mi landing overshoot
8/11/62	*Vostok 3	Andrian G. Nikolayev	94:22	Vostok 3 and 4 made 1st group flight
8/12/62	*Vostok 4	Pavel R. Popovich	70:57	On 1st orbit, it came within 3 mi of Vostok 3
10/3/62	Mercury-Atlas 8	Walter M. Schirra Jr.	9:13	Landed 5 mi from target
5/15/63	Mercury-Atlas 9	L. Gordon Cooper	34:19	1st U.S. evaluation of effects of one day in space on a person; 22 orbits
6/14/63	*Vostok 5	Valery F. Bykovsky	119:06	Vostok 5 and 6 made 2nd group flight
6/16/63	*Vostok 6	Valentina V. Tereshkova	70:50	**1st woman in space**; passed within 3 mi of Vostok 5
10/12/64	*Voskhod 1	Vladimir M. Komarov, Konstantin P. Feoktistov, Boris B. Yegorov	24:17	1st 3-person orbital flight; 1st without space suits
3/18/65	*Voskhod 2	Pavel I. Belyayev, Aleksei A. Leonov	26:02	Leonov made **1st "space walk"** (10 min)
3/23/65	Gemini-Titan 3	Grissom (2), John W. Young	4:53	1st piloted spacecraft to change its orbital path
6/3/65	Gemini-Titan 4	James A. McDivitt, Edward H. White 2nd	97:56	White was 1st American to "walk in space" (36 min)
8/21/65	Gemini-Titan 5	Cooper (2), Charles Conrad Jr.	190:55	Longest-duration human flight to date
12/15/65	Gemini-Titan 6A	Schirra (2), Thomas P. Stafford	25:51	Completed 1st U.S. space rendezvous, with Gemini 7
12/4/65	Gemini-Titan 7	Frank Borman, James A. Lovell	330:35	Longest-duration Gemini flight
3/16/66	Gemini-Titan 8	Neil A. Armstrong, David R. Scott	10:41	1st docking of one space vehicle with another; mission aborted, control malfunction; 1st Pacific landing
6/3/66	Gemini-Titan 9A	Stafford (2), Eugene A. Cernan	72:21	Performed simulation of lunar module rendezvous
7/18/66	Gemini-Titan 10	Young (2), Michael Collins	70:47	1st use of Agena target vehicle's propulsion systems; 1st orbital docking
9/12/66	Gemini-Titan 11	Conrad (2), Richard F. Gordon Jr.	71:17	1st tethered flight; highest Earth-orbit altitude (850 mi)
11/11/66	Gemini-Titan 12	Lovell (2), Edwin E. "Buzz" Aldrin Jr.	94:34	Final Gemini mission; 5-hr EVA
4/23/67	*Soyuz 1	Komarov (2)	26:40	Crashed on reentry, killing Komarov
10/11/68	Apollo-Saturn 7	Schirra (3), Donn F. Eisele, R. Walter Cunningham	260:09	1st piloted flight of Apollo spacecraft command-service module only; live TV footage of crew
12/21/68	Apollo-Saturn 8	Borman (2), Lovell (3), William A. Anders	147:00	**1st lunar orbit** and piloted lunar return reentry (command-service module only); views of lunar surface televised to Earth
1/14/69	*Soyuz 4	Vladimir A. Shatalov	71:21	Docked with Soyuz 5
1/15/69	*Soyuz 5	Boris V. Volyanov, Aleksei S. Yeliseyev, Yevgeny V. Khrunov	72:54	Docked with 4; Yeliseyev and Khrunov transferred to Soyuz 4 via a spacewalk
3/3/69	Apollo-Saturn 9	McDivitt (2), D. Scott (2), Russell L. Schweickart	241:00	1st piloted flight of lunar module
5/18/69	Apollo-Saturn 10	Stafford (3), Young (3), Cernan (2)	192:03	1st lunar module orbit of Moon, 50,000 ft from Moon surface
7/16/69	Apollo-Saturn 11	Armstrong (2), Collins (2), Aldrin (2)	195:18	**1st lunar landing** made by Armstrong and Aldrin (7/20); collected 48.5 lb of soil, rock samples; lunar stay time 21:36:21
10/11/69	*Soyuz 6	Georgi S. Shonin, Valery N. Kubasov	118:43	1st welding of metals in space
10/12/69	*Soyuz 7	Anatoly V. Flipchenko, Vladislav N. Volkov, Viktor V. Gorbatko	118:40	Space lab construction test made; Soyuz 6, 7, and 8: 1st time 3 spacecraft, 7 crew members orbited the Earth at once
10/13/69[2]	*Soyuz 8	Shatalov (2), Yeliseyev (2)	118:51	Part of space lab construction team
11/14/69	Apollo-Saturn 12	Conrad (3), Richard F. Gordon Jr. (2), Alan L. Bean	244:36	Conrad and Bean made **2nd Moon landing** (11/18); collected 74.7 lb of samples, lunar stay time 31:31
4/11/70	Apollo-Saturn 13	Lovell (4), Fred W. Haise Jr., John L. Swigert Jr.	142:54	Aborted after service module oxygen tank ruptured; crew returned in lunar module
6/1/70	*Soyuz 9	Nikolayev (2), Vitaliy I. Sevastyanov	424:59	Longest human spaceflight to date
1/31/71	Apollo-Saturn 14	A. Shepard (2), Stuart A. Roosa, Edgar D. Mitchell	216:01	Shepard and Mitchell made **3rd Moon landing** (2/3); collected 96 lb of lunar samples; lunar stay 33:31
4/19/71[2]	*Salyut 13	(Occupied by Soyuz 11 crew)		**1st space station**
4/22/71[2]	*Soyuz 10	Shatalov (3), Yeliseyev (3), Nikolay N. Rukavishnikov	47:46	1st successful docking with a space station; failed to enter space station
6/6/71	*Soyuz 11	Georgi T. Dobrovolskiy, V. Volkov (2), Viktor I. Patsayev	570:22	Docked and entered Salyut 1 space station; crew died during reentry from loss of pressurization

Launch Date	Mission[1]	Crew (no. of flights)	Duration (hr:min)	Remarks
7/26/71	Apollo-Saturn 15	D. Scott (3), James B. Irwin, Alfred M. Worden	295:12	Scott and Irwin made **4th Moon landing** (7/30); 1st lunar rover use; 1st deep space walk; 170 lb of samples; 66:55 stay
4/16/72	Apollo-Saturn 16	Young (4), Charles M. Duke Jr., Thomas K. Mattingly 2nd	265:51	Young and Duke made **5th Moon landing** (4/20); collected 213 lb of lunar samples; lunar stay 71:2
12/7/72	Apollo-Saturn 17	Cernan (3), Ronald E. Evans, Harrison H. Schmitt	301:51	Cernan and Schmitt made 6th and **last lunar landing** (12/11); collected 243 lb of samples; record lunar stay over 75 hrs
5/14/73[2]	Skylab 14	(Occupied by Skylab 2, 3, and 4 crews)		**1st U.S. space station**
5/25/73	Skylab 2	Conrad (4), Joseph P. Kerwin, Paul J. Weitz	672:49	1st Amer. piloted orbiting space station; crew repaired damage caused in boost
7/28/73	Skylab 3	Bean (2), Owen K. Garriott, Jack R. Lousma	1,427:09	Crew systems and operational tests; scientific activities; 3 EVAs, 13:44
11/16/73	Skylab 4	Gerald P. Carr, Edward G. Gibson, William Pogue	2,017:15	Final Skylab mission
7/15/75	*Soyuz 19 (ASTP)	Leonov (2), Kubasov (2)	143:31	U.S.-USSR joint flight; crews linked up in space (7/17), conducted experiments, shared meals, held a joint news conf.
7/15/75	Apollo (ASTP)	Vance Brand, Stafford (4), Donald K. Slayton	217:28	Joint flight with Soyuz 19
12/10/77[2]	*Soyuz 26	Yuri V. Romanenko, Georgiy M. Grechko (2)	2,314:00	1st multiple docking to a space station (Soyuz 26 and 27 docked at Salyut 6)
1/10/78[2]	*Soyuz 27	Vladimir A. Dzhanibekov	142:59	*See Soyuz 26*
3/2/78[2]	*Soyuz 28	Aleksei A. Gubarev (2), Vladimir Remek	190:16	1st international crew launch; Remek was 1st Czech in space
4/12/81	Columbia (STS-1)	Young (5), Robert L. Crippen	54:21	**1st space shuttle** to fly into Earth's orbit
11/12/81	Columbia (STS-2)	Joe H. Engle, Richard H. Truly	54:13	1st scientific payload; 1st reuse of space shuttle
11/11/82	Columbia (STS-5)	Brand (2), Robert Overmyer, William Lenoir, Joseph Allen	122:14	1st 4-person crew
6/18/83	Challenger (STS-7)	Crippen (3), Frederick Hauck, Sally K. Ride, John M. Fabian, Norman Thagard	146:24	Ride was **1st U.S. woman in space**; 1st 5-person crew
6/27/83[2]	*Soyuz T-9	Vladimir A. Lyakhov (3), Aleksandr Pavlovich Aleksandrov	3,585:46	Docked at Salyut 7; 1st construction in space
8/30/83	Challenger (STS-8)	Truly (2), Daniel Brandenstein, William Thornton, Guion Bluford, Dale Gardner	145:09	Bluford was **1st African-American in space**
11/28/83	Columbia (STS-9)	Young (6), Brewster Shaw Jr., Robert Parker, Garriott (2), Byron Lichtenberg, Ulf Merbold	247:47	1st 6-person crew; 1st Spacelab mission
2/3/84	Challenger (41-B)	Brand (3), Robert Gibson, Ronald McNair, Bruce McCandless, Robert Stewart	191:16	1st untethered EVA
2/8/84	*Soyuz T-10B	Leonid Kizim, Vladimir Solovyov, Oleg Atkov	1,510:43	Docked with Salyut 7; crew set space duration record of 237 days
4/3/84	*Soyuz T-11	Yury Malyshev (2), Gennady Strekalov (3), Rakesh Sharma	4,365:48	Docked with Salyut 7; Sharma 1st Indian in space
4/6/84	Challenger (41-C)	Crippen (4), Francis R. Scobee, George D. Nelson, Terry J. Hart, James D. van Hoften	167:40	1st in-orbit satellite repair
7/17/84[2]	*Soyuz T-12	Dzhanibekov (4), Svetlana Y. Savitskaya (2), Igor P. Volk	283:14	Docked at Salyut 7; Savitskaya was 1st woman to perform EVA
8/30/84	Discovery (41-D)	Henry W. Hartsfield (2), Michael L. Coats, Richard M. Mullane, Steven A. Hawley, Judith A. Resnik, Charles D. Walker	144:56	1st flight of U.S. nonastronaut (Walker)
10/5/84	Challenger (41-G)	Crippen (4), Jon A. McBride, Kathryn D. Sullivan, Ride (2), Marc Garneau, David C. Leestma, Paul D. Scully-Power	197:24	1st 7-person crew
11/8/84	Discovery (51-A)	Hauck (2); David M. Walker, Dr. Anna L. Fisher, J. Allen (2), D. Gardner (2)	191:45	1st satellite retrieval/repair
4/12/85	Discovery (51-D)	Karol J. Bobko, Donald E. Williams, Jake Garn, C. Walker (2), Jeffrey A. Hoffman, S. David Griggs, M. Rhea Seddon	167:55	Garn (R, UT) was 1st U.S. senator in space
6/17/85	Discovery (51-G)	Brandenstein (2), John O. Creighton, Shannon W. Lucid, Steven R. Nagel, Fabian (2), Prince Sultan Salman al-Saud, Patrick Baudry	169:39	Launched 3 satellites; Salman al-Saud was 1st Arab in space; Baudry was 1st French person on U.S. mission
10/3/85	Atlantis (51-J)	Bobko (3), Ronald J. Grabe, David C. Hilmers, Stewart (2), William A. Pailes	97:47	1st Atlantis flight
10/30/85	Challenger (61-A)	Hartsfield (3), Nagel (2), Buchli (2), Bluford (2), Bonnie J. Dunbar, Wubbo J. Ockels, Richard Furrer, Ernst Messerschmid	168:45	1st 8-person crew; 1st German Spacelab mission
1/12/86	Columbia (61-C)	R. Gibson (2), Charles F. Bolden Jr., Hawley (2), G. Nelson (2), Franklin R. Chang-Diaz, Robert J. Cenker, Bill Nelson	146:04	B. Nelson was 1st U.S. representative in space; material and astronomy experiments conducted
1/28/86	Challenger (51-L)	Scobee (2), Michael J. Smith, Resnik (2), Ellison S. Onizuka (2), Ronald E. McNair, Gregory B. Jarvis, Christa McAuliffe	—	**Exploded 73 sec after liftoff**; all aboard were killed
2/20/86[2]	*Mir3	—	—	*Mir* **space station** with 6 docking ports launched
3/13/86[2]	*Soyuz T-15	Kizim (3), Solovyov (2)	3,000:01	Ferry between stations; docked at *Mir*
2/5/87	*Soyuz TM-2	Romanenko (3), Aleksandr I. Laveikin	7,835:38	Romanenko set endurance record, since broken
7/22/87	*Soyuz TM-3	Aleksandr Viktorenko, Aleksandr Pavlovich Aleksandrov (2), Mohammed Faris	3,847:16	Docked with *Mir*; Faris 1st Syrian in space

Launch Date	Mission[1]	Crew (no. of flights)	Duration (hr:min)	Remarks
12/21/87	*Soyuz TM-4	V. Titov (2), Muso Manarov, Anatoly Levchenko	8,782:39	Docked with *Mir*
6/7/88	*Soyuz TM-5	Viktor Savinykh (3), Anatoly Solovyev, Aleksandr Panayotov Aleksandrov	236:13	Docked with *Mir*; Aleksandrov 1st Bulgarian in space
9/29/88	Discovery (STS-26)	Hauck (3), Richard O. Covey (2), Hilmers (2), G. Nelson (2), John M. Lounge (2)	97:00	1st shuttle flight since Challenger explosion 1/28/86
5/4/89	Atlantis (STS-30)	D. Walker (2), Grabe (2), Thagard (2), Mary L. Cleave (2), Mark C. Lee	96:56	Launched Venus orbiter *Magellan*
10/18/89	Atlantis (STS-34)	Donald E. Williams (2), Michael J. McCulley, Lucid (2), Chang-Diaz (2), Ellen S. Baker	119:39	Launched Jupiter probe and orbiter *Galileo*
4/24/90	Discovery (STS-31)	McCandless (2), Sullivan (2), Loren J. Shriver (2), Bolden (2), Hawley (3)	121:16	**Launched Hubble Space Telescope**
10/6/90	Discovery (STS-41)	Richard N. Richards (2), Robert D. Cabana, Bruce E. Melnick, William M. Shepherd (2), Thomas D. Akers	98:10	Launched *Ulysses* spacecraft to investigate interstellar space and the Sun
5/18/91	*Soyuz TM-12	Anatoly Artsebarskiy, Sergei Krikalev (2) (to *Mir*), Helen Sharman	3,471:22	Docked with *Mir*; Sharman 1st from United Kingdom in space
3/17/92	*Soyuz TM-14	Viktorenko (3) (to *Mir*), Alexandr Kaleri (to *Mir*), Klaus-Dietrich Flade, Aleksandr Volkov (3) (from *Mir*), Krikalev (2) (from *Mir*)	3,495:11	First human CIS space mission; docked with *Mir* 3/19; Viktorenko and Kaleri to *Mir*; Volkov and Krikalev from *Mir*; Krikalev was in space 313 days
5/7/92	Endeavour (STS-49)	Brandenstein (4), Kevin C. Chilton, Melnick (2), Pierre J. Thuot (2), Richard J. Hieb (2), Kathryn Thornton (2), Akers (2)	213:30	1st 3-person EVA; satellite recovery and redeployment
9/12/92	Endeavour (STS-47)	R. Gibson (4), Curtis L. Brown Jr., Lee (2), Jay Apt (2), N. Jan Davis, Mae Carol Jemison, Mamoru Mohri	190:30	Jemison was 1st black woman in space; Lee and Davis 1st married couple to travel together in space; 1st Japanese Spacelab
6/21/93	Endeavour (STS-57)	Grabe (4), Brian J. Duffy (2), G. David Low (3), Nancy J. Sherlock, Peter J. K. Wisoff, Janice E. Voss	239:46	Carried Spacelab commercial payload module
12/2/93	Endeavour (STS-61)	Covey (3), Kenneth D. Bowersox (2), Claude Nicollier (2), Story Musgrave (5), Akers (3), K. Thornton (3), Hoffman (4)	259:58	Hubble Space Telescope repaired; Akers set new U.S. EVA duration record (29 hr, 40 min)
2/3/94	Discovery (STS-60)	Bolden (3), Kenneth S. Reightier Jr. (2), Davis (2), Chang-Diaz (3), Ronald M. Sega, Krikalev (3)	199:10	Krikalev was 1st Russian on U.S. shuttle
7/1/94	*Soyuz TM-19	Yuri I. Malenchenko, Talgat A. Musabayev, Merbold (2) (from *Mir*)	3,022:53	Docked with *Mir*; Merbold from *Mir*
9/9/94	Discovery (STS-64)	Richards (4), L. Blaine Hammond Jr. (2), Jerry M. Linenger, Susan J. Helms (2), Carl J. Meade (3), Lee (3)	262:50	Performed atmospheric research; 1st untethered EVA in over 10 years
2/3/95	Discovery (STS-63)	James D. Wetherbee (2), Eileen M. Collins, Bernard A. Harris (2), C. Michael Foale (2), Janice E. Voss (2), V. Titov (4)	198:29	*Discovery* and Russian space station rendezvous
3/2/95	Endeavour (STS-67)	Stephen S. Oswald (3), William G. Gregory, Samuel T. Durrance (2), Ronald Parise (2), Wendy B. Lawrence, Tamara E. Jernigan (3), John M. Grunsfeld	399:09	Shuttle data made available on the Internet; astronomy research conducted
3/14/95	*Soyuz TM-21	Thagard (5), Vladimir Dezhurov, Strekalov (5)	2,688[5]	Docked with *Mir* 3/16/95; Thagard was 1st Amer. on the Russ. spacecraft; Valery Polyakov returned to Earth, 3/22/95, after record stay in space (439 days)
6/27/95	Atlantis (STS-71)	R. Gibson (5), Charles J. Precourt (2), E. Baker (3), Gregory J. Harbaugh (3), Dunbar (4), Solovyev (4) (to *Mir*), Nikolai M. Budarin (to *Mir*), Thagard (5) (from *Mir*), Strekalov (from *Mir*), Dezhurov (from *Mir*)	269:47	**1st shuttle-*Mir* docking;** exchanged crew members with *Mir*; Thagard, with his stay on *Mir*, had spent 115 days in space
11/12/95	Atlantis (STS-74)	Kenneth D. Cameron (3), James D. Halsell Jr. (2), Chris Hadfield, Jerry L. Ross (5), William S. McArthur (2)	196:30	2nd shuttle-*Mir* docking (11/15-11/18); erected a 15-ft permanent docking tun-nel to *Mir* for future use by U.S. orbiters
2/22/96	Columbia (STS-75)	Andrew M. Allen (3), Scott J. Horowitz, Chang-Diaz (5), Umberto Guidoni, Hoffman (5), Maurizio Cheli, Nicollier (3)	377:40	Lost an Italian satellite when its tether was severed; microgravity experiments performed; singe marks found on 2 O-rings
3/22/96	Atlantis (STS-76)	Chilton (3), Richard A. Searfoss (2), Sega (2), Michael R. Clifford (3), Linda Godwin (3), Lucid (5) (to *Mir*)	221:15	3rd shuttle-*Mir* docking (5 days); Lucid to *Mir*; 2-person EVA
9/16/96	Atlantis (STS-79)	Apt (4), Terry Wilcutt (2), WilliamReaddy (3), Akers (4), Carl E. Walz (3), Lucid (5) (from *Mir*), John E. Blaha (5) (to *Mir*)	243:19	Docked with *Mir* 9/18/96; exchanged crew members; Lucid set U.S. and women's duration in space record (188 days)
11/19/96	Columbia (STS-80)	Kenneth D. Cockrell (3), Kent V. Rominger (2), Jernigan (4), Thomas D. Jones (3), Musgrave (6)	423:53	Longest-duration shuttle flight; Musgrave was oldest person to fly in space; 2 science satellites deployed and retrieved
1/12/97	Atlantis (STS-81)	Michael A. Baker (4), Brent W. Jett (2), Wisoff (3), Grunsfeld (2), Marsha Ivins (4), Linenger (2) (to *Mir*), Blaha (5) (from *Mir*)	243:30	Docked with *Mir* 1/14-1/19/97; Linenger to *Mir*; Blaha from *Mir*, spent 128 days in space
2/11/97	Discovery (STS-82)	Bowersox (4), Horowitz (2), Joe Tanner (2), Hawley (4), Harbaugh (4), Lee (4), Steve Smith (2)	238:47	Increased capabilities of Hubble Space Telescope; 5 EVAs used to service it
5/15/97	Atlantis (STS-84)	Precourt (3), E. Collins (2), Jean-François Clervoy (2), Carlos Noriega, Ed Lu, Elena Kondakova, Foale (4) (to *Mir*), Linenger (2) (from *Mir*)	**221:20**	Docked with *Mir* 5/16-5/21; Foale to *Mir*; Linenger from *Mir*, 132 days in space, 2nd-longest time for an American; stay on *Mir* marked by troubles incl. fire 2/23
8/5/97	*Soyuz TM-26	Solovyev (5), Pavel Vinogradov	4,743:35	Docked with *Mir* 8/7/97; repaired damaged space station

Launch Date	Mission[1]	Crew (no. of flights)	Duration (hr:min)	Remarks
8/7/97	Discovery (STS-85)	Brown (4), Rominger (3), Davis (3), Robert L. Curbeam Jr., Stephen K. Robinson, Bjarni V. Tryggvason	284:27	Deployed and retrieved satellite designed to study Earth's middle atmosphere; demonstrated robotic arm
9/25/97	Atlantis (STS-86)	Wetherbee (4), Michael J. Bloomfield, V. Titov (4), Scott Parazynski (2), Jean-Loup Chrétien (3), Lawrence (2), David A. Wolf (2) (to Mir), Foale (4) (from Mir)	236:24	Docked with Mir 9/27-10/3/97; delivered new computer to Mir; Wolf to Mir; Foale from Mir; stay on Mir marked by major collision with cargo ship 6/25
1/22/98	Endeavour (STS-89)	Wilcutt (3), Joe F. Edwards Jr., Dunbar (5), Michael P. Anderson, James F. Reilly II, Salizhan Sharipov, Andrew Thomas (2) (to Mir), Wolf (2) (from Mir)	211:48	Docked with Mir 1/24-1/29/98; delivered water and cargo; Thomas to Mir; Wolf from Mir, 128 days in space
1/29/98	*Soyuz TM-27	Musabayev (2), Budarin (2), Leopold Eyharts	4,923:36	Docked with Mir 1/31/98
4/17/98	Columbia (STS-90)	Searfoss (3), Scott D. Altman, Richard M. Linnehan (2), Dafydd Rhys Williams, Kathryn P. Hire, Jay C. Buckey, James A. Pawelczyk	381:50	Studied effects of microgravity on the nervous systems of the crew and over 2,000 live animals; 1st surgery in space on animals meant to survive
6/2/98	Discovery (STS-91)	Precourt (4), Dominic L. Gorie, Lawrence (3), Chang-Diaz (6), Janet L. Kavandi, Valery Ryumin (4), A. Thomas (2) (from Mir)	235:53	Final docking mission with Mir; Thomas from Mir, 141 days in space
10/29/98	Discovery (STS-95)	Brown (5), Steven W. Lindsey (2), Parazynski (3), Robinson (2), Pedro Duque, Chiaki Mukai (2), Glenn (2)	213:44	Sen. John Glenn (D, OH), 77, was **oldest person to fly in space**; Duque was 1st Spaniard in space; experiments to study aging performed on Glenn
12/4/98	Endeavour (STS-88)	Cabana (4), Frederick W. Sturckow, Nancy J. Currie (3), Ross (6), James H. Newman (3), Krivalev (4)	283:18	**1st assembly of International Space Station (ISS)**; attached U.S.-built Unity connecting module to Russian-built Zarya control module; 1st crew to enter ISS
7/23/99	Columbia (STS-93)	E. Collins (3), Jeffrey S. Ashby, Hawley (5), Catherine G. Coleman (2), Michel Tognini (2)	118:50	Collins was 1st woman to command a space shuttle; deployed Chandra X-ray Observatory telescope
12/19/99	Discovery (STS-103)	Brown (6), Scott Kelly, S. Smith (3), Foale (5), Grunsfeld (3), Nicollier (4), Clervoy (3)	191:10	Replaced equipment on and upgraded Hubble Space Telescope; 3 EVAs
2/11/00	Endeavour (STS-99)	Kevin Kregel (4), Gorie (2), Kavandi (2), Janice E. Voss (5), Mohri (2), Gerhard P.J. Thiele	269:38	Used radar to make most complete topographic map of Earth's surface ever produced
5/19/00	Atlantis (STS-101)	Halsell (5), Horowitz (3), Helms (4), Yury Usachev (3), James S. Voss (4), Mary Ellen Weber (2), Jeffrey N. Williams	236:09	Serviced and resupplied ISS; boosted orbit of ISS to an altitude of about 238 mi; 1 EVA
9/8/00	Atlantis (STS-106)	Wilcutt (4), Altman (2), Lu (2), Richard A. Mastracchio, Daniel C. Burbank, Malenchenko (2), Boris V. Morukov	283:10	Prepared ISS for 1st permanent crew; 1 EVA by all 7 crew members
10/11/00	Discovery (STS-92)	Duffy (4), Pamela A. Melroy, Koichi Wakata (2), Leroy Chiao (3), Wisoff (4), Michael Lopez-Alegria (2), McArthur (3)	309:43	Installed framework structure on ISS, setting the stage for future additions; 4 EVAs
10/31/00	2*Soyuz TM-204	Shepherd (4), Yuri Gidzenko (2), Krikalev (5)	—	Established **1st permanent manning of ISS** with 3-person crew for a 4-month stay
11/30/00	Endeavour (STS-97)	Jett (3), Bloomfield (2), Tanner (3), Marc Garneau (2), Noriega (2)	259:57	Delivered 17-ton solar arrays, batteries, and radiators to ISS; 3 EVAs
2/7/01	Atlantis (STS-98)	Cockrell (4), Ivins (5), Jones (4), Curbeam (2), Mark L. Polansky	309:20	Installed U.S. Destiny Laboratory Module on the ISS; 3 EVAs
3/8/01	Discovery (STS-102)	Wetherbee (5), James M. Kelly, Helms (4) (to ISS), James S. Voss (5) (to ISS), Paul Richards, Andrew S.W. Thomas (2), Usachev (4) (to ISS), Shepherd (4) (from ISS), Gidzenko (2) (from ISS), Krikalev (5) (from ISS)	307:49	Transported 2nd permanent crew (Voss, Helms, Usachev) to ISS and returned 1st crew to Earth; 2 EVAs
4/19/01	Endeavour (STS-100)	Rominger (5), John L. Phillips, Hadfield (2), Ashby (2), Parazynski (4), Guidoni (2), Yuri V. Lonchakov	285:30	Installed the Canadarm2, a robotic arm, and delivered supplies to ISS; 2 EVAs
7/12/01	Atlantis (STS-104)	Lindsey (3), Charles O. Hobaugh, Michael L. Gernhardt (4), Kavandi (3), Reilly (2)	259:58	Installed a Joint Airlock, with nitrogen and oxygen tanks to permit future spacewalks from the ISS; 3 EVAs
8/10/01	Discovery (STS-105)	Horowitz (4), Sturckow (2), Daniel Barry (3), Patrick G. Forrester, Culbertson (3) (to ISS), Dezhurov (2) (to ISS), Mikhail Tyurin (to ISS), Usachev (4), Voss (5) (from ISS), Helms (5) (from ISS)	285:13	Transported Expedition Three crew to ISS (Culbertson, Tyurin, Dezhurov) and returned Expedition Two crew to Earth; 2 EVAs
12/5/01	Endeavour (STS-108)	Gorie (3), Mark Kelly, Godwin (4), Daniel Tani, Yury Onufrienko (2) (to ISS), Daniel Bursch (4) (to ISS), Walz (4) (to ISS), Culbertson (3) (from ISS), Dezhurov (2) (from ISS), Tyurin (from ISS)	283:36	Transported Expedition Four crew to ISS (Onufrienko, Bursch, Walz) and returned Expedition Three crew to Earth; deployed STARSHINE 2 satellite; 1 EVA
3/1/02	Columbia (STS-109)	Altman (2), Duane G. Carey, Grunsfeld (4), Currie (4), Linnehan (3), Newman (4), Michael J. Massimino	262:10	Installed powerful new camera and upgraded other equipment on Hubble Space Telescope; 5 EVAs
4/8/02	Atlantis (STS-110)	Bloomfield (3), Stephen N. Frick, Rex J. Walheim, Ellen Ochoa (4), Lee M.E. Morin, Ross (7), S. Smith (4)	259:42	Installed S0 Truss, backbone for expansion of ISS; Ross set records with 7th spaceflight, 9th spacewalk; 4 EVAs
6/5/02	Endeavour (STS-111)	Cockrell (4), Paul Lockhart, Chang-Diaz (7), Philippe Perrin, Valery Korzun (2) (to ISS), Peggy Whitson (to ISS), Sergei Treschev (to ISS), Onufrienko (2) (from ISS), Bursch (4) (from ISS), Walz (4) (from ISS)	332:35	Transported Expedition Five crew to ISS (Korzun, Whitson, Treschev) and returned Expedition Four crew to Earth; brought platform for ISS robot arm; 3 EVAs
10/7/02	Atlantis (STS-112)	Ashby (3), Melroy (2), Wolf (3), Sandy Magnus, Piers Sellers, Fyodor Yurchikhin	259:58	Installed S1 Truss to ISS; 3 EVAs

Launch Date	Mission[1]	Crew (no. of flights)	Duration (hr:min)	Remarks
11/23/02	Endeavour (STS-113)	Wetherbee (6), Lockhart (2), Lopez-Alegria (3), John Herrington, Bowersox (5) (to ISS), Budarin (3) (to ISS), Don Pettit (to ISS), Korzun (2) (from ISS), Whitson (from ISS), Treschev (from ISS)	330:47	Delivered Expedition Six crew to ISS (Bowersox, Budarin, Pettit) and returned Expedition Five crew to Earth; installed P1 Truss to ISS; 3 EVAs
1/16/03	Columbia (STS-107)	Rick Husband (2), William McCool, Michael Anderson (2), David Brown, Kalbana Chawla (2), Laurel Clark, Ilan Ramon	382:20	Entire crew lost when Columbia burned up during reentry, 2/1/03 (see box below)

Note: As of Sept. 2003, there have been 113 space shuttle flights, 88 since the 1986 *Challenger* explosion. Both totals include the final *Columbia* flight; the *Columbia* completed 28 flights, counting the mission on which it was lost. There are 3 remaining shuttles: the *Discovery* (30 flights), the *Atlantis* (26), and the *Endeavour* (19); the *Challenger* completed 9 missions in all. Four Soviets are known to have died in spaceflights: Komarov was killed on *Soyuz 1* (1967) when the parachute lines tangled during descent; the 3-person *Soyuz 11* crew (1971) was asphyxiated. Six Americans and an Israeli astronaut died aboard the *Columbia*; 7 Americans died in the *Challenger* explosion, and 3 astronauts—Virgil I. Grissom, Edward H. White, and Roger B. Chaffee—died in the Jan. 27, 1967, Apollo 1 fire on the ground at Cape Kennedy, FL. (1) For space shuttle flights, the mission name is in parentheses following the name of the orbiter. (2) Launch date. (3) Space stations, such as the *Salyuts* and *Mir*, were used to house crews starting in 1971. (4) Skylab 1 deteriorated and fell from orbit without burning up upon entering the atmosphere. Pieces fell on Australia and into the Indian Ocean; no one was injured. (5) The approximate crew duration for Thagard's stay. Crew did not return together.

Columbia Disaster

The space shuttle *Columbia* broke apart and burned up Feb. 1, 2003, on its reentry into Earth's atmosphere, killing all 7 astronauts aboard. A special panel, the Columbia Accident Investigation Board, issued a report Aug. 26 sharply criticizing the "organizational culture" of NASA, saying that complacency and a reduced focus on safety issues had contributed to the disaster. The specific cause, the board found, was a hole knocked in the heat shield on *Columbia*'s left wing by a chunk of foam insulation that had broken off from one of the large external fuel tanks about 82 seconds after liftoff and hit the wing at a speed of 545 mph. During reentry, hot gasses entered the hole, melting *Columbia*'s structure and causing its breakup. Engineers had observed the chunk of foam and suggested that observations be made to see if it had caused damage, but none were. The board contended that a rescue mission could possibly have been mounted if the foam-caused damage had been investigated.

After the *Columbia* accident, the other space shuttles were grounded. The board, which voiced support for continued human spaceflight, endorsed the space shuttle program's continuation with reservations, saying that shuttles could fly again after NASA carried out a number of significant improvements, and that they should be replaced as soon as possible. NASA officials indicated the shuttle might be ready to fly again by the summer of 2004, although with a reduced schedule.

International Space Station

The International Space Station (ISS) is considered the largest cooperative scientific project in history.

16 cooperating nations: U.S., Russia, Canada, Belgium, Denmark, France, Germany, Italy, Netherlands, Norway, Spain, Sweden, Switzerland, United Kingdom, Japan, and Brazil

The station when completed:
- mass of 1,040,000 lb
- 356' x 290', with almost an acre of solar panels
- internal volume roughly equivalent to passenger cabin of a 747 jumbo jet
- 6 laboratories; living space for up to 7 people

Assembly:
- 11/20/98: U.S.-owned, Russian-built *Zarya* ("sunrise") control module launched by rocket—1st step in assembly of station
- 12/4/98: U.S.-built *Unity* connecting module launched on space shuttle *Endeavour*; shuttle crew attached *Unity* and *Zarya*
- 5/27/99: space shuttle *Discovery* launched, bringing supplies; 1st docking with ISS
- 7/26/00: Russian-built *Zvezda* ("star") service module, primary Russian contribution to ISS, connected to station

- 11/2/00: 1st permanent crew arrives for 4-month stay
- 2/9/01: U.S. Destiny Laboratory Module delivered
- 4/21/01: A robotic arm, Canadarm2, delivered
- 4/11/02: The S0 Truss, backbone of future expansion of the ISS, installed
- 2/1/03 *Columbia* disaster puts assembly on indefinite hold; resupply problems force crew size to be cut from 3 to 2, pending resumption of shuttle flights

Examples of research conducted or planned:
- growing living cells in an environment free of gravity
- studying the effects on humans of long-term exposure to reduced gravity
- studying large-scale long-term changes in Earth's environment by observing Earth from orbit

---

Summary of Worldwide Successful Launches, 1957-2002

Source: National Aeronautics and Space Administration

Year	Total[1]	Russia[2]	U.S.	Japan	ESA[3]	China	France	India	U.K.	Germany	Canada	Israel
1957-59	24	6	18	—	—	—	—	—	—	—	—	—
1960-69	1,035	399	614	—	2	—	4	—	1	—	—	—
1970-79	1,366	1,028	247	18	5	8	14	1	6	3	4	—
1980-89	1,431	1,132	191	26	14	16	5	9	4	7	5	—
1990-99	1,045	542	300	23	55	33	16	11	7	6	4	—
2000	81	35	29	0	12	5	0	0	0	0	0	—
2001	57	23	23	1	7	1	0	2	0	0	0	—
2002	61	23	18	3	11	4	0	1	0	0	0	1
TOTAL	5,100	3,188	1,440	71	106	67	39	24	18	16	13	1

(1) Includes launches sponsored by countries not shown. (2) Figures covering 1957-96 apply to the Soviet Union, or, after 1991, to the Commonwealth of Independent States. (3) European Space Agency.

Notable Proposed Space Missions

Source: National Aeronautics and Space Administration

Planned Launch date	Mission	Purpose
Dec. 2003	Gravity Probe B (GP-B)	Attempt to prove Einstein's Theory of General Relativity by measuring minute "twisting" in space-time caused by rotation of Earth
Feb. 2004	International Rosetta Mission	Rendezvous with comet 46 P/Wirtanen in 2011 to study the object's nucleus and environment
Mar. 2004	Messenger	Orbit and map Mercury after 5-year flight, including 2 flybys of Venus and 2 of Mercury
Jan. 2006	New Horizons (Pluto)	After a gravity boost from Jupiter in 2007, fly by Pluto in 2015, then go on to explore one or more Kuiper Belt objects
2007	Planck-Herschel Satellite	Study the origins of the Universe and "dark matter"; collect data to study whether the Universe is finite or infinite

Notable U.S. Planetary Science Missions

Source: National Aeronautics and Space Administration

Spacecraft	Launch date (Coordinated Universal Time)	Mission	Remarks
Mariner 2	Aug. 27, 1962	Venus	Passed within 22,000 mi of Venus 12/14/62; contact lost 1/3/63 at 54 million mi
Ranger 7	July 28, 1964	Moon	Yielded over 4,000 photos of lunar surface
Mariner 4	Nov. 28, 1964	Mars	Passed behind Mars 7/14/65; took 22 photos from 6,000 mi
Ranger 8	Feb. 17, 1965	Moon	Yielded over 7,000 photos of lunar surface
Surveyor 3	Apr. 17, 1967	Moon	Scooped and tested lunar soil
Mariner 5	June 14, 1967	Venus	In solar orbit; closest Venus flyby 10/19/67
Mariner 6	Feb. 24, 1969	Mars	Came within 2,000 mi of Mars 7/31/69; collected data, photos
Mariner 7	Mar. 27, 1969	Mars	Came within 2,000 mi of Mars 8/5/69
Mariner 9	May 30, 1971	Mars	First craft to orbit Mars 11/13/71; sent back over 7,000 photos
Pioneer 10	Mar. 2, 1972	Jupiter	Passed Jupiter 12/4/73; exited the planetary system 6/13/83; transmission ended 3/31/97 at 6.39 billion mi
Pioneer 11	Apr. 5, 1973	Jupiter, Saturn	Passed Jupiter 12/3/74; Saturn 9/1/79; discovered an additional ring and 2 moons around Saturn; operating in outer solar system; transmission ended 9/95
Mariner 10	Nov. 3, 1973	Venus, Mercury	Passed Venus 2/5/74; arrived Mercury 3/29/74. 1st time gravity of 1 planet (Venus) used to whip spacecraft toward another (Mercury)
Viking 1	Aug. 20, 1975	Mars	Landed on Mars 7/20/76; did scientific research, sent photos; functioned 6 years
Viking 2	Sept. 9, 1975	Mars	Landed on Mars 9/3/76; functioned 3 years
Voyager 1	Sept. 5, 1977	Jupiter, Saturn	Encountered Jupiter 3/5/79, provided evidence of Jupiter ring; passed near Saturn 11/12/80; passed Pioneer 10 to become most distant human-made object 2/17/98
Voyager 2	Aug. 20, 1977	Jupiter, Saturn, Uranus, Neptune	Encountered Jupiter 7/9/79; Saturn 8/25/81; Uranus 1/24/86; Neptune 8/25/89
Pioneer Venus 1	May 20, 1978	Venus	Entered Venus orbit 12/4/78; spent 14 years studying planet; ceased operating 10/19/92
Pioneer Venus 2	Aug. 8, 1978	Venus	Encountered Venus 12/9/78; probes impacted on surface
Magellan	May 4, 1989	Venus	Landed on Venus 8/10/90; orbited and mapped Venus; monitored geological activity on surface; ceased operating 10/11/94
Galileo	Oct. 18, 1989	Jupiter	Used Earth's gravity to propel it toward Jupiter; encountered Venus Feb. 1990; encountered Jupiter 12/7/95; released probe to Jovian surface; encountered moons Ganymede, Europa, Io, and Callisto; disintegrated in Jovian atmosphere 9/21/03
Mars Observer	Sept. 25, 1992	Mars	Communication was lost 8/21/93
Near Earth Asteroid Rendezvous (NEAR)	Feb. 17, 1996	Asteroid Eros	Rendezvoused with Eros 4/00; began orbiting and studying the asteroid; communication ceased 2/28/01
Mars Global Surveyor	Nov. 7, 1996	Mars	Began orbiting Mars 9/11/97; began 2-year mapping survey of entire Martian surface 3/9/99; discovered magnetism on planet; observed Martian moon Phobos; discovered evidence of liquid water in geologically recent past 6/22/00
Mars Pathfinder	Dec. 4, 1996	Mars	Landed on Mars 7/4/97; rover Sojourner made measurements of the Martian climate and soil composition, sending thousands of surface images; ceased operating 9/27/97
Cassini	Oct. 15, 1997	Saturn	Scheduled to reach Saturn in 2004; 4-year mission to study planet's atmosphere, rings, and moons; probe will land on moon Titan
Lunar Prospector	Jan. 6, 1998	Moon	Began orbiting Moon 1/11/98; mapped abundance of 11 elements on Moon's surface; discovered evidence of water-ice at both lunar poles; made 1st precise gravity map of entire lunar surface; crashed into crater near Moon's south pole 7/31/99 to end mission
Mars Climate Orbiter	Dec. 11, 1998	Mars	Communication was lost 9/23/99
Mars Polar Lander	Jan. 3, 1999	Mars	Communication was lost 12/3/99
Stardust	Feb. 7, 1999	Comet Wild-2	Scheduled to reach comet in 2004; to gather dust samples and return them to Earth in 2006; flew by asteroid Annefrank 11/04/02
2001 Mars Odyssey	Apr. 7, 2001	Mars	Reached Mars 10/24/01; mission through 8/04 to study climate and geologic history.
Genesis	Aug. 8, 2001	Sun	Scheduled to travel to the Sun, collect particles from solar wind and return them to Earth in 2004.
Mars Rovers	June 7 & July 10, 2003	Mars	Twin rovers scheduled to land on Mars Jan. 2004 to explore geology of planet, focusing on history of water

Passenger Traffic at World Airports, 2002[1]

Source: Airports Council International

Airport Location (Name)[1]	Passenger Arrivals and Departures	Airport Location (Name)[1]	Passenger Arrivals and Departures
London, UK (Heathrow)	63,338,641	Munich, Germany (Munich)	23,163,720
Tokyo/Haneda, Japan (Tokyo Intl.)	61,079,478	Sydney, Australia (Kingsford Smith)	22,797,724
Frankfurt, Germany (Rhein/Main)	48,450,357	Barcelona, Spain (El Prat)	21,345,090
Paris, France (Charles De Gaulle)	48,350,172	Seoul, South Korea (Kimpo Intl.)	21,057,093
Amsterdam, Netherlands (Schiphol)	40,736,009	Mexico City, Mexico (Mexico City)	20,521,147
Madrid, Spain (Barajas)	33,913,456	Fukuoka, Japan (Fukuoka)	19,523,495
Hong Kong, China (Hong Kong Intl.)	33,882,463	Taipei, Taiwan (Chiang Kai-Shek)	19,228,411
Bangkok, Thailand (Bangkok Intl.)	32,182,980	Manchester, UK (Manchester)	19,022,485
London, UK (Gatwick)	29,628,423	Sapporo, Japan (Chitose)	18,832,451
Singapore (Changi)	28,979,344	Copenhagen, Denmark (Copenhagen)	18,197,606
Tokyo, Japan (Narita)	28,883,606	Zurich, Switzerland (Zurich)	17,902,073
Beijing, China (Beijing Capital Intl.)	27,159,665	Palma De Mallorca, Spain (Palma de Mallorca)	17,828,762
Toronto, Ontario (Lester B. Pearson Intl.)	25,930,363	Osaka, Japan (Itami)	17,627,571
Rome, Italy (Fiumicino)	25,340,383	Milan, Italy (Malpensa)	17,441,250
Paris, France (Orly)	23,169,725	Osaka, Japan (Kansai)	17,373,731

(1) Excludes U.S. airports (see page 710), and Airports not participating in Airports Council Intl. Airport Traffic Statistics collection.

Passenger Traffic at U.S. Airports, 2002

Source: Airports Council International-North America

AIRPORT	Passenger Arrivals and Departures	AIRPORT	Passenger Arrivals and Departures	AIRPORT	Passenger Arrivals and Departures
Hartsfield Atlanta (ATL) ...	76,876,128	Houston (IAH)	33,905,253	Seattle-Tacoma (SEA)	26,690,843
Chicago O'Hare (ORD) ...	66,565,952	Minneapolis/St. Paul (MSP).	32,628,331	Orlando (MCO)	26,653,672
Los Angeles (LAX)	56,223,843	Detroit (DTW)	32,477,694	St. Louis (STL)	25,626,114
Dallas/Ft. Worth (DFW) ...	52,828,573	San Francisco (SFO).....	31.456,422	Philadelphia (PHL)	24,799.470
Denver (DEN)............	35,651,098	Miami (MIA)	30,060,241	Charlotte (CLT)	23,597,926
Phoenix Sky Harbor (PHX)	35,547,167	JFK-New York (JFK)	29,943,084	Boston Logan (BOS)......	22,696,141
Las Vegas (LAS)	35,009,011	Newark (EWR)..........	29,202,654		

U.S. Scheduled Airline Traffic, 1990-2002

Source: Courtesy of Air Transport Association of America, Inc. Reprinted with permission.
Copyright ©2003 by Air Transport Association of America, Inc. All rights reserved.
(in thousands, except where otherwise noted)

	1990	1995	2000	2001*	2002
Revenue passengers enplaned	465,600	547,800	666,200	622,100	611,700
Revenue passenger miles	457,926,000	540,656,000	692,757,000	651,700,000	639,587,000
Available seat miles..................	733,375,000	807,078,000	956,950,000	930,511,000	892,745,000
% of seating utilized.................	62.4	67.0	72.4	70.0	71.6
Cargo traffic (ton miles)................	12,549,000	16,921,000	23,888,000	22,003,000	24,509,000
Passenger revenue	$58,453,000	$69,594,000	$93,622,000	$80,947,000	$73,281,000
Net profit............................	–$3,921,000	$2,314,000	$2,486,000	–$8,275,000	–$11,295,000
Employees	545,809	546,987	679,967	671,969	601,356

*Revenues and profit measures include aid payments from the U.S. government after Sept. 2001 terrorist attacks.

Leading U.S. Passenger Airlines, 2002

Source: Courtesy of Air Transport Association of America, Inc. Reprinted with permission.
©2003 by Air Transport Association of America, Inc. All rights reserved.
(in thousands)

Airline	Passengers	Airline	Passengers	Airline	Passengers	Airline	Passengers
American	94,048	America West......	19,426	Atlantic Southeast ..	8,329	Aloha	4,367
Delta..............	90,799	Alaska	14,138	American Trans Air ..	7,846	Frontier	3,722
Southwest	72,448	American Eagle	11,835	JetBlue............	5,672	Spirit.............	3,672
United	68,350	AirTran	9,654	Mesaba	5,587	Midwest Express	2,164
Northwest	51,743	Continental Express..	9,212	Hawaiian	5,183	Trans States........	2,018
US Airways.........	47,155	Comair...........	8,732	Horizon Air	4,815	National	1,910
Continental........	39,486						

U.S. Airline Safety, Scheduled Commercial Carriers, 1985-2002

Source: Courtesy of Air Transport Association of America, Inc. Reprinted with permission.
Copyright © 2003 by Air Transport Association of America, Inc. All rights reserved.

	Departures (millions)	Fatal accidents	Fatalities	Accident rate[2]		Departures (millions)	Fatal accidents	Fatalities	Accident rate[2]
1985......	6.1	4	197	0.066	1994	7.8	4	239	0.051
1986[1].....	6.9	2	5	0.014	1995	8.1	2	166	0.025
1987[1].....	7.3	4	231	0.041	1996	7.9	3	342	0.038
1988[1].....	7.3	3	285	0.027	1997	9.9	3	3	0.030
1989......	7.3	8	131	0.110	1998	10.5	1	1[3]	0.009
1990......	7.8	6	39	0.077	1999	10.9	2	12	0.018
1991......	7.5	4	162	0.053	2000	11.0	3	92	0.027
1992......	7.5	4	33	0.053	2001[1].....	9.8	6	531	0.020
1993......	7.7	1	1	0.013	2002	10.1	0	0	0.000

(1) Sabotage-caused accidents are included in the number of fatal accidents and fatalities, but not in the calculation of accident rates.
(2) Fatal accidents per 100,000 departures. (3) On-ground employee fatality.

Aircraft Operating Statistics, 2002

Source: Courtesy of Air Transport Association of America, Inc. Reprinted with permission.
Copyright © 2003 by Air Transport Association of America, Inc. All rights reserved. Figures are averages for most commonly used models.

	No. of seats	Speed airborne (mph)	Flight length (mi)	Fuel (gal per hr)	Operating cost per hr		No. of seats	Speed airborne (mph)	Flight length (mi)	Fuel (gal per hr)	Operating cost per hr
B747-200/300* ..	370	520	3,148	3,625	$9,153	B727-200*	148	430	644	1,289	$4,075
B747-400*	367	534	3,960	3,411	8,443	B727-100*	-	417	468	989	13,667
B747-100*.....	-	503	2,022	1,762	3,852	A320	146	454	1,065	767	2,359
B747-F*	-	506	2,512	3,593	7,138	B737-900.....	141	409	646	703	2,595
L-1011	325	494	2,023	1,981	8,042	MD-80	134	432	791	953	2,718
DC-10*	286	497	1,637	2,405	7,374	B737-700LR	132	441	879	740	1,692
B767-400	265	495	1,682	1,711	3,124	B737-300/700 ..	132	403	542	723	2,388
B-777	263	525	3,515	2,165	5,105	A319	122	442	904	666	1,913
A330..........	261	509	3,559	1,407	3,076	A310-200*	-	455	847	1,561	8,066
MD-11*	261	515	2,485	2,473	7,695	B737-100/200 ..	119	396	465	824	2,377
A300-600*	235	460	947	1,638	6,518	B717-200.....	112	339	175	573	3,355
B757-300	235	472	1,309	985	2,345	B737-500.....	110	407	576	756	2,347
B767-300ER* ..	207	497	2,122	1,579	4,217	DC-9	101	387	496	826	2,071
DC-8*	-	437	686	1,712	8,065	F-100	87	398	587	662	2,303
B757-200*	181	464	1,175	1,045	3,312	B737-200C	55	387	313	924	3,421
B767-200ER..	175	487	1,987	1,404	3,873	ERJ-145	50	360	343	280	1,142
A321	169	454	1,094	673	1,347	CRJ-145	49	397	486	369	1,433
B737-800/900..	151	454	1,035	770	2,248	ERJ-135	37	357	382	267	969
MD-90	150	446	886	825	2,716	SD 340B	33	230	202	84	644

* Data includes cargo operations.

WORLD ALMANAC QUICK QUIZ

Rank these U.S. airports by number of passenger arrivals and departures in 2002, highest to lowest:

    (a) JFK-New York   (b) Atlanta   (c) Dallas/Ft. Worth   (d) Chicago

For the answer look in this chapter, or see page 1008.

Some Notable Aviation Firsts[1]

1903 — On Dec. 17, near Kitty Hawk, NC, brothers Wilbur and Orville Wright made the 1st human-carrying, powered flight. Each made 2 flights; the longest, about 852 ft, lasted 59 sec.

1907 — U.S. airplane manufacturing company formed by Glenn H. Curtiss.

1908 — 1st airplane passenger, Lt. Frank P. Lahm, rode with Wilbur Wright in a brief (6 min, 24 sec) flight.

1911 — 1st transportation of mail by airplane officially approved by the U.S. Postal Service began on Sept. 23. It lasted one week. In 1918, limited scheduled air mail service began. By 1921, scheduled transcontinental airmail service began between New York City and San Francisco.

1914 — 1st scheduled passenger airline service began. It operated between St. Petersburg and Tampa, FL.

1919 — 1st airline food, a basket lunch, was served as part of a commercial airline service.

1930 — Ellen Church became 1st flight attendant.

1939 — On Aug. 27, the German Heinkel He 178 made the 1st successful flight powered by a jet engine.

(1) Excludes notable around-the-world and international trips.

1947 — Mach 1, the sound barrier, was broken by Amer. Chuck Yeager in a Bell X-1 rocket-powered aircraft.

1947 — Largest airplane ever flown, Howard Hughes's "Spruce Goose," flew 1 mi at an altitude of 80 ft.

1953 — Jacqueline Cochran became 1st woman to fly faster than sound.

1960 — Convair B-58, 1st supersonic bomber, was introduced.

1968 — The supersonic speed of Mach 2 was accomplished for 1st time, in a Tupolev Tu-144. The plane had an approximate maximum speed of 1,200 mph.

1970 — The Tupolev Tu-144, during commercial transport, exceeded Mach 2. It reached about 1,335 mph at 53,475 ft.

1976 — The Concorde began 1st scheduled supersonic commercial service.

1977 — The Gossamer Condor successfully demonstrated human-powered flight, completing figure-8 course of 1.15 miles.

1979 — The human-powered Gossamer Albatross crossed the English Channel in 2 hr, 49 min.

Some Notable Around-the-World and Intercontinental Trips

Aviator or Craft	From/To	Miles	Time	Date
Nellie Bly	New York/New York		72d 06h 11m	1889
George Francis Train	New York/New York		67d 12h 03m	1890
Charles Fitzmorris	Chicago/Chicago		60d 13h 29m	1901
J. W. Willis Sayre	Seattle/Seattle		54d 09h 42m	1903
J. Alcock-A.W. Brown [1]	Newfoundland/Ireland	1,960	16h 12m	June 14-15, 1919
2 U.S. Army airplanes	Seattle/Seattle	26,103	35d 01h 11m	1924
Richard E. Byrd, Floyd Bennett [2]	Spitsbergen (Nor.)/N. Pole	1,545	15h 30m	May 9, 1926
Amundsen-Ellsworth-Nobile Polar Expedition (in a dirigible)	Spitsbergen (Nor.)/over N. Pole to Teller, Alaska		80h	May 11-14,1926
E.S. Evans and L. Wells (*New York World*)	New York/New York	18,410[3]	28d 14h 36m 05s	June 16-July 14, 1926
Charles Lindbergh[4]	New York/Paris	3,610	33h 29m 30s	May 20-21, 1927
Amelia Earhart, W. Stultz, L. Gordon	Newfoundland/Wales		20h 40m	June 17-18, 1928
Graf Zeppelin	Friedrichshafen, Ger./Lakehurst, NJ	6,630	4d 15h 46m	Oct. 11-15, 1928
Graf Zeppelin	Friedrichshafen, Ger./Lakehurst, NJ	21,700	20d 04h	Aug. 14-Sept. 4, 1929
Wiley Post and Harold Gatty (Monoplane Winnie Mae)	New York/New York	15,474	8d 15h 51m	July 1, 1931
C. Pangborn-H. Herndon Jr.[5]	Misawa, Japan/Wenatchee, Wash..	4,458	41h 34m	Oct. 3-5, 1931
Amelia Earhart [6]	Newfoundland/Ireland	2,026	14h 56m	May 20-21, 1932
Wiley Post (Monoplane Winnie Mae)[7]	New York/New York	15,596	115h 36m 30s	July 15-22, 1933
Hindenburg Zeppelin	Lakehurst, NJ/Frankfort, Ger.		42h 53m	Aug. 9-11, 1936
Howard Hughes and 4 assistants	New York/New York	14,824	3d 19h 08m 10s	July 10-13, 1938
America, Pan American 4-engine Lockheed Constellation[8]	New York/New York	22,219	101h 32m	June 17-30, 1947
Col. Edward Eagan	New York/New York	20,559	147h 15m	Dec. 13, 1948
USAF B-50 Lucky Lady II (Capt. James Gallagher) [9]	Ft. Worth, TX/Ft. Worth, TX	23,452	94h 01m	Mar. 2, 1949
Col. D. Schilling, USAF [10]	England/Limestone, ME	3,300	10h 01m	Sept. 22, 1950
C.F. Blair Jr.	Norway/Alaska	3,300	10h 29m	May 29, 1951
Canberra Bomber [11]	N. Ireland/Newfoundland	2073	04h 34m	Aug. 26, 1952
	Newfoundland/N. Ireland	2073	03h 25m	Aug. 26, 1952
3 USAF B-52 Strato-fortresses [12]	Merced, CA/CA	24,325	45h 19m	Jan. 15-18, 1957
USSR TU-114 [13]	Moscow/New York	5,092	11h 06m	June 28, 1959
Peter Gluckmann (solo)	San Francisco/San Francisco	22,800	29d	Aug. 22-Sept. 20, 1959
Sue Snyder	Chicago/Chicago	21,219	62h 59m	June 22-24, 1960
Robert & Joan Wallick	Manila/Manila	23,129	5d 06h 17m 10s	June 2-7, 1966
Trevor K. Brougham	Darwin, Australia/Darwin	24,800	5d 05h 57m	Aug. 5-10, 1972
Arnold Palmer	Denver/Denver	22,985	57h 7m 12s	May 17-19, 1976
Boeing 747[14]	San Francisco/San Francisco	26,382	57h 25m 42s	Oct. 28-31, 1977
Richard Rutan & Jeana Yeager[15]	Edwards AFB, CA	24,986	09d 03m 44s	Dec. 14-23, 1986
Concorde	New York/New York	1,114 mph	31h 27m 49s	Aug. 15-16, 1995
Col. Douglas L. Raaberg and crew, B1 bomber[16]	Dyess AFB, Abilene, TX/ Dyess AFB	6,250	36h 13m 36s	June 3, 1995
Linda Finch[17]	Oakland, CA/Oakland, CA	26,000	73d	Mar. 17-May 28, 1997
Bertrand Piccard, Brian Jones[18]	Switzerland/Egypt	29,054.6	19d 21h 55m	Mar. 1-21, 1999
Steve Fossett[19]	Australia/Australia	21,109.6	14d 20h 01m	June 19-July 4, 2002

(1) Nonstop transatlantic flight. (2) Claim of reaching N. Pole in dispute; if claim is untrue, then Amundsen-Ellsworth-Nobile were the first to fly over N. Pole. (3) Includes mileage by train and auto, 4,110; by plane, 6,300; by steamship, 8,000. (4) Solo transatlantic flight in the Ryan monoplane "Spirit of St. Louis." (5) Nonstop transpacific flight. (6) First woman's transoceanic solo flight. Earhart disappeared in the Pacific in 1937 while attempting an around-the-world flight. (7) First to fly solo around N circumference of the world and first to fly twice around the world. (8) Inception of regular commercial global air service. (9) First nonstop round-the-world flight, refueled 4 times in flight. (10) Nonstop jet transatlantic flight. (11) Transatlantic round trip on same day. (12) First nonstop global flight by jet planes; refueled in flight by KC-97 aerial tankers; average speed approx. 525 mph. (13) Nonstop between Moscow and New York. (14) Speed record around the world over both Earth's poles. (15) Circled Earth nonstop without refueling. (16) Refueled in flight 6 times. Tested B-1B bomber by bombing 3 pre-arranged target sites on 3 continents. (17) Followed the intended around-the-world flight route (1937) of Amelia Earhart. (18) First to circumnavigate the globe nonstop in a balloon. (19) First solo circumnavigation of the globe nonstop in a balloon; time, dates and distance are for complete flight, which exceeded circumnavigation because winds prevented landing.

COMPUTERS AND THE INTERNET

About Personal Computers

A personal computer, or PC, is a relatively small computer used by one person at a time. Portable PCs compact enough to fit on a person's lap are known as **laptops** or (in the case of lighter models) **notebooks**. Special software called the **operating system** enables you to operate the computer system's physical parts, or hardware. The most common operating systems used on PCs are Microsoft Windows, the Macintosh OS, and Linux.

(The term "personal computer" is also sometimes used more narrowly to refer just to machines conforming to the standard developed by IBM for personal computers, which uses a microprocessor made by Intel, or a compatible processor, and an operating system such as Windows or Linux that can work with that processor.)

The heart of a PC is its microprocessor, or **central processing unit**, contained on a chip of silicon. The microprocessor carries out arithmetic and logical operations specified by computer programs. PCs have several places where data and instructions are kept, among them:

- **ROM** (Read Only Memory), a type of memory in which once information is written, it cannot be changed, but only read. ROM may be used to keep information that always needs to be available, such as the instructions for loading the operating system when you turn your computer on.
- **RAM** (Random Access Memory), computer memory where data and programs are temporarily kept when they are being worked on; its contents are lost when the computer is turned off.
- **Hard drive**, a hardware device containing one or more disks for long-term storage of data and programs; information placed on a hard disk will remain there until erased or deleted. Information on a hard drive is accessed more slowly than information in RAM.

A PC usually offers several ways to put information into it and get information out. **Input devices** generally include a keyboard and a mouse (or its equivalent for a laptop, such as a trackball, pointing stick, or touch pad). There may also be a microphone and some sort of device for connecting the PC to other computers on a local network or to distant computers via, say, the Internet. A modem is a common device for connecting to the Internet via a telephone line. Game players' computer systems tend to include a joystick or similar control device. These days, most computers also have a CD-ROM drive, for reading information from CD-ROM discs. Some systems may include a scanner, for capturing the content of printed materials. **Output devices** typically include a video monitor, a printer, speakers, and, again, a connection to the Internet or to a local network. Many computers have one or more additional devices from which information may be input and to which information may be output, such as a floppy drive, a CD-RW drive (similar to a CD-ROM drive, but information can be written to the disk as well as read from it), and/or a DVD drive. All such devices connected to the computer proper (basically the microprocessor and associated circuitry and memory) are called **peripherals**.

Commonly used measures for the **capacity or power** of a PC include the speed of the microprocessor, expressed in megahertz (MHz), millions of cycles per second, or in gigahertz (GHz), billions of cycles per second; the size of the RAM, expressed in megabytes, or millions of bytes; and the size of the hard drive, expressed in gigabytes, or billions of bytes. Generally speaking, the bigger these numbers are, the more capable the machine. In mid-2003, average-priced desktop PCs (i.e., in the $800-$1,500 range) typically offered 256 or 512 megabytes of RAM, processor speeds in the neighborhood of 2 gigahertz or more, and hard drives with 40 to 120 gigabytes storage capacity. (A caveat: technological improvements mean these numbers will be outdated fairly quickly.)

Computer Milestones

Devices for performing calculations are nothing new—the abacus, a frame with wires on which beads are moved back and forth (still used today in some parts of the world), traces its origins back to ancient times. But the marvels of electronic miniaturization that are modern PCs are a relatively recent development. They are the descendents of vacuum-tube devices introduced in the early 20th century.

Among early **landmark events in computer history** are:

- In 1623 the **1st mechanical calculator**, capable of adding, subtracting, multiplying, and dividing was developed by the German mathematician Wilhelm Schikard; the only 2 models Schikard made, however, were destroyed in a fire.
- In 1642, French mathematician Blaise Pascal built the 1st of more than 4 dozen copies of an adding and subtracting machine that he invented.
- In 1790, French inventor Joseph Marie Jacquard devised a new control system for looms. He "programmed" the loom, communicating desired weaving operations to the machine via patterns of holes in paper cards.
- The British mathematician and scientist Charles Babbage used the Jacquard punch-card system in his design for a sophisticated, programmable **"Analytical Engine"** that contained some of the basic features of today's computers. Babbage's conception was beyond the capabilities of the technology of his time, and the machine remained unfinished at his death in 1871.
- The **1890 U.S. census** was expedited by the rapid processing of huge amounts of data with an electrical punch-card tabulating machine developed by American inventor Herman Hollerith, whose company in 1924 became International Business Machines (IBM).
- On the eve of World War II researchers experimented with ways to speed up computation, since calculators using solely mechanical components were too slow. One approach was to use **electromechanical relays**, which basically are electrically controlled switches.
- In 1940, Bell Laboratories mathematician George Stibitz completed the 1st electromechanical relay-based calculator. In the same year Stibitz provided the 1st demonstration of remote operation of a computer, using a teletype to transmit problems to his machine and to receive the results.
- In 1941, German engineer Konrad Zuse completed the relay-based Z3, the 1st fully functional digital computer to be controlled by a program. In 1944, the **1st large-scale automatic digital computer**, the Mark I, built by IBM and Harvard Professor Howard Aiken, went into operation; this relay-based machine was 55 feet long and 8 feet high.
- Efforts were also under way to develop **fully electronic machines**, using vacuum tubes, which can operate much more quickly than relays.
- Between 1937 and 1942 the 1st rudimentary vacuum-tube calculator was built by the physicist John Vincent Atanasoff and his assistant Clifford Berry at Iowa State College (now University).
- More substantial electronic machines were the Colossus, developed by the British in 1943 to break German codes, and the **Eniac** (for Electronic Numerical Integrator and Computer), a 30-ton room-sized computer with over 18,000 vacuum tubes, built by physicist John Mauchly and engineer J. Presper Eckert at the University of Pennsylvania for the U.S. Army and completed in 1946. The Colossus was a special-purpose machine; its capabilities were powerful (for its time) but limited. Eniac was a general-purpose machine and could be programmed to do different tasks, although programming could take a couple of days, since cables had to be plugged in and switches set by hand.
- In 1951, Eckert and Mauchly's **Univac** ("Universal Automatic Computer") became the 1st computer commercially available in the U.S.; the 1st customer: the Census Bureau. CBS-TV used a Univac in 1952 to predict the results of the presidential election.

The invention of the **transistor** in 1947 and the **integrated circuit** in 1958 paved the way for the development of the **microprocessor** (an entire computer processing unit on a chip), the 1st commercial example of which was the Intel 4004 in 1971. These advances allowed computers to become smaller, speedier, more reliable, and more powerful. In fact, a prediction made in 1965 by engineer and Intel cofounder Gordon Moore that the number of transistors that could be put on a computer chip would double every year (revised in 1975 to every 18 months) has largely held true, coming to be known as "Moore's Law."

•In 1975 the **1st widely marketed personal computer**, the MITS Altair 8800, was introduced in kit form, with no keyboard and no video display, for under $400. In the same year Microsoft was founded by Bill Gates and Paul Allen.

•In 1976 the **1st PC word-processing program**, the Electric Pencil, was written.

•In 1977 the **Apple II** was introduced by Apple Computer, which had been formed the previous year by Steven Jobs and Stephen Wozniak. Capable of displaying text and graphics in color, the machine enjoyed phenomenal success.

•In 1981, **IBM** unveiled its "Personal Computer," which used Microsoft's DOS (disk operating system).

•In 1984, Apple Computer introduced the 1st **Macintosh**. The easy-to-use Macintosh came with a proprietary operating system and was the 1st popular computer to have a GUI (graphical user interface) and a mouse—features originally developed by the Xerox Corporation.

•In 1990, Microsoft released **Windows** 3.0, the 1st workable version of its own GUI.

•In 1991, **Linux**, based on the Unix operating system used in high-power computers, was invented for the PC by Helsinki Univ. student Linus Torvalds and made available for free.

•In 1996 the **Palm Pilot**, the 1st widely successful handheld computer and personal information manager, arrived.

•In 1997 the IBM computer Deep Blue beat world chess champion Garry Kasparov in a 6-game match, 3.5-2.5.

•In 2001, Apple introduced a new Unix-based operating system called OS X for the Macintosh.

•By Apr. 2002, according to computer industry research firm Gartner Dataquest, **1 billion personal computers** (PCs), including desktop and laptop machines of all types, had been shipped by manufacturers since 1975, when the 1st commercially successful PC went on sale. The next billion were expected to ship within 5 or 6 years.

•As of early 2003, Apple had only about 3% of the overall U.S. personal computer market, with machines using the Microsoft Windows operating system accounting for almost all the rest.

About the Internet

The **Internet** is a vast and rapidly growing computer network of computer networks. In 1994, a total of 3 million people (most of them in the U.S.) made use of it; by 2002 there were some 650 million users worldwide. In 2002, according to Nielsen//NetRatings, some 166 million Americans had access to the Internet from their homes, the largest number of any country in the world. The market research firm IDC projects that worldwide daily Internet traffic initiated by end users, which in 2002 averaged an estimated 180 petabits (180 quadrillion bits, where a bit is the smallest unit of computer information, representing a 1 or 0), will exceed 5,000 petabits by 2007. This means Internet users would daily move over the Internet more than 60,000 times as much information as is contained in the Library of Congress. According to estimates by Global Reach, English was the native language of about 35% of the 650 people online in early 2003; the 2nd-most-common language was Chinese, with nearly 12%.

Data compiled by InternetWorldStats.com indicated that in 2003 the country or territory with the largest proportion of Internet users among its population was Sweden, at 67%; Hong Kong was close behind, followed by the Netherlands, Denmark, and the U.S.

The Internet is not owned or funded by any one institution, organization, or government. It has no CEO and is not a commercial service. Its development is guided by the Internet Society (ISOC), composed of volunteers. The ISOC appoints the Internet Architecture Board (IAB), which oversees issues of standards, network resources, etc. Other volunteer groups are the Internet Engineering Task Force (IETF), which develops standards, and the Internet Research Task Force (IRTF), which carries out research on the Internet's long-term future.

Internet Developments

The Internet grew out of a series of developments in the academic, governmental, and information technology communities. Here are some **major historical highlights**:

•In 1969, ARPANET, an experimental 4-computer network, was established by the Advanced Research Projects Agency (ARPA) of the U.S. Defense Dept. so that research scientists could communicate.

•By 1971, ARPANET linked about 2 dozen computers ("hosts") at 15 sites, including MIT and Harvard. By 1981, there were over 200 hosts.

•In 1978 the first **spam**, or junk e-mail, message was sent over ARPANET.

•During the 1980s, more and more computers using different operating systems were connected. In 1983, the military portion of ARPANET was moved onto the MILNET, and ARPANET was disbanded in 1990.

•In the late 1980s, the National Science Foundation's NSFNET began its own network and allowed everyone to access it. It was, however, mainly the domain of "techies," computer-science graduates, and professors.

•In 1988, Internet Relay Chat (IRC) was developed by Finnish student Jarkko Oikarinen, enabling people to communicate via the Internet in "real time." It 1st drew world attention as a source of up-to-date information in the 1991 Persian Gulf War.

•1988 saw the 1st known case of large-scale damage caused by a **computer virus** spread via the Internet--a "worm" crafted by Cornell University graduate student Robert Morris, Jr., infected thousands of computers, shutting many down and causing millions of dollars of damage.

•In 1989 the 1st commercial ISP supplying dial-up Internet access appeared, known as The World.

•In 1989-90 the **World Wide Web** was invented by Tim Berners-Lee as an environment in which scientists at the European Center for Nuclear Research in Switzerland could share information. It gradually evolved into a medium with text, graphics, audio, animation, and video.

•In 1991 commercial traffic was admitted to the NSFNET. 1991 saw release of the 1st **browser**, or software for accessing the World Wide Web. In 1993, the U.S. National Center for Supercomputing Applications released versions of Mosaic, the 1st graphical Web browser, for Microsoft Windows, Unix systems running the X Window GUI, and the Apple Macintosh.

•In 1994, **Netscape** Communications released the Netscape Navigator browser. **Microsoft** released its Internet Explorer browser the following year but initially failed to make a dent in Netscape's dominance of the browser market. But by 1998, Netscape's market share had fallen below 50%, while Internet Explorer's exceeded 25%.

•In 1996 a group of universities launched Internet2, an advanced, high-performance network for the research community. It provided a test bed for development of new capabilities that might find use in the commercial Internet.

The release of the free **Napster** file-sharing service in 1999 enabled users to easily exchange files containing music or other content without regard to copyright restrictions. In 2001, a court ordered Napster, whose users numbered in the millions, to suspend operations because it fostered massive copyright violations; Napster users, however, switched to other file-sharing services, such as Morpheus and KaZaA, to exchange files of copyrighted music. In Sept. 2003 the Recording Industry Association of America filed suits against hundreds of people for allegedly violating copyright law by downloading pirated music.

•In 2000 a federal district judge found Microsoft guilty of antitrust violations; he ordered the company split into 2 parts, but implementation of the penalty was stayed pending appeal. In 2001 the Justice Dept., Microsoft, and several states agreed on a settlement that avoided the break up of the company but bound Microsoft to make portions of its Windows operating system code available to competitors so they could design their products to work with Windows; the accord also included safeguards against Microsoft retaliating against computer makers that chose not to bundle Microsoft products with their machines.

•By mid-2003 all states except Massachusetts had settled with the company. Also in 2003, Microsoft settled a separate lawsuit—brought by Netscape owner, AOL—by agreeing to pay AOL $760 million and let the Internet service provider use Internet Explorer free of charge for 7 years. By mid-2003, Internet Explorer held over 94% of the browser market, according to market researchers.

•In mid-2003 Niue, a self-governing Pacific island associated with New Zealand, became the 1st "country" to offer free nationwide **wireless access** to the Internet (using Wi-Fi technology). This technology was becoming increasingly widespread.

•In mid-2003, **spam** was estimated to account for half of all e-mail.

•Worldwide economic damage due to **viruses** and **hacker attacks** reached a record $32.8 billion for the month of Aug. 2003, according to an estimate by the digital risk assessment company mi2g.

How the Internet Works

The 2 most popular aspects of the Internet are electronic mail, or e-mail, and the **World Wide Web**, which may be thought of as a graphical environment that can be navigated through **hyperlinks**—from one site you click on hyperlinks to go to related sites. The Internet in general involves 3 basic elements: server, client, and network. A **server** is a computer program that makes data available to other programs on the same or other computers—it "serves" them. A **client** is a computer that requests data from a server. A **network** is an interconnected system in which multiple computers can communicate, via copper wire, coaxial cable, fiber-optic cable, radio waves, etc. When you use a **browser** to go to a site on the World Wide Web, you access the site's files.

Here are the steps in opening and accessing a file:

•In the browser, specify the address, or **URL**, of the website.

•The browser sends your request to the server of your **Internet service provider** (ISP), the company that supplies your connection to the Internet.

•That server sends the request to the server at the URL.

•The file is sent to the ISP's server, which sends the file back to the browser, which displays the file.

Internet Resources

Domains. A domain is the fundamental part of an address on the Internet, such as a website address or an e-mail address. Since 1998 the system of domain names has been overseen by a nonprofit corporation called the Internet Corporation for Assigned Names and Numbers (ICANN). Numerous companies offer domain registration services; examples include VeriSign, Register.com, and BulkRegister.com.

The final part of a domain name, known as the **top-level domain**, is its most basic part. For example, in *The World Almanac's* e-mail address—Walmanac@waegroup.com—com is the top-level domain. ("Walmanac" is *The World Almanac's* "username.") The top-level domains include:

Domain	What It Is
.aero	an organization in the air-transport industry
.biz	a business
.com	generally a commercial organization, business, or company
.coop	a nonprofit business cooperative, such as a rural electric coop
.edu	a 4-year higher-educational institution
.gov	a nonmilitary U.S. federal governmental entity, usually federal
.info	an informational site for an individual or organization, without restriction
.int	an international organization
.mil	a U.S. military organization
.museum	a museum
.name	an individual
.net	suggested for a network administration, but actually used by a wide variety of sites
.org	suggested for a nonprofit organization, but actually used by a wide variety of sites
.pro	a professional, such as an accountant, lawyer, or physician

The top-level domain us is also available to persons, organizations, and entities in the U.S. Generally speaking, country codes are used for most top-level domains outside the U.S.—for example, jp in Japan, uk in the United Kingdom, and ru in Russia.

FAQs. Frequently Asked Questions documents contain answers to common questions. A huge collection of FAQs can be found at the site www.faqs.org/faqs.

FTP. File Transfer Protocol is a simple method of transferring files on the Internet. Using FTP, you log on to a remote site, find files, and copy them to your computer. Sites that offer FTP capability can be accessed with special programs and also often with browsers. The address for such a site when accessed through a browser typically begins with ftp://.

HTTP. Hypertext Transfer Protocol is the file-exchange method underlying the World Wide Web. A website address begins with http:// (or https:// for "secure" sites that protect the confidentiality of information you may transmit over the Web).

Newsgroups. Newsgroups, a classic institution of the Internet, are found on the part of the Internet called Usenet. In a newsgroup, messages concerning a particular topic are posted in a public forum. You can simply read the postings, or you can post something yourself.

Online Activities

Communication via e-mail, online chat, or instant messaging is the most widely used application of the Internet. A relatively new form of communication that attracted attention in 2003 was the online personal journal, or **blog**. (The name derives from "Web log.") As of mid-2003, according to Blogcount.com, the estimated total number of active blogs approached 3 million, most of them in the U.S. While many blogs could be of little interest to anyone not a friend of the author, others attract more attention. A blog published anonymously by an Iraqi living in Baghdad drew considerable notice during the 2003 Iraq war.

The Net is a major source of reference **information** on health and medicine, government, and a plethora of other topics. Many people rely on it for up-to-the-minute news. The Internet is also a vehicle for such activities as distributing music, broadcasting radio, gambling, and conducting business.

Forrester Research predicts that U.S. online **retail sales** will rise from an estimated $95.7 billion in 2003 to $229.9 billion in 2008, when they will account for some 10% of total U.S. retail sales. In 2003, travel services—such as hotels, airline tickets, and car rentals—were a leading component of online sales, totaling an estimated $27 billion, but according to Forrester, the next 5 years would see particularly strong growth in the food and beverage sector. **B2B ecommerce**, or business conducted between companies via the Internet, is even more substantial. According to eMarketer estimates, revenues from B2B ecommerce were expected to exceed $1.4 trillion worldwide by the end of 2003, reaching $2.7 trillion in 2004. (By comparison, in 2000, ecommerce totaled just $278.19 billion worldwide, according to eMarketer.) In the U.S. alone, B2B ecommerce revenues were predicted to total $721 billion by the end of 2003 and $1.01 trillion in 2004.

Safety and Security on the Internet

Common sense dictates some basic security rules:

•Do not give out your phone number, address, or other personal information, unless needed for a transaction at a site you trust.

•Be careful about giving out credit card numbers.

•If you feel someone is being threatening or dangerous, inform your Internet service provider.

Viruses. There is always a risk of acquiring a computer **virus**. In a general sense, a virus is chunk of computer code designed to produce an unexpected event. Some viruses may merely display a whimsical message on your screen. Some may wreak havoc in your system. Your system can pick up a virus from a program downloaded from the Internet or elsewhere via modem (or received on a disk); a virus can also be communicated via e-mail, as was the case with Klez.E, SoBig.E, and BugBear.B, the most common viruses at mid-2003.

You should have **antivirus software** installed on your computer, keep it up to date, and try to keep abreast of reports of new viruses. Be careful about opening e-mail from unknown correspondents, and if you have programs with a macro capability (macros are bits of auxiliary coding that are meant to play a helpful role but can be taken advantage of by some viruses), make sure the programs' macro virus protection (if any) is turned on. Keep macros disabled if you do not know what you might want to use them for. If you have a high-speed Internet connection that is always on, you should use protective "firewall" software to guard your system against attacks by hackers; in fact, a firewall is a wise precaution even for those who use a dial-up modem.

Some viruses propagate with the help of a carrier program. Others, such as **worms**, do not. A worm may or may not damage files, but reproduces itself with the help of the infected computer's resources. Klez, SoBig, and BugBear are examples of worms. A worm typically installs a "back door" on the infected system, giving access to a hacker; attempts to turn off any antivirus program on the system; and tries to log the user's keystrokes. The term **Trojan horse** is used for malicious computer code that is concealed within harmless code or data and is capable of taking control at some point and causing damage.

Filtering. Such browsers as Internet Explorer, Netscape Navigator, and Opera, as well as some search engines, contain features that let you filter the content that can be viewed on your computer. Special filtering software is also available, and some ISPs, such as AOL and MSN, make it possible for you to restrict the type of content seen on screen.

Parents can find more information on protecting their children while online at the websites of several U.S. government agencies, such as the FBI (www.fbi.gov/publications/pguide/pguide.htm). Another helpful site is www.safekids.com.

Spam. Junk e-mail, or spam, has surged in the past few years. Many sellers of goods or services love spam because it provides an extremely inexpensive form of marketing. For recipients, however, these unsolicited ads can be a time-wasting annoyance or worse—spam may hawk pornography or products dangerous to health, may seek to defraud the recipient, or may carry a destructive computer virus. Net administrators worry that the flood of spam may cause delays or even a breakdown in the flow of Internet traffic. Estimates vary, but according to Ferris Research, the total cost of spam to U.S. organizations in 2003, including such costs as lost productivity and the use of technical resources and staff time to deal with the e-mail flood, could be expected to exceed $10 billion. Brightmail, a maker of antispam software, estimated that by June 2003 spam accounted for over 48% of e-mail traffic, up from 8% in 2001.

While filtering software can help reduce the deluge of spam—some e-mail programs include filters—experts also recommend that you be wary of revealing your e-mail address as you surf the Web. As of mid-2003, several antispamming measures were under discussion in Congress.

Portals and Search Engines

Many people have a favorite site that they go to 1st when logging on to the World Wide Web. A convenient choice for such a site is a **portal**, a gateway site offering a search engine but also a variety of other features, which may include free e-mail, chat, instant messaging, news services, stock updates, weather reports, real estate listings, yellow pages, people finders, maps, TV and movie listings, shopping, tools to create and post your own Web page, and perhaps even a language translation service. Many portals permit you to customize the opening screen. Another common feature is a personal calendar to help you schedule activities.

Leading portals include:

AltaVista	www.altavista.com
AOL	www.aol.com
Excite	www.excite.com
Go.com	www.go.com
Lycos	www.lycos.com
MSN	www.msn.com
Netscape.com	www.netscape.com
Yahoo!	www.yahoo.com

By using the portal's **search engine** you can locate information and, in some cases, images on sites throughout a large part of the Internet. No search engine covers the entire Web completely, and some portals offer a list of search engines to choose from. Search engines typically allow you to find occurrences of a particular key word or words. Search engines use different methods for finding, indexing, and retrieving information. Some store only the title and URL of sites; others index every word of a site's content. Some give extra weight to words in titles or other key positions, or to sites for which more hyperlinks exist on the Web. Some search engines also can retrieve images or other nontext files on the Net. Many search engines work with the help of a program called a "spider," "crawler," or "bot." This visits sites across the Web and extracts information that can be used to create the search engine's index.

In addition to a search engine that requires you to submit key words, some portals also offer a subject guide—a menulike "directory," generally compiled by humans. You drill down through the directory to find a subcategory with websites of interest. Yahoo! is a popular example.

Among other search engines and directories:

AllTheWeb.com (www.alltheweb.com) is very up-to-date; it claims to refresh its index every 7 to 11 days. Its search results are available via HotBot and the Lycos portal.

Ask Jeeves (www.ask.com) provides a directory but also responds to questions entered in plain English.

Google (www.google.com) has more than 3 billion Web pages indexed. Its search results, which rely largely on link popularity in ranking sites, are also available via the AOL, Netscape.com, and Yahoo! portals. Google's features include newsgroup searches and the ability to retrieve an archived copy of a webpage made at the time the page was indexed (the page may since have changed its content or gone offline).

HotBot (www.hotbot.com), owned by Lycos, offers useful advanced options.

Open Directory (dmoz.org) aims to cope with the vast size of the Web and produce the most comprehensive directory by using volunteer editors. Its information is used by such services as AOL, Netscape, Ask Jeeves, and Excite.

Teoma (www.teoma.com), owned by Ask Jeeves, groups search results into topics and also supplies links to related resources.

A **meta-search engine** submits your request to several different search engines at the same time. However, meta-search engines typically do not exhaust each of the search engines' databases, and they may be unable to transmit complicated search requests. Among the better-known meta-search engines are **Dogpile** (www.dogpile.com); **Ixquick** (www.ixquick.com); **Queryserver** (www.queryserver.com); and **Vivísimo** (www.vivisimo.com).

Large segments of the Web are not readily searchable by general-purpose search engines. Special search tools include those available via the Direct Search site (www.freepint.com/gary/direct.htm). Another helpful site is Invisibleweb.com (www.invisibleweb.com).

For more information about search engines, including links to specialized search tools, go to **Search Engine Watch**, at www.searchenginewatch.com.

The **Internet Archive** may be of help if you are looking for Web pages that existed in the past—say, previous versions of a current page or a website that has disappeared. The Archive's "Wayback Machine" (www.archive.com), holds more than 10 billion old pages.

► **IT'S A FACT:** A new technology called Wi-Fi, short for wireless fidelity, allows people to link to other computers, peripherals (e.g., printers), and the Internet from their computers without plugging in any wires. Designed to be faster than cable modems (11 megabits per second in its current version; up to 54 Mbps with newer standards), this popular technology works like a cell phone, connecting computers to a base station (but the range is much less than that of a cell phone—base station needs to be within a few hundred feet). Engineering specifications (802.11) set by the Institute of Electrical and Electronic Engineers are designed to ensure that different Wi-Fi products will work together. In addition to its use in homes and offices, Wi-Fi is becoming increasingly available in airports, hotels and other public venues.

Internet Lingo

The following abbreviations are sometimes used on the Internet documents and in e-mail.

BTW	By the way	**GTG**	Got to go	**OTOH**	On the other hand
F2F	Face to face; a personal meeting	**HHOK**	Ha, ha—only kidding	**PLS**	Please
FCOL	For crying out loud	**IMHO**	In my humble opinion	**ROTFL**	Rolling on the floor laughing
FWIW	For what it's worth	**IMO**	In my opinion	**TAFN**	That's all for now
GOK	God only knows	**LOL**	Laughing out loud	**TTFN**	Ta-ta for now

Emoticons, or **smileys**, are a series of typed characters that, when turned sideways, resemble a face and express an emotion. Here are some smileys often encountered on the Internet.

:-)	Smile	:-D	Laugh	:-(	Unhappy	:-b..	Drooling
;-)	Wink	:-*	Kiss	:-o	Shouting	{*}	A hug and a kiss

Internet Directory to Selected Sites

The Websites listed are but a sampling of what is available. For some others, see the following *World Almanac* features: the Where to Get Help directory (Health), the Business Directory (Consumer Information), the Sports Directory, Travel and Tourism, Associations and Societies, 100 Most Populous U.S. Cities, States of the U.S., U.S. Government, and Nations of the World. You may also find suggested websites of interest in the free monthly World Almanac E-Newsletter, available at www.worldalmanac.com. (Addresses are subject to change, and sites or products are not endorsed by *The World Almanac*.)

You must type an address exactly as written. You may be unable to connect to a site because (1) you have mistyped the address, (2) the site is busy, or (3) it has moved or no longer exists.

Online Service Providers
America Online
www.aol.com
AT&T WorldNet Service
www.att.net
CompuServe
www.compuserve.com
EarthLink
www.earthlink.net
Microsoft Network
www.msn.com
Juno
www.juno.com

Directories
Addresses.com
www.addresses.com
Bigfoot (e-mail addresses and white page listings)
www.bigfoot.com
InfoSpace, the Ultimate Directory
www.infospace.com
People Search
people.yahoo.com
Switchboard, the People and Business Directory
www.switchboard.com
WhoWhere?
www.whowhere.lycos.com

Security and Screening
The National Fraud Information Center
www.fraud.org
SET Secure Electronic Transaction
www.setco.org

What's New on the Internet
Internet Scout Project (latest resources for researchers)
scout.cs.wisc.edu
Nerd World: Media (what's new in computer world)
www.nerdworld.com/whatsnew.html
Yahoo! What's New (listing of every new site each day; sometimes thousands)
dir.yahoo.com/new

Auctions
eBay
www.ebay.com
uBid Online Auction
www.ubid.com
Yahoo! Auctions
auctions.shopping.yahoo.com

Audio/Video
MP3.com
www.mp3.com
Real Networks
www.real.com

Bookstores
Amazon.com Inc.
www.amazon.com
Barnes and Noble
www.barnesandnoble.com

The Complete Guide to Online Bookstores
www.bookarea.com
Powell's City of Books
www.powells.com

Chat Sites
America Online
www.aim.com/community/chats/allchats.html
Excite
communicate.excite.com
IVILLAGE: The Women's Network
www.ivillage.com
Lycos
chat.lycos.com
Yahoo
chat.yahoo.com

Children's Sites
(See also Family Resources)
Children's Television Workshop
www.sesameworkshop.org
Judy Blume's Home Base
www.judyblume.com
The Newbery Medal
www.ala.org/alsc/newbery.html
Peace Corps Kids World
www.peacecorps.gov/kids
Rock and Roll Hall of Fame and Museum
www.rockhall.com
Seussville
www.seussville.com
SuperSite for Kids
www.bonus.com
Weekly Reader
www.weeklyreader.com
White House for Kids
www.whitehouse.gov/kids
World Almanac for Kids
www.worldalmanacforkids.com
Yahooligans (for homework help sites)
www.yahooligans.com

Economic Data
Bureau of Economic Analysis
www.bea.doc.gov
Bureau of Labor Statistics
www.bls.gov
Economics Statistics Briefing Room
www.whitehouse.gov/fsbr/esbr.html
Economy at a Glance
stats.bls.gov/eag/
Office of Management and Budget
www.access.gpo.gov/usbudget
Statistical Abstract of the United States (a sampling)
www.census.gov/statab/www
STAT-USA/Internet (a subscription-based government service)
www.stat-usa.gov/stat-usa.html

Entertainment
Eonline
www.eonline.com
The Internet Movie Database
www.imdb.com
Movies.com
www.movies.go.com
The Movie Times
www.the-movie-times.com
Variety
www.variety.com

Family Resources
(See also Children's Sites)
Babies Online
www.babiesonline.com
BabyCenter
www.babycenter.com
Family.Com
family.go.com
KidsHealth.org
www.kidshealth.org
KidSource Online
www.kidsource.com
ParenthoodWeb
www.parenthood.com
Parent Soup
www.parentsoup.com
ParentsPlace.com
www.parentsplace.com
Screen It! Entertainment Reviews for Parents
www.screenit.com
Zero to Three
www.zerotothree.com

Greeting Cards, Electronic
Blue Mountain Arts
www.bluemountain.com
Egreetings Network
www.egreetings.com

E-CARDS
www.ecards.com
1001 Postcards
www.postcards.org
123 Greetings
www.123greetings.com

Health
CenterWatch Clinical Trials Listing Service
www.centerwatch.com
drkoop.com
www.drkoop.com
Drugstore.com
www.drugstore.com
Healthfinder
www.healthfinder.gov
Mayo Clinic Health Oasis
www.mayohealth.org
Medscape
www.medscape.com
The Merck Manual
www.merck.com
National Institutes of Health
health.nih.gov
U.S. National Library of Medicine
www.nlm.nih.gov

WebMD
www.webmd.com

Job Search Sites
CareerBuilder
www.careerbuilder.com
Hotjobs
hotjobs.yahoo.com
Monster.com
www.monster.com

Money Management
Internal Revenue Service
www.irs.gov
Wall Street Journal
www.wsj.com
American Stock Exchange
www.amex.com
E*TRADE
www.etrade.com
MarketWatch
cbs.marketwatch.com
NASDAQ
www.nasdaq.com
New York Stock Exchange
www.nyse.com
Priceline
www.priceline.com
Mortgage Calculator
www.weichert.com
Retirement Calculator
www.retirementcalc.com

Music
All Music Guide
www.allmusic.com
MusicMoz (open music project)
www.musicmoz.com
BBC Music
www.bbc.co.uk/music
Classical Net
www.classical.net

News
The Associated Press
www.ap.org
BBC Online
www.bbc.co.uk
Cable News Network
www.cnn.com
The Los Angeles Times
www.latimes.com
MSNBC
www.msnbc.com
The New York Times on the Web
www.nytimes.com
Reuters
www.reuters.com
USA Today
www.usatoday.com
Washington Post
www.washingtonpost.com
World Press Review Online
www.worldpress.org

Reference
About.com
www.about.com
BookWire
www.bookwire.com

CIA Publications and Reports
www.odci.gov/cia/publications
Explore the Internet; The Library of Congress
lcweb.loc.gov/
Libweb—Library Servers via WWW
sunsite.berkeley.edu/Libweb
Merriam-Webster Network Editions
www.m-w.com

yourDictionary.com
www.yourdictionary.com
Refdesk
www.refdesk.com
Roget's Thesaurus
www.thesaurus.com

Sports
ESPN
www.espn.go.com
Sporting News

www.sportingnews.com
Sports Illustrated
www.sportsillustrated.cnn.com
Sports Network
www.sportsnetwork.com
Weather
National Weather Service Home Page
www.nws.noaa.gov

National Center for Environmental Prediction
(includes links to Storm Prediction Center and other sites)
www.ncep.noaa.gov
Weather Channel
www.weather.com

Most-Visited Websites, August 2003

Source: comScore Media Metrix, Inc.

Rank	Website*	Visitors[1]	Rank	Website*	Visitors[1]
1.	AOL Time Warner Network—Proprietary & WWW	111,117	11.	Excite Network	28,002
2.	MSN—Microsoft Sites	110,673	12.	Viacom Online	27,299
3.	Yahoo! Sites	108,240	13.	InfoSpace Network	26,979
4.	eBay	63,608	14.	Walt Disney Internet Group (WDIG)	25,131
5.	Google Sites	54,709	15.	CNET Networks	25,014
6.	Terra Lycos	51,880	16.	Real.com Network	22,541
7.	About/Primedia	42,680	17.	Classmates.com Sites	21,254
8.	Amazon Sites	35,494	18.	The Weather Channel	20,480
9.	Gator Network	34,263	19.	Overture	19,071
10.	Symantec	28,524	20.	eUniverse Network	18,646

*In some cases, represents an aggregation of commonly owned domain names. (1) Number of visitors, in thousands, who visited website at least once in August 2003, according to a comScore Media Metrix sample.

Percent of U.S. Households With Internet Access, 2001, by Selected Characteristics

Percent of U.S. Households With a Computer, 2001, by Selected Characteristics

Source: National Telecommunications and Information Administration, U.S. Dept. of Commerce

TOTAL		**50.5**
Race	White, not Hispanic	55.4
	Black, not Hispanic	30.8
	Hispanic	32.0
	Asian, Pacific Islander	68.1
Household type	Married couple with children under 18	71.6
	Male householder with children under 18	44.9
	Female householder w. children under 18	40.0
	Family households without children	53.2
	Nonfamily households	35.0
Location	Urban	51.1
	Central city	45.7
	Rural	48.7
Annual income	$5,000 or less	20.5
	$5,000-9,999	14.4
	$10,000-14,999	19.4
	$15,000-19,999	23.6
	$20,000-24,999	31.8
	$25,000-34,999	42.2
	$35,000-49,999	56.4
	$50,000-74,999	71.4
	$75,000+	85.4

TOTAL		**56.5**
Race	White, not Hispanic	61.1
	Black, not Hispanic	37.1
	Hispanic	40.0
	Asian, Pacific Islander	72.7
Household Type	Married couple with child under 18	78.9
	Male household with child under 18	55.1
	Female household w. child under 18	49.2
	Family households without children	58.8
	Nonfamily households	39.2
Location	Urban	56.7
	Central city	51.5
	Rural	55.6
Annual income	$5,000 or less	25.9
	$5,000-9,999	19.2
	$10,000-14,999	25.7
	$15,000-19,999	31.8
	$20,000-24,999	40.1
	$25,000-34,999	49.7
	$35,000-49,999	64.3
	$50,000-74,999	77.7
	$75,000+	89.0

Top-Selling Software, 2003

Source: NPD Techworld Data, Reston, VA
(based on unit U.S. sales, Jan.-July 2003[1])

All Software
1. TurboTax 2002 Deluxe, Intuit
2. Norton Antivirus 2003, Symantec
3. TurboTax 2002, Intuit
4. TurboTax 2002 Multi State 45, Intuit
5. Taxcut 2002 Deluxe, Block Financial
6. Taxcut 2002 State, Block Financial
7. Taxcut 2002, Block Financial
8. Checksoft Express, Elibrium
9. MS Windows XP Home Ed. Upgrade, Microsoft
10. Norton Internet Security 2003, Symantec

Games
1. Command & Conquer: Generals, Electronic Arts
2. The Sims: Superstar Expansion Pack, Electronic Arts
3. Sim City 4, Electronic Arts
4. The Sims Deluxe, Electronic Arts
5. Warcraft III: Frozen Throne Expansion Pack, Vivendi Universal Publishing
6. The Sims: Unleashed Expansion Pack, Electronic Arts
7. Battlefield 1942, Electronic Arts
8. MS Zoo Tycoon, Microsoft

9. Battlefield 1942: Road To Rome Expansion Pack, Electronic Arts
10. Warcraft III: Reign Of Chaos, Vivendi Universal Publishing

System Utilities
1. Norton Antivirus 2003, Symantec
2. Norton Internet Security 2003, Symantec
3. Norton System Works 2003, Symantec
4. Norton Antivirus 2003 Upgrade, Symantec
5. Norton Internet Security 2003 Upgrade, Symantec

Home Education Software
1. Mavis Beacon Teaches Typing 15.0, Riverdeep Interactive
2. Adventure Workshop 1st-3rd Grade, Riverdeep Interactive
3. Instant Immersion Spanish JC, Topics Entertainment
4. Dora The Explorer Backpack Adventure, Atari
5. Instant Immersion Spanish, Topics Entertainment
6. Dora The Explorer Lost City Adventure, Atari
7. Adventure Workshop 4th-6th Grade, Riverdeep Interative
8. Adventure Workshop Preschool-1st Grade, Riverdeep Interactive
9. Blue's ABC Time Activities JC, Atari
10. Blues's Preschool, Atari

> **IT'S A FACT:** U.S. customers spent over $300 million on online dating/personals services in 2002, according to comScore Networks, a market research firm. The number represented a more than 3-fold increase from the previous year, and outpaced other categories such as games and entertainment/lifestyles websites.

Personal Productivity Software

1. MS Streets & Trips 2003, Microsoft
2. Easy CD & DVD Creator 6.0, Roxio
3. Home & Office Suite Deluxe, Valusoft/THQ
4. Home and Business Attorney, Block Financial
5. Kiplinger's Willpower, Block Financial
6. MS Works 7.0, Microsoft
7. DVD X Copy, 321 Studios
8. MS Works Suite 2003, Microsoft
9. Punch Home Design Pro Suite Platinum, Punch Software
10. Serene Scene Marine Acquarium 2.0, Encore

Business Software

1. MS Office XP Student & Teacher Ed, Microsoft
2. McAfee SpamKiller 4.0, Network Associates
3. Ad Subtract, Valusoft/THQ
4. Act! 6.0, Interact Commerce

5. MS Office XP, Microsoft
6. MS Office XP Pro, Microsoft
7. Pop-up Stopper Companion 3.0, Panicware
8. pcAnywhere 10.5 Host & Remote, Symantec
9. Print Shop CD Label Creator, Riverdeep Interactive
10. MS Office XP Pro Upgrade, Microsoft

Finance Software

1. TurboTax 2002 Deluxe, Intuit
2. TurboTax 2002, Intuit
3. TurboTax 2002 Multi State 45, Intuit
4. Taxcut 2002 Deluxe, Block Financial
5. Taxcut 2002 State, Block Financial
6. Taxcut 2002, Block Financial
7. Checksoft Express, Elibrium
8. Quicken 2003, Intuit
9. TurboTax 2002 CA State, Intuit
10. TurboTax 2002 Home & Business, Intuit

(1) Some widely used software is often bundled with computers when sold; these are not included in sales figures above.

Glossary of Computer and Internet Terms

Source: *Microsoft Press® Computer Dictionary, Third Edition* with updates. Copyright 1997, 1998, 1999, 2000, 2001, 2002 by Microsoft Press. Reproduced by permission of Microsoft Press. All rights reserved.

Acrobat A commercial program from Adobe that converts a fully formatted document created on a Windows, Macintosh, MS-DOS, or UNIX platform into a Portable Document Format (PDF) file that can be viewed on several different platforms. Acrobat enables users to send documents that contain distinctive typefaces, color, graphics, and photographs electronically to recipients, regardless of the application used to create the originals. Recipients need the Acrobat reader, which is available for free, to view the files.

application A program designed to assist in the performance of a specific task, such as word processing, accounting, or inventory management.

artificial intelligence (AI) The branch of computer science concerned with enabling computers to simulate such aspects of human intelligence as speech recognition, deduction, inference, creative response, and the ability to learn from experience.

ASCII Pronounced "askee." An acronym for American Standard Code for Information Interchange, a coding scheme using 7 or 8 bits that assigns numeric values to up to 256 characters, including letters, numerals, punctuation marks, control characters, and other symbols.

backup (noun; back up (verb) As a noun, a duplicate copy of a program, a disk, or data. As a verb, to make a duplicate copy of a program, a disk, or data.

bandwidth Data transfer capacity of a digital communications system.

baud rate Speed at which a modem can transmit data.

BBS An abbreviation for bulletin board system, a computer system equipped with one or more modems or other means of network access that serves as an information and message-passing center for remote users.

binary The binary number system has 2 as its base, so values are expressed as combinations of 2 digits, 0 and 1. These 2 digits can represent the logical values true and false as well as numerals, and they can be represented in an electronic device by the 2 states on and off, recognized as 2 voltage levels. Therefore, the binary number system is at the heart of digital computing.

bit Short for binary digit; the smallest unit of information handled by a computer. One bit expresses a 1 or a 0 in a binary numeral, or a true or a false logical condition, and is represented physically by an element such as a high or low voltage at one point in a circuit or a small spot on a disk magnetized one way or the other.

boot The process of starting or resetting a computer.

browser *See* **Web browser.**

bug An error in coding or logic that causes a program to malfunction or to produce incorrect results. Also, a recurring physical problem that prevents a system or set of components from working together properly.

bulletin board system *See* **BBS.**

byte A unit of data, today almost always consisting of 8 bits. A byte can represent a single character, such as a letter, a digit, or a punctuation mark.

CD-ROM Acronym for compact disc read-only memory, a form of storage characterized by high capacity (roughly 650 megabytes) and the use of laser optics rather than magnetic means for reading data.

central processing unit (CPU) The computational and control unit of a computer; the device that interprets and executes instructions.

chat room The informal term for a data communication channel that links computers and permits users to "converse", often about a particular subject that interests them, by sending text messages to one another in real time.

chip *See* **integrated circuit.**

client On a local area network, a computer that accesses shared network resources provided by another computer (called a server). *See also* **server.**

computer Any machine that does three things: accepts structured input, processes it according to prescribed rules, and produces the results as output.

cookie A block of data that a Web server stores on a client system. When a user returns to the same Web site, the browser sends a copy of the cookie back to the server. Cookies are used to identify users, to instruct the server to send a customized version of the requested Web page, to submit account information for the user, and for other administrative purposes.

CPU *See* **central processing unit.**

crash The failure of either a program or a disk drive. A program crash results in the loss of all unsaved data and can leave the operating system unstable enough to require restarting the computer.

cursor A special on-screen indicator, such as a blinking underline or rectangle, that marks the place of which keystrokes will appear when typed.

cyberspace The universe of environments, such as the Internet, in which persons interact by means of connected computers.

cyberspeak Terminology and language (often jargon, slang, and acronyms) relating to the Internet—computer-connected—environment, that is, cyberspace..

database A file composed of records, each of which contains fields, together with a set of operations for searching, sorting, recombining, and other functions.

data compression A means of reducing the space or bandwidth needed to store or transmit a block of data.

debug To detect, locate, and correct logical or syntactical errors in a program or malfunctions in hardware.

defragger A software utility for reuniting parts of a file that have become fragmented through rewriting and updating.

desktop publishing The use of a computer and specialized software to combine text and graphics to create a document that can be printed on either a laser printer or a typesetting machine.

dial-up access Connection to a data communications network through the public switched telecommunication network.

digital certificate 1. An assurance that software downloaded from the Internet comes from a reputable source. 2. A user identity card or "driver's license" for cyberspace. Issued by a certificate authority.

digital subscriber line Any of a family of high-bandwidth data communications technologies that can achieve high transmission speeds over standard twisted-pair copper wires originating from telephone companies. Envisioned as a means of enabling high-speed networking and Internet access, DSL, or xDSL, is the collective term for a number of technologies including ADSL, RADSL, IDSL, SDSL, HDSL, and VDSL.

digital video disc The next generation of optical disc storage technology. With digital video disc technology video, audio, and computer data can be encoded onto a compact disc (CD). A digital video disc can store greater amounts of data than traditional CDs.

directory service A service on a network that returns mail addresses of other users or enables a user to locate hosts and services.

disk A round, flat piece of flexible plastic (floppy disk) or inflexible metal (hard disk) coated with a magnetic material that can be electrically influenced to hold information recorded in digital (binary) format.

disk drive An electromechanical device that reads from and writes to disks.

disk operating system Abbreviated DOS. A generic term describing any operating system that is loaded from disk devices when the system is started or rebooted.

distance learning Broadly, any educational or learning process or system in which the teacher/instructor is separated geographically or in time from his or her students; or in which students are separated from other students or educational resources.

DOS *See* **disk operating system.**

download In communications, to transfer a copy of a file from a remote computer to the requesting computer by means of a modem or network. *See also* **upload.**

DVD *See* **digital video disc.**

dynamic HTML A technology designed to add richness, interactivity, and graphical interest to Web pages by providing those pages with the ability to change and update themselves in response to user actions, without the need for repeated downloads from a server.

encryption The process of encoding data to prevent unauthorized access, especially during transmission. The U.S. National Bureau of Standards created a complex encryption standard, DES (Data Encryption Standard), that provides almost unlimited ways to encrypt documents.

FAQ An abbreviation for Frequently Asked Questions, a document listing common questions and answers on a particular subject. FAQs are often posted on Internet newsgroups where new participants ask the same questions that regular readers have answered many times.

fatal exception error A Windows message signaling that an unrecoverable error, one that causes the system to halt, has occurred. Data being processed when the error occurs is usually lost, and the computer must be rebooted.

field A location in a record in which a particular type of data is stored.

file A complete, named collection of information, such as a program, a set of data used by a program, or a user-created document.

firewall A security system intended to protect an organization's network against external threats, such as hackers, from another network. *See also* **proxy server.**

flame An abusive or personally insulting e-mail message or newsgroup posting.

format In general, the structure or appearance of a unit of data. As a verb, to change the appearance of selected text or the contents of a selected cell in a spreadsheet.

forum A medium provided by an online service or BBS for users to carry on written discussions of a topic by posting messages and replying to them.

FTP An abbreviation for File Transfer Protocol, the protocol used for copying files to and from remote computer systems on a network using TCP/IP such as the Internet.

gigabyte Abbreviated GB; 1024 megabytes. *See* **megabyte.**

graphical user interface Abbreviated GUI (pronounced "gooey"). A type of environment that represents programs, files, and options by means of icons, menus, and dialog boxes on the screen. The user can select and activate these options by pointing and clicking with a mouse or, often, with the keyboard. *See also* **icon.**

hacker A computerphile—a person who is engrossed in computer technology and programming or who likes to examine the code of operating systems and other programs to see how they work. Also, a person who uses computer expertise for illicit ends, such as for gaining access to computer systems without permission and tampering with programs and data.

hard copy Printed output on paper, film, or other permanent medium.

hit Retrieval of a document, such as a home page, from a website.

home page A document intended to serve as a starting point in a hypertext system, especially the World Wide Web. Also, an entry page for a set of Web pages and other files in a website.

host The main computer in a system of computers or terminals connected by communications links.

HTML An abbreviation for HyperText Markup Language, the markup language used for documents on the World Wide Web.

HTTP An abbreviation for HyperText Transfer Protocol, the client/server protocol used to access information on the Web.

hyperlink A connection between an element in a hypertext document, such as a word, phrase, symbol, or image, and a different element in the document, another hypertext document, a file, or a script. The user activates the link by clicking on the linked element, which is usually highlighted.

hypermedia The integration of any combination of text, graphics, sound, and video into a primarily associative system of information storage and retrieval in which users jump from subject to related subject.

hypertext Text linked together in a complex, nonsequential web of associations in which the user can browse through related topics.

icon A small image displayed on the screen to represent an object that can be manipulated by the user.

import To bring information from one system or program into another.

instant messaging A service that alerts users when friends or colleagues are on line and allows them to communicate with each other in real time through private online chat areas.

integrated circuit Also called a chip. A device consisting of a number of connected circuit elements, such as transistors, and resistors, fabricated on a single chip of silicon crystal or other semiconductor material.

interactive Characterized by conversational exchange of input and output, as when a user enters a question or command the system immediately responds.

intranet A TCP/IP network designed for information processing within a company or organization. It usually employs Web pages for information dissemination and Internet applications, such as Web browsers.

IP address Short for Internet Protocol address, a 32-bit (4-byte) binary number that uniquely identifies a host (computer) connected to the Internet to other Internet hosts, for communication through the transfer of packets.

Java A programming language, developed by Sun Microsystems, Inc., that can be run on any platform.

kilobyte Abbreviated K, KB, or Kbyte; 1,024 bytes.

LAN Rhymes with "can." Acronym for local area network, a group of computers and other devices dispersed over a limited area and connected by a link that enables any device to interact with any other on the network.

laptop A small, portable computer that runs on either batteries or AC power, designed for use during travel. Laptops have flat screens and small keyboards.

legacy system A computer, software program, network, or other computer equipment that remains in use after a business or organization installs new systems.

link *See* **hyperlink.**

local area network *See* **LAN.**

logon The process of identifying oneself to a computer after connecting to it over a communications line. Also called *login.*

lurk To receive and read articles or messages in a newsgroup or other online conference without contributing anything to the ongoing conversation.

mailing list A list of names and e-mail addresses that are grouped under a single name. When a user places the name of the mailing list in a mail client's To: field, the client automatically sends the same message to the machine where the mailing list resides, and that machine sends the message to all the addresses on the list.

mainframe computer A high-level computer designed for the most intensive computational tasks.

markup language A set of codes in a text file that instruct a printer or video display how to format, index, and link the contents of the file. Examples of markup languages are HTML (HyperText Markup Language), which is used in Web pages, and SGML (Standard Generalized Markup Language), which is used for typesetting and desktop publishing purposes and in electronic documents.

megabyte Abbreviated MB. Usually 1,048,576 bytes (2^{20}); sometimes interpreted as 1 million bytes.

memory Circuitry that allows information to be stored and retrieved. In common usage it refers to the fast semiconductor storage (RAM) directly connected to the processor. *See also* **RAM.**

menu A list of options from which a program user can make a selection in order to perform a desired action, such as choosing a command or applying a format.

microcomputer A computer built around a single-chip microprocessor.

microprocessor A central processing unit (CPU) on a single chip. *See also* **integrated circuit.**

minicomputer A mid-level computer built to perform complex computations while dealing efficiently with input and output from users connected via terminals.

modem A communications device that enables a computer to transmit information over a standard telephone line.

monitor The device on which images generated by the computer's video adapter are displayed.

motherboard The main circuit board containing the primary components of a computer system.

mouse A common pointing device. It has a flat-bottomed casing designed to be gripped by one hand.

multimedia The combination of sound, graphics, animation, and video.

multitasking A mode of operation offered by an operating system in which a computer works on more than one task at a time.

Net Short for Internet.

network A group of computers and associated devices that are connected by communications facilities.

newsgroup A forum on the Internet for threaded discussions on a specified range of subjects. A newsgroup consists of articles and follow-up posts. *See* **post, thread.**

online Activated and ready for operating; capable of communicating with or being controlled by a computer.

operating system The software that controls the allocation and usage of hardware resources such as memory, CPU time, disk space, and peripheral devices.

optical scanner An input device that uses light-sensing equipment to scan paper or another medium, translating the pattern of light and dark or color into a digital signal that can be manipulated by either optical character recognition software or graphics software.

packet A unit of information transmitted as a whole from one device to another on a network.

palmtop A portable personal computer whose size enables it to be held in one hand while it is operated with the other hand. A major difference between palmtop computers and laptop computers is that palmtops are usually powered by off-the-shelf batteries such as AA cells.

password A unique string of characters that a user types in as an identification code.

PC Abbreviation for personal computer, a microcomputer that conforms to the standard developed by IBM for personal computers, which uses an Intel microprocessor (or one that is compatible); also used as a general term for any microcomputer.

PDA Acronym for Personal Digital Assistant. A lightweight palmtop computer designed to provide specific functions like personal organization (calendar, note taking, database, calculator, and so on) as well as communications. More advanced models also offer multimedia features.

PDF Acronym for Portable Document Format. The Adobe specification for electronic documents that use the Adobe Acrobat family of servers and readers.

peripheral A device, such as a disk drive, printer, modem, or joystick, that is connected to a computer and is controlled by the computer's microprocessor.

personal computer See PC.

pixel Short for picture element; also called pel. One spot in a rectilinear grid of thousands of such spots that are individually "painted" to form an image produced on the screen by a computer or on paper by a printer.

portal A website that serves as a gateway to the Internet. A portal is a collection of links, content, and services designed to guide users to information they are likely to find interesting—news, weather, entertainment, commerce sites, chat rooms, and so on.

post To submit an article in a newsgroup or other online conference. See thread.

program A sequence of instructions that can be executed by a computer.

protocol A set of rules or standards designed to enable computers to communicate with one another and to exchange information with as little error as possible.

proxy server A firewall component that manages Internet traffic to and from a local area network and can provide other features, e.g., document caching and access control.

RAM Pronounced "ram." An acronym for random access memory. Semiconductor-based memory that can be read and written by the CPU or other hardware devices.

ROM 1. Acronym for read-only-memory. A semiconductor circuit into which code or data is permanently installed by the manufacturing process. 2. Any semiconductor circuit serving as a memory that contains instructions or data that can be read but not modified.

routing table In data communications, a table of information that provides network hardware (bridges and routers) with the directions needed to forward packets of data to locations on other networks.

RTF An acronym for rich text format. RTF is used for transferring formatted documents between applications, even those applications running on different platforms, such as between IBM and compatibles and Apple Macintoshes.

search engine On the Internet, a program that searches for keywords in files and documents.

server On a local area network (LAN), a computer running software that controls access to the network and its resources, such as printers and disk drives. On the Internet or other network, a computer or program that responds to commands from a client. See client, LAN.

SGML Acronym for Standard Generalized Markup Language. An information-management standard adopted by the International Organization for Standardization (ISO) in 1986 as a means of providing platform- and application-independent documents that retain formatting, indexing, and linked information. SGML provides a grammar-like mechanism for users to define the structure of their documents, and the tags they will use to denote the structure in individual documents.

sleep mode A power management mode that shuts down all unnecessary computer operations to save energy; also known as suspend mode.

snail mail A phrase popular on the Internet for referring to mail services provided by the United States Postal Service and similar agencies in other countries.

software Computer programs; instructions that make hardware work.

spam An unsolicited e-mail message sent to many recipients at one time, or a news article posted simultaneously to many newsgroups. Electronic junk mail.

spreadsheet program An application commonly used for budgets, forecasting, and other finance-related tasks that organizes data values using cells, where the relationships between cells are defined by formulas.

stream To transfer data continuously, beginning to end, in a steady flow. Many aspects of computing rely on the ability to stream data; file input and output, for example, and communications. On the Internet, streaming enables users to begin accessing and using a file before it has been transmitted in its entirety.

supercomputer A large, extremely fast, and expensive computer used for complex or sophisticated calculations.

surf To browse among collections of information on the Internet, in newsgroups, and especially the World Wide Web.

system administrator The person responsible for administering use of a multiuser computer system, communications system, or both.

TCP/IP An abbreviation for Transmission Control Protocol/Internet Protocol, a protocol developed by the Department of Defense for communications between computers. It has become the de facto standard for data transmission over networks, including the Internet.

telecommute To work in one location (often, at home) and communicate with a main office at a different location through a personal computer.

thread In electronic mail and Internet newsgroups, a series of messages and replies related to a specific topic.

upload In communications, the process of transferring a copy of a file from a local computer to a remote computer by means of a modem or network.

URL An abbreviation for Uniform Resource Locator, an address for a resource on the Internet.

Usenet A worldwide network of Unix systems that has a decentralized administration and is used as a bulletin board system by special-interest discussion groups.

user interface The portion of a program with which a user interacts.

user-friendly Easy to learn and easy to use.

virus An intrusive program that infects computer files by inserting in those files copies of itself.

voice recognition The capability of a computer to understand the spoken word for the purpose of receiving commands and data input from the speaker.

WAN See wide area network

Web See World Wide Web.

Web browser A client application that enables a user to view HTML documents, follow the hyperlinks among them, transfer files, and execute some programs.

webcasting Popular term for broadcasting information via the World Wide Web, using push and pull technologies to move selected information from a server to a client.

webmaster The person or persons responsible for creating and maintaining a site on the World Wide Web.

website A group of related HTML documents and associated files, scripts, and databases that is served up by an HTTP server on the World Wide Web.

WebTV® Trademark name for technology from Microsoft and WebTV Networks that provide consumers with the ability to access the Internet on a television by means of a set-top box equipped with a modem.

wide area network (WAN) A communications network that connects geographically separated areas.

window In applications and graphical interfaces, a portion of the screen that can contain its own document or message.

word processor A program for manipulating text-based documents; the electronic equivalent of paper, pen, typewriter, eraser, and, most likely, dictionary and thesaurus.

workstation A combination of input, output, and computing hardware used for work by an individual.

World Wide Web (WWW) The total set of interlinked hypertext documents residing on Web, or HTTP, servers all around the world.

WYSIWYG Pronounced "wizzywig." An acronym for "What you see is what you get." A display method that shows documents and graphics characters on the screen as they will appear when printed.

XML Acronym for eXtensible Markup Language. A condensed form of SGML, the Standard Generalized markup Language. XML lets Web developers and designers create customized tags that offer greater flexibility in organizing and presenting information than is possible with the older HTML document coding system.

Zip drive A disk drive developed by Iomega that uses 3.5-inch removable disks (Zip disks) capable of storing 100 megabytes of data apiece. See also disk drive.

WORLD ALMANAC QUICK QUIZ

Which U.S. Census first used an electrical punch-card machine produced by a company that eventually became IBM?

(a) 1890 Census   (b) 1910 Census   (c)1930 Census   (d) 1950 Census

For the answer look in this chapter, or see page 1008.

CONSUMER INFORMATION

Business Directory

Listed below are major U.S. corporations offering products and services to consumers. Information as of Sept. 2003. Alphabetization is by first key word. Listings generally include examples of products offered.

Company Name; Address; Telephone Number; Website; Top Executive; Business, Products, or Services.

Abbott Laboratories; 100 Abbott Park Rd., Abbott Park, IL 60064; (847) 937-6100; www.abbott.com; Miles D. White; develops, manufactures, and sells broad line of health care prods., including pharmaceutical, nutritional, and hospital prods.

Aetna, Inc.; 151 Farmington Ave., Hartford, CT 06156; (203) 273-0123; www.aetna.com; John W. Rowe; health insurance, financial services.

AFLAC; 1932 Wynnton Rd., Columbus, GA 31999; (706) 323-3431; www.aflac.com; Daniel Amos; health and life insurance.

Alaska Air Group; 19300 Pacific Hwy. S., Seattle, WA 98188; (206) 431-7040; www.alaskaair.com; William Ayer; air travel (Alaska Air, Horizon Air).

Alberto-Culver; 2525 Armitage Ave., Melrose Park, IL 60160; (708) 450-3000; www.alberto.com; Leonard H. Lavin; hair care (VO5), consumer prods. (Mrs. Dash, Sugar Twin), personal care prods. (St. Ives), Sally Beauty Supply stores.

Albertson's, Inc.; 250 Parkcenter Blvd., Boise, ID 83726; (208) 395-6200; www.albertsons.com; Lawrence R. Johnston; supermarkets; largest retail food and drug co. in the U.S.

Allegheny Technologies, Inc.; 1000 Six PPG Place, Pittsburgh, PA 15222-5479; (412) 394-2800; www.alleghenytechnologies.com; James L. Murdy; electronics, aerospace, industrial; specialty metals.

Allied Waste Industries; 15800 N. Greenway-Hayden Loop, Suite 100, Scottsdale, AZ 85260; (480) 627-2700; www.alliedwaste.com; Thomas Van Weelden; solid waste management.

Allstate Corp.; Allstate Plaza, Northbrook, IL 60062; (847) 402-5000; www.allstate.com; Edward Liddy; property/casualty, life insurance.

Altria Group, Inc.; 120 Park Ave., NY, NY 10017; (917) 663-4000; www.aitria.com; www.kraft.com. Louis C. Camilleri; cigarettes (largest U.S. tobacco company; Marlboro, Merit, Virginia Slims); beer (Miller, Molson, Red Dog); Kraft Foods products (Jell-O, Maxwell House, Kool-Aid, Oscar Mayer, Tang, Cheez Whiz and Velveeta., Post cereals, Tombstone Pizza, and Toblerone chocolate); Nabisco products (Oreo, Chips Ahoy! cookies, Ritz, Triscuit crackers, Mallomars). (Philip Morris Companies, Inc., changed its name to Altria, 1/27/03).

Aluminum Co. of America (Alcoa); 201 Isabella St., Pittsburgh, PA 15212; (412) 553-4545; www.alcoa.com; Alain Belda; world's largest aluminum producer.

Amazon.com Inc.; 1200 12th Ave. S., Suite 1200 Seattle, WA 98144; (206) 266-1000; www.amazon.com; Jeff Bezos; on-line books, electronics, camera/photo, and home and garden seller.

Amerada Hess Corp.; 1185 Ave. of the Americas, NY, NY 10036; (212) 997-8500; www.hess.com; J. B. Hess; integrated international oil co.

American Electric Power; 1 Riverside Plaza, Columbus, OH 43215; (614) 223-1000; www.aep.com; E. Linn Draper Jr.; utilities.

American Express Co.; 200 Vesey St., NY, NY 10285; (212) 640-2000; www.americanexpress.com; Kenneth Chenault; travel, financial, and information services.

American Greetings Corp.; 1 American Rd., Cleveland, OH 44144; (216) 252-7300; www.americangreetings.com; Zev Weiss; greeting cards, stationery, party goods, gift items.

American Home Products: see Wyeth.

American Intl. Group; 70 Pine St., NY, NY 10270; (212) 770-7000; www.aig.com; Maurice R. Greenberg; insurance, financial services.

American Standard; One Centennial Ave., P.O. Box 6820, Piscataway, NJ 08854; (732) 980-3000; www.americanstandard.com; Frederic M. Poses; bathroom and kitchen fixtures and fittings, air conditioning systems, vehicle control systems.

AMR Corp.; PO Box 619616, Dallas/Ft. Worth Airport, TX 75261; (817) 963-1234; www.amrcorp.com; Gerard J. Arpey; Donald J. Carty; air transportation (American Airlines, American Eagle).

Anheuser-Busch Cos., Inc.; 1 Busch Pl., St. Louis, MO 63118; (314) 577-2000; www.anheuser-busch.com; August A. Busch 3rd; world's largest brewer (Budweiser, Michelob, BudLight, Busch, O'Doul's), aluminum can manuf. and recycling, theme parks.

AOL Time Warner Inc.: see Time Warner, Inc.

Apple Computer, Inc.; 1 Infinite Loop, Cupertino, CA 95014-2084; (408) 996-1010; www.apple.com; Steve Jobs; manuf. of personal computers, software, peripherals.

Aramark Corp.; Aramark Tower, 1101 Market St., Philadelphia, PA 19107; (215) 238-3000; www.aramark.com; Joseph Neubauer; food and support services, uniforms and career apparel, child care and early education.

Archer Daniels Midland Co.; 4666 Faries Pkwy., Decatur, IL 62525; (217) 424-5200; www.admworld.com; G. Allen Andreas; agricultural commodities and prods.

Armstrong World Industries, Inc.; 2500 Columbia Ave., Lancaster, PA 17603; (717) 397-0611; www.armstrong.com; Michael D. Lockhart; interior furnishings, specialty prods.

Arvinmeritor Industries, Inc.; 2135 West Maple Road, Troy, MI 48084; (248) 435-1000; www.arvinmeritor.com; Larry Yost; auto emission and ride control systems.

Ashland Inc.; 50 E. River Center, PO Box 391, Covington, KY 41012; (859) 815-3333; www.ashland.com; James J. O'Brien; petroleum producer and refiner (Valvoline), chemicals, road construction.

AT&T Corp.; One AT&T Way, Bedminster, NJ 07921; (908) 221-2000; www.att.com; David W. Dorman; communications, global information management.

AutoNation; 110 S.E. 6th St., Ft. Lauderdale, FL 33301; (954) 769- 6000; www.autonation.com; Michael Jackson; new and used auto vehicles, auto parts, maintenance, and repair, auto protection products.

Avon Prods., Inc.; 1345 Ave. of Americas, NY, NY 10105; (212) 282-5000; www.avon.com; Andrea Jung; cosmetics, fragrances, toiletries, fashion jewelry, gift items, casual apparel, lingerie.

Bank of America Corp.; Bank of America Corporate Center, 100 N. Tryon St., Charlotte, NC 28255; (704) 386-5000; www.bankofamerica.com; Kenneth D. Lewis; major U.S. bank.

Bank One Corp.; 1 Bank One Plaza, Chicago, IL 60670; (302) 732-4000; www.bankone.com; James Dimon; banking and financial services, credit card services, investment management.

Bausch & Lomb Inc.; One Bausch & Lomb Place, Rochester, NY 14604; (716) 338-6000; www.bausch.com; Ronald L. Zarrella; vision and health-care prods., accessories.

Baxter International Inc.; 1 Baxter Pkwy., Deerfield, IL 60015; (847) 948-2000; www.baxter.com; H. M. Kraemer Jr.; health care prods. & services.

Bear Stearns Cos. Inc.; 383 Madison Ave., NY, NY 10179; (212) 272-2000; www.bearstearns.com; James E. Cayne; investment banking, securities trading, brokerage.

Becton, Dickinson & Co.; 1 Becton Dr., Franklin Lakes, NJ 07417; (201) 847-6800; www.bd.com; E.J. Ludwig; medical, laboratory, diagnostic prods.

BellSouth Corp.; 1155 Peachtree St. NE, Atlanta, GA 30309; (404) 249-2000; www.bellsouth.com; F. Duane Ackerman; telephone service in southern U.S.

Berkshire Hathaway Inc.; 1440 Kiewit Plaza, Omaha, NE 68131; www.berkshirehathaway.com; Warren E. Buffett; subsidiaries include GEICO Direct insurance, Johns Manville building materials, Fruit of the Loom underwear, International Dairy Queen restaurants/desserts; Shaw carpets, Benjamin Moore paints.

Best Buy Co., Inc.; P.O. Box 9312, Minneapolis, MN 55344; (612) 291-1000; www.bestbuy.com; Richard Schulze; retailer of software, appliances, electronics, cameras, home office equipment.

Black & Decker Corp.; 701 E. Joppa Rd., Towson, MD 21204; (410) 716-3900; www.blackanddecker.com; Nolan D. Archibald; manuf. power tools, household prods. (Kwikset, Price Pfister), small appliances (Black & Decker).

H & R Block, Inc.; 4400 Main St., Kansas City, MO 64111; (816) 753-6900; www.hrblock.com; Mark A. Ernst; tax return preparation.

Boeing Co.; 100 N. Riverside, Chicago, IL 60606; (312) 544-2140; www.boeing.com; Philip M. Condit; leading manufacturer of commercial, jet aircraft.

Boise Cascade Corp.; 1111 W. Jefferson St., Boise, ID 83728; (208) 384-6161; www.bc.com; George J. Harad; distributor of office products & building materials; paper, wood prods.

Borden, Inc.; 180 E. Broad St., Columbus OH 43215-3707; (614) 225-4000; C. Robert Kidder; snacks (Wise, Cheez Doodles), adhesives (Elmer's, Krazy Glue), pasta (Prince, Creamette, Goodman's), pasta sauce (Aunt Millie's, Classico), Wyler's bouillon, Soup Starter, Corning Consumer Prods. (Corningware, Corelle, Pyrex, Revere); chemicals; consumer adhesives (Elmer's). Owned by KKR Investments, Inc. (www.kkr.com).

Bristol-Myers Squibb Co.; 345 Park Ave., NY, NY 10154; (212) 546-4000; www.bms.com; Peter R. Dolan; drugs (Bufferin, Comtrex, Excedrin, Pravachol, TAXOL), nutritionals (Enfamil infant formula, Boost energy drink).

Brown-Forman Corp.; PO Box 1080, Louisville, KY 40201-1080; (502) 585-1100; www.brown-forman.com; Owsley Brown 2nd; distilled spirits (Jack Daniel's, Southern Comfort), wines (Bolla, Fetzer, Korbel), china and crystal (Dansk, Lenox), Gorham, Kirk Steiff silver prods., Hartmann luggage.

Brown Shoe Co., Inc.; 8300 Maryland Ave., P.O. Box 29, St. Louis, MO 63166; (314) 854-4000; www.brownshoe.com; Ronald A. Fromm; manuf. and retailer (Famous Footwear) of women's, men's, and children's shoes (Buster Brown, Naturalizer, Dr. Scholl's).

Brunswick Corp.; 1 N. Field Ct., Lake Forest, IL 60045; (847) 735-4700; www.brunswickcorp.com; George Buckley; largest U.S. maker of leisure and recreation prods., marine, camping, fitness and fishing equip., bowling centers and equip.

Burger King Corp.; One Whopper Way, 5505 Blue Lagoon Dr., Miami, FL 33126; (305) 378-3000; www.burgerking.com; Bradley D. Blum; quick-serve restaurants.

Burlington Industries; 3330 West Friendly Ave., Greensboro, NC 27410; (336) 379-2000; www.burlington.com; George Henderson III; fabrics and textile products.

Burlington Northern Santa Fe Inc.; 2650 Lou Menk Dr., Ft. Worth, TX 76161-0057; (817) 352-1000; www.bnsf.com; Matthew Rose; one of the largest U.S. rail transportation cos.

Campbell Soup Co.; Campbell Pl., Camden, NJ 08103; (609) 342-4800; www.campbellsoup.com; Douglas R. Conant; soups, Franco-American spaghetti, V8 vegetable juice, Prego spaghetti sauce, Pepperidge Farm, Pace sauces.

Caterpillar Inc.; 100 N.E. Adams St., Peoria, IL 61629; (309) 675-1000; www.cat.com; Glen A. Barton; world's largest producer of earth moving equip.

Chase Manhattan Corp.: see JPMorgan Chase & Co. Inc.

ChevronTexaco Corp.; 6001 Bollinger Canyon Rd., San Ramon, CA 94853; (925) 842-1000; www.chevrontexaco.com; David J. O'Reilly; 2nd-largest U.S.-based oil co.

Chiquita Brands International, Inc.; 250 E. 5th St., Cincinnati, OH 45202; (513) 784-8000; www.chiquita.com; Cyrus F. Friedham Jr.; bananas, fruits, vegetables.

Church & Dwight Co., Inc.; 469 N. Harrison St., Princeton, NJ 08543; (609) 683-5900; www.churchdwight.com; R.A. Davies 3rd; world's largest producer of sodium bicarbonate (Arm & Hammer); household products (Brillo, Fresh'n Soft, other Arm & Hammer products); personal care products (Arrid antiperspirant, Pearl Drops, Nair, Trojan condoms, First Response pregnancy test).

CIGNA Corp.; 1 Liberty Pl., Philadelphia, PA 19103; (215) 761-1000; www.cigna.com; H. Edward Hanway; insurance holding co.

Circuit City Stores, Inc.; 9950 Mayland Dr., Richmond, VA 23233-1464; (804) 527-4000; www.circuitcity.com; Alan McCollough; retailer of electronic, audio/video equip., consumer appliances; new and used-car stores (CarMax).

Cisco Systems; 170 West Tasman Dr., San Jose, CA 95134; (408) 526-4000; www.cisco.com; John Chambers; networking and communication products.

Citigroup; 399 Park Ave., NY, NY 10043; (212) 559-1000; www.citigroup.com; Sanford I. Weill; diversified financial services.

Liz Claiborne, Inc.; 1440 Broadway, New York, NY 10018; (212) 354-4900; www.lizclaiborne.com; P. Charron; apparel, accessories.

Clorox Co.; 1221 Broadway, Oakland, CA 94612; (510) 271-7000; www.clorox.com; Gerald E. Johnston; retail consumer prods. (Clorox, Formula 409, Pine-Sol, S.O.S., Soft Scrub cleansers; Armor All, STP, Rain Dance automotive prods.; Scoop Away, Fresh Step cat litters; Kingsford charcoal briquets; Combat insecticide; Hidden Valley dressing; K.C. Masterpiece barbecue sauce; Brita water systems)

Coca-Cola Co.; 1 Coca-Cola Plaza, Atlanta, GA 30313; (404) 676-2121; www.cocacola.com; Douglas N. Daft; world's largest soft drink co. (Coca-Cola, Sprite, Nestea), world's largest dist. of juice prods. (Minute Maid, Hi-C, Fruitopia).

Colgate-Palmolive Co.; 300 Park Ave., NY, NY 10022; (212) 310-2000; www.colgate.com; Reuben Mark; soap (Palmolive, Irish Spring), detergent (Fab, Ajax), toothpaste (Colgate), Hill's pet food.

Compaq Computer Corp.: see Hewlett-Packard Co.

CompUSA Inc.; 14951 N. Dallas Pkwy., Dallas, TX 75254; (972) 982-4000; www.compusa.com; Hal Compton; largest U.S. superstore retailer of microcomputers and peripherals.

Computer Sciences Corp.; 2100 E. Grand Ave., El Segundo, CA 90245; (310) 615-0311; www.csc.com; Van B. Honeycutt; technology services.

ConAgra; 1 ConAgra Dr., Omaha, NE 68102; (402) 595-4000; www.conagra.com; Bruce Rohde; 2nd-largest U.S. food processor (Armour, Bumble Bee, Butterball, Chef Boyardee, Healthy Choice frozen dinners, Egg Beaters, Reddi-Wip).

ConocoPhillips Co.; 600 North Dairy Ashford, P.O. Box 2197, Houston, TX 77252; (281) 293-1000; www.conocophillips.com; James J. Mulva; oil and petrochemical co. Formed by merger of Conoco and Phillips Petroleum, 8/30/02. Third-largest U.S. integrated energy company.

Continental Airlines, Inc.; 1600 Smith St. HQS11, Houston, TX 77002; (713) 324-5242; www.continental.com; Gordon M. Bethune; air transportation.

Adolph Coors Co.; 311 Tenth St., Golden, CO 80401; (303) 279-6565; www.coors.com; Peter Coors; brewer (Coors, Killian's, Zima).

Corning Inc.; 1 Riverfront Plaza, Corning, NY 14831; (607) 974-9000; www.corning.com; James R. Houghton; telecommunications, specialty materials, optical fiber and cable.

Costco Wholesale Corp.; 999 Lake Dr., Issaquah, WA 98027; (425) 313-8100; www.costco.com; James D. Sinegal; wholesale-membership warehouses.

Crane Co.; 100 First Stamford Place, Stamford, CT 06902; (203) 363-7300; www.craneco.com; Robert S. Evans; manuf. fluid control devices, vending machines, fiberglass panels, aircraft brakes.

A. T. Cross Co.; 1 Albion Rd., Lincoln, RI 02865; (401) 333-1200; www.cross.com; David Whalen; writing instruments.

Crown Cork & Seal Co.; 1 Crown Way, Philadelphia, PA 19154-4599; (215) 698-5100; www.crowncork.com; John W. Conway; world's leading supplier of packaging prods.

CSX Corp.; 500 Water St., C900, Jacksonville, FL 32202; (904) 633-1000; www.csx.com; Michael J. Ward; rail, ocean, barge freight transport.

CVS Corp.; 1 CVS Dr., Woonsocket, RI 02895; (401) 765-1500; www.CVS.com; Thomas M. Ryan; drugstore chain.

Dana Corp.; 4500 Dorr St., Toledo, OH 43615; (419) 535-4500; www.dana.com; Joseph M. Magliochetti; truck and auto parts, supplies.

Darden Restaurants; 5900 Lake Ellenor Dr., Orlando, FL 32809; (407) 245-4000; www.darden.com; Joe Lee; chain restaurants (Red Lobster, Olive Garden, Bahama Breeze, Smokey Bones BBQ Sports Bar).

Deere & Co.; One John Deere Pl., Moline, IL 61265; (309) 765-8000; www.deere.com; Robert W. Lane; world's largest manuf. of farm equip.; industrial equip.; lawn and garden tractors.

Dell Computer Corp.; 1 Dell Way, Round Rock, TX 78682; (512) 338-4400; www.dell.com; Michael S. Dell; laptop and desktop computers.

Delphi Corp.; 5725 Delphi Dr., Troy, MI 48098; (248) 813-2000; www.delphi.com; J.T. Battenburg III; automotive systems, audio systems, mobile electronics.

Delta Air Lines, Inc.; P.O. Box 20706, Atlanta, GA 30320; (404) 715-2600; www.delta.com; Leo F. Mullin; air transportation.

Dial Corp.; 15501 N. Dial Blvd., Scottsdale, AZ 85260-1619; (602) 754-3425; www.dialcorp.com; Herbert Baum; consumer prods. (Dial, Coast soap, Purex detergent, Armour Star meats, Renuzit air fresheners).

Diebold, Inc; 5995 Mayfair Rd., P.O. Box 3077, North Canton, OH 44720; (330) 490-4000; www.diebold.com; Walden W. O'Dell; manuf. ATMs, security systems and prods.

Dillard's; 1600 Cantrell Rd., Little Rock, AR 72201; (501) 376-5200; www.dillards.com; William Dillard 2nd; 2nd-largest dept. store chain in U.S.

Walt Disney Co.; 500 S. Buena Vista St., Burbank, CA 91521-7320; (818) 560-1000; www.disney.com; Michael D. Eisner; motion pictures, television (ESPN, ABC, SoapNet, Disney Channel, Lifetime), radio stations, theme parks (Walt Disney World, Disneyland) and resorts, publishing, recordings, retailing (Disney Stores).

Dole Food Co., Inc.; One Dole Drive, Westlake Village, CA 91362; (818) 879-6600; www.dole.com; David H. Murdock; food prods., fresh fruits and vegetables.

R. R. Donnelley & Sons Co.; 77 W. Wacker Dr., Chicago, IL 60601-1696; (312) 326-8000; www.rrdonnelley.com; William L. Davis; commercial printer, digital media.

Dow Chemical Co.; 2030 Dow Center, Midland, MI 48674; (517) 636-1000; www.dow.com; William S. Stavropoulos; chemicals, plastics (world's 2nd-largest chemical co. after merger, 2/7/01, with Union Carbide).

Dow Jones & Co., Inc.; 200 Liberty St., NY, NY 10281; (212) 416-2000; www.dowjones.com; John Chambers; financial news service, publishing (Wall Street Journal, Barron's, Ottaway Newspapers).

Dun & Bradstreet Corp.; 103 JFK Parkway, Short Hills, NJ 07078; (973) 921-5500; www.dnb.com; Allen Z. Loren.; business information, publishing ("Yellow Pages" phone books).

Duracell: see Gillette.

E. I. du Pont de Nemours & Co. (Dupont); 1007 Market St., Wilmington, DE 19898; (302) 774-1000; www.dupont.com; Charles Holliday; largest U.S. chemical co.; petroleum, consumer prods.

▶ **IT'S A FACT:** In 1935, Fred Lazarus Jr., co-founder of Federated Department Stores, Inc., pursuaded President Franklin D. Roosevelt to move Thanksgiving from the last Thursday in November to the fourth Thursday of that month in order to expand the holiday shopping season, and thereby improve business. The move was made official in 1941 by an act of Congress.

Eastman Kodak Co.; 343 State St., Rochester, NY 14650-0205; (585) 724-4000; www.kodak.com; D. Carp; world's largest producer of photographic prods.

Eaton Corp.; 1111 Superior Ave., Cleveland, OH 44114; (216) 523-5000; www.eaton.com; Alexander Cutler; manuf. of vehicle powertrain components, controls.

Edison Intl.; 2244 Walnut Grove Ave., P.O. Box 800, Rosemead, CA 91770; (626) 302-2222; www.edisonx.com; John Bryson; electric utilities.

Electronic Data Systems; 5400 Legacy Dr., Plano, TX 75024; (972) 604-6000; www.eds.com; Michael Jordan; management consulting, e-solutions, software.

El Paso Corp.; 1001 Louisiana Street, Houston, TX 77002; (713) 420-2600; www.elpaso.com; Ronald L. Kuehn Jr.; diversified energy company primarily engaged in interstate transmission of natural gas.

Emerson Electric Co.; 8000 West Florissant Avenue, St. Louis, MO 63136; (314) 553-2000; www.gotoemerson.com; David Farr; electrical, electronics prods. & systems.

Energizer Holdings Inc.; 533 Maryville Univ. Dr., St. Louis, MO 63141; www.energizer.com; J. Patrick Mulcahy; batteries, flashlights, lanterns.

Exxon Mobil Corp.; 5959 Las Colinas Blvd., Irving, TX 75039-2298; (972) 444-1000; www.exxonmobil.com; Lee Raymond; world's largest publicly owned integrated oil co.

Fannie Mae; 3900 Wisconsin Ave. NW, Washington, DC 20016; (202) 752-7000; www.fanniemae.com; Franklin Raines; largest U.S. provider of residential mortgage funds.

Fedders Corp.; 505 Martinsville Road, PO Box 813, Liberty Corner, NJ 07938; (908) 604-8686; www.fedders.com; Salvatore Giordano Jr; manuf. of room air conditioners (Fedders, Airtemp), dehumidifiers.

Federated Dept. Stores; 7 W. 7th St., Cincinnati, OH 45202; (513) 579-7000; www.Federated-fds.com; James Zimmerman; full-line dept. stores Macy's, Bloomingdale's, Burdines.

FedEx Corp.; 942 S. Shady Grove Rd., Memphis, TN 38120; (901) 369-3600; www.fedex.com; F. W. Smith; express delivery service.

First Data Corp.; 6200 S. Quebec St., Greenwood Village, CO, 30328; (303) 967-8000; www.firstdata.com; Charles Fote; info. retrieval, data processing.

FleetBoston Financial Corp.; 100 Federal St., 10034F, Boston, MA 02110; (617) 434-2200; www.fleet.com; Charles Gifford; financial services company.

Fleetwood Enterprises, Inc.; 3125 Myers St., Riverside, CA 92503; (909) 351-3500; www.fleetwood.com; Edward B. Candill; manufactured homes, recreational vehicles.

Fleming Cos. Inc.; P.O. Box 299013, Lewisville, TX 75029; (972) 906-8000; www.fleming.com; Peter S. Willmott; one of largest U.S. wholesale food distrib.

Fluor Corp.; One Enterprise Dr., Aliso Viejo, CA 92656; (949) 349-2000; www.fluor.com; Alan L. Boeckmann; largest international engineering and construction co. in U.S.

Foot Locker, Inc.; formerly Venator Group, 112 West 34th St., NY, NY 10120; (212) 720-3700; www.footlocker-inc.com; Matthew D. Serra; operates retail stores: shoes (Kinney), apparel (Eastbay), athletic footwear (Foot Locker), athletic merchandise (Champs).

Ford Motor Co.; American Rd., Dearborn, MI 48121; (313) 322-3000; www.ford.com; William Clay Ford Jr.; 2nd-largest auto manufacturer, motor vehicle sales (Ford, Lincoln-Mercury, Volvo), rentals (Hertz).

Fortune Brands, Inc.; 300 Tower Parkway, Lincolnshire, IL 60069; (847) 484-4400; www.fortunebrands.com.index/cfm; Norman H. Wesley; spirits and wine (Jim Beam), hardware, office prods. (Swingline), golf and leisure prods. (Titleist, Cobra, FootJoy).

Freddie Mac; 8200 Jones Branch Dr., McLean, VA 22102; (703) 903-2000; www.freddiemac.com; Gregory Parseghian; residential mortgage provider.

Fruit of the Loom, Inc.; 1 Fruit of the Loom Dr., Bowling Green, KY 42102-9015; (270) 781-6400; www.fruit.com; John B. Holland; manuf. of underwear, activewear. A subsidiary of Berkshire Hathaway, acquired 4/30/02.

Gannett Co., Inc.; 7950 Jones Branch Dr., McLean, VA 22107; (703) 854-6000; www.gannett.com; D.H. McCorkindale; newspaper publishing (*USA Today*), network and cable TV.

The Gap, Inc.; Two Folsom St., San Francisco, CA 94105; (415) 952-4400; www.gap.com; Donald G. Fisher; casual and activewear retailer (Gap, Banana Republic, Old Navy).

Gateway; 14303 Gateway Pl., Poway, CA 92064; (858) 848-3401; www.gateway.com; Theodore Waitt; personal computers.

General Dynamics; 3190 Fairview Park Drive, Falls Church, VA 22042; (703) 876-3000; www.generaldynamics.com; Nicholas D. Chabraja; nuclear submarines (Trident, Seawolf), armored vehicles, combat systems, computing devices, defense systems.

General Electric Co.; 3135 Easton Tpke., Fairfield, CT 06431; (203) 373-2211; www.ge.com; Jeffrey Immelt; electrical, electronic equip., radio and television broadcasting (NBC), aircraft engines, power generation, appliances.

General Mills, Inc.; Number One General Mills Blvd., PO Box 1113, Minneapolis, MN 55440; (763) 764-7600; www.general mills.com; S. W. Sanger; foods (Total, Wheaties, Cheerios, Chex, Hamburger Helper, Betty Crocker, Bisquick).

General Motors; 100 Renaissance Center, Detroit, MI 48243; (313) 556-5000; www.gm.com; G. Richard Wagoner Jr.; world's largest auto manuf. (Chevrolet, Pontiac, Cadillac, Buick).

Genuine Parts Co.; 2999 Circle 75 Pkwy., Atlanta, GA 30339; (770) 953-1700; www.genpt.com; Larry L. Prince; distributes auto replacement parts (NAPA).

Georgia-Pacific Corp.; 133 Peachtree St. NE, Atlanta, GA 30303; (404) 652-4000; www.gp.com; A. D. Correll; manuf. of paper and wood prods.

Gillette; Prudential Tower Bldg., Boston, MA 02199; (617) 421-7000; www.gillette.com; James M. Kilts; personal care prods. (Sensor, Atra razors, Oral-B toothbrushes, Right Guard, Soft & Dri), appliances (Braun), batteries (Duracell).

Goldman Sachs Group; 85 Broad Street, NY, NY 10004; (212) 902-1000; www.gs.com; Henry M. Paulson Jr.; investment banking, asset management, securities services.

The Goodyear Tire & Rubber Co.; 1144 E. Market St., Akron, OH 44316; (330) 796-2121; www.goodyear.com; Robert Keegan; world's largest rubber manuf.; tires and other auto prods.

W. R. Grace & Co.; 7500 Grace Dr., Columbia, MD 21044; (410) 531-4000; www.grace.com; Paul J. Norris; chemicals, construction prods.

Great Atlantic & Pacific Tea Co. (A&P); 2 Paragon Dr., Montvale, NJ 07645; (201) 573-9700; www.aptea.com; Christian Haub; supermarkets (A&P, Waldbaum's, Kohl's, Dominion).

Halliburton Co.; 5 Houston Center, 1401 McKinney, Houston, TX 77010; (713) 759-2600; www.halliburton.com; Dave Lesar; energy, engineering, and construction services.

Harley-Davidson, Inc.; 3700 W. Juneau Avenue, Milwaukee, WI 53208; (414) 343-4680; www.harley-davidson.com; Jeffrey Bleustein; manuf. of motorcycles, parts, and accessories.

Harrah's Entertainment, Inc.; One Harrah's Court, Las Vegas, NV 89119; (702) 407-6000; www.harrahs.com; Philip G. Satre; casino-hotels and riverboats.

Hartford Financial Services Group, Inc.; Hartford Plaza, 690 Asylum Ave., Hartford, CT 06115; (860) 547-5000; www.the hartford.com; Ramani Ayer; insurance, financial services.

Hartmarx; 101 N. Wacker Dr., Chicago, IL 60606; (312) 372-6300; www.hartmarx.com; Elbert O. Hand; apparel manuf. (Hart Schaffner & Marx, Hickey Freeman, Claiborne, Tommy Hilfiger, Pierre Cardin, Perry Ellis).

Hasbro, Inc.; 1027 Newport Ave., Pawtucket, RI 02862; (401) 431-8697; www.hasbro.com; Alan G. Hassenfeld; toy and game manuf. (Milton Bradley, Playskool, G. I. Joe, Parker Bros., Tiger Electronics, Play-Doh).

HCA Inc.; 1 Park Plaza, Nashville, TN 37203; (615) 344-9551; www.hcahealthcare.com; Jack O. Bovender Jr.; largest hospital mgmt. co. in the U.S.

H. J. Heinz Co.; 600 Grant St., Pittsburgh, PA 15219; (412) 456-5700; www.heinz.com; William R. Johnson; foods (StarKist, Ore-Ida, 57 Varieties), pet food (Kibbles 'n Bits, 9 Lives), Weight Watchers.

Hershey Foods Corp.; 100 Crystal A Dr., Hershey, PA 17033; (717) 534-6799; www.hersheys.com; Richard H. Lenny; largest U.S. producer of chocolate and confectionery prods. (Reese's, Kit Kat, Mounds, Almond Joy, Cadbury, Jolly Rancher, Twizzlers, Milk Duds, Good & Plenty).

Hewlett-Packard Co.; 3000 Hanover St., Palo Alto, CA 94304; (650) 857-1501; www.hp.com; Carly Fiorina; manuf. computers, electronic prods. and systems. (On 5/3/02 Hewlett-Packard acquired Compaq Computer Co.)

Hillenbrand Industries, Inc.; 700 State Rte. 46 E, Batesville, IN 47006; (812) 934-7000; www.hillenbrand.com; R.J. Hillenbrand; manuf. caskets, adjustable hospital beds.

Hilton Hotels Corp.; 9336 Civic Center Dr., Beverly Hills, CA 90210; (310) 278-4321; www.hilton.com; Stephen F. Bollenbach; hotels, casinos.

Home Depot, Inc.; 2455 Paces Ferry Rd. NW, Atlanta, GA 30339; (770) 433-8211; www.homedepot.com; Robert L. Nardelli; retail building supply, home improvement warehouse stores.

Honeywell Inc.; 101 Columbia Road, Morristown, NJ 07962; (973) 455-2000; www.honeywell.com; David Cote; merger in 12/99 with AlliedSignal Corp. industrial and home control systems, aerospace guidance systems.

Hormel Foods Corp.; 1 Hormel Pl., Austin, MN 55912-3680; (507) 437-5611; www.hormel.com; Joel W. Johnson; meat processor, pork and beef prods. (SPAM, Dinty Moore, Little Sizzlers).

Houghton Mifflin Co.; 222 Berkeley St., Boston, MA 02116; (617) 351-5000; www.hmco.com; Sylvia Metayer; publisher of textbooks, reference, general interest books.

Huffy Corp.; 225 Byers Rd., Miamisburg, OH 45342; (937) 866-6251; www.huffy.com; Don R. Graber; largest U.S. bicycle manuf., sports and hardware equip.

Humana, Inc.; 500 W. Main Street, PO Box 1438, Louisville, KY 40202; (502) 580-1000; www.humana.com; David A. Jones; managed healthcare service provider, related specialty products.

Illinois Toolworks; 3600 West Lake Ave., Glenview, IL 60025; (847) 724-7500; www.itwinc.com; W. James Farrell; food equip. (Hobart), home appliances and cookware (West Bend).

Ingersoll-Rand; 200 Chestnut Ridge Road, Woodcliff Lake, NJ 07675; (201) 573-0123; www.irco.com; Herbert L. Henkel; industrial machinery.

Intel Corp.; 2200 Mission College Blvd., Santa Clara, CA 95052-8119; (408) 765-8080; www.intel.com; A. S. Grove; manuf. integrated circuits (Pentium).

International Business Machines Corp. (IBM); One New Orchard Rd., Armonk, NY 10504; (914) 499-1900; www.ibm.com; Samuel Palmisano; world's largest supplier of advanced information processing technology equip., services.

International Paper Co.; 400 Atlantic St., Stamford, CT 06921; (203) 541-8000; www.internationalpaper.com; John T. Dillon; world's largest paper/forest prods. co., chemicals, packaging.

International Steel Group-Bethlehem; 3250 Interstate Dr., 2nd Fl., Richfield, OH 44286; www.bethsteel.com; Rodney B. Mott; steel & steel prods.

Interstate Bakeries Corp.; 12 E. Armour Blvd., Kansas City, MO 64111; (816) 502-4000; www.interstatebakeries corp.com; Charles A. Sullivan; baked goods wholesaler, distributor (Wonder, Hostess, Dolly Madison, Beefsteak, Home Pride).

J. Crew Group, Inc.; 770 Broadway, NY, NY 10003; (212) 209-2500; www.jcrew.com; Millard S. Drexler; apparel and accessories, retail and mail order.

Jet Blue Airways; 118-29 Queens Blvd., Forest Hills, NY 11375; (800) JETBLUE; www.jetblue.com; David Neeleman; air travel.

Jo-Ann Stores, Inc.; 5555 Darrow Rd., Hudson, OH 44236; (330) 656-2600; www.joann.com; Alan Rosskamm; nation's largest specialty fabric and craft stores (Jo-Ann Fabric and Crafts, Jo-Ann etc.).

Johnson Controls, Inc.; 5757 N. Green Bay Avenue, Milwaukee, WI 53201; (414) 524-1200; www.johnsoncontrols.com; James H. Keyes; fire protection services, auto seats and batteries.

Johnson & Johnson; 1 Johnson & Johnson Plaza, New Brunswick, NJ 08933; (732) 524-0400; www.jnj.com; William Weldon; surgical dressings (Band-Aid), pharmaceuticals (Tylenol), toiletries (Neutrogena).

S.C. Johnson & Son, Inc.; 1525 Howe St., Racine, WI 53403; (262) 260-2000; www.scjohnson.com; William D. Perez; cleaning and other household prods. (Johnson's Wax, Windex, pledge, Fantastik, Raid, Off!, Shout, Glade, Scrubbing Bubbles, Ziploc bags).

Jostens Inc.; 5501 Norman Center Dr., Minneapolis, MN 55437; (612) 830-3300; www.jostens.com; Bob Buhrmaster; school rings, yearbooks, plaques.

JPMorgan Chase & Co. Inc; 270 Park Ave., NY, NY 10017; (212) 270-6000; www.jpmorganchase.com; William Harrison Jr.; global financial firm.

Kellogg Co.; One Kellogg Sq., Battle Creek, MI 49016; (269) 961-2000; www.kelloggs.com; Carlos Gutierrez; world's largest mfgr. of ready-to-eat cereals, other food prods. (Frosted Flakes, Rice Krispies, Froot Loops, Pop-Tarts, Nutri-Grain, Eggo).

Kelly Services, Inc.; 999 West Big Beaver Rd., Troy, MI 48084; (248) 362-4444; www.kellyservices.com; Terence Adderley; temporary staffing services.

Kimberly-Clark Corp.; PO Box 619100, Dallas, TX 75261-9100; (972) 281-1200; www.kimberly-clark.com; Thomas Falk; personal care prods. (Kleenex, Scott, Cottonelle, Huggies, Viva, Kotex).

King World Productions, Inc.; 1700 Broadway, 33rd Floor, NY, NY 10019; (212) 315-4000; www.kingworld.com; Roger King; distributor of TV programs (*Oprah Winfrey Show, Wheel of Fortune, Jeopardy!, Inside Edition*).

Kmart Corp.; 3100 W. Big Beaver Rd., Troy, MI 48084; (248) 643-1000; www.kmart.com; Julian C. Day; discount stores.

Knight Ridder, Inc.; 50 W. San Fernando Street, San Jose, CA 95113-2413; (408) 938-7700; www.knightridder.com; P.A. Ridder; newspaper publishing.

Kraft Foods, Inc.: *see* Altria Group, Inc.

Kroger Co.; 1014 Vine St., Cincinnati, OH 45202; (513) 762-4000; www.kroger.com; Joseph A. Pichler; largest U.S. retail grocery chain, convenience stores, mall jewelry stores.

(Estee) Lauder Cos.; 767 5th Ave., NY, NY 10153; (212) 572-4200; www.esteelauder.com; Leonard A. Lauder; cosmetics (Clinique), fragrance prods. (Aramis, Aveda, Tommy Hilfiger).

La-Z-Boy Inc.; 1284 N. Telegraph Rd., Monroe, MI 48162; (734) 242-1444; www.lazboy.com; Patrick H. Norton; reclining chairs, other furniture.

Leggett & Platt, Inc.; No. 1 Leggett Rd., Carthage, MO 64836; (417) 358-8131; www.leggett.com; Felix E. Wright; furniture and furniture components, industrial materials, automotive seating suspension, train and cable control systems.

Lehman Bros. Holdings, Inc.; 745 7th Ave., NY, NY 10019; (212) 526-7000; www.lehman.com; Richard S. Fuld Jr.; investment bank.

Levi Strauss & Co;; 1155 Battery St., San Francisco, CA 94111; (415) 501-6000; www.levistrauss.com; Robert D. Haas; blue jeans, casual sportswear.

Liberty Mutual Group; 175 Berkeley St., Boston, MA 02116; (617) 357-9500; www.libertymutual.com; Edmund F. Kelly; auto, home, and life insurance.

Eli Lilly and Company; Lilly Corporate Center, Indianapolis, IN 46285; (317) 276-2000; www.lilly.com; Sidney Taurel; pharmaceuticals (Axid, Ceclor, Prozac) and animal health prods.

The Limited, Inc.; 3 Limited Pkwy., P.O. Box 16000, Columbus, OH 43216; (614) 479-7000; www.limited.com; Leslie H. Wexner; apparel stores (Lane Bryant, Lerner, Limited, Express, Victoria's Secret, Henri Bendel), home decor (White Barn Candle Co., Bath & Body Works).

L.L.Bean, Inc.; Freeport, ME 04033-0001; (800) 441-5713; www.llbean.com; Leon Gorman; outdoor apparel and footwear.

Lockheed Martin Corp.; 6801 Rockledge Dr., Bethesda, MD 20817; (301) 897-6000; www.lockheedmartin.com; Vance Coffman; commercial and military aircraft, electronics, missiles.

Loews Corp.; 667 Madison Ave., NY, NY 10021; (212) 521-2000; www.loews.com; James S. Tisch; tobacco prods. (Kent, True, Newport), watches (Bulova), hotels, insurance (CNA Financial), offshore drilling (Diamond).

Longs Drug Stores, Inc.; 141 N. Civic Dr., P.O. Box 5222, Walnut Creek, CA 94596; (925) 937-1170; www.longs.com; Robert M. Long; drug store chain.

Lowe's Cos., Inc.; 1605 Curtis Bridge Rd., N. Wilkesboro, NC 28656; (336) 658-4000; www.lowes.com; Robert L. Tillman; building materials and home improvement superstores.

Luby's, Inc.; 2211 NE Loop 410, PO Box 33069, San Antonio, TX 78265; (210) 654-9000; www.lubys.com; Christopher Pappas; operates cafeterias in S and SW.

Lucent Technologies, Inc.; 600 Mountain Ave., Murray Hill, NJ 07974; (908) 582-8500; www.lucent.com; Patricia Russo; leading developer, designer, and manuf. of telecommunications systems, software, and prods.

Mandalay Resort Group; 3950 Las Vegas Boulevard South, Las Vegas, NV 89119; (702) 632-6700; www.mandalay resortgroup.org; Michael Ensign; casino-resort operator (Excalibur, Luxor).

Manpower Inc.; 5301 N. Ironwood Rd., Milwaukee, WI 53217; (414) 961-1000; www.manpower.com; Jeffrey A. Joerres; 2nd-largest non-gov't. employment services co. in the world.

Marathon Oil Corp.; 555 San Felipe Rd., Houston, TX 77056; (713) 629-6600; www.marathon.com; Clarence P. Cazalot Jr.; integrated oil co. (Became independent co. 1/1/02 after being separated from USX-Marathon Group; United States Steel Corp. created as a result of a spin-off from USX.)

Marriott International, Inc.; Marriott Drive, Washington, DC 20058; (301) 380-3000; www.marriott.com; John Willard Marriott Jr; hotels, retirement communities, food service dist.

Masco Corp.; 21001 Van Born Rd., Taylor, MI 48180; (313) 274-7400; www.masco.com; Richard A. Manoogian; manuf. kitchen, bathroom prods. (Delta, Peerless faucets; Fieldstone, Merillat cabinets).

Mass Mutual Financial Group; 1295 State St., Springfield, MA 01111; (800) 767-1000; www.massmutual.com; Robert J. O'Connell; financial planning and investment, life insurance.

Mattel, Inc.; 333 Continental Blvd., El Segundo, CA 90245; (310) 252-2000; www.mattel.com; Robert A. Eckert; largest U.S. toymaker (Barbie, Fisher-Price, Hot Wheels, Matchbox, American Girls).

May Department Stores Co.; 611 Olive St., St. Louis, MO 63101; (314) 342-6300; www.maycompany.com; Gene S. Kahn; department stores (Hecht's, Lord & Taylor, Filene's, Foley's).

Maytag Corp.; 403 W. Fourth St. N., Newton, IA 50208; (641) 792-7000; www.maytagcorp.com; Ralph F. Hake; major appliance mfgr. (Magic Chef, Admiral, Jenn-Air), Hoover vacuum cleaners, floor care systems.

McDonald's Corp.; McDonald's Plaza, Oak Brook, IL 60523; (630) 623-3000; www.mcdonalds.com; Jim Cantalupo; fastfood restaurants.

McGraw-Hill Cos.; 1221 Ave. of the Americas, NY, NY 10020; (212) 512-2000; www.mcgraw-hill.com; Harold (Terry) McGraw 3rd; book, textbooks, magazine publishing (*Business Week*), information and financial services (Standard & Poor's), TV stations.

McKesson Corp.; 1 Post St., San Francisco, CA 94104; (415) 983-8300; www.mckesson.com; John Hammergren; distributor of drugs and toiletries and provides software and services in U.S.; bottled water.

Mead Westvaco Corp.; One High Ridge Park, Stamford, CT 06905; (203) 461-7400; www.meadwestvaco.com; John A. Luke Jr.; printing and writing paper, paperboard, packaging, shipping containers.

Medtronic, Inc.; 710 Medtronic Pkwy., Minneapolis, MN 55432; (763) 514-4000; www.medtronic.com; Art Collins; world's largest manuf. of implantable biomedical devices.

Merck & Co., Inc.; PO Box 100, Whitehouse Station, NJ 08889-0100; (908) 423-1000; www.merck.com; Raymond V. Gilmartin; pharmaceuticals (Pepcid, Zocor), animal health care prods.

Meredith Corp.; 1716 Locust St., Des Moines, IA 50336; (515) 284-3000; www.meredith.com; William T. Kerr; magazine publishing (*Better Homes and Gardens, Ladies' Home Journal*), book publishing, broadcasting.

Merrill Lynch & Co., Inc.; 4 World Financial Ctr., NY, NY 10080; (212) 449-1000; www.ml.com; Stan O' Neal; securities broker, financial services.

Metropolitan Life Ins. Co.; One Madison Ave., NY, NY 10010; (212) 578-2211; www.metlife.com; Bob H. Benmosche; insurance, financial services.

MGM Mirage Resorts, Inc.; 3400 S. Las Vegas Blvd., Las Vegas, NV 89109; (702) 791-7111; www.mirage.com; J. Terrence Lanni; hotel-casino operator (Mirage, Treasure Island, Golden Nugget).

Microsoft Corp.; One Microsoft Way, Redmond, WA 98052-6399; (425) 882-8080; www.microsoft.com; William H. Gates; largest independent software maker (Windows, Word, Excel).

Mobil Corp.; see Exxon Mobil Corp.

MONY Group, Inc.; 1740 Broadway, NY, NY 10019; (212) 708-2000; www.mony.com; Michael Roth; life insurance, annuity, and investment products.

Motorola, Inc.; 1303 E. Algonquin Rd., Schaumburg, IL 60196; (847) 576-5000; www.motorola.com; Christopher B. Galvin; electronic equipment and components; integrated communication devices.

Morgan Stanley Dean Witter & Co.; 1585 Broadway, NY, NY 10036; (212) 761-4000; www.msdw.com; Phillip J. Purcell; diversified financial services, major U.S. credit-card issuer.

Nabisco: see Philip Morris Cos. Inc.

National Semiconductor Corp.; 2900 Semiconductor Dr., P.O. Box 58090; Santa Clara, CA 95052-8090; (408) 721-5000; www.national.com; Brian L. Halla; manuf. of semiconductors, integrated circuits.

Nationwide Mutual Insurance Company; One Nationwide Plaza, Columbus, OH 43215; (800) 882-2822; www.nationwide.com; W.G. Jurgensen; life insurance and financial services.

Navistar Intl. Corp.; 4201 Winfield Rd., PO Box 1488, Warrenville, IL 60555; (630) 735-2143; www.navistar.com; John R. Horne; manuf. heavy-duty trucks, parts, school buses.

NCR Corp.; 1700 S. Patterson Blvd., Dayton, OH 45479; (937) 445-5000; www.ncr.com; Mark Hurd; computer hardware and software, computer services and supplies.

Nestlé Purina PetCare; formerly Ralston Purina; Checkerboard Sq., St. Louis, MO 63164; (314) 982-2161; www.purina.com; W. Patrick McGinnis; world's largest producer of dog and cat food (Purina, Alpo, Fancy Feast) and some baked goods. Owned by Nestlé SA in Switzerland.

Nestlé USA, Inc.; 800 North Brand Blvd., Glendale, CA 91203; (818) 549-6000; www.nestleusa.com; Joe Weller; candy (Baby Ruth, Raisinets), beverages (Nestea, Juicy Juice), frozen foods (Stouffer's); owned by Nestlé SA in Switzerland.

Newell Rubbermaid Inc.; Newell Center, 29 E. Stephenson St., Freeport, IL 61032; (815) 235-4171; www.newellco.com; Joseph Galli Jr.; cookware (Calphalon, WearEver); hair accessories (Goody); glassware (Anchor Hocking); kitchen products (Rubbermaid); window treatments (Levolor, Kirsch); home storage (Lee Ravan); writing instruments (Eberhard Faber, Sanford, Sharpie); address card files (Rolodex); infant and juvenile prods (Little Tikes, Graco, Century).

New York Times Co.; 229 W. 43rd St., NY, NY 10036; (212) 556-1234; www.nytco.com; A. O. Sulzberger Jr.; newspapers (*Boston Globe*), radio and TV stations, magazines (*Golf Digest*).

Nike, Inc.; 1 Bowerman Dr., Beaverton, OR 97005; (503) 671-6453; www.NikeBiz.com; Philip H. Knight; athletic and leisure footware, apparel.

Nordstrom, Inc.; 1617 6th Ave., Seattle, WA 98101; (206) 628-2111; www.nordstrom.com; Blake W. Nordstrom; upscale dept. store chain.

Norfolk Southern Corp.; Three Commercial Pl., Norfolk, VA 23510; (757) 629-2600; www.nscorp.com; David R. Goode; operates railway, freight carrier.

Northrop Grumman Corp;; 1840 Century Park East, Los Angeles, CA 90067; (310) 553-6262; www.northgrum.com; Ronald D. Sugar; aircraft, electronics, data systems, information systems, missiles. (Northrop Grumman acquired TRW, 12/12/02.)

Northwest Airlines Corp.; 2700 Lone Oak Pkwy., Eagan, MN 55121; (612) 726-2111; www.nwa.com; Richard H. Anderson; air transportation.

Northwestern Mutual Life Insurance Co.; 720 E. Wisconsin Ave., Milwaukee, WI 53202; (414) 271-1444; www.northwesternmutual.com; Edward J. Zore; life insurance, investment products and services, annuities.

Occidental Petroleum Corp.; 10889 Wilshire Blvd., Los Angeles, CA 90024; (310) 208-8800; www.oxy.com; Ray R. Irani; oil, natural gas, chemicals, plastics, fertilizers.

Office Depot.; 2200 Old Germantown Rd., Delray Beach, FL 33445; (561) 278-4800; www.officedepot.com; Bruce Nelson; retail office supply stores.

Omnicom Group Inc.; 437 Madison Ave., NY, NY 10022; (212) 415-3600; www.omnicomgroup.com; John Wren; advertising, market services, interactive/digital media.

Oracle Corp.; 500 Oracle Pkwy., Redwood Shores, CA 94065; www.oracle.com; Lawrence Ellison; database and file management software.

Owens Corning; 1 Owens Corning Parkway, Toledo, OH 43659; (419) 248-8000; www.owenscorning.com; David T. Brown; world leader in advanced glass, composite materials.

Owens-Illinois; 1 SeaGate, Toledo, OH 43666; (419) 247-5000; J. H. Lemieux; www.o-i.com; one of the world's largest producer of glass and plastic packaging.

Pacific Gas & Electric Corp. (PG&E); One Market, Spear Tower, Ste. 2400, San Francisco, CA 94105; (415) 267-7000; www.pgecorp.com; Robert D. Glynn Jr.; energy supplier.

PaineWebber Group, Inc.: see UBS PaineWebber Group, Inc.

Park Place Entertainment; 3930 Howard Hughes Pkwy., Las Vegas, NV 89109; (702) 699-5000; www.parkplace.com; Stephen Bollenbach; casino/hotel operators (Caesars, Paris, Bally's, Flamingo, Hilton, Grand Casino, Conrad).

J.C. Penney Co.; 6501 Legacy Dr., Plano, TX 75024; (972) 431-1000; www.jcpenney.com; Allen Questrom; dept. stores, catalog sales, drug stores (Eckerd, Fay's), insurance.

Pennzoil-Quaker State Co.(SOPUS Products); Pennzoil Pl., P.O. Box 2967, Houston, TX 77252-2967; (800) 990-9811; www.pennzoil.com; motor, gear, and transmission oils; grease; air and oil filters; cleaning and hydraulic fluids. Acquired by Royal Dutch/Shell Group (based in Neth.) 10/1/2002; U.S. affiliate is Shell Oil Company.

PepsiCo, Inc.; 700 Anderson Hill Rd., Purchase, NY 10577; (914) 253-2000; www.pepsico.com; Steven S. Reinemund; soft drinks (Pepsi-Cola, Mountain Dew), fruit juice (Tropicana), FritoLay snacks (Ruffles, Lay's, Fritos, Doritos, Rold Gold), Quaker Oats.

Pfizer, Inc.; 235 E. 42nd St., NY, NY 10017; (212) 733-2323; www.pfizer.com; Henry McKinnell; pharmaceuticals (Celebrex, Diflucan, Viagra, Zithromax), hospital, agricultural, chemical prods., consumer prods. (Visine, Desitin, Benadryl, Listerine, Lubriderm, Schick, Sudafed, Zantac 75, BENGAY). (Co. merged with Warner-Lambert 6/19/01; acquired Pharmacia Corp. 4/16/03)

Pharmacia Corp.: see Pfizer, Inc.

Philip Morris Cos. Inc.: see Altria Group, Inc.

Phillips-Van Heusen Corp.; 200 Madison Ave., NY, NY 10016; (212) 381-3500; www.pvh.com; Bruce Klatsky; designer of dress shirts, sportswear, and footwear (IZOD, Geoffrey Beene, DKNY, Kenneth Cole). (Company acquired Calvin Klein 2/12/03.)

Pillowtex Corp.; 1 Lake Circle Dr., Kannopolis, NC 28081; (704) 939-2000; www.pillowtex.com; Mike Gannaway; household textile prods.

Pitney Bowes, Inc.; 1 Elmcroft Rd., Stamford, CT 06926; (203) 356-5000; www.pb.com; Michael J. Critelli; world's largest mfgr. of postage meters, and mailing equip.

Polaroid Corp.; 1265 Main St., Bldg. W3, Waltham, MA 02451; (781) 386-2000; www.polaroid.com; Michael Pocock; photographic equip. and supplies, optical goods.

Polo Ralph Lauren Corp.; 650 Madison Ave., NY, NY 10022; (212) 318-7000; www.polo.com; Ralph Lauren; men's and women's apparel.

PPG Industries, Inc.; 1 PPG Place, Pittsburgh, PA 15272; (412) 434-3131; www.ppg.com; Raymond W. LeBoeuf; glass prods., silicas, fiberglass, chemicals; world's leading supplier of automobile/industrial coatings.

Procter & Gamble Co.; 1 Procter & Gamble Plaza, Cincinnati, OH 45202; (513) 983-1100; www.pg.com; Alan Lafley; soaps and detergents (Ivory, Cheer, Tide, Mr. Clean, Comet, Zest); toiletries (Crest, Scope, Head & Shoulders, Noxzema, Oil of Olay, Old Spice); pharmaceuticals (NyQuil, Pepto-Bismol, Vicks cough medicines); foods (Folgers coffee, Pringles); paper prods. (Charmin toilet tissues, Bounty towels, Tampax tampons, Pampers & Luvs disposable diapers); Cover Girl and Max Factor cosmetics, Clairol haircare.

Prudential Financial, Inc.; 751 Broad St., Newark, NJ 07102; (973) 802-6000; www.prudential.com; Arthur F. Ryan; insurance, financial services.

Publix Super Markets; 3300 Airport Rd., Lakeland, FL 33815; (863) 688-1188; www.publix.com; Charles Jenkins Jr.; chain of supermarkets.

Quaker Oats Co.: *see* PepsiCo, Inc.

Qwest Communications, Inc.; 1801 California St., Denver, CO 80202; (303) 992-1400; www.qwest.com; Richard Notebaert; provides telecommunications, wireless, and directory services for most of western and southwestern U.S.

Radio Shack, formerly Tandy Corp.; 100 Throckmorton St., Suite 1800, Fort Worth, TX 76102; (817) 415-3011; www.radioshack.com; Leonard H. Roberts; consumer electronics retailer (Computer City, Radio Shack).

Ralcorp Holdings, Inc.; 800 Market St., St. Louis, MO 63101; (314) 877-7000; www.ralcorp.com; Joe R. Micheletto; private-label breakfast cereals, snack foods, baby food (Beech-Nut).

Ralston Purina: *see* Nestlé Purina PetCare.

Raytheon Co.; 141 Spring St., Lexington, MA 02421; (781) 862-6600; www.raytheon.com; Daniel P. Burnham; defense systems, electronics.

Reader's Digest Assn., Inc.; Reader's Digest Road, Pleasantville, NY 10570; (914) 238-1000; www.rd.com; Thomas Ryder; direct-mail marketer of magazines, books, music and video prods.

Reebok Intl., Ltd.; 1895 J.W. Foster Blvd., Canton, MA 02021; (781) 401-5000; www.reebok.com; Paul Fireman; athletic and leisure footwear, apparel.

Revlon, Inc.; 625 Madison Ave., NY, NY 10022; (212) 527-4000; www.revlon.com; Ronald O. Perelman; cosmetics, beauty aids, skin care.

Rite Aid Corp.; 30 Hunter Lane, Camp Hill, PA 17011-2404; (717) 761-2633; www.riteaid.com; Mary F. Sammons; discount drug stores.

RJ Reynolds Tobacco; 401 N. Main St., Winston-Salem, NC 27102; (336) 741-5500; www.rjrt.com; Andrew J. Schindler; 2nd-largest U.S. producer of cigarettes (Winston, Salem, Camel).

Rockwell Auto; 777 E. Wisconsin Ave., Suite 1400, Milwaukee, WI 53202; (414) 212-5200; www.rockwell.com; Don H. Davis; diversified high-tech. co. (world leader in electronic controls).

Rohm & Haas Co.; 100 Independence Mall West, Philadelphia, PA 19106; (215) 592-3000; www.rohmhaas.com; J. Michael Fitzpatrick; adhesives and sealants, process chemicals, automotive coatings; salt (Morton, Windsor).

Ryder System, Inc.; 3600 NW 82nd Ave., Miami, FL 33166; (305) 500-3726; www.ryder.com; Gregory T. Swienton; truckleasing service.

Safeway Inc.; 5918 Stoneridge Mall Rd., Pleasanton, CA 94588-3229; (925) 467-3000; www.safeway.com; Steven A. Burd; supermarkets.

Sara Lee Corp.; Three First National Plaza, Chicago, IL 60602; (312) 726-2600; www.saralee.com; C. Steven McMillan; baked goods, fresh and processed meats (Ball Park, Jimmy Dean, Hillshire Farms, Kahn's), hosiery, intimate apparel, and knitwear (Hanes, L'eggs, Playtex, Champion).

SBC Communications, Inc.; 175 E. Houston, San Antonio, TX 78205; (210) 821-4105; www.sbc.com; Edward Whitacre Jr.; telephone services (Ameritech, Southwestern Bell, Pacific Bell).

Schering-Plough Corp.; 2000 Galloping Hill, Kenilworth, NJ 07033; (908) 298-4000; www.sch-plough.com; Fred Hassan; pharmaceuticals (Claritin, Proventil), consumer prods. (Afrin, Coppertone), animal health prods.

Seagate Technology; 920 Disc Dr., Scotts Valley, CA 95066; (405) 324-4770; www.seagate.com; Stephen J. Luczo; manuf. disk drives.

Sears, Roebuck and Co.; 3333 Beverly Rd., Hoffman Estates, IL 60179; (847) 286-2500; www.sears.com; Alan J. Lacy; 2nd-largest U.S. retailer, department, specialty stores.

Shaw Industries, Inc.: *see* Berkshire Hathaway Inc.

Sherwin-Williams Co.; 101 Prospect Ave. NW, Cleveland, OH 44115-1075; (216) 566-2000; www.sherwin.com; Jack Breen; largest North American paint and varnish producer (Dutch Boy, Pratt & Lambert, Martha Stewart, Minwax).

Smithfield Foods, Inc.; 200 Commerce St., Smithfield, VA 23430; (757) 365-3000; www.smithfieldfoods.com; Joseph Luter III; pork and processed meat products.

J. M. Smucker Co.; One Strawberry Lane, Orrville, OH 44667; (330) 682-3000; www.smuckers.com; Timothy P. Smucker; preserves, jams, jellies (Dickinson's), toppings (Magic Shell), syrups, juices, Jif peanut butter, Crisco oil

Smurfit-Stone Container Corp.; 150 N. Michigan Ave., Chicago, IL 60601; (312) 346-6600; www.smurfit-stone.net; Patrick J. Moore; industry leader for corrugated containers, paper bags and sacks.

Southwest Airlines Co.; P.O. Box 36611, Dallas, TX 75235; (214) 792-4000; www.southwest.com; Colleen Barrett; air transportation.

Sprint Corp.; 6200 Sprint Pkwy., Overland Park, KS 66251; (913) 624-3000; www.sprint.com; Gary Forsee; long-distance and local telecommunications.

Staples, Inc; 500 Staples Dr., Framingham, MA 01702; (508) 253-5000; www.staples.com; Ron Sargent; office-supply superstores.

Starbucks Corp.; 2401 Utah Ave. S., P.O. Box 34067, Seattle, WA 98134; (206) 447-1575; www.starbucks.com; Orin Smith; coffee and tea producers, retail coffee and tea stores.

Starwood Hotels and Resorts Worldwide; 1111 Westchester Ave., White Plains, NY 10604; (914) 640-8100; www.starwood.com; Barry S. Sternlicht; hotels and leisure company (Westin, Sheraton, W Hotels).

State Farm Mutual Automobile Ins. Co.; 1 State Farm Plaza, Bloomington, IL 61701; (309) 766-2311; www.statefarm.com; Edward B. Rust Jr.; major insurance co.

Stride Rite Corp.;; 191 Spring St., P.O. Box 9191, Lexington, MA 02420; (617) 824-6000; www.striderite. com; David Chamberlain; high-quality children's footwear (Keds, Sperry Top-Sider) and eyewear.

Sun Microsystems, Inc.; 4150 Network Circle, Santa Clara, CA 95054; (650) 960-1300; www.sun.com; Scott G. McNealy; supplier of network-based distributed computer systems (Java programming language).

Sunoco, Inc.; 1801 Market St., Philadelphia, PA 19103-1699; (215) 977-3000; www.sunocoinc.com; J.D. Drosdick; energy resources co., markets Sunoco gasoline.

SUPERVALU Inc.; 11840 Valley View Rd., Eden Prairie, MN 55340; (952) 828-4000; www.supervalu.com; Jeff Noddie; food wholesaler, retailer.

Sysco Corp.; 1390 Enclave Pkwy, Houston, TX 77077-2099; (281) 584-1390; www.sysco.com; Richard J. Schneiders; leading U.S. food distributor.

Target Corp.; 1000 Nicollet Mall, Minneapolis, MN 55403; (612) 370-6948; www.targetcorp.com; Robert J. Ulrich; department, specialty stores (Target, Marshall Field's, Mervyn's California).

Tenneco Automotive, Inc.; 500 N. Field Drive, Lake Forest, IL 60045; (847) 482-5000; www.tenneco-automotive.com; Mark P. Frissora; automotive parts (Monroe, Walker).

Texaco Inc.: *see* ChevronTexaco Corp.

Texas Instruments Inc.; 12500 TI Blvd., Dallas, TX 75266; (972) 995-3773; www.ti.com; T. J. Engibous; electronics, semiconductors, software

Textron, Inc.; 40 Westminster St., Providence, RI 02903; (401) 421-2800; www.textron.com; Lewis B. Campbell; aerospace, industrial, automotive prods., financial services.

3M Company; 3M Center, St. Paul, MN 55144-1000; (612) 733-1110; www.3m.com; W. James McNerney Jr.; abrasives, adhesives, electrical, health care, cleaning (Scotch-Brite, O-Cel-O sponges), printing, consumer prods. (Scotch Tape, Post-it).

TIAA-CREF; 730 Third Ave., NY, NY 10017; (800) 842-2733; www.tiaa-cref.org; John H. Biggs; financial services provider.

Timberland Company; 200 Domain Dr., Stratham, NH 03885; (603) 772-9500; www.timberland.com; Jeffrey Swartz; footwear, apparel, accessories.

Time Warner Inc.; 75 Rockefeller Plaza, New York, NY 10019; (212) 484-8000; www.timewarner.com; Stephen Richard D. Parsons; world's largest Internet online service; magazine publishing (*Time, Sports Illustrated, Fortune, Money, People, DC Comics*), TV and CATV (WB Network, HBO, Cinemax, CNN, TBS, TNT), book publishing (Little, Brown; Warner Books), motion pictures (Warner Bros., New Line Cinema), recordings, sports teams (Atlanta Braves, Atlanta Hawks), retailing (Warner Bros. stores). (America Online and Time Warner completed the largest corporate merger in history in 2001, becoming the largest media company in the U.S. Dropped "AOL" from name, 9/18/03.)

The TJX Cos., Inc.; 770 Cochituate Rd., Framingham, MA 01701; (508) 390-1000; www.tjx.com; Edmond English; world's largest off-price apparel retailer (T.J. Maxx, Marshalls).

Tootsie Roll Industries, Inc.; 7401 S. Cicero Ave., Chicago, IL 60629; (773) 838-3400; www.tootsie.com; Ellen and Melvin Gordon; candy (Tootsie Roll, Mason Dots, Charms, Sugar Daddy, Charleston Chew, Junior Mints).

Toro Co.; 8111 Lyndale Ave. S, Bloomington, MN 55420; (952) 888-8801; www.toro.com; Kendrick B. Melrose; lawn and turf maintenance (Lawn-Boy), snow removal equipment, lighting and irrigation systems.

Toys "R" Us; 461 From Rd., Paramus, NJ 07652; (201) 262-7800; www.toysrus.com; John J. Eyler Jr.; world's largest children's specialty retailer (Toys "R" Us, Kids "R" Us, Babies "R" Us, Imaginarium).

Transamerica Corp.; 1150 South Olive St. Los Angeles, CA 90015; (213) 742-2111; www.transamerica.com; Ron F. Wagley; insurance, financial services; wholly owned subsidiary of Netherlands-based AEGON.

Triarc Cos., Inc.; 280 Park Ave., NY, NY 10017; (212) 451-3000; www.triarc.com; Nelson Peltz; fast-food restaurants (Arby's), beverages (Royal Crown, Mystic, Nehi, Stewart's).

Tribune Co.; 435 N. Michigan Ave., Chicago, IL 60611; (312) 222-9100; www.tribune.com; Dennis J. Fitzsimmons; newspapers (*Los Angeles Times, Chicago Tribune, Newsday*), magazines (*Field & Stream, Popular Science*), broadcasting (incl. WGN-TV and 23 other stations), Chicago Cubs baseball team.

Trinity Industries, Inc.; PO Box 568887, 2525 Stemmons Freeway, Dallas, TX 75207; (214) 631-4420; www.trin.net; Timothy R. Wallace; manufactures metal prods., rail and freight prods.

TRW Inc.: *see* Northrop Grumman.

TWA: *see* AMR Corp.

Tyco Intl., Ltd.; 273 Corporate Dr., Portsmouth, NH 03801; (603) 334-3900; www.tyco.com; Edward Breen; fire protection systems, pipes, power cables, medical supplies, packaging.

Tyson Foods, Inc.; 2210 West Oaklawn, Springdale, AR 72764; (501) 290-4000; www.tysonfoodsinc.com; John Tyson; fresh and processed poultry and beef, pork, and seafood prods. (Holly Farms, Weaver, Louis Kemp, IBP).

UAL Corp.; 1200 E. Algonquin Rd., Elk Grove Twp., IL 60007; (847) 700-4000; www.ual.com; Glenn Tilton; air transportation (United Airlines).

UBS PaineWebber Group, Inc.; 1285 Ave. of the Americas, NY, NY 10019; (212) 713-2000; www.ubspainewebber.com; Joseph J. Grano Jr.; financial services.

Unilever Bestfoods North America; 700 Sylvan Ave., Englewood Cliffs, NJ 07632; (201) 894-4000; www.bestfoods.com; Jim Rice; food (Hellmann's mayonnaise, Knorr soups, Ragu pasta sauce, Wish-Bone salad dressing, Lipton Tea, Skippy Peanut Butter, Slim-Fast). Owned by Unilever NV (Neth.) and Unilever PLC (UK).

Union Carbide Corp.: *see* Dow Chemical Co.

Union Pacific Corp.; 1416 Dodge St., Omaha, NE, 68179; (402) 271-5000; www.up.com; Richard Davidson; largest railroad, trucking co. in U.S.; Fenix, telecommunications, software.

Unisys Corp.; Unisys Way, Blue Bell, PA 19424-0001; (215) 986-4011; www.unisys.com; Lawrence A. Weinbach; designs, manuf. computer information systems and related prods..

UnitedHealth Group Corp.; 9900 Bren Rd. East, Minnetonka, MN 55343; (612) 936-1300; www.unitedhealthgroup.com; William W. McGuire; owns, manages health maintenance organizations.

United Parcel Service of America, Corp.; 55 Glenlake Pkwy. NE, Atlanta, GA 30328; (404) 828-6000; www.ups.com; Michael L. Eskew; courier services.

United States Steel Corp.; 600 Grant St., Pittsburgh, PA 15219-2800; (412) 433-1121; www.ussteel.com; Thomas J. Usher; steel, tin prods. (Became separate co. 1/1/02 as a result of a spin-off from USX-Marathon Group; rest of corp. became Marathon Oil Corp.)

United Technologies Corp.; One Financial Plaza, Hartford, CT 06101; (860) 728-7000; www.utc.com; George David; aerospace, industrial prods. and services (Otis Elevator, Pratt & Whitney, Sikorsky Aircraft).

Unocal Corp.; 2141 Rosecrans Ave., Ste. 4000, El Segundo, CA 90245; (310) 726-7731; www.unocal.com; Charles R. Williamson; integrated oil co.

US Airways Group, Inc.; 2345 Crystal Dr., Arlington, VA 22227; (703) 872-7000; www.usairways.com; David N. Siegel; air transportation.

UST Inc.; 100 W. Putnam Ave., Greenwich, CT 06830; (203) 661-1100; www.ustinc.com; Vincent A. Gierer Jr.; smokeless tobacco (Copenhagen, Skoal), pipe tobacco, wine (Chateau St. Michelle, Conn Creek, Columbia Crest).

Verizon Communications; 1095 Avenue of the Americas, New York, NY 10036; (212) 395-2121; www.verizon.com; Charles R. Lee, Ivan Seidenberg; largest U.S. wireline and wireless provider; world's lgst. provider of print and on-line directory info. (co. formed from merger of Bell Atlantic and GTE, 6/30/00.)

V.F. Corp.; 105 Corporate Center Blvd., Greensboro, NC 27408; (336) 547-6000; www.vfc.com; Mackey J. McDonald; apparel (Lee, Wrangler jeans, Vanity Fair, Healthtex, Jantzen).

Viacom, Inc.; 1515 Broadway, NY, NY 10036; (212) 258-6000; www.viacom.com; Sumner Redstone; TV broadcast stations and cable systems, channels (CBS, UPN, TNN, BET, Comedy Central, Showtime, MTV, VH1, Nickelodeon); book publishing (Simon & Schuster); produces, distributes movies, TV shows (Paramount); video stores (Blockbuster), theme parks.

Visteon Corp.; 17000 Rotunda Dr., Dearborn, MI 48120; (800) VISTEON; www.visteon.com; Peter J. Pestillo; automotive parts manufacturing, architectural glass.

Wachovia Corp.; One Wachovia Center, Charlotte, NC 28288; (704) 374-6565; www.wachovia.com; G. Kennedy Thompson; financial services provider.

Walgreen Co.; 200 Wilmot Rd., Deerfield, IL 60015; (847) 940-2500; www.walgreens.com; David W. Bernauer; nation's largest drugstore chain.

Wal-Mart Stores, Inc.; 702 SW 8th St., Bentonville, AR 72716; (479) 273-4000; www.walmart.com; S. Robson Walton; world's largest retailer; discount stores, wholesale clubs.

Washington Post Co.; 1150 15th St. NW, Washington, DC 20071; (202) 334-6000; www.washpostco.com; Donald E. Graham; newspapers, *Newsweek* magazine, TV and CATV stations, Stanley H. Kaplan Educational Centers.

Waste Management; 1001 Fannin, Suite 4000, Houston, TX 77002; (713) 512-6200; www.wm.com; Maurice Myers; N. America's largest solid waste collection and disposal co.

Wells Fargo & Co.; 420 Montgomery St., San Francisco, CA 94163; (800) 411-4932; www.wellsfargo.com; R. Kovacevich; bank holding co.

Wendy's Intl., Inc;; 4288 W. Dublin-Granville Rd., Dublin, OH 43017; (614) 764-3100; www.wendys.com; John T. Schuessler; quick-service restaurants.

Weyerhaeuser Co.; 33663 Weyerhauser Way, Federal Way, WA 98063; (253) 924-2345; www.weyerhaeuser.com; Steven R. Rogel; world's largest private owner of softwood timber, distrib. paper and wood prods.

Whirlpool Corp.; 2000 N. M-63, Benton Harbor, MI 49022; (616) 923-5000; www.whirlpoolcorp.com; David Whitwam; world's largest manuf. of major home appliances (KitchenAid, Kenmore, Roper).

Whitman Corp.; 3501 Algonquin Road, Rolling Meadows, IL 60008; (847) 818-5000; www.whitmancorp.com; Robert C. Pohlad; beverage bottler and distributor (Pepsi-Cola).

Winn-Dixie Stores, Inc.; 5050 Edgewood Ct., Jacksonville, FL 32254; (904) 783-5000; www.winn-dixie.com; Frank Lazaran; supermarkets (Winn Dixie, Save Rite, Thrift Way).

Winnebago Industries, Inc.; PO Box 152, Forest City, IA 50436; (641) 585-3535; www.winnebagoind.com; Bruce D. Hertzke; manuf. and financing of motor homes, recreational vehicles.

WorldCom, Inc.; 500 Clinton Ctr. Dr., Clinton, MS 39056; (877) 624-9266; www.wcom.com; John Sidgmore (temporary); long-distance telephone service; filed for bankruptcy, 7/21/02.

WRC Media Inc.; 512 Seventh Ave., New York, NY 10018; (212) 768-0455; www.wrcmedia.com; Martin E. Kenney Jr.; publisher of educational and reference media; World Almanac, Facts On File News Services, Funk & Wagnalls, Gareth Stevens Publishing, CompassLearning, Weekly Reader, American Guidance, ChildU.

Wm. Wrigley Jr. Co.; 410 N. Michigan Ave., Chicago, IL 60611; (312) 644-2121; www.wrigley.com; William Wrigley Jr.; world's largest mfgr. of chewing gum.

Wyeth, formerly American Home Products; 5 Giralda Farms, Madison, NJ 07940; (973) 660-5000; www.wyeth.com; Robert Essner; prescription and over-the-counter drugs (Advil, Anacin, Chap Stick, Robitussin).

Xerox Corp.; 800 Long Ridge Road, Stamford, CT 06904; (203) 968-3000; www.xerox.com; Anne Mulcahy; copiers, printers, document publishing equip.

Yahoo! Inc.; 701 First Ave. Sunnyvale, CA 94089; (408) 349-3300; www.yahoo.com; Terry Semel; global internet media company.

Yum! Brands, Inc.; 1441 Gardiner Lane, Louisville, KY 40213; (502) 874-8300; www.yum.com; David C. Novak; quick-serve restaurants (Pizza Hut, KFC, Taco Bell).

Who Owns What: Familiar Consumer Products and Services

Listed here are some consumer brands and their (U.S.) parent companies. Excluded are many brands whose parent companies have the same or a similar name (e.g., Colgate is Colgate-Palmolive Co.). For company contact information, see Business Directory on previous pages.

ABC broadcasting: Walt Disney
Admiral appliances: Maytag
Advil: Wyeth
Ajax cleanser: Colgate-Palmolive
Almond Joy candy bar: Hershey
American Girl: Mattel
Anacin: Wyeth
Arm & Hammer: Church & Dwight
Arrid antiperspirant: Church & Dwight
Aunt Jemima Pancake mix: PepsiCo (Quaker Oats)
Aunt Millie's pasta sauce: Borden
Banana Republic stores: The Gap
Band-Aids: Johnson & Johnson
Barbie dolls: Mattel
Ben-Gay: Pfizer
Betty Crocker prods.: General Mills
Blockbuster video stores: Viacom
Boston Market: H.J. Heinz
Bounty paper towels: Procter & Gamble
Brillo soap pads: Church & Dwight
Brita water systems: Clorox
Budweiser beer: Anheuser-Busch
Bufferin: Bristol-Myers Squibb
Bulova watches: Loews
Business Week magazine: McGraw-Hill
Buster Brown shoes: Brown Shoe
Butterball: ConAgra
Cadbury: Hershey
Cap'n Crunch cereal: PepsiCo (Quaker Oats)
Calphalon cookware: Newell Rubbermaid
CBS Broadcasting: Viacom
Chap Stick: Wyeth
Charmin toilet tissue: Procter & Gamble
Cheer detergent: Procter & Gamble
Cheerios cereal: General Mills
Cheez Whiz: Altria (Kraft)
Chef Boyardee: ConAgra
Chips Ahoy!: Altria (Nabisco)
Cinemax: Time Warner
Clairol hair prods.: Procter & Gamble
Clinique: Estee Lauder
CNN: Time Warner
Combat insecticides: Clorox
Comet cleanser: Procter & Gamble
Coppertone sun care prods.: Schering-Plough
Crest toothpaste: Procter & Gamble
Crisco shortening: J.M. Smucker
DC Comics: Time Warner
Desitin Ointment: Pfizer
Doritos chips: PepsiCo
Duracell batteries: Gillette
Dutch Boy paints: Sherwin-Williams
Efferdent dental cleanser: Pfizer
Elmer's glue: Borden
ESPN: Walt Disney
Excedrin: Bristol-Myers Squibb
Fab detergent: Colgate-Palmolive
Fantastik: S.C. Johnson
Field & Stream: Time Warner
Fisher Price Toys: Mattel
Folger's coffee: Procter & Gamble
Formula 409 spray cleaner: Clorox
Franco-American spaghetti: Campbell Soup
Frito-Lays snacks: PepsiCo
Fruitopia drinks: Coca-Cola
Gatorade: PepsiCo
Glad Prods.: Clorox
Godiva chocolate: Campbell Soup
Haagen-Dazs: General Mills

Halcion: Pfizer
Halls coughdrops: Pfizer
Hamburger Helper: General Mills
Hanes hosiery: Sara Lee
HBO: Time Warner
Head and Shoulders shampoo: Procter & Gamble
Healthtex: V.F. Corp.
Hellmann's mayonnaise: Unilever Bestfoods
Hertz car rental: Ford
Hi-C fruit drinks: Coca-Cola
Hidden Valley prods.: Clorox
Hillshire Farms meats: Sara Lee
Holly Farms: Tyson Foods
Hostess cakes: Interstate Bakeries
Huggies diapers: Kimberly-Clark
Ivory soap: Procter & Gamble
Jack Daniel's Whiskey: Brown-Forman
Java programming language: Sun Microsystems
Jell-O: Altria (Kraft)
Jenn-Air stoves: Maytag
Jif peanut butter: J.M. Smucker
Jim Beam bourbon: Fortune Brands
Keds footwear: Stride Rite
Kent cigarettes: Loews
KFC restaurants: Yum! Brands
Kibbles 'n Bits pet foods: H. J. Heinz
Kinney shoe stores: Foot Locker
KitchenAid appliances: Whirlpool
Kit Kat candy: Hershey
Kleenex: Kimberly-Clark
Knorr soups: Unilever Bestfoods
Kool-Aid: Altria (Kraft)
Krazy Glue: Borden
Kwikset doorknobs: Black & Decker
Ladies Home Journal magazine: Meredith
Lee jeans: V.F. Corp.
L'eggs hosiery: Sara Lee
Lenox china: Brown-Forman
LifeSavers candy: Altria (Kraft)
Lipton tea: Unilever Bestfoods
Listerine mouthwash: Pfizer
Lord & Taylor: May Dept. Stores
Marlboro cigarettes: Altria (Philip Morris)
Max Factor beauty products: Procter & Gamble
Maxwell House coffee: Altria (Kraft)
Metamucil: Procter & Gamble
Michelob beer: Anheuser-Busch
Miller beer: Altria (Philip Morris)
Milton Bradley games: Hasbro
Minute Maid juices: Coca-Cola
Monroe automotive parts: Tenneco Automotive
MTV: Viacom
Nature Valley granola bars: General Mills
NBC broadcasting: General Electric
Neutrogena soap: Johnson & Johnson
Newsweek magazine: Washington Post
Nickelodeon TV: Viacom
9 Lives cat food: H.J. Heinz
Oil of Olay: Procter & Gamble
Old Navy Clothing: The Gap
Oreo cookies: Altria (Nabisco)
Oscar Mayer meats: Altria (Kraft)
Pampers: Procter & Gamble
Parker Bros. games: Hasbro
People magazine: Time Warner
Pepperidge Farm prods.: Campbell Soup
Pepto-Bismol: Procter & Gamble

Philadelphia Cream Cheese: Altria (Kraft)
Pine-Sol cleaner: Clorox
Pizza Hut restaurants: Yum! Brands
Planters nuts: Altria (Kraft)
Playskool toys: Hasbro
Playtex apparel: Sara Lee
Post cereals: Altria (Kraft)
Post-it notes: 3M
Prego pasta sauce: Campbell Soup
Prozac: Eli Lilly
Ragu sauce: Unilever Bestfoods
Reese's candy: Hershey
Rice-A-Roni: PepsiCo (Quaker Oats)
Rice Krispies: Kellogg
Right Guard deodorant: Gillette
Ritz crackers: Altria (Nabisco)
Robitussin: Wyeth
Rogaine hair growth aide: Pfizer
Ruffles chips: PepsiCo
Schick razors: Energizer
Scope mouthwash: Procter & Gamble
Scotch tape: 3M
Scott tissue: Kimberly-Clark
Simon & Schuster publishing: Viacom
Skippy peanut butter: Unilever Bestfoods
Slimfast: Unilever Bestfoods
SnackWell's cookies: Altria (Nabisco)
S.O.S. cleanser: Clorox
Southern Comfort liquor: Brown-Forman
SPAM meat: Hormel Foods
Sports Illustrated magazine: Time Warner
Sprite soda: Coca-Cola
StarKist tuna: H.J. Heinz
Sugar Twin: Alberto-Culver
Swanson broth: Campbell Soup
Swiffer: Procter & Gamble
Taco Bell restaurants: Yum! Brands
Tampax tampons: Procter & Gamble
Thomas' English muffins: Unilever Bestfoods
Tide detergent: Procter & Gamble
Time magazine: Time Warner
Titleist: Fortune Brands
Tombstone pizza: Altria (Kraft)
Triscuits: Altria (Nabisco)
Trojan condoms: Church & Dwight
Tropicana juice: PepsiCo
Tylenol: Johnson & Johnson
Ultra Brite toothpaste: Colgate-Palmolive
USA Today newspaper: Gannett
V8 vegetable juice: Campbell Soup
Vanity Fair apparel: V.F. Corp.
Velveeta cheese prods.: Altria (Kraft)
VH-1: Viacom
Viagra: Pfizer
Vicks cough medicines: Procter & Gamble
Victoria's Secret stores: The Limited
Visine eye drops: Pfizer
Wall Street Journal: Dow Jones
Weekly Reader: WRC Media
Weight Watchers: H.J. Heinz
Wheaties cereal: General Mills
Windex: S.C. Johnson
Windows software applications: Microsoft
Wise snacks: Borden
Wonderbra: Sara Lee
Wonder bread: Interstate Bakeries
The World Almanac: WRC Media
Zest soap: Procter & Gamble
Ziploc storage bags: S.C. Johnson

Top Brands in Selected Categories, 2001-2002

Source: Information Resources, Inc., a Chicago-based marketing research company; figures for 12-month period ending 8/11/02.

Ready-to-Eat Cold Cereals

	Sales	Market Share (%)
Private Label	$544,039,808	7.9
General Mills Cheerios	333,025,248	4.9
Kelloggs Frosted Flakes	281,109,824	4.1
General Mills Honey Nut Cheerios	229,125,408	3.3
Cinnamon Toast Crunch	189,967,904	2.8

Toothpaste[1]

	Sales	Market Share (%)
Crest	$277,630,784	22.2
Colgate	170,529,680	13.6
Colgate Total	103,354,072	8.2
Aquafresh	89,731,256	7.2
Crest Multicare	64,826,536	5.2

Ground Coffee (excluding Decaf)

	Sales	Market Share (%)
Folgers	$349,179,584	21.6
Maxwell House	273,306,848	16.9
Private Label	129,805,656	8.0
Maxwell House Master Blend	128,839,048	8.0
Starbucks	113,367,488	7.0

(1) Excludes Wal-Mart Sales.

Cookies[1]

	Sales	Market Share (%)
Nabisco Oreos	$524,557,312	13.4
Nabisco Chips Ahoy!	352,624,672	9.0
Private Label	334,307,040	8.5
Keebler Chips Deluxe	158,515,680	4.0
Nabisco Newtons	136,476,848	3.5

Top 10 Shopping Websites

Source: comScore Media Metrix, Inc.

Rank	Website address[1]	Visitors[2]	Rank	Website address[1]	Visitors[2]
1.	www.ebay.com	62,319,000	6.	www.americangreetings.com	12,809,000
2.	www.amazon.com	36,900,000	7.	www.adobe.com	11,176,000
3.	www.shopping.yahoo.com	21,235,000	8.	www.dell.com	10,931,000
4.	www.dealtime.com	16,113,000	9.	www.ticketmaster.com	10,095,000
5.	www.walmart.com	13,293,000	10.	www.hewlettpackard.com	9,802,000

(1) May include affiliated websites not shown. (2) Visited website at least once in July 2003.

The Cost of Raising a Child Born in 2002

Source: Center for Nutrition Policy and Promotion, U.S. Dept. of Agriculture

Estimated annual expenditures in 2002 dollars for a child born in 2002, by income group, for each year to age 17. Estimates are for the younger child in a 2-parent family with 2 children, for the overall U.S.

Year	Lowest	Income group[1] Middle	Highest	Year	Lowest	Income group[1] Middle	Highest
2002	$6,620	$9,230	$13,750	2012	$9,390	$12,840	$18,730
2003	6,830	9,530	14,190	2013	9,690	13,250	19,330
2004	7,050	9,830	14,640	2014	11,190	14,750	21,190
2005	7,450	10,420	15,440	2015	11,550	15,230	21,870
2006	7,690	10,750	15,940	2016	11,920	15,710	22,550
2007	7,940	11,100	16,450	2017	12,160	16,520	23,980
2008	8,290	11,440	16,740	2018	12,550	17,050	24,750
2009	8,550	11,810	17,280	2019	12,950	17,600	25,540
2010	8,830	12,180	17,830				
2011	9,100	12,440	18,150	TOTAL	$169,750	$231,680	$338,370

(1) In 2002, lowest annual income is less than $39,700 (average in this range = $24,800); middle income is $39,700-$66,900 (average = $52,900); highest income is $66,900 or more (average = $100,100).

Median Price of Existing Single-Family Homes, by Metropolitan Area, 2001-2003

Source: National Association of REALTORS®

Median prices are based on all transactions within the time period shown.

Metropolitan Area	2001	2002	2nd Qtr 2003
Akron, OH	$113,600	$115,300	$119,600
Albany/Schenectady/Troy, NY	121,600	130,500	143,300
Albuquerque, NM	133,300	133,800	140,100
Amarillo, TX	90,200	91,900	97,600
Orange Cnty. (Anaheim/ Santa Ana MSA), CA	355,600	412,700	471,700
Appleton/Oshkosh/ Neenah, WI	105,100	112,700	115,900
Atlanta, GA	138,800	146,500	151,400
Atlantic City, NJ	125,700	143,600	164,600
Aurora/Elgin, IL	178,200	193,300	213,000
Austin/San Marcos, TX	152,000	156,500	161,200
Baltimore, MD	158,200	179,600	204,200
Baton Rouge, LA	114,000	116,900	123,000
Beaumont/Port Arthur, TX	84,000	84,300	87,300
Biloxi/Gulfport, MS	96,000	100,200	108,600
Birmingham, AL	133,600	137,400	141,900
Boise City, ID	130,000	123,200	128,400
Boston, MA	$356,600	$395,900	$409,100
Bradenton, FL	137,800	150,000	170,400
Buffalo/Niagara Falls, NY	84,100	85,000	90,400
Canton, OH	107,800	109,000	116,100
Cedar Rapids, IA	115,700	118,800	122,900
Champaign/Urbana/Rantoul, IL	100,400	107,100	122,700
Charleston, SC	150,800	159,400	169,000
Charleston, WV	104,700	107,200	111,500
Charlotte/Gastonia/ Rock Hill, NC/SC	145,300	149,100	153,300
Chattanooga, TN/GA	107,300	112,300	119,300
Chicago, IL	198,500	220,900	241,900
Cincinnati, OH/KY/IN	130,200	134,100	140,000
Colorado Springs, CO	173,300	176,900	181,700
Columbia, SC	115,800	119,500	122,900
Columbus, OH	135,700	140,300	152,200
Corpus Christi, TX	91,600	94,400	104,600
Dallas, TX	131,100	135,200	139,900

Metropolitan Area	2001	2002	2nd Qtr 2003	Metropolitan Area	2001	2002	2nd Qtr 2003
Davenport/Moline/ Rock Island, IA/IL	$89,600	$95,000	$107,200	Oklahoma City, OK	$95,000	$100,100	$100,200
Dayton/Springfield, OH	106,900	112,600	114,500	Omaha, NE/IA	117,100	122,400	128,200
Daytona Beach, FL	93,700	108,300	122,800	Orlando, FL	124,100	136,600	137,700
Denver, CO	218,300	228,100	237,900	Pensacola, FL	105,000	112,200	114,400
Des Moines, IA	125,300	130,200	131,200	Peoria, IL	88,600	88,000	95,700
El Paso, TX	85,800	88,900	93,000	Philadelphia, PA/NJ	134,800	146,100	167,700
Eugene/Springfield, OR	134,600	143,700	150,700	Phoenix, AZ	139,400	143,800	152,500
Fargo/Moorhead, ND/MN	99,500	107,700	116,800	Pittsburgh, PA	97,800	101,500	110,600
Ft. Lauderdale/Hollywood/ Pompano Beach, FL	168,100	197,000	222,200	Portland, ME	158,000	180,000	197,400
Ft. Myers/Cape Coral, FL	NA	133,600	152,300	Portland, OR	172,300	180,400	191,600
Ft. Wayne, IN	93,900	94,900	97,000	Providence, RI	158,000	193,200	228,900
Gainesville, FL	118,000	130,000	144,700	Raleigh/Durham, NC	168,200	172,200	173,800
Gary/Hammond, IN	114,100	114,300	120,400	Reno, NV	165,100	183,200	203,500
Grand Rapids, MI	121,100	125,300	130,500	Richland/Kennewick/Pasco, WA	NA	140,800	147,200
Green Bay, WI	123,800	130,100	142,000	Richmond/Petersburg, VA	133,300	142,300	156,800
Greensboro/Winston-Salem/ High Point, NC	132,700	135,800	140,800	Riverside/San Bernardino, CA	156,700	176,500	212,600
Greenville/Spartanburg, SC	124,500	125,300	131,100	Rochester, NY	92,200	93,800	98,200
Hartford, CT	167,300	175,900	198,500	Rockford, IL	101,500	106,900	112,100
Honolulu, HI	299,900	335,000	375,000	Sacramento, CA	173,200	209,500	243,600
Houston, TX	122,400	132,800	136,900	Saginaw/Bay City/Midland, MI	84,700	NA	NA
Indianapolis, IN	116,900	116,800	122,300	Saint Louis, MO/IL	116,200	117,000	123,300
Jackson, MS	NA	NA	114,800	Salt Lake City/Ogden, UT	147,600	148,800	152,700
Jacksonville, FL	109,900	117,800	130,800	San Antonio, TX	103,800	110,400	122,300
Kalamazoo, MI	112,300	117,800	NA	San Diego, CA	298,600	364,200	407,000
Kansas City, MO/KS	135,700	137,400	144,700	San Francisco Bay Area, CA	475,900	517,100	560,200
Knoxville, TN	117,200	118,400	141,300	Sarasota, FL	NA	176,200	203,900
Lake County, IL	178,900	195,800	217,800	Seattle, WA	245,400	254,000	273,800
Lansing/East Lansing, MI	119,500	126,400	137,900	Shreveport, LA	88,000	90,300	102,600
Las Vegas, NV	149,100	159,800	177,100	Sioux Falls, SD	113,900	116,700	126,800
Lexington/Fayette, KY	121,700	127,100	131,400	South Bend/Mishawaka, IN	92,800	91,000	91,000
Lincoln, NE	117,400	122,400	132,900	Spokane, WA	108,000	108,700	117,400
Little Rock-N. Little Rock, AR	95,100	95,700	105,200	Springfield, IL	87,300	90,600	97,100
Los Angeles Area, CA	241,400	286,000	337,200	Springfield, MA	127,400	139,800	150,700
Louisville, KY/IN	NA	125,200	131,200	Springfield, MO	92,300	NA	NA
Madison, WI	162,500	177,000	181,700	Syracuse, NY	86,100	86,400	92,800
Melbourne/Titusville/ Palm Bay, FL	98,400	112,700	130,100	Tacoma, WA	159,500	170,400	176,000
Memphis, TN/AR/MS	125,100	129,400	135,000	Tallahassee, FL	129,700	136,900	135,100
Miami/Hialeah, FL	162,700	189,800	NA	Tampa/St. Petersburg/ Clearwater, FL	123,600	133,500	138,600
Milwaukee, WI	149,400	173,800	186,100	Toledo, OH	110,600	109,600	114,100
Minneapolis/St. Paul, MN/WI	167,400	185,000	197,100	Topeka, KS	88,700	89,000	100,700
Mobile, AL	106,900	114,900	119,600	Trenton, NJ	165,300	179,500	212,300
Montgomery, AL	NA	113,600	120,900	Tucson, AZ	128,800	146,400	159,200
Nashville, TN	130,000	NA	NA	Tulsa, OK	110,000	106,700	111,500
New Haven/Meriden, CT	168,000	192,300	213,500	Washington, DC/MD/VA	213,900	250,200	285,700
New Orleans, LA	117,400	123,500	133,200	Waterloo/Cedar Falls, IA	84,500	87,800	93,100
New York/N. New Jersey/ Long Island, NY/NJ/CT	258,200	309,800	350,900	W. Palm Beach/Boca Raton/ Delray Beach, FL	149,500	NA	233,600
Norfolk/Virginia Bch/ Newport News, VA	NA	NA	134,300	Wichita, KS	94,900	98,100	98,500
				Wilmington, DE/NJ/MD	136,500	150,100	161,300
				Worcester, MA	152,600	187,700	205,000
				United States	**$147,800**	**$158,300**	**$168,900**

NA = Not available.

Housing Affordability, U.S., 1990-2003
Source: National Association of REALTORS®

Year	Median priced existing home	Average mortgage rate[1]	Monthly principal & interest payment	Payment as percentage of median income
1990	$92,000	10.04%	$648	22.0%
1991	97,100	9.30	642	21.4
1992	99,700	8.11	591	19.3
1993	103,100	7.16	558	18.1
1994	107,200	7.47	598	18.5
1995	110,500	7.85	639	18.9
1996	115,800	7.71	661	18.8
1997	121,800	7.68	693	18.7
1998	128,400	7.10	690	17.4
1999	133,300	7.33	733	18.0
2000	139,000	8.03	818	19.3
2001	147,800	7.03	789	18.4
2002	158,100	6.55	804	18.3
2003[2]	182,100	5.39	817	18.3

(1) All figures assume a down payment of 20% of the home price. Based on effective rate on loans closed on existing homes for the period shown. (2) Preliminary, as of July.

U.S. Home Ownership Rates, by Selected Characteristics, 1997, 2003[1]

Source: Bureau of the Census, U.S. Dept. of Commerce

Region	1997	2003	Race/Ethnicity	1997	2003
Northeast	62.4%	64.2%	White, non-Hispanic	72.1%	75.2%
Midwest	70.3	72.8	Black	44.4	47.3
South	68.1	69.9	Hispanic	43.3	46.2
West	59.9	63.2	Other	52.7	55.8

Age			Income		
Under 35	38.6%	41.9%	Median family income or more	80.8%	83.6%
35-44	66.3	67.8	Below median family income	50.0	51.6
45-54	75.6	76.3			
55-64	80.3	81.6			
65+	79.1	80.2	**TOTAL U.S. RATE**	**65.7%**	**68.0%**

(1) in 2003, figures are for 2nd quarter of the year. Not seasonally-adjusted.

Mortgage Loan Calculator

Source: HSH Associates, www.hsh.com

This table allows you to calculate the monthly principal and interest payment for each $1,000 of your mortgage. Divide your loan amount by 1,000 and multiply the result by the factor located at the intersection of the interest rate and term you are considering.

Example: For a 30-year mortgage at 6%, the payment factor would be 5.996. If the mortgage amount is $250,000, divide this by 1,000 to find a value of 250. That $250,000 times the 5.996 (payment factor) gives you a monthly principal and interest payment of $1,499 per month. Please be aware that this is approximate, as the factor you are using is only 3 decimal places (your mortgage lender will likely use a payment factor which is more precise than that). Also, this is only your P&I payment; your actual monthly payment will include property taxes, insurance, and other possible costs). **Hint:** You can calculate payments for interest rates not shown by finding the factor between 2 given interest rates. For example, the factor for 5.125% is ½ the difference between 5% and 5.25%; so subtract 5.368 from 5.522. Take the result (0.154), divide it by 2 (0.077) then add it to the 5% factor (5.368) to get 5.445, your factor for a 5.125% interest rate.

INTEREST RATE	MORTGAGE TERM IN YEARS							
	5	10	15	20	25	30	35	40
3.00	17.969	9.656	6.906	5.546	4.742	4.216	3.849	3.580
3.25	18.080	9.772	7.027	5.672	4.873	4.352	3.989	3.725
3.50	18.192	9.889	7.149	5.800	5.006	4.490	4.133	3.874
3.75	18.304	10.006	7.272	5.929	5.141	4.631	4.279	4.025
4.00	18.417	10.125	7.397	6.060	5.278	4.774	4.428	4.179
4.25	18.530	10.244	7.523	6.192	5.417	4.919	4.579	4.336
4.50	18.643	10.364	7.650	6.326	5.558	5.067	4.733	4.496
4.75	18.757	10.485	7.778	6.462	5.701	5.216	4.889	4.658
5.00	18.871	10.607	7.908	6.600	5.846	5.368	5.047	4.822
5.25	18.986	10.729	8.039	6.738	5.992	5.522	5.207	4.989
5.50	19.101	10.853	8.171	6.879	6.141	5.678	5.370	5.158
5.75	19.217	10.977	8.304	7.021	6.291	5.836	5.535	5.329
6.00	19.333	11.102	8.439	7.164	6.443	5.996	5.702	5.502
6.25	19.449	11.228	8.574	7.309	6.597	6.157	5.871	5.677
6.50	19.566	11.355	8.711	7.456	6.752	6.321	6.042	5.855
6.75	19.683	11.482	8.849	7.604	6.909	6.486	6.214	6.034
7.00	19.801	11.611	8.988	7.753	7.068	6.653	6.389	6.214
7.25	19.919	11.740	9.129	7.904	7.228	6.822	6.565	6.397
7.50	20.038	11.870	9.270	8.056	7.390	6.992	6.742	6.581
7.75	20.157	12.001	9.413	8.209	7.553	7.164	6.922	6.766
8.00	20.276	12.133	9.557	8.364	7.718	7.338	7.103	6.953
8.25	20.396	12.265	9.701	8.521	7.885	7.513	7.285	7.141
8.50	20.517	12.399	9.847	8.678	8.052	7.689	7.469	7.331
8.75	20.637	12.533	9.994	8.837	8.221	7.867	7.654	7.522
9.00	20.758	12.668	10.143	8.997	8.392	8.046	7.840	7.714
9.25	20.880	12.803	10.292	9.159	8.564	8.227	8.027	7.907
9.50	21.002	12.940	10.442	9.321	8.737	8.409	8.216	8.101
9.75	21.124	13.077	10.594	9.485	8.911	8.592	8.406	8.296
10.00	21.247	13.215	10.746	9.650	9.087	8.776	8.597	8.491
10.25	21.370	13.354	10.900	9.816	9.264	8.961	8.789	8.688
10.50	21.494	13.493	11.054	9.984	9.442	9.147	8.981	8.886
10.75	21.618	13.634	11.209	10.152	9.621	9.335	9.175	9.084
11.00	21.742	13.775	11.366	10.322	9.801	9.523	9.370	9.283
11.25	21.867	13.917	11.523	10.493	9.982	9.713	9.565	9.483
11.50	21.993	14.060	11.682	10.664	10.165	9.903	9.761	9.683
11.75	22.118	14.203	11.841	10.837	10.348	10.094	9.958	9.884
12.00	22.244	14.347	12.002	11.011	10.532	10.286	10.155	10.085

How to Obtain Birth, Death, Marriage, Divorce Records

The pamphlet "Where to Write for Vital Records: Births, Deaths, Marriages, and Divorces" (Stock # 017-022-01539-1) is available from the U.S. Government Printing Office (GPO) at a cost of $4.25. Orders can also be placed by calling (866) 512-1800, by e-mail at orders@gpo.gov, or on the website bookstore.gpo.gov. The complete pamphlet can also be accessed online at www.cdc.gov/nchs/howto/w2w/w2welcom.htm

TELECOMMUNICATIONS

Worldwide Telecommunications: Market Data (1990-2003)

Source: © International Telecommunication Union

	1990	1991	1992	1993	1994	1995	1996	1997	1998	1999	2000	2001	2002[3]	2003[4]
Total market revenue (billions of U.S. $)[1]	$508	$523	$580	$605	$675	$779	$885	$946	$1,015	$1,123	$1,210	$1,232	$1,295	$1,370
Intl. phone traffic (billions of minutes)[2]	33	38	43	49	57	63	71	79	89	100	118	127	135	140
Main telephone lines (millions)	520	546	572	604	643	689	738	792	846	905	983	1,053	1,129	1,210
Mobile cellular subscribers (millions)	11	16	23	34	56	91	145	215	318	490	740	955	1,155	1,329

(1) Revenue from installation, subscription, and local, trunk, and international call charges. (2) From 1994 including traffic between countries of the former Soviet Union. (3) Estimate. (4) Projection.

Worldwide Use of Cellular Telephones, Year-end 2002

Source: © International Telecommunication Union; estimated; top countries or regions ranked by number of subscribers per 100 pop.

Country/Region	Number of subscribers (thousands)	per 100 pop.	Country/Region	Number of subscribers (thousands)	per 100 pop.	Country/Region	Number of subscribers (thousands)	per 100 pop.
Taiwan	23,905	106	Singapore	3,295	79	Slovakia	2,923	55
Luxembourg	455	101	Martinique	320	79	Seychelles	44	54
Israel	6,334	95	Ireland	2,969	76	Aruba	53	50
Italy	52,316	93	United Arab Emirates	2,428	76	Guernsey	32	50
Hong Kong	6,297	93	Germany	59,200	72	United States	140,766	49
Iceland	260	90	Netherlands	11,700	72	Croatia	2,278	47
Sweden	7,915	89	Guadeloupe	324	70	Lithuania	1,632	47
Czech Republic	8,610	85	Malta	277	70	Qatar	267	44
Finland	4,400	85	Jersey	61	70	Chile	6,446	43
United Kingdom	49,921	84	Korea, South	32,342	68	Latvia	917	39
Greece	9,240	84	France	38,585	65	Canada	11,849	38
Norway	3,842	84	Hungary	6,562	65	Virgin Islands (U.S.)	41	38
Slovenia	1,667	84	Estonia	881	65	Poland	14,000	36
Austria	6,760	83	Australia	12,579	64	Turkey	23,374	35
Denmark	4,478	83	Macao	276	63	Malaysia	8,500	35
Spain	33,475	82	Japan	79,083	62	Puerto Rico	1,211	32
Portugal	8,528	82	New Zealand	2,436	62	Antigua & Barbuda	25	32
Belgium	8,135	79	Cyprus	418	60	Greenland	17	30
Switzerland	5,734	79	Bahrain	389	58	WORLD	1,143,647	19

U.S. Cellular Telephone Subscribership, 1985–2002[1]

Source: The CTIA Semi-Annual Wireless Industry Survey. Used with permission of CTIA; in thousands of subscribers[2]

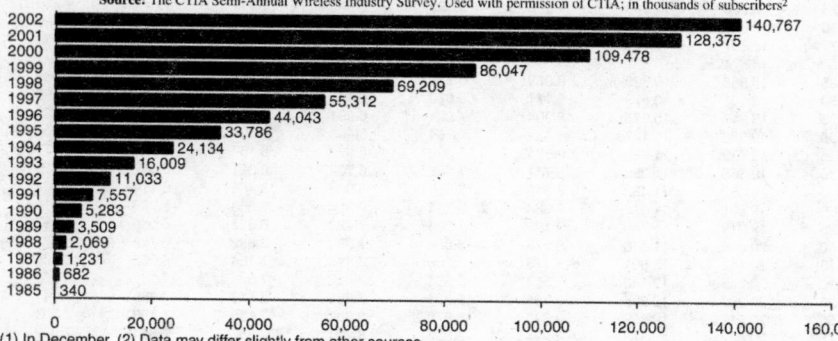

Year	Subscribers
2002	140,767
2001	128,375
2000	109,478
1999	86,047
1998	69,209
1997	55,312
1996	44,043
1995	33,786
1994	24,134
1993	16,009
1992	11,033
1991	7,557
1990	5,283
1989	3,509
1988	2,069
1987	1,231
1986	682
1985	340

(1) In December. (2) Data may differ slightly from other sources.

U.S. Sales and Household Penetration, Selected Products[1], 1985-2002

Source: Consumer Electronics Association

	1985 Sales[2]	1985 % of all households	1990 Sales[2]	1990 % of all households	1995 Sales[2]	1995 % of all households	2000 Sales[2]	2000 % of all households	2002 Sales[2]	2002 % of all households
Cordless telephones	$280	11	$842	28	$1,141	55	$1,307	80	$1,261	81
Pagers	—	—	118	1	300	11	750	23	810	17
Modems/fax modems	10	0	191	2.7	770	16	1,564	55	1,365	56
Telephone answering devices	325	7	827	35	1,077	57	984	75	1,060	78
Cellular phones	116	0.10	1,098	5	2,574	29	8,995	60	8,835	66

(1) Data may differ slightly from other sources. (2) In millions of dollars.

In July 2003 the Federal Trade Commission created a Do Not Call Registry, allowing people to submit phone numbers to a national list, to make them off limits to most telemarketers. Over 50 million people had signed up by Oct. 1, but court rulings delayed enforcement of the system. On Oct. 7 a circuit appeals court allowed enforcement to proceed; starting Oct. 9, new registrations could be made on-line at DONOTCALL.GOV or by phoning 1-888-382-1222 toll-free. But the future of the system remained unclear.

Telephone Area Codes, by Number

As of Sept. 2003. For area codes listed by place, see pages 383-416.

Area Code	Location or Service	Area Code	Location or Service	Area Code	Location or Service	Area Code	Location or Service
201	New Jersey	402	Nebraska	612	Minnesota	810	Michigan
202	District of Columbia	403	Alberta	613	Ontario	811	Business Office
203	Connecticut	404	Georgia	614	Ohio	812	Indiana
204	Manitoba	405	Oklahoma	615	Tennessee	813	Florida
205	Alabama	406	Montana	616	Michigan	814	Pennsylvania
206	Washington	407	Florida	617	Massachusetts	815	Illinois
207	Maine	408	California	618	Illinois	816	Missouri
208	Idaho	409	Texas	619	California	817	Texas
209	California	410	Maryland	620	Kansas	818	California
210	Texas	411	Directory Assistance	623	Arizona	819	Quebec
211	Community Info.	412	Pennsylvania	626	California	828	North Carolina
212	New York	413	Massachusetts	630	Illinois	830	Texas
213	California	414	Wisconsin	631	New York	831	California
214	Texas	415	California	636	Missouri	832	Texas
215	Pennsylvania	416	Ontario	641	Iowa	843	South Carolina
216	Ohio	417	Missouri	646	New York	845	New York
217	Illinois	418	Quebec	647	Ontario	847	Illinois
218	Minnesota	419	Ohio	649	Turks & Caicos Islands	848	New Jersey
219	Indiana	423	Tennessee	650	California	850	Florida
224	Illinois	425	Washington	651	Minnesota	856	New Jersey
225	Louisiana	430	Texas	660	Missouri	857	Massachusetts
228	Mississippi	432	Texas	661	California	858	California
229	Georgia	434	Virginia	662	Mississippi	859	Kentucky
231	Michigan	435	Utah	664	Montserrat	860	Connecticut
234	Ohio	440	Ohio	670	N. Mariana Islands	862	New Jersey
239	Florida	441	Bermuda	671	Guam	863	Florida
240	Maryland	443	Maryland	678	Georgia	864	South Carolina
242	Bahamas	450	Quebec	682	Texas	865	Tennessee
246	Barbados	456	Inbound International	700	IC Services	866	Toll-Free Service
248	Michigan	469	Texas	701	North Dakota	867	Yukon, NW Terr., Nunavut
250	British Columbia	473	Grenada	702	Nevada		
251	Alabama	478	Georgia	703	Virginia	868	Trinidad & Tobago
252	North Carolina	479	Arkansas	704	North Carolina	869	St. Kitts & Nevis
253	Washington	480	Arizona	705	Ontario	870	Arkansas
254	Texas	484	Pennsylvania	706	Georgia	876	Jamaica
256	Alabama	500	Personal Comm. Serv.	707	California	877	Toll-Free Service
260	Indiana	501	Arkansas	708	Illinois	878	Pennsylvania
262	Wisconsin	502	Kentucky	709	Newfoundland	880	Toll-Free Service
264	Anguilla	503	Oregon	710	U.S. Government	881	Toll-Free Service
267	Pennsylvania	504	Louisiana	711	TRS Access	882	Toll-Free Service
268	Antigua/Barbuda	505	New Mexico	712	Iowa	888	Toll-Free Service
269	Michigan	506	New Brunswick	713	Texas	900	Premium Service
270	Kentucky	507	Minnesota	714	California	901	Tennessee
276	Virginia	508	Massachusetts	715	Wisconsin	902	Nova Scotia
281	Texas	509	Washington	716	New York	903	Texas
284	British Virgin Islands	510	California	717	Pennsylvania	904	Florida
289	Ontario	511	Traffic Info.	718	New York	905	Ontario
301	Maryland	512	Texas	719	Colorado	906	Michigan
302	Delaware	513	Ohio	720	Colorado	907	Alaska
303	Colorado	514	Quebec	724	Pennsylvania	908	New Jersey
304	West Virginia	515	Iowa	727	Florida	909	California
305	Florida	516	New York	731	Tennessee	910	North Carolina
306	Saskatchewan	517	Michigan	732	New Jersey	911	Emergency
307	Wyoming	518	New York	734	Michigan	912	Georgia
308	Nebraska	519	Ontario	740	Ohio	913	Kansas
309	Illinois	520	Arizona	754	Florida	914	New York
310	California	530	California	757	Virginia	915	Texas
311	Non-Emergency Access	540	Virginia	758	St. Lucia	916	California
312	Illinois	541	Oregon	760	California	917	New York
313	Michigan	551	New Jersey	763	Minnesota	918	Oklahoma
314	Missouri	559	California	765	Indiana	919	North Carolina
315	New York	561	Florida	767	Dominica	920	Wisconsin
316	Kansas	562	California	770	Georgia	925	California
317	Indiana	563	Iowa	772	Florida	928	Arizona
318	Louisiana	567	Ohio	773	Illinois	931	Tennessee
319	Iowa	570	Pennsylvania	774	Massachusetts	936	Texas
320	Minnesota	571	Virginia	775	Nevada	937	Ohio
321	Florida	573	Missouri	778	British Columbia	939	Puerto Rico
323	California	574	Indiana	780	Alberta	940	Texas
325	Texas	580	Oklahoma	781	Massachusetts	941	Florida
330	Ohio	585	New York	784	St. Vincent & Gren.	947	Michigan
334	Alabama	586	Michigan	785	Kansas	949	California
336	North Carolina	600	(Canadian Services)	786	Florida	952	Minnesota
337	Louisiana	601	Mississippi	787	Puerto Rico	954	Florida
339	Massachusetts	602	Arizona	800	Toll-Free Service	956	Texas
340	U.S. Virgin Islands	603	New Hampshire	801	Utah	970	Colorado
345	Cayman Islands	604	British Columbia	802	Vermont	971	Oregon
347	New York	605	South Dakota	803	South Carolina	972	Texas
351	Massachusetts	606	Kentucky	804	Virginia	973	New Jersey
352	Florida	607	New York	805	California	978	Massachusetts
360	Washington	608	Wisconsin	806	Texas	979	Texas
361	Texas	609	New Jersey	807	Ontario	980	North Carolina
386	Florida	610	Pennsylvania	808	Hawaii	985	Louisiana
401	Rhode Island	611	Repair Service	809	Dominican Republic	989	Michigan

Codes for International Direct Dial Calling From the U.S.

Basic station-to-station calls: 011 + country code (as shown) + city code (if required) + local number.

Person-to-person, operator-assisted, collect, credit card calls; calls billed to another number: 01 + country code (below) + city code (if required) + local number.

Selected city codes given below. For further information, contact your long distance company.

Country/Territory	Code	Country/Territory	Code	Country/Territory	Code	Country/Territory	Code
Afghanistan	93	Saskatchewan	306*	Iran	98	Poland	48
Albania	355	Yukon Territory	867*	Iraq	964	Portugal	351
Algeria	213	Cape Verde	238	Ireland	353	Puerto Rico	787*/
American Samoa	684	Cayman Islands	345*	Israel	972		939*
Andorra	376	Central African Rep.	236	Italy	39	Qatar	974
Angola	244	Chad Republic	235	Jamaica	876*	Reunion Island	262
Anguilla	264*	Chile	56	Japan	81	Romania	40
Antarctica (Scott Base		China	86	Jordan	962	Russia	7
and Casey Base)	672	Hong Kong	852	Kazakhstan	7	Rwanda	250
Antigua & Barbuda	268*	Macao	853	Kenya	254	St. Kitts & Nevis	869*
Argentina	54	Christmas and the		Kiribati	686	St. Lucia	758*
Armenia	374	Cocos Islands	61	Korea, North	850	St. Maarten	590
Aruba	297	Colombia	57	Korea, South	82	St. Pierre and Miquelon	508
Ascension Island	247	Comoros	269	Kuwait	965	St. Vincent & the	
Australia	61	Congo, Dem. Rep.	243	Kyrgyzstan	996	Grenadines	784*
Austria	43	Congo Republic	242	Laos	856	Samoa (formerly	
Azerbaijan	994	Cook Islands	682	Latvia	371	Western Samoa)	685
Bahamas	242*	Costa Rica	506	Lebanon	961	San Marino	378
Bahrain	973	Côte d'Ivoire	225	Lesotho	266	São Tomé & Príncipe	239
Bangladesh	880	Croatia	385	Liberia	231	Saudi Arabia	966
Barbados	246*	Cuba	53	Libya	218	Senegal	221
Belarus	375	Curacao	599	Liechtenstein	423	Serbia & Montenegro	381
Belgium	32	Cyprus	357	Lithuania	370	Seychelles	248
Belize	501	Czech Republic	420	Luxembourg	352	Sierra Leone	232
Benin	229	Denmark	45	Macedonia	389	Singapore	65
Bermuda	441*	Diego Garcia	246	Madagascar	261	Slovakia	421
Bhutan	975	Djibouti	253	Malawi	265	Slovenia	386
Bolivia	591	Dominica	767*	Malaysia	60	Solomon Islands	677
Bosnia & Herzegovina	387	Dominican Republic	809*	Maldives	960	Somalia	252
Botswana	267	East Timor	670	Mali	223	South Africa	27
Brazil	55	Ecuador	593	Malta	356	Spain	34
Brunei	673	Egypt	20	Marshall Islands	692	Sri Lanka	94
Bulgaria	359	El Salvador	503	Mauritania	222	Sudan	249
Burkina Faso	226	Equatorial Guinea	240	Mauritius	230	Suriname	597
Burundi	257	Estonia	372	Mayotte Island	269	Swaziland	268
Cambodia	855	Ethiopia	251	Mexico	52	Sweden	46
Cameroon	237	Falkland Islands	500	Micronesia	691	Switzerland	41
Canada	1	Faroe Islands	298	Moldova	373	Syria	963
Alberta	403*/	Fiji	679	Monaco	377	Taiwan	886
	780*	Finland	358	Mongolia	976	Tajikistan	992
British Columbia	250*/	France	33	Montserrat	664*	Tanzania	255
	778	French Antilles	596	Morocco	212	Thailand	66
British Columbia		French Guiana	594	Mozambique	258	Togo	228
(lower mainland)	604*	French Polynesia	689	Myanmar	95	Tonga	676
Vancouver	604*	Gabon	241	Namibia	264	Trinidad & Tobago	868*
Manitoba	204*	Gambia, The	220	Nauru	674	Tunisia	216
New Brunswick	506*	Georgia	995	Nepal	977	Turkey	90
Newfoundland	709*	Germany	49	Netherlands	31	Turkmenistan	993
NW Territories	867*	Ghana	233	Netherlands Antilles	599	Turks & Caicos Isls.	649*
Nova Scotia	902*	Gibraltar	350	New Caledonia	687	Tuvalu	688
Nunavut	867*	Greece	30	New Zealand	64	Uganda	256
Ontario		Greenland	299	Nicaragua	505	Ukraine	380
London	519*	Grenada	473*	Niger	227	United Arab Emirates	971
Niagara Falls	289*	Guadeloupe	590	Nigeria	234	United Kingdom	44
North Bay	705*	Guam	671*	Niue	683	Uruguay	598
Ottawa	613*	Guantanamo Bay	53	N. Mariana Isls.	670	Uzbekistan	998
Thunder Bay	807*	Guatemala	502	Norway	47	Vanuatu	678
Toronto Metro.	416/	Guinea	224	Oman	968	Vatican City	39
	647*	Guinea-Bissau	245	Pakistan	92	Venezuela	58
Toronto Vicinity	905*	Guyana	592	Palau	680	Vietnam	84
Prince Edward Isl.	902*	Haiti	509	Panama	507	Virgin Islands, British	284*
Quebec		Honduras	504	Papua New Guinea	675	Virgin Islands, U.S.	340*
Montreal	514*	Hungary	36	Paraguay	595	Yemen	967
Montreal N. and		Iceland	354	Peru	51	Zambia	260
S. Shore	450*	India	91	Philippines	63	Zimbabwe	263
Quebec City	418*	Indonesia	62				
Sherbrooke	819*						

* These numbers are area codes. Follow Domestic Dialing instructions: dial "1" + area code + number you are calling.

Selected city codes: Beijing, 10; Brasilia, 61; Buenos Aires, 11; Dhaka, 2; Dublin, 1; Islamabad, 51; Jakarta, 21; Jerusalem, 2; Lagos, 1; London, 20; Madrid, 91; Mexico City, 55; New Delhi, 11; Paris, 1; Rome, 06; Tokyo, 3.

POSTAL INFORMATION

Basic U.S. Postal Service

The Postal Reorganization Act, creating a government-owned postal service under the executive branch and replacing the old Post Office Department, was signed into law by Pres. Richard Nixon, Aug. 12, 1970. The service officially came into being on July 1, 1971. The U.S. Postal Service is governed by an 11-person Board of Governors. Nine of the members are appointed by the president with Senate approval. These 9 choose a postmaster general. The board and the postmaster general choose the 11th member, who serves as deputy postmaster general. An independent Postal Rate Commission of 5 members, appointed by the president, reviews and rules on proposed postal rate increases submitted by the Board of Governors.

U.S. Domestic Rates

(Domestic rates apply to the U.S., to its territories and possessions, and to APOs and FPOs. Many changes in domestic postal rates, fees, services, and terminology took effect June 30, 2002.)

First-Class Mail

First-Class Mail includes written matter such as letters, postal cards, and postcards (private mailing cards), plus all other matter wholly or partly in writing, whether sealed or unsealed, except book manuscripts, periodical articles and music, manuscript copy accompanying proofsheets or corrected proofsheets of the same, and the writing authorized by law on matter of other classes. Also included: matter sealed or closed against inspection, bills, and statements of accounts.

Written letters and matter sealed against inspection cost 37¢ for first ounce or fraction, 23¢ for each additional ounce or fraction up to and including 13 ounces. U.S. Postal Service cards cost 23¢ for postage, with a 2¢ fee for the card. Private postcards postage is 23¢. Presort and automation-compatible mail can qualify for lower rates if certain piece minimums, mailing permits, and other requirements are met.

Express Mail

Express Mail provides guaranteed expedited service for any mailable article (up to 70 lbs and not over 108 in. in combined length and girth). Offers next day delivery by noon to most destinations; no extra charge for Saturday, Sunday, or holiday delivery. Second-day service is available to locations not on the Next Day Delivery Network. The basic rate for Express Mail weighing up to 8 oz is $13.65. All rates include insurance up to $100, shipment receipt, and record of delivery at the destination post office. Express Mail tracking is available on the USPS Web site (www.usps.com).

Express Mail Flat Rate: $13.65, regardless of weight, if matter fits into a special Postal Service flat-rate envelope.

Pickup service is available for $12.50 per stop, regardless of the number of pieces or service used (e.g., Express Mail, Priority Mail, or Parcel Post can be picked up together).

Contact your local post office for further information.

Standard Mail

Standard Mail is limited to items less than 16 ounces such as solicitations, newsletters, advertising materials, books, cassettes, and other merchandise. A minimum volume of 200 pieces or 50 lbs of such items is necessary, and specific bulk mail preparation and sortation requirements apply.

The minimum rate per piece for pieces 3.3 ounces or less is $0.268 for basic letters and $0.344 for basic nonletters. Contact your post office for the discounts offered for auto-

mation, presorted, carrier route, destination entry, and other discounts. Separate rates are available for some nonprofit organizations.

Any mailer who uses a permit imprint is required to pay a one-time $150 fee plus an annual (calendar year) fee of $150. Additional standards apply to mailings of nonidentical-weight pieces.

Priority Mail

Due to expeditious handling and transportation, Priority Mail is delivered in 2-3 days, on average. Priority Mail may include packages up to 70 lbs and not over 108 in. in length and girth combined, whether sealed or unsealed, including written and other First Class material.

Parcels weighing less than 15 lb and measuring over 84 in., but less than 108 in., in length and girth combined cost the same as a 15-lb parcel mailed to the same zone. Pickup service costs an additional $12.50 per stop.

Priority Mail Flat Rate: $3.85, regardless of weight, if matter fits into a special Postal Service flat-rate envelope.

Priority Mail Rates
(single-piece zone rate)

Weight not over (lbs)	ZONES					
	1-3	4	5	6	7	8
1	$3.85	$3.85	$3.85	$3.85	$3.85	$3.85
2	3.95	4.55	4.90	5.05	5.40	5.75
3	4.75	6.05	6.85	7.15	7.85	8.55
4	5.30	7.05	8.05	8.50	9.45	10.35
5	5.85	8.00	9.30	9.85	11.00	12.15
6	6.30	8.85	9.90	10.05	11.30	12.30
7	6.80	9.80	10.65	11.00	12.55	14.05
8	7.35	10.75	11.45	11.95	13.80	15.75
9	7.90	11.70	12.20	12.90	15.05	17.50
10	8.40	12.60	13.00	14.00	16.30	19.20
11	8.95	13.35	13.75	15.15	17.55	20.90
12	9.50	14.05	14.50	16.30	18.80	22.65
13	10.00	14.75	15.30	17.50	20.05	24.35
14	10.55	15.45	16.05	18.60	21.25	26.05
15[1]	11.05	16.20	16.85	19.75	22.50	27.80

(1) See postmaster for pieces greater than 15 lbs.

Periodicals

Periodicals include newspapers and magazines.

For the general public, the applicable Package Services or First-Class postage is paid for periodicals.

For publishers, rates vary according to (1) whether item is sent to same county, (2) percentage of editorial and advertising matter, (3) whether the publishing org. is nonprofit or produces educational material for use in classrooms, (4) weight, (5) distance, (6) level of presort, (7) automation compatibility.

Package Services

Package Services, formerly "Standard Mail (B)," is any mailable matter that is not included in First-Class or Periodicals (unless permitted or required by regulations). There are currently four subclasses of Package Services: Parcel Post, Bound Printed Matter, Media Mail (formerly "Special Standard Mail"), and Library Mail.

The post office determines charges for Package Services according to the weight of the package in pounds and the zone distance shipped (Media Mail and Library Mail rates are determined by weight alone). There is no minimum weight; see separate headings for maximum weight. Presort and automation-compatible mail for all Package Services can qualify for lower rates if certain piece minimums, mail-

ing permits, and other requirements are met. Contact your local post office for further information. Package Services is not sealed against postal inspection.

Parcel Post

Parcel Post is any Package Services not mailed as Bound Print Matter, Media Mail, or Library Mail. Any Package Services matter may be mailed at the Parcel Post rates, subject to these basic standards: not to exceed 70 lbs or 108 in. in combined length and girth (packages over 108 in., but not more than 130 in. in combined length and girth are subject to oversize rates). All fractions of a pound are counted as a full pound.

> **IT'S A FACT:** Possibly the hardest-to-reach address in the U.S. is Supai, AZ, a small Havasupai Indian Reservation (some 600 people) deep below the south rim of the Grand Canyon. It's the last remaining site for mule-train mail delivery in the nation. Helicopters and air drops are impractical there, so the only way to bring mail and supplies there is down a winding 8-mile trail; the Postal Service makes the trip 5 times a week, even through wind and rain, carrying about a ton of cargo per week.

Parcel Post Basic Rate Schedule

(Inter BMC/ASF ZIP codes only, machinable[1] parcels, no discount, no surcharge)

Weight not over (lbs)	ZONES 1 & 2	3	4	5	6	7	8
1	$3.69	$3.75	$3.75	$3.75	$3.75	$3.75	$3.75
2	3.85	3.85	4.14	4.14	4.49	4.49	4.49
3	4.65	4.65	5.55	5.65	5.71	5.77	6.32
4	4.86	5.20	6.29	6.93	7.14	7.20	7.87
5	5.03	5.71	6.94	7.75	8.58	8.64	9.43
6	5.63	6.01	7.44	8.50	9.52	9.90	11.49
7	5.80	6.28	7.91	9.20	10.35	11.39	12.83
8	5.98	6.53	8.30	9.84	11.11	12.54	15.04
9	6.11	6.76	8.74	10.45	11.83	13.38	17.04
10	6.28	7.57	9.10	11.01	12.50	14.17	18.14
11	6.41	7.80	9.47	11.54	13.13	14.92	19.15
12	6.54	8.01	9.80	12.04	13.72	15.62	20.10
13	6.67	8.19	10.12	12.51	14.28	16.27	20.99
14	6.80	8.42	10.43	12.95	14.81	16.90	21.84
15	6.92	8.61	10.73	13.38	15.31	17.49	22.64
16	7.02	8.79	11.00	13.78	15.79	18.05	23.41
17	7.15	8.94	11.28	14.16	16.24	18.59	24.13
18	7.25	9.11	11.52	14.52	16.68	19.09	24.82
19	7.37	9.28	11.77	14.87	17.09	19.58	25.48
20[2]	7.46	9.43	11.98	15.20	17.48	20.05	26.12

(1) Machinable parcels must be: not less than 6 in. long, 3 in. high, and .25 in. thick or more than 34 in. long, 17 in. high, and 17 in. thick; at least 6 oz. but not more than 35 lbs. (2) Consult postmaster for pieces greater than 20 lbs.

Bound Printed Matter

(minimum weight: none; maximum weight: 15 lbs)

Applies to advertising, promotional, directory, or editorial material that is bound by permanent fastening and consists of sheets of which at least 90% are imprinted by any process other than handwriting or typewriting. Does not include stationery (or pads of blank forms) or personal correspondence. Packages must not exceed 108 in. in combined length and girth, marked "Bound Printed Matter" or "BPM."

Bound Printed Matter Rates

(zone rate for flat single pieces; parcels pay 8¢ more)

Weight not over (lbs)	ZONES 1&2	3	4	5	6	7	8
1.0	$1.79	$1.84	$1.88	$1.96	$2.03	$2.12	$2.29
1.5	1.79	1.84	1.88	1.96	2.03	2.12	2.29
2.0	1.86	1.92	1.98	2.08	2.18	2.30	2.52
2.5	1.93	2.01	2.08	2.21	2.33	2.48	2.76
3.0	2.00	2.09	2.18	2.33	2.48	2.66	2.99
3.5	2.07	2.18	2.28	2.46	2.63	2.84	3.23
4.0	2.14	2.26	2.38	2.58	2.78	3.02	3.46
4.5	2.21	2.35	2.48	2.71	2.93	3.20	3.70
5.0	2.28	2.43	2.58	2.83	3.08	3.38	3.93
6.0	2.42	2.60	2.78	3.08	3.38	3.74	4.40
7.0	2.56	2.77	2.98	3.33	3.68	4.10	4.87
8.0	2.70	2.94	3.18	3.58	3.98	4.46	5.34
9.0	2.84	3.11	3.38	3.83	4.28	4.82	5.81
10.0	2.98	3.28	3.58	4.08	4.58	5.18	6.28
11.0	3.12	3.45	3.78	4.33	4.88	5.54	6.75
12.0	3.26	3.62	3.98	4.58	5.18	5.90	7.22
13.0	3.40	3.79	4.18	4.83	5.48	6.26	7.69
14.0	3.54	3.96	4.38	5.08	5.78	6.62	8.16
15.0	3.68	4.13	4.58	5.33	6.08	6.98	8.63

Media Mail

(minimum weight: none; maximum weight: 70 lbs)

Formerly "Special Standard Mail." Applies to books of at least 8 printed pages; 16-mm or narrower-width films; printed music; printed test materials; sound recordings, playscripts, and manuscripts for books; printed educational charts; loose-leaf pages and binders consisting of medical information; computer-readable media. Advertising restrictions apply. Packages must be marked "Media Mail" and may not exceed 108 in. in combined length and girth. Contact your local post office for further information.

Rates are calculated by weight only. Single-piece rates are: $1.42, up to 1 lb; 42¢ for each additional pound or fraction, to 7 lbs; additional pounds thereafter, 30¢ each.

Library Mail

(minimum weight: none; maximum weight: 70 lbs)

Applies to books, printed music, bound academic theses, periodicals, sound recordings, museum materials, and other library materials mailed between schools, colleges, universities, public libraries, museums, veteran and fraternal organizations, and nonprofit religious, educational, scientific, and labor organizations or associations (or to or from these organizations). Advertising restrictions apply. All packages must be marked "Library Mail," and may not exceed 108 in. in combined length and girth. Contact your local post office for further information.

Rates are calculated by weight only. Single-piece rates are: $1.35, up to 1 lb; 40¢ for each additional pound or fraction, to 7 lbs; additional pounds thereafter, 29¢ each.

Domestic Mail Special Services

Special Handling

Provides preferential handling, but not preferential delivery, to the extent practicable in dispatch and transportation. Available for First-Class Mail, Priority Mail, and Package Services for the following surcharge: up to 10 lb, $5.95; over 10 lb, $8.25 Pieces must be marked "Special Handling."

Registered Mail

Provides sender with mailing receipt, and a delivery record is maintained. Only matter prepaid with postage at First Class postage rates may be registered. Stamps or meter stamps must be attached. The face of the article must be at least 5" long, 3½" high. The mailer is required to declare the value of mail presented for registration.

Declared Value	Registration Fee[1]
$0.00	$7.50
$0.01 to $100.00	8.00
$100.01 to $500.00	8.85
$500.01 to $1,000.00	9.70
$1,000.01 to $2,000.00	10.55
$2,000.01 to $3,000.00	11.40
$3,000.01 to $4,000.00	12.25
$4,000.01 to $5,000.00	13.10
$5,000.01 to $6,000.00	13.95
$6,000.01 to $7,000.00	14.80
$7,000.01 to $8,000.00	15.65
$8,000.01 to $9,000.00	16.50
$9,000.01 to $10,000.00	17.35

(1) Fee for articles with declared value over $0.00 includes insurance; fee is in addition to postage.

C.O.D.: Unregistered: Applicable to First Class, Priority Mail, Express Mail, and Package Services. Items must be sent as bona fide orders or be in conformity with agreements between senders and addressees. Maximum amount collectible is $1,000. **Registered:** For details, consult postmaster.

Certified mail: Available for any matter having no intrinsic value on which First Class or Priority Mail postage is paid. A receipt is furnished at the time of mailing, and evidence of delivery is obtained. Basic fee is $2.30 in addition to regular postage. Return receipt and restricted delivery available upon payment of additional fees. No indemnity.

Insured Mail

Applicable to Standard Mail, Package Services, and First-Class or Priority Mail items eligible to be mailed as Package Services. Matter for sale addressed to prospective purchasers who have not ordered it or authorized its sending cannot be insured. Note: for Express Mail, insurance is included up to $100. Add $1.00 per $100 or fraction thereof over $100 up to $5,000.

Declared Value	Insured Mail Fee[1]
$0.01 to $50.00	$1.30
$50.01 to $100.00	2.20
$100.01 to $200.00	3.20
$200.01 to $300.00	4.20
$300.01 to $400.00	5.20
$400.01 to $500.00	6.20
$500.01 to $600.00	7.20
$600.01 to $700.00	8.20
$700.01 to $800.00	$9.20
$800.01 to $900.00	10.20
$900.01 to $1,000.00	11.20

$1,000.01 to $5,000.00 11.20 plus $1.00 per $100 or fraction thereof over $1,000 in desired coverage
(1) In addition to postage. (Maximum liability is $5,000.) See postmaster for details on bulk discounts.

Delivery Confirmation

Applies to First-Class Mail parcels, Priority Mail and Package Services. Available for purchase at the time of mailing only. Provides mailer with the date and time an article was delivered and, if delivery was attempted but not successful, the date and time of the attempt. Electronic confirmation is available for barcoded matter.

Manual confirmation is available for retail purchasers on the Internet (www.usps.com) or toll-free by phone (800-222-1811).

Priority Mail fees: manual, 45¢; electronic, free. First-Class Mail parcels and Package Services fees: manual, 55¢; electronic, 13¢.

Forwarding Addresses

To obtain a forwarding address, the mailer must write on the envelope or cover the words "Address Correction Requested." The destination post office then will check for a forwarding address on file and provide it for 70¢ per manual correction, 20¢ per automated correction.

International Mail Special Services

Registration: Available to practically all countries for letter-post items only. Fee $7.50. The maximum indemnity payable—generally only in case of complete loss (of both contents and wrapper)—is $40.45. To Canada only, the fee is $8.00, providing indemnity for loss up to $100, $8.85 for loss up to $500, and $9.70 for loss up to $1,000. Contact your post office for more details.

Return Receipt: Shows to whom and when delivered; Fee: $1.75 (must be purchased at time of mailing).

Special Delivery: Not available as of June 1997.

Air Mail: Available daily to practically all countries.

Aerogrammes — Aerogrammes are letter sheets that can be folded into the form of an envelope and sealed. Intended for personal communication only and may not include enclosures. Fee: 70¢ from U.S. to all countries.

Air mail postcards (single) — 50¢ to Canada and Mexico; 70¢ to all other countries.

International Reply Coupons (IRC): Provide foreign addressees with a prepaid means of responding to communications initiated by a U.S. sender. Each IRC is equivalent to the destination country's minimum postage rate for an unregistered airmail letter. Fee: $1.75 per coupon.

Restricted Delivery: Available to many countries for registered mail; some limitations. Fee: $3.50.

Insurance: Available to many countries for loss of or damage to items paid at parcel post rate. Consult postmaster for indemnity limits for individual countries.

Limit of indemnity Not over	Fees	
	Canada[1]	All other countries[1]
$ 50	$1.30	$1.85
100	2.20	2.60
200	3.20	3.60
300	4.20	4.60
400	5.20	5.60
500	6.20	6.60
600	7.20	7.60
700	8.20	8.60
800		9.60
900		10.60
1,000[2]		11.60

(1) Not all countries insure items up to the amounts listed in the table. Canada does not insure items for more than $675. (2) For amounts more than $1,000, add $1.00 for each $100 or fraction.

Post Office-Authorized 2-Letter State Abbreviations

The abbreviations below are approved by the U.S. Postal Service for use in addresses.

Alabama....AL	Hawaii....HI	Missouri....MO	Pennsylvania....PA
Alaska....AK	Idaho....ID	Montana....MT	Puerto Rico....PR
American Samoa....AS	Illinois....IL	Nebraska....NE	Rhode Island....RI
Arizona....AZ	Indiana....IN	Nevada....NV	South Carolina....SC
Arkansas....AR	Iowa....IA	New Hampshire....NH	South Dakota....SD
California....CA	Kansas....KS	New Jersey....NJ	Tennessee....TN
Colorado....CO	Kentucky....KY	New Mexico....NM	Texas....TX
Connecticut....CT	Louisiana....LA	New York....NY	Utah....UT
Delaware....DE	Maine....ME	North Carolina....NC	Vermont....VT
District of Columbia..DC	Marshall Islands[1]....MH	North Dakota....ND	Virgin Islands....VI
Federated States	Maryland....MD	Northern Mariana Is...MP	Virginia....VA
of Micronesia[1]....FM	Massachusetts....MA	Ohio....OH	Washington....WA
Florida....FL	Michigan....MI	Oklahoma....OK	West Virginia....WV
Georgia....GA	Minnesota....MN	Oregon....OR	Wisconsin....WI
Guam....GU	Mississippi....MS	Palau[1]....PW	Wyoming....WY

(1) Although an independent nation, this country is currently subject to domestic rates and fees.

Canadian Province and Territory Postal Abbreviations

Source: Canada Post

Alberta....AB	Newfoundland	Nunavut....NU	Quebec....QC[1]
British Columbia....BC	and Labrador....NF	Ontario....ON	Saskatchewan....SK
Manitoba....MB	Northwest Territories.NT	Prince Edward Island PE	Yukon Territory....YT
New Brunswick....NB	Nova Scotia....NS		

(1) PQ is also acceptable.

SOCIAL SECURITY

Social Security Programs

Source: Social Security Administration; World Almanac research; data as of Sept. 2003.

Old-Age, Survivors, and Disability Insurance; Medicare; Supplemental Security Income

Social Security Benefits

Social Security benefits are based on a worker's primary insurance amount (PIA), which is related by law to the average indexed monthly earnings (AIME) on which Social Security contributions have been paid. The full PIA is payable to a retired worker who becomes entitled to benefits at age 65 and to an entitled disabled worker at any age. Spouses and children of retired or disabled workers and survivors of deceased workers receive set proportions of the PIA subject to a family maximum amount. The PIA is calculated by applying varying percentages to succeeding parts of the AIME. The formula is adjusted annually to reflect changes in average annual wages.

Automatic increases in Social Security benefits are initiated for December of each year, assuming the Consumer Price Index (CPI) for the 3rd calendar quarter of the year increased relative to the base quarter, which is either the 3rd calendar quarter of the preceding year or the quarter in which an increase legislated by Congress became effective. The size of the benefit increase is determined by the percentage rise of the CPI between the quarters measured.

The average monthly benefit payable to all retired workers amounted to $895 in Dec. 2002. The average benefit for disabled workers in that month amounted to $834.

Minimum and maximum monthly retired-worker benefits payable to individuals who retired at age 65[1]

	Minimum benefit[2]		Maximum benefit[2]	
Year attaining age 65	Paid at retirement	Payable as of Dec. 2001	Payable at retirement	Payable effective Dec. 2001
1970	$64.00	$326.50	(3)	(4)
1980	133.90	326.50	$572.00	$1,397.80
1990	(5)	(5)	975.00	1,395.30
1993	(5)	(5)	1,128.80	1,414.50
1994	(5)	(5)	1,147.50	1,401.50
1995	(5)	(5)	1,199.10	1,424.70
1996	(5)	(5)	1,248.90	1,493.30
1997	(5)	(5)	1,326.60	1,422.20
1998	(5)	(5)	1,342.80	1,480.40
1999	(5)	(5)	1,373.10	1,494.40
2000	(5)	(5)	1,434.80	1,526.30
2001	(5)	(5)	1,536.70	1,576.60
2002	(5)	(5)	1,660.50	1,683.70

(1) Assumes retirement at beginning of year. (2) The final benefit amount payable is rounded to next lower $1 (if not already a multiple of $1). (3) Benefits $196.40 for women and $189.80 for men. (4) Benefits $1,003.40 for women and $968.90 for men. (5) Minimum eliminated for workers who reached age 62 after 1981.

Amount of Work Required

To qualify for benefits, the worker generally must have worked a certain length of time in covered employment. Just how long depends on when the worker reaches age 62 or, if earlier, when he or she dies or becomes disabled.

A person is fully insured who has 1 quarter of coverage for every year after 1950 (or year age 21 is reached, if later) up to but not including the year the worker reaches 62, dies, or becomes disabled. In 2003, a person earns 1 quarter of coverage for each $890 of annual earnings in covered employment, up to 4 quarters per year.

The law permits special monthly payments under the Social Security program to certain very old persons who are not eligible for regular benefits since they had little or no opportunity to earn work credits during their working lifetime (so-called special age-72 beneficiaries).

To receive disability benefits, the worker, in addition to being fully insured, must generally have credit for 20 quarters of coverage out of the 40 calendar quarters before he or she became disabled. A disabled blind worker need meet only the fully insured requirement. Persons disabled before age 31 can qualify with a briefer period of coverage. Certain survivor benefits are payable if the deceased worker had 6 quarters of coverage in the 13 quarters preceding death.

Work credit for fully insured status for benefits

Born after 1929; die, become disabled, or reach age 62 in	Years needed	Born after 1929; die, become disabled, or reach age 62 in	Years needed
1983	8	1987	9
1984	8 1/2	1988	9 1/4
1985	8 1/2	1989	9 1/2
1986	8 3/4	1990	9 3/4
		1991 and after	10

Contribution and benefit base

Calendar year	OASDI[1]	HI[2]	Calendar year	OASDI[1]	HI[2]
1990	$51,300	$51,300	1998	$68,400	no limit
1992	55,500	130,200	1999	72,600	no limit
1993	57,600	135,000	2000	76,200	no limit
1994	60,600	no limit	2001	80,400	no limit
1995	61,200	no limit	2002	84,900	no limit
1996	62,700	no limit	2003	87,000	no limit
1997	65,400	no limit	2004	88,500 (est.)	no limit

(1) Old-Age, Survivors, and Disability Ins. (2) Hospital Ins.

Tax-rate schedule

(percentage of covered earnings)

Year	Total (for employees and employers, each)	OASDI	HI
1979-80	6.13	5.08	1.05
1981	6.65	5.35	1.30
1982-83	6.70	5.40	1.30
1984	7.00	5.70	1.30
1985	7.05	5.70	1.35
1986-87	7.15	5.70	1.45
1988-89	7.51	6.06	1.45
1990 and after	7.65	6.20	1.45
For self-employed			
1979-80	8.10	7.05	1.05
1981	9.30	8.00	1.30
1982-83	9.35	8.05	1.30
1984	14.00	11.40	2.60
1985	14.10	11.40	2.70
1986-87	14.30	11.40	2.90
1988-89	15.02	12.12	2.90
1990 and after	15.30	12.40	2.90

What Aged Workers Receive

When a person has enough work in covered employment and reaches retirement age (currently age 65 for full benefit, age 62 for reduced benefit), he or she may retire and receive monthly old-age benefits. The age when unreduced benefits become payable will increase gradually from 65 to 67 over a 21-year period beginning with workers age 62 in the year 2000 (reduced benefits will still be available as early as age 62, but with a larger reduction at that age).

Beginning with year 2000, the retirement earnings test has been eliminated beginning with the month in which the beneficiary reaches full-benefit retirement age (FRA). A person at and above FRA will not have benefits reduced because of earnings. In the calendar year in which a beneficiary reaches FRA, benefits are reduced $1 for every $3 of earnings above the limit allowed by law ($30,720 in 2003), but this reduction is only to months prior to attainment of FRA. For years before the year when the beneficiary attains FRA, the reduction in benefits is $1 for every $2 of earnings over the annual exempt amount ($11,520 for year 2003).

For workers who reached age 65 between 1982 and 1989, Social Security benefits are raised by 3% for each year for which the worker between ages 65 and 70 (72 before 1984) failed to receive benefits, whether because of earnings from work or because the worker had not applied for benefits. The delayed retirement credit is 1% per year for workers who reached age 65 before 1982. The delayed retirement credit will rise to 8% per year by 2008. The rate for workers who reached age 65 in 1998-99 is 5.5%; 2000-2001 6.0%; 2002-2003, 6.5%; 2004-2005, 7.0%; 2006-2007, 7.5%.

Effective Dec. 2002, the special benefit for persons aged 72 or over who do not meet the regular coverage requirements became $226.80 a month. Like other monthly benefits, these payments are subject to cost-of-living increases.

They are not made to persons on the public assistance or supplemental security income rolls.

For workers retiring before age 65, benefits are permanently reduced 5/9 of 1% for each month before FRA, up to 36 months. If the number of months exceeds 36, then the benefit is further reduced 5/12 of 1% per month. For example, when FRA reaches 67, for workers who retire at exactly age 62, there are a total of 60 months of reduction. The reduction for the first 36 months is 5/9 of 36%, or 20%. The reduction for the remaining 24 months is 5/12 of 24%, or 10%. Thus, when the FRA reaches 67, the amount of reduction at age 62 will be 30%. The nearer to age 65 the worker is when he or she begins collecting a benefit, the larger the benefit will be. The nearer to the FRA the worker is when he or she begins collecting a benefit, the larger the benefit will be.

Benefits for Worker's Spouse

The spouse of a worker who is getting Social Security retirement or disability payments may become entitled to an insurance benefit of one-half of the worker's PIA, when he or she reaches 65. Reduced spouse's benefits are available at age 62 and are permanently reduced 25/36 of 1% for each month before FRA, up to 36 months. If the number of months exceeds 36, then the benefit is further reduced 5/12 of 1% per month. Benefits are also payable to the aged divorced spouse of an insured worker if he or she was married to the worker for at least 10 years.

Benefits for Children of Workers

If a retired or disabled worker has a child under age 18, the child will normally get a benefit equal to half of the worker's unreduced benefit. So will the worker's spouse, even if under age 62, if he or she is caring for an entitled child of the worker who is under 16 or became disabled before age 22. However, total benefits paid on a worker's earnings record are subject to a maximum. (Total monthly benefits paid to the family of a worker who retired in Jan. 2003 at age 65 and always had the maximum earnings creditable under Social Security cannot exceed $3,047.)

When entitled children reach age 18, their benefits generally stop, but a child disabled before age 22 may get a benefit as long as the disability meets the definition in the law. Benefits will be paid until age 19 to a child attending elementary or secondary school full-time.

Benefits may also be paid to a grandchild or step-grandchild of a worker or of his or her spouse, in special circumstances.

OASDI	May 2003	May 2002	May 2001	May 2000
Monthly beneficiaries, total (in thousands)[1] ..	46,771	46,190	45,683	45,132
Aged 65 and over, total ...	33,179	32,953	32,762	32,434
Retired workers	26,680	26,352	26,055	25,644
Survivors and dependents .	6,498	6,601	6,707	6,790
Under age 65, total.......	13,592	13,236	12,921	12,697
Retired workers	2,645	2,660	2,626	2,564
Disabled workers	5,702	5,337	5,119	4,944
Survivors and dependents .	8,579	5,198	5,176	5,189
Total monthly benefits (in millions)	$38,244	$36,883	$35,170	$33,212

(1) Totals may not add because of rounding or incomplete enumeration.

What Disabled Workers Receive

A worker who becomes unable to work may be eligible for a monthly disability benefit. Benefits continue until it is determined that the individual is no longer disabled. When a disabled-worker beneficiary reaches age 65, the disability benefit becomes a retired-worker benefit.

Benefits generally like those for dependents of retired-worker beneficiaries may be paid to dependents of disabled beneficiaries. However, the maximum family benefit in disability cases is generally lower than in retirement cases.

Survivor Benefits

If an insured worker should die, one or more types of benefits may be payable to survivors, again subject to a maximum family benefit as described above.

1. If claiming benefits at age 65, the surviving spouse will receive a benefit equal to 100% of the deceased worker's PIA. Benefits claimed before FRA are reduced for age with a maximum reduction of 28.5 percent at age 60. However, for those whose spouses claimed their benefits before age 65, these are limited to the reduced amount the worker would be getting if alive, but not less than 82% of the worker's PIA. Remarriage after the worker's death ends the surviving spouse's benefit rights. However, if the widow(er) marries and the marriage is ended, he or she regains benefit rights. (A marriage after age 60, age 50 if disabled, is deemed not to have occurred for benefit purposes.) Survivor benefits may also be paid to a divorced spouse if the marriage lasted for at least 10 years.

Disabled widows and widowers may under certain circumstances qualify for benefits after attaining age 50 at the rate of 71.5% of the deceased worker's PIA. The widow or widower must have become totally disabled before or within 7 years after the spouse's death or the last month in which he or she received mother's or father's insurance benefits.

2. There is a benefit for each child until the child reaches age 18. The monthly benefit for each child of a deceased worker is ¾ of the amount the worker would have received if he or she had lived and drawn full retirement benefits. A child with a disability that began before age 22 may also receive benefits. Also, a child may receive benefits until reaching age 19 if he or she is in full-time attendance at an elementary or secondary school.

3. There is a mother's or father's benefit for the widow(er) if children of the worker under age 16 are in his or her care. The benefit is 75% of the PIA, and it continues until the youngest child reaches age 16, at which time payments stop even if the child's benefit continues. However, if the widow(er) has a disabled child beneficiary age 16 or over in care, benefits may continue.

4. Dependent parents may be eligible for benefits if they have been receiving at least half their support from the worker before his or her death, have reached age 62, and (except in certain circumstances) have not remarried since the worker's death. Each parent gets 75% of the worker's PIA; if only one parent survives, the benefit is 82%.

5. A lump sum cash payment of $255 is made when there is a spouse who was living with the worker or a spouse or child eligible for immediate monthly survivor benefits.

Self-Employed Workers

A self-employed person who has net earnings of $400 or more in a year must report such earnings for Social Security tax and credit purposes. The person reports net returns from the business. Income from real estate, savings, dividends, loans, pensions, or insurance policies are not included unless it is part of the business.

A self-employed person receives 1 quarter of coverage for each $890 (for 2003), up to a maximum of 4 quarters.

The nonfarm self-employed have the option of reporting their earnings as 2/3 of their gross income from self-employment, but not more than $1,600 a year and not less than their actual net earnings. This option can be used only if actual net earnings from self-employment income are less than $1,600, and may be used only 5 times. Also, the self-employed person must have actual net earnings of $400 or more in 2 of the 3 taxable years immediately preceding the year in which he or she uses the option.

When a person has both taxable wages and earnings from self-employment, wages are credited for Social Security purposes first; only as much self-employment income as brings total earnings up to the current taxable maximum becomes subject to the self-employment tax.

Farm Owners and Workers

Self-employed farmers whose gross annual earnings from farming are $2,400 or less may report 2/3 of their gross earnings instead of net earnings for Social Security purposes. Farmers whose gross income is over $2,400 and whose net earnings are less than $1,600 can report $1,600. Cash or crop shares received from a tenant or share farmer count if the owner participated materially in production or management. The self-employed farmer pays contributions at the same rate as other self-employed persons.

Agricultural employees. A worker's earnings from farm work count toward benefits (1) if the employer pays the worker $150 or more in cash during the year; or (2) if the employer spends $2,500 or more in the year for agricultural labor. Under these rules a person gets credit for 1 calendar quarter for each $890 in cash pay in 2003.

Foreign farm workers admitted to the U.S. on a temporary basis are not covered.

Household Workers

Anyone 18 or older employed as maid, cook, laundry worker, nurse, babysitter, chauffeur, gardener, or other worker in the house of another is covered by Social Security if paid $1,400 or more in cash in calendar year 2003 by any one employer. Room and board do not count, but transportation costs count if paid in cash. The job need not be regular or full-time. The employee should get a Social Security card at the Social Security office and show it to the employer.

The employer deducts the amount of the employee's Social Security tax from the worker's pay, adds an identical amount as the employer's Social Security tax, and sends the total amount to the federal government.

Medicare Coverage

The Medicare health insurance program provides acute-care coverage for Social Security and Railroad Retirement beneficiaries age 65 and over, for persons entitled for 24 months to receive Social Security or Railroad Retirement disability benefits, and for certain persons with end-stage kidney disease. What follows is a basic description and may not cover all circumstances.

The basic Medicare plan, available nationwide, is a fee-for-service arrangement, where the beneficiary may use any provider accepting Medicare; some services are not covered and there are some out-of-pocket costs.

Under "Medicare + Choice," persons eligible for Medicare may have the option of getting services through a health maintenance organization (HMO) or other managed care plan. Any such plan must provide at least the same benefits, except for hospice services, and may provide added benefits—such as lower or no deductibles and coverage for some prescription drugs—but is usually subject to restrictions in choice of health care providers. In some plans services by outside providers are still covered for an extra out-of-pocket cost. Also available as options in some areas are Medicare-approved private fee-for-service plans and Medicare medical savings accounts.

Hospital insurance (Part A). The basic hospital insurance program pays covered services for hospital and posthospital care including the following:

- All necessary inpatient hospital care for the first 60 days of each benefit period, except for a deductible ($840 in 2003). For days 61-90, Medicare pays for services over and above a coinsurance amount ($210 per day in 2003). After 90 days, the beneficiary has 60 reserve days for which Medicare helps pay. The coinsurance amount for reserve days was $420 in 2003.
- Up to 100 days' care in a skilled-nursing facility in each benefit period. Hospital insurance pays for all covered services for the first 20 days; for the 21-100th day, the beneficiary pays coinsurance ($105 a day in 2003).
- Part-time home health care provided by nurses or other health workers.
- Limited coverage of hospice care for individuals certified to be terminally ill.

There is a premium for this insurance in certain cases.

Medical insurance (Part B). Elderly persons can receive benefits under this supplementary program only if they sign up for them and agree to a monthly premium ($58.70 if you sign up upon being eligible in 2003). The federal government pays the rest of the cost. The medical insurance program usually pays 80% of the approved amount (after the first $100 in each calendar year) for the following services:

- Covered services received from a doctor in his or her office, in a hospital, in a skilled-nursing facility, at home, or in other locations.
- Medical and surgical services, including anesthesia.

- Diagnostic tests and procedures that are part of the patient's treatment.
- Radiology and pathology services by doctors while the individual is a hospital inpatient or outpatient.
- Other services such as X rays, services of a doctor's office nurse, drugs and biologicals that cannot be self-administered, transfusions of blood and blood components, medical supplies, physical/occupational therapy and speech pathology services.

In addition to the above, certain other tests or preventive measures are now covered without an additional premium. These include mammograms, bone mass measurement, colo-rectal cancer screening, and flu shots. Outpatient prescription drugs are generally not covered under the basic plan, nor are routine physical exams, dental care, hearing aids, or routine eye care. There is limited coverage for non-hospital treatment of mental illness.

To get medical insurance protection, persons approaching age 65 may enroll in the 7-month period that includes 3 months before the 65th birthday, the month of the birthday, and 3 months after the birthday, but if they wish coverage to begin in the month they reach age 65, they must enroll in the 3 months before their birthday. Persons not enrolling within their first enrollment period may enroll later, during the first 3 months of each year (coverage begins July 1), but their premium may be 10% higher for each 12-month period elapsed since they first could have enrolled.

The monthly premium is deducted from the cash benefit for persons receiving Social Security, Railroad Retirement, or Civil Service retirement benefits. Income from the medical premiums and the federal matching payments are put in a Supplementary Medical Insurance Trust Fund, from which benefits and administrative expenses are paid.

Further details are available on the Internet at www.medicare.gov or by calling 1-800-638-6833.

Medicare card. Persons qualifying for hospital insurance under Social Security receive a health insurance card similar to cards now used by Blue Cross and other health insurers. The card indicates whether the individual has taken out medical insurance protection. It is to be shown to the hospital, skilled-nursing facility, home health agency, doctor, or whoever provides the covered services.

Payments are generally made only in the 50 states, Puerto Rico, Virgin Islands, Guam, and American Samoa.

Social Security Financing

Social Security is paid for by a tax on certain earnings (for 2003, on earnings up to $87,000) for Old Age, Survivors, and Disability Insurance and on all earnings (no upper limit) for Hospital Insurance with the Medicare Program; the taxable earnings base for OASDI has been adjusted annually to reflect increases in average wages. The employed worker and his or her employer share Social Security taxes equally.

Employers remit amounts withheld from employee wages for Social Security and income taxes to the Internal Revenue Service; employer Social Security taxes are also payable at the same time. (Self-employed workers pay Social Security taxes when filing their regular income tax forms.) The Social Security taxes (along with revenues arising from partial taxation of the Social Security benefits of certain high-income people) are transferred to the Social Security Trust Funds—the Federal Old-Age and Survivors Insurance (OASI) Trust Fund, the Federal Disability Insurance (DI) Trust Fund, and the Federal Hospital Insurance (HI) Trust Fund; they can be used only to pay benefits, the cost of rehabilitation services, and administrative expenses. Money not immediately needed for these purposes is by law invested in obligations of the federal government, which must pay interest on the money borrowed and must repay the principal when the obligations are redeemed or mature.

Supplemental Security Income

On Jan. 1, 1974, the Supplemental Security Income (SSI) program established by the 1972 Social Security Act amendments replaced the former federal grants to states for aid to the needy aged, blind, and disabled in the 50 states and the District of Columbia. The program provides both for federal payments, based on uniform national standards and eligibility requirements, and for state supplementary payments varying from state to state. The Social Security Administration administers the federal payments financed from general funds of the Treasury—and the state supplements as well, if the state elects to have its supplementary program federally administered. States may supplement the federal payment for all recipients and must supplement it for persons otherwise adversely affected by the transition from the former public assistance programs. In May 2003, the number of persons receiving federally administered payments was 6,836,665 and the payments totaled $3.0 billion.

The maximum monthly federal SSI payment for individuals with no other countable income, living in their own household, was $552 in 2003. For couples it was $829.

Social Security Statement

On Oct. 1, 1999, the Social Security Administration initiated the mailing of an annual *Social Security Statement* to all workers age 25 and older not already receiving benefits. Workers will automatically receive statements about 3 months before their birth month. The statement provides estimates of potential monthly Social Security retirement, disability, and survivor benefits as well as a record of lifetime earnings. The statement also provides workers an easy way to determine whether their earnings are accurately posted in Social Security records.

For further information contact the Social Security Administration toll-free at 1-800-772-1213 or visit its website at www.socialsecurity.gov

Examples of Monthly Benefits Available

Description of benefit or beneficiary	For low earnings ($15,628 in 2003)[1]	For avg. earnings ($34,730 in 2003)[2]	For max. earnings ($87,000 in 2003)
Primary insurance amount (worker retiring at 65)	$709.10	$1,171.10	$1,741.10
Maximum family benefit (worker retiring at 65)	1,063.6	2,133.60	3,047.00
Maximum family disability benefit (worker disabled at 55; in 2000)*	1,048.90	1,843.80	2,857.20
Disabled worker (worker disabled at 55)			
Worker alone	746.30	1,229.20	1,9.4080
Worker, spouse, and 1 child	1,048.00	1,843.00	2,856.00
Retired worker claiming benefits at age 62:			
Worker alone[3]	572.00	942.00	1,404.00
Worker with spouse claiming benefits at—			
Age 65 or over	945.00	1,556.00	2,319.00
Age 62[3]	839.00	1,402.00	2,060.00
Widow or widower claiming benefits at—			
Age 65 or over[4]	709.00	1,171.00	1,741.00
Age 60 (spouse died at 65 without receiving reduced benefits)	506.00	837.00	1,244.00
Disabled widow or widower claiming benefits at age 50-59[5]	506.00	837.00	1,244.00
1 surviving child	531.00	878.00	1,305.00
Widow or widower age 65 or over and 1 child[6]	1,240.00	2,049.00	3,046.00
Widowed mother or father and 1 child[6]	1,062.00	1,756.00	2,610.00
Widowed mother or father and 2 children[6]	1,062.00	2,133.00	3,045.00

Effective Jan. 2003. *Assumes work beginning at age 22. (1) 45% of average. (2) Estimate. (3) Assumes maximum reduction. (4) A widow(er)'s benefit amount is limited to the amount the spouse would have been receiving if still living, but not less than 82.5% of the Primary Insurance Amount (PIA). (5) Effective Jan. 1984, disabled widow(er)s claiming a benefit at ages 50-59 receive a benefit equal to 71.5% of the PIA. (6) Based on worker dying at age 65.

Social Security Trust Funds

Old-Age and Survivors Insurance Trust Fund, 1940-2002

(in millions)

Fiscal year[1]	Total	INCOME Net contributions[2]	Income from taxing benefits	Payments from the Treasury fund[3]	Net interest[4]	Total	DISBURSEMENTS Benefit payments[5]	Administrative expenses	Transfers to Railroad Retirement program	Net increase in fund	Fund at end of period
1940	$368	$325	—	—	$43	$62	$35	$26	—	$306	$2,031
1950	2,928	2,667	—	$4	257	1,022	961	61	—	1,905	13,721
1960	11,382	10,866	—	—	516	11,198	10,677	203	$318	184	20,324
1970	32,220	30,256	—	449	1,515	29,848	28,798	471	579	2,371	32,454
1980	105,841	103,456	—	540	1,845	107,678	105,083	1,154	1,442	-1,837	22,823
1990	286,653	267,530	$4,848	-2,089	16,363	227,519	222,987	1,563	2,969	59,134	214,197
1996	363,741	321,557	6,471	7	35,706	308,217	302,861	1,802	3,554	575,096	589,121
1997	397,169	349,946	7,426	2	39,795	322,073	316,257	2,128	3,688	67,916	567,395
1998	424,848	371,207	9,149	1	44,491	332,324	326,762	1,899	3,662	92,524	681,645
1999	457,040	396,352	10,899	—	49,788	339,874	334,383	1,809	3,681	117,167	798,812
2000	484,228	418,219	12,476	—	53,532	353,396	347,868	1,990	3,538	130,832	893,003
2001	513,800	440,800	11,800	—	61,200	373,000	367,000	2,100	3,300	140,800	1,033,800
2002	529,300	448,100	13,600	—	68,100	389,500	383,900	2,100	3,500	139,700	1,173,600

(1) Fiscal years 1980 and later consist of the 12 months ending on Sept. 30 of each year. Fiscal years prior to 1977 consisted of the 12 months ending on June 30 of each year. (2) Beginning in 1983, includes transfers from general fund of Treasury representing contributions that would have been paid on deemed wage credits for military service in 1957 and later, if such credits were considered covered wages. (3) Includes payments (a) in 1947-52 and in 1967 and later, for costs of noncontributory wage credits for military service performed before 1957; (b) in 1972-83, for costs of deemed wage credits for military service performed after 1956; and (c) in 1969 and later, for costs of benefits to certain uninsured persons who attained age 72 before 1968. (4) Net interest includes net profits or losses on marketable investments. Beginning in 1967, administrative expenses were charged currently to the trust fund on an estimated basis, with a final adjustment, including interest, made in the next fiscal year. The amounts of these interest adjustments are included in net interest. For years prior to 1967, the method of accounting for administrative expenses is described in the 1970 Annual Report. Beginning in Oct. 1973, the figures shown include relatively small amounts of gifts to the fund. During 1983-91, interest paid from the trust fund to the general fund on advance tax transfers is reflected. (5) Beginning in 1967, includes payments for vocational rehabilitation services furnished to disabled persons receiving benefits because of their disabilities. Beginning in 1983, amounts are reduced by amount of reimbursement for unnegotiated benefit checks.

Disability Insurance Trust Fund, 1970-2002
(in millions)

Fiscal year[1]	INCOME					DISBURSEMENTS				Net increase in fund	Fund at end of period
	Total	Net contributions[2]	Income from taxation of benefits	Payments from the Treasury fund[3]	Net interest[4]	Total	Benefit payments[5]	Administrative expenses	Transfers to Railroad Retirement program		
1970....	$4,774	$4,481	—	$16	$277	$3,259	$3,085	$164	$10	$1,514	$5,614
1980....	13,871	13,255	—	130	485	15,872	15,515	368	-12	2,001	3,629
1990....	28,791	28,539	$144	-775	883	25,616	24,829	707	80	3,174	11,079
1996....	60,710	57,325	373	—	3,012	45,351	44,189	1,160	2	15,359	52,924
1997....	60,499	56,037	470	—	3,992	47,034	45,695	1,280	59	13,465	66,389
1998....	64,357	58,966	558	—	4,832	49,931	48,207	1,567	157	14,425	80,815
1999....	69,541	63,203	661	—	5,677	53,035	51,381	1,519	135	16,507	97,321
2000....	77,023	70,001	756	-836	6,266	56,008	54,174	1,608	159	21,014	113,752
2001....	82,100	74,600	700	—	7,600	69,900	58,200	1,800	*	22,100	135,900
2002....	85,700	76,100	900	—	8,700	66,400	64,200	2,00	200	19,400	155,300

* Less than $50 million. (1) Fiscal years 1977 and later consist of the 12 months ending Sept. 30 of each year. Fiscal years prior to 1977 consisted of the 12 months ending June 30 of each year. (2) Beginning in 1983, includes transfers from general fund of Treasury representing contributions that would have been paid on deemed wage credits for military service in 1957 and later, if such credits were considered to be covered wages. (3) Includes payments (a) for costs of noncontributory wage credits for military service performed before 1957; and (b) in 1972-83, for costs of deemed wage credits for military service performed after 1956. (4) Net interest includes net profits or losses on marketable investments. Administrative expenses are charged currently to the trust fund on an estimated basis, with a final adjustment, including interest, made in the following fiscal year. Figures shown include relatively small amounts of gifts to the fund. During the years 1983-91, interest paid from the trust fund to the general fund on advance tax transfers is reflected. (5) Includes payments for vocational rehabilitation services. Beginning in 1983, amounts are reduced by amount of reimbursement for unnegotiated benefit checks. NOTE: Totals may not add because of rounding.

Supplementary Medical Insurance Trust Fund (Medicare), 1975-2002
(in millions)

Fiscal year[1]	INCOME				DISBURSEMENTS			Balance in fund at end of year[5]
	Premium from participants	Government contributions[2]	Interest and other income[3]	Total Income	Benefit payments[4]	Administrative expenses	Total disbursements	
1975....	$1,887	$2,330	$105	$4,322	$3,765	$405	$4,170	$1,424
1980....	2,928	6,932	415	10,275	10,144	593	10,737	4,532
1990....	11,494[6]	33,210	1,434[6]	46,138[6]	41,498	1,524[6]	43,022[6]	14,527[6]
1995....	19,244	36,988	1,937	58,169	63,491	1,722	65,213	13,874
1996....	18,931	61,702	1,392	82,025	67,176	1,771	68,946	26,953
1997....	19,141	59,471	2,193	80,806	71,133	1,420	72,553	35,206
1998....	19,427	59,919	2,608	81,955	74,837[7]	1,435	76,272	40,889
1999....	20,160	62,185	2,933	85,278	79,000[7]	1,510	80,518	45,649
2000....	20,515	65,561	3,164	89,239	87,212[7]	1,780	88,992	45,896
2001....	22,307	69,838	3,191	95,336	97,466[7]	1,986	99,452	41,780
2002....	24,427	78,318	2,960	105,705	106,995[7]	1,830	108,825	38,659

(1) Fiscal year 1975 consists of the 12 months ending on June 30, 1975; fiscal years 1980 and later consist of the 12 months ending on Sept. 30 of each year. (2) General fund matching payments, plus certain interest-adjustment items. (3) Other income includes recoveries of amounts reimbursed from the trust fund that are not obligations of the trust fund and other miscellaneous income. (4) Includes costs of Peer Review Organizations from 1983 to 2001, and costs of Quality Improvement Organizations beginning in 2002. (5) The financial status of the program depends on both the assets and the liabilities of the program. (6) Includes the impact of the Medicare Catastrophic Coverage Act of 1988. (7) Benefit payments less monies transferred from the HI trust fund for home health agency costs, as provided for by PL 105-33. NOTE: Totals do not necessarily equal sums of rounded components.

Hospital Insurance Trust Fund (Medicare), 1975-2002
(in millions)

Fisc. year[1]	INCOME								DISBURSEMENTS			Net increase in fund	Fund at end of year
	Payroll taxes	Income from taxation of benefits	Transfers from railroad retirement acct.	Reimbursment for uninsured persons	Premiums from voluntary enrollees[2]	Pymts. for military wage credits	Interest on investments and other income[2]	Total income	Benefit pymts.[3]	Administrative expense[4]	Total disbursements		
1975	$11,291	—	$132	$481	$6	$48	$609	$12,568	$10,353	$259	$10,612	$1,956	$9,870
1980	23,244	—	244	697	17	141	1,072	25,415	23,790	497	24,288	1,127	14,490
1990	70,655	—	367	413	113	107	7,908	79,563	65,912	774	66,687	12,876	95,631
1995	98,053	3,913	396	462	998	61	10,963	114,847	113,583	1,300	114,883	-36	129,520
1996	106,934	4,069	401	419	1,107	-2,293[5]	10,496	121,135	124,088	1,229	125,317	-4,182	125,338
1997	112,725	3,558	419	481	1,279	70	10,017	128,548	136,175	1,661	137,836	-9,287	116,050
1998	121,913	5,067	419	34	1,320	67	9,382	138,203	135,487[6]	1,653	137,140	1,063	117,113
1999	134,385	6,552	430	652	1,401	71	9,523	153,015	129,463[6]	1,978	131,441	21,574	138,687
2000	137,738	8,787	465	470	1,392	2	10,827	159,681	127,934[6]	2,340	130,284	29,397	168,084
2001	151,931	4,903	470	453	1,440	-1,175[7]	12,993	171,014	139,356[6]	2,368	141,723	29,290	197,374
2002	151,951	10,946	425	442	1,525	0	14,850	179,762	145,566[6]	2,464	148,031	31,731	229,105

(1) Fiscal year 1975 consists of the 12 months ending on June 30, 1975; fiscal years 1980 and later consist of the 12 months ending Sept. 30 of each year. (2) Other income includes recoveries of amounts reimbursed from the trust fund that are not obligations of the trust fund, receipts from the fraud and abuse control program, and a small amount of miscellaneous income. (3) Includes costs of Peer Review Organizations (beginning with the implementation of the Prospective Payment System on Oct. 1, 1983) and costs of Quality Improvement Organizations beginning in 2002. (4) Includes costs of experiments and demonstration projects. Beginning in 1997, includes fraud and abuse control expenses, as provided for by PL 104-191. (5) Includes the lump-sum general revenue adjustment of $-2,366 mil, as provided for by PL 98-21. (6) Includes monies transferred to the SMI trust fund for home health agency costs, as provided for by PL 105-33. (7) Includes the lump-sum general review adjustment of -$1,117 million, as provided for by sec. 151 of PL 98-21. NOTE: Totals do not necessarily equal sums of rounded components.

TAXES

Federal Income Tax

Source: George W. Smith III, CPA, Managing Partner, George W. Smith & Company, P.C

On June 7, 2001, Pres. George W. Bush signed into law his 1st major tax bill, the $1.35 trillion Tax Relief Act. On Mar. 9, 2002, he signed the Job Creation and Worker Assistance Act. On May 28, 2003, in the East Room of the White House, he signed a 3rd major tax bill, the Jobs and Growth Tax Relief Reconciliation Act.

Jobs and Growth Tax Relief Reconciliation Act of 2003

This 10-year, $350 billion package was the 3rd-largest tax cut in U.S. history.

Rate Reductions. The Tax Relief Act of 2001 reduced the top individual tax rates for years 2002-2003 to 27%, 30%, 35%, and 38.6%. Two years later the rates have been reduced to 25%, 28%, and 33%, with a maximum top rate of 35%, starting in 2003. Unless Congress decides otherwise, the rates will revert to pre-2001 levels after 2010.

Child Tax Credit. The 2001 law had increased the maximum tax credit for each qualifying dependent child under age 17 from $500 to $600 initially, and up to $1,000 phased in over a 10-year period. The 2003 legislation advanced the credit for 2003 and 2004 to $1,000. To stimulate the economy, advance refunds of up to $400 per child, about 25 million checks, were mailed in July and Aug. 2003 to qualifying individuals. Under present law, the credit reverts to $500 after 2010.

Dividend Income. Some of the toughest congressional debates involved cutting taxes on corporate dividends paid to individuals. Previously, dividends were taxed as normal income, and so the tax rate could go as high as 38.6%. The 2003 law dropped the maximum rate to 15% for dividends paid after 2002. For taxpayers in the 10% and 15% tax brackets the rates were reduced to 5%. After 2008 dividends will be taxed at the rates they were prior to 2003.

Capital Gains. The maximum capital gains tax rate was reduced from 20% to 15% starting May 6, 2003. The lower 10% rate drops to 5%. To qualify, the appreciated asset must be held for more than one year. This provision expires at the end of 2008. Higher capital gains rates on collectibles and certain real estate remain unchanged.

Recent Federal Tax Rate Cuts			
	Pre-2001 Rates	After 2001 Cuts[1]	After 2003 Cuts[2]
Top Bracket...	39.6%	38.6%	35%
Next.........	36%	35%	33%
Next.........	31%	30%	28%
Next.........	28%	27%	25%
Next.........	15%	15%	15%
Lowest.......	same	10%	10%
(1) Effective July 1, 2001. (2) Effective Jan. 1, 2003.			

Deductions. Starting in 2003 the basic standard deduction for married couples filing jointly increases to twice the standard deduction for single filers. The law also expands the 15% bracket for joint returns to twice the size of the 15% bracket for single returns. After 2004, the law reverts to the provisions of the 2001 Tax Act.

Business Assets. Section 179 of the tax code allows a taxpayer to expense up to $25,000 of the cost of qualifying depreciable property such as machinery and equipment. Congress increased the maximum to $100,000 through 2005. The deduction now begins to phase out if the annual cost of property exceeds $400,000.

Depreciation. Taxpayers can now elect an additional first-year depreciation of 50% for qualified property acquired after May 5, 2003, and before Jan. 1, 2005. A $4,600 deduction allowed under the 2002 law for certain new passenger automobiles in their first year of purchase was increased to $7,650.

Job Creation and Worker Assistance Act of 2002

This measure contains over $120 billion in current tax cuts and incentives.

Classroom Materials. Under the 2002 law, elementary and secondary school teachers, principals, and counselors who buy school books or other teaching materials and supplies with their own money can deduct up to $250 of these expenses. Taxpayers do not have to itemize to take this deduction, but it is repealed after 2003.

Operating Loss. Businesses and individuals with an operating loss in 2001 and 2002 were allowed to carry it back 5 years instead of 2; after 2002, however, the 2-year rule again applies.

Depreciation. Under this law, businesses that purchase new qualifying property after Sept. 10, 2001, but before Sept. 10, 2004, can now take a first-year depreciation deduction equal to 30% of the property's basis. This act also provides higher dollar deductions for new vehicles placed in service after Sept. 10, 2001, and before Sept. 10, 2004. See 2003 law for the changes.

Other Measures. The definition of qualified foster care payments excludable from income has been expanded. Miscellaneous Income, Form 1099, may now be sent to recipients electronically. The new regulations also clarify when a taxpayer can qualify as head of household or surviving spouse if a child was kidnapped or is missing.

The Economic Growth and Tax Relief Reconciliation Act of 2001 (Tax Relief Act)

This massive, 10-year tax package added 440 changes to the Internal Revenue Tax Code. In addition to changes mentioned above, here are some other highlights.

Dependent Care. Starting in 2003, the maximum expense eligible for the dependent care tax credit was increased from $2,400 to $3,000 for one qualifying child or other dependent incapable of self-care, and from $4,800 to $6,000 for 2 or more. The phase-out limitations for higher income also increase.

Adoption. As of 2003, the maximum adoption credit goes to $10,160 per child and the exclusion from income of employer-provided adoption assistance starts to phase out at $152,390. A credit can be claimed for a special needs adoption whether or not the taxpayer has qualified adoption expenses.

Education. The legislation increases the maximum annual contributions allowed to a Coverdell Education Savings Account, formerly known as the Education IRA, from $500 to $2,000 for elementary and secondary education expenses, whether for a public, private, or religious school. Qualifying distributions are not taxable. The phase-out maximum for joint filers increases to twice that of single filers. Contributions *are* taxable, but income earned is not.

Student Loans. The income phase-out range for the interest deduction on student loans increases to $50,000-$65,000 for single taxpayers and $100,000-$130,000 for married taxpayers. Beginning in 2003, these limitations are to be adjusted annually for inflation. The legislation also repeals the 60-month time limitation for the number of months during which interest paid is deductible.

College. This law created a $3,000 educational deduction for qualified college tuition and related expenses. Generally, any accredited public, nonprofit, or proprietary post-secondary institution is considered an eligible education institution. The expenses are deductible even if the taxpayer does not itemize. The amount increases to $4,000 for 2004 and 2005, but there are phase-outs for higher-income taxpayers. This deduction is repealed after 2005.

Joint Filers. The standard deduction available to married taxpayers filing a joint return will gradually increase over a 5-year period starting in 2005 until 2009, when the amount reaches 200% of that allowed for single taxpayers. The recent Jobs Tax Relief Act advanced these dates to 2003.

Higher Income. The phasing out of the personal exemption and Schedule A itemized deductions for higher income taxpayers will be reduced by 1/3 in 2006 and 2007, 2/3 for 2008 and 2009, and totally eliminated in 2010.

Estate Exclusion. The estate tax exclusion was increased from $675,000 to $1 million in 2002 and 2003, to $1.5 million in 2004 and 2005, to $2 million in 2006 through 2008, and to $3.5 million in 2009. All estate taxes are repealed for the year 2010.

IT'S A FACT: The IRS web site (www.irs.gov) now allows taxpayers to check the status of their refunds at anytime from anywhere. You will need to type in your expected refund amount, social security number, and filing status.

Recent Legislation, IRS Rulings, Other Tax Matters

Alimony. The U.S. Tax Court in 2003 ruled that a taxpayer could not deduct alimony payments made to a former spouse prior to divorce because the payments were voluntary and not legally required.

Weight Loss. The Internal Revenue Service (IRS) now allows a medical deduction for costs of certain weight-loss programs. Participation must be for treatment of a physician-diagnosed disease including obesity. No deduction is allowed for purely cosmetic reasons or special diet foods.

Eye Surgery. The cost of certain kinds of eye surgery (radial keratomy, lasik, etc.) to improve vision now is allowed as a medical deduction.

Smoking. Taxpayers can deduct two types of treatments for quitting cigarette smoking as a medical expense: (1) participation in a smoking-cessation program, and (2) prescription drugs to alleviate the effects of nicotine withdrawal. Over-the-counter products such as nicotine patches and chewing gum remain nondeductible.

Spouse's Half. A "tenancy by the entireties" is a form of co-ownership that applies only in the case of a married couple. The U.S. Circuit Court of Appeals in 2003 ruled in favor of the IRS stating that it could levy on and sell property held by the taxpayer with a spouse.

Frequent Flyers. A recent IRS announcement states, "The IRS will not assert that any taxpayer has understated his federal tax liability by reason of the receipt or personal use of frequent flyer miles or other in-kind promotional benefits attributable to the taxpayer's business or official travel."

Garage Sale. Revenues received from a garage sale usually do not result in taxable income. In most cases, the item that was sold cost more than the revenue received. Nor are losses deductible.

Day Camp. If both spouses work, the cost of summer day camp may qualify for the child care credit.

Divorce. Legal fees paid to collect taxable alimony or to seek tax advice during a divorce are deductible on Schedule A. Fees paid related to the settlement of assets are personal expenses and not deductible.

Tax-Free Income. Rental income (for instance, for personal residences rented to players in a major golf tournament) is not taxable if the taxpayer's residence is rented for fewer than 15 days during the year. Expenses attributed to the rental income are not deductible.

Whoops. Penalties and fines paid to a governmental agency or department are not deductible. This includes parking and speeding tickets, also penalties for late filing of a tax return.

Frivolous Returns. An IRS news release dated Apr. 3, 2002, states, "Taxpayers who file frivolous income tax returns face a $500 penalty and may be subject to civil penalties of 20-75% of the underpaid tax. Those who pursue frivolous tax cases in the courts may face a penalty of up to $25,000, in addition to the taxes, interest, and civil penalties that they may owe."

Tax Highlights

Medical Insurance. The page-1, Form-1040 70% deduction for medical insurance premiums paid in 2002 for self-employed individuals, spouses, and dependents becomes a 100% page-1 deduction for 2003. For more information call the IRS at 1-800-829-3676 and ask for their free Publication 535, Business Expenses.

Death Benefits. Qualified accelerated death benefits paid under a life insurance contract to terminally ill persons (certified as expected to die within 24 months) are excludable from gross income. A similar exclusion applies to the sale or assignment of insurance death benefits to another person. Starting in 2003 accelerated death benefits paid to a chronically ill person under a long-term care rider are tax-free up to $220 per day. The dollar amount is indexed annually for inflation.

Sale of Residence. Married couples filing jointly who lived in their principal residence for at least 2 years during a 5-year period can exclude up to $500,000 in gain from the sale of their residence. This deduction is reusable every 2 years. Single taxpayers can exclude a gain up to $250,000. Married couples who do not share a principal residence but continue to file a joint return also may claim up to $250,000 for a qualifying sale or exchange of each spouse's principal residence.

Homeowners who have lived in their home fewer than 2 years and must sell because of a change in place of work can prorate the exclusion based on amount of time lived there.

House Closing Points. The IRS has ruled that taxpayers need not deduct points in the year of purchase of a home; they may amortize the points over the life of the loan.

Home Office. A deduction is allowed for taxpayers who set up an office at home to take care of the administrative or management side of their business, but the rules are complicated. The instructions on Form 8829, Expenses for Business Use of Your Home, provide guidance.

Domestic Workers. The annual threshold dollar amount for reporting and paying Social Security and federal unemployment taxes on domestic employees, including nannies and housekeepers, increased to $1,400 in 2003. Household workers under 18 are exempt unless household work is their principal occupation. Household employers must apply for an employer federal ID number and issue W-2 wage statements.

Mileage. The mileage allowance deduction for driving to obtain medical treatment or for automobile costs incurred in a job-related move dropped from 13 cents to 12 cents per mile in 2003. For use of a car in volunteer work for qualified charities the deduction remains at 14 cents. Starting in 2003 the standard mileage rate for business use of autos, including leased cars, decreased from 36.5 cents to 36 cents.

Investments. Investors can take a miscellaneous deduction on Schedule A for investment and custodial fees, trust administration fees, cost of investment advice, and financial newspapers and reports and other expenses incurred in managing their investment portfolio. However, they cannot deduct expenses for attending a convention, seminar, or similar meeting.

Innocent Spouse Relief. The IRS Reform Act of 1998 provides a separate liability section for taxpayers who are divorced, legally separated, or living apart for at least 12 months. In effect, this legislation prevents a spouse from being held liable for the other spouse's tax liability and misdeeds.

Gifting. An individual can now make tax-free gifts of up to $11,000 each to as many individuals as he or she chooses.

Children's Income. Parents may elect to include on their income tax return the dividend and interest income of a dependent child under age 14 whose unearned income is more than $750 and gross income is less than $7,500. Form 8814, Parent's Election to Report Child's Interest and Dividends, must be attached to the parents' tax return. The election is not available if estimated tax payments were made or investments were sold in the child's name during the year.

Full-Time Student. A taxpayer may not claim a dependency exemption in 2003 for an individual who qualifies as a full-time student and is over age 23 at the end of the year, unless the child's gross income is less than $3,050.

Responsibility. If a dependent child with taxable income cannot file an income tax return, the parent, guardian, or other legally responsible person must file a return for the child.

Hobbies. Qualifying long-term gains for collectibles such as art, antiques, jewelry, stamps, and coins are taxed at a maximum 28%.

Filing and Payment Dates

Filing Dates. The due date for filing a 2003 Form 1040, 1040A, or 1040EZ U.S. Individual Income Tax Return is Thurs., Apr. 15, 2004.

Estimated Taxes. Due dates for filing individual quarterly federal estimated tax payments, Form 1040-ES for 2004 are: 1st quarter, Thurs., Apr. 15. 2nd quarter, Tues., June 15; 3rd quarter, Wed., Sept. 15; 4th quarter, Mon., Jan. 17, 2005. Different filing dates may apply for state and local quarterly estimated tax payments.

WORLD ALMANAC QUICK QUIZ

According to Tax Foundation figures for 2002, which of the 50 states gets the most money from the federal government per dollar of federal tax paid? Which gets the least?

  (a) New Mexico   (b) New Jersey
  (c) Arkansas   (d) Vermont

For the answer look in this chapter, or see page 1008.

Refunds. Individuals can call the IRS toll-free at 1-800-829-4477 for a recorded message to check on the status of their expected refund. Taxpayers may have refunds deposited directly into their bank account. The average refund received through June 30, 2003, was $1,967, up 2.1% from a year earlier. The total dollar amount of refunds was $187 billion. About 95.1 million taxpayers received refunds.

Need More Time? Individuals who cannot file their 2003 tax return by the due date may apply for a 4-month extension. Although the extension is automatic, Form 4868 must be filed no later than Apr. 15, 2004, to qualify. Extensions also may be obtained by calling 1-800-796-1074. Approximately 8.5 million individuals filed for the 4-month extension for 2003. An estimated 3 million taxpayers asked for an additional 2-month extension through October 15, 2003.

Payments. Taxpayers may use their VISA, MasterCard, Discover, or American Express credit cards for payments. To pay by credit card, call 1-888-2-PAY-TAX. There is a "convenience fee" charged by the credit card company based on the size of the payment. Estimated tax payments also can be paid this way or via the Internet, instead of filing Form 1040-ES payment vouchers.

Installment Payments. Depending on the amount of tax owed, taxpayers may apply for monthly installment payments by attaching Form 9465 to their tax return. There is a nominal filing fee if the request is approved.

Timely Postmark. When a taxpayer's return is mailed on time, the IRS must accept the postmark as the filing date even if the IRS receives it weeks later. The postmark of qualified couriers such as UPS and FedEx also is proof of timely mailing. Caution: When the return is mailed after the filing due date, or after the extended due date, the IRS considers a return as filed on the date it is received by the IRS, not the date of postmark.

Statute of Limitations. Taxpayers have until Apr. 15, 2004, to file their 2000 federal tax return to claim a refund. After that date any tax or withholding refund for 2000, including the refundable earned income tax credit they may have coming, will be lost . . . forever.

Filing Penalties. The IRS can levy 2 potential penalties when a return is filed after the due date with a balance owing: one is for failing to file a timely tax return, the other is for failure to pay the tax when due. Interest will be charged on any unpaid tax balance.

Precaution. To protect the taxpayer's privacy, social security numbers no longer appear on mailing labels.

Services. Free IRS tax forms, information on tax legislation, or relevant court decisions, and other information and resources are available from the IRS via the following:

Tax Questions: 1-800-829-1040
Internet website: www.irs.gov
Telnet: iris.irs.gov
File Transfer Protocol: ftp.irs.gov
Fax: 1-703-368-9694
Forms/Publications: 1-800-829-3676

English/Spanish. The IRS provides videotaped instructions both in English and Spanish at participating libraries. Many IRS publications and tax forms including instructions also are printed in Spanish. For more information, call 1-800-TAX-FORM and ask for the free IRS Publication 1SP, Derechos del Contribuyente.

Hearing Impaired. The IRS telephone service for hearing impaired persons is available for taxpayers with access to TDD equipment. The toll-free number is 1-800-829-4059.

Individual Income Tax Rates for Year 2003

Tax Rate	Single Taxable Income
10%	$1 to $7,000
15%	$7,001 to 28,400
25%	$28,401 to $68,800
28%	$68,801 to $143,300
33%	$143,301 to $311,950
35%	More than $311,950

Tax Rate	Married Filing Separately Taxable Income
10%	$1 to $7,000
15%	$7,001 to $28,400
25%	$28,401 to $57,325
28%	$57,326 to $87,350
33%	$87,351 to $155,975
35%	More than $155,975

Tax Rate	Married Filing Jointly or Qualifying Widow(er) Taxable Income
10%	$1 to $14,000
15%	$14,001 to $56,800
25%	$56,801 to $114,650
28%	$114,651 to $174,700
33%	$174,701 to $311,950
35%	More than $311,950

Tax Rate	Head of Household Taxable Income
10%	$1 to $10,000
15%	$10,001 to $38,050
25%	$38,051 to $98,250
28%	$98,251 to $159,100
33%	$159,101 to $311,950
35%	More than $311,950

Tax Rate	Estates and Trusts Taxable Income
15%	$0 to $1,900
25%	$1,901 to $4,500
28%	$4,501 to $6,850
33%	$6,851 to $9,350
35%	More than $9,300

"Kiddie Tax." If a child under age 14 has net investment income exceeding $1,500 for 2003, the excess is taxed at the parents' top marginal tax rate.

Exemptions

Dollar Amounts. The personal exemption amount for each taxpayer, spouse, and dependent for 2003 is $3,050, up from $3,000 for 2002 and $2,900 for 2001. These exemption amounts are adjusted each year for any cost of living increase.

Phaseout. The exemption deduction for higher income taxpayers begins to be phased out when their income exceeds certain threshold dollar amounts. These threshold amounts are adjusted annually for any cost of living increase. Each exemption is reduced by 2% for each $2,500 ($1,250 for married persons filing separately) or fraction thereof by which adjusted gross income for year 2003 exceeds the following:

Married filing jointly	$209,250
Qualifying widow(er)	$209,250
Head of household	$174,400
Single	$139,500
Married filing separately	$104,625

Exemptions for the year 2003 are fully phased out when adjusted gross income is more than $122,500 ($61,250 for married filing separately) over the above threshold amount. These phase out regulations will be completely repealed after 2010.

Standard Deduction

The standard deduction is a flat dollar amount that is subtracted from the adjusted gross income (AGI) of taxpayers who do not itemize deductions. The amount allowed depends on filing status and is adjusted annually for inflation.

2003 Standard Deduction Amount

Single	$4,700
Married filing jointly or qualifying widow(er)	$9,500
Married filing separately	$4,700
Head of household	$7,000

These figures are not applicable if an individual can be claimed as a dependent on another person's tax return.

Standard Deduction for Dependents. An individual reported as a dependent on another person's 2003 income tax return generally may claim on his or her own tax return only the greater of $750 or the sum of $250 plus earned income not to exceed $4,750. A blind dependent may add $1,150 to this amount. Earned income includes wages, salaries, commissions and tips, net profit from self-employment, and any part of a scholarship or fellowship grant that must be included in gross income.

Taxpayers who are 65 or older and/or blind may claim an additional standard deduction:

2003 Additional Standard Deduction Amount

Single or head of household, 65 or older OR blind	$1,150
Single or head of household, 65 or older AND blind	$2,300
Married filing jointly or qualifying widow(er), 65 or older OR blind (per person)	$950
Married filing jointly or qualifying widow(er), 65 or older AND blind (per person)	$1,900
Married filing separately, 65 or older OR blind	$950
Married filing separately, 65 or older AND blind	$1,900

Adjustments to Income

Traditional IRA. The maximum tax-deferred Individual Retirement Arrangement (IRA) deduction for a married couple filing jointly is $6,000 through 2004, but not to exceed total earned income if less than $6,000. Each spouse can contribute up to $3,000 annually even if one spouse had little or no income. Individuals age 50 or older can fund an additional "catch-up" amount of $500 through 2005. However, there are income limitations and phase-outs.

Withdrawals. There is a 10% early withdrawal penalty for IRA distributions before age 59¾ unless it qualifies for one of the following exceptions:
- Distributions paid to the beneficiary after the death of the owner.
- Payments paid due to the disability of the owner.
- Part of a series of substantially equal periodic payments.
- Payments made to an employee following separation from employment after age 55. This exception does not apply if a qualified distribution from a pension plan is rolled into an IRA.
- Used to pay certain unreimbursed medical expenses.
- Used to pay certain qualifying higher education expenses.
- Used to pay certain qualified first time home buyer acquisition costs (up to $10,000).

Roth IRA. Although contributions paid into a Roth IRA are not deductible, distributions of funds including investment earnings held in the account for 5 years or longer and distributed after age 59¾ are free both of income tax and the 10% early withdrawal penalty at the time of distribution.

Funds paid from the Roth IRA after the 5-year exclusion period to an estate or decedent's beneficiary on or after an individual's death, including funds paid to an individual who is disabled, are tax and penalty free regardless of age.

Withdrawals from a Roth IRA held less than 5 years can be subject both to income tax and the 10% withdrawal penalty regardless of age. However, earnings withdrawn for "qualified higher education expenses" of the taxpayer, spouse, or any child or grandchild of the taxpayer or spouse are taxable but not subject to the early withdrawal penalty.

For more information on IRAs call the IRS at 1-800-829-3676 for a free copy of Publication 590, Individual Retirement Arrangements (IRA).

Moving Expenses. Taxpayers who change jobs or are transferred usually can deduct part of their moving expenses, including travel and the cost of moving of household goods, but not meals. Starting in 2003, the mileage rate for automobiles used in the move was decreased to 12 cents per mile. To take a deduction, the new job must be at least 50 miles farther from the former home than the old job. Employees must work full-time for at least 39 weeks during the first 12 months after they arrive in the general area of their new job.

Itemized Deductions

If the total amount of itemized deductions is more than the standard deduction, taxpayers generally should itemize their deductions on Schedule A, Form 1040. The following examples are just a few of the deductions that may be itemized; some are subject to income limitations.
- Most **medical expenses**, but only the amount that exceeds 7.5% of the taxpayer's adjusted gross income. Medicines, birth control pills, and insulin qualify if prescribed by a doctor. Cosmetic surgery for congenital abnormality, for personal injury from an accident or trauma, or for a disfiguring disease is also allowed as a medical deduction.
- **Long-term care** insurance premiums as a medical expense, up to certain annual limits based on age. The maximum premium allowed in 2003 is: $250 if age 40 or less; $470 from 41 to 50; $940, 51 to 60; $2,510, 61 to 70, and $3,130 if over age 70. Any long-term benefits received under a qualifying policy are tax-free, subject to per diem restrictions.
- **Mortgage interest** paid on a primary residence or a second home. However, there are limitations on mortgages in excess of $1,000,000. Borrowers generally can also deduct points paid on their principal-home mortgage loan. Interest on home equity loans is also deductible, but only covering the first $100,000 of equity debt. Credit card interest is not deductible.

State and local income taxes, real estate **taxes**, and personal property taxes, but not sales and transfer taxes.
- Casualty and theft **losses**, subject to the $100 and 10% limitation rule for each occurrence.
- **Charitable contributions**. Taxpayers deducting individual contributions of $250 or more must obtain written substantiation from the charity. If the amount is $75 or more, the charity must provide a breakdown of the payment indicating how much was a deductible contribution and what (if any) was the nondeductible value of goods, meals, or services received.

Certain miscellaneous expenses are deductible, but only the amount that exceeds 2% of adjusted gross income. Miscellaneous deductions include investment expenses (not to exceed net investment income), union and professional dues, cost of tax preparation, and safe-deposit box rental fees. Other deductible expenses include employment fees paid to agencies for resumes, postage, travel, and other out-of-pocket expenditures to look for a new job. These expenses must be related to the individual's present occupation and are deductible even if he or she does not get the job.

Unreimbursed employee business expenses such as travel, automobile, telephone, and gifts, also are deductible. However, only 50% of the cost of customer meals and entertainment is.

Threshold Reduction. Many itemized deductions otherwise allowed are further reduced by the smaller of these two figures: 3% of a taxpayer's 2003 adjusted gross income in excess of the threshold amount of $139,500 ($69,750 for married taxpayers filing separately) OR 80% of the amount of these itemized deductions otherwise allowable for the year. These dollar amounts are adjusted for cost-of-living increases each year.

This provision does not apply to medical expenses, investment interest expense, casualty losses, or gambling expenses.

The threshold reduction is phased out starting in 2006 by the Tax Relief Act of 2001 and completely repealed after 2009.

Business Expenses

Business Equipment. The election to expense currently the cost of certain business machinery and other assets instead of depreciating them over a period of years is called a Section 179 Expense Election. The maximum annual dollar amount was increased in 2003 from $25,000 to $100,000.

Software. Off-the-shelf computer software now can be expensed.

Commercial Vehicles. The Section 179 tax provision now allows businesses to expense up to $100,000 of the cost of heavy sport-utility vehicles (SUVs) weighing over 6,000 lbs. loaded.

Dues. Dues paid to social, athletic, luncheon, sporting, and country clubs, including airport and hotel clubs, are not deductible. Dues paid to the Chamber of Commerce, business economic clubs, and trade associations remain deductible.

Tax Credits

A tax deduction reduces a taxpayer's taxable income, whereas tax credits are reductions in the amount of tax owed, dollar-for-dollar.

Adoption Credit. Starting in 2003 the adoption credit for qualified expenses increases to $10,160. The phase-out of the credit begins at $152,390 of adjusted gross income. The credit limit is per person, not per year, and is adjusted annually for inflation.

Earned Income Credit. Lower-income workers who maintain a household may be eligible for a refundable earned income credit. The credit is based on total earned income such as wages, commissions, and tips. The Tax Relief Act of 2001 further simplified the rules by redefining earned income, extending the definition of qualifying children to include descendents of stepchildren, and eliminating the one-year residency requirement for foster children.

The phaseout range of the earned income credit increased for joint filers by an additional $1,000 starting in 2002 up to a maximum increase of $3,000 in 2008. Starting in 2009 the credit will be adjusted annually for the cost of living. After 2010 all these changes will be repealed.

Refunds. Individuals may qualify for the earned income credit even if they are not required to file a return. However, a tax return must be filed to receive the refund. The IRS will assist individuals filing for the credit if they would like help.

Education Credits. The Hope Scholarship Credit applies to qualified tuition and expenses for the first 2 years of postsecondary education in a degree or certificate program at an eligible institution. However, it does not apply to room and board or cost of books. The credit can be as high as $1,500.

The Lifetime Learning Credit is available for taxpayers whose postsecondary education expenses are not eligible for the Hope credit. The credit is 20% of tuition and other qualifying expenses paid for by the taxpayer, spouse, or dependents. Starting in 2003, taxpayers can deduct up to $2,000 ($10,000 of expenses x 20%) for all entitled students who are enrolled in an eligible educational institution.

The Lifetime Learning Credit is allowed only for years in which the Hope credit is not used. Neither credit may be taken in any year in which funds are withdrawn from a Coverdell education savings account for the same expenses. The credit begins to phase out for higher income levels.

These credits are deducted from the individual's federal income tax and reported on Form 8863, Education Credits (Hope and Lifetime Learning Credits). Any credit exceeding the individual's tax liability is nonrefundable.

Taxable Social Security Benefits

Earnings Limitations. Starting in 2003, persons aged 62 to 65 lose $1 of their Social Security benefits for every $2 of earned income over $11,520. But persons 65 or over receiving Social Security benefits no longer are subject to an earnings limitation.

Taxable Benefits. Up to 50% of Social Security benefits may be taxable income if the person's total income is: over $25,000 but less than $34,000 for a single individual, head of household, qualifying widow(er), or a married person who is filing separately if spouses lived apart all year; or over $32,000 but less than $44,000 for married individuals filing jointly.

For incomes exceeding these maximums, 85% of Social Security benefits may become taxable. If a taxpayer is married and filing separately and lived with a spouse at any time during the year, the percentage amounts are reduced to zero.

Good News. *Social Security benefits are not taxable if they are the only income received during the year.*

Retirement Planning

The SIMPLE Plan. A popular retirement plan, the Savings Incentive Match Plan for Employees (SIMPLE), is available for businesses with 100 or fewer employees, including self-employed individuals. It is generally easier to implement and more cost-effective to administer than a traditional 401(k) plan.

For 2003, employees can defer up to $8,000 in compensation, an increase of $1,000 from 2002. There is an additional $1,000 catch-up for individuals age 50 and over. The Tax Relief Act of 2001 increases the amount annually thereafter by $1,000 until $10,000 is reached in 2005. A SIMPLE retirement plan can operate either as an IRA or as a 401(k). The tax liability on these amounts is deferred until a future date when the taxpayer draws the money out of the account.

Profit-Sharing Plans. This plan limits the total employer and employee contributions to the lesser of 25% of compensation or $40,000.

Age 70¾ Plus. The owner of a traditional IRA or a SIMPLE plan must begin receiving distributions from the IRA or SIMPLE by Apr. 1 of the calendar year following the year in which he or she reaches age 70¾, even if the individual is not retired. However, any employee who works beyond age 70¾ and is not a 5% or more owner of the business can continue to defer profit sharing and pension plan distributions.

Retired and Moved. States may not impose an income tax on retirement income if the person is no longer a resident.

IRS Tax Audit

The IRS projects that well over 130 million individual income tax returns will be filed in the year 2004. Fewer than 1 out of every 100 will be selected for audit.

The IRS said it audited 743,881 tax returns during 2002. Needless to say, the agency is very good at selecting returns that will yield additional taxes. If the IRS concludes that you owe more and you disagree with the findings, you can meet with a supervisor. If you still do not agree, you can appeal to a separate Appeals Office or to the U.S. Tax Court.

For more information about audits, call the IRS at 1-800-829-3676 for its free Publication 556, Examination of Returns, Appeal Rights, and Claims for Refund. Or visit www.irs.gov

Your Rights as a Taxpayer

Congress has enacted "taxpayer bill of rights" legislation and created an Office of the Taxpayer Advocate within the IRS, with authority to order IRS personnel to issue refund checks and meet deadlines for resolving disputes. Taxpayers Advocates can be contacted at 1-877-777-4778 (1-800-829-4059 for TTY/TDD). The IRS must pay legal fees if the taxpayer wins the case and the IRS cannot show it was "substantially justified" in pursuing it.

To confidentially report misconduct, waste, fraud, or abuse by an IRS employee, you can call 1-800-366-4484.

For more information ask for IRS Publication 1, Your Rights as a Taxpayer, by calling 1-800-TAX-FORM for a free copy.

Alternative Minimum Tax

The Alternative Minimum Tax (AMT) was established in 1969 to prevent people with very high incomes from using special tax breaks to pay little or no federal income tax. It was never indexed for inflation and, also because of various changes in the tax law, it affects more and more middle-income taxpayers every year, requiring them to pay higher taxes and do extra paperwork. The IRS estimates that about 2.7 million individuals are now impacted by the tax, and it is projected that the number could reach more than 30 million by 2010.

Many tax breaks—such as for incentive stock options or accelerated depreciation on certain kinds of property—do mostly hit wealthy taxpayers or businesses, but affected middle-class taxpayers can also lose the benefits of certain very ordinary deductions, such as for state and local income taxes.

The IRS provides a worksheet in the Form 1040A and 1040 instructions to help you determine whether you are hit by the AMT. If so, you need to fill out Form 6251, Alternative Minimum Tax, to figure out how much tax you owe.

Federal Outlays to States Per Dollar of Tax Revenue Received

Source: The Tax Foundation
(figures for fiscal year 2002; ranked highest to lowest)

State	Outlay	State	Outlay	State	Outlay	State	Outlay	State	Outlay
District of Columbia	$6.44	Arkansas	$1.55	Maryland	$1.22	Ohio	$1.03	Delaware	$0.85
New Mexico	2.37	Oklahoma	1.52	Arizona	1.21	Georgia	1.01	Colorado	0.78
North Dakota	2.07	Virginia	1.50	Nebraska	1.19	Florida	1.01	Minnesota	0.77
Alaska	1.91	Kentucky	1.50	Utah	1.14	Indiana	1.00	Illinois	0.77
Mississippi	1.89	Louisiana	1.48	Kansas	1.13	Oregon	0.98	California	0.76
West Virginia	1.82	South Carolina	1.34	Vermont	1.13	Texas	0.92	Massachusetts	0.75
Montana	1.67	Maine	1.34	Pennsylvania	1.09	Wisconsin	0.88	Nevada	0.74
Alabama	1.64	Missouri	1.34	Rhode Island	1.08	Michigan	0.88	New Hampshire	0.66
South Dakota	1.61	Idaho	1.31	North Carolina	1.07	Washington	0.87	Connecticut	0.65
Hawaii	1.57	Tennessee	1.26	Wyoming	1.06	New York	0.85	New Jersey	0.62
		Iowa	1.23						

Tax Burden in Selected Countries[1]

Source: Organization for Economic Cooperation and Development, 2002

Country	Income tax (%)	Social Security (%)	Total payment[2] (%)	Country	Income tax (%)	Social Security (%)	Total payment[2] (%)	Country	Income tax (%)	Social Security (%)	Total payment[2] (%)
Denmark	33	11	43	France	13	13	27	New Zealand	20	0	20
Belgium	28	14	41	Canada	19	7	26	Slovak Republic	7	13	19
Germany	21	21	41	Australia	24	0	24	Spain	13	6	19
Finland	26	6	32	Czech Republic	11	13	24	Greece	1	16	17
Poland	6	25	31	United States	17	8	24	Portugal	6	11	17
Sweden	23	7	30	United Kingdom	16	8	23	Ireland	11	5	16
Turkey	15	15	30	Iceland	22	0	22	Japan	6	10	16
Netherlands	7	22	29	Luxembourg	8	14	22	Korea	2	7	9
Norway	21	8	29	Switzerland	10	12	22	Mexico	2	2	4
Austria	11	18	29								
Hungary	17	13	29								
Italy	19	9	28								

(1) Does not include taxes not listed, such as sales tax or VAT. Rates shown apply to a single person with average earnings. (2) Totals may not add due to rounding.

State Government Personal Income Tax Rates, 2003

Source: Reproduced with permission from *CCH State Tax Guide*, published and copyrighted by CCH Inc., 2700 Lake Cook Road, Riverwoods, IL 60015
Below are basic state tax rates on taxable income, for 2003 unless otherwise indicated. Alaska, Florida, Nevada, South Dakota, Texas, Washington, and Wyoming did not have state income taxes and are thus not listed. Tax rates apply in stages—for example, a single person in Arizona making $60,000 in taxable income would pay 2.87% on the first $10,000 of income, 3.2% on the next $15,000, etc. For further details, see notes at end of table.

Alabama
Single, Head of household, & Married filing separately
$0 to $500	2%
$501 to $3,000	4%
$3,001 and over	5%

Married filing jointly
$0 to $1,000	2%
$1,001 to $6,000	4%
$6,001 and over	5%

Arizona[1]
Single & Married filing separately
$0 to $10,000	2.87%
$10,001 to $25,000	3.2%
$25,001 to $50,000	3.74%
$50,001 to $150,000	4.72%
$150,001 and over	5.04%

Married filing jointly and Head of household
$0 to $20,000	2.87%
$20,001 to $50,000	3.2%
$50,001 to $100,000	3.74%
$100,001 to $300,000	4.72%
$300,001 and over	5.04%

Arkansas[2,3]
Single, Head of household, Married filing jointly, & Married filing separately
$0 to $3,299	1%
$3,300 to $6,599	2.5%
$6,600 to $9,899	3.5%
$9,900 to $16,499	4.5%
$16,500 to $27,499	6%
$27,500 and over	7%

California[1,2]
Single or Married filing separately
$0 to $5,962	1%
$5,963 to $14,133	2%
$14,134 to $22,306	4%
$22,307 to $30,965	6%
$30,966 to $39,133	8%
$39,134 and over	9.3%

Head of household
$0 to $11,930	1%
$11,931 to $28,267	2%
$28,268 to $36,437	4%
$36,438 to $45,096	6%
$45,097 to $53,267	8%
$53,268 and over	9.3%

Married filing jointly
$0 to $11,924	1%
$11,925 to $28,266	2%
$28,267 to $44,612	4%
$44,613 to $61,930	6%
$61,931 to $78,266	8%
$78,267 and over	9.3%

Colorado
4.63% of federal taxable income.

Connecticut
Single & Married filing separately
$0 to $10,000	3%
$10,001 and over	5%

Head of household
$0 to $16,000	3%
$16,001 and over	5%

Married filing jointly
$0 to $20,000	3%
$20,001 and over	5%

Delaware
Single, Head of household, Married filing jointly, & Married filing separately
$2,000 to $5,000	2.2%
$5,001 to $10,000	3.9%
$10,001 to $20,000	4.8%
$20,001 to $25,000	5.2%
$25,001 to $60,000	5.55%
$60,001 and over	5.95%

District of Columbia
Single, Head of household, Married filing jointly, & Married filing separately
$0 to $10,000	5%
$10,001 to $30,000	7.5%
$30,001 and over	9.3%

Georgia
Single
$0 to $750	1%
$751 to $2,250	2%
$2,251 to $3,750	3%
$3,751 to $5,250	4%
$5,251 to $7,000	5%
$7,001 and over	6%

Head of household & Married filing jointly
$0 to $1,000	1%
$1,001 to $3,000	2%
$3,001 to $5,000	3%
$5,001 to $7,000	4%
$7,001 to $10,000	5%
$10,001 and over	6%

Married filing separately
$0 to $500	1%
$501 to $1,500	2%
$1,501 to $2,500	3%
$2,501 to $3,500	4%
$3,501 to $5,000	5%
$5,001 and over	6%

Hawaii
Single & Married filing separately
$0 to $2,000	1.4%
$2,001 to $4,000	3.2%
$4,001 to $8,000	5.5%
$8,001 to $12,000	6.4%
$12,001 to $16,000	6.8%
$16,001 to $20,000	7.2%
$20,001 to $30,000	7.6%
$30,001 to $40,000	7.9%
$40,001 and over	8.25%

Head of household
$0 to $3,000	1.4%
$3,001 to $6,000	3.2%
$6,001 to $12,000	5.5%
$12,001 to $18,000	6.4%
$18,001 to $24,000	6.8%
$24,001 to $30,000	7.2%
$30,001 to $45,000	7.6%
$45,001 to $60,000	7.9%
$60,001 and over	8.25%

Married filing jointly
$0 to $4,000	1.4%
$4,001 to $8,000	3.2%
$8,001 to $16,000	5.5%
$16,001 to $24,000	6.4%
$24,001 to $32,000	6.8%
$32,001 to $40,000	7.2%
$40,001 to $60,000	7.6%
$60,001 to $80,000	7.9%
$80,001 and over	8.25%

Idaho[1,2]
Single & Married filing separately
$0 to $1,104	1.6%
$1,105 to $2,207	3.6%
$2,208 to $3,311	4.1%
$3,312 to $4,415	5.1%
$4,416 to $5,518	6.1%
$5,519 to $8,278	7.1%
$8,279 to $22,074	7.4%
$22,075 and over	7.8%

Head of household & Married filing jointly
$0 to $2,208	1.6%
$2,209 to $4,414	3.6%
$4,415 to $6,622	4.1%
$6,623 to $8,830	5.1%
$8,831 to $11,036	6.1%
$11,037 to $16,556	7.1%
$16,557 to $44,148	7.4%
$44,149 and over	7.8%

Illinois
3% of taxable net income

Indiana
3.4% of adjusted gross income

Iowa[2,3]
Single, Head of household, Married filing jointly, & Married filing separately
$0 to $1,211	0.36%
$1,212 to $2,422	0.72%
$2,423 to $4,844	2.43%
$4,845 to $10,899	4.5%

$10,900 to $18,165	6.12%
$18,166 to $24,200	6.48%
$24,201 to $36,330	6.8%
$36,331 to $54,495	7.92%
$54,496 and over	8.98%

Kansas
Single, Head of household, & Married filing separately
$0 to $15,000	3.5%
$15,001 to $30,000	6.25%
$30,001 and over	6.45%

Married filing jointly
$0 to $30,000	3.5%
$30,001 to $60,000	6.25%
$60,001 and over	6.45%

Kentucky
Single, Head of household, Married filing jointly, & Married filing separately
$0 to $3,000	2%
$3,001 to $4,000	3%
$4,001 to $5,000	4%
$5,001 to $8,000	5%
$8,001 and over	6%

Louisiana[1]
Single, Head of household, Married filing jointly, & Married filing separately
$0 to $12,500	2%
$12,501 to $25,000	4%
$25,001 and over	6%

Maine[2,3]
Single & Married filing separately
$0 to $4,250	2%
$4,251 to $8,450	4.5%
$8,451 to $16,950	7%
$16,951 and over	8.5%

Head of household
$0 to $6,400	2%
$6,401 to $12,700	4.5%
$12,701 to $25,450	7%
$25,451 and over	8.5%

Married filing jointly
$0 to $8,500	2%
$8,501 to $16,950	4.5%
$16,951 to $33,950	7%
$33,951 and over	8.5%

Maryland
Single, Head of household, Married filing jointly, & Married filing separately
$0 to $1,000	2%
$1,001 to $2,000	3%
$2,001 to $3,000	4%
$3,001 and over	4.75%

Massachusetts
Interest, dividends, short-term capital gains	12%
Several classes of capital gain income	0% to 5%
All other income	5.3%

Michigan
4% of taxable income

Minnesota[2]
Single
$0 to $19,010	5.35%
$19,011 to $62,440	7.05%
$62,441 and over	7.85%

Head of household
$0 to $23,400	5.35%
$23,401 to $94,030	7.05%
$94,031 and over	7.85%

Married filing jointly
$0 to $27,780	5.35%
$27,781 to $110,390	7.05%
$110,391 and over	7.85%

Married filing separately
$0 to $13,890	5.35%
$13,891 to $55,200	7.05%
$55,201 and over	7.85%

Mississippi
Single, Head of household, Married filing jointly, & Married filing separately
$0 to $5,000	3%
$5,001 to $10,000	4%

$10,001 and over	5%

Missouri
Single, Head of household, Married filing jointly, & Married filing separately
$0 to $1,000	1.5%
$1,001 to $2,000	2%
$2,001 to $3,000	2.5%
$3,001 to $4,000	3%
$4,001 to $5,000	3.5%
$5,001 to $6,000	4%
$6,001 to $7,000	4.5%
$7,001 to $8,000	5%
$8,001 to $9,000	5.5%
$9,001 and over	6%

Montana[2,3]
Single, Head of household, Married filing jointly, & Married filing separately
$0 to $2,199	2%
$2,200 to $4,399	3%
$4,400 to $8,699	4%
$8,700 to $13,099	5%
$13,100 to $17,399	6%
$17,400 to $21,799	7%
$21,800 to $30,499	8%
$30,500 to $43,499	9%
$43,500 to $76,199	10%
$76,200 and over	11%

Nebraska
Single
$0 to $2,400	2.56%
$2,401 to $17,000	3.57%
$17,001 to $26,500	5.12%
$26,501 and over	6.84%

Head of household
$0 to $3,800	2.56%
$3,801 to $24,000	3.57%
$24,001 to $35,000	5.12%
$35,001 and over	6.84%

Married filing jointly
$0 to $4,000	2.56%
$4,001 to $30,000	3.57%
$30,001 to $46,750	5.12%
$46,751 and over	6.84%

Married filing separately
$0 to $2,000	2.56%
$2,001 to $15,000	3.57%
$15,001 to $23,375	5.12%
$23,376 and over	6.84%

New Hampshire
5% on interest and dividends only

New Jersey
Single & Married filing separately
$0 to $20,000	1.4%
$20,001 to $35,000	1.75%
$35,001 to $40,000	3.5%
$40,001 to $75,000	5.525%
$75,001 and over	6.37%

Head of household & Married filing jointly
$0 to $20,000	1.4%
$20,001 to $50,000	1.75%
$50,001 to $70,000	2.45%
$70,001 to $80,000	3.5%
$80,001 to $150,000	5.525%
$150,001 and over	6.37%

New Mexico[1]
Single
$0 to $5,500	1.7%
$5,501 to $11,000	3.2%
$11,001 to $16,000	4.7%
$16,001 to $26,000	6%
$26,001 to $42,000	7.1%
$42,001 and over	7.7%

Head of household
$0 to $7,000	1.7%
$7,001 to $14,000	3.2%
$14,001 to $20,000	4.7%
$20,001 to $33,000	6%
$33,001 to $53,000	7.1%
$53,001 and over	7.7%

Married filing jointly
$0 to $8,000	1.7%
$8,001 to $16,000	3.2%
$16,001 to $24,000	4.7%

$24,001 to $40,000 . . . . . 6%
$40,001 to $64,000 . . . 7.1%
$64,001 and over 7.7%
Married filing separately
$0 to $4,000 . . . . 1.7%
$4,001 to $8,000. . . . . . 3.2%
$8,001 to $12,000. . . . . 4.7%
$12,001 to $20,000. . . . . 6%
$20,001 to $32,000. . . . 7.1%
$32,001 and over 7.7%

New York
Single & Married filing separately
$0 to $8,000 . . . . 4%
$8,001 to $11,000 . . . . 4.5%
$11,001 to $13,000 . . 5.25%
$13,001 to $20,000 . . . 5.9%
$20,001 to $100,000. 6.85%
$100,001 to $500,000. 7.5%
$500,001 and over7.7%
Head of household
$0 to $11,000 . . . . 4%
$11,001 to $15,000. . . . 4.5%
$15,001 to $17,000. . . 5.25%
$17,001 to $30,000. . . . 5.9%
$30,001 to $125,000. 6.85%
$125,001 to $500,000. 7.5%
$500,001 and over . . . 7.7%
Married filing jointly
$0 to $16,000. . . . . 4%
$16,001 to $22,000. . . . 4.5%
$22,001 to $26,000. . . 5.25%
$26,001 to $40,000. . . . 5.9%
$40,001 to $150,000. 6.85%
$150,001 to $500,000. 7.5%
$500,001 and over . . . 7.7%

North Carolina
Single
$0 to $12,750 . . . . . . 6%
$12,751 to $60,000. . . . . 7%
$60,001 to $120,000. 7.75%
$120,001 and over . . 8.25%
Head of household
$0 to $17,000 . . . . . . 6%
$17,001 to $80,000. . . . . 7%
$80,001 to $160,000. 7.75%
$160,001 and over . . 8.25%
Married filing jointly
$0 to $21,250. . . . . . . 6%
$21,251 to $100,000. . . . 7%
$100,001 to $200,000 7.75%
$200,001 and over . . 8.25%
Married filing separately
$0 to $10,625 . . . . . . 6%
$10,626 to $50,000. . . . . 7%
$50,001 to $100,000. 7.75%
$100,001 and over . . 8.25%

North Dakota[2,3]
Single
$0 to $28,400 . . . . . . 2.1%
$28,401 to $68,800. . 3.92%
$68,801 to $143,500. 4.34%
$143,501 to $311,950 5.04%
$311,951 and over . . 5.54%
Head of Household
$0 to $38,050 . . . . . . 2.1%
$38,051 to $98,250. . 3.92%
$98,251 to $159,100. 4.34%
$159,101 to $311,950 5.04%
$311,951 and over . . 5.54%
Married filing jointly
$0 to $47,450. . . . . . . 2.1%
$47,451 to $114,650. 3.92%
$114,651 to $174,700 4.34%
$174,701 to $311,950 5.04%
$311,951 and over . . 5.54%
Married filing separately
$0 to $23,725. . . . . . . 2.1%
$23,726 to $57,325. . 3.92%
$57,326 to $87,350. . 4.34%
$87,351 to $155,975. 5.04%
$155,976 and over . . 5.54%

Ohio
Single, Head of household, Married filing jointly, & Married filing separately
$0 to $5,000 . . . . . 0.743%
$5,001 to $10,000. . . 1.486%
$10,001 to $15,000. . 2.972%
$15,001 to $20,000. . 3.715%
$20,001 to $40,000. . 4.457%
$40,001 to $80,000. . 5.201%
$80,001 to $100,000 5.943%
$100,001 to $200,000. 6.9%
$200,001 and over . . . 7.5%

Oklahoma
Single & Married filing separately
$0 to $1,000 . . . . 0.5%
$1,001 to $2,500. . . . . . 1%
$2,501 to $3,750. . . . . . 2%
$3,751 to $4,900. . . . . . 3%
$4,901 to $6,200. . . . . . 4%
$6,201 to $7,700. . . . . . 5%
$7,701 to $10,000. . . . . 6%
$10,001 and over 7%
Head of household & Married filing jointly
$0 to $2,000 . . . . 0.5%
$2,001 to $5,000. . . . . . 1%
$5,001 to $7,500. . . . . . 2%
$7,501 to $9,800. . . . . . 3%
$9,801 to $12,200. . . . . 4%
$12,201 to $15,000. . . . 5%
$15,001 to $21,000. . . . 6%
$21,001 and over 7%

Oregon[2,3]
Single & Married filing separately
$0 to $2,550 . . . . .5%
$2,551 to $6,350. . . . . . .7%
$6,351 and over 9%
Married filing jointly and Head of household
$0 to $5,100 . . . . .5%
$5,101 to $12,700. . . . . .7%
$12,701 and over 9%

Pennsylvania
2.8% of taxable compensation, net profits, net gains from the sale of property, rent, royalties, dividends, interest, etc.

Rhode Island
Generally, 25% of the federal income tax rates, including capital gains and other special rates for types of income in effect before enactment of the 2001 Economic Growth and Tax Relief Reconciliation Act

South Carolina[2,3]
Single, Head of household, Married filing jointly, & Married filing separately
$0 to $2,460 . . . . 2.5%
$2,461 to $4,920. . . . . . 3%
$4,921 to $7,380. . . . . . 4%
$7,381 to $9,840. . . . . . 5%
$9,841 to $12,300. . . . . 6%
$12,301 and over 7%

Tennessee
6% of interest and dividends

Utah
Single & Married filing separately
$0 to $863. . . . . 2.3%
$864 to $1,726 . . . . . . 3.3%
$1,727 to $2,588. . . . . 4.2%
$2,589 to $3,450. . . . . 5.2%
$3,451 to $4,313. . . . . . .6%
$4,314 and over 7%
Head of household & Married filing jointly
$0 to $1,726 . . . . 2.3%
$1,727 to $3,450. . . . . 3.3%
$3,451 to $5,176. . . . . 4.2%
$5,177 to $6,900. . . . . 5.2%
$6,901 to $8,626. . . . . . .6%
$8,627 and over 7%

Vermont[2,3]
Single
$0 to $27,950 . . . . . . 3.6%
$27,951 to $67,700. . . 7.2%
$67,701 to $141,250. . 8.5%
$141,251 to $307,050. 9.0%
$307,051 and over 9.5%
Head of Household
$0 to $37,450 . . . . . . 3.6%
$37,451 to $96,700. . . 7.2%
$96,701 to $156,600. . 8.5%
$156,601 to $307,050. 9.0%
$307,051 and over . . . 9.5%
Married filing jointly
$0 to $46,700. . . . . . . 3.6%
$46,701 to $112,850. . 7.2%
$112,851 to $171,950. 8.5%
$171,951 to $307,050. 9.0%
$307,051 and over . . . 9.5%
Married filing separately
$0 to $23,350. . . . . . . 3.6%
$23,351 to $56,425. . . 7.2%
$56,426 to $85,975. . . 8.5%
$85,976 to $153,525. . 9.0%
$153,526 and over . . . 9.5%

Virginia
Single, Head of household, Married filing jointly, & Married filing separately
$0 to $3,000 . . . . .2%
$3,001 to $5,000. . . . . . .3%
$5,001 to $17,000. . . . . .5%
$17,001 and over 5.75%

West Virginia
Single, Head of household, & Married filing jointly
$0 to $10,000 . . . . .3%
$10,001 to $25,000. . . . .4%
$25,001 to $40,000. . . 4.5%
$40,001 to $60,000. . . . .6%
$60,001 and over 6.5%
Married filing separately
$0 to $5,000 . . . . .3%
$5,001 to $12,500. . . . . .4%
$12,501 to $20,000. . . 4.5%
$20,001 to $30,000. . . . .6%
$30,001 and over 6.5%

Wisconsin[1,2]
Single and Head of household
$0 to $8,430 . . . . 4.6%
$8,431 to $16,860. . . 6.15%
$16,861 to $126,420. . 6.5%
$126,421 and over . . 6.75%
Married filing jointly
$0 to $11,240 . . . . . . 4.6%
$11,241 to $22,480. . 6.15%
$22,481 to $168,560. . 6.5%
$168,561 and over . . 6.75%
Married filing separately
$0 to $5,620 . . . . 4.6%
$5,621 to $11,240. . . 6.15%
$11,241 to $84,280. . . 6.5%
$84,281 and over . . . 6.75%

(1) Community property states in which one-half of the community income is usually taxable to each spouse. (2) Brackets indexed for inflation annually. (3) 2003 adjusted brackets not currently available. Bracketed rates listed are for 2002. **Colorado:** Alternative minimum tax imposed. Qualified taxpayers may pay alternative tax of 0.5% of gross receipts from sales. **Connecticut:** Resident estates and trusts are subject to the 5% income tax rate on all of their income. Additional state minimum tax imposed on resident individuals, trusts, and estates is equal to the amount by which the minimum tax exceeds the basic income tax (the lesser of (a) 19% of adjusted federal tentative minimum tax, or (b) 5.5% of adjusted federal alternative minimum taxable income). Separate provisions apply for non- and part-year-resident individuals, trusts and estates. **District of Columbia:** Minimum tax is $100. **Idaho:** Each person (joint returns deemed one person) filing a return pays additional $10. **Illinois:** Additional personal property replacement tax of 1.5% of net income is imposed on partnerships, trusts, and S corporations. **Indiana:** Counties may impose an adjusted gross income tax on residents at .5%, .75% or 1% and at .25% on nonresidents or a county option income tax at rates ranging between .2% and 1%, with the rate on nonresidents equal to one-fourth of the rate on residents. **Iowa:** An alternative minimum tax is imposed equal to 75% of the maximum state individual income tax rate for the tax year of the state alternative minimum taxable income. **Louisiana:** The amount of tax due is determined from tax tables. These amounts are doubled (rates remain the same) for taxpayers filing joint returns. **Maine:** Additional state minimum tax is imposed equal to the amount by which the state minimum tax (27% of adjusted federal tentative minimum tax) exceeds Maine income tax liability, other than withholding tax liability. **Michigan:** Persons with business activity allocated or apportioned to Michigan are also subject to a single business tax on an adjusted tax base. **Minnesota:** A 6.4% alternative minimum tax is imposed. **Montana:** Minimum tax, $1. **Nebraska:** The tax rates in the schedules are determined by multiplying the primary rate set by the legislature by the following factors for the brackets, from lowest to highest bracket. For tax years beginning on January 1, 2003, and before January 1, 2004, the respective factors are: 0.6932, 0.9646, 1.3846, and 1.848. For tax years beginning before January 1, 2003, and for tax years beginning on or after January 1, 2004, the respective factors are: 0.6784, 0.9432, 1.3541, and 1.8054. The figure obtained for each bracket is rounded to the nearest tenth of 1%. One rate schedule is to be established for each federal filing status (Sec. 77-2715.02). **New Mexico:** Qualified taxpayers may pay alternative tax of 0.75% of gross receipts for New Mexico sales. **New York:** Applicable to taxable years beginning after 2002 and before 2006, the tax table benefit is the difference between the amount of taxable income in the tax table in Sec. 601(a) not subject to the 2nd-highest rate of tax for the taxable year multiplied by such rate and (b) the 2nd-highest dollar-denominated tax for such amount set forth in the tax table applicable to the taxable year in Sec. 601(a) less the tax table benefit in Sec. 601(d)(1). The fraction is as follows: the numerator is the lessor of $50,000 or the excess of sate adjusted gross income for the taxable year over $150,000, and the denominator is $50,000. Also applicable to taxable years beginning 2002 and before 2006, the tax table benefit is the difference between the amount of taxable income in the tax table in Sec. 601(a) not subject to the 2nd-highest rate of tax for the taxable year multiplied by such rate and (b) the 2nd-highest dollar-denominated tax for such amount set forth in the tax table applicable to the taxable year in Sec. 601(a) less the sum of tax table benefits in Sec. 601(d)(1) and (2). For taxpayers with adjusted gross income over $500,000, the fraction is one. **Oklahoma:** Rates given are for taxpayers not deducting federal income tax. Rates for married individuals filing jointly, surviving spouses and heads of households deducting federal income tax range from .50% of the first $2,000 to 10% of income over $24,000. For single individuals and married individuals filing separately deducting federal income tax, rates range from .50% of the first $1,000 to 10% of income over $16,000. **Wisconsin:** A temporary recycling surcharge is imposed on individuals, estates, partnerships, trusts, and exempt trusts, except those entities engaged only in farming, at the rate of the greater of $25 or .2173% of net business income. The maximum surcharge is $9,800. An individual, estate, trust, exempt trust, or partnership engaged in farming is subject to a surcharge of $25.

TRAVEL AND TOURISM

Tourism Trends

After falling by 0.5% in 2001, world tourist arrivals regained momentum in 2002 and grew by 2.8%, according to the World Tourism Organization based in Madrid, Spain. Worldwide, there were 703 million international tourist arrivals in 2002, 19 million more than in 2001. Worldwide tourism receipts rose by 3.2%, from $459 billion in 2001 to $474 billion in 2002. Europe commanded the largest share of the tourism market, about 57% of the world total, with 399.8 million international tourist arrivals, a slight increase of 2.3%. With 19% of the world total, Asia and the Pacific overtook the Americas for the second-largest share, growing by 8.4% with about 131 million arrivals in 2002. Africa saw 29 million arrivals, up 2.8%, mainly in the south. The Middle East had 27.6 million arrivals, an 18.4% increase from 2001. With about 115 million arrivals, the Americas were the only regions that experienced a decline in tourism in 2002, down by about 4.3% from 2001.

In the first half of 2003, the SARS outbreak and the war in Iraq led to decreased tourism arrivals, especially in Asia and North America. The International Air Transport Assoc., which measures air passenger traffic in revenue passenger kilometers, reported a 6.5% decline in passenger traffic in Jan.-July 2003, compared with the same period in 2002. Asia and North America had the largest such declines, at –15.5% and –10.6%, respectively. According to the Air Transport Assoc. of America, air passenger traffic in the U.S. (measured in revenue passenger miles) fell 2.3% in 2002, but had stabilized by Aug. 2003. The Travel Industry Assoc. of America reported that average airfares in the U.S. had risen 1.2% in Aug. 2003, compared with Aug. 2002 levels.

World Tourism Receipts, 1990-2002

Source: World Tourism Organization

(in billions; figures rounded)

1990 . . . . . $264	1993 . . . . $323	1995 . . . $405	1997 . . . $443	1999 . . . . $455	2001 . . . . $459
1991 278	1994 356	1996 439	1998 . . . 445	2000 473	2002 474
1992 317					

World's Top 10 Tourist Destinations, 2002

Source: World Tourism Organization

(number of arrivals in millions; excluding same-day visitors)

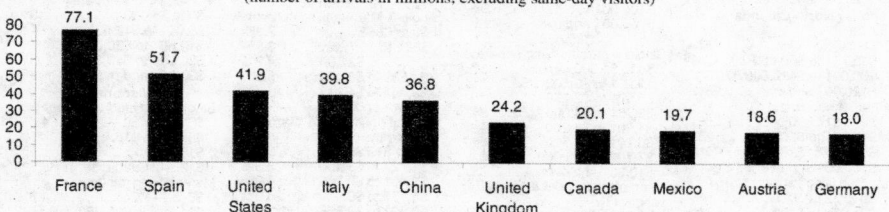

France 77.1, Spain 51.7, United States 41.9, Italy 39.8, China 36.8, United Kingdom 24.2, Canada 20.1, Mexico 19.7, Austria 18.6, Germany 18.0

Top Countries in Tourism Earnings, 2002

Source: World Tourism Organization

International tourism receipts (excluding transportation); in billions of dollars

Rank	Country	Receipts 2001	Receipts 2002	% change		Rank	Country	Receipts 2001	Receipts 2002	% change
1.	United States	$72.3	$66.5	–7.4		9.	Hong Kong, China . .	$8.2	$10.1	22.2
2.	Spain	32.9	33.6	2.2		10.	Greece	9.1	9.7	3.1
3.	France	29.6	32.3	7.8		11.	Mexico	8.4	8.9	5.4
4.	Italy	25.9	26.9	4.3		12.	Canada	10.8	8.7	–19.3
5.	China[1]	17.8	20.4	14.6		13.	Turkey	8.9	8.5	4.8
6.	Germany	17.2	19.2	4.0		14.	Australia	7.6	8.1	6.1
7.	United Kingdom . . .	15.9	17.8	9.5		15.	Thailand	7.0	7.9	11.7
8.	Austria	12.0	11.2	11.1						

(1) Excluding Hong Kong.

Average Number of Vacation Days per Year, Selected Countries

Source: World Tourism Organization

Country	Days	Country	Days	Country	Days
Italy	42	Brazil	34	Korea	25
France	37	United Kingdom	28	Japan	25
Germany	35	Canada	26	United States	13

International Travel to the U.S., 1986-2002

Source: Tourism Industries, International Trade Administration, Dept. of Commerce

(Visitors each year are in millions; some figures are revised and may differ from other sources.)

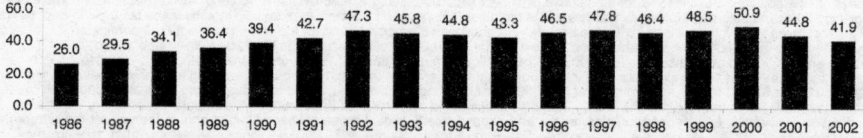

1986: 26.0, 1987: 29.5, 1988: 34.1, 1989: 36.4, 1990: 39.4, 1991: 42.7, 1992: 47.3, 1993: 45.8, 1994: 44.8, 1995: 43.3, 1996: 46.5, 1997: 47.8, 1998: 46.4, 1999: 48.5, 2000: 50.9, 2001: 44.8, 2002: 41.9

International Visitors to the U.S., 2001[1]

Source: Tourism Industries, International Trade Administration, Dept. of Commerce

Country of origin	Visitors (thousands)	Expenditures (millions)[2]	Expenditures per visitor	Country of origin	Visitors (thousands)	Expenditures (millions)[2]	Expenditures per visitor
Canada........	13,507	$6,484	$480	South Korea....	618	$1,928	$3,120
Mexico........	9,558	5,320	557	Venezuela.....	555	1,824	3,286
United Kingdom.	4,097	9,191	2,243	Brazil.........	551	1,862	3,379
Japan.........	4,083	8,899	2,180	Italy..........	472	1,181	2,502
Germany......	1,314	2,965	2,256				
France........	876	2,284	2,607	All countries...	44,898	$73.12 bil[3]	$1,629

(1) Excludes cruise travel. (2) Excludes international passenger fare payments. (3) Does not include international traveler spending on U.S. carriers for transactions made outside the U.S.

Traveler Spending in the U.S., 1987-2002

Source: Tourism Industries, International Trade Administration, Dept. of Commerce

(in billions)

	Domestic Travelers	International Travelers		Domestic Travelers	International Travelers		Domestic Travelers	International Travelers
1987.....	$235	$31	1993.....	$323	$58	1998	$425	$71
1988.....	258	38	1994.....	340	58	1999	458	75
1989.....	273	47	1995.....	360	63	2000	488	82
1990.....	291	43	1996.....	385	70	2001	464	72
1991.....	296	48	1997.....	406	73	2002	NA	67*
1992.....	306	55						

* Preliminary figure. NA = Not available

U.S. Domestic Leisure Travel Volume, 1994-2002

Source: "Tourism Works for America," 2003 edition, Travel Industry Assn. of America

(in millions of person-trips of 50 mi or more, one-way)

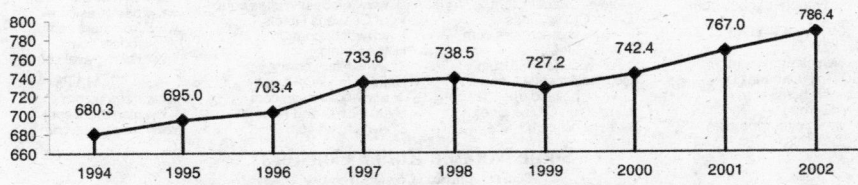

1994	1995	1996	1997	1998	1999	2000	2001	2002
680.3	695.0	703.4	733.6	738.5	727.2	742.4	767.0	786.4

Top U.S. States by Domestic Traveler Spending, 2001

Source: Travel Industry Assn. of America

(billions of dollars)

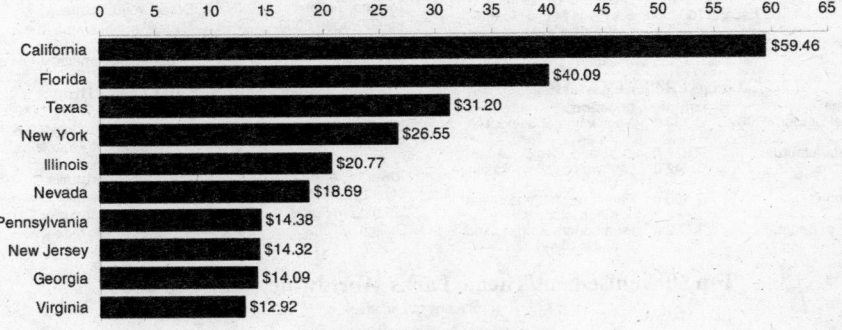

State	Spending
California	$59.46
Florida	$40.09
Texas	$31.20
New York	$26.55
Illinois	$20.77
Nevada	$18.69
Pennsylvania	$14.38
New Jersey	$14.32
Georgia	$14.09
Virginia	$12.92

Top 15 Travel Websites

Source: comScore Media Metrix

Rank		Visitors[1]	Rank		Visitors[1]	Rank		Visitors[1]
1.	www.mapquest.com..	75,307,000	6.	hotels.com sites.....	14,560,000	11.	travel.yahoo.com....	6,249,000
2.	www.expedia.com...	32,252,000	7.	www.hotwire.com...	9,383,000	12.	delta.com.........	5,968,000
3.	www.orbitz.com.....	19,083,000	8.	AOL Proprietary Travel	8,720,000	13.	www.aa.com.......	4,662,000
4.	Trip Network, Inc....	15,581,000	9.	www.priceline.com...	7,699,000	14.	tripadvisor.com.....	3,950,000
5.	www.travelocity.com..	14,693,000	10.	www.southwest.com .	7,596,000	15.	www.ual.com.......	3,758,000

(1) Number of users who visited at least once in July 2003.

WORLD ALMANAC QUICK QUIZ

In which of these countries do workers enjoy the highest average number of annual vacation days?

(a) France   (b) Korea   (c) Italy   (d) United Kingdom

For the answer look in this chapter, or see page 1008.

▶ **IT'S A FACT:** According to Cruise Lines International Assoc., the number of passengers from North America taking cruises each year increased from 1.43 million in 1980 to 7.64 million in 2002. The average cruise in 2002 lasted 7 days.

Travel Websites

The following websites are among those that may be of use in planning trips and making arrangements. Websites listed under "Maps" enable the user to plot a route to a destination. Inclusion here does not represent endorsement by *The World Almanac*.

AIRLINES
American Airlines
  www.aa.com
America West Airlines
  www.americawest.com
Continental Airlines
  www.continental.com
Delta Air Lines
  www.delta.com
Northwest Airlines
  www.nwa.com
Southwest Airlines
  www.southwest.com
United Airlines
  www.ual.com
USAirways
  www.usair.com

BUSES
Gray Line Worldwide
  www.grayline.com
Greyhound Lines
  www.greyhound.com
Peter Pan Bus Lines
  www.peterpanbus.com

TRAINS
Amtrak
  www.amtrak.com
BC Rail (Canada)
  www.bcrail.com
Rail Europe
  www.raileurope.com

CAR RENTALS
Alamo Rent A Car
  www.goalamo.com
Avis Rent-A-Car
  www.avis.com
Budget Rent A Car
  www.budget.com
Dollar Rent A Car
  www.dollarcar.com
Enterprise Rent-A-Car
  www.enterprise.com
Hertz
  www.hertz.com
National Car Rental
  www.nationalcar.com
Rent-A-Wreck
  www.rentawreck.com
Thrifty Rent-A-Car
  www.thrifty.com

CRUISE LINES
Carnival Cruise Lines
  www.carnival.com
Celebrity Cruises
  www.celebrity.com
Costa Cruise Lines
  www.costacruises.com
Cunard Line
  www.cunardline.com
Holland America Line
  www.hollandamerica.com
Norwegian Cruise Line
  www.ncl.com

Princess Cruises
  www.princess.com
Royal Caribbean Int'l.
  www.rccl.com
Windjammer Barefoot Cruises
  www.windjammer.com

HOTELS/RESORTS
Best Western Int'l.
  www.bestwestern.com
Choice Hotels Int'l.,
  Clarion Hotels & Resorts,
  Comfort Inns,
  Econo Lodges,
  MainStay Suites,
  Quality Inns,
  Rodeway Inns,
  Sleep Inns
  www.hotelchoice.com
Days Inn of America
  www.daysinn.com
Doubletree Hotels
  www.doubletree.com
Embassy Suites
  www.embassysuites.com
Four Seasons Hotels
  www.fshr.com
Hilton Hotels
  www.hilton.com
Holiday Inn Worldwide
  www.holidayinn.com
Hyatt Hotels and Resorts
  www.hyatt.com

Hotels.com
  www.hotels.com
Inter-Continental Hotels
  www.interconti.com
Loews Hotels
  www.loewshotels.com
Marriott Int'l.
  www.marriott.com
Radisson Hotels Int'l.
  www.radisson.com
Sheraton Hotels & Resorts
  www.sheraton.com
Westin Hotels & Resorts
  www.westin.com
Wyndham Hotels & Resorts
  www.wyndham.com

TRAVEL PLANNING
www.travelocity.com
www.priceline.com
www.expedia.com
www.itn.net (American Express)
www.lowestfare.com
www.cheaptickets.com
www.bestfares.com
www.frommers.com
www.fodors.com
www.libertytravel.com

MAPS
www.freetrip.com
www.mapquest.com
www.mapsonus.com

Some Notable Roller Coasters

Source: American Coasters Network

Fastest Roller Coasters

Name	Speed	Location
Top Thrill Dragster	120 mph	Cedar Point; Sandusky, OH
Dodonpa	107 mph	Fujikyu Highland; Yamanashi, Japan
Tower of Terror	100 mph	Dreamworld; Australia
Superman The Escape	100 mph	Six Flags Magic Mountain; Valencia, CA
Steel Dragon 2000	95 mph	Nagashima Spaland; Mie, Japan

Longest Roller Coasters

Name	Length	Location
Steel Dragon 2000	8,133 ft	Nagashima Spaland; Mie, Japan
Daidarasaurus	7,677 ft	Expoland, Osaka, Japan
Ultimate	7,442 ft	Lightwater Valley; Yorkshire, UK
Beast	7,400 ft	Paramount's Kings Island; Kings Island, OH
Son of Beast	7,032 ft	Paramount's Kings Island; Kings Island, OH

Tallest Roller Coasters

Name	Drop	Location
Top Thrill Dragster	420 ft	Cedar Point; Sandusky, OH
Superman The Escape	415 ft	Six Flags Magic Mountain; Valencia, CA
Tower of Terror	377 ft	Dreamworld; Australia
Steel Dragon 2000	318 ft	Nagashima Spaland; Mie, Japan
Millennium Force	310 ft	Cedar Point; Sandusky, OH

Roller Coasters With Longest Drop

Name	Drop	Location
Top Thrill Dragster	400 ft	Cedar Point; Sandusky, OH
Superman The Escape	328 ft	Six Flags Magic Mountain; Valencia, CA
Tower of Terror	328 ft	Dreamworld; Australia
Steel Dragon 2000	307 ft	Nagashima Spaland; Mie, Japan
Millennium Force	300 ft	Cedar Point; Sandusky, OH
Goliath	255 ft	Six Flags Magic Mountain; Valencia, CA

Top 50 Amusement/Theme Parks Worldwide, Year-end 2002

(ranked by attendance)

Source: Amusement Business

Rank	Park and Location	Country	Attendance
1.	Magic Kingdom at Walt Disney World, Lake Buena Vista, FL	United States	14,044,800*
2.	Tokyo Disneyland	Japan	13,000,000*
3.	Disneyland, Anaheim, CA	United States	12,720,000*
4.	Tokyo Disneysea	Japan	12,000,000*
5.	Disneyland Paris, Marne-La-Vallee	France	10,300,000*
6.	Everland, Kyonggi-Do	South Korea	9,335,000
7.	Lotte World, Seoul	South Korea	9,100,000*
8.	Epcot at Walt Disney World, Lake Buena Vista, FL	United States	8,289,000*
9.	Disney-MGM Studios at Walt Disney World, Lake Buena Vista, FL	United States	8,031,000*
10.	Universal Studios, Osaka	Japan	8,010,000*
11.	Disney's Animal Kingdom at Walt Disney World, Lake Buena Vista, FL	United States	7,305,586*
12.	Universal Studios at Universal Orlando, FL	United States	6,852,600*
13.	Blackpool (England) Pleasure Beach	United Kingdom	6,400,000*
14.	Islands of Adventure at Universal Orlando, FL	United States	6,072,000*
15.	Universal Studios Hollywood, Universal City, CA	United States	5,200,000*
16.	Yokohama Hakkeijima Sea Paradise	Japan	5,065,400*

Rank	Park and Location	Country	Attendance
17.	Seaworld Florida, Orlando, FL	United States	5,000,000*
18.	Disney's California Adventure, Anaheim, CA	United States	4,700,000*
19.	Busch Gardens, Tampa Bay, FL	United States	4,500,000*
	Adventuredome at Circus Circus, Las Vegas, NV	United States	4,500,000*
21.	Seaworld California, San Diego, CA	United States	4,000,000*
22.	Tivoli Gardens, Copenhagen	Denmark	3,800,000
23.	Knott's Berry Farm, Buena Park, CA	United States	3,624,890*
24.	Huis Ten Bosch, Seasebo City	Japan	3,550,000
25.	Morey's Piers, Wildwood, NJ	United States	3,400,000*
26.	Ocean Park, Hong Kong	China	3,380,000
27.	Europa-Park, Rust	Germany	3,300,000*
28.	Cedar Point, Sandusky, OH	United States	3,250,000*
	Six Flags Great Adventure, Jackson, NJ	United States	3,250,000*
30.	Universal's Mediterrania, Salou	Spain	3,200,000*
31.	Paramount's Kings Island, Kings Island, OH	United States	3,182,500*
32.	Six Flags Magic Mountain, Valencia, CA	United States	3,100,000*
	Liseburg, Gothenburg	Sweden	3,100,000*
34.	Efteling, Kaatsheuvel	The Netherlands	3,030,000
35.	Santa Cruz Beach Boardwalk, CA	United States	3,000,000*
36.	Seoul Land, Kyonggi-Do.	South Korea	2,950,000*
37.	Gardaland, Castelnuovo Del Garda	Italy	2,900,000
38.	La Feria De Chapultapec, Mexico City	Mexico	2,890,000
39.	Paramount Canada's Wonderland, Maple, Ontario	Canada	2,826,250*
40.	Walt Disney Studios Park, Marne-La-Valee	France	2,800,000*
41.	Suzuka Circuit	Japan	2,742,600*
42.	Six Flags Great America, Gurnee, IL	United States	2,700,000*
43.	Six Flags Over Texas, Arlington, TX.	United States	2,675,000*
44.	Hersheypark, Hershey, PA	United States	2,629,000
45.	Busch Gardens, Williamsburg, VA	United States	2,600,000*
46.	Six Flags Mexico, Mexico City	Mexico	2,525,000*
47.	Camp Snoopy at Mall of America, Bloomington, MN	United States	2,520,000*
48.	Nagashima Spa Land, Kuwana	Japan	2,500,000
	Alton Towers, Staffordshire.	England	2,500,000
	Bakken, Klampenborg	Denmark	2,500,000*

*Estimated attendance.

Passports, Health Regulations, and Travel Warnings for Foreign Travel

Source: Bureau of Consular Affairs, U.S. Dept. of State

Passports are issued by the U.S. Department of State to citizens and nationals of the U.S. to provide documentation for foreign travel. For U.S. citizens traveling on business or as tourists, especially in Europe, a U.S. passport is often sufficient to gain admission for a limited stay. For many countries, however, a **visa** must also be obtained before entering. It is the responsibility of the traveler to check in advance and obtain any required visas from the appropriate embassies or nearest consulates.

Each country has its own specific guidelines concerning length and purpose of visit, etc. Some may require visitors to display proof that they have (1) sufficient funds to stay for the intended time period, (2) onward/return tickets, and/or (3) at least 6-months remaining validity on their U.S. passports.

Some countries, including **Canada, Mexico,** and some **Caribbean** islands, do not require a passport or a visa for limited stays. However, they do require proof of U.S. citizenship, and may have other requirements. Apart from governmental requirements, some airlines and cruiselines to these locations require passengers to have passports in order to board. For further information, check with the embassy or nearest consulate of the country you plan to visit and the airline or cruiseline you plan to use.

How to Obtain a Passport

Those who have never been issued a passport in their own name, and those who do not meet all the requirements for application by mail, must apply in person at one of 5,000+ designated passport acceptance facilities across the U.S. Those leaving the country or in need of a passport for a foreign visa within 14 days must appear by appointment at one of 13 Regional Passport Agencies. If abroad, application at a U.S. embassy or consulate is required.

A DS-11 Application for Passport is the form to use when appling in person. All persons, including infants, are now required to obtain passports in their own name. For children under 14, there are special additional requirements: (1) Both parents/guardians must have identification and sign the application in person, and (2) birth/citizenship evidence must include proof of parental relationship to the child, such as parents' names on the child's certified birth certificate. Visit travel.state.gov or call the NPIC for questions.

Persons who (1) possess their most recent, undamaged passport, which (2) was issued within the last 15 years and; (3) after their 16th birthday, and (4) whose name has not changed or who have proper documentation for their name change, may be eligible to apply for a new passport by mail. The form DS-82, *Application for Passport by Mail*, must be completed and mailed to the address shown on the form, together with the previous passport, 2 recent identical photographs (see below), and a fee of $55.

Proof of citizenship—A valid passport previously issued to the applicant, or one in which he or she was included (prior to the individual passport requirement), may be accepted as proof of U.S. citizenship. If the applicant has no prior passport and was born in the U.S., a certified copy of the birth certificate generally must be presented. It must generally show the given name and surname, the date and place of birth, and that the birth record was filed shortly after birth. A delayed birth certificate (filed more than 1 year after date of birth) is acceptable if it shows that acceptable secondary evidence was used for creating this record.

If a birth certificate is not obtainable, a notice from a state registrar must be submitted stating that no birth record exists. It must be accompanied by the best obtainable secondary evidence, such as a baptismal certificate or hospital birth record.

A naturalized citizen with no previous passport must present a Certificate of Naturalization issued by the Bureau of Citizenship and Immigration (BCIS) in the Dept. of Homeland Security (formerly the Immigration and Naturalization Service). A person born abroad claiming U.S. citizenship through either a native-born or a naturalized citizen parent must normally submit a Certificate of Citizenship issued by the BCIS or a Consular Report of Birth or Certification of Birth Abroad issued by the Dept. of State. If such a document has not been obtained, evidence of citizenship of the parent(s) through whom citizenship is claimed and evidence that would establish the parent/child relationship must be submitted. Additionally, if citizenship is derived through birth to a citizen parent(s), the applicant must submit parents' marriage certificate, plus an affidavit from parent(s) showing periods and places of residence or presence in the U.S. and abroad, specifying periods spent abroad in the employment of the U.S. government, including the armed forces, or with certain international organizations. If citizenship is derived through naturalization of parents, evidence of admission to the U.S. for permanent residence also is required.

It is important to apply for a passport as far in advance as possible. Passport acceptance facilities and agencies are busiest between March and August. It can take several weeks to receive a passport. Visit travel.state.gov or call the NPIC for information about expedited service.

Photographs—Passport applicants must submit 2 identical photographs that are recent (taken within the last 6 months) and a good current likeness. They should be 2 x 2 in. in size. The image size, from bottom of chin to top of head (including hair), should not be less than 1 in. or more than 1-3/8 in. Photographs should be portrait-type prints. They must be clear, front view, full face, with a plain white or off-white background.

Identity—Applicants must establish their identity to the satisfaction of the accepting agent. Generally, acceptable documents of identity include a previous U.S. passport, a Certificate of Naturalization, a Certificate of Citizenship, a valid driver's license, or a government identification card. Applicants may not use a Social Security card, learner's or temporary driver's license, credit card, or expired ID card. Extremely old documents cannot be used by themselves.

Applicants unable to establish identity must present some documentation in their own name and be accompanied by a person who has known them at least 2 years and is a U.S. citizen or legal U.S. permanent resident alien. That person must sign an affidavit before the individual who executes the application, and must establish his or her own identity.

Fees—For persons under 16 years of age, the basic fee is $40, for a 5-year passport. For persons 16 and older, the basic fee is $55 for a 10-year passport. For all first-time passports there is an additional $30 execution fee. To receive a passport within 10 days or less, an additional $60 expedite fee is required; plus two-way overnight delivery is strongly recommended. Fees are nonrefundable. There is no execution fee when using form DS-82, *Application for Passport by Mail.* **Forms are available on-line** at travel.state.gov

Passport loss—The loss or theft of a valid passport should be reported immediately. In the U.S., call 1-202-955-0430. Voice mail is available after business hours. If abroad, contact the nearest U.S. embassy or consulate. The DS-64, *Statement Regarding Lost or Stolen Passport,* is available on-line at travel.state.gov

General Information—For up-to-date passport and international travel information, visit the Consular Affairs website (www.travel.state.gov), or call the National Passport Information Center at 1-977-487-2778 (TDD/TYY: 1-888-874-7793). Customer service representatives are available from 8 A.M. to 8 P.M., Eastern Time, Mon.-Fri., excluding Federal Holidays.

Health Regulations

Under the regulations adopted by the World Health Organization, a country may require International Certificates of Vaccination against yellow fever. A cholera immunization may be required for travelers from infected areas. Check with health care providers or your records to see that other immunizations (e.g., for tetanus and polio) are up-to-date.

Other preventative measures, including prophylactic medication for malaria are advisable for travel to some countries. No immunizations are needed to return to the U.S. An increasing number of countries have regulations regarding AIDS testing, particularly for longtime visitors. Detailed information and recommendations are included in *Health Information for International Travel,* the "Yellow Book," published every 2 years by the Centers for Disease Control (CDC). It can be ordered from the Public Health Foundation for $29 by going to bookstore.phf.org/cat24.htm, or by calling 1-877-252-1200. Information may also be obtained from your local health department or physician, or by calling the Centers for Disease Control and Prevention at 1-877-FYI-TRIP (1-877-394-8747). The more technically oriented *International Travel and Health* is available from the World Health Organization for $22.50, with portions of the book accessible for free online, at www.who.int./ith

Travel Warnings

Travel Warnings are issued when the State Dept. decides, based on relevant information, to recommend that Americans avoid travel to a certain country; these are subject to change. As of Oct. 1, 2003, travel warnings were in effect for: Afghanistan, Algeria, Angola, Bosnia and Herzegovina, Burundi, Central African Rep., Colombia, Côte d'Ivoire, Dem. Rep. of the Congo, Indonesia, Iran, Iraq, Israel (incl. West Bank and Gaza), Kenya, Lebanon, Liberia, Libya, Nigeria, Pakistan, Saudi Arabia, Somalia, Sudan, Tajikistan, Yemen, Zimbabwe. For current information, visit www.travel.state.gov

Customs Exemptions for Travelers

Source: U.S. Customs and Border Protection, Department of Homeland Security

U.S. residents returning after a stay abroad of at least 48 hours are usually granted customs exemptions of **$800 each** (this and all exemptions figured according to fair retail value). The duty-free articles must accompany the traveler at the time of return, be for personal or household use, have been acquired as an incident of the trip, and be properly declared to Customs. No more than 1 liter of alcoholic beverages or more than 100 cigars and 200 cigarettes (1 carton) may be included in the $800 exemption. The exemption for alcoholic beverages holds only if the returning resident is at least 21 years old at the time of arrival. Cuban cigars may be included only if purchased in Cuba **while on authorized travel.**

If a U.S. resident arrives directly or indirectly from a U.S. island possession—American Samoa, Guam, or U.S. Virgin Islands—a customs exemption of **$1,200 is allowed.** Up to 1,000 cigarettes may be included, but only 200 of them may have been purchased elsewhere. If a U.S. resident returns from any one of the following places, **the exemption is $600:** Antigua and Barbuda, Aruba, Bahamas, Barbados, Belize, British Virgin Islands, Costa Rica, Dominica, Dominican Republic, El Salvador, Grenada, Guatemala, Guyana, Haiti, Honduras, Jamaica, Montserrat, Netherlands Antilles, Nicaragua, Panama, St. Kitts and Nevis, St. Lucia, St. Vincent and the Grenadines, Trinidad and Tobago.

The $800, $1,200, or $600 exemption may be granted only if the exemption has not been used in whole or part within the preceding 30-day period and only if the stay abroad was for at least 48 hours. The 48-hr absence requirement does not apply to travelers returning from Mexico or U.S. Virgin Islands. Travelers who cannot claim the $800, $600, or $1,200 exemption because of the 30-day or 48-hr provisions may bring in free of duty and tax articles acquired abroad for personal or household use up to a value of **$200.**

There are also allowances for goods when shipped. Goods shipped for personal use may be imported free of duty and tax if the total value is no more than $200. This exemption does not apply to perfume containing alcohol if it is valued at more than $5 retail, to alcoholic beverages, or to cigars and cigarettes. The $200 mail exemption does not apply to merchandise subject to absolute or tariff-rate quotas unless the item is for personal use. Tailor-made suits ordered from Hong Kong, however, are subject to quota/visa requirements even if imported for personal use.

Bona fide gifts of not more than $100 in value, when shipped, can be received in the U.S. free of duty and tax, provided that the same person does not receive more than $100 in gift shipments in one day. The limit is increased to $200 for bona fide gift items shipped from U.S. Virgin Islands, American Samoa, or Guam. (Shipping of alcoholic beverages, including wine and beer, by mail is prohibited by U.S. postal laws.) These gifts are not declared by the traveler upon return to the U.S.

The U.S. Customs and Border Protection booklet "Know Before You Go" answers frequently asked customs questions and is available free by writing U.S. Customs and Border Protection, KBYG, PO Box 7407, Washington, DC 20044, or by visiting the agency's website at www.cbp.gov

NATIONS OF THE WORLD

As of mid-2003, there were 193 nations in the world. This number includes 2 nations that are not members of the United Nations—Taiwan and Vatican City (the Holy See). The 193 nations are profiled below, in alphabetical order. Certain regions and territories that are not independent nations can be found under the entry for the governing nation. Following the nation profiles you will find comparative statistics, information on the UN and other international organizations, and other information about nations.

Sources: U.S. Census Bureau: Intl. Data Base; U.S. Central Intelligence Agency: *The World Factbook;* U.S. Dept. of Energy; U.S. Dept. of State. UN Education, Scientific, and Cultural Org. (UNESCO); UN Food and Agriculture Org.; FAO Statistical Database and *Yearbook of Fishery Statistics;* Intl. Monetary Fund; Intl. Telecommunication Union (for telephone and internet data); UN Population Division: *World Population Prospects* and *World Urbanization Prospects;* UN Statistics Division: *Statistical Yearbook.* World Tourism Organization. Intl. Institute for Strategic Studies: *The Military Balance.*

Note: Because of rounding or incomplete enumeration, some percentages may not add to 100%. FY = fiscal year. **National population and health** figures are mid-2003 estimates, unless otherwise noted. Percentage of urban population is for mid-year 2001. **City** populations, except capitals, are 2001 estimates for **urban agglomerations,** i.e., whole metropolitan areas, for 2000. All capital populations are estimates for 2001. Where indicated, the latest available population of the city proper is also given. **GDP** estimates are based on purchasing power parity calculations, which involve use of intl. dollar price weights applied to quantities of goods and services produced. **Tourism** figures represent receipts from international tourism. **Budget** figures are for expenditures, unless otherwise noted. **Motor vehicle** statistics are for 2000 unless otherwise noted; comm. (commercial) vehicles include trucks and buses. **Passenger** statistics are for 1999, and **Airport** figures include total number with paved runways in 2002. **TV** and **radio** figures are for 1999, and **daily newspapers** are for 1998, except where noted. **Telephone** and **internet** data are for 2002, unless otherwise noted. **Literacy** rates given generally measure the percent of population able to read and write on a lower elementary school level, not the (smaller) percent able to read instructions necessary for a job or license. Figures for **gold reserves, international reserves less gold, and consumer prices** are for 2002, except where noted. **Embassy addresses** are for Wash., DC, area code (202), unless otherwise noted.

For further details and later information on developments around the world, see the front-of-the-book Feature section and the Chronology of the Year's Events. See pages 497-512 for full-color maps and flags of all nations.

Afghanistan
Transitional Islamic State of Afghanistan

People: Population: 23,897,000. **Age distrib.** (%): <15: 42; 65+: 2.8. **Pop. density:** 96 per sq. mi. **Urban:** 22%. **Ethnic groups:** Pashtun 44%, Tajik 25%, Hazara 10%, Uzbek 8%. **Principal languages:** Dari (Afghan Persian), Pashtu (both official); Turkic (incl. Uzbek, Turkmen); Balochi, Pashai, many others. **Chief religion:** Muslim (official, Sunni 85%, Shi'a 15%).

Geography: Area (total): 250,001 sq. mi. **Location:** In SW Asia, NW of the Indian subcontinent. **Neighbors:** Pakistan on E, S; Iran on W; Turkmenistan, Tajikistan, Uzbekistan on N. The NE tip touches China. **Topography:** The country is landlocked and mountainous, much of it over 4,000 ft. above sea level. The Hindu Kush Mts. tower 16,000 ft. above Kabul and reach a height of 25,000 ft. to the E. Trade with Pakistan flows through the 35-mile-long Khyber Pass. The climate is dry, with extreme temperatures, and there are large desert regions, though mountain rivers produce intermittent fertile valleys. **Capital:** Kabul, 2,734,000.

Government: Type: Transitional administration. **Head of state and gov.:** Pres. Hamid Karzai; b Dec. 24, 1957; in office: June 19, 2002. **Local divisions:** 32 provinces. **Defense budget** (2002): $250 mil. **Active troops:** 60,000.

Economy: Industries: textiles, soap, furniture, shoes. **Chief crops:** wheat, fruits, nuts, wool. **Natural resources:** nat. gas, oil, coal, copper, chromite, talc, barite, sulfur, lead, zinc, iron ore, salt, gems. **Arable land:** 12%. **Livestock** (2002): chickens: 6.50 mil.; goats: 5 mil.; sheep: 11 mil. **Fish catch** (2002 est.): 800 metric tons. **Electricity prod.** (2001): 0.34 bil. kWh. **Labor force:** agri. 80%, ind. 10%, services 10%.

Finance: Monetary unit: Afghani (AFA) (Sept. 2003: 42.79 = $1 U.S.). **GDP** (2002 est.): $19 bil. **Per capita GDP:** $700. **Imports** (2001): $1.3 bil.; partners (1999): Pakistan 19%, Japan 16%, Kenya 9%, South Korea 7%. **Exports** (2001 est.): $1.2 bil.; partners (1999): Pakistan 32%, India 8%, Belgium 7%, Germany 5%. **Tourism** (1998): $1 mil. **Budget** (2003 plan est.): $550 mil.

Transport: Railroad: Length: 15 mi. **Motor vehicles:** 6,200 pass. cars, 7,000 comm. vehicles. **Civil aviation:** 80.2 mil pass.-mi.; 10 airports.

Communications: TV sets: 14 per 1,000 pop. **Radios:** 132 per 1,000 pop. **Telephone lines:** 29,000 main lines. **Daily newspaper circ.:** 5.6 per 1,000 pop.

Health: Life expectancy: 47.7 male; 46.2 female. **Births** (per 1,000 pop.): 40.6. **Deaths** (per 1,000 pop.): 17.2. **Natural inc.:** 2.35%. **Infant mortality** (per 1,000 live births): 142.5.

Education: Compulsory: ages 7-12. **Literacy** (1999 est.): 36%. **Major Intl. Organizations:** UN (FAO, IBRD, ILO, IMF, WHO). **Embassy:** 2341 Wyoming Ave. NW 20008; 234-3770. **Websites:** www.embassyofafghanistan.org www.afghanistan mfa.net

Afghanistan, occupying a favored invasion route since antiquity, has been variously known as Ariana or Bactria (in ancient times) and Khorasan (in the Middle Ages). Foreign empires alternated rule with local emirs and kings until the 18th century, when a unified kingdom was established. In 1973, a military coup ushered in a republic.

Pro-Soviet leftists took power in a bloody 1978 coup and concluded an economic and military treaty with the USSR. In Dec. 1979 the USSR began a massive airlift into Kabul and backed a new coup, leading to installation of a more pro-Soviet leader. Soviet troops fanned out over Afghanistan and waged a protracted guerrilla war with Muslim rebels, in which some 15,000 Soviet troops reportedly died.

A UN-mediated agreement was signed Apr. 14, 1988, providing for withdrawal of Soviet troops, a neutral Afghan state, and repatriation of refugees. Afghan rebels rejected the pact, vowing to continue fighting while "Soviets and their puppets" remained in Afghanistan. The Soviets completed their troop withdrawal Feb. 15, 1989; fighting between Afghan rebels and government forces ensued.

Communist Pres. Najibullah resigned Apr. 16, 1992, as competing guerrilla forces advanced on Kabul. The rebels achieved power Apr. 28, ending 14 years of Soviet-backed regimes. More than 2 million Afghans had been killed and 6 million had left the country since 1979.

Following the rebel victory there were clashes between moderates and Islamic fundamentalist forces. Burhanuddin Rabbani, a guerrilla leader, became president June 28, 1992, but fierce fighting continued around Kabul and elsewhere. The Taliban, an insurgent Islamic fundamentalist faction, gained increasing control and in Sept. 1996 captured Kabul and set up a government. The Taliban executed former President Najibullah and empowered Islamic religious police to enforce codes of dress and behavior that were especially restrictive to women. Rabbani and other ousted leaders fled to the north.

Victories in the northern cities of Mazar-e Sharif, Aug. 8, 1998, and Taloqan, Aug. 8-11, 1998, gave the Taliban control over more than 90% of the country; the killing of several Iranian diplomats during the Mazar-e Sharif takeover further heightened tensions with Iran. On Aug. 20, 1998, U.S. cruise missiles struck SE of Kabul, hitting facilities the U.S. said were terrorist training camps run by a wealthy Saudi, Osama bin Laden. The UN imposed sanctions Nov. 14, 1999, when Afghanistan refused to turn over bin Laden to the U.S. for prosecution; a UN ban on all military aid to the Taliban took effect Jan. 19, 2001. By March, aid agencies reported that drought and continued warfare had put more than 1 million people at risk of famine. Meanwhile, the Taliban launched a campaign to destroy non-Islamic antiquities.

Ahmed Shah Massoud, leader of the anti-Taliban resistance, died Sept. 9, 2001, of wounds sustained in a suicide bombing by assassins posing as journalists. After the Sept. 11 attacks on the World Trade Center and Pentagon, the U.S., blaming bin Laden, demanded that the Taliban surrender him and shut down his al-Qaeda terrorist network. When the Taliban refused, the U.S., with British assistance, began bombing Afghanistan Oct. 7. Supported by the U.S., the opposition Northern Alliance recaptured Mazar-e Sharif Nov. 9 and took Kabul 4 days later; the Taliban forces abandoned Kandahar, their last stronghold, to S tribesmen Dec. 7. A power-sharing agreement signed in Bonn, Germany, Dec. 5 by 4 anti-Taliban factions, including the Northern Alliance, provided for an interim government headed by Hamid Karzai, a Pashtun tribal leader; the UN authorized Dec. 20 a multinational security force. Meanwhile, U.S. and allied forces continued to hunt for bin Laden, whose fate remained unknown, and other top al-Qaeda and Taliban officials.

At a conference in Tokyo, Jan. 21-22, 2002, donor countries and agencies pledged more than $4.5 bil in aid to Afghanistan over 5 years. In March 2002, the U.S. launched Operation Anaconda to hunt down Taliban in the mountains of the SE. Meeting June 13 in Kabul, a traditional council (loya jirga) chose Karzai to head a new transitional government. An errant U.S. air strike on the night of June 30-July 1 apparently killed 48 people celebrating a wedding at Kakarak, N of Kandahar. Gunmen July 6 assassinated Vice Pres. Haji Abdul Qadir, a Pashtun. A car bomb in Kabul killed 26 people Sept. 5; in Kandahar that same day, Karzai, guarded by U.S. troops, survived an assassination attempt. Continued lawlessness allowed for a dramatic increase in opium production by the end of 2002.

Although the U.S. announced the end of major combat operations in Afghanistan, May 1, 2003, resistance continued. Four German peacekeepers died when a car bomb detonated near their vehicle, June 7, and clashes in the SE between U.S. forces and Taliban and tribal fighters intensified July-Sept. Attacks against aid workers forced the UN to suspend humanitarian operations Aug. 10 in many southern regions. NATO officially assumed control of peacekeeping forces (ISAF) Aug. 11. As of Sept. 2003, about 9,000 U.S. troops and a NATO security force of 5,500 remained in the country, but a lack foreign aid hampered reconstruction efforts.

Albania
Republic of Albania

People: Population: 3,166,000. **Age distrib.** (%): <15: 28.8; 65+: 7.2. **Pop. density:** 299 per sq. mi. **Urban:** 43%. **Ethnic groups:** Albanian 95%, Greek 3%. **Principal languages:** Albanian (Tosk is the official dialect), Greek. **Chief religions:** Muslim 70%, Albanian Orthodox 20%, Roman Catholic 10%.

Geography: Area: 11,100 sq. mi. (total); 10,578 sq. mi. (land). **Location:** SE Europe, on SE coast of Adriatic Sea. **Neighbors:** Greece on S, Yugoslavia on N, Macedonia on E. **Topography:** Apart from a narrow coastal plain, Albania consists of hills and mountains covered with scrub forest, cut by small E-W rivers. **Capital:** Tirana, 299,000.

Government: Type: Republic. **Head of state:** Pres. Alfred Moisiu; b Dec. 1, 1929; in office: July 24, 2002. **Head of gov.:** Prime Min. Fatos Nano; b 1952; in office: July 31, 2002. **Local divisions:** 36 districts, 1 municipality. **Defense budget** (2001): $42.4 mil. **Active troops:** 27,000.

Economy: Industries: food proc., textiles, clothing, lumber. **Chief crops:** wheat, corn, potatoes, sugar beets, grapes. **Natural resources:** oil, nat. gas, coal, chromium, copper, timber, nickel, hydropower. **Crude oil reserves** (2002): 165 mil. bbls. **Arable land:** 21%. **Livestock** (2002): cattle: 700,000; chickens: 4.30 mil.; goats: 1.03 mil.; pigs: 110,000; sheep: 1.80 mil. **Fish catch** (2002): 3,596 metric tons. **Electricity prod.** (2001): 5.29 bil. kWh. **Labor force:** agri. 50%, ind. and services 50%.

Finance: Monetary unit: Lek (ALL) (Sept. 2003: 128.49 = $1 U.S.). **GDP** (2002 est.): $14 bil. **Per capita GDP:** $4,500. **Imports** (2002): $1.5 bil.; partners (2001): Italy 32%, Greece 26%, Turkey 6%, Germany 6%. **Exports** (2002): $340 mil.; partners (2001): Italy 71%, Greece 12%, Germany 7%, Yugoslavia 3%. **Tourism** (1999): $211 mil. **Budget** (2002 est.): $1.5 bil. **Intl. reserves less gold:** $617 mil. **Gold:** 80,000 oz t. **Consumer prices:** 7.8%.

Transport: Railroad: Length: 278 mi. **Motor vehicles:** 114,500 pass. cars, 43,000 comm. vehicles. **Civil aviation:** 4.3 mil pass.-mi.; 4 airports. **Chief ports:** Durres, Sarande, Vlore.

Communications: TV sets: 146 per 1,000 pop. **Radios:** 259 per 1,000 pop. **Telephone lines:** 220,000. **Daily newspaper circ.:** 36 per 1,000 pop. **Internet:** 10,000 users.

Health: Life expectancy: 69.5 male; 75.4 female. **Births** (per 1,000 pop.): 18.2. **Deaths** (per 1,000 pop.): 6.5. **Natural inc.:** 1.17%. **Infant mortality** (per 1,000 live births): 37.3.

Major Intl. Organizations: UN (IBRD, ILO, IMF, IMO, WHO), OSCE.

Education: Compulsory: ages 6-13. **Literacy:** 86.5%.

Embassy: 2100 S St. NW 20008; 223-4942.

Websites: www.keshilliministrave.al; www.president.al

Ancient Illyria was conquered by Romans, Slavs, and Turks (15th century); the latter Islamized the population. Independent Albania was proclaimed in 1912, republic was formed in 1920. King Zog I ruled 1925-39, until Italy invaded.

Communist partisans took over in 1944, allied Albania with USSR, then broke with USSR in 1960 over de-Stalinization. Strong political alliance with China followed, leading to several billion dollars in aid, which was curtailed after 1974. China cut off aid in 1978 when Albania attacked its policies after the death of Chinese ruler Mao Zedong. Large-scale purges of officials occurred during the 1970s.

Enver Hoxha, the nation's ruler for 4 decades, died Apr. 11, 1985. Eventually the new regime introduced some liberalization, including measures in 1990 providing for freedom to travel abroad. Efforts were begun to improve ties with the outside world. Mar. 1991 elections left the former Communists in power, but a general strike and urban opposition led to the formation of a coalition cabinet including non-Communists.

Albania's former Communists were routed in elections Mar. 1992, amid economic collapse and social unrest. Sali Berisha was elected as the first non-Communist president since World War II. Berisha's party claimed a landslide victory in disputed parliamentary elections, May 26 and June 2, 1996. Public protests over the collapse of fraudulent investment schemes in Jan. 1997 led to armed rebellion and anarchy. The UN Security Council, Mar. 28, authorized a 7,000-member force to restore order. Socialists and their allies won parliamentary elections, June 29 and July 6, and international peacekeepers completed their pullout by Aug. 11, 1997. During NATO's air war against Yugoslavia, Mar.-June 1999, Albania hosted some 465,000 Kosovar refugees.

Algeria
People's Democratic Republic of Algeria

People: Population: 31,800,000. **Age distrib.** (%): <15: 33.5; 65+: 4.1. **Pop. density:** 35 per sq. mi. **Urban:** 58%. **Ethnic groups:** Arab-Berber 99%. **Principal languages:** Arabic (official), French, Berber dialects. **Chief religion:** Sunni Muslim (official) 99%.

Geography: Area (total): 919,594 sq. mi. **Location:** In NW Africa, from Mediterranean Sea into Sahara Desert. **Neighbors:** Morocco on W; Mauritania, Mali, Niger on S; Libya, Tunisia on E. **Topography:** The Tell, located on the coast, comprises fertile plains 50-100 miles wide, with a moderate climate and adequate rain. Two major chains of the Atlas Mts., running roughly E-W and reaching 7,000 ft., enclose a dry plateau region. Below lies the Sahara, mostly desert with major mineral resources. **Capital:** Algiers (El Djazair), 2,861,000.

Government: Type: Republic. **Head of state:** Pres. Abdelaziz Bouteflika; b Mar. 2, 1937; in office: Apr. 27, 1999. **Head of gov.:** Prime Min. Ahmed Ouyahia; b July 2, 1952; in office: May 5, 2003. **Local divisions:** 48 provinces. **Defense budget:** (2001) $2.1 bil. **Active troops:** 136,700.

Economy: Industries: oil, nat. gas, light industries, mining, petrochemical, food proc. **Chief crops:** wheat, barley, oats, grapes, olives, citrus. **Natural resources:** oil, nat. gas, iron ore, phosphates, uranium, lead, zinc. **Crude oil reserves** (2002): 9.2 bil. bbls. **Arable land:** 3%. **Livestock** (2002): cattle: 1.70 mil.; chickens: 110 mil.; goats: 3.50 mil.; pigs: 6,000; sheep: 19.30 mil. **Fish catch** (2002 est.): 100,281 metric tons. **Electricity prod.** (2001): 24.69 bil. kWh. **Labor force:** government 29%, agri. 25%, construct. and public works 15%, ind. 11%, other 20%.

Finance: Monetary unit: Dinar (DZD) (Sept. 2003: 80.42 = $1 U.S.). **GDP** (2002 est.): $167 bil. **Per capita GDP:** $5,300. **Imports** (2002): $10.6 bil.; partners (2000): France 29%, U.S. 9%, Italy 8%, Germany 6%. **Exports** (2002 est.): $19.5 bil.; partners (2000): Italy 23%, Spain 13%, U.S. 13%, France 11%. **Tourism** (1998): $24 mil. **Budget** (2001 est.): $18.8 bil. **Intl. reserves less gold:** $17.09 bil. **Gold:** 5.58 mil. oz t. **Consumer prices:** 1.4%.

Transport: Railroad: 2,995 mi. **Motor vehicles:** 1,721,800 pass. cars, 1,010,500 comm. vehicles. **Civil aviation:** 1.86 bil pass.-mi.; 54 airports. **Chief ports:** Algiers, Annaba, Oran.

Communications: TV sets: 107 per 1,000 pop. **Radios:** 242 per 1,000 pop. **Telephone lines:** 1,880,000. **Daily newspaper circ.:** 26.5 per 1,000 pop. **Internet:** 500,000 users.

Health: Life expectancy: 69.1 male; 72.0 female. **Births** (per 1,000 pop.): 21.9. **Deaths** (per 1,000 pop.): 5.1. **Natural inc.:** 1.69%. **Infant mortality** (per 1,000 live births): 37.7.

Education: Compulsory: ages 6-15. **Literacy:** 70%.

Major Intl. Organizations: UN (FAO, IBRD, ILO, IMF, IMO, WHO), AL, AU, OPEC.

Embassy: 2118 Kalorama Rd. NW 20008; 265-2800.

Website: www.algeria-us.org

Earliest known inhabitants were ancestors of Berbers, followed by Phoenicians, Romans, Vandals, and, finally, Arabs. Turkey ruled 1518 to 1830, when France took control.

Large-scale European immigration and French cultural inroads did not prevent an Arab nationalist movement from launching guerrilla war. Peace, and French withdrawal, was negotiated with French Pres. Charles de Gaulle. One million Europeans left. Independence came July 5, 1962. Ahmed Ben Bella was the victor of infighting and ruled until 1965, when an army coup installed Col. Houari Boumedienne as leader; Boumedienne led until his death from a blood disease, 1978.

In 1967, Algeria declared war on Israel, broke ties with U.S., and moved toward eventual military and political ties with the USSR. Some 500 died in riots protesting economic hardship in 1988. In 1989, voters approved a new constitution, which cleared the way for a multiparty system.

The government canceled the Jan. 1992 elections that Islamic fundamentalists were expected to win, and banned all nonreligious activities at Algeria's 10,000 mosques. Pres. Mohammed Boudiaf was assassinated June 29, 1992. There were repeated attacks on high-ranking officials, security forces, foreigners, and others by militant Muslim fundamentalists over the next 7 years; progovernment death squads also were active.

Liamine Zeroual won the presidential election of Nov. 16, 1995. A new constitution banning Islamic political parties and increasing the president's powers passed in a referendum on Nov. 28, 1996. Pro-government parties won the parliamentary election of June 6, 1997. Abdelaziz Bouteflika, who became president after a flawed election on Apr. 15, 1999, made peace with rebels and won approval for an amnesty plan in a referendum on Sept. 16; by then, some 100,000 people had died in the civil war. Some 100 people died and thousands were injured in violent protests Apr.-June 2001, chiefly by Algeria's Berber minority. Floods in Nov. killed over 700 people. An earthquake in N Algeria, May 21, 2003, claimed over 2,200 lives and left about 200,000 people homeless.

IT'S A FACT: What is the biggest country in Africa? The answer is Sudan or Algeria, depending on what kind of area you are talking about. The total area of Sudan is 967,500 sq. miles, somewhat greater than Algeria's total area of 919,600 sq. miles. But if you consider only the land area (not counting inland water), Sudan's area shrinks to 917,000 sq. miles. Algeria, for its part, is mostly desert, and has no inland water area to subtract. So, Algeria's land area is the same as its total area, making it larger than Sudan in that respect.

Andorra
Principality of Andorra

People: Population: 69,150. **Age distrib.** (%): <15: 15.2; 65+: 12.9. **Pop. density:** 397 per sq. mi. **Urban:** 92%. **Ethnic groups:** Spanish 43%, Andorran 33%, Portuguese 11%, French 7%. **Principal languages:** Catalan (official), Castilian Spanish, French. **Chief religion:** Predominantly Roman Catholic.

Geography: Area (total): 181 sq. mi. **Location:** SW Europe, in Pyrenees Mts. **Neighbors:** Spain on S, France on N. **Topography:** High mountains and narrow valleys cover the country. **Capital:** Andorra la Vella, 21,000.

Government: Type: Parliamentary co-principality. **Heads of state:** President of France & Bishop of Urgel (Spain), as co-princes. **Head of gov.:** Marc Forné Molné; b Dec. 30, 1946; in office: Dec. 21, 1994. **Local divisions:** 7 parishes. **Defense budget:** Responsibility of France and Spain.

Economy: Industries: tourism, cattle raising, timber, tobacco, banking. **Chief crops:** tobacco, rye, wheat, barley, oats. **Natural resources:** hydropower, mineral water, timber, iron ore, lead. **Arable land:** 2%. **Labor force:** agri. 1%, ind. 21%, services 78%.

Finance: Monetary unit: Franc (ADF) (Sept. 2003: 7.47 = $1 U.S.). Andorran Peseta (ADP) (Sept. 2003: 186.17 = $1 U.S.). **GDP** (2000 est.): $1.3 bil. **Per capita GDP:** $19,000. **Imports** (1998): $1.077 bil.; partners (1998): Spain 48%, France 35%, U.S. 2.3%. **Exports** (1998): $58 mil.; partners (1998): France 34%, Spain 58%. **Budget** (1997): $342 mil.

Transport: Motor vehicles: 35,358 pass. cars, 4,238 comm. vehicles.

Communications: TV sets: 440 per 1,000 pop. **Radios:** 229 per 1,000 pop. **Telephone lines:** 35,000. **Daily newspaper circ.:** 60 per 1,000 pop. **Internet:** 7,000 users.

Health: Life expectancy: 80.6 male; 86.6 female. **Births** (per 1,000 pop.): 9.7. **Deaths** (per 1,000 pop.): 5.7. **Natural inc.:** 0.39%. **Infant mortality** (per 1,000 live births): 4.1.

Education: Literacy: 100%.

Major Intl. Organizations: UN.

Embassy: 2 UN Plaza, 25th floor, New York, NY 10017; (212) 750-8064.

Website: www.andorra.ad

Andorra was a co-principality, with joint sovereignty by France and the bishop of Urgel, from 1278 to 1993.

Tourism, especially skiing, is the economic mainstay. A free port, allowing for an active trading center, draws some 13 million tourists annually. Andorran voters chose to end a feudal system that had been in place for 715 years and adopt a parliamentary system of government Mar. 14, 1993.

Angola
Republic of Angola

People: Population: 13,625,000. **Age distrib.** (%): <15: 43.3; 65+: 2.8. **Pop. density:** 28 per sq. mi. **Urban:** 35%. **Ethnic groups:** Ovimbundu 37%, Kimbundu 25%, Bakongo 13%. **Principal languages:** Portuguese (official), Bantu and other African languages. **Chief religions:** Indigenous beliefs 47%, Roman Catholic 38%, Protestant 15%.

Geography: Area (total): 481,353 sq. mi. **Location:** In SW Africa on Atlantic coast. **Neighbors:** Namibia on S, Zambia on E, Congo-Kinshasa (formerly Zaire) on N; Cabinda, an enclave separated from rest of country by short Atlantic coast of Congo-Kinshasa, borders Congo-Brazzaville. **Topography:** Most of Angola consists of a plateau elevated 3,000 to 5,000 feet above sea level, rising from a narrow coastal strip. There is also a temperate highland area in the west-central region, a desert in the S, and a tropical rain forest covering Cabinda. **Capital:** Luanda, 2,819,000.

Government: Type: Republic. **Head of state:** Pres. José Eduardo dos Santos; b Aug. 28, 1942; in office: Sept. 20, 1979. **Head of gov.:** Prime Min. Fernando da Piedade Dias dos Santos; b Mar. 5, 1952; in office: Dec. 6, 2002. **Local divisions:** 18 provinces. **Defense budget:** (2002) $250 mil. **Active troops:** 100,000.

Economy: Industries: oil, mining, cement, metals, fish & food proc. **Chief crops:** bananas, sugarcane, coffee, sisal. **Natural resources:** oil, diamonds, iron ore, phosphates, copper, feldspar, gold, bauxite, uranium. **Livestock** (2002): cattle: 4.04 mil.; chickens: 6.80 mil.; goats: 2.15 mil.; pigs: 800,000; sheep: 350,000. **Crude oil reserves** (2002): 5.4 bil. bbls. **Arable land:** 2%. **Fish catch** (2002): 252,518 metric tons. **Electricity prod.** (2001): 1.45 bil. kWh. **Labor force:** agri. 85%, ind. and services 15%.

Finance: Monetary unit: New Kwanza (AON) (Sept. 2003: 58.17 = $1 U.S.). **GDP** (2002 est.): $16.9 bil. **Per capita GDP:** $1,600. **Imports** (2001): $2.7 bil.; partners (2000): EU 47.4%, South Korea 16%, South Africa 15.9%, U.S. 11.3%. **Exports** (2001 est.): $7 bil.; partners (2000): U.S. 44.5%, EU 17.3%, China 22.7%, South Korea 8.1%. **Tourism** (1999): $18 mil. **Budget** (1992 est.):

$2.5 bil. **Intl. reserves less gold:** $276 mil. **Consumer prices** (change in 2000): 325%.

Transport: Railroad: Length: 1,722 mi. **Motor vehicles** (1998): 28,200 pass. cars, 30,600 comm. vehicles. **Civil aviation:** 329.9 mil pass.-mi.; 32 airports. **Chief ports:** Cabinda, Lobito, Luanda.

Communications: TV sets: 15 per 1,000 pop. **Radios:** 67 per 1,000 pop. **Telephone lines:** 85,000. **Daily newspaper circ.:** 11 per 1,000 pop. **Internet:** 41,000 users.

Health: Life expectancy: 36.1 male; 37.8 female. **Births** (per 1,000 pop.): 45.6. **Deaths** (per 1,000 pop.): 25.8. **Natural inc.:** 1.97%. **Infant mortality** (per 1,000 live births): 193.8.

Education: Compulsory: ages 6-9. **Literacy** (1998 est.): 42%.

Major Intl. Organizations: UN (FAO, IBRD, ILO, IMF, IMO, WHO, WTrO), AU.

Embassy: 1615 M St. NW, Suite 900, 20036; 785-1156.

Website: www.angola.org

From the early centuries AD to 1500, Bantu tribes penetrated most of the region. Portuguese came in 1583, allied with the Bakongo kingdom in the north, and developed the slave trade. Large-scale colonization did not begin until the 20th century, when 400,000 Portuguese immigrated.

A guerrilla war began in 1961 lasted until 1975, when Portugal granted independence. Fighting then erupted between three rival rebel groups—the National Front, based in Zaire (now Congo), the Soviet-backed Popular Movement for the Liberation of Angola (MPLA), and the National Union for the Total Independence of Angola (UNITA), aided by the U.S. and South Africa.

Cuban troops and Soviet aid helped the MPLA win control of most of the country by 1976, although fighting continued through the 1980s. A peace accord between the MPLA government and UNITA was signed May 1, 1991.

Elections were held in Sept. 1992, but fighting again broke out, as UNITA rejected the results. UNITA signed a new peace treaty with the government, Nov. 20, 1994, but the rebels were slow to demobilize. The UN Security Council voted, Aug. 28, 1997, to impose sanctions on UNITA. In Aug. 1998, Angola sent thousands of troops into Congo-Kinshasa (formerly Zaire) to support Laurent Kabila's regime. The UN ended its mission in Angola in Mar. 1999, as the civil war continued.

As of 2001, the UN estimated that the war with UNITA had claimed some 1 million lives and left another 2.5 million people homeless. More than 250 died when UNITA rebels ambushed a train Aug. 10. Rebel leader Jonas Savimbi was killed by government troops Feb. 22, 2002. UNITA agreed to a truce Apr. 4. Fighting continued, however, between government forces and separatist guerrillas in oil-rich Cabinda.

Antigua and Barbuda

People: Population: 67,897. **Age distrib.** (%): <15: 28; 65+: 4.7. **Pop. density:** 400 per sq. mi. **Urban:** 37%. **Ethnic groups:** Black, British, Portuguese, Lebanese, Syrian. **Principal languages:** English (official), local dialects. **Chief religions:** Predominantly Protestant; some Roman Catholic.

Geography: Area (total): 171 sq. mi. **Location:** Eastern Caribbean. **Neighbors:** St. Kitts & Nevis to W, Guadeloupe (Fr.) to S. **Topography:** These are mostly low-lying and limestone coral islands. Antigua is mostly hilly with an indented coast; Barbuda is a flat island with a large lagoon on the W. **Capital:** Saint John's, (2001) 24,000.

Government: Type: Constitutional monarchy with British-style parliament. **Head of state:** Queen Elizabeth II; represented by Gov.-Gen. James Carlisle; b Aug. 5, 1937; in office: June 10, 1993. **Head of gov.:** Prime Min. Lester Bird; b Feb. 21, 1938; in office: Mar. 9, 1994. **Local divisions:** 6 parishes, 2 dependencies. **Defense budget:** (2002) $4 mil. **Active troops:** 170.

Economy: Industries: tourism, constr., light mfg. **Chief crops:** cotton, fruits, vegetables. **Arable land:** 18%. **Livestock** (2002): cattle: 14,000; chickens: 95,000; goats: 34,500; pigs: 5,000; sheep: 18,000. **Fish catch** (2002): 1,583 metric tons. **Electricity prod.** (2001): 0.11 bil. kWh. **Labor force:** commerce and services 82%, agri. 11%, ind. 7%.

Finance: Monetary unit: East Caribbean Dollar (XCD) (Sept. 2003: 2.66 = $1 U.S.). **GDP** (2002 est.): $750 mil. **Per capita GDP:** $11,000. **Imports** (2000): $357 mil.; partners: U.S. 27%, UK 16%, Canada 4%, OECS 3%. **Exports** (2000 est.): $40 mil.; partners: OECS 26%, Barbados 15%, Guyana 4%, Trinidad and Tobago 2%. **Tourism** (1999): $291 mil. **Budget** (2000 est.): $145.9 mil. **Intl. reserves less gold:** $64 mil.

Transport: Railroad: Length: 48 mi. **Motor vehicles** (1998): 24,000 pass. cars. **Civil aviation:** 171.5 mil pass.-mi.; 2 airports.

Communications: TV sets: 493 per 1,000 pop. **Radios:** 545 per 1,000 pop. **Telephone lines:** 37,300. **Daily newspaper circ.:** 91 per 1,000 pop. **Internet:** 7,000 users.

Health: Life expectancy: 69.0 male; 73.8 female. **Births** (per 1,000 pop.): 18.2. **Deaths** (per 1,000 pop.): 5.6. **Natural inc.:** 1.26%. **Infant mortality** (per 1,000 live births): 20.9.

Education: Compulsory: ages 5-16. **Literacy** (1992): 90%.

Major Intl. Organizations: UN (FAO, IBRD, ILO, IMF, IMO, WHO, WTrO), Caricom, the Commonwealth, OAS, OECS.

Embassy: 3216 New Mexico Ave. NW 20016; 362-5211.

Website: www.antigua-barbuda.com

Columbus landed on Antigua in 1493. The British colonized it in 1632.

The British associated state of Antigua achieved independence as Antigua and Barbuda on Nov. 1, 1981. The government maintains close relations with the U.S., United Kingdom, and Venezuela. The country was hit hard by Hurricane Luis, Sept. 1995. About 3,000 refugees fleeing a volcanic eruption on Montserrat have settled in Antigua since 1995.

Argentina
Argentine Republic

People: Population: 38,428,000. **Age distrib.** (%): <15: 26.3; 65+: 10.5. **Pop. density:** 36 per sq. mi. **Urban:** 88%. **Ethnic groups:** European 97%, Amerindian 3%. **Principal languages:** Spanish (official), English, Italian, German, French. **Chief religion:** Roman Catholic 92% (official).

Geography: Area: 1,068,301 sq. mi. (total); 1,056,641 sq. mi. (land); second largest country in South America. **Location:** Occupies most of southern South America. **Neighbors:** Chile on W; Bolivia, Paraguay on N; Brazil, Uruguay on NE. **Topography:** Mountains in the W are: the Andean, Central, Misiones, and Southern ranges. Aconcagua is the highest peak in the western hemisphere, alt. 22,834 ft. E of the Andes are heavily wooded plains, called the Gran Chaco in the N, and the fertile, treeless Pampas in the central region. Patagonia, in the S, is bleak and arid. Rio de la Plata, an estuary in the NE, 170 by 140 mi., is mostly fresh water, from 2,485-mi Parana and 1,000-mi Uruguay rivers. **Capital:** Buenos Aires (the Senate has approved moving the capital to the Patagonia Region). **Cities (urban aggr.):** Buenos Aires, 12,106,000, (2000 city proper: 2 mil.); Cordoba, 1,368,000; Rosario, 1,279,000.

Government: Type: Republic. **Head of state and gov.:** Pres. Néstor Kirchner; b Feb. 25, 1950; in office: May 25, 2003. **Local divisions:** 23 provinces, 1 federal district. **Defense budget:** (2002) $0.94 bil. **Active troops:** 69,900.

Economy: Industries: food proc., vehicles, consumer durables, textiles, chemicals. **Chief crops:** sunflower seeds, lemons, soybeans, grapes, corn. **Natural resources:** lead, zinc, tin, copper, iron ore, mang., oil, uranium. **Crude oil reserves** (2002): 3.0 bil. bbls. **Arable land:** 9%. **Livestock** (2002): cattle: 50.37 mil.; chickens: 110.50 mil.; goats: 3.55 mil.; pigs: 4.25 mil.; sheep: 14 mil. **Fish catch** (2002): 924,662 metric tons. **Electricity prod.** (2001): 97.17 bil. kWh.

Finance: Monetary unit: Peso (ARS) (Sept. 2003: 2.95 = $1 U.S.). **GDP** (2002 est.): $391 bil. **Per capita GDP:** $10,200. **Imports** (2001): $20.3 bil.; partners (2000): Brazil 25.1%, U.S. 18.7%, Germany 5%, China 4%. **Exports** (2001): $26.7 bil.; partners (2000): Brazil 26.5%, U.S. 11.8%, Chile 10.6%, Spain 3.5%. **Tourism:** $2.9 bil. **Budget** (2000 est.): $48 bil. **Intl. reserves less gold:** $7.72 bil. **Gold:** 10,000 oz t. **Consumer prices:** 25.9%.

Transport: Railroad: Length: 20,968 mi. **Motor vehicles:** 6.05 mil pass. cars, 1.0 mil comm. vehicles. **Civil aviation:** 8.71 bil pass.-mi.; 145 airports. **Chief ports:** Buenos Aires, Bahia Blanca, La Plata.

Communications: TV sets: 293 per 1,000 pop. **Radios:** 681 per 1,000 pop. **Telephone lines:** 8,009,400. **Daily newspaper circ.:** 37.3 per 1,000 pop. **Internet:** 4,100,000 users.

Health: Life expectancy: 71.7 male; 79.4 female. **Births** (per 1,000 pop.): 17.5. **Deaths** (per 1,000 pop.): 7.6. **Natural inc.:** 0.99%. **Infant mortality** (per 1,000 live births): 16.2.

Education: Compulsory: ages 6-14. **Literacy:** 97.1%.

Major Intl. Organizations: UN (FAO, IBRD, ILO, IMF, IMO, WHO, WTrO), OAS.

Embassy: 1600 New Hampshire Ave. NW 20009; 238-6400.

Websites: http://www.un.int/argentina/english/index.htm
www.congenargentinany.com

Nomadic Indians roamed the Pampas when Spaniards arrived, 1515-16, led by Juan Diaz de Solis. Nearly all the Indians were killed by the late 19th century. The colonists won independence, 1816, and a long period of disorder ended in a strong centralized government.

Large-scale Italian, German, and Spanish immigration in the decades after 1880 spurred modernization. Social reforms were enacted in the 1920s, but military coups prevailed 1930-46, until the election of Gen. Juan Perón as president.

Perón, with his wife, Eva Duarte (d 1952), effected labor reforms, but also suppressed speech and press freedoms, closed religious schools, and ran the country into debt. A 1955 coup exiled Perón, who was followed by a series of military and civilian regimes. Perón returned in 1973, and was once more elected president. He died 10 months later, succeeded by his wife Isabel, who had been elected vice president, and who became the first woman head of state in the western hemisphere.

A military junta ousted Mrs. Perón in 1976 amid charges of corruption. Under a continuing state of siege, the army conducted a "dirty war" against guerrillas and leftists in which an estimated 30,000 people "disappeared." On Dec. 9, 1985, after a trial of 5 months and nearly 1,000 witnesses, 5 former junta members were found guilty of murder and human rights abuses.

Argentine troops seized control of the British-held Falkland Islands on Apr. 2, 1982. Both countries had claimed sovereignty over the islands, located 250 miles off the Argentine coast, since 1833. The British dispatched a task force and declared a total air and sea blockade around the Falklands. Fighting began May 1; several hundred lost their lives as the result of the destruction of a British destroyer and the sinking of an Argentine cruiser.

British troops landed on East Falkland Island May 21 and eventually surrounded Stanley, the capital city and Argentine stronghold. The Argentine troops surrendered, June 14; Argentine Pres. Leopoldo Galtieri resigned June 17.

Democratic rule returned in 1983 as Raul Alfonsin's Radical Civic Union party gained an absolute majority in the presidential electoral college and Congress. By 1989 the nation was plagued by severe financial and political problems, as hyperinflation sparked looting and rioting in several cities. The government of Perónist Pres. Carlos Saúl Menem, installed 1989, introduced harsh economic measures to curtail inflation, control government spending, and restructure the foreign debt.

About 100 people were killed in the terrorist bombing of a Jewish cultural center in Buenos Aires, July 18, 1994. Following passage of a new constitution in Aug. 1994, Menem was reelected president on May 14, 1995. A pact restoring commercial air links between Argentina and the Falklands was signed July 14, 1999.

Buenos Aires Mayor Fernando de la Rúa won the presidential election Oct. 24, 1999. A prolonged recession and a debt of more than $130 billion left Argentina facing an economic crisis in 2001, which austerity measures and IMF aid failed to remedy. After widespread rioting and looting Dec. 19, de la Rúa resigned. A 2-week period of protests and political upheavals abated when Congress, Jan. 1, 2002, chose a Peronist, Eduardo Alberto Duhalde, to finish de la Rúa's term. Duhalde devalued the peso by cutting its ties with the U.S. dollar. Further economic decline and renewed protests led Duhalde July 2 to schedule an early presidential election for Mar. 2003; another Peronist, Néstor Kirchner, took office May 25, 2003, after Menem pulled out of a runoff election. Kirchner moved to end corruption and human rights abuses among the military and police. A new IMF aid deal, approved Sept. 10, rescued Argentina from default.

Armenia
Republic of Armenia

People: Population: 3,061,000. **Age distrib.** (%): <15: 22.2; 65+: 10.1. **Pop. density:** 266 per sq. mi. **Urban:** 67%. **Ethnic groups:** Armenian 93%, Russian 2%. **Principal languages:** Armenian (official), Russian. **Chief religions:** Armenian Apostolic 94%, other Christian 4%, Yezidi 2%.

Geography: Area: 11,506 sq. mi. (total); 10,965 sq. mi. (land). **Location:** SW Asia. **Neighbors:** Georgia on N, Azerbaijan on E, Iran on S, Turkey on W. **Topography:** Mountainous with many peaks above 10,000 ft. **Capital:** Yerevan, 1,420,000.

Government: Type: Republic. **Head of state:** Pres. Robert Kocharian; b Aug. 31, 1954; in office: Apr. 9, 1998. **Head of gov.:** Prime Min. Andranik Markarian; b June 12, 1951; in office: May 12, 2000. **Local divisions:** 10 provinces, 1 city. **Defense budget:** (2002) $62 mil. **Active troops:** 44,610.

Economy: Industries: machine tools & machines, electric motors, tires, knitted wear. **Chief crops:** grapes, vegetables. **Natural resources:** gold, copper, molybd., zinc, alumina. **Arable land:** 17%. **Livestock** (2002): cattle: 520,000; chickens: 4.50 mil.; goats: 20,000; pigs: 98,000; sheep: 549,000. **Fish catch** (2002): 2,197 metric tons. **Electricity prod.** (2001): 6.48 bil. kWh. **Labor force:** agri. 45%, services 30%, ind. 25%.

Finance: Monetary unit: Dram (AMD) (Sept. 2003: 554.8 = $1 U.S.). **GDP** (2002 est.): $12.6 bil. **Per capita GDP:** $3,800. **Imports** (2001): $868.6 mil.; partners (2000): Russia 15%, U.S. 12%, Belgium 10%, Iran 9%. **Exports** (2001 est.): $338.5 mil.; partners (2000): Belgium 23%, Russia 15%, U.S. 13%, Iran 10%. **Tourism:** $45 mil. **Budget** (2003 est.): $482 mil. **Intl. reserves less gold:** $313 mil. **Gold:** 40,000 oz t. **Consumer prices:** 1.1%.

Transport: Railroad: Length: 529 mi. **Civil aviation:** 397.1 mil pass.-mi.; 8 airports.

Communications: TV sets: 241 per 1,000 pop. **Radios:** 239 per 1,000 pop. **Telephone lines:** 531,500. **Daily newspaper circ.:** 6.9 per 1,000 pop. **Internet:** 70,000 users.

Health: Life expectancy: 62.4 male; 71.2 female. **Births** (per 1,000 pop.): 12.6. **Deaths** (per 1,000 pop.): 10.2. **Natural inc.:** 0.24%. **Infant mortality** (per 1,000 live births): 40.9.

Education: Compulsory: ages 7-17. **Literacy:** 98.6%.

Major Intl. Organizations: UN (FAO, IBRD, ILO, IMF, WHO), CIS, OSCE.

Embassy: 2225 R St. NW 20008; 319-1976.

Website: www.gov.am/en

Ancient Armenia extended into parts of what are now Turkey and Iran. Present-day Armenia was set up as a Soviet republic

Apr. 2, 1921. It joined Georgian and Azerbaijan SSRs Mar. 12, 1922, to form the Transcaucasian SFSR, which became part of the USSR Dec. 30, 1922. Armenia became a constituent republic of the USSR Dec. 5, 1936. An earthquake struck Armenia Dec. 7, 1988; approximately 55,000 were killed and several cities and towns were left in ruins.

Armenia declared independence Sept. 23, 1991, and became an independent state when the USSR disbanded Dec. 26, 1991.

Fighting between mostly Christian Armenia and mostly Muslim Azerbaijan escalated in 1992 and continued through 1993. Each country claimed Nagorno-Karabakh, an enclave in Azerbaijan that has a majority population of ethnic Armenians. A temporary cease-fire was announced in May 1994, with Armenian forces in control of the enclave. Voters approved, July 5, 1995, a new constitution increasing presidential powers. Pres. Levon Ter-Petrosian won reelection on Sept. 22, 1996, amid claims of fraud; he resigned Feb. 3, 1998, in a conflict over Nagorno-Karabakh. Robert Kocharian, a nationalist born in the disputed region, won the presidency on Mar. 30, 1998. Gunmen stormed Parliament Oct. 27, 1999, killing Prime Min. Vazgen Sarkissian and 7 others. Kocharian won a 2d term Mar. 5, 2003, in a runoff vote viewed as flawed by opposition groups and Western observers.

Australia
Commonwealth of Australia

People: Population: 19,731,000. **Age distrib.** (%): <15: 20.4; 65+: 12.6. **Pop. density:** 7 per sq. mi. **Urban:** 91%. **Ethnic groups:** White 92%, Asian 7%, Aborigine and other 1%. **Principal languages:** English (official), Aboriginal languages. **Chief religions:** Anglican 26%, Roman Catholic 26%, other Christian 24%. **Geography: Area:** 2,967,907 sq. mi. (total); 2,941,297 sq. mi. (land). **Location:** SE of Asia, Indian O. is W and S, Pacific O. (Coral, Tasman seas) is E; they meet N of Australia in Timor and Arafura seas. Tasmania lies 150 mi. S of Victoria state, across Bass Strait. **Neighbors:** Nearest are Indonesia, Papua New Guinea on N; Solomons, Fiji, and New Zealand on E. **Topography:** An island continent. The Great Dividing Range along the E coast has Mt. Kosciusko, 7,310 ft. The W plateau rises to 2,000 ft., with arid areas in the Great Sandy and Great Victoria deserts. The NW part of Western Australia and Northern Terr. are arid and hot. The NE has heavy rainfall and Cape York Peninsula has jungles. **Capital:** Canberra, 387,000. **Cities (urban aggr.):** Sydney, 3,907,000; Melbourne, 3,232,000; Brisbane, 1,622,000; Perth, 1,329,000; Adelaide, 1,064,000.

Government: Type: Democratic, federal state system. **Head of state:** Queen Elizabeth II, represented by Gov.-Gen. Michael Jeffery; b 1937; in office; Aug. 11, 2003. **Head of gov.:** Prime Min. John Howard; b July 26, 1939; in office: Mar. 11, 1996. **Local divisions:** 6 states, 2 territories. **Defense budget** (2002): $7.6 bil. **Active troops:** 50,920.

Economy: Industries: mining, industrial & transp. equip., food proc., chemicals, steel. **Chief crops:** wheat, barley, sugarcane, fruits. **Natural resources:** bauxite, coal, iron ore, copper, tin, silver, uranium, nickel, tungsten, mineral sands, lead, zinc, diamonds, nat. gas, oil. **Crude oil reserves** (2002): 3.5 bil. bbls. **Other resources:** Wool (world's leading producer), beef. **Arable land:** 6%. **Livestock** (2002): cattle: 28.77 mil.; chickens: 93 mil.; goats: 200,000; pigs: 2.76 mil.; sheep: 113 mil. **Fish catch** (2002): 236,282 metric tons. **Electricity prod.** (2001): 198.25 bil. kWh. **Labor force:** services 73%, ind. 22%, agri. 5%.

Finance: Monetary unit: Australian Dollar (AUD) (Sept. 2003: 1.56 = $1 U.S.). **GDP** (2002 est.): $528 bil. **Per capita GDP:** $27,000. **Imports** (2002): $68 bil.; partners (1999): U.S. 63%, Netherlands 11%, Netherlands Antilles 3%, Japan. **Exports** (2002 est.): $66.3 bil.; partners (2001): Developing countries 45.6%, Japan 19.7%, ASEAN 13.3%, EU 11.7%. **Tourism:** $8.44 bil. **Budget** (2001 est.): $84.1 bil. **Intl. reserves less gold:** $15.22 bil. **Gold:** 2.56 mil oz t. **Consumer prices:** 3.0%.

Transport: Railroad: Length: 21,014 mi. **Motor vehicles (1998):** 9.56 mil pass. cars, 2.18 mil comm. vehicles. **Civil aviation:** 46.96 bil pass.-mi.; 294 airports. **Chief ports:** Sydney, Melbourne, Brisbane, Adelaide, Fremantle, Geelong.

Communications: TV sets: 716 per 1,000 pop. **Radios:** 1,391 per 1,000 pop. **Telephone lines:** 10,590,000. **Daily newspaper circ.:** 293 per 1,000 pop. **Internet:** 8,400,000 users.

Health: Life expectancy: 77.3 male; 83.1 female. **Births** (per 1,000 pop.): 12.6. **Deaths** (per 1,000 pop.): 7.3. **Natural inc.:** 0.52%. **Infant mortality** (per 1,000 live births): 4.8.

Education: Compulsory: ages 5-15. **Literacy** (1996 est.): 100%.

Major Intl. Organizations: UN and all of its specialized agencies, APEC, the Commonwealth, OECD.

Embassy: 1601 Massachusetts Ave. NW 20036; 797-3000.

Website: www.gov.au

Australia harbors many plant and animal species not found elsewhere, including kangaroos, koalas, platypuses, dingos (wild dogs), Tasmanian devils (raccoon-like marsupials), wombats (bear-like marsupials), and barking and frilled lizards.

Capt. James Cook explored the E coast in 1770, when the continent was inhabited by a variety of different tribes. The first settlers, beginning in 1788, were mostly convicts, soldiers, and

government officials. By 1830, Britain had claimed the entire continent, and the immigration of free settlers began to accelerate. The Commonwealth was proclaimed Jan. 1, 1901. Northern Terr. was granted limited self-rule July 1, 1978.

State/Territory, Capital	Area (sq. mi.)	Population (2002 est.)
New South Wales, Sydney	309,500	6,257,351
Victoria, Melbourne	87,900	4,888,234
Queensland, Brisbane	666,990	3,729,028
Western Australia, Perth	975,100	1,934,494
South Australia, Adelaide	379,900	1,522,456
Tasmania, Hobart	26,200	473,365
Australian Capital Terr., Canberra	900	322,234
Northern Terr., Darwin	519,800	197,724

Racially discriminatory immigration policies were abandoned in 1973, after 3 million Europeans (half British) had entered since 1945. The 50,000 aborigines and 150,000 part-aborigines are mostly detribalized, but there are several preserves in the Northern Territory. They remain economically disadvantaged.

Australia's agricultural success makes the country among the top exporters of beef, lamb, wool, and wheat. Major mineral deposits have been developed, largely for export. Industrialization has been completed. The nation endured a deep recession 1990-93 but has rebounded strongly.

The Labor Party won a majority in Feb. 1983 general elections and was reelected in 1984, 1987, 1990, and 1993. After an election that focused mainly on economic issues, conservatives swept into power in elections Mar. 2, 1996.

Prime Min. John Howard retained power, but with a reduced majority, in parliamentary elections Oct. 3, 1998. Australia led an international peacekeeping force into East Timor in Sept. 1999. In a referendum Nov. 6, voters rejected a proposal that would have made Australia a republic. Sydney hosted the Summer Olympics Sept. 15-Oct. 1, 2000. Howard won a 3rd term in the elections of Nov. 10, 2001. Australian troops fought in U.S.-led military operations in Afghanistan (2001) and Iraq (2003); 2,000 Australian peacekeepers began arriving in the Solomon Is., July 24, 2003.

Australian External Territories

Norfolk Isl., area 13 sq. mi., pop. (2001 Norfolk census) 1,574, was taken over, 1914. The soil is very fertile, suitable for citrus, bananas, and coffee. Many of the inhabitants are descendants of the *Bounty* mutineers, moved to Norfolk 1856 from Pitcairn Isl. Australia offered the island limited home rule in 1978.

Coral Sea Isls. Territory, area 1 sq. mi., is administered from Norfolk Isl.

Territory of Ashmore and Cartier Isls., area 2 sq. mi., in the Indian O., came under Australian authority 1934 and are administered as part of Northern Territory. **Heard Isl. and McDonald Isls.,** area 159 sq. mi., are administered by the Dept. of Science.

Cocos (Keeling) Isls., 27 small coral islands in the Indian O. 1,750 mi. NW of Australia. Pop. (2002 est.) 600; area 5 sq. mi. The residents voted to become part of Australia, Apr. 1984.

Christmas Isl., area 52 sq. mi. (2002 est.) 1,436; 230 mi. S of Java, was transferred by Britain in 1958. It has phosphate deposits.

Australian Antarctic Territory was claimed by Australia in 1933, including 2,362,000 sq. mi. of territory S of 60th parallel S Lat. and between 160th-45th meridians E Long. It does not include Adelie Coast.

Austria
Republic of Austria

People: Population: 8,116,000. **Age distrib.** (%): <15: 16.4; 65+: 15.4. **Pop. density:** 254 per sq. mi. **Urban:** 67%. **Ethnic groups:** German 88%. **Principal languages:** German (official), Serbo-Croatian, Slovenian. **Chief religions:** Roman Catholic 78%, Protestant 5%.

Geography: Area: 32,378 sq. mi. (total); 31,945 sq. mi. (land). **Location:** In S Central Europe. **Neighbors:** Switzerland, Liechtenstein on W; Germany, Czech Rep. on N; Slovakia, Hungary on E; Slovenia, Italy on S. **Topography:** Austria is primarily mountainous, with the Alps and foothills covering the western and southern provinces. The eastern provinces and Vienna are located in the Danube River Basin. **Capital:** Vienna, 2,066,000.

Government: Type: Federal republic. **Head of state:** Pres. Thomas Klestil; b Nov. 4, 1932; in office: July 8, 1992. **Head of gov.:** Chancellor Wolfgang Schüssel; b June 7, 1945; in office: Feb. 4, 2000. **Local divisions:** 9 bundeslaender (states), each with a legislature. **Defense budget** (2002): $1.7 bil. **Active troops:** 34,600.

Economy: Industries: constr., machinery, vehicles & parts, food, chemicals. **Chief crops:** grains, potatoes, sugar beets, grapes. **Natural resources:** iron ore, oil, timber, magnesite, lead, coal, lignite, copper, hydropower. **Crude oil reserves** (2002): 86 mil. bbls. **Arable land:** 17%. **Livestock** (2002): cattle: 2.12 mil.; chickens: 11 mil.; goats: 59,000; pigs: 3.44 mil.; sheep: 321,000. **Fish catch** (2002): 2,755 metric tons. **Electricity prod.** (2001): 58.75 bil. kWh. **Labor force:** services 67%, ind. and crafts 29%, agri. and forestry 4%.

Finance: Monetary unit: Euro (EUR) (Sept. 2003: 0.92 = $1 U.S.). **GDP** (2002 est.): $226 bil. **Per capita GDP:** $27,700. **Imports** (2002): $68 bil.; partners (2001): Developing countries

31.7%, EU 21.6%, U.S. 18.9%, ASEAN 14.8%. **Exports** (2001): $70 bil.; partners (2000): EU 63%, Switzerland 5%, U.S. 5%, Hungary 4%. **Tourism:** $11.44 bil. **Budget** (2001 est.): $54 bil. **Intl. reserves less gold:** $7.12 bil. **Gold:** 10.21 mil oz t. **Consumer prices:** 1.8%.

Transport: Railroad: Length: 3,787 mi. **Motor vehicles:** 4.1 mil pass. cars, 770,000 comm. vehicles. **Civil aviation:** 8.31 bil pass.-mi.; 24 airports. **Chief ports:** Linz, Vienna, Enns, Krems.

Communications: TV sets: 526 per 1,000 pop. **Radios:** 751 per 1,000 pop. **Telephone lines:** 3,810,000. **Daily newspaper circ.:** 296 per 1,000 pop. **Internet:** 3,340,000 users.

Health: Life expectancy: 75.0 male; 81.5 female. **Births** (per 1,000 pop.): 9.4. **Deaths** (per 1,000 pop.): 9.7. **Natural inc.:** -0.03%. **Infant mortality** (per 1,000 live births): 4.3.

Education: Compulsory: ages 6-15. **Literacy:** 98%.

Major Intl. Organizations: UN and all of its specialized agencies, EU, OECD, OSCE.

Embassy: 3524 International Ct. NW 20008; 895-6700.

Website: www.austria.gv.at/e

Rome conquered Austrian lands from Celtic tribes around 15 BC. In 788 the territory was incorporated into Charlemagne's empire. By 1300, the House of Hapsburg had gained control; they added vast territories in all parts of Europe to their realm in the next few hundred years.

Austrian dominance of Germany was undermined in the 18th century and ended by Prussia by 1866. But the Congress of Vienna, 1815, confirmed Austrian control of a large empire in southeast Europe consisting of Germans, Hungarians, Slavs, Italians, and others. The dual Austro-Hungarian monarchy was established in 1867, giving autonomy to Hungary and almost 50 years of peace.

World War I, started after the June 28, 1914, assassination of Archduke Franz Ferdinand, the Hapsburg heir, by a Serbian nationalist, destroyed the empire. By 1918 Austria was reduced to a small republic, with the borders it has today.

Nazi Germany invaded Austria Mar. 13, 1938. The republic was reestablished in 1945, under Allied occupation. Full independence and neutrality were restored in 1955. Austria joined the European Union Jan. 1, 1995. The rise of the right-wing, anti-immigrant Austrian Freedom Party challenged the dominance of the Austrian Social Democratic Party in the late 1990s. When Freedom Party members joined the cabinet, Feb. 4, 2000, the EU imposed political sanctions on Austria, Feb. 4-Sept. 12, 2000. Party support plummeted in elections Nov. 24, 2002.

Azerbaijan
Azerbaijani Republic

People: Population: 8,370,000. **Age distrib.** (%): <15: 28.3; 65+: 7.4. **Pop. density:** 250 per sq. mi. **Urban:** 52%. **Ethnic groups:** Azeri 90%, Dagestani 3%, Russian 3%, Armenian 2%. **Principal languages:** Azeri (official), Russian, Armenian. **Chief religions:** Muslim 93%, Russian Orthodox 3%, Armenian Orthodox 2%.

Geography: Area: 33,436 sq. mi. (total); 33,243 sq. mi. (land). **Location:** SW Asia. **Neighbors:** Russia, Georgia on N; Iran on S; Armenia on W; Caspian Sea on E. **Topography:** The Great Caucasus Mts. in N, Karabakh Upland in W border the Kur-Abas lowland; climate is arid except in the subtropical SE. **Capital:** Baku, 1,964,000.

Government: Type: Republic. **Head of state:** Pres. Haydar A. Aliyev; b May 10, 1923; in office: June 30, 1993. **Head of gov.:** Prime Min. Ilham Aliyev; b Dec. 24, 1961; in office: Aug. 4, 2003. **Local division:** 59 rayons, 11 cities, 1 autonomous republic. **Defense budget:** (2002) $118 mil. **Active troops:** 72,100.

Economy: Industries: oil products, oil field equip., steel, iron ore, cement. **Chief crops:** cotton, grain, rice, grapes. **Natural resources:** oil, nat. gas, iron ore, nonferrous metals, alumina. **Crude oil reserves** (2002): 1.2 bil. bbls. **Arable land:** 18%. **Livestock** (2002): cattle: 2.07 mil.; chickens: 14.38 mil.; goats: 565,600; pigs: 18,000; sheep: 5.90 mil. **Fish catch** (2002): 11,063 metric tons. **Electricity prod.** (2001): 18.23 bil. kWh. **Labor force:** agri. and forestry 41%, ind. 7%, services 52%.

Finance: Monetary unit: Manat (AZM) (Sept. 2003: 4,892 = $1 U.S.). **GDP** (2002 est.): $27 bil. **Per capita GDP:** $3,500. **Imports** (2002): $1.8 bil.; partners (2001): U.S. 16.1%, Russia 10.7%, Turkey 10.4%, Kazakhstan 7%. **Exports** (2002 est.): $2 bil.; partners (2001): Italy 57.2%, Israel 7.1%, Georgia 4.5%, Russia 3.4%. **Tourism** (1999): $81 mil. **Budget** (2001): $807 mil. **Intl. reserves less gold:** $531 mil. **Consumer prices:** 2.8%.

Transport: Railroad: Length: 1,320 mi. **Motor vehicles:** 332,100 pass. cars; 133,400 comm. vehicles. **Civil aviation:** 381.5 mil. pass.-mi.; 27 airports. **Chief port:** Baku.

Communications: TV sets: 257 per 1,000 pop. **Radios:** 23 per 1,000 pop. **Telephone lines:** 989,200. **Daily newspaper circ.:** 27 per 1,000 pop. **Internet:** 300,000 users.

Health: Life expectancy: 59.0 male; 67.6 female. **Births** (per 1,000 pop.): 19.3. **Deaths** (per 1,000 pop.): 9.7. **Natural inc.:** 0.96%. **Infant mortality** (per 1,000 live births): 82.4.

Education: Compulsory: ages 6-16. **Literacy** (2002): 100%.

Major Intl. Organizations: UN (FAO, IBRD, ILO, IMF, IMO, WHO), CIS, OSCE.

Embassy: 927 15th St. NW, Suite 700, 20035; 842-0001.

Website: www.president.az

Azerbaijan was the home of Scythian tribes and part of the Roman Empire. Overrun by Turks in the 11th century and conquered by Russia in 1806 and 1813, it joined the USSR Dec. 30, 1922, and became a constituent republic in 1936. Azerbaijan declared independence Aug. 30, 1991, and became an independent state when the Soviet Union disbanded Dec. 26, 1991.

Fighting between mostly Muslim Azerbaijan and mostly Christian Armenia escalated in 1992 and continued in 1993 and 1994. Each country claimed Nagorno-Karabakh, an enclave in Azerbaijan with a majority population of ethnic Armenians. A temporary cease-fire was announced in May 1994, with Armenian forces in control of the enclave.

A National Council ousted Communist Pres. Mutaibov and took power May 19, 1992. Abulfez Elchibey became the nation's first democratically elected president June 7, but was ousted from office by Surat Huseynov, commander of a private militia, June 30, 1993. Huseynov became prime minister, and Haydar Aliyev, a pro-Russian former Communist, became president. Huseynov fled the country after his supporters staged an unsuccessful coup attempt Oct. 1994. Voters approved a new constitution expanding presidential powers, Nov. 12, 1995. Pres. Aliyev was reelected Oct. 11, 1998, but international monitors called the election seriously flawed. In Dec. 2001, a presidential decree made Latin script obligatory for the Azerbaijani language, replacing the Cyrillic alphabet used during Soviet rule.

The ailing Aliyev had his son named prime minister Aug. 4, 2003.

The Bahamas
Commonwealth of The Bahamas

People: Population: 314,000. **Age distrib.** (%): <15: 29; 65+: 6.3. **Pop. density:** 406 per sq. mi. **Urban:** 89%. **Ethnic groups:** Black 85%, White 12%. **Principal languages:** English, Creole (among Haitian immigrants). **Chief religions:** Baptist 32%, Anglican 20%, Roman Catholic 19%, other Christian 24%.

Geography: Area: 5,382 sq. mi. (total); 3,888 sq. mi. (land). **Location:** In Atlantic O., E of Florida. **Neighbors:** Nearest are U.S. on W, Cuba on S. **Topography:** Nearly 700 islands (29 inhabited) and over 2,000 islets in the W Atlantic O. extend 760 mi. NW to SE. **Capital:** Nassau. **Cities (urban aggr.):** (2001 est.): Nassau, 220,000; Grand Bahama, 40,898.

Government: Type: Independent commonwealth. **Head of state:** Queen Elizabeth II, represented by Gov.-Gen. Dame Ivy Dumont; b Oct. 2, 1930; in office: Nov. 13, 2001. **Head of gov.:** Prime Min. Perry Christie; b Aug. 21,1943; in office: May 3, 2002. **Local divisions:** 21 districts. **Defense budget:** (2002) $26 mil. **Active troops:** 860.

Economy: Industries: tourism, banking, cement, oil refining & shipment, salt, rum. **Chief crops:** citrus, vegetables. **Natural resources:** salt, aragonite, timber. **Arable land:** 1%. **Livestock** (2002): cattle: 700; chickens: 3.45 mil.; goats: 13,852; pigs: 5,000; sheep: 6,000. **Fish catch** (2002): 9,303 metric tons. **Electricity prod.:** 1.56 bil. kWh. **Labor force:** tourism 50%, other services 40%, ind. 5%, agri. 5%.

Finance: Monetary unit: Bahamian Dollar (BSD) (Sept. 2003: 1.00 = $1 U.S.). **GDP** (2002 est.): $5.2 bil. **Per capita GDP:** $17,000. **Imports** (2000): $1.88 bil.; partners (2001): U.S. 16.1%, Russia 10.7%, Turkey 10.4%, Kazakhstan 7.0%. **Exports** (2000): $535.8 mil.; partners (2000): U.S. 28.2%, France 16.5%, Germany 14.1%, UK 12.4%. **Tourism** (1999): $1.5 bil. **Budget** (2000): $956.5 mil. **Intl. reserves less gold:** $280 mil. **Consumer prices:** 2.2%.

Transport: Motor vehicles (1998): 67,400 pass. cars, 16,800 comm. vehicles. **Civil aviation:** 227.4 mil pass.-mi.; 30 airports. **Chief ports:** Nassau, Freeport.

Communications: TV sets: 243 per 1,000 pop. **Radios:** 739 per 1,000 pop. **Telephone lines:** 126,600. **Daily newspaper circ.:** 125 per 1,000 pop. **Internet:** 21,200 users.

Health: Life expectancy: 62.3 male; 69.2 female. **Births** (per 1,000 pop.): 18.6. **Deaths** (per 1,000 pop.): 8.7. **Natural inc.:** 0.99%. **Infant mortality** (per 1,000 live births): 26.2.

Education: Compulsory: ages 5-16. **Literacy:** 95.6%.

Major Intl. Organizations: UN (FAO, IBRD, ILO, IMF, IMO, WHO), Caricom, the Commonwealth, OAS.

Embassy: 2220 Massachusetts Ave. NW 20008; 319-2660.

Websites: www.bahamas.gov.bs; www.bahamas.com

Christopher Columbus first set foot in the New World on San Salvador (Watling Isl.) in 1492, when Arawak Indians inhabited the islands. British settlement began in 1647; the islands became a British colony in 1783. Internal self-government was granted in 1964; full independence within the Commonwealth was attained July 10, 1973. International banking and investment management have become major industries alongside tourism.

Bahrain
Kingdom of Bahrain

People: Population: 724,000. **Age distrib. (%):** <15: 29.2; 65+: 3.1. **Pop. density:** 3,029 per sq. mi. **Urban:** 93%. **Ethnic groups:** Arab 73%, Asian 19%, Iranian 8%. **Principal languages:** Arabic (official), English, Farsi, Urdu. **Chief religion:** Muslim (official; Shi'a 70%, Sunni 30%).

Geography: Area (total): 257 sq. mi. **Location:** SW Asia, in Persian Gulf. **Neighbors:** Nearest are Saudi Arabia on W, Qatar on E. **Topography:** Bahrain Island, and several adjacent, smaller islands, are flat, hot, and humid, with little rain. **Capital:** Manama, 150,000.

Government: Type: Constitutional monarchy. **Head of state:** King Hamad bin Isa al-Khalifa; b Jan. 28, 1950; in office: as emir Mar. 6, 1999; as king Feb. 14, 2002. **Head of gov.:** Prime Min. Khalifa bin Sulman al-Khalifa; b 1936; in office: Jan. 19, 1970. **Local divisions:** 12 municipalities. **Defense budget:** (2001) $215 mil. **Active troops:** 10,700.

Economy: Industries: oil proc. & refining, aluminum smelting, offshore banking, ship repair. **Chief crops:** fruit, vegetables. **Natural resources:** oil, nat. gas, fish, pearls. **Crude oil reserves** (2002): 125 mil. bbls. **Arable land:** 1%. **Livestock** (2002): cattle: 11,000; chickens: 465,000; goats: 16,300; sheep: 18,000. **Fish catch** (2002): 11,230 metric tons. **Electricity prod.** (2001): 6.26 bil. kWh. **Labor force:** ind., commerce, and service 79%, government 20%, agri. 1%.

Finance: Monetary unit: Dinar (BHD) (Sept. 2003: 0.38 = $1 U.S.). **GDP** (2002 est.): $9.8 bil. **Per capita GDP:** $14,000. **Imports** (2001): $4.5 bil.; partners (2000): Saudi Arabia 28.7%, U.S. 12.5%, UK 6.6%, France 6%. **Exports** (2001): $5.5 bil.; partners (2000): India 8.4%, U.S. 3.9%, Saudi Arabia 3.4%, Japan 2.8%. **Tourism** (1999): $408 mil. **Budget** (2002 est.): $2.2 bil. **Intl. reserves less gold:** $1.3 bil. **Gold:** 150,000 oz t. **Consumer prices:** 1.2%.

Transport: Motor vehicles (1999): 169,600 pass. cars, 35,700 comm. vehicles. **Civil aviation:** 1.76 bil pass.-mi.; 3 airports. **Chief ports:** Manama, Sitrah.

Communications: TV sets: 446 per 1,000 pop. **Radios:** 64 per 1,000 pop. **Telephone lines:** 175,400. **Daily newspaper circ.:** 117 per 1,000 pop. **Internet:** 165,000 users.

Health: Life expectancy: 71.3 male; 76.2 female. **Births** (per 1,000 pop.): 19.0. **Deaths** (per 1,000 pop.): 4.0. **Natural inc.:** 1.50%. **Infant mortality** (per 1,000 live births): 18.6.

Education: Free, compulsory: ages 6-17. **Literacy:** 89.1%.

Major Intl. Organizations: UN (FAO, IBRD, ILO, IMF, IMO, WHO, WTrO), AL.

Embassy: 3502 International Dr. NW 20008; 342-0741.

Website: www.bahrain.gov.bh/english/index.asp

Long ruled by the Khalifa family, Bahrain was a British protectorate from 1861 to Aug. 15, 1971, when it regained independence.

Pearls, shrimp, fruits, and vegetables were the mainstays of the economy until oil was discovered in 1932. By the 1970s, oil reserves were depleted; international banking flourished.

Bahrain took part in the 1973-74 Arab oil embargo against the U.S. and other nations. The government bought controlling interest in the oil industry in 1975. Shiite dissidents have clashed with the Sunni-led government since 1996.

Emir Hamad bin Isa al-Khalifa proclaimed himself king Feb. 14, 2002. Local elections in May marked the 1st time Bahraini women were allowed to vote and run for office.

Bangladesh
People's Republic of Bangladesh

People: Population: 146,736,000. **Age distrib. (%):** <15: 33.8; 65+: 3.4. **Pop. density:** 2,838 per sq. mi. **Urban:** 26%. **Ethnic groups:** Bengali 98%. **Principal languages:** Bangla (official, also known as Bengali), English. **Chief religions:** Muslim 83% (official), Hindu 16%.

Geography: Area: 55,599 sq. mi. (total); 51,703 sq. mi. (land). **Location:** In S Asia, on N bend of Bay of Bengal. **Neighbors:** India nearly surrounds country on W, N, E; Myanmar on SE. **Topography:** The country is mostly a low plain cut by the Ganges and Brahmaputra rivers and their delta. The land is alluvial and marshy along the coast, with hills only in the extreme SE and NE. A tropical monsoon climate prevails, among the rainiest in the world. **Capital:** Dhaka. **Cities (urban aggr.):** Dhaka, 13,181,000; Chittagong, 3,651,000; Khulna, 1,442,000.

Government: Type: Parliamentary democracy. **Head of state:** Pres. Iajuddin Ahmed; b Feb. 1,1931; in office: Sept. 6, 2002. **Head of gov.:** Prime Min. Khaleda Zia; b Aug. 15,1945; in office: Oct. 10, 2001. **Local divisions:** 6 divisions. **Defense budget** (2002): $678 mil. **Active troops:** 137,000.

Economy: Industries: cotton textiles, jute, garments, tea processing, newsprint, cement, chemical fertilizer, light engineering,

sugar. **Chief crops:** rice, jute, tea, wheat, sugarcane, potatoes, tobacco. **Natural resources:** nat. gas, timber, coal. **Crude oil reserves** (2002): 57 mil. bbls. **Arable land:** 73%. **Livestock** (2002): cattle: 23.90 mil.; chickens: 140 mil.; goats: 34.10 mil.; sheep: 1.13 mil. **Fish catch** (2002 est.): 1,687,000 metric tons. **Electricity prod.** (2001): 15.33 bil. kWh. **Labor force:** agri. 63%, services 26%, ind. 11%.

Finance: Monetary unit: Taka (BDT) (Sept. 2003: 60.23 = $1 U.S.). **GDP** (2002 est.): $239 bil. **Per capita GDP:** $1,700. **Imports** (2001): $8.7 bil.; partners (2000): India 10.5%, EU 9.5%, Japan 9.5%, Singapore 8.5%. **Exports** (2001): $6.6 bil.; partners (2000): U.S. 31.8%, Germany 10.9%, UK 7.9%, France 5.2%. **Tourism:** $59 mil. **Budget** (2000 est.): $6.8 bil. **Intl. reserves less gold:** $1.24 bil. **Gold:** 110,000 oz t. **Consumer prices:** 6.8%.

Transport: Railroad: Length: 1,706 mi. **Motor vehicles** (1998): 65,000 pass. cars, 145,900 comm. vehicles. **Civil aviation:** 2.18 bil pass.-mi.; 15 airports. **Chief ports:** Chittagong, Dhaka, Mongla Port.

Communications: TV sets: 7 per 1,000 pop. **Radios:** 50 per 1,000 pop. **Telephone lines:** 682,000. **Daily newspaper circ.:** 53.4 per 1,000 pop. **Internet:** 204,000 users.

Health: Life expectancy: 61.5 male; 61.2 female. **Births** (per 1,000 pop.): 29.9. **Deaths** (per 1,000 pop.): 8.6. **Natural inc.:** 2.13%. **Infant mortality** (per 1,000 live births): 66.1.

Education: Compulsory: ages 6-10. **Literacy:** 43.1%.

Major Intl. Organizations: UN (FAO, IBRD, ILO, IMF, IMO, WHO, WTrO), the Commonwealth.

Embassy: 3510 International Dr. NW 20007; 202-244-2745.

Website: www.bangladeshgov.org

Muslim invaders conquered the formerly Hindu area in the 12th century. British rule lasted from the 18th century to 1947, when East Bengal became part of Pakistan.

Charging West Pakistani domination, the Awami League, based in the East, won National Assembly control in 1971. Assembly sessions were postponed; riots broke out. Pakistani troops attacked Mar. 25; Bangladesh independence was proclaimed the next day. In the ensuing civil war, one million died and 10 million fled to India.

War between India and Pakistan broke out Dec. 3, 1971. Pakistan surrendered in the East on Dec. 16. Mujibur Rahman, known as Sheikh Mujib, became prime minister; he was killed in a coup Aug. 15, 1975. During the 1970s the country moved into the Indian and Soviet orbits in response to U.S. support of Pakistan, and much of the economy was nationalized.

On May 30, 1981, Pres. Ziaur Rahman was killed in an unsuccessful coup attempt by army rivals. Vice Pres. Abdus Sattar assumed the presidency but was ousted in a coup led by army chief of staff Gen. H. M. Ershad, Mar. 1982. Ershad declared Bangladesh an Islamic Republic in 1988; a parliamentary system of government was adopted in 1991.

Bangladesh is subject to devastating storms and floods that kill thousands. A cyclone struck Apr. 1991, killing over 131,000 people and causing $2.7 billion in damages. Chronic destitution in the densely crowded population has been worsened by the decline of jute as a world commodity. Pollution of surface water and naturally occurring contamination of groundwater by arsenic have caused widespread health problems.

Political turmoil led to the resignation, Mar. 30, 1996, of Prime Minister Khaleda Zia, the widow of Ziaur Rahman. Sheikh Mujib's daughter, Hasina Wazed (known as Sheikh Hasina), led the country after the June 12, 1996 election. Bangladesh and India signed a treaty, Dec. 12, resolving their long-standing dispute over the use of water from the Ganges River. A cyclone in May 1997 left an estimated 800,000 people homeless. Floods in July-Sept. 1998 inundated much of the country, killed over 1,400 people (many through disease), and stranded at least 30 million.

An interim government was installed July 2001 pending national elections. Khaleda Zia returned to power following the parliamentary elections of Oct. 1, 2001.

Barbados

People: Population: 270,000. **Age distrib. (%):** <15: 21.4; 65+: 8.8. **Pop. density:** 1,626 per sq. mi. **Urban:** 51%. **Ethnic groups:** Black 90%, White 4%. **Principal languages:** English. **Chief religions:** Protestant 67%, Roman Catholic 4%.

Geography: Area (total): 166 sq. mi. **Location:** In Atlantic O., farthest E of West Indies. **Neighbors:** Nearest are St. Lucia and St. Vincent & the Grenadines to the W. **Topography:** The island lies alone in the Atlantic almost completely surrounded by coral reefs. Highest point is Mt. Hillaby, 1,115 ft. **Capital:** Bridgetown, 136,000.

Government: Type: Parliamentary democracy. **Head of state:** Queen Elizabeth II, represented by Gov.-Gen. Sir Clifford Husbands; b Aug. 5, 1926; in office: June 1, 1996. **Head of gov.:** Prime Min. Owen Arthur; b Oct. 17, 1949; in office: Sept. 7, 1994.

Local divisions: 11 parishes and Bridgetown. **Defense budget** (2002): $13 mil. **Active troops:** 610.

Economy: Industries: tourism, sugar, light mfg., component assembly. **Chief crops:** sugarcane, vegetables, cotton. **Natural resources:** oil, fish, nat. gas. **Crude oil reserves** (2002): 3 mil. bbls. **Other resources:** Fish. **Arable land:** 37%. **Livestock** (2002): cattle: 21,000; chickens: 3.50 mil.; goats: 5,000; pigs: 35,000; sheep: 42,000. **Fish catch** (2002): 2,676 metric tons. **Electricity prod.** (2001): 0.78 bil. kWh. **Labor force:** services 75%, ind. 15%, agri. 10%.

Finance: Monetary unit: Barbados Dollar (BBD) (Sept. 2003: 1.98 = $1 U.S.). **GDP** (2002 est.): $4 bil. **Per capita GDP:** $14,500. **Imports** (2000): $1.16 bil.; partners (2000): U.S. 40.8%, Caribbean Community 19.8%, UK 8.1%, Japan 5.2%. **Exports** (2000): $272 mil.; partners (2000): Caribbean Community 43.2%, U.S. 15.3%, UK 13.2%. **Tourism:** $745 mil. **Budget** (2000 est.): $886 mil. **Intl. reserves less gold** $492 mil. **Consumer prices:** .1%.

Transport: Motor vehicles (1999): 62,100 pass. cars; 9,400 comm. vehicles. **Civil aviation:** 1 airport. **Chief port:** Bridgetown.

Communications: TV sets: 290 per 1,000 pop. **Radios:** 651 per 1,000 pop. **Telephone lines** (2000): 129,000. **Daily newspaper circ.:** 155 per 1,000 pop. **Internet:** 15,000 users.

Health: Life expectancy: 69.6 male; 74.1 female. **Births** (per 1,000 pop.): 13.2. **Deaths** (per 1,000 pop.): 9.0. **Natural inc.:** 0.41%. **Infant mortality** (per 1,000 live births): 12.7.

Education: Compulsory: ages 5-16. **Literacy** (2002): 97%.

Major Intl. Organizations: UN (FAO, IBRD, ILO, IMF, IMO, WHO, WTrO), Caricom, the Commonwealth, OAS.

Embassy: 2144 Wyoming Ave. NW 20008; 939-9200.

Website: www.barbados.gov.bb

Barbados was probably named by Portuguese sailors in reference to bearded fig trees. An English ship visited in 1605, and British settlers arrived on the uninhabited island in 1627. Slaves worked the sugar plantations until slavery was abolished in 1834. Self-rule came gradually, with full independence proclaimed Nov. 30, 1966. British traditions have remained.

Belarus
Republic of Belarus

People: Population: 9,895,000. **Age distrib.** (%): <15: 17.3; 65+: 14.1. **Pop. density:** 123 per sq. mi. **Urban:** 70%. **Ethnic groups:** Belarusian 81%, Russian 11%. **Principal languages:** Belarusian, Russian. **Chief religions:** Eastern Orthodox 80%, other 20%.

Geography: Area (total): 80,155 sq. mi. **Location:** E Europe. **Neighbors:** Poland on W; Latvia, Lithuania on N; Russia on E; Ukraine on S. **Topography:** Belarus is a landlocked country consisting mostly of hilly lowland with significant marsh areas in S. **Capital:** Minsk, 1,664,000.

Government: Type: Republic. **Head of state:** Pres. Aleksandr Lukashenko; b Aug. 30, 1954; in office: July 20,1994. **Head of gov.:** Prime Min. Syarhey Sidorski; b 1954; in office: July 10, 2003 (acting). **Local divisions:** 6 oblasts and 1 municipality. **Defense budget** (2002): $176.7 mil. **Active troops:** 79,800.

Economy: Industries: machine tools, tractors, trucks, earthmovers, motorcycles. **Chief crops:** grain, potatoes, vegetables, sugar beets, flax. **Natural resources:** timber, peat, oil, nat. gas, granite, dolomitic limestone, marl, chalk, sand, gravel, clay. **Crude oil reserves** (2002): 198 mil. bbls. **Arable land:** 29%. **Livestock** (2002): cattle: 4.08 mil.; chickens: 33 mil.; goats: 62,000; pigs: 3.37 mil.; sheep: 83,000. **Fish catch** (2002): 5,609 metric tons. **Electricity prod.** (2001): 24.4 bil. kWh. **Labor force:** 41% services; 40% ind. & const.; 19% agric. & forestry.

Finance: Monetary unit: Ruble (BYR) (Sept. 2003: 2,093.00 = $1 U.S.). **GDP** (2002 est.): $85 bil. **Per capita GDP:** $8,200. **Imports** (2001): $8.1 bil.; partners (2000): Russia 65%, Germany 7%, Poland 3%. **Exports** (2001): $7.5 bil.; partners (2000): Russia 51%, Ukraine 8%, Poland 4%, Germany 3%. **Tourism:** $17 mil. **Budget** (1997): $4.1 bil. **Intl. reserves less gold:** $455 mil. **Consumer prices:** 42.5%.

Transport: Railroad: Length: 3,432 mi. **Motor vehicles:** 1.45 mil pass. cars, 10,000 comm. vehicles. **Civil aviation:** 210.0 pass.-mi.; 28 airports. **Chief port:** Mazyr.

Communications: TV sets: 331 per 1,000 pop. **Radios:** 292 per 1,000 pop. **Telephone lines:** 2,967,200. **Daily newspaper circ.:** 151.1 per 1,000 pop. **Internet:** 808,700 users.

Health: Life expectancy: 62.5 male; 74.6 female. **Births** (per 1,000 pop.): 10.2. **Deaths** (per 1,000 pop.): 14.1. **Natural inc.:** -0.39%. **Infant mortality** (per 1,000 live births): 13.9.

Education: Compulsory: ages 6-14. **Literacy:** 99.6%.

Major Intl. Organizations: UN (IBRD, ILO, IMF, WHO), CIS, OSCE.

Embassy: 1619 New Hampshire Ave. NW 20009; 986-1604.

Website: www.belarusembassy.org

The region was subject to Lithuanians and Poles in medieval times, and was a prize of war between Russia and Poland beginning in 1503. It became part of the USSR in 1922, although the western part of the region was controlled by Poland. Belarus was overrun by German armies in 1941; recovered by Soviet troops in 1944. Following World War II, Belarus increased in area through Soviet annexation of part of NE Poland. Belarus declared independence Aug. 25, 1991. It became an independent state when the Soviet Union disbanded Dec. 26, 1991.

A new constitution was adopted, Mar. 15, 1994, and a new president was chosen in elections concluding July 1. Russia and Belarus signed a pact Apr. 2, 1996, linking their political and economic systems. An authoritarian constitution enacted in Nov. gave Pres. Aleksandr Lukashenko vast new powers. Lukashenko's insistence on tightening ties with Russia resulted in the signing of new accords in 1997 and 1998. Opponents charged harassment and fraud in the presidential election of Sept. 9, 2001, won by Lukashenko.

Belgium
Kingdom of Belgium

People: Population: 10,318,000. **Age distrib.** (%): <15: 17.3; 65+: 17.1. **Pop. density:** 884 per sq. mi. **Urban:** 97%. **Ethnic groups:** Fleming 58%, Walloon 31%. **Principal languages:** Dutch, French, German (all official); Flemish, Luxembourgish. **Chief religions:** Roman Catholic 75%, Protestant, other 25%.

Geography: Area: 11,780 sq. mi. (total); 11,672 sq. mi. (land) **Location:** in W Europe, on North Sea. **Neighbors:** France on W and S, Luxembourg on SE, Germany on E, Netherlands on N. **Topography:** Mostly flat, the country is trisected by the Scheldt and Meuse, major commercial rivers. The land becomes hilly and forested in the SE (Ardennes) region. **Capital:** Brussels, 1,134,000.

Government: Type: Parliamentary democracy under a constitutional monarch. **Head of state:** King Albert II; b June 6, 1934; in office: Aug. 9, 1993. **Head of gov.:** Premier Guy Verhofstadt; b Apr. 11, 1953; in office: July 12, 1999. **Local divisions:** 10 provinces and Brussels. **Defense budget** (2002): $2.7 bil. **Active troops:** 39,260.

Economy: Industries: engineering & metal products, motor vehicle assembly, proc. food & beverages, chemicals, textiles, glass, oil, coal. **Chief crops:** sugar beets, vegetables, fruits, grain, tobacco. **Natural resources:** coal, nat. gas. **Arable land:** 24%. **Livestock** (incl. Luxembourg) (2002): cattle: 3.11 mil.; chickens: 52 mil.; goats: 23,000; pigs: 6.85 mil.; sheep: 160,000. **Fish catch** (2002): 31,839 metric tons. **Electricity prod.** (2001): 74.28 bil. kWh. **Labor force:** services 73%, ind. 25%, agri. 2%.

Finance: Monetary unit: Euro (EUR) (Sept. 2003: 0.92 = $1 U.S.). **GDP** (2002 est.): $297.6 bil. **Per capita GDP:** $29,000. **Imports** (2001): $152 bil.; partners (2001): EU 68.7%, , U.S. 7.2%. **Exports** (2002 est.): $162 bil.; partners (2001): EU 75.3%, U.S. 5.6%. **Tourism** (1999): $7.04 bil. **Budget** (2000): $106 bil. **Intl. reserves less gold:** $8.72 bil. **Gold:** 8.29 mil oz t. **Consumer prices:** 1.6%.

Transport: Railroad: Length: 2,126 mi. **Motor vehicles:** 4.68 mil pass. cars, 563,200 comm. vehicles. **Civil aviation:** 10.99 bil pass.-mi.; 25 airports. **Chief ports:** Antwerp (one of the world's busiest), Zeebrugge, Ghent.

Communications: TV sets: 532 per 1,000 pop. **Radios:** 797 per 1,000 pop. **Telephone lines:** 5,132,400. **Daily newspaper circ.:** 160 per 1,000 pop. **Internet:** 3,400,000 users.

Health: Life expectancy: 75.0 male; 81.8 female. **Births** (per 1,000 pop.): 10.5. **Deaths** (per 1,000 pop.): 10.1. **Natural inc.:** 0.04%. **Infant mortality** (per 1,000 live births): 4.6.

Education: Compulsory: ages 6-18. **Literacy:** 98%.

Major Intl. Organizations: UN and all of its specialized agencies, EU, NATO, OECD, OSCE.

Embassy: 3330 Garfield St. NW 20008; 333-6900.

Website: www.belgium.be/

Belgium derives its name from the Belgae, the first recorded inhabitants, probably Celts. The land was conquered by Julius Caesar, and was ruled for 1800 years by conquerors, including Rome, the Franks, Burgundy, Spain, Austria, and France. After 1815, Belgium was made a part of the Netherlands, but it became an independent constitutional monarchy in 1830.

Belgian neutrality was violated by Germany in both world wars. King Leopold III surrendered to Germany, May 28, 1940. After the war, he was forced by political pressure to abdicate in favor of his son, King Baudouin. Baudouin was succeeded by his brother, Albert II, Aug. 9, 1993.

The Flemings of northern Belgium speak Dutch, while French is the language of the Walloons in the south. The language difference has been a perennial source of controversy and led to antagonism between the 2 groups. Parliament has passed measures aimed at transferring power from the central government to 3 regions—Wallonia, Flanders, and Brussels. Constitutional changes in 1993 made Belgium a federal state. Sabena, the national airline, went bankrupt Nov. 6, 2001.

Belize

People: Population: 256,000. **Age distrib.** (%): <15: 41.6; 65+: 3.5. **Pop. density:** 29 per sq. mi. **Urban:** 48%. **Ethnic groups:** Mestizo 49%, Creole 25%, Maya 11%, Garifuna 6%. **Principal languages:** English (official), Spanish, Mayan, Garifuna (Carib), Creole. **Chief religions:** Roman Catholic 50%, Protestant 27%.

Geography: Area: 8,867 sq. mi. (total); 8,805 sq. mi. (land). **Location:** Eastern coast of Central America. **Neighbors:** Mexico on N, Guatemala on W and S. **Topography:** Belize has swampy lowlands in N, Maya Mts. in S, coral reefs and cays near coast. Climate is tropical. **Capital:** Belmopan, 9,000.

Government: Type: Parliamentary democracy. **Head of state:** Queen Elizabeth II, represented by Gov.-Gen. Sir Colville Young; b Nov. 20, 1932; in office: Nov. 17, 1993. **Head of gov.:** Prime Min. Said Musa; b Mar. 19, 1944; in office: Aug. 28, 1998. **Local divisions:** 6 districts. **Defense budget** (2002): $18.5 mil. **Active troops:** 1,050.

Economy: Industries: clothing, food proc., tourism, constr. **Chief crops:** bananas, coca, citrus, sugarcane. **Natural resources:** timber, fish, hydropower. **Arable land:** 2%. **Livestock** (2002): cattle: 64,000; chickens: 1.40 mil.; goats: 1,600; pigs: 25,000; sheep: 3,000. **Fish catch** (2002): 18,830 metric tons. **Electricity prod.** (2001): 0.2 bil. kWh. **Labor force:** agri. 27%, ind. 18%, services 55%.

Finance: Monetary unit: Belize Dollar (BZD) (Sept. 2003: 1.96 = $1 U.S.). **GDP** (2002 est.): $1.3 bil. **Per capita GDP:** $4,900. **Imports** (2001): $505 mil.; partners (1999): U.S. 51%, Mexico 12%, Central America 5%, UK 4%. **Exports** (2001 est.): $239.6 mil.; partners (1999): EU 45%, U.S. 42%, Caricom 6%, Canada 1%. **Tourism** (1999): $112 mil. **Budget** (2002) $209 mil. **Intl. reserves less gold:** $84 mil. **Consumer prices:** 2.2%.

Transport: Motor vehicles: 21,500 pass. cars, 3,900 comm. vehicles. **Civil aviation: 4** airports. **Chief ports:** Belize City, Big Creek.

Communications: TV sets: 183 per 1,000 pop. **Radios:** 594 per 1,000 pop. **Telephone lines:** 31,600. **Internet:** 22,000 users.

Health: Life expectancy: 65.2 male; 69.6 female. **Births** (per 1,000 pop.): 30.5. **Deaths** (per 1,000 pop.): 6.1. **Natural inc.:** 2.44%. **Infant mortality** (per 1,000 live births): 27.1.

Education: Compulsory: ages 5-14. **Literacy:** 94.1%.

Major Intl. Organizations: UN (FAO, IBRD, ILO, IMF, IMO, WHO, WTrO), Caricom, the Commonwealth, OAS.

Embassy: 2535 Massachusetts Ave. NW 20008; 332-9636.

Website: www.belize.gov.bz

Belize (formerly British Honduras) was Britain's last colony on the American mainland; independence was achieved Sept. 21, 1981. Relations with neighboring Guatemala, initially tense, have improved in recent years. Belize has become a center for drug trafficking between Colombia and the U.S.

Benin
Republic of Benin

People: Population: 6,736,000. **Age distrib.** (%): <15: 47.2; 65+: 2.3. **Pop. density:** 158 per sq. mi. **Urban:** 43%. **Ethnic groups:** 42 groups, incl. Fon, Adja, Yoruba, and Bariba. **Principal languages:** French (official), Fon, Yoruba, various tribal languages. **Chief religions:** Indigenous beliefs 50%, Christian 30%, Muslim 20%.

Geography: Area: 43,483 sq. mi. (total); 42,711 sq. mi. (land). **Location:** In W Africa on Gulf of Guinea. **Neighbors:** Togo on W; Burkina Faso, Niger on N; Nigeria on E. **Topography:** Most of Benin is flat and covered with dense vegetation. The coast is hot, humid, and rainy. **Capital:** Porto-Novo 225,000. **Cities (urban aggr., 1994 est.):** Cotonou 750,000.

Government: Type: Republic. **Head of state and gov.:** Pres. Mathieu Kerekou; b Sept. 2, 1933; in office: Apr. 4, 1996. **Local divisions:** 6 departments. **Defense budget** (2002): $47 mil. **Active troops:** 4,550.

Economy: Industries: textiles, food proc., chemical prod., constr. materials. **Chief crops:** cotton, corn, cassava, yams, beans. **Natural resources:** oil, limestone, marble, timber. **Crude oil reserves** (2002): 8 mil. bbls. **Arable land:** 13%. **Livestock** (2002): cattle: 1.52 mil.; chickens: 30 mil.; goats: 1.20 mil.; pigs: 460,000; sheep: 655,000. **Fish catch** (2002): 38,415 metric tons. **Electricity prod.** (2001): 0.27 bil. kWh.

Finance: Monetary unit: CFA Franc BCEAO (XOF) (Sept. 2003: 605.18 = $1 U.S.). **GDP** (2002 est.): $7.3 bil. **Per capita GDP:** $1,070. **Imports** (2000): $437.6 mil.; partners (2001): France, US, China, Cote d'Ivoire. **Exports** (2000): $35.3 mil.; partners (2001): Brazil, France, Indonesia, Thailand. **Tourism** (1998): $33 mil. **Budget** (2001) $561.8 mil. **Intl. reserves less gold:** $453 mil. **Consumer prices:** 2.5%.

Transport: Railroad: Length: 359 mi. **Motor vehicles (1998):** 7,300 pass. cars, 6,200 comm. vehicles. **Civil aviation:** 146.0 mil pass.-mi.; 1 airport. **Chief port:** Cotonou.

Communications: TV sets: 44 per 1,000 pop. **Radios:** 448 per 1,000 pop. **Telephone lines:** 59,300. **Daily newspaper circ.:** 2.2 per 1,000 pop. **Internet:** 25,000 users.

Health: Life expectancy: 50.4 male; 51.8 female. **Births** (per 1,000 pop.): 43.2. **Deaths** (per 1,000 pop.): 13.7. **Natural inc.:** 2.95%. **Infant mortality** (per 1,000 live births): 86.8.

Education: Compulsory: ages 6-11. **Literacy** (2002): 37%.

Major Intl. Organizations: UN (FAO, IBRD, ILO, IMF, IMO, WHO, WTrO), AU.

Embassy: 2124 Kalorama Rd. NW 20008; 232-6656.

Websites: www.gouv.bj; www.benintourism.com

The Kingdom of Abomey, rising to power in wars with neighboring kingdoms in the 17th century, came under French domination in the late 19th century and was incorporated into French West Africa by 1904.

Under the name Dahomey, the country gained independence Aug. 1, 1960; it became Benin in 1975. In the fifth coup since independence Col. Ahmed Kerekou took power in 1972; two years later he declared a socialist state with a "Marxist-Leninist" philosophy. In Dec. 1989, Kerekou announced Marxism-Leninism would no longer be the state ideology.

In Mar. 1991, Kerekou lost to Nicéphore Soglo in Benin's first free presidential election in 30 years. Kerekou defeated Soglo in Mar. 1996 to reclaim the presidency. He won reelection in a runoff Mar. 22, 2001.

Bhutan
Kingdom of Bhutan

People: Population: 2,257,000. **Age distrib.** (%): <15: 39.8; 65+: 4. **Pop. density:** 124 per sq. mi. **Urban:** 7%. **Ethnic groups:** Bhote 50%, Nepalese 35%, indigenous tribes 15%. **Principal languages:** Dzongkha (official); Tibetan, Nepalese dialects. **Chief religions:** Lamaistic Buddhist 75% (official), Hindu 25%.

Geography: Area (total): 18,147 sq. mi. **Location:** S Asia, in eastern Himalayan Mts. **Neighbors:** India on W (Sikkim) and S, China on N. **Topography:** Bhutan is comprised of very high mountains in the N, fertile valleys in the center, and thick forests in the Duar Plain in the S. **Capital:** Thimphu 32,000.

Government: Type: Monarchy. **Head of state and gov.:** King Jigme Singye Wangchuk; b Nov. 11, 1955; in office: July 21, 1972. **Head of gov.:** Prime Min. **Lyonpo Jigme Thinley;** b 1952; in office: Aug. 30, 2003. **Local divisions:** 18 districts. **Defense budget** (2002): $19 mil. **Active troops:** NA.

Economy: Industries: cement, wood products, proc. fruits, alcoholic beverages, calcium carbide. **Chief crops:** rice, corn, root crops, citrus, grains. **Natural resources:** timber, hydropower, gypsum, calcium carbide. **Livestock** (2002): cattle: 321,000; chickens: 310,000; goats: 31,300; pigs: 41,000; sheep: 23,000. **Fish catch** (2002 est.): 330 metric tons. **Arable land:** 2%. **Electricity prod.** (2001): 1.9 bil. kWh. **Labor force:** agri. 93%, services 5%, ind. and commerce 2%.

Finance: Monetary unit: Ngultrum (BTN) (Sept. 2003: 45.61 = $1 U.S.). **GDP** (2002 est.): $2.7 bil. **Per capita GDP:** $1,300. **Imports** (2000): $196 mil.; partners: India 77%, Japan, UK, Germany. **Exports** (2000 est.): $154 mil.; partners: India 94%, Bangladesh. **Tourism:** $9 mil. **Budget** (1996 est.): $152 mil. **Intl. reserves less gold:** $236 mil. **Consumer prices:** 2.5%.

Transport: Civil aviation: 25.5 mil pass.-mi.; 1 airport.

Communications: TV sets: 6 per 1,000 pop. **Radios:** 19 per 1,000 pop. **Telephone lines:** 19,600. **Internet:** 10,000 users.

Health: Life expectancy: 53.9 male; 53.3 female. **Births** (per 1,000 pop.): 34.8. **Deaths** (per 1,000 pop.): 13.5. **Natural inc.:** 2.14%. **Infant mortality** (per 1,000 live births): 104.7.

Education: Compulsory: ages 6-16. **Literacy** (2002): 42.2%.

Major Intl. Organizations: UN (FAO, IBRD, IMF, WHO).

Embassy: (Consulate-General): 2 UN Plaza, 27th Fl., New York, NY 10017; 212-826-1919

Website: www.kingdomofbhutan.com

The region came under Tibetan rule in the 16th century. British influence grew in the 19th century. A Buddhist monarchy was set up in 1907. According to a 1910 treaty, Britain guided Bhutan's external affairs, while the country remained internally self-governing. Upon independence, India assumed Britain's role in a 1949 revision of the treaty. Isolated for much of its history, Bhutan took tentative steps toward modernization in the 1990s.

Bolivia
Republic of Bolivia

People: Population: 8,808,000. **Age distrib.** (%): <15: 37.8; 65+: 4.5. **Pop. density:** 21 per sq. mi. **Urban:** 63%. **Ethnic groups:** Quechua 30%, Mestizo 30%, Aymara 25%, white 15%. **Principal languages:** Spanish, Quechua, Aymara (all official) **Chief religion:** Roman Catholic 95% (official).

Geography: Area: 424,164 sq. mi. (total); 418,685 sq. mi. (land). **Location:** In W central South America, in the Andes Mts. (one of 2 landlocked countries in South America). **Neighbors:** Peru and Chile on W, and Paraguay on S, Brazil on E and N. **Topography:** The great central plateau, at an altitude of 12,000 ft., over 500 mi. long, lies between two great cordilleras having 3 of the highest peaks in South America. Lake Titicaca, on Peruvian border, is highest lake in world on which steamboats ply (12,506 ft.), is the highest lake in the world. The E central region has semitropical forests; the llanos, or Amazon-Chaco lowlands are in E. **Capitals:** La Paz (administrative), Sucre (judicial). **Cities (urban aggr.):** La Paz, 1,499,000; Santa Cruz, 1,062,000, Sucre: 183,000.

Government: Type: Republic. **Head of state and gov.:** Pres. Gonzalo Sánchez de Lozada; b July 1, 1930: in office: Aug. 6, 2002. **Local divisions:** 9 departments. **Defense budget:** (2001) $138 mil. **Active troops:** 31,500.

Economy: Industries: mining, smelting, oil, food & beverages, tobacco, handicrafts, clothing. **Chief crops:** soybeans, coffee, coca, cotton, corn, sugarcane, rice, potatoes, timber. **Natural resources:** tin, nat. gas, oil, zinc, tungsten, antimony, silver, iron, lead, gold, timber, hydropower. **Crude oil reserves** (2002): 441 mil. bbls. **Other resources:** Timber. **Arable land:** 2%. **Livestock** (2002): cattle: 6.48 mil.; chickens: 74.50 mil.; goats: 1.50 mil.; pigs: 2.85 mil.; sheep: 8.90 mil. **Fish catch** (2002): 6,260 metric tons. **Electricity prod.** (2001): 3.9 bil. kWh.

Finance: Monetary unit: Boliviano (BOB) (Sept. 2003: 7.96 = $1 U.S.). **GDP** (2002 est.): $21 bil. **Per capita GDP:** $2,500. **Imports** (2001): $1.5 bil.; partners (2000): U.S. 24%, Argentina 17%, Brazil 15%, Chile 9%. **Exports** (2001 est.): $1.2 bil.; partners (2000): U.S. 32%, Colombia 18%, UK 15%, Brazil 15%. **Tourism:** $160 mil. **Budget** (2002 est.): $4 bil. **Intl. reserves less gold:** $427 mil. **Gold:** 910,000 oz t. **Consumer prices:** .9%.

Transport: Railroad: Length: 2,293 mi. **Motor vehicles:** 304,600 pass. cars, 151,700 comm. vehicles. **Civil aviation:** 1.15 bil pass.-mi.; 12 airports.

Communications: TV sets: 118 per 1,000 pop. **Radios:** 675 per 1,000 pop. **Telephone lines:** 563,900. **Daily newspaper circ.:** 55 per 1,000 pop. **Internet:** 180,000 users.

Health: Life expectancy: 62.2 male; 67.5 female. **Births** (per 1,000 pop.): 25.5. **Deaths** (per 1,000 pop.): 7.9. **Natural inc.:** 1.76%. **Infant mortality** (per 1,000 live births): 56.1.

Education: Compulsory: ages 6-13. **Literacy:** 87.2%.

Major Intl. Organizations: UN (FAO, IBRD, ILO, IMF, IMO, WHO, WTrO), OAS.

Embassy: 3014 Massachusetts Ave. NW 20008; 483-4410.

The Incas conquered the region from earlier Indian inhabitants in the 13th century. Spanish rule began in the 1530s and lasted until Aug. 6, 1825. The country is named after Simon Bolivar, independence fighter.

Websites: www.bolivia.gov.bo; www.bolivia-usa.org

In a series of wars, Bolivia lost its Pacific coast to Chile, the oil-bearing Chaco to Paraguay, and rubber-growing areas to Brazil, 1879-1935.

Economic unrest, especially among the militant mine workers, has contributed to continuing political instability. A reformist government under Victor Paz Estenssoro, 1951-64, nationalized tin mines and attempted to improve conditions for the Indian majority but was overthrown by a military junta. A long series of coups and countercoups continued until constitutional government was restored in 1982.

U.S. pressure on the government to reduce the country's coca output, the raw material for cocaine, has led to clashes between police and coca growers and increased anti-U.S. feeling among Bolivians. Gen. Hugo Banzer Suárez, who ruled as a dictator, 1971-78, became president in Aug. 1997. 105 people died in earthquakes near Aiquile May 22, 1998. Stricken with cancer, Banzer resigned and was succeeded Aug. 7, 2001, by Vice-Pres. Jorge Quiroga Ramirez. After an inconclusive presidential election June 30, 2002, Congress Aug. 4 chose Gonzalo Sánchez de Lozada, a U.S.-educated mining executive, as head of state. He revamped his cabinet and rescinded a proposed tax hike after violent clashes in La Paz, Feb. 12-14, 2003, killed at least 30 people.

Bosnia and Herzegovina

People: Population: 4,161,000. **Age distrib.** (%): <15: 19.8; 65+: 9.6. **Pop. density:** 211 per sq. mi. **Urban:** 43%. **Ethnic groups:** Bosniak 48%, Serbian 37%, Croatian 14%. **Principal languages:** Bosnian (official), Croatian, Serbian. **Chief religions:** Muslim 40%, Orthodox 31%, Roman Catholic 15%, Protestant 4%.

Geography: Area (total): 19,741 sq. mi. **Location:** On Balkan Peninsula in SE Europe. **Neighbors:** Yugoslavia on E and SE, Croatia on N and W. **Topography:** Hilly with some mountains. About 36% of the land is forested. **Capital:** Sarajevo 552,000.

Government: Type: Federal republic. **Heads of state:** Collective presidency with rotating leadership. **Head of gov.:** Chrm. of Council Ministers Adnan Terzic; b 1960; in office: Dec. 23, 2002. **Local divisions:** Muslim-Croat Federation, divided into 10 cantons; Republika Srpska. **Defense budget** (2002): $130 mil. **Active troops:** 13,200.

Economy: Industries: steel, mining, vehicle assembly, textiles, tobacco products, wooden furniture, tank & aircraft assembly, domestic appliances. **Chief crops:** wheat, corn, fruits, vegetables. **Natural resources:** coal, iron, bauxite, mang., timber, copper, chromium, lead, zinc, hydropower. **Arable land:** 14%. **Livestock** (2002): cattle: 440,000; chickens: 4.70 mil.; pigs 300,000; sheep: 670,000. **Fish catch** (2002 est.): 2,500 metric tons. **Electricity prod.** (2001): 9.98 bil. kWh.

Finance: Monetary unit: Converted Marka (BAM) (Sept. 2003: 1.79 = $1 U.S.). **GDP** (2002 est.): $7.3 bil. **Per capita GDP:** $1,900. **Imports** (2001): $3.1 bil.; partners: Croatia, Slovenia, Germany, Italy. **Exports** (2001 est.): $1.1 bil.; partners: Croatia Switzerland Italy Germany **Tourism:** $17 mil. **Budget** (1999 est.): $2.2 bil. **Intl. reserves less gold:** $972 mil.

Transport: Railroad: Length: 634 mi. **Chief port:** Bosanski Brod. **Civil aviation:** 26.1 mil pass.-mi.; 14 airports.

Communications: TV sets: 112 per 1,000 pop. **Radios:** 245 per 1,000 pop. **Telephone lines:** 490,200. **Daily newspaper circ.:** 152 per 1,000 pop. **Internet:** 100,000 users.

Health: Life expectancy: 69.6 male; 75.2 female. **Births** (per 1,000 pop.): 12.7. **Deaths** (per 1,000 pop.): 8.2. **Natural inc.:** 0.44%. **Infant mortality** (per 1,000 live births): 22.7.

Education: Free, compulsory: ages 7-15. **Literacy:** (1991): 86%.

Major Intl. Organizations: UN (FAO, IBRD, ILO, IMF, IMO, WHO), OSCE.

Embassy: 2109 E St. NW, 20037; 337-1500.

Website: www.fbihvlada.gov.ba/engleski

Bosnia was ruled by Croatian kings c. AD 958, and by Hungary 1000-1200. It became organized c. 1200 and later took control of Herzegovina. The kingdom disintegrated from 1391, with the southern part becoming the independent duchy Herzegovina. It was conquered by Turks in 1463 and made a Turkish province. The area was placed under control of Austria-Hungary in 1878, and made part of the province of **Bosnia and Herzegovina,** which was formally annexed to Austria-Hungary 1908; Bosnia became a province of Yugoslavia in 1918. It was reunited with Herzegovina as a federated republic in the 1946 Yugoslavian constitution.

Bosnia and Herzegovina declared sovereignty Oct. 15, 1991. A referendum for independence was passed Feb. 29, 1992. Ethnic Serbs' opposition to the referendum spurred violent clashes and bombings. The U.S. and EU recognized the republic Apr. 7. Fierce three-way fighting continued between Bosnia's Serbs, Muslims, and Croats. Serb forces massacred thousands of Bosnian Muslims and engaged in "ethnic cleansing" (the expulsion of Muslims and other non-Serbs from areas under Bosnian Serb control). The capital, Sarajevo, was surrounded and besieged by Bosnian Serb forces. Muslims and Croats in Bosnia reached a cease fire Feb. 23, 1994, and signed an accord, Mar. 18, to create a Muslim-Croat confederation in Bosnia. However, by mid-1994, Bosnian Serbs controlled over 70% of the country.

As fighting continued in 1995, the balance of power began to shift toward the Muslim-Croat alliance. Massive NATO air strikes at Bosnian Serb targets beginning Aug. 30 triggered a new round of peace talks, and the siege of Sarajevo was lifted Sept. 15. The new talks produced an agreement in principle to create autonomous regions within Bosnia, with the Serb region (Republika Srpska) constituting 49% of the country. A Croat-Muslim offensive in Sept. recaptured significant territory, leaving Bosnian Serbs in control of approximately half that percentage.

A peace agreement initialed in Dayton, Ohio, Nov. 21, 1995, was signed in Paris, Dec. 14, by leaders of Bosnia, Croatia, and Serbia. Some 60,000 NATO troops (about 20,000 from the U.S.) moved in to police the accord. Meanwhile, a UN tribunal began bringing charges against suspected war criminals. Elections were held Sept. 14, 1996, for a 3-person collective presidency, for seats in a federal parliament, and for regional offices. In Dec. a revamped NATO "stabilization force" (SFOR) of over 30,000 members (more than 8,000 from the U.S.) received an 18-month mandate, which was later extended.

In a landmark verdict Aug. 2, 2001, the UN tribunal found Radislav Krstic, a Bosnian Serb general, guilty of genocide for the mass killing of over 7,000 Muslims at Srebrenica in 1995. By Jan. 2003, SFOR's troop strength in Bosnia had been reduced to less than 13,000.

Botswana
Republic of Botswana

People: Population: 1,785,000. **Age distrib.** (%): <15: 40; 65+: 4.2. **Pop. density:** 8 per sq. mi. **Urban:** 49%. **Ethnic groups:** Tswana 79%, Kalanga 11%, Basarwa 3%. **Principal languages:** English (official), Setswana. **Chief religions:** Indigenous beliefs 85%, Christian 15%.

Geography: Area: 231,804 sq. mi. (total); 226,012 sq. mi. (land). **Location:** In southern Africa. **Neighbors:** Namibia on N and W, South Africa on S, Zimbabwe on NE; Botswana claims border with Zambia on N. **Topography:** The Kalahari Desert, supporting nomadic Bushmen and wildlife, spreads over SW; there are swamplands and farming areas in N, and rolling plains in E where livestock are grazed. **Capital:** Gaborone 225,000.

Government: Type: Parliamentary republic. **Head of state and gov.:** Pres. Festus Mogae; b Aug. 21, 1939; in office: Apr. 1, 1998. **Local divisions:** 10 districts, 4 town councils. **Defense budget** (2002): $277 mil. **Active troops:** 9,000.

Economy: Industries: diamonds, copper, nickel, salt, soda ash, potash, proc., textiles. **Chief crops:** sorghum, maize, millet, beans, sunflowers. **Natural resources:** diamonds, copper, nickel, salt, soda ash, potash, coal, iron ore, silver. **Arable land:** 1%. **Livestock** (2002): cattle: 2.40 mil.; chickens: 4 mil.; goats: 2.25 mil.; pigs: 7,000; sheep: 370,000. **Fish catch** (2002): 118 metric tons. **Electricity prod.** (2001): 0.41 bil. kWh.

Finance: Monetary unit: Pula (BWP) (Sept. 2003: 4.85 = $1 U.S.). **GDP** (2002 est.): $15.1 bil. **Per capita GDP:** $9,500. **Imports** (2001): $2.1 bil.; partners (1999): Southern African Customs Union 77%, EFTA 9%, Zimbabwe 4%. **Exports** (2001 est.): $2.5 bil.; partners (1999): EFTA 85%, Southern African Customs Union 10%, Zimbabwe 2%. **Tourism** (1999): $234 mil. **Budget** (2002) $2.4 bil. **Intl. reserves less gold:** $4.03 bil. **Consumer prices:** 8.1%.

Transport: Railroad: Length: 552 mi. **Motor vehicles (1999):** 44,500 pass. cars, 67,900 comm. vehicles. **Civil aviation:** 41.6 mil pass.-mi.; 10 airports.

Communications: TV sets: 21 per 1,000 pop. **Radios:** 154 per 1,000 pop. **Telephone lines:** 142,600. **Daily newspaper circ.:** 27 per 1,000 pop. **Internet:** 50,000 users.

Health: Life expectancy: 32.2 male; 32.3 female. **Births** (per 1,000 pop.): 25.5. **Deaths** (per 1,000 pop.): 31.0. **Natural inc.:** -0.55%. **Infant mortality** (per 1,000 live births): 67.3.

Education: Compulsory: ages 6-15. **Literacy:** 79.8%.

Major Intl. Organizations: UN (FAO, IBRD, ILO, IMF, WHO, WTrO), the Commonwealth, AU.

Embassy: 1531-3 New Hampshire Ave. NW 20036; 244-4990.

Website: www.gov.bw

First inhabited by bushmen, then Bantus, the region became the British protectorate of Bechuanaland in 1886, halting encroachment by Boers and Germans from the south and southwest. The country became fully independent Sept. 30, 1966, as Botswana. Cattle raising and mining (diamonds, copper, nickel) have contributed to economic growth; economy is closely tied to South Africa. According to UN estimates, more than one-third of the adult population has HIV/AIDS.

Brazil
Federative Republic of Brazil

People: Population: 178,470,000. **Age distrib.** (%): <15: 28; 65+: 5.6. **Pop. density:** 55 per sq. mi. **Urban:** 82%. **Ethnic groups:** European 55%, Creole 38%, African 6%. **Principal languages:** Portuguese (official), Spanish, English, French. **Chief religion:** Roman Catholic (nominal) 80%.

Geography: Area: 3,286,486 sq. mi. (total); 3,265,074 sq. mi. (land), largest country in South America. **Location:** Occupies E half of South America. **Neighbors:** French Guiana, Suriname, Guyana, Venezuela on N; Colombia, Peru, Bolivia, Paraguay, on W; Uruguay on S. **Topography:** Brazil's Atlantic coastline stretches 4,603 miles. In N is the heavily wooded Amazon basin covering half the country. Its network of rivers is navigable for 15,814 mi. The Amazon itself flows 2,093 miles in Brazil, all navigable. The NE region is semiarid scrubland, heavily settled and poor. The S central region, favored by climate and resources, has almost half of the population, produces 75% of farm goods and 80% of industrial output. The narrow coastal belt includes most of the major cities. Almost the entire country has a tropical or semitropical climate. **Capital:** Brasília. **Cities (urban aggr.):** São Paulo, 17,962,000, (2001 city est.: 10.4 mil.); Rio de Janeiro, 10,652,000; Belo Horizonte, 4,224,000, Brasília, 2,073,000.

Government: Type: Federal republic. **Head of state and gov.:** Luiz Inacio Lula da Silva; b. Oct. 27, 1945; in office: Jan. 1, 2003. **Local divisions:** 26 states, 1 federal district (Brasília). **Defense budget** (2002): $9.1 bil. **Active troops:** 287,600.

Economy: Industries: textiles, shoes, chemicals, cement, lumber, iron ore, steel, aircraft, motor vehicles & parts. **Chief crops:** coffee, soybeans, wheat, rice, corn, sugarcane, cocoa, citrus. **Natural resources:** bauxite, gold, iron ore, mang., nickel, phosphates, platinum, tin, uranium, oil, hydropower, timber. **Crude oil reserves** (2002): 8.5 bil. bbls. **Arable land:** 5%. **Livestock** (2002): cattle: 176 mil.; chickens: 1.05 bil.; goats: 9 mil.; pigs: 30 mil.; sheep: 15.50 mil. **Fish catch** (2002 est.): 980,000 metric tons. **Electricity prod.** (2001): 321.17 bil. kWh. **Labor force:** services 53%, agri. 23%, ind. 24%.

Finance: Monetary unit: Real (BRL) (Sept. 2003: 3.03 = $1 U.S.). **GDP** (2002 est.): $1.3 tril. **Per capita GDP:** $7,600. **Imports** (2001): $57.7 bil.; partners (2001): U.S. 23.2%, Argentina 11.2%, Germany 8.7%, Japan 5.5%. **Exports** (2001 est.): $57.8 bil.; partners (2001): U.S. 24.4%, Argentina 11.2%, Germany 8.7%, Japan 5.5%. **Tourism:** $4.23 bil. **Budget** (2000) $91.6 bil. **Intl. reserves less gold:** $27.72 bil. **Gold:** 440.00 oz t. **Consumer prices:** 8.4%.

Transport: Railroad: Length: 19,339 mi. **Motor vehicles** (1998): 10.83 mil pass. cars, 2.43 mil comm. vehicles. **Civil aviation:** 26.2 bil pass.-mi.; 665 airports. **Chief ports:** Santos, Rio de Janeiro, Vitoria, Salvador, Rio Grande, Recife.

Communications: TV sets: 333 per 1,000 pop. **Radios:** 434 per 1,000 pop. **Telephone lines:** 38,810,000. **Daily newspaper circ.:** 43.2 per 1,000 pop. **Internet:** 14,300,000 users.

Health: Life expectancy: 67.2 male; 75.3 female. **Births** (per 1,000 pop.): 17.7. **Deaths** (per 1,000 pop.): 6.1. **Natural inc.:** 1.15%. **Infant mortality** (per 1,000 live births): 31.7.

Education: Compulsory: ages 7-14. **Literacy:** 86.4%.

Major Intl. Organizations: UN and most of its specialized agencies, OAS.

Embassy: 3006 Massachusetts Ave. NW 20008; 238-2700.

Website: www.brasilemb.org

Pedro Alvares Cabral, a Portuguese navigator, is generally credited as the first European to reach Brazil, in 1500. The country was thinly settled by various Indian tribes. Only a few have survived to the present, mostly in the Amazon basin.

In the next centuries, Portuguese colonists gradually pushed inland, bringing along large numbers of African slaves. (Slavery was not abolished until 1888.) The King of Portugal, fleeing before Napoleon's army, moved the seat of government to Brazil in 1808. Brazil thereupon became a kingdom under Dom Joao VI. After his return to Portugal, his son Pedro proclaimed the independence of Brazil, Sept. 7, 1822, and was crowned emperor. The second emperor, Dom Pedro II, was deposed in 1889, and a republic proclaimed, called the United States of Brazil. In 1967 the country was renamed the Federative Republic of Brazil.

A military junta took control in 1930; dictatorial power was assumed by Getulio Vargas, until finally forced out by the military in 1945. A democratic regime prevailed 1945-64, during which time the capital was moved from Rio de Janeiro to Brasília. In 1964, Pres. Joao Belchoir Marques Goulart instituted economic policies that aggravated Brazil's inflation; he was overthrown by an army revolt. The next 5 presidents were all military leaders. Censorship was imposed, and much of the opposition was suppressed amid charges of torture.

Since 1930, successive governments have pursued industrial and agricultural growth and interior area development. Exploiting vast Natural resources and a huge labor force, Brazil became the leading industrial power of Latin America by the 1970s, while agricultural output soared. By the 1990s, Brazil had one of the world's largest economies; income was poorly distributed, however, and more than one out of four Brazilians continued to survive on less than $1 a day. Despite protective environmental legislation, development has destroyed much of the Amazon ecosystem. Brazil hosted delegates from 178 countries at the Earth Summit, June 3-14, 1992.

Democratic presidential elections were held in 1985 as the nation returned to civilian rule. Fernando Collor de Mello was elected president in Dec. 1989. In Sept. 1992, Collor was impeached for corruption. He resigned on Dec. 29 as his trial was beginning, and Itamar Franco, who had been acting president, was sworn in as president. In elections held on Oct. 3, 1994, Fernando Henrique Cardoso was elected president. Reelected Oct. 4, 1998, he guided Brazil through a series of financial crises. New presidential elections were set for Oct. 2002.

A new civil code guaranteeing legal equality for women was enacted Aug. 15, 2001. The IMF approved a $30 bil. loan to Brazil Aug. 7, 2002; by then, Brazil's debt already exceeded $260 bil. Luiz Inacio Lula da Silva, a union leader and reformer, won a presidential runoff Oct. 27 with 61.3% of the vote. Brazil's space program suffered a setback when a rocket exploded on its launchpad Aug. 22, 2003, killing 21 people.

Brunei
State of Brunei Darussalam

People: Population: 358,000. **Age distrib.** (%): <15: 30.2; 65+: 2.8. **Pop. density:** 176 per sq. mi. **Urban:** 73%. **Ethnic groups:** Malay 67%, Chinese 15%, indigenous 6%. **Principal languages:** Malay (official), English, Chinese. **Chief religions:** Muslim (official) 67%, Buddhist 13%, Christian 10%; indigenous beliefs, other 10%.

Geography: Area: 2,228 sq. mi. (total); 2,035 sq. mi. (land). **Location:** In SE Asia, on the N coast of the island of Borneo; it is surrounded on its landward side by the Malaysian state of Sarawak. **Topography:** Brunei has a narrow coastal plain, with mountains in E, hilly lowlands in W. There are swamps in W and NE. **Climate** is tropical. **Capital:** Bandar Seri Begawan, (1999 met. area est.) 46,000.

Government: Type: Independent sultanate. **Head of state and gov.:** Sultan Sir Muda Hassanal Bolkiah Mu'izzadin Waddaulah; b July 15, 1946; in office: Jan. 1, 1984 (sultan since Oct. 5, 1967). **Local divisions:** 4 districts. **Defense budget** (2002): $267 mil. **Active troops:** 7,000.

Economy: Industries: oil, oil refining, nat. gas liquefaction, constr. **Chief crops:** rice, vegetables, fruits. **Natural resources:** oil, nat. gas, timber. **Arable land:** 1%. **Livestock** (2002): cattle: 3,000; chickens: 5 mil.; goats: 2,449; pigs: 6,000; sheep: 3,000. **Fish catch** (2002): 1,591 metric tons. **Electricity prod.** (2001): 2.5 bil. kWh. **Labor force:** government 48%, production of oil, natural gas, services, and construct. 42%, agri., forestry, and fishing 10%.

Finance: Monetary unit: Dollar (BND) (Sept. 2003: 1.77 = $1 U.S.). **GDP** (2002 est.): $6.5 bil. **Per capita GDP:** $18,600. **Imports** (2000): $1.4 bil.; partners (1999): Singapore 34%, UK 15%, Malaysia 15%, U.S. 5%. **Exports** (2000 est.): $3 bil.; partners (1999): Japan 42%, U.S. 17%, South Korea 14%, Thailand 3%. **Tourism** (1998): $37 mil. **Budget** (1997 est.): $2.6 bil.

Transport: Railroad: Length: 8 mi. **Motor vehicles** (1999): 176,000 pass. cars, 19,400 comm. vehicles. **Civil aviation:** 1.59 bil pass.-mi.; 1 airport.

Communications: TV sets: 637 per 1,000 pop. **Radios:** 302 per 1,000 pop. **Telephone lines:** 88,400. **Daily newspaper circ.:** 69 per 1,000 pop. **Internet:** 35,000 users.

Health: Life expectancy: 71.9 male; 76.8 female. **Births** (per 1,000 pop.): 19.7. **Deaths** (per 1,000 pop.): 3.4. **Natural inc.:** 1.63%. **Infant mortality** (per 1,000 live births): 13.5.

Education: Compulsory: ages 5-16. **Literacy:** 91.8%.

Major Intl. Organizations: UN and some of its specialized agencies, APEC, ASEAN, the Commonwealth.

Embassy: 3520 International Court NW 20008; 202-237-1838.

Website: www.gov.bn

The Sultanate of Brunei was a powerful state in the early 16th century, with authority over all of the island of Borneo as well as parts of the Sulu Islands and the Philippines. In 1888, a treaty placed the state under the protection of Great Britain.

Brunei became a fully sovereign and independent state on Jan. 1, 1984. Much of the country's oil wealth has been squandered in recent years by members of the royal family.

Bulgaria
Republic of Bulgaria

People: Population: 7,897,000. **Age distrib.** (%): <15: 14.6; 65+: 16.9. **Pop. density:** 185 per sq. mi. **Urban:** 67%. **Ethnic groups:** Bulgarian 84%, Turk 10%, Roma 5%. **Principal languages:** Bulgarian (official), Turkish. **Chief religions:** Bulgarian Orthodox 84%, Muslim 12%.

Geography: Area: 42,823 sq. mi. (total); 42,684 sq. mi. (land). **Location:** SE Europe, in E Balkan Peninsula on Black Sea. **Neighbors:** Romania on N; Yugoslavia, Macedonia on W; Greece, Turkey on S. **Topography:** The Stara Planina (Balkan) Mts. stretch E-W across the center of the country, with the Danubian plain on N, the Rhodope Mts. on SW, and Thracian Plain on SE. **Capital:** Sofia 1,187,000.

Government: Type: Republic. **Head of state:** Pres. Georgi Parvanov; b June 28, 1957; in office: Jan. 22, 2002. **Head of gov.:** Prime Min. Simeon Sakskoburggotski (Simeon II); b June 16, 1937; in office: July 24, 2001. **Local divisions:** 9 provinces. **Defense budget** (2002): $431 mil. **Active troops:** 68,450.

Economy: Industries: utilities, food. beverages, tobacco, machinery, metals, chemicals. **Chief crops:** vegetables, fruits, tobacco, wine, wheat, barley, sunflowers, sugar beets. **Natural resources:** bauxite, copper, lead, zinc, coal, timber. **Crude oil reserves** (2002): 15 mil. bbls. **Arable land:** 37%. **Livestock** (2002): cattle: 640,000; chickens: 15 mil.; goats: 675,000; pigs: 1.14 mil.; sheep: 2.29 mil. **Fish catch** (2002): 8,140 metric tons. **Electricity prod.** (2001): 41.38 bil. kWh. **Labor force:** agri. 26%, ind. 31%, services 43%.

Finance: Monetary unit: Lev (BGL) (Sept. 2003: 1.80 = $1 U.S.). **GDP** (2002 est.): $50.6 bil. **Per capita GDP:** $6,600. **Imports** (2002): $6.9 bil.; partners (2001): Russia 19.9%, Germany 15.3%, Italy 9.6%, France 6.0%. **Exports** (2002 est.): $5.3 bil.; partners (2001): Italy 14%, Turkey 10%, Germany 9%, Greece 8%. **Tourism:** $1.07 bil. **Budget** (2001 est.): $5.68 bil. **Intl. reserves less gold:** $3.24 bil. **Gold:** 1.28 mil oz t. **Consumer prices:** 5.8%.

Transport: Railroad: Length: 2,668 mi. **Motor vehicles:** 1.99 mil pass. cars, 301,700 comm. vehicles. **Civil aviation:** 939.5 mil pass.-mi.; 128 airports. **Chief ports:** Burgas, Varna.

Communications: TV sets: 429 per 1,000 pop. **Radios:** 537 per 1,000 pop. **Telephone lines:** 2,922,000. **Daily newspaper circ.:** 257 per 1,000 pop. **Internet:** 605,000 users.

Health: Life expectancy: 68.3 male; 75.6 female. **Births** (per 1,000 pop.): 8.0. **Deaths** (per 1,000 pop.): 14.3. **Natural inc.:** -0.63%. **Infant mortality** (per 1,000 live births): 13.7.

Education: Compulsory: ages 7-15. **Literacy:** 98.6%.

Major Intl. Organizations: UN (FAO, IBRD, ILO, IMF, IMO, WHO, WTrO), OSCE.

Embassy: 1621 22d St. NW 20008; 202-387-0174.

Website: www.government.bg/English

Bulgaria was settled by Slavs in the 6th century. Turkic Bulgars arrived in the 7th century, merged with the Slavs, became Christians by the 9th century, and set up powerful empires in the 10th and 12th centuries. The Ottomans prevailed in 1396 and remained for 500 years.

An 1876 revolt led to an independent kingdom in 1908. Bulgaria expanded after the first Balkan War but lost its Aegean coastline in World War I, when it sided with Germany. Bulgaria joined the Axis in World War II but withdrew in 1944. Communists took power with Soviet aid; monarchy was abolished Sept. 8, 1946.

On Nov. 10, 1989, Communist Party leader and head of state Todor Zhivkov, who had held power for 35 years, resigned. Zhivkov was imprisoned, Jan. 1990, and convicted, Sept. 1992, of corruption and abuse of power. In Jan. 1990, Parliament voted to revoke the constitutionally guaranteed dominant role of the Communist Party. A new constitution took effect July 13, 1991. An economic austerity program was launched in May 1996. Former Prime Min. Andrei Lukanov, a longtime Communist leader, was assassinated Oct. 2 in Sofia. Petar Stoyanov won a presidential runoff election Nov. 3.

Bulgaria's deteriorating economy provoked nationwide strikes and demonstrations in Jan. 1997. The Union of Democratic Forces, an anti-Communist group, won national elections on Apr. 19, 1997. The UDF lost the elections of June 17, 2001, to a party headed by the former king, Simeon II. Socialist opposition leader Georgi Parvanov won a presidential runoff vote Nov. 18.

Burkina Faso

People: Population: 13,002,000. **Age distrib.** (%): <15: 47.3; 65+: 2.9. **Pop. density:** 123 per sq. mi. **Urban:** 17%. **Ethnic groups:** Mossi (approx. 40%), Gurunsi, Senufo, Lobi, Bobo, Mande, Fulani. **Principal languages:** French (official), Sudanic languages. **Chief religions:** Muslim 50%, indigenous beliefs 40%, Christian (mainly Roman Catholic) 10%.

Geography: Area: 105,869 sq. mi. (total); 105,715 sq. mi. (land). **Location:** In W Africa, S of the Sahara. **Neighbors:** Mali on NW; Niger on NE; Benin, Togo, Ghana, Côte d'Ivoire on S. **Topography:** Landlocked Burkina Faso is in the savanna region of W Africa. The N is arid, hot, and thinly populated. **Capital:** Ouagadougou, 862,000.

Government: Type: Republic. **Head of state:** Pres. Blaise Compaoré; b 1951; in office: Oct. 15, 1987. **Head of gov.:** Prime Min. Paramanga Ernest Yonli; b 1956; in office: Nov. 7, 2000. **Local divisions:** 45 provinces. **Defense budget** (2002): $38 mil. **Active troops:** 10,200.

Economy: Industries: cotton, beverages, agric. proc., soap, cigarettes, textiles, gold. **Chief crops:** peanuts, shea nuts, sesame, cotton, sorghum, millet. **Natural resources:** mang., limestone, marble, gold, antimony, copper, nickel. bauxite, lead, phosphates, zinc, silver. **Arable land:** 13%. **Livestock** (2002): cattle: 4.80 mil.; chickens: 23 mil.; goats: 8.70 mil.; pigs: 630,000; sheep: 6.80 mil. **Fish catch** (2002 est.): 8,505 metric tons. **Electricity prod.** (2001): 0.28 bil. kWh. **Labor force:** agri. 90%.

Finance: Monetary unit: CFA Franc BCEAO (XOF) (Sept. 2003: 605.18 = $1 U.S.). **GDP** (2002 est.): $13.6 bil. **Per capita GDP:** $1,080. **Imports** (2001): $580 mil.; partners (2000): Cote d'Ivoire 25.1%, Venezuela 23.4%, France 17.0%. **Exports** (2001 est.): $265 mil.; partners (2000): Venezuela 14.7%, Benelux 12.2%, Italy 9.6%, France 7.0%. **Tourism** (1998): $42 mil. **Budget** (1995 est.): $492 mil. **Intl. reserves less gold:** $231 mil. **Consumer prices:** 2.2%.

Transport: Railroad: Length: 386 mi. **Motor vehicles** (1998): 35,500 pass. cars, 19,500 comm. vehicles. **Civil aviation:** 167.1 mil pass.-mi.; 2 airports.

Communications: TV sets: 11 per 1,000 pop. **Radios:** 34 per 1,000 pop. **Telephone lines:** 57,600. **Daily newspaper circ.:** 1.3 per 1,000 pop. **Internet:** 19,000 users.

Health: Life expectancy: 43.0 male; 45.9 female. **Births** (per 1,000 pop.): 44.8. **Deaths** (per 1,000 pop.): 18.8. **Natural inc.:** 2.60%. **Infant mortality** (per 1,000 live births): 99.8.

Education: Compulsory: ages 6-16. **Literacy:** 26.6%.

Major Intl. Organizations: UN and many of its specialized agencies, AU.

Embassy: 2340 Massachusetts Ave. NW 20008; 332-5577.

Website: www.burkinaembassy-usa.org

The Mossi tribe entered the area in the 11th to 13th centuries. Their kingdoms ruled until they were defeated by the Mali and Songhai empires.

French control came by 1896, but Upper Volta (renamed Burkina Faso on Aug. 4, 1984) was not established as a separate territory until 1947. Full independence came Aug. 5, 1960, and a pro-French government was elected. The military seized power in 1980. A 1987 coup established the current regime, which instituted a multiparty democracy in the early 1990s.

Several hundred thousand farm workers migrate each year to Côte d'Ivoire and Ghana. Burkina Faso is heavily dependent on foreign aid.

Burma
(See Myanmar)

Burundi
Republic of Burundi

People: Population: 6,825,000. **Age distrib.** (%): <15: 46.5; 65+: 2.8. **Pop. density:** 689 per sq. mi. **Urban:** 9%. **Ethnic groups:** Hutu 85%, Tutsi 14%, Twa (Pygmy) 1%. **Principal languages:** Kirundi, French (both official); Swahili. **Chief religions:** Roman Catholic 62%, indigenous beliefs 23%, Muslim 10%, Protestant 5%.

Geography: Area: 10,745 sq. mi. (total); 9,904 sq. mi. (land). **Location:** In central Africa. **Neighbors:** Rwanda on N, Dem. Rep. of the Congo (formerly Zaire) on W, Tanzania on E and S. **Topography:** Much of the country is grassy highland, with mountains reaching 8,900 ft. The southernmost source of the White Nile is located in Burundi. Lake Tanganyika is the second deepest lake in the world. **Capital:** Bujumbura 346,000.

Government: Type: In transition. **Head of state and gov.:** Pres. Domitien Ndayizeye; b May 2, 1953; in office: Apr. 30, 2003. **Local divisions:** 15 provinces. **Defense budget** (2002): $33 mil. **Active troops:** 45,500.

Economy: Industries: light consumer goods, component assembly, constr., food proc. **Chief crops:** coffee, cotton, tea, corn, sorghum, sweet potatoes, bananas. **Natural resources:** nickel, uranium, rare earth oxides, peat, cobalt, copper, platinum, vanadium, hydropower. **Arable land:** 44%. **Livestock** (2002): cattle: 315,000; chickens: 4.70 mil.; goats: 600,000; pigs: 70,000; sheep: 230,000. **Fish catch** (2002 est.): 9,064 metric tons. **Electricity prod.** (2001): 0.16 bil. kWh. **Labor force:** 93% agric.

Finance: Monetary unit: Franc (BIF) (Sept. 2003: 1,096.50 = $1 U.S.). **GDP** (2002 est.): $3.8 bil. **Per capita GDP:** $600. **Imports** (2001): $125 mil.; partners (2000 est.): EU 37.6%, Tanzania 10.3%, Zambia 4.3%, India 3.4%. **Exports** (2001 est.): $24 mil.; partners (2000 est.): EU 52.5%, U.S. 11.5%, Kenya 11.5%, Switzerland 4.9%. **Tourism:** $1 mil. **Budget** (2000 est.): $176 mil. **Intl. reserves less gold:** $43 mil. **Gold** (2000): 20,000 oz t. **Consumer prices:** -1.4%.

Transport: Motor vehicles (1998): 8,200 pass. cars, 11,800 comm. vehicles. **Civil aviation** (1998): 5.0 mil pass.-mi.; 1 airport. **Chief port:** Bujumbura.

Communications: TV sets: 15 per 1,000 pop. **Radios:** 152 per 1,000 pop. **Telephone lines:** 20,000. **Daily newspaper circ.:** .2 per 1,000 pop. **Internet:** 6,000 users.

Health: Life expectancy: 42.5 male; 43.9 female. **Births** (per 1,000 pop.): 39.7. **Deaths** (per 1,000 pop.): 17.8. **Natural inc.:** 2.19%. **Infant mortality** (per 1,000 live births): 71.5.

Education: Compulsory: ages 7-12. **Literacy:** 51.6%.

Major Intl. Organizations: UN (FAO, IBRD, ILO, IMF, WHO, WTrO), AU.

Embassy: 2233 Wisconsin Ave. NW , Suite 212, 20007; 342-2574.

Website: www.burundi.gov.bi

The pygmy Twa were the first inhabitants, followed by Bantu Hutus, who were conquered in the 16th century by the Tutsi (Watusi), probably from Ethiopia. Under German control in 1899, the area fell to Belgium in 1916, which exercised successively a League of Nations mandate and UN trusteeship over Ruanda-Urundi (now the two countries of Rwanda and Burundi). Burundi became independent July 1, 1962.

An unsuccessful Hutu rebellion in 1972-73 left 10,000 Tutsi and 150,000 Hutu dead. Over 100,000 Hutu fled to Tanzania and Zaire (now Congo). In the 1980s, Burundi's Tutsi-dominated regime pledged itself to ethnic reconciliation and democratic reform. In the nation's first democratic presidential election, in June 1993, a Hutu, Melchior Ndadaye, was elected. He was killed in an attempted coup, Oct. 21, 1993. At least 150,000 Burundians died as a result of ethnic conflict during the next three years. Pres. Cyprien Ntaryamira, elected Jan. 1994, was killed with the president of Rwanda in a mysterious plane crash, Apr. 6. The incident sparked massive carnage in Rwanda; violence in Burundi, initially far more limited, intensified in 1995. Ethnic strife continued after a military coup, July 25, 1996. Former South African Pres. Nelson Mandela mediated peace talks from Dec. 1999; most warring groups signed a draft peace treaty in Arusha, Tanzania, Aug. 28, 2000. Coup attempts were suppressed Apr. 18 and July 23, 2001. A power-sharing government headed by Buyoya was sworn in Nov. 1, but clashes with rebels continued. Domitien Ndayizeye, a Hutu, became president Apr. 30, 2003.

Cambodia
Kingdom of Cambodia

People: Population: 14,144,000. **Age distrib.** (%): <15: 40.7; 65+: 3.5. **Pop. density:** 208 per sq. mi. **Urban:** 18%. **Ethnic groups:** Khmer 90%, Vietnamese 5%, Chinese 1%. **Principal languages:** Khmer (official), French, English. **Chief religion:** Theravada Buddhist 95% (official).

Geography: Area: 69,900 sq. mi. (total); 68,155 sq. mi. (land). **Location:** SE Asia, on Indochina Peninsula. **Neighbors:** Thailand on W and N, Laos on NE, Vietnam on E. **Topography:** The central area, formed by the Mekong R. basin and Tonle Sap lake, is level. Hills and mountains are in SE, a long escarpment separates the country from Thailand on NW. 76% of the area is forested. **Capital:** Phnom Penh 1,109,000.

Government: Type: Constitutional monarchy. **Head of state:** King Norodom Sihanouk; b Oct. 31, 1922; in office: Sept. 24, 1993. **Head of gov.:** Prime Min. Hun Sen; b Apr. 4, 1952; in office: Nov. 30, 1998. **Local divisions:** 20 provinces and 3 municipalities. **Defense budget** (2002): $248 mil. **Active troops:** 125,000.

Economy: Industries: tourism, garments, rice milling, fishing, wood & wood products, rubber, cement, gem mining, textiles. **Chief crops:** rice, rubber, corn, vegetables. **Natural resources:** timber, gems, iron ore, mang., phosphates. **Arable land:** 13%. **Livestock** (2002): cattle: 2.87 mil.; chickens: 15.25 mil.; pigs: 2.11 mil. **Fish catch** (2002 est.): 412,700 metric tons. **Electricity prod.** (2001): 0.12 bil. kWh. **Labor force:** agri. 80%.

Finance: Monetary unit: Riel (KHR) (Sept. 2003: 3,989.80 = $1 U.S.). **GDP** (2002 est.): $19.7 bil. **Per capita GDP:** $1,500. **Imports** (2000): $1.4 bil.; partners (2000): Singapore 22.5%, Thailand 19.8%, Hong Kong 15.6%, China 4.9%. **Exports** (2000 est.): $1.05 bil.; partners (2000): U.S. 46.4%, Vietnam 26.1%, Germany 5.6%, Singapore 5.0%. **Tourism:** $228 mil. **Budget** (2001 est.): $607 mil. **Intl. reserves less gold:** $571 mil. **Gold:** 400,000 oz t. **Consumer prices:** 3.2%.

Transport: Railroad: Length: 375 mi. **Motor vehicles:** 8,300 pass. cars, 3,100 comm. vehicles. **Civil aviation:** 5 airports. **Chief port:** Kampong Saom (Sihanoukville).

Communications: TV sets: 9 per 1,000 pop. **Radios:** 128 per 1,000 pop. **Telephone lines:** 33,500. **Daily newspaper circ.:** 1.7 per 1,000 pop. **Internet:** 30,000 users.

Health: Life expectancy: 55.5 male; 60.5 female. **Births** (per 1,000 pop.): 27.3. **Deaths** (per 1,000 pop.): 9.3. **Natural inc.:** 1.80%. **Infant mortality** (per 1,000 live births): 75.9.

Education: Compulsory: ages 6-12. **Literacy:** 69.9%.

Major Intl. Organizations: UN (FAO, IBRD, ILO, IMF, IMO, WHO, WTrO), ASEAN.

Embassy: 4530 16th St. NW 20011; 726-7742.

Website: www.cambodia.gov.kh

Early kingdoms dating from that of Funan in the 1st century AD culminated in the great Khmer empire that flourished from the 9th century to the 13th, encompassing present-day Thailand, Cambodia, Laos, and southern Vietnam. The peripheral areas were lost to invading Siamese and Vietnamese, and France established a protectorate in 1863. Independence came in 1953.

Prince Norodom Sihanouk, king 1941-1955 and head of state from 1960, tried to maintain neutrality. Relations with the U.S. were broken in 1965, after South Vietnam planes attacked Vietcong forces within Cambodia. Relations were restored in 1969, after Sihanouk charged Viet Communists with arming Cambodian insurgents.

In 1970, pro-U.S. Prem. Lon Nol seized power, demanding removal of 40,000 North Viet troops; the monarchy was abolished. Sihanouk formed a government-in-exile in Beijing, and open war began between the government and Communist Khmer Rouge guerrillas. The U.S. provided heavy military and economic aid.

Khmer Rouge forces captured Phnom Penh Apr. 17, 1975. The new government evacuated all cities and towns, and shuffled the rural population, sending virtually the entire population to clear jungle, forest, and scrub. Over one million people were killed in executions and enforced hardships.

Severe border fighting broke out with Vietnam in 1978 and developed into a full-fledged Vietnamese invasion. Formation of a Vietnamese-backed government was announced, Jan. 8, 1979, one day after the Vietnamese capture of Phnom Penh. Thousands of refugees flowed into Thailand, and widespread starvation was reported.

On Jan. 10, 1983, Vietnam launched an offensive against rebel forces in the west. They overran a refugee camp, Jan. 31, driving 30,000 residents into Thailand. In March, Vietnam launched a major offensive against camps on the Cambodian-Thailand border, engaged Khmer Rouge guerrillas, and crossed the border, instigating clashes with Thai troops. Vietnam withdrew nearly all its troops by Sept. 1989.

Following UN-sponsored elections in Cambodia that ended May 28, 1993, the 2 leading parties agreed to share power in an interim government until a new constitution was adopted. On Sept. 21, a constitution reestablishing a monarchy was adopted by the National Assembly. It took effect Sept. 24, with Sihanouk as king. The Khmer Rouge, which had boycotted the elections, opposed the new government, and armed violence continued in the mid-1990s. Ieng Sary, a Khmer Rouge leader, broke with the guerrillas, formed a rival group, and announced his support for the monarchy in Aug. 1996, as Khmer Rouge strength rapidly diminished.

Co-Prime Min. Hun Sen staged a coup July 5, 1997, ousting his rival, Prince Norodom Ranariddh. Pol Pot, the Khmer Rouge leader who held power during the late 1970s, was denounced by his former comrades at a show trial, July 25, and sentenced to house arrest; he died Apr. 15, 1998. Hun Sen's party won parliamentary elections on July 26. Cambodia was formally admitted to ASEAN on Apr. 30, 1999. Hun Sen's party retained power in parliamentary elections July 27, 2003.

Cameroon
Republic of Cameroon

People: Population: 16,018,000. **Age distrib.** (%): <15: 42.1; 65+: 3.4. **Pop. density:** 88 per sq. mi. **Urban:** 50%. **Ethnic groups:** Highlanders 31%, Equatorial Bantu 19%, Kirdi 11%, Fulani 10%, NW Bantu 8%, E Nigritic 7%. **Principal languages:** English, French (both official); 24 African language groups. **Chief religions:** Indigenous beliefs 40%, Christian 40%, Muslim 20%.

Geography: Area: 183,568 sq. mi. (total); 181,252 sq. mi. (land). **Location:** Between W and central Africa. **Neighbors:** Nigeria on NW; Chad, Central African Republic on E; Congo, Gabon, Equatorial Guinea on S. **Topography:** A low coastal plain with rain forests is in S; plateaus in center lead to forested mountains in W, including Mt. Cameroon, 13,435 ft.; grasslands in N lead to marshes around Lake Chad. **Capital:** Yaoundé. **Cities** (urban agg.): Douala, 1,642,000; Yaoundé, 1,481,000.

Government: Type: Republic. **Head of state:** Pres. Paul Biya; b Feb. 13, 1933; in office: Nov. 6, 1982. **Head of gov.:** Prime Min. Peter Mafani Musonge; b Dec. 3, 1942; in office: Sept. 19, 1996. **Local divisions:** 10 provinces. **Defense budget:** (2002) $132 mil. **Active troops:** 23,100.

Economy: Industries: oil prod. & refining, food proc., light consumer goods, textiles, lumber. **Chief crops:** coffee, cocoa, cotton, rubber, bananas, oilseed, grains. **Natural resources:** oil, bauxite, iron ore, timber, hydropower. **Arable land:** 13%. **Livestock** (2002): cattle: 5.90 mil.; chickens: 30 mil.; goats: 4.40 mil.; pigs: 1.35 mil.; sheep: 3.80 mil. **Fish catch** (2002 est.): 111,081 metric tons. **Electricity prod.** (2001): 3.61 bil. kWh. **Labor force:** agri. 70%, ind. and commerce 13%, other 17%.

Finance: Monetary unit: CFA Franc BEAC (XAF) (Sept. 2003: 597.03 = $1 U.S.). **GDP** (2002 est.): $27 bil. **Per capita GDP:** $1,700. **Imports** (2000): $1.5 bil.; partners (2000 est.): France 29%, Germany 7%, U.S. 6%, Japan 6%. **Exports** (2000 est.): $2.1 bil.; partners (2000 est.): Italy 24%, France 18%, Netherlands 10%. **Tourism** (1998): $40 mil. **Budget** (2001 est.): $2.1 bil. **Intl. reserves less gold:** $463 mil. **Gold:** 30,000 oz t. **Consumer prices:** 2.8%.

Transport: Railroad: Length: 626 mi. **Motor vehicles:** 115,900 pass. cars, 47,400 comm. vehicles. **Civil aviation:** 371.0 mil pass.-mi.; 11 airports. **Chief ports:** Douala, Kribi.

Communications: TV sets: 34 per 1,000 pop. **Radios:** 163 per 1,000 pop. **Telephone lines:** 101,400. **Daily newspaper circ.:** 6.7 per 1,000 pop. **Internet:** 45,000 users.

Health: Life expectancy: 47.2 male; 49.0 female. **Births** (per 1,000 pop.): 35.5. **Deaths** (per 1,000 pop.): 15.3. **Natural inc.:** 2.02%. **Infant mortality** (per 1,000 live births): 70.1.

Education: Compulsory: ages 6-12. **Literacy:** 79%.

Major Intl. Organizations: UN (FAO, IBRD, ILO, IMF, IMO, WHO, WTrO), the Commonwealth, AU.

Embassy: 2349 Massachusetts Ave. NW 20008; 265-8790.

Websites: www.prc.cm; www.camnet.cm/mintour/tourisme

Portuguese sailors were the first Europeans to reach Cameroon, in the 15th century. The European and American slave trade was very active in the area. German control lasted from 1884 to 1916, when France and Britain divided the territory, later receiving League of Nations mandates and UN trusteeships. French Cameroon became independent Jan. 1, 1960; one part of British Cameroon joined Nigeria in 1961, the other part joined Cameroon. Stability has allowed for development of roads, railways, agriculture, and petroleum production.

Pres. Paul Biya retained his office in Oct. 1992 elections, but the results were widely disputed. A new constitution won legislative approval in Dec. 1995. Fraud charges accompanied legislative elections, May 17, 1997, which Biya's party won.

Canada

People: Population: 31,510,000. **Age distrib.** (%): <15: 18.7; 65+: 12.9. **Pop. density:** 9 per sq. mi. **Urban:** 79%. **Ethnic groups:** British 28%, French 23%, other European 15%, Amerindian 2%. **Principal languages:** English, French (both official). **Chief religions:** Roman Catholic 46%, Protestant 36%, other 18%.

Geography: Area: 3,851,806 sq. mi. (total); 3,560,234 sq. mi. (land), the largest country in land size in the western hemisphere. **Topography:** Canada stretches 3,426 miles from east to west and extends southward from the North Pole to the U.S. border. Its seacoast includes 36,356 miles of mainland and 115,133 miles of islands, including the Arctic islands almost from Greenland to near the Alaskan border. **Climate:** While generally temperate, varies from freezing winter cold to blistering summer heat. **Capital:** Ottawa, 1,094,000. **Cities (urban aggr.):** Toronto, 4.75 mil; Montreal, 3.5 mil; Vancouver, 2.0 mil; Ottawa-Hull, 1.1 mil; Edmonton, 944,000; Calgary, 953,000.

Government: Type: Confederation with parliamentary democracy. **Head of state:** Queen Elizabeth II, represented by Gov.-Gen. Adrienne Clarkson; b Feb. 10, 1939; in office: Oct. 7, 1999. **Head of gov.:** Prime Min. Jean Chrétien; b Jan. 11, 1934; in office: Nov. 4, 1993. **Local divisions:** 10 provinces, 3 territories. **Defense budget** (2002): $7.6 bil. **Active troops:** 52,300.

Economy: Industries: transp. equip., chemicals, minerals, food & fish products, wood & paper products, oil & nat. gas. **Chief crops:** wheat, barley, oilseed, tobacco, fruits, vegetables. **Natural resources:** iron ore, nickel, zinc, copper, gold, lead, molybd., potash, silver, fish, timber, wildlife, coal, oil, nat. gas, hydropower. **Crude oil reserves** (2002): 4.9 bil. bbls. **Arable land:** 5%. **Livestock** (2002): cattle: 13.70 mil.; chickens: 158 mil.; goats: 30,000; pigs: 14.37 mil.; sheep: 994,000. **Fish catch** (2002): 1,201,955 metric tons. **Electricity prod.** (2001): 566.31 bil. kWh. **Labor force:** services 74%, manufact. 15%, construct. 5%, agri. 3%, other 3%.

Finance: Monetary unit: Dollar (CAD) (Sept. 2003: 1.38 = $1 U.S.). **GDP** (2002 est.): $923 bil. **Per capita GDP:** $29,400. **Imports** (2002): $229 bil.; partners (2001): U.S. 72.7%, UK 3.4%, other EU 3.2%, Japan 3.0%. **Exports** (2002 est.): $260.5 bil.; partners (2000): U.S. 84.6%, Japan 2.2%, UK 1.6%, other EU 2.2%. **Tourism:** $10.77 bil. **Budget** (2001 est.): $161.4 bil. **Intl. reserves less gold:** $27.2 bil. **Gold:** 600,000 mil oz t. **Consumer prices:** 2.2%.

Transport: Railroad: Length: 22,440 mi. **Motor vehicles:** 16.86 mil pass. cars, 668,000 comm. vehicles. **Civil aviation:** 40.59 bil pass.-mi.; 507 airports. **Chief ports:** Halifax, Montreal, Quebec, Saint John, Toronto, Vancouver.

Communications: TV sets: 709 per 1,000 pop. **Radios:** 1,038 per 1,000 pop. **Telephone lines:** 19,962,100. **Daily newspaper circ.:** 159 per 1,000 pop. **Internet:** 16,200,000 users.

Health: Life expectancy: 76.4 male; 83.4 female. **Births** (per 1,000 pop.): 11.0. **Deaths** (per 1,000 pop.): 7.6. **Natural inc.:** 0.34%. **Infant mortality** (per 1,000 live births): 4.9.

Education: Compulsory: ages 6-16. **Literacy** (1994): 97%.

Major Intl. Organizations: UN and all of its specialized agencies, APEC, the Commonwealth, NATO, OAS, OECD, OSCE.

Embassy: 501 Pennsylvania Ave. NW 20001; 682-1740.

Websites: www.statcan.ca, canada.gc.ca

Provinces/Territories	Area (sq. mi.)	Population (2001 cen.)*
Alberta	255,287	2,974,807
British Columbia	365,948	3,907,738
Manitoba	250,947	1,119,583
New Brunswick	28,355	729,498
Newfoundland & Labrador	156,649	512,930
Nova Scotia	21,425	908.007
Ontario	412,581	11,410,046
Prince Edward Island	2,185	135,294
Quebec	594,860	7,237,479
Saskatchewan	251,866	978,933
Northwest Territories	503,951	37,360
Yukon Territory	186,661	28,674
Nunavut	818,959	26,745

*Excludes incompletely enumerated Indian reserves or settlements.

French explorer Jacques Cartier, who reached the Gulf of St. Lawrence in 1534, is generally regarded as Canada's founder. But English seaman John Cabot sighted Newfoundland in 1497, and Vikings are believed to have reached the Atlantic coast centuries before either explorer.

Canadian settlement was pioneered by the French who established Quebec City (1608) and Montreal (1642) and declared New France a colony in 1663.

Britain acquired Acadia (later Nova Scotia) in 1717 and, through military victory over French forces in Canada, captured Quebec (1759) and obtained control of the rest of New France in 1763. The French, through the Quebec Act of 1774, retained the rights to their own language, religion, and civil law. The British presence in Canada increased during the American Revolution when many colonials, proudly calling themselves United Empire Loyalists, moved north to Canada. Fur traders and explorers led Canadians westward across the continent. Sir Alexander Mackenzie reached the Pacific in 1793 and scrawled on a rock by the ocean, "from Canada by land."

In Upper and Lower Canada (later called Ontario and Quebec) and in the Maritimes, legislative assemblies appeared in the 18th century and reformers called for responsible government. But the War of 1812 intervened. The war, a conflict between Great Britain and the United States fought mainly in Upper Canada, ended in a stalemate in 1814.

In 1837 political agitation for more democratic government culminated in rebellions in Upper and Lower Canada. Britain sent Lord Durham to investigate; in a famous report (1839), he recommended union of the 2 parts into one colony called Canada. The union lasted until Confederation, July 1, 1867, when proclamation of the British North America (BNA) Act (now known as the Constitution Act, 1867) launched the Dominion of Canada, consisting of Ontario, Quebec, and the former colonies of Nova Scotia and New Brunswick.

Since 1840 the Canadian colonies had held the right to internal self-government. The BNA Act, which was the basis for the country's written constitution, established a federal system of government on the model of a British parliament and cabinet structure under the crown. Canada was proclaimed a self-governing Dominion within the British Empire in 1931. With the ratification of the Constitution Act, 1982, Canada severed its last formal legislative link with Britain by obtaining the right to amend its constitution.

The so-called Meech Lake Agreement was signed (subject to provincial ratification) June 3, 1987. The accord would have assured constitutional protection for Quebec's efforts to preserve its French language and culture. Critics charged it did not make any provision for other minority groups and it gave Quebec too much power, which might enable Quebec to override the nation's 1982 Charter of Rights and Freedoms (an integral part of the constitution). The accord died June 22, 1990.

Its failure sparked a separatist revival in Quebec, which culminated in Aug. 1992 in the Charlottetown agreement. This called for changes to the constitution, such as recognition of Quebec as a "distinct society" within the Canadian confederation. It was defeated in a national referendum Oct. 26, 1992.

Canada became the first nation to ratify the North American Free Trade Agreement between Canada, Mexico, and the U.S. June 23, 1993. It went into effect Jan. 1, 1994.

On Feb. 24, 1993, Brian Mulroney resigned as prime minister after more than 8 years in office; he was succeeded by Kim Campbell. In elections Oct. 25, 1993, the ruling Conservatives were defeated in a landslide that left them only 2 of the 295 seats in the House of Commons. Jean Chrétien became prime minister. In a Quebec referendum held Oct. 30, 1995, proponents of secession lost by a razor-thin margin. The elections of June 2, 1997, left the Liberals with a slim majority.

On Jan. 7, 1998, the government apologized to native peoples for 150 years of mistreatment and pledged to set up a "healing fund." Canada's highest court ruled, Aug. 20, that Quebec cannot secede unilaterally, even if a majority of the province approves. Nunavut ("Our Land"), carved from Northwest Territories as a homeland for the Inuit, was established Apr. 1, 1999.

Victory by the Liberals in national elections Nov. 27, 2000, made Chrétien the 1st Canadian prime minister in over 50 years to head a 3rd successive majority government. Chrétien stated Aug. 21, 2002, that he would not seek a 4th term in 2004.

Canada sent 5 warships in Oct. 2001, and 850 troops in Feb. 2002, to join U.S. counterterrorism operations in Afghanistan. Four Canadian soldiers conducting a training exercise near Kandahar were accidentally killed Apr. 17 by U.S. forces. Canada's first war casualties since its participation in the Korean War. The Canadian government contributed $100 mil. for humanitarian and reconstruction efforts in Afghanistan in Jan. 2002, and in Mar. 2003 pledged $250 mil more. Relations between Canada and the U.S. cooled after Prime Min. Chrétien refused to contribute troops to the U.S.-led invasion of Iraq in Mar. 2003.

A SARS outbreak killed more than 40 people in the Toronto area in 2003, and cost the city and national economy millions of dollars in lost revenues. The Ontario Court of Appeal ruled June 10 that provincial governments must extend full marriage rights to same-sex couples. A massive power blackout in the Northeast, Aug. 14, cut power to parts of Ontario and Manitoba, including Ottawa and Toronto.

Prime Ministers of Canada

Canada is a constitutional monarchy with a parliamentary system of government. It is also a federal state. Canada's official head of state, Queen Elizabeth II, is represented by a resident Governor-General. However, in practice the nation is governed by the Prime Minister, leader of the party that commands the support of a majority of the House of Commons, dominant chamber of Canada's bicameral Parliament.

Name	Party	Term
Sir John A. Macdonald	Conservative	1867-1873
Alexander Mackenzie	Liberal	1873-1878
Sir John A. Macdonald	Conservative	1878-1891
Sir John J. C. Abbott	Conservative	1891-1892
Sir John S. D. Thompson	Conservative	1892-1894
Sir Mackenzie Bowell	Conservative	1894-1896
Sir Charles Tupper	Conservative	1896[1]
Sir Wilfrid Laurier	Liberal	1896-1911
Sir Robert Laird Borden	Cons./Union.[2]	1911-1920
Arthur Meighen	Unionist	1920-1921
W. L. Mackenzie King	Liberal	1921-1926
Arthur Meighen	Conservative	1926[3]
W. L. Mackenzie King	Liberal	1926-1930
Richard Bedford Bennett	Conservative	1930-1935
W. L. Mackenzie King	Liberal	1935-1948
Louis St. Laurent	Liberal	1948-1957
John G. Diefenbaker	Prog. Cons.	1957-1963
Lester Bowles Pearson	Liberal	1963-1968
Pierre Elliott Trudeau	Liberal	1968-1979
Joe Clark	Prog. Cons.	1979-1980
Pierre Elliott Trudeau	Liberal	1980-1984
John Napier Turner	Liberal	1984[4]
Brian Mulroney	Prog. Cons.	1984-1993
Kim Campbell	Prog. Cons.	1993[5]
Jean Chrétien	Liberal	1993-

(1) May-July. (2) Conservative 1911-1917, Unionist 1917-1920. (3) June-Sept. (4) June-Sept. (5) June-Oct.

Cape Verde
Republic of Cape Verde

People: Population: 463,000. **Age distrib.** (%): <15: 41.9; 65+: 6.6. **Pop. density:** 298 per sq. mi. **Urban:** 64%. **Ethnic groups:** Creole 71%, African 28%, European 1%. **Principal languages:** Portuguese (official), Crioulo. **Chief religions:** Roman Catholic (infused with indigenous beliefs); Protestant (mostly Church of the Nazarene).

Geography: Area (total): 1,557 sq. mi. **Location:** In Atlantic O., off W tip of Africa. **Neighbors:** Nearest are Mauritania, Senegal to E. **Topography:** Cape Verde Islands are 15 in number, volcanic in origin (active crater on Fogo). The landscape is eroded and stark, with vegetation mostly in interior valleys. **Capital:** Praia 82,000.

Government: Type: Republic. **Head of state:** Pres. Pires; b Apr. 29, 1934; in office: Mar. 22, 2001. **Head of gov.:** Prime Min. José Maria Neves; b Mar. 28, 1960; in office: Feb. 1, 2001. **Local divisions:** 16 districts. **Defense budget** (2002): $5 mil. **Active troops:** 1,200.

Economy: Industries: food & beverages, fish proc., shoes & garments, salt mining, ship repair. **Chief crops:** bananas, corn, beans, sweet potatoes, sugarcane, coffee, peanuts. **Natural resources:** salt, basalt rock, limestone, kaolin, fish. **Arable land:** 11%. **Livestock** (2002): cattle: 22,000; chickens: 480,000; goats: 110,000; pigs: 200,000; sheep: 8,000 **Fish catch** (2002): 9,653 metric tons. **Electricity prod.** (2001): 0.04 bil. kWh.

Finance: Monetary unit: Escudo (CVE) (Sept. 2003: 101.72 = $1 U.S.). **GDP** (2002 est.): $600 mil. **Per capita GDP:** $1,400. **Imports** (2001): $218 mil.; partners (1999): Portugal 52%, Germany 7%, France 4%, UK 3%. **Exports** (2001 est.): $27.3 mil.; partners (1999): Portugal 45%, UK 20%, Germany 20%, Guinea-Bissau 5%. **Tourism** (1999): $23 mil. **Budget** (2000) $198 mil. **Intl. reserves less gold:** $27 mil. **Consumer prices** (changes in 2001): 3.7%.

Transport: Motor vehicles (1999): 13,500 pass. cars, 3,100 comm. vehicles. **Civil aviation:** 207.5 mil pass.-mi.; 6 airports. **Chief ports:** Mindelo, Praia.

Communications: TV sets: 5 per 1,000 pop. **Radios:** 183 per 1,000 pop. **Telephone lines:** 70,200. **Internet:** 16,000 users.

Health: Life expectancy: 66.5 male; 73.2 female. **Births** (per 1,000 pop.): 27.0. **Deaths** (per 1,000 pop.): 6.9. **Natural inc.:** 2.01%. **Infant mortality** (per 1,000 live births): 50.5.

Education: Compulsory: ages 6-12. **Literacy:** 76.6%.

Major Intl. Organizations: UN (FAO, IBRD, ILO, IMF, IMO, WHO), AU.

Embassy: 3415 Massachusetts Ave. NW 20007; 965-6820.

Websites: www.governo.cv; www.capeverdeusa.org

The uninhabited Cape Verdes were discovered by the Portuguese in 1456 or 1460. The first Portuguese colonists landed in 1462; African slaves were brought soon after, and most Cape Verdeans descend from both groups. Cape Verde independence came July 5, 1975. Antonio Mascarenhas Monteiro won the nation's first free presidential election Feb. 17, 1991; he was reelected without opposition five years later. Pedro Pires won a presidential runoff election Feb. 25, 2001.

Central African Republic

People: Population: 3,865,000. **Age distrib.** (%): <15: 43; 65+: 3.8. **Pop. density:** 16 per sq. mi. **Urban:** 42%. **Ethnic groups:** Baya 33%, Banda 27%, Mandjia 13%, Sara 10%, Mboum 7%, M'Baka 4%, Yakoma 4%. **Principal languages:** French (official), Sangho (national), tribal languages. **Chief religions:** Indigenous beliefs 35%, Protestant 25%, Roman Catholic 25%, Muslim 15%.

Geography: Area (total): 240,535 sq. mi. **Location:** In central Africa. **Neighbors:** Chad on N, Cameroon on W, Congo-Brazzaville and Congo-Kinshasa (formerly Zaire) on S, Sudan on E. **Topography:** Mostly rolling plateau, average altitude 2,000 ft., with rivers draining S to the Congo and N to Lake Chad. Open, well-watered savanna covers most of the area, with an arid area in NE, and tropical rain forest in SW. **Capital:** Bangui 666,000.

Government: Type: In transition. **Head of state:** Pres. François Bozizé; b Oct. 14, 1946; in office: Mar. 15, 2003. **Head of gov.:** Prime Min. Abel Goumba; Sept. 18, 1926; in office: Mar. 23, 2003. **Local divisions:** 14 prefectures, 2 economic prefectures, 1 commune. **Defense budget** (2002): $21 mil. **Active troops:** 2,550.

Economy: Industries: diamond mining, sawmills, breweries, textiles, footwear, bicycle & motorcycle assembly. **Chief crops:** cotton, coffee, tobacco, cassava, yams, millet, corn, bananas. **Natural resources:** diamonds, uranium, timber, gold, oil, hydropower. **Arable land:** 3%. **Livestock** (2002): cattle: 3.10 mil.; chickens: 4.20 mil.; goats: 2.60 mil.; pigs: 680,000; sheep: 220,000. **Fish catch** (2002 est.): 15,125 metric tons. **Electricity prod.** (2001): 0.11 bil. kWh.

Finance: Monetary unit: CFA Franc BEAC (XAF) (Sept. 2003: 597.03 = $1 U.S.). **GDP** (2002 est.): $4.7 bil. **Per capita GDP:** $1,300. **Imports** (2000): $154 mil.; partners (1999): France 35%, Cameroon 13%, Benelux, C'ote d'Ivoire. **Exports** (2000 est.): $172 mil.; partners (2001): Portugal 38%, Germany 12%, Thailand, Costa Rica. **Tourism** (1998): $6 mil. **Intl. reserves less gold:** $91 mil. **Gold:** 100,000 oz t. **Consumer prices:** 3.4%.

Transport: Motor vehicles (1995): 8,900 pass. cars, 3,500 comm. vehicles. **Civil aviation:** 146.0 mil. pass.-mi.; 3 airport. **Chief port:** Bangui.

Communications: TV sets: 6 per 1,000 pop. **Radios:** 83 per 1,000 pop. **Telephone lines:** 8,900. **Daily newspaper circ.:** 1.8 per 1,000 pop. **Internet:** 3,000 users.

Health: Life expectancy: 40.2 male; 43.3 female. **Births** (per 1,000 pop.): 35.9. **Deaths** (per 1,000 pop.): 19.7. **Natural inc.:** 1.62%. **Infant mortality** (per 1,000 live births): 93.3.

Education: Compulsory: ages 6-14. **Literacy:** 51%.

Major Intl. Organizations: UN (FAO, IBRD, ILO, IMF, WHO, WTrO), AU.

Embassy: 1618 22d St. NW 20008; 483-7800.

Website: www.embassy.org/embassies/cf.html

Various Bantu tribes migrated through the region for centuries before French control was asserted in the late 19th century, when the region was named Ubangi-Shari. Complete independence was attained Aug. 13, 1960.

All political parties were dissolved in 1960, and the country became a center for Chinese political influence in Africa. Relations with China were severed after 1965. Pres. Jean-Bedel Bokassa, who seized power in a 1965 military coup, proclaimed himself constitutional emperor of the renamed Central African Empire Dec. 1976.

Bokassa's rule was characterized by ruthless authoritarianism and human rights violations. He was ousted in a bloodless coup aided by the French government, Sept. 20, 1979. In 1981, Gen. André Kolingba became head of state in another bloodless coup. Multiparty legislative and presidential elections were held in Oct. 1992 but were canceled by the government when Kolingba was losing. New elections, held in Aug. and Sept. 1993, led to the replacement of Kolingba with a civilian government under Pres. Ange-Félix Patassé. France sent in troops to suppress army mutinies in 1996 and 1997. Patassé loyalists won a narrow majority in legislative elections on Nov. 22 and Dec. 13, 1998, and he was reelected to a 2nd 6-year term on Sept. 19, 1999. After thwarting several coup attempts, Patassé was ousted Mar. 15, 2003, by rebels under former army chief François Bozizé.

Chad
Republic of Chad

People: Population: 8,598,000. **Age distrib. (%): <15:** 47.8; **65+:** 2.8. **Pop. density:** 18 per sq. mi. **Urban:** 24%. **Ethnic groups:** About 200 groups; largest are Arabs in N and Sara in S. **Principal languages:** French, Arabic (both official), Sara, more than 120 different languages and dialects. **Chief religions:** Muslim 51%, Christian 35%, animist 7%, other 7%.

Geography: Area: 495,755 sq. mi. (total); 486,179 sq. mi. (land). **Location:** In central N Africa. **Neighbors:** Libya on N; Niger, Nigeria, Cameroon on W; Central African Republic on S; Sudan on E. **Topography:** Wooded savanna, steppe, and desert in the S; part of the Sahara in the N. Southern rivers flow N to Lake Chad, surrounded by marshland. **Capital:** N'Djamena, 735,000.

Government: Type: Republic. **Head of state:** Pres. Idriss Déby; b 1952; in office: Dec. 4, 1990. **Head of gov.:** Prime Min. Moussa Faki; in office: June 24, 2003. **Local divisions:** 14 prefectures. **Defense budget** (2002): $14 mil. **Active troops:** 30,350.

Economy: Industries: cotton textiles, meatpacking, beer brewing, sodium carbonate, soap, cigarettes, constr. materials. **Chief crops:** cotton, sorghum, millet, peanuts, rice, potatoes, cassava. **Natural resources:** oil, uranium, natron, kaolin, fish. **Arable land:** 3%. **Livestock** (2002): cattle: 5.90 mil.; chickens: 5 mil.; goats: 5.50 mil.; pigs: 24,000; sheep: 2.43 mil. **Fish catch** (2002 est.): 84,000 metric tons. **Electricity prod.** (2001): 0.09 bil. kWh. **Labor force:** agri. more than 80%.

Finance: Monetary unit: CFA Franc BEAC (XAF) (Sept. 2003: 597.03 = $1 U.S.). **GDP** (2002 est.): $10 bil. **Per capita GDP:** $1,100. **Imports** (2000 est.): $223 mil.; partners (1999): France 40%, Cameroon 13%, Nigeria 12%, India 5%. **Exports** (2000 est.): $172 mil.; partners (2001): Portugal 38%, Germany 12%. **Tourism** (1998): $10 mil. **Budget** (1998 est.): $218 mil. **Intl. reserves less gold:** $161 mil. **Gold:** 100,000 oz t. **Consumer prices:** 5.2%.

Transport: Motor vehicles (1995): 8,700 pass. cars, 12,400 comm. vehicles. **Civil aviation:** 146.0 mil pass.-mi.; 7 airports.

Communications: TV sets: 1 per 1,000 pop. **Radios:** 236 per 1,000 pop. **Telephone lines:** 11,000. **Daily newspaper circ.:** .2 per 1,000 pop. **Internet:** 4,000 users.

Health: Life expectancy: 47.0 male; 50.1 female. **Births** (per 1,000 pop.): 47.1. **Deaths** (per 1,000 pop.): 16.4. **Natural inc.:** 3.07%. **Infant mortality** (per 1,000 live births): 95.7.

Education: Compulsory: ages 6-11. **Literacy:** 47.5%.

Major Intl. Organizations: UN (FAO, IBRD, ILO, IMF, WHO, WTrO), AU.

Embassy: 2002 R St. NW 20009; 462-4009.

Website: www.chadembassy.org

Chad was the site of paleolithic and neolithic cultures before the Sahara Desert formed. A succession of kingdoms and Arab slave traders dominated Chad until France took control around 1900. Independence came Aug. 11, 1960.

Northern Muslim rebels have fought animist and Christian southern government and French troops from 1966, despite numerous cease-fires and peace pacts.

Libyan troops entered the country at the request of a pro-Libyan Chad government, Dec. 1980. The troops were withdrawn from Chad in Nov. 1981. Rebel forces, led by Hissène Habré, captured the capital and forced Pres. Goukouni Oueddei to flee the country in June 1982.

In 1983, France sent some 3,000 troops to Chad to assist Pres. Habré in opposing Libyan-backed rebels. France and Libya agreed to a simultaneous withdrawal of troops from Chad in Sept. 1984, but Libyan forces remained in the north until Mar. 1987, when Chad forces drove them from their last major stronghold. In Dec. 1990, Habré was overthrown by a Libyan-supported insurgent group, the Patriotic Salvation Movement.

On Feb. 3, 1994, the World Court dismissed a long-standing territorial claim by Libya to the mineral-rich Aozou Strip, on the Libyan border. Libyan troops reportedly withdrew at the end of May. Following approval of a new constitution in March 1996, Chad's first multiparty presidential election was held in June and July. The U.S. Peace Corps withdrew from Chad in Apr. 1998 because of continuing clashes between rebels and Chad government forces.

Pres. Idriss Déby won reelection May 20, 2001, to another 5-year term.

Chile
Republic of Chile

People: Population: 15,805,000. **Age distrib. (%): <15:** 26.9; **65+:** 7.5. **Pop. density:** 55 per sq. mi. **Urban:** 86%. **Ethnic groups:** European and Mestizo 95%, Amerindian 3%. **Principal languages:** Spanish (official), Araucanian. **Chief religions:** Roman Catholic 89%, Protestant 11%.

Geography: Area: 292,260 sq. mi. (total); 289,113 sq. mi. (land). **Location:** Occupies western coast of S South America. **Neighbors:** Peru on N, Bolivia on NE, on E. **Topography:** Andes Mts. on E border incl. some of the world's highest peaks; on W is 2,650-mile Pacific coast. Width varies between 100 and 250 miles. In N is Atacama Desert, in center are agricultural regions, in S, forests and grazing lands. **Capital:** Santiago, 5,551,000.

Government: Type: Republic. **Head of state and gov.:** Pres. Ricardo Lagos Escobar; b Mar. 2, 1938; in office: Mar. 11, 2000. **Local divisions:** 13 regions. **Defense budget** (2002): $1.1 bil. **Active troops:** 80,500.

Economy: Industries: copper, other minerals, foodstuffs, fish proc., iron, steel, wood & wood products, transp. equip., cement, textiles. **Chief crops:** wheat, corn, grapes, beans, sugar beets, potatoes, fruit. **Natural resources:** copper, timber, iron ore, nitrates, prec. metals, molybd., hydropower. **Crude oil reserves** (2002): 150 mil. bbls. **Arable land:** 5%. **Livestock** (2002): cattle: 4.10 mil.; chickens: 76 mil.; goats: 900,000; pigs: 2.75 mil.; sheep: 4.10 mil. **Fish catch** (2002): 4,363,239 metric tons. **Electricity prod.** (2001): 41.66 bil. kWh. **Labor force:** agri. 14%, ind. 27%, services 59%.

Finance: Monetary unit: Peso (CLP) (Sept. 2003: 712.51 = $1 U.S.). **GDP** (2002 est.): $151 bil. **Per capita GDP:** $10,000. **Imports** (2001): $18 bil.; partners (2000): U.S. 19%, Argentina 16%, Brazil 7%, China 6%. **Exports** (2001): $18.5 bil.; partners (2000): U.S. 17%, Japan 14%, UK 6%, Brazil 5%. **Tourism** (1999): $827 mil. **Budget** (2001 est.): $17 bil. **Intl. reserves less gold:** $11.28 bil. **Gold:** 10,000 oz. t. **Consumer prices:** 2.5%.

Transport: Railroad: Length: 4,164 mi. **Motor vehicles** (1999): 1.32 mil. pass. cars, 691,100 comm. vehicles. **Civil aviation:** 6.62 bil pass.-mi.; 71 airports. **Chief ports:** Valparaiso, Arica, Antofagasta.

Communications: TV sets: 240 per 1,000 pop. **Radios:** 354 per 1,000 pop. **Telephone lines:** 3,467,200. **Daily newspaper circ.:** 98 per 1,000 pop. **Internet:** 3,102,200 users.

Health: Life expectancy: 73.0 male; 79.8 female. **Births** (per 1,000 pop.): 16.1. **Deaths** (per 1,000 pop.): 5.6. **Natural inc.:** 1.05%. **Infant mortality** (per 1,000 live births): 8.9.

Education: Compulsory: ages 6-14. **Literacy:** 96.2%.

Major Intl. Organizations: UN and all of its specialized agencies, APEC, OAS.

Embassy: 1732 Massachusetts Ave. NW 20036; 785-1746.

Website: www.chile-usa.org

Northern Chile was under Inca rule before the Spanish conquest, 1536-40. The southern Araucanian Indians resisted until the late 19th century. Independence was gained 1810-18, under José de San Martin and Bernardo O'Higgins; the latter, as supreme director 1817-23, sought social and economic reforms until deposed. Chile defeated Peru and Bolivia in 1836-39 and 1879-84, gaining mineral-rich northern land.

In 1970, Salvador Allende Gossens, a Marxist, became president with a third of the national vote. His government improved conditions for the poor, but illegal and violent actions by extremist supporters of the government, the regime's failure to attain majority support, and poorly planned socialist economic programs led to political and financial chaos.

A military junta seized power Sept. 11, 1973, and said Allende had killed himself. The junta, headed by Gen. Augusto Pinochet Ugarte, named a mostly military cabinet and announced plans to "exterminate Marxism." Repression continued during the 1980s with little sign of any political liberalization.

In a plebiscite held Oct. 5, 1988, voters rejected the incumbent president, Pinochet. He agreed to presidential elections. In Dec. 1989 voters elected a civilian president, although Pinochet continued to head the army until Mar. 10, 1998. In Mar. 1994 a Chilean human rights group estimated that human rights violations had claimed more than 3,100 lives during Pinochet's rule. Attempts to prosecute him failed when he was declared mentally unfit to stand trial by courts in Britain and Chile. Ricardo Lagos Escobar, Chile's 1st Socialist president since the 1973 coup, took office Mar. 11, 2000. Chile and the U.S. signed a free trade accord June 6, 2003.

Tierra del Fuego is the largest (18,800 sq. mi.) island in the archipelago of the same name at the southern tip of South America, an area of majestic mountains, tortuous channels, and high winds. It was visited 1520 by Magellan and named Land of Fire because of its many Indian bonfires. Part of the island is in Chile, part in Argentina. Punta Arenas, on a mainland peninsula, is a center of sheep raising and the world's southernmost city (pop. about 70,000); Puerto Williams is the southernmost settlement.

China
People's Republic of China
(Statistical data do not include Hong Kong or Macao.)

People: Population: 1,304,196,000. **Age distrib. (%): <15:** 24.3; **65+:** 7.3. **Pop. density:** 362 per sq. mi. **Urban:** 37%. **Ethnic groups:** 56 groups; Han 92%. Also Zhuang, Manchu, Hui, Miao, Uygur, Yi, Tujia, Tong, Tibetan, Mongol, et al. **Principal languages:** Mandarin (official), Yue (Cantonese), Wu (Shanghaiese), Minbei (Fuzhou), Minnan (Hokkien-Taiwanese), Xiang, Gan, Hakka, minority languages. **Chief religions:** Officially atheist; Buddhism, Taoism, some Muslims, Christians.

Geography: Area: 3,705,404 sq. mi. (total); 3,600,944 sq. mi. (land). **Location:** Occupies most of the habitable mainland of E Asia. **Neighbors:** Mongolia on N; Russia on NE and NW; Afghanistan, Pakistan, Tajikistan, Kyrgystan, Kazakhstan on W; India, Nepal, Bhutan, Myanmar, Laos, Vietnam on S; North Korea on NE. **Topography:** Two-thirds of the vast territory is mountainous or desert; only one-tenth is cultivated. Rolling topography rises to high elevations in the N in the Daxinganlingshanmai separating Manchuria and Mongolia; the Tien Shan in Xinjiang; the Himalayan and Kunlunshanmai in the SW and in Tibet. Length is 1,860 mi. from N to S, width E to W is more than 2,000 mi. The eastern half of China is one of the world's best-watered lands. Three great river systems, the Chang (Yangtze), Huang (Yellow), and Xi, provide water for vast farmlands. **Capital:** Beijing. **Cities (urban aggr.):** Shanghai 12,887,000; Beijing 10,836,000; Tianjin 9,156,000; Chongqing 4,900,000; Shenyang 4,828,000; Guangzhou 3,893,000.

Government: Type: Communist Party-led state. **Head of state:** Pres. Hu Jintao; b Dec. 1942; in office: Mar. 15, 2003 (also gen. secy of Communist Party since Nov. 15, 2002). **Head of gov.:** Premier Wen Jiabao; b. Sept. 1942; in office: Mar. 16, 2003. **Local divisions:** 22 provinces (not including Taiwan), 5 autonomous regions, and 4 municipalities, plus the special administrative regions of Hong Kong (as of July 1, 1997) and Macao (as of Dec. 20, 1999). **Defense budget** (2002): $20 bil. **Active troops:** 2,270,000.

Economy: Industries: iron, steel, coal, machine building, armaments, textiles & apparel, oil, cement, chemical fertilizers. **Chief crops:** rice, wheat, potatoes, sorghum, peanuts, tea. **Natural resources:** coal, iron ore, oil, nat. gas, mercury, tin, tungsten, antimony, manganese, molybd., vanadium, magnetite, aluminum, lead, zinc, uranium, hydropower. **Crude oil reserves** (2002): 24.0 bil. bbls. **Arable land:** 10%. **Livestock** (2002): cattle: 106.18 mil.; chickens: 3.92 bil.; goats: 161.49 mil.; pigs: 464.70 mil.; sheep: 136.97 mil. **Fish catch** (2002): 42,579,490 metric tons. **Electricity prod.** (2001): 1,420.35 bil. kWh. **Labor force:** agri. 50%, ind. 22%, services 28%.

Finance: Monetary unit: Yuan Renminbi (CNY) (Sept. 2003: 8.29 = $1 U.S.). **GDP** (2002 est.): $5.7 tril. **Per capita GDP:** $4,400. **Imports** (2002): $268.6 bil.; partners (2001): Japan 17.6%, Taiwan 11.2%, U.S. 10.8%, South Korea 9.6%. **Exports** (2002 est.): $312.8 bil.; partners (2001): U.S. 20.4%, Hong Kong 17.5%, Japan 16.9%, South Korea 4.7%. **Tourism:** $16.23 bil. **Budget** (2002 est.): $267.1 bil. **Intl. reserves less gold:** $214.14 bil. **Gold:** 19.3 mil oz t. **Consumer prices:** –0.8%.

Transport: Railroad: Length: 41,957 mi. **Motor vehicles** (1998): 6.55 mil pass. cars, 6.28 mil comm. vehicles. **Civil aviation:** 77.35 bil pass.-mi.; 351 airports. **Chief ports:** Shanghai, Qinhuangdao, Dalian, Guangzhou (Canton).

Communications: TV sets: 291 per 1,000 pop. **Radios:** 342 per 1,000 pop. **Telephone lines:** 214,420,000. **Daily newspaper circ.:** 23 per 1,000 pop. **Internet:** 59,100,000 users.

Health: Life expectancy: 70.3 male; 74.3 female. **Births** (per 1,000 pop.): 13.0. **Deaths** (per 1,000 pop.): 6.7. **Natural inc.:** 0.62%. **Infant mortality** (per 1,000 live births): 25.3.

Education: Compulsory: ages 6-14. **Literacy:** 86%.

Major Intl. Organizations: UN (FAO, IBRD, ILO, IMF, IMO, WHO, WTrO), APEC.

Embassy: 2300 Conn. Ave. NW 20008; 328-2500.

Website: www.china.org.cn/english/index.htm

Remains of various humanlike creatures who lived as early as several hundred thousand years ago have been found in many parts of China. Neolithic agricultural settlements dotted the Huang (Yellow) R. basin from about 5000 BC. Their language, religion, and art were the sources of later Chinese civilization.

Bronze metallurgy reached a peak and Chinese pictographic writing, similar to today's, was in use in the more developed culture of the Shang Dynasty (c. 1500 BC-c. 1000 BC), which ruled much of North China.

A succession of dynasties and interdynastic warring kingdoms ruled China for the next 3,000 years. They expanded Chinese political and cultural domination to the south and west, and developed a brilliant technologically and a culturally advanced society. Rule by foreigners (Mongols in the Yuan Dynasty, 1271-1368, and Manchus in the Ch'ing Dynasty, 1644-1911) did not alter the underlying culture.

A period of relative stagnation left China vulnerable to internal and external pressures in the 19th century. Rebellions left tens of millions dead, and Russia, Japan, Britain, and other powers exercised political and economic control in large parts of the country. China became a republic Jan. 1, 1912, following the Wuchang Uprising inspired by Dr. Sun Yat-sen, founder of the Kuomintang (Nationalist) party. By 1928, the Kuomintang, led by Chiang Kai-shek, succeeded in nominal reunification of China. About the same time, a bloody purge of Communists from the ranks of the Kuomintang fomented hostilities between the two groups that would continue for decades.

For over 50 years, 1894-1945, China was involved in conflicts with Japan. In 1895, China ceded Korea, Taiwan, and other areas. On Sept. 18, 1931, Japan seized the Northeastern Provinces (Manchuria) and set up a puppet state called Manchukuo. The border province of Jehol was cut off as a buffer state in 1933. Taking advantage of Chinese dissension, Japan invaded China proper July 7, 1937. On Nov. 20 the retreating Nationalist government moved its capital to Chongqing (Chungking) from Nanking (Nanjing), which Japanese troops then ravaged Dec. 13.

From 1939 the Sino-Japanese War (1937-45) became part of the broader world conflict. After its defeat in World War II, Japan

gave up all seized land, and internal conflicts involving the Kuomintang, Communists, and other factions resumed. China came under the domination of Communist armies, 1949-1950. The Kuomintang government moved to Taiwan, Dec. 8, 1949.

The Chinese People's Political Consultative Conference convened Sept. 21, 1949; The People's Republic of China was proclaimed in Beijing (Peking) Oct. 1, 1949, under Mao Zedong. China and the USSR signed a 30-year treaty of "friendship, alliance and mutual assistance," Feb. 15, 1950. The U.S. refused recognition of the new regime. On Nov. 26, 1950, the People's Republic sent armies into Korea against U.S. troops and forced a stalemate in the Korean War.

After an initial period of consolidation, 1949-52, industry, agriculture, and social and economic institutions were forcibly molded according to Maoist ideals. However, frequent drastic changes in policy and violent factionalism interfered with economic development. In 1957, Mao admitted an estimated 800,000 people had been executed 1949-54; opponents claimed much higher figures.

The Great Leap Forward, 1958-60, tried to force the pace of economic development through intensive labor on huge new rural communes, and through emphasis on ideological purity. The program caused resistance and was largely abandoned.

By the 1960s, relations with the USSR deteriorated, with disagreements on borders, ideology, and leadership of world Communism. The USSR canceled aid accords, and China, with Albania, launched anti-Soviet propaganda drives.

The Great Proletarian Cultural Revolution, 1965, was an attempt to oppose pragmatism and bureaucratic power and instruct a new generation in revolutionary principles. Massive purges took place. A program of forcibly relocating millions of urban teenagers into the countryside was launched. By 1968 the movement had run its course; many purged officials returned to office in subsequent years, and reforms that had placed ideology above expertise were gradually weakened.

On Oct. 25, 1971, the UN General Assembly ousted the Taiwan government from the UN and seated the People's Republic in its place. The U.S. had supported the mainland's admission but opposed Taiwan's expulsion.

U.S. Pres. Richard Nixon visited China Feb. 21-28, 1972, on invitation from Premier Zhou Enlai, ending years of antipathy between the 2 nations. China and the U.S. opened liaison offices in each other's capitals, May-June 1973. The U.S., Dec. 15, 1978, formally recognized the People's Republic of China as the sole legal government of China; diplomatic relations between the 2 nations were established, Jan. 1, 1979.

Mao died Sept. 9, 1976. By 1978, Vice Premier Deng Xiaoping had consolidated his power, succeeding Mao as "paramount leader" of China. The new ruling group modified Maoist policies in education, culture, and industry, and sought better ties with non-Communist countries. During this "reassessment" of Mao's policies his widow, Jiang Qing, and other "Gang of Four" leftists were convicted of "committing crimes during the 'Cultural Revolution,'" Jan. 25, 1981.

By the mid-1980s, China had enacted far-reaching economic reforms, deemphasizing centralized planning and incorporating market-oriented incentives. Some 100,000 students and workers staged a march in Beijing to demand political reforms, May 4, 1989. The demonstrations continued during a visit to Beijing by Soviet leader Mikhail Gorbachev May 15-18; it was the first Sino-Soviet summit since 1959. As the unrest spread, martial law was imposed, May 20. Troops entered Beijing, June 3-4, and crushed the pro-democracy protests, as tanks and armored personnel carriers rolled through Tiananmen Square. It is estimated that 5,000 died, 10,000 were injured, and hundreds of students and workers were arrested.

Floods in July and Aug. 1998 killed at least 3,000 and caused an estimated $20 bil. in damage. NATO bombs hit the Chinese embassy in Belgrade, Yugoslavia, on May 7, 1999, killing 3 people and wounding 27, for which the U.S. paid compensation. The government banned a popular religious sect, the Falun Gong, July 22, after it staged the largest unauthorized demonstrations in Beijing since 1989. The U.S. and China signed a major trade agreement Nov. 15. Portugal returned Macao to China Dec. 20, 1999.

Beijing was chosen, July 13, 2001, to host the 2008 Summer Olympics. Admission to the WTrO Dec. 11 marked an economic milestone, though protested by many human rights and labor organizations. Hu Jintao was named Communist Party general secretary at the 16th party congress, Nov. 15, 2002, and elected president by the 10th National People's Congress, Mar. 15, 2003. A SARS epidemic beginning in late 2002 killed 349 people in mainland China by Aug. 2003. More than 1 million adults have HIV/AIDS, a rapidly growing problem in China. In Aug. 2003, China assumed an unprecedented diplomatic role when it hosted talks between North and South Korea, the U.S., Russia, and Japan regarding N. Korea's nuclear weapons program.

Manchuria. Home of the Manchus, rulers of China 1644-1911, Manchuria has accommodated millions of Chinese settlers in the 20th century. Under Japanese rule 1931-45, the area became industrialized. The region is divided into the 3 NE provinces of Heilongjiang, Jilin, and Liaoning.

Autonomous Regions

Guangxi Zhuang is in SE China, bounded on N by Guizhou and Hunan provinces, E and S by Guangdong, on SW by Vietnam, and on W by Yunnan. It produces rice in the river valleys and has valuable forest products. Pop. (2000): 44.89 mil

Inner Mongolia was organized by the People's Republic in 1947. Its boundaries have undergone frequent changes, reaching its greatest extent in 1956 (and restored in 1979), with an area of 454,600 sq. mi., allegedly in order to dilute the minority Mongol population. Chinese settlers outnumber the Mongols more than 10 to 1. Pop. (2000): 23.76 mil. Capital: Hohhot.

Ningxia Hui, in N central China, is about 60,000 sq. mi., pop. (2000): 5.62 mil. Capital: Yinchuan. Situated mainly of the semiarid Inner Mongolian plateau region with desert areas in the N. The Huang He (Yellow R.) flows across the N furnishes water for irrigation. Coal is mined in the E. Modern industry is relatively undeveloped and only one railroad crosses the region. The majority of the population is Han, and the Hui (Chinese Muslims) constitute about one-third of the population. The region experienced a significant population boom from 1950-80, which has now stabilized.

Xinjiang Uygur, in Central Asia, is 635,900 sq. mi., pop. (2000): 19.25 mil (75% Uygurs, a Turkic Muslim group, with a heavy Chinese increase in recent years). Capital: Urumqi. It is China's richest region in strategic minerals. China has moved to crack down on Uygur separatists, whom Beijing regards as terrorists.

Tibet, 471,700 sq. mi., is a thinly populated region of high plateaus and massive mountains, the Himalayas on the S, the Kunluns on the N. High passes connect with India and Nepal; roads lead into China proper. Capital: Lhasa. Average altitude is 15,000 ft. Jiachan, 15,870 ft., is believed to be the highest inhabited town on earth. Agriculture is primitive. Pop. (2000): 2.62 mil (of whom about 500,000 are Chinese). Another 4 million Tibetans form the majority of the population of vast adjacent areas that have long been incorporated into China.

China ruled all of Tibet from the 18th century, but independence came in 1911. China reasserted control in 1951, and a Communist government was installed in 1953, revising the theocratic Lamaist Buddhist rule. Serfdom was abolished, but all land remained collectivized.

A Tibetan uprising within China in 1956 spread to Tibet in 1959. The rebellion was crushed with Chinese troops, and Buddhism was almost totally suppressed. The Dalai Lama and 100,000 Tibetans fled to India.

Hong Kong

Hong Kong (Xianggang), located at the mouth of the Zhu Jiang (Pearl R.) in SE China, 90 mi. S of Canton (Guangzhou), was a British dependency from 1842 until July 1, 1997, when it became a Special Administrative Region of China. Its nucleus is Hong Kong Isl., 31 sq. mi., occupied by the British in 1841 and formally ceded to them in 1842, on which is located the seat of government. Opposite is Kowloon Peninsula, 3 sq. mi., and Stonecutters Isl., added to the territory in 1860. An additional 355 sq. mi. known as the New Territories, a mainland area and islands, were leased from China, 1898, for 99 years. Area 604,249 sq. mi. (total); 600,543 sq. mi. (land); pop. (2003 est.) 7,394,170, including fewer than 20,000 British.

Hong Kong is a major center for trade and banking. Per capita GDP, $25,400 (2000 est.), is among the highest in the world. Principal industries are textiles and apparel; also tourism ($7.21 bil expenditures in 1999), electronics, shipbuilding, iron and steel, fishing, cement, and small manufactures. Hong Kong's spinning mills are among the best in the world.

Hong Kong harbor was long an important British naval station and one of the world's great transshipment ports. The colony was often a place of refuge for exiles from mainland China. It was occupied by Japan during World War II.

From 1949 to 1962 Hong Kong absorbed more than a million refugees fleeing Communist China. Starting in the 1950s, cheap labor led to a boom in light manufacturing, while liberal tax policies attracted foreign investment; Hong Kong became one of the wealthiest, most productive areas in the Far East. Poor living and working conditions and low wages for many led to political unrest in the 1960s, but legislation and public works programs raised the standard of living by the 1970s.

With the end of the 99-year lease on the New Territories drawing near, Britain and China signed an agreement, Dec. 19, 1984, under which all of Hong Kong was to be returned to China in 1997; under this agreement Hong Kong was to be allowed to keep its capitalist system for 50 years. In Dec. 1996, an electoral college appointed by China chose a shipping magnate, Tung Chee-hwa, to be Hong Kong's chief executive when it reverted to Chinese control.

Following the transfer of government on July 1, Hong Kong retained its street names and its currency, the Hong Kong dollar (HK$7.80 = $1 U.S.), but without the queen's picture. Official languages remained Chinese (Cantonese dialect) and English. Pro-democracy candidates did well in May 24, 1998, elections, despite having been excluded from the provisional gov't. in 1997. A SARS outbreak in 2003 claimed almost 300 lives and damaged the economy.

A controversial anti-subversion security bill introduced Sept. 2002 was revised and published by the government in May 2003. Hundreds of thousands turned out to protest the legislation July 1, the largest demonstrations in Hong Kong since protests against the Tiananmen square incident in 1989, and the largest ever against the territorial government. Security Secretary Regina Ip, who strongly supported the bill, and Financial Secretary Antony Leung, accused of financial improprieties, both resigned July 16. The bill was offically withdrawn by Chief Executive Tung Sept. 5, 2003.

Macao

Macao, area of 10 sq. mi., is an enclave, a peninsula and 2 small islands, at the mouth of the Xi (Pearl) R. in China. It was established as a Portuguese trading colony in 1557. In 1849, Portugal claimed sovereignty over the territory; this claim was accepted by China in an 1887 treaty. Portugal granted broad autonomy in 1976. Under a 1987 agreement, Macao reverted to China Dec. 20, 1999. As in the case of Hong Kong, the Chinese government guaranteed Macao it would not interfere in its way of life and capitalist system for a period of 50 years. Pop. (2003 est.): 469,903.

Colombia
Republic of Colombia

People: Population: 44,222,000. **Age distrib. (%):** <15: 31.6; 65+: 4.8. **Pop. density:** 110 per sq. mi. **Urban:** 76%. **Ethnic groups:** Mestizo 58%, European 20%, Creole 14%, Black 4%, Black-Amerindian 1%, Amerindian 3%. **Principal languages:** Spanish (official). **Chief religion:** Roman Catholic 90%.

Geography: Area: 439,735 sq. mi. (total); 401,044 sq. mi. (land). **Location:** At the NW corner of South America. **Neighbors:** Panama on NW, Ecuador and Peru on S, Brazil and Venezuela on E. **Topography:** Three ranges of Andes—Western, Central, and Eastern Cordilleras—run through the country from N to S. The eastern range consists mostly of high tablelands, densely populated. The Magdalena R. rises in the Andes, flows N to Caribbean, through a rich alluvial plain. Sparsely settled plains in E are drained by Orinoco and Amazon systems. **Capital:** Bogotá (Full name: Santa Fe de Bogotá.) **Cities (urban aggr.):** Bogotá 6,957,000; Medellín 2,866,000; Cali 2,233,000; Barranquilla 1,683,000.

Government: Type: Republic. **Head of state and gov.:** Pres. Álvaro Uribe Vélez; b July 4, 1952; in office: Aug. 7, 2002. **Local divisions:** 32 departments, capital district of Bogota. **Defense budget:** (2002) $1.7 bil. **Active troops:** 158,000.

Economy: Industries: textiles, food proc., oil, clothing & footwear, beverages, chemicals, cement, mining. **Chief crops:** coffee, cut flowers, bananas, rice, tobacco, corn, sugarcane, cocoa. **Natural resources:** oil, nat. gas, coal, iron ore, nickel, gold, copper, emeralds, hydropower. **Crude oil reserves** (2002): 1.8 bil. bbls. **Arable land:** 4%. **Livestock** (2002): cattle: 27 mil.; chickens: 108 mil.; goats: 1.02 mil.; pigs: 2.35 mil.; sheep: 2.25 mil. **Fish catch** (2002 est.): 190,000 metric tons. **Electricity prod.** (2001): 42.99 bil. kWh. **Labor force:** services 46%, agric. 30%, ind. 24%. **Finance: Monetary unit:** Peso (COP) (Sept. 2003: 2,900.30 = $1 U.S.) **GDP** (2002 est.): $268 bil. **Per capita GDP:** $6,500. **Imports** (2001): $12.7 bil.; partners (2001 est.): U.S. 35%, EU 16%, Andean Community of Nations 15%, Japan 5%. **Exports** (2001 est.): $12.3 bil.; partners (2001 est.): U.S. 43%, Andean Community of Nations 22%, EU 14%. **Tourism:** $1.03 bil. **Budget** (2001 est.): $25.6 bil. **Intl. reserves less gold:** $7.89 bil. **Gold:** 330,000 oz t. **Consumer prices:** 6.3%.

Transport: Railroad: Length: 2,053 mi. **Motor vehicles** (1998): 725,400 pass. cars, 420,900 comm. vehicles. **Civil aviation:** 4.88 bil pass.-mi.; 96 airports. **Chief ports:** Buenaventura, Barranquilla, Cartagena.

Communications: TV sets: 279 per 1,000 pop. **Radios:** 539 per 1,000 pop. **Telephone lines:** 7,766,000. **Daily newspaper circ.:** 46 per 1,000 pop. **Internet:** 1,982,000 users

Health: Life expectancy: 67.3 male; 75.1 female. **Births** (per 1,000 pop.): 21.6. **Deaths** (per 1,000 pop.): 5.6. **Natural inc.:** 1.60%. **Infant mortality** (per 1,000 live births): 22.5.

Education: Compulsory: ages 5-14. **Literacy:** 92.5%.

Major Intl. Organizations: UN (FAO, IBRD, ILO, IMF, IMO, WHO, WTrO), OAS.

Embassy: 2118 Leroy Pl. NW 20008; 387-8338.

Websites: www.colombiaemb.org; www.turismocolombia.com

Spain subdued the local Indian kingdoms (Funza, Tunja) by the 1530s and ruled Colombia and neighboring areas as New Granada for 300 years. Independence was won by 1819. Venezuela and Ecuador broke away in 1829-30, and Panama withdrew in 1903.

Colombia is plagued by rural and urban violence. "La Violencia" of 1948-58 claimed 200,000 lives; since 1989, political violence has resulted in more than 35,000 deaths. Attempts at land and social reform and progress in industrialization have not reduced massive social problems.

The government's increased activity against local drug traffickers sparked a series of retaliation killings. On Aug. 18, 1989, Luis Carlos Galán, the ruling party's presidential hopeful for the 1990 election, was assassinated. In 1990, 2 other presidential candidates were assassinated, as drug traffickers carried on a campaign of intimidation.

Charges that Ernesto Samper Pizano's 1994 campaign received money from the Cali drug cartel engulfed his administration in scandal, although the legislature voted, June 12, 1996, not to impeach him. Andrés Pastrana Arango, son of former Pres. Misael Pastrana Borrero (in office 1970-74), won a presidential runoff election, June 21, 1998. An earthquake Jan. 25, 1999, in western Colombia killed at least 1,185 people and left 250,000 homeless. At least 5 million people in more than 700 cities took part in protests Oct. 24 against continuing violence and human rights abuses.

The U.S. authorized $1.3 billion in antidrug aid to Colombia Aug. 22, 2000. Right-wing paramilitaries launched a campaign Dec. 22 against suspected left-wing guerrillas. Legislation expanding the powers of the military was signed Aug. 13, 2001. The collapse of talks with the rebels in Feb. 2002 brought an upsurge of fighting. A hardliner, Álvaro Uribe Vélez, whose father had been killed by leftist rebels in 1983, won a presidential election May 26. A wave of guerrilla violence as he took office led Uribe to declare a "state of unrest" Aug. 12. Police powers were increased Sept. 10 as part of a new government offensive.

Comoros
Union of Comoros

People: Population: 768,000. **Age distrib.** (%): <15: 42.9; 65+: 2.9. **Pop. density:** 917 per sq. mi. **Urban:** 34%. **Ethnic groups:** Antalote, Cafre, Makoa, Oimatsaha, Sakalava (all are mostly an African-Arab mix). **Principal languages:** Arabic, French (both official), Shikomoro (a blend of Swahili and Arabic). **Chief religion:** Muslim 98% (official).

Geography: Area (total): 838 sq. mi. **Location:** 3 islands—Grande Comore (Njazidja), Anjouan (Nzwani), and Moheli (Mwali)—in the Mozambique Channel between NW Madagascar and SE Africa. **Neighbors:** Nearest are Mozambique on W, Madagascar on E. **Topography:** The islands are of volcanic origin, with an active volcano on Grande Comore. **Capital:** Moroni (2001 met. est.) 49,000.

Government: Type: In transition. **Head of state and gov.:** Pres. Azali Assoumani; b Jan. 1,1959; in office: May 26, 2002. **Local divisions:** 3 main islands with 4 municipalities.

Economy: Industries: tourism, perfume distillation. **Chief crops:** vanilla, cloves, perfume essences, copra, coconuts, bananas, cassava. **Arable land:** 35%. **Livestock** (2002): cattle: 52,000; chickens: 490,000; goats: 115,000; sheep: 21,000 **Fish catch** (2002): 12,180 metric tons. **Electricity prod.** (2001): 0.02 bil. kWh. **Labor force:** agri. 80%.

Finance: Monetary unit: Franc (KMF) (Sept. 2003: 449.79 = $1 U.S.). **GDP** (2002 est.): $441 mil. **Per capita GDP:** $720. **Imports** (2001): $44.9 mil.; partners (1999): France 34%, South Africa 14%, Kenya 7%, Pakistan 4%. **Exports** (2001 est.): $35.3 mil.; partners (1999): France 46%, U.S. 18%, Singapore 5%, Germany 9%. **Tourism:** $19 mil. **Budget** (1997): $53 mil. **Intl. reserves less gold:** $59 mil.

Transport: Civil aviation (1996):1.9 mil pass.-mi.; 4 airports. **Chief ports:** Fomboni, Moroni, Moutsamoudou.

Communications: TV sets: **4 per 1,000 pop. Radios:** 141 per 1,000 pop. **Telephone lines:** 10,300. **Internet:** 3,200 users.

Health: Life expectancy: 58.9 male; 63.5 female. **Births** (per 1,000 pop.): 38.5. **Deaths** (per 1,000 pop.): 8.9. **Natural inc.:** 2.96%. **Infant mortality** (per 1,000 live births): 79.5.

Education: Compulsory: ages 6-14. **Literacy:** 56.5%.

Major Intl. Organizations: UN (FAO, IBRD, ILO, IMF, WHO), AL, AU.

Embassy: 420 E. 50th St., New York, NY 10022; 212-750-1637.

Website: www.presidence-rfic.com

The islands were controlled by Muslim sultans until the French acquired them 1841-1909. They became a French overseas territory in 1947. A 1974 referendum favored independence, with only the Christian island of Mayotte preferring association with France. The French National Assembly decided to allow each of the islands to decide its own fate. The Comore Chamber of Deputies declared independence July 6, 1975, with Ahmed Abdallah as president. In a referendum in 1976, Mayotte voted to remain French.

A leftist regime that seized power from Abdallah in 1975 was deposed in a pro-French 1978 coup in which he regained the presidency. In Nov. 1989, Pres. Abdallah was assassinated; soon after, a multiparty system was instituted. A Sept. 1995 military coup, assisted by French mercenaries, ousted Pres. Said Mohamed Djohar. French troops invaded, Oct. 4, and forced coup leaders to surrender. Djohar returned from exile in Jan. 1996, and in Mar. a new presidential election was held. A hijacked Ethiopian Airlines

Boeing 767 crashed offshore on Nov. 23, killing 123 of the 175 people on board.

Attempts to work out a new constitutional relationship between Grande Comore, Anjouan, and Moheli have been ongoing since Anjouan and Moheli seceded from the Comoros in 1997. Unrest on Grande Comore culminated in a military coup, Apr. 30, 1999. Anjouans endorsed secession in a disputed vote Jan. 23, 2000. Irregularities marred the presidential runoff election of Apr. 14, 2002, won by Azali Assoumani, who led the 1999 coup; each of the 3 islands also elected its own president in 2002.

Congo (formerly Zaire)
Democratic Republic of the Congo

(Congo, officially Democratic Republic of the Congo, is also known as Congo-Kinshasa. It should not be confused with Republic of the Congo, commonly called Congo Republic, and also known as Congo-Brazzaville.)

People: Population: 52,771,000. **Age distrib.** (%): <15: 48.2; 65+: 2.5. **Pop. density:** 60 per sq. mi. **Urban:** 31%. **Ethnic groups:** Over 200 groups. Four largest, the Mongo, Luba, Kongo (all Bantu), and Mangbetu-Azande (Hamitic), make up 45% of pop. **Principal languages:** French (official), Lingala, Kingswana (a swahili dialect), Tshiluba. **Chief religions:** Roman Catholic 50%, Protestant 20%, Kimbanguist 10%, Muslim 10%.

Geography: Area: 905,567 sq. mi. (total): 875,525 sq. mi. (land). **Location:** in central Africa. **Neighbors:** Congo-Brazzaville on W; Central African Republic, Sudan on N; Uganda, Rwanda, Burundi, Tanzania on E; Zambia, Angola on S. **Topography:** Congo includes the bulk of the Congo R. basin. The vast central region is a low-lying plateau covered by rain forest. Mountainous terraces in the W, savannas in the S and SE, grasslands toward the N, and the high Ruwenzori Mts. on the E surround the central region. A short strip of territory borders the Atlantic O. **Capital:** Kinshasa. **Cities** (urban aggr.): Kinshasa 5,064,000; Lubumbashi 965,000.

Government: Type: In transition. **Head of state and gov.:** Pres. Joseph Kabila; b June 24, 1971; in office: Jan. 26, 2001. **Local divisions:** 10 provinces, 1 city. **Defense budget** (2002): $400 mil. **Active troops:** 81,400.

Economy: Industries: mining, mineral proc., textiles, footwear, cigarettes, proc. foods & beverages, cement. **Chief crops:** coffee, sugar, rubber, tea, quinine, cassava, bananas, root crops, corn, fruits, wood products. **Natural resources:** cobalt, copper, cadmium, oil, diamonds, gold, silver, zinc, mang., tin, germanium, uranium, radium, bauxite, iron ore, coal, hydropower, timber. **Crude oil reserves** (2002): 1.5 bil. bbls. **Arable land:** 3%. **Livestock** (2002): cattle: 765,000; chickens: 19.59 mil.; goats: 4 mil.; pigs: 953,000; sheep: 897,000. **Fish catch** (2002 est.): 208,848 metric tons. **Electricity prod.** (2001): 5.24 bil. kWh. **Labor force:** 65% agric., 16% ind., 19% serv.

Finance: Monetary unit: franc (CDF) (Sept. 2003: 407.95 = $1 U.S.). **GDP** (2002 est.): $34 bil. **Per capita GDP:** $610. **Imports** (2002): $890 mil.; partners (2000): South Africa 18.2%, Belgium 16.4%, Nigeria 11.8%, France 5.9%. **Exports** (2002): $1.2 bil.; partners (2000): Belgium 59.7%, U.S. 12.9%, Zimbabwe 7.4%, France 6.9%. **Tourism** (1998): $2 mil. **Budget** (1996 est.): $244 mil. **Consumer prices:** 32%.

Transport: Railroad: Length: 3,193 mi. **Motor vehicles:** 330,000 pass. cars, 200,000 comm. vehicles. **Civil aviation:** mil pass.-mi.; 24 airports. **Chief ports:** Matadi, Boma, Kinshasa.

Communications: TV sets: 2 per 1,000 pop. **Radios:** 376 per 1,000 pop. **Telephone lines:** 20,000. **Daily newspaper circ.:** 2.7 per 1,000 pop. **Internet:** 6,000 users.

Health: Life expectancy: 46.8 male; 51.1 female. **Births** (per 1,000 pop.): 45.1. **Deaths** (per 1,000 pop.): 14.9. **Natural inc.:** 3.03%. **Infant mortality** (per 1,000 live births): 96.6.

Education: Compulsory: ages 6-15. **Literacy:** 83.8%.

Major Intl. Organizations: UN and most of its specialized agencies, AU.

Embassy: 1800 New Hampshire Ave. NW 20009; 234-7690.

Website: www.embassy.org/embassies/zr.htm l

The earliest inhabitants of Congo may have been the pygmies, followed by Bantus from the E and Nilotic tribes from the N. The large Bantu Bakongo kingdom ruled much of Congo and Angola when Portuguese explorers visited in the 15th century.

Leopold II, king of the Belgians, formed an international group to exploit the Congo region in 1876. In 1877 Henry M. Stanley explored the Congo, and in 1878 the king's group sent him back to organize the region and win over the native chiefs. The Conference of Berlin, 1884-85, organized the Congo Free State with Leopold as king and chief owner. Exploitation of native laborers on the rubber plantations caused international criticism and led to granting of a colonial charter, 1908; the colony became known as the Belgian Congo. Millions of Congolese are believed to have died between 1880 and 1920 as a result of slave labor and other causes under European rule.

Belgian and Congolese leaders agreed Jan. 27, 1960, the Congo would become independent in June. In the first general elections, May 31, the National Congolese movement of Patrice Lumumba won a plurality in the National Assembly. He was appointed premier June 21, and formed a coalition cabinet. The Republic of the Congo was proclaimed June 30.

Widespread violence caused Europeans and others to flee. The UN Security Council, Aug. 9, 1960, called on Belgium to withdraw its troops and sent a UN contingent. Pres. Joseph Kasavubu removed Lumumba as premier in Sept.; Lumumba was murdered Jan. 17, 1961.

The last UN troops left the Congo June 30, 1964, and Moise Tshombe became president.

On Sept. 7, 1964, leftist rebels set up a "People's Republic" in Stanleyville (now Kisangani). Tshombe hired foreign mercenaries and sought to rebuild the Congolese Army. In Nov. and Dec. 1964 rebels killed scores of white hostages and thousands of Congolese; Belgian paratroopers, dropped from U.S. transport planes, rescued hundreds. By July 1965 the rebels had lost their effectiveness.

In late 1965 Gen. Joseph D. Mobutu was named president. He later changed his name to Mobutu Sese Seko and ruled as a dictator. The country became the Democratic Republic of the Congo (1966) and the Republic of Zaire (1971).

Economic decline and government corruption plagued Zaire in the 1980s and worsened in the 1990s. In 1990, Pres. Mobutu announced an end to a 20-year ban on multiparty politics. He sought to retain power despite mounting international pressure and internal opposition.

During 1994, Zaire was inundated with refugees from the massive ethnic bloodshed in Rwanda. Ethnic violence spread to E Zaire in 1996. In Oct. militant Hutus, who dominated in the refugee camps, fought against rebels (mostly Tutsis) in Zaire, precipitating intervention by government troops. As a result of the fighting, Rwandan refugees abandoned the camps; hundreds of thousands returned to Rwanda, while hundreds of thousands more were dispersed throughout E Zaire. The rebels, led by Gen. Laurent Kabila—a former Marxist and longtime opponent of Mobutu—gained momentum and began to move W across Zaire. As turmoil engulfed his nation, Mobutu stayed in W Europe during the latter part of 1996.

With Mobutu out of the country, the Zairean army put up little resistance; rebels were aided by several of Mobutu's enemies, notably Rwanda and Uganda. Mobutu returned to Zaire in March 1997, but attempts to negotiate with Kabila were ineffectual. On May 17, Kabila's troops entered Kinshasa and Mobutu went into exile. The country again assumed the name Democratic Republic of the Congo. Mobutu died Sept. 7 in Rabat, Morocco.

Kabila, who ruled by decree, alienated UN officials, international aid donors, and former allies. Rebels assisted by Rwanda and Uganda threatened Kinshasa in Aug. 1998, but the assault was turned back with help from Angola, Namibia, and Zimbabwe. Rebel groups agreed to a cease-fire on Aug. 31, 1999, but the truce was widely violated. Kabila was assassinated Jan. 16, 2001, apparently by one of his bodyguards, and was succeeded by his son Joseph.

A volcanic eruption in E Congo near Goma, Jan. 17, 2002, engulfed much of the city in lava and left thousands homeless.

Congo and Rwanda signed a peace agreement July 30, 2002, seeking to end the Congolese civil war.

The overall death toll from the civil war and related causes was estimated at 3.3 million through Nov. 2002. By then the war had apparently begun to wind down, with agreements by Rwanda and Uganda to pull out their remaining troops. A power-sharing accord signed Apr. 2, 2003, led to the installation of a new Congolese government in July. A UN peacekeeping force (MONUC), established in the Congo in 1999, still remained in 2003 numbering about 7,000.

Congo Republic
Republic of the Congo

(Congo Republic, officially Republic of the Congo, is also known as Congo-Brazzaville. It should not be confused with Democratic Republic of the Congo [formerly Zaire], now commonly called Congo, and also known as Congo-Kinshasa.)

People: Population: 3,724,000. **Age distrib.** (%): <15: 42.4; 65+: 3.3. **Pop. density:** 28 per sq. mi. **Urban:** 66%. **Ethnic groups:** Kongo 48%, Sangha 20%, M'Bochi 12%, Teke 17%. **Principal languages:** French (official), Lingala, Monokutuba, Kikongo, many local languages and dialects. **Chief religions:** Christian 50%, animist 48%, Muslim 2%.

Geography: Area: 132,047 sq. mi. (total); 131,854 sq. mi. (land). **Location:** In W central Africa. **Neighbors:** Gabon and Cameroon on W, Central African Republic on N, Congo-Kinshasa (formerly Zaire) on E, Angola on SW. **Topography:** Much of the Congo is covered by thick forests. A coastal plain leads to the fertile Niari Valley. The center is a plateau; the Congo R. basin consists of flood plains in the lower and savanna in the upper portion. **Capital:** Brazzaville 1,360,000.

Government: Type: Republic. **Head of state and gov.:** Pres. Denis Sassou-Nguesso; b 1943; in office: Oct. 25, 1997. **Local divisions:** 10 regions, 6 communes. **Defense budget** (2002): $90 mil. **Active troops:** 10,000.

Economy: Industries: oil, cement, lumber, brewing, sugar, palm oil. **Chief crops:** cassava, sugar, rice, corn, peanuts, vegetables, coffee, cocoa. **Natural resources:** oil, timber, potash, lead, zinc, uranium, copper, phosphates, nat. gas, hydropower. **Crude oil reserves** (2002): 187 mil. bbls. **Livestock** (2002): cattle: 90,000; chickens: 1.90 mil.; goats: 280,000; pigs: 46,000; sheep: 96,000. **Fish catch** (2002 est.): 42,200 metric tons. **Electricity prod.:** 0.36 bil. kWh.

Finance: Monetary unit: CFA Franc BEAC (XAF) (Sept. 2003: 597.03 = $1 U.S.). **GDP** (2002 est.): $2.5 bil. **Per capita GDP:** $900. **Imports** (2002): $730 mil.; partners (2001): France 20.5%, Italy 10.9%, U.S. 9.5%, Belgium 5.1%, South Africa 2.5%. **Exports:** (2002): $2.4 bil; partners (2001) U.S. 17.2%, S. Korea 12.7%, China 9.9%, Germany 5.6%, France 2.4%. **Tourism:** $11 mil. **Budget** (1997 est.): $970 mil. **Intl. reserves less gold:** $23 mil. **Gold:** 100,000 oz t. **Consumer prices:** 4.4%.

Transport: Railroad: Length: 556 mi. **Motor vehicles** (1998): 29,000 pass. cars, 16,600 comm. vehicles. **Civil aviation:** 4 airports. **Chief ports:** Pointe-Noire, Brazzaville.

Communications: TV sets: 13 per 1,000 pop. **Radios:** 126 per 1,000 pop. **Telephone lines:** 22,000 main lines. **Daily newspaper circ.:** 8 per 1,000 pop. **Internet:** 1,000 users

Health: Life expectancy: 49.0 male; 51.0 female. **Births** (per 1,000 pop.): 29.5. **Deaths** (per 1,000 pop.): 14.2. **Natural inc.:** 1.53%. **Infant mortality** (per 1,000 live births): 95.3.

Education: Compulsory: ages 6-15. **Literacy:** 65.5%.

Major Intl. Organizations: UN (FAO, IBRD, ILO, IMF, IMO, WHO), AU.

Embassy: 4891 Colorado Ave. NW 20011; 726-5500.

Website: www.embassyofcongo.org

The Loango Kingdom flourished in the 15th century, as did the Anzico Kingdom of the Batekes; by the late 17th century they had become weakened. By 1885, France established control of the region, then called the Middle Congo. Republic of the Congo gained independence Aug. 15, 1960.

After a 1963 coup sparked by trade unions, the country adopted a Marxist-Leninist stance, with the USSR and China vying for influence. France remained a dominant trade partner and source of technical assistance, however, and French-owned private enterprise retained a major economic role. In 1970, the country was renamed People's Republic of the Congo.

In 1990, Marxism was renounced and opposition parties were legalized. In 1991 the country's name was changed back to Republic of the Congo, and a new constitution was approved. A democratically elected government came into office in 1992. Factional fighting broke out in Brazzaville, June 5, 1997, and intensified during the summer, devastating the capital. Troops loyal to former Marxist dictator Denis Sassou-Nguesso took control of the city Oct. 15. He claimed a lopsided victory in the presidential election of Mar. 10, 2002. The government and "Ninja" rebels in the Pool Region agreed to a cease-fire Mar. 17, 2003.

Costa Rica
Republic of Costa Rica

People: Population: 4,173,000. **Age distrib.** (%): <15: 30.8; 65+: 5.3. **Pop. density:** 213 per sq. mi. **Urban:** 60%. **Ethnic groups:** European and Mestizo 94%, black 3%, Amerindian 1%, Chinese 1%. **Principal languages:** Spanish (official), English spoken around Puerto Limon. **Chief religions:** Roman Catholic 76% (official), Protestant 14%.

Geography: Area: 19,730 sq. mi. (total); 19,560 sq. mi. (land). **Location:** In Central America. **Neighbors:** Nicaragua on N, Panama on S. **Topography:** Lowlands by the Caribbean are tropical. The interior plateau, with an altitude of about 4,000 ft., is temperate. **Capital:** San José, 983,000.

Government: Type: Republic. **Head of state and gov.:** Pres. Abel Pacheco; b Dec. 22, 1933; in office: May 8, 2002. **Local divisions:** 7 provinces. **Defense budget:** $76 mil. **Active troops:** N/A.

Economy: Industries: microprocessors, food proc., textiles and clothing, constr. materials, fertilizer, plastics. **Chief crops:** coffee, pineapples, bananas, sugar, corn, rice, beans, potatoes, timber. **Natural resources:** hydropower. **Arable land:** 6%. **Livestock** (2002): cattle: 1.22 mil.; chickens: 17 mil.; goats: 1,650; pigs: 475,000; sheep: 3,000. **Fish catch** (2002): 45,253 metric tons. **Electricity prod.** (2001): 6.84 bil. kWh. **Labor force:** agri. 20%, ind. 22%, services 58%.

Finance: Monetary unit: Colon (CRC) (Sept. 2003: 416.50 = $1 U.S.). **GDP** (2002 est.): $32.3 bil. **Per capita GDP:** $8,500. **Imports** (2001): $6.5 bil.; partners (2000): U.S. 53.2%, EU 10.3%, Mexico 6.2%, Venezuela 5.3%. **Exports** (2001): $5 bil.; partners (2000): U.S. 51.8%, EU 20%, Central America 10.6%, Puerto Rico 2.8%. **Tourism:** $1.1 bil. **Budget** (2000 est.): $2.35 bil. **Intl. reserves less gold:** $1.10 bil. **Consumer prices:** 9.2%.

Transport: Railroad: Length: 590 mi. **Motor vehicles** (1999): 326,500 pass. cars, 169,800 comm. vehicles. **Civil aviation:** 1.33 bil pass.-mi.; 30 airports. **Chief ports:** Limon, Puntarenas, Golfito.

Communications: TV sets: 229 per 1,000 pop. **Radios:** 774 per 1,000 pop. **Telephone lines:** 1,038,000. **Daily newspaper circ.:** 94 per 1,000 pop. **Internet:** 384,000 users.

Health: Life expectancy: 73.9 male; 79.1 female. **Births** (per 1,000 pop.): 19.4. **Deaths** (per 1,000 pop.): 4.3. **Natural inc.:** 1.51%. **Infant mortality** (per 1,000 live births): 10.6.

Education: Compulsory: ages 5-15. **Literacy:** 96%.

Major Intl. Organizations: UN (FAO, IBRD, ILO, IMF, IMO, WHO, WTrO), OAS.

Embassy: 2114 S St. NW 20008; 234-2945.

Websites: www.costarica-embassy.org
www.visitcostarica.com

Guaymi Indians inhabited the area when Spaniards arrived, 1502. Independence came in 1821. Costa Rica seceded from the Central American Federation in 1838. Since the civil war of 1948-49, there has been little violent social conflict, and free political institutions have been preserved. During 1993 there was an unusual wave of kidnappings and hostage-taking, some of it related to the international cocaine trade.

Costa Rica, though still a largely agricultural country, has achieved a relatively high standard of living, and land ownership is widespread. Tourism is growing rapidly.

Côte d'Ivoire
Republic of Ivory Coast

People: Population: 16,631,000. **Age distrib.** (%): <15: 46; 65+: 2.2. **Pop. density:** 135 per sq. mi. **Urban:** 44%. **Ethnic groups:** Akan 42%, Voltaiques (Gur) 18%, N Mandes 17%, Krous 11%, S Mandes 10%. **Principal languages:** French (official), Dioula, many native dialects. **Chief religions:** Muslim 35-40%, Christian 20-30%, indigenous beliefs 25-40%.

Geography: Area: 124,502 sq. mi. (total); 122,780 sq. mi. (land). **Location:** On S coast of W Africa. **Neighbors:** Liberia, Guinea on W; Mali, Burkina Faso on N; Ghana on E. **Topography:** Forests cover the W half of the country, and range from a coastal strip to halfway to the N on the E. A sparse inland plain leads to low mountains in NW. **Capital:** Yamoussoukro (official); Abidjan (de facto). **Cities (urban aggr.):** Abidjan 3,956,000.

Government: Type: In transition. **Head of state:** Pres. Laurent Gbagbo; b May 31, 1945; in office: Oct. 26, 2000. **Head of gov.:** Prime Min. Seydou Diarra; b Nov. 23, 1933; in office: Feb. 10, 2003. **Local divisions:** 45 provinces. **Defense budget** (2002): $90 mil. **Active troops:** 17,050.

Economy: Industries: foodstuffs, beverages, wood products, oil refining, truck & bus assembly, textiles, fertilizer, building materials, electricity. **Chief crops:** coffee, cocoa beans, bananas, palm kernels. **Natural resources:** oil, nat. gas, diamonds, mang., iron ore, cobalt, bauxite, copper, hydropower. **Crude oil reserves** (2002): 100 mil. bbls. **Arable land:** 8%. **Livestock** (2002): cattle: 1.41 mil.; chickens: 29.40 mil.; goats: 1.13 mil.; pigs: 336,000; sheep: 1.45 mil. **Fish catch** (2002): 74,581 metric tons. **Electricity prod.** (2001): 4.61 bil. kWh. **Labor force:** 51% agric.; 12% manuf. & mining.

Finance: Monetary unit: CFA Franc BCEAO (XOF) (Sept. 2003: 605.18 = $1 U.S.). **GDP** (2002 est.): $24.5 bil. **Per capita GDP:** $1,500. **Imports** (2001): $2.4 bil.; partners (1999): France 26%, Nigeria 10%, China 7%, Italy 5%. **Exports** (2001 est.): $3.6 bil.; partners (1999): France 13%, U.S. 8%, Netherlands 7%, Germany 7%. **Tourism** (1999): $108 mil. **Budget** (2001 est.): $2.4 bil. **Intl. reserves less gold:** $1.37 mil. **Consumer prices:** 3.1%.

Transport: Railroad: Length: 410 mi. **Motor vehicles** (1998): 78,100 pass. cars, 36,300 comm. vehicles. **Civil aviation:** 236.7 mil pass.-mi.; 7 airports. **Chief ports:** Abidjan, Dabou, San-Pédro.

Communications: TV sets: 65 per 1,000 pop. **Radios:** 161 per 1,000 pop. **Telephone lines:** 336,100. **Daily newspaper circ.:** 17 per 1,000 pop. **Internet:** 90,000 users.

Health: Life expectancy: 40.3 male; 45.0 female. **Births** (per 1,000 pop.): 40.0. **Deaths** (per 1,000 pop.): 18.4. **Natural inc.:** 2.16%. **Infant mortality** (per 1,000 live births): 98.3.

Education: Compulsory: ages 6-15. **Literacy:** 50.9%.

Major Intl. Organizations: UN and all of its specialized agencies, AU.

Embassy: 2424 Massachusetts Ave. NW 20008; 797-0300.

Website: www.presidence.gov.ci

A French protectorate from 1842, Côte d'Ivoire became independent in 1960. It is the most prosperous of all the tropical African nations, as a result of diversification of agriculture for export, close ties to France, and encouragement of foreign investment. About 20% of the population are workers from neighboring countries. Côte d'Ivoire officially changed its name from Ivory Coast in Oct. 1985.

Students and workers protested, Feb. 1990, demanding the ouster of longtime Pres. Félix Houphouët-Boigny. Côte d'Ivoire held its first multiparty presidential election Oct. 1990, and Houphouët-Boigny retained his office. He died Dec. 7, 1993. The National Assembly named a successor, Henri Konan Bédié, who was reelected Oct. 22, 1995; he was ousted in a military coup Dec. 24, 1999. The coup leader, Robert Guéi, apparently lost a presidential vote Oct. 22, 2000, but claimed victory anyway. After mass protests, he fled, and Laurent Gbagbo became president.

Guéi was killed in Abidjan Sept. 19, 2002, after a mutiny broke out there and in Bouaké and Korhogo. French troops Sept. 25 rescued 160 students (100 from the U.S.) trapped in Bouaké. Fueled by the conflict in neighboring Liberia, fighting in Côte d'Ivoire continued for months, despite the presence of 3,000 French peacekeepers. Agreement on power sharing was reached in Mar. 2003, and Gbagbo and former rebel leaders held a ceremony July 5, declaring that the war was over.

Croatia
Republic of Croatia

People: Population: 4,428,000. **Age distrib.** (%): <15: 18.3; 65+: 15.4. **Pop. density:** 203 per sq. mi. **Urban:** 58%. **Ethnic groups:** Croat 78%, Serb 12%, Bosniak 1%. **Principal languages:** Croatian (official), Serbian. **Chief religions:** Roman Catholic 88%, Orthodox 5%.

Geography: Area: 21,831 sq. mi. (total); 21,782 sq. mi. (land). **Location:** SE Europe, on the Balkan Peninsula. **Neighbors:** Slovenia, Hungary on N; Bosnia and Herzegovina, Yugoslavia on E. **Topography:** Flat plains in NE; highlands, low mtns. along Adriatic coast. **Capital:** Zagreb 1,081,000.

Government: Type: Parliamentary democracy. **Head of state:** Pres. Stipe Mesic; b Dec. 24, 1934; in office: Feb. 18, 2000. **Head of gov.:** Prime Min. Ivica Racan; b Feb. 24, 1944; in office: Jan. 27, 2000. **Local divisions:** 21 counties. **Defense budget** (2002): $599 mil. **Active troops:** 51,000.

Economy: Industries: chemicals, plastics, machine tools, fabricated metal, electronics. **Chief crops:** wheat, corn, sugar beets, sunflower seeds, barley. **Natural resources:** oil, coal, bauxite, iron ore, calcium, natural asphalt, silica, mica, clays, salt, hydropower. **Crude oil reserves** (2002): 92 mil. bbls. **Arable land:** 21%. **Livestock** 2002: cattle: 438,000; chickens: 10.80 mil.; goats: 93,000; pigs: 1.30 mil.; sheep: 528,000. **Fish catch** (2002): 28,256 metric tons. **Electricity prod.** (2001): 12.12 bil. kWh. **Labor force:** 31.1% industry & mining.

Finance: Monetary unit: Kuna (HRK) (Sept. 2003: 7.24 = $1 U.S.). **GDP** (2002 est.): $38.9 bil. **Per capita GDP:** $8,800. **Imports** (2002): $9.7 bil.; partners (2001): Germany 17.1%, Italy 16.9%, Slovenia 7.9%, Russia 7.2%. **Exports** (2002 est.): $5.1 bil.; partners (2001): Italy 23.7%, Germany 14.8%, Bosnia and Herzegovina 12%, Slovenia 9.1%. **Tourism:** $2.76 bil. **Budget** (2001 est.): $9 bil. **Intl. reserves less gold:** $4.33 bil. **Consumer prices:** 2.0%.

Transport: Railroad: Length: 1,694 mi. **Motor vehicles:** 1.12 mil. pass. cars, 127,200 comm. vehicles. **Civil aviation:** 348.0 mil pass.-mi.; 16 airports. **Chief ports:** Rijeka, Split, Dubrovnik.

Communications: TV sets: 286 per 1,000 pop. **Radios:** 337 per 1,000 pop. **Telephone lines:** 1,879,000. **Daily newspaper circ.:** 115 per 1,000 pop. **Internet:** 789,000 users.

Health: Life expectancy: 70.8 male; 78.2 female. **Births** (per 1,000 pop.): 12.8. **Deaths** (per 1,000 pop.): 11.3. **Natural inc.:** 0.15%. **Infant mortality** (per 1,000 live births): 6.9.

Education: Compulsory: ages 7-15. **Literacy:** 98.5%.

Major Intl. Organizations: UN (FAO, IBRD, ILO, IMF, IMO, WHO), OSCE.

Embassy: 2343 Massachusetts Ave. NW 20008; 588-5899.

Website: www.crotiaemb.org

From the 7th century the area was inhabited by Croats, a south Slavic people. It was formed into a kingdom under Tomislav in 924, and joined with Hungary in 1102. The Croats became westernized and separated from Slavs under Austro-Hungarian influence. The Croats retained autonomy under the Hungarian crown. Slavonia was taken by Turks in the 16th century; the northern part was restored by the Treaty of Karlowitz in 1699. Croatia helped Austria put down the Hungarian revolution 1848-49 and as a result was set up with Slavonia as the separate Austrian crownland of Croatia and Slavonia, which was reunited to Hungary as part of Ausgleich in 1867. It united with other Yugoslav areas to proclaim the Kingdom of Serbs, Croats, and Slovenes in 1918. At the reorganization of Yugoslavia in 1929, Croatia and Slavonia became Savska county, which in 1939 was united with Primorje county to form the county of Croatia. A nominally independent state between 1941 and 1945, it became a constituent republic in the 1946 constitution.

On June 25, 1991, Croatia declared independence from Yugoslavia. Fighting began between ethnic Serbs and Croats, with the former gaining control of about 30% of Croatian territory. A cease-fire was declared in Jan. 1992, but new hostilities broke out in 1993. A cease-fire with Serb rebels forming a self-declared republic of Krajina was agreed to Mar. 30, 1994. Croatian government troops recaptured most of the Serb-held territory Aug. 1995. Pres. Franjo Tudjman signed a peace accord with leaders of Bosnia and Serbia in Paris, Dec. 14. Tudjman won reelection June 15, 1997; international monitors called the vote "free but not fair." The last Serb-held enclave, E Slavonia, returned to Croatian control Jan. 15, 1998.

Tudjman died Dec. 10, 1999. Stipe Mesic, a moderate, won a presidential runoff election Feb. 7, 2000.

Cuba
Republic of Cuba

People: Population: 11,300,000. **Age distrib.** (%): <15: 20.6; 65+: 10.1. **Pop. density:** 264 per sq. mi. **Urban:** 76%. **Ethnic groups:** Creole 51%, White 37%, Black 11%, Chinese 1%. **Principal languages:** Spanish (official). **Chief religions:** Roman Catholic, Santeria.

Geography: Area (total): 42,803 sq. mi. **Location:** In the Caribbean, westernmost of West Indies. **Neighbors:** Bahamas and U.S. to N, Mexico to W, Jamaica to S, Haiti to E. **Topography:** The coastline is about 2,500 miles. The N coast is steep and rocky, the S coast low and marshy. Low hills and fertile valleys cover more than half the country. Sierra Maestra, in the E, is the highest of 3 mountain ranges. **Capital:** Havana 2,268,000.

Government: Type: Communist state. **Head of state and gov.:** Pres. Fidel Castro Ruz; b Aug. 13, 1926; in office: Dec, 3, 1976 (formerly prime min. since Feb. 16, 1959). **Local divisions:** 14 provinces, 1 special municipality. **Defense budget** (2001): $37.7 mil. **Active troops:** 46,000.

Economy: Industries: sugar, oil, tobacco, chemicals, constr., services. **Chief crops:** sugar, tobacco, citrus, coffee, rice. **Natural resources:** cobalt, nickel, iron ore, copper, mang., salt, timber, silica, oil. **Crude oil reserves** (2002): 750 mil. bbls. **Arable land:** 24%. **Livestock** (2002): cattle: 4.40 mil.; chickens: 13.30 mil.; goats: 240,000; pigs: 2.70 mil.; sheep: 310,000. **Fish catch** (2002 est.): 110,330 metric tons. **Electricity prod.** (2001): 14.39 bil. kWh. **Labor force:** agri. 24%, ind. 25%, services 51%.

Finance: Monetary unit: Peso (CUP) (Sept. 2003: 2.35 = $1 U.S.). **GDP** (2002 est.): $25.9 bil. **Per capita GDP:** $2,300. **Imports** (2001): $4.8 bil.; partners (2001): Spain 12.7%, France 6.5%, Canada 5.7%, China 5.3%. **Exports** (2002 est.): $1.8 bil.; partners (2001): Netherlands 22.4%, Russia 13.3%, Canada 13.3%, Spain 7.3%. **Tourism:** $1.76 bil. **Budget** (2000 est.): $15.6 bil.

Transport: Railroad: Length: 2,987 mi. **Motor vehicles:** 16,500 pass. cars, 30,000 comm. vehicles. **Civil aviation:** 2.31 bil pass.-mi.; 70 airports. **Chief ports:** Havana, Matanzas, Cienfuegos, Santiago de Cuba.

Communications: TV sets: 248 per 1,000 pop. **Radios:** 352 per 1,000 pop. **Telephone lines:** 574,400. **Daily newspaper circ.:** 118 per 1,000 pop. **Internet:** 120,000 users.

Health: Life expectancy: 74.4 male; 79.4 female. **Births** (per 1,000 pop.): 11.9. **Deaths** (per 1,000 pop.): 7.4. **Natural inc.:** 0.45%. **Infant mortality** (per 1,000 live births): 7.2.

Education: Compulsory: ages 6-14. **Literacy:** 97%.

Major Intl. Organizations: UN (FAO, ILO, IMO, WHO, WTrO).

Some 50,000 Indians lived in Cuba when it was reached by Columbus in 1492. Its name derives from the Indian Cubanacan. Except for British occupation of Havana, 1762-63, Cuba remained Spanish until 1898. A slave-based sugar plantation economy developed from the 18th century, aided by early mechanization of milling. Sugar remains the chief product and chief export despite government attempts to diversify.

Websites: www.cubagov.cu/ingles/default.htm
www.travel. state.gov/cuba.html

A ten-year uprising ended in 1878 with guarantees of rights by Spain, which Spain failed to carry out. A full-scale movement under Jose Marti began Feb. 24, 1895.

The U.S. declared war on Spain in Apr. 1898, after the sinking of the USS *Maine* in Havana harbor, and defeated it in the Spanish-American War. Spain gave up all claims to Cuba. U.S. troops withdrew in 1902, but under 1903 and 1934 agreements, the U.S. leases a site at Guantánamo Bay in the SE as a naval base. U.S. and other foreign investments acquired a dominant role in the economy. In 1952, former Pres. Fulgencio Batista seized control and established a dictatorship, which grew increasingly harsh and corrupt. Fidel Castro assembled a rebel band in 1956; guerrilla fighting intensified in 1958. Batista fled Jan. 1, 1959, and in the resulting political vacuum Castro took power, becoming premier Feb. 16.

The government began a program of sweeping economic and social changes, without restoring promised liberties. Opponents were imprisoned, and some were executed. Some 700,000 Cubans emigrated in the first years after the Castro takeover, mostly to the U.S.

Cattle and tobacco lands were nationalized, while a system of cooperatives was instituted. By 1960 all banks and industrial companies had been nationalized, including over $1 billion worth of U.S.-owned properties, mostly without compensation.

Poor sugar crops resulted in farm collectivization, tight labor controls, and rationing, despite continued aid from the USSR and other Communist nations. A U.S.-imposed export embargo in 1962 severely damaged the economy.

In 1961, some 1,400 Cubans, trained and backed by the U.S. Central Intelligence Agency, unsuccessfully tried to invade and overthrow the regime. In the fall of 1962, the U.S. learned the USSR had brought nuclear missiles to Cuba. After an Oct. 22 warning from Pres. John F. Kennedy, the missiles were removed.

In 1977, Cuba and the U.S. signed agreements to exchange diplomats, without restoring full ties, and to regulate offshore fishing. In 1978 and 1980, the U.S. agreed to accept political prisoners released by Cuba, some of whom were criminals and mental patients. A 1987 agreement provided for 20,000 Cubans to emigrate to the U.S. each year; Cuba agreed to take back some 2,500 jailed in the U.S. since 1980.

In 1975-78, Cuba sent troops to aid one faction in the Angola civil war; the last Cuban troops were withdrawn by May 1991. Cuba's involvement in Central America, Africa, and the Caribbean contributed to poor relations with the U.S.

Cuba's economy, dependent on aid from other Communist countries, was severely shaken by the collapse of the Communist bloc in the late 1980s. Stiffer trade sanctions enacted by the U.S. in 1992 made things worse. Antigovernment demonstrations in Aug. 1994 prompted Castro to loosen emigration restrictions. A new U.S.-Cuba accord in Sept. ended the exodus of "boat people" after more than 30,000 had left Cuba. In another policy shift, the U.S. announced May 2, 1995, it would admit 20,000 Cuban refugees held at the Guantánamo base but would send further boat people back to Cuba.

The U.S. imposed additional sanctions after Cuba, Feb. 24, 1996, shot down 2 aircraft operated by an anti-Castro exile group based in Miami. Cuba blamed exile groups for bombings at Havana tourist hotels, July-Sept. 1997. Pope John Paul II visited Cuba, Jan. 21-25, 1998; he called for an end to U.S. trade sanctions, while pressing Castro to release political prisoners and allow political and religious freedom. U.S. restrictions on travel with Cuba were eased in 1999. On June 28, 2000, Elián González was returned to Cuba to live with his father, ending a 7-month legal battle that began when the boy was rescued off Florida from a shipwreck in which his mother was killed; the boy's Miami relatives had sought to keep him in the U.S.

The U.S., Jan. 11, 2002, began using the base at Guantánamo Bay to detain prisoners captured in Afghanistan. Visiting Havana May 12-17, former U.S. Pres. Jimmy Carter called for democratic reforms and for lifting the U.S. trade embargo. In one of its largest crackdowns in recent years, Cuba arrested about 78 dissidents in Mar. 2003. On Apr. 11, the government executed 3 men who nine days earlier had hijacked a ferry in Havana bay in a failed attempt to escape to the U.S. Both the crackdown and executions were denounced worldwide.

Cyprus
Republic of Cyprus
(Figures below marked with a # do not include Turkish-held area—Turkish Republic of Northern Cyprus.)

People: Population: 802,000. **Age distrib.** (%): <15: 22.4; 65+: 11. **Pop. density:** 225 per sq. mi. **Urban:** 70%. **Ethnic groups:** Greek 85%, Turkish 12%. **Principal languages:** Greek, Turkish (both official), English. **Chief religions:** Greek Orthodox 78%, Muslim 18%.

Geography: Area: 3,571 sq. mi. (land); 3,568 sq. mi. (land). **Location:** In eastern Mediterranean Sea, off Turkish coast. **Neighbors:** Nearest are Turkey on N, Syria and Lebanon on E. **Topography:** Two mountain ranges run E-W, separated by a wide, fertile plain. **Capital:** Nicosia 199,000.

Government: Type: Republic. **Head of state and gov.:** Pres. Tassos Papadopoulos; b Jan. 7, 1934; in office: Feb. 28, 2003. **Local divisions:** 6 districts. **Defense budget** (2001): $321 mil. **Active troops:** 10,000.

Economy: Industries: food, beverages, textiles, chemicals, metal products, tourism. **Chief crops:** potatoes, citrus, vegetables, barley, grapes, olives. **Natural resources:** copper, pyrites, asbestos, gypsum, timber, salt, marble, clay earth pigment. **Arable land:** 12%. **Livestock** (2002): cattle: 54,000; chickens: 3.40 mil.; goats: 447,100; pigs: 445,000; sheep: 297,000. **Fish catch** (2002): 77,686 metric tons. **Electricity prod.** (2001): 3.4 bil. kWh. **Labor force:** Greek Cypriot area: services 73%, ind. 22%, agri. 5%; Turkish Cypriot area: services 56.4%, ind. 22.8%, agri. 20.8%.

Finance: Monetary unit: Pound (CYP) (Sept. 2003: 0.54 = $1 U.S.). **GDP** (2002 est.): Greek area: $9.4 bil., Turkish area: $787 mil. **Per capita GDP:** Greek area: $15,000, Turkish area: $6,000. **Imports** (2001): Greek Cypriot area: $3.5 bil.; Turkish Cypriot area: $424.9 mil.; partners: Greek Cypriot area (2000): EU 52%, U.S. 10%. Turkish Cypriot area (1999): Turkey 59%, UK 13%, other EU 13%. **Exports** (2001 est.): Turkish Cypriot area (1999): $50.7 mil.; Greek Cypriot area: $851 mil.; partners (2000): Turkish Cypriot area: Turkey 51%, UK 31%, other EU 16.5% Greek Cypriot area: EU 36%, Russia 8%, Syria 7%, Lebanon 5%. **Tourism:** $1.89 bil. **Budget** (2003 est.): $3.7 bil. Greek area; 432.8 mil turkish. **Intl. reserves less gold:** $2.22 bil. **Gold:** 460,000 mil. oz t. **Consumer prices:** 2.8%.

Transport: Motor vehicles: 267,600 pass. cars, 119,600 comm. vehicles. **Civil aviation:** 1.67 bil pass.-mi.; 13 airports. **Chief ports:** Famagusta, Limassol.

Communications: Television sets: 154 per 1000 pop. **Radios:** 406 per 1,000 pop. **Telephone lines:** 427,400. **Daily newspaper circ.:** 102.5 per 1,000 pop. **Internet:** 210,000 users.

Health: Life expectancy: 74.9 male; 79.7 female. **Births** (per 1,000 pop.): 12.8. **Deaths** (per 1,000 pop.): 7.6. **Natural inc.:** 0.51%. **Infant mortality** (per 1,000 live births): 7.5.

Education: Compulsory: ages 6-14. **Literacy:** 97.6%.

Major Intl. Organizations: UN (FAO, IBRD, ILO, IMF, IMO, WHO, WTrO), the Commonwealth, OSCE.
Embassy: 2211 R St. NW 20008; 462-5772.
Websites: www.cyprusembassy.net
www.embassy.org/embassies/cy.html

Agitation for enosis (union) with Greece increased after World War II, with the Turkish minority opposed, and broke into violence in 1955-56. In 1959, Britain, Greece, Turkey, and Cypriot leaders approved a plan for an independent republic, with constitutional guarantees for the Turkish minority and permanent division of offices on an ethnic basis. Greek and Turkish Communal Chambers dealt with religion, education, and other matters.

Archbishop Makarios III, formerly the leader of the enosis movement, was elected president, and full independence became final Aug. 16, 1960. Further communal strife led the United Nations to send a peacekeeping force in 1964; its mandate has been repeatedly renewed.

The Cypriot National Guard, led by officers from the army of Greece, seized the government July 15, 1974. On July 20, Turkey invaded the island; Greece mobilized its forces but did not intervene. A cease-fire was arranged but collapsed. By Aug. 16, Turkish forces had occupied the NE 40% of the island, despite the presence of UN peacekeeping forces.

Turkish Cypriots voted overwhelmingly, June 8, 1975, to form a separate Turkish Cypriot federated state. A president and assembly were elected in 1976. Some 200,000 Greeks have been expelled from the Turkish-controlled area, replaced by thousands of Turks, some from the mainland. Face-to-face talks between the Greek and Turkish Cypriot leaders resumed Dec. 4, 2001, for the 1st time in 4 years. Turkish Cyprus opened its border with Greek Cyprus Apr. 23, 2003, for the 1st time since partition.

Turkish Republic of Northern Cyprus

A declaration of independence was announced by Turkish-Cypriot leader Rauf Denktash, Nov. 15, 1983. The state is not internationally recognized, although it does have trade relations with some countries. Area of TRNC: 1,295 sq mi.; pop. (2001 est.): 208,886, 99% Turkish; capital: Lefkosa (Nicosia).

Czech Republic

People: Population: 10,236,000. **Age distrib.** (%): <15: 15.7; 65+: 14. **Pop. density:** 337 per sq.mi. **Urban:** 75%. **Ethnic groups:** Czech 81%, Moravian 13%, Slovak 3%. **Principal languages:** Czech (official), German, Polish, Romani. **Chief religions:** Atheist 40%, Roman Catholic 39%, Protestant 5%, Orthodox 3%.
Geography: Area: 30,450 sq. mi. (total); 29,836 sq. mi. (land). **Location:** In E central Europe. **Neighbors:** Poland on N, Germany on N and W, Austria on S, Slovakia on E and SE. **Topography:** Bohemia, in W, is a plateau surrounded by mountains; Moravia is hilly. **Capital:** Prague 1,202,000.
Government: Type: Republic. **Head of state:** Vaclav Klaus; b June 19, 1941; in office: mar. 7, 2003. **Head of gov.:** Prime Min. Vladimir Spidla; b Apr. 22, 1951; in office: July 12, 2002. **Local divisions:** 73 districts, 4 municipalities. **Defense budget** (2002): $1.6 bil. **Active troops:** 49,450.
Economy: Industries: metallurgy, machinery, motor vehicles, glass, armaments. **Chief crops:** wheat, potatoes, sugar beets, hops, fruit. **Natural resources:** coal, kaolin, clay, graphite, timber. **Arable land:** 41%. **Crude oil reserves** (2002): 15 mil. bbls. **Livestock** (2002): cattle: 1.52 mil.; chickens: 16.56 mil.; goats: 13,574; pigs: 3.44 mil.; sheep: 96,000. **Fish catch** (2002): 24,744 metric tons. **Electricity prod.** (2001): 70.04 bil. kWh. **Labor force:** agri. 5%, ind. 35%, services 60%.
Finance: Monetary unit: Koruna (CZK) (Sept. 2003: 29.92 = $1 U.S.). **GDP** (2002 est.): $155.9 bil. **Per capita GDP:** $15,300. **Imports** (2002): $41.7 bil.; partners (2001): Germany 32.9%, Slovakia 6.4%, Russia 6.0%, Italy 5.8%. **Exports** (2002) $38 bil.; partners (2001): Germany 35.4%, Slovakia 7.3%, UK 5.5%, Austria 5.3%. **Tourism:** $2.87 bil. **Budget** (2001 est.): $18 bil. **Intl. reserves less gold:** $17.33 bil. **Gold:** 440,000 oz t. **Consumer prices:** 1.8%.
Transport: Railroad: Length: 5,868 mi. **Motor vehicles:** 3.72 mil pass. cars, 595,800 comm. vehicles. **Civil aviation:** 1.78 bil pass.-mi.; 44 airports. **Chief ports:** Decin, Prague, Ustinad Labem.
Communications: TV sets: 487 per 1,000 pop. Radios: 803 per 1,000 pop. **Telephone lines:** 3,860,800. **Daily newspaper circ.:** 254 per 1,000 pop. **Internet:** 1,500,000 users
Health: Life expectancy: 71.7 male; 78.9 female. **Births** (per 1,000 pop.): 9.0. **Deaths** (per 1,000 pop.): 10.7. **Natural Inc.:** -0.17%. **Infant mortality** (per 1,000 live births): 5.4.
Education: Compulsory: ages 6-15. **Literacy** (1999 est.): 99.9%.
Major Intl. Organizations: UN (FAO, IBRD, ILO, IMF, IMO, WHO, WTrO), NATO, OECD, OSCE.
Embassy: 3900 Spring of Freedom St. NW 20008; 202-274-9100.
Website: www.czech.cz

Bohemia and Moravia were part of the Great Moravian Empire in the 9th century and later became part of the Holy Roman Empire. Under the kings of Bohemia, Prague in the 14th century was the cultural center of Central Europe. Bohemia and Hungary became part of Austria-Hungary.

In 1914-18 Thomas G. Masaryk and Eduard Benes formed a provisional government with the support of Slovak leaders including Milan Stefanik. They proclaimed the Republic of Czechoslovakia Oct. 28, 1918.

Czechoslovakia

By 1938 Nazi Germany had worked up disaffection among German-speaking citizens in Sudetenland and demanded its cession. British Prime Min. Neville Chamberlain, with the acquiescence of France, signed with Hitler at Munich, Sept. 30, 1938, an agreement to the cession, with a guarantee of peace by Hitler and Mussolini. Germany occupied Sudetenland Oct. 1-2.

Hitler on Mar. 15, 1939, dissolved Czechoslovakia, made protectorates of Bohemia and Moravia, and supported the autonomy of Slovakia, proclaimed independent Mar. 14, 1939.

Soviet troops with some Czechoslovak contingents entered eastern Czechoslovakia in 1944 and reached Prague in May 1945; Benes returned as president. In May 1946 elections, the Communist Party won 38% of the votes, and Benes accepted Klement Gottwald, a Communist, as prime minister.

In Feb. 1948, the Communists seized power in advance of scheduled elections. In May 1948 a new constitution was approved. Benes refused to sign it. On May 30 the voters were offered a one-slate ballot and the Communists won full control. Benes resigned June 7 and Gottwald became president. The country was renamed the Czechoslovak Socialist Republic. A harsh Stalinist period followed, with complete and violent suppression of all opposition.

In Jan. 1968 a liberalization movement spread through Czechoslovakia. Antonin Novotny, long the Stalinist ruler, was deposed as party leader and succeeded by Alexander Dubcek, a Slovak, who supported democratic reforms. On Mar. 22 Novotny resigned as president and was succeeded by Gen. Ludvik Svoboda. On Apr. 6, Prem. Joseph Lenart resigned and was succeeded by Oldrich Cernik, a reformer.

In July 1968 the USSR and 4 Warsaw Pact nations demanded an end to liberalization. On Aug. 20, the Soviet, Polish, East German, Hungarian, and Bulgarian armies invaded Czechoslovakia. Despite demonstrations and riots by students and workers, press censorship was imposed, liberal leaders were ousted from office and promises of loyalty to Soviet policies were made by some oldline Communist Party leaders.

On Apr. 17, 1969, Dubcek resigned as leader of the Communist Party and was succeeded by Gustav Husak. In Jan. 1970, Cernik was ousted. Censorship was tightened, and the Communist Party expelled a third of its members. In 1973, amnesty was offered to some of the 40,000 who fled the country after the 1968 invasion, but repressive policies continued.

More than 700 leading Czechoslovak intellectuals and former party leaders signed a human rights manifesto in 1977, called Charter 77, prompting a renewed crackdown by the regime.

The police crushed the largest antigovernment protests since 1968, when tens of thousands of demonstrators took to the streets of Prague, Nov. 17, 1989. As protesters demanded free elections, the Communist Party leadership resigned Nov. 24; millions went on strike Nov. 27.

On Dec. 10, 1989, the first cabinet in 41 years without a Communist majority took power; Vaclav Havel, playwright and human rights campaigner, was chosen president, Dec. 29. In Mar. 1990 the country was officially renamed the Czech and Slovak Federal Republic. Havel failed to win reelection July 3, 1992; his bid was blocked by a Slovak-led coalition.

Slovakia declared sovereignty, July 17. Czech and Slovak leaders agreed, July 23, on a basic plan for a peaceful division of Czechoslovakia into 2 independent states.

Czech Republic

Czechoslovakia split into 2 separate states—the Czech Republic and Slovakia—on Jan. 1, 1993. Havel was elected president of the Czech Republic on Jan. 26. Record floods in July 1997 caused more than $1.7 billion in damage. The country became a full member of NATO on Mar. 12, 1999. Floods Aug. 2002 damaged cultural treasures in Prague. Vaclav Klaus was chosen Feb. 28, 2003, to replace the retiring Havel. Czech voters June 13-14 endorsed joining the EU in 2004.

Denmark
Kingdom of Denmark

People: Population: 5,364,000. **Age distrib.** (%): <15: 18.7; 65+: 14.9. **Pop. density:** 328 per sq. mi. **Urban:** 85%. **Ethnic groups:** Mainly Danish; German minority in S. **Principal languages:** Danish (official), Faroese, Greenlandic (an Inuit dialect), German. **Chief religion: Chief religions:** Evangelical Lutheran 95% (official), other Christian 3%, Muslim 2%.
Geography: Area: 16,639 sq. mi. (total); 16,368 sq. mi. (land). **Location:** In N Europe, separating the North and Baltic seas. **Neighbors:** Germany on S, Norway on NW, Sweden on NE. **Topography:** Denmark consists of the Jutland Peninsula and about 500 islands, 100 inhabited. The land is flat or gently rolling and is almost all in productive use. **Capital:** Copenhagen 1,332,000.

Government: Type: Constitutional monarchy. **Head of state:** Queen Margrethe II; b Apr. 16, 1940; in office: Jan. 14, 1972. **Head of gov.:** Prime Min. Anders Fogh Rasmussen; b Jan. 26, 1953; in office: Nov. 27, 2001. **Local divisions:** 14 counties, 2 kommunes. **Defense budget** (2002): $2.4 bil. **Active troops:** 22,700.

Economy: Industries: food proc., machinery, textiles & clothing, chemicals, electronics, constr., furniture. **Chief crops:** barley, wheat, potatoes, sugar beets. **Natural resources:** oil, nat. gas, fish, salt, limestone, stone, gravel, sand. **Crude oil reserves** (2002): 1.1 bil. bbls. **Arable land:** 60%. **Livestock** (2002): cattle: 1.92 mil.; chickens: 20 mil.; pigs:12.99 mil.; sheep: 154,000. **Fish catch** (2002): 1,552,012 metric tons. **Electricity prod.** (2001): 35.47 bil. kWh. **Labor force:** services 79%, ind. 17%, agri. 4%.

Finance: Monetary unit: Krone (DKK) (Sept. 2003: 6.85 = $1 U.S.). **GDP** (2002 est.): $155.5 bil. **Per capita GDP:** $29,000. **Imports** (2002): $47.9 bil.; partners (2001): EU 69.9%, U.S. 4.2%. **Exports** (2002 est.): $56.3 bil.; partners (2001): EU 64.7%, U.S. 6.9%, Norway 5.5%. **Tourism:** $4.03 bil. **Budget** (2001 est.): $51.3 bil. **Intl. reserves less gold:** $19.85 bil. **Gold:** 2.14 mil oz t. **Consumer prices:** 2.4%.

Transport: Railroad: Length: 1,776 mi. **Motor vehicles** (1998): 1.82 mil. pass. cars, 371,500 comm. vehicles. **Civil aviation:** 3.66 bil pass.-mi.; 28 airports. **Chief ports:** Copenhagen, Alborg, Arhus, Odense.

Communications: TV sets: 776 per 1,000 pop. **Radios:** 1,325 per 1,000 pop. **Telephone lines:** 3,739,200. **Daily newspaper circ.:** 306.1 per 1,000 pop. **Internet:** 2,500,000 users.

Health: Life expectancy: 74.5 male; 79.9 female. **Births** (per 1,000 pop.): 11.5. **Deaths** (per 1,000 pop.): 10.7. **Natural inc.:** 0.08%. **Infant mortality** (per 1,000 live births): 4.9.

Education: Compulsory: ages 7-16. **Literacy:** 100%.

Major Intl. Organizations: UN and all of its specialized agencies, EU, NATO, OECD, OSCE.

Embassy: 3200 Whitehaven St. NW 20008; 234-4300.

Website: www.denmark.dk

The origin of Copenhagen dates back to ancient times, when the fishing and trading place named Havn (port) grew up on a cluster of islets, but Bishop Absalon (1128-1201) is regarded as the actual founder of the city.

Danes formed a large component of the Viking raiders in the early Middle Ages. The Danish kingdom was a major power until the 17th century, when it lost its land in southern Sweden. Norway was separated in 1815, and Schleswig-Holstein in 1864. Northern Schleswig was returned in 1920.

Voters ratified the Maastricht Treaty, the basic document of the European Union, in May 1993, after rejecting it in 1992. On Sept. 28, 2000, Danes voted not to join the euro currency zone.

The **Faroe Islands** in the North Atlantic, about 300 mi. NW of the Shetlands, and 850 mi. from Denmark proper, 18 inhabited, have an area of 540 sq. mi. and pop. (2003 est.) of 46,345. They are an administrative division of Denmark, self-governing in most matters. Torshavn is the capital. Fish is a primary export (571,255 metric tons in 2002).

Greenland (Kalaallit Nunaat)

Greenland, a huge island between the North Atlantic and the Polar Sea, is separated from the North American continent by Davis Strait and Baffin Bay. Its total area is 836,330 sq. mi., 84% of which is ice-capped. Most of the island is a lofty plateau 9,000 to 10,000 ft. in altitude. The average thickness of the cap is 1,000 ft. The population (2003 est.) is 56,385. Under the 1953 Danish constitution the colony became an integral part of the realm with representatives in the Folketing (Danish legislature). The Danish parliament, 1978, approved home rule for Greenland, effective May 1, 1979. With home rule, Greenlandic place names came into official use. The technically correct name for Greenland is now Kalaallit Nunaat; the official name for its capital is Nuuk, rather than Godthab. Fish is the principal export (158,485 metric tons in 2001).

Djibouti
Republic of Djibouti

People: Population: 703,000. **Age distrib.** (%): <15: 42.6; 65+: 2.9. **Pop. density:** 83 per sq. mi. **Urban:** 84%. **Ethnic groups:** Somali 60%, Afar 35%. **Principal languages:** French, Arabic (both official); Somali, Afar. **Chief religions:** Muslim 94%, Christian 6%.

Geography: Area: 8,880 sq. mi. (total); 8,873 sq. mi. (land). **Location:** On E coast of Africa, separated from Arabian Peninsula by the strategically vital strait of Bab el-Mandeb. **Neighbors:** Ethiopia on W and SW, Eritrea on NW, Somalia on SE. **Topography:** The territory, divided into a low coastal plain, mountains behind, and an interior plateau, is arid, sandy, and desolate. The climate is generally hot and dry. **Capital:** Djibouti 542,000.

Government: Type: Republic. **Head of state:** Pres. Ismail Omar Guelleh; b Nov. 27, 1947; in office: May 8, 1999. **Head of gov.:** Prime Min. Dileita Mohamed Dileita; b Mar. 12, 1958; in office: Mar. 7, 2001. **Local divisions:** 5 districts. **Defense budget** (2002): $22 mil. **Active troops:** 9,850.

Economy: Industries: constr., agricult. proc. **Chief crops:** fruits, vegetables. **Natural resources:** geothermal areas. **Livestock** (2002): cattle: 269,000; chickens: 513,000; sheep: 465,000.

Fish catch (2002 est.): 350 metric tons. **Electricity prod.** (2001): 0.18 bil. kWh. **Labor force:** agri. 75%, ind. 11%, services 14%.

Finance: Monetary unit: Franc (DJF) (Sept. 2003: 180.43 = $1 U.S.). **GDP** (2002 est.): $619 mil. **Per capita GDP:** $1,300. **Imports** (1999): $440 mil.; partners (1998): France 13%, Ethiopia 12%, Italy 9%, Saudi Arabia 6%. **Exports** (1999 est.): $260 mil.; partners (1998): Somalia 53%, Yemen 23%, Ethiopia 5%. **Tourism** (1997): $4 mil. **Budget** (1999 est.): $182 mil. **Intl. reserves less gold:** $54 mil.

Transport: Railroad: Length: 62 mi. **Motor vehicles** (1994): 13,500 pass. cars, 3,000 comm. vehicles. **Civil aviation:** 3 airports. **Chief port:** Djibouti.

Communications: TV sets: 48 per 1,000 pop. **Radios:** 86 per 1,000 pop. **Telephone lines:** 10,100. **Daily newspaper circ.:** 8 per 1,000 pop. **Internet:** 4,500 users.

Health: Life expectancy: 41.8 male; 44.5 female. **Births** (per 1,000 pop.): 40.8. **Deaths** (per 1,000 pop.): 19.5. **Natural inc.:** 2.13%. **Infant mortality** (per 1,000 live births): 107.0.

Education: Compulsory: ages 6-11. **Literacy:** 67.9%.

Major Intl. Organizations: UN (FAO, IBRD, ILO, IMF, IMO, WHO, WTrO), AL, AU.

Embassy: Suite 515, 1156 15th St. NW 20005; 331-0270.

Website: www.office-tourisme.dj

France gained control of the territory in stages between 1862 and 1900. As French Somaliland it became an overseas territory of France in 1945; in 1967 it was renamed the French Territory of the Afars and the Issas.

Ethiopia and Somalia have renounced their claims to the area, but each has accused the other of trying to gain control. There were clashes between Afars (ethnically related to Ethiopians) and Issas (related to Somalis) in 1976. Immigrants from both countries continued to enter the country up to independence, which came June 27, 1977.

French aid is the mainstay of the economy, as well as assistance from Arab countries. A peace accord Dec. 1994 ended a 3-year-long uprising by Afar rebels. As of Aug. 2003 some 2,700 French and 1,500 U.S. troops were based in Djibouti.

Dominica
Commonwealth of Dominica

People: Population: 70,000. **Age distrib.** (%): <15: 28.3; 65+: 7.9. **Pop. density:** 240 per sq. mi. **Urban:** 71%. **Ethnic groups:** Black, Creole, White, Carib Amerindian. **Principal languages:** English (official), French patois. **Chief religions:** Roman Catholic 77%, Protestant 15%.

Geography: Area (total): 291 sq. mi. **Location:** In Eastern Caribbean, most northerly Windward Isl. **Neighbors:** Guadeloupe to N, Martinique to S. **Topography:** Mountainous, a central ridge running from N to S, terminating in cliffs; volcanic in origin, with numerous thermal springs; rich deep topsoil on leeward side, red tropical clay on windward coast. **Capital:** Roseau 26,000.

Government: Type: Parliamentary democracy. **Head of state:** Pres. Vernon Lorden Shaw; b May 13, 1930; in office: Oct. 6, 1998. **Head of gov.:** Prime Min. Pierre Charles; b June 30,1954; in office: Oct. 3, 2000. **Local divisions:** 10 parishes.

Economy: Industries: soap, coconut oil, tourism, copra, furniture, cement blocks, shoes. **Chief crops:** bananas, citrus, mangoes, coconuts, cocoa. **Natural resources:** timber, hydropower. **Arable land:** 9%. **Livestock** (2002): cattle: 13,000; chickens: 190,000; goats: 9,700; pigs: 5,000; sheep: 8,000. **Fish catch** (2002 est.): 1,157 metric tons. **Electricity prod.** (2001): 0.07 bil. kWh. **Labor force:** agri. 40%, ind. and commerce 32%, services 28%.

Finance: Monetary unit: East Caribbean Dollar (XCD) (Sept. 2003: 2.66 = $1 U.S.). **GDP** (2002 est.): $380 mil. **Per capita GDP:** $5,400. **Imports** (2000): $132 mil.; partners (1996 est.): U.S. 41%, Caricom countries 25%, UK 13%, Netherlands. **Exports** (2000 est.): $49 mil.; partners (1996 est.): Caricom countries 47%, UK 36%, U.S. 7%. **Tourism** (1999): $49 mil. **Budget** (2001) $84.4 mil. **Intl. reserves less gold:** $33 mil. **Consumer prices:** .2%.

Transport: Motor vehicles (1998): 8,700 pass. cars, 3,400 comm. vehicles. **Civil aviation:** 2 airports. **Chief port:** Roseau.

Communications: TV sets: 232 per 1,000 pop. **Radios:** 648 per 1,000 pop. **Telephone lines** (1999): 25,400. **Internet:** 12,500 users.

Health: Life expectancy: 71.2 male; 77.2 female. **Births** (per 1,000 pop.): 16.8. **Deaths** (per 1,000 pop.): 7.0. **Natural inc.:** 0.98%. **Infant mortality** (per 1,000 live births): 15.3.

Education: Compulsory: ages 5-17. **Literacy:** 94%.

Major Intl. Organizations: UN (FAO, IBRD, ILO, IMF, IMO, WHO, WTrO), Caricom, the Commonwealth, OAS, OECS.

Embassy: 3216 New Mexico Ave. NW 20016; 364-6781.

Website: www.ndcdominica.dm

A British colony since 1805, Dominica was granted self-government in 1967. Independence was achieved Nov. 3, 1978.

Hurricane David struck, Aug. 30, 1979, devastating the island and destroying the banana plantations, Dominica's economic mainstay. Coups were attempted in 1980 and 1981.

Dominica participated in the 1983 U.S.-led invasion of nearby Grenada.

Dominican Republic

People: Population: 8,745,000. **Age distrib.** (%): <15: 33.7; 65+: 5. **Pop. density:** 468 per sq. mi. **Urban:** 66%. **Ethnic groups:** Creole 73%, White 16%, Black 11%. **Principal languages:** Spanish (official). **Chief religion:** Roman Catholic 95%.

Geography: Area: 18,815 sq. mi. (total); 18,680 sq. mi. (land). **Location:** In West Indies, sharing isl. of Hispaniola with Haiti. **Neighbors:** Haiti on W, Puerto Rico (U.S.) to E. **Topography:** The Cordillera Central range crosses the center of the country, rising to over 10,000 ft., highest in the Caribbean. The Cibao Valley to the N is major agricultural area. **Capital:** Santo Domingo. **Cities (urban aggr.):** Santo Domingo 2,629,000; Santiago de los Caballeros 804,000.

Government: Type: Republic. **Head of state and gov.:** Pres. Hipólito Mejía; b Feb. 22, 1941; in office: Aug. 16, 2000. **Local divisions:** 29 provinces and national district. **Defense budget** (2001): $145 mil. **Active troops:** 24,500.

Economy: Industries: tourism, sugar proc., mining, textiles, cement, tobacco. **Chief crops:** sugarcane, coffee, cotton, cocoa, tobacco, rice, beans. **Natural resources:** nickel, bauxite, gold, silver. **Arable land:** 21%. **Livestock** (2002): cattle: 2.22 mil.; chickens: 47.38 mil.; goats: 187,425; pigs: 566,000; sheep: 106,000. **Fish catch** (2002): 15,864 metric tons. **Electricity prod.** (2001): 9.19 bil. kWh. **Labor force:** services and government 58.7%, ind. 24.3%, agri. 17%.

Finance: Monetary unit: Peso (DOP) (Sept. 2003: 32.08 = $1 U.S.). **GDP** (2002 est.): $53 bil. **Per capita GDP:** $6,100. **Imports** (2001): $8.7 bil.; partners (2000 est.): U.S. 60.5%, Japan 10.4%, Mexico 4.7%, Venezuela 3%. **Exports** (2001 est.): $5.5 bil.; partners (2000 est.): U.S. 87.3%, Netherlands 1.1%, Canada 0.7%, France 0.7%. **Tourism:** $2.92 bil. **Budget** (2001 est.): $3.2 bil. **Intl. reserves less gold:** $345 mil. **Gold:** 20,000 oz t. **Consumer prices:** 5.2%.

Transport: Railroad: Length: 470 mi. **Motor vehicles:** 495,600 pass. cars, 283,000 comm. vehicles. **Civil aviation:** 3.1 mil pass.-mi.; 13 airports. **Chief ports:** Santo Domingo, San Pedro de Macorís, Puerto Plata.

Communications: TV sets: 96 per 1,000 pop. **Radios:** 178 per 1,000 pop. **Telephone lines:** 955,100. **Daily newspaper circ.:** 153 per 1,000 pop. **Internet:** 186,000 users.

Health: Life expectancy: 66.4 male; 69.6 female. **Births** (per 1,000 pop.): 23.9. **Deaths** (per 1,000 pop.): 6.9. **Natural inc.:** 1.71%. **Infant mortality** (per 1,000 live births): 34.2.

Education: Compulsory: ages 6-14. **Literacy:** 84.7%.

Major Intl. Organizations: UN (FAO, IBRD, ILO, IMF, IMO, WHO, WTrO), OAS.

Embassy: 1715 22nd St. NW 20008; 332-6280.

Website: www.presidencia.gov.do/Ingles/welcome.htm

Carib and Arawak Indians inhabited the island of Hispaniola when Columbus landed in 1492. The city of Santo Domingo, founded 1496, is the oldest settlement by Europeans in the hemisphere and has the supposed ashes of Columbus in an elaborate tomb in its ancient cathedral.

The western third of the island was ceded to France in 1697. Santo Domingo itself was ceded to France in 1795. Haitian leader Toussaint L'Ouverture seized it, 1801. Spain returned intermittently 1803-21, as several native republics came and went. Haiti ruled again, 1822-44; Spanish occupation occurred 1861-63.

The country was occupied by U.S. Marines from 1916 to 1924, when a constitutionally elected government was installed.

In 1930, Gen. Rafael Leonidas Trujillo Molina was elected president. Trujillo ruled brutally until his assassination in 1961. Pres. Joaquín Balaguer, appointed by Trujillo in 1960, resigned under pressure in 1962.

Juan Bosch, elected president in the first free elections in 38 years, was overthrown in 1963. On Apr. 24, 1965, a revolt was launched by followers of Bosch and others, including a few Communists. Four days later U.S. Marines intervened against pro-Bosch forces. Token units were later sent by 5 South American countries as a peacekeeping force. A provisional government supervised a June 1966 election, in which Balaguer defeated Bosch. Balaguer remained in office for most of the next 28 years, but his May 1994 reelection was widely denounced as fraudulent. He cut short his term and on June 30, 1996, Leonel Fernández Reyna was elected.

Hurricane Georges struck Sept. 22, 1998, causing extensive property damage and claiming more than 200 lives. The leftist candidate, Hipólito Mejía, won a presidential vote May 16, 2000.

East Timor
Democratic Republic of Timor-Leste

People: Population: 778,000 **Age distrib.** (%): NA. **Pop. density:** 138 per sq. mi. **Urban:** 8%. **Ethnic groups:** Austronesian, Papuan. **Principal languages:** Tetum, Portuguese (both official); Indonesian, English, other native languages. **Chief religions:** Roman Catholic 90%, Muslim 4%, Protestant 3%.

Geography: Area (total): 5,794 sq. mi. **Location:** E half of Timor Is. in the SW Pacific O. **Neighbors:** Indonesia (West Timor) on W. **Topography:** Terrain is rugged, rising to 9,721 ft at Mt. Ramelau. **Capital:** Dili (2002 est.): 140,000.

Government: Head of state: Pres. Xanana Gusmão; b June 20, 1946; in office: May 20, 2002. **Head of gov.:** Prime Min. Mari Alkatiri; b Nov. 26, 1949; in office: May 20, 2002. **Active troops:** 636.

Economy: Industries: printing, soap, handicrafts, clothing. **Chief crops:** coffee, rice, maize, cassava, sweet potatoes. **Natural resources:** gold, oil, nat. gas, mang., marble. **Livestock** (2002): 2.10 mil.; goats: 235,000; pigs: 300,000; sheep: 36,000.

Finance: Monetary unit: U.S. dollar and Indonesian Rupiah (Sept. 2002: 9,010 = $1 U.S.). **GDP** (2001 est.): $440 mil. **Per capita GDP:** $500. **Imports** (2001): $237 mil.; partners: NA. **Exports** (2001 est.): $8 mil.; partners: NA. **Budget** (2003 est.): $97 mil.

Transport: Civil aviation: 3 airports. **Chief port:** Dili.

Health: Life expectancy: 63.0 male; 67.6 female. **Births** (per 1,000 pop.): 27.8. **Deaths** (per 1,000 pop.): 6.4. **Natural inc.:** 2.13%. **Infant mortality** (per 1,000 live births): 50.5.

Education: Literacy (2001): 48%.

Major Intl. Organizations: UN.

Website: www.gov.east-timor.org

The collapse of Portuguese rule in East Timor led to an outbreak of factional fighting in Aug. 1975 and an invasion by Indonesia in Dec. Indonesia annexed East Timor as a 27th province in 1976, despite international condemnation. In over 2 decades some 200,000 Timorese died as a result of civil war, famine, and persecution by Indonesian authorities. In a referendum held Aug. 30, 1999, under UN auspices, Timorese voted overwhelmingly for independence. Pro-Indonesian militias then went on a rampage, terrorizing the population. Under pressure, the government allowed entrance of an international peacekeeping force, which began arriving in Sept.; a UN interim administration formally took command Oct. 26, 1999.

Pro-independence forces won elections for a constituent assembly Aug. 30, 2001. Xanana Gusmão, a former guerrilla leader, won the presidential election Apr. 14, 2002. East Timor became independent May 20 and entered the UN Sept. 27.

Ecuador
Republic of Ecuador

People: Population: 13,003,000. **Age distrib.** (%): <15: 35.4; 65+: 4.4. **Pop. density:** 122 per sq. mi. **Urban:** 63%. **Ethnic groups:** Mestizo 65%, Amerindian 25%, Black 3%. **Principal languages:** Spanish (official), Amerindian languages (especially Quechua). **Chief religion:** Roman Catholic 95%.

Geography: Area: 109,483 sq. mi. (total); 106,888 sq. mi. (land). **Location:** In NW South America, on Pacific coast, astride the Equator. **Neighbors:** Colombia on N, Peru on E and S. **Topography:** Two ranges of Andes run N and S, splitting the country into 3 zones: hot, humid lowlands on the coast; temperate highlands between the ranges; and rainy, tropical lowlands to the E. **Capital:** Quito. **Cities (urban aggr.):** Guayaquil, 2,118,000; Quito: 1,616,000.

Government: Type: Republic. **Head of state and gov.:** Pres. Lucio Gutiérrez Borbúa; b Mar. 23, 1957; in office: Jan. 15, 2003. **Local divisions:** 21 provinces. **Defense budget** (2002): $507 mil. **Active troops:** 59,500.

Economy: Industries: oil, food proc., textiles, metal work, paper & wood products. **Chief crops:** bananas, coffee, cocoa, rice, potatoes, cassava, plantains, sugarcane. **Natural resources:** oil, fish, timber, hydropower. **Crude oil reserves** (2002): 2.1 bil. bbls. **Arable land:** 6%. **Livestock** (2002): cattle: 5.60 mil.; chickens: 140 mil.; goats: 275,000; pigs: 2.40 mil.; sheep: 1.98 mil. **Fish catch** (2002): 654,539 metric tons. **Electricity prod.** (2001): 10.74 bil. kWh. **Labor force:** agri. 30%, ind. 25%, services 45%.

Finance: Monetary unit: U.S. dollar. **GDP** (2002 est.): $41.7 bil. **Per capita GDP:** $3,100. **Imports** (2001): $4.8 bil.; partners (2000): U.S. 25%, Colombia 13%, Japan 8%, Venezuela 8%. **Exports** (2001 est.): $4.8 bil.; partners (2000): U.S. 38%, Peru 6%, Chile 5%, Colombia 5%. **Tourism:** $402 mil. **Budget** (2001 est.): planned $5.6 bil. **Intl. reserves less gold:** $526 mil. **Gold:** 850,000 oz t. **Consumer prices:** 12.5%.

Transport: Railroad: Length: 600 mi. **Motor vehicles** (1999): 322,300 pass. cars, 272,000 comm. vehicles. **Civil aviation:** 862.5 mil pass.-mi.; 61 airports. **Chief ports:** Guayaquil, Manta, Esmeraldas, Puerto Bolivar.

Communications: TV sets: 213 per 1,000 pop. **Radios:** 406 per 1,000 pop. **Telephone lines:** 1,426,200. **Daily newspaper circ.:** 43.4 per 1,000 pop. **Internet:** 503,300 users.

Health: Life expectancy: 69.1 male; 74.9 female. **Births** (per 1,000 pop.): 24.9. **Deaths** (per 1,000 pop.): 5.3. **Natural inc.:** 1.97%. **Infant mortality** (per 1,000 live births): 32.0.

Education: Compulsory: ages 5-14. **Literacy:** 92.5%.

Major Intl. Organizations: UN (FAO, IBRD, ILO, IMF, WHO, WTrO), OAS.

Embassy: 2535 15th St. NW 20009; 234-7200.

Website: www.ecuador.org

The region, which was the northern Inca empire, was conquered by Spain in 1533. Liberation forces defeated the Spanish May 24, 1822, near Quito. Ecuador became part of the Great Colombia Republic but seceded, May 13, 1830.

Since 1972, the economy has revolved around petroleum exports; oil revenues have declined since 1982, causing severe economic problems. Ecuador suspended interest payments for 1987 on its estimated $8.2 billion foreign debt following a Mar. 5-6 earthquake that left 20,000 homeless and destroyed a stretch of the country's main oil pipeline.

Ecuadoran Indians staged protests in the 1990s to demand greater rights. A border war with Peru flared from Jan. 26, 1995, until a truce took effect Mar. 1. Vice-Pres. Alberto Dahik resigned and fled Ecuador, Oct. 11, 1995, to avoid arrest on corruption charges. Elected president in a runoff, July 7, 1996, Abdalá Bucaram—a populist known as El Loco, or "The Crazy One"—imposed stiff price increases and other austerity measures. His rising unpopularity and erratic behavior led the National Congress, Feb. 6, 1997, to dismiss him for "mental incapacity." Bucaram went into exile, and Congress, on Feb. 11, confirmed its leader, Fabian Alarcón, as president for 18 months. Voters endorsed the actions in a referendum May 25.

Jamil Mahuad Witt, mayor of Quito, won a presidential runoff election July 12, 1998. In Sept. 1998 and Mar. 1999 he imposed emergency measures to cope with a continuing economic crisis. Opposed by Indian groups and military leaders, he was ousted Jan. 21, 2000, and succeeded by Vice-Pres. Gustavo Noboa Bejarano. Noboa went ahead with a plan introduced by Mahuad to replace the sucre with the U.S. dollar as Ecuador's currency. Lucio Gutiérrez Borbúa, a leader in the 2000 coup, won a presidential runoff Nov. 24, 2002. Noboa, under investigation for financial mismanagement, went into exile Aug. 23, 2003.

The **Galápagos Islands,** pop. (2001 est.) 16,000, about 600 mi. to the W, are the home of huge tortoises and other unusual animals. The oil tanker *Jessica* ran aground Jan. 16, 2001, off San Cristóbal Is., spilling some 185,000 gallons of fuel.

Egypt
Arab Republic of Egypt

People: Population: 71,931,000. **Age distrib.** (%): <15: 33.96; 65+: 3.86. **Pop. density:** 187 per sq. mi. **Urban:** 43%. **Ethnic groups:** Egyptian Arab 99%. **Principal languages:** Arabic (official); English, French. **Chief religions:** Muslim (official; mostly Sunni) 94%, Coptic Christian and other 6%.

Geography: Area: 386,662 sq. mi. (total); 384,345 sq. mi. (land). **Location:** Northeast corner of Africa. **Neighbors:** Libya on W, Sudan on S, Israel and Gaza Strip on E. **Topography:** Almost entirely desolate and barren, with hills and mountains in E and along Nile. The Nile Valley, where most of the people live, stretches 550 miles. **Capital:** Cairo. **Cities (urban aggr.):** Cairo 9,586,000; Alexandria 3,506,000.

Government: Type: Republic. **Head of state:** Pres. Hosni Mubarak; b May 4, 1928; in office: Oct. 14, 1981. **Head of gov.:** Prime Min. Atef Obeid; b Apr. 14, 1932; in office: Oct. 5, 1999. **Local divisions:** 26 governorates. **Defense budget** (2002): $3.0 bil. **Active troops:** 443,000.

Economy: Industries: textiles, food proc., tourism, chemicals, hydrocarbons, constr., cement, metals. **Chief crops:** cotton, rice, corn, wheat, beans, fruits, vegetables. **Natural resources:** oil, nat. gas, iron ore, phosphates, mang., limestone, gypsum, talc, asbestos, lead, zinc. **Crude oil reserves** (2002): 2.9 bil. bbls. **Arable land:** 2%. **Livestock** (2002): cattle: 3.80 mil.; chickens: 88 mil.; goats: 3.47 mil.; pigs: 30,000; sheep: 4.67 mil. **Fish catch** (2002): 771,515 metric tons. **Electricity prod.** (2001): 75.23 bil. kWh. **Labor force:** agri. 29%, ind. 22%, services 49%.

Finance: Monetary unit: Pound (EGP) (Sept. 2003: 6.18 = $1 U.S.). **GDP** (2002 est.): $268 bil. **Per capita GDP:** $3,900. **Imports** (2001): $164 bil.; partners (2000): EU 36%, U.S. 18%, Asian countries 13%, Middle East 5%. **Exports** (2001 est.): $7.1 bil.; partners (2000): EU 43%, U.S. 15%, Middle East 11%, Asian countries 9%. **Tourism:** $4.35 bil. **Budget** (2001): $26.2 bil. **Intl. reserves less gold:** $9.74 bil. **Gold:** 2.43 mil oz t. **Consumer prices:** 2.7%.

Transport: Railroad: Length: 3,079 mi. **Motor vehicles:** 1.7 mil pass. cars, 600,000 comm. vehicles. **Civil aviation:** 5.64 bil pass.-mi.; 71 airports. **Chief ports:** Alexandria, Port Said, Suez, Damietta.

Communications: TV sets: 170 per 1,000 pop. **Radios:** 317 per 1,000 pop. **Telephone lines:** 6,688,400. **Daily newspaper circ.:** 32.4 per 1,000 pop. **Internet:** 600,000 users.

Health: Life expectancy: 67.9 male; 73.0 female. **Births** (per 1,000 pop.): 24.4. **Deaths** (per 1,000 pop.): 5.4. **Natural inc.:** 1.90%. **Infant mortality** (per 1,000 live births): 35.3.

Education: Compulsory: ages 6-13. **Literacy:** 57.7%.

Major Intl. Organizations: UN (FAO, IBRD, ILO, IMF, IMO, WHO, WTrO), AL, AU.

Embassy: 3521 International Ct. NW 20008; 895-5400.

Website: www.sis.gov.eg

Archaeological records of ancient Egyptian civilization date back to 4000 BC. A unified kingdom arose around 3200 BC and extended its way south into Nubia and as far north as Syria. A high culture of rulers and priests was built on an economic base of serfdom, fertile soil, and annual flooding of the Nile.

Imperial decline facilitated conquest by Asian invaders (Hyksos, Assyrians). The last native dynasty fell in 341 BC to the Persians, who were in turn replaced by Greeks (Alexander and the Ptolemies), Romans, Byzantines, and Arabs, who introduced Islam and

the Arabic language. The ancient Egyptian language is preserved only in Coptic Christian liturgy.

Egypt was ruled as part of larger Islamic empires for several centuries. The Mamluks, a military caste of Caucasian origin, ruled Egypt from 1250 until defeat by the Ottoman Turks in 1517. Under Turkish sultans the khedive as hereditary viceroy had wide authority. Britain intervened in 1882 and took control of administration, though nominal allegiance to the Ottoman Empire continued until 1914.

The country was a British protectorate from 1914 to 1922. A 1936 treaty strengthened Egyptian autonomy, but Britain retained bases in Egypt and a condominium over the Sudan. Britain fought German and Italian armies from Egypt, 1940-42. In 1951 Egypt abrogated the 1936 treaty; the Sudan became independent in 1956.

The uprising of July 23, 1952 was led by the Society of Free Officers, who named Maj. Gen. Mohammed Naguib commander in chief and forced King Farouk to abdicate. When the republic was proclaimed June 18, 1953, Naguib became its first president and premier. Lt. Col. Gamal Abdel Nasser removed Naguib and became premier in 1954. In 1956, he was voted president. Nasser died in 1970 and was replaced by Vice Pres. Anwar Sadat.

The Aswan High Dam, completed 1971, provides irrigation for more than a million acres of land. Artesian wells, drilled in the Western Desert, reclaimed 43,000 acres, 1960-66.

When the state of Israel was proclaimed in 1948, Egypt joined other Arab nations invading Israel and was defeated.

After terrorist raids across its border, Israel invaded Egypt's Sinai Peninsula, Oct. 29, 1956. Egypt rejected a cease-fire demand by Britain and France; on Oct. 31 the 2 nations dropped bombs and on Nov. 5-6 landed forces. Egypt and Israel accepted a UN cease-fire; fighting ended Nov. 7.

A UN Emergency Force guarded the 117-mile-long border between Egypt and Israel until May 19, 1967, when it was withdrawn at Nasser's demand. Egyptian troops entered the Gaza Strip and the heights of Sharm el Sheikh and 3 days later closed the Strait of Tiran to all Israeli shipping. Full-scale war broke out June 5; before it ended under a UN cease-fire June 10, Israel had captured Gaza and the Sinai Peninsula, controlled the east bank of the Suez Canal, and reopened the gulf. After sporadic fighting, Israel and Egypt agreed, Aug. 7, 1970, to a new cease-fire.

In a surprise attack Oct. 6, 1973, Egyptian forces crossed the Suez Canal into the Sinai. (At the same time, Syrian forces attacked Israelis on the Golan Heights.) Egypt was supplied by a USSR military airlift; the U.S. responded with an airlift to Israel. Israel counterattacked, crossed the canal, surrounded Suez City. A UN cease-fire took effect Oct. 24.

Under an agreement signed Jan. 18, 1974, Israeli forces withdrew from the canal's W bank; limited numbers of Egyptian forces occupied a strip along the E bank. A second accord was signed in 1975, with Israel yielding Sinai oil fields. Pres. Sadat's surprise visit to Jerusalem, Nov. 1977, opened the prospect of peace with Israel. On Mar. 26, 1979, Egypt and Israel signed a formal peace treaty, ending 30 years of war, and establishing diplomatic relations. Israel returned control of the Sinai to Egypt in Apr. 1982.

Tension between Muslim fundamentalists and Christians in 1981 caused street riots and culminated in a nationwide security crackdown in Sept. Pres. Sadat was assassinated on Oct. 6; he was succeeded by Hosni Mubarak.

Egypt was a political and military supporter of the Allied forces in their defeat of Iraq in the Persian Gulf War, 1991.

Egypt saw a rising tide of Islamic fundamentalist violence in the 1990s. Egyptian security forces conducted raids against Islamic militants, some of whom were executed for terrorism. Naguib Mahfouz, winner of the 1988 Nobel Prize for Literature, was stabbed by Islamic militants Oct. 14, 1994. Pres. Mubarak escaped assassination in Ethiopia, June 26, 1995; Egypt blamed Sudan for the attack. On Nov. 17, 1997, near Luxor, Muslim extremists killed 58 foreign tourists and 4 Egyptians.

Mubarak, who was grazed by a knife-wielding assailant Sept. 6, 1999, was confirmed by popular vote Sept. 26 for a 4th presidential term. An EgyptAir jetliner bound from New York to Cairo plunged into the Atlantic near Nantucket Is., Oct. 31, 1999, killing all 217 people on board. Fire on a train bound from Cairo to Luxor, Feb. 20, 2002, left more than 360 people dead.

The **Suez Canal,** 103 mi. long, links the Mediterranean and Red seas. It was built by a French corporation 1859-69, but Britain obtained controlling interest in 1875. The last British troops were removed June 13, 1956. On July 26, Egypt nationalized the canal.

El Salvador
Republic of El Salvador

People: Population: 6,515,000. **Age distrib.** (%): <15: 37.4; 65+: 5.1. **Pop. density:** 814 per sq. mi. **Urban:** 62%. **Ethnic groups:** Mestizo 90%, White 9%, Amerindian 1%. **Principal languages:** Spanish (official), Nahua. **Chief religions:** Roman Catholic 83%, many Protestant groups.

Geography: Area: 8,124 sq. mi. (total); 8,000 sq. mi. (land). **Location:** In Central America. **Neighbors:** Guatemala on W, Honduras on N. **Topography:** A hot Pacific coastal plain in the south rises to a cooler plateau and valley region, densely populated. The

N is mountainous, including many volcanoes. **Capital:** San Salvador 1,381,000.

Government: Type: Republic. **Head of state and gov.:** Pres. Francisco Flores; b Oct. 17, 1959; in office: June 1, 1999. **Local divisions:** 14 departments. **Defense budget** (2002): $109 mil. **Active troops:** 16,800.

Economy: Industries: food proc., beverages, oil, chemicals, fertilizer, textiles, furniture, light metals. **Chief crops:** coffee, sugar, corn, rice, beans, oilseed, cotton, sorghum. **Natural resources:** hydropower, geothermal power, oil. **Arable land:** 27%. **Livestock** (2002): cattle: 1.04 mil.; chickens: 8.10 mil.; goats: 15,200; pigs: 150,000; sheep: 5,000. **Fish catch** (2002): 18,142 metric tons. **Electricity prod.** (2001): 3.73 bil. kWh. **Labor force:** agri. 30%, ind. 15%, services 55%.

Finance: Monetary unit: Colon (SVC) (Sept. 2003: 8.70 = $1 U.S.). **GDP** (2002 est.): $30 bil. **Per capita GDP:** $4,700. **Imports** (2001): $5 bil.; partners (2000): U.S. 50%, Guatemala 10%, EU 7%, Mexico 5%. **Exports** (2001): $2.9 bil.; partners (2000): U.S. 65%, Guatemala 11%, Honduras 8%, EU 5%. **Tourism:** $254 mil. **Budget** (2001 est.): $2.5 bil. **Intl. reserves less gold:** $1.19 bil. **Gold:** .47 mil. oz t. **Consumer prices:** 1.9%.

Transport: Railroad: Length: 349 mi. **Motor vehicles:** 148,000 pass. cars, 250,800 comm. vehicles. **Civil aviation:** 3.16 bil pass.-mi.; 4 airports. **Chief ports:** La Union, Acajutla, La Libertad.

Communications: TV sets: 191 per 1,000 pop. **Radios:** 478 per 1,000 pop. **Telephone lines:** 667,700. **Daily newspaper circ.:** 28.3 per 1,000 pop. **Internet:** 300,000 users.

Health: Life expectancy: 67.02 male; 74.4 female. **Births** (per 1,000 pop.): 27.9. **Deaths** (per 1,000 pop.): 6.0. **Natural inc.:** 2.20%. **Infant mortality** (per 1,000 live births): 26.8.

Education: Compulsory: ages 7-15. **Literacy:** 80.2%.

Major intl. Organizations: UN (FAO, IBRD, ILO, IMF, IMO, WHO, WTrO), OAS.

Embassy: 2308 California St. NW 20008; 265-9671.

Website: www.elsalvador.org (Spanish & English)

El Salvador became independent of Spain in 1821, and of the Central American Federation in 1839.

A fight with Honduras in 1969 over the presence of 300,000 Salvadoran workers left 2,000 dead.

A military coup overthrew the government of Pres. Carlos Humberto Romero in 1979, but the ruling military-civilian junta failed to quell a rebellion by leftist insurgents, armed by Cuba and Nicaragua. Extreme right-wing death squads organized to eliminate suspected leftists were blamed for thousands of deaths in the 1980s. The Reagan administration staunchly supported the government with military aid. The 12-year civil war ended Jan. 16, 1992, as the government and leftist rebels signed a formal peace treaty. The civil war had taken the lives of some 75,000 people. The treaty provided for military and political reforms.

Nine soldiers, including 3 officers, were indicted Jan. 1990 in the Nov. 1989 slaying of 6 Jesuit priests in San Salvador. Two of the officers received maximum 30-year jail sentences. They were released Mar. 20, 1993, when the National Assembly passed a sweeping amnesty.

Francisco Flores, candidate of the right-wing ARENA party, won the presidential election of Mar. 7, 1999. Earthquakes Jan. 13 and Feb. 13, 2001, left more than 1,150 people dead.

Equatorial Guinea
Republic of Equatorial Guinea

People: Population: 494,000. **Age distrib.** (%): <15: 42.4; 65+: 3.8. **Pop. density:** 46 per sq. mi. **Urban:** 49%. **Ethnic groups:** Fang 83%, Bubi 10%. **Principal languages:** Spanish, French (both official), Fang, Bubi, pidgin English, Portuguese Creole, Ibo. **Chief religions:** nominally Christian and predominantly Roman Catholic, pagan practices.

Geography: Area (total): 10,831 sq. mi. **Location:** Bioko Isl. off W Africa coast in Gulf of Guinea, and Rio Muni, mainland enclave. **Neighbors:** Gabon on S, Cameroon on E and N. **Topography:** Bioko Isl. consists of 2 volcanic mountains and a connecting valley. Rio Muni, with over 90% of the area, has a coastal plain and low hills beyond. **Capital:** Malabo 33,000.

Government: Type: Republic. **Head of state:** Pres. Teodoro Obiang Nguema Mbasogo; b June 5, 1942; in office: Oct. 10, 1979. **Head of gov.:** Prime Min. Cándido Muatetema Rivas; b Feb. 2, 1960; in office: Mar. 4, 2001. **Local divisions:** 7 provinces. **Defense budget** (2002): $4.5 mil. **Active troops:** 1,320.

Economy: Industries: oil, fishing, sawmilling, nat. gas. **Chief crops:** coffee, cocoa, rice, yams, cassava, bananas. **Natural resources:** oil, timber, gold, mang., uranium. **Crude oil reserves** (2002): 12 mil. bbls. **Arable land:** 5%. **Livestock** (2002): cattle: 5,000; chickens: 320,000; goats: 9,000; pigs: 6,000; sheep: 38,000. **Fish catch** (2002 est.): 3,500 metric tons. **Electricity prod.** (2001): 0.02 bil. kWh.

Finance: Monetary unit: CFA Franc BEAC (XAF) (Sept. 2003: 597.03 = $1 U.S.). **GDP** (2002 est.): $1.3 bil. **Per capita GDP:** $2,700. **Imports** (2001): $736 mil.; partners (1999): U.S. 60%, France 12%, Spain 8%, Italy 6%. **Exports** (2001 est.): $2.1 bil.;

partners (1999): China 24%, Japan 7%, U.S. 7%, South Korea 5%. **Tourism** (1998): $2 mil. **Budget** (2001 est.): $158 mil. **Intl. reserves less gold:** $65 mil.

Transport: Motor vehicles: 4,000 pass. cars, 3,600 comm. vehicles. **Civil aviation:** 2.5 mil pass.-mi.; 2 airport. **Chief ports:** Malabo, Bata.

Communications: TV sets: 116 per 1,000 pop. **Radios:** 429 per 1,000 pop. **Telephone lines:** 8,800. **Daily newspaper circ.:** 4.9 per 1,000 pop. **Internet:** 1,700 users.

Health: Life expectancy: 52.6 male; 56.9 female. **Births** (per 1,000 pop.): 36.9. **Deaths** (per 1,000 pop.): 12.5. **Natural inc.:** 2.19%. **Infant mortality** (per 1,000 live births): 89.0.

Education: Compulsory: ages 7-11. **Literacy:** 85.7%.

Major Intl. Organizations: UN (FAO, IBRD, ILO, IMF, IMO, WHO), AU.

Embassy: 2020 16th St. NW 20009; 202-518-5700.

Website: www.embassy.org/embassies/gq.html

Fernando Po (now Bioko) Island was reached by Portugal in the late 15th century and ceded to Spain in 1778. Independence came Oct. 12, 1968. Riots occurred in 1969 over disputes between the island and the more backward Rio Muni province on the mainland. Masie Nguema Biyogo, a mainlander, became president for life in 1972.

Masie's reign was one of the most brutal in Africa, resulting in a bankrupted nation. Most of the nation's 7,000 Europeans emigrated. He was ousted in a military coup, Aug. 1979, and Teodoro Mbasogo, leader of the coup, became president. His regime eventually agreed to elections, held Nov. 21, 1993. These were nominally won by the ruling party, but boycotted by opposition parties that maintained the rules were rigged. Elections for president, Feb. 25, 1996 and Dec. 15, 2002, were similarly condemned. Oil sales to the U.S. have boomed in recent years.

Eritrea
State of Eritrea

People: Population: 4,141,000. **Age distrib.** (%): <15: 42.9; 65+: 3.2. **Pop. density:** 88 per sq. mi. **Urban:** 19%. **Ethnic groups:** Tigrinya 50%, Tigre and Kunama 40%, Afar 4%, Saho 3%. **Principal languages:** Arabic, Tigrinya (both official); Afar, Amharic, Tigre, Kunama, other Cushitic languages. **Chief religions:** Muslim, Coptic Christian, Roman Catholic, Protestant.

Geography: Area (total): 46,842 sq. mi. **Location:** In E Africa, on SW coast of Red Sea. **Neighbors:** Ethiopia on S, Djibouti on SE, Sudan on W. **Topography:** Includes many islands of the Dahlak Archipelago, low coastal plains in S, mountain range with peaks to 9,000 ft. in N. **Capital:** Asmara 503,000.

Government: Type: In transition. **Head of state and gov.:** Isaias Afwerki; b Feb. 2, 1946; in office: May 24, 1993. **Local divisions:** 8 provinces. **Defense budget** (2002): $120 mil. **Active troops:** 172,000.

Economy: Industries: food proc., beverages, clothing, textiles. **Chief crops:** sorghum, lentils, vegetables, corn, cotton, tobacco, coffee, sisal. **Natural resources:** gold, potash, zinc, copper, salt, fish. **Arable land:** 12%. **Livestock** (2002): cattle: 2.20 mil.; chickens: 1.30 mil.; goats: 1.70 mil.; sheep: 1.57 mil. **Fish catch** (2002): 8,820 metric tons. **Electricity prod.** (2001): 0.22 bil. kWh. **Labor force:** agri. 80%, ind. and services 20%.

Finance: Monetary unit: Nakfa (ERN) (Sept. 2003: 9.67 = $1 U.S.). **GDP** (2002 est.): $3.3 bil. **Per capita GDP:** $740. **Imports** (2000): $470.5 mil.; partners (1998): Italy 17.4%, UAE 16.2%, Germany 5.7%, UK 4.5%. **Exports** (2000): $34.8 mil.; partners (1998): Sudan 27.2%, Ethiopia 26.5%, Japan 13.2%, UAE 7.3%. **Tourism:** $36 mil. **Budget** (2000 est.): $615.7 mil.

Transport: Railroad: Length: 197 mi. **Civil aviation:** 4 airports. **Chief ports:** Mitsiwa, Aseb.

Communications: TV sets: 16 per 1,000 pop. **Radios:** 484 per 1,000 pop. **Telephone lines:** 35,900. **Internet:** 9,000 users.

Health: Life expectancy: 51.5 male; 54.9 female. **Births** (per 1,000 pop.): 39.4. **Deaths** (per 1,000 pop.): 13.2. **Natural inc.:** 2.62%. **Infant mortality** (per 1,000 live births): 76.3.

Education: Compulsory: ages 7-13. **Literacy:** 58.6%.

Major Intl. Organizations: UN (FAO, IBRD, ILO, IMF, IMO, WHO), AU.

Embassy: 1708 New Hampshire Ave. NW 20009; 319-1991.

Website: www.embassy.org/embassies/er.html

Eritrea was part of the Ethiopian kingdom of Aksum. It was an Italian colony from 1890 to 1941, when it was captured by the British. Following a period of British and UN supervision, Eritrea was awarded to Ethiopia as part of a federation in 1952. Ethiopia annexed Eritrea as a province in 1962. This led to a 31-year struggle for independence, which ended when Eritrea formally declared itself an independent nation May 24, 1993. A constitution was ratified in 1997 but not implemented. A border war with Ethiopia which erupted in June 1998 intensified in May 2000, as Ethiopian troops plunged into W Eritrea; a cease-fire signed June 18 provided for UN peacekeepers to patrol a buffer zone on Eritrean territory. A peace treaty was signed Dec. 12, 2000. An international tribunal adjudicated the boundary dispute Apr. 2002.

Estonia
Republic of Estonia

People: Population: 1,323,000. **Age distrib.** (%): <15: 16.4; 65+: 15.1. **Pop. density:** 76 per sq. mi. **Urban:** 69%. **Ethnic groups:** Estonian 65%, Russian 28%. **Principal languages:** Estonian (official), Russian, Ukrainian, Finnish. **Chief religions:** Evangelical Lutheran, Russian Orthodox, Estonian Orthodox.

Geography: Area: 17,462 sq. mi. (total); 16,684 sq. mi. (land). **Location:** E Europe, bordering the Baltic Sea and Gulf of Finland. **Neighbors:** Russia on E, Latvia on S. **Topography:** Estonia is a marshy lowland with numerous lakes and swamps; about 40% forested. Elongated hills show evidence of former glaciation. More than 800 islands on Baltic coast. **Capital:** Tallinn 401,000.

Government: Type: Republic. **Head of state:** Pres. Arnold Rüütel; b May 10, 1928; in office: Oct. 8, 2001. **Head of gov.:** Prime Min. Juhan Parts; b Aug. 27, 1966; in office: Apr. 10, 2003. **Local divisions:** 15 counties. **Defense budget** (2002): $131 mil. **Active troops:** 5,510.

Economy: Industries: engineering, electronics, timber, wood products, textiles, telecom. **Chief crops:** potatoes, vegetables. **Natural resources:** oil shale, peat, phosphorite, clay, limestone, sand, dolomite, sea mud. **Arable land:** 25%. **Livestock** (2002): cattle: 261,000; chickens: 2.30 mil.; pigs: 345,000; sheep: 29,000. **Fish catch** (2002): 105,634 metric tons. **Electricity prod.** (2001): 7.94 bil. kWh. **Labor force:** ind. 20%, agri. 11%, services 69%.

Finance: Monetary unit: Kroon (EEK) (Sept. 2003: 14.44 = $1 U.S.). **GDP** (2002 est.): $15.2 bil. **Per capita GDP:** $10,900. **Imports** (2002): $4.4 bil.; partners (2001): Finland 18%, Germany 11%, Sweden 9%, China 9%. **Exports** (2002) $3.4 bil.; partners (2001): Finland 33.8%, Sweden 14%, Latvia 6.9%, Germany 6.9%. **Tourism:** $505 mil. **Budget** (2002 est.): $1.89 bil. **Intl. reserves less gold:** $736 mil. **Gold:** 10,000 oz t. **Consumer prices:** 3.6%.

Transport: Railroad: Length: 601 mi. **Motor vehicles:** 463,900 pass. cars, 88,200 comm. vehicles. **Civil aviation:** 139.8 mil pass.-mi.; 14 airports. **Chief port:** Tallinn.

Communications: TV sets: 567 per 1,000 pop. **Radios:** 992 per 1,000 pop. **Telephone lines:** 475,000. **Daily newspaper circ.:** 174 per 1,000 pop. **Internet:** 560,000 users.

Health: Life expectancy: 64.4 male; 76.6 female. **Births** (per 1,000 pop.): 9.2. **Deaths** (per 1,000 pop.): 13.4. **Natural inc.:** -0.42%. **Infant mortality** (per 1,000 live births): 12.0.

Education: Compulsory: ages 7-15. **Literacy:** 99.8%.

Major Intl. Organizations: UN (FAO, IBRD, ILO, IMF, IMO, WHO), OSCE.

Embassy: 1730 M Street NW, Suite 503, 20036; 588-0101.

Website: www.riik.ee/en/valitsus/

Estonia was a province of imperial Russia before World War I, and was independent between World Wars I and II. It was conquered by the USSR in 1940 and incorporated as the Estonian SSR. Estonia declared itself an "occupied territory," and proclaimed a free nation Mar. 1990. During an abortive Soviet coup, Estonia declared immediate full independence, Aug. 20, 1991; the Soviet Union recognized its independence in Sept. 1991. The first free elections in over 50 years were held Sept. 20, 1992. The last occupying Russian troops were withdrawn by Aug. 31, 1994. In a referendum Sept. 14, 2003, Estonian voters endorsed joining the EU in May 2004.

Ethiopia
Federal Democratic Republic of Ethiopia

People: Population: 70,678,000. **Age distrib.** (%): <15: 47.2; 65+: 2.8. **Pop. density:** 163 per sq. mi. **Urban:** 16%. **Ethnic groups:** Oromo 40%, Amhara and Tigre 32%, Sidamo 9%, Shankella 6%, Somali 6%, Afar 4%, Gurage 2%. **Principal languages:** Amharic, Tigrinya, Oromigna, Guaragigna, Somali, Arabic, over 200 other languages. **Chief religions:** Muslim 45-50%, Ethiopian Orthodox 35%-40%, animist 12%.

Geography: Area: 435,186 sq. mi. (total); 432,312 sq. mi. (land). **Location:** In East Africa. **Neighbors:** Sudan on W, Kenya on S, Somalia and Djibouti on E, Eritrea on N. **Topography:** A high central plateau, between 6,000 and 10,000 ft. high, rises to higher mountains near the Great Rift Valley, cutting in from the SW. The Blue Nile and other rivers cross the plateau, which descends to plains on both W and SE. **Capital:** Addis Ababa 2,753,000.

Government: Type: Federal republic. **Head of state:** Pres. Girma Wolde Giorgis; b Dec. 1924; in office: Oct. 8, 2001. **Head of gov.:** Prime Min. Meles Zenawi; b May 8, 1955; in office: Aug. 23, 1995. **Local divisions:** 9 states, 2 charted cities. **Defense budget** (2002): $481 mil. **Active troops:** 252,500.

Economy: Industries: food proc., beverages, textiles, chemicals, metals proc., cement. **Chief crops:** cereals, coffee, oilseed, sugarcane, potatoes. **Natural resources:** gold, platinum, copper, potash, nat. gas, hydropower. **Arable land:** 12%. **Crude oil reserves** (2002): 0.4 mil. bbls. **Livestock** (2002): cattle: 34.50 mil.; chickens: 55.80 mil.; goats: 17 mil.; pigs: 25,000; sheep: 22.50 mil. **Fish catch** (2002): 15,390 metric tons. **Electricity prod.** (2001): 1.71 bil. kWh. **Labor force:** agri. and animal husbandry 80%, government and services 12%, ind. and construct. 8%.

Finance: Monetary unit: Birr (ETB) (Sept. 2003: 8.86 = $1 U.S.). **GDP** (2002 est.): $50.6 bil. **Per capita GDP:** $750. **Imports** (2000): $1.54 bil.; partners (2000 est.): Saudi Arabia 25%, U.S. 9%, Italy 7%, Russia 4%. **Exports** (2000 est.): $442 mil.; partners (2000 est.): Germany 18%, Japan 11%, Djibouti 11%, Saudi Arabia 8%. **Tourism** (1998): $24 mil. **Budget** (2002 est.): $1.9 bil. **Intl. reserves less gold:** $649 mil. **Gold:** 250,000 oz t. **Consumer prices:** 1.6%.

Transport: Railroad: Length: 423 mi. **Motor vehicles** (1999): 71,000 pass. cars, 34,600 comm. vehicles. **Civil aviation:** 1.53 bil pass.-mi.; 14 airports.

Communications: TV sets: 5 per 1,000 pop. **Radios:** 185 per 1,000 pop. **Telephone lines:** 368,200. **Daily newspaper circ.:** .4 per 1,000 pop. **Internet:** 50,000 users.

Health: Life expectancy: 40.4 male; 42.1 female. **Births** (per 1,000 pop.): 39.8. **Deaths** (per 1,000 pop.): 20.2. **Natural inc.:** 1.96%. **Infant mortality** (per 1,000 live births): 103.2.

Education: Compulsory: ages 7-13. **Literacy:** 42.7%.

Major Intl. Organizations: UN (FAO, IBRD, ILO, IMF, IMO, WHO), AU.

Embassy: 3506 International Dr. NW 20008; 202-364-1200.

Websites: ethiospokes.net ; www.ethiopianembassy.org

Ethiopian culture was influenced by Egypt and Greece. The ancient monarchy was invaded by Italy in 1880 but maintained its independence until another Italian invasion in 1936. British forces freed the country in 1941.

The last emperor, Haile Selassie I, established a parliament and judiciary system in 1931 but barred all political parties.

A series of droughts in the 1970s killed hundreds of thousands. An army mutiny, strikes, and student demonstrations led to the dethronement of Selassie in 1974; he died Aug. 1975, while being held by the ruling junta. The junta pledged to form a one-party socialist state and instituted a successful land reform; opposition was violently suppressed. The influence of the Coptic Church, embraced in AD 330, was curbed, and the monarchy was abolished in 1975.

The regime, torn by bloody coups, faced uprisings by tribal and political groups in part aided by Sudan and Somalia. Ties with the U.S., once a major ally, deteriorated, while cooperation accords were signed with the USSR in 1977. In 1978, Soviet advisers and Cuban troops helped defeat Somalian forces. Ethiopia and Somalia signed a peace agreement in 1988.

A worldwide relief effort began in 1984, as an extended drought threatened the country with famine; up to a million people may have died as a result of starvation and disease.

The Ethiopian People's Revolutionary Democratic Front (EPRDF), an umbrella group of 6 rebel armies, launched a major push against government forces, Feb. 1991. In May, Pres. Mengistu Haile Mariam resigned and left the country. The EPRDF took over and set up a transitional government. Ethiopia's first multiparty general elections were held in 1995.

Eritrea, a province on the Red Sea, declared its independence May 24, 1993. Fighting along the border with Eritrea, which erupted in June 1998, intensified in May 2000, as Ethiopian forces plunged into Eritrean territory; a cease-fire was signed June 18 and a peace treaty Dec. 12. The war displaced 350,000 Ethiopians and is estimated to have cost the country nearly $3 billion. A collapse of crop prices in 2001, followed by drought in 2002-03, led to severe food shortages.

Fiji
Republic of the Fiji Islands

People: Population: 839,000. **Age distrib.** (%): <15: 32.5; 65+: 3.7. **Pop. density:** 119 per sq. mi. **Urban:** 50%. **Ethnic groups:** Fijian 51%, Indian 44%. **Principal languages:** English (official), Fijian, Hindustani. **Chief religions:** Christian 52%, Hindu 38%, Muslim 8%.

Geography: Area (total): 7,054 sq. mi. **Location:** In western South Pacific O. **Neighbors:** Nearest are Vanuatu to W, Tonga to E. **Topography:** 322 islands (106 inhabited), many mountainous, with tropical forests and large fertile areas. Viti Levu, the largest island, has over half the total land area. **Capital:** Suva (2001): 203,000.

Government: Type: Republic. **Head of state:** Pres. Ratu Josefa Iloilo; b Dec. 29, 1920; in office: July 18, 2000. **Head of gov.:** Prime Min. Matti Vanhanen; b Nov. 4, 1955; in office: June 24, 2003. **Local divisions:** 4 divisions comprising 14 provinces and 1 dependency. **Defense budget** (2002): $30 mil. **Active troops:** 3,500.

Economy: Industries: tourism, sugar, clothing, copra, gold & silver prod. **Chief crops:** sugarcane, coconuts, cassava, rice, sweet potatoes, bananas. **Natural resources:** timber, fish, gold, copper, oil, hydropower. **Arable land:** 10%. **Livestock** (2002): cattle: 340,000; chickens: 3.70 mil.; goats: 245,749; pigs: 137,000; sheep: 7,000. **Fish catch** (2002): 44,689 metric tons. **Electricity prod.** (2001): 0.52 bil. kWh. **Labor force:** agri., including subsistence agri. 70%.

Finance: Monetary unit: Fiji Dollar (FJD) (Sept. 2003: 1.92 = $1 U.S.). **GDP** (2002 est.): $4.7 bil. **Per capita GDP:** $5,500. **Imports** (2000): $833 mil.; partners (2000): Australia 46.2%, NZ 13.1%, Singapore 6.6%, Japan 4.5%. **Exports** (2000): $572 mil.;

partners (2000): Australia 24.9%, U.S. 20.8%, UK 14.4%, Japan 5.1%. **Tourism:** $171 mil. **Budget** (2000 est.): $531.4 mil. **Intl. reserves less gold:** $264 mil. **Consumer prices** (change in 2001): 4.3%.

Transport: Railroad: Length: 371 mi. **Motor vehicles:** (1998): 51,700 pass. cars, 48,600 comm. vehicles. **Civil aviation:** 1.34 bil pass.-mi.; 3 airports. **Chief ports:** Suva, Lautoka.

Communications: TV sets: 110 per 1,000 pop. **Radios:** 677 per 1,000 pop. **Telephone lines:** 92,200. **Daily newspaper circ.:** 46 per 1,000 pop. **Internet:** 22,000 users.

Health: Life expectancy: 66.4 male; 71.4 female. **Births** (per 1,000 pop.): 23.1. **Deaths** (per 1,000 pop.): 5.7. **Natural inc.:** 1.74%. **Infant mortality** (per 1,000 live births): 13.4.

Education: Compulsory: ages 6-15. **Literacy:** 93.7%.

Major Intl. Organizations: UN (FAO, IBRD, ILO, IMF, IMO, WHO, WTrO), the Commonwealth.

Embassy: 2233 Wisconsin Ave. NW, Suite 240, 20007; 337-8320.

Website: www.fiji.gov.fj

A British colony since 1874, Fiji became an independent parliamentary democracy Oct. 10, 1970. Cultural differences between the Indian community (descendants of contract laborers brought to the islands in the 19th century) and indigenous Fijians have led to political polarization.

In 1987, a military coup ousted the government; order was restored May 21 under a compromise granting Lt. Col. Sitiveni Rabuka, the coup's leader, increased power. Rabuka staged a second coup Sept. 25 and declared Fiji a republic. Civilian government was restored in Dec. A new constitution favoring indigenous Fijians was issued July 25, 1990; amendments enacted in July 1997 made the constitution more equitable.

Fiji's 1st Indian prime minister, Mahendra Chaudhry, took office May 19, 1999. He and other government officials were taken captive May 19, 2000, by indigenous Fijian gunmen led by George Speight. The hostage crisis led to a military takeover, May 29. Release of the last remaining hostages in July 2000 coincided with the installation of an interim military-backed government. Speight was charged with treason (sentenced to life in prison Feb. 18, 2002). The government was reconstituted in Mar. 2001 after an appellate court ruled it illegal. Voting ending Sept. 1, 2001, returned caretaker Prime Min. Laisenia Qarase to office.

Finland
Republic of Finland

People: Population: 5,207,000. **Age distrib.** (%): <15: 17.9; 65+: 15.2. **Pop. density:** 44 per sq. mi. **Urban:** 59%. **Ethnic groups:** Finnish 93%, Swedish 6%. **Principal languages:** Finnish, Swedish (both official); Russian, Sami. **Chief religion:** Evangelical Lutheran 89%.

Geography: Area: 130,128 sq. mi. (total); 117,943 sq. mi. (land). **Location:** In northern Europe. **Neighbors:** Norway on N, Sweden on W, Russia on E. **Topography:** South and central Finland are generally flat areas with low hills and many lakes. The N has mountainous areas, 3,000-4,000 ft. above sea level. **Capital:** Helsinki 936,000.

Government: Type: Constitutional republic. **Head of state:** Pres. Tarja Halonen; b Dec. 24, 1943; in office: Mar. 1, 2000. **Head of gov.:** Prim Min. Matti Vanhanen, b Nov. 4, 1955; in office: June 24, 2003. **Local divisions:** 6 laanit (provinces). **Defense budget** (2002): $1.7 bil. **Active troops:** 31,850.

Economy: Industries: metal products, electronics, shipbuilding, paper, copper refining, foodstuffs, chemicals, textiles, clothing. **Chief crops:** barley, wheat, sugar beets, potatoes. **Natural resources:** timber, copper, zinc, iron ore, silver. **Arable land:** 8%. **Livestock** (2002): cattle: 1.03 mil.; chickens: 6 mil.; goats: 8,000; pigs: 1.30 mil.; sheep: 100,000. **Fish catch** (2001): 165,835 metric tons. **Electricity prod.** (2001): 71.2 bil. kWh. **Labor force:** public services 32%, ind. 22%, commerce 14%, finance, insurance, and business services 10%, agri. and forestry 8%, transport and communications 8%, construct. 6%.

Finance: Monetary unit: Euro (EUR) (Sept. 2003: 0.92 = $1 U.S.). **GDP** (2002 est.): $1.5 tril. **Per capita GDP:** $26,200. **Imports** (2002): $31.8 bil.; partners (2001): Germany 14.5%, Sweden 10.2%, Russia 9.6%, U.S. 6.9%. **Exports** (2002) $40.1 bil.; partners (2001): Germany 12.4%, U.S. 9.7%, UK 9.6%, Sweden 8.4%. **Tourism:** $1.4 bil. **Budget** (2000 est.): $31 bil. **Intl. reserves less gold:** $6.83 bil. **Gold:** 1.58 mil oz t. **Consumer prices:** 1.7%.

Transport: Railroad: Length: 3,644 mi. **Motor vehicles:** 2.13 mil pass. cars, 314,200 comm. vehicles. **Civil aviation:** 4.85 bil pass.-mi.; 74 airports. **Chief ports:** Helsinki, Turku, Rauma, Kotka.

Communications: TV sets: 643 per 1,000 pop. **Radios:** 1,564 per 1,000 pop. **Telephone lines:** 2,850,000. **Daily newspaper circ.:** 454.6 per 1,000 pop. **Internet:** 2,650,000 users.

Health: Life expectancy: 74.3 male; 81.7 female. **Births** (per 1,000 pop.): 10.5. **Deaths** (per 1,000 pop.): 9.8. **Natural inc.:** 0.07%. **Infant mortality** (per 1,000 live births): 3.7.

Education: Compulsory: ages 7-16. **Literacy** (1997): 100%.

Major Intl. Organizations: UN (FAO, IBRD, ILO, IMF, IMO, WHO, WTrO), EU, OECD, OSCE.

Embassy: 3301 Massachusetts Ave. NW 20008; 298-5800.

Website: www.finland.fi

The early Finns probably migrated from the Ural area at about the beginning of the Christian era. Swedish settlers brought the country into Sweden, 1154 to 1809, when Finland became an autonomous grand duchy of the Russian Empire. Russian exactions created a strong national spirit; on Dec. 6, 1917, Finland declared its independence and in 1919 became a republic.

On Nov. 30, 1939, the Soviet Union invaded, and the Finns were forced to cede 16,173 sq. mi. of territory. After World War II, further cessions were exacted. In 1948, Finland signed a treaty of mutual assistance with the USSR; Finland and Russia nullified this treaty with a new pact in Jan. 1992.

Following approval by Finnish voters in an advisory referendum Oct. 16, 1994, Finland joined the European Union effective Jan. 1, 1995.

Aland or **Ahvenanmaa,** constituting an autonomous province, is a group of small islands, 590 sq. mi., in the Gulf of Bothnia, 25 mi. from Sweden, 15 mi. from Finland. Mariehamn is the principal port.

France
French Republic

People: Population: 60,144,000. **Age distrib.** (%): <15: 18.5; 65+: 16.3. **Pop. density:** 285 per sq. mi. **Urban:** 76%. **Ethnic groups:** French, with Slavic, N African, Indochinese, Basque minorities. **Principal languages:** French (official), Italian, Breton, Alsatian (German), Corsican, Gascon, Portuguese, Provençal, Dutch, Flemish, Catalan, Basque, Romani. **Chief religions:** Roman Catholic 83%-88%, Muslim 5%-10%.

Geography: Area: 211,209 sq. mi. (total); 210,669 sq. mi. (land). **Location:** In western Europe, between Atlantic O. and Mediterranean Sea. **Neighbors:** Spain on S; Italy, Switzerland, Germany on E; Luxembourg, Belgium on N. **Topography:** A wide plain covers more than half of the country, in N and W, drained to W by Seine, Loire, Garonne rivers. The Massif Central is a mountainous plateau in center. In E are Alps (Mt. Blanc is tallest in W Europe, 15,771 ft.), the lower Jura range, and the forested Vosges. The Rhone flows from Lake Geneva to Mediterranean. Pyrenees are in SW, on border with Spain. **Capital:** Paris. **Cities (urban aggr.):** Paris 9,658,000 (1997 city proper, est.: 2,152,000); Lyon 1,353,000; Marseilles 1,290,000; Lille 991,000.

Government: Type: Republic. **Head of state:** Pres. Jacques Chirac; b Nov. 29, 1932; in office: May 17, 1995. **Head of gov.:** Prime Min. Jean-Pierre Raffarin; b Aug. 3, 1948; in office: May 6, 2002. **Local divisions:** 22 administrative regions containing 96 departments. **Defense budget** (2002): $29.5 bil. **Active troops:** 260,400.

Economy: Industries: machinery, chemicals, automobiles, metallurgy, aircraft, electronics, textiles, food proc. tourism. **Chief crops:** wheat, cereals, sugar beets, potatoes, wine grapes. **Natural resources:** coal, iron ore, bauxite, zinc, potash, timber, fish. **Crude oil reserves** (2002): 140 mil. bbls. **Other resources:** Timber, dairy. **Arable land:** 33%. **Livestock** (2002): cattle: 20.28 mil.; chickens: 240 mil.; goats: 1.20 mil.; pigs: 14.80 mil.; sheep: 9.21 mil. **Fish catch** (2002): 858,246 metric tons. **Electricity prod.** (2001): 520.15 bil. kWh. **Labor force:** services 71%, ind. 25%, agri. 4%.

Finance: Monetary unit: Euro (EUR) (Sept. 2003: 0.92 = $1 U.S.). **GDP** (2002 est.): $1.5 tril. **Per capita GDP:** $25,700. **Imports** (2002): $303.7 bil.; partners (2001): EU 58.6%, U.S. 8.9%. **Exports** (2002) $307.8 bil.; partners (2001): EU 61.3%, U.S. 8.7%. **Tourism:** $29.9 bil. **Budget** (2002 est.): $330 bil. **Intl. reserves less gold:** $20.86 bil. **Gold:** 97.25 mil oz t. **Consumer prices:** 1.9%.

Transport: Railroad: Length: 19,846 mi. **Motor vehicles** (1999): 27.48 mil pass. cars, 5.79 mil comm. vehicles. **Civil aviation:** 63.04 bil pass.-mi.; 273 airports. **Chief ports:** Marseille, Le Havre, Bordeaux, Rouen.

Communications: TV sets: 620 per 1,000 pop. **Radios:** 946 per 1,000 pop. **Telephone lines:** 33,928,700. **Daily newspaper circ.:** 218 per 1,000 pop. **Internet:** 18,716,000 users.

Health: Life expectancy: 75.6 male; 83.1 female. **Births** (per 1,000 pop.): 12.5. **Deaths** (per 1,000 pop.): 9.1. **Natural inc.:** 0.35%. **Infant mortality** (per 1,000 live births): 4.4.

Education: Compulsory: ages 6-16. **Literacy** (1994): 99%.

Major Intl. Organizations: UN and most of its specialized agencies, EU, NATO, OECD, OSCE.

Embassy: 4101 Reservoir Rd. NW 20007; 944-6000.

Website: www.ambafrance–us.org

Celtic Gaul was conquered by Julius Caesar 58-51 BC; Romans ruled for 500 years. Under Charlemagne, Frankish rule extended over much of Europe. After his death France emerged as one of the successor kingdoms.

The monarchy was overthrown by the French Revolution (1789-93) and succeeded by the First Republic; followed by the First Empire under Napoleon (1804-15), a monarchy (1814-48), the Second Republic (1848-52), the Second Empire (1852-70), the Third Republic (1871-1946), the Fourth Republic (1946-58), and the Fifth Republic (1958 to present).

France suffered severe losses in manpower and wealth in the First World War, when it was invaded by Germany. By the Treaty of Versailles, France exacted return of Alsace and Lorraine, provinces seized by Germany in 1871. Germany invaded France again in May 1940, and signed an armistice with a government based in Vichy. After France was liberated by the Allies in Sept. 1944, Gen. Charles de Gaulle became head of the provisional government, serving until 1946.

De Gaulle again became premier in 1958, during a crisis over Algeria, and obtained voter approval for a new constitution, ushering in the Fifth Republic. He became president Jan. 1959. Using strong executive powers, he promoted French economic and technological advances in the context of the European Economic Community and guarded French foreign policy independence.

France had withdrawn from Indochina in 1954, and from Morocco and Tunisia in 1956. Most of its remaining African territories, including Algeria, were freed 1958-62. In 1966, France withdrew all its troops from the integrated military command of NATO, though 60,000 remained stationed in Germany.

In May 1968 rebellious students in Paris and other centers rioted, battled police, and were joined by workers who launched nationwide strikes. The government awarded pay increases to the strikers May 26. De Gaulle resigned from office in Apr. 1969, after losing a nationwide referendum on constitutional reform. Georges Pompidou, who was elected to succeed him, continued De Gaulle's emphasis on French independence from the U.S. and Soviet Union. After Pompidou's death, in 1974, Valery Giscard d'Estaing was elected president; he continued the basically conservative policies of his predecessors.

On May 10, 1981, France elected François Mitterrand, a Socialist, president. Under Mitterrand the government nationalized 5 major industries and most private banks. After 1986, however, when rightists won a narrow victory in the National Assembly, Mitterrand chose conservative Jacques Chirac as premier. A 2-year period of "cohabitation" ensued, and France began to pursue a privatization program in which many state-owned companies were sold. After Mitterrand was elected to a 2nd 7-year term in 1988, he appointed a Socialist as premier. The center-right won a large majority in 1993 legislative elections, ushering in another period of "cohabitation" with a conservative premier.

In 1993, France set tighter rules for entry into the country and made it easier for the government to expel foreigners. In 1994, France sent troops to Rwanda in an effort to help protect civilians there from ongoing massacres. The international terrorist known as Carlos the Jackal (Ilich Ramirez Sánchez) was arrested in Sudan in Aug. 1994 and extradited to France, where he had been sentenced in absentia to life imprisonment.

Former conservative Prime Min. Jacques Chirac won the presidency in a runoff May 7, 1995. A series of terrorist bombings and bombing attempts began in summer 1995; Islamic extremists, opposed to France's support of the Algerian government and its struggle with Islamic fundamentalists, were believed responsible. In Sept. 1995, France stirred widespread protests by resuming nuclear tests in the South Pacific, after a 3-year moratorium; the tests ended Jan. 1996.

Chirac cut government spending to help the French economy meet the budgetary goals set for the introduction of a common European currency. With unemployment at nearly 13%, legislative elections completed June 1, 1997, produced a decisive victory for the leftist parties. The result was a new period of "cohabitation," this time between a conservative president and a Socialist prime minister, Lionel Jospin. France contributed 7,000 troops to the NATO-led security force (KFOR) that entered Kosovo in June 1999.

French voters, disaffected by government scandals, shocked the political establishment in the 1st round of presidential voting Apr. 21, 2002, by giving far-right leader Jean-Marie Le Pen, leader of the far-right National Front, a 2nd place finish with 16.9% of the vote; Chirac won only 19.9%, and Jospin was 3rd, with 16.2%. Chirac easily won the May 5 runoff, with 82%, and his center-right allies won parliamentary elections June 9 and 16.

Although France contributed several hundred troops to the NATO force in Afghanistan, relations with the U.S. soured in Mar. 2003 when Chirac led a movement to block the UN Security Council from backing a U.S.-led invasion of Iraq. According to estimates in late Sept., nearly 15,000 people, mainly elderly, died as a result of a heat wave in Aug. 2003.

The island of **Corsica**, in the Mediterranean W of Italy and N of Sardinia, is a territorial collectivity and region of France comprising 2 departments. It elects a total of 2 senators and 3 deputies to the French Parliament. Area: 3,369 sq. mi.; pop. (2001 census): 260,149. The capital is Ajaccio, birthplace of Napoleon I. Violence by Corsican separatist groups has hurt tourism, a leading industry on the island. Corsicans rejected, 51-49%, a limited autonomy plan in a referendum July 6, 2003.

Overseas Departments

French Guiana is on the NE coast of South America with Suriname on the W and Brazil on the E and S. Its area is 35,135 sq. mi. (total); 34,421 sq. mi. (land).; pop. (2003 est.) 186,917. Guiana sends one senator and 2 deputies to the French Parliament. Guiana is administered by a prefect and has a Council General of 16 elected members; capital is Cayenne.

The famous penal colony, Devil's Island, was phased out between 1938 and 1951. The European Space Agency maintains a satellite-launching center (established by France in 1964) in the city of Kourou.

Immense forests of rich timber cover 88% of the land. Fishing (especially shrimp), forestry, and gold mining are the most important industries.

Guadeloupe, in the West Indies' Leeward Islands, consists of 2 large islands, Basse-Terre and Grande-Terre, separated by the Salt River, plus Marie Galante and the Saintes group to the S and, to the N, Desirade, St. Barthelemy, and over half of St. Martin (the Netherlands' portion is called St. Maarten). A French possession since 1635, the department is represented in the French Parliament by 2 senators and 4 deputies; administration consists of a prefect (governor) as well as an elected general and regional councils.

Area of the islands is 687 sq. mi. (total); 659 sq. mi. (land); pop. (2003 est.) 440,189, mainly descendants of slaves; capital is Basse-Terre on Basse-Terre Island. The land is fertile; sugar, rum, and bananas are exported. Tourism is an important industry.

Martinique, the northernmost of the Windward Islands, in the West Indies, has been a possession since 1635, and a department since Mar. 1946. It is represented in the French Parliament by 2 senators and 4 deputies. The island was the birthplace of Napoleon's Empress Josephine.

It has an area of 425 sq. mi. (total); 409 sq. mi. (land); pop. (2003 est.) 425,966, mostly descendants of slaves. The capital is Fort-de-France (pop. 1991: 101,000). It is a popular tourist stop. The chief exports are rum, bananas, and petroleum products.

Réunion is a volcanic island in the Indian O. about 420 mi. E of Madagascar, and has belonged to France since 1665. Area, 972 sq. mi. (total); 968 sq. mi. (land); pop. (2003 est.) 755,171, 30% of French extraction. Capital: Saint-Denis. The chief export is sugar. It elects 5 deputies, 3 senators to the French Parliament.

Overseas Territorial Collectivities

Mayotte, claimed by Comoros and administered by France, voted in 1976 to become a territorial collectivity of France. An island NW of Madagascar, area is 144 sq. mi., pop. (2003 est.) 178,437. The capital is Mamoutzou.

St. Pierre and Miquelon, formerly an overseas territory (1816-1976) and department (1976-85), made the transition to territorial collectivity in 1985. It consists of 2 groups of rocky islands near the SW coast of Newfoundland, inhabited by fishermen. The exports are chiefly fish products. The St. Pierre group has an area of 10 sq. mi.; Miquelon, 83 sq. mi. Total pop. (2003 est.) 6,976. The capital is St. Pierre.

Both Mayotte and St. Pierre and Miquelon elect a deputy and a senator to the French Parliament.

Overseas Territories

Territory of **French Polynesia** comprises 130 islands widely scattered among 5 archipelagos in the South Pacific; administered by a Council of Ministers (headed by a president). Territorial Assembly and the Council have headquarters at Papeete, on Tahiti, one of the **Society Islands** (which include the **Windward** and **Leeward** islands). Two deputies and a senator are elected to the French Parliament.

Other groups are the **Marquesas Islands**, the **Tuamotu Archipelago**, including the **Gambier Islands**, and the **Austral Islands.**

Total area of the islands administered from Tahiti is 1,609 sq. mi. (total); 1,413 sq. mi. (land); pop. (2003 est.) 262,125, more than half on Tahiti. Tahiti is picturesque and mountainous with a productive coastline bearing coconuts, citrus, pineapples, and vanilla. Cultured pearls are also produced.

Tahiti was visited by Capt. James Cook in 1769 and by Capt. Bligh in the *Bounty*, 1788-89. Its beauty impressed Herman Melville, Paul Gauguin, and Charles Darwin. Tahitians angered by French nuclear testing rioted Sept. 1995.

Territory of the **French Southern and Antarctic Lands** comprises **Adelie Land**, on Antarctica, and 4 island groups in the Indian O. **Area:** 3,023 sq. mi. (total); 3,023 sq. mi. (land).

Adelie, reached 1,840, has a research station, a coastline of 185 mi., and tapers 1,240 mi. inland to the South Pole. The U.S. does not recognize national claims in Antarctica. There are 2 huge glaciers, Ninnis, 22 mi. wide, 99 mi. long, and Mentz, 11 mi. wide, 140 mi. long. The Indian O. groups are:

Kerguelen Archipelago, visited 1772, consists of one large and 300 small islands. The chief is 87 mi. long, 74 mi. wide, and has Mt. Ross, 6,429 ft. tall. Principal research station is Port-aux-Français. Seals often weigh 2 tons; there are blue whales, coal, peat, semiprecious stones. **Crozet Archipelago**, reached 1772, covers 195 sq. mi. Eastern Island rises to 6,560 ft. **Saint Paul**, in southern Indian O., has warm springs with earth at places heating to 120° to 390° F. **Amsterdam** is nearby; both produce cod and rock lobster.

Territory of **New Caledonia** and Dependencies is a group of islands in the Pacific O. about 1,115 mi. E of Australia and approx. the same distance NW of New Zealand. Dependencies are the

Loyalty Islands, Isle of Pines, Belep Archipelago, and **Huon Islands.**

The largest island, New Caledonia, is 6,530 sq. mi. Total area of the territory is 7,359 sq. mi. (total); 7,172 sq. mi. (land); population (2003 est.) 210,798. The group was acquired by France in 1853.

The territory is administered by a High Commissioner. There is a popularly elected Territorial Congress. Two deputies and a senator are elected to the French Parliament. Capital: Noumea.

Mining is the chief industry. New Caledonia is one of the world's largest nickel producers. Other minerals found are chrome, iron, cobalt, manganese, silver, gold, lead, and copper. Agricultural products include yams, sweet potatoes, potatoes, manioc (cassava), corn, and coconuts.

In 1987, New Caledonian voters chose by referendum to remain within the French Republic. There were clashes between French and Melanesians (Kanaks) in 1988. An agreement Apr. 21, 1998, between France and rival New Caledonian factions specified a 15- to 20-year period of "shared sovereignty." The French constitution was amended, July 6, to allow the territory a gradual increase in autonomy, and New Caledonian voters approved the plan Nov. 8, 1998, by a 72% majority.

Territory of the **Wallis and Futuna Islands** comprises 2 island groups in the SW Pacific S of Tuvalu, N of Fiji, and W of Western Samoa; became an overseas territory July 29, 1961. The islands have a total area of 106 sq. mi. and population (2003 est.) of 15,734. **Alofi,** attached to Futuna, is uninhabited. Capital: Mata-Utu. Chief products are copra, yams, taro roots, bananas, and coconuts. A senator and a deputy are elected to the French Parliament.

Gabon
Gabonese Republic

People: Population: 1,329,000. **Age distrib.** (%): <15: 33.3; 65+: 6.1. **Pop. density:** 13 per sq. mi. **Urban:** 82%. **Ethnic groups:** Fang, Bapounou, Nzebi, Obamba, European. **Principal languages:** French (official), Fang, Myene, Nzebi, Bapounou/Eschira, Bandjabi. **Chief religion:** Christian 55%-75%.

Geography: Area: 103,347 sq. mi. (total); 99,486 sq. mi. (land). **Location:** On Atlantic coast of W central Africa. **Neighbors:** Equatorial Guinea and Cameroon on N, Congo on E and S. **Topography:** Heavily forested, the country consists of coastal lowlands; plateaus in N, E, and S; mountains in N, SE, and center. The Ogooue R. system covers most of Gabon. **Capital:** Libreville 573,000.

Government: Type: Republic. **Head of state:** Pres. Omar Bongo; b Dec. 30, 1935; in office: Dec. 2, 1967. **Head of gov.:** Prime Min. Jean-François Ntoutoume-Emane; b Oct. 6, 1939; in office: Jan. 23, 1999. **Local divisions:** 9 provinces. **Defense budget** (2002): $125 mil. **Active troops:** 4,700.

Economy: Industries: food & beverages, textiles, lumber, cement, oil, mining, chemicals, ship repair. **Chief crops:** cocoa, coffee, sugar, palm oil, rubber. **Natural resources:** oil, mang., uranium, gold, timber, iron, hydropower. **Crude oil reserves** (2002): 2.5 bil. bbls. **Arable land:** 1%. **Livestock** (2002): cattle: 36,000; chickens: 3.20 mil.; goats: 91,000; pigs: 213,000; sheep: 198,000 **Fish catch** (2002): 40,559 metric tons. **Electricity prod.** (2001): 0.8 bil. kWh. **Labor force:** agri. 60%, services 25%, ind. 15%.

Finance: Monetary unit: CFA Franc BEAC (XAF) (Sept. 2003: 597.03 = $1 U.S.). **GDP** (2002 est.): $7 bil. **Per capita GDP:** $5,700. **Imports** (2001): $921 mil.; partners (2000): France 62%, Cote d'Ivoire 7%, U.S. 5%, Belgium 3%. **Exports** (2001 est.): $2.5 bil.; partners (2000): U.S. 51%, France 17%, China 8%, Netherlands Antilles 4%. **Tourism:** $7 mil. **Budget** (2002 est.): $1.8 bil. **Intl. reserves less gold:** $103 mil. **Gold:** 10,000 oz t. **Consumer prices** (change in 2000): .5%.

Transport: Railroad: Length: 403 mi. **Motor vehicles** (1998): 23,000 pass. cars, 10,000 comm. vehicles. **Civil aviation:** 485.9 bil pass.-mi.; 10 airports. **Chief ports:** Port-Gentil, Owendo, Libreville.

Communications: TV sets: 251 per 1,000 pop. **Radios:** 501 per 1,000 pop. **Telephone lines:** 37,200. **Daily newspaper circ.:** 29 per 1,000 pop. **Internet:** 25,000 users.

Health: Life expectancy: 55.5 male; 58.8 female. **Births** (per 1,000 pop.): 36.5. **Deaths** (per 1,000 pop.): 11.2. **Natural inc.:** 2.54%. **Infant mortality** (per 1,000 live births): 55.1.

Education: Compulsory: ages 6-16. **Literacy** (2002): 63%.

Major Intl. Organizations: UN (FAO, IBRD, ILO, IMF, IMO, WHO, WTrO), AU.

Embassy: Suite 200, 2034 20th St. NW 20009; 797-1000.

Website: www.embassy.org/embassies/ga.html

France established control over the region in the second half of the 19th century. Gabon became independent Aug. 17, 1960. A multiparty political system was introduced in 1990, and a new constitution was enacted Mar. 14, 1991. However, the reelection of longtime Pres. Omar Bongo, on Dec. 5, 1993, prompted rioting and charges of vote fraud; another Bongo victory on Dec. 6, 1998, was likewise allegedly marred by irregularities.

Gabon is one of the most prosperous black African countries, thanks to abundant natural resources, foreign private investment, and government development programs.

The Gambia
Republic of The Gambia

People: Population: 1,426,000. **Age distrib.** (%): <15: 45.1; 65+: 2.6. **Pop. density:** 1,844 per sq. mi. **Urban:** 31%. **Ethnic groups:** Mandinka 42%, Fula 18%, Wolof 16%, Jola 10%, Serahuli 9%. **Principal languages:** English (official), Mandinka, Wolof, Fula, other native dialects. **Chief religions:** Muslim 90%, Christian 9%.

Geography: Area: 4,363 sq. mi. (total); 3,861 sq. mi. (land). **Location:** On Atlantic coast near W tip of Africa. **Neighbors:** Surrounded on 3 sides by Senegal. **Topography:** A narrow strip of land on each side of the lower Gambia R. **Capital:** Banjul 418,000.

Government: Type: Republic. **Head of state and gov.:** Yahya Jammeh; b May 25, 1965; in office: July 23, 1994. **Local divisions:** 5 divisions, 1 city. **Defense budget** (2002): $2.4 mil. **Active troops:** 800.

Economy: Industries: peanuts, fish, hides, tourism, beverages, agric. machinery, woodworking, metalworking, clothing. **Chief crops:** peanuts, millet, sorghum, rice, corn, sesame, cassava, palm kernels. **Natural resources:** fish. **Livestock** (2002): cattle: 323,000; chickens: 586,000; goats: 228,404; pigs: 8,000; sheep: 129,000. **Fish catch** (2002): 34,527 metric tons. **Electricity prod.** (2001): 0.09 bil. kWh. **Labor force:** agri. 75%, ind., commerce, and services 19%, government 6%.

Finance: Monetary unit: Dalasi (GMD) (Sept. 2003: 28.44 = $1 U.S.). **GDP** (2002 est.): $2.6 bil. **Per capita GDP:** $1,800. **Imports** (2001): $200.3 mil.; partners (2000): China 18%, UK 10%, Netherlands 8%, France 6%, Brazil 6%. **Exports** (2001): $139.2 mil.; partners (2000): Benelux 26%, Japan 15%, UK 14%, Brazil 7%. **Tourism** (1998): $49 mil. **Budget** (2001 est.): $80.9 mil. **Intl. reserves less gold:** $79 mil. **Consumer prices** (change in 2000): 0.8%.

Transport: Motor vehicles (1998): 6,400 pass. cars, 3,500 comm. vehicles. **Civil aviation:** .; 1 airport. **Chief port:** Banjul.

Communications: TV Sets: 3 per 1,000 pop. **Radios:** 394 per 1,000 pop. **Telephone lines:** 35,000. **Daily newspaper circ.:** 1.7 per 1,000 pop. **Internet:** 18,000 users.

Health: Life expectancy: 52.4 male; 56.4 female. **Births** (per 1,000 pop.): 40.8. **Deaths** (per 1,000 pop.): 12.4. **Natural inc.:** 2.84%. **Infant mortality** (per 1,000 live births): 74.9.

Education: Free: ages 7-13. **Literacy:** 40.1%.

Major Intl. Organizations: UN (FAO, IBRD, ILO, IMF, IMO, WHO, WTrO), the Commonwealth, AU.

Embassy: Suite 1000, 1155 15th St. NW 20005; 785-1399.

Websites: www.statehouse.gm; www.visitthegambia.gm

The tribes of Gambia were at one time associated with the West African empires of Ghana, Mali, and Songhay. The area became Britain's first African possession in 1588.

Independence came Feb. 18, 1965; republic status within the Commonwealth was achieved in 1970. The country suffered from severe famine in the 1970s. After a coup attempt in 1981, The Gambia formed the confederation of Senegambia with Senegal that lasted until 1989.

On July 23, 1994, after 24 years in power, Pres. Dawda K. Jawara was deposed in a bloodless coup by a military officer, Yahya Jammeh. Jammeh barred political activity, detained potential opponents, and governed by decree. A new constitution was approved by referendum, Aug. 8, 1996. On Sept. 27 Jammeh won the presidential election. Parliamentary balloting on Jan. 2, 1997, completed the nominal return to civilian rule, but Jammeh retained a firm grip on power. He followed his reelection win on Oct. 18, 2001, with a new crackdown on dissidents.

Georgia

People: Population: 5,126,000. **Age distrib.** (%): <15: 19; 65+: 12.8. **Pop. density:** 190 per sq. mi. **Urban:** 57%. **Ethnic groups:** Georgian 70%, Armenian 8%, Russian 6%, Azeri 6%. **Principal languages:** Georgian (official), Russian, Armenian, Azeri, Abkhaz (official in Abkhazia). **Chief religions:** Georgian Orthodox 65%, Muslim 11%, Russian Orthodox 10%, Armenian Apostolic 8%.

Geography: Area (total): 26,911 sq. mi. **Location:** SW Asia, on E coast of Black Sea. **Neighbors:** Russia on N and NE, Turkey and Armenia on S, Azerbaijan on SE. **Topography:** Separated from Russia on NE by main range of the Caucasus Mts. **Capital:** Tbilisi 1,406,000.

Government: Type: Republic. **Head of state and gov.:** Pres. Eduard A. Shevardnadze; b Jan. 25, 1928; in office: Mar. 10, 1992. **Local divisions:** 53 rayons, 9 cities, and 2 autonomous republics. **Defense budget** (2002): $32 mil. **Active troops:** 17,500.

Economy: Industries: steel, aircraft, machine tools, appliances, mining, chemicals. **Chief crops:** citrus, grapes, tea, vegetables, potatoes. **Natural resources:** timber, hydropower, mang., iron ore, copper, coal, oil. **Crude oil reserves** (2002): 35 mil. bbls. **Arable land:** 9%. **Livestock** (2002): cattle: 1.20 mil.; chickens: 8.50 mil.; goats: 110,000; pigs: 465,000; sheep: 577,000. **Fish**

catch (2002): 1,910 metric tons. **Electricity prod.** (2001): 7.27 bil. kWh. **Labor force:** ind. 20%, agri. 40%, services 40%.

Finance: Monetary unit: Lari (GEL) (Sept. 2003: 2.14 = $1 U.S.). **GDP** (2002 est.): $15 bil. Per capita **GDP** (2001 est.): $3,100. **Imports** (2002): $750 mil.; partners (2001): Turkey 15.3%, Russia 13.3%, Azerbaijan 10.7%, Germany 10.1%. **Exports** (2002 est.): $515 mil.; partners (2001): Russia 23.0%, Turkey 21.5%, Azerbaijan 3.3%, U.S. 3.0%. **Tourism** (1999): $400 mil. **Budget** (2001 est.): $554 mil. **Intl. reserves less gold:** $145 mil. **Consumer prices:** 5.6%.

Transport: Railroad: Length: 984 mi. **Motor vehicles:** 244,900 pass. cars, 66,800 comm. vehicles. **Civil aviation:** 190.8 mil pass.-mi.; 22 airports. **Chief ports:** Batumi, Sukhumi.

Communications: TV sets: 516 per 1,000 pop. **Radios:** 590 per 1,000 pop. **Telephone lines:** 648,500. **Internet:** 73,500 users.

Health: Life expectancy: 61.3 male; 68.4 female. **Births** (per 1,000 pop.): 11.8. **Deaths** (per 1,000 pop.): 14.7. **Natural inc.:** -0.29%. **Infant mortality** (per 1,000 live births): 51.2.

Education: Compulsory: ages 6-14. **Literacy** (1999 est.): 99%.

Major Intl. Organizations: UN (FAO, IBRD, ILO, IMF, IMO, WHO), CIS, OSCE.

Embassy: Suite 300, 1615 New Hampshire Ave. NW 20009; 393-5959.

Website: www.parliament.ge

The region, which contained the ancient kingdoms of Colchis and Iberia, was Christianized in the 4th century and conquered by Arabs in the 8th century. It expanded to include an area from the Black Sea to the Caspian and parts of Armenia and Persia before its disintegration under the impact of Mongol and Turkish invasions. Annexation by Russia in 1801 led to the Russian war with Persia, 1804-1813. Georgia entered the USSR in 1922 and became a constituent republic in 1936.

Georgia declared independence Apr. 9, 1991. It became an independent state when the Soviet Union disbanded Dec. 26, 1991. There was fighting during 1991 between rebel forces and loyalists of Pres. Zviad Gamsakhurdia, who fled the capital Jan. 6, 1992. The ruling Military Council picked former Soviet Foreign Minister Eduard A. Shevardnadze to chair a newly created State Council. An attempted coup by forces loyal to Gamsakhurdia was crushed June 24, 1992. Shevardnadze was later elected president. Gamsakhurdia died Jan. 1994, reportedly by suicide.

In Abkhazia, an autonomous republic within Georgia, ethnic Abkhazis, reportedly aided by Russia, launched a bloody military campaign and, by late 1993, had gained control of much of the region. A cease-fire providing for Russian peacekeepers was signed in Moscow May 14, 1994. Intermittent clashes continued into the late 1990s.

On Feb. 3, 1994, Georgia signed agreements with Russia for economic and military cooperation. On Mar. 1, Georgia's Supreme Council ratified membership by Georgia in the Commonwealth of Independent States.

Shevardnadze was wounded by a car bomb Aug. 29, 1995, while on his way to Parliament to sign a new constitution. He was reelected president Nov. 5. Shevardnadze escaped another assassination attempt, Feb. 9, 1998, when gunmen ambushed his motorcade. A mutiny by more than 200 soldiers opposed to Shevardnadze was crushed Oct. 19. He won another 5-year presidential term Apr. 9, 2000. Chechen rebels based in Pankisi Gorge, NE of Tbilisi, have launched attacks against Russian troops in Chechnya, heightening tensions with Russia.

Germany
Federal Republic of Germany

People: Population: 82,476,000. **Age distrib.** (%): <15: 15.4; 65+: 17. **Pop. density:** 610 per sq. mi. **Urban:** 88%. **Ethnic groups:** German 92%, Turkish 2%. **Principal languages:** German (official), Turkish, Italian, Greek, English, Danish, Dutch, Slavic languages. **Chief religions:** Protestant 34%, Roman Catholic 34%, Muslim 4%.

Geography: Area: 137,846 sq. mi. (total); 134,836 sq. mi. (land). **Location:** In central Europe. **Neighbors:** Denmark on N; Netherlands, Belgium, Luxembourg, France on W; Switzerland, Austria on S; Czech Rep., Poland on E. **Topography:** Germany is flat in N, hilly in center and W, and mountainous in Bavaria in the S. Chief rivers are Elbe, Weser, Ems, Rhine, and Main, all flowing toward North Sea, and Danube, flowing toward Black Sea. **Capital:** Berlin. **Cities (urban aggr.):** Rhein-Ruhr North (including Essen) 6.53 mil.; Rhein Main (Frankfurt am Mein) 3.68 mil.; Berlin 3.31 mil; Rhein-Ruhr Middle (Dusseldorf) 3.23 mil.; Rhein-Ruhr South (Cologne) 3.05 mil.; Stuttgart 2.67 mil. **Cities (proper):** Berlin 3.39 mil.; Hamburg 1.7 mil.; Munich 1.19 mil.; Cologne 963,200; Frankfurt am Mein 644,700.

Government: Type: Federal republic. **Head of state:** Pres. Johannes Rau; b Jan. 16, 1931; in office: July 1, 1999. **Head of gov.:** Chan. Gerhard Schröder; b Apr. 7, 1944; in office: Oct. 27, 1998. **Local divisions:** 16 laender (states). **Defense budget** (2002): $24.9 bil. **Active troops:** 296,000.

Economy: Industries: iron, steel, coal, cement, chemicals, machinery, vehicles, machine tools, electronics, food & beverages, shipbuilding. **Chief crops:** potatoes, wheat, barley, sugar beets, fruit, cabbages. **Natural resources:** iron ore, coal, potash,

timber, lignite, uranium, copper, nat. gas, salt, nickel. **Crude oil reserves** (2002): 364 mil. bbls. **Arable land:** 33%. **Livestock** (2002): cattle: 14.23 mil.; chickens: 109.99 mil.; goats: 160,000; pigs: 25.96 mil.; sheep: 2.18 mil. **Fish catch** (2002): 264,691 metric tons. **Electricity prod.** (2001): 544.83 bil. kWh. **Labor force:** ind. 33.4%, agri. 2.8%, services 63.8%.

Finance: Monetary unit: Euro (EUR) (Sept. 2003: 0.92 = $1 U.S.). **GDP** (2002 est.): $2.2 tril. **Per capita GDP:** $26,600. **Imports** (2002): $487.3 bil.; partners (2001): France 9.4%, Netherlands 8.4%, U.S. 8.3%, UK 6.9%. **Exports** (2002 est.): $608 bil.; partners (2001): France 11.1%, U.S. 10.6%, UK 8.4%, Netherlands 6.2%. **Tourism:** $17.81 bil. **Budget** (2001 est.): $825 bil. **Intl. reserves less gold:** $37.64 bil. **Gold:** 110.79 mil oz t. **Consumer prices:** 1.3%.

Transport: Railroad: Length: 27,340 mi. **Motor vehicles:** 42.84 mil pass., 3.17 mil comm. vehicles. **Civil aviation:** 65.00 bil pass.-mi.; 328 airports. **Chief ports:** Hamburg, Bremen, Bremerhaven, Lubeck, Rostock.

Communications: TV sets: 581 per 1,000 pop. **Radios:** 948 per 1,000 pop. **Telephone lines:** 53,720,000. **Daily newspaper circ.:** 305.2 per 1,000 pop. **Internet:** 35,000,000 users.

Health: Life expectancy: 75.5 male; 81.6 female. **Births** (per 1,000 pop.): 8.6. **Deaths** (per 1,000 pop.): 10.3. **Natural inc.:** -0.17%. **Infant mortality** (per 1,000 live births): 4.2.

Education: Compulsory: ages 6-18. **Literacy** (1993): 100%.

Major Intl. Organizations: UN and all of its specialized agencies, EU, NATO, OECD, OSCE.

Embassy: 4645 Reservoir Rd. NW 20007; 298-4000.

Website: www.germany-info.org

Germany is a central European nation originally composed of numerous states, with a common language and traditions, that were united in one country in 1871; Germany was split into 2 countries from the end of World War II until 1990, when it was reunified.

History and government. Germanic tribes were defeated by Julius Caesar, 55 and 53 BC, but Roman expansion N of the Rhine was stopped in AD 9. Charlemagne, ruler of the Franks, consolidated Saxon, Bavarian, Rhenish, Frankish, and other lands; after him the eastern part became the German Empire. The Thirty Years' War, 1618-1648, split Germany into small principalities and kingdoms. After Napoleon, Austria contended with Prussia for dominance, but lost the Seven Weeks' War to Prussia, 1866. Otto von Bismarck, Prussian chancellor, formed the North German Confederation, 1867.

In 1870 Bismarck maneuvered Napoleon III into declaring war. After the quick defeat of France, Bismarck formed the **German Empire** and on Jan. 18, 1871, in Versailles, proclaimed King Wilhelm I of Prussia German emperor (Deutscher kaiser).

The German Empire reached its peak before World War I in 1914, with 208,780 sq. mi., plus a colonial empire. After that war Germany ceded Alsace-Lorraine to France; West Prussia and Posen (Poznan) province to Poland; part of Schleswig to Denmark; lost all colonies and ports of Memel and Danzig.

Republic of Germany, 1919-1933, adopted the Weimar constitution; met reparation payments and elected Friedrich Ebert and Gen. Paul von Hindenburg presidents.

Third Reich, 1933-1945, Adolf Hitler led the National Socialist German Workers' (Nazi) party after World War I. In 1923 he attempted to unseat the Bavarian government and was imprisoned. Pres. von Hindenburg named Hitler chancellor Jan. 30, 1933; on Aug. 3, 1934, the day after Hindenburg's death, the cabinet joined the offices of president and chancellor and made Hitler fuehrer (leader). Hitler abolished freedom of speech and assembly, and began a long series of persecutions climaxed by the murder of millions of Jews and others.

He repudiated the Versailles treaty and reparations agreements, remilitarized the Rhineland (1936), and annexed Austria (Anschluss, 1938). At Munich he made an agreement with Neville Chamberlain, British prime minister, which permitted Germany to annex part of Czechoslovakia. He signed a nonaggression treaty with the USSR, 1939 and declared war on Poland Sept. 1, 1939, precipitating World War II. With total defeat near, Hitler committed suicide in Berlin Apr. 1945. The victorious Allies voided all acts and annexations of Hitler's Reich.

Division of Germany. Germany was sectioned into 4 zones of occupation, administered by the Allied Powers (U.S., USSR, U.K., and France). The USSR took control of many E German states. The territory E of the so-called Oder-Neisse line was assigned to, and later annexed by, Poland. Northern East Prussia (now Kaliningrad) was annexed by the USSR. Greater Berlin, which lost not part of the Soviet zone, was administered by the 4 occupying powers under the Allied Command. In 1948 the USSR withdrew, established its single command in East Berlin, and cut off supplies. The Western Allies utilized a gigantic airlift to bring food to West Berlin, 1948-49.

In 1949, 2 separate German states were established; in May the zones administered by the Western Allies became West Germany; in Oct. the Soviet sector became East Germany. West Berlin was considered an enclave of West Germany, although its status was disputed by the Soviet bloc.

East Germany. The German Democratic Republic (East Germany) was proclaimed in the Soviet sector of Berlin Oct. 7, 1949.

It was declared fully sovereign in 1954, but Soviet troops remained on grounds of security and the 4-power Potsdam agreement.

Coincident with the entrance of West Germany into the European defense community in 1952, the East German government decreed a prohibited zone 3 miles deep along its 600-mile border with West Germany and cut Berlin's telephone system in two. Berlin was further divided by erection of a fortified wall in 1961, after over 3 million East Germans had fled to the West.

East Germany suffered severe economic problems at least until the mid-1960s. Then a "new economic system" was introduced, easing central planning controls and allowing factories to make profits provided they were reinvested in operations or redistributed to workers as bonuses. By the early 1970s, the economy of East Germany was highly industrialized, and the nation was credited with the highest standard of living among Warsaw Pact countries. But growth slowed in the late 1970s, because of shortages of natural resources and labor, and a huge debt to lenders in the West. Comparison with the lifestyle in the West caused many young people to emigrate.

The government firmly resisted following the USSR's policy of glasnost, but by Oct. 1989, was faced with nationwide demonstrations demanding reform. Pres. Erich Honecker, in office since 1976, was forced to resign, Oct. 18. On Nov. 4, the border with Czechoslovakia was opened and permission granted for refugees to travel to the West. On Nov. 9, the East German government announced its decision to open the border with the West, signaling the end of the "Berlin Wall," which was the supreme emblem of the cold war. On Aug. 23, 1990, the East German parliament agreed to formal unification with West Germany; this occurred Oct. 3.

West Germany. The Federal Republic of Germany (West Germany) was proclaimed May 23, 1949, in Bonn, after a constitution had been drawn up by a consultative assembly formed by representatives of the 11 laender (states) in the French, British, and American zones. Later reorganized into 9 units, the laender numbered 10 with the addition of the Saar, 1957. Berlin also was granted land (state) status, but the 1945 occupation agreements placed restrictions on it.

The occupying powers, the U.S., Britain, and France, restored civil status, Sept. 21, 1949. The Western Allies ended the state of war with Germany in 1951 (the U.S. resumed diplomatic relations July 2), while the USSR did so in 1955. The powers lifted controls and the republic became fully independent May 5, 1955.

Dr. Konrad Adenauer, Christian Democrat, was made chancellor Sept. 15, 1949, reelected 1953, 1957, 1961. Willy Brandt, heading a coalition of Social Democrats and Free Democrats, became chancellor Oct. 21, 1969. Brandt resigned May 1974 because of a spy scandal.

In 1970 Brandt signed friendship treaties with the USSR and Poland. In 1971, the U.S., Britain, France, and the USSR signed an agreement on Western access to West Berlin. In 1972 East and West Germany signed their first formal treaty, implementing the agreement easing access to West Berlin. In 1973 a West Germany-Czechoslovakia pact normalized relations and nullified the 1938 "Munich Agreement."

West Germany experienced strong economic growth from the 1950s through the 1980s. The country led Europe in provisions for worker participation in the management of industry.

In 1989 the changes in the East German government and opening of the Berlin Wall sparked talk of reunification of the 2 Germanys. In 1990, under Chancellor Helmut Kohl's leadership, West Germany moved rapidly to reunite with East Germany.

A New Era. As Communism was being rejected in East Germany, talks began concerning German reunification. At a meeting in Ottawa, Feb. 1990, the foreign ministers of the World War II "Big Four" Allied nations and of East Germany and West Germany reached agreement on a format for high-level talks on German reunification.

In May 1990, NATO ministers adopted a package of proposals on reunification, including the inclusion of the united Germany as a full member of NATO and the barring of the new Germany from having its own nuclear, chemical, or biological weapons. In July, the USSR agreed to conditions that would allow Germany to become a member of NATO.

The 2 nations agreed to monetary unification under the West German mark beginning in July. The merger of the 2 Germanys took place Oct. 3, and the first all-German elections since 1932 were held Dec. 2. Eastern Germany received over $1 trillion in public and private funds from western Germany between 1990 and 1995. In 1991, Berlin again became the capital of Germany; the legislature, most administrative offices, and most foreign embassies had shifted from Bonn to Berlin by late 1999.

Germany's highest court ruled, July 12, 1994, that German troops could participate in international military missions abroad, when approved by Parliament. Ceremonies were held marking the final withdrawal of Russian troops from Germany, Aug. 31. Ceremonies were held the following week marking the final withdrawal of American, British, and French troops from Berlin. General elections Oct. 16 left Chancellor Helmut Kohl's governing coalition with a slim parliamentary majority. On Oct. 31, 1996, after more than 14 years in office, Kohl surpassed Adenauer as Germany's longest-serving chancellor in the 20th century.

Unemployment hit a postwar high of 12.6% in Jan. 1998. The Kohl era ended with the defeat of the Christian Democrats in parliamentary elections Sept. 27; Gerhard Schröder, of the Social Democratic Party, became chancellor. Germany contributed 8,500 troops to the NATO-led security force (KFOR) that entered Kosovo in June 1999. Kohl resigned as honorary party chairman Jan. 18, 2000, amid allegations of illegal fund-raising. Kohl reached an agreement with prosecutors Feb. 8, 2001, in which he acknowledged committing a "breach of trust" and agreed to pay a fine, but did not plead guilty to any criminal charges.

Despite a stagnant economy, Schröder's coalition of Social Democrats and Greens retained a slim majority in the elections of Sept. 22, 2002; the prime minister was apparently aided by his government's response to devastating summer floods and by his criticism of U.S. policy toward Iraq. In early 2003, Germany worked with France and Russia to block the UN Security Council from endorsing the U.S.-led invasion of Iraq. Over 2,000 troops were serving with Coalition forces and the NATO peacekeeping force (ISAF) in Afghanistan.

Helgoland, an island of 130 acres in the North Sea, was taken from Denmark by a British Naval Force in 1807 and later ceded to Germany to become part of Schleswig-Holstein province in return for rights in East Africa. The heavily fortified island was surrendered to UK, May 23, 1945, demilitarized in 1947, and returned to West Germany, Mar. 1, 1952. It is a free port.

Ghana
Republic of Ghana

People: Population: 20,922,000. **Age distrib.** (%): <15: 40.4; 65+: 3.5. **Pop. density:** 236 per sq. mi. **Urban:** 36%. **Ethnic groups:** Akan 44%, Moshi-Dagomba 16%, Ewe 13%, Ga 8%, Gurma 3%, Yoruba 1%. **Principal languages:** English (official); about 75 African languages incl. Akan, Moshi-Dagomba, Ewe, and Ga. **Chief religions:** Christian 63%, indigenous beliefs 21%, Muslim 16%.

Geography: Area: 92,456 sq. mi. (total); 89,166 sq. mi. (land). **Location:** On southern coast of W Africa. **Neighbors:** Côte d'Ivoire on W, Burkina Faso on N, Togo on E. **Topography:** Most of Ghana consists of low fertile plains and scrubland, cut by rivers and by the artificial Lake Volta. **Capital:** Accra 1,925,000.

Government: Type: Republic. **Head of state and gov.:** Pres. John Agyekum Kufuor; b Dec. 8, 1938; in office: Jan. 7, 2001. **Local divisions:** 10 regions. **Defense budget** (2002): $42 mil. **Active troops:** 7,000.

Economy: Industries: mining, lumbering, light mfg., aluminum smelting, food proc. **Chief crops:** cocoa, rice, coffee, cassava, peanuts, corn, shea nuts, bananas. **Natural resources:** gold, timber, diamonds, bauxite, mang., fish, rubber, hydropower. **Crude oil reserves** (2002): 17 mil. bbls. **Arable land:** 12%. **Livestock** (2002): cattle: 1.30 mil.; chickens: 20.47 mil.; goats: 3.10 mil.; pigs: 324,000; sheep: 2.74 mil. **Fish catch** (2002): 451,287 metric tons. **Electricity prod.** (2001): 8.8 bil. kWh. **Labor force:** agri. 60%, ind. 15%, services 25%.

Finance: Monetary unit: Cedi (GHC) (Sept. 2003: 8,825.60 = $1 U.S.). **GDP** (2002 est.): $42.5 bil. **Per capita GDP:** $2,100. **Imports** (2000): $2.83 bil.; partners (1998): UK, Nigeria, US, Germany. **Exports** (2000): $1.94 bil.; partners (1998): Togo, UK, Italy, Netherlands. **Tourism** (1999): $304 mil. **Budget** (2001 est.): $1.975 bil. **Intl. reserves less gold:** $397 mil. **Gold:** 280,000 oz t. **Consumer prices:** 14.8%.

Transport: Railroad: Length: 592 mi. **Motor vehicles** (1998): 32,600 pass. cars, 38,400 comm. vehicles. **Civil aviation:** 681.6 mil pass.-mi.; 7 airports. **Chief ports:** Tema, Takoradi.

Communications: TV sets: 115 per 1,000 pop. **Radios:** 680 per 1,000 pop. **Telephone lines:** 242,100. **Daily newspaper circ.:** 14 per 1,000 pop. **Internet:** 40,500 users.

Health: Life expectancy: 55.7 male; 57.4 female. **Births** (per 1,000 pop.): 25.8. **Deaths** (per 1,000 pop.): 10.5. **Natural inc.:** 1.53%. **Infant mortality** (per 1,000 live births): 53.0.

Education: Compulsory: ages 6-14. **Literacy:** 74.8%.

Major Intl. Organizations: UN and all of its specialized agencies, the Commonwealth, AU.

Embassy: 3512 International Dr. NW 20008; 686-4520.

Website: www.ghana.gov.gh

Named for an African empire along the Niger River, AD 400-1240, Ghana was ruled by Britain for 113 years as the Gold Coast. The UN in 1956 approved merger with the British Togoland trust territory. Independence came Mar. 6, 1957, and republic status within the Commonwealth in 1960.

Pres. Kwame Nkrumah built hospitals and schools, promoted development projects like the Volta R. hydroelectric and aluminum plants but ran the country into debt, jailed opponents, and was accused of corruption. A 1964 referendum gave Nkrumah dictatorial powers and set up a one-party socialist state. Nkrumah was overthrown in 1966 by a police-army coup, which expelled Chinese and East German teachers and technicians. Elections were held in 1969, but 4 further coups occurred in 1972, 1978, 1979, and 1981. The 1979 and 1981 coups, led by Flight Lieut. Jerry Rawlings, were followed by suspension of the constitution and banning of political parties. A new constitution, allowing multiparty politics, was approved in April 1992.

In Feb. 1993 more than 1,000 people were killed in ethnic clashes in northern Ghana. Rawlings won the presidential election of Dec. 7, 1996. Kofi Annan, a career UN diplomat from Ghana, became UN secretary general on Jan. 1, 1997. Opposition leader John Agyekum Kufuor won a runoff vote Dec. 28, 2000, and was sworn in Jan. 7, 2001, marking Ghana's 1st peaceful transfer of power from one elected president to another; as of mid-2003 some 70,000 Liberian refugees, over 19,000 Sierra Leoneans, and nearly 6,000 Ivorians remained in Guinea

Greece
Hellenic Republic

People: Population: 10,976,000. **Age distrib.** (%): <15: 14.8; 65+: 18.1. **Pop. density:** 217 per sq. mi. **Urban:** 60%. **Ethnic groups:** Greek 98%. **Principal languages:** Greek (official), English, French. **Chief religions:** Greek Orthodox 98% (official), Muslim 1%.

Geography: Area: 50,942 sq. mi. (total); 50,502 sq. mi. (land). **Location:** Occupies southern end of Balkan Peninsula in SE Europe. **Neighbors:** Albania, Macedonia, Bulgaria on N; Turkey on E. **Topography:** About three-quarters of Greece is nonarable, with mountains in all areas. Pindus Mts. run through the country N to S. The heavily indented coastline is 9,385 mi. long. Of over 2,000 islands, only 169 are inhabited, among them Crete, Rhodes, Milos, Kerkira (Corfu), Chios, Lesbos, Samos, Euboea, Delos, Mykonos. **Capital:** Athens 3,120,000 (1999 city proper: 748,110).

Government: Type: Parliamentary republic. **Head of state:** Pres. Konstantinos Stephanopoulos; b Aug. 15, 1926; in office: Mar. 8, 1995. **Head of gov.:** Prime Min. Costas Simitis; b June 23, 1936; in office: Jan. 18, 1996. **Local divisions:** 13 regions comprising 51 prefectures. **Defense budget** (2002): $3.5 bil. **Active troops:** 177,600.

Economy: Industries: tourism, food & tobacco proc., textiles, chemicals, metal products, mining, oil. **Chief crops:** wheat, corn, barley, sugar beets, olives, tomatoes, grapes. **Natural resources:** bauxite, lignite, magnesite, oil, marble, hydropower potential. **Crude oil reserves** (2002): 9 mil. bbls. **Arable land:** 19%. **Livestock** (2002): cattle: 585,000; chickens: 28 mil.; goats: 5.02 mil.; pigs: 938,000; sheep: 9.21 mil. **Fish catch** (2002): 192,190 metric tons. **Electricity prod.** (2001): 49.79 bil. kWh. **Labor force:** ind. 20%, agri. 20%, services 60%.

Finance: Monetary unit: Euro (EUR) (Sept. 2003: 0.92 = $1 U.S.). **GDP** (2002 est.): $201.1 bil. **Per capita GDP:** $19,000. **Imports** (2002): $31.4 bil.; partners (1999): EU 66.2%. **Exports** (2002) $12.6 bil.; partners (1999): EU 51.6%, U.S. 5.7%. **Tourism:** $9.22 bil. **Budget** (1998 est.): $47.6 bil. **Intl. reserves less gold:** $5.95 bil. **Gold:** 3.94 mil oz t. **Consumer prices:** 3.6%.

Transport: Railroad: Length: 1,598 mi. **Motor vehicles** (1999): 2.93 mil pass. cars, 1.05 mil. comm. vehicles. **Civil aviation:** 5.16 bil pass.-mi.; 66 airports. **Chief ports:** Piraeus, Thessaloníki, Patrai.

Communications: TV sets: 480 per 1,000 pop. **Radios:** 475 per 1,000 pop. **Telephone lines:** 5,607,700. **Daily newspaper circ.:** 22.4 per 1,000 pop. **Internet:** 2,000,000 users.

Health: Life expectancy: 76.3 male; 81.7 female. **Births** (per 1,000 pop.): 9.8. **Deaths** (per 1,000 pop.): 9.9. **Natural inc.:** -0.01%. **Infant mortality** (per 1,000 live births): 6.1.

Education: Compulsory: ages 6-14. **Literacy:** 97.5%.

Major Intl. Organizations: UN (FAO, IBRD, ILO, IMF, IMO, WHO, WTrO), EU, NATO, OECD, OSCE.

Embassy: 2221 Massachusetts Ave. NW 20008; 939-5800.

Website: www.greekembassy.org

The achievements of ancient Greece in art, architecture, science, mathematics, philosophy, drama, literature, and democracy became legacies for succeeding ages. Greece reached the height of its glory and power, particularly in the Athenian city-state, in the 5th century BC. Greece fell under Roman rule in the 2d and 1st centuries BC. In the 4th century AD it became part of the Byzantine Empire and, after the fall of Constantinople to the Turks in 1453, part of the Ottoman Empire.

Greece won its war of independence from Turkey 1821-1829, and became a kingdom. A republic was established 1924; the monarchy was restored, 1935, and George II, King of the Hellenes, resumed the throne. In Oct. 1940, Greece rejected an ultimatum from Italy. Nazi support resulted in its defeat and occupation by Germans, Italians, and Bulgarians. By the end of 1944 the invaders withdrew. Communist resistance forces were defeated by Royalist and British troops. A plebiscite again restored the monarchy.

Communists waged guerrilla war 1947-49 against the government but were defeated with the aid of the U.S. A period of reconstruction and rapid development followed, mainly with conservative governments under Premier Constantine Karamanlis. The Center Union, led by George Papandreou, won elections in 1963 and 1964, but King Constantine, who acceded in 1964, forced Papandreou to resign. A period of political maneuvers ended in the military takeover of April 21, 1967, by Col. George Pap-

adopoulos. King Constantine tried to reverse the consolidation of the harsh dictatorship Dec. 13, 1967, but failed and fled to Italy. Papadopoulos was ousted Nov. 25, 1973.

Greek army officers serving in the National Guard of Cyprus staged a coup on the island July 15, 1974. Turkey invaded Cyprus a week later, precipitating the collapse of the Greek junta, which was implicated in the Cyprus coup. Democratic government returned (and in 1975 the monarchy was abolished).

The 1981 electoral victory of the Panhellenic Socialist Movement (Pasok) of Andreas Papandreou brought substantial changes in Greece's internal and external policies. A scandal centered on George Kostokas, a banker and publisher, led to the arrest or investigation of leading Socialists, implicated Papandreou, and contributed to the defeat of the Socialists at the polls in 1989. However, Papandreou, who was narrowly acquitted Jan. 1992 of corruption charges, led the Socialists to a comeback victory in general elections Oct. 10, 1993.

Tensions between Greece and the Former Yugoslav Republic of Macedonia eased when the 2 countries agreed to normalize relations Sept. 13, 1995. The ailing Papandreou was replaced as prime minister by Costas Simitis, Jan. 18, 1996. Simitis led the Socialists to victory in the election of Sept. 22. The International Olympic Committee, Sept. 5, 1997, chose Athens to host the Summer Games in 2004. An earthquake that shook Athens Sept. 7, 1999, killed at least 143 people and left over 60,000 homeless. The Socialists retained power by a narrow margin in the elections of Apr. 9, 2000.

Police in 2002 cracked down on the November 17 terrorist movement, blamed for 23 killings since the mid-1970s.

Grenada

People: Population: 89,000. **Age distrib.** (%): <15: 35.9; 65+: 3.8. **Pop. density:** 682 per sq. mi. **Urban:** 38%. **Ethnic groups:** Black 82%, Creole 13%. **Principal languages:** English (official), French patois. **Chief religions:** Roman Catholic 53%, Anglican 14%, other Protestant 33%.

Geography: Area (total): 133 sq. mi. **Location:** In Caribbean, 90 mi. N of Venezuela. **Neighbors:** Venezuela, Trinidid & Tobago to S; St. Vincent & the Grenadines to N. **Topography:** Main island is mountainous; country includes Carriacou and Petit Martinique islands. **Capital:** Saint George's 36,000.

Government: Type: Parliamentary democracy. **Head of state:** Queen Elizabeth II, represented by Gov.-Gen. Daniel Williams; b Nov. 4, 1935; in office: Aug. 8, 1996. **Head of gov.:** Prime Min. Keith Mitchell; b Nov. 12, 1946; in office: June 22, 1995. **Local divisions:** 6 parishes, 1 dependency.

Economy: Industries: food, beverages, textiles, light assembly operations, tourism, constr. **Chief crops:** bananas, cocoa, nutmeg, mace, citrus, avocados. **Natural resources:** timber. **Arable land:** 15%. **Livestock** (2002): cattle: 4,000; chickens: 150,000; goats: 7,100; pigs: 6,000; sheep: 13,000. **Fish catch** (2002): 2,247 metric tons. **Electricity prod.** (2001): 0.14 bil. kWh. **Labor force:** services 62%, agri. 24%, ind. 14%.

Finance: Monetary unit: East Caribbean Dollar (XCD) (Sept. 2003: 2.66 = 1 U.S.). **GDP** (2002 est.): $440 mil. **Per capita GDP:** $5,000. **Imports** (2000): $270 mil.; partners (1999): U.S. 31.2%, Caricom 23.6%, UK 13.8%, Japan 7.1%. **Exports** (2000 est.): $78 mil.; partners (1999): Caricom 32.3%, UK 20%, U.S. 13%, Netherlands 8.8%. **Tourism** (1999): $63 mil. **Budget** (1997): $102.1 mil. **Intl. reserves less gold:** $65 mil. **Consumer prices** (change in 1999): 0.2%.

Transport: Motor vehicles: 15,500 pass. cars, 3,900 comm. vehicles. **Civil aviation:** 3 airports. **Chief ports:** Saint George's, Grenville.

Communications: TV sets: 376 per 1,000 pop. **Radios:** 613 per 1,000 pop. **Telephone lines:** 33,500. **Internet:** 6,500 users.

Health: Life expectancy: 62.7 male; 66.3 female. **Births** (per 1,000 pop.): 22.9. **Deaths** (per 1,000 pop.): 7.5. **Natural inc.:** 1.54%. **Infant mortality** (per 1,000 live births): 14.6.

Education: Compulsory: ages 5-16. **Literacy** (1994): 85%.

Major Intl. Organizations: UN (FAO, IBRD, ILO, IMF, WHO, WTrO), Caricom, the Commonwealth, OAS, OECS.

Embassy: 1701 New Hampshire Ave. NW 20009; 265-2561.

Website: www.grenadagrenadines.com

Columbus sighted Grenada in 1498. First European settlers were French, 1650. The island was held alternately by France and England until final British occupation, 1784. Grenada became fully independent Feb. 7, 1974, during a general strike. It is the smallest independent nation in the western hemisphere.

On Oct. 14, 1983, a military coup ousted Prime Minister Maurice Bishop, who was put under house arrest, later freed by supporters, rearrested, and, finally, on Oct. 19, executed. U.S. forces, with a token force from 6 area nations, invaded Grenada, Oct. 25. Resistance from the Grenadian army and Cuban advisors was quickly overcome as most people welcomed the invading forces. U.S. troops left Grenada in June 1985. Cuban Pres. Castro received an enthusiastic greeting when visiting Grenada Aug. 2-3, 1998.

Guatemala
Republic of Guatemala

People: Population: 12,347,000. **Age distrib.** (%): <15: 41.8; 65+: 3.7. **Pop. density:** 295 per sq. mi. **Urban:** 40%. **Ethnic groups:** Mestizo 55%, Amerindian 43%. **Principal languages:** Spanish (official); more than 20 Amerindian languages, incl. Quiche, Cakchiquel, Kekchi, Mam, Garifuna, and Xinca. **Chief religions:** Mostly Roman Catholic; some Protestant, indigenous Mayan beliefs.

Geography: Area: 42,043 sq. mi. (total); 41,865 sq. mi. (land). **Location:** In Central America. **Neighbors:** Mexico on N and W, El Salvador on S, Honduras and Belize on E. **Topography:** The central highland and mountain areas are bordered by the narrow Pacific coast and the lowlands and fertile river valleys on the Caribbean. There are numerous volcanoes in S, more than half a dozen over 11,000 ft. **Capital:** Guatemala City 3,366,000.

Government: Type: Republic. **Head of state and gov.:** Pres. Alfonso Portillo Cabrera; b Sept. 24, 1951; in office: Jan. 14, 2000. **Local divisions:** 22 departments. **Defense budget** (2002): $186 mil. Active troops: 31,400.

Economy: Industries: sugar, textiles, clothing, furniture, chemicals, oil, metals, rubber, tourism. **Chief crops:** sugarcane, corn, bananas, coffee, beans, cardamom. **Natural resources:** oil, nickel, rare woods, fish, chicle, hydropower. **Crude oil reserves** (2002): 526 mil. bbls. **Arable land:** 12%. **Livestock** (2002): cattle: 2.54 mil.; chickens: 35 mil.; goats: 111,500; pigs: 1.45 mil.; sheep: 552,000. **Fish catch** (2002 est.): 14,300 metric tons. **Electricity prod.** (2001): 6.24 bil. kWh. **Labor force:** agri. 50%, ind. 15%, services 35%.

Finance: Monetary unit: Quetzal (GTQ) (Sept. 2003: 8.17 = $1 U.S.). **GDP** (2002 est.): $48 bil. **Per capita GDP:** $3,700. **Imports** (2001): $4.9 bil.; partners (2000): U.S. 35.2%, Mexico 12.6%, South Korea 7.9%, El Salvador 6.4%. **Exports** (2001): $2.9 bil.; partners (2000): U.S. 57%, El Salvador 8.7%, Costa Rica 3.7%, Nicaragua 2.8%. **Tourism:** $518 mil. **Budget** (2002 est.): $2.7 bil. **Intl. reserves less gold:** $1.69 bil. **Gold:** 22,000 oz t. **Consumer prices:** 8.0%.

Transport: Railroad: Length: 549 mi. **Motor vehicles** (1998): 646,500 pass. cars, 21,200 comm. vehicles. **Civil aviation:** 212.5 mil pass.-mi.; 11 airports. **Chief ports:** Puerto Barrios, San Jose.

Communications: TV sets: 61 per 1,000 pop. **Radios:** 79 per 1,000 pop. **Telephone lines:** 756,000. **Daily newspaper circ.:** 33 per 1,000 pop. **Internet:** 200,000 users

Health: Life expectancy: 64.3 male; 66.2 female. **Births** (per 1,000 pop.): 35.1. **Deaths** (per 1,000 pop.): 6.8. **Natural inc.:** 2.83%. **Infant mortality** (per 1,000 live births): 37.9.

Education: Compulsory: ages 5-15. **Literacy:** 70.6%.

Major Intl. Organizations: UN (FAO, IBRD, ILO, IMF, IMO, WHO, WTrO), OAS.

Embassy: 2220 R St. NW 20008; 745-4952.

Website: www.guatemala-embassy.org

The old Mayan Indian empire flourished in what is today Guatemala for over 1,000 years before the Spanish.

Guatemala was a Spanish colony 1524-1821; briefly a part of Mexico and then of the U.S. of Central America, the republic was established in 1839.

Since 1945 when a liberal government was elected to replace the long-term dictatorship of Jorge Ubico, the country has seen a variety of military and civilian governments and periods of civil war. Dissident army officers seized power Mar. 23, 1982, denouncing a presidential election as fraudulent and pledging to restore "authentic democracy" to the nation. Political violence caused large numbers of Guatemalans to seek refuge in Mexico. Another military coup occurred Oct. 8, 1983. The nation returned to civilian rule in 1986.

The crisis-ridden government of Pres. Jorge Serrano Elías was ousted by the military June 1, 1993. Ramiro de León Carpio was elected president by Congress June 6. A conservative businessman, Alvaro Arzú Irigoyen, won the presidency, Jan. 7, 1996. On Sept. 19 the Guatemalan government and leftist rebels approved a peace accord; the final agreement was signed Dec. 29. During more than 35 years of armed conflict, some 200,000 people were killed or "disappeared" (and are presumed dead); most of these casualties were attributed to the government and its paramilitary allies.

Violent episodes in 1998 included the daylight ambush of a busload of U.S. college students, Jan. 16, resulting in the rape of five young women, and the murder of Bishop Juan José Gerardi, a human rights activist, Apr. 26. U.S. Pres. Bill Clinton, on a visit to Guatemala Mar. 10, 1999, apologized for aid the U.S. had given to forces which he said "engaged in violence and widespread repression." Candidates of the right-wing populist Guatemalan Republican Front won control of Congress, Nov. 7, 1999, and the presidency, Dec. 26. Drought and weak export prices during 2001-02 worsened the plight of Guatemala's poor, who make up 80% of the population.

Guinea
Republic of Guinea

People: Population: 8,480,000. **Age distrib.** (%): <15: 42.8; 65+: 2.7. **Pop. density:** 89 per sq. mi. **Urban:** 28%. **Ethnic groups:** Peuhl 40%, Malinke 30%, Soussou 20%. **Principal languages:** French (official); many African languages. **Chief religions:** Muslim 85%, Christian 8%, indigenous beliefs 7%.

Geography: Area (total): 94,926 sq. mi. **Location:** On Atlantic coast of W Africa. **Neighbors:** Guinea-Bissau, Senegal, Mali on N; Côte d'Ivoire on E; Liberia on S. **Topography:** A narrow coastal belt leads to the mountainous middle region, the source of the Gambia, Senegal, and Niger rivers. Upper Guinea, farther inland, is a cooler upland. The SE is forested. **Capital:** Conakry 1,272,000.

Government: Type: Republic. **Head of state:** Pres. Gen. Lansana Conté; b 1934; in office: Apr. 5, 1984. **Head of gov.:** Prime Min. Lamine Sidimé; b 1944; in office: Mar. 8. 1999. **Local divisions:** 4 administrative regions, 1 special zone. **Defense budget** (2002): $43 mil. **Active troops:** 9,700.

Economy: Industries: bauxite, gold, diamonds, aluminum refining, light mfg., agric. proc. **Chief crops:** rice, coffee, pineapples, palm kernels, cassava, bananas, sweet potatoes. **Natural resources:** bauxite, iron ore, diamonds, gold, uranium, hydropower, fish. **Arable land:** 2%. **Livestock** (2002): cattle: 2.68 mil.; chickens: 11.86 mil.; goats: 1.01 mil.; pigs: 98,000; sheep: 892,000. **Fish catch** (2002 est.): 90,000 metric tons. **Electricity prod.** (2001): 0.79 bil. kWh. **Labor force:** agri. 80%, ind. and services 20%.

Finance: Monetary unit: Franc (GNF) (Sept. 2003: 2,056.00 = $1 U.S.). **GDP** (2002 est.): $15.9 bil. **Per capita GDP:** $2,000. **Imports** (2000): $555.2 mil.; partners: France, US, Belgium, Cote d'Ivoire. **Exports** (2000): $694.5 mil.; partners: Belgium, US, Ireland, Russia. **Tourism:** $12 mil. **Budget** (2000 est.): $472.4 mil. **Intl. reserves less gold:** $126 mil.

Transport: Railroad: Length: 675 mi. **Motor vehicles** (1995): 23,200 pass. cars, 13,000 comm. vehicles. **Civil aviation:** 58.4 mil pass.-mi.; 5 airports. **Chief port:** Conakry.

Communications: TV sets: 47 per 1,000 pop. **Radios:** 52 per 1,000 pop. **Telephone lines:** 25,500. **Internet:** 15,000 users.

Health: Life expectancy: 48.3 male; 50.8 female. **Births** (per 1,000 pop.): 42.5. **Deaths** (per 1,000 pop.): 15.7. **Natural inc.:** 2.68%. **Infant mortality** (per 1,000 live births): 93.3.

Education: Compulsory: ages 7-12. **Literacy** (2002): 36%.

Major Intl. Organizations: UN and most of its specialized agencies, AU.

Embassy: 2112 Leroy Pl. NW 20008; 483-9420.

Part of the ancient West African empires, Guinea fell under French control 1849-98. Under Sékou Touré, it opted for full independence in 1958, and France withdrew all aid.

Website: www.embassy.org/gn.html

Touré turned to Communist nations for support and set up a militant one-party state. Thousands of opponents were jailed in the 1970s, in the aftermath of an unsuccessful Portuguese invasion. Many were tortured and killed.

The military took control in a bloodless coup after the March 1984 death of Touré. A new constitution was approved in 1991, but movement toward democracy was slow. When presidential elections were finally held, in Dec. 1993, the incumbent, Gen. Lansana Conté, was the official winner; outside monitors called the elections flawed. Parliamentary elections June 11, 1995, raised similar complaints. Conté suppressed an army mutiny in Conakry, Feb. 2-3, 1996, and won reelection in Dec. 1998.

Fighting in early 2001 along the border with Liberia and Sierra Leone created a refugee crisis; as of mid-2003, some 70,000 Liberian refugees, over 19,000 Sierra Leoneans, and nearly 6,000 Ivorians remained in Guinea.

Guinea-Bissau
Republic of Guinea-Bissau

People: Population: 1,493,000. **Age distrib.** (%): <15: 41.9; 65+: 2.9. **Pop. density:** 138 per sq. mi. **Urban:** 32%. **Ethnic groups:** Balanta 30%, Fula 20%, Manjaca 14%, Mandinga 13%, Papel 7%. **Principal languages:** Portuguese (official), Crioulo, African languages. **Chief religions:** Indigenous beliefs 50%, Muslim 45%, Christian 5%.

Geography: Area: 13,946 sq. mi. (total); 10,811 sq. mi. (land). **Location:** On Atlantic coast of W Africa. **Neighbors:** Senegal on N, Guinea on E and S. **Topography:** A swampy coastal plain covers most of the country; to the east is a low savanna region. **Capital:** 292,000.

Government: Type: In transition. **Head of state and gov.:** Pres. Veríssimo Correia Seabra; in office: Sept. 14, 2003 (interim). **Local divisions:** 9 regions. **Defense budget** (2002): $3 mil. **Active troops:** 9,250.

Economy: Industries: agric. proc., beer, soft drinks. **Chief crops:** rice, corn, beans, cassava, cashew nuts, peanuts, palm kernels, cotton. **Natural resources:** fish, timber, phosphates, bauxite, oil. **Arable land:** 11%. **Livestock** (2002): cattle: 515,000; chickens: 1.40 mil.; goats: 325,000; pigs: 350,000; sheep: 285,000. **Fish catch** (2002 est.): 5,000 metric tons. **Electricity prod.** (2001): 0.06 bil. kWh. **Labor force:** agri. 82%.

Finance: Monetary unit: CFA Franc BCEAO (XOF) (Sept. 2003: 605.18 = $1 U.S.) **GDP** (2002 est.): $1.1 bil. **Per capita GDP:** $800. **Imports** (2000): $55.2 mil.; partners (2000): Portugal 30%, Senegal 14.6%, Thailand 8.5%, China 5.7%. **Exports** (2000 est.): $80 mil.; partners (2000): India 51.4%, Italy 2.7%, South Korea 2.0%, Belgium 2.0%. **Tourism:** $12 mil. **Budget:** NA. **Intl. reserves less gold:** $76 mil. **Consumer prices:** .9%.

Transport: Motor vehicles (1995): 3,500 pass. cars, 2,500 comm. vehicles. **Civil aviation** (1998): 6.2 mil pass.-mi.; 3 airports. **Chief port:** Bissau.

Communications: Radios: 43 per 1,000 pop. **Telephone lines:** 12,000. **Daily newspaper circ.:** 5.4 per 1,000 pop. **Internet:** 4,000 users.

Health: Life expectancy: 45.1 male; 48.9 female. **Births** (per 1,000 pop.): 38.4. **Deaths** (per 1,000 pop.): 16.6. **Natural inc.:** 2.18%. **Infant mortality** (per 1,000 live births): 110.3.

Education: Compulsory: ages 7-12. **Literacy** (2002): 55%.

Major Intl. Organizations: UN (FAO, IBRD, ILO, IMF, IMO, WHO, WTrO), AU.

Embassy: 15929 Yukon Lane, Rockville, MD 20855; 301-947-3958.

Website: embassy.org/embassies/gw.html

Portuguese mariners explored the area in the mid-15th century; the slave trade flourished in the 17th and 18th centuries, and colonization began in the 19th.

Beginning in the 1960s, an independence movement waged a guerrilla war and formed a government in the interior that had international support. Independence came Sept. 10, 1974, after the Portuguese regime was overthrown.

The November 1980 coup gave Vieira absolute power. Vieira eventually initiated political liberalization; multiparty elections were held July 3, 1994. An army uprising June 7, 1998, triggered a civil war, with Senegal and Guinea aiding the Vieira regime. After a peace accord signed on Nov. 2 broke down, rebel troops ousted Vieira on May 7, 1999. Elections Nov. 28-29, 1999, and Jan. 16, 2000, brought a return of civilian rule. Top military officers staged an apparently bloodless coup Sept. 14, 2003.

Guyana
Co-operative Republic of Guyana

People: Population: 765,000 **Age distrib.** (%): <15: 27.6; 65+: 5. **Pop. density:** 10 per sq. mi. **Urban:** 37%. **Ethnic groups:** East Indian 50%, black 36%, Amerindian 7%. **Principal languages:** English (official), Amerindian dialects, Creole, Hindi, Urdu. **Chief religions:** Christian 50%, Hindu 35%, Muslim 10%.

Geography: Area: 83,000 sq. mi. (total); 76,004 sq. mi. (land). **Location:** On N coast of South America. **Neighbors:** Venezuela on W, Brazil on S, Suriname on E. **Topography:** Dense tropical forests cover much of the land, although a flat coastal area up to 40 mi. wide, where 90% of the population lives, provides rich alluvial soil for agriculture. A grassy savanna divides the 2 zones. **Capital:** Georgetown (2001 est.): 280,000.

Government: Type: Republic. **Head of state:** Pres. Bharrat Jagdeo; b Jan. 23, 1964; in office: Aug. 11, 1999. **Head of gov.:** Prime Min. Samuel Hinds; b Dec. 27, 1943; in office: Dec. 22, 1997. **Local divisions:** 10 regions. **Defense budget** (2002): $5.7 mil. **Active troops:** 1,600.

Economy: Industries: bauxite, sugar, rice milling, timber, textiles, gold mining. **Chief crops:** sugar, rice, wheat, vegetable oils. **Natural resources:** bauxite, gold, diamonds, hardwood timber, shrimp, fish. **Arable land:** 2%. **Livestock** (2002): cattle: 220,000; chickens: 12.50 mil.; goats: 79,000; pigs: 20,000; sheep: 130,000. **Fish catch** (2002): 54,013 metric tons. **Electricity prod.** (2001): 0.85 bil. kWh. **Labor force:** 39% agric., forestry, fishing; 24% mining, manuf., const.

Finance: Monetary unit: Dollar (GYD) (Sept. 2003: 178.10 = $1 U.S.) **GDP** (2002 est.): $2.7 bil. **Per capita GDP:** $4,000. **Imports** (2000): $585 mil.; partners (1999): U.S. 29%, Trinidad and Tobago 18%, Netherlands Antilles 16%, UK 7%. **Exports** (2000): $505 mil.; partners (1999): Canada 22%, U.S. 22%, UK 18%, Netherlands Antilles 11%. **Tourism** (1999): $59 mil. **Budget** (2000): $235.2 mil. **Intl. reserves less gold:** $209 mil. **Consumer prices:** 5.3%.

Transport: Railroad: Length: 116 **Motor vehicles:** 24,000 pass. cars, 9,000 comm. vehicles. **Civil aviation:** 172.1 mil pass.-mi.; 48 airports. **Chief port:** Georgetown.

Communications: TV sets: 70 per 1,000 pop. **Radios:** 468 per 1,000 pop. **Telephone lines:** 80,400. **Daily newspaper circ.:** 47 per 1,000 pop. **Internet:** 95,000 users.

Health: Life expectancy: 60.5 male; 65.8 female. **Births** (per 1,000 pop.): 17.9. **Deaths** (per 1,000 pop.): 9.3. **Natural inc.:** 0.86%. **Infant mortality** (per 1,000 live births): 37.6.

Education: Compulsory: ages 6-15. **Literacy:** 98.8%.

Major Intl. Organizations: UN (FAO, IBRD, ILO, IMF, IMO, WHO, WTrO), Caricom, the Commonwealth, OAS.

Embassy: 2490 Tracy Place NW 20008; 265-6900.

Website: guyana.org/govt/embassy.html

Guyana became a Dutch possession in the 17th century, but sovereignty passed to Britain in 1815. Indentured servants from India soon outnumbered African slaves. Ethnic tension has affected political life.

Guyana became independent May 26, 1966. A Venezuelan claim to the western half of Guyana was suspended in 1970 but renewed in 1982; an agreement was reached in 1989. The Suriname border is disputed. The government has nationalized most of the economy, which has remained severely depressed.

The Port Kaituma ambush of U.S. Rep. Leo J. Ryan and others investigating mistreatment of American followers of the Rev. Jim Jones's People's Temple cult triggered a mass suicide-execution of 911 cultists at Jonestown in the jungle, Nov. 18, 1978.

The People's National Congress, the party in power since Guyana became independent, was voted out of office with the election of Cheddi Jagan in Oct. 1992. When Pres. Jagan died Mar. 6, 1997, Prime Min. Samuel Hinds succeeded him; his widow, Janet Jagan, became prime min. Mar. 17. She won the presidency in a disputed election Dec. 15. She resigned because of ill health Aug. 11, 1999, and was succeeded by Bharrat Jagdeo, then 35, who became the youngest head of state in the Americas. He was re-elected Mar. 19, 2001.

Haiti
Republic of Haiti

People: Population: 8,326,000. **Age distrib.** (%): <15: 39.5; 65+: 4.2. **Pop Density:** 782 per sq. mi. **Urban:** 36%. **Ethnic groups:** Black 95%, Creole and other 5%. **Principal languages:** French, Creole (both official). **Chief religions:** Roman Catholic 80%, Protestant 16%; Voodoo widely practiced.

Geography: Area: 10,714 sq. mi. (total); 10,641 sq. mi. (land). **Location:** In Caribbean, occupies western third of Isl. of Hispaniola. **Neighbors:** Dominican Republic on E, Cuba to W. **Topography:** About two-thirds of Haiti is mountainous. Much of the rest is semiarid. Coastal areas are warm and moist. **Capital:** Port-au-Prince 1,838,000.

Government: Type: Republic. **Head of state:** Pres. Jean-Baptiste Aristide; b July 15, 1953; in office Feb. 7, 2001. **Head of gov.:** Yvon Neptune; b Nov. 8, 1946; in office: Mar. 12, 2002. **Local divisions:** 9 departments. **Defense budget** (2002): $40 mil. **Active troops:** NA.

Economy: Industries: sugar refining, flour milling, textiles, cement, light assembly. **Chief crops:** coffee, mangoes, sugarcane, rice, corn, sorghum. **Natural resources:** bauxite, copper, calcium carbonate, gold, marble, hydropower. **Arable land:** 20%. **Livestock** (2002): cattle: 1.44 mil.; chickens: 5.50 mil.; goats: 1.94 mil.; pigs: 1 mil.; sheep: 152,000. **Fish catch** (2002 est.): 5,000 metric tons. **Electricity prod.** (2001): 0.58 bil. kWh. **Labor force:** agri. 66%, services 25%, ind. 9%.

Finance: Monetary unit: Gourde (HTG) (Sept. 2003: 38.70 = $1 U.S.) **GDP** (2002 est.): $12 bil. **Per capita GDP:** $1,700. **Imports** (2001): $977.5 mil.; partners (2000): U.S. 60%, EU 10.5%, Dominican Republic 3.7%. **Exports** (2001): $326.6 mil.; partners (2000): U.S. 90%, EU 6%. **Tourism** (1999): $55 mil. **Budget** (2001 est.): $361 mil. **Intl. reserves less gold:** $60 mil. **Consumer prices:** 9.9%.

Transport: Railroad: Length: 25 mi. **Motor vehicles** (1999): 93,000 pass. cars, 61,600 comm. vehicles. **Civil aviation:** 2 airports. **Chief ports:** Port-au-Prince, Les Cayes, Cap-Haitien.

Communications: TV sets: 5 per 1,000 pop. **Radios:** 53 per 1,000 pop. **Telephone lines:** 130,000. **Daily newspaper circ.:** 2.5 per 1,000 pop. **Internet:** 80,000 users.

Health: Life expectancy: 50.4 male; 52.9 female. **Births** (per 1,000 pop.): 34.1. **Deaths** (per 1,000 pop.): 13.4. **Natural inc.:** 2.07%. **Infant mortality** (per 1,000 live births): 76.0.

Education: Compulsory: ages 6-11. **Literacy:** 52.9%.

Major Intl. Organizations: UN and most of its specialized agencies, OAS.

Embassy: 2311 Massachusetts Ave. NW 20008; 332-4090.

Website: www.haiti.org

Haiti, visited by Columbus, 1492, and a French colony from 1697, attained its independence, 1804, following the rebellion led by former slave Toussaint L'Ouverture. Following a period of political violence, the U.S. occupied the country 1915-34.

Francois Duvalier was elected president in Sept. 1957; in 1964 he was named president for life. Upon his death in 1971, he was succeeded by his son, Jean Claude. Drought in 1975-77 brought famine, and Hurricane Allen in 1980 destroyed most of the rice, bean, and coffee crops. Following several weeks of unrest, President Jean Claude Duvalier fled Haiti aboard a U.S. Air Force jet Feb. 7, 1986, ending the 28-year dictatorship by the Duvalier family.

> **IT'S A FACT:** The nation of Haiti, which gained its independence from France in 1804, is the second-oldest independent nation (after the U.S.) in the Western Hemisphere.

A military-civilian council headed by Gen. Henri Namphy assumed control. In 1987, voters approved a new constitution, but the Jan. 1988 elections were marred by violence and boycotted by the opposition. Gen. Namphy seized control, June 20, but was ousted by a military coup in Sept.

Father Jean-Bertrand Aristide was elected president Dec. 1990. In Sept. 1991, Aristide was arrested by the military and expelled from the country. Some 35,000 Haitian refugees were intercepted by the U.S. Coast Guard as they tried to enter the U.S., 1991-92. Most were returned to Haiti. There was a new upsurge of refugees starting in late 1993.

The UN imposed a worldwide oil, arms, and financial embargo on Haiti June 23, 1993. The embargo was suspended when the military agreed to Aristide's return to power on Oct. 30, but the military effectively blocked his return. After renewed sanctions, the UN Security Council authorized, July 31, 1994, an invasion of Haiti by a multinational force. With U.S. troops already en route, an invasion was averted, Sept. 18, by a new agreement for military leaders to step down and Aristide to resume office. As part of the agreement, thousands of U.S. troops began arriving in Haiti, Sept. 19. Aristide returned to Haiti and was restored in office Oct. 15. A UN peacekeeping force exercised responsibility in Haiti from Mar. 31, 1995 to Nov. 30, 1997.

Aristide transferred power to his elected successor, René Préval, on Feb. 7, 1996. Prime Min. Rosny Smarth announced his resignation June 9, 1997, and quit running the government Oct. 20, but Préval and Parliament deadlocked for another 17 months until a successor was appointed by presidential decree. At least 140 people died and more than 160,000 became homeless when Hurricane Georges struck Haiti Sept. 22, 1998.

Aristide's Lavalas Family party swept parliamentary and local elections, May 21 and June 9, 2000. Aristide won the presidency Nov. 26, 2000, in an election boycotted by opposition groups. A coup attempt Dec. 17, 2001, was suppressed.

Honduras
Republic of Honduras

People: Population: 6,941,000. **Age distrib.** (%): <15: 41.8; 65+: 3.6. **Pop. density:** 161 per sq. mi. **Urban:** 54%. **Ethnic groups:** Mestizo 90%, Amerindian 7%, Black 2%, White 1%. **Principal languages:** Spanish (official), Garifuna, Amerindian dialects. **Chief religion:** Roman Catholic 97%.

Geography: Area: 43,278 sq. mi. (total); 43,201 sq. mi. (land). **Location:** In Central America. **Neighbors:** Guatemala on W, El Salvador and Nicaragua on S. **Topography:** The Caribbean coast is 500 mi. long. Pacific coast, on Gulf of Fonseca, is 40 mi. long. Honduras is mountainous, with wide fertile valleys and rich forests. **Capital:** Tegucigalpa 980,000.

Government: Type: Republic. **Head of state:** Pres. Ricardo Maduro; b Apr. 20, 1946; in office: Jan. 27, 2002. **Local divisions:** 18 departments. **Defense budget** (2002): $115 mil. **Active troops:** 8,300.

Economy: Industries: sugar, coffee, textiles, clothing, wood products. **Chief crops:** bananas, coffee, citrus. **Natural resources:** timber, gold, silver, copper, lead, zinc, iron ore, antimony, coal, fish, hydropower. **Arable land:** 15%. **Livestock** (2002): cattle: 1.73 mil.; chickens: 19 mil.; goats: 32,000; pigs: 480,000; sheep: 14,000. **Fish catch** (2002): 16,451 metric tons. **Electricity prod.** (2001): 3.78 bil. kWh. **Labor force:** agri. 34%, ind. 21%, services 45%.

Finance: Monetary unit: Lempira (HNL) (Sept. 2003: 18.07 = $1 U.S.). **GDP** (2002 est.): $17.6 bil. **Per capita GDP:** $2,600. **Imports** (2001): $2.7 bil.; partners (2000): U.S. 46.1%, Guatemala 8.2%, El Salvador 6.6%, Mexico 4.7%. **Exports** (2001 est.): $2 bil.; partners (2000): U.S. 39.9%, El Salvador 9.2%, Germany 7.9%, Belgium 5.8%. **Tourism:** $240 mil. **Budget** (1999 est.): $411.9 mil. **Intl. reserves less gold:** $1.12 bil. **Gold:** 20,000 oz t. **Consumer prices:** 7.7%.

Transport: Railroad: Length: 370 mi. **Motor vehicles:** (1998): 17,200 pass. cars, 53,900 comm. vehicles. **Civil aviation:** mil pass.-mi.; 12 airports. **Chief ports:** Puerto Cortes, La Ceiba.

Communications: TV sets: 95 per 1,000 pop. **Radios:** 410 per 1,000 pop. **Telephone lines:** 322,500. **Daily newspaper circ.:** 55 per 1,000 pop. **Internet:** 200,000 users.

Health: Life expectancy: 65.3 male; 68.1 female. **Births** (per 1,000 pop.): 31.7. **Deaths** (per 1,000 pop.): 6.4. **Natural inc.:** 2.52%. **Infant mortality** (per 1,000 live births): 30.0.

Education: Free, compulsory: ages 7-13. **Literacy:** 76.2%.

Major Intl. Organizations: UN, (FAO, IBRD, ILO, IMF, IMO, WHO, WTrO), OAS.

Embassy: 3007 Tilden St. NW, Suite 4M, 20008; 966-7702.

Website: www.hondurasemb.com

Mayan civilization flourished in Honduras in the 1st millennium AD. Columbus arrived in 1502. Honduras became independent after freeing itself from Spain, 1821, and from the Fed. of Central America, 1838.

Gen. Oswaldo Lopez Arellano, president for most of the period 1963-75 by virtue of one election and 2 coups, was ousted by the army in 1975 over charges of pervasive bribery by United Brands Co. of the U.S. An elected civilian government took power in 1982.

Some 3,200 U.S. troops were sent to Honduras after the Honduran border was violated by Nicaraguan forces, Mar. 1988.

Already one of the poorest countries in the western hemisphere, Honduras was devastated in late Oct. 1998 by Hurricane Mitch, which killed at least 5,600 people and caused more than $850 million in damage to crops and livestock. Ricardo Maduro, a businessman who pledged to crack down on crime, was elected president Nov. 25, 2001.

Hungary
Republic of Hungary

People: Population: 9,877,000. **Age distrib.** (%): <15: 16.4; 65+: 14.8. **Pop. density:** 277 per sq. mi. **Urban:** 65%. **Ethnic groups:** Hungarian 90%, Roma 4%, German 3%, Serb 2%. **Principal languages:** Hungarian (official), Romani, German, Slavic languages, Romanian. **Chief religions:** Roman Catholic 68%, Protestant 25%.

Geography: Area: 35,919 sq. mi. (total); 35,653 sq. mi. (land). **Location:** In E central Europe. **Neighbors:** Slovakia, Ukraine on N; Austria on W; Slovenia, Yugoslavia, Croatia on S; Romania on E. **Topography:** The Danube R. forms the Slovak border in the NW, then swings S to bisect the country. The eastern half of Hungary is mainly a great fertile plain, the Alfold; the W and N are hilly. **Capital:** Budapest, 1,812,000.

Government: Type: Parliamentary democracy. **Head of state:** Pres. Ferenc Mádl; b Jan. 29, 1931; in office: Aug. 4, 2000. **Head of gov.:** Prime Min. Péter Medgyessy; b Oct. 19, 1942; in office: May 27, 2002. **Local divisions:** 19 counties, 20 urban counties, 1 capital. **Defense budget** (2002): $1.08 bil. **Active troops:** 33,400.

Economy: Industries: mining, metallurgy, constr. materials, proc. foods, textiles, pharm., auto. **Chief crops:** wheat, corn, sunflower seed, potatoes, sugar beets. **Natural resources:** bauxite, coal, nat. gas, fertile soils. **Crude oil reserves** (2002): 111 mil. bbls. **Arable land:** 51%. **Livestock** (2002): cattle: 783,000; chickens: 34.34 mil.; goats: 227,000; pigs: 4.82 mil.; sheep: 1.14 mil. **Fish catch** (2002): 19,694 metric tons. **Electricity prod.** (2001): 34.39 bil. kWh. **Labor force:** services 65%, ind. 27%, agri. 8%.

Finance: Monetary unit: Forint (HUF) (Sept. 2003: 236.89 = $1 U.S.). **GDP** (2002 est.): $134.7 bil. **Per capita GDP:** $13,300. **Imports** (2002): $33.9 bil.; partners (2001): Germany 26.4%, Italy 8.3%, Austria 7.9%, Russia 6.8%. **Exports** (2002 est.): $31.4 bil.; partners (2001): Germany 34.9%, Austria 8.7%, Italy 5.9%, U.S. 5.6%. **Tourism:** $3.42 bil. **Budget** (2000 est.): $14.4 bil. **Intl. reserves less gold:** $7.61 bil. **Gold:** 100,000 oz t. **Consumer prices:** 5.3%.

Transport: Railroad: Length: 4,890 mi. **Motor vehicles:** 2.36 mil pass. cars, 384,300 comm. vehicles. **Civil aviation:** 1.78 bil. pass.-mi.; 17 airport.

Communications: TV sets: 447 per 1,000 pop. **Radios:** 690 per 1,000 pop. **Telephone lines:** 3,666,400. **Daily newspaper circ.:** 46.3 per 1,000 pop. **Internet:** 1,600,000 users.

Health: Life expectancy: 67.8 male; 76.8 female. **Births** (per 1,000 pop.): 9.3. **Deaths** (per 1,000 pop.): 13.0. **Natural inc.:** -0.37%. **Infant mortality** (per 1,000 live births): 8.6.

Education: Compulsory: ages 7-16. **Literacy:** 99.4%.

Major Intl. Organizations: UN (FAO, IBRD, ILO, IMF, IMO, WHO, WTrO), NATO, OECD, OSCE.

Embassy: 3910 Shoemaker St. NW 20008; 202-362-6730.

Website: www.huembwas.org

Earliest settlers, chiefly Slav and Germanic, were overrun by Magyars from the E. Stephen I (997-1038) was made king by Pope Sylvester II in AD 1000. The country suffered repeated Turkish invasions in the 15th-17th centuries. After the defeats of the Turks, 1686-1697, Austria dominated, but Hungary obtained concessions until it regained internal independence in 1867, with the emperor of Austria as king of Hungary in a dual monarchy with a single diplomatic service. Defeated with the Central Powers in 1918, Hungary lost Transylvania to Romania, Croatia and Bacska to Yugoslavia, Slovakia and Carpatho-Ruthenia to Czechoslovakia, all of which had large Hungarian minorities. A republic under Michael Karolyi and a bolshevist revolt under Bela Kun were followed by a vote for a monarchy in 1920 with Admiral Nicholas Horthy as regent.

Hungary joined Germany in World War II, and was allowed to annex most of its lost territories. Russian troops captured the country, 1944-1945. By terms of an armistice with the Allied powers Hungary agreed to give up territory acquired by the 1938 dismemberment of Czechoslovakia and to return to its borders of 1937.

A republic was declared Feb. 1, 1946; Zoltan Tildy was elected president. In 1947 the Communists forced Tildy out. Premier Imre Nagy, who had been in office since mid-1953, was ousted for his moderate policy of favoring agriculture and consumer production, April 18, 1955.

In 1956, popular demands to oust Erno Gero, Communist Party secretary, and for formation of a government by Nagy, resulted in the latter's appointment Oct. 23; demonstrations against Communist rule developed into open revolt. On Nov. 4 Soviet forces launched a massive attack against Budapest with 200,000 troops, 2,500 tanks and armored cars.

About 200,000 persons fled the country. Thousands were arrested and executed, including Nagy in June 1958. In spring 1963 the regime freed many captives from the 1956 revolt.

Hungarian troops participated in the 1968 Warsaw Pact invasion of Czechoslovakia. Major economic reforms were launched early in 1968, switching from a central planning system to one based on market forces and profit.

In 1989 Parliament passed legislation legalizing freedom of assembly and association as Hungary shifted away from communism. In Oct. the Communist Party was formally dissolved. The last Soviet troops left Hungary June 19, 1991. Hungary became a full member of NATO on Mar. 12, 1999. Hungarian voters Apr. 12, 2003, endorsed joining the EU in 2004.

Iceland
Republic of Iceland

People: Population: 290,000. **Age distrib. (%):** <15: 23; 65+: 11.9. **Pop. density:** 7 per sq. mi. **Urban:** 93%. **Ethnic groups:** Icelandic 94%. **Principal languages:** Icelandic (official) **Chief religion:** Evangelical Lutheran 93% (official).

Geography: Area: 39,768 sq. mi. (total); 38,707 sq. mi. (land). **Location:** Isl. at N end of Atlantic O. **Neighbors:** Nearest is Greenland (Den.), to W. **Topography:** Recent volcanic origin. Three-quarters of the surface is wasteland: glaciers, lakes, a lava desert. There are geysers and hot springs, and the climate is moderated by the Gulf Stream. **Capital:** Reykjavík 175,000.

Government: Type: Constitutional republic. **Head of state:** Pres. Olafur Ragnar Grimsson; b May 14, 1943; in office: Aug. 1, 1996. **Head of gov.:** Prime Min. David Oddsson; Jan. 17, 1948; in office: Apr. 30, 1991. **Local divisions:** 23 counties, 14 independent towns. **Defense budget:** Icelandic Defense Force provided by the U.S.

Economy: Industries: fish proc., aluminum smelting, ferrosilicon prod., tourism. **Chief crops:** potatoes, turnips. **Natural resources:** fish, hydropower, geothermal power, diatomite. **Livestock** (2002): cattle: 71,000; chickens: 180,000; goats: 438; pigs: 44,000; sheep: 470,000. **Fish catch** (2002): 1,985,086 metric tons. **Electricity prod.** (2001): 7.89 bil. kWh. **Labor force:** agri. 5.1%, fishing and fish processing 11.8%, manufact. 12.9%, construct. 10.7%, other services 59.5%.

Finance: Monetary unit: Krona (ISK) (Sept. 2003: 81.72 = $1 U.S.). **GDP** (2002 est.): $7 bil. **Per capita GDP:** $25,000. **Imports** (2002): $2 bil.; partners (2001): Germany 12.2%, U.S. 11.1%, Denmark 8.6%, Norway 7.8%. **Exports** (2002) $2 bil.; partners (2001): UK 18.2%, Germany 14.9%, Netherlands 10.9 U.S. 10.3%. **Tourism** (1998): $227 mil. **Budget** (1999): $3.3 bil. **Intl. reserves less gold:** $324 mil. **Gold:** 60,000 oz t. **Consumer prices:** 5.2%.

Transport: Motor vehicles: 158,900 pass. cars, 21,100 comm. vehicles. **Civil aviation:** 2.55 bil. pass.-mi.; 13 airports. **Chief port:** Reykjavik.

Communications: TV sets: 505 per 1,000 pop. **Radios:** 1,075 per 1,000 pop. **Telephone lines:** 190,600. **Daily newspaper circ.:** 365 per 1,000 pop. **Internet:** 175,000 users.

Health: Life expectancy: 77.5 male; 82.2 female. **Births** (per 1,000 pop.): 14.1. **Deaths** (per 1,000 pop.): 7.0. **Natural inc.:** 0.72%. **Infant mortality** (per 1,000 live births): 3.5.

Education: Compulsory: ages 6-16. **Literacy** (1997 est.): 99.9%.

Major Intl. Organizations: UN (FAO, IBRD, ILO, IMF, IMO, WHO, WTrO), EFTA, NATO, OECD, OSCE.

Embassy: Suite 1200, 1156 15th St. NW 20005; 265-6653.

Website: www.iceland.org

Iceland was an independent republic from 930 to 1262, when it joined with Norway. Its language has maintained its purity for 1,000 years. Danish rule lasted from 1380-1918; the last ties with the Danish crown were severed in 1941. The Althing, or assembly, is the world's oldest surviving parliament.

India
Republic of India

People: Population: 1,065,462,000. **Age distrib. (%):** <15: 32.7; 65+: 4.7. **Pop. density:** 928 per sq. mi. **Urban:** 28%. **Ethnic groups:** Indo-Aryan 72%, Dravidian 25%. **Principal languages:** Hindi, English, Bengali, Telugu, Marathi, Tamil, Urdu, Gujarati, Malayalam, Kannada, Oriya, Punjabi, Assamese, Kashmiri, Sindhi, and Sanskrit (all official); Hindustani, a mix of Hindi and Urdu spoken in the north, is popular but not official. **Chief religions:** Hindu 82%, Muslim 12%, Christian 2%, Sikh 2%.

Geography: Area: 1,269,345 sq. mi. (total); 1,147,954 sq. mi. (land). **Location:** Occupies most of the Indian subcontinent in S Asia. **Neighbors:** Pakistan on W; China, Nepal, Bhutan on N; Myanmar, Bangladesh on E. **Topography:** The Himalaya Mts., highest in world, stretch across India's northern borders. Below, the Ganges Plain is wide, fertile, and among the most densely populated regions of the world. The area below includes the Deccan Peninsula. Close to one quarter of the area is forested. The climate varies from tropical heat in S to near-Arctic cold in N. Rajasthan Desert is in NW; NE Assam Hills get 400 in. of rain a year. **Capital:** New Delhi (2001 city est.) 300,000. **Cities (urban aggr.):** Mumbai (Bombay) 16,086,000; Kolkata (Calcutta) 13,058,000;

Delhi 12,987,000; Hyderabad 5,445,000; Chennai (Madras) 6,353,000; Bangalore 5,567,000.

Government: Type: Federal republic. **Head of state:** Pres. A. P. J. Abdul Kalam; b Oct. 15, 1931; in office: July 25, 2002. **Head of gov.:** Prime Min. Atal Bihari Vajpayee; b Dec. 25, 1924; in office Mar. 19, 1998. **Local divisions:** 28 states, 6 union territories, 1 national capital territory. **Defense budget** (2002): $15.6 bil. **Active troops:** 1,298,000

Economy: Industries: textiles, chemicals, food proc., steel, transp. equip., cement, mining, oil, machinery, software. **Chief crops:** rice, wheat, oilseed, cotton, jute, tea, sugarcane, potatoes. **Natural resources:** coal, iron ore, mang., mica, bauxite, titanium ore, chromite, nat. gas, diamonds, oil, limestone. **Crude oil reserves** (2002): 4.8 bil. bbls. **Arable land:** 56%. **Livestock** (2002): cattle: 219.64 mil.; chickens: 413.40 mil.; goats: 123.50 mil.; pigs: 17.50 mil.; sheep: 58.20 mil. **Fish catch** (2002): 5,965,230 metric tons. **Electricity prod.** (2001): 533.34 bil. kWh. **Labor force:** agri. 60%, services 23%, ind. 17%.

Finance: Monetary unit: Rupee (INR) (Sept. 2003: 45.93 = $1 U.S.). **GDP** (2002 est.): $2.7 tril. **Per capita GDP:** $2,540. **Imports** (2001): $53.8 bil.; partners (2000): UK 6.3%, U.S. 6.0%, Belgium 5.7%, Japan 3.5%. **Exports** (2001): $44.5 bil.; partners (2000): U.S. 20.9%, UK 5.2%, Germany 4.3%, Japan 4.0%. **Tourism:** $3.3 bil. **Budget** (2002 est.): $78.2 bil. **Intl. reserves less gold:** $49.77 bil. **Gold:** 11.50 mil oz t. **Consumer prices:** 4.4%.

Transport: Railroad: Length: 39,577 mi. **Motor vehicles** (1998): 5.06 mil pass. cars, 7.54 mil comm. vehicles. **Civil aviation:** 15.05 bil pass.-mi.; 232 airports. **Chief ports:** Kolkata (Calcutta), Mumbai (Bombay), Chennai (Madras), Vishakhapatnam, Kandla.

Communications: TV sets: 75 per 1,000 pop. **Radios:** 120 per 1,000 pop. **Telephone lines:** 41,420,000. **Daily newspaper circ.:** 48.1 per 1,000 pop. **Internet:** 16,580,000 users.

Health: Life expectancy: 62.9 male; 64.4 female. **Births** (per 1,000 pop.): 23.3. **Deaths** (per 1,000 pop.): 8.5. **Natural inc.:** 1.48%. **Infant mortality** (per 1,000 live births): 59.6.

Education: Theoretically compulsory in 23 states to age 14. **Literacy:** 59.5%.

Major Intl. Organizations: UN (FAO, IBRD, ILO, IMF, IMO, WHO, WTrO), the Commonwealth.

Embassy: 2107 Massachusetts Ave. NW 20008; 939-7000.

Websites: www.nic.in; www.indianembassy.org

India has one of the oldest civilizations in the world. Excavations trace the Indus Valley civilization back for at least 5,000 years. Paintings in the mountain caves of Ajanta, richly carved temples, the Taj Mahal in Agra, and the Kutab Minar in Delhi are among relics of the past.

Aryan tribes, speaking Sanskrit, invaded from the NW around 1500 BC, and merged with the earlier inhabitants to create classical Indian civilization.

Asoka ruled most of the Indian subcontinent in the 3d century BC, and established Buddhism. But Hinduism revived and eventually predominated. During the Gupta kingdom, 4th-6th century AD, science, literature, and the arts enjoyed a "golden age."

Arab invaders established a Muslim foothold in the W in the 8th century, and Turkish Muslims gained control of North India by 1200. The Mogul emperors ruled 1526-1857.

Vasco da Gama established Portuguese trading posts 1498-1503. The Dutch followed. The British East India Co. sent Capt. William Hawkins, 1609, to get concessions from the Mogul emperor for spices and textiles. Operating as the East India Co. the British gained control of most of India. The British parliament assumed political direction; under Lord Bentinck, 1828-35, rule by rajahs was curbed. After the Sepoy troops mutinied, 1857-58, the British supported the native rulers.

Nationalism grew rapidly after World War I. The Indian National Congress and the Muslim League demanded constitutional reform. A leader emerged in Mohandas K. Gandhi (called Mahatma, or Great Soul), born Oct. 2, 1869, assassinated Jan. 30, 1948. He advocated self-rule, nonviolence, and removal of the caste system of untouchability. In 1930 he launched a program of civil disobedience, including a boycott of British goods and rejection of taxes without representation.

In 1935 Britain gave India a constitution providing a bicameral federal congress. Muhammad Ali Jinnah, head of the Muslim League, sought creation of a Muslim nation, Pakistan.

The British government partitioned British India into the dominions of India and Pakistan. India became a member of the UN in 1945, a self-governing member of the Commonwealth in 1947, and a democratic republic, Jan. 26, 1950. More than 12 million Hindu and Muslim refugees crossed the India-Pakistan borders in a mass transferral of some of the 2 peoples during 1947; about 200,000 were killed in communal fighting.

After Pakistan troops began attacks on Bengali separatists in East Pakistan, Mar. 25, 1971, some 10 million refugees fled into India. India and Pakistan went to war Dec. 3, 1971, on both the East and West fronts. Pakistan troops in the east surrendered Dec. 16; Pakistan agreed to a cease-fire in the west Dec. 17.

Indira Gandhi, India's prime minister since Jan. 1966, invoked emergency powers in June 1975. Thousands of opponents were arrested and press censorship imposed. These and other actions, including enforcement of coercive birth control measures in some areas, were widely resented. Opposition parties, united in the Janata coalition, turned Gandhi's New Congress Party from power in federal and state parliamentary elections in 1977.

Gandhi became prime minister for the second time, Jan. 14, 1980. She was assassinated by 2 of her Sikh bodyguards Oct. 31, 1984, in response to the government suppression of a Sikh uprising in Punjab in June 1984, which included an assault on the Golden Temple at Amritsar, the holiest Sikh shrine. Widespread rioting followed the assassination; thousands of Sikhs were killed and some 50,000 left homeless. Rajiv, Indira Gandhi's son, replaced her as prime minister. He was swept from office in 1989 amid charges of incompetence and corruption, and assassinated May 21, 1991, while campaigning to recapture the prime ministership.

A gas leak at a Union Carbide chemical plant in Bhopal, in Dec. 1984, eventually killed an estimated 14,000 people. A lawsuit settled in 1989 provided $470 mil. in compensation to victims; in 2002 an Indian High Court upheld a culpable homicide conviction against former UC chairman Warren Anderson.

Sikhs ignited several violent clashes during the 1980s. The government's May 1987 decision to bring the state of Punjab under rule of the central government led to violence. Many died during a government siege of the Golden Temple, May 1988. In Assam in NW India, thousands were killed in ethnic violence in Feb. 1993.

Nationwide riots followed the destruction of a 16th-century mosque by Hindu militants in Dec. 1992. In the biggest wave of criminal violence in Indian history, a series of bombs jolted Bombay and Calcutta, Mar. 12-19, 1993, killing over 300.

Corruption scandals dominated Indian politics in the mid-1990s. Mother Teresa of Calcutta, renowned for her work among the poor, died Sept. 5, 1997. India's 1st lowest-caste Pres., K. R. Narayanan, took office July 25. The Hindu nationalist Bharatiya Janata Party (BJP) won enough seats in parliamentary elections, Feb. 1998, to form a government. Atal Bihari Vajpayee was sworn in as prime minister Mar. 19. India conducted a series of nuclear tests in mid-May, drawing worldwide condemnation and raising tensions with Pakistan.

An alliance led by Vajpayee won a majority in legislative elections, Sept. 5-Oct. 3, 1999. A cyclone that hit the state of Orissa, E India, on Oct. 29, 1999, left some 10,000 people dead. A powerful earthquake in Gujarat state on Jan. 26, 2001, claimed more than 20,000 lives and left more than 166,00 people injured. India blamed Pakistani-sponsored terrorist groups for an Oct. 1 suicide attack on the state legislature in Jammu and Kashmir (see below), in which at least 40 people died, and a Dec. 13 assault on the Indian parliament in New Delhi Dec. 13, which left 13 people dead. Hindu-Muslim clashes in Gujarat Feb. 27-Mar. 11, 2002, claimed more than 700 lives. A. P. J. Abdul Kalam, a Muslim scientist who spearheaded India's nuclear weapons program, became president July 25.

Two bombs in Mumbai, Aug. 25, 2003, killed more than 50 people; Indian authorities blamed Muslim militants. According to UN estimates, about 4 million Indians have HIV/AIDS.

Sikkim, bordered by Tibet, Bhutan, and Nepal, formerly British protected, became a protectorate of India in 1950. Area, 2,740 sq. mi; pop. (2001 census) 540,493; capital: Gangtok. In Sept. 1974, India's parliament voted to make Sikkim an associate Indian state, absorbing it into India.

Kashmir is a predominantly Muslim region in the NW that borders India, Pakistan, Afghanistan, and China. Originally a Hindu kingdom, Muslim rule began in 1341; after almost 200 years under the Moguls, the area was incorporated into British India in 1846. Fighting broke out in the region between India and Pakistan in 1947 following independence from Britain. A cease-fire was negotiated by the UN Jan. 1, 1949; it gave Pakistan control of one-third of the area as Azad Kashmir, in the west and northwest, and India the remaining two-thirds, as the Indian state of **Jammu and Kashmir.** It is India's only Muslim-majority state. Area: 39,146 sq. mi.; pop. 10,000,000, 2001 cens.; capitals: Srinagar (summer) and Jammu (winter). Fighting returned to the area during the 1965 and 1971 wars with Pakistan. China occupied about 14,000 sq. miles in the Ladakh district after a war with India in 1962.

In the 1990s there were repeated clashes between Indian army troops and Muslim separatist fighters triggered by India's decision to impose central government rule. The clashes strained relations between India and Pakistan, which India charged was aiding the separatists; the heaviest fighting in more than 2 decades took place during May-June 1999. As 2002 began, some 1 million Indian and Pakistani troops faced each other across the "line of control" that divides Kashmir. Tensions escalated when Muslin gunmen May 14 killed 34 people, many of them women and children, at an army base near Jammu, and Pakistan conducted missile tests May 25-28. U.S. mediation in June helped ease the crisis. Legislative elections were held Sept.-Oct. 2002. The official number of conflict-related deaths since 1990 is about 34,000; the actual number could be twice as large.

France, 1952-54, peacefully yielded to India its 5 colonies, former French India, comprising Pondicherry, Karikal, Mahe, Yanaon (which became **Pondicherry Union Territory,** area 190 sq. mi; pop. (2001 census) 973,829 and Chandernagor (which was incorporated into the state of **West Bengal).**

Indonesia
Republic of Indonesia

People: Population: 219,883,000. **Age distrib.** (%): <15: NA; 65+: NA. **Pop. density:** 314 per sq. mi. **Urban:** 42%. **Ethnic groups:** Javanese 45%, Sundanese 14%, Madurese 8%, Malay 8%. **Principal languages:** Bahasa Indonesia (official, modified form of Malay), English, Dutch, Javanese, other dialects. **Chief religions:** Muslim 88%, Protestant 5%, Roman Catholic 3%, Hindu 2%, Buddhist 1%.

Geography: Area: 741,099 sq. mi. (total); 705,192 sq. mi. (land). **Location:** Archipelago SE of Asian mainland along the Equator. **Neighbors:** Malaysia on N, Papua New Guinea on E. **Topography:** Indonesia comprises over 13,500 islands (6,000 inhabited), including Java (one of the most densely populated areas in the world with over 2,000 persons per sq. mi.), Sumatra, Kalimantan (most of Borneo), Sulawesi (Celebes), and West Irian (Irian Jaya, the W half of New Guinea). Also: Bangka, Billiton, Madura, Bali, Timor. The mountains and plateaus on the major islands have a cooler climate than the tropical lowlands. **Capital:** Jakarta. **Cities (urban aggr.):** Jakarta 11,429,000, (2000 city proper: 8.8 mil); Bandung 3,409,000; Surabaja 2,461,000.

Government: Type: Republic. **Head of state and gov.:** Megawati Sukarnoputri; b Jan. 23, 1947; in office: July 23, 2001. **Local divisions:** 30 provinces, 2 special regions, 1 capital district. **Defense budget** (2002): $1.12 bil. **Active troops:** 297,000.

Economy: Industries: oil & nat. gas, textiles, apparel & footwear, mining, cement, fertilizers, plywood, rubber. **Chief crops:** rice, cassava, peanuts, rubber, cocoa, coffee, palm oil, copra. **Natural resources:** oil, tin, nat. gas, nickel, timber, bauxite, copper, coal, gold, silver. **Crude oil reserves** (2002): 5.0 bil. bbls. **Arable land:** 10%. **Livestock** (2002): cattle: 11.20 mil.; chickens: 870 mil.; goats: 12.40 mil.; pigs: 6 mil.; sheep: 7.35 mil. **Fish catch** (2002): 5,068,106 metric tons. **Electricity prod.** (2001): 95.78 bil. kWh. **Labor force:** agri. 45%, ind. 16%, services 39%.

Finance: Monetary unit: Rupiah (IDR) (Sept. 2003: 8,474.40 = $1 U.S.). **GDP** (2002 est.): $663 bil. **Per capita GDP:** $3,100. **Imports** (2001): $38.1 bil.; partners (2000 est.): Japan 16.3%, Singapore 11.4%, U.S. 10.2%, South Korea 6.3%. **Exports** (2001 est.): $56.5 bil.; partners (2000 est.): Japan 23.4%, U.S. 13.6%, Singapore 10.7%, South Korea 7%. **Tourism:** $5.75 bil. **Budget** (2000 est.): $30 bil. **Intl. reserves less gold:** $22.78 bil. **Gold:** 3.10 mil oz t. **Consumer prices:** 11.5%.

Transport: Railroad: Length: 4,013 mi. **Motor vehicles:** 3.04 mil pass. cars, 2.37 mil comm. vehicles. **Civil aviation:** 9.04 bil pass.-mi.; 153 airports. **Chief ports:** Jakarta, Surabaya, Palembang, Semarang, Ujungpandang.

Communications: TV sets: 143 per 1,000 pop. **Radios:** 155 per 1,000 pop. **Telephone lines:** 7,632,600. **Daily newspaper circ.:** 22.8 per 1,000 pop. **Internet:** 4,000,000 users.

Health: Life expectancy: 66.5 male; 71.5 female. **Births** (per 1,000 pop.): 21.5. **Deaths** (per 1,000 pop.): 6.3. **Natural inc.:** 1.52%. **Infant mortality** (per 1,000 live births): 38.1.

Education: Compulsory: ages 7-15. **Literacy:** 88.5%.

Major Intl. Organizations: UN and all of its specialized agencies, APEC, ASEAN, OPEC.

Embassy: 2020 Massachusetts Ave. NW 20036; 775-5200.

Websites: www.dfa-deplu.go.id
www.embassyofindonesia.org

Hindu and Buddhist civilization from India reached Indonesia nearly 2,000 years ago, taking root especially in Java. Islam spread along the maritime trade routes in the 15th century, and became predominant by the 16th century. The Dutch replaced the Portuguese as the area's most important European trade power in the 17th century, securing territorial control over Java by 1750. The outer islands were not finally subdued until the early 20th century, when the full area of present-day Indonesia was united under one rule for the first time.

Following Japanese occupation, 1942-45, nationalists led by Sukarno and Hatta declared independence. The Netherlands ceded sovereignty Dec. 27, 1949, after 4 years of fighting. A republic was declared, Aug. 17, 1950, with Sukarno as president. West Irian, on New Guinea, remained under Dutch control. After the Dutch in 1957 rejected proposals for new negotiations over West Irian, Indonesia stepped up the seizure of Dutch property. In 1963 the UN turned the area over to Indonesia, which promised a plebiscite. In 1969, voting by tribal chiefs favored staying with Indonesia, despite an uprising and widespread opposition.

Sukarno suspended Parliament in 1960, and was named president for life in 1963. He made close alliances with Communist governments. Russian-armed Indonesian troops staged raids in 1964 and 1965 into Malaysia, whose formation Sukarno had opposed. (In 1966 Indonesia and Malaysia signed an agreement ending hostility.)

In 1965 an attempted coup in which several military officers were murdered was successfully put down. The regime blamed the coup on the Communist Party, some of whose members were known to have been involved. In its wake more than 300,000 alleged Communists were killed in army-initiated massacres.

Parliament reelected Suharto to a 7th consecutive 5-year term Mar. 10, 1998, as a severe economic downturn focused public anger on nepotism, cronyism, and corruption in the Suharto regime.

Price increases in May sparked mass protests and then mob violence in Jakarta and other cities, claiming some 500 lives. Suharto resigned May 21 and was succeeded by his vice-president, Bacharuddin Jusuf Habibie. Abdurrahman Wahid, leader of Indonesia's largest Muslim organization, was elected president Oct. 20, 1999. In Aug. 2000, under pressure from the legislature, he agreed to share power with Vice-Pres. Megawati Sukarnoputri, the daughter of the late Pres. Sukarno. Charging Wahid with incompetence and corruption, the legislature ousted him July 23, 2001, and Megawati became Indonesia's 1st woman president.

Clashes between Muslims and Christians in the Maluku (Molucca) Is. have claimed more than 2,500 lives since Jan. 1999; in addition, some 550 people, many refugees from the fighting, died when their ferry sank June 29, 2000. Ethnic violence in Kalimantan, Borneo, killed more than 400 in Feb. 2001. Separatists in Aceh, NW Sumatra, fought repeatedly against government troops during the 1980s and '90s; when peace talks broke down in May 2003, the Indonesian military launched a new offensive to put down the independence movement there. East Timor, a former Portuguese colony that Indonesia invaded in Dec. 1975 and controlled until Oct. 1999, became a fully independent country May 20, 2002.

Investigators blamed Jemaah Islamiah, an Islamic terrorist group linked with al-Qaeda, for bombings that killed 202 people, mostly foreign tourists, at nightclubs in Bali, Oct. 12, 2002, and 12 people at a Marriott hotel in Jakarta, Aug. 5, 2003. In mid-Aug., an Indonesian known as Hambali, a founder of Jemaah Islamiah and suspected al-Qaeda ally, was arrested in Thailand on charges of allegedly organizing the Bali and Marriott hotel bombings. Prominent Muslim cleric Abu Bakar Bashir was sentenced to 4 years in jail for treason, Sept. 2, but links to the group were not proven. By Sept., 3 militants had been sentenced to death for their roles in the Bali bombings, and several suspects awaited trial.

Iran
Islamic Republic of Iran

People: Population: 68,920,000. **Age distrib. (%):** <15: 31.6; 65+: 4.7. **Pop. density:** 109 per sq. mi. **Urban:** 65%. **Ethnic groups:** Persian 51%, Azeri 24%, Gilaki/Mazandarani 8%, Kurd 7%, Arab 3%, Lur 2%, Balochi 2%, Turkmen 2%. **Principal languages:** Farsi/Persian (official), Kurdish, Pashto, Luri, Balochi, Gilaki, Mazandarami; Azeri and Turkic languages; Arabic, Turkish. **Chief religion:** Muslim (official; Shi'a 89%, Sunni 10%).

Geography: Area: 636,296 sq. mi. (total); 631,663 sq. mi. (land). **Location:** Between the Middle East and S Asia. **Neighbors:** Turkey, Iraq on W; Armenia, Azerbaijan, Turkmenistan on N; Afghanistan, Pakistan on E. **Topography:** Interior highlands and plains surrounded by high mountains, up to 18,000 ft. Large salt deserts cover much of area, but there are many oases and forest areas. Most of the population inhabits the N and NW. **Capital:** Tehran. **Cities** (urban aggr.): Tehran 7,038,000; Esfahan 1,381,000; Mashhad 1,990,000.

Government: Type: Islamic republic. **Religious head:** Ayatollah Sayyed Ali Khamenei; b 1939; in office: June 4, 1989. **Head of state and gov.:** Pres. Mohammad Khatami; b 1943; in office: Aug. 3, 1997. **Local divisions:** 25 provinces. **Defense budget (2002):** $4.1 bil. **Active troops:** 520,000.

Economy: Industries: oil, petrochems., textiles, constr. materials, food proc., metal fabricating, armaments. **Chief crops:** wheat, rice, other grains, sugar beets, fruits, nuts, cotton. **Natural resources:** oil, nat. gas, coal, chromium, copper, iron ore, lead, mang., zinc, sulfur. **Crude oil reserves** (2002): 89.7 bil. bbls. **Arable land:** 10%. **Livestock** (2002): cattle: 8.74 mil.; chickens: 270 mil.; goats: 25.76mil.; sheep: 53.90 mil. **Fish catch** (2002): 399,000 metric tons. **Electricity prod.** (2001): 124.58 bil. kWh. **Labor force:** agri. 30%, ind. 25%, services 45%.

Finance: Monetary unit: Rial (IRR) (Sept. 2003: 7,900.00 = $1 U.S.). **GDP** (2002 est.): $456 bil. **Per capita GDP:** $7,000. **Imports** (2002): $19.6 bil.; partners (1999): Germany 11%, Italy 8.3%, China 6.1%, Japan 5.3%. **Exports** (2002 est.): $24 bil.; partners (1999): Japan 20.5%, Italy 7%, UAE 5.9%, France 4.7%. **Tourism:** $850 mil. **Budget** (2002 est.): $31.6 bil. **Consumer prices:** 14.3%.

Transport: Railroad: Length: 3,809 mi. **Motor vehicles** (1998): 684,500 pass. cars, 355,100 comm. vehicles. **Civil aviation:** 4.88 bil pass.-mi.; 122 airports. **Chief port:** Bandar-e Abbas.

Communications: TV sets: 154 per 1,000 pop. **Radios:** 265 per 1,000 pop. **Telephone lines:** 13,075,000. **Daily newspaper circ.:** 28 per 1,000 pop. **Internet:** 1,005,000 users.

Health: Life expectancy: 68.0 male; 70.7 female. **Births** (per 1,000 pop.): 17.2. **Deaths** (per 1,000 pop.): 5.5. **Natural Inc.:** 1.17%. **Infant mortality** (per 1,000 live births): 44.2.

Education: Compulsory: ages 6-11. **Literacy:** 79.4%.

Major Intl. Organizations: UN (FAO, IBRD, ILO, IMF, IMO, WHO), OPEC.

Websites: www.daftar.org; www.un.int/iran

Iran was once called Persia. The Iranians, who supplanted an earlier agricultural civilization, came from the E during the 2d millennium BC; they were an Indo-European group related to the Aryans of India.

In 549 BC Cyrus the Great united the Medes and Persians in the Persian Empire, conquered Babylonia in 538 BC, and restored Jerusalem to the Jews. Alexander the Great conquered Persia in 333 BC, but Persians regained independence in the next century under the Parthians, themselves succeeded by Sassanian Persians in AD 226. Arabs brought Islam to Persia in the 7th century, replacing the indigenous Zoroastrian faith. After Persian political and cultural autonomy was reasserted in the 9th century, arts and sciences flourished.

Turks and Mongols ruled Persia in turn from the 11th century to 1502, when Ismael I established the Iranian Safavid dynasty, and made Shiite Islam the offical religion. The dynasty lasted until 1722. The British and Russian empires vied for influence in the 19th century; Afghanistan was severed from Iran by Britain in 1857.

Reza Khan, a miltary officer, became prime min., 1923, and shah in 1925. He began modernization, curbed foreign influence, and officially changed the country's name from Persia to Iran in 1935. Fearing the shah's Axis sympathies, British and Soviet troops forced him to abdicate, 1941; succeeded by his son, Mohammad Reza Pahlavi. With U.S. backing, he brought economic and social change to Iran, (the "White Revolution"), but repression, often severe, of conservative Islamic opposition intensified. Violent protests in 1978 eventually forced the shah to depart, Jan. 16, 1979. He appointed Prime Min. Shahpur Bakhtiar to head a regency council in his absence. Shiite leader Ayatollah Ruhollah Khomeini, exiled by the shah in 1963, returned to Tehran, Feb. 1, and by Feb. 11 pro-Khomeini foces had defeated gov. troops. Khomeini then established an Islamic theocracy.

Iranian militants seized the U.S. embassy, Nov. 4, 1979, and took hostages including 62 Americans. Despite international condemnations and U.S. efforts, including an abortive Apr. 1980 rescue attempt, the crisis continued. The U.S. broke diplomatic relations with Iran, Apr. 7. The shah died in Egypt, July 27. The hostage drama ended Jan. 20, 1981, when an accord, involving the release of frozen Iranian assets, was reached.

A dispute over the Shatt al-Arab waterway situated between Iran and Iraq led to a long and costly war between the 2 countries, beginning Sept. 22, 1980. Iraqi troops occupied Iranian territory, including the port city of Khorramshahr in October. Iranian troops recaptured the city and drove Iraqi troops back across the border, May 1982. In Nov. 1986 it became known that the U.S., which had generally sided with Iraq during the war, had secretly shipped arms to Iran to gain that country's help in obtaining the release of U.S. hostages held by terrorists in Lebanon. The revelation sparked a major scandal in the Reagan administration.

A U.S. Navy warship shot down an Iranian commercial airliner, July 3, 1988, after mistaking it for an F-14 fighter jet; all 290 aboard the plane died. In Aug. 1988, Iran agreed to accept a UN resolution calling for a cease-fire with Iraq.

An earthquake struck northern Iran June 21, 1990, killing more than 45,000, injuring 100,000, and leaving 400,000 homeless. Some one million Kurdish refugees fled from Iraq to Iran following the Persian Gulf War. To curb Iran's alleged support for international terrorism, the U.S. in 1996 authorized sanctions on foreign companies that invest there.

Mohammad Khatami, a moderate Shiite Muslim cleric, was elected president on May 23, 1997, winning nearly 70% of the vote. During the next 3 years, hardline Islamists clashed repeatedly and sometimes violently with reformers, who won a majority in parliamentary elections Feb. 18 and May 5, 2000. Inviting rapprochement with Iran, the U.S. eased some sanctions Mar. 18. Khatami was reelected June 8, 2001, with a 77% majority, Khatami continued to face resistance from religious conservatives.

The U.S.-led war in Iraq, beginning Mar. 2003, contributed to a new period of instability in Iran, which the U.S. suspected was developing nuclear weapons and harboring members of al-Qaeda. In June, armed Islamist vigilantes harassed students who were holding pro-democracy protests in Tehran and other cities.

Iraq
Republic of Iraq

People: Population: 25,175,000. **Age distrib. (%):** <15: 41.1; 65+: 3. **Pop. density:** 150 per sq. mi. **Urban:** 67%. **Ethnic groups:** Arab 75%-80%, Kurdish 15%-20%. **Principal languages:** Arabic (official), Kurdish (official in Kurdish regions), Assyrian, Armenian. **Chief religion:** Muslim (official; Shi'a 60%-65%, Sunni 32%-37%)

Geography: Area: 168,754 sq. mi. (total); 166,859 sq. mi. (land). **Location:** In the Middle East, occupying most of historic Mesopotamia. **Neighbors:** Jordan and Syria on W, Turkey on N, Iran on E, Kuwait and Saudi Arabia on S. **Topography:** Mostly an alluvial plain, including the Tigris and Euphrates rivers, descending from mountains in N to desert in SW. Persian Gulf region is marshland. **Capital:** Baghdad. **Cities (urban aggr.):** Baghdad 4,958,000; Arbil 2,369,000; Basra (city est.) 1,337,000; Mosul 1,131,000.

Government: Type: In transition. **U.S. Military Commander:** Gen. John Abizaid; b Apr. 1, 1951; in office: July 7, 2003. **U.S. Civil Administrator:** L. Paul Bremer; b Sept. 30, 1941; appointed: May 6, 2003. **Governing Council:** 25-member body with rotating presidency. **Local divisions:** 18 governorates (3 in Kurdish Autonomous Region). **Defense budget** (2001): $1.4 bil. **Active troops:** NA.

Economy: Industries: oil, chemicals, textiles, constr. materials, food proc. **Chief crops:** wheat, barley, rice, vegetables, dates, cotton. **Natural resources:** oil, nat. gas, phosphates, sulfur. **Arable land:** 12%. **Crude oil reserves** (2002): 112.5 bil. bbls. **Livestock** (2002): cattle: 1.35 mil.; chickens: 23 mil.; goats: 1.60 mil.; sheep: 6.78 mil. **Fish catch** (2002 est.): 22,800 metric tons. **Electricity prod.** (2001): 36.01 bil. kWh.

Finance: Monetary unit: Dinar (IQD) (Sept. 2003: 0.32 = $1 U.S.). **GDP** (2002 est.): $58 bil. **Per capita GDP:** $2,400. **Imports** (2001): $11 bil.; partners (2000): France 22.5%, Australia 22%, China 5.8%, Russia 5.8%. **Exports** (2001 est.): $15.8 bil.; partners (2000): U.S. 46.2%, Italy 12.2%, France 9.6%, Spain 8.6%. **Tourism** (1998): 13 mil. **Budget:** NA. **Tourism** (1998): $13 mil.

Transport: Railroad: Length: 1,453 mi. **Motor vehicles** (1995): 680,100 pass. cars, 319,900 comm. vehicles. **Civil aviation:** mil pass.-mi.; 77 airports. **Chief port:** Basra.

Communications: TV sets: 82 per 1,000 pop. **Radios:** 229 per 1,000 pop. **Telephone lines:** 1,860,000. **Daily newspaper circ.:** 19 per 1,000 pop.

Health: Life expectancy: 66.7 male; 69.0 female. **Births** (per 1,000 pop.): 33.7. **Deaths** (per 1,000 pop.): 5.8. **Natural inc.:** 2.78%. **Infant mortality** (per 1,000 live births): 55.2.

Education: Compulsory: ages 5-11. **Literacy:** 40.4%.

Major Intl. Organizations: UN (FAO, IBRD, ILO, IMF, IMO, WHO), AL, OPEC.

Website: www.embassy.org/embassies/iq.html

The Tigris-Euphrates valley, formerly called Mesopotamia, was the site of one of the earliest civilizations in the world. The Sumerian city-states of 3,000 BC originated the culture later developed by the Semitic Akkadians, Babylonians, and Assyrians.

Mesopotamia ceased to be a separate entity after the Persian, Greek, and Arab conquests. The latter founded Baghdad, from where the caliph ruled a vast empire in the 8th and 9th centuries. Mongol and Turkish conquests led to a decline in population, economy, cultural life, and the irrigation system.

Britain secured a League of Nations mandate over Iraq after World War I. Independence under a king came in 1932. Rebellious army officers killed King Faisal II, July 14, 1958, and established a leftist, pan-Arab republic, which pursued close ties with the USSR. Successive regimes were increasingly dominated by the Baath Arab Socialist Party. In the 1973 Arab-Israeli war Iraq sent forces to aid Syria. A Baath leader, Saddam Hussein, became president of Iraq, July 16, 1979. Within a month of assuming power, Saddam Hussein instituted a bloody purge in the wake of a reported coup attempt against the new regime. He ruled as a dictator for more than 2 decades. In 1980, Iraq invaded Iran, precipitating a long and costly war with huge casualties. See also *Iran.*

A local faction of the international Baath Arab Socialist party has ruled by decree since 1968. The USSR and Iraq signed an aid pact in 1972, and arms were sent along with several thousand advisers. The 1978 execution of 21 Communists and a shift of trade to the West signalled a more neutral policy, straining relations with the USSR. In the 1973 Arab-Israeli war Iraq sent forces to aid Syria. Within a month of assuming power, Saddam Hussein instituted a bloody purge in the wake of a reported coup attempt against the new regime.

Years of battling with the Kurdish minority resulted in total defeat for the Kurds in 1975, when Iran withdrew support. The fighting led to Iraqi bombing of Kurdish villages in Iran, causing relations with Iran to deteriorate.

After skirmishing intermittently for 10 months over the sovereignty of the disputed Shatt al-Arab waterway that divides the two countries, Iraq and Iran entered into open warfare on Sept. 22, 1980. In the following days, there was heavy ground fighting around Abadan and the port of Khorramshahr, as Iraq launched an attack on Iran's oil-rich province of Khuzistan.

Israeli planes destroyed a nuclear reactor near Baghdad June 7, 1981, claiming it could be used to produce nuclear weapons. Hussein used poison gas against the rebellious Iraqi Kurdish minority in 1988, killing large numbers.

Iraq attacked and overran Kuwait Aug. 2, 1990, sparking an international crisis.

Backed by the UN, a U.S.-led coalition launched air and missile attacks on Iraq, Jan. 16, 1991. The coalition began a ground attack to retake Kuwait Feb. 23. Iraqi forces showed little resistance and were soundly defeated in 4 days. Some 175,000 Iraqis were taken prisoner, and casualties were estimated at over 85,000. As part of the cease-fire agreement, Iraq agreed to scrap all poison gas and germ weapons and allow UN observers to inspect the sites. UN trade sanctions would remain in effect until Iraq complied with all terms.

In Feb. 1991, Iraqi troops drove Kurdish insurgents and civilians to the borders of Iran and Turkey, causing a refugee crisis. The U.S. and allies established havens inside Iraq for the Kurds. The U.S. launched a missile attack aimed at Iraq's intelligence headquarters in Baghdad June 26, 1993, citing evidence that Iraq had sponsored a plot to kill former Pres. George Bush. Iraqi cooperation with UN weapons inspection teams was intermittent throughout the 1990s.

In Aug. 1995, two of Saddam Hussein's sons-in-law, who held high positions in the Iraqi military, defected to Jordan; both were killed after returning to Iraq in Feb. 1996. On Dec. 9 the UN allowed Baghdad to begin selling limited amounts of oil for food and medicine.

Iraqi resistance to UN access to suspected weapons sites touched off diplomatic crises during 1997-98, culminating in intensive U.S. and British aerial bombardment of Iraqi military targets, Dec. 16-19, 1998. After 2 years of intermittent activity, U.S. and British warplanes struck harder at sites near Baghdad on Feb. 16, 2001.

In a speech before the UN, Sept. 12, 2002, U.S. Pres. George Bush accused Iraq of repeatedly violating UN resolutions to eliminate weapons of mass destruction, refrain from supporting terrorism, and end repression. "Under Security Council Resolution 1441, approved Nov. 8, Iraq allowed UN inspectors to search for banned weapons, while the U.S. and Britain built up troops in the Persian Gulf. Despite opposition from France, Germany, Russia, and other members of the Security Council, a U.S.-led coalition launched an invasion of Iraq on the evening of Mar. 19 (EST). By Apr. 6 the British controlled Basra and other areas in the S, and the U.S. entered Baghdad Apr. 7. Hussein had disappeared, the Iraqi government had collapsed, and most of Iraq's armed forces had dissolved into the civilian population. On May 1, Pres. Bush declared that major combat there was over.

According to an Associated Press survey of hospitals, there were at least 3,240 Iraqi civilian war-related deaths in the first month of the war; estimates from other sources, through Sept., ranged as high as 7,000 or more. The number of Iraqi military dead was unknown. U.S. forces had lost 138 service members from all causes, 112 in combat-related deaths, by May 1.

By late August the number of total U.S. deaths since May exceeded the number before May 1. Difficulties in establishing law and order persisted, and guerrilla attacks continued; there were 79 U.S. combat-related deaths between May 1 and Sept. 21. A 25-member Iraqi Governing Council was appointed July 13 and named a cabinet Sept. 1. Two of Hussein's sons, Uday and Qusay, were killed July 22 by U.S. troops in Mosul.

Iraqi resistance activities widened with the bombings of the Jordanian embassy, Aug. 7, the UN headquarters in Baghdad, Aug. 19, killing UN special envoy Sergio Vieira de Mello and 21 others, and a blast in Najaf Aug. 29 that killed at least 83 people, including Ayatollah Mohammad Bakir al-Hakim, an influential Shiite leader. After a second bombing at its Baghdad headquarters Sept. 22, the UN scaled back its presence in Iraq. Iraqi Council member Akila al-Hashemi died Sept. 25, several days after her car was ambushed. As of Sept. 2003, allied occupation forces numbered 150,000 from the U.S. and 20,000 from the U.K. and other countries.

Ireland

People: Population: 3,956,000. **Age distrib. (%):** <15: 21.3; 65+: 11.4. **Pop. density:** 149 per sq. mi. **Urban:** 59%. **Ethnic groups:** Celtic; English minority. **Principal languages:** English, Irish Gaelic (both official); Irish Gaelic spoken by small number in western areas. **Chief religions:** Roman Catholic 92%, Anglican 3%.

Geography: Area: 27,135 sq. mi. (total); 26,599 sq. mi. (land). **Location:** In the Atlantic O. just W of Great Britain. **Neighbors:** United Kingdom (Northern Ireland) on E. **Topography:** Ireland consists of a central plateau surrounded by isolated groups of hills and mountains. The coastline is heavily indented by the Atlantic O. **Capital:** Dublin 993,000.

Government: Type: Parliamentary republic. **Head of state:** Pres. Mary McAleese; b June 27, 1951; in office: Nov. 11, 1997. **Head of gov.:** Prime Min. Bertie Ahern; b Sept. 12, 1951; in office: June 26, 1997. **Local divisions:** 26 counties. **Defense budget** (2002): $724 mil. **Active troops:** 10,460.

Economy: Industries: food products, brewing, textiles, clothing, pharm., chemicals. **Chief crops:** turnips, barley, potatoes, sugar beets; wheat. **Natural resources:** zinc, lead, nat. gas, barite, copper, gypsum, limestone, dolomite, peat, silver. **Arable land:** 13%. **Livestock** (2002): cattle: 7.19 mil.; chickens: 11.30 mil.; pigs: 1.76 mil.; sheep: 7.40 mil. **Fish catch** (2002): 417,244 metric tons. **Electricity prod.** (2001): 23.53 bil. kWh. **Labor force:** agri. 8%, ind. 29%, services 63%.

Finance: Monetary unit: Euro (EUR) (Sept. 2003: 0.92 = $1 U.S.). **GDP** (2002 est.): $118.5 bil. **Per capita GDP:** $30,500. **Imports** (2002): $48.3 bil.; partners (2000): EU 61.4%, U.S. 16.2%, Japan 4%. **Exports** (2002 est.): $85.3 bil.; partners (2000): EU 62.8%, U.S. 17.1%. **Tourism:** $3.57 bil. **Budget** (2002) $30.5 bil. **Intl. reserves less gold:** $3.98 bil. **Gold:** 180,000 oz t. **Consumer prices:** 4.7%.

Transport: Railroad: Length: 2,059 mi. **Motor vehicles** (1999): 1.28 mil pass. cars, 193,100 comm. vehicles. **Civil aviation:** 6.85 bil pass.-mi.; 16 airports. **Chief ports:** Dublin, Cork.

Communications: TV sets: 406 per 1,000 pop. **Radios:** 697 per 1,000 pop. **Telephone lines:** 1,860,000. **Daily newspaper circ.:** 150 per 1,000 pop. **Internet:** 1,065,000 users.

Health: Life expectancy: 74.6 male; 80.3 female. **Births** (per 1,000 pop.): 14.6. **Deaths** (per 1,000 pop.): 7.9. **Natural inc.:** 0.67%. **Infant mortality** (per 1,000 live births): 5.3.

Education: Compulsory: ages 6-15. **Literacy** (1993): 100%.
Major Intl. Organizations: UN (FAO, IBRD, ILO, IMF, IMO, WHO, WTrO), EU, OECD, OSCE.
Embassy: 2234 Massachusetts Ave. NW 20008; 462-3939.
Websites: www.irlgov.ie/; www.irelandemb.org

Celtic tribes invaded the islands about the 4th century BC; their Gaelic culture and literature flourished and spread to Scotland and elsewhere in the 5th century AD, the same century in which St. Patrick converted the Irish to Christianity. Invasions by Norsemen began in the 8th century, ended with defeat of the Danes by the Irish King Brian Boru in 1014. English invasions started in the 12th century; for over 700 years the Anglo-Irish struggle continued with bitter rebellions and savage repressions.

The Easter Monday Rebellion in 1916 failed but was followed by guerrilla warfare and harsh reprisals by British troops called the "Black and Tans." The Dail Eireann (Irish parliament) reaffirmed independence in Jan. 1919. The British offered dominion status to Ulster (6 counties) and southern Ireland (26 counties) Dec. 1921. The constitution of the Irish Free State, a British dominion, was adopted Dec. 11, 1922. Northern Ireland remained part of the United Kingdom.

A new constitution adopted by plebiscite came into operation Dec. 29, 1937. It declared the name of the state Eire in the Irish language (Ireland in English) and declared it a sovereign democratic state. On Dec. 21, 1948, an Irish law declared the country a republic rather than a dominion and withdrew it from the Commonwealth. The British Parliament recognized both actions, 1949, but reasserted its claim to incorporate the 6 northeastern counties in the U.K. This claim has not been recognized by Ireland (*see United Kingdom—Northern Ireland*).

Irish governments have favored peaceful unification of all Ireland and cooperated with Britain against terrorist groups. On Dec. 15, 1993, Irish and British governments agreed on outlines of a peace plan to resolve the Northern Ireland issue. On Aug. 31, 1994, the Irish Republican Army announced a cease-fire; when peace talks lagged, however, the IRA returned to its terror campaign on Feb. 9, 1996. The IRA proclaimed a new cease-fire as of July 20, 1997, and peace talks resumed Sept. 15.

Ireland's first woman president, Mary Robinson, resigned Sept. 12 to become UN high commissioner for human rights. She was succeeded by Mary McAleese, a law professor from Northern Ireland and the first northerner to hold the office. After negotiators in Northern Ireland approved a peace settlement on Good Friday, April 10, 1998, voters in the Irish Republic endorsed the accord on May 22. Irish voters rejected, June 7, 2001, then reversed themselves and approved, Oct. 19, 2002, a plan calling for EU expansion.

Israel
State of Israel

People: Population: 6,433,000. **Age distrib.** (%): <15: 27.1; 65+: 9.9. **Pop. density:** 820 per sq. mi. **Urban:** 92%. **Ethnic groups:** Jewish 80%, Arab and other 20%. **Principal languages:** Hebrew, Arabic (both official), English. **Chief religions:** Jewish 80%, Muslim (mostly Sunni) 15%, Christian 2%.
Geography: Area: 8,019 sq. mi. (total); 7,849 sq. mi. (land). **Location:** Middle East, on E end of Mediterranean Sea. **Neighbors:** Lebanon on N; Syria, West Bank, and Jordan on E; Gaza Strip and Egypt on W. **Topography:** The Mediterranean coastal plain is fertile and well-watered. In the center is the Judean Plateau. A triangular-shaped semi-desert region, the Negev, extends from south of Beersheba to an apex at the head of the Gulf of Aqaba. The E border drops sharply into the Jordan Rift Valley, including Lake Tiberias (Sea of Galilee) and the Dead Sea, which is c.1,300 ft. below sea level, lowest point on the earth's surface. **Capital:** Jerusalem (most countries maintain their embassy in Tel Aviv). **Cities (urban aggr.):** Jerusalem (2001 est.) 661,000; Tel Aviv-Yafo 2,001,000; Haifa (1997 est.) 255,300.
Government: Type: Republic. **Head of state:** Pres. Moshe Katsav; b 1945; in office: Aug. 1, 2000. **Head of gov.:** Prime Min. Ariel Sharon; b 1928; in office: Mar. 7, 2001. **Local divisions:** 6 districts. **Defense budget** (2002): $9.4 bil. **Active troops:** 161,500.
Economy: Industries: high-tech products, wood & paper products, potash & phosphates, food, beverages, tobacco. **Chief crops:** citrus, vegetables, cotton. **Natural resources:** timber, potash, copper ore, nat. gas, phosphate rock, magnesium bromide, clays, sand. **Crude oil reserves** (2002): 4 mil. bbls. **Arable land:** 17%. **Livestock** (2002): cattle: 390,000; chickens: 30 mil.; goats: 65,000; pigs: 155,000; sheep: 392,000. **Fish catch** (2002 est.): 25,100 metric tons. **Electricity prod.** (2001): 42.24 bil. kWh. **Labor force:** public services 31.2%, manufact. 20.2%, finance and business 13.1%, commerce 12.8%, construct. 7.5%, personal and other services 6.4%, transport, storage, and communications 6.2%, agri., forestry, and fishing 2.6%.
Finance: Monetary unit: New Shekel (ILS) (Sept. 2003: 4.45 = $1 U.S.). **GDP** (2002 est.): $122 bil. **Per capita GDP:** $19,000. **Imports** (2002): $30.8 bil.; partners (2001): U.S. 23.5%, Benelux 10.2%, Germany 7.9%, uk 6.7%. **Exports** (2002 est.): $28 bil.; partners (2001): U.S. 42.8%, Benelux 7.4%, Hong Kong 6.8%, Germany 4.8%. **Tourism:** $3.10 bil. **Budget** (2002 est.): $45.1 bil. **Intl. reserves less gold:** $17.71 bil. **Consumer prices:** 5.6%.

Transport: Railroad: Length: 402 mi. **Motor vehicles:** 1.40 mil pass. cars, 328,000 comm. vehicles. **Civil aviation:** 8.40 bil pass.-mi.; 28 airports. **Chief ports:** Haifa, Ashdod, Elat.
Communications: TV sets: 328 per 1,000 pop. **Radios:** 524 per 1,000 pop. **Telephone lines:** 3,100,000. **Daily newspaper circ.:** 290 per 1,000 pop. **Internet:** 2,000,000 users.
Health: Life expectancy: 77.0 male; 81.2 female. **Births** (per 1,000 pop.): 18.7. **Deaths** (per 1,000 pop.): 6.2. **Natural inc.:** 1.25%. **Infant mortality** (per 1,000 live births): 7.4.
Education: Free, compulsory: ages 5-15. **Literacy:** 95.4%.
Major Intl. Organizations: UN (FAO, IBRD, ILO, IMF, IMO, WHO, WTrO).
Embassy: 3514 International Dr. NW 20008; 364-5500.
Websites: www.israel.org; www.israelemb.org

Occupying the SW corner of the ancient Fertile Crescent, Israel contains some of the oldest known evidence of agriculture and of primitive town life. A more advanced civilization emerged in the 3d millennium BC. The Hebrews probably arrived early in the 2d millennium BC. Under King David and his successors (c.1000 BC-597 BC), Judaism was developed and secured. After conquest by Babylonians, Persians, and Greeks, an independent Jewish kingdom was revived, 168 BC, but Rome took effective control in the next century, suppressed Jewish revolts in AD 70 and AD 135, and renamed Judea Palestine, after the earlier coastal inhabitants, the Philistines.

Arab invaders conquered Palestine in 636. The Arabic language and Islam prevailed within a few centuries, but a Jewish minority remained. The land was ruled from the 11th century as a part of non-Arab empires by Seljuks, Mamluks, and Ottomans (with a crusader interval, 1098-1291).

After 4 centuries of Ottoman rule, during which the population declined to a low of 350,000 (1785), the land was taken in 1917 by Britain, which pledged in the Balfour Declaration to support a Jewish national homeland there. In 1920 a British Palestine Mandate was recognized; in 1922 the land east of the Jordan was detached.

Jewish immigration, begun in the late 19th century, swelled in the 1930s with refugees from the Nazis; heavy Arab immigration from Syria and Lebanon also occurred. Arab opposition to Jewish immigration turned violent in 1920, 1921, 1929, and 1936. The UN General Assembly voted in 1947 to partition Palestine into an Arab and a Jewish state. Britain withdrew in May 1948.

Israel was declared an independent state May 14, 1948; the Arabs rejected partition. Egypt, Jordan, Syria, Lebanon, Iraq, and Saudi Arabia invaded, but failed to destroy the Jewish state, which gained territory. Separate armistices with the Arab nations were signed in 1949; Jordan occupied the West Bank, Egypt occupied Gaza; neither granted Palestinian autonomy.

After persistent terrorist raids, Israel invaded Egypt's Sinai, Oct. 29, 1956, aided briefly by British and French forces. A UN cease-fire was arranged Nov. 6.

An uneasy truce between Israel and the Arab countries, supervised by a UN Emergency Force, prevailed until May 19, 1967, when the UN force withdrew at Egypt's demand. Egyptian forces reoccupied the Gaza Strip and closed the Gulf of Aqaba to Israeli shipping. In a 6-day war that started June 5, the Israelis took the Gaza Strip, occupied the Sinai Peninsula to the Suez Canal, and captured East Jerusalem, Syria's Golan Heights, and Jordan's West Bank. The fighting was halted June 10 by UN-arranged cease-fire agreements.

Egypt and Syria attacked Israel, Oct. 6, 1973 (on Yom Kippur, the most solemn day on the Jewish calendar). Israel counter-attacked, driving the Syrians back, and crossed the Suez Canal. A cease-fire took effect Oct. 24 and a UN peacekeeping force went to the area. Under a disengagement agreement signed Jan. 18, 1974, Israel withdrew from the canal's west bank.

Israeli forces raided Entebbe, Uganda, July 3, 1976, and rescued 103 hostages who had been seized by Arab and German terrorists.

In 1977, the conservative opposition, led by Menachem Begin, was voted into office for the first time. Egypt's Pres. Anwar al-Sadat visited Jerusalem Nov. 1977, and on Mar. 26, 1979, Egypt and Israel signed a formal peace treaty, ending 30 years of war. Israel returned the Sinai to Egypt in 1982.

Israel invaded S Lebanon, Mar. 1978, following a Lebanon-based terrorist attack in Israel. Israel withdrew in favor of a 6,000-man UN force, but continued to aid Lebanese Christian militiamen.

On June 7, 1981, Israeli jets destroyed an Iraqi atomic reactor near Baghdad that, Israel claimed, would have enabled Iraq to manufacture nuclear weapons. Israeli forces invaded Lebanon, June 6, 1982, to destroy PLO strongholds there. After massive Israeli bombing of West Beirut, the PLO agreed to evacuate the city. Israeli troops entered West Beirut after newly elected Lebanese Pres. Bashir Gemayel was assassinated on Sept. 14. Israel drew widespread condemnation when Lebanese Christian forces, Sept. 16, entered two West Beirut refugee camps and slaughtered hundreds of Palestinian refugees.

In 1989, violence escalated over the Israeli military occupation of the West Bank and Gaza Strip. In a series of uprisings known as the 1st intifada, Palestinian protesters defied Israeli troops, who forcibly retaliated.

During the Persian Gulf War in early 1991, Iraq fired a series of Scud missiles at Israel. The Labor Party of Yitzhak Rabin won a clear victory in elections held June 23, 1992.

Ongoing peace talks led to historic agreements between Israel and the PLO, Sept. 1993. The PLO recognized Israel's right to exist; Israel recognized the PLO as the Palestinians' representative; the two sides then signed, Sept. 13, an agreement for limited Palestinian self-rule and the West Bank and Gaza.

Israel and Jordan signed, July 25, 1994, in Washington, DC, a declaration ending their 46-year state of war. A formal peace treaty was signed Oct. 26.

Arab and Jewish extremists repeatedly challenged the peace process. A Jewish gunman opened fire on Arab worshippers at a mosque in Hebron, Feb. 25, 1994, killing at least 29 before he himself was killed. On Nov. 4, 1995, an Orthodox Jewish Israeli assassinated Rabin as he left a peace rally in Tel Aviv.

Support for Rabin's successor, Shimon Peres, was shaken by a series of suicide bombings and rocket attacks against Israel by Islamic militants. Emphasizing security issues, the candidate of the conservative Likud bloc, Benjamin Netanyahu, was elected prime minister on May 29.

On Sept. 24, 1996, Israel opened a tunnel entrance near a sacred Muslim site in Jerusalem, setting off several days of violence between Israeli soldiers and Palestinian demonstrators and police. Pres. Bill Clinton hosted a summit meeting between Netanyahu and PLO leader Yasir Arafat soon after, and peace talks were resumed.

Under an interim accord brokered by Clinton and signed by Netanyahu and PLO leader Yasir Arafat at the White House, Oct. 23, 1998, Israel yielded more West Bank territory to the Palestinians, in exchange for new security guarantees. Negotiations bogged down, however, and full implementation did not begin until Sept. 1999. In the interim, Netanyahu lost by a landslide to the Labor party candidate, Ehud Barak, in the general election of May 17.

Israel pulled virtually all its troops out of S Lebanon by May 24, 2000. Marathon summit talks in the U.S. between Barak and Arafat, July 11-25, failed. A 2nd intifada began in late Sept. in Israel and the Palestinian territories. Barak called new elections for prime minister but lost Feb. 6, 2001, to Ariel Sharon, a hardliner. The bloodshed intensified during the summer, as Palestinian suicide bombers launched attacks on Israeli civilians and Israel launched offensives against Palestinian-controlled territory and carried out an assassination campaign against suspected terrorists.

Israel launched a major West Bank offensive Mar. 29, 2002, 2 days after a suicide bomber killed 26 Israeli Jews at a Passover celebration in Netanya. Fighting was particularly fierce at the Jenin refugee camp, where 23 Israeli troops and at least 50 Palestinians were killed. Israel withdrew in early May but, after another wave of suicide bombings, reoccupied much of the West Bank June 21-27. In June 2002 the Israeli government began building a controversial security barrier in the West Bank to restrict Palestinian access to Israel.

Pres. George W. Bush met with Sharon and Palestinian Prime Minister Mahmoud Abbas at Aqaba, Jordan, June 4, 2003, seeking support for a U.S. "road map" for Middle East peace. Palestinian militant groups agreed to a temporary cease-fire June 29; the truce broke down Aug. 19 after a bus bombing in Jerusalem, killing 6 children and 14 others. Israel Sept. 1 vowed "all-out war" against Hamas terrorists. Abbas resigned as prime minister. Sept. 6, citing a power struggle with Arafat. Ahmed Qurei, a leading member of the Fatah movement, accepted the position Sept. 10. Following two more bombings Sept. 9, Israel declared its intention to "remove" Arafat.

Since Sept. 2000, the conflict has claimed the lives of nearly 800 Israelis and over 2,300 Palestinians.

Gaza Strip

The Gaza Strip, also known as Gaza, extends NE from the Sinai Peninsula for 40 km (25 mi), with the Mediterranean Sea to the W and Israel to the E. The Palestinian Authority is responsible for civil government, but Israel retains control over security. Nearly all the inhabitants are Palestinian Arabs, more than 35% of whom live in refugee camps. Population (2003 est) 1,274,868. Area: 139 sq. mi.

Israel captured Gaza from Egypt in the 1967 war. It remained under Israeli occupation until May 1994, when the Israeli Defense Forces withdrew. Agreements between Israel and the PLO in 1993 and 1994 provided for interim self-rule in Gaza, pending the completion of final status negotiations.

West Bank

Located W of the Jordan R. and Dead Sea, the West Bank is bounded by Jordan on the E and by Israel on the N, W, and S. The Palestinian Authority administers several major cities, but Israel retains control over much land, including Jewish settlements. Population (2003 est) 2,237,194. Area: 2,200 sq. mi.

Israel captured the West Bank from Jordan in the 1967 war. A 1974 Arab summit conference designated the PLO as sole representative of West Bank Arabs. In 1988 Jordan cut legal and administrative ties with the territory. Jericho was returned to Palestinian control in May 1994. An accord between Israel and the PLO expanding Palestinian self-rule in the West Bank was signed Sept. 28, 1995. Later agreements gave Palestinians full or shared control of 40% of West Bank territory.

Italy
Italian Republic

People: Population: 57,423,000. **Age distrib. (%):** <15: 14.1; 65+: 18.6. **Pop. density:** 506 per sq. mi. **Urban:** 67%. **Ethnic groups:** Mostly Italian; small minorities of German, Slovene, Albanian. **Principal languages:** Italian (official), German, French, Slovenian, Albanian. **Chief religion:** Predominately Roman Catholic.

Geography: Area: 116,305 sq. mi. (total); 113,522 sq. mi. (land). **Location:** In S Europe, jutting into Mediterranean Sea. **Neighbors:** France on W, Switzerland and Austria on N, Slovenia on E. **Topography:** Occupies a long boot-shaped peninsula, extending SE from the Alps into the Mediterranean, with the islands of Sicily and Sardinia offshore. The alluvial Po Valley drains most of N. The rest of the country is rugged and mountainous, except for intermittent coastal plains, like the Campania, S of Rome. Apennine Mts. run down through center of peninsula. **Capital:** Rome. **Cities (urban aggr.):** Milan 4,251,000; Naples 3,012,000; Rome 2,651,000; Turin 1,294,000.

Government: Type: Republic. **Head of state:** Pres. Carlo Azeglio Ciampi; b Dec. 9, 1920; in office: May 18, 1999. **Head of gov.:** Prime Min. Silvio Berlusconi; b Sept. 29, 1936; in office: June 11, 2001. **Local divisions:** 20 regions divided into 94 provinces. **Defense budget (2002):** $19.4 bil. **Active troops:** 216,800

Economy: Industries: tourism, machinery, iron & steel, chemicals, food proc., textiles, autos. **Chief crops:** fruits, vegetables, grapes, potatoes, sugar beets, soybeans, grain, olives. **Natural resources:** mercury, potash, marble, sulfur, nat. gas, oil, fish, coal. **Crude oil reserves** (2002): 622 mil. bbls. **Arable land:** 31%. **Livestock** (2002): cattle 7.21 mil.; chickens: 100 mil.; goats: 1.33 mil.; pigs: 8.41 mil.; sheep: 10.95 mil. **Fish catch** (2002): 528,666 metric tons. **Electricity prod.** (2001): 258.84 bil. kWh. **Labor force:** services 63%, ind. 32%, agri. 5%.

Finance: Monetary unit: Euro (EUR) (Sept. 2003: 0.92 = $1 U.S.). **GDP** (2002 est.): $1.4 tril. **Per capita GDP:** $25,000. **Imports** (2002): $238.2 bil.; partners (2001): EU 56.5%, U.S. 4.9%. **Exports** (2002 est.): $259.2 bil.; partners (2001): EU 53.8%, U.S. 9.7%. **Tourism:** $27.4 bil. **Budget** (2001 est.): $517 bil. **Intl. reserves less gold:** $21.04 bil. **Gold:** 78.83 mil oz t. **Consumer prices:** 2.5%.

Transport: Railroad: Length: 12,294 mi. **Motor vehicles** (1999): 31.95 mil pass. cars, 3.41 mil comm. vehicles. **Civil aviation:** 24.56 bil pass.-mi.; 96 airports. **Chief ports:** Genoa, Venice, Trieste, Palermo, Naples, La Spezia.

Communications: TV sets: 492 per 1,000 pop. **Radios:** 880 per 1,000 pop. **Telephone lines:** 27,452,000. **Daily newspaper circ.:** 104 per 1,000 pop. **Internet:** 17,000,000 users.

Health: Life expectancy: 76.5 male; 82.5 female. **Births** (per 1,000 pop.): 9.2. **Deaths** (per 1,000 pop.): 10.1. **Natural inc.:** -0.09%. **Infant mortality** (per 1,000 live births): 6.2.

Education: Compulsory: ages 6-14. **Literacy:** 98.6%.

Major Intl. Organizations: UN and all of its specialized agencies, EU, NATO, OECD, OSCE.

Embassy: 3000 Whitehaven St. NW 20008; 202-612-4400. **Websites:** www.italyemb.org; www.travel.it

Rome emerged as the major power in Italy after 500 BC, dominating the Etruscans to the N and Greeks to the S. Under the Empire, which lasted until the 5th century AD, Rome ruled most of Western Europe, the Balkans, the Middle East, and N Africa. In 1988, archaeologists unearthed evidence showing Rome as a dynamic society in the 6th and 7th centuries BC.

After the Germanic invasions, lasting several centuries, a high civilization arose in the city-states of the N, culminating in the Renaissance. But German, French, Spanish, and Austrian intervention prevented the unification of the country. In 1859 Lombardy came under the crown of King Victor Emmanuel II of Sardinia. By plebiscite in 1860, Parma, Modena, Romagna, and Tuscany joined, followed by Sicily and Naples, and by the Marches and Umbria. The first Italian Parliament declared Victor Emmanuel king of Italy Mar. 17, 1861. Mantua and Venetia were added in 1866 as an outcome of the Austro-Prussian war. The Papal States were taken by Italian troops Sept. 20, 1870, on the withdrawal of the French garrison. The states were annexed to the kingdom by plebiscite. Italy recognized Vatican City as independent Feb. 11, 1929.

Fascism appeared in Italy Mar. 23, 1919, led by Benito Mussolini, who took over the government at the invitation of the king Oct. 28, 1922. Mussolini acquired dictatorial powers. He made war on Ethiopia and proclaimed Victor Emmanuel III emperor, defied the sanctions of the League of Nations, sent troops to fight for Franco against the Republic of Spain, and joined Germany in World War II.

After Fascism was overthrown in 1943, Italy declared war on Germany and Japan and contributed to the Allied victory. It surrendered conquered lands and lost its colonies. Mussolini was killed by partisans Apr. 28, 1945. Victor Emmanuel III abdicated May 9, 1946; his son Humbert II was king until June 10, when Italy became a republic after a referendum, June 2-3.

Since World War II, Italy has enjoyed growth in industrial output and living standards, in part a result of membership in the European Community (now European Union). Political stability has not kept pace with economic prosperity, and organized crime and corruption have been persistent problems.

Christian Democratic leader and former Prime Min. Aldo Moro was abducted and murdered in 1978 by Red Brigade terrorists. The wave of left-wing political violence, including other kidnappings and assassinations, continued into the 1980s.

In the early 1990s, scandals implicated some of Italy's most prominent politicians. In Mar. 1994 voting, under reformed election rules, right-wing parties won a majority, dislodging Italy's long-powerful Christian Democratic Party. After a series of short-lived governments, a coalition of center-left parties won the election of Apr. 21, 1996. Italy led a 7,000-member international peacekeeping force in Albania, Apr.-Aug. 1997. Two earthquakes in central Italy Sept. 26 killed 11 people, left about 12,000 homeless, and damaged priceless frescoes in Assisi.

On Feb. 3, 1998, a low-flying U.S. military aircraft severed a gondola cable at a ski resort in N Italy, killing 20 people. Implementation of a deficit reduction plan enabled Italy to qualify in May to adopt the euro, a common European currency. Italy contributed 2,000 troops to the NATO-led security force (KFOR) that entered Kosovo in June 1999. Turin was chosen June 19 to host the Winter Olympics in 2006.

Supporters of Silvio Berlusconi, a multibillionaire media magnate, won the parliamentary elections of May 13, 2001. An earthquake Oct. 31, 2002, in San Giuliano di Puglia, killed 26 schoolchildren. Berlusconi backed the U.S.-led war in Iraq, Mar.-Apr. 2003. On trial for bribing judges in the 1980s, he was helped when Parliament passed a bill in June immunizing top government leaders from prosecution while they held office. Over 4,100 elderly Italians died because of a severe summer heat wave.

Sicily, 9,926 sq. mi., pop. (2001 est.) 4,866,200 is an island 180 by 120 mi., seat of a region that embraces the island of **Pantelleria,** 32 sq. mi., and the **Lipari** group, 44 sq. mi., including 2 active volcanoes: **Vulcano,** 1,637 ft., and **Stromboli,** 3,038 ft. From prehistoric times Sicily has been settled by various peoples; a Greek state had its capital at Syracuse. Rome took Sicily from Carthage 215 BC. **Mt. Etna,** an 11,053-ft. active volcano, is its tallest peak.

Sardinia, 9,301 sq. mi., pop. (2001 est.) 1,599,500, lies in the Mediterranean, 115 mi. W of Italy and $7\frac{1}{2}$ mi. S of Corsica. It is 160 mi. long, 68 mi. wide, and mountainous, with mining of coal, zinc, lead, copper. In 1720 Sardinia was added to the possessions of the Dukes of Savoy in Piedmont and Savoy to form the Kingdom of Sardinia. Giuseppe Garibaldi is buried on the nearby isle of Caprera. **Elba,** 86 sq. mi., lies 6 mi. W of Tuscany. Napoleon I lived in exile on Elba 1814-1815.

Jamaica

People: Population: 2,651,000. **Age distrib.** (%): <15: 29.1; 65+: 6.8. **Pop. density:** 634 per sq. mi. **Urban:** 57%. **Ethnic groups:** Black 91%, mixed 7%, East Indian and other 2%. **Principal languages:** English, patois English. **Chief religions:** Protestant 61%, Roman Catholic 4%, spiritual cults and other 35%.

Geography: Area: 4,244 sq. mi. (total); 4,182 sq. mi. (land). **Location:** In West Indies. **Neighbors:** Nearest are Cuba to N, Haiti to E. **Topography:** Four-fifths of Jamaica is covered by mountains. **Capital:** Kingston 672,000.

Government: Type: Parliamentary democracy. **Head of state:** Queen Elizabeth II, represented by Gov.-Gen. Sir Howard Cooke; b Nov. 13, 1915; in office: Aug. 1, 1991. **Head of gov.:** Prime Min. Percival J. Patterson; b Apr. 10, 1935; in office: Mar. 30, 1992. **Local divisions:** 14 parishes. **Defense budget** (2002): $37 mil. **Active troops:** 2,830.

Economy: Industries: tourism, bauxite, textiles, food proc., light manufactures, rum, cement, metal, paper, chemical products. **Chief crops:** sugarcane, bananas, coffee, citrus, potatoes. **Natural resources:** bauxite, gypsum, limestone. **Arable land:** 14%. **Livestock** (2002): cattle: 400,000; chickens: 11 mil.; goats: 440,000; pigs: 180,000; sheep: 1,000. **Fish catch** (2002 est.): 10,212 metric tons. **Electricity prod.** (2001): 6.27 bil. kWh. **Labor force:** services 60%, agri. 21%, ind. 19%.

Finance: Monetary unit: Jamaican Dollar (JMD) (Sept. 2003: 60.10 = $1 U.S.). **GDP** (2002 est.): $10 bil. **Per capita GDP:** $3,900. **Imports** (2001): $3.1 bil.; partners (1999): U.S. 47.8%, Caricom countries 12.4%, Latin America 7.2%, EU 4.7%. **Exports** (2001 est.): $1.6 bil.; partners (1999): U.S. 35.7%, EU 15.9%, UK 13%, Canada 10.5%. **Tourism:** $1.33 bil. **Budget** (2000 est.): $2.56 bil. **Intl. reserves less gold:** $1.12 bil. **Consumer prices:** 7.1%.

Transport: Railroad: Length: 169 mi. **Motor vehicles** (1997): 156,800 pass. cars, 56,100 comm. vehicles. **Civil aviation:** 2.17 bil pass.-mi.; 11 airports. **Chief ports:** Kingston, Montego Bay.

Communications: TV sets: 191 per 1,000 pop. **Radios:** 796 per 1,000 pop. **Telephone lines:** 532,100. **Daily newspaper circ.:** 62 per 1,000 pop. **Internet:** 100,000 users.

Health: Life expectancy: 73.8 male; 78.0 female. **Births** (per 1,000 pop.): 17.4. **Deaths** (per 1,000 pop.): 5.4. **Natural inc.:** 1.19%. **Infant mortality** (per 1,000 live births): 13.3.

Education: Compulsory: ages 6-12. **Literacy:** 87.9%.

Major Intl. Organizations: UN (FAO, IBRD, ILO, IMF, IMO, WHO, WTrO), Caricom, the Commonwealth, OAS.

Embassy: 1520 New Hampshire Ave. NW 20036; 452-0660. **Websites:** www.cabinet.gov.jm; www.emjamusa.org

Jamaica was visited by Columbus, 1494, and ruled by Spain (under whom Arawak Indians died out) until seized by Britain, 1655. Jamaica won independence Aug. 6, 1962.

In 1974 Jamaica sought an increase in taxes paid by U.S. and Canadian bauxite mines. The socialist government acquired 50% ownership of the companies' Jamaican interests in 1976, and was reelected that year. Rudimentary welfare state measures were passed. Relations with the U.S. improved in the 1980s when Jamaican politics entered a more conservative phase. Violent clashes between government forces and West Kingston slum residents claimed at least 20 lives July 7-10, 2001.

Japan

People: Population: 127,654,000. **Age distrib.** (%): <15: 14.5; 65+: 18. **Pop. density:** 838 per sq. mi. **Urban:** 79%. **Ethnic groups:** Japanese 99%; Korean, Chinese, and other 1%. **Principal languages:** Japanese (official), Ainu, Korean. **Chief religions:** Shinto and Buddhist, observed together by 84%.

Geography: Area: 145,883 sq. mi. (total); 144,689 sq. mi. (land). **Location:** Archipelago off E coast of Asia. **Neighbors:** Russia to N, South Korea to W. **Topography:** Japan consists of 4 main islands: Honshu ("mainland"), 87,805 sq. mi.; Hokkaido, 30,144 sq. mi.; Kyushu, 14,114 sq. mi.; and Shikoku, 7,049 sq. mi. The coast, deeply indented, measures 16,654 mi. The northern islands are a continuation of the Sakhalin Mts. The Kunlun range of China continues into southern islands, the ranges meeting in the Japanese Alps. In a vast transverse fissure crossing Honshu E-W rises a group of volcanoes, mostly extinct or inactive, including 12,388 ft. Mt. Fuji (Fujiyama) near Tokyo. **Capital:** Tokyo. **Cities (urban aggr.):** Tokyo 26,546,000 (1998 city proper: 7,854,000); Osaka 11,013,000, (1998 city proper: 2,599,642); Nagoya 3,157,000; Sapporo 1,813,000; Kyoto 1,849,000.

Government: Type: Parliamentary democracy. **Head of state:** Emp. Akihito; b Dec. 23, 1933; in office: Jan. 7, 1989. **Head of gov.:** Prime Min. Junichiro Koizumi; b Jan. 8, 1942; in office: Apr. 26, 2001. **Local divisions:** 47 prefectures. **Defense budget** (2002): $42.6 bil. **Active troops:** 239,900.

Economy: Industries: motor vehicles, electronic equip., machine tools, steel & nonferrous metals, ships, chemicals, textiles, proc. foods. **Chief crops:** rice, sugar beets, vegetables, fruit. **Natural resources:** fish. **Crude oil reserves** (2002): 59 mil. bbls. **Arable land:** 11%. **Livestock** (2002): cattle: 4.56 mil.; chickens: 294 mil.; goats: 35,000; pigs: 9.61 mil.; sheep: 11,000. **Fish catch** (2002): 5,521,100 metric tons. **Electricity prod.** (2001): 1,036.8 bil. kWh. **Labor force:** services 70%, ind. 25%, agri. 5%.

Finance: Monetary unit: Yen (JPY) (Sept. 2003: 116.00 = $1 U.S.). **GDP** (2002 est.): $3.5 tril. **Per capita GDP:** $28,000. **Imports** (2002): $292.1 bil.; partners (2001 est.): U.S. 18.1%, China 16.6%, South Korea 4.9%, Taiwan 4.1%. **Exports** (2002 est.): $383.8 bil.; partners (2001): U.S. 30.1%, China 7.7%, South Korea 6.3%, Taiwan 6.0%. **Tourism:** $3.74 bil. **Budget** (2001 est.): $718 bil. **Intl. reserves less gold:** $339.23 bil. **Gold:** 24.6 mil oz t. **Consumer prices:** −0.9%.

Transport: Railroad: Length: 14,698 mi. **Motor vehicles:** 52.74 mil pass. cars, 18.46 mil comm. vehicles. **Civil aviation:** 101.16 bil pass.-mi.; 141 airports. **Chief ports:** Tokyo, Kobe, Osaka, Nagoya, Chiba, Kawasaki, Hakodate.

Communications: TV sets: 719 per 1,000 pop. **Radios:** 956 per 1,000 pop. **Telephone lines:** 74,567,000. **Daily newspaper circ.:** 578 per 1,000 pop. **Internet:** 57,200,000 users.

Health: Life expectancy: 77.6 male; 84.4 female. **Births** (per 1,000 pop.): 9.6. **Deaths** (per 1,000 pop.): 8.6. **Natural inc.:** 0.11%. **Infant mortality** (per 1,000 live births): 3.3.

Education: Compulsory: ages 6-15. **Literacy** (2002): 100%.

Major Intl. Organizations: UN and all its specialized agencies, APEC, OECD.

Embassy: 2520 Massachusetts Ave. NW 20008; 238-6700. **Websites:** www.us.emb-japan.go.jp; www.jnto.go.jp

According to Japanese legend, the empire was founded by Emperor Jimmu, 660 BC, but earliest records of a unified Japan date from 1,000 years later. Chinese influence was strong in the formation of Japanese civilization. Buddhism was introduced before the 6th century AD.

A feudal system, with locally powerful noble families and their samurai warrior retainers, dominated from 1192. Central power was held by successive families of shoguns (military dictators), 1192-1867, until recovered by Emperor Meiji, 1868. The Portuguese and Dutch had minor trade with Japan in the 16th and 17th centuries; U.S. Commodore Matthew C. Perry opened the country to U.S. trade in a treaty ratified 1854. Industrialization was begun in the late 19th century. Japan fought China, 1894-95, gaining Taiwan. After war with Russia, 1904-5, Russia ceded S half of Sakhalin and gave concessions in China. Japan annexed Korea 1910.

In World War I Japan ousted Germany from Shandong in China and took over German Pacific islands. Japan took Manchuria in 1931 and launched full-scale war in China in 1937. Japan launched war against the U.S. by attacking Pearl Harbor Dec. 7, 1941. The U.S. dropped atomic bombs on Hiroshima, Aug. 6, and Nagasaki, Aug. 9, 1945. Japan surrendered Aug. 14, 1945.

In a new constitution adopted May 3, 1947, Japan renounced the right to wage war; the emperor gave up claims to divinity; the

Diet became the sole law-making authority. The U.S. and 48 other non-Communist nations signed a peace treaty and the U.S. a bilateral defense agreement with Japan, in San Francisco Sept. 8, 1951, restoring Japan's sovereignty as of April 28, 1952.

Rebuilding after World War II, Japan emerged as one of the most powerful economies in the world, and as a leader in technology.The U.S. and Western Europe criticized Japan for its restrictive policy on imports, which eventually allowed Japan to accumulate huge trade surpluses.

On June 26, 1968, the U.S. returned to Japanese control the Bonin Isls., Volcano Isls. (including Iwo Jima), and Marcus Isls. On May 15, 1972, Okinawa, the other Ryukyu Isls., and the Daito Isls. were returned by the U.S.; it was agreed the U.S. would continue to maintain military bases on Okinawa.

The Recruit scandal, the nation's worst political scandal since World War II, which involved illegal political donations and stock trading, led to the resignation of Premier Noboru Takeshita in May 1989. Following new political and economic scandals, the ruling Liberal Democratic Party (LDP) was denied a majority in general elections July 18, 1993. On June 29, 1994, Tomiichi Murayama became Japan's first Socialist premier since 1947-48.

An earthquake in the Kobe area in Jan. 1995 claimed more than 5,000 lives, injured nearly 35,000, and caused over $90 billion in property damage. On Mar. 20, a nerve gas attack in the Tokyo subway (blamed on a religious cult) killed 12 and injured thousands. Public anger at the rape of a 12-year-old Okinawa schoolgirl by 3 U.S. servicemen, Sept. 4, led the U.S. to begin reducing its military presence there.

Murayama resigned as prime minister, Jan. 5, 1996, and was replaced by Ryutaro Hashimoto of the LDP. Hashimoto signed a joint security declaration with U.S. Pres. Bill Clinton in Tokyo, Apr. 17, 1996. Nagano hosted the Winter Olympics, Feb. 7-22, 1998.

With Japan mired in a lengthy recession, the LDP suffered a sharp rebuke in elections for parliament's upper house, July 12, 1998. Hashimoto resigned, and on July 24, the LDP chose Keizo Obuchi as prime minister. After Obuchi had a stroke Apr. 3, 2000, an LDP stalwart, Yoshiro Mori, succeeded him on Apr. 5. Obuchi died May 14. Parliamentary elections June 25 left the LDP and its allies with a reduced majority in the lower house. The unpopular Mori was replaced as LDP leader and prime minister in Apr. 2001 by Junichiro Koizumi, a populist reformer. Koizumo was reelected as LDP party leader, Sept. 20.

Jordan
Hashemite Kingdom of Jordan

People: Population: 5,473,000. **Age distrib.** (%): <15: 36.6; 65+: 3.4. **Pop. density:** 155 per sq. mi. **Urban:** 79%. **Ethnic groups:** Arab 98%, Armenian 1%, Circassian 1%. **Principal languages:** Arabic (official), English. **Chief religions:** Muslim (official; mostly Sunni) 92%, Christian 6%.

Geography: Area: 35,637 sq. mi. (total); 35,510 sq. mi. (land). **Location:** In Middle East. **Neighbors:** Israel and West Bank on W, Saudi Arabia on S, Iraq on E, Syria on N. **Topography:** About 88% of Jordan is arid. Fertile areas are in W. Only port is on short Aqaba Gulf coast. Country shares Dead Sea (about 1,300 ft. below sea level) with Israel. **Capital:** Amman 1,181,000.

Government: Type: Constitutional monarchy. **Head of state:** King Abdullah II; b Jan. 30, 1962; in office: Feb. 7, 1999. **Head of gov.:** Prime Min. Ali Abu al-Ragheb; b 1946; in office: June 19, 2000. **Local divisions:** 12 governorates. **Defense budget** (2002): $1.0 bil. **Active troops:** 100,240.

Economy: Industries: phosphates, oil refining, cement, potash, light mfg. **Chief crops:** wheat, barley, citrus, tomatoes, melons, olives. **Natural resources:** phosphates, potash, shale oil. **Crude oil reserves** (2002): 1 mil. bbls. **Arable land:** 4%. **Livestock** (2002): cattle: 67,000; chickens: 24 mil.; goats: 550,000; sheep: 1.90 mil. **Fish catch** (2002): 1,060 metric tons. **Electricity prod.** (2001): 7.09 bil. kWh. **Labor force:** services 82.5%, ind. 12.5%, agri. 5%.

Finance: Monetary unit: Dinar (JOD) (Sept. 2003: 0.71 = $1 U.S.). **GDP** (2002 est.): $22.8 bil. **Per capita GDP:** $4,300. **Imports** (2002): $4.4 bil.; partners (2001): Germany 8.8%, U.S. 7.8%, Italy 5.6%, France 5.5%. **Exports** (2002 est.): $2.5 bil.; partners (2001): India 11.4%, U.S. 9.6%, Saudi Arabia 5.6%, Israel 3.7%. **Tourism:** $722 mil. **Budget** (2002 est.): $3 bil. **Intl. reserves less gold:** $2.93 bil. **Gold:** 410,000 oz t. **Consumer prices:** 1.8%.

Transport: Railroad: Length: 421 mi. **Motor vehicles:** 255,800 pass. cars, 104,500 comm. vehicles. **Civil aviation:** 2.61 bil pass.-mi.; 15 airports. **Chief port:** Al Aqabah.

Communications: TV sets: 83 per 1,000 pop. **Radios:** 271 per 1,000 pop. **Telephone lines:** 680,000. **Daily newspaper circ.:** 55.8 per 1,000 pop. **Internet:** 234,000 users.

Health: Life expectancy: 75.4 male; 80.5 female. **Births** (per 1,000 pop.): 23.7. **Deaths** (per 1,000 pop.): 2.6. **Natural inc.:** 2.11%. **Infant mortality** (per 1,000 live births): 18.9.

Education: Compulsory: ages 6-15. **Literacy:** 91.3%.

Major Intl. Organizations: UN (FAO, IBRD, ILO, IMF, IMO, WHO), AL.

Embassy: 3504 International Dr. NW 20008; 966-2664.

Websites: www.nic.gov.jo
www.jordanembassyus.org/new/index.shtml

From ancient times to 1922 the lands to the E of the Jordan River were culturally and politically united with the lands to the W. Arabs conquered the area in the 7th century; the Ottomans took control in the 16th. Britain's 1920 Palestine Mandate covered both sides of the Jordan. In 1921, Abdullah, son of the ruler of Hejaz in Arabia, was installed by Britain as emir of an autonomous Transjordan, covering two-thirds of Palestine. An independent kingdom was proclaimed, 1946.

During the 1948 Arab-Israeli war the West Bank and East Jerusalem were added to the kingdom, which changed its name to Jordan. All these territories were lost to Israel in the 1967 war, which swelled the number of Arab refugees on the East Bank.

Some 700,000 refugees entered Jordan following Iraq's invasion of Kuwait, Aug. 1990. Jordan was viewed as supporting Iraq during the 1990-1991 Persian Gulf crisis.

Jordan and Israel officially agreed, July 25, 1994, to end their state of war; a formal peace treaty was signed Oct. 26. Following a prolonged bout with cancer, King Hussein died Feb. 7, 1999; his eldest son and designated successor immediately assumed the throne as Abdullah II.

Kazakhstan
Republic of Kazakhstan

People: Population: 15,433,000. **Age distrib.** (%): <15: 26; 65+: 7.5. **Pop. density:** 15 per sq. mi. **Urban:** 56%. **Ethnic groups:** Kazakh 53%, Russian 30%, Ukrainian 4%, Uzbek 3%, German 2%, Uighur 1%. **Principal languages:** Kazakh, Russian (both official); Ukrainian, German, Uzbek. **Chief religions:** Muslim 47%, Russian Orthodox 44%.

Geography: Area: 1,049,155 sq. mi. (total); 1,030,815 sq. mi. (land). **Location:** In Central Asia. **Neighbors:** Russia on N; China on E; Kyrgyzstan, Uzbekistan, Turkmenistan on S; Caspian Sea on W. **Topography:** Extends from the lower reaches of Volga in Europe to the Altay Mts. on the Chinese border. **Capital:** Astana. **Cities** (urban aggr.): Alma-Ata 1,130,000; Astana 328,000.

Government: Type: Republic. **Head of state:** Pres. Nursultan A. Nazarbayev; b July 6, 1940; in office: Apr. 1990. **Head of gov.:** Prime Min. Daniyal Akhmetov; b June 15, 1954; in office: June 13, 2003. **Local divisions:** 14 oblystar, 1 city. **Defense budget** (2002): $226 mil. **Active troops:** 60,000.

Economy: Industries: mining and oil producer, agric. machinery, electric motors, constr. materials. **Chief crops:** wheat, cotton, wool. **Natural resources:** oil, nat. gas, coal, iron ore, mang., chrome ore, nickel, cobalt, copper, molybd., lead, zinc, bauxite, gold, uranium. **Crude oil reserves** (2002): 5.4 bil. bbls. **Arable land:** 12%. **Livestock** (2002): cattle: 4.19 mil.; chickens: 20 mil.; goats: 1.15 mil.; pigs: 1.10 mil.; sheep: 9.12 mil. **Fish catch** (2002): 31,071 metric tons. **Electricity prod.** (2001): 52.43 bil. kWh. **Labor force:** ind. 30%, agri. 20%, services 50%.

Finance: Monetary unit: Tenge (KZT) (Sept. 2003: 153.44 = $1 U.S.). **GDP** (2002 est.): $105 bil. **Per capita GDP:** $6,300. **Imports** (2001): $8.2 bil.; partners (2000): Russia 48.7%, Germany 6.6%, U.S. 5.5%. **Exports** (2001 est.): $10.5 bil.; partners (2000): Russia 19.5%, China 7.3%, Germany 6.2%. **Tourism** (1999): $363 mil. **Budget** (2001 est.): $5.1 bil. **Intl. reserves less gold:** $1.88 bil. **Gold:** 1.71 mil oz t. **Consumer prices:** 5.8%.

Transport: Railroad: Length: 8,451 mi. **Motor vehicles** (1999): 987,700 pass. cars, 257,400 comm. vehicles. **Civil aviation:** 917.8 mil pass.-mi.; 60 airports. **Chief ports:** Aqtau, Atyrau.

Communications: TV sets: 240 per 1,000 pop. **Radios:** 395 per 1,000 pop. **Telephone lines:** 1,939,600. **Internet:** 150,000 users.

Health: Life expectancy: 58.2 male; 69.1 female. **Births** (per 1,000 pop.): 18.4. **Deaths** (per 1,000 pop.): 10.8. **Natural inc.:** 0.76%. **Infant mortality** (per 1,000 live births): 58.7.

Education: Compulsory: ages 7-17. **Literacy** (2002): 98%.

Major Intl. Organizations: UN (IBRD, ILO, IMF, IMO, WHO), CIS, OSCE.

Embassy: 1401 16th St. NW 20036; 232-5488.

Websites: www.un.int/kazakhstan; www.president.kz

The region came under the Mongols' rule in the 13th century and gradually came under Russian rule, 1730-1853. It was admitted to the USSR as a constituent republic 1936. Kazakhstan declared independence Dec. 16, 1991. It became an independent state when the Soviet Union dissolved Dec. 26, 1991. The party chief, Nursultan Nazarbayev, was elected president unopposed. In legislative elections Mar. 7, 1994, criticized by international monitors, his party won a sweeping victory. Kazakhstan agreed, Feb. 14, to dismantle nuclear missiles and adhere to the 1968 Nuclear Nonproliferation Treaty; the U.S. pledged increased aid. Private land ownership was legalized Dec. 26, 1995.

Astana (formerly Akmola) was dedicated as the nation's new capital on June 9, 1998.

Pres. Nazarbayev won reelection to a 7-year term Jan. 10, 1999, after his leading opponent, former Prime Min. Akezhan Kazhegeldin, was barred on a technicality.

Kenya
Republic of Kenya

People: Population: 31,987,000. **Age distrib.** (%): <15: 41.1; 65+: 2.8. **Pop. density:** 146 per sq. mi. **Urban:** 34%. **Ethnic groups:** Kikuyu 22%, Luhya 14%, Luo 13%, Kalenjin 12%, Kamba 11%, Kisii 6%, Meru 6%. **Principal languages:** English, Swahili (both official); numerous indigenous languages. **Chief religions:** Protestant 45%, Roman Catholic 33%, indigenous beliefs 10%, Muslim 10%.

Geography: Area: 224,962 sq. mi. (total); 219,788 sq. mi. (land). **Location:** E Africa, on coast of Indian O. **Neighbors:** Uganda on W, Tanzania on S, Somalia on E, Ethiopia on N, Sudan on NW. **Topography:** The northern three-fifths of Kenya is arid. To the S, a low coastal area and a plateau varying from 3,000 to 10,000 ft. The Great Rift Valley enters the country N-S, flanked by high mountains. **Capital:** Nairobi. **Cities** (urban aggr.): Nairobi 2,343,000; Mombasa (1991 est.) 600,000.

Government: Type: Republic. **Head of state and gov.:** Pres. Mwai Kibaki; b Nov. 15, 1931; in office: Dec. 30, 2002. **Local divisions:** Nairobi and 7 provinces. **Defense budget** (2002): $268 mil. **Active troops:** 24,400.

Economy: Industries: light consumer goods, agric. proc., oil refining, cement, tourism. **Chief crops:** coffee, tea, corn, wheat, sugarcane, fruit. **Natural resources:** gold, limestone, soda ash, salt barites, rubies, fluorspar, garnets, wildlife, hydropower. **Arable land:** 7%. **Livestock** (2002): cattle: 12.50 mil.; chickens: 32 mil.; goats: 9 mil.; pigs: 315,000; sheep: 6.50 mil. **Fish catch** (2002): 165,160 metric tons. **Electricity prod.** (2001): 4.03 bil. kWh. **Labor force:** agri. 75%-80%.

Finance: Monetary unit: Shilling (KES) (Sept. 2003: 77.07 = $1 U.S.). **GDP** (2002 est.): $32 bil. **Per capita GDP:** $1,020. **Imports** (2001): $3.1 bil.; partners (2000): UK 12%, UAE 9.8%, Japan 6.5%, India 4.4%. **Exports** (2001 est.): $1.8 bil.; partners (2000): UK 13.5%, Tanzania 12.5%, Uganda 12.0%, Germany 5.5%. **Tourism:** $304 mil. **Budget** (2000 est.): $2.97 bil. **Intl. reserves less gold:** $786 mil. **Consumer prices:** 2.0%.

Transport: Railroad: Length: 1,726 mi. **Motor vehicles:** 244,800 pass. cars, 217,800 comm. vehicles. **Civil aviation:** 1.56 bil pass.-mi.; 19 airports. **Chief ports:** Mombasa, Kisumu, Lamu.

Communications: TV sets: 22 per 1,000 pop. **Radios:** 216 per 1,000 pop. **Telephone lines:** 328,100. **Daily newspaper circ.:** 9.4 per 1,000 pop. **Internet:** 500,000 users.

Health: Life expectancy: 45.0 male; 45.4 female. **Births** (per 1,000 pop.): 28.8. **Deaths** (per 1,000 pop.): 16.0. **Natural inc.:** 1.28%. **Infant mortality** (per 1,000 live births): 63.4.

Education: Compulsory: ages 6-13. **Literacy:** 85.1%.

Major Intl. Organizations: UN and all of its specialized agencies, the Commonwealth, AU.

Embassy: 2249 R St. NW 20008; 387-6101.

Website: www.statehouse.go.ke

Arab colonies exported spices and slaves from the Kenya coast as early as the 8th century. Britain obtained control in the 19th century. Kenya won independence Dec. 12, 1963, 4 years after the end of the violent Mau Mau uprising.

Kenya had steady growth in industry and agriculture under a modified private enterprise system, and enjoyed a relatively free political life. But stability was shaken in 1974-75, with opposition charges of corruption and oppression. Jomo Kenyatta, the country's leader since independence, died Aug. 22, 1978. He was succeeded by his vice president, Daniel arap Moi.

During the first half of the 1990s, Kenya suffered widespread unemployment and high inflation. Tribal clashes in the western provinces claimed thousands of lives and left tens of thousands homeless. Pres. Moi won a third term in Dec. 1992 elections, which were marred by violence and fraud. Clashes in the Mombasa region, Aug. 1997, left more than 40 people dead. Pres. Moi was re-elected Dec. 29, in an election again plagued by irregularities.

A truck bomb explosion at the U.S. embassy in Nairobi, Aug. 7, 1998, killed more than 200 people and injured about 5,000. The U.S. blamed the attack and a near-simultaneous embassy bombing in Tanzania on al-Qaeda. After a trial in New York City, 4 conspirators were convicted May 29, 2001. In Mombasa, Nov. 28, 2002, terrorists linked with al-Qaeda killed 12 Kenyans and 3 Israeli tourists at an Israeli-owned hotel and narrowly missed shooting down an Israeli-bound jet.

Constitutionally barred from seeking a 3rd term, Moi was succeeded Dec. 30, 2002, by Mwai Kibaki, the presidential candidate of the opposition Democratic Party.

Kiribati
Republic of Kiribati

People: Population: 98,500. **Age distrib.** (%): <15: 40.2; 65+: 3.2. **Pop. density:** 356 per sq. mi. **Urban:** 39%. **Ethnic groups:** Micronesian. **Principal languages:** English (official), I-Kiribati. **Chief religions:** Roman Catholic 52%, Protestant 40%.

Geography: Area (total): 313 sq. mi. **Location:** 33 Micronesian islands (the Gilbert, Line, and Phoenix groups) in the mid-Pacific scattered in a 2-mil sq. mi. chain around the point where the International Date Line formerly cut the Equator. In 1997 the Date Line was moved to follow Kiribati's E border. **Neighbors:** Nearest are Nauru to SW, Tuvalu and Tokelau Isls. to S. **Topography:** Except

Banaba (Ocean) Isl., all are low-lying, with soil of coral sand and rock fragments, subject to erratic rainfall. **Capital:** South Tarawa: 32,000.

Government: Type: Republic. **Head of state and gov.:** Anote Tong; in office: July 10, 2003. Pres. Teburoro Tito; b Aug. 25, 1953; in office: Oct. 1, 1994. **Local divisions:** 3 units, 6 districts.

Economy: Industries: fishing, handicrafts. **Chief crops:** copra, taro, breadfruit, sweet potatoes. **Natural resources:** phosphates. **Livestock** (2002): 400,000; pigs: 12,000; sheep: 189,000. **Fish catch** (2002): 32,393 metric tons. **Electricity prod.** (2001): 0.01 bil. kWh.

Finance: Monetary unit: Australian Dollar (Sept. 2003: 1.56 = $1 U.S.). **GDP** (2001 est.): $79 mil. **Per capita GDP:** $840. **Imports** (1999): $44 mil.; partners (2000): Australia, Japan, Fiji, Poland. **Exports** (1998): $6 mil.; partners (2000): Japan, Bangladesh, US, Australia. **Tourism** (1999): $2 mil. **Budget** (2000 est.): $37.2 mil.

Transport: Civil aviation (1998): 6.8 mil pass.-mi.; 4 airports. **Chief port:** Tarawa.

Communications: TV sets: 23 per 1,000 pop. **Radios:** 341 per 1,000 pop. **Telephone lines:** 3,600. **Internet:** 2,000 users.

Health: Life expectancy: 58.0 male; 64.0 female. **Births** (per 1,000 pop.): 31.2. **Deaths** (per 1,000 pop.): 8.6. **Natural inc.:** 2.26%. **Infant mortality** (per 1,000 live births): 51.3.

Education: Compulsory: ages 6-15. **Literacy** (2002): 90%

Major Intl. Organizations: UN (IBRD, IMF, WHO), the Commonwealth.

Website: www.tskl.net.ki/Kiribati

A British protectorate since 1892, the Gilbert and Ellice Islands colony was completed with the inclusion of the Phoenix Islands, 1937. Tarawa Atoll was the scene of some of the bloodiest fighting in the Pacific during World War II.

Self-rule was granted 1971; the Ellice Islands separated from the colony 1975 and became independent Tuvalu, 1978. Kiribati (pronounced *Kiribass*) independence was attained July 12, 1979. Under a treaty of friendship the U.S. relinquished its claims to several Line and Phoenix islands, including Christmas (Kiritimati), Canton, and Enderbury. Kiribati was admitted to the UN Sept. 14, 1999.

Korea, North
Democratic People's Republic of Korea

People: Population: 22,664,000. **Age distrib.** (%): <15: 25.4; 65+: 7.2. **Pop. density:** 488 per sq. mi. **Urban:** 61%. **Ethnic group:** Korean. **Principal languages:** Korean (official). **Chief religions:** Activities almost non-existent; traditionally Buddhist, Confucianist, Chondogyo.

Geography: Area: 46,541 sq. mi. (total); 46,491 sq. mi. (land). **Location:** In northern E Asia. **Neighbors:** China and Russia on N, South Korea on S. **Topography:** Mountains and hills cover nearly all the country, with narrow valleys and small plains in between. The N and the E coasts are the most rugged areas. **Capital:** Pyongyang. **Cities (urban aggr.):** Pyongyang 3,197,000; Nampo 1,046,000.

Government: Type: Communist state. **Leader:** Kim Jong Il; b Feb. 16, 1942; officially assumed post Oct. 8, 1997. **Local divisions:** 9 provinces, 3 special cities. **Defense budget** (2002): $1.04 bil. **Active troops:** 1,082,000.

Economy: Industries: armaments, machine building, electric power, chemicals, mining, metallurgy, textiles. **Chief crops:** rice, corn, potatoes, soybeans. **Natural resources:** coal, lead, tungsten, zinc, graphite, magnesite, iron ore, copper, gold, pyrites, salt, fluorspar, hydropower. **Arable land:** 14%. **Livestock** (2002): cattle: 570,000; chickens: 16.89 mil.; goats: 2.57 mil.; pigs: 3.14 mil.; sheep: 600. **Fish catch** (2002 est.): 263,700 metric tons. **Electricity prod.** (2001): 30.01 bil. kWh. **Labor force:** agri. 36%, nonagricultural 64%.

Finance: Monetary unit: Won (KPW) (Sept. 2003: 2.20 = $1 U.S.). **GDP** (2002 est.): $22 bil. **Per capita GDP:** $1,000. **Imports** (2001): $1.874 bil.; partners (2000): China 26.7%, South Korea 16.2%, Japan 12.3%. **Exports** (2001 est.): $826 mil.; partners (2000): Japan 36.3%, South Korea 21.5%, China 5.2%. **Budget** NA.

Transport: Railroad: Length: 3,107 mi. **Civil Aviation:** 110.6 mil. pass.-mi.; 34 airports. **Chief ports:** Chongjin, Hamhung, Nampo.

Communications: TV sets: 55 per 1,000 pop. **Radios:** 146 per 1,000 pop. **Telephone lines** (1998): 23,257,000. **Daily newspaper circ.:** 199 per 1,000 pop.

Health: Life expectancy: 68.1 male; 73.6 female. **Births** (per 1,000 pop.): 17.6. **Deaths** (per 1,000 pop.): 6.9. **Natural inc.:** 1.07%. **Infant mortality** (per 1,000 live births): 25.7.

Labor force: agri. 36%, other 64%.

Education: Compulsory: ages 6-17. **Literacy:** 99%

Major Intl. Organizations: UN (FAO, IMO, WHO).

The Democratic People's Republic of Korea was founded May 1, 1948, in the zone occupied by Russian troops after World War II. Its armies tried to conquer the south, 1950. After 3 years of fighting, with Chinese and U.S. intervention, a cease-fire was proclaimed. For the next four decades, a hardline Communist regime headed by Kim Il Sung kept tight control over the nation's political, economic, and cultural life. The nation used its abundant mineral and hydroelectric resources to develop its military strength and heavy industry.

In Mar. 1993, North Korea became the first nation to formally withdraw from the Nuclear Nonproliferation Treaty, the international pact designed to limit the spread of nuclear weapons. The nation suspended its withdrawal in June in reaction to threats of UN economic sanctions, but was widely believed to be developing nuclear weapons. The U.S. and North Korea reached an interim agreement, Aug. 13, 1994, intended to resolve the nuclear issue, and further negotiations followed.

Kim Il Sung died July 8, 1994. He was succeeded by his son, Kim Jong Il. North Korea at this time suffered from defections by high officials, a deteriorating economy, and severe food shortages in the late 1990s.

On Sept. 17, 1999, the U.S. eased travel and trade restrictions on North Korea after Pyongyang agreed to suspend long-range missile testing. A first-ever summit conference in Pyongyang between North and South Korean leaders, June 13-15, 2000, marked an unexpected improvement in relations between the 2 Koreas, and brought an end to many U.S. sanctions. In Sept. 2002, Japanese Prime Min. Junichiro Koizumi became the 1st Japanese prime minister to visit North Korea; there, in a landmark summit, North Korea agreed to begin normalizing relations, and admitted for the 1st time that its agents had helped to kidnap 11 Japanese in the late 1970s.

Relations with the U.S. deteriorated after Pres. George Bush, in a speech Jan. 31, 2002, included North Korea with Iraq and Iran as part of an "axis of evil." The U.S. insisted that North Korea dismantle its nuclear weapons program, while North Korea demanded a nonaggression treaty and economic aid from the U.S. Six-nation talks sponsored by China, Aug. 27-29, 2003, failed to resolve the dispute. The North Korean legislature Sept. 3 approved further development of a nuclear deterrent.

Korea, South
Republic of Korea

People: Population: 47,700,000. **Age distrib.** (%): <15: 21.4; 65+: 7.6. **Pop. density:** 1,258 per sq. mi. **Urban:** 83%. **Ethnic group:** Korean. **Principal languages:** Korean (official). **Chief religions:** Christian 49%, Buddhist 47%, Confucianist 3%.

Geography: Area: 38,023 sq. mi. (total); 37,911 sq. mi. (land). **Location:** In northern E Asia. **Neighbors:** North Korea on N. **Topography:** The country is mountainous, with a rugged east coast. The western and southern coasts are deeply indented, with many islands and harbors. **Capital:** Seoul. **Cities (urban aggr.):** Seoul 9,862,000; Pusan 3,830,000; Inch'on 2,884,000; Taegu 2,675,000.

Government: Type: Republic. **Head of state:** Pres. Roh Moo Hyun; b Aug. 6, 1946; in office: Feb. 25, 2003. **Head of gov.:** Prime Min. Goh Kun; b 1938; in office: Feb. 26, 2003. **Head of gov.:** Prime Min. Kim Suk Soo; b 1932; in office: Sept. 10, 2002 (acting). **Local divisions:** 9 provinces, 6 special cities. **Defense budget** (2002): $14.1 bil. **Active troops:** 686,000.

Economy: Industries: electronics, autos, chemicals, shipbuilding, steel, textiles, clothing, footwear, food proc. **Chief crops:** rice, root crops, barley, vegetables, fruit. **Natural resources:** coal, tungsten, graphite, molybd., lead, hydropower potential. **Arable land:** 19%. **Livestock** (2002): cattle: 1.95 mil.; chickens: 107 mil.; goats: 430,000; pigs: 8.81 mil. **Fish catch** (2002): 2,282,486 metric tons. **Electricity prod.** (2001): 290.67 bil. kWh. **Labor force:** services 69%, ind. 21.5%, agri. 9.5%.

Finance: Monetary unit: Won (KRW) (Sept. 2003: 1,174.90 = $1 U.S.). **GDP** (2002 est.): $931 bil. **Per capita GDP:** $19,400. **Imports** (2002): $146.6 bil.; partners (2001): Japan 18.9%, U.S. 15.9%, China 9.4%, Saudi Arabia 5.7%. **Exports** (2002 est.): $159.2 bil.; partners (2001): U.S. 20.7%, China 12.1%, Japan 11.0%, Hong Kong 6.3%. **Tourism:** $6.61 bil. **Budget** (2000): $95.7 bil. **Intl. reserves less gold:** $89.26 bil. **Gold:** 440,000 oz t. **Consumer prices:** 2.8%.

Transport: Railroad: Length: 1,941 mi. **Motor vehicles** (1999): 7.84 mil pass. cars, 3.29 mil comm. vehicles. **Civil aviation:** 34.87 bil pass.-mi.; 69 airports. **Chief ports:** Pusan, Inch'on.

Communications: TV sets: 364 per 1,000 pop. **Radios:** 1,039 per 1,000 pop. **Telephone lines:** 26,270,000. **Daily newspaper circ.:** 393 per 1,000 pop. **Internet:** 23,527,000 users

Health: Life expectancy: 71.7 male; 79.3 female. **Births** (per 1,000 pop.): 12.6. **Deaths** (per 1,000 pop.): 6.0. **Natural inc.:** 0.66%. **Infant mortality** (per 1,000 live births): 7.3.

Education: Free, compulsory: ages 6-12. **Literacy:** 98%.

Major Intl. Organizations: UN (FAO, IBRD, ILO, IMF, IMO, WHO, WTrO), APEC, OECD.

Embassy: 2450 Massachusetts Ave. NW 20008; 939-5600.

Websites: www.korea.net; www.cwd.go.kr

Korea, once called the Hermit Kingdom, has a recorded history since the 1st century BC. It was united in a kingdom under the Silla Dynasty, AD 668. It was at times associated with the Chinese empire; the treaty that concluded the Sino-Japanese war of 1894-95 recognized Korea's complete independence. In 1910 Japan forcibly annexed Korea as Chosun.

At the Potsdam conference, July 1945, the 38th parallel was designated as the line dividing the Soviet and the American occupation. Russian troops entered Korea Aug. 10, 1945; U.S. troops entered Sept. 8, 1945. The Soviet military organized socialists and Communists and blocked efforts to let the Koreans unite their country.

The South Koreans formed the Republic of Korea in May 1948 with Seoul as the capital. Dr. Syngman Rhee was chosen president. A separate, Communist regime was formed in the N; its army attacked the S in June 1950, initiating the Korean War. UN troops, under U.S. command, supported the S in the war, which ended in an armistice (July 1953) leaving Korea divided by a "no-man's land" along the 38th parallel.

Rhee's authoritarian rule became increasingly unpopular, and a movement spearheaded by college students forced his resignation Apr. 26, 1960. In an army coup May 16, 1961, Gen. Park Chung Hee became chairman of a ruling junta. He was elected president, 1963; a 1972 referendum allowed him to be reelected for an unlimited series of 6-year terms. Park was assassinated by the chief of the Korean CIA, Oct. 26, 1979. In May 1980, Gen. Chun Doo Hwan, head of military intelligence, reinstated full martial law and ordered the brutal suppression of pro-democracy demonstrations in Kwangju.

In July 1972 South and North Korea agreed on a common goal of reunifying the 2 nations by peaceful means. But there was no sign of a thaw in relations between the two regimes until 1985, when they agreed to discuss economic issues.

On June 10, 1987, middle-class office workers, shopkeepers, and business executives joined with students in antigovernment protests in Seoul calling for democratic reforms. Following weeks of rioting and violence, Chun, July 1, agreed to permit election of the next president by direct popular vote and other reforms. In Dec., Roh Tae Woo was elected president. In 1990, the nation's 3 largest political parties merged; some 100,000 students protested the merger as undemocratic.

Kim Young Sam took office in 1993 as the first civilian president since 1961. Convicted of mutiny, treason, and corruption, Chun was sentenced to death by a Seoul court, Aug. 26, 1996, for his role in the 1979 coup and 1980 Kwangju massacre; Roh received a 22-1/2 year prison sentence. On Dec. 16, Chun's term was reduced to life in prison, and Roh's to 17 years.

The collapse in Jan. 1997 of the Hanbo steel firm triggered a new round of corruption scandals. With currency and stock values plummeting, the nation averted default by agreeing, Dec. 4, on a $57 billion bailout from the IMF. Kim Dae Jung, a longtime dissident, won the presidential election Dec. 18. Chun and Roh were released and pardoned Dec. 22, 1997.

At an unprecedented summit meeting in Pyongyang, June 13-15, 2000, Pres. Kim Dae Jung and North Korean leader Kim Jong Il agreed to work for reconciliation and eventual reunification of their 2 countries. On Oct. 13, 2000, Kim Dae Jung was named the winner of the 2000 Nobel Peace Prize. Embarrassed by a naval clash with North Korea June 29, 2002, and by corruption probes targeting his family, he revamped his cabinet July 11. Roh Moo Hyun, candidate of the ruling Millennium Democratic Party, won a presidential election Dec. 19. The legislature, controlled by opposition parties, rejected 2 of his nominees for prime min., July 31 and Aug. 28.

A subway fire in Taegu, Feb. 18, 2003, killed 198 people; the arsonist was given a life term, and 8 subway officials charged with negligence also received prison sentences. Typhoon Maemi battered Pusan and other areas Sept. 12-13, 2003, leaving more than 90 people dead and causing at least $1 billion in damage.

Kuwait
State of Kuwait

People: Population: 2,521,000. **Age distrib.** (%): <15: 28.3; 65+: 2.5. **Pop. density:** 366 per sq. mi. **Urban:** 96%. **Ethnic groups:** Arab 80%, South Asian 9%, Iranian 4%. **Principal languages:** Arabic (official), English. **Chief religion:** Muslim 85% (official; Sunni 70%, Shi'a 30%).

Geography: Area (total): 6,880 sq. mi. **Location:** In Middle East, at N end of Persian Gulf. **Neighbors:** Iraq on N, Saudi Arabia on S. **Topography:** The country is flat, very dry, and extremely hot. **Capital:** Kuwait City: 888,000.

Government: Type: Constitutional monarchy. **Head of state:** Emir Sheikh Jabir al-Ahmad al-Jabir as-Sabah; b 1928; in office: Jan. 1, 1978. **Head of gov.:** Prime Min. Sheikh Sabah al-Ahmad as-Sabah; b 1929; in office: July 13, 2003. **Local divisions:** 5 governorates. **Defense budget:** (2002) $3.9 bil. **Active troops:** 15,500.

Economy: Industries: oil, petrochems., desalination, food proc., constr. materials. **Natural resources:** oil, fish, shrimp, nat. gas. **Crude oil reserves** (2002): 96.5 bil. bbls. **Livestock** (2002): cattle: 15,000; chickens: 32.46 mil.; goats: 130,000; sheep: 630,000. **Fish catch** (2002): 6,041 metric tons. **Electricity prod.** (2001): 31.49 bil. kWh. **Labor force:** 50% gov't. and social services; 40% services; 10% industry and agric.

Finance: Monetary unit: Dinar (KWD) (Sept. 2003: 0.30 = $1 U.S.). **GDP** (2002 est.): $34.2 bil. **Per capita GDP:** $15,000. **Imports** (2001): $7.4 bil.; partners (2000): U.S. 12%, Japan 8%, UK 8%, Germany 7%. **Exports** (2001 est.): $16.2 bil.; partners (2000): Japan 23%, U.S. 14%, South Korea 13%, Singapore 7%. **Tourism** (1999): $243 mil. **Budget** (2003): $17.5 bil. **Intl. reserves less gold:** $6.77 bil. **Gold:** 2.54 mil oz t. **Consumer prices:** 1.4%.

Transport: Motor vehicles (1999): 624,000 pass. cars, 130,000 comm. vehicles. **Civil aviation:** 3.83 bil pass.-mi.; 3 airports. **Chief port:** Mina al-Ahmadi.

Communications: TV sets: 480 per 1,000 pop. **Radios:** 633 per 1,000 pop. **Telephone lines:** 472,400. **Daily newspaper circ.:** 374 per 1,000 pop. **Internet:** 200,000 users.

Health: Life expectancy: 75.7 male; 77.6 female. **Births** (per 1,000 pop.): 21.8. **Deaths** (per 1,000 pop.): 2.5. **Natural inc.:** 1.94%. **Infant mortality** (per 1,000 live births): 10.6.

Education: Compulsory: ages 6-14. **Literacy:** 83.5%.

Major Intl. Organizations: UN (FAO, IBRD, ILO, IMF, IMO, WHO, WTrO), AL, OPEC.

Embassy: 2940 Tilden St. NW 20008; 966-0702.

Website: www.kuwait-info.org

Kuwait is ruled by the Sabah dynasty, founded 1759. Britain ran foreign relations and defense from 1899 until independence in 1961. The majority of the population is non-Kuwaiti, with many Palestinians, and cannot vote.

Oil is the fiscal mainstay, providing most of Kuwait's income. Oil pays for free medical care, education, and social security. There are no taxes, except customs duties.

Kuwait was attacked and overrun by Iraqi forces Aug. 2, 1990. The emir and senior members of the ruling family fled to Saudi Arabia to establish a government in exile. On Aug. 28, Iraq announced that Kuwait was its 19th province. Following several weeks of aerial attacks on Iraq and Iraqi forces in Kuwait, a U.S.-led coalition began a ground attack Feb. 23, 1991. By Feb. 27, Iraqi forces were routed and Kuwait liberated.

Former U.S. Pres. George Bush visited Kuwait, Apr. 14-16, 1993. Kuwaiti authorities arrested 14 Iraqis and Kuwaitis for allegedly plotting to assassinate him during his visit; 13 were convicted and sentenced to prison or death, June 4, 1994. The UN Security Council ruled, Sept. 27, 2000, that Iraq had to pay the Kuwait Petroleum Corp. $15.9 billion for damage to Kuwaiti oil fields during the Persian Gulf War. Iraq recognized Kuwait's territorial integrity Mar. 28, 2002. N Kuwait was used by U.S. and British troops as a staging area prior to the Mar. 2003 invasion of Iraq.

Kyrgyzstan
Kyrgyz Republic

People: Population: 5,138,000. **Age distrib.** (%): <15: 34.4; 65+: 6.2. **Pop. density:** 67 per sq. mi. **Urban:** 34%. **Ethnic groups:** Kyrgyz 52%, Russian 18%, Uzbek 13%, Ukrainian 3%, German 2%. **Principal languages:** Kyrgyz, Russian (both official); Uzbek. **Chief religions:** Muslim 75%, Russian Orthodox 20%.

Geography: Area: 76,641 sq. mi. (total); 73,861 sq. mi. (land). **Location:** In Central Asia. **Neighbors:** Kazakhstan on N, China on E, Uzbekistan on W, Tajikistan on S. **Topography:** Kyrgyzstan is a landlocked country nearly covered by Tien Shan and Pamir Mts.; avg. elevation 9,020 ft. A large lake, Issyk-Kul, in NE is 1 mi. above sea level. **Capital:** Bishkek: 736,000.

Government: Type: Republic. **Head of state:** Pres. Askar Akayev; b Nov. 10, 1944; in office: Oct. 28, 1990. **Head of gov.:** Prime Min. Nikolay Tanayev; b Nov. 5, 1945; in office: May 30, 2002. **Local divisions:** 6 oblasts, 1 city. **Defense budget** (2002): $23.5 mil. **Active troops:** 10,900.

Economy: Industries: small machinery, textiles, food proc., cement, shoes, timber, refrigerators, furniture, electric motors. **Chief crops:** tobacco, cotton, potatoes, vegetables, grapes, fruits & berries. **Natural resources:** hydropower, gold, rare earth metals, coal, oil, nat. gas, nepheline, mercury, bismuth, lead, zinc. **Crude oil reserves** (2002): 40 mil. bbls. **Arable land:** 7%. **Livestock** (2002): cattle: 979,000; chickens: 3.40 mil.; goats: 645,745; pigs: 81,000; sheep: 3.13 mil. **Fish catch** (2002): 201 metric tons. **Electricity prod.** (2001): 13.45 bil. kWh. **Labor force:** agri. 55%, ind. 15%, services 30%.

Finance: Monetary unit: Som (KGS) (Sept. 2003: 43.24 = $1 U.S.). **GDP** (2002 est.): $13.5 bil. **Per capita GDP:** $2,800. **Imports** (2001): $420 mil.; partners (2000): Russia 23.9%, Uzbekistan 13.5%, Kazakhstan 10.3%, U.S. 9.7%. **Exports** (2001 est.): $475 mil.; partners (2000): Germany 28.7%, Uzbekistan 17.7%, Russia 12.9%, China 8.7%. **Tourism** (1998): $8 mil. **Budget** (1999 est.): $238.7 mil. **Intl. reserves less gold:** $212 mil. **Gold:** 80,000 oz t. **Consumer prices:** 2.1%.

Transport: Railroad: Length: 230 mi. **Motor vehicles:** 189,800 pass. cars. **Civil aviation:** 330.6 mil pass.-mi.; 18 airports. **Chief ports:** Ysyk-Kol.

Communications: TV sets: 49 per 1,000 pop. **Radios:** 113 per 1,000 pop. **Telephone lines:** 394,800. **Daily newspaper circ.:** 11 per 1,000 pop. **Internet:** 152,000 users.

Health: Life expectancy: 59.5 male; 68.0 female. **Births** (per 1,000 pop.): 26.1. **Deaths** (per 1,000 pop.): 9.1. **Natural inc.:** 1.70%. **Infant mortality** (per 1,000 live births): 75.3.

Education: Compulsory: ages 7-16. **Literacy** (1993): 97%.

Major Intl. Organizations: UN (FAO, IBRD, ILO, IMF, WHO), CIS, OSCE.

Embassy: 1732 Wisconsin Ave. NW, 20007; 338-5141.

Website: www.kyrgyzstan.org

The region was inhabited around the 13th century by the Kyrgyz. It was annexed to Russia 1864. After 1917, it was nominally a Kara-Kyrgyz autonomous area, which was reorganized 1926, and made a constituent republic of the USSR in 1936. Kyrgyzstan declared independence Aug. 31, 1991. It became an independent

state when the USSR disbanded Dec. 26, 1991. A constitution was adopted May 5, 1993.

Reelected Dec. 24, 1995, Pres. Askar Akayev gained approval by referendum of a constitutional amendment expanding his presidential powers, Feb. 10, 1996. Amendments restricting the powers of parliament and allowing private ownership of land were ratified by referendum Oct. 17, 1998. Akayev won a 3d 5-year term in the Oct. 29, 2000, election. The U.S. military presence in Kyrgyzstan has been expanding since Dec. 2001.

Laos
Lao People's Democratic Republic

People: Population: 5,657,000. **Age distrib.** (%): <15: 42.5; 65+: 3.3. **Pop. density:** 63 per sq. mi. **Urban:** 20%. **Ethnic groups:** Lao Loum 68%, Lao Theung 22%, Lao Soung (incl. Hmong and Yao) 9%. **Principal languages:** Lao (official), French, English, and various ethnic languages. **Chief religions:** Buddhist 60%, animist and other 40%.

Geography: Area: 91,429 sq. mi. (total); 89,112 sq. mi. (land). **Location:** In Indochina Peninsula in SE Asia. **Neighbors:** Myanmar and China on N, Vietnam on E, Cambodia on S, Thailand on W. **Topography:** Landlocked, dominated by jungle. High mountains along eastern border are the source of the E-W rivers slicing across the country to the Mekong R., which defines most of the western border. **Capital:** Vientiane 663,000.

Government: Type: Communist. **Head of state:** Pres. Khamtai Siphandon; b Feb. 8, 1924; in office: Feb. 24, 1998. **Head of gov.:** Prime Min. Boungnang Vorachith; b Aug. 15, 1937; in office: Mar. 27, 2001. **Local divisions:** 16 provinces, 1 municipality, 1 special zone. **Defense budget** (2001): $15.8 mil. **Active troops:** 29,100.

Economy: Industries: mining, timber, electric power, agric. proc., constr., garments, tourism. **Chief crops:** sweet potatoes, vegetables, corn, coffee, sugarcane. **Natural resources:** timber, hydropower, gypsum, tin, gold, gemstones. **Arable land:** 3%. **Livestock** (2002): cattle: 1.15 mil.; chickens: 15 mil.; goats: 240,000; pigs: 1.43 mil. **Fish catch** (2002 est.): 80,000 metric tons. **Electricity prod.** (2001): 1.32 bil. kWh. **Labor force:** agri. 80%.

Finance: Monetary unit: Kip (LAK) (Sept. 2003: 7,872.60 = $1 U.S.). **GDP** (2002 est.): $9.9 bil. **Per capita GDP:** $1,700. **Imports** (2000): $540 mil.; partners (2000): Thailand 52%, Singapore 3.9%, Japan 1.6%, Hong Kong 1.5%. **Exports** (2001 est.): $325 mil.; partners (2000): Thailand 20%, France 7.5%, Germany 5.9%, UK 4.1%. **Tourism** (2001): $114 mil. **Budget** (1999 est.): $462 mil. **Intl. reserves less gold:** $141 mil. **Gold:** 17,100 oz t. **Consumer prices:** 10.6%.

Transport: Motor vehicles: 9,000 pass. cars, 9,000 comm. vehicles. **Civil aviation:** 48.5 mil pass.-mi.; 9 airports.

Communications: TV sets: 10 per 1,000 pop. **Radios:** 145 per 1,000 pop. **Telephone lines:** 61,900. **Daily newspaper circ.:** 3.7 per 1,000 pop. **Internet:** 15,000 users.

Health: Life expectancy: 52.3 male; 56.3 female. **Births** (per 1,000 pop.): 36.9. **Deaths** (per 1,000 pop.): 12.4. **Natural inc.:** 2.45%. **Infant mortality** (per 1,000 live births): 88.9.

Education: Compulsory: ages 6-10. **Literacy:** 52.8%.

Major Intl. Organizations: UN (FAO, IBRD, ILO, IMF, WHO), ASEAN.

Embassy: 2222 S St. NW 20008; 332-6416.

Website: www.laoembassy.com/discover/index.htm

Laos became a French protectorate in 1893, but regained independence as a constitutional monarchy July 19, 1949.

Conflicts among neutralist, Communist, and conservative factions created a chaotic political situation. Armed conflict increased after 1960.

The 3 factions formed a coalition government in June 1962, with neutralist Prince Souvanna Phouma as premier. A 14-nation conference in Geneva signed agreements, 1962, guaranteeing neutrality and independence. By 1964 the Pathet Lao had withdrawn from the coalition, and, with aid from North Vietnamese troops, renewed sporadic attacks. U.S. planes bombed the Ho Chi Minh trail, supply line from North Vietnam to Communist forces in Laos and South Vietnam.

In 1970 the U.S. stepped up air support and military aid. After Pathet Lao military gains, Souvanna Phouma in May 1975 ordered government troops to cease fighting; the Pathet Lao took control. The Lao People's Democratic Republic was proclaimed Dec. 3, 1975.

From the mid-1970s through the 1980s, the Laotian government relied on Vietnam for military and financial aid. Since easing its foreign investment laws in 1988, Laos has attracted more than $5 billion from Thailand, the U.S., and other nations. Laos was admitted to ASEAN on July 23, 1997.

Latvia
Republic of Latvia

People: Population: 2,307,000. **Age distrib.** (%): <15: 15.8; 65+: 15.6. **Pop. density:** 93 per sq. mi. **Urban:** 60%. **Ethnic groups:** Latvian 58%, Russian 30%, Belarusian 4%, Ukrainian 3%, Polish 2%, Lithuanian 1%. **Principal languages:** Latvian (official), Russian, Belorusian, Ukrainian, Polish. **Chief religions:** Lutheran, Roman Catholic, Russian Orthodox.

Geography: Area: 24,938 sq. mi. (total); 24,552 sq. mi. (land). **Location:** E Europe, on the Baltic Sea. **Neighbors:** Estonia on N, Lithuania and Belarus on S, Russia on E. **Topography:** Latvia is a lowland with numerous lakes, marshes and peat bogs. Principal river, W. Dvina (Daugava), rises in Russia. There are glacial hills in E. **Capital:** Riga 756,000.

Government: Type: Republic. **Head of state:** Pres. Vaira Vike-Freiberga; b Dec. 1, 1937; in office: July 8, 1999. **Head of gov.:** Prime Min. Einars Repse; Dec. 9, 1961; in office: Nov. 7, 2002. **Local divisions:** 26 counties, 7 municipalities. **Defense budget** (2002): $116 mil. **Active troops:** 5,500.

Economy: Industries: vehicles, railroad cars, synthetics, agric. machinery, fertilizers, washing machines. **Chief crops:** grain, sugar beets, potatoes, other vegetables. **Natural resources:** peat, limestone, dolomite, hydropower, wood, amber. **Arable land:** 27%. **Livestock** (2002): cattle: 385,000; chickens: 3.62 mil.; goats: 11,500; pigs: 429,000; sheep: 29,000. **Fish catch** (2002): 125,896 metric tons. **Electricity prod.** (2001): 4.37 bil. kWh. **Labor force:** agri. 15%, ind. 25%, services 60%.

Finance: Monetary unit: Lats (LVL) (Sept. 2003: 0.58 = $1 U.S.). **GDP** (2002 est.): $20 bil. **Per capita GDP:** $8,300. **Imports** (2002): $3.9 bil.; partners (2001 est.): Germany 17%, Russia 9%, Lithuania 8%, Finland 8%. **Exports** (2002) $2.3 bil.; partners (2001 est.): Germany 17%, UK 16%, Sweden 10%, Lithuania 8%. **Tourism:** $131 mil. **Budget** (2002 est.): $2.6 bil. **Intl. reserves less gold:** $913 mil. **Gold:** 250,000 mil. oz t. **Consumer prices:** 2.0%.

Transport: Railroad: Length: 1,499 mi. **Motor vehicles:** 556,800 pass. cars, 108,600 comm. vehicles. **Civil aviation:** 82.0 mil pass.-mi.; 22 airports. **Chief port:** Riga.

Communications: TV sets: 757 per 1,000 pop. **Radios:** 701 per 1,000 pop. **Telephone lines:** 701,200. **Daily newspaper circ.:** 247 per 1,000 pop. **Internet:** 310,000 users.

Health: Life expectancy: 63.5 male; 75.5 female. **Births** (per 1,000 pop.): 8.6. **Deaths** (per 1,000 pop.): 14.7. **Natural inc.:** -0.62%. **Infant mortality** (per 1,000 live births): 14.6.

Education: Compulsory: ages 7-15. **Literacy:** 99.8%.

Major Intl. Organizations: UN (FAO, IBRD, ILO, IMF, IMO, WHO), OSCE.

Embassy: 4325 17th St. NW 20011; 726-8213.

Website: www.latvia-usa.org

Prior to 1918, Latvia was occupied by the Russians and Germans. It was an independent republic, 1918-39. The Aug. 1939 Soviet-German agreement assigned Latvia to the Soviet sphere of influence. It was officially accepted as part of the USSR on Aug. 5, 1940. It was overrun by the German army in 1941, but retaken in 1945.

During an abortive Soviet coup, Latvia declared independence, Aug. 21, 1991. The Soviet Union recognized Latvia's independence in Sept. 1991. The last Russian troops in Latvia withdrew by Aug. 31, 1994. Responding to international pressure, Latvian voters on Oct. 3, 1998, eased citizenship laws that had discriminated against some 500,000 ethnic Russians. On June 17, 1999, the legislature elected Vaira Vike-Freiberga as Latvia's 1st woman president. In a referendum Sept. 20, 2003, voters endorsed Latvia's entry into the EU in May 2004.

Lebanon
Lebanese Republic

People: Population: 3,653,000. **Age distrib.** (%): <15: 27.3; 65+: 6.8. **Pop. density:** 925 per sq. mi. **Urban:** 90%. **Ethnic groups:** Arab 95%, Armenian 4%. **Principal languages:** Arabic (official), French, English, Armenian. **Chief religions:** Muslim 70%, Christian 30%.

Geography: Area: 4,015 sq. mi. (total); 3,950 sq. mi. (land). **Location:** In Middle East, on E end of Mediterranean Sea. **Neighbors:** Syria on E, Israel on S. **Topography:** There is a narrow coastal strip, and 2 mountain ranges running N-S enclosing the fertile Beqaa Valley. The Litani R. runs S through the valley, turning W to empty into the Mediterranean. **Capital:** Beirut: 2,115,000.

Government: Type: Republic. **Head of state:** Pres. Emile Lahoud; b 1936; in office: Nov. 24, 1998. **Head of gov.:** Prime Min. Rafiq al-Hariri; b 1944; in office: Oct. 23, 2000. **Local divisions:** 5 governorates. **Defense budget** (2002): $536 mil. **Active troops:** 71,830.

Economy: Industries: banking, food proc., jewelry, cement, textiles, mineral & chemical products. **Chief crops:** citrus, grapes, tomatoes, apples, vegetables, potatoes, olives, tobacco. **Natural resources:** limestone, iron ore, salt, water. **Arable land:** 21%. **Livestock** (2002): cattle: 74,000; chickens: 32.50 mil.; goats: 450,000; pigs: 64,000; sheep: 385,000. **Fish catch** (2002): 3,970 metric tons. **Electricity prod.** (2001): 6.73 bil. kWh. **Labor force:** 62% services; 31% industry; 7% agric.

Finance: Monetary unit: Pound (LBP) (Sept. 2003: 1552.70 = $1 U.S.). **GDP** (2002 est.): $19.3 bil. **Per capita GDP:** $5,400. **Imports** (2001): $6.6 bil.; partners (2000): Italy 11%, France 8%, Germany 8%, U.S. 7%. **Exports** (2001 est.): $700 mil.; partners (2000): Saudi Arabia 11%, UAE 11%, Switzerland 7%, U.S. 7%. **Tourism:** $742 mil. **Budget** (2001 est.): $5.9 bil. **Intl. reserves less gold:** $5.33 bil. **Gold:** 9.22 mil oz t.

Transport: Railroad: Length: 248 mi. **Motor vehicles** (1998): 1.34 mil pass. cars, 95,400 comm. vehicles. **Civil aviation:** 800.3 mil pass.-mi.; 5 airports. **Chief ports:** Beirut, Tripoli, Sidon.

Communications: TV sets: 355 per 1,000 pop. **Radios:** 907 per 1,000 pop. **Telephone lines:** 678,800. **Newspaper circ.:** 107 per 1,000 pop. **Internet:** 400,000 users.

Health: Life expectancy: 69.6 male; 74.6 female. **Births** (per 1,000 pop.): 19.7. **Deaths** (per 1,000 pop.): 6.3. **Natural inc.:** 1.34%. **Infant mortality** (per 1,000 live births): 26.4.

Education: Compulsory: ages 3-12. **Literacy:** 87.4%.

Major Intl. Organizations: UN (FAO, IBRD, ILO, IMF, IMO, WHO), AL.

Embassy: 2560 28th St. NW 20008; 939-6300.

Websites: www.lebanonembassyus.org
www.embassy.org/embassies/lb.html

Formed from 5 former Turkish Empire districts, Lebanon became an independent state Sept. 1, 1920, administered under French mandate 1920-41. French troops withdrew in 1946.

Under the 1943 National Covenant, all public positions were divided among the various religious communities, with Christians in the majority. By the 1970s, Muslims became the majority and demanded a larger political and economic role.

U.S. Marines intervened, May-Oct. 1958, during a Syrian-aided revolt. Continued raids against Israeli civilians, 1970-75, brought Israeli attacks against guerrilla camps and villages. Israeli troops occupied S Lebanon, Mar. 1978, and again in Apr. 1980.

An estimated 60,000 were killed and billions of dollars in damage inflicted in a 1975-76 civil war. Palestinian units and leftist Muslims fought against the Maronite militia, the Phalange, and other Christians. Several Arab countries provided political and arms support to the various factions, while Israel aided Christian forces. Up to 15,000 Syrian troops intervened in 1976 to fight Palestinian groups. A cease-fire was mainly policed by Syria.

New clashes between Syrian troops and Christian forces erupted, Apr. 1, 1981. By Apr. 22, fighting had also broken out between two Muslim factions. In July, Israeli air raids on Beirut killed or wounded some 800 persons.

Israeli forces invaded Lebanon June 6, 1982, in a coordinated land, sea, and air attack aimed at crushing strongholds of the Palestine Liberation Organization (PLO). Israeli and Syrian forces engaged in the Bekaa Valley. By June 14, Israeli troops had encircled Beirut. On Aug. 21, the PLO evacuated west Beirut after massive Israeli bombings there. Israeli troops entered west Beirut following the Sept. 14 assassination of newly elected Lebanese Pres. Bashir Gemayel. On Sept. 16, Lebanese Christian troops entered 2 refugee camps and massacred hundreds of Palestinian refugees. An agreement May 17, 1983, between Lebanon, Israel, and the U.S. (but not Syria) provided for the withdrawal of Israeli troops; at least 30,000 Syrian troops remained in Lebanon, and Israeli forces continued to occupy a "security zone" in the south.

In 1983, terrorist bombings became a way of life in Beirut as some 50 people were killed in an explosion at the U.S. Embassy, Apr. 18; 241 U.S. servicemen and 58 French soldiers died in separate Muslim suicide attacks, Oct. 23.

Kidnapping of foreign nationals by Islamic militants became common in the 1980s. U.S., British, French, and Soviet citizens were victims. All were released by 1992.

A treaty signed May 22, 1991, between Lebanon and Syria recognized Lebanon as a separate state for the first time since the 2 countries gained independence in 1943.

Israeli forces conducted air raids and artillery strikes against guerrilla bases and villages in S Lebanon, causing over 200,000 to flee their homes July 25-29, 1993. Some 500,000 civilians fled their homes in Apr. 1996 when Israel again struck suspected guerrilla bases in the south. Pope John Paul II visited Lebanon May 10-11, 1997. During May-June 1998 the nation held its 1st municipal elections in 35 years. With Syria's approval, the legislature unanimously elected Lebanese armed forces chief Emile Lahoud as president Oct. 15.

Israel withdrew virtually all its troops from S Lebanon by May 24, 2000, leaving Hezbollah, an Iranian-backed guerrilla group, in control of much of the region. By mid-2003 Syria had reduced its troop presence in Lebanon to about 15,000

Lesotho
Kingdom of Lesotho

People: Population: 1,802,000. **Age distrib.** (%): <15: 39; 65+: 4.7. **Pop. density:** 154 per sq. mi. **Urban:** 29%. **Ethnic groups:** Sotho 99%. **Principal languages:** Sesotho, English (both official), Zulu, Xhosa. **Chief religions:** Christian 80%, indigenous beliefs 20%.

Geography: Area (total): 11,720 sq. mi. **Location:** In southern Africa. **Neighbors:** Completely surrounded by Republic of South Africa. **Topography:** Landlocked and mountainous, altitudes from 5,000 to 11,000 ft. **Capital:** Maseru: 271,000.

Government: Type: Modified constitutional monarchy. **Head of state:** King Letsie III; b July 17, 1963; in office: Feb. 7, 1996. **Head of gov.:** Pakalitha Mosisili; b Mar. 14, 1945; in office: May 29, 1998. **Local divisions:** 10 districts. **Defense budget** (2002): $22 mil. **Active troops:** 2,000.

Economy: Industries: food, beverages, textiles, apparel, handicrafts. **Chief crops:** corn, wheat, sorghum, barley. **Natural resources:** water, diamonds, other minerals. **Arable land:** 11%. **Livestock** (2002): cattle: 510,000; chickens: 1.70 mil.; goats: 570,000; pigs: 60,000; sheep: 730,000. **Fish catch** (2002): 32 metric tons. **Electricity prod.** (2001): 0.0 bil. kWh. **Labor force:** 86% of resident population engaged in subsistence agri.; roughly 35% of the active male wage earners work in South Africa.

Finance: Monetary unit: Loti (LSL) (Sept. 2003: 7.27 = $1 U.S.). **GDP** (2002 est.): $5.6 bil. **Per capita GDP:** $2,700. **Imports** (2001): $720 mil.; partners (1999): South African Customs Union 89.5%, Asia 7%. **Exports** (2001 est.): $250 mil.; partners (1999): South African Customs Union 53.9%, North America 45.6%. **Tourism** (1999): $19 mil. **Budget** (2000 est.): $80 mil. **Intl. reserves less gold:** $299 mil. **Consumer prices:** 33.8%.

Transport: Railroad: Length: 2 mi. **Motor vehicles:** 5,000 pass. cars, 18,000 comm. vehicles. **Civil aviation:** 4 airports.

Communications: TV sets: 16 per 1,000 pop. **Radios:** 52 per 1,000 pop. **Telephone lines:** 34,000. **Daily newspaper circ.:** 7.6 per 1,000 pop. **Internet:** 5,000 users.

Health: Life expectancy: 36.8 male; 37.1 female. **Births** (per 1,000 pop.): 27.3. **Deaths** (per 1,000 pop.): 24.6. **Natural inc.:** 0.27%. **Infant mortality** (per 1,000 live births): 86.2.

Education: Compulsory: ages 6-13. **Literacy:** 84.8%.

Major Intl. Organizations: UN (FOA, IBRD, ILO, IMF, WHO, WTrO), the Commonwealth, AU.

Embassy: 2511 Massachusetts Ave. NW 20008; 797-5533.

Website: www.embassy.org/embassies/ls.html

Lesotho (once called Basutoland) became a British protectorate in 1868 when Chief Moshesh sought protection against the Boers. Independence came Oct. 4, 1966. Elections were suspended in 1970. Most of Lesotho's GNP is provided by citizens working in South Africa. Livestock raising is the chief industry; diamonds are the chief export.

South Africa imposed a blockade, Jan. 1, 1986, because Lesotho had given sanctuary to anti-apartheid groups. The blockade sparked a Jan. 20 military coup, and was lifted, Jan. 25, when the new leaders agreed to expel the rebels.

In Mar. 1990, King Moshoeshoe was exiled by the military government. Letsie III became king Nov. 12. In Mar. 1993, Ntsu Mokhehle, a civilian, was elected prime minister, ending 23 years of military rule. After a series of violent disturbances, the king dismissed the Mokhele government Aug. 17, 1994: constitutional rule was restored Sept. 14. Letsie abdicated and Moshoeshoe was reinstated Jan. 25, 1995.

Moshoeshoe died in an automobile accident, Jan. 15, 1996. Letsie was reinstated Feb. 7; his formal coronation was Oct. 31, 1997. South Africa and Botswana sent troops Sept. 22, 1998, to help suppress violent antigovernment protests.

According to UN estimates, nearly more than 30% of the adult population has HIV/AIDS.

Liberia
Republic of Liberia

People: Population: 3,367,000. **Age distrib.** (%): <15: 43.3; 65+: 3.5. **Pop. density:** 91 per sq. mi. **Urban:** 46%. **Ethnic groups:** Kpelle, Bassa, Dey, and other tribes 95%; Americo-Liberians 2.5%, Caribbean 2.5%. **Principal languages:** English (official), Mande, West Atlantic, and Kwa languages. **Chief religions:** Indigenous beliefs 40%, Christian 40%, Muslim 20%.

Geography: Area: 43,000 sq. mi. (total); 37,189 sq. mi. (land). **Location:** On SW coast of W Africa. **Neighbors:** Sierra Leone on W, Guinea on N, Côte d'Ivoire on E. **Topography:** Marshy Atlantic coastline rises to low mountains and plateaus in the forested interior; 6 major rivers flow in parallel courses to the ocean. **Capital:** Monrovia 491,000.

Government: Type: In transition. **Head of state and gov.:** Pres. Moses Blah; b Apr. 18, 1947; in office: Aug. 11, 2003 (interim). **Local divisions:** 13 counties. **Defense budget** (2002): $15 mil. **Active troops:** 11-15,000.

Economy: Industries: rubber & palm oil proc., timber, diamonds. **Chief crops:** rubber, coffee, cocoa, rice, cassava, palm oil, sugarcane, bananas. **Natural resources:** iron ore, timber, diamonds, gold, hydropower. **Arable land:** 1%. **Livestock** (2002): cattle: 36,000; chickens: 4 mil.; goats: 220,000; pigs: 130,000; sheep: 210,000. **Fish catch** (2002): 11,300 metric tons. **Electricity prod.** (2001): 0.47 bil. kWh. **Labor force:** agri. 70%, ind. 8%, services 22%.

Finance: Monetary unit: Liberian Dollar (LRD) (Sept. 2003: 1.00 = $1 U.S.). **GDP** (2002 est.): $3.5 bil. **Per capita GDP:** $1,100. **Imports** (2000): $170 mil.; partners (2000): France 29.1%, South Korea (20.6%, Japan 15.8%, Singapore 8.4%. **Exports** (2000 est.): $55 mil.; partners (2000): Belgium 38.5%, Germany 17.6%, Italy 6.0%, U.S. 5.8%. **Budget** (2000): $90.5 mil. **Intl. reserves less gold:** $2 mil.

Transport: Railroad: Length: 304 mi. **Motor vehicles** (1998): 17,400 pass. cars, 10,700 comm. vehicles. **Civil aviation:** 2 airports. **Chief ports:** Monrovia, Buchanan, Greenville, Harper.

Communications: TV sets: 26 per 1,000 pop. **Radios:** 329 per 1,000 pop. **Telephone lines:** 6,700 main lines. **Daily newspaper circ.:** 17 per 1,000 pop.

Health: Life expectancy: 47.0 male; 49.3 female. **Births** (per 1,000 pop.): 45.3. **Deaths** (per 1,000 pop.): 17.8. **Natural inc.:** 2.74%. **Infant mortality** (per 1,000 live births): 132.2.

Education: Compulsory: ages 6-16. **Literacy:** 57.5%.

Major Intl. Organizations: UN and most of its specialized agencies, AU.

Embassy: 5201 16th St. NW 20011; 723-0437.

Website: www.liberian-connection.com/embassy.htm

Liberia was founded in 1822 by U.S. black freedmen who settled at Monrovia with the aid of colonization societies. It became a republic July 26, 1847, with a constitution modeled on that of the U.S. Descendants of freedmen dominated politics.

Under Pres. William V. S. Tubman, Liberia was a founding member of the UN in 1945. Tubman died in 1971 and was succeeded by his vice-president, William R. Tolbert, Jr. Charging rampant corruption, an Army Redemption Council of enlisted men staged a bloody predawn coup, April 12, 1980, in which Pres. Tolbert was killed and replaced as head of state by Sgt. Samuel Doe. Doe was chosen president in a disputed election, and survived a subsequent coup, in 1985.

A civil war began Dec. 1989. In Sept. 1990, Pres. Doe was captured and put to death. Despite the introduction of peacekeeping forces from several countries, factional fighting intensified, and a series of cease-fires failed. Factional fighting devastated Monrovia in Apr. 1996.

On Sept. 3, 1996, Ruth Perry became modern Africa's first female head of state, leading another transitional government. By then, the civil war had claimed more than 150,000 lives and uprooted over half the population.

Former rebel leader Charles Taylor was elected president July 19, 1997, in Liberia's 1st national election in 12 years. The UN imposed sanctions May 4, 2001, to punish Liberia for aiding the Revolutionary United Front (RUF) insurgency in Sierra Leone. Taylor declared a state of emergency Feb. 8, 2002, after Liberian rebels launched raids near Monrovia.

A U.N.-sponsored war crimes tribunal indicted Taylor June 4, 2003, for his role in Sierra Leone. With rebels again threatening Monrovia, Taylor resigned Aug. 11 and went into exile. Under a power-sharing agreement, Vice-Pres. Moses Blah then became interim president, as West African and U.S. troops sought to enforce a cease-fire. The UN authorized a 15,000-member peacekeeping force (UNMIL) Sept. 19 to help stabilize the nation.

Libya
Great Socialist People's Libyan Arab Jamahiriya

People: Population: 5,551,000. **Age distrib.** (%): <15: 35; 65+: 4. **Pop. density:** 8 per sq. mi. **Urban:** 88%. **Ethnic groups:** Arab-Berber 97%. **Principal languages:** Arabic (official), Italian, English. **Chief religion:** Muslim (official; mostly Sunni) 97%.

Geography: Area (total): 679,362 sq. mi. **Location:** On Mediterranean coast of N Africa. **Neighbors:** Tunisia, Algeria on W; Niger, Chad on S; Sudan, Egypt on E. **Topography:** Desert and semidesert regions cover 92% of the land, with low mountains in N, higher mountains in S, and a narrow coastal zone. **Capital:** Tripoli. **Cities (urban aggr.):** Benghazi 829,000; Tripoli 1,776,000.

Government: Type: Islamic Arabic Socialist "Mass-State." **Head of state and gov.:** Col. Muammar al-Qaddafi; b Sept. 1942; in power: Sept. 1969. **Local divisions:** 25 municipalities. **Defense budget** (2001): $1.2 bil. **Active troops:** 76,000.

Economy: Industries: oil, food proc., textiles, handicrafts, cement. **Chief crops:** wheat, barley, olives, dates, citrus, vegetables, peanuts, soybeans. **Natural resources:** oil, nat. gas, gypsum. **Crude oil reserves** (2002): 29.5 bil. bbls. **Arable land:** 1%. **Livestock** (2002): cattle: 220,000; chickens: 25 mil.; goats: 1.95 mil.; sheep: 5.20 mil. **Fish catch** (2002 est.): 33,339 metric tons. **Electricity prod.** (2001): 20.18 bil. kWh. **Labor force:** services 54%, ind. 29%, agri. 17%.

Finance: Monetary unit: Dinar (LYD) (Sept. 2003: 1.22 = $1 U.S.). **GDP** (2002 est.): $41 bil. **Per capita GDP:** $7,600. **Imports** (2001): $8.7 bil.; partners (2000): Italy 25%, Germany 10%, UK 8%, France 7%. **Exports** (2001 est.): $13.1 bil.; partners (2000): Italy 42%, Germany 19%, Spain 13%, Turkey 6%. **Tourism** (1999): $28 mil. **Budget** (2002 est.): $8.6 bil. **Intl. reserves less gold:** $10.86 bil. **Gold:** 4.62 mil oz t.

Transport: Motor vehicles (1997): 859,000 pass. cars, 362,400 comm. vehicles. **Civil aviation:** 234.3 mil pass.-mi.; 58 airports. **Chief ports:** Tripoli, Banghazi.

Communications: TV sets: 139 per 1,000 pop. **Radios:** 259 per 1,000 pop. **Telephone lines:** 610,000. **Daily newspaper circ.:** 14 per 1,000 pop. **Internet:** 20,000 users.

Health: Life expectancy: 73.9 male; 78.3 female. **Births** (per 1,000 pop.): 27.4. **Deaths** (per 1,000 pop.): 3.5. **Natural inc.:** 2.39%. **Infant mortality** (per 1,000 live births): 26.8.

Education: Compulsory: ages 6-14. **Literacy:** 82.6%.

Major Intl. Organizations: UN (FAO, IBRD, ILO, IMF, IMO, WHO), AL, AU, OPEC.

Website: www.libya–un.org

First settled by Berbers, Libya was ruled in succession by Carthage, Rome, the Vandals, and the Ottomans. Italy ruled from 1912, and Britain and France after WW II. Libya became an independent constitutional monarchy Jan. 2, 1952. In 1969 a junta led by Col. Muammar al-Qaddafi seized power.

Libya and Egypt fought several air and land battles along their border in July 1977. Chad charged Libya with military occupation of its uranium-rich northern region in 1977. Libyan troops were driven from their last major stronghold by Chad forces in 1987, leaving over $1 billion in military equipment behind.

Libya reportedly helped arm violent revolutionary groups in Egypt and Sudan and aided terrorists of various nationalities, and was blamed for aiding the attacks on the Rome and Vienna airports in Dec. 1985. The U.S. and Libya clashed, Jan.-Mar. 1986, over access to the Gulf of Sidra, which Libya claimed as territorial waters. The U.S. accused Qaddafi of ordering the Apr. 5 bombing of a West Berlin discotheque, which killed 3, including a U.S. serviceman. In response, the U.S. sent warplanes to attack terrorist-related targets in Tripoli and Banghazi, Libya, Apr. 14.

Libyan agents were accused of planting bombs that blew up Pan Am Flight 103 over Lockerbie, Scotland, killing 270 people Dec. 21, 1988; and UTA Flight 772 over Niger, killing 170 people Sept. 19, 1989. The UN imposed sanctions, Apr. 15, 1992, for Libya's failure to cooperate in the Lockerbie and UTA cases.

UN sanctions were suspended after Libya, Apr. 5, 1999, handed over two Lockerbie suspects for trial in the Netherlands under Scottish law. One of the two defendants, a Libyan intelligence official, Abdel Basset Ali al-Meghri, was convicted of murder Jan. 31, 2001. After prolonged negotiations, Libya agreed in 2003 to renounce terrorism and settle compensation cases for the families of the Lockerbie and UTA bombing victims. The UN lifted sanctions, Sept. 12, 2003.

Liechtenstein
Principality of Liechtenstein

People: Population: 33,000. **Age distrib.** (%): <15: 18.3; 65+: 11.2. **Pop. density:** 533 per sq. mi. **Urban:** 22%. **Ethnic groups:** Alemannic 86%; Italian, Turkish, and other 14%. **Principal languages:** German (official), Alemannic dialect. **Chief religions:** Roman Catholic 80%, Protestant 7%.

Geography: Area (total): 62 sq. mi. **Location:** Central Europe, in the Alps. **Neighbors:** Switzerland on W, Austria on E. **Topography:** The Rhine Valley occupies one-third of the country, the Alps cover the rest. **Capital:** Vaduz: 5,000.

Government: Type: Hereditary constitutional monarchy. **Head of state:** Prince Hans-Adam II; b Feb. 14, 1945; in office: Nov. 13, 1989. **Head of gov.:** Otmar Hasler; b Sept. 28, 1953; in office: Apr. 5, 2001. **Local divisions:** 11 communes.

Economy: Industries: electronics, metallurgy, textiles, ceramics, pharm., food products, precision instruments, tourism. **Chief crops:** wheat, barley, corn, potatoes. **Natural resources:** hydropower. **Arable land:** 24%. **Livestock:** (2002): cattle: 6,000; goats: 280; pigs: 3,000; sheep: 3,000. **Labor force:** ind. 47.4%, services 51.3%, agri. 1.3%.

Finance: Monetary unit: Swiss Franc (CHF) (Sept. 2003: 1.42 = $1 U.S.). **GDP** (1999 est.): $825 mil. **Per capita GDP** (1999 est.): $25,000. **Imports** (1996): $917.3 mil.; partners: EU countries, Switzerland. **Exports** (1996): $2.47 bil.; partners: EU 62.6%, U.S. 18.9%, Switzerland 15.7%. **Budget** (1998 est.): $414.1 mil.

Transport: Railroad: Length: 11 mi.

Communications: TV sets: 469 per 1,000 pop. **Radios:** 656 per 1,000 pop. **Daily newspaper circ.:** 602 per 1,000 pop.

Health: Life expectancy: 75.6 male; 82.9 female. **Births** (per 1,000 pop.): 10.9. **Deaths** (per 1,000 pop.): 6.9. **Natural inc.:** 0.41%. **Infant mortality** (per 1,000 live births): 4.9.

Education: Compulsory: ages 7-16. **Literacy** (1997): 100%.

Major Intl. Organizations: UN (WTrO), EFTA, OSCE.

Website: www.news.li

Liechtenstein became sovereign in 1806. Austria administered Liechtenstein's ports up to 1920; Switzerland has administered its postal services since 1921. Liechtenstein is united with Switzerland by a customs and monetary union. Taxes are low; many international corporations have headquarters there. Foreign workers comprise 60% of the labor force.

Lithuania
Republic of Lithuania

People: Population: 3,444,000. **Age distrib.** (%): <15: 18.2; 65+: 13.8. **Pop. density:** 137 per sq. mi. **Urban:** 69%. **Ethnic groups:** Lithuanian 81%, Russian 9%, Polish 7%, Belarusian 2%. **Principal languages:** Lithuanian (official), Belorusian, Russian, Polish. **Chief religion:** Predominantly Roman Catholic.

Geography: Area: 25,174 sq. mi. **Location:** In E Europe, on SE coast of Baltic. **Neighbors:** Latvia on N, Belarus on E, S, Poland and Russia on W. **Topography:** Lithuania is a lowland with hills in W and S; fertile soil; many small lakes and rivers, with marshes espec. in N and W. **Capital:** Vilnius. **Cities (urban aggr.):** Vilnius 579,000; Kaunas 412,639.

Government: Type (total): Republic. **Head of state: Pres. Rolandas Paksas; b June 10, 1956; in office: Feb. 26, 2003. Head of gov.:** Prime Min. Algirdas Brazauskas; b Sept. 22, 1932; in office: July 3, 2001. **Local divisions:** 10 provinces. **Defense budget** (2002): $230 mil. **Active troops:** 13,510.

Economy: Industries: machine tools, electric motors, large appliances, oil refining, shipbuilding. **Chief crops:** grain, potatoes,

sugar beets, flax, vegetables. **Natural resources:** peat. **Crude oil reserves** (2002): 12 mil. bbls. **Arable land:** 35%. **Livestock** (2002): cattle: 752,000; chickens: 6.58 mil.; goats: 23,700; pigs: 1.01 mil.; sheep: 12,000. **Fish catch** (2002): 153,932 metric tons. **Electricity prod.** (2001): 14.62 bil. kWh. **Labor force:** ind. 30%, agri. 20%, services 50%.

Finance: Monetary unit: Litas (LTL) (Sept. 2003: 3.19 = $1 U.S.). **GDP** (2002 est.): $29.2 bil. **Per capita GDP:** $8,400. **Imports** (2002): $6.8 bil.; partners (2001): Russia 25.3%, Germany 17.2%, Poland 4.9%, Italy 4.2%. **Exports** (2002 est.): $5.4 bil.; partners (2001): UK 13.8%, Latvia 12.6%, Germany 12.6%, Russia 11%. **Tourism:** $391 mil. **Budget** (2001 est.): $1.77 bil. **Intl. reserves less gold:** $1.73 bil. **Gold:** 190,000 oz t. **Consumer prices:** .3%.

Transport: Railroad: Length: 1,241 mi. **Motor vehicles:** 1.17 mil. pass. cars, 113,700 comm. vehicles. **Civil aviation:** 169.0 mil pass.-mi; 22 airports. **Chief port:** Klaipeda.

Communications: TV sets: 422 per 1,000 pop. **Radios:** 502 per 1,000 pop. **Telephone lines:** 935,900. **Daily newspaper circ.:** 29.3 per 1,000 pop. **Internet:** 250,000 users.

Health: Life expectancy: 63.8 male; 75.7 female. **Births** (per 1,000 pop.): 10.5. **Deaths** (per 1,000 pop.): 12.9. **Natural inc.:** -0.24%. **Infant mortality** (per 1,000 live births): 14.2.

Education: Compulsory: ages 7-15. **Literacy:** 99.6%.

Major Intl. Organizations: UN (FAO, IBRD, ILO, IMF, IMO, WHO), OSCE.

Embassy: 2622 16th St. NW 20009; 234-5860.

Websites: www.ltembassyus.org

Lithuania was occupied by the German army, 1914-18. It was annexed by the Soviet Russian army, but the Soviets were overthrown, 1919. Lithuania was a democratic republic until 1926, when the regime was ousted by a coup. In 1939 the Soviet-German treaty assigned most of Lithuania to the Soviet sphere of influence. Lithuania was annexed by the USSR Aug. 3, 1940.

Lithuania formally declared its independence from the Soviet Union Mar. 11, 1990. During an abortive Soviet coup in Aug., the Western nations recognized Lithuania's independence, which was ratified by the Soviet Union in Sept. 1991.

The last Russian troops withdrew on Aug. 31, 1993. Lithuania applied to join the European Union, Dec. 8, 1995. The conservative Homeland Union defeated the former Communists in parliamentary elections Oct. 20 and Nov. 10, 1996. A Lithuanian-American, Valdas Adamkus, won the presidency in a runoff election Jan. 4, 1998. Parliamentary elections Oct. 8, 2000, dealt conservatives a major setback. Adamkus lost to Rolandas Paksas in a runoff election, Jan. 5, 2003. Voters approved a referendum May 11, to join the EU in May 2004.

Luxembourg
Grand Duchy of Luxembourg

People: Population: 453,000. **Age distrib.** (%): <15: 18.9; 65+: 14.1. **Pop. density:** 454 per sq. mi. **Urban:** 92%. **Ethnic groups:** Mixture of French and German. **Principal languages:** Luxembourgish (national); German, French (official). **Chief religion:** Majority is Roman Catholic; 1979 law forbids collection of such statistics.

Geography: Area (total): 998 sq. mi. **Location:** In W Europe. **Neighbors:** Belgium on W, France on S, Germany on E. **Topography:** Heavy forests (Ardennes) cover N, S is a low, open plateau. **Capital:** Luxembourg-Ville: 82,000.

Government: Type: Constitutional monarchy. **Head of state:** Grand Duke Henri; b Apr. 16, 1955; in office: Oct. 7, 2000. **Head of gov.:** Prime Min. Jean-Claude Juncker; b Dec. 9, 1954; in office: Jan. 19, 1995. **Local divisions:** 3 districts. **Defense budget** (2002): $145 mil. **Active troops:** 900.

Economy: Industries: banking, iron & steel, food proc., chemicals, metal products, engineering, tires, glass, aluminum. **Chief crops:** barley, oats, potatoes, wheat, fruits, grapes. **Natural resources:** iron ore. **Arable land:** 24%. **Electricity prod.** (2001): 0.46 bil. kWh. **Labor force:** services 90.1%, ind. 8%, agri. 1.9%.

Finance: Monetary unit: Euro (EUR) (Sept. 2003: 0.92 = $1 U.S.). **GDP** (2002 est.): $20 bil. **Per capita GDP:** $44,000. **Imports** (2000): $10.25 bil.; partners (2001): EU 86.7%, , U.S. 5.8%. **Exports** (2000): $7.85 bil.; partners (2001): EU 84.7%, U.S. 3.5%. **Tourism** (1999): $2.2 bil. **Budget** (2002 est.): $5.5 bil. **Intl. reserves less gold:** $112 mil. **Gold:** 80,000 oz t. **Consumer prices:** 2.1%.

Transport: Railroad: Length: 170 mi. **Motor vehicles** (1999): 253,400 pass. cars, 53,600 comm. vehicles. **Civil aviation:** 458.6 mil pass.-mi; 1 airport. **Chief port:** Mertert.

Communications: TV sets: 599 per 1,000 pop. **Radios:** 683 per 1,000 pop. **Telephone lines:** 346,800. **Daily newspaper circ.:** 332 per 1,000 pop. **Internet:** 165,000 users.

Health: Life expectancy: 74.4 male; 81.2 female. **Births** (per 1,000 pop.): 11.9. **Deaths** (per 1,000 pop.): 8.8. **Natural inc.:** 0.31%. **Infant mortality** (per 1,000 live births): 4.7.

Education: Compulsory: ages 6-15. **Literacy** (2000 est.): 100%.

Major Intl. Organizations: UN (FAO, IBRD, ILO, IMF, IMO, WHO, WTrO), EU, NATO, OECD, OSCE.

Embassy: 2200 Massachusetts Ave. NW 20008; 265-4171.

Websites: www.gouvernement.lu; www.luxembourg-usa.org

Luxembourg, founded about 963, was ruled by Burgundy, Spain, Austria, and France from 1448 to 1815. It left the Germanic Confederation in 1866. Overrun by Germany in 2 world wars, Luxembourg ended its neutrality in 1948, when a customs union with Belgium and Netherlands was adopted.

Macedonia
Former Yugoslav Republic of Macedonia

People: Population (total): 2,056,000. **Age distrib.** (%): <15: 22.4; 65+: 10.4. **Pop. density:** 207 per sq. mi. **Urban:** 59%. **Ethnic groups:** Macedonian 67%, Albanian 23%, Turkish 4%, Roma 2%, Serb 2%. **Principal languages:** Macedonian (official), Albanian, Turkish, Romani, Serbo-Croatian. **Chief religions:** Macedonian Orthodox 67%, Muslim 30%.

Geography: Area: 9,781 sq. mi. (total); 9,597 sq. mi. (land). **Location:** In SE Europe. **Neighbors:** Bulgaria on E, Greece on S, Albania on W, Serbia on N. **Topography:** Macedonia is a landlocked, mostly mountainous country, with deep river valleys, 3 large lakes; country is bisected by Vardar R. **Capital:** Skopje: 437,000.

Government: Type: Republic. **Head of state:** Pres. Boris Trajkovski; b June 25, 1956; in office: Dec. 15, 1999. **Head of gov.:** Prime Min. Branko Crvenkovski; b Oct. 12, 1962; in office: Nov. 1, 2002. **Local divisions:** 123 municipalities. **Defense budget** (2002): $115 mil. **Active troops:** 12,300.

Economy: Industries: mining, textiles, wood products, tobacco, food proc., buses. **Chief crops:** rice, tobacco, wheat, corn, millet, cotton, sesame. **Natural resources:** chromium, lead, zinc, mang., tungsten, nickel, iron ore, asbestos, sulfur, timber. **Arable land:** 24%. **Livestock** (2002): cattle: 265,000; chickens: 3.35 mil.; pigs: 200,000; sheep: 1.20 mil. **Fish catch** (2002): 1,181 metric tons. **Electricity prod.** (2001): 6.47 bil. kWh.

Finance: Monetary unit: (MKD) Denar (Sept. 2003: 53.8 = $1 U.S.). **GDP** (2002 est.): $10 bil. **Per capita GDP:** $5,000. **Imports** (2002): $1.6 bil.; partners (2000): Germany 12.6%, Greece 10.9%, Yugoslavia 9.3%, Russia 8.3%. **Exports** (2002 est.): $1 bil.; partners (2001): Serbia and Montenegro 23.1%, Germany 20.6%, Greece 8.8%, Italy 8.6%. **Tourism** (1998): $15 mil. **Budget** (2001 est.): $1.02 bil. **Intl. reserves less gold:** $531 mil. **Gold:** 200,000 oz t. **Consumer prices:** .1%.

Transport: Railroad: Length: 434 mi. **Motor vehicles:** 300,000 pass. cars, 23,300 comm. vehicles. **Civil aviation:** 372.2 mil pass.-mi; 10 airports.

Communications: TV sets: 273 per 1,000 pop. **Radios:** 550 per 1,000 pop. **Telephone lines:** 538,500. **Daily newspaper circ.:** 21 per 1,000 pop. **Internet:** 70,000 users.

Health: Life expectancy: 72.2 male; 76.9 female. **Births** (per 1,000 pop.): 13.2. **Deaths** (per 1,000 pop.): 7.8. **Natural inc.:** 0.54%. **Infant mortality** (per 1,000 live births): 12.1.

Education: Free, compulsory: ages 7-15. **Literacy:** NA.

Major Intl. Organizations: UN (FAO, IBRD, ILO, IMF, IMO, WHO).

Embassy: 3050 K St. NW 20007; 337-3063.

Website: www.gov.mk

Macedonia, as part of a larger region also called Macedonia, was ruled by Muslim Turks from 1389 to 1912, when native Greeks, Bulgarians, and Slavs won independence. Serbia received the largest part of the territory, with the rest going to Greece and Bulgaria. In 1913, the area was incorporated into Serbia, which in 1918 became part of the Kingdom of Serbs, Croats, and Slovenes (later Yugoslavia). In 1946, Macedonia became a constituent republic of Yugoslavia.

Macedonia declared its independence Sept. 8, 1991, and was admitted to the UN under a provisional name in 1993. A UN force, which included several hundred U.S. troops, was deployed there to deter the warring factions in Bosnia from carrying their dispute into other areas of the Balkans.

In Feb. 1994 both Russia and the U.S. recognized Macedonia. Greece, which objected to Macedonia's use of what it considered a Hellenic name and symbols, imposed a trade blockade on the landlocked nation; the 2 countries agreed to normalize relations Sept. 13, 1995. A car bombing, Oct. 3, seriously injured Pres. Kiro Gligorov. Macedonia and Yugoslavia signed a treaty normalizing relations Apr. 8, 1996.

By the end of NATO's air war against Yugoslavia, Mar.-June 1999, Macedonia had a Kosovar refugee population of more than 250,000; over 90% had been repatriated by Sept. 1. Boris Trajkovski, candidate of the ruling center-right coalition, won a presidential runoff vote Nov. 14.

Ethnic Albanian guerrillas launched an offensive Mar. 2001 in NW Macedonia. An accord signed Aug. 13 paved the way for the introduction of a NATO peacekeeping force. A law broadening the rights of ethnic Albanians was enacted Jan. 24, 2002. A 320-member EU force replaced the NATO peacekeepers Mar. 31, 2003.

Madagascar
Republic of Madagascar

People: Population: 17,404,000. **Age distrib.** (%): <15: 45; 65+: 3.2. **Pop. density:** 78 per sq. mi. **Urban:** 30%. **Ethnic groups:** Mainly Malagasy (Indonesian-African); also Cotiers, French, Indian, Chinese. **Principal languages:** Malagasy, French

(both official). **Chief religions:** Indigenous beliefs 52%, Christian 41%, Muslim 7%.

Geography: Area: 226,657 sq. mi. (total); 224,534 sq. mi. (land). **Location:** In the Indian O., off the SE coast of Africa. **Neighbors:** Comoro Isls. to NW, Mozambique to W. **Topography:** Humid coastal strip in the E, fertile valleys in the mountainous center plateau region, and a wider coastal strip on the W. **Capital:** Antananarivo 1,689,000.

Government: Type: Republic. **Head of state:** Pres. Marc Ravalomanana; b Dec. 12, 1949; in office: Feb. 22, 2002 (de facto). **Head of gov.:** Prime Min. Jacques Sylla; b 1946; in office: Feb. 26, 2002 (de facto). **Local divisions:** 6 provinces. **Defense budget** (2002): $48.9 mil. **Active troops:** 13,500.

Economy: Industries: meat proc., soap, brewing, hides, sugar, textiles, glassware, cement, autos. **Chief crops:** coffee, vanilla, sugarcane, cloves, cocoa, rice, cassava, beans, bananas, peanuts. **Natural resources:** graphite, chromite, coal, bauxite, salt, quartz, tar sands, gemstones, mica, fish, hydropower. **Arable land:** 4%. **Livestock** (2002): cattle: 10.30 mil.; chickens: 19 mil.; goats: 1.35 mil.; pigs: 850,000; sheep: 790,000. **Fish catch** (2002): 143,332 metric tons. **Electricity prod.** (2001): 0.83 bil. kWh.

Finance: Monetary unit: Malagasy Franc (MGF) (Sept. 2003: 6,216.40 = $1 U.S.). **GDP** (2002): $12.6 bil. **Per capita GDP:** $760. **Imports** (2000): $919 mil.; partners: France 38%, Hong Kong 10%, China 5%, Singapore 5%. **Exports** (2000): $680 mil.; partners (2000): France 41%, U.S. 21%, Germany 7%, Japan 4%. **Tourism:** $116 mil. **Budget** (1998 est.): $735 mil. **Intl. reserves less gold:** $267 mil. **Consumer prices:** 15.9%.

Transport: Railroad: Length: 555 mi. **Motor vehicles** (1998): 64,000 pass. cars, 9,100 comm. vehicles. **Civil aviation:** 644.4 mil pass.-mi; 29 airports. **Chief ports:** Toamasina, Antsiranana, Mahajanga, Toliara, Antsohimbondrona.

Communications: TV sets: 23 per 1,000 pop. **Radios:** 209 per 1,000 pop. **Telephone lines:** 58,400. **Daily newspaper circ.:** 4.6 per 1,000 pop. **Internet:** 35,000 users.

Health: Life expectancy: 53.8 male; 58.5 female. **Births** (per 1,000 pop.): 42.2. **Deaths** (per 1,000 pop.): 11.9. **Natural inc.:** 3.03%. **Infant mortality** (per 1,000 live births): 80.2.

Education: Compulsory: ages 6-14. **Literacy:** 68.9%.

Major Intl. Organizations: UN (FAO, IBRD, ILO, IMF, IMO, WHO, WTrO), AU.

Embassy: 2374 Massachusetts Ave. NW 20008; 265-5525.

Website: www.embassy.org/madagascar

Madagascar was settled 2,000 years ago by Malayan-Indonesian people, whose descendants still predominate. A unified kingdom ruled the 18th and 19th centuries. The island became a French protectorate, 1885, and a colony 1896. Independence came June 26, 1960.

Discontent with inflation and French domination led to a coup in 1972. The new regime nationalized French-owned financial interests, closed French bases and a U.S. space-tracking station, and obtained Chinese aid. The government conducted a program of arrests, expulsion of foreigners, and repression of strikes, 1979.

In 1990, Madagascar ended a ban on multiparty politics that had been in place since 1975. Albert Zafy was elected president in 1993, ending the 17-year rule of Adm. Didier Ratsiraka. After Zafy was impeached by the legislature, Madagascar's constitutional court removed him from office, Sept. 5, 1996. Prime Min. Norbert Ratsirahonana then became interim president pending national elections, Nov. 3 and Dec. 29, in which Ratsiraka edged Zafy. A cholera epidemic, exacerbated by cyclones in Feb. and Apr. 2000, claimed at least 1,600 lives.

Marc Ravalomanana won a power struggle with Ratsiraka that followed a disputed presidential election Dec. 16, 2001.

Malawi
Republic of Malawi

People: Population: 12,105,000. **Age distrib.** (%): <15: 44; 65+: 2.8. **Pop. density:** 333 per sq. mi. **Urban:** 15%. **Ethnic groups:** Chewa, Nyanja, Tumbuka, Yao, Lomwe, Sena, Tonga, Ngoni, Ngonde. **Principal languages:** Chichewa, English (both official), several African languages. **Chief religions:** Protestant 55%, Roman Catholic 20%, Muslim 20%.

Geography: Area: 45,745 sq. mi. (total); 36,324 sq. mi. (land). **Location:** In SE Africa. **Neighbors:** Zambia on W, Mozambique on S and E, Tanzania on N. **Topography:** Malawi stretches 560 mi. N-S along Lake Malawi (Lake Nyasa), most of which belongs to Malawi. High plateaus and mountains line the Rift Valley the length of the nation. **Capital:** Lilongwe. **Cities (urban aggr., 1998 est.):** Blantyre 2,000,000; Lilongwe 523,000.

Government: Type: Republic. **Head of state and gov.:** Pres. Bakili Muluzi; b Mar. 17, 1943; in office: May 21, 1994. **Local divisions:** 3 regions, 26 districts. **Defense budget** (2002): $5.9 mil. **Active troops:** 5,300.

Economy: Industries: tobacco, tea, sugar, wood products, cement, consumer goods. **Chief crops:** tobacco, sugarcane, cotton, tea, corn, potatoes, cassava, sorghum. **Natural resources:** limestone, hydropower, uranium, coal, bauxite. **Arable land:** 18%. **Livestock** (2002): cattle: 6.82 mil.; chickens: 25.50 mil.; goats: 8.85 mil.; pigs: 85,000; sheep: 6.15 mil. **Fish catch** (2002): 41,187 metric tons. **Electricity prod.** (2001): 0.77 bil. kWh. **Labor force:** agri. 86%.

Finance: Monetary unit: Kwacha (MWK) (Sept. 2003: 109.27 = $1 U.S.). **GDP** (2002 est.): $7.2 bil. **Per capita GDP:** $670. **Imports** (2001): $463.6 mil.; partners (2000): South Africa 40%, UK 11%, Zimbabwe 7%, Japan 5%. **Exports** (2001): $415.5 mil.; partners (2000): South Africa 18%, Germany 13%, U.S. 13%, UK 10%. **Tourism:** $27 mil. **Budget** (1999 est.): $523 mil. **Intl. reserves less gold:** $121 mil. **Gold:** 10,000 oz t. **Consumer prices:** 14.7%.

Transport: Railroad: Length: 495 mi. **Motor vehicles** (1996): 1,600 pass. cars, 1,900 comm. vehicles. **Civil aviation:** 139.2 mil pass.-mi; 6 airports.

Communications: TV sets: 3 per 1,000 pop. Radios: 476 per 1,000 pop. **Telephone lines:** 73,100. **Daily newspaper circ.:** 3 per 1,000 pop. **Internet:** 27,000 users.

Health: Life expectancy: 37.6 male; 38.4 female. **Births** (per 1,000 pop.): 44.7. **Deaths** (per 1,000 pop.): 22.6. **Natural inc.:** 2.21%. **Infant mortality** (per 1,000 live births): 105.2.

Education: Compulsory: ages 6-14. **Literacy:** 62.7%.

Major Intl. Organizations: UN (FAO, IBRD, ILO, IMF, IMO, WHO, WTrO), the Commonwealth, AU.

Embassy: 2408 Massachusetts Ave. NW 20008; 797-1007.

Website: www.malawi.gov.mw

Bantus came to the land in the 16th century, Arab slavers in the 19th. The area became the British protectorate Nyasaland in 1891. It became independent July 6, 1964, and a republic in 1966. After 3 decades as a one-party state under Pres. Hastings Kamuzu Banda, Malawi adopted a new constitution and, in multiparty elections held May 17, 1994, chose a new leader, Bakili Muluzi. Banda was acquitted, Dec. 23, 1995, of complicity in the deaths of 4 political opponents in 1983; he died Nov. 25, 1997.

According to UN estimates, 15% of the adult population has HIV/AIDS, and AIDS has orphaned at least 470,000 children.

Malaysia

People: Population: 24,425,000. **Age distrib.** (%): <15: 34.1; 65+: 4.3. **Pop. density:** 193 per sq. mi. **Urban:** 58%. **Ethnic groups:** Malay and other indigenous 58%, Chinese 24%, Indian 8%. **Principal languages:** Malay (official), English, Chinese dialects, Tamil, Telugu, Malayalam, Panjabi, Thai, Iban, and Kadazan in East. **Chief religions:** Muslim (official) 60%, Buddhist 19%, Christian 9%, Hindu 6%, Confucianist/Taoist 3%.

Geography: Area: 127,317 sq. mi. (total); 126,854 sq. mi. (land). **Location:** On the SE tip of Asia, plus the N coast of the island of Borneo. **Neighbors:** Thailand on N, Indonesia on S. **Topography:** Most of W Malaysia is covered by tropical jungle, including the central mountain range that runs N-S through the peninsula. The western coast is marshy, the eastern, sandy. E Malaysia has a wide, swampy coastal plain, with interior jungles and mountains. **Capital:** Kuala Lumpur 1,410,000.

Government: Type: Federal parliamentary democracy with a constitutional monarch. **Head of state:** Paramount Ruler Syed Sirajuddin Syed Putra Jamalullail; b May 16, 1943; in office: Dec. 13, 2001. **Head of gov.:** Prime Min. Datuk Seri Mahathir bin Mohamad; b Dec. 20, 1925; in office: July 16, 1981. **Local divisions:** 13 states, 2 federal territories. **Defense budget** (2002): $2.9 bil. **Active troops:** 100,000.

Economy: Industries: rubber & palm oil proc., light mfg., electronics, tin, mining, timber, oil. **Chief crops:** rubber, palm oil, cocoa, rice, coconuts, pepper. **Natural resources:** tin, oil, timber, copper, iron ore, nat. gas, bauxite. **Crude oil reserves** (2002): 3.0 bil. bbls. **Arable land:** 3%. **Livestock** (2002): cattle: 755,000; chickens: 130 mil.; goats: 215,000; pigs: 2.10 mil.; sheep: 170,000. **Fish catch** (2002): 1,392,891 metric tons. **Electricity prod.** (2001): 68.34 bil. kWh. **Labor force:** local trade and tourism 28%, manufact. 27%, agri., forestry, and fisheries 16%, services 10%, government 10%, construct. 9%.

Finance: Monetary unit: Ringgit (MYR) (Sept. 2003: 3.80 = $1 U.S.). **GDP** (2002 est.): $210 bil. **Per capita GDP:** $9,300. **Imports** (2001): $76.9 bil.; partners (2001 est.): Japan 20%, U.S. 17%, Singapore 13%, Taiwan 5%. **Exports** (2001 est.): $94.4 bil.; partners (2001 est.): U.S. 20%, Singapore 17%, Japan 14%, Hong Kong 4.5%. **Tourism:** $4.56 bil. **Budget** (2001): $27.2 bil. **Intl. reserves less gold:** $25.17 bil. **Consumer prices:** 1.8%.

Transport: Railroad: Length: 1,119 mi. **Motor vehicles:** 350,400 pass. cars, 36,800 comm. vehicles. **Civil aviation:** 20.95 bil pass.-mi; 35 airports. **Chief ports:** Kuantan, Kelang, Kota Kinabalu, Kuching.

Communications: TV sets: 174 per 1,000 pop. **Radios:** 434 per 1,000 pop. **Telephone lines:** 4,710,000 . **Daily newspaper circ.:** 158 per 1,000 pop. **Internet:** 6,500,000 users.

Health: Life expectancy: 69.0 male; 74.5 female. **Births** (per 1,000 pop.): 23.7. **Deaths** (per 1,000 pop.): 5.1. **Natural inc.:** 1.86%. **Infant mortality** (per 1,000 live births): 19.0.

Education: Compulsory: ages 6-16. **Literacy:** 88.9%.

Major Intl. Organizations: UN (FAO, IBRD, ILO, IMF, IMO, WHO, WTrO), APEC, ASEAN, the Commonwealth.

Embassy: 3516 International Court NW 20008; 202-572-9700.

Websites: www.embassy.org/embassies/my.html
www.tourism.gov.my/

European traders appeared in the 16th century; Britain established control in 1867. Malaysia was created Sept. 16, 1963. It included Malaya (which had become independent in 1957 after the suppression of Communist rebels), plus the formerly British Singapore, Sabah (N Borneo), and Sarawak (NW Borneo). Singapore was separated in 1965, in order to end tensions between Chinese, the majority in Singapore, and Malays in control of the Malaysian government.

A monarch is elected by a council of hereditary rulers of the Malayan states every 5 years.

Abundant natural resources have bolstered prosperity, and foreign investment has aided industrialization. Work on a new federal capital at Putrajaya, south of Kuala Lumpur, began in 1995. However, sagging stock and currency prices forced the postponement of major development projects in Sept. 1997.

As the recession deepened and political unrest grew, Prime Min. Mahathir bin Mohamad imposed new currency controls and fired his popular deputy prime minister, Anwar bin Ibrahim, Sept. 2, 1998. Anwar, who then called for Mahathir's resignation, was arrested Sept. 20; he was convicted of corruption, Apr. 14, 1999, and sentenced to 6 years in prison. Another conviction, Aug. 8, 2000, for sodomy, resulted in an additional 9-year sentence.

Maldives
Republic of Maldives

People: Population: 318,000. **Age distrib.** (%): <15: 45.3; 65+: 3. **Pop. density:** 2,745 per sq. mi. **Urban:** 28%. **Ethnic groups:** Dravidian, Sinhalese, Arab. **Principal languages:** Divehi (Sinhala dialect, Arabic script; official), English. **Chief religion:** Muslim (official; mostly Sunni).

Geography: Area (total): 116 sq. mi. **Location:** In the Indian O., SW of India. **Neighbors:** Nearest is India on N. **Topography:** 19 atolls with 1,190 islands, 198 inhabited. None of the islands are over 5 sq. mi. in area, and all are nearly flat. **Capital:** Male: 84,000.

Government: Type: Republic. **Head of state and gov.:** Pres. Maumoon Abdul Gayoom; b Dec. 29, 1937; in office: Nov. 11, 1978. **Local divisions:** 19 atolls and Male. **Defense budget:** $36 mil. **Active troops:** NA.

Economy: Industries: fish proc., tourism, shipping, boat building, coconut proc., garments. **Chief crops:** coconuts, corn, sweet potatoes. **Natural resources:** fish. **Arable land:** 10%. **Fish catch** (2002): 125,814 metric tons. **Electricity prod.** (2001): 0.12 bil. kWh. **Labor force:** agri. 22%, ind. 18%, services 60%.

Finance: Monetary unit: Rufiyaa (MVR) (Sept. 2003: 12.69 = $1 U.S.). **GDP** (2002 est.): $1.3 bil. **Per capita GDP:** $3,900. **Imports** (2000): $372 mil.; partners: Singapore, India, Sri Lanka, Japan. **Exports** (2000 est.): $88 mil.; partners: US, UK, Sri Lanka, Japan. **Tourism:** $344 mil. **Budget** (2002 est.): $282 mil. **Intl. reserves less gold:** $98 mil. **Consumer prices:** .9%.

Transport: Motor vehicles: 300 pass. cars, 400 comm. vehicles. **Civil aviation:** 311.3 mil pass.-mi; 2 airports. **Chief ports:** Male, San.

Communications: TV sets: 38 per 1,000 pop. **Radios:** 129 per 1,000 pop. **Telephone lines:** 28,700. **Daily newspaper circ.:** 12 per 1,000 pop. **Internet:** 15,000 users.

Health: Life expectancy: 62.1 male; 64.6 female. **Births** (per 1,000 pop.): 36.7. **Deaths** (per 1,000 pop.): 7.7. **Natural inc.:** 2.91%. **Infant mortality** (per 1,000 live births): 60.1.

Education: Compulsory: ages 6-12. **Literacy:** 97.2%.

Major Intl. Organizations: UN (FAO, IBRD, IMF, IMO, WHO, WTrO), the Commonwealth.

Website: www.un.int/maldives

The islands have been a British protectorate since 1887. The country became independent July 26, 1965. Long a sultanate, the Maldives became a republic in 1968. Natural resources and tourism are being developed; however, the Maldives remains one of the world's poorest countries. Tourism and fishing are the most important sectors of the economy.

Mali
Republic of Mali

People: Population: 13,007,000. **Age distrib.** (%): <15: 47.2; 65+: 3. **Pop. density:** 28 per sq. mi. **Urban:** 31%. **Ethnic groups:** Mande 50% (Bambara, Malinke, Soninke), Peul 17%, Voltaic 12%, Tuareg and Moor 10%, Songhai 6%. **Principal languages:** French (official); Bambara and other African languages. **Chief religions:** Muslim 90%, indigenous beliefs 9%.

Geography: Area: 478,766 sq. mi. (total); 471,044 sq. mi. (land). **Location:** In the interior of W Africa. **Neighbors:** Mauritania, Senegal on W; Guinea, Côte d'Ivoire, Burkina Faso on S; Niger on E; Algeria on N. **Topography:** A landlocked grassy plain in the upper basins of the Senegal and Niger rivers, extending N into the Sahara. **Capital:** Bamako: 1,161,000.

Government: Type: Republic. **Head of state:** Pres. Amadou Toumani Touré; b Nov. 4, 1948; in office: June 8, 2002. **Head of gov.:** Prime Min. Ahmed Mohamed Ag Hamani; in office: June 9, 2002. **Local divisions:** 8 regions, 1 capital district. **Defense budget** (2002): $69 mil. **Active troops:** 7,350.

Economy: Industries: food proc., constr., phosphates, gold. **Chief crops:** cotton, millet, rice, corn, vegetables, peanuts. **Natural resources:** gold, phosphates, kaolin, salt, limestone, uranium, hydropower. **Arable land:** 2%. **Livestock** (2002): cattle: 6.82 mil.; chickens: 25.50 mil.; goats: 8.85 mil.; pigs: 85,000; sheep: 6.15

mil. **Fish catch** (2002 est.): 100,035 metric tons. **Electricity prod.** (2001): 0.48 bil. kWh. **Labor force:** agri. and fishing 80%.

Finance: Monetary unit: CFA Franc BCEAO (XOF) (Sept. 2003: 605.18 = $1 U.S.). **GDP** (2002 est.): $9.8 bil. **Per capita GDP:** $860. **Imports** (2001): $600 mil.; partners (2000): Cote d'Ivoire 21%, France 12.4%, Senegal 4%, Germany 4%. **Exports** (2001 est.): $575 mil.; partners (2000): Brazil 10.6%, South Korea 9.9%, Italy 7.3%, Canada 7%. **Tourism:** $50 mil. **Budget** (2002 est.): $828 mil. **Intl. reserves less gold:** $437 mil. **Consumer prices:** 5.0%.

Transport: Railroad: Length: 453 mi. **Motor vehicles:** (1998): 6,300 pass. cars, 7,600 comm. vehicles. **Civil aviation:** 146.0 mil pass.-mi; 7 airports. **Chief port:** Koulikoro.

Communications: TV sets: 13 per 1,000 pop. **Radios:** 55 per 1,000 pop. **Telephone lines:** 49,900. **Daily newspaper circ.:** 1.2 per 1,000 pop. **Internet:** 30,000 users.

Health: Life expectancy: 44.7 male; 46.2 female. **Births** (per 1,000 pop.): 47.8. **Deaths** (per 1,000 pop.): 19.2. **Natural inc.:** 2.86%. **Infant mortality** (per 1,000 live births): 119.2.

Education: Compulsory: ages 7-15. **Literacy:** 46.4%.

Major Intl. Organizations: UN and most of its specialized agencies, AU.

Embassy: 2130 R St. NW 20008; 332-2249.

Website: www.maliembassy-usa.org

Until the 15th century the area was part of the great Mali Empire. Timbuktu (Tombouctou) was a center of Islamic study. French rule was secured, 1898. The Sudanese Rep. and Senegal became independent as the Mali Federation June 20, 1960, but Senegal withdrew, and the Sudanese Rep. was renamed Mali.

Mali signed economic agreements with France and, in 1963, with Senegal. In 1968, a coup ended the socialist regime. Famine struck in 1973-74, killing as many as 100,000 people. Drought conditions returned in the 1980s.

The military, Mar. 26, 1991, overthrew the government of Pres. Moussa Traoré, who had been in power since 1968. Oumar Konare, a coup leader, was elected president, Apr. 26, 1992. A peace accord between the government and a Tuareg rebel group was signed in June 1994. Konare and his party won a series of flawed elections, Apr.-Aug. 1997. Twice condemned to death for crimes committed in office, Traoré had his sentences commuted to life imprisonment in Dec. 1997 and Sept. 1999.

Amadou Toumani Touré, who led the 1991 coup, won a presidential runoff election May 12, 2002.

Malta
Republic of Malta

People: Population: 394,000. **Age distrib.** (%): <15: 19.7; 65+: 12.8. **Pop. density:** 3,179 per sq. mi. **Urban:** 91%. **Ethnic group:** Maltese, other Mediterranean. **Principal languages:** Maltese (a Semitic dialect), English (both official). **Chief religion:** Roman Catholic 91% (official).

Geography: Area (total):122 sq. mi. **Location:** In center of Mediterranean Sea. **Neighbors:** Nearest is Italy on N. **Topography:** Island of Malta is 95 sq. mi.; other islands in the group: Gozo, 26 sq. mi.; Comino, 1 sq. mi. The coastline is heavily indented. Low hills cover the interior. **Capital:** Valletta: 82,000.

Government: Type: Parliamentary democracy. **Head of state:** Pres. Guido de Marco; b July 22, 1931; in office: Apr. 4, 1999. **Head of gov.:** Prime Min. Edward Fenech-Adami; b Feb. 7, 1934; in office: Sept. 6, 1998. **Local divisions:** 3 regions comprising 67 local councils. **Defense budget** (2002): $28 mil. **Active troops:** 2,140.

Economy: Industries: tourism, electronics, shipbuilding, food & beverages, textiles. **Chief crops:** potatoes, cauliflower, grapes, wheat, barley, tomatoes, citrus. **Natural resources:** limestone, salt. **Arable land:** 38%. **Livestock** (2002): cattle: 19,000; chickens: 820,000; goats: 9,000; pigs: 69,000; sheep: 16,000. **Fish catch** (2002): 2,117 metric tons. **Electricity prod.** (2001): 1.77 bil. kWh. **Labor force:** ind. 24%, services 71%, agri. 5%.

Finance: Monetary unit: Lira (MTL) (Sept. 2003: 0.41=1 U.S.). **GDP** (2002 est.): $7 bil. **Per capita GDP:** $17,000. **Imports** (2001): $2.8 bil.; partners (2001): Italy 19.9%, France 15.0%, U.S. 11.6%, UK 10.0%. **Exports** (2001): $2 bil.; partners (2001): U.S. 20.2%, Germany 14.1%, France 10.2%, UK 8.8%. **Tourism:** $650 mil. **Budget** (2002) $1.6 bil. **Intl. reserves less gold:** $1.63 bil. **Gold** (2000): 10,000 oz t. **Consumer prices:** 2.2%.

Transport: Motor vehicles: 211,300 pass. cars, 52,600 comm. vehicles. **Civil aviation:** 1.44 bil pass.-mi; 1 airport. **Chief ports:** Valletta, Marsaxlokk.

Communications: TV sets: 549 per 1,000 pop. **Radios:** 669 per 1,000 pop. **Telephone lines:** 207,300. **Daily newspaper circ.:** 133 per 1,000 pop. **Internet:** 99,000 users.

Health: Life expectancy: 75.9 male; 81.1 female. **Births** (per 1,000 pop.): 12.8. **Deaths** (per 1,000 pop.): 7.8. **Natural inc.:** 0.5%. **Infant mortality** (per 1,000 live births): 5.6.

Education: Compulsory: ages 5-16. **Literacy:** 92.8%.

Major Intl. Organizations: UN (FAO, IBRD, ILO, IMF, IMO, WHO, WTrO), the Commonwealth, OSCE.

Embassy: 2017 Connecticut Ave. NW 20008; 462-3611.

Website: www.gov.mt

Malta was ruled by Phoenicians, Romans, Arabs, Normans, the Knights of Malta, France, and Britain (since 1814). It became inde-

pendent Sept. 21, 1964. Malta became a republic in 1974. The withdrawal of the last British sailors, Apr. 1, 1979, ended 179 years of British military presence on the island. From 1971 to 1987 and again from 1996 to 1998, Malta was governed by the socialist Labour Party. The Nationalist Party, which held office 1987-96 and favors Malta's entry into the EU, returned to power after elections Sept. 5, 1998. In a referendum Mar. 8, 2003, voters approved accession to the EU in 2004; the Nationalists won a parliamentary majority in elections Apr. 12.

Marshall Islands
Republic of the Marshall Islands

People: Population: 56,000. **Age distrib.** (%): <15: 49.1; 65+: 2. **Pop. density:** 807 per sq. mi. **Urban:** 66%. **Ethnic groups:** Micronesian. **Principal languages:** English, Marshallese (both official); Malay-Polynesian dialects, Japanese. **Chief religion:** Mostly Protestant.

Geography: Area (total): 70 sq. mi. **Location:** In N Pacific Ocean; composed of two 800-mi-long parallel chains of coral atolls. **Neighbors:** Nearest are Micronesia to W, Nauru and Kiribati to S. **Topography:** Marshall Islands are low coral limestone and sand islands. **Capital:** Majuro: 25,000.

Government: Type: Republic. **Head of state and gov.:** Pres. Kessai Note; b 1950; in office: Jan. 10, 2000. **Local divisions:** 33 municipalities.

Economy: Industries: copra, fish, tourism, handicrafts, wood, pearls. **Chief crops:** coconuts, tomatoes, melons, taro, breadfruit, fruits. **Natural resources:** fish, minerals. **Fish catch** (2002): 37,098 metric tons. **Labor force:** agri. 21.4%, ind. 20.9%, services 57.7%.

Finance: Monetary unit: U.S. Dollar. **GDP** (2001 est.): $115 mil. **Per capita GDP** (2001 est.): $1,600. **Imports** (2000): $54 mil.; partners: U.S., Japan, Australia, NZ. **Exports** (2000): $9 mil.; partners: U.S., Japan, Australia. **Tourism:** (1999): $4 mil. **Budget** (1999): $40 mil.

Transport: Civil aviation: 7.5 mil pass.-mi; 4 airports. **Chief port:** Majuro.

Communications: Telephone lines: 4,200. **internet:** 900 users.

Health: Life expectancy: 67.5 male; 71.4 female. **Births** (per 1,000 pop.): 34.2. **Deaths** (per 1,000 pop.): 5.0. **Natural inc.:** 2.92%. **Infant mortality** (per 1,000 live births): 31.6.

Education: Compulsory: ages 6-14. **Literacy** (1999): 93.7%.

Major Intl. Organizations: UN (IBRD, IMF, WHO).

Embassy: 2433 Massachusetts Ave. NW 20008; 234-5414.

Website: www.rmiembassyus.org

The Marshall Islands were a German possession until World War I and were administered by Japan between the World Wars. After WW II, they were administered as part of the UN Trust Territory of the Pacific Islands by the U.S.

The Marshall Islands secured international recognition as an independent nation on Sept. 17, 1991. Amata Kabua, the islands' first and only president since 1979, died Dec. 19, 1996. His cousin Imata Kabua, elected president Jan. 13, 1997, was succeeded by Kessai Note on Jan. 10, 2000.

Mauritania
Islamic Republic of Mauritania

People: Population: 2,893,000. **Age distrib.** (%): <15: 46.1; 65+: 2.2. **Pop. density:** 7 per sq. mi. **Urban:** 59%. **Ethnic groups:** Mixed Maur/Black 40%, Maur 30%, Black 30%. **Principal languages:** Hassaniya Arabic, Wolof (both official); Fulani, Pulaar, Soninke (all national); French. **Chief religion:** Predominantly Muslim (official).

Geography: Area: 397,955 sq. mi. (total); 397,839 sq. mi. (land). **Location:** In NW Africa. **Neighbors:** Morocco on N, Algeria and Mali on E, Senegal on S. **Topography:** The fertile Senegal R. valley in the S gives way to a wide central region of sandy plains and scrub trees. The N is arid and extends into the Sahara. **Capital:** Nouakchott: 626,000.

Government: Type: Islamic republic. **Head of state:** Pres. Maaouya Ould Sidi Ahmed Taya; b 1941; in office: Apr. 18, 1992. **Head of gov.:** Prime Min. Sghair Ould M'Bareck; b 1954; in office: July 6, 2003. **Local divisions:** 12 regions, 1 capital district. **Defense budget** (2002): $26 mil. **Active troops:** 15,750.

Economy: Industries: fish proc., iron ore, gypsum. **Chief crops:** dates, millet, sorghum, rice, corn. **Natural resources:** iron ore, gypsum, copper, phosphate, diamonds, gold, oil, fish. **Livestock** (2002): cattle: 1.50 mil.; chickens: 4.10 mil.; goats: 5.10 mil.; pigs: 14,000; sheep: 7.60 mil. **Fish catch** (2002 est.): 83,596 metric tons. **Electricity Prod.:** (2001): 0.16 bil. kWh. **Labor force:** agri. 50%, services 40%, ind. 10%.

Finance: Monetary unit: Ouguiya (MRO) (Sept. 2003: 274.40=1 U.S.). **GDP** (2002 est.): $5.3 bil. **Per capita GDP:** $1,900. **Imports** (2000): $335 mil.; partners (2000): France 33%, U.S. 10%, Spain 9%, Algeria 6%. **Exports** (2000): $359 mil.; partners (2000): France 18%, Japan 16%, Italy 13%, Spain 10%. **Tourism** (1999): $28 mil. **Budget** (2002 est.): $378 mil. **Intl. reserves less gold:** $291 mil. **Gold:** 10,000 oz t. **Consumer prices:** 3.8%.

▲ ROAD TO PEACE
Pres. George W. Bush met with Israeli
Prime Min. Ariel Sharon (left) and
Palestinian Prime Min. Mahmoud Abbas
in Jordan June 4 to discuss implementing
Bush's proposed "road map" for peace in
the Middle East. Amid renewed violence,
Abbas resigned Sept. 6.

▲ DIVIDING WALL
Palestinians wait to cross through a
370-mile barrier, combining walls,
fences, razor-wire, and trenches,
being built by Israeli authorities for
security reasons. Palestinians argued
that the barrier, which often runs
deep into the West Bank, was
cutting off thousands from land
and jobs on the other side.

▲ NUCLEAR THREAT
North Korean leader Kim Jong Il,
seen with his top generals in April.
The U.S. was working with Asian
nations to seek to contain North
Korea's nuclear weapons
development program.

▲ WAITING AND HOPING
A U.S. Marine stands guard, and Liberians wait,
as 15 U.S. Navy Seals (off camera) land on the
beach to join African peacekeepers in the
capital city of Monrovia, Aug. 18. With Pres.
Charles Taylor gone into exile and rebel factions
continuing peace talks, Liberians hoped to
begin recovery after 14 years of civil war.

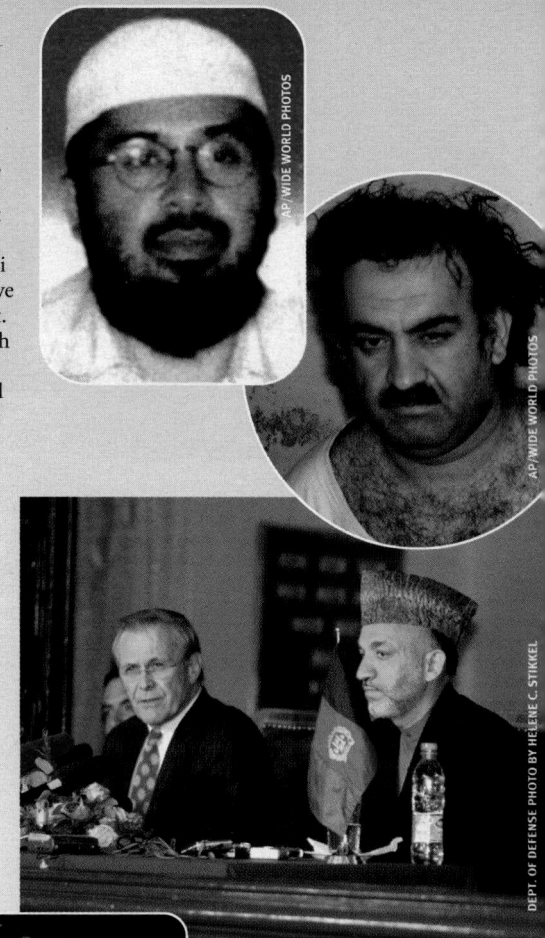

AL-QAEDA ARRESTS
The U.S. and other countries continued to hunt down suspected top al-Qaeda operatives. Riduan Isamuddin, or Hambali (left), captured in Thailand Aug. 14, was thought to be the mastermind behind the Oct. 2002 bombings in Bali that killed over 200, and to have played a major role in the Sept. 11, 2001, attacks. Khalid Sheikh Mohammed (right), caught in Pakistan Mar. 1, was an alleged mastermind of the Sept. 11 attacks. ▶

AFGHANISTAN IN FLUX
U.S. Sec. of Defense Donald Rumsfeld, left, in the Afghan capital of Kabul, May 1, announces an end to "major combat" operations there, as Afghan Pres. Hamid Karzai looks on. A year and a half after the ouster of Taliban militia by U.S. forces, reconstruction efforts were proceeding slowly; security remained fragile, despite the presence of some 8,000 U.S. soldiers and 5,500 international peacekeeping troops. ▶

◀ SARS FEARS
At an April ballet class in Hong Kong, students wore masks to protect themselves from severe acute respiratory syndrome (SARS), a contagious disease that started in China and spread around the globe, afflicting more than 8,400 people. Largely contained by July, SARS had caused more than 900 deaths through mid-August.

AP/WIDE WORLD PHOTOS

◀ CANADA BACKS GAY MARRIAGE
A lesbian couple outside Parliament Hill in Ottawa, Canada, on June 10, the day the Ontario Court of Appeal ordered that full marriage rights be extended to gay couples.

AP/WIDE WORLD PHOTOS

HEAT WAVE

A sweltering heat wave hit Europe in July and August, with many places seeing temperatures over 100°F for the first time since weather records were begun in the late 1800s. Thousands died across the continent, including an estimated 10,000 or more in France alone. The heat lowered water levels in the Rhine, as seen here in Düsseldorf, Germany. ▶

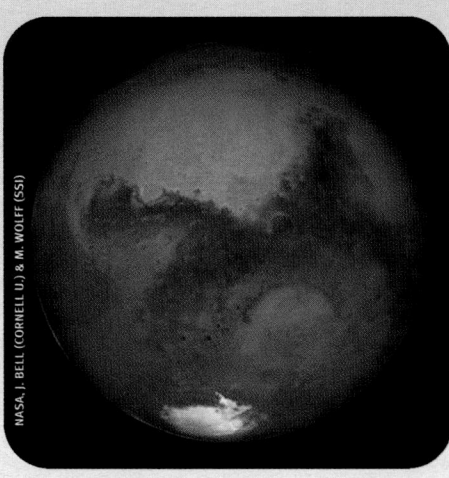

NASA, J. BELL (CORNELL U.) & M. WOLFF (SSI)

◀ MARS
In August, Mars made its closest approach to Earth in nearly 60,000 years, bringing out millions of skywatchers hoping to catch a glimpse of the red planet in the night sky. This picture was taken by the Hubble Space Telescope on Aug. 27, the day Mars was closest of all, at 34,647,420 miles.

▲ HERE'S HARRY
Harry Potter and the Order of the Phoenix, the long-awaited fifth book in the popular children's series by British author J.K. Rowling (inset), went on sale June 21 just after midnight.

▲ TRADING QUESTIONS
Homemaking entrepreneur Martha Stewart (left) was indicted in U.S. District Court in Manhattan June 4 on charges related to her sale of ImClone stock in Dec. 2001 just before an adverse ruling by the FDA became public. Sam Waksal (right), former chairman and CEO of the biotech company, was sentenced June 10 to 7 years, 3 months in prison and fined $4 million for securities fraud, obstruction of justice, and perjury.

▲ FIRST MEMOIRS
Former First Lady Sen. Hillary Rodham Clinton (D, NY) signs copies of her memoir, *Living History*, at a New York City bookstore. The book, chronicling her White House years, sold 200,000 copies on the first day it was released, June 9.

▲ DIFFICULT TIMES
New York Times executive editor Howell Raines (center) and managing editor Gerald Boyd (left), seen here entering a staff meeting, resigned after a scandal involving ex-reporter Jayson Blair (inset), who the paper said had "committed frequent acts of journalistic fraud."

▲ SUPERSTAR ACCUSED
Lakers basketball star Kobe Bryant with his wife Vanessa at a news conference in Los Angeles, July 18, after he was charged with sexually assaulting a 19-year-old woman in Eagle, CO. Bryant admitted adultery but denied charges of rape.

▲ FUGITIVE FOUND
Alleged 1996 Olympic Park bomber and anti-abortion activist Eric Robert Rudolph (center) leaves the Murphy, NC, sheriff's department for arraignment in federal court June 2 in Asheville. The object of a 5-year intensive manhunt, Rudolph was caught May 31 near Murphy.

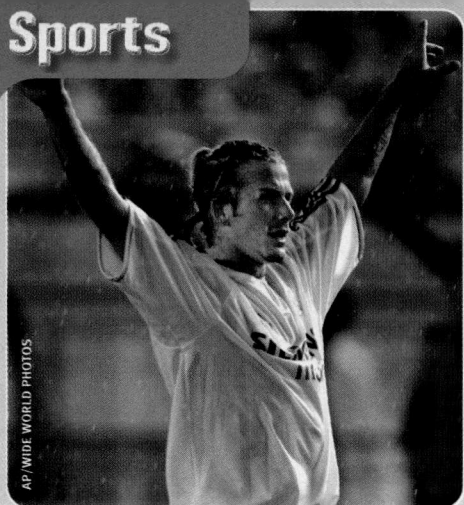

AP/WIDE WORLD PHOTOS

LUCY NICHOLSON/REUTERS/LANDOV

▲ **BECKHAM BENDS IT**

In only his 2nd game with his new team, Real Madrid, English soccer mega-star David Beckham scored a goal in Tokyo Aug. 5 with his trademark curving free kick—of the film *Bend It Like Beckham* fame.

▲ **TIM'S WORLD**

San Antonio center Tim Duncan, named NBA MVP in 2002 and 2003, powered the Spurs past the New Jersey Nets June 15 to win their 2nd NBA title in 5 years.

AP/WIDE WORLD PHOTOS

AP/WIDE WORLD PHOTOS

▲ **DRIVE FOR FIVE**

Lance Armstrong (in yellow jersey) held off Germany's Jan Ullrich by 61 seconds to win the Tour de France July 27, for a record-tying 5th time in a row.

▲ **SUPER BUCS**

The Tampa Bay defense intercepted Oakland 5 times in their 48-21 win in Super Bowl XXXVII on Jan. 26. Safety Dexter Jackson picked off 2 key passes in the 1st half—and the Super Bowl MVP Award.

▲ WHERE THE BOYS WERE
Annika Sorenstam became the 1st woman in 58 years to compete on the PGA Tour when she teed off at the Colonial, in Fort Worth, TX, May 22. She missed the cut by 4 strokes, but went on to complete an LPGA career Grand Slam, winning the LPGA June 8 and the Women's British Open on Aug. 3.

▲ PHENOM LEBRON
LeBron James, the top U.S. high school (St. Vincent-St. Mary's) basketball player, became only the 2nd prep player to be selected #1 in the NBA Draft, June 26. The 6' 8" forward went to the Cleveland Cavaliers.

▲ SERENA SUPREME
Serena Williams defeated her sister, Venus, to take her 2nd straight Wimbledon title July 5. It was her 2nd Grand Slam of the year and the 5th time since early 2002 she beat Venus in a Grand Slam final.

Sports

AP/WIDE WORLD PHOTOS

▲ 300 W'S
Future Hall-of-Fame pitcher Roger Clemens, in his 20th season, got the 300th win and 4,000th strikeout of his career against the St. Louis Cardinals, June 13 at Yankee Stadium.

AP/WIDE WORLD PHOTOS

▲ PHELPS PHANTASTIC
At the World Swimming Championships in Barcelona, Spain, 18-year-old American Michael Phelps set 5 individual world records—1 more than Mark Spitz set at the 1972 Olympics. Phelps set marks in the 100 butterfly, 200 butterfly, 200 individual medley (twice), and the 400 individual medley.

◄ SIMPLY SMASHING
In only her 3rd marathon, 28-year-old British running sensation Paula Radcliffe lowered her own world record by nearly 2 minutes (1:53), clocking 2 hours, 15 minutes, 25 seconds at the London Marathon, Apr. 13.

2·15·25
TIMEX
FLORA LONDON MARATHON 2003

AP/WIDE WORLD PHOTOS

Transport: Railroad: Length: 437 mi. **Motor vehicles (1998):** 5,400 pass. cars, 6,600 comm. vehicles. **Civil aviation:** 180.2 mil pass.-mi; 10 airports. **Chief ports:** Nouakchott, Nouadhibou.

Communications: TV sets: 95 per 1,000 pop. **Radios:** 146 per 1,000 pop. **Telephone Lines:** 32,000. **Daily newspaper circ.:** .5 per 1,000 pop. **Internet:** 10,000 users.

Health: Life expectancy: 49.8 male; 54.1 female. **Births (per 1,000 pop.):** 42.2. **Deaths** (per 1,000 pop.): 13.0. **Natural inc.:** 2.91%. **Infant mortality** (per 1,000 live births): 73.8.

Education: Compulsory: ages 6-14. **Literacy:** 41.7%.

Major Intl. Organizations: UN (FAO, IBRD, ILO, IMF, IMO, WHO, WTrO), AL, AU.

Embassy: 2129 Leroy Pl. NW 20008; 232-5700.

Website: www.mauritania.mr

Mauritania was a French protectorate from 1903. It became independent Nov. 28, 1960 and annexed the south of former Spanish Sahara (now Western Sahara) in 1976. Saharan guerrillas of the Polisario Front stepped up attacks in 1977; 8,000 Moroccan troops and French bomber raids aided the government. Mauritania signed a peace treaty with the Polisario Front, 1979, resumed diplomatic relations with Algeria while breaking a defense treaty with Morocco, and renounced sovereignty over its share of Western Sahara. Opposition parties were legalized and a new constitution approved in 1991.

Although slavery has been repeatedly abolished, most recently in 1980, thousands of Mauritanians continued to live under conditions of servitude.

Mauritius
Republic of Mauritius

People: Population: 1,221,000. **Age distrib.** (%): <15: 25.4; 65+: 6.3. **Pop. density:** 1,710 per sq. mi. **Urban:** 42%. **Ethnic groups:** Indo-Mauritian 68%, Creole 27%, Sino-Mauritian 3%, Franco-Mauritian 2%. **Principal languages:** English (official), Creole, French, Hindi, Urdu, Hakka, Bhojpuri. **Chief religions:** Hindu 52%, Christian 28%, Muslim 17%.

Geography: Area: 788 sq. mi. (total); 784 sq. mi. (land). **Location:** In the Indian O., 500 mi. E of Madagascar. **Neighbors:** Nearest is Madagascar to W. **Topography:** A volcanic island nearly surrounded by coral reefs. A central plateau is encircled by mountain peaks. **Capital:** Port Louis: 176,000.

Government: Type: Republic. **Head of state:** Pres. Karl Auguste Offmann; b Nov. 25, 1940; in office: Feb. 25, 2002. **Head of gov.:** Prime Min. Anerood Jugnauth; b Mar. 29, 1930; in office: Sept. 17, 2000. **Local divisions:** 9 districts, 3 dependencies. **Defense budget** (2001): $9 mil.

Economy: Industries: sugar & food proc., textiles, clothing, chemicals. **Chief crops:** sugarcane, tea, corn, potatoes, bananas. **Natural resources:** fish. **Arable land:** 49%. **Livestock** (2002): cattle: 28,000; chickens: 7.70 mil.; goats: 95,000; sheep: 7,000. **Fish catch** (2002): 10,753 metric tons. **Electricity prod.** (2001): 1.31 bil. kWh. **Labor force:** construct. and ind. 36%, services 24%, agri. and fishing 14%, trade, restaurants, hotels 16%, transportation and communication 7%, finance 3%.

Finance: Monetary unit: Rupee (MUR) (Sept. 2003: 29.19=1 U.S.). **GDP** (2002 est.): $13.2 bil. **Per capita GDP:** $11,000. **Imports** (2001): $2 bil.; partners (2000 est.): South Africa 20%, France 19%, India 9%, Hong Kong 5%. **Exports** (2001 est.): $1.6 bil.; partners (2000 est.): UK 25.8%, France 20.8%, U.S. 16%, South Africa 10.9%. **Tourism:** $585 mil. **Budget** (1999 est.): $1.2 bil. **Intl. reserves less gold:** $903 mil. **Gold:** 60,000 oz t. **Consumer prices:** 6.7%.

Transport: Motor vehicles: 87,500 pass. cars, 34,200 comm. vehicles. **Civil aviation:** 2.53 bil pass.-mi; 2 airports. **Chief port:** Port Louis.

Communications: TV sets: 248 per 1,000 pop. **Radios:** 371 per 1,000 pop. **Telephone lines:** 327,200. **Daily newspaper circ.:** 71.7 per 1,000 pop. **Internet:** 180,000 users.

Health: Life expectancy: 67.8 male; 75.9 female. **Births (per 1,000 pop.):** 16.1. **Deaths** (per 1,000 pop.): 6.8. **Natural inc.:** 0.93%. **Infant mortality** (per 1,000 live births): 16.1.

Education: Compulsory: ages 6-12. **Literacy:** 85.6%.

Major Intl. Organizations: UN and all of its specialized agencies. the Commonwealth, AU.

Embassy: 4301 Connecticut Ave. NW, Suite 441, 20008; 244-1491.

Website: www.gov.mu

Mauritius was uninhabited when settled in 1638 by the Dutch, who introduced sugarcane. France took over in 1721, bringing African slaves. Britain ruled from 1810 to Mar. 12, 1968, bringing Indian workers for the sugar plantations.

Mauritius formally severed its association with the British crown Mar. 12, 1992.

Mexico
United Mexican States

People: Population: 103,457,000. **Age distrib.** (%): <15: 32.8; 65+: 4.5. **Pop. density:** 139 per sq. mi. **Urban:** 75%. **Ethnic groups:** Mestizo 60%, Amerindian 30%, White 9%. **Principal languages:** Spanish (official), Náhuatl, Maya, Zaptec, Otomi, Miztec,

other indigenous. **Chief religions:** Roman Catholic 89%, Protestant 6%.

Geography: Area: 761,605 sq. mi. (total); 742,489 sq. mi. (land). **Location:** In southern North America. **Neighbors:** U.S. on N, Guatemala and Belize on S. **Topography:** The Sierra Madre Occidental Mts. run NW-SE near the west coast; the Sierra Madre Oriental Mts. run near the Gulf of Mexico. They join S of Mexico City. Between the 2 ranges lies the dry central plateau, 5,000 to 8,000 ft. alt., rising toward the S, with temperate vegetation. Coastal lowlands are tropical. About 45% of land is arid. **Capital:** Mexico City. **Cities (urban aggr.):** Mexico City 18,268,000; Guadalajara 3,697,000; Monterrey 3,267,000; Puebla 1,888,000.

Government: Type: Federal republic. **Head of state and gov.:** Pres. Vicente Fox Quesada; b July 2, 1942; in office: Dec. 1, 2000. **Local divisions:** 31 states, 1 federal district. **Defense budget** (2002): $3.2 bil. **Active troops:** 192,770.

Economy: Industries: food & beverages, tobacco, chemicals, iron & steel, oil, mining, textiles, clothing, autos, consumer durables, tourism. **Chief crops:** corn, wheat, soybeans, rice, beans, cotton, coffee, fruit, tomatoes. **Natural resources:** oil, silver, copper, gold, lead, zinc, nat. gas, timber. **Crude oil reserves** (2002): 26.9 bil. bbls. **Arable land:** 12%. **Livestock** (2002): cattle: 585,000; chickens: 28 mil.; goats: 5.02 mil.; pigs: 938,000; sheep: 9.21 mil. **Fish catch** (2002): 1,474,667 metric tons. **Electricity prod.** (2001): 198.56 bil. kWh. **Labor force:** agri. 20%, ind. 24%, services 56%.

Finance: Monetary unit: Peso (MXN) (Sept. 2003: 10.94=1 U.S.). **GDP** (2002 est.): $900 bil. **Per capita GDP:** $9,000. **Imports** (2001): $168 bil.; partners (2001 est.): U.S. 68.4%, Japan 4.7%, Germany 3.6%, Canada 2.5%. **Exports** (2001): $159 bil.; partners (2001 est.): U.S. 88.4%, Canada 2%, Germany 0.9%, Spain 0.8%. **Tourism:** $8.3 bil. **Budget** (2001 est.): $140 bil. **Intl. reserves less gold:** $37.22 bil. **Gold:** 220,000 oz t. **Consumer prices:** 5.0%.

Transport: Railroad: Length: 11,185 mi. **Motor vehicles:** 10.44 mil pass. cars, 5.04 mil comm. vehicles. **Civil aviation:** 17.30 bil pass.-mi; 231 airports. **Chief ports:** Coatzacoalcos, Mazatlan, Tampico, Veracruz.

Communications: TV sets: 272 per 1,000 pop. **Radios:** 329 per 1,000 pop. **Telephone lines:** 14,941,600. **Daily newspaper circ.:** 97 per 1,000 pop. **Internet:** 4,663,400 users.

Health: Life expectancy: 69.3 male; 75.5 female. **Births (per 1,000 pop.):** 21.9. **Deaths** (per 1,000 pop.): 5.0. **Natural inc.:** 1.70%. **Infant mortality** (per 1,000 live births): 23.7.

Education: Compulsory: ages 6-15. **Literacy:** 92.2%.

Major Intl. Organizations: UN (FAO, IBRD, ILO, IMF, IMO, WHO, WTrO), APEC, OAS, OECD.

Embassy: 1911 Pennsylvania Ave. NW 20006; 728-1600.

Website: www.presidencia.gob.mx/?NLang=en

Mexico was the site of advanced Indian civilizations. The Mayas, an agricultural people, moved up from Yucatan, built immense stone pyramids, invented a calendar. The Toltecs were overcome by the Aztecs, who founded Tenochtitlan AD 1325, now Mexico City. Hernando Cortes, Spanish conquistador, destroyed the Aztec empire, 1519-21.

After 3 centuries of Spanish rule the people rose, under Fr. Miguel Hidalgo y Costilla, 1810, Fr. Morelos y Payon, 1812, and Gen. Agustin Iturbide, who made himself emperor as Agustin I, 1821. A republic was declared in 1823.

Mexican territory extended into the present American Southwest and California until Texas revolted and established a republic in 1836; the Mexican legislature refused recognition but was unable to enforce its authority there. After numerous clashes, the U.S.-Mexican War, 1846-48, resulted in the loss by Mexico of the lands north of the Rio Grande.

French arms supported an Austrian archduke on the throne of Mexico as Maximilian I, 1864-67, but pressure from the U.S. forced France to withdraw. Dictatorial rule by Porfirio Diaz, president 1877-80, 1884-1911, led to a period of rebellion and factional fighting. A new constitution, Feb. 5, 1917, brought social reform.

The Institutional Revolutionary Party (PRI) dominated politics from 1929 until the late 1990s. Radical opposition, including some guerrilla activity, was contained by strong measures. Some gains in agriculture, industry, and social services were achieved, but much of the work force remained jobless or underemployed. Although prospects brightened with the discovery of vast oil reserves, inflation and a drop in world oil prices aggravated Mexico's economic problems in the 1980s.

Mexico reached agreement with the U.S. and Canada on the North American Free Trade Agreement (NAFTA) Aug. 12, 1992; it took effect Jan. 1, 1994.

Guerrillas of the Zapatista National Liberation Army (EZLN) launched an uprising, Jan. 1, 1994, in southern Mexico. A tentative peace accord was reached Mar. 2. The presidential candidate of the governing PRI, Luis Donaldo Colosio Murrieta, was assassinated at a political rally in Tijuana, Mar. 23. The new PRI candidate, Ernesto Zedillo Ponce de León, won election Aug. 21 and was inaugurated Dec. 1, 1994.

An austerity plan and pledges of aid from the U.S. saved Mexico's currency from collapse in early 1995. Popular Revolutionary Army guerrillas launched coordinated attacks on government targets in Aug. 1996. In elections July 6, 1997, the PRI failed to win a congressional majority for the first time since 1929. An armed gang massacred 45 peasants in Chiapas on Dec. 22, 1997. In the presidential election of July 2, 2000, the PRI lost for the 1st time in over 7 decades; the winner, opposition candidate Vicente Fox Quesada, took office Dec. 1, 2000. Fox's National Action Party suffered a setback in midterm elections, July 6, 2003.

Micronesia
Federated States of Micronesia

People: Population: 109,000. **Age distrib.** (%): <15: NA; 65+: NA. **Pop. density:** 141 per sq. mi. **Urban:** 29%. **Ethnic groups:** Nine distinct Micronesian and Polynesian groups. **Principal languages:** English (official), Trukese, Pohnpeian, Yapese, Kosrean, Ulithian, Woleaian, Nukuoro, Kapingamaranelectricity prod.: gi. **Chief religions:** Roman Catholic 50%, Protestant 47%.

Geography: Area (total): 271 sq. mi. **Location:** Consists of 607 islands in the W Pacific Ocean. **Topography:** The country includes both high mountainous islands and low coral atolls; volcanic outcroppings on Pohnpei, Kosrae, and Truk. Climate is tropical. **Capital:** Palikir, on Pohnpei; (1994 island pop.) 33,372.

Government: Type: Republic. **Head of state and gov.:** Pres. Joseph J. Urusemal; b Mar. 19, 1952; in office: May 11, 2003. **Local divisions:** 4 states.

Economy: Industries: tourism, constr., fish proc., handicrafts. **Chief crops:** black pepper, fruits & vegetables, coconuts, cassava, sweet potatoes. **Natural resources:** timber, fish, minerals. **Livestock** (2002): cattle: 14,000; chickens: 185,000; goats: 4,000; pigs: 32,000. **Fish catch** (2002 est.): 18,062 metric tons. **Electricity prod.:** NA. **Labor force:** two-thirds are government employees.

Finance: Monetary unit: U.S. Dollar. **GDP** (2002 est.): $277 mil. **Per capita GDP:** $2,000. **Imports:** $149 mil.; partners: U.S., Australia, Japan. **Exports:** $22 mil.; partners: Japan, U.S., Guam. **Budget** (1998 est.): $160 mil. **Intl. reserves less gold:** $86 mil.

Transport: 6 airports. **Chief ports:** Colonia (Yap), Kolonia (Pohnpei), Lele, Moen.

Communications: TV sets 20 per 1,000 pop. **Radios:** 70 per 1,000 pop. **Telephone lines:** 10,100. **Internet:** 5,000 users.

Health: Life expectancy: 66.7 male; 70.6 female. **Births** (per 1,000 pop.): 27.1. **Deaths** (per 1,000 pop.): 6.0. **Natural inc.:** 2.11%. **Infant mortality** (per 1,000 live births): 33.5.

Education: Compulsory: ages 6-13. **Literacy** (1991): 90%.

Major Intl. Organizations: UN (IBRD, IMF, WHO).

Embassy: 1725 N St. NW 20036; 223-4383.

Websites: www.fsmgov.org; www.fsmembassy.org

The Federated States of Micronesia, formerly known as the Caroline Islands, was ruled successively by Spain, Germany, Japan, and the U.S. It was internationally recognized as an independent nation Sept. 17, 1991. Tropical Storm Chata'an July 1-2, 2002, left 47 people dead and over 1,000 homeless in Chuuk.

Moldova
Republic of Moldova

People: Population: 4,267,000. **Age distrib.** (%): <15: 21.7; 65+: 10.1. **Pop. density:** 328 per sq. mi. **Urban:** 41%. **Ethnic groups:** Moldovan/Romanian 65%, Ukrainian 14%, Russian 13%. **Principal languages:** Moldovan (official.), Russian, Gagauz (a Turkish dialect). **Chief religion:** Eastern Orthodox 99%.

Geography: Area: 13,067 sq. mi. (total); 12,885 sq. mi. (land). **Location:** In E Europe. **Neighbors:** Romania on W; Ukraine on N, E, and S. **Topography:** The country is landlocked; mainly hilly plains, with steppelands in S near the Black Sea. **Capital:** Kishinev 662,000.

Government: Type: Republic. **Head of state:** Pres. Vladimir Voronin; b May 25, 1941; in office: Apr. 7, 2001. **Head of gov.:** Prime Min. Vasile Tarlev; b Oct. 9, 1963; in office: Apr. 19, 2001. **Local divisions:** 21 cities and towns, 48 urban settlements, more than 1,600 villages. **Defense budget** (2002): $6.9 mil. **Active troops:** 7,210.

Economy: Industries: food proc., agric. machinery, foundry equip. **Chief crops:** vegetables, grapes, grain, sunflower seed, tobacco. **Natural resources:** lignite, phosphorite, gypsum, limestone. **Arable land:** 53%. **Livestock** (2002): cattle: 412,000; chickens: 14.12 mil.; goats: 111,700; pigs: 449,000; sheep: 858,000. **Fish catch** (2002): 1,576 metric tons. **Electricity prod.** (2001): 3.39 kWh. **Labor force:** agri. 40%, ind. 14%, other 46%.

Finance: Monetary unit: Leu (MDL) (Sept. 2003: 13.68=1 U.S.). **GDP** (2002 est.): $11 bil. **Per capita GDP:** $2,500. **Imports** (2002): $980 mil.; partners (2001): Ukraine 18%, Russia 15.1%, Romania 13.1%, Germany 10.5%. **Exports** (2002 est.): $590 mil.; partners (2001): Russia 43%, Ukraine 10.1%, Italy 8.1%, Germany 7.2%. **Tourism:** $4 mil. **Budget** (1998 est.): $594 mil. **Intl. reserves less gold:** $198 mil. **Consumer prices:** 5.1%.

Transport: Railroad: Length: 825 mi. **Motor vehicles:** 232,300 pass. cars, 6,900 comm. vehicles. **Civil aviation:** 60.3 mil pass.-mi; 8 airport.

Communications: TV sets: 297 per 1,000 pop. **Radios:** 742 per 1,000 pop. **Telephone lines:** 639,200. **Daily newspaper circ.:** 150.8 per 1,000 pop. **Internet:** 60,000 users.

Health: Life expectancy: 60.6 male; 69.4 female. **Births** (per 1,000 pop.): 14.3. **Deaths** (per 1,000 pop.): 12.7. **Natural inc.:** 0.16%. **Infant mortality** (per 1,000 live births): 41.6.

Education: Compulsory: ages 7-16. **Literacy:** 99.1%.

Major Intl. Organizations: UN (FAO, IBRD, ILO, IMF, WHO, WTrO), CIS, OSCE.

Embassy: 2101 S St. NW 20008; 667-1130.

Website: www.moldova.org

In 1918, Romania annexed all of Bessarabia that Russia had acquired from Turkey in 1812 by the Treaty of Bucharest. In 1924, the Soviet Union established the Moldavian Autonomous Soviet Socialist Republic on the eastern bank of the Dniester. It was merged with the Romanian-speaking districts of Bessarabia in 1940 to form the Moldavian SSR.

During World War II, Romania, allied with Germany, occupied the area. It was recaptured by the USSR in 1944. Moldova declared independence Aug. 27, 1991. It became an independent state when the USSR disbanded Dec. 26, 1991.

Fighting erupted Mar. 1992 in the Dnestr (Dniester) region between Moldovan security forces and Slavic separatists—ethnic Russians and ethnic Ukrainians—who feared Moldova would merge with neighboring Romania. In a plebiscite on Mar. 6, 1994, voters in Moldova supported independence, without unification with Romania.

Defying the Moldovan government, voters in the breakaway Dnestr region held legislative elections and approved a separatist constitution Dec. 24, 1995. Petru Lucinschi, a former Communist, won a presidential runoff election Dec. 1, 1996. A peace accord with Dnestr separatists was signed in Moscow May 8, 1997. The Communists won the most seats in parliamentary elections Mar. 22, 1998, but a coalition of three center-right parties formed the government. New elections Feb. 25, 2001, brought a decisive Communist victory.

Monaco
Principality of Monaco

People: Population: 32,000. **Age distrib.** (%): <15: 15.5; 65+: 22.4. **Pop. density:** c. 40,000 per sq. mi. **Urban:** 100%. **Ethnic groups:** French 47%, Monegasque 16%, Italian 16%. **Principal languages:** French (official), English, Italian, Monegasque. **Chief religion:** Roman Catholic 90% (official).

Geography: Area (total): about 3/4 sq. mi. **Location:** On the NW Mediterranean coast. **Neighbors:** France to W, N, E. **Topography:** Monaco-Ville sits atop a high promontory, the rest of the principality rises from the port up the hillside. **Capital:** Monaco-ville: 34,000.

Government: Type: Constitutional monarchy. **Head of state:** Prince Rainier III; b May 31, 1923; in office: May 9, 1949. **Head of gov.:** Min. of State Patrick Leclercq; b 1938; in office: Jan. 5, 2000. **Local divisions:** 4 quarters.

Economy: Industries: tourism, constr., light industrial products. **Chief crops:** none. **Natural resources:** none. **Fish catch** (2002): 3 metric tons.

Finance: Monetary unit: Euro (EUR) (Sept. 2003: 0.92=1 U.S.). **GDP** (1999 est.): $870 mil. **Per capita GDP:** $27,000. **Imports/Exports:** Integrated with France. **Budget** (1995): $531 mil.

Transport: Railroad: Length: 1 mi. **Motor vehicles:** 17,000 pass. cars, 4,000 comm. vehicles. **Civil aviation:** 1.2 mil pass.-mi. **Chief port:** Monaco.

Communications: TV sets: 758 per 1,000 pop. **Radios:** 1,030 per 1,000 pop. **Daily newspaper circ.:** 251 per 1,000 pop.

Health: Life expectancy: 75.2 male; 83.4 female. **Births** (per 1,000 pop.): 9.6. **Deaths** (per 1,000 pop.): 12.9. **Natural inc.:** -0.33%. **Infant mortality** (per 1,000 live births): 5.7.

Education: Compulsory: ages 6-15. **Literacy:** 99%.

Major Intl. Organizations: UN (IMO, WHO), OSCE.

Website: www.monaco-consulate.com

An independent principality for over 300 years, Monaco has belonged to the House of Grimaldi since 1297, except during the French Revolution. It was placed under the protectorate of Sardinia in 1815, and under France, 1861. The Prince of Monaco was an absolute ruler until the 1911 constitution. Monaco was admitted to the UN on May 28, 1993.

Monaco's fame as a tourist resort is widespread. It is noted for its mild climate, magnificent scenery, and elegant casinos.

Mongolia

People: Population: 2,594,000. **Age distrib.** (%): <15: 32; 65+: 3.9. **Pop. density:** 4 per sq. mi. **Urban:** 57%. **Ethnic groups:** Mongol 85%, Turkic 7%, Tungusic 5%. **Principal languages:** Khalkha Mongol, Turkic, Russian. **Chief religion:** Tibetan Buddhist Lamaism 96%.

Geography: Area: 604,249 sq. mi. (total); 600.543 sq. mi. (land). **Location:** In E Central Asia. **Neighbors:** Russia on N, China on E, W, and S. **Topography:** Mostly a high plateau with mountains, salt lakes, and vast grasslands. Arid lands in the S are part of the Gobi Desert. **Capital:** Ulan Bator: 761,000.

Government: Type: Republic. **Head of state:** Pres. Natsagiyn Bagabandi; b Apr. 22, 1950; in office: June 20, 1997. **Head of gov.:** Nambaryn Enkhbayar; b June 1, 1958; in office: July 26,

2000. **Local divisions:** 18 provinces, 3 municipalities. **Defense budget** (2002): $24.6 mil. **Active troops:** 9,100.

Economy: Industries: constr. materials, mining, oil, food, beverages. **Chief crops:** wheat, barley, potatoes, forage crops. **Natural resources:** oil, coal, copper, molybd., tungsten, phosphates, tin, nickel, zinc, fluorspar, gold, silver, iron. **Arable land:** 1%. **Livestock** (2002): cattle: 2.05 mil.; chickens: 60,000; goats: 8.86 mil.; pigs: 15,000; sheep: 11.80 mil. **Fish catch** (2002): 117 metric tons. **Electricity prod.** (2001): 2.23 bil. kWh. **Labor force:** primarily herding/agricultural.

Finance: Monetary unit: Tugrik (MNT) (Sept. 2003: 1120.37=1 U.S.). **GDP** (2002 est.): $5 bil. **Per capita GDP:** $1,840. **Imports** (2000): $614.5 mil.; partners (2000): Russia 34%, China 21%, Japan 12%, South Korea 9%. **Exports** (2000): $466.1 mil.; partners (2000): U.S., Antigua and Barbuda. **Tourism** (1999): $28 mil. **Budget** (2001 est.): $427 mil. **Intl. reserves less gold:** $257mil. **Gold:** 140,000 oz t. **Consumer prices** (change in 2001): 8.0%.

Transport: Railroad: Length: 1,128 mi. **Motor vehicles:** 21,000 pass. cars, 27,000 comm. vehicles. **Civil aviation:** 270.9 mil pass.-mi; 10 airports.

Communications: TV sets: 58 per 1,000 pop. **Radios:** 142 per 1,000 pop. **Telephone lines:** 124,300. **Daily newspaper circ.:** 27 per 1,000 pop. **Internet:** 40,000 users.

Health: Life expectancy: 61.6 male; 66.1 female. **Births** (per 1,000 pop.): 21.4. **Deaths** (per 1,000 pop.): 7.2. **Natural inc.:** 1.42%. **Infant mortality** (per 1,000 live births): 57.2.

Education: Compulsory: ages 8-15. **Literacy:** 99%.

Major Intl. Organizations: UN (FAO, IBRD, ILO, IMF, IMO, WHO, WTrO).

Embassy: 2833 M St. NW 20007; 333-7117.

Websites: www.pmis.gov.mn/indexeng.php
www.mongoliatourism.gov.mn

One of the world's oldest countries, Mongolia reached the zenith of its power in the 13th century when Genghis Khan and his successors conquered all of China and extended their influence as far west as Hungary and Poland. In later centuries, the empire dissolved and Mongolia became a province of China.

With the advent of the 1911 Chinese revolution, Mongolia, with Russian backing, declared its independence. A Communist regime was established July 11, 1921.

In 1990, the Mongolian Communist Party yielded its monopoly on power but won election in July. A new constitution took effect Feb. 12, 1992. A democratic alliance won legislative elections, June 30, 1996. Natsagiyn Bagabandi, a former Communist, won the presidential election of May 18, 1997. A protracted political crisis took a violent turn Oct. 2, 1998, with the murder of Sanjaasuregiyn Zorig, a popular cabinet member seeking to become prime minister. The former Communists won 72 of 76 seats in parliamentary elections, July 2, 2000. Pres. Bagabandi was reelected May 20, 2001.

Morocco
Kingdom of Morocco

People: Population: 30,566,000. **Age distrib.** (%): <15: 33.8; 65+: 4.7. **Pop. density:** 177 per sq. mi. **Urban:** 56%. **Ethnic groups:** Arab-Berber 99%. **Principal languages:** Arabic (official), Berber dialects, French, Spanish, English. **Chief religion:** Muslim 99% (official).

Geography: Area: 172,414 sq. mi. (total); 172,317 sq. mi. (land). **Location:** On NW coast of Africa. **Neighbors:** Western Sahara on S, Algeria on E. **Topography:** Consists of 5 natural regions: mountain ranges (Riff in the N, Middle Atlas, Upper Atlas, and Anti-Atlas); rich plains in the W; alluvial plains in SW; well-cultivated plateaus in the center; a pre-Sahara arid zone extending from SE. **Capital:** Rabat. **Cities (urban aggr.):** Casablanca 3,357,000; Rabat 1,668,000; Fès 907,000.

Government: Type: Constitutional monarchy. **Head of state:** King Mohammed VI; b Aug. 21, 1963; in office: July 23, 1999. **Head of gov.:** Prime Min. Driss Jettou; b May 24, 1945; in office: Oct. 9, 2002. **Local divisions:** 16 regions. **Defense budget** (2002): $1.7 bil. **Active troops:** 196,300.

Economy: Industries: mining, food proc., leather goods, textiles, constr., tourism. **Chief crops:** barley, wheat, citrus, grapes, vegetables, olives. **Natural resources:** phosphates, iron ore, mang., lead, zinc, fish, salt. **Crude oil reserves** (2002): 2 mil. bbls. **Arable land:** 21%. **Livestock** (2002): cattle: 2.66 mil.; chickens: 137 mil.; goats: 5.20 mil.; pigs: 8,000; sheep: 17.30 mil. **Fish catch** (2002): 1,084,638 metric tons. **Electricity prod.** (2001): 13.35 bil. kWh. **Labor force:** agri. 50%, services 35%, ind. 15%.

Finance: Monetary unit: Dirham (MAD) (Sept. 2003: 10.14=1 U.S.). **GDP** (2002 est.): $115 bil. **Per capita GDP:** $3,900. **Imports** (2001): $12.4 bil.; partners (2000): France 25%, Spain 11%, Germany 6%, Italy 6%. **Exports** (2001 est.): $8.2 bil.; partners (2000): France 26%, Spain 10%, UK 8%, Italy 6%. **Tourism:** $2.04 bil. **Budget** (2001 est.): $14.6 bil. **Intl. reserves less gold:** $7.45 bil. **Gold:** 710,000 oz t. **Consumer prices:** 2.8%.

Transport: Railroad: Length: 1,185 mi. **Motor vehicles** (1999): 1.16 mil pass. cars, 400,300 comm. vehicles. **Civil aviation:** 4.11 bil pass.-mi; 26 airports. **Chief ports:** Tangier, Casablanca, Kenitra.

Communications: TV sets: 165 per 1,000 pop. **Radios:** 247 per 1,000 pop. **Telephone lines:** 1,127,400. **Daily newspaper circ.:** 26.1 per 1,000 pop. **Internet:** 500,000 users.

Health: Life expectancy: 67.8 male; 72.4 female. **Births** (per 1,000 pop.): 23.3. **Deaths** (per 1,000 pop.): 5.8. **Natural inc.:** 1.75%. **Infant mortality** (per 1,000 live births): 44.9.

Education: Compulsory: ages 6-14. **Literacy:** 51.7%.

Major Intl. Organizations: UN (FAO, IBRD, ILO, IMF, IMO, WHO, WTrO), AL.

Embassy: 1601 21st St. NW 20009; 462-7979.

Website: www.mincom.gov.ma/

Berbers were the original inhabitants, followed by Carthaginians and Romans. Arabs conquered in 683. In the 11th and 12th centuries, a Berber empire ruled all NW Africa and most of Spain from Morocco.

Part of Morocco came under Spanish rule in the 19th century; France controlled the rest in the early 20th. Tribal uprisings lasted from 1911 to 1933. The country became independent Mar. 2, 1956. Tangier, an internationalized seaport, was turned over to Morocco, 1956. Ifni, a Spanish enclave, was ceded in 1969. Morocco annexed the disputed territory of Western Sahara during the second half of the 1970s.

King Hassan II assumed the throne in 1961, reigning until his death on July 23, 1999; he was immediately succeeded by his eldest son. Political reforms in the 1990s included the establishment of a bicameral legislature in 1997.

Five terrorist attacks in Casablanca May 16, 2003, left about 40 people dead, including 10 suicide bombers; the government blamed Salafia Jihadia, an extremist group connected with al-Qaeda.

Western Sahara

Western Sahara, formerly the protectorate of Spanish Sahara, is bounded the in N by Morocco, the NE by Algeria, the E and S by Mauritania, and on the W by the Atlantic Ocean. Phosphates are the major resource. Population (2003 est.): 261,794; capital: Laayoune (El Aaiun). Area: 102,600 sq mi.

Spain withdrew from its protectorate in Feb. 1976. On Apr. 14, 1976, Morocco annexed over 70,000 sq. mi, with the remainder annexed by Mauritania. A guerrilla movement, the Polisario Front, which had proclaimed the region independent Feb. 27, launched attacks with Algerian support. After Mauritania signed a treaty with Polisario on Aug. 5, 1979, Morocco occupied Mauritania's portion of Western Sahara.

After years of bitter fighting, Morocco controlled the main urban areas, but Polisario guerrillas moved freely in the vast, sparsely populated deserts. The 2 sides implemented a cease-fire in 1991, when a UN peacekeeping force was deployed. A peace plan developed by former U.S. Sec. of State James A. Baker III was endorsed by the UN Security Council, July 31, 2003; it was accepted by Polisario but rejected by Morocco.

Mozambique
Republic of Mozambique

People: Population: 18,863,000. **Age distrib.** (%): <15: 42.5; 65+: 2.8. **Pop. density:** 62 per sq. mi. **Urban:** 33%. **Ethnic groups:** Shangaan, Chokwe, Manyika, Sena, Makua. **Principal languages:** Portuguese (official) and dialects, English. **Chief religions:** Indigenous beliefs 50%, Christian 30%, Muslim 20%.

Geography: Area: 309,495 sq. mi. (total); 302,739 sq. mi. (land). **Location:** On SE coast of Africa. **Neighbors:** Tanzania on N; Malawi, Zambia, Zimbabwe on W; South Africa, Swaziland on S. **Topography:** Coastal lowlands comprise nearly half the country with plateaus rising in steps to the mountains along the western border. **Capital:** Maputo 1,134,000.

Government: Type: Republic. **Head of state:** Pres. Joaquim Chissano; b Oct. 22, 1939; in office: Oct. 19, 1986. **Head of gov.:** Prime Min. Pascoal Mocumbi; b Apr. 10, 1941; in office: Dec. 21, 1994. **Local divisions:** 10 provinces. **Defense budget** (2002): $69 mil. **Active troops:** 10,000–11,500.

Economy: Industries: food, beverages, chemicals, oil products, textiles, cement. **Chief crops:** cotton, cashews, sugarcane, tea, cassava, corn, coconuts, sisal, trop. fruits. **Natural resources:** coal, titanium, nat. gas, hydropower, tantalum, graphite. **Arable land:** 4%. **Livestock** (2002): cattle: 1.32 mil.; chickens: 28 mil.; goats: 392,000; pigs: 180,000; sheep: 125,000. **Fish catch** (2002): 32,512 metric tons. **Electricity prod.** (2001): 7.19 bil. kWh. **Labor force:** agri. 81%, ind. 6%, services 13%.

Finance: Monetary unit: Metical (MZM) (Sept. 2003: 23,355.00=1 U.S.). **GDP** (2002 est.): $19.2 bil. **Per capita GDP:** $1,000. **Imports** (2001): $1.254 bil.; partners (2000): South Africa 33.5%, Portugal 4.8%, U.S. 4.2%, Australia 3.8%. **Exports** (2001 est.): $746 mil.; partners (2000): South Africa 12.7%, Zimbabwe 12.2%, Spain 10.6%, Portugal 10.0%. **Budget** (2001 est.): $1.025 bil. **Intl. reserves less gold:** $603 mil. **Gold:** 70,000 oz t. **Consumer prices:** 16.8%.

Transport: Railroad: Length: 1,946 mi. **Motor vehicles** (1998): 27,200 pass. cars, 14,500 comm. vehicles. **Civil aviation:** 202.6 mil pass.-mi; 22 airports. **Chief ports:** Maputo, Beira, Nacala, Inhambane.

Communications: TV sets: 5 per 1,000 pop. **Radios:** 40 per 1,000 pop. **Telephone lines:** 89,500. **Daily newspaper circ.:** 2.3 per 1,000 pop. **Internet:** 30,000 users.

Health: Life expectancy: 31.0 male; 31.6 female. **Births** (per 1,000 pop.): 38.2. **Deaths** (per 1,000 pop.): 30.0. **Natural inc.:** 0.82%. **Infant mortality** (per 1,000 live births): 199.0.

Education: Compulsory: ages 6-12. **Literacy:** 47.8%.

Major Intl. Organizations: UN (FAO, IBRD, ILO, IMF, IMO, WHO, WTrO), the Commonwealth, AU.

Embassy: 1990 M St. NW, Suite 570, 20036; 293-7146.

Website: www.mozambique.mz/eindex.htm

The first Portuguese post on the Mozambique coast was established in 1505, on the trade route to the East. Mozambique became independent June 25, 1975, after a ten-year war against Portuguese colonial domination. The 1974 revolution in Portugal had paved the way for the orderly transfer of power to Frelimo (Front for the Liberation of Mozambique). Frelimo took over local administration Sept. 20, 1974, although opposed, in part violently, by some blacks and whites.

The new government, led by Maoist Pres. Samora Machel, provided for a gradual transition to a Communist system. Economic problems included the emigration of most of the country's whites, a politically untenable economic dependence on white-ruled South Africa, and a large external debt.

In the 1980s, severe drought and civil war caused famine and heavy loss of life. Pres. Machel was killed in a plane crash just inside the South African border, Oct. 19, 1986.

The ruling party formally abandoned Marxist-Leninism in 1989, and a new constitution, effective Nov. 30, 1990, provided for multiparty elections and a free-market economy.

On Oct. 4, 1992, a peace agreement was signed aimed at ending hostilities between the government and the rebel Mozambique National Resistance (MNR). Repatriation of 1.7 million Mozambican refugees officially ended June 1995. In Mar. 1999 the heaviest floods in 4 decades left nearly 200,000 people stranded. Even worse flooding in Feb.-Mar. 2000 claimed more than 600 lives, displaced over 1 million people, and devastated the economy. A train crash May 25, 2002, in S Mozambique killed 196 people.

Myanmar *(formerly* Burma)
Union of Myanmar

People: Population: 49,485,000. **Age distrib.** (%): <15: 28.6; 65+: 4.8. **Pop. density:** 195 per sq. mi. **Urban:** 28%. **Ethnic groups:** Burman 68%, Shan 9%, Karen 7%, Rakhine 4%, Chinese 3%, Indian 2%, Mon 2%. **Principal languages:** Burmese (official); many ethnic minority languages. Chief religions: Buddhist 89%, Christian 4%, Muslim 4%, Animist 1%.

Geography: Area: 261,970 sq. mi. (total); 253,955 sq. mi. (land). **Location:** Between S and SE Asia, on Bay of Bengal. **Neighbors:** Bangladesh, India on W; China, Laos, Thailand on E. **Topography:** Mountains surround Myanmar on W, N, and E, and dense forests cover much of the nation. N-S rivers provide habitable valleys and communications, especially the Irrawaddy, navigable for 900 miles. The country has a tropical monsoon climate. **Capital:** Yangon (Rangoon). **Cities (urban aggr.):** Yangon 4,504,000; Mandalay 770,000.

Government: Type: Military. **Head of State:** Gen. Than Shwe; b Feb. 2, 1933; in office: Apr. 24, 1992. **Head of gov.:** Khin Nyunt; b Oct. 11, 1939; in office: Aug. 25, 2003. **Local divisions:** 7 states, 7 divisions. **Defense budget** (2002): $555 mil. **Active troops:** 444,000.

Economy: Industries: agric. proc., apparel, wood & wood products, mining, constr. materials. **Chief crops:** rice, beans, sesame, peanuts, sugarcane. **Natural resources:** oil, timber, tin, antimony, zinc, copper, tungsten, lead, coal, marble, limestone, gemstones, nat. gas, hydropower. **Crude oil reserves** (2001): 0.2 bil bbls. **Arable land:** 15%. **Livestock** (2002): cattle: 11.55 mil.; chickens: 57.13 mil.; goats: 1.54 mil.; pigs: 4.50 mil.; sheep: 432,000. **Fish catch** (2002): 1,288,134 metric tons. **Electricity prod.** (2001): 6.14 bil. kWh. **Labor force:** agri. 70%, ind. 7%, services 23%.

Finance: Monetary unit: Kyat (MMK) (Sept. 2003: 6.45=1 U.S.). **GDP** (2002 est.): $70 bil. **Per capita GDP:** $1,660. **Imports** (2001): $2.2 bil.; partners (2000 est.): China 26%, Singapore 23%, South Korea 15%, Japan 10%. **Exports** (2001): $1.8 bil.; partners (2000 est.): U.S. 27%, India 16%, China 7%, Japan 6%. **Tourism** (1999): $35 mil. **Budget** (1997): $12.2 bil. **Intl. reserves less gold:** $346 mil. **Gold:** 230,000 oz t. **Consumer prices:** 57.1%.

Transport: Railroad: Length: 2,480 mi. **Motor vehicles:** 173,900 pass. cars, 90,400 comm. vehicles. **Civil aviation:** 220.6 mil pass.-mi; 8 airports. **Chief ports:** Bassein, Moulmein.

Communications: TV sets: 7 per 1,000 pop. **Radios:** 72 per 1,000 pop. **Telephone lines:** 295,200. **Daily newspaper circ.:** 9.1 per 1,000 pop. **Internet:** 10,000 users.

Health: Life expectancy: 54.1 male; 57.6 female. **Births** (per 1,000 pop.): 19.2. **Deaths** (per 1,000 pop.): 12.2. **Natural inc.:** 0.70%. **Infant mortality** (per 1,000 live births): 70.4.

Education: Compulsory: ages 5-9. **Literacy** (1995 est.): 83.1%.

Major Intl. Organizations: UN (FAO, IBRD, ILO, IMF, IMO, WHO, WTrO), ASEAN.

Embassy: 2300 S St. NW 20008; 332-9044.

Websites: www.myanmar-tourism.com; www.myanmar.com

The Burmese arrived from Tibet before the 9th century, displacing earlier cultures, and a Buddhist monarchy was established by the 11th. Burma was conquered by the Mongol dynasty of China in 1272, then ruled by Shans as a Chinese tributary, until the 16th century.

Britain subjugated Burma in 3 wars, 1824-84, and ruled the country as part of India until 1937, when it became self-governing. Independence outside the Commonwealth was achieved Jan. 4, 1948.

Gen. Ne Win dominated politics from 1962 to 1988, first as military ruler then as constitutional president. His regime drove Indians from the civil service and Chinese from commerce. Economic socialization was advanced, isolation from foreign countries enforced. In 1987 Burma, once the richest nation in SE Asia, was granted less-developed status by the UN.

Ne Win resigned July 1988, following waves of antigovernment riots. Rioting and street violence continued, and in Sept. the military seized power, under Gen. Saw Maung. In 1989 the country's name was changed to Myanmar.

The first free multiparty elections in 30 years took place May 27, 1990, with the main opposition party winning a decisive victory, but the military refused to hand over power. A key opposition leader, Aung San Suu Kyi, awarded the Nobel Peace Prize in 1991, was held under house arrest from July 20, 1989, to July 10, 1995; after her release, the military government continued to restrict her activities and to harass and imprison her supporters. New U.S. economic sanctions took effect on May 21, 1997. Myanmar was admitted to ASEAN July 23, 1997.

Confined again in Sept. 2000, Aung San Suu Kyi was freed May 6, 2002. She was rearrested May 30, 2003, as part of a broader government crackdown on dissidents. The regime has been accused of committing many human rights abuses in its attempt to stay in power.

Namibia
Republic of Namibia

People: Population: 1,987,000. **Age distrib.** (%): <15: 42.6; 65+: 3.7. **Pop. density:** 6 per sq. mi. **Urban:** 31%. **Ethnic groups:** Ovambo 50%, Kavangos 9%, Herero 7%, Damara 7% White 6%, mixed 7%. **Principal languages:** English (official), Afrikaans, German, Oshivambo, Herero, Nama. **Chief religions:** Lutheran 50%, other Christian 30%, indigenous beliefs 10-20%.

Geography: Area (total): 318,695 sq. mi. **Location:** In S Africa on the coast of the Atlantic Ocean. **Neighbors:** Angola on N, Botswana on E, South Africa on S. **Topography:** Three distinct regions incl. Namib desert along the Atlantic coast, a mountainous central plateau with woodland savanna, and Kalahari desert in E. True forests are found in NE. There are 4 rivers, but little other surface water. **Capital:** Windhoek: 216,000.

Government: Type: Republic. **Head of state:** Pres. Sam Nujoma; b May 12, 1929; in office: Mar. 21, 1990. **Head of gov.:** Prime Min. Theo-Ben Gurirab; b Jan. 23, 1939; in office: Aug. 28, 2002. **Local divisions:** 13 regions. **Defense budget** (2002): $84 mil. **Active troops:** 9,000.

Economy: meatpacking, fish proc., dairy products, mining. **Chief crops:** millet, sorghum, peanuts. **Natural resources:** diamonds, copper, uranium, gold, lead, tin, lithium, cadmium, zinc, salt, vanadium, nat. gas, hydropower, fish. **Arable land:** 1%. **Livestock** (2002): cattle: 2.51 mil.; chickens: 2.35 mil.; goats: 1.77 mil.; pigs: 22,000; sheep: 2.37 mil. **Fish catch** (2002): 547,542 metric tons. **Electricity prod.** (2001): 0.03 bil. kWh. **Labor force:** agri. 47%, ind. 20%, services 33%.

Finance: Monetary unit: Namibia Dollar (NAD) (Sept. 2003: 7.45=1 U.S.). **GDP** (2002 est.): $12.6 bil. **Per capita GDP:** $6,900. **Imports** (2001): $1.71 bil.; partners (1997 est.): South Africa 81%, U.S. 4%, Germany 2%. **Exports** (2001 est.): $1.58 bil.; partners (1998 est.): UK 43%, South Africa 26%, Spain 14%, France 8%. **Tourism** (1998): $288 mil. **Budget** (1998): $950 mil. **Intl. reserves less gold:** $238 mil. **Consumer prices:** 11.3%.

Transport: Railroad: Length: 2,480 mi. **Motor vehicles:** 62,500 pass. cars, 66,500 comm. vehicles. **Civil aviation:** 340.5 mil pass.-mi; 21 airports. **Chief ports:** Luderitz, Walvis Bay.

Communications: TV sets: 38 per 1,000 pop. **Radios:** 143 per 1,000 pop. **Telephone lines:** 117,400. **Daily newspaper circ.:** 19 per 1,000 pop. **Internet:** 45,000 users.

Health: Life expectancy: 44.3 male; 41.2 female. **Births** (per 1,000 pop.): 34.1. **Deaths** (per 1,000 pop.): 19.2. **Natural inc.:** 1.49%. **Infant mortality** (per 1,000 live births): 68.4.

Education: Compulsory: ages 6-16. **Literacy:** 84%.

Major Intl. Organizations: UN (FAO, IBRD, ILO, IMF, IMO, WHO, WTrO), the Commonwealth, AU.

Embassy: 1605 New Hampshire Ave. NW 20009; 986-0540.

Websites: www.opm.gov.na; www.met.gov.na

Namibia was declared a German protectorate in 1890 and officially called South-West Africa. South Africa seized the territory from Germany in 1915 during World War I; the League of Nations gave South Africa a mandate over the territory in 1920. In 1966, the Marxist South-West Africa People's Organization (SWAPO) launched a guerrilla war for independence. The UN General Assembly named the area Namibia in 1968.

After many years of guerrilla warfare and failed diplomatic efforts, South Africa, Angola, and Cuba signed a U.S.-mediated agreement Dec. 22, 1988, to end South African administration of Namibia and provide for a cease-fire and transition to independence, in accordance with a 1978 UN plan. A separate accord between Cuba and Angola provided for a phased withdrawal of Cuban troops from Namibia. A constitution providing for multiparty government was adopted Feb. 9, 1990, and Namibia gained independence Mar. 21.

Walvis Bay, the principal deepwater port, had been turned over to South African administration in 1922. It remained in South African hands after independence, but South Africa turned control of the port back to Namibia, as of Mar. 1, 1994. Separatist violence flared in the Caprivi Strip in the late 1990s.

The UN recently estimated that 22.5% of the adult population has HIV/AIDS.

Nauru
Republic of Nauru

People: Population: 13,000. **Age distrib.** (%): <15: 39.6; 65+: 1.7. **Pop. density:** 1,550 per sq. mi. **Urban:** 100%. **Ethnic groups:** Nauruan 58%, other Pacific Islander 26%, Chinese 8%, European 8%. **Principal languages:** Nauruan (official), English. **Chief religions:** Protestant 66%, Roman Catholic 33%.

Geography: Area: 8 sq. mi. **Location:** In W Pacific O. just S of the Equator. **Neighbors:** Nearest is Kiribati to E. **Topography:** Mostly a plateau bearing high-grade phosphate deposits, surrounded by a sandy shore and coral reef in concentric rings. **Capital:** Govt. offices in Yaren district.

Government: Type: Republic. **Head of state and gov.:** Pres. René Harris; b 1948; in office: Aug. 8, 2003. **Local divisions:** 14 districts.

Economy: Industries: phosphate mining, offshore banking, coconut products. **Chief crops:** coconuts. **Natural resources:** phosphates, fish. **Livestock:** (2002): cattle: 5,000; pigs: 3,000. **Fish catch** (2002 est.): 400 metric tons. **Electricity prod.** (2001): 0.03 bil. kWh. **Labor force:** employed in mining phosphates, public administration, education, and transportation.

Finance: Monetary unit: Australian Dollar (AUD) (Sept. 2003: 1.56 = $1 U.S.). **GDP** (2001 est.): $60 mil. **Per capita GDP:** $5,000. **Imports** (1991): $21.1 mil.; partners (2000): Australia, U.S., UK, Indonesia. **Exports** (1991): $25.3 mil.; partners (2000): NZ, Australia, South Korea, U.S. **Budget** (1996): $64.8 mil.

Transport: Railroad: Length: 3 mi. **Civil aviation:** 157.8 mil pass.-mi.; 1 airport. **Chief port:** Nauru.

Communications: TV sets: 1 per 1,000 pop. **Radios:** 45 per 1,000 pop.

Health: Life expectancy: 58.4 male; 65.7 female. **Births** (per 1,000 pop.): 26.1. **Deaths** (per 1,000 pop.): 7.1. **Natural inc.:** 1.90%. **Infant mortality** (per 1,000 live births): 10.3.

Education: Compulsory: ages 6-16.

Major Intl. Organizations: UN (WHO), the Commonwealth.

Website: www.nauruembassy.org

The island was discovered in 1798 by the British but was formally annexed to the German Empire in 1886. After World War I, Nauru became a League of Nations mandate administered by Australia. During World War II the Japanese occupied the island and shipped 1,200 Nauruans to the fortress island of Truk as slave laborers.

In 1947 Nauru was made a UN trust territory, administered by Australia. It became an independent republic Jan. 31, 1968, and was admitted to the UN Sept. 14, 1999.

Phosphate exports have provided Nauru with per capita revenues that are among the highest in the Third World. Phosphate reserves, however, are nearly depleted, and environmental damage from strip-mining has been severe. Lax banking practices have made Nauru a haven for money laundering; the country has also raised funds by selling passports to noncitizens.

Nepal
Kingdom of Nepal

People: Population: 25,164,000. **Age distrib.** (%): <15: 40; 65+: 3.6. **Pop. density:** 476 per sq. mi. **Urban:** 12%. **Ethnic groups:** Newar, Indian, Gurung, Magar, Tamang, Rai, Limbu, Sherpa, Tharu. **Principal languages:** Nepali (official); about 30 dialects and 12 other languages. **Chief religions:** Hinduism 86% (official), Buddhism 8%, Muslim 4%.

Geography: Area: 54,363 sq. mi. (total); 52,819 sq. mi. (land). **Location:** Astride the Himalaya Mts. **Neighbors:** China on N, India on S. **Topography:** The Himalayas stretch across the N, the hill country with its fertile valleys extends across the center, while the S border region is part of the flat, subtropical Ganges Plain. **Capital:** Kathmandu. **Cities (urban aggr.):** Kathmandu 755,000; (1995 metro. est.) Lalitpur 190,000; Biratnagar 132,000.

Government: Type: Constitutional monarchy. **Head of state:** King Gyanendra Bir Bikram Shah Dev; b July 7, 1947; in office: June 4, 2001. **Head of gov.:** Prime Min. Surya Bahadur Thapa; b Mar. 21, 1928; in office: June 5, 2003. **Local divisions:.** Local divisions: 5 regions subdivided into 14 zones. **Defense budget** (2002): $70 mil. **Active troops:** 51,000.

Economy: Industries: tourism, carpets, textiles, rice, jute, sugar, oilseed. **Chief crops:** rice, corn, wheat, sugarcane. **Natural re-**sources: quartz, water, timber, hydropower, lignite, copper, cobalt, iron ore. **Arable land:** 17%. **Livestock** (2002): cattle: 6.98 mil.; chickens: 21.37 mil.; goats: 6.61 mil.; pigs: 934,000; sheep: 840,000. **Fish catch** (2002): 33,270 metric tons. **Electricity prod.** (2001): 1.76 bil. kWh. **Labor force:** agri. 81%, services 16%, ind. 3%.

Finance: Monetary unit: Rupee (NPR) (Sept. 2003: 77.33=1 U.S.). **GDP** (2002 est.): $36 bil. **Per capita GDP:** $1,400. **Imports** (2001): $1.6 bil.; partners: India 39%, Singapore 10%, China/Hong Kong 9%. **Exports:** (2001 est.): $757 mil.; partners (2001): India 48%, U.S. 26%, Germany 11%. **Tourism** (1999): $168 mil. **Budget** (1999 est.): $1.1 bil. **Intl. reserves less gold:** $749 mil. **Gold:** 150,000 oz t. **Consumer prices:** 2.8%.

Transport: Railroad: Length: 37 mi. **Motor vehicles** (1999): 49,400 pass. cars, 185,800 comm. vehicles. **Civil aviation:** 635.7 mil pass.-mi; 9 airports.

Communications: TV sets: 6 per 1,000 pop. **Radios:** 38 per 1,000 pop. **Telephone lines:** 327,700. **Daily newspaper circ.:** 11 per 1,000 pop. **Internet:** 60,000 users.

Health: Life expectancy: 59.4 male; 58.6 female. **Births** (per 1,000 pop.): 32.5. **Deaths** (per 1,000 pop.): 9.8. **Natural inc.:** 2.26%. **Infant mortality** (per 1,000 live births): 70.6.

Education: Compulsory: ages 6-10. **Literacy:** 45.2%.

Major Intl. Organizations: UN (FAO, IBRD, ILO, IMF, IMO, WHO).

Embassy: 2131 Leroy Pl. NW 20008; 667-4550.

Website: www.nepalembassyusa.org

Nepal was originally a group of petty principalities, the inhabitants of one of which, the Gurkhas, became dominant about 1769. In 1951 King Tribhubana Bir Bikram, member of the Shah family, ended the system of rule by hereditary premiers of the Ranas family, who had kept the kings virtual prisoners, and established a cabinet system of government.

Virtually closed to the outside world for centuries, Nepal is now linked to India and Pakistan by roads and air service and to Tibet by road. Polygamy, child marriage, and the caste system were officially abolished in 1963.

The government announced the legalization of political parties in 1990. Elections on Nov. 15, 1994, led to the installation of Nepal's first Communist government, which held power until a no-confidence vote Sept. 10, 1995.

Nine members of Nepal's royal family, including King Birendra and Queen Aishwarya, died as the result of a massacre on the night of June 1, 2001. An official inquiry blamed the carnage on a 10th member of the family, Crown Prince Dipendra, who reportedly shot himself that night and died 3 days later, allowing Birendra's brother Gyanendra to assume the throne. A Maoist insurgency has claimed at least 8,000 lives since 1996. A seven-month ceasefire collapsed in Aug. 2003 and violence continued.

Netherlands
Kingdom of the Netherlands

People: Population: 16,149,000. **Age distrib.** (%): <15: 18.3; 65+: 13.8. **Pop. density:** 1,232 per sq. mi. **Urban:** 90%. **Ethnic groups:** Dutch 83%. **Principal languages:** Dutch (official), Frisian, Flemish. **Chief religions:** Roman Catholic 31%, Protestant 21%, Muslim 4%.

Geography: Area: 16,033 sq. mi. (total); 13,082 sq. mi. (land) **Location:** In NW Europe on North Sea. **Neighbors:** Germany on E, Belgium on S. **Topography:** The land is flat, an average alt. of 37 ft. above sea level, with much land below sea level reclaimed and protected by some 1,500 miles of dikes. Since 1920 the government has been draining the IJsselmeer, formerly the Zuider Zee. **Capital:** Amsterdam. **Cities (urban aggr.):** Amsterdam 1,105,151; Rotterdam 1,078,000; The Hague 442,799.

Government: Type: Parliamentary democracy under a constitutional monarch. **Head of state:** Queen Beatrix; b Jan. 31, 1938; in office: Apr. 30, 1980. **Head of gov.:** Prime Min. Jan Peter Balkenende; b May 7, 1956; in office: July 22, 2002. **Seat of govt.:** The Hague. **Local divisions:** 12 provinces. **Defense budget** (2001): $6.6 bil. **Active troops:** 49,580.

Economy: Industries: agro industries, metal & engineering products, electrical machinery & equip., chemicals, oil, constr., microelectronics, fishing. **Chief crops:** grains, potatoes, sugar beets, fruits, vegetables. **Natural resources:** nat. gas, oil. **Crude oil reserves** (2002): 107 mil. bbls. **Arable land:** 25%. **Livestock** (2002): cattle: 4.05 mil.; chickens: 98 mil.; goats: 215,000; pigs: 13 mil.; sheep: 1.30 mil. **Fish catch** (2002): 570,226 metric tons. **Electricity prod.** (2001): 88.32 bil. kWh. **Labor force:** services 73%, ind. 23%, agri. 4%.

Finance: Monetary unit: Euro (EUR) (Sept. 2003: 0.92=1 U.S.). **GDP** (2002 est.): 434 bil.; $2.4 bil. **Per capita GDP:** $26,900. **Imports** (2001): $201.1 bil.; partners (2001): EU 54.6%, U.S. 9.9%. **Exports** (2002) $221.9 bil.; partners (2001): EU 77.6%. **Tourism:** $6.95 bil. **Budget** (2001 est.): $134 bil. **Intl. reserves less gold:** $7.03 bil. **Gold:** 27.38 mil oz t. **Consumer prices:** 3.5%.

Transport: Railroad: Length: 1,745 mi. **Motor vehicles** (1999): 6.12 mil pass. cars, 806,000 comm. vehicles. **Civil aviation:** 43.57 bil pass.-mi; 21 airports. **Chief ports:** Rotterdam, Amsterdam, Ijmuiden.

Communications: TV sets: 540 per 1,000 pop. **Radios:** 980 per 1,000 pop. **Telephone lines:** 10,003,000. **Daily newspaper circ.:** 306 per 1,000 pop. **Internet:** 8,590,000 users.

Health: Life expectancy: 75.9 male; 81.8 female. **Births** (per 1,000 pop.): 11.3. **Deaths** (per 1,000 pop.): 8.7. **Natural inc.:** 0.27%. **Infant mortality** (per 1,000 live births): 4.3.

Education: Compulsory: ages 6-18. **Literacy** (2000 est.): 99%.

Major Intl. Organizations: UN and all of its specialized agencies, EU, NATO, OECD, OSCE.

Embassy: 4200 Linnean Ave. NW 20008; 244-5300.

Website: www.netherlands-embassy.org

Julius Caesar conquered the region in 55 BC, when it was inhabited by Celtic and Germanic tribes.

After the empire of Charlemagne fell apart, the Netherlands (Holland, Belgium, Flanders) split among counts, dukes, and bishops, passed to Burgundy and thence to Charles V of Spain. His son, Philip II, tried to check the Dutch drive toward political freedom and Protestantism (1568-1573). William the Silent, prince of Orange, led a confederation of the northern provinces, called Estates, in the Union of Utrecht, 1579. The Estates retained individual sovereignty, but were represented jointly in the States-General, a body that had control of foreign affairs and defense. In 1581 they repudiated allegiance to Spain. The rise of the Dutch republic to naval, economic, and artistic eminence came in the 17th century.

The United Dutch Republic ended 1795 when the French formed the Batavian Republic. Napoleon made his brother Louis king of Holland, 1806; Louis abdicated 1810 when Napoleon annexed Holland. In 1813 the French were expelled. In 1815 the Congress of Vienna formed a kingdom of the Netherlands, including Belgium, under William I. In 1830, the Belgians seceded and formed a separate kingdom.

The constitution, promulgated 1814, and subsequently revised, provides for a hereditary constitutional monarchy.

The Netherlands maintained its neutrality in World War I, but was invaded and brutally occupied by Germany, 1940-45.

In 1949, after several years of fighting, the Netherlands granted independence to Indonesia. In 1963, West New Guinea (now Irian Jaya) was turned over to Indonesia. Immigration from former Dutch colonies has been substantial.

The murder May 6, 2002, of right-wing populist leader Pim Fortuyn, 9 days before legislative elections, marked the 1st political assassination in modern Dutch history.

Netherlands Dependencies

The **Netherlands Antilles,** constitutionally on a level of equality with the Netherlands homeland within the kingdom, consist of 2 groups of islands in the West Indies. **Curaçao** and **Bonaire** are near the coast of Venezuela; **St. Eustatius, Saba,** and the southern part of **St. Maarten** are SE of Puerto Rico. The northern two-thirds of St. Maarten belongs to French Guadeloupe; the French call the island St. Martin. Total area of the 2 groups is 371 sq. mi., including Bonaire (111), Curaçao (171), St. Eustatius (8), Saba (5), St. Maarten (Dutch part) (13). St. Maarten suffered extensive damage from Hurricane Luis, Sept. 1995. Total pop. of the Netherlands Antilles (2003 est.) was 216,226. Willemstad, on Curaçao, is the capital. The principal industry is the refining of crude oil from Venezuela. Tourism is also an important industry, as is shipbuilding.

Aruba, about 26 mi. W of Curaçao, was separated from the Netherlands Antilles on Jan. 1, 1986; it is an autonomous member of the Netherlands, the same status as the Netherland Antilles. Area 75 sq. mi.; pop. (2003 est.) 70,844; capital Oranjestad. Chief industries are oil refining and tourism.

New Zealand

People: Population: 3,875,000. **Age distrib.** (%): <15: 22.2; 65+: 11.5. **Pop. density:** 37 per sq. mi. **Urban:** 86%. **Ethnic groups:** New Zealand European 75%, Maori 10%, other European 5%, Pacific Islander 4%. **Principal languages:** English, Maori (both official). **Chief religions:** Protestant 52%, Roman Catholic 15%.

Geography: Area (total): 103,738 sq. mi. **Location:** In SW Pacific O. **Neighbors:** Nearest are Australia on W, Fiji and Tonga on N. **Topography:** Each of the 2 main islands (North and South Isls.) is mainly hilly and mountainous. The east coasts consist of fertile plains, especially the broad Canterbury Plains on South Isl. A volcanic plateau is in center of North Isl. South Isl. has glaciers and 15 peaks over 10,000 ft. **Capital:** Wellington. **Cities (urban agg.):** Auckland 1,102,000; Wellington 345,000; Christchurch 331,443.

Government: Type: Parliamentary democracy. **Head of state:** Queen Elizabeth II, represented by Gov.-Gen. Dame Silvia Cartwright; b Nov. 7, 1943; in office: Apr. 4, 2001. **Head of gov.:** Prime Min. Helen Clark; b Feb. 26, 1950; in office: Dec. 10, 1999. **Local divisions:** 93 counties, 9 districts, 3 town districts. **Defense budget** (2002): $697 mil. **Active troops:** 8,710.

Economy: Industries: food proc., wood & paper products, textiles, machinery, transp. equip., banking & insurance, tourism, mining. **Chief crops:** wheat, barley, potatoes, fruits, vegetables. **Natural resources:** nat. gas, iron ore, sand, coal, timber, hydropower, gold, limestone. **Crude oil reserves** (2002): 90 mil. bbls. **Arable land:** 9%. **Livestock** (2002): cattle: 2.30 mil.; chickens: 17.50 mil.; goats: 6,600; pigs: 405,000; sheep: 4,000. **Fish catch**

(2002): 637,134 metric tons. **Electricity prod.** (2001): 37.51 bil. kWh. **Labor force:** services 65%, ind. 25%, agri. 10%.

Finance: Monetary unit: New Zealand Dollar (NZD) (Sept. 2003: 1.76=1 U.S.). **GDP** (2002 est.): $78.8 bil. **Per capita GDP:** $20,200. **Imports** (2001): $12.5 bil.; partners (2000): Australia 22.5%, U.S. 17.5%, Japan 11%, UK 4%. **Exports** (2001 est.): $14.2 bil.; partners (2000): Australia 20.4%, U.S. 14.5%, Japan 13.5%, UK 5.4%. **Tourism:** $2.07 bil. **Budget** (2002) $31.2 bil. **Intl. reserves less gold:** $2.75 bil. **Consumer prices:** 2.7%.

Transport: Railroad: Length: 2,428 mi. **Motor vehicles:** 1.91 mil pass. cars, 438,100 comm. vehicles. **Civil aviation:** 12.01 bil pass.-mi; 46 airports. **Chief ports:** Auckland, Christchurch, Wellington, Dunedin, Tauranga.

Communications: TV sets: 516 per 1,000 pop. **Radios:** 997 per 1,000 pop. **Telephone lines:** 1,765,000. **Daily newspaper circ.:** 207 per 1,000 pop. **Internet:** 1,908,000 users.

Health: Life expectancy: 75.3 male; 81.4 female. **Births** (per 1,000 pop.): 14.1. **Deaths** (per 1,000 pop.): 7.5. **Natural inc.:** 0.66%. **Infant mortality** (per 1,000 live births): 6.1.

Education: Compulsory: ages 5-16. **Literacy** (1997): 100%.

Major Intl. Organizations: UN (FAO, IBRD, ILO, IMF, IMO, WHO, WTrO), APEC, the Commonwealth, OECD.

Embassy: 37 Observatory Cir. NW 20008; 328-4800.

Websites: www.govt.nz; www.stats.govt.nz/statsweb.nsf

The Maoris, a Polynesian group from the eastern Pacific, reached New Zealand before and during the 14th century. The first European to sight New Zealand was Dutch navigator Abel Janszoon Tasman, but Maoris refused to allow him to land. British Capt. James Cook explored the coasts, 1769-1770.

British sovereignty was proclaimed in 1840, with organized settlement beginning in the same year. Representative institutions were granted in 1853. Maori Wars ended in 1870 with British victory. The colony became a dominion in 1907, and is an independent member of the Commonwealth.

A progressive tradition in politics dates back to the 19th century, when New Zealand was internationally known for social experimentation; much of the nation's economy has been deregulated in recent years. The National Party, led by Jim Bolger, won general elections in 1990 and 1993. After inconclusive elections, Oct. 12, 1996, Bolger remained as prime minister, heading a National/New Zealand First party coalition. When Bolger lost his party's support, Jenny Shipley became the nation's first female prime minister, Dec. 8, 1997. The Labour Party won the general elections of Nov. 27, 1999, and July 27, 2002.

The native Maoris number nearly 15% of the population. Six of 120 members of the House of Representatives are elected directly by the Maori people. The legislature legalized prostitution July 2003. New Zealand contributed troops to the Aus.-led force in the Solomon Islands.

New Zealand comprises **North Island,** 44,702 sq. mi.; **South Island,** 58,384 sq. mi.; **Stewart Island,** 674 sq. mi.; **Chatham Islands,** 372 sq. mi.; and several groups of smaller islands.

In 1965, the **Cook Islands** (pop., 2003 est., 21,008; area 93 sq. mi.), located halfway between New Zealand and Hawaii, became self-governing although New Zealand retains responsibility for defense and foreign affairs. **Niue** attained the same status in 1974; it lies 400 mi. to W (pop., 1995 est., 1,800; area 100 sq. mi.). **Tokelau** (pop., 2003 est., 1,418; area 4 sq. mi.) comprises 3 atolls 300 mi. N of Samoa.

Ross Dependency, administered by New Zealand since 1923, comprises 160,000 sq. mi. of Antarctic territory.

Nicaragua
Republic of Nicaragua

People: Population: 5,466,000. **Age distrib.** (%): <15: 38.3; 65+: 3. **Pop. density:** 118 per sq. mi. **Urban:** 57%. **Ethnic groups:** Mestizo 69%, White 17%, Black 9%, Amerindian 5%. **Principal languages:** Spanish (official); indigenous languages, English on Atlantic coast. **Chief religion:** Roman Catholic 85%.

Geography: Area: 49,998 sq. mi. (total); 46,430 sq. mi. (land). **Location:** In Central America. **Neighbors:** Honduras on N, Costa Rica on S. **Topography:** Both Caribbean and Pacific coasts are over 200 mi. long. The Cordillera Mts., with many volcanic peaks, run NW-SE through the middle of the country. Between this and a volcanic range to the E lie Lakes Managua and Nicaragua. **Capital:** Managua 1,039,000.

Government: Type: Republic. **Head of state and gov.:** Pres. Enrique Bolaños Geyer; b May 13, 1928; in office Jan. 10, 2002. **Local divisions:** 15 departments, 2 autonomous regions. **Defense budget** (2002): $23 mil. **Active troops:** 14,000.

Economy: Industries: food proc., chemicals, machinery & metal products, textiles, clothing, oil refining & distribution, beverages, footwear, wood. **Chief crops:** coffee, bananas, sugarcane, cotton, rice, corn, tobacco, sesame, soya. **Natural resources:** gold, silver, copper, tungsten, lead, zinc, timber, fish. **Arable land:** 9%. **Livestock** (2002): cattle: 2.26 mil.; chickens: 24 mil.; goats: 6.90 mil.; pigs: 39,000; sheep: 4.50 mil. **Fish catch** (2002): 28,520 metric tons. **Electricity prod.** (2001): 2.55 bil. kWh. **Labor force:** services 43%, agri. 42%, ind. 15%.

Finance: Monetary unit: Gold Cordoba (NIO) (Sept. 2003: 15.09=1 U.S.). **GDP** (2002 est.): $12.8 bil. **Per capita GDP:**

$2,500. **Imports** (2001): $1.6 bil.; partners (2000): U.S. 23.9%, Costa Rica 11.4%, Venezuela 9.9%, Guatemala 7.9%. **Exports** (2001 est.): $609.5 mil.; partners (2000): U.S. 57.7%, Germany 5.3%, Canada 4.2%, Costa Rica 3.3%. **Tourism:** $116 mil. **Budget** (2000 est.): $908 mil. **Intl. reserves less gold:** $330 mil. **Gold:** 20,000 oz t. **Consumer prices:** 4.0%.

Transport: Railroad: Length: 4 mi. **Motor vehicles** (1999): 65,100 pass. cars, 82,900 comm. vehicles. **Civil aviation:** 41.6 mil pass.-mi; 11 airports. **Chief ports:** Corinto, Puerto Sandino, San Juan del Sur.

Communications: TV sets: 69 per 1,000 pop. **Radios:** 270 per 1,000 pop. **Telephone lines:** 171,600. **Daily newspaper circ.:** 30 per 1,000 pop. **Internet:** 90,000 users.

Health: Life expectancy: 67.7 male; 71.8 female. **Births** (per 1,000 pop.): 26.3. **Deaths** (per 1,000 pop.): 4.7. **Natural inc.:** 2.16%. **Infant mortality** (per 1,000 live births): 31.4.

Education: Compulsory: ages 7-12. **Literacy:** 67.5%.

Major Intl. Organizations: UN and most of its specialized agencies, OAS.

Embassy: 1627 New Hampshire Ave. NW 20009; 939-6570.

Nicaragua, inhabited by various Indian tribes, was conquered by Spain in 1552. After gaining independence from Spain, 1821, Nicaragua was united for a short period with Mexico, then with the United Provinces of Central America, finally becoming an independent republic, 1838.

Website: www.consuladodenicaragua.com

U.S. Marines occupied the country at times in the early 20th century, the last time from 1926 to 1933.

Gen. Anastasio Somoza Debayle was elected president in 1967. He resigned in 1972, but was re-elected president in 1974. Martial law was imposed in Dec. 1974, after officials were kidnapped by the Marxist Sandinista guerrillas. Violent opposition spread to nearly all classes in 1978; nationwide strikes called against the government touched off a civil war, which ended when Somoza fled Nicaragua and the Sandinistas took control of Managua in July 1979. Somoza was assassinated in Paraguay, Sept. 17, 1980.

Relations with the U.S. were strained as a result of Nicaragua's aid to leftist guerrillas in El Salvador and U.S. backing of anti-Sandinista contra guerrilla groups. In 1983 the contras launched a major offensive; the Sandinistas imposed rule by decree. In 1985 the U.S. House rejected Pres. Reagan's request for military aid to the contras. The subsequent diversion of funds to the contras from the proceeds of a secret arms sale to Iran caused a major scandal in the U.S.

In a stunning upset, Violeta Barrios de Chamorro defeated Sandinista leader Daniel Ortega Saavedra in national elections, Feb. 25, 1990. Arnoldo Alemán Lacayo, a conservative former mayor of Managua, defeated Ortega in the presidential election of Oct. 20, 1996. Up to 2,000 people died in W Nicaragua Oct. 30, 1998, in a mudslide caused by rains from Hurricane Mitch. Drought and a drop in coffee prices plunged Nicaragua into an economic crisis in 2001. Enrique Bolaños Geyer, a conservative businessman, defeated Ortega in a presidential election Nov. 4. Bolaños Aug. 7, 2002, accused Alemán of having stolen nearly $95 million while he was president.

Niger
Republic of Niger

People: Population: 11,972,000. **Age distrib.** (%): <15: 47.9; 65+: 2.3. **Pop. density:** 24 per sq. mi. **Urban:** 21%. **Ethnic groups:** Hausa 56%, Djerma 22%, Fula 9%, Tuareg 8%, Beri Beri (Kanouri) 4%. **Principal languages:** French (official); Hausa, Djerma, Fulani (all national). **Chief religion:** Muslim 80%.

Geography: Area: 489,191 sq. mi. (total); 489,075 sq. mi. (land). **Location:** In the interior of N Africa. **Neighbors:** Libya, Algeria on N; Mali, Burkina Faso on W; Benin, Nigeria on S; Chad on E. **Topography:** Mostly arid desert and mountains. A narrow savanna in the S and the Niger R. basin in the SW contain most of the population. **Capital:** Niamey; 821,000.

Government: Type: Republic. **Head of state:** Pres. Tandja Mamadou; b 1938; in office: Dec. 22, 1999. **Head of gov.:** Prime Min. Hama Amadou; b 1950; in office: Jan. 3, 2000. **Local divisions:** 7 departments, 1 capital district. **Defense budget** (2002): $33 mil. **Active troops:** 5,300.

Economy: Industries: uranium mining, cement, brick, textiles, food proc., chemicals. **Chief crops:** cowpeas, cotton, peanuts, millet, sorghum, cassava, rice. **Natural resources:** uranium, coal, iron ore, tin, phosphates, gold, oil. **Arable land:** 3%. **Livestock** (2002): cattle: 2.26 mil.; chickens: 24 mil.; goats: 6.90 mil.; pigs: 39,000; sheep: 4.50 mil. **Fish catch** (2002): 20,821 metric tons. **Electricity prod.** (2001): 0.24 bil. kWh. **Labor force:** agri. 90%, ind. and commerce 6%, government 4%.

Finance: Monetary unit: CFA Franc BCEAO (XOF) (Sept. 2003: 605.18=1 U.S.). **GDP** (2002 est.): $8.8 bil. **Per capita GDP:** $830. **Imports** (2001): $331 mil.; partners (2000): France 16.8%, Cote d'Ivoire 13.4%, U.S. 9.6%, Nigeria 7.6%. **Exports** (2001 est.): $246 mil.; partners (2000): France 43.4%, Nigeria 35.0%, Spain 4.5%, U.S. 3.9%. **Tourism** (1999): $24 mil. **Budget** (2002 est.): $320 mil. **Intl. reserves less gold:** $98 mil. **Consumer prices:** 2.6%.

Transport: Motor vehicles (1995): 16,000 pass. cars, 18,000 comm. vehicles. **Civil aviation:** 146.0 mil pass.-mi; 9 airports.

Communications: TV sets: 15 per 1,000 pop. **Radios:** 36 per 1,000 pop. **Telephone lines:** 21,700. **Daily newspaper circ.:** .2 per 1,000 pop. **Internet:** 12,000 users.

Health: Life expectancy: 42.3 male; 42.1 female. **Births** (per 1,000 pop.): 49.5. **Deaths** (per 1,000 pop.): 21.7. **Natural inc.:** 2.78%. **Infant mortality** (per 1,000 live births): 123.6.

Education: Compulsory: ages 7-12. **Literacy:** 17.6%.

Major Intl. Organizations: UN (FAO, IBRD, ILO, IMF, WHO, WTrO), AU.

Embassy: 2204 R St. NW 20008; 483-4224.

Website: www.nigerembassyusa.org

Niger was part of ancient and medieval African empires. European explorers reached the area in the late 18th century. The French colony of Niger was established 1900-22, after the defeat of Tuareg fighters, who had invaded the area from the N a century before. The country became independent Aug. 3, 1960. The next year it signed a bilateral agreement with France.

In 1993, Niger held its first free and open elections since independence; an opposition leader, Mahamane Ousmane, won the presidency. A peace accord Apr. 24, 1995, ended a Tuareg rebellion that began in 1990. A coup, Jan. 27, 1996, followed by a disputed presidential election in July, left the military in control of Niger. On Apr. 9, 1999, Gen. Ibrahim Bare Mainassara, Niger's president since 1996, was assassinated, apparently by members of his security team. Elections were held Oct. 17 and Nov. 24, 1999, under a new constitution, approved by referendum July 18, that provided for a return to civilian rule.

Nigeria
Federal Republic of Nigeria

People: Population: 124,009,000. **Age distrib.** (%): <15: 43.6; 65+: 2.8. **Pop. density:** 353 per sq. mi. **Urban:** 45%. **Ethnic groups:** More than 250; Hausa and Fulani 29%, Yoruba 21%, Igbo (Ibo) 18%, Ijaw 10%. **Principal languages:** English (official); Hausa, Yoruba, Igbo (Ibo), Fulani. **Chief religions:** Muslim 50%, Christian 40%, indigenous beliefs 10%.

Geography: Area: 356,669 sq. mi. (total); 351,649 sq. mi. (land). **Location:** On the S coast of W Africa. **Neighbors:** Benin on W, Niger on N, Chad and Cameroon on E. **Topography:** 4 E-W regions divide Nigeria: a coastal mangrove swamp 10-60 mi. wide, a tropical rain forest 50-100 mi. wide, a plateau of savanna and open woodland, and semidesert in the N. **Capital:** Abuja. **Cities (urban aggr.):** Lagos 8,665,000; Ibadan 1,549,000; Ogbomosho 809,000; Abuja 420,000.

Government: Type: Republic. **Head of state and gov.:** Pres. Olusegun Obasanjo; b Mar. 5, 1937; in office: May 29, 1999. **Local divisions:** 36 states, 1 capital territory. **Defense budget** (2002): $529 mil. **Active troops:** 78,500.

Economy: Industries: crude oil, mining, palm oil, peanuts, cotton, rubber. **Chief crops:** cocoa, peanuts, palm oil, corn, rice, sorghum, millet, cassava, yams, rubber. **Natural resources:** natural gas, oil, tin, columbite, iron ore, coal, limestone, lead, zinc. **Crude oil reserves** (2002): 24.0 bil. bbls. **Arable land:** 33%. **Livestock** (2002): cattle: 19.50 mil.; chickens: 130 mil.; goats: 26 mil.; pigs: 5.10 mil.; sheep: 21 mil. **Fish catch** (2002): 476,544 metric tons. **Electricity prod.** (2001): 15.67 bil. kWh. **Labor force:** agri. 70%, ind. 10%, services 20%.

Finance: Monetary unit: Naira (NGN) (Sept. 2003: 135.61=1 U.S.). **GDP** (2002 est.): $113.5 bil. **Per capita GDP:** $875. **Imports** (2001): $13.7 bil.; partners (2000): UK 11%, U.S. 9%, France 9%, Germany 7%. **Exports** (2001 est.): $20.3 bil.; partners (2000): U.S. 46%, Spain 11%, India 6%, France 5%. **Tourism** (1998): $142 mil. **Budget** (2000 est.): $3.6 bil. **Intl. reserves less gold:** $5.39 bil. **Gold:** 690,000 oz t. **Consumer prices:** 12.9%.

Transport: Railroad: Length: 2,210 mi. **Motor vehicles** (1997): 52,300 pass. cars, 13,500 comm. vehicles. **Civil aviation:** 348.0 mil pass.-mi; 36 airports. **Chief ports:** Port Harcourt, Lagos, Warri, Calabar.

Communications: TV sets: 69 per 1,000 pop. **Radios:** 226 per 1,000 pop. **Telephone lines:** 702,000. **Daily newspaper circ.:** 24 per 1,000 pop. **Internet:** 200,000 users.

Health: Life expectancy: 50.9 male; 51.1 female. **Births** (per 1,000 pop.): 38.8. **Deaths** (per 1,000 pop.): 13.8. **Natural inc.:** 2.50%. **Infant mortality** (per 1,000 live births): 71.4.

Education: Compulsory: ages 6-12. **Literacy:** 68%.

Major Intl. Organizations: UN (FAO, IBRD, ILO, IMF, IMO, WHO, WTrO), the Commonwealth, AU, OPEC.

Embassy: 1333 16th St. NW 20036; 986-8400.

Website: www.nigeriaembassyusa.org

Early cultures in Nigeria date back to at least 700 BC. From the 12th to the 14th centuries, more advanced cultures developed in the Yoruba area, at Ife, and in the north, where Muslim influence prevailed. Portuguese and British slavers appeared from the 15th-16th centuries. Britain seized Lagos, 1861, and gradually extended control inland until 1900. Nigeria became independent Oct. 1, 1960, and a republic Oct. 1, 1963.

On May 30, 1967, the Eastern Region seceded, proclaiming itself the Republic of Biafra, plunging the country into civil war. Casualties in the war were estimated at over 1 million, including many "Biafrans" (mostly Ibos) who died of starvation despite international efforts to provide relief. The secessionists, after steadily losing ground, capitulated Jan. 12, 1970.

Nigeria emerged as one of the world's leading oil exporters in the 1970s, but much of the revenue has been squandered through corruption and mismanagement.

After 13 years of military rule, the nation made a peaceful return to civilian government, Oct. 1979. Military rule resumed, Dec. 31, 1983; a second coup came in 1985.

Headed by Gen. Ibrahim Babangida, the military regime held elections June 12, 1993, but annulled the vote June 23 when it appeared that Moshood Abiola would win. Riots followed and many were killed. Babangida resigned and appointed a civilian to head an interim government, Aug. 26, but that government was ousted Nov. 17 in a coup led by Gen. Sani Abacha. On June 11, 1994, Abiola declared himself president; he was jailed June 23.

Abacha's brutal rule ended June 8, 1998, when he died of an apparent heart attack. Abiola died in prison July 7, as Abacha's successor, Gen. Abdulsalam Abubakar, was reportedly preparing to free him. Abiola's death sparked riots in Lagos and other cities; on July 20, Abubakar promised early elections and a return to civilian rule. Olusegun Obasanjo (a former military ruler) won the presidential vote Feb. 27, 1999, Nigeria's 1st civilian government in 15 years.

An oil fire that exploded from a ruptured pipeline in S. Nigeria, Oct. 17, 1998, killed at least 700 people who were scavenging for fuel. The imposition of strict Islamic law in northern states led to clashes, Jan.-Mar. 2000, in which at least 800 people died. U.S. Pres. Bill Clinton visited Nigeria Aug. 26-27, 2000, the 1st visit there by a U.S. head of state in 22 years. Clashes between Muslims and Christians Sept. 7-12 and Oct. 13-14 claimed an estimated 600 lives; another 200 people died when soldiers went on a rampage in SE Nigeria Oct. 22-24.

At least 1,000 people were killed Jan. 27, 2002, when an army weapons depot in Lagos exploded; many of the victims drowned in a drainage canal while fleeing the blasts.

By 2002, the strict Islamic legal code of sharia had been adopted by about one-third of Nigeria's 36 states. Controversy over Nigeria's plans to host a Miss World pageant sparked sectarian riots in Kaduna, Nov. 20-24, leaving more than 200 people dead and 1,100 injured. Obasanjo won reelection Apr. 19, 2003. In Aug., Nigeria contributed several hundred troops to the ECOWAS peacekeeping force in Liberia.

Norway
Kingdom of Norway

People: Population: 4,533,000. **Age distrib. (%):** <15: 20; 65+: 15. **Pop. density:** 38 per sq. mi. **Urban:** 75%. **Ethnic groups:** Norwegian, Sami. **Principal languages:** Norwegian (official), Sami, Finnish. Chief religion: Evangelical Lutheran 86% (official).

Geography: Area: 125,182 sq. mi. (total); 118,865 sq. mi. (land). **Location:** W part of Scandinavian peninsula in NW Europe (extends farther north than any European land). **Neighbors:** Sweden, Finland, Russia on E. **Topography:** A highly indented coast is lined with tens of thousands of islands. Mountains and plateaus cover most of the country, which is only 25% forested. **Capital:** Oslo. **Cities (urban aggr.):** Oslo 787,000 (city proper 2000 est., 507,467); Bergen (1996 est.) 223,773.

Government: Type: Hereditary constitutional monarchy. **Head of state:** King Harald V; b Feb. 21, 1937; in office: Jan. 17, 1991. **Head of gov.:** Prime Min. Kjell Magne Bondevik; b Sept. 3, 1947; in office: Oct. 19, 2001. **Local divisions:** 19 provinces. **Defense budget** (2002): $3.8 bil. **Active troops:** 26,600.

Economy: Industries: oil & gas, food proc., shipbuilding, pulp & paper products, metals, chemicals, timber, mining, textiles, fishing. **Chief crops:** barley, wheat, potatoes. **Natural resources:** oil, copper, nat. gas, pyrites, nickel, iron ore, zinc, lead, fish, timber, hydropower. **Crude oil reserves** (2002): 9.4 bil. bbls. **Arable land:** 3%. **Livestock** (2002): cattle: 973,000; chickens: 3.20 mil.; goats: 52,000; pigs: 400,000; sheep: 2.50 mil. **Fish catch** (2002): 3,199,404 metric tons. **Electricity prod.** (2001): 120.1 bil. kWh. **Labor force:** services 74%, ind. 22%, agri., forestry, and fishing 4%.

Finance: Monetary unit: Kroner (NOK) (Sept. 2003: 7.60=1 U.S.). **GDP** (2002 est.): $143 bil. **Per capita GDP:** $31,800. **Imports** (2002): $37.3 bil.; partners (2001): EU 66.5%, U.S. 7%. **Exports** (2002 est.): $68.2 bil.; partners (2001): EU 76.8%, U.S. 7.9%. **Tourism** (1999): $2.23 bil. **Budget** (2000 est.): $57.6 bil. **Intl. reserves less gold:** $15.21 bil. **Gold:** 1.18 mil oz t. **Consumer prices:** 1.3%.

Transport: Railroad: Length: 2,489 mi. **Motor vehicles:** 1.85 mil pass. cars, 451,000 comm. vehicles. **Civil aviation:** 6.14 bil pass.-mi; 66 airports. **Chief ports:** Bergen, Stavanger, Oslo, Kristiansand.

Communications: TV sets: 653 per 1,000 pop. **Radios:** 917 per 1,000 pop. **Telephone lines:** 3,325,000. **Daily newspaper circ.:** 586.6 per 1,000 pop. **Internet:** 2,300,000 users.

Health: Life expectancy: 76.2 male; 82.2 female. **Births** (per 1,000 pop.): 12.2. **Deaths** (per 1,000 pop.): 9.7. **Natural inc.:** 0.25%. **Infant mortality** (per 1,000 live births): 3.9.

Education: Compulsory: ages 6-16. **Literacy:** 100%.

Major Intl. Organizations: UN and all of its specialized agencies, EFTA, NATO, OECD, OSCE.

Embassy: 2720 34th St. NW 20008; 333-6000.
Website: odin.dep.no/odin/engelsk/index-b-n-a.html

The first ruler of Norway was Harald the Fairhaired, who came to power in AD 872. Between 800 and 1000, Norway's Vikings raided and occupied widely dispersed parts of Europe.

The country was united with Denmark 1381-1814, and with Sweden, 1814-1905. In 1905, the country became independent with Prince Charles of Denmark as king.

Norway remained neutral during World War I. Germany attacked Norway Apr. 9, 1940, and held it until liberation May 8, 1945. The country abandoned its neutrality after the war, and joined NATO. In a referendum Nov. 28, 1994, Norwegian voters rejected European Union membership.

Abundant hydroelectric resources provided the base for industrialization, giving Norway one of the highest living standards in the world. The country is a leading producer and exporter of crude oil, with extensive reserves in the North Sea. Norway's merchant marine is one of the world's largest.

Svalbard is a group of mountainous islands in the Arctic O., area 23,957 sq. mi., pop. (2003 est.) 2,811. The largest, Spitsbergen (formerly called West Spitsbergen), 15,060 sq. mi., seat of the governor, is about 370 mi. N of Norway. By a treaty signed in Paris, 1920, major European powers recognized the sovereignty of Norway, which incorporated it in 1925.

Jan Mayen, area 144 sq. mi., is a volcanic island located about 565 mi. WNW of Norway; it was annexed in 1929.

Oman
Sultanate of Oman

People: Population: 2,851,000. **Age distrib. (%):** <15: 41.9; 65+: 2.4. **Pop. density:** 35 per sq. mi. **Urban:** 77%. **Ethnic groups:** Arab, Baluchi, South Asian, African. **Principal languages:** Arabic (official), English, Baluchi, Urdu, Indian dialects. **Chief religion:** Muslim 75% (official; mostly Ibadhi).

Geography: Area (total): 82,031 sq. mi. **Location:** On SE coast of Arabian peninsula. **Neighbors:** United Arab Emirates, Saudi Arabia, Yemen on W. **Topography:** Oman has a narrow coastal plain up to 10 mi. wide, a range of barren mountains reaching 9,900 ft., and a wide, stony, mostly waterless plateau, avg. alt. 1,000 ft. Also, an exclave at the tip of the Musandam peninsula controls access to the Persian Gulf. **Capital:** Muscat: 540,000.

Government: Type: Absolute monarchy. **Head of state and gov.:** Sultan Qabus bin Said; b Nov. 18, 1940; in office: July 23, 1970 (also prime min. since Jan. 2, 1972). **Local divisions:** 6 regions and 2 governorates. **Defense budget** (2002): $2.3 bil. **Active troops:** 41,700.

Economy: Industries: oil, gas, constr., cement, copper. **Chief crops:** dates, limes, bananas, alfalfa, vegetables. **Natural resources:** oil, copper, asbestos, marble, limestone, chromium, gypsum, nat. gas. **Crude oil reserves** (2002): 5.5 bil. bbls. **Livestock** (2001): cattle: 290,000; chickens: 3.40 mil.; goats: 980,000; sheep: 335,000. **Fish catch** (2002 est.): 128,544 metric tons. **Electricity prod.** (2001): 9.27 bil. kWh.

Finance: Monetary unit: Rial (OMR) (Sept. 2003: 0.39=1 U.S.). **GDP** (2002 est.): $22.4 bil. **Per capita GDP:** $8,300. **Imports** (2001): $5.4 bil.; partners (2001): UAE 23%, Japan 16%, UK 13%, Italy 7%, Germany 5%, U.S. 5%. **Exports** (2001 est.): $10.9 bil.; partners (2001): Japan 21%, Thailand 18%, China 16%, South Korea 12%. **Tourism** (1999): $104 mil. **Budget** (2000 est.): $6.9 bil. **Intl. reserves less gold:** $2.33 bil. **Gold** (2001): 290,000 oz t. **Consumer prices:** –.7%.

Transport: Motor vehicles (1999): 310,400 pass. cars, 117,600 comm. vehicles. **Civil aviation:** 2.13 bil pass.-mi; 6 airports. **Chief ports:** Matrah, Mina' al Fahl.

Communications: TV sets: 575 per 1,000 pop. **Radios:** 607 per 1,000 pop. **Telephone lines:** 235,300. **Daily newspaper circ.:** 29 per 1,000 pop. **Internet:** 120,000 users.

Health: Life expectancy: 70.4 male; 74.9 female. **Births** (per 1,000 pop.): 37.5. **Deaths** (per 1,000 pop.): 4.0. **Natural inc.:** 3.35%. **Infant mortality** (per 1,000 live births): 21.0.

Education: Literacy: 75.8%.

Major Intl. Organizations: UN (FAO, IBRD, ILO, IMF, IMO, WHO), AL.

Embassy: 2535 Belmont Rd. NW 20008; 387-1980.
Website: www.omanet.com

Oman was originally called Muscat and Oman. A long history of rule by other lands, including Portugal in the 16th century, ended with the ouster of the Persians in 1744. By the early 19th century, Muscat and Oman was one of the most important countries in the region, controlling much of the Persian and Pakistan coasts, and also ruling far-away Zanzibar, which was separated in 1861 under British mediation.

British influence was confirmed in a 1951 treaty, and Britain helped suppress an uprising by traditionally rebellious interior tribes against control by Muscat in the 1950s.

On July 23, 1970, Sultan Said bin Taimur was overthrown by his son, who changed the nation's name to Sultanate of Oman.

Oil is the major source of income.

Oman opened its air bases to Western forces following the Iraqi invasion of Kuwait on Aug. 2, 1990. Oman served as a base for U.S. aircraft in the Afghanistan war, 2001.

Pakistan
Islamic Republic of Pakistan

People: Population: 153,578,000. **Age distrib.** (%): <15: 39.9; 65+: 4.1. **Pop. density:** 511 per sq. mi. **Urban:** 33%. **Ethnic groups:** Punjabi, Sindhi, Pashtun, Balochi. **Principal languages:** English, Urdu (both official); Punjabi, Sindhi, Siraiki, Pashtu, Balochi, Hindko, Brahui, Burushaski. **Chief religions:** Muslim 97% (official; Sunni 77%, Shi'a 20%).

Geography: Area: 310,403 sq. mi. (total); 300,665 sq. mi. (land). **Location:** In W part of South Asia. **Neighbors:** Iran on W, Afghanistan and China on N, India on E. **Topography:** The Indus R. rises in the Hindu Kush and Himalaya Mts. in the N (highest is K2, or Godwin Austen, 28,250 ft., 2d highest in world), then flows over 1,000 mi. through fertile valley and empties into Arabian Sea. Thar Desert, Eastern Plains flank Indus Valley. **Capital:** Islamabad. **Cities (urban aggr.):** Karachi 10,032,000; Lahore 5,452,000; Faisalabad 2,142,000; Islamabad 636,000.

Government: Type: Republic with strong military influence. **Head of state:** Pres. Pervez Musharraf; b Aug. 11,1943; in office: Oct. 5, 1999 (as pres. from June 20, 2001). **Head of gov.:** Mir Zafarullah Khan Jamali; b Jan. 1, 1944; in office: Nov. 23, 2002. **Local divisions:** 4 provinces and 1 capital territory, plus federally administered tribal areas. **Defense budget** (2002): $2.6 bil. **Active troops:** 620,000.

Economy: Industries: textiles, food proc., beverages, constr. materials, clothing, paper products. **Chief crops:** cotton, wheat, rice, sugarcane, fruits. **Natural resources:** nat. gas, oil, coal, iron ore, copper, salt, limestone. **Crude oil reserves** (2002): 298 mil. bbls. **Arable land:** 27%. **Livestock** (2002): cattle: 22.86 mil.; chickens: 155 mil.; goats: 50.90 mil.; sheep:24.40 mil. **Fish catch** (2002): 623,425 metric tons. **Electricity prod.** (2001): 66.96 bil. kWh. **Labor force:** agri. 44%, ind. 17%, services 39%.

Finance: Monetary unit: Rupee (PKR) (Sept. 2003: 60.06=1 U.S.). **GDP** (2002 est.): $311 bil. **Per capita GDP** (2001): $2,100. **Imports** (2001): $9.2 bil.; partners (2000): Kuwait 11.7%, UAE 10.7%, Saudi Arabia 10.5%, U.S. 6%. **Exports** (2001): $8.8 bil.; partners (2000): U.S. 24.8%, UK 6.5%, UAE 6.2%, Hong Kong 5.9%. **Tourism:** $86 mil. **Budget** (2002 est.): $14.8 bil. **Intl. reserves less gold:** $5.94 bil. **Gold:** 2.09 mil oz t. **Consumer prices:** 3.3%.

Transport: Railroad: Length: 5,072 mi. **Motor vehicles:** 1.07 mil. pass. cars, 434,500 comm. vehicles. **Civil aviation:** 6.50 bil pass.-mi; 87 airports. **Chief port:** Karachi.

Communications: TV sets: 105 per 1,000 pop. **Radios:** 94 per 1,000 pop. **Telephone lines:** 3,690,000. **Daily newspaper circ.:** 27.2 per 1,000 pop. **Internet:** 500,000 users.

Health: Life expectancy: 61.3 male; 63.1 female. **Births** (per 1,000 pop.): 29.6. **Deaths** (per 1,000 pop.): 8.8. **Natural inc.:** 2.08%. **Infant mortality** (per 1,000 live births): 76.5.

Education: Compulsory: ages 5-9. **Literacy:** 45.7%.

Major Intl. Organizations: UN (FAO, IBRD, ILO, IMF, IMO, WHO, WTrO).

Embassy: 2315 Massachusetts Ave. NW 20008; 939-6200.

Website: www.pakistan-embassy.org/index.asp

Present-day Pakistan shares the 5,000-year history of the India-Pakistan subcontinent. At present-day Harappa and Mohenjo Daro, the Indus Valley Civilization, with large cities and elaborate irrigation systems, flourished c. 4,000-2,500 BC. Aryan invaders from the NW conquered the region around 1,500 BC, forging the Vedic civilization that dominated the region for over a thousand years.

Other invaders from the W followed, including the Persians, Macedonians (led by Alexander the Great), and Sassanians. The first Arab invasion, AD 712, introduced Islam. Present-day Pakistan and India were part of the Mogul empire from 1526 to 1857. Muslim power faded by the end of the 19th cent. as the British gained control of the N and NW areas of the subcontinent.

After World War I, the Muslims of British India began agitation for minority rights in elections. Muhammad Ali Jinnah (1876-1948) was the principal architect of Pakistan. A leader of the Muslim League from 1916, he worked for dominion status for India; from 1940 he advocated a separate Muslim state.

When the British withdrew Aug. 14, 1947, the Islamic majority areas of India acquired self-government as Pakistan, with dominion status in the Commonwealth. Pakistan was divided into 2 sections, West Pakistan and East Pakistan. The 2 areas were nearly 1,000 mi. apart on opposite sides of India.

In Oct. 1958, Gen. Mohammad Ayub Khan took power in a coup. He was elected president in 1960. Ultimately he resigned in 1969, after violent rioting and unrest, most of it in East Pakistan, which demanded autonomy. The government was turned over to Gen. Agha Mohammad Yahya Kahn and martial law was declared.

The Awami League, which had sought regional autonomy for East Pakistan for several years, won a majority in Dec. 1970 elections to a constituent assembly. In March 1971, Yahya postponed the assembly. Rioting and strikes broke out in the East.

On Mar. 25, 1971, government troops launched attacks in the East. The Easterners, aided by India, proclaimed the independent nation of Bangladesh. In months of widespread fighting, countless thousands were killed. Some 10 million Easterners fled into India. Full-scale war between India and Pakistan had spread to both the East and West fronts by Dec. 3. Pakistan troops in the East surrendered Dec. 16; Pakistan agreed to a cease-fire in the West Dec. 17. On July 3, 1972, Pakistan and India signed a pact agreeing to withdraw troops from their borders and seek peaceful solutions to all problems.

Zulfikar Ali Bhutto, leader of the Pakistan People's Party, which had won the most West Pakistan votes in Dec. 1970 elections, became president Dec. 20. Bhutto was overthrown in a military coup July 1977. Convicted of complicity in a 1974 political murder, he was executed Apr. 4, 1979. Over 3 million Afghan refugees flooded into Pakistan after the USSR invaded Afghanistan Dec. 1979; over 1.2 million remained in 1999.

Pres. Mohammad Zia ul-Haq was killed when his plane exploded in Aug. 1988. Following Nov. elections, Benazir Bhutto, daughter of Zulfikar Ali Bhutto, was named prime minister, becoming the first woman leader of a Muslim nation. She was accused of corruption and dismissed by the president, Aug. 1990; her party was soundly defeated in Oct. 1990 elections, and Nawaz Sharif became prime minister. She regained power after elections in Oct. 1993. Opposition to Bhutto centered around Karachi, which was crippled by violent strikes and ethnic clashes during 1995 and 1996. Accusing the Bhutto government of corruption and mismanagement, Pres. Farooq Leghari appointed a caretaker prime minister Nov. 5, 1996. Elections on Feb. 3, 1997, gave Sharif a parliamentary majority.

Responding to nuclear weapons tests by India, Pakistan conducted its own tests, May 28-30, 1998; the U.S. imposed economic sanctions on both countries.

In mid-1999, Muslim infiltrators, apparently including Pakistani troops, seized Indian-held positions in the disputed territory of Kashmir, which witnessed its heaviest fighting in over 2 decades (see India). After meeting with Pres. Bill Clinton on July 4, Sharif agreed to a Pakistani pullback. Growing conflict between Sharif and the military climaxed in his firing on Oct. 12 of army chief Gen. Pervez Musharraf, whose supporters staged a bloodless coup. Musharraf assumed the presidency June 20, 2001.

Following the Sept. 11, 2001, terrorist attack on the U.S., Pres. Musharraf, Sept. 19, pledged cooperation with the U.S. in actions against the Taliban and al-Qaeda in neighboring Afghanistan; in return, the U.S. offered Pakistan financial aid and debt relief. To defuse mounting tensions with India, Musharraf in late Dec. 2001 ordered the arrest of members of Islamic militant groups that India blamed for a Dec. 13 attack on the parliament in New Delhi. Guerrilla violence in Kashmir and Pakistani missile tests May 25-28, 2002, heightened fears of war with India, but the crisis was eased in June with U.S. mediation.

A referendum Apr. 30, 2002, extended Musharraf's rule for another 5 years; many observers called the vote rigged. Musharraf amended the constitution Aug. 21 to increase the military's formal role in governing the country. Legislative elections Oct. 10 showed a surge of support for Muslim fundamentalist parties.

During 2002-03 there was evidence of growing al-Qaeda and Taliban activity within Pakistan. Militants kidnapped Wall Street Journal reporter Daniel Pearl Jan. 23, 2002, and eventually killed him; 4 Islamic extremists were convicted July 15. Several alleged al-Qaeda operatives, including Ramzi bin al-Shibh, believed to have been a close associate of Sept. 11 ringleader Mohamed Atta, were captured in a shootout in Karachi, Sept. 11, 2002. The alleged mastermind of the Sept. 11 attack, Khalid Sheikh Mohammed, was apprehended in Rawalpindi, Mar. 1, 2003. A suicide raid on a Shiite mosque in Quetta, July 4, left at least 53 people dead, including the 3 attackers.

Palau
Republic of Palau

People: Population: 20,000. **Age distrib.** (%): <15: 26.8; 65+: 4.6. **Pop. density:** 111 per sq. mi. **Urban:** 69%. **Ethnic groups:** Palauan (Micronesian/Malayan/Melanesian mix) 70%, Asian 28%, White 2%. **Principal languages:** English (official); Palauan, Sonsorolese, Tobi, Angaur, Japanese (all official in certain states). **Chief religions:** Roman Catholic 49%, Modekngei 30%.

Geography: Area (total): 177 sq. mi. **Location:** Archipelago (26 islands, more than 300 islets) in the W Pacific Ocean, about 530 mi SE of the Philippines. **Neighbors:** Micronesia to E, Indonesia to S. **Topography:** Palau is comprised of a mountainous main island and low coral atolls, usually fringed with large barrier reefs. **Capital:** Koror: 14,000. (Note: a new capital is being built in Babelthuap.)

Government: Type: Republic. **Head of state and gov.:** Pres. Tommy Remengesau; b 1956; in office: Jan. 19, 2001. **Local divisions:** 18 states.

Economy: Industries: tourism, handicrafts, constr., garment making. **Chief crops:** coconuts, copra, cassava, sweet potatoes. **Natural resources:** timber, gold & other minerals, fish. **Fish catch** (2002 est.): 2,002 metric tons. **Labor force:** agr. 20%.

Finance: Monetary unit: U.S. Dollar. **GDP** (2001 est.): $174 mil. **Per capita GDP** (2001 est.): $9,000. **Imports** (1999): $126 mil.; partners: U.S. **Exports** (1999): $11 mil.; partners: U.S., Japan, Singapore. **Budget** (1999 est.): $80.8 mil.

Transport: 1 airport.

Communications: TV sets: 98 per 1,000 pop. **Radios:** 550 per 1,000 pop.

Health: Life expectancy: 66.4 male; 72.8 female. **Births** (per 1,000 pop.): 19.0. **Deaths** (per 1,000 pop.): 7.0. **Natural inc.:** 1.20%. **Infant mortality** (per 1,000 live births): 15.8.

Education: Compulsory: ages 6-14. **Literacy** (1990): 98%.

Major Intl. Organizations: UN (WHO).

Embassy: 1800 K St. NW, # 714, 20006; 452-6814.

Spain acquired the Palau Islands in 1886 and sold them to Germany in 1899. Japan seized them in 1914. American forces occupied the islands in 1944; in 1947, they became part of the U.S.-administered UN Trust Territory of the Pacific Islands. In 1981 Palau became an autonomous republic; in 1993 the republic ratified a compact of free association with the U.S., which provides financial aid in return for U.S. use of Palauan military facilities over 15 years. Palau became an independent nation on Oct. 1, 1994. Vice-Pres. Tommy Remengesau won the presidential election held Nov. 7, 2000.

Website: www.palauembassy.com

Panama
Republic of Panama

People: Population: 3,120,000. **Age distrib.** (%): <15: 29.6; 65+: 6.1. **Pop. density:** 106 per sq. mi. **Urban:** 57%. **Ethnic groups:** Mestizo 70%, Amerindian-West Indian 14%, White 10%, Amerindian 6%. **Principal languages:** Spanish (official), English. **Chief religions:** Roman Catholic 85%, Protestant 15%.

Geography: Area: 30,193 sq. mi. (total); 29,340 sq. mi. (land). **Location:** In Central America. **Neighbors:** Costa Rica on W, Colombia on E. **Topography:** 2 mountain ranges run the length of the isthmus. Tropical rain forests cover the Caribbean coast and eastern Panama. **Capital:** Panama City 1,202,000.

Government: Type: Republic. **Head of state and gov.:** Pres. Minerva Elisa Moscoso; b July 1, 1948; in office: Sept. 1, 1999. **Local divisions:** 9 provinces, 3 territories. **Defense budget** (2001): $135 mil. **Active troops:** Nil. (11,800 paramilitary).

Economy: Industries: constr., oil refining, brewing, constr. materials, sugar milling. **Chief crops:** bananas, rice, corn, coffee, sugarcane. **Natural resources:** copper, mahogany, shrimp, hydropower. **Arable land:** 7%. **Livestock** (2002): cattle: 1.53 mil.; chickens: 14.13 mil.; goats: 6,165; pigs: 280,000 **Fish catch** (2002 est.): 237,394 metric tons. **Electricity prod.** (2001): 4.04 bil. kWh. **Labor force:** agri. 20.8%, ind. 18%, services 61.2%.

Finance: Monetary unit: Balboa (PAB) (Sept. 2003: 1.00=1 U.S.). **GDP** (2002 est.): $17.3 bil. **Per capita GDP:** $6,000. **Imports** (2001): $6.7 bil.; partners (2000 est.): U.S. 33.1%, Ecuador 7.2%, Venezuela 6.6%, Japan 5.5%. **Exports** (2001 est.): $5.9 bil.; partners (2000 est.): U.S. 45.9%, Sweden 8.1%, Benelux 5.3%, Costa Rica 5.1%. **Tourism** (1999): $576 mil. **Budget** (2000 est.): $2 bil. **Intl. reserves less gold:** $870 mil. **Consumer prices:** 1.0%.

Transport: Railroad: Length: 221 mi. **Motor vehicles** (1998): 212,600 pass. cars, 68,400 comm. vehicles. **Civil aviation:** 1.05 bil pass.-mi; 41 airports. **Chief ports:** Balboa, Cristobal.

Communications: TV sets: 192 per 1,000 pop. **Radios:** 299 per 1,000 pop. **Telephone lines:** 376,500. **Daily newspaper circ.:** 62 per 1,000 pop. **Internet:** 120,000 users.

Health: Life expectancy: 70.0 male; 74.8 female. **Births** (per 1,000 pop.): 20.8. **Deaths** (per 1,000 pop.): 6.3. **Natural inc.:** 1.45%. **Infant mortality** (per 1,000 live births): 21.4.

Education: Compulsory: ages 6-11. **Literacy:** 92.6%.

Major Intl. Organizations: UN (FAO, IBRD, ILO, IMF, IMO, WHO), OAS.

Embassy: 2862 McGill Terrace NW 20008; 483-1407.

Websites: www.presidencia.gob.pa
www.consuladogeneraldepanama.com

The coast of Panama was sighted by Rodrigo de Bastidas, sailing with Columbus for Spain in 1501, and was visited by Columbus in 1502. Vasco Nunez de Balboa crossed the isthmus and "discovered" the Pacific Ocean, Sept. 13, 1513. Spanish colonies were ravaged by Francis Drake, 1572-95, and Henry Morgan, 1668-71. Morgan destroyed the old city of Panama which had been founded in 1519. Freed from Spain, Panama joined Colombia in 1821.

Panama declared its independence from Colombia Nov. 3, 1903, with U.S. recognition. In support of Panama, U.S. naval forces deterred action by Colombia. Panama granted use, occupation, and control of the Canal Zone to the U.S. by treaty, ratified Feb. 26, 1904. In 1978, a new treaty provided for a gradual takeover by Panama of the canal, and withdrawal of U.S. troops, to be completed before the end of the century. U.S. payments were substantially increased in the interim.

President Delvalle was ousted by the National Assembly, Feb. 26, 1988, after he tried to fire the head of the Panama Defense Forces, Gen. Manuel Antonio Noriega, who was under U.S. federal indictment on drug charges. U.S. troops invaded Panama Dec. 20, 1989, and Noriega surrendered Jan. 3, 1990.

On Aug. 30, 1998, voters rejected a constitutional change that would have allowed Pres. Ernesto Pérez Balladares to run for re-election in 1999. Mireya Moscoso, widow of former Pres. Arnulfo Arias, was elected president May 2, 1999, becoming Panama's first female head of state. The U.S. handed over control of the Panama Canal to Panama Dec. 31, 1999.

Papua New Guinea
Independent State of Papua New Guinea

People: Population: 5,711,000. **Age distrib.** (%): <15: 38.6; 65+: 3.7. **Pop. density:** 33 per sq. mi. **Urban:** 18%. **Ethnic groups:** Melanesian, Papuan, Negrito, Micronesian, Polynesian. **Principal languages:** English (official), pidgin English, Motu; 715 indigenous languages. **Chief religions:** Indigenous beliefs 34%, Roman Catholic 22%, Protestant 44%.

Geography: Area: 178,703 sq. mi. (total); 174,850 sq. mi. (land). **Location:** SE Asia, occupying E half of island of New Guinea and about 600 nearby islands. **Neighbors:** Indonesia (West Irian) on W, Australia on S. **Topography:** Thickly forested mts. cover much of the center of the country, with lowlands along the coasts. Included are some islands of Bismarck and Solomon groups, such as the Admiralty Isls., New Ireland, New Britain, and Bougainville. **Capital:** Port Moresby: 259,000.

Government: Type: Parliamentary democracy. **Head of state:** Queen Elizabeth II, represented by Gov.-Gen. Albert Kipalan; elected: Sept. 18, 2003; scheduled to take office: Nov. 13, 2003. **Head of gov.:** Prime Min. Sir Michael Somare; b Apr. 9, 1936; in office: Aug. 5, 2002. **Local divisions:** 20 provinces. **Defense budget** (2002): $27 mil. **Active troops:** 3,100.

Economy: Industries: copra & palm oil proc., wood products, mining. **Chief crops:** coffee, cocoa, coconuts, palm kernels, tea, rubber, sweet potatoes. **Natural resources:** gold, copper, silver, nat. gas, timber, oil, fish. **Crude oil reserves** (2002): 238 mil. bbls. **Livestock** (2002): cattle: 89,000; chickens: 3.80 mil.; goats: 2,400; pigs: 1.65 mil.; sheep: 7,000. **Fish catch** (2002 est.): 122,434 metric tons. **Electricity prod.** (2001): 1.5 bil. kWh. **Labor force:** agri. 85%.

Finance: Monetary unit: Kina (PGK) (Sept. 2003: 3.42=1 U.S.). **GDP** (2002 est.): $1.2 bil. **Per capita GDP:** $2,300. **Imports** (2001): $1.024 bil.; partners (2000): Australia 50%, Singapore 20%, Japan 4%, NZ 4%. **Exports** (2001 est.): $1.8 bil.; partners (2000): Australia 30%, Japan 11%, China 6%, Germany 4%. **Tourism** (1999): $76 mil. **Budget** (2000 est.): $1.1 bil. **Intl. reserves less gold:** $236 mil. **Gold:** 60,000 oz t. **Consumer prices:** 11.8%.

Transport: Motor vehicles (1998): 21,700 pass. cars, 89,700 comm. vehicles. **Civil aviation:** 398.3 bil pass.-mi; 21 airports. **Chief ports:** Port Moresby, Lae.

Communications: TV sets: 13 per 1,000 pop. **Radios:** 91 per 1,000 pop. **Telephone lines:** 62,000. **Daily newspaper circ.:** 15 per 1,000 pop. **Internet:** 50,000 users.

Health: Life expectancy: 62.1 male; 66.4 female. **Births** (per 1,000 pop.): 31.1. **Deaths** (per 1,000 pop.): 7.6. **Natural inc.:** 2.34%. **Infant mortality** (per 1,000 live births): 54.8.

Education: Compulsory: ages 6-14. **Literacy:** 66%.

Major Intl. Organizations: UN (FAO, IBRD, ILO, IMF, IMO, WHO, WTrO), the Commonwealth, APEC.

Embassy: 1779 Massachusetts Ave NW, 20036; 745-3680.

Websites: www.pngonline.gov.pg; www.pngembassy.org

Human remains have been found in the interior of New Guinea dating back at least 10,000 years and possibly much earlier. Successive waves of peoples probably entered the country from Asia through Indonesia. The indigenous population consists of a huge number of tribes, many living in almost complete isolation with mutually unintelligible languages.

Europeans visited in the 15th century, but actual land claims did not begin until the 19th century, when the Dutch took control of the island's western half. The southern half of eastern New Guinea was first claimed by Britain in 1884, and transferred to Australia in 1905. The northern half was claimed by Germany in 1884, but captured in World War I by Australia, which was first granted a League of Nations mandate and then a UN trusteeship over the area. The 2 territories were administered jointly after 1949, given self-government Dec. 1, 1973, and became independent Sept. 16, 1975.

Secessionist rebels clashed with government forces on Bougainville beginning in 1988; a truce signed Oct. 10, 1997, brought a halt to the fighting, which had claimed an estimated 20,000 lives. The country suffered from a severe drought in 1997. A tsunami killed at least 3,000 people July 17, 1998. A Bougainville autonomy agreement was signed Aug. 30, 2001. Army mutinies were suppressed in Mar. 2001 and Mar. 2002.

Paraguay
Republic of Paraguay

People: Population: 5,878,000. **Age distrib.** (%): <15: 38.7; 65+: 4.7. **Pop. density:** 38 per sq. mi. **Urban:** 57%. **Ethnic groups:** Mestizo 95%. **Principal languages:** Spanish, Guaraní (both official). **Chief religions:** Roman Catholic 90%.

Geography: Area: 157,047 sq. mi. (total); 153,398 sq. mi. (land). **Location:** Landlocked country in central South America. **Neighbors:** Bolivia on N, Argentina on S, Brazil on E. **Topography:** Paraguay R. bisects the country. To E are fertile plains, wooded slopes, grasslands. To W is the Gran Chaco plain, with marshes and scrub trees. Extreme W is arid. **Capital:** Asunción 1,302,000.

Government: Type: Republic. **Head of state and gov.:** Pres. Nicanor Duarte Frutos; b Oct. 11, 1956; in office: Aug. 15, 2003.

Local divisions: 18 departments and capital city. **Defense budget** (2001): $64 mil. **Active troops:** 18,600.

Economy: Industries: sugar, cement, textiles, beverages, wood products. **Chief crops:** cotton, sugarcane, soybeans, corn, wheat, tobacco, cassava. **Natural resources:** hydropower, timber, iron ore, mang., limestone. **Arable land:** 6%. **Livestock** (2002): cattle: 9.90 mil.; chickens: 15.50 mil.; goats: 125,000; pigs: 2.75 mil.; sheep: 407,000. **Fish catch** (2002 est.): 25,110 metric tons. **Electricity prod.** (2001): 44.89 bil. kWh. **Labor force:** agri. 45%.

Finance: Monetary unit: Guaraní (PYG) (Sept. 2003: 6,365.80=1 U.S.). **GDP** (2002 est.): $25 bil. **Per capita GDP:** $4,200. **Imports** (2001): $2.7 bil.; partners (2000): Argentina 25.4%, Brazil 24.5%, Uruguay 3.8%. **Exports** (2001 est.): $2.2 bil.; partners (2000): Brazil 39%, Uruguay 14%, Argentina 11%. **Tourism:** $66 mil. **Budget** (1999 est.): $2 bil. **Intl. reserves less gold:** $463 mil. **Gold:** 30,000 oz t. **Consumer prices:** 10.5%.

Transport: Railroad: Length: 603 mi. **Motor vehicles (1993):** 250,700 pass. cars, 37,700 comm. vehicles. **Civil aviation:** 151.6 mil pass.-mi; 11 airports. **Chief port:** Asunción.

Communications: TV sets: 205 per 1,000 pop. **Radios:** 182 per 1,000 pop. **Telephone lines:** 273,200. **Daily newspaper circ.:** 43 per 1,000 pop. **Internet:** 100,000 users.

Health: Life expectancy: 71.9 male; 77.0 female. **Births** (per 1,000 pop.): 30.1. **Deaths** (per 1,000 pop.): 4.6. **Natural inc.:** 2.55%. **Infant mortality** (per 1,000 live births): 27.7.

Education: Compulsory: ages 6-14. **Literacy:** 94%.

Major Intl. Organizations: UN (FAO, IBRD, ILO, IMF, IMO, WHO, WTrO), OAS.

Embassy: 2400 Massachusetts Ave. NW, 20008; 483-6960.

Website: www.paraguay.com

The Guaraní Indians were settled farmers speaking a common language before the arrival of Europeans. Visited by Sebastian Cabot in 1527 and settled as a Spanish possession in 1535, Paraguay gained its independence from Spain in 1811. It lost much of its territory to Brazil, Uruguay, and Argentina in the War of the Triple Alliance, 1865-1870. Large areas were won from Bolivia in the Chaco War, 1932-35.

Gen. Alfredo Stroessner, who had ruled since 1954, was ousted in a military coup led by Gen. Andrés Rodríguez on Feb. 3, 1989. Rodríguez was elected president May 1. Juan Carlos Wasmosy was elected president May 9, 1993, becoming the nation's first civilian head of state in many years.

A prolonged power struggle involving a popular military leader, Gen. Lino César Oviedo, who was accused of insubordination, culminated in his surrender Dec. 12, 1997. He was freed Aug. 18, 1998, following the inauguration of Pres. Raúl Cubas Grau, Oviedo's successor as Colorado Party nominee.

The assassination of Vice Pres. Luis María Argaña, Mar. 23, 1999, by an unidentified gunman, was widely attributed to Cubas and triggered protests and an impeachment vote; Cubas resigned Mar. 28 and was succeeded by Senate leader Luis Ángel González Macchi. An attempted military coup was suppressed May 18, 2000.

Mass protests over the depressed economy led to the proclamation of a state of emergency July 15, 2002. Nicanor Duarte Frutos won the presidency, Apr. 27, 2003, maintaining 55 years of uninterrupted Colorado Party rule.

Peru
Republic of Peru

People: Population: 27,167,000. **Age distrib.** (%): <15: 34; 65+: 4.9. **Pop. density:** 55 per sq. mi. **Urban:** 73%. **Ethnic groups:** Amerindian 45%, Mestizo 37%, White 15%. **Principal languages:** Spanish, Quechua (both official); Aymara. **Chief religions:** Roman Catholic 90% (official).

Geography: Area: 496,226 sq. mi. (total); 494,210 sq. mi. (land). **Location:** On the Pacific coast of South America. **Neighbors:** Ecuador, Colombia on N; Brazil, Bolivia on E; Chile on S. **Topography:** An arid coastal strip, 10 to 100 mi. wide, supports much of the population thanks to widespread irrigation. The Andes cover 27% of land area. The uplands are well-watered, as are the eastern slopes reaching the Amazon basin, which covers half the country with its forests and jungles. **Capital:** Lima. **Cities (urban aggr.):** Lima 7,594,000; Arequipa 710,103; Callao 424,294.

Government: Type: Republic. **Head of state:** Pres. Alejandro Toledo; b Mar. 28, 1946; in office: July 28, 2001. **Head of gov.:** Prime Min.Beatriz Merino; in office: June 28, 2003. **Local divisions:** 12 regions, 24 departments, 1 constitutional province. **Defense budget** (2002): $762 mil. **Active troops:** 110,000.

Economy: Industries: mining, oil, fishing, textiles, clothing, food proc. **Chief crops:** coffee, cotton, sugarcane, rice, wheat, potatoes, corn, plantains, coca. **Natural resources:** copper, silver, gold, oil, timber, fish, iron ore, coal, phosphate, potash, hydropower, nat. gas. **Crude oil reserves** (2002): 323 mil. bbls. **Arable land:** 3%. **Livestock** (2002): cattle: 4.95 mil.; chickens: 90 mil.; goats: 2.01 mil.; pigs: 2.80 mil.; sheep: 14.30 mil. **Fish catch** (2002): 7,995,507 metric tons. **Electricity prod.** (2001): 20.59 bil. kWh. **Labor force:** agri., mining and quarrying, manufact., construct., transport, services.

Finance: Monetary unit: Nuevo Sol (PEN) (Sept. 2003: 3.61=1 U.S.). **GDP** (2002 est.): $132 bil. **Per capita GDP:** $4,800. **Imports** (2001): $7.4 bil.; partners (2000): U.S. 27%, Chile 8%, Spain 6%, Venezuela 4%. **Exports** (2001 est.): $7.3 bil.; partners (2000): U.S. 28%, UK 8%, Switzerland 8%, China 6%. **Tourism:** $1.0 bil. **Budget** (2002 est.): $10.4 bil. **Intl. reserves less gold:** $6.87 bil. **Gold:** 1.11 mil oz t. **Consumer prices:** .2%.

Transport: Railroad: Length: 1,306 mi. **Motor vehicles:** 731,300 pass. cars, 459,600 comm. vehicles. **Civil aviation:** 988.0 bil pass.-mi; 49 airports. **Chief ports:** Callao, Chimbote, Matarani, Salaverry.

Communications: TV sets: 147 per 1,000 pop. **Radios:** 273 per 1,000 pop. **Telephone lines:** 2,022,300. **Daily newspaper circ.:** 85 per 1,000 pop. **Internet:** 2,000,000 users.

Health: Life expectancy: 68.5 male; 73.4 female. **Births** (per 1,000 pop.): 22.8. **Deaths** (per 1,000 pop.): 5.7. **Natural inc.:** 1.71%. **Infant mortality** (per 1,000 live births): 37.0.

Education: Compulsory: ages 6-16. **Literacy:** 90.9%.

Major Intl. Organizations: UN and all of its specialized agencies, APEC, OAS.

Embassy: 1700 Massachusetts Ave. NW 20036; 833-9860.

Website: travel.peru.com/travel/English

The powerful Inca empire had its seat at Cuzco in the Andes and covered most of Peru, Bolivia, and Ecuador, as well as parts of Colombia, Chile, and Argentina. Building on the achievements of 800 years of Andean civilization, the Incas had a high level of skill in architecture, engineering, textiles, and social organization.

A civil war had weakened the empire when Francisco Pizarro, Spanish conquistador, began raiding Peru for its wealth, 1532. In 1533 he seized the ruling Inca, Atahualpa, filled a room with gold as a ransom, then executed him and enslaved the natives.

Lima was the seat of Spanish viceroys until the Argentine liberator, José de San Martín, captured it in 1821; Spanish forces were ultimately routed by Simón Bolívar, 1824.

On Oct. 3, 1968, a military coup ousted Pres. Fernando Belaunde Terry. In 1968-74, the military government started socialist programs. Food shortages, escalating foreign debt, and strikes led to another coup, Aug. 29, 1976.

After 12 years of military rule, Peru returned to democratic leadership in 1980 but was plagued by economic problems and by leftist Shining Path (Sendero Luminoso) guerrillas. Conflict between guerrillas and government troops, 1980-2000, killed more than 69,000 people, mostly Andean Indians.

Elected president in June 1990, Alberto Fujimori, the son of Japanese immigrants, dissolved the National Congress, suspended parts of the constitution, and initiated press censorship, Apr. 5, 1992. The leader of Shining Path was captured Sept. 12.

With the economy booming and signs of significant progress in curtailing guerrilla activity, Fujimori won reelection Apr. 9, 1995. Repressive antiterrorism tactics, however, drew international criticism. On Dec. 17, 1996, leftist Tupac Amaru guerrillas infiltrated a reception at the Japanese ambassador's residence in Lima and took hundreds of hostages, most of whom were later released. Peruvian soldiers stormed the embassy Apr. 22, 1997, rescuing 71 of the remaining hostages; 1 hostage, 2 soldiers, and all 14 guerrillas were killed. Fujimori's path to a 3rd term was cleared when his lone remaining challenger withdrew, charging electoral fraud, 6 days before a runoff vote on May 28, 2000. Scandals involving his top aide and intelligence chief, Vladimiro Montesinos, led Fujimori to resign his office Nov. 20, while on a visit to Japan; instead of accepting his resignation, Congress ousted him as "morally unfit."

Alejandro Toledo won a presidential runoff election June 3, 2001. Montesinos was captured in Venezuela June 23 and extradited to Peru and sentenced on abuse of power charges July 1, 2002. Charges were filed Sept. 5 against the exiled Fujimori, alleging his complicity in the killings by a paramilitary death squad of at least 25 people during 1991-92.

Fireworks explosions killed 291 people in a crowded Lima commercial district Dec. 29, 2001. A sagging economy and resurgent rebel activity eroded Toledo's popularity in 2003. On June 28, he named Peru's 1st female prime minister, Beatriz Moreno.

Philippines
Republic of the Philippines

People: Population: 79,999,000. **Age distrib.** (%): <15: 36.6; 65+: 3.7. **Pop. density:** 695 per sq. mi. **Urban:** 59%. **Ethnic groups:** Christian Malay 91.5%, Muslim Malay 4%, Chinese 1.5%. **Principal languages:** Filipino, English (both official); many dialects. **Chief religions:** Roman Catholic 83%, Protestant 9%, Muslim 5%.

Geography: Area: 115,831 sq. mi. (total); 115,124 sq. mi. (land). **Location:** An archipelago off the SE coast of Asia. **Neighbors:** Nearest are Malaysia and Indonesia on S, Taiwan on N. **Topography:** The country consists of some 7,100 islands stretching 1,100 mi. N-S. About 95% of area and population are on 11 largest islands, which are mountainous, except for the heavily indented coastlines and for the central plain on Luzon. **Capital:** Manila. **Cities (urban aggr.):** Manila 10,069,000; Quezon City 2,160,000; Davao 1,146,000.

Government: Type: Republic. **Head of state and gov.:** Pres. Gloria Macapagal Arroyo; b Apr. 5, 1947; in office: Jan. 20, 2001. **Local divisions:** 72 provinces, 61 chartered cities. **Defense budget** (2002): $1.4 bil. **Active troops:** 106,000.

Economy: Industries: textiles, pharm., chemicals, wood products, food proc., electronics. **Chief crops:** rice, coconuts, corn, sugarcane, bananas, pineapples. **Natural resources:** timber, oil, nickel, cobalt, silver, gold, salt, copper. **Crude oil reserves** (2002): 178 mil. bbls. **Arable land:** 19%. **Livestock** (2002): cattle: 2.55 mil.; chickens: 125.72 mil.; goats: 6.97 mil.; pigs: 11.65 mil.; sheep: 30,000. **Fish catch** (2002): 2,379,874 metric tons. **Electricity prod.** (2001): 45.21 bil. kWh. **Labor force:** agri. 39.8%, government and social services 19.4%, services 17.7%, manufact. 9.8%, construct. 5.8%, other 7.5%.

Finance: Monetary unit: Peso (PHP) (Sept. 2003: 54.83=1 U.S.). **GDP** (2002 est.): $356 bil. **Per capita GDP:** $4,200. **Imports** (2000): $30 bil.; partners (2000): Japan 19%; U.S. 16%, EU 9%, South Korea 8%. **Exports** (2000): $37 bil.; partners (2000): U.S. 30%, Japan 15%, Netherlands 8%, Singapore 8%. **Tourism** (1999): $2.53 bil. **Budget** (2002 est.): $15 bil. **Intl. reserves less gold:** $9.67 bil. **Gold:** 8.73 mil oz t. **Consumer prices:** 3.1%.

Transport: Railroad: Length: 557 mi. **Motor vehicles (1999):** 2.08 mil. pass. cars, 276,600 comm. vehicles. **Civil aviation:** 6.40 bil pass.-mi; 82 airports. **Chief ports:** Cebu, Manila, Iloilo, Davao.

Communications: TV sets: 110 per 1,000 pop. **Radios:** 161 per 1,000 pop. **Telephone lines:** 3,889,900. **Daily newspaper circ.:** 79 per 1,000 pop. **Internet:** 2,000,000 users.

Health: Life expectancy: 66.4 male; 72.3 female. **Births** (per 1,000 pop.): 26.3. **Deaths** (per 1,000 pop.): 5.6. **Natural inc.:** 2.07%. **Infant mortality** (per 1,000 live births): 25.0.

Education: Compulsory: ages 6-12. **Literacy:** 95.9%.

Major Intl. Organizations: UN (FAO, IBRD, ILO, IMF, IMO, WHO, WTrO), ASEAN.

Embassy: 1600 Massachusetts Ave. NW 20036; 467-9300.

Websites: www.philippineembassy-usa.org; www.gov.ph

The Malay peoples of the Philippine Islands, whose ancestors probably migrated from Southeast Asia, were mostly hunters, fishers, and unsettled cultivators.

The archipelago was visited by Magellan, 1521. The Spanish founded Manila, 1571. The islands, named for King Philip II of Spain, were ceded by Spain to the U.S. for $20 million, 1898, following the Spanish-American War. U.S. troops suppressed a guerrilla uprising in a brutal 6-year war, 1899-1905.

Japan attacked the Philippines Dec. 8, 1941, and occupied the islands during WW II. On July 4, 1946, independence was proclaimed in accordance with an act passed by the U.S. Congress in 1934. A republic was established.

On Sept. 21, 1972, Pres. Ferdinand Marcos declared martial law. Marcos proclaimed a new constitution, Jan. 17, 1973, with himself as president. His wife, Imelda, received wide powers in 1978 to supervise planning and development. Political corruption was widespread. Martial law was lifted Jan. 17, 1981, but Marcos retained broad emergency powers. He was reelected in June to a new 6-year term as president.

The assassination of prominent opposition leader Benigno S. Aquino Jr., Aug. 21, 1983, sparked demonstrations calling for the resignation of Marcos. After a bitter presidential campaign, amid allegations of widespread election fraud, Marcos was declared the victor Feb. 16, 1986, over Corazon Aquino, widow of the slain opposition leader. With his support collapsing, Marcos fled the country Feb. 25.

Recognized as president by the U.S. and other nations, Aquino was plagued by a weak economy, widespread poverty, Communist and Muslim insurgencies, and lukewarm military support. Rebel troops seized military bases and TV stations and bombed the presidential palace, Dec. 1, 1989. Government forces defeated the attempted coup aided by air cover provided by U.S. F-4s. Aquino endorsed Fidel Ramos in the May 1992 presidential election, which he won.

The U.S. vacated the Subic Bay Naval Station at the end of 1992, ending its long military presence in the Philippines.

The government signed a cease-fire agreement, Jan. 30, 1994, with Muslim separatist guerrillas, but some rebels refused to abide by the accord. A new treaty providing for expansion and development of an autonomous Muslim region on Mindanao was signed Sept. 2, 1996, formally ending a rebellion that had claimed more than 120,000 lives since 1972.

Running as a populist, Joseph (Erap) Estrada, a former movie actor, won the presidential election of May 11, 1998. Charged with bribery and corruption, he was impeached Nov. 13, 2000. When the Supreme Court ruled the presidency vacant Jan. 20, 2001, Vice-Pres. Gloria Macapagal Arroyo became president.

As part of the war on terrorism, the U.S. assisted Filipino troops in combating Abu Sayyaf, an Islamic guerrilla group; the leader of the extremists, Abu Sabaya, was killed June 21, 2002. A resurgence of terrorism on Mindanao in 2003 included bombings at Davao's airport, Mar. 4, and ferry terminal, Apr. 2. A mutiny by some 300 troops in Manila, July 27, was suppressed.

Poland
Republic of Poland

People: Population: 38,587,000. **Age distrib.** (%): <15: 17.9; 65+: 12.6. **Pop. density:** 328 per sq. mi. **Urban:** 63%. **Ethnic groups:** Polish 98%, German 1%. **Principal languages:** Polish (official), Ukrainian, German. **Chief religion:** Roman Catholic 95%.

Geography: Area: 120,728 sq. mi. (total); 117,555 sq. mi. (land). **Location:** On the Baltic Sea in E central Europe. **Neighbors:** Germany on W; Czech Rep., Slovakia on S; Lithuania, Belarus, Ukraine on E; Russia on N. **Topography:** Mostly lowlands forming part of the Northern European Plain. The Carpathian Mts. along the S border rise to 8,200 ft. **Capital:** Warsaw. **Cities** (urban aggr., 1997): Katowice 3,494,000; Warsaw 2,282,000; Lodz 1,053,000; Krakow 859,000.

Government: Type: Republic. **Head of state:** Pres. Aleksander Kwasniewski; b Nov. 15, 1954; in office: Dec. 23, 1995. **Head of gov.:** Prime Min. Leszek Miller; b July 3, 1946; in office: Oct. 19, 2001. **Local divisions:** 16 provinces. **Defense budget** (2002): $3.5 bil. **Active troops:** 163,000.

Economy: Industries: machinery, iron & steel, coal, chemicals, shipbuilding, food proc., glass, beverages, textiles. **Chief crops:** potatoes, fruits, vegetables, wheat. **Natural resources:** coal, sulfur, copper, nat. gas, silver, lead, salt. **Crude oil reserves** (2002): 115 mil. bbls. **Arable land:** 47%. **Livestock** (2002): cattle: 5.50 mil.; chickens: 50.69 mil.; pigs:18.71 mil.; sheep: 340,000. **Fish catch** (2002): 261,376 metric tons. **Electricity prod.** (2001): 134.96 bil. kWh. **Labor force:** ind. 22.1%, agri. 27.5%, services 50.4%.

Finance: Monetary unit: Zloty (PLN) (Sept. 2003: 4.02=1 U.S.). **GDP** (2002 est.): $368.1 bil. **Per capita GDP:** $9,500. **Imports** (2002): $43.4 bil.; partners (2001): Germany 23.9%, Russia 8.8%, Italy 8.2%, France 6.8%. **Exports** (2002 est.): $32.4 bil.; partners (2001): Germany 34.3%, Italy 5.4%, France 5.4%, UK 5.0%. **Tourism** (1999): $6.10 bil. **Budget** (1999): $52.3 bil. **Intl. reserves less gold:** $21.07 bil. **Gold:** 3.31 mil oz t. **Consumer prices:** 1.9%.

Transport: Railroad: Length: 14,553 mi. **Motor vehicles** (1999): 9.28 mil. pass. cars, 1.78 mil comm. vehicles. **Civil aviation:** 2.88 bil pass.-mi; 88 airports. **Chief ports:** Gdansk, Gdynia, Ustka, Szczecin.

Communications: TV sets: 387 per 1,000 pop. **Radios:** 522 per 1,000 pop. **Telephone lines:** 11,400,000. **Daily newspaper circ.:** 107.7 per 1,000 pop. **Internet:** 3,800,000 users.

Health: Life expectancy: 69.8 male; 78.3 female. **Births** (per 1,000 pop.): 10.5. **Deaths** (per 1,000 pop.): 10.0. **Natural inc.:** 0.05%. **Infant mortality** (per 1,000 live births): 9.0.

Education: Compulsory: ages 7-15. **Literacy:** 99.8%.

Major Intl. Organizations: UN (FAO, IBRD, ILO, IMF, IMO, WHO, WTrO), NATO, OECD, OSCE.

Embassy: 2640 16th St. NW 20009; 234-3800.

Websites: www.polandembassy.org; www.poland.pl

Slavic tribes in the area were converted to Latin Christianity in the 10th century. Poland was a great power from the 14th to the 17th centuries. In 3 partitions (1772, 1793, 1795) it was apportioned among Prussia, Russia, and Austria. Overrun by the Austro-German armies in World War I, it declared its independence on Nov. 11, 1918, and was recognized as independent by the Treaty of Versailles, June 28, 1919. Large territories to the east were taken in a war with Russia, 1921.

Germany and the USSR invaded Poland Sept. 1-27, 1939, and divided the country. During the war, some 6 million Polish citizens, half of them Jews, were killed by the Nazis. With Germany's defeat, a Polish government-in-exile in London was recognized by the U.S., but the USSR pressed the claims of a rival group. The election of 1947 was completely dominated by the Communists.

In compensation for 69,860 sq. mi. ceded to the USSR, in 1945 Poland received approx. 40,000 sq. mi. of German territory E of the Oder-Neisse line comprising Silesia, Pomerania, West Prussia, and part of East Prussia.

In 12 years of rule by Stalinists, large estates were abolished, industries nationalized, schools secularized, and Roman Catholic prelates jailed. Farm production fell off. Harsh working conditions caused a riot in Poznan, June 28-29, 1956. A new Politburo, committed to a more independent Polish Communism, was named Oct. 1956, with Wladyslaw Gomulka as first secretary of the party. Collectivization of farms ended. Gomulka agreed to permit religious liberty and religious publications, provided the church kept out of politics.

In Dec. 1970 workers in port cities rioted because of price rises and new incentive wage rules. On Dec. 20 Gomulka resigned as party leader; he was succeeded by Edward Gierek. The rules were dropped and price rises revoked.

After 2 months of labor turmoil had crippled the country, the Polish government, Aug. 30, 1980, met the demands of striking workers at the Lenin Shipyard, Gdansk. Government concessions included the right to form independent trade unions and the right to strike. By 1981, 9.5 mil workers had joined the independent trade union (Solidarity). As Solidarity's demands grew bolder, the government, spurred by fear of Soviet intervention, imposed martial law Dec. 13. Lech Walesa and other Solidarity leaders were arrested.

On Apr. 5, 1989, an accord was reached between the government and opposition factions on political and economic reforms, including free elections. Candidates endorsed by Solidarity swept the parliamentary elections, June 4. Lech Walesa became president Dec. 22, 1990.

A radical economic program designed to transform the economy into a free-market system led to inflation and unemployment. In Sept. 1993, former Communists and other leftists won a majority in the lower house of Parliament. Walesa lost to a former Communist, Aleksander Kwasniewski, in a presidential runoff election, Nov. 19, 1995.

A new constitution was approved by referendum May 25, 1997. Flooding in July caused more than $1 billion in property damage. Solidarity won parliamentary elections held Sept. 21. Poland became a full member of NATO on Mar. 12, 1999. Pres. Kwasniewski was reelected Oct. 8, 2000. The former Communists won a plurality in parliamentary voting Sept. 23, 2001.

In a referendum June 7-8, 2003, voters approved joining the EU in 2004. Poland, a close U.S. ally, assumed command Sept. 3 of a 9,000-member multinational force in south-central Iraq.

Portugal
Portuguese Republic

People: Population: 10,062,000. **Age distrib.** (%): <15: 16.9; 65+: 15.8. **Pop. density:** 284 per sq. mi. **Urban:** 66%. **Ethnic groups:** Mainly Portuguese. **Principal languages:** Portuguese (official). **Chief religion:** Roman Catholic 94%.

Geography: Area: 35,672 sq. mi. (total); 35,502 sq. mi. (land), incl. the Azores and Madeira Islands. **Location:** At SW extreme of Europe. **Neighbors:** Spain on N, E. **Topography:** Portugal N of Tajus R., which bisects the country NE-SW, is mountainous, cool and rainy. To the S there are drier, rolling plains, and a warm climate. **Capital:** Lisbon. **Cities (urban agg.):** Lisbon 3,942,000; Porto 1,940,000.

Government: Type: Republic. **Head of state:** Pres. Jorge Sampaio; b Sept. 18, 1939; in office: Mar. 9, 1996. **Head of gov.:** Prime Min. José Manuel Durão Barroso; b b Mar. 23, 1956; in office: Apr. 6, 2002. **Local divisions:** 18 districts, 2 autonomous regions. **Defense budget** (2002): $1.3 bil. **Active troops:** 43,600.

Economy: Industries: textiles, footwear, wood and paper products, metalworking, oil refining, chemicals, fish proc, wine, tourism. **Chief crops:** grain, potatoes, olives, grapes. **Natural resources:** fish, cork, tungsten, iron ore, uranium ore, marble, hydropower. **Arable land:** 26%. **Livestock** (2002): cattle: 1.40 mil.; chickens: 35 mil.; goats: 565,000; pigs: 2.39 mil.; sheep: 3.48 mil. **Fish catch** (2002): 199,038 metric tons. **Electricity prod.** (2001): 44.32 bil. kWh. **Labor force:** services 60%, ind. 30%, agri. 10%.

Finance: Monetary unit: Euro (EUR) (Sept. 2003: 0.92=1 U.S.). **GDP** (2002 est.): $182 bil. **Per capita GDP:** $18,000. **Imports** (2001): $39 bil.; partners (2001): EU 74.2%, U.S. 3.8%, Japan 1.9%. **Exports** (2001): $25.9 bil.; partners (2001): EU 79.7%, U.S. 5.8%. **Tourism:** $5.21 bil. **Budget** (2001 est.): $48 bil. **Intl. reserves less gold:** $8.22 bil. **Gold:** 19.03 mil oz t. **Consumer prices:** 3.5%.

Transport: Railroad: Length: 1,771 mi. **Motor vehicles** (1999): 4.93 mil pass. cars, 1.6 mil. comm. vehicles. **Civil aviation:** 6.26 bil pass.-mi; 40 airports. **Chief ports:** Lisbon, Setubal, Leixoes.

Communications: TV sets: 567 per 1,000 pop. **Radios:** 306 per 1,000 pop. **Telephone lines:** 4,361,000. **Daily newspaper circ.:** 32 per 1,000 pop. **Internet:** 2.5 mil.

Health: Life expectancy: 72.9 male; 80.1 female. **Births** (per 1,000 pop.): 11.5. **Deaths** (per 1,000 pop.): 10.2. **Natural inc.:** 0.12%. **Infant mortality** (per 1,000 live births): 5.7.

Education: Compulsory: ages 6-14. **Literacy:** 93.3%.
Major Intl. Organizations: UN (FAO, IBRD, ILO, IMF, IMO, WHO, WTrO), EU, NATO, OECD, OSCE.
Embassy: 2125 Kalorama Rd. NW 20008; 328-8610.
Website: www.presidenciarepublica.pt/en/main.html

Portugal, an independent state since the 12th century, was a kingdom until a revolution in 1910 drove out King Manoel II and a republic was proclaimed.

From 1932 a strong, repressive government was headed by Premier Antonio de Oliveira Salazar. Illness forced his retirement in Sept. 1968.

On Apr. 25, 1974, the government was seized by a military junta led by Gen. Antonio de Spinola, who became president. The new government reached agreements providing independence for Guinea-Bissau, Mozambique, Cape Verde Islands, Angola, and São Tomé and Príncipe. Banks, insurance companies, and other industries were nationalized.

Parliament approved, June 1, 1989, a package of reforms that did away with the socialist economy and created a "democratic" economy, denationalizing industries. Portugal returned Macao to China on Dec. 20, 1999.

Azores Islands, in the Atlantic, 740 mi. W of Portugal, have an area of 868 sq. mi. and a pop. (1993 est.) of 238,000. A 1951 agreement gave the U.S. rights to use defense facilities in the Azores. The **Madeira Islands,** 350 mi. off the NW coast of Africa, have an area of 306 sq. mi. and a pop. (1993 est.) of 437,312. Both groups were offered partial autonomy in 1976.

Qatar
State of Qatar

People: Population: 610,000. **Age distrib.** (%): <15: 25.2; 65+: 2.7. **Pop. density:** 144 per sq. mi. **Urban:** 93%. **Ethnic groups:** Arab 40%, Pakistani 18%, Indian 18%, Iranian 10%. **Principal languages:** Arabic (official), English. **Chief religion:** Muslim 95% (official).

Geography: Area (total): 4,416 sq. mi. **Location:** Middle East, occupying peninsula on W coast of Persian Gulf. **Neighbors:** Saudi Arabia on S. **Topography:** Mostly a flat desert, with some limestone ridges; vegetation of any kind is scarce. **Capital:** Doha: 285,000.

Government: Type: Traditional monarchy. **Head of state:** Emir Hamad bin Khalifa ath-Thani; b 1950; in office: June 27, 1995. **Head of gov.:** Prime Min. Abdullah bin Khalifa ath-Thani; b 1959; in office: Oct. 29, 1996. **Local divisions:** 9 municipalities. **Defense budget** (2001): $1.6 bil. **Active troops:** 12,400.

Economy: Industries: oil prod. & refining, fertilizers, petrochems., constr. materials. **Chief crops:** fruits, vegetables. **Natural resources:** oil, nat. gas, fish. **Crude oil reserves** (2002): 15.2 bil. bbls. **Livestock** (2002): cattle: 15,000; chickens: 4 mil.; goats: 179,000; sheep: 215,000. **Fish catch** (2002): 8,607 metric tons. **Electricity prod.** (2001): 9.26 bil. kWh. **Arable land:** 1%.

Finance: Monetary unit: Rial (QAR) (Sept. 2003: 3.64=1 U.S.). **GDP** (2002 est.): $17.2 bil. **Per capita GDP:** $21,500. **Imports** (2001): $3.5 bil.; partners (1998): UK 10%, Japan 8%, Germany 6%, Italy 6%. **Exports** (2001 est.): $11 bil.; partners (1999): Japan 43%, Singapore 8%, South Korea 6%, U.S. 4%. **Tourism:** $5.17 bil. **Budget** (2002 est.): $5.5 bil. **Intl. reserves less gold:** $1.15 bil. **Gold:** 20,000 oz t. **Consumer prices:** 1.0%.

Transport: Motor vehicles: 199,600 pass. cars, 92,900 comm. vehicles. **Civil aviation:** 1.76 bil pass.-mi; 2 airports. **Chief ports:** Doha, Umm Sáid.

Communications: TV sets: 866 per 1,000 pop. **Radios:** 450 per 1,000 pop. **Telephone lines:** 176,500. **Daily newspaper circ.:** 146 per 1,000 pop. **Internet:** 50,500 users.

Health: Life expectancy: 70.7 male; 75.8 female. **Births** (per 1,000 pop.): 15.7. **Deaths** (per 1,000 pop.): 4.4. **Natural inc.:** 1.13%. **Infant mortality** (per 1,000 live births): 20.0.

Education: Compulsory: ages 6-11. **Literacy:** 82.5%.
Major Intl. Organizations: UN (FAO, IBRD, ILO, IMF, IMO, WHO, WTrO), AL, OPEC.
Embassy: 4200 Wisconsin Ave. NW, Suite 200, 20016; 274-1600.
Websites: www.embassy.org/embassies/qa.html
www.qatar- info.com

Qatar was under Bahrain's control until the Ottoman Turks took power, 1872 to 1915. In a treaty signed 1916, Qatar gave Great Britain responsibility for its defense and foreign relations. After Britain announced it would remove its military forces from the Persian Gulf area by the end of 1971, Qatar sought a federation with other British-protected states in the area; this failed and Qatar declared itself independent, Sept. 1, 1971. Crown Prince Hamad bin Khalifa ath-Thani ousted his father, Emir Khalifa bin Hamad ath-Thani, June 27, 1995. In municipal elections held Mar. 8, 1999, women participated for the 1st time as candidates and voters.

Oil and natural gas revenues give Qatar a per capita income among the world's highest. Military ties with the U.S. have been expanding; Camp As-Sayliyah, a base near Doha, served as a command center for the U.S.-led invasion of Iraq, Mar. 2003. The influential Arab news network Al-Jazeera is based in Qatar.

Romania

People: Population: 22,334,000. **Age distrib.** (%): <15: 17.4; 65+: 13.8. **Pop. density:** 251 per sq. mi. **Urban:** 55%. **Ethnic groups:** Romanian 90%, Hungarian, Roma, and others 10%. **Principal languages:** Romanian (official), Hungarian, German, Romani. **Chief religions:** Romanian Orthodox 70%, Roman Catholic 6%, Protestant 6%.

Geography: Area: 91,699 sq. mi. (total); 88,935 sq. mi. (land). **Location:** SE Europe, on the Black Sea. **Neighbors:** Moldova on E, Ukraine on N, Hungary and Serbia and Montenegro on W, Bulgaria on S. **Topography:** The Carpathian Mts. encase the northcentral Transylvanian plateau. There are wide plains S and E of the mountains, through which flow the lower reaches of the rivers of the Danube system. **Capital:** Bucharest 1,998,000.

Government: Type: Republic. **Head of state:** Pres. Ion Iliescu; b Mar. 3, 1930; in office: Dec. 20, 2000. **Head of gov.:** Prime Min. Adrian Nastase; b June 22, 1950; in office: Dec. 28, 2000. **Local divisions:** 40 counties, 1 municipality. **Defense budget** (2002): $1.1 bil. **Active troops:** 99,200.

Economy: Industries: textiles & footwear, light machinery, auto assembly, mining, timber. **Chief crops:** wheat, corn, sugar beets, sunflower seed, potatoes, grapes. **Natural resources:** oil, timber, nat. gas, coal, iron ore, salt, hydropower. **Crude oil reserves** (2002): 956 mil. bbls. **Arable land:** 41%. **Livestock** (2002): cattle: 2.72 mil.; chickens: 70.10 mil.; goats: 520,000; pigs: 3.95 mil.; sheep: 7.30 mil. **Fish catch** (2002): 18,455 metric tons. **Electricity prod.** (2001): 50.86 bil. kWh. **Labor force:** agri. 40%, ind. 25%, services 35%.

Finance: Monetary unit: Lei (ROL) (Sept. 2003: 35,477.00=1 U.S.). **GDP** (2002 est.): $166 bil. **Per capita GDP:** $7,400. **Imports** (2001): $14.4 bil.; partners (2000): Italy 19%, Germany 15%, Russia 9%, France 6%. **Exports** (2001 est.): $11.5 bil.; partners (2000): Italy 22%, Germany 16%, France 7%, Turkey 6%. **Tourism:** $364 mil. **Budget** (1999 est.): $12.4 bil. **Intl. reserves less gold:** $5.3 bil. **Gold:** 3.39 mil oz t. **Consumer prices:** 22.5%.

Transport: Railroad: Length: 7,074 mi. **Motor vehicles** (1999): 2.98 mil pass. cars; 489,00 comm. vehicles. **Civil aviation:** 1.09 bil pass.-mi; 26 airports. **Chief ports:** Constanta, Braila.

Communications: TV sets: 312 per 1,000 pop. **Radios:** 335 per 1,000 pop. **Telephone lines:** 4,116,000. **Daily newspaper circ.:** 300 per 1,000 pop. **Internet:** 1,800,000 users.

Health: Life expectancy: 66.9 male; 74.6 female. **Births** (per 1,000 pop.): 10.8. **Deaths** (per 1,000 pop.): 12.3. **Natural inc.:** -0.15%. **Infant mortality** (per 1,000 live births): 18.4.

Education: Compulsory: ages 7-14. **Literacy:** 98.4%.

Major Intl. Organizations: UN (FAO, IBRD, ILO, IMF, IMO, WHO, WTrO), OSCE.

Embassy: 1607 23rd St. NW 20008; 332-4846.

Websites: www.roembus.org; www.gov.ro/engleza/index.html
Romania's earliest known people merged with invading Proto-Thracians, preceding by centuries the Dacians. The Dacian kingdom was occupied by Rome, AD 106-271; people and language were Romanized. The principalities of Wallachia and Moldavia, dominated by Turkey, were united in 1859, became Romania in 1861. In 1877 Romania proclaimed independence from Turkey, and became an independent state by the Treaty of Berlin, 1878; a kingdom under Carol I, 1881; and a constitutional monarchy with a bicameral legislature, 1886.

Romania helped Russia in its war with Turkey, 1877-78. After World War I it acquired Bessarabia, Bukovina, Transylvania, and Banat. In 1940 it ceded Bessarabia and Northern Bukovina to the USSR, part of southern Dobrudja to Bulgaria, and northern Transylvania to Hungary.

In 1941, Prem. Marshal Ion Antonescu led Romania in support of Germany against the USSR. In 1944 he was overthrown by King Michael and Romania joined the Allies.

After occupation by Soviet troops a People's Republic was proclaimed, Dec. 30, 1947; Michael was forced to abdicate.

On Aug. 22, 1965, a new constitution proclaimed Romania a Socialist Republic. Pres. Nicolae Ceausescu maintained an independent course in foreign affairs, but his domestic policies were repressive. All industry was state-owned, and state farms and cooperatives owned almost all arable land.

On Dec. 16, 1989, security forces opened fire on antigovernment demonstrators in Timisoara; hundreds were buried in mass graves. Ceausescu declared a state of emergency as protests spread to other cities. On Dec. 21, in Bucharest, security forces fired on protesters. Army units joined the rebellion, Dec. 22, and a group known as the Council of National Salvation announced that it had overthrown the government. Fierce fighting took place between the army, which backed the new government, and forces loyal to Ceausescu.

Ceausescu and his wife were captured and, following a trial in which they were found guilty of genocide, were executed Dec. 25, 1989. Former Communists dominated the government in succeeding years. A new constitution providing for a multiparty system took effect Dec. 8, 1991. Many of Romania's state-owned companies were privatized in 1996. The former Communists were swept from power in elections Nov. 3 and 17, 1996, but made a comeback in balloting Nov. 26 and Dec. 10, 2000.

Russia
Russian Federation

People: Population: 143,246,000. **Age distrib.** (%): <15: 16.7; 65+: 13.1. **Pop. density:** 22 per sq. mi. **Urban:** 73%. **Ethnic groups:** Russian 82%, Tatar 4%, Ukrainian 3%, Chuvash 1%, Bashkir 1%, Belarusian 1%, Moldavian 1%. **Principal languages:** Russian (official), many others. **Chief religions:** Russian Orthodox, Muslim.

Geography: Area: 6,592,767 sq. mi. (total); 6,562,110 sq. mi. (land), more than 76% of total area of the former USSR and the largest country in the world. **Location:** Stretches from E Europe across N Asia to the Pacific O. **Neighbors:** Finland, Norway, Estonia, Latvia, Belarus, Ukraine on W; Georgia, Azerbaijan, Kazakhstan, China, Mongolia, North Korea on S; Kaliningrad exclave bordered by Poland on the S, Lithuania on the N and E. **Topography:** Russia contains every type of climate except the distinctly tropical, and has a varied topography. The European portion is a low plain, grassy in S, wooded in N, with Ural Mts. on the E, and

Caucasus Mts. on the S. Urals stretch N-S for 2,500 mi. The Asiatic portion is also a vast plain, with mountains on the S and in the E; tundra covers extreme N, with forest belt below; plains, marshes are in W, desert in SW. **Capital:** Moscow. **Cities (urban aggr.):** Moscow 8,316,000; St. Petersburg 4,635,000; Nizhniy Novgorod 1,332,000; Novosibirsk 1,321,000.

Government: Type: Federal republic. **Head of state:** Vladimir Putin; b Oct. 7, 1952; in office: May 7, 2000. **Head of gov.:** Prime Min. Mikhail Kasyanov; b Dec. 8, 1957; in office: May 17, 2000. **Local divisions:** 21 autonomous republics, 68 autonomous territories and regions. **Defense budget** (2002): $8.3 bil. **Active troops:** 988,100.

Economy: Industries: coal, oil, gas, chemicals, metals; light machinery, shipbuilding; transp., communic. equip., agric. machinery, constr. equip., electric power equip., medical & scientific instruments, consumer durables, textiles. **Chief crops:** grain, sugar beets, sunflower seed, vegetables, fruits. **Natural resources:** oil, nat. gas, coal, minerals, timber. **Crude oil reserves** (2002): 48.6 bil. bbls. **Arable land:** 8%. **Livestock** (2002): cattle: 26.93 mil.; chickens: 345 mil.; goats: 1.80 mil.; pigs: 15.92 mil.; sheep: 13 mil. **Fish catch** (2002): 3,718,268 metric tons. **Electricity prod.** (2001): 846.46 bil. kWh. **Labor force:** agri. 12.3%, ind. 22.7%, services 65%.

Finance: Monetary unit: Rouble (RUB) (Sept. 2003: 30.60=1 U.S. NOTE: On Jan 1, 1998, Russia eliminated 3 digits from the ruble.) **GDP** (2002 est.): $1.4 tril. **Per capita GDP:** $9,300. **Imports** (2001): $60.7 bil.; partners (2001): Germany 13.2%, Belarus 9.6%, Ukraine 9.3%, U.S. 7.6%. **Exports** (2002 est.): $104.6 bil.; partners (2001): Germany 9.3%, U.S. 8.3%, Italy 7.5%, China 5.6%. **Tourism:** $7.51 bil. **Budget** (2002 est.): $62 bil. **Intl. reserves less gold:** $32.4 bil. **Gold:** 12.46 mil oz t. **Consumer prices:** 15.8%.

Transport: Railroad: Length: 54,157 mi. **Motor vehicles:** 20.35 mil pass. cars, 3.23 mil comm. vehicles. **Civil aviation:** 28.50 bil pass.-mi; 471 airports. **Chief ports:** St. Petersburg, Murmansk, Arkhangelsk.

Communications: TV sets: 421 per 1,000 pop. **Radios:** 417 per 1,000 pop. **Telephone lines:** 35,500,000. **Daily newspaper circ.:** 105 per 1,000 pop. **Internet:** 6,000,000 users.

Health: Life expectancy: 62.5 male; 73.1 female. **Births** (per 1,000 pop.): 10.1. **Deaths** (per 1,000 pop.): 14.0. **Natural inc.:** -0.39%. **Infant mortality** (per 1,000 live births): 19.5.

Education: Compulsory: ages 6-15. **Literacy:** 99.6%.

Major Intl. Organizations: UN (IBRD, ILO, IMF, IMO, WHO), APEC, CIS, OSCE.

Embassy: 2650 Wisconsin Ave. NW 20007; 298-5700.

Website: www.russianembassy.org

History. Slavic tribes began migrating into Russia from the W in the 5th century AD. The first Russian state, founded by Scandinavian chieftains, was established in the 9th century, centering in Novgorod and Kiev. In the 13th century the Mongols overran the country. It recovered under the grand dukes and princes of Muscovy, or Moscow, and by 1480 freed itself from the Mongols. Ivan the Terrible was the first to be formally proclaimed Tsar (1547). Peter the Great (1682-1725) extended the domain and, in 1721, founded the Russian Empire.

Western ideas and the beginnings of modernization spread through the huge Russian empire in the 19th and early 20th centuries. But political evolution failed to keep pace.

Military reverses in the 1905 war with Japan and in World War I led to the breakdown of the Tsarist regime. The 1917 Revolution began in March with a series of sporadic strikes for higher wages by factory workers. A provisional democratic government under Prince Georgi Lvov was established but was quickly followed in May by the second provisional government, led by Alexander Kerensky. The Kerensky government and the freely-elected Constituent Assembly were overthrown in a Communist coup led by Vladimir Ilyich Lenin Nov. 7.

Soviet Union

Lenin's death Jan. 21, 1924, resulted in an internal power struggle from which Joseph Stalin eventually emerged on top. Stalin secured his position at first by exiling opponents, but from the 1930s to 1953, he resorted to a series of "purge" trials, mass executions, and mass exiles to work camps. These measures resulted in millions of deaths, according to most estimates.

Germany and the Soviet Union signed a non-aggression pact Aug. 1939; Germany launched a massive invasion of the Soviet Union, June 1941. Notable heroic episode was the "900 days" siege of Leningrad (now St. Petersburg), lasting to Jan. 1944, and causing a million deaths; the city was never taken. Russian winter counterthrusts, 1941-42 and 1942-43, stopped the German advance. Turning point was the failure of German troops to take and hold Stalingrad (now Volgograd), Sept. 1942 to Feb. 1943. With British and U.S. Lend-Lease aid and sustaining great casualties, the Russians drove the German forces from eastern Europe and the Balkans in the next 2 years.

After Stalin died, Mar. 5, 1953, Nikita Khrushchev was elected first secretary of the Central Committee. In 1956 he condemned Stalin and "de-Stalinization" began.

Under Khrushchev the open antagonism of Poles and Hungarians toward domination by Moscow was brutally suppressed in 1956. He advocated peaceful co-existence with the capitalist countries, but continued arming the Soviet Union with nuclear weapons. He aided the Cuban revolution under Fidel Castro but withdrew Soviet missiles from Cuba during confrontation by U.S. Pres. Kennedy, Sept.-Oct. 1962. Khrushchev was suddenly deposed, Oct. 1964, and replaced by Leonid I. Brezhnev.

In Aug. 1968 Russian, Polish, East German, Hungarian, and Bulgarian military forces invaded Czechoslovakia to put a curb on liberalization policies of the Czech government.

Massive Soviet military aid to North Vietnam in the late 1960s and early 1970s helped assure Communist victories throughout Indo-China. Soviet arms aid and advisers were sent to several African countries in the 1970s.

In Dec. 1979, Soviet forces entered Afghanistan to support that government against rebels. In Apr. 1988, the Soviets agreed to withdraw their troops, ending a futile 8-year war.

Mikhail Gorbachev was chosen gen. secy. of the Communist Party, Mar. 1985. He held 4 summit meetings with U.S. Pres. Ronald Reagan. In 1987, in Washington, a treaty was signed eliminating intermediate-range nuclear missiles from Europe.

In 1987, Gorbachev initiated a program of reforms, including expanded freedoms and the democratization of the political process, through openness (*glasnost*) and restructuring (*perestroika*). The reforms were opposed by some Eastern bloc countries and many old-line Communists in the USSR. Gorbachev faced economic problems as well as ethnic and nationalist unrest in the republics.

When an apparent coup against Gorbachev became known on Aug. 19, 1991, the pres. of the Russian Republic, Boris Yeltsin, denounced it and called for a general strike. Some 50,000 demonstrated at the Russian Parliament in support of Yeltsin. By Aug. 21, the coup had failed and Gorbachev was restored as president. On Aug. 24, Gorbachev resigned as leader of the Communist Party. Several republics declared their independence, including Russia, Ukraine, and Kazakhstan. On Aug. 29, the Soviet Parliament voted to suspend all activities of the Communist Party.

The Soviet Union officially broke up Dec. 26, 1991, one day after Gorbachev resigned. The Soviet hammer and sickle flying over the Kremlin was lowered and replaced by the flag of Russia, ending the domination of the Communist Party over all areas of national life since 1917.

Russian Federation

In a first major step in radical economic reform, Russia eliminated state subsidies of most goods and services, Jan. 1992. The effect was to allow prices to soar far beyond the means of ordinary workers. In June, Pres. Yeltsin and U.S. Pres. George Bush agreed to massive arms reductions.

Russia launched a drive to privatize thousands of large and medium-sized state-owned enterprises in 1993. Yeltsin narrowly survived an impeachment vote by the Congress of People's Deputies, Mar. 28. He received strong support from voters in a referendum Apr. 25, but he continued to face a legislature dominated by conservatives and former Communists. On Sept. 21, 1993, Yeltsin called for early elections and dissolved Parliament, which in turn declared him deposed. Yeltsin legislators then barricaded themselves in the Parliament building. On Oct. 3, anti-Yeltsin forces attacked some facilities in Moscow and broke into the Parliament building. Yeltsin ordered the army to attack and seize the building. 140 people were killed in the fighting, according to medical authorities.

Yeltsin remained in power, and in a referendum Dec. 12, 1993, a new constitution was approved. In Dec. 1994 the Russian government sent troops into the breakaway republic of Chechnya. Grozny, the Chechen capital, fell in Feb. 1995 after heavy fighting, but Chechen rebels continued to resist.

Despite poor health, Yeltsin won a presidential runoff election over a Communist opponent, July 3, 1996. On Aug. 14, after rebels embarrassed the Russian military by retaking Grozny, Yeltsin gave his security chief, Alexander Lebed, broad powers to negotiate an end to the Chechnya war. Lebed and Chechen leaders signed a peace accord Aug. 31. On Oct. 17, Yeltsin dismissed Lebed for insubordination. Russian troops remaining in Chechnya were pulled out Jan. 1997. On May 27, Yeltsin signed a "founding act" increasing cooperation with NATO and paving the way for NATO to admit Eastern European nations.

During 1998-99, Yeltsin made numerous cabinet changes, seeking to cope with a deepening economic crisis; the cabinet upheavals triggered repeated confrontations with Parliament. Russia's economic crisis deepened throughout 1998; in Aug. the ruble plummeted and the country defaulted on its debt. Yeltsin dismissed Prime Min. Viktor Chernomyrdin on Mar. 23 and Chernomyrdin's successor, Sergei Kiriyenko, on Aug. 23. Each move triggered a confrontation with parliament. Yevgeny Primakov became premier Sept. 11, 1998; in subsequent cabinet upheavals, Sergei Stepashin took over on May 19, 1999, followed by Vladimir Putin on Aug. 16. Disagreements over the war in Kosovo, Mar.-June 1999, strained relations with the U.S. and NATO. Russia moved forcibly in Aug. to suppress Islamic rebels in Dagestan; the conflict soon spread to neighboring Chechnya, where Russia launched a full-scale assault. A series of 5 bombings in Moscow and Dagestan, which the Russian government attributed to Chechen rebels, killed over 300 people.

Yeltsin unexpectedly resigned Dec. 31, 1999, naming Putin as his interim successor. Russian troops took control of Grozny in early Feb. 2000. Putin defeated 10 opponents in a presidential election Mar. 26. The Russian parliament ratified 2 nuclear weapons treaties, the START II arms-reduction accord Apr. 14 and the Comprehensive Test Ban Treaty Apr. 21. A reorganization plan announced May 17 sought to reassert Moscow's control over Russia's regional governments. The Russian nuclear submarine *Kursk* sank in the Barents Sea Aug. 12, killing 118 sailors.

Russia and China signed a 20-year friendship and cooperation treaty July 16, 2001. Putin and Bush signed May 24, 2002, an agreement calling for a 2/3 reduction in nuclear weapons stockpiles. However, Russia pulled out of the START II treaty Jun. 14 after the U.S. withdrew from the 1972 ABM Treaty June 13 to develop a missile defense program. Russia joined a new partnership agreement with NATO May 28.

As Russian forces continued their campaign against Islamic separatists in Chechnya, some 50 Chechen guerrillas seized more than 800 hostages in a Moscow theater, Oct. 23, 2002; 129 hostages and nearly all the guerrillas were killed Oct. 26 when Russian special forces used knockout gas in retaking the theater. Russia, which supported the U.S.-led war in Afghanistan in 2001, sided with France and Germany in blocking UN Security Council endorsement of the U.S.-led invasion of Iraq, Mar. 2003.

Rwanda
Rwandese Republic

People: Population: 8,387,000. **Age distrib. (%):** <15: 41.7; 65+: 2.9. **Pop. density:** 871 per sq. mi. **Urban:** 6%. **Ethnic groups:** Hutu 84%, Tutsi 15%, Twa (Pygmy) 1%. **Principal languages:** Kinyarwanda, French, English (all official); Swahili. **Chief religions:** Roman Catholic 57%, Protestant 26%, Adventist 11%, Muslim 5%.

Geography: Area: 10,169 sq. mi. (total); 9,632 sq. mi. (land). **Location:** In E central Africa. **Neighbors:** Uganda on N, Congo (formerly Zaire) on W, Burundi on S, Tanzania on E. **Topography:** Grassy uplands and hills cover most of the country, with a chain of volcanoes in the NW. The source of the Nile R. has been located in the headwaters of the Kagera (Akagera) R., SW of Kigali. **Capital:** Kigali: 412,000.

Government: Type: Republic. **Head of state:** Pres. Paul Kagame; b Oct. 1957; in office: Apr. 22, 2000 (de facto from Mar. 24). **Head of gov.:** Prime Min. Bernard Makuza; b 1961; in office: Mar. 8, 2000. **Local divisions:** 12 prefectures subdivided into 155 communes. **Defense budget** (2002): $52 mil. **Active troops:** 60,000-75,000.

Economy: Industries: cement, agric. products. **Chief crops:** coffee, tea, pyrethrum (insecticide made from chrysanthemums), bananas. **Natural resources:** gold, tin, tungsten, methane, hydropower. **Crude oil reserves** (2002): 48.6 bil. bbls. **Arable land:** 35%. **Livestock** (2002): cattle: 800,000; chickens: 1.20 mil.; goats: 700,000; pigs: 180,000; sheep: 260,000. **Fish catch** (2002): 7,263 metric tons. **Electricity prod.** (2001): 0.1 bil. kWh. **Labor force:** agric. 90%.

Finance: Monetary unit: Franc (RWF) (Sept. 2003: 535.80=1 U.S.). **GDP** (2002 est.): $9 bil. **Per capita GDP:** $1,200. **Imports** (2001): $248 mil.; partners (2000 est.): Kenya 29.4%, EU 28%, U.S. 10%, India 4.4%. **Exports** (2001 est.): $61 mil.; partners (2000 est.): EU 56.9%, Pakistan 12.3%, U.S. 9.2%, China 4.4%. **Tourism:** $17 mil. **Budget** (2001 est.): $445 mil. **Intl. reserves less gold:** $179 mil. **Consumer prices:** 2.5%.

Transport: Motor vehicles: 10,700 pass. cars, 16,300 comm. vehicles. **Civil aviation:** ; 4 airports. **Chief ports:** Gisenyi, Cyangugu.

Communications: TV sets: .09 per 1,000 pop. **Radios:** 101 per 1,000 pop. **Telephone lines:** 21,500. **Daily newspaper circ.:** 0.1 per 1,000 pop. **Internet:** 20,000 users.

Health: Life expectancy: 38.5 male; 40.2 female. **Births** (per 1,000 pop.): 40.1. **Deaths** (per 1,000 pop.): 21.7. **Natural inc.:** 1.84%. **Infant mortality** (per 1,000 live births): 102.6.

Education: Compulsory: ages 7-12. **Literacy:** 70.4%.

Major Intl. Organizations: UN (FAO, IBRD, ILO, IMF, WHO, WTrO), AU.

Embassy: 1714 New Hampshire Ave. NW 20009; 232-2882.

Website: www.rwanda1.com

For centuries, the Tutsi (an extremely tall people) dominated the Hutu (90% of the population). A civil war broke out in 1959 and Tutsi power was ended. Many Tutsi went into exile. A referendum in 1961 abolished the monarchic system. Rwanda, which had been part of the Belgian UN trusteeship of Rwanda-Urundi, became independent July 1, 1962.

In 1963 Tutsi exiles invaded in an unsuccessful coup; a large-scale massacre of Tutsi followed. Rivalries among Hutu led to a bloodless coup July 1973 in which Juvénal Habyarimana took power. After an invasion and coup attempt by Tutsi exiles in 1990, a multiparty democracy was established.

Renewed ethnic strife led to an Aug. 1993 peace accord between the government and rebels of the Tutsi-led Rwandan Patriotic Front (RPF). But after Habyarimana and the president of Burundi were killed Apr. 6, 1994, in a suspicious plane crash, massive violence broke out. More than 1 million may have died in massacres, mostly of Tutsi by Hutu militias, and in civil warfare as the RPF sought power. About 2 million Tutsi and Hutu fled to camps in Zaire (now Congo) and other countries, where many died of cholera and other natural causes. French troops under a UN mandate moved into SW Rwanda June 23 to establish a so-called safe zone. The RPF claimed victory, installing a government in July led by a moderate Hutu president. French troops pulled out Aug. 22. A UN peacekeeping mission ended Mar. 8, 1996, but the Rwandan government and a UN-sponsored tribunal in Tanzania continued to gather evidence against those responsible for genocide. More than 1 million refugees (mostly Hutu) flooded back to Rwanda from Tanzania and Zaire in Nov. and Dec. 1996.

Firing squads in Rwanda on Apr. 24, 1998, executed 22 people convicted of genocide. Former Prime Min. Jean Kambanda pleaded guilty May 1 before the UN tribunal and received a life sentence Sept. 4, 1998. Maj. Gen. Paul Kagame, leader of the RPF, was sworn in as Rwanda's 1st Tutsi president Apr. 22, 2000. A Belgian court June 8, 2001, convicted 2 Roman Catholic nuns and 2 other Rwandans for their role in the 1994 genocide.

Rwanda and the Congo signed an accord July 30, 2002, in which Rwanda agreed to withdraw troops from the Congo and the Congo agreed to stop harboring Hutu guerrillas. Rwandan voters in 2003 approved a new constitution, May 26, and reelected Pres. Kagame, Aug. 25.

Saint Kitts and Nevis
Federation of Saint Kitts and Nevis

People: Population: 39,000. **Age distrib.** (%): <15: 29.4; 65+: 8.7. **Pop. density:** 385 per sq. mi. **Urban:** 34%. **Ethnic group:** Black, British, Portuguese, Lebanese. **Principal languages:** English (official). **Chief religions:** Anglican, other Protestant, Roman Catholic.

Geography: Area (total): 101 sq. mi. **Location:** In the N part of the Leeward group of the Lesser Antilles in the E Caribbean Sea. **Neighbors:** Antigua and Barbuda to E. **Topography:** St. Kitts has forested volcanic slopes; Nevis rises from beaches to central peak. Climate is tropical moderated by sea breezes. **Capital:** Basseterre: 12,000.

Government: Type: Constitutional monarchy. **Head of state:** Queen Elizabeth II, represented by Gov-Gen. Sir Cuthbert M. Sebastian; b Oct. 22, 1921; in office: Jan. 1, 1996. **Head of gov.:** Prime Min. Denzil Llewellyn Douglas; b Jan. 14, 1953; in office: July 7, 1995. **Local divisions:** 14 parishes.

Economy: Industries: sugar proc., tourism, cotton, salt, copra, clothing, footwear, beverages. **Chief crops:** sugarcane, rice, yams, vegetables, bananas. **Arable land:** 22%. **Livestock** (2002): cattle: 4,000; chickens: 60,000; goats: 14,400; pigs: 5,000; sheep: 14,000. **Fish Catch** (2002): 596 metric tons. **Electricity prod.** (2001): 0.1 bil. kWh. **Labor force:** agri. 21.7%, services 53.6%, ind., commerce, and manufact. 24.7%.

Finance: Monetary unit: East Caribbean Dollar (XCD) (Sept. 2003: 2.66=1 U.S.). **GDP** (2002 est.): $339 mil. **Per capita GDP:** $8,800. **Imports** (2000): $141.3 mil.; partners (1995 est.): U.S. 42.4%, Caricom countries 17.2%, UK 11.3%. **Exports** (2000 est.): $51.7 mil.; partners (1995 est.): U.S. 68.5%, UK 22.3%, Caricom countries 5.5%. **Tourism** (1999): $70 mil. **Budget** (2003): $128.2 mil. **Intl. reserves less gold:** $48 mil. **Consumer prices** (change in 1999): 3.9%.

Transport: Railroad: Length: 36 mi. **Motor vehicles** (1999): 7,700 pass. cars, 3,900 comm. vehicles. Civil aviation: 2 airports. **Chief ports:** Basseterre, Charlestown.

Communications: TV sets: 256 per 1,000 pop. **Radios:** 718 per 1,000 pop. **Telephone lines** (1999): 23,500. **Internet:** 5,000 users

Health: Life expectancy: 68.8 male; 74.6 female. **Births** (per 1,000 pop.): 18.5. **Deaths** (per 1,000 pop.): 8.9. **Natural inc.:** 0.96%. **Infant mortality** (per 1,000 live births): 15.4.

Education: Compulsory: ages 5-17. **Literacy** (1992): 90%.
Major Intl. Organizations: UN (FAO, IBRD, ILO, IMF, WHO, WTrO), Caricom, the Commonwealth, OAS, OECS.

Embassy: 3216 New Mexico Ave., NW 20016; 686-2636.
Website: www.stkittsnevis.net

St. Kitts (formerly St. Christopher; known by the natives as Liamuiga) and Nevis were reached (and named) by Columbus in 1493. They were settled by Britain in 1623, but ownership was disputed with France until 1713. They were part of the Leeward Islands Federation, 1871-1956, and the Federation of the West Indies, 1958-62. The colony achieved self-government as an Associated State of the UK in 1967, and became fully independent Sept. 19, 1983. A secession referendum on Nevis, Aug. 10, 1998, fell short of the two-thirds majority required.

Saint Lucia

People: Population: 149,000. **Age distrib.** (%): <15: 31.6; 65+: 5.3. **Pop. density:** 632 per sq. mi. **Urban:** 38%. **Ethnic groups:** Black 90%, mixed 6%, East Indian 3%, White 1%. **Principal languages:** English (official), French patois. **Chief religions:** Roman Catholic 90%, Protestant 10%.

Geography: Area: 238 sq. mi. (total); 234 sq. mi. (land). **Location:** In E Caribbean, 2d largest of the Windward Isls. **Neighbors:** Martinique to N, St. Vincent to S. **Topography:** Mountainous, vol-

canic in origin; Soufriere, a volcanic crater, in the S. Wooded mountains run N-S to Mt. Gimie, 3,145 ft., with streams through fertile valleys. **Capital:** Castries: 57,000.

Government: Type: Parliamentary democracy. **Head of state:** Queen Elizabeth II, represented by Gov.-Gen. Calliopa Pearlette Louisy; b June 8, 1946; in office: Sept. 17, 1997. **Head of gov.:** Prime Min. Kenny Anthony; b Jan. 8, 1951; in office: May 24, 1997. **Local divisions:** 11 quarters.

Economy: Industries: clothing, electronic components, beverages, cardboard, tourism, lime & coconut proc. **Chief crops:** bananas, coconuts, vegetables, citrus, root crops, cocoa. **Natural resources:** timber, pumice, mineral springs, geothermal areas. **Arable land:** 8%. **Livestock** (2002): cattle: 12,000; chickens: 240,000; goats: 9,800; pigs: 15,000; sheep: 13,000 **Fish Catch** (2002): 1,984 metric tons. **Electricity prod.** (2001): 0.12 bil. kWh. **Labor force:** agri. 21.7, services 53.6%, ind., commerce, and manufact. 24.7%.

Finance: Monetary unit: East Caribbean Dollar (XCD) (Sept. 2003: 2.66=1 U.S.). **GDP** (2002 est.): $866 mil. **Per capita GDP:** $5,400. **Imports** (2000): $319.4 mil.; partners (1995): U.S. 36%, Caricom countries 22%, UK 11%, Japan 5%. **Exports** (2000 est.): $68.3 mil.; partners (1995): UK 50%, U.S. 24%, Caricom countries 16%. **Tourism** (1999): $311 mil. **Budget** (2000 est.): $146.7 mil. **Intl. reserves less gold:** $69 mil. **Consumer prices** (change in 2001): 0.1%.

Transport: Motor vehicles (1996): 13,500 pass. cars, 10,800 comm. vehicles. **Civil aviation:** 2 airports. **Chief ports:** Castries, Vieux Fort.

Communications: TV sets: 368 per 1,000 pop. **Radios:** 750 per 1,000 pop. **Telephone lines** (1999): 44,500 main lines.

Health: Life expectancy: 69.5 male; 76.9 female. **Births** (per 1,000 pop.): 20.9. **Deaths** (per 1,000 pop.): 5.2. **Natural inc.:** 1.57%. **Infant mortality** (per 1,000 live births): 14.4.

Education: Compulsory: ages 3-16. **Literacy** (1993): 80%.
Major Intl. Organizations: UN (FAO, IBRD, ILO, IMF, IMO, WHO, WTrO), Caricom, the Commonwealth, OAS, OECS.

Embassy: 3216 New Mexico Ave. NW 20016; 364-6792.
Website: www.stlucia.gov.lc

St. Lucia was ceded to Britain by France at the Treaty of Paris, 1814. Self-government was granted with the West Indies Act, 1967. Independence was attained Feb. 22, 1979.

Saint Vincent and the Grenadines

People: Population: 120,000. **Age distrib.** (%): <15: 28.9; 65+: 6.3. **Pop. density:** 917 per sq. mi. **Urban:** 56%. **Ethnic groups:** Black 66%, mixed 19%, East Indian 6%, Carib Amerindian 2%. **Principal languages:** English (official), French patois. **Chief religions:** Anglican 47%, Methodist 28%, Roman Catholic 13%.

Geography: Area: 150 sq. mi. **Location:** In the E Caribbean, St. Vincent (133 sq. mi.) and the northern islets of the Grenadines form a part of the Windward chain. **Neighbors:** St. Lucia to N, Barbados to E, Grenada to S. **Topography:** St. Vincent is volcanic, with a ridge of thickly wooded mountains running its length. **Capital:** Kingstown: 28,000.

Government: Constitutional monarchy. **Head of State:** Queen Elizabeth II, represented by Gov.-Gen. Frederick Ballantyne; in office: Sept. 2, 2002. **Head of gov.:** Prime Min. Ralph Gonsalves; b Aug. 8, 1946; in office: Mar. 29, 2001. **Local divisions:** 6 parishes.

Economy: Industries: food proc., cement, furniture, clothing, starch. **Chief crops:** bananas, coconuts, sweet potatoes, spices. **Natural resources:** hydropower. **Arable land:** 10%. **Livestock** (2002): cattle: 6,000; chickens: 200,000; goats: 6,000; pigs: 10,000; sheep: 13,000. **Fish catch** (2002): 45,778 metric tons. **Electricity prod.** (2001): 0.09 bil. kWh. **Labor force:** agri. 26%, ind. 17%, services 57%.

Finance: Monetary unit: East Caribbean Dollar (Sept. 2003: 2.66 = $1 U.S.). **GDP** (2002 est.): $339 mil. **Per capita GDP:** $2,900. **Imports** (2000): $185.6 mil.; partners (1995): U.S. 36%, Caricom countries 28%, UK 13%. **Exports** (2000 est.): $53.7 mil.; partners (1995): Caricom countries 49%, UK 16%, U.S. 10%. **Tourism** (1999): $77 mil. **Budget** (2000 est.): $85.8 mil. **Intl. reserves less gold:** $39 mil. **Consumer prices:** 0.8%.

Transport: Motor vehicles: 9,100 pass. cars, 4,000 comm. vehicles. **Civil aviation:** 5 airports. **Chief port:** Kingstown.

Communications: TV sets: 230 per 1,000 pop. **Radios:** 688 per 1,000 pop. **Telephone lines** (1999): 26,100. **Daily newspaper circ.:** 9 per 1,000 pop. **Internet:** 5,500 users.

Health: Life expectancy: 71.3 male; 74.9 female. **Births** (per 1,000 pop.): 17.2. **Deaths** (per 1,000 pop.): 6.1. **Natural inc.:** 1.11%. **Infant mortality** (per 1,000 live births): 15.7.

Education: Compulsory: ages 5-15. **Literacy** (1994): 82%.
Major Intl. Organizations: UN (FAO, IBRD, ILO, IMF, IMO, WHO, WTrO), Caricom, the Commonwealth, OAS, OECS.

Embassy: 3216 New Mexico Ave. NW 20016; 364-6730.
Website: www.embsvg.com

Columbus landed on St. Vincent on Jan. 22, 1498 (St. Vincent's Day). Britain and France both laid claim to the island in the 17th and 18th centuries; the Treaty of Versailles, 1783, finally ceded it to Britain. Associated State status was granted 1969; independence was attained Oct. 27, 1979.

Samoa
(*formerly* Western Samoa)
Independent State of Samoa

People: Population: 178,000. **Age distrib.** (%): <15: 30.6; 65+: 5.9. **Pop. density:** 162 per sq. mi. **Urban:** 22%. **Ethnic groups:** Samoan 92.5%, Euronesians 7%. **Principal languages:** Samoan, English (both official). **Chief religion:** Christian 99.7%.

Geography: Area: 1,137 sq. mi. (total); 1,133 sq. mi. (land). **Location:** In the S Pacific O. **Neighbors:** Nearest are Fiji to SW, Tonga to S. **Topography:** Main islands, Savaii (659 sq. mi.) and Upolu (432 sq. mi.), both ruggedly mountainous, and small islands Manono and Apolima. **Capital:** Apia, 35,000.

Government: Type: Constitutional monarchy. **Head of state:** Malietoa Tanumafili II; b Jan. 4, 1913; in office: Jan. 1, 1962. **Head of gov.:** Prime Min. Tuilaepa Sailele Malielegaoi; b Apr. 14, 1945; in office: Nov. 23, 1998. **Local divisions:** 11 districts.

Economy: Industries: food proc., building materials, auto parts. **Chief crops:** coconuts, bananas, taro, yams. **Natural resources:** timber, fish, hydropower. **Arable land:** 19%. **Livestock** (2002): cattle: 28,000; chickens: 450,000; pigs: 201,000. **Fish catch** (2002 est.): 12,966 metric tons. **Electricity Prod.:** (2001): 0.11 bil. kWh. **Labor force:** agri. 65%, services 30%, ind. 5%.

Finance: Monetary unit: Tala (WST) (Sept. 2003: 3.01=1 U.S.). **GDP** (2002 est.): $1 bil. **Per capita GDP:** $5,600. **Imports** (2000): $90 mil.; partners (2000): Australia 27%, U.S. 26%, New Zealand 14%, Fiji 12%. **Exports** (2000): $17 mil.; partners (2000): Australia 62%, Indonesia 13%, U.S. 11%, American Samoa 3%. **Tourism:** $40 mil. **Budget** (2001): $119 mil. **Intl. reserves less gold:** $46 mil. **Consumer prices** (change in 2000): 1.0%.

Transport: Motor vehicles (1997): 1,200 pass. cars, 1,400 comm. vehicles. **Civil aviation:** 151.6 mil pass. mi; 3 airports. **Chief ports:** Apia, Asau.

Communications: TV sets: 56 per 1,000 pop. **Radios:** 1,035 per 1,000 pop. **Telephone lines:** 10,300. **Internet:** 4,000 users.

Health: Life expectancy: 67.4 male; 73.0 female. **Births** (per 1,000 pop.): 15.4. **Deaths** (per 1,000 pop.): 6.4. **Natural inc.:** 0.90%. **Infant mortality** (per 1,000 live births): 29.7.

Education: Compulsory: ages 5-14. **Literacy:** 99.7%.

Major Intl. Organizations: UN (FAO, IBRD, IMF, IMO, WHO), the Commonwealth.

Embassy: 820 2nd Ave., Suite 400D, New York, NY 10017; (212) 599-6196.

Website: www.samoa.ws/govtsamoapress/

Samoa (formerly known as Western Samoa to distinguish it from American Samoa, a small U.S. territory) was a German colony, 1899 to 1914, when New Zealand landed troops and took over. It became a New Zealand mandate under the League of Nations and, in 1945, a New Zealand UN Trusteeship.

An elected local government took office in Oct. 1959, and the country became fully independent Jan. 1, 1962.

San Marino
Republic of San Marino

People: Population: 28,000. **Age distrib.** (%): <15: 16.1; 65+: 16.4. **Pop. density:** 1,214 per sq. mi. **Urban:** 90%. **Ethnic groups:** Sammarinese, Italian **Principal language:** Italian (official). **Chief religion:** Predominantly Roman Catholic.

Geography: Area (total): 24 sq. mi. **Location:** In N central Italy near Adriatic coast. **Neighbors:** Completely surrounded by Italy. **Topography:** The country lies on the slopes of Mt. Titano. **Capital:** San Marino: 5,000.

Government: Type: Republic. **Heads of state and gov.:** Two co-regents appt. every 6 months. **Local divisions:** 9 castelli.

Economy: Industries: tourism, banking, textiles, electronics, ceramics, cement, wine. **Chief crops:** wheat, grapes, corn, olives. **Natural resources:** building stone. **Arable land:** 17%. **Labor force:** services 57%, ind. 42%, agri. 1%.

Finance: Monetary unit: Euro (EUR) (Sept. 2003: 0.92=1 U.S.). **GDP** (2001 est.): $940 mil. **Per capita GDP:** $34,600. **Imports:** trade data are included with the statistics for Italy. **Budget** (2000 est.): $400 mil.

Transport: Motor vehicles (1997): 24,825 pass. cars, 4,149 comm. vehicles.

Communications: TV sets: 875 per 1,000 pop. **Radios:** 1,346 per 1,000 pop. **Daily newspaper circ.:** 69.2 per 1,000 pop.

Health: Life expectancy: 77.9 male; 85.3 female. **Births** (per 1,000 pop.): 10.5. **Deaths** (per 1,000 pop.): 7.9. **Natural inc.:** 0.26%. **Infant mortality** (per 1,000 live births): 6.0.

Education: Compulsory: ages 6-14. **Literacy** (1997): 99%.

Major Intl. Organizations: UN (ILO, IMF, WHO), OSCE.

Website: www.sanmarinosite.com

San Marino claims to be the oldest state in Europe and to have been founded in the 4th century. A Communist-led coalition ruled 1947-57; a similar coalition ruled 1978-86. It has had a treaty of friendship with Italy since 1862.

São Tomé and Príncipe
Democratic Republic of São Tomé and Príncipe

People: Population: 161,000. **Age distrib.** (%): <15: 47.7; 65+: 4. **Pop. density:** 434 per sq. mi. **Urban:** 48%. **Ethnic groups:** Mestizo, Black, Portuguese. **Principal languages:** Portuguese (official), Creole, Fang. **Chief religions:** Predominantly Roman Catholic.

Geography: Area: 386 sq. mi. (total); 386 sq. mi. (land). **Location:** In the Gulf of Guinea about 125 miles off W central Africa. **Neighbors:** Gabon, Equatorial Guinea to E. **Topography:** São Tomé and Príncipe islands, part of an extinct volcano chain, are both covered by lush forests and croplands. **Capital:** São Tomé: 67,000.

Government: Type: Republic. **Head of state:** Pres. Fradique Melo de Menezes; b. Mar. 21, 1942; in office: Sept. 3, 2001. **Head of gov.:** Prime Min. Maria das Neves; b 1958; in office: Oct. 7, 2002. **Local divisions:** 2 provinces.

Economy: Industries: light constr., textiles, soap, beer; fish proc. **Chief crops:** cocoa, coconuts, palm kernels, cinnamon, pepper, coffee. **Natural resources:** fish, hydropower. **Arable land:** 2%. **Livestock** (2002): cattle: 4,000; chickens: 350,000; goats: 4,800; pigs: 2,000; sheep: 3,000. **Fish catch** (2002 est.): 3,500 metric tons. **Electricity prod.** (2001): 0.02 bil. kWh. **Labor force:** mainly agri. and fishing.

Finance: Monetary unit: Dobra (STD) (Sept. 2003: 8,700.00=1 U.S.). **GDP** (2002 est.): $200 mil. **Per capita GDP:** $1,200. **Imports** (2000): $40 mil.; partners (1999): Portugal 43%, France 15.7%, UK 13.7%. **Exports** (2000 est.): $4.1 mil.; partners (1999): Portugal 33.3%, Netherlands 8.3%, Spain 8.3%. **Tourism** (1998): $2 mil. **Budget** (1993 est.): $114 mil. **Intl. reserves less gold:** $13 mil.

Transport: Civil aviation: 8.1 mil pass.-mi; 2 airports. **Chief ports:** São Tomé, Santo Antonio.

Communications: TV sets: 229 per 1,000 pop. **Radios:** 319 per 1,000 pop. **Telephone lines:** 5,400. **Internet:** 9,000 users.

Health: Life expectancy: 64.8 male; 67.8 female. **Births** (per 1,000 pop.): 41.9. **Deaths** (per 1,000 pop.): 7.1. **Natural inc.:** 3.48%. **Infant mortality** (per 1,000 live births): 46.0.

Education: Compulsory: ages 7-15. **Literacy** (1991 est.): 79.3%.

Major Intl. Organizations: UN (FAO, IBRD, ILO, IMF, IMO, WHO), AU.

Website: www.stome.com

The islands were discovered in 1471 by the Portuguese, who brought the first settlers—convicts and exiled Jews. Sugar planting was replaced by the slave trade as the chief economic activity until coffee and cocoa were introduced in the 19th century.

Portugal agreed, 1974, to turn the colony over to the Gabon-based Movement for the Liberation of São Tomé and Príncipe, which proclaimed as first president its East German-trained leader, Manuel Pinto da Costa. Independence came July 12, 1975. Democratic reforms were instituted in 1987. In 1991 Miguel Trovoada won the first free presidential election following da Costa's withdrawal. A military coup that ousted Trovoada Aug. 15, 1995, was reversed a week later after Angolan mediation. Trovoada defeated da Costa in a presidential runoff election, July 21, 1996.

Fradique de Menezes, a wealthy cocoa exporter, easily beat da Costa in the presidential election of July 29, 2001. The government was ousted in a military coup July 16, 2003, but restored to power July 23. The country, long one of the world's poorest, is expected to reap billions of dollars from oil development in the Gulf of Guinea.

Saudi Arabia
Kingdom of Saudi Arabia

People: Population: 24,217,000. **Age distrib.** (%): <15: 42.4; 65+: 2.8. **Pop. density:** 29 per sq. mi. **Urban:** 87%. **Ethnic groups:** Arab 90%, Afro-Asian 10% **Principal languages:** Arabic (official). **Chief religion:** Muslim (official).

Geography: Area (total): 756,984 sq. mi. **Location:** Occupies most of Arabian Peninsula in Mid-East. **Neighbors:** Kuwait, Iraq, Jordan on N; Yemen, Oman on S; United Arab Emirates, Qatar on E. **Topography:** Bordered by Red Sea on the W. The highlands on W, up to 9,000 ft., slope as an arid, barren desert to the Persian Gulf on the E. **Capital:** Riyadh. **Cities (urban aggr.):** Riyadh 4,761,000; Jeddah 3,192,000; Mecca 1,335,000.

Government: Type: Monarchy with council of ministers. **Head of state and gov.:** King Fahd ibn Abdul Aziz; b 1923; in office: June 13, 1982 (prime min. since 1982). **Local divisions:** 13 provinces. **Defense budget** (2002): $21.3 bil. **Active troops:** 124,500.

Economy: Industries: oil prod. & refining, petrochems., cement, construction, fertilizers, plastics. **Chief crops:** wheat, barley, tomatoes, melons, dates, citrus. **Natural resources:** oil, nat. gas, iron ore, gold, copper. **Crude oil reserves** (2002): 261.8 bil. bbls. **Arable land:** 2%. **Livestock** (2002): cattle: 307,000; chickens: 160 mil.; goats: 4.53 mil.; sheep: 7.93 mil. **Fish catch** (2002): 57,385 metric tons. **Electricity prod.** (2001): 122.4 bil. kWh. **Labor force:** agri. 12%, ind. 25%, services 63%.

Finance: Monetary unit: Riyal (SAR) (Sept. 2003: 3.75=1 U.S.). **GDP** (2002 est.): $242 bil. **Per capita GDP:** $10,500. **Im-**

ports (2001): $29.7 bil.; partners (2000): U.S. 21.1%, Japan 9.4%, Germany 7.4%, UK 7.3%. **Exports** (2001): $66.9 bil.; partners (2000): U.S. 17.4%, Japan 17.3%, South Korea 11.7%, Singapore 5.3%. **Tourism** (1998): $1.46 bil. **Budget** (2003 est.): $56.5 bil. **Intl. reserves less gold:** $15.16 bil. **Gold:** 4.60 mil oz t. **Consumer prices:** –0.5%.

Transport: Railroad: Length: 865 mi. **Motor vehicles** (1998): 7.05 mil pass. cars, **Civil aviation:** 12.19 bil pass.-mi; 71 airports. **Chief ports:** Jiddah, Ad Dammam.

Communications: TV sets: 263 per 1,000 pop. **Radios:** 321 per 1,000 pop. **Telephone lines:** 3,232,900. **Daily newspaper circ.:** 318.1 per 1,000 pop. **Internet:** 1,600,000 users.

Health: Life expectancy: 67.0 male; 70.6 female. **Births** (per 1,000 pop.): 37.2. **Deaths** (per 1,000 pop.): 5.8. **Natural inc.:** 3.14%. **Infant mortality** (per 1,000 live births): 47.9.

Education: Compulsory: ages 6-11. **Literacy:** 78.8%.

Major Intl. Organizations: UN (FAO, IBRD, ILO, IMF, IMO, WHO), AL, OPEC.

Embassy: 601 New Hampshire Ave. NW 20037; 202-337-4076.

Website: www.saudiembassy.net

Before Muhammad, Arabia was divided among numerous warring tribes and small kingdoms and was at times dominated by larger Arabian and non-Arabian kingdoms. It was united for the first time by Muhammad, in the early 7th century AD. His successors conquered the entire Near East and North Africa, bringing Islam and the Arabic language. But Arabia itself soon returned to its former status.

Nejd, in central Arabia, long an independent state and center of the Wahhabi sect, fell under Turkish rule in the 18th century. In 1913 Ibn Saud, founder of the Saudi dynasty, overthrew the Turks and captured the Turkish province of Hasa in E Arabia; he took the Hejaz region in W Arabia in 1925 and most of Asir, in SW Arabia, by 1926. The discovery of oil in the 1930s transformed the new country.

Ibn Saud reigned until his death, Nov. 1953. Subsequent kings have been sons of Ibn Saud. The king exercises authority together with a Council of Ministers. The Islamic religious code is the law of the land. Alcohol and public entertainments are restricted, and women have an inferior legal status. There is no constitution and no parliament, although a Consultative Council was established by the king in 1993.

Saudi Arabia has often allied itself with the U.S. and other Western nations, and billions of dollars of advanced arms have been purchased from Britain, France, and the U.S.; however, Western support for Israel has often strained relations. Saudi units fought against Israel in the 1948 and 1973 Arab-Israeli wars. Beginning with the 1967 Arab-Israeli war, Saudi Arabia provided large annual financial gifts to Egypt; aid was later extended to Syria, Jordan, and Palestinian groups, as well as to other Islamic countries.

King Faisal played a leading role in the 1973-74 Arab oil embargo against the U.S. and other nations. Crown Prince Khalid was proclaimed king on Mar. 25, 1975, after the assassination of Faisal. Fahd became king on June 13, 1982, following Khalid's death.

The Hejaz contains the holy cities of Islam—Medina, where the Mosque of the Prophet enshrines the tomb of Muhammad, and Mecca, his birthplace. More than 2 million Muslims make pilgrimage to Mecca annually. In 1987, Iranians making a pilgrimage to Mecca clashed with anti-Iranian pilgrims and Saudi police; more than 400 were killed. Some 1,426 Muslim pilgrims died July 2, 1990, in a stampede in a pedestrian tunnel leading to Mecca. Nearly 300 pilgrims were killed in a stampede in Mecca, May 26, 1994. More than 340 pilgrims died in a tent fire near Mecca, Apr. 15, 1997.

Following Iraq's attack on Kuwait, Aug. 2, 1990, Saudi Arabia accepted the Kuwait royal family and more than 400,000 Kuwaiti refugees. King Fahd invited Western and Arab troops to deploy on its soil in support of Saudi defense forces. During the Persian Gulf War, 28 U.S. soldiers were killed when an Iraqi missile hit their barracks in Dhahran, Feb. 25, 1991. The nation's northern Gulf coastline suffered severe pollution as a result of Iraqi sabotage of Kuwaiti oil fields. Islamic extremists were blamed for truck bombs that killed 7 (5 from the U.S.) at a military training center in Riyadh, Nov. 13, 1995, and 19 Americans at a base in Dhahran, June 25, 1996. U.S. officials repeatedly chided the Saudi government for failing to cooperate fully in the investigation.

The presence of 15 Saudis among the 19 al-Qaeda hijackers who took part in the Sept. 11, 2001, attacks on the U.S. raised new tensions between the U.S. and Saudi governments, and some blamed the Saudi government for allowing Muslim extremism to flourish in Saudi Arabia. Policy differences over Iraq and the Israeli-Palestinian dispute were further irritants. Al-Qaeda was blamed for 4 nighttime suicide bombings of Western targets in Riyadh, May 12-13, 2003, in which 34 people died, including 9 of the attackers. The U.S. completed a pull-out of its combat forces in Sept.

With King Fahd ailing, his half-brother, Crown Prince Abdullah, has taken a leading role in recent years.

Senegal
Republic of Senegal

People: Population: 10,095,000. **Age distrib.** (%): <15: 43.5; 65+: 3.1. **Pop. density:** 136 per sq. mi. **Urban:** 48%. **Ethnic groups:** Wolof 43%, Pular 24%, Serer 15%, Jola 4%, Mandinka 3%, Soninke 1%. **Principal languages:** French (official), Wolof, Pulaar, Jola, Mandinka. **Chief religions:** Muslim 94%, Christian 5%.

Geography: Area: 75,749 sq. mi. (total); 74,132 sq. mi. (land). **Location:** At W extreme of Africa. **Neighbors:** Mauritania on N, Mali on E, Guinea and Guinea-Bissau on S; surrounds Gambia on three sides. **Topography:** Low rolling plains cover most of Senegal, rising somewhat in the SE. Swamp and jungles are in SW. **Capital:** Dakar 2,160,000.

Government: Type: Republic. **Head of state:** Pres. Abdoulaye Wade; b May 29, 1926; in office: Apr. 1, 2000. **Head of gov.:** Prime Min. Idrissa Seck; b Aug. 9, 1959; in office: Nov. 4, 2002. **Local divisions:** 10 regions. **Defense budget** (2002): $67 mil. **Active troops:** 9,400.

Economy: Industries: food & fish proc., phosphate mining, fertilizer. **Chief crops:** peanuts, millet, corn, sorghum, rice, cotton. **Natural resources:** fish, phosphates, iron ore. **Arable land:** 12%. **Livestock:** (2002): cattle: 3.23 mil.; chickens: 45 mil.; goats: 4 mil.; pigs: 280,000; sheep: 4.82 mil. **Fish catch** (2002): 405,560 metric tons. **Electricity Prod.:** (2001): 1.52 bil. kWh. **Labor force:** agri. 70%.

Finance: Monetary unit: CFA Franc BCEAO (XOF) (Sept. 2003: 605.18=1 U.S.). **GDP** (2002 est.): $16.2 bil. **Per capita GDP:** $1,500. **Imports** (2001): $1.3 bil.; partners (2000): France 27%, Nigeria 19%, Germany 4%, U.S. 4%. **Exports** (2001): $1 bil.; partners (2000): France 19%, Italy 12%, Spain 6%, Cote d'Ivoire 2%. **Tourism** (1999): $166 mil. **Budget** (2002 est.): $1.373 bil. **Intl. reserves less gold:** $469 mil. **Consumer prices:** 2.2%.

Transport: Railroad: Length: 563 mi. **Motor vehicles** (1995): 106,000 pass. cars, 48,00 comm. vehicles. **Civil aviation:** 149.8 mil pass.-mi; 9 airports. **Chief ports:** Dakar, Saint-Louis.

Communications: TV sets: 41 per 1,000 pop. **Radios:** 141 per 1,000 pop. **Telephone lines:** 224,600. **Daily newspaper circ.:** 5.3 per 1,000 pop. **Internet:** 105,000 users.

Health: Life expectancy: 54.8 male; 58.0 female. **Births** (per 1,000 pop.): 36.2. **Deaths** (per 1,000 pop.): 10.9. **Natural inc.:** 2.54%. **Infant mortality** (per 1,000 live births): 57.6.

Education: Compulsory: ages 7-12. **Literacy:** 40.2%.

Major Intl. Organizations: UN and all of its specialized agencies, AU.

Embassy: 2112 Wyoming Ave. NW 20008; 234-0540.

Website: www.gouv.sn

Portuguese settlers arrived in the 15th century, but French control grew from the 17th century. The last independent Muslim state was subdued in 1893. Dakar became the capital of French West Africa.

Independence as part, along with the Sudanese Rep., of the Mali Federation, came June 20, 1960. Senegal withdrew Aug. 20. French political and economic influence remained strong.

Senegal, Dec. 17, 1981, signed an agreement with The Gambia for confederation of the 2 countries, without loss of individual sovereignty, under the name of Senegambia. The confederation collapsed in 1989, although in 1991 the 2 nations signed a friendship and cooperation treaty.

Separatists in Casamance Province of S Senegal have clashed with government forces since 1982. Senegal sent troops in June 1998 to help the Guinea-Bissau government suppress an army uprising. Forty years of Socialist Party rule ended when Abdoulaye Wade, leader of the Senegalese Democratic Party, won a presidential runoff election Mar. 19, 2000. A Senegalese ferry capsized off the coast of The Gambia Sept. 26, 2002, killing at least 1,150 people.

Serbia and Montenegro
(formerly Yugoslavia)

People: Population: 10,527,000. **Age distrib.** (%): <15: 19.6; 65+: 15.1. **Pop. density:** 267 per sq. mi. **Urban:** 52%. **Ethnic groups:** Serb 63%, Albanian 17%, Montenegrin 5%, Hungarian 3%. **Principal languages:** Serbian (official), Albanian. **Chief religions:** Orthodox 65%, Muslim 19%, Roman Catholic 4%.

Geography: Area: 39,518 sq. mi. (total); 39,435 sq. mi. (land). **Location:** On the Balkan Peninsula in SE Europe. **Neighbors:** Croatia, Bosnia and Herzegovina on W; Hungary on N; Romania, Bulgaria on E; Albania, Macedonia on S. **Topography:** Terrain varies widely, with fertile plains drained by the Danube and other rivers in N, limestone basins in E, ancient mountains and hills in SE, and very high coastline in Montenegro along SW. **Capital:** Belgrade. **Cities (urban aggr.):** Belgrade 1,687,000.

Government: Type: Federal republic. **Head of state and gov.:** Pres. Svetozar Marovic; b Mar. 31, 1955; in office: Mar. 7, 2003. **Head of gov.:** Prime Min. Dragisa Pesic; b 1954; in office: July 24, 2001. **Local divisions:** 2 republics, 2 autonomous provinces. **Defense budget** (2002): $721 mil. **Active troops:** 74,500.

Economy: Industries: aircraft, vehicle, & other machine building; metallurgy, mining, consumer goods, electronics, oil products, chemicals. **Chief crops:** cereals, fruits, vegetables, tobacco, olives. **Natural resources:** oil, gas, coal, antimony, copper, lead, zinc, nickel, gold, pyrite, chrome, hydropower. **Crude oil reserves** (2002): 78 mil. bbls. **Livestock** (2002): cattle: 1.83 mil.; chickens: 21.10 mil.; goats: 174,385; pigs: 3.33 mil.; sheep: 1.45 mil. **Fish catch** (2002): 3,557 metric tons. **Electricity prod.** (2001): 31.71 bil. kWh. **Labor force:** N/A

Finance: Monetary unit: Dinar (YUN) (Sept. 2003: 57.61=1 U.S.). **GDP** (2002 est.): $25.3 bil. **Per capita GDP:** $2,370. **Imports** (2002): $5.3 bil.; partners (2001): Russia 14.2%, Germany 12.2%, Italy 10.3%, Greece 4.5%. **Exports** (2002 est.): $2.2 bil.; partners (2001): Italy 16.4%, Bosnia and Herzegovina 13.1%, Germany 12.1%, Macedonia 9.2%. **Tourism** (1999): $17 mil. **Budget** (2001 est.): $4.3 bil.

Transport: Railroad: Length: 2,522 mi. **Motor vehicles:** 1.00 mil pass. cars, 331,000 comm. vehicles. **Civil aviation:** ; 19 airports. **Chief ports:** Bar, Novi Sad.

Communications: TV sets: 277 per 1,000 pop. **Radios:** 296 per 1,000 pop. **Telephone lines:** 2,493,000. **Daily newspaper circ.:** 107 per 1,000 pop. **Internet:** 640,000 users.

Health: Life expectancy: 71.0 male; 77.2 female. **Births** (per 1,000 pop.): 12.7. **Deaths** (per 1,000 pop.): 10.6. **Natural inc.:** 0.21%. **Infant mortality** (per 1,000 live births): 16.9.

Education: Compulsory: ages 7-14. **Literacy** (2002): 98%.

Major Intl. Organizations: Currently suspended from UN and its agencies.

Embassy: 2410 California St. NW 20008; 202-332-0333.

Website: www.gov.yu

Serbia, which had since 1389 been a vassal principality of Turkey, was established as an independent kingdom by the Treaty of Berlin, 1878. Montenegro, independent since 1389, also obtained international recognition in 1878. After the Balkan wars, Serbia's boundaries were enlarged by the annexation of Old Serbia and Macedonia, 1913.

When the Austro-Hungarian empire collapsed after World War I, the Kingdom of Serbs, Croats, and Slovenes was formed from the former provinces of Croatia, Dalmatia, Bosnia, Herzegovina, Slovenia, Vojvodina, and the independent state of Montenegro. The name became Yugoslavia in 1929.

Nazi Germany invaded in 1941. Many Yugoslav partisan troops continued to operate. Among these were the Chetniks led by Draja Mikhailovich, who fought other partisans led by Josip Broz, known as Marshal Tito. Tito, backed by the USSR and Britain from 1943, was in control by the time the Germans had been driven from Yugoslavia in 1945. Mikhailovich was executed July 17, 1946, by the Tito regime.

A constituent assembly proclaimed Yugoslavia a republic Nov. 29, 1945. It became a federal republic Jan. 31, 1946, with Tito, a Communist, heading the government. Tito rejected Stalin's policy of dictating to all Communist nations, and he accepted economic and military aid from the West.

Pres. Tito died May 4, 1980. After his death, Yugoslavia was governed by a collective presidency, with a rotating succession. On Jan. 22, 1990, the Communist Party renounced its leading role in society.

Croatia and Slovenia formally declared independence June 25, 1991. In Croatia, fighting began between Croats and ethnic Serbs. Serbia sent arms and medical supplies to the Serb rebels in Croatia. Croatian forces clashed with Yugoslav army units and their Serb supporters.

The republics of Serbia and Montenegro proclaimed a new "Federal Republic of Yugoslavia" Apr. 17, 1992. Serbia, under Pres. Slobodan Milosevic, was the main arms supplier to ethnic Serb fighters in Bosnia and Herzegovina. The UN imposed sanctions May 30 on the newly reconstituted Yugoslavia as a means of ending the bloodshed in Bosnia.

A peace agreement initialed in Dayton, Ohio, Nov. 21, 1995, was signed in Paris, Dec. 14, by Milosevic and leaders of Bosnia and Croatia. In May 1996, a UN tribunal in the Netherlands began trying suspected war criminals from the former Yugoslavia. The UN lifted sanctions against Yugoslavia Oct. 1, 1996, after elections were held in Bosnia. Mass protests erupted when Milosevic refused to accept opposition victories in local elections Nov. 17; non-Communist governments took office in Belgrade and other cities in Feb. 1997. Barred from running for a 3d term as Serbian president, Milosevic had himself inaugurated as president of Yugoslavia on July 23, 1997.

Defeated in a presidential election Sept. 24, 2000, by opposition leader Vojislav Kostunica, Milosevic initially refused to accept the result. A rising tide of mass demonstrations forced him to resign Oct. 6, and Kostunica was sworn in the next day. Charged with corruption and abuse of power, Milosevic surrendered to Serbian authorities Apr. 1, 2001. He was extradited June 28, 2001, to The Hague, where a UN tribunal had indicted him for war crimes. A pact to reconstitute Yugoslavia as a new union of Serbia and Montenegro was signed Mar. 14, 2002, and took effect Feb. 4, 2003. Zoran Djindjic, premier of the Republic of Serbia, was assassinated in Belgrade, Mar. 12; the murder triggered a roundup of more than 4,500 people associated with organized crime or the Milosevic regime.

Kosovo: A nominally autonomous province in southern Serbia (4,203 sq. mi.), with a population of about 2,000,000, mostly Albanians. The capital is Pristina. Revoking provincial autonomy, Ser-

bia began ruling Kosovo by force in 1989. Albanian secessionists proclaimed an independent Republic of Kosovo in July 1990. Guerrilla attacks by the Kosovo Liberation Army in 1997 brought a ferocious counteroffensive by Serbian authorities.

Fearful that the Serbs were employing "ethnic cleansing" tactics, as they had in Bosnia, the U.S. and its NATO allies sought to pressure the Yugoslav government. When Milosevic refused to comply, NATO launched an air war against Yugoslavia, Mar.-June 1999; the Serbs retaliated by terrorizing the Kosovars and forcing hundreds of thousands to flee, mostly to Albania and Macedonia. A 50,000-member multinational force (KFOR) entered Kosovo in June, and most of the Kosovar refugees had returned by Sept. 1. As of 2003, Kosovo was under UN administration, with a NATO-led security force of about 30,000.

Vojvodina: A nominally autonomous province in northern Serbia (8,304 sq. mi.), with a population of about 2,000,000, mostly Serbian. The capital is Novi Sad.

Seychelles
Republic of Seychelles

People: Population: 80,000. **Age distrib.** (%): <15: 27.8; 65+: 6.2. **Pop. density:** 457 per sq. mi. **Urban:** 65%. **Ethnic groups:** Mainly Seychellois (mix of French, African, and Asian). **Principal languages:** English, French, Creole (all official). **Chief religions:** Roman Catholic 87%, Anglican 7%.

Geography: Area (total): 176 sq. mi. **Location:** In the Indian O. 700 miles NE of Madagascar. **Neighbors:** Nearest are Madagascar on SW, Somalia on NW. **Topography:** A group of 86 islands, about half of them composed of coral, the other half granite, the latter predominantly mountainous. **Capital:** Victoria: 30,000.

Government: Type: Republic. **Head of state and gov.:** Pres. France-Albert René, b. Nov. 16, 1935; in office: June 5, 1977. **Local divisions:** 23 districts. **Defense budget** (2002): $11 mil. **Active troops:** 450.

Economy: Industries: fishing, tourism, coconut & vanilla proc., rope, boats. **Chief crops:** coconuts, cinnamon, vanilla, sweet potatoes, cassava, bananas. **Natural resources:** fish, copra, cinnamon. **Arable land:** 2%. **Livestock** (2002): cattle: 2,000; chickens: 570,000; goats: 5,250; pigs: 19,000. **Fish catch** (2002): 47,832 metric tons. **Electricity prod.** (2001): 0.16 bil. kWh. **Labor force:** ind. 19%, services 71%, agri. 10%.

Finance: Monetary unit: Rupee (SCR) (Sept. 2003: 5.23=1 U.S.). **GDP** (2002 est.): $626 mil. **Per capita GDP:** $7,800. **Imports** (2001): $360.2 mil.; partners (1999): Italy 13.3%, South Africa 10.7%, France 9.9%, UK 8.0%. **Exports** (2001): $182.6 mil.; partners (1999): UK 48.1%, Italy 23.1%, France 14.8%, Netherlands 2.7%. **Tourism:** $110 mil. **Budget** (1998 est.): $262 mil. **Intl. reserves less gold:** $51 mil. **Consumer prices:** .2%.

Transport: Motor vehicles (1999): 6,400 pass. cars, 2,200 comm. vehicles. **Civil aviation:** 456.7 bil pass.-mi; 7 airports. **Chief port:** Victoria.

Communications: TV sets: 214 per 1,000 pop. **Radios:** 560 per 1,000 pop. **Telephone lines:** 21,400. **Daily newspaper circ.:** 45 per 1,000 pop. **Internet:** 9,000 users.

Health: Life expectancy: 65.8 male; 76.9 female. **Births** (per 1,000 pop.): 16.9. **Deaths** (per 1,000 pop.): 6.5. **Natural inc.:** 1.04%. **Infant mortality** (per 1,000 live births): 16.4.

Education: Compulsory: ages 6-15. **Literacy** (2002): 84%.

Major Intl. Organizations: UN (FAO, IBRD, ILO, IMF, IMO, WHO), the Commonwealth, AU.

Embassy: 800 2d Ave., Suite 400, New York, NY 10017; 212-687-9766.

Website: www.seychelles-online.com.sc/seychelles.html

The islands were occupied by France in 1768, and seized by Britain in 1794. Ruled as part of Mauritius from 1814, the Seychelles became a separate colony in 1903. The ruling party had opposed independence as impractical, but pressure from the AU and the UN became irresistible, and independence was declared June 29, 1976. The first president was ousted in a coup a year later by a socialist leader. A new constitution, approved June 1993, provided for a multiparty state.

Sierra Leone
Republic of Sierra Leone

People: Population: 4,971,000. **Age distrib.** (%): <15: 44.7; 65+: 3.2. **Pop. density:** 180 per sq. mi. **Urban:** 37%. **Ethnic groups:** Temne 30%, Mende 30%, other tribes 30%; Creole 10%. **Principal languages:** English (official), Mende in S, Temne in N, Krio (English Creole). **Chief religions:** Muslim 60%, indigenous beliefs 30%, Christian 10%.

Geography: Area: 27,699 sq. mi. (total); 27,653 sq. mi. (land). **Location:** On W coast of W Africa. **Neighbors:** Guinea on N and E, Liberia on S. **Topography:** The heavily-indented, 210-mi. coastline has mangrove swamps. Behind are wooded hills, rising to a plateau and mountains in the E. **Capital:** Freetown: 837,000.

Government: Type: Republic. **Head of state and gov.:** Ahmad Tejan Kabbah; b Feb. 16, 1932; in office: Mar. 10, 1998. **Local divisions:** 3 provinces, 1 area. **Defense budget** (2002): $18 mil. **Active troops:** 13–14,000.

Economy: Industries: diamonds, light mfg., oil refining. **Chief crops:** rice, coffee, cocoa, palm kernels & oil, peanuts. **Natural resources:** diamonds, titanium ore, bauxite, iron ore, gold, chromite. **Arable land:** 7%. **Livestock** (2002): cattle: 400,000; chickens: 6 mil.; goats: 200,000; pigs: 52,000; sheep: 365,000. **Fish catch** (2002): 75,240 metric tons. **Electricity Prod.:** (2001): 0.25 bil. kWh.

Finance: Monetary unit: Leone (SLL) (Sept. 2003: 1,930.10=1 U.S.). **GDP** (2002 est.): $2.8 bil. **Per capita GDP:** $580. **Imports** (2000): $145 mil.; partners (2000): Czech Republic 26.7%, UK 26.6%, U.S. 5.1%, Netherlands 4.6%. **Exports** (2000 est.): $65 mil.; partners (2000): NZ 33.7%, Belgium 32.6%, U.S. 7.4%, France 5.1%. **Tourism:** 12 mil. **Budget** (2000 est.): $351 mil. **Intl. reserves less gold:** $62 mil. **Consumer prices:** −3.3%.

Transport: Railroad: Length: 52 mi. **Motor vehicles** (1998): 32,400 pass. cars, 11,900 comm. vehicles. **Civil aviation:** 18.6 mil pass.-mi; 1 airport. **Chief ports:** Freetown, Bonthe.

Communications: TV sets: 13 per 1,000 pop. **Radios:** 274 per 1,000 pop. **Telephone lines:** 22,700. **Daily newspaper circ.:** 4.7 per 1,000 pop. **Internet:** 7,000 users.

Health: Life expectancy: 40.3 male; 45.4 female. **Births** (per 1,000 pop.): 43.9. **Deaths** (per 1,000 pop.): 20.7. **Natural inc.:** 2.32%. **Infant mortality** (per 1,000 live births): 146.9.

Education: Literacy (2002): 31%.

Major Intl. Organizations: UN (FAO, IBRD, ILO, IMF, IMO, WHO, WTrO), the Commonwealth, AU.

Embassy: 1701 19th St. NW 20009; 939-9261.

Website: www.Sierra-Leone.org

Freetown was founded in 1787 by the British government as a haven for freed slaves. Their descendants, known as Creoles, number more than 60,000.

Successive steps toward independence followed the 1951 constitution. Ten years later, full independence arrived Apr. 27, 1961. Sierra Leone declared itself a republic Apr. 19, 1971. A one-party state approved by referendum in 1978 brought political stability, but mismanagement and corruption plagued the economy.

Mutinous soldiers ousted Pres. Joseph Momoh Apr. 30, 1992. Another coup, Jan. 16, 1996, paved the way for multiparty elections and a return to civilian rule. A peace accord, signed Nov. 30 with the Revolutionary United Front (RUF), brought a temporary halt to a civil war that had claimed over 10,000 lives in 5 years.

A coup on May 25, 1997, was met with widespread international opposition. Armed intervention by Nigeria restored Pres. Ahmad Tejan Kabbah to power on Mar. 10, 1998, but RUF rebels mounted a guerrilla counteroffensive, reportedly killing thousands of civilians and mutilating thousands more. The Kabbah government signed a power-sharing agreement with the RUF on July 7, 1999. The accord collapsed in early May 2000, as RUF guerrillas took more than 500 UN peacekeepers hostage. Rebel leader Foday Sankoh was captured in Freetown May 17. The hostages were freed by the end of May, and 233 more UN personnel behind rebel lines were rescued July 15. A UN-sponsored disarmament program in 2001 reduced the level of violence. The UN authorized establishment of a war crimes tribunal Jan. 3, 2002. Government and rebel leaders declared an official end to the war Jan. 18. Kabbah won the May 14 presidential election. Sankoh, an indicted war criminal, died in UN custody July 29, 2003.

Singapore
Republic of Singapore

People: Population: 4,253,000. **Age distrib.** (%): <15: 17.6; 65+: 7.1. **Pop. density:** 17,653 per sq. mi. **Urban:** 100%. **Ethnic groups:** Chinese 77%, Malay 14%, Indian 8%. **Principal languages:** Chinese, Malay, Tamil, English (all official). **Chief religions:** Buddhist, Muslim, Christian, Taoist, Hindu.

Geography: Area: 267 sq. mi. (total); 264 sq. mi. (land). **Location:** Off tip of Malayan Peninsula in SE Asia. **Neighbors:** Nearest are Malaysia on N, Indonesia on S. **Topography:** Singapore is a flat, formerly swampy island. The nation includes 40 nearby islets. **Capital:** Singapore 4,108,000.

Government: Type: Republic. **Head of state:** Pres. S. R. Nathan; b July 3, 1924; in office: Sept. 1, 1999. **Head of gov.:** Prime Min. Goh Chok Tong; b May 20, 1941; in office: Nov. 28, 1990. **Defense budget** (2002): $4.8 bil. **Active troops:** 60,500.

Economy: Industries: electronics, chemicals, financial services, oil drilling equip., oil refining, rubber proc. **Chief crops:** rubber, copra, fruit, orchids, vegetables. **Natural resources:** fish. **Arable land:** 2%. **Livestock** (2002): cattle: 200; chickens: 2 mil.; goats: 300; pigs: 190,000. **Fish catch** (2002): 8,704 metric tons. **Electricity prod.** (2001): 30.48 bil. kWh. **Labor force:** financial, business, and other services 35%, manufact. 21%, construct. 13%, transportation and communication 9%, other 22%.

Finance: Monetary unit: Singapore Dollar (SGD) (Sept. 2003: 1.76=1 U.S.). **GDP** (2002 est.): $105 bil. **Per capita GDP:** $24,000. **Imports** (2001): $116 bil.; partners (2000): Japan 17%, Malaysia 17%, U.S. 15%, China 5%. **Exports** (2001 est.): $122 bil.; partners (2000): Malaysia 18%, U.S. 17%, Hong Kong 8%, Japan 7.5%. **Tourism:** $6.37 bil. **Budget** (2000 est.): $19.5 bil. **International reserves:** $60.33 bil. **Consumer prices:** −0.4%.

Transport: Railroad: Length: 24 mi. **Motor vehicles:** 413,500 pass. cars, 137,200 comm. vehicles. **Civil aviation:** 40.68 bil pass.-mi; 9 airports. **Chief port:** Singapore.

Communications: TV sets: 341 per 1,000 pop. **Radios:** 744 per 1,000 pop. **Telephone lines:** 1,930,200. **Daily newspaper circ.:** 324 per 1,000 pop. **Internet:** 2,247,000 users.

Health: Life expectancy: 77.5 male; 83.6 female. **Births** (per 1,000 pop.): 12.8. **Deaths** (per 1,000 pop.): 4.3. **Natural inc.:** 0.84%. **Infant mortality** (per 1,000 live births): 3.57.

Education: Literacy: 93.2%.

Major Intl. Organizations: UN (IBRD, ILO, IMF, IMO, WHO, WTrO), the Commonwealth, APEC, ASEAN.

Embassy: 3501 International Pl. NW 20008; 537-3100.

Website: www.gov.sg

Founded in 1819 by Sir Thomas Stamford Raffles, Singapore was a British colony until 1959, when it became autonomous within the Commonwealth. On Sept. 16, 1963, it joined with Malaya, Sarawak, and Sabah to form the Federation of Malaysia. Tensions between Malayans, dominant in the federation, and ethnic Chinese, dominant in Singapore, led to an accord under which Singapore became a separate nation, Aug. 9, 1965.

Singapore is one of the world's largest ports. Standards in health, education, and housing are generally high. International banking has grown rapidly in recent years. The government, dominated by a single party, has taken strong actions to suppress dissent.

In Dec. 2001, the government thwarted an alleged plot to blow up the U.S. Embassy; in Sept. 2002, authorities reported arrests of 21 militants identified as members of Jemaah Islamiah, a radical Muslim group active in Southeast Asia. A SARS epidemic killed 33 people, Feb.-May 2003. After subsiding, a new case was confirmed Sept. 10.

Slovakia
Slovak Republic

People: Population: 5,402,000. **Age distrib.** (%): <15: 18.3; 65+: 11.6. **Pop. density:** 287 per sq. mi. **Urban:** 58%. **Ethnic groups:** Slovak 86%, Hungarian 11%, Roma 2%. **Principal languages:** Slovak (official), Hungarian. **Chief religions:** Roman Catholic 60%, Protestant 8%, Orthodox 4%.

Geography: Area: 18,859 sq. mi. (total); 18,842 sq. mi. (land). **Location:** In E central Europe. **Neighbors:** Poland on N, Hungary on S, Austria and Czech Rep. on W, Ukraine on E. **Topography:** Mountains (Carpathians) in N, fertile Danube plane in S. **Capital:** Bratislava. **Cities (urban aggr.):** Bratislava 464,000; (1997 est.): Kosice 242,000.

Government: Type: Republic. **Head of state:** Rudolf Schuster; b Jan. 4, 1934; in office: June 15, 1999. **Head of gov.:** Prime Min. Mikulás Dzurinda; b Feb. 4, 1955; in office: Oct. 30, 1998. **Local divisions:** 8 departments. **Defense budget** (2002): $450 mil. **Active troops:** 26,200.

Economy: Industries: metals; food & beverages; electricity, gas, coke, oil, nuclear fuels. **Chief crops:** grains, potatoes, sugar beets, hops, fruit. **Natural resources:** coal, lignite, iron ore, copper, mang., salt. **Crude oil reserves** (2002): 9 mil. bbls. **Arable land:** 31%. **Livestock** (2002): cattle: 645,000; chickens: 15.03 mil.; goats: 51,400; pigs: 1.52 mil.; sheep: 366,000. **Fish catch** (2002): 2,530 metric tons. **Electricity prod.** (2001): 30.29 bil. kWh. **Labor force:** ind. 29.3%, agri. 8.9%, construct. 8%, transport and communication 8.2%, services 45.6%.

Finance: Monetary unit: Koruna (SKK) (Sept. 2003: 38.74=1 U.S.). **GDP** (2002 est.): $66 bil. **Per capita GDP:** $12,200. **Imports** (2001): $15.4 bil.; partners (2001): EU 49.8%, Czech Republic 15.1%, Russia 14.8%. **Exports** (2002 est.): $12.9 bil.; partners (2001): EU 59.9%, Czech Republic 16.6%. **Tourism:** $432 mil. **Budget** (1999): $5.6 bil. **Intl. reserves less gold:** $6.48 bil. **Gold:** 1.13 mil. oz t. **Consumer prices:** 3.3%.

Transport: Railroad: Length: 2,274 mi. **Motor vehicles:** 1.27 mil. pass. cars, 153,200 comm. vehicles. **Civil aviation:** 72.7 mil pass.-mi; 20 airports. **Chief ports:** Bratislava, Komarno.

Communications: TV sets: 418 per 1,000 pop. **Radios:** 967 per 1,000 pop. **Telephone lines:** 1,402,700. **Daily newspaper circ.:** 174.6 per 1,000 pop. **Internet:** 862,800 users

Health: Life expectancy: 70.4 male; 78.6 female. **Births** (per 1,000 pop.): 10.1. **Deaths** (per 1,000 pop.): 9.2. **Natural inc.:** 0.09%. **Infant mortality** (per 1,000 live births): 8.6.

Education: Compulsory: ages 6-15. **Literacy** (1994): 100%.

Major Intl. Organizations: UN (FAO, IBRD, ILO, IMF, IMO, WHO, WTrO), OSCE.

Embassy: 3523 International Ct. NW 20008; 202-237-1054. **Website:** www.government.gov.sk/english/

Slovakia was originally settled by Illyrian, Celtic, and Germanic tribes and was incorporated into Great Moravia in the 9th century. It became part of Hungary in the 11th century. Overrun by Czech Hussites in the 15th century, it was restored to Hungarian rule in 1526. The Slovaks disassociated themselves from Hungary after World War I and joined the Czechs of Bohemia to form the Republic of Czechoslovakia, Oct. 28, 1918.

Germany invaded Czechoslovakia, 1939, and declared Slovakia independent. Slovakia rejoined Czechoslovakia in 1945.

Czechoslovakia split into 2 separate states—the Czech Republic and Slovakia—on Jan. 1, 1993. A prolonged parliamentary standoff left the country without a president for much of 1998.

Prime Min. Vladimir Meciar, a nationalist, suffered a setback in legislative elections Sept. 25-26, 1998, and was defeated in a presidential runoff vote by Rudolf Schuster, May 29, 1999. A center-right coalition governed Slovakia after parliamentary elections Sept. 20-21, 2002. In a referendum May 16-17, 2003, Slovak voters endorsed joining the EU in 2004.

Slovenia
Republic of Slovenia

People: Population: 1,984,000. **Age distrib. (%):** <15: 15.7; 65+: 14.5. **Pop. density:** 254 per sq. mi. **Urban:** 49%. **Ethnic groups:** Slovene 88%, Croat 3%, Serb 2%, Bosniak 1%. **Principal languages:** Slovenian (official), Serbo-Croatian. **Chief religion:** Roman Catholic 71%.

Geography: Area: 7,827 sq. mi. (total); 7,780 sq. mi. (land). **Location:** In SE Europe. **Neighbors:** Italy on W, Austria on N, Hungary on NE, Croatia on SE, S. **Topography:** Mostly hilly; 42% of the land is forested. **Capital:** Ljubljana: 250,000.

Government: Type: Republic. **Head of state:** Pres. Janez Drnovsek; b May 17, 1950; in office: Dec. 22, 2002. **Head of gov.:** Prime Min. Anton Rop; Dec. 27, 1960; in office: Dec. 11, 2002. **Head of gov.:** Prime Min. Janez Drnovsek; b May 17, 1950; in office: Nov. 17, 2000. **Local divisions:** 136 municipalities, 11 urban municipalities. **Defense budget** (2002): $313 mil. **Active troops:** 9,000.

Economy: Industries: metallurgy, electronics, trucks, electric power equip., wood products, textiles, chemicals, machine tools. **Chief crops:** potatoes, hops, wheat, sugar beets, corn, grapes. **Natural resources:** lignite, lead, zinc, mercury, uranium, silver, hydropower, timber. **Livestock** (2002): cattle: 477,000; chickens: 7.15 mil.; goats: 22,000; pigs: 600,000; sheep: 94,000. **Fish catch** (2002): 3,089 metric tons. **Electricity prod.** (2001): 13.69 bil. kWh.

Finance: Monetary unit: Tolar (SIT) (Sept. 2003: 221.49=1 U.S.). **GDP** (2002 est.): $36 bil. **Per capita GDP:** $18,000. **Imports** (2002): $11.1 bil.; partners (2001): Germany 19.6%, Italy 18.0%, France 10.8%, Austria 8.5%. **Exports** (2002) $10.3 bil.; partners (2001): Germany 26.0%, Italy 12.4%, Croatia 8.6%, Austria 7.4%. **Tourism:** 1999. **Budget** (1997 est.): $8.32 bil. **Intl. reserves less gold:** $5.13 bil. oz t. **Consumer prices:** 7.5%.

Transport: Railroad: Length: 746 mi. **Motor vehicles:** 868,300 pass. cars, 56,800 comm. vehicles. **Civil aviation:** 320.0 mil pass.-mi; 6 airports. **Chief ports:** Izola, Koper, Piran.

Communications: TV sets: 362 per 1,000 pop. **Radios:** 404 per 1,000 pop. **Telephone lines:** 811,400. **Daily newspaper circ.:** 170.6 per 1,000 pop. **Internet:** 800,000 users.

Health: Life expectancy: 71.7 male; 79.6 female. **Births** (per 1,000 pop.): 9.2. **Deaths** (per 1,000 pop.): 10.2. **Natural Inc.:** -0.09%. **Infant mortality** (per 1,000 live births): 4.4.

Education: Compulsory: ages 7-14. **Literacy:** 99.7%.

Major Intl. Organizations: UN (FAO, IBRD, ILO, IMF, IMO, WHO, WTrO), OSCE.

Embassy: 1525 New Hampshire Ave. NW 20036; 667-5363. **Website:** www.sigov.si

The Slovenes settled in their current territory during the period from the 6th to the 8th century. They fell under German domination as early as the 9th century. Modern Slovenian political history began after 1848 when the Slovenes, who were divided among several Austrian provinces, began their struggle for political and national unification. In 1918 a majority of Slovenes became part of the Kingdom of Serbs, Croats, and Slovenes, later renamed Yugoslavia.

Slovenia declared independence June 25, 1991, and joined the UN May 22, 1992. In a referendum Mar. 23, 2003, voters endorsed membership in the EU and NATO, both effective 2004.

Solomon Islands

People: Population: 477,000. **Age distrib.** (%): <15: 43.4; 65+: 3.1. **Pop. density:** 45 per sq. mi. **Urban:** 20%. **Ethnic groups:** Melanesian 93%, Polynesian 4%, Micronesian, European, and others 3%. **Principal languages:** English (official), Melanesian pidgin, and 120 indigenous languages. **Chief religions:** Anglican 45%, Roman Catholic 18%, other Christian 35%.

Geography: Area: 10,985 sq. mi. (total); 10,633 sq. mi. (land). **Location:** Melanesian Archipelago in the W Pacific O. **Neighbors:** Nearest is Papua New Guinea to W. **Topography:** 10 large

volcanic and rugged islands and 4 groups of smaller ones. **Capital:** Honiara: 78,000.

Government: Type: In transition. Head of state: Queen Elizabeth II, represented by Gov.-Gen. Sir John Lapli; b 1955; in office: July 7, 1999. **Head of gov.:** Prime Min. Sir Allan Kemakeza; b 1951; in office: Dec. 17, 2001. **Local divisions:** 9 provinces and Honiara.

Economy: Industries: tuna, mining, timber. **Chief crops:** cocoa, beans, coconuts, palm kernels, rice, potatoes. **Natural resources:** fish, timber, gold, bauxite, phosphates, lead, zinc, nickel. **Arable land:** 1%. **Livestock** (2002): cattle: 5.30 mil.; chickens: 3.30 mil.; goats: 12.50 mil.; pigs: 4,000; sheep: 13.20 mil. **Electricity prod.** (2001): 0.03 bil. kWh. **Fish catch** (2002 est.): 30,090 metric tons. **Labor force:** agri. 75%, ind. 5%, services 20%.

Finance: Monetary unit: Dollar (SBD) (Sept. 2003: 7.41=1 U.S.). **GDP** (2001 est.): $800 mil. **Per capita GDP:** $1,700. **Imports** (1999): $152 mil.; partners (2000): Australia 27%, Singapore 25%, NZ 5.5%, Japan 5.3%. **Exports** (1999 est.): $165 mil.; partners (2000): Japan 22%, China 15%, Philippines 13%, South Korea 12%. **Tourism** (1999): $6 mil. **Budget** (1997 est.): $168 mil. **Intl. reserves less gold:** $13 mil. **Consumer prices:** (change in 1999): 8.3%.

Transport: Civil aviation: 49.7 mil pass.-mi; 2 airports. **Chief port:** Honiara.

Communications: TV sets: 16 per 1,000 pop. **Radios:** 141 per 1,000 pop. **Telephone lines:** 6,600. **Internet:** 2,200 users.

Health: Life expectancy: 69.6 male; 74.7 female. **Births** (per 1,000 pop.): 32.5. **Deaths** (per 1,000 pop.): 4.1. **Natural Inc.:** 2.83%. **Infant mortality** (per 1,000 live births): 22.9.

Education: Literacy (1994): 54%.

Major Intl. Organizations: UN (FAO, IBRD, ILO, IMF, IMO, WHO, WTrO), the Commonwealth.

Embassy: 800 Second Ave., Suite 400L, New York, NY 10017; (212) 599-6193.

Website: www.commerce.gov.sb

The Solomon Islands were sighted in 1568 by an expedition from Peru. Britain established a protectorate in the 1890s over most of the group, inhabited by Melanesians.

The islands saw major World War II battles. Self-government came Jan. 2, 1976, and independence was formally attained July 7, 1978.

A coup attempt June 5, 2000, sparked factional fighting in Honiara. During the next 3 years, violence, lawlessness, and corruption became widespread. To restore order, a 2,225-member intervention force, led by Australia and authorized by the Pacific Islands Forum, began arriving in Honiara July 24, 2003.

Somalia

People: Population: 9,890,000. **Age distrib.** (%): <15: 44.7; 65+: 2.7. **Pop. density:** 41 per sq. mi. **Urban:** 28%. **Ethnic groups:** Somali 85%, Bantu and other 15%. **Principal languages:** Somali, Arabic (both official); Italian, English. **Chief religion:** Sunni Muslim (official).

Geography: Area: 246,201 sq. mi. (total); 242,216 sq. mi. (land). **Location:** Occupies the eastern horn of Africa. **Neighbors:** Djibouti, Ethiopia, Kenya on W. **Topography:** The coastline extends for 1,700 mi. Hills cover the N; the center and S are flat. **Capital:** Mogadishu 1,212,000.

Government: Type: In transition. **Head of state:** Abdiqassim Salad Hassan; b 1942; in office: Aug. 27, 2000. **Head of gov.:** Prime Min. Hassan Abshir Farah; b June 20, 1945; in office: Nov. 12, 2001. Local divisions: 18 regions. **Defense budget** (2002): $15 mil. **Active troops:** Nil.

Economy: Industries: a few light industries, incl. sugar refining, textiles, wireless communication. **Chief crops:** bananas, sorghum, corn, coconuts, rice. **Natural resources:** uranium, iron ore, tin, gypsum, bauxite, copper, salt, nat. gas, oil. **Arable land:** 2%. **Livestock** (2002): cattle: 5.30 mil.; chickens: 3.30 mil.; goats: 12.50 mil.; pigs: 4,000; sheep: 13.20 mil. **Fish catch** (2002 est.): 20,000 metric tons. **Electricity prod.** (2001): 0.25 bil. kWh. **Labor force:** agri. 71%, ind. and services 29%.

Finance: Monetary unit: Shilling (SOS) (Sept. 2003: 2,620.00=1 U.S.). **GDP** (2001 est.): $4.1 bil. **Per capita GDP:** $550. **Imports** (1999): $314 mil.; partners (2000): Djibouti 27%, Kenya 12%, India 9%. **Exports** (1999 est.): $186 mil.; partners (2000): Saudi Arabia 29%, UAE 29%, Yemen 28%. **Budget:** NA

Transport: Motor vehicles (1995): 12,000 pass. cars, 12,000 comm. vehicles. **Civil aviation:** ; 6 airports. **Chief ports:** Mogadishu, Berbera.

Communications: TV sets: 14 per 1,000 pop. **Radios:** 53 per 1,000 pop. **Telephone lines:** 15,000 main lines. **Daily newspaper circ.:** 1.2 per 1,000 pop.

Health: Life expectancy: 45.7 male; 49.1 female. **Births** (per 1,000 pop.): 46.4. **Deaths** (per 1,000 pop.): 17.6. **Natural inc.:** 2.88%. **Infant mortality** (per 1,000 live births): 120.3.

Education: Compulsory: ages 6-14. **Literacy** (2001 est.): 37.8%.

Major Intl. Organizations: UN (FAO, IBRD, ILO, IMF, IMO, WHO), AL, AU.

Website: travel.state.gov/somalia.html

British Somaliland (present-day N Somalia) was formed in the 19th century, as was Italian Somaliland (now central and S Somalia). Italy lost its African colonies in World War II. In 1949, the UN approved eventual independence for the former Italian colony (designated the UN Trust Territory of Somalia) after a 10-year period under Italian administration.

British Somaliland gained independence, June 26, 1960, and by prearrangement, merged July 1 with the trust territory of Somalia to create the independent Somali Republic (Somalia).

On Oct. 16, 1969, Pres. Abdi Rashid Ali Shirmarke was assassinated. On Oct. 21, a military group led by Maj. Gen. Muhammad Siad Barre seized power. In 1970, Barre declared the country a socialist state—the Somali Democratic Republic.

Somalia has laid claim to Ogaden, the huge eastern region of Ethiopia, peopled mostly by Somalis. Ethiopia battled Somali rebels in 1977. Some 11,000 Cuban troops with Soviet arms defeated Somali army troops and ethnic Somali rebels in Ethiopia, 1978. As many as 1.5 million refugees entered Somalia. Guerrilla fighting in Ogaden continued until 1988, when a peace agreement was reached with Ethiopia.

The civil war intensified again and Barre was forced to flee the capital, Jan. 1991. Fighting between rival factions caused 40,000 casualties in 1991 and 1992, and by mid-1992 the civil war, drought, and banditry combined to produce a famine that threatened some 1.5 million people with starvation.

In Dec. 1992 the UN accepted a U.S. offer of troops to safeguard food delivery to the starving. The UN took control of the multinational relief effort from the U.S. May 4, 1993. While the operation helped alleviate the famine, efforts to reestablish order foundered, and there were significant U.S. and other casualties; a failed mission Oct. 3-4 left 18 U.S. troops and more than 500 Somalis dead. The U.S. withdrew its peacekeeping forces Mar. 25, 1994.

When the last UN troops pulled out Mar. 3, 1995, Mogadishu had no functioning central government, and armed factions controlled different regions. By 1999 a joint police force was operating in the capital, but much of the country, especially in S Somalia, faced continued violence and food shortages. U.S. officials believe Somalia has been a base of operations for al-Qaeda terrorists.

South Africa
Republic of South Africa

People: Population: 45,026,000. **Age distrib. (%):** <15: 31.6; 65+: 5. **Pop. density:** 96 per sq. mi. **Urban:** 58%. **Ethnic groups:** Black 75%, White 14%, mixed 8%, Indian 3%. **Principal languages:** Afrikaans, English, Ndebele, Pedi, Sotho, Swazi, Tsonga, Tswana, Venda, Xhosa, Zulu (all official). **Chief religions:** Christian 68%, indigenous beliefs and animist 29%.

Geography: Area: (total): 471,010 sq. mi. **Location:** At the southern extreme of Africa. **Neighbors:** Namibia, Botswana, Zimbabwe on N; Mozambique, Swaziland on E; surrounds Lesotho. **Topography:** The large interior plateau reaches close to the country's 2,700-mi. coastline. There are few major rivers or lakes; rainfall is sparse in W, more plentiful in E. **Capitals:** Cape Town (legislative), Pretoria (administrative), and Bloemfontein (judicial). **Cities (urban aggr.):** Cape Town 2,993,000; Durban 2,391,000; Johannesburg 2,950,000; Pretoria 1,590,000; Bloemfontein 364,000.

Government: Type: Republic. **Head of state and gov.:** Pres. Thabo Mvuyelwa Mbeki; b: June 18, 1942; in office: June 16 1999. **Local divisions:** 9 provinces. **Defense budget** (2002): $1.8 bil. **Active troops:** 60,000.

Economy: Industries: mining (espec. platinum, gold, chromium), auto assembly, metalworking, machinery, textiles, chemicals, fertilizer, foodstuffs. **Chief crops:** corn, wheat, sugarcane, fruits, vegetables. **Natural resources:** gold, chromium, antimony, coal, iron ore, mang., nickel, phosphates, tin, uranium, diamonds, platinum, copper, vanadium, salt, nat. gas. **Crude oil reserves** (2002): 16 mil. bbls. **Arable land:** 10%. **Livestock** (2002): cattle: 13.72 mil.; chickens: 119 mil.; goats: 6.85 mil.; pigs: 1.60 mil.; sheep: 29.09 mil. **Fish catch** (2002): 759,522 metric tons. **Electricity Prod.:** (2001): 195.64 bil. kWh. **Labor force:** agri. 30%, ind. 25%, services 45%.

Finance: Monetary unit: Rand (ZAR) (Sept. 2003: 7.27=1 U.S.). **GDP** (2002 est.): $432 bil. **Per capita GDP:** $10,000. **Imports** (2001): $28.1 bil.; partners (2001 est.): EU 41%, U.S. 11.4%, Saudi Arabia 7.3%, Japan 7%. **Exports** (2001 est.): $32.3 bil.; partners (2001 est.): EU 33%, U.S. 20%, Japan 6%, Mozambique 2.5%. **Tourism** (1999): $2.53 bil. **Budget** (2003) $24.7 bil. **Intl. reserves less gold:** $4.34 bil. **Gold:** 5.58 mil oz t. **Consumer prices:** 8.9%.

Transport: Railroad: Length: 12,666 mi. **Motor vehicles** (1999): 3.97 mil pass. cars, 2.25 mil comm. vehicles. **Civil aviation:** 11.82 bil pass.-mi; 143 airports. **Chief ports:** Durban, Cape Town, East London, Port Elizabeth.

Communications: TV sets: 138 per 1,000 pop. **Radios:** 355 per 1,000 pop. **Telephone lines:** 4,895,000. **Daily newspaper circ.:** 32 per 1,000 pop. **Internet:** 3,100,000 users.

Health: Life expectancy: 46.6 male; 46.5 female. **Births** (per 1,000 pop.): 18.9. **Deaths** (per 1,000 pop.): 18.4. **Natural inc.:** 0.05%. **Infant mortality** (per 1,000 live births): 60.8.

Education: Compulsory: ages 7-15. **Literacy:** 86.4%.

Major Intl. Organizations: UN (FAO, IBRD, ILO, IMF, IMO, WHO, WTrO), the Commonwealth, AU.

Embassy: 3051 Massachusetts Ave. NW 20008; 232-4400. **Website:** www.gov.za

Bushmen and Hottentots were the original inhabitants. Bantus, including Zulu, Xhosa, Swazi, and Sotho, had occupied the area from NE to S South Africa before the 17th century.

The Cape of Good Hope area was settled by Dutch, beginning in the 17th century. Britain seized the Cape in 1806. Many Dutch trekked north and founded 2 republics, Transvaal and Orange Free State. Diamonds were discovered, 1867, and gold, 1886. The Dutch (Boers) resented encroachments by the British and others; the Anglo-Boer War followed, 1899-1902. Britain won and, effective May 31, 1910, created the Union of South Africa, incorporating 2 British colonies (Cape and Natal) with Transvaal and Orange Free State. After a referendum, the Union became the Republic of South Africa, May 31, 1961, and withdrew from the Commonwealth.

With the election victory of Daniel Malan's National Party in 1948, the policy of separate development of the races, or apartheid, an already existing unofficially, became official. Under apartheid, blacks were severely restricted to certain occupations, and paid far lower wages than whites for similar work. Only whites could vote or run for public office. Persons of Asian Indian ancestry and those of mixed race (Coloureds) had limited political rights. In 1959 the government passed acts providing for the eventual creation of several Bantu nations, or Bantustans.

Protests against apartheid were brutally suppressed. At Sharpeville on Mar. 21, 1960, 69 black protesters were killed by government troops. At least 600 persons, mostly Bantus, were killed in 1976 riots protesting apartheid. In 1981, South Africa launched military operations in Angola and Mozambique to combat guerrilla groups.

A new constitution was approved by referendum, Nov. 1983, extending the parliamentary franchise to the Coloured and Asian minorities. Laws banning interracial sex and marriage were repealed in 1985.

In 1986, Nobel Peace Prize winner Bishop Desmond Tutu called for Western nations to apply sanctions against South Africa to force an end to apartheid. Pres. P. W. Botha announced in Apr. the end to the nation's system of racial pass laws and offered blacks an advisory role in government. On May 19, South Africa attacked 3 neighboring countries—Zimbabwe, Botswana, Zambia—to strike at guerrilla strongholds of the black nationalist African National Congress (ANC). A nationwide state of emergency was declared June 12, giving almost unlimited power to the security forces.

Some 2 million South African black workers staged a massive strike, June 6-8, 1988. Pres. Botha, head of the government since 1978, resigned Aug. 14, 1989, and was replaced by F. W. de Klerk. In 1990 the government lifted its ban on the ANC. Black nationalist leader Nelson Mandela was freed Feb. 11 after more than 27 years in prison. In Feb. 1991, Pres. de Klerk announced plans to end all apartheid laws.

In 1993 negotiators agreed on basic principles for a new democratic constitution. South Africa's partially self-governing black territories, or "homelands," were dissolved and incorporated into a national system of 9 provinces. In elections Apr. 26-29, 1994, the ANC won 62.7% of the vote, making Mandela president. The National Party won 20.4%. The Inkatha Freedom Party won 10.5% and control of the legislature in a mainly Zulu province. By then, fighting between the ANC and Inkatha (aided, during the apartheid era, by South African defense forces) had killed more than 14,000 people in the Zulu region since the mid-1980s.

In 1995, Mandela appointed a truth commission, led by Desmond Tutu, to document human rights abuses under apartheid. A post-apartheid constitution, modified to meet the objections of the Constitutional Court, became law Dec. 10, 1996, with provisions to take effect over a 3-year period.

The ANC won a landslide victory in elections held June 2, 1999. ANC leader Thabo Mbeki, Mandela's deputy president, thus became South Africa's 2d popularly elected president.

The UN recently estimated that about 5 million South Africans, including 20% of all adults, have HIV/AIDS. South Africa was the site, in July 2000, of an international AIDS conference. Pharmaceutical firms, Apr. 19, 2001, dropped their challenge to a 1997 law that allowed cheaper, generic versions of patented AIDS drugs to be imported. Johannesburg hosted the UN World Summit on Sustainable Development, Aug. 26-Sept. 4, 2002.

Spain
Kingdom of Spain

People: Population: 41,060,000. **Age distrib. (%):** <15: 14.5; 65+: 17.4. **Pop. density:** 213 per sq. mi. **Urban:** 78%. **Ethnic groups:** Castilian, Catalan, Basque, Galician. **Principal languages:** Castilian Spanish (official), Catalan, Galician, Basque. **Chief religion:** Roman Catholic 94%.

Geography: Area: 194,897 sq. mi. (total); 192,874 sq. mi. (land). **Location:** In SW Europe. **Neighbors:** Portugal on W, France on N. **Topography:** The interior is a high, arid plateau broken by mountain ranges and river valleys. The NW is heavily watered, the S has lowlands and a Mediterranean climate. **Capital:** Madrid. **Cities (urban agg.):** Madrid 3,969,000, (1998 city proper: 2,881,506); Barcelona 2,729,000; Valencia 754,000.

Government: Type: Constitutional monarchy. **Head of state:** King Juan Carlos I de Borbon y Borbon; b Jan. 5, 1938; in office: Nov. 22, 1975. **Head of gov.:** Prime Min. José María Aznar; b Feb. 25, 1953; in office: May 5, 1996. **Local divisions:** 17 autonomous communities. **Defense budget** (2002): $7.1 bil. **Active troops:** 177,950.

Economy: Industries: textiles & apparel, food & beverages, metals, chemicals, shipbuilding, autos, machine tools, tourism. **Chief crops:** grain, vegetables, olives, grapes, sugar beets, citrus. **Natural resources:** coal, lignite, iron ore, uranium, mercury, pyrites, fluorspar, gypsum, zinc, lead, tungsten, copper, kaolin, potash, hydropower. **Crude oil reserves** (2002): 21 mil. bbls. **Arable land:** 30%. **Livestock** (2002): cattle: 6.41 mil.; chickens: 128 mil.; goats: 3.11 mil.; pigs: 23.86 mil.; sheep: 24.30 mil. **Fish catch** (2002): 1,397,467 metric tons. **Electricity prod.** (2001): 222.55 bil. kWh. **Labor force:** services 64%, manufact., mining, and construct. 29%, agri. 7%.

Finance: Monetary unit: (EUR) (Sept. 2003: 0.92=1 U.S.) **GDP** (2002 est.): $828 bil. **Per capita GDP:** $20,700. **Imports** (2002): $156.6 bil.; partners: EU 63.9%, OPEC 7.3%, U.S. 4.6%, Japan 2.5%, Latin America 4.2%. **Exports** (2002 est.): $122.2 bil.; partners (2001): EU 71.3%, Latin America 6.1%, U.S. 4.4%. **Tourism:** $31 bil. **Budget** (2000 est.): $109 bil. **Intl. reserves less gold:** $25 bil. **Gold:** 16.83 mil oz t. **Consumer prices:** 3.1%.

Transport: Railroad: Length: 9,427 mi. **Motor vehicles** (1999): 16.85 mil pass. cars, 3.79 mil comm. vehicles. **Civil aviation:** 27.45 bil pass.-mi; 93 airports. **Chief ports:** Barcelona, Bilbao, Valencia, Cartagena.

Communications: TV sets: 555 per 1,000 pop. **Radios:** 331 per 1,000 pop. **Telephone lines:** 18,705,600. **Daily newspaper circ.:** 100 per 1,000 pop. **Internet:** 7,856,000 users.

Health: Life expectancy: 75.9 male; 82.8 female. **Births** (per 1,000 pop.): 10.1. **Deaths** (per 1,000 pop.): 9.5. **Natural inc.:** 0.06%. **Infant mortality** (per 1,000 live births): 4.5.

Education: Compulsory: ages 6-16. **Literacy:** 97.9%.

Major Intl. Organizations: UN and all of its specialized agencies, EU, NATO, OECD, OSCE.

Embassy: 2375 Pennsylvania Ave. NW 20037; 452-0100.

Website: www.spainemb.org/ingles/indexing.htm

Initially settled by Iberians, Basques, and Celts, Spain was successively ruled (wholly or in part) by Carthage, Rome, and the Visigoths. Muslims invaded Iberia from North Africa in 711. Reconquest of the peninsula by Christians from the N laid the foundations of modern Spain. In 1469 the kingdoms of Aragon and Castile were united by the marriage of Ferdinand II and Isabella I. Moorish rule ended with the fall of the kingdom of Granada, 1492. Spain's large Jewish community was expelled the same year.

Spain obtained a colonial empire with the "discovery" of America by Columbus, 1492, the conquest of Mexico by Cortes, and Peru by Pizarro. It also controlled the Netherlands and parts of Italy and Germany. Spain lost its American colonies in the early 19th century. It lost Cuba, the Philippines, and Puerto Rico during the Spanish-American War, 1898.

Primo de Rivera became dictator in 1923. King Alfonso XIII revoked the dictatorship, 1930, but was forced to leave the country in 1931. A republic was proclaimed, which disestablished the church, curtailed its privileges, and secularized education. During 1936-39 a Popular Front composed of socialists, Communists, republicans, and anarchists governed Spain.

Army officers under Francisco Franco revolted against the government, 1936. In a destructive 3-year war, in which some one million died, Franco received massive help and troops from Italy and Germany, while the USSR, France, and Mexico supported the republic. The war ended Mar. 28, 1939. Franco was named caudillo, leader of the nation. Spain was officially neutral in World War II, but its cordial relations with fascist countries caused its exclusion from the UN until 1955.

In July 1969, Franco and the Cortes (Parliament) designated Prince Juan Carlos as the future king and chief of state. After Franco's death, Nov. 20, 1975, Juan Carlos was sworn in as king. In free elections June 1977, moderates and democratic socialists emerged as the largest parties.

In 1981 a coup attempt by right-wing military officers was thwarted by the king. The Socialist Workers' Party, under Felipe González Márquez, won 4 consecutive general elections, from 1982 to 1993, but lost to a coalition of conservative and regional parties in the election of Mar. 3, 1996.

Catalonia and the Basque country were granted autonomy, Jan. 1980, following overwhelming approval in home-rule referendums. Basque extremists, however, have pushed for independence. The militant Basque separatist group ETA proclaimed a cease-fire as of Sept. 18, 1998, but announced an end to the truce Nov. 28, 1999. The Popular Party of conservative Prime Min. José María Aznar won a majority in the parliamentary election of Mar. 12, 2000. Aznar, going against Spanish public opinion, openly supported the U.S.-led invasion of Iraq, Mar. 2003.

The **Balearic Islands** in the W Mediterranean, 1,927 sq. mi., are a province of Spain; they include **Majorca** (Mallorca; capital Palma de Mallorca), **Minorca, Cabrera, Ibiza,** and **Formentera.** The **Canary Islands,** 2,807 sq. mi., in the Atlantic W of Morocco, form 2 provinces, and include the islands of **Tenerife, Palma, Gomera, Hierro, Grand Canary, Fuerteventura,** and **Lanzarote;**

Las Palmas and Santa Cruz are thriving ports. **Ceuta** and **Melilla,** small Spanish enclaves on Morocco's Mediterranean coast, gained limited autonomy in Sept. 1994.

Spain has sought the return of Gibraltar, in British hands since 1704.

Sri Lanka
Democratic Socialist Republic of Sri Lanka

People: Population: 19,065,000. **Age distrib.** (%): <15: 25.6; 65+: 6.7. **Pop. density:** 763 per sq. mi. **Urban:** 23%. **Ethnic groups:** Sinhalese 74%, Tamil 18%, Moor 7%. **Principal languages:** Sinhala, Tamil (both official); English. **Chief religions:** Buddhist 70%, Hindu 15%, Christian 8%, Muslim 7%.

Geography: Area: 25,332 sq. mi. (total); 24,996 sq. mi. (land). **Location:** In Indian O. off SE coast of India. **Neighbors:** India on NW. **Topography:** The coastal area and the northern half are flat; the S-central area is hilly and mountainous. **Capital:** Colombo: 681,000.

Government: Type: Republic. **Head of state:** Pres. Chandrika Bandaranaike Kumaratunga; b June 29, 1945; in office: Nov. 12, 1994. **Head of gov.:** Prime Min. Ranil Wickremesinghe; b Mar. 24, 1949; in office: Dec. 9, 2001. **Local divisions:** 8 provinces. **Defense budget** (2002): $645 mil. **Active troops:** 157,900.

Economy: Industries: rubber proc., tea & coconut prod., clothing, cement, oil refining, textiles, tobacco. **Chief crops:** rice, sugarcane, grains, oilseed, spices, tea, rubber. **Natural resources:** limestone, graphite, mineral sands, gems, phosphates, clay, hydropower. **Arable land:** 14%. **Livestock** (2002): cattle: 1.57 mil.; chickens: 10.66 mil.; goats: 492,600; pigs: 68,000; sheep: 12,000. **Fish catch** (2002): 288,010 metric tons. **Electricity prod.** (2001): 6.36 bil. kWh. **Labor force:** services 45%, agri. 38%, ind. 17%.

Finance: Monetary unit: Rupee (LKR) (Sept. 2003: 96.76=1 U.S.). **GDP** (2002 est.): $73.7 bil. **Per capita GDP:** $3,700. **Imports** (2001): $6 bil.; partners (2000): Japan 9%, India 8%, Hong Kong 7%, Singapore 7%. **Exports** (2001): $4.9 bil.; partners (2000): U.S. 39%, UK 13%, Middle East 8%, Germany 4%. **Tourism:** $253 mil. **Budget** (2001 est.): $4.1 bil. **Intl. reserves less gold:** $1.2 bil. **Gold:** 630,000 oz t. **Consumer prices:** 9.6%.

Transport: Railroad: Length: 909 mi. **Motor vehicles** (1999): 309,500 pass. cars, 227,100 comm. vehicles. **Civil aviation:** 3.20 bil pass.-mi; 14 airports. **Chief ports:** Colombo, Trincomalee, Galle.

Communications: TV sets: 102 per 1,000 pop. **Radios:** 211 per 1,000 pop. **Telephone lines:** 883,100. **Daily newspaper circ.:** 29 per 1,000 pop. **Internet:** 200,000 users.

Health: Life expectancy: 70.1 male; 75.3 female. **Births** (per 1,000 pop.): 16.1. **Deaths** (per 1,000 pop.): 6.5. **Natural inc.:** 0.97%. **Infant mortality** (per 1,000 live births): 15.2.

Education: Compulsory: ages 5-13. **Literacy:** 92.3%.

Major Intl. Organizations: UN (FAO, IBRD, ILO, IMF, IMO, WHO, WTrO), the Commonwealth.

Embassy: 2148 Wyoming Ave. NW 20008; 483-4025.

Website: www.slembassyusa.org

The island was known to the ancient world as Taprobane (Greek for copper-colored) and later as Serendip (from Arabic). Colonists from N India subdued the indigenous Veddahs about 543 BC; their descendants, the Buddhist Sinhalese, still form most of the population. Hindu descendants of Tamil immigrants from S India account for about one-fifth of the population.

Parts were occupied by the Portuguese in 1505 and the Dutch in 1658. The British seized the island in 1796. As Ceylon it became an independent member of the Commonwealth in 1948, and the Republic of Sri Lanka May 22, 1972.

Prime Min. W. R. D. Bandaranaike was assassinated Sept. 25, 1959. In new elections, the Freedom Party was victorious under Mrs. Sirimavo Bandaranaike, widow of the former prime minister. After May 1970 elections, Mrs. Bandaranaike became prime minister again. In 1971 the nation suffered economic problems and terrorist activities by ultra-leftists, thousands of whom were executed. Massive land reform and nationalization of foreign-owned plantations were undertaken in the mid-1970s. Mrs. Bandaranaike was ousted in 1977 elections. Presidential powers were increased in 1978 in an effort to restore stability.

Tensions between Sinhalese and Tamil separatists erupted into violence in the early 1980s. More than 64,000 died in the civil war, which continued through the late 1990s; another 20,000, mostly young Tamils, "disappeared" after they were taken into custody by government security forces.

Pres. Ranasinghe Premadasa was assassinated May 1, 1993, by a Tamil rebel. Mrs. Bandaranaike's daughter, Chandrika Bandaranaike Kumaratunga, became prime minister after the Aug. 16, 1994, general elections. Elected president Nov. 9, Kumaratunga appointed her mother prime minister. Kumaratunga, who was injured in a suicide bomb attack at a campaign rally Dec. 18, 1999, won a 2nd 6-year term 3 days later. In failing health, Mrs. Bandaranaike resigned Aug. 10 and died Oct. 10, 2000.

Facing a possible no-confidence motion, Pres. Kumaratunga suspended parliament July 10, 2001. Elections Dec. 5 resulted in a victory for the United National Party, headed by Ranil Wickremesinghe. A truce accord intended to bring an end to the 18-year-long civil war was signed Feb. 22, 2002. Severe monsoon flooding in the S and SW, May 2003, killed at least 265 people.

Sudan
Republic of the Sudan

People: Population: 33,610,000. **Age distrib.** (%): <15: 44.2; 65+: 2.2. **Pop. density:** 37 per sq. mi. **Urban:** 37%. **Ethnic groups:** Black 52%, Arab 39%, Beja 6%. **Principal languages:** Arabic (official), Nubian, Ta Bedawie; Nilotic, Sudanic dialects; English. **Chief religions:** Sunni Muslim 70%, indigenous beliefs 25%, Christian 5%.

Geography: Area: 967,498 sq. mi. (total); 917,378 sq. mi. (land). **Location:** At the E end of Sahara desert zone. **Neighbors:** Egypt on N; Libya, Chad, Central African Republic on W; Congo (formerly Zaire), Uganda, Kenya on S; Ethiopia, Eritrea on E. **Topography:** The N consists of the Libyan Desert in the W, and the mountainous Nubia Desert in E, with narrow Nile valley between. The center contains large, fertile, rainy areas with fields, pasture, and forest. The S has rich soil, heavy rain. **Capital:** Khartoum. **Cities (urban aggr.):** Khartoum 2,853,000; Omdurman (1993) 1,271,403.

Government: Type: Republic with strong military influence. **Head of state and gov.:** Pres. Gen. Omar Hassan Ahmad Al-Bashir; b Jan. 1, 1944; in office: June 30, 1989. **Local divisions:** 26 states. **Defense budget** (2002): $387 mil. **Active troops:** 117,000.

Economy: Industries: oil, cotton ginning, textiles, cement, edible oils, sugar. **Chief crops:** cotton, peanuts, sorghum, millet, wheat, gum arabic, sugarcane. **Natural resources:** oil, iron ore, copper, chromium ore, zinc, tungsten, mica, silver, gold, hydropower. **Crude oil reserves** (2002): 563 mil. bbls. **Arable land:** 5%. **Livestock** (2002): cattle: 38.33 mil.; chickens: 37.50 mil.; goats: 40 mil.; sheep: 47.04 mil. **Fish catch** (2002): 59,000 metric tons. **Electricity prod.** (2001): 2.39 bil. kWh. **Labor force:** agri. 80%, ind. and commerce 7%, government 13%.

Finance: Monetary unit: Dinar (SDD) (Sept. 2003: 259.99=1 U.S.). **GDP** (2002 est.): $52.9 bil. **Per capita GDP:** $1,420. **Imports** (2001): $1.6 bil.; partners (2000): China 12%, Saudi Arabia 10%, UK 10%, Germany 7%. **Exports** (2001 est.): $2.1 bil.; partners (2000): Japan 25%, China 19%, Saudi Arabia 14%, Germany 4%. **Tourism** (1999): $2 mil. **Budget** (2001 est.): $1.9 bil. **Intl. reserves less gold:** $324 mil. **Consumer prices** (change in 2001): 6.4%.

Transport: Railroad: Length: 3,725 mi. **Motor vehicles** (1995): 30,800 pass. cars, 35,900 comm. vehicles. **Civil aviation:** 430.6 bil. pass.-mi; 12 airports. **Chief port:** Port Sudan.

Communications: TV sets: 173 per 1,000 pop. **Radios:** 480 per 1,000 pop. **Telephone lines:** 671,800. **Daily newspaper circ.:** 27 per 1,000 pop. **Internet:** 84,000 users.

Health: Life expectancy: 56.6 male; 58.9 female. **Births** (per 1,000 pop.): 36.5. **Deaths** (per 1,000 pop.): 9.6. **Natural inc.:** 2.69%. **Infant mortality** (per 1,000 live births): 65.6.

Education: Compulsory: ages 6-14. **Literacy:** 61.1%.

Major Intl. Organizations: UN (FAO, IBRD, ILO, IMF, IMO, WHO), AL, AU.

Embassy: 2210 Massachusetts Ave. NW 20008; 338-8565.

Website: www.sudanembassy.org

Northern Sudan, ancient Nubia, was settled by Egyptians in antiquity. The population was converted to Coptic Christianity in the 6th century. Arab conquests brought Islam to the area in the 15th century.

In the 1820s Egypt took over Sudan, defeating the last of earlier empires, including the Fung. In the 1880s a revolution was led by Muhammad Ahmad, who called himself the Mahdi (leader of the faithful), and his followers, the dervishes.

In 1898 an Anglo-Egyptian force crushed the Mahdi's successors. In 1951 the Egyptian Parliament abrogated its 1899 and 1936 treaties with Great Britain and amended its constitution to provide for a separate Sudanese constitution. Sudan voted for complete independence effective Jan. 1, 1956.

In 1969, a Revolutionary Council took power, but a civilian premier and cabinet were appointed; the government announced it would create a socialist state

Economic problems plagued the nation in the 1980s and 1990s, aggravated by civil war and influxes of refugees from neighboring countries. After 16 years in power, Pres. Jaafar al-Nimeiry was overthrown in a bloodless coup, Apr. 6, 1985. Sudan held its first democratic parliamentary elections in 18 years in 1986, but the elected government was overthrown in a bloodless coup June 30, 1989.

In the mid-1980s, rebels in the south (populated largely by black Christians and followers of tribal religions) took up arms against government domination by northern Sudan, mostly Arab-Muslim. War and related famine cost an estimated 2 million lives and displaced millions of southerners. In 1993, Amnesty International accused Sudan of "ethnic cleansing" against the Nuba people in the South. A preliminary peace pact was signed July 20, 2002, but talks broke off Sept. 2; another truce accord was reached Oct. 15.

A new constitution based on Islamic law took effect June 30, 1998. On Aug. 20, in retaliation for bombings in Kenya and Tanzania, U.S. missiles destroyed a Khartoum pharmaceutical plant the U.S. alleged was associated with terrorist activities; independent inquiries later cast some doubt on the U.S. claim. Embroiled in a power struggle, Pres. Omar Hassan Ahmad Al-Bashir dissolved

parliament and declared a state of emergency Dec. 12, 1999. The main opposition parties boycotted presidential and legislative elections Dec. 13-22, 2000, won by Bashir.

Suriname
Republic of Suriname

People: Population: 436,000. **Age distrib.** (%): <15: 31.1; 65+: 5.8. **Pop. density:** 7 per sq. mi. **Urban:** 75%. **Ethnic groups:** East Indians 37%, Creole 31%, Javanese 15%, Maroons 10%, Amerindian 2%, Chinese 2%, White 1%. **Principal languages:** Dutch (official), English, Sranang Tongo (an English Creole), Hindustani, Javanese. **Chief religions:** Hindu 27%, Protestant 25%, Roman Catholic 23%, Muslim 20%.

Geography: Area: 63,039 sq. mi. (total); 62,344 sq. mi. (land). **Location:** On N shore of South America. **Neighbors:** Guyana on W, Brazil on S, French Guiana on E. **Topography:** A flat Atlantic coast, where dikes permit agriculture. Inland is a forest belt; to the S, largely unexplored hills cover 75% of the country. **Capital:** Paramaribo: 240,000.

Government: Type: Republic. **Head of state and gov.:** Pres. Runaldo Ronald Venetiaan; b June 18, 1936; in office: Aug. 12, 2000. **Local divisions:** 10 districts. **Defense budget** (2002): $9.2 mil. **Active troops:** 1,840.

Economy: Industries: mining, oil, lumber, food proc., fishing. **Chief crops:** rice, bananas, palm kernels, coconuts, plantains, peanuts. **Natural resources:** timber, hydropower, fish, kaolin, shrimp, bauxite, gold, nickel, copper, platinum, iron ore. **Crude oil reserves** (2002): 74 mil. bbls. **Livestock** (2002): cattle: 136,000; chickens: 3.90 mil.; goats: 7,000; pigs: 24,000; sheep: 8,000. **Fish catch** (2002): 19,337 metric tons. **Electricity prod.** (2001): 1.96 bil. kWh.

Finance: Monetary unit: Guilder (SRG) (Sept. 2003: 2502.40=1 U.S.). **GDP** (2002 est.): $1.5 bil. **Per capita GDP:** $3,500. **Imports** (1999): $525 mil.; partners (1999): U.S. 35%, Netherlands 15%, Trinidad and Tobago 12%, Japan. **Exports** (2000): $399 mil.; partners (1999): U.S. 23%, Norway 19%, Netherlands 11%. **Tourism** (1999): $53 mil. **Budget** (1997 est.): $403 mil. **Intl. reserves less gold:** $78 mil. **Gold:** 20,000 mil. oz t. **Consumer prices** (change in 1999): 98.9%.

Transport: Railroad: Length: 103 mi. **Motor vehicles:** 61,400 pass. cars, 23,500 comm. vehicles. **Civil aviation:** 451.1 bil pass.-mi; 5 airports. **Chief ports:** Paramaribo, New Nickerie, Albina.

Communications: TV sets: 241 per 1,000 pop. **Radios:** 728 per 1,000 pop. **Telephone lines:** 77,400. **Daily newspaper circ.:** 67.6 per 1,000 pop. **Internet:** 14,500 users.

Health: Life expectancy: 66.8 male; 71.8 female. **Births** (per 1,000 pop.): 19.4. **Deaths** (per 1,000 pop.): 6.8. **Natural inc.:** 1.26%. **Infant mortality** (per 1,000 live births): 24.7.

Education: Compulsory: ages 7-12. **Literacy** (2002): 93%.

Major Intl. Organizations: UN (FAO, IBRD, ILO, IMF, IMO, WHO, WTrO), Caricom, OAS.

Embassy: 4301 Connecticut Ave., Suite 460, NW 20008; 244-7488.

Website: www.surinameembassy.org

The Netherlands acquired Suriname in 1667 from Britain, in exchange for New Netherlands (New York). The 1954 Dutch constitution raised the colony to a level of equality with the Netherlands and the Netherlands Antilles. Independence was granted Nov. 25, 1975, despite objections from East Indians. Some 40% of the population (mostly East Indians) immigrated to the Netherlands in the months before independence.

The National Military Council took control of the government, Feb. 1982. Civilian rule was restored in 1987, but political turmoil continued until 1992, disrupting the nation's economy.

Swaziland
Kingdom of Swaziland

People: Population: 1,077,000. **Age distrib.** (%): <15: 45.5; 65+: 2.6. **Pop. density:** 162 per sq. mi. **Urban:** 27%. **Ethnic groups:** African 97%, European 3% **Principal languages:** English, siSwati (both official). **Chief religions:** Christian 60%, Muslim 10%, indigenous and other 30%.

Geography: Area: 6,704 sq. mi. (total); 6,642 sq. mi. (land). **Location:** In southern Africa, near Indian O. coast. **Neighbors:** South Africa on N, W, S; Mozambique on E. **Topography:** The country descends from W-E in broad belts, becoming more arid in the low veld region, then rising to a plateau in the E. **Capitals:** Mbabane (administrative), Lobamba (legislative). **Cities (urban aggr.):** Mbabane: 80,000.

Government: Type: Constitutional monarchy. **Head of state:** King Mswati III; b Apr. 19, 1968; in office: Apr. 25, 1986. **Head of gov.:** Prime Min. Barnabas Sibusiso Dlamini; b May 15, 1942; in office: July 26, 1996. **Local divisions:** 4 districts.

Economy: Industries: coal mining, pulp, sugar, soft drinks, textiles, apparel. **Chief crops:** sugarcane, cotton, corn, tobacco, rice, citrus. **Natural resources:** asbestos, coal, clay, cassiterite, hydropower, timber, gold, diamonds, quarry stone, talc. **Arable land:** 11%. **Livestock** (2002): cattle: 615,000; chickens: 3.20 mil.; goats: 445,000; pigs: 34,000; sheep: 32,000. **Fish catch** (2002 est.): 142 metric tons. **Electricity prod.** (2001): 0.35 bil. kWh. **Labor force:** private sector: 70%, public sector: 30%.

Finance: Monetary unit: Lilangeni (SZL) (Sept. 2003: 7.35=1 U.S.). **GDP** (2002 est.): $4.8 bil. **Per capita GDP:** $4,400. **Imports** (2001): $850 mil.; partners (2000): South Africa 89%, EU 5%, Japan 2%, Singapore 2%. **Exports** (2001): $702 mil.; partners (1999): South Africa 72%, EU 12%, UK 6%, Mozambique 4%. **Tourism** (1999): $35 mil. **Budget** (2002 est.): $506.9 mil. **Intl. reserves less gold:** $203 mil. **Consumer prices** (changes in 2001): 5.9%.

Transport: Railroad: Length: 185 mi. **Motor vehicles** (1997): 31,900 pass. cars, 39,700 comm. vehicles. **Civil aviation:** 8.1 mil pass.-mi; 1 airport.

Communications: TV sets: 112 per 1,000 pop. **Radios:** 168 per 1,000 pop. **Telephone lines:** 35,100. **Daily newspaper circ.:** 17 per 1,000 pop. **Internet:** 20,000 users.

Health: Life expectancy: 41.0 male; 37.9 female. **Births** (per 1,000 pop.): 29.4. **Deaths** (per 1,000 pop.): 21.1. **Natural inc.:** 0.83%. **Infant mortality** (per 1,000 live births): 67.4.

Education: Compulsory: ages 6-12. **Literacy:** 81.6%.

Major Intl. Organizations: UN (FAO, IBRD, ILO, IMF, WHO, WTrO), the Commonwealth, AU.

Embassy: 3400 International Dr. NW 20008; 362-6683.

Website: www.gov.sz

The royal house of Swaziland traces back 400 years, and is one of Africa's last ruling dynasties. The Swazis, a Bantu people, were driven to Swaziland from lands to the N by the Zulus in 1820. Their autonomy was later guaranteed by Britain and Transvaal (later part of South Africa), with Britain assuming control after 1903. Independence came Sept. 6, 1968. In 1973 the king repealed the constitution and assumed full powers.

A new constitution banning political parties took effect Oct. 13, 1978. A shrinking economy and the AIDS crisis have fueled student and labor unrest in recent years. The UN has estimated that about 33% of the adult population has HIV/AIDS.

Sweden
Kingdom of Sweden

People: Population: 8,876,000. **Age distrib.** (%): <15: 18; 65+: 17.3. **Pop. density:** 56 per sq. mi. **Urban:** 83%. **Ethnic groups:** Swedish 89%, Finnish 2%; Sami and others 9%. **Principal languages:** Swedish (official), Sami, Finnish. **Chief religion:** Lutheran 87%.

Geography: Area: 173,732 sq. mi. (total); 158,662 sq. mi. (land). **Location:** On Scandinavian Peninsula in N Europe. **Neighbors:** Norway on W, Denmark on S (across Kattegat), Finland on E. **Topography:** Mountains along NW border cover 25% of Sweden, flat or rolling terrain covers the central and southern areas, which include several large lakes. **Capital:** Stockholm. **Cities (urban aggr.):** Stockholm 1,626,000; Göteborg 778,000.

Government: Type: Constitutional monarchy. **Head of state:** King Carl XVI Gustaf; b Apr. 30, 1946; in office: Sept. 19, 1973. **Head of gov.:** Prime Min. Goran Persson; b June 20, 1949; in office: Mar. 21, 1996. **Local divisions:** 21 counties. **Defense budget** (2002): $4.5 bil. **Active troops:** 33,900.

Economy: Industries: iron & steel, precision equip., wood & paper products, proc. foods, autos. **Chief crops:** barley, wheat, sugar beets. **Natural resources:** zinc, iron ore, lead, copper, silver, timber, uranium, hydropower. **Arable land:** 7%. **Livestock** (2002): cattle: 1.64 mil.; chickens: 7.40 mil.; goats: 1.88 mil.; sheep: 427,000. **Fish catch** (2002): 318,589 metric tons. **Electricity prod.** (2001): 152.91 bil. kWh. **Labor force:** agri. 2%, ind. 24%, services 74%.

Finance: Monetary unit: Krona (SEK) (Sept. 2003: 8.43=1 U.S.). **GDP** (2002 est.): $227.4 bil. **Per capita GDP:** $25,400. **Imports** (2002): $68.6 bil.; partners (2001): EU 66.3%, , Norway 8.5%, U.S. 6.7%. **Exports** (2002 est.): $80.6 bil.; partners (2001): EU 54.6%, U.S. 10.5%, Norway 8.6%. **Tourism:** $4.11 bil. **Budget** (2001 est.): $110 bil. **Intl. reserves less gold:** $12.6 bil. **Gold:** 5.96 mil oz t. **Consumer prices:** 2.2%.

Transport: Railroad: Length: 7,967 mi. **Motor vehicles:** 4.0 mil pass. cars, 388,600 comm. vehicles. **Civil aviation:** 6.59 bil pass.-mi; 145 airports. **Chief ports:** Göteborg, Stockholm, Malmö.

Communications: TV sets: 551 per 1,000 pop. **Radios:** 932 per 1,000 pop. **Telephone lines:** 6,441,000. **Daily newspaper circ.:** 430.4 per 1,000 pop. **Internet:** 5,125,000 users.

Health: Life expectancy: 77.3 male; 82.8 female. **Births** (per 1,000 pop.): 9.7. **Deaths** (per 1,000 pop.): 10.6. **Natural inc.:** -0.09%. **Infant mortality** (per 1,000 live births): 3.4.

Education: Compulsory: ages 7-16. **Literacy** (2002): 100%.

Major Intl. Organizations: UN and all of its specialized agencies, EU, OECD, OSCE.

Embassy: 1501 M St. NW 20005; 467-2600.

Website: www.swedish-embassy.org

The Swedes have lived in present-day Sweden for at least 5,000 years, longer than nearly any other European people. Gothic tribes from Sweden played a major role in the disintegration of the Roman Empire. Other Swedes helped create the first Russian state in the 9th century.

The Swedes were Christianized from the 11th century, and a strong centralized monarchy developed. A parliament, the Riksdag, was first called in 1435, the earliest parliament on the European continent, with all classes of society represented.

Swedish independence from rule by Danish kings (dating from 1397) was secured by Gustavus I in a revolt, 1521-23; he built up the government and military and established the Lutheran Church. In the 17th century Sweden was a major European power, gaining most of the Baltic seacoast, but its international position subsequently declined.

The Napoleonic wars, 1799-1815, in which Sweden acquired Norway (it became independent 1905), were the last in which Sweden participated. Armed neutrality was maintained in both world wars.

More than 4 decades of Social Democratic rule ended in the 1976 parliamentary elections; the party returned to power in the 1982 elections. After Prime Min. Olof Palme was shot to death in Stockholm, Feb. 28, 1986, Ingvar Carlsson took office. Carl Bildt, a non-Socialist, became prime minister Oct. 1991, with a mandate to restore Sweden's economic competitiveness. The Social Democrats returned to power following 1994 elections.

Swedish voters approved membership in the European Union Nov. 13, 1994, and Sweden entered the EU as of Jan. 1, 1995. Carlsson retired and was succeeded by Goran Persson in Mar. 1996. Persson and his Social Democrats led coalition governments after the elections of Sept. 20, 1998, and Sept. 15, 2002. Foreign Min. Anna Lindh died Sept. 11, 2003, after being stabbed in a Stockholm department store. Swedish voters Sept. 14 rejected adoption of the euro currency.

Switzerland
Swiss Confederation

People: Population: 7,169,000. **Age distrib.** (%): <15: 16.8; 65+: 15.5. **Pop. density:** 467 per sq. mi. **Urban:** 68%. **Ethnic groups:** German 65%, French 18%, Italian 10%, Romansch 1%. **Principal languages:** German, French, Italian (all official); Romansch (semi-official). **Chief religions:** Roman Catholic 46%, Protestant 40%.

Geography: Area: 15,942 sq. mi. (total); 15,355 sq. mi. (land). **Location:** In the Alps Mts. in central Europe. **Neighbors:** France on W, Italy on S, Austria on E, Germany on N. **Topography:** The Alps cover 60% of the land area; the Jura, near France, 10%. Running between, from NE to SW, are midlands, 30%. **Capitals:** Bern (administrative), Lausanne (judicial). **Cities (urban aggr.):** Zurich 939,000; Basel 166,700; Geneva 398,910; Bern 316,000.

Government: Type: Federal republic. **Head of state and gov.:** The president is elected by the Federal Assembly to a nonrenewable 1-year term. **Local divisions:** 20 full cantons, 6 half cantons. **Defense budget** (2002): $3.3 bil. **Active troops:** 3,500.

Economy: Industries: machinery, chemicals, watches, textiles, precision instruments. **Chief crops:** grains, fruits, vegetables. **Natural resources:** hydropower, timber, salt. **Arable land:** 10%. **Livestock** (2002): cattle: 1.59 mil.; chickens: 7.16 mil.; goats: 67,500; pigs: 1.54 mil.; sheep: 441,000. **Fish catch** (2002): 2,850 metric tons. **Electricity prod.** (2001): 68.68 bil. kWh. **Labor force:** services 69.1%, ind. 26.3%, agri. 4.6%.

Finance: Monetary unit: Franc (CHF) (Sept. 2003: 1.42=1 U.S.). **GDP** (2002 est.): $231 bil. **Per capita GDP:** $31,700. **Imports** (2002): $94.4 bil.; partners (2001): EU 79.9%, U.S. 5.1%. **Exports** (2002 est.): $100.3 bil.; partners (2001): EU 61%, U.S. 10.6%, Japan 3.9%. **Tourism:** $7.3 bil. **Budget** (2001 est.): $30 bil. **Intl. reserves less gold:** $29.54 bil. **Gold:** 61.62 mil oz t. **Consumer prices:** 0.6%.

Transport: Railroad: Length: 2,738 mi. **Motor vehicles:** 3.55 mil pass. cars, 318,800 comm. vehicles. **Civil aviation:** 20.70 bil pass.-mi; 41 airports. **Chief port:** Basel.

Communications: TV sets: 457 per 1,000 pop. **Radios:** 979 per 1,000 pop. **Telephone lines:** 5,335,000. **Daily newspaper circ.:** 369.6 per 1,000 pop. **Internet:** 2,375,000 users.

Health: Life expectancy: 77.1 male; 83.0 female. **Births** (per 1,000 pop.): 9.6. **Deaths** (per 1,000 pop.): 8.8. **Natural inc.:** 0.08%. **Infant mortality** (per 1,000 live births): 4.4.

Education: Compulsory: ages 7-15. **Literacy** (1994): 100%.

Major Intl. Organizations: UN and most of its specialized agencies, EFTA, OECD, OSCE.

Embassy: 2900 Cathedral Ave. NW 20008; 745-7900.

Websites: www.eda.admin.ch/eda/e/home.ht
www.myswitzer land.com

Switzerland, the former Roman province of Helvetia, traces its modern history to 1291, when 3 cantons created a defensive league. Other cantons were subsequently admitted to the Swiss Confederation, which obtained its independence from the Holy Roman Empire through the Peace of Westphalia (1648). The cantons were joined under a federal constitution in 1848, with large powers of local control retained by each.

Switzerland has maintained an armed neutrality since 1815, and has not been involved in a foreign war since 1515. It is the seat of many UN and other international agencies but did not become a full member of the UN until Sept. 10, 2002.

Switzerland is a world banking center. In an effort to crack down on criminal transactions, the nation's strict bank-secrecy rules have been eased since 1990. Stung by charges that assets seized by the Nazis and deposited in Swiss banks in World War II had not been properly returned, the government announced, March 5, 1997, a $4.7 billion fund to compensate victims of the Holocaust and other catastrophies. Swiss banks agreed Aug. 12, 1998, to pay $1.25 billion in reparations. Abortion was decriminalized by a June 2, 2002 referendum.

Syria
Syrian Arab Republic

People: Population: 17,800,000. **Age distrib.** (%): <15: 39.3; 65+: 3.2. **Pop. density:** 250 per sq. mi. **Urban:** 52%. **Ethnic groups:** Arab 90%, Kurds, Armenians, and other 10%. **Principal languages:** Arabic (official); Kurdish, Armenian. **Chief religions:** Sunni Muslim 74%, other Muslims 16%, Christian 10%.

Geography: Area: 71,498 sq. mi. (total); 71,062 sq. mi. (land). **Location:** Middle East, at E end of Mediterranean Sea. **Neighbors:** Lebanon and Israel on W, Jordan on S, Iraq on E, Turkey on N. **Topography:** Syria has a short Mediterranean coastline, then stretches E and S with fertile lowlands and plains, alternating with mountains and large desert areas. **Capital:** Damascus. **Cities (urban aggr.):** Damascus 2,195,000; Aleppo 2,229,000; Homs 811,000.

Government: Type: Republic (under military regime). **Head of state:** Pres. Bashar al-Assad; b Sept. 1965; in office: July 17, 2000. **Head of gov.:** Prime Min. Muhammad Naji al-Otari; in office: Sept. 10, 2003. **Local divisions:** 14 provinces. **Defense budget** (2002): $1.0 bil. **Active troops:** 319,000.

Economy: Industries: oil, textiles, food proc., beverages, tobacco, phosphate mining. **Chief crops:** wheat, barley, cotton, lentils, chickpeas, olives, sugar beets. **Natural resources:** oil, phosphates, chrome, manag., asphalt, iron ore, salt, marble, gypsum, hydropower. **Crude oil reserves** (2002): 2.5 bil. bbls. **Arable land:** 28%. **Livestock** (2002): cattle: 900,000; chickens: 22.50 mil.; goats: 1.08 mil.; pigs: 770; sheep: 13 mil. **Fish catch** (2002): 14,171 metric tons. **Electricity prod.** (2001): 23.26 bil. kWh. **Labor force:** agri. 40%, ind. 20%, services 40%.

Finance: Monetary unit: Pound (SYP) (Sept. 2003: 47.82=1 U.S.). **GDP** (2002 est.): $59.4 bil. **Per capita GDP:** $3,500. **Imports** (2001): $4 bil.; partners (2000 est.): Italy 9%, Germany 7%, France 5%, Lebanon 5%. **Exports** (2001): $5 bil.; partners (2000 est.): Germany 27%, Italy 12%, France 10%, Turkey 10%. **Tourism:** $474 mil. **Budget** (2002 est.): $7 bil. **Gold:** 830,000 oz t. **Consumer prices** (change in 2001): 0.4%.

Transport: Railroad: Length: 1,709 mi. **Motor vehicles** (1999): 180,700 pass. cars, 313,500 comm. vehicles. **Civil aviation:** 799.7 bil pass.-mi; 24 airports. **Chief ports:** Latakia, Tartus.

Communications: TV sets: 68 per 1,000 pop. **Radios:** 278 per 1,000 pop. **Telephone lines:** 1,710,000. **Daily newspaper circ.:** 20 per 1,000 pop. **Internet:** 60,000 users.

Health: Life expectancy: 68.2 male; 70.7 female. **Births** (per 1,000 pop.): 29.5. **Deaths** (per 1,000 pop.): 5.0. **Natural inc.:** 2.45%. **Infant mortality** (per 1,000 live births): 31.7.

Education: Compulsory: ages 6-11. **Literacy:** 76.9%.

Major Intl. Organizations: UN (FAO, IBRD, ILO, IMF, IMO, WHO), AL.

Embassy: 2215 Wyoming Ave. NW 20008; 232-6313.
Website: www.syria-net.com

Syria was the center of the Seleucid empire, but later became absorbed in the Roman and Arab empires. Ottoman rule prevailed for 4 centuries, until the end of World War I.

The state of Syria was formed from former Turkish districts, separated by the Treaty of Sevres, 1920, and divided into the states of Syria and Greater Lebanon. Both were administered under a French League of Nations mandate 1920-1941.

Syria was proclaimed a republic by the occupying French Sept. 16, 1941, and exercised full independence Apr. 17, 1946. Syria joined the Arab invasion of Israel in 1948.

Syria joined Egypt Feb. 1958 in the United Arab Republic but seceded Sept. 1961. The Socialist Baath party and military leaders seized power Mar. 1963. The Baath, a pan-Arab organization, became the only legal party. The government has been dominated by the Alawite minority.

In the Arab-Israeli war of June 1967, Israel seized and occupied the Golan Heights, from which Syria had shelled Israeli settlements. On Oct. 6, 1973, Syria joined Egypt in an attack on Israel. Syrian troops entered Lebanon in 1976, during the Lebanese civil war and remained a strong presence in the country. They fought Palestinian guerrillas and, later, Christian militiamen. Syria sided with Iran during the Iran-Iraq war, 1980-88.

Following Israel's invasion of Lebanon, June 6, 1982, Israeli planes destroyed 17 Syrian antiaircraft missile batteries in the Bekaa Valley, June 9. Some 25 Syrian planes were downed during the engagement. Israel and Syria agreed to a cease-fire June 11. Syria's role in promoting international terrorism led to strained relations with the U.S. and Great Britain.

Syria condemned the Aug. 1990 Iraqi invasion of Kuwait and sent troops to help Allied forces in the Gulf War. In 1991, Syria accepted U.S. proposals for the terms of an Arab-Israeli peace conference. Syria subsequently participated in negotiations with Israel, but progress toward peace was slow.

Former Prime Min. Mahmoud Al-Zoubi killed himself May 21, 2000, after being charged with corruption. Hafez al-Assad, president of Syria since 1971, died June 10, 2000, and was succeeded by his son Bashar al-Assad. Following the invasion of Iraq, Mar. 2003, the U.S. pressured Syria to rein in extremist groups and deny safe haven to fugitive Iraqi leaders. The Syrian troop presence in Lebanon was subsequently reduced to 15,000 from about 35,000.

Taiwan
Republic of China

People: Population: 22,603,000. **Age distrib.** (%): <15: 21; 65+: 9. **Pop. density:** 1,815 per sq. mi. **Urban:** 75%. **Ethnic groups:** Taiwanese 84%, mainland Chinese 14%, Aborigine 2%. **Principal languages:** Mandarin Chinese (official), Taiwanese (Min), Hakka dialects. **Chief religions:** Buddhist, Confucian, and Taoist 93%; Christian 5%.

Geography: Area: 13,892 sq. mi. (total); 12,456 sq. mi. (land). **Location:** Off SE coast of China, between East and South China seas. **Neighbors:** Nearest is China. **Topography:** A mountain range forms the backbone of the island; the eastern half is very steep and craggy, the western slope is flat, fertile, and well cultivated. **Capital:** Taipei. **Cities (urban aggr., 1997 est.):** Taipei 2,595,699; Kaohsiung 1,434,907; Taichung 881,870.

Government: Type: Democracy. **Head of state:** Pres. Chen Shui-bian; b 1950; in office: May 20, 2000. **Head of gov.:** Prime Min. Yu Shyi-kun; b Apr. 25, 1948; in office: Feb. 1, 2002. **Local divisions:** 16 counties, 5 municipalities, 2 special municipalities (Taipei, Kaohsiung). **Defense budget** (2002): $7.0 bil. **Active troops:** 370,000.

Economy: Industries: electronics, oil refining, chemicals, textiles, iron & steel, machinery, cement, food proc. **Chief crops:** rice, corn, vegetables, fruit, tea. **Natural resources:** coal, nat. gas, limestone, marble, asbestos. **Crude oil reserves** (2002): 4 mil. bbls. **Arable land:** 24%. **Fish catch** (1997): 1.04 mil metric tons. **Electricity prod.** (2001): 151.11 bil. kWh. **Labor force:** services 58%, ind. 35%, agri. 7%.

Finance: Monetary unit: Dollar (TWD) (Sept. 2003: 34.17=1 U.S.). **GDP** (2002 est.): $406 bil. **Per capita GDP:** $18,000. **Imports** (2001): $109 bil.; partners (2000): Japan 27.5%, U.S. 17.9%, Europe 13.6%. South Korea 6.4%. **Exports** (2001): $122 bil.; partners (2000): U.S. 23.5%, Hong Kong 21.1%, Europe 16%, ASEAN 12.2%. **Tourism** (1999): $3.57 bil. **Budget** (2002) $36.1 bil.

Transport: Railroad: Length: 688 mi. **Motor vehicles** (1997): 4.40 mil pass. cars, 833,545 comm. vehicles. **Civil aviation:** 22.8 bil pass.-mi; 37 airports. **Chief ports:** Kaohsiung, Chilung (Keelung), Hualien, Taichung.

Communications: TV sets: 327 per 1,000 pop. **Radios:** 402 per 1,000 pop. **Telephone lines:** 13,099,400. **Daily newspaper circ.:** 20.2 per 1,000 pop. **Internet:** 8,590,000 users.

Health: Life expectancy: 74.1 male; 79.9 female. **Births** (per 1,000 pop.): 12.7. **Deaths** (per 1,000 pop.): 6.2. **Natural inc.:** 0.65%. **Infant mortality** (per 1,000 live births): 6.7.

Education: Free, compulsory: ages 6-15. **Literacy** (1998): 94%.

Major Intl. Organizations: APEC.
Embassy: 4201 Wisconsin Avenue NW 20016; 202-895-1800
Website: www.taiwan.gov.tw/ENGLISH/

Large-scale Chinese immigration began in the 17th century. The island came under mainland control after an interval of Dutch rule, 1620-62. Taiwan (also called Formosa) was ruled by Japan 1895-1945. Two million Kuomintang supporters fled to the island in 1949, establishing Taiwan as the seat of the Republic of China. The U.S., upon recognizing the People's Republic of China, Dec. 15, 1978, severed diplomatic ties with Taiwan. The U.S. and Taiwan maintain contact via quasi-official agencies.

Land reform, government planning, U.S. aid and investment, and free universal education brought huge advances in industry, agriculture, and living standards. In 1987 martial law was lifted after 38 years, and in 1991 the 43-year period of emergency rule ended. Taiwan held its first direct presidential election Mar. 23, 1996. An earthquake on Sept. 21, 1999, killed more than 2,300 people and injured thousands more. Five decades of Nationalist Party rule ended with the presidential election of Mar. 18, 2000, won by Chen Shui-bian, leader of the pro-independence Democratic Progressive Party.

Both the Taipei and Beijing governments long considered Taiwan an integral part of China, although Taiwanese officials appeared to signal a departure from that policy in July 1999. Taiwan has resisted Beijing's efforts at reunification, including military pressure, even as investment ties with mainland China have expanded. On Jan. 26, 2003, for the 1st time since 1949, a commercial passenger flight originating in Taiwan made a scheduled landing on the mainland. Taiwan has one of the world's strongest economies and is among the 10 leading capital exporters.

A SARS epidemic killed 180 people, Feb.-June 2003.

The **Penghu Isls.** (Pescadores), 49 sq. mi., pop. (1996 est.) 90,142, lie between Taiwan and the mainland. **Quemoy** and **Matsu,** pop. (1996 est.) 53,286, lie just off the mainland.

Tajikistan
Republic of Tajikistan

People: Population: 6,245,000. **Age distrib.** (%): <15: 40.4; 65+: 4.7. **Pop. density:** 113 per sq. mi. **Urban:** 28%. **Ethnic groups:** Tajik 65%, Uzbek 25%, Russian 4%. **Principal languages:** Tajik (official), Russian. **Chief religions:** Sunni Muslim 85%, Shi'a Muslim 5%.

Geography: Area: 55,251 sq. mi. (total); 55,097 sq. mi. (land). **Location:** Central Asia. **Neighbors:** Uzbekistan on N and W, Kyrgyzstan on N, China on E, Afghanistan on S. **Topography:** Mountainous region that contains the Pamirs, Trans-Alai mountain system. **Capital:** Dushanbe: 522,000.

Government: Type: Republic. **Head of state:** Pres. Imomali Rakhmonov; b Oct. 5, 1952; in office: Nov. 19, 1994. **Head of gov.:** Akil Akilov; b 1944; in office: Dec. 20, 1999. **Local divisions:** 2 viloyats, 1 autonomous viloyat. **Defense budget** (2002): $14.8 mil. **Active troops:** 6,000.

Economy: Industries: metals, chemicals & fertilizers, cement, vegetable oil, machine tools. **Chief crops:** cotton, grain, fruits, grapes, vegetables. **Natural resources:** hydropower, oil, uranium, mercury, lignite, lead, zinc, antimony, tungsten, silver, gold. **Crude oil reserves** (2002): 12 mil. bbls. **Arable land:** 6%. **Livestock** (2002): cattle: 1.10 mil.; chickens: 1 mil.; goats: 625,300; pigs: 500; sheep: 1.69 mil. **Fish catch (2002): 236 metric tons. Electricity prod.** (2001): 14.18 bil. kWh. **Labor force:** agri. 67.2%, ind. 7.5%, services 25.3%.

Finance: Monetary unit: Somoni (TJS) (Sept. 2003: 3.23=1 U.S.). **GDP** (2002 est.): $8 bil. **Per capita GDP:** $1,250. **Imports** (2001): $700 mil.; partners (2000): Uzbekistan 27%, Russia 16%, Europe 12%. **Exports** (2001 est.): $640 mil.; partners (2000): Europe 43%, Russia 30%, Uzbekistan 13%. **Budget** (2002) $520 mil.

Transport: Railroad: Length: 300 mi. **Motor vehicles:** 117,100 pass. cars, 16,800 comm. vehicles. **Civil aviation:** 142.3 mil pass.-mi; 13 airport.

Communications: TV sets: 328 per 1,000 pop. **Radios:** 143 per 1,000 pop. **Telephone lines:** 232,700. **Daily newspaper circ.:** 20 per 1,000 pop. **Internet:** 3,500 users

Health: Life expectancy: 61.4 male; 67.5 female. **Births** (per 1,000 pop.): 32.8. **Deaths** (per 1,000 pop.): 8.5. **Natural inc.:** 2.43%. **Infant mortality** (per 1,000 live births): 113.4.

Education: Compulsory: ages 7-16. **Literacy:** 99.4%.

Major International Organizations: UN (FAO, IBRD, ILO, IMF, WHO), CIS, OSCE.

Website: www.tajikistan.tajnet.com/english/index.html

There were settled societies in the region from about 3000 BC. Throughout history, it has undergone invasions by Iranians (Arabs who converted the population to Islam), Mongols, Uzbeks, Afghans, and Russians. The USSR gained control of the region 1918-25. In 1924, the Tajik ASSR was created within the Uzbek SSR. The Tajik SSR was proclaimed in 1929.

Tajikistan declared independence Sept. 9, 1991. Factional fighting led to the installation of a pro-Communist regime, Jan. 1993. A new constitution establishing a presidential system was approved by referendum Nov. 6, 1994.

Clashes between Muslim rebels, reportedly armed by Afghanistan, and troops loyal to the government and supported by Russia, claimed an estimated 55,000 lives by mid-1997, despite a series of peace accords. Constitutional changes including legalization of Islamic political parties were approved by referendum Sept. 26, 1999. Pres. Imomali Rakhmonov won a Nov. 6 election called "a farce" by human-rights observers. Voters approved, June 22, 2003, constitutional changes giving Rakhmonov the right to serve as president until 2020.

Tanzania
United Republic of Tanzania

People: Population: 36,977,000. **Age distrib.** (%): <15: 44.6; 65+: 2.9. **Pop. density:** 108 per sq. mi. **Urban:** 33%. **Ethnic groups:** Mainland: Bantu 95%; Zanzibar: Arab, African, mixed. **Principal languages:** Swahili, English (both official), Arabic, many local languages. **Chief religions:** Christian 30%, Muslim 35%, indigenous beliefs 35%; Zanzibar is 99% Muslim.

Geography: Area: 364,900 sq. mi. (total); 342,101 sq. mi. (land). **Location:** On coast of E Africa. **Neighbors:** Kenya, Uganda on N; Rwanda, Burundi, Congo (formerly Zaire) on W; Zambia, Malawi, Mozambique on S. **Topography:** Hot, arid central plateau, surrounded by the lake region in the W, temperate highlands in N and S, the coastal plains. Mt. Kilimanjaro, 19,340 ft., is highest in Africa. **Capital:** Dodoma. **Cities** (urban aggr.): Dar-es-Salaam 2,347,000; Dodoma 180,000.

Government: Type: Republic. **Head of state:** Pres. Benjamin William Mkapa; b Nov. 12, 1938; in office: Nov. 23, 1995. **Head of gov.:** Prime Min. Frederick Tluway Sumaye; b May 29, 1950; in office: Nov. 28, 1995. **Local divisions:** 25 regions. **Defense budget** (2002): $141 mil. **Active troops:** 27,000.

Economy: Industries: agric. proc., diamond & gold mining, oil refining, shoes. **Chief crops:** coffee, sisal, tea, cotton, pyrethrum (insecticide from chrysanthemums), cashews. **Natural resources:** hydropower, tin, phosphates, iron ore, coal, diamonds, gemstones, gold, nat. gas, nickel. **Arable land:** 3%. **Livestock** (2002):

cattle: 17 mil.; chickens: 30 mil.; goats: 11.64 mil.; pigs: 450,000; sheep: 3.40 mil. **Fish catch** (2002): 336,200 metric tons. **Electricity prod.** (2001): 2.91 bil. kWh. **Labor force:** agri. 80%, ind. and services 20%.

Finance: Monetary unit: Shilling (TZS) (Sept. 2003: 1,069.10=1 U.S.). **GDP** (2002 est.): $22.5 bil. **Per capita GDP:** $630. **Imports** (2001): $1.55 bil.; partners (2000): South Africa 11.5%, Japan 9.3%, UK 7.0%, Australia 6.2%. **Exports** (2001): $827 mil.; partners (2000): UK 22.0%, India 14.8%, Germany 9.9%, Netherlands 6.9%. **Tourism:** $739 mil. **Budget** (2001 est.): $1.38 bil. **Intl. reserves less gold:** $1.13 bil. **Consumer prices:** 4.6%.

Transport: Railroad: Length: 2,218 mi. **Motor vehicles** (1999): 13,800 pass. cars; 42,500 comm. vehicles. **Civil aviation:** 109.4 mil pass.-mi; 11 airports. **Chief ports:** Dar-es-Salaam, Mtwara, Tanga.

Communications: TV sets: 21 per 1,000 pop. **Radios:** 280 per 1,000 pop. **Telephone lines:** 148,500. **Daily newspaper circ.:** 3.9 per 1,000 pop. **Internet:** 100,000 users.

Health: Life expectancy: 43.3 male; 45.8 female. **Births** (per 1,000 pop.): 39.5. **Deaths** (per 1,000 pop.): 17.4. **Natural inc.:** 2.21%. **Infant mortality** (per 1,000 live births): 103.7.

Education: Compulsory: ages 7-13. **Literacy:** 78.2%.

Major Intl. Organizations: UN and all of its specialized agencies, the Commonwealth, AU.

Embassy: 2139 R St. NW 20008; 202-939-6125.

Website: www.tanzania.go.tz/index2E.html

The Republic of Tanganyika in E Africa and the island Republic of Zanzibar, off the coast of Tanganyika, both of which had recently gained independence, joined into a single nation, the United Republic of Tanzania, Apr. 26, 1964. Zanzibar retains internal self-government.

Until resigning as president in 1985, Julius K. Nyerere, a former Tanganyikan independence leader, dominated Tanzania's politics, which emphasized government planning and control of the economy, with single-party rule. In 1992 the constitution was amended to establish a multiparty system. Privatization of the economy was undertaken in the 1990s.

At least 500 people died when an overcrowded Tanzanian ferry sank in Lake Victoria, May 21, 1996. About 460,000 Rwandan refugees, mostly Hutu, returned from Tanzania to Rwanda in Dec. 1996. A bomb at the U.S. embassy in Dar-es-Salaam, Aug. 7, 1998, killed 11 people and injured at least 70 others. The U.S. blamed the attack and a near-simultaneous embassy bombing in Kenya on Islamic terrorists associated with Osama bin Laden. After a trial in New York City, 4 conspirators were convicted May 29, 2001.

Former Pres. Nyerere died in London Oct. 14, 1999. President since 1995, Benjamin Mkapa was reelected Oct. 29, 2000. Over 280 people died in a train wreck June 24, 2002, SE of Dodoma.

Tanganyika. Arab colonization and slaving began in the 8th century AD; Portuguese sailors explored the coast by about 1500. Other Europeans followed.

In 1885 Germany established German East Africa of which Tanganyika formed the bulk. It became a League of Nations mandate and, after 1946, a UN trust territory, both under Britain. It became independent Dec. 9, 1961, and a republic within the Commonwealth a year later.

Zanzibar, the Isle of Cloves, lies 23 mi. off mainland Tanzania; area 640 sq. mi. and pop. (2002) 622,459. The island of **Pemba,** 25 mi. to the NE, area 380 sq. mi. and pop. (2002) 362,166 is included in the administration.

Chief industry is cloves and clove oil production, of which Zanzibar and Pemba produce most of the world's supply.

Zanzibar was for centuries the center for Arab slave traders. Portugal ruled the region for 2 centuries until ousted by Arabs around 1700. Zanzibar became a British Protectorate in 1890; independence came Dec. 10, 1963. Revolutionary forces overthrew the Sultan Jan. 12, 1964. The new government ousted Western diplomats and newsmen, slaughtered thousands of Arabs, and nationalized farms. Union with Tanganyika followed.

Thailand
Kingdom of Thailand

People: Population: 62,833,000. **Age distrib.** (%): <15: 23.3; 65+: 6.8. **Pop. density:** 318 per sq. mi. **Urban:** 20%. **Ethnic groups:** Thai 75%, Chinese 14%. **Principal languages:** Thai, Chinese, Malay, Khmer. **Chief religions:** Buddhism 95% (official), Muslim 4%.

Geography: Area: 198,456 sq. mi. (total); 197,595 sq. mi. (land). **Location:** On Indochinese and Malayan peninsulas in SE Asia. **Neighbors:** Myanmar on W and N, Laos on N, Cambodia on E, Malaysia on S. **Topography:** A plateau dominates the NE third of Thailand, dropping to the fertile alluvial valley of the Chao Phraya R. in the center. Forested mountains are in the N, with narrow fertile valleys. The S peninsula region is covered by rain forests. **Capital:** Bangkok 7,527,000.

Government: Type: Constitutional monarchy. **Head of state:** King Bhumibol Adulyadej; b Dec. 5, 1927; in office: June 9, 1946. **Head of gov.:** Prime Min. Thaksin Shinawatra; b July 26, 1949; in office: Feb. 18, 2001. **Local divisions:** 76 provinces. **Defense budget** (2002): $1.9 bil. **Active troops:** 306,000.

Economy: Industries: tourism; textiles & garments, agric. proc., beverages, tobacco, cement, light mfg.; electric appliances & components, computers & parts. **Chief crops:** rice, cassava, rubber, corn, sugarcane, coconuts, soybeans. **Natural resources:** tin, rubber, nat. gas, tungsten, tantalum, timber, lead, fish, gypsum, lignite, fluorite. **Crude oil reserves** (2002): 516 mil. bbls. **Arable land:** 34%. **Livestock** (2002): cattle: 4.64 mil.; chickens: 250 mil.; goats: 150,000; pigs: 6.69 mil.; sheep: 43,000. **Fish catch** (2002): 3,605,544 metric tons. **Electricity prod.** (2001): 97.6 bil. kWh. **Labor force:** agri. 54%, ind. 15%, services 31%.

Finance: Monetary unit: Baht (THB) (Sept. 2003: 40.89=1 U.S.). **GDP** (2002 est.): $429 bil. **Per capita GDP:** $6,900. **Imports** (2001): $62.3 bil.; partners (2000): Japan 24%, U.S. 11%, Singapore 10%, Malaysia 6%. **Exports** (2001 est.): $65.3 bil.; partners (2000): U.S. 23%, Japan 14%, Singapore 8%, China 6%. **Tourism:** $7.12 bil. **Budget** (2000 est.): $21 bil. **Intl. reserves less gold:** $27.99 bil. **Gold:** 2.50 mil oz t. **Consumer prices:** 0.6%.

Transport: Railroad: Length: 2,530 mi. **Motor vehicles** (1999): 2.65 mil pass. cars, 4.07 mil comm. vehicles. **Civil aviation:** 23.83 bil pass.-mi; 62 airports. **Chief ports:** Bangkok, Sattahip.

Communication: TV sets: 274 per 1,000 pop. **Radios:** 234 per 1,000 pop. **Telephone lines:** 6,042,500. **Daily newspaper circ.:** 63 per 1,000 pop. **Internet:** 4,800,000 users.

Health: Life expectancy: 69.1 male; 73.5 female. **Births** (per 1,000 pop.): 16.4. **Deaths** (per 1,000 pop.): 6.9. **Natural inc.:** 0.95%. **Infant mortality** (per 1,000 live births): 21.8.

Education: Compulsory: ages 6-14. **Literacy:** 96%.

Major Intl. Organizations: UN (FAO, IBRD, ILO, IMF, IMO, WHO, WTrO), ASEAN, APEC.

Embassy: 1024 Wisconsin Ave., Suite 401, NW 20007; 944-3600.

Website: www.thaigov.go.th/index-eng.htm

Thais began migrating from southern China during the 11th century. A unified Thai kingdom was established in 1350.

Thailand, known as Siam until 1939, is the only country in SE Asia never taken over by a European power, thanks to King Mongkut and his son King Chulalongkorn. Ruling successively from 1851 to 1910, they modernized the country and signed trade treaties with Britain and France. A bloodless revolution in 1932 limited the monarchy. Thailand was an ally of Japan during World War II and of the U.S. during the postwar period.

The military took over the government in a bloody 1976 coup. Chatchai Choonhavan was chosen prime minister in a democratic election, Aug. 1988. In Feb. 1991, the military ousted Choonhavan in a bloodless coup. A violent crackdown on street demonstrations in May 1992 led to more than 50 deaths. AIDS reached epidemic proportions in Thailand in the mid-1990s.

A steep downturn in the economy forced Thailand to seek more than $15 billion in emergency international loans in Aug. 1997. A new constitution won legislative approval Sept. 27. As the economic crisis deepened, Chuan Leekpai became prime minister Nov. 9, 1997, and implemented financial reforms. By the end of the 1990s, according to UN estimates, more than 750,000 people in Thailand had HIV/AIDS.

Following elections in Jan. 2001, Thaksin Shinawatra, a wealthy former telecommunications executive, became prime minister. Thailand's Constitutional Court acquitted him Aug. 3 of corruption while he was deputy prime minister in 1997. On Feb. 1, 2003, Thaksin launched a nationwide crackdown on methamphetamines; human rights observers criticized police tactics in the drug war, which killed more than 2,200 people by Aug.

Togo
Togolese Republic

People: Population: 4,909,000. **Age distrib.** (%): <15: 45.1; 65+: 2.5. **Pop. density:** 234 per sq. mi. **Urban:** 34%. **Ethnic groups:** 37 African tribes; largest are Ewe, Mina, and Kabre. **Principal languages:** French (official); Ewe, Mina in S; Kabye, Dagomba in N. **Chief religions:** Indigenous beliefs 51%, Christian 29%, Muslim 20%.

Geography: Area: 21,925 sq. mi. (total); 20,998 sq. mi. (land). **Location:** On S coast of W Africa. **Neighbors:** Ghana on W, Burkina Faso on N, Benin on E. **Topography:** A range of hills running SW-NE splits Togo into 2 savanna plains regions. **Capital:** Lomé: 732,000.

Government: Type: Republic. **Head of state:** Pres. Gnassingbé Eyadéma; b Dec. 26, 1937; in office: Apr. 14, 1967. **Head of gov.:** Prime Min. Koffi Sama; b 1944; in office: June 29, 2002. **Local divisions:** 5 regions. **Defense budget** (2002): $33 mil. **Active troops:** 9,450.

Economy: Industries: phosphates mining, agric. proc., cement, handicrafts. **Chief crops:** coffee, cocoa, cotton, yams, cassava, corn. **Natural resources:** phosphates, limestone, marble. **Arable land:** 38%. **Livestock** (2002): cattle: 277,000; chickens: 8.50 mil.; goats: 1.42 mil.; pigs: 289,000; sheep: 1.70 mil. **Fish catch** (2002): 23,283 metric tons. **Electricity prod.** (2001): 0.1 bil. kWh. **Labor force:** agri. 65%, ind. 5%, services 30%.

Finance: Monetary unit: CFA Franc BCEAO (XOF) (Sept. 2003: 605.18=1 U.S.). **GDP** (2002 est.): $8 bil. **Per capita GDP:**

$1,500. **Imports** (2001): $420 mil.; partners (2000): Ghana 26%, France 11%, China 7%, Cote d'Ivoire 7%. **Exports** (2001): $306 mil.; partners (2000): Benin 12%, Nigeria 9%, Belgium 5%, Ghana 4%. **Tourism** (1999): $6 mil. **Budget** (1997 est.): $252 mil. **Intl. reserves less gold:** $151 mil. **Consumer prices:** 3.1%.

Transport: Railroad: Length: 326 mi. **Motor vehicles** (1998): 74,700 pass. cars, 34,600 comm. vehicles. **Civil aviation:** 146.0 mil pass.-mi; 2 airports. **Chief port:** Lomé.

Communications: TV sets: 22 per 1,000 pop. **Radios:** 244 per 1,000 pop. **Telephone lines:** 51,200. **Daily newspaper circ.:** 3.6 per 1,000 pop. **Internet:** 200,000 users.

Health: Life expectancy: 51.5 male; 55.5 female. **Births** (per 1,000 pop.): 35.2. **Deaths** (per 1,000 pop.): 11.5. **Natural inc.:** 2.37%. **Infant mortality** (per 1,000 live births): 68.7.

Education: Compulsory: ages 6-15. **Literacy:** 60.9%.

Major Intl. Organizations: UN (FAO, IBRD, ILO, IMF, IMO, WHO, WTrO), AU.

Embassy: 800 Second Ave., Suite 400B, New York, NY 10017.

Website: www.republicoftogo.com

In Jan. 1993 police fired on protesters, killing at least 22. Some 25,000 people fled to Ghana and Benin as a result of civil unrest. In Jan. 1994 at least 40 people were killed when gunmen reportedly attacked an army base. Further violence marred Togo's 1st multiparty legislative elections, held Feb. 1994.

In office since 1967, Pres. Gnassingbé Eyadéma is Africa's longest-serving head of state. He was reelected June 1, 2003, in a vote that, like previous elections, was viewed as undemocratic.

Tonga
Kingdom of Tonga

People: Population: 104,000. **Age distrib.** (%): <15: 39.5; 65+: 4.1. **Pop. density:** 376 per sq. mi. **Urban:** 33%. **Ethnic groups:** Polynesian. **Principal languages:** Tongan, English (both official). **Chief religions:** Wesleyan 41%, Roman Catholic 16%, Mormon 14%.

Geography: Area: 289 sq. mi. (total); 277 sq. mi. (land). **Location:** In western South Pacific O. **Neighbors:** Nearest are Fiji to W, Samoa to NE. **Topography:** Tonga comprises 170 volcanic and coral islands, 36 inhabited. **Capital:** Nuku'alofa: 33,000.

Government: Type: Constitutional monarchy. **Head of state:** King Taufa'ahau Tupou IV; b July 4, 1918; in office: Dec. 16, 1965. **Head of gov.:** Prime Min. Prince Ulukalala Lavaka Ata; b July 12, 1959; in office: Jan. 3, 2000. **Local divisions:** 5 divisions, 23 districts.

Economy: Industries: tourism, fishing. **Chief crops:** squash, coconuts, copra, bananas, vanilla, cocoa. **Natural resources:** fish. **Arable land:** 24%. **Livestock** (2002): cattle: 11,000; chickens: 300,000; goats: 12,500; pigs: 81,000. **Fish catch** (2002): 4,673 metric tons. **Electricity prod.** (2001): 0.03 bil. kWh. **Labor force:** agri. 65%.

Finance: Monetary unit: Pa'anga (TOP) (Sept. 2003: 2.17=1 U.S.). **GDP** (2001 est.): $236 mil. **Per capita GDP:** $2,200. **Imports** (2000): $70 mil.; partners (2000 est.): New Zealand 29.8%, Japan 18.6%, Australia 12.7%, U.S. 12.7%. **Exports** (2000 est.): $9.3 mil.; partners (2000 est.): Japan 50.4%, U.S. 31.6%, NZ 4.1%, Australia 2.1%. **Tourism:** $9 mil. **Budget** (2000): $52.4 mil. **Intl. reserves less gold:** $20 mil. **Consumer prices:** 10.4%.

Transport: Motor vehicles (1999): 10,800 pass. cars, 4,000 comm. vehicles. **Civil aviation:** 11.8 mil pass.-mi; 1 airport. **Chief port:** Nuku'alofa.

Communications: TV sets: 61 per 1,000 pop. **Radios:** 663 per 1,000 pop. **Telephone lines:** 11,200. **Daily newspaper circ.:** 72 per 1,000 pop. **Internet:** 2,900 users.

Health: Life expectancy: 66.4 male; 71.4 female. **Births** (per 1,000 pop.): 24.5. **Deaths** (per 1,000 pop.): 5.5. **Natural inc.:** 1.90%. **Infant mortality** (per 1,000 live births): 13.4.

Education: Compulsory: ages 6-14. **Literacy** (1996 est.): 98.5%.

Major Intl. Organizations: UN (FAO, IBRD, IMF, WHO), the Commonwealth.

Embassy: 800 Second Ave., Suite 400B, New York, NY 10017

Website: www.pmo.gov.to

The islands were first settled by the Dutch in the early 17th century. A series of civil wars ended in 1845 with establishment of the Tupou dynasty. In 1900 Tonga became a British protectorate. On June 4, 1970, Tonga became independent and a member of the Commonwealth. It joined the UN on Sept. 14, 1999.

Trinidad and Tobago
Republic of Trinidad and Tobago

People: Population: 1,303,000. **Age distrib.** (%): <15: 23; 65+: 6.8. **Pop. density:** 658 per sq. mi. **Urban:** 75%. **Ethnic groups:** Black 40%, East Indian 40%, mixed 18%. **Principal languages:** English (official), Hindi, French, Spanish, Chinese. **Chief religions:** Roman Catholic 29%, Hindu 24%, Protestant 14%, Muslim 6%.

Geography: Area: 1,980 sq. mi. **Location:** In Caribbean, off E coast of Venezuela. **Neighbors:** Nearest is Venezuela to SW. **Topography:** Three low mountain ranges cross Trinidad E-W, with a well-watered plain between N and central ranges. Parts of E and

W coasts are swamps. Tobago, 116 sq. mi., lies 20 mi. NE. **Capital:** Port-of-Spain: 54,000.

Government: Type: Parliamentary democracy. **Head of state:** Pres. George Maxwell Richards; b 1931; in office: Mar. 17, 2003. **Head of gov.:** Prime Min. Patrick Augustus Mervyn Manning; b Aug. 17, 1946; in office: Dec. 24, 2001. **Local divisions:** 8 counties, 3 municipalities, 1 ward. **Defense budget** (2002): $67 mil. **Active troops:** 2,700.

Economy: Industries: oil, chemicals, tourism, food proc. **Chief crops:** cocoa, sugarcane, rice, citrus, coffee, vegetables. **Natural resources:** oil, nat. gas, asphalt. **Crude oil reserves** (2002): 716 mil. bbls. **Arable land:** 15%. **Livestock** (2002): cattle: 37,000; chickens: 16.50 mil.; goats: 60,500; pigs: 42,000; sheep: 13,000. **Fish catch** (2002): 11,415 metric tons. **Electricity prod.** (2001): 5.32 bil. kWh. **Labor force:** construct. and utilities 12.4%, manufact., mining, and quarrying 14%, agri. 9.5%, services 64.1%.

Finance: Monetary unit: Tobago Dollar (TTD) (Sept. 2003: 6.12=1 U.S.). **GDP** (2002 est.): $11.1 bil. **Per capita GDP:** $9,500. **Imports** (2001): $3.5 bil.; partners (1999): U.S. 39.8%, Venezuela 11.9%, EU 11%, Caricom 4.8%. **Exports** (2001 est.): $4.1 bil.; partners (1999): U.S. 45.9%, Caricom countries 26.1%, Latin America 9.5%, EU 5.7%. **Tourism** (1999): $210 mil. **Budget** (1998): $1.6 bil. **Intl. reserves less gold:** $1.49 bil. **Gold:** 60,000 mil. oz t. **Consumer prices:** 4.2%.

Transport: Motor vehicles (1999): 229,400 pass. cars, 53,900 comm. vehicles. **Civil aviation:** 1.69 bil pass.-mi; 3 airports. **Chief ports:** Port-of-Spain, Scarborough.

Communications: TV sets: 337 per 1,000 pop. **Radios:** 532 per 1,000 pop. **Telephone lines:** 325,100. **Daily newspaper circ.:** 123 per 1,000 pop. **Internet:** 138,000 users.

Health: Life expectancy: 67.1 male; 72.2 female. **Births** (per 1,000 pop.): 12.7. **Deaths** (per 1,000 pop.): 8.7. **Natural inc.:** 0.40%. **Infant mortality** (per 1,000 live births): 25.0.

Education: Compulsory: ages 5-11. **Literacy:** 98.6%.

Major Intl. Organizations: UN (FAO, IBRD, ILO, IMF, IMO, WHO, WTrO), Caricom, the Commonwealth, OAS.

Embassy: 1708 Massachusetts Ave. NW 20036; 467-6490.

Websites: www.gov.tt; www.visittnt.com

Columbus sighted Trinidad in 1498. A British possession since 1802, Trinidad and Tobago won independence Aug. 31, 1962. It became a republic in 1976.

The nation is one of the most prosperous in the Caribbean. Oil production has increased with offshore finds. Middle Eastern oil is refined and exported, mostly to the U.S.

In July 1990, some 120 Muslim extremists captured the Parliament building and TV station and took about 50 hostages, including Prime Min. Arthur N. R. Robinson, who was beaten, shot in the legs, and tied to explosives. After a 6-day siege, the rebels surrendered.

Basdeo Panday, the country's first prime minister of East Indian ancestry, took office Nov. 9, 1995. Robinson became president on Mar. 19, 1997. Patrick Manning of the People's National Movement became prime minister after elections Dec. 10, 2001. George Maxwell Richards, a former university dean, succeeded Robinson as president, Mar. 17, 2003.

Tunisia
Republic of Tunisia

People: Population: 9,832,000. **Age distrib.** (%): <15: 27.8; 65+: 6.3. **Pop. density:** 164 per sq. mi. **Urban:** 66%. **Ethnic groups:** Arab 98%, European 1%, Jewish and other 1%. **Principal languages:** Arabic (official), French prevalent. **Chief religion:** Muslim 98% (official; mostly Sunni).

Geography: Area: 63,170 sq. mi. (total); 59,985 sq. mi. (land). **Location:** On N coast of Africa. **Neighbors:** Algeria on W, Libya on E. **Topography:** The N is wooded and fertile. The central coastal plains are given to grazing and orchards. The S is arid, approaching Sahara Desert. **Capital:** Tunis 1,927,000.

Government: Type: Republic. **Head of state:** Pres. Gen. Zine al-Abidine Ben Ali; b Sept. 3, 1936; in office: Nov. 7, 1987. **Head of gov.:** Prime Min. Mohamed Ghannouchi; b Aug. 18, 1941; in office: Nov. 17, 1999. **Local divisions:** 23 governorates. **Defense budget** (2002): $429 mil. **Active troops:** 35,000.

Economy: Industries: oil, mining, tourism, textiles, footwear, agribusiness. **Chief crops:** olives, grain, tomatoes, citrus, sugar beets, dates, almonds. **Natural resources:** oil, phosphates, iron ore, lead, zinc, salt. **Crude oil reserves** (2002): 308 mil. bbls. **Arable land:** 19%. **Livestock** (2002): cattle: 760,000; chickens: 43 mil.; goats: 1.45 mil.; pigs: 6,000; sheep: 6.93 mil. **Fish catch** (2002): 100,350 metric tons. **Electricity prod.** (2001): 10.48 bil. kWh. **Labor force:** services 55%, ind. 23%, agri. 22%.

Finance: Monetary unit: Dinar (TND) (Sept. 2003: 1.34=1 U.S.). **GDP** (2002 est.): $63 bil. **Per capita GDP:** $6,500. **Imports** (2001): $8.9 bil.; partners (2000): France 30%, Italy 21%, Germany 11%, Spain 4%. **Exports** (2001 est.): $6.6 bil.; partners (2000): France 28%, Italy 21%, Germany 14%, Belgium 6%. **Tourism:** $1.5 bil. **Budget** (2002 est.): $5.7 bil. **Intl. reserves less gold:** $1.69 bil. **Gold:** 220,000 oz t. **Consumer prices:** 2.7%.

Transport: Railroad: Length: 1,347 mi. **Motor vehicles** (1999): 482,700 pass. cars, 250,300 comm. vehicles. **Civil aviation:** 1.72 bil pass.-mi; 14 airports. **Chief ports:** Tunis, Sfax, Bizerte.

Communications: TV sets: 190 per 1,000 pop. **Radios:** 158 per 1,000 pop. **Telephone lines:** 1,200,000. **Daily newspaper circ.:** 31 per 1,000 pop. **Internet:** 505,500 users.

Health: Life expectancy: 72.8 male; 76.2 female. **Births** (per 1,000 pop.): 16.5. **Deaths** (per 1,000 pop.): 5.0. **Natural inc.:** 1.15%. **Infant mortality** (per 1,000 live births): 26.9.

Education: Compulsory: ages 6-16. **Literacy:** 74.2%.

Major Intl. Organizations: UN (FAO, IBRD, ILO, IMF, IMO, WHO, WTrO), AL, AU.

Embassy: 1515 Massachusetts Ave. NW 20005; 862-1850.

Websites: www.ministeres.tn; www.tourismtunisia.com

Site of ancient Carthage and a former Barbary state under the suzerainty of Turkey, Tunisia became a protectorate of France under a treaty signed May 12, 1881. The nation became independent Mar. 20, 1956, and ended the monarchy the following year. Habib Bourguiba, an independence leader, served as president until 1987, when he was deposed by his prime minister, Zine al-Abidine Ben Ali.

Tunisia has actively repressed Islamic fundamentalism. A synagogue blast on Djerba Is., Apr. 11, 2002, apparently set off by al-Qaeda, killed 17 people, including 12 German tourists.

Turkey
Republic of Turkey

People: Population: 71,325,000. **Age distrib.** (%): <15: 27.8; 65+: 6.3. **Pop. density:** 240 per sq. mi. **Urban:** 66%. **Ethnic groups:** Turkish 80%, Kurdish 20%. **Principal languages:** Turkish (official), Kurdish, Arabic, Armenian, Greek. **Chief religion:** Muslim 99.8% (mostly Sunni).

Geography: Area: 301,383 sq. mi. (total); 297,592 sq. mi. (land). **Location:** Occupies Asia Minor, stretches into continental Europe; borders on Mediterranean and Black seas. **Neighbors:** Bulgaria, Greece on W; Georgia, Armenia on N; Iran on E; Iraq, Syria on S. **Topography:** Central Turkey has wide plateaus, with hot, dry summers and cold winters. High mountains ring the interior on all but W, with more than 20 peaks over 10,000 ft. Rolling plains are in W; mild, fertile coastal plains are in S, W. **Capital:** Ankara. **Cities (urban aggr.):** Istanbul 8,953,000; Ankara 3,208,000; Izmir 2,214,000.

Government: Type: Republic. **Head of state:** Pres. Ahmet Necdet Sezer; b Sept. 13, 1941; in office: May 16, 2000. **Head of gov.:** Prime Min. Recep Tayyip Erdogan; b Feb. 26, 1954; in office: Mar. 14, 2003. **Local divisions:** 80 provinces. **Defense budget** (2002): $5.8 bil. **Active troops:** 514,850.

Economy: Industries: textiles, food proc., autos, mining, steel, oil, constr. **Chief crops:** tobacco, cotton, grain, olives, sugar beets, citrus. **Natural resources:** antimony, coal, chromium, mercury, copper, borate, sulfur, iron ore, hydropower. **Crude oil reserves** (2002): 296 mil. bbls. **Arable land:** 32%. **Livestock** (2002): cattle: 10.55 mil.; chickens: 217.58 mil.; goats: 7.02 mil.; pigs: 3,000; sheep: 26.97 mil. **Fish catch** (2002): 594,971 metric tons. **Electricity prod.** (2001): 116.57 bil. kWh. **Labor force:** agri. 39.7%, services 37.9%, ind. 22.4%.

Finance: Monetary unit: Lira (TRL) (Sept. 2003: 1,418,031.00=1 U.S.). **GDP** (2002 est.): $468 bil. **Per capita GDP:** $7,000. **Imports** (2002): $43.9 bil.; partners (2001 est.): Germany 12.9%, Italy 8.4%, Russia 8.3%, U.S. 7.9%. **Exports** (2002) $37.6 bil.; partners (2001): Germany 17.2%, U.S. 10.0%, Italy 7.5%, UK 6.9%. **Tourism:** $7.64 bil. **Budget** (2002): $69.1 bil. **Intl. reserves less gold:** $19.91 bil. **Gold:** 3.73 mil oz t. **Consumer prices** (change in 2000): 45.0%.

Transport: Railroad: Length: 5,348 mi. **Motor vehicles** (1999): 4.07 mil pass. cars, 730,700 comm. vehicles. **Civil aviation:** 8.30 bil pass.-mi; 86 airports. **Chief ports:** Istanbul, Izmir, Mersin.

Communications: TV sets: 328 per 1,000 pop. **Radios:** 510 per 1,000 pop. **Telephone lines:** 18,914,900. **Daily newspaper circ.:** 111 per 1,000 pop. **Internet:** 4,900,000 users.

Health: Life expectancy: 69.4 male; 74.3 female. **Births** (per 1,000 pop.): 17.6. **Deaths** (per 1,000 pop.): 6.0. **Natural inc.:** 1.16%. **Infant mortality** (per 1,000 live births): 44.2.

Education: Compulsory: ages 6-14. **Literacy:** 86.5%.

Major Intl. Organizations: UN (FAO, IBRD, ILO, IMF, IMO, WHO, WTrO), NATO, OECD, OSCE.

Embassy: 2525 Massachusetts Ave. NW 20008; 202-612-6700.

Website: www.turkey.org

Ancient inhabitants of Turkey were among the world's first agriculturalists. Such civilizations as the Hittite, Phrygian, and Lydian flourished in Asiatic Turkey (Asia Minor), as did much of Greek civilization. After the fall of Rome in the 5th century, Constantinople (now Istanbul) was the capital of the Byzantine Empire for 1,000 years. It fell in 1453 to Ottoman Turks, who ruled a vast empire for over 400 years.

Just before World War I, Turkey, or the Ottoman Empire, ruled what is now Syria, Lebanon, Iraq, Jordan, Israel, Saudi Arabia, Yemen, and islands in the Aegean Sea.

Turkey joined Germany and Austria in World War I, and its defeat resulted in the loss of much territory and the fall of the sultanate. A republic was declared Oct. 29, 1923, with Mustafa Kemal (later Kemal Ataturk) as its first president. Ataturk led Turkey until his death in 1938. The Caliphate (spiritual leadership of Islam) was renounced in 1924.

Long embroiled with Greece over Cyprus, off Turkey's south coast, Turkey invaded the island July 20, 1974, after Greek officers seized the Cypriot government as a step toward unification with Greece. Turkey sought a new government for Cyprus, with Greek Cypriot and Turkish Cypriot zones. In reaction to Turkey's moves, the U.S. cut off military aid in 1975. Turkey, in turn, suspended the use of most U.S. bases. Aid was restored in 1978. There was a military takeover, Sept. 12, 1980.

Religious and ethnic tensions and active left and right extremists have caused endemic violence. The military formally transferred power to an elected Parliament in 1983. Martial law, imposed in 1978, was lifted in 1984.

Turkey was a member of the Allied forces that ousted Iraq from Kuwait, 1991. In the aftermath of the war, millions of Kurdish refugees fled to Turkey's border to escape Iraqi forces. The Turkish government mounted sporadic offensives against separatist Kurds in this border area and in N Iraq, causing heavy casualties among guerrillas and civilians.

Kurdish militants, demanding an independent state for the Kurds, raided Turkish diplomatic missions in some 25 Western European cities June 24, 1993. Tansu Ciller officially became Turkey's first woman prime minister July 5, 1993. The Welfare Party, an Islamic group, gained strength in the 1990s but was unable to form a government until June 1996, when it came to power in coalition with Ciller's True Path Party.

The pro-Islamic government resigned June 18, 1997, under pressure from the military. The European Union rebuffed Turkey's membership bid Dec. 12, 1997. The military stepped up its campaign against Islamic fundamentalism in 1998.

Kurdish rebel leader Abdullah Öcalan was captured Feb. 15, 1999; convicted of terrorism June 29, he was sentenced to death by a Turkish security court. His organization, the Kurdistan Workers' Party, announced Aug. 5 that it would abandon its 14-year-old armed insurgency. A major earthquake Aug. 17 in NW Turkey killed over 17,000 people and injured thousands more. Another quake in the same region Nov. 12 claimed at least 675 lives.

The IMF announced $7.5 billion in emergency loans Dec. 6, 2000, to help Turkey cope with a severe financial crisis. The death penalty was abolished Aug. 3, 2002, and Öcalan's sentence was commuted to life in prison Oct. 3. The Justice and Development Party, an Islamic group headed by Recep Tayyip Erdogan, won a plurality in parliamentary elections Nov. 3. During the U.S.-led invasion of Iraq, Mar.-Apr. 2003, Turkey, a NATO ally, refused to allow coalition forces to launch attacks on N Iraq from Turkish soil.

Turkmenistan

People: Population: 4,867,000. **Age distrib. (%):** <15: 37.3; 65+: 4.1. **Pop. density:** 26 per sq. mi. **Urban:** 45%. **Ethnic groups:** Turkmen 77%, Uzbek 9%, Russian 7%, Kazakh 2%. **Principal languages:** Turkmen, Russian, Uzbek. **Chief religions:** Muslim 89%, Eastern Orthodox 9%.

Geography: Area (total): 188,456 sq. mi. **Neighbors:** Kazakhstan on N, Uzbekistan on N and E, Afghanistan and Iran on S. **Topography:** The Kara Kum Desert occupies 80% of the area. Bordered on W by Caspian Sea. **Capital:** Ashgabat: 558,000.

Government: Type: Republic with authoritarian rule. **Head of state and gov.:** Pres. Saparmurad Niyazov; b Feb. 18, 1940; in office: Oct. 27, 1990. **Local divisions:** 5 regions. **Defense budget** (2001): $163 mil. **Active troops:** 17,500.

Economy: Industries: nat. gas, oil, oil products, textiles, food proc. **Chief crops:** cotton, grain. **Natural resources:** oil, nat. gas, coal, sulfur, salt. **Crude oil reserves** (2002): 546 mil. bbls. **Arable land:** 3%. **Livestock** (2002): cattle: 860,000; chickens: 4.80 mil.; goats: 375,000; pigs: 45,000; sheep: 6 mil. **Fish catch** (2002): 12,792 metric tons. **Electricity prod.** (2001): 10.18 bil. kWh. **Labor force:** agri. 48%, ind. 15%, services 37%.

Finance: Monetary unit: Manat (TMM) (Sept. 2003: 5,016 = $1 U.S.). **GDP** (2002 est.): $26 bil. **Per capita GDP:** $5,500. **Imports** (2001): $2.3 bil.; partners (1999): Turkey 17%, Ukraine 12%, Russia 11%, UAE 8%. **Exports** (2001 est.): $2.7 bil.; partners (1999): Ukraine 27%, Iran 14%, Turkey 11%, Italy 9%. **Tourism** (1998): $192 mil. **Budget** (1999 est.): $658.2 mil.

Transport: Railroad: Length: 1,516 mi. **Civil aviation:** 397.7 bil pass.-mi; 13 airports. **Chief port:** Turkmenbashi.

Communications: TV sets: 198 per 1,000 pop. **Radios:** 289 per 1,000 pop. **Telephone lines:** 387,600. **Internet:** 8,000 users.

Health: Life expectancy: 57.7 male; 64.8 female. **Births** (per 1,000 pop.): 28.0. **Deaths** (per 1,000 pop.): 8.9. **Natural inc.:** 1.92%. **Infant mortality** (per 1,000 live births): 73.2.

Education: Literacy (2002): 100%.

Major Intl. Organizations: UN (FAO, IBRD, ILO, IMF, IMO, WHO), CIS, OSCE.

Embassy: 2207 Massachusetts Ave., NW 20008; 588-1500.
Website: www.turkmenistanembassy.org

The region has been inhabited by Turkic tribes since the 10th century. It became part of Russian Turkestan in 1881, and a constituent republic of the USSR in 1925. Turkmenistan declared independence Oct. 27, 1991, and became an independent state when the USSR disbanded Dec. 26, 1991.

Extensive oil and gas reserves place Turkmenistan in a more favorable economic position than other former Soviet republics. A new rail line linking Iran and Turkmenistan was inaugurated May 13, 1996. Political power centered around the former Communist Party apparatus, and Pres. Saparmurad Niyazov became the object of a personality cult. An alleged coup plot Nov. 25, 2002, triggered a crackdown on Niyazov's political opponents.

Tuvalu

People: Population: 11,300. **Age distrib. (%):** <15: 32.6; 65+: 5.1. **Pop. density:** 1,126 per sq. mi. **Urban:** 53%. **Ethnic group:** Polynesian 96%, Micronesian 4%. **Principal languages:** Tuvaluan, English, Samoan, Kiribati (on the island of Nui). **Chief religions:** Church of Tuvalu (Congregationalist) 97%.

Geography: Area (total): 10 sq. mi. **Location:** 9 islands forming a NW-SE chain 360 mi. long in the SW Pacific O. **Neighbors:** Nearest are Kiribati to N, Fiji to S. **Topography:** The islands are all low-lying atolls, nowhere more than 15 ft. above sea level, composed of coral reefs. **Capital:** Funafuti: 5,000.

Government: Type: Parliamentary democracy. **Head of state:** Queen Elizabeth II, represented by Gov.-Gen. Faimalaga Luka; in office: Sept. 9, 2003. **Head of gov.:** Prime Min. Saufatu Sopoanga; in office: Aug. 2, 2002.

Economy: Industries: fishing, tourism, copra. **Chief crops:** coconuts. **Natural resources:** fish. **Livestock** (2002): chickens: 40,000; pigs: 13,000. **Fish catch** (2002 est.): 500 metric tons. **Labor force:** people make a living mainly through exploitation of the sea, reefs, and atolls and from wages sent home by those abroad.

Finance: Monetary unit: Australian Dollar (AUD) (Sept. 2003: 1.56 = $1 U.S.). **GDP** (2000 est.): $12 mil. **Per capita GDP:** $1,100. **Imports** (1998): $7.2 mil.; partners (2000): Fiji, Australia, Portugal, NZ. **Exports** (1997): $276,000; partners (2000): Sweden, Fiji Iceland, Germany. **Budget** (2000): $11.2 mil.

Transport: Civil aviation: 1 airport. **Chief port:** Funafuti.

Communications: TV sets: 9 per 1,000 pop. **Radios:** 364 per 1,000 pop.

Health: Life expectancy: 65.2 male; 69.6 female. **Births** (per 1,000 pop.): 21.6. **Deaths** (per 1,000 pop.): 7.3. **Natural inc.:** 1.42%. **Infant mortality** (per 1,000 live births): 21.3.

Education: Compulsory: ages 7-14. **Literacy** (1996): 55%.
Major Intl. Organizations: UN, WHO, the Commonwealth.
Website: www.tuvaluislands.com

The Ellice Islands separated from the British Gilbert and Ellice Islands Colony in 1975 and became Tuvalu; independence came Oct. 1, 1978. In 2000, Tuvalu joined the United Nations.

Uganda
Republic of Uganda

People: Population: 25,827,000. **Age distrib. (%):** <15: 50.9; 65+: 2.1. **Pop. density:** 335 per sq. mi. **Urban:** 15%. **Ethnic groups:** Baganda 17%, Ankole 8%, Basoga 8%, Iteso 8%, Bakiga 7%; many other groups. **Principal languages:** English (official), Swahili, Ganda, many Bantu and Nilotic languages. Arabic. **Chief religions:** Roman Catholic 33%, Protestant 33%, Muslim 16%, indigenous beliefs 18%.

Geography: Area: 91,135 sq. mi. (total); 77,108 sq. mi. (land). **Location:** In E Central Africa. **Neighbors:** Sudan on N, Congo (formerly Zaire) on W, Rwanda and Tanzania on S, Kenya on E. **Topography:** Most of Uganda is a high plateau 3,000-6,000 ft. high, with high Ruwenzori range in W (Mt. Margherita 16,763 ft.), volcanoes in SW; NE is arid, W and SW rainy. Lakes Victoria, Edward, Albert form much of borders. **Capital:** Kampala 1,274,000.

Government: Type: Republic. **Head of state:** Pres. Yoweri Kaguta Museveni; Aug. 15, 1944; in office: Jan. 29, 1986. **Head of gov.:** Prime Min. Apollo Nsibambi; b Nov. 27, 1938; in office: Apr. 5, 1999. **Local divisions:** 39 districts. **Defense budget** (2002): $140 mil. **Active troops:** 50,000–60,000.

Economy: Industries: sugar, brewing, tobacco, cotton textiles, cement. **Chief crops:** coffee, tea, cotton, tobacco, cassava, potatoes. **Natural resources:** copper, cobalt, hydropower, limestone, salt. **Arable land:** 25%. **Livestock** (2002): cattle: 5.90 mil.; chickens: 25.50 mil.; goats: 6.20 mil.; pigs: 1.55 mil.; sheep: 1.10 mil. **Fish catch** (2002): 223,086 metric tons. **Electricity prod.** (2001): 1.93 bil. kWh. **Labor force:** agri. 82%, ind. 5%, services 13%.

Finance: Monetary unit: Shilling (UGS) (Sept. 2003: 1,996.37=1 U.S.). **GDP** (2002 est.): $31 bil. **Per capita GDP:** $1,260. **Imports** (2001): $1.26 bil.; partners (2000): Kenya 43.1%, U.S. 7%, India 6.8%, South Africa 6.1%. **Exports** (2001): $367 mil.; partners (2000): Germany 12%, Netherlands 10.2%, U.S. 8.7%, Spain 8%. **Tourism** (1999): $149 mil. **Budget** (1999 est.): $1.04 bil. **Intl. reserves less gold:** $687 mil. **Consumer prices:** –0.3%.

Transport: Railroad: Length: 771 mi. **Motor vehicles:** 49,000 pass. cars, 74,300 comm. vehicles. **Civil aviation:** 221.2 mil pass.-mi; 4 airports. **Chief ports:** Entebbe, Jinja.

Communications: TV sets: 28 per 1,000 pop. **Radios:** 130 per 1,000 pop. **Telephone lines:** 55,000. **Daily newspaper circ.:** 2.1 per 1,000 pop. **Internet:** 60,000 users.

Health: Life expectancy: 43.4 male; 46.4 female. **Births** (per 1,000 pop.): 46.6. **Deaths** (per 1,000 pop.): 17.0. **Natural inc.:** 2.96%. **Infant mortality** (per 1,000 live births): 87.9.

Education: Literacy: 69.9%.

Major Intl. Organizations: UN (FAO, IBRD, ILO, IMF, WHO, WTrO), the Commonwealth, AU.

Embassy: 5911 16th St. NW 20011; 726-7100.

Website: www.government.go.ug

Britain obtained a protectorate over Uganda in 1894. The country became independent Oct. 9, 1962, and a republic within the Commonwealth a year later. In 1967, the traditional kingdoms, including the powerful Buganda state, were abolished and the central government strengthened.

Gen. Idi Amin seized power from Prime Min. Milton Obote in 1971. During his eight years of dictatorial rule, he was responsible for the deaths of up to 300,000 of his opponents. In 1972 he expelled nearly all of Uganda's 45,000 Asians. Amin was named president for life in 1976. Tanzanian troops and Ugandan exiles and rebels ousted Amin, Apr. 11, 1979.

Obote held the presidency from Dec. 1980 until his ouster in a military coup July 27, 1985. Guerrilla war and rampant human rights abuses plagued Uganda under Obote's regime.

Conditions improved after Yoweri Museveni took power in Jan. 1986. In 1993 the government authorized restoration of the Buganda and other monarchies, but only for ceremonial purposes. Under a constitution ratified Oct. 1995, nonparty presidential and legislative elections were held in 1996. Uganda helped Laurent Kabila seize power in the Congo (formerly Zaire) in 1997 but sent troops in 1998 to aid insurgents seeking his ouster. A withdrawal agreement was made Sept. 6, 2002. Museveni faced several regional insurgencies in the late 1990s.

At least 330 members of the Movement for the Restoration of the Ten Commandments of God died in a church fire in Kanungu, Mar. 17, 2000; in all, over 900 deaths were associated with the cult. An ebola virus outbreak Oct.-Dec. 2000 killed more than 150 people. Pres. Museveni won reelection Mar. 12, 2001. Idi Amin died in exile in Saudi Arabia, Aug. 16, 2003.

Ukraine

People: Population: 48,523,000. **Age distrib.** (%): <15: 16.8; 65+: 14.5. **Pop. density:** 208 per sq. mi. **Urban:** 68%. **Ethnic groups:** Ukrainian 78%, Russian 17%. **Principal languages:** Ukrainian (official), Russian, Romanian, Polish, Hungarian. **Chief religions:** Ukrainian Orthodox (Kiev patriarchate and Russian patriarchate), Autocephalous Orthodox, Ukrainian Greek Catholic.

Geography: Area (total): 233,090 sq. mi. **Location:** In E Europe. **Neighbors:** Belarus on N; Russia on NE and E; Moldova and Romania on SW; Hungary, Slovakia, and Poland on W. **Topography:** Part of the E European plain. Mountainous areas include the Carpathians in the SW and Crimean chain in the S. Arable black soil constitutes a large part of the country. **Capital:** Kiev. **Cities (urban aggr.):** Kiev (Kyiv) 2,488,000; Kharkov 1,416,000; Dnepropetrovsk 1,069,000.

Government: Type: Republic. **Head of state:** Pres. Leonid Danylovich Kuchma; b Aug. 9, 1938; in office: July 19, 1994. **Head of gov.:** Prime Min. Viktor Yanukovych; b July 9, 1950: in office: Nov. 21, 2002. **Local divisions:** 24 oblasts, 2 municipalities, 1 autonomous republic. **Defense budget** (2002): $631 mil. **Active troops:** 302,300.

Economy: Industries: coal, electric power, metals, machinery & transp. equip., chemicals, sugar. **Chief crops:** grain, sugar beets, sunflower seeds, vegetables. **Natural resources:** iron ore, coal, mang., nat. gas, oil, salt, sulfur, graphite, titanium, magnesium, kaolin, nickel, mercury, timber. **Crude oil reserves** (2002): 395 mil. bbls. **Arable land:** 58%. **Livestock** (2002): cattle: 9.60 mil.; chickens: 146 mil.; goats: 911,900; pigs: 8.48 mil.; sheep: 963,000. **Fish catch** (2002): 382,297 metric tons. **Electricity Prod.:** (2001): 164.69 bil. kWh. **Labor force:** ind. 32%, agri. 24%, services 44%.

Finance: Monetary unit: Hryvnia (UAH) (Sept. 2003: 5.60=1 U.S.). **GDP** (2002 est.): $218 bil. **Per capita GDP:** $4,500. **Imports** (2001): $17.1 bil.; partners (2001 est.): Russia 36.9%, Turkmenistan 10.5%, Germany 8.7%, U.S. **Exports** (2001 est.): $17.3 bil.; partners (2001 est.): Russia 22.6%, Turkey 6.2%, Italy 5.1%, Germany. **Tourism** (1999): $2.12 bil. **Budget** (2002 est.): $11.1 bil. **Intl. reserves less gold:** $3.12 bil. **Gold:** 500,000 oz t. **Consumer prices** (change in 1999): 22.7%.

Transport: Railroad: Length: 13,987 mi. **Motor vehicles:** 5.25 mil pass. cars. **Civil aviation:** 815.2 bil pass.-mi; 182 airports. **Chief ports:** Odesa, Kiev, Berdiansk.

Communications: TV sets: 433 per 1,000 pop. **Radios:** 882 per 1,000 pop. **Telephone lines:** 10,669,600. **Daily newspaper circ.:** 99.5 per 1,000 pop. **Internet:** 600,000 users.

Health: Life expectancy: 61.1 male; 72.2 female. **Births** (per 1,000 pop.): 9.9. **Deaths** (per 1,000 pop.): 16.4. **Natural inc.:** - 0.65%. **Infant mortality** (per 1,000 live births): 20.9.

Education: Compulsory: ages 6-15. **Literacy:** 99.7%.

Major Intl. Organizations: UN (IBRD, ILO, IMF, IMO, WHO), CIS, OSCE.

Embassy: 3350 M St. NW 20007; 333-0606.

Websites: www.ukremb.com; www.kmu.gov.ua/control/en

Trypilians flourished along the Dnieper River, Ukraine's main artery, from 6000-1000 BC. Ukrainians' Slavic ancestors inhabited modern Ukrainian territory well before the first century AD.

In the 9th century, the princes of Kiev established a strong state called Kievan Rus, which included much of present-day Ukraine. A strong dynasty was established, with ties to virtually all major European royal families. St. Vladimir the Great, ruler of Kievan Rus, accepted Christianity as the national faith in 988. At the crossroads of European trade routes, Kievan Rus reached its zenith under Yaroslav the Wise (1019-1054). Internal conflicts led to the disintegration of the Ukrainian state by the 13th century. Mongol rule was supplanted by Poland and Lithuania in the 14th and 15th centuries. The N Black Sea coast and Crimea came under the control of the Turks in 1478.

Ukrainian Cossacks, starting in the late 16th century, waged numerous wars of liberation against the occupiers of Ukraine: Russia, Poland, and Turkey. By the late 18th century, Ukrainian independence was lost. Ukraine's neighbors once again divided its territory. At the turn of the 19th century, Ukraine was occupied by Russia and Austria-Hungary.

An independent Ukrainian National Republic was proclaimed on January 22, 1918. In 1921, Ukraine's neighbors occupied and divided Ukrainian territory. In 1922, Ukraine became a constituent republic of the USSR as the Ukrainian SSR. In 1932-33, the Soviet government engineered a man-made famine in eastern Ukraine, resulting in the deaths of 7-10 million Ukrainians.

In March 1939, independent Carpatho-Ukraine was the first European state to wage war against Nazi-led aggression in the region. During World War II the Ukrainian nationalist underground fought both Nazi and Soviet forces. Restoration of Ukrainian independence was declared June 30, 1941. Over 5 million Ukrainians died in the war. With the reoccupation of Ukraine by Soviet troops in 1944 came a renewed wave of mass arrests, executions, and deportations.

The world's worst nuclear power plant disaster occurred in Chernobyl, Ukraine, in April 1986; many thousands were killed or disabled as a result of the radiation leak. The plant was finally shut down Dec. 15, 2000.

Ukrainian independence was restored in Dec. 1991 with the dissolution of the Soviet Union. In the post-Soviet period Ukraine was burdened with a deteriorating economy. Following a 1994 accord with Russia and the U.S., Ukraine's large nuclear arsenal was transferred to Russia for destruction. A new constitution legalizing private property and establishing Ukrainian as the sole official language was approved by parliament June 29, 1996. In May 1997, Russia and Ukraine resolved disputes over the Black Sea fleet and the future of Sevastopol and signed a long-delayed treaty of friendship. President since 1994, Leonid Kuchma won a 2nd 5-year term in a runoff vote Nov. 14, 1999; a referendum expanding his powers passed Apr. 16, 2000.

A blast from an errant Ukrainian missile caused a Russian jetliner to plunge into the Black Sea Oct. 4, 2001, killing all 78 people on board. A Russian Su-27 fighter plane crashed at a military airshow in W. Ukraine, Jul. 2002, killing 83.

United Arab Emirates

People: Population: 2,995,000. **Age distrib.** (%): <15: 27.7; 65+: 2.6. **Pop. density:** 93 per sq. mi. **Urban:** 87%. **Ethnic groups:** Arab and Iranian 42%, Indian 50%. **Principal languages:** Arabic (official), Persian, English, Hindi, Urdu. **Chief religion:** Muslim 96% (official; Shi'a 16%).

Geography: Area (total): 32,000 sq. mi. **Location:** Middle East, on the S shore of the Persian Gulf. **Neighbors:** Saudi Arabia on W and S, Oman on E. **Topography:** A barren, flat coastal plain gives way to uninhabited sand dunes on the S. Hajar Mts. are on E. **Capital:** Abu Dhabi 471,000.

Government: Type: Federation of emirates. **Head of state:** Pres. Zaid ibn Sultan an-Nahayan; b 1918; in office: Dec. 2, 1971. **Head of gov.:** Prime Min. Sheik Maktum ibn Rashid al-Maktum; b 1946; in office: Nov. 20, 1990. **Local divisions:** 7 autonomous emirates: Abu Dhabi, Ajman, Dubai, Fujaira, Ras al-Khaimah, Sharjah, Umm al-Qaiwain. **Defense budget** (2002): $1.6 bil. **Active troops:** 41,500.

Economy: Industries: oil, fishing, petrochems., constr. materials, boat building, handicrafts, pearling. **Chief crops:** dates, vegetables, watermelons. **Natural resources:** oil, nat. gas. **Crude oil reserves** (2002): 97.8 bil. bbls. **Livestock** (2002): cattle: 96,000; chickens: 16.90 mil.; goats: 1.28 mil.; sheep: 510,000. **Fish catch** (2002 est.): 110,000 metric tons. **Electricity Prod.:** (2001): 37.75 bil. kWh. **Labor force:** services 78%, ind. 15%, agri. 7%.

Finance: Monetary unit: Dirham (AED) (Sept. 2003: 3.67=1 U.S.). **GDP** (2002 est.): $53 bil. **Per capita GDP:** $22,000. **Imports** (2000): $28.6 bil.; partners (1999): Japan 9%, UK 8%, U.S. 8%, Italy 6%. **Exports** (2000 est.): $47.6 bil.; partners (1999): Japan 30%, India 7%, Singapore 6%, South Korea 4%. **Budget** (2000 est.): $22 bil. **Intl. reserves less gold:** $11.20 bil. **Gold:** 40,000 oz t.

Transport: Motor vehicles (1999): 346,300 pass. cars, 89,300 comm. vehicles. **Civil aviation:** 11.28 bil pass.-mi; 22 airports. **Chief ports:** Ajman, Das Island.

Communications: TV sets: 309 per 1,000 pop. **Radios:** 355 per 1,000 pop. **Telephone lines:** 1,093,700. **Daily newspaper circ.:** 156 per 1,000 pop. **Internet:** 1,175,600 users.

Health: Life expectancy: 72.3 male; 77.4 female. **Births** (per 1,000 pop.): 18.5. **Deaths** (per 1,000 pop.): 4.0. **Natural inc.:** 1.45%. **Infant mortality** (per 1,000 live births): 15.6.

Education: Compulsory: ages 5-11. **Literacy:** 77.9%.

Major Intl. Organizations: UN (FAO, IBRD, ILO, IMF, IMO, WHO, WTrO), AL, OPEC.

Embassy: Suite 700, 1255 22nd Street NW, 20037, 202-243-2400.

Websites: www.uae.gov.ae; www.uaeinteract.com

The 7 "Trucial Sheikdoms" gave Britain control of defense and foreign relations in the 19th century. They merged to become an independent state Dec. 2, 1971.

The Abu Dhabi Petroleum Co. was fully nationalized in 1975. Oil revenues have given the UAE one of the highest per capita GDPs in the world. International banking has grown in recent years.

United Kingdom
United Kingdom of Great Britain and Northern Ireland

People: Population: 59,251,000. **Age distrib.** (%): <15: 18.7; 65+: 15.8. **Pop. density:** 635 per sq. mi. **Urban:** 90%. **Ethnic groups:** English 81.5%, Scottish 9.6%, Irish 2.4%, Welsh 1.9%, Ulster 1.9%, West Indian, Indo-Pakistani, and other 2.8%. **Principal languages:** English (official), Welsh and Scottish Gaelic. **Chief religions:** Christian 72%, Muslim 3%, many others.

Geography: Area: 94,525 sq. mi. (total); 93,278 sq. mi. (land). **Location:** Off the NW coast of Europe, across English Channel, Strait of Dover, and North Sea. **Neighbors:** Ireland to W, France to SE. **Topography:** England is mostly rolling land, rising to Uplands of southern Scotland; Lowlands are in center of Scotland, granite Highlands are in N. Coast is heavily indented, especially on W. British Isles have milder climate than N Europe due to the Gulf Stream and ample rainfall. Severn, 220 mi., and Thames, 215 mi., are longest rivers. **Capital:** London. **Cities (urban aggr.):** London 7,640,000; Birmingham 2,272,000; Manchester 2,252,000 Leeds 1,433,000; Liverpool 915,000.

Government: Type: Constitutional monarchy. **Head of state:** Queen Elizabeth II; b Apr. 21, 1926; in office: Feb. 6, 1952. **Head of gov.:** Prime Min. Tony Blair; b May 6, 1953; in office: May 2, 1997. **Local divisions:** 467 local authorities, including England: 387; Wales: 22; Scotland: 32; Northern Ireland: 26. **Defense budget** (2001): $35.4 bil. **Active troops:** 210,450.

Economy: Industries: machine tools, electric power equip., automation equip., railroad equip., shipbuilding, aircraft, vehicles, electronics & comm. equip., metals, chemicals, coal, oil. **Chief crops:** cereals, oilseed, potatoes, vegetables. **Natural resources:** coal, oil, nat. gas, tin, limestone, iron ore, salt, clay, chalk, gypsum, lead, silica. **Crude oil reserves** (2002): 4.9 bil. bbls. **Arable land:** 25%. **Livestock** (2002): cattle: 10.43 mil.; chickens: 168 mil.; goats: 5.53 mil.; sheep: 33 mil. **Fish catch** (2002): 911,622 metric tons. **Electricity Prod.:** (2001): 360.93 bil. kWh. **Labor force:** agri. 1%, ind. 25%, services 74%.

Finance: Monetary unit: Pound (GBP) (Sept. 2003: .64 = $1 U.S.). **GDP** (2002 est.): $1.5 tril. **Per capita GDP:** $25,300. **Imports** (2002): $330.1 bil.; partners (2001): EU 51.7%, , U.S. 13.2%. **Exports** (2002 est.): $286.3 bil.; partners (2001): EU 58.1%, U.S. 15.4%. **Tourism:** $19.54 bil. **Budget** (2001): $540 bil. **Intl. reserves less gold:** $28.95 bil. **Gold:** 10.09 mil oz t. **Consumer prices:** 1.6%.

Transport: Railroad: Length: 10,487 mi. **Motor vehicles** (1999): 24.59 mil pass. cars, 3.33 mil comm. vehicles. **Civil aviation:** 95.50 bil pass.-mi; 334 airports. **Chief ports:** London, Liverpool, Cardiff, Belfast.

Communications: TV sets: 661 per 1,000 pop. **Radios:** 1,437 per 1,000 pop. **Telephone lines:** 35,290,000. **Daily newspaper circ.:** 329 per 1,000 pop. **Internet:** 24,000,000 users.

Health: Life expectancy: 75.7 male; 80.7 female. **Births** (per 1,000 pop.): 11.0. **Deaths** (per 1,000 pop.): 10.2. **Natural inc.:** 0.08%. **Infant mortality** (per 1,000 live births): 5.3.

Education: Compulsory: ages 5-16. **Literacy** (2000 est.): 99%.

Major Intl. Organizations: UN and all of its specialized agencies, the Commonwealth, EU, NATO, OECD, OSCE.

Embassy: 3100 Massachusetts Ave. NW 20008; 588-6500.

Website: www.britainusa.com

The United Kingdom of Great Britain and Northern Ireland comprises England, Wales, Scotland, and Northern Ireland.

Queen and Royal Family. The ruling sovereign is Elizabeth II of the House of Windsor, b Apr. 21, 1926, elder daughter of King George VI. She succeeded to the throne Feb. 6, 1952, and was crowned June 2, 1953. She was married Nov. 20, 1947, to Lt. Philip Mountbatten, b June 10, 1921, former Prince of Greece. He was created Duke of Edinburgh, and given the title H.R.H., Nov. 19, 1947; he was named Prince of the United Kingdom and Northern Ireland Feb. 22, 1957. Prince Charles Philip Arthur George, b Nov. 14, 1948, is the Prince of Wales and heir apparent. His 1st son, William Philip Arthur Louis, b June 21, 1982, is second in line to the throne.

Parliament is the legislative body for the UK, with certain powers over dependent units. It consists of 2 houses: The **House of Commons** has 659 members, elected by direct ballot and divided

as follows: England 529; Wales 40; Scotland 72; Northern Ireland 18. Following a drastic reduction in the number of hereditary peerages, the **House of Lords** (Sept. 2003) comprised 91 hereditary peers, 569 life peers, and 2 archbishops and 23 bishops of the Church of England, for a total of 685.

Resources and Industries. Great Britain's major occupations are manufacturing and trade. Metals and metal-using industries contribute more than 50% of exports. Of about 60 million acres of land in England, Wales, and Scotland, 46 million are farmed, of which 17 million are arable, the rest pastures.

Large oil and gas fields have been found in the North Sea. Commercial oil production began in 1975. There are large deposits of coal.

Britain imports all of its cotton, rubber, sulphur, about 80% of its wool, half of its food and iron ore, also certain amounts of paper, tobacco, chemicals. Manufactured goods made from these basic materials have been exported since the industrial age began. Main exports are machinery, chemicals, textiles, clothing, autos and trucks, iron and steel, locomotives, ships, jet aircraft, farm machinery, drugs, radio, TV, radar and navigation equipment, scientific instruments, arms, whisky.

Religion and Education. The Church of England is Protestant Episcopal. The queen is its temporal head, with rights of appointments to archbishoprics, bishoprics, and other offices. There are 2 provinces, Canterbury and York, each headed by an archbishop. The most famous church is Westminster Abbey (1050-1760), site of coronations, tombs of Elizabeth I, Mary, Queen of Scots, kings, poets, and of the Unknown Warrior.

The most celebrated British universities are Oxford and Cambridge, each dating to the 13th century. There are about 70 other universities.

History. Britain was part of the continent of Europe until about 6,000 BC, but migration across the English Channel continued long afterward. Celts arrived 2,500 to 3,000 years ago. Their language survives in Welsh, and Gaelic enclaves.

England was added to the Roman Empire in AD 43. After the withdrawal of Roman legions in 410, waves of Jutes, Angles, and Saxons arrived from German lands. They contended with Danish raiders for control from the 8th through 11th centuries. The last successful invasion was by French speaking Normans in 1066, who united the country with their dominions in France.

Opposition by nobles to royal authority forced King John to sign the Magna Carta in 1215, a guarantee of rights and the rule of law. In the ensuing decades, the foundations of the parliamentary system were laid.

English dynastic claims to large parts of France led to the Hundred Years War, 1338-1453, and the defeat of England. A long civil war, the War of the Roses, lasted 1455-85, and ended with the establishment of the powerful Tudor monarchy. A distinct English civilization flourished. The economy prospered over long periods of domestic peace unmatched in continental Europe. Religious independence was secured when the Church of England was separated from the authority of the pope in 1534.

Under Queen Elizabeth I, England became a major naval power, leading to the founding of colonies in the new world and the expansion of trade with Europe and the Orient. Scotland was united with England when James VI of Scotland was crowned James I of England in 1603.

A struggle between Parliament and the Stuart kings led to a bloody civil war, 1642-49, and the establishment of a republic under the Puritan Oliver Cromwell. The monarchy was restored in 1660, but the "Glorious Revolution" of 1688 confirmed the sovereignty of Parliament: a Bill of Rights was granted 1689.

In the 18th century, parliamentary rule was strengthened. Technological and entrepreneurial innovations led to the Industrial Revolution. The 13 North American colonies were lost, but replaced by growing empires in Canada and India. Britain's role in the defeat of Napoleon, 1815, strengthened its position as the leading world power.

The extension of the franchise in 1832 and 1867, the formation of trade unions, and the development of universal public education were among the drastic social changes that accompanied the spread of industrialization and urbanization in the 19th century. Large parts of Africa and Asia were added to the empire during the reign of Queen Victoria, 1837-1901.

Though victorious in World War I, Britain suffered huge casualties and economic dislocation. Ireland became independent in 1921, and independence movements became active in India and other colonies. The country suffered major bombing damage in World War II, but held out against Germany single-handedly for a year after France fell in 1940.

Industrial growth continued in the postwar period, but Britain lost its leadership position to other powers. Labor governments passed socialist programs nationalizing some basic industries and expanding social security. Prime Min. Margaret Thatcher's Conservative government, however, tried to increase the role of private enterprise. In 1987, Thatcher became the first British leader in 160 years to be elected to a 3d consecutive term as prime minister. Falling on unpopular times, she resigned as prime minister in Nov. 1990. Her successor, John Major, led Conservatives to an upset victory at the polls, Apr. 9, 1992.

The UK supported the UN resolutions against Iraq and sent military forces to the Persian Gulf War. The Channel Tunnel linking Britain to the Continent was inaugurated May 6, 1994. Britain's relations with the European Union, and France especially, were frayed in 1996 when the EU banned British beef because of the threat of "mad cow" disease.

On May 1, 1997, the Labour Party swept into power in a landslide victory, the largest of any party since 1935. Labour Party leader Tony Blair, 43, became Britain's youngest prime minister since 1812. Diana, Princess of Wales, died in a car crash in Paris, Aug. 31. Britain played a leading role in the NATO air war against Yugoslavia, Mar.-June 1999, and contributed 12,000 troops to the multinational security force in Kosovo (KFOR).

Blair led Labour to another landslide election victory June 7, 2001. After the Sept. 11 attack on the U.S., Britain took an important role in the U.S.-led war against terrorism. The U.K. participated in the bombing of Afghanistan that began Oct. 7.

Overcoming dissent within his own cabinet, Blair committed British troops to the U.S.-led invasion of Iraq, Mar.-Apr. 2003. Forces from the U.K. then remained to occupy S Iraq. Blair's credibility was undermined after the death of arms expert David Kelly fueled controversy over whether a prewar dossier about Iraq's weapons capabilities had been modified to provide a rationale for war. A parliamentary inquiry Sept. 11 cleared Blair of wrongdoing. Blair testified Aug. 28 in front of a judicial inquiry investigating Kelly's death, which, as of Sept. 15, was still ongoing.

Wales

The Principality of Wales in western Britain has an area of 8,019 sq. mi. and a population (2001) of 2,903,200. Cardiff is the capital, pop. (2001 est.; city proper) 305,000.

Less than 20% of Wales residents speak English and Welsh; about 32,000 speak Welsh solely. A 1979 referendum rejected, 4-1, the creation of an elected Welsh assembly; a similar proposal passed by a thin margin on Sept. 18, 1997. Elections were held May 6, 1999.

Early Anglo-Saxon invaders drove Celtic peoples into the mountains of Wales, terming them Waelise (Welsh, or foreign). There they developed a distinct nationality. Members of the ruling house of Gwynedd in the 13th century fought England but were crushed, 1283. Edward of Caernarvon, son of Edward I of England, was created Prince of Wales, 1301.

Scotland

Scotland, a kingdom now united with England and Wales in Great Britain, occupies the northern 37% of the main British island, and the Hebrides, Orkney, Shetland, and smaller islands. Length 275 mi., breadth approx. 150 mi., area 30,418 sq. mi., population (2002) 5,064,000.

The Lowlands, a belt of land approximately 60 mi. wide from the Firth of Clyde to the Firth of Forth, divide the farming region of the Southern Uplands from the granite Highlands of the North; they contain 75% of the population and most of the industry. The Highlands, famous for hunting and fishing, have been opened to industry by many hydroelectric power stations.

Edinburgh, pop. (2001 est., city proper) 449,000, is the capital. Glasgow, pop. (2001 est.; city proper) 579,000, is Britain's greatest industrial center. It is a shipbuilding complex on the Clyde and an ocean port. Aberdeen, pop. (1996 est.) 227,430, NE of Edinburgh, is a major port, center of granite industry, fish-processing, and North Sea oil exploration. Dundee, pop. (1996 est.) 150,250, NE of Edinburgh, is an industrial and fish-processing center. About 90,000 persons speak Gaelic as well as English.

History. Scotland was called Caledonia by the Romans who battled early Celtic tribes and occupied southern areas from the 1st to the 4th centuries. Missionaries from Britain introduced Christianity in the 4th century; St. Columba, an Irish monk, converted most of Scotland in the 6th century.

The Kingdom of Scotland was founded in 1018. William Wallace and Robert Bruce both defeated English armies 1297 and 1314, respectively.

In 1603 James VI of Scotland, son of Mary, Queen of Scots, succeeded to the throne of England as James I, and effected the Union of the Crowns. In 1707 Scotland received representation in the British Parliament, resulting from the union of former separate Parliaments. Its executive in the British cabinet is the Secretary of State for Scotland. The growing Scottish National Party urges independence. A 1979 referendum on the creation of an elected Scottish assembly was defeated, but a proposal to create a regional legislature with limited taxing authority passed by a landslide Sept. 11, 1997. Elections were held May 6, 1999.

Memorials of Robert Burns, Sir Walter Scott, John Knox, and Mary, Queen of Scots, draw many tourists, as do the beauties of the Trossachs, Loch Katrine, Loch Lomond, and abbey ruins.

Industries. Engineering products are the most important industry, with growing emphasis on office machinery, autos, electronics, and other consumer goods. Oil has been discovered offshore in the North Sea, stimulating on-shore support industries.

Scotland produces fine woolens, worsteds, tweeds, silks, fine linens, and jute. It is known for its special breeds of cattle and sheep. Fisheries have large hauls of herring, cod, whiting. Whisky is the biggest export.

The Hebrides are a group of c. 500 islands, 100 inhabited, off the W coast. The Inner Hebrides include **Skye, Mull,** and **Iona,** the last famous for the arrival of St. Columba, AD 563. The Outer Hebrides include **Lewis** and **Harris.** Industries include sheep raising and weaving. The **Orkney Islands,** c. 90, are to the NE. The capital is Kirkwall, on Pomona Isl. Fish curing, sheep raising, and weaving are occupations. NE of the Orkneys are the 200 **Shetland Islands,** 24 inhabited, home of Shetland pony. The Orkneys and Shetlands are centers for the North Sea oil industry.

Northern Ireland

Northern Ireland was constituted in 1920 from 6 of the 9 counties of Ulster, the NE corner of Ireland. Area 5,452 sq. mi., pop. (1996 est.) 1,663,300. Capital and chief industrial center, Belfast, pop. (2001 est.; city proper) 277,000.

Industries. Shipbuilding, including large tankers, has long been an important industry, centered in Belfast, the largest port. Linen manufacture is also important, along with apparel, rope, and twine. Growing diversification has added engineering products, synthetic fibers, and electronics. There are large numbers of cattle, hogs, and sheep. Potatoes, poultry, and dairy foods are also produced.

Government. An act of the British Parliament, 1920, divided Northern from Southern Ireland, each with a parliament and government. When Ireland became a dominion, 1921, and later a republic, Northern Ireland chose to remain a part of the United Kingdom. It elects 18 members to the House of Commons.

During 1968-69, large demonstrations were conducted by Roman Catholics who charged they were discriminated against in voting rights, housing, and employment. The Catholics, a minority comprising about a third of the population, demanded abolition of property qualifications for voting in local elections. Violence and terrorism intensified, involving branches of the Irish Republican Army (outlawed in the Irish Republic), Protestant groups, police, and British troops.

A succession of Northern Ireland prime ministers pressed reform programs but failed to satisfy extremists on both sides. Between 1969 and 1994 more than 3,000 were killed in sectarian violence, many in England itself. Britain suspended the Northern Ireland parliament Mar. 30, 1972, and imposed direct British rule. A coalition government was formed in 1973 when moderates won election to a new one-house Assembly. But a Protestant general strike overthrew the government in 1974 and direct rule was resumed.

The agony of Northern Ireland was dramatized in 1981 by the deaths of 10 Irish nationalist hunger strikers in Maze Prison near Belfast. In 1985 the Hillsborough agreement gave the Rep. of Ireland a voice in the governing of Northern Ireland; the accord was strongly opposed by Ulster loyalists. On Dec. 12, 1993, Britain and Ireland announced a declaration of principles to resolve the Northern Ireland conflict.

On Aug. 31, 1994, the IRA announced a cease-fire, saying it would rely on political means to achieve its objectives; the IRA resumed its terrorist tactics on Feb. 9, 1996. Reinstatement of the IRA cease-fire as of July 20, 1997, led to the resumption of peace talks Sept. 15.

A settlement reached on Good Friday, April 10, 1998, provided for restoration of home rule and election of a 108-member assembly with safeguards for minority rights. Both Ireland and Great Britain agreed to give up their constitutional claims on Northern Ireland. The accord was approved May 22 by voters in Northern Ireland and the Irish Republic, and elections to the assembly were held June 25. IRA dissidents seeking to derail the agreement were responsible for a bomb at Omagh Aug. 15 that killed 29 people and injured over 330.

London transferred authority to a Northern Ireland power-sharing government Dec. 2, 1999. Delays in IRA disarmament led to several suspensions of self-government, most recently from Oct. 15, 2002; the IRA broke off disarmament talks Oct. 30.

Education and Religion. Northern Ireland is about 58% Protestant, 42% Roman Catholic. Education is compulsory between the ages of 5 and 16 years.

Channel Islands

The Channel Islands, area 75 sq. mi., pop. (2003 est.) 145,000, off the NW coast of France, the only parts of the one-time Dukedom of Normandy belonging to England, are Jersey, Guernsey and the dependencies of Guernsey—Alderney, Brechou, Great Sark, Little Sark, Herm, Jethou and Lihou. Jersey and Guernsey have separate legal existences and lieutenant governors named by the Crown. The islands were the only British soil occupied by German troops in World War II.

Isle of Man

The Isle of Man, area 221 sq. mi., pop. (2003 est.) 74,261, is in the Irish Sea, 20 mi. from Scotland, 30 mi. from Cumberland. It is rich in lead and iron. The island has its own laws and a lieutenant governor appointed by the Crown. The Tynwald (legislature) consists of the Legislative Council, partly elected, and House of Keys, elected. Capital: Douglas. Farming, tourism, and fishing (kippers, scallops) are chief occupations. Man is famous for the Manx tailless cat.

Gibraltar

Gibraltar, a dependency on the southern coast of Spain, guards the entrance to the Mediterranean. The Rock of Gibraltar has been in British possession since 1704. The Rock is 2.75 mi. long, 3/4 of a mi. wide and 1,396 ft. in height; a narrow isthmus connects it with the mainland. Pop. (2003 est.) 27,776.

Gibraltar has historically been an object of contention between Britain and Spain. Residents voted with near unanimity to remain under British rule, in a 1967 referendum held in pursuance of a UN resolution on decolonization. A new constitution, May 30, 1969, increased Gibraltarian control of domestic affairs (the UK continues to handle defense and internal security matters). Following a 1984 agreement between Britain and Spain, the border, closed by Spain in 1969, was fully reopened in Feb. 1985. A UN General Assembly resolution requested Britain to end Gibraltar's colonial status by Oct. 1, 1996. A plan for the U.K. and Spain to share sovereignty was rejected by Gibraltar voters, Nov. 7, 2002.

British West Indies

Swinging in a vast arc from the coast of Venezuela NE, then N and NW toward Puerto Rico are the Leeward Islands, forming a coral and volcanic barrier sheltering the Caribbean from the open Atlantic. Many of the islands are self-governing British possessions. Universal suffrage was instituted 1951-54; ministerial systems were set up 1956-1960.

The **Leeward Islands** still associated with the UK are **Montserrat**, area 39 sq. mi., pop. (2002 est.) 4,500, capital Plymouth; the **British Virgin Islands**, 59 sq. mi., pop. (2003 est.) 21,730, capital Road Town; and **Anguilla**, the most northerly of the Leeward Islands, 39 sq. mi., pop. (2003 est.) 12,738, capital The Valley. Montserrat has been devastated by the Soufrière Hills volcano, which began erupting July 18, 1995.

The three **Cayman Islands**, a dependency, lie S of Cuba, NW of Jamaica. Pop. (2003 est.) 41,934, most of it on Grand Cayman. It is a free port; in the 1970s Grand Cayman became a tax-free refuge for foreign funds and branches of many Western banks were opened there. Total area 101 sq. mi., capital Georgetown.

The **Turks and Caicos Islands** are a dependency at the SE end of the Bahama Islands. Of about 30 islands, only 6 are inhabited; area 166 sq. mi., pop. (2003 est.) 19,350; capital Grand Turk. Salt, shellfish, and conch shells are the main exports.

Bermuda

Bermuda is a British dependency governed by a royal governor and an assembly, dating from 1620, the oldest legislative body among British dependencies. Capital is Hamilton.

It is a group of about 150 small islands of coral formation, 20 inhabited, comprising 20.0 sq. mi. in the western Atlantic, 580 mi. E of North Carolina. Pop. (2003 est.) 64,482 (about 61% of African descent). Pop. density is high.

The U.S. maintains a NASA tracking facility; a U.S. naval air base was closed in 1995.

Tourism is the major industry; Bermuda boasts many resort hotels. The government raises most revenue from import duties. Exports: petroleum products, medicine. In a referendum Aug. 15, 1995, voters rejected independence by nearly a 3-to-1 majority.

Hurricane Fabian, the most potent storm to reach Bermuda in 50 years, struck Sept. 5, 2003; 4 people were missing and presumed dead, and damage was estimated at over $300 million.

South Atlantic

The **Falkland Islands**, a dependency, lie 300 mi. E of the Strait of Magellan at the southern end of South America.

The Falklands or Islas Malvinas include 2 large islands and about 200 smaller ones, area 4,700 sq. mi., pop. (2003 est.) 2,967, capital Stanley. The licensing of foreign fishing vessels has become the major source of revenue. Sheep-grazing is a main industry; wool is the principal export. There are indications of large oil and gas deposits. The islands are also claimed by Argentina, though 97% of inhabitants are of British origin. Argentina invaded the islands Apr. 2, 1982. The British responded by sending a task force to the area, landing their main force on the Falklands, May 21, and forcing an Argentine surrender at Port Stanley, June 14. A pact resuming commercial air service with Argentina was signed July 14, 1999.

British Antarctic Territory, south of 60° S lat., formerly a dependency of the Falkland Isls., was made a separate colony in 1962 and includes the **South Shetland Islands,** the **South Orkneys**, and the Antarctic Peninsula. A chain of meteorological stations is maintained.

South Georgia and the South Sandwich Islands, formerly administered by the Falklands Isls., became a separate dependency in 1985. South Georgia, 1,450 sq. mi., with no permanent population, is about 800 mi. SE of the Falklands; the South Sandwich Isls., 130 sq. mi., are uninhabited, about 470 mi. SE of South Georgia.

St. Helena, an island 1,200 mi. off the W. coast of Africa and 1,800 mi. E of South America, 47 sq. mi. and pop. (2003 est.) 7,367. Flax, lace, and rope-making are the chief industries. After Napoleon Bonaparte was defeated at Waterloo the Allies exiled

him to St. Helena, where he lived from Oct. 16, 1815, to his death, May 5, 1821. Capital is Jamestown.

Tristan da Cunha is the principal of a group of islands of volcanic origin, total area 40 sq. mi., halfway between the Cape of Good Hope and South America. A volcanic peak 6,760 ft. high erupted in 1961. The 262 inhabitants were removed to England, but most returned in 1963. The islands are dependencies of St. Helena. Pop. (2002) 284.

Ascension is an island of volcanic origin, 34 sq. mi. in area, 700 mi. NW of St. Helena, through which it is administered. It is a communications relay center for Britain, and has a U.S. satellite tracking center. Pop. (2002) was 1,050, half of them communications workers. The island is noted for sea turtles.

Hong Kong
(*See* China/Hong Kong)

British Indian Ocean Territory

Formed Nov. 1965, embracing islands formerly dependencies of Mauritius or Seychelles: the Chagos Archipelago (including Diego Garcia), Aldabra, Farquhar, and Des Roches. The latter 3 were transferred to Seychelles, which became independent in 1976. Area 23 sq. mi. No permanent civilian population remains; the U.K. and the U.S. maintain a military presence.

Pacific Ocean

Pitcairn Island is in the Pacific, halfway between South America and Australia. The island was discovered in 1767 by Philip Carteret but was not inhabited until 23 years later when the mutineers of the *Bounty* landed there. The area is 18 sq. mi. and 2003 pop. was 47. It is a British dependency and is administered by a British High Commissioner in New Zealand and a local Council. The uninhabited islands of **Henderson, Ducie,** and **Oeno** are in the Pitcairn group.

United States
United States of America

People: Population: 294,043,000. (incl. 50 states & Dist. of Columbia). (Note: U.S. pop. figures may differ elsewhere in *The World Almanac*.) **Age distrib.** (%): <15: 21; 65+: 12.6. **Pop. density:** 83 per sq. mi. **Urban:** 75%. **Ethnic groups:** White 75.1%, Black 12.3%, Asian 3.6%, Amerindian and Alaska native 0.9%. (Hispanics of any race or group 12.5%.) **Principal languages:** English, Spanish. **Chief religions:** Protestant 56%, Roman Catholic 28%, Jewish 2%

Geography: Area: 3,717,810 sq. mi. (total); 3,536,292 sq. mi. (land) (incl. 50 states and DC). **Topography:** Vast central plain, mountains in west, hills and low mountains in east. **Capital:** Washington, D.C.: 3,997,000

Government: Federal republic, strong democratic tradition. **Head of state and gov.:** Pres. George W. Bush; b July 6, 1946; in office: Jan. 20, 2001. **Local divisions:** 50 states and Dist. of Columbia. **Defense budget** (2002): $350.7 bil. **Active troops:** 1,414,000.

Economy: Industries: oil, steel, motor vehicles, aerospace, telecom., chemicals, electronics, food proc., consumer goods, lumber, mining. **Chief crops:** wheat, corn, fruits, vegetables, cotton. **Natural resources:** coal, copper, lead, molybd., phosphates, uranium, bauxite, gold, iron, mercury, nickel, potash, silver, tungsten, zinc, oil, nat. gas, timber. **Crude oil reserves** (2002): 22.4 bil. bbls. **Arable land:** 19%. **Livestock** (2002): cattle: 96.70 mil.; chickens: 1.83 bil.; goats: 1.25 mil.; pigs: 59.14 mil.; sheep: 6.69 mil. **Fish catch** (2002): 5,405,404 metric tons. **Electricity prod.** (2001): 3,719.49 bil. kWh. **Labor force:** managerial, professional 31%, technical, sales, admin. support 28.9%, services 13.6%, manufact., mining, transportation, and crafts 24.1%, farming, forestry, and fishing 2.4%.

Finance: GDP (2002 est.): $10.4 tril. **Per capita GDP:** $37,600. **Imports** (2001): $1.148 trillion partners (2001): Canada 19%, Mexico 11.5%, Japan 11.1%, China 8.9%. **Exports** (2001 est.): $723 bil.; partners (2001): Canada 22.4%, Mexico 13.9%, Japan 7.9%, UK 5.6%. **Tourism:** $85.15 bil. **Budget** (2002 est.): $2.052 trillion. **Intl. reserves less gold:** $49.99 bil. **Gold:** 262 mil oz t. **Consumer prices:** 1.6%.

Transport: Railroad: Length: 132,000 mi. **Motor vehicles:** 211.94 mil pass. cars, 8.52 mil comm. vehicles. **Civil aviation:** 646.00 bil pass.-mi; 5,131 airports.

Communications: TV sets: 844 per 1,000 pop. **Radios:** 2,116 per 1,000 pop. **Telephone lines:** 190,000,000. **Daily newspaper circ.:** 212 per 1,000 pop. **Internet:** 155,000,000 users.

Health: Life expectancy: 74.4 male; 80.1 female. **Births** (per 1,000 pop.): 14.1. **Deaths** (per 1,000 pop.): 8.4. **Natural inc.:** 0.57%. **Infant mortality** (per 1,000 live births): 6.8.

Education: Free, compulsory: ages 6-17. **Literacy** (1994): 97%.

Major Intl. Organizations: UN (FAO, IBRD, ILO, IMF, IMO, WHO, WTrO), APEC, NATO, OAS, OECD, OSCE.

Websites: www.census.gov; www.whitehouse.gov
www.first gov.gov

See also **United States History chapter.**

Uruguay
Oriental Republic of Uruguay

People: Population: 3,415,000. **Age distrib.** (%): <15: 24.4; 65+: 13. **Pop. density:** 51 per sq. mi. **Urban:** 92%. **Ethnic groups:** White 88%, Mestizo 8%, Black 4%. **Principal languages:** Spanish (official), Portunol/Brazilero (Portuguese-Spanish). **Chief religion:** Roman Catholic 66%.

Geography: Area: 68,039 sq. mi. (total); 67,035 sq. mi. (land). **Location:** In southern South America, on the Atlantic O. **Neighbors:** Argentina on W, Brazil on N. **Topography:** Uruguay is composed of rolling, grassy plains and hills, well watered by rivers flowing W to Uruguay R. **Capital:** Montevideo 1,329,000.

Government: Type: Republic. **Head of state and gov.:** Pres. Jorge Batlle Ibáñez; b Oct. 25, 1927: in office: Mar. 1, 2000. **Local divisions:** 19 departments. **Defense budget** (2002): $206 mil. **Active troops:** 23,900.

Economy: Industries: food proc., electrical machinery, transp. equip., oil products, textiles. **Chief crops:** rice, wheat, corn, barley. **Natural resources:** hydropower, minor minerals, fisheries. **Arable land:** 7%. **Livestock** (2001): cattle: 10.80 mil.; chickens: 13.00 mil.; goats: 14,800; pigs: 380,000; sheep: 13.03 mil. **Fish catch** (2002): 105,051 metric tons. **Electricity prod.** (2001): 7.96 bil. kWh. **Labor force:** agri. 14%, ind. 16%, services 70%.

Finance: Monetary unit: Peso (UYP) (Sept. 2003: 27.68=1 U.S.). **GDP** (2002 est.): $26.5 bil. **Per capita GDP:** $7,800. **Imports** (2001): $2.9 bil.; partners (2001 est.): Mercosur partners: 44%, EU 18%, U.S. 9%. **Exports** (2001 est.): $2.24 bil.; partners (2001 est.): Mercosur partners: 40%, EU 20%, U.S. 8%. **Tourism:** $652 mil. **Budget** (2000): $4.6 bil. **Intl. reserves less gold:** $566 mil. **Gold:** 10,000 oz t. **Consumer prices:** 14.0%.

Transport: Railroad: Length: 1,860 mi. **Motor vehicles** (1999): 662,300 pass. cars, 57,800 comm. vehicles. **Civil aviation:** 521.3 mil pass.-mi; 15 airports. **Chief port:** Montevideo.

Communications: TV sets: 531 per 1,000 pop. **Radios:** 603 per 1,000 pop. **Telephone lines:** 946,500. **Daily newspaper circ.:** 293 per 1,000 pop. **Internet:** 400,000 users.

Health: Life expectancy: 72.5 male; 79.4 female. **Births** (per 1,000 pop.): 17.2. **Deaths** (per 1,000 pop.): 9.0. **Natural inc.:** 0.82%. **Infant mortality** (per 1,000 live births): 13.8.

Education: Compulsory: ages 6-15. **Literacy:** 98%.

Major intl. Organizations: UN (FAO, IBRD, ILO, IMF, IMO, WHO, WTrO), OAS.

Embassy: 2715 M St. NW 20007; 331-1313.

Website: uruguay.usembassy.gov

Spanish settlers began to supplant the indigenous Charrua Indians in 1624. Portuguese from Brazil arrived later, but Uruguay was attached to the Spanish Viceroyalty of Rio de la Plata in the 18th century. Rebels fought against Spain beginning in 1810. An independent republic was declared Aug. 25, 1825.

Terrorist activities led Pres. Juan María Bordaberry to agree to military control of his administration Feb. 1973. In June he abolished Congress and set up a Council of State in its place. Bordaberry was removed by the military in a 1976 coup. Civilian government was restored in 1985.

Socialist measures were adopted in the early 1900s. The state retains a dominant role in the power, telephone, railroad, cement, oil-refining, and other industries, although some privatization began in the early 2000s. Uruguay's standard of living remains one of the highest in South America, and political and labor conditions among the freest. The U.S. agreed Aug. 4, 2002, to provide a short-term loan of $1.5 billion to help Uruguay weather a financial crisis.

Uzbekistan
Republic of Uzbekistan

People: Population: 26,093,000. **Age distrib.** (%): <15: 35.5; 65+: 4.7. **Pop. density:** 151 per sq. mi. **Urban:** 37%. **Ethnic groups:** Uzbek 80%, Russian 6%, Tajik 5%, Kazakh 3%, Karakalpak 3%, Tatar 2%. **Principal languages:** Uzbek (official), Russian, Tajik. **Chief religions:** Muslim 88% (mostly Sunni), Eastern Orthodox 9%.

Geography: Area: 172,742 sq. mi. (total); 164,248 sq. mi. (land). **Location:** Central Asia. **Neighbors:** Kazakhstan on N and W, Kyrgyzstan and Tajikistan on E, Afghanistan and Turkmenistan on S. **Topography:** Mostly plains and desert. **Capital:** Tashkent 2,157,000.

Government: Type: Republic. **Head of state:** Pres. Islam A. Karimov; b Jan. 30, 1938; in office: Mar. 24, 1990. **Head of gov.:** Prime Min. Utkir Sultanov; b July 14, 1939; in office: Dec. 21, 1995. **Local divisions:** 12 regions, 1 autonomous republic, 1 city. **Defense budget** (2002): $106 mil. **Active troops:** 50,000–55,000.

Economy: Industries: textiles, food proc., machine building, metallurgy, nat. gas, chemicals. **Chief crops:** cotton, vegetables, fruits, grain. **Natural resources:** nat. gas, oil, coal, gold, uranium, silver, copper, lead, zinc, tungsten, molybd. **Crude oil reserves** (2002): 594 mil. bbls. **Arable land:** 9%. (2002): cattle: 5.40 mil.; chickens: 14.50 mil.; goats: 830,000; pigs: 90,000; sheep: 8.22 mil. **Fish catch** (2002): 8,152 metric tons. **Electricity prod.** (2001): 44.49 bil. kWh. **Labor force:** agri. 44%, ind. 20%, services 36%.

Finance: Monetary unit: Som (UZS) (Sept. 2003: 976.00=1 U.S.). **GDP** (2002 est.): $65 bil. **Per capita GDP:** $2,500. **Imports** (2001): $2.5 bil.; partners (2002): Russia 15.8%, South Korea 9.8%, U.S. 8.7%, Germany 8.6%. **Exports** (2001 est.): $2.8 bil.; partners (2000): Russia 16.7%, Switzerland 8.3%, UK 7.2%, Ukraine 4.7%. **Tourism** (1998): $21 mil. **Budget** (1999 est.): $4.1 bil.

Transport: Railroad: Length: 2,272 mi. **Motor vehicles:** 865,000 pass. cars, 14,500 comm. vehicles. **Civil aviation:** 2.07 bil pass.-mi; 27 airports. **Chief port:** Termiz.

Communications: TV sets: 280 per 1,000 pop. **Radios:** 465 per 1,000 pop. **Telephone lines:** 1,663,000. **Daily newspaper circ.:** 3.3 per 1,000 pop. **Internet:** 275,000 users.

Health: Life expectancy: 60.5 male; 67.6 female. **Births** (per 1,000 pop.): 26.1. **Deaths** (per 1,000 pop.): 8.0. **Natural inc.:** 1.81%. **Infant mortality** (per 1,000 live births): 71.5.

Education: Compulsory: ages 6-14. **Literacy:** 99.3%.

Major intl. Organizations: UN (IBRD, ILO, IMF, WHO), CIS, OSCE.

Embassy: 1746 Massachusetts Ave. NW 20036; 887-5300.

The region was overrun by the Mongols under Genghis Khan in 1220. In the 14th century, Uzbekistan became the center of a native empire—that of the Timurids. In later centuries Muslim feudal states emerged. Russian military conquest began in the 19th century.

Website: www.uzbekistan.org

The Uzbek SSR became a Soviet Union republic in 1925. Uzbekistan declared independence Aug. 29, 1991. It became an independent republic when the Soviet Union disbanded Dec. 26, 1991. Subsequently, the government of Uzbekistan was led by former Communists. U.S. forces used bases in Uzbekistan during military action in Afghanistan in 2001. A pact tightening military and economic ties with the U.S. was signed Mar. 12, 2002.

Vanuatu
Republic of Vanuatu

People: Population: 212,000. **Age distrib.** (%): <15: 35.6; 65+: 3.3. **Pop. density:** 37 per sq. mi. **Urban:** 22%. **Ethnic groups:** Melanesian 98%, French, Vietnamese, Chinese, other Pacific Islanders. **Principal languages:** Bislama, English, French (all official); more than 100 local languages. **Chief religions:** Presbyterian 37%, Anglican 15%, Roman Catholic 15%, indigenous beliefs 8%, other Christian 10%.

Geography: Area (total): 4,710 sq. mi. **Location:** SW Pacific, 1,200 mi. NE of Brisbane, Australia. **Neighbors:** Fiji to E, Solomon Isls. to NW. **Topography:** Dense forest with narrow coastal strips of cultivated land. **Capital:** Vila; 31,000.

Government: Type: Republic. **Head of state:** Pres. John Bani; b. July 1, 1941; in office: Mar. 24, 1999. **Head of gov.:** Prime Min. Edward Natapei; b 1954; in office: Apr. 13, 2001. **Local divisions:** 6 provinces

Economy: Industries: food & fish freezing, wood proc., meat canning. **Chief crops:** copra, coconuts, cocoa, coffee, taro, yams. **Natural resources:** mang., timber, fish. **Arable land:** 2%. **Livestock** (2002): cattle: 151,000; chickens: 340,000; goats: 12,000; pigs: 62,000. **Fish catch** (2002 est.): 26,690 metric tons. **Electricity prod.** (2001): 0.04 bil. kWh. **Labor force:** agri. 65%, services 30%, ind. 5%.

Finance: Monetary unit: Vatu (VUV) (Sept. 2003: 128.10=1 U.S.). **GDP** (2002 est.): $563 mil. **Per capita GDP:** $2,900. **Imports** (2000): $87.5 mil.; partners (2000): Australia 28%, Singapore 14%, New Zealand 8%, Japan 4%. **Exports** (2000): $22.8 mil.; partners (2000): Japan 32%, Belgium 17%, U.S. 17%, Germany 8%. **Tourism:** $58 mil. **Budget** (1996 est.): $99.8 mil. **Intl. reserves less gold:** $27 mil. **Consumer prices** (change in 2001): 3.7%.

Transport: Motor vehicles: (1998): 2,700 pass. cars, 3,800 comm. vehicles. **Civil aviation:** 110.6 mil pass.-mi; 3 airports. **Chief ports:** Forai, Port-Vila.

Communications: TV sets: 12 per 1,000 pop. **Radios:** 350 per 1,000 pop. **Telephone lines:** 7,100. **Internet:** 5,500 users.

Health: Life expectancy: 60.3 male; 63.2 female. **Births** (per 1,000 pop.): 24.3. **Deaths** (per 1,000 pop.): 8.1. **Natural inc.:** 1.61%. **Infant mortality** (per 1,000 live births): 58.1.

Education: Compulsory: ages 6-12. **Literacy** (1997): 53%.

Major intl. Organizations: UN (FAO, IBRD, IMF, IMO, WHO), the Commonwealth.

Website: www.vanuatugovernment.gov.vu

The Anglo-French condominium of the New Hebrides, administered jointly by France and Great Britain since 1906, became the independent Republic of Vanuatu on July 30, 1980.

Vatican City (The Holy See)

People: Population: 900. **Urban:** 100%. **Ethnic groups:** Italian, Swiss, other. **Principal languages:** Latin (official), Italian, French, Monastic Sign Language, various others. **Chief religion:** Roman Catholic.

Geography: Area (total): 108.7 acres. **Location:** In Rome, Italy. **Neighbors:** Completely surrounded by Italy.

Monetary unit: Euro (EUR) (Sept. 2003: 0.92=1 U.S.).

Apostolic Nunciature in U.S.: 3339 Massachusetts Ave. NW 20008; 333-7121.

Website: www.vatican.va

The popes for many centuries, with brief interruptions, held temporal sovereignty over mid-Italy (the so-called Papal States), comprising an area of some 16,000 sq. mi., with a population in the 19th century of more than 3 million. This territory was incorporated in the new Kingdom of Italy (1861), the sovereignty of the pope being confined to the palaces of the Vatican and the Lateran in Rome and the villa of Castel Gandolfo, by an Italian law, May 13, 1871. This law also guaranteed to the pope and his successors a yearly indemnity of over $620,000. The allowance, however, remained unclaimed.

A Treaty of Conciliation, a concordat, and a financial convention were signed Feb. 11, 1929, by Cardinal Gasparri and Premier Mussolini. The documents established the independent state of Vatican City and gave the Roman Catholic church special status in Italy. The treaty (Lateran Agreement) was made part of the Constitution of Italy (Article 7) in 1947. Italy and the Vatican signed an agreement in 1984 on revisions of the concordat; the accord eliminated Roman Catholicism as the state religion and ended required religious education in Italian schools.

Vatican City includes the Basilica of Saint Peter, the Vatican Palace and Museum covering over 13 acres, the Vatican gardens, and neighboring buildings between Viale Vaticano and the church. Thirteen buildings in Rome, outside the boundaries, enjoy extraterritorial rights; these buildings house congregations or officers necessary for the administration of the Holy See.

The legal system is based on the code of canon law, the apostolic constitutions, and laws especially promulgated for the Vatican City by the pope. The Secretariat of State represents the Holy See in its diplomatic relations. By the Treaty of Conciliation the pope is pledged to a perpetual neutrality unless his mediation is specifically requested. This, however, does not prevent the defense of the Church whenever it is persecuted.

The present sovereign of the State of Vatican City is the Supreme Pontiff John Paul II, born Karol Wojtyla in Wadowice, Poland, May 18, 1920, elected Oct. 16, 1978 (the first non-Italian to be elected pope in 456 years).

The U.S. restored formal relations in 1984 after the U.S. Congress repealed an 1867 ban on diplomatic relations with the Vatican. The Vatican and Israel agreed to establish formal relations Dec. 30, 1993.

Venezuela
Bolivarian Republic of Venezuela

People: Population: 25,699,000. **Age distrib.** (%): <15: 31.6; 65+: 4.8. **Pop. density:** 75 per sq. mi. **Urban:** 87%. **Ethnic groups:** Spanish, Italian, Portuguese, Arab, German, Black, indigenous. **Principal languages:** Spanish (official); numerous indigenous dialects. **Chief religion:** Roman Catholic 96%.

Geography: Area: 352,144 sq. mi. (total); 340,561 sq. mi. (land). **Location:** On Caribbean coast of South America. **Neighbors:** Colombia on W, Brazil on S, Guyana on E. **Topography:** Flat coastal plain and Orinoco Delta are bordered by Andes Mts. and hills. Plains, called llanos, extend between mountains and Orinoco. Guiana Highlands and plains are S of Orinoco, which stretches 1,600 mi. and drains 80% of Venezuela. **Capital:** Caracas. **Cities (urban aggr.):** Caracas 3,177,000; Maracaibo 1,901,000; Valencia 1,893,000.

Government: Type: Federal republic. **Head of state and gov.:** Pres. Hugo Rafael Chávez Frías; b July 28, 1954; in office: Feb. 2, 1999. **Local divisions:** 22 states, 1 federal district (Caracas), 1 federal dependency (72 islands). **Defense budget** (2002): $1.1 bil. **Active troops:** 82,300.

Economy: Industries: oil, iron, constr. materials, food proc., textiles, steel, aluminum, auto assembly. **Chief crops:** corn, sorghum, sugarcane, rice, bananas, vegetables, coffee. **Natural resources:** oil, nat. gas, iron ore, gold, bauxite, other minerals, hydropower, diamonds. **Crude oil reserves** (2002): 77.7 bil bbls. **Arable land:** 4%. **Livestock** (2002): cattle: 16 mil.; chickens: 115 mil.; goats: 4 mil.; pigs: 5.65 mil.; sheep: 820,000. **Fish catch** (2002): 434,569 metric tons. **Electricity prod.** (2001): 87.6 bil. kWh. **Labor force:** services 64%, ind. 23%, agri. 13%.

Finance: Monetary unit: Bolívar (VEB) (Sept. 2003: 1,599.50=1 U.S.). **GDP** (2002 est.): $132.8 bil. **Per capita GDP:** $5,500. **Imports** (2001): $18.4 bil.; partners (2000): U.S. 35.8%, Colombia 6.8%, Brazil 4.5%, Germany 3.9%. **Exports** (2001): $29.5 bil.; partners (2000): U.S. 60%, Brazil 5.5%, Colombia 3.5%, Italy 3.5%. **Tourism** (1999): $656 mil. **Budget** (2000 est.): $27 bil. **Intl. reserves less gold:** $6.24 bil. **Gold:** 10.56 mil oz t. **Consumer prices:** 22.4%.

Transport: Railroad: Length: 424 mi. **Motor vehicles** (1996): 1.39 mil pass. cars, 664,600 comm. vehicles. **Civil aviation:** 3.14 bil pass.-mi; 127 airports. **Chief ports:** Maracaibo, La Guaira, Puerto Cabello.

Communications: TV sets: 185 per 1,000 pop. **Radios:** 296 per 1,000 pop. **Telephone lines:** 2,841,800. **Daily newspaper circ.:** 206 per 1,000 pop. **Internet:** 1,274,400 users.

Health: Life expectancy: 70.8 male; 77.1 female. **Births** (per 1,000 pop.): 19.8. **Deaths** (per 1,000 pop.): 4.9. **Natural inc.:** 1.49%. **Infant mortality** (per 1,000 live births): 23.8.

Education: Free, compulsory: ages 6-12. **Literacy:** 93.4%.

Major Intl. Organizations: UN (FAO, IBRD, ILO, IMF, IMO, WHO, WTrO), OAS, OPEC.
Embassy: 1099 30th St. NW 20007; 342-2214.
Website: www.embavenez-us.org

Columbus first set foot on the South American continent on the peninsula of Paria, Aug. 1498. Alonso de Ojeda, 1499, was the first European to see Lake Maracaibo. He called the land Venezuela, or Little Venice, because the Indians had houses on stilts. Spain dominated Venezuela until Simón Bolívar's victory near Carabobo in June 1821. The republic was formed after secession from the Colombian Federation in 1830.

Military strongmen ruled Venezuela for most of the 20th century. They promoted the oil industry; some social reforms were implemented. Since 1959, the country has had democratically elected governments.

Venezuela helped found the Organization of Petroleum Exporting Countries (OPEC). The government, Jan. 1, 1976, nationalized the oil industry with compensation. Oil accounts for most of Venezuela's export earnings; the economy suffered a severe cash crisis in the 1980s and 1990s as a result of depressed oil revenues. Government attempts to reduce dependence on oil have met with limited success.

An attempted coup by midlevel military officers was thwarted by loyalist troops Feb. 4, 1992. A second coup attempt was thwarted in Nov. Pres. Carlos Andrés Pérez was removed from office on corruption charges, May 1993; he was convicted, May 1996, of mismanaging a $17 million secret government fund.

A 1992 coup leader, Hugo Chávez, who ran as a populist, was elected president Dec. 6, 1998. Voters on Dec. 15 approved a new constitution greatly increasing his powers. Floods and mudslides in Dec. 1999 killed, by official estimates, at least 30,000 people.

Popular among the poor, Chávez alienated some middle- and upper-class Venezuelans with his program of economic and political reform, and his foreign policy antagonized the U.S. Gunfire erupted at a mass protest Apr. 11, 2002, in Caracas, killing at least 17 people. Chávez was forced to relinquish power, but when an interim government issued decrees suspending democratic institutions, Chávez loyalists rebelled; the coup fell apart, and the president reclaimed his office Apr. 14.

Opponents of Chávez mounted a crippling general strike, Dec. 2002-Feb. 2003, which ended after mediation by the OAS and former U.S. president Jimmy Carter. Several dissidents were killed later that month. The Colombian and Spanish embassies in Caracas were bombed Feb. 25. Chávez and opposition groups pledged, May 29, 2003, to halt the tide of political violence. Opponents presented petitions with over 3 mil. signatures Aug. 20, demanding a vote to recall Chávez. The petitions were rejected by an electoral commission on a technicality.

Vietnam
Socialist Republic of Vietnam

People: Population: 81,377,000. **Age distrib.** (%): <15: 31.6; 65+: 5.5. **Pop. density:** 648 per sq. mi. **Urban:** 25%. **Ethnic groups:** Vietnamese 85%-90%, Chinese, Hmong, Thai, Khmer, Cham. **Principal languages:** Vietnamese (official), French, Chinese, English. **Chief religions:** Buddhist, Taoist, Roman Catholic, indigenous beliefs.

Geography: Area: 127,244 sq. mi. (total); 125,622 sq. mi. (land). **Location:** SE Asia, on the E coast of the Indochinese Peninsula. **Neighbors:** China on N, Laos and Cambodia on W. **Topography:** Vietnam is long and narrow, with a 1,400-mi. coast. About 32% of country is readily arable, including the densely settled Red R. valley in the N, narrow coastal plains in center, and the wide, often marshy Mekong R. Delta in the S. The rest consists of semi-arid plateaus and barren mountains, with some stretches of tropical rain forest. **Capital:** Hanoi. **Cities (urban aggr.):** Ho Chi Minh City 4,619,000; Hanoi 3,822,000; Hai Phong 1,676,000.

Government: Type: Communist. **Head of state:** Pres. Tran Duc Luong; b May 1937; in office: Sept. 24, 1997. **Head of gov.:** Prime Min. Phan Van Khai; b Dec. 1933; in office: Sept. 25, 1997. **Local divisions:** 58 provinces, 3 cities, 1 capital region. **Defense budget** (2002): $2.34 bil. **Active troops:** 484,000.

Economy: Industries: food proc., garments, shoes, machinery, mining. **Chief crops:** rice, corn, potatoes, rubber, soybeans, coffee, tea. **Natural resources:** phosphates, coal, mang., bauxite, chromate, oil, nat. gas, timber, hydropower. **Crude oil reserves** (2002): 600 mil bbls. **Arable land:** 17%. **Livestock** (2002): cattle: 4.30 mil.; chickens: 155 mil.; goats: 560,600; pigs: 21.74 mil. **Fish catch** (2002 est.): 2,009,623 metric tons. **Electricity prod.** (2001): 29.8 bil. kWh. **Labor force:** agri. 63%, ind. and services 37%.

Finance: Monetary unit: Dong (VND) (Sept. 2003: 16,089.00=1 U.S.). **GDP** (2002 est.): $183 bil. **Per capita GDP:** $2,250. **Imports** (2001): $15.3 bil.; partners (2000): Singapore 17.7%, Japan 14.4%, Taiwan 12.1%, South Korea 11.1%. **Exports** (2001 est.): $15.1 bil.; partners (2000): Japan 18.1%, China 10.6%, Australia 8.8%, Singapore 6.1%. **Tourism** (1998): $86 mil. **Budget** (1999): $5.6 bil. **Intl. reserves less gold:** $3.03 bil. **Consumer prices:** 3.8%.

Transport: Railroad: Length: 1,619 mi. **Motor vehicles** (1999): 57,800 comm. vehicles. **Civil aviation:** 2.38 bil pass.-mi; 24 airports. **Chief ports:** Ho Chi Minh City, Haiphong, Da Nang.

Communications: TV sets: 184 per 1,000 pop. **Radios:** 107 per 1,000 pop. **Telephone lines:** 5,567,100. **Daily newspaper circ.:** 4 per 1,000 pop. **Internet:** 1,500,000 users.
Health: Life expectancy: 67.6 male; 72.7 female. **Births** (per 1,000 pop.): 19.6. **Deaths** (per 1,000 pop.): 6.2. **Natural inc.:** 1.34%. **Infant mortality** (per 1,000 live births): 30.8.
Education: Compulsory: ages 6-10. **Literacy:** 94%.
Major Intl. Organizations: UN (FAO, IBRD, ILO, IMF, IMO, WHO), APEC, ASEAN.
Embassy: Suite 400, 1233 20th St. NW 20037; 861-0737.
Website: www.vietnamembassy-usa.org

Vietnam's recorded history began in Tonkin before the Christian era. Settled by Viets from central China, Vietnam was held by China, 111 BC-AD 939, and was a vassal state during subsequent periods. Vietnam defeated the armies of Kublai Khan, 1288. Conquest by France began in 1858 and ended in 1884 with the protectorates of Tonkin and Annam in the N and the colony of Cochin-China in the S.

Japan occupied Vietnam in 1940; nationalist aims gathered force. A number of groups formed the Vietminh (Independence) League, headed by Ho Chi Minh, Communist guerrilla leader. In Aug. 1945 the Vietminh forced out Bao Dai, former emperor of Annam, head of a Japan-sponsored regime. France, seeking to reestablish colonial control, battled Communist and nationalist forces, 1946-1954, and was defeated at Dienbienphu, May 8, 1954. Meanwhile, on July 1, 1949, Bao Dai had formed a State of Vietnam, with himself as chief of state, with French approval. China backed Ho Chi Minh.

A cease-fire signed in Geneva July 21, 1954, provided for a buffer zone, withdrawal of French troops from the North, and elections to determine the country's future. Under the agreement the Communists gained control of territory north of the 17th parallel, with its capital at Hanoi and Ho Chi Minh as president. South Vietnam came to comprise the 39 southern provinces. Some 900,000 North Vietnamese fled to South Vietnam.

On Oct. 26, 1955, Ngo Dinh Diem, premier of the interim government of South Vietnam, proclaimed the Republic of Vietnam and became its first president.

The North adopted a constitution Dec. 31, 1959, based on Communist principles and calling for reunification of all Vietnam. North Vietnam sought to take over South Vietnam beginning in 1954. Fighting persisted from 1956, with the Communist Vietcong, aided by North Vietnam, pressing war in the South. Northern aid to Vietcong guerrillas was intensified in 1959, and large-scale troop infiltration began in 1964, with Soviet and Chinese arms assistance. Large Northern forces were stationed in border areas of Laos and Cambodia.

A serious political conflict arose in the South in 1963 when Buddhists denounced authoritarianism and brutality. This paved the way for a military coup Nov. 1-2, 1963, which overthrew Diem. Several other military coups followed.

In 1964, the U.S. began air strikes against North Vietnam. Beginning in 1965, the raids were stepped up and U.S. troops became combatants. U.S. troop strength in Vietnam, which reached a high of 543,400 in Apr. 1969, was ordered reduced by President Nixon in a series of withdrawals, beginning in June 1969. U.S. bombings were resumed in 1972-73.

A cease-fire agreement was signed in Paris Jan. 27, 1973 by the U.S., North and South Vietnam, and the Vietcong. It was never implemented.

North Vietnamese forces attacked remaining government outposts in the Central Highlands in the first months of 1975. Government retreats turned into a rout, and the Saigon regime surrendered April 30. North Vietnam assumed control, and began transforming society along Communist lines.

The war's toll included—Combat deaths: U.S. 47,369; South Vietnam more than 200,000; other allied forces 5,225. Total U.S. fatalities numbered more than 58,000. Vietnamese civilian casualties were more than a million. Displaced war refugees in South Vietnam totaled more than 6.5 million.

The country was officially reunited July 2, 1976. The Northern capital, flag, anthem, emblem, and currency were applied to the new state. Nearly all major government posts went to officials of the former Northern government.

Heavy fighting with Cambodia took place, 1977-80, amid mutual charges of aggression and atrocities against civilians. Increasing numbers of Vietnamese civilians, ethnic Chinese, escaped the country, via the sea or the overland route across Cambodia. Vietnam launched an offensive against Cambodian refugee strongholds along the Thai-Cambodian border in 1985; they also engaged Thai troops.

Relations with China soured as 140,000 ethnic Chinese left Vietnam charging discrimination; China cut off economic aid. Reacting to Vietnam's invasion of Cambodia, China attacked 4 Vietnamese border provinces, Feb. 1979.

Vietnam announced reforms aimed at reducing central control of the economy in 1987, as many of the old revolutionary followers of Ho Chi Minh were removed from office.

Citing Vietnamese cooperation in returning remains of U.S. soldiers killed in the Vietnam War, the U.S. announced an end, Feb. 3, 1994, to a 19-year-old U.S. embargo on trade with Vietnam. The U.S. extended full diplomatic recognition to Vietnam July 11, 1995.

The Communist Party replaced the country's ill and aging leadership in Sept. 1997.

Floods in central Vietnam, Oct.-Nov. 1999, killed some 550 people and left over 600,000 families homeless. The U.S. and Vietnam signed a comprehensive trade deal July 13, 2000. U.S. Pres. Bill Clinton made a historic visit to Vietnam Nov. 17-19. Nong Duc Manh, a moderate, was named to head the Communist Party Apr. 22, 2001.

Western Samoa
See Samoa

Yemen
Republic of Yemen

People: Population: 20,010,000. **Age distrib.** (%): <15: 47; 65+: 2.9. **Pop. density:** 98 per sq. mi. **Urban:** 25%. **Ethnic groups:** Mainly Arab; Afro-Arab, South Asian, European. **Principal languages:** Arabic (official). **Chief religion:** Muslim (official; Sunni 60% and Shi'a 40%).

Geography: Area (total): 203,850 sq. mi. **Location:** Middle East, on the S coast of the Arabian Peninsula. **Neighbors:** Saudi Arabia on N, Oman on the E. **Topography:** A sandy coastal strip leads to well-watered fertile mountains in interior. **Capital:** Sana'a. **Cities** (urban aggr.): Sana'a 1,410,000; Aden (1995 est.): 562,000.

Government: Type: Republic. **Head of state:** Pres. Ali Abdullah Saleh; b. 1942; in office: July 17, 1978. **Head of gov.:** Prime Min. Abd-al-Qadir Bajamal; b 1946; in office: Apr. 4, 2001. **Local divisions:** 17 governorates and capital region. **Defense budget** (2002): $515 mil. **Active troops:** 66,500

Economy: Industries: oil prod. & refining, cotton textiles, leather goods, food proc. **Chief crops:** grain, fruits, vegetables, pulses, coffee, cotton. **Natural resources:** oil, fish, salt, marble, coal, gold, lead, nickel, copper. **Crude oil reserves** (2002): 4.0 bil bbls. **Arable land:** 3%. **Livestock** (2002): cattle: 1.34 mil.; chickens: 29.60 mil.; goats: 4.25 mil.; sheep: 4.80 mil. **Fish catch** (2002): 142,198 metric tons. **Electricity prod.** (2001): 3.01 bil. kWh. **Labor force:** most are employed in agric. and herding.

Finance: Monetary unit: Rial (YER) (Sept. 2003: 177 = $1 U.S.). **GDP** (2002 est.): $15.7 bil. **Per capita GDP:** $840. **Imports** (2001): $3 bil.; partners (1999): Saudi Arabia 10%, UAE 8%, France 7%, U.S. 7%. **Exports** (2001 est.): $3.9 bil.; partners (1999): Thailand 34%, China 26%, South Korea 14%, Singapore 9%. **Tourism:** $76 mil. **Budget** (2001 est.): $3.1 bil. **Intl. reserves less gold:** $3.24 bil. **Gold:** 50,000 oz t. **Consumer prices** (change in 1998): 7.9%.

Transport: Motor vehicles (1999): 380,600 pass. cars, 422,100 comm. vehicles. **Civil aviation:** 640.6 bil pass.-mi; 16 airports. **Chief ports:** Ai Hudaydah, Al Mukalla, Aden.

Communications: TV sets: 286 per 1,000 pop. **Radios:** 64 per 1,000 pop. **Telephone lines:** 423,200. **Daily newspaper circ.:** 15 per 1,000 pop. **Internet:** 17,000 users.

Health: Life expectancy: 59.2 male; 62.9 female. **Births** (per 1,000 pop.): 43.2. **Deaths** (per 1,000 pop.): 9.0. **Natural inc.:** 3.42%. **Infant mortality** (per 1,000 live births): 65.0.

Education: Compulsory: ages 6-14. **Literacy** (1994): 50.2%.

Major Intl. Organizations: UN (FAO, IBRD, ILO, IMF, IMO, WHO), AL.

Embassy: Suite 705, 2600 Virginia Ave. NW 20037; 965-4760.

Website: www.yemenembassy.org

Yemen's territory once was part of the ancient Kingdom of Sheba, or Saba, a prosperous link in trade between Africa and India. The Bible speaks of its gold, spices, and precious stones as gifts borne by the Queen of Sheba to King Solomon.

Yemen became independent in 1918, after years of Ottoman Turkish rule, but remained politically and economically backward. Imam Ahmed ruled 1948-1962. Army officers headed by Brig. Gen. Abdullah al-Salal declared the country to be the Yemen Arab Republic, Sept. 1962.

The Imam Ahmed's heir, the Imam Mohamad al-Badr, fled to the mountains where tribesmen joined royalist forces; internal warfare between them and the republican forces continued. About 150,000 people died in the fighting. In April 1970 hostilities ended with an agreement between Yemen and Saudi Arabia, which had aided the royalists. On June 13, 1974, an army group, led by Col. Ibrahim al-Hamidi, seized the government. He was killed in 1977.

Meanwhile, South Yemen won independence from Britain in 1967, formed out of the British colony of Aden and the British protectorate of South Arabia. It became the Arab world's only Marxist state, taking the name People's Democratic Republic of Yemen in 1970 and signing a friendship treaty with the USSR in 1979 that allowed for the stationing of Soviet troops.

More than 300,000 Yemenis fled from the south to the north after independence, contributing to 2 decades of hostility between the 2 states that flared into warfare twice in the 1970s.

An Arab League-sponsored agreement between North and South Yemen on unification of the 2 countries was signed Mar. 29, 1979. An agreement providing for widespread political and economic cooperation was signed in 1988.

The 2 countries were formally united May 21, 1990, but regional clan-based rivalries led to full-scale civil war in 1994. Secessionists declared a breakaway state in S Yemen, May 21, 1994, but northern troops captured the former southern capital of Aden in July. A new constitution was approved Sept. 28.

A dispute between Yemen and Eritrea over the Hanish Isls. in the Red Sea, which led to armed clashes in 1995, was resolved by arbitration in 1998.

Yemen, the ancestral home of Osama bin Laden, has been caught in a crossfire between the U.S. and Islamic extremists. While on a refueling stop in Aden, Oct. 12, 2000, the destroyer U.S.S. *Cole* was bombed, leaving 17 Americans dead and more than 3 dozen injured; the U.S. government blamed the attack on terrorists associated with Osama bin Laden. The U.S. sent troops in 2002 to help track down members of al-Qaeda. A missile fired Nov. 3, 2002, from an unmanned CIA surveillance aircraft killed 6 suspected al-Qaeda members, including an American. Three U.S. missionaries were slain at a Baptist hospital in Jibla, Dec. 30; the gunman, an Islamic militant, received a death sentence May 10, 2003.

Yugoslavia
See Serbia and Montenegro

Zaire
See Congo

Zambia
Republic of Zambia

People: Population: 10,812,000. **Age distrib.** (%): <15: 47.1; 65+: 2.5. **Pop. density:** 38 per sq. mi. **Urban:** 40%. **Ethnic groups:** More than 70 groups; largest are Bemba, Tonga, Ngoni, and Lozi. **Principal languages:** English (official), Bemba, Kaonda, Lozi, Lunda, Luvale, Nyanja, Tonga, 70 others. **Chief religions:** Christian 50%-75%, Muslim and Hindu 24%-49%.

Geography: Area: 290,586 sq. mi. (total); 285,995 sq. mi. (land). **Location:** In S central Africa. **Neighbors:** Congo (formerly Zaire) on N; Tanzania, Malawi, Mozambique on E; Zimbabwe, Namibia on S; Angola on W. **Topography:** Zambia is mostly high plateau country covered with thick forests, and drained by several important rivers, including the Zambezi. **Capital:** Lusaka 1,718,000.

Government: Type: Republic. **Head of state and gov.:** Pres. Levy Patrick Mwanawasa; b Sept. 3, 1948; in office: Jan. 2, 2002. **Local divisions:** 9 provinces. **Defense budget** (2002): $23 mil. **Active troops:** 21,600.

Economy: Industries: copper mining & proc., constr., foodstuffs. **Chief crops:** corn, sorghum, rice, peanuts, sunflower seeds. **Natural resources:** copper, cobalt, zinc, lead, coal, emeralds, gold, silver, uranium, hydropower. **Arable land:** 7%. **Livestock** (2002): cattle: 2.40 mil.; chickens: 30 mil.; goats: 1.27 mil.; pigs: 340,000; sheep: 150,000. **Fish catch** (2002 est.): 69,200 metric tons. **Electricity prod.** (2001): 7.75 bil. kWh. **Labor force:** agric. 85%, ind. 6%, services 9%.

Finance: Monetary unit: Kwacha (ZMK) (Sept. 2003: 4,930.00=1 U.S.). **GDP** (2002 est.): $8.9 bil. **Per capita GDP:** $890. **Imports** (2001): $12.05 bil.; partners (2000): South Africa 67.1%, UK 9.8%, Zimbabwe 7.5%, U.S. 5.9%. **Exports** (2001 est.): $876 mil.; partners (2000): UK 25.2%, South Africa 24.5%, Switzerland 9.4%, Malawi 7.5%. **Tourism:** $91 mil. **Budget** (2001 est.): $1.25 bil. **Intl. reserves less gold:** $394 mil. **Consumer prices** (change in 1997): 24.8%.

Transport: Railroad: Length: 1,340 mi. **Motor vehicles** (1996): 3,700 pass. cars, 3,900 comm. vehicles. **Civil aviation:** 21.1 mil pass.-mi; 11 airports. **Chief port:** Mpulungu.

Communications: TV sets: 145 per 1,000 pop. **Radios:** 160 per 1,000 pop. **Telephone lines:** 88,500. **Daily newspaper circ.:** 12 per 1,000 pop. **Internet:** 52,400 users.

Health: Life expectancy: 35.3 male; 35.3 female. **Births** (per 1,000 pop.): 39.5. **Deaths** (per 1,000 pop.): 24.3. **Natural inc.:** 1.52%. **Infant mortality** (per 1,000 live births): 99.3.

Education: Compulsory: ages 7-13. **Literacy:** 80.6%.

Major Intl. Organizations: UN (FAO, IBRD, ILO, IMF, WHO, WTrO), the Commonwealth, AU.

Embassy: 2419 Massachusetts Ave. NW 20008; 265-9717.

Website: www.state.gov.zm

As Northern Rhodesia, the country was under the administration of the South Africa Company, 1889 until 1924, when the office of governor was established, and, subsequently, a legislature. The country became an independent republic within the Commonwealth Oct. 24, 1964.

As part of a program of government participation in major industries, a government corporation in 1970 took over 51% of the ownership of 2 foreign-owned copper-mining companies. Privately-held land and other enterprises were nationalized in 1975. In the 1980s and 1990s lowered copper prices hurt the economy and severe drought caused famine.

Food riots erupted in June 1990, as the nation suffered its worst violence since independence. Elections held Oct. 1991 brought an end to one-party rule. The new government sought to sell state enterprises, including the copper industry. Pres. Frederick Chiluba won reelection Nov. 18, 1996, but international observers cited harassment of opposition parties. A coup attempt was suppressed Oct. 28, 1997.

Thwarted in his effort to change the constitution to allow himself to run for a 3d term, Chiluba endorsed Levy Patrick Mwanawasa, who won a disputed election Dec. 27, 2001. Chiluba was arrested Feb. 24, 2003, on charges that he stole government funds while he was president.

According to UN estimates, about 21.5% of the adult population has HIV/AIDS. Food shortages threatened more than 2 million Zambians in 2002; the government refused to distribute shipments of U.S. food because the grain was genetically modified.

Zimbabwe
Republic of Zimbabwe

People: Population: 12,891,000. **Age distrib.** (%): <15: 37.9; 65+: 3.7. **Pop. density:** 86 per sq. mi. **Urban:** 36%. **Ethnic groups:** Shona 82%, Ndebele 14%. **Principal languages:** English (official), Shona, Sindebele, numerous dialects. **Chief religions:** Syncretic (Christian-indigenous mix) 50%, Christian 25%, indigenous beliefs 24%.

Geography: Area: 150,804 sq. mi. (total); 149,294 sq. mi. (land). **Location:** In southern Africa. **Neighbors:** Zambia on N, Botswana on W, South Africa on S, Mozambique on E. **Topography:** Zimbabwe is high plateau country, rising to mountains on eastern border, sloping down on the other borders. **Capital:** Harare. **Cities (urban aggr.):** Harare 1,868,000; Bulawayo 824,000.

Government: Type: Republic. **Head of state and gov.:** Pres. Robert Mugabe; b Feb. 21, 1924; in office: Dec. 31, 1987. **Local divisions:** 8 provinces, 2 cities. **Defense budget** (2002): $631 mil. **Active troops:** 36,000

Economy: Industries: mining, steel, wood products, cement, chemicals. **Chief crops:** corn, cotton, tobacco, wheat, coffee. **Natural resources:** coal, chromium ore, asbestos, gold, nickel, copper, iron ore, vanadium, lithium, tin, platinum. **Arable land:** 7%. **Livestock** (2002): cattle: 5.70 mil.; chickens: 20 mil.; goats: 2.97 mil.; pigs: 604,000; sheep: 535,000. **Fish catch** (2002 est.): 13,200 metric tons. **Electricity prod.** (2001): 6.74 bil. kWh. **Labor force:** agri. 66%, services 24%, ind. 10%.

Finance: Monetary unit: Zimbabwe Dollar (ZWD) (Sept. 2003: 813.57=1 U.S.). **GDP** (2002 est.): $27 bil. **Per capita GDP:** $2,400. **Imports** (2001): $1.5 bil.; partners (2000 est.): South Africa 46.3%, UK 7.2%, Germany 2.5%, U.S. 2.8%. **Exports** (2001 est.): $2.1 bil.; partners (2000): South Africa 12.1%, UK 8.5%, Japan 7.7%, Germany 6.1%. **Tourism:** $202 mil. **Budget** (2000) $2.6 bil. **Intl. reserves less gold:** $61 mil. **Gold:** 140,000 oz t. **Consumer prices:** 140.1%.

Transport: Railroad: Length: 1,912 mi. **Motor vehicles:** 544,500 pass. cars, 67,700 comm. vehicles. **Civil aviation:** 570.4 bil pass.-mi; 17 airports. **Chief ports:** Binga, Kariba.

Communications: TV sets: 35 per 1,000 pop. **Radios:** 389 per 1,000 pop. **Telephone lines:** 287,900. **Daily newspaper circ.:** 19 per 1,000 pop. **Internet:** 500,000 users.

Health: Life expectancy: 40.1 male; 37.9 female. **Births** (per 1,000 pop.): 30.3. **Deaths** (per 1,000 pop.): 22.0. **Natural inc.:** 0.83%. **Infant mortality** (per 1,000 live births): 66.5.

Education: Compulsory: ages 6-12. **Literacy:** 90.7%.

Major Intl. Organizations: UN (FAO, IBRD, ILO, IMF, WHO, WTrO), the Commonwealth, AU.

Embassy: 1608 New Hampshire Ave. NW 20009; 332-7100.

Website: www.zimembassy-usa.org

Britain took over the area as Southern Rhodesia in 1923 from the British South Africa Co. (which, under Cecil Rhodes, had conquered it by 1897) and granted internal self-government. Under a 1961 constitution, voting was restricted to keep whites in power. On Nov. 11, 1965, Prime Min. Ian D. Smith announced his country's unilateral declaration of independence.

Britain termed the act illegal and demanded that the country (known as Rhodesia until 1980) broaden voting rights to provide for eventual rule by the black African majority. The UN imposed sanctions and, in May 1968, a trade embargo. Intermittent negotiations between the government and various black nationalist groups failed to prevent increasing guerrilla warfare.

In the country's first universal-franchise election, Apr. 21, 1979, Bishop Abel Muzorewa's United African National Council gained a bare majority of the black-dominated Parliament. A cease-fire was accepted by all parties, Dec. 5. Independence as Zimbabwe was finally achieved Apr. 18, 1980.

On Mar. 6, 1992, Pres. Robert Mugabe declared a national disaster because of drought and appealed to foreign donors for food, money, and medicine. An economic adjustment program caused widespread hardship. Mugabe was reelected Mar. 1996 after opposition candidates withdrew. A land redistribution campaign launched by Mugabe triggered violent attacks in Apr. 2000 against some white farmers; whites made up less than 1% of the population but held 70% of the land. Mugabe's opponents gained in legislative elections June 24-25, 2000. International observers criticized Mugabe for relying on fraud and intimidation to win the presidential election of Mar. 9-11, 2002. The EU, the U.S., and the Commonwealth have imposed sanctions on the Mugabe regime.

The UN recently estimated that nearly 34% of the adult population has HIV/AIDS.

National Rankings by Population, Area, Population Density, 2003

Source: *United Nations World Population Prospects: The 2002 Revision* for all pop. figures of 100,000 or more; other pop. figs (not released by UN) from Bureau of the Census, U.S. Dept. of Commerce

As of mid-2003, according to revised UN projections based on medium-fertility assumptions, the world had an estimated population of 6,301,463,000. China was the most populous nation, with 1/5 of the world total. India, the 2nd-largest, passed the 1-billion mark in 1999. Russia is the largest country in land area.

	Largest Populations			Largest Populations			Smallest Populations	
Rank	Country	Population	Rank	Country	Population	Rank	Country	Population
1.	China[1]	1,304,196,000	11.	Mexico	103,457,000	1.	Vatican City	900
2.	India	1,065,462,000	12.	Germany	82,476,000	2.	Tuvalu	11,000
3.	United States	294,043,000	13.	Vietnam	81,377,000	3.	Nauru	13,000
4.	Indonesia	219,883,000	14.	Philippines	79,999,000	4.	Palau	20,000
5.	Brazil	178,470,000	15.	Egypt	71,931,000	5.	San Marino	28,000
6.	Pakistan	153,578,000	16.	Turkey	71,325,000	6.	Monaco	32,000
7.	Bangladesh	146,736,000	17.	Ethiopia	70,678,000	7.	Liechtenstein	33,000
8.	Russia	143,246,000	18.	Iran	68,920,000	8.	Saint Kitts and Nevis	39,000
9.	Japan	127,654,000	19.	Thailand	62,833,000	9.	Marshall Islands	56,000
10.	Nigeria	124,009,000	20.	France	60,144,000	10.	Antigua and Barbuda	68,000

(1) Excluding Hong Kong, pop. 7,049,000, and Macao, pop. 464,000. Includes Taiwan, for which UN does not give sep. figure.

	Largest Land Areas			Smallest Land Areas	
Rank	Country	Area (sq km)	Rank	Country	Area (sq km)
1.	Russia	17,075,400	1.	Vatican City	0.4
2.	China	9,326,411	2.	Monaco	2
3.	Canada	9,220,970	3.	Nauru	21
4.	United States	9,166,601	4.	Tuvalu	26
5.	Brazil	8,456,511	5.	San Marino	60
6.	Australia	7,617,931	6.	Liechtenstein	161
7.	India	2,973,190	7.	Marshall Islands	181
8.	Argentina	2,736,690	8.	Saint Kitts and Nevis	261
9.	Kazakhstan	2,717,300	9.	Maldives	300
10.	Algeria	2,381,741	10.	Malta	321

	Most Densely Populated			Most Sparsely Populated	
Rank	Country	Persons per sq km	Rank	Country	Persons per sq km
1.	Monaco	16,065.0	1.	Mongolia	1.7
2.	Singapore	6,815.7	2.	Namibia	2.4
3.	Vatican City	2,045.5	3.	Australia	2.6
4.	Malta	1,227.4	4.	Suriname	2.7
5.	Bahrain	1,169.6	5.	Mauritania	2.8
6.	Bangladesh	1,095.8	6.	Iceland	2.9
7.	Maldives	1,060.0	7.	Botswana	3.0
8.	The Gambia	711.9	8.	Libya	3.2
9.	Taiwan	700.6	9.	Canada	3.4
10.	Mauritius	660.4	10.	Guyana	3.9

Current Population and Projections for All Countries: 2003, 2025, and 2050

Source: *United Nations World Population Prospects: The 2002 Revision* for all pop. figures of 100,000 or more; other pop. figs (not released by UN) from Bureau of the Census, U.S. Dept. of Commerce

(midyear figures, in thousands)

COUNTRY	2003	2025	2050	COUNTRY	2003	2025	2050
Afghanistan	23,897	44,940	69,517	China[1]	1,304,196	1,445,100	1,395,182
Albania	3,166	3,629	3,670	Colombia	44,222	58,157	67,491
Algeria	31,800	42,429	48,667	Comoros	768	1,266	1,816
Andorra*	70	78	69	Congo (Brazzaville)	3,724	6,750	10,643
Angola	13,625	25,162	43,131	Congo (Kinshasa)	52,771	95,448	151,644
Antigua and Barbuda*	68	75	69	Costa Rica	4,173	5,621	6,512
Argentina	38,428	47,043	52,805	Côte d'Ivoire	16,631	22,140	27,572
Armenia	3,061	2,866	2,334	Croatia	4,428	4,088	3,587
Australia	19,731	23,205	25,560	Cuba	11,300	11,479	10,074
Austria	8,116	7,979	7,376	Cyprus	802	892	892
Azerbaijan	8,370	10,222	10,942	Czech Republic	10,236	9,806	8,553
Bahamas	314	374	395	East Timor	778	1,197	1,433
Bahrain	724	1,034	1,270	Denmark	5,364	5,469	5,273
Bangladesh	146,736	208,268	254,599	Djibouti	703	992	1,395
Barbados	270	283	258	Dominica*	70	78	82
Belarus	9,895	8,950	7,539	Dominican Republic	8,745	10,955	11,876
Belgium	10,318	10,516	10,221	Ecuador	13,003	16,704	18,724
Belize	256	356	421	Egypt	71,931	103,165	127,407
Benin	6,736	11,120	15,602	El Salvador	6,515	8,418	9,793
Bhutan	2,257	3,701	5,288	Equatorial Guinea	494	812	1,177
Bolivia	8,808	12,495	15,748	Eritrea	4,141	7,261	10,539
Bosnia and Herzegovina	4,161	4,183	3,564	Estonia	1,323	1,017	657
Botswana	1,785	1,614	1,380	Ethiopia	70,678	116,006	170,987
Brazil	178,470	216,372	233,140	Fiji	839	965	969
Brunei	358	527	685	Finland	5,207	5,289	4,941
Bulgaria	7,897	6,609	5,255	France	60,144	64,165	64,230
Burkina Faso	13,002	24,527	42,373	Gabon	1,329	1,915	2,488
Burundi	6,825	12,328	19,459	Gambia	1,426	2,177	2,905
Cambodia	14,144	21,899	29,567	Georgia	5,126	4,429	3,472
Cameroon	16,018	20,831	24,948	Germany	82,476	81,959	79,145
Canada	31,510	36,128	39,085	Ghana	20,922	30,618	39,548
Cape Verde	463	666	812	Greece	10,976	10,707	9,814
Central African Republic	3,865	5,193	6,563	Grenada*	89	96	87
Chad	8,598	15,770	25,359	Guatemala	12,347	19,456	26,166
Chile	15,805	19,651	21,805	Guinea	8,480	13,704	19,591

COUNTRY	2003	2025	2050
Guinea-Bissau	1,493	2,774	4,719
Guyana	765	724	507
Haiti	8,326	10,670	12,429
Honduras	6,941	10,115	12,630
Hungary	9,877	8,865	7,589
Iceland	290	325	330
India	1,065,462	1,369,284	1,531,438
Indonesia	219,883	270,113	293,797
Iran	68,920	90,927	105,485
Iraq	25,175	41,707	57,932
Ireland	3,956	4,668	4,996
Israel	6,433	8,598	9,989
Italy	57,423	52,939	44,875
Jamaica	2,651	3,263	3,669
Japan	127,654	123,444	109,722
Jordan	5,473	8,116	10,154
Kazakhstan	15,433	15,388	13,941
Kenya	31,987	39,917	43,984
Kiribati*	99	158	235
Korea North	22,664	24,665	24,966
Korea, South	47,700	50,165	46,418
Kuwait	2,521	3,930	4,926
Kyrgyzstan	5,138	6,484	7,235
Laos	5,657	8,635	11,448
Latvia	2,307	1,857	1,331
Lebanon	3,653	4,554	4,946
Lesotho	1,802	1,608	1,377
Liberia	3,367	6,081	9,821
Libya	5,551	7,785	9,248
Liechtenstein*	33	38	36
Lithuania	3,444	3,035	2,526
Luxembourg	453	580	716
Macedonia	2,056	2,199	2,156
Madagascar	17,404	30,249	46,292
Malawi	12,105	18,245	25,949
Malaysia	24,425	33,479	39,551
Maldives	318	559	819
Mali	13,007	25,679	45,998
Malta	394	418	402
Marshall Islands*	56	83	103
Mauritania	2,893	4,973	7,497
Mauritius	1,221	1,415	1,461
Mexico	103,457	129,866	140,228
Micronesia, Fed. States of	109	122	158
Moldova	4,267	4,096	3,580
Monaco*	32	35	33
Mongolia	2,594	3,368	3,773
Morocco	30,566	40,721	47,064
Mozambique	18,863	25,350	31,275
Myanmar	49,485	59,760	64,493
Namibia	1,987	2,350	2,654
Nauru*	13	18	23
Nepal	25,164	37,831	50,810
Netherlands	16,149	17,123	16,954
New Zealand	3,875	4,379	4,512
Nicaragua	5,466	8,318	10,868
Niger	11,972	25,722	53,037
Nigeria	124,009	192,115	258,478
Norway	4,533	4,859	4,895
Oman	2,851	4,785	6,812
Pakistan	153,578	249,766	348,700
Palau*	20	24	26
Panama	3,120	4,290	5,140

COUNTRY	2003	2025	2050
Papua New Guinea	5,711	8,443	11,110
Paraguay	5,878	9,173	12,111
Peru	27,167	35,622	41,105
Philippines	79,999	108,589	126,965
Poland	38,587	37,337	33,004
Portugal	10,062	9,834	9,027
Qatar	610	790	874
Romania	22,334	20,806	18,063
Russian Federation	143,246	124,428	101,456
Rwanda	8,387	12,509	16,973
Saint Kitts and Nevis*	39	46	52
Saint Lucia	149	167	163
Saint Vincent and the Grenadines	120	130	129
Samoa	178	224	254
San Marino*	28	35	35
São Tomé and Príncipe	161	254	349
Saudi Arabia	24,217	39,751	54,738
Senegal	10,095	15,663	21,589
Serbia and Montenegro	10,527	10,230	9,371
Seychelles*	80	88	90
Sierra Leone	4,971	7,593	10,339
Singapore	4,253	4,905	4,538
Slovakia	5,402	5,397	4,948
Slovenia	1,984	1,859	1,569
Solomon Islands	477	783	1,071
Somalia	9,890	20,978	39,669
South Africa	45,026	42,962	40,243
Spain	41,060	40,369	37,336
Sri Lanka	19,065	21,464	21,172
Sudan	33,610	47,536	60,133
Suriname	436	486	459
Swaziland	1,077	1,042	948
Sweden	8,876	9,055	8,700
Switzerland	7,169	6,801	5,810
Syrian Arab Republic	17,800	26,979	34,174
Taiwan[2]	22,603	24,636	23,204
Tajikistan	6,245	8,193	9,552
Tanzania	36,977	53,435	69,112
Thailand	62,833	73,869	77,079
Togo	4,909	7,551	10,005
Tonga	104	121	122
Trinidad and Tobago	1,303	1,340	1,221
Tunisia	9,832	12,037	12,887
Turkey	71,325	88,995	97,759
Turkmenistan	4,867	6,549	7,541
Tuvalu*	11	16	20
Uganda	25,827	54,883	103,248
Ukraine	48,523	40,775	31,749
United Arab Emirates	2,995	3,944	4,112
United Kingdom	59,251	63,287	66,166
United States of America	294,043	358,030	408,695
Uruguay	3,415	3,875	4,128
Uzbekistan	26,093	33,774	37,818
Vanuatu	212	327	435
Vatican City	(3)	NA	NA
Venezuela	25,699	35,252	41,733
Vietnam	81,377	104,649	117,693
Yemen	20,010	43,204	84,385
Zambia	10,812	14,401	18,528
Zimbabwe	12,891	12,857	12,658
WORLD	**6,305,252**	**7,851,261**	**8,911,714**

*The UN does not list 2003 estimates for countries with populations below 100,000. Figures are from the Bureau of the Census, U.S. Dept. of Commerce. (1) Excludes Hong Kong, population 7,049,000, and Macao, population 464,000. Includes Taiwan, for which UN does not give separate figure. (2) The UN does not recognize Taiwan. Figures are from Bureau of the Census. (3) 2003 population is estimated to be 900. Future estimates do not exist.

Population of the World's Largest Cities

Source: United Nations, Dept. for Economic and Social Information and Policy Analysis

Population figures are revised UN estimates and projections for "urban agglomerations"—that is, contiguous densely populated urban areas, not demarcated by administrative boundaries. Data may differ from figures for cities elsewhere in *The World Almanac*.

Rank	City, Country	Pop. (thousands) 2000	Pop. (thousands) projected) 2015	Annual growth rate (percent) 1995-2000	Percentage increase for: 1975-2000	Percentage increase for: 2000-2015[1]	Pop. of city as percentage of nation's 2000 pop.
1.	Tokyo, Japan	26,444	27,190	0.51	34	3	21
2.	Mexico City, Mexico	18,066	20,434	1.52	69	13	18
3.	São Paulo, Brazil	17,962	21,229	1.81	74	18	10
4.	New York City, U.S.	16,732	17,944	0.48	5	7	6
5.	Mumbai (Bombay), India	16,086	22,577	2.80	119	40	2
6.	Los Angeles, U.S.	13,213	14,494	1.28	48	10	5
7.	Kolkata (Calcutta), India	13,058	16,747	1.90	66	28	1
8.	Shanghai, China	12,887	13,598	−0.34	13	6	1
9.	Dhaka, Bangladesh	12,519	22,766	6.62	476	82	10
10.	Delhi, India	12,441	20,884	4.65	181	68	1

Rank	City, Country	Pop. (thousands) 2000	Pop. (thousands, projected) 2015	Annual growth rate (percent) 1995-2000	Percentage increase for: 1975-2000	Percentage increase for: 2000-2015[1]	Pop. of city as percentage of nation's 2000 pop.
11.	Buenos Aires, Argentina	12,024	13,185	0.70	31	10	33
12.	Jakarta, Indonesia	11,018	17,268	4.05	129	57	5
13.	Osaka, Japan	11,013	11,013	-0.05	12	0	9
14.	Beijing, China	10,839	11,671	0.02	27	8	1
15.	Karachi, Pakistan	10,032	16,197	3.69	151	61	7

(1) Projected.

The World's Refugees, 2002

Source: *World Refugee Survey 2003*, U.S. Committee for Refugees, a nonprofit corp.

These estimates are conservative and have been rounded. Totals include individuals granted asylum and those who had pending asylum claims as of year-end 2002. Figures generally do not include those who have achieved permanent resettlement.

(as of Dec. 31, 2002; only countries estimated to host 50,000 or more refugees are listed)

Place of asylum	Origin of Most	Number
AFRICA		3,029,000
Algeria	Western Sahara, Palestinians . . .	85,000*
Central African Republic	Sudan, Dem. Rep. of the Congo . .	50,000
Democratic Republic of the Congo . .	Angola, Sudan, Burundi, Uganda, Central African Republic, Rep. of the Congo	274,000
Republic of the Congo .	Democratic Rep. of the Congo, Angola, Rwanda, Central African Republic	118,000*
Côte d'Ivoire . . .	Liberia	50,000*
Egypt	Palestinians, Sudan, Somalia	78,000*
Ethiopia	Sudan, Somalia, Eritrea	115,000*
Guinea	Sierra Leone, Côte d'Ivoire	182,000*
Kenya	Somalia, Sudan, Ethiopia	221,000*
Liberia	Sierra Leone, Côte d'Ivoire	65,000
Sierra Leone . . .	Liberia	60,000*
South Africa . . .	Dem. Rep. of the Congo, Somalia, Angola	65,000
Sudan	Eritrea, Uganda, Ethiopia	287,000*
Tanzania	Burundi, Democratic Rep. of the Congo, Rwanda, Somalia	516,000*
Uganda	Sudan, Rwanda, Democratic Rep. of the Congo	221,000
Zambia	Angola, Democratic Rep. of the Congo	247,000*
EUROPE		859,900
Germany	Serbia and Montenegro (Kosovo), Bosnia and Herzegovina	104,000*

Place of asylum	Origin of Most	Number
United Kingdom		79,200
Serbia and Montenegro . . Croatia, Bosnia and Herzegovina		353,000
AMERICAS AND THE CARIBBEAN		756,500
Canada		78,400
United States . . .	El Salvador, Guatemala, Haiti, Cuba, Colombia, Nicaragua . . .	638,000**
EAST ASIA AND THE PACIFIC		875,900
China	Vietnam, North Korea	396,000
Malaysia	Philippines	59,000
Thailand	Myanmar	336,000
MIDDLE EAST		5,289,400
Gaza Strip	Palestinians	879,000
Iran	Afghanistan, Iraq	2,208,500*
Iraq	Palestinians, Iran, Turkey	134,700
Jordan	Palestinians, Iraq	155,000
Kuwait	Palestinians, Iraq	65,000
Lebanon	Palestinians, Iraq	409,000
Saudi Arabia . .	Palestinians, Iraq	245,400
Syria	Palestinians, Iraq	482,000
West Bank	Palestinians	627,000
Yemen	Somalia, Ethiopia, Iraq	81,700
SOUTH AND CENTRAL ASIA		2,188,000
Bangladesh	Myanmar	122,100*
India	Sri Lanka, China (Tibet), Myanmar, Bhutan, Afghanistan	332,300
Nepal	Bhutan, China (Tibet)	132,000
Pakistan	Afghanistan, India	1,518,000*
TOTAL		13,000,000

* Estimates vary widely in number reported. **Approximate number of refugees based on cases reported.

Principal Sources of Refugees, 2002

Sources: *World Refugee Survey 2003*, U.S. Committee for Refugees (as of Dec. 31, 2002)

Afghanistan	3,500,000*	Sierra Leone	130,000	Nigeria	30,000*
Palestinians	3,000,000*	Guatemala	129,000**	East Timor	29,000
Myanmar	510,000*	Bhutan	127,000	Georgia	26,000
Sudan	475,000	Western Sahara	110,000*	Rep. of the Congo	25,000
Angola	410,000	North Korea	100,000*	Cote d'Ivoire	25,000
Dem. Rep. of the Congo	410,000	Serbia and Montenegro	74,000*	Uganda	25,000
Burundi	400,000	Colombia	59,000	Ethiopia	20,000
Vietnam	302,000	Philippines	59,000	Cambodia	17,000
Somalia	300,000	Russian Federation	59,000	Central African Republic	15,000
Iraq	294,000*	Tajikistan	53,000*	Nicaragua	13,000
Eritrea	290,000*	Rwanda	50,000*	Ukraine	13,000
Liberia	280,000*	Mauritania	45,000*	Armenia	12,000
Croatia	251,000*	Turkey	44,000	Indonesia	12,000
El Salvador	203,000*	India	39,000	Albania	10,000
China	178,000	Iran	38,000	Algeria	10,000
Bosnia and Herzegovina . . .	160,000	Cuba	34,000	Ghana	10,000
Sri Lanka	155,000	Haiti	33,000	Pakistan	10,000

*Estimates vary widely in number reported. **Includes asylum seekers with cases pending in U.S.

Estimated HIV Infection and Reported AIDS Cases, Year-end 2002

Source: UNAIDS, Joint United Nations Program on HIV/AIDS

The spread of AIDS (acquired immune deficiency syndrome) has had a major impact on life expectancies in sub-Saharan Africa and parts of Asia. In Botswana, for instance, life expectancy at birth has dropped to its pre-1950 level (about 35 years), due primarily to AIDS. In June 2001, the UN General Assembly held its 1st-ever special session devoted to a health issue, producing a Declaration of Commitment on HIV/AIDS. Among stated goals was a 25% reduction in HIV (human immunodeficiency virus) among people 15 to 24 in the most affected countries by 2005, and globally by 2010. The 13th International Conference on AIDS and STIs (sexually transmitted infections) took place Sept. 21-26, 2003, in Namibia. The role armed forces play in spreading AIDS was the main topic addressed.

The number of people living with HIV/AIDS worldwide as of Dec. 2002 was an estimated 42 million, with the largest number in sub-Saharan Africa. The total includes about 3.2 million children (under 15 years old); most children are believed to have acquired HIV from their mother before or at birth, or through breast feeding. UNAIDS estimates that nearly 5 million new HIV infections occurred in 2002 and that about 3.1 million people died of AIDS that year, including 610,000 children.

Studies, primarily in industrialized nations, have indicated that about 60% of adults infected by HIV develop AIDS within 12-13 years of becoming infected; development of the disease may be more rapid in Third World countries.

Since the start of the global epidemic in the late 1970s, HIV has infected more than 60 million people; an estimated 24.8 million people have died of AIDS, including 4.9 million children.

Current, New HIV/AIDS Cases and Deaths by Region, Year-end 2002

Region	Current cases[1]	Percent[2]	New Cases 2002	Est. Deaths
Sub-Saharan Africa	29,400,000	70	3,500,000	2,400,000
South/Southeast Asia	6,000,000	14.3	700,000	440,000
Latin America	1,500,000	3.6	150,000	60,000
East Asia/Pacific	1,200,000	2.9	270,000	45,000
Eastern Europe/Central Asia	1,200,000	2.9	250,000	25,000
North America	980,000	2.3	45,000	15,000
Western Europe	570,000	1.4	30,000	8,000
North Africa/Middle East	550,000	1.3	83,000	37,000
Caribbean	440,000	1.0	60,000	42,000
Australia and New Zealand	15,000	—	500	<100
WORLD[3]	**42,000,000**	**100**	**5,000,000**	**3,100,000**

(1) Adults and children living with HIV/AIDS. (2) Percentage of total number of people worldwide living with HIV. (3) Details do not add to total because of rounding. (—) Dash means less than 1%.

Major International Organizations

African Union (AU), inaugurated July 9, 2002, in Durban, South Africa, following disbanding of the Organization of African Unity, and consisting of the same 35 members; i.e., all countries of Africa, including the territory of Western Sahara. The new organization was intended to focus on fighting poverty and corruption in Africa. The founders provided for a peer review committee to oversee member states' adherence to standards of good government, respect for human rights, and financial transparency. The AU's founding document authorized the organization to intervene to stop genocide, war crimes, or human rights abuses within individual member nations. **Headquarters:** Ethiopia. **Website:** www.africa-union.org

Asia-Pacific Economic Cooperation (APEC), founded Nov. 1989 as a forum to further cooperation on trade and investment between nations of the region and the rest of the world. Members in 2003 were Australia, Brunei, Canada, Chile, China, Hong Kong, Indonesia, Japan, Malaysia, Mexico, New Zealand, Papua New Guinea, Peru, Philippines, Russia, Singapore, South Korea, Taiwan, Thailand, U.S., and Vietnam. **Headquarters:** Singapore. **Website:** www.apecsec.org.sg

Association of Southeast Asian Nations (ASEAN), formed Aug. 8, 1967, to promote economic, social, and cultural cooperation and development among states of the Southeast Asian region. Members in 2003 were Brunei, Cambodia, Indonesia, Laos, Malaysia, Myanmar, Philippines, Singapore, Thailand, and Vietnam. **Headquarters:** Jakarta. **Website:** www.asean.or.id

Caribbean Community and Common Market (CARICOM), established July 4, 1973. Its aim is to further cooperation in economics, health, education, culture, science and technology, and tax administration, as well as the coordination of foreign policy. Members in 2003 were Antigua and Barbuda, Bahamas (Community only), Barbados, Belize, Dominica, Grenada, Guyana, Haiti, Jamaica, Montserrat, Saint Kitts and Nevis, Saint Lucia, Saint Vincent and the Grenadines, Suriname, and Trinidad and Tobago. **Headquarters:** Georgetown, Guyana. **Website:** www.caricom.org

The Commonwealth, originally called the British Commonwealth of Nations, then the Commonwealth of Nations; an association of nations and dependencies that were once parts of the former British Empire. The British monarch is the symbolic head of the Commonwealth.

There are 54 independent nations in the Commonwealth. As of 2003, regular members included the United Kingdom and 15 other nations recognizing the British monarch, represented by a governor-general, as their head of state: Antigua and Barbuda, Australia, Bahamas, Barbados, Belize, Canada, Grenada, Jamaica, New Zealand, Papua New Guinea, Saint Kitts and Nevis, Saint Lucia, Saint Vincent and the Grenadines, the Solomon Islands, and Tuvalu. Also members in good standing were 36 countries with their own heads of state: Bangladesh, Botswana, Brunei, Cameroon, Cyprus, Dominica, Fiji, The Gambia, Ghana, Guyana, India, Kenya, Kiribati, Lesotho, Malawi, Malaysia, Maldives, Malta, Mauritius, Mozambique, Namibia, Nauru, Nigeria, Samoa, Seychelles, Sierra Leone, Singapore, South Africa, Sri Lanka, Swaziland, Tanzania, Tonga, Trinidad and Tobago, Uganda, Vanuatu, and Zambia.

Pakistan has been suspended from the councils of the Commonwealth since Oct. 1999, following a military coup. Zimbabwe was suspended in Mar. 2002, following election and land redistribution controversies; the suspension was renewed in 2003. The Commonwealth facilitates consultation among members through meetings of ministers and through a permanent Secretariat. **Headquarters:** London. **Website:** www.thecommonwealth.org

Commonwealth of Independent States (CIS), an alliance established in Dec. 1991, made up of former Soviet constituent republics. Members in 2003 were 12 of the 15: Armenia, Azerbaijan, Belarus, Georgia, Kazakhstan, Kyrgyzstan, Moldova, Russia, Tajikistan, Turkmenistan, Ukraine, and Uzbekistan. Policy is set through coordinating bodies such as a Council of Heads of State and Council of Heads of Government. **Capital** of the commonwealth: Minsk, Belarus. **Website:** www.cis.minsk.by

European Free Trade Association (EFTA), created May 3, 1960, to promote expansion of free trade. By Dec. 31, 1966, tariffs and quotas between member nations had been eliminated. Members entered into free trade agreements with the EU in 1972 and 1973. In 1992, EFTA and EU agreed to create a single market—with free flow of goods, services, capital, and labor—among nations of the 2 organizations. Members in 2003 were Iceland, Liechtenstein, Norway, and Switzerland. Many former EFTA members are now EU members. **Headquarters:** Geneva. **Website:** www.efta.int

European Union (EU)—known as the European Community (EC) until 1994; the name covers 3 organizations with common membership: the European Economic Community (Common Market), European Coal and Steel Community, and European Atomic Energy Community (Euratom). Austria, Finland, and Sweden entered the EU on Jan. 1, 1995. The 15 full members in 2003 were Austria, Belgium, Denmark, Finland, France, Germany, Greece, Ireland, Italy, Luxembourg, Netherlands, Portugal, Spain, Sweden, and UK. Ten nations—Cyprus, the Czech Republic, Estonia, Hungary, Latvia, Lithuania, Malta, Poland, Slovakia, and Slovenia—signed an accession treaty Apr. 16-17, 2003. They were scheduled to join the union in May 2004. Some 70 nations in Africa, the Caribbean, and the Pacific are affiliated under the Lomé Convention. **Website:** europa.eu.int

► **IT'S A FACT:** The UN Population Division has been lowering its population projections, based partly on present and anticipated declines in fertility rates and partly on estimates that the AIDS epidemic in the most heavily affected countries will be more severe and prolonged than had been expected. (Projections from other sources vary.) The UN in early 2003 lowered its projected 2050 world population figure from 9.3 billion to 8.9 billion. By 2050, countries with the highest AIDS rates—Botswana, Lesotho, South Africa, and Swaziland—are expected to have lower populations than today.

A merger of the 3 communities' executives went into effect July 1, 1967. The Council of the Union, European Commission, European Parliament, and European Courts of Justice and of Auditors comprise the permanent structure. The EU aims to integrate the economies, coordinate social developments, and bring about political union of the member states. Effective Dec. 31, 1992, there are no restrictions on the movement of goods, services, capital, workers, and tourists within the EU. There are also common agricultural, fisheries, and nuclear research policies.

Leaders of member nations (12 at the time) met Dec. 9-11, 1991, in Maastricht, the Netherlands. They committed the organization to launching a common currency (the euro) by 1999; sought to establish common foreign policies; laid the groundwork for a common defense policy; gave the organization a leading role in social policy (Britain was not included in this plan); pledged increased aid for poorer member nations; and slightly increased the powers of the 567-member European Parliament. The treaties went into effect Nov. 1, 1993, following ratification by all 12 members.

In June 1998 the European Central Bank was established. In Jan. 1999, 11 of the 15 EU countries began using the euro for some purposes: Austria, Belgium, Finland, France, Germany, Ireland, Italy, Luxembourg, Netherlands, Portugal, and Spain. By Feb. 2002, national currencies in these 11 countries and Greece were removed from circulation and replaced with the euro as the only currency of legal tender. EU peacekeeping forces replaced NATO troops in Macedonia, Mar. 31, 2003, the first such mission for the organization.

Group of Eight (G-8), established Sept. 22, 1985; organization of 7 major industrial democracies (Canada, France, Germany, Italy, Japan, UK, and U.S.) and (later) Russia, meeting periodically to discuss economic and other issues. At its annual economic summit in May 1998, the name was changed to G-8 from G-7. The 7 were still free to meet without Russia on some issues, especially those relating to global finance. The 2004 annual G-8 summit was to be hosted in the U.S. at Sea Island, GA, June 8-10.

International Criminal Police Organization (Interpol), created June 13, 1956, to promote mutual assistance among all police authorities within the limits of the law existing in the different countries. There were 181 members (independent nations), plus 14 subbureaus (dependencies) in 2003. **Website:** www.interpol.com

League of Arab States (Arab League), created Mar. 22, 1945. The League promotes economic, social, political, and military cooperation, mediates disputes, and represents Arab states in certain international negotiations. Members in 2003 were Algeria, Bahrain, Comoros, Djibouti, Egypt, Iraq, Jordan, Kuwait, Lebanon, Libya, Mauritania, Morocco, Oman, Palestine (considered an independent state by the League), Qatar, Saudi Arabia, Somalia, Sudan, Syria, Tunisia, United Arab Emirates, and Yemen. **Headquarters:** Cairo. **Website:** www.arableagueonline.org

North Atlantic Treaty Organization (NATO), created by treaty (signed Apr. 4, 1949; in effect Aug. 24, 1949). Members in 2003 were Belgium, Canada, Czech Republic, Denmark, France, Germany, Greece, Hungary, Iceland, Italy, Luxembourg, Netherlands, Norway, Poland, Portugal, Spain, Turkey, U.K, and U.S. Members agreed to settle disputes by peaceful means, to develop their capacity to resist armed attack, to regard an attack on one as an attack on all, and take necessary action to repel an attack under Article 51 of the UN Charter. **Headquarters:** Brussels. **Website:** www.nato.int

The NATO structure consists of the North Atlantic Council (NAC), the Defense Planning Committee, the Military Committee (realigned in June 2003 and consisting of 2 commands: Allied Command Operations, and Allied Command Transformation), the Nuclear Planning Group, and the Canada-U.S. Regional Planning Group. France detached itself from the military command structure in 1966.

With the end of the cold war in the early 1990s, members put greater stress on political action and on creating a rapid deployment force to react to local crises. By the mid-1990s, 27 nations, including Russia and other former Soviet republics, had joined with NATO in the so-called Partnership for Peace (PfP; drafted Dec. 1993), which provided for limited joint military exercises, peace-keeping missions, and information exchange. NATO has proceeded gradually toward extending full membership to former Eastern bloc nations. On Mar. 12, 1999, 3 former Warsaw Pact members, Hungary, Poland, and the Czech Republic, formally became members. NATO and Russia signed a cooperation pact May 28, 2002, forming NATO-Russia Council, and NATO invited 7 former eastern-bloc nations to join the alliance, Nov. 21.

In Dec. 1995, a NATO-led multinational force (SFOR) was deployed to help keep the peace in Bosnia and Herzegovina; in 1999, another force (KFOR) was deployed in Kosovo.

Following the terrorist attacks on the U.S., the NATO Council agreed, Sept. 12, 2001, to invoke for the first time Article 5 of the treaty, which stipulates mutual defense of alliance members. NATO assumed control of the International Security Assistance Force in Afghanistan (ISAF), Aug. 2003, marking the first time NATO led a mission outside Europe. As of Sept. 2003, the ISAF numbered 5,500.

Organization of African Unity (OAU), formed May 25, 1963, by 32 African countries. Disbanded July, 2002, and re-formed as the African Union (AU).

Organization of American States (OAS), formed in Bogotá, Colombia, Apr. 30, 1948. It has a Permanent Council, Inter-American Council for Integral Development, Juridical Committee, and Commission on Human Rights. The Permanent Council can call meetings of foreign ministers to deal with urgent security matters. A General Assembly meets annually.

Members in 2003 were Antigua and Barbuda, Argentina, Bahamas, Barbados, Belize, Bolivia, Brazil, Canada, Chile, Colombia, Costa Rica, Cuba, Dominica, Dominican Republic, Ecuador, El Salvador, Grenada, Guatemala, Guyana, Haiti, Honduras, Jamaica, Mexico, Nicaragua, Panama, Paraguay, Peru, Saint Kitts and Nevis, Saint Lucia, Saint Vincent and the Grenadines, Suriname, Trinidad and Tobago, U.S., Uruguay, and Venezuela. In 1962, the OAS suspended Cuba from participation in activities but not from membership. **Headquarters:** Washington, DC. **Website:** www.oas.org

Organization for Economic Cooperation and Development (OECD), established Sept. 30, 1961, to promote the economic and social welfare of all its member countries and to stimulate efforts on behalf of developing nations. The OECD also collects and disseminates economic and environmental information. Members in 2003 were Australia, Austria, Belgium, Canada, Czech Republic, Denmark, Finland, France, Germany, Greece, Hungary, Iceland, Ireland, Italy, Japan, Luxembourg, Mexico, Netherlands, New Zealand, Norway, Poland, Portugal, Slovak Republic, South Korea, Spain, Sweden, Switzerland, Turkey, United Kingdom, and the United States. **Headquarters:** Paris. **Website:** www.oecd.org

Organization of Petroleum Exporting Countries (OPEC), created Sept. 14, 1960. This group made up of most—but not all—major petroleum exporting nations, seeks to stabilize the oil market and set world oil prices by controlling production. Members in 2003 were Algeria, Indonesia, Iran, Iraq, Kuwait, Libya, Nigeria, Qatar, Saudi Arabia, United Arab Emirates, and Venezuela. **Headquarters:** Vienna. **Website:** www.opec.org

Organization for Security and Cooperation in Europe (OSCE), established in 1972 as the Conference on Security and Cooperation in Europe; name adopted Jan. 1, 1995. The group, formed by NATO and Warsaw Pact members, seeks improved East-West relations through a commitment to nonaggression and human rights as well as cooperation in economics, science and technology, cultural exchange, and environmental protection. There were 55 member states in 2003. **Headquarters:** Vienna. **Website:** www.osce.org

IT'S A FACT: Pakistan and Bangladesh contributed the largest numbers of troops and civilian police to UN peacekeeping forces as of July 2003, with 3,910 and 3,137 people, respectively. Other contributions included 519 from the United States, 334 from Russia, and 305 from China.

United Nations

The 58th regular session of United Nations General Assembly opened Sept. 16, 2003, attended by world leaders and other delegates from 191 nations.

UN headquarters is in New York, NY, between First Ave. and Roosevelt Drive and E. 42d St. and E. 48th St.

The 6 main organs of the UN are the: General Assembly, Security Council, Economic and Social Council, Trusteeship Council, International Court of Justice, and Secretariat. The UN family is much larger, encompassing 15 agencies and several programs and bodies.

The UN Dept. of Public Information maintains its own news service, which can be accessed at www.un.org/news. It also publishes the *UN Chronicle*, available at www.un.org/chronicle. The UN has a post office originating its own stamps.

Proposals to establish an organization of nations for maintenance of world peace led to convening of the United Nations Conference on International Organization at San Francisco, Apr. 25-June 26, 1945, where the UN charter was drawn up. It was signed June 26 by 50 nations, and by Poland, one of the original 51 members, on Oct. 15, 1945. It came into effect Oct. 24, 1945, upon ratification by the permanent members of the Security Council and a majority of other signatories.

Purposes: To maintain international peace and security; to develop friendly relations among nations; to achieve international cooperation in solving economic, social, cultural, and humanitarian problems and in promoting respect for human rights and basic freedoms; to be a center for harmonizing the actions of nations in attaining these common ends.

Visitors to the UN: Headquarters is open to the public every day except Thanksgiving, Christmas, and New Year's Day. Guided tours are given approximately every half hour from 9:30 AM to 4:45 PM weekdays; 10 AM to 4:30 PM weekends. The UN is closed weekends in Jan. and Feb.

Groups of 12 or more should write to the Group Program Unit, Public Services Section, Room GA-63, United Nations, New York, NY 10017, or telephone (212) 963-4440. Children under 5 not permitted on tours.

Roster of the United Nations

The 191 members of the United Nations, with the years in which they became members; as of Oct. 2003.

Member	Year	Member	Year	Member	Year	Member	Year
Afghanistan	1946	Dominica	1978	Liberia	1945	Saint Vincent and the	
Albania	1955	Dominican Republic	1945	Libya	1955	Grenadines	1980
Algeria	1962	East Timor	2002	Liechtenstein	1990	Samoa (formerly	
Andorra	1993	Ecuador	1945	Lithuania	1991	Western Samoa)	1976
Angola	1976	Egypt[3]	1945	Luxembourg	1945	San Marino	1992
Antigua and Barbuda	1981	El Salvador	1945	Macedonia[5]	1993	São Tomé and Príncipe	1975
Argentina	1945	Equatorial Guinea	1968	Madagascar	1960	Saudi Arabia	1945
Armenia	1992	Eritrea	1993	Malawi	1964	Senegal	1960
Australia	1945	Estonia	1991	Malaysia[6]	1957	Serbia and Montenegro[8]	1945
Austria	1955	Ethiopia	1945	Maldives	1965	Seychelles	1976
Azerbaijan	1992	Fiji	1970	Mali	1960	Sierra Leone	1961
Bahamas	1973	Finland	1955	Malta	1964	Singapore[6]	1965
Bahrain	1971	France	1945	Marshall Islands	1991	Slovakia[2]	1993
Bangladesh	1974	Gabon	1960	Mauritania	1961	Slovenia	1992
Barbados	1966	Gambia, The	1965	Mauritius	1968	Solomon Islands	1978
Belarus	1945	Georgia	1992	Mexico	1945	Somalia	1960
Belgium	1945	Germany	1973	Micronesia	1991	South Africa[9]	1945
Belize	1981	Ghana	1957	Moldova	1992	Spain	1955
Benin	1960	Greece	1945	Monaco	1993	Sri Lanka	1955
Bhutan	1971	Grenada	1974	Mongolia	1961	Sudan	1956
Bolivia	1945	Guatemala	1945	Morocco	1956	Suriname	1975
Bosnia & Herzegovina	1992	Guinea	1958	Mozambique	1975	Swaziland	1968
Botswana	1966	Guinea-Bissau	1974	Myanmar (Burma)	1948	Sweden	1946
Brazil	1945	Guyana	1966	Namibia	1990	Switzerland	2002
Brunei	1984	Haiti	1945	Nauru	1999	Syria[3]	1945
Bulgaria	1955	Honduras	1945	Nepal	1955	Tajikistan	1992
Burkina Faso	1960	Hungary	1955	Netherlands	1945	Tanzania[10]	1961
Burundi	1962	Iceland	1946	New Zealand	1945	Thailand	1946
Cambodia	1955	India	1945	Nicaragua	1945	Togo	1960
Cameroon	1960	Indonesia[4]	1950	Niger	1960	Tonga	1999
Canada	1945	Iran	1945	Nigeria	1960	Trinidad and Tobago	1962
Cape Verde	1975	Iraq	1945	Norway	1945	Tunisia	1956
Central African Rep.	1960	Ireland	1955	Oman	1971	Turkey	1945
Chad	1960	Israel	1949	Pakistan	1947	Turkmenistan	1992
Chile	1945	Italy	1955	Palau	1994	Tuvalu	2000
China[1]	1945	Jamaica	1962	Panama	1945	Uganda	1962
Colombia	1945	Japan	1956	Papua New Guinea	1975	Ukraine	1945
Comoros	1975	Jordan	1955	Paraguay	1945	United Arab Emirates	1971
Congo, Democratic		Kazakhstan	1992	Peru	1945	United Kingdom	1945
Rep. of the (Zaire)	1960	Kenya	1963	Philippines	1945	United States	1945
Congo, Republic of the	1960	Kiribati	1999	Poland	1945	Uruguay	1945
Costa Rica	1945	Korea, North	1991	Portugal	1955	Uzbekistan	1992
Côte d'Ivoire	1960	Korea, South	1991	Qatar	1971	Vanuatu	1981
Croatia	1992	Kuwait	1963	Romania	1955	Venezuela	1945
Cuba	1945	Kyrgyzstan	1992	Russia[7]	1945	Vietnam	1977
Cyprus	1960	Laos	1955	Rwanda	1962	Yemen[11]	1947
Czech Republic[2]	1993	Latvia	1991	Saint Kitts and Nevis	1983	Zambia	1964
Denmark	1945	Lebanon	1945	Saint Lucia	1979	Zimbabwe	1980
Djibouti	1977	Lesotho	1966				

(1) The General Assembly voted in 1971 to expel the Chinese government on Taiwan and admit the Beijing government. (2) Czechoslovakia, which split into Czech Republic and Slovakia on Jan. 1, 1993, was a UN member from 1945 to 1992. (3) Egypt and Syria were original members. In 1958, the United Arab Republic was established by a union of Egypt and Syria and continued as one single member of the UN. In 1961, Syria resumed its separate membership. (4) Indonesia withdrew from the UN in 1965 and rejoined in 1966. (5) Admitted under the provisional name of The Former Yugoslav Republic of Macedonia. (6) Malaya joined the UN in 1957. In 1963, its name was changed to Malaysia following the accession of Singapore, Sabah, and Sarawak. Singapore became an independent UN member in 1965. (7) The USSR was an original member from 1945. After the USSR's dissolution in 1991, Russia informed the UN it would be continuing the USSR's membership in the Security Council and all other UN organs with the support of the Commonwealth of Independent States (comprised of most of the former Soviet republics). (8) The Socialist Federal Republic of Yugoslavia became a member in 1945. After 4 of its 6 republics (Bosnia and Herzegovina, Croatia, Macedonia, and Slovenia) declared independence in 1991-92, the 2 remaining republics, Montenegro and Serbia, reconstituted themselves as the Federal Republic of

Yugoslavia, which assumed Yugoslavia's UN seat Apr. 8, 1992. In Sept. 1992, the General Assembly decided the Federal Republic of Yugoslavia could not automatically take the seat of the former Yugoslavia. Membership was granted in Nov. 2000 by a vote of the General Assembly. In Feb. 2003, Yugoslavia changed its name to Serbia and Montenegro. (9) In 1994, the General Assembly admitted the South African delegation, which had been rejected for 24 years because of apartheid. (10) Tanganyika was a member from 1961 and Zanzibar from 1963. Following the ratification in 1964 of Articles of Union between Tanganyika and Zanzibar, the United Republic of Tanganyika and Zanzibar continued as a single member of the UN, later changing its name to United Republic of Tanzania. (11) The Yemen Arab Republic was admitted in 1947; the People's Republic of Yemen, in 1967. The 2 nations merged in 1990. **NOTE:** China (Taiwan) and Vatican City are not members. Vatican City is a permanent observer.

United Nations Secretaries General

Took Office	Secretary, Nation	Took Office	Secretary, Nation	Took Office	Secretary, Nation
1946	Trygve Lie, Norway	1972	Kurt Waldheim, Austria	1992	Boutros Boutros-Ghali, Egypt
1953	Dag Hammarskjold, Sweden	1982	Javier Perez de Cuellar, Peru	1997	Kofi Annan, Ghana
1961	U Thant, Burma				

U.S. Representatives to the United Nations

The U.S. Representative to the United Nations is the chief of the U.S. Mission to the United Nations in New York and holds the rank and status of Ambassador Extraordinary and Plenipotentiary (A.E.P.). Year given is the year each took office.

Year	Representative	Year	Representative	Year	Representative
1946	Edward R. Stettinius, Jr.	1968	James Russell Wiggins	1981	Jeane J. Kirkpatrick
1946	Herschel V. Johnson (act.)	1969	Charles W. Yost	1985	Vernon A. Walters
1947	Warren R. Austin	1971	George H. W. Bush	1989	Thomas R. Pickering
1953	Henry Cabot Lodge, Jr.	1973	John A. Scali	1992	Edward J. Perkins
1960	James J. Wadsworth	1975	Daniel P. Moynihan	1993	Madeleine K. Albright
1961	Adlai E. Stevenson	1976	William W. Scranton	1997	Bill Richardson
1965	Arthur J. Goldberg	1977	Andrew Young	1999	Richard C. Holbrooke
1968	George W. Ball	1979	Donald McHenry	2001	John D. Negroponte

Organization of the United Nations

The United Nations consists of 6 principal organs, 15 agencies, and many programs and other bodies. The 6 principal organs are the General Assembly, the Security Council, the Secretariat, the Economic and Social Council, the Trusteeship Council, and the Intl. Court for Justice.

General Assembly. The General Assembly is composed of representatives of all the member nations. Each nation is entitled to one vote. The General Assembly meets in regular annual sessions and in special session when convoked at the request of the Security Council or a majority of UN members. On important questions a two-thirds majority of members present and voting is required; on other questions a simple majority is sufficient.

The General Assembly must approve the UN budget and apportion expenses among members. A member in arrears can lose its vote if the amount of arrears equals or exceeds the amount of the contributions due for the preceding 2 full years. **Website:** www.un.org/ga

Security Council. The Security Council consists of 15 members, 5 with permanent seats. The remaining 10 are elected for 2-year terms by the General Assembly. **Website:** www.un.org/docs/sc

Permanent members of the Council are: China, France, Russia, United Kingdom, and the United States. Nonpermanent members are: (with terms expiring Dec. 31, 2003) Bulgaria, Cameroon, Guinea, Mexico, and Syria; (with terms expiring Dec. 31, 2004): Angola, Chile, Germany, Pakistan, Spain.

The Security Council has the primary responsibility within the UN for maintaining international peace and security. The Council may investigate any dispute that threatens international peace and security.

Any member of the UN at UN headquarters may, if invited by the Council, participate in its discussions, and a nation not a member of the UN may appear if it is a party to a dispute. Decisions on procedural questions are made by an affirmative vote of 9 members. On all other matters the affirmative vote of 9 members must include the concurring votes of all permanent members (giving them veto power). A party to a dispute must refrain from voting.

The Security Council directs the various peacekeeping forces deployed throughout the world.

Secretariat. The Secretariat is an international staff of about 8,900 that carries out the day-today operations of the UN and is headed by the secretary general. The secretary general is the chief administrative officer of the UN, and is appointed by the General Assembly, on the recommendation of the Security Council, for a five-year, renewable term. The Secretary General reports to the General Assembly and may bring to the attention of the Security Council any matter that threatens international peace.

Economic and Social Council. The Economic and Social Council consists of 54 members elected by the General Assembly for 3-year terms. The council is responsible for carrying out UN functions with regard to international economic, social, cultural, educational, health, and related matters. It meets once a year. **Website:** www.un.org/esa

Trusteeship Council. The administration of trust territories was under UN supervision; however, all 11 Trust Territories have attained their right to self-determination. The work of the Council was suspended May 1994.

Budget: The General Assembly approved a total budget for the biennium 2003-2004 of $2.17 billion.

International Court of Justice (World Court). The International Court of Justice is the principal judicial organ of the UN. All members are ipso facto parties to the statute of the Court. The Court has jurisdiction over cases the parties submit to it and matters especially provided for in the charter or in treaties. It gives advisory opinions and renders judgments. In disputes between nations, the Court's decisions are binding only between parties concerned and in respect to a particular dispute. If any party to a case fails to heed a judgment, the other party may have recourse to the Security Council.

The 15 judges are elected for 9-year terms by the General Assembly and the Security Council. Retiring judges are eligible for reelection. The Court remains permanently in session, except during vacations. All questions are decided by majority. The International Court of Justice sits in The Hague, Netherlands. **Website:** www.icj-cij.org

The text of the **UN Charter** may be obtained from the Public Inquiries Unit, Department of Public Information, United Nations, New York, NY 10017. (212) 963-4475. **Website:** www.un.org/aboutUN/charter/index.html

---

WORLD ALMANAC QUICK QUIZ

Which country was the largest source of refugees in 2002?
(a) Myanmar   (b) Afghanistan   (c) Dem. Republic of the Congo   (d) Sudan
For the answer look in this chapter, or see page 1008.

Ongoing UN Peacekeeping Missions, 2003

Source: United Nations Cartographic Section, Map No. 4000(E) Rev. 19

(Year given is the year each mission began operation)

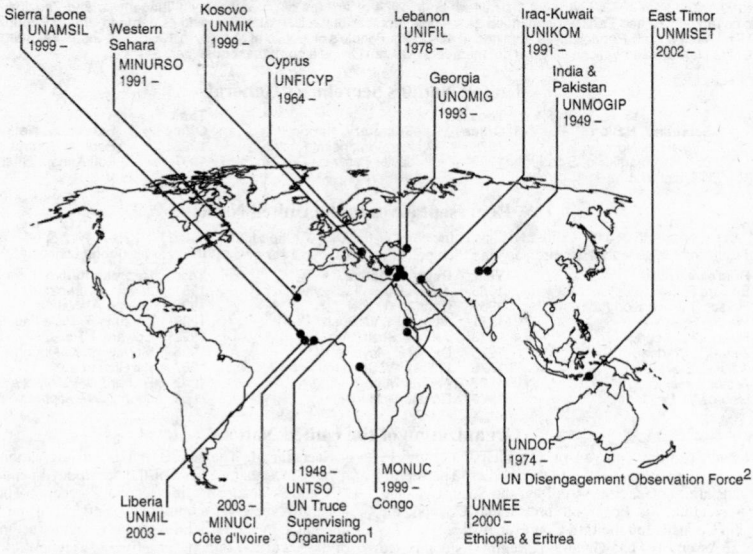

(1) Functions in 5 Mideast nations. (2) Golan Heights.

Selected Specialized and Related Agencies

These specialized and related agencies are autonomous, with their own memberships and organs, and at the same time have a functional relationship or working agreement with the UN (headquarters), except for UNICEF and UNHCR, which report directly to the Economic and Social Council and to the General Assembly.

Food and Agriculture Organization (FAO) aims to increase production from farms, forests, and fisheries; improve food distribution and marketing, nutrition, and the living conditions of rural people. (Viale delle Terme di Caracalla, 00100 Rome, Italy.) **Website:** www.fao.org

International Atomic Energy Agency (IAEA) aims to promote the safe, peaceful uses of atomic energy. (Vienna International Centre, PO Box 100, Wagramer Strasse 5, A-1400, Vienna, Austria.) **Website:** www.iaea.org

International Civil Aviation Org. (ICAO) promotes international civil aviation standards and regulations. (999 University St., Montreal, Quebec, Canada H3C 5H7.) **Website:** www.icao.org

International Fund for Agricultural Development (IFAD) aims to mobilize funds for agricultural and rural projects in developing countries. (107 Via del Seratico, 00142 Rome, Italy.) **Website:** www.ifad.org

Industrial Development Org. (UNIDO) helps developing nations and those in transition pursue sustainable industrial development while promoting economic, environmental, and labor practices. (Vienna Intl. Centre, 1400-A Vienna, Austria.) **Website:** www.unido.org

International Labor Org. (ILO) aims to promote employment; improve labor conditions and living standards. (4 route des Morillons, CH-1211 Geneva 22, Switzerland.)

International Maritime Org. (IMO) aims to promote cooperation on technical matters affecting international shipping. (4 Albert Embankment, London SE1 7SR, U.K.) **Website:** www.imo.org

International Monetary Fund (IMF) aims to promote international monetary cooperation and currency stabilization and expansion of international trade. (700 19th St., NW, Washington, DC 20431.) **Website:** www.imf.org

International Telecommunication Union (ITU) establishes regulations for radio, telegraph, telephone, and space

radio-communications, and allocates radio frequencies. (Place des Nations, 1211 Geneva 20, Switzerland.) **Website:** www.itu.int

Office of the High Commissioner for Human Rights (OHCHR) seeks to uphold human rights standards by monitoring areas of concern, investigating abuses, and working with gov. institutions to improve conditions. (8-14 Avenue de la Paix, 1211 Geneva 10, Switzerland.) **Website:** www.unhchr.com

United Nations Children's Fund (UNICEF) provides financial aid and development assistance to programs for children and mothers in developing countries. (3 UN Plaza, New York, NY 10017.) **Website:** www.unicef.org

United Nations Educational, Scientific, and Cultural Org. (UNESCO) aims to promote collaboration among nations through education, science, and culture. After a 19-year boycott, the United States rejoined the organization on Sept. 29, 2003. (7 Place de Fontenoy, 75352 Paris 07 SP, France.) **Website:** www.unesco.org

United Nations High Commissioner for Refugees (UN-HCR) provides essential assistance for refugees. (UN High Comm. for Refugees, 2500 CH-1211, Geneva 2, Switzerland.) **Website:** www.unhcr.int

Universal Postal Union (UPU) aims to perfect postal services and promote international collaboration. (Case Postale 13, 3000 Berne 15 Switzerland.) **Website:** www.upu.int

World Bank Group encompasses 5 development institutions focused on worldwide poverty reduction. The **International Bank for Reconstruction and Development (IBRD)** provides loans and technical assistance for projects in developing member countries; encourages cofinancing for projects from other public and private sources. The **International Development Association (IDA)** provides funds for development projects on concessionary terms to the poorer developing member countries. The **International**

Finance Corporation (IFC) promotes the growth of the private sector in developing member countries; encourages the development of local capital markets; stimulates the international flow of private capital. The **Multilateral Investment Guarantee Agency (MIGA)** promotes investment in developing countries; guarantees investments to protect investors from noncommercial risks, such as nationalization; advises governments on attracting private investment. The **International Center for Settlement of Investment Disputes (ICSID)** provides conciliation and arbitration services for disputes between foreign investors and host governments which arise out of an investment. (1818 H St., NW, Washington, DC 20433.) **Website:** www.worldbank. org

World Health Org. (WHO) aims to aid the attainment of the highest possible level of health. (Avenue Appia 20, CH-1211 Geneva 27, Switzerland.) **Website:** www.who.int

World Intellectual Property Org. (WIPO) seeks to protect, through international cooperation, literary, industrial,

scientific, and artistic works. (34, Chemin des Columbettes, 1211 Geneva, Switzerland.) **Website:** www.wipo.org

World Meteorological Org. (WMO) aims to coordinate and improve world meteorological work. (7 bis Avenue de la Paix, CP 2300, 1211 Geneva 2, Switzerland.) **Website:** www.wmo.ch

World Tourism Org. (WTO) promotes development of responsible, sustainable, and universally accessible tourism, and provides incentives for environmental and cultural protection. (Capitan Haya 42, Madrid, Spain.) **Website:** www.world-tourism.org

World Trade Org. (WTrO) replacing the General Agreement on Tariffs and Trade (GATT), administers trade agreements and treaties, examines the trade regimes of members, keeps track of various trade measures and statistics, and attempts to settle trade disputes. (Centre William Rappard, 154 Rue de Lausanne, CH 1211 Geneva 21, Switzerland.) **Website:** www.wto.org

International Criminal Court (ICC)

The International Criminal Court was created when 120 nations signed the Rome Statute on July 17, 1998. Its mission is to try individuals accused of genocide, war crimes, or other crimes against humanity, as has been undertaken in the past by temporary tribunals. The statute came into force July 1, 2002, 60 days after the 60th nation ratified it. As of Sept. 2003, 92 nations were members of the ICC, although China, Japan, Russia, and the U.S. had not joined. The U.S. expressed opposition to some provisions of the ICC, mainly regarding liability of its military in peace-keeping situations.

The ICC, unlike the World Court, is not an organ of the UN, but an independent international agency with its own

budget and administration. It consists of 18 judges elected by member nations. A president and 1st and 2nd vice presidents are elected for 3-year, renewable terms by an absolute majority of the judges. A Registry handles the nonjudicial aspects of administration. The Office of the Prosecutor will review, investigate, and, when necessary, prosecute cases referred to it by a state or by the UN Security Council.

Jurisdiction is limited to member nations, and only when their courts are deemed either inoperable or unfit for fair trial. The court, which as of Sept. 2003 was not fully operational, will hear cases in The Hague, Netherlands. **Website:** www.icc-cpi.int

Geneva Conventions

The Geneva Conventions are 4 international treaties governing the protection of civilians in time of war, the treatment of prisoners of war, and the care of the wounded and sick in the armed forces. The first convention, covering the sick and wounded, was concluded in Geneva, Switzerland, in 1864; it was amended and expanded in 1906. A third convention, in 1929, covered prisoners of war. Outrage at the treatment of prisoners and civilians during World War II by some belligerents, notably Germany and Japan, prompted the conclusion, in Aug. 1949, of 4 new conventions. Three of these restated and strengthened the previous conventions, and the fourth codified general principles of international law governing the treatment of civilians in wartime.

The 1949 convention for civilians provided for special safeguards for wounded persons, children under 15 years of

age, pregnant women, and the elderly. Discrimination on racial, religious, national, or political grounds was forbidden. Torture, collective punishment, reprisals, unwarranted destruction of property, and forced use of civilians for an occupier's armed forces were also prohibited. Also included was a pledge to treat prisoners humanely, feed them adequately, and deliver relief supplies to them. They were not to be forced to disclose more than minimal information. Two additional protocols were adopted in June 1977 dealing with the protection of war victims, especially civilians, and protection for non-international conflicts.

Most countries have formally accepted all or most of the humanitarian conventions as binding. However, there is no permanent machinery in place to apprehend, try, or punish violators.

Major Foreign Development Aid Donors, 2001-2002

Source: Organization for Economic Cooperation and Development; ranked by percent of GNI (Gross National Income) in 2002.

In 2002, the U.S. gave the highest total amount of development aid but ranked 22nd by percent of GNP.

Country	ODA[1], as% of GNI 2001	2002	ODA[1] in U.S. dollars (millions) 2001	2002	Country	ODA[1], as% of GNI 2001	2002	ODA[1] in U.S. dollars (millions) 2001	2002
1. Denmark	1.03	0.96	$1,634	$1,632	12. Canada	0.22	0.28	$1,533	$2,013
2. Norway	0.80	0.91	1,346	1,746	13. Germany	0.27	0.27	4,990	5,359
3. Netherlands	0.82	0.82	3,172	3,377	14. Spain	0.30	0.25	1,737	1,608
4. Luxembourg	0.82	0.78	1,41	1,43	Australia	0.25	0.25	873	962
5. Sweden	0.77	0.74	1,666	1,754	16. Portugal	0.25	0.24	268	282
6. Belgium	0.37	0.42	867	1,061	17. Austria	0.29	0.23	533	475
7. Ireland	0.33	0.41	287	397	Japan	0.23	0.23	9,847	9,220
8. France	0.32	0.36	4,198	5,182	New Zealand	0.25	0.23	112	124
9. Finland	0.32	0.35	389	466	20. Greece	0.17	0.22	202	295
10. Switzerland	0.34	0.32	908	933	21. Italy	0.15	0.20	1,627	2,313
11. United Kingdom	0.32	0.30	4,579	4,749	22. United States	0.11	0.12	11,429	12,900

(1) ODA = official development assistance.

Top 10 Recipients of U.S. Development Aid, 2000-2001

Source: Organization for Economic Cooperation and Development

Country	Millions of U.S. $ (avg. 2000-2001)	Country	Millions of U.S. $ (avg. 2000-2001)	Country	Millions of U.S. $ (avg. 2000-2001)
1. Russia	$834	5. Ukraine	$246	8. Yugoslavia	$159
2. Egypt	808	6. Colombia	228	9. Indonesia	158
3. Israel	568	7. Jordan	173	10. Peru	158
4. Pakistan	438				

SPORTS

Sports Highlights of 2003

On **Jan. 3**, Ohio State (14-0) won the **NCAA football national title**, upsetting top-ranked defending champion Miami (FL), 31-24 in double-overtime at the Fiesta Bowl in Tempe, AZ. For Ohio State, underdogs by 11.5 points, it was their 1st national title since 1968, and 5th overall. Ohio St. quarterback Craig Krenzel and defensive back Mike Doss were named MVPs of the game. The loss snapped Miami's 34-game winning streak.

The Tampa Bay Buccaneers won their 1st NFL Championship **Jan. 27**, defeating the Oakland Raiders, 48-21, at **Super Bowl XXXVII** in San Diego. Safety Dexter Jackson, who had 2 key interceptions, was named the game's MVP. The Buccaneers intercepted Oakland quarterback Rich Gannon, the NFL's regular season MVP, a record 5 times—returning 3 for touchdowns (2 by Dwight Smith, and 1 by Derrick Brooks).

In the **women's NCAA basketball final** on **Apr. 8**, Connecticut captured its 2nd-straight title, defeating Oklahoma, 82-70. Connecticut's Diana Taurasi was named Most Outstanding Player of the Final Four. In the **men's NCAA tournament**, Syracuse topped Kansas, 81-78, for the national championship on Apr. 7. Syracuse freshman Carmelo Anthony was named Most Outstanding Player of the Final Four.

In the **London Marathon** on **Apr. 13**, Great Britain's Paula Radcliffe smashed her own world best for the marathon, winning in 2 hrs., 15 mins., and 25 secs. She had set the previous record of 2:17:18 at the Chicago Marathon in Oct. 2002.

Sweden's **Annika Sorenstam** became the 1st woman in 58 years to play in a PGA event when she teed off at the Colonial PGA Tournament in Fort Worth, TX, on **May 22**. (Babe Zaharias played in the Los Angeles Open in 1945.) Sorenstam shot a 1-over-par 71 in the 1st round, then slipped to 5 over par and missed the cut for the final 2 rounds by 4 strokes. Kenny Perry won the Colonial with a final score of 261, a tournament record 19-under-par.

Yankee **Roger Clemens** became the 21st pitcher in Major League history to win 300 games with a 5-2 win over the St. Louis Cardinals in New York on **June 13**. Clemens got Edgar Renteria to miss a 3-2 pitch in the 2nd inning for his 4,000th career strikeout. He finished the season with 310 wins and 4,099 strikeouts (3rd all-time).

The San Antonio Spurs won their 2nd **NBA Championship** in 5 years (1999), defeating the New Jersey Nets 88-77, in the 6th and deciding game at the SBC Center in San Antonio on **June 15**. San Antonio's Tim Duncan had 21 points, 20 rebounds, 10 assists, and 8 blocked shots in the game. Three of Duncan's blocks came in a 5:30 stretch of the 4th quarter in which San Antonio outscored New Jersey, 19-0, to take control of the game. Duncan, the regular season MVP, was also named MVP of the Finals.

At the FINA **World Swimming Championships (July 20-27)** in Barcelona, Spain, American Michael Phelps won 3 individual gold medals and set 5 world records in 6 days. Phelps set 2 records in the 200 meter individual medley, 1 in the 200 butterfly, 1 in the 100 butterfly, and 1 in the 400 individual medley. The 18-year-old Phelps eclipsed Mark Spitz's feat of 4 world records in the 1972 Olympics.

On **July 27**, **Lance Armstrong** won the Tour de France for the 5th straight year—tying a record for consecutive victories set by Spain's Miguel Indurain (1991-95). Armstrong finished the 3-week, 2,130-mile tour with an overall time of 83 hrs., 41 mins., 12 secs. The 1997 Tour winner, Jan Ullrich of Germany, was 1:01 behind, the closest any rider has come in Armstrong's 5 wins.

On **Sept. 14**, Baltimore running back Jamal Lewis set a new **NFL single-game rushing record** of 295 yards on 30 carries in the Ravens' 33-13 win over the Cleveland Browns. Lewis scored on runs of 82 and 63 yards in the game. The previous record of 278 yards was set by Cincinnati's Corey Dillon in 2000.

In the **Berlin Marathon Sept. 28**, Kenyan Paul Tergat set a new men's world best, winning in 2 hrs., 4 mins., and 55 secs. Countryman Sammy Korir, hired as a pace-setter, finished 1 sec. behind. Both broke the previous world record of 2:05:38 set by Moroccan-born American Khalid Khannouchi in the London Marathon in April.

In the **Women's World Cup** soccer final **Oct. 12** in Carson, CA, Germany defeated Sweden, 2-1, in overtime to win its 1st title. The U.S. took 3rd with a 3-1 win over Canada. German forward Birgit Prinz won the Golden Ball as top player in the tournament, and her 7 goals earned her the Golden Shoe as top scorer. Germany defeated the U.S., 3-0, on Oct. 5.

Two classic **Major League Baseball League Championship Series** came to a head in 7th games Oct. 15-16. The Florida Marlins, under 72-year-old manager Jack McKeon, beat the Chicago Cubs at Wrigley Field, 9-6, for the NL pennant. The Cubs, who had led the series 3-1, had not reached the World Series since 1945 and had not won it since 1908. The New York Yankees and the Boston Red Sox played their decisive 7th game Oct. 16. The Red Sox, who had not won the World Series since 1918, were seeking their 1st AL pennant since 1986.

Sports Quotes of 2003

"I think what we've had here is a little social concern in the NFL. The media has been very desirous that a black quarterback do well. There is a little hope invested in McNabb, and he got a lot of credit for the performance of this team that he didn't deserve. The defense carried this team."—**Rush Limbaugh**, commentator for ESPN's *Sunday NFL Countdown*, on Philadelphia quarterback Donovan McNabb

"To have these two milestones I was able to achieve tonight, it was really special. Everybody can stop chasing me around the country."—Yankees pitcher **Roger Clemens**, on striking out his 4,000th batter and winning his 300th game, after unsuccessful tries in New York, Detroit, and Chicago

"When I was watching Muhammad Ali, I remember that I wanted him to quit even when he came back and won fights. It was the same with Sugar Ray Leonard. I was saying, what is it that makes those guys go on? Is it money, fame, glory? I'm still trying to find out."—Heavyweight boxing champion **Lennox Lewis**, 37, on his possible retirement

"I will never sit here and say I'm the greatest ever. I've done what I've done in the game. I've won a number of majors—I think that's kind of the answer to everything."—**Pete Sampras**, winner of a record 14 Grand Slam tennis titles, on his retirement

"We asked for an alligator, we paid for an alligator, and unfortunately we did not get an alligator."—Univ. of Florida spokesman **Steve McClain**, on the fact that a crocodile appears on the 2003 Florida Gators football media guide

"This has been a Tour of too many problems, too many close calls. I wish it would stop. I wish I could just have some uneventful days. Anyway, I had a good day today."—**Lance Armstrong**, who fell off his bike, before remounting and winning stage 15 and eventually his 5th Tour de France

"Why should we want to face an easier team? I'm not afraid to fail."—Yankee shortstop **Derek Jeter**, on whether he'd rather face injury-depleted Oakland or Boston in the American League Championship Series

Miscellaneous Sports Facts

Bad Mama! Pam Reed, a 5'3", 42-year-old mother of 5 from Arizona, took 28 hrs., 26 mins., and 52 secs. to win her 2nd-straight Badwater Ultramarathon in July 2003. She's the only woman ever to win outright the 135-mile race from California's Death Valley to halfway up 14,495-foot Mt. Whitney.

Twice as Nice. On July 29, 2003, switch-hitter Bill Mueller of the Boston Red Sox became the only player in Major League history to hit a grand slam from both sides of the plate in the same game (and in consecutive at-bats) in Boston's 14-7 win over the Texas Rangers.

Sammy Slammin'. Since the beginning of the 1994 season, the Chicago Cubs' Sammy Sosa has hit 469 home runs—the most in a 10-year span by any player in Major League history.

One Tough Joe. Joe Kulak completed a Grand Slam of ultrarunning by finishing 4 major U.S. 100-mile races (Western States 100, Vermont 100, Leadville Trail 100, and the Wasatch Front 100) in a cumulative time of 78 hrs., 22 mins., 47 secs. Kulak won the Vermont race in 14:55:26.

In the Pink. Soccer superstar David Beckham bared it all for his fans, July 1, when his 90-minute physical exam for his new team, Real Madrid, was televised live worldwide.

Squeezin' in. The Univ. of Michigan set a new NCAA football single-game attendance mark of 111,726 at a 38-0 win over Notre Dame on Sept. 13—even though Michigan Stadium's official capacity is 107,501. About 250 members of the school bands were moved to the field to open up more seats. The record total includes fans, ushers, working media, and bands.

Summer Olympic Games
Sites of Summer Olympic Games

1896 Athens, Greece	**1924** Paris, France	**1960** Rome, Italy	**1988** Seoul, South Korea
1900 Paris, France	**1928** Amsterdam,Netherlands	**1964** Tokyo, Japan	**1992** Barcelona, Spain
1904 St. Louis, U.S.	**1932** Los Angeles, U.S.	**1968** Mexico City, Mexico	**1996** Atlanta, U.S.
1906 Athens, Greece	**1936** Berlin, Germany	**1972** Munich, W. Germany	**2000** Sydney, Australia
1908 London, England	**1948** London, England	**1976** Montreal, Canada	**2004** Athens, Greece
1912 Stockholm, Sweden	**1952** Helsinki, Finland	**1980** Moscow, USSR	**2008** Beijing, China
1920 Antwerp, Belgium	**1956** Melbourne, Australia	**1984** Los Angeles, U.S.	

Games not recognized by International Olympic Committee. Games VI (1916), XII (1940), and XIII (1944) were not celebrated.

The 2004 Summer Olympic Games

Athens, Greece, Aug. 13-29, 2004

The Olympic Games were born in ancient Greece and the first modern Games were held in Athens in 1896. In 2004, 10,500 athletes representing 201 National Olympic Commitees were expected compete in 301 events in 28 sports at the 28th Olympiad. No new sports or demonstration sports were scheduled to be introduced in, but, for the first time, women will compete in wrestling. The emblem of the Athens Olympics is an olive wreath, which was the award given to winners in the ancient games. The mascots are Phevos and Athena, named for two ancient Greek gods. Pheyos is the god of light and music; Athena is the goddess of wisdom and patron of the city of Athens. For further information, see the official website for the Athens games: www.athens2004.com or visit the Olympic Movement website at www.olympic.org

Summer Olympic Games in 2000

Sydney, Australia, Sept. 15-Oct. 1, 2000

About 11,000 athletes from 199 countries competed in 300 events in 28 sports at the 2000 Summer Games. New sports introduced in Sydney included synchronized diving, trampoline, taekwondo, and triathlon. For the 1st time, women also competed in water polo, weight lifting, the pole vault, the hammer throw, and the modern pentathlon.

Australia's Cathy Freeman won the women's 400m dash, becoming the 1st Aborigine to earn an individual gold medal. U.S. sprinter Marion Jones won 3 golds and 2 bronze medals, the most ever in track and field by a woman at a single Olympics. American wrestler Rulon Gardner provided the biggest upset of the Games when he defeated 3-time Olympic champion Aleksandr Karelin of Russia in the Greco-Roman super heavyweight final. The U.S. baseball team won its 1st-ever gold medal. In swimming, Sydney hometown favorite Ian Thorpe helped set 3 relay world records and improved his own record in the 400m freestyle.

Summer Olympic Games Champions, 1896-2000
(indicates Olympic record; w indicates wind-aided)

The 1980 games were boycotted by 62 nations, including the U.S. The 1984 games were boycotted by the USSR and by most Eastern bloc nations. E and W Germany competed separately, 1968-88. The 1992 Unified Team consisted of 12 former Soviet republics. The 1992 Independent Olympic Participants (I.O.P.) were from Serbia, Montenegro, and Macedonia.

TRACK AND FIELD—Men
100-Meter Run

1896	Thomas Burke, United States	12.0s
1900	Francis W. Jarvis, United States	11.0s
1904	Archie Hahn, United States	11.0s
1908	Reginald Walker, South Africa	10.8s
1912	Ralph Craig, United States	10.8s
1920	Charles Paddock, United States	10.8s
1924	Harold Abrahams, Great Britain	10.6s
1928	Percy Williams, Canada	10.8s
1932	Eddie Tolan, United States	10.3s
1936	Jesse Owens, United States	10.3s
1948	Harrison Dillard, United States	10.3s
1952	Lindy Remigino, United States	10.4s
1956	Bobby Morrow, United States	10.5s
1960	Armin Hary, Germany	10.2s
1964	Bob Hayes, United States	10.0s
1968	Jim Hines, United States	9.95s
1972	Valery Borzov, USSR	10.14s
1976	Hasely Crawford, Trinidad	10.06s
1980	Allan Wells, Great Britain	10.25s
1984	Carl Lewis, United States	9.99s
1988	Carl Lewis, United States	9.92s
1992	Linford Christie, Great Britain	9.96s
1996	Donovan Bailey, Canada	9.84s*
2000	Maurice Greene, United States	9.87s

200-Meter Run

1900	Walter Tewksbury, United States	22.2s
1904	Archie Hahn, United States	21.6s
1908	Robert Kerr, Canada	22.6s
1912	Ralph Craig, United States	21.7s
1920	Allan Woodring, United States	22.0s
1924	Jackson Scholz, United States	21.6s
1928	Percy Williams, Canada	21.8s
1932	Eddie Tolan, United States	21.2s
1936	Jesse Owens, United States	20.7s
1948	Mel Patton, United States	21.1s
1952	Andrew Stanfield, United States	20.7s
1956	Bobby Morrow, United States	20.6s
1960	Livio Berruti, Italy	20.5s
1964	Henry Carr, United States	20.3s
1968	Tommie Smith, United States	19.83s
1972	Valeri Borzov, USSR	20.00s
1976	Donald Quarrie, Jamaica	20.23s

200-Meter Run

1980	Pietro Mennea, Italy	20.19s
1984	Carl Lewis, United States	19.80s
1988	Joe DeLoach, United States	19.75s
1992	Mike Marsh, United States	20.01s
1996	Michael Johnson, United States	19.32s*
2000	Konstantinos Kenteris, Greece	20.09s

400-Meter Run

1896	Thomas Burke, United States	54.2s
1900	Maxey Long, United States	49.4s
1904	Harry Hillman, United States	49.2s
1908	Wyndham Halswelle, Great Brit., walkover	50.0s
1912	Charles Reidpath, United States	48.2s
1920	Bevil Rudd, South Africa	49.6s
1924	Eric Liddell, Great Britain	47.6s
1928	Ray Barbuti, United States	47.8s
1932	William Carr, United States	46.2s
1936	Archie Williams, United States	46.5s
1948	Arthur Wint, Jamaica	46.2s
1952	George Rhoden, Jamaica	45.9s
1956	Charles Jenkins, United States	46.7s
1960	Otis Davis, United States	44.9s
1964	Michael Larrabee, United States	45.1s
1968	Lee Evans, United States	43.86s
1972	Vincent Matthews, United States	44.66s
1976	Alberto Juantorena, Cuba	44.26s
1980	Viktor Markin, USSR	44.60s
1984	Alonzo Babers, United States	44.27s
1988	Steven Lewis, United States	43.87s
1992	Quincy Watts, United States	43.50s
1996	Michael Johnson, United States	43.49s*
2000	Michael Johnson, United States	43.84s

800-Meter Run

1896	Edwin Flack, Australia	2m. 11s
1900	Alfred Tysoe, Great Britain	2m. 1.2s
1904	James Lightbody, United States	1m. 56s
1908	Mel Sheppard, United States	1m. 52.8s
1912	James Meredith, United States	1m. 51.9s
1920	Albert Hill, Great Britain	1m. 53.4s
1924	Douglas Lowe, Great Britain	1m. 52.4s
1928	Douglas Lowe, Great Britain	1m. 51.8s
1932	Thomas Hampson, Great Britain	1m. 49.8s
1936	John Woodruff, United States	1m. 52.9s
1948	Mal Whitfield, United States	1m. 49.2s

800-Meter Run

1952	Mal Whitfield, United States	1m. 49.2s
1956	Thomas Courtney, United States	1m. 47.7s
1960	Peter Snell, New Zealand	1m. 46.3s
1964	Peter Snell, New Zealand	1m. 45.1s
1968	Ralph Doubell, Australia	1m. 44.3s
1972	Dave Wottle, United States	1m. 45.9s
1976	Alberto Juantorena, Cuba	1m. 43.50s
1980	Steve Ovett, Great Britain	1m. 45.40s
1984	Joaquim Cruz, Brazil	1m. 43.00s
1988	Paul Ereng, Kenya	1m. 43.45s
1992	William Tanui, Kenya	1m. 43.66s
1996	Vebjoern Rodal, Norway	1m. 42.58s*
2000	Nils Schumann, Germany	1m. 45.08

1,500-Meter Run

1896	Edwin Flack, Australia	4m. 33.2s
1900	Charles Bennett, Great Britain	4m. 6.2s
1904	James Lightbody, United States	4m. 5.4s
1908	Mel Sheppard, United States	4m. 3.4s
1912	Arnold Jackson, Great Britain	3m. 56.8s
1920	Albert Hill, Great Britain	4m. 1.8s
1924	Paavo Nurmi, Finland	3m. 53.6s
1928	Harry Larva, Finland	3m. 53.2s
1932	Luigi Beccali, Italy	3m. 51.2s
1936	Jack Lovelock, New Zealand	3m. 47.8s
1948	Henri Eriksson, Sweden	3m. 49.8s
1952	Joseph Barthel, Luxembourg	3m. 45.2s
1956	Ron Delany, Ireland	3m. 41.2s
1960	Herb Elliott, Australia	3m. 35.6s
1964	Peter Snell, New Zealand	3m. 38.1s
1968	Kipchoge Keino, Kenya	3m. 34.9s
1972	Pekka Vasala, Finland	3m. 36.3s
1976	John Walker, New Zealand	3m. 39.17s
1980	Sebastian Coe, Great Britain	3m. 38.4s
1984	Sebastian Coe, Great Britain	3m. 32.53s
1988	Peter Rono, Kenya	3m. 35.96s
1992	Fermin Cacho Ruiz, Spain	3m. 40.12s
1996	Noureddine Morceli, Algeria	3m. 35.78s
2000	Noah Ngeny, Kenya	3m. 32.07s*

5,000-Meter Run

1912	Hannes Kolehmainen, Finland	14m. 36.6s
1920	Joseph Guillemot, France	14m. 55.6s
1924	Paavo Nurmi, Finlands	14m. 31.2
1928	Willie Ritola, Finland	14m. 38s
1932	Lauri Lehtinen, Finland	14m. 30s
1936	Gunnar Hockert, Finland	14m. 22.2s
1948	Gaston Reiff, Belgium	14m. 17.6s
1952	Emil Zatopek, Czechoslovakia	14m. 6.6s
1956	Vladimir Kuts, USSR	13m. 39.6s
1960	Murray Halberg, New Zealand	13m. 43.4s
1964	Bob Schul, United States	13m. 48.8s
1968	Mohamed Gammoudi, Tunisia	14m. 05.0s
1972	Lasse Viren, Finland	13m. 26.4s
1976	Lasse Viren, Finland	13m. 24.76s
1980	Miruts Yifter, Ethiopia	13m. 21.0s
1984	Said Aouita, Morocco	13m. 05.59s*
1988	John Ngugi, Kenya	13m. 11.70s
1992	Dieter Baumann, Germany	13m. 12.52s
1996	Venuste Niyongabo, Burundi	13m. 07.96s
2000	Millon Wolde, Ethiopia	13m. 35.49s

10,000-Meter Run

1912	Hannes Kolehmainen, Finland	31m. 20.8s
1920	Paavo Nurmi, Finland	31m. 45.8s
1924	Willie Ritola, Finland	30m. 23.2s
1928	Paavo Nurmi, Finland	30m. 18.6s
1932	Janusz Kusocinski, Poland	30m. 11.4s
1936	Ilmari Salminen, Finland	30m. 15.4s
1948	Emil Zatopek, Czechoslovakia	29m. 59.6s
1952	Emil Zatopek, Czechoslovakia	29m. 17.0s
1956	Vladimir Kuts, USSR	28m. 45.6s
1960	Pyotr Bolotnikov, USSR	28m. 32.2s
1964	Billy Mills, United States	28m. 24.4s
1968	Naftali Temu, Kenya	29m. 27.4s
1972	Lasse Viren, Finland	27m. 38.4s
1976	Lasse Viren, Finland	27m. 40.4s
1980	Miruts Yifter, Ethiopia	27m. 42.7s
1984	Alberto Cova, Italy	27m. 47.54s
1988	Brahim Boutaib, Morocco	27m. 21.46s
1992	Khalid Skah, Morocco	27m. 46.70s
1996	Haile Gebrselassie, Ethiopia	27m. 07.34s*
2000	Haile Gebrselassie, Ethiopia	27m. 18.20s

110-Meter Hurdles

1896	Thomas Curtis, United States	17.6s
1900	Alvin Kraenzlein, United States	15.4s
1904	Frederick Schule, United States	16.0s
1908	Forrest Smithson, United States	15.0s
1912	Frederick Kelly, United States	15.1s
1920	Earl Thomson, Canada	14.8s

110-Meter Hurdles

1924	Daniel Kinsey, United States	15.0s
1928	Sydney Atkinson, South Africa	14.8s
1932	George Saling, United States	14.6s
1936	Forrest Towns, United States	14.2s
1948	William Porter, United States	13.9s
1952	Harrison Dillard, United States	13.7s
1956	Lee Calhoun, United States	13.5s
1960	Lee Calhoun, United States	13.8s
1964	Hayes Jones, United States	13.6s
1968	Willie Davenport, United States	13.33s
1972	Rod Milburn, United States	13.24s
1976	Guy Drut, France	13.30s
1980	Thomas Munkelt, E. Germany	13.39s
1984	Roger Kingdom, United States	13.20s
1988	Roger Kingdom, United States	12.98s
1992	Mark McCoy, Canada	13.12s
1996	Allen Johnson, United States	12.95s*
2000	Anier Garcia, Cuba	13.00s

400-Meter Hurdles

1900	J.W.B. Tewksbury, United States	57.6s
1904	Harry Hillman, United States	53.0s
1908	Charles Bacon, United States	55.0s
1920	Frank Loomis, United States	54.0s
1924	F. Morgan Taylor, United States	52.6s
1928	Lord Burghley, Great Britain	53.4s
1932	Robert Tisdall, Ireland	51.7s
1936	Glenn Hardin, United States	52.4s
1948	Roy Cochran, United States	51.1s
1952	Charles Moore, United States	50.8s
1956	Glenn Davis, United States	50.1s
1960	Glenn Davis, United States	49.3s
1964	Rex Cawley, United States	49.6s
1968	Dave Hemery, Great Britain	48.12s
1972	John Akii-Bua, Uganda	47.82s
1976	Edwin Moses, United States	47.64s
1980	Volker Beck, E. Germany	48.70s
1984	Edwin Moses, United States	47.75s
1988	Andre Phillips, United States	47.19s
1992	Kevin Young, United States	46.78s*
1996	Derrick Adkins, United States	47.54s
2000	Angelo Taylor, United States	47.50s

400-Meter Relay

1912	Great Britain	42.4s
1920	United States	42.2s
1924	United States	41.0s
1928	United States	41.0s
1932	United States	40.0s
1936	United States	39.8s
1948	United States	40.6s
1952	United States	40.1s
1956	United States	39.5s
1960	Germany (U.S. disqualified)	39.5s
1964	United States	39.0s
1968	United States	38.24s
1972	United States	38.19s
1976	United States	38.33s
1980	USSR	38.26s
1984	United States	37.83s
1988	USSR (U.S. disqualified)	38.19s
1992	United States	37.40s*
1996	Canada	37.69s
2000	United States	37.61s

1,600-Meter Relay

1908	United States	3m. 29.4s
1912	United States	3m. 16.6s
1920	Great Britain	3m. 22.2s
1924	United States	3m. 16s
1928	United States	3m. 14.2s
1932	United States	3m. 8.2s
1936	Great Britain	3m. 9s
1948	United States	3m. 10.4s
1952	Jamaica	3m. 03.9s
1956	United States	3m. 04.8s
1960	United States	3m. 02.2s
1964	United States	3m. 00.7s
1968	United States	2m. 56.16s
1972	Kenya	2m. 59.8s
1976	United States	2m. 58.65s
1980	USSR	3m. 01.1s
1984	United States	2m. 57.91s
1988	United States	2m. 56.16s
1992	United States	2m. 55.74s*
1996	United States	2m. 55.99s
2000	United States	2m. 56.35s

3,000-Meter Steeplechase

1920	Percy Hodge, Great Britain	10m. 0.4s
1924	Willie Ritola, Finland	9m. 33.6s

3,000-Meter Steeplechase

1928	Toivo Loukola, Finland	9m. 21.8s
1932	Volmari Iso-Hollo, Finland	10m. 33.4s
	(About 3,450 m; extra lap by error.)	
1936	Volmari Iso-Hollo, Finland	9m. 3.8s
1948	Thore Sjoestrand, Sweden	9m. 4.6s
1952	Horace Ashenfelter, United States	8m. 45.4s
1956	Chris Brasher, Great Britain	8m. 41.2s
1960	Zdzislaw Krzyszkowiak, Poland	8m. 34.2s
1964	Gaston Roelants, Belgium	8m. 30.8s
1968	Amos Biwott, Kenya	8m. 51s
1972	Kipchoge Keino, Kenya	8m. 23.6s
1976	Anders Garderud, Sweden	8m. 08.2s
1980	Bronislaw Malinowski, Poland	8m. 09.7s
1984	Julius Korir, Kenya	8m. 11.8s
1988	Julius Kariuki, Kenya	8m. 05.51s*
1992	Matthew Birir, Kenya	8m. 08.84s
1996	Joseph Keter, Kenya	8m. 07.12s
2000	Reuben Kosgei, Kenya	8m. 21.43s

20-Kilometer Walk

1956	Leonid Spirin, USSR	1h. 31m. 27.4s
1960	Vladimir Golubnichy, USSR	1h. 33m. 7.2s
1964	Kenneth Mathews, Great Britain	1h. 29m. 34.0s
1968	Vladimir Golubnichy, USSR	1h. 33m. 58.4s
1972	Peter Frenkel, E. Germany	1h. 26m. 42.4s
1976	Daniel Bautista, Mexico	1h. 24m. 40.6s
1980	Maurizio Damilano, Italy	1h. 23m. 35.5s
1984	Ernesto Canto, Mexico	1h. 23m. 13.0s
1988	Josef Pribilinec, Czechoslovakia	1h. 19m. 57.0s
1992	Daniel Plaza Montero, Spain	1h. 21m. 45.0s
1996	Jefferson Perez, Ecuador	1h. 20m.7s
2000	Robert Korzeniowski, Poland	1h. 18m. 59.0s*

50-Kilometer Walk

1932	Thomas W. Green, Great Britain	4h. 50m. 10s
1936	Harold Whitlock, Great Britain	4h. 30m. 41.4s
1948	John Ljunggren, Sweden	4h. 41m. 52s
1952	Giuseppe Dordoni, Italy	4h. 28m. 07.8s
1956	Norman Read, New Zealand	4h. 30m. 42.8s
1960	Donald Thompson, Great Britain	4h. 25m. 30s
1964	Abdon Pamich, Italy	4h. 11m. 12.4s
1968	Christoph Hohne, E. Germany	4h. 20m. 13.6s
1972	Bern Kannenberg, W. Germany	3h. 56m. 11.6s
1980	Hartwig Gauter, E. Germany	3h. 49m. 24.0s
1984	Raul Gonzalez, Mexico	3h. 47m. 26.0s
1988	Vayachselav Ivanenko, USSR	3h. 38m. 29.0s*
1992	Andrei Perlov, Unified Team	3h. 50m. 13.0s
1996	Robert Korzeniowski, Poland	3h. 43m. 30s
2000	Robert Korzeniowski, Poland	3h. 42m. 22s

Marathon

1896	Spiridon Loues, Greece	2h. 58m. 50s
1900	Michel Theato, France	2h. 59m. 45s
1904	Thomas Hicks, United States	3h. 28m. 63s
1908	John J. Hayes, United States	2h. 55m. 18.4s
1912	Kenneth McArthur, South Africa	2h. 36m. 54.8s
1920	Hannes Kolehmainen, Finland	2h. 32m. 35.8s
1924	Albin Stenroos, Finland	2h. 41m. 22.6s
1928	A.B. El Ouafi, France	2h. 32m. 57s
1932	Juan Zabala, Argentina	2h. 31m. 36s
1936	Kijung Son, Japan (Korean)	2h. 29m. 19.2s
1948	Delfo Cabrera, Argentina	2h. 34m. 51.6s
1952	Emil Zatopek, Czechoslovakia	2h. 23m. 03.2s
1956	Alain Mimoun, France	2h. 25m.
1960	Abebe Bikila, Ethiopia	2h. 15m. 16.2s
1964	Abebe Bikila, Ethiopia	2h. 12m. 11.2s
1968	Mamo Wolde, Ethiopia	2h. 20m. 26.4s
1972	Frank Shorter, United States	2h. 12m. 19.8s
1976	Waldemar Cierpinski, E. Germany	2h. 09m. 55s
1980	Waldemar Cierpinski, E. Germany	2h. 11m. 03s
1984	Carlos Lopes, Portugal	2h. 09m. 21s*
1988	Gelindo Bordin, Italy	2h. 10m. 32s
1992	Hwang Young-Cho, S. Korea	2h. 13m. 23s
1996	Josia Thugwane, South Africa	2h. 12m. 36s
2000	Gezahgne Abera, Ethiopia	2h. 10m. 11s

High Jump

1896	Ellery Clark, United States	1.81m. (5'11¼")
1900	Irving Baxter, United States	1.90m. (6' 2¾")
1904	Samuel Jones, United States	1.80m. (5' 11")
1908	Harry Porter, United States	1.90m. (6' 2¾ ")
1912	Alma Richards, United States	1.93m. (6' 4")
1920	Richmond Landon, United States	1.93m. (6' 4")
1924	Harold Osborn, United States	1.98m. (6' 6")
1928	Robert W. King, United States	1.94m. (6' 4¼")
1932	Duncan McNaughton, Canada	1.97m. (6' 5½")
1936	Cornelius Johnson, United States	2.03m. (6' 8")
1948	John L. Winter, Australia	1.98m. (6' 6")
1952	Walter Davis, United States	2.04m. (6' 8¼")
1956	Charles Dumas, United States	2.12m. (6' 11½")
1960	Robert Shavlakadze, USSR	2.16m. (7' 1")
1964	Valery Brumel, USSR	2.18m. (7' 1¾")
1968	Dick Fosbury, United States	2.24m. (7' 4¼")
1972	Jüri Tarmak, USSR	2.23m. (7' 3¾")
1976	Jacek Wszola, Poland	2.25m. (7' 4½")
1980	Gerd Wessig, E. Germany	2.36m. (7' 8¾")
1984	Dietmar Mögenburg, W. Germany	2.35m. (7' 8½")
1988	Hennady Avdeyenko, USSR	2.38m. (7' 9¾")
1992	Javier Sotomayor Sanabria, Cuba	2.34m. (7' 8")
1996	Charles Austin, United States	2.39m. (7' 10")*
2000	Sergey Kliugin, Russia	2.35m. (7' 8½")

Long Jump

1896	Ellery Clark, United States	6.35m. (20' 10")
1900	Alvin Kraenzlein, United States	7.18m. (23' 6¾")
1904	Meyer Prinstein, United States	7.34m. (24' 1")
1908	Frank Irons, United States	7.48m. (24' 6½")
1912	Albert Gutterson, United States	7.60m. (24' 11¼")
1920	William Petterssen, Sweden	7.15m. (23' 5½")
1924	William DeHart Hubbard, U.S.	7.44m. (24' 5")
1928	Edward B. Hamm, United States	7.73m. (25' 4½")
1932	Edward Gordon, United States	7.64m. (25' ¾")
1936	Jesse Owens, United States	8.06m. (26' 5½")
1948	Willie Steele, United States	7.82m. (25' 8")
1952	Jerome Biffle, United States	7.57m. (24' 10")
1956	Gregory Bell, United States	7.83m. (25' 8¼")
1960	Ralph Boston, United States	8.12m. (26' 7¾")
1964	Lynn Davies, Great Britain	8.07m. (26' 5¾")
1968	Bob Beamon, United States	8.90m. (29' 2½")*
1972	Randy Williams, United States	8.24m. (27' ½")
1976	Arnie Robinson, United States	8.35m. (27' 4¾")
1980	Lutz Dombrowski, E. Germany	8.54m. (28' ¼")
1984	Carl Lewis, United States	8.54m. (28' ¼")
1988	Carl Lewis, United States	8.72m. (28' 7½")
1992	Carl Lewis, United States	8.67m. (28' 5½")
1996	Carl Lewis, United States	8.50m. (27' 10¾")
2000	Ivan Pedroso, Cuba	8.55m. (28' ¾")

Triple Jump

1896	James Connolly, United States	13.71m.(44' 11¾")
1900	Meyer Prinstein, United States	14.47m.(47' 5¾")
1904	Meyer Prinstein, United States	14.35m.(47' 1")
1908	Timothy Ahearne, G.B.-Ireland	14.92m.(48' 11½")
1912	Gustaf Lindblom, Sweden	14.76m.(48' 5")
1920	Vilho Tuulos, Finland	14.50m.(47' 7")
1924	Anthony Winter, Australia	15.52m.(50' 11")
1928	Mikio Oda, Japan	15.21m.(49' 11")
1932	Chuhei Nambu, Japan	15.72m.(51' 7")
1936	Naoto Tajima, Japan	16.00m.(52' 6")
1948	Arne Ahman, Sweden	15.40m.(50' 6¼")
1952	Adhemar Ferreira da Silva, Brazil	16.22m.(53' 2¾")
1956	Adhemar Ferreira da Silva, Brazil	16.35m.(53' 7¾")
1960	Jozef Schmidt, Poland	16.81m.(55' 1½")
1964	Jozef Schmidt, Poland	16.85m.(55' 3½")
1968	Viktor Saneyev, USSR	17.39m.(57' ¾")
1972	Viktor Saneyev, USSR	17.35m.(56' 11¼")
1976	Viktor Saneyev, USSR	17.29m.(56' 8¾")
1980	Jaak Uudmae, USSR	17.35m.(56' 11")
1984	Al Joyner, United States	17.26m.(56' 7½")
1988	Khristo Markov, Bulgaria	17.61m.(57' 9½")
1992	Mike Conley, United States	18.17m.(59' 7½")w
1996	Kenny Harrison, United States	18.09m.(59' 4¼")*
2000	Jonathan Edwards, Britain	17.71m.(58' 1¼")

Discus Throw

1896	Robert Garrett, United States	29.15m.(95' 7")
1900	Rudolf Bauer, Hungary	36.04m.(118' 3")
1904	Martin Sheridan, United States	39.28m.(128' 10")
1908	Martin Sheridan, United States	40.89m.(134' 1")
1912	Armas Taipale, Finland	45.21m.(148' 3")
1920	Elmer Niklander, Finland	44.68m.(146' 7")
1924	Clarence Houser, United States	46.15m.(151' 4")
1928	Clarence Houser, United States	47.32m.(155' 3")
1932	John Anderson, United States	49.49m.(162' 4")
1936	Ken Carpenter, United States	50.48m.(165' 7")
1948	Adolfo Consolini, Italy	52.78m.(173' 2")
1952	Sim Iness, United States	55.03m.(180' 6")
1956	Al Oerter, United States	56.36m.(184' 11")
1960	Al Oerter, United States	59.18m.(194' 2")
1964	Al Oerter, United States	61.00m.(200' 1")
1968	Al Oerter, United States	64.78m.(212' 6")
1972	Ludvik Danek, Czechoslovakia	64.40m.(211' 3")
1976	Mac Wilkins, United States	67.50m.(221' 5")
1980	Viktor Rashchupkin, USSR	66.64m.(218' 8")
1984	Rolf Dannenberg, W. Germany	66.60m.(218' 6")
1988	Jurgen Schult, E. Germany	68.82m.(225' 9")
1992	Romas Ubartas, Lithuania	65.12m.(213' 8")
1996	Lars Riedel, Germany	69.40m.(227' 8")*
2000	Virgilijus Alekna, Lithuania	69.30m.(227' 4")

Hammer Throw

1900	John Flanagan, United States	49.73m.(163' 1")
1904	John Flanagan, United States	51.22m.(168' 0")
1908	John Flanagan, United States	51.92m.(170' 4")
1912	Matt McGrath, United States	54.74m.(179' 7")
1920	Pat Ryan, United States	52.86m.(173' 5")
1924	Fred Tootell, United States	53.28m.(174' 10")
1928	Patrick O'Callaghan, Ireland	51.38m.(168' 7")
1932	Patrick O'Callaghan, Ireland	53.92m.(176' 11")
1936	Karl Hein, Germany	56.48m.(185' 4")
1948	Imre Németh, Hungary	56.06m.(183' 11")
1952	József Csérmák, Hungary	60.34m.(197' 11")
1956	Harold Connolly, United States	63.18m.(207' 3")
1960	Vasily Rudenkov, USSR	67.10m.(202' 0")
1964	Romuald Klim, USSR	69.74m.(228' 10")
1968	Gyula Zsivótsky, Hungary	73.36m.(240' 8")
1972	Anatoly Bondarchuk, USSR	75.50m.(247' 8")
1976	Yuri Syedykh, USSR	77.52m.(254' 4")
1980	Yuri Syedykh, USSR	81.80m.(268' 4")
1984	Juha Tiainen, Finland	78.08m.(256' 2")
1988	Sergei Litvinov, USSR	84.80m.(278' 2")*
1992	Andrey Abduvaliyev, Unified Team.	82.54m.(270' 9")
1996	Balázs Kiss, Hungary	81.24m.(266' 6")
2000	Szymon Ziolkowski, Poland	80.02m.(262' 6")

Javelin Throw

1908	Erik Lemming, Sweden	54.82m. (179' 10")
1912	Erik Lemming, Sweden	60.64m. (198' 11")
1920	Jonni Myyrä, Finland	64.78m. (215' 10")
1924	Jonni Myyrä, Finland	62.96m. (206' 7")
1928	Eric Lundkvist, Sweden	66.60m. (218' 6")
1932	Matti Järvinen, Finland	72.70m. (238' 6")
1936	Gerhard Stöck, Germany	71.84m. (235' 8")
1948	Kai Tapio Rautavaara, Finland	69.76m. (228' 11")
1952	Cy Young, United States	73.78m. (242' 1")
1956	Egil Danielsen, Norway	85.70m. (281' 2")
1960	Viktor Tsibulenko, USSR	84.64m. (277' 8")
1964	Pauli Nevala, Finland	82.66m. (271' 2")
1968	Janis Lusis, USSR	90.10m. (295' 7")
1972	Klaus Wolfermann, W. Germany	90.48m. (296' 10")
1976	Miklós Németh, Hungary	94.58m. (310' 4")
1980	Dainis Kula, USSR	91.20m. (299' 2")
1984	Arto Härkönen, Finland	86.76m. (284' 8")
1988	Tapio Korjus, Finland	84.28m. (276' 6")
1992	Jan Zelezny, Czechoslovakia (a)	89.66m. (294' 2")
1996	Jan Zelezny, Czech Republic	88.16m. (289' 3")
2000	Jan Zelezny, Czech Republic	90.17m. (295' 9½")*

(a) New records were kept after javelin was modified in 1986.

Pole Vault

1896	William Welles Hoyt, United States	3.30m.(10' 10")
1900	Irving Baxter, United States	3.30m.(10' 10")
1904	Charles Dvorak, United States	3.50m.(11' 6")
1908	A. C. Gilbert, United States	
	Edward Cooke Jr., United States	3.71m (12' 2")
1912	Harry Babcock, United States	3.95m.(12' 11½")
1920	Frank Foss, United States	4.09m.(13' 5")
1924	Lee Barnes, United States	3.95m.(12' 11½")
1928	Sabin W. Carr, United States	4.20m.(13' 9¼")
1932	William Miller, United States	4.31m.(14' 1¾")
1936	Earle Meadows, United States	4.35m.(14' 3¼")
1948	Guinn Smith, United States	4.30m.(14' 1¼")
1952	Robert Richards, United States	4.55m.(14' 11¼")
1956	Robert Richards, United States	4.56m.(14' 11½")
1960	Don Bragg, United States	4.70m.(15' 5")
1964	Fred Hansen, United States	5.10m.(16' 8¾")
1968	Bob Seagren, United States	5.40m.(17' 8½")
1972	Wolfgang Nordwig, E. Germany	5.50m.(18' ½")
1976	Tadeusz Slusarski, Poland	5.50m.(18' ½")
1980	Wladyslaw Kozakiewicz, Poland	5.78m.(18' 11½")
1984	Pierre Quinon, France	5.75m.(18' 10¼")
1988	Sergei Bubka, USSR	5.90m.(19' 4¼")
1992	Maksim Tarassov, Unified Team	5.80m.(19' ¼")
1996	Jean Galfione, France	5.92m.(19' 5")*
2000	Nick Hysong, United States	5.90m.(19' 4¼")

16-lb. Shot Put

1896	Robert Garrett, United States	11.22m.(36' 9¾")
1900	Richard Sheldon, United States	14.10m.(46' 3¼")
1904	Ralph Rose, United States	14.81m.(48' 7")
1908	Ralph Rose, United States	14.21m.(46' 7½")
1912	Pat McDonald, United States	15.34m.(50' 4")
1920	Ville Pörhölä, Finland	14.81m.(48' 7¼")
1924	L. Clarence Houser, United States	14.99m.(49' 2¼")
1928	John Kuck, United States	15.87m.(52' ¾")
1932	Leo Sexton, United States	16.00m.(52' 6")
1936	Hans Woellke, Germany	16.20m.(53' 1¾")
1948	Wilbur Thompson, United States	17.12m.(56' 2")
1952	W. Parry O'Brien, United States	17.41m.(57' 1½")
1956	W. Parry O'Brien, United States	18.57m.(60' 11¼")

16-lb. Shot Put

1960	William Nieder, United States	19.68m.(64' 6¾")
1964	Dallas Long, United States	20.33m.(66' 8½")
1968	Randy Matson, United States	20.54m.(67' 4¾")
1972	Wladyslaw Komar, Poland	21.18m.(69' 6")
1976	Udo Beyer, E. Germany	21.05m.(69' ¾")
1980	Vladimir Kyselyov, USSR	21.35m.(70' ½")
1984	Alessandro Andrei, Italy	21.26m.(69' 9")
1988	Ulf Timmermann, E. Germany	22.47m.(73' 8¾")*
1992	Michael Stulce, United States	21.70m.(71' 2½")
1996	Randy Barnes, United States	21.62m.(70' 11¼")
2000	Arsi Harju, Finland	21.29m.(69' 10¼")

Decathlon (not held 1908)

1904	Thomas Kiely, Ireland	6,036 pts.
1912	Hugo Wieslander, Sweden (a)	7,724.49 pts.
1920	Helge Lovland, Norway	6,804.35 pts.
1924	Harold Osborn, United States	7,710.77 pts.
1928	Paavo Yrjola, Finland	8,053.29 pts.
1932	James Bausch, United States	8,462.23 pts.
1936	Glenn Morris, United States	7,900 pts.
1948	Robert Mathias, United States	7,139 pts.
1952	Robert Mathias, United States	7,887 pts.
1956	Milton Campbell, United States	7,937 pts.
1960	Rafer Johnson, United States	8,392 pts.
1964	Willi Holdorf, Germany (b)	7,887 pts.
1968	Bill Toomey, United States	8,193 pts.
1972	Nikolai Avilov, USSR	8,454 pts.
1976	Bruce Jenner, United States	8,617 pts.
1980	Daley Thompson, Great Britain	8,495 pts.
1984	Daley Thompson, Great Britain (c)	8,798 pts.*
1988	Christian Schenk, E. Germany	8,488 pts.
1992	Robert Zmelik, Czechoslovakia	8,611 pts.
1996	Dan O'Brien, United States	8,824 pts.
2000	Erki Nool, Estonia	8,641 pts.

(a) Jim Thorpe of the U.S. won the 1912 Decathlon with 8,413 pts. but was disqualified and had to return his medals because he had played pro baseball prior to the Olympics. The IOC in 1982 posthumously restored his decathlon and pentathlon golds. (b) Former point systems used prior to 1964. (c) Scoring change effective Apr. 1985; Thompson's readjusted score is 8,847 pts.

TRACK AND FIELD—Women

(* indicates Olympic record; w indicates wind-aided)

100-Meter Run

1928	Elizabeth Robinson, United States	12.2s
1932	Stella Walsh, Poland (a)	11.9s
1936	Helen Stephens, United States	11.5s
1948	Francina Blankers-Koen, Netherlands	11.9s
1952	Marjorie Jackson, Australia	11.5s
1956	Betty Cuthbert, Australia	11.5s
1960	Wilma Rudolph, United States	11.0s
1964	Wyomia Tyus, United States	11.4s
1968	Wyomia Tyus, United States	11.08s
1972	Renate Stecher, E. Germany	11.07s
1976	Annegret Richter, W. Germany	11.08s
1980	Lyudmila Kondratyeva, USSR	11.06s
1984	Evelyn Ashford, United States	10.97s
1988	Florence Griffith-Joyner, United States	10.54sw
1992	Gail Devers, United States	10.82s
1996	Gail Devers, United States	10.94s
2000	Marion Jones, United States	10.75s

(a) A 1980 autopsy determined that Walsh was a man.

200-Meter Run

1948	Francina Blankers-Koen, Netherlands	24.4s
1952	Marjorie Jackson, Australia	23.7s
1956	Betty Cuthbert, Australia	23.4s
1960	Wilma Rudolph, United States	24.0s
1964	Edith McGuire, United States	23.0s
1968	Irena Szewinska, Poland	22.5s
1972	Renate Stecher, E. Germany	22.40s
1976	Barbel Eckert, E. Germany	22.37s
1980	Barbel Wockel, E. Germany	22.03s
1984	Valerie Brisco-Hooks, United States	21.81s
1988	Florence Griffith-Joyner, United States	21.34s*
1992	Gwen Torrence, United States	21.81s
1996	Marie-Jose Perec, France	22.12s
2000	Marion Jones, United States	21.84s

400-Meter Run

1964	Betty Cuthbert, Australia	52.0s
1968	Colette Besson, France	52.0s
1972	Monika Zehrt, E. Germany	51.08s
1976	Irena Szewinska, Poland	49.29s
1980	Marita Koch, E. Germany	48.88s
1984	Valerie Brisco-Hooks, United States	48.83s
1988	Olga Bryzgina, USSR	48.65s
1992	Marie-Jose Perec, France	48.83s

400-Meter Run

1996	Marie-Jose Perec, France	48.25s*
2000	Cathy Freeman, Australia	49.11s

800-Meter Run

1928	Lina Radke, Germany	2m. 16.8s
1960	Ludmila Shevtsova, USSR	2m. 4.3s
1964	Ann Packer, Great Britain	2m. 1.1s
1968	Madeline Manning, United States	2m. 0.9s
1972	Hildegard Falck, W. Germany	1m. 58.6s
1976	Tatyana Kazankina, USSR	1m. 54.94s
1980	Nadezhda Olizarenko, USSR	1m. 53.43s*
1984	Doina Melinte, Romania	1m. 57.60s
1988	Sigrun Wodars, E. Germany	1m. 56.10s
1992	Ellen Van Langen, Netherlands	1m. 55.54s
1996	Svetlana Masterkova, Russia	1m. 57.73s
2000	Maria Mutola, Mozambique	1m. 56.15s

1,500-Meter Run

1972	Lyudmila Bragina, USSR	4m. 01.4s
1976	Tatyana Kazankina, USSR	4m. 05.48s
1980	Tatyana Kazankina, USSR	3m. 56.6s
1984	Gabriella Dorio, Italy	4m. 03.25s
1988	Paula Ivan, Romania	3m. 53.96s*
1992	Hassiba Boulmerka, Algeria	3m. 55.30s
1996	Svetlana Masterkova, Russia	4m. 00.83s
2000	Nouria Benida Merah, Algeria	4m. 05.10s

3,000-Meter Run

1984	Maricica Puica, Romania	8m. 35.96s
1988	Tatyana Samolenko, USSR	8m. 26.53s*
1992	Elena Romanova, Unified Team	8m. 46.04s

5,000-Meter Run

1996	Wang Junxia, China	14m. 59.88s
2000	Gabriela Szabo, Romania	14m. 40.79s*

10,000-Meter Run

1988	Olga Boldarenko, USSR	31m. 44.69s
1992	Derartu Tulu, Ethiopia	31m. 06.02s
1996	Fernanda Ribeiro, Portugal	31m. 01.63s
2000	Derartu Tulu, Ethiopia	30m. 17.49s*

100-Meter Hurdles

1972	Annelie Ehrhardt, E. Germany	12.59s
1976	Johanna Schaller, E. Germany	12.77s
1980	Vera Komisova, USSR	12.56s
1984	Benita Brown-Fitzgerald, United States	12.84s
1988	Jordanka Donkova, Bulgaria	12.38s*
1992	Paraskevi Patoulidou, Greece	12.64s
1996	Ludmila Enquist, Sweden	12.58s
2000	Olga Shishigina, Kazakhstan	12.65s

400-Meter Hurdles

1984	Nawal el Moutawakil, Morocco	54.61s
1988	Debra Flintoff-King, Australia	53.17s
1992	Sally Gunnell, Great Britain	53.23s
1996	Deon Hemmings, Jamaica	52.82s*
2000	Irina Privalova, Russia	53.02s

1,600-Meter Relay

1972	East Germany	3m. 23s
1976	East Germany	3m. 19.23s
1980	USSR	3m. 20.02s
1984	United States	3m. 18.29s
1988	USSR	3m. 15.17s*
1992	Unified Team	3m. 20.20s
1996	United States	3m. 20.91s
2000	United States	3m. 22.62s

400-Meter Relay

1928	Canada	48.4s
1932	United States	46.9s
1936	United States	46.9s
1948	Netherlands	47.5s
1952	United States	45.9s
1956	Australia	44.5s
1960	United States	44.5s
1964	Poland	43.6s
1968	United States	42.88s
1972	West Germany	42.81s
1976	East Germany	42.55s
1980	East Germany	41.60s*
1984	United States	41.65s
1988	United States	41.98s
1992	United States	42.11s
1996	United States	41.95s
2000	Bahamas	41.95s

10 Kilometer Walk

1992	Chen Yueling, China	44m. 32s
1996	Elena Nikolayeva, Russia	41m. 49s*

20 Kilometer Walk

2000	Wang Liping, China	1m. 29.05s*

Marathon

1984	Joan Benoit, United States	2h. 24m. 52s

Marathon

1988	Rosa Mota, Portugal	2h. 25m. 40s
1992	Valentina Yegorova, Unified Team	2h. 32m. 41s
1996	Fatuma Roba, Ethiopia	2h. 26m. 05s
2000	Naoko Takahashi, Japan	2h. 23m. 14s*

High Jump

1928	Ethel Catherwood, Canada	1.59m. (5' 2½")
1932	Jean Shiley, United States	1.65m. (5' 5")
1936	Ibolya Csák, Hungary	1.60m. (5' 3")
1948	Alice Coachman, U. S.	1.68m. (5' 6")
1952	Esther Brand, South Africa	1.67m. (5' 5¾")
1956	Mildred L. McDaniel, U. S.	1.76m. (5' 9¼")
1960	Iolanda Balas, Romania	1.85m. (6' ¾")
1964	Iolanda Balas, Romania	1.90m. (6' 2¾ ")
1968	Miloslava Resková, Czech.	1.82m. (5' 11½")
1972	Ulrike Meyfarth, W. Germany	1.92m. (6' 3½")
1976	Rosemarie Ackermann, E. Ger.	1.93m. (6' 4")
1980	Sara Simeoni, Italy	1.97m. (6' 5½")
1984	Ulrike Meyfarth, W. Germany	2.02m. (6' 7½")
1988	Louise Ritter, United States	2.03m. (6' 8")
1992	Heike Henkel, Germany	2.02m. (6' 7½")
1996	Stefka Kostadinova, Bulgaria	2.05m. (6' 8¾")
2000	Yelena Yelesina, Russia	2.01m. (6' 7")

Long Jump

1948	Olga Gyarmati, Hungary	5.69m. (18' 8")
1952	Yvette Williams, New Zealand	6.24m. (20' 5¼")
1956	Elzbieta Krzesinska, Poland	6.35m. (20' 10")
1960	Vira Krepkina, USSR	6.37m. (20' 10¾)
1964	Mary Rand, Great Britain	6.76m. (22' 2¼")
1968	Viorica Viscopoleanu, Romania	6.82m. (22' 4½")
1972	Heidemarie Rosendahl, W. Ger.	6.78m. (22' 3")
1976	Angela Voigt, E. Germany	6.72m. (22' ¾")
1980	Tatyana Kolpakova, USSR	7.06m. (23' 2")
1984	Anisoara Cusmir-Stanciu, Rom.	6.96m. (22' 10")
1988	Jackie Joyner-Kersee, United States.	7.40m. (24' 3½")*
1992	Heike Drechsler, Germany	7.14m. (23' 5¼")
1996	Chioma Ajunwa, Nigeria	7.12m. (23' 4½")
2000	Heike Drechsler, Germany	6.99m. (22' 11¼")

Triple Jump

1996	Inessa Kravets, Ukraine	15.33m. (50' 3½")*
2000	Tereza Marinova, Bulgaria	15.20m. (49' 10½")

Discus Throw

1928	Halina Konopacka, Poland	39.62m. (130' 0")
1932	Lillian Copeland, United States	40.58m. (133' 2")
1936	Gisela Mauermayer, Germany	47.62m. (156' 3")
1948	Micheline Ostermeyer, France	41.92m. (137' 6")
1952	Nina Ponomareva, USSR	51.42m. (168' 8")
1956	Olga Fikotová, Czech.	53.68m. (176' 1")
1960	Nina Ponomareva, USSR	55.10m. (180' 9")
1964	Tamara Press, USSR	57.26m. (187' 10")
1968	Lia Manoliu, Romania	58.28m. (191' 2")
1972	Faina Melnik, USSR	66.62m. (218' 7")
1976	Evelin Jahl, E. Germany	69.00m. (226' 4")
1980	Evelin Jahl, E. Germany	69.96m. (229' 6")
1984	Ria Stalman, Netherlands.	65.36m. (214' 5")
1988	Martina Hellmann, E. Germany	72.30m. (237' 2")*
1992	Maritza Martén Garcia, Cuba	70.06m. (229' 10")
1996	Ilke Wyludda, Germany	69.66m. (228' 6")
2000	Ellina Zvereva, Belarus	68.40m. (224' 5")

Hammer Throw

2000	Kamila Skolimowska, Poland	71.16m. (233' 5¾")*

Pole Vault

2000	Stacy Dragila, United States	4.60m. (15' 1")*

Shot Put (8 lb., 13 oz.)

1948	Micheline Ostermeyer, France	13.75m. (45' 1½")
1952	Galina Zybina, USSR	15.28m. (50' 1½")
1956	Tamara Tyshkyevich, USSR	16.59m. (54' 5¼")
1960	Tamara Press, USSR	17.32m. (56' 10")
1964	Tamara Press, USSR	18.14m. (59' 6¼")
1968	Margitta Gummel, E. Germany	19.61m. (64' 4")
1972	Nadezhda Chizova, USSR	21.03m. (69' 0")
1976	Ivanka Khristova, Bulgaria	21.16m. (69' 5¼")
1980	Ilona Slupianek, E. Germany	22.41m. (73' 6¼")*
1984	Claudia Losch, W. Germany	20.49m. (67' 2¼")
1988	Natalya Lisovskaya, USSR	22.24m. (72' 11¾")
1992	Svetlana Krivelyova, Unified Team.	21.06m. (69' 1¼")
1996	Astrid Kumbernuss, Germany	20.56m. (67' 5½")
2000	Yanina Karolchik, Belarus	20.56m. (67' 5½")

Javelin Throw

1932	"Babe" Didrikson, United States	43.68m. (143' 4")
1936	Tilly Fleischer, Germany	45.18m. (148' 3")
1948	Herma Bauma, Austria	45.56m. (149' 6")
1952	Dana Zátopková, Czech.	50.46m. (165' 7")
1956	Inese Jaunzeme, USSR	53.86m. (176' 8")
1960	Elvira Ozolina, USSR	55.98m. (183' 8")
1964	Mihaela Penes, Romania	60.54m. (198' 7")

Javelin Throw

1968	Angéla Németh, Hungary	60.36m.	(198' 0")
1972	Ruth Fuchs, E. Germany	63.88m.	(209' 7")
1976	Ruth Fuchs, E. Germany	65.94m.	(216' 4")
1980	Maria Colón Ruenes, Cuba	68.40m.	(224' 5")
1984	Tessa Sanderson, Great Britain	69.56m.	(228' 2")
1988	Petra Felke, E. Germany	74.68m.	(245' 0")
1992	Silke Renke, Germany	68.34m.	(224' 2")
1996	Heli Rantanen, Finland	67.94m.	(222' 11")
2000	Trine Hattestad, Norway (a)	68.91m.	(226' 1")*

(a) New records were kept after javelin was modified in 1999.

Heptathlon

1984	Glynis Nunn, Australia	6,390 pts.
1988	Jackie Joyner-Kersee, U.S.	7,291 pts.*
1992	Jackie Joyner-Kersee, U.S.	7,044 pts.
1996	Ghada Shouaa, Syria	6,780 pts.
2000	Denise Lewis, Britain	6,584 pts.

SWIMMING AND DIVING—Men
(* indicates Olympic record)

50-Meter Freestyle

1988	Matt Biondi, U.S.	22.14
1992	Aleksandr Popov, Unified Team	21.91*
1996	Aleksandr Popov, Russia	22.13
2000	Anthony Ervin, U.S.	21.98
2000	Gary Hall Jr., U.S.	21.98

100-Meter Freestyle

1896	Alfred Hajos, Hungary	1:22.2
1904	Zoltan de Halmay, Hungary (100 yards)	1:02.8
1908	Charles Daniels, U.S.	1:05.6
1912	Duke P. Kahanamoku, U.S.	1:03.4
1920	Duke P. Kahanamoku, U.S.	1:01.4
1924	John Weissmuller, U.S.	59.0
1928	John Weissmuller, U.S.	58.6
1932	Yasuji Miyazaki, Japan	58.2
1936	Ferenc Csik, Hungary	57.6
1948	Wally Ris, U.S.	57.3
1952	Clark Scholes, U.S.	57.4
1956	Jon Henricks, Australia	55.4
1960	John Devitt, Australia	55.2
1964	Don Schollander, U.S.	53.4
1968	Mike Wenden, Australia	52.2
1972	Mark Spitz, U.S.	51.22
1976	Jim Montgomery, U.S.	49.99
1980	Jorg Woithe, E. Germany	50.40
1984	Rowdy Gaines, U.S.	49.80
1988	Matt Biondi, U.S.	48.63
1992	Aleksandr Popov, Unified Team	49.02
1996	Aleksandr Popov, Russia	48.74
2000	Pieter van den Hoogenband, Netherlands	48.30

200-Meter Freestyle

1968	Mike Wenden, Australia	1:55.2
1972	Mark Spitz, U.S.	1:52.78
1976	Bruce Furniss, U.S.	1:50.29
1980	Sergei Kopliakov, USSR	1:49.81
1984	Michael Gross, W. Germany	1:47.44
1988	Duncan Armstrong, Australia	1:47.25
1992	Yevgeny Sadovyi, Unified Team	1:46.70
1996	Danyon Loader, New Zealand	1:47.63
2000	Pieter van den Hoogenband, Netherlands	1:45.35*

400-Meter Freestyle

1904	C. M. Daniels, U.S. (440 yards)	6:16.2
1908	Henry Taylor, Great Britain	5:36.8
1912	George Hodgson, Canada	5:24.4
1920	Norman Ross, U.S.	5:26.8
1924	John Weissmuller, U.S.	5:04.2
1928	Albert Zorilla, Argentina	5:01.6
1932	Clarence Crabbe, U.S.	4:48.4
1936	Jack Medica, U.S.	4:44.5
1948	William Smith, U.S.	4:41.0
1952	Jean Boiteux, France	4:30.7
1956	Murray Rose, Australia	4:27.3
1960	Murray Rose, Australia	4:18.3
1964	Don Schollander, U.S.	4:12.2
1968	Mike Burton, U.S.	4:09.0
1972	Brad Cooper, Australia	4:00.27
1976	Brian Goodell, U.S.	3:51.93
1980	Vladimir Salnikov, USSR	3:51.31
1984	George DiCarlo, U.S.	3:51.23
1988	Ewe Dassler, E. Germany	3:46.95
1992	Yevgeny Sadovyi, Unified Team	3:45.00
1996	Danyon Loader, New Zealand	3:47.97
2000	Ian Thorpe, Australia	3:40.59*

1,500-Meter Freestyle

1908	Henry Taylor, Great Britain	22:48.4
1912	George Hodgson, Canada	22:00.0

1,500-Meter Freestyle

1920	Norman Ross, U.S.	22:23.2
1924	Andrew Charlton, Australia	20:06.6
1928	Arne Borg, Sweden	19:51.8
1932	Kusuo Kitamura, Japan	19:12.4
1936	Noboru Terada, Japan	19:13.7
1948	James McLane, U.S.	19:18.5
1952	Ford Konno, U.S.	18:30.3
1956	Murray Rose, Australia	17:58.9
1960	Jon Konrads, Australia	17:19.6
1964	Robert Windle, Australia	17:01.7
1968	Mike Burton, U.S.	16:38.9
1972	Mike Burton, U.S.	15:52.58
1976	Brian Goodell, U.S.	15:02.40
1980	Vladimir Salnikov, USSR	14:58.27
1984	Michael O'Brien, U.S.	15:05.20
1988	Vladimir Salnikov, USSR	15:00.40
1992	Kieren Perkins, Australia	14:43.48*
1996	Kieren Perkins, Australia	14:56.40
2000	Grant Hackett, Australia	14:48.33

100-Meter Backstroke

1904	Walter Brack, Germany (100 yds.)	1:16.8
1908	Arno Bieberstein, Germany	1:24.6
1912	Harry Hebner, U.S.	1:21.2
1920	Warren Kealoha, U.S.	1:15.2
1924	Warren Kealoha, U.S.	1:13.2
1928	George Kojac, U.S.	1:08.2
1932	Masaji Kiyokawa, Japan	1:08.6
1936	Adolph Kiefer, U.S.	1:05.9
1948	Allen Stack, U.S.	1:06.4
1952	Yoshi Oyakawa, U.S.	1:05.4
1956	David Thiele, Australia	1:02.2
1960	David Thiele, Australia	1:01.9
1968	Roland Matthes, E. Germany	58.7
1972	Roland Matthes, E. Germany	56.58
1976	John Naber, U.S.	55.49
1980	Bengt Baron, Sweden	56.33
1984	Rick Carey, U.S.	55.79
1988	Daichi Suzuki, Japan	55.05
1992	Mark Tewksbury, Canada	53.98
1996	Jeff Rouse, U.S.	54.10
2000	Lenny Krayzelburg, U.S.	53.72*

200-Meter Backstroke

1964	Jed Graef, U.S.	2:10.3
1968	Roland Matthes, E. Germany	2:09.6
1972	Roland Matthes, E. Germany	2:02.82
1976	John Naber, U.S.	1:59.19
1980	Sandor Wladar, Hungary	2:01.93
1984	Rick Carey, U.S.	2:00.23
1988	Igor Polianski, USSR	1:59.37
1992	Martin Lopez-Zubero, Spain	1:58.47
1996	Brad Bridgewater, U.S.	1:58.54
2000	Lenny Krayzelburg, U.S.	1:56.76*

100-Meter Breaststroke

1968	Don McKenzie, U.S.	1:07.7
1972	Nobutaka Taguchi, Japan	1:04.94
1976	John Hencken, U.S.	1:03.11
1980	Duncan Goodhew, Great Britain	1:03.44
1984	Steve Lundquist, U.S.	1:01.65
1988	Adrian Moorhouse, Great Britain	1:02.04
1992	Nelson Diebel, U.S.	1:01.50
1996	Fred Deburghgraeve, Belgium	1:00.60
2000	Domenico Fioravanti, Italy	1:00.46*

200-Meter Breaststroke

1908	Frederick Holman, Great Britain	3:09.2
1912	Walter Bathe, Germany	3:01.8
1920	Haken Malmroth, Sweden	3:04.4
1924	Robert Skelton, U.S.	2:56.6
1928	Yoshiyuki Tsuruta, Japan	2:48.8
1932	Yoshiyuki Tsuruta, Japan	2:45.4
1936	Tetsuo Hamuro, Japan	2:41.5
1948	Joseph Verdeur, U.S.	2:39.3
1952	John Davies, Australia	2:34.4
1956	Masura Furukawa, Japan	2:34.7
1960	William Mulliken, U.S.	2:37.4
1964	Ian O'Brien, Australia	2:27.8
1968	Felipe Munoz, Mexico	2:28.7
1972	John Hencken, U.S.	2:21.55
1976	David Wilkie, Great Britain	2:15.11
1980	Robertas Zhulpa, USSR	2:15.85
1984	Victor Davis, Canada	2:13.34
1988	Jozsef Szabo, Hungary	2:13.52
1992	Mike Barrowman, U.S.	2:10.16*
1996	Norbert Rozsa, Hungary	2:12.57
2000	Domenico Fioravanti, Italy	2:10.87

100-Meter Butterfly

1968	Doug Russell, U.S.	55.9
1972	Mark Spitz, U.S.	54.27
1976	Matt Vogel, U.S.	54.35
1980	Par Arvidsson, Sweden	54.92
1984	Michael Gross, W. Germany	53.08
1988	Anthony Nesty, Suriname	53.00
1992	Pablo Morales, U.S.	53.32
1996	Denis Pankratov, Russia	52.27
2000	Lars Froelander, Sweden	52.00

200-Meter Butterfly

1956	William Yorzyk, U.S.	2:19.3
1960	Michael Troy, U.S.	2:12.8
1964	Kevin J. Berry, Australia	2:06.6
1968	Carl Robie, U.S.	2:08.7
1972	Mark Spitz, U.S.	2:00.70
1976	Mike Bruner, U.S.	1:59.23
1980	Sergei Fesenko, USSR	1:59.76
1984	Jon Sieben, Australia	1:57.04
1988	Michael Gross, W. Germany	1:56.94
1992	Mel Stewart, U.S.	1:56.26
1996	Denis Pankratov, Russia	1:56.51
2000	Tom Malchow, U.S.	1:55.35*

200-Meter Individual Medley

1968	Charles Hickcox, U.S.	2:12.0
1972	Gunnar Larsson, Sweden	2:07.17
1984	Alex Baumann, Canada	2:01.42
1988	Tamas Darnyi, Hungary	2:00.17
1992	Tamas Darnyi, Hungary	2:00.76
1996	Attila Czene, Hungary	1:59.91
2000	Massimiliano Rosolino, Italy	1:58.98*

400-Meter Individual Medley

1964	Dick Roth, U.S.	4:45.4
1968	Charles Hickcox, U.S.	4:48.4
1972	Gunnar Larsson, Sweden	4:31.98
1976	Rod Strachan, U.S.	4:23.68
1980	Aleksandr Sidorenko, USSR	4:22.89
1984	Alex Baumann, Canada	4:17.41
1988	Tamas Darnyi, Hungary	4:14.75
1992	Tamas Darnyi, Hungary	4:14.23
1996	Tom Dolan, U.S.	4:14.90
2000	Tom Dolan, U.S.	4:11.76*

400-Meter Freestyle Relay

1964	United States	3:31.2
1968	United States	3:31.7
1972	United States	3:26.42
1984	United States	3:19.03
1988	United States	3:16.53
1992	United States	3:16.74
1996	United States	3:15.41
2000	Australia	3:13.67*

800-Meter Freestyle Relay

1908	Great Britain	10:55.6
1912	Australia	10:11.6
1920	United States	10:04.4
1924	United States	9:53.4
1928	United States	9:36.2
1932	Japan	8:58.4
1936	Japan	8:51.5
1948	United States	8:46.0
1952	United States	8:31.1
1956	Australia	8:23.6
1960	United States	8:10.2
1964	United States	7:52.1
1968	United States	7:52.33
1972	United States	7:35.78
1976	United States	7:23.22
1980	USSR	7:23.50
1984	United States	7:15.69
1988	United States	7:12.51
1992	Unified Team	7:11.95
1996	United States	7:14.84
2000	Australia	7:07.05*

400-Meter Medley Relay

1960	United States	4:05.4
1964	United States	3:58.4
1968	United States	3:54.9
1972	United States	3:48.16
1976	United States	3:42.22
1980	Australia	3:45.70
1984	United States	3:39.30
1988	United States	3:36.93
1992	United States	3:36.93
1996	United States	3:34.84
2000	United States	3:33.73*

Springboard Diving

		Points
1908	Albert Zurner, Germany	85.5
1912	Paul Guenther, Germany	79.23

Springboard Diving

		Points
1920	Louis Kuehn, U.S.	675.40
1924	Albert White, U.S.	97.46
1928	Pete Desjardins, U.S.	185.04
1932	Michael Galitzen, U.S.	161.38
1936	Richard Degener, U.S.	163.57
1948	Bruce Harlan, U.S.	163.64
1952	David Browning, U.S.	205.29
1956	Robert Clotworthy, U.S.	159.56
1960	Gary Tobian, U.S.	170.00
1964	Kenneth Sitzberger, U.S.	159.90
1968	Bernie Wrightson, U.S.	170.15
1972	Vladimir Vasin, USSR	594.09
1976	Phil Boggs, U.S.	619.52
1980	Aleksandr Portnov, USSR	905.02
1984	Greg Louganis, U.S.	754.41
1988	Greg Louganis, U.S.	730.80
1992	Mark Lenzi, U.S.	676.53
1996	Xiong Ni, China.	701.46
2000	Xiong Ni, China.	708.72

Platform Diving

		Points
1904	Dr. G.E. Sheldon, U.S.	112.75
1908	Hjalmar Johansson, Sweden	183.75
1912	Erik Adlerz, Sweden	73.94
1920	Clarence Pinkston, U.S.	100.67
1924	Albert White, U.S.	97.46
1928	Pete Desjardins, U.S.	98.74
1932	Harold Smith, U.S.	124.80
1936	Marshall Wayne, U.S.	113.58
1948	Sammy Lee, U.S.	130.05
1952	Sammy Lee, U.S.	156.28
1956	Joaquin Capilla, Mexico	152.44
1960	Robert Webster, U.S.	165.56
1964	Robert Webster, U.S.	148.58
1968	Klaus Dibiasi, Italy	164.18
1972	Klaus Dibiasi, Italy	504.12
1976	Klaus Dibiasi, Italy	600.51
1980	Falk Hoffmann, E. Germany	835.65
1984	Greg Louganis, U.S.	710.91
1988	Greg Louganis, U.S.	638.61
1992	Sun Shuwei, China.	677.31
1996	Dmitri Sautin, Russia	692.34
2000	Tian Liang, China.	724.53

SWIMMING AND DIVING—Women
(* indicates Olympic record)

50-Meter Freestyle

1988	Kristin Otto, E. Germany.	25.49
1992	Yang Wenyi, China.	24.76
1996	Amy Van Dyken, U.S.	24.87
2000	Inge de Bruijn, Netherlands	24.32

100-Meter Freestyle

1912	Fanny Durack, Australia	1:22.2
1920	Ethelda Bleibtrey, U.S.	1:13.6
1924	Ethel Lackie, U.S.	1:12.4
1928	Albina Osipowich, U.S.	1:11.0
1932	Helene Madison, U.S.	1:06.8
1936	Hendrika Mastenbroek, Holland	1:05.9
1948	Greta Andersen, Denmark	1:06.3
1952	Katalin Szoke, Hungary	1:06.8
1956	Dawn Fraser, Australia	1:02.0
1960	Dawn Fraser, Australia	1:01.2
1964	Dawn Fraser, Australia	59.5
1968	Jan Henne, U.S.	1:00.0
1972	Sandra Neilson, U.S.	58.59
1976	Kornelia Ender, E. Germany.	55.65
1980	Barbara Krause, E. Germany	54.79
1984	(tie) Carrie Steinseifer, U.S.	55.92
	Nancy Hogshead, U.S.	55.92
1988	Kristin Otto, E. Germany.	54.93
1992	Zhuang Yong, China.	54.64
1996	Li Jingyi, China.	54.50
2000	Inge de Bruijn, Netherlands	53.83

200-Meter Freestyle

1968	Debbie Meyer, U.S.	2:10.5
1972	Shane Gould, Australia.	2:03.56
1976	Kornelia Ender, E. Germany.	1:59.26
1980	Barbara Krause, E. Germany	1:58.33
1984	Mary Wayte, U.S.	1:59.23
1988	Heike Friedrich, E. Germany	1:57.65*
1992	Nicole Haislett, U.S.	1:57.90
1996	Claudia Poll, Costa Rica.	1:58.16
2000	Susie O'Neill, Australia	1:58.24

400-Meter Freestyle

1924	Martha Norelius, U.S.	6:02.2
1928	Martha Norelius, U.S.	5:42.8
1932	Helene Madison, U.S.	5:28.5
1936	Hendrika Mastenbroek, Netherlands	5:26.4
1948	Ann Curtis, U.S.	5:17.8

400-Meter Freestyle (continued)

1952	Valerie Gyenge, Hungary	5:12.1
1956	Lorraine Crapp, Australia	4:54.6
1960	Susan Chris von Saltza, U.S.	4:50.6
1964	Virginia Duenkel, U.S.	4:43.3
1968	Debbie Meyer, U.S.	4:31.8
1972	Shane Gould, Australia	4:19.44
1976	Petra Thuemer, E. Germany	4:09.89
1980	Ines Diers, E. Germany	4:08.76
1984	Tiffany Cohen, U.S.	4:07.10
1988	Janet Evans, U.S.	4:03.85*
1992	Dagmar Hase, Germany	4:07.18
1996	Michelle Smith, Ireland	4:07.25
2000	Brooke Bennett, U.S.	4:05.80

800-Meter Freestyle

1968	Debbie Meyer, U.S.	9:24.0
1972	Keena Rothhammer, U.S.	8:53.68
1976	Petra Thuemer, E. Germany	8:37.14
1980	Michelle Ford, Australia	8:28.90
1984	Tiffany Cohen, U.S.	8:24.95
1988	Janet Evans, U.S.	8:20.20
1992	Janet Evans, U.S.	8:25.52
1996	Brooke Bennett, U.S.	8:27.89
2000	Brooke Bennett, U.S.	8:19.67*

100-Meter Backstroke

1924	Sybil Bauer, U.S.	1:23.2
1928	Marie Braun, Netherlands	1:22.0
1932	Eleanor Holm, U.S.	1:19.4
1936	Dina Senff, Netherlands	1:18.9
1948	Karen Harup, Denmark	1:14.4
1952	Joan Harrison, South Africa	1:14.3
1956	Judy Grinham, Great Britain	1:12.9
1960	Lynn Burke, U.S.	1:09.3
1964	Cathy Ferguson, U.S.	1:07.7
1968	Kaye Hall, U.S.	1:06.2
1972	Melissa Belote, U.S.	1:05.78
1976	Ulrike Richter, E. Germany	1:01.83
1980	Rica Reinisch, E. Germany	1:00.86
1984	Theresa Andrews, U.S.	1:02.55
1988	Kristin Otto, E. Germany	1:00.89
1992	Krisztina Egerszegi, Hungary	1:00.68
1996	Beth Botsford, U.S.	1:01.19
2000	Diana Mocanu, Romania	1:00.21*

200-Meter Backstroke

1968	Pokey Watson, U.S.	2:24.8
1972	Melissa Belote, U.S.	2:19.19
1976	Ulrike Richter, E. Germany	2:13.43
1980	Rica Reinisch, E. Germany	2:11.77
1984	Jolanda De Rover, Netherlands	2:12.38
1988	Krisztina Egerszegi, Hungary	2:09.29
1992	Krisztina Egerszegi, Hungary	2:07.06*
1996	Krisztina Egerszegi, Hungary	2:07.83
2000	Diana Mocanu, Romania	2:08.16

100-Meter Breaststroke

1968	Djurdjica Bjedov, Yugoslavia	1:15.8
1972	Cathy Carr, U.S.	1:13.58
1976	Hannelore Anke, E. Germany	1:11.16
1980	Ute Geweniger, E. Germany	1:10.22
1984	Petra Van Staveren, Netherlands	1:09.88
1988	Tania Dangalakova, Bulgaria	1:07.95
1992	Elena Roudkovskaia, Unified Team	1:08.00
1996	Penny Heyns, South Africa	1:07.73
2000	Megan Quann, U.S.	1:07.05

200-Meter Breaststroke

1924	Lucy Morton, Great Britain	3:33.2
1928	Hilde Schrader, Germany	3:12.6
1932	Clare Dennis, Australia	3:06.3
1936	Hideko Maehata, Japan	3:03.6
1948	Nelly Van Vliet, Netherlands	2:57.2
1952	Eva Szekely, Hungary	2:51.7
1956	Ursula Happe, Germany	2:53.1
1960	Anita Lonsbrough, Great Britain	2:49.5
1964	Galina Prozumenschikova, USSR	2:46.4
1968	Sharon Wichman, U.S.	2:44.4
1972	Beverly Whitfield, Australia	2:41.71
1976	Marina Koshevaia, USSR	2:33.35
1980	Lina Kachushite, USSR	2:29.54
1984	Anne Ottenbrite, Canada	2:30.38
1988	Silke Hoerner, E. Germany	2:26.71
1992	Kyoko Iwasaki, Japan	2:26.65
1996	Penny Heyns, South Africa	2:25.41
2000	Agnes Kovacs, Hungary	2:24.35

100-Meter Butterfly

1956	Shelley Mann, U.S.	1:11.0
1960	Carolyn Schuler, U.S.	1:09.5
1964	Sharon Stouder, U.S.	1:04.7
1968	Lynn McClements, Australia	1:05.5

100-Meter Butterfly

1972	Mayumi Aoki, Japan	1:03.34
1976	Kornelia Ender, E. Germany	1:00.13
1980	Caren Metschuck, E. Germany	1:00.42
1984	Mary T. Meagher, U.S.	59.26
1988	Kristin Otto, E. Germany	59.00
1992	Qian Hong, China	58.62
1996	Amy Van Dyken, U.S.	59.13
2000	Inge de Bruijn, Netherlands	56:61*

200-Meter Butterfly

1968	Ada Kok, Netherlands	2:24.7
1972	Karen Moe, U.S.	2:15.57
1976	Andrea Pollack, E. Germany	2:11.41
1980	Ines Geissler, E. Germany	2:10.44
1984	Mary T. Meagher, U.S.	2:06.90
1988	Kathleen Nord, E. Germany	2:09.51
1992	Summer Sanders, U.S.	2:08.67
1996	Susan O'Neill, Australia	2:07.76
2000	Misty Hyman, U.S.	2:05.88*

200-Meter Individual Medley

1968	Claudia Kolb, U.S.	2:24.7
1972	Shane Gould, Australia	2:23.07
1984	Tracy Caulkins, U.S.	2:12.64
1988	Daniela Hunger, E. Germany	2:12.59
1992	Lin Li, China	2:11.65
1996	Michelle Smith, Ireland	2:13.93
2000	Yana Klochkova, Ukraine	2:10.68*

400-Meter Individual Medley

1964	Donna de Varona, U.S.	5:18.7
1968	Claudia Kolb, U.S.	5:08.5
1972	Gail Neall, Australia	5:02.97
1976	Ulrike Tauber, E. Germany	4:42.77
1980	Petra Schneider, E. Germany	4:36.29
1984	Tracy Caulkins, U.S.	4:39.24
1988	Janet Evans, U.S.	4:37.76
1992	Krisztina Egerszegi, Hungary	4:36.54
1996	Michelle Smith, Ireland	4:39.18
2000	Yana Klochkova, Ukraine	4:33.59*

400-Meter Freestyle Relay

1912	Great Britain	5:52.8
1920	United States	5:11.6
1924	United States	4:58.8
1928	United States	4:47.6
1932	United States	4:38.0
1936	Netherlands	4:36.0
1948	United States	4:29.2
1952	Hungary	4:24.4
1956	Australia	4:17.1
1960	United States	4:08.9
1964	United States	4:03.8
1968	United States	4:02.5
1972	United States	3:55.19
1976	United States	3:44.82
1980	East Germany	3:42.71
1984	United States	3:43.43
1988	East Germany	3:40.63
1992	United States	3:39.46
1996	United States	3:39.29
2000	United States	3:36.61*

800-Meter Freestyle Relay

1996	United States	7:59.87
2000	United States	7:57.80*

400-Meter Medley Relay

1960	United States	4:41.1
1964	United States	4:33.9
1968	United States	4:28.3
1972	United States	4:20.75
1976	East Germany	4:07.95
1980	East Germany	4:06.67
1984	United States	4:08.34
1988	East Germany	4:03.74
1992	United States	4:02.54
1996	United States	4:02.88
2000	United States	3:58.30*

Springboard Diving Points

1920	Aileen Riggin, U.S.	539.90
1924	Elizabeth Becker, U.S.	474.50
1928	Helen Meany, U.S.	78.62
1932	Georgia Coleman U.S.	87.52
1936	Marjorie Gestring, U.S.	89.27
1948	Victoria M. Draves, U.S.	108.74
1952	Patricia McCormick, U.S.	147.30
1956	Patricia McCormick, U.S.	142.36
1960	Ingrid Kramer, Germany	155.81

Springboard Diving Points

1964	Ingrid Engel-Kramer, Germany	145.00
1968	Sue Gossick, U.S.	150.77
1972	Micki King, U.S.	450.03
1976	Jenni Chandler, U.S.	506.19
1980	Irina Kalinina, USSR	725.91
1984	Sylvie Bernier, Canada	530.70
1988	Gao Min, China	580.23
1992	Gao Min, China	572.40
1996	Fu Mingxia, China	547.68
2000	Fu Mingxia, China	609.42

Platform Diving Points

1912	Greta Johansson, Sweden	39.90
1920	Stefani Fryland-Clausen, Denmark	34.60
1924	Caroline Smith, U.S.	33.20
1928	Elizabeth B. Pinkston, U.S.	31.60

Platform Diving Points

1932	Dorothy Poynton, U.S.	40.26
1936	Dorothy Poynton Hill, U.S.	33.93
1948	Victoria M. Draves, U.S.	8.87
1952	Patricia McCormick, U.S.	79.37
1956	Patricia McCormick, U.S.	84.85
1960	Ingrid Kramer, Germany	91.28
1964	Lesley Bush, U.S.	99.80
1968	Milena Duchkova, Czech.	109.59
1972	Ulrika Knape, Sweden	390.00
1976	Elena Vaytsekhouskaya, USSR	406.59
1980	Martina Jaschke, E. Germany	596.25
1984	Zhou Jihong, China	435.51
1988	Xu Yanmei, China	445.20
1992	Fu Mingxia, China	461.43
1996	Fu Mingxia, China	521.58
2000	Laura Wilkinson, U.S.	543.75

BOXING

Lt. Flyweight (48 kg/106 lbs)

1968	Francisco Rodriguez, Venezuela
1972	Gyorgy Gedo, Hungary
1976	Jorge Hernandez, Cuba
1980	Shamil Sabyrov, USSR
1984	Paul Gonzalez, U.S.
1988	Ivailo Hristov, Bulgaria
1992	Rogelio Marcelo, Cuba
1996	Daniel Petrov, Bulgaria
2000	Brahim Asloum, France

Flyweight (51 kg/112 lbs)

1904	George Finnegan, U.S.
1920	William Di Gennara, U.S.
1924	Fidel LaBarba, U.S.
1928	Antal Kocsis, Hungary
1932	Istvan Enekes, Hungary
1936	Willi Kaiser, Germany
1948	Pascual Perez, Argentina
1952	Nathan Brooks, U.S.
1956	Terence Spinks, Great Britain
1960	GyulaTorok, Hungary
1964	Fernando Atzori, Italy
1968	Ricardo Delgado, Mexico
1972	Georgi Kostadinov, Bulgaria
1976	Leo Randolph, U.S.
1980	Peter Lessov, Bulgaria
1984	Steve McCrory, U.S.
1988	Kim Kwang Sun, S. Korea
1992	Su Choi Choi, N. Korea
1996	Maikro Romero, Cuba
2000	Wijan Ponlid, Thailand

Bantamweight (54 kg /119 lbs)

1904	Oliver Kirk, U.S.
1908	A. Henry Thomas, Great Britain
1920	Clarence Walker, South Africa
1924	William Smith, South Africa
1928	Vittorio Tamagnini, Italy
1932	Horace Gwynne, Canada
1936	Ulderico Sergo, Italy
1948	Tibor Csik, Hungary
1952	Pentti Hamalainen, Finland
1956	Wolfgang Behrendt, E. Germany
1960	Oleg Grigoryev, USSR
1964	Takao Sakurai, Japan
1968	Valery Sokolov, USSR
1972	Orlando Martinez, Cuba
1976	Yong-Jo Gu, N. Korea
1980	Juan Hernandez, Cuba
1984	Maurizio Stecca, Italy
1988	Kennedy McKinney, U.S.
1992	Joel Casamayor, Cuba
1996	Istvan Kovacs, Hungary
2000	Guillermo Rigondeaux, Cuba

Featherweight (57 kg/125 lbs)

1904	Oliver Kirk, U.S.
1908	Richard Gunn, Great Britain
1920	Paul Fritsch, France
1924	John Fields, U.S.
1928	Lambertus van Klaveren, Netherlands
1932	Carmelo Robledo, Argentina
1936	Oscar Casanovas, Argentina
1948	Ernesto Formenti, Italy
1952	Jan Zachara, Czechoslovakia
1956	Vladimir Safronov, USSR
1960	Francesco Musso, Italy
1964	Stanislav Stephashkin, USSR
1968	Antonin Roldan, Mexico

1972	Boris Kousnetsov, USSR
1976	Angel Herrera, Cuba
1980	Rudi Fink, E. Germany
1984	Meldrick Taylor, U.S.
1988	Giovanni Parisi, Italy
1992	Andreas Tews, Germany
1996	Somluck Kamsing, Thailand
2000	Bekzat Sattarkhanov, Kazakhstan

Lightweight (60 kg/132 lbs)

1904	Harry Spanger, U.S.
1908	Frederick Grace, Great Britain
1920	Samuel Mosberg, U.S.
1924	Hans Nielsen, Denmark
1928	Carlo Orlandi, Italy
1932	Lawrence Stevens, South Africa
1936	Imre Harangi, Hungary
1948	Gerald Dreyer, South Africa
1952	Aureliano Bolognesi, Italy
1956	Richard McTaggart, Great Britain
1960	Kazimierz Pazdzior, Poland
1964	Jozef Grudzien, Poland
1968	Ronald Harris, U.S.
1972	Jan Szczepanski, Poland
1976	Howard Davis, U.S.
1980	Angel Herrera, Cuba
1984	Pernell Whitaker, U.S.
1988	Andreas Zuelow, E. Germany
1992	Oscar De La Hoya, U.S.
1996	Hocine Soltani, Algeria
2000	Mario Kindelan, Cuba

Lt. Welterweight (63.5 kg/139 lbs)

1952	Charles Adkins, U.S.
1956	Vladimir Yengibaryan, USSR
1960	Bohumil Nemecek, Czechoslovakia
1964	Jerzy Kulej, Poland
1968	Jerzy Kulej, Poland
1972	Ray Seales, U.S.
1976	Ray Leonard, U.S.
1980	Patrizio Oliva, Italy
1984	Jerry Page, U.S.
1988	Viatcheslav Janovski, USSR
1992	Hector Vinent, Cuba
1996	Hector Vinent, Cuba
2000	Mahamadkadyz Abdullaev, Uzbekistan

Welterweight (67 kg/147 lbs)

1904	Albert Young, U.S.
1920	Albert Schneider, Canada
1924	Jean Delarge, Belgium
1928	Edward Morgan, New Zealand
1932	Edward Flynn, U.S.
1936	Sten Suvio, Finland
1948	Julius Torma, Czechoslovakia
1952	Zygmunt Chychia, Poland
1956	Nicolae Linca, Romania
1960	Giovanni Benvenuti, Italy
1964	Marian Kasprzyk, Poland
1968	Manfred Wolke, E. Germany
1972	Emilio Correa, Cuba
1976	Jochen Bachfeld, E. Germany
1980	Andres Aldama, Cuba
1984	Mark Breland, U.S.
1988	Robert Wangila, Kenya
1992	Michael Carruth, Ireland
1996	Oleg Saitov, Russia
2000	Oleg Saitov, Russia

Lt. Middleweight (71 kg/156 lbs)

1952	Laszlo Papp, Hungary
1956	Laszlo Papp, Hungary
1960	Wilbert McClure, U.S.
1964	Boris Lagutin, USSR
1968	Boris Lagutin, USSR
1972	Dieter Kottysch, W. Germany
1976	Jerzy Rybicki, Poland
1980	Armando Martinez, Cuba
1984	Frank Tate, U.S.
1988	Park Si Hun, S. Korea
1992	Juan Lemus, Cuba
1996	David Reid, U.S.
2000	Yermakhan Ibraimov, Kazakhstan

Middleweight (75 kg/165 lbs)

1904	Charles Mayer, U.S.
1908	John Douglas, Great Britain
1920	Harry Mallin, Great Britain
1924	Harry Mallin, Great Britain
1928	Piero Toscani, Italy
1932	Carmen Barth, U.S.
1936	Jean Despeaux, France
1948	Laszlo Papp, Hungary
1952	Floyd Patterson, U.S.
1956	Gennady Schatkov, USSR
1960	Edward Crook, U.S.
1964	Valery Popenchenko, USSR
1968	Christopher Finnegan, Great Britain
1972	Vyacheslav Lemechev, USSR
1976	Michael Spinks, U.S.
1980	Jose Gomez, Cuba
1984	Joon-Sup Shin, S. Korea
1988	Henry Maske, E. Germany
1992	Ariel Hernandez, Cuba
1996	Ariel Hernandez, Cuba
2000	Jorge Gutierrez, Cuba

Lt. Heavyweight (81 kg/178 lbs)

1920	Edward Eagan, U.S.
1924	Harry Mitchell, Great Britain
1928	Victor Avendano, Argentina
1932	David Carstens, South Africa
1936	Roger Michelot, France
1948	George Hunter, South Africa
1952	Norvel Lee, U.S.
1956	James Boyd, U.S.
1960	Cassius Clay, U.S.
1964	Cosimo Pinto, Italy
1968	Dan Poznyak, USSR
1972	Mate Parlov, Yugoslavia
1976	Leon Spinks, U.S.
1980	Slobodan Kacar, Yugoslavia
1984	Anton Josipovic, Yugoslavia
1988	Andrew Maynard, U.S.
1992	Torsten May, Germany
1996	Vassili Jirov, Kazakhstan
2000	Alexander Lebziak, Russia

Heavyweight (91 kg/201 lbs)

1984	Henry Tillman, U.S.
1988	Ray Mercer, U.S.
1992	Felix Savon, Cuba
1996	Felix Savon, Cuba
2000	Felix Savon, Cuba

Super Heavyweight (91+ kg/201+ lbs)
(known as heavyweight, 1904-80)

1904	Samuel Berger, U.S.	1932	Santiago Lovell, Argentina	1972	Teofilo Stevenson, Cuba
1908	Albert Oldham, Great Britain	1936	Herbert Runge, Germany	1976	Teofilo Stevenson, Cuba
1920	Ronald Rawson, Great Britain	1948	Rafael Iglesias, Argentina	1980	Teofilo Stevenson, Cuba
1924	Otto von Porat, Norway	1952	H. Edward Sanders, U.S.	1984	Tyrell Biggs, U.S.
1928	Arturo Rodriguez Jurado, Argentina	1956	T. Peter Rademacher, U.S.	1988	Lennox Lewis, Canada
		1960	Franco De Piccoli, Italy	1992	Roberto Balado, Cuba
		1964	Joe Frazier, U.S.	1996	Vladimir Klitchko, Ukraine
		1968	George Foreman, U.S.	2000	Audley Harrison, Britain

Winter Olympic Games

Sites of Winter Olympic Games

1924 Chamonix, France	1952 Oslo, Norway	1968 Grenoble, France	1992 Albertville, France
1928 St. Moritz, Switzerland	1956 Cortina d'Ampezzo, Italy	1972 Sapporo, Japan	1994 Lillehammer, Norway
1932 Lake Placid, New York		1976 Innsbruck, Austria	1998 Nagano, Japan
1936 Garmisch-Partenkirchen, Germany	1960 Squaw Valley, California	1980 Lake Placid, New York	2002 Salt Lake City, Utah
1948 St. Moritz, Switzerland	1964 Innsbruck, Austria	1984 Sarajevo, Yugoslavia	2006 Turin, Italy
		1988 Calgary, Canada	2010 Vancouver, Canada

Winter Olympic Games in 2002—Highlights
Salt Lake City, Utah, Feb. 8-24, 2002

Over 16 days, 2,200 athletes from 77 nations competed in Salt Lake City. Some 2.1 billion viewers worldwide made these the most watched Winter Games ever.

Pairs figure skating was surrounded by controversy when Russia's Yelena Berezhnaya and Anton Sikharulidze were awarded the gold after Canadians Jamie Sale and David Pelletier skated a seemingly flawless long program. An investigation found that a French judge had been pressured to vote for the Russians in exchange for a 1st-place vote for a French pair in ice dancing, and the IOC awarded a 2nd gold medal to Sale and Pelletier. The gold in women's figure skating went to 16-year-old Sarah Hughes. Croatia's Janica Kostelic became the 1st alpine skier to win 4 medals, 3 gold, in a single Olympics. Americans Jill Bakken and Vonetta Flowers won the 1st-ever women's bobsled event—Flowers was the 1st African-American to win a Winter Olympic medal. American Jim Shea Jr. won gold in the skeleton, an event not held in 44 years. In men's ice hockey, the U.S. team took the silver, losing to Canada, 5-2, in the final, the best U.S. finish since 1980. Canada also won gold in women's ice hockey, defeating the U.S., 3-2.

As in 1998, Germany led the medal count. For the U.S., 2nd by 1, the 34 medals (10 gold) was a Winter Games record.

2002 Final Medal Standings

	Gold	Silver	Bronze	Total		Gold	Silver	Bronze	Total
Germany	12	16	7	35	Croatia	3	1	0	4
United States	10	13	11	34	South Korea	2	2	0	4
Norway	11	7	6	24	Estonia	1	1	1	3
Canada	6	3	8	17	Bulgaria	0	1	2	3
Austria	2	4	11	17	Australia	2	0	0	2
Russia	6	6	4	16	Spain	2	0	0	2
Italy	4	4	4	12	Czech Republic	1	0	1	2
France	4	5	2	11	Great Britain	1	0	1	2
Switzerland	3	2	6	11	Japan	0	1	1	2
Netherlands	3	5	0	8	Poland	0	1	1	2
China	2	2	4	8	Belarus	0	0	1	1
Finland	4	2	1	7	Slovenia	0	0	1	1
Sweden	0	2	4	6	**TOTAL**	**79**	**78**	**77**	**234**

Winter Olympic Games Champions, 1924-2002

In 1992, the Unified Team represented the former Soviet republics of Russia, Ukraine, Belarus, Kazakhstan, and Uzbekistan.

Alpine Skiing

	Men's Downhill	Time
1948	Henri Oreiller, France	2:55.0
1952	Zeno Colo, Italy	2:30.8
1956	Toni Sailer, Austria	2:52.2
1960	Jean Vuarnet, France	2:06.0
1964	Egon Zimmermann, Austria	2:18.16
1968	Jean-Claude Killy, France	1:59.85
1972	Bernhard Russi, Switzerland	1:51.43
1976	Franz Klammer, Austria	1:45.73
1980	Leonhard Stock, Austria	1:45.50
1984	Bill Johnson, U.S.	1:45.49
1988	Pirmin Zurbriggen, Switzerland	1:59.63
1992	Patrick Ortlieb, Austria	1:50.37
1994	Tommy Moe, U.S.	1:45.75
1998	Jean-Luc Cretier, France	1:50.11
2002	Fritz Strobl, Austria	1:39.13

	Men's Super Giant Slalom	Time
1988	Franck Piccard, France	1:39.66
1992	Kjetil-Andre Aamodt, Norway	1:13.04
1994	Markus Wasmeier, Germany	1:32.53
1998	Hermann Maier, Austria	1:34.82
2002	Kjetil Andre Aamodt, Norway	1:21.58

	Men's Giant Slalom	Time
1952	Stein Eriksen, Norway	2:25.0
1956	Toni Sailer, Austria	3:00.1
1960	Roger Staub, Switzerland	1:48.3
1964	Francois Bonlieu, France	1:46.71
1968	Jean-Claude Killy, France	3:29.28
1972	Gustavo Thoeni, Italy	3:09.62
1976	Heini Hemmi, Switzerland	3:26.97

	Men's Giant Slalom	Time
1980	Ingemar Stenmark, Sweden	2:40.74
1984	Max Julen, Switzerland	2:41.18
1988	Alberto Tomba, Italy	2:06.37
1992	Alberto Tomba, Italy	2:06.98
1994	Markus Wasmeier, Germany	2:52.46
1998	Hermann Maier, Austria	2:38.51
2002	Stephan Eberharter, Austria	2:23.28

	Men's Slalom	Time
1948	Edi Reinalter, Switzerland	2:10.3
1952	Othmar Schneider, Austria	2:00.0
1956	Toni Sailer, Austria	3:14.7
1960	Ernst Hinterseer, Austria	2:08.9
1964	Josef Stiegler, Austria	2:11.13
1968	Jean-Claude Killy, France	1:39.73
1972	Francisco Fernandez-Ochoa, Spain	1:49.27
1976	Piero Gros, Italy	2:03.29
1980	Ingemar Stenmark, Sweden	1:44.26
1984	Phil Mahre, U.S.	1:39.41
1988	Alberto Tomba, Italy	1:39.47
1992	Finn Christian Jagge, Norway	1:44.39
1994	Thomas Stangassinger, Austria	2:02.02
1998	Hans-Petter Buraas, Norway	1:49.31
2002	Jean-Pierre Vidal, France	1:41.06

	Men's Combined	Time
1936	Franz-Pfnuer, Germany	99.25 (pts.)
1948	Henri Oreiller, France	3.27 (pts.)
1988	Hubert Strolz, Austria	36.55 (pts.)
1992	Josef Polig, Italy	14.58 (pts.)
1994	Lasse Kjus, Norway	3:17.53
1998	Mario Reiter, Austria	3:08.06
2002	Kjetil Andre Aamodt, Norway	3:17.56

Women's Downhill	Time
1948 Hedi Schlunegger, Switzerland.	2:28.3
1952 Trude Jochum-Beiser, Austria	1:47.1
1956 Madeleine Berthod, Switzerland	1:40.7
1960 Heidi Biebl, Germany	1:37.6
1964 Christl Haas, Austria	1:55.39
1968 Olga Pall, Austria	1:40.87
1972 Marie-Theres Nadig, Switzerland	1:36.68
1976 Rosi Mittermaier, W. Germany	1:46.16
1980 Annemarie Moser-Proell , Austria.	1:37.52
1984 Michela Figini, Switzerland	1:13.36
1988 Marina Kiehl, W. Germany	1:25.86
1992 Kerrin Lee-Gartner, Canada	1:52.55
1994 Katja Seizinger, Germany.	1:35.93
1998 Katja Seizinger, Germany.	1:28.89
2002 Carole Montillet, France	1:39.56

Women's Super Giant Slalom	Time
1988 Sigrid Wolf, Austria	1:19.03
1992 Deborah Compagnoni, Italy	1:21.22
1994 Diann Roffe (Steinrotter), U.S.	1:22.15
1998 Picabo Street, U.S.	1:18.02
2002 Daniela Ceccarelli, Italy	1:13.59

Women's Giant Slalom	Time
1952 Andrea Mead Lawrence, U.S.	2:06.8
1956 Ossi Reichert, Germany	1:56.5
1960 Yvonne Ruegg, Switzerland	1:39.9
1964 Marielle Goitschel, France	1:52.24
1968 Nancy Greene, Canada	1:51.97
1972 Marie-Theres Nadig, Switzerland	1:29.90
1976 Kathy Kreiner, Canada	1:29.13
1980 Hanni Wenzel, Liechtenstein (2 runs)	2:41.66
1984 Debbie Armstrong, U.S.	2:20.98
1988 Vreni Schneider, Switzerland	2:06.49
1992 Pernilla Wiberg, Sweden.	2:12.74
1994 Deborah Compagnoni, Italy	2:30.97
1998 Deborah Compagnoni, Italy	2:50.59
2002 Janica Kostelic, Croatia	2:30.01

Women's Slalom	Time
1948 Gretchen Fraser, U.S.	1:57.2
1952 Andrea Mead Lawrence, U.S.	2:10.6
1956 Renee Colliard, Switzerland	1:52.3
1960 Anne Heggtveit, Canada.	1:49.6
1964 Christine Goitschel, France.	1:29.86
1968 Marielle Goitschel, France	1:25.86
1972 Barbara Ann Cochran, U.S.	1:31.24
1976 Rosi Mittermaier, W. Germany	1:30.54
1980 Hanni Wenzel, Liechtenstein	1:25.09
1984 Paoletta Magoni, Italy	1:36.47
1988 Vreni Schneider, Switzerland	1:36.69
1992 Petra Kronberger, Austria	1:32.68
1994 Vreni Schneider, Switzerland	1:56.01
1998 Hilde Gerg, Germany	1:32.40
2002 Janica Kostelic, Croatia	1:46.10

Women's Combined	Time
1936 Christl Cranz, Germany	97.06 (pts.)
1948 Trude Beiser-Jochum, Austria	6.58 (pts.)
1988 Anita Wachter, Austria	29.25 (pts.)
1992 Petra Kronberger, Austria	2.55 (pts.)
1994 Pernilla Wiberg, Sweden.	3:05.16
1998 Katja Seizinger, Germany.	2:40.74
2002 Janica Kostelic, Croatia	2:43.28

Biathlon

Men's 10 Kilometers	Time
1980 Frank Ullrich, E. Germany	32:10.69
1984 Eirik Kvalfoss, Norway	30:53.80
1988 Frank-Peter Roetsch, E. Germany	25:08.10
1992 Mark Kirchner, Germany.	26:02.30
1994 Serguei Tchepikov, Russia	28:07.00
1998 Ole Einar Bjoerndalen, Norway.	27:16.20
2002 Ole Einar Bjoerndalen, Norway.	24:51.3

Men's 12.5 Kilometers	Time
2002 Ole Einar Bjoerndalen, Norway.	32:34.6

Men's 20 Kilometers	Time
1960 Klas Lestander, Sweden	1:33:21.6
1964 Vladimir Melanin, USSR	1:20:26.8
1968 Magnar Solberg, Norway	1:13:45.9
1972 Magnar Solberg, Norway	1:15:55.50
1976 Nikolai Kruglov, USSR	1:14:12.26
1980 Anatoly Aljabiev, USSR	1:08:16.31
1984 Peter Angerer, W. Germany	1:11:52.7
1988 Frank-Peter Roetsch, E. Germany	0:56:33.33
1992 Yevgeny Redkine, Unified Team	0:57:34.4
1994 Serguei Tarasov, Russia.	0:57:25.3
1998 Halvard Hanevold, Norway	0:56:16.4
2002 Ole Einar Bjoerndalen, Norway.	0:51:03.3

Men's 30-Kilometer Relay	Time
1968 USSR, Norway, Sweden (40 km)	2:13:02.4
1972 USSR, Finland, E. Germany (40 km)	1:51:44.92
1976 USSR, Finland, E. Germany (40 km)	1:57:55.64
1980 USSR, E. Germany, W. Germany	1:34:03.27
1984 USSR, Norway, W. Germany.	1:38:51.70
1988 USSR, W. Germany, Italy	1:22:30.00
1992 Germany, Unified Team, Sweden	1:24:43.50
1994 Germany, Russia, France	1:30:22.1
1998 Germany, Norway, Russia	1:19:43.3
2002 Norway, Germany, France	1:23:42.3

Women's 7.5 Kilometers	Time
1992 Anfissa Restsova, Unified Team	24:29.20
1994 Myriam Bedard, Canada	26:08.8
1998 Galina Koukleva, Russia	23:08.0
2002 Kati Wilhelm, Germany	20:41.4

Women's 10 Kilometers	Time
2002 Olga Pyleva, Russia.	31:07.7

Women's 15 Kilometers	Time
1992 Antje Misersky, Germany.	51:47.2
1994 Myriam Bedard, Canada	52:06.6
1998 Ekaterina Dafovska, Bulgaria.	54:52.0
2002 Andrea Henkel, Germany.	47:29.1

Women's 22.5-Kilometer Relay	Time
1992 France, Germany, Unified Team	1:15:55.6

Women's 30-Kilometer Relay	Time
1994 Russia, Germany, France	1:47:19.5
1998 Germany, Russia, Norway	1:40:13.6
2002 Germany, Norway, Russia	1:27:55.0

Bobsledding
(Driver in parentheses)

4-Man Bob	Time
1924 Switzerland (Eduard Scherrer)	5:45.54
1928 United States (William Fiske) (5-man)	3:20.50
1932 United States (William Fiske)	7:53.68
1936 Switzerland (Pierre Musy)	5:19.85
1948 United States (Francis Tyler)	5:20.10
1952 Germany (Andreas Ostler)	5:07.84
1956 Switzerland (Franz Kapus)	5:10.44
1964 Canada (Victor Emery).	4:14.46
1968 Italy (Eugenio Monti) (2 races)	2:17.39
1972 Switzerland (Jean Wicki)	4:43.07
1976 E. Germany (Meinhard Nehmer)	3:40.43
1980 E. Germany (Meinhard Nehmer)	3:59.92
1984 E. Germany (Wolfgang Hoppe)	3:20.22
1988 Switzerland (Ekkehard Fasser)	3:47.51
1992 Austria (Ingo Appelt)	3:53.90
1994 Germany (Wolfgang Hoppe)	3:27.28
1998 Germany II (Christoph Langen)	2:39.41
2002 Germany II (Andre Lange)	3:07.51

2-Man Bob	Time
1932 United States (Hubert Stevens)	8:14.74
1936 United States (Ivan Brown)	5:29.29
1948 Switzerland (F. Endrich).	5:29.20
1952 Germany (Andreas Ostler)	5:24.54
1956 Italy (Dalla Costa).	5:30.14
1964 Great Britain (Anthony Nash)	4:21.90
1968 Italy (Eugenio Monti)	4:41.54
1972 W. Germany (Wolfgang Zimmerer)	4:57.07
1976 E. Germany (Meinhard Nehmer)	3:44.42
1980 Switzerland (Erich Schaerer)	4:09.36
1984 E. Germany (Wolfgang Hoppe)	3:25.56
1988 USSR (Janis Kipours)	3:54.19
1992 Switzerland (Gustav Weber)	4:03.26
1994 Switzerland (Gustav Weber)	3:30.81
1998 Canada (Pierre Lueders), Italy (Guenther Huber) (tie)	3:37.24
2002 Germany II (Christoph Langen)	3:10.11

2-Woman Bob	Time
2002 United States II (Jill Bakken)	1:37.76

Curling
Men
1998 Switzerland, Canada, Norway
2002 Norway, Canada, Switzerland

Women
1998 Canada, Denmark, Sweden
2002 Britain, Switzerland, Canada

Figure Skating
Men's Singles
1908# Ulrich Salchow, Sweden
1920# Gillis Grafstrom, Sweden
1924 Gillis Grafstrom, Sweden
1928 Gillis Grafstrom, Sweden
1932 Karl Schaefer, Austria
1936 Karl Schaefer, Austria

Men's Singles
1948 Richard Button, U.S.
1952 Richard Button, U.S.
1956 Hayes Alan Jenkins, U.S.
1960 David W. Jenkins, U.S.
1964 Manfred Schnelldorfer, Germany
1968 Wolfgang Schwartz, Austria
1972 Ondrej Nepela, Czechoslovakia
1976 John Curry, Great Britain
1980 Robin Cousins, Great Britain
1984 Scott Hamilton, U.S.
1988 Brian Boitano, U.S.
1992 Viktor Petrenko, Unified Team
1994 Aleksei Urmanov, Russia
1998 Ilya Kulik, Russia
2002 Alexei Yagudin, Russia
(#) Event was held at Summer Olympics.

Women's Singles
1908# Madge Syers, Great Britain
1920# Magda Julin-Mauroy, Sweden
1924 Herma von Szabo-Planck, Austria
1928 Sonja Henie, Norway
1932 Sonja Henie, Norway
1936 Sonja Henie, Norway
1948 Barbara Ann Scott, Canada
1952 Jeanette Altwegg, Great Britan
1956 Tenley Albright, U.S.
1960 Carol Heiss, U.S.
1964 Sjoukje Dijkstra, Netherlands
1968 Peggy Fleming, U.S.
1972 Beatrix Schuba, Austria
1976 Dorothy Hamill, U.S.
1980 Anett Poetzsch, E. Germany
1984 Katarina Witt, E. Germany
1988 Katarina Witt, E. Germany
1992 Kristi Yamaguchi, U.S.
1994 Oksana Baiul, Ukraine
1998 Tara Lipinski, U.S.
2002 Sarah Hughes, U.S.
(#) Event was held at Summer Olympics.

Pairs
1908# Anna Hubler & Heinrich Burger, Germany
1920# Ludovika & Walter Jakobsson, Finland
1924 Helene Engelman & Alfred Berger, Austria
1928 Andree Joly & Pierre Brunet, France
1932 Andree Joly & Pierre Brunet, France
1936 Maxi Herber & Ernst Baier, Germany
1948 Micheline Lannoy & Pierre Baugniet, Belgium
1952 Ria and Paul Falk, Germany
1956 Elisabeth Schwartz & Kurt Oppelt, Austria
1960 Barbara Wagner & Robert Paul, Canada
1964 Ludmila Beloussova & Oleg Protopopov, USSR
1968 Ludmila Beloussova & Oleg Protopopov, USSR
1972 Irina Rodnina & Alexei Ulanov, USSR
1976 Irina Rodnina & Aleksandr Zaitzev, USSR
1980 Irina Rodnina & Aleksandr Zaitzev, USSR
1984 Elena Valova & Oleg Vassiliev, USSR
1988 Ekaterina Gordeeva & Sergei Grinkov, USSR
1992 Natalia Mishkutienok & Artur Dimitriev, Unified Team
1994 Ekaterina Gordeeva & Sergei Grinkov, Russia
1998 Oksana Kazakova & Artur Dmitriev, Russia
2002 Elena Berezhnaya & Anton Sikharulidze, Russia;
     Jamie Sale & David Pelletier, Canada (tie)
(#) Event was held at Summer Olympics.

Ice Dancing
1976 Ludmila Pakhomova & Aleksandr Gorschkov, USSR
1980 Natalya Linichuk & Gennadi Karponosov, USSR
1984 Jayne Torvill & Christopher Dean, Great Britain
1988 Natalia Bestemianova & Andrei Bukin, USSR
1992 Marina Klimova & Sergei Ponomarenko, Unified Team
1994 Pasha Grishuk & Evgeny Platov, Russia
1998 Pasha Grishuk & Evgeny Platov, Russia
2002 Marina Anissina & Gwendal Peizerat, France

Freestyle Skiing
Men's Moguls

		Points
1992	Edgar Grospiron, France	25.81
1994	Jean-Luc Brassard, Canada	27.24
1998	Jonny Moseley, U.S.	26.93
2002	Janne Lahtela, Finland	27.97

Men's Aerials

		Points
1994	Andreas Schoenbaechler, Switzerland	234.67
1998	Eric Bergout, U.S.	255.64
2002	Ales Valenta, Czech Republic	257.02

Women's Moguls

		Points
1992	Donna Weinbrecht, U.S.	23.69
1994	Stine Lise Hattestad, Norway	25.97
1998	Tae Satoya, Japan	25.06
2002	Kari Traa, Norway	25.94

Women's Aerials

		Points
1994	Lina Tcherjazova, Uzbekistan	166.84
1998	Nikki Stone, U.S.	193.00
2002	Alisa Camplin, Australia	193.47

Ice Hockey
MEN
1920# Canada, U.S., Czechoslovakia
1924 Canada, U.S., Great Britain
1928 Canada, Sweden, Switzerland
1932 Canada, U.S., Germany
1936 Great Britain, Canada, U.S.
1948 Canada, Czechoslovakia, Switzerland
1952 Canada, U.S., Sweden
1956 USSR, U.S., Canada
1960 U.S., Canada, USSR
1964 USSR, Sweden, Czechoslovakia
1968 USSR, Czechoslovakia, Canada
1972 USSR, U.S., Czechoslovakia
1976 USSR, Czechoslovakia, W. Germany
1980 U.S., USSR, Sweden
1984 USSR, Czechoslovakia, Sweden
1988 USSR, Finland, Sweden
1992 Unified Team, Canada, Czechoslovakia
1994 Sweden, Canada, Finland
1998 Czech Republic, Russia, Finland
2002 Canada, U.S., Russia
(#) Event was held at Summer Olympics.

WOMEN
1998 U.S., Canada, Finland
2002 Canada, U.S., Sweden

Luge
Men's Singles

		Time
1964	Thomas Keohler, E. Germany	3:26.77
1968	Manfred Schmid, Austria	2:52.48
1972	Wolfgang Scheidel, E. Germany	3:27.58
1976	Detlef Guenther, E. Germany	3:27.688
1980	Bernhard Glass, E. Germany	2:54.796
1984	Paul Hildgartner, Italy	3:04.258
1988	Jens Mueller, E. Germany	3:05.548
1992	Georg Hackl, Germany	3:02.363
1994	Georg Hackl, Germany	3:21.571
1998	Georg Hackl, Germany	3:18.436
2002	Armin Zoeggeler, Italy	2:57.941

Women's Singles

		Time
1964	Ortun Enderlein, Germany	3:24.67
1968	Erica Lechner, Italy	2:28.66
1972	Anna M. Muller, E. Germany	2:59.18
1976	Margit Schumann, E. Germany	2:50.621
1980	Vera Zozulya, USSR	2:36.537
1984	Steffi Martin, E. Germany	2:46.570
1988	Steffi Walter, E. Germany	3:03.973
1992	Doris Neuner, Austria	3:06.696
1994	Gerda Weissensteiner, Italy	3:15.517
1998	Silke Kraushaar, Germany	3:23.779
2002	Sylke Otto, Germany	2:52.464

Men's Doubles

		Time
1964	Austria	1:41.62
1968	E. Germany	1:35.85
1972	Italy, E. Germany (tie)	1:28.35
1976	E. Germany	1:25.604
1980	E. Germany	1:19.331
1984	W. Germany	1:23.620
1988	E. Germany	1:31.940
1992	Germany	1:32.053
1994	Italy	1:36.720
1998	Germany	1:41.105
2002	Germany	1:26.082

Skeleton
Men

		Time
1928	Jennison Heaton, U.S.	3:01.8
1948	Nino Bibbia, Italy	5:23.2
2002	Jim Shea, U.S.	1:41.96

Women

		Time
2002	Tristan Gale, U.S.	1:45.11

Nordic Skiing
Cross-Country Events

Men's 1.5 Kilometers (0.93 miles)

		Time
2002	Tor Arne Hetland, Norway	2:56.9

Men's 10 Kilometers (6.2 miles)

		Time
1992	Vegard Ulvang, Norway	27:36.0
1994	Bjoern Daehlie, Norway	24:20.1
1998	Bjoern Daehlie, Norway	27:24.5
2002	Johann Muehlegg, Spain	49:20.4

Men's 15 Kilometers (9.3 miles)	Time
1924 Thorleif Haug, Norway	1:14:31
1928 Johan Grottumsbraaten, Norway	1:37:01
1932 Sven Utterstrom, Sweden	1:23:07
1936 Erik-August Larsson, Sweden	1:14:38
1948 Martin Lundstrom, Sweden	1:13:50
1952 Hallgeir Brenden, Norway	1:01:34
1956 Hallgeir Brenden, Norway	0:49:39.0
1960 Haakon Brusveen, Norway	0:51:55.5
1964 Eero Maentyranta, Finland	0:50:54.1
1968 Harald Groenningen, Norway	0:47:54.2
1972 Sven-Ake Lundback, Sweden	0:45:28.24
1976 Nikolai Balukov, USSR	0:43:58.47
1980 Thomas Wassberg, Sweden	0:41:57.63
1984 Gunde Svan, Sweden	0:41:25.6
1988 Mikhail Deviatiarov, USSR	0:41:18.9
1992 Bjoern Daehlie, Norway	0:38:01.9
1994 Bjoern Daehlie, Norway	0:35:48.8
1998 Thomas Alsgaard, Norway	1:07:01.7
2002 Andrus Veerpalu, Estonia	0:37:07.4

(Note: approx. 18-km course 1924-1952)

Men's 30 Kilometers (18.6 miles)	Time
1956 Veikko Hakulinen, Finland	1:44:06.0
1956 Veikko Hakulinen, Finland	1:44:06.0
1960 Sixten Jernberg, Sweden	1:51:03.9
1964 Eero Maentyranta, Finland	1:30:50.7
1968 Franco Nones, Italy	1:35:39.2
1972 Vyacheslav Vedenine, USSR	1:36:31.15
1976 Sergei Saveliev, USSR	1:30:29.38
1980 Nikolai Zimyatov, USSR	1:27:02.80
1984 Nikolai Zimyatov, USSR	1:28:56.3
1988 Aleksei Prokourorov, USSR	1:24:26.3
1992 Vegard Ulvang, Norway	1:22:27.8
1994 Thomas Alsgaard, Norway	1:12:26.4
1998 Mika Myllae, Finland	1:33:55.8
2002 Johann Muehlegg, Spain	1:09:28.9

Men's 50 Kilometers (31.2 miles)	Time
1924 Thorleif Haug, Norway	3:44:32.0
1928 Per Erik Hedlund, Sweden	4:52:03.0
1932 Veli Saarinen, Finland	4:28:00.0
1936 Elis Wiklund, Sweden	3:30:11.0
1948 Nils Karlsson, Sweden	3:47:48.0
1952 Veikko Hakulinen, Finland	3:33:33.0
1956 Sixten Jernberg, Sweden	2:50:27.0
1960 Kalevi Hamalainen, Finland	2:59:06.3
1964 Sixten Jernberg, Sweden	2:43:52.6
1968 Ole Ellefsaeter, Norway	2:28:45.8
1972 Paal Tyldum, Norway	2:43:14.75
1976 Ivar Formo, Norway	2:37:30.05
1980 Nikolai Zimyatov, USSR	2:27:24.60
1984 Thomas Wassberg, Sweden	2:15:55.8
1988 Gunde Svan, Sweden	2:04:30.9
1992 Bjoern Daehlie, Norway	2:03:41.5
1994 Vladimir Smirnov, Kazakhstan	2:07:20.3
1998 Bjoern Daehlie, Norway	2:05:08.2
2002 Mikhail Ivanov, Russia	2:06:20.8

Men's 40-Kilometer Relay	Time
1936 Finland, Norway, Sweden	2:41:33.0
1948 Sweden, Finland, Norway	2:32:08.0
1952 Finland, Norway, Sweden	2:20:16.0
1956 USSR, Finland, Sweden	2:15:30.0
1960 Finland, Norway, USSR	2:18:45.6
1964 Sweden, Finland, USSR	2:18:34.6
1968 Norway, Sweden, Finland	2:08:33.5
1972 USSR, Norway, Switzerland	2:04:47.94
1976 Finland, Norway, USSR	2:07:59.72
1980 USSR, Norway, Finland	1:57:03.46
1984 Sweden, USSR, Finland	1:55:06.30
1988 Sweden, USSR, Czechoslovakia	1:43:58.60
1992 Norway, Italy, Finland	1:39:26.00
1994 Italy, Norway, Finland	1:41:15.00
1998 Norway, Italy, Finland	1:40:55.70
2002 Norway, Italy, Germany	1:32:45.5

Women's 1.5 Kilometers (0.93 miles)	Time
2002 Julia Tchepalova, Russia	3:10.6

Women's 5 Kilometers (3.1 miles)	Time
1964 Claudia Boyarskikh, USSR	17:50.5
1968 Toini Gustafsson, Sweden	16:45.2
1972 Galina Koulacova, USSR	17:00.50
1976 Helena Takalo, Finland	15:48.69
1980 Raisa Smetanina, USSR	15:06.92
1984 Marja-Liisa Haemaelainen, Finland	17:04.0
1988 Marjo Matikainen, Finland	15:04.0
1992 Marjut Lukkarinen, Finland	14:13.8
1994 Ljubov Egorova, Russia	14:08.8
1998 Larissa Lazutina, Russia	17:37.9
2002 Olga Danilova, Russia	24:52.1

Women's 10 Kilometers (6.2 miles)	Time
1952 Lydia Wideman, Finland	41:40.0
1956 Lyubov Kosyreva, USSR	38:11.0
1960 Maria Gusakova, USSR	39:46.6
1964 Claudia Boyarskikh, USSR	40:24.3
1968 Toini Gustafsson, Sweden	36:46.5
1972 Galina Koulacova, USSR	34:17.82
1976 Raisa Smetanina, USSR	30:13.41
1980 Barbara Petzold, E. Germany	30:31.54
1984 Marja-Liisa Haemaelainen, Finland	31:44.2
1988 Vida Ventsene, USSR	30:08.3
1992 Lyubov Egorova, Unified Team	25:53.7
1994 Lyubov Egorova, Russia	27:30.1
1998 Larissa Lazutina, Russia	46:06.9
2002 Bente Skari, Norway	28:05.6

Women's 15 Kilometers (9.3 miles)	Time
1992 Lyubov Egorova, Unified Team	42:20.8
1994 Manuela Di Centa, Italy	39:44.5
1998 Olga Danilova, Russia	46:55.4
2002 Stefania Belmondo, Italy	39:54.4

Women's 30 Kilometers (18.6 miles)	Time
1992 Stefania Belmondo, Italy	1:22:30.1
1994 Manuela Di Centa, Italy	1:25:41.6
1998 Julija Tchepalova, Russia	1:22:01.5
2002 Gabriella Paruzzi, Italy	1:30:57.1

Women's 20-Kilometer Relay	Time
1956 Finland, USSR, Sweden (15 km)	1:09:01.0
1960 Sweden, USSR, Finland (15 km)	1:04:21.4
1964 USSR, Sweden, Finland (15 km)	0:59:20.2
1968 Norway, Sweden, USSR (15 km)	0:57:30.0
1972 USSR, Finland, Norway (15 km)	0:48:46.15
1976 USSR, Finland, E. Germany	1:07:49.75
1980 E. Germany, USSR, Norway	1:02:11.1
1984 Norway, Czechoslovakia, Finland	1:06:49.7
1988 USSR, Norway, Finland	0:59:51.1
1992 United Team, Norway, Italy	0:59:34.8
1994 Russia, Norway, Italy	0:57:12.5
1998 Russia, Norway, Italy	0:55:13.5
2002 Germany, Norway, Switzerland	0:49:30.6

Combined Cross-Country & Jumping (Men)

7.5 Kilometer Nordic Combined
2002 Samppa Lajunen, Finland

15 Kilometer Nordic Combined
1924	Thorleif Haug, Norway
1928	Johan Grottumsbraaten, Norway
1932	Johan Grottumsbraaten, Norway
1936	Oddbjorn Hagen, Norway
1948	Heikki Hasu, Finland
1952	Simon Slattvik, Norway
1956	Sverre Stenersen, Norway
1960	Georg Thoma, W. Germany
1964	Tormod Knutsen, Norway
1968	Franz Keller, W. Germany
1972	Ulrich Wehling, E. Germany
1976	Ulrich Wehling, E. Germany
1980	Ulrich Wehling, E. Germany
1984	Tom Sandberg, Norway
1988	Hippolyt Kempf, Switzerland
1992	Fabrice Guy, France
1994	Fred Barre Lundberg, Norway
1998	Bjarte Engen Vik, Norway
2002	Samppa Lajunen, Finland

Team Nordic Combined
1988	W. Germany, Switzerland, Austria
1992	Japan, Norway, Austria
1994	Japan, Norway, Switzerland
1998	Norway, Finland, France
2002	Finland, Germany, Austria

Medals based on combination of points for jumping events and time for cross-country events.

Ski Jumping (Men)

Normal Hill	Points
1964 Veikko Kankkonen, Finland	229.9
1968 Jiri Raska, Czechoslovakia	216.5
1972 Yukio Kasaya, Japan	244.2
1976 Hans-Georg Aschenbach, E. Germany	252.0
1980 Toni Innauer, Austria	266.3
1984 Jens Weissflog, E. Germany	215.2
1988 Matti Nykaenen, Finland	230.5
1992 Ernst Vettori, Austria	222.8
1994 Espen Bredesen, Norway	282.0
1998 Jani Soininen, Finland	234.5
2002 Simon Ammann, Switzerland	269.0

Large Hill	Points
1924 Jacob Tullin Thams, Norway	18.960
1928 Alfred Andersen, Norway	19.208
1932 Birger Ruud, Norway	228.1
1936 Birger Ruud, Norway	232.0
1948 Petter Hugsted, Norway	228.1
1952 Arnfinn Bergmann, Norway	226.0
1956 Antti Hyvarinen, Finland	227.0
1960 Helmut Recknagel, E. Germany	227.2
1964 Toralf Engan, Norway	230.7
1968 Vladimir Beloussov, USSR	231.3
1972 Wojciech Fortuna, Poland	219.9
1976 Karl Schnabl, Austria	234.8
1980 Jouko Tormanen, Finland	271.0
1984 Matti Nykaenen, Finland	231.2
1988 Matti Nykaenen, Finland	224.0
1992 Toni Nieminen, Finland	239.5
1994 Jens Weissflog, Germany	274.5
1998 Kazuyoshi Funaki, Japan	272.3
2002 Simon Ammann, Switzerland	281.4

Team Large Hill	Points
1988 Finland, Yugoslavia, Norway	634.4
1992 Finland, Austria, Czechoslovakia	644.4
1994 Germany, Japan, Austria	970.1
1998 Japan, Germany, Austria	933.0
2002 Germany, Finland, Slovenia	974.1

Snowboarding

Men's Giant Slalom	Time
1998 Ross Rebagliati, Canada	2:03.96
2002 Philipp Schoch, Switzerland	

Men's Halfpipe	Points
1998 Gian Simmen, Switzerland	85.2
2002 Ross Powers	46.1

Women's Giant Slalom	Time
1998 Karine Ruby, France	2:17.34
2002 Isabelle Blanc, France	

Women's Halfpipe	Points
1998 Nicola Thost, Germany	74.6
2002 Kelly Clark, U.S.	47.9

Speed Skating
*indicates Olympic record

Men's 500 Meters	Time[1]
1924 Charles Jewtraw, U.S.	0:44.0
1928 Thunberg, Finland & Evensen, Norway (tie)	0:43.4
1932 John A. Shea, U.S.	0:43.4
1936 Ivar Ballangrud, Norway	0:43.4
1948 Finn Helgesen, Norway	0:43.1
1952 Kenneth Henry, U.S.	0:43.2
1956 Evgeniy Grishin, USSR	0:40.2
1960 Evgeniy Grishin, USSR	0:40.2
1964 Terry McDermott, U.S.	0:40.1
1968 Erhard Keller, W. Germany	0:40.3
1972 Erhard Keller, W. Germany	0:39.44
1976 Evgeny Kulikov, USSR	0:39.17
1980 Eric Heiden, U.S.	0:38.03
1984 Sergei Fokichev, USSR	0:38.19
1988 Uwe-Jens Mey, E. Germany	0:36.45
1992 Uwe-Jens Mey, Germany	0:37.14
1994 Aleksandr Golubev, Russia	0:36.33
1998 Hiroyasu Shimizu, Japan	0:35.59
2002 Casey FitzRandolph, U.S.	0:34.42*

(1) Better time of two runs. Medals based on combined times.

Men's 1,000 Meters	Time
1976 Peter Mueller, U.S.	1:19.32
1980 Eric Heiden, U.S.	1:15.18
1984 Gaetan Boucher, Canada	1:15.80
1988 Nikolai Guiliaev, USSR	1:13.03
1992 Olaf Zinke, Germany	1:14.85
1994 Dan Jansen, U.S.	1:12.43
1998 Ids Postma, Netherlands	1:10.64
2002 Gerard van Velde, Netherlands	1:07.18*

Men's 1,500 Meters	Time
1924 Clas Thunberg, Finland	2:20.8
1928 Clas Thunberg, Finland	2:21.1
1932 John A. Shea, U.S.	2:57.5
1936 Charles Mathiesen, Norway	2:19.2
1948 Sverre Farstad, Norway	2:17.6
1952 Hjalmar Andersen, Norway	2:20.4
1956 Grishin & Mikhailov, both USSR (tie)	2:08.6
1960 Aas, Norway & Grishin, USSR (tie)	2:10.4
1964 Ants Anston, USSR	2:10.3
1968 Cornelis Verkerk, Netherlands	2:03.4
1972 Ard Schenk, Netherlands	2:02.96
1976 Jan Egil Storholt, Norway	1:59.38

Men's 1,500 Meters	Time
1980 Eric Heiden, U.S.	1:55.44
1984 Gaetan Boucher, Canada	1:58.36
1988 Andre Hoffmann, E. Germany	1:52.06
1992 Johann Koss, Norway	1:54.81
1994 Johann Koss, Norway	1:51.29
1998 Aadne Sondral, Norway	1:47.87
2002 Derek Parra, U.S.	1:43.95*

Men's 5,000 Meters	Time
1924 Clas Thunberg, Finland	8:39.0
1928 Ivar Ballangrud, Norway	8:50.5
1932 Irving Jaffee, U.S.	9:40.8
1936 Ivar Ballangrud, Norway	8:19.6
1948 Reidar Liaklev, Norway	8:29.4
1952 Hjalmar Andersen, Norway	8:10.6
1956 Boris Shilkov, USSR	7:48.7
1960 Viktor Kosichkin, USSR	7:51.3
1964 Knut Johannesen, Norway	7:38.4
1968 F. Anton Maier, Norway	7:22.4
1972 Ard Schenk, Netherlands	7:23.61
1976 Sten Stensen, Norway	7:24.48
1980 Eric Heiden, U.S.	7:02.29
1984 Sven Tomas Gustafson, Sweden	7:12.28
1988 Tomas Gustafson, Sweden	6:44.63
1992 Geir Karlstad, Norway	6:59.97
1994 Johann Koss, Norway	6:34.96
1998 Gianni Romme, Netherlands	6:22.20
2002 Jochem Uytdehaage, Netherlands	6:14.66*

Men's 10,000 Meters	Time
1924 Julius Skutnabb, Finland	18:04.8
1928 Event not held because of thawing of ice	
1932 Irving Jaffee, U.S.	19:13.6
1936 Ivar Ballangrud, Norway	17:24.3
1948 Ake Seyffarth, Sweden	17:26.3
1952 Hjalmar Andersen, Norway	16:45.8
1956 Sigvard Ericsson, Sweden	16:35.9
1960 Knut Johannesen, Norway	15:46.6
1964 Jonny Nilsson, Sweden	15:50.1
1968 Jonny Hoeglin, Sweden	15:23.6
1972 Ard Schenk, Netherlands	15:01.35
1976 Piet Kleine, Netherlands	14:50.59
1980 Eric Heiden, U.S.	14:28.13
1984 Igor Malkov, USSR	14:39.90
1988 Tomas Gustafson, Sweden	13:48.20
1992 Bart Veldkamp, Netherlands	14:12.12
1994 Johann Koss, Norway	13:30.55
1998 Gianni Romme, Netherlands	13:15.33
2002 Jochem Uytdehaage, Netherlands	12:58.92*

Women's 500 Meters	Time[1]
1960 Helga Haase, Germany	0:45.9
1964 Lydia Skoblikova, USSR	0:45.0
1968 Ludmila Titova, USSR	0:46.1
1972 Anne Henning, U.S.	0:43.33
1976 Sheila Young, U.S.	0:42.76
1980 Karin Enke, E. Germany	0:41.78
1984 Christa Rothenburger, E. Germany	0:41.02
1988 Bonnie Blair, U.S.	0:39.10
1992 Bonnie Blair, U.S.	0:40.33
1994 Bonnie Blair, U.S.	0:39.25
1998 Catriona Le May-Doan, Canada	0:38.21
2002 Catriona Le May Doan, Canada	0:37.30

(1) Better time of two runs. Medals based on combined times.

Women's 1,000 Meters	Time
1960 Klara Guseva, USSR	1:34.1
1964 Lydia Skoblikova, USSR	1:33.2
1968 Carolina Geijssen, Netherlands	1:32.6
1972 Monika Pflug, W. Germany	1:31.40
1976 Tatiana Averina, USSR	1:28.43
1980 Natalya Petruseva, USSR	1:24.10
1984 Karin Enke, E. Germany	1:21.61
1988 Christa Rothenburger, E. Germany	1:17.65
1992 Bonnie Blair, U.S.	1:21.90
1994 Bonnie Blair, U.S.	1:18.74
1998 Marianne Timmer, Netherlands	1:16.51
2002 Chris Witty, U.S.	1:13.83*

Women's 1,500 Meters	Time
1960 Lydia Skoblikova, USSR	2:52.2
1964 Lydia Skoblikova, USSR	2:22.6
1968 Kaija Mustonen, Finland	2:22.4
1972 Dianne Holum, U.S.	2:20.85
1976 Galina Stepanskaya, USSR	2:16.58
1980 Anne Borckink, Netherlands	2:10.95
1984 Karin Enke, E. Germany	2:03.42
1988 Yvonne van Gennip, Netherlands	2:00.68
1992 Jacqueline Boerner, Germany	2:05.87
1994 Emese Hunyady, Austria	2:02.19
1998 Marianne Timmer, Netherlands	1:57.58
2002 Anni Friesinger, Germany,	1:54.02*

Women's 3,000 Meters		Time
1960	Lydia Skoblikova, USSR	5:14.3
1964	Lydia Skoblikova, USSR	5:14.9
1968	Johanna Schut, Netherlands	4:56.2
1972	Christina Baas-Kaiser, Netherlands	4:52.14
1976	Tatiana Averina, USSR	4:45.19
1980	Bjoerg Eva Jensen, Norway	4:32.13
1984	Andrea Schoene, E. Germany	4:24.79
1988	Yvonne van Gennip, Netherlands	4:11.94
1992	Gunda Niemann, Germany	4:19.90
1994	Svetlana Bazhanova, Russia	4:17.43
1998	Gunda Niemann-Stirnemann, Germany	4:07.29
2002	Claudia Pechstein, Germany,	3:57.70*

Women's 5,000 Meters		Time
1988	Yvonne van Gennip, Netherlands	7:14.13
1992	Gunda Niemann, Germany	7:31.57
1994	Claudia Pechstein, Germany	7:14.37
1998	Claudia Pechstein, Germany	6:59.61
2002	Claudia Pechstein, Germany	6:46.91*

Short-Track Speed Skating
indicates Olympic record

Men's 500 Meters		Time
1998	Takafumi Nishitani, Japan	42.862
2002	Marc Gagnon, Canada	41.802*

Men's 1,000 Meters		Time
1992	Kim Ki-Hoon, S. Korea	1:30.76
1994	Kim Ki-Hoon, S. Korea	1:34.57

Men's 1,000 Meters		Time
1998	Dong-Sung Kim, S. Korea	1:32.375
2002	Steven Bradbury, Australia	1:29.109

Men's 1,500 Meters		Time
2002	Apolo Anton Ohno, U.S.	2:18.541

Men's 5,000-Meter Relay		Time
1992	S. Korea, Canada, Japan	7:14.02
1994	Italy, U.S., Australia	7:11.74
1998	Canada, S. Korea, China	7:06.075
2002	Canada, Italy, China	6:51.579

Women's 500 Meters		Time
1992	Cathy Turner, U.S.	47.04
1994	Cathy Turner, U.S.	45.98
1998	Annie Perreault, Canada	46.568
2002	Yang Yang (A)	44.187

Women's 1,000 Meters		Time
1998	Chun Lee-Kyung, S. Korea	1:42.776
2002	Yang Yang (A), China	1:36.391

Women's 1,500 Meters		Time
2002	Gi-Hyun Ko, S. Korea	2:31.581

Women's 3,000 Meter Relay		Time
1992	Canada, U.S., Unified Team	4:36.62
1994	S. Korea, Canada, U.S.	4:26.64
1998	S. Korea, China, Canada	4:16.26
2002	S. Korea, China, Canada	4:12.793*

Olympic Information

The modern Olympic Games, first held in Athens, Greece, in 1896, were the result of efforts by Baron Pierre de Coubertin, a French educator, to promote interest in education and culture and to foster better international understanding through love of athletics. His source of inspiration was the ancient Greek Olympic Games, most notable of the 4 Panhellenic celebrations. The games were combined patriotic, religious, and athletic festivals held every 4 years. The first such recorded festival was held in 776 BC, the date from which the Greeks began to keep their calendar by "Olympiads," or 4-year spans between the games.

Baron de Coubertin enlisted 13 nations to send athletes to the first modern Olympics in 1896; now athletes from nearly 200 nations and territories compete in the Summer Olympics. The Winter Olympic Games were started in 1924.

Symbol: Five rings or circles, linked together to represent the sporting friendship of all peoples. They also symbolize 5 geographic areas—Europe, Asia, Africa, Australia, and America. Each ring is a different color—blue, yellow, black, green, or red.

Flag: The symbol of the 5 rings on a plain white background.

Creed: "The most important thing in the Olympic Games is not to win but to take part, just as the most important thing in life is not the triumph but the struggle. The essential thing is not to have conquered but to have fought well."

Motto: "Citius, Altius, Fortius." Latin meaning "swifter, higher, stronger."

Oath: "In the name of all competitors I promise that we will take part in these Olympic Games, respecting and abiding by the rules which govern them, in the true spirit of sportsmanship for the glory of sport and the honor of our teams."

Flame: The modern version of the flame was adopted in 1936. The torch used to kindle it is first lit by the sun's rays at Olympia, Greece, then carried to the site of the Games by relays of runners. Ships and planes are used when necessary.

Paralympics

The first Olympic games for the disabled were held in Rome after the 1960 Summer Olympics; use of the name "paralympic" began with the 1964 games in Tokyo. The Paralympics are held by the Olympic host country in the same year and usually same city or venue. A goal of the Paralympics is to provide elite competition to athletes with functional disabilities that prevent their involvement in the Olympics. In 1976 the first Winter Paralympic Games were held, in Ornskoldsvik, Sweden.

The VIII Paralympic Winter Games were held Mar. 7-16, 2002, in Salt Lake City, Utah. Some 417 athletes from 35 countries competed in Alpine and Nordic skiing and ice sledge hockey. The U.S. led the medal standings with 43 (10 gold), followed by Germany, 33 (17 gold), and Austria 29 (9 gold). U.S. highlights included a gold medal for the sledge hockey team after a 4-3 overtime shootout victory over Norway and 4 gold medals for Alpine skier Sarah Will.

The XII Paralympic Games were scheduled for Sept. 17-28, 2004, in Athens, Greece. The IX Paralympic Winter Games were to be held Mar. 10-19, 2006, in Torino, Italy, where wheelchair curling was to be contested for the first time.

Special Olympics

Special Olympics is an international program of year-round sports training and athletic competition dedicated to "empowering individuals with mental retardation." All 50 U.S. states, Washington, DC, and Guam have chapter offices. In addition, there are accredited Special Olympics programs in nearly 150 countries. Persons wishing to volunteer or find out more about Special Olympics can contact Special Olympics International Headquarters, 1325 G St. NW, Suite 500, Washington, DC 20005, or access the Special Olympics website at www.specialolympics.org

Special Olympics: 2003 World Summer Games, 2005 World Winter Games

The 11th Special Olympics World Summer Games were held June 21-29, 2003, in Dublin, Ireland. More than 7,000 athletes, 3,000 coaches and official delegates, and 28,000 friends and family members attended the first Special Olympic World Games outside the U.S. Competition included Aquatics, Athletics, Badminton, Bocce, Bowling, Cycling, Equestrian Sports, Golf, Gymnastics (Artistic and Rhythmic), Power lifting, Rollerskating, Table Tennis, and Tennis. Scheduled team sports were Basketball, Handball, Sailing, Soccer, and Volleyball. Kayaking and Pitch-and-Putt (a form of golf) were to be included as demonstration sports.

The 8th Special Olympics World Winter Games were scheduled to be held Feb. 26 through Mar. 5, 2005, in Nagano, Japan. About 2,500 athletes from 80 countries are to compete in these, the first Special Olympics World Games to be held in Asia. In addition to the athletes, more than 10,000 people—coaches, volunteers, family, and friends—were expected to attend. The competition will include Alpine Skiing, Cross-Country Skiing, Floor Hockey, Figure Skating, Speed Skating, Snowshoeing, and Snowboarding, all to be held in the same venues used at the 1998 Olympic Games.

TRACK AND FIELD
World Track and Field Outdoor Records
As of Oct. 2003

The International Amateur Athletic Federation, the world body of track and field, recognizes only records in metric distances, except for the mile. *Pending ratification. **World best; marathon records not officially recognized by IAAF.

Men's Records
Running

Event	Record	Holder	Country	Date	Where made
100 meters	9.78 s.	Tim Montgomery	U.S.	Sept. 14, 2002	Paris, France
200 meters	19.32 s.	Michael Johnson	U.S.	Aug. 1, 1996	Atlanta, GA
400 meters	43.18 s.	Michael Johnson	U.S.	Aug. 26, 1999	Seville, Spain
800 meters	1 m., 41.11 s.	Wilson Kipketer	Denmark	Aug. 24, 1997	Cologne, Germany
1,000 meters	2 m., 11.96 s.	Noah Ngeny	Kenya	Sept. 5, 1999	Rieti, Italy
1,500 meters	3 m., 26.00 s.	Hicham El Guerrouj	Morocco	July 14, 1998	Rome, Italy
1 mile	3 m., 43.13 s.	Hicham El Guerrouj	Morocco	July 7, 1999	Rome, Italy
2,000 meters	4 m., 44.79 s.	Hicham El Guerrouj	Morocco	Sept. 7, 1999	Berlin, Germany
3,000 meters	7 m., 20.67 s.	Daniel Komen	Kenya	Sept. 1, 1996	Rieti, Italy
5,000 meters	12 m., 39.36 s.	Haile Gebrselassie	Ethiopia	June 13, 1998	Helsinki, Finland
10,000 meters	26 m., 22.75 s.	Haile Gebrselassie	Ethiopia	June 1,1998	Hengelo, Netherlands
20,000 meters	56 m., 55.6 s.	Arturo Barrios	Mexico	Mar. 30, 1991	La Flèche, France
25,000 meters	1 hr., 13 m., 55.8 s.	Toshihiko Seko	Japan	Mar. 22, 1981	Christchurch, NZ
3,000 meter stpl.	7 m., 53.17 s.*	Brahim Boulami	Morocco	Aug. 16, 2002	Zurich, Switzerland
Marathon**	2 hr., 4 m., 55 s.	Paul Tergat	Kenya	Sept. 28, 2003	Berlin, Germany

Hurdles

Event	Record	Holder	Country	Date	Where made
110 meters	12.91 s.	Colin Jackson	Gr. Britain	Aug. 20, 1993	Stuttgart, Germany
400 meters	46.78 s.	Kevin Young	U.S.	Aug. 6, 1992	Barcelona, Spain

Relay Races

Event	Record	Holder	Country	Date	Where made
400 mtrs. (4x100)	37.40 s.	(Marsh, Burrell, Mitchell, Lewis)	U.S.	Aug. 8, 1992	Barcelona, Spain
		(Drummond, Cason, Mitchell, Burrell)	U.S.	Aug. 21, 1993	Stuttgart, Germany
800 mtrs. (4x200)	1 m., 18.68 s.	(Marsh, Burrell, Heard, Lewis)	U.S.	Apr. 17, 1994	Walnut, CA
1,600 mtrs. (4x400)	2 m., 54.20 s.	(Young, Pettigrew, Washington, Johnson)	U.S.	July 22, 1998	Long Island, NY
3,200 mtrs. (4x800)	7 m., 03.89 s.	(Elliott, Cook, Cram, Coe)	Gr. Britain	Aug. 30, 1982	London, England

Field Events

Event	Record	Holder	Country	Date	Where made
High jump	2.45m (8' ½")	Javier Sotomayor	Cuba	July 27, 1993	Salamanca, Spain
Long jump	8.95m (29' 4½")	Mike Powell	U.S.	Aug. 30, 1991	Tokyo, Japan
Triple jump	18.29m (60' ¼")	Jonathan Edwards	Gr. Britain	Aug. 7, 1995	Göteborg, Sweden
Pole vault	6.14m (20' 1¾")	Sergei Bubka	Ukraine	July 31, 1994	Sestriere, Italy
16-lb. shot put	23.12m (75' 10¼")	Randy Barnes	U.S.	May 20, 1990	Los Angeles, CA
Discus	74.08m (243' 0")	Juergen Schult	E. Germany	June 6, 1986	Neubrandenburg, Germany
Javelin	98.48m (323' 1")	Jan Zelezny	Czech Rep.	May 25, 1996	Jena, Germany
16-lb. hammer	86.74m (284' 7")	Yuri Sedykh	USSR	Aug. 30, 1986	Stuttgart, W. Germany
Decathlon	9,026 pts.	Roman Sebrle	Czech Rep.	May 27, 2001	Götzis, Austria

Women's Records
Running

Event	Record	Holder	Country	Date	Where made
100 meters	10.49 s.	Florence Griffith Joyner	U.S.	July 16, 1988	Indianapolis, IN
200 meters	21.34 s.	Florence Griffith Joyner	U.S.	Sept. 29, 1988	Seoul, S. Korea
400 meters	47.60 s.	Marita Koch	E. Germany	Oct. 6, 1985	Canberra, Australia
800 meters	1 m., 53.28 s.	Jarmila Kratochvilova	Czech Rep.	July 26, 1983	Munich, Germany
1,000 meters	2 m., 28.98 s.	Svetlana Masterkova	Russia	Aug. 23, 1996	Brussels, Belgium
1,500 meters	3 m., 50.46 s.	Qu Yunxia	China	Sept. 11, 1993	Beijing, China
1 mile	4 m., 12.56 s.	Svetlana Masterkova	Russia	Aug. 14, 1996	Zurich, Switzerland
2,000 meters	5 m., 25.36 s.	Sonia O'Sullivan	Ireland	July 8, 1994	Edinburgh, Scotland
3,000 meters	8 m., 06.11 s.	Junxia Wang	China	Sept. 13, 1993	Beijing, China
3,000 meter stpl.	9 m., 8.33 s.*	Gulnara Samitova	Russia	Aug. 10, 2002	Tula, Russia
5,000 meters	14 m., 28.09 s.	Bo Jiang	China	Oct. 23, 1997	Shanghai, China
10,000 meters	29 m., 31.78 s.	Junxia Wang	China	Sept. 8, 1993	Beijing, China
20,000 meters	1 h., 05m. 26.6 s.	Tegla Loroupe	Kenya	Sept. 3, 2000	Borgholzhausen, Germany
30,000 meters	1 h., 45 m., 50 s.*	Tegla Loroupe	Kenya	June 6, 2003	Warstein, Germany
Marathon	2 h., 15 m., 25	Paula Radcliffe	Gr. Britain	April 13, 2003	London, England

Hurdles

Event	Record	Holder	Country	Date	Where made
100 meters	12.21 s.	Yordanka Donkova	Bulgaria	Aug. 20, 1988	Stara Zagora, Bulgaria
400 meters	52.34 s.	Yuliya Pechonkina	Russia	Aug. 10, 2003	Tula, Russia

Relay Races

Event	Record	Holder	Country	Date	Where made
400 mtrs. (4×100)	.41.37 s.	(Gladisch, Rieger, Auerswald, Goehr)	E. Germany	. Oct. 6, 1985. .	. Canberra, Australia
800 mtrs. (4×200)	.1 m., 27.46 s.....	U.S. "Blue" (Jenkins, Clarke, Richardson, Jamieson)	U.S.	...... Sept. 28, 2000	. Philadelphia, PA
1,600 mtrs. (4×400)	3 m., 15.17 s.....	(Ledovskaya, Nazarova, Pinigina, Bryzgina)	USSR	..... Oct. 1, 1988. ..	. Seoul, S. Korea
3,200 mtrs. (4×800)	7 m., 50.17 s.....	(Olizarenko, Gurina, Borisova, Podyalovskaya)	USSR	...... Aug. 5, 1984	. . Moscow, USSR

Field Events

Event	Record	Holder	Country	Date	Where made
High jump.......	.2.09m (6' 10¼")	... Stefka Kostadinova	Bulgaria.	.... Aug. 30, 1987	....Rome, Italy
Long jump	.7.52m (24' 8¼")	... Galina Chistyakova	USSR	...... June 11, 1988. ..	....Leningrad
Triple jump.......	15.50m (50' 10¼")	... Inessa Kravets...........	Ukraine	.... Aug. 10, 1995	....Göteborg, Sweden
Pole vault........	4.82m* (15' 9¾")	.. Yelena Isinbayeva	Russia	.... July 13, 2003.....	....Gateshead, England
Shot put	22.63m (74' 3")	... Natalya Lisovskaya	USSR	...... June 7, 1987	...Moscow, Russia
Discus	76.80m (252' 0")	... Gabriele Reinsch	E. Germany.	July 9, 1988......	....Neubrandenburg,Germany
Hammer	76.07m (249' 7")	.. Mihaela Melinte	Romania	.. Aug. 29, 1999	...Rüdlingen, Switzerland
Javelin	71.54m (234' 8")	.. Osleidys Menéndez	Cuba	.... July 1, 2001......	.Réthymno, Greece
Heptathlon	7,291 pts.	Jackie Joyner-Kersee	U.S.	.... Sept. 23-24, 1988	. .Seoul, S. Korea

World Track and Field Indoor Records

As of Oct. 2003

The International Amateur Athletic Federation first recognized world indoor track and field records on Jan. 1, 1987. World indoor bests set prior to Jan. 1, 1987, are subject to approval as world records providing they meet the IAAF world records criteria, including drug testing. Criteria for indoor and outdoor records are the same, except that a track performance cannot be set on an indoor track larger than 200 meters. (a)=altitude. *Pending ratification.

Men's Records

Event	Record	Holder	Country	Date	Where made
50 meters	.5.56 (a)	... Donovan Bailey	Canada	. Feb. 9, 1996 ..	.Reno, NV
	5.56	.. Maurice Greene	U.S.	. Feb. 13, 1999	.Los Angeles, CA
60 meters	.6.39	... Maurice Greene	U.S.	. Mar. 3, 2001 ..	.Atlanta, GA
	6.39	... Maurice Greene	U.S.	. Feb. 3, 1998 ..	.Madrid, Spain
200 meters	.19.92	.. Frankie Fredericks	Namibia	. Feb. 18, 1996 ..	.Lievin, France
400 meters	44.63	.. Michael Johnson	U.S.	. Mar. 4, 1995 ..	.Atlanta, GA
800 meters	1:42.67..........	.. Wilson Kipketer	Denmark ..	. Mar. 9, 1997 ..	.Paris, France
1,000 meters	2:14.96..........	.. Wilson Kipketer	Denmark ..	. Feb. 20, 2000	Birmingham, England
1,500 meters	3:31.18..........	.. Hicham El Guerrouj	Morocco ..	. Feb. 2, 1997 ..	.Stuttgart, Germany
1 mile	3:48.45..........	.. Hicham El Guerrouj	Morocco ..	. Feb. 12, 1997 ..	.Ghent, Belgium
3,000 meters	7:24.90..........	.. Daniel Komen	Kenya ..	. Feb. 6, 1998 ..	.Budapest, Hungary
5,000 meters	12:50.38.........	.. Haile Gebrselassie	Ethiopia ..	. Feb. 14, 1999 ..	.Birmingham, England
50-meter hurdles ..	. 6.25	.. Mark McKoy	Canada ..	. Mar. 5, 1986 ..	.Kobe, Japan
60-meter hurdles ..	. 7.30	.. Colin Jackson	Gr. Britain ..	. Mar. 6, 1994 ..	.Sindelfingen, Germany
High jump.......	.2.43m (7' 11½")	.. Javier Sotomayor	Cuba ..	. Mar. 4, 1989 ..	.Budapest, Hungary
Pole vault........	6.15m (20' 2")	... Sergei Bubka	Ukraine ..	. Feb. 21, 1993 ..	.Donyetsk, Ukraine
Long jump	.8.79m (28' 10¼")	.. Carl Lewis	U.S. ..	. Jan. 27, 1984 ..	.New York, NY
Triple jump.......	17.83 (58' 6")	... Aliecer Urrutia	Cuba ..	. Mar. 1, 1997 ..	.Sindelfingen, Germany
Shot put	22.66m (74' 4¼")	.. Randy Barnes	U.S. ..	. Jan. 20, 1989 ..	.Los Angeles, CA

Women's Records

Event	Record	Holder	Country	Date	Where made
50 meters	.5.96	.. Irina Privalova	Russia	. Feb. 9, 1995 ..	.Madrid, Spain
60 meters	.6.92	.. Irina Privalova	Russia	. Feb. 9, 1995 ..	.Madrid, Spain
		Irina Privalova	Russia	. Feb. 11, 1993 ..	.Madrid, Spain
200 meters	21.87	.. Merlene Ottey.	Jamaica	. Feb. 13, 1993 ..	.Lievin, France
400 meters	49.59	.. Jarmila Kratochvilova	Czechoslov. ..	. Mar. 7, 1982 ..	.Milan, Italy
800 meters	1:55.82*	.. Jolanda Ceplak	Slovenia	. Mar. 3, 2002 ..	.Vienna, Austria
1,000 meters	2:30.94..........	.. Maria Mutola	Mozambique	. Feb. 25, 1999 ..	.Stockholm, Sweden
1,500 meters	3:59.98*	.. Regina Jacobs	U.S.	. Feb. 1, 2003 ..	.Boston, MA
1 mile	4:17.14..........	.. Doina Melinte	Romania	. Feb. 9, 1990 ..	.E. Rutherford, NJ
3,000 meters	8:29.15..........	.. Berhane Adere	Ethiopia	. Mar. 3, 2002 ..	.Stuttgart, Germany
5,000 meters	14:47.35..........	.. Gabriela Szabo	Romania	. Feb. 13, 1999 ..	.Dortmund, Germany
50-meter hurdles ..	. 6.58	.. Cornelia Oschkenat	E. Germany ..	. Feb. 20, 1988 ..	.Berlin, Germany
60-meter hurdles ..	. 7.69	.. Lyudmila Engquist	USSR ..	. Feb. 4, 1990 ..	.Chelyabinsk, USSR
High jump.......	.2.07m (6' 9½")	.. Heike Henkel	Germany ..	. Feb. 8, 1992 ..	.Karlsruhe, Germany
Pole vault........	4.80* m (15' 9")	.. Svetlana Feofanova	Russia ..	. Mar. 16, 2003 ..	.Birmingham, England
Long jump	.7.37m (24' 2¼")	.. Heike Drechsler	E. Germany ..	. Feb. 13, 1988 ..	.Vienna, Austria
Triple jump.......	15.16m (49' 9")	... Ashia Hansen	Gr. Britain ..	. Feb. 28, 1998 ..	.Valencia, Spain
Shot put	22.50m (73' 10")	.. Helena Fibingerova	Czechoslovakia .	. Feb. 19, 1977 .	.Jablonec, Czechoslovakia

▶ **IT'S A FACT:** Held in 1900, 1904, 1906, 1908, 1912, and 1920, Tug-of-war has the distinction of being the discontinued sport to make the most appearances as a medal sport in the Summer Olympic Games. Polo has been contested 5 times; rugby, 4 times; golf, lacrosse, and rackets, twice.

BASEBALL

Major League Baseball 2003: Storied Cubs, Red Sox Come Close

Third baseman Aaron Boone homered off Boston's Tim Wakefield in the 11th inning of Game 7 of the American League Championship Series for a 7-6 win in New York that sent the Yankees into their 39th World Series. Yankee closer Mariano Rivera, who notched 2 saves and a win in the ALCS, was the series MVP. Hopes for a historic World Series match-up between the Chicago Cubs, who last won it all in 1908, and Boston (1918 champs) had been dashed the previous night when the Florida Marlins defeated the Cubs, 9-6, in Game 7 of the NLCS. After leading 3 games to 1, the Cubs lost 3 straight, including the final 2 at home. Marlin catcher Ivan Rodriguez, who had an NLCS-record 10 RBI, was MVP. In the regular season, Atlanta won 101 games and a record 12th straight NL East title, San Francisco won 100 games and the NL West, and the resurgent Cubs held off Houston to win the NL Central by a game. The surprising 91-71 Florida Marlins, who had won just 79 games in 2002, overtook Philadelphia to win the NL wildcard by 5 games. The Yankees tied for the season's best record with 101 wins and the AL East title. Oakland won the AL West and Minnesota topped the AL Central, with Boston nabbing the AL wildcard. Detroit lost 119 games, breaking Philadelphia's AL record of 117 losses set in 1916. Since 1900, only the 1962 New York Mets (40-120) had lost more games. The Tigers won their final 2 games over Minnesota. Dodger Eric Gagne broke the Major League record of 54 consecutive saves (over 2 years) and finished the season with 63 straight. The AL defeated the NL, 7-6, in the All-Star Game at Chicago's U.S. Cellular Field to earn the league the home-field advantage in the World Series under new rules adopted for 2003. The financially strapped Montreal Expos were 13-9 in 22 home games played in San Juan, PR, in an effort to generate more revenue and extend Major League Baseball to the Caribbean. San Francisco's Barry Bonds hit 45 home runs, 2 short of Willie Mays's 3rd-ranking career total of 660.

Major League Pennant Winners, 1901–1968

	National League						American League			
Year	Winner	Won	Lost	Pct	Manager	Year	Winner	Won	Lost	Pct	Manager
1901	Pittsburgh	90	49	.647	Clarke	1901	Chicago	83	53	.610	Griffith
1902	Pittsburgh	103	36	.741	Clarke	1902	Philadelphia	83	53	.610	Mack
1903	Pittsburgh	91	49	.650	Clarke	1903	Boston	91	47	.659	Collins
1904	New York	106	47	.693	McGraw	1904	Boston	95	59	.617	Collins
1905	New York	105	48	.686	McGraw	1905	Philadelphia	92	56	.622	Mack
1906	Chicago	116	36	.763	Chance	1906	Chicago	93	58	.616	Jones
1907	Chicago	107	45	.704	Chance	1907	Detroit	92	58	.613	Jennings
1908	Chicago	99	55	.643	Chance	1908	Detroit	90	63	.588	Jennings
1909	Pittsburgh	110	42	.724	Clarke	1909	Detroit	98	54	.645	Jennings
1910	Chicago	104	50	.675	Chance	1910	Philadelphia	102	48	.680	Mack
1911	New York	99	54	.647	McGraw	1911	Philadelphia	101	50	.669	Mack
1912	New York	103	48	.682	McGraw	1912	Boston	105	47	.691	Stahl
1913	New York	101	51	.664	McGraw	1913	Philadelphia	96	57	.627	Mack
1914	Boston	94	59	.614	Stallings	1914	Philadelphia	99	53	.651	Mack
1915	Philadelphia	90	62	.592	Moran	1915	Boston	101	50	.669	Carrigan
1916	Brooklyn	94	60	.610	Robinson	1916	Boston	91	63	.591	Carrigan
1917	New York	98	56	.636	McGraw	1917	Chicago	100	54	.649	Rowland
1918	Chicago	84	45	.651	Mitchell	1918	Boston	75	51	.595	Barrow
1919	Cincinnati	96	44	.686	Moran	1919	Chicago	88	52	.629	Gleason
1920	Brooklyn	93	60	.604	Robinson	1920	Cleveland	98	56	.636	Speaker
1921	New York	94	59	.614	McGraw	1921	New York	98	55	.641	Huggins
1922	New York	93	61	.604	McGraw	1922	New York	94	60	.610	Huggins
1923	New York	95	58	.621	McGraw	1923	New York	98	54	.645	Huggins
1924	New York	93	60	.608	McGraw	1924	Washington	92	62	.597	Harris
1925	Pittsburgh	95	58	.621	McKechnie	1925	Washington	96	55	.636	Harris
1926	St. Louis	89	65	.578	Hornsby	1926	New York	91	63	.591	Huggins
1927	Pittsburgh	94	60	.610	Bush	1927	New York	110	44	.714	Huggins
1928	St. Louis	95	59	.617	McKechnie	1928	New York	101	53	.656	Huggins
1929	Chicago	98	54	.645	McCarthy	1929	Philadelphia	104	46	.693	Mack
1930	St. Louis	92	62	.597	Street	1930	Philadelphia	102	52	.662	Mack
1931	St. Louis	101	53	.656	Street	1931	Philadelphia	107	45	.704	Mack
1932	Chicago	90	64	.584	Grimm	1932	New York	107	47	.695	McCarthy
1933	New York	91	61	.599	Terry	1933	Washington	99	53	.651	Cronin
1934	St. Louis	95	58	.621	Frisch	1934	Detroit	101	53	.656	Cochrane
1935	Chicago	100	54	.649	Grimm	1935	Detroit	93	58	.616	Cochrane
1936	New York	91	62	.597	Terry	1936	New York	102	51	.667	McCarthy
1937	New York	95	57	.625	Terry	1937	New York	102	52	.662	McCarthy
1938	Chicago	89	63	.586	Hartnett	1938	New York	99	53	.651	McCarthy
1939	Cincinnati	97	57	.630	McKechnie	1939	New York	106	45	.702	McCarthy
1940	Cincinnati	100	53	.654	McKechnie	1940	Detroit	90	64	.584	Baker
1941	Brooklyn	100	54	.649	Durocher	1941	New York	101	53	.656	McCarthy
1942	St. Louis	106	48	.688	Southworth	1942	New York	103	51	.669	McCarthy
1943	St. Louis	105	49	.682	Southworth	1943	New York	98	56	.636	McCarthy
1944	St. Louis	105	49	.682	Southworth	1944	St. Louis	89	65	.578	Sewell
1945	Chicago	98	56	.636	Grimm	1945	Detroit	88	65	.575	O'Neill
1946	St. Louis	98	58	.628	Dyer	1946	Boston	104	50	.675	Cronin
1947	Brooklyn	94	60	.610	Shotton	1947	New York	97	57	.630	Harris
1948	Boston	91	62	.595	Southworth	1948	Cleveland	97	58	.626	Boudreau
1949	Brooklyn	97	57	.630	Shotton	1949	New York	97	57	.630	Stengel
1950	Philadelphia	91	63	.591	Sawyer	1950	New York	98	56	.636	Stengel
1951	New York	98	59	.624	Durocher	1951	New York	98	56	.636	Stengel
1952	Brooklyn	96	57	.627	Dressen	1952	New York	95	59	.617	Stengel
1953	Brooklyn	105	49	.682	Dressen	1953	New York	99	52	.656	Stengel
1954	New York	97	57	.630	Durocher	1954	Cleveland	111	43	.721	Lopez
1955	Brooklyn	98	55	.641	Alston	1955	New York	96	58	.623	Stengel
1956	Brooklyn	93	61	.604	Alston	1956	New York	97	57	.630	Stengel
1957	Milwaukee	95	59	.617	Haney	1957	New York	98	56	.636	Stengel
1958	Milwaukee	92	62	.597	Haney	1958	New York	92	62	.597	Stengel

Year	National League Winner	Won	Lost	Pct	Manager	Year	American League Winner	Won	Lost	Pct	Manager
1959	Los Angeles	88	68	.564	Alston	1959	Chicago	94	60	.610	Lopez
1960	Pittsburgh	95	59	.617	Murtaugh	1960	New York	97	57	.630	Stengel
1961	Cincinnati	93	61	.604	Hutchinson	1961	New York	109	53	.673	Houk
1962	San Francisco	103	62	.624	Dark	1962	New York	96	66	.593	Houk
1963	Los Angeles	99	63	.611	Alston	1963	New York	104	57	.646	Houk
1964	St. Louis	93	69	.574	Keane	1964	New York	99	63	.611	Berra
1965	Los Angeles	97	65	.599	Alston	1965	Minnesota	102	60	.630	Mele
1966	Los Angeles	95	67	.586	Alston	1966	Baltimore	97	63	.606	Bauer
1967	St. Louis	101	60	.627	Schoendienst	1967	Boston	92	70	.568	Williams
1968	St. Louis	97	65	.599	Schoendienst	1968	Detroit	103	59	.636	Smith

Major League Pennant Winners, 1969-2003
National League

Year	East Winner	W	L	Pct	Manager	West Winner	W	L	Pct	Manager	Pennant Winner
1969	N.Y. Mets	100	62	.617	Hodges	Atlanta	93	69	.574	Harris	New York
1970	Pittsburgh	89	73	.549	Murtaugh	Cincinnati	102	60	.630	Anderson	Cincinnati
1971	Pittsburgh	97	65	.599	Murtaugh	San Francisco	90	72	.556	Fox	Pittsburgh
1972	Pittsburgh	96	59	.619	Virdon	Cincinnati	95	59	.617	Anderson	Cincinnati
1973	N.Y. Mets	82	79	.509	Berra	Cincinnati	99	63	.611	Anderson	New York
1974	Pittsburgh	88	74	.543	Murtaugh	Los Angeles	102	60	.630	Alston	Los Angeles
1975	Pittsburgh	92	69	.571	Murtaugh	Cincinnati	108	54	.667	Anderson	Cincinnati
1976	Philadelphia	101	61	.623	Ozark	Cincinnati	102	60	.630	Anderson	Cincinnati
1977	Philadelphia	101	61	.623	Ozark	Los Angeles	98	64	.605	Lasorda	Los Angeles
1978	Philadelphia	90	72	.556	Ozark	Los Angeles	95	67	.586	Lasorda	Los Angeles
1979	Pittsburgh	98	64	.605	Tanner	Cincinnati	90	71	.559	McNamara	Pittsburgh
1980	Philadelphia	91	71	.562	Green	Houston	93	70	.571	Virdon	Philadelphia
1981(a)	Philadelphia	34	21	.618	Green	Los Angeles	36	21	.632	Lasorda	(c)
1981(b)	Montreal	30	23	.566	Williams, Fanning	Houston	33	20	.623	Virdon	Los Angeles
1982	St. Louis	92	70	.568	Herzog	Atlanta	89	73	.549	Torre	St. Louis
1983	Philadelphia	90	72	.556	Corrales, Owens	Los Angeles	91	71	.562	Lasorda	Philadelphia
1984	Chicago	96	65	.596	Frey	San Diego	92	70	.568	Williams	San Diego
1985	St. Louis	101	61	.623	Herzog	Los Angeles	95	67	.586	Lasorda	St. Louis
1986	N.Y. Mets	108	54	.667	Johnson	Houston	96	66	.593	Lanier	New York
1987	St. Louis	95	67	.586	Herzog	San Francisco	90	72	.556	Craig	St. Louis
1988	N.Y. Mets	100	60	.625	Johnson	Los Angeles	94	67	.584	Lasorda	Los Angeles
1989	Chicago	93	69	.571	Zimmer	San Francisco	92	70	.568	Craig	San Francisco
1990	Pittsburgh	95	67	.586	Leyland	Cincinnati	91	71	.562	Piniella	Cincinnati
1991	Pittsburgh	98	64	.605	Leyland	Atlanta	94	68	.580	Cox	Atlanta
1992	Pittsburgh	96	66	.593	Leyland	Atlanta	98	64	.605	Cox	Atlanta
1993	Philadelphia	97	65	.599	Fregosi	Atlanta	104	58	.642	Cox	Philadelphia

Year	Division	Winner	W	L	Pct	Manager	Playoffs	Pennant Winner
1994(d)	East	Montreal	74	40	.649	Alou	—	—
	Central	Cincinnati	66	48	.579	Johnson		
	West	Los Angeles	58	56	.509	Lasorda		
1995	East	Atlanta	90	54	.625	Cox	Atlanta 3, Colorado* 1	Atlanta
	Central	Cincinnati	85	59	.590	Johnson	Cincinnati 3, Los Angeles 0	
	West	Los Angeles	78	66	.542	Lasorda	Atlanta 4, Cincinnati 0	
1996	East	Atlanta	96	66	.593	Cox	Atlanta, Los Angeles* 0	Atlanta
	Central	St. Louis	88	74	.543	La Russa	St. Louis 3, San Diego 0	
	West	San Diego	91	71	.562	Bochy	Atlanta 4, St. Louis 3	
1997	East	Atlanta	101	61	.623	Cox	Atlanta 3, Houston 0	Florida* (e)
	Central	Houston	84	78	.519	Dierker	Florida* 3, San Francisco 0	
	West	San Francisco	90	72	.556	Baker	Florida* 4, Atlanta 2	
1998	East	Atlanta	106	56	.654	Cox	Atlanta 3, Chicago* 0	San Diego
	Central	Houston	102	60	.630	Dierker	San Diego 3, Houston 1	
	West	San Diego	97	64	.602	Bochy	San Diego 4, Atlanta 2	
1999	East	Atlanta	103	59	.636	Cox	Atlanta 3, Houston 1	Atlanta
	Central	Houston	97	65	.599	Dierker	New York* 3, Arizona 1	
	West	Arizona	100	62	.617	Showalter	Atlanta 4, New York 2	
2000	East	Atlanta	95	67	.586	Cox	St. Louis 3, Atlanta 0	New York* (f)
	Central	St. Louis	95	67	.586	La Russa	New York* 3, San Francisco 1	
	West	San Francisco	97	65	.599	Baker	New York* 4, St. Louis 1	
2001	East	Atlanta	88	74	.543	Cox	Atlanta 3, Houston 0	Arizona
	Central	Houston	93	69	.574	Dierker	Arizona 3, St. Louis* 2	
	West	Arizona	92	70	.568	Brenly	Arizona 4, Atlanta 1	
2002	East	Atlanta	101	59	.631	Cox	St. Louis 3, Arizona 0	San Francisco* (g)
	Central	St. Louis	97	65	.599	La Russa	San Francisco* 3, Atlanta 2	
	West	Arizona	98	64	.605	Brenly	San Francisco 4, St. Louis 1	
2003	East	Atlanta	101	61	.623	Cox	Chicago 3, Atlanta 2	Florida*(i)
	Central	Chicago	88	74	.543	Baker	Florida* 3, San Francisco 2	
	West	San Francisco	100	61	.621	Alou	Florida* 4, Chicago 3	

American League

Year	East Winner	W	L	Pct	Manager	West Winner	W	L	Pct	Manager	Pennant Winner
1969	Baltimore	109	53	.673	Weaver	Minnesota	97	65	.599	Martin	Baltimore
1970	Baltimore	108	54	.667	Weaver	Minnesota	98	64	.605	Rigney	Baltimore
1971	Baltimore	101	57	.639	Weaver	Oakland	101	60	.627	Williams	Baltimore
1972	Detroit	86	70	.551	Martin	Oakland	93	62	.600	Williams	Oakland
1973	Baltimore	97	65	.599	Weaver	Oakland	94	68	.580	Williams	Oakland
1974	Baltimore	91	71	.562	Weaver	Oakland	90	72	.556	Dark	Oakland

Year	East Winner	W	L	Pct	Manager	West Winner	W	L	Pct	Manager	Pennant Winner
1975	Boston	95	65	.594	Johnson	Oakland	98	64	.605	Dark	Boston
1976	New York	97	62	.610	Martin	Kansas City	90	72	.556	Herzog	New York
1977	New York	100	62	.617	Martin	Kansas City	102	60	.630	Herzog	New York
1978	New York	100	63	.613	Martin, Lemon	Kansas City	92	70	.568	Herzog	New York
1979	Baltimore	102	57	.642	Weaver	California	88	74	.543	Fregosi	Baltimore
1980	New York	103	59	.636	Howser	Kansas City	97	65	.599	Frey	Kansas City
1981(a)	New York	34	22	.607	Michael	Oakland	37	23	.617	Martin	(c)
1981(b)	Milwaukee	31	22	.585	Rodgers	Kansas City	30	23	.566	Frey, Howser	New York
1982	Milwaukee	95	67	.586	Rodgers, Kuenn	California	93	69	.574	Mauch	Milwaukee
1983	Baltimore	98	64	.605	Altobelli	Chicago	99	63	.611	La Russa	Baltimore
1984	Detroit	104	58	.642	Anderson	Kansas City	84	78	.519	Howser	Detroit
1985	Toronto	99	62	.615	Cox	Kansas City	91	71	.562	Howser	Kansas City
1986	Boston	95	66	.590	McNamara	California	92	70	.568	Mauch	Boston
1987	Detroit	98	64	.605	Anderson	Minnesota	85	77	.525	Kelly	Minnesota
1988	Boston	89	73	.549	McNamara, Morgan	Oakland	104	58	.642	La Russa	Oakland
1989	Toronto	89	73	.549	Williams, Gaston	Oakland	99	63	.611	La Russa	Oakland
1990	Boston	88	74	.543	Morgan	Oakland	103	59	.636	La Russa	Oakland
1991	Toronto	91	71	.562	Gaston	Minnesota	95	67	.586	Kelly	Minnesota
1992	Toronto	96	66	.593	Gaston	Oakland	96	66	.593	La Russa	Toronto
1993	Toronto	95	67	.586	Gaston	Chicago	94	68	.580	Lamont	Toronto

Year	Division	Winner	W	L	Pct	Manager	Playoffs	Pennant Winner
1994(d)	East	New York	70	43	.619	Showalter	—	—
	Central	Chicago	67	46	.593	Lamont		
	West	Texas	52	62	.456	Kennedy		
1995	East	Boston	86	58	.597	Kennedy	Cleveland 3, Boston 0	Cleveland
	Central	Cleveland	100	44	.694	Hargrove	Seattle 3, New York* 2	
	West	Seattle	79	66	.545	Piniella	Cleveland 4, Seattle 2	
1996	East	New York	92	70	.568	Torre	Baltimore* 3, Cleveland 1	New York
	Central	Cleveland	99	62	.615	Hargrove	New York 3, Texas 1	
	West	Texas	90	72	.556	Oates	New York 4, Baltimore* 1	
1997	East	Baltimore	98	64	.605	Johnson	Baltimore 3, Seattle 1	Cleveland
	Central	Cleveland	86	75	.534	Hargrove	Cleveland 3, New York* 2	
	West	Seattle	90	72	.556	Piniella	Cleveland 4, Baltimore 2	
1998	East	New York	114	48	.704	Torre	New York 3, Texas 0	New York
	Central	Cleveland	89	73	.549	Hargrove	Cleveland 3, Boston* 1	
	West	Texas	88	74	.543	Oates	New York 4, Cleveland 2	
1999	East	New York	98	64	.605	Torre	New York 3, Texas 0	New York
	Central	Cleveland	97	65	.599	Hargrove	Boston* 3, Cleveland 2	
	West	Texas	95	67	.586	Oates	New York 4, Boston* 1	
2000	East	New York	87	74	.540	Torre	New York 3, Oakland 2	New York
	Central	Chicago	95	67	.586	Manuel	Seattle* 3, Chicago 0	
	West	Oakland	91	70	.565	Howe	New York 4, Seattle* 2	
2001	East	New York	95	65	.594	Torre	Seattle 3, Cleveland 2	New York
	Central	Cleveland	91	71	.562	Manuel	New York 3, Oakland 2	
	West	Seattle	116	46	.716	Piniella	New York 4, Seattle* 1	
2002	East	New York	103	58	.640	Torre	Anaheim* 3, New York 1	Anaheim* (h)
	Central	Minnesota	94	67	.584	Gardenhire	Minnesota 3, Oakland 2	
	West	Oakland	103	59	.636	Howe	Anaheim* 4, Minnesota 1	
2003	East	New York	101	61	.623	Torre	New York 3, Minnesota 1	New York
	Central	Minnesota	90	72	.556	Gardenhire	Boston* 3, Oakland 2	
	West	Oakland	96	66	.593	Macha	New York 4, Boston* 3	

*Wild card team. (a) First half. (b) Second half. (c) Montreal, L.A., N.Y. Yankees, and Oakland won the divisional playoffs. (d) In Aug. 1994, a players' strike began that caused the cancellation of the remainder of the season, the playoffs, and the World Series. Teams listed as division "winners" for 1994 were leading their divisions at the time of the strike. (e) Florida manager: Jim Leyland. (f) New York manager Bobby Valentine. (g) San Francisco manager: Dusty Baker. (h) Anaheim manager: Mike Scioscia. (i) Florida manager: Jack McKeon.

Home Run Leaders

Note: Asterisk (*) indicates the all-time single-season record for each league.

	National League			American League	
Year	Player, Team	HR	Year	Player, Team	HR
1901	Sam Crawford, Cincinnati	16	1901	Napoleon Lajoie, Philadelphia	13
1902	Thomas Leach, Pittsburgh	6	1902	Socks Seybold, Philadelphia	16
1903	James Sheckard, Brooklyn	9	1903	Buck Freeman, Boston	13
1904	Harry Lumley, Brooklyn	9	1904	Harry Davis, Philadelphia	10
1905	Fred Odwell, Cincinnati	9	1905	Harry Davis, Philadelphia	8
1906	Timothy Jordan, Brooklyn	12	1906	Harry Davis, Philadelphia	12
1907	David Brain, Boston	10	1907	Harry Davis, Philadelphia	8
1908	Timothy Jordan, Brooklyn	12	1908	Sam Crawford, Detroit	7
1909	Red Murray, New York	7	1909	Ty Cobb, Detroit	9
1910	Fred Beck, Boston; Frank Schulte, Chicago	10	1910	Jake Stahl, Boston	10
1911	Frank Schulte, Chicago	21	1911	J. Franklin Baker, Philadelphia	9
1912	Henry Zimmerman, Chicago	14	1912	J. Franklin Baker, Philadelphia; Tris Speaker, Boston	10
1913	Gavvy Cravath, Philadelphia	19	1913	J. Franklin Baker, Philadelphia	13
1914	Gavvy Cravath, Philadelphia	19	1914	J. Franklin Baker, Philadelphia	9
1915	Gavvy Cravath, Philadelphia	24	1915	Robert Roth, Chicago-Cleveland	7
1916	Dave Robertson, N.Y.; Fred (Cy) Williams, Chi.	12	1916	Wally Pipp, New York	12
1917	Dave Robertson, N.Y.; Gavvy Cravath, Phi.	12	1917	Wally Pipp, New York	9
1918	Gavvy Cravath, Philadelphia	8	1918	Babe Ruth, Boston; Tilly Walker, Philadelphia	11
1919	Gavvy Cravath, Philadelphia	12	1919	Babe Ruth, Boston	29
1920	Cy Williams, Philadelphia	15	1920	Babe Ruth, New York	54
1921	George Kelly, New York	23	1921	Babe Ruth, New York	59
1922	Rogers Hornsby, St. Louis	42	1922	Ken Williams, St. Louis	39

Year	National League — Player, Team	HR	Year	American League — Player, Team	HR
1923	Cy Williams, Philadelphia	41	1923	Babe Ruth, New York	41
1924	Jacques Fournier, Brooklyn	27	1924	Babe Ruth, New York	46
1925	Rogers Hornsby, St. Louis	39	1925	Bob Meusel, New York	33
1926	Hack Wilson, Chicago	21	1926	Babe Ruth, New York	47
1927	Hack Wilson, Chicago; Cy Williams, Philadelphia	30	1927	Babe Ruth, New York	60
1928	Hack Wilson, Chicago; Jim Bottomley, St. Louis	31	1928	Babe Ruth, New York	54
1929	Chuck Klein, Philadelphia	43	1929	Babe Ruth, New York	46
1930	Hack Wilson, Chicago	56	1930	Babe Ruth, New York	49
1931	Chuck Klein, Philadelphia	31	1931	Babe Ruth, Lou Gehrig, both New York	46
1932	Chuck Klein, Philadelphia; Mel Ott, New York	38	1932	Jimmie Foxx, Philadelphia	58
1933	Chuck Klein, Philadelphia	28	1933	Jimmie Foxx, Philadelphia	48
1934	Rip Collins, St. Louis; Mel Ott, New York	35	1934	Lou Gehrig, New York	49
1935	Walter Berger, Boston	34	1935	Jimmie Foxx, Philadelphia; Hank Greenberg, Detroit	36
1936	Mel Ott, New York	33	1936	Lou Gehrig, New York	49
1937	Mel Ott, New York; Joe Medwick, St. Louis	31	1937	Joe DiMaggio, New York	46
1938	Mel Ott, New York	36	1938	Hank Greenberg, Detroit	58
1939	John Mize, St. Louis	28	1939	Jimmie Foxx, Boston	35
1940	John Mize, St. Louis	43	1940	Hank Greenberg, Detroit	41
1941	Dolph Camilli, Brooklyn	34	1941	Ted Williams, Boston	37
1942	Mel Ott, New York	30	1942	Ted Williams, Boston	36
1943	Bill Nicholson, Chicago	29	1943	Rudy York, Detroit	34
1944	Bill Nicholson, Chicago	33	1944	Nick Etten, New York	22
1945	Tommy Holmes, Boston	28	1945	Vern Stephens, St. Louis	24
1946	Ralph Kiner, Pittsburgh	23	1946	Hank Greenberg, Detroit	44
1947	Ralph Kiner, Pittsburgh; John Mize, New York	51	1947	Ted Williams, Boston	32
1948	Ralph Kiner, Pittsburgh; John Mize, New York	40	1948	Joe DiMaggio, New York	39
1949	Ralph Kiner, Pittsburgh	54	1949	Ted Williams, Boston	43
1950	Ralph Kiner, Pittsburgh	47	1950	Al Rosen, Cleveland	37
1951	Ralph Kiner, Pittsburgh	42	1951	Gus Zernial, Chicago-Philadelphia	33
1952	Ralph Kiner, Pittsburgh; Hank Sauer, Chicago	37	1952	Larry Doby, Cleveland	32
1953	Ed Mathews, Milwaukee	47	1953	Al Rosen, Cleveland	43
1954	Ted Kluszewski, Cincinnati	49	1954	Larry Doby, Cleveland	32
1955	Willie Mays, New York	51	1955	Mickey Mantle, New York	37
1956	Duke Snider, Brooklyn	43	1956	Mickey Mantle, New York	52
1957	Hank Aaron, Milwaukee	44	1957	Roy Sievers, Washington	42
1958	Ernie Banks, Chicago	47	1958	Mickey Mantle, New York	42
1959	Ed Mathews, Milwaukee	46	1959	Rocky Colavito, Cleve.; Harmon Killebrew, Wash.	42
1960	Ernie Banks, Chicago	41	1960	Mickey Mantle, New York	40
1961	Orlando Cepeda, San Francisco	46	1961	Roger Maris, New York	*61
1962	Willie Mays, San Francisco	49	1962	Harmon Killebrew, Minnesota	48
1963	Hank Aaron, Milwaukee; Willie McCovey, S.F.	44	1963	Harmon Killebrew, Minnesota	45
1964	Willie Mays, San Francisco	47	1964	Harmon Killebrew, Minnesota	49
1965	Willie Mays, San Francisco	52	1965	Tony Conigliaro, Boston	32
1966	Hank Aaron, Atlanta	44	1966	Frank Robinson, Baltimore	49
1967	Hank Aaron, Atlanta	39	1967	Carl Yastrzemski, Boston; Harmon Killebrew, Minn.	44
1968	Willie McCovey, San Francisco	36	1968	Frank Howard, Washington	44
1969	Willie McCovey, San Francisco	45	1969	Harmon Killebrew, Minnesota	49
1970	Johnny Bench, Cincinnati	45	1970	Frank Howard, Washington	44
1971	Willie Stargell, Pittsburgh	48	1971	Bill Melton, Chicago	33
1972	Johnny Bench, Cincinnati	40	1972	Dick Allen, Chicago	37
1973	Willie Stargell, Pittsburgh	44	1973	Reggie Jackson, Oakland	32
1974	Mike Schmidt, Philadelphia	36	1974	Dick Allen, Chicago	32
1975	Mike Schmidt, Philadelphia	38	1975	George Scott, Milwaukee; Reggie Jackson, Oakland	36
1976	Mike Schmidt, Philadelphia	38	1976	Graig Nettles, New York	32
1977	George Foster, Cincinnati	52	1977	Jim Rice, Boston	39
1978	George Foster, Cincinnati	40	1978	Jim Rice, Boston	46
1979	Dave Kingman, Chicago	48	1979	Gorman Thomas, Milwaukee	45
1980	Mike Schmidt, Philadelphia	48	1980	Reggie Jackson, New York; Ben Oglivie, Milwaukee	41
1981	Mike Schmidt, Philadelphia	31	1981	Bobby Grich, California; Tony Armas, Oakland; Dwight Evans, Boston; Eddie Murray, Baltimore	22
1982	Dave Kingman, New York	37	1982	Gorman Thomas, Milwaukee; Reggie Jackson, Cal.	39
1983	Mike Schmidt, Philadelphia	40	1983	Jim Rice, Boston	39
1984	Mike Schmidt, Phi.; Dale Murphy, Atlanta	36	1984	Tony Armas, Boston	43
1985	Dale Murphy, Atlanta	37	1985	Darrell Evans, Detroit	40
1986	Mike Schmidt, Philadelphia	37	1986	Jesse Barfield, Toronto	40
1987	Andre Dawson, Chicago	49	1987	Mark McGwire, Oakland	49
1988	Darryl Strawberry, New York	39	1988	Jose Canseco, Oakland	42
1989	Kevin Mitchell, San Francisco	47	1989	Fred McGriff, Toronto	36
1990	Ryne Sandberg, Chicago	40	1990	Cecil Fielder, Detroit	51
1991	Howard Johnson, New York	38	1991	Cecil Fielder, Detroit; Jose Canseco, Oakland	44
1992	Fred McGriff, San Diego	35	1992	Juan Gonzalez, Texas	43
1993	Barry Bonds, San Francisco	46	1993	Juan Gonzalez, Texas	46
1994	Matt Williams, San Francisco	43	1994	Ken Griffey Jr., Seattle	40
1995	Dante Bichette, Colorado	40	1995	Albert Belle, Cleveland	50
1996	Andres Galarraga, Colorado	47	1996	Mark McGwire, Oakland	52
1997[1]	Larry Walker, Colorado	49	1997[1]	Ken Griffey Jr., Seattle	56
1998	Mark McGwire, St. Louis	70	1998	Ken Griffey Jr., Seattle	56
1999	Mark McGwire, St. Louis	65	1999	Ken Griffey Jr., Seattle	48
2000	Sammy Sosa, Chicago	50	2000	Troy Glaus, Anaheim	47
2001	Barry Bonds, San Francisco	*73	2001	Alex Rodriguez, Texas	52
2002	Sammy Sosa, Chicago	49	2002	Alex Rodriguez, Texas	57
2003	Jim Thome, Philadelphia	47	2003	Alex Rodriguez, Texas	47

(1) In 1997, Mark McGwire hit 58 home runs; 34 with the Oakland Athletics (AL) and 24 with the St. Louis Cardinals (NL).

Runs Batted In Leaders

Note: Asterisk (*) indicates the all-time single-season record for each league since beginning of "modern" era in 1901.

	National League			American League	
Year	Player, Team	RBI	Year	Player, Team	RBI
1907	Sherwood Magee, Philadelphia	85	1907	Ty Cobb, Detroit	116
1908	Honus Wagner, Pittsburgh	109	1908	Ty Cobb, Detroit	108
1909	Honus Wagner, Pittsburgh	100	1909	Ty Cobb, Detroit	107
1910	Sherwood Magee, Philadelphia	123	1910	Sam Crawford, Detroit	120
1911	Frank Schulte, Chicago	121	1911	Ty Cobb, Detroit	144
1912	Henry Zimmerman, Chicago	103	1912	J. Franklin Baker, Philadelphia	133
1913	Gavvy Cravath, Philadelphia	128	1913	J. Franklin Baker, Philadelphia	126
1914	Sherwood Magee, Philadelphia	103	1914	Sam Crawford, Detroit	104
1915	Gavvy Cravath, Philadelphia	115	1915	Sam Crawford, Detroit; Robert Veach, Detroit	112
1916	Henry Zimmerman, Chicago-NewYork	83	1916	Del Pratt, St. Louis	103
1917	Henry Zimmerman, New York	102	1917	Robert Veach, Detroit	103
1918	Sherwood Magee, Philadelphia	76	1918	Robert Veach, Detroit	78
1919	Hi Myers, Boston	73	1919	Babe Ruth, Boston	114
1920	George Kelly, N.Y.; Rogers Hornsby, St. Louis	94	1920	Babe Ruth, New York	137
1921	Rogers Hornsby, St. Louis	126	1921	Babe Ruth, New York	171
1922	Rogers Hornsby, St. Louis	152	1922	Ken Williams, St. Louis	155
1923	Emil Meusel, New York	125	1923	Babe Ruth, New York	131
1924	George Kelly, New York	136	1924	Goose Goslin, Washington	129
1925	Rogers Hornsby, St. Louis	143	1925	Bob Meusel, New York	138
1926	Jim Bottomley, St. Louis	120	1926	Babe Ruth, New York	145
1927	Paul Waner, Pittsburgh	131	1927	Lou Gehrig, New York	175
1928	Jim Bottomley, St. Louis	136	1928	Babe Ruth, New York; Lou Gehrig, New York	142
1929	Hack Wilson, Chicago	159	1929	Al Simmons, Philadelphia	157
1930	Hack Wilson, Chicago	*191	1930	Lou Gehrig, New York	174
1931	Chuck Klein, Philadelphia	121	1931	Lou Gehrig, New York	*184
1932	Don Hurst, Philadelphia	143	1932	Jimmie Foxx, Philadelphia	169
1933	Chuck Klein, Philadelphia	120	1933	Jimmie Foxx, Philadelphia	163
1934	Mel Ott, New York	135	1934	Lou Gehrig, New York	165
1935	Walter Berger, Boston	130	1935	Hank Greenberg, Detroit	170
1936	Joe Medwick, St. Louis	138	1936	Hal Trosky, Cleveland	162
1937	Joe Medwick, St. Louis	154	1937	Hank Greenberg, Detroit	183
1938	Joe Medwick, St. Louis	122	1938	Jimmie Foxx, Boston	175
1939	Frank McCormick, Cincinnati	128	1939	Ted Williams, Boston	145
1940	John Mize, St. Louis	137	1940	Hank Greenberg, Detroit	150
1941	Adolph Camilli, Brooklyn	120	1941	Joe DiMaggio, New York	125
1942	John Mize, New York	110	1942	Ted Williams, Boston	137
1943	Bill Nicholson, Chicago	128	1943	Rudy York, Detroit	118
1944	Bill Nicholson, Chicago	122	1944	Vern Stephens, St. Louis	109
1945	Dixie Walker, Brooklyn	124	1945	Nick Etten, New York	111
1946	Enos Slaughter, St. Louis	130	1946	Hank Greenberg, Detroit	127
1947	John Mize, New York	138	1947	Ted Williams, Boston	114
1948	Stan Musial, St. Louis	131	1948	Joe DiMaggio, New York	155
1949	Ralph Kiner, Pittsburgh	127	1949	Ted Williams, Bos.; Vern Stephens, Bos.	159
1950	Del Ennis, Philadelphia	126	1950	Walt Dropo, Bos.; Vern Stephens, Bos.	144
1951	Monte Irvin, New York	121	1951	Gus Zernial, Chicago-Philadelphia	129
1952	Hank Sauer, Chicago	121	1952	Al Rosen, Cleveland	105
1953	Roy Campanella, Brooklyn	142	1953	Al Rosen, Cleveland	145
1954	Ted Kluszewski, Cincinnati	141	1954	Larry Doby, Cleveland	126
1955	Duke Snider, Brooklyn	136	1955	Ray Boone, Detroit; Jackie Jensen, Boston	116
1956	Stan Musial, St. Louis	109	1956	Mickey Mantle, New York	130
1957	Hank Aaron, Milwaukee	132	1957	Roy Sievers, Washington	114
1958	Ernie Banks, Chicago	129	1958	Jackie Jensen, Boston	122
1959	Ernie Banks, Chicago	143	1959	Jackie Jensen, Boston	112
1960	Hank Aaron, Milwaukee	126	1960	Roger Maris, New York	112
1961	Orlando Cepeda, San Francisco	142	1961	Roger Maris, New York	142
1962	Tommy Davis, Los Angeles	153	1962	Harmon Killebrew, Minnesota	126
1963	Hank Aaron, Milwaukee	130	1963	Dick Stuart, Boston	118
1964	Ken Boyer, St. Louis	119	1964	Brooks Robinson, Baltimore	118
1965	Deron Johnson, Cincinnati	130	1965	Rocky Colavito, Cleveland	108
1966	Hank Aaron, Atlanta	127	1966	Frank Robinson, Baltimore	122
1967	Orlando Cepeda, St. Louis	111	1967	Carl Yastrzemski, Boston	121
1968	Willie McCovey, San Francisco	105	1968	Ken Harrelson, Boston	109
1969	Willie McCovey, San Francisco	126	1969	Harmon Killebrew, Minnesota	140
1970	Johnny Bench, Cincinnati	148	1970	Frank Howard, Washington	126
1971	Joe Torre, St. Louis	137	1971	Harmon Killebrew, Minnesota	119
1972	Johnny Bench, Cincinnati	125	1972	Dick Allen, Chicago	113
1973	Willie Stargell, Pittsburgh	119	1973	Reggie Jackson, Oakland	117
1974	Johnny Bench, Cincinnati	129	1974	Jeff Burroughs, Texas	118
1975	Greg Luzinski, Philadelphia	120	1975	George Scott, Milwaukee	109
1976	George Foster, Cincinnati	121	1976	Lee May, Baltimore	109
1977	George Foster, Cincinnati	149	1977	Larry Hisle, Minnesota	119
1978	George Foster, Cincinnati	120	1978	Jim Rice, Boston	139
1979	Dave Winfield, San Diego	118	1979	Don Baylor, California	139
1980	Mike Schmidt, Philadelphia	121	1980	Cecil Cooper, Milwaukee	122
1981	Mike Schmidt, Philadelphia	91	1981	Eddie Murray, Baltimore	78
1982	Dale Murphy, Atlanta; Al Oliver, Montreal	109	1982	Hal McRae, Kansas City	133
1983	Dale Murphy, Atlanta	121	1983	Cecil Cooper, Milwaukee; Jim Rice, Boston	126
1984	Gary Carter, Montreal; Mike Schmidt, Phi.	106	1984	Tony Armas, Boston	123
1985	Dave Parker, Cincinnati	125	1985	Don Mattingly, New York	145
1986	Mike Schmidt, Philadelphia	119	1986	Joe Carter, Cleveland	121
1987	Andre Dawson, Chicago	137	1987	George Bell, Toronto	134
1988	Will Clark, San Francisco	109	1988	Jose Canseco, Oakland	124
1989	Kevin Mitchell, San Francisco	125	1989	Ruben Sierra, Texas	119
1990	Matt Williams, San Francisco	122	1990	Cecil Fielder, Detroit	132

Year	National League Player, Team	RBI	Year	American League Player, Team	RBI
1991	Howard Johnson, New York	117	1991	Cecil Fielder, Detroit	133
1992	Darren Daulton, Philadelphia	109	1992	Cecil Fielder, Detroit	124
1993	Barry Bonds, San Francisco	123	1993	Albert Belle, Cleveland	129
1994	Jeff Bagwell, Houston	116	1994	Kirby Puckett, Minnesota	112
1995	Dante Bichette, Colorado	128	1995	Albert Belle, Cleveland; Mo Vaughn, Boston	126
1996	Andres Galarraga, Colorado	150	1996	Albert Belle, Cleveland	148
1997	Andres Galarraga, Colorado	140	1997	Ken Griffey Jr., Seattle	147
1998	Sammy Sosa, Chicago	158	1998	Juan Gonzalez, Texas	157
1999	Mark McGwire, St. Louis	147	1999	Manny Ramirez, Cleveland	165
2000	Todd Helton, Colorado	147	2000	Edgar Martinez, Seattle	145
2001	Sammy Sosa, Chicago	160	2001	Bret Boone, Seattle	141
2002	Lance Berkman, Houston	128	2002	Alex Rodriguez, Texas	142
2003	Preston Wilson, Colorado	141	2003	Carlos Delgado, Toronto	145

Batting Champions

Note: Asterisk (*) indicates the all-time single-season record for each league since the beginning of the "modern" era in 1901.

Year	National League Player	Team	Avg.	Year	American League Player	Team	Avg.
1901	Jesse C. Burkett	St. Louis	.382	1901	Napoleon Lajoie	Philadelphia	.426*
1902	Clarence Beaumont	Pittsburgh	.357	1902	Ed Delahanty	Washington	.376
1903	Honus Wagner	Pittsburgh	.355	1903	Napoleon Lajoie	Cleveland	.355
1904	Honus Wagner	Pittsburgh	.349	1904	Napoleon Lajoie	Cleveland	.381
1905	James Seymour	Cincinnati	.377	1905	Elmer Flick	Cleveland	.306
1906	Honus Wagner	Pittsburgh	.339	1906	George Stone	St. Louis	.358
1907	Honus Wagner	Pittsburgh	.350	1907	Ty Cobb	Detroit	.350
1908	Honus Wagner	Pittsburgh	.354	1908	Ty Cobb	Detroit	.324
1909	Honus Wagner	Pittsburgh	.339	1909	Ty Cobb	Detroit	.377
1910	Sherwood Magee	Philadelphia	.331	1910[1]	Ty Cobb	Detroit	.385
1911	Honus Wagner	Pittsburgh	.334	1911	Ty Cobb	Detroit	.420
1912	Henry Zimmerman	Chicago	.372	1912	Ty Cobb	Detroit	.410
1913	Jacob Daubert	Brooklyn	.350	1913	Ty Cobb	Detroit	.390
1914	Jacob Daubert	Brooklyn	.329	1914	Ty Cobb	Detroit	.368
1915	Larry Doyle	New York	.320	1915	Ty Cobb	Detroit	.369
1916	Hal Chase	Cincinnati	.339	1916	Tris Speaker	Cleveland	.386
1917	Edd Roush	Cincinnati	.341	1917	Ty Cobb	Detroit	.383
1918	Zach Wheat	Brooklyn	.335	1918	Ty Cobb	Detroit	.382
1919	Edd Roush	Cincinnati	.321	1919	Ty Cobb	Detroit	.384
1920	Rogers Hornsby	St. Louis	.370	1920	George Sisler	St. Louis	.407
1921	Rogers Hornsby	St. Louis	.397	1921	Harry Heilmann	Detroit	.394
1922	Rogers Hornsby	St. Louis	.401	1922	George Sisler	St. Louis	.420
1923	Rogers Hornsby	St. Louis	.384	1923	Harry Heilmann	Detroit	.403
1924	Rogers Hornsby	St. Louis	*.424	1924	Babe Ruth	New York	.378
1925	Rogers Hornsby	St. Louis	.403	1925	Harry Heilmann	Detroit	.393
1926	Eugene Hargrave	Cincinnati	.353	1926	Henry Manush	Detroit	.378
1927	Paul Waner	Pittsburgh	.380	1927	Harry Heilmann	Detroit	.398
1928	Rogers Hornsby	Boston	.387	1928	Goose Goslin	Washington	.379
1929	Lefty O'Doul	Philadelphia	.398	1929	Lew Fonseca	Cleveland	.369
1930	Bill Terry	New York	.401	1930	Al Simmons	Philadelphia	.381
1931	Chick Hafey	St. Louis	.349	1931	Al Simmons	Philadelphia	.390
1932	Lefty O'Doul	Brooklyn	.368	1932	Dale Alexander	Detroit-Boston	.367
1933	Chuck Klein	Philadelphia	.368	1933	Jimmie Foxx	Philadelphia	.356
1934	Paul Waner	Pittsburgh	.362	1934	Lou Gehrig	New York	.363
1935	Arky Vaughan	Pittsburgh	.385	1935	Buddy Myer	Washington	.349
1936	Paul Waner	Pittsburgh	.373	1936	Luke Appling	Chicago	.388
1937	Joe Medwick	St. Louis	.374	1937	Charlie Gehringer	Detroit	.371
1938	Ernie Lombardi	Cincinnati	.342	1938	Jimmie Foxx	Boston	.349
1939	John Mize	St. Louis	.349	1939	Joe DiMaggio	New York	.381
1940	Debs Garms	Pittsburgh	.355	1940	Joe DiMaggio	New York	.352
1941	Pete Reiser	Brooklyn	.343	1941	Ted Williams	Boston	.406
1942	Ernie Lombardi	Boston	.330	1942	Ted Williams	Boston	.356
1943	Stan Musial	St. Louis	.357	1943	Luke Appling	Chicago	.328
1944	Dixie Walker	Brooklyn	.357	1944	Lou Boudreau	Cleveland	.327
1945	Phil Cavarretta	Chicago	.355	1945	George Stirnweiss	New York	.309
1946	Stan Musial	St. Louis	.365	1946	Mickey Vernon	Washington	.353
1947	Harry Walker	St.L.-Phi.	.363	1947	Ted Williams	Boston	.343
1948	Stan Musial	St. Louis	.376	1948	Ted Williams	Boston	.369
1949	Jackie Robinson	Brooklyn	.342	1949	George Kell	Detroit	.343
1950	Stan Musial	St. Louis	.346	1950	Billy Goodman	Boston	.354
1951	Stan Musial	St. Louis	.355	1951	Ferris Fain	Philadelphia	.344
1952	Stan Musial	St. Louis	.336	1952	Ferris Fain	Philadelphia	.327
1953	Carl Furillo	Brooklyn	.344	1953	Mickey Vernon	Washington	.337
1954	Willie Mays	New York	.345	1954	Roberto Avila	Cleveland	.341
1955	Richie Ashburn	Philadelphia	.338	1955	Al Kaline	Detroit	.340
1956	Hank Aaron	Milwaukee	.328	1956	Mickey Mantle	New York	.353
1957	Stan Musial	St. Louis	.351	1957	Ted Williams	Boston	.388
1958	Richie Ashburn	Philadelphia	.350	1958	Ted Williams	Boston	.328
1959	Hank Aaron	Milwaukee	.355	1959	Harvey Kuenn	Detroit	.353
1960	Dick Groat	Pittsburgh	.325	1960	Pete Runnels	Boston	.320
1961	Roberto Clemente	Pittsburgh	.351	1961	Norm Cash	Detroit	.361
1962	Tommy Davis	Los Angeles	.346	1962	Pete Runnels	Boston	.326
1963	Tommy Davis	Los Angeles	.326	1963	Carl Yastrzemski	Boston	.321
1964	Roberto Clemente	Pittsburgh	.339	1964	Tony Oliva	Minnesota	.323
1965	Roberto Clemente	Pittsburgh	.329	1965	Tony Oliva	Minnesota	.321
1966	Matty Alou	Pittsburgh	.342	1966	Frank Robinson	Baltimore	.316
1967	Roberto Clemente	Pittsburgh	.357	1967	Carl Yastrzemski	Boston	.326
1968	Pete Rose	Cincinnati	.335	1968	Carl Yastrzemski	Boston	.301

National League				American League			
Year	Player	Team	Avg.	Year	Player	Team	Avg.
1969	Pete Rose	Cincinnati	.348	1969	Rod Carew	Minnesota	.332
1970	Rico Carty	Atlanta	.366	1970	Alex Johnson	California	.329
1971	Joe Torre	St. Louis	.363	1971	Tony Oliva	Minnesota	.337
1972	Billy Williams	Chicago	.333	1972	Rod Carew	Minnesota	.318
1973	Pete Rose	Cincinnati	.338	1973	Rod Carew	Minnesota	.350
1974	Ralph Garr	Atlanta	.353	1974	Rod Carew	Minnesota	.364
1975	Bill Madlock	Chicago	.354	1975	Rod Carew	Minnesota	.359
1976	Bill Madlock	Chicago	.339	1976	George Brett	Kansas City	.333
1977	Dave Parker	Pittsburgh	.338	1977	Rod Carew	Minnesota	.388
1978	Dave Parker	Pittsburgh	.334	1978	Rod Carew	Minnesota	.333
1979	Keith Hernandez	St. Louis	.344	1979	Fred Lynn	Boston	.333
1980	Bill Buckner	Chicago	.324	1980	George Brett	Kansas City	.390
1981	Bill Madlock	Pittsburgh	.341	1981	Carney Lansford	Boston	.336
1982	Al Oliver	Montreal	.331	1982	Willie Wilson	Kansas City	.332
1983	Bill Madlock	Pittsburgh	.323	1983	Wade Boggs	Boston	.361
1984	Tony Gwynn	San Diego	.351	1984	Don Mattingly	New York	.343
1985	Willie McGee	St. Louis	.353	1985	Wade Boggs	Boston	.368
1986	Tim Raines	Montreal	.334	1986	Wade Boggs	Boston	.357
1987	Tony Gwynn	San Diego	.370	1987	Wade Boggs	Boston	.363
1988	Tony Gwynn	San Diego	.313	1988	Wade Boggs	Boston	.366
1989	Tony Gwynn	San Diego	.336	1989	Kirby Puckett	Minnesota	.339
1990	Willie McGee	St. Louis	.335	1990	George Brett	Kansas City	.329
1991	Terry Pendleton	Atlanta	.319	1991	Julio Franco	Texas	.341
1992	Gary Sheffield	San Diego	.330	1992	Edgar Martinez	Seattle	.343
1993	Andres Galarraga	Colorado	.370	1993	John Olerud	Toronto	.363
1994	Tony Gwynn	San Diego	.394	1994	Paul O'Neill	New York	.359
1995	Tony Gwynn	San Diego	.368	1995	Edgar Martinez	Seattle	.356
1996	Tony Gwynn	San Diego	.353	1996	Alex Rodriguez	Seattle	.358
1997	Tony Gwynn	San Diego	.372	1997	Frank Thomas	Chicago	.347
1998	Larry Walker	Colorado	.363	1998	Bernie Williams	New York	.339
1999	Larry Walker	Colorado	.379	1999	Nomar Garciaparra	Boston	.357
2000	Todd Helton	Colorado	.372	2000	Nomar Garciaparra	Boston	.372
2001	Larry Walker	Colorado	.350	2001	Ichiro Suzuki	Seattle	.350
2002	Barry Bonds	San Francisco	.370	2002	Manny Ramirez	Boston	.349
2003	Albert Pujols	St. Louis	.359	2003	Bill Mueller	Boston	.326

(1) Some baseball researchers have concluded that Ty Cobb actually hit .382 in 1910 while Napoleon Lajoie, Cleveland, hit .383.

Cy Young Award Winners

Year	Player, Team	Year	Player, Team	Year	Player, Team
1956	Don Newcombe, Dodgers	1976	(NL) Randy Jones, Padres	1991	(NL) Tom Glavine, Braves
1957	Warren Spahn, Braves		(AL) Jim Palmer, Orioles		(AL) Roger Clemens, Red Sox
1958	Bob Turley, Yankees	1977	(NL) Steve Carlton, Phillies	1992	(NL) Greg Maddux, Cubs
1959	Early Wynn, White Sox		(AL) Sparky Lyle, Yankees		(AL) Dennis Eckersley, A's
1960	Vernon Law, Pirates	1978	(NL) Gaylord Perry, Padres	1993	(NL) Greg Maddux, Braves
1961	Whitey Ford, Yankees		(AL) Ron Guidry, Yankees		(AL) Jack McDowell, White Sox
1962	Don Drysdale, Dodgers	1979	(NL) Bruce Sutter, Cubs	1994	(NL) Greg Maddux, Braves
1963	Sandy Koufax, Dodgers		(AL) Mike Flanagan, Orioles		(AL) David Cone, Royals
1964	Dean Chance, Angels	1980	(NL) Steve Carlton, Phillies	1995	(NL) Greg Maddux, Braves
1965	Sandy Koufax, Dodgers		(AL) Steve Stone, Orioles		(AL) Randy Johnson, Mariners
1966	Sandy Koufax, Dodgers	1981	(NL) Fernando Valenzuela, Dodgers	1996	(NL) John Smoltz, Braves
1967	(NL) Mike McCormick, Giants		(AL) Rollie Fingers, Brewers		(AL) Pat Hentgen, Blue Jays
	(AL) Jim Lonborg, Red Sox	1982	(NL) Steve Carlton, Phillies	1997	(NL) Pedro Martinez, Expos
1968	(NL) Bob Gibson, Cardinals		(AL) Pete Vuckovich, Brewers		(AL) Roger Clemens, Blue Jays
	(AL) Dennis McLain, Tigers	1983	(NL) John Denny, Phillies	1998	(NL) Tom Glavine, Braves
1969	(NL) Tom Seaver, Mets		(AL) LaMarr Hoyt, White Sox		(AL) Roger Clemens, Blue Jays
	(AL) (tie) Dennis McLain, Tigers	1984	(NL) Rick Sutcliffe, Cubs	1999	(NL) Randy Johnson,
	Mike Cuellar, Orioles		(AL) Willie Hernandez, Tigers		Diamondbacks
1970	(NL) Bob Gibson, Cardinals	1985	(NL) Dwight Gooden, Mets		(AL) Pedro Martinez, Red Sox
	(AL) Jim Perry, Twins		(AL) Bret Saberhagen, Royals	2000	(NL) Randy Johnson,
1971	(NL) Ferguson Jenkins, Cubs	1986	(NL) Mike Scott, Astros		Diamondbacks
	(AL) Vida Blue, A's		(AL) Roger Clemens, Red Sox		(AL) Pedro Martinez, Red Sox
1972	(NL) Steve Carlton, Phillies	1987	(NL) Steve Bedrosian, Phillies	2001	(NL) Randy Johnson,
	(AL) Gaylord Perry, Indians		(AL) Roger Clemens, Red Sox		Diamondbacks
1973	(NL) Tom Seaver, Mets	1988	(NL) Orel Hershiser, Dodgers		(AL) Roger Clemens, Yankees
	(AL) Jim Palmer, Orioles		(AL) Frank Viola, Twins	2002	(NL) Randy Johnson, Diamondbacks
1974	(NL) Mike Marshall, Dodgers	1989	(NL) Mark Davis, Padres		(AL) Barry Zito, A's
	(AL) Jim (Catfish) Hunter, A's		(AL) Bret Saberhagen, Royals		
1975	(NL) Tom Seaver, Mets	1990	(NL) Doug Drabek, Pirates		
	(AL) Jim Palmer, Orioles		(AL) Bob Welch, A's		

Most Valuable Player

(As selected by the Baseball Writers' Assoc. of America. Prior to 1931, MVP honors were named by various sources.)

National League

Year	Player, team	Year	Player, team	Year	Player, team
1931	Frank Frisch, St. Louis	1942	Mort Cooper, St. Louis	1953	Roy Campanella, Brooklyn
1932	Chuck Klein, Philadelphia	1943	Stan Musial, St. Louis	1954	Willie Mays, N.Y.
1933	Carl Hubbell, New York	1944	Martin Marion, St. Louis	1955	Roy Campanella, Brooklyn
1934	Dizzy Dean, St. Louis	1945	Phil Cavarretta, Chicago	1956	Don Newcombe, Brooklyn
1935	Gabby Hartnett, Chicago	1946	Stan Musial, St. Louis	1957	Hank Aaron, Milwaukee
1936	Carl Hubbell, N.Y.	1947	Bob Elliott, Boston	1958	Ernie Banks, Chicago
1937	Joe Medwick, St. Louis	1948	Stan Musial, St. Louis	1959	Ernie Banks, Chicago
1938	Ernie Lombardi, Cincinnati	1949	Jackie Robinson, Brooklyn	1960	Dick Groat, Pittsburgh
1939	Bucky Walters, Cincinnati	1950	Jim Konstanty, Philadelphia	1961	Frank Robinson, Cincinnati
1940	Frank McCormick, Cincinnati	1951	Roy Campanella, Brooklyn	1962	Maury Wills, L.A.
1941	Dolph Camilli, Brooklyn	1952	Hank Sauer, Chicago	1963	Sandy Koufax, L.A.

Year	Player, team	Year	Player, team	Year	Player, team
1964	Ken Boyer, St. Louis	1977	George Foster, Cincinnati	1990	Barry Bonds, Pittsburgh
1965	Willie Mays, San Francisco	1978	Dave Parker, Pittsburgh	1991	Terry Pendleton, Atlanta
1966	Roberto Clemente, Pittsburgh	(tie)	Keith Hernandez, St. Louis	1992	Barry Bonds, Pittsburgh
1967	Orlando Cepeda, St. Louis	1980	Mike Schmidt, Philadelphia	1993	Barry Bonds, San Francisco
1968	Bob Gibson, St. Louis	1981	Mike Schmidt, Philadelphia	1994	Jeff Bagwell, Houston
1969	Willie McCovey, San Francisco	1982	Dale Murphy, Atlanta	1995	Barry Larkin, Cincinnati
1970	Johnny Bench, Cincinnati	1983	Dale Murphy, Atlanta	1996	Ken Caminiti, San Diego
1971	Joe Torre, St. Louis	1984	Ryne Sandberg, Chicago	1997	Larry Walker, Colorado
1972	Johnny Bench, Cincinnati	1985	Willie McGee, St. Louis	1998	Sammy Sosa, Chicago
1973	Pete Rose, Cincinnati	1986	Mike Schmidt, Philadelphia	1999	Chipper Jones, Atlanta
1974	Steve Garvey, L.A.	1987	Andre Dawson, Chicago	2000	Jeff Kent, San Francisco
1975	Joe Morgan, Cincinnati	1988	Kirk Gibson, L.A.	2001	Barry Bonds, San Francisco
1976	Joe Morgan, Cincinnati	1989	Kevin Mitchell, San Francisco	2002	Barry Bonds, San Francisco

American League

Year	Player, team	Year	Player, team	Year	Player, team
1931	Lefty Grove, Philadelphia	1955	Yogi Berra, N.Y.	1979	Don Baylor, California
1932	Jimmie Foxx, Philadelphia	1956	Mickey Mantle, N.Y.	1980	George Brett, Kansas City
1933	Jimmie Foxx, Philadelphia	1957	Mickey Mantle, N.Y.	1981	Rollie Fingers, Milwaukee
1934	Mickey Cochrane, Detroit	1958	Jackie Jensen, Boston	1982	Robin Yount, Milwaukee
1935	Hank Greenberg, Detroit	1959	Nellie Fox, Chicago	1983	Cal Ripken, Jr., Baltimore
1936	Lou Gehrig, N.Y.	1960	Roger Maris, N.Y.	1984	Willie Hernandez, Detroit
1937	Charley Gehringer, Detroit	1961	Roger Maris, N.Y.	1985	Don Mattingly, N.Y.
1938	Jimmie Foxx, Boston	1962	Mickey Mantle, N.Y.	1986	Roger Clemens, Boston
1939	Joe DiMaggio, N.Y.	1963	Elston Howard, N.Y.	1987	George Bell, Toronto
1940	Hank Greenberg, Detroit	1964	Brooks Robinson, Baltimore	1988	Jose Canseco, Oakland
1941	Joe DiMaggio, N.Y.	1965	Zoilo Versalles, Minnesota	1989	Robin Yount, Milwaukee
1942	Joe Gordon, N.Y.	1966	Frank Robinson, Baltimore	1990	Rickey Henderson, Oakland
1943	Spurgeon Chandler, N.Y.	1967	Carl Yastrzemski, Boston	1991	Cal Ripken, Jr., Baltimore
1944	Hal Newhouser, Detroit	1968	Denny McLain, Detroit	1992	Dennis Eckersley, Oakland
1945	Hal Newhouser, Detroit	1969	Harmon Killebrew, Minnesota	1993	Frank Thomas, Chicago
1946	Ted Williams, Boston	1970	John (Boog) Powell, Baltimore	1994	Frank Thomas, Chicago
1947	Joe DiMaggio, N.Y.	1971	Vida Blue, Oakland	1995	Mo Vaughn, Boston
1948	Lou Boudreau, Cleveland	1972	Dick Allen, Chicago	1996	Juan Gonzalez, Texas
1949	Ted Williams, Boston	1973	Reggie Jackson, Oakland	1997	Ken Griffey Jr., Seattle
1950	Phil Rizzuto, N.Y.	1974	Jeff Burroughs, Texas	1998	Juan Gonzalez, Texas
1951	Yogi Berra, N.Y.	1975	Fred Lynn, Boston	1999	Ivan Rodriguez, Texas
1952	Bobby Shantz, Philadelphia	1976	Thurman Munson, N.Y.	2000	Jason Giambi, Oakland
1953	Al Rosen, Cleveland	1977	Rod Carew, Minnesota	2001	Ichiro Suzuki, Seattle
1954	Yogi Berra, N.Y.	1978	Jim Rice, Boston	2002	Miguel Tejada, Oakland

Rookie of the Year

(As selected by the Baseball Writers' Assoc. of America)

1947—Combined selection—Jackie Robinson, Brooklyn, 1b; 1948—Combined selection—Alvin Dark, Boston, N.L., ss

National League

Year	Player, team	Year	Player, team	Year	Player, team
1949	Don Newcombe, Brooklyn, p	1968	Johnny Bench, Cincinnati, c	1985	Vince Coleman, St. Louis, of
1950	Sam Jethroe, Boston, of	1969	Ted Sizemore, L.A., 2b	1986	Todd Worrell, St. Louis, p
1951	Willie Mays, N.Y., of	1970	Carl Morton, Montreal, p	1987	Benito Santiago, San Diego, c
1952	Joe Black, Brooklyn, p	1971	Earl Williams, Atlanta, c	1988	Chris Sabo, Cincinnati, 3b
1953	Jim Gilliam, Brooklyn, 2b	1972	Jon Matlack, N.Y., p	1989	Jerome Walton, Chicago, of
1954	Wally Moon, St. Louis, of	1973	Gary Matthews, S.F., of	1990	Dave Justice, Atlanta, 1b
1955	Bill Virdon, St. Louis, of	1974	Bake McBride, St. Louis, of	1991	Jeff Bagwell, Houston, 1b
1956	Frank Robinson, Cincinnati, of	1975	John Montefusco, S.F., p	1992	Eric Karros, L.A., 1b
1957	Jack Sanford, Philadelphia, p	1976	Butch Metzger, San Diego, p	1993	Mike Piazza, L.A., c
1958	Orlando Cepeda, S.F., 1b	(tie)	Pat Zachry, Cincinnati, p	1994	Raul Mondesi, L.A., of
1959	Willie McCovey, S.F., 1b	1977	Andre Dawson, Montreal, of	1995	Hideo Nomo, L.A., p
1960	Frank Howard, L.A., of	1978	Bob Horner, Atlanta, 3b	1996	Todd Hollandsworth, L.A., of
1961	Billy Williams, Chicago, of	1979	Rick Sutcliffe, L.A., p	1997	Scott Rolen, Philadelphia, 3b
1962	Ken Hubbs, Chicago, 2b	1980	Steve Howe, L.A., p	1998	Kerry Wood, Chicago, p
1963	Pete Rose, Cincinnati, 2b	1981	Fernando Valenzuela, L.A., p	1999	Scott Williamson, Cincinnati, p
1964	Richie Allen, Philadelphia, 3b	1982	Steve Sax, L.A., 2b	2000	Rafael Furcal, Atlanta, ss
1965	Jim Lefebvre, L.A., 2b	1983	Darryl Strawberry, N.Y., of	2001	Albert Pujols, St. Louis, of
1966	Tommy Helms, Cincinnati, 2b	1984	Dwight Gooden, N.Y., p	2002	Jason Jennings, Colorado, P
1967	Tom Seaver, N.Y., p				

American League

Year	Player, team	Year	Player, team	Year	Player, team
1949	Roy Sievers, St. Louis, of	1968	Stan Bahnsen, N.Y., p	1985	Ozzie Guillen, Chicago, ss
1950	Walt Dropo, Boston, of	1969	Lou Piniella, Kansas City, of	1986	Jose Canseco, Oakland, of
1951	Gil McDougald, N.Y., 3b	1970	Thurman Munson, N.Y., c	1987	Mark McGwire, Oakland, 1b
1952	Harry Byrd, Philadelphia, p	1971	Chris Chambliss, Cleveland, 1b	1988	Walt Weiss, Oakland, ss
1953	Harvey Kuenn, Detroit, ss	1972	Carlton Fisk, Boston, c	1989	Gregg Olson, Baltimore, p
1954	Bob Grim, N.Y., p	1973	Al Bumbry, Baltimore, of	1990	Sandy Alomar, Jr., Cleveland, c
1955	Herb Score, Cleveland, p	1974	Mike Hargrove, Texas, 1b	1991	Chuck Knoblauch, Minnesota, 2b
1956	Luis Aparicio, Chicago, ss	1975	Fred Lynn, Boston, of	1992	Pat Listach, Milwaukee, ss
1957	Tony Kubek, N.Y., if-of	1976	Mark Fidrych, Detroit, p	1993	Tim Salmon, California, of
1958	Albie Pearson, Washington, of	1977	Eddie Murray, Baltimore, dh	1994	Bob Hamelin, Kansas City, dh
1959	Bob Allison, Washington, of	1978	Lou Whitaker, Detroit, 2b	1995	Marty Cordova, Minnesota, of
1960	Ron Hansen, Baltimore, ss	1979	John Castino, Minnesota, 3b	1996	Derek Jeter, N.Y., ss
1961	Don Schwall, Boston, p	(tie)	Alfredo Griffin, Toronto, ss	1997	Nomar Garciaparra, Boston, ss
1962	Tom Tresh, N.Y., if-of	1980	Joe Charboneau, Cleveland, of	1998	Ben Grieve, Oakland, of
1963	Gary Peters, Chicago, p	1981	Dave Righetti, N.Y., p	1999	Carlos Beltran, Kansas City, of
1964	Tony Oliva, Minnesota, of	1982	Cal Ripken, Jr., Baltimore, ss	2000	Kazuhiro Sasaki, Seattle, p
1965	Curt Blefary, Baltimore, of	1983	Ron Kittle, Chicago, of	2001	Ichiro Suzuki, Seattle, of
1966	Tommie Agee, Chicago, of	1984	Alvin Davis, Seattle, 1b	2002	Eric Hinske, Toronto, 3b
1967	Rod Carew, Minnesota, 2b				

WORLD ALMANAC EDITORS' PICKS
2003 All-World Baseball Team

The editors of *The World Almanac* have chosen the following as the best players at each position based on 2003 regular season performance.

Position	World Almanac 2003 Best	Position	World Almanac 2003 Best
1st base	Todd Helton (Colorado Rockies)	Catcher	Javy Lopez (Atlanta Braves)
2nd base	Brett Boone (Seattle Mariners)	Right-handed starting pitcher	Mark Prior (Chicago Cubs)
3rd base	Scott Rolen (St. Louis Cardinals)	Left-handed starting pitcher	Jamie Moyer (Seattle Mariners)
Shortstop	Alex Rodriguez (Texas Rangers)	Right-handed relief pitcher	Eric Gagne (Los Angeles Dodgers)
Left field	Albert Pujols (St. Louis Cardinals)	Left-handed relief pitcher	Billy Wagner (Houston Astros)
Center field	Vernon Wells (Toronto Blue Jays)	Designated hitter	Rafael Palmeiro (Texas Rangers)
Right field	Gary Sheffield (Atlanta Braves)		

Manager of the Year

1983	(NL) Tommy Lasorda, L.A.	1990	(NL) Jim Leyland, Pittsburgh	1997	(NL) Dusty Baker, San Francisco	
	(AL) Tony La Russa, Chicago		(AL) Jeff Torborg, Chicago		(AL) Davey Johnson, Baltimore	
1984	(NL) Jim Frey, Chicago	1991	(NL) Bobby Cox, Atlanta	1998	(NL) Larry Dierker, Houston	
	(AL) Sparky Anderson, Detroit		(AL) Tom Kelly, Minnesota		(AL) Joe Torre, N.Y.	
1985	(NL) Whitey Herzog, St. Louis	1992	(NL) Jim Leyland, Pittsburgh	1999	(NL) Jack McKeon, Cincinnati	
	(AL) Bobby Cox, Toronto		(AL) Tony La Russa, Oakland		(AL) Jimy Williams, Boston	
1986	(NL) Hal Lanier, Houston	1993	(NL) Dusty Baker, San Francisco	2000	(NL) Dusty Baker, San Francisco	
	(AL) John McNamara, Boston		(AL) Gene Lamont, Chicago		(AL) Jerry Manuel, Chicago	
1987	(NL) Buck Rodgers, Montreal	1994	(NL) Felipe Alou, Montreal	2001	(NL) Larry Bowa, Philadelphia	
	(AL) Sparky Anderson, Detroit		(AL) Buck Showalter, N.Y.		(AL) Lou Piniella, Seattle	
1988	(NL) Tommy Lasorda, L.A.	1995	(NL) Don Baylor, Colorado	2002	(NL) Tony La Russa, St. Louis	
	(AL) Tony La Russa, Oakland		(AL) Lou Piniella, Seattle		(AL) Mike Scioscia, Anaheim	
1989	(NL) Don Zimmer, Chicago	1996	(NL) Bruce Bochy, San Diego			
	(AL) Frank Robinson, Blatimore		(AL) (tie) Joe Torre, N.Y. Johnny Oates, Texas			

The Rawlings Gold Glove Awards: 2002 and All-Time Leaders

American League

Kenny Rogers, Texas, p	Alex Rodriguez, Texas, ss
Bengie Molina, Anaheim, c	Darin Erstad, Anaheim, of
John Olerud, Seattle, 1b	Ichiro Suzuki, Seattle, of
Bret Boone, Seattle, 2b	Torii Hunter, Minnesota, of
Eric Chavez, Oakland, 3b	

National League

Greg Maddux, Atlanta, p	Edgar Renteria, St. Louis, ss
Brad Ausmus, Houston, c	Andruw Jones, Atlanta, of
Todd Helton, Colorado, 1b	Larry Walker, Colorado, of
Fernando Vina, St. Louis, 2b	Jim Edmonds, St Louis, of
Scott Rolen, St. Louis, 3b	

The following are the players at each position who have won the most Gold Gloves since the award was instituted in 1957.

Pitcher:	Jim Kaat 16	Second base:	Roberto Alomar 10	Shortstop:	Ozzie Smith 13
	Greg Maddux 13		Ryne Sandberg 9		Luis Aparicio 9
Catcher:	Johnny Bench 10		Bill Mazeroski 8	Outfield:	Roberto Clemente 12
	Ivan Rodriguez 10		Frank White 8		Willie Mays. 12
First base:	Keith Hernandez 11	Third base:	Brooks Robinson 16		Al Kaline 10
	Don Mattingly 9		Mike Schmidt 10		Ken Griffey Jr. 10

National League Final Standings, 2003

Eastern Division

	W	L	Pct.	GB	Home	Road	vs. East	vs. Central	vs. West	vs. AL
Atlanta	101	61	.623	—	55-26	46-35	41-35	27-12	23-9	10-5
Florida*	91	71	.562	10.0	53-28	38-43	48-28	19-20	15-17	9-6
Philadelphia	86	76	.531	15.0	49-32	37-44	39-37	21-18	18-14	8-7
Montreal	83	79	.512	18.0	52-29	31-50	35-41	20-16	19-13	9-9
New York	66	95	.410	34.5	34-46	32-49	27-49	17-22	17-14	5-10

Central Division

	W	L	Pct.	GB	Home	Road	vs. East	vs. Central	vs. West	vs. AL
Chicago	88	74	.543	—	44-37	44-37	15-15	47-37	17-13	9-9
Houston	87	75	.537	1.0	48-33	39-42	13-17	49-35	14-16	11-7
St. Louis	85	77	.525	3.0	48-33	37-44	17-13	46-38	12-18	10-8
Pittsburgh	75	87	.463	13.0	39-42	36-45	15-18	39-45	16-17	5-7
Cincinnati	69	93	.426	19.0	35-46	34-47	14-19	34-50	14-19	7-5
Milwaukee	68	94	.420	20.0	31-50	37-44	14-22	37-47	12-18	5-7

Western Division

	W	L	Pct.	GB	Home	Road	vs. East	vs. Central	vs. West	vs. AL
San Francisco	100	61	.621	—	57-24	43-37	14-17	23-13	53-23	10-8
Los Angeles	85	77	.525	15.5	46-35	39-42	16-16	23-13	35-41	11-7
Arizona	84	78	.519	16.5	45-36	39-42	16-16	23-16	34-42	11-4
Colorado	74	88	.457	26.5	49-32	25-56	11-21	19-20	35-41	9-6
San Diego	64	98	.395	36.5	35-46	29-52	10-22	13-23	33-43	8-10

*Wild card team.

National League Statistics, 2003

(Individual Statistics: Batting—at least 150 at-bats; Pitching—at least 70 innings or 10 saves; *changed teams within NL during season; entry includes statistics for more than 1 team; # changed teams to or from AL during season; entry includes only NL stats)

Team Batting

Team	BAT	AB	R	H	HR	RBI
Atlanta	.284	5670	907	1608	235	872
St. Louis	.279	5672	876	1580	196	827
Pittsburgh	.267	5581	753	1492	163	711
Colorado	.267	5518	853	1472	198	814
Florida	.266	5490	751	1459	157	709
San Francisco	.264	5456	755	1440	180	713
Arizona	.263	5570	717	1467	152	696
Houston	.263	5583	805	1466	191	763
Philadelphia	.261	5543	791	1448	166	757
San Diego	.261	5531	678	1442	128	641
Chicago	.259	5519	724	1431	172	691
Montreal	.258	5437	711	1404	144	682
Milwaukee	.256	5548	714	1423	196	685
New York	.247	5341	642	1317	124	607
Cincinnati	.245	5509	694	1349	182	669
Los Angeles	.243	5458	574	1328	124	544

Team Pitching

Team	ERA	IP	H	SO	BB	SV
Los Angeles	3.16	1457.2	1254	1289	526	58
San Francisco	3.73	1437.1	1349	1006	546	43
Chicago	3.83	1456.1	1304	1404	617	36
Arizona	3.84	1455.0	1379	1291	526	42
Houston	3.86	1450.0	1350	1139	565	50
Montreal	4.01	1437.2	1467	1028	463	42
Florida	4.04	1445.1	1415	1132	530	36
Philadelphia	4.04	1443.2	1386	1060	536	33
Atlanta	4.10	1456.1	1425	992	555	51
New York	4.48	1413.1	1497	907	576	38
St. Louis	4.60	1463.2	1544	969	508	41
Pittsburgh	4.64	1444.1	1527	926	502	44
San Diego	4.87	1431.1	1458	1091	611	31
Milwaukee	5.02	1452.0	1590	1034	575	44
Cincinnati	5.09	1446.1	1578	932	590	30
Colorado	5.20	1420.0	1629	866	552	34

Arizona Diamondbacks

BATTERS	BA	AB	R	H	HR	RBI	SO	SB
C. Baerga	.343	207	31	71	4	39	20	1
A. Cintron	.317	448	70	142	13	51	33	2
L. Gonzalez	.304	579	92	176	26	104	67	5
R. Mondesi#	.302	162	27	49	8	22	31	5
S. Finley	.287	516	82	148	22	70	94	15
R. Hammock	.282	195	30	55	8	28	44	3
L. Overbay	.276	254	23	70	4	28	67	1
D. Bautista	.275	284	29	78	4	36	50	3
C. Moeller	.268	239	29	64	7	29	59	1
S. Hillenbrand#	.267	330	40	88	17	59	44	0
M. Kata	.257	288	42	74	7	29	53	3
J. Spivey	.255	365	52	93	13	50	95	4
C. Counsell	.234	303	40	71	3	21	32	11
Q. McCracken	.227	203	17	46	0	18	34	5
R. Barajas	.218	220	19	48	3	28	43	0
PITCHERS	W-L	ERA	IP	H	BB	SO	SV	
J. Valverde	2-1	2.15	50.1	24	26	71	10	
O. Villarreal	10-7	2.57	98.0	80	46	80	0	
M. Mantei	5-4	2.62	55.0	37	18	68	29	
B. Webb	10-9	2.84	180.2	140	68	172	0	
C. Schilling	8-9	2.95	168.0	144	32	194	0	
M. Batista	10-9	3.54	193.1	197	60	142	0	
R. Johnson	6-8	4.26	114.0	125	27	125	0	
E. Dessens	8-8	5.07	175.2	212	57	113	0	
Manager-Bob Brenly								

Atlanta Braves

BATTERS	BA	AB	R	H	HR	RBI	SO	SB
G. Sheffield	.330	576	126	190	39	132	55	18
J. Lopez	.328	457	89	150	43	109	90	0
M. Giles	.316	551	101	174	21	69	80	14
C. Jones	.305	555	103	169	27	106	83	2
J. Franco	.294	197	28	58	5	31	43	0
R. Furcal	.292	664	130	194	15	61	76	25
A. Jones	.277	595	101	165	36	116	125	4
V. Castilla	.277	542	65	150	22	76	86	1
R. Fick	.269	409	52	110	11	80	47	1
M. DeRosa	.263	266	40	70	6	22	49	1
D. Bragg	.241	162	21	39	0	9	38	2
H. Blanco	.199	151	11	30	1	13	21	0
PITCHERS	W-L	ERA	IP	H	BB	SO	SV	
J. Smoltz	0-2	1.12	64.1	48	8	73	45	
R. Ortiz	21-7	3.81	212.1	177	102	149	0	
M. Hampton	14-8	3.84	190.0	186	78	110	0	
G. Maddux	16-11	3.96	218.1	225	33	124	0	
H. Ramirez	12-4	4.00	182.1	181	72	100	0	
S. Reynolds	11-9	5.43	167.1	191	59	94	0	
Manager-Bobby Cox								

Chicago Cubs

BATTERS	BA	AB	R	H	HR	RBI	SO	SB
M. Grudzielanek	.314	481	73	151	3	38	64	6
C. Patterson	.298	329	49	98	13	55	77	16
K. Lofton*	.296	547	97	162	12	46	51	30
T. Goodwin	.287	171	26	49	1	12	33	19
E. Karros	.286	336	37	96	12	40	46	1
R. Martinez	.283	293	30	83	3	34	50	0
M. Alou	.280	565	83	158	22	91	67	3
S. Sosa	.279	517	99	144	40	103	143	0
R. Simon*	.276	410	47	113	16	72	37	0
A. Ramirez*	.272	607	75	165	27	106	99	2
D. Miller	.233	352	34	82	9	36	91	1
P. Bako	.229	188	19	43	0	17	47	0
A. Gonzalez	.228	536	71	122	20	59	123	3
T. Womack*	.226	349	43	79	2	22	47	13
H. Choi	.218	202	31	44	8	28	71	1
T. O'Leary	.218	174	18	38	5	28	31	3
PITCHERS	W-L	ERA	IP	H	BB	SO	SV	
M. Prior	18-6	2.43	211.1	183	50	245	0	
J. Borowski	2-2	2.63	68.1	53	19	66	33	
C. Zambrano	13-11	3.11	214.0	188	94	168	0	
K. Wood	14-11	3.20	211.0	152	100	266	0	
K. Farnsworth	3-2	3.30	76.1	53	36	92	0	
M. Clement	14-12	4.11	201.2	169	79	171	0	
S. Estes	8-11	5.73	152.1	182	83	103	0	
Manager-Dusty Baker								

Cincinnati Reds

BATTERS	BA	AB	R	H	HR	RBI	SO	SB
J. Guillen	.337	315	52	106	23	63	63	1
S. Casey	.291	573	71	167	14	80	58	4
D. Jimenez#	.290	290	34	84	7	31	43	7
B. Larkin	.282	241	39	68	2	18	32	2
A. Boone	.273	403	61	110	18	65	74	15
A. Kearns	.264	292	39	77	15	58	68	5
J. Castro	.253	320	28	81	9	33	58	2
K. Griffey	.247	166	34	41	13	26	44	1
R. Mateo	.242	207	16	50	3	18	53	0
R. Olmedo	.239	230	24	55	0	17	46	1
J. LaRue	.230	379	52	87	16	50	111	3
W. Pena	.218	165	20	36	5	16	53	3
R. Taylor	.217	180	17	39	5	19	68	7
R. Branyan	.216	176	22	38	9	26	69	0
A. Dunn	.215	381	70	82	27	57	126	8
F. Lopez	.213	197	28	42	2	13	59	8
PITCHERS	W-L	ERA	IP	H	BB	SO	SV	
F. Heredia#	5-2	3.00	72.0	61	28	41	1	
S. Williamson#	5-3	3.19	42.1	34	25	53	21	
C. Reitsma	9-5	4.29	84.0	92	19	53	12	
P. Wilson	8-10	4.64	166.2	190	50	93	0	
J. Riedling	2-3	4.90	101.0	107	47	65	1	
D. Graves	4-15	5.33	169.0	204	41	60	2	
J. Haynes	2-12	6.30	94.1	118	57	49	0	
R. Dempster	3-7	6.54	115.2	134	70	84	0	
Manager-Bob Boone, Dave Miley								

Colorado Rockies

BATTERS	BA	AB	R	H	HR	RBI	SO	SB
T. Helton	.358	583	135	209	33	117	72	0
J. Payton	.302	600	93	181	28	89	77	6
L. Walker	.284	454	86	129	16	79	87	7
P. Wilson	.282	600	94	169	36	141	139	14
R. Belliard	.277	447	73	124	8	50	71	7
G. Norton	.263	179	19	47	6	31	47	2
C. Stynes	.255	443	71	113	11	73	76	3
J. Uribe	.253	316	45	80	10	33	60	7
C. Johnson	.230	356	49	82	20	61	84	1
G. Zaun	.229	166	15	38	4	21	21	1
M. Bellhorn#	.221	249	27	55	2	26	78	5
PITCHERS	W-L	ERA	IP	H	BB	SO	SV	
B. Fuentes	3-3	2.75	75.1	64	34	82	4	
J. Speier	3-1	4.05	73.1	73	23	66	9	
S. Chacon	11-8	4.60	137.0	124	58	93	0	
D. Oliver	13-11	5.04	180.1	201	61	88	0	
J. Jennings	12-13	5.11	181.1	212	88	119	0	
J. Jimenez	2-10	5.22	101.2	137	32	45	20	
D. Stark	3-3	5.83	78.2	98	33	30	0	
A. Cook	4-6	6.02	124.0	160	57	43	0	
Manager-Clint Hurdle								

Florida Marlins

BATTERS	BA	AB	R	H	HR	RBI	SO	SB
L. Castillo	.314	545	99	187	6	39	60	21
J. Pierre	.305	668	100	204	1	41	35	65
I. Rodriguez	.297	511	90	152	16	85	92	10
M. Lowell	.276	492	76	136	32	105	78	3
D. Lee	.271	539	91	146	31	92	131	21

BATTERS	BA	AB	R	H	HR	RBI	SO	SB
J. Encarnacion	.270	601	80	162	19	94	82	19
M. Cabrera	.268	314	39	84	12	62	84	0
A. Gonzalez	.256	528	52	135	18	77	106	0
T. Hollandsworth	.254	228	32	58	3	20	55	2

PITCHERS	W-L	ERA	IP	H	BB	SO	SV
J. Beckett	9-8	3.04	142.0	132	56	152	0
D. Willis	14-6	3.30	160.2	148	58	142	0
M. Redman	14-9	3.59	190.2	172	61	151	0
B. Looper	6-4	3.68	80.2	82	29	56	28
B. Penny	14-10	4.13	196.1	195	56	138	0
C. Pavano	12-13	4.30	201.0	204	-49	133	0
M. Tejera	3-4	4.67	81.0	82	36	58	2

Manager-Jeff Torborg, Jack McKeon

Houston Astros

BATTERS	BA	AB	R	H	HR	RBI	SO	SB
R. Hidalgo	.309	514	91	159	28	88	104	9
J. Kent	.297	505	77	150	22	93	85	6
M. Ensberg	.291	385	69	112	25	60	60	7
L. Berkman	.288	538	110	155	25	93	108	5
J. Bagwell	.278	605	109	168	39	100	119	11
C. Biggio	.264	628	102	166	15	62	116	8
G. Blum	.262	420	51	110	10	52	50	0
A. Everett	.256	387	51	99	8	51	66	8
J. Vizcaino	.249	189	14	47	3	26	22	0
O. Merced	.231	212	20	49	3	26	33	3
B. Ausmus	.229	450	43	103	4	47	66	5

PITCHERS	W-L	ERA	IP	H	BB	SO	SV
B. Wagner	1-4	1.78	86.0	52	23	105	44
O. Dotel	6-4	2.48	87.0	53	31	97	4
R. Oswalt	10-5	2.97	127.1	116	29	108	0
B. Lidge	6-3	3.60	85.0	60	42	97	1
T. Redding	10-14	3.68	176.0	179	65	116	0
R. Stone	6-4	3.69	83.0	76	31	47	1
W. Miller	14-13	4.13	187.1	168	77	161	0
R. Villone	6-6	4.13	106.2	91	48	91	0
J. Robertson	15-9	5.10	160.2	180	64	99	0

Manager-Jimy Williams

Los Angeles Dodgers

BATTERS	BA	AB	R	H	HR	RBI	SO	SB
B. Jordan	.299	224	28	67	6	28	30	1
J. Cabrera	.282	347	43	98	6	37	62	6
S. Green	.280	611	84	171	19	85	112	6
P. LoDuca	.273	568	64	155	7	52	54	0
C. Izturis	.251	558	47	140	1	40	70	10
D. Roberts	.250	388	56	97	2	16	39	40
A. Cora	.249	477	39	119	4	34	59	4
F. McGriff	.249	297	32	74	13	40	66	0
A. Beltre	.240	559	50	134	23	80	103	2
J. Burnitz*	.239	464	63	111	31	77	112	5
M. Kinkade	.216	162	25	35	5	14	38	1

PITCHERS	W-L	ERA	IP	H	BB	SO	SV
E. Gagne	2-3	1.20	82.1	37	20	137	55
P. Quantrill	2-5	1.75	77.1	61	15	44	1
G. Mota	6-3	1.97	105.0	78	26	99	1
W. Alvarez	6-2	2.37	95.0	80	23	82	1
K. Brown	14-9	2.39	211.0	184	56	185	0
H. Nomo	16-13	3.09	218.1	175	98	177	0
K. Ishii	9-7	3.86	147.0	129	101	140	0
O. Perez	12-12	4.52	185.1	191	46	141	0
A. Ashby	3-10	5.18	73.0	90	17	41	0

Manager-Jim Tracy

Milwaukee Brewers

BATTERS	BA	AB	R	H	HR	RBI	SO	SB
S. Podsednik	.314	558	100	175	9	58	91	43
G. Jenkins	.296	487	81	144	28	95	120	0
A. Sanchez#	.282	163	15	46	0	10	28	8
B. Clark	.273	315	33	86	6	40	40	13
R. Sexson	.272	606	97	165	45	124	151	2
E. Perez	.271	350	26	95	11	45	47	0
W. Helms	.261	476	56	124	23	67	131	0
K. Ginter	.257	358	51	92	14	44	87	1
J. Vander Wal	.257	327	50	84	14	45	104	1
K. Osik	.249	241	22	60	2	21	44	0
R. Clayton	.228	483	49	110	11	39	92	5

PITCHERS	W-L	ERA	IP	H	BB	SO	SV
D. Kolb	1-2	1.96	41.1	34	19	39	21
B. Sheets	11-13	4.45	220.2	232	43	157	0
M. Kinney	10-13	5.19	190.2	201	80	152	0
W. Franklin	10-13	5.50	194.2	201	94	116	0
G. Rusch	1-12	6.42	123.1	171	45	93	1

Manager-Ned Yost

Montreal Expos

BATTERS	BA	AB	R	H	HR	RBI	SO	SB
V. Guerrero	.330	394	71	130	25	79	53	9
J. Vidro	.310	509	77	158	15	65	50	3
O. Cabrera	.297	626	95	186	17	80	64	24
W. Cordero	.278	436	57	121	16	71	90	1
B. Wilkerson	.268	504	78	135	19	77	155	13
J. Carroll	.260	227	31	59	1	10	39	5
E. Chavez	.251	483	66	121	5	47	59	18
H. Mateo	.240	154	29	37	0	7	38	11
J. Macias	.239	272	31	65	4	22	45	4
R. Calloway	.238	340	36	81	9	52	80	9
B. Schneider	.230	335	34	77	9	46	75	0
M. Barrett	.208	226	33	47	10	30	37	0
F. Tatis	.194	175	15	34	2	15	40	2

PITCHERS	W-L	ERA	IP	H	BB	SO	SV
L. Ayala	10-3	2.92	71.0	65	13	46	5
L. Hernandez	15-10	3.20	233.1	225	57	178	0
J. Vazquez	13-12	3.24	230.2	198	57	241	0
T. Ohka	10-12	4.16	199.0	233	45	118	0
Z. Day	9-8	4.18	131.1	132	59	61	0
C. Vargas	6-8	4.34	114.0	111	41	62	0
R. Biddle	5-8	4.65	71.2	71	40	54	34
T. Tucker	2-3	4.73	80.0	90	20	47	0

Manager-Frank Robinson

New York Mets

BATTERS	BA	AB	R	H	HR	RBI	SO	SB
J. Reyes	.307	274	47	84	5	32	36	13
J. Phillips	.298	403	45	120	11	58	50	0
C. Floyd	.290	365	57	106	18	68	66	3
M. Piazza	.286	234	37	67	11	34	40	0
T. Perez	.269	346	32	93	4	42	29	5
R. Cedeno	.267	484	70	129	7	37	86	14
R. Alomar#	.262	263	34	69	2	22	40	6
T. Wigginton	.255	573	73	146	11	71	124	12
V. Wilson	.242	269	28	65	8	39	56	1
J. McEwing	.241	278	31	67	1	16	57	3
T. Clark	.232	254	29	59	16	43	73	0
R. Gonzalez	.230	217	28	50	2	21	34	3
R. Sanchez#	.207	174	11	36	0	12	18	1

PITCHERS	W-L	ERA	IP	H	BB	SO	SV
D. Weathers	1-6	3.08	87.2	87	40	75	7
A. Benitez	3-3	3.10	49.1	41	24	50	21
S. Trachsel	16-10	3.78	204.2	204	65	111	0
J. Seo	9-12	3.82	188.1	193	46	110	0
A. Leiter	15-9	3.99	180.2	176	94	139	0
T. Glavine	9-14	4.52	183.1	205	66	82	0

Manager-Art Howe

Philadelphia Phillies

BATTERS	BA	AB	R	H	HR	RBI	SO	SB
M. Lieberthal	.313	508	68	159	13	81	59	0
M. Byrd	.303	495	86	150	7	45	94	11
B. Abreu	.300	577	99	173	20	101	126	22
P. Polanco	.289	492	87	142	14	63	38	14
J. Thome	.266	578	111	154	47	131	182	0
T. Perez	.265	298	39	79	5	33	54	0
J. Rollins	.263	628	85	165	8	62	113	20
R. Ledee	.247	255	37	63	13	46	59	0
K. Stinnett	.237	186	14	44	3	19	52	0
P. Burrell	.209	522	57	109	21	64	142	0
D. Bell	.195	297	32	58	4	37	40	0

PITCHERS	W-L	ERA	IP	H	BB	SO	SV
R. Cormier	8-0	1.70	84.2	54	25	67	1
V. Padilla	14-12	3.62	208.2	196	62	133	0
K. Millwood	14-12	4.01	222.0	210	68	169	0
R. Wolf	16-10	4.23	200.0	176	78	177	0
B. Myers	14-9	4.43	193.0	205	76	143	0
C. Silva	3-1	4.43	87.1	92	37	48	1
B. Duckworth	4-7	4.94	93.0	98	44	68	0
M. Williams*	1-7	6.14	63.0	66	41	39	28
J. Mesa	5-7	6.52	58.0	71	31	45	24

Manager-Larry Bowa

Pittsburgh Pirates

BATTERS	BA	AB	R	H	HR	RBI	SO	SB
T. Redman	.330	230	36	76	3	19	18	7
J. Kendall	.325	587	84	191	6	58	40	8
M. Stairs	.292	305	49	89	20	57	64	0
R. Sanders	.285	453	74	129	31	87	110	15
R. Mackowiak	.270	174	20	47	6	19	53	6
C. Wilson	.262	309	49	81	18	48	89	3
J. Wilson	.256	558	58	143	9	62	74	5
A. Nunez	.248	311	37	77	4	35	53	9
J. Reboulet	.241	261	37	63	3	25	47	2
J. Hernandez*	.225	519	58	117	13	57	177	2

PITCHERS	W-L	ERA	IP	H	BB	SO	SV
K. Wells	10-9	3.28	197.1	171	76	147	0
J. Suppan#	10-7	3.57	141.0	147	31	78	0
J. Tavarez	3-3	3.66	83.2	75	27	39	11
B. Meadows	2-1	4.72	76.1	91	11	38	1
S. Torres	7-5	4.76	121.0	128	42	84	2
J. D'Amico	9-16	4.77	175.1	204	42	100	0
K. Benson	5-9	4.97	105.0	127	36	68	0
J. Fogg	10-9	5.26	142.0	166	40	71	0
O. Perez*	4-10	5.47	126.2	129	77	141	0

Manager-Lloyd McClendon

St. Louis Cardinals

BATTERS	BA	AB	R	H	HR	RBI	SO	SB
A. Pujols	.359	591	137	212	43	124	65	5
E. Renteria	.330	587	96	194	13	100	54	34
J. Drew	.289	287	60	83	15	42	48	2
S. Rolen	.286	559	98	160	28	104	104	13
E. Perez	.285	253	47	72	11	41	53	5
B. Hart	.277	296	46	82	4	28	64	3
J. Edmonds	.275	447	89	123	39	89	127	1
T. Martinez	.273	476	66	130	15	69	71	1
O. Palmeiro	.271	317	37	86	3	33	31	3
M. Matheny	.252	441	43	111	8	47	81	1
F. Vina	.251	259	35	65	4	23	24	4
K. Robinson	.250	208	19	52	1	16	27	6
M. Cairo	.245	261	41	64	5	32	30	4

PITCHERS	W-L	ERA	IP	H	BB	SO	SV
J. Isringhausen	0-1	2.36	42.0	31	18	41	22
M. Morris	11-8	3.76	172.1	164	39	120	0
W. Williams	18-9	3.87	220.2	220	55	153	0
G. Stephenson	7-13	4.59	174.1	167	60	91	0
M. DeJean#	5-8	4.68	82.2	86	39	71	19
D. Haren	3-7	5.08	72.2	84	22	43	0
B. Tomko	13-9	5.28	202.2	252	57	114	0
J. Simontacchi	9-5	5.56	126.1	153	41	74	1
J. Fassero	1-7	5.68	77.2	93	34	55	3

Manager-Tony La Russa

San Diego Padres

BATTERS	BA	AB	R	H	HR	RBI	SO	SB
M. Loretta	.314	589	74	185	13	72	62	5
B. Giles*	.299	492	93	147	20	88	58	4
S. Burroughs	.286	517	62	148	7	58	75	7
P. Nevin	.279	226	30	63	13	46	44	2
L. Merloni#	.272	151	20	41	1	17	33	2
G. Matthews Jr. #	.271	306	50	83	4	22	66	12
X. Nady	.267	371	50	99	9	39	74	6
M. Kotsay	.266	482	64	128	7	38	82	6
B. Buchanan	.263	198	29	52	8	29	51	6
R. Vazquez	.261	422	56	110	3	30	88	10
R. Klesko	.252	397	47	100	21	67	83	2
G. Bennett	.238	307	26	73	2	42	48	3

PITCHERS	W-L	ERA	IP	H	BB	SO	SV
R. Beck	3-2	1.78	35.1	25	11	32	20
S. Linebrink	3-2	3.31	92.1	93	36	68	0
A. Eaton	9-12	4.08	183.0	173	68	146	0
J. Peavy	12-11	4.11	194.2	173	82	156	0
B. Lawrence	10-15	4.19	210.2	206	57	116	0
L. Hackman	2-2	5.17	76.2	78	36	48	0
K. Jarvis	4-8	5.87	92.0	113	32	49	0

Manager-Bruce Bochy

San Francisco Giants

BATTERS	BA	AB	R	H	HR	RBI	SO	SB
B. Bonds	.341	390	111	133	45	90	58	7
A. Galarraga	.301	272	36	82	12	42	61	1
M. Grissom	.300	587	82	176	20	79	82	11
R. Durham	.285	410	61	117	8	33	82	7
B. Santiago	.279	401	53	112	11	56	69	0
R. Aurilia	.277	505	65	140	13	58	82	2
J. Snow	.273	330	48	90	8	51	55	1
Y. Torrealba	.260	200	22	52	4	29	39	1
E. Alfonzo	.259	514	56	133	13	81	41	5
N. Perez	.256	328	27	84	1	31	23	3
E. Young*	.251	475	80	119	15	34	44	27
J. Cruz	.250	539	90	135	20	68	121	5
P. Feliz	.247	235	31	58	16	48	53	2

PITCHERS	W-L	ERA	IP	H	BB	SO	SV
J. Schmidt	17-5	2.34	207.2	152	46	208	0
M. Herges*	3-2	2.62	79.0	68	29	68	3
T. Worrell	4-4	2.87	78.1	74	28	65	38
J. Nathan	12-4	2.96	79.0	51	33	83	0
J. Williams	7-5	3.30	131.0	116	49	88	0
J. Brower	8-5	3.96	100.0	90	39	65	2
D. Moss#	9-7	4.70	115.0	121	63	57	0
K. Rueter	10-5	4.53	147.0	170	47	41	0
J. Foppert	8-9	5.03	111.0	103	69	101	0

Manager-Felipe Alou

American League Final Standings, 2003

Eastern Division

	W	L	Pct.	GB	Home	Road	vs. East	vs. Central	vs. West	vs. NL
New York	101	61	.623	—	50-32	51-29	47-29	23-9	18-18	13-5
Boston*	95	67	.586	6.0	53-28	42-39	41-35	24-12	19-13	11-7
Toronto	86	76	.531	15.0	41-40	45-36	37-39	22-14	17-15	10-8
Baltimore	71	91	.438	30.0	40-40	31-51	31-45	14-18	21-15	5-13
Tampa Bay	63	99	.389	38.0	36-45	27-54	34-42	12-20	14-22	3-15

Central Division

	W	L	Pct.	GB	Home	Road	vs. East	vs. Central	vs. West	vs. NL
Minnesota	90	72	.556	—	48-33	42-39	17-15	43-33	20-16	10-8
Chicago	86	76	.531	4.0	51-30	35-46	21-15	42-34	13-19	10-8
Kansas City	83	79	.512	7.0	40-40	43-39	12-20	46-30	16-20	9-9
Cleveland	68	94	.420	22.0	38-43	30-51	14-18	35-41	13-23	6-12
Detroit	43	119	.265	47.0	23-58	20-61	9-27	24-52	6-26	4-14

Western Division

	W	L	Pct.	GB	Home	Road	vs. East	vs. Central	vs. West	vs. NL
Oakland	96	66	.593	—	57-24	39-42	28-13	25-20	34-24	9-9
Seattle	93	69	.574	3.0	50-31	43-38	18-23	32-13	33-25	10-8
Anaheim	77	85	.475	19.0	45-37	32-48	15-30	26-15	25-33	11-7
Texas	71	91	.438	25.0	43-38	28-53	22-23	21-20	24-34	4-14

*Wild card team.

American League Team Statistics, 2003

(Individual Statistics: Batting—at least 150 at-bats; Pitching—at least 70 innings or 10 saves; *changed teams within AL during season, entry includes statistics for more than one team; # changed teams to or from NL during season, entry includes only AL stats)

Team Batting

Team	BAT	AB	R	H	HR	RBI
Boston	.289	5769	961	1667	238	932
Toronto	.279	5661	894	1580	190	853
Minnesota	.277	5655	801	1567	155	755
Kansas City	.274	5568	836	1526	162	781
Seattle	.271	5561	795	1509	139	759
NewYork	.271	5605	877	1518	230	845
Anaheim	.268	5487	736	1473	150	687
Baltimore	.268	5665	743	1516	152	695
Texas	.266	5664	826	1506	239	799
Tampa Bay	.265	5654	715	1501	137	678
Chicago	.263	5487	791	1445	220	766
Oakland	.254	5497	768	1398	176	742
Cleveland	.254	5572	699	1413	158	660
Detroit	.240	5466	591	1312	153	553

Team Pitching

Team	ERA	IP	H	SO	BB	SV
Oakland	3.63	1441.2	1336	1018	499	48
Seattle	3.76	1441.0	1340	1001	466	38
New York	4.02	1462.0	1512	1119	375	49
Chicago	4.17	1431.0	1364	1056	518	36
Cleveland	4.21	1459.1	1477	943	501	34
Anaheim	4.28	1431.1	1444	980	486	39
Minnesota	4.41	1462.0	1526	997	402	45
Boston	4.48	1464.2	1503	1141	488	36
Toronto	4.69	1435.0	1560	984	485	36
Baltimore	4.76	1449.2	1579	981	526	41
Tampa Bay	4.93	1436.2	1454	877	639	30
Kansas City	5.05	1438.2	1569	865	566	36
Detroit	5.30	1438.2	1616	764	557	27
Texas	5.67	1433.1	1625	1009	603	43

Anaheim Angels

BATTERS	BA	AB	R	H	HR	RBI	SO	SB
G. Anderson	.315	638	80	201	29	116	83	6
B. Fullmer	.306	206	32	63	9	35	31	5
C. Figgins	.296	240	34	71	0	27	38	13
J. DaVanon	.282	330	56	93	12	43	59	17
B. Molina	.281	409	37	115	14	71	31	1
T. Salmon	.275	528	78	145	19	72	93	3
E. Owens	.270	241	29	65	1	20	24	11
A. Kennedy	.269	449	71	121	13	49	73	22
S. Spiezio	.265	521	69	138	16	83	66	6
D. Eckstein	.252	452	59	114	3	31	45	16
D. Erstad	.252	258	35	65	4	17	40	9
T. Glaus	.248	319	53	79	16	50	73	7
S. Wooten	.243	272	25	66	7	32	45	0

PITCHERS	W-L	ERA	IP	H	BB	SO	SV
B. Donnelly	2-2	1.58	74.0	55	24	79	3
B. Weber	5-1	2.69	80.1	84	22	46	0
S. Shields	5-6	2.85	148.1	138	38	111	1
F. Rodriguez	8-3	3.03	86.0	50	35	95	2
T. Percival	0-5	3.47	49.1	33	23	48	33
J. Washburn	10-15	4.43	207.1	205	54	118	0
J. Lackey	10-16	4.63	204.0	223	66	151	0
R. Ortiz	16-13	5.20	180.0	209	63	94	0
A. Sele	7-11	5.77	121.2	135	58	53	0

Manager-Mike Scioscia

Baltimore Orioles

BATTERS	BA	AB	R	H	HR	RBI	SO	SB
M. Mora	.317	344	68	109	15	48	71	6
L. Bigbie	.303	287	43	87	9	31	60	7
L. Matos	.303	439	70	133	13	45	90	15
B. Surhoff	.295	319	32	94	5	41	29	2
J. Gibbons	.277	625	80	173	23	100	89	0
B. Fordyce	.273	348	28	95	6	31	44	2
J. Hairston	.271	218	25	59	2	21	25	14
B. Roberts	.270	460	65	124	5	41	58	23
D. Segui	.263	224	26	59	5	25	47	1
D. Cruz	.250	548	61	137	14	65	49	1
G. Gil	.237	169	22	40	3	16	34	0
T. Batista	.235	631	76	148	26	99	102	4
G. Matthews Jr. #	.204	162	21	33	2	20	29	0

PITCHERS	W-L	ERA	IP	H	BB	SO	SV
S. Ponson#	14-6	3.77	148.0	147	43	100	0
E. DuBose	3-6	3.79	73.2	60	25	44	0
P. Hentgen	7-8	4.09	160.2	150	58	100	1
J. Johnson	10-10	4.18	189.2	216	80	118	0
J. Julio	0-7	4.38	61.2	60	34	52	36
R. Helling#	7-8	5.71	138.2	156	40	86	0
R. Lopez	7-10	5.82	147.0	188	43	103	0
O. Daal	4-11	6.34	93.2	134	30	53	0

Manager-Mike Hargrove

Boston Red Sox

BATTERS	BA	AB	R	H	HR	RBI	SO	SB
B. Mueller	.326	524	85	171	19	85	77	1
M. Ramirez	.325	569	117	185	37	104	94	3
T. Nixon	.306	441	81	135	28	87	96	4
S. Hillenbrand#	.303	185	20	56	3	38	26	1
N. Garciaparra	.301	658	120	198	28	105	61	19
G. Kapler	.291	158	29	46	4	23	23	4
D. Ortiz	.288	448	79	129	31	101	83	0
T. Walker	.283	587	92	166	13	85	54	1
K. Millar	.276	544	83	150	25	96	108	3
J. Damon	.273	608	103	166	12	67	74	30
J. Varitek	.273	451	63	123	25	85	106	3
D. Jackson	.261	161	34	42	1	13	28	16
D. Mirabelli	.258	163	23	42	6	18	36	0

PITCHERS	W-L	ERA	IP	H	BB	SO	SV
P. Martinez	14-4	2.22	186.2	147	47	206	0
B. Kim #	8-5	3.18	79.1	70	18	69	16
M. Timlin	6-4	3.55	83.2	77	9	65	2
T. Wakefield	11-7	4.09	202.1	193	71	169	1
D. Lowe	17-7	4.47	203.1	216	72	110	0
J. Burkett	12-9	5.15	181.2	202	47	107	0
C. Fossum	6-5	5.47	79.0	82	34	63	1

Manager-Grady Little

Chicago White Sox

BATTERS	BA	AB	R	H	HR	RBI	SO	SB
M. Ordonez	.317	606	95	192	29	99	73	9
C. Lee	.291	623	100	181	31	113	91	18
C. Everett	.287	526	93	151	28	92	84	8
A. Rowand	.287	157	22	45	6	24	21	0
S. Alomar	.268	194	22	52	5	26	17	0
F. Thomas	.267	546	87	146	42	105	115	0
J. Crede	.261	536	68	140	19	75	75	1
T. Graffanino	.260	250	51	65	7	23	37	8
D. Jimenez	.255	271	35	69	7	26	46	4
R. Alomar#	.253	253	42	64	3	17	37	6
J. Valentin	.237	503	79	119	28	74	114	8
M. Olivo	.237	317	37	75	6	27	80	6
P. Konerko	.234	444	49	104	18	65	50	0
B. Daubach	.230	183	26	42	6	21	54	1

PITCHERS	W-L	ERA	IP	H	BB	SO	SV
D. Marte	4-2	1.58	79.2	50	34	87	11
E. Loaiza	21-9	2.90	226.1	196	56	207	0
T. Gordon	7-6	3.16	74.0	57	31	91	12
B. Colon	15-13	3.87	242.0	223	67	173	0
M. Buehrle	14-14	4.14	230.1	250	61	119	0
J. Garland	12-13	4.51	191.2	188	74	108	0
B. Koch	5-5	5.77	53.0	59	28	42	11
D. Wright	1-7	6.15	86.1	91	46	47	1

Manager-Jerry Manuel

Cleveland Indians

BATTERS	BA	AB	R	H	HR	RBI	SO	SB
M. Bradley	.321	377	61	121	10	56	73	17
V. Martinez	.289	159	15	46	1	16	21	1
J. Gerut	.279	480	66	134	22	75	70	4
C. Crisp	.266	414	55	110	3	27	51	15
E. Burks	.263	198	27	52	6	28	46	1
C. Blake	.257	557	80	143	17	67	109	7
T. Hafner	.254	291	35	74	14	40	81	2
B. Broussard	.249	386	53	96	16	55	75	5
M. Lawton	.249	374	57	93	15	53	47	10
R. Ludwick*	.247	162	17	40	7	26	48	2
J. Bard	.244	303	25	74	8	36	53	0
O. Vizquel	.244	250	43	61	2	19	20	8
T. Laker	.241	162	17	39	3	21	38	2
J. Peralta	.227	242	24	55	4	21	65	1
J. McDonald	.215	214	21	46	1	14	31	3
B. Phillips	.208	370	36	77	6	33	77	4

PITCHERS	W-L	ERA	IP	H	BB	SO	SV
D. Riske	2-2	2.29	74.2	52	20	82	8
C. Sabathia	13-9	3.60	197.2	190	66	141	0
D. Baez	2-9	3.81	75.2	65	23	66	25
J. Westbrook	7-10	4.33	133.0	142	56	58	0
J. Davis	8-11	4.68	165.1	172	47	85	0
T. Mulholland	3-4	4.91	99.0	117	37	42	0
B. Traber	6-9	5.24	111.2	132	40	88	0

Manager-Eric Wedge

Detroit Tigers

BATTERS	BA	AB	R	H	HR	RBI	SO	SB
D. Young	.297	562	78	167	29	85	130	2
A. Sanchez#	.289	394	43	114	1	22	46	44
W. Morris	.272	346	37	94	6	37	42	4
K. Witt	.263	270	25	71	10	26	68	1
C. Pena	.248	452	51	112	18	50	123	4
C. Monroe	.240	425	51	102	23	70	89	4
E. Munson	.240	313	28	75	18	50	61	3
B. Higginson	.235	469	61	110	14	52	73	8
R. Santiago	.225	444	41	100	2	29	66	10
O. Infante	.222	221	24	49	0	8	37	6
A. Torres	.220	168	23	37	1	9	35	5
S. Halter	.217	360	33	78	12	30	77	2
B. Inge	.203	330	32	67	8	30	79	4

PITCHERS	W-L	ERA	IP	H	BB	SO	SV
N. Cornejo	6-17	4.67	194.2	236	58	46	0
C. Spurling	1-3	4.68	77.0	78	22	38	3
M. Roney	1-9	5.45	100.2	102	48	47	0
J. Bonderman	6-19	5.56	162.0	193	58	108	0
M. Maroth	9-21	5.73	193.1	231	50	87	0
W. Ledezma	3-7	5.79	84.0	99	35	49	0
G. Knotts	3-8	6.0	95.1	111	47	51	0
A. Bernero#	1-12	6.08	100.2	104	41	54	0

Manager-Alan Trammell

Kansas City Royals

BATTERS	BA	AB	R	H	HR	RBI	SO	SB
C. Beltran	.307	521	102	160	26	100	81	41
R. Ibanez	.294	608	95	179	18	90	81	8
M. Sweeney	.293	392	62	115	16	83	56	3
J. Randa	.291	502	80	146	16	72	61	1
A. Berroa	.287	567	92	163	17	73	100	21
A. Guiel	.277	354	63	98	15	52	63	3
K. Harvey	.266	485	50	129	13	64	94	2
M. Tucker	.262	389	61	102	13	55	88	8
D. Relaford	.254	500	70	127	8	59	70	20
M. DiFelice	.254	189	29	48	3	25	30	1
B. Mayne	.245	372	39	91	6	36	59	0
C. Febles	.235	196	31	46	0	11	30	8

PITCHERS	W-L	ERA	IP	H	BB	SO	SV
A. Levine*	3-6	2.79	71.0	67	29	30	1
D. May	10-8	3.77	210.0	197	53	115	0
B. Anderson*	14-11	3.78	197.2	212	43	87	0
J. Affeldt	7-6	3.93	126.0	126	38	98	4
M. MacDougal	3-5	4.08	64.0	64	32	57	27
R. Hernandez	7-5	4.61	91.2	87	37	48	0
D. Carrasco	6-5	4.82	80.1	82	40	57	2
J. Lima	8-3	4.91	73.1	80	26	32	0
J. Grimsley	2-6	5.16	75.0	88		58	0

PITCHERS	W-L	ERA	IP	H	BB	SO	SV
K. Snyder	1-6	5.17	85.1	94	21	39	0
K. Wilson	6-3	5.33	72.2	92	16	42	0
K. Appier*	8-9	5.40	111.2	120	43	55	0
C. George	9-6	7.11	93.2	120	44	39	0

Manager-Tony Pena

Minnesota Twins

BATTERS	BA	AB	R	H	HR	RBI	SO	SB
A. Pierzynski	.312	487	63	152	11	74	55	3
S. Stewart*	.307	573	90	176	13	73	66	4
J. Jones	.304	517	76	157	16	69	105	13
D. Mientkiewicz	.300	487	67	146	11	65	55	4
C. Koskie	.292	469	76	137	14	69	113	11
M. LeCroy	.287	345	39	99	17	64	82	0
C. Guzman	.268	534	78	143	3	53	79	18
L. Rivas	.259	475	69	123	8	43	65	17
G. Gomez	.251	175	14	44	1	15	13	2
T. Hunter	.250	581	83	145	26	102	106	6
D. Mohr	.250	348	50	87	10	36	106	5
D. Hocking	.239	188	22	45	3	22	37	0
PITCHERS	W-L	ERA	IP	H	BB	SO	SV	
L. Hawkins	9-3	1.86	77.1	69	15	75	2	
E. Guardado	3-5	2.89	65.1	50	14	60	41	
J. Santana	12-3	3.07	158.1	127	47	169	0	
J. Rincon	5-6	3.68	85.2	74	38	63	0	
B. Radke	14-10	4.49	212.1	242	28	120	0	
K. Rogers	13-8	4.57	195.0	227	50	116	0	
K. Lohse	14-11	4.61	201.0	211	45	130	0	
R. Reed	6-12	5.07	135.0	155	29	71	0	
J. Mays	8-8	6.30	130.0	159	39	50	0	

Manager-Ron Gardenhire

New York Yankees

BATTERS	BA	AB	R	H	HR	RBI	SO	SB
D. Jeter	.324	482	87	156	10	52	88	11
A. Soriano	.290	682	114	198	38	91	130	35
H. Matsui	.287	623	82	179	16	106	86	2
N. Johnson	.284	324	60	92	14	47	57	5
J. Posada	.281	481	83	135	30	101	110	2
R. Sierra*	.270	307	33	83	9	43	47	2
J. Rivera	.266	173	22	46	7	26	27	0
B. Williams*	.263	445	77	117	15	64	61	5
K. Garcia*	.262	244	25	64	11	35	52	0
R. Mondesi#	.258	361	56	93	16	49	66	17
A. Boone*	.254	189	31	48	6	31	30	8
R. Ventura#	.251	283	31	71	9	42	62	0
J. Giambi	.250	535	97	134	41	107	140	2
T. Zeile#	.210	186	29	39	6	23	36	0
PITCHERS	W-L	ERA	IP	H	BB	SO	SV	
M. Rivera	5-2	1.66	70.2	61	10	63	40	
J. Contreras	7-2	3.30	71.0	52	30	72	0	
M. Mussina	17-8	3.40	214.2	192	40	195	0	
R. Clemens	17-9	3.91	211.2	199	58	190	0	
A. Pettitte	21-8	4.02	208.1	227	50	180	0	
D. Wells	15-7	4.14	213.0	242	20	101	0	
J. Weaver	7-9	5.99	159.1	211	47	93	0	

Manager-Joe Torre

Oakland Athletics

BATTERS	BA	AB	R	H	HR	RBI	SO	SB
E. Chavez	.282	588	94	166	29	101	89	8
M. Tejada	.278	636	98	177	27	106	65	10
R. Hernandez	.273	483	70	132	21	78	79	0
B. McMillon	.268	153	15	41	6	26	36	0
J. Guillen#	.265	170	25	45	8	23	32	0
E. Byrnes	.263	414	64	109	12	51	71	10
E. Durazo	.259	537	92	139	21	77	105	1
S. Hatteberg	.253	541	63	137	12	61	53	0
M. Ellis	.248	553	78	137	9	52	94	6
T. Long	.245	486	64	119	14	61	67	4
C. Singleton	.245	306	38	75	1	36	55	7
J. Dye	.172	221	28	38	4	20	42	1
PITCHERS	W-L	ERA	IP	H	BB	SO	SV	
K. Foulke	9-1	2.08	86.2	57	20	88	43	
T. Hudson	16-7	2.70	240.0	197	61	162	0	
C. Bradford	7-4	3.04	77.0	67	30	62	2	
M. Mulder	15-9	3.13	186.2	180	40	128	0	
B. Zito	14-12	3.30	231.2	186	88	146	0	
J. Halama	3-5	4.22	108.2	117	36	51	0	
T. Lilly	12-10	4.34	178.1	179	58	147	0	
R. Harden	5-4	4.46	74.2	72	40	67	0	
S. Sparks	0-6	4.88	107.0	114	37	54	2	

Manager-Ken Macha

Seattle Mariners

BATTERS	BA	AB	R	H	HR	RBI	SO	SB
I. Suzuki	.312	679	111	212	13	62	69	34
R. Winn	.295	600	103	177	11	75	108	23
B. Boone	.294	622	111	183	35	117	125	16
E. Martinez	.294	497	72	146	24	98	95	0
R. Sanchez#	.294	170	22	50	0	11	21	1
C. Guillen	.276	388	63	107	7	52	64	4
J. Olerud	.269	539	64	145	10	83	67	0
M. Cameron	.253	534	74	135	18	76	137	17
W. Bloomquist	.250	196	30	49	1	14	39	4
D. Wilson	.241	316	32	76	4	43	52	0
B. Davis	.236	246	25	58	6	42	61	0
M. McLemore	.233	309	34	72	2	37	71	5
J. Cirillo	.205	258	24	53	2	23	32	1
PITCHERS	W-L	ERA	IP	H	BB	SO	SV	
S. Hasegawa	2-4	1.48	73.0	62	18	32	16	
J. Mateo	4-0	3.15	85.2	69	13	71	1	
J. Moyer	21-7	3.27	215.0	199	66	129	0	
R. Franklin	11-13	3.57	212.0	199	61	99	0	
J. Pineiro	16-11	3.78	211.2	192	76	151	0	
K. Sasaki	1-2	4.05	33.1	31	15	29	10	
F. Garcia	12-14	4.51	201.1	196	71	144	0	
G. Meche	15-13	4.59	186.1	187	63	130	0	

Manager-Bob Melvin

Tampa Bay Devil Rays

BATTERS	BA	AB	R	H	HR	RBI	SO	SB
A. Huff	.311	636	91	198	34	107	80	2
R. Baldelli	.289	637	89	184	11	78	128	27
C. Crawford	.281	630	80	177	5	54	102	55
T. Lee	.275	542	75	149	19	70	97	6
J. Lugo	.275	433	58	119	15	53	88	10
M. Anderson	.270	482	59	130	6	67	60	19
D. Rolls	.255	373	43	95	7	46	84	11
T. Hall	.253	463	50	117	12	47	40	0
A. Martin	.252	238	19	60	3	26	51	2
B. Grieve	.230	165	28	38	4	17	41	0
PITCHERS	W-L	ERA	IP	H	BB	SO	SV	
T. Harper	4-8	3.77	93.0	86	31	64	1	
J. Gonzalez	6-11	3.91	156.1	131	69	97	0	
V. Zambrano	12-10	4.21	188.1	165	106	132	0	
L. Carter	7-5	4.33	79.0	72	19	47	26	
J. Colome	3-7	4.50	74.0	69	46	69	2	
J. Sosa	5-12	4.62	128.2	137	60	72	0	
R. Bell	5-4	5.52	101.0	103	39	44	0	
J. Kennedy	3-12	6.13	133.2	167	47	111	0	

Manager-Lou Piniella

Texas Rangers

BATTERS	BA	AB	R	H	HR	RBI	SO	SB
M. Young	.306	666	106	204	14	72	103	13
B. Hlalock	.300	567	89	170	29	90	97	2
A. Rodriguez	.298	607	124	181	47	118	126	17
J. Gonzalez	.294	327	49	96	24	70	73	1
D. Glanville#	.272	195	22	53	4	14	25	4
R. Palmeiro	.260	561	92	146	38	112	77	2
M. Teixeira	.259	529	66	137	26	84	120	1
E. Diaz	.257	334	30	86	4	35	32	3
L. Nix	.255	184	25	47	8	30	53	3
S. Spencer*	.251	395	39	99	12	49	92	2
T. Greene	.229	205	25	47	10	20	47	0
R. Christenson	.176	165	22	29	2	16	44	2
PITCHERS	W-L	ERA	IP	H	BB	SO	SV	
F. Cordero	5-8	2.94	82.2	70	38	90	15	
U. Urbina#	0-4	4.19	38.2	33	18	41	26	
J. Thomson	13-14	4.85	217.0	234	49	136	0	
R. Dickey	9-8	5.09	116.2	135	38	94	1	
J. Benoit	8-5	5.49	105.0	99	51	87	0	
R. Rodriguez	3-9	5.73	81.2	89	28	41	0	
I. Valdes	9-8	6.10	115.0	148	29	47	0	
C. Lewis	10-9	7.30	127.0	163	70	88	0	

Manager-Buck Showalter

Toronto Blue Jays

BATTERS	BA	AB	R	H	HR	RBI	SO	SB
V. Wells	.317	678	118	215	33	117	80	4
G. Myers	.307	329	51	101	15	52	57	0
C. Delgado	.302	570	117	172	42	145	137	0
F. Catalanotto	.299	489	83	146	13	59	62	2
R. Johnson	.294	412	79	121	10	52	67	5
M. Bordick	.274	343	39	94	5	54	60	3
O. Hudson	.268	474	54	127	9	57	87	5
J.Phelps	.268	396	57	106	20	66	115	1
C.Woodward	.261	349	49	91	7	45	72	1
T. Wilson	.258	256	37	66	5	35	80	0
D. Berg	.255	161	26	41	4	18	34	0
B. Kielty*	.244	427	71	104	13	57	92	8
E. Hinske	.243	449	74	109	12	63	104	12
PITCHERS	W-L	ERA	IP	H	BB	SO	SV	
R. Halladay	22-7	3.25	266.0	253	32	204	0	
A. Lopez	1-3	3.42	73.2	58	34	64	14	
K. Escobar	13-9	4.29	180.1	189	78	159	4	
M. Hendrickson	9-9	5.51	158.1	207	40	76	0	
C. Politte	1-5	5.66	49.1	52	17	40	12	
C. Lidle	12-15	5.75	192.2	216	60	112	0	
T. Sturtze	7-6	5.94	89.1	107	43	54	0	

Manager-Carlos Tosca

National Baseball Hall of Fame and Museum, Cooperstown, NY[1]

#Aaron, Hank
Alexander, Grover Cleveland
Alston, Walt
Anderson, Sparky
Anson, Cap
Aparicio, Luis
Appling, Luke
Ashburn, Richie
Averill, Earl
Baker, Home Run
Bancroft, Dave
#Banks, Ernie
Barlick, Al
Barrow, Edward G.
Beckley, Jake
Bell, Cool Papa
#Bench, Johnny
Bender, Chief
Berra, Yogi
Bottomley, Jim
Boudreau, Lou
Bresnahan, Roger
#Brett, George
#Brock, Lou
Brouthers, Dan
Brown, Mordecai (Three Finger)
Bulkeley, Morgan C.
Bunning, Jim
Burkett, Jesse C.
Campanella, Roy
#Carew, Rod
Carey, Max
#Carlton, Steve
*Carter, Gary
Cartwright, Alexander
Cepeda, Orlando
Chadwick, Henry
Chance, Frank
Chandler, Happy
Charleston, Oscar
Chesbro, John
Chylak, Nestor

Clarke, Fred
Clarkson, John
#Clemente, Roberto
Cobb, Ty[2]
Cochrane, Mickey
Collins, Eddie
Collins, James
Combs, Earle
Comiskey, Charles A.
Conlan, Jocko
Connolly, Thomas H.
Connor, Roger
Coveleski, Stan
Crawford, Sam
Cronin, Joe
Cummings, Candy
Cuyler, Kiki
Dandridge, Ray
Davis, George "Gorgeous"
Day, Leon
Dean, Dizzy
Delahanty, Ed
Dickey, Bill
DiHigo, Martin
DiMaggio, Joe
#Doby, Larry
Doerr, Bobby
Drysdale, Don
Duffy, Hugh
Durocher, Leo
Evans, Billy
Evers, John
Ewing, Buck
Faber, Urban
#Feller, Bob
Ferrell, Rick
Fingers, Rollie
Fisk, Carlton
Flick, Elmer H.
Ford, Whitey
Foster, Andrew (Rube)
Foster, Bill

Fox, Nellie
Foxx, Jimmie
Frick, Ford
Frisch, Frank
Galvin, Pud
#Gehrig, Lou
Gehringer, Charles
#Gibson, Bob
Gibson, Josh
Giles, Warren
Gomez, Lefty
Goslin, Goose
Greenberg, Hank
Griffith, Clark
Grimes, Burleigh
Grove, Lefty
Hafey, Chick
Haines, Jesse
Hamilton, Bill
Hanlon, Ned
Harridge, Will
Harris, Bucky
Hartnett, Gabby
Heilmann, Harry
Herman, Billy
Hooper, Harry
Hornsby, Rogers
Hoyt, Waite
Hubbard, Cal
Hubbell, Carl
Huggins, Miller
Hulbert, William
Hunter, Catfish
Irvin, Monte
#Jackson, Reggie
Jackson, Travis
Jenkins, Ferguson
Jennings, Hugh
Johnson, Byron
Johnson, William (Judy)
Johnson, Walter[2]
Joss, Addie
#Kaline, Al
Keefe, Timothy

Keeler, William
Kell, George
Kelley, Joe
Kelly, George
Kelly, King
Killebrew, Harmon
Kiner, Ralph
Klein, Chuck
Klem, Bill
#Koufax, Sandy
Lajoie, Napoleon
Landis, Kenesaw M.
Lasorda, Tom
Lazzeri, Tony
Lemon, Bob
Leonard, Buck
Lindstrom, Fred
Lloyd, Pop
Lombardi, Ernie
Lopez, Al
Lyons, Ted
Mack, Connie
MacPhail, Larry
MacPhail, Lee
#Mantle, Mickey
Manush, Henry
Maranville, Rabbit
Marichal, Juan
Marquard, Rube
Mathews, Eddie
Mathewson, Christy[2]
#Mays, Willie
Mazeroski, Bill
McCarthy, Joe
McCarthy, Thomas
#McCovey, Willie
McGinnity, Joe
McGowan, Bill
McGraw, John
McKechnie, Bill
McPhee, John "Bid"
Medwick, Joe
Mize, Johnny
#Morgan, Joe

*#Murray, Eddie
#Musial, Stan
Newhouser, Hal
Nichols, Kid
Niekro, Phil
O'Rourke, James "Orator"
Ott, Mel
Paige, Satchel
#Palmer, Jim
Pennock, Herb
Perez, Tony
Perry, Gaylord
Plank, Ed
#Puckett, Kirby
Radbourn, Charlie
Reese, Pee Wee
Rice, Sam
Rickey, Branch
Rixey, Eppa
Rizzuto, Phil (Scooter)
Roberts, Robin
#Robinson, Brooks
#Robinson, Frank
#Robinson, Jackie
Robinson, Wilbert
Rogan, Joe "Bullet"
Roush, Edd
Ruffing, Red
Rusie, Amos
#Ruth, Babe[2]
#Ryan, Nolan
Schalk, Ray
#Schmidt, Mike
Schoendienst, Red
#Seaver, Tom
Selee, Frank
Sewell, Joe
Simmons, Al
Sisler, George
Slaughter, Enos
Smith, Hilton
#Smith, Ozzie
Snider, Duke

#Spahn, Warren
Spalding, Albert
Speaker, Tris
#Stargell, Willie
Stearnes, Norman "Turkey"
Stengel, Casey
Sutton, Don
Terry, Bill
Thompson, Sam
Tinker, Joe
Traynor, Pie
Vance, Dazzy
Vaughan, Arky
Veeck, Bill
Waddell, Rube
Wagner, Honus[2]
Wallace, Roderick
Walsh, Ed
Waner, Lloyd
Waner, Paul
Ward, John
Weaver, Earl
Weiss, George
Welch, Mickey
Wells, Willie
Wheat, Zach
Wilhelm, Hoyt
Williams, Billy
Williams, Smokey Joe
#Williams, Ted
Williams, Vic
Wilson, Hack
#Winfield, Dave
Wright, George
Wright, Harry
Wynn, Early
#Yastrzemski, Carl
Yawkey, Tom
Young, Cy
Youngs, Ross
#Yount, Robin

(1) Player must generally be retired for five complete seasons before being eligible for induction. (2) Players inducted in 1936 (the year the Hall of Fame began). # Denotes players chosen in first year of Hall of Fame eligibility or under special circumstances earlier. *Denotes 2003 inductees. **NOTE:** Four players, Babe Ruth (1936), Lou Gehrig (1939), Joe DiMaggio (1955), and Roberto Clemente (1973), were inducted less than five years after retirement or, in Clemente's case, death.

Major League Leaders in 2003

American League

Batting: Bill Mueller, Boston, .326; Manny Ramírez, Boston, .325; Derek Jeter, New York, .324; Vernon Wells, Toronto, .317; Magglio Ordóñez, Chicago, .317; Garret Anderson, Anaheim, .315.

Runs: Álex Rodríguez, Texas, 124; Nomar Garciaparra, Boston, 120; Vernon Wells, Toronto, 118; Manny Ramírez, Boston, 117; Carlos Delgado, Toronto, 117; Alfonso Soriano, New York, 114.

Runs Batted In: Carlos Delgado, Toronto, 145; Álex Rodríguez, Texas, 118; Vernon Wells, Toronto, 117; Bret Boone, Seattle, 117; Garret Anderson, Anaheim, 116; Carlos Lee, Chicago, 113.

Hits: Vernon Wells, Toronto, 215; Ichiro Suzuki, Seattle, 212; Michael Young, Texas, 204; Garret Anderson, Anaheim, 201; Nomar Garciaparra, Boston, 197; Alfonso Soriano, New York, 196; Aubrey Huff, Tampa Bay, 198.

Doubles: Garret Anderson, Anaheim, 49; Vernon Wells, Toronto, 49; Aubrey Huff, Tampa Bay, 46; Magglio Ordóñez, Chicago, 46; Bill Mueller, Boston, 45; Eric Hinske, Toronto, 45; Shannon Stewart, Minnesota, 44.

Triples: Cristian Guzmán, Minnesota, 14; Nomar Garciaparra, Boston, 13; Carlos Beltrán, Kansas City, 10; Carl Crawford,

Tampa Bay, 9; Eric Byrnes, Oakland, 9; Michael Young, Texas, 9; Luis Rivas, Minnesota, 9.

Home Runs: Álex Rodríguez, Texas, 47; Carlos Delgado, Toronto, 42; Frank Thomas, Chicago, 42; Jason Giambi, New York, 41; Alfonso Soriano, New York, 38; Rafael Palmeiro, Texas, 38; Manny Ramírez, Boston, 37.

Stolen Bases: Carl Crawford, Tampa Bay, 55; Álex Sánchez, Detroit, 44; Carlos Beltrán, Kansas City, 41; Alfonso Soriano, New York, 35; Ichiro Suzuki, Seattle, 34

Pitching: Roy Halladay, Toronto, 22-7, .759, 3.25; Andy Pettitte, New York, 21-8, .724, 4.02; Esteban Loaiza, Chicago, 21-9, .700, 2.90; Jamie Moyer, Seattle, 21-7, .750, 3.27; Mike Mussina, New York, 17-8, .708, 3.40; Derek Lowe, Boston, 17-7, .680, 4.47; Roger Clemens, New York, 17-9, .654, 3.91; Ramón Ortiz, Anaheim, 16-13, .552, 5.20; Tim Hudson, Oakland, 16-7, .696, 2.70; Joel Piñeiro, Seattle, 16-11, .593, 3.78.

Strikeouts: Esteban Loaiza, Chicago, 207; Pedro Martínez, Boston, 206; Roy Halladay, Toronto, 204; Mike Mussina, New York, 195; Roger Clemens, New York, 190.

Saves: Keith Foulke, Oakland, 43; Eddie Guardado, Minnesota, 41; Mariano Rivera, New York, 40; Jorge Julio, Baltimore, 36; Troy Percival, Anaheim, 33.

National League

Batting: Albert Pujols, St. Louis, .359; Todd Helton, Colorado, .358; Barry Bonds, San Francisco, .341; Gary Sheffield, Atlanta, .330; Edgar Rentería, St. Louis, .330; Jason Kendall, Pittsburgh, .325.

Runs: Albert Pujols, St. Louis, 137; Todd Helton, Colorado, 135; Rafael Furcal, Atlanta, 130; Gary Sheffield, Atlanta, 126; Barry Bonds, San Francisco, 111; Jim Thome, Philadelphia, 111; Lance Berkman, Houston, 110.

Runs Batted In: Preston Wilson, Colorado, 141; Gary Sheffield, Atlanta, 132; Jim Thome, Philadelphia, 131; Albert Pujols, St. Louis, 124; Richie Sexson, Milwaukee, 124; Todd Helton, Colorado, 117.

Hits: Albert Pujols, St. Louis, 212; Todd Helton, Colorado, 209; Juan Pierre, Florida, 204; Rafael Furcal, Atlanta, 194; Edgar Rentería, St. Louis, 194; Jason Kendall, Pittsburgh, 191.

Doubles: Albert Pujols, St. Louis, 51; Todd Helton, Colorado, 49; Scott Rolen, St. Louis, 49; Shawn Green, Los Angeles, 49; Marcus Giles, Atlanta, 49; Edgar Rentería, St. Louis, 47; Orlando Cabrera, Montreal, 47.

Triples: Steve Finley, Arizona, 10; Rafael Furcal, Atlanta, 10; Scott Podsednik, Milwaukee, 8; Kenny Lofton, Chicago, 8; 4 players tied with 7.

Home Runs: Jim Thome, Philadelphia, 47; Barry Bonds, San Francisco, 45; Richie Sexson, Milwaukee, 45; Javy López, Atlanta, 43; Albert Pujols, St. Louis, 43; Sammy Sosa, Chicago, 40.

Stolen Bases: Juan Pierre, Florida, 65; Scott Podsednik, Milwaukee, 43; Dave Roberts, Los Angeles, 40; Edgar Rentería, St. Louis, 34; Kenny Lofton, Chicago, 30.

Pitching: Russ Ortiz, Atlanta, 21-7, .750, 3.81; Mark Prior, Chicago, 18-6, .750, 2.43; Woody Williams, St. Louis, 18-9, .667, 3.87; Jason Schmidt, San Francisco, 17-5, .773, 2.34; Steve Trachsel, New York, 16-10, .615, 3.78; Randy Wolf, Philadelphia, 16-10, .615, 4.23; Greg Maddux, Atlanta, 16-11, .593, 3.96; Hideo Nomo, Los Angeles, 16-13, .552, 3.09.

Strikeouts: Kerry Wood, Chicago, 266; Mark Prior, Chicago, 245; Javier Vázquez, Montreal, 241; Jason Schmidt, San Francisco, 208; Curt Schilling, Arizona, 194.

Saves: Eric Gagne, Los Angeles, 55; John Smoltz, Atlanta, 45; Billy Wagner, Houston, 44; Tim Worrell, San Francisco, 38; Rocky Biddle, Montreal, 34.

50 Home Run Club

Only Mark McGwire and Barry Bonds have ever hit 70 or more home runs in a season. Five players—including Babe Ruth and Roger Maris—have hit 60 or more, a feat Sammy Sosa accomplished for the 3d time in 2001. These 5 are at the pinnacle of a select group of players to have hit 50 or more homers in a season. The following list shows each time a player achieved this mark.

HR	Player, team	Year	HR	Player, team	Year
73	Barry Bonds, San Francisco Giants	2001	54	Babe Ruth, N.Y. Yankees	1928
70	Mark McGwire, St. Louis Cardinals	1998	54	Ralph Kiner, Pittsburgh Pirates	1949
66	Sammy Sosa, Chicago Cubs	1998	54	Mickey Mantle, N.Y. Yankees	1961
65	Mark McGwire, St. Louis Cardinals	1999	52	Mickey Mantle, N.Y. Yankees	1956
64	Sammy Sosa, Chicago Cubs	2001	52	Willie Mays, San Francisco Giants	1965
63	Sammy Sosa, Chicago Cubs	1999	52	George Foster, Cincinnati Reds	1977
61	Roger Maris, N.Y. Yankees	1961	52	Mark McGwire, Oakland A's	1996
60	Babe Ruth, N.Y. Yankees	1927	52	Alex Rodriguez, Texas Rangers	2001
59	Babe Ruth, N.Y. Yankees	1921	52	Jim Thome, Cleveland Indians	2002
58	Jimmie Foxx, Philadelphia Athletics	1932	51	Ralph Kiner, Pittsburgh Pirates	1947
58	Hank Greenberg, Detroit Tigers	1938	51	Johnny Mize, N.Y. Giants	1947
58	Mark McGwire, Oakland A's/St. Louis Cardinals	1997	51	Willie Mays, N.Y. Giants	1955
57	Luis Gonzalez, Arizona Diamondbacks	2001	51	Cecil Fielder, Detroit Tigers	1990
57	Alex Rodriguez, Texas Rangers	2002	50	Jimmie Foxx, Boston Red Sox	1938
56	Hack Wilson, Chicago Cubs	1930	50	Albert Belle, Cleveland Indians	1995
56	Ken Griffey Jr., Seattle Mariners	1997	50	Brady Anderson, Baltimore Orioles	1996
56	Ken Griffey Jr., Seattle Mariners	1998	50	Greg Vaughn, San Diego Padres	1998
54	Babe Ruth, N.Y. Yankees	1920	50	Sammy Sosa, Chicago Cubs	2000

Earned Run Average Leaders

	National League					American League			
Year	Player, team	G	IP	ERA	Year	Player, team	G	IP	ERA
1977	John Candelaria, Pittsburgh	33	231	2.34	1977	Frank Tanana, California	31	241	2.54
1978	Craig Swan, New York	29	207	2.43	1978	Ron Guidry, New York	35	274	1.74
1979	J. R. Richard, Houston	38	292	2.71	1979	Ron Guidry, New York	33	236	2.78
1980	Don Sutton, Los Angeles	32	212	2.21	1980	Rudy May, New York	41	175	2.47
1981	Nolan Ryan, Houston	21	149	1.69	1981	Steve McCatty, Oakland	22	186	2.32
1982	Steve Rogers, Montreal	35	277	2.40	1982	Rick Sutcliffe, Cleveland	34	216	2.96
1983	Atlee Hammaker, San Francisco	23	172	2.25	1983	Rick Honeycutt, Texas	25	174	2.42
1984	Alejandro Pena, Los Angeles	28	199	2.48	1984	Mike Boddicker, Baltimore	34	261	2.79
1985	Dwight Gooden, New York	35	276	1.53	1985	Dave Stieb, Toronto	36	265	2.48
1986	Mike Scott, Houston	37	275	2.22	1986	Roger Clemens, Boston	33	254	2.48
1987	Nolan Ryan, Houston	34	211	2.76	1987	Jimmy Key, Toronto	36	261	2.76
1988	Joe Magrane, St. Louis	24	165	2.18	1988	Allan Anderson, Minnesota	30	202	2.45
1989	Scott Garrelts, San Francisco	30	193	2.28	1989	Bret Saberhagen, Kansas City	36	262	2.16
1990	Danny Darwin, Houston	48	162	2.21	1990	Roger Clemens, Boston	31	228	1.93
1991	Dennis Martinez, Montreal	31	222	2.39	1991	Roger Clemens, Boston	35	271	2.62
1992	Bill Swift, San Francisco	30	164	2.08	1992	Roger Clemens, Boston	32	246	2.41
1993	Greg Maddux, Atlanta	36	267	2.36	1993	Kevin Appier, Kansas City	34	238	2.56
1994	Greg Maddux, Atlanta	25	202	1.56	1994	Steve Ontiveros, Oakland	27	115	2.65
1995	Greg Maddux, Atlanta	28	209	1.63	1995	Randy Johnson, Seattle	30	214	2.48
1996	Kevin Brown, Florida	32	233	1.89	1996	Juan Guzman, Toronto	27	187	2.93
1997	Pedro Martinez, Montreal	31	241	1.90	1997	Roger Clemens, Toronto	34	264	2.05
1998	Greg Maddux, Atlanta	34	251	2.22	1998	Roger Clemens, Toronto	33	234	2.65
1999	Randy Johnson, Arizona	35	271	2.48	1999	Pedro Martinez, Boston	31	213	2.07
2000	Kevin K. Brown, Los Angeles	33	230	2.58	2000	Pedro Martinez, Boston	29	217	1.74
2001	Randy Johnson, Arizona	35	249	2.49	2001	Freddy Garcia, Seattle	34	238	3.05
2002	Randy Johnson, Arizona	35	260	2.32	2002	Pedro Martinez, Boston	30	199	2.26
2003	Jason Schmidt, San Francisco	29	207	2.34	2003	Pedro Martinez, Boston	29	186	2.22

ERA is computed by multiplying earned runs allowed by 9, then dividing by innings pitched.

Strikeout Leaders

Note: Asterisk (*) indicates the all-time single-season record for each league.

	National League			American League	
Year	Pitcher, Team	SO	Year	Pitcher, Team	SO
1901	Noodles Hahn, Cincinnati	239	1901	Cy Young, Boston	158
1902	Vic Willis, Boston	225	1902	Rube Waddell, Philadelphia	210
1903	Christy Mathewson, New York	267	1903	Rube Waddell, Philadelphia	302
1904	Christy Mathewson, New York	212	1904	Rube Waddell, Philadelphia	349
1905	Christy Mathewson, New York	206	1905	Rube Waddell, Philadelphia	287
1906	Fred Beebe, Chicago-St. Louis	171	1906	Rube Waddell, Philadelphia	196
1907	Christy Mathewson, New York	178	1907	Rube Waddell, Philadelphia	232
1908	Christy Mathewson, New York	259	1908	Ed Walsh, Chicago	269
1909	Orval Overall, Chicago	205	1909	Frank Smith, Chicago	177
1910	Earl Moore, Philadelphia	185	1910	Walter Johnson, Washington	313
1911	Rube Marquard, New York	237	1911	Ed Walsh, Chicago	255
1912	Grover Alexander, Philadelphia	195	1912	Walter Johnson, Washington	303

	National League			American League	
Year	Pitcher, Team	SO	Year	Pitcher, Team	SO
1913	Tom Seaton, Philadelphia	168	1913	Walter Johnson, Washington	243
1914	Grover Alexander, Philadelphia	214	1914	Walter Johnson, Washington	225
1915	Grover Alexander, Philadelphia	241	1915	Walter Johnson, Washington	203
1916	Grover Alexander, Philadelphia	167	1916	Walter Johnson, Washington	228
1917	Grover Alexander, Philadelphia	201	1917	Walter Johnson, Washington	188
1918	Hippo Vaughn, Chicago	148	1918	Walter Johnson, Washington	162
1919	Hippo Vaughn, Chicago	141	1919	Walter Johnson, Washington	147
1920	Grover Alexander, Chicago	173	1920	Stan Coveleski, Cleveland	133
1921	Burleigh Grimes, Brooklyn	136	1921	Walter Johnson, Washington	143
1922	Dazzy Vance, Brooklyn	134	1922	Urban Shocker, St. Louis	149
1923	Dazzy Vance, Brooklyn	197	1923	Walter Johnson, Washington	130
1924	Dazzy Vance, Brooklyn	262	1924	Walter Johnson, Washington	158
1925	Dazzy Vance, Brooklyn	221	1925	Lefty Grove, Philadelphia	116
1926	Dazzy Vance, Brooklyn	140	1926	Lefty Grove, Philadelphia	194
1927	Dazzy Vance, Brooklyn	184	1927	Lefty Grove, Philadelphia	174
1928	Dazzy Vance, Brooklyn	200	1928	Lefty Grove, Philadelphia	183
1929	Pat Malone, Chicago	166	1929	Lefty Grove, Philadelphia	170
1930	Bill Hallahan, St. Louis	177	1930	Lefty Grove, Philadelphia	209
1931	Bill Hallahan, St. Louis	159	1931	Lefty Grove, Philadelphia	175
1932	Dizzy Dean, St. Louis	191	1932	Red Ruffing, New York	190
1933	Dizzy Dean, St. Louis	199	1933	Lefty Gomez, New York	163
1934	Dizzy Dean, St. Louis	195	1934	Lefty Gomez, New York	158
1935	Dizzy Dean, St. Louis	190	1935	Tommy Bridges, Detroit	163
1936	Van Lingle Mungo, Brooklyn	238	1936	Tommy Bridges, Detroit	175
1937	Carl Hubbell, New York	159	1937	Lefty Gomez, New York	194
1938	Clay Bryant, Chicago	135	1938	Bob Feller, Cleveland	240
1939	Claude Passeau, Philadelphia-Chicago	137	1939	Bob Feller, Cleveland	246
	Bucky Walters, Cincinnati				
1940	Kirby Higbe, Philadelphia	137	1940	Bob Feller, Cleveland	261
1941	John Vander Meer, Cincinnati	202	1941	Bob Feller, Cleveland	260
1942	John Vander Meer, Cincinnati	186	1942	Tex Hughson, Boston	113
				Bobo Newsom, Washington	
1943	John Vander Meer, Cincinnati	174	1943	Allie Reynolds, Cleveland	151
1944	Bill Voiselle, New York	161	1944	Hal Newhouser, Detroit	187
1945	Preacher Roe, Pittsburgh	148	1945	Hal Newhouser, Detroit	212
1946	Johnny Schmitz, Cincinnati	135	1946	Bob Feller, Cleveland	348
1947	Ewell Blackwell, Cincinnati	193	1947	Bob Feller, Cleveland	196
1948	Harry Brecheen, St. Louis	149	1948	Bob Feller, Cleveland	164
1949	Warren Spahn, Boston	151	1949	Virgil Trucks, Detroit	153
1950	Warren Spahn, Boston	191	1950	Bob Lemon, Cleveland	170
1951	Warren Spahn, Boston	164	1951	Vic Raschi, New York	164
	Don Newcombe, Brooklyn				
1952	Warren Spahn, Boston	183	1952	Allie Reynolds, New York	160
1953	Robin Roberts, Philadelphia	198	1953	Billy Pierce, Chicago	186
1954	Robin Roberts, Philadelphia	185	1954	Bob Turley, Baltimore	185
1955	Sam Jones, Chicago	198	1955	Herb Score, Cleveland	245
1956	Sam Jones, Chicago	176	1956	Herb Score, Cleveland	263
1957	Jack Sanford, Philadelphia	188	1957	Early Wynn, Cleveland	184
1958	Sam Jones, St. Louis	225	1958	Early Wynn, Chicago	179
1959	Don Drysdale, Los Angeles	242	1959	Jim Bunning, Detroit	201
1960	Don Drysdale, Los Angeles	246	1960	Jim Bunning, Detroit	201
1961	Sandy Koufax, Los Angeles	269	1961	Camilo Pacual, Minnesota	221
1962	Don Drysdale, Los Angeles	232	1962	Camilo Pacual, Minnesota	206
1963	Sandy Koufax, Los Angeles	306	1963	Camilo Pacual, Minnesota	202
1964	Bob Veale, Pittsburgh	250	1964	Al Downing, New York	217
1965	Sandy Koufax, Los Angeles	'382	1965	Sam McDowell, Cleveland	325
1966	Sandy Koufax, Los Angeles	317	1966	Sam McDowell, Cleveland	225
1967	Jim Bunning, Philadelphia	253	1967	Jim Lonborg, Boston	246
1968	Bob Gibson, St. Louis	268	1968	Sam McDowell, Cleveland	283
1969	Ferguson Jenkins, Chicago	273	1969	Sam McDowell, Cleveland	279
1970	Tom Seaver, New York	283	1970	Sam McDowell, Cleveland	304
1971	Tom Seaver, New York	289	1971	Mickey Lolich, Detroit	308
1972	Steve Carlton, Philadelphia	310	1972	Nolan Ryan, California	329
1973	Tom Seaver, New York	251	1973	Nolan Ryan, California	'383
1974	Steve Carlton, Philadelphia	240	1974	Nolan Ryan, California	367
1975	Tom Seaver, New York	243	1975	Frank Tanana, California	269
1976	Tom Seaver, New York	235	1976	Nolan Ryan, California	327
1977	Phil Niekro, Atlanta	262	1977	Nolan Ryan, California	341
1978	J.R. Richard, Houston	303	1978	Nolan Ryan, California	260
1979	J.R. Richard, Houston	313	1979	Nolan Ryan, California	223
1980	Steve Carlton, Philadelphia	286	1980	Len Barker, Cleveland	187
1981	Fernando Valenzuela, Los Angeles	180	1981	Len Barker, Cleveland	127
1982	Steve Carlton, Philadelphia	286	1982	Floyd Bannister, Seattle	209
1983	Steve Carlton, Philadelphia	275	1983	Jack Morris, Detroit	232
1984	Dwight Gooden, New York	276	1984	Mark Langston, Seattle	204
1985	Dwight Gooden, New York	268	1985	Bert Blyleven, Cleveland-Minnesota	206
1986	Mike Scott, Houston	306	1986	Mark Langston, Seattle	245
1987	Nolan Ryan, Houston	270	1987	Mark Langston, Seattle	262
1988	Nolan Ryan, Houston	228	1988	Roger Clemens, Boston	291
1989	Jose DeLeon, St. Louis	201	1989	Nolan Ryan, Texas	301
1990	David Cone, New York	233	1990	Nolan Ryan, Texas	232
1991	David Cone, New York	241	1991	Roger Clemens, Boston	241
1992	John Smoltz, Atlanta	215	1992	Randy Johnson, Seattle	241
1993	Jose Rijo, Cincinnati	227	1993	Randy Johnson, Seattle	308
1994	Andy Benes, San Diego	189	1994	Randy Johnson, Seattle	204
1995	Hideo Nomo, Los Angeles	236	1995	Randy Johnson, Seattle	294
1996	John Smoltz, Atlanta	276	1996	Roger Clemens, Boston	257

	National League			American League	
Year	**Pitcher, Team**	**SO**	**Year**	**Pitcher, Team**	**SO**
1997	Curt Schilling, Philadelphia	319	1997	Roger Clemens, Toronto	292
1998	Curt Schilling, Philadelphia	300	1998	Roger Clemens, Toronto	271
1999	Randy Johnson, Arizona	364	1999	Pedro Martinez, Boston	313
2000	Randy Johnson, Arizona	347	2000	Pedro Martinez, Boston	284
2001	Randy Johnson, Arizona	372	2001	Hideo Nomo, Boston	220
2002	Randy Johnson, Arizona	334	2002	Pedro Martinez, Boston	239
2003	Kerry Wood, Chicago	266	2003	Esteban Loaiza	207

Victory Leaders

Note: Asterisk (*) indicates the all-time single-season record for each league in the "modern" era beginning in 1901.

	National League			American League	
Year	**Pitcher, Team**	**Wins**	**Year**	**Pitcher, Team**	**Wins**
1901	Bill Donavan, Brooklyn	25	1901	Cy Young, Boston	33
1902	Jack Chesbro, Pittsburgh	28	1902	Cy Young, Boston	32
1903	Joe McGinnity, New York	31	1903	Cy Young, Boston	28
1904	Joe McGinnity, New York	35	1904	Jack Chesbro, New York	*41
1905	Christy Mathewson, New York	31	1905	Rube Waddell, Philadelphia	27
1906	Joe McGinnity, New York	27	1906	Al Orth, New York	27
1907	Christy Mathewson, New York	24	1907	Doc White, Chicago	27
1908	Christy Mathewson, New York	*37	1908	Ed Walsh, Chicago	40
1909	Mordecai Brown, Chicago	27	1909	George Mullin, Detroit	29
1910	Christy Mathewson, New York	27	1910	Jack Coombs, Philadelphia	31
1911	Grover Alexander, Chicago	28	1911	Jack Coombs, Philadelphia	28
1912	Rube Marquard, New York	26	1912	Joe Wood, Boston	34
1913	Tom Seaton, Philadelphia	27	1913	Walter Johnson, Washington	36
1914	Grover Alexander, Philadelphia	27	1914	Walter Johnson, Washington	28
1915	Grover Alexander, Philadelphia	31	1915	Walter Johnson, Washington	27
1916	Grover Alexander, Philadelphia	33	1916	Walter Johnson, Washington	25
1917	Grover Alexander, Philadelphia	30	1917	Eddie Cicotte, Chicago	28
1918	Hippo Vaughn, Chicago	22	1918	Walter Johnson, Washington	23
1919	Jesse Barnes, New York	25	1919	Eddie Cicotte, Chicago	29
1920	Grover Alexander, Philadelphia	27	1920	Jim Bagby, Cleveland	31
1921	Burleigh Grimes, Brooklyn	22	1921	Urban Shocker, St. Louis	27
1922	Eppa Rixey, Cincinnati	25	1922	Eddie Rommel, Philadelphia	27
1923	Dolf Luque, Cincinnati	27	1923	George Uhle, Cleveland	26
1924	Dazzy Vance, Brooklyn	28	1924	Walter Johnson, Washington	23
1925	Dazzy Vance, Brooklyn	22	1925	Eddie Rommel, Philadelphia	21
1926	Flint Rhem, St. Louis	20	1926	George Uhle, Cleveland	27
1927	Charlie Root, Chicago	26	1927	Ted Lyons, Chicago	22
1928	Burleigh Grimes, Pittsburgh	25	1928	George Pipgras, New York	24
1929	Pat Malone, Chicago	22	1929	George Earnshaw, Philadelphia	24
1930	Pat Malone, Chicago	20	1930	Lefty Grove, Philadelphia	28
1931	Heine Meine, Pittsburgh	19	1931	Lefty Grove, Philadelphia	31
1932	Lon Warneke, Chicago	22	1932	Alvin Crowder, Washington	26
1933	Carl Hubbell, New York	23	1933	Lefty Grove, Philadelphia	24
1934	Dizzy Dean, St. Louis	30	1934	Lefty Gomez, New York	26
1935	Dizzy Dean, St. Louis	28	1935	Wes Ferrell, Boston	25
1936	Carl Hubbell, New York	26	1936	Tommy Bridges, Detroit	23
1937	Carl Hubbell, New York	22	1937	Lefty Gomez, New York	21
1938	Bill Lee, Chicago	22	1938	Red Ruffing, New York	21
1939	Bucky Walters, Cincinnati	27	1939	Bob Feller, Cleveland	24
1940	Bucky Walters, Cincinnati	22	1940	Bob Feller, Cleveland	27
1941	Whit Wyatt, Brooklyn	22	1941	Bob Feller, Cleveland	25
1942	Mort Cooper, St. Louis	22	1942	Tex Hughson, Boston	22
1943	Rip Sewell, Pittsburgh	21	1943	Dizzy Trout, Detroit	20
1944	Bucky Walters, Cincinnati	23	1944	Hal Newhouser, Detroit	29
1945	Red Barrett, Boston-St. Louis	23	1945	Hal Newhouser, Detroit	25
1946	Howie Pollet, St. Louis	21	1946	Hal Newhouser, Detroit	26
1947	Ewell Blackwell, Cincinnati	22	1947	Bob Feller, Cleveland	20
1948	Johnny Sain, Boston	24	1948	Hal Newhouser, Detroit	21
1949	Warren Spahn, Boston	21	1949	Mel Parnell, Boston	25
1950	Warren Spahn, Boston	21	1950	Bob Lemon, Cleveland	23
1951	Sal Maglie, New York	23	1951	Bob Feller, Cleveland	22
1952	Robin Roberts, Philadelphia	28	1952	Bobby Shantz, Philadelphia	24
1953	Warren Spahn, Milwaukee	23	1953	Bob Porterfield, Washington	22
1954	Robin Roberts, Philadelphia	23	1954	Early Wynn, Cleveland	23
1955	Robin Roberts, Philadelphia	23	1955	Frank Sullivan, Boston	18
1956	Don Newcombe, Brooklyn	27	1956	Frank Lary, Detroit	21
1957	Warren Spahn, Milwaukee	21	1957	Billy Pierce, Chicago	20
1958	Warren Spahn, Milwaukee	22	1958	Bob Turley, New York	21
1959	Warren Spahn, Milwaukee	21	1959	Early Wynn, Chicago	22
1960	Warren Spahn, Milwaukee	21	1960	Jim Perry, Cleveland	18
1961	Warren Spahn, Milwaukee	21	1961	Whitey Ford, New York	25
1962	Don Drysdale, Los Angeles	25	1962	Ralph Terry, New York	23
1963	Juan Marichal, San Francisco	25	1963	Whitey Ford, New York	24
1964	Larry Jackson, Chicago	24	1964	Gary Peters, Chicago	20
1965	Sandy Koufax, Los Angeles	26	1965	Mudcat (Jim) Grant, Minnesota	21
1966	Sandy Koufax, Los Angeles	27	1966	Jim Kaat, Minnesota	25
1967	Mike McCormick, San Francisco	22	1967	Earl Wilson, Detroit	22
1968	Juan Marichal, San Francisco	26	1968	Denny McLain, Detroit	31
1969	Tom Seaver, New York	25	1969	Denny McLain, Detroit	24
1970	Gaylord Perry, San Francisco	23	1970	Jim Perry, Minnesota	24
1971	Fergie Jenkins, Chicago	24	1971	Mickey Lolich, Detroit	25
1972	Steve Carlton, Philadelphia	27	1972	Wilbur Wood, Chicago	24
1973	Ron Bryant, San Francisco	24	1973	Wilbur Wood, Chicago	24
1974	Phil Niekro, Atlanta	20	1974	Fergie Jenkins, Texas	25

National League

Year	Pitcher, Team	Wins
1975	Tom Seaver, New York	22
1976	Randy Jones, San Diego	22
1977	Steve Carlton, Philadelphia	23
1978	Gaylord Perry, San Diego	21
1979	Phil Niekro, Atlanta	21
1980	Steve Carlton, Philadelphia	24
1981	Tom Seaver, Cincinnati	14
1982	Steve Carlton, Philadelphia	23
1983	John Denny, Philadelphia	19
1984	Joaquin Andujar, St. Louis	20
1985	Dwight Gooden, New York	24
1986	Fernando Valenzuela, Los Angeles	21
1987	Rick Sutcliffe, Chicago	18
1988	Danny Jackson, Cincinnati	23
1989	Mike Scott, Houston	20
1990	Doug Drabek, Pittsburgh	22
1991	John Smiley, Pittsburgh	20
1992	Greg Maddux, Chicago	20
1993	Tom Glavine, Atlanta	22
1994	Greg Maddux, Atlanta	16
1995	Greg Maddux, Atlanta	19
1996	John Smoltz, Atlanta	24
1997	Denny Neagle, Atlanta	20
1998	Tom Glavine, Atlanta	20
1999	Mike Hampton, Houston	22
2000	Tom Glavine, Atlanta	21
2001	Matt Morris, St. Louis; Curt Schilling, Arizona	22
2002	Randy Johnson, Arizona	24
2003	Russ Ortiz, Atlanta	21

American League

Year	Pitcher, Team	Wins
1975	Jim Palmer, Baltimore	23
1976	Jim Palmer, Baltimore	22
1977	Jim Palmer, Baltimore	20
1978	Ron Guidry, New York	25
1979	Mike Flanagan, Baltimore	23
1980	Steve Stone, Baltimore	25
1981	Pete Vuckovich, Milwaukee	14
1982	La Marr Hoyt, Chicago	19
1983	La Marr Hoyt, Chicago	24
1984	Mike Boddicker, Baltimore	20
1985	Ron Guidry, New York	22
1986	Roger Clemens, Boston	24
1987	Dave Stewart, Oakland; Roger Clemens, Boston	20
1988	Frank Viola, Minnesota	24
1989	Bret Saberhagen, Kansas City	23
1990	Bob Welch, Oakland	27
1991	Bill Gullickson, Detroit	20
1992	Jack Morris, Toronto	21
1993	Jack McDowell, Chicago	22
1994	Jimmy Key, New York	17
1995	Mike Mussina, Baltimore	19
1996	Andy Pettitte, New York	21
1997	Roger Clemens, Toronto	21
1998	Rick Helling, Texas; Roger Clemens, Toronto	20
1999	Pedro Martinez, Boston	23
2000	David Wells, Toronto	20
2001	Mark Mulder, Oakland	21
2002	Barry Zito, Oakland	23
2003	Roy Halladay	22

All-Time World Series Career Leaders

Batting Leaders

Batter	Hits	AB	Avg.
1. Bobby Brown	18	41	0.439
2. Paul Molitor	23	55	0.418
3. Pepper Martin	23	55	0.418
4. J.T. Snow	11	27	0.407
5. Hal McRae	18	45	0.400

Batter	Hits	AB	Avg.
6. Lou Brock	34	87	0.391
7. Marquis Grissom	30	77	0.390
8. Troy Glaus	10	26	0.385
9. George Brett	19	51	0.373
10. Thurman Munson	25	67	0.373

Games Played

Yogi Berra	75
Mickey Mantle	65
Elston Howard	54
Hank Bauer	53
Gil McDougald	53
Phil Rizzuto	52
Joe DiMaggio	51
Frankie Frisch	50
Pee Wee Reese	44
Roger Maris	41
Babe Ruth	41

Hits

Yogi Berra	71
Mickey Mantle	59
Frankie Frisch	58
Joe DiMaggio	54
Hank Bauer	46
PeeWee Reese	46
Phil Rizzuto	45
Gil McDougald	45
Lou Gehrig	43
Elston Howard	42
Babe Ruth	42
Eddie Collins	42

Runs

Mickey Mantle	42
Yogi Berra	41
Babe Ruth	37
Lou Gehrig	30
Joe DiMaggio	27
Roger Maris	26
Elston Howard	25
Gil McDougald	23
Jackie Robinson	22
Derek Jeter	22

Runs Batted In

Mickey Mantle	40
Yogi Berra	39
Lou Gehrig	35
Babe Ruth	33
Joe DiMaggio	30
Bill Skowron	29
Duke Snider	26
Reggie Jackson	24
Hank Bauer	24
Bill Dickey	24
Gil McDougald	24

Home Runs

Mickey Mantle	18
Babe Ruth	15
Yogi Berra	12
Duke Snider	11
Reggie Jackson	10
Lou Gehrig	10
Joe DiMaggio	8
Bill Skowron	8
Frank Robinson	8
Hank Bauer	7
Gil McDougald	7
Goose Goslin	7

Stolen Bases

Lou Brock	14
Eddie Collins	14
Frank Chance	10
Dave Lopes	10
Phil Rizzuto	10
Frank Frisch	9
Honus Wagner	9
Johnny Evers	8
Roberto Alomar	7
Rickey Henderson	7
Pepper Martin	7
Joe Morgan	7
Joe Tinker	7

Pitching Leaders

Games Pitched

Whitey Ford	22
Rollie Fingers	16
Allie Reynolds	15
Mike Stanton	15
Bob Turley	15
Clay Carroll	14
Mariano Rivera	14
Clem Labine	13
Mark Wohlers	13
Waite Hoyt	12
Catfish Hunter	12
Art Nehf	12

Wins

Whitey Ford	10
Bob Gibson	7
Allie Reynolds	7
Red Ruffing	7
Chief Bender	6
Lefty Gomez	6
Waite Hoyt	6
Three Finger Brown	5
Jack Coombs	5
Catfish Hunter	5
Herb Pennock	5
Vic Raschi	5
Christy Mathewson	5

Strikeouts

Whitey Ford	94
Bob Gibson	92
Allie Reynolds	62
Sandy Koufax	61
Red Ruffing	61
Chief Bender	59
George Earnshaw	56
John Smoltz	52
Waite Hoyt	49
Christy Mathewson	48

Saves

Mariano Rivera	8
Rollie Fingers	6
Johnny Murphy	4
Allie Reynolds	4
John Wetteland	4
Robb Nen	4

World Series Results, 1903-2002

1903 Boston AL 5, Pittsburgh NL 3	1937 New York AL 4, New York NL 1	1970 Baltimore AL 4, Cincinnati NL 1
1904 No series	1938 New York AL 4, Chicago NL 0	1971 Pittsburgh NL 4, Baltimore AL 3
1905 New York NL 4, Philadelphia AL 1	1939 New York AL 4, Cincinnati NL 0	1972 Oakland AL 4, Cincinnati NL 3
1906 Chicago AL 4, Chicago NL 2	1940 Cincinnati NL 4, Detroit AL 3	1973 Oakland AL 4, New York NL 3
1907 Chicago NL 4, Detroit AL 0, 1 tie	1941 New York AL 4, Brooklyn NL 1	1974 Oakland AL 4, Los Angeles NL 1
1908 Chicago NL 4, Detroit AL 1	1942 St. Louis NL 4, New York AL 1	1975 Cincinnati NL 4, Boston AL 3
1909 Pittsburgh NL 4, Detroit AL 3	1943 New York AL 4, St. Louis NL 1	1976 Cincinnati NL 4, New York AL 0
1910 Philadelphia AL 4, Chicago NL 1	1944 St. Louis NL 4, St. Louis AL 2	1977 New York AL 4, Los Angeles NL 2
1911 Philadelphia AL 4, New York NL 2	1945 Detroit AL 4, Chicago NL 3	1978 New York AL 4, Los Angeles NL 2
1912 Boston AL 4, New York NL 3, 1 tie	1946 St. Louis NL 4, Boston AL 3	1979 Pittsburgh NL 4, Baltimore AL 3
1913 Philadelphia AL 4, New York NL 1	1947 New York AL 4, Brooklyn NL 3	1980 Philadelphia NL 4, Kansas City AL 2
1914 Boston NL 4, Philadelphia AL 0	1948 Cleveland AL 4, Boston NL 2	1981 Los Angeles NL 4, New York AL 2
1915 Boston AL 4, Philadelphia NL 1	1949 New York AL 4, Brooklyn NL 1	1982 St. Louis NL 4, Milwaukee AL 3
1916 Boston AL 4, Brooklyn NL 1	1950 New York AL 4, Philadelphia NL 0	1983 Baltimore AL 4, Philadelphia NL 1
1917 Chicago AL 4, New York NL 2	1951 New York AL 4, New York NL 2	1984 Detroit AL 4, San Diego NL 1
1918 Boston AL 4, Chicago NL 2	1952 New York AL 4, Brooklyn NL 3	1985 Kansas City AL 4, St. Louis NL 3
1919 Cincinnati NL 5, Chicago AL 3	1953 New York AL 4, Brooklyn NL 2	1986 New York NL 4, Boston AL 3
1920 Cleveland AL 5, Brooklyn NL 2	1954 New York NL 4, Cleveland AL 0	1987 Minnesota AL 4, St. Louis NL 3
1921 New York NL 5, New York AL 3	1955 Brooklyn NL 4, New York AL 3	1988 Los Angeles NL 4, Oakland AL 1
1922 New York NL 4, New York AL 0, 1 tie	1956 New York AL 4, Brooklyn NL 3	1989 Oakland AL 4, San Francisco NL 0
1923 New York AL 4, New York NL 2	1957 Milwaukee NL 4, New York AL 3	1990 Cincinnati NL 4, Oakland AL 0
1924 Washington AL 4, New York NL 3	1958 New York AL 4, Milwaukee NL 3	1991 Minnesota AL 4, Atlanta NL 3
1925 Pittsburgh NL 4, Washington AL 3	1959 Los Angeles NL 4, Chicago AL 2	1992 Toronto AL 4, Atlanta NL 2
1926 St. Louis NL 4, New York AL 3	1960 Pittsburgh NL 4, New York AL 3	1993 Toronto AL 4, Philadelphia NL 2
1927 New York AL 4, Pittsburgh NL 0	1961 New York AL 4, Cincinnati NL 1	1994 No series
1928 New York AL 4, St. Louis NL 0	1962 New York AL 4, San Francisco NL 3	1995 Atlanta NL 4, Cleveland AL 2
1929 Philadelphia AL 4, Chicago NL 1	1963 Los Angeles NL 4, New York AL 0	1996 New York AL 4, Atlanta NL 2
1930 Philadelphia AL 4, St. Louis NL 2	1964 St. Louis NL 4, New York AL 3	1997 Florida NL 4, Cleveland AL 3
1931 St. Louis NL 4, Philadelphia AL 3	1965 Los Angeles NL 4, Minnesota AL 3	1998 New York AL 4, San Diego NL 0
1932 New York AL 4, Chicago NL 0	1966 Baltimore AL 4, Los Angeles NL 0	1999 New York AL 4, Atlanta NL 0
1933 New York NL 4, Washington AL 1	1967 St. Louis NL 4, Boston AL 3	2000 New York AL 4, New York NL 1
1934 St. Louis NL 4, Detroit AL 3	1968 Detroit AL 4, St. Louis NL 3	2001 Arizona NL 4, New York AL 3
1935 Detroit AL 4, Chicago NL 2	1969 New York NL 4, Baltimore AL 1	2002 Anaheim AL 4, San Francisco NL 3
1936 New York AL 4, New York NL 2		

World Series MVP

Year	Player, Position, Team	Year	Player, Position, Team	Year	Player, Position, Team
1955	Johnny Podres, p, Brooklyn	1972	Gene Tenace, c, Oakland	1987	Frank Viola, p, Minnesota
1956	Don Larsen, p, New York, AL	1973	Reggie Jackson, of, Oakland	1988	Orel Hershiser, p, LA
1957	Lew Burdette, p, Milwaukee, NL	1974	Rollie Fingers, p, Oakland	1989	Dave Stewart, p, Oakland
1958	Bob Turley, p, NY AL	1975	Pete Rose, 3b, Cincinnati	1990	Jose Rijo, p, Cincinnati
1959	Larry Sherry, p, LA	1976	Johnny Bench, c, Cincinnati	1991	Jack Morris, p, Minnesota
1960[1]	Bobby Richardson, 2b, NY, AL	1977	Reggie Jackson, of, NY, AL	1992	Pat Borders, c, Toronto
1961	Whitey Ford, p, NY, AL	1978	Bucky Dent, ss, NY, AL	1993	Paul Molitor, dh, Toronto
1962	Ralph Terry, p, NY, AL	1979	Willie Stargell, 1b, Pittsburgh	1994	no series
1963	Sandy Koufax, p, Los Angeles, NL	1980	Mike Schmidt, 3b, Philadelphia	1995	Tom Glavine, p, Atlanta
1964	Bob Gibson, p, St. Louis	1981	Ron Cey, 3b, LA	1996	John Wetteland, p, NY, AL
1965	Sandy Koufax, p, Los Angeles, NL		Pedro Guerrero, of, LA	1997	Livan Hernandez, p, Florida
1966	Frank Robinson, of, Baltimore		Steve Yeager, c, LA	1998	Scott Brosius, 3b, NY, AL
1967	Bob Gibson, p, St. Louis	1982	Darrell Porter, c, St. Louis	1999	Mariano Rivera, p, NY, AL
1968	Mickey Lolich, p, Detroit	1983	Rick Dempsey, c, Baltimore	2000	Derek Jeter, ss, NY, AL
1969	Donn Clendenon, 1b, NY, NL	1984	Alan Trammell, ss, Detroit	2001	Curt Schilling, p, Arizona
1970	Brooks Robinson, 3b, Baltimore	1985	Bret Saberhagen, p, Kansas City		Randy Johnson, p, Arizona
1971	Roberto Clemente, of, Pittsburgh	1986	Ray Knight, 3b, NY, NL	2002	Troy Glaus, 3b, Anaheim

(1) Bobby Richardson won the MVP although Pittsburgh beat New York.

World Series Won-Lost Records, by Franchise[1]

Team	Wins	Losses	Team	Wins	Losses
New York Yankees	26	12	Toronto Blue Jays	2	0
Philadelphia/Kansas City/Oakland A's	9	5	New York Mets	2	2
St. Louis Cardinals	9	6	Chicago White Sox	2	2
Brooklyn/Los Angeles Dodgers	6	12	Cleveland Indians	2	3
Pittsburgh Pirates	5	2	Chicago Cubs	2	8
Boston Red Sox	5	4	LA/California/Anaheim Angels	1	0
Cincinnati Reds	5	4	Arizona Diamondbacks	1	0
New York/San Francisco Giants	5	12	Florida Marlins	1	0
Detroit Tigers	4	5	Kansas City Royals	1	1
Washington Senators/Minnesota Twins	3	3	Philadelphia Phillies	1	4
St. Louis Browns/Baltimore Orioles	3	4	Seattle Pilots/Milwaukee Brewers	0	1
Boston/Milwaukee/Atlanta Braves	3	6	San Diego Padres	0	2

(1) Through 2002.

All-Time Major League Leaders

(*player active in 2003 season)

Games		At Bats		Runs Batted In		Runs	
Pete Rose	3,562	Pete Rose	14,053	Hank Aaron	2,297	Rickey Henderson*	2,295
Carl Yastrzemski	3,308	Hank Aaron	12,364	Babe Ruth	2,213	Ty Cobb	2,246
Hank Aaron	3,298	Carl Yastrzemski	11,988	Lou Gehrig	1,995	Hank Aaron	2,174
Rickey Henderson*	3,081	Cal Ripken Jr.	11,551	Stan Musial	1,951	Babe Ruth	2,174
Ty Cobb	3,035	Ty Cobb	11,434	Ty Cobb	1,937	Pete Rose	2,165
Eddie Murray	3,026	Eddie Murray	11,336	Jimmie Foxx	1,922	Willie Mays	2,062
Stan Musial	3,026	Robin Yount	11,008	Eddie Murray	1,917	Stan Musial	1,949
Cal Ripken Jr.	3,001	Dave Winfield	11,003	Willie Mays	1,903	Barry Bonds	1,941
Willie Mays	2,992	Stan Musial	10,972	Cap Anson	1,879	Lou Gehrig	1,888
Dave Winfield	2,973	Rickey Henderson*	10,961	Mel Ott	1,860	Tris Speaker	1,882

Stolen Bases

Rickey Henderson*.	1,406
Lou Brock	938
Billy Hamilton	912
Ty Cobb	892
Tim Raines	808
Vince Coleman	752
Eddie Collins	744
Arlie Latham	739
Max Carey	738
Honus Wagner	722

Triples

Sam Crawford	309
Ty Cobb	295
Honus Wagner	252
Jake Beckley	243
Roger Connor	233
Tris Speaker	222
Fred Clarke	220
Dan Brouthers	205
Joe Kelley	194
Paul Waner	191

Doubles

Tris Speaker	792
Pete Rose	746
Stan Musial	725
Ty Cobb	724
George Brett	665
Nap Lajoie	657
Carl Yastrzemski	646
Honus Wagner	640
Hank Aaron	624
Paul Molitor	605
Paul Waner	605

Walks

Rickey Henderson*.	2,190
Barry Bonds	2,070
Babe Ruth	2,174
Ted Williams	2,019
Barry Bonds*	1,922
Joe Morgan	1,865
Carl Yastrzemski	1,845
Mickey Mantle	1,733
Mel Ott	1,708
Eddie Yost	1,614
Darrell Evans	1,605

Strikeouts

Nolan Ryan	5,714
Steve Carlton	4,136
Roger Clemens*	4,099
Randy Johnson*	3,871
Bert Blyleven	3,701
Tom Seaver	3,640
Don Sutton	3,574
Gaylord Perry	3,534
Walter Johnson	3,509
Phil Niekro	3,342

Saves

Lee Smith	478
John Franco*	424
Dennis Eckersley	390
Jeff Reardon	367
Trevor Hoffman*	352
Randy Myers	347
Rollie Fingers	341
John Wetteland	330
Roberto Hernandez*.	320
Rick Aguilera	318

Shutouts

Walter Johnson	110
Grover Alexander	90
Christy Mathewson	79
Cy Young	76
Eddie Plank	69
Warren Spahn	63
Nolan Ryan	61
Tom Seaver	61
Bert Blyleven	60
Don Sutton	58

Losses

Cy Young	316
Jim Galvin	308
Nolan Ryan	292
Walter Johnson	279
Phil Niekro	274
Gaylord Perry	265
Don Sutton	256
Jack Powell	254
Eppa Rixey	251
Bert Blyleven	250

All-Time Home Run Leaders

Player	HR	Player	HR	Player	HR	Player	HR
Hank Aaron	755	Willie McCovey	521	Carl Yastrzemski	452	Joe Carter	396
Babe Ruth	714	Ted Williams	521	Dave Kingman	442	Graig Nettles	390
Willie Mays	660	Ernie Banks	512	Andre Dawson	438	Johnny Bench	389
Barry Bonds*	658	Ed Mathews	512	Cal Ripken Jr.	431	Dwight Evans	385
Frank Robinson	586	Mel Ott	511	Juan Gonzalez*	429	Harold Baines	384
Mark McGwire	583	Eddie Murray	504	Billy Williams	426	Frank Howard	382
Harmon Killebrew	573	Lou Gehrig	493	Jeff Bagwell*	419	Jim Rice	382
Reggie Jackson	563	Fred McGriff*	491	Frank Thomas*	418	Jim Thome*	381
Mike Schmidt	548	Ken Griffey Jr.*	481	Darrell Evans	414	Albert Belle	381
Sammy Sosa*	539	Stan Musial	475	Duke Snider	407	Orlando Cepeda	380
Mickey Mantle	536	Willie Stargell	475	Al Kaline	399	Norm Cash	377
Jimmie Foxx	534	Dave Winfield	465	Andres Galarraga*	398	Tony Perez	379
Rafael Palmeiro*	528	Jose Canseco	462	Dale Murphy	398		

Players With 3,000 Major League Hits

Player	Hits	Player	Hits	Player	Hits	Player	Hits
Pete Rose	4,256	Paul Molitor	3,319	George Brett	3,154	Rickey Henderson*	3,055
Ty Cobb	4,189	Eddie Collins	3,315	Paul Waner	3,152	Rod Carew	3,053
Hank Aaron	3,771	Willie Mays	3,283	Robin Yount	3,142	Lou Brock	3,023
Stan Musial	3,630	Eddie Murray	3,255	Tony Gwynn	3,141	Wade Boggs	3,010
Tris Speaker	3,514	Nap Lajoie	3,242	Dave Winfield	3,110	Al Kaline	3,007
Carl Yastrzemski	3,419	Cal Ripken Jr.	3,184	Cap Anson[1]	3,056	Roberto Clemente	3,000
Honus Wagner	3,415						

Pitchers With 300 Major League Wins

Cy Young	511	Pud Galvin	360	Nolan Ryan	324	Roger Clemens	310
Walter Johnson	417	Tim Keefe	342	Don Sutton	324	Charley Radbourn	309
Grover Alexander	373	Steve Carlton	329	Phil Niekro	318	Mickey Welch	307
Christy Mathewson	373	John Clarkson	328	Gaylord Perry	314	Lefty Grove	300
Warren Spahn	363	Eddie Plank	326	Tom Seaver	311	Early Wynn	300
Kid Nichols	361						

(1) According to revised stats from Total Baseball, the official encyclopedia of Major League Baseball.

All-Time Major League Single-Season Leaders

(*player active in 2003 season; records for "modern" era beginning 1901)

Home Runs

Barry Bonds* (2001)	73
Mark McGwire (1998)	70
Sammy Sosa* (1998)	66
Mark McGwire (1999)	65
Sammy Sosa* (2001)	64

Batting Average

Nap Lajoie (1901)	.426
Rogers Hornsby (1924)	.424
George Sisler (1922)	.420
Ty Cobb (1911)	.420
Ty Cobb (1912)	.409

Earned Run Average

Dutch Leonard (1914)	0.96
Mordecai Brown (1906)	1.04
Bob Gibson (1968)	1.12
Walter Johnson (1913)	1.14
Christy Mathewson (1909)	1.14

Runs

Babe Ruth (1921)	177
Lou Gehrig (1936)	167
Lou Gehrig (1931)	163
Babe Ruth (1928)	163
Chuck Klein (1930)	158
Babe Ruth (1920, 1927)	158

Stolen Bases

Rickey Henderson* (1982)	130
Lou Brock (1974)	118
Vince Coleman (1985)	110
Vince Coleman (1987)	109
Rickey Henderson* (1983)	108

Wins

Jack Chesbro (1904)	41
Ed Walsh (1908)	40
Christy Mathewson (1908)	37
Walter Johnson (1913)	36
Joe McGinnity (1904)	35

Hits

George Sisler (1920)	257
Bill Terry (1930)	254
Lefty O'Doul (1929)	254
Al Simmons (1925)	253
Chuck Klein (1930)	250
Rogers Hornsby (1922)	250

Walks (Batter)

Barry Bonds* (2002)	198
Barry Bonds* (2001)	177
Babe Ruth (1923)	170
Mark McGwire (1998)	162
Ted Williams (1949)	162
Ted Williams (1947)	162

Strikeouts

Nolan Ryan (1973)	383
Sandy Koufax (1965)	382
Randy Johnson* (2001)	372
Nolan Ryan (1974)	367
Randy Johnson* (1999)	364

Runs Batted In

Hack Wilson (1930)	191
Lou Gehrig (1931)	184
Hank Greenberg (1937)	183
Jimmie Foxx (1938)	175
Lou Gehrig (1927)	175

Strikeouts (Batter)

Bobby Bonds (1970)	189
Jose Hernandez* (2002)	188
Preston Wilson* (2000)	187
Bobby Bonds (1969)	187
Rob Deer (1987)	186
Jim Thome* (2001)	185
Jose Hernandez* (2001)	185
Pete Incaviglia (1986)	185

Saves

Bobby Thigpen (1990)	57
Eric Gagne* (2003)	55
John Smoltz* (2002)	55
Trevor Hoffman* (1998)	53
Randy Myers (1993)	53
Eric Gagne* (2002)	52

Official Major League Perfect Games Since 1900

Date	Pitcher	Teams	Date	Pitcher	Teams
5/5/04	Cy Young	Boston 3 vs. Phil. 0 (AL)	5/15/81	Len Barker	Clev. 3 vs. Toronto 0 (AL)
10/2/08	Addie Joss	Clev. 1 vs. Chicago 0 (AL)	9/30/84	Mike Witt	Calif.1 at Texas 0 (AL)
4/30/22	Charlie Robertson	Chicago 2 at Detroit 0 (AL)	9/16/88	Tom Browning	Cincinnati 1 vs. L.A. 0 (NL)
10/8/56	Don Larsen	N.Y. 2 vs. Brooklyn 0 (AL)*	7/28/91	Dennis Martinez	Montreal 2 vs. L.A. 0 (NL)
6/21/64	Jim Bunning	Phil. 6 at N.Y. 0 (NL)	7/28/94	Kenny Rogers	Texas 4 vs. California 0 (AL)
9/9/65	Sandy Koufax	L.A. 1 vs. Chicago 0 (NL)	5/17/98	David Wells	N.Y. 4 vs. Minn. 0 (AL)
5/8/68	Catfish Hunter	Oakland 4 vs. Minn.0 (AL)	7/18/99	David Cone	N.Y. 6 vs. Montreal 0 (AL)

*World Series Game

Most Career Major League No Hitters

No.	Pitcher
7	Nolan Ryan
4	Sandy Koufax
3	Larry Corcoran, Bob Feller, Cy Young
2	Jim Bunning, Steve Busby, Carl Erskine, Bob Forsch, Pud Galvin, Ken Holtzman, Addie Joss, Dutch Leonard, Jim Maloney, Christy Mathewson, Hideo Nomo, Allie Reynolds, Frank Smith, Warren Spahn, Bill Stoneman, Virgil Trucks, Johnny Vander Meer, Ed Walsh, Don Wilson

All-Star Baseball Games, 1933-2003

Year	Winner, Score	Host team	Year	Winner, Score	Host team	Year	Winner, Score	Host team
1933*	American, 4-2	Chicago (AL)	1959*	National, 5-4	Pittsburgh	1981	National, 5-4	Cleveland
1934*	American, 9-7	New York (NL)	1959*	American, 5-3	Los Angeles	1982	National, 4-1	Montreal
1935*	American, 4-1	Cleveland	1960*	National, 5-3	Kansas City	1983	American, 13-3	Chicago (AL)
1936*	National, 4-3	Boston (NL)	1960*	National, 6-0	New York (AL)	1984	National, 3-1	San Francisco
1937*	American, 8-3	Washington	1961*	National, 5-4³	San Francisco	1985	National, 6-1	Minnesota
1938*	National, 4-1	Cincinnati	1961*	Called–rain, 1-1	Boston	1986	American, 3-2	Houston
1939*	American, 3-1	New York (AL)	1962*	National, 3-1³	Washington	1987	National, 2-0⁵	Oakland
1940*	National, 4-0	St. Louis (NL)	1962*	American, 9-4	Chicago (NL)	1988	American, 2-1	Cincinnati
1941*	American, 7-5	Detroit	1963*	National, 5-3	Cleveland	1989	American, 5-3	California
1942*	American, 3-1	New York (NL)	1964*	National, 7-4	New York (NL)	1990	American, 2-0	Chicago (NL)
1943	American, 5-3	Philadelphia (AL)	1965*	National, 6-5	Minnesota	1991	American, 4-2	Toronto
1944	National, 7-1	Pittsburgh	1966*	National, 2-1³	St. Louis	1992	American, 13-6	San Diego
1945	(Not played)		1967*	National, 2-1⁴	California	1993	American, 9-3	Baltimore
1946*	American, 12-0	Boston (AL)	1968	National, 1-0	Houston	1994	National, 8-7³	Pittsburgh
1947*	American, 2-1	Chicago (NL)	1969*	National, 9-3	Washington	1995	National, 3-2	Texas
1948*	American, 5-2	St. Louis (AL)	1970	National, 5-4²	Cincinnati	1996	National, 6-0	Philadelphia
1949*	American, 11-7	Brooklyn	1971	American, 6-4	Detroit	1997	American, 3-1	Cleveland
1950*	National, 4-3¹	Chicago (AL)	1972	National, 4-3³	Atlanta	1998	American, 13-8	Colorado
1951*	National, 8-3	Detroit	1973	National, 7-1	Kansas City	1999	American, 4-1	Boston
1952*	National, 3-2	Philadelphia (NL)	1974	National, 7-2	Pittsburgh	2000	American, 6-3	Atlanta
1953*	National, 5-1	Cincinnati	1975	National, 6-3	Milwaukee	2001	American, 4-1	Seattle
1954*	American, 11-9	Cleveland	1976	National, 7-1	Philadelphia	2002	Hack Wilson	191
1955*	National, 6-5²	Milwaukee	1977	National, 7-5	New York (AL)		(1930)	
1956*	National, 7-3	Washington	1978	National, 7-3	San Diego	2003	Lou Gehrig	184
1957*	American, 6-5	St. Louis	1979	National, 7-6	Seattle		(1931)	
1958*	American, 4-3	Baltimore	1980	National, 4-2	Los Angeles			

*Denotes day game. (1) 14 innings. (2) 12 innings. (3) 10 innings. (4) 15 innings. (5) 13 innings. (6) Game called in the 11th inning when both teams ran out of pitchers. (7) Under rule change, league winning All-Star games earned World Series home-field advantage.

Major League Franchise Shifts and Additions

1953—Boston Braves (NL) became Milwaukee Braves.
1954—St. Louis Browns (AL) became Baltimore Orioles.
1955—Philadelphia Athletics (AL) became Kansas City Athletics.
1958—New York Giants (NL) became San Francisco Giants.
1958—Brooklyn Dodgers (NL) became L.A. Dodgers.
1961—Washington Senators (AL) became Minnesota Twins.
1961—L.A. Angels (renamed California Angels in 1965 and Anaheim Angels in 1997) enfranchised by the American League.
1961—Washington Senators enfranchised by the American League (a new team, replacing the former Washington club, whose franchise was moved to Minneapolis-St. Paul).
1962—Houston Colt .45's (renamed the Houston Astros in 1965) enfranchised by the National League.
1962—New York Mets enfranchised by the National League.
1966—Milwaukee Braves (NL) became Atlanta Braves.
1968—Kansas City Athletics (AL) became Oakland Athletics.
1969—Kansas City Royals and Seattle Pilots enfranchised by the American League; Montreal Expos and San Diego Padres enfranchised by the National League.
1970—Seattle Pilots became Milwaukee Brewers.
1971—Washington Senators became Texas Rangers (Dallas-Fort Worth area).
1977—Toronto Blue Jays and Seattle Mariners enfranchised by the American League.
1993—Colorado Rockies (Denver) and Florida Marlins (Miami) enfranchised by the National League.
1998—Tampa Bay Devil Rays began play in the American League; Arizona Diamondbacks (Phoenix) began play in the National League (both teams enfranchised in 1995). Milwaukee Brewers moved from the AL to the NL.

Baseball Stadiums[1]
National League

Team	Stadium (year opened)	Surface	Home run distances (ft.)			Seating capacity
			LF	Center	RF	
Arizona Diamondbacks	Bank One Ballpark (1998)	Grass	330	407	334	49,033
Atlanta Braves	Turner Field (1997)	Grass	335	401	330	50,062
Chicago Cubs	Wrigley Field (1914)	Grass	355	400	353	38,902
Cincinnati Reds	Great American Ballpark (2003)	Grass	328	404	325	42,059
Colorado Rockies	Coors Field (1995)	Grass	347	415	350	50,381
Florida Marlins	Pro Player Stadium (1987)	Grass	325	410	345	42,531
Houston Astros	Minute Maid Park (2000)	Grass	315	435	326	42,000
Los Angeles Dodgers	Dodger Stadium (1962)	Grass	330	395	330	56,000
Milwaukee Brewers	Miller Park (2001)	Grass	342	400	356	43,000
Montreal Expos	Olympic Stadium (1976)	Artificial	325	404	325	46,500
New York Mets	Shea Stadium (1964)	Grass	338	410	338	55,775
Philadelphia Phillies	Veterans Stadium (1971)	Artificial	330	408	330	62,409

National League

Team	Stadium (year opened)	Surface	Home run distances (ft.) [1]			Seating capacity
			LF	Center	RF	
Pittsburgh Pirates............	PNC Park (2001)	Grass	325	399	320	38,365
St. Louis Cardinals...........	Busch Stadium (1966)	Grass	330	402	330	49,625
San Diego Padres	Qualcomm Stadium (1967)............	Grass	327	405	330	56.133
San Francisco Giants........	Pacific Bell Park (2000).	Grass	335	404	307	41,059

American League

Team	Stadium (year opened)	Surface	LF	Center	RF	Seating capacity
Anaheim Angels.............	Edison Intl. Field of Anaheim (1966)	Grass	333	408	333	45,050
Baltimore Orioles	Oriole Park at Camden Yards (1992)	Grass	333	400	318	48,876
Boston Red Sox............	Fenway Park (1912)	Grass	310	420	302	33,871
Chicago White Sox..........	U.S. Cellular Field (1991)	Grass	347	400	347	45,936
Cleveland Indians...........	Jacobs Field (1994)	Grass	325	405	325	43,368
Detroit Tigers	Comerica Park (2000)...............	Grass	345	402	330	40,000
Kansas City Royals	Kauffman Stadium (1973)............	Grass	330	400	330	40,625
Minnesota Twins............	Hubert H. Humphrey Metrodome (1982)	Artificial	343	408	327	48,678
New York Yankees	Yankee Stadium (1923)	Grass	318	408	314	55,070
Oakland A's	Network Associates Coliseum (1968)......	Grass	330	400	330	43,662
Seattle Mariners	Safeco Field (1999)	Grass	331	405	327	47,116
Tampa Bay Devil Rays	Tropicana Field (1990)	Artificial	315	407	322	45,200
Texas Rangers	The Ballpark in Arlington (1994)........	Grass	332	400	325	49,166
Toronto Blue Jays...........	SkyDome (1989).	Artificial	328	400	328	50,516

(1) As of 2003 season.

Little League World Series

The Little League World Series is played annually in Williamsport, PA. Pitcher Yuutaro Tanaka hit a home run and struck out 14 batters to lead Japan's Tokyo Musashi-Fuchu team to a 10-1 win over East Boynton Beach (FL) in the 2003 Little League World Series final, Aug. 25. Florida teams have been to the LLWS a record 8 times without a championship.

Year	Winning / Losing Team	Score	Year	Winning / Losing Team	Score
1947	Williamsport, PA; Lock Haven, PA	16-7	1976	Tokyo, Japan; Campbell, CA	10-3
1948	Lock Haven, PA; St. Petersburg, FL.	6-5	1977	Taiwan; El Cajon, CA....................	7-2
1949	Hammonton, NJ; Pensacola, FL	5-0	1978	Taiwan; Danville, CA....................	11-1
1950	Houston, TX; Bridgeport, CT...............	2-1	1979	Taiwan; Campbell, CA....................	2-1
1951	Stamford, CT; Austin, TX..................	3-0	1980	Taiwan; Tampa, FL......................	4-3
1952	Norwalk, CT; Monongahela, PA.	4-3	1981	Taiwan; Tampa, FL......................	4-2
1953	Birmingham, AL; Schenectady, NY	1-0	1982	Kirkland, WA; Taiwan....................	6-0
1954	Schenectady, NY; Colton, CA.	7-5	1983	Marietta, GA; Dominican Rep..............	3-1
1955	Morrisville, PA; Merchantville, NJ	4-3	1984	South Korea; Altamonte Springs, FL.	6-2
1956	Roswell, NM; Delaware, NJ	3-1	1985	South Korea; Mexico	7-1
1957	Mexico; La Mesa, CA....................	4-0	1986	Taiwan; Tucson, AZ.....................	12-0
1958	Mexico; Kankakee, IL....................	10-1	1987	Chinese Taipei; Irvine, CA................	21-1
1959	Hamtramck, MI; Auburn, CA	12-0	1988	Chinese Taipei; Pearl City, HI	10-0
1960	Levittown, PA; Ft. Worth, TX	5-0	1989	Trumbull, CT; Chinese Taipei..............	5-2
1961	El Cajon, CA; El Campo, TX	4-2	1990	Chinese Taipei; Shippensburg, PA	9-0
1962	San Jose, CA; Kankakee, IL	3-0	1991	Chinese Taipei; Danville, CA..............	11-0
1963	Granada Hills, CA; Stratford, CT	2-1	1992	Long Beach, CA; Philippines*	6-0
1964	Staten Island, NY; Mexico	4-0	1993	Long Beach, CA; Panama.................	3-2
1965	Windsor Locks, CT; Ontario, Canada.	3-1	1994	Venezuela; Northridge, CA	4-3
1966	Houston, TX; W. New York, NJ.............	8-2	1995	Taiwan; Spring, TX	17-3
1967	Tokyo, Japan; Chicago, IL	4-1	1996	Taiwan; Cranston, RI....................	13-3
1968	Osaka, Japan; Richmond, VA	1-0	1997	Mexico; Mission Viejo, CA................	5-4
1969	Taiwan; Santa Clara, CA	5-0	1998	Toms River, NJ; Japan.	12-9
1970	Wayne, NJ; Campbell, CA	2-0	1999	Japan; Phenix City, AL	5-0
1971	Taiwan; Gary, IN.......................	12-3	2000	Venezuela; Bellaire, TX..................	3-2
1972	Taiwan; Hammond, IN	6-0	2001	Japan; Apopka, FL......................	2-1
1973	Taiwan; Tucson, AZ	12-0	2002	Louisville, KY; Japan....................	1-0
1974	Taiwan; Red Bluff, CA	12-1	2003	Japan; East Boynton Beach, FL	10-1
1975	Lakewood, NJ; Tampa, FL.................	4-3			

*Philippines won 15-4, but was disqualified for using ineligible players. Long Beach was awarded title by forfeit 6-0 (1 run per inning).

NCAA Baseball Division I Champions

Year	Champion	Year	Champion	Year	Champion
1947	California	1961	USC	1976	Arizona
1948	Southern California	1962	Michigan	1977	Arizona St.
		1963	USC	1978	USC
1949	Texas	1964	Minnesota	1979	Cal. St.-Fullerton
1950	Texas	1965	Arizona St.	1980	Arizona
1951	Oklahoma	1966	Ohio St.	1981	Arizona St.
1952	Holy Cross	1967	Arizona St.	1982	Miami (FL)
1953	Michigan	1968	USC	1983	Texas
1954	Missouri	1969	Arizona St.	1984	Cal. St.-Fullerton
1955	Wake Forest	1970	USC	1985	Miami (FL)
1956	Minnesota	1971	USC	1986	Arizona
1957	California	1972	USC	1987	Stanford
1958	USC	1973	USC	1988	Stanford
1959	Oklahoma St.	1974	USC	1989	Wichita St.
1960	Minnesota	1975	Texas		
1990	Georgia				
1991	LSU				
1992	Pepperdine				
1993	LSU				
1994	Oklahoma				
1995	Cal. St.-Fullerton				
1996	LSU				
1997	LSU				
1998	USC				
1999	Miami (FL)				
2000	LSU				
2001	Miami (FL)				
2002	Texas				
2003	Rice				

NCAA Women's Softball Division I Champions

Year	Champion	Year	Champion	Year	Champion	Year	Champion
1982	UCLA	1988	UCLA	1994	Arizona	1999	UCLA
1983	Texas A&M	1989	UCLA	1995	UCLA	2000	Oklahoma
1984	UCLA	1990	UCLA	1996	Arizona	2001	Arizona
1985	UCLA	1991	Arizona	1997	Arizona	2002	California
1986	Cal St. Fullerton	1992	UCLA	1998	Fresno St.	2003	UCLA
1987	Texas A&M	1993	Arizona				

NATIONAL BASKETBALL ASSOCIATION
2002-2003 Season: Spurs Champs, NBA Greats Retire, League Expands

The San Antonio Spurs defeated the New Jersey Nets, 4 games to 2, in the 2003 NBA Finals to win their 2nd championship. Center Tim Duncan, the NBA MVP for the 2nd straight year, was also named MVP of the Finals for a 2nd time (1999). The L.A. Lakers, who failed in their bid to win 4 straight NBA titles (losing to the Spurs, 4-2, in the Western Conference semifinals) signed free-agent veterans Karl Malone and Gary Payton on July 16. Malone, 40, had a career average of 25.4 points per game and was 2nd all-time in career points and 7th in rebounds.

Five players on the NBA's "50 Greatest Players" list retired in 2002-2003. Patrick Ewing, who played 15 of his 17 seasons in New York, retired in Sept. 2002, followed by Houston's Hakeem Olajuwan in Nov. Utah guard John Stockton retired at the end of the 2003 season. Michael Jordan, 40, who came out of retirement in 2001 to play 2 seasons for Washington, also retired in May. San Antonio's David Robinson retired after winning the NBA title in June. In Jan. the NBA approved its 30th franchise, to begin play in the 2004-2005 season in Charlotte, NC. In June, owner Robert Johnson announced Bobcats as the team's name. On June 25, LeBron James (Cleveland) became only the 2nd high school player picked 1st in the NBA Draft.

Final Standings, 2002-2003 Season

(playoff seedings in parentheses; in each conference the 2 division winners automatically get the number 1 and 2 seeds)

Eastern Conference
Atlantic Division

	W	L	Pct	GB
New Jersey(2)	49	33	.598	—
Philadelphia (4)	48	34	.585	1
Boston (6)	44	38	.537	5
Orlando (8)	42	40	.512	7
Washington	37	45	.451	12
New York	37	45	.451	12
Miami	25	57	.305	24

Central Division

	W	L	Pct	GB
Detroit (1)	50	32	.610	—
Indiana (3)	48	34	.585	2
New Orleans (5)	47	35	.573	3
Milwaukee (7)	42	40	.512	8
Atlanta	35	47	.427	15
Chicago	30	52	.366	20
Toronto	24	58	.293	26
Cleveland	17	65	.207	33

Western Conference
Midwest Division

	W	L	Pct	GB
San Antonio (1)	60	22	.732	—
Dallas (3)	60	22	.732	—
Minnesota (4)	51	31	.622	9
Utah (7)	47	35	.573	13
Houston	43	39	.524	17
Memphis	28	54	.341	32
Denver	17	65	.207	43

Pacific Division

	W	L	Pct	GB
Sacramento (2)	59	23	.720	—
L.A. Lakers (5)	50	32	.610	9
Portland (6)	50	32	.610	9
Phoenix (8)	44	38	.537	15
Golden State	40	42	.488	19
Seattle	38	44	.463	21
L.A. Clippers	27	55	.329	32

NBA Regular Season Individual Highs in 2002-2003

Minutes, game: 55, 4 players tied (Shareef Abdur-Rahim, Ricky Davis, Tracy McGrady, Jalen Rose).

Points, game: 55, Kobe Bryant, L.A. Lakers v. Wash., March 28.

Field goals, game: 19, 4 players tied (Kobe Bryant, Shaquille O'Neal, Gary Payton, Wally Szczerbiak).

FG attempts, game: 47, Kobe Bryant, L.A. Lakers at Bos., Nov. 7.

3-pointers, game: 12, Kobe Bryant, L.A. Lakers v. Seattle, Jan. 7.

3-pt. attempts, game: 18, Kobe Bryant, L.A. Lakers v. Seattle, Jan. 7.

Free throws, game: 20, Paul Pierce, Boston at N.Y., Nov. 2.

FT attempts, game: 22, Karl Malone, Utah at Orlando, Mar. 12.

Rebounds, game: 25, Tim Duncan, San Ant. at Miami, Feb. 1.

Assists, game: 18, Jason Kidd, N.J. v. Memphis, Mar. 22; Gary Payton, Seattle at Houston, Nov. 5.

Steals, game: 9, Allen Iverson, Phil. v. L.A. Lakers, Dec. 20.

Blocks, game: 10, Jermaine O'Neal, Ind. v. Toronto, Jan. 22; Ben Wallace, Det. v. Miami, Nov. 20

Minutes, season: 3,485; Allen Iverson, Philadelphia.

Off. rebounds, season: 293, Ben Wallace, Detroit.

Def. rebounds, season: 858, Kevin Garnett, Minnesota.

Personal fouls, season: 344, Kurt Thomas, New York.

2003 NBA Playoff Results

Eastern Conference
New Jersey defeated Milwaukee 4 games to 2
Boston defeated Indiana 4 games to 2
Philadelphia defeated New Orleans 4 games to 2
Detroit defeated Orlando 4 games to 3
New Jersey defeated Boston 4 games to 0
Detroit defeated Philadelphia 4 games to 2
New Jersey defeated Detroit 4 games to 0

Western Conference
Sacramento defeated Utah 4 games to 1
San Antonio defeated Phoenix 4 games to 2
L.A. Lakers defeated Minnesota 4 games to 2
Dallas defeated Portland 4 games to 3
San Antonio defeated L.A. Lakers 4 games to 2
Dallas defeated Sacramento 4 games to 3
San Antonio defeated Dallas 4 games to 2

Championship
San Antonio defeated New Jersey 4 games to 2 [101-89, 85-87, 84-79, 76-77, 93-83, 88-77].

Spurs Supreme in 2003

The San Antonio Spurs won their 2nd NBA Championship in 5 years, defeating the New Jersey Nets, 88-77, in the 6th and deciding game at the SBC Center in San Antonio on June 15. San Antonio's Tim Duncan had 21 points, 20 rebounds, 10 assists, and 8 blocked shots in the game. In the 4th quarter, Duncan blocked 3 shots over a span of 5:30 in which San Antonio outscored New Jersey, 19-0, to take control of the game. Duncan, the regular season MVP, was also named MVP of the Finals. All-Star guard Jason Kidd led the Nets in the NBA Finals for a 2nd straight year, with 21 points. Kenyon Martin, who averaged 16.7 points a game during the season, was held to 6 by Duncan.

NBA Finals Composite Box Scores

San Antonio	FG M-A	FT M-A	Reb O-T	Ast	Avg	New Jersey	FG M-A	FT M-A	Reb O-T	Ast	Avg
Tim Duncan	54-109	37-54	23-102	32	24.2	Jason Kidd	44-121	20-24	14-37	47	19.7
Tony Parker	32-83	14-23	2-19	25	14.0	Kenyon Martin	36-105	16-24	15-60	13	14.7
David Robinson	22-36	21-30	15-44	4	10.8	Richard Jefferson	30-72	19-24	8-39	11	13.2
Stephen Jackson	23-61	6-12	4-25	16	10.3	Kerry Kittles	23-61	12-15	6-25	8	10.8
Manu Ginobili	16-46	17-21	9-27	12	8.7	Lucious Harris	11-36	15-19	7-16	7	6.5
Malik Rose	19-43	8-8	10-23	4	7.7	Aaron Williams	11-26	6-8	10-21	4	5.6
Speedy Claxton	14-25	9-12	1-6	9	6.2	Rodney Rogers	10-31	5-6	4-10	3	4.7
Bruce Bowen	7-30	2-2	2-19	5	3.3	Jason Collins	7-21	8-10	15-28	6	3.7
Steve Kerr	3-4	1-2	1-1	2	2.0	Dikembe Mutombo	5-10	4-4	7-17	0	2.3
Kevin Willis	3-9	2-2	7-9	0	1.6	Anthony Johnson	5-9	0-0	0-1	1	2.2
Danny Ferry	0-0	0-0	0-0	0	0.0	Brian Scalabrine	0-0	0-0	0-1	0	0.0
Steve Smith	0-1	0-0	0-0	0	0.0	Tamar Slay	0-0	0-0	0-0	0	0.0

NBA Finals MVP

Year	Player	Year	Player	Year	Player
1969	Jerry West, Los Angeles	1980	Magic Johnson, Los Angeles	1992	Michael Jordan, Chicago
1970	Willis Reed, New York	1981	Cedric Maxwell, Boston	1993	Michael Jordan, Chicago
1971	Lew Alcindor (Kareem Abdul-Jabbar), Milwaukee	1982	Magic Johnson, Los Angeles	1994	Hakeem Olajuwon, Houston
1972	Wilt Chamberlain, Los Angeles	1983	Moses Malone, Philadelphia	1995	Hakeem Olajuwon, Houston
1973	Willis Reed, New York	1984	Larry Bird, Boston	1996	Michael Jordan, Chicago
1974	John Havlicek, Boston	1985	Kareem Abdul-Jabbar, L.A. Lakers	1997	Michael Jordan, Chicago
1975	Rick Barry, Golden State	1986	Larry Bird, Boston	1998	Michael Jordan, Chicago
1976	Jo Jo White, Boston	1987	Magic Johnson, L.A. Lakers	1999	Tim Duncan, San Antonio
1977	Bill Walton, Portland	1988	James Worthy, L.A. Lakers	2000	Shaquille O'Neal, L.A. Lakers
1978	Wes Unseld, Washington	1989	Joe Dumars, Detroit	2001	Shaquille O'Neal, L.A. Lakers
1979	Dennis Johnson, Seattle	1990	Isiah Thomas, Detroit	2002	Shaquille O'Neal, L.A. Lakers
		1991	Michael Jordan, Chicago	2003	Tim Duncan, San Antonio

NBA Finals All-Time Statistical Leaders

(at the end of the 2003 NBA season finals; *denotes active in 2002-2003)

Scoring Average (Minimum 10 games)

	G	FG	FT	Pts.	Avg		G	FG	FT	Pts.	Avg
Rick Barry	10	138	87	363	36.3	Hakeem Olajuwon	17	187	91	467	27.5
*Shaquille O'Neal	19	253	144	650	34.2	Elgin Baylor	44	442	277	1,161	26.4
*Michael Jordan	35	438	258	1,176	33.6	*Tim Duncan	11	105	72	282	25.6
Jerry West	55	612	455	1,679	30.5	Julius Erving	22	216	128	561	25.5
Bob Pettit	25	241	227	709	28.4	Joe Fulks	11	84	104	272	24.7

Games Played

Bill Russell	70
Sam Jones	64
Kareem Abdul-Jabbar	56
Jerry West	55
Tom Heinsohn	52

Rebounds

Bill Russell	1,718
Wilt Chamberlain	862
Elgin Baylor	593
Kareem Abdul-Jabbar	507
Tom Heinsohn	473

Assists

Magic Johnson	584
Bob Cousy	400
Bill Russell	315
Jerry West	306
Dennis Johnson	228

NBA Scoring Leaders

Year	Scoring champion	Pts	Avg	Year	Scoring champion	Pts	Avg
1947	Joe Fulks, Philadelphia	1,389	23.2	1975	Bob McAdoo, Buffalo	2,831	34.5
1948	Max Zaslofsky, Chicago	1,007	21.0	1976	Bob McAdoo, Buffalo	2,427	31.1
1949	George Mikan, Minneapolis	1,698	28.3	1977	Pete Maravich, New Orleans	2,273	31.1
1950	George Mikan, Minneapolis	1,865	27.4	1978	George Gervin, San Antonio	2,232	27.2
1951	George Mikan, Minneapolis	1,932	28.4	1979	George Gervin, San Antonio	2,365	29.6
1952	Paul Arizin, Philadelphia	1,674	25.4	1980	George Gervin, San Antonio	2,585	33.1
1953	Neil Johnston, Philadelphia	1,564	22.3	1981	Adrian Dantley, Utah	2,452	30.7
1954	Neil Johnston, Philadelphia	1,759	24.4	1982	George Gervin, San Antonio	2,551	32.3
1955	Neil Johnston, Philadelphia	1,631	22.7	1983	Alex English, Denver	2,326	28.4
1956	Bob Pettit, St. Louis	1,849	25.7	1984	Adrian Dantley, Utah	2,418	30.6
1957	Paul Arizin, Philadelphia	1,817	25.6	1985	Bernard King, New York	1,809	32.9
1958	George Yardley, Detroit	2,001	27.8	1986	Dominique Wilkins, Atlanta	2,366	30.3
1959	Bob Pettit, St. Louis	2,105	29.2	1987	Michael Jordan, Chicago	3,041	37.1
1960	Wilt Chamberlain, Philadelphia	2,707	37.9	1988	Michael Jordan, Chicago	2,868	35.0
1961	Wilt Chamberlain, Philadelphia	3,033	38.4	1989	Michael Jordan, Chicago	2,633	32.5
1962	Wilt Chamberlain, Philadelphia	4,029	50.4	1990	Michael Jordan, Chicago	2,753	33.6
1963	Wilt Chamberlain, San Francisco	3,586	44.8	1991	Michael Jordan, Chicago	2,580	31.5
1964	Wilt Chamberlain, San Francisco	2,948	36.5	1992	Michael Jordan, Chicago	2,404	30.1
1965	Wilt Chamberlain, San Francisco, Phil.	2,534	34.7	1993	Michael Jordan, Chicago	2,541	32.6
1966	Wilt Chamberlain, Philadelphia	2,649	33.5	1994	David Robinson, San Antonio	2,383	29.8
1967	Rick Barry, San Francisco	2,775	35.6	1995	Shaquille O'Neal, Orlando	2,315	29.3
1968	Dave Bing, Detroit	2,142	27.1	1996	Michael Jordan, Chicago	2,465	30.4
1969	Elvin Hayes, San Diego	2,327	28.4	1997	Michael Jordan, Chicago	2,431	29.6
1970	Jerry West, Los Angeles	2,309	31.2	1998	Michael Jordan, Chicago	2,357	28.7
1971	Lew Alcindor (Kareem Abdul-Jabbar), Milwaukee	2,596	31.7	1999	Allen Iverson, Philadelphia	1,284	26.8
1972	Kareem Abdul-Jabbar, Milwaukee	2,822	34.8	2000	Shaquille O'Neal, L.A. Lakers	2,344	29.7
1973	Nate Archibald, Kans. City-Omaha	2,719	34.0	2001	Allen Iverson, Philadelphia	2,207	31.1
1974	Bob McAdoo, Buffalo	2,261	30.6	2002	Allen Iverson, Philadelphia	1,883	31.4
				2003	Tracy McGrady, Orlando	2,407	32.1

NBA Most Valuable Player

Year	Player	Year	Player	Year	Player
1956	Bob Pettit, St. Louis	1972	Kareem Abdul-Jabbar, Milwaukee	1988	Michael Jordan, Chicago
1957	Bob Cousy, Boston	1973	Dave Cowens, Boston	1989	Magic Johnson, L.A. Lakers
1958	Bill Russell, Boston	1974	Kareem Abdul-Jabbar, Milwaukee	1990	Magic Johnson, L.A. Lakers
1959	Bob Pettit, St. Louis	1975	Bob McAdoo, Buffalo	1991	Michael Jordan, Chicago
1960	Wilt Chamberlain, Philadelphia	1976	Kareem Abdul-Jabbar, L.A. Lakers	1992	Michael Jordan, Chicago
1961	Bill Russell, Boston	1977	Kareem Abdul-Jabbar, L.A. Lakers	1993	Charles Barkley, Phoenix
1962	Bill Russell, Boston	1978	Bill Walton, Portland	1994	Hakeem Olajuwon, Houston
1963	Bill Russell, Boston	1979	Moses Malone, Houston	1995	David Robinson, San Antonio
1964	Oscar Robertson, Cincinnati	1980	Kareem Abdul-Jabbar, L.A. Lakers	1996	Michael Jordan, Chicago
1965	Bill Russell, Boston	1981	Julius Erving, Philadelphia	1997	Karl Malone, Utah
1966	Wilt Chamberlain, Philadelphia	1982	Moses Malone, Houston	1998	Michael Jordan, Chicago
1967	Wilt Chamberlain, Philadelphia	1983	Moses Malone, Philadelphia	1999	Karl Malone, Utah
1968	Wilt Chamberlain, Philadelphia	1984	Larry Bird, Boston	2000	Shaquille O'Neal, L.A. Lakers
1969	Wes Unseld, Baltimore	1985	Larry Bird, Boston	2001	Allen Iverson, Philadelphia
1970	Willis Reed, New York	1986	Larry Bird, Boston	2002	Tim Duncan, San Antonio
1971	Lew Alcindor (Kareem Abdul-Jabbar), Milwaukee	1987	Magic Johnson, L.A. Lakers	2003	Tim Duncan, San Antonio

NBA Champions, 1947-2003

Year	Eastern Conference	Western Conference	Champion	Coach	Runner-up
	Regular season			**Playoffs**	
1947	Washington Capitols	Chicago Stags	Philadelphia	Ed Gottlieb	Chicago
1948	Philadelphia Warriors	St. Louis Bombers	Baltimore	Buddy Jeannette	Philadelphia
1949	Washington Capitols	Rochester	Minneapolis	John Kundla	Washington
1950	Syracuse	Minneapolis	Minneapolis	John Kundla	Syracuse
1951	Philadelphia Warriors	Minneapolis	Rochester	Lester Harrison	New York
1952	Syracuse	Rochester	Minneapolis	John Kundla	New York
1953	New York	Minneapolis	Minneapolis	John Kundla	New York
1954	New York	Minneapolis	Minneapolis	John Kundla	Syracuse
1955	Syracuse	Ft. Wayne	Syracuse	Al Cervi	Ft. Wayne
1956	Philadelphia Warriors	Ft. Wayne	Philadelphia	George Senesky	Ft. Wayne
1957	Boston	St. Louis	Boston	Red Auerbach	St. Louis
1958	Boston	St. Louis	St. Louis	Alex Hannum	Boston
1959	Boston	St. Louis	Boston	Red Auerbach	Minneapolis
1960	Boston	St. Louis	Boston	Red Auerbach	St. Louis
1961	Boston	St. Louis	Boston	Red Auerbach	St. Louis
1962	Boston	Los Angeles	Boston	Red Auerbach	Los Angeles
1963	Boston	Los Angeles	Boston	Red Auerbach	Los Angeles
1964	Boston	San Francisco	Boston	Red Auerbach	San Francisco
1965	Boston	Los Angeles	Boston	Red Auerbach	Los Angeles
1966	Philadelphia	Los Angeles	Boston	Red Auerbach	Los Angeles
1967	Philadelphia	San Francisco	Philadelphia	Alex Hannum	San Francisco
1968	Philadelphia	St. Louis	Boston	Bill Russell	Los Angeles
1969	Baltimore	Los Angeles	Boston	Bill Russell	Los Angeles
1970	New York	Atlanta	New York	Red Holzman	Los Angeles

Year	Atlantic	Central	Midwest	Pacific	Champion	Coach	Runner-up
1971	New York	Baltimore	Milwaukee	Los Angeles	Milwaukee	Larry Costello	Baltimore
1972	Boston	Baltimore	Milwaukee	Los Angeles	Los Angeles	Bill Sharman	New York
1973	Boston	Baltimore	Milwaukee	Los Angeles	New York	Red Holzman	Los Angeles
1974	Boston	Capital	Milwaukee	Los Angeles	Boston	Tom Heinsohn	Milwaukee
1975	Boston	Washington	Chicago	Golden State	Golden State	Al Attles	Washington
1976	Boston	Cleveland	Milwaukee	Golden State	Boston	Tom Heinsohn	Phoenix
1977	Philadelphia	Houston	Denver	Los Angeles	Portland	Jack Ramsay	Philadelphia
1978	Philadelphia	San Antonio	Denver	Portland	Washington	Dick Motta	Seattle
1979	Washington	San Antonio	Kansas City	Seattle	Seattle	Len Wilkens	Washington
1980	Boston	Atlanta	Milwaukee	Los Angeles	Los Angeles	Paul Westhead	Philadelphia
1981	Boston	Milwaukee	San Antonio	Phoenix	Boston	Bill Fitch	Houston
1982	Boston	Milwaukee	San Antonio	Los Angeles	Los Angeles	Pat Riley	Philadelphia
1983	Philadelphia	Milwaukee	San Antonio	Los Angeles	Philadelphia	Billy Cunningham	Los Angeles
1984	Boston	Milwaukee	Utah	Los Angeles	Boston	K.C. Jones	Los Angeles
1985	Boston	Milwaukee	Denver	L.A. Lakers	L.A. Lakers	Pat Riley	Boston
1986	Boston	Milwaukee	Houston	L.A. Lakers	Boston	K.C. Jones	Houston
1987	Boston	Atlanta	Dallas	L.A. Lakers	L.A. Lakers	Pat Riley	Boston
1988	Boston	Detroit	Denver	L.A. Lakers	L.A. Lakers	Pat Riley	Detroit
1989	New York	Detroit	Utah	L.A. Lakers	Detroit	Chuck Daly	L.A. Lakers
1990	Philadelphia	Detroit	San Antonio	L.A. Lakers	Detroit	Chuck Daly	Portland
1991	Boston	Chicago	San Antonio	Portland	Chicago	Phil Jackson	L.A. Lakers
1992	Boston	Chicago	Utah	Portland	Chicago	Phil Jackson	Portland
1993	New York	Chicago	Houston	Phoenix	Chicago	Phil Jackson	Phoenix
1994	New York	Atlanta	Houston	Seattle	Houston	Rudy Tomjanovich	New York
1995	Orlando	Indiana	San Antonio	Phoenix	Houston	Rudy Tomjanovich	Orlando
1996	Orlando	Chicago	San Antonio	Seattle	Chicago	Phil Jackson	Seattle
1997	Miami	Chicago	Utah	Seattle	Chicago	Phil Jackson	Utah
1998	Miami	Chicago	Utah	L.A. Lakers	Chicago	Phil Jackson	Utah
1999	Miami	Indiana	San Antonio	Portland	San Antonio	Gregg Popovich	New York
2000	Miami	Indiana	Utah	L.A. Lakers	L.A. Lakers	Phil Jackson	Indiana
2001	Philadelphia	Milwaukee	San Antonio	L.A. Lakers	L.A. Lakers	Phil Jackson	Philadelphia
2002	New Jersey	Detroit	San Antonio	Sacramento	L.A. Lakers	Phil Jackson	New Jersey
2003	New Jersey	Detroit	San Antonio	Sacramento	San Antonio	Gregg Popovich	New Jersey

NBA Coach of the Year, 1963-2003

1963 Harry Galiatin, St. Louis Hawks	1976 Bill Fitch, Cleveland Cavaliers	1990 Pat Riley, Los Angeles Lakers
1964 Alex Hannum, San Francisco Warriors	1977 Tom Nissalke, Houston Rockets	1991 Don Chaney, Houston Rockets
1965 Red Auerbach, Boston Celtics	1978 Hubie Brown, Atlanta Hawks	1992 Don Nelson, Golden State Warriors
1966 Dolph Schayes, Philadelphia 76ers	1979 Cotton Fitzsimmons, Kansas City Kings	1993 Pat Riley, New York Knicks
1967 Johnny Kerr, Chicago Bulls	1980 Bill Fitch, Boston Celtics	1994 Lenny Wilkens, Atlanta Hawks
1968 Richie Guerin, St. Louis Hawks	1981 Jack McKinney, Indiana Pacers	1995 Del Harris, Los Angeles Lakers
1969 Gene Shue, Baltimore Bullets	1982 Gene Shue, Washington Bullets	1996 Phil Jackson, Chicago Bulls
1970 Red Holzman, New York Knicks	1983 Don Nelson, Milwaukee Bucks	1997 Pat Riley, Miami Heat
1971 Dick Motta, Chicago Bulls	1984 Frank Layden, Utah Jazz	1998 Larry Bird, Indiana Pacers
1972 Bill Sharman, Los Angeles Lakers	1985 Don Nelson, Milwaukee Bucks	1999 Mike Dunleavy, Portland Trail Blazers
1973 Tom Heinsohn, Boston Celtics	1986 Mike Fratello, Atlanta Hawks	2000 Glenn "Doc" Rivers, Orlando Magic
1974 Ray Scott, Detroit Pistons	1987 Mike Schuler, Portland Trail Blazers	2001 Larry Brown, Philadelphia 76ers
1975 Phil Johnson, Kansas City-Omaha Kings	1988 Doug Moe, Denver Nuggets	2002 Rick Carlisle, Detroit Pistons
	1989 Cotton Fitzsimmons, Phoenix Suns	2003 Gregg Popovich, San Antonio

NBA All-League and All-Defensive Teams, 2002-2003

	All-League Team			All-Defensive Team	
First team	**Second team**		**Position**	**First team**	**Second team**
Tim Duncan, San Antonio	Dirk Nowitzki, Dallas		Forward	Kevin Garnett, Minnesota	Ron Artest, Indiana
Kevin Garnett, Minnesota	Chris Webber, Sacramento		Forward	Tim Duncan, San Antonio	Bruce Bowen, San Antonio
Shaquille O'Neal, L.A. Lakers	Ben Wallace, Detroit		Center	Ben Wallace, Detroit	Shaquille O'Neal, L.A. Lakers
Kobe Bryant, L.A. Lakers	Jason Kidd, New Jersey		Guard	Doug Christie, Sacramento	Jason Kidd, New Jersey
Tracy McGrady, Orlando	Allen Iverson, Philadelphia		Guard	Kobe Bryant, L.A. Lakers	Eric Snow, Philadelphia

NBA Statistical Leaders, 2002-2003

Scoring Average
(Minimum 70 games or 1,400 pts)

	G	FG	FT	Pts	Avg
Tracy McGrady, Orlando	75	829	576	2,407	32.1
Kobe Bryant, L.A. Lakers	82	868	601	2,461	30.0
Allen Iverson, Philadelphia	82	804	570	2,262	27.6
Shaquille O'Neal, L.A. Lakers	67	695	451	1,841	27.5
Paul Pierce, Boston	79	663	604	2,048	25.9
Dirk Nowitzki, Dallas	80	690	483	2,011	25.1
Tim Duncan, San Antonio	81	714	450	1,884	23.3
Chris Webber, Sacramento	67	661	215	1,542	23.0
Kevin Garnett, Minnesota	82	743	377	1,883	23.0
Ray Allen, Seattle	76	598	316	1,713	22.5
Allan Houston, New York	82	652	363	1,845	22.5

3-Point Field Goal Percentage
(Minimum 55 3-point field goals made)

	FG	FGA	Pct
Bruce Bowen, San Antonio	101	229	.441
Michael Redd, Milwaukee	182	416	.438
Wesley Person, Memphis	100	231	.433
David Wesley, New Orleans	134	316	.424
Wally Szczerbiak, Minnesota	61	145	.421
Steve Nash, Dallas	111	269	.413
Matt Harpring, Utah	66	160	.413
Anthony Peeler, Minnesota	87	212	.410
Mike Bibby, Sacramento	56	137	.409
Eddie Jones, Miami	98	241	.407
Jon Barry, Detroit	87	214	.407

Rebounds per Game
(Minimum 70 games or 800 rebounds)

	G	Off	Def	Tot	Avg
Ben Wallace, Detroit	73	293	833	1,126	15.4
Kevin Garnett, Minnesota	82	244	858	1,102	13.4
Tim Duncan, San Antonio	81	259	784	1,043	12.9
Jermaine O'Neal, Indiana	77	202	594	796	10.3
Brian Grant, Miami	82	241	596	837	10.2
Troy Murphy, Golden State	79	228	578	806	10.2
Dirk Nowitzki, Dallas	80	81	710	791	9.9
Shawn Marion, Phoenix	81	199	574	773	9.5
Jerome Williams, Toronto	71	231	419	650	9.2
P.J. Brown, New Orleans	78	243	458	701	9.0
Donyell Marshall, Chicago	78	234	465	699	9.0

Assists per Game
(Minimum 70 games or 400 assists)

	G	No	Avg
Jason Kidd, New Jersey	80	711	8.9
Jason Williams, Memphis	76	631	8.3
Gary Payton, Milwaukee	80	663	8.3
Stephon Marbury, Phoenix	81	654	8.1
John Stockton, Utah	82	629	7.7
Jamaal Tinsley, Indiana	73	548	7.5
Jason Terry, Atlanta	81	600	7.4
Steve Nash, Dallas	82	598	7.3
Andre Miller, L.A. Clippers	80	537	6.7
Eric Snow, Philadelphia	82	544	6.6

Field Goal Percentage
(Minimum 300 field goals made)

	FGM	FGA	Pct
Eddy Curry, Chicago	335	573	.585
Shaquille O'Neal, L.A. Lakers	695	1,211	.574
Carlos Boozer, Cleveland	331	618	.536
P.J. Brown, New Orleans	319	601	.531
Radoslav Nesterovic, Minnesota	400	762	.525
Nene Hilario, Denver	321	619	.519
Tim Duncan, San Antonio	714	1,392	.513
Matt Harpring, Utah	521	1,020	.511
Pau Gasol, Memphis	569	1,116	.510
Brian Grant, Miami	344	676	.509

Steals per Game
(Minimum 70 games or 125 steals)

	G	No	Avg
Allen Iverson, Philadelphia	82	225	2.74
Ron Artest, Indiana	69	159	2.30
Shawn Marion, Phoenix	81	185	2.28
Doug Christie, Sacramento	80	180	2.25
Jason Kidd, New Jersey	80	179	2.24
Kobe Bryant, L.A. Lakers	82	181	2.21
Paul Pierce, Boston	79	139	1.76
Caron Butler, Miami	78	137	1.76
Steve Francis, Houston	81	141	1.74
Jamaal Tinsley, Indiana	73	125	1.71

Free Throw Percentage
(Minimum 125 free throws made)

	FTM	FTA	Pct
Allan Houston, New York	363	395	.919
Ray Allen, Seattle	316	345	.916
Steve Nash, Dallas	308	339	.909
Troy Hudson, Minnesota	208	231	.900
Reggie Miller, Indiana	207	230	.900
Jason Terry, Atlanta	259	292	.887
Dirk Nowitzki, Dallas	483	548	.881
Chauncey Billups, Detroit	318	362	.878
Jerry Stackhouse, Washington	455	518	.878
Darrell Armstrong, Orlando	165	188	.878
Glenn Robinson, Atlanta	268	306	.876

Blocked Shots per Game
(Minimum 70 games or 100 blocked shots)

	G	Blk	Avg
Theo Ratliff, Atlanta	81	262	3.23
Ben Wallace, Detroit	73	230	3.15
Tim Duncan, San Antonio	81	237	2.93
Elton Brand, L.A. Clippers	62	158	2.55
Adonal Foyle, Golden State	82	205	2.50
Shaquille O'Neal, L.A. Lakers	67	159	2.37
Jermaine O'Neal, Indiana	77	178	2.31
Andrei Kirilenko, Utah	80	175	2.19
Shawn Bradley, Dallas	81	170	2.10
Erick Dampier, Golden State	82	154	1.88
Zydrunas Ilgauskas, Cleveland	81	152	1.88
Keon Clark, Sacramento	80	150	1.88

NBA Rookie of the Year

Year	Player	Year	Player	Year	Player
1953	Don Meineke, Ft. Wayne	1971	Dave Cowens, Boston;	1988	Mark Jackson, New York
1954	Ray Felix, Baltimore		Geoff Petrie, Portland (tie)	1989	Mitch Richmond, Golden State
1955	Bob Pettit, Milwaukee	1972	Sidney Wicks, Portland	1990	David Robinson, San Antonio
1956	Maurice Stokes, Rochester	1973	Bob McAdoo, Buffalo	1991	Derrick Coleman, New Jersey
1957	Tom Heinsohn, Boston	1974	Ernie DiGregorio, Buffalo	1992	Larry Johnson, Charlotte
1958	Woody Sauldsberry, Philadelphia	1975	Keith Wilkes, Golden State	1993	Shaquille O'Neal, Orlando
1959	Elgin Baylor, Minneapolis	1976	Alvan Adams, Phoenix	1994	Chris Webber, Golden State
1960	Wilt Chamberlain, Philadelphia	1977	Adrian Dantley, Buffalo	1995	Grant Hill, Detroit;
1961	Oscar Robertson, Cincinnati	1978	Walter Davis, Phoenix		Jason Kidd, Dallas (tie)
1962	Walt Bellamy, Chicago	1979	Phil Ford, Kansas City	1996	Damon Stoudamire, Toronto
1963	Terry Dischinger, Chicago	1980	Larry Bird, Boston	1997	Allen Iverson, Philadelphia
1964	Jerry Lucas, Cincinnati	1981	Darrell Griffith, Utah	1998	Tim Duncan, San Antonio
1965	Willis Reed, New York	1982	Buck Williams, New Jersey	1999	Vince Carter, Toronto
1966	Rick Barry, San Francisco	1983	Terry Cummings, San Diego	2000	Elton Brand, Chicago;
1967	Dave Bing, Detroit	1984	Ralph Sampson, Houston		Steve Francis, Houston (tie)
1968	Earl Monroe, Baltimore	1985	Michael Jordan, Chicago	2001	Mike Milier, Orlando
1969	Wes Unseld, Baltimore	1986	Patrick Ewing, New York	2002	Pau Gasol, Memphis
1970	Lew Alcindor, Milwaukee	1987	Chuck Person, Indiana	2003	Amaré Stoudemire, Phoenix

NBA Defensive Player of the Year

1983 Sidney Moncrief, Milwaukee	1990 Dennis Rodman, Detroit	1997 Dikembe Mutombo, Atlanta
1984 Sidney Moncrief, Milwaukee	1991 Dennis Rodman, Detroit	1998 Dikembe Mutombo, Atlanta
1985 Mark Eaton, Utah	1992 David Robinson, San Antonio	1999 Alonzo Mourning, Miami
1986 Alvin Robertson, San Antonio	1993 Hakeem Olajuwon, Houston	2000 Alonzo Mourning, Miami
1987 Michael Cooper, L.A. Lakers	1994 Hakeem Olajuwon, Houston	2001 Dikembe Mutombo, Philadelphia
1988 Michael Jordan, Chicago	1995 Dikembe Mutombo, Denver	2002 Ben Wallace, Detroit
1989 Mark Eaton, Utah	1996 Gary Payton, Seattle	2003 Ben Wallace, Detroit

NBA Sixth Man Award

1983 Bobby Jones, Philadelphia	1990 Ricky Pierce, Milwaukee	1997 John Starks, New York
1984 Kevin McHale, Boston	1991 Detlef Schrempf, Seattle	1998 Danny Manning, Phoenix
1985 Kevin McHale, Boston	1992 Detlef Schrempf, Seattle	1999 Darrell Armstrong, Orlando
1986 Bill Walton, Boston	1993 Clifford Robinson, Portland	2000 Rodney Rogers, Phoenix
1987 Ricky Pierce, Milwaukee	1994 Dell Curry, Charlotte	2001 Aaron McKie, Philadelphia
1988 Roy Tarpley, Dallas	1995 Anthony Mason, New York	2002 Corliss Williamson, Detroit
1989 Eddie Johnson, Phoenix	1996 Toni Kukoc, Chicago	2003 Bobby Jackson, Sacramento

2003 NBA Player Draft, First-Round Picks

(held June 25, 2003)

Team	Player, College/Team	Team	Player, College/Team
1. Cleveland	Lebron James, G/F, St. Vincent-St. Mary HS (OH)	16. Boston	Troy Bell[6], G, Boston College
2. Detroit[1]	Darko Milicic, F, Hemofarm Vrsac (Serbia-Montenegro)	17. Phoenix	Zarko Cabarkapa, F, Buducnost (Serbia-Montenegro)
3. Denver	Carmelo Anthony, F, Syracuse	18. New Orleans	David West, F, Xavier
4. Toronto	Chris Bosh, F, Georgia Tech	19. Utah	Aleksandar Pavlovic, F, Buducnost (Serbia-Montenegro)
5. Miami	Dwyane Wade, G, Marquette	20. Boston[7]	Dahntay Jones[8], F, Duke
6. L.A. Clippers	Chris Kaman, C, Central Michigan	21. Atlanta[9]	Boris Diaw, F, Pau Orthenz (France)
7. Chicago	Kirk Hinrich, G, Kansas	22. New Jersey	Zoran Planinic, G, Cibona Zagreb (Croatia)
8. Milwaukee[2]	T.J. Ford, G, Texas	23. Portland	Travis Outlaw, F, Starkville HS (MS)
9. New York	Mike Sweetney, F, Georgetown	24. L.A. Lakers	Brian Cook, F, Illinois
10. Washington	Jarvis Hayes, F, Georgia	25. Detroit	Carlos Delfino, F, Skipper Bologna (Italy)
11. Golden State	Mickael Pietrus, G/F, Pau Orthenz (France)	26. Minnesota	Ndudi Ebi, F, Westbury Christian HS (TX)
12. Seattle	Nick Collison, F, Kansas	27. Memphis[10]	Kendrick Perkins[11], C, Ozen HS (TX)
13. Memphis[3]	Marcus Banks[4], G, UNLV	28. San Antonio	Leandrinho Barbosa[12], G, Bauru Tilibra (Brazil)
14. Seattle[5]	Luke Ridnour, G, Oregon	29. Dallas	Josh Howard, F, Wake Forest
15. Orlando	Reece Gaines, G, Louisville		

(1) From Memphis. (2) From Atlanta. (3) From Houston. (4) Rights traded to Boston. (5) From Milwaukee. (6) Rights traded to Memphis. (7) From Philadelphia. (8) Rights traded to Memphis. (9) From Indiana. (10) From Sacramento through Orlando. (11) Rights traded to Boston. (12) Rights traded to Phoenix.

Number-One First-Round NBA Draft Picks, 1966-2003

Year	Team	Player, college	Year	Team	Player, college
1966	New York	Cazzie Russell, Michigan	1985	New York	Patrick Ewing, Georgetown
1967	Detroit	Jimmy Walker, Providence	1986	Cleveland	Brad Daugherty, North Carolina
1968	Houston	Elvin Hayes, Houston	1987	San Antonio	David Robinson, Navy
1969	Milwaukee	Lew Alcindor[1], UCLA	1988	L.A. Clippers	Danny Manning, Kansas
1970	Detroit	Bob Lanier, St. Bonaventure	1989	Sacramento	Pervis Ellison, Louisville
1971	Cleveland	Austin Carr, Notre Dame	1990	New Jersey	Derrick Coleman, Syracuse
1972	Portland	LaRue Martin, Loyola-Chicago	1991	Charlotte	Larry Johnson, UNLV
1973	Philadelphia	Doug Collins, Illinois St.	1992	Orlando	Shaquille O'Neal, LSU
1974	Portland	Bill Walton, UCLA	1993	Orlando	Chris Webber[3], Michigan
1975	Atlanta	David Thompson[2], N.C. State	1994	Milwaukee	Glenn Robinson, Purdue
1976	Houston	John Lucas, Maryland	1995	Golden State	Joe Smith, Maryland
1977	Milwaukee	Kent Benson, Indiana	1996	Philadelphia	Allen Iverson, Georgetown
1978	Portland	Mychal Thompson, Minnesota	1997	San Antonio	Tim Duncan, Wake Forest
1979	L.A. Lakers	Magic Johnson, Michigan St.	1998	L.A. Clippers	Michael Olowokandi, Pacific
1980	Golden State	Joe Barry Carroll, Purdue	1999	Chicago Bulls	Elton Brand, Duke
1981	Dallas	Mark Aguirre, DePaul	2000	New Jersey	Kenyon Martin, Cincinnati
1982	L.A. Lakers	James Worthy, North Carolina	2001	Washington	Kwame Brown, Glynn Academy (HS)
1983	Houston	Ralph Sampson, Virginia	2002	Houston	Yao Ming, Shanghai Sharks (China)
1984	Houston	Akeem Olajuwon, Houston	2003	Cleveland	LeBron James, St. Vincent-St. Mary (HS)

(1) Later Kareem Abdul-Jabbar. (2) Signed with Denver of the ABA. (3) Traded to Golden State.

All-Time NBA Statistical Leaders

(At the end of the 2002-2003 season. *Player active in 2002-2003 season.)

Scoring Average (Minimum 400 games or 10,000 points)				Free Throw Percentage (Minimum 1,200 free throws made)			
	G	Pts.	Avg		FTA	FTM	Pct.
*Michael Jordan	1,072	32,292	30.1	Mark Price	2,362	2,135	.904
Wilt Chamberlain	1,045	31,419	30.1	Rick Barry	4,243	3,818	.900
*Shaquille O'Neal	742	20,475	27.6	Calvin Murphy	3,864	3,445	.892
Elgin Baylor	846	23,149	27.4	Scott Skiles	1,741	1,548	.889
Jerry West	932	25,192	27.0	*Reggie Miller	6,593	5,841	.886
*Allen Iverson	487	13,170	27.0	Larry Bird	4,471	3,960	.886
Bob Pettit	792	20,880	26.4	Bill Sharman	3,559	3,143	.883
George Gervin	791	20,708	26.2	*Ray Allen	2,215	1,954	.882
Oscar Robertson	1,040	26,710	25.7	Jeff Hornacek	3,390	2,973	.877
*Karl Malone	1,434	36,374	25.4	Ricky Pierce	3,871	3,389	.875

Field Goal Percentage
(Minimum 2,000 field goals made)

	FGA	FGM	Pct.
Artis Gilmore	9,570	5,732	.599
Mark West	4,356	2,528	.580
*Shaquille O'Neal	14,072	8,116	.577
Steve Johnson	4,965	2,841	.572
Darryl Dawkins	6,079	3,477	.572
James Donaldson	5,442	3,105	.571
Jeff Ruland	3,734	2,105	.564
Kareem Abdul-Jabbar	28,307	15,837	.559
Kevin McHale	12,334	6,830	.554
Bobby Jones	6,199	3,412	.550

3-Point Field Goal Percentage
(Minimum 250 3-point field goals made)

	3-FGA	3-FGM	Pct.
*Steve Kerr	1,599	726	.454
*Hubert Davis	1,650	728	.441
*Michael Redd	617	270	.438
Drazen Petrovic	583	255	.437
Tim Legler	603	260	.431
B.J. Armstrong	1,026	436	.425
*Steve Nash	1,361	569	.418
*Wesley Person	2,527	1,054	.417
*Pat Garrity	1,242	513	.413
Dana Barros	2,652	1,090	.411

Games Played

Robert Parish	1,611
Kareem Abdul-Jabbar	1,560
*John Stockton	1,504
*Karl Malone	1,434
*Kevin Willis	1,342
Moses Malone	1,329
Buck Williams	1,307
Elvin Hayes	1,303
Sam Perkins	1,286
A.C. Green	1,278
*Charles Oakley	1,275

Field Goals Attempted

Kareem Abdul-Jabbar	28,307
*Karl Malone	25,810
*Michael Jordan	24,537
Elvin Hayes	24,272
John Havlicek	23,930
Wilt Chamberlain	23,497
Dominique Wilkins	21,589
Alex English	21,036
Hakeem Olajuwon	20,991
Elgin Baylor	20,171

Points

Kareem Abdul-Jabbar	38,387
*Karl Malone	36,374
*Michael Jordan	32,292
Wilt Chamberlain	31,419
Moses Malone	27,409
Elvin Hayes	27,313
Hakeem Olajuwon	26,946
Oscar Robertson	26,710
Dominique Wilkins	26,668
John Havlicek	26,395

Minutes Played

Kareem Abdul-Jabbar	57,446
*Karl Malone	53,479
Elvin Hayes	50,000
Wilt Chamberlain	47,859
*John Stockton	47,764
John Havlicek	46,471
Robert Parish	45,704
Moses Malone	45,071
Hakeem Olajuwon	44,222
Oscar Robertson	43,886

Field Goals Made

Kareem Abdul-Jabbar	15,837
*Karl Malone	13,335
Wilt Chamberlain	12,681
*Michael Jordan	12,192
Elvin Hayes	10,976
Hakeem Olajuwon	10,749
Alex English	10,659
John Havlicek	10,513
Dominique Wilkins	9,963
Patrick Ewing	9,702

Rebounds

Wilt Chamberlain	23,924
Bill Russell	21,620
Kareem Abdul-Jabbar	17,440
Elvin Hayes	16,279
Moses Malone	16,212
Robert Parish	14,715
*Karl Malone	14,601
Nate Thurmond	14,464
Walt Bellamy	14,241
Wes Unseld	13,769

Personal Fouls

Kareem Abdul-Jabbar	4,657
*Karl Malone	4,462
Robert Parish	4,443
*Charles Oakley	4,413
Hakeem Olajuwon	4,383
Buck Williams	4,267
Elvin Hayes	4,193
Otis Thorpe	4,146
*Kevin Willis	4,047
James Edwards	4,042

3- Point Field Goals Attempted

*Reggie Miller	5,854
*Tim Hardaway	4,345
Dale Ellis	4,269
Vernon Maxwell	3,931
Mookie Blaylock	3,816
Dan Majerle	3,798
*Glen Rice	3,868
John Starks	3,591
Mitch Richmond	3,417
*Nick Van Exel	3,717

Assists

*John Stockton	15,806
*Mark Jackson	10,215
Magic Johnson	10,141
Oscar Robertson	9,887
Isiah Thomas	9,061
*Rod Strickland	7,704
*Gary Payton	7,590
Maurice Cheeks	7,392
Lenny Wilkens	7,211
Terry Porter	7,160

Blocked Shots

Hakeem Olajuwon	3,830
Kareem Abdul-Jabbar	3,189
Mark Eaton	3,064
*David Robinson	2,954
Patrick Ewing	2,894
*Dikembe Mutombo	2,873
Tree Rollins	2,542
Robert Parish	2,361
Manute Bol	2,086
George T. Johnson	2,082

3- Point Field Goals Made

*Reggie Miller	2,330
Dale Ellis	1,719
*Tim Hardaway	1,542
*Glen Rice	1,554
Dan Majerle	1,360
Mitch Richmond	1,326
Terry Porter	1,297
Mookie Blaylock	1,283
Vernon Maxwell	1,256
Dell Curry	1,245

Steals

*John Stockton	3,265
*Michael Jordan	2,514
Maurice Cheeks	2,310
*Scottie Pippen	2,286
Clyde Drexler	2,207
Hakeem Olajuwon	2,162
*Gary Payton	2,147
Alvin Robertson	2,112
Mookie Blaylock	2,075
*Karl Malone	2,035

All-Time NBA Coaching Victories
(At the end of the 2002-2003 season. *Active through 2002-2003 season.)

Coach	W-L	Pct.	Coach	W-L	Pct.
Lenny Wilkens*	1,292-1,114	.537	Gene Shue	784-861	.477
Pat Riley*	1,110-569	.661	Phil Jackson*	776-290	.728
Don Nelson*	1,096-828	.570	George Karl*	708-499	.587
Bill Fitch	944-1,106	.460	John MacLeod	707-657	.518
Red Auerbach	938-479	.662	Red Holzman	696-604	.535
Dick Motta	935-1,017	.479	Chuck Daly	638-437	.593
Larry Brown*	879-685	.562	Doug Moe	628-529	.543
Jerry Sloan*	875-521	.627	Rick Adelman*	603-384	.611
Jack Ramsay	864-783	.525	Mike Fratello	572-465	.552
Cotton Fitzsimmons	832-775	.518	Alvin Attles	557-518	.518

WORLD ALMANAC QUICK QUIZ

In addition to Wilt Chamberlain in 1960, who is the only other NBA player to be named Rookie of the Year and MVP in the same year?

(a) Michael Jordan   (b) Larry Bird
(c) Tim Duncan   (d) Wes Unseld

For the answer look in this chapter, or see page 1008.

Basketball Hall of Fame, Springfield, MA

(2003 inductees have an asterisk*)

PLAYERS

Abdul-Jabbar, Kareem
Archibald, Nate
Arizin, Paul
Barlow, Thomas
Barry, Rick
Baylor, Elgin
Beckman, John
Bellamy, Walt
Belov, Sergei
Bing, Dave
Bird, Larry
Blazejowski, Carol
Borgmann, Bennie
Bradley, Bill
Brennan, Joseph
Cervi, Al
Chamberlain, Wilt
Cooper, Charles
Cosic, Kresimir
Cousy, Bob
Cowens, Dave
Crawford, Joan
Cunningham, Billy
Curry, Denise
Davies, Bob
DeBernardi, Forrest
DeBusschere, Dave
Denhart, Dutch
Donovan, Anne
Endacott, Paul
English, Alex
Erving, Julius (Dr. J)
Foster, Bud
Frazier, Walt
Friedman, Max
Fulks, Joe
Gale, Lauren
Gallatin, Harry
Gates, Pop
Gervin, George
Gola, Tom
Goodrich, Gail
Greer, Hal
Gruenig, Ace
Hagan, Cliff
Hanson, Victor
Harris-Stewart, Luisa
Havlicek, John
Hawkins, Connie
Hayes, Elvin
Haynes, Marques
Heinsohn, Tom

Holman, Nat
Houbregs, Bob
Howell, Bailey
Hyatt, Chuck
Issel, Dan
Jeannette, Buddy
Johnson, Earvin "Magic"
Johnson, William
Johnston, Neil
Jones, K.C.
Jones, Sam
Krause, Moose
Kurland, Bob
Lanier, Bob
Lapchick, Joe
*Lemon, Meadowlark
Lieberman-Cline, Nancy
*Lloyd, Earl
Lovellette, Clyde
Lucas, Jerry
Luisetti, Hank
Macauley, Ed
Malone, Moses
Maravich, Pete
Martin, Slater
McAdoo, Bob
McCracken, Branch
McCracken, Jack
McDermott, Bobby
McGuire, Dick
McHale, Kevin
*Meneghin, Dino
Meyers, Ann
Mikan, George
Mikkelsen, Vern
Miller, Cheryl
Monroe, Earl
Murphy, Calvin
Murphy, Stretch
Page, Pat
*Parish, Robert
Petrovic, Drazen
Pettit, Bob
Phillip, Andy
Pollard, Jim
Ramsey, Frank
Reed, Willis
Risen, Arnie
Robertson, Oscar
Roosma, John S.
Russell, Bill
Russell, Honey

Schayes, Adolph
Schmidt, Ernest
Schommer, John
Sedran, Barney
Semjonova, Uljana
Sharman, Bill
Steinmetz, Christian
Thomas, Isiah
Thompson, Cat
Thompson, David
Thurmond, Nate
Twyman, Jack
Unseld, Wes
Vandivier, Fuzzy
Wachter, Edward
Walton, Bill
Wanzer, Bobby
West, Jerry
White, Nera
Wilkens, Lenny
Wooden, John
Yardley, George

COACHES

Allen, Forrest (Phog)
Anderson, Harold
Auerbach, Red
*Barmore, Leon
Barry, Sam
Blood, Ernest
Brown, Larry
Cann, Howard
Carlson, Dr. H. C.
Carnesecca, Lou
Carnevale, Ben
Carril, Pete
Case, Everett
Chaney, John
Conradt, Jody
Crum, Denny
Daly, Chuck
Dean, Everett
Diaz-Miguel, Antonio
Diddle, Edgar
Drake, Bruce
Gaines, Clarence
Gardner, Jack
Gill, Slats
Gomelsky, Aleksandr
Hannum, Alex
Harshman, Marv
Haskins, Don
Hickey, Edgar
Hobson, Howard
Holzman, Red

Iba, Hank
Julian, Alvin
Keaney, Frank
Keogan, George
Knight, Bob
Krzyzewski, Mike
Kundla, John
Lambert, Ward
Litwack, Harry
Loeffler, Kenneth
Lonborg, Dutch
McCutchan, Arad
McGuire, Al
McGuire, Frank
McLendon, John
Meanwell, Dr. W. E.
Meyer, Ray
Miller, Ralph
Moore, Billie
Newell, Pete
Nikolic, Aleksandar
Olson, Lute
Ramsay, Jack
Rubini, Cesare
Rupp, Adolph
Sachs, Leonard
Shelton, Everett
Smith, Dean
Summitt, Pat
Taylor, Fred
Thompson, John
Wade, Margaret
Watts, Stan
Wilkens, Lenny
Wooden, John
Woolpert, Phil
Wootten, Morgan
*Worthy, James
Yow, Kay

TEAMS

First Team
Original Celtics
Buffalo Germans
NY Renaissance
Harlem Globetrotters

REFEREES

Enright, James
Hepbron, George
Hoyt, George
Kennedy, Matthew
Leith, Lloyd
Mihalik, Red
Nucatola, John

Quigley, Ernest
Shirley, J. Dallas
Strom, Earl
Tobey, David
Walsh, David

CONTRIBUTORS

Abbott, Senda B.
Bee, Clair
Biasone, Danny
Brown, Walter
Bunn, John
Douglas, Bob
Duer, Al O.
Embry, Wayne
Fagan, Cliff
Fisher, Harry
Fleisher, Larry
Gottlieb, Edward
Gulick, Dr. L. H.
Harrison, Lester
*Heary, Francis "Chick"
Hepp, Dr. Ferenc
Hickox, Edward
Hinkle, Tony
Irish, Ned
Jones, R. W.
Kennedy, Walter
Liston, Emil
Mokray, Bill
Morgan, Ralph
Morgenweck, Frank
Naismith, Dr. James
Newton, C. M.
O'Brien, John
O'Brien, Larry
Olsen, Harold
Podoloff, Maurice
Porter, H. V.
Reid, William
Ripley, Elmer
St. John, Lynn
Saperstein, Abe
Schabinger, Arthur
Stagg, Amos Alonzo
Stankovich, Boris
Steitz, Edward
Taylor, Chuck
Teague, Bertha
Tower, Oswald
Trester, Arthur
Wells, Clifford
Wilke, Lou
Zollner, Fred

NBA Home Courts[1]

Team	Name (built)	Capacity
Atlanta	Philips Arena (1999)	20,000
Boston	FleetCenter (1995)	18,624
Chicago	United Center (1994)	21,500
Cleveland	Gund Arena (1994)	20,562
Dallas	American Airlines Center (2001)	19,200
Denver	Pepsi Center (1999)	19,099
Detroit	The Palace of Auburn Hills (1988)	22,076
Golden State	Arena in Oakland[2] (1966)	19,596
Houston	Compaq Center[3] (1975)	16,285
Indiana	Conseco Fieldhouse (1999)	18,345
L.A. Clippers	Staples Center (1999)	19,060
L.A. Lakers	Staples Center (1999)	19,282
Memphis	The Pyramid (1991)	20,142
Miami	American Airlines Arena (1999)	19,600
Milwaukee	Bradley Center (1988)	18,600
Minnesota	Target Center (1990)	19,006
New Jersey	Continental Airlines Arena[4] (1981)	20,049
New Orleans	New Orleans Arena (1999)	18,500
New York	Madison Square Garden (1968)	19,763
Orlando	TD Waterhouse Centre[5] (1989)	17,248
Philadelphia	First Union Center[6] (1996)	20,444
Phoenix	America West Arena (1992)	19,023
Portland	The Rose Garden (1995)	19,980
Sacramento	ARCO Arena (1988)	17,317
San Antonio	SBC Center (2002)	18,500
Seattle	KeyArena at Seattle Center[7] (1962)	17,072
Toronto	Air Canada Centre (1999)	19,800
Utah	Delta Center (1991)	19,911
Washington	MCI Center (1997)	20,674

(1) At the end of the 2002-2003 season. (2) Oakland Coliseum Arena, 1966-96; renovated and renamed in 1997. (3) The Summit, 1975-97; the 18,300-seat Houston Arena was scheduled to open for the 2003-2004 season. (4) Brendan Byrne/Meadowlands Arena, 1981-96. (5) Orlando Arena, 1989-2000. (6) CoreStates Center, 1996-98. (7) Seattle Center Coliseum, 1962-94; renovated, expanded, and renamed in 1995.

WOMEN'S PROFESSIONAL BASKETBALL

WNBA 2004: Detroit Shocks L.A. for First Title, League Reorganizes

A year after posting the worst record in the WNBA, the Detroit Shock denied the Los Angeles Sparks a three-peat with an 83-78 win in the deciding Game 3 of the WNBA Finals, Sept. 16 at the Palace of Auburn Hills in Michigan. Detroit center Ruth Riley scored a career-high 27 points and was named MVP of the Finals. The Shock became only the 3rd champion in WNBA history after 4-time winners Houston and Los Angeles.

After the 2002 season, 2 WNBA franchises folded and 2 others relocated. An October decision by the NBA board of governors altered ownership rights for WNBA teams, permitting non-NBA owners in non-NBA cities. Citing financial difficulties, the Miami Sol announced soon after that it would cease operations. The Portland Fire made a similar announcement in December. By November, the parent company of the NBA's San Antonio Spurs had the 6,000 season ticket deposits required to obtain a WNBA franchise, and the Utah Starzz relocated to San Antonio to become the Silver Stars. In Jan. 2003, the WNBA announced the Orlando Miracle's move to the Mohegan Sun Casino in Uncasville, CT, to become the Connecticut Sun. In a dispersal draft held Apr. 24, Miami's Ruth Riley was selected first by Detroit.

WNBA Final Standings, 2003 Season

x-clinched playoff berth; y-clinched top seed

Eastern Conference	W-L	Pct	GB	Western Conference	W	Pct	GB
y- Detroit	25- 9	0.735	0.0	y- Los Angeles	24-10	0.706	0.0
x- Charlotte	18-16	0.529	7.0	x- Houston	20-14	0.588	4.0
x-Connecticut	18-16	0.529	7.0	x-Sacramento	19-15	0.559	5.0
x-Cleveland	17-17	0.500	8.0	x-Minnesota	18-16	0.529	6.0
Indiana	16-18	0.471	9.0	Seattle	18-16	0.529	6.0
New York	16-18	0.471	9.0	San Antonio	12-22	0.353	12.0
Washington	9-25	0.265	16.0	Phoenix	8-26	0.235	16.0

2002 WNBA Playoffs

(Playoff seeding in parentheses; Conference winner automatically gets top seed)

Eastern Conference
Detroit (1) defeated Cleveland (4) 2 games to 1
Connecticut (3) defeated Charlotte (2) 2 games to 0
Detroit defeated Connecticut 2 games to 0

Western Conference
Los Angeles (1) defeated Minnesota (4) 2 games to 1
Sacramento (3) defeated Houston (2) 2 games to 1
Los Angeles defeated Sacramento 2 games to 1

WNBA Championship (Best of 3)
Detroits defeated Los Angeles 2 games to 1 [63-75, 62-61, 83-78].

2002 All-WNBA Teams

First Team	Position	Second Team
Lisa Leslie, Los Angeles	Center	Cheryl Ford, Detroit
Lauren Jackson, Seattle	Forward	Sheryl Swoopes, Houston
Tamika Catchings, Indiana	Forward	Swin Cash, Detroit
Katie Smith, Minnesota	Guard	Nikki Teasley, Los Angeles
Sue Bird, Seattle	Guard	Deanna Nolan, Detroit

WNBA Statistical Leaders and Awards in 2003

Minutes played — 1,210, Tamika Catchings, Indiana
Total points — 698, Lauren Jackson, Seattle
Points per game — 21.2, Lauren Jackson, Seattle
Highest field goal % — .668, Tamika Williams, Minnesota
Highest 3-pt. field goal % — .469, Becky Hammon, New York
Highest free throw % — .951, Becky Hammon, New York
Total rebounds — 334, Cheryl Ford, Detroit
Rebounds per game — 10.9, Chamique Holdsclaw, Washington

Total assists — 229, Ticha Penicheiro, Sacramento
Assists per game — 6.7, Ticha Penicheiro, Sacramento
Total steals — 77, Sheryl Swoopes, Houston
Steals per game — 2.48, Sheryl Swoopes, Houston
Total blocked shots — 100, Margo Dydek, San Antonio
Coach of the year — Bill Laimbeer, Detroit
Defensive player of year — Sheryl Swoopes, Houston
Most improved player of the year — Michelle Snow, Houston

WNBA Champions

	Regular season			Playoffs	
Year	Eastern Conference	Western Conference	Champion	Coach	Runner-up
1997	Houston Comets	Phoenix Mercury	Houston	Van Chancellor	New York
1998	Cleveland Rockers	Houston Comets	Houston	Van Chancellor	Phoenix
1999	New York Liberty	Houston Comets	Houston	Van Chancellor	New York
2000	New York Liberty	Los Angeles Sparks	Houston	Van Chancellor	New York
2001	Cleveland Rockers	Los Angeles Sparks	Los Angeles	Michael Cooper	Charlotte
2002	New York Liberty	Los Angeles Sparks	Los Angeles	Michael Cooper	New York
2003	Detroit Shock	Los Angeles Sparks	Detroit	Bill Laimbeer	Los Angeles

WNBA Scoring Leaders

Year	Scoring champion	Pts	Avg	Year	Scoring champion	Pts	Avg
1997	Cynthia Cooper, Houston	621	22.2	2001	Katie Smith, Minnesota	739	23.1
1998	Cynthia Cooper, Houston	680	22.7	2002	Chamique Holdsclaw, Washington	397	19.9
1999	Cynthia Cooper, Houston	686	22.1	2003	Lauren Jackson, Seattle	698	21.2
2000	Sheryl Swoopes, Houston	643	20.7				

WNBA Finals MVP

1997	Cynthia Cooper, Houston
1998	Cynthia Cooper, Houston
1999	Cynthia Cooper, Houston
2000	Cynthia Cooper, Houston
2001	Lisa Leslie, Los Angeles
2002	Lisa Leslie, Los Angeles
2003	Ruth Riley, Detroit

WNBA Most Valuable Player

1997	Cynthia Cooper, Houston
1998	Cynthia Cooper, Houston
1999	Yolanda Griffith, Sacramento
2000	Sheryl Swoopes, Houston
2001	Lisa Leslie, Los Angeles
2002	Sheryl Swoopes, Houston
2003	Lauren Jackson, Seattle

WNBA Rookie of the Year

1997	no award
1998	Tracy Reid, Charlotte
1999	Chamique Holdsclaw, Washington
2000	Betty Lennox, Minnesota
2001	Jackie Stiles, Portland
2002	Tamika Catchings, Indiana
2003	Cheryl Ford, Detroit

COLLEGE BASKETBALL

Men's Final NCAA Division I Conference Standings, 2002-2003

(*conference tournament champion)

America East

	Conf W	Conf L	All W	All L
Boston U.	13	3	20	11
Vermont*	11	5	21	12
Hartford	10	6	17	13
Binghamton	9	7	14	13
Northeastern	8	8	16	15
Maine	8	8	14	16
Stony Brook	7	9	13	16
MD Baltimore Co.	5	13	7	20
Albany	3	13	7	21
New Hampshire	3	13	5	23

Atlantic Coast

	Conf W	Conf L	All W	All L
Wake Forest	13	3	25	6
Duke*	12	5	26	7
Maryland	11	5	21	10
North Carolina St.	9	8	18	13
Georgia Tech	7	9	16	15
North Carolina	6	10	19	16
Virginia	6	10	16	16
Clemson	5	11	15	13
Florida St.	4	12	14	15

Atlantic Sun

	Conf W	Conf L	All W	All L
Troy State*	14	2	26	6
Mercer	14	2	23	6
Belmont	12	4	17	12
Central Florida	11	5	21	11
Georgia St	8	8	14	15
Jacksonville	8	8	13	16
Stetson	4	12	6	20
Fla Atlantic	3	13	7	21
Gardner Webb	2	14	5	24
Campbell	1	15	5	22
David Lipscomb	0	0	8	20

Atlantic 10
East Division

	Conf W	Conf L	All W	All L
St. Joseph's	12	4	23	7
Rhode Island	10	6	20	11
Temple	10	6	18	16
Massachusetts	6	10	12	18
Fordham	3	13	4	24
St. Bonaventure	1	15	7	22

West Division

	Conf W	Conf L	All W	All L
Xavier	15	1	26	6
Dayton*	14	2	25	6
Richmond	10	6	16	13
La Salle	6	10	13	16
George Washington	5	11	12	17
Duquesne	4	12	10	20

Big East
East Division

	Conf W	Conf L	All W	All L
Connecticut	10	6	23	10
Boston College	10	6	19	12
Providence	8	8	18	14
Villanova	8	8	15	16
St. John's	7	9	21	13
Miami (FL)	4	12	11	17
Virginia Tech	4	12	11	18

West Division

	Conf W	Conf L	All W	All L
Syracuse	13	3	30	5
Pittsburgh*	13	3	28	5
Notre Dame	10	6	24	10
Seton Hall	10	6	17	13
Georgetown	6	10	19	15
West Virginia	5	11	14	15
Rutgers	4	12	12	16

Big Sky

	Conf W	Conf L	All W	All L
Weber St.*	14	0	26	6
Eastern Wash.	9	5	18	13
Idaho St.	7	7	15	14
Montana	7	7	13	17
Northern Arizona	6	8	15	13
Sacramento St.	5	9	12	17
Montana St.	5	9	11	16
Portland St.	3	11	5	22

Big South

	Conf W	Conf L	All W	All L
Winthrop	11	3	20	10
Charleston Southern	8	6	14	14
Liberty	8	6	14	15
UNC Asheville*	7	7	15	17
Radford	6	8	10	20
Coast Carolina	5	9	13	15
High Point	3	11	7	20
Virginia Mil. Inst.	3	13	10	20
Birmingham Southern	0	0	19	9

Big 10

	Conf W	Conf L	All W	All L
Wisconsin	12	4	24	8
Illinois*	11	5	25	7
Purdue	10	6	19	11
Michigan St.	10	6	22	13
Michigan	10	6	17	13
Indiana	8	8	21	13
Minnesota	8	8	19	14
Ohio St.	7	9	17	15
Iowa	7	9	17	14
Northwestern	3	13	12	17
Penn St.	2	14	7	21

Big 12

	Conf W	Conf L	All W	All L
Kansas	14	2	30	8
Texas	13	3	26	7
Oklahoma*	13	4	27	7
Oklahoma St.	10	6	22	10
Colorado	9	7	20	12
Missouri	9	8	22	11
Texas Tech	6	10	22	13
Texas A&M	6	10	14	14
Iowa St.	5	11	17	14
Baylor	5	11	14	14
Kansas St.	4	12	13	17
Nebraska	3	13	11	19

Big West

	Conf W	Conf L	All W	All L
Santa Barbara	14	4	18	14
UC Irvine	13	5	20	9
Utah St.*	12	6	23	9
Cal Poly	10	8	16	13
Idaho	9	9	13	15
CS-Northridge	8	10	14	15
Fullerton St.	8	10	10	19
U of the Pacific	7	11	12	16
UC Riverside	5	13	6	18
Long Beach St.	4	14	5	22

Colonial Athletic Association

	Conf W	Conf L	All W	All L
NC Wilmington*	15	3	24	7
Va. Commonwealth	12	6	18	10
Drexel	12	6	19	12
George Mason	11	7	16	12
Delaware	9	9	15	14
Old Dominion	9	9	12	15
James Madison	8	10	13	17
William & Mary	7	11	12	16
Hofstra	6	12	8	21
Towson	1	17	4	24

Conference USA
American Division

	Conf W	Conf L	All W	All L
Marquette	14	2	27	6
Louisville*	11	5	25	7
Saint Louis	9	7	16	14
Cincinnati	9	7	17	12
DePaul	8	8	16	13
Charlotte	8	8	13	15
East Carolina	3	13	12	15

National Division

	Conf W	Conf L	All W	All L
Memphis	13	3	23	7
Tulane	8	8	16	15
UAB	8	8	21	13
USF	7	9	15	14
Houston	6	10	8	20
Southern Miss.	5	11	13	16
TCU	3	13	9	19

Horizon

	Conf W	Conf L	All W	All L
Butler	14	2	27	6
Wisc. Milwaukee*	13	3	24	8
Illinois (Chi.)	12	4	21	9
Detroit	9	7	18	12
Loyola Chi.	9	7	15	16
Wright St.	4	12	10	18
Wisc. Green Bay	4	12	10	20
Youngstown State	4	12	9	20
Cleveland St.	3	13	8	22

Ivy Group[1]

	Conf W	Conf L	All W	All L
Pennsylvania	14	0	22	6
Brown	12	2	17	12
Princeton	10	4	16	11
Yale	8	6	14	13
Harvard	4	10	12	15
Cornell	4	10	9	18
Dartmouth	4	10	8	19
Columbia	0	14	2	25

Metro Atlantic Athletic

	Conf W	Conf L	All W	All L
Manhattan*	14	4	23	7
Fairfield	13	5	19	12
Siena	12	6	21	11
Niagara	12	6	17	12
Iona	11	7	17	12
Marist	8	10	13	16
Rider	7	11	12	16
Canisius	6	12	10	18
St. Peter's	6	12	10	19
Loyola MD	1	17	4	24

Mid-American
East Division

	Conf W	Conf L	All W	All L
Kent St.	12	6	21	10
Miami (OH)	11	7	13	15
Akron	9	9	14	14
Marshall	9	9	14	15
Ohio	8	10	14	16
Buffalo	2	16	5	23

West Division

	Conf W	Conf L	All W	All L
Central Mich.*	14	4	25	7
Northern Illinois	11	7	17	14
Western Mich.	10	8	20	11
Eastern Mich.	8	10	14	14
Bowling Green	8	10	13	16
Ball St.	8	10	12	17
Toledo	7	11	13	16

Mid Continent

	Conf W	Conf L	All W	All L
Valparaiso	12	2	20	11
Oakland	10	4	17	11
Indiana-Purdue*	10	4	20	14
Oral Roberts	9	5	18	10
UMKC	7	7	9	20
Southern Utah	5	9	11	17
Western Illinois	3	11	7	21
Centenary	0	0	14	14
Chicago St.	0	14	3	27

Mid-Eastern Athletic

	Conf W	Conf L	All W	All L
South Carolina St.*	15	3	20	11
Hampton	13	5	19	11
Delaware St.	13	5	15	12
Florida A&M	11	7	17	12
Coppin St.	11	7	11	17
Norfolk St.	10	8	14	15
Howard	9	9	13	17
Morgan St.	6	12	7	22
Bethune-Cookman	5	13	8	22
MD Eastern Shore	5	13	5	23
N. Carolina A&T	1	17	1	26

Missouri Valley

	Conf W	Conf L	All W	All L
Southern Illinois	16	2	24	7
Creighton*	15	3	29	5
Wichita St.	12	6	18	12
SMS	12	6	17	12
Evansville	8	10	12	16
Bradley	8	10	12	18
Northern Iowa	7	11	11	17
Drake	5	13	10	20
Illinois St.	5	13	8	21
Indiana St.	2	16	7	24

Mountain West

	Conf W	Conf L	All W	All L
Utah	11	3	25	8
BYU	11	3	23	9
UNLV	8	6	21	11
Wyoming	8	6	21	11
San Diego St.	6	8	16	14
Colorado St.*	5	9	19	14
New Mexico	4	10	10	18
Air Force	3	11	12	16

Northeast	Conf. W	L	All W	L
Wagner*	14	4	21	11
Monmouth (N.J.)	13	5	15	13
Central Conn.	12	6	15	13
Quinnipiac	10	8	17	12
St. Francis (PA)	10	8	14	14
Fair Dickinson	9	9	15	14
St. Francis (NY)	9	9	14	16
Robert Morris	7	11	10	17
LIU Brooklyn	7	11	9	19
Mt. St. Marys	6	12	11	16
Sacred Heart	6	12	8	21
Ohio Valley				
Austin Peay*	13	3	23	8
Morehead St.	13	3	20	9
Tennessee Tech	11	5	20	12
Jacksonville St.	10	6	20	9
Murray St.	9	7	17	12
Eastern Illinois	9	7	14	15
Samford	9	7	13	15
Tenn. Martin	7	9	14	14
Eastern Kentucky	5	11	11	17
SE Missouri St.	5	11	11	19
Tennessee St.	0	16	2	25
Pacific-10				
Arizona	17	1	28	4
Stanford	14	4	24	9
California	13	5	22	9
Arizona St.	11	7	20	12
Oregon*	10	8	23	10
Oregon St.	6	12	13	15
USC	6	12	13	17
UCLA	6	12	10	19
Washington	5	13	10	17
Washington St.	2	16	7	20
Patriot				
Holy Cross*	13	1	26	5
American	9	5	16	14
Colgate	9	5	14	14
Lehigh	8	6	16	12
Bucknell	7	7	14	15
Lafayette	6	8	13	16
Navy	4	10	8	20
Army	0	14	5	22

Southeastern East Division	Conf. W	L	All W	L
Kentucky*	16	0	32	4
Florida	12	4	25	8
Georgia	11	5	19	8
Tennessee	9	7	17	12
South Carolina	5	11	12	16
Vanderbilt	3	13	11	18
West Division				
Mississippi St.	9	7	21	10
LSU	8	8	21	11
Auburn	8	8	22	12
Alabama	7	9	17	12
Mississippi	4	12	14	15
Arkansas	4	12	9	19
Southern North Division				
Appalachian St.*	11	5	19	10
East Tenn. St.	11	5	20	11
Davidson	11	5	17	10
Elon University	8	6	12	15
Western Carolina	6	10	9	19
NC Greensboro	3	13	7	22
South Division				
Coll Of Charltn	13	3	25	8
UT-Chattanooga	11	5	21	9
Georgia Southern	8	8	16	13
Wofford	8	8	14	15
Furman	8	8	14	17
The Citadel	3	13	8	20
Southland				
Sam Houston St.*	17	3	23	7
Stephen F. Austin	16	4	21	8
Texas Arlington	13	7	16	13
Texas St.	11	9	17	12
McNeese St.	10	10	15	14
Lamar	10	10	13	14
Louisiana Monroe	10	10	12	16
SE Louisiana	9	11	11	16
Tex San Antonio	7	13	10	17
Northwestern St.	6	14	6	21
Nicholls St.	1	19	3	25
Southwest Athletic				
Prairie View	14	4	17	12
Miss. Valley St.	13	5	15	14
Texas Southern*	11	7	18	13

	Conf. W	L	All W	L
Alabama St.	11	7	14	15
Alcorn St.	10	8	14	19
Grambling	9	9	12	18
Jackson St.	9	9	10	18
Southern	5	13	9	20
Alabama A&M	4	14	8	19
Ark Pine Bluff	4	14	4	24
Sun Belt East Division				
Western Kentucky*	12	2	24	9
Middle Tenn. St.	9	5	16	14
Arkansas-Little Rock	8	6	19	11
Arkansas St.	6	8	13	15
Florida Int'l	1	13	8	21
West Division				
La Lafayette	12	3	20	10
New Mexico St.	9	6	20	9
Denver	7	8	17	15
New Orleans	7	8	15	14
South Alabama	7	8	14	14
North Texas	2	13	7	21
West Coast				
Gonzaga	12	2	24	9
San Diego*	10	4	18	12
San Francisco	9	5	15	14
Pepperdine	7	7	15	13
St. Mary's (CA)	6	8	15	15
Santa Clara	4	10	13	15
Portland	4	10	11	17
Loyola Marymount	4	10	11	20
Western Athletic Conference				
Fresno St.	13	5	20	8
Tulsa*	12	6	23	10
SMU	11	7	17	13
Nevada	11	7	18	14
Rice	11	7	19	10
Hawai'i	9	9	19	12
La. Tech	9	9	12	15
Boise St.	7	11	13	16
SJSU	4	14	7	21
UTEP	3	15	6	24
Independents				
TX A&M Corp Chris	—	—	14	15
TX Pan American	—	—	10	20
IPFW	—	—	9	21
Savannah St.	—	—	3	24

(1) Conference does not hold a tournament. (2) Trans America Athletic Conference, 1979-2001.

All-Time Winningest Division I College Teams by Percentage
(through 2002-2003 season)

TEAM	Yrs	Won	Lost	Pct.	TEAM	Yrs	Won	Lost	Pct.
Kentucky	100	1849	572	0.764	Utah	95	1492	775	0.658
Indiana	103	1540	525	0.746	Arkansas	80	1377	742	0.650
N. Carolina	93	1808	666	0.731	Temple	107	1608	874	0.648
UNLV	45	928	363	0.719	Louisville	89	1431	778	0.648
Kansas	105	1801	753	0.705	Weber State	41	756	413	0.647
UCLA	84	1520	672	0.693	Notre Dame	98	1529	838	0.646
Duke	98	1706	775	0.688	Illinois	98	1458	798	0.646
St. John's-NY	96	1662	763	0.685	Arizona	98	1438	788	0.646
Syracuse	102	1602	737	0.685	Pennsylvania	103	1555	876	0.640
W. Kentucky	84	1466	723	0.670	DePaul	80	1242	716	0.634

Major College Basketball Tournaments

The National Invitation Tournament (NIT), first played in 1938, is the nation's oldest basketball tournament. The first National Collegiate Athletic Association (NCAA) national championship tournament was played one year later. Selections for both tournaments are made in March, with the NCAA selecting first from among the top Division I teams.

National Invitation Tournament Champions

Year	Champion	Year	Champion	Year	Champion	Year	Champion	Year	Champion
1938	Temple	1952	LaSalle	1965	St. John's	1978	Texas	1991	Stanford
1939	Long Island Univ.	1953	Seton Hall	1966	Brigham Young	1979	Indiana	1992	Virginia
1940	Colorado	1954	Holy Cross	1967	Southern Illinois	1980	Virginia	1993	Minnesota
1941	Long Island Univ.	1955	Duquesne	1968	Dayton	1981	Tulsa	1994	Villanova
1942	West Virginia	1956	Louisville	1969	Temple	1982	Bradley	1995	Virginia Tech
1943	St. John's	1957	Bradley	1970	Marquette	1983	Fresno State	1996	Nebraska
1944	St. John's	1958	Xavier (Ohio)	1971	North Carolina	1984	Michigan	1997	Michigan
1945	De Paul	1959	St. John's	1972	Maryland	1985	UCLA	1998	Minnesota
1946	Kentucky	1960	Bradley	1973	Virginia Tech	1986	Ohio State	1999	California
1947	Utah	1961	Providence	1974	Purdue	1987	So. Mississippi	2000	Wake Forest
1948	St. Louis	1962	Dayton	1975	Princeton	1988	Connecticut	2001	Tulsa
1949	San Francisco	1963	Providence	1976	Kentucky	1989	St. John's	2002	Memphis
1950	CCNY	1964	Bradley	1977	St. Bonaventure	1990	Vanderbilt	2003	St. John's
1951	Brigham Young								

2003 MEN'S NCAA BASKETBALL TOURNAMENT

EAST

```
(1) Oklahoma 71
(16) South Carolina St. 54        Oklahoma 74
                                                      Oklahoma 65
(8) California 76 (OT)            California 65
(9) NC St. 74                                                          Oklahoma 47
(5) Mississippi St. 46
(12) Butler 47                    Butler 79             Butler 54
(4) Louisville 86                 Louisville 71
(13) Austin Peay 64                                                                    Syracuse 95
(6) Oklahoma St. 77
(11) Pennsylvania 63              Oklahoma St. 56
                                                      Syracuse 79
(3) Syracuse 76                   Syracuse 68
(14) Manhattan 65                                                      Syracuse 63
(7) St. Joseph's 63
(10) Auburn 65 (OT)               Auburn 68             Auburn 78
(2) Wake Forest 76                Wake Forest 62
(15) E. Tennessee St. 73
```

SOUTH

```
(1) Texas 82
*(16) UNC Asheville 61            Texas 77
                                                      Texas 82
(8) LSU 56                        Purdue 67
(9) Purdue 80                                                          Texas 85
(5) Connecticut 58
(12) BYU 53                       Connecticut 85        Connecticut 78
(4) Stanford 77                   Stanford 74
(13) San Diego 69                                                                      Texas 84
(6) Maryland 75
(11) UNC Wilmington 73            Maryland 77
                                                      Maryland 58
(3) Xavier 71                     Xavier 64
(14) Troy St. 59                                                       Michigan St. 76
(7) Michigan St. 79
(10) Colorado 64                  Michigan St. 68       Michigan St. 60
(2) Florida 85                    Florida 46
(15) Sam Houston St. 55
```

MIDWEST

```
(1) Kentucky 95
(16) IUPUI 64                     Kentucky 74
                                                      Kentucky 63
(8) Oregon 58                     Utah 54
(9) Utah 60                                                            Kentucky 69
(5) Wisconsin 81
(12) Weber St. 74                 Wisconsin 61          Wisconsin 57
(4) Dayton 71                     Tulsa 60
(13) Tulsa 84                                                                          Marquette 61
(6) Missouri 72
(11) Southern Illinois 71         Missouri 92
                                                      Marquette 77
(3) Marquette 72                  Marquette 101 (OT)
(14) Holy Cross 68                                                    Marquette 83
(7) Indiana 67
(10) Alabama 62                   Indiana 52            Pittsburgh 74
(2) Pittsburgh 87                 Pittsburgh 74
(15) Wagner 61
```

WEST

```
(1) Arizona 80
(16) Vermont 51                   Arizona 96 (2 OT)
                                                      Arizona 88
(8) Cincinnati 69                 Gonzaga 95
(9) Gonzaga 74                                                         Arizona 75
(5) Notre Dame 70
(12) UW-Milwaukee 69              Notre Dame 68         Notre Dame 71
(4) Illinois 65                   Illinois 60
(13) Western Kentucky 60                                                               Kansas 94
(6) Creighton 73
(11) Central Michigan 79          Central Michigan 60
                                                      Duke 65
(3) Duke 67                       Duke 86
(14) Colorado St. 57                                                  Kansas 78
(7) Memphis 71
(10) Arizona St. 84               Arizona St. 76        Kansas 69
(2) Kansas 64                     Kansas 108
(15) Utah St. 61
```

Syracuse 81
Kansas 78

*UNC Asheville defeated Texas Southern, 92-84 (OT), in a special play-in game on Mar. 18 to earn the 16th seed in the South.

2003 Men's NCAA Tournament: Fab Freshmen Lead Syracuse to 1st Title

The Syracuse Orangemen (30-5) defeated the Kansas Jayhawks (30-8), 81-78, for the national title in the New Orleans Superdome on Apr. 7, 2003. Syracuse standout freshman Carmelo Anthony led all scorers with 20 points in the game and was named Most Outstanding Player of the Final Four. Gerry McNamara, another freshman, hit 6 three-pointers as Syracuse scored 53 points in the 1st half, a record for an NCAA final. Syracuse, which led by as many as 18 points in the first half, survived a late rally by Kansas to give Jim Boeheim his 1st title in 27 years as coach of his alma mater. Just 17 days later, on Apr. 24, Anthony declared himself an early entry candidate for the NBA Draft. The 6'8", 220-lb. forward was selected 3rd overall by the Denver Nuggets in June.

NCAA Division I Champions

Year	Champion	Coach	Final opponent	Score	Outstanding player	Site
1939	Oregon	Howard Hobson	Ohio St.	46-33	None	Evanston, IL
1940	Indiana	Branch McCracken	Kansas	60-42	Marvin Huffman, Indiana	Kansas City, MO
1941	Wisconsin	Harold Foster	Washington St.	39-34	John Kotz, Wisconsin	Kansas City, MO
1942	Stanford	Everett Dean	Dartmouth	53-38	Howard Dallmar, Stanford	Kansas City, MO
1943	Wyoming	Everett Shelton	Georgetown	46-34	Ken Sailors, Wyoming	New York, NY
1944	Utah	Vadal Peterson	Dartmouth	42-40[1]	Arnold Ferrin, Utah	New York, NY
1945	Oklahoma St.[2]	Henry Iba	NYU	49-45	Bob Kurland, Oklahoma St.	New York, NY
1946	Oklahoma St.[2]	Henry Iba	North Carolina	43-40	Bob Kurland, Oklahoma St.	New York, NY
1947	Holy Cross	Alvin Julian	Oklahoma	58-47	George Kaftan, Holy Cross	New York, NY
1948	Kentucky	Adolph Rupp	Baylor	58-42	Alex Groza, Kentucky	New York, NY
1949	Kentucky	Adolph Rupp	Oklahoma St.	46-36	Alex Groza, Kentucky	Seattle, WA
1950	CCNY	Nat Holman	Bradley	71-68	Irwin Dambrot, CCNY	New York, NY
1951	Kentucky	Adolph Rupp	Kansas St.	68-58	None	Minneapolis, MN
1952	Kansas	Forrest Allen	St. John's	80-63	Clyde Lovellette, Kansas	Seattle, WA
1953	Indiana	Branch McCracken	Kansas	69-68	B.H. Born, Kansas	Kansas City, MO
1954	La Salle	Kenneth Loeffler	Bradley	92-76	Tom Gola, La Salle	Kansas City, MO
1955	San Francisco	Phil Woolpert	LaSalle	77-63	Bill Russell, San Francisco	Kansas City, MO
1956	San Francisco	Phil Woolpert	Iowa	83-71	Hal Lear, Temple	Evanston, IL
1957	North Carolina	Frank McGuire	Kansas	54-53[1]	Wilt Chamberlain, Kansas	Kansas City, MO
1958	Kentucky	Adolph Rupp	Seattle	84-72	Elgin Baylor, Seattle	Louisville, KY
1959	California	Pete Newell	West Virginia	71-70	Jerry West, West Virginia	Louisville, KY
1960	Ohio St.	Fred Taylor	California	75-55	Jerry Lucas, Ohio St.	San Francisco, CA
1961	Cincinnati	Edwin Jucker	Ohio St.	70-65[1]	Jerry Lucas, Ohio St.	Kansas City, MO
1962	Cincinnati	Edwin Jucker	Ohio St.	71-59	Paul Hogue, Cincinnati	Louisville, KY
1963	Loyola (IL)	George Ireland	Cincinnati	60-58[1]	Art Heyman, Duke	Louisville, KY
1964	UCLA	John Wooden	Duke	98-83	Walt Hazzard, UCLA	Kansas City, MO
1965	UCLA	John Wooden	Michigan	91-80	Bill Bradley, Princeton	Portland, OR
1966	Texas-El Paso[3]	Don Haskins	Kentucky	72-65	Jerry Chambers, Utah	College Park, MD
1967	UCLA	John Wooden	Dayton	79-64	Lew Alcindor, UCLA	Louisville, KY
1968	UCLA	John Wooden	North Carolina	78-55	Lew Alcindor, UCLA	Los Angeles, CA
1969	UCLA	John Wooden	Purdue	92-72	Lew Alcindor, UCLA	Louisville, KY
1970	UCLA	John Wooden	Jacksonville	80-69	Sidney Wicks, UCLA	College Park, MD
1971	UCLA	John Wooden	Villanova*	68-62	Howard Porter, Villanova*	Houston, TX
1972	UCLA	John Wooden	Florida St.	81-76	Bill Walton, UCLA	Los Angeles, CA
1973	UCLA	John Wooden	Memphis St.	87-66	Bill Walton, UCLA	St. Louis, MO
1974	North Carolina St.	Norm Sloan	Marquette	76-64	David Thompson, N.C. St.	Greensboro, NC
1975	UCLA	John Wooden	Kentucky	92-85	Richard Washington, UCLA	San Diego, CA
1976	Indiana	Bob Knight	Michigan	86-68	Kent Benson, Indiana	Philadelphia, PA
1977	Marquette	Al McGuire	North Carolina	67-59	Butch Lee, Marquette	Atlanta, GA
1978	Kentucky	Joe Hall	Duke	94-88	Jack Givens, Kentucky	St. Louis, MO
1979	Michigan St.	Jud Heathcote	Indiana St.	75-64	Magic Johnson, Michigan St.	Salt Lake City, UT
1980	Louisville	Denny Crum	UCLA*	59-54	Darrell Griffith, Louisville	Indianapolis, IN
1981	Indiana	Bob Knight	North Carolina	63-50	Isiah Thomas, Indiana	Philadelphia, PA
1982	North Carolina	Dean Smith	Georgetown	63-62	James Worthy, N. Carolina	New Orleans, LA
1983	North Carolina St.	Jim Valvano	Houston	54-52	Hakeem Olajuwon, Houston	Albuquerque, NM
1984	Georgetown	John Thompson	Houston	84-75	Patrick Ewing, Georgetown	Seattle, WA
1985	Villanova	Rollie Massimino	Georgetown	66-64	Ed Pinckney, Villanova	Lexington, KY
1986	Louisville	Denny Crum	Duke	72-69	Pervis Ellison, Louisville	Dallas, TX
1987	Indiana	Bob Knight	Syracuse	74-73	Keith Smart, Indiana	New Orleans, LA
1988	Kansas	Larry Brown	Oklahoma	83-79	Danny Manning, Kansas	Kansas City, MO
1989	Michigan	Steve Fisher	Seton Hall	80-79[1]	Glen Rice, Michigan	Seattle, WA
1990	UNLV	Jerry Tarkanian	Duke	103-73	Anderson Hunt, UNLV	Denver, CO
1991	Duke	Mike Krzyzewski	Kansas	72-65	Christian Laettner, Duke	Indianapolis, IN
1992	Duke	Mike Krzyzewski	Michigan	71-51	Bobby Hurley, Duke	Minneapolis, MN
1993	North Carolina	Dean Smith	Michigan	77-71	Donald Williams, N. Carolina	New Orleans, LA
1994	Arkansas	Nolan Richardson	Duke	76-72	Corliss Williamson, Arkansas	Charlotte, NC
1995	UCLA	Jim Harrick	Arkansas	89-78	Ed O'Bannon, UCLA	Seattle, WA
1996	Kentucky	Rick Pitino	Syracuse	76-67	Tony Delk, Kentucky	E. Rutherford, NJ
1997	Arizona	Lute Olson	Kentucky	84-79[1]	Miles Simon, Arizona	Indianapolis, IN
1998	Kentucky	Tubby Smith	Utah	78-69	Jeff Sheppard, Kentucky	San Antonio, TX
1999	Connecticut	Jim Calhoun	Duke	77-74	Richard Hamilton, Connecticut	St. Petersburg, FL
2000	Michigan St.	Tom Izzo	Florida	89-76	Mateen Cleaves, Michigan St.	Indianapolis, IN
2001	Duke	Mike Krzyzewski	Arizona	82-72	Shane Battier, Duke	Minneapolis, MN
2002	Maryland	Gary Williams	Indiana	64-52	Juan Dixon, Maryland	Atlanta, GA
2003	Syracuse	Jim Boeheim	Kansas	81-78	Carmelo Anthony	New Orleans, LA

*Declared ineligible after the tournament. (1) Overtime. (2) Then known as Oklahoma A&M. (3) Then known as Texas Western.

Top Division I Career Scorers

(minimum 1,500 points; ranked by average)

Player, school	Years	Points	Avg.	Player, school	Years	Points	Avg.
Pete Maravich, LSU	1968-70	3,667	44.2	Frank Selvy, Furman	1952-54	2,538	32.5
Austin Carr, Notre Dame	1969-71	2,560	34.6	Rick Mount, Purdue	1968-70	2,323	32.3
Oscar Robertson, Cincinnati	1958-60	2,973	33.8	Darrell Floyd, Furman	1954-56	2,281	32.1
Calvin Murphy, Niagara	1968-70	2,548	33.1	Nick Werkman, Seton Hall	1962-64	2,273	32.0
Dwight Lamar, SW Louisiana	1972-73	1,862	32.7	Willie Humes, Idaho State	1970-71	1,510	31.5

John R. Wooden Award

Awarded to the nation's outstanding college basketball player by the Los Angeles Athletic Club.

1977	Marques Johnson, UCLA	1986	Walter Berry, St. John's	1995	Ed O'Bannon, UCLA
1978	Phil Ford, North Carolina	1987	David Robinson, Navy	1996	Marcus Camby, Massachusetts
1979	Larry Bird, Indiana State	1988	Danny Manning, Kansas	1997	Tim Duncan, Wake Forest
1980	Darrell Griffith, Louisville	1989	Sean Elliott, Arizona	1998	Antawn Jamison, North Carolina
1981	Danny Ainge, Brigham Young	1990	Lionel Simmons, La Salle	1999	Elton Brand, Duke
1982	Ralph Sampson, Virginia	1991	Larry Johnson, UNLV	2000	Kenyon Martin, Cincinnati
1983	Ralph Sampson, Virginia	1992	Christian Laettner, Duke	2001	Shane Battier, Duke
1984	Michael Jordan, North Carolina	1993	Calbert Cheaney, Indiana	2002	Jay Williams, Duke
1985	Chris Mullin, St. John's	1994	Glenn Robinson, Purdue	2003	T.J. Ford, Texas

Most Coaching Victories in the NCAA Tournament Through 2003

(Coaches active in 2002-2003 season in **bold**)

Coach, School(s), First/Last appearance	Wins	Tourns.	Coach, School(s), First/Last appearance	Wins	Tourns.
Dean Smith, North Carolina, 1967/1997	65	27	John Thompson, Georgetown, 1975/1997	34	20
Mike Krzyzewski, Duke, 1984/2003	60	19	**Jim Boeheim**, Syracuse, 1977/2003	38	22
John Wooden, UCLA, 1950/1975	47	16	**Eddie Sutton**, Creighton, Arkansas, Kentucky,		
Denny Crum, Louisville, 1972/2000	42	23	Oklahoma St., 1974/2003	33	24
Bob Knight, Indiana, Texas Tech, 1973/2002	42	25	Jerry Tarkanian, Long Beach St., UNLV,		
Lute Olson, Iowa, Arizona, 1979/2003	42	24	Fresno St.,1970/2001	32*	15

*Does not include 6 wins in the 1971-73 tournaments which were later vacated for NCAA rule violations.

Women's College Basketball

2003 Women's NCAA Tournament: UConn Cruises to 2nd Straight Title

Top-ranked defending national champion Connecticut (31-1) captured its 2nd-straight title, defeating Tennessee (28-4), 73-68, at the Georgia Dome in Atlanta on Apr. 8. The Huskies have met and beaten the Volunteers 3 times in the NCAA championship game (1995, 2000, 2003). Connecticut Junior Diana Taurasi, the only returning starter from the 2001-2002 undefeated team, led all scorers in the final with 28 points. Taurasi, who won the Wade Trophy as the nation's top basketball player, was also named Most Outstanding Player of the Final Four.

NCAA Division I Women's Champions

Year	Champion	Coach	Final opponent	Score	Outstanding player	Site
1982	Louisiana Tech	Sonja Hogg	Cheyney	76-62	Janice Lawrence, La. Tech	Norfolk, VA
1983	USC	Linda Sharp	Louisiana Tech	69-67	Cheryl Miller, USC	Norfolk, VA
1984	USC	Linda Sharp	Tennessee	72-61	Cheryl Miller, USC	Los Angeles, CA
1985	Old Dominion	Marianne Stanley	Georgia	70-65	Tracy Claxton, Old Dominion	Austin, TX
1986	Texas	Jody Conradt	USC	97-81	Clarissa Davis, Texas	Lexington, KY
1987	Tennessee	Pat Summitt	Louisiana Tech	67-44	Tonya Edwards, Tennessee	Austin, TX
1988	Louisiana Tech	Leon Barmore	Auburn	56-54	Erica Westbrooks, La. Tech	Tacoma, WA
1989	Tennessee	Pat Summitt	Auburn	76-60	Bridgette Gordon, Tennessee	Tacoma, WA
1990	Stanford	Tara VanDerveer	Auburn	88-81	Jennifer Azzi, Stanford	Knoxville, TN
1991	Tennessee	Pat Summitt	Virginia	70-67*	Dawn Staley, Virginia	New Orleans, LA
1992	Stanford	Tara VanDerveer	W. Kentucky	78-62	Molly Goodenbour, Stanford	Los Angeles, CA
1993	Texas Tech	Marsha Sharp	Ohio St.	84-82	Sheryl Swoopes, Texas Tech	Atlanta, GA
1994	North Carolina	Sylvia Hatchell	Louisiana Tech	60-59	Charlotte Smith, North Carolina	Richmond, VA
1995	Connecticut	Geno Auriemma	Tennessee	70-64	Rebecca Lobo, Connecticut	Minneapolis, MN
1996	Tennessee	Pat Summitt	Georgia	83-65	Michelle Marciniak, Tennessee	Charlotte, NC
1997	Tennessee	Pat Summitt	Old Dominion	68-59	Chamique Holdsclaw, Tennessee	Cincinnati, OH
1998	Tennessee	Pat Summitt	Louisiana Tech	93-75	Chamique Holdsclaw, Tennessee	Kansas City, MO
1999	Purdue	Carolyn Peck	Duke	62-45	Ukari Figgs, Purdue	San Jose, CA
2000	Connecticut	Geno Auriemma	Tennessee	71-52	Shea Ralph, Connecticut	Philadelphia, PA
2001	Notre Dame	Muffet McGraw	Purdue	68-66	Ruth Riley, Notre Dame	St. Louis, MO
2002	Connecticut	Geno Auriemma	Oklahoma	82-70	Swin Cash, Connecticut	San Antonio, TX
2003	Connecticut	Geno Auriemma	Tennessee	73-68	Diana Taurasi, Connecticut	Atlanta, GA

* Overtime.

Wade Trophy

Awarded by National Assn. for Girls and Women in Sport for academics, community service, and player performance.

Year	Player, school	Year	Player, school	Year	Player, school
1978	Carol Blazejowski, Montclair St.	1988	Teresa Weatherspoon,	1997	DeLisha Milton, Florida
1979	Nancy Lieberman, Old Dominion		Louisiana Tech	1998	Chamique Holdsclaw,
1980	Nancy Lieberman, Old Dominion	1989	Clarissa Davis, Texas		Tennessee
1981	Lynette Woodard, Kansas	1990	Jennifer Azzi, Stanford	1999	Stephanie White-McCarty,
1982	Pam Kelly, Louisiana Tech	1991	Daedra Charles, Tennessee		Purdue
1983	LaTaunya Pollard, Long Beach St.	1992	Susan Robinson, Penn St.	2000	Edwina Brown, Texas
1984	Janice Lawrence, Louisiana Tech	1993	Karen Jennings, Nebraska	2001	Jackie Stiles, SW Missouri St.
1985	Cheryl Miller, USC	1994	Carol Ann Shudlick, Minnesota	2002	Sue Bird, Connecticut
1986	Kamie Ethridge, Texas	1995	Rebecca Lobo, Connecticut	2003	Diana Taurasi, Connecticut
1987	Shelly Pennefeather, Villanova	1996	Jennifer Rizzotti, Connecticut		

Top Division I Women's Career Scorers

(Minimum 1,500 points; ranked by average)

Player, school	Years	Points	Avg.	Player, school	Years	Points	Avg.
Patricia Hoskins, Miss. Valley St.	1985-89	3,122	28.4	Valorie Whiteside, Appalachian St.	1984-88	2,944	25.4
Sandra Hodge, New Orleans	1981-84	2,860	26.7	Joyce Walker, LSU	1981-84	2,906	24.8
Jackie Stiles, SW Missouri St.	1997-2001	3,393	26.3	Tarcha Hollis, Grambling	1988-91	2,058	24.2
Lorri Bauman, Drake	1981-84	3,115	26.0	Korie Hlede, Duquesne	1994-98	2,631	24.1
Andrea Congreaves, Mercer	1989-93	2,796	25.9	Erma Jones, Bethune-Cookman	1982-84	2,095	24.1
Cindy Blodgett, Maine	1994-98	3,005	25.5	Karen Pelphrey, Marshall	1983-86	2,746	24.1

2003 WOMEN'S NCAA BASKETBALL TOURNAMENT

EAST REGIONAL

(1) Connecticut 91
(16) Boston U. 44
   Connecticut 81
(8) Michigan St. 47
(9) TCU 50
   TCU 66
    Connecticut 70
(5) Boston Coll. 73
(12) Old Dominion 72
   Boston Coll. 86 (OT)
(4) Vanderbilt 54
(13) Liberty 44
   Vanderbilt 85
    Boston Coll. 49
     Connecticut 73

(6) Arizona 47
(11) Notre Dame 59
   Notre Dame 59
(3) Kansas St. 79
(14) Harvard 69
   Kansas St. 53
    Notre Dame 47
(7) Virginia Tech 61
(10) Georgia Tech 59
   Virginia Tech 62
(2) Purdue 66
(15) Valparaiso 51
   Purdue 80
    Purdue 66
     Purdue 64

      Connecticut 71

WEST REGIONAL

(1) LSU 86
(16) SW Texas St. 50
   LSU 80
(8) Wisc.-Green Bay 78
(9) Washington 65
   Wisc.-Green Bay 69
    LSU 69
(5) LA Tech 94
(12) Pepperdine 60
   LA Tech 74
(4) Ohio St. 66
(13) Weber St. 44
   Ohio St. 61
    LA Tech 63
     LSU 60

(6) Minnesota 68
(11) Tulane 48
   Minnesota 68
(3) Stanford 82
(14) Western Michigan 66
   Stanford 56
    Minnesota 60
(7) Arkansas 71
(10) Cincinnati 57
   Arkansas 67
(2) Texas 90
(15) Hampton 64
   Texas 50
    Texas 73
     Texas 78

      Texas 69

MIDEAST REGIONAL

(1) Tennessee 95
(16) Alabama St. 43
   Tennessee 81
(8) Virginia 72
(9) Illinois 56
   Virginia 51
    Tennessee 86
(5) South Carolina 68
(12) Chattanooga 54
   South Carolina 67
(4) Penn St. 64
(13) Holy Cross 33
   Penn St. 77
    Penn St. 58
     Tennessee 73

(6) Colorado 84
(11) BYU 45
   Colorado 86
(3) North Carolina 72
(14) Austin Peay 70
   North Carolina 67
    Colorado 51
(7) George Washington 71
(10) Oklahoma 61
   G. Washington 57
(2) Villanova 51
(15) St. Francis (PA) 36
   Villanova 70
    Villanova 53
     Villanova 49

      Tennessee 66

MIDWEST REGIONAL

(1) Duke 66
(16) Georgia St. 48
   Duke 65
(8) Utah 73
(9) DePaul 64
   Utah 54
    Duke 66
(5) Georgia 80
(12) Charlotte 61
   Georgia 74
(4) Rutgers 64
(13) Western Kentucky 52
   Rutgers 64
    Georgia 63
     Duke 57

(6) New Mexico 91 (OT)
(11) Miami (FL) 85
   New Mexico 73
(3) Mississippi St. 73
(14) Manhattan 47
   Mississippi St. 61
    New Mexico 48
(7) UC Santa Barbara 71
(10) Xavier 62
   UCSB 68
(2) Texas Tech 67
(15) SW Missouri St. 59
   Texas Tech 72
    Texas Tech 71
     Texas Tech 51

      Duke 56

Connecticut
Tennessee 68

NATIONAL FOOTBALL LEAGUE

NFL 2002-2003: Bucs Super, Records for Smith, Rice, & Harrison

In the 1st title game to match the top defense against the top offense, the Tampa Bay Buccaneers defeated the Oakland Raiders, 48-21, in Super Bowl XXXVII in San Diego Jan. 26, 2003. The Raiders, with NFL MVP quarterback Rich Gannon, led the league in passing (279.7 yards/game) and total offense (398.8 yards/game). The Buccaneers allowed only 196 points in 2002, the 4th-lowest total since the NFL went to a 16-game schedule in 1978.

Dallas running back Emmitt Smith passed Hall-of-Famer Walter Payton (16,726) as the NFL's all-time rushing leader on Oct. 27, 2002. Smith finished the season with 17,162 career yards. Payton (21,264) was also passed by Oakland's Jerry Rice as the all-time leader in total yards from scrimmage. By the end of 2002, Rice had amassed 22,242 yds. Rice (203) and Smith (164) were the NFL's all-time leading TD scorers. Indianapolis receiver Marvin Harrison set an NFL single-season record with 143 catches, breaking Herman Moore's 1995 mark by 20. Baltimore cornerback Chris McAlister's 107-yd. return of a missed 57-yd. field goal by Denver kicker Jason Elam on Sept. 30 was the longest scoring play in NFL history.

Final 2002 Standings

American Football Conference

East Division

	W	L	T	Pct.	Pts.	Opp.	Div.
NY Jets	9	7	0	.562	359	336	4-2
New England	9	7	0	.562	381	346	4-2
Miami	9	7	0	.562	378	301	2-4
Buffalo	8	8	0	.500	379	397	2-4

North Division

	W	L	T	Pct.	Pts.	Opp.	Div.
Pittsburgh	10	5	1	.656	390	345	6-0
Cleveland*	9	7	0	.562	344	320	3-3
Baltimore	7	9	0	.438	316	354	3-3
Cincinnati	2	14	0	.125	279	456	0-6

South Division

	W	L	T	Pct.	Pts.	Opp.	Div.
Tennessee	11	5	0	.688	367	324	6-0
Indianapolis*	10	6	0	.625	349	313	4-2
Jacksonville	6	10	0	.375	328	315	1-5
Houston	4	12	0	.250	213	356	1-5

West Division

	W	L	T	Pct.	Pts.	Opp.	Div.
Oakland	11	5	0	.688	450	304	4-2
Denver	9	7	0	.562	392	344	3-3
San Diego	8	8	0	.500	333	367	3-3
Kansas City	8	8	0	.500	467	399	2-4

National Football Conference

East Division

	W	L	T	Pct.	Pts.	Opp.	Div.
Philadelphia	12	4	0	.750	415	241	5-1
NY Giants*	10	6	0	.625	320	279	5-1
Washington	7	9	0	.438	307	365	1-5
Dallas	5	11	0	.312	217	329	1-5

North Division

	W	L	T	Pct.	Pts.	Opp.	Div.
Green Bay	12	4	0	.750	398	328	5-1
Minnesota	6	10	0	.375	390	442	4-2
Chicago	4	12	0	.250	281	379	2-4
Detroit	3	13	0	.188	306	451	1-5

South Division

	W	L	T	Pct.	Pts.	Opp.	Div.
Tampa Bay	12	4	0	.750	346	196	4-2
Atlanta*	9	6	1	.594	402	314	4-2
New Orleans	9	7	0	.562	432	388	3-3
Carolina	7	9	0	.438	258	302	1-5

West Division

	W	L	T	Pct.	Pts.	Opp.	Div.
San Francisco	10	6	0	.625	367	351	5-1
St. Louis	7	9	0	.438	316	369	4-2
Seattle	7	9	0	.438	355	369	2-4
Arizona	5	11	0	.312	262	417	1-5

* Wild card team.

AFC Playoffs—NY Jets 41, Indianapolis 0; Pittsburgh 36, Cleveland 33; Tennessee 34, Pittsburgh 31; Oakland 30, NY Jets 10; Championship: Oakland 41, Tennessee 24.

NFC Playoffs—San Francisco 39, NY Giants 38; Atlanta 27, Green Bay 7; Philadelphia 20, Atlanta 6; Tampa Bay 31, San Francisco 6; Championship: Tampa Bay 27, Philadelphia 10.

Super Bowl—Tampa Bay 48, Oakland 21.

National Football League Champions

Year	East Winner (W-L-T)	West Winner (W-L-T)	Playoff
1933	New York Giants (11-3-0)	Chicago Bears (10-2-1)	Chicago Bears 23, New York 21
1934	New York Giants (8-5-0)	Chicago Bears (13-0-0)	New York 30, Chicago Bears 13
1935	New York Giants (9-3-0)	Detroit Lions (7-3-2)	Detroit 26, New York 7
1936	Boston Redskins (7-5-0)	Green Bay Packers (10-1-1)	Green Bay 21, Boston 6
1937	Washington Redskins (8-3-0)	Chicago Bears (9-1-1)	Washington 28, Chicago Bears 21
1938	New York Giants (8-2-1)	Green Bay Packers (8-3-0)	New York 23, Green Bay 17
1939	New York Giants (9-1-1)	Green Bay Packers (9-2-0)	Green Bay 27, New York 0
1940	Washington Redskins (9-2-0)	Chicago Bears (8-3-0)	Chicago Bears 73, Washington 0
1941	New York Giants (8-3-0)	Chicago Bears (10-1-1)(a)	Chicago Bears 37, New York 9
1942	Washington Redskins (10-1-1)	Chicago Bears (11-0-0)	Washington 14, Chicago Bears 6
1943	Washington Redskins (6-3-1)	Chicago Bears (8-1-1)	Chicago Bears, 41, Washington 21
1944	New York Giants (8-1-1)	Green Bay Packers (8-2-0)	Green Bay 14, New York 7
1945	Washington Redskins (8-2-0)	Cleveland Rams (9-1-0)	Cleveland 15, Washington 14
1946	New York Giants (7-3-1)	Chicago Bears (8-2-1)	Chicago Bears 24, New York 14
1947	Philadelphia Eagles (8-4-0)(a)	Chicago Cardinals (9-3-0)	Chicago Cardinals 28, Philadelphia 21
1948	Philadelphia Eagles (9-2-1)	Chicago Cardinals (11-1-0)	Philadelphia 7, Chicago Cardinals 0
1949	Philadelphia Eagles (11-1-0)	Los Angeles Rams (8-2-2)	Philadelphia 14, Los Angeles 0
1950	Cleveland Browns (10-2-0)(a)	Los Angeles Rams (9-3-0)(a)	Cleveland 30, Los Angeles 28
1951	Cleveland Browns (11-1-0)	Los Angeles Rams (8-4-0)	Los Angeles 24, Cleveland 17
1952	Cleveland Browns (8-4-0)	Detroit Lions (9-3-0)(a)	Detroit 17, Cleveland 7
1953	Cleveland Browns (11-1-0)	Detroit Lions (10-2-0)	Detroit 17, Cleveland 16
1954	Cleveland Browns (9-2-1)	Detroit Lions (9-2-1)	Cleveland 56, Detroit 10
1955	Cleveland Browns (9-2-1)	Los Angeles Rams (8-3-1)	Cleveland 38, Los Angeles 14
1956	New York Giants (8-3-1)	Chicago Bears (9-2-1)	New York 47, Chicago Bears 7
1957	Cleveland Browns (9-2-1)	Detroit Lions (8-4-0)(a)	Detroit 59, Cleveland 14
1958	New York Giants (9-3-0)(a)	Baltimore Colts (9-3-0)	Baltimore 23, New York 17(b)
1959	New York Giants (10-2-0)	Baltimore Colts (9-3-0)	Baltimore 31, New York 16
1960	Philadelphia Eagles (10-2-0)	Green Bay Packers (8-4-0)	Philadelphia 17, Green Bay 13
1961	New York Giants (10-3-1)	Green Bay Packers (11-3-0)	Green Bay 37, New York 0
1962	New York Giants (12-2-0)	Green Bay Packers (13-1-0)	Green Bay 16, New York 7
1963	New York Giants (11-3-0)	Chicago Bears (11-1-2)	Chicago 14, New York 10
1964	Cleveland Browns (10-3-1)	Baltimore Colts (12-2-0)	Cleveland 27, Baltimore 0
1965	Cleveland Browns (11-3-0)	Green Bay Packers (10-3-1)(a)	Green Bay 23, Cleveland 12
1966	Dallas Cowboys (10-3-1)	Green Bay Packers (12-2-0)	Green Bay 34, Dallas 27

(a) Won divisional playoff. (b) Won at 8:15 of sudden death overtime period.

Year	Conference	Division	Winner (W-L-T)	Playoffs(c)	Year
1967	East	Century	Cleveland Browns (9-5-0)	Dallas 52, Cleveland 14	1967
		Capitol	Dallas Cowboys (9-5-0)		
	West	Central	Green Bay Packers (9-4-1)	Green Bay 28, Los Angeles 7	
		Coastal	Los Angeles Rams (11-1-2)(a)	Green Bay 21, Dallas 17	
1968	East	Century	Cleveland Browns (10-4-0)	Cleveland 31, Dallas 20	1968
		Capitol	Dallas Cowboys (12-2-0)		
	West	Central	Minnesota Vikings (8-6-0)	Baltimore 24, Minnesota 14	
		Coastal	Baltimore Colts (13-1-0)	Baltimore 34, Cleveland 0	
1969	East	Century	Cleveland Browns (10-3-1)	Cleveland 38, Dallas 14	1969
		Capitol	Dallas Cowboys (11-2-1)		
	West	Central	Minnesota Vikings (12-2-0)	Minnesota 23, Los Angeles 20	
		Coastal	Los Angeles Rams (11-3-0)	Minnesota 27, Cleveland 7	
1970	American	Eastern	Baltimore Colts (11-2-1)	Baltimore 17, Cincinnati 0	1970
		Central	Cincinnati Bengals (8-6-0)	Oakland 21, Miami* 14	
		Western	Oakland Raiders (8-4-2)	Baltimore 27, Oakland 17	
	National	Eastern	Dallas Cowboys (10-4-0)	Dallas 5, Detroit* 0	
		Central	Minnesota Vikings (12-2-0)	San Francisco 17, Minnesota 14	
		Western	San Francisco 49ers (10-3-1)	Dallas 17, San Francisco 10	
1971	American	Eastern	Miami Dolphins (10-3-1)	Miami 27, Kansas City* 24	1971
		Central	Cleveland Browns (9-5-0)	Baltimore 20, Cleveland 3	
		Western	Kansas City Chiefs (10-3-1)	Miami 21, Baltimore 0	
	National	Eastern	Dallas Cowboys (11-3-0)	Dallas 20, Minnesota 12	
		Central	Minnesota Vikings (11-3-0)	San Francisco 24, Washington* 20	
		Western	San Francisco 49ers (9-5-0)	Dallas 14, San Francisco 3	
1972	American	Eastern	Miami Dolphins (14-0-0)	Miami 20, Cleveland* 14	1972
		Central	Pittsburgh Steelers (11-3-0)	Pittsburgh 13, Oakland 7	
		Western	Oakland Raiders (10-3-1)	Miami 21, Pittsburgh 17	
	National	Eastern	Washington Redskins (11-3-0)	Washington 16, Green Bay 3	
		Central	Green Bay Packers (10-4-0)	Dallas* 30, San Francisco 28	
		Western	San Francisco 49ers (8-5-1)	Washington 26, Dallas* 3	
1973	American	Eastern	Miami Dolphins (12-2-0)	Miami 34, Cincinnati 16	1973
		Central	Cincinnati Bengals (10-4-0)	Oakland 33, Pittsburgh* 14	
		Western	Oakland Raiders (9-4-1)	Miami 27, Oakland 10	
	National	Eastern	Dallas Cowboys (10-4-0)	Dallas 27, Los Angeles 16	
		Central	Minnesota Vikings (12-2-0)	Minnesota 27, Washington* 20	
		Western	Los Angeles Rams (12-2-0)	Minnesota 27, Dallas 10	
1974	American	Eastern	Miami Dolphins (11-3-0)	Oakland 28, Miami 26	1974
		Central	Pittsburgh Steelers (10-3-1)	Pittsburgh 32, Buffalo* 14	
		Western	Oakland Raiders (12-2-0)	Pittsburgh 24, Oakland 13	
	National	Eastern	St. Louis Cardinals (10-4-0)	Minnesota 30, St. Louis 14	
		Central	Minnesota Vikings (10-4-0)	Los Angeles 19, Washington* 10	
		Western	Los Angeles Rams (10-4-0)	Minnesota 14, Los Angeles 10	
1975	American	Eastern	Baltimore Colts (10-4-0)	Pittsburgh 28, Baltimore 10	1975
		Central	Pittsburgh Steelers (12-2-0)	Oakland 31, Cincinnati* 28	
		Western	Oakland Raiders (11-3-0)	Pittsburgh 16, Oakland 10	
	National	Eastern	St. Louis Cardinals (11-3-0)	Dallas* 17, Minnesota 14	
		Central	Minnesota Vikings (12-2-0)	Los Angeles 35, St. Louis 23	
		Western	Los Angeles Rams (12-2-0)	Dallas* 37, Los Angeles 7	
1976	American	Eastern	Baltimore Colts (11-3-0)	Pittsburgh 40, Baltimore 14	1976
		Central	Pittsburgh Steelers (10-4-0)	Oakland 24, New England* 21	
		Western	Oakland Raiders (13-1-0)	Oakland 24, Pittsburgh 7	
	National	Eastern	Dallas Cowboys (11-3-0)	Minnesota 35, Washington* 20	
		Central	Minnesota Vikings (11-2-1)	Los Angeles 14, Dallas 12	
		Western	Los Angeles Rams (10-3-1)	Minnesota 24, Los Angeles 13	
1977	American	Eastern	Baltimore Colts (10-4-0)	Oakland* 37, Baltimore 31	1977
		Central	Pittsburgh Steelers (9-5-0)	Denver 34, Pittsburgh 21	
		Western	Denver Broncos (12-2-0)	Denver 20, Oakland* 17	
	National	Eastern	Dallas Cowboys (12-2-0)	Dallas 37, Chicago* 7	
		Central	Minnesota Vikings (9-5-0)	Minnesota 14, Los Angeles 7	
		Western	Los Angeles Rams (10-4-0)	Dallas 23, Minnesota 6	
1978	American	Eastern	New England Patriots (11-5-0)	Pittsburgh 33, Denver 10	1978
		Central	Pittsburgh Steelers (14-2-0)	Houston* 31, New England 14	
		Western	Denver Broncos (10-6-0)	Pittsburgh 34, Houston* 5	
	National	Eastern	Dallas Cowboys (12-4-0)	Dallas 27, Atlanta* 20	
		Central	Minnesota Vikings (8-7-1)	Los Angeles 34, Minnesota 10	
		Western	Los Angeles Rams (12-4-0)	Dallas 28, Los Angeles 0	
1979	American	Eastern	Miami Dolphins (10-6-0)	Houston* 17, San Diego 14	1979
		Central	Pittsburgh Steelers (12-4-0)	Pittsburgh 34, Miami 14	
		Western	San Diego Chargers (12-4-0)	Pittsburgh 27, Houston* 13	
	National	Eastern	Dallas Cowboys (11-5-0)	Tampa Bay 24, Philadelphia* 17	
		Central	Tampa Bay Buccaneers (10-6-0)	Los Angeles 21, Dallas 19	
		Western	Los Angeles Rams (9-7-0)	Los Angeles 9, Tampa Bay 0	
1980	American	Eastern	Buffalo Bills (11-5-0)	San Diego 20, Buffalo 14	1980
		Central	Cleveland Browns (11-5-0)	Oakland* 14, Cleveland 12	
		Western	San Diego Chargers (11-5-0)	Oakland* 34, San Diego 27	
	National	Eastern	Philadelphia Eagles (12-4-0)	Philadelphia 31, Minnesota 16	
		Central	Minnesota Vikings (9-7-0)	Dallas* 30, Atlanta 27	
		Western	Atlanta Falcons (12-4-0)	Philadelphia 20, Dallas* 7	
1981	American	Eastern	Miami Dolphins (11-4-1)	San Diego 41, Miami 38	1981
		Central	Cincinnati Bengals (12-4-0)	Cincinnati 28, Buffalo* 21	
		Western	San Diego Chargers (10-6-0)	Cincinnati 27, San Diego 7	
	National	Eastern	Dallas Cowboys (12-4-0)	Dallas 38, Tampa Bay 0	
		Central	Tampa Bay Buccaneers (9-7-0)	San Francisco 38, N.Y. Giants* 24	
		Western	San Francisco 49ers (13-3-0)	San Francisco 28, Dallas 27	
1982 (d)	American		Los Angeles Raiders (8-1-0)	Strike-shortened season (see	1982 (d)
	National		Washington Redskins (8-1-0)	playoff results after footnote)	
1983	American	Eastern	Miami Dolphins (12-4-0)	Seattle* 27, Miami 20	1983
		Central	Pittsburgh Steelers (10-6-0)	L.A. Raiders 38, Pittsburgh 10	
		Western	Los Angeles Rams (12-4-0)	L.A. Raiders 30, Seattle* 14	
	National	Eastern	Washington Redskins (14-2-0)	Washington 51, L.A. Rams* 7	
		Central	Detroit Lions (9-7-0)	San Francisco 24, Detroit 23	
		Western	San Francisco 49ers (10-6-0)	Washington 24, San Francisco 21	

Year	Conference	Division	Winner (W-L-T)	Playoffs(c)	Year
1984	American	Eastern	Miami Dolphins (14-2-0)	Miami 31, Seattle* 10	1984
		Central	Pittsburgh Steelers (9-7-0)	Pittsburgh 24, Denver 17	
		Western	Denver Broncos (13-3-0)	Miami 45, Pittsburgh 28	
	National	Eastern	Washington Redskins (11-5-0)	Chicago 23, Washington 19	
		Central	Chicago Bears (10-6-0)	San Francisco 21, N.Y. Giants* 10	
		Western	San Francisco 49ers (15-1-0)	San Francisco 23, Chicago 0	
1985	American	Eastern	Miami Dolphins (12-4-0)	New England* 27, L.A. Raiders 20	1985
		Central	Cleveland Browns (8-8-0)	Miami 24, Cleveland 21	
		Western	Los Angeles Raiders (12-4-0)	New England* 31, Miami 14	
	National	Eastern	Dallas Cowboys (10-6-0)	Chicago 21, N.Y. Giants* 0	
		Central	Chicago Bears (15-1-0)	L.A. Rams 20, Dallas 0	
		Western	Los Angeles Rams (11-5-0)	Chicago 24, L.A. Rams 0	
1986	American	Eastern	New England Patriots (11-5-0)	Denver 22, New England 17	1986
		Central	Cleveland Browns (12-4-0)	Cleveland 23, N.Y. Jets* 20	
		Western	Denver Broncos (11-5-0)	Denver 23, Cleveland 20	
	National	Eastern	New York Giants (14-2-0)	N.Y. Giants 49, San Francisco 3	
		Central	Chicago Bears (14-2-0)	Washington* 27, Chicago 13	
		Western	San Francisco 49ers (10-5-1)	N.Y. Giants 17, Washington* 0	
1987	American	Eastern	Indianapolis Colts (9-6-0)	Cleveland 38, Indianapolis 21	1987
		Central	Cleveland Browns (10-5-0)	Denver 34, Houston* 10	
		Western	Denver Broncos (10-4-1)	Denver 38, Cleveland 33	
	National	Eastern	Washington Redskins (11-4-0)	Washington 21, Chicago 17	
		Central	Chicago Bears (11-4-0)	Minnesota* 36, San Francisco 24	
		Western	San Francisco 49ers (13-2-0)	Washington 17, Minnesota* 10	
1988	American	Eastern	Buffalo Bills (12-4-0)	Buffalo 17, Houston* 10	1988
		Central	Cincinnati Bengals (12-4-0)	Cincinnati 21, Seattle 13	
		Western	Seattle Seahawks (9-7-0)	Cincinnati 21, Buffalo 10	
	National	Eastern	Philadelphia Eagles (10-6-0)	Chicago 20, Philadelphia 12	
		Central	Chicago Bears (12-4-0)	San Francisco 34, Minnesota* 9	
		Western	San Francisco 49ers (10-6-0)	San Francisco 28, Chicago 3	
1989	American	Eastern	Buffalo Bills (9-7-0)	Cleveland 34, Buffalo 30	1989
		Central	Cleveland Browns (9-6-1)	Denver 24, Pittsburgh* 23	
		Western	Denver Broncos (11-5-0)	Denver 37, Cleveland 21	
	National	Eastern	New York Giants (12-4-0)	San Francisco 41, Minnesota 13	
		Central	Minnesota Vikings (10-6-0)	L.A. Rams* 19, N.Y. Giants 13	
		Western	San Francisco 49ers (14-2-0)	San Francisco 30, L.A. Rams* 3	
1990	American	Eastern	Buffalo Bills (13-3-0)	L.A. Raiders 20, Cincinnati 10	1990
		Central	Cincinnati Bengals (9-7-0)	Buffalo 44, Miami* 34	
		Western	Los Angeles Raiders (12-4-0)	Buffalo 51, L.A. Raiders 3	
	National	Eastern	New York Giants (13-3-0)	San Francisco 28, Washington* 10	
		Central	Chicago Bears (11-5-0)	N.Y. Giants 31, Chicago 3	
		Western	San Francisco 49ers (14-2-0)	N.Y. Giants 15, San Francisco 13	
1991	American	Eastern	Buffalo Bills (13-3-0)	Denver 26, Houston 24	1991
		Central	Houston Oilers (11-5-0)	Buffalo 37, Kansas City* 14	
		Western	Denver Broncos (12-4-0)	Buffalo 10, Denver 7	
	National	Eastern	Washington Redskins (14-2-0)	Washington 24, Atlanta* 7	
		Central	Detroit Lions (12-4-0)	Detroit 38, Dallas* 6	
		Western	New Orleans Saints (11-5-0)	Washington 41, Detroit 10	
1992	American	Eastern	Miami Dolphins (11-5-0)	Miami 31, San Diego 0	1992
		Central	Pittsburgh Steelers (11-5-0)	Buffalo* 24, Pittsburgh 3	
		Western	San Diego Chargers (11-5-0)	Buffalo* 29, Miami 10	
	National	Eastern	Dallas Cowboys (13-3-0)	Dallas 34, Philadelphia* 10	
		Central	Minnesota Vikings (11-5-0)	San Francisco 20, Washington* 13	
		Western	San Francisco 49ers (14-2-0)	Dallas 30, San Francisco 20	
1993	American	Eastern	Buffalo Bills (12-4-0)	Buffalo 29, L.A. Raiders* 23	1993
		Central	Houston Oilers (12-4-0)	Kansas City 28, Houston 20	
		Western	Kansas City Chiefs (11-5-0)	Buffalo 30, Kansas City 13	
	National	Eastern	Dallas Cowboys (12-4-0)	Dallas 27, Green Bay* 17	
		Central	Detroit Lions (10-6-0)	San Francisco 44, N.Y. Giants* 3	
		Western	San Francisco 49ers (10-6-0)	Dallas 38, San Francisco 21	
1994	American	Eastern	Miami Dolphins (10-6-0)	Pittsburgh 29, Cleveland* 9	1994
		Central	Pittsburgh Steelers (12-4-0)	San Diego 22, Miami 21	
		Western	San Diego Chargers (11-5-0)	San Diego 17, Pittsburgh 13	
	National	Eastern	Dallas Cowboys (12-4-0)	San Francisco 44, Chicago* 15	
		Central	Minnesota Vikings (10-6-0)	Dallas 35, Green Bay* 9	
		Western	San Francisco 49ers (13-3-0)	San Francisco 38, Dallas 28	
1995	American	Eastern	Buffalo Bills (10-6-0)	Indianapolis* 10, Kansas City 7	1995
		Central	Pittsburgh Steelers (11-5-0)	Pittsburgh 40, Buffalo 21	
		Western	Kansas City Chiefs (13-3-0)	Pittsburgh 20, Indianapolis* 16	
	National	Eastern	Dallas Cowboys (12-4-0)	Dallas 30, Philadelphia* 11	
		Central	Green Bay Packers (11-5-0)	Green Bay 27, San Francisco 17	
		Western	San Francisco 49ers (11-5-0)	Dallas 38, Green Bay 27	
1996	American	Eastern	New England Patriots (11-5-0)	Jacksonville* 30, Denver 27	1996
		Central	Pittsburgh Steelers (10-6-0)	New England 28, Pittsburgh 3	
		Western	Denver Broncos (13-3-0)	New England 20, Jacksonville* 6	
	National	Eastern	Dallas Cowboys (10-6-0)	Green Bay 35, San Francisco* 14	
		Central	Green Bay Packers (13-3-0)	Carolina 26, Dallas 17	
		Western	Carolina Panthers (12-4-0)	Green Bay 30, Carolina 13	
1997	American	Eastern	New England Patriots (10-6-0)	Pittsburgh 7, New England 6	1997
		Central	Pittsburgh Steelers (11-5-0)	Denver* 14, Kansas City 10	
		Western	Kansas City Chiefs (13-3-0)	Denver* 24, Pittsburgh 21	
	National	Eastern	New York Giants (10-5-1)	San Francisco 38, Minnesota* 22	
		Central	Green Bay Packers (13-3-0)	Green Bay 21, Tampa Bay* 7	
		Western	San Francisco 49ers (13-3-0)	Green Bay 23, San Francisco 10	
1998	American	Eastern	N.Y. Jets (12-4-0)	Denver 38, Miami* 3	1998
		Central	Jacksonville Jaguars (11-5-0)	N.Y. Jets 34, Jacksonville 24	
		Western	Denver Broncos (14-2-0)	Denver 23, N.Y. Jets 10	
	National	Eastern	Dallas Cowboys (10-6-0)	Atlanta 20, San Francisco* 18	
		Central	Minnesota Vikings (15-1-0)	Minnesota 41, Arizona* 21	
		Western	Atlanta Falcons (14-2-0)	Atlanta 30, Minnesota 27 (OT)	

Year	Conference	Division	Winner (W-L-T)	Playoffs(c)	Year
1999	American	Eastern	Indianapolis Colts (13-3-0)	Jacksonville 62, Miami* 7	1999
		Central	Jacksonville Jaguars (14-2-0)	Tennessee* 19, Indianapolis 16	
		Western	Seattle Seahawks (9-7-0)	Tennessee* 33, Jacksonville 14	
	National	Eastern	Washington Redskins (10-6-0)	Tampa Bay 14, Washington 13	
		Central	Tampa Bay Buccaneers (11-5-0)	St. Louis 49, Minnesota* 37	
		Western	St. Louis Rams (13-3-0)	St. Louis 11, Tampa Bay 6	
2000	American	Eastern	Miami Dolphins (11-5-0)	Oakland 27, Miami 0	2000
		Central	Tennessee Titans (13-3-0)	Baltimore* 24, Tennessee 10	
		Western	Oakland Raiders (12-4-0)	Baltimore* 16, Oakland 3	
	National	Eastern	N.Y. Giants (12-4-0)	Minnesota 34, New Orleans 16	
		Central	Minnesota Vikings (11-5-0)	N.Y. Giants 20, Philadelphia* 10	
		Western	New Orleans Saints (10-6-0)	N.Y. Giants 41, Minnesota 0	
2001	American	Eastern	New England Patriots (11-5-0)	New England 16, Oakland 13	2001
		Central	Pittsburgh Steelers (13-3-0)	Pittsburgh 27, Baltimore* 10	
		Western	Oakland Raiders (10-6-0)	New England 24, Pittsburgh 17	
	National	Eastern	Philadelphia Eagles (11-5-0)	Philadelphia 33, Chicago 19	
		Central	Chicago Bears (13-3-0)	St. Louis 45, Green Bay* 17	
		Western	St. Louis Rams (14-2-0)	St. Louis 29, Philadelphia 24	
2002	American	East	N.Y. Jets (9-7-0)		2002
		North	Pittsburgh Steelers (10-5-1)	Oakland 30, N.Y. Jets 10	
		South	Tennessee Titans (11-5-0)	Tennessee 34, Pittsburgh 31	
		West	Oakland Raiders (11-5-0)	Oakland 41, Tennessee 24	
	National	East	Philadelphia Eagles (12-4-0)		
		North	Green Bay Packers (12-4-0)	Philadelphia 20, Atlanta* 6	
		South	Tampa Bay Buccaneers (12-4-0)	Tampa Bay 31, San Francisco 6	
		West	San Francisco 49ers (10-6-0)	Tampa Bay 27, Philadelphia 10	

*Wild card team. (c) From 1978 on, only the final 2 conference playoff rounds are shown. (d) A strike shortened the 1982 season from 16 to 9 games. The top 8 teams in each conference played in a tournament to determine the conference champion. See below. **AFC playoffs**—Miami 28, New England 13; L.A. Raiders 27, Cleveland 10; N.Y. Jets 44, Cincinnati 17; San Diego 31, Pittsburgh 28; N.Y. Jets 17, L.A. Raiders 14; Miami 34, San Diego 13; Miami 14 N.Y. Jets 0. **NFC playoffs**—Washington 31, Detroit 7; Green Bay 41, St. Louis 16; Dallas 30, Tampa Bay 17; Minnesota 30, Atlanta 24; Washington 21, Minnesota 7; Dallas 37, Green Bay 26; Washington 31, Dallas 17. **AFC Champion**—Miami Dolphins. **NFC Champion**—Washington Redskins.

Super Bowl XXXVII: Tampa Bay 48, Oakland 21

On Jan. 26, 2003, the Tampa Bay Buccaneers outscored and out-muscled the Oakland Raiders, 48-21, in Super Bowl XXXVII in San Diego, CA. With an impressive Super Bowl win, Tampa Bay shed its reputation as a perennial loser. The Buccaneers' defense all but shut down the Raider offense with 5 sacks and 5 interceptions, and held Oakland to 19 rushing yards. Free safety Dexter Jackson earned MVP honors by twice intercepting Rich Gannon, the league's MVP. On offense, Tampa Bay quarterback Brad Johnson and wide receiver Keenan McCardell connected for 2 touchdowns, helping stretch the Buccaneers' lead to 23 points in the 3rd quarter. The Raiders did mount a late comeback, scoring 18 unanswered points to cut their deficit to 34-21. But Tampa Bay kept the pressure on Gannon, forcing him to throw 2 4th-quarter interceptions that were returned for touchdowns.

Score by Quarters

Oakland	3	0	6	12—21
Tampa Bay	3	17	14	14—48

Scoring

Oakland—Janikowski 40 yd. field goal
Tampa Bay—Gramatica 31 yd. field goal
Tampa Bay—Gramatica 43 yd. field goal
Tampa Bay—Alstott 2 yd. run (Gramatica kick)
Tampa Bay—McCardell 5 yd. pass from Johnson (Gramatica kick)
Tampa Bay—McCardell 8 yd. pass from Johnson (Gramatica kick)
Tampa Bay—Smith 44 yd. interception return (Gramatica kick)
Oakland—Porter 39 yd. pass from Gannon (pass failed)
Oakland—Johnson 13 yd. return of blocked punt (pass failed)
Oakland—Rice 48 yd. pass from Gannon (pass failed)
Tampa Bay—Brooks 44 yd. interception return (Gramatica kick)
Tampa Bay—Smith 50 yd. interception return (Gramatica kick)

Individual Statistics

Rushing—Oakland: Garner 7-41, Crockett 2-6, Gannon 2-3. Tampa Bay: Pittman 29-124, Alstott 10-15, Johnson 1-10, Stecker 1-1, Tupa 1-0.

Passing—Oakland: Gannon 24-44, 272 yds, 2 TD, 5 Int. Tampa Bay: Johnson 18-34 215 yds, 2 TD, 1 Int.

Receiving—Oakland:Garner 7-51, Rice 5-77, Jolley 5-59, Porter 4-62, Brown 1-9, Ritchie 1-7, Wheatley 1-7. Tampa Bay: Johnson 6-69, Alstott 5-43, Jurevicius 4-78, McCardell 2-13, Dilger 1-12.

Team Statistics

	Oak	TB
First downs	11	24
Total net yards	269	365
Rushes-yards	11-19	42-150
Passing yards, net	250	215
Punt returns-yards	3-29	1-25
Kickoff returns-yards	9-149	4-90
Interception returns-yards	1-12	5-172
Att.-comp.-int.	24-44-5	18-34-1
Field goals made-attempts	1-1	2-2
Sacked-yards lost	5-22	0-0
Punts-average	5-39	5-31
Fumbles-lost	1-0	1-0
Penalties-yards	7-51	5-41
Time of possession	22:46	37:14

Attendance—67,603. **Time**—3:50.

Super Bowl Results

	Year	Winner	Loser	Winning coach	Site
I	1967	Green Bay Packers, 35	Kansas City Chiefs, 10	Vince Lombardi	Los Angeles Coliseum, CA
II	1968	Green Bay Packers, 33	Oakland Raiders, 14	Vince Lombardi	Orange Bowl, Miami, FL
III	1969	New York Jets, 16	Baltimore Colts, 7	Weeb Ewbank	Orange Bowl, Miami, FL
IV	1970	Kansas City Chiefs, 23	Minnesota Vikings, 7	Hank Stram	Tulane Stadium, New Orleans, LA
V	1971	Baltimore Colts, 16	Dallas Cowboys, 13	Don McCafferty	Orange Bowl, Miami, FL
VI	1972	Dallas Cowboys, 24	Miami Dolphins, 3	Tom Landry	Tulane Stadium, New Orleans, LA
VII	1973	Miami Dolphins, 14	Washington Redskins, 7	Don Shula	Los Angeles Coliseum, CA
VIII	1974	Miami Dolphins, 24	Minnesota Vikings, 7	Don Shula	Rice Stadium, Houston, TX
IX	1975	Pittsburgh Steelers, 16	Minnesota Vikings, 6	Chuck Noll	Tulane Stadium, New Orleans, LA
X	1976	Pittsburgh Steelers, 21	Dallas Cowboys, 17	Chuck Noll	Orange Bowl, Miami, FL
XI	1977	Oakland Raiders, 32	Minnesota Vikings, 14	John Madden	Rose Bowl, Pasadena, CA
XII	1978	Dallas Cowboys, 27	Denver Broncos, 10	Tom Landry	Superdome, New Orleans, LA
XIII	1979	Pittsburgh Steelers, 35	Dallas Cowboys, 31	Chuck Noll	Orange Bowl, Miami, FL
XIV	1980	Pittsburgh Steelers, 31	Los Angeles Rams, 19	Chuck Noll	Rose Bowl, Pasadena, CA
XV	1981	Oakland Raiders, 27	Philadelphia Eagles, 10	Tom Flores	Superdome, New Orleans, LA
XVI	1982	San Francisco 49ers, 26	Cincinnati Bengals, 21	Bill Walsh	Silverdome, Pontiac, MI
XVII	1983	Washington Redskins, 27	Miami Dolphins, 17	Joe Gibbs	Rose Bowl, Pasadena, CA
XVIII	1984	Los Angeles Raiders, 38	Washington Redskins, 9	Tom Flores	Tampa Stadium, FL
XIX	1985	San Francisco 49ers, 38	Miami Dolphins, 16	Bill Walsh	Stanford Stadium, Palo Alto, CA
XX	1986	Chicago Bears, 46	New England Patriots, 10	Mike Ditka	Superdome, New Orleans, LA
XXI	1987	New York Giants, 39	Denver Broncos, 20	Bill Parcells	Rose Bowl, Pasadena, CA

	Year	Winner	Loser	Winning coach	Site
XXII	1988	Washington Redskins, 42	Denver Broncos, 10	Joe Gibbs	San Diego Stadium, CA
XXIII	1989	San Francisco 49ers, 20	Cincinnati Bengals, 16	Bill Walsh	Joe Robbie Stadium, Miami, FL
XXIV	1990	San Francisco 49ers, 55	Denver Broncos, 10	George Seifert	Superdome, New Orleans, LA
XXV	1991	New York Giants, 20	Buffalo Bills, 19	Bill Parcells	Tampa Stadium, FL
XXVI	1992	Washington Redskins, 37	Buffalo Bills, 24	Joe Gibbs	Metrodome, Minneapolis, MN
XXVII	1993	Dallas Cowboys, 52	Buffalo Bills, 17	Jimmy Johnson	Rose Bowl, Pasadena, CA
XXVIII	1994	Dallas Cowboys, 30	Buffalo Bills, 13	Jimmy Johnson	Georgia Dome, Atlanta, GA
XXIX	1995	San Francisco 49ers, 49	San Diego Chargers, 26	George Seifert	Joe Robbie Stadium, Miami, FL
XXX	1996	Dallas Cowboys, 27	Pittsburgh Steelers, 17	Barry Switzer	Sun Devil Stadium, Tempe, AZ
XXXI	1997	Green Bay Packers, 35	New England Patriots, 21	Mike Holmgren	Superdome, New Orleans, LA
XXXII	1998	Denver Broncos, 31	Green Bay Packers, 24	Mike Shanahan	Qualcomm Stadium, San Diego, CA
XXXIII	1999	Denver Broncos, 34	Atlanta Falcons, 19	Mike Shanahan	Pro Player Stadium, Miami, FL
XXXIV	2000	St. Louis Rams, 23	Tennessee Titans, 16	Dick Vermeil	Georgia Dome, Atlanta, GA
XXXV	2001	Baltimore Ravens, 34	New York Giants, 7	Brian Billick	Raymond James Stad., Tampa, FL
XXXVI	2002	New England Patriots, 20	St. Louis Rams, 17	Bill Belichick	Superdome, New Orleans, LA
XXXVII	2003	Tampa Bay Buccaneers, 48	Oakland Raiders, 21	Jon Gruden	Qualcomm Stadium, San Diego, CA

Super Bowl Single-Game Statistical Leaders

Passing Yards

	Year	Att/Comp	Yds	TDs
Kurt Warner, Rams	2000	45/24	414	2
Kurt Warner, Rams	2002	44/28	365	1
Joe Montana, 49ers	1989	36/23	357	2

Passing Touchdowns

	Year	Att/Comp	Yds	TDs
Steve Young, 49ers	1995	36/24	325	6
Joe Montana, 49ers	1990	29/22	297	5
Troy Aikman, Cowboys	1993	30/22	273	4
Doug Williams, Redskins	1988	29/18	340	4
Terry Bradshaw, Steelers	1979	30/17	318	4

Receiving Yards

	Year	Recept.	Yds	TDs
Jerry Rice, 49ers	1989	11	215	1
Ricky Sanders, Redskins	1988	9	193	2
Lynn Swann, Steelers	1976	4	161	1

Scoring

	Year	Points	
Terrell Davis, Broncos	1998	18	3 TDs
Jerry Rice, 49ers	1995	18	3 TDs
Ricky Watters, 49ers	1995	18	3 TDs
Jerry Rice, 49ers	1990	18	3 TDs
Roger Craig, 49ers	1985	18	3 TDs
Don Chandler, Packers	1968	15	4 FG, 3PATs

Rushing Yards

	Year	Attempts	Yds	TDs
Timmy Smith, Redskins	1988	22	204	2
Marcus Allen, Raiders	1984	20	191	2
John Riggins, Redskins	1983	38	166	1

Super Bowl MVPs

1967	Bart Starr, Green Bay	1980	Terry Bradshaw, Pittsburgh
1968	Bart Starr, Green Bay	1981	Jim Plunkett, Oakland
1969	Joe Namath, N.Y. Jets	1982	Joe Montana, San Francisco
1970	Len Dawson, Kansas City	1983	John Riggins, Washington
1971	Chuck Howley, Dallas	1984	Marcus Allen, L.A. Raiders
1972	Roger Staubach, Dallas	1985	Joe Montana, San Francisco
1973	Jake Scott, Miami	1986	Richard Dent, Chicago
1974	Larry Csonka, Miami	1987	Phil Simms, N.Y. Giants
1975	Franco Harris, Pittsburgh	1988	Doug Williams, Washington
1976	Lynn Swann, Pittsburgh	1989	Jerry Rice, San Francisco
1977	Fred Biletnikoff, Oakland	1990	Joe Montana, San Francisco
1978	Randy White, Harvey Martin, Dallas	1991	Ottis Anderson, N.Y. Giants
1979	Terry Bradshaw, Pittsburgh		

1992	Mark Rypien, Washington
1993	Troy Aikman, Dallas
1994	Emmitt Smith, Dallas
1995	Steve Young, San Francisco
1996	Larry Brown, Dallas
1997	Desmond Howard, Green Bay
1998	Terrell Davis, Denver
1999	John Elway, Denver
2000	Kurt Warner, St. Louis
2001	Ray Lewis, Baltimore
2002	Tom Brady, New England
2003	Dexter Jackson, Tampa Bay

American Football Conference Leaders

(American Football League, 1960-69)

Passing[1]						Receiving			
Player, team	Att	Com	YG	TD	Year	Player, team	Rec.	YG	TD
Jack Kemp, L.A. Chargers	406	211	3,018	20	1960	Lionel Taylor, Denver	92	1,235	12
George Blanda, Houston	362	187	3,330	36	1961	Lionel Taylor, Denver	100	1,176	4
Len Dawson, Dallas Texans	310	189	2,759	29	1962	Lionel Taylor, Denver	77	908	4
Tobin Rote, San Diego	286	170	2,510	20	1963	Lionel Taylor, Denver	78	1,101	10
Len Dawson, Kansas City	354	199	2,879	30	1964	Charley Hennigan, Houston	101	1,546	8
John Hadl, San Diego	348	174	2,798	20	1965	Lionel Taylor, Denver	85	1,131	6
Len Dawson, Kansas City	284	159	2,527	26	1966	Lance Alworth, San Diego	73	1,383	13
Daryle Lamonica, Oakland	425	220	3,228	30	1967	George Sauer, N.Y. Jets	75	1,189	6
Len Dawson, Kansas City	224	131	2,109	17	1968	Lance Alworth, San Diego	68	1,312	10
Greg Cook, Cincinnati	197	106	1,854	15	1969	Lance Alworth, San Diego	64	1,003	4
Daryle Lamonica, Oakland	356	179	2,516	22	1970	Marlin Briscoe, Buffalo	57	1,036	8
Bob Griese, Miami	263	145	2,089	19	1971	Fred Biletnikoff, Oakland	61	929	9
Earl Morrall, Miami	150	83	1,360	11	1972	Fred Biletnikoff, Oakland	58	802	7
Ken Stabler, Oakland	260	163	1,997	14	1973	Fred Willis, Houston	57	371	1
Ken Anderson, Cincinnati	328	213	2,667	18	1974	Lydell Mitchell, Baltimore Colts	72	544	2
Ken Anderson, Cincinnati	377	228	3,169	21	1975	Reggie Rucker, Cleveland	60	770	3
						Lydell Mitchell, Baltimore Colts	60	554	4
Ken Stabler, Oakland	291	194	2,737	27	1976	MacArthur Lane, Kansas City	66	686	1
Bob Griese, Miami	307	180	2,252	22	1977	Lydell Mitchell, Baltimore Colts	71	620	4
Terry Bradshaw, Pittsburgh	368	207	2,915	28	1978	Steve Largent, Seattle	71	1,168	8
Dan Fouts, San Diego	530	332	4,082	24	1979	Joe Washington, Baltimore Colts	82	750	3
Brian Sipe, Cleveland	554	337	4,132	30	1980	Kellen Winslow, San Diego	89	1,290	9
Ken Anderson, Cincinnati	479	300	3,754	29	1981	Kellen Winslow, San Diego	88	1,075	10
Ken Anderson, Cincinnati	309	218	2,495	12	1982	Kellen Winslow, San Diego	54	721	6
Dan Marino, Miami	296	173	2,210	20	1983	Todd Christensen, L.A. Raiders	92	1,247	12
Dan Marino, Miami	564	362	5,084	48	1984	Ozzie Newsome, Cleveland	89	1,001	5
Ken O'Brien, N.Y. Jets	488	297	3,888	25	1985	Lionel James, San Diego	86	1,027	6
Dan Marino, Miami	623	378	4,746	44	1986	Todd Christensen, L.A. Raiders	95	1,153	8
Bernie Kosar, Cleveland	389	241	3,033	22	1987	Al Toon, N.Y. Jets	68	976	5
Boomer Esiason, Cincinnati	388	223	3,572	28	1988	Al Toon, N.Y. Jets	93	1,067	5
Boomer Esiason, Cincinnati	455	258	3,525	28	1989	Andre Reed, Buffalo	88	1,312	9
Jim Kelly, Buffalo	346	219	2,829	24	1990	Haywood Jeffires, Houston	74	1,048	8
						Drew Hill, Houston	74	1,019	5

Passing[1]					Year	Receiving			
Player, team	Att	Com	YG	TD		Player, team	Rec.	YG	TD
Jim Kelly, Buffalo	474	304	3,844	33	1991	Haywood Jeffires, Houston	100	1,181	7
Warren Moon, Houston	346	224	2,521	18	1992	Haywood Jeffires, Houston	90	913	9
John Elway, Denver	551	348	4,030	25	1993	Reggie Langhorne, Indianapolis	85	1,038	3
Dan Marino, Miami	615	385	4,453	30	1994	Ben Coates, New England	96	1,174	7
Jim Harbaugh, Indianapolis	314	200	2,575	17	1995	Carl Pickens, Cincinnati	99	1,234	17
John Elway, Denver	466	287	3,328	26	1996	Carl Pickens, Cincinnati	100	1,180	12
Mark Brunell, Jacksonville	435	264	3,281	18	1997	Tim Brown, Oakland	104	1,408	5
Vinny Testaverde, N.Y. Jets	421	259	3,256	29	1998	O.J. McDuffie, Miami	90	1,050	7
Peyton Manning, Indianapolis	533	331	4,135	26	1999	Jimmy Smith, Jacksonville	116	1,636	6
Brian Griese, Denver	336	216	2,688	19	2000	Marvin Harrison, Indianapolis	102	1,413	14
Rich Gannon, Oakland	549	361	3,828	27	2001	Marvin Harrison, Indianapolis	109	1,524	15
Chad Pennington, N.Y. Jets	399	275	3,120	22	2002	Marvin Harrison, Indianapolis	143	1,722	11

Scoring					Year	Rushing			
Player, team	TD	PAT	FG	Pts		Player, team	Yds	Att	TD
Gene Mingo, Denver	6	33	18	123	1960	Abner Haynes, Dallas Texans	875	156	9
Gino Cappelletti, Boston	8	48	17	147	1961	Billy Cannon, Houston	948	200	6
Gene Mingo, Denver	4	32	27	137	1962	Cookie Gilchrist, Buffalo	1,096	214	13
Gino Cappelletti, Boston	2	35	22	113	1963	Clem Daniels, Oakland	1,099	215	3
Gino Cappelletti, Boston	7	36	25	155	1964	Cookie Gilchrist, Buffalo	981	230	6
Gino Cappelletti, Boston	9	27	17	132	1965	Paul Lowe, San Diego	1,121	222	7
Gino Cappelletti, Boston	6	35	16	119	1966	Jim Nance, Boston	1,458	299	11
George Blanda, Oakland	0	56	20	116	1967	Jim Nance, Boston	1,216	269	7
Jim Turner, N.Y. Jets	0	43	34	145	1968	Paul Robinson, Cincinnati	1,023	238	8
Jim Turner, N.Y. Jets	0	33	32	129	1969	Dick Post, San Diego	873	182	6
Jan Stenerud, Kansas City	0	26	30	116	1970	Floyd Little, Denver	901	209	3
Garo Yepremian, Miami	0	33	28	117	1971	Floyd Little, Denver	1,133	284	6
Bobby Howfield, N.Y. Jets	0	40	27	121	1972	O.J. Simpson, Buffalo	1,251	292	6
Roy Gerela, Pittsburgh	0	36	29	123	1973	O.J. Simpson, Buffalo	2,003	332	12
Roy Gerela, Pittsburgh	0	33	20	93	1974	Otis Armstrong, Denver	1,407	263	9
O.J. Simpson, Buffalo	23	0	0	138	1975	O.J. Simpson, Buffalo	1,817	329	16
Toni Linhart, Baltimore Colts	0	49	20	109	1976	O.J. Simpson, Buffalo	1,503	290	8
Errol Mann, Oakland	0	39	20	99	1977	Mark van Eeghen, Oakland	1,273	324	7
Pat Leahy, N.Y. Jets	0	41	22	107	1978	Earl Campbell, Houston	1,450	302	13
John Smith, New England	0	46	23	115	1979	Earl Campbell, Houston	1,697	368	19
John Smith, New England	0	51	26	129	1980	Earl Campbell, Houston	1,934	373	13
Jim Breech, Cincinnati	0	49	22	115	1981	Earl Campbell, Houston	1,376	361	10
Nick Lowery, Kansas City	0	37	26	115					
Marcus Allen, L.A. Raiders	14	0	0	84	1982	Freeman McNeil, N.Y. Jets	786	151	6
Gary Anderson, Pittsburgh	0	38	27	119	1983	Curt Warner, Seattle	1,446	335	13
Gary Anderson, Pittsburgh	0	45	24	117	1984	Earnest Jackson, San Diego	1,179	296	8
Gary Anderson, Pittsburgh	0	40	33	139	1985	Marcus Allen, L.A. Raiders	1,759	380	11
Tony Franklin, New England	0	44	32	140	1986	Curt Warner, Seattle	1,481	319	13
Jim Breech, Cincinnati	0	25	24	97	1987	Eric Dickerson, L.A. Rams-Ind.	1,288*	283	6
Scott Norwood, Buffalo	0	33	32	129	1988	Eric Dickerson, Indianapolis	1,659	388	14
David Treadwell, Denver	0	39	27	120	1989	Christian Okoye, Kansas City	1,480	370	12
Nick Lowery, Kansas City	0	37	34	139	1990	Thurman Thomas, Buffalo	1,297	271	11
Pete Stoyanovich, Miami	0	28	31	121	1991	Thurman Thomas, Buffalo	1,407	288	7
Pete Stoyanovich, Miami	0	34	30	124	1992	Barry Foster, Pittsburgh	1,690	390	11
Jeff Jaeger, L.A. Raiders	0	27	35	132	1993	Thurman Thomas, Buffalo	1,315	355	6
John Carney, San Diego	0	33	34	135	1994	Chris Warren, Seattle	1,545	333	9
Norm Johnson, Pittsburgh	0	39	34	141	1995	Curtis Martin, New England	1,487	368	14
Cary Blanchard, Indianapolis	0	27	36	135	1996	Terrell Davis, Denver	1,538	345	13
Mike Hollis, Jacksonville	0	41	31	134	1997	Terrell Davis, Denver	1,750	369	15
Steve Christie, Buffalo	0	41	33	140	1998	Terrell Davis, Denver	2,008	392	21
Mike Vanderjagt, Indianapolis	0	43	34	145	1999	Edgerrin James, Indianapolis	1,553	369	13
Matt Stover, Baltimore	0	30	35	135	2000	Edgerrin James, Indianapolis	1,709	387	13
Mike Vanderjagt, Indianapolis	0	41	28	125	2001	Priest Holmes, Kansas City	1,555	325	8
Priest Holmes, Kansas City	0	0	0	144	2002	Ricky Williams, Miami	1,853	383	16

*Includes 277 yards after being traded to NFC; 1,011 yards led AFC. (1) Based on quarterback ranking points.

National Football Conference Leaders

(National Football League, 1960-69)

Passing[1]					Year	Receiving			
Player, team	Att	Com	YG	TD		Player, team	Rec.	YG	TD
Milt Plum, Cleveland	250	151	2,297	21	1960	Raymond Berry, Baltimore Colts	74	1,298	10
Milt Plum, Cleveland	302	177	2,416	18	1961	Jim Phillips, L.A. Rams	78	1,092	5
Bart Starr, Green Bay	285	178	2,438	12	1962	Bobby Mitchell, Washington	72	1,384	11
Y.A. Tittle, N.Y. Giants	367	221	3,145	36	1963	Bobby Joe Conrad, St. Louis Cardinals	73	967	10
Bart Starr, Green Bay	272	163	2,144	15	1964	Johnny Morris, Chicago	93	1,200	10
Rudy Bukich, Chicago	312	176	2,641	20	1965	Dave Parks, San Francisco	80	1,344	12
Bart Starr, Green Bay	251	156	2,257	14	1966	Charley Taylor, Washington	72	1,119	12
Sonny Jurgensen, Washington	508	288	3,747	31	1967	Charley Taylor, Washington	70	990	9
Earl Morrall, Baltimore Colts	317	182	2,909	26	1968	Clifton McNeil, San Francisco	71	994	7
Sonny Jurgensen, Washington	442	274	3,102	22	1969	Dan Abramowicz, New Orleans	73	1,015	7
John Brodie, San Francisco	378	223	2,941	24	1970	Dick Gordon, Chicago	71	1,026	13
Roger Staubach, Dallas	211	126	1,882	15	1971	Bob Tucker, N.Y. Giants	59	791	4
Norm Snead, N.Y. Giants	325	196	2,307	17	1972	Harold Jackson, Philadelphia	62	1,048	4
Roger Staubach, Dallas	286	179	2,428	23	1973	Harold Carmichael, Philadelphia	67	1,116	9
Sonny Jurgensen, Washington	167	107	1,185	11	1974	Charles Young, Philadelphia	63	696	3
Fran Tarkenton, Minnesota	425	273	2,994	25	1975	Chuck Foreman, Minnesota	73	691	9
James Harris, L.A. Rams	158	91	1,460	8	1976	Drew Pearson, Dallas	58	806	6
Roger Staubach, Dallas	361	210	2,620	18	1977	Ahmad Rashad, Minnesota	51	681	2
Roger Staubach, Dallas	413	231	3,190	25	1978	Rickey Young, Minnesota	88	704	5
Roger Staubach, Dallas	461	267	3,586	27	1979	Ahmad Rashad, Minnesota	80	1,156	9
Ron Jaworski, Philadelphia	451	257	3,529	27	1980	Earl Cooper, San Francisco	83	567	4
Joe Montana, San Francisco	488	311	3,565	19	1981	Dwight Clark, San Francisco	85	1,105	4
Joe Theismann, Washington	252	161	2,033	13	1982	Dwight Clark, San Francisco	60	913	5

Passing[1]

Player, team	Att	Com	YG	TD	Year
Steve Bartkowski, Atlanta	432		3,167	22	1983
		274			
Joe Montana, San Francisco	432	279	3,630	28	1984
Joe Montana, San Francisco	494	303	3,653	27	1985
Tommy Kramer, Minnesota	372	208	3,000	24	1986
Joe Montana, San Francisco	398	266	3,054	31	1987
Wade Wilson, Minnesota	332	204	2,746	15	1988
Joe Montana, San Francisco	386	271	3,521	26	1989
Phil Simms, N.Y. Giants	311	184	2,284	15	1990
Steve Young, San Francisco	279	180	2,517	17	1991
Steve Young, San Francisco	402	268	3,465	25	1992
Steve Young, San Francisco	462	314	4,023	29	1993
Steve Young, San Francisco	461	324	3,969	35	1994
Brett Favre, Green Bay	570	359	4,413	38	1995
Steve Young, San Francisco	316	214	2,410	14	1996
Steve Young, San Francisco	356	241	3,029	19	1997
Randall Cunningham, Minnesota	425	259	3,704	34	1998
Kurt Warner, St. Louis	499	325	4,353	41	1999
Trent Green, St. Louis	240	145	2,063	16	2000
Kurt Warner, St. Louis	546	375	4,830	36	2001
Brad Johnson, Tampa Bay	451	281	3,049	22	2002

Receiving

Year	Player, team	Rec	YG	TD
1983	Roy Green, St. Louis Cardinals	78	1,227	14
	Charlie Brown, Washington	78	1,225	8
	Earnest Gray, N.Y. Giants	78	1,139	5
1984	Art Monk, Washington	106	1,372	7
1985	Roger Craig, San Francisco	92	1,016	6
1986	Jerry Rice, San Francisco	86	1,570	15
1987	J.T. Smith, St. Louis Cardinals	91	1,117	8
1988	Henry Ellard, L.A. Rams	86	1,414	10
1989	Sterling Sharpe, Green Bay	90	1,423	12
1990	Jerry Rice, San Francisco	100	1,502	13
1991	Michael Irvin, Dallas	93	1,523	8
1992	Sterling Sharpe, Green Bay	108	1,461	13
1993	Sterling Sharpe, Green Bay	112	1,274	11
1994	Cris Carter, Minnesota	122	1,256	7
1995	Herman Moore, Detroit	123	1,686	14
1996	Jerry Rice, San Francisco	108	1,254	8
1997	Herman Moore, Detroit	104	1,293	8
1998	Frank Sanders, Arizona	89	1,145	3
1999	Muhsin Muhammad, Carolina	96	1,253	8
2000	Muhsin Muhammad, Carolina	102	1,183	6
2001	David Boston, Arizona	98	1,598	8
2002	Randy Moss, Minnesota	106	1,347	7

Scoring

Player, team	TD	PAT	FG	Pts	Year
Paul Hornung, Green Bay	15	41	15	176	1960
Paul Hornung, Green Bay	10	41	15	146	1961
Jim Taylor, Green Bay	19	0	0	114	1962
Don Chandler, N.Y. Giants	0	52	18	106	1963
Lenny Moore, Baltimore Colts	20	0	0	120	1964
Gale Sayers, Chicago	22	0	0	132	1965
Bruce Gossett, L.A. Rams	0	29	28	113	1966
Jim Bakken, St. Louis Cardinals	0	36	27	117	1967
Leroy Kelly, Cleveland	20	0	0	120	1968
Fred Cox, Minnesota	0	43	26	121	1969
Fred Cox, Minnesota	0	35	30	125	1970
Curt Knight, Washington	0	27	29	114	1971
Chester Marcol, Green Bay	0	29	33	128	1972
David Ray, L.A. Rams	0	40	30	130	1973
Chester Marcol, Green Bay	0	19	25	94	1974
Chuck Foreman, Minnesota	22	0	0	132	1975
Mark Moseley, Washington	0	31	22	97	1976
Walter Payton, Chicago	16	0	0	96	1977
Frank Corral, L.A. Rams	0	31	29	118	1978
Mark Moseley, Washington	0	39	25	114	1979
Ed Murray, Detroit	0	35	27	116	1980
Ed Murray, Detroit	0	46	25	121	1981
Rafael Septien, Dallas	0	40	27	121	
Wendell Tyler, L.A. Rams	13	0	0	78	1982
Mark Moseley, Washington	0	62	33	161	1983
Ray Wersching, San Francisco	0	56	25	131	1984
Kevin Butler, Chicago	0	51	31	144	1985
Kevin Butler, Chicago	0	36	28	120	1986
Jerry Rice, San Francisco	23	0	0	138	1987
Mike Cofer, San Francisco	0	40	27	121	1988
Mike Cofer, San Francisco	0	49	29	136	1989
Chip Lohmiller, Washington	0	41	30	131	1990
Chip Lohmiller, Washington	0	56	31	149	1991
Morten Andersen, New Orleans	0	33	29	120	1992
Chip Lohmiller, Washington	0	30	30	120	
Jason Hanson, Detroit	0	28	34	130	1993
Fuad Reveiz, Minnesota	0	30	34	132	1994
Emmitt Smith, Dallas	22	0	0	132	
Emmitt Smith, Dallas	25	0	0	150	1995
John Kasay, Carolina	0	34	37	145	1996
Richie Cunningham, Dallas	0	24	34	126	1997
Gary Anderson, Minnesota	0	59	35	164	1998
Jeff Wilkins, St. Louis	0	64	20	124	1999
Marshall Faulk, St. Louis	26	0	0	156	2000
Marshall Faulk, St. Louis	21	0	0	128	2001
Jay Feely, Atlanta	0	42	32	138	2002

(1) Based on quarterback ranking points.

Rushing

Year	Player, team	Yds	Att	TD
1960	Jim Brown, Cleveland	1,257	215	9
1961	Jim Brown, Cleveland	1,408	305	8
1962	Jim Taylor, Green Bay	1,474	272	19
1963	Jim Brown, Cleveland	1,863	291	12
1964	Jim Brown, Cleveland	1,446	280	7
1965	Jim Brown, Cleveland	1,544	289	17
1966	Gale Sayers, Chicago	1,231	229	8
1967	Leroy Kelly, Cleveland	1,205	235	11
1968	Leroy Kelly, Cleveland	1,239	248	16
1969	Gale Sayers, Chicago	1,032	236	8
1970	Larry Brown, Washington	1,125	237	5
1971	John Brockington, Green Bay	1,105	216	4
1972	Larry Brown, Washington	1,216	285	8
1973	John Brockington, Green Bay	1,144	265	3
1974	Lawrence McCutcheon, L.A. Rams	1,109	236	3
1975	Jim Otis, St. Louis Cardinals	1,076	269	5
1976	Walter Payton, Chicago	1,390	311	13
1977	Walter Payton, Chicago	1,852	339	14
1978	Walter Payton, Chicago	1,395	333	11
1979	Walter Payton, Chicago	1,610	369	14
1980	Walter Payton, Chicago	1,460	317	6
1981	George Rogers, New Orleans	1,674	378	13
1982	Tony Dorsett, Dallas	745	177	5
1983	Eric Dickerson, L.A. Rams	1,808	390	18
1984	Eric Dickerson, L.A. Rams	2,105	379	14
1985	Gerald Riggs, Atlanta	1,719	397	10
1986	Eric Dickerson, L.A. Rams	1,821	404	11
1987	Charles White, L.A. Rams	1,374	324	11
1988	Herschel Walker, Dallas	1,514	361	5
1989	Barry Sanders, Detroit	1,470	280	14
1990	Barry Sanders, Detroit	1,304	255	13
1991	Emmitt Smith, Dallas	1,563	365	12
1992	Emmitt Smith, Dallas	1,713	373	18
1993	Emmitt Smith, Dallas	1,486	283	9
1994	Barry Sanders, Detroit	1,883	331	7
1995	Emmitt Smith, Dallas	1,773	377	25
1996	Barry Sanders, Detroit	1,553	307	11
1997	Barry Sanders, Detroit	2,053	335	11
1998	Jamal Anderson, Atlanta	1,846	410	14
1999	Stephen Davis, Washington	1,405	290	17
2000	Robert Smith, Minnesota	1,521	295	7
2001	Stephen Davis, Washington	1,432	356	5
2002	Deuce McAllister, New Orleans	1,388	325	13

2002 NFL Individual Leaders
American Football Conference

PASSING	Att	Comp	Pct comp	Yds	Yds/Att	Long	TD	Pct TD	Int	Rating points
Chad Pennington, N.Y. Jets	275	399	68.9	3,120	7.82	47	22	5.5	6	104.2
Rich Gannon, Oakland	418	618	67.6	4,689	7.59	75	26	4.2	10	97.3
Trent Green, Kansas City	287	470	61.1	3,690	7.85	99	26	5.5	13	92.6
Peyton Manning, Indianapolis	392	591	66.3	4,200	7.11	69	27	4.6	19	88.8
Drew Bledsoe, Buffalo	375	610	61.5	4,359	7.15	73	24	3.9	15	86.0
Tom Brady, New England	373	601	62.1	3,764	6.26	49	28	4.7	14	85.7
Mark Brunell, Jacksonville	245	416	58.9	2,788	6.70	79	17	4.1	7	85.7
Brian Griese, Denver	291	436	66.7	3,214	7.37	82	15	3.4	15	85.6
Jay Fiedler, Miami	179	292	61.3	2,024	6.93	59	14	4.8	9	85.2
Tommy Maddox, Pittsburgh	234	377	62.1	2,836	7.52	72	20	5.3	16	85.2

RUSHING	Att	Yds	Avg	Long	TD
Ricky Williams, Miami	383	1,853	4.8	63	16
LaDainian Tomlinson, San Diego	372	1,683	4.5	76	14
Priest Holmes, Kansas City	313	1,615	5.2	56	21
Clinton Portis, Denver	273	1,508	5.5	59	15
Travis Henry, Buffalo	325	1,438	4.4	34	13
Jamal Lewis, Baltimore	308	1,327	4.3	75	6
Fred Taylor, Jacksonville	287	1,314	4.6	63	8
Corey Dillon, Cincinnati	314	1,311	4.2	67	7
Eddie George, Tennessee	343	1,165	3.4	35	12
Curtis Martin, N.Y. Jets	261	1,094	4.2	35	7

RECEIVING	Catches	Yds	Avg	Long	TD
Marvin Harrison, Indianapolis	143*	1,722	12.0	69	11
Hines Ward, Pittsburgh	112	1,329	11.9	72	12
Eric Moulds, Buffalo	100	1,287	12.9	70	10
Troy Brown, New England	97	890	9.2	38	3
Peerless Price, Buffalo	94	1,252	13.3	73	9
Jerry Rice, Oakland	92	1,211	13.2	75	7
Charlie Garner, Oakland	91	941	10.3	69	4
Laveranues Coles, Washington	89	1,264	14.2	43	5
Rod Smith, Denver	89	1,027	11.5	46	5
Tim Brown, Oakland	81	930	11.5	45	2
Jimmy Smith, Jacksonville	80	1,027	12.8	47	7

SCORING—KICKERS	PAT	FG	Long	Pts
Sebastian Janikowski, Oakland	50/50	26/33	51	128
Jason Elam, Denver	42/43	26/36	55	120
Morten Andersen, Kansas City	51/51	22/26	50	117
Adam Vinatieri, New England	36/36	27/30	57	117
Mike Hollis, N.Y. Giants	40/40	25/33	54	115
Olindo Mare, Miami	42/43	24/31	53	114

SCORING—NON-KICKERS	TD	Rush	Rec.	2 Pt	Pts
Priest Holmes, Kansas City	24	21	3	0	144
Ricky Williams, Miam	17	16	1	0	102
Clinton Portis, Denver	17	15	2	0	102
LaDainian Tomlinson, San Diego	15	14	1	0	90

*NFL record.

SCORING—NON-KICKERS	TD	Rush	Rec.	2 Pt	Pts
Eddie George, Tennessee	14	12	2	1	86
Travis Henry, Buffalo	14	13	1	0	84

INTERCEPTIONS	No.	Yds	Avg	Long	TD
Rod Woodson, Oakland	8	225	28.1	98	2
Greg Wesley, Kansas City	6	170	28.3	50	0
Marlon McCree, Jacksonville	6	129	21.5	53	0
Nate Clements, Buffalo	6	82	13.7	42	1
Patrick Surtain, Miami	6	79	13.2	40	1
Lance Schulters, Tennessee	6	56	9.3	28	0

KICKOFF RETURNS	No.	Yds	Avg	Long	TD
Kevin Faulk, New England	26	725	27.9	87	2
Chad Morton, Washington	58	1,509	26.0	98	2
Reuben Droughns, Denver	20	516	25.8	53	0
Brandon Bennett, Cincinnati	49	1,231	25.1	94	1
Marcus Knight, Oakland	29	705	24.3	65	0

PUNT RETURNS	No.	Yds	Avg	Long	TD
Santana Moss, N.Y. Jets	25	413	16.5	63	2
Dennis Northcutt, Cleveland	25	367	14.7	87	2
Dante Hall, Kansas City	29	390	13.4	90	2
Bobby Shaw, Buffalo	25	310	12.4	69	1
Deltha O'Neal, Denver	30	251	8.4	53	0

PUNTING	No.	Yds	Long	Avg
Chris Hanson, Jacksonville	81	3,583	64	44.2
Brian Moorman, Buffalo	66	2,844	84	43.1
Shane Lechler, Oakland	53	2,251	70	42.5
Craig Hentrich, Tennessee	65	2,725	56	41.9
Chris Gardocki, Cleveland	79	3,305	59	41.8

SACKS	No.
Jason Taylor, Miami	18.5
Dwight Freeney, Indianapolis	13.0
Rod Coleman, Oakland	11.0
John Abraham, N.Y. Jets	10.0
Kevin Carter, Tennessee	10.0
Adewale Ogunleye, Miami	9.5

National Football Conference

PASSING	Att	Comp	Pct comp	Yds	Yds/Att.	Long	TD	Pct TD	Int	Rating points
Brad Johnson, Tampa Bay	281	451	62.3	3,049	6.76	76	22	4.9	6	92.9
Matt Hasselbeck, Seattle	267	419	63.7	3,075	7.34	49	15	3.6	10	87.8
Donovan McNabb, Philadelpia	211	361	58.4	2,289	6.34	59	17	4.7	6	86.0
Jeff Garcia, San Francisco	328	528	62.1	3,344	6.33	76	21	4.0	10	85.6
Brett Favre, Green Bay	341	551	61.9	3,658	6.64	85	27	4.9	16	85.6
Kerry Collins, N.Y. Giants	335	545	61.5	4,073	7.47	82	19	3.5	14	85.4
Michael Vick, Atlanta	231	421	54.9	2,936	6.97	74	16	3.8	8	81.6
Aaron Brooks, New Orleans	283	528	53.6	3,572	6.77	64	27	5.1	15	80.1
Jim Miller, Tampa Bay	180	314	57.3	1,944	6.19	54	13	4.1	9	77.5
Rodney Peete, Carolina	223	381	58.5	2,630	6.90	69	15	3.9	14	77.4

RUSHING	Att	Yds	Avg	Long	TD
Deuce McAllister, New Orleans	325	1,388	4.3	62	13
Tiki Barber, N.Y. Giants	304	1,387	4.6	70	11
Michael Bennett, Minnesota	255	1,296	5.1	85	5
Ahman Green, Green Bay	286	1,240	4.3	43	7
Shaun Alexander, Seattle	295	1,175	4.0	58	16
Duce Staley, Philadelpia	269	1,029	3.8	57	5
James Stewart, Detroit	231	1,021	4.4	56	4
Emmitt Smith, Dallas	254	975	3.8	30	5
Garrison Hearst, San Francisco	215	972	4.5	40	8
Marshall Faulk, St. Louis	212	953	4.5	44	8

RECEIVING	Catches	Yds	Avg	Long	TD
Randy Moss, Minnesota	106	1,347	12.7	60	7
Terrell Owens, San Francisco	100	1,300	13.0	76	13
Marty Booker, Chicago	97	1,183	12.2	54	6
Torry Holt, St. Louis	91	1,302	14.3	58	4
Joe Horne, New Orleans	88	1,312	14.9	63	7
Amani Toomer, N.Y. Giants	82	1,343	16.4	82	8
Marshall Faulk, St. Louis	80	537	6.7	40	2
Isaac Bruce, St. Louis	79	1,075	13.6	34	7
Koren Robinson, Seattle	78	1,240	15.9	83	5
Keyshawn Johnson, Tampa Bay	76	1,088	14.3	76	5

SCORING—KICKERS	PAT	FG	Long	Pts
Jay Feely, Atlanta	42/43	32/40	52	138
David Akers, Philadelphia	43/43	30/34	51	133
John Carney, New Orleans	37/37	31/35	48	130
Ryan Longwell, Green Bay	44/44	28/34	49	128
Martin Gramatica, Tampa Bay	32/32	32/39	53	128
Matt Bryant, N.Y. Giants	30/32	26/32	47	108

SCORING—NON-KICKERS	TD	Rush	Rec.	2 Pt	Pts
Shaun Alexander, Seattle	18	16	2	00	108
Deuce McAllister, New Orleans	16	13	3	00	96
Terrell Owens, San Francisco	14	1	13	00	84
Moe Williams, Minnesota	11	11	0	00	66

SCORING—NON-KICKERS	TD	Rush	Rec.	2 Pt	Pts
Tiki Barber, N.Y. Giants	11	11	0	00	66
Daunte Culpepper, Minnesota	10	10	0	1	62

INTERCEPTIONS	No.	Yds	Avg	Long	TD
Brian Kelly, Tampa Bay	8	68	8.5	31	0
Darren Sharper, Green Bay	7	233	33.3	89	1
Tony Parrish, San Francisco	7	204	29.1	60	0
Seven players tied with 5					

KICKOFF RETURNS	No.	Yds	Avg	Long	TD
MarTay Jenkins, Atlanta	20	559	28.0	95	1
Brian Mitchell, N.Y. Giants	43	1,162	27.0	57	0
Eddie Drummond, Detroit	40	1,039	26.0	91	0
Michael Lewis, New Orleans	70	1,807	25.8	97	2
Aaron Stecker, Tampa Bay	37	934	25.2	67	0

PUNT RETURNS	No.	Yds	Avg	Long	TD
Jimmy Williams, San Francisco	20	336	16.8	89	1
Michael Lewis, New Orleans	44	625	14.2	83	1
Brian Mitchell, N.Y. Giants	46	567	12.3	76	1
Allen Rossum, Atlanta	24	288	12.0	36	0
Bobby Engram, Seattle	21	224	10.7	61	1

PUNTING	No.	Yds	Long	Avg
Todd Sauerbrun, Carolina	104	4,735	67	45.5
Scott Player, Arizona	88	3,864	58	43.9
Sean Landeta, St. Louis	52	2,229	63	42.9
Tom Tupa, Tampa Bay	90	3,856	71	42.8
Brad Maynard, Chicago	87	3,679	75	42.3

SACKS	No.
Simeon Rice, Tampa Bay	15.5
Andre Carter, San Francisco	12.5
Hugh Douglas, Philadelphia	12.5
Kabeer Gbaja-Biamila, Green Bay	12.0
Leonard Little, St. Louis	12.0
Julius Peppers, Carolina	12.0

First-Round Selections in the 2003 NFL Draft

Team	Player	Pos	College	Team	Player	Pos	College
1. Cincinnati	Carson Palmer	QB	USC	17. Arizona[8]	Bryant Johnson	WR	Penn St.
2. Detroit	Charles Rogers	WR	Michigan St.	18. Arizona[9]	Calvin Pace	DE	Wake Forest
3. Houston	Andre Johnson	WR	Miami (FL)	19. Baltimore[10]	Kyle Boller	QB	California
4. N.Y. Jets[1]	Dewayne Robertson	DT	Kentucky	20. Denver	George Foster	OT	Georgia
5. Dallas	Terence Newman	CB	Kansas St.	21. Cleveland	Jeff Faine	C	Notre Dame
6. New Orleans[2]	Johnathan Sullivan	DT	Georgia	22. Chicago[11]	Rex Grossman	QB	Florida
7. Jacksonville	Byron Leftwich	QB	Marshall	23. Buffalo[12]	Willis McGahee	RB	Miami (FL)
8. Carolina	Jordan Gross	OT	Utah	24. Indianapolis	Dallas Clark	TE	Iowa
9. Minnesota[3]	Kevin Williams	DE	Oklahoma St.	25. N.Y. Giants	William Joseph	DT	Miami (FL)
10. Baltimore	Terrell Suggs	DE	Arizona St.	26. San Francisco	Kwame Harris	OT	Stanford
11. Seattle	Marcus Trufant	CB	Washington St.	27. Kansas City[13]	Larry Johnson	RB	Penn St.
12. St. Louis[4]	Jimmy Kennedy	DT	Penn St.	28. Tennessee	Andre Woolfolk	CB	Oklahoma
13. New England	Ty Warren	DT	Texas A&M	29. Green Bay	Nick Barnett	LB	Oregon St.
14. Chicago[5]	Michael Haynes	DE	Penn St.	30. San Diego[14]	Sammy Davis	CB	Texas A&M
15. Philadelphia[6]	Jerome McDougle	DE	Miami (FL)	31. Oakland	Nnamdi Asomugha	CB	California
16. Pittsburgh[7]	Troy Polamalu	SS	USC	32. Oakland[15]	Tyler Brayton	DE	Colorado

(1) From Chicago. (2) From Arizona. (3) Passed at #7, exercised pick at #9. (4) From Washington through N.Y. Jets and Chicago. (5) From Buffalo through New England. (6) From San Diego. (7) From Kansas City. (8) From New Orleans. (9) From Miami through New Orleans. (10) From New England. (11) From N.Y. Jets. (12) From Atlanta. (13) From Pittsburgh. (14) From Philadelphia. (15) From Tampa Bay.

Number One NFL Draft Choices, 1936-2003

Year	Team	Player, Pos., College	Year	Team	Player, Pos., College
1936	Philadelphia	Jay Berwanger, HB, Chicago	1970	Pittsburgh	Terry Bradshaw, QB, La.Tech
1937	Philadelphia	Sam Francis, FB, Nebraska	1971	New England	Jim Plunkett, QB, Stanford
1938	Cleveland Rams	Corbett Davis, FB, Indiana	1972	Buffalo	Walt Patulski, DE, Notre Dame
1939	Chicago Cards	Ki Aldrich, C, TCU	1973	Houston	John Matuszak, DE, Tampa
1940	Chicago Cards	George Cafego, HB, Tennessee	1974	Dallas	Ed "Too Tall" Jones, DE, Tenn. St.
1941	Chicago Bears	Tom Harmon, HB, Michigan	1975	Atlanta	Steve Bartkowski, QB, Cal.
1942	Pittsburgh	Bill Dudley, HB, Virginia	1976	Tampa Bay	Lee Roy Selmon, DE, Oklahoma
1943	Detroit	Frank Sinkwich, HB, Georgia	1977	Tampa Bay	Ricky Bell, RB, USC
1944	Boston Yanks	Angelo Bertelli, QB, Notre Dame	1978	Houston	Earl Campbell, RB, Texas
1945	Chicago Cards	Charley Trippi, HB, Georgia	1979	Buffalo	Tom Cousineau, LB, Ohio St.
1946	Boston Yanks	Frank Dancewicz, QB, Notre Dame	1980	Detroit	Billy Sims, RB, Oklahoma
1947	Chicago Bears	Bob Fenimore, HB, Okla. A&M	1981	New Orleans	George Rogers, RB, S.Carolina
1948	Washington	Harry Gilmer, QB, Alabama	1982	New England	Kenneth Sims, DT, Texas
1949	Philadelphia	Chuck Bednarik, C, Penn	1983	Baltimore Colts	John Elway, QB, Stanford
1950	Detroit	Leon Hart, E, Notre Dame	1984	New England	Irving Fryar, WR, Nebraska
1951	N.Y. Giants	Kyle Rote, HB, SMU	1985	Buffalo	Bruce Smith, DE, Va.Tech
1952	L.A. Rams	Bill Wade, QB, Vanderbilt	1986	Tampa Bay	Bo Jackson, RB, Auburn
1953	San Francisco	Harry Babcock, E, Georgia	1987	Tampa Bay	Vinny Testaverde, QB, Miami (FL)
1954	Cleveland	Bobby Garrett, QB, Stanford	1988	Atlanta	Aundray Bruce, LB, Auburn
1955	Baltimore Colts	George Shaw, QB, Oregon	1989	Dallas	Troy Aikman, QB, UCLA
1956	Pittsburgh	Gary Glick, DB, Col. A&M	1990	Indianapolis	Jeff George, QB, Illinois
1957	Green Bay	Paul Hornung, QB, Notre Dame	1991	Dallas	Russell Maryland, DL, Miami (FL)
1958	Chicago Cards	King Hill, QB, Rice	1992	Indianapolis	Steve Emtman, DL, Washington
1959	Green Bay	Randy Duncan, QB, Iowa	1993	New England	Drew Bledsoe, QB, Washington St.
1960	L.A. Rams	Billy Cannon, HB, LSU	1994	Cincinnati	Dan Wilkinson, DT, Ohio St.
1961	Minnesota	Tommy Mason, HB, Tulane	1995	Cincinnati	Ki-Jana Carter, RB, Penn State
1962	Washington	Ernie Davis, HB, Syracuse	1996	N.Y. Jets	Keyshawn Johnson, WR, USC
1963	L.A. Rams	Terry Baker, QB, Oregon St.	1997	St. Louis	Orlando Pace, T, Ohio St.
1964	San Francisco	Dave Parks, E, Texas Tech	1998	Indianapolis	Peyton Manning, QB, Tennessee
1965	N.Y. Giants	Tucker Frederickson, HB, Auburn	1999	Cleveland	Tim Couch, QB, Kentucky
1966	Atlanta	Tommy Nobis, LB, Texas	2000	Cleveland	Courtney Brown, DE, Penn State
1967	Baltimore Colts	Bubba Smith, DT, Michigan St.	2001	Atlanta	Michael Vick, QB, Virginia Tech
1968	Minnesota	Ron Yary, T, USC	2002	Houston	David Carr, QB, Fresno St.
1969	Buffalo	O.J. Simpson, RB, USC	2003	Cincinnati	Carson Palmer, QB, USC

NFL MVP, Defensive Player of the Year, and Rookie of the Year

The Most Valuable Player and Defensive Player of the Year are two of many awards given out annually by the Associated Press. Rookie of the Year is one of many awards given out annually by *The Sporting News.* Many other organizations give out annual awards honoring the NFL's best players.

Most Valuable Player

1957 Jim Brown, Cleveland	1972 Larry Brown, Washington	1988 Boomer Esiason, Cincinnati
1958 Gino Marchetti, Baltimore Colts	1973 O.J. Simpson, Buffalo	1989 Joe Montana, San Francisco
1959 Charley Conerly, N.Y. Giants	1974 Ken Stabler, Oakland	1990 Joe Montana, San Francisco
1960 Norm Van Brocklin, Philadelphia;	1975 Fran Tarkenton, Minnesota	1991 Thurman Thomas, Buffalo
Joe Schmidt, Detroit	1976 Bert Jones, Baltimore	1992 Steve Young, San Francisco
1961 Paul Hornung, Green Bay	1977 Walter Payton, Chicago	1993 Emmitt Smith, Dallas
1962 Jim Taylor, Green Bay	1978 Terry Bradshaw, Pittsburgh	1994 Steve Young, San Francisco
1963 Y.A. Tittle, N.Y. Giants	1979 Earl Campbell, Houston	1995 Brett Favre, Green Bay
1964 John Unitas, Baltimore Colts	1980 Brian Sipe, Cleveland	1996 Brett Favre, Green Bay
1965 Jim Brown, Cleveland	1981 Ken Anderson, Cincinnati	1997 (tie) Brett Favre, Green Bay;
1966 Bart Starr, Green Bay	1982 Mark Moseley, Washington	Barry Sanders, Detroit
1967 John Unitas, Baltimore Colts	1983 Joe Theismann, Washington	1998 Terrell Davis, Denver
1968 Earl Morrall, Baltimore Colts	1984 Dan Marino, Miami	1999 Kurt Warner, St. Louis
1969 Roman Gabriel, L.A. Rams	1985 Marcus Allen, L.A. Raiders	2000 Marshall Faulk, St. Louis
1970 John Brodie, San Francisco	1986 Lawrence Taylor, N.Y. Giants	2001 Kurt Warner, St. Louis
1971 Alan Page, Minnesota	1987 John Elway, Denver	2002 Rich Gannon, Oakland

Defensive Player of the Year

1966	Larry Wilson, St. Louis	1979	Lee Roy Selmon, Tampa Bay	1991	Pat Swilling, New Orleans
1967	Deacon Jones, Los Angeles	1980	Lester Hayes, Oakland	1992	Junior Seau, San Diego
1968	Deacon Jones, Los Angeles	1981	Joe Klecko, N.Y. Jets	1993	Bruce Smith, Buffalo
1969	Dick Butkus, Chicago	1982	Mark Gastineau, N.Y. Jets	1994	Deion Sanders, San Francisco
1970	Dick Butkus, Chicago	1983	Jack Lambert, Pittsburgh	1995	Bryce Paup, Buffalo
1971	Carl Eller, Minnesota	1984	Mike Haynes, L.A. Raiders	1996	Bruce Smith, Buffalo
1972	Joe Greene, Pittsburgh	1985	Howie Long, L.A. Raiders; Andre	1997	Dana Stubblefield, San Francisco
1973	Alan Page, Minnesota		Tippett, New England	1998	Reggie White, Green Bay
1974	Joe Greene, Pittsburgh	1986	Lawrence Taylor, N.Y. Giants	1999	Warren Sapp, Tampa Bay
1975	Curley Culp, Houston	1987	Reggie White, Philadelphia	2000	Ray Lewis, Baltimore
1976	Jerry Sherk, Cleveland	1988	Mike Singletary, Chicago	2001	Michael Strahan, NY Giants
1977	Harvey Martin, Dallas	1989	Tim Harris, Green Bay	2002	Derrick Brooks, Tampa Bay
1978	Randy Gradishar, Denver	1990	Bruce Smith, Buffalo		

Rookie of the Year

1964	Charley Taylor, Washington	1975	NFC: Steve Bartkowski, Atlanta	1987	Robert Awalt, St. Louis
1965	Gale Sayers, Chicago		AFC: Robert Brazile, Houston	1988	Keith Jackson, Philadelphia
1966	Tommy Nobis, Atlanta	1976	NFC: Sammy White, Minnesota	1989	Barry Sanders, Detroit
1967	Mel Farr, Detroit		AFC: Mike Haynes, New England	1990	Richmond Webb, Miami
1968	Earl McCulloch, Detroit	1977	NFC: Tony Dorsett, Dallas	1991	Mike Croel, Denver
1969	Calvin Hill, Dallas		AFC: A. J. Duhe, Miami	1992	Santana Dotson, Tampa Bay
1970	NFC: Bruce Taylor, San Francisco	1978	NFC: Al Baker, Detroit	1993	Jerome Bettis, L.A. Rams
	AFC: Dennis Shaw, Buffalo		AFC: Earl Campbell, Houston	1994	Marshall Faulk, Indianapolis
1971	NFC: John Brockington, Green Bay	1979	NFC: Ottis Anderson, St. Louis	1995	Curtis Martin, New England
	AFC: Jim Plunkett, New England		AFC: Jerry Butler, Buffalo	1996	Eddie George, Houston
1972	NFC: Chester Marcol, Green Bay	1980	Billy Sims, Detroit	1997	Warrick Dunn, Tampa Bay
	AFC: Franco Harris, Pittsburgh	1981	George Rogers, New Orleans	1998	Randy Moss, Minnesota
1973	NFC: Chuck Foreman, Minnesota	1982	Marcus Allen, L.A. Raiders	1999	Edgerrin James, Indianapolis
	AFC: Boobie Clark, Cincinnati	1983	Dan Marino, Miami	2000	Brian Urlacher, Chicago
1974	NFC: Wilbur Jackson, San Francisco	1984	Louis Lipps, Pittsburgh	2001	Kendrell Bell, Pittsburgh
	AFC: Don Woods, San Diego	1985	Eddie Brown, Cincinnati	2002	Clinton Portis, Denver
		1986	Rueben Mayes, New Orleans		

The Sporting News 2002 NFL All-Pro Team

Offense—Quarterback: Rich Gannon, Oakland. Running Backs: Priest Holmes, Kansas City; Ricky Williams, Miami. Wide Receivers: Marvin Harrison, Indianapolis; Terrell Owens, San Francisco. Tight End: Tony Gonzalez, Kansas City. Tackles: Jonathan Ogden, Baltimore; Tra Thomas, Philadelphia. Guards: Alan Faneca, Pittsburgh; Will Shields, Kansas City. Center: Kevin Mawae, NY Jets.

Defense—Linebackers: Derrick Brooks, Tampa Bay; Joey Porter, Pittsburgh; Brian Urlacher, Chicago. Defensive Ends: Simeon Rice, Tampa Bay; Jason Taylor, Miami. Defensive Tackles: La'Roi Glover, Dallas; Warren Sapp, Tampa Bay. Cornerbacks: Aaron Glenn, Houston; Patrick Surtain, Miami. Safeties: Brian Dawkins, Philadelphia; Darren Sharper, Green Bay.

Special Teams—Kicker: David Akers, Philadelphia. Punter: Todd Sauerbrun, Carolina. Punt Returner: Santana Moss, NY Jets. Kick Returner: Michael Lewis, New Orleans.

All-Time NFL Coaching Victories

(at end of 2002 season; ranked by career wins; *active in 2002)

Coach	Years	Teams	Regular Season W	L	T	Pct	Career W	L	T	Pct
Don Shula	33	Colts, Dolphins	328	156	6	.676	347	173	6	.665
George Halas	40	Bears	318	148	31	.671	324	151	31	.671
Tom Landry	29	Cowboys	250	162	6	.605	270	178	6	.601
Curly Lambeau	33	Packers, Cardinals, Redskins	226	132	22	.624	229	134	22	.623
Chuck Noll	23	Steelers	193	148	1	.566	209	156	1	.572
Dan Reeves*	22	Broncos, Giants, Falcons	187	155	2	.547	198	164	2	.547
Chuck Knox	22	Rams, Bills, Seahawks	186	147	1	.558	193	158	1	.550
Paul Brown	21	Browns, Bengals	166	100	6	.621	170	109	6	.607
Bud Grant	18	Vikings	158	96	5	.620	168	108	5	.607
Marty Schottenheimer*	17	Browns, Chiefs, Redskins, Chargers	161	101	1	.614	166	112	1	.597
Steve Owen	23	Giants	155	108	17	.598	155	108	17	.584
Marv Levy	17	Chiefs, Bills	143	112	0	.561	154	120	0	.562
Bill Parcells	15	Giants, Patriots, Jets	138	100	1	.579	149	106	1	.584
Joe Gibbs	12	Redskins	124	60	0	.674	140	65	0	.683
Hank Stram	17	Chiefs, Saints	131	97	10	.571	136	100	10	.573
Weeb Ewbank	20	Colts, Jets	130	129	7	.502	134	130	7	.507
Mike Ditka	14	Bears, Saints	121	95	0	.560	127	101	0	.557
Jim Mora	15	Saints, Colts	125	106	0	.541	125	112	0	.527
George Seifert*	11	49ers, Panthers	114	62	0	.648	124	67	0	.649
Sid Gillman	18	Rams, Chargers, Oilers	122	99	7	.550	123	104	7	.541

All-Time Professional (NFL and AFL) Football Records

(at end of 2002 season; *active in 2002; (a) includes AFL statistics)

Leading Lifetime Scorers

Player	Yrs	TD	PAT	FG	Total	Player	Yrs	TD	PAT	FG	Total
Gary Anderson*	21	0	741	494	2,223	Matt Bahr	17	0	522	300	1,422
Morten Andersen*	21	0	695	486	2,153	Mark Moseley	16	0	482	300	1,382
George Blanda (a)	26	9	943	335	2,002	Jim Bakken	17	0	534	282	1,380
Norm Johnson	18	0	638	366	1,736	Fred Cox	15	0	519	282	1,365
Nick Lowery	18	0	562	383	1,711	Lou Groza	17	1	641	234	1,349
Jan Stenerud (a)	19	0	580	373	1,699	John Carney*	15	0	368	321	1,331
Eddie Murray	19	0	538	352	1,594	Steve Christie*	13	0	399	299	1,296
Al Del Greco	17	0	543	347	1,584	Jim Breech	14	0	517	243	1,246
Pat Leahy	18	0	558	304	1,470	Pete Stoyanovich	12	0	420	272	1,236
Jim Turner (a)	16	1	521	304	1,439	Matt Stover*	12	0	366	288	1,230

Leading Lifetime Touchdown Scorers

Player	Yrs	Rush	Rec	Ret	Total	Player	Yrs	Rush	Rec	Ret	Total
Jerry Rice*	18	10	192	1	203	Tim Brown*	15	1	97	4	102
Emmitt Smith*	13	153	11	0	164	Steve Largent	14	1	100	0	101
Marcus Allen	16	123	21	1	145	Franco Harris	13	91	9	0	100
Cris Carter*	16	0	130	1	131	Eric Dickerson	11	90	6	0	96
Jim Brown	9	106	20	0	126	Jim Taylor	10	83	10	0	93
Walter Payton	13	110	15	0	125	Tony Dorsett	12	77	13	1	91
Marshall Faulk*	9	87	33	0	120	Bobby Mitchell	11	18	65	8	91
John Riggins	14	104	12	0	116	Ricky Watters	10	78	13	0	91
Lenny Moore	12	63	48	2	113	Leroy Kelly	10	74	13	3	90
Barry Sanders	10	99	10	0	109	Charley Taylor	13	11	79	0	90
Don Hutson	11	3	99	3	105						

Most Points, Season — 176, Paul Hornung, Green Bay Packers, 1960 (15 TDs, 41 PATs, 15 FGs).
Most Points, Game — 40, Ernie Nevers, Chicago Cardinals vs. Chicago Bears, Nov. 28, 1929 (6 TDs, 4 PATs).
Most Touchdowns, Season — 26, Marshall Faulk, St. Louis Rams, 2000 (18 rushing, 8 receiving).
Most Touchdowns, Game — 6, Ernie Nevers, Chicago Cardinals vs. Chicago Bears, Nov. 28, 1929 (6 rushing); Dub Jones, Cleveland Browns vs. Chicago Bears, Nov. 25, 1951 (4 rushing, 2 pass receptions); Gale Sayers, Chicago Bears vs. San Francisco 49ers, Dec. 12, 1965 (4 rushing, 1 pass reception, 1 punt return).
Most Points After TD, Season — 66, Uwe von Schamann, Miami Dolphins, 1984.
Most Consecutive Points After TD — 371, Jason Elam, Denver Broncos, 1993-2002.
Most Field Goals, Season — 39, Olindo Mare, Miami Dolphins, 1999.
Most Field Goals, Game — 7, Jim Bakken, St. Louis Cardinals vs. Pittsburgh Steelers, Sept. 24, 1967; Rich Karlis, Minnesota vs. L.A. Rams, Nov. 5, 1989 (OT); Chris Boniol, Dallas vs. Green Bay, Nov. 18, 1996.
Most Field Goals Career — 494, Gary Anderson, Pitts. Steelers-Phil. Eagles-SF 49ers-Minn. Vikings, 1982-2002.
Longest Field Goal — 63 yds., Tom Dempsey, New Orleans Saints vs. Detroit Lions, Nov. 8, 1970; Jason Elam, Denver Broncos vs. Jacksonville Jaguars, Oct. 25, 1998.

Defensive Records

Most Interceptions, Career — 81, Paul Krause, Washington Redskins-Minnesota Vikings, 1964-79.
Most Interceptions, Season — 14, Dick "Night Train" Lane, L. A. Rams, 1952.
Most Touchdowns, Career — 12, Rod Woodson, Pittsburgh Steelers-San Francisco 49ers-Baltimore Ravens-Oakland Raiders, 1987-2002.
Most Touchdowns, Season — 4, Ken Houston, Houston Oilers, 1971; Jim Kearney, Kansas City Chiefs, 1972; Eric Allen, Philadelphia Eagles, 1993.
Most Sacks, Career (Since 1982) — 198, Reggie White, Philadelphia Eagles-Green Bay Packers, 1985-2000.
Most Sacks, Season (Since 1982) — 22.5, Michael Strahan, N.Y. Giants, 2002.
Most Sacks, Game (Since 1982) — 7, Derrick Thomas, Kansas City Chiefs vs. Seattle Seahawks, Nov. 11, 1990.

Leading Lifetime Rushers
(ranked by rushing yards)

Player	Yrs	Att	Yards	Avg	Long	TD	Player	Yrs	Att	Yards	Avg	Long	TD
Emmitt Smith*	13	4,052	17,162	4.2	75	153	John Riggins	14	2,916	11,352	3.9	66	104
Walter Payton	13	3,838	16,726	4.4	76	110	O.J. Simpson (a)	11	2,404	11,236	4.7	94	61
Barry Sanders	10	3,062	15,269	5.0	85	99	Ricky Watters	10	2,622	10,643	4.1	57	78
Eric Dickerson	11	2,996	13,259	4.4	85	90	Marshall Faulk*	9	2,367	10,395	4.4	71	87
Tony Dorsett	12	2,936	12,739	4.3	99	77	Curtis Martin*	8	2,604	10,361	4.0	70	71
Jim Brown	9	2,359	12,312	5.2	80	106	Ottis Anderson	14	2,562	10,273	4.0	76	81
Marcus Allen	16	3,022	12,243	4.1	61	123	Earl Campbell	8	2,187	9,407	4.3	81	74
Franco Harris	13	2,949	12,120	4.1	75	91	Eddie George*	7	2,421	8,978	3.7	76	59
Thurman Thomas	13	2,877	12,074	4.2	80	65	Terry Allen	10	2,152	8,614	4.0	55	73
Jerome Bettis*	10	2,873	11,542	4.0	71	62	Jim Taylor	10	1,941	8,597	4.4	84	83

Most Yards Gained, Season — 2,105, Eric Dickerson, L.A. Rams, 1984.
Most Yards Gained, Game — 278, Corey Dillon, Cincinnati Bengals vs. Denver Broncos, Oct. 22, 2000.
Most Touchdowns Rushing, Career — 153, Emmitt Smith, Dallas Cowboys, 1990-2002.
Most Touchdowns Rushing, Season — 25, Emmitt Smith, Dallas Cowboys, 1995.
Most Touchdowns Rushing, Game — 6, Ernie Nevers, Chicago Cardinals vs. Chicago Bears, Nov. 28, 1929.
Most Rushing Attempts, Game — 45, Jamie Morris, Washington Redskins vs. Cincinnati Bengals, Dec. 17, 1988 (overtime).
Longest Run From Scrimmage — 99 yds., Tony Dorsett, Dallas Cowboys vs. Minnesota Vikings, Jan. 3, 1983 (touchdown).

Leading Lifetime Receivers
(ranked by number of receptions)

Player	Yrs	No.	Yards	Avg	Long	TD	Player	Yrs	No.	Yards	Avg	Long	TD
Jerry Rice*	18	1,456	21,597	14.8	96	192	Shannon Sharpe*	13	753	9,290	12.3	82	54
Cris Carter*	16	1,101	13,899	12.6	80	130	Michael Irvin	12	750	11,904	15.9	87	65
Tim Brown*	15	1,018	14,167	13.9	80	97	Charlie Joiner (a)	18	750	12,146	16.2	87	65
Andre Reed	16	951	13,198	13.9	83	87	Andre Rison	12	743	10,205	13.7	80	84
Art Monk	16	940	12,721	13.5	79	68	Gary Clark	11	699	10,856	15.5	84	65
Irving Fryar	17	851	12,785	15.0	80	84	Terance Mathis*	13	689	8,809	12.8	81	63
Steve Largent	14	819	13,089	16.0	74	100	Herman Moore*	12	670	9,174	13.7	93	62
Henry Ellard	16	814	13,777	16.9	81	65	Marvin Harrison*	7	665	8,800	13.2	78	73
Larry Centers*	13	808	6,691	8.3	50	27	Jimmy Smith*	9	664	9,287	14.0	75	51
James Lofton	16	764	14,004	18.3	80	75	Ozzie Newsome	13	662	7,980	12.1	74	47

Most Yards Gained, Career — 21,597, Jerry Rice, San Francisco 49ers, Oakland Raiders, 1985-2002.
Most Yards Gained, Season — 1,848, Jerry Rice, San Francisco 49ers, 1995.
Most Yards Gained, Game — 336, Willie "Flipper" Anderson, L. A. Rams vs. New Orleans, Nov. 26, 1989 (overtime).
Most Pass Receptions, Season — 143, Marvin Harrison, Indianapolis Colts, 2002.
Most Pass Receptions, Game — 20, Terrell Owens, San Francisco 49ers vs. Chicago Bears, Dec. 17, 2000 (283 yards).
Most Touchdown Receptions, Career — 192, Jerry Rice, San Francisco 49ers, Oakland Raiders, 1985-2002.
Most Touchdown Receptions, Season — 22, Jerry Rice, San Francisco 49ers, 1987.
Most Touchdown Receptions, Game — 5, Bob Shaw, Chicago Cardinals vs. Baltimore Colts, Oct. 2, 1950; Kellen Winslow, San Diego Chargers vs. Oakland Raiders, Nov. 22, 1981; Jerry Rice, San Francisco 49ers vs. Atlanta Falcons, Oct. 14, 1990.

Leading Lifetime Passers

(minimum 1,500 attempts; ranked by quarterback rating points)

Player	Yrs	Att	Comp	Yds	TD	Int	Pts[1]	Player	Yrs	Att	Comp	Yds	TD	Int	Pts[1]
Kurt Warner* . . .	5	1,623	1,083	14,082	101	64	98.2	Jim Kelly	11	4,779	2,874	35,467	237	175	84.4
Steve Young . . .	15	4,149	2,667	33,124	232	107	96.8	Trent Green* . . .	5	1,743	1,006	12,977	82	53	84.2
Joe Montana . . .	15	5,391	3,409	40,551	273	139	92.3	Brian Griese* . . .	5	1,678	1,044	11,763	71	53	84.1
Jeff Garcia* . . .	4	1,968	1,224	13,704	95	43	89.9	Roger Staubach	11	2,958	1,685	22,700	153	109	83.4
Brett Favre*	12	5,993	3,652	42,285	314	188	86.7	Neil Lomax	8	3,153	1,817	22,771	136	90	82.7
Dan Marino	17	8,358	4,967	61,361	420	252	86.4	Sonny Jurgensen	18	4,262	2,433	32,224	255	189	82.63
Peyton Manning*	5	2,817	1,749	20,618	138	100	85.9	Len Dawson (a) .	19	3,741	2,136	28,711	239	183	82.56
Rich Gannon* . . .	14	3,913	2,367	26,945	171	98	85.3	Ken Anderson . .	16	4,475	2,654	32,838	197	160	81.85
Mark Brunell* . . .	9	3,561	2,142	25,309	142	86	85.1	Bernie Kosar . .	12	3,365	1,994	23,301	124	87	81.82
Brad Johnson* . .	9	2,831	1,747	19,428	114	74	84.6	Steve McNair* . .	8	2,780	1,634	19,422	108	76	81.73

(1) Rating points based on performances in the following categories: Percentage of completions, percentage of touchdown passes, percentage of interceptions, and average gain per pass attempt.

Most Yards Gained, Career — 61,361, Dan Marino, Miami Dolphins, 1983-99.
Most Yards Gained, Season — 5,084, Dan Marino, Miami Dolphins, 1984.
Most Yards Gained, Game — 554, Norm Van Brocklin, L. A. Rams vs N.Y. Yanks, Sept. 18, 1951 (27 completions in 41 attempts).
Most Touchdowns Passing, Career — 420, Dan Marino, Miami Dolphins, 1983-99.
Most Touchdowns Passing, Season — 48, Dan Marino, Miami Dolphins, 1984.
Most Touchdowns Passing, Game — 7, Sid Luckman, Chicago Bears vs. N.Y. Giants, Nov. 14, 1943; Adrian Burk, Phil. Eagles vs. Washington Redskins, Oct. 17, 1954; George Blanda, Houston Oilers vs. N.Y. Titans, Nov. 19, 1961; Y.A. Tittle, N.Y. Giants vs. Washington Redskins, Oct. 28, 1962; Joe Kapp, Minnesota Vikings vs. Baltimore Colts, Sept. 28, 1969.
Most Passes Completed, Career — 4,967, Dan Marino, Miami Dolphins, 1983-99.
Most Passes Completed, Season — 418 Rich Gannon, Oakland, 2002.
Most Passes Completed, Game — 45, Drew Bledsoe, New England Patriots vs. Minnesota Vikings, Nov. 13, 1994 (overtime).

National Football League Franchise Origins

(founding year, league; home stadium location; subsequent history)

Arizona Cardinals—1920, American Professional Football Association (APFA)[1]. Chicago, 1920-59; St. Louis, 1960-87; Tempe, AZ, 1988-present.
Atlanta Falcons—1996, NFL. Atlanta, 1966-present.
Baltimore Ravens—1996, NFL. Baltimore, 1996-present.
Buffalo Bills—1969, American Football League (AFL)[2]. Buffalo, 1960-72; Orchard Park, NY, 1972-present.
Carolina Panthers—1995, NFL. Clemson, SC, 1995; Charlotte, NC, 1996-present.
Chicago Bears—1920 APFA. Decatur, IL, 1920; Chicago, 1921-present.
Cincinnati Bengals—1968, AFL. Cincinnati, 1968-present.
Cleveland Browns—1946, All-America Football Conference (AAFC)[3]. Cleveland, 1946-95; 1999-present.
Dallas Cowboys—1960, NFL. Dallas, 1960-70; Irving, TX, 1971-present.
Denver Broncos—1960, AFL. Denver, 1960-present.
Detroit Lions—1930, NFL. Portsmouth, OH, 1930-33; Detroit, 1934-74; Pontiac, MI, 1975-present.
Green Bay Packers—1921, APFA. Green Bay, WI, 1921-present.
Houston Texans—2002, NFL. Houston 2002-present.
Indianapolis Colts—1953, NFL. Baltimore, 1953-83; Indianapolis, 1984-present.
Jacksonville Jaguars—1995, NFL. Jacksonville, FL, 1995-present.
Kansas City Chiefs—1960, AFL. Dallas, 1960-62; Kansas City, 1963-present.

Miami Dolphins—1966, AFL. Miami, 1966-present.
Minnesota Vikings—1961, NFL. Bloomington, MN, 1961-81; Minneapolis, 1982-present.
New England Patriots—1960, AFL. Boston, 1960-70; Foxboro, MA, 1982-present.
New Orleans Saints—1967, NFL. New Orleans, 1967-present.
New York Giants—1925, NFL. New York, 1925-73, 1975; New Haven, CT, 1973-74; E. Rutherford, NJ, 1976-present.
New York Jets—1960, AFL. New York, 1960-83; E. Rutherford, NJ, 1984-present.
Oakland Raiders—1960, AFL. Oakland, CA, 1960-81, 1995-present; Los Angeles, 1982-94.
Philadelphia Eagles—1933, NFL. Piladelphia, 1933-present.
Pittsburgh Steelers—1933, NFL. Pittsburgh, 1933-present.
St. Louis Rams—1937, NFL. Cleveland, 1936-45; Los Angeles, 1946-79; Anaheim, 1980-94; St. Louis, 1995-present.
San Diego Chargers—1960, AFL. Los Angeles, 1960; San Diego, 1961-present.
Seattle Seahawks—1976, NFL. Seattle, 1976-present.
San Francisco 49ers—1946, AAFC. San Francisco, 1946-present.
Tampa Bay Buccaneers—1976, NFL. Tampa, 1976-present.
Tennessee Titans—1960, AFL. Houston, 1969-96; Memphis, 1997; Nashville, 1998-present.
Washington Redskins—1932, NFL. Boston, 1932-36; Washinton, DC, 1937-96; Landover, MD, 1997-present.

(1) The American Professional Football Association (APFA) was formed in 1920 to standardize the rules of professional football. In 1922, the name was changed to the National Football League. (2) The most successful of 4 separate leagues called the "American Football League" (1926; 1936-37; 1940-41; 1960-69). Congress approved an NFL/AFL merger in 1966. Baltimore, Cleveland, and Pittsburgh agreed to join the 10 incoming AFL teams to form the American Football Conference. The NFL began play in 1970 with 26 teams. (3) The All-America Football Conference, 1946-49. In 1950, 3 of its teams joined the NFL (Baltimore, Cleveland, and San Francisco). The Baltimore franchise failed, but the NFL awarded the city a 2nd one, also called the Colts, in 1953.

American Football League Champions

Year	Eastern Division	Western Division	Championship
1960	Houston Oilers (10-4-0)	Los Angeles Chargers (10-4-0)	Houston 24, Los Angeles 16
1961	Houston Oilers (10-3-1)	San Diego Chargers (12-2-0)	Houston 10, San Diego 3
1962	Houston Oilers (11-3-0)	Dallas Texans (11-3-0)	Dallas 20, Houston 17 (2 overtimes)
1963	Boston Patriots (7-6-1)(a)	San Diego Chargers (11-3-0)	San Diego 51, Boston 10
1964	Buffalo Bills (12-2-0)	San Diego Chargers (8-5-1)	Buffalo 20, San Diego 7
1965	Buffalo Bills (10-3-1)	San Diego Chargers (9-2-3)	Buffalo 23, San Diego 0
1966	Buffalo Bills (9-4-1)	Kansas City Chiefs (11-2-1)	Kansas City 31, Buffalo 7
1967	Houston Oilers (9-4-1)	Oakland Raiders (13-1-0)	Oakland 40, Houston 7
1968	New York Jets (11-3-0)	Oakland Raiders (12-2-0)(b).	New York 27, Oakland 23
1969	New York Jets (10-4-0)	Oakland Raiders (12-1-1)	Kansas City 17, Oakland 7 (c)

(a) Defeated Buffalo Bills in divisional playoff. (b) Defeated Kansas City Chiefs in divisional playoff. (c) Kansas City Chiefs defeated N.Y. Jets and Oakland Raiders defeated Houston Oilers in divisional playoffs.

Pro Football Hall of Fame, Canton, Ohio

(Asterisks indicate 2003 inductees.)

Herb Adderley	Tony Dorsett	Jimmy Johnson	Hugh McElhenny	Don Shula
George Allen	John "Paddy" Driscoll	John Henry Johnson	Johnny "Blood" McNally	O.J. Simpson
*Marcus Allen	Bill Dudley	Charlie Joiner	Mike Michalske	Mike Singletary
Lance Alworth	Glen "Turk" Edwards	David "Deacon" Jones	Wayne Millner	Jackie Slater
Doug Atkins	Weeb Ewbank	Stan Jones	Bobby Mitchell	Jackie Smith
Morris "Red" Badgro	Tom Fears	Henry Jordan	Ron Mix	John Stallworth
Lem Barney	Jim Finks	Sonny Jurgensen	Joe Montana	Bart Starr
Cliff Battles	Ray Flaherty	Jim Kelly	Lenny Moore	Roger Staubach
Sammy Baugh	Len Ford	Leroy Kelly	Marion Motley	Ernie Stautner
Chuck Bednarik	Dr. Daniel Fortmann	Walt Kiesling	Mike Munchak	Jan Stenerud
Bert Bell	Dan Fouts	Frank "Bruiser" Kinard	Anthony Munoz	Dwight Stephenson
Bobby Bell	Frank Gatski	Paul Krause	George Musso	*Hank Stram
Raymond Berry	Bill George	Earl "Curly" Lambeau	Bronko Nagurski	Ken Strong
*Elvin Bethea	Joe Gibbs	Jack Lambert	Joe Namath	Joe Stydahar
Charles Bidwill	Frank Gifford	Tom Landry	Earle "Greasy" Neale	Lynn Swann
Fred Biletnikoff	Sid Gillman	Dick "Night Train" Lane	Ernie Nevers	Fran Tarkenton
George Blanda	Otto Graham	Jim Langer	Ozzie Newsome	Charley Taylor
Mel Blount	Red Grange	Willie Lanier	Ray Nitschke	Jim Taylor
Terry Bradshaw	Bud Grant	Steve Largent	Chuck Noll	Lawrence "LT" Taylor
Jim Brown	Joe Greene	Yale Lary	Leo Nomellini	Jim Thorpe
Paul Brown	Forrest Gregg	Dante Lavelli	Merlin Olsen	Y.A. Tittle
Roosevelt Brown	Bob Griese	Bobby Layne	Jim Otto	George Trafton
Willie Brown	Lou Groza	Alphonse "Tuffy"	Steve Owen	Charley Trippi
Buck Buchanan	Joe Guyon	Leemans	Alan Page	Emlen Tunnell
Nick Buoniconti	George Halas	Marv Levy	Clarence "Ace" Parker	Clyde "Bulldog" Turner
Dick Butkus	Jack Ham	Bob Lilly	Jim Parker	Johnny Unitas
Earl Campbell	Dan Hampton	Larry Little	Walter Payton	Gene Upshaw
Tony Canadeo	John Hannah	*James Lofton	Joe Perry	Norm Van Brocklin
Joe Carr	Franco Harris	Vince Lombardi	Pete Pihos	Steve Van Buren
Dave Casper	Mike Haynes	Howie Long	Hugh "Shorty" Ray	Doak Walker
Guy Chamberlin	Ed Healey	Ronnie Lott	Dan Reeves	Bill Walsh
Jack Christiansen	Mel Hein	Sid Luckman	Mel Renfro	Paul Warfield
Earl "Dutch" Clark	Ted Hendricks	Roy "Link" Lyman	John Riggins	Bob Waterfield
George Connor	Wilbur "Pete" Henry	Tom Mack	Jim Ringo	Mike Webster
Jim Conzelman	Arnold Herber	John Mackey	Andy Robustelli	Arnie Weinmeister
Lou Creekmur	Bill Hewitt	Tim Mara	Art Rooney	Randy White
Larry Csonka	Clarke Hinkle	Wellington Mara	Dan Rooney	Dave Wilcox
Al Davis	Elroy "Crazylegs"	Gino Marchetti	Pete Rozelle	Bill Willis
Willie Davis	Hirsch	George Preston	Bob St. Clair	Larry Wilson
Len Dawson	Paul Hornung	Marshall	Gale Sayers	Kellen Winslow
*Joe DeLamielleure	Ken Houston	Ollie Matson	Joe Schmidt	Alex Wojciechowicz
Eric Dickerson	Cal Hubbard	Don Maynard	Tex Schramm	Willie Wood
Dan Dierdorf	Sam Huff	George McAfee	Lee Roy Selmon	Ron Yary
Mike Ditka	Lamar Hunt	Mike McCormack	Billy Shaw	Jack Youngblood
Art Donovan	Don Hutson	Tommy McDonald	Art Shell	

NFL Stadiums[1]

Team—Stadium, Location, Turf (Year Built)	Capacity	Team—Stadium, Location, Turf (Year Built)	Capacity
Bears—New Soldier Field[2], Champaign, IL, G (1924) .	61,500	Giants—Giants Stad., E. Rutherford, NJ, G (1976)...	79,466
Bengals—Paul Brown Stad., Cincinnati, OH, G (2000).	65,600	Jaguars—ALLTEL Stad.[7], Jacksonville, FL, G (1946).	73,000
Bills—Ralph Wilson Stad., Orchard Park, NY, A (1973) .	73,967	Jets—Giants Stad., E. Rutherford, NJ, G (1976)......	79,466
Broncos—Invesco Field at Mile High, Denver, CO,		Lions—Ford Field, Detroit, MI, A (2002)	65,000
G (2001)	76,125	Packers—Lambeau Field[8], Green Bay, WI, G (1957) .	72,515
Browns—Cleveland Browns Stad., Cleveland, OH,		Panthers—Ericsson Stad., Charlotte, NC, G (1996) .	73,258
G (1999)	73,300	Patriots—Gillette Stad., Foxboro, MA, G (2002)....	68,000
Buccaneers—Raymond James Stad., Tampa, FL,		Raiders—Network Associates Coliseum[9], Oakland,	
G (1998)	65,657	CA, G (1966)	63,132
Cardinals—Sun Devil Stad., Tempe, AZ, G (1958) ...	73,014	Rams—Edward Jones Dome[10], St. Louis, MO, A	
Chargers—Qualcomm Stad.3, San Diego, CA,		(1995).	66,000
G (1967)	71,500	Ravens—Ravens Stad.[11], Baltimore, MD, SG (1998) .	69,354
Chiefs—Arrowhead Stad., Kansas City, MO, G (1972).	79,451	Redskins—FedEx Field[12], Landover, MD, G (1997) ...	80,116
Colts—RCA Dome 4, Indianapolis, IN, A (1983)......	56,127	Saints—Louisiana Superdome, New Orleans, LA, G (1975) .	69,703
Cowboys—Texas Stad., Irving, TX, A (1971)........	65,675	Seahawks—Seahawks Stad., Seattle, WA, A (2002) ..	67,000
Dolphins—Pro Player Stad.5, Miami, FL, G (1987) ...	75,192	Steelers—Heinz Field, Pittsburgh, PA, A (2001)	64,450
Eagles—Lincoln Financial Field, Philadelphia, PA,		Texans—Reliant Stadium, Houston, TX, G (2002)	69,500
G (2003)	65,352	Titans—The Coliseum13, Nashville, TN, G (1999)	67,000
Falcons—Georgia Dome, Atlanta, GA, A (1992)	71,228	Vikings—Hubert H. Humphrey Metrodome, Minn., MN,	
49ers—3Com Park[6], San Francisco, CA, G (1960)....	69,734	A (1982)	64,121

G=Grass. A=Artificial turf. SG=Sport Grass (hybrid of artificial and natural turf). (1) As of the start of the 2003 season. (2) Renovation in 2002 replaced interior of stadium (3) Formerly San Diego Stadium (1967-80), San Diego Jack Murphy Stadium (1981-97). (4) Formerly the Hoosier Dome (1983-94). (5) Formerly Joe Robbie Stadium (1987-96). (6) Formerly Candlestick Park; full name: 3Com Park at Candlestick Point. (7) Formerly Jacksonville Municipal Stadium (1946-97). (8) Formerly City Stadium (1957-65). Renovation completed in 2003, added 11,625 seats. (9) Formerly Oakland/Alameda County Coliseum. (10) Formerly Trans World Dome (1995-2001); full name: Edward Jones Dome at America's Center. (11) Formerly PSINet Stadium (1998-2002); Ravens Stadium (2002-2003). (12) Formerly Jack Kent Cooke Stadium (1997-99). (13) Formerly Adelphia Col. (1999-2002).

Future Sites of the Super Bowl

(Information subject to change.)

No.	Site	Date	No.	Site	Date
XXXVIII	Reliant Stadium, Houston, TX	Feb. 1, 2004	XL	Ford Field, Detroit, MI	Feb. 5, 2006
XXXIX	ALLTEL Stadium, Jacksonville, FL	Feb. 6, 2005	XLI	Pro Player Stadium, Miami, FL	2007; date not set

COLLEGE FOOTBALL
Ohio State Goes 14-0, Wins Fiesta Bowl and 2002 National Title

The No. 2 Ohio State Buckeyes defeated the top-ranked Miami (FL) Hurricanes, 31-24, in double overtime Jan. 3, 2003, in Tempe, AZ, for their 4th national championship. Heavily favored, the defending champion Hurricanes entered the contest with a 34-game winning streak. The game was closely played throughout, and overtime was needed after Miami's Todd Sievers kicked a 40-yard field goal at the end of regulation, making the score 17-17. Miami had the ball first and quickly scored as Ken Dorsey connected with tight end Kellen Winslow Jr. Miami appeared to have won, after Ohio State failed to score on 4th down. But, a pass interference penalty was called on Miami, and Ohio State quarterback Craig Krenzel scored 3 plays later. Maurice Clarett then ran a touchdown for the Buckeyes up to the 1-yard line, but could not score on 4th down as a blitzing Ohio State defense caused an errant pass by Miami's Ken Dorsey to end the game.

National College Football Champions, 1936-2002

The unofficial champion as selected by the AP poll of writers and USA Today/ESPN (until 1991, UPI; 1991-1996 USA Today/CNN) poll of coaches. In years the polls disagreed, both teams are listed (AP winner first). The AP poll started in 1936; the UPI poll in 1950.

1936 Minnesota	1950 Oklahoma	1964 Alabama	1977 Notre Dame
1937 Pittsburgh	1951 Tennessee	1965 Alabama, Mich. St.	1978 Alabama, USC
1938 Texas Christian	1952 Michigan St.	1966 Notre Dame	1979 Alabama
1939 Texas A&M	1953 Maryland	1967 USC	1980 Georgia
1940 Minnesota	1954 Ohio St., UCLA	1968 Ohio St.	1981 Clemson
1941 Minnesota	1955 Oklahoma	1969 Texas	1982 Penn St.
1942 Ohio St.	1956 Oklahoma	1970 Nebraska, Texas	1983 Miami (FL)
1943 Notre Dame	1957 Auburn, Ohio St.	1971 Nebraska	1984 Brigham Young
1944 Army	1958 Louisiana St.	1972 USC	1985 Oklahoma
1945 Army	1959 Syracuse	1973 Notre Dame,	1986 Penn St.
1946 Notre Dame	1960 Minnesota	Alabama	1987 Miami (FL)
1947 Notre Dame	1961 Alabama	1974 Oklahoma, USC	1988 Notre Dame
1948 Michigan	1962 USC	1975 Oklahoma	1989 Miami (FL)
1949 Notre Dame	1963 Texas	1976 Pittsburgh	1990 Colorado, GA Tech
1991 Miami (FL), Washington			
1992 Alabama			
1993 Florida St.			
1994 Nebraska			
1995 Nebraska			
1996 Florida			
1997 Michigan, Nebraska			
1998 Tennessee			
1999 Florida St.			
2000 Oklahoma			
2001 Miami (FL)			
2002 Ohio State			

2002 Final Associated Press and USA Today/ESPN NCAA Football Rankings
Associated Press Poll

1. Ohio St. (14-0)	6. Texas (11-2)	11. Alabama (10-3)
2. Miami (FL) (12-1)	7. Kansas St. (11-2)	12. N. Carolina St. (11-3)
3. Georgia (13-1)	8. Iowa (11-2)	13. Maryland (11-3)
4. S. California (11-2)	9. Michigan (10-3)	14. Auburn (9-4)
5. Oklahoma (12-2)	10. Washington St. (10-3)	15. Boise St. (12-1)

16. Penn St. (9-4)	21. Florida St. (9-5)
17. Notre Dame (10-3)	22. Virginia (9-5)
18. Virginia Tech (10-4)	23. TCU (10-2)
19. Pittsburgh (9-4)	24. Marshall (11-2)
20. Colorado (9-5)	25. West Virginia (9-4)

USA Today/ESPN Coaches' Poll

1. Ohio St. (14-0)	6. Kansas St. (11-2)	11. North Carolina (11-3)
2. Miami (FL) (12-1)	7. Texas (11-2)	12. Boise St. (12-1)
3. Georgia (13-1)	8. Iowa (11-2)	13. Maryland (11-3)
4. S. California (11-2)	9. Michigan (10-3)	14. Virginia Tech (10-4)
5. Oklahoma (12-2)	10. Washington St. (10-3)	15. Penn St. (9-4)

16. Auburn (9-4)	21. Colorado (9-5)
17. Notre Dame (10-3)	22. TCU (10-2)
18. Pittsburgh (9-4)	23. Florida St. (9-5)
19. Marshall (11-2)	24. Florida (8-5)
20. West Virginia (9-4)	25. Virginia (9-5)

Note: Team records include bowl games. The American Football Coaches Assoc. prohibits coaches from voting for schools on major NCAA probation. the NCAA placed the Univ. of Alabama on 5-year probation Feb. 1, 2002, for recruiting violations.

Annual Results of Major Bowl Games
(Dates indicate year the game was played; bowl games are generally played in late December or early January.)

Rose Bowl, Pasadena, CA

1902	(Jan.) Michigan 49, Stanford 0	1946 Alabama 34, USC 14
1916	Washington St. 14, Brown 0	1947 Illinois 45, UCLA 14
1917	Oregon 14, Pennsylvania 0	1948 Michigan 49, USC 0
1918-19	Service teams	1949 Northwestern 20, California 14
1920	Harvard 7, Oregon 6	1950 Ohio St. 17, California 14
1921	California 28, Ohio St. 0	1951 Michigan 14, California 6
1922	Wash. & Jeff. 0, California 0	1952 Illinois 40, Stanford 7
1923	USC 14, Penn St. 3	1953 USC 7, Wisconsin 0
1924	Navy 14, Washington 14	1954 Mich. St. 28, UCLA 20
1925	Notre Dame 27, Stanford 10	1955 Ohio St. 20, USC 7
1926	Alabama 20, Washington 19	1956 Mich. St. 17, UCLA 14
1927	Alabama 7, Stanford 7	1957 Iowa 35, Oregon St. 19
1928	Stanford 7, Pittsburgh 6	1958 Ohio St. 10, Oregon 7
1929	Georgia Tech 8, California 7	1959 Iowa 38, California 12
1930	USC 47, Pittsburgh 14	1960 Washington 44, Wisconsin 8
1931	Alabama 24, Wash. St. 0	1961 Washington 17, Minnesota 7
1932	USC 21, Tulane 12	1962 Minnesota 21, UCLA 3
1933	USC 35, Pittsburgh 0	1963 USC 42, Wisconsin 37
1934	Columbia 7, Stanford 0	1964 Illinois 17, Washington 7
1935	Alabama 29, Stanford 13	1965 Michigan 34, Oregon St. 7
1936	Stanford 7, SMU 0	1966 UCLA 14, Mich. St. 12
1937	Pittsburgh 21, Washington 0	1967 Purdue 14, USC 13
1938	California 13, Alabama 0	1968 USC 14, Indiana 3
1939	USC 7, Duke 3	1969 Ohio St. 27, USC 16
1940	USC 14, Tennessee 0	1970 USC 10, Michigan 3
1941	Stanford 21, Nebraska 13	1971 Stanford 27, Ohio St. 17
1942*	Oregon St. 20, Duke 16	1972 Stanford 13, Michigan 12
1943	Georgia 9, UCLA 0	1973 USC 42, Ohio St. 17
1944	USC 29, Washington 0	1974 Ohio St. 42, USC 21
1945	USC 25, Tennessee 0	

1975 USC 18, Ohio St. 17
1976 UCLA 23, Ohio St. 10
1977 USC 14, Michigan 6
1978 Washington 27, Michigan 20
1979 USC 17, Michigan 10
1980 USC 17, Ohio St. 16
1981 Michigan 23, Washington 6
1982 Washington 28, Iowa 0
1983 UCLA 24, Michigan 14
1984 UCLA 45, Illinois 9
1985 USC 20, Ohio St. 17
1986 UCLA 45, Iowa 28
1987 Arizona St. 22, Michigan 15
1988 Mich. St. 20, USC 17
1989 Michigan 22, USC 14
1990 USC 17, Michigan 10
1991 Washington 46, Iowa 34
1992 Washington 34, Michigan 14
1993 Michigan 38, Washington 31
1994 Wisconsin 21, UCLA 16
1995 Penn St. 38, Oregon 20
1996 USC 41, Northwestern 32
1997 Ohio St. 20, Arizona St. 17
1998 Michigan 21, Wash. St. 16
1999 Wisconsin 38, UCLA 31
2000 Wisconsin 17, Stanford 9
2001 Washington 34, Purdue 24
2002 Miami (FL) 37, Nebraska 14
2003 Oklahoma, 34, Washington St. 14

*Played at Durham, NC.

Orange Bowl, Miami, FL

1935	(Jan.) Bucknell 26, Miami (FL) 0	1941 Mississippi St. 14, Georgetown 7
1936	Catholic U. 20, Mississippi 19	1942 Georgia 40, TCU 26
1937	Duquesne 13, Mississippi St. 12	1943 Alabama 37, Boston Coll. 21
1938	Auburn 6, Michigan St. 0	1944 LSU 19, Texas A&M 14
1939	Tennessee 17, Oklahoma 0	1945 Tulsa 26, Georgia Tech 12
1940	Georgia Tech 21, Missouri 7	1946 Miami (FL) 13, Holy Cross 6

1947 Rice 8, Tennessee 0
1948 Georgia Tech 20, Kansas 14
1949 Texas 41, Georgia 28
1950 Santa Clara 21, Kentucky 13
1951 Clemson 15, Miami (FL) 14
1952 Georgia Tech 17, Baylor 14

1953 Alabama 61, Syracuse 6
1954 Oklahoma 7, Maryland 0
1955 Duke 34, Nebraska 7
1956 Oklahoma 20, Maryland 6
1957 Colorado 27, Clemson 21
1958 Oklahoma 48, Duke 21
1959 Oklahoma 21, Syracuse 6
1960 Georgia 14, Missouri 0
1961 Missouri 21, Navy 14
1962 LSU 25, Colorado 7
1963 Alabama 17, Oklahoma 0
1964 Nebraska 13, Auburn 7
1965 Texas 21, Alabama 17
1966 Alabama 39, Nebraska 28
1967 Florida 27, Georgia Tech 12
1968 Oklahoma 26, Tennessee 24
1969 Penn St. 15, Kansas 14

1970 Penn St. 10, Missouri 3
1971 Nebraska 17, LSU 12
1972 Nebraska 38, Alabama 6
1973 Nebraska 40, Notre Dame 6
1974 Penn St. 16, LSU 9
1975 Notre Dame 13, Alabama 11
1976 Oklahoma 14, Michigan 6
1977 Ohio St. 27, Colorado 10
1978 Arkansas 31, Oklahoma 6
1979 Oklahoma 31, Nebraska 24
1980 Oklahoma 24, Florida St. 7
1981 Oklahoma 18, Florida St. 17
1982 Clemson 22, Nebraska 15
1983 Nebraska 21, LSU 20
1984 Miami (FL) 31, Nebraska 30
1985 Washington 28, Oklahoma 17
1986 Oklahoma 25, Penn St. 10

1987 Oklahoma 42, Arkansas 8
1988 Miami (FL) 20, Oklahoma 14
1989 Miami (FL) 23, Nebraska 3
1990 Notre Dame 21, Colorado 6
1991 Colorado 10, Notre Dame 9
1992 Miami (FL) 22, Nebraska 0
1993 Florida St. 27, Nebraska 14
1994 Florida St. 18, Nebraska 16
1995 Nebraska 24, Miami (FL) 17
1996 Florida St. 31, Notre Dame 26
1996 (Dec.) Nebraska 41, Virginia Tech 21
1998 (Jan.) Nebraska 42, Tennessee 17
1999 Florida 31, Syracuse 10
2000 Michigan 35, Alabama 34 (OT)
2001 Oklahoma 13, Florida St. 2
2002 Florida 56, Maryland 23
2003 USC 38, Iowa 17

Sugar Bowl, New Orleans, LA

1935 (Jan.) Tulane 20, Temple 14
1936 TCU 3, LSU 2
1937 Santa Clara 21, LSU 14
1938 Santa Clara 6, LSU 0
1939 TCU 15, Carnegie Tech 7
1940 Texas A&M 14, Tulane 13
1941 Boston Col. 19, Tennessee 13
1942 Fordham 2, Missouri 0
1943 Tennessee 14, Tulsa 7
1944 Georgia Tech 20, Tulsa 18
1945 Duke 29, Alabama 26
1946 Oklahoma A&M 33, St. Mary's 13
1947 Georgia 20, N. Carolina 10
1948 Texas 27, Alabama 7
1949 Oklahoma 14, N. Carolina 6
1950 Oklahoma 35, LSU 0
1951 Kentucky 13, Oklahoma 7
1952 Maryland 28, Tennessee 13
1953 Georgia Tech 24, Mississippi 7
1954 Georgia Tech 42, West Virginia 19
1955 Navy 21, Mississippi 0
1956 Georgia Tech 7, Pittsburgh 0
1957 Baylor 13, Tennessee 7

1958 Mississippi 39, Texas 7
1959 LSU 7, Clemson 0
1960 Mississippi 21, LSU 0
1961 Mississippi 14, Rice 6
1962 Alabama 10, Arkansas 3
1963 Mississippi 17, Arkansas 13
1964 Alabama 12, Mississippi 7
1965 LSU 13, Syracuse 10
1966 Missouri 20, Florida 18
1967 Alabama 34, Nebraska 7
1968 LSU 20, Wyoming 13
1969 Arkansas 16, Georgia 2
1970 Mississippi 27, Arkansas 22
1971 Tennessee 34, Air Force 13
1972 Oklahoma 40, Auburn 22
1972 (Dec.) Oklahoma 14, Penn St. 0
1973 Notre Dame 24, Alabama 23
1974 Nebraska 13, Florida 10
1975 Alabama 13, Penn St. 6
1977 (Jan.) Pittsburgh 27, Georgia 3
1978 Alabama 35, Ohio St. 6
1979 Alabama 14, Penn St. 7
1980 Alabama 24, Arkansas 9

1981 Georgia 17, Notre Dame 10
1982 Pittsburgh 24, Georgia 20
1983 Penn St. 27, Georgia 23
1984 Auburn 9, Michigan 7
1985 Nebraska 28, LSU 10
1986 Tennessee 35, Miami (FL) 7
1987 Nebraska 30, LSU 15
1988 Syracuse 16, Auburn 16
1989 Florida St. 13, Auburn 7
1990 Miami (FL) 33, Alabama 25
1991 Tennessee 23, Virginia 22
1992 Notre Dame 39, Florida 28
1993 Alabama 34, Miami (FL) 13
1994 Florida 41, West Virginia 7
1995 Florida St. 23, Florida 17
1995 (Dec.) Virginia Tech 28, Texas 10
1997 (Jan.) Florida 52, Florida St. 20
1998 Florida St. 31, Ohio St. 14
1999 Ohio St. 24, Texas A&M 14
2000 Florida St. 46, Virginia Tech 29
2001 Miami (FL) 37, Florida 20
2002 LSU 47, Illinois 34
2003 Georgia 26, Florida St. 13

Cotton Bowl, Dallas, TX

1937 (Jan.) TCU 16, Marquette 6
1938 Rice 28, Colorado 14
1939 St. Mary's 20, Texas Tech 13
1940 Clemson 6, Boston Coll. 3
1941 Texas A&M 13, Fordham 12
1942 Alabama 29, Texas A&M 21
1943 Texas 14, Georgia Tech 7
1944 Randolph Field 7, Texas 7
1945 Oklahoma A&M 34, TCU 0
1946 Texas 40, Missouri 27
1947 Arkansas 0, LSU 0
1948 SMU 13, Penn St. 13
1949 SMU 21, Oregon 13
1950 Rice 27, North Carolina 13
1951 Tennessee 20, Texas 14
1952 Kentucky 20, TCU 7
1953 Texas 16, Tennessee 0
1954 Rice 28, Alabama 6
1955 Georgia Tech 14, Arkansas 6
1956 Mississippi 14, TCU 13
1957 TCU 28, Syracuse 27
1958 Navy 20, Rice 7
1959 TCU 0, Air Force 0

1960 Syracuse 23, Texas 14
1961 Duke 7, Arkansas 6
1962 Texas 12, Mississippi 7
1963 LSU 13, Texas 0
1964 Texas 28, Navy 6
1965 Arkansas 10, Nebraska 7
1966 LSU 14, Arkansas 7
1966 (Dec.) Georgia 24, SMU 9
1968 (Jan.) Texas A&M 20, Alabama 16
1969 Texas 36, Tennessee 13
1970 Texas 21, Notre Dame 17
1971 Notre Dame 24, Texas 11
1972 Penn St. 30, Texas 6
1973 Texas 17, Alabama 13
1974 Nebraska 19, Texas 3
1975 Penn St. 41, Baylor 20
1976 Arkansas 31, Georgia 10
1977 Houston 30, Maryland 21
1978 Notre Dame 38, Texas 10
1979 Notre Dame 35, Houston 34
1980 Houston 17, Nebraska 14
1981 Alabama 30, Baylor 2

1982 Texas 14, Alabama 12
1983 SMU 7, Pittsburgh 3
1984 Georgia 10, Texas 9
1985 Boston Coll. 45, Houston 28
1986 Texas A&M 36, Auburn 16
1987 Ohio St. 28, Texas A&M 12
1988 Texas A&M 35, Notre Dame 10
1989 UCLA 17, Arkansas 3
1990 Tennessee 31, Arkansas 27
1991 Miami (FL) 46, Texas 3
1992 Florida St. 10, Texas A&M 2
1993 Notre Dame 28, Texas A&M 3
1994 Notre Dame 24, Texas A&M 21
1995 USC. 55, Texas Tech 14
1996 Colorado 38, Oregon 6
1997 Brigham Young 19, Kansas St. 15
1998 UCLA 29, Texas A&M 23
1999 Texas 38, Mississippi St. 11
2000 Arkansas 27, Texas 6
2001 Kansas St. 35, Tennessee 21
2002 Oklahoma 10, Arkansas 3
2003 Texas 35, LSU 20

Sun Bowl, El Paso, TX (John Hancock Bowl, 1989-93)

1936 (Jan.) Hardin-Simmons 14,
    New Mexico St. 14
1937 Hardin-Simmons 34, Texas Mines 6
1938 West Virginia 7, Texas Tech 6
1939 Utah 26, New Mexico 0
1940 Catholic U. 0, Arizona St. 0
1941 Western Reserve 26, Arizona St. 13
1942 Tulsa 6, Texas Tech 0
1943 2d Air Force 13, Hardin-Simmons 7
1944 Southwestern (TX) 7, New Mexico 0
1945 Southwestern (TX) 35,
    Univ. of Mexico 0
1946 New Mexico 34, Denver 24
1947 Cincinnati 18, Virginia Tech 6
1948 Miami (OH) 13, Texas Tech 12
1949 West Virginia 21, Texas Mines 12
1950 Texas Western 33, Georgetown 20
1951 West Texas St. 14, Cincinnati 13
1952 Texas Tech 25, Pacific (CA) 14
1953 Pacific (CA) 26, S. Mississippi 7
1954 Texas Western 37, S. Miss. 14
1955 Texas Western 47, Florida St. 20
1956 Wyoming 21, Texas Tech 14
1957 Geo. Washington 13, TX Western 0

1958 Louisville 34, Drake 20
1958 (Dec.) Wyoming 14,
    Hardin-Simmons 6
1959 New Mexico St. 28, N. Texas St. 8
1960 New Mexico St. 20, Utah St. 13
1961 Villanova 17, Wichita 9
1962 West Texas St. 15, Ohio U. 14
1963 Oregon 21, SMU 14
1964 Georgia 7, Texas Tech 0
1965 Texas Western 13, TCU 12
1966 Wyoming 28, Florida St. 20
1967 UTEP 14, Mississippi 7
1968 Auburn 34, Arizona 10
1969 Nebraska 45, Georgia 6
1970 Georgia Tech. 17, Texas Tech 9
1971 LSU 33, Iowa St. 15
1972 North Carolina 32, Texas Tech 28
1973 Missouri 34, Auburn 17
1974 Mississippi St. 26,
    North Carolina 24
1975 Pittsburgh 33, Kansas 19
1977 (Jan.) Texas A&M 37, Florida 14
1977 (Dec.) Stanford 24, LSU 14
1978 Texas 42, Maryland 0

1979 Washington 14, Texas 7
1980 Nebraska 31, Mississippi St. 17
1981 Oklahoma 40, Houston 14
1982 North Carolina 26, Texas 10
1983 Alabama 28, SMU 7
1984 Maryland 28, Tennessee 27
1985 Georgia 13, Arizona 13
1986 Alabama 28, Washington 6
1987 Oklahoma St. 35, West Virginia 33
1988 Alabama 29, Army 28
1989 Pittsburgh 31, Texas A&M 28
1990 Michigan St. 17, USC 16
1991 UCLA 6, Illinois 3
1992 Baylor 20, Arizona 15
1993 Oklahoma 41, Texas Tech 10
1994 Texas 35, North Carolina 31
1995 Iowa 38, Washington 18
1996 Stanford 38, Michigan St. 0
1997 Arizona St. 17, Iowa 7
1998 TCU 28, USC 19
1999 Oregon 24, Minnesota 20
2000 Wisconsin 21, UCLA 20
2001 Washington St. 33, Purdue 27
2002 Purdue 34, Washington 24

Fiesta Bowl, Tempe, AZ

1971 (Dec.) Arizona St. 45, Florida St. 38	1983 Arizona St. 32, Oklahoma 21	1994 Arizona 29, Miami (FL) 0
1972 Arizona St. 49, Missouri 35	1984 Ohio St. 28, Pittsburgh 23	1995 Colorado 41, Notre Dame 24
1973 Arizona St. 28, Pittsburgh 7	1985 UCLA 39, Miami (FL) 37	1996 Nebraska 62, Florida 24
1974 Okla. St. 16, Brigham Young 6	1986 Michigan 27, Nebraska 23	1997 Penn St. 38, Texas 15
1975 Arizona St. 17, Nebraska 14	1987 Penn St. 14, Miami (FL) 10	1997 (Dec.) Kansas St. 35, Syracuse 18
1976 Oklahoma 41, Wyoming 7	1988 Florida St. 31, Nebraska 28	1999 (Jan.) Tennessee 23, Florida St. 16
1977 Penn St. 42, Arizona St. 30	1989 Notre Dame 34, W. Virginia 21	2000 Nebraska 31, Tennessee 21
1978 UCLA 10, Arkansas 10	1990 Florida St. 41, Nebraska 17	2001 Oregon St. 41, Notre Dame 9
1979 Pittsburgh 16, Arizona 10	1991 Louisville 34, Alabama 7	2002 Oregon 38, Colorado 16
1980 Penn St. 31, Ohio St. 19	1992 Penn St. 42, Tennessee 17	2003 Ohio St. 31, Miami 24 (2 OT)
1982 (Jan.) Penn St. 26, USC 10	1993 Syracuse 26, Colorado 22	

Gator Bowl, Jacksonville, FL

1946 (Jan.) Wake Forest 26, S. Carolina 14	1965 (Dec.) GA Tech 31, Texas Tech 21	1984 Oklahoma St. 21, S. Carolina 14
1947 Oklahoma 34, N. Carolina St. 13	1966 Tennessee 18, Syracuse 12	1985 Florida St. 34, Oklahoma St. 23
1948 Maryland 20, Georgia 20	1967 Penn St. 17, Florida St. 17	1986 Clemson 27, Stanford 21
1949 Clemson 24, Missouri 23	1968 Missouri 35, Alabama 10	1987 LSU 30, S. Carolina 13
1950 Maryland 20, Missouri 7	1969 Florida 14, Tennessee 13	1989 (Jan.) Georgia 34, Michigan St. 27
1951 Wyoming 20, Washington & Lee 7	1971 (Jan.) Auburn 35, Mississippi 28	1989 (Dec.) Clemson 27, W. Virginia 7
1952 Miami (FL) 14, Clemson 0	1971 (Dec.) Georgia 7, N. Carolina 3	1991 (Jan.) Michigan 35, Mississippi 3
1953 Florida 14, Tulsa 13	1972 Auburn 24, Colorado 3	1991 (Dec.) Oklahoma 48, Virginia 14
1954 Texas Tech 35, Auburn 13	1973 Texas Tech 28, Tennessee 19	1992 Florida 27, N. Carolina St. 10
1954 (Dec.) Auburn 33, Baylor 13	1974 Auburn 27, Texas 3	1993 Alabama 24, N. Carolina 10
1955 Vanderbilt 25, Auburn 13	1975 Maryland 13, Florida 0	1994 Tennessee 45, Virginia Tech 23
1956 Georgia Tech 21, Pittsburgh 14	1976 Notre Dame 20, Penn St. 9	1996 (Jan.) Syracuse 41, Clemson 0
1957 Tennessee 3, Texas A&M 0	1977 Pittsburgh 34, Clemson 3	1997 N. Carolina 20, W. Virginia 13
1958 Mississippi 7, Florida 3	1978 Clemson 17, Ohio St. 15	1998 N. Carolina 42, Virginia Tech 3
1960 (Jan.) Arkansas 14, Georgia Tech 7	1979 N. Carolina 17, Michigan 15	1999 Georgia Tech 35, Notre Dame 28
1960 (Dec.) Florida 13, Baylor 12	1980 Pittsburgh 37, S. Carolina 9	2000 Miami (FL) 28, Georgia Tech 13
1961 Penn St. 30, Georgia Tech 15	1981 N. Carolina 31, Arkansas 27	2001 Virginia Tech 41, Clemson 20
1962 Florida 17, Penn St. 7	1982 Florida St. 31, West Virginia 12	2002 Florida St. 30, Virginia Tech 17
1963 N. Carolina 35, Air Force 0	1983 Florida 14, Iowa 6	2003 N. Carolina St. 28, Notre Dame 6
1965 (Jan.) Florida St. 36, Okla.19		

Liberty Bowl, Memphis, TN

1959 (Dec.) Penn St. 7, Alabama 0	1974 Tennessee 7, Maryland 3	1989 Mississippi 42, Air Force 29
1960 Penn St. 41, Oregon 12	1975 USC 20, Texas A&M 0	1990 Air Force 23, Ohio St. 11
1961 Syracuse 15, Miami (FL) 14	1976 Alabama 36, UCLA 6	1991 Air Force 38, Mississippi St. 15
1962 Oregon St. 6, Villanova 0	1977 Nebraska 21, N. Carolina 17	1992 Mississippi 13, Air Force 0
1963 Mississippi St. 16, N. Carolina St. 12	1978 Missouri 20, LSU 15	1993 Louisville 18, Michigan St. 7
1964 Utah 32, West Virginia 6	1979 Penn St. 9, Tulane 6	1994 Illinois 30, East Carolina 0
1965 Mississippi 13, Auburn 7	1980 Purdue 28, Missouri 25	1995 East Carolina 19, Stanford 13
1966 Miami (FL) 14, Virginia Tech 7	1981 Ohio St. 31, Navy 28	1996 Syracuse 30, Houston 17
1967 N. Carolina St. 14, Georgia 7	1982 Alabama 21, Illinois 15	1997 So. Mississippi 41, Pittsburgh 7
1968 Mississippi 34, Virginia Tech 17	1983 Notre Dame 19, Boston Coll. 18	1998 Tulane 41, Brigham Young 27
1969 Colorado 47, Alabama 33	1984 Auburn 21, Arkansas 15	1999 So. Mississippi 23, Colorado St. 17
1970 Tulane 17, Colorado 3	1985 Baylor 21, LSU 7	2000 Colorado St. 22, Louisville 17
1971 Tennessee 14, Arkansas 13	1986 Tennessee 21, Minnesota 14	2001 Louisville 28, BYU 10
1972 Georgia Tech 31, Iowa St. 30	1987 Georgia 20, Arkansas 17	2002 TCU 17, Colorado St. 3
1973 N. Carolina St. 31, Kansas 18	1988 Indiana 34, S. Carolina 10	

Capital One Bowl, Orlando, FL
(Florida Citrus Bowl 1984-2002, Tangerine Bowl, 1947-1983)

1947 (Jan.) Catawba 31, Maryville 6	1964 E. Carolina 14, Massachusetts 13	1984 Georgia 17, Florida St. 17
1948 Catawba 7, Marshall 0	1965 E. Carolina 31, Maine 0	1985 Ohio St. 10, Brigham Young 7
1949 Murray St. 21, Sul Ross St. 21	1966 Morgan St. 14, West Chester 6	1987 (Jan.) Auburn 16, USC 7
1950 St. Vincent 7, Emory & Henry 6	1967 Tenn.-Martin 25, West Chester 8	1988 Clemson 35, Penn St. 10
1951 Morris Harvey 35, Emory & Henry 14	1968 Richmond 49, Ohio U. 42	1989 Clemson 13, Oklahoma 6
1952 Stetson 35, Arkansas St. 20	1969 Toledo 56, Davidson 33	1990 Illinois 31, Virginia 21
1953 East Texas St. 33, Tenn. Tech 0	1970 Toledo 40, William & Mary 12	1991 Georgia Tech 45, Nebraska 21
1954 East Texas St. 7, Arkansas St. 7	1971 Toledo 28, Richmond 3	1992 California 37, Clemson 13
1955 Neb.-Omaha 7, E. Kentucky 6	1972 Tampa 21, Kent St. 18	1993 Georgia 21, Ohio St. 14
1956 Juniata 6, Missouri Valley 6	1973 Miami (OH) 16, Florida 7	1994 Penn St. 31, Tennessee 13
1957 West Texas St. 20, So. Miss. 13	1974 Miami (OH) 21, Georgia 10	1995 Alabama 24, Ohio St. 17
1958 East Texas St. 10, So. Miss. 9	1975 Miami (OH) 20, S. Carolina 7	1996 Tennessee 20, Ohio St. 14
1958 (Dec.) East Texas St. 26, Missouri Valley 7	1976 Okla. St. 49, Brigham Young 21	1997 Tennessee 48, Northwestern 28
1960 (Jan.) Middle Tennessee 21, Presbyterian 12	1977 Florida St. 40, Texas Tech 17	1998 Florida 21, Penn St. 6
1960 (Dec.) Citadel 27, Tenn. Tech 0	1978 N. Carolina St. 30, Pittsburgh 17	1999 Michigan 45, Arkansas 31
1961 Lamar 21, Middle Tennessee 14	1979 LSU 34, Wake Forest 10	2000 Michigan St. 37, Florida 34
1962 Houston 49, Miami (OH) 21	1980 Florida 35, Maryland 20	2001 Michigan 31, Auburn 28
1963 Western Ky. 27, Coast Guard 0	1981 Missouri 19, So. Mississippi 17	2002 Tennessee 45, Michigan 17
	1982 Auburn 33, Boston College 26	2003 Auburn 13, Penn St. 9
	1983 Tennessee 30, Maryland 23	

Peach Bowl, Atlanta, GA

1968 (Dec.) LSU 31, Florida St. 27	1981 (Jan.) Miami (FL) 20, Virginia Tech 10	1993 N. Carolina 21, Mississippi St. 17
1969 W. Virginia 14, S. Carolina 3	1981 (Dec.) W. Virginia 26, Florida 6	1993 (Dec.) Clemson 14, Kentucky 13
1970 Arizona St. 48, N. Carolina 26	1982 Iowa 28, Tennessee 22	1995 (Jan.) N. Carolina St. 28, Miss. St. 24
1971 Mississippi 41, Georgia Tech 18	1983 Florida St. 28, N. Carolina 3	1995 (Dec.) Virginia 34, Georgia 27
1972 N. Carolina St. 49, W. Virginia 13	1984 Virginia 27, Purdue 22	1996 LSU 10, Clemson 7
1973 Georgia 17, Maryland 16	1985 Army 31, Illinois 29	1998 (Jan.) Auburn 21, Clemson 17
1974 Vanderbilt 6, Texas Tech 6	1986 Va. Tech 25, N. Carolina St. 24	1998 (Dec.) Georgia 35, Virginia 33
1975 W. Virginia 13, N. Carolina St. 10	1988 (Jan.) Tennessee 28, Indiana 22	1999 Mississippi St. 17, Clemson 7
1976 Kentucky 21, N. Carolina 0	1988 (Dec.) N. Carolina St. 28, Iowa 23	2000 LSU 28, Georgia Tech 14
1977 N. Carolina St. 24, Iowa St. 14	1989 Syracuse 19, Georgia 18	2001 North Carolina 16, Auburn 10
1978 Purdue 41, Georgia Tech. 21	1990 Auburn 27, Indiana 23	2002 Maryland 30, Tennessee 3
1979 Baylor 24, Clemson 18	1992 (Jan.) E. Carolina 37, NC St. 34	

Other Bowl Results, Late 2002- Early 2003

Alamo Bowl, San Antonio, TX: Wisconsin 31, Colorado 28 (OT)

Continental Tire Bowl, Charlotte, NC: Virginia 48, West Virginia 22

GMAC Bowl, Mobile, AL.: Marshall 38, Louisville 15

Hawaii Bowl, Honolulu, HI: Tulane 36, Hawaii 28

Holiday Bowl, San Diego, CA: Kansas State 34, Arizona State 27

Houston Bowl, Houston, TX: Oklahoma State 33, Southern Miss 23

Humanitarian Bowl, Boise, ID: Boise State 34, Iowa State 16

Independence Bowl, Shreveport, LA: Mississippi 27, Nebraska 23

Insight Bowl, Tempe, AZ.: Pittsburgh 38, Oregon State 13

Las Vegas Bowl, Las Vegas, NV: UCLA 27, New Mexico 13

Motor City Bowl, Detroit, MI: Boston College 51, Toledo 25

Music City Bowl, Nashville, TN: Minnesota 29, Arkansas 14

New Orleans Bowl, New Orleans, LA: North Texas 24, Cincinnati 19

Outback Bowl, Tampa, FL: Michigan 38, Florida 30

San Francisco Bowl, San Francisco, CA: Virginia Tech 20, Air Force 13

Seattle Bowl, Seattle, WA: Wake Forest 38, Oregon 17

Silicon Valley Classic, San Jose, CA: Fresno State 30, Georgia Tech 21

Tangerine Bowl, Orlando, FL: Texas Tech 55, Clemson 15

All-Time NCAA Division I-A Statistical Leaders

(at end of 2002 season)

Career Rushing Yards

Player, team	Yrs	Carries	Yds	Avg
Ron Dayne, Wisconsin	1996-99	1,115	6,397	5.74
Ricky Williams, Texas	1995-98	1,011	6,279	6.21
Tony Dorsett, Pittsburgh	1973-76	1,074	6,082	5.66
Charles White, USC	1976-79	1,023	5,598	5.47
Travis Prentice, Miami (OH)	1996-99	1,138	5,596	4.92

Career Passing Yards

Player, team	Yrs	Comp/Att	Yds
Ty Detmer, BYU	1988-91	958/1,530	15,031
Tim Rattay, Louisiana Tech	1997-99	1,015/1,552	12,746
Chris Redman, Louisville	1996-99	1,031/1,679	12,541
Kliff Kingsbury, Texas Tech.	1999-02	1,231/1,883	12,429
Todd Santos, San Diego St.	1984-87	910/1,484	11,425

Career Rushing Yard/Game (min. 2,500 yds.)

Player, team	Yrs	Carries	Yds	Avg/Game
Ed Marinaro, Cornell	1969-71	918	4,715	174.6
O.J. Simpson, USC	1967-68	621	3,124	164.4
Herschel Walker, Georgia	1980-82	994	5,259	159.4
LeShon Johnson, N. Illinois	1992-93	592	3,314	150.6
Ron Dayne, Wisconsin	1996-99	1,115	6,397	148.8

Career Receiving Yards

Player, team	Yrs	Rec	Yds	Avg
Trevor Insley, Nevada	1996-99	298	5,005	16.8
Marcus Harris, Wyoming	1993-96	259	4,518	17.4
Ryan Yarborough, Wyoming	1990-93	229	4,357	19.0
Troy Edwards, Louisiana Tech	1996-98	280	4,352	15.5
Aaron Turner, Pacific (CA)	1989-92	266	4,345	16.3

Selected College Division I Football Teams in 2002

(2002 record does not include bowl games or Division I-AA playoff games; coaches at the start of 2003 season)

Team	Nickname	Team colors	Conference	Coach	2002 record (W-L)
Air Force	Falcons	Blue & silver	Mountain West.	Fisher DeBerry	8-5
Akron	Zips	Blue & gold	Mid-American	Lee Owens	4-8
Alabama	Crimson Tide	Crimson & white	Southeastern	Dennis Franchione	10-3
Arizona	Wildcats	Cardinal & navy	Pacific Ten	John Mackovic	4-8
Arizona State	Sun Devils	Maroon & gold	Pacific Ten	Dirk Koetter	8-6
Arkansas	Razorbacks	Cardinal & white	Southeastern	Houston Nutt	9-5
Arkansas State	Indians	Scarlet & black	Big West	Joe Hollis	6-7
Army	Cadets, Black Knights	Black, gold, gray	Conference USA	Todd Berry	1-11
Auburn	Tigers	Burnt orange & navy	Southeastern	Tommy Tuberville	9-4
Ball State	Cardinals	Cardinal & white	Mid-American	Bill Lynch	6-6
Baylor	Bears	Green & gold	Big Twelve	Kevin Steele	3-9
Boston College	Eagles	Maroon & gold	Big East	Tom O'Brien	9-4
Bowling Green	Falcons	Orange & brown	Mid-American	Urban Meyer	9-3
Brigham Young (BYU)	Cougars	Royal blue, white, tan.	Mountain West.	Gary Crowton	5-7
Brown	Bears	Brown, cardinal, white	Ivy League	Phil Estes	2-8
California	Golden Bears	Blue & gold	Pacific Ten	Jeff Tedford	7-5
Central Michigan	Chippewas	Maroon & gold	Mid-American	Mike DeBord	4-8
Cincinnati	Bearcats	Red & black	Conference USA	Rick Minter	7-7
Citadel	Bulldogs	Blue & white	Southern	Ellis Johnson	3-9
Clemson	Tigers	Purple & orange	Atlantic Coast	Tommy Bowden	7-6
Colgate	Red Raiders	Maroon, gray, & white	Patriot League	Dick Biddle	9-3
Colorado	Buffaloes	Silver, gold, & black	Big Twelve	Gary Barnett	9-5
Colorado State	Rams	Green & gold	Mountain West.	Sonny Lubick	10-4
Columbia	Lions	Columbia blue & white	Ivy League	Ray Tellier	1-9
Connecticut	Huskies	Blue & white	Independent	Randy Edsall	6-6
Cornell	Big Red	Carnelian & white	Ivy League	Tim Pendergast	4-6
Dartmouth	Big Green	Dartmouth green & white	Ivy League	John Lyons	3-7
Delaware	Fightin' Blue Hens	Blue & gold	Atlantic Ten	Harold Raymond	6-6
Delaware State	Hornets	Red & blue	Mid-Eastern Athletic	Ben Blacknall	4-8
Duke	Blue Devils	Royal blue & white	Atlantic Coast	Carl Franks	2-10
East Carolina	Pirates	Purple & gold	Conference USA	Steve Logan	4-8
East Tennessee State	Buccaneers	Blue & gold	Southern	Paul Hamilton	4-8
Eastern Illinois	Panthers	Blue & gray	Ohio Valley	Bob Spoo	8-4
Eastern Kentucky	Colonels	Maroon & white	Ohio Valley	Roy Kidd	8-4
Eastern Michigan	Eagles	Dark green & white	Mid-American	Jeff Woodruff	3-9
Eastern Washington	Eagles	Red & white	Big Sky	Paul Wulff	6-5
Florida	Gators	Orange & blue	Southeastern	Ron Zook	8-5
Florida A&M	Rattlers	Orange & green	Mid-Eastern Athletic	Billy Joe	7-5
Florida State	Seminoles	Garnet & gold	Atlantic Coast	Bobby Bowden	9-5
Fresno State	Bulldogs	Cardinal & blue	Western Athletic	Pat Hill	9-5
Furman	Paladins	Purple & white	Southern	Bobby Johnson	8-4
Georgia	Bulldogs	Red & black	Southeastern	Mark Richt	13-1
Georgia Southern	Eagles	Blue & white	Southern	Paul Johnson	11-3
Georgia Tech	Yellow Jackets	Old gold & white	Atlantic Coast	Chan Gailey	7-6
Grambling State	Tigers	Black & gold	Southwestern	Doug Williams	11-2
Harvard	Crimson	Crimson, black, white	Ivy League	Tim Murphy	7-3
Holy Cross	Crusaders	Royal purple	Patriot League	Dan Allen	4-8
Houston	Cougars	Scarlet & white	Conference USA	Dana Dimel	5-7
Howard	Bison	Blue, white & red	Mid-Eastern Athletic	Steve Wilson	6-5
Idaho	Vandals	Silver & gold	Big West	Tom Cable	2-10
Idaho State	Bengals	Orange & black	Big Sky	Larry Lewis	8-3

Team	Nickname	Team colors	Conference	Coach	2002 record (W-L)
Illinois	Fighting Illini	Orange & blue	Big Ten	Ron Turner	5-7
Illinois State	Redbirds	Red & white	Gateway	Denver Johnson	6-5
Indiana	Hoosiers	Cream & crimson	Big Ten	Gerry DiNardo	3-9
Indiana State	Sycamores	Blue & white	Gateway	Tim McGuire	5-7
Iowa	Hawkeyes	Old gold & black	Big Ten	Kirk Ferentz	11-2
Iowa State	Cyclones	Cardinal & gold	Big Twelve	Dan McCarney	7-7
Jackson State	Tigers	Blue & white	Southwestern	Robert Hughes	7-4
James Madison	Dukes	Purple & gold	Atlantic Ten	Mickey Matthews	5-7
Kansas	Jayhawks	Crimson & blue	Big Twelve	Mark Mangino	2-10
Kansas State	Wildcats	Purple & white	Big Twelve	Bill Snyder	11-2
Kent State	Golden Flashes	Navy blue & gold	Mid-American	Dean Pees	3-9
Kentucky	Wildcats	Blue & white	Southeastern	Guy Morriss	7-5
Lafayette	Leopards	Maroon & white	Patriot League	Frank Tavani	7-5
Lehigh	Mountain Hawks	Brown & white	Patriot League	Pete Lembo	8-4
Liberty	Flames	Red, white, blue	Independent	Ken Karcher	2-9
Louisiana-Lafayette	Ragin' Cajuns	Vermilion & white	Independent	Rickey Bustle	3-9
Louisiana-Monroe	Indians	Maroon & gold	Independent	Bobby Keasler	3-9
Louisiana State (LSU)	Fighting Tigers	Purple & gold	Southeastern	Nick Saban	8-5
Louisiana Tech	Bulldogs	Red & blue	Independent	Jack Bicknell III	4-8
Louisville	Cardinals	Red, black, white	Conference USA	John L. Smith	7-6
Maine	Black Bears	Blue & white	Atlantic Ten	Jack Cosgrove	11-3
Marshall	Thundering Herd	Green & white	Mid-American	Bob Pruett	11-2
Maryland	Terrapins	Red, white, black, gold	Atlantic Coast	Ralph Friedgen	11-3
Massachusetts	Minutemen	Maroon & white	Atlantic Ten	Mark Whipple	8-4
McNeese State	Cowboys	Blue & gold	Southland	Tommy Tate	13-2
Memphis	Tigers	Blue & gray	Conference USA	Tommy West	3-9
Miami (Florida)	Hurricanes	Orange, green, white	Big East	Larry Coker	12-1
Miami (Ohio)	RedHawks	Red & white	Mid-American	Terry Hoeppner	7-5
Michigan	Wolverines	Maize & blue	Big Ten	Lloyd Carr	10-3
Michigan State	Spartans	Green & white	Big Ten	Bobby Williams	4-8
Middle Tennessee St.	Blue Raiders	Blue & white	Independent	Andy McCollum	4-8
Minnesota	Golden Gophers	Maroon & gold	Big Ten	Glen Mason	8-5
Mississippi	Rebels	Cardinal red & navy	Southeastern	David Cutcliffe	7-6
Mississippi State	Bulldogs	Maroon & white	Southeastern	Jackie Sherrill	3-9
Mississippi Valley	Delta Devils	Green & white	Southwestern	LaTraia Jones	5-6
Missouri	Tigers	Old gold & black	Big Twelve	Gary Pinkel	5-7
Montana	Grizzlies	Copper, silver, gold	Big Sky	Joe Glenn	11-3
Montana State	Bobcats	Blue & gold	Big Sky	Mike Kramer	7-6
Morehead State	Eagles	Blue & gold	Independent	Matt Ballard	9-3
Morgan State	Bears	Blue & orange	Mid-Eastern Athletic	Stanley Mitchell	7-5
Murray State	Racers	Blue & gold	Ohio Valley	Joe Pannunzio	7-5
Navy	Midshipmen	Navy blue & gold	Independent	Paul Johnson	2-10
Nebraska	Cornhuskers	Scarlet & cream	Big Twelve	Frank Solich	7-7
Nevada	Wolf Pack	Silver & blue	Western Athletic	Chris Tormey	5-7
Nev.-Las Vegas (UNLV)	Runnin' Rebels	Scarlet & gray	Mountain West	John Robinson	5-7
New Hampshire	Wildcats	Blue & white	Atlantic Ten	Sean McDonnell	3-8
New Mexico	Lobos	Cherry & silver	Mountain West	Rocky Long	7-7
New Mexico State	Aggies	Crimson & white	Big West	Tony Samuel	7-5
Nicholls St.	Colonels	Red & gray	Southland	Daryl Daye	7-4
North Carolina	Tar Heels	Carolina blue & white	Atlantic Coast	John Bunting	3-9
North Carolina A & T	Aggies	Blue & gold	Mid-Eastern Athletic	Bill Hayes	4-8
North Carolina State	Wolfpack	Red & white	Atlantic Coast	Chuck Amato	11-3
North Texas	Mean Green	Green & white	Big West	Darrell Dickey	8-5
Northeastern	Huskies	Red & black	Atlantic Ten	Don Brown	10-3
Northern Arizona	Lumberjacks	Blue & gold	Big Sky	Jerome Souers	6-5
Northern Illinois	Huskies	Cardinal & black	Mid-American	Joe Novak	8-4
Northern Iowa	Panthers	Purple & old gold	Gateway	Mark Farley	5-6
Northwestern	Wildcats	Purple & white	Big Ten	Randy Walker	3-9
Northwestern State	Demons	Purple, white, & orange	Southland	Steve Roberts	9-4
Notre Dame	Fighting Irish	Gold & blue	Independent	Tyrone Willingham	10-3
Ohio	Bobcats	Hunter green & white	Mid-American	Brian Knorr	4-8
Ohio State	Buckeyes	Scarlet & gray	Big Ten	Jim Tressel	14-0
Oklahoma	Sooners	Crimson & cream	Big Twelve	Bob Stoops	12-2
Oklahoma State	Cowboys	Orange & black	Big Twelve	Les Miles	8-5
Oregon	Ducks	Green & yellow	Pacific Ten	Mike Bellotti	7-6
Oregon State	Beavers	Orange & black	Pacific Ten	Dennis Erickson	8-5
Penn State	Nittany Lions	Blue & white	Big Ten	Joe Paterno	9-4
Pennsylvania	Quakers	Red & blue	Ivy League	Al Bagnoli	9-1
Pittsburgh	Panthers	Blue & gold	Big East	Walt Harris	9-4
Princeton	Tigers	Orange & black	Ivy League	Roger Hughes	6-4
Purdue	Boilermakers	Old gold & black	Big Ten	Joe Tiller	7-6
Rhode Island	Rams	Light & dark blue, white	Atlantic Ten	Tim Stowers	3-9
Rice	Owls	Blue & gray	Western Athletic	Ken Hatfield	4-7
Richmond	Spiders	Red & white	Atlantic Ten	Jim Reid	4-7
Rutgers	Scarlet Knights	Scarlet	Big East	Greg Schiano	1-11
Sam Houston State	Bearkats	Orange & white	Southland	Ron Randleman	4-7
Samford	Bulldogs	Crimson & blue	Independent	Pete Hurt	4-7
San Diego State	Aztecs	Scarlet & black	Mountain West	Tom Craft	4-7
San Jose State	Spartans	Gold, white, blue	Western Athletic	Fitz Hill	6-7
South Carolina	Gamecocks	Garnet & black	Southeastern	Lou Holtz	5-7
South Carolina State	Bulldogs	Garnet & blue	Mid-Eastern Athletic	Willie E. Jeffries	7-5
SE Missouri State	Indians	Red & white	Ohio Valley	Tim Billings	8-4
Southern California (USC)	Trojans	Cardinal & gold	Pacific Ten	Pete Carroll	11-2
Southern Illinois	Salukis	Maroon & white	Gateway	Jerry Kill	4-8
Southern Methodist (SMU)	Mustangs	Red & blue	Western Athletic	Mike Cavan	3-9
Southern Mississippi	Golden Eagles	Black & gold	Conference USA	Jeff Bower	7-6
SW Missouri State	Bears	Maroon & white	Gateway	Randy Ball	4-7
SW Texas State	Bobcats	Maroon & gold	Southland	Manny Matsakis	4-7
Stanford	Cardinal	Cardinal & white	Pacific Ten	Buddy Teevens	2-9
Stephen F. Austin	Lumberjacks	Purple & white	Southland	Mike Santiago	6-5

Team	Nickname	Team colors	Conference	Coach	2002 record (W-L)
Syracuse	Orangemen	Orange	Big East	Paul Pasqualoni	4-8
Temple	Owls	Cherry & white	Big East	Bobby Wallace	4-8
Tennessee	Volunteers	Orange & white	Southeastern	Phillip Fulmer	8-5
Tennessee-Chattanooga	Mocs	Navy blue & gold	Southern	Rodney Allison	2-10
Tennessee-Martin	Skyhawks	Orange, white, blue	Ohio Valley	Sam McCorkle	2-10
Tennessee State	Tigers	Royal blue & white	Ohio Valley	James Reese	2-10
Tennessee Tech	Golden Eagles	Purple & gold	Ohio Valley	Mike Hennigan	5-7
Texas	Longhorns	Burnt orange & white	Big Twelve	Mack Brown	11-2
Texas A & M	Aggies	Maroon & white	Big Twelve	R. C. Slocum	6-6
Texas Christian (TCU)	Horned Frogs	Purple & white	Western Athletic	Gary Patterson	10-2
Texas Southern	Tigers	Maroon & gray	Southwestern	Bill Thomas	4-7
Texas Tech	Red Raiders	Scarlet & black	Big Twelve	Mike Leach	9-5
Toledo	Rockets	Blue & gold	Mid-American	Tom Amstutz	9-5
Troy State	Trojans	Cardinal & black	Southland	Larry Blakeney	4-8
Tulane	Green Wave	Olive green & sky blue	Conference USA	Chris Scelfo	8-5
Tulsa	Golden Hurricane	Blue, gold, crimson	Western Athletic	Keith Burns	1-11
UCLA	Bruins	Blue & gold	Pacific Ten	Bob Toledo	8-5
Utah	Utes	Crimson & white	Mountain West	Ron McBride	5-6
Utah State	Aggies	Navy blue & white	Big West	Mick Dennehy	4-7
UTEP (Texas-El Paso)	Miners	Orange, blue, silver	Western Athletic	Gary Nord	2-10
Vanderbilt	Commodores	Black & gold	Southeastern	Bobby Johnson	2-10
Villanova	Wildcats	Blue & white	Atlantic Ten	Andy Talley	11-4
Virginia	Cavaliers	Burnt Orange & blue	Atlantic Coast	Al Groh	9-5
Virginia Military Inst. (VMI)	Keydets	Red, white, yellow	Southern	Cal McCombs	6-6
Virginia Tech	Hokies	Burnt orange & maroon	Big East	Frank Beamer	10-4
Wake Forest	Demon Deacons	Old gold & black	Atlantic Coast	Jim Grobe	7-6
Washington	Huskies	Purple & gold	Pacific Ten	Rick Neuheisel	7-6
Washington State	Cougars	Crimson & gray	Pacific Ten	Mike Price	10-3
Weber State	Wildcats	Royal purple & white	Big Sky	Jerry Graybeal	3-8
West Virginia	Mountaineers	Old gold & blue	Big East	Rich Rodriquez	9-4
Western Carolina	Catamounts	Purple & gold	Southern	Bill Bleil	5-6
Western Illinois	Leathernecks	Purple & gold	Gateway	Don Patterson	11-2
Western Kentucky	Hilltoppers	Red & white	Ohio Valley	Jack Harbaugh	12-3
Western Michigan	Broncos	Brown & gold	Mid-American	Gary Darnell	4-8
William & Mary	Tribe	Green, gold, silver	Atlantic Ten	Jimmye Laycock	6-5
Wisconsin	Badgers	Cardinal & white	Big Ten	Barry Alvarez	8-6
Wyoming	Cowboys	Brown & gold	Mountain West	Vic Koenning	2-10
Yale	Bulldogs, Elis	Yale blue & white	Ivy League	Jack Siedlecki	6-4
Youngstown State	Penguins	Red & white	Gateway	Jon Heacock	7-4

Heisman Trophy Winners

Awarded annually to the nation's outstanding college football player by the Downtown Athletic Club.

1935 Jay Berwanger, Chicago, HB	1958 Pete Dawkins, Army, HB	1981 Marcus Allen, USC, RB
1936 Larry Kelley, Yale, E	1959 Billy Cannon, LSU, HB	1982 Herschel Walker, Georgia, RB
1937 Clinton Frank, Yale, HB	1960 Joe Bellino, Navy, HB	1983 Mike Rozier, Nebraska, RB
1938 David O'Brien, Texas Christian, QB	1961 Ernest Davis, Syracuse, HB	1984 Doug Flutie, Boston College, QB
1939 Nile Kinnick, Iowa, HB	1962 Terry Baker, Oregon St., QB	1985 Bo Jackson, Auburn, RB
1940 Tom Harmon, Michigan, HB	1963 Roger Staubach, Navy, QB	1986 Vinny Testaverde, Miami, QB
1941 Bruce Smith, Minnesota, HB	1964 John Huarte, Notre Dame, QB	1987 Tim Brown, Notre Dame, WR
1942 Frank Sinkwich, Georgia, HB	1965 Mike Garrett, USC, HB	1988 Barry Sanders, Oklahoma St., RB
1943 Angelo Bertelli, Notre Dame, QB	1966 Steve Spurrier, Florida, QB	1989 Andre Ware, Houston, QB
1944 Leslie Horvath, Ohio St., QB	1967 Gary Beban, UCLA, QB	1990 Ty Detmer, BYU, QB
1945 Felix Blanchard, Army, FB	1968 O. J. Simpson, USC, RB	1991 Desmond Howard, Michigan, WR
1946 Glenn Davis, Army, HB	1969 Steve Owens, Oklahoma, RB	1992 Gino Torretta, Miami, QB
1947 John Lujack, Notre Dame, QB	1970 Jim Plunkett, Stanford, QB	1993 Charlie Ward, Florida St., QB
1948 Doak Walker, SMU, HB	1971 Pat Sullivan, Auburn, QB	1994 Rashaan Salaam, Colorado, RB
1949 Leon Hart, Notre Dame, E	1972 Johnny Rodgers, Nebraska, RB-WR	1995 Eddie George, Ohio St., RB
1950 Vic Janowicz, Ohio St., HB	1973 John Cappelletti, Penn St., RB	1996 Danny Wuerffel, Florida, QB
1951 Richard Kazmaier, Princeton, HB	1974 Archie Griffin, Ohio St., RB	1997 Charles Woodson, Michigan, CB
1952 Billy Vessels, Oklahoma, HB	1975 Archie Griffin, Ohio St., RB	1998 Ricky Williams, Texas, RB
1953 John Lattner, Notre Dame, HB	1976 Tony Dorsett, Pittsburgh, RB	1999 Ron Dayne, Wisconsin, RB
1954 Alan Ameche, Wisconsin, FB	1977 Earl Campbell, Texas, RB	2000 Chris Weinke, Florida St., QB
1955 Howard Cassady, Ohio St., HB	1978 Billy Sims, Oklahoma, RB	2001 Eric Crouch, Nebraska, QB
1956 Paul Hornung, Notre Dame, QB	1979 Charles White, USC, RB	2002 Carson Palmer, USC, QB
1957 John Crow, Texas A & M, HB	1980 George Rogers, S. Carolina, RB	

Outland Award Winners

Honoring the outstanding interior lineman selected by the Football Writers Association of America.

1946 George Connor, Notre Dame, T	1965 Tommy Nobis, Texas, G	1984 Bruce Smith, Virginia Tech, DT
1947 Joe Steffy, Army, G	1966 Loyd Phillips, Arkansas, T	1985 Mike Ruth, Boston College, NG
1948 Bill Fischer, Notre Dame, G	1967 Ron Yary, Southern Cal, T	1986 Jason Buck, BYU, DT
1949 Ed Bagdon, Michigan St., G	1968 Bill Stanfill, Georgia, T	1987 Chad Hennings, Air Force, DT
1950 Bob Gain, Kentucky, T	1969 Mike Reid, Penn St., DT	1988 Tracy Rocker, Auburn, DT
1951 Jim Weatherall, Oklahoma, T	1970 Jim Stillwagon, Ohio St., MG	1989 Mohammed Elewonibi, BYU, G
1952 Dick Modzelewski, Maryland, T	1971 Larry Jacobson, Nebraska, DT	1990 Russell Maryland, Miami (FL), DT
1953 J. D. Roberts, Oklahoma, G	1972 Rich Glover, Nebraska, MG	1991 Steve Emtman, Washington, DT
1954 Bill Brooks, Arkansas, G	1973 John Hicks, Ohio St., OT	1992 Will Shields, Nebraska, G
1955 Calvin Jones, Iowa, G	1974 Randy White, Maryland, DE	1993 Rob Waldrop, Arizona, NG
1956 Jim Parker, Ohio St., G	1975 Lee Roy Selmon, Oklahoma, DT	1994 Zach Wiegert, Nebraska, OT
1957 Alex Karras, Iowa, T	1976 Ross Browner, Notre Dame, DE	1995 Jonathan Ogden, UCLA, OT
1958 Zeke Smith, Auburn, G	1977 Brad Shearer, Texas, DT	1996 Orlando Pace, Ohio St., OT
1959 Mike McGee, Duke, T	1978 Greg Roberts, Oklahoma, G	1997 Aaron Taylor, Nebraska, OT
1960 Tom Brown, Minnesota, G	1979 Jim Ritcher, North Carolina St., C	1998 Kris Farris, UCLA, OT
1961 Merlin Olsen, Utah St., T	1980 Mark May, Pittsburgh, OT	1999 Chris Samuels, Alabama, OT
1962 Bobby Bell, Minnesota, T	1981 Dave Rimington, Nebraska, C	2000 John Henderson, Tennessee, DT
1963 Scott Appleton, Texas, T	1982 Dave Rimington, Nebraska, C	2001 Bryant McKinnie, Miami (FL), OT
1964 Steve Delong, Tennessee, T	1983 Dean Steinkuhler, Nebraska, G	2002 Rien Long, Washington St., DT

All-Time Division I-A Percentage Leaders

(Classified as Division I-A for the last 10 years; record includes bowl games; ties computed as half won and half lost)

	Years	Won	Lost	T	Pct.	Bowl Games** W	L	T		Years	Won	Lost	T	Pct.	Bowl Games** W	L	T
Notre Dame...	114	791	250	42	0.750	13	12	0	Miami (FL)*...	76	496	283	19	0.633	15	12	0
Michigan...	123	823	269	36	0.746	18	16	0	LSU...	109	636	368	47	0.627	16	17	1
Alabama.....	108	754	284	43	0.717	29	19	3	Auburn*...	110	626	374	47	0.620	15	12	2
Oklahoma...	108	725	282	53	0.709	23	12	1	Arizona St....	90	502	303	24	0.620	10	9	1
Texas........	110	766	306	33	0.708	20	20	2	Colorado...	113	630	384	36	0.617	11	14	0
Ohio St......	113	745	292	53	0.708	15	19	0	Florida......	96	582	354	40	0.617	14	16	0
Nebraska.....	113	771	308	40	0.707	20	21	0	C. Michigan*...	102	519	317	36	0.616	0	2	0
Tennessee...	106	726	300	52	0.698	23	20	0	Army........	113	622	393	51	0.607	2	2	0
Penn St.......	116	753	322	41	0.693	23	12	2	Texas A&M...	108	623	396	48	0.606	13	14	0
USC.........	110	695	296	54	0.691	26	15	0	UCLA........	84	499	323	37	0.602	12	11	1
Florida St.*...	56	409	194	17	0.673	18	11	2	Syracuse...	113	652	422	49	0.602	12	8	1
Washington...	113	632	347	50	0.638	14	14	1	Michigan St....	106	572	382	44	0.595	7	9	0
Georgia*...	109	662	367	54	0.636	20	15	3	Arkansas...	109	610	409	40	0.595	10	20	3
Miami (OH)*...	114	611	342	44	0.635	5	2	0									

*Includes games that were forfeited or changed by action of NCAA Council and/or Committee on Infractions. **Includes major bowl games only; that is, those where team's opponent was classified as a major college team that season or at the time of the bowl game.

College Football Coach of the Year

The Division I-A Coach of the Year has been selected by the American Football Coaches Assn. since 1935 and selected by the Football Writers Assn. of America since 1957. When polls disagree, both winners are indicated.

1935 Lynn Waldorf, Northwestern
1936 Dick Harlow, Harvard
1937 Edward Mylin, Lafayette
1938 Bill Kern, Carnegie Tech
1939 Eddie Anderson, Iowa
1940 Clark Shaughnessy, Stanford
1941 Frank Leahy, Notre Dame
1942 Bill Alexander, Georgia Tech
1943 Amos Alonzo Stagg, Pacific
1944 Carroll Widdoes, Ohio St.
1945 Bo McMillin, Indiana
1946 Earl "Red" Blaik, Army
1947 Fritz Crisler, Michigan
1948 Bennie Oosterbaan, Michigan
1949 Bud Wilkinson, Oklahoma
1950 Charlie Caldwell, Princeton
1951 Chuck Taylor, Stanford
1952 Biggie Munn, Michigan St.
1953 Jim Tatum, Maryland
1954 Henry "Red" Sanders, UCLA
1955 Duffy Daugherty, Michigan St.
1956 Bowden Wyatt, Tennessee
1957 Woody Hayes, Ohio St.
1958 Paul Dietzel, LSU
1959 Ben Schwartzwalder, Syracuse
1960 Murray Warmath, Minnesota
1961 Paul "Bear" Bryant, Ala. (AFCA);
     Darrell Royal, Texas (FWAA)
1962 John McKay, USC

1963 Darrell Royal, Texas
1964 Ara Parseghian, Notre Dame, &
     Frank Broyles, Arkansas (AFCA);
     Ara Parseghian (FWAA)
1965 Tommy Prothro, UCLA (AFCA);
     Duffy Daugherty, Mich. St. (FWAA)
1966 Tom Cahill, Army
1967 John Pont, Indiana
1968 Joe Paterno, Penn St. (AFCA);
     Woody Hayes, Ohio St. (FWAA)
1969 Bo Schembechler, Michigan
1970 Charles McClendon, LSU, & Darrell
     Royal, Texas (AFCA); Alex Agase,
     Northwestern (FWAA)
1971 Paul "Bear" Bryant, Alabama (AFCA);
     Bob Devaney, Nebraska (FWAA)
1972 John McKay, USC
1973 Paul "Bear" Bryant, Alabama
     (AFCA); Johnny Majors, Pittsburgh
     (FWAA)
1974 Grant Teaff, Baylor
1975 Frank Kush, Arizona St. (AFCA);
     Woody Hayes, Ohio St. (FWAA)
1976 Johnny Majors, Pittsburgh
1977 Don James, Washington (AFCA);
     Lou Holtz, Arkansas (FWAA)
1978 Joe Paterno, Penn St.
1979 Earle Bruce, Ohio St.
1980 Vince Dooley, Georgia

1981 Danny Ford, Clemson
1982 Joe Paterno, Penn St.
1983 Ken Hatfield, Air Force (AFCA);
     Howard Schnellenberger,
     Miami (FL) (FWAA)
1984 LaVell Edwards, Brigham Young
1985 Fisher De Berry, Air Force
1986 Joe Paterno, Penn St.
1987 Dick MacPherson, Syracuse
1988 Don Nehlen, W. Virginia (AFCA);
     Lou Holtz, Notre Dame (FWAA)
1989 Bill McCartney, Colorado
1990 Bobby Ross, Georgia Tech
1991 Don James, Washington
1992 Gene Stallings, Alabama
1993 Barry Alvarez, Wisconsin (AFCA);
     Terry Bowden, Auburn (FWAA)
1994 Tom Osborne, Nebraska (AFCA);
     Rich Brooks, Oregon (FWAA)
1995 Gary Barnett, Northwestern
1996 Bruce Snyder, Arizona St.
1997 Mike Price, Washington St.
1998 Phillip Fulmer, Tennessee
1999 Frank Beamer, Virginia Tech
2000 Bob Stoops, Oklahoma
2001 Larry Coker, Miami (FL) & Ralph
     Friedgen, Maryland (AFCA); Ralph
     Friedgen, Maryland (FWAA)
2002 Jim Tressel, Ohio St.

All-Time Division I-A Coaching Victories (Including Bowl Games)

*Joe Paterno	336	*Lou Holtz	238	Dan McGugin	197	Gil Dobie	180
*Bobby Bowden	332	Hayden Fry	232	Fielding Yost	196	Carl Snavely	180
Paul "Bear" Bryant	323	Jess Neely	207	Howard Jones	194	Jerry Claiborne	179
Glenn "Pop" Warner	319	Warren Woodson	203	John Cooper	192	*Jackie Sherrill	178
Amos Alonzo Stagg	314	Don Nehlen	202	John Vaught	190	Ben Schwartzwalder	178
LaVell Edwards	257	Eddie Anderson	201	George Welsh	189	Frank Kush	176
Tom Osborne	255	Vince Dooley	201	John Heisman	185	Don James	176
Woody Hayes	238	Jim Sweeney	200	Johnny Majors	185	Ralph Jordan	176
Bo Schembechler	234	Dana X. Bible	198	Darrell Royal	184		

Coaches active in 2002 are denoted by an asterisk(*). Eddie Robinson of Grambling State Univ. (Div. I-AA), who retired after the 1997 season, holds the record for most college football victories, with 408.

NCAA Div. I-A Football Conference Champions (1980-2002)

Atlantic Coast

1980	North Carolina
1981	Clemson
1982	Clemson
1983	Maryland
1984	Maryland
1985	Maryland
1986	Clemson
1987	Clemson
1988	Clemson
1989	Virginia, Duke
1990	Georgia Tech
1991	Clemson
1992	Florida St.
1993	Florida St.
1994	Florida St.
1995	Virginia, Florida St.
1996	Florida St.
1997	Florida St.
1998	Florida St., Georgia Tech
1999	Florida St.
2000	Florida St.
2001	Maryland
2002	Florida St.

Big 12*

1996	Texas
1997	Nebraska
1998	Texas A&M
1999	Nebraska
2000	Oklahoma
2001	Colorado
2002	Oklahoma

Big East

1991	Miami (FL), Syracuse
1992	Miami (FL)
1993	West Virginia
1994	Miami (FL)
1995	Virginia Tech, Miami (FL)
1996	Virginia Tech, Miami (FL), Syracuse
1997	Syracuse
1998	Syracuse
1999	Virginia Tech
2000	Miami (FL)
2001	Miami (FL)
2002	Miami (FL)

Big Ten

1980	Michigan
1981	Iowa, Ohio St.
1982	Michigan
1983	Illinois
1984	Ohio St.
1985	Iowa
1986	Michigan, Ohio St.
1987	Michigan St.
1988	Michigan
1989	Michigan
1990	Iowa, Ill., Mich., Mich. St.
1991	Michigan
1992	Michigan
1993	Ohio St., Wisconsin
1994	Penn St.
1995	Northwestern
1996	Ohio St., Northwestern
1997	Michigan
1998	Ohio St., Wisconsin, Michigan
1999	Wisconsin
2000	Michigan, Northwestern, Purdue
2001	Illinois
2002	Iowa, Ohio St.

Big West**
1980 Long Beach St.
1981 San Jose St.
1982 Fresno St.
1983 Cal St.-Fullerton
1984 Cal St.-Fullerton
1985 Fresno St.
1986 San Jose St.
1987 San Jose St.
1988 Fresno St.
1989 Fresno St.
1990 San Jose St.
1991 San Jose St., Fresno St.
1992 Nevada
1993 SW Louisiana, Utah St.
1994 Nevada, SW Louisiana, UNLV
1995 Nevada
1996 Nevada, Utah St.
1997 Nevada, Utah St.
1998 Idaho
1999 Boise St.
2000 Boise St.

Conference USA
1996 So. Mississippi, Houston
1997 So. Mississippi
1998 Tulane
1999 So. Mississippi
2000 Louisville
2001 Louisville
2002 Cincinnati, TCU

Mid-American Athletic
1980 Central Michigan
1981 Toledo
1982 Bowling Green
1983 Northern Illinois
1984 Toledo
1985 Bowling Green
1986 Miami (OH)
1987 E. Michigan
1988 W. Michigan
1989 Ball St.
1990 Central Michigan
1991 Bowling Green
1992 Bowling Green
1993 Ball St.
1994 Central Michigan
1995 Toledo
1996 Ball St.
1997 Marshall
1998 Marshall
1999 Marshall
2000 Marshall
2001 Toledo
2002 Marshall

Mountain West***
1999 BYU, Colorado St., Utah
2000 Colorado St.
2001 BYU
2002 Colorado St.

Pacific Ten
1980 Washington
1981 Washington
1982 UCLA
1983 UCLA
1984 USC
1985 UCLA
1986 Arizona St.
1987 UCLA, USC
1988 USC
1989 USC
1990 Washington
1991 Washington
1992 Washington, Stanford
1993 UCLA, Arizona, USC
1994 Oregon
1995 USC, Washington
1996 Arizona St.
1997 Washington St., UCLA
1998 UCLA
1999 Stanford
2000 Washington, Oregon St., Oregon
2001 Oregon
2002 USC, Washington St.

Southeastern
1980 Georgia
1981 Georgia, Alabama
1982 Georgia
1983 Auburn
1984 Florida (title vacated)
1985 Tennessee
1986 LSU
1987 Auburn
1988 Auburn, LSU
1989 Ala., Tenn., Auburn
1990 Tennessee
1991 Florida
1992 Alabama
1993 Florida
1994 Florida
1995 Florida
1996 Florida
1997 Tennessee
1998 Tennessee
1999 Alabama
2000 Florida
2001 LSU
2002 Georgia

Sun Belt**
2001 LSU
2002 North Texas

Western Athletic
1980 Brigham Young (BYU)
1981 Brigham Young
1982 Brigham Young
1983 Brigham Young
1984 Brigham Young
1985 BYU, Air Force
1986 San Diego St.
1987 Wyoming
1988 Wyoming
1989 Brigham Young
1990 Brigham Young
1991 Brigham Young
1992 Hawaii, BYU, Fresno St.
1993 Wyoming, Fresno St., BYU
1994 Colorado St.
1995 Colorado St., Air Force, Utah, BYU
1996 Brigham Young
1997 Colorado St.
1998 Air Force
1999 Fresno St., Hawaii, TCU
2000 Texas Christian, UTEP
2001 Louisiana Tech
2002 Boise St.

(*) In 1996 all former Big Eight teams joined with 4 of the 8 Southwest Conf. teams to form the Big 12. (**) In 2001, former Big West teams Ark. St., Idaho, New Mexico St., and N. Texas joined La.-Lafayette, La.-Monroe (Southland), and Middle Tenn. (Ohio Valley) to form the Sun Belt Conf. Boise St. moved to the WAC, and Utah St. became an independent. (***) In 1999, 8 Western Athletic teams formed the Mountain West Conf.

NCAA Div. I-AA Football Conference Champions (1990-2002)

Atlantic 10
1990 Massachusetts
1991 Delaware, Villanova
1992 Delaware
1993 Boston U.
1994 New Hampshire
1995 Delaware
1996 William & Mary
1997 Villanova
1998 Richmond
1999 J. Madison, Mass.
2000 Delaware, Richmond
2001 Hofstra, Maine, Villanova, Will. & Mary
2002 Maine, Northeastern

Big Sky
1990 Nevada
1991 Nevada
1992 Idaho, Eastern Wash.
1993 Montana
1994 Boise St.
1995 Montana
1996 Montana
1997 Eastern Wash.
1998 Montana
1999 Montana
2000 Montana
2001 Montana
2002 Idaho St., Montana, Montana St.

Big South
2002 Gardner-Webb

Gateway
1990 Northern Iowa
1991 Northern Iowa
1992 Northern Iowa
1993 Northern Iowa
1994 Northern Iowa
1995 N. Iowa, Eastern Ill.
1996 Northern Iowa
1997 Western Illinois
1998 Western Illinois
1999 Illinois St.
2000 Western Illinois
2001 Northern Iowa
2002 W. Illinois, W. Kentucky

Ivy Group
1990 Cornell, Dartmouth
1991 Dartmouth
1992 Dartmouth, Princeton
1993 Penn
1994 Penn
1995 Princeton
1996 Dartmouth
1997 Harvard
1998 Penn
1999 Brown, Yale
2000 Penn
2001 Harvard
2002 Pennsylvania

Metro Atlantic
1993 Iona
1994 Marist, St. John's (NY)
1995 Duquesne
1996 Duquesne
1997 Georgetown
1998 Fairfield, Georgetown
1999 Duquesne
2000 Duquesne
2001 Duquesne
2002 Duquesne

Mid-East Athletic
1990 Florida A&M
1991 North Carolina A&T
1992 North Carolina A&T
1993 Howard
1994 South Carolina St.
1995 Florida A&M
1996 Florida A&M
1997 Hampton
1998 Florida A&M, Hampton
1999 North Carolina A&T
2000 Florida A&M
2001 Florida A&M
2002 Bethune-Cookman

Northeast
1996 R. Morris, Monmouth
1997 Robert Morris
1998 R.Morris, Monmouth
1999 Robert Morris
2000 Robert Morris
2001 Sacred Heart
2002 Albany (NY)

Ohio Valley
1990 E. Ky., Middle Tenn.
1991 Eastern Kentucky
1992 Middle Tennessee
1993 Eastern Kentucky
1994 Eastern Kentucky
1995 Murray St.
1996 Murray St.
1997 Eastern Kentucky
1998 Tennessee St.
1999 Tennessee St.
2000 Western Kentucky
2001 Eastern Illinois
2002 Eastern Illinois

Patriot
1990 Holy Cross
1991 Holy Cross
1992 Lafayette
1993 Lehigh
1994 Lafayette
1995 Lehigh
1996 Bucknell
1997 Colgate
1998 Lehigh
1999 Colgate, Lehigh
2000 Lehigh
2001 Lehigh
2002 Colgate, Fordham

Pioneer
1993 Dayton
1994 Dayton, Butler
1995 Drake
1996 Dayton
1997 Dayton
1998 Drake
1999 Dayton
2000 Dayton, Drake, Valparaiso
2001 Dayton
2002 Dayton

Southern
1990 Furman
1991 Appalachian St.
1992 Citadel
1993 Georgia Southern
1994 Marshall
1995 Appalachian St.
1996 Marshall
1997 Georgia Southern
1998 Georgia Southern
1999 Appalachian St., GA Southern, Furman
2000 Georgia Southern
2001 Georgia Southern
2002 Georgia Southern

Southland
1990 La.-Monroe
1991 McNeese St.
1992 La.-Monroe
1993 McNeese St.
1994 North Texas
1995 McNeese St.
1996 Troy St.
1997 McNeese St., Northwestern St.
1998 Northwestern St.
1999 Troy St., S. F. Austin
2000 Troy St.
2001 Sam Houston St., McNeese St.
2002 McNeese St.

Southwestern Athletic
1990 Jackson St.
1991 Alabama St.
1992 Alcorn St.
1993 Southern U.
1994 Grambling, Alcorn St.
1995 Jackson St.
1996 Jackson St.
1997 Southern U.
1998 Southern U.
1999 Southern U.
2000 Grambling
2001 Grambling
2002 Grambling

NATIONAL HOCKEY LEAGUE

2002-2003: Devils Bring Stanley Cup Home; Ducks Surprise; Roy Retires

The New Jersey Devils, under coach Pat Burns, skated to their 3rd NHL championship in 9 seasons, defeating the Anaheim Mighty Ducks, 3-0, in Game 7 of the Stanley Cup Finals at home at Continental Airlines Arena on June 9. New Jersey goalie Martin Brodeur recorded his 3rd shutout of the finals and set an NHL record with his 7th in the postseason. Home ice provided the winning edge as the home team won all 7 games for the 3rd time in NHL history. For Anaheim (who finished the season with 95 points, up from 69 in 2001-2002), the loss ended an improbable playoff run in which the 7th seed eliminated defending champion Detroit in the 1st round (4-0), and then defeated top-seeded Dallas, 4-2. In the finals, goalie Jean-Sebastien Giguere became only the 5th player on a losing team to win the Conn Smythe Trophy as playoff MVP. Colorado goalie Patrick Roy, 37, retired May 28. The NHL's winningest goalie (551) ended his 18-year career with many records including games played (1,029), playoff victories (151), playoff games (247), and playoff shutouts (23). Roy won the Stanley Cup 4 times, twice each with Montreal and Colorado, and is the only 3-time Conn Smythe winner.

Final Standings 2002-2003

(playoff seeding in parentheses; division winners automatically seeded 1, 2, or 3; overtime losses [OTL] worth 1 point.)

Eastern Conference

Atlantic Division

	W	L	T	OTL	GF	GA	Pts
New Jersey (2)	46	20	10	6	216	166	108
Philadelphia (4) ..	45	20	13	4	211	166	107
N.Y. Islanders (8)..	35	34	11	2	224	231	83
N.Y. Rangers	32	36	10	4	210	231	78
Pittsburgh	27	44	6	5	189	255	65

Northeast Division

	W	L	T	OTL	GF	GA	Pts
Ottawa (1)	52	21	8	1	263	182	113
Toronto (5)	44	28	7	3	236	208	98
Boston (7)	36	31	11	4	245	237	87
Montreal	30	35	8	9	206	234	77
Buffalo	27	37	10	8	190	219	72

Southeast Division

	W	L	T	OTL	GF	GA	Pts
Tampa Bay (3)	36	25	16	5	219	210	93
Washington (6)....	39	29	8	6	224	220	92
Atlanta	31	39	7	5	226	284	74
Florida	24	36	13	9	176	237	70
Carolina	22	43	11	6	171	240	61

Western Conference

Central Division

	W	L	T	OTL	GF	GA	Pts
Detroit (2)	48	20	10	4	269	203	110
St. Louis (5)......	41	24	11	6	253	222	99
Chicago	30	33	13	6	207	226	79
Nashville	27	35	13	7	183	206	74
Columbus	29	42	8	3	213	263	69

Northwest Division

	W	L	T	OTL	GF	GA	Pts
Colorado (3)	42	19	13	8	251	194	105
Vancouver (4)	45	23	13	1	264	208	104
Minnesota (6)	42	29	10	1	198	178	95
Edmonton(8)	36	26	11	9	231	230	92
Calgary	29	36	13	4	186	228	75

Pacific Division

	W	L	T	OTL	GF	GA	Pts
Dallas (1)	46	17	15	4	245	169	111
Anaheim (7)	40	27	9	6	203	193	95
Los Angeles	33	37	6	6	203	221	78
Phoenix	31	35	11	5	204	230	78
San Jose	28	37	8	9	214	239	73

2003 Stanley Cup Playoff Results

Eastern Conference

Ottawa defeated N.Y. Islanders 4 games to 1
New Jersey defeated Boston 4 games to 1
Tampa Bay defeated Washington 4 games to 2
Philadelphia defeated Toronto 4 games to 3
Ottawa defeated Philadelphia 4 games to 2
New Jersey defeated Tampa Bay 4 games to 1
New Jersey defeated Ottawa 4 games to 3

Western Conference

Dallas defeated Edmonton 4 games to 2
Anaheim defeated Detroit 4 games to 0
Minnesota defeated Colorado 4 games to 3
Vancouver defeated St. Louis 4 games to 3
Anaheim defeated Dallas 4 games to 2
Minnesota defeated Vancouver 4 games to 3
Anaheim defeated Minnesota 4 games to 0

Finals

New Jersey defeated Anaheim 4 games to 3 [3-0, 3-0, 2-3 (OT), 0-1 (OT), 6-3, 2-5, 3-0].

Stanley Cup Champions Since 1927

Year	Champion	Coach	Final opponent	Year	Champion	Coach	Final opponent
1927	Ottawa	Dave Gill	Boston	1966	Montreal	Toe Blake	Detroit
1928	N.Y. Rangers	Lester Patrick	Montreal	1967	Toronto	Punch Imlach	Montreal
1929	Boston	Cy Denneny	N.Y. Rangers	1968	Montreal	Toe Blake	St. Louis
1930	Montreal	Cecil Hart	Boston	1969	Montreal	Claude Ruel	St. Louis
1931	Montreal	Cecil Hart	Chicago	1970	Boston	Harry Sinden	St. Louis
1932	Toronto	Dick Irvin	N.Y. Rangers	1971	Montreal	Al MacNeil	Chicago
1933	N.Y. Rangers	Lester Patrick	Toronto	1972	Boston	Tom Johnson	N.Y. Rangers
1934	Chicago	Tommy Gorman	Detroit	1973	Montreal	Scotty Bowman	Chicago
1935	Montreal Maroons	Tommy Gorman	Toronto	1974	Philadelphia	Fred Shero	Boston
1936	Detroit	Jack Adams	Toronto	1975	Philadelphia	Fred Shero	Buffalo
1937	Detroit	Jack Adams	N.Y. Rangers	1976	Montreal	Scotty Bowman	Philadelphia
1938	Chicago	Bill Stewart	Toronto	1977	Montreal	Scotty Bowman	Boston
1939	Boston	Art Ross	Toronto	1978	Montreal	Scotty Bowman	Boston
1940	N.Y. Rangers	Frank Boucher	Toronto	1979	Montreal	Scotty Bowman	N.Y. Rangers
1941	Boston	Cooney Weiland	Detroit	1980	N.Y. Islanders	Al Arbour	Philadelphia
1942	Toronto	Hap Day	Detroit	1981	N.Y. Islanders	Al Arbour	Minnesota
1943	Detroit	Jack Adams	Boston	1982	N.Y. Islanders	Al Arbour	Vancouver
1944	Montreal	Dick Irvin	Chicago	1983	N.Y. Islanders	Al Arbour	Edmonton
1945	Toronto	Hap Day	Detroit	1984	Edmonton	Glen Sather	N.Y. Islanders
1946	Montreal	Dick Irvin	Boston	1985	Edmonton	Glen Sather	Philadelphia
1947	Toronto	Hap Day	Montreal	1986	Montreal	Jean Perron	Calgary
1948	Toronto	Hap Day	Detroit	1987	Edmonton	Glen Sather	Philadelphia
1949	Toronto	Hap Day	Detroit	1988	Edmonton	Glen Sather	Boston
1950	Detroit	Tommy Ivan	N.Y. Rangers	1989	Calgary	Terry Crisp	Montreal
1951	Toronto	Joe Primeau	Montreal	1990	Edmonton	John Muckler	Boston
1952	Detroit	Tommy Ivan	Montreal	1991	Pittsburgh	Bob Johnson	Minnesota
1953	Montreal	Dick Irvin	Boston	1992	Pittsburgh	Scotty Bowman	Chicago
1954	Detroit	Tommy Ivan	Montreal	1993	Montreal	Jacques Demers	Los Angeles
1955	Detroit	Jimmy Skinner	Montreal	1994	N.Y. Rangers	Mike Keenan	Vancouver
1956	Montreal	Toe Blake	Detroit	1995	New Jersey	Jacques Lemaire	Detroit
1957	Montreal	Toe Blake	Boston	1996	Colorado	Marc Crawford	Florida
1958	Montreal	Toe Blake	Boston	1997	Detroit	Scotty Bowman	Philadelphia
1959	Montreal	Toe Blake	Toronto	1998	Detroit	Scotty Bowman	Washington
1960	Montreal	Toe Blake	Toronto	1999	Dallas	Ken Hitchcock	Buffalo
1961	Chicago	Rudy Pilous	Detroit	2000	New Jersey	Larry Robinson	Dallas
1962	Toronto	Punch Imlach	Chicago	2001	Colorado	Bob Hartley	New Jersey
1963	Toronto	Punch Imlach	Detroit	2002	Detroit	Scotty Bowman	Carolina
1964	Toronto	Punch Imlach	Detroit	2003	New Jersey	Pat Burns	Anaheim
1965	Montreal	Toe Blake	Chicago				

Individual Leaders, 2002-2003

Points
Peter Forsberg, Colorado, 106; Markus Naslund, Vancouver, 104; Joe Thornton, Boston, 101; Milan Hejduk, Colorado, 98; Todd Bertuzzi, Vancouver, 97.

Goals
Milan Hejduk, Colorado, 50; Markus Naslund, Vancouver, 48; Todd Bertuzzi, Vancouver, 46; Marian Hossa, Ottawa, 45; Glen Murray, Boston, 44.

Assists
Peter Forsberg, Colorado, 77; Joe Thornton, Boston, 65; Mario Lemieux, Pittsburgh, 63; Mike Modano, Dallas, 57; Pavol Demitra, St. Louis, 57; Vaclav Prospal, Tampa Bay, 57; Brad Richards, Tampa Bay, 57; Markus Naslund, Vancouver, 56; Paul Kariya, Anaheim, 56.

Power-play goals
Todd Bertuzzi, Vancouver, 25; Markus Naslund, Vancouver, 24; Dany Heatley, Atlanta, 19; Milan Hejduk, Colorado, 18; Mats Sundin, Toronto, 16; 4 players tied with 15.

Shorthanded goals
Shawn Bates, N.Y. Islanders, 6; Brian Rolston, Boston, 5; Martin Rucinsky, St. Louis, 4; Curtis Brown, Buffalo, 4; Kirk Maltby, Detroit, 4; Matt Cooke, Vancouver, 4; 14 players tied with 3.

Shooting percentage
(minimum 82 shots)
Milan Hejduk, Colorado, 20.50; Alexander Mogilny, Toronto, 20.00; Brenden Morrow, Dallas, 20.00; Scott Mellanby, St. Louis, 19.70; Marian Hossa, Ottawa, 19.70; Todd Bertuzzi, Vancouver, 18.90; Eric Boguniecki, St. Louis, 18.80.

Plus/Minus
Peter Forsberg, Colorado, 52; Milan Hejduk, Colorado, 52; Nicklas Lidstrom, Detroit, 40; Jere Lehtinen, Dallas, 39; Derian Hatcher, Dallas, 37; Mike Modano, Dallas, 34.

Penalty minutes
Jody Shelley, Columbus, 249; Reed Low, St. Louis, 234; Matt Johnson, Minnesota, 201; Wade Belak, Toronto, 196; Peter Worrell, Florida, 193.

Goaltending Leaders
(minimum 25 games)
Goals against average
Marty Turco, Dallas, 1.72; Roman Cechmanek, Philadelphia, 1.83; Dwayne Roloson, Minnesota, 2.00; Martin Brodeur, New Jersey, 2.02; Patrick Lalime, Ottawa, 2.16.

Wins
Martin Brodeur, New Jersey, 41; Patrick Lalime, Ottawa, 39; Ed Belfour, Toronto, 37; Patrick Roy, Colorado, 35; Jean-Sebastian Giguere, Anaheim, 34.

Save percentage
Marty Turco, Dallas, .932; Dwayne Roloson, Minnesota, .927; Roman Cechmanek, Philadelphia, .925; Manny Legace, Detroit, .925; Emmanuel Fernandez, Minnesota, .924; Ed Belfour, Toronto, .922.

Shutouts
Martin Brodeur, New Jersey, 9; Patrick Lalime, Ottawa, 8; Jean-Sebastian Giguere, Anaheim, 8; Jocelyn Thibault, Chicago, 8; Marty Turco, Dallas, 7; Ed Belfour, Toronto, 7; Roman Cechmanek, Philadelphia, 6; Robert Luongo, Florida, 6; 5 players tied with 5.

 IT'S A FACT: In the history of the NHL, seven goalies have been credited with a total of 9 goals. Philadelphia's Ron Hextall (1987, 1989) and New Jersey's Martin Brodeur (1997, 2000) each scored twice. The 1st was New York Islander Billy Smith in 1979. The most recent was San Jose's Evgeni Nabokov in 2002.

All-Time Leading Scorers

Player	Goals	Assists	Points	Player	Goals	Assists	Points	Player	Goals	Assists	Points
Wayne Gretzky.	894	1,963	2,857	Phil Esposito . . .	717	873	1,590	Adam Oates* . . .	339	1,063	1,402
Gordie Howe . .	801	1,049	1,850	Ray Bourque . . .	410	1,169	1,579	Jari Kurri	601	797	1,398
Mark Messier* .	676	1,168	1,844	Paul Coffey . . .	396	1,135	1,531	John Bucyk . . .	556	813	1,369
Marcel Dionne .	731	1,040	1,771	Stan Mikita. . . .	541	926	1,467	Guy Lafleur . . .	560	793	1,353
Ron Francis* . .	536	1,222	1,758	Bryan Trottier . .	524	901	1,425	Denis Savard . .	473	865	1,338
Mario Lemieux*	682	1,010	1,692	Doug Gilmour* . .	450	964	1,414	Mike Gartner . . .	708	627	1,335
Steve Yzerman*	660	1,010	1,670	Dale Hawerchuk	518	891	1,409				

Note: Through end of 2002-2003 season. *Active in the 2002-2003 season.

Most NHL Goals in a Season

Player	Team	Season	Goals	Player	Team	Season	Goals
Wayne Gretzky	Edmonton	1981-82	92	Jari Kurri	Edmonton.	1984-85	71
Wayne Gretzky	Edmonton	1983-84	87	Brett Hull	St. Louis	1991-92	70
Brett Hull	St. Louis	1990-91	86	Mario Lemieux	Pittsburgh	1987-88	70
Mario Lemieux	Pittsburgh	1988-89	85	Bernie Nicholls	Los Angeles	1988-89	70
Phil Esposito	Boston	1971-72	76	Mike Bossy	N.Y. Islanders . . .	1978-79	69
Alexander Mogilny	Buffalo.	1992-93	76	Mario Lemieux	Pittsburgh	1992-93	69
Teemu Selanne	Winnipeg.	1992-93	76	Mario Lemieux	Pittsburgh	1995-96	69
Wayne Gretzky	Edmonton	1984-85	73	Mike Bossy	N.Y. Islanders . . .	1980-81	68
Brett Hull	St. Louis	1989-90	72	Phil Esposito	Boston	1973-74	68
Wayne Gretzky	Edmonton	1982-83	71	Jari Kurri	Edmonton.	1985-86	68

Hart Memorial Trophy (MVP)

1927	Herb Gardiner, Montreal	1953	Gordie Howe, Detroit	1979	Bryan Trottier, N.Y. Islanders
1928	Howie Morenz, Montreal	1954	Al Rollins, Chicago	1980	Wayne Gretzky, Edmonton
1929	Roy Worters, N.Y. Americans	1955	Ted Kennedy, Toronto	1981	Wayne Gretzky, Edmonton
1930	Nels Stewart, Montreal Maroons	1956	Jean Beliveau, Montreal	1982	Wayne Gretzky, Edmonton
1931	Howie Morenz, Montreal	1957	Gordie Howe, Detroit	1983	Wayne Gretzky, Edmonton
1932	Howie Morenz, Montreal	1958	Gordie Howe, Detroit	1984	Wayne Gretzky, Edmonton
1933	Eddie Shore, Boston	1959	Andy Bathgate, N.Y. Rangers	1985	Wayne Gretzky, Edmonton
1934	Aurel Joliat, Montreal	1960	Gordie Howe, Detroit	1986	Wayne Gretzky, Edmonton
1935	Eddie Shore, Boston	1961	Bernie Geoffrion, Montreal	1987	Wayne Gretzky, Edmonton
1936	Eddie Shore, Boston	1962	Jacques Plante, Montreal	1988	Mario Lemieux, Pittsburgh
1937	Babe Siebert, Montreal	1963	Gordie Howe, Detroit	1989	Wayne Gretzky, Los Angeles
1938	Eddie Shore, Boston	1964	Jean Beliveau, Montreal	1990	Mark Messier, Edmonton
1939	Toe Blake, Montreal	1965	Bobby Hull, Chicago	1991	Brett Hull, St. Louis
1940	Ebbie Goodfellow, Detroit	1966	Bobby Hull, Chicago	1992	Mark Messier, N.Y. Rangers
1941	Bill Cowley, Boston	1967	Stan Mikita, Chicago	1993	Mario Lemieux, Pittsburgh
1942	Tom Anderson, N.Y. Americans	1968	Stan Mikita, Chicago	1994	Sergei Fedorov, Detroit
1943	Bill Cowley, Boston	1969	Phil Esposito, Boston	1995	Eric Lindros, Philadelphia
1944	Babe Pratt, Toronto	1970	Bobby Orr, Boston	1996	Mario Lemieux, Pittsburgh
1945	Elmer Lach, Montreal	1971	Bobby Orr, Boston	1997	Dominik Hasek, Buffalo
1946	Max Bentley, Chicago	1972	Bobby Orr, Boston	1998	Dominik Hasek, Buffalo
1947	Maurice Richard, Montreal	1973	Bobby Clarke, Philadelphia	1999	Jaromir Jagr, Pittsburgh
1948	Buddy O'Connor, N.Y. Rangers	1974	Phil Esposito, Boston	2000	Chris Pronger, St. Louis
1949	Sid Abel, Detroit	1975	Bobby Clarke, Philadelphia	2001	Joe Sakic, Colorado
1950	Chuck Rayner, N.Y. Rangers	1976	Bobby Clarke, Philadelphia	2002	Jose Theodore, Montreal
1951	Milt Schmidt, Boston	1977	Guy Lafleur, Montreal	2003	Peter Forsberg, Colorado
1952	Gordie Howe, Detroit	1978	Guy Lafleur, Montreal		

Calder Memorial Trophy (Rookie of the Year)

1933 Carl Voss, Detroit	1957 Larry Regan, Boston	1981 Peter Stastny, Quebec
1934 Russ Blinco, Montreal Maroons	1958 Frank Mahovlich, Toronto	1982 Dale Hawerchuk, Winnipeg
1935 Dave Schriner, N.Y. Americans	1959 Ralph Backstrom, Montreal	1983 Steve Larmer, Chicago
1936 Mike Karakas, Chicago	1960 Bill Hay, Chicago	1984 Tom Barrasso, Buffalo
1937 Syl Apps, Toronto	1961 Dave Keon, Toronto	1985 Mario Lemieux, Pittsburgh
1938 Cully Dahlstrom, Chicago	1962 Bobby Rousseau, Montreal	1986 Gary Suter, Calgary
1939 Frank Brimsek, Boston	1963 Kent Douglas, Toronto	1987 Luc Robitaille, Los Angeles
1940 Kilby Macdonald, N.Y. Rangers	1964 Jacques Laperriere, Montreal	1988 Joe Nieuwendyk, Calgary
1941 John Quilty, Montreal	1965 Roger Crozier, Detroit	1989 Brian Leetch, N.Y. Rangers
1942 Grant Warwick, N.Y. Rangers	1966 Brit Selby, Toronto	1990 Sergei Makarov, Calgary
1943 Gaye Stewart, Toronto	1967 Bobby Orr, Boston	1991 Ed Belfour, Chicago
1944 Gus Bodnar, Toronto	1968 Derek Sanderson, Boston	1992 Pavel Bure, Vancouver
1945 Frank McCool, Toronto	1969 Danny Grant, Minnesota	1993 Teemu Selanne, Winnipeg
1946 Edgar Laprade, N.Y. Rangers	1970 Tony Esposito, Chicago	1994 Martin Brodeur, New Jersey
1947 Howie Meeker, Toronto	1971 Gilbert Perreault, Buffalo	1995 Peter Forsberg, Quebec
1948 Jim McFadden, Detroit	1972 Ken Dryden, Montreal	1996 Daniel Alfredsson, Ottawa
1949 Pentti Lund, N.Y. Rangers	1973 Steve Vickers, N.Y. Rangers	1997 Bryan Berard, N.Y. Islanders
1950 Jack Gelineau, Boston	1974 Denis Potvin, N.Y. Islanders	1998 Sergei Samsonov, Boston
1951 Terry Sawchuk, Detroit	1975 Eric Vail, Atlanta	1999 Chris Drury, Colorado
1952 Bernie Geoffrion, Montreal	1976 Bryan Trottier, N.Y. Islanders	2000 Scott Gomez, New Jersey
1953 Gump Worsley, N.Y. Rangers	1977 Willi Plett, Atlanta	2001 Evgeni Nabokov, San Jose
1954 Camille Henry, N.Y. Rangers	1978 Mike Bossy, N.Y. Islanders	2002 Dany Heatley, Atlanta
1955 Ed Litzenberger, Chicago	1979 Bobby Smith, Minnesota	2003 Barret Jackman, St. Louis
1956 Glenn Hall, Detroit	1980 Ray Bourque, Boston	

Conn Smythe Trophy (MVP in Playoffs)

1965 Jean Beliveau, Montreal	1978 Larry Robinson, Montreal	1991 Mario Lemieux, Pittsburgh
1966 Roger Crozier, Detroit	1979 Bob Gainey, Montreal	1992 Mario Lemieux, Pittsburgh
1967 Dave Keon, Toronto	1980 Bryan Trottier, N.Y. Islanders	1993 Patrick Roy, Montreal
1968 Glenn Hall, St. Louis	1981 Butch Goring, N.Y. Islanders	1994 Brian Leetch, N.Y. Rangers
1969 Serge Savard, Montreal	1982 Mike Bossy, N.Y. Islanders	1995 Claude Lemieux, New Jersey
1970 Bobby Orr, Boston	1983 Billy Smith, N.Y. Islanders	1996 Joe Sakic, Colorado
1971 Ken Dryden, Montreal	1984 Mark Messier, Edmonton	1997 Mike Vernon, Detroit
1972 Bobby Orr, Boston	1985 Wayne Gretzky, Edmonton	1998 Steve Yzerman, Detroit
1973 Yvan Cournoyer, Montreal	1986 Patrick Roy, Montreal	1999 Joe Nieuwendyk, Dallas
1974 Bernie Parent, Philadelphia	1987 Ron Hextall, Philadelphia	2000 Scott Stevens, New Jersey
1975 Bernie Parent, Philadelphia	1988 Wayne Gretzky, Edmonton	2001 Patrick Roy, Colorado
1976 Reg Leach, Philadelphia	1989 Al MacInnis, Calgary	2002 Nicklas Lidstrom, Detroit
1977 Guy Lafleur, Montreal	1990 Bill Ranford, Edmonton	2003 Jean-Sebastien Giguere, Anaheim

Lady Byng Memorial Trophy (Most Gentlemanly Player)

1925 Frank Nighbor, Ottawa	1952 Sid Smith, Toronto	1978 Butch Goring, Los Angeles
1926 Frank Nighbor, Ottawa	1953 Red Kelly, Detroit	1979 Bob MacMillan, Atlanta
1927 Billy Burch, N.Y. Americans	1954 Red Kelly, Detroit	1980 Wayne Gretzky, Edmonton
1928 Frank Boucher, N.Y. Rangers	1955 Sid Smith, Toronto	1981 Rick Kehoe, Pittsburgh
1929 Frank Boucher, N.Y. Rangers	1956 Earl Reibel, Detroit	1982 Rick Middleton, Boston
1930 Frank Boucher, N.Y. Rangers	1957 Andy Hebenton, N.Y. Rangers	1983 Mike Bossy, N.Y. Islanders
1931 Frank Boucher, N.Y. Rangers	1958 Camille Henry, N.Y. Rangers	1984 Mike Bossy, N.Y. Islanders
1932 Joe Primeau, Toronto	1959 Alex Delvecchio, Detroit	1985 Jari Kurri, Edmonton
1933 Frank Boucher, N.Y. Rangers	1960 Don McKenney, Boston	1986 Mike Bossy, N.Y. Islanders
1934 Frank Boucher, N.Y. Rangers	1961 Red Kelly, Toronto	1987 Joe Mullen, Calgary
1935 Frank Boucher, N.Y. Rangers	1962 Dave Keon, Toronto	1988 Mats Naslund, Montreal
1936 Doc Romnes, Chicago	1963 Dave Keon, Toronto	1989 Joe Mullen, Calgary
1937 Marty Barry, Detroit	1964 Ken Wharram, Chicago	1990 Brett Hull, St. Louis
1938 Gordie Drillon, Toronto	1965 Bobby Hull, Chicago	1991 Wayne Gretzky, Los Angeles
1939 Clint Smith, N.Y. Rangers	1966 Alex Delvecchio, Detroit	1992 Wayne Gretzky, Los Angeles
1940 Bobby Bauer, Boston	1967 Stan Mikita, Chicago	1993 Pierre Turgeon, N.Y. Islanders
1941 Bobby Bauer, Boston	1968 Stan Mikita, Chicago	1994 Wayne Gretzky, Los Angeles
1942 Syl Apps, Toronto	1969 Alex Delvecchio, Detroit	1995 Ron Francis, Pittsburgh
1943 Max Bentley, Chicago	1970 Phil Goyette, St. Louis	1996 Paul Kariya, Anaheim
1944 Clint Smith, Chicago	1971 John Bucyk, Boston	1997 Paul Kariya, Anaheim
1945 Bill Mosienko, Chicago	1972 Jean Ratelle, N.Y. Rangers	1998 Ron Francis, Pittsburgh
1946 Toe Blake, Montreal	1973 Gil Perreault, Buffalo	1999 Wayne Gretzky, N.Y. Rangers
1947 Bobby Bauer, Boston	1974 John Bucyk, Boston	2000 Pavol Demitra, St. Louis
1948 Buddy O'Connor, N.Y. Rangers	1975 Marcel Dionne, Detroit	2001 Joe Sakic, Colorado
1949 Bill Quackenbush, Detroit	1976 Jean Ratelle, N.Y.R.-Boston	2002 Ron Francis, Carolina
1950 Edgar Laprade, N.Y. Rangers	1977 Marcel Dionne, Los Angeles	2003 Alexander Mogilny, Toronto
1951 Red Kelly, Detroit		

James Norris Memorial Trophy (Outstanding Defenseman)

1954 Red Kelly, Detroit	1971 Bobby Orr, Boston	1988 Ray Bourque, Boston
1955 Doug Harvey, Montreal	1972 Bobby Orr, Boston	1989 Chris Chelios, Montreal
1956 Doug Harvey, Montreal	1973 Bobby Orr, Boston	1990 Ray Bourque, Boston
1957 Doug Harvey, Montreal	1974 Bobby Orr, Boston	1991 Ray Bourque, Boston
1958 Doug Harvey, Montreal	1975 Bobby Orr, Boston	1992 Brian Leetch, N.Y. Rangers
1959 Tom Johnson, Montreal	1976 Denis Potvin, N.Y. Islanders	1993 Chris Chelios, Chicago
1960 Doug Harvey, Montreal	1977 Larry Robinson, Montreal	1994 Ray Bourque, Boston
1961 Doug Harvey, Montreal	1978 Denis Potvin, N.Y. Islanders	1995 Paul Coffey, Detroit
1962 Doug Harvey, N.Y. Rangers	1979 Denis Potvin, N.Y. Islanders	1996 Chris Chelios, Chicago
1963 Pierre Pilote, Chicago	1980 Larry Robinson, Montreal	1997 Brian Leetch, N.Y. Rangers
1964 Pierre Pilote, Chicago	1981 Randy Carlyle, Pittsburgh	1998 Rob Blake, Los Angeles
1965 Pierre Pilote, Chicago	1982 Doug Wilson, Chicago	1999 Al MacInnis, St. Louis
1966 Jacques Laperriere, Montreal	1983 Rod Langway, Washington	2000 Chris Pronger, St. Louis
1967 Harry Howell, N.Y. Rangers	1984 Rod Langway, Washington	2001 Nicklas Lidstrom, Detroit
1968 Bobby Orr, Boston	1985 Paul Coffey, Edmonton	2002 Nicklas Lidstrom, Detroit
1969 Bobby Orr, Boston	1986 Paul Coffey, Edmonton	2003 Nicklas Lidstrom, Detroit
1970 Bobby Orr, Boston	1987 Ray Bourque, Boston	

Maurice "Rocket" Richard Trophy (Most Goals)

1999 Teemu Selanne, Anaheim	2001 Pavel Bure, Florida	2003 Milan Hejduk, Colorado
2000 Pavel Bure, Florida	2002 Jarome Iginla, Calgary	

Art Ross Trophy (Leading Points Scorer)

1927 Bill Cook, N.Y. Rangers	1953 Gordie Howe, Detroit	1979 Bryan Trottier, N.Y. Islanders
1928 Howie Morenz, Montreal	1954 Gordie Howe, Detroit	1980 Marcel Dionne, Los Angeles
1929 Ace Bailey, Toronto	1955 Bernie Geoffrion, Montreal	1981 Wayne Gretzky, Edmonton
1930 Cooney Weiland, Boston	1956 Jean Beliveau, Montreal	1982 Wayne Gretzky, Edmonton
1931 Howie Morenz, Montreal	1957 Gordie Howe, Detroit	1983 Wayne Gretzky, Edmonton
1932 Harvey Jackson, Toronto	1958 Dickie Moore, Montreal	1984 Wayne Gretzky, Edmonton
1933 Bill Cook, N.Y. Rangers	1959 Dickie Moore, Montreal	1985 Wayne Gretzky, Edmonton
1934 Charlie Conacher, Toronto	1960 Bobby Hull, Chicago	1986 Wayne Gretzky, Edmonton
1935 Charlie Conacher, Toronto	1961 Bernie Geoffrion, Montreal	1987 Wayne Gretzky, Edmonton
1936 Dave Schriner, N.Y. Americans	1962 Bobby Hull, Chicago	1988 Mario Lemieux, Pittsburgh
1937 Dave Schriner, N.Y. Americans	1963 Gordie Howe, Detroit	1989 Mario Lemieux, Pittsburgh
1938 Gordie Drillon, Toronto	1964 Stan Mikita, Chicago	1990 Wayne Gretzky, Los Angeles
1939 Toe Blake, Montreal	1965 Stan Mikita, Chicago	1991 Wayne Gretzky, Los Angeles
1940 Milt Schmidt, Boston	1966 Bobby Hull, Chicago	1992 Mario Lemieux, Pittsburgh
1941 Bill Cowley, Boston	1967 Stan Mikita, Chicago	1993 Mario Lemieux, Pittsburgh
1942 Bryan Hextall, N.Y. Rangers	1968 Stan Mikita, Chicago	1994 Wayne Gretzky, Los Angeles
1943 Doug Bentley, Chicago	1969 Phil Esposito, Boston	1995 Jaromir Jagr, Pittsburgh
1944 Herbie Cain, Boston	1970 Bobby Orr, Boston	1996 Mario Lemieux, Pittsburgh
1945 Elmer Lach, Montreal	1971 Phil Esposito, Boston	1997 Mario Lemieux, Pittsburgh
1946 Max Bentley, Chicago	1972 Phil Esposito, Boston	1998 Jaromir Jagr, Pittsburgh
1947 Max Bentley, Chicago	1973 Phil Esposito, Boston	1999 Jaromir Jagr, Pittsburgh
1948 Elmer Lach, Montreal	1974 Phil Esposito, Boston	2000 Jaromir Jagr, Pittsburgh
1949 Roy Conacher, Chicago	1975 Bobby Orr, Boston	2001 Jaromir Jagr, Pittsburgh
1950 Ted Lindsay, Detroit	1976 Guy Lafleur, Montreal	2002 Jarome Iginla, Calgary
1951 Gordie Howe, Detroit	1977 Guy Lafleur, Montreal	2003 Peter Forsberg, Colorado
1952 Gordie Howe, Detroit	1978 Guy Lafleur, Montreal	

Frank J. Selke Trophy (Best Defensive Forward)

1978 Bob Gainey, Montreal	1987 Dave Poulin, Philadelphia	1995 Ron Francis, Pittsburgh
1979 Bob Gainey, Montreal	1988 Guy Carbonneau, Montreal	1996 Sergei Federov, Detroit
1980 Bob Gainey, Montreal	1989 Guy Carbonneau, Montreal	1997 Michael Peca, Buffalo
1981 Bob Gainey, Montreal	1990 Rick Meagher, St. Louis	1998 Jere Lehtinen, Dallas
1982 Steve Kasper, Boston	1991 Dirk Graham, Chicago	1999 Jere Lehtinen, Dallas
1983 Bobby Clarke, Philadelphia	1992 Guy Carbonneau, Montreal	2000 Steve Yzerman, Detroit
1984 Doug Jarvis, Washington	1993 Doug Gilmour, Toronto	2001 John Madden, New Jersey
1985 Craig Ramsay, Buffalo	1994 Sergei Federov, Detroit	2002 Michael Peca, N.Y. Islanders
1986 Troy Murray, Chicago		2003 Jere Lehtinen, Dallas

Vezina Trophy (Outstanding Goalie)*

1927 George Hainsworth, Montreal	1954 Harry Lumley, Toronto	1979 Dryden, Larocque, Montreal
1928 George Hainsworth, Montreal	1955 Terry Sawchuk, Detroit	1980 Sauve, Edwards, Buffalo
1929 George Hainsworth, Montreal	1956 Jacques Plante, Montreal	1981 Sevigny, Larocque, Herron,
1930 Tiny Thompson, Boston	1957 Jacques Plante, Montreal	Montreal
1931 Roy Worters, N.Y. Americans	1958 Jacques Plante, Montreal	1982 Bill Smith, N.Y. Islanders
1932 Charlie Gardiner, Chicago	1959 Jacques Plante, Montreal	1983 Pete Peeters, Boston
1933 Tiny Thompson, Boston	1960 Jacques Plante, Montreal	1984 Tom Barrasso, Buffalo
1934 Charlie Gardiner, Chicago	1961 John Bower, Toronto	1985 Pelle Lindbergh, Philadelphia
1935 Lorne Chabot, Chicago	1962 Jacques Plante, Montreal	1986 John Vanbiesbrouck, N.Y. Rangers
1936 Tiny Thompson, Boston	1963 Glenn Hall, Chicago	1987 Ron Hextall, Philadelphia
1937 Normie Smith, Detroit	1964 Charlie Hodge, Montreal	1988 Grant Fuhr, Edmonton
1938 Tiny Thompson, Boston	1965 Sawchuk, Bower, Toronto	1989 Patrick Roy, Montreal
1939 Frank Brimsek, Boston	1966 Worsley, Hodge, Montreal	1990 Patrick Roy, Montreal
1940 Dave Kerr, N.Y. Rangers	1967 Hall, DeJordy, Chicago	1991 Ed Belfour, Chicago
1941 Turk Broda, Toronto	1968 Worsley, Vachon, Montreal	1992 Patrick Roy, Montreal
1942 Frank Brimsek, Boston	1969 Hall, Plante, St. Louis	1993 Ed Belfour, Chicago
1943 Johnny Mowers, Detroit	1970 Tony Esposito, Chicago	1994 Dominik Hasek, Buffalo
1944 Bill Durnan, Montreal	1971 Giacomin, Villemure, N.Y. Rangers	1995 Dominik Hasek, Buffalo
1945 Bill Durnan, Montreal	1972 Esposito, Smith, Chicago	1996 Jim Carey, Washington
1946 Bill Durnan, Montreal	1973 Ken Dryden, Montreal	1997 Dominik Hasek, Buffalo
1947 Bill Durnan, Montreal	1974 Bernie Parent, Philadelphia;	1998 Dominik Hasek, Buffalo
1948 Turk Broda, Toronto	Tony Esposito, Chicago	1999 Dominik Hasek, Buffalo
1949 Bill Durnan, Montreal	1975 Bernie Parent, Philadelphia	2000 Olaf Kolzig, Washington
1950 Bill Durnan, Montreal	1976 Ken Dryden, Montreal	2001 Dominik Hasek, Buffalo
1951 Al Rollins, Toronto	1977 Dryden, Larocque, Montreal	2002 Jose Theodore, Montreal
1952 Terry Sawchuk, Detroit	1978 Dryden, Larocque, Montreal	2003 Martin Brodeur, New Jersey
1953 Terry Sawchuk, Detroit		

*Before 1982, awarded to the goalie or goalies who played a minimum of 25 games for the team that allowed the fewest goals; since 1982, awarded to the outstanding goalie, as determined by a vote of NHL general managers.

National Hockey Hall of Fame, Toronto, Ontario

(2003 inductees have an asterisk*)

PLAYERS

Abel, Sid	Bentley, Doug	Bucyk, John	Cook, Bun	Dumart, Woody
Adams, Jack	Bentley, Max	Burch, Billy	Coulter, Art	Dunderdale, Tommy
Apps, Syl	Blake, Toe	Cameron, Harry	Cournoyer, Yvan	Durnan, Bill
Armstrong, George	Boivin, Leo	Cheevers, Gerry	Cowley, Bill	Dutton, Red
Bailey, Ace	Boon, Dickie	Clancy, King	Crawford, Rusty	Dye, Babe
Bain, Dan	Bossy, Mike	Clapper, Dit	Darragh, Jack	Esposito, Phil
Baker, Hobey	Bouchard, Butch	Clarke, Bobby	Davidson, Scotty	Esposito, Tony
Barber, Bill	Boucher, Frank	Cleghorn, Sprague	Day, Hap	Farrel, Arthur
Barry, Marty	Boucher, George	Colville, Neil	Delvecchio, Alex	Federko, Bernie
Bathgate, Andy	Bower, Johnny	Conacher, Charlie	Denneny, Cy	Fetisov, Viacheslav
Bauer, Bobby	Bowie, Dubbie	Conacher, Lionel	Dionne, Marcel	Flaman, Fernie
Beliveau, Jean	Broadbent, Punch	Conacher, Roy	Drillon, Gordie	Foyston, Frank
Benedict, Clint	Broda, Turk	Connell, Alex	Drinkwater, Graham	Fredrickson, Frank
		Cook, Bill	Dryden, Ken	*Fuhr, Grant

Gadsby, Bill
Gainey, Bob
Gardiner, Chuck
Gardiner, Herb
Gardiner, Jimmy
Gartner, Mike
Geoffrion, Bernie
Gerard, Eddie
Giacomin, Eddie
Gilbert, Rod
Gillies, Clark
Gilmour, Billy
Goheen, Moose
Goodfellow, Ebbie
Goulet, Michel
Grant, Mike
Green, Shorty
Gretzky, Wayne
Griffis, Si
Hainsworth, George
Hall, Glenn
Hall, Joe
Harvey, Doug
Hawerchuk, Dale
Hay, George
Hern, Riley
Hextall, Bryan
Holmes, Hap
Hooper, Tom
Horner, Red
Horton, Tim
Howe, Gordie
Howe, Syd
Howell, Harry
Hull, Bobby
Hutton, Bouse
Hyland, Harry
Irvin, Dick
Jackson, Busher
Johnson, Ching
Johnson, Ernie
Johnson, Tom
Joliat, Aurel
Keats, Duke
Kelly, Red
Kennedy, Ted
Keon, Dave
Kurri, Jari
Lach, Elmer
Lafleur, Guy
*LaFontaine, Pat
Lalonde, Newsy
Langway, Rod
Laperriere, Jacques

Lapointe, Guy
Laprade, Edgar
Laviolette, Jack
LeSueur, Percy
Lehman, Hughie
Lemaire, Jacques
Lemieux, Mario
Lewis, Herbie
Lindsay, Ted
Lumley, Harry
MacKay, Mickey
Mahovlich, Frank
Malone, Joe
Mantha, Sylvio
Marshall, Jack
Maxwell, Fred
McDonald, Lanny
McGee, Frank
McGimsie, Billy
McNamara, George
Mikita, Stan
Moore, Dickie
Moran, Paddy
Morenz, Howie
Mosienko, Bill
Mullen, Joe
Nighbor, Frank
Noble, Reg
O'Connor, Buddy
Oliver, Harry
Olmstead, Bert
Orr, Bobby
Parent, Bernie
Park, Brad
Patrick, Lester
Patrick, Lynn
Perreault, Gilbert
Phillips, Tom
Pilote, Pierre
Pitre, Didier
Plante, Jacques
Potvin, Denis
Pratt, Babe
Primeau, Joe
Pronovost, Marcel
Pulford, Bob
Pulford, Harvey
Quackenbush, Bill
Rankin, Frank
Ratelle, Jean
Rayner, Chuck
Reardon, Kenny
Richard, Henri
Richard, Maurice

Richardson, George
Roberts, Gordie
Robinson, Larry
Ross, Art
Russel, Blair
Russell, Ernie
Ruttan, Jack
Salming, Borje
Savard, Denis
Savard, Serge
Sawchuk, Terry
Scanlan, Fred
Schmidt, Milt
Schriner, Sweeney
Seibert, Earl
Seibert, Oliver
Shore, Eddie
Shutt, Steve
Siebert, Babe
Simpson, Joe
Sittler, Darryl
Smith, Alf
Smith, Billy
Smith, Clint
Smith, Hooley
Smith, Tommy
Stanley, Allan
Stanley, Barney
Stastny, Peter
Stewart, Jack
Stewart, Nels
Stuart, Bruce
Stuart, Hod
Taylor, Cyclone
Thompson, Tiny
Tretiak, Vladislav
Trihey, Harry
Trottier, Bryan
Ullman, Norm
Vezina, Georges
Walker, Jack
Walsh, Marty
Watson, Harry (Moose)
Watson, Harry Percival
Weiland, Cooney
Westwick, Harry
Whitcroft, Fred
Wilson, Phat
Worsley, Gump
Worters, Roy

BUILDERS
Adams, Charles
Adams, Weston

Ahearn, Bunny
Ahearn, Frank
Allan, Sir Montagu
Allen, Keith
Arbour, Al
Ballard, Harold
Bauer, Father David
Bickell, J.P.
Bowman, Scotty
Brown, George
Brown, Walter
Buckland, Frank
Bush, Walter, Jr.
Butterfield, Jack
Calder, Frank
Campbell, Angus
Campbell, Clarence
Cattarinich, Joseph
Dandurand, Leo
Dilio, Frank
Dudley, George
Dunn, James
Francis, Emile
Gibson, Jack
Gorman, Tommy
Griffiths, Frank
Hanley, Bill
Hay, Charles
Hendy, Jim
Hewitt, Foster
Hewitt, William
Hume, Fred
*Ilitch, Mike
Imlach, Punch
Ivan, Tommy
Jennings, William
Johnson, Bob
Juckes, Gordon
Kilpatrick, John
Knox, Seymour
LeBel, Robert
Leader, Al
Lockhart, Thomas
Loicq, Paul
Mariucci, John
Mathers, Frank
McLaughlin, Frederic
Milford, Jake
Molson, Sen. Hartland
Morrison, Ian "Scotty"
Murray, Pere Athol
Neilson, Roger
Nelson, Francis

Norris, Bruce
Norris, James
Norris, James Sr.
Northey, William
O'Brien, J. Ambrose
O'Neill, Brian Francis
Page, Frederick
Patrick, Craig
Patrick, Frank
Pickard, Allan
Pilous, Rudy
Poile, Bud
Pollock, Sam
Raymond, Sen. Donat
Robertson, John Ross
Robinson, Claude
Ross, Phillip
Sabetzki, Gunther
Sather, Glen
Selke, Frank
Sinden, Harry
Smith, Frank
Smythe, Conn
Snider, Ed
Stanley, Lord (of Preston)
Sutherland, Capt. James T.
Tarasov, Anatoli
Torrey, Bill
Turner, Lloyd
Tutt, William
Voss, Carl
Waghorne, Fred
Wirtz, Arthur
Wirtz, Bill
Ziegler, John A., Jr.

REFEREES AND LINESMEN
Armstrong, Neil
Ashley, John
Chadwick, Bill
D'Amico, John
Elliott, Chaucer
Hayes, George
Hewitson, Bobby
Ion, Mickey
Pavelich, Matt
Rodden, Mike
Smeaton, Cooper
Storey, Red
Udvari, Frank
Van Hellemond, Andy

NHL Home Ice[1]

Team	Name (built)	Capacity	Team	Name (built)	Capacity
Anaheim	The Arrowhead Pond of Anaheim (1993)	17,174	Montreal	Le Centre Bell[6] (1996)	21,273
Atlanta	Philips Arena (1999)	18,750	Nashville	Gaylord Entertainment Center[7] (1996)	17,500
Boston	FleetCenter (1995)	17,565	New Jersey	Continental Airlines Arena[8] (1981)	19,040
Buffalo	HSBC Arena[2] (1996)	18,690	N.Y. Islanders	Nassau Veterans Memorial Col. (1972)	16,297
Calgary	Pengrowth Saddledome (1983)	17,104	N.Y. Rangers	Madison Square Garden (1968)	18,200
Carolina	RBC Center[3] (1999)	18,730	Ottawa	Corel Centre (1996)	18,500
Chicago	United Center (1994)	20,500	Philadelphia	First Union Center (1996)	19,519
Colorado	Pepsi Center (1999)	18,007	Phoenix	America West Arena (1992)	16,210
Columbus	Nationwide Arena (2000)	18,500	Pittsburgh	Mellon Arena[9] (1961)	17,537
Dallas	American Airlines Center (1980)	18,000	St. Louis	Savvis Center[10] (1994)	21,000
Detroit	Joe Louis Arena (1979)	19,983	San Jose	HP Pavilion[11] (1993)	17,483
Edmonton	Skyreach Centre[4] (1974)	17,100	Tampa Bay	St. Pete Times Forum[12] (1996)	19,758
Florida	Office Depot Center[5] (1998)	19,250	Toronto	Air Canada Centre (1999)	18,800
Los Angeles	Staples Center (1999)	18,500	Vancouver	GM Place (1995)	18,422
Minnesota	Xcel Energy Arena (2000)	18,600	Washington	MCI Center (1997)	19,700

(1) At the end of the 2002-2003 season. (2) Marine Midland Arena, 1996-2000. (3) Entertainment & Sports Arena, 1996-2002. (4) Northlands Col., 1974-79; Edmonton Col., 1979-98. (5) National Car Rental Center, 1998-2002. (6) Le Centre Molson, 1996-2002. (7) Nashville Arena, 1997-1999. (8) Brendan Byrne/Meadowlands Arena, 1981-96. (9) Civic Arena, 1961-99. (10) Kiel Center, 1994-2000. (11) San Jose Arena, 1993-2000; Compaq Center, 2001. (12) Ice Palace, 1996-2002.

NCAA HOCKEY CHAMPIONS

Year	Team	Year	Team	Year	Team	Year	Team
1948	Michigan	1962	Michigan Tech	1976	Minnesota	1990	Wisconsin
1949	Boston College	1963	North Dakota	1977	Wisconsin	1991	N. Michigan
1950	Colorado College	1964	Michigan	1978	Boston Univ.	1992	Lake Superior St.
1951	Michigan	1965	Michigan Tech	1979	Minnesota	1993	Maine
1952	Michigan	1966	Michigan State	1980	North Dakota	1994	Lake Superior St.
1953	Michigan	1967	Cornell	1981	Wisconsin	1995	Boston Univ.
1954	RPI	1968	Denver	1982	North Dakota	1996	Michigan
1955	Michigan	1969	Denver	1983	Wisconsin	1997	North Dakota
1956	Michigan	1970	Cornell	1984	Bowling Green	1998	Michigan
1957	Colorado College	1971	Boston Univ.	1985	RPI	1999	Maine
1958	Denver	1972	Boston Univ.	1986	Michigan State	2000	North Dakota
1959	North Dakota	1973	Wisconsin	1987	North Dakota	2001	Boston College
1960	Denver	1974	Minnesota	1988	Lake Superior St.	2002	Minnesota
1961	Denver	1975	Michigan Tech	1989	Harvard	2003	Minnesota

SOCCER
2003 Women's World Cup

Germany defeated Sweden, 2-1, in overtime, in the final of the Women's World Cup Oct. 12, 2003, at the Home Depot Center in Carson, CA. Substitute Nia Kuenzer's header in the 8th minute of overtime gave Germany its 1st World Cup title. Germany's best previous finishes had been 2nd in 1995 and 3rd in 1991. German forward Birgit Prinz won the Golden Ball as top player in the tournament, and her 7 goals earned her the Golden Shoe as top scorer. Germany's Maren Meinert and Brazil's Katia each scored 4 goals. The U.S. defeated Canada, 3-1, in the 3rd-place game Oct. 11. Shannon Boxx, Kristine Lilly, and Tiffeny Milbrett each scored for the U.S. The U.S., shocked by Germany 3-0 in the semifinals, had won 2 World Cup titles and finished 3rd twice. FIFA, soccer's world governing body, had announced in May that the Women's World Cup—scheduled to be held in China from Sept. 23 through Oct. 11—would move to the U.S. over concerns about Severe Acute Respiratory Syndrome (SARS). The 2007 Women's World Cup was then scheduled for China.

2003 First Round Standings

COUNTRY (Group A)	W	L	T	GF	GA	Pts	COUNTRY (Group C)	W	L	T	GF	GA	Pts
United States	3	0	0	11	1	9	Germany	3	0	0	13	2	9
Sweden	2	1	0	5	3	6	Canada	2	1	0	7	5	6
North Korea	1	2	0	3	4	3	Japan	1	2	0	7	6	3
Nigeria	0	3	0	0	11	0	Argentina	0	3	0	1	15	0

COUNTRY (Group B)	W	L	T	GF	GA	Pts	COUNTRY (Group D)	W	L	T	GF	GA	Pts
Brazil	2	0	1	8	2	7	China	2	0	1	3	1	7
Norway	2	1	0	10	5	6	Russia	2	1	0	5	2	6
France	1	1	1	2	3	4	Ghana	1	2	0	2	5	3
South Korea	0	3	0	1	11	0	Australia	0	2	1	3	5	1

2003 First Round Women's World Cup Results

Sept. 20
Norway 2, France 0 (A)
North Korea 3, Nigeria 0 (A)
Germany 4, Canada 1 (C)
Japan 6, Argentina 0 (C)

Sept. 21
United States 3, Sweden 1 (B)
Brazil 3, South Korea 0 (B)
Russia 2, Australia 1 (E)
China 1, Ghana 0 (E)

Sept. 24
Brazil 4, Norway 1 (B)
Germany 3, Japan 0 (C)
France 1, South Korea 0 (B)
Canada 3, Argentina 0 (C)

Sept. 25
Sweden 1, North Korea 0 (A)
United States 5, Nigeria 0 (A)
Russia 3, Ghana 0 (E)
China 1, Australia 1 (E)

Sept. 27
Norway 7, South Korea 1 (D)
France 1, Brazil 1 (B)
Germany 6, Argentina 1 (B)
Canada 3, Japan 1 (D)

Sept. 28
Sweden 3, Nigeria 0 (C)
United States 3, North Korea 0 (C)
Ghana 2, Australia 1 (F)
China 1, Russia 0 (F)

Final Round Results

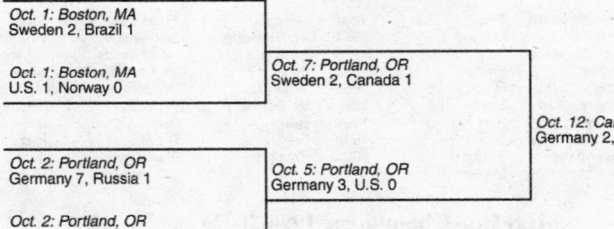

Oct. 1: Boston, MA
Sweden 2, Brazil 1

Oct. 1: Boston, MA
U.S. 1, Norway 0

Oct. 7: Portland, OR
Sweden 2, Canada 1

Oct. 2: Portland, OR
Germany 7, Russia 1

Oct. 2: Portland, OR
Canada 1, China 0

Oct. 5: Portland, OR
Germany 3, U.S. 0

Oct. 12: Carson, CA
Germany 2, Sweden 1 (OT)

Third Place Final
Oct. 11: Carson, CA
U.S. 3, Canada 1

Women's World Cup, 1991-2003

Year	Winner	Final Opponent	Score	Site	Third Place
1991	U.S.	Norway	2-1	China	Germany
1995	Norway	Germany	2-0	Sweden	U.S.
1999	U.S.	China	0-0*	Pasadena, CA	Brazil
2003	Germany	Sweden	2-1 (OT)	Carson, CA	U.S.

* U.S. 5-4, penalty kicks

2002 Women's United Soccer Association

In the WUSA Founder's Cup championship game, Aug. 24, 2002, in San Diego, CA, the Washington Freedom defeated the Atlanta Beat in overtime, 2-1. MVP Abby Wambach scored both goals for Washington, the 2nd 6 minutes into overtime. Boston Breaker forward Maren Meinert was named the MVP of the WUSA season. San Diego's Joy Fawcett was Defender of the Year, and Briana Scurry was Goalkeeper of the Year. Christine Latham of the Washington Spirit was named Rookie of the Year, and the Coach of the Year was Pia Sundhage (Philadelphia).

On Sept. 15, just 5 days before the start of the 2003 Women's World Cup, the Women's United Soccer Association announced that it would fold. Though some top players had taken pay cuts, the league reportedly had a deficit of about $16 million. Lack of TV ratings and sponsorship spelled doom for the league, which saw its average attendance fall from more than 8,000 per game in its inaugural year (2001) to 6,700 in 2003.

2002 Men's World Cup

Soccer superpower Brazil won 7 straight matches, including a 2-0 win over Germany on June 30, to claim a record 5th World Cup. Favorites France, Argentina, and Portugal failed to advance to the 2nd round, while the U.S. had an unexpectedly strong showing, defeating Mexico, 2-0, before losing 1-0 to Germany in the quarterfinals. Co-host South Korea also played well, finishing 4th overall. A total of 198 teams vied for the 29 of 32 spots in the competition. (Co-hosts Japan and S. Korea, and 1998 winner France had automatic bids.) Brazilian forward Ronaldo won the Golden Shoe for most goals, 8, including 2 in the final. Germany's Oliver Kahn became the 1st goalkeeper to win the Golden Ball as the tournament's best player. The next World Cup was scheduled to be held in 12 German cities in 2006. Berlin was scheduled to host the finals.

Final Round Results

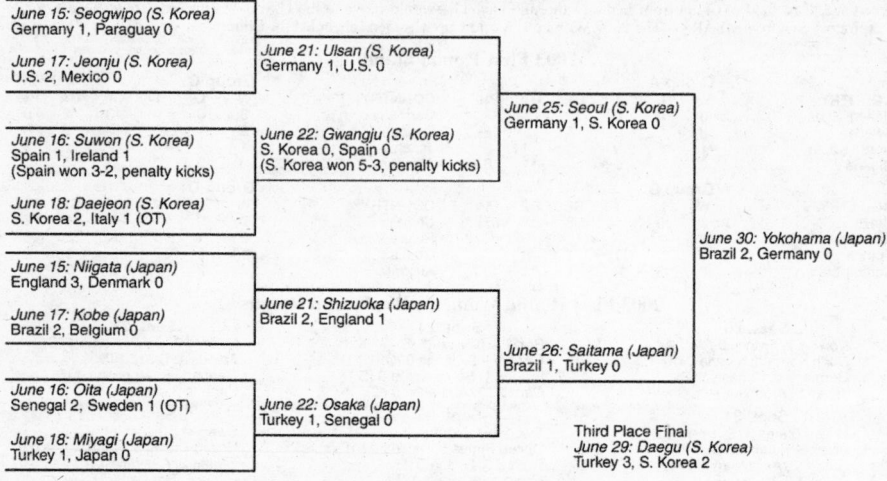

```
June 15: Seogwipo (S. Korea)
Germany 1, Paraguay 0
                                June 21: Ulsan (S. Korea)
June 17: Jeonju (S. Korea)      Germany 1, U.S. 0
U.S. 2, Mexico 0
                                                        June 25: Seoul (S. Korea)
                                                        Germany 1, S. Korea 0
June 16: Suwon (S. Korea)       June 22: Gwangju (S. Korea)
Spain 1, Ireland 1              S. Korea 0, Spain 0
(Spain won 3-2, penalty kicks)  (S. Korea won 5-3, penalty kicks)

June 18: Daejeon (S. Korea)
S. Korea 2, Italy 1 (OT)
                                                                    June 30: Yokohama (Japan)
                                                                    Brazil 2, Germany 0
June 15: Niigata (Japan)
England 3, Denmark 0
                                June 21: Shizuoka (Japan)
June 17: Kobe (Japan)           Brazil 2, England 1
Brazil 2, Belgium 0
                                                        June 26: Saitama (Japan)
                                                        Brazil 1, Turkey 0
June 16: Oita (Japan)
Senegal 2, Sweden 1 (OT)        June 22: Osaka (Japan)
                                Turkey 1, Senegal 0
June 18: Miyagi (Japan)                                 Third Place Final
Turkey 1, Japan 0                                       June 29: Daegu (S. Korea)
                                                        Turkey 3, S. Korea 2
```

Men's World Cup, 1930-2002

Year	Winner	Final opponent	Site	Year	Winner	Final opponent	Site
1930	Uruguay	Argentina	Uruguay	1974	W. Germany	Netherlands	W. Germany
1934	Italy	Czechoslovakia	Italy	1978	Argentina	Netherlands	Argentina
1938	Italy	Hungary	France	1982	Italy	W. Germany	Spain
1950	Uruguay	Brazil	Brazil	1986	Argentina	W. Germany	Mexico
1954	W. Germany	Hungary	Switzerland	1990	W. Germany	Argentina	Italy
1958	Brazil	Sweden	Sweden	1994	Brazil	Italy	U.S.
1962	Brazil	Czechoslovakia	Chile	1998	France	Brazil	France
1966	England	W. Germany	England	2002	Brazil	Germany	Japan/S. Korea
1970	Brazil	Italy	Mexico				

MLS Cup Champions, 1996-2002

Year	Winner	Final opponent	Score	Site	MVP
1996	Washington, DC	Los Angeles	3–2 (OT)	Foxboro, MA	Marco Etcheverry
1997	Washington, DC	Colorado	2–1	Washington, DC	Jaime Moreno
1998	Chicago	Washington, DC	2–0	Pasadena, CA	Peter Nowak
1999	Washington, DC	Los Angeles	2–0	Foxboro, MA	Ben Olsen
2000	Kansas City	Chicago	1-0	Washington, DC	Tony Meola
2001	San Jose	Los Angeles	2-1 (OT)	Columbus, OH	Dwayne DeRosario
2002	Los Angeles	New England	1-0 (OT)	Foxboro, MA	Carlos Ruiz

NCAA Soccer Champions, 1982-2002

Year[1]	Men	Women	Year[1]	Men	Women
1982	Indiana	North Carolina	1993	Virginia	North Carolina
1983	Indiana	North Carolina	1994	Virginia	North Carolina
1984	Clemson	North Carolina	1995	Wisconsin	Notre Dame
1985	UCLA	George Mason	1996	St. John's (NY)	North Carolina
1986	Duke	North Carolina	1997	UCLA	North Carolina
1987	Clemson	North Carolina	1998	Indiana	Florida
1988	Indiana	North Carolina	1999	Indiana	North Carolina
1989	Santa Clara (tie, 2 OT)	Virginia, North Carolina	2000	Connecticut	North Carolina
1990	UCLA	North Carolina	2001	North Carolina	Santa Clara
1991	Virginia	North Carolina	2002	UCLA	Portland
1992	Virginia	North Carolina			

(1) NCAA Championships began in 1959 for men, in 1982 for women.

GOLF

Men's All-Time Major Professional Championship Leaders

(Through the 2003 season; *active PGA player; (a)=amateur.)

Player	Masters	U.S. Open	British Open	PGA	Total
Jack Nicklaus*	1963, '65-66, '72, '75, '86	1962, '67, '72, '80	1966, '70, '78	1963, '71, '73, '75, '80	18
Walter Hagen	—	1914, '19	1922, '24, '28-29	1921, '24-27	11
Ben Hogan	1951, '53	1948, '50-51, '53	1953	1946, '48	9
Gary Player	1961, '74, '78	1965	1959, '68, '74	1962, '72	9
Tom Watson*	1977, '81	1982	1975, '77, '80, '82-83	—	8
Tiger Woods*	1997, 2001, 2002	2000, 2002	2000	1999, 2000	8
Bobby Jones (a)	—	1923, '26, '29-30	1926-27, '30	—	7
Arnold Palmer	1958, '60, '62, '64	1960	1961-62	—	7
Gene Sarazen	1935	1922, '32	1932	1922-23, '33	7
Sam Snead	1949, '52, '54	—	1946	1942, '49, '51	7
Harry Vardon	—	1900	1896, '98-99, 1903, '11, '14	—	7
Nick Faldo*	1989-90, '96	—	1987, '90, '92	—	6
Lee Trevino	—	1968, '71	1971-72	1974, '84	6

Professional Golfers' Association Leading Money Winners, by Year

Year	Player	Earnings	Year	Player	Earnings	Year	Player	Earnings
1946	Ben Hogan	$42,556	1965	Jack Nicklaus	$140,752	1984	Tom Watson	$476,260
1947	Jimmy Demaret	27,936	1966	Billy Casper	121,944	1985	Curtis Strange	542,321
1948	Ben Hogan	36,812	1967	Jack Nicklaus	188,988	1986	Greg Norman	653,296
1949	Sam Snead	31,593	1968	Billy Casper	205,168	1987	Curtis Strange	925,941
1950	Sam Snead	35,758	1969	Frank Beard	175,223	1988	Curtis Strange	1,147,644
1951	Lloyd Mangrum	26,088	1970	Lee Trevino	157,037	1989	Tom Kite	1,395,278
1952	Julius Boros	37,032	1971	Jack Nicklaus	244,490	1990	Greg Norman	1,165,477
1953	Lew Worsham	34,002	1972	Jack Nicklaus	320,542	1991	Corey Pavin	979,430
1954	Bob Toski	65,819	1973	Jack Nicklaus	308,362	1992	Fred Couples	1,344,188
1955	Julius Boros	65,121	1974	Johnny Miller	353,201	1993	Nick Price	1,478,557
1956	Ted Kroll	72,835	1975	Jack Nicklaus	323,149	1994	Nick Price	1,499,927
1957	Dick Mayer	65,835	1976	Jack Nicklaus	266,438	1995	Greg Norman	1,654,959
1958	Arnold Palmer	42,407	1977	Tom Watson	310,653	1996	Tom Lehman	1,780,159
1959	Art Wall, Jr.	53,167	1978	Tom Watson	362,429	1997	Tiger Woods	2,066,833
1960	Arnold Palmer	75,262	1979	Tom Watson	462,636	1998	David Duval	2,591,031
1961	Gary Player	64,540	1980	Tom Watson	530,808	1999	Tiger Woods	6,616,585
1962	Arnold Palmer	81,448	1981	Tom Kite	375,699	2000	Tiger Woods	9,188,321
1963	Arnold Palmer	128,230	1982	Craig Stadler	446,462	2001	Tiger Woods	5,687,777
1964	Jack Nicklaus	113,284	1983	Hal Sutton	426,668	2002	Tiger Woods	6,912,625

Masters Golf Tournament Winners

Year	Winner	Year	Winner	Year	Winner	Year	Winner
1934	Horton Smith	1953	Ben Hogan	1970	Billy Casper	1987	Larry Mize
1935	Gene Sarazen	1954	Sam Snead	1971	Charles Coody	1988	Sandy Lyle
1936	Horton Smith	1955	Cary Middlecoff	1972	Jack Nicklaus	1989	Nick Faldo
1937	Byron Nelson	1956	Jack Burke	1973	Tommy Aaron	1990	Nick Faldo
1938	Henry Picard	1957	Doug Ford	1974	Gary Player	1991	Ian Woosnam
1939	Ralph Guldahl	1958	Arnold Palmer	1975	Jack Nicklaus	1992	Fred Couples
1940	Jimmy Demaret	1959	Art Wall Jr.	1976	Ray Floyd	1993	Bernhard Langer
1941	Craig Wood	1960	Arnold Palmer	1977	Tom Watson	1994	Jose Maria Olazabal
1942	Byron Nelson	1961	Gary Player	1978	Gary Player	1995	Ben Crenshaw
1943-45	not played	1962	Arnold Palmer	1979	Fuzzy Zoeller	1996	Nick Faldo
1946	Herman Keiser	1963	Jack Nicklaus	1980	Seve Ballesteros	1997	Tiger Woods
1947	Jimmy Demaret	1964	Arnold Palmer	1981	Tom Watson	1998	Mark O'Meara
1948	Claude Harmon	1965	Jack Nicklaus	1982	Craig Stadler	1999	Jose Maria Olazabal
1949	Sam Snead	1966	Jack Nicklaus	1983	Seve Ballesteros	2000	Vijay Singh
1950	Jimmy Demaret	1967	Gay Brewer, Jr.	1984	Ben Crenshaw	2001	Tiger Woods
1951	Ben Hogan	1968	Bob Goalby	1985	Bernhard Langer	2002	Tiger Woods
1952	Sam Snead	1969	George Archer	1986	Jack Nicklaus	2003	Mike Weir

United States Open Winners

(First contested in 1895)

Year	Winner	Year	Winner	Year	Winner	Year	Winner
1934	Olin Dutra	1954	Ed Furgol	1971	Lee Trevino	1988	Curtis Strange
1935	Sam Parks, Jr.	1955	Jack Fleck	1972	Jack Nicklaus	1989	Curtis Strange
1936	Tony Manero	1956	Cary Middlecoff	1973	Johnny Miller	1990	Hale Irwin
1937	Ralph Guldahl	1957	Dick Mayer	1974	Hale Irwin	1991	Payne Stewart
1938	Ralph Guldahl	1958	Tommy Bolt	1975	Lou Graham	1992	Tom Kite
1939	Byron Nelson	1959	Billy Casper	1976	Jerry Pate	1993	Lee Janzen
1940	Lawson Little	1960	Arnold Palmer	1977	Hubert Green	1994	Ernie Els
1941	Craig Wood	1961	Gene Littler	1978	Andy North	1995	Corey Pavin
1942-45	Not Played	1962	Jack Nicklaus	1979	Hale Irwin	1996	Steve Jones
1946	Lloyd Mangrum	1963	Julius Boros	1980	Jack Nicklaus	1997	Ernie Els
1947	L. Worsham	1964	Ken Venturi	1981	David Graham	1998	Lee Janzen
1948	Ben Hogan	1965	Gary Player	1982	Tom Watson	1999	Payne Stewart
1949	Cary Middlecoff	1966	Billy Casper	1983	Larry Nelson	2000	Tiger Woods
1950	Ben Hogan	1967	Jack Nicklaus	1984	Fuzzy Zoeller	2001	Retief Goosen
1951	Ben Hogan	1968	Lee Trevino	1985	Andy North	2002	Tiger Woods
1952	Julius Boros	1969	Orville Moody	1986	Ray Floyd	2003	Jim Furyk
1953	Ben Hogan	1970	Tony Jacklin	1987	Scott Simpson		

> **IT'S A FACT:** Annika Sorenstam made news when she became the 1st woman in 58 years to play on the PGA tour at the Colonial in May, but 3 other women also took on the men in 2003. Suzy Whaley played in the Greater Hartford Open in July, 13-year-old Michelle Wie played in the Nationwide Tour's Boise Open in September, and Jan Stephenson teed up at Turtle Bay on the Champion's Tour in October.

British Open Winners
(First contested in 1860)

Year	Winner	Year	Winner	Year	Winner	Year	Winner
1934	Henry Cotton	1956	Peter Thomson	1972	Lee Trevino	1988	Seve Ballesteros
1935	Alf Perry	1957	Bobby Locke	1973	Tom Weiskopf	1989	Mark Calcavecchia
1936	Alf Padgham	1958	Peter Thomson	1974	Gary Player	1990	Nick Faldo
1937	T.H. Cotton	1959	Gary Player	1975	Tom Watson	1991	Ian Baker-Finch
1938	R.A. Whitcombe	1960	Kel Nagle	1976	Johnny Miller	1992	Nick Faldo
1939	Richard Burton	1961	Arnold Palmer	1977	Tom Watson	1993	Greg Norman
1940-45	not played	1962	Arnold Palmer	1978	Jack Nicklaus	1994	Nick Price
1946	Sam Snead	1963	Bob Charles	1979	Seve Ballesteros	1995	John Daly
1947	Fred Daly	1964	Tony Lema	1980	Tom Watson	1996	Tom Lehman
1948	Henry Cotton	1965	Peter Thomson	1981	Bill Rogers	1997	Justin Leonard
1949	Bobby Locke	1966	Jack Nicklaus	1982	Tom Watson	1998	Mark O'Meara
1950	Bobby Locke	1967	Roberto de Vicenzo	1983	Tom Watson	1999	Paul Lawrie
1951	Max Faulkner	1968	Gary Player	1984	Seve Ballesteros	2000	Tiger Woods
1952	Bobby Locke	1969	Tony Jacklin	1985	Sandy Lyle	2001	David Duval
1953	Ben Hogan	1970	Jack Nicklaus	1986	Greg Norman	2002	Ernie Els
1954	Peter Thomson	1971	Lee Trevino	1987	Nick Faldo	2003	Ben Curtis
1955	Peter Thomson						

PGA Championship Winners
(First contested in 1916)

Year	Winner	Year	Winner	Year	Winner	Year	Winner
1934	Paul Runyan	1952	James Turnesa	1970	Dave Stockton	1987	Larry Nelson
1935	Johnny Revolta	1953	Walter Burkemo	1971	Jack Nicklaus	1988	Jeff Sluman
1936	Denny Shute	1954	Melvin Harbert	1972	Gary Player	1989	Payne Stewart
1937	Denny Shute	1955	Doug Ford	1973	Jack Nicklaus	1990	Wayne Grady
1938	Paul Runyan	1956	Jack Burke	1974	Lee Trevino	1991	John Daly
1939	Henry Picard	1957	Lionel Hebert	1975	Jack Nicklaus	1992	Nick Price
1940	Byron Nelson	1958	Dow Finsterwald	1976	Dave Stockton	1993	Paul Azinger
1941	Victor Ghezzi	1959	Bob Rosburg	1977	Lanny Wadkins	1994	Nick Price
1942	Sam Snead	1960	Jay Hebert	1978	John Mahaffey	1995	Steve Elkington
1943	not played	1961	Jerry Barber	1979	David Graham	1996	Mark Brooks
1944	Bob Hamilton	1962	Gary Player	1980	Jack Nicklaus	1997	Davis Love III
1945	Byron Nelson	1963	Jack Nicklaus	1981	Larry Nelson	1998	Vijay Singh
1946	Ben Hogan	1964	Bob Nichols	1982	Ray Floyd	1999	Tiger Woods
1947	Jim Ferrier	1965	Dave Marr	1983	Hal Sutton	2000	Tiger Woods
1948	Ben Hogan	1966	Al Geiberger	1984	Lee Trevino	2001	David Toms
1949	Sam Snead	1967	Don January	1985	Hubert Green	2002	Rich Beem
1950	Chandler Harper	1968	Julius Boros	1986	Bob Tway	2003	Shaun Micheel
1951	Sam Snead	1969	Ray Floyd				

Women's All-Time Major Professional Championship Leaders
(Through the 2003 season; *active LPGA player.)

Player	Nabisco[1]	LPGA	U.S. Open[2]	du Maurier[3]/ British Open	Titleholders[4]	Western Open[5]	Total
Patty Berg .... —	—	—	1946	—	1937-39, '48, '53, '55, '57	1941, '43, '48, '51, '55, '57-58	15
Mickey Wright...... —	—	1958, '60-61, '63	1958-59, '61, '64	—	1961-62	1962-63, '66	13
Louise Suggs ..... —	—	1957	1949, '52	—	1946, '54, '56, '59	1946-47, '49, '53	11
Babe Zaharias ..... —	—	—	1948, '50, '54	—	1947, '50, '52	1940, '44-45, '50	10
Betsy Rawls ...... —	—	1959, '69	1951, '53, '57, '60	—	—	1952, '59	8
Juli Inkster*........ 1984, '89		1999, 2000	1999, 2002	1984	—	—	7
Pat Bradley*....... 1986		1986	1981	1980, '85-86	—	—	6
Betsy King*....... 1987, '90, '97		1992	1989-90	—	—	—	6
Patty Sheehan* 1996		1983-84, '93	1992, '94	—	—	—	6
Kathy Whitworth.... —		1967, '71, '75	—	—	1965-66	1967	6
Karrie Webb*[3] 2000		2001	2000-2001	1999[3], 2002	—	—	6
Annika Sorenstam*[3]. 2001-02		2003	1995-96	2003	—	—	6

Tournaments: (1) Nabisco Championship, formerly Nabisco Dinah Shore (1982-1999), designated major in 1983. (2) U.S. Women's Open. (3) In 2001, the British Open replaced the du Maurier Classic as the LPGA's 4th major. Webb won the 2002 Brit. Open; Sorenstam won in 2003. (4) Titleholders Championship; major from 1930 to 1972. (5) Western Open; major from 1937 to 1967.

Ladies Professional Golf Association Leading Money Winners

Year	Player	Earnings	Year	Player	Earnings	Year	Player	Earnings
1954	Patty Berg	$16,011	1971	Kathy Whitworth	$41,181	1987	Ayako Okamoto	$466,034
1955	Patty Berg	16,492	1972	Kathy Whitworth	65,063	1988	Sherri Turner	347,255
1956	Marlene Hagge	20,235	1973	Kathy Whitworth	82,854	1989	Betsy King	654,132
1957	Patty Berg	16,272	1974	JoAnne Carner	87,094	1990	Beth Daniel	863,578
1958	Beverly Hanson	12,629	1975	Sandra Palmer	94,805	1991	Pat Bradley	763,118
1959	Betsy Rawls	26,774	1976	Judy Rankin	150,734	1992	Dottie Mochrie	693,335
1960	Louise Suggs	16,892	1977	Judy Rankin	122,890	1993	Betsy King	595,992
1961	Mickey Wright	22,236	1978	Nancy Lopez	189,813	1994	Laura Davies	687,201
1962	Mickey Wright	21,641	1979	Nancy Lopez	215,987	1995	Annika Sorenstam	666,533
1963	Mickey Wright	31,269	1980	Beth Daniel	231,000	1996	Karrie Webb	1,002,000
1964	Mickey Wright	29,800	1981	Beth Daniel	206,977	1997	Annika Sorenstam	1,236,789
1965	Kathy Whitworth	28,658	1982	JoAnne Carner	310,399	1998	Annika Sorenstam	1,092,748
1966	Kathy Whitworth	33,517	1983	JoAnne Carner	291,404	1999	Karrie Webb	1,591,959
1967	Kathy Whitworth	32,937	1984	Betsy King	266,771	2000	Karrie Webb	1,876,853
1968	Kathy Whitworth	48,379	1985	Nancy Lopez	416,472	2001	Annika Sorenstam	2,105,868
1969	Carol Mann	49,152	1986	Pat Bradley	492,021	2002	Annika Sorenstam	2,863,904
1970	Kathy Whitworth	30,235						

Nabisco Championship Winners[1]

Year	Winner	Year	Winner	Year	Winner	Year	Winner
1983	Amy Alcott	1989	Juli Inkster	1995	Nanci Bowen	2000	Karrie Webb
1984	Juli Inkster	1990	Betsy King	1996	Patty Sheehan	2001	Annika Sorenstam
1985	Alice Miller	1991	Amy Alcott	1997	Betsy King	2002	Annika Sorenstam
1986	Pat Bradley	1992	Dottie Pepper	1998	Pat Hurst	2003	Patricia Meunier-
1987	Betsy King	1993	Helen Alfredsson	1999	Dottie Pepper		Lebouc
1988	Amy Alcott	1994	Donna Andrews				

(1) Formerly the Colgate Dinah Shore (1972-81), the Nabisco Dinah Shore (1982-99). Designated as a major championship in 1983.

LPGA Championship Winners

Year	Winner	Year	Winner	Year	Winner	Year	Winner
1955	Beverly Hanson	1968	Sandra Post	1980	Sally Little	1992	Betsy King
1956	Marlene Hagge	1969	Betsy Rawls	1981	Donna Caponi	1993	Patty Sheehan
1957	Louise Suggs	1970	Shirley Englehorn	1982	Jan Stephenson	1994	Laura Davies
1958	Mickey Wright	1971	Kathy Whitworth	1983	Patty Sheehan	1995	Kelly Robbins
1959	Betsy Rawls	1972	Kathy Ahern	1984	Patty Sheehan	1996	Laura Davies
1960	Mickey Wright	1973	Mary Mills	1985	Nancy Lopez	1997	Chris Johnson
1961	Mickey Wright	1974	Sandra Haynie	1986	Pat Bradley	1998	Se Ri Pak
1962	Judy Kimball	1975	Kathy Whitworth	1987	Jane Geddes	1999	Juli Inkster
1963	Mickey Wright	1976	Betty Burfeindt	1988	Sherri Turner	2000	Juli Inkster
1964	Mary Mills	1977	Chako Higuchi	1989	Nancy Lopez	2001	Karrie Webb
1965	Sandra Haynie	1978	Nancy Lopez	1990	Beth Daniel	2002	Se Ri Pak
1966	Gloria Ehret	1979	Donna Caponi	1991	Meg Mallon	2003	Annika Sorenstam
1967	Kathy Whitworth						

U.S. Women's Open Winners

Year	Winner	Year	Winner	Year	Winner	Year	Winner
1946	Patty Berg	1961	Mickey Wright	1975	Sandra Palmer	1990	Betsy King
1947	Betty Jameson	1962	Murle Lindstrom	1976	JoAnne Carner	1991	Meg Mallon
1948	"Babe" Zaharias	1963	Mary Mills	1977	Hollis Stacy	1992	Patty Sheehan
1949	Louise Suggs	1964	Mickey Wright	1978	Hollis Stacy	1993	Lauri Merten
1950	"Babe" Zaharias	1965	Carol Mann	1979	Jerilyn Britz	1994	Patty Sheehan
1951	Betsy Rawls	1966	Sandra Spuzich	1980	Amy Alcott	1995	Annika Sorenstam
1952	Louise Suggs	1967	Catherine Lacoste	1981	Pat Bradley	1996	Annika Sorenstam
1953	Betsy Rawls		(amateur)	1982	Janet Alex	1997	Alison Nicholas
1954	"Babe" Zaharias	1968	Susie Maxwell Berning	1983	Jan Stephenson	1998	Se Ri Pak
1955	Fay Crocker	1969	Donna Caponi	1984	Hollis Stacy	1999	Juli Inkster
1956	Mrs. K. Cornelius	1970	Donna Caponi	1985	Kathy Baker	2000	Karrie Webb
1957	Betsy Rawls	1971	JoAnne Carner	1986	Jane Geddes	2001	Karrie Webb
1958	Mickey Wright	1972	Susie Maxwell Berning	1987	Laura Davies	2002	Juli Inkster
1959	Mickey Wright	1973	Susie Maxwell Berning	1988	Liselotte Neumann	2003	Hilary Lunke
1960	Betsy Rawls	1974	Sandra Haynie	1989	Betsy King		

Women's British Open[1]

Year	Winner	Year	Winner	Year	Winner
2001	Se Ri Pak	2002	Karrie Webb	2003	Annika Sorenstam

(1) First held as the Ladies' British Open in 1976; became the LPGA's 4th major championship in 2001, replacing the du Maurier Classic.

du Maurier Classic Winners[1]

Year	Winner	Year	Winner	Year	Winner	Year	Winner
1979	Amy Alcott	1985	Pat Bradley	1991	Nancy Scranton	1996	Laura Davies
1980	Pat Bradley	1986	Pat Bradley	1992	Sherri Steinhauer	1997	Colleen Walker
1981	Jan Stephenson	1987	Jody Rosenthal	1993	Brandie Burton	1998	Brandie Burton
1982	Sandra Haynie	1988	Sally Little	1994	Martha Nause	1999	Karrie Webb
1983	Hollis Stacy	1989	Tammie Green	1995	Jenny Lidback	2000	Meg Mallon
1984	Juli Inkster	1990	Cathy Johnston				

(1) Formerly the Peter Jackson Classic (1974-82). Designated a major championship from 1979-2000.

International Golf

Ryder Cup

Began as a biennial team competition between pro golfers from the U.S. and Great Britain. The British team was expanded in 1973 to include players from Ireland and in 1979 to include players from the rest of Europe. The 2004 Cup was scheduled for Sept. 14-19, at Oakland Hills CC, Bloomfield Hills, MI.

Year	Winner	Year	Winner	Year	Winner	Year	Winner
1927	U.S., 9½-2½	1951	U.S., 9½-2½	1969	Draw, 16-16	1987	Europe, 15-13
1929	Britain-Ireland, 7-5	1953	U.S., 6½-5½	1971	U.S., 18½-13½	1989	Draw, 14-14
1931	U.S., 9-3	1955	U.S., 8-4	1973	U.S., 19-13	1991	U.S., 14½-13½
1933	Britain, 6½-5½	1957	Britain-Ireland, 7½-4½	1975	U.S., 21-11	1993	U.S., 15-13
1935	U.S., 9-3	1959	U.S., 8½-3½	1977	U.S., 12½-7½	1995	Europe, 14½-13½
1937	U.S., 8-4	1961	U.S., 14½-9½	1979	U.S., 17-11	1997	Europe, 14½-13½
1939-45	Not played	1963	U.S., 23-9	1981	U.S., 18½-9½	1999	U.S., 14½-13½
1947	U.S., 11-1	1965	U.S., 19½-12½	1983	U.S., 14½-13½	2002	Europe, 15½-12½
1949	U.S., 7-5	1967	U.S., 23½-8½	1985	Europe, 16½-11½		

Solheim Cup

The Solheim Cup began in 1990 as a biennial team competition between pro women golfers from Europe and the U.S. In the Sept. 14 final round of the 2003 Cup in Sweden, Europe reached the 14½ points needed to win with 5 matches in progress. In an unprecedented move, the trailing players conceded, and all the golfers walked off the course. Competition moved to odd years in 2003 to alternate with the Ryder Cup, which was postponed and moved permanently to even years after the Sept. 2001 terrorist attacks. The 2005 Cup was scheduled to be held Sept. 9-11, at Crooked Stick Golf Club in Carmel, IN.

Year	Winner	Year	Winner	Year	Winner	Year	Winner
1990	U.S., 11½-4½	1994	U.S., 13-7	1998	U.S., 16-12	2002	U.S., 15½-12½
1992	Europe, 11½-6½	1996	U.S., 17-11	2000	Europe, 14½-11½	2003	Europe, 17½-10½

TENNIS

Australian Open Singles Champions, 1969-2003

(First contested 1905 for men, 1922 for women. Became an Open Championship in 1969.)
*2 tournaments held in 1977 (Jan. & Dec.). **In 1986 tournament moved to Jan. 1987; no championship in 1986.

Men's Singles

Year	Champion	Final Opponent
1969	Rod Laver	Andres Gimeno
1970	Arthur Ashe	Dick Crealy
1971	Ken Rosewall	Arthur Ashe
1972	Ken Rosewall	Mal Anderson
1973	John Newcombe	Onny Parun
1974	Jimmy Connors	Phil Dent
1975	John Newcombe	Jimmy Connors
1976	Mark Edmondson	John Newcombe
1977*	Roscoe Tanner	Guillermo Vilas
	Vitas Gerulaitis	John Lloyd
1978	Guillermo Vilas	John Marks
1979	Guillermo Vilas	John Sadri
1980	Brian Teacher	Kim Warwick
1981	Johan Kriek	Steve Denton
1982	Johan Kriek	Steve Denton
1983	Mats Wilander	Ivan Lendl
1984	Mats Wilander	Kevin Curren
1985**	Stefan Edberg	Mats Wilander
1987	Stefan Edberg	Pat Cash
1988	Mats Wilander	Pat Cash
1989	Ivan Lendl	Miloslav Mecir
1990	Ivan Lendl	Stefan Edberg
1991	Boris Becker	Ivan Lendl
1992	Jim Courier	Stefan Edberg
1993	Jim Courier	Stefan Edberg
1994	Pete Sampras	Todd Martin
1995	Andre Agassi	Pete Sampras
1996	Boris Becker	Michael Chang
1997	Pete Sampras	Carlos Moya
1998	Petr Korda	Marcelo Rios
1999	Yevgeny Kafelnikov	Thomas Enqvist
2000	Andre Agassi	Yevgeny Kafelnikov
2001	Andre Agassi	Arnaud Clement
2002	Thomas Johansson	Marat Safin
2003	Andre Agassi	Rainer Schuettler

Women's Singles

Year	Champion	Final Opponent
1969	Margaret Smith Court	Billie Jean King
1970	Margaret Smith Court	Kerry Melville Reid
1971	Margaret Smith Court	Evonne Goolagong
1972	Virginia Wade	Evonne Goolagong
1973	Margaret Smith Court	Evonne Goolagong
1974	Evonne Goolagong	Chris Evert
1975	Evonne Goolagong	Martina Navratilova
1976	Evonne Goolagong	Renata Tomanova
1977*	Kerry Reid	Dianne Balestrat
	Evonne Goolagong	Helen Gourlay
1978	Chris O'Neill	Betsy Nagelsen
1979	Barbara Jordan	Sharon Walsh
1980	Hana Mandlikova	Wendy Turnbull
1981	Martina Navratilova	Chris Evert Lloyd
1982	Chris Evert Lloyd	Martina Navratilova
1983	Martina Navratilova	Kathy Jordan
1984	Chris Evert Lloyd	Helena Sukova
1985**	Martina Navratilova	Chris Evert Lloyd
1987	Hana Mandlikova	Martina Navratilova
1988	Steffi Graf	Chris Evert
1989	Steffi Graf	Helena Sukova
1990	Steffi Graf	Mary Joe Fernandez
1991	Monica Seles	Jana Novotna
1992	Monica Seles	Mary Joe Fernandez
1993	Monica Seles	Steffi Graf
1994	Steffi Graf	Arantxa Sánchez Vicario
1995	Mary Pierce	Arantxa Sánchez Vicario
1996	Monica Seles	Anke Huber
1997	Martina Hingis	Mary Pierce
1998	Martina Hingis	Conchita Martínez
1999	Martina Hingis	Amelie Mauresmo
2000	Lindsay Davenport	Martina Hingis
2001	Jennifer Capriati	Martina Hingis
2002	Jennifer Capriati	Martina Hingis
2003	Serena Williams	Venus Williams

French Open Singles Champions, 1968-2003

(First contested 1891 for men, 1897 for women. Became an Open Championship in 1968.)

Men's Singles

Year	Champion	Final Opponent
1968	Ken Rosewall	Rod Laver
1969	Rod Laver	Ken Rosewall
1970	Jan Kodes	Zeljko Franulovic
1971	Jan Kodes	Ilie Nastase
1972	Andres Gimeno	Patrick Proisy
1973	Ilie Nastase	Nikki Pilic
1974	Bjorn Borg	Manuel Orantes
1975	Bjorn Borg	Guillermo Vilas
1976	Adriano Panatta	Harold Solomon
1977	Guillermo Vilas	Brian Gottfried
1978	Bjorn Borg	Guillermo Vilas
1979	Bjorn Borg	Victor Pecci
1980	Bjorn Borg	Vitas Gerulaitis
1981	Bjorn Borg	Ivan Lendl
1982	Mats Wilander	Guillermo Vilas
1983	Yannick Noah	Mats Wilander
1984	Ivan Lendl	John McEnroe
1985	Mats Wilander	Ivan Lendl
1986	Ivan Lendl	Mikael Pernfors
1987	Ivan Lendl	Mats Wilander
1988	Mats Wilander	Henri Leconte
1989	Michael Chang	Stefan Edberg
1990	Andres Gomez	Andre Agassi
1991	Jim Courier	Andre Agassi
1992	Jim Courier	Petr Korda
1993	Sergi Bruguera	Jim Courier
1994	Sergi Bruguera	Alberto Berasategui
1995	Thomas Muster	Michael Chang
1996	Yevgeny Kafelnikov	Michael Stich
1997	Gustavo Kuerten	Sergei Bruguera
1998	Carlos Moya	Alex Corretja
1999	Andre Agassi	Andrei Medvedev
2000	Gustavo Kuerten	Magnus Norman
2001	Gustavo Kuerten	Alex Corretja
2002	Albert Costa	Juan Carlos Ferrero
2003	Juan Carlos Ferrero	Martin Verkerk

Women's Singles

Year	Champion	Final Opponent
1968	Nancy Richey	Ann Jones
1969	Margaret Smith Court	Ann Jones
1970	Margaret Smith Court	Helga Niessen
1971	Evonne Goolagong	Helen Gourlay
1972	Billie Jean King	Evonne Goolagong
1973	Margaret Smith Court	Chris Evert
1974	Chris Evert	Olga Morozova
1975	Chris Evert	Martina Navratilova
1976	Sue Barker	Renata Tomanova
1977	Mima Jausovec	Florenza Mihai
1978	Virginia Ruzici	Mima Jausovec
1979	Chris Evert Lloyd	Wendy Turnbull
1980	Chris Evert Lloyd	Virginia Ruzici
1981	Hana Mandlikova	Sylvia Hanika
1982	Martina Navratilova	Andrea Jaeger
1983	Chris Evert Lloyd	Mima Jausovec
1984	Martina Navratilova	Chris Evert Lloyd
1985	Chris Evert Lloyd	Martina Navratilova
1986	Chris Evert Lloyd	Martina Navratilova
1987	Steffi Graf	Martina Navratilova
1988	Steffi Graf	Natalia Zvereva
1989	Arantxa Sánchez Vicario	Steffi Graf
1990	Monica Seles	Steffi Graf
1991	Monica Seles	Arantxa Sánchez Vicario
1992	Monica Seles	Steffi Graf
1993	Steffi Graf	Mary Joe Fernandez
1994	Arantxa Sánchez Vicario	Mary Pierce
1995	Steffi Graf	Arantxa Sánchez Vicario
1996	Steffi Graf	Arantxa Sánchez Vicario
1997	Iva Majoli	Martina Hingis
1998	Arantxa Sánchez Vicario	Monica Seles
1999	Steffi Graf	Martina Hingis
2000	Mary Pierce	Conchita Martinez
2001	Jennifer Capriati	Kim Clijsters
2002	Serena Williams	Venus Williams
2003	Justine Henin-Hardenne	Kim Clijsters

U.S. Open Champions, 1925-2003

(Became an Open Championship in 1970.)

Men's Singles		Women's Singles	
(First contested 1881)		(First contested 1887)	
Year	Champion — Final Opponent	Year	Champion — Final Opponent

Year	Champion	Final Opponent	Year	Champion	Final Opponent
1925	Bill Tilden	William Johnston	1925	Helen Willis	Kathleen McKane
1926	Rene Lacoste	Jean Borotra	1926	Molla B. Mallory	Elizabeth Ryan
1927	Rene Lacoste	Bill Tilden	1927	Helen Wills	Betty Nuthall
1928	Henri Cochet	Francis Hunter	1928	Helen Wills	Helen Jacobs
1929	Bill Tilden	Francis Hunter	1929	Helen Wills	M. Watson
1930	John Doeg	Francis Shields	1930	Betty Nuthall	L. A. Harper
1931	H. Ellsworth Vines	George Lott	1931	Helen Wills Moody	E. B. Whittingstall
1932	H. Ellsworth Vines	Henri Cochet	1932	Helen Jacobs	Carolin A. Babcock
1933	Fred Perry	John Crawford	1933	Helen Jacobs	Helen Wills Moody
1934	Fred Perry	Wilmer Allison	1934	Helen Jacobs	Sarah H. Palfrey
1935	Wilmer Allison	Sidney Wood	1935	Helen Jacobs	Sarah Palfrey Fabyan
1936	Fred Perry	Don Budge	1936	Alice Marble	Helen Jacobs
1937	Don Budge	Baron G. von Cramm	1937	Anita Lizana	Jadwiga Jedrzejowska
1938	Don Budge	C. Gene Mako	1938	Alice Marble	Nancye Wynne
1939	Robert Riggs	S. Welby Van Horn	1939	Alice Marble	Helen Jacobs
1940	Don McNeill	Robert Riggs	1940	Alice Marble	Helen Jacobs
1941	Robert Riggs	F. L. Kovacs	1941	Sarah Palfrey Cooke	Pauline Betz
1942	F. R. Schroeder Jr.	Frank Parker	1942	Pauline Betz	Louise Brough
1943	Joseph Hunt	Jack Kramer	1943	Pauline Betz	Louise Brough
1944	Frank Parker	William Talbert	1944	Pauline Betz	Margaret Osborne
1945	Frank Parker	William Talbert	1945	Sarah Palfrey Cooke	Pauline Betz
1946	Jack Kramer	Thomas Brown Jr.	1946	Pauline Betz	Doris Hart
1947	Jack Kramer	Frank Parker	1947	Louise Brough	Margaret Osborne
1948	Pancho Gonzales	Eric Sturgess	1948	Margaret Osborne duPont	Louise Brough
1949	Pancho Gonzales	F. R. Schroeder Jr.	1949	Margaret Osborne duPont	Doris Hart
1950	Arthur Larsen	Herbert Flam	1950	Margaret Osborne duPont	Doris Hart
1951	Frank Sedgman	E. Victor Seixas Jr.	1951	Maureen Connolly	Shirley Fry
1952	Frank Sedgman	Gardnar Mulloy	1952	Maureen Connolly	Doris Hart
1953	Tony Trabert	E. Victor Seixas Jr.	1953	Maureen Connolly	Doris Hart
1954	E. Victor Seixas Jr.	Rex Hartwig	1954	Doris Hart	Louise Brough
1955	Tony Trabert	Ken Rosewall	1955	Doris Hart	Patricia Ward
1956	Ken Rosewall	Lewis Hoad	1956	Shirley Fry	Althea Gibson
1957	Malcolm Anderson	Ashley Cooper	1957	Althea Gibson	Louise Brough
1958	Ashley Cooper	Malcolm Anderson	1958	Althea Gibson	Darlene Hard
1959	Neale A. Fraser	Alejandro Olmedo	1959	Maria Bueno	Christine Truman
1960	Neale A. Fraser	Rod Laver	1960	Darlene Hard	Maria Bueno
1961	Roy Emerson	Rod Laver	1961	Darlene Hard	Ann Haydon
1962	Rod Laver	Roy Emerson	1962	Margaret Smith	Darlene Hard
1963	Rafael Osuna	F. A. Froehling 3rd	1963	Maria Bueno	Margaret Smith
1964	Roy Emerson	Fred Stolle	1964	Maria Bueno	Carole Graebner
1965	Manuel Santana	Cliff Drysdale	1965	Margaret Smith	Billie Jean Moffitt
1966	Fred Stolle	John Newcombe	1966	Maria Bueno	Nancy Richey
1967	John Newcombe	Clark Graebner	1967	Billie Jean King	Ann Haydon Jones
1968	Arthur Ashe	Tom Okker	1968	Virginia Wade	Billie Jean King
1969	Rod Laver	Tony Roche	1969	Margaret Smith Court	Nancy Richey
1970	Ken Rosewall	Tony Roche	1970	Margaret Smith Court	Rosemary Casals
1971	Stan Smith	Jan Kodes	1971	Billie Jean King	Rosemary Casals
1972	Ilie Nastase	Arthur Ashe	1972	Billie Jean King	Kerry Melville
1973	John Newcombe	Jan Kodes	1973	Margaret Smith Court	Evonne Goolagong
1974	Jimmy Connors	Ken Rosewall	1974	Billie Jean King	Evonne Goolagong
1975	Manuel Orantes	Jimmy Connors	1975	Chris Evert	Evonne Goolagong
1976	Jimmy Connors	Bjorn Borg	1976	Chris Evert	Evonne Goolagong
1977	Guillermo Vilas	Jimmy Connors	1977	Chris Evert	Wendy Turnbull
1978	Jimmy Connors	Bjorn Borg	1978	Chris Evert	Pam Shriver
1979	John McEnroe	Vitas Gerulaitis	1979	Tracy Austin	Chris Evert Lloyd
1980	John McEnroe	Bjorn Borg	1980	Chris Evert Lloyd	Hana Mandlikova
1981	John McEnroe	Bjorn Borg	1981	Tracy Austin	Martina Navratilova
1982	Jimmy Connors	Ivan Lendl	1982	Chris Evert Lloyd	Hana Mandlikova
1983	Jimmy Connors	Ivan Lendl	1983	Martina Navratilova	Chris Evert Lloyd
1984	John McEnroe	Ivan Lendl	1984	Martina Navratilova	Chris Evert Lloyd
1985	Ivan Lendl	John McEnroe	1985	Hana Mandlikova	Martina Navratilova
1986	Ivan Lendl	Miloslav Mecir	1986	Martina Navratilova	Helena Sukova
1987	Ivan Lendl	Mats Wilander	1987	Martina Navratilova	Steffi Graf
1988	Mats Wilander	Ivan Lendl	1988	Steffi Graf	Gabriela Sabatini
1989	Boris Becker	Ivan Lendl	1989	Steffi Graf	Martina Navratilova
1990	Pete Sampras	Andre Agassi	1990	Gabriela Sabatini	Steffi Graf
1991	Stefan Edberg	Jim Courier	1991	Monica Seles	Martina Navratilova
1992	Stefan Edberg	Pete Sampras	1992	Monica Seles	Arantxa Sanchez Vicario
1993	Pete Sampras	Cedric Pioline	1993	Steffi Graf	Helena Sukova
1994	Andre Agassi	Michael Stich	1994	Arantxa Sanchez Vicario	Steffi Graf
1995	Pete Sampras	Andre Agassi	1995	Steffi Graf	Monica Seles
1996	Pete Sampras	Michael Chang	1996	Steffi Graf	Monica Seles
1997	Patrick Rafter	Greg Rusedski	1997	Martina Hingis	Venus Williams
1998	Patrick Rafter	Mark Philippoussis	1998	Lindsay Davenport	Martina Hingis
1999	Andre Agassi	Todd Martin	1999	Serena Williams	Martina Hingis
2000	Marat Safin	Pete Sampras	2000	Venus Williams	Lindsay Davenport
2001	Lleyton Hewitt	Pete Sampras	2001	Venus Williams	Serena Williams
2002	Pete Sampras	Andre Agassi	2002	Serena Williams	Venus Williams
2003	Andy Roddick	Juan Carlos Ferrero	2003	Justine Henin-Hardenne	Kim Clijsters

All-England Champions, Wimbledon, 1925-2003
(Became an Open Championship in 1968.)

Men's Singles
(First contested 1877)

Year	Champion	Final Opponent
1925	Rene Lacoste	Jean Borotra
1926	Jean Borotra	Howard Kinsey
1927	Henri Cochet	Jean Borotra
1928	Rene Lacoste	Henri Cochet
1929	Henri Cochet	Jean Borotra
1930	Bill Tilden	Wilmer Allison
1931	Sidney B. Wood	Francis X. Shields
1932	Ellsworth Vines	Henry Austin
1933	Jack Crawford	Ellsworth Vines
1934	Fred Perry	Jack Crawford
1935	Fred Perry	Gottfried von Cramm
1936	Fred Perry	Gottfried von Cramm
1937	Donald Budge	Gottfried von Cramm
1938	Donald Budge	Henry Austin
1939	Bobby Riggs	Elwood Cooke
1940-45	Not held	Not held
1946	Yvon Petra	Geoff E. Brown
1947	Jack Kramer	Tom P. Brown
1948	Bob Falkenburg	John Bromwich
1949	Ted Schroeder	Jaroslav Drobny
1950	Budge Patty	Frank Sedgman
1951	Dick Savitt	Ken McGregor
1952	Frank Sedgman	Jaroslav Drobny
1953	Vic Seixas	Kurt Nielsen
1954	Jaroslav Drobny	Ken Rosewall
1955	Tony Trabert	Kurt Nielsen
1956	Lew Hoad	Ken Rosewall
1957	Lew Hoad	Ashley Cooper
1958	Ashley Cooper	Neale Fraser
1959	Alex Olmedo	Rod Laver
1960	Neale Fraser	Rod Laver
1961	Rod Laver	Chuck McKinley
1962	Rod Laver	Martin Mulligan
1963	Chuck McKinley	Fred Stolle
1964	Roy Emerson	Fred Stolle
1965	Roy Emerson	Fred Stolle
1966	Manuel Santana	Dennis Ralston
1967	John Newcombe	Wilhelm Bungert
1968	Rod Laver	Tony Roche
1969	Rod Laver	John Newcombe
1970	John Newcombe	Ken Rosewall
1971	John Newcombe	Stan Smith
1972	Stan Smith	Ilie Nastase
1973	Jan Kodes	Alex Metreveli
1974	Jimmy Connors	Ken Rosewall
1975	Arthur Ashe	Jimmy Connors
1976	Bjorn Borg	Ilie Nastase
1977	Bjorn Borg	Jimmy Connors
1978	Bjorn Borg	Jimmy Connors
1979	Bjorn Borg	Roscoe Tanner
1980	Bjorn Borg	John McEnroe
1981	John McEnroe	Bjorn Borg
1982	Jimmy Connors	John McEnroe
1983	John McEnroe	Chris Lewis
1984	John McEnroe	Jimmy Connors
1985	Boris Becker	Kevin Curren
1986	Boris Becker	Ivan Lendl
1987	Pat Cash	Ivan Lendl
1988	Stefan Edberg	Boris Becker
1989	Boris Becker	Stefan Edberg
1990	Stefan Edberg	Boris Becker
1991	Michael Stich	Boris Becker
1992	Andre Agassi	Goran Ivanisevic
1993	Pete Sampras	Jim Courier
1994	Pete Sampras	Goran Ivanisevic
1995	Pete Sampras	Boris Becker
1996	Richard Krajicek	MaliVai Washington
1997	Pete Sampras	Cedric Pioline
1998	Pete Sampras	Goran Ivanisevic
1999	Pete Sampras	Andre Agassi
2000	Pete Sampras	Patrick Rafter
2001	Goran Ivanisevic	Patrick Rafter
2002	Lleyton Hewitt	David Nalbandian
2003	Roger Federer	Mark Philippoussis

Women's Singles
(First contested 1884)

Year	Champion	Final Opponent
1925	Suzanne Lenglen	Joan Fry
1926	Kathleen McKane Godfree	Lili de Alvarez
1927	Helen Wills	Lili de Alvarez
1928	Helen Wills	Lili de Alvarez
1929	Helen Wills	Helen Jacobs
1930	Helen Wills Moody	Elizabeth Ryan
1931	Cilly Aussem	Hilde Kranwinkel
1932	Helen Wills Moody	Helen Jacobs
1933	Helen Wills Moody	Dorothy Round
1934	Dorothy Round	Helen Jacobs
1935	Helen Wills Moody	Helen Jacobs
1936	Helen Jacobs	Hilde Kranwinkel Sperling
1937	Dorothy Round	Jadwiga Jedrzejowska
1938	Helen Wills Moody	Helen Jacobs
1939	Alice Marble	Kay Stammers
1940-45	Not held	Not held
1946	Pauline Betz	Louise Brough
1947	Margaret Osborne	Doris Hart
1948	Louise Brough	Doris Hart
1949	Louise Brough	Margaret Osborne duPont
1950	Louise Brough	Margaret Osborne duPont
1951	Doris Hart	Shirley Fry
1952	Maureen Connolly	Louise Brough
1953	Maureen Connolly	Doris Hart
1954	Maureen Connolly	Louise Brough
1955	Louise Brough	Beverly Fleitz
1956	Shirley Fry	Angela Buxton
1957	Althea Gibson	Darlene Hard
1958	Althea Gibson	Angela Mortimer
1959	Maria Bueno	Darlene Hard
1960	Maria Bueno	Sandra Reynolds
1961	Angela Mortimer	Christine Truman
1962	Karen Hantze-Susman	Vera Sukova
1963	Margaret Smith	Billie Jean Moffitt
1964	Maria Bueno	Margaret Smith
1965	Margaret Smith	Maria Bueno
1966	Billie Jean King	Maria Bueno
1967	Billie Jean King	Ann Haydon Jones
1968	Billie Jean King	Judy Tegart
1969	Ann Haydon-Jones	Billie Jean King
1970	Margaret Smith Court	Billie Jean King
1971	Evonne Goolagong	Margaret Smith Court
1972	Billie Jean King	Evonne Goolagong
1973	Billie Jean King	Chris Evert
1974	Chris Evert	Olga Morozova
1975	Billie Jean King	Evonne Goolagong Cawley
1976	Chris Evert	Evonne Goolagong Cawley
1977	Virginia Wade	Betty Stove
1978	Martina Navratilova	Chris Evert
1979	Martina Navratilova	Chris Evert Lloyd
1980	Evonne Goolagong	Chris Evert Lloyd
1981	Chris Evert Lloyd	Hana Mandlikova
1982	Martina Navratilova	Chris Evert Lloyd
1983	Martina Navratilova	Andrea Jaeger
1984	Martina Navratilova	Chris Evert Lloyd
1985	Martina Navratilova	Chris Evert Lloyd
1986	Martina Navratilova	Hana Mandlikova
1987	Martina Navratilova	Steffi Graf
1988	Steffi Graf	Martina Navratilova
1989	Steffi Graf	Martina Navratilova
1990	Martina Navratilova	Zina Garrison
1991	Steffi Graf	Gabriela Sabatini
1992	Steffi Graf	Monica Seles
1993	Steffi Graf	Jana Novotna
1994	Conchita Martinez	Martina Navratilova
1995	Steffi Graf	Arantxa Sánchez Vicario
1996	Steffi Graf	Arantxa Sánchez Vicario
1997	Martina Hingis	Jana Novotna
1998	Jana Novotna	Nathalie Tauziat
1999	Lindsay Davenport	Steffi Graf
2000	Venus Williams	Lindsay Davenport
2001	Venus Williams	Justine Henin
2002	Serena Williams	Venus Williams
2003	Serena Williams	Venus Williams

Davis Cup Challenge Round, 1900-2002

Year	Result	Year	Result	Year	Result
1900	United States 3, British Isles 0	1906	British Isles 5, United States 0	1912	British Isles 3, Australasia 2
1901	Not held	1907	Australasia 3, British Isles 2	1913	United States 3, British Isles 2
1902	United States 3, British Isles 2	1908	Australasia 3, United States 2	1914	Australasia 3, United States 2
1903	British Isles 4, United States 1	1909	Australasia 5, United States 0	1915-18	Not held
1904	British Isles 5, Belgium 0	1910	Not held	1919	Australasia 4, British Isles 1
1905	British Isles 5, United States 0	1911	Australasia 5, United States 0	1920	United States 5, Australasia 0

Year	Result	Year	Result	Year	Result
1921	United States 5, Japan 0	1952	Australia 4, United States 1	1978	United States 4, Great Britain 1
1922	United States 4, Australasia 1	1953	Australia 3, United States 2	1979	United States 5, Italy 0
1923	United States 4, Australasia 1	1954	United States 3, Australia 2	1980	Czechoslovakia 4, Italy 1
1924	United States 5, Australasia 0	1955	Australia 5, United States 0	1981	United States 3, Argentina 1
1925	United States 5, France 0	1956	Australia 5, United States 0	1982	United States 4, France, 1
1926	United States 4, France 1	1957	Australia 3, United States 2	1983	Australia 3, Sweden 2
1927	France 3, United States 2	1958	United States 3, Australia 2	1984	Sweden 4, United States 1
1928	France 4, United States 1	1959	Australia 3, United States 2	1985	Sweden 3, W. Germany 2
1929	France 3, United States 2	1960	Australia 4, Italy 1	1986	Australia 3, Sweden 2
1930	France 4, United States 1	1961	Australia 5, Italy 0	1987	Sweden 5, India 0
1931	France 3, Great Britain 2	1962	Australia 5, Mexico 0	1988	W. Germany 4, Sweden 1
1932	France 3, United States 2	1963	United States 3, Australia 2	1989	W. Germany 3, Sweden 2
1933	Great Britain 3, France 2	1964	Australia 3, United States 2	1990	United States 3, Australia 2
1934	Great Britain 4, United States 1	1965	Australia 4, Spain 1	1991	France 3, United States 1
1935	Great Britain 5, United States 0	1966	Australia 4, India 1	1992	United States 3, Switzerland 1
1936	Great Britain 3, Australia 2	1967	Australia 4, Spain 1	1993	Germany 4, Australia 1
1937	United States 4, Great Britain 1	1968	United States 4, Australia	1994	Sweden 4, Russia 1
1938	United States 3, Australia 2	1969	United States 5, Romania 0	1995	United States 3, Russia 2
1939	Australia 3, United States 2	1970	United States 5, W. Germany 0	1996	France 3, Sweden 2
1940-45	Not held	1971	United States 3, Romania 2	1997	Sweden 5, United States 0
1946	United States 5, Australia 0	1972	United States 3, Romania 2	1998	Sweden 4, Italy 1
1947	United States 4, Australia 1	1973	Australia 5, United States 0	1999	Australia 3, France 2
1948	United States 5, Australia 0	1974	South Africa (default by India)	2000	Spain 3, Australia 1
1949	United States 4, Australia 1	1975	Sweden 3, Czechoslovakia 2	2001	France 3, Australia 2
1950	Australia 4, United States 1	1976	Italy 4, Chile 1	2002	Russia 3, France 2
1951	Australia 3, United States 2	1977	Australia 3, Italy 1		

All-Time Grand Slam Singles Titles Leaders

Men	Australian Open	French Open[3]	Wimbledon	U.S. Open	Total
Pete Sampras[1]	1994, '97	—	1993-95, 1997-2000	1990, '93, '95-96, 2002	14
Roy Emerson	1961, '63-67	1963, '67	1964-65	1961, '64	12
Bjorn Borg	—	1974-75, 1978-81	1976-80	—	11
Rod Laver	1960, '62, '69	1962, '69	1961-62, '68-69	1962, '69	11
Bill Tilden	—	—	1920-21, '30	1920-25, '29	10
Andre Agassi[2]	1995, 2000, '01, '03	1999	1992	1994, '99	8
Jimmy Connors	1974	—	1974, '82	1974, '76, '78, '82-83	8
Ivan Lendl	1989-90	1984, '86-87	—	1985-87	8
Fred Perry	1934	1935	1934-36	1933-34, '36	8
Ken Rosewall	1953, '55, '71-72	1953, '68	—	1956, '70	8
Women					
Margaret Smith Court	1960-66, '69-71, '73	1962, '64, '69-70, '73	1963, '65, '70	1962, '65, '69-70, '73	24
Steffi Graf	1988-90, '94	1987-88, '93, '95-96, 99	1988-89, '91-93, '95-96	1988-89, '93, '95-96	22
Helen Wills Moody	—	1928-30, '32	1927-30, '32-33, '35, '38	1923-25, '27-29, '31	19
Chris Evert Lloyd	1982, '84	1974-75, '79-80, '83, '85-86	1974, '76, '81	1975-78, '80, '82	18
Martina Navratilova	1981, '83, '85	1982, '84	1978-79, '82-87, '90	1983-84, '86-87	18
Billie Jean King	1968	1972	1966-68, '72-73, '75	1967, '71-72, '74	12
Suzanne Lenglen	—	1920-23, '25-26	1919-23, '25	—	12
Maureen Connolly	1953	1953-54	1952-54	1951-53	9
Monica Seles[2]	1991-93, '96	1990-92	—	1991-92	9

(1) Retired Aug. 2003. (2) Active player in 2003. (3) Prior to 1925, French Open entry was limited to members of French clubs.

RIFLE AND PISTOL INDIVIDUAL CHAMPIONSHIPS
Source: National Rifle Association

National Outdoor Rifle and Pistol Championships in 2003

Pistol—GYSG Brian H. Zins, USMC, Quantico, VA, 2665-148x

Civilian Pistol—Steve F. Reiter, Sparks, NV, 2643-132x

Woman Pistol—Judy Tant, East Lansing, MI, 2577-78x

Smallbore Rifle Prone—Paul T. Gideon, Gambier, OH, 6397-507x

Civilian Smallbore Rifle Prone—Paul T. Gideon, Gambier, OH, 6397-507x

Woman Smallbore Rifle Prone—Carolyn Millard-Sparks, Atlanta, GA, 6397-505x

Smallbore Rifle NRA 3-Position—Maj. Michael A. Anti, USA, Ft. Benning, GA, 2297-100x

Civilian Smallbore Rifle NRA 3-Position—Jamie L. Beyerle, Lebanon, PA, 2292-82x

Woman Smallbore Rifle NRA 3-Position—Jamie L. Beyerle, Lebanon, PA, 2292-82x

High Power Rifle—G. David Tubb, Canadian, TX, 2389-138x

Civilian High Power Rifle—G. David Tubb, Canadian, TX, 2389-138x

Woman High Power Rifle—SSGT Julia L. Watson, USMC, Quantico, VA, 2356-88x

High Power Rifle Long Range—Nancy H. Tompkins-Gallager, Prescott, AZ, 1241-76x

Woman High Power Rifle Long Range—Nancy H. Tompkins-Gallager, Prescott, AZ, 1241-76x

National Indoor Rifle and Pistol Championships in 2003

Smallbore Rifle 4-Position—Maj. Michael A. Anti, USA, Ft. Benning, GA, 1189-86x

Woman Smallbore Rifle 4-Position—Kristina Fehlings, Fairfax, VA, 795-69x

Smallbore Rifle NRA 3-Position—Matthew Emmons, Browns Mills, NJ, 1189-86x

Woman Smallbore Rifle NRA 3-Position—Jamie Beyerle, Lebanon, PA, 1183-71x

Intn'l Smallbore Rifle—Matthew Emmons, Browns Mills, NJ, 1189-96x

Woman Intn'l Smallbore Rifle—Jamie Beyerle, Lebanon, PA, 1189-85x

Air Rifle—Jamie Beyerle, Lebanon, PA, 593

Woman Air Rifle—Jamie Beyerle, Lebanon, PA, 593

Conventional Pistol—Thomas Rose, Columbus, GA, 887-38x

Woman Conventional Pistol—Rosemary Lyman, Whitefish, MT, 856-22x

Intn'l Free Pistol—Jay Williams, Vancouver, WA, 540

Woman Intn'l Free Pistol—Laura Tyler, Craig, CO, 492

Intn'l Standard Pistol—Eric Weeldreyer, Kalamazoo, MI, 573

Woman Intn'l Standard Pistol—Frances Spear, Harpusville, NY, 541

Air Pistol—John Zurek, Phoenix, AZ, 575

Woman Air Pistol—Laura Tyler, Craig, CO, 547

NRA Bianchi Cup National Action Pistol Championships in 2003

Action Pistol—Doug Koenig, Albertus, PA, 1920.183

Woman Action Pistol—Vera Koo, Menlo Park, CA, 1894.141

Junior Action Pistol—Joshua Sweeney, Cessnock, Australia, 1898.154

AUTO RACING
Indianapolis 500 Winners

Year	Winner, Car (Chassis-Engine)	MPH[1]	Year	Winner, Car (Chassis-Engine)	MPH[1]
1911	Ray Harroun, Marmon	74.602	1960	Jim Rathmann, Watson-Offy	138.767
1912	Joe Dawson, National	78.719	1961	A.J. Foyt Jr., Trevis-Offy	139.130
1913	Jules Goux, Peugeot	75.933	1962	Rodger Ward, Watson-Offy	140.293
1914	Rene Thomas, Delage	82.474	1963	Parnelli Jones, Watson-Offy	143.137
1915	Ralph DePalma, Mercedes	89.840	1964	A.J. Foyt Jr., Watson-Offy	147.350
1916	Dario Resta, Peugeot	84.001	1965	Jim Clark, Lotus-Ford	150.686
1917-18—Not held			1966	Graham Hill, Lola-Ford	144.317
1919	Howdy Wilcox, Peugeot	88.050	1967	A.J. Foyt Jr., Coyote-Ford	151.207
1920	Gaston Chevrolet, Frontenac	88.618	1968	Bobby Unser, Eagle-Offy	152.882
1921	Tommy Milton, Frontenac	89.621	1969	Mario Andretti, Hawk-Ford	156.867
1922	Jimmy Murphy, Duesenberg-Miller	94.484	1970	Al Unser, P.J. Colt-Ford	155.749
1923	Tommy Milton, Miller	90.954	1971	Al Unser, P.J. Colt-Ford	157.735
1924	L.L. Corum-Joe Boyer, Duesenberg	98.234	1972	Mark Donohue, McLaren-Offy	162.962
1925	Peter DePaolo, Duesenberg	101.127	1973	Gordon Johncock, Eagle-Offy	159.036
1926	Frank Lockhart, Miller	95.904	1974	Johnny Rutherford, McLaren-Offy	158.589
1927	George Souders, Duesenberg	97.545	1975	Bobby Unser, Eagle-Offy	149.213
1928	Louie Meyer, Miller	99.482	1976	Johnny Rutherford, McLaren-Offy	148.725
1929	Ray Keech, Miller	97.585	1977	A.J. Foyt Jr., Coyote-Foyt	161.331
1930	Billy Arnold, Summers-Miller	100.448	1978	Al Unser, Lola-Cosworth	161.363
1931	Louis Schneider, Stevens-Miller	96.629	1979	Rick Mears, Penske-Cosworth	158.899
1932	Fred Frame, Wetteroth-Miller	104.144	1980	Johnny Rutherford, Chaparral-Cosworth	142.862
1933	Louie Meyer, Miller	104.162	1981	Bobby Unser, Penske-Cosworth	139.084
1934	Bill Cummings, Miller	104.863	1982	Gordon Johncock, Wildcat-Cosworth	162.029
1935	Kelly Petillo, Wetteroth-Offy	106.240	1983	Tom Sneva, March-Cosworth	162.117
1936	Louie Meyer, Stevens-Miller	109.069	1984	Rick Mears, March-Cosworth	163.612
1937	Wilbur Shaw, Shaw-Offy	113.580	1985	Danny Sullivan, March-Cosworth	152.982
1938	Floyd Roberts, Wetteroth-Miller	117.200	1986	Bobby Rahal, March-Cosworth	170.722
1939	Wilbur Shaw, Maserati	115.035	1987	Al Unser, March-Cosworth	162.175
1940	Wilbur Shaw, Maserati	114.277	1988	Rick Mears, Penske-Chevy Indy V8	144.809
1941	Floyd Davis-Mauri Rose, Wetteroth-Offy	115.117	1989	Emerson Fittipaldi, Penske-Chevy Indy V8.	167.581
1942-45—Not held			1990	Arie Luyendyk, Lola-Chevy Indy V8	185.981*
1946	George Robson, Adams-Sparks	114.820	1991	Rick Mears, Penske-Chevy Indy V8	176.457
1947	Mauri Rose, Deidt-Offy	116.338	1992	Al Unser Jr., Galmer-Chevy Indy V8A	134.477
1948	Mauri Rose, Deidt-Offy	119.814	1993	Emerson Fittipaldi, Penske-Chevy Indy V8C	157.207
1949	Bill Holland, Deidt-Offy	121.327	1994	Al Unser Jr., Penske-Mercedes Benz	160.872
1950	Johnnie Parsons, Kurtis-Offy	124.002	1995	Jacques Villeneuve, Reynard-Ford Cosworth XB.	153.616
1951	Lee Wallard, Kurtis-Offy	126.244	1996	Buddy Lazier, Reynard-Ford Cosworth	147.956
1952	Troy Ruttman, Kuzma-Offy	128.922	1997	Arie Luyendyk, G Force-Aurora	145.827
1953	Bill Vukovich, KK500A-Offy	128.740	1998	Eddie Cheever, Dallara-Aurora	145.155
1954	Bill Vukovich, KK500A-Offy	130.840	1999	Kenny Brack, Dallara-Aurora	153.176
1955	Bob Sweikert, KK500C-Offy	128.213	2000	Juan Montoya, G Force-Aurora	167.607
1956	Pat Flaherty, Watson-Offy	128.490	2001	Helio Castroneves, Reynard-Honda	131.294
1957	Sam Hanks, Salih-Offy	135.601	2002	Helio Castroneves, Reynard-Honda	166.499
1958	Jimmy Bryan, Salih-Offy	133.791	2003	Gil de Ferran, Dallara-Toyota	156.291
1959	Rodger Ward, Watson-Offy	135.857			

(1) Average speed. *Race record. **Note:** The race was less than 500 mi in the following years: 1916 (300 mi), 1926 (400 mi), 1950 (345 mi), 1973 (332.5 mi), 1975 (435 mi), 1976 (255 mi).

CART Champ Car World Series PPG Cup Winners
(U.S. Auto Club Champions prior to 1979; Championship Auto Racing Teams [CART] Champions, 1979-2002)

Year	Driver	Year	Driver	Year	Driver	Year	Driver	Year	Driver
1959	Roger Ward	1968	Bobby Unser	1977	Tom Sneva	1986	Bobby Rahal	1995	Jacques Villeneuve
1960	A. J. Foyt	1969	Mario Andretti	1978	Tom Sneva	1987	Bobby Rahal		
1961	A. J. Foyt	1970	Al Unser	1979	Rick Mears	1988	Danny Sullivan	1996	Jimmy Vasser
1962	Rodger Ward	1971	Joe Leonard	1980	Johnny Rutherford	1989	Emerson Fittipaldi	1997	Alex Zanardi
1963	A. J. Foyt	1972	Joe Leonard	1981	Rick Mears	1990	Al Unser Jr.	1998	Alex Zanardi
1964	A. J. Foyt	1973	Roger McCluskey	1982	Rick Mears	1991	Michael Andretti	1999	Juan Montoya
1965	Mario Andretti	1974	Bobby Unser	1983	Al Unser	1992	Bobby Rahal	2000	Gil de Ferran
1966	Mario Andretti	1975	A. J. Foyt	1984	Mario Andretti	1993	Nigel Mansell	2001	Gil de Ferran
1967	A. J. Foyt	1976	Gordon Johncock	1985	Al Unser	1994	Al Unser Jr.	2002	Cristiano da Matta

Notable One-Mile Land Speed Records

Andy Green, a Royal Air Force pilot, broke the sound barrier and set the first supersonic world speed record on land, Oct. 15, 1997, in Black Rock Desert, NV. Green, driving a car built by Richard Noble, had 2 runs at an average speed of 763.035 mph, as calculated according to the rules of the Federation Internationale Automobiliste (FIA). This record and speed exceeded the speed of sound, calculated at 751.251 mph for that place and time.

Date	Driver	Car	MPH	Date	Driver	Car	MPH
1/26/06	Marriott	Stanley (Steam)	127.659	11/19/37	Eyston	Thunderbolt 1	311.42
3/16/10	Oldfield	Benz	131.724	9/16/38	Eyston	Thunderbolt 1	357.5
4/23/11	Burman	Benz	141.732	8/23/39	Cobb	Railton	368.9
2/12/19	DePalma	Packard	149.875	9/16/47	Cobb	Railton-Mobil	394.2
4/27/20	Milton	Dusenberg	155.046	8/05/63	Breedlove	Spirit of America	407.45
4/28/26	Parry-Thomas	Thomas Spl.	170.624	10/27/64	Arfons	Green Monster	536.71
3/29/27	Seagrave	Sunbeam	203.790	11/15/65	Breedlove	Spirit of America	600.601
4/22/28	Keech	White Triplex	207.552	10/23/70	Gabelich	Blue Flame	622.407
3/11/29	Seagrave	Irving-Napier	231.446	10/09/79	Barrett	Budweiser Rocket	638.637*
2/05/31	Campbell	Napier-Campbell	246.086	10/04/83	Noble	Thrust 2	633.468
2/24/32	Campbell	Napier-Campbell	253.96	9/25/97	Green	Thrust SSC	714.144
2/22/33	Campbell	Napier-Campbell	272.109	10/15/97	Green	Thrust SSC	763.035
9/03/35	Campbell	Bluebird Special	301.13				

*Not recognized as official by sanctioning bodies.

2003 Le Mans 24 Hours Race

For the 1st time in 73 years, British carmaker Bentley won the "24 Hours of Le Mans" race held June 14, 2003. Bentley held the top 2 spots for nearly 22 hours. The winning No. 7 car averaged 214.4 km/hour (133.2 mph) for a record 377 laps (5,146.05 km/3,197.61 miles) around the 8.48-mile (13.65-km) track, eclipsing the 375-lap mark set by Audi in 2002. Audi, which also won Le Mans in 2000 and 2001, finished 3rd and 4th. Driver Tom Kristensen (Denmark) won a record 4th straight race. After winning 5 times between 1924 and 1930, Bentley retired from Le Mans until 2001. Bentley finished 3rd that year and 4th in 2002. It was the 1st win for the Bentley team's other drivers, Rinaldo Capello (Italy) and Guy Smith (UK).

> ▶ **IT'S A FACT:** British auto racer Graham Hill (1929-1975) is the only driver whose career includes a Formula One World Championship (1962, 1968), and wins at both the Indianapolis 500 (1966), and the 24 Hours of Le Mans (1972).

World Formula One Grand Prix Champions, 1950-2003

Year	Driver	Year	Driver	Year	Driver
1950	Nino Farini, Italy	1968	Graham Hill, England	1986	Alain Prost, France
1951	Juan Fangio, Argentina	1969	Jackie Stewart, Scotland	1987	Nelson Piquet, Brazil
1952	Alberto Ascari, Italy	1970	Jochen Rindt, Austria	1988	Ayrton Senna, Brazil
1953	Alberto Ascari, Italy	1971	Jackie Stewart, Scotland	1989	Alain Prost, France
1954	Juan Fangio, Argentina	1972	Emerson Fittipaldi, Brazil	1990	Ayrton Senna, Brazil
1955	Juan Fangio, Argentina	1973	Jackie Stewart, Scotland	1991	Ayrton Senna, Brazil
1956	Juan Fangio, Argentina	1974	Emerson Fittipaldi, Brazil	1992	Nigel Mansell, Britain
1957	Juan Fangio, Argentina	1975	Niki Lauda, Austria	1993	Alain Prost, France
1958	Mike Hawthorne, England	1976	James Hunt, England	1994	Michael Schumacher, Germany
1959	Jack Brabham, Australia	1977	Niki Lauda, Austria	1995	Michael Schumacher, Germany
1960	Jack Brabham, Australia	1978	Mario Andretti, United States	1996	Damon Hill, England
1961	Phil Hill, United States	1979	Jody Scheckter, South Africa	1997	Jacques Villeneuve, Canada
1962	Graham Hill, England	1980	Alan Jones, Australia	1998	Mika Hakkinen, Finland
1963	Jim Clark, Scotland	1981	Nelson Piquet, Brazil	1999	Mika Hakkinen, Finland
1964	John Surtees, England	1982	Keke Rosberg, Finland	2000	Michael Schumacher, Germany
1965	Jim Clark, Scotland	1983	Nelson Piquet, Brazil	2001	Michael Schumacher, Germany
1966	Jack Brabham, Australia	1984	Niki Lauda, Austria	2002	Michael Schumacher, Germany
1967	Denis Hulme, New Zealand	1985	Alain Prost, France	2003	Michael Schumacher, Germany

NASCAR Racing

Winston Cup Champions, 1949-2002

Year	Driver	Year	Driver	Year	Driver	Year	Driver	Year	Driver
1949	Red Byron	1960	Rex White	1971	Richard Petty	1982	Darrell Waltrip	1993	Dale Earnhardt
1950	Bill Rexford	1961	Ned Jarrett	1972	Richard Petty	1983	Bobby Allison	1994	Dale Earnhardt
1951	Herb Thomas	1962	Joe Weatherly	1973	Benny Parsons	1984	Terry Labonte	1995	Jeff Gordon
1952	Tim Flock	1963	Joe Weatherly	1974	Richard Petty	1985	Darrell Waltrip	1996	Terry Labonte
1953	Herb Thomas	1964	Richard Petty	1975	Richard Petty	1986	Dale Earnhardt	1997	Jeff Gordon
1954	Lee Petty	1965	Ned Jarrett	1976	Cale Yarborough	1987	Dale Earnhardt	1998	Jeff Gordon
1955	Tim Flock	1966	David Pearson	1977	Cale Yarborough	1988	Bill Elliott	1999	Dale Jarrett
1956	Buck Baker	1967	Richard Petty	1978	Cale Yarborough	1989	Rusty Wallace	2000	Bobby Labonte
1957	Buck Baker	1968	David Pearson	1979	Richard Petty	1990	Dale Earnhardt	2001	Jeff Gordon
1958	Lee Petty	1969	David Pearson	1980	Dale Earnhardt	1991	Dale Earnhardt	2002	Tony Stewart
1959	Lee Petty	1970	Bobby Isaac	1981	Darrell Waltrip	1992	Alan Kulwicki		

NASCAR Rookie of the Year, 1958-2002

Year	Driver	Year	Driver	Year	Driver	Year	Driver	Year	Driver
1958	Shorty Rollins	1967	Donnie Allison	1976	Skip Manning	1985	Ken Schrader	1994	Jeff Burton
1959	Richard Petty	1968	Pete Hamilton	1977	Ricky Rudd	1986	Alan Kulwicki	1995	Ricky Craven
1960	David Pearson	1969	Dick Brooks	1978	Ronnie Thomas	1987	Davey Allison	1996	Johnny Benson
1961	Woodie Wilson	1970	Bill Dennis	1979	Dale Earnhardt	1988	Ken Bouchard	1997	Mike Skinner
1962	Tom Cox	1971	Walter Ballard	1980	Jody Riley	1989	Dick Trickle	1998	Kenny Irwin
1963	Billy Wade	1972	Larry Smith	1981	Ron Bouchard	1990	Rob Moroso	1999	Tony Stewart
1964	Doug Cooper	1973	Lennie Pond	1982	Geoff Bodine	1991	Bobby Hamilton	2000	Matt Kenseth
1965	Sam McQuagg	1974	Earl Ross	1983	Sterling Martin	1992	Jimmy Hensley	2001	Kevin Harvick
1966	James Hylton	1975	Bruce Hill	1984	Rusty Wallace	1993	Jeff Gordon	2002	Ryan Newman

Daytona 500 Winners, 1959-2003

Year	Driver, car	Avg. MPH	Year	Driver, car	Avg. MPH
1959	Lee Petty, Oldsmobile	135.521	1982	Bobby Allison, Buick	153.991
1960	Junior Johnson, Chevrolet	124.740	1983	Cale Yarborough, Pontiac	155.979
1961	Marvin Panch, Pontiac	149.601	1984	Cale Yarborough, Chevrolet	150.994
1962	Fireball Roberts, Pontiac	152.529	1985	Bill Elliott, Ford	172.265
1963	Tiny Lund, Ford	151.566	1986	Geoff Bodine, Chevrolet	148.124
1964	Richard Petty, Plymouth	154.334	1987	Bill Elliott, Ford	176.263
1965	Fred Lorenzen, Ford (a)	141.539	1988	Bobby Allison, Buick	137.531
1966	Richard Petty, Plymouth (b)	160.627	1989	Darrell Waltrip, Chevrolet	148.466
1967	Mario Andretti, Ford	146.926	1990	Derrike Cope, Chevrolet	165.761
1968	Cale Yarborough, Mercury	143.251	1991	Ernie Irvan, Chevrolet	148.148
1969	Lee Roy Yarborough, Ford	160.875	1992	Davey Allison, Ford	160.256
1970	Pete Hamilton, Plymouth	149.601	1993	Dale Jarrett, Chevrolet	154.972
1971	Richard Petty, Plymouth	144.456	1994	Sterling Marlin, Chevrolet	156.931
1972	A. J. Foyt, Mercury	161.550	1995	Sterling Marlin, Chevrolet	141.710
1973	Richard Petty, Dodge	157.205	1996	Dale Jarrett, Ford	154.308
1974	Richard Petty, Dodge (c)	140.894	1997	Jeff Gordon, Chevrolet	148.295
1975	Benny Parsons, Chevrolet	153.649	1998	Dale Earnhardt, Chevrolet	172.712
1976	David Pearson, Mercury	152.181	1999	Jeff Gordon, Chevrolet	161.551
1977	Cale Yarborough, Chevrolet	153.218	2000	Dale Jarrett, Ford	155.669
1978	Bobby Allison, Ford	159.730	2001	Michael Waltrip, Chevrolet	161.783
1979	Richard Petty, Oldsmobile	143.977	2002	Ward Burton, Dodge	142.971
1980	Buddy Baker, Oldsmobile	177.602	2003	Michael Waltrip, Chevrolet (d)	133.870
1981	Richard Petty, Buick	169.651			

(a) 322.5 mi. (b) 495 mi. (c) 450 mi. (d) 272.5 mi.

BOXING

Champions by Classes

There are many governing bodies in boxing, including the World Boxing Council, World Boxing Assn., International Boxing Federation, World Boxing Org., U.S. Boxing Assn., North American Boxing Federation, and European Boxing Union. Others are recognized by TV networks and the print media. All the governing bodies have their own champions and various boxing divisions.

The following are the recognized champions—as of Oct. 15, 2003—in the principal divisions of the WBA, WBC, and IBF.

Class, Weight limit	WBA	WBC	IBF
Heavyweight	Roy Jones Jr., U.S.	Lennox Lewis, U.K.	Chris Byrd, U.S.
Cruiserweight (190 lb)	Jean-Marc Mormeck, France	Wayne Braithwaite, U.S.	James Toney, U.S.
Light Heavyweight (175 lb)	Medhi Sahnoune, France	Antonio Tarver, U.S.	Antonio Tarver., U.S.
Super Middleweight (168 lb)	Sven Ottke, Germany[1]	Markus Beyer, Germany	Sven Ottke, Germany
Middleweight (160 lb)	Bernard Hopkins, U.S.[2]	Bernard Hopkins, U.S.	Bernard Hopkins, U.S.
Jr. Middleweight (154 lb)	Shane Mosley, U.S.[3]	Shane Mosley, U.S.	Ronald Wright, U.S.
Welterweight (147 lb)	Ricardo Mayorga, Nicaragua[4]	Ricardo Mayorga, Nicaragua	Cory Spinks, U.S.
Jr. Welterweight (140 lb)	Kostya Tszyu, Australia[5]	Kostya Tszyu, Australia	Kostya Tszyu, Australia
Lightweight (135 lb)	Leonard Dorin, Canada	Floyd Mayweather, U.S.	Vacant
Jr. Lightweight (130 lb)	Acelino Freitas, Brazil[6]	Jesus Chavez, U.S.	Carlos Hernandez, El Salvador
Featherweight (126 lb)	Derrick Gainer, U.S.	Erik Morales, Mexico	Juan Manuel Marquez, Mexico
Jr. Featherweight (122 lb)	Mahyar Monshipor, France	Oscar Larios, Mexico.	Manny Pacquiao, Philippines
Bantamweight (118 lb)	Johnny Bredahl, Denmark	Veeraphol Sahaprom, Thailand	Rafael Marquez, Mexico
Jr. Bantamweight (115 lb)	Alexander Munoz, Venezuela	Masanori Tokuyama, Japan	Luis Perez, Nicaragua
Flyweight (112 lb)	Eric Morel, U.S./P.R.	P.S. Wonjongkam, Thailand	Irene Pacheco, Colombia
Jr. Flyweight (108 lb)	Rosendo Alvarez, Nicaragua	Jorge Arce, Mexico	Victor Burgos, Mexico
Strawweight (105 lb)	Noel Arambulent, Venezuela	Jose Antonio Aguirre, Mexico	Daniel Reyes, Colombia

Note: The WBA designates multiple title holders as "Super World Champs" and permits a concurrent "World" champ: (1) Anthony Mundine, Australia. (2) William Joppy, U.S. (3) Alex Garcia, Mexico. (4) Jose Rivera, U.S. (5) Vivian Harris, Guyana. (6) Yodsanan Nanthachai, Thailand.

Ring Champions by Years

(*abandoned the title or was stripped of it; IBF champions listed only for heavyweight division)

Heavyweights

1882-1892	John L. Sullivan (a)	1964-1967	Cassius Clay* (Muhammad Ali) (d)	1990	"Buster" Douglas (WBA, WBC, IBF)
1892-1897	James J. Corbett (b)	1970-1973	Joe Frazier		
1897-1899	Robert Fitzsimmons	1973-1974	George Foreman	1990-1992	Evander Holyfield (WBA, WBC, IBF)
1899-1905	James J. Jeffries* (c)	1974-1978	Muhammad Ali		
1905-1906	Marvin Hart	1978-1979	Muhammad Ali* (WBA)	1992-1993	Riddick Bowe (WBA, IBF,WBC*)
1906-1908	Tommy Burns	1978	Leon Spinks* (WBA) (e);	1992-1994	Lennox Lewis (WBC)
1908-1915	Jack Johnson		Ken Norton (WBC)	1993-1994	Evander Holyfield (WBA, IBF)
1915-1919	Jess Willard	1978-1983	Larry Holmes* (WBC) (f)	1994	Michael Moorer (WBA, IBF)
1919-1926	Jack Dempsey	1979-1980	John Tate (WBA)	1994-1995	Oliver McCall (WBC);
1926-1928	Gene Tunney*	1980-1982	Mike Weaver (WBA)		George Foreman (WBA*, IBF*)
1928-1930	Vacant	1982-1983	Michael Dokes (WBA)	1995	Frans Botha* (IBF)
1930-1932	Max Schmeling	1983-1984	Gerrie Coetzee (WBA)	1995-1996	Bruce Seldon (WBA);
1932-1933	Jack Sharkey	1983-1985	Larry Holmes (IBF) (f)		Frank Bruno (WBC)
1933-1934	Primo Carnera	1984	Tim Witherspoon (WBC)	1996	Mike Tyson (WBC*, WBA)
1934-1935	Max Baer	1984-1985	Greg Page (WBA)	1996-1997	Michael Moorer (IBF)
1935-1937	James J. Braddock	1984-1986	Pinklon Thomas (WBC)	1996-1999	Evander Holyfield (WBA, IBF)
1937-1949	Joe Louis*	1985-1986	Tony Tubbs (WBA)	1997-2001	Lennox Lewis (WBC)
1949-1951	Ezzard Charles	1985-1987	Michael Spinks* (IBF)	1999-2001	Lennox Lewis (WBA*, WBC, IBF)
1951-1952	Joe Walcott	1986	Tim Witherspoon (WBA);		
1952-1956	Rocky Marciano*		Trevor Berbick (WBC)	2000-2001	Evander Holyfield (WBA)
1956-1959	Floyd Patterson	1986-1987	Mike Tyson (WBC); James	2001-2003	John Ruiz (WBA)
1959-1960	Ingemar Johansson		"Bonecrusher" Smith (WBA)	2001	Hasim Rahman (WBC, IBF);
1960-1962	Floyd Patterson	1987	Tony Tucker (IBF)		Lennox Lewis (WBC, IBF*)
1962-1964	Sonny Liston	1987-1990	Mike Tyson (WBC, WBA, IBF)	2002	Chris Byrd (IBF)
				2003	Roy Jones Jr. (WBA)

(a) London Prize Ring (bare knuckle champion). (b) First Marquis of Queensberry champion. (c) Jeffries vacated title (1905), designated Marvin Hart and Jack Root as logical contenders. Hart def. Root in 12 rounds (1905), in turn was def. by Tommy Burns (1906), who claimed the title. Jack Johnson def. Burns (1908) and was recognized as champ. Johnson won the title by defeating Jeffries in the latter's attempted comeback (1910). (d) Title declared vacant by the WBA and others in 1967 after Ali refused military induction. Joe Frazier recognized as champ by 6 states, Mexico, and South America. Jimmy Ellis declared champ by the WBA. Frazier KOd Ellis, Feb. 16, 1970. (e) After Spinks defeated Ali, the WBC recognized Ken Norton as champ. Ali def. Spinks in 1978 rematch for WBA title, retired in 1979. (f) Holmes relinquished WBC title in Dec. 1983, to fight as champ of the new IBF.

Light Heavyweights

1903	Jack Root, George Gardner	1962-1963	Harold Johnson	1987	Leslie Stewart (WBA)
1903-1905	Bob Fitzsimmons	1963-1965	Willie Pastrano	1987-1991	Virgil Hill (WBA)
1905-1912	Philadelphia Jack O'Brien*	1965-1966	Jose Torres	1987	Thomas Hearns* (WBC)
1912-1916	Jack Dillon	1966-1968	Dick Tiger	1987-1988	Don Lalonde (WBC)
1916-1920	Battling Levinsky	1968-1974	Bob Foster*	1988	Sugar Ray Leonard* (WBC)
1920-1922	George Carpentier	1974-1977	John Conteh (WBC)	1989	Dennis Andries (WBC)
1922-1923	Battling Siki	1974-1978	Victor Galindez (WBA)	1989-1990	Jeff Harding (WBC)
1923-1925	Mike McTigue	1977-1978	Miguel Cuello (WBC)	1990-1991	Dennis Andries (WBC)
1925-1926	Paul Berlenbach	1978	Mate Parlov (WBC)	1991-1994	Jeff Harding (WBC)
1926-1927	Jack Delaney*	1978-1979	Mike Rossman (WBA);	1991-1992	Thomas Hearns (WBA)
1927-1929	Tommy Loughran*		Marvin Johnson (WBC)	1992	Iran Barkley* (WBA)
1930-1934	Maxey Rosenbloom	1979-1981	Matthew Saad Muhammad (WBC)	1992-1997	Virgil Hill (WBA)
1934-1935	Bob Olin			1994-1995	Mike McCallum (WBC)
1935-1939	John Henry Lewis*	1979-1980	Marvin Johnson (WBA)	1995-1996	Fabrice Tiozzo* (WBC)
1939	Melio Bettina	1980-1981	Eddie Mustafa Muhammad (WBA)	1996-1997	Roy Jones Jr. (WBC)
1939-1941	Billy Conn*			1997	Montell Griffin (WBC);
1941	Anton Christoforidis (won NBA title)	1981-1983	Michael Spinks (WBA); Dwight Braxton (WBC)		Roy Jones Jr. (WBC); Darius Michalczewski*(WBA)
1941-1948	Gus Lesnevich, Freddie Mills	1983-1985	Michael Spinks*	1997-1998	Lou Del Valle (WBA)
1948-1950	Freddie Mills	1985-1986	J. B. Williamson (WBC)	1998-2003	Roy Jones Jr. (WBA*, WBC*)
1950-1952	Joey Maxim	1986-1987	Marvin Johnson (WBA);	2003	Mehdi Sahnoune (WBA)
1952-1962	Archie Moore		Dennis Andries (WBC)		Antonio Tarver (WBC)

Middleweights

1884-1891	Jack "Nonpareil" Dempsey
1891-1897	Bob Fitzsimmons*
1897-1907	Tommy Ryan*
1907-1908	Stanley Ketchel; Billy Papke
1908-1910	Stanley Ketchel
1911-1913	vacant
1913	Frank Klaus; George Chip
1914-1917	Al McCoy
1917-1920	Mike O'Dowd
1920-1923	Johnny Wilson
1923-1926	Harry Greb
1926-1931	Tiger Flowers; Mickey Walker
1931-1932	Gorilla Jones (NBA)
1932-1937	Marcel Thil
1938	Al Hostak (NBA); Solly Krieger (NBA)
1939-1940	Al Hostak (NBA)
1941-1947	Tony Zale
1947-1948	Rocky Graziano
1948	Tony Zale; Marcel Cerdan
1949-1951	Jake LaMotta
1951	Ray Robinson; Randy Turpin; Ray Robinson*
1953-1955	Carl (Bobo) Olson
1955-1957	Ray Robinson
1957	Gene Fullmer; Ray Robinson
1957-1958	Carmen Basilio
1958	Ray Robinson
1959	Gene Fullmer (NBA); Ray Robinson (NY)
1960	Gene Fullmer (NBA); Paul Pender (NY and MA)
1961	Gene Fullmer (NBA); Terry Downes (NY, MA, Europe)
1962	Gene Fullmer; Dick Tiger (NBA); Paul Pender (NY and MA)*
1963	Dick Tiger (universal)
1963-1965	Joey Giardello
1965-1966	Dick Tiger
1966-1967	Emile Griffith
1967	Nino Benvenuti
1967-1968	Emile Griffith
1968-1970	Nino Benvenuti
1970-1977	Carlos Monzon*
1977-1978	Rodrigo Valdez
1978-1979	Hugo Corro
1979-1980	Vito Antuofermo
1980	Alan Minter
1980-1987	Marvin Hagler
1987	Sugar Ray Leonard* (WBC)
1987-1989	Sumbu Kalambay (WBA)
1987-1988	Thomas Hearns (WBC)
1988-1989	Iran Barkley (WBC)
1989-1990	Roberto Duran* (WBC)
1989-1991	Mike McCallum (WBA)
1990-1993	Julian Jackson (WBC)
1992-1993	Reggie Johnson (WBA)
1993-1995	Gerald McClellan* (WBC)
1993-1994	John David Jackson (WBA)
1994-1997	Jorge Castro (WBA)
1995	Julian Jackson (WBC)
1995-1996	Quincy Taylor (WBC); Shinji Takehara (WBA)
1996-1998	Keith Holmes (WBC)
1996-1997	William Joppy (WBA)
1997	Julio Cesar Green (WBA)
1998-2001	William Joppy (WBA)
1998-1999	Hassine Cherifi (WBC)
1999-2001	Keith Holmes (WBC)
2001	Felix Trinidad (WBA); Bernard Hopkins (WBC, WBA)

Welterweights

1892-1894	Mysterious Billy Smith
1894-1896	Tommy Ryan
1896	Kid McCoy*
1900	Rube Ferns; Matty Matthews
1901	Rube Ferns
1901-1904	Joe Walcott
1904-1906	Dixie Kid; Joe Walcott; Honey Mellody
1907-1911	Mike Sullivan
1911-1915	Vacant
1915-1919	Ted Lewis
1919-1922	Jack Britton
1922-1926	Mickey Walker
1926	Pete Latzo
1927-1929	Joe Dundee
1929	Jackie Fields
1930	Jack Thompson; Tommy Freeman
1931	Tommy Freeman; Jack Thompson; Lou Brouillard
1932	Jackie Fields
1933	Young Corbett; Jimmy McLarnin
1934	Barney Ross; Jimmy McLarnin
1935-1938	Barney Ross
1938-1940	Henry Armstrong
1940-1941	Fritzie Zivic
1941-1946	Fred Cochrane
1946	Marty Servo*
1946-1951	Ray Robinson* (a)
1951	Johnny Bratton (NBA)
1951-1954	Kid Gavilan
1954-1955	Johnny Saxton
1955	Tony De Marco
1955-1956	Carmen Basilio
1956	Johnny Saxton
1956-1957	Carmen Basilio*
1958	Virgil Akins
1958-1960	Don Jordan
1960-1961	Benny Paret
1961	Emile Griffith
1961-1962	Benny Paret
1962-1963	Emile Griffith
1963	Luis Rodriguez
1963-1966	Emile Griffith*
1966-1969	Curtis Cokes
1969-1970	Jose Napoles
1970-1971	Billy Backus
1971-1975	Jose Napoles
1975-1976	John Stracey (WBC); Angel Espada (WBA)
1976-1979	Carlos Palomino (WBC)
1976-1980	Jose Cuevas (WBA)
1979	Wilfredo Benitez (WBC)
1979-1980	Sugar Ray Leonard (WBC)
1980	Roberto Duran (WBC)
1980-1981	Thomas Hearns (WBA)
1980-1982	Sugar Ray Leonard*
1983-1985	Donald Curry (WBA); Milton McCrory (WBC)
1985-1986	Donald Curry
1986-1987	Lloyd Honeyghan (WBC)
1987	Mark Breland (WBA)
1987-1988	Marlon Starling (WBA); Jorge Vaca (WBC)
1988-1989	Tomas Molinares (WBA); Lloyd Honeyghan (WBC)
1989-1990	Marlon Starling (WBC); Mark Breland (WBA)
1990-1991	Maurice Blocker (WBC); Aaron Davis (WBA)
1991	Simon Brown (WBC)
1991-1992	Meldrick Taylor (WBA)
1991-1993	Buddy McGirt (WBC)
1992-1994	Crisanto Espana (WBA)
1993-1997	Pernell Whitaker (WBC)
1994-1998	Ike Quartey (WBA*)
1997-1999	Oscar De La Hoya (WBC*)
1998	James Page (WBA*)
1999-2000	Felix Trinidad (WBC*)
2000	Oscar De La Hoya (WBC*)
2000-2002	Shane Mosley (WBC)
2001-2002	Andrew Lewis (WBA)
2002	Ricardo Mayorga (WBA)
2002-2003	Vernon Forrest (WBC)
2003	Ricardo Mayorga (WBA, WBC)

(a) Robinson gained the title by defeating Tommy Bell in an elimination agreed to by the New York Commission and the National Boxing Association. Both claimed Robinson waived his title when he won the middleweight crown from LaMotta in 1951.

Lightweights

1896-1899	Kid Lavigne
1899-1902	Frank Erne
1902-1908	Joe Gans
1908-1910	Battling Nelson
1910-1912	Ad Wolgast
1912-1914	Willie Ritchie
1914-1917	Freddie Welsh
1917-1925	Benny Leonard*
1925	Jimmy Goodrich; Rocky Kansas
1926-1930	Sammy Mandell
1930	Al Singer; Tony Canzoneri
1930-1933	Tony Canzoneri
1933-1935	Barney Ross*
1935-1936	Tony Canzoneri
1936-1938	Lou Ambers
1938	Henry Armstrong
1939	Lou Ambers
1940	Lew Jenkins
1941-1943	Sammy Angott
1944	S. Angott (NBA); J. Zurita (NBA)
1945-1951	Ike Williams (NBA: later universal)
1951-1952	James Carter
1952	Lauro Salas; James Carter
1953-1954	James Carter
1954	Paddy De Marco; James Carter
1955	James Carter; Bud Smith
1956	Bud Smith; Joe Brown
1956-1962	Joe Brown
1962-1965	Carlos Ortiz
1965	Ismael Laguna
1965-1968	Carlos Ortiz
1968-1969	Teo Cruz
1969-1970	Mando Ramos
1970	Ismael Laguna
1970-1972	Ken Buchanan (WBA)
1971-1972	Pedro Carrasco (WBC)
1972-1979	Roberto Duran* (WBA)
1972	Mando Ramos (WBC); Chango Carmona (WBC)
1972-1974	Rodolfo Gonzalez (WBC)
1974-1976	Ishimatsu Suzuki (WBC)
1976-1978	Esteban De Jesus (WBC)
1979-1981	Jim Watt (WBC)
1979-1980	Ernesto Espana (WBA)
1980-1981	Hilmer Kenty (WBA)
1981	Sean O'Grady (WBA); Claude Noel (WBA)
1981-1983	Alexis Arguello* (WBC)
1981-1982	Arturo Frias (WBA)
1982-1984	Ray Mancini (WBA)
1983-1984	Edwin Rosario (WBC)
1984-1986	Livingstone Bramble (WBA)
1984-1985	Jose Luis Ramirez (WBC)
1985-1986	Hector (Macho) Camacho (WBC)
1986-1987	Edwin Rosario (WBA)
1987-1988	Julio Cesar Chavez (WBA); Jose Luis Ramirez (WBC)
1988-1989	Julio Cesar Chavez (WBA, WBC)
1989-1990	Edwin Rosario (WBA); Pernell Whitaker (WBC)
1990	Juan Nazario (WBA)
1990-1992	Pernell Whitaker*
1992	Joey Gamache (WBA)
1992-1996	Miguel Angel Gonzalez* (WBC)
1992-1993	Tony Lopez (WBA)
1993	Dingaan Thobela (WBA)
1993-1998	Orzubek Nazarov (WBA)
1996-1997	Jean-Baptiste Mendy (WBC)
1997-1998	Steve Johnston (WBC)
1998-1999	Jean-Baptiste Mendy (WBA); Cesar Bazan (WBC)
1999	Julian Lorcy (WBA); Stefano Zoff (WBA)
1999-2000	Gilberto Serrano (WBA); Steve Johnston (WBC)
2000-2001	Takanori Hatakeyama (WBA);
2000-2002	Jose Luis Castillo (WBC)
2001	Julien Lorcy (WBA)
2001-2002	Raul Balbi (WBA)
2002	Leonard Dorin (WBA); Floyd Mayweather (WBC)

Featherweights

1892-1900	George Dixon (disputed)	
1900-1901	Terry McGovern;	
	Young Corbett*	
1901-1912	Abe Attell	
1912-1923	Johnny Kilbane	
1923	Eugene Criqui;	
	Johnny Dundee	
1923-1925	Johnny Dundee*	
1925-1927	Kid Kaplan*	
1927-1928	Benny Bass;	
	Tony Canzoneri	
1928-1929	Andre Routis	
1929-1932	Battling Battalino*	
1932-1934	Tommy Paul (NBA)	
1933-1936	Freddie Miller	
1936-1937	Petey Sarron	
1937-1938	Henry Armstrong*	
1938-1940	Joey Archibald (a)	
1940-1941	Harry Jeffra	
1942-1948	Willie Pep	
1948-1949	Sandy Saddler	
1949-1950	Willie Pep	
1950-1957	Sandy Saddler*	
1957-1959	Hogan (Kid) Bassey	

1959-1963	Davey Moore
1963-1964	Sugar Ramos
1964-1967	Vicente Saldivar*
1968	Paul Rojas (WBA)
1968-1969	Jose Legra (WBC)
1968-1971	Shozo Saijyo (WBA)
1969-1970	Johnny Famechon (WBC)
1970	Vicente Salvidar (WBC)
1970-1972	Kuniaki Shibata (WBC)
1971-1972	Antonio Gomez (WBA)
1972	Clemente Sanchez* (WBC)
1972-1974	Ernesto Marcel* (WBA)
1972-1973	Jose Legra (WBC)
1973-1974	Eder Jofre* (WBC)
1974	Ruben Olivares (WBA)
1974-1975	Bobby Chacon (WBC)
1974-1976	Alexis Arguello* (WBA)
1975	Ruben Olivares (WBA)
1975-1976	David Kotey (WBC)
1976-1980	Danny Lopez (WBC)
1977	Rafael Ortega (WBA)
1977-1978	Cecilio Lastra (WBA)
1978-1985	Eusebio Pedrosa (WBA)
1980-1982	Salvador Sanchez (WBC)

1982-1984	Juan LaPorte (WBC)
1984	Wilfredo Gomez (WBC)
1984-1988	Azumah Nelson (WBC)
1985-1986	Barry McGuigan (WBA)
1986-1987	Steve Cruz (WBA)
1987-1991	Antonio Esparragoza (WBA)
1988-1990	Jeff Fenech* (WBC)
1990-1991	Marcos Villasana (WBC)
1991-1993	Park Yung Kyun (WBC);
	Paul Hodkinson (WBC)
1993	Goyo Vargas (WBC)
1993-1995	Kevin Kelley (WBC)
1993-1996	Eloy Rojas (WBA)
1995	Alejandro Gonzalez (WBC)
1995-1996	Manuel Medina (WBC)
1995-1999	Luisito Espinosa (WBC)
1996-1997	Wilfredo Vasquez* (WBA)
1998	Freddie Norwood (WBA)
1998-1999	Antonio Ceremeno (WBA)
1999	Cesar Soto (WBC);
	Naseem Hamed* (WBC);
	Freddie Norwood (WBA)
2000-2001	Guty Espadas (WBC)
2000	Derrick Gainer (WBA)
2001-2002	Erik Morales (WBC)(b)

(a) After Petey Scalzo knocked out Archibald in an overweight match and was refused a title bout, the NBA named Scalzo champion. NBA title succession: Scalzo, 1938-1941; Richard Lemos, 1941; Jackie Wilson, 1941-1943; Jackie Callura, 1943; Phil Terranova, 1943-1944; Sal Bartolo, 1944-1946. (b) Marco Antonio Barrera won a unanimous dec. over Morales on June 22, 2002, but refused the WBC title. Morales regained WBC title with unanimous dec. over Paulie Ayala on Nov. 16, 2002.

History of Heavyweight Championship Bouts

(bouts in which title changed hands)

1889—July 8—John L. Sullivan def. Jake Kilrain, 75, Richburg, MS. (Last championship bare knuckles bout.)

1892—Sept. 7—James J. Corbett def. John L. Sullivan, 21, New Orleans. (Big gloves used for first time.)

1897—Bob Fitzsimmons def. James J. Corbett, 14, Carson City, NV.

1899—June 9, James J. Jeffries def. Bob Fitzsimmons, 11, Coney Island, NY. (Jeffries retired as champion in 1905.)

1905—July 3, Marvin Hart KOd Jack Root, 12, Reno, NV. (Jeffries refereed and gave the title to Hart. Jack O'Brien also claimed the title.)

1906—Feb. 23, Tommy Burns def. Marvin Hart, 20, Los Angeles.

1908—Dec. 26, Jack Johnson KOd Tommy Burns, 14, Sydney, Australia. (Police halted contest.)

1915—April 5, Jess Willard KOd Jack Johnson, 26, Havana, Cuba.

1919—July 4, Jack Dempsey def. Jess Willard, Toledo, OH. (Willard failed to answer bell for 4th round.)

1926—Sept. 23, Gene Tunney def. Jack Dempsey, 10, Philadelphia. (Tunney retired as champion in 1928.)

1930—June 12, Max Schmeling def. Jack Sharkey, 4, NY. (Sharkey fouled Schmeling in a bout generally considered to have resulted in the election of a successor to Tunney.)

1932—June 21, Jack Sharkey def. Max Schmeling, 15, NY.

1933—June 29, Primo Carnera KOd Jack Sharkey, 6, NY.

1934—June 14, Max Baer KOd Primo Carnera, 11, NY.

1935—June 13, James J. Braddock def. Max Baer, 15, NY.

1937—June 22, Joe Louis KOd James J. Braddock, 8, Chicago. (Louis retired as champion in 1949.)

1949—June 22, Ezzard Charles def. Joe Walcott, 15, Chicago; NBA recognition only.

1951—July 18, Joe Walcott KOd Ezzard Charles, 7, Pittsburgh.

1952—Sept. 23, Rocky Marciano KOd Joe Walcott, 13, Philadelphia. (Marciano retired as champion in 1956.)

1956—Nov. 30, Floyd Patterson KOd Archie Moore, 5, Chicago.

1959—June 26, Ingemar Johansson KOd Floyd Patterson, 3, NY.

1960—June 20, Floyd Patterson KOd Ingemar Johansson, 5, NY. (Patterson was 1st heavyweight to regain title.)

1962—Sept. 25, Sonny Liston KOd Floyd Patterson, 1, Chicago.

1964—Feb. 25, Cassius Clay (Muhammad Ali) KOd Sonny Liston, 7, Miami Beach, FL. (In 1967, Ali was stripped of his title by the WBA and others for refusing military service.)

1970—Feb. 16, Joe Frazier KOd Jimmy Ellis, 5, NY. (Frazier def. Ali in 15 rounds, Mar. 8, 1971, in NY.)

1973—Jan. 22, George Foreman KOd Joe Frazier, 2, Kingston, Jamaica

1974—Oct. 30, Muhammad Ali KOd George Foreman, 8, Kinshasa, Zaire.

1978—Feb. 15, Leon Spinks def. Muhammad Ali, 15, Las Vegas. (WBC recognized Ken Norton as champion after Spinks refused to fight him before his rematch with Ali.); June 9, (WBC) Larry Holmes def. Ken Norton, 15, Las Vegas. (Holmes gave up title in Dec. 1983.); Sept. 15, (WBA) Muhammad Ali def. Leon Spinks, 15, New Orleans. (Ali retired as champion in 1979.)

1979—Oct. 20, (WBA) John Tate def. Gerrie Coetzee, 15, Pretoria, South Africa.

1980—Mar. 31, (WBA) Mike Weaver KOd John Tate, 15, Knoxville.

1982—Dec. 10, (WBA) Michael Dokes KOd Mike Weaver, 1, Las Vegas.

1983—Sept. 23, (WBA) Gerrie Coetzee KOd Michael Dokes, 10, Richfield, OH; in Dec., Larry Holmes relinquished the WBC title and was named champion of the newly formed IBF.

1984—Mar. 9, (WBC) Tim Witherspoon def. Greg Page, 12, Las Vegas; Aug. 31, (WBC) Pinklon Thomas def. Tim Witherspoon, 12, Las Vegas; Dec. 2, (WBA) Greg Page KOd Gerrie Coetzee, 8, Sun City, Bophuthatswana.

1985—Apr. 29, (WBA) Tony Tubbs def. Greg Page, 15, Buffalo, NY; Sept. 21, (IBF) Michael Spinks def. Larry Holmes, 15, Las Vegas. (Spinks relinquished title in Feb. 1987.)

1986—Jan. 17, (WBA) Tim Witherspoon def. Tony Tubbs, 15, Atlanta, GA; Mar. 23, (WBC) Trevor Berbick def. Pinklon Thomas, 12, Miami; Nov. 22, (WBC) Mike Tyson KOd Trevor Berbick, 2, Las Vegas; Dec. 12, (WBA) James "Bonecrusher" Smith KOd Tim Witherspoon, 1, NY.

1987—Mar. 7, (WBA, WBC) Mike Tyson def. James "Bonecrusher" Smith, 12, Las Vegas; May 30, (IBF) Tony Tucker KOd James "Buster" Douglas, 10, Las Vegas; Aug. 1, (WBA, WBC, IBF) Mike Tyson def. Tony Tucker, 12, Las Vegas. (Tyson became undisputed champion.)

1990—Feb. 11, (WBA, WBC, IBF) James "Buster" Douglas KOd Mike Tyson, 10, Tokyo; Oct. 25, (WBA, WBC, IBF) Evander Holyfield KOd James "Buster" Douglas, 3, Las Vegas.

1992—Nov. 13, (WBA, WBC, IBF) Riddick Bowe def. Evander Holyfield, 12, Las Vegas. (Lennox was later named WBC champion when Bowe refused to fight him.)

1993—Nov. 6, (WBA, IBF) Evander Holyfield def. Riddick Bowe, 12, Las Vegas.

1994—Apr. 22, (WBA, IBF) Michael Moorer def. Evander Holyfield, 12, Las Vegas; Sept. 24, (WBC) Oliver McCall KOd Lennox Lewis, 2, London; Nov. 5, (WBA, IBF) George Foreman KOd Michael Moorer, 10, Las Vegas. (In Mar. 1995, Foreman was stripped of the WBA title. In June, Foreman relinquished the IBF title.)

1995—Sept. 2, (WBC) Frank Bruno def. Oliver McCall, 12, London; Dec. 9, (IBF) Frans Botha def. Axel Schulz, 12, Las Vegas. (Botha was subsequently stripped of title.)

1996—Mar. 16, (WBC) Mike Tyson KOd Frank Bruno, 3, Las Vegas; June 22, (IBF) Michael Moorer def. Axel Schulz, 12, Dortmund, Germany; Sept. 7, (WBA, WBC) Mike Tyson KOd Bruce Seldon, 1, Las Vegas. (Tyson was subsequently stripped of WBC title.); Nov. 9, (WBA) Evander Holyfield KOd Mike Tyson, 11, Las Vegas.

1997—Feb. 7, (WBC) Lennox Lewis KOd Oliver McCall, 5, Las Vegas; Nov. 8, (IBF) Evander Holyfield def. Michael Moorer, 8, Las Vegas.

1999—Nov. 13, (WBA, WBC, IBF) Lennox Lewis def. Evander Holyfield, 12, Las Vegas. (Lewis became undisputed champion. In April 2000, Lewis was stripped of his WBA title.)

2000—Aug. 12, (WBA) Evander Holyfield def. John Ruiz, 12, Las Vegas.

2001—Mar. 3, (WBA) John Ruiz def. Evander Holyfield, 12, Las Vegas; Apr. 21, (WBC, IBF) Hasim Rahman KOd Lennox Lewis, 5, Brakpan, South Africa; Nov. 17, (WBC, IBF) Lennox Lewis KOd Hasim Rahman, 4, Las Vegas.

2002—Dec. 14, (IBF) Chris Byrd def. Evander Holyfield, 12, Atlantic City.

2003—Mar. 1, (WBA) Roy Jones Jr. def. John Ruiz, 12, Las Vegas.

THOROUGHBRED RACING

Triple Crown Winners

Since 1920, colts have carried 126 lb. in triple crown events; fillies, 121 lb.

(Kentucky Derby, Preakness, and Belmont Stakes)

Year	Horse	Jockey	Trainer	Year	Horse	Jockey	Trainer
1919	Sir Barton	J. Loftus	H. G. Bedwell	1946	Assault	W. Mehrtens	M. Hirsch
1930	Gallant Fox	E. Sande	J. Fitzsimmons	1948	Citation	E. Arcaro	H. A. Jones
1935	Omaha	W. Sanders	J. Fitzsimmons	1973	Secretariat	R. Turcotte	L. Laurin
1937	War Admiral	C. Kurtsinger	G. Conway	1977	Seattle Slew	J. Cruguet	W. H. Turner Jr.
1941	Whirlaway	E. Arcaro	B. A. Jones	1978	Affirmed	S. Cauthen	L. S. Barrera
1943	Count Fleet	J. Longden	G. D. Cameron				

Kentucky Derby

Churchill Downs, Louisville, KY; inaug. 1875; distance 1-1/4 mi; 1-1/2 mi until 1896. 3-year-olds.
Best time: 1:59 2/5, by Secretariat, 1973; 2003 time: 2:01.19.

Year	Winner	Jockey	Year	Winner	Jockey	Year	Winner	Jockey
1875	Aristides	O. Lewis	1918	Exterminator	W. Knapp	1961	Carry Back	J. Sellers
1876	Vagrant	R. Swim	1919	Sir Barton	J. Loftus	1962	Decidedly	W. Hartack
1877	Baden Baden	W. Walker	1920	Paul Jones	T. Rice	1963	Chateaugay	B. Baeza
1878	Day Star	Carter	1921	Behave Yourself	C. Thompson	1964	Northern Dancer	W. Hartack
1879	Lord Murphy	C. Schauer	1922	Morvich	A. Johnson	1965	Lucky Debonair	W. Shoemaker
1880	Fonso	G. Lewis	1923	Zev	E. Sande	1966	Kauai King	D. Brumfield
1881	Hindoo	J. McLaughlin	1924	Black Gold	J. D. Mooney	1967	Proud Clarion	R. Ussery
1882	Apollo	B. Hurd	1925	Flying Ebony	E. Sande	1968	Dancer's Image#	R. Ussery
1883	Leonatus	W. Donohue	1926	Bubbling Over	A. Johnson	1969	Majestic Prince	W. Hartack
1884	Buchanan	I. Murphy	1927	Whiskery	L. McAtee	1970	Dust Commander	M. Manganello
1885	Joe Cotton	E. Henderson	1928	Reigh Count	C. Lang	1971	Canonero II	G. Avila
1886	Ben Ali	P. Duffy	1929	Clyde Van Dusen	L. McAtee	1972	Riva Ridge	R. Turcotte
1887	Montrose	I. Lewis	1930	Gallant Fox	E. Sande	1973	Secretariat	R. Turcotte
1888	Macbeth II	G. Covington	1931	Twenty Grand	C. Kurtsinger	1974	Cannonade	A. Cordero
1889	Spokane	T. Kiley	1932	Burgoo King	E. James	1975	Foolish Pleasure	J. Vasquez
1890	Riley	I. Murphy	1933	Brokers Tip	D. Meade	1976	Bold Forbes	A. Cordero
1891	Kingman	I. Murphy	1934	Cavalcade	M. Garner	1977	Seattle Slew	J. Cruguet
1892	Azra	A. Clayton	1935	Omaha	W. Saunders	1978	Affirmed	S. Cauthen
1893	Lookout	E. Kunze	1936	Bold Venture	I. Hanford	1979	Spectacular Bid	R. Franklin
1894	Chant	F. Goodale	1937	War Admiral	C. Kurtsinger	1980	Genuine Risk*	J. Vasquez
1895	Halma	J. Perkins	1938	Lawrin	E. Arcaro	1981	Pleasant Colony	J. Velasquez
1896	Ben Brush	W. Simms	1939	Johnstown	J. Stout	1982	Gato del Sol	E. Delahoussaye
1897	Typhoon II	F. Garner	1940	Gallahadion	C. Bierman	1983	Sunny's Halo	E. Delahoussaye
1898	Plaudit	W. Simms	1941	Whirlaway	E. Arcaro	1984	Swale	L. Pincay
1899	Manuel	F. Taral	1942	Shut Out	W. D. Wright	1985	Spend a Buck	A. Cordero
1900	Lieut. Gibson	J. Boland	1943	Count Fleet	J. Longden	1986	Ferdinand	W. Shoemaker
1901	His Eminence	J. Winkfield	1944	Pensive	C. McCreary	1987	Alysheba	C. McCarron
1902	Alan-a-Dale	J. Winkfield	1945	Hoop, Jr.	E. Arcaro	1988	Winning Colors*	G. Stevens
1903	Judge Himes	H. Booker	1946	Assault	W. Mehrtens	1989	Sunday Silence	P. Valenzuela
1904	Elwood	F. Prior	1947	Jet Pilot	E. Guerin	1990	Unbridled	C. Perret
1905	Agile	J. Martin	1948	Citation	E. Arcaro	1991	Strike the Gold	C. Antley
1906	Sir Huon	R. Troxler	1949	Ponder	S. Brooks	1992	Lil E. Tee	P. Day
1907	Pink Star	A. Minder	1950	Middleground	W. Boland	1993	Sea Hero	J. Bailey
1908	Stone Street	A. Pickens	1951	Count Turf	C. McCreary	1994	Go for Gin	C. McCarron
1909	Wintergreen	V. Powers	1952	Hill Gail	E. Arcaro	1995	Thunder Gulch	G. Stevens
1910	Donau	F. Herbert	1953	Dark Star	H. Moreno	1996	Grindstone	J. Bailey
1911	Meridian	G. Archibald	1954	Determine	R. York	1997	Silver Charm	G. Stevens
1912	Worth	C.H. Shilling	1955	Swaps	W. Shoemaker	1998	Real Quiet	K. Desormeaux
1913	Donerail	R. Goose	1956	Needles	D. Erb	1999	Charismatic	C. Antley
1914	Old Rosebud	J. McCabe	1957	Iron Liege	W. Hartack	2000	Fusaichi Pegasus	K. Desormeaux
1915	Regret*	J. Notter	1958	Tim Tam	I. Valenzuela	2001	Monarchos	J. Chavez
1916	George Smith	J. Loftus	1959	Tomy Lee	W. Shoemaker	2002	War Emblem	V. Espinoza
1917	Omar Khayyam	C. Borel	1960	Venetian Way	W. Hartack	2003	Funny Cide	J. Santos

*Regret, Genuine Risk, and Winning Colors are the only fillies to have won the Derby. # Dancer's Image was disqualified from purse money after tests disclosed that he had run with a pain-killing drug, phenylbutazone, in his system. All wagers were paid on Dancer's Image. Forward Pass was awarded first place money. The Kentucky Derby has been won 5 times by 2 jockeys: Eddie Arcaro, 1938, 1941, 1945, 1948, and 1952; and Bill Hartack, 1957, 1960, 1962, 1964, and 1969. It was won 4 times by Willie Shoemaker, 1955, 1959, 1965, and 1986; and 3 times by each of 4 jockeys: Isaac Murphy, 1884, 1890, and 1891; Earle Sande, 1923, 1925, and 1930; Angel Cordero, 1974, 1976, and 1985; and Gary Stevens, 1988, 1995, and 1997.

Top 10 Fastest Winning Times for the Kentucky Derby

(Official Kentucky Derby times measured in fifths of a second.)

Time	Horse	Jockey	Year	Time	Horse	Jockey	Year
1m. 59 2/5 s.	Secretariat	Ron Turcotte	1973	2m. 1 1/5 s.	Thunder Gulch	Gary Stevens	1995
1m. 59 4/5 s.	Monarchos	Jorge Chavez	2001		Affirmed	Steve Cauthen	1978
2m.	Northern Dancer	Bill Hartack	1964		Lucky Debonair	Bill Shoemaker	1965
2m. 1/5 s.	Spend a Buck	Angel Cordero Jr.	1985	2m. 1 2/5 s.	Whirlaway	Eddie Arcaro	1941
2m. 2/5 s.	Decidedly	Bill Hartack	1962	2m. 1 3/5 s.	Bold Forbes	Angel Cordero Jr.	1976
2m. 3/5 s.	Proud Clarion	Robert Ussery	1967		Hill Gail	Eddie Arcaro	1952
2m. 1 s.	Funny Cide	Jose Santos	2003		Middleground	William Boland	1950
	War Emblem	Victor Espinoza	2002				
	Fusaichi Pegasus	Kent Desormeaux	2000				
	Grindstone	Jerry Bailey	1996				

Preakness Stakes

Pimlico Race Course, Baltimore, MD; inaug. 1873; distance 1-3/16 mi. 3-year-olds.
Best time: 1:53 2/5, by Tank's Prospect (1985) and Louis Quatorze (1996); 2003 time: 1:55.61.

Year	Winner	Jockey	Year	Winner	Jockey	Year	Winner	Jockey
1873	Survivor	G. Barbee	1919	Sir Barton	J. Loftus	1962	Greek Money	J.L. Rotz
1874	Culpepper	M. Donohue	1920	Man o' War	C. Kummer	1963	Candy Spots	W. Shoemaker
1875	Tom Ochiltree	L. Hughes	1921	Broomspun	F. Coltiletti	1964	Northern Dancer	W. Hartack
1876	Shirley	G. Barbee	1922	Pillory	L. Morris	1965	Tom Rolfe	R. Turcotte
1877	Cloverbrook	C. Holloway	1923	Vigil	B. Marinelli	1966	Kauai King	D. Brumfield
1878	Duke of Magenta	C. Holloway	1924	Nellie Morse	J. Merimee	1967	Damascus	W. Shoemaker
1879	Harold	L. Hughes	1925	Coventry	C. Kummer	1968	Forward Pass	I. Valenzuela
1880	Grenada	L. Hughes	1926	Display	J. Maiben	1969	Majestic Prince	W. Hartack
1881	Saunterer	W. Costello	1927	Bostonian	A. Abel	1970	Personality	E. Belmonte
1882	Vanguard	W. Costello	1928	Victorian	R. Workman	1971	Canonero II	G. Avila
1883	Jacobus	G. Barbee	1929	Dr. Freeland	L. Schaefer	1972	Bee Bee Bee	E. Nelson
1884	Knight of Ellerslie	S. H. Fisher	1930	Gallant Fox	E. Sande	1973	Secretariat	R. Turcotte
1885	Tecumseh	J. McLaughlin	1931	Mate	G. Ellis	1974	Little Current	M. Rivera
1886	The Bard	S. H. Fisher	1932	Burgoo King	E. James	1975	Master Derby	D. McHargue
1887	Dunboyne	W. Donohue	1933	Head Play	C. Kurtsinger	1976	Elocutionist	J. Lively
1888	Refund	F. Littlefield	1934	High Quest	R. Jones	1977	Seattle Slew	J. Cruguet
1889	Buddhist	G. Anderson	1935	Omaha	W. Saunders	1978	Affirmed	S. Cauthen
1890	Montague	W. Martin	1936	Bold Venture	G. Woolf	1979	Spectacular Bid	R. Franklin
1894	Assignee	F. Taral	1937	War Admiral	C. Kurtsinger	1980	Codex	A. Cordero
1895	Belmar	F. Taral	1938	Dauber	M. Peters	1981	Pleasant Colony	J. Velasquez
1896	Margrave	H. Griffin	1939	Challedon	G. Seabo	1982	Aloma's Ruler	J. Kaenel
1897	Paul Kauvar	C. Thorpe	1940	Bimelech	F.A. Smith	1983	Deputed	
1898	Sly Fox	W. Simms	1941	Whirlaway	E. Arcaro		Testamony	D. Miller
1899	Half Time	R. Clawson	1942	Alsab	B. James	1984	Gate Dancer	A. Cordero
1900	Hindus	H. Spencer	1943	Count Fleet	J. Longden	1985	Tank's Prospect	P. Day
1901	The Parader	F. Landry	1944	Pensive	C. McCreary	1986	Snow Chief	A. Solis
1902	Old England	L. Jackson	1945	Polynesian	W.D. Wright	1987	Alysheba	C. McCarron
1903	Flocarline	W. Gannon	1946	Assault	W. Mehrtens	1988	Risen Star	E. Delahoussaye
1904	Bryn Mawr	E. Hildebrand	1947	Faultless	D. Dodson	1989	Sunday Silence	P. Valenzuela
1905	Cairngorm	W. Davis	1948	Citation	E. Arcaro	1990	Summer Squall	P. Day
1906	Whimsical	W. Miller	1949	Capot	T. Atkinson	1991	Hansel	J. Bailey
1907	Don Enrique	G. Mountain	1950	Hill Prince	E. Arcaro	1992	Pine Bluff	C. McCarron
1908	Royal Tourist	E. Dugan	1951	Bold	E. Arcaro	1993	Prairie Bayou	M. Smith
1909	Effendi	W. Doyle	1952	Blue Man	C. McCreary	1994	Tabasco Cat	P. Day
1910	Layminster	R. Estep	1953	Native Dancer	E. Guerin	1995	Timber Country	P. Day
1911	Watervale	E. Dugan	1954	Hasty Road	J. Adams	1996	Louis Quatorze	P. Day
1912	Colonel Holloway	C. Turner	1955	Nashua	E. Arcaro	1997	Silver Charm	G. Stevens
1913	Buskin	J. Butwell	1956	Fabius	W. Hartack	1998	Real Quiet	K. Desormeaux
1914	Holiday	A. Schuttinger	1957	Bold Ruler	E. Arcaro	1999	Charismatic	C. Antley
1915	Rhine Maiden	D. Hoffman	1958	Tim Tam	I. Valenzuela	2000	Red Bullet	J. Bailey
1916	Damrosch	L. McAtee	1959	Royal Orbit	W. Harmatz	2001	Point Given	G. Stevens
1917	Kalitan	E. Haynes	1960	Bally Ache	R. Ussery	2002	War Emblem	V. Espinoza
1918	War Cloud	J. Loftus	1961	Carry Back	J. Sellers	2003	Funny Cide	J. Santos
	Jack Hare	Jr. C. Peak						

Belmont Stakes

Belmont Park, Elmont, NY; inaug. 1867; distance 1-1/2 mi. 3-year-olds. Best time: 2:24, Secretariat, 1973; 2003 time: 2:28.26.

Year	Winner	Jockey	Year	Winner	Jockey	Year	Winner	Jockey
1867	Ruthless	J. Gilpatrick	1904	Delhi	G. Odom	1943	Count Fleet	J. Longden
1868	General Duke	R. Swim	1905	Tanya	E. Hildebrand	1944	Bounding Home	G. L. Smith
1869	Fenian	C. Miller	1906	Burgomaster	L. Lyne	1945	Pavot	E. Arcaro
1870	Kingfisher	W. Dick	1907	Peter Pan	G. Mountain	1946	Assault	W. Mehrtens
1871	Harry Bassett	W. Miller	1908	Colin	J. Notter	1947	Phalanx	R. Donoso
1872	Joe Daniels	J. Rowe	1909	Joe Madden	E. Dugan	1948	Citation	E. Arcaro
1873	Springbok	J. Rowe	1910	Sweep	J. Butwell	1949	Capot	T. Atkinson
1874	Saxon	G. Barbee	1913	Prince Eugene	R. Troxler	1950	Middleground	W. Boland
1875	Calvin	R. Swim	1914	Luke McLuke	M. Buxton	1951	Counterpoint	D. Gorman
1876	Algerine	W. Donohue	1915	The Finn	G. Byrne	1952	One Count	E. Arcaro
1877	Cloverbrook	C. Holloway	1916	Friar Rock	E. Haynes	1953	Native Dancer	E. Guerin
1878	Duke of Magenta	L. Hughes	1917	Hourless	J. Butwell	1954	High Gun	E. Guerin
1879	Spendthrift	S. Evans	1918	Johren	F. Robinson	1955	Nashua	E. Arcaro
1880	Grenada	L. Hughes	1919	Sir Barton	J. Loftus	1956	Needles	D. Erb
1881	Saunterer	T. Costello	1920	Man o' War	C. Kummer	1957	Gallant Man	W. Shoemaker
1882	Forester	J. McLaughlin	1921	Grey Lag	E. Sande	1958	Cavan	P. Anderson
1883	George Kinney	J. McLaughlin	1922	Pillory	C. H. Miller	1959	Sword Dancer	W. Shoemaker
1884	Panique	J. McLaughlin	1923	Zev	E. Sande	1960	Celtic Ash	W. Hartack
1885	Tyrant	P. Duffy	1924	Mad Play	E. Sande	1961	Sherluck	B. Baeza
1886	Inspector	B.J. McLaughlin	1925	American Flag	A. Johnson	1962	Jaipur	W. Shoemaker
1887	Hanover	J. McLaughlin	1926	Crusader	A. Johnson	1963	Chateaugay	B. Baeza
1888	Sir Dixon	J. McLaughlin	1927	Chance Shot	E. Sande	1964	Quadrangle	M. Ycaza
1889	Eric	W. Hayward	1928	Vito	C. Kummer	1965	Hail to All	J. Sellers
1890	Burlington	S. Barnes	1929	Blue Larkspur	M. Garner	1966	Amberoid	W. Boland
1891	Foxford	E. Garrison	1930	Gallant Fox	E. Sande	1967	Damascus	W. Shoemaker
1892	Patron	W. Hayward	1931	Twenty Grand	C. Kurtsinger	1968	Stage Door Johnny	H. Gustines
1893	Comanche	W. Simms	1932	Faireno	T. Malley	1969	Arts and Letters	B. Baeza
1894	Henry of Navarre	W. Simms	1933	Hurryoff	M. Garner	1970	High Echelon	J. L. Rotz
1895	Belmar	F. Taral	1934	Peace Chance	W. D. Wright	1971	Pass Catcher	W. Blum
1896	Hastings	H. Griffin	1935	Omaha	W. Saunders	1972	Riva Ridge	R. Turcotte
1897	Scottish Chieftain	J. Scherrer	1936	Granville	J. Stout	1973	Secretariat	R. Turcotte
1898	Bowling Brook	F. Littlefield	1937	War Admiral	C. Kurtsinger	1974	Little Current	M. Rivera
1899	Jean Bereaud	R. R. Clawson	1938	Pasteurized	J. Stout	1975	Avatar	W. Shoemaker
1900	Ildrim	N. Turner	1939	Johnstown	J. Stout	1976	Bold Forbes	A. Cordero
1901	Commando	H. Spencer	1940	Bimelech	F. A. Smith	1977	Seattle Slew	J. Cruguet
1902	Masterman	J. Bullman	1941	Whirlaway	E. Arcaro	1978	Affirmed	S. Cauthen
1903	Africander	J. Bullman	1942	Shut Out	E. Arcaro	1979	Coastal	R. Hernandez

Year	Winner	Jockey	Year	Winner	Jockey	Year	Winner	Jockey
1980	Temperence Hill	E. Maple	1988	Risen Star	E. Delahoussaye	1996	Editor's Note	R. Douglas
1981	Summing	G. Martens	1989	Easy Goer	P. Day	1997	Touch Gold	C. McCarron
1982	Conquistador Cielo	L. Pincay	1990	Go and Go	M. Kinane	1998	Victory Gallop	G. Stevens
1983	Caveat	L. Pincay	1991	Hansel	J. Bailey	1999	Lemon Drop Kid	J. Santos
1984	Swale	L. Pincay	1992	A.P. Indy	E. Delahoussaye	2000	Commendable	P. Day
1985	Creme Fraiche	E. Maple	1993	Colonial Affair	J. Krone	2001	Point Given	G. Stevens
1986	Danzig Connection	C. McCarron	1994	Tabasco Cat	P. Day	2002	Sarava	E. Prado
1987	Bet Twice	C. Perret	1995	Thunder Gulch	G. Stevens	2003	Empire Maker	J. Bailey

Annual Leading Jockey — Money Won[1]

Year	Jockey	Earnings	Year	Jockey	Earnings	Year	Jockey	Earnings
1957	Bill Hartack	$3,060,501	1973	Laffit Pincay, Jr.	$4,093,492	1988	Jose Santos	$14,877,298
1958	Willie Shoemaker	2,961,693	1974	Laffit Pincay, Jr.	4,251,060	1989	Jose Santos	13,838,389
1959	Willie Shoemaker	2,843,133	1975	Braulio Baeza	3,695,198	1990	Gary Stevens	13,881,198
1960	Willie Shoemaker	2,123,961	1976	Angel Cordero, Jr.	4,709,500	1991	Chris McCarron	14,441,083
1961	Willie Shoemaker	2,690,819	1977	Steve Cauthen	6,151,750	1992	Kent Desormeaux	14,193,006
1962	Willie Shoemaker	2,916,844	1978	Darrel McHargue	6,029,885	1993	Mike Smith	14,024,815
1963	Willie Shoemaker	2,526,925	1979	Laffit Pincay, Jr.	8,193,535	1994	Mike Smith	15,979,820
1964	Willie Shoemaker	2,649,553	1980	Chris McCarron	7,663,300	1995	Jerry Bailey	16,311,876
1965	Braulio Baeza	2,582,702	1981	Chris McCarron	8,397,604	1996	Jerry Bailey	19,465,376
1966	Braulio Baeza	2,951,022	1982	Angel Cordero, Jr.	9,483,590	1997	Jerry Bailey	18,320,743
1967	Braulio Baeza	3,088,888	1983	Angel Cordero, Jr.	10,116,697	1998	Gary Stevens	19,622,855
1968	Braulio Baeza	2,835,108	1984	Chris McCarron	12,045,813	1999	Pat Day	18,092,845
1969	Jorge Velasquez	2,542,315	1985	Laffit Pincay, Jr.	13,353,299	2000	Pat Day	17,479,838
1970	Laffit Pincay, Jr.	2,626,526	1986	Jose Santos	11,329,297	2001	Jerry Bailey	22,597,720
1971	Laffit Pincay, Jr.	3,784,377	1987	Jose Santos	12,375,433	2002	Jerry Bailey	22,871,814
1972	Laffit Pincay, Jr.	3,225,827						

(1) Total earnings for all horses that jockey raced in year listed; does not reflect jockey's earnings.

Breeders' Cup

The Breeders' Cup was inaugurated in 1984 and consists of 7 races at one track on one day late in the year to determine Thoroughbred racing's champion contenders. It has been held at the following locations:

1984 Hollywood Park, CA	1991 Churchill Downs, KY	1997 Hollywood Park, CA
1985 Aqueduct Racetrack, NY	1992 Gulfstream Park, FL	1998 Churchill Downs, KY
1986 Santa Anita Park, CA	1993 Santa Anita Park, CA	1999 Gulfstream Park, FL
1987 Hollywood Park, CA	1994 Churchill Downs, KY	2000 Churchill Downs, KY
1988 Churchill Downs, KY	1995 Belmont Park, NY	2001 Belmont Park, NY
1989 Gulfstream Park, FL	1996 Woodbine Racetrack, Ontario	2002 Arlington Park, IL
1990 Belmont Park, NY		

Juvenile
Distances: 1 mi 1984-85, 1987; 1-1/16 mi 1986 and since 1988

Year		Jockey	Year		Jockey	Year		Jockey
1984	Chief's Crown	D. MacBeth	1991	Arazi	P. Valenzuela	1997	Favorite Trick	P. Day
1985	Tasso	L. Pincay, Jr.	1992	Gilded Time	C. McCarron	1998	Answer Lively	J. Bailey
1986	Capote	L. Pincay, Jr.	1993	Brocco	G. Stevens	1999	Anees	G. Stevens
1987	Success Express	J. Santos	1994	Timber Country	P. Day	2000	Macho Uno	J. Bailey
1988	Is It True	L. Pincay, Jr.	1995	Unbridled's Song	M. Smith	2001	Johannesburg	M. Kinane
1989	Rhythm	C. Perret	1996	Boston Harbor	J. Bailey	2002	Vindication	M. Smith
1990	Fly So Free	J. Santos						

Juvenile Fillies
Distances: 1 mi 1984-85, 1987; 1-1/16 mi 1986 and since 1988

Year		Jockey	Year		Jockey	Year		Jockey
1984	*Outstandingly	W. Guerra	1991	Pleasant Stage	E. Delahoussaye	1997	Countess Diana	S. Sellers
1985	Twilight Ridge	J. Velasquez	1992	Eliza	P. Valenzuela	1998	Silverbulletday	G. Stevens
1986	Brave Raj	P. Valenzuela	1993	Phone Chatter	L. Pincay, Jr.	1999	Cash Run	J. Bailey
1987	Epitome	P. Day	1994	Flanders	P. Day	2000	Caressing	J. Velazquez
1988	Open Mind	A. Cordero, Jr.	1995	My Flag	J. Bailey	2001	Tempera	D. Flores
1989	Go for Wand	R. Romero	1996	Storm Song	C. Perret	2002	Storm Flag Flying	J. Velazquez
1990	Meadow Star	J. Santos						

*By disqualification.

Sprint
Distance: 6 furlongs

Year		Jockey	Year		Jockey	Year		Jockey
1984	Eillo	C. Perret	1991	Sheikh Albadou	P. Eddery	1997	Elmhurst	C. Nakatani
1985	Precisionist	C. McCarron	1992	Thirty Slews	E. Delahoussaye	1998	Reraise	C. Nakatani
1986	Smile	J. Vasquez	1993	Cardmania	E. Delahoussaye	1999	Artax	A. Chaves
1987	Very Subtle	P. Valenzuela	1994	Cherokee Run	M. Smith	2000	Kona Gold	A. Solis
1988	Gulch	A. Cordero, Jr.	1995	Desert Stormer	K. Desormeaux	2001	Squirtle Squirt	J. Bailey
1989	Dancing Spree	A. Cordero, Jr.	1996	Lit De Justice	C. Nakatani	2002	Orientate	J. Bailey
1990	Safely Kept	C. Perret						

Mile

Year		Jockey	Year		Jockey	Year		Jockey
1984	Royal Heroine	F. Toro	1991	Opening Verse	P. Valenzuela	1997	Spinning World	C. Asmussen
1985	Cozzene	W. Guerra	1992	Lure	M. Smith	1998	Da Hoss	J. Velazquez
1986	Last Tycoon	Y. St.-Martin	1993	Lure	M. Smith	1999	Silic	C. Nakatani
1987	Miesque	F. Head	1994	Barathea	L. Dettori	2000	War Chant	G. Stevens
1988	Miesque	F. Head	1995	Ridgewood Pearl	J. Murtagh	2001	Val Royal	J. Valdivia Jr.
1989	Steinlen	J. Santos	1996	Da Hoss	G. Stevens	2002	Domedriver	T. Thulliez
1990	Royal Academy	L. Piggott						

Filly & Mare Turf
Distance: 1-3/8 mi 1999-2000, 1-1/4 mi 2002

Year		Jockey	Year		Jockey	Year		Jockey
1999	Soaring Softly	J. Bailey	2001	Banks Hill	O. Peslier	2002	Starine	J. Velazquez
2000	Perfect Sting	J. Bailey						

Distaff

Distances: 1-1/4 mi 1984-87; 1-1/8 mi since 1988

Year		Jockey	Year		Jockey	Year		Jockey
1984	Princess Rooney	E. Delahoussaye	1991	Dance Smartly	P. Day	1997	Ajina	M. Smith
1985	Life's Magic	A. Cordero, Jr.	1992	Paseana	C. McCarron	1998	Escena	G. Stevens
1986	Lady's Secret	P. Day	1993	Hollywood Wildcat	E. Delahoussaye	1999	Beautiful Pleasure	J. Chaves
1987	Sacahuista	R. Romero	1994	One Dreamer	G. Stevens	2000	Spain	V. Espinoza
1988	Personal Ensign	R. Romero	1995	Inside Information	M. Smith	2001	Unbridled Elaine	P. Day
1989	Bayakoa	L. Pincay, Jr.	1996	Jewel Princess	C. Nakatani	2002	Azeri	M. Smith
1990	Bayakoa	L. Pincay, Jr.						

Turf

Distance: 1-1/2 mi

Year		Jockey	Year		Jockey	Year		Jockey
1984	Lashkari	Y. St-Martin	1990	In The Wings	G. Stevens	1997	Chief Bearhart	J. Santos
1985	Pebbles	P. Eddery	1991	Miss Alleged	E. Legrix	1998	Buck's Boy	S. Sellers
1986	Manila	J. Santos	1992	Fraise	P. Valenzuela	1999	Daylami	L. Dettori
1987	Theatrical	P. Day	1993	Kotashaan	K. Desormeaux	2000	Kalanisi	J. Murtagh
1988	Great Communicator	R. Sibille	1994	Tikkanen	M. Smith	2001	Fantastic Light	L. Dettori
1989	Prized	E. Delahoussaye	1995	Northern Spur	C. McCarron	2002	High Chaparral	M. Kinane
			1996	Pilsudski	W. Swinburn			

Classic

Distance: 1-1/4 mi

Year		Jockey	Year		Jockey	Year		Jockey
1984	Wild Again	P. Day	1991	Black Tie Affair	J. Bailey	1997	Skip Away	M. Smith
1985	Proud Truth	J. Velasquez	1992	A.P. Indy	E. Delahoussaye	1998	Awesome Again	P. Day
1986	Skywalker	L. Pincay, Jr.	1993	Arcangues	J. Bailey	1999	Cat Thief	P. Day
1987	Ferdinand	W. Shoemaker	1994	Concern	J. Bailey	2000	Tiznow	C. McCarron
1988	Alysheba	C. McCarron	1995	Cigar	J. Bailey	2001	Tiznow	C. McCarron
1989	Sunday Silence	C. McCarron	1996	Alphabet Soup	C. McCarron	2002	Volponi	P. Johnson
1990	Unbridled	P. Day						

Eclipse Awards

The Eclipse Awards, honoring the Horse of the Year and other champions of the sport, began in 1971 and are sponsored by the *Daily Racing Form*, the Thoroughbred Racing Associations, and the National Turf Writers Assn. Prior to 1971, the *DRF* (1936-70) and the TRA (1950-70) issued separate selections for Horse of the Year.

Eclipse Awards for 2002

Horse of the Year—Azari
2-year-old colt or gelding—Vindication
2-year-old filly—Storm Flag Flying
3-year-old colt or gelding—War Emblem
3-year-old filly—Farda Amigat

Older male (4-year-olds & up)— Left Bank
Older female (4-year-olds & up)—Azeri
Male turf horse—High Chaparral
Turf filly or mare—Golden Apples
Sprinter—Orientate

Steeplechase horse—Flat Top
Trainer—Bobby Frankel
Jockey—Jerry Bailey
Apprentice jockey—Jeremy Rose
Breeder—Juddmonte Farms
Owner—Richard Englander

Horse of the Year

1936	Granville	1953	Tom Fool	1969	Arts and Letters	1986	Lady's Secret
1937	War Admiral	1954	Native Dancer	1970	Fort Marcy (DRF)	1987	Ferdinand
1938	Seabiscuit	1955	Nashua		Personality (TRA)	1988	Alysheba
1939	Challedon	1956	Swaps	1971	Ack Ack	1989	Sunday Silence
1940	Challedon	1957	Bold Ruler (DRF)	1972	Secretariat	1990	Criminal Type
1941	Whirlaway		Dedicate (TRA)	1973	Secretariat	1991	Black Tie Affair
1942	Whirlaway	1958	Round Table	1974	Forego	1992	A.P. Indy
1943	Count Fleet	1959	Sword Dancer	1975	Forego	1993	Kotashaan
1944	Twilight Tear	1960	Kelso	1976	Forego	1994	Holy Bull
1945	Busher	1961	Kelso	1977	Seattle Slew	1995	Cigar
1946	Assault	1962	Kelso	1978	Affirmed	1996	Cigar
1947	Armed	1963	Kelso	1979	Affirmed	1997	Favorite Trick
1948	Citation	1964	Kelso	1980	Spectacular Bid	1998	Skip Away
1949	Capot	1965	Roman Brother (DRF)	1981	John Henry	1999	Charismatic
1950	Hill Prince		Moccasin (TRA)	1982	Conquistador Cielo	2000	Tiznow
1951	Counterpoint	1966	Buckpasser	1983	All Along	2001	Point Given
1952	One Count (DRF)	1967	Damascus	1984	John Henry	2002	Azeri
	Native Dancer (TRA)	1968	Dr. Fager	1985	Spend A Buck		

HARNESS RACING

Harness Horse of the Year

(Chosen by the U.S. Trotting Assn. and the U.S. Harness Writers Assn.)

1947	Victory Song	1961	Adios Butler	1975	Savoir	1989	Matt's Scooter
1948	Rodney	1962	Su Mac Lad	1976	Keystone Ore	1990	Beach Towel
1949	Good Time	1963	Speedy Scot	1977	Green Speed	1991	Precious Bunny
1950	Proximity	1964	Bret Hanover	1978	Abercrombie	1992	Artsplace
1951	Pronto Don	1965	Bret Hanover	1979	Niatross	1993	Staying Together
1952	Good Time	1966	Bret Hanover	1980	Niatross	1994	Cam's Card Shark
1953	Hi Lo's Forbes	1967	Nevele Pride	1981	Fan Hanover	1995	CR Kay Suzie
1954	Stenographer	1968	Nevele Pride	1982	Cam Fella	1996	Continentalvictory
1955	Scott Frost	1969	Nevele Pride	1983	Cam Fella	1997	Malabar Man
1956	Scott Frost	1970	Fresh Yankee	1984	Fancy Crown	1998	Moni Maker
1957	Torpid	1971	Albatross	1985	Nihilator	1999	Moni Maker
1958	Emily's Pride	1972	Albatross	1986	Forrest Skipper	2000	Gallo Blue Chip
1959	Bye Bye Byrd	1973	Sir Dalrae	1987	Mack Lobell	2001	Bunny Lake
1960	Adios Butler	1974	Delmonica Hanover	1988	Mack Lobell	2002	Real Desire

The Hambletonian (3-year-old trotters)

Year	Winner	Driver	Year	Winner	Driver	Year	Winner	Driver
1965	Egyptian		1979	Legend Hanover	George Sholty	1992	Alf Palema	Mickey McNicholl
	Candor	Del Cameron	1980	Burgomeister	Bill Haughton	1993	American	
1966	Kerry Way	Frank Ervin	1981	Shiaway St. Pat	Ray Remmen		Winner	Ron Pierce
1967	Speedy Streak	Del Cameron	1982	Speed Bowl	Tommy Haughton	1994	Victory Dream	Michel Lachance
1968	Nevele Pride	Stanley Dancer	1983	Duenna	Stanley Dancer	1995	Tagliabue	John Campbell
1969	Lindy's Pride	Howard Beissinger	1984	Historic Freight	Ben Webster	1996	Continental-	
1970	Timothy T	John Simpson, Sr.	1985	Prakas	Bill O'Donnell		victory	Michel Lachance
1971	Speedy Crown	Howard Beissinger	1986	Nuclear		1997	Malabar Man	Malvern Burroughs
1972	Super Bowl	Stanley Dancer		Kosmos	Ulf Thoresen	1998	Muscles Yankee	John Campbell
1973	Flirth	Ralph Baldwin	1987	Mack Lobell	John Campbell	1999	Self Possessed	Mike Lachance
1974	Christopher T	Bill Haughton	1988	Armbro Goal	John Campbell	2000	Yankee Paco	Trevor Ritchie
1975	Bonefish	Stanley Dancer	1989	Park Avenue		2001	Scarlet Knight	Stefan Melander
1976	Steve Lobell	Bill Haughton		Joe	Ron Waples	2002	Chip Chip	
1977	Green Speed	Bill Haughton	1990	Harmonious	John Campbell		Hooray	Eric Ledford
1978	Speedy Somolli	Howard Beissinger	1991	Giant Victory	Jack Moiseyev	2003	Amigo Hall	Mike Lachance

NCAA WRESTLING CHAMPIONS

Year	Champion	Year	Champion	Year	Champion	Year	Champion	Year	Champion
1964	Oklahoma State	1972	Iowa State	1980	Iowa	1988	Arizona State	1996	Iowa
1965	Iowa State	1973	Iowa State	1981	Iowa	1989	Oklahoma State	1997	Iowa
1966	Oklahoma State	1974	Oklahoma	1982	Iowa	1990	Oklahoma State	1998	Iowa
1967	Michigan State	1975	Iowa	1983	Iowa	1991	Iowa	1999	Iowa
1968	Oklahoma State	1976	Iowa	1984	Iowa	1992	Iowa	2000	Iowa
1969	Iowa State	1977	Iowa State	1985	Iowa	1993	Iowa	2001	Minnesota
1970	Iowa State	1978	Iowa	1986	Iowa	1994	Oklahoma State	2002	Minnesota
1971	Oklahoma State	1979	Iowa	1987	Iowa State	1995	Iowa	2003	Oklahoma State

CHESS
World Chess Champions
Source: U.S. Chess Federation
Official world champions since the title was first used are as follows:

1866-1894 Wilhelm Steinitz, Austria	**1963-1969** Tigran Petrosian, USSR
1894-1921 Emanuel Lasker, Germany	**1969-1972** Boris Spassky, USSR
1921-1927 Jose R. Capablanca, Cuba	**1972-1975** Bobby Fischer, U.S. (b)
1927-1935 Alexander A. Alekhine, France	**1975-1985** Anatoly Karpov, USSR
1935-1937 Max Euwe, Netherlands	**1985-1993** Garry Kasparov, USSR/Russia (c)
1937-1946 Alexander A. Alekhine, France (a)	**1993-1995** Garry Kasparov, Russia (PCA) (d)
1948-1957 Mikhail Botvinnik, USSR	**1993-1999** Anatoly Karpov, Russia (FIDE)
1957-1958 Vassily Smyslov, USSR	**1999** Aleksandr Khalifman, Russia (FIDE)
1958-1959 Mikhail Botvinnik, USSR	**2000** Viswanathan Anand, India (FIDE) (e)
1960-1961 Mikhail Tal, USSR	**2002-** Ruslan Ponomariov, Ukraine (FIDE)
1961-1963 Mikhail Botvinnik, USSR	

(a) After Alekhine died in 1946, the title was vacant until 1948, when Botvinnik won the 1st championship match sanctioned by the International Chess Federation (FIDE). (b) Defaulted championship after refusal to accept FIDE rules for a championship match, Apr. 1975. (c) Kasparov broke with FIDE, Feb. 26, 1993. FIDE stripped Kasparov of his title Mar. 23. Kasparov defeated Nigel Short of Great Britain in a world championship match played Sept.-Oct. 1993 under the auspices of a new organization the two had founded, the Professional Chess Association (PCA). FIDE held a championship match between Anatoly Karpov (Russia) and Jan Timman (the Netherlands), which Karpov won in Nov. 1993. (d) The PCA folded in 1995. (e) In Nov. 2000, Vladimir Kramnik (Russia) defeated Garry Kasparov (Russia), widely recognized as the unofficial world champion, 8½-6½, at the Braingames World Chess Championships in London.

Recent matches: In Jan. 2002, 18-year-old Ruslan Ponomariov (Ukraine) def. Vassily Ivanchuk (Ukraine), 4½-2½, in Moscow, Russia, to become the youngest world chess champion. (Anand had lost to Ivanchuk in the semifinals.) On Feb. 8, 2003, a 6-game match between former world chess champion Garry Kasparov and Deep Junior, a computer program, ended in a draw. Each won 1 game, with the other 4 drawn.

FIDE encountered obstacles in its plan under the 2002 Prague Agreement to unify the World Chess title. Current FIDE champion Ruslan Ponomariov was to play Garry Kasparov, rated #1 player in the world, in Sept. 2003, but Ponomariov failed to agree with FIDE on terms for the match by an Aug. 28 deadline. On Aug. 29, FIDE announced plans instead for a 128-player knockout World Championship tournament in Nov.-Dec. 2003 (Ponomariov would retain the title until then), with the winner to play Kasparov in 2004. FIDE also announced plans to sponsor a match in Nov. 2003 between Vladimir Kramnik, the 2000 Braingames champion, and Peter Leko, winner of the 2002 Dortmund Sparkassen Chess Meeting. (A planned match between the two in spring 2003, to be sponsored by the London-based Einstein Group, new owners of the rights to the Braingames chess title, had fallen through because of financial problems.) If these events proceeded as planned, the next step would be unification match in spring 2004 between the winner of the Kramnik-Leko match and the winner of the match between Kasparov and the FIDE champion emerging from the Oct.-Nov. championships. **Further information:** More information on chess and chess champions may be accessed on the U.S. Chess Federation's Internet site: www.uschess.org

BOWLING
Professional Bowlers Association
Hall of Fame

PERFORMANCE			WALTER RAY	Dick Evans	Don McCune
Bill Allen	Gary Dickinson	Johnny Petraglia	Williams Jr.	Raymond Firestone	Mike McGrath
Glenn Allison	Mike Durbin	Dick Ritger	Wayne Zahn	E. A. "Bud" Fisher	Steve Nagy
Earl Anthony	Buzz Fazio	Mark Roth		Jim Fitzgerald	Keijiro Nakano
Mike Aulby	Dave Ferraro	Carmen Salvino		Skee Foremsky	Chuck Pezzano
Joe Berardi	Jim Godman	Ernie Schlegel	**MERITORIOUS**	Lou Frantz	Jack Reichert
Ray Bluth	Billy Hardwick	Harry Smith	**SERVICE**	Harry Golden	Joe Richards
Parker Bohn III	Marshall Hollman	Dave Soutar	Glenn Allison	John Guenther	Jim St. John
Roy Buckley	Tommy Hudson	Jim Stefanich	Joe Antenora	Ted Hoffman Jr.	Chris Schenkel
Nelson Burton Jr.	Dave Husted	Brian Voss	John Archibald	Joe Joseph	Ernie Schlegel
Don Carter	Don Johnson	Wayne Webb	Barry Asher	John Jowdy	Teata Semiz
Pat Colwell	Joe Joseph	Dick Weber	Tom Baker	Joe Kelley	Lorraine Stilzlein
Steve Cook	Larry Laub	Pete Weber	Chuck Clemens	Larry Lichstein	Bob Strampe
Dave Davis	Amleto Monacelli	Billy Welu	Eddie Elias	Mike Limongello	Al Thompson
	David Ozio	Mark Williams	Frank Esposito	Andy Marzich	Roger Zeller
	George Pappas				

Tournament of Champions

Year	Winner	Year	Winner	Year	Winner	Year	Winner
1965	Billy Hardwick	1975	Dave Davis	1984	Mike Durbin	1993	George Branham, 3rd
1966	Wayne Zahn	1976	Marshall Holman	1985	Mark Williams	1994	Norm Duke
1967	Jim Stefanich	1977	Mike Berlin	1986	Marshall Holman	1996	Dave D'Entremont
1968	Dave Davis	1978	Earl Anthony	1987	Pete Weber	1997	John Gant
1969	Jim Godman	1979	George Pappas	1988	Mark Williams	1998	Bryan Goebel
1970	Don Johnson	1980	Wayne Webb	1989	Del Ballard, Jr.	1999	Jason Couch
1971	Johnny Petraglia	1981	Steve Cook	1990	Dave Ferraro	2000	Jason Couch
1972	Mike Durbin	1982	Mike Durbin	1991	David Ozio	2001	Walter Ray Williams Jr.
1973	Jim Godman	1983	Joe Berardi	1992	Marc McDowell	2002	Jason Couch
1974	Earl Anthony						

PBA Leading Money Winners

Total winnings are from PBA, ABC Masters, and BPAA All-Star tournaments only and do not include numerous other tournaments or earnings from special television shows and matches. In 2001, the PBA began an Oct.-Mar. season schedule. After 2000, year shown is year the season ended.

Year	Bowler	Amount	Year	Bowler	Amount	Year	Bowler	Amount
1962	Don Carter	$49,972	1976	Earl Anthony	$110,833	1990	Amleto Monacelli	$204,775
1963	Dick Weber	46,333	1977	Mark Roth	105,583	1991	David Ozio	225,585
1964	Bob Strampe	33,592	1978	Mark Roth	134,500	1992	Marc McDowell	174,215
1965	Dick Weber	47,674	1979	Mark Roth	124,517	1993	Walter Ray Williams Jr.	296,370
1966	Wayne Zahn	54,720	1980	Wayne Webb	116,700	1994	Norm Duke	273,753
1967	Dave Davis	54,165	1981	Earl Anthony	164,735	1995	Mike Aulby	219,792
1968	Jim Stefanich	67,377	1982	Earl Anthony	134,760	1996	Walter Ray Williams Jr.	241,330
1969	Billy Hardwick	64,160	1983	Earl Anthony	135,605	1997	Walter Ray Williams Jr.	240,544
1970	Mike McGrath	52,049	1984	Mark Roth	158,712	1998	Walter Ray Williams Jr.	238,225
1971	Johnny Petraglia	85,065	1985	Mike Aulby	201,200	1999	Parker Bohn III	240,912
1972	Don Johnson	56,648	1986	Walter Ray Williams Jr	145,550	2000	Norm Duke	143,325
1973	Don McCune	69,000	1987	Pete Weber	175,491	2002	Parker Bohn III	245,200
1974	Earl Anthony	99,585	1988	Brian Voss	225,485	2003	Walter Ray Williams Jr.	419,700
1975	Earl Anthony	107,585	1989	Mike Aulby	298,237			

Leading PBA Averages by Year

Year	Bowler	Average	Year	Bowler	Average	Year	Bowler	Average
1962	Don Carter	212.84	1976	Mark Roth	215.97	1990	Amleto Monacelli	218.15
1963	Billy Hardwick	210.34	1977	Mark Roth	218.17	1991	Norm Duke	218.20
1964	Ray Bluth	210.51	1978	Mark Roth	219.83	1992	Dave Ferraro	219.70
1965	Dick Weber	211.89	1979	Mark Roth	221.66	1993	Walter Ray Williams Jr.	222.98
1966	Wayne Zahn	208.66	1980	Earl Anthony	218.53	1994	Norm Duke	222.83
1967	Wayne Zahn	212.34	1981	Mark Roth	216.69	1995	Mike Aulby	225.49
1968	Jim Stefanich	211.89	1982	Marshall Holman	212.84	1996	Walter Ray Williams Jr.	225.37
1969	Bill Hardwick	212.95	1983	Earl Anthony	216.64	1997	Walter Ray Williams Jr.	222.00
1970	Nelson Burton Jr.	214.90	1984	Marshall Holman	213.91	1998	Walter Ray Williams Jr.	226.13
1971	Don Johnson	213.97	1985	Mark Baker	213.71	1999	Parker Bohn III	228.04
1972	Don Johnson	215.29	1986	John Gant	214.37	2000	Chris Barnes	220.93
1973	Earl Anthony	215.79	1987	Marshall Holman	216.80	2002	Parker Bohn III	221.54
1974	Earl Anthony	219.39	1988	Mark Roth	218.03	2003	Walter Ray Williams Jr.	224.94
1975	Earl Anthony	219.06	1989	Pete Weber	215.43			

American Bowling Congress

ABC Masters Tournament Champions

Year	Winner	Year	Winner	Year	Winner
1980	Neil Burton, St. Louis, MO	1988	Del Ballard, Jr., Richardson, TX	1996	Ernie Schlegel, Vancouver, WA
1981	Randy Lightfoot, St. Charles, MO	1989	Mike Aulby, Indianapolis, IN	1997	Jason Queen, Decatur, IL
1982	Joe Berardi, Brooklyn, NY	1990	Chris Warren, Dallas, TX	1998	Mike Aulby, Indianapolis, IN
1983	Mike Lastowski, Havre de Grace, MD	1991	Doug Kent, Canandaigua, NY	1999	Brian Boghosian, Middletown, CT
1984	Earl Anthony, Dublin, CA	1992	Ken Johnson, N. Richmond Hills, TX	2000	Mika Koivuniemi, Finland
1985	Steve Wunderlich, St. Louis, MO	1993	Norm Duke, Oklahoma City, OK	2001	Parker Bohn III, Jackson, NJ
1986	Mark Fahy, Chicago, IL	1994	Steve Fehr, Cincinnati, OH	2002	Brett Wolfe, Reno, NV
1987	Rick Steelsmith, Wichita, KS	1995	Mike Aulby, Indianapolis, IN	2003	Bryon Smith, Roseburg, OR

Champions in 2003

Regular Singles: Ron Bahr, Topeka, KS
Regular Doubles: Sean Rash, Anchorage, AK & Derek Sapp, Keokuk, IA
Regular All Events: Steve Kloempken, Ogden, UT
Regular Team: Bowler's Edge Pro Shop, Menasha, WI

Classified Singles: George L. Blackburn, Sallisaw, OK
Classified Doubles: Ray L. Burke, Gig Harbor, WA & G. Slim Slater, Federal Way, WA
Classified All Events: Donald P. Grogan Jr., Seneca, SC
Classified Team: Garden Center Lanes 4, Alexandra, MN

Most Sanctioned 300 Games

Name	Games	Name	Games	Name	Games
Jeff Carter, Springfield, IL	76	Bob Learn Jr., Erie, PA	58	Mike Whalin, Cincinnati, OH	53
Joe Jimenez, Saginaw, MI	71	Jim Tomek Jr., Camp Hill, PA	57	John Chacko Jr., Larksville, PA	53
Chris Hayward, Toledo, OH	66	Frank Massengale Jr., Hixon, TN	57	Randy Lightfoot, St. Charles, MO	51
Jerry Kessler, Dayton, OH	62	Randy Choat, Granite City, IL	56	Ralph Burley Jr., Dayton, OH	51
Dean Wolf, Reading, PA	62	Bob Buckery, McAdoo, PA	56	John Wilcox Jr., Lewisburg, PA	51
Jeff Ripic, Endicott, NY	62	Jim Johnson Jr., Tampa, FL	54	Gregory Spafford, St. Joseph, MO	50
Robert Faragon, Albany, NY	61	John Delp III, West Lawn, PA	54	Gordon Childers, Benton, AR	50
Jeff Jensen, Wichita, KS	60				

Women's International Bowling Congress

Champions in 2003

Queens Tournament: Wendy Macpherson, Henderson, NV
Classic Singles: Michelle Feldman, Skaneateles, NY
Classic Doubles: Karen Collura, Toronto, ON & Connie Ward, Hamilton, ON
Classic All Events: Michelle Feldman, Skaneateles, NY
Classic Team: Barry Asher's Embroidery, Yorba Linda, CA

Div. I Singles: Debra Lewis, Kalamazoo, MI
Div. I Doubles: Frostenia Milner & Rhonda Terry, Greensboro, NC
Div. I All Events: Mindy Molstad, Wheaton, IL
Div. I Team: Caveman Bowl, Grants Pass, OR

Most Sanctioned 300 Games

Tish Johnson, Panorama City, CA 35	Vicki Fischel, Wheat Ridge, CO 23	Kim Terrell, San Francisco, CA 20
Jodi Musto, Schenectady, NY. 29	Debbie McMullen, Denver, CO 23	Marianne DiRupo, Succasunna, NJ . . . 20
Aleta Sill, Dearborn, MI 27	Anne-Marie Duggan, Edmond, OK. . . . 21	Shannon Duplantis, New Orleans, LA. . 19
Leanne Barrette, Yukon, OK. 25	Jodi Hughes, Greenville, SC. 21	Mandy Wilson, Dayton, OH. 18
Dede Davidson, Woodland Hills, CA . . 25	Cheryl Daniels, Detroit, MI 21	Kim Adler, Palm City, FL 18
Altramese Webb, Detroit, MI 24	Carolyn Dorin-Ballard, N. Richland	Cindy Coburn-Carroll, Tonawanda, NY. 17
Jeanne Naccarato, Tacoma, WA 23	Hills, TX 21	Jackie Mitskavich, DuBois, PA 16

FIGURE SKATING
U.S. and World Individual Champions, 1952-2003

U.S. Champions			World Champions	
MEN	**WOMEN**	**YEAR**	**MEN**	**WOMEN**
Dick Button	Tenley Albright	1952	Dick Button, U.S.	Jacqueline du Bief, France
Hayes Jenkins	Tenley Albright	1953	Hayes Jenkins, U.S.	Tenley Albright, U.S.
Hayes Jenkins	Tenley Albright	1954	Hayes Jenkins, U.S.	Gundi Busch, W. Germany
Hayes Jenkins	Tenley Albright	1955	Hayes Jenkins, U.S.	Tenley Albright, U.S.
Hayes Jenkins	Tenley Albright	1956	Hayes Jenkins, U.S.	Carol Heiss, U.S.
Dave Jenkins	Carol Heiss	1957	Dave Jenkins, U.S.	Carol Heiss, U.S.
Dave Jenkins	Carol Heiss	1958	Dave Jenkins, U.S.	Carol Heiss, U.S.
Dave Jenkins	Carol Heiss	1959	Dave Jenkins, U.S.	Carol Heiss, U.S.
Dave Jenkins	Carol Heiss	1960	Alain Giletti, France	Carol Heiss, U.S.
Bradley Lord	Laurence Owen	1961	none	none
Monty Hoyt	Barbara Roles Pursley	1962	Don Jackson, Canada	Sjoukje Dijkstra, Netherlands
Tommy Litz	Lorraine Hanlon	1963	Don McPherson, Canada	Sjoukje Dijkstra, Netherlands
Scott Allen	Peggy Fleming	1964	Manfred Schnelldorfer, W. Germany	Sjoukje Dijkstra, Netherlands
Gary Visconti	Peggy Fleming	1965	Alain Calmat, France	Petra Burka, Canada
Scott Allen	Peggy Fleming	1966	Emmerich Danzer, Austria	Peggy Fleming, U.S.
Gary Visconti	Peggy Fleming	1967	Emmerich Danzer, Austria	Peggy Fleming, U.S.
Tim Wood	Peggy Fleming	1968	Emmerich Danzer, Austria	Peggy Fleming, U.S.
Tim Wood	Janet Lynn	1969	Tim Wood, U.S.	Gabriele Seyfert, E. Germany
Tim Wood	Janet Lynn	1970	Tim Wood, U.S.	Gabriele Seyfert, E. Germany
John Misha Petkevich	Janet Lynn	1971	Ondrej Nepela, Czechoslovakia	Beatrix Schuba, Austria
Ken Shelley	Janet Lynn	1972	Ondrej Nepela, Czechoslovakia	Beatrix Schuba, Austria
Gordon McKellen, Jr.	Janet Lynn	1973	Ondrej Nepela, Czechoslovakia	Karen Magnussen, Canada
Gordon McKellen, Jr.	Dorothy Hamill	1974	Jan Hoffmann, E. Germany	Christine Errath, E. Germany
Gordon McKellen, Jr.	Dorothy Hamill	1975	Sergei Volkov, USSR	Dianne de Leeuw, Neth.-U.S.
Terry Kubicka	Dorothy Hamill	1976	John Curry, Gr. Britain	Dorothy Hamill, U.S.
Charles Tickner	Linda Fratianne	1977	Vladimir Kovalev, USSR	Linda Fratianne, U.S.
Charles Tickner	Linda Fratianne	1978	Charles Tickner, U.S.	Anett Poetzsch, E. Germany
Charles Tickner	Linda Fratianne	1979	Vladimir Kovalev, USSR	Linda Fratianne, U.S.
Charles Tickner	Linda Fratianne	1980	Jan Hoffmann, E. Germany	Anett Poetzsch, E. Germany
Scott Hamilton	Elaine Zayak	1981	Scott Hamilton, U.S.	Denise Biellmann, Switzerland
Scott Hamilton	Rosalynn Sumners	1982	Scott Hamilton, U.S.	Elaine Zayak, U.S.
Scott Hamilton	Rosalynn Sumners	1983	Scott Hamilton, U.S.	Rosalynn Sumners, U.S.
Scott Hamilton	Rosalynn Sumners	1984	Scott Hamilton, U.S.	Katarina Witt, E. Germany
Brian Boitano	Tiffany Chin	1985	Aleksandr Fadeev, USSR	Katarina Witt, E. Germany
Brian Boitano	Debi Thomas	1986	Brian Boitano, U.S.	Debi Thomas, U.S.
Brian Boitano	Jill Trenary	1987	Brian Orser, Canada	Katarina Witt, E. Germany
Brian Boitano	Debi Thomas	1988	Brian Boitano, U.S.	Katarina Witt, E. Germany
Christopher Bowman	Jill Trenary	1989	Kurt Browning, Canada	Midori Ito, Japan
Todd Eldredge	Jill Trenary	1990	Kurt Browning, Canada	Jill Trenary, U.S.
Todd Eldredge	Tonya Harding	1991	Kurt Browning, Canada	Kristi Yamaguchi, U.S.
Christopher Bowman	Kristi Yamaguchi	1992	Viktor Petrenko, Ukraine	Kristi Yamaguchi, U.S.
Scott Davis	Nancy Kerrigan	1993	Kurt Browning, Canada	Oksana Baiul, Ukraine
Scott Davis	vacant[1]	1994	Elvis Stojko, Canada	Yuka Sato, Japan
Todd Eldredge	Nicole Bobek	1995	Elvis Stojko, Canada	Chen Lu, China
Rudy Galindo	Michelle Kwan	1996	Todd Eldredge, U.S.	Michelle Kwan, U.S.
Todd Eldredge	Tara Lipinski	1997	Elvis Stojko, Canada	Tara Lipinski, U.S.
Todd Eldredge	Michelle Kwan	1998	Alexei Yagudin, Russia	Michelle Kwan, U.S.
Michael Weiss	Michelle Kwan	1999	Alexei Yagudin, Russia	Maria Butyrskaya, Russia
Michael Weiss	Michelle Kwan	2000	Alexei Yagudin, Russia	Michelle Kwan, U.S.
Timothy Goebel	Michelle Kwan	2001	Yevgeny Plushchenko, Russia	Michelle Kwan, U.S.
Todd Eldredge	Michelle Kwan	2002	Alexei Yagudin, Russia	Irina Slutskaya, Russia
Michael Weiss	Michelle Kwan	2003	Yevgeny Plushchenko, Russia	Michelle Kwan, U.S.

(1) Tonya Harding was stripped of title.

SKIING
World Cup Alpine Champions, 1967-2003

Men

1967	Jean Claude Killy, France	1979	Peter Luescher, Switzerland	1992	Paul Accola, Switzerland
1968	Jean Claude Killy, France	1980	Andreas Wenzel, Liechtenstein	1993	Marc Girardelli, Luxembourg
1969	Karl Schranz, Austria	1981	Phil Mahre, U.S.	1994	Kjetil Andre Aamodt, Norway
1970	Karl Schranz, Austria	1982	Phil Mahre, U.S.	1995	Alberto Tomba, Italy
1971	Gustavo Thoeni, Italy	1983	Phil Mahre, U.S.	1996	Lasse Kjus, Norway
1972	Gustavo Thoeni, Italy	1984	Pirmin Zurbriggen, Switzerland	1997	Luc Alphand, France
1973	Gustavo Thoeni, Italy	1985	Marc Girardelli, Luxembourg	1998	Hermann Maier, Austria
1974	Piero Gros, Italy	1986	Marc Girardelli, Luxembourg	1999	Lasse Kjus, Norway
1975	Gustavo Thoeni, Italy	1987	Pirmin Zurbriggen, Switzerland	2000	Hermann Maier, Austria
1976	Ingemar Stenmark, Sweden	1988	Pirmin Zurbriggen, Switzerland	2001	Hermann Maier, Austria
1977	Ingemar Stenmark, Sweden	1989	Marc Girardelli, Luxembourg	2002	Stephan Eberharter, Austria
1978	Ingemar Stenmark, Sweden	1990	Pirmin Zurbriggen, Switzerland	2003	Stephan Eberharter, Austria
		1991	Marc Girardelli, Luxembourg		

Women

1967	Nancy Greene, Canada
1968	Nancy Greene, Canada
1969	Gertrud Gabl, Austria
1970	Michele Jacot, France
1971	Annemarie Proell, Austria
1972	Annemarie Proell, Austria
1973	Annemarie Proell, Austria
1974	Annemarie Proell, Austria
1975	Annemarie Proell, Austria
1976	Rose Mittermaier, W. Germany
1977	Lise-Marie Morerod, Switzerland
1978	Hanni Wenzel, Liechtenstein
1979	Annemarie Proell Moser, Austria
1980	Hanni Wenzel, Liechtenstein
1981	Marie-Theres Nadig, Switzerland
1982	Erika Hess, Switzerland
1983	Tamara McKinney, U.S.
1984	Erika Hess, Switzerland
1985	Michela Figini, Switzerland
1986	Maria Walliser, Switzerland
1987	Maria Walliser, Switzerland
1988	Michela Figini, Switzerland
1989	Vreni Schneider, Switzerland
1990	Petra Kronberger, Austria
1991	Petra Kronberger, Austria
1992	Petra Kronberger, Austria
1993	Anita Wachter, Austria
1994	Vreni Schneider, Switzerland
1995	Vreni Schneider, Switzerland
1996	Katja Seizinger, Germany
1997	Pernilla Wiberg, Sweden
1998	Katja Seizinger, Germany
1999	Alexandra Meissnitzer, Austria
2000	Renate Goetschl, Austria
2001	Janica Kostelic, Croatia
2002	Michaela Dorfmeister, Austria
2003	Janica Kostelic, Croatia

LACROSSE
Lacrosse Champions in 2003

Major League Lacrosse—Villanova, PA, Aug. 24: Long Island Lizards 15, Baltimore Bayhawks 14.
U.S. Club Lacrosse Association Championship—Haverford, PA, June 8: Single Source Solutions 10, M.A.B. Philadelphia 8.
National Lacrosse League Championship—Rochester, NY, May 3: Toronto Rock 8, Rochester Knighthawks 6.

NCAA Men's Division I Championship—Baltimore, MD, May 26: Virginia 9, Johns Hopkins 7.
NCAA Women's Division I Championship—Syracuse, NY, May 18: Princeton 8, Virginia 7.

2003 Men's NCAA Division I All-America Team

Attack: Kyle Barrie, Johns Hopkins; Ryan Boyle, Princeton; Mike Powell, Syracuse.
Midfield: Kevin Cassese, Duke; Adam Doneger, Johns Hopkins; Chris Fiore, Cornell; Chris Rotelli, Virginia.
Defense: Damien Davis, Princeton; Ryan McClay, Cornell; Michael Howley, Maryland.
Goal: Tillman Johnson, Virginia.
Coach of the Year: Jim Stagnitta, Rutgers.

2003 Women's NCAA Division I All-America Team

Attack: Sarah Averson, Cornell; Suzanne Eyler, Loyola; Sonia Judd, Maryland; Whitney Miller, Princeton; Wick Stanwick, Georgetown.
Midfield: Lauren Aumiller, Virginia; Kelly Coppedge, Maryland; Alex Fiore, Princeton; Kate Kaiser, Duke; Theresa Sherry, Princeton; Lisa Staedt, James Madison.
Defense: Rachael Becker, Princeton; Michi Ellers, Georgetown; Marianne Gioffre, Loyola; Tiffany Schummer, Virginia.
Goal: Alexis Venechanos, Maryland.
Coach of the Year: Chris Sailer, Princeton.

NCAA Division I Lacrosse Champions 1982-2003

Year[1]	Men	Women	Year[1]	Men	Women	Year[1]	Men	Women
1982	North Carolina	Massachusetts	1990	vacated	Harvard	1997	Princeton	Maryland
1983	Syracuse	Delaware	1991	North Carolina	Virginia	1998	Princeton	Maryland
1984	Johns Hopkins	Temple	1992	Princeton	Maryland	1999	Virginia	Maryland
1985	Johns Hopkins	New Hampshire	1993	Syracuse	Virginia	2000	Syracuse	Maryland
1986	North Carolina	Maryland	1994	Princeton	Princeton	2001	Princeton	Maryland
1987	Johns Hopkins	Penn St.	1995	Syracuse	Maryland	2002	Syracuse	Princeton
1988	Syracuse	Temple	1996	Princeton	Maryland	2003	Virginia	Princeton
1989	Syracuse	Penn St.						

(1) NCAA Championships began in 1971 for men, in 1982 for women.

SWIMMING
World Swimming Records
(Long course, as of Oct. 1, 2003. * pending FINA ratification)

Men's Records

Freestyle

Distance	Time	Holder	Country	Where made	Date
50 meters	0:21.64	Alexander Popov	Russia	Moscow, Russia	June 16, 2000
100 meters	0:47.84	Pieter van den Hoogenband	Netherlands	Sydney, Australia	Sept. 19, 2000
200 meters	1:44.06	Ian Thorpe	Australia	Fukuoka, Japan	July 25, 2001
400 meters	3:40.08	Ian Thorpe	Australia	Manchester, England	July 30, 2002
800 meters	7:39.16	Ian Thorpe	Australia	Fukuoka, Japan	July 24, 2001
1,500 meters	14:34:56	Grant Hackett	Australia	Fukuoka, Japan	July 29, 2001

Breaststroke

Distance	Time	Holder	Country	Where made	Date
50 meters	0:27.18	Oleg Lisogor	Ukraine	Berlin, Germany	Aug. 2, 2002
100 meters	0:59.78	Kosuke Kitajima	Japan	Barcelona, Spain	July 21, 2003
200 meters	2:09.42	Kosuke Kitajima	Japan	Barcelona, Spain	July 24, 2003

Butterfly

Distance	Time	Holder	Country	Where made	Date
50 meters	0:23.43	Michael Welsh	Australia	Barcelona, Spain	July 21, 2003
100 meters	0:50.98	Ian Crocker	U.S.	Barcelona, Spain	July 26, 2003
200 meters	1:53.93	Michael Phelps	U.S.	Barcelona, Spain	July 22, 2003

Backstroke

Distance	Time	Holder	Country	Where made	Date
50 meters	0:24.80	Thomas Rupprath	Germany	Barcelona, Spain	July 27, 2003
100 meters	0:53.60	Lenny Krayzelburg	U.S.	Sydney, Australia	Aug. 24, 1999
200 meters	1:55.15	Aaron Peirsol	U.S.	Minneapolis, MN	Mar. 20, 2002

Individual Medley

Distance	Time	Holder	Country	Where made	Date
200 meters	1:55.94	Michael Phelps	U.S.	Maryland, U.S.	Aug. 9, 2003
400 meters	4.09.09	Michael Phelps	U.S.	Barcelona, Spain	July 27, 2003

Medley Relay

Distance	Time	Holder	Country	Where made	Date
400 m. (4×100)	3:31.54	(Peirsol, Crocker, Phelps, Lezak)	U.S.	Barcelona, Spain	July 27, 2003

Freestyle Relays

Distance	Time	Holder	Country	Where made	Date
400 m. (4×100)	3:13.67	(Klim, Fydler, Callus, Thorpe)	Australia	Sydney, Australia	Sept. 16, 2000
800 m. (4×200)	7:04.66	(Hackett, Klim, Kirby, Thorpe)	Australia	Fukuoka, Japan	July 27, 2001

Women's Records
Freestyle

Distance	Time	Holder	Country	Where made	Date
50 meters	0:24.13	Inge de Bruijn	Netherlands	Sydney, Australia	Sept. 22, 2000
100 meters	0:53.77	Inge de Bruijn	Netherlands	Sydney, Australia	Sept. 20, 2000
200 meters	1:56.64	Franziska Van Almsick	Germany	Berlin, Germany	Aug. 3, 2002
400 meters	4:03.85	Janet Evans	U.S.	Seoul, South Korea	Sept. 22, 1988
800 meters	8:16.22	Janet Evans	U.S.	Tokyo, Japan	Aug. 20, 1989
1,500 meters	15:52.10	Janet Evans	U.S.	Orlando, FL	Mar. 26, 1988

Breaststroke

50 meters	0:30.57	Zoe Baker	U.K.	Manchester, England	July 30, 2002
100 meters	1:06.37	Jones Leisel	Australia	Barcelona, Spain	July 21, 2003
200 meters	2:22.99	Hui Qi	China	Hangzhou, China	Apr. 13, 2001
	2:22.99	Amanda Beard	U.S.	Barcelona, Spain	July 25, 2003

Butterfly

50 meters	0:25.57	Anna-Karin Kammerling	Sweden	Berlin, Germany	July 30, 2000
100 meters	0:56.61	Inge de Bruijn	Netherlands	Sydney, Australia	Sept. 17, 2000
200 meters	2:05.78	Otylia Jedrzejczak	Poland	Berlin, Germany	Aug. 4, 2002

Backstroke

50 meters	0:28.25	Sandra Voelker	Germany	Berlin, Germany	June 17, 2000
100 meters	0:59.58	Natalie Coughlin	U.S.	Ft. Lauderdale, FL	Aug. 13, 2002
200 meters	2:06.62	Kristina Egerszegi	Hungary	Athens, Greece	Aug. 25, 1991

Individual Medley

200 meters	2:09.72	Yanyan Wu	China	Shanghai, China	Oct. 17, 1997
400 meters	4:33.59	Yana Klochkova	Ukraine	Sydney, Australia	Sept. 16, 2000

Freestyle Relays

400 m. (4×100)	3:36.00	(Meissner, Dallman, Volker, van Almsick)	Germany	Berlin, Germany	July 29, 2002
800 m. (4×200)	7:55.47	(Stellmach, Strauss, Mohring, Friedrich)	E. Germany	Strasbourg, France	Aug. 18, 1987

Medley Relay

400 m. (4×100)	3:58.30	(Bedford, Quann, Thompson, Torres)	U.S.	Sydney, Australia	Sept. 23, 2000

YACHTING
The America's Cup in 2003

In the 31st America's Cup the Swiss boat *Alinghi* swept 2-time defending champion *Team New Zealand*, 5-0, in the best-of-nine series. For the 1st time in its 152-year history, the Cup resides on the European continent, in landlocked Switzerland. New Zealand's troubles began 2 months after their last Cup win, when skipper Russell Coutts defected to the Swiss. By 2003, a third of New Zealand's sailors and designers had left to work for other teams. Coutts is undefeated in America's Cup races and won a record 14th on Mar. 2. He was the only captain to win a Cup with 2 different countries.

In the Hauraki Gulf off the coast of Auckland, New Zealand, the Kiwis were in trouble from the start, breaking down early and withdrawing from the 1st race. A broken mast forced the New Zealand boat to withdraw again in the 4th race—postponed 6 times for too little wind, then too much. In the 3 races in which both boats finished, *Alinghi* won by an average of 25 seconds. The next America's Cup will most likely take place in 2007, in either the Mediterranean or the Atlantic.

Competition for the America's Cup grew out of the first contest to establish a world yachting championship, one of the carnival features of the London Exposition of 1851. The race covered a 60-mile course around the Isle of Wight; the prize was a cup worth about $500, donated by the Royal Yacht Squadron of England, known as the "America's Cup" because it was first won by the U.S. yacht *America*.

Winners of the America's Cup

1851 America	1937 Ranger defeated Endeavour II, England, (4-0)
1870 Magic defeated Cambria, England, (1-0)	1958 Columbia defeated Sceptre, England, (4-0)
1871 Columbia (first three races) and Sappho (last two races) defeated Livonia, England, (4-1)	1962 Weatherly defeated Gretel, Australia, (4-1)
1876 Madeline defeated Countess of Dufferin, Canada, (2-0)	1964 Constellation defeated Sovereign, England, (4-0)
1881 Mischief defeated Atalanta, Canada, (2-0)	1967 Intrepid defeated Dame Pattie, Australia, (4-0)
1885 Puritan defeated Genesta, England, (2-0)	1970 Intrepid defeated Gretel II, Australia, (4-1)
1886 Mayflower defeated Galatea, England, (2-0)	1974 Courageous defeated Southern Cross, Australia, (4-0)
1887 Volunteer defeated Thistle, Scotland, (2-0)	1977 Courageous defeated Australia, Australia, (4-0)
1893 Vigilant defeated Valkyrie II, England, (3-0)	1980 Freedom defeated Australia, Australia, (4-1)
1895 Defender defeated Valkyrie III, England, (3-0)	1983 Australia II, Australia, defeated Liberty, (4-3)
1899 Columbia defeated Shamrock, England, (3-0)	1987 Stars & Stripes defeated Kookaburra III, Australia, (4-0)
1901 Columbia defeated Shamrock II, England, (3-0)	1988 Stars & Stripes defeated New Zealand, New Zealand, (2-0)
1903 Reliance defeated Shamrock III, England, (3-0)	1992 America[3] defeated Il Moro di Venezia, Italy, (4-1)
1920 Resolute defeated Shamrock IV, England, (3-2)	1995 Black Magic 1, New Zealand, defeated Young America, (5-0)
1930 Enterprise defeated Shamrock V, England, (4-0)	2000 New Zealand, NZ, defeated Luna Rossa, Italy, (5-0)
1934 Rainbow defeated Endeavour, England, (4-2)	2003 Alinghi, Switzerland, defeated Team New Zealand, NZ, (5-0)

POWER BOATING
American Power Boat Assn. Gold Cup Champions, 1978-2003

Year	Boat	Driver	Year	Boat	Driver	Year	Boat	Driver
1978	Atlas Van Lines	Bill Muncey	1987	Miller American	Chip Hanauer	1996	Pico American Dream	Dave Villwock
1979	Atlas Van Lines	Bill Muncey	1988	Circus Circus	Chip Hanauer			
1980	Miss Budweiser	Dean Chenoweth	1989	Miss Budweiser	Tom D'Eath	1997	Miss Budweiser	Dave Villwock
1981	Miss Budweiser	Dean Chenoweth	1990	Miss Budweiser	Tom D'Eath	1998	Miss Budweiser	Dave Villwock
1982	Atlas Van Lines	Chip Hanauer	1991	Winston Eagle	Mark Tate	1999	Miss PICO	Chip Hanauer
1983	Atlas Van Lines	Chip Hanauer	1992	Miss Budweiser	Chip Hanauer	2000	Miss Budweiser	Dave Villwock
1984	Atlas Van Lines	Chip Hanauer	1993	Miss Budweiser	Chip Hanauer	2001	Miss Tubby's Subs	Mike Hanson
1985	Miller American	Chip Hanauer	1994	Smokin' Joe's	Mark Tate	2002	Miss Budweiser	Dave Villwock
1986	Miller American	Chip Hanauer	1995	Miss Budweiser	Chip Hanauer	2003	Miss Fox Hills	Mitch Evans

GYMNASTICS
2003 World Gymnastics Championships

At the World Gymnastic Championships, held in Anaheim, CA, Aug. 16-24, the U.S. women won their 1st-ever team gold medal. Americans Chellsie Memmel and Hollie Vise tied for the gold in the uneven bars. The U.S. men took the team silver behind China. For the U.S., Paul Hamm won the all-around title and tied for the gold in the floor exercise.

RODEO
Pro Rodeo Cowboy All-Around Champions, 1977-2002

Year	Winner	Money won	Year	Winner	Money won
1977	Tom Ferguson, Miami, OK	$76,730	1990	Ty Murray, Stephenville, TX.	$213,772
1978	Tom Ferguson, Miami, OK	103,734	1991	Ty Murray, Stephenville, TX.	244,230
1979	Tom Ferguson, Miami, OK	96,272	1992	Ty Murray, Stephenville, TX.	225,992
1980	Paul Tierney, Rapid City, SD	105,568	1993	Ty Murray, Stephenville, TX.	297,896
1981	Jimmie Cooper, Monument, NM	105,862	1994	Ty Murray, Stephenville, TX.	246,170
1982	Chris Lybbert, Coyote, CA.	123,709	1995	Joe Beaver, Huntsville, TX.	141,753
1983	Roy Cooper, Durant, OK.	153,391	1996	Joe Beaver, Huntsville, TX.	166,103
1984	Dee Pickett, Caldwell, ID.	122,618	1997	Dan Mortensen, Manhattan, MT	184,559
1985	Lewis Feild, Elk Ridge, UT	130,347	1998	Ty Murray, Stephenville, TX.	264,673
1986	Lewis Feild, Elk Ridge, UT	166,042	1999	Fred Whitfield, Hockley, TX	217,819
1987	Lewis Feild, Elk Ridge, UT	144,335	2000	Joe Beaver, Huntsville, TX.	225,396
1988	Dave Appleton, Arlington, TX	121,546	2001	Cody Ohl, Stephensville, TX	296,419
1989	Ty Murray, Odessa, TX.	134,806	2002	Trevor Brazile, Anson, TX	273,997

DOGS
Westminster Kennel Club, 1989-2003

Year	Best-in-show	Breed	Owner(s)
1989	Ch. Royal Tudor's Wild As The Wind	Doberman	Sue & Art Kemp, Richard & Carolyn Vida, Beth Wilhite
1990	Ch. Wendessa Crown Prince	Pekingese	Ed Jenner
1991	Ch. Whisperwind on a Carousel	Poodle	Joan & Frederick Hartsock
1992	Ch. Registry's Lonesome Dove	Fox Terrier	Marion & Sam Lawrence
1993	Ch. Salilyn's Condor	English Springer Spaniel	Donna & Roger Herzig
1994	Ch. Chidley Willum	Norwich Terrier	Ruth Cooper & Patricia Lussier
1995	Ch. Gaelforce Post Script	Scottish Terrier	Dr. Vandra Huber & Dr. Joe Kinnarney
1996	Ch. Clussexx Country Sunrise	Clumber Spaniel	Judith & Richard Zaleski
1997	Ch. Parsifal Di Casa Netzer	Standard Schnauzer	Rita Holloway & Gabrio Del Torre
1998	Ch. Fairewood Frolic	Norwich Terrier	Sandina Kennels
1999	Ch. Loteki Supernatural Being	Papillon	John Oulton
2000	Ch. Salilyn 'N Erin's Shameless	English Springer Spaniel	Carl Blain, Fran Sunseri, & Julia Gasow
2001	Ch. Special Times Just Right	Bichons Frises	Cecilia Ruggles, E. McDonald, & F. Werneck
2002	Ch. Surrey Spice Girl	Poodle (Miniature)	Ron L. & Barbara Scott
2003	Ch. Torum's Scarf Michael	Kerry Blue Terrier	Marilu Hanson

2003 Iditarod Trail Sled Dog Race

Robert Sorlie, of Norway, won his 1st Iditarod sled dog race, Mar. 13, in only his 2nd time racing the event (he finished 9th in 2002). The 1,100-mile course from Anchorage to Nome, AK, had to be rerouted several times due to lack of snow. Some 400 miles of trail were affected. Sorlie was the 1st non-American winner in race history. His winning time was 9 days, 15 hours, 47 minutes.

MARATHONS
Boston Marathon, 2003, and 1972-2003

In the 107th Boston Marathon, Apr. 21, Robert Kipkoech Cheruiyot (Kenya) won in 2 hours, 10 minutes, and 11 seconds. The top 5 runners were all from Kenya. Benjamin Kosgei Kimutai (2:10:34) and Martin Lel (2:11:11) finished 2nd and 3rd. Kenyan Rogers Rop, the 2002 champion, finished 7th. Russia's Svetlana Zakharova was the women's champion, with a winning time of 2:25:20. Lyubov Denisova, also from Russia, finished 2nd in 2:26:51. Third went to Kenya's Joyce Chepchumba Koech (2:27:20).

Boston Marathon Winners
All times in hour:minute:second format. *Course records.

Men's Winner	Time	Year	Women's Winner	Time
Olavi Suomalainen, Finland	2:15:39	1972	Nina Kuscsik, U.S.	3:10:26
Jon Anderson, U.S.	2:16:03	1973	Jacqueline Hansen, U.S.	3:05:59
Neil Cusack, Ir.	2:13:39	1974	Michiko Gorman, U.S.	2:47:11
Bill Rodgers, U.S.	2:09:55	1975	Liane Winter, West Ger.	2:42:24
Jack Fultz, U.S.	2:20:19	1976	Kim Merritt, U.S.	2:47:10
Jerome Drayton, Can.	2:14:46	1977	Michiko Gorman, U.S.	2:48:33
Bill Rodgers, U.S.	2:10:13	1978	Gayle S. Barron, U.S.	2:44:52
Bill Rodgers, U.S.	2:09:27	1979	Joan Benoit, U.S.	2:35:15
Bill Rodgers, U.S.	2:12:11	1980	Jacqueline Gareau, Can.	2:34:28
Toshihiko Seko, Japan	2:09:26	1981	Allison Roe, N. Zealand	2:26:46
Alberto Salazar, U.S.	2:08:52	1982	Charlotte Teske, West Ger.	2:29:33
Greg Myer, U.S.	2:09:00	1983	Joan Benoit, U.S.	2:22:43
Geoff Smith, G.B.	2:10:34	1984	Lorraine Moller, N. Zealand	2:29:28
Geoff Smith, G.B.	2:14:05	1985	Lisa Larsen Weidenbach, U.S.	2:34:06
Robert de Castella, Australia	2:07:51	1986	Ingrid Kristiansen, Nor.	2:24:55
Toshihiko Seko, Japan	2:11:50	1987	Rosa Mota, Portugal	2:25:21
Ibrahim Hussein, Ken.	2:08:43	1988	Rosa Mota, Portugal	2:24:30
Abebe Mekonnen, Eth.	2:09:06	1989	Ingrid Kristiansen, Nor.	2:24:33
Gelindo Bordin, Italy	2:08:19	1990	Rosa Mota, Portugal	2:25:24
Ibrahim Hussein, Kenya	2:11:06	1991	Wanda Panfil, Poland	2:24:18
Ibrahim Hussein, Kenya	2:08:14	1992	Olga Markova, CIS	2:23:43
Cosmas Ndeti, Kenya	2:09:33	1993	Olga Markova, CIS	2:25:27
Cosmas Ndeti, Kenya	2:07:15*	1994	Uta Pippig, Germany	2:21:45*
Cosmas Ndeti, Kenya	2:09:22	1995	Uta Pippig, Germany	2:25:11

Men's Winner	Time	Year	Women's Winner	Time
Moses Tanui, Kenya	2:09:15	1996	Uta Pippig, Germany	2:27:12
Lameck Aguta, Kenya	2:10:34	1997	Fatuma Roba, Ethiopia	2:26:23
Moses Tanui, Kenya	2:07:34	1998	Fatuma Roba, Ethiopia	2:23:21
Joseh Chebet, Kenya	2:09:52	1999	Fatuma Roba, Ethiopia	2:23:25
Elijah Lagat, Kenya	2:09:47	2000	Catherine Ndereba, Kenya	2:26:11
Lee Bong-ju, S. Korea	2:09:43	2001	Catherine Ndereba, Kenya	2:23:53
Rodgers Rop, Kenya	2:09:02	2002	Margaret Okayo, Kenya	2:20:43
Robert K. Cheruiyot, Kenya	2:10:11	2003	Svetlana Zakharova, Russia	2:25:20

Boston Marathon Winners, 1897-1971

The 1st Boston Marathon was held in 1897. Women were officially accepted into the race in 1972.

Year	Winner	Time	Year	Winner	Time
1897	John J. McDermott, New York	2:55:10	1935	John A. Kelley, Massachusetts	2:32:07
1898	Ronald J. MacDonald, Canada	2:42:00	1936	Ellison M. Brown, Rhode Island	2:33:40
1899	Lawrence Brignolia, Massachusetts	2:54:38	1937	Walter Young, Canada	2:33:20
1900	John Caffery, Canada	2:39:44	1938	Leslie S. Pawson, Rhode Island	2:35:34
1901	John Caffery, Canada	2:29:23	1939	Ellison M. Brown, Rhode Island	2:28:51
1902	Sammy Mellor, New York	2:43:12	1940	Gerard Cote, Canada	2:28:28
1903	John Lorden , Massachusetts	2:41:29	1941	Leslie S. Pawson, Rhode Island	2:30:38
1904	Michael Spring, New York	2:38:04	1942	Joe Smith, Massachusetts	2:26:51
1905	Frederick Lorz, New York	2:38:25	1943	Gerard Cote, Canada	2:28:25
1906	Tim Ford, Massachusetts	2:45:45	1944	Gerard Cote, Canada	2:31:50
1907	Thomas Longboat, Canada	2:24:24	1945	John A. Kelley, Massachusetts	2:30:40
1908	Thomas Morrissey, New York	2:25:43	1946	Stylianos Kyriakides, Greece	2:29:27
1909	Henri Renaud, New Hampshire	2:53:36	1947	Yun Bok Suh, Korea	2:25:39
1910	Fred Cameron, Canada	2:28:52	1948	Gerard Cote, Canada	2:31:02
1911	Clarence DeMar, Massachusetts	2:21:39	1949	Karl Leandersson, Sweden	2:31:50
1912	Michael Ryan, New York	2:21:18	1950	Kee Yong Ham, Korea	2:32:39
1913	Fritz Carlson, Minnesota	2:25:14	1951	Shigeki Tanaka, Japan	2:27:45
1914	James Duffy, Canada	2:25:14	1952	Doroteo Flores, Guatamela	2:31:53
1915	Edouard Fabre, Canada	2:31:41	1953	Keizo Yamada, Japan	2:18:51
1916	Arthur Roth, Massachusetts	2:27:16	1954	Veikko Karvonen, Finland	2:20:39
1917	Bill Kennedy, New York	2:28:37	1955	Hideo Hamamura, Japan	2:18:22
1918	Military Relay, Camp Devens	2:29:53	1956	Antti Viskari, Finland	2:14:14
1919	Carl Linder, Massachusetts	2:29:13	1957	John J. Kelley, Connecticut	2:20:05
1920	Peter Trivoulides, New York	2:29:31	1958	Franjo Mihalic, Yugoslavian	2:25:54
1921	Frank Zuna, New York	2:18:57	1959	Eino Oksanen, Finland	2:22:42
1922	Clarence DeMar, Massachusetts	2:18:10	1960	Paavo Kotila, Finland	2:20:54
1923	Clarence DeMar, Massachusetts	2:23:47	1961	Eino Oksanen, Finland	2:23:39
1924	Clarence DeMar, Massachusetts	2:29:40	1962	Eino Oksanen, Finland	2:23:48
1925	Charles Mellor, Illinois	2:33:00	1963	Aurele Vandendriessche, Belgium	2:18:58
1926	John C. Miles, Canada	2:25:40	1964	Aurele Vandendriessche, Belgium	2:19:59
1927	Clarence DeMar, Massachusetts	2:40:22	1965	Morio Shigematsu, Japan	2:16:33
1928	Clarence DeMar, Massachusetts	2:37:07	1966	Kenji Kemihara, Japan	2:17:11
1929	John C. Miles, Canada	2:33:08	1967	David McKenzie, New Zealand	2:15:45
1930	Clarence DeMar, Massachusetts	2:34:48	1968	Amby Burfoot, Connecticut	2:22:17
1931	James P. Henigan, Massachusetts	2:46:45	1969	Yoshiaki Unetani, Japan	2:13:49
1932	Paul DeBruyn, Germany	2:33:36	1970	Ron Hill, Great Britain	2:10:30
1933	Leslie S. Pawson, Rhode Island	2:31:01	1971	Alvaro Mejia, Colombia	2:18:45
1934	Dave Komonen, Canada	2:32:53			

New York City Marathon

All time in hour:minute:second format; *Course record.

Men's Winner	Time	Year	Women's Winner	Time
Gary Muhrcke, U.S.	2:31:38	1970	no finisher	—
Norman Higgins, U.S.	2:22:54	1971	Beth Bonner, U.S.	2:55:22
Sheldon Karlin, U.S.	2:27:52	1972	Nina Kuscsik, U.S.	3:08:41
Tom Fleming, U.S.	2:19:25	1973	Nina Kuscsik, U.S.	2:57:07
Norbert Sander, U.S.	2:26:30	1974	Katherine Switzer, U.S.	3:07:29
Tom Fleming, U.S.	2:19:27	1975	Kim Merritt, U.S.	2:46:14
Bill Rodgers, U.S.	2:10:10	1976	Miki Gorman, U.S.	2:39:11
Bill Rodgers, U.S.	2:11:28	1977	Miki Gorman, U.S.	2:43:10
Bill Rodgers, U.S.	2:12:12	1978	Grete Waitz, Norway	2:32:30
Bill Rodgers, U.S.	2:11:42	1979	Grete Waitz, Norway	2:27:33
Alberto Salazar, U.S.	2:09:41	1980	Grete Waitz, Norway	2:25:42
Alberto Salazar, U.S.	2:08:13	1981	Allison Roe, N. Zealand	2:25:29
Alberto Salazar, U.S.	2:09:29	1982	Grete Waitz, Norway	2:27:14
Rod Dixon, N.Z.	2:08:59	1983	Grete Waitz, Norway	2:27:00
Orlando Pizzolato, Italy	2:14:53	1984	Grete Waitz, Norway	2:29:30
Orlando Pizzolato, Italy	2:11:34	1985	Grete Waitz, Norway	2:28:34
Gianni Poli, Italy	2:11:06	1986	Grete Waitz, Norway	2:28:06
Ibrahim Hussein, Kenya	2:11:01	1987	Priscilla Welch, G.B.	2:30:17
Steve Jones, G.B.	2:08:20	1988	Grete Waitz, Norway	2:28:07
Juma Ikangaa, Tanz.	2:08:01	1989	Ingrid Kristiansen, Norway	2:25:30
Douglas Wakiihuri, Ken.	2:12:39	1990	Wanda Panfil, Poland	2:30:45
Salvador Garcia, Mexico	2:09:28	1991	Liz McColgan, G.B.	2:27:32
Willie Mtolo, S. Afr.	2:09:29	1992	Lisa Ondieki, Australia	2:24:40*
Andres Espinosa, Mex.	2:10:04	1993	Uta Pippig, Germany	2:26:24
German Silva, Mexico	2:11:21	1994	Tegla Loroupe, Kenya	2:27:37
German Silva, Mexico	2:11:00	1995	Tegla Loroupe, Kenya	2:28:06
Giacomo Leone, Italy	2:09:54	1996	Anuta Catuna, Romania	2:28:43
John Kagwe, Kenya	2:08:12	1997	F. Rochat-Moser, Switzerland	2:28:43
John Kagwe, Kenya	2:08:45	1998	Franca Fiacconi, Italy	2:25:17
Joseph Chebet, Kenya	2:09:14	1999	Adriana Fernandez, Mex.	2:25:06
Abdelkhader El Mouaziz, Morocco	2:10:09	2000	Ludmila Petrova, Russia	2:25:45
Tesfaye Jifar, Ethiopia	2:07:43*	2001	Margaret Okayo, Kenya	2:24:21*
Rodgers Rop, Kenya	2:08:07	2002	Joyce Chepchumba, Kenya	2:25:56

Other Marathon Results in 2003

Los Angeles Marathon—Mar. 2. Men: Mark Yatich, Kenya, 2:09:52. Women: Tatyana Pozdnyakora, Ukraine, 2:29:40.

Paris Marathon—Apr. 6. Men: Mike Rotich, Kenya, 2:06:32. Women: Beatrice Omwanza, Kenya, 2:27:44.

Rotterdam Marathon—Apr. 13. Men: William Kiplagat, Kenya, 2:07:42. Women: Olivera Jevtic, Serbia and Montenegro, 2:25:23.

London Marathon—Apr. 13. Men: Gezahegne Abera, Ethiopia, 2:07:56. Women: Paula Radcliffe, U.K., 2:15:25 (world best).

Berlin Marathon—Sept. 28. Men: Paul Tergat, Kenya, 2:04:55 (world best); 2nd Sammy Korir, Kenya, 2:04:56. Women: Naoko Takahashi, Japan, 2:21:49.

Chicago Marathon—Oct. 12. Men: Evans Rutto, Kenya, 2:05:05. Women: Svetlzna Zakharova, Russsia, 2:23:07.

Ironman Triathlon World Championships

The Ironman Triathlon World Championships—a 2.4-mile ocean swim, 112-mile bike ride and 26.2-mile run—are held annually at Kailua-Kona, Hawaii. On Oct. 19, 2002, the men's race was won by American Tim DeBoom in 8:29:56. Switzerland's Natascha Badmann won the women's race in 9:07:54. All times in hour:minute:second format. *Course records.

Men's Winner	Time	Year	Women's Winner	Time
Gordon Haller, U.S.	11:46:58	1978	no finisher	—
Tom Warren, U.S.	11:15:56	1979	Lyn Lemaire, U.S.	12:55:00
Dave Scott, U.S.	9:24:33	1980	Robin Beck, U.S.	11:21:24
John Howard, U.S.	9:38:29	1981	Linda Sweeney, U.S.	12:00:32
Dave Scott, U.S.	9:08:23	1982	Julie Leach, U.S.	10:54:08
Dave Scott, U.S.	9:05:57	1983	Sylviane Puntous, Canada	10:43:36
Dave Scott, U.S.	8:54:20	1984	Sylvanie Puntous, Canada	10:25:13
ScottTinley, U.S.	8:50:54	1985	Joanne Ernst, U.S.	10:25:22
Dave Scott, U.S.	8:28:37	1986	Paula Newby-Fraser, Zimbabwe	9:49:14
Dave Scott, U.S.	8:34:13	1987	Erin Baker, New Zealand	9:35:25
Scott Molina, U.S.	8:31:00	1988	Paula Newby-Fraser, Zimbabwe	9:01:01
Mark Allen, U.S.	8:09:15	1989	Paula Newby-Fraser, Zimbabwe	9:00:56
Mark Allen, U.S.	8:28:17	1990	Erin Baker, New Zealand	9:13:42
Mark Allen, U.S.	8:18:32	1991	Paula Newby-Fraser, Zimbabwe	9:07:52
Mark Allen, U.S.	8:09:08	1992	Paula Newby-Fraser, Zimbabwe	8:55:28*
Mark Allen, U.S.	8:07:45	1993	Paula Newby-Fraser, Zimbabwe	8:58:23
Greg Welch, Australia	8:20:27	1994	Paula Newby-Fraser, Zimbabwe	9:20:14
Mark Allen, U.S.	8:20:34	1995	Karen Smyers, U.S.	9:16:46
Luc Van Lierde, Belgium	8:04:08*	1996	Paula Newby-Fraser, Zimbabwe	9:06:49
Thomas Hellriegel, Germany	8:33:01	1997	Heather Fuhr, Canada	9:31:43
Peter Reid, Canada	8:24:20	1998	Natascha Badmann, Switz.	9:24:16
Luc Van Lierde, Belgium	8:17:17	1999	Lori Bowden, U.S.	9:13:02
Peter Reid, Canada	8:21:01	2000	Natascha Badmann, Switz.	9:26:16
Timothy Deboom, U.S.	8:31:18	2001	Natascha Badmann, Switz.	9:28:37
Timothy Deboom, U.S.	8:29:56	2002	Natascha Badmann, Switz.	9:07:54

CYCLING

2003 Tour de France

In the 100th anniversary Tour de France, the world's premier cycling event, American Lance Armstrong rode into Paris in the 20th stage on July 27 wearing the leader's yellow jersey for the 5th straight year—tying a record for consecutive victories set by Spain's Miguel Indurain (1991-95). Armstrong finished the 23-day, 2,130-mile tour with an overall time of 83 hrs., 41 mins., 12 secs, defeating Germany's Jan Ullrich by only 61 secs., his narrowest margin ever. Ullrich, the 1997 winner, was runner-up for the 5th time. Armstrong and the U.S. Postal Service team finished 4th in the team competition. Team CSC, led by American Tyler Hamilton, won the team title. Hamilton broke his collarbone in a 35-rider crash in the 1st stage, but went on to finish 4th overall and won the 16th stage.

Tour de France Winners, 1980-2003

Year	Winner	Year	Winner	Year	Winner
1980	Zoop Zoetemelk, The Netherlands	1988	Pedro Delgado, Spain	1996	Bjarne Riis, Denmark
1981	Bernard Hinault, France	1989	Greg LeMond, U.S.	1997	Jan Ullrich, Germany
1982	Bernard Hinault, France	1990	Greg LeMond, U.S.	1998	Marco Pantani, Italy
1983	Laurent Fignon, France	1991	Miguel Indurain, Spain	1999	Lance Armstrong, U.S.
1984	Laurent Fignon, France	1992	Miguel Indurain, Spain	2000	Lance Armstrong, U.S.
1985	Bernard Hinault, France	1993	Miguel Indurain, Spain	2001	Lance Armstrong, U.S.
1986	Greg LeMond, U.S.	1994	Miguel Indurain, Spain	2002	Lance Armstrong, U.S.
1987	Stephen Roche, Ireland	1995	Miguel Indurain, Spain	2003	Lance Armstrong, U.S.

SULLIVAN AWARD

James E. Sullivan Memorial Trophy Winners

The James E. Sullivan Memorial Trophy, named after the former president of the Amateur Athletic Union (AAU) and inaugurated in 1930, is awarded annually by the AAU to the athlete who "by his or her performance, example and influence as an amateur, has done the most during the year to advance the cause of sportsmanship."

Year	Winner	Sport	Year	Winner	Sport	Year	Winner	Sport
1930	Bobby Jones	Golf	1943	Gilbert Dodds	Track	1957	Bobby Joe Morrow	Track
1931	Barney Berlinger	Track	1944	Ann Curtis	Swimming	1958	Glenn Davis	Track
1932	Jim Bausch	Track	1945	Doc Blanchard	Football	1959	Parry O'Brien	Track
1933	Glenn Cunningham	Track	1946	Arnold Tucker	Football	1960	Rafer Johnson	Track
1934	Bill Bonthron	Track	1947	John Kelly, Jr.	Rowing	1961	Wilma Rudolph Ward	Track
1935	Lawson Little	Golf	1948	Robert Mathias	Track	1962	James Beatty	Track
1936	Glenn Morris	Track	1949	Dick Button	Skating	1963	John Pennel	Track
1937	Don Budge	Tennis	1950	Fred Wilt	Track	1964	Don Schollander	Swimming
1938	Don Lash	Track	1951	Rev. Robert Richards	Track	1965	Bill Bradley	Basketball
1939	Joe Burk	Rowing	1952	Horace Ashenfelter	Track	1966	Jim Ryun	Track
1940	Greg Rice	Track	1953	Dr. Sammy Lee	Diving	1967	Randy Matson	Track
1941	Leslie MacMitchell	Track	1954	Mal Whitfield	Track	1968	Debbie Meyer	Swimming
1942	Cornelius Warmerdam	Track	1955	Harrison Dillard	Track	1969	Bill Toomey	Track
			1956	Patricia McCormick	Diving	1970	John Kinsella	Swimming

Year	Winner	Sport	Year	Winner	Sport	Year	Winner	Sport
1971	Mark Spitz	Swimming	1984	Greg Louganis	Diving	1993	Charlie Ward	Football, Basketball
1972	Frank Shorter	Track	1985	Joan Benoit Samuelson	Marathon	1994	Dan Jansen	Speed Skating
1973	Bill Walton	Basketball	1986	Jackie Joyner-Kersee	Track	1995	Bruce Baumgartner	Wrestling
1974	Rick Wohlhutter	Track	1987	Jim Abbott	Baseball	1996	Michael Johnson	Track
1975	Tim Shaw	Swimming	1988	Florence Griffith Joyner	Track	1997	Peyton Manning	Football
1976	Bruce Jenner	Track	1989	Janet Evans	Swimming	1998	Chamique Holdsclaw	Basketball
1977	John Naber	Swimming	1990	John Smith	Wrestling	1999	Coco Miller and Kelly Miller	Basketball
1978	Tracy Caulkins	Swimming	1991	Mike Powell	Track	2000	Rulon Gardner	Wrestling
1979	Kurt Thomas	Gymnastics	1992	Bonnie Blair	Speed Skating	2001	Michelle Kwan	Figure Skating
1980	Eric Heiden	Speed Skating				2002	Sarah Hughes	Figure Skating
1981	Carl Lewis	Track						
1982	Mary Decker	Track						
1983	Edwin Moses	Track						

FISHING
Selected IGFA Saltwater & Freshwater All-Tackle World Records
Source: International Game Fish Association; records confirmed to Sept. 19, 2003

Saltwater Fish Records

Species	Weight	Where caught	Date	Angler
Albacore	88 lbs. 2 oz.	Canary Islands, Spain	Nov. 19, 1977	Siegfried Dickemann
Amberjack, greater	155 lbs. 12 oz.	Bermuda	Aug. 16, 1992	Larry Trott
Barracuda, great	85 lbs.	Christmas Island, Kiribati	Apr. 11, 1992	John W. Helfrich
Barracuda, Mexican	21 lbs.	Phantom Isle, Costa Rica	Mar. 27, 1987	E. Greg Kent
Barracuda, Pacific	26 lbs. 8 oz.	Playa Matapalo, Costa Rica	Jan. 3, 1999	Doug Hettinger
Bass, barred sand	13 lbs. 3 oz.	Huntington Beach, CA	Aug. 29, 1988	Robert Halal
Bass, black sea	10 lbs. 4 oz.	Virginia Beach, VA	Jan. 1, 2000	Allan P. Paschall
Bass, giant sea	563 lbs. 8 oz.	Anacapa Island, CA	Aug. 20, 1968	James D. McAdam Jr.
Bass, striped	78 lbs. 8 oz.	Atlantic City, NJ	Sept. 21, 1982	Albert R. McReynolds
Bluefish	31 lbs. 12 oz.	Hatteras Inlet, NC	Jan. 30, 1972	James M. Hussey
Bonefish	19 lbs.	Zululand, South Africa	May 26, 1962	Brian W. Batchelor
Bonito, Atlantic	18 lbs. 4 oz.	Faial Island, Azores	July 8, 1953	D. Gama Higgs
Bonito, Pacific	21 lbs. 3 oz.	Malibu, CA	July 30, 1978	Gino M. Picciolo
Cabezon	23 lbs.	Juan De Fuca Strait, WA	Aug. 4, 1990	Wesley S. Hunter
Cobia	135 lbs. 9 oz.	Shark Bay, Australia	July 9, 1985	Peter W. Goulding
Cod, Atlantic	98 lbs. 12 oz.	Isle of Shoals, NH	June 8, 1969	Alphonse J. Bielevich
Cod, Pacific	35 lbs.	Unalaska Bay, AK	June 16, 1999	Jim Johnson
Conger	133 lbs. 4 oz.	Berry Head, S. Devon, England	June 5, 1995	Vic Evans
Dolphin	88 lbs.	Exuma, Bahamas	May 5, 1998	Richard D. Evans
Drum, black	113 lbs. 1 oz.	Lewes, DE	Sept. 15, 1975	Gerald M. Townsend
Drum, red	94 lbs. 2 oz.	Avon, NC	Nov. 7, 1984	David G. Deuel
Eel, American	9 lbs. 4 oz.	Cape May, NJ	Nov. 9, 1995	Jeff Pennick
Eel, marbled	36 lbs. 1 oz.	Hazelmere Dam, South Africa	June 10, 1984	Ferdie Van Nooten
Flounder, southern	20 lbs. 9 oz.	Nassau Sound, FL	Dec. 23, 1983	Larenza W. Mungin
Flounder, summer	22 lbs. 7 oz.	Montauk, NY	Sept. 15, 1975	Charles Nappi
Grouper, Goliath	680 lbs.	Fernandina Beach, FL	May 20, 1961	Lynn Joyner
Grouper, Warsaw	436 lbs. 12 oz.	Gulf of Mexico, Destin, FL	Dec. 22, 1985	Steve Haeusler
Halibut, Atlantic	355 lbs. 6 oz.	Valevag, Norway	Oct. 20, 1997	Odd Arve Gunderstad
Halibut, California	58 lbs. 9 oz.	Santa Rosa Island, CA	June 26, 1999	Roger W. Borrell
Halibut, Pacific	459 lbs.	Dutch Harbor, AK	June 11, 1996	Jack Tragis
Jack, crevalle	58 lbs. 6 oz.	Barra do Kwanza, Angola	Dec. 10, 2000	Nuno Abohbot Po da Silva
Jack, horse-eye	29 lbs. 8 oz.	Ascencion Island, South Atlantic	May 28, 1993	Mike Hanson
Jack, Pacific crevalle	39 lbs.	Playa Zancudo, Costa Rica	Mar. 3, 1997	Ingrid Callaghan
Kawakawa	29 lbs.	Clarion Island, Mexico	Dec. 17, 1986	Ronald Nakamura
Lingcod	76 lbs. 9 oz.	Gulf of Alaska, AK	Aug. 11, 2001	Antwan D. Tinsley
Mackerel, cero	17 lbs. 2 oz.	Islamorada, FL	Apr. 5, 1986	G. Michael Mills
Mackerel, king	93 lbs.	San Juan, PR	Apr. 18, 1999	Steve Perez Graulau
Mackerel, Spanish	13 lbs.	Ocracoke Inlet, NC	Nov. 4, 1987	Robert Cranton
Marlin, Atlantic blue	1,402 lbs. 2 oz.	Vitoria, Brazil	Feb. 29, 1992	Paulo Roberto A. Amorim
Marlin, black	1,560 lbs.	Cabo Blanco, Peru	Aug. 4, 1953	Alfred C. Glassell Jr.
Marlin, Pacific blue	1,376 lbs.	Kaaiwi Pt., Kona, HI	May 31, 1982	Jay W. deBeaubien
Marlin, striped	494 lbs.	Tutukaka, New Zealand	Jan. 16, 1986	Bill Boniface
Marlin, white	181 lbs. 14 oz.	Vitoria, Brazil	Dec. 8, 1979	Evandro Luiz Coser
Permit	60 lbs. 0 oz.	Ilha do Mel, Paranagua, Brazil	Dec. 14, 2002	Renato P. Fiedler
Pollack, European	27 lbs. 6 oz.	Salcombe, Devon, England	Jan. 16, 1986	Robert Samuel Milkins
Pollock	50 lbs.	Salstraumen, Norway	Nov. 30, 1995	Thor-Magnus Lekang
Pompano, African	50 lbs. 8 oz.	Daytona Beach, FL	Apr. 21, 1990	Tom Sargent
Roosterfish	114 lbs.	La Paz, Baja Cal., Mexico	June 1, 1960	Abe Sackheim
Runner, blue	11 lbs. 2 oz.	Dauphin Isl., AL	June 28, 1997	Stacey Michelle Moiren
Runner, rainbow	37 lbs. 9 oz.	Clarion Island, Mexico	Nov. 21, 1991	Tom Pfleger
Sailfish, Atlantic	141 lbs. 1 oz.	Luanda, Angola	Feb. 19, 1994	Alfredo de Sousa Neves
Sailfish, Pacific	221 lbs.	Santa Cruz Island, Ecuador	Feb. 12, 1947	C. W. Stewart
Seabass, white	83 lbs. 12 oz.	San Felipe, Mexico	Mar. 31, 1953	L. C. Baumgardner
Seatrout, spotted	17 lbs. 7 oz.	Ft. Pierce, FL	May 11, 1995	Craig F. Carson
Shark, bigeye thresher	802 lbs.	Tutukaka, New Zealand	Feb. 8, 1981	Dianne North
Shark, bignose	369 lbs. 14 oz.	Markham R., Papua New Guinea	Oct. 23, 1993	Lester J. Rohrlach
Shark, blue	528 lbs.	Montauk Point, NY	Aug. 9, 2001	Joe Seidel
Shark, great hammerhead	991 lbs.	Sarasota, FL	May 30, 1982	Allen Ogle
Shark, Greenland	1,708 lbs. 9 oz.	Trondheimsfjord, Norway	Oct. 18, 1987	Terje Nordtvedt
Shark, porbeagle	507 lbs.	Caithness, Scotland	Mar. 9, 1993	Christopher Bennett
Shark, shortfin mako	1,221 lbs.	Chatham, MA	July 21, 2001	Luke Sweeney
Shark, tiger	1,780 lbs.	Cherry Grove, SC	June 14, 1964	Walter Maxwell
Shark, white	2,664 lbs.	Ceduna, S.A., Australia	Apr. 21, 1959	Alfred Dean
Sheepshead	21 lbs. 4 oz.	New Orleans, LA	Apr. 16, 1982	Wayne Desselle
Skipjack, black	26 lbs.	Thetis Bank, Baja Cal., Mexico	Oct. 23, 1991	Clifford Hamaishi
Snapper, cubera	121 lbs. 8 oz.	Cameron, LA	July 5, 1982	Mike Hebert
Snapper, red	50 lbs. 4 oz.	Gulf of Mexico, LA	June 23, 1996	Capt. Doc Kennedy

Species	Weight	Where caught	Date	Angler
Snook, common	53 lbs. 10 oz.	Parismina Ranch, Costa Rica	Oct. 18, 1978	Gilbert Ponzi
Spearfish, Mediterranean	90 lbs. 13 oz.	Madeira Island, Portugal	June 2, 1980	Joseph Larkin
Swordfish	1,182 lbs.	Iquique, Chile	May 7, 1953	L. B. Marron
Tarpon	286 lbs. 9 oz.	Rubane, Guinea-Bissau	Mar. 20, 2003	Max Domecq
Tautog	25 lbs.	Ocean City, NJ	Jan. 20, 1998	Anthony R. Monica
Trevally, bigeye	31 lbs. 8 oz.	Poivre Isl., Seychelles	Apr. 23, 1997	Les Sampson
Trevally, giant	145 lbs. 8 oz.	Makena, Maui, HI	Mar. 28, 1991	Russell Mori
Tuna, Atlantic bigeye	392 lbs. 6 oz.	Canary Islands, Spain	July 15, 1996	Dieter Vogel
Tuna, blackfin	45 lbs. 8 oz.	Key West, FL	May 4, 1996	Sam J. Burnett
Tuna, bluefin	1,496 lbs.	Aulds Cove, Nova Scotia	Oct. 26, 1979	Ken Fraser
Tuna, longtail	79 lbs. 2 oz.	Montague Isl., N.S.W., Australia	Apr. 12, 1982	Tim Simpson
Tuna, Pacific bigeye	435 lbs.	Cabo Blanco, Peru	Apr. 17, 1957	Dr. Russel V. A. Lee
Tuna, skipjack	45 lbs. 4 oz.	Flathead Bank, Baja Cal., Mexico	Nov. 16, 1996	Brian Evans
Tuna, southern bluefin	348 lbs. 5 oz.	Whakatane, New Zealand	Jan. 16, 1981	Rex Wood
Tuna, yellowfin	388 lbs. 12 oz.	San Benedicto Island, Mexico	Apr. 1, 1977	Curt Wiesenhutter
Tunny, little	35 lbs. 2 oz.	Cap de Garde, Algeria	Dec. 14, 1988	Jean Yves Chatard
Wahoo	158 lbs. 8 oz.	Loreto, Baja Cal., Mexico	June 10, 1996	Keith Winter
Weakfish	19 lbs. 2 oz.	Jones Beach Inlet, NY	Oct. 11, 1984	Dennis Roger Rooney
		Delaware Bay, DE	May 20, 1989	William E. Thomas
Yellowtail, California	88 lbs. 3 oz.	Alijos Rocks, Baja Cal., Mexico	June 21, 2000	Ronald Tadashi Fujii
Yellowtail, southern	114 lbs. 10 oz.	Tauranga, New Zealand	Feb. 5, 1984	Mike Godfrey
		White Island, New Zealand	Jan. 9, 1987	David Lugton

Freshwater Fish Records

Species	Weight	Where caught	Date	Angler
Barramundi	83 lbs. 7 oz.	Lake Tinaroo, N. Queensland, Australia	Sept. 23, 1999	David Powell
Bass, largemouth	22 lbs. 4 oz.	Montgomery Lake, GA	June 2, 1932	George W. Perry
Bass, rock	3 lbs.	York River, Ontario	Aug. 1, 1974	Peter Gulgin
	3 lbs.	Lake Erie, PA	June 18, 1998	Herbert G. Ratner, Jr.
Bass, shoal	8 lbs. 12 oz.	Apalachicola River, FL	Jan. 28, 1995	Carl W. Davis
Bass, smallmouth	10 lbs. 14 oz.	Dale Hollow Lake, TN	Apr. 24, 1969	John T. Gorman
Bass, white	6 lbs. 13 oz.	Lake Orange, VA	July 31, 1989	Ronald L. Sprouse
Bass, whiterock	27 lbs. 5 oz.	Greers Ferry Lake, AR	April 24, 1997	Jerald C. Shaum
Bass, yellow	2 lbs. 9 oz.	Waverly, TN	Feb. 27, 1998	John T. Chappell
Bluegill	4 lbs. 12 oz.	Ketona Lake, AL	Apr. 9, 1950	T. S. Hudson
Bowfin	21 lbs. 8 oz.	Florence, SC	Jan. 29, 1980	Robert L. Harmon
Bream	13 lbs. 3 oz.	Hagbvan Creek, Sweden	May 11, 1984	Luis Kilian Rasmussen
Buffalo, bigmouth	70 lbs. 5 oz.	Bastrop, LA	Apr. 21, 1980	Delbert Sisk
Buffalo, black	63 lbs. 6 oz.	Mississippi River, IA	Aug. 14, 1999	Jim Winters
Buffalo, smallmouth	82 lbs. 3 oz.	Athens Lake, AR	June 6, 1993	Randy Collins
Bullhead, brown	6 lbs. 5 oz.	Lake Mahopac, NY	Sept. 8, 2002	Ray Lawrence
Bullhead, yellow	4 lbs. 4 oz.	Mormon Lake, AZ	May 11, 1984	Emily Williams
Burbot	18 lbs. 11 oz.	Angenmanalren, Sweden	Oct. 22, 1996	Margit Agren
Carp, common	75 lbs. 11 oz.	Lac de St. Cassien, France	May 21, 1987	Leo van der Gugten
Catfish, blue	116 lbs. 12 oz.	Mississippi R., AR	Aug 3, 2001	Charles Ashley Jr.
Catfish, channel	58 lbs.	Santee-Cooper Res., SC	July 7, 1964	W. B. Whaley
Catfish, flathead	123 lbs. 9 oz.	Independence, KS	May 14, 1998	Ken Paulie
Catfish, white	21 lbs. 8 oz.	Gorton Pond, CT	Apr. 22, 2001	Thomas Urquhart
Char, Arctic	32 lbs. 9 oz.	Tree River, Canada	July 30, 1981	Jeffrey L. Ward
Crappie, white	5 lbs. 3 oz.	Enid Dam, MS	July 31, 1957	Fred L. Bright
Dolly Varden	20 lbs. 14oz.	Wulik R., AK	July 7, 2001	Raz Reid
Dorado	51 lbs. 5 oz.	Toledo (Corrientes), Argentina	Sept. 27, 1984	Armando Giudice
Drum, freshwater	54 lbs. 8 oz.	Nickajack Lake, TN	Apr. 20, 1972	Benny E. Hull
Gar, alligator	279 lbs.	Rio Grande, TX	Dec. 2, 1951	Bill Valverde
Gar, Florida	10 lbs.	Everglades, FL	Jan. 28, 2002	Herbert G. Ratner Jr.
Gar, longnose	50 lbs. 5 oz.	Trinity River, TX	July 30, 1954	Townsend Miller
Gar, shortnose	5 lbs. 12 oz.	Ren Lake, IL	July 16, 1995	Donna K. Willmert
Gar, spotted	9 lbs. 12 oz.	Lake Mexia, TX	Apr. 7, 1994	Rick Rivard
Grayling, Arctic	5 lbs. 15 oz.	Katseyedie River, N.W.T.	Aug. 16, 1967	Jeanne P. Branson
Inconnu	53 lbs.	Pah River, AK	Aug. 20, 1986	Lawrence E. Hudnall
Kokanee	9 lbs. 6 oz.	Okanagan Lake, Vernon, B.C.	June 18, 1988	Norm Kuhn
Muskellunge	67 lbs. 8 oz.	Lake Court Oreilles, WI	July 24, 1949	Cal Johnson
Muskellunge, tiger	51 lbs. 3 oz.	Lac Vieux-Desert, MI	July 16, 1919	John Knobla
Perch, Nile	230 lbs.	Lake Nasser, Egypt	Dec. 20, 2000	William Toth
Perch, white	3 lbs. 1 oz.	Forest Hill Park, NJ	May 6, 1989	Edward Tango
Perch, yellow	4 lbs. 3 oz.	Bordentown, NJ	May, 1865	Dr. C. C. Abbot
Pickerel, chain	9 lbs. 6 oz.	Homerville, GA	Feb. 17, 1961	Baxley McQuaig Jr.
Pike, northern	55 lbs. 1 oz.	Lake of Grefeern, W. Germany	Oct. 16, 1986	Lothar Louis
Redhorse, greater	9 lbs. 3 oz.	Salmon River, Pulaski, NY	May 11, 1985	Jason Wilson
Redhorse, silver	11 lbs. 7 oz.	Plum Creek, WI	May 29, 1985	Neal Long
Salmon, Atlantic	79 lbs. 2 oz.	Tana River, Norway	1928	Henrik Henriksen
Salmon, chinook	97 lbs. 4 oz.	Kenai River, AK	May 17, 1985	Les Anderson
Salmon, chum	35 lbs.	Edye Pass, BC	July 11, 1995	Todd A. Johansson
Salmon, coho	33 lbs. 4 oz.	Salmon River, Pulaski, NY	Sept. 27, 1989	Jerry Lifton
Salmon, pink	14 lbs. 13 oz.	Monroe, WA	Sept. 30, 2001	Alexander Minerich
Salmon, sockeye	15 lbs. 3 oz.	Kenai River, AK	Aug. 9, 1987	Stan Roach
Sauger	8 lbs. 12 oz.	Lake Sakakawea, ND	Oct. 6, 1971	Mike Fischer
Shad, American	11 lbs. 4 oz.	Connecticut River, MA	May 19, 1986	Bob Thibodo
Sturgeon, beluga	224 lbs. 13 oz.	Guryev, Kazakhstan	May 3, 1993	Merete Lehne
Sturgeon, white	468 lbs.	Benicia, CA	July 9, 1983	Joey Pallotta 3d
Sunfish, green	2 lbs. 2 oz.	Stockton Lake, MO	June 18, 1971	Paul M. Dilley
Sunfish, redbreast	1 lb. 12 oz.	Suwannee River, FL	May 29, 1984	Alvin Buchanan
Sunfish, redear	5 lbs. 7oz.	Diverson Canal, GA	Nov. 6, 1998	Amos M. Gay
Tigerfish, giant	97 lbs.	Zaire River, Kinshasa, Zaire	July 9, 1988	Raymond Houtmans
Tilapia, Nile	13 lbs. 3 oz.	Antelope Isl., Karibe, Zimbabwe	July 5, 2002	Sorel van Rooyen
Trout, Apache	5 lb. 3 oz.	Apache Res., AZ	May 29, 1991	John Baldwin
Trout, brook	14 lbs. 8 oz.	Nipigon River, Ontario	July, 1916	Dr. W. J. Cook

Species	Weight	Where caught	Date	Angler
Trout, bull	32 lbs.	Lake Pend Oreille, ID	Oct. 27, 1949	N. L. Higgins
Trout, cutthroat	41 lbs.	Pyramid Lake, NV	Dec., 1925	John Skimmerhorn
Trout, golden	11 lbs.	Cooks Lake, WY	Aug. 5, 1948	Charles S. Reed
Trout, lake	72 lbs.	Great Bear Lake, N.W.T.	Aug. 9, 1995	Lloyd E. Bull
Trout, rainbow	42 lbs. 2 oz.	Bell Island, AK	June 22, 1970	David Robert White
Trout, tiger	20 lbs. 13 oz.	Lake Michigan, WI	Aug. 12, 1978	Pete M. Friedland
Walleye	25 lbs.	Old Hickory Lake, TN	Aug. 2, 1960	Mabry Harper
Warmouth	2 lbs. 7 oz.	Yellow River, Holt, FL	Oct. 19, 1985	Tony D. Dempsey
Whitefish, lake	14 lbs. 6 oz.	Meaford, Ontario	May 21, 1984	Dennis M. Laycock
Whitefish, mountain	5 lbs. 8 oz.	Elbow River, Calgary, AB	Aug. 1, 1995	Randy G. Woo
Whitefish, round	6 lbs.	Putahow R., Manitoba, Can.	June 14, 1984	Allan J. Ristori
Zander	25 lbs. 2 oz.	Trosa, Sweden	June 12, 1986	Harry Lee Tennison

DIRECTORY OF SPORTS ORGANIZATIONS
Major League Baseball
Commissioner's Office 245 Park Ave., 31st Fl., New York, NY 10167
Website: www.mlb.com

American League

Anaheim Angels
2000 Gene Autry Way
Anaheim, CA 92806

Baltimore Orioles
333 W. Camden St.
Baltimore, MD 21201

Boston Red Sox
4 Yawkey Way
Boston, MA 02215

Chicago White Sox
333 W. 35th St.
Chicago, IL 60616

Cleveland Indians
2401 Ontario St.
Cleveland, OH 44115

Detroit Tigers
2100 Woodward Ave.
Detroit, MI 48201

Kansas City Royals
1 Royal Way
Kansas City, MO 64141

Minnesota Twins
34 Kirby Puckett Place
Minneapolis, MN 55415

New York Yankees
161st St. and River Ave.
Bronx, NY 10451

Oakland Athletics
7000 Coliseum Way
Oakland, CA 94621

Seattle Mariners
83 King St.
Seattle, WA 98104

Tampa Bay Devil Rays
One Tropicana Dr.
St. Petersburg, FL 33705

Texas Rangers
1000 Ballpark Way
Arlington, TX 76011

Toronto Blue Jays
1 Blue Jays Way, Ste 3200
Toronto, ON M5V 1J1

National League

Arizona Diamondbacks
401 E. Jefferson St.
Phoenix, AZ 85001

Atlanta Braves
755 Hank Aaron Drive
Atlanta, GA 30302

Chicago Cubs
1060 W. Addison
Chicago, IL 60613

Cincinnati Reds
100 Cinergy Field
Cincinnati, OH 45202

Colorado Rockies
2001 Blake St.
Denver, CO 80205

Florida Marlins
2269 Dan Marino Blvd.
Miami, FL 33056

Houston Astros
501 Crawford St.
Houston, TX 77002

Los Angeles Dodgers
1000 Elysian Park Ave.
Los Angeles, CA 90012

Milwaukee Brewers
One Brewers Way
Milwaukee, WI 53214

Montreal Expos
4549 Ave. Pierre de
Coubertin
Montreal, QC H1V 3N7

New York Mets
123-01 Roosevelt Ave.
Flushing, NY 11368

Philadelphia Phillies
3501 S. Broad St.
Philadelphia, PA 19148

Pittsburgh Pirates
115 Federal St.
Pittsburgh, PA 15212

St. Louis Cardinals
250 Stadium Plaza
St. Louis, MO 63102

San Diego Padres
8880 Rio San Diego Dr.,
Ste. 400
San Diego, CA 92112

San Francisco Giants
24 Willie Mays Plaza
San Francisco, CA 94107

National Basketball Association
League Office, Olympic Tower, 645 5th Ave., New York, NY 10022
Website: www.nba.com

Atlanta Hawks
One CNN Center, Ste. 405,
South Tower
Atlanta, GA 30303

Boston Celtics
151 Merrimac St.
Boston, MA 02114

Chicago Bulls
1901 W. Madison St.
Chicago, IL 60612

Cleveland Cavaliers
1 Center Court
Cleveland, OH 44115

Dallas Mavericks
2909 Taylor St.
Dallas, TX 75226

Denver Nuggets
1000 Chopper Cr.
Denver, CO 80204

Detroit Pistons
Two Championship Dr.
Auburn Hills, MI 48326

Golden State Warriors
1011 Broadway
Oakland, CA 94607

Houston Rockets
Two Greenway Plaza,
Ste. 400
Houston, TX 77046

Indiana Pacers
125 S. Pennsylvania St.
Indianapolis, IN 46204

Los Angeles Clippers
1111 S. Figueroa St.,
Ste. 1100
Los Angeles, CA 90015

Los Angeles Lakers
555 Nash St.
El Segundo, CA 90245

Memphis Grizzlies
One Auction Ave.
Memphis, TN 38105

Miami Heat
601 Biscayne Blvd.
Miami, FL 33132

Milwaukee Bucks
1001 N. 4th St.
Milwaukee, WI 53203

Minnesota Timberwolves
600 1st Ave. North
Minneapolis, MN 55403

New Jersey Nets
390 Murray Hill Parkway
E. Rutherford, NJ 07073

New Orleans Hornets
1501 Girod St.
New Orleans, LA 70113

New York Knickerbockers
Two Pennsylvania Plaza
New York, NY 10121

Orlando Magic
Two Magic Place
8701 Maitland Summit Blvd.
Orlando, FL 32810

Philadelphia 76ers
3601 S. Broad St.
Philadelphia, PA 19148

Phoenix Suns
201 E. Jefferson
Phoenix, AZ 85004

Portland Trail Blazers
One Center Ct.
Portland, OR 97227

Sacramento Kings
One Sports Parkway
Sacramento, CA 95834

San Antonio Spurs
100 Montana St.
San Antonio, TX 78203

Seattle SuperSonics
351 Elliott Ave., West
Suite 500
Seattle, WA 98119

Toronto Raptors
40 Bay St., Ste. 400
Toronto, ON M5J 2X2

Utah Jazz
301 W. South Temple
Salt Lake City, UT 84101

Washington Wizards
601 F St., NW
Washington, DC 20004

National Hockey League
League Headquarters, 1251 Ave. of the Americas, 47th Fl., New York, NY 10020
Website: www.nhl.com

Mighty Ducks of Anaheim
2695 E. Katella Ave.
Anaheim, CA 92806

Atlanta Thrashers
1 CNN Ctr., 12th Fl., S. Tower
Atlanta, GA 30348

Boston Bruins
One FleetCenter, Ste. 250
Boston, MA 02114

Buffalo Sabres
HSBC Arena
One Seymour H. Knox III Plaza
Buffalo, NY 14203

Calgary Flames
PO Box 1540, Station M
Calgary, AB T2P 3B9

Carolina Hurricanes
1400 Edwards Mill Rd.
Raleigh, NC 27607

Chicago Blackhawks
1901 W. Madison St.
Chicago, IL 60612

Colorado Avalanche
1000 Chopper Cr.
Denver, CO 80204

Columbus Blue Jackets
200 W. Nationwide Blvd.
Columbus, OH 43215

Dallas Stars
211 Cowboys Parkway
Irving, TX 75063

Detroit Red Wings
600 Civic Center Dr.
Detroit, MI 48226

Edmonton Oilers
11230 110 St.
Edmonton, AB T5G 3H7

Florida Panthers
One Panther Parkway
Sunrise, FL 33323

Los Angeles Kings
1111 S. Figueroa St.
Los Angeles, CA 90015

Minnesota Wild
444 Cedar St., Ste. 900
St. Paul, MN 55101

Montreal Canadiens
1260 rue de La Gauchetière
St. W
Montreal, QC H3B 5E8

Nashville Predators
501 Broadway
Nashville, TN 37203

New Jersey Devils
50 Rte. 120 N. PO Box 504
E. Rutherford, NJ 07073

New York Islanders
Nassau Veterans Memorial
Coliseum
1255 Hempstead Tpke.
Uniondale, NY 11553

New York Rangers
Two Pennsylvania Plaza,
14th Fl.
New York, NY 10121

Ottawa Senators
1000 Palladium Dr.
Kanata, ON K2V 1A5

Philadelphia Flyers
First Union Center
3601 South Broad St.
Philadelphia, PA 19148

Phoenix Coyotes
9375 E. Bell Rd.
Scottsdale, AZ 85260

Pittsburgh Penguins
66 Mario Lemieux Place
Pittsburgh, PA 15219

St. Louis Blues
1401 Clark Ave.
St. Louis, MO 63103

San Jose Sharks
525 W. Santa Clara St.
San Jose, CA 95113

Tampa Bay Lightning
401 Channelside Dr.
Tampa, FL 33602

Toronto Maple Leafs
40 Bay St., Ste. 400
Toronto, ON M5J 2X2

Vancouver Canucks
800 Griffiths Way
Vancouver, BC V6B 6G1

Washington Capitals
401 9th St. NW Ste. 750
Washington, DC 20004

National Football League

League Office, 280 Park Ave., New York, NY 10017
Website: www.nfl.com

Arizona Cardinals
8701 S. Hardy Dr.
Tempe, AZ 85284

Atlanta Falcons
4400 Falcon Parkway
Flowery Branch, GA 30542

Baltimore Ravens
200 St. Paul Pl., Ste. 2400
Baltimore, MD 21202

Buffalo Bills
One Bills Drive
Orchard Park, NY 14127

Carolina Panthers
800 S. Mint St.
Charlotte, NC 28202

Chicago Bears
1000 Football Dr.
Lake Forest, IL 60045

Cincinnati Bengals
One Paul Brown Stadium Dr.
Cincinnati, OH 45202

Cleveland Browns
76 Lou Groza Blvd.
Berea, OH 44017

Dallas Cowboys
One Cowboys Parkway
Irving, TX 75063

Denver Broncos
13655 Broncos Parkway
Englewood, CO 80112

Detroit Lions
1200 Featherstone Rd.
Pontiac, MI 48342

Green Bay Packers
1265 Lombardi Ave.
Green Bay, WI 54307

Houston Texans
One Reliant Park
Houston, TX 77054

Indianapolis Colts
7001 W. 56th St.
Indianapolis, IN 46254

Jacksonville Jaguars
One ALLTELL Stadium
Place
Jacksonville, FL 32202

Kansas City Chiefs
One Arrowhead Drive
Kansas City, MO 64129

Miami Dolphins
7500 SW 30th St.
Davie, FL 33329

Minnesota Vikings
9520 Viking Dr.
Eden Prairie, MN 55344

New England Patriots
60 Washington St.
Foxboro, MA 02035

New Orleans Saints
1500 Podras St.
New Orleans, LA 70112

New York Giants
Giants Stadium
E. Rutherford, NJ 07073

New York Jets
1000 Fulton Ave.
Hempstead, NY 11550

Oakland Raiders
1220 Harbor Bay Parkway
Alameda, CA 94502

Philadelphia Eagles
3501 S. Broad St.
Philadelphia, PA 19148

Pittsburgh Steelers
3400 S. Water St.
Pittsburgh, PA 15203

St. Louis Rams
One Rams Way
St. Louis, MO 63045

San Diego Chargers
4020 Murphy Rd.
PO Box 609609
San Diego, CA 92160

San Francisco 49ers
4949 Centennial Blvd.
Santa Clara, CA 95054

Seattle Seahawks
11220 NE 53d St.
Kirkland, WA 98033

Tampa Bay Buccaneers
One Buccaneer Place
Tampa, FL 33607

Tennessee Titans
460 Great Circle Rd.
Nashville, TN 37228

Washington Redskins
21300 Redskin Park Dr.
Ashburn, VA 20147

Other Sports Organizations

Amateur Athletic Union, PO Box 22409, Lake Buena Vista, FL 32830
Website: www.aausports.org

Amateur Softball Assn.
2801 NE 50th St.
Oklahoma City, OK 73111
www.softball.org

American Kennel Club
260 Madison Ave., 4th Fl.
New York, NY 10016
www.akc.org

Canadian Football League
50 Wellington St. E. 3rd Fl.
Toronto, Ont. M5E 1C8
www.cfl.ca

CART (Championship Auto
Racing Teams)
5350 Lakeview Pkwy.
South Dr., Building 36
Indianapolis, IN 46268
www.cart.com

Intl. Game Fish Assn.
300 Gulf Stream Way
Dania Beach, FL 33004
www.igfa.org

LPGA
100 International Golf Dr.
Daytona Beach, FL 32124
www.lpga.com

Little League Baseball
PO Box 3485
Williamsport, PA 17701
www.littleleague.org

Major League Soccer
110 E. 42d St., 10th Fl.
New York, NY 10017
www.mlsnet.com

NASCAR
P.O. Box 2875
Daytona Beach, FL 32120
www.nascar.com

NCAA (National Collegiate
Athletic Association)
700 W. Washington St.
PO Box 6222
Indianapolis, IN 46206
www.ncaa.org

National Rifle Assn.
11250 Waples Mill Rd.
Fairfax, VA 22030
www.nra.org

Pro Bowlers Assn.
719 Second Ave., Ste. 701
Seattle, WA 98104
www.pbatour.com

PGA
100 Ave. of the Champions
Box 109601
Palm Beach Gardens, FL
33410
www.pga.com

Pro Rodeo Cowboys Assn.
101 Pro Rodeo Dr.
Colorado Springs, CO 80919
www.prorodeo.com

Special Olympics
1325 G St., NW, Ste. 500
Washington, DC 20005
www.specialolympics.org

Thoroughbred Racing Assn.
420 Fair Hill Dr.
Elkton, MD 21921
www.tra-online.com

USA Equestrian
4047 Iron Works Pkwy.
Lexington, KY 40511
www.equestrian.org

USA Swimming
One Olympic Plaza
Colorado Springs, CO 80909
www.usa-swimming.org

USA Track & Field
1 RCA Dome, Ste. 140
Indianapolis, IN 46225
www.usatf.org

U.S. Auto Club
4910 W. 16th St.
Speedway, IN 46224
www.usacracing.com

U.S. Figure Skating Assn.
20 First St.
Colorado Springs, CO 80906
www.usfsa.org

U.S. Olympic Committee
One Olympic Plaza
Colorado Springs, CO 80909
www.usoc.org

U.S. Skiing Assn.
1500 Kearns Blvd.
PO Box 100
Park City, UT 84060
www.usskiteam.com

U.S. Soccer Federation
1801 S. Prairie Ave.
Chicago, IL 60616
www.ussoccer.com

U.S. Tennis Assn.
70 W. Red Oak Lane
West Harrison, NY 10604
www.usta.com

U.S. Trotting Assn.
750 Michigan Ave.
Columbus, OH 43215
www.ustrotting.com

WNBA
Olympic Tower
645 5th Ave.
New York, NY 10022
www.wnba.com

NOTABLE SPORTS PERSONALITIES

Henry (Hank) Aaron, b. 1934: Milwaukee-Atlanta outfielder; hit record 755 home runs, led NL 4 times; record 2,297 RBIs.

Kareem Abdul-Jabbar, b. 1947: Milwaukee, L.A. Lakers center; MVP 6 times; all-time leading NBA scorer, 38,387 points.

Andre Agassi, b. 1970: won: Wimbledon, '92; U.S. Open, '94; Austral. Open, '95, 2000-01, 2003; French Open, '99.

Troy Aikman, b. 1966: quarterback; led Dallas Cowboys to Super Bowl wins in 1993-94, 1996; Super Bowl MVP, 1993.

Amy Alcott, b. 1956: golfer, 29 career wins (5 majors), inducted into World Golf Hall of Fame in 1999.

Grover Cleveland "Pete" Alexander (1887-1950): pitcher; won 373 NL games; pitched 16 shutouts, 1916.

Muhammad Ali, b. 1942: 3-time heavyweight champion.

Gary Anderson, b. 1959: kicker, NFL's career points leader, with 2,223 through the end of the 2002 seaon.

Sparky Anderson, b. 1934: only manager to win World Series in the NL (Cincinnati, 1975-76) and the AL (Detroit, 1984).

Mario Andretti (1938-2001): won Daytona 500 (1967), Indy 500 (1969); Formula 1 world title (1978).

Earl Anthony (1938-2001): bowler, won record 6 PBA Championships (1973-75, 1981-83), 41 career PBA tournaments.

Eddie Arcaro, (1916-97): only jockey to win racing's Triple Crown twice, 1941,1948; rode 4,779 winners in his career.

Henry Armstrong (1912-88): boxer, held feather-, welter-, light-weight titles simultaneously, 1937-38.

Lance Armstrong, b. 1971: cyclist, 5-time winner of the Tour de France (1999-2003).

Arthur Ashe (1943-93): tennis, won U.S. Open (1968); Wimbledon (1975); died of AIDS.

Evelyn Ashford, b.1957: sprinter, won 100m gold (1984) and silver (1988); member of 5 U.S. Olympic teams (1976-1992).

Red Auerbach, b. 1917: coached Boston to 9 NBA titles.

Tracy Austin, b. 1962: youngest player to win U.S. Open tennis title (age 16 in 1979), 2-time AP Female Athlete of the Year.

Ernie Banks, b. 1931: Chicago Cubs slugger; hit 512 NL homers; twice MVP; never played in World Series.

Roger Bannister, b. 1929: British physician, ran first sub 4-minute mile, May 6, 1954 (3 min. 59.4 sec.).

Charles Barkely, b. 1963: NBA MVP, 1993; 4th player ever to surpass 20,000 pts, 10,000 rebounds, and 4,000 assists.

Rick Barry, b. 1944: NBA scoring leader, 1967; ABA, 1969.

Sammy Baugh, b. 1914: Washington Redskins quarterback; held numerous records upon retirement after 16 pro seasons.

Elgin Baylor, b. 1934: L.A. Lakers forward; 10-time all-star.

Bob Beamon, b. 1946: Olympic long jump gold medalist in 1968; world record jump of 29' 2½" stood until 1991.

Boris Becker, b. 1967: German tennis star; won U.S. Open 1989; Wimbledon champ 3 times.

David Beckham, b. 1975: English soccer star; captain of 2002 World Cup team.

Jean Beliveau, b. 1931: Montreal Canadiens center; scored 507 goals; twice MVP.

Johnny Bench, b. 1947: Cincinnati Reds catcher; MVP twice; led league in home runs twice, RBIs 3 times.

Patty Berg, b. 1918: won more than 80 golf tournaments; AP Woman Athlete-of-the-Year 3 times.

Yogi Berra, b. 1925: Yankee catcher (1946-63); 3-time MVP.

Abebe Bikila (1932-73): Ethiopian runner, won consecutive Olympic marathon gold medals in 1960 (barefoot), 1964.

Matt Biondi, b. 1965: swimmer, won 5 golds, 1988 Olympics.

Larry Bird, b. 1956: Boston Celtics forward; chosen MVP 1984-86; 1998 coach of the year with Indiana Pacers.

Bonnie Blair, b. 1964: speed skater won 5 individual gold medals in 3 Olympics (1988, '92, '94).

George Blanda, b. 1927: quarterback, kicker; 26 years as active player, scored 2,002 career points.

Fanny Blankers-Koen, b. 1918: track, won 4 golds in 1948.

Wade Boggs, b. 1958: AL batting champ, 1983, 1985-88; reached 3,000 career hits, 1999 (3,010).

Barry Bonds, b. 1964: outfielder, hit record 73 homers in 2001; NL MVP 1990, 1992-93, 2001-02; 4th all-time in home runs (658).

Bjorn Borg, b. 1956: led Sweden to first Davis Cup, 1975; Wimbledon champion 5 times.

Mike Bossy, b. 1957: N.Y. Islanders right wing scored more than 50 goals 8 times.

Ray Bourque, b. 1960: Boston defenseman,1979-2000, 5-time Norris Trophy winner; won Stanley Cup with Colorado, 2001.

Bill Bradley, b. 1943: All-America at Princeton; led NY Knicks to 2 NBA titles (1970, '73); U.S. senator, 1979-97.

Terry Bradshaw, b. 1948: quarterback, led Pittsburgh to 4 Super Bowl wins (1975-76, 1979-80); NFL MVP, 1978.

George Brett, b. 1953: Kansas City Royals infielder, led AL in batting, 1976, 1980, 1990; MVP, 1980.

Lou Brock, b. 1939: St. Louis Cardinals outfielder, stole NL record 118 bases, 1974; led NL 8 times.

Jim Brown, b. 1936: Clev. fullback, 12,312 yds.; 3-time MVP.

Paul Brown (1908-91): football owner, coach; led eponymous Cleveland Browns to 3 NFL championships.

Paul "Bear" Bryant (1913-83): college football coach with 323 wins; led Alabama to 5 national titles (1961, '64, '65, '78, '79).

Sergei Bubka, b. 1963: Ukrainian pole vaulter; first to clear 20 feet; gold medal, 1988 Olympics.

Don Budge, (1915-2000): won numerous amateur and pro tennis titles; "grand slam," 1938.

Maria Bueno, b. 1939: tennis, 4 U.S. titles, 3 Wimbledon.

Dick Butkus, b. 1942: Chicago Bears linebacker, twice chosen best NFL defensive player.

Dick Button, b. 1929: figure skater; won 1948, 1952 Olympic gold medals; world titlist, 1948-52.

Walter Camp, (1859-1925): Yale football player, coach, athletic director; established many rules.

Roy Campanella (1921-93): Hall of Fame catcher for the Brooklyn Dodgers (1948-57); 3-time NL MVP.

Earl Campbell, b. 1955: NFL running back; MVP 1978-79.

Jennifer Capriati, b. 1976: won Australian (2001-02) and French Opens (2001), at 14 in 1990 was youngest top-10 player.

Rod Carew, b. 1945: AL infielder; 7 batting titles, 1977 MVP.

Steve Carlton, b. 1944: NL pitcher; won 20 games 5 times, Cy Young award 4 times.

Billy Casper, b. 1931: PGA Player-of-the-Year 3 times; U.S. Open champ twice.

Tracy Caulkins, b. 1963: swimmer, won 3 Olympic golds, 1984; set 63 U.S. and 5 world records; won 48 individual U.S. titles.

Wilt Chamberlain (1936-99): center; was NBA leading scorer 7 times, MVP 4 times; scored 100 pts. in a game, 1962.

Bobby Clarke, b. 1949: Philadelphia Flyers center; led team to 2 Stanley Cup championships; MVP 3 times.

Roger Clemens, b. 1962: pitcher, 1986 AL MVP; only 6-time Cy Young winner (1986-87, '91, '97-98; 2001); twice struck out record 20 batters in a game; won 300 games.

Roberto Clemente (1934-72): Pittsburgh Pirates outfielder; won 4 batting titles; MVP, 1966; killed in plane crash.

Ty Cobb (1886-1961): Detroit Tigers outfielder; had record .367 lifetime batting average, 12 batting titles.

Sebastian Coe, b. 1956: British runner, won Olympic 1,500m gold medal and 800m silver medal in 1980 and 1984.

Nadia Comaneci, b. 1961: Romanian gymnast, won 3 gold medals, achieved 7 perfect scores, 1976 Olympics.

Maureen Connolly (1934-69): won tennis "grand slam," 1953; AP Woman-Athlete-of-the-Year 3 times.

Jimmy Connors, b. 1952: tennis, 5 U.S. titles, 2 Wimbledon.

Cynthia Cooper, b. 1963: basketball, 4-time MVP of the WNBA finals and 2-time league MVP for the Houston Comets.

James J. Corbett (1866-1933): heavyweight champion, 1892-97; credited with being the first "scientific" boxer.

Angel Cordero, b. 1942: leading money winner, 1976, 1982-83; rode 3 Kentucky Derby winners.

Howard Cosell (1920-95): commentator for ABC's *Monday Night Football* and *Wide World of Sports.*

Margaret Smith Court, b. 1942: Australian tennis great, won 24 grand slam events.

Bob Cousy, b. 1928: Boston guard; 6 NBA titles; 1957 MVP.

Bjoern Daehlie, b. 1967: Norwegian cross-country skier; won record 8 Winter Olympic gold medals.

Lindsay Davenport, b. 1976: tennis, won Olympic gold (1996), U.S. Open (1998), Wimbledon (1999), Austral. Open (2000).

Dizzy Dean (1911-74): colorful pitcher for St. Louis Cardinals "Gashouse Gang" in the 30s; MVP, 1934.

Mary Decker Slaney, b. 1958: runner, has held 7 separate American records from the 800m to 10,000m.

Oscar De La Hoya, b. 1972: won IBF lightweight (1995); WBC super lightweight (1996) and welterweight (1997, 2000) titles.

Donna de Varona, b. 1947: 2 Olympic swimming golds,1964; 1st female sportscaster at a major network (ABC), 1965.

Jack Dempsey (1895-1983): heavyweight champ, 1919-26.

Gail Devers, b. 1966: Olympic 100m gold medalist, 1992, '96.

Eric Dickerson, b. 1960: NFL record 2,105 rushing yds.,1984.

Joe DiMaggio (1914-99): N.Y. Yankees outfielder; hit safely in record 56 consecutive games, 1941; AL MVP 3 times.

Tony Dorsett, b. 1954: Heisman winner who led the Dallas Cowboys to an NFL title in his rookie year (1977).

Tim Duncan, b. 1976: San Antonio center, 2-time NBA Finals MVP (1999, 2003); NBA MVP, 2002-03.

Roberto Duran, b. 1951: Panamanian boxer, held titles at 3 weights; lost 1980 "no mas" fight to Sugar Ray Leonard.

Leo Durocher (1906-91): manager, won 3 NL pennants (Brooklyn-1941, NY Giants-1951, '54) and 1954 World Series.

Dale Earnhardt (1951-2001): 7-time NASCAR Winston Cup champ; died in a last-lap crash at 2001 Daytona 500.

Stefan Edberg, b. 1966: U.S. singles champ, 1991, 1992; Wimbledon champ, 1988, 1990.

Gertrude Ederle, b. 1906: first woman to swim English Channel, broke existing men's record, 1926.

Teresa Edwards, b. 1964: basketball, 5-time Olympian; gold medalist in 1984, '88, '96, 2000 and bronze medal in 1992.

Hicham El Guerrouj, b. 1974: Moroccan runner, holds world records in mile (3:43.13) and 1500m (3:26.0).

John Elway, b. 1960: quarterback; led Denver Broncos to 2 Super Bowl wins, 1998, 1999; regular-season MVP, 1987.

Julius Erving, b. 1950: 3-time ABA MVP, 1981 NBA MVP.

Phil Esposito, b. 1942: NHL scoring leader 5 times.

Janet Evans, b. 1971: 4 Olympic swimming golds, 1988-92.

Lee Evans, b. 1947: Olympic 400m gold medalist in 1968 with a 43.86 sec. world record not broken until 1988.

Chris Evert, b. 1954: U.S. Open tennis champ 6 times, Wimbledon champ 3 times.

Ray Ewry (1873-1937): track-and-field star, won 8 gold medals, 1900, 1904, and 1908 Olympics.

Nick Faldo, b. 1957: won Masters, British Open 3 times each.

Juan Fangio (1911-95): Argentinian, 5-time World Grand Prix driving champ (1951, 1954-57).

Marshall Faulk, b. 1973: 2000 NFL MVP, record 26 TDs in 2001; 2-time Off. Player of the Year (2000-01).

Brett Favre, b. 1969: led Green Bay to Super Bowl win, 1997; NFL regular-season MVP, 1995, 1996; co-MVP, 1997.

Bob Feller, b. 1918: Cleveland Indians pitcher; won 266 games; pitched 3 no-hitters, 12 one-hitters.

Rollie Fingers, b. 1946: pitcher, 341 career saves; AL MVP, Cy Young Award, 1981; World Series MVP, 1974.

Peggy Fleming, b. 1948: world figure skating champion, 1966-68; gold medalist, 1968 Olympics.

Whitey Ford, b. 1928: N.Y. Yankees pitcher, won record 10 World Series games.

George Foreman, b. 1949: heavyweight champion, 1973-74, 1994-95; at 45, the oldest to win a heavyweight title.

Dick Fosbury, b. 1947: high jumper; won 1968 Olympic gold medal; developed the "Fosbury Flop."

Dan Fouts, b. 1951: quarterback (San Diego), 5th in career passing yards (43,040); TV analyst on *Monday Night Football.*

Jimmie Foxx (1907-67): Red Sox, Athletics slugger; MVP 3 times; triple crown, 1933.

A. J. Foyt, b. 1935: won Indy 500 4 times; U.S. Auto Club champ 7 times.

Joe Frazier, b. 1944: heavyweight champion, 1970-73.

Walt Frazier, b. 1945: Hall of Fame guard for N.Y. Knicks NBA championship teams (1970, '73).

Haile Gebrselassie, b. 1973: Ethiopian, world record holder in 5,000m and 10,000m; 10,000m gold medalist in 1996, 2000.

Lou Gehrig (1903-41): N.Y. Yankees 1st baseman; MVP, 1927, 1936; triple crown, 1934; AL record 184 RBIs, 1931.

George Gervin, b. 1952: top NBA scorer, 1978-80, 1982.

Althea Gibson, (1927-2003) 2-time U.S. and Wimbledon champ.

Bob Gibson, b. 1935: St. Louis Cardinals pitcher; won Cy Young award twice; struck out 3,117 batters.

Josh Gibson (1911-47): Hall of Fame catcher, known as "Babe Ruth of the Negro Leagues"; credited with as many as 84 homers in 1 season and about 800 in his career.

Marc Girardelli, b. 1963: skier (Lux.), won 5 World Cup titles.

Jeff Gordon, b. 1971: race car driver, youngest to win NASCAR Winston Cup 3 times (1995, 1997-98).

Steffi Graf, b. 1969: German; won tennis "grand slam," 1988; U.S. Open 5 times; Wimbledon champ 7 times.

Otto Graham, b. 1921: Cleveland quarterback, 4-time all-pro.

Red Grange (1903-91): All-America at Univ. of Illinois, 1923-25; played for Chicago Bears, 1925-35.

Joe Greene, b. 1946: Pittsburgh Steelers lineman; twice NFL outstanding defensive player.

Wayne Gretzky, b. 1961: top scorer in NHL history with record 894 goals, 1,963 assists, 2,857 points; MVP, 1980-87, 1989.

Bob Griese, b. 1945: All-Pro quarterback led Miami Dolphins to 17-0 season (1972) and 2 Super Bowl titles (1973-74).

Ken Griffey Jr., b. 1969: outfielder, led AL in homers 1994, 1997-1999; 1997 AL MVP; 10 gold gloves.

Archie Griffin, b. 1954: Ohio State running back is the only 2-time winner of the Heisman Trophy (1974-75).

Florence Griffith Joyner, (1959-98): sprinter; won 3 gold medals at 1988 Olympics; Olympic record for 100m.

Lefty Grove (1900-75): pitcher; won 300 AL games.

Janet Guthrie, b. 1938: 1st woman driver in Indy 500 (1977).

Tony Gwynn, b. 1960: 8-time NL batting champ, 1984, 1987-89, 1994-97; 3,141 career hits.

Walter Hagen (1892-1969): golf; 5 PGA, 4 British Open titles.

George Halas (1895-1983): founder-coach of Chicago Bears; won 5 NFL championships.

Dorothy Hamill, b. 1956: figure skater, gold medalist at the Olympics and World championships in 1976.

Scott Hamilton, b. 1958: U.S. and world figure skating champion, 1981-84; Olympic gold medalist, 1984.

Mia Hamm, b. 1972: led U.S. to World Cup (1991, '99) and Olympic ('96) titles; most career goals in women's soccer.

Franco Harris, b. 1950: running back, led Steelers to 4 Super Bowls (1975-76, 1979-80); 1,000+ yds. in a season 8 times.

Bill Hartack, b. 1932: jockey, rode 5 Kentucky Derby winners.

Dominik Hasek, b. 1965: Buffalo Sabres goalie; won Vezina Trophy, 1994-95, 1997-99, 2001; NHL MVP, 1997-98.

John Havlicek, b. 1940: Boston forward scored 26,395 NBA points.

Eric Heiden, b. 1958: speed skater, won 5 Olympic golds, 1980.

Rickey Henderson, b. 1958: outfielder, 1990 AL MVP; record 130 stolen bases, 1982; all-time leader in steals , runs, and walks.

Sonja Henie (1912-69): world champion figure skater, 1927-36; Olympic gold medalist, 1928, 1932, 1936.

Martina Hingis, b. 1980: won Australian Open, Wimbledon, and U.S. Open; youngest No. 1 player (16 yrs., 6 m.) in 1997.

Ben Hogan (1912-97): golfer, won 4 U.S. Open championships, 2 PGA, 2 Masters.

Chamique Holdsclaw, b. 1977: basketball, 2-time national player of the year, led Tennessee to 3 NCAA titles (1996-98).

Evander Holyfield, b. 1962: 4-time heavyweight champion.

Rogers Hornsby (1896-1963): NL 2nd baseman; batted record .424 in 1924; twice won triple crown.

Paul Hornung, b. 1935: Green Bay Packers runner-placekicker, scored record 176 points, 1960.

Gordie Howe, b. 1928: hockey forward; NHL MVP 6 times; scored 801 goals in 26 NHL seasons.

Carl Hubbell (1903-88): N.Y. Giants pitcher; 20-game winner 5 consecutive years, 1933-37.

Sarah Hughes, b. 1985: figure skater, won Olympic gold, 2002; silver at U.S. and bronze at World Championships, 2001.

Bobby Hull, b. 1939: NHL all-star 10 times; MVP, 1965-66.

Brett Hull, b. 1964: St. Louis Blues forward; led NHL in goals, 1990-92; MVP, 1991.

Catfish Hunter (1946-99): pitched perfect game, 1968; 20-game winner 5 times.

Don Hutson (1913-97): Packers receiver, caught 99 TD passes; 2-time NFL MVP.

Julie Inkster, b. 1960: Hall of Fame golfer, 2nd to win all 4 of LPGA's modern majors; won 7 career major titles.

Phil Jackson, b. 1945: won 9 NBA titles as coach of Bulls and Lakers; 1973 title as a NY Knick.

Reggie Jackson, b. 1946: slugger; led AL in home runs 4 times; MVP, 1973; hit 5 World Series home runs, 1977.

"Shoeless" Joe Jackson (1889-1951): outfielder, 3rd highest career batting average (.356); one of the "Black Sox" banned for allegedly throwing 1919 World Series.

Jaromir Jagr, b. 1972: Czech hockey player, NHL MVP in 1999; Art Ross Trophy (leading scorer) 1995, 1998-2001.

Bruce Jenner, b. 1949: Olympic decathlon gold medalist, 1976.

Lynn Jennings, b. 1960: runner, 3-time World and 9-time U.S. cross country champ; bronze at 1992 Olympics (10,000m).

Earvin (Magic) Johnson, b. 1959: NBA MVP, 1987, 1989, 1990; Playoff MVP, 1980, 1982, 1987; 2nd in career assists.

Jack Johnson (1878-1946): heavyweight champion, 1908-15.

Michael Johnson, b. 1967: 5-time Olympic gold medalist (1996, 2000); world and Olympic record holder, 200m and 400m.

Randy Johnson, b. 1963: 5-time Cy Young winner; strikeout leader: 1993-94, 1998-2002; 3,871 career strikeouts (4th).

Walter Johnson (1887-1946): Washington Senators pitcher; won 416 games; record 110 shutouts.

Bobby Jones (1902-71): won "grand slam of golf" 1930; U.S. Amateur champ 5 times, U.S. Open champ 4 times.

David "Deacon" Jones, b.1938: 5-time All-Pro with LA Rams (1965-69); quarterback "sack" specialist credited with inventing the term.

Marion Jones, b. 1975: 2000 Olympic 100m, 200m, 1,600m relay gold medalist, bronze in long jump and 400m relay.

Roy Jones Jr., b. 1969: undisputed Light heavyweight champ.

Michael Jordan, b. 1963: leading NBA scorer 1987-93, 1996-98; MVP, 1988, 1991-92, '96, '98; Playoff MVP, 1991-93, 1996-98; ESPN Athlete of the Century.

Dorothy Kamenshek, b. 1925: led Rockford (IL) Peaches to 4 All-American Girls Baseball League titles in the 1940s.

Jackie Joyner-Kersee, b. 1962: Olympic gold medalist in heptathlon (1988 , '92) and long jump (1988).

Harmon Killebrew, b. 1936: Minnesota Twins slugger; led AL in home runs 6 times; 573 lifetime.

Jean Claude Killy, b. 1943: French skier; 3 1968 Olympic golds.

Ralph Kiner, b. 1922: Pittsburgh Pirates slugger, led NL in home runs 7 consecutive years, 1946-52.

Billie Jean King, b. 1943: U.S. singles champ 4 times; Wimbledon champ 6 times; beat Bobby Riggs, 1973.

Bob Knight, b. 1940: basketball coach, led Indiana U. to NCAA title in 1976, '81, '87.

Olga Korbut, b. 1955: Soviet gymnast; 3 1972 Olympic golds.

Sandy Koufax, b. 1935: 3-time Cy Young winner; lowest ERA in NL, 1962-66; pitched 4 no-hitters, one a perfect game.

Ingrid Kristiansen, b. 1956: Norwegian, only runner ever to hold world records in 5,000m, 10,000m, and marathon.

Julie Krone, b. 1963: winningest female jockey, only woman to ride a winner in a Triple Crown race (Belmont, 1993).

Michelle Kwan, b.1980: figure skater, 7 U.S. and 5 World titles; silver medalist at 1998 Olympics, bronze in 2002.

Guy Lafleur, b. 1951: 3-time NHL scoring leader; 1977-78 MVP.

Kennesaw Mountain Landis (1866-1944): 1st commissioner of baseball (1920-44); banned the 8 "Black Sox" involved in the fixing of the 1919 World Series.

Tom Landry (1924-2000): Dallas Cowboys head coach, 1960-88; won 2 Super Bowls (1972, '78); 3rd in career wins (270).

Dick "Night train" Lane (1928-2002): Hall of Fame defensive back, intercepted an NFL single-season record 14 passes (1952).

Don Larsen, b. 1929: As NY Yankee, pitched only World Series perfect game, Oct. 8, 1956—a 2-0 win over Brooklyn.

Rod Laver, b. 1938: Australian; won tennis "grand slam" twice, 1962, 1969; Wimbledon champ 4 times.

Mario Lemieux, b. 1965: 6-time NHL leading scorer; MVP, 1988, 1993, 1996; Playoff MVP, 1991-92.

Greg Lemond, b. 1961: 3-time Tour de France winner (1986, '89-90); first American to win the event.

Ivan Lendl, b. 1960: U.S. Open tennis champ, 1985-87.

Sugar Ray Leonard, b. 1956: boxer, held titles in 5 different weight classes.

Carl Lewis, b. 1961: track-and-field star, won 9 Olympic gold medals in sprinting and the long jump.

Lennox Lewis, b. 1965: Brit. heavyweight champ, 1997-2003.

Tara Lipinski, b. 1982: youngest figure skater to win U.S. and world championships, 1997, and Winter Olympic gold, 1998.

Vince Lombardi (1913-70): Green Bay Packers coach, led team to 5 NFL championships and 2 Super Bowl victories.

Nancy Lopez, b. 1957: Hall of Fame golfer, 4-time LPGA Player of the Year, 3-time winner of the LPGA Championship.

Greg Louganis, b. 1960: won Olympic gold medals in both springboard and platform diving, 1984, 1988.

Joe Louis (1914-81): heavyweight champion, 1937-49.

Sid Luckman (1916-98): Chicago Bears quarterback; led team to 4 NFL championships; MVP, 1943.

Connie Mack (1862-1956): Philadelphia Athletics manager, 1901-50; won 9 pennants, 5 championships.

John Madden, b. 1936: won Super Bowl as coach of the Oakland Raiders (1977); NFL TV analyst since 1982.

Greg Maddux, b. 1966: NL pitcher, won 4 consecutive Cy Young awards, 1992-95.

Karl Malone, b. 1963: Utah Jazz forward; was MVP, 1997, 1999; 14-time All-Star; 36,374 career points (2nd all-time).

Moses Malone, b. 1955: NBA center, MVP, 1979, 1982-83.

Mickey Mantle (1931-95): N.Y. Yankees outfielder; triple crown, 1956; 18 World Series home runs; MVP 3 times.

Pete Maravich (1948-88): guard, scored NCAA record 44.2 ppg during collegiate career; led NBA in scoring, 1977.

Rocky Marciano (1923-69): heavyweight champion, 1952-56; retired undefeated.

Dan Marino, b. 1961: Miami quarterback; set NFL record of 5,084 yds passing and 48 touchdowns, 1984; career leader, TDs, yds passing.

Roger Maris (1934-85): N.Y. Yankees outfielder; hit AL record 61 home runs, 1961; MVP, 1960 and 1961.

Eddie Mathews, b : Milwaukee-Atlanta 3rd baseman, hit 512 career home runs.

Christy Mathewson (1880-1925): pitcher, won 373 games.

Bob Mathias, b. 1930: decathlon gold medalist, 1948, 1952.

Willie Mays, b. 1931: N.Y.-S.F. Giants center fielder; hit 660 home runs, led NL 4 times; had 3,283 hits; twice MVP.

Willie McCovey, b. 1938: S.F. Giants slugger; hit 521 home runs; led NL 3 times; MVP, 1969.

John McEnroe, b. 1959: U.S. Open tennis champ, 1979-81, 1984; Wimbledon champ, 1981, 1983-84.

John McGraw (1873-1934): N.Y. Giants manager, led team to 10 pennants, 3 championships.

Mark McGwire, b. 1963: hit then-record 70 home runs in 1998; 583 career home runs (5th).

Tamara McKinney, b. 1962: 1st U.S. skier to win overall Alpine World Cup championship (1983).

Mary T. Meagher, b. 1964: swimmer, "Madame Butterfly" won 3 Olympic gold medals in 1984.

Mark Messier, b. 1961: center, chosen NHL MVP, 1990, 1992; Conn Smythe Trophy, 1984.

Debbie Meyer, b. 1952: 1st swimmer to win 3 individual Olympic golds (1968).

George Mikan, b. 1924: Minn. Lakers center, considered the best basketball player of the first half of the 20th century.

Stan Mikita, b. 1940: Chicago Black Hawks center, led NHL in scoring 4 times; MVP twice.

Billy Mills, b. 1938: runner, upset winner of the 1964 Olympic 10,000m; only American man ever to win the event.

Joe Montana, b. 1956: S.F. 49ers quarterback; Super Bowl MVP, 1982, 1985, 1990.

Archie Moore (1913-98): light-heavyweight champ, 1952-62.

Howie Morenz (1902-37): Montreal Canadiens forward, considered best hockey player of first half of the 20th century.

Edwin Moses, b. 1955: undefeated in 122 consecutive 400m hurdles races, 1977-87; Olympic gold medalist, 1976, '84.

Shirley Muldowney, b. 1940: 1st woman to race National Hot Rod Assoc. Top Fuel dragsters; 3-time NHRA points champ.

Eddie Murray, b. 1956: durable slugger; 3rd player to combine 3,000+ hits with 500+ home runs.

Stan Musial, b. 1920: St. Louis Cardinals star; won 7 NL batting titles; MVP 3 times.

Bronko Nagurski (1908-90): Chicago Bears fullback and tackle; gained more than 4,000 yds. rushing.

Joe Namath, b. 1943: Jets quarterback, 1969 Super Bowl MVP.

Martina Navratilova, b. 1956: Wimbledon champ 9 times, U.S. Open champ 1983-84, 1986-87.

Byron Nelson, b. 1912: won 11 consecutive golf tournaments in 1945; twice Masters and PGA titlist.

Ernie Nevers (1903-76): Stanford star, selected as best college fullback to play between 1919-69.

Paula Newby-Fraser, b. 1972: 8-time Ironman Triathlon World Champ; holds course record.

John Newcombe, b. 1943: Australian; twice U.S. Open tennis champ; Wimbledon titlist 3 times.

Jack Nicklaus, b. 1940: PGA Player-of-the-Year, 1967, 1972; leading money winner 8 times; won 18 majors (6 Masters).

Chuck Noll, b. 1931: Pittsburgh coach; won 4 Super Bowls.

Paavo Nurmi (1897-1973): Finnish distance runner, won 6 Olympic gold medals, 1920, 1924, 1928.

Al Oerter, b. 1936: discus thrower, won gold medal at 4 consecutive Olympics, 1956-68.

Hakeem Olajuwon, b. 1963: Houston center; NBA MVP, 1994, Playoffs MVP, 1994-95; career blocked shot leader.

Barney Oldfield, (1878-1946): pioneer auto racer was first to drive a car 60 mph (1903).

Shaquille O'Neal, b. 1972: center, led L.A. Lakers to NBA titles, 2000-2002; 2000, 2002 Finals MVP; 2000 NBA MVP.

Bobby Orr, b. 1948: Boston Bruins defenseman; Norris Trophy 8 times; led NHL in scoring twice, assists 5 times.

Mel Ott (1909-1958): N.Y. Giants outfielder hit 511 home runs; led NL 6 times.

Jesse Owens (1913-80): track and field star, won 4 1936 Olympic gold medals.

Satchel Paige (1906-82): pitcher, starred in Negro leagues, 1924-48; entered major leagues at age 42.

Arnold Palmer, b. 1929: golf's first $1 million winner; won 4 Masters, 2 British Opens.

Jim Palmer, b. 1945: Baltimore Orioles pitcher; Cy Young award 3 times; 20-game winner 8 times.

Joe Paterno, b. 1926: winningest NCAA Div. I football coach, 336 wins through 2002; led Penn St. to natl. titles, 1982, 1986.

Floyd Patterson, b. 1935: 2-time heavyweight champion.

Walter Payton (1954-1999): Chicago Bears running back; most rushing yards in NFL history; top NFC rusher, 1976-80.

Pelé, b. 1940: soccer star, led Brazil to 3 World Cup titles (1958, '62, '70); scored 1,281 goals in 22-year career.

Bob Pettit, b. 1932: first NBA player to score 20,000 points; twice NBA scoring leader.

Richard Petty, b. 1937: NASCAR national champ 7 times; 7-time Daytona 500 winner.

Laffit Pincay Jr., b. 1946: jockey, leading money-winner 1970-74, 1979, 1985.

Jacques Plante (1929-86): goalie; 7 Vezina trophies; first goalie to wear a mask in a game.

Gary Player, b. 1936: South African golfer, won 3 Masters, 3 British Opens, 2 PGA Championships, and the U.S. Open.

Steve Prefontaine, (1951-75): runner, 1st to win 4 NCAA titles in same event (5,000m, 1970-73); died in auto accident.

Kirby Puckett, b. 1961: Minnesota Twins outfielder; won AL batting title, 1989; led AL in hits, 1987-89, 1992; RBIs, 1994.

Paula Radcliffe, b. 1973: Brit. runner, set marathon world best of 2:15:25 in London, 2003.

Willis Reed, b. 1942: N.Y. Knicks center; MVP, 1970; Playoff MVP, 1970, 1973.

Mary Lou Retton, b. 1973: Brit. runner set marathon world best of 2:15:25 in London 2003.

Jerry Rice, b. 1962: receiver, 1989 Super Bowl MVP; NFL record for career touchdowns (203), receptions (1,456).

Maurice Richard, (1921-2000): Montreal Canadiens forward scored 544 regular season goals, 82 playoff goals.

Branch Rickey (1881-1965): executive; helped break baseball's color barrier, 1947; initiated farm system, 1919.

Cal Ripken Jr., b. 1960: Baltimore shortstop; AL MVP 1983, 1991; most consecutive games played (2,632).

Oscar Robertson, b. 1938: guard; averaged career 25.7 points per game; 3rd most career assists; MVP, 1964.

Brooks Robinson, b. 1937: Baltimore Orioles 3rd baseman; played in 4 World Series; MVP, 1964; 16 gold gloves.

Frank Robinson, b. 1935: MVP in both NL and AL; triple crown, 1966; 586 career home runs; first black manager in majors.

Jackie Robinson (1919-72): broke baseball's color barrier with Brooklyn Dodgers, 1947; MVP, 1949.

Sugar Ray Robinson (1920-89): middleweight champion 5 times, welterweight champion.

Knute Rockne (1888-1931): Notre Dame football coach, 1918-31; revolutionized game by stressing forward pass.

Bill Rodgers, b. 1947: runner, won Boston and New York City marathons 4 time each, 1975-80.

Pete Rose, b. 1941: won 3 NL batting titles; hit safely in 44 consecutive games, 1978; has most career hits, 4,256; banned from baseball for alleged gambling, 1989.

Ken Rosewall, b. 1934: Australian; 2-time U.S. Open champ, 8 grand slam singles titles.

Patrick Roy, b. 1965: Montreal-Colorado goalie; only 3-time NHL Playoffs MVP (Conn Smythe Trophy), 1986, '93, 2001.

Wilma Rudolph (1940-94): sprinter, won 3 1960 Olympic golds.

Adolph Rupp (1901-77): NCAA basketball coach; led Kentucky to 4 national titles, 1948-49, 1951, 1958.

Bill Russell, b. 1934: Boston Celtics center, led team to 11 NBA titles; MVP 5 times; first black coach of major pro sports team.

Babe Ruth (1895-1948): N.Y. Yankees outfielder; hit 60 home runs, 1927; 714 lifetime; led AL 12 times.

Johnny Rutherford, b. 1938: auto racer, won 3 Indy 500s.

Nolan Ryan, b. 1947: pitcher; holds season (383), career (5,714) strikeout records; won 324 games (7 no-hitters).

Pete Sampras, b. 1971: tennis star; 1st man in Open era to win 7 Wimbledons; most career Grand Slam wins (14).

Joan Benoit Samuelson, b. 1968: won 1st Olympic women's marathon (1984), Boston Marathon (1979, '83).

Barry Sanders, b. 1968: rushed for 2,053 yards in 1997; led NFL in rushing, 1990, 1994, 1996, 1997.

Gene Sarazen, (1902-99): won PGA championship 3 times, U.S. Open twice; developed the sand wedge.

Gale Sayers, b. 1943: Chicago back, twice led NFL in rushing.

Mike Schmidt, b. 1949: Phillies 3rd baseman; led NL in home runs 8 times; 548 lifetime; NL MVP, 1980, 1981, 1986.

Michael Schumacher, b. 1969: German driver, 6-time Formula 1 world champ (1994-95, 2000-2003).

Tom Seaver, b. 1944: pitcher; won NL Cy Young award 3 times; won 311 major league games.

Monica Seles, b. 1973: won U.S. ('91-92), Australian ('91-93, '96), French ('90-92) Opens; stabbed on court by fan, 1993.

Patty Sheehan, b. 1956: Hall of Fame golfer, 3 LPGA Championships (1983-84, '93).

Willie Shoemaker (1931-2003): jockey; rode 4 Kentucky Derby and 5 Belmont Stakes winners; leading career money winner.

Eddie Shore (1902-85): Boston Bruins defenseman; MVP 4 times, first-team all-star 7 times.

Frank Shorter, b. 1947: runner, only American to win men's Olympic marathon (1972) since 1908; silver medalist in 1976.

Don Shula, b. 1930: all-time winningest NFL coach (347 games).

Al Simmons (1902-56): AL outfielder batted .334 lifetime.

O. J. Simpson, b. 1947: running back; rushed for 2,003 yds., 1973; AFC leading rusher 4 times; acquitted of murder, 1995.

George Sisler (1893-1973): St. Louis Browns 1st baseman; had record 257 hits, 1920; batted .340 lifetime.

Dean Smith, b. 1931: basketball coach, most career Division I wins (879); led North Carolina to 2 NCAA titles (1982, '93).

Emmitt Smith, b. 1969: Dallas running back; NFL and Super Bowl MVP, 1993; record 25 rushing touchdowns, 1995.

Lee Smith, b. 1957: relief pitcher, all-time save leader, 478.

Conn Smythe (1895-1980): won 7 Stanley Cups as Toronto GM (1929-1961); playoff MVP award named in his honor.

Sam Snead (1912-2002): PGA and Masters champ 3 times each, record 82 PGA tournament victories.

Annika Sorenstam, b. 1970: golfer, set LPGA 18-hole record of 59 (−13), and 72-hole record of 27-under-par in Mar. 2001.

Sammy Sosa, b. 1968: Cubs outfielder; 66 homers, NL MVP, 1998; 1st to hit 60+ homers 3 times (63 in 1999, 64 in 2001).

Warren Spahn, b. 1921: pitcher; won 363 NL games; 20-game winner 13 times; Cy Young award, 1957.

Tris Speaker (1885-1958): AL outfielder; batted .345 over 22 seasons; hit record 792 career doubles.

Mark Spitz, b. 1950: swimmer, won 7 golds at 1972 Olympics.

Amos Alonzo Stagg (1862-1965): football innovator; Univ. of Chicago football coach for 41 years, 5 undefeated seasons.

Bart Starr, b. 1934: Green Bay Packers quarterback, led team to 5 NFL titles and 2 Super Bowl victories.

Roger Staubach, b. 1942: Dallas Cowboys quarterback; leading NFC passer 5 times.

Casey Stengel (1890-1975): managed Yankees to 10 pennants, 7 championships, 1949-60.

Jackie Stewart, b. 1939: Scot auto racer, 27 Grand Prix wins.

John Stockton b. 1962: Utah Jazz guard; NBA career leader in assists, steals; NBA assists leader, 1988-96.

Picabo Street, b. 1971: skier, 2-time World Cup downhill champion (1995-96); Olympic super G gold medalist in 1998.

Louise Suggs, b. 1923: U.S. Women's Open champ, 1949, '52; 11 major victories, ranks 3rd all-time.

John L. Sullivan (1858-1918): last bareknuckle heavyweight champion, 1882-1892.

Pat Summit, b. 1952: basketball coach, led Tennessee Lady Vols to 6 NCAA titles (1987, '89, '91, '96-98).

Fran Tarkenton, b. 1940: quarterback, Minnesota, N.Y. Giants, 2nd in career touchdown passes; 1975 Player of the Year.

Lawrence Taylor, b. 1959: linebacker; led N.Y. Giants to 2 Super Bowl titles; played in 10 Pro Bowls.

Frank Thomas, b. 1968: Chicago White Sox 1st baseman; was AL MVP, 1993-94; won AL batting title, 1997.

Jenny Thompson, b. 1973: swimmer, most decorated U.S. woman with 10 Olympic medals (8 gold) in 1992, 1996, 2000.

Daley Thompson, b. 1958: British decathlete, Olympic gold medalist in 1980, '84.

Jim Thorpe (1888-1953): football All-America, 1911, 1912; won pentathlon and decathlon, 1912 Olympics.

Bill Tilden (1893-1953): won 7 U.S. tennis titles, 3 Wimbledon.

Y. A. Tittle, b. 1926: N.Y. Giants quarterback; MVP, 1961, 1963.

Alberto Tomba, b. 1966: Italian skier, all-time Olympic alpine medalist (3 golds, 2 silver).

Lee Trevino, b. 1939: golfer, won U.S., British Open twice.

Bryan Trottier, b. 1956: center for 6 Stanley Cup champs.

Gene Tunney, (1897-1978): heavyweight champion, 1926-28.

Mike Tyson, b. 1966: Undisputed heavyweight champ, 1987-1990; at 19, youngest to win a heavyweight title (WBC, 1986).

Wyomia Tyus, b. 1945: Olympic 100m gold medalist, 1964, '68.

Johnny Unitas, (1933-2002): Baltimore Colts quarterback; passed for more than 40,000 yds; MVP, 1957, 1967.

Al Unser, b. 1939: Indy 500 winner 4 times.

Bobby Unser, b. 1934: Indy 500 winner 3 times.

Norm Van Brocklin (1926-83): quarterback; passed for game record 554 yds., 1951; MVP, 1960.

Amy Van Dyken, b. 1973: swimmer, first American woman to win 4 gold medals in one Olympics (1996).

Lasse Viren, b. 1949: Finnish runner; Olympic 5,000m and 10,000m gold medalist in 1972 and 1976.

Honus Wagner (1874-1955): Pittsburgh Pirates shortstop, won 8 NL batting titles.

Grete Waitz, b. 1953: Norwegian, 9-time winner of the New York City Marathon (1978-80, 1982-86, '88).

"Jersey" Joe Walcott, (1914-94): boxer, became heavyweight champion at age 37, 1951-52.

Bill Walton, b. 1952: center led Portland Trail Blazers to 1977 NBA title; MVP, 1978; NBA TV commentator.

Kurt Warner, b. 1971: St. Louis Rams quarterback, NFL MVP 1999, 2001; Super Bowl MVP, 2000.

Tom Watson, b. 1949: 6-time PGA Player of the Year, won 5 British Opens, 2 Masters, U.S. Open.

Karrie Webb, b. 1974: Australian golfer; youngest (26 yrs. 6 mos.) to win career Grand Slam, 1999-2001.

Johnny Weissmuller (1903-84): swimmer; won 52 national championships, 5 Olympic gold medals; set 67 world records.

Jerry West, b. 1938: L.A. Lakers guard; had career average 27 points per game; first team all-star 10 times.

Byron "Whizzer" White (1917-2002): running back, led NCAA in scoring and rushing at Colorado (1937), led NFL in rushing twice (1938, '40); Supreme Court justice, 1962-93.

Reggie White, b. 1961: defensive end, all-time NFL sack leader.

Kathy Whitworth, b. 1939: 7-time LPGA Player of the Year (1966-69, 1971-73); 88 tour wins most on LPGA or PGA tour.

Lenny Wilkens, b. 1937: winningest coach in NBA history; in Hall of Fame as player and coach.

Serena Williams, b. 1981: 2-time Wimbledon, U.S. Open champ; Australian (2003); French Open (2002).

Ted Williams (1918-2002): Boston Red Sox outfielder; won 6 batting titles, two triple crowns; hit .406 in 1941.

Venus Williams, b. 1980: Wimbledon, U.S. Open, Olympic champ (2000); Wimbledon, U.S. Open champ (2001).

Helen Willis Moody (1905-98): tennis star; won U.S. Open 7 times, Wimbledon 8 times.

Katarina Witt, b. 1965: German figure skater; won Olympic gold medal, 1984, 1988; world champ, 1984-84, 1987-88.

John Wooden, b. 1910: UCLA basketball coach; 10 NCAA titles.

Tiger Woods, b. 1975: golfer, youngest ever to win the sport's career Grand Slam (all 4 majors), at age 24, when he won the British Open, 2000; 8 major titles.

Mickey Wright, b. 1935: won LPGA and U.S. Open championship 4 times; 82 career wins including 13 majors.

Kristi Yamaguchi, b. 1971: figure skater; won national, world, and Olympic titles in 1992.

Carl Yastrzemski, b. 1939: Boston Red Sox slugger; won 3 batting titles; triple crown, 1967.

Cy Young (1867-1955): pitcher, won record 511 games.

Steve Young, b. 1961: 49ers quarterback; led NFL in passing, 1991-94, 1996, 1997; Super Bowl MVP, 1995.

Babe Didrikson Zaharias (1914-56): track star; won 2 1932 Olympic gold medals; won numerous golf tournaments.

Emil Zátopek (1922-2000): Czech runner won 3 gold medals at 1952 Olympics (5,000m, 10,000m, and marathon).

GENERAL INDEX

Note: Page numbers in **boldface** indicate key reference. Page numbers in *italics* indicate photos.

QUICK REFERENCE INDEX

SPORTS QUICK REFERENCE INDEX

FOR COMPLETE INDEX, SEE PAGES 979-1007.

WORLD ALMANAC QUICK QUIZ—ANSWERS

73–c; 80–c; 88–d; 99–b; 102–1-b, 2-c, 3-a, 4-d; 120–; 148–d; 150–c, a, d, b; 160–c; 171–b; 177–c, a, d, b; 202–a-3, b-4, c-1, d-2; 206–c; 232–c; 259–d; 262–a; 283–c; 293–b; 297–d; 327–b; 334–a, b, d, c; 341–b; 353–d; 365–c; 442–b; 446–a, c, b, d; 451–a; 480–c; 496–c; 515–a; 519–d, c, a, b; 528–b, d, a, c; 536–c, b, d, a; 557–b; 565–b; 611–c; 622–c; 632–d; 645–b; 647–a; 682–c, a, d, b; 685–a; 690–d; 694–c; 701–a; 702–a; 711–b, d, c, a; 720–a; 724–c; 744–most (a), least (b); 751–c; 761–d; 773–b; 828–d; 836–c; 861–b; 910–d

The #1 Bestselling American Reference Book of All Time

THE WORLD ALMANAC 2004

"#1 in coverage, currency, and usability."
— *BOOKLIST/RBB, AMERICAN LIBRARY ASSOCIATION, MAY 2003*

▶ **Get More Familiar with Your World:** Authoritative, up-to-date information on population, nations, states, economy, environment, education, sports, health, computers, history, presidents, personalities, awards, religion, sciences, the sun, and everything under it

▶ **Remember 2003:** Color photo scrapbook, authoritative chronology, Top Ten news stories, obituaries, quotes, and offbeat news of the year

▶ **Compare Your Opinions with the Experts:** Check out our Editors' Picks all-time rankings for films, music, history, and more; then send in your votes for next year's *World Almanac* (see page 1007 for details)

▶ **Get Yourself or a Loved One into the Right College:** A special essay by the editors of the Fiske Guides for college entrance

▶ **Understand Baby Boomers:** A statistical profile and memories timeline, with essays by Wendy Wasserstein and Joyce Maynard

▶ **Use It All the Time:** 2004 planning calendar; 2004 presidential election information; 2004 tax guide; business and associations directories; anti-terrorism preparation; crossword puzzle reference; mortgage-rate, mileage, and metric calculators; health and nutrition information; ZIP and area codes

"The most useful reference book known to modern man."
— *LOS ANGELES TIMES*

"Useful to any human being on the planet...the world's most powerful reference."
— *SEATTLE TIMES*

"It's the best in the business."
— *MANCHESTER UNION LEAD*

Still only $11.95

Distributed by
St. Martin's Press
Printed In U.S.A.

ISBN 0-88687-910-8

51195

9 780886 879105
EAN